ARCTIC OCEAN
Barents Sea
Kara Sea
Laptev Sea
East Siberian Sea
RUSSIA
FINLAND
ESTONIA
LATVIA
LITHUANIA
BELARUS
UKRAINE
MOLDOVA
ROMANIA
BULGARIA
KOSOVO
SERBIA
MACEDONIA
GREECE
Black Sea
GEORGIA
ARMENIA
AZERBAIJAN
TURKEY
CYPRUS
SYRIA
LEBANON
ISRAEL
JORDAN
IRAQ
IRAN
KUWAIT
BAHRAIN
QATAR
SAUDI ARABIA
UNITED ARAB EMIRATES
OMAN
YEMEN
Persian Gulf
Arabian Sea
Red Sea
EGYPT
SUDAN
SOUTH SUDAN
ERITREA
DJIBOUTI
Somaliland
ETHIOPIA
SOMALIA
UGANDA
KENYA
DEMOCRATIC REPUBLIC OF THE CONGO
RWANDA
BURUNDI
TANZANIA
MALAWI
ZAMBIA
MOZAMBIQUE
ZIMBABWE
BOTSWANA
SWAZILAND
LESOTHO
SOUTH AFRICA
COMORO ISLANDS
MADAGASCAR
SEYCHELLES
MAURITIUS
Réunion
Caspian Sea
Aral Sea
KAZAKHSTAN
UZBEKISTAN
TURKMENISTAN
KYRGYZSTAN
TAJIKISTAN
AFGHANISTAN
PAKISTAN
INDIA
NEPAL
BHUTAN
BANGLADESH
MALDIVES
SRI LANKA
Bay of Bengal
MONGOLIA
PEOPLE'S REPUBLIC OF CHINA
DEMOCRATIC PEOPLE'S REPUBLIC OF KOREA
REPUBLIC OF KOREA
Sea of Japan
JAPAN
Yellow Sea
East China Sea
TAIWAN
Hong Kong
Macau
MYANMAR (BURMA)
LAOS
THAILAND
VIETNAM
CAMBODIA
South China Sea
PHILIPPINES
Spratly Islands
BRUNEI
MALAYSIA
SINGAPORE
Celebes Sea
EAST INDIES
INDONESIA
TIMOR-LESTE
PAPUA NEW GUINEA
Sea of Okhotsk
Bering Sea
Aleutian Islands
PACIFIC OCEAN
Northern Marianas
Philippine Sea
Guam
PALAU
Caroline Islands
FEDERATED STATES OF MICRONESIA
MARSHALL ISLANDS
Gilbert Islands
NAURU
KIRIBATI
Phoenix Islands
MELANESIA
SOLOMON ISLANDS
TUVALU
Wallis & Futuna
VANUATU
FIJI
TONGA
Coral Sea
New Caledonia
Norfolk Island
Great Barrier Reef
INDIAN OCEAN
AUSTRALIA
Tasman Sea
North Islands
Chatham Islands
NEW ZEALAND
South Islands
ANTARCTICA

POLITICAL HANDBOOK OF THE WORLD 2014

POLITICAL HANDBOOK OF THE WORLD 2014

Edited by Tom Lansford

Los Angeles | London | New Delhi
Singapore | Washington DC

Los Angeles | London | New Delhi
Singapore | Washington DC

FOR INFORMATION:

CQ Press
SAGE Publications, Inc.
2455 Teller Road
Thousand Oaks, California 91320
E-mail: order@sagepub.com

SAGE Publications Ltd.
1 Oliver's Yard
55 City Road
London EC1Y 1SP
United Kingdom

SAGE Publications India Pvt. Ltd.
B 1/I 1 Mohan Cooperative Industrial Area
Mathura Road, New Delhi 110 044
India

SAGE Publications Asia-Pacific Pte. Ltd.
3 Church Street
#10-04 Samsung Hub
Singapore 049483

Printed in the United States of America.

Print ISBN: 978-1-4833-3328-1
ISSN: 0193-175X

Publishing history continues on page 1835, which is to be considered an extension of the copyright page.

Project management and editorial services provided by MTM Publishing, Inc.
435 West 23rd Street, #8C
New York NY 10011
www.mtmpublishing.com

President: Valerie Tomaselli
VP, Book Development: Hilary Poole
Editorial Assistant: Jenna Vaccaro
Editor-in-Chief: Tom Lansford
Contributing Editors: Brian Beary, Jack Covarrubias, James Frusetta, Elizabeth M. Hewitt, J. Stephen Hoadley, Thomas C. Muller, B. Jared Pack, Ann Robertson, Mark E. Sedgwick

Sponsoring Editor: Andrew Boney
Production Editor: Tracy Buyan
Copy Editors: Lana Arndt, Karin Rathert, Terri Lee Paulsen, Pam Schroeder
Typesetter: C&M Digitals (P) Ltd.
Proofreader: Theresa Kay
Cover Designer: Michael Dubowe
Marketing Manager: Carmel Schrire

14 15 16 17 18 10 9 8 7 6 5 4 3 2 1

CONTENTS

INTERGOVERNMENTAL ORGANIZATIONS

APPENDIXES

INTERGOVERNMENTAL ORGANIZATION ABBREVIATIONS

Country membership in an intergovernmental organization is given in one of two locations: Appendix C lists membership of the United Nations and its specialized and related agencies; non-UN memberships are listed at the end of each country section, under Intergovernmental Representation, using the abbreviations below. An asterisk indicates a nonofficial abbreviation. In the individual country sections, associate memberships are in italics.

ADB	Asian Development Bank
AfDB*	African Development Bank
APEC	Asia-Pacific Economic Cooperation
ASEAN	Association of Southeast Asian Nations
AU	African Union
Caricom	Caribbean Community and Common Market
CEUR*	Council of Europe
CIS	Commonwealth of Independent States
Comesa	Common Market for Eastern and Southern Africa
CWTH*	Commonwealth
EBRD	European Bank for Reconstruction and Development
ECOWAS	Economic Community of West African States
EFTA	European Free Trade Association
EIB	European Investment Bank
EU	European Union
GCC	Gulf Cooperation Council
G-7	Group of Seven
G-8	Group of Eight
G-20	Group of Twenty
IADB*	Inter-American Development Bank
ICC	International Criminal Court
IEA	International Energy Agency
IOM	International Organization for Migration
LAS	League of Arab States (Arab League)
Mercosur	Southern Cone Common Market
*NAM	Nonaligned Movement
NATO	North Atlantic Treaty Organization
OAS	Organization of American States
OECD	Organization for Economic Cooperation and Development
OIC*	Organization of the Islamic Conference
OPEC	Organization of the Petroleum Exporting Countries
OSCE	Organization for Security and Cooperation in Europe
PIF	Pacific Islands Forum
SAARC	South Asian Association for Regional Cooperation
SADC	Southern African Development Community
SCO	Shanghai Cooperation Organization
WEU	Western European Union
WTO	World Trade Organization

PREFACE

Africa and the Middle East were plagued by political instability throughout 2013. An Islamist insurrection in northern Mali prompted an international military intervention in January by soldiers from France and the Economic Community of West African States (ECOWAS). Although a peace agreement was signed in June, fighting continued into the fall. Popular unrest in Jordan prompted King Abdullah II to replace Prime Minister Hamadi Jebali with Ali Laarayedh. In March, a coup in the Central Africa Republic (CAR) deposed President François Bozizé. Rebel leader Michel Djotodia was subsequently proclaimed leader of the country, though he was not recognized as the legitimate president of the CAR by the international community. Egyptian President Mohamed Morsi was overthrown by the military on July 2 and replaced by an interim leader, Abdi Mansour. Morsi's subsequent arrest led to clashes between the military-led regime and supporters of the ousted president.

The bloody Syrian civil war continued through 2013. In March allegations emerged that the regime had used chemical weapons against rebels. In September a United Nations (UN) inspection team found that the nerve agent sarin had been used in an attack in August in the city of Ghouta. Under threat of military action by the United States and other Western powers, the regime of Bashir al-Assad agreed to a Russia plan to destroy its stockpile of chemical weapons under the supervision of the UN. Meanwhile fighting continued. By October international rights groups estimated that more than 115,000 had been killed in the violence that had also created more than 6 million displaced persons. By November more than 2 million Syrians had fled to neighboring states, overwhelming aid resources and prompting a massive humanitarian crisis. An outbreak of polio in Syria further underscored the deteriorating conditions in the country.

Afghanistan and Pakistan continued to fight antigovernment insurgencies led by the Taliban in 2013. In Pakistan, efforts to negotiate a settlement with the Taliban were undermined by U.S. drone attacks. From 2001 to November 2013 the United States had conducted 282 drone strikes, killing more than 2,500 Pakistanis, including a significant number of civilians. However the United States substantially reduced the number of attacks, from a peak of 90 in 2010 to 46 in 2012 and 20 in 2013. Meanwhile facing a proposed 2014 withdrawal of U.S. military forces, Afghanistan and the United States continued to negotiate over a post-2014 international security presence in the country. As of November, the United States had 47,000 troops in Afghanistan.

Efforts to reduce violence around the world and slow the $70 billion annual conventional arms trade resulted in the Arms Trade Treaty, adopted by the UN General Assembly on April 2, 2013. The accord aimed to create cross-border verification mechanisms to ensure that weapons were not sold to terrorists, organized crime, or those engaged in human rights violations. Meanwhile officials in the United States were shocked by the release of more than 200,000 classified documents by security contractor Edward Snowden in May. The documents revealed that U.S. electronic surveillance was far more extensive than most people realized and included the collection of e-mails, texts, and other electronic communications. The release of the documents created considerable tension between the United States and some of its closest allies when it was discovered that the U.S. government had collected personal communications from a range of world leaders, including German Chancellor Angela Merkel.

Across the globe, new leaders took office in 2013. On March 13 the National People's Congress elected Xi Jinping president of China, following the ten-year tenure of Hu Jintao. Xi entered office with pledges to curb corruption and expand economic opportunities. Longtime Venezuelan President Hugo Chávez died in office on March 5 and was replaced by Vice President Nicolás Maduro, who went on to win election in his own right in bitterly contested balloting on April 14. Maduro continued the main policies of his predecessor. Pakistan reached an important milestone as for the first time in its history a parliament completed its full term and peacefully turned over power following elections on May 11 in which the Pakistan Muslim League-Nawaz won a majority. Party leader Muhammad Nawaz Sharif subsequently became prime minister on June 5. In Australia the September 7 electoral victory of a center-right coalition ended six years of rule by the Labor Party and made Liberal Party leader Tony Abbott prime minister. A host of other countries, ranging from Iceland to Paraguay to Kenya, elected new leaders in 2013, while the monarchs of Belgium, the Netherlands, and Qatar abdicated in favor of younger successors.

The election of moderate cleric Hassan Rouhani as president of Iran on June 14, 2013, offered the potential to reduce the isolation of the Islamic republic. With an economy crippled by international economic sanctions because of Iran's nuclear program, Rouhani signaled a willingness to negotiate with foreign powers, led by the United States. On November 24 an interim agreement was announced whereby sanctions would be lifted in exchange for restrictions on Iran's nuclear program and UN inspections of atomic facilities. The breakthrough was in marked contrast to the position of North Korea, which began the year with its third nuclear weapons test in February amid global condemnation. Pyongyang rebuffed international efforts to negotiate over its nuclear weapons program.

Catholics around the world were surprised by the February 2013 resignation of Pope Benedict XVI, who became the first pontiff to voluntarily leave office since 1294. He was succeeded by Jorge Mario Bergoglio of Argentina, who became Pope Francis on March 13. Francis was the first pope from the Western Hemisphere and the first Jesuit to hold the Church's highest office.

In many nations, familiar leaders remained in power following elections. Benjamin Netanyahu was returned as prime minister of Israel after balloting in January 2013. On April 18 Giorgio Napolitano became the first president in Italian history to be reelected. In July incumbent Prime Minister Hun Sen was reelected in Cambodia following legislative balloting that was criticized by opposition groups and international observers. Meanwhile Robert Mugabe, the leader of Zimbabwe since 1980, was reelected president in polling that was condemned by Western powers but was praised by neighboring states. One result was that limited economic sanctions against Zimbabwe remained in place after the elections.

The global economy continued its slow recovery in 2013. According to the International Monetary Fund (IMF), after growing 3.2 percent in 2012, the world's economy expanded by an estimated 3.2 percent in 2013. Growth remained constrained in the advanced economies of North America, Western Europe, and Japan, rising by 1.5 percent in 2012 and an estimated 1.2 percent the following year. Within the European Union (EU) combined GDP declined by 0.3 percent in 2012 and was estimated to be flat, with 0 percent growth, in 2013. The EU and IMF were forced to provide another bailout package for Cyprus in 2013, while Croatia became the EU's newest member in July of that year. Economic expansion in emerging markets also slowed, falling from 4.9 percent in 2012 to an estimated 4.5 percent in 2013. China led the emerging economies with growth of 7.7 percent in 2012 and an estimated 7.6 percent in 2013. Latin America and the Caribbean saw growth of 2.9 percent in 2012, slowing to 2.7 percent the next year. The economies of the Middle East, North Africa, Afghanistan, and Pakistan expanded by 4.6 percent in 2012 but only grew by an estimated 2.3 percent in 2013. Sub-Saharan Africa was the one region where growth rates expanded, rising from 4.9 percent to an estimated 5.0 percent.

Governments faced increasing pressure from slow economic growth and rising population figures. By November of 2013 the world's population was estimated to be 7.12 billion by the U.S. Census Bureau. The most populous countries were predominately developing nations: China, 1.35 billion; India, 1.22 billion; the United States, 316 million; Indonesia, 251 million; and Brazil, 201 million. With an aging population fueling fears of a potential worker shortage, China in November 2013 announced it would begin to relax its one-child policy to allow some couples to have a second child.

Climate change remained a major concern, especially among islands and coastal nations. The continued development of superstorms, such as Typhoon Haiyan, which devastated areas of the Philippines and Southeast Asia in November 2013, reinforced concerns over the impact of climate change on global weather patterns. Negotiations at the Conference of the Parties (COP 19) to the UN Framework Convention on Climate Change Kyoto Protocol in Warsaw, Poland, in November resulted in an agreement on the basic principles for a new climate change accord to be finalized in Paris in 2015. However, nongovernmental organizations were critical of the summit for failing to include more specific commitments by states.

***

The handbook first appeared in 1928 when the Council on Foreign Relations published *A Political Handbook of the World*, edited by Malcolm W. Davis and Walter H. Mallory. A more complete publishing history of the handbook can be found on page 1835. This is the ninth edition of the handbook to be published by CQ Press, an imprint of SAGE Publications. The handbook is also available in an enhanced online edition.

Individual country entries are arranged alphabetically, based on their customary names in English. Official names are also provided in both English and the national language or languages. If a country has related territories, they are treated together at the end of the entry on that country—for example, Northern Ireland is treated at the end of the entry on the United Kingdom. In the case of politically divided China and Korea, a discussion of matters pertaining to the nation as a whole is followed by separate entries on the People's Republic of China and Taiwan, in the first instance, and on the Democratic People's Republic of Korea (North Korea) and on the Republic of Korea (South Korea), in the second. We have included one territory without a permanent population and government (Antarctica). At the end of the country entries, we have also included an entry on the Palestinian Authority/Palestinian Liberation Organization (PA/PLO).

The handbook covers significant events and national elections through 2013. This information is incorporated within the regular text wherever possible or in headnotes at the beginning of the country entries for elections that occurred at the end of the year. Each entry begins with information on a country's political status, area, population, major urban centers, languages, currency, and head of state and chief executive. Demographic and economic information is presented in the section titled "The Country," while political background, constitution and government, foreign relations, and current issues are examined in "Government and Politics." "Political Parties and Groups" provides extensive analyses of formal parties, political groupings, and any antigovernment or illegal formations. Each entry ends with an overview of the nation's legislature, a current cabinet list, and a brief intergovernmental representation section, including a membership list of intergovernmental organizations for the respective country.

The intergovernmental organizations selected for treatment are presented in a separate alphabetical sequence based on their official (or, in a few cases, customary) names in English. A list of member countries of most organizations is printed within each entry. This section is limited to groups that have membership composed of more than two states, governing bodies that meet with some degree of regularity, and permanent secretariats or other continuing means for implementing collective decisions.

We gratefully acknowledge the Research Foundation of the State University of New York at Binghamton for its longtime support of this work and its integral role from 1975 to 2005 in maintaining the handbook's legacy of consistently high editorial standards. We are also thankful for the continuing assistance from Binghamton University and its Political Science Department. We would also like to acknowledge the work of the contributing editors, without whom the handbook would not be possible: Brian Beary, Jack Covarrubias, James Frusetta, Elizabeth Hewitt, Stephen Hoadley, Tom Muller, B. Jared Pack, Ann Robertson, and Mark Sedgwick. Once again this year, MTM Publishing was integral to the handbook, and we wish to extend a special thanks to Hilary Poole for her diligence and efforts in bringing the project to fruition. Finally, Tom Lansford expresses his gratitude and love to his muses—Gina, Ella, and Kate.

GOVERNMENTS

AFGHANISTAN

Islamic Republic of Afghanistan

Da Afğānistān Islāmī Jomhoriyat

Political Status: Republic established following military coup that overthrew traditional monarchy in July 1973; constitution of 1977 abolished and the Democratic Republic of Afghanistan announced following left-wing coup of April 27, 1978; successor regime established following coup of December 27, 1979, but effectively overthrown on April 16, 1992; successor regime effectively overthrown by the Taliban in September 1996 but claimed to remain legitimate government; interim administration installed in December 2001 following overthrow of the Taliban; transitional government installed in June 2002; new constitution providing for multiparty democracy approved by a *Loya Jirga* (Grand National Council) on January 4, 2004; permanent government of the renamed Islamic Republic of Afghanistan established by inauguration of the president on December 7, 2004, and the cabinet on December 23.

Area: 249,999 sq. mi. (647,497 sq. km).

Population: 33,463,634 (2012E—UN); 31,108,077 (2013E—U.S. Census). Nomads and refugees in western Pakistan and northern Iraq at one time totaled more than 5 million, many of whom have returned to Afghanistan.

Major Urban Centers (2011E—UN): KABUL (3,052,000), Kandahar (374,200), Herat (410,700), Mazar-i-Sharif (346,500).

Official Languages: Pushtu, Dari (Persian); in addition, the 2004 constitution authorized six minority languages (Baluchi, Nuristani, Pamiri, Pashai, Turkmen, and Uzbek) to serve as official third languages in the areas where the majority speaks them.

Monetary Unit: Afghani (market rate November 1, 2013: 56.77 afghanis = $1US).

President: Hamid KARZAI (nonparty); appointed chair of a new interim administration at the UN-sponsored Bonn Conference on December 5, 2001, and inaugurated on December 22 for a six-month term (for a detailed description of the complicated issue of the leadership of Afghanistan prior to Karzai's inauguration, see the 2000–2002 *Handbook*); elected president of a new transitional government by an "emergency" *Loya Jirga* on June 13, 2002, and inaugurated on June 19 for a term that was initially scheduled not to exceed two years; elected by popular vote on October 9, 2004, and sworn in for a five-year term on December 7. (President Karzai's term was scheduled to expire on May 21, 2009, but new presidential elections were postponed until August 20 due to security concerns and organizational difficulties. The Supreme Court proposed that Karzai remain in his post until the election.) Reelected on August 20, 2009, and inaugurated for a five-year term on November 19 (see Government and politics, below).

Vice Presidents: Mohammad Qasim FAHIM (First Vice President) and Mohammad Karim KHALILI (Second Vice President); elected on August 20, 2010, and inaugurated on November 19 for a term concurrent with that of the president.

THE COUNTRY

Strategically located between the Middle East, Central Asia, and the Indian subcontinent, Afghanistan is a land marked by physical and social diversity. Physically, the landlocked country ranges from the high mountains of the Hindu Kush in the northeast to low-lying deserts along the western border. Pushtuns (alternatively Pashtuns or Pathans) constitute the largest of the population groups at 42 percent, followed by Tajiks, 27 percent, who speak Dari (an Afghan variant of Persian); others include Uzbeks, 9 percent; Hazaras, 9 percent; Aimak, 3 percent; Turkmen, 3 percent; and Baluchis, 2 percent. The Kuchi peoples, primarily Pushtuns and Baluchis who maintain a centuries-old nomadic lifestyle, reportedly number 1.3–1.5 million. Tribal distinctions (except among the Tajiks) may cut across ethnic cleavages, while religion is a major unifying factor. Approximately 98 percent of the people profess Islam (80 percent Sunni and the remainder Shiite [mostly from the Hazara population]). Prior to the Taliban takeover in 1996, women constituted a growing percentage of the paid workforce in urban areas, particularly in health services and education, although female participation in government was minuscule. In the countryside the role of women has for a long time been heavily circumscribed by traditional Islamic fundamentalist strictures, which the Taliban movement also imposed on the urban population. Governments since 2001 have all included women, while a significant number of seats were reserved for women in the National Assembly. However, the status of women had not improved nearly as much as had been anticipated following the fall of the Taliban, with rape, abduction, and forced marriage still commonplace, particularly beyond Kabul. In 2012, the UN, in its annual Gender Index, ranked Afghanistan 141st out of 146 countries in women's equality and opportunity.

Afghanistan is one of the world's poorest countries. Nearly 80 percent of the labor force is engaged in agriculture (largely at a subsistence level). Current government subsidies are aimed at the production of pomegranates, nuts, grapes, apricots, and saffron for export. The country's extensive mineral deposits are largely unexploited, except for natural gas. Industry is virtually nonexistent. One major source of income is opium; as much as 90 percent of the world's heroin reportedly originates in Afghanistan. About 12 percent of the population reportedly was engaged in opium activities, valued at about $1.4 billion annually, compared to "legal" exports valued at less than $600 million. Most of the opium production is currently concentrated in the south and southwest. Government poppy eradication efforts have been moderately successful elsewhere, although many former poppy farmers have reportedly turned to cultivating cannabis, of which Afghanistan is now also one of the world's leading exporters. After declining between 2007 and 2010, opium production rose significantly from 2011 into 2013.

The rate of childhood death (mostly from preventable diseases) is among the highest in the world although it has declined by a third since the fall of the Taliban. The illiteracy rate is estimated to be more than 60 percent. Nearly all girls and two-thirds of boys reportedly did not attend school under the Taliban regime, the former in large part because of the Taliban policy against education for women. Life expectancy is only 45 years, an estimated 50 percent of the population lives in poverty, and 75 percent of the population lacks access to safe water. In addition, much of the country has inadequate electrical grids, sewerage, roads, and other public services. Economic development is hampered by the fact that much of the nation's wealth is concentrated in the hands of powerful warlords backed by private militias.

Although private foreign investors remained leery of ongoing security problems and perceived deep-seated corruption at all levels of authority, in general, the transitional government received praise for its "crisis management" during 2002–2004 (for an overview of Afghanistan's economy prior to 2001, please see the 2011 *Handbook*). Following its installation in late 2004, the new permanent administration pledged to pursue long-term stability and economic expansion through the promotion of free-market activity. However, the government continued to rely on foreign aid for 90 percent of its budget and on foreign troops for its security.

A survey in 2006 indicated that oil and gas reserves might be significantly larger than anticipated, while deposits of coal, copper, gold, gemstones, iron ore, and marble also awaited exploitation. Further studies in 2010 revealed that Afghanistan may have up to $1 trillion in mineral wealth, mainly gold, cobalt, and lithium. However, private investment slumped by 50 percent in 2007 as a consequence of the Taliban insurgency, which continued to rely on "taxes" on opium for much of its financing.

The IMF warned in 2008 that corruption was rampant in many sectors, particularly the judiciary. The IMF also criticized the government for failing to enact tax reforms deemed necessary to support the "anemic" private sector. However, a state-owned Chinese company announced plans to invest $3 billion over the next five years to exploit what was believed to be the second largest copper deposit in the world.

An Afghan Support Conference in June 2008 pledged an additional $15–20 billion for development, although participants acknowledged that much aid to date had been wasted. In January 2010 the IMF announced that through the Heavily Indebted Poor Countries (HIPC) initiative, 96 percent of Afghanistan's external debt, or $11.6 billion, would be forgiven. By 2010 the United States had emerged as Afghanistan's main trading partner, followed by India and Pakistan.

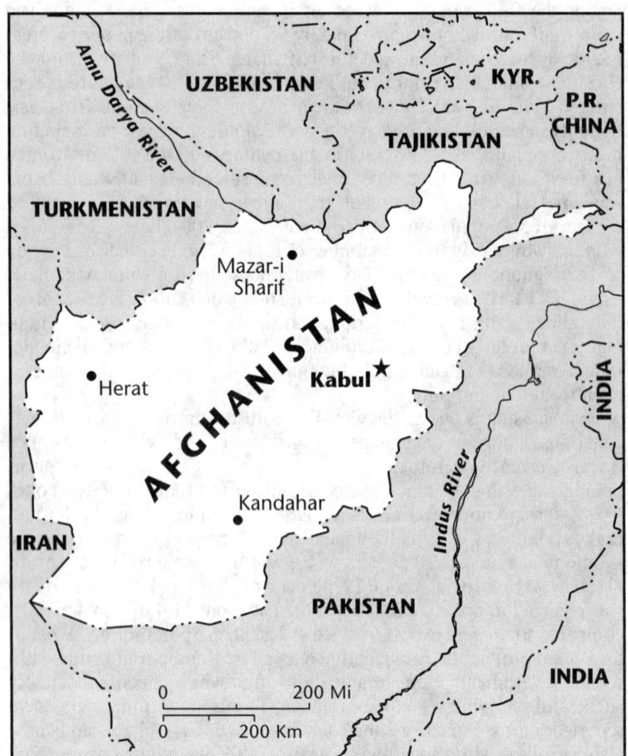

The IMF reported that annual GDP growth between 2009 and 2011 averaged 12.6 percent, while inflation grew by a yearly average of 10.5 percent. Meanwhile, the government estimated that more than 2 million people remained unemployed as economic revitalization efforts suffered from an intensified insurgency by the Taliban. The 2013 UN Human Development Index ranked Afghanistan 175th out of 186 countries in terms of quality-of-life measurements such as education, life expectancy, standard of living, and literacy. In 2012 GDP rose by 10.2 percent, while inflation was 4.4 percent, and GDP per capita was $622.

GOVERNMENT AND POLITICS

Political background. The history of Afghanistan reflects the interplay of a number of political forces, the most important of which traditionally were the monarchy, the army, religious and tribal leaders, and foreign powers. The existence of the country as a political entity is normally dated from 1747, when the Persians were overthrown and Ahmad Shah DURANI established the foundations of an Afghan empire. His successors, however, proved relatively ineffective in the face of dynastic and tribal conflicts coupled in the 19th century with increasingly frequent incursions by the Russians and British. The latter wielded decisive influence during the reign of ABDUR RAHMAN Khan and in 1898 imposed acceptance of the Durand line, which established the country's southern and eastern borders but which, by ignoring the geographic distribution of the Pushtun tribes, also laid the foundation for subsequent conflict over establishment of a Pushtunistan state. Emir AMANULLAH succeeded in forcing the British to relinquish control over Afghan foreign affairs in 1919 and attempted to implement such reforms as modern education, women's rights, and increased taxation before being forced to abdicate under pressure from traditional leaders.

The outbreak of World War II severely damaged the economy: markets were lost, and access to imports and credit was cut off. Subsequently, dissent among intellectuals and failure to resolve the Pushtunistan issue led to a crisis of leadership. Prince Sardar Mohammad DAOUD, designated prime minister in 1953, succeeded in obtaining economic aid from both the United States and the Soviet Union, while modernization of the army helped to alleviate the threat posed by tribes hostile to the government. Politically, however, Daoud was autocratic, ignoring the legislature, jailing his critics, and suppressing opposition publications. His dismissal in 1963 was followed by a series of moves toward a more modern political system, including the promulgation of a new constitution in 1964 and the holding of parliamentary elections in 1965. Nevertheless, problems were subsequently encountered, including recurrent famine; a worsening financial situation; increased restiveness on the part of the small, educated middle class; and a sense of impatience with civilian rule. The distress led in 1973 to a military coup, the overthrow of the monarch (Mohammad ZAHIR SHAH), and the return of Daoud as president of a newly proclaimed republic.

On April 27, 1978, in the wake of unrest stemming from the assassination of a prominent opposition leader in Kabul, the Daoud regime was overthrown in a left-wing coup led by the deputy air force commander, Col. Abdul KHADIR. On April 30 a newly constituted Revolutionary Council designated Nur Mohammad TARAKI, secretary general of the formerly outlawed People's Democratic Party of Afghanistan (PDPA), as its president and announced the establishment of the Democratic Republic of Afghanistan, with Taraki as prime minister. On March 27, 1979, Taraki yielded the office of prime minister to party hard-liner Hafizullah AMIN while remaining titular head of state by virtue of his presidency of the Revolutionary Council.

It was officially announced on September 16, 1979, that the PDPA Central Committee had unanimously elected Amin as its secretary general, and shortly thereafter the Revolutionary Council designated him to succeed Taraki as president. While Kabul radio reported on October 9 that Taraki had died after "a severe and prolonged illness," foreign observers generally assumed that the former president had succumbed on September 17 to wounds received three days earlier during an armed confrontation at the presidential palace. Subsequent reports suggested that a Soviet-backed effort by Taraki to remove the widely disliked Amin as part of a conciliatory policy toward rebel Muslim tribesmen had, in effect, backfired. Such suspicions intensified when the Soviet Union airlifted some 4,000–5,000 troops to Kabul on December 25–26, which resulted in Amin's death and replacement on December 27 by his longtime PDPA rival, Babrak KARMAL, theretofore living under Soviet protection in Czechoslovakia. Karmal proved scarcely more acceptable to the rebels than Amin, however, his regime being supported primarily by the continued presence of Soviet military personnel (estimated to number more than 110,000 by mid-1982). During the ensuing three years, the level of Soviet military involvement increased because of continued resistance throughout the country by mujahidin (holy warriors) guerrillas (funded in part by the United States), operating largely from rural bases and supplied from Pakistan, where more than 3 million Afghans had sought refuge. However, in 1985 a semblance of constitutional government was restored. A partially elected *Loya Jirga* was convened on April 23, the first such assemblage in eight years. It promptly endorsed the Soviet presence, while elections for local village councils were held from August through October, despite disruptions attributable to mujahidin activity. Based in Peshawar, Pakistan, the seven leading mujahidin groups formed an Islamic Alliance of Afghan Holy Warriors (*Ittehad-i-Islami Afghan Mujahidin*) in May 1985 to coordinate resistance to the Moscow-backed regime in Kabul.

On May 4, 1986, after a visit to the Soviet Union for what were described as medical reasons, Karmal stepped down as PDPA secretary general in favor of the former head of the state intelligence service, Mohammad NAJIBULLAH (Najib). On November 20 Karmal asked to be relieved of his remaining government and party posts, being succeeded as head of the Revolutionary Council by Haji Mohammad CHAMKANI, who was, however, designated only on an acting basis.

In December 1986 the PDPA Central Committee endorsed Najibullah's plan for "national reconciliation," calling for a cease-fire, political liberalization, and the formation of a coalition government. Although the seven-party mujahidin alliance refused to negotiate and intense fighting continued, the government promoted its democratization campaign in 1987 by legalizing additional political parties, drafting a new constitution providing for an elected national legislature, and conducting local elections. However, in practical terms there was little challenge to Najibullah's consolidation of power: the Revolutionary Council on September 30, 1987, unanimously elected him as its president, and on November 30 the *Loya Jirga,* having approved the new constitution, named him as the first president of the republic ("Democratic" having been deleted from the country's name).

On April 14, 1988, Afghanistan, Pakistan, the Soviet Union, and the United States concluded a series of agreements providing for a Soviet troop withdrawal within one year. Elections to the new National Assembly (*Meli Shura*) were held the same month, although the government was unable to convince the mujahidin to participate. On May 26 the Revolutionary Council dissolved itself in deference to the assembly, and, in a further effort by the government to reduce the appearance of PDPA dominance, Mohammad Hasan SHARQ, who was not a PDPA member, was appointed chair of the Council of Ministers to replace Soltan Ali KESHTMAND.

The Soviet troop withdrawal was completed on February 15, 1989, prompting significant political moves by both the government and mujahidin. Najibullah quickly dropped all non-PDPA members from the Council of Ministers; concurrently, a state of emergency was declared, and a new 20-member Supreme Council for the Defense of the Homeland was created to serve, under Najibullah's leadership, as the "supreme military and political organ" for the duration of the emergency. On February 21 Keshtmand effectively resumed the duties of prime minister through his appointment as chair of the Council of Ministers' Executive Committee.

For their part, the mujahidin vowed to continue their resistance until an Islamic administration was installed in Kabul. On February 24, 1989, the rebels proclaimed a "free Muslim state" under an Afghan Interim Government (AIG) headed by Imam Sibghatullah MOJADEDI as president and Abdul Rasul SAYAF as prime minister. However, the widespread belief that the rebels would quickly vanquish the Najibullah regime proved incorrect, despite two reported coup plots in December and a nearly successful uprising led (in apparent collusion with rebel fundamentalist Gulbuddin HEKMATYAR) by the hard-line defense minister, Lt. Gen. Shahnawaz TANAI, in March 1990.

On May 7, 1990, President Najibullah named Fazil Haq KHALIQYAR, a former minister-advisor in the Executive Council, to succeed Keshtmand as prime minister. Half of the members of the cabinet subsequently named by Khaliqyar were described as politically "neutral." On May 28–29 the *Loya Jirga* convened in Kabul to reiterate its commitment to private sector development and to ratify a number of reform-oriented constitutional amendments.

On May 27, 1991, Najibullah announced that his government was prepared to observe a cease-fire with the mujahidin to permit implementation of a peace plan advanced by UN secretary general Javier Pérez de Cuéllar that would entail an end to external involvement in Afghan affairs and provide for nationwide balloting to choose a new government. Two months later, the AIG stated that it "had recognized positive points" in the UN proposal. Consequently, on September 1 the United States and the Soviet Union declared that they were halting arms supplies to the combatants. Trilateral discussions among U.S., Soviet, and mujahidin representatives were subsequently held on the transfer of power to an interim regime that would oversee elections within two years. The fundamentalists, however, continued to call for Najibullah's immediate removal and the scheduling of an earlier poll.

On March 19, 1992, mujahidin hard-liners rejected an offer by Najibullah to yield effective authority to an interim administration, reiterating their demand that he resign. By early April, on the other hand, a pronounced shift in the balance of power had emerged in the strategic northern city of Mazar-i-Sharif, where local militias were forming alliances with moderate mujahidin units. The realignment cut across both government and insurgent groupings, inaugurating a new cleavage between southern Pushtun fundamentalists led by Hekmatyar and non-Pushtun northerners under the command of Ahmed Shah MASOUD.

On April 16, 1992, Najibullah submitted his resignation and sought refuge at the UN office in Kabul after four of his top generals had deserted to Masoud. Within a week, the eastern city of Jalalabad became the last provincial capital to fall to joint mujahidin, militia, and former government forces (including supporters of both Hekmatyar and Masoud), who thereupon initiated a successful assault on Kabul. On April 24 the leaders of six rebel groups met in Peshawar, Pakistan, to announce the formation of a 51-member Islamic Jihad Council (IJC), headed by Imam Mojadedi, to assume power in the capital. After two months the IJC was to be replaced by an interim administration under Burhanuddin RABBANI, with Hekmatyar as prime minister and Masoud as defense minister. However, Hekmatyar instead launched an attack on his erstwhile allies. In three days of heavy fighting, Hekmatyar's troops were unable to defeat the Masoud coalition, and on April 28 Mojadedi arrived to proclaim the formation of an Islamic republic. Meanwhile, Hekmatyar's forces continued to ring Kabul's southern and eastern outskirts, threatening to launch another offensive if Masoud did not break with the non-mujahidin northerners (particularly with Gen. Abdul Rashid DOSTAM, an Uzbek, who had served under the former Communist regime). Subsequently, on May 25, Masoud and Hekmatyar agreed to halt hostilities and hold elections in six months. Even while they were talking, however, clashes were reported between units loyal to Hekmatyar and Dostam. In early June, fighting also broke out between Iranian-backed Hazara Shiites and Saudi Arabian–backed Sunni units loyal to Masoud. Reportedly the Shiites had demanded a minimum of eight ministerial posts in the Mojadedi government.

Although initially indicating that he wished to continue as acting president beyond his two-month mandate, Mojadedi stepped down on June 28, 1992, in favor of Rabbani. Concurrently, Hekmatyar agreed to the appointment of his deputy, Ustad FARID, as prime minister of an interim cabinet. Formally invested on July 6, Farid was forced from office a month later, after heavy fighting had erupted in Kabul between pro- and anti-Rabbani groups, including a massive artillery bombardment by Hekmatyar's forces that caused more than 1,800 deaths.

On October 31, 1992, a Leadership Council, self-appointed five months earlier and chaired by Rabbani, extended the interim president's mandate beyond its four-month limit, permitting Rabbani to convene a Council of Resolution and Settlement in late December that elected him to a two-year term as head of state. Thereafter, Kabul was the scene of renewed fighting, culminating in a peace accord concluded by Rabbani and Hekmatyar in Islamabad, Pakistan, on March 7, 1993. The pact was endorsed by all but one of the major mujahidin leaders. On March 8 Hekmatyar accepted appointment as prime minister, although differences immediately arose over the assignment of portfolios. On May 24, after further fighting in Kabul, a new cease-fire was announced, under which Masoud agreed to resign as defense minister and turn the ministry over to a tripartite commission. The principal obstacle having been overcome, a coalition cabinet was reportedly sworn in at an undisclosed location on June 17. However, the new administration was never effectively implemented in view of continued conflict between forces loyal to Rabbani and Hekmatyar, with General Dostam switching sides to join forces with Hekmatyar in fighting in Kabul and elsewhere in early 1994.

In late June 1994 Rabbani's troops succeeded in sweeping most Hekmatyar and Dostam units from the capital, and in mid-July the Organization of the Islamic Conference (OIC) reported that all parties had agreed to a peace process. Concurrently, however, reports circulated that Pakistan's Inter-Services Intelligence (ISI) was supplying large quantities of arms and ammunition to Hekmatyar, who commenced a systematic bombardment of Kabul after the Supreme Court had extended Rabbani's presidential mandate for an additional six months without granting a similar extension of Hekmatyar's prime ministerial mandate.

On August 28, 1994, Maulawi Mohammad Nabi MOHAMMAD of the moderate Islamic Revolutionary Movement was named chair of a *Loya Jirga* convening commission in preparation for national elections. On November 6 Rabbani and his supporters accepted a modified version of a UN peace plan that called for a commission on which the principal mujahidin units would have equal representation, with Rabbani subsequently announcing his willingness to step down as soon as "reliable mechanisms for a transfer of power" were in place.

Meanwhile the balance of power within Afghanistan was disrupted by an incursion of several thousand young Taliban (Islamic students) supported by Pakistan's fundamentalist *Jamiat-ul-Ulema-e-Islam* (Assembly of Islamic Clergy) and led by Maulana Fazlur RAHMAN. In November 1994 Taliban forces captured the city of Kandahar and initiated an antidrug crusade throughout the opium-growing province of Helmand. The success of the new group appeared to reflect a major shift by Pakistan's ISI away from Hekmatyar and gave rise to speculation that the new element in Afghanistan's domestic turmoil might force a truce between Hekmatyar and Rabbani.

After winning control of a third of the country's provinces, the Taliban by late February 1995 had driven Hekmatyar from his base in Charosyab, ten miles south of Kabul, and proceeded to advance on the capital. However, on March 11 the student militia suffered its first major defeat at the hands of Rabbani and Masoud and was subsequently forced to yield Charosyab to government forces. Routed in the east, the Taliban launched an offensive against the western city of Herat. That initiative also failed when Masoud dispatched a number of fighter-bombers and some 2,000 troops to aid in the city's defense. Further Taliban defeats followed, while the anti-Rabbani mujahidin front collapsed with Hekmatyar's withdrawal to the eastern city of Jalalabad and Dostam's unwillingness to commit his forces to battle.

On June 9, 1995, a truce was declared between government and Taliban forces. However, the Taliban mounted a major offensive in September that yielded the capture of Herat. On November 7 President Rabbani offered to resign if the Taliban agreed to a cease-fire and "foreign interference" (presumably by Pakistan in support of the Taliban) were to end. Thereafter, fighting intensified in the vicinity of Kabul, followed by peace talks in which the government succeeded in reaching an accommodation with Hekmatyar (although not with his erstwhile mujahidin allies) providing for joint military action against the Taliban and for governmental power-sharing. Under a peace accord signed on May 24, 1996, the supporters of Rabbani and Hekmatyar undertook to cooperate on the organization of new elections and to establish "genuine Islamic government," with Rabbani continuing as president and Hekmatyar being restored to the premiership. In accordance with the agreement, Hekmatyar was formally reappointed prime minister on June 26. Among the first actions of the restored prime minister were the closure of cinemas and the banning of music on radio and television on Sundays, on the grounds that such activities were contrary to Islamic precepts. However, underscoring the potential for a new round of conflict, Hekmatyar's former anti-Rabbani mujahidin allies suspended Hekmatyar from membership of the coordination council established by the four main fundamentalist movements in 1994 under the leadership of former interim president Sibghatullah Mojadedi (leader of the National Liberation Front).

More ominously for the new government, the predominantly Sunni Taliban guerrillas, still strongly backed by Pakistan, continued to make military advances in July and August 1996, and by early September they controlled 18 of the country's 30 provinces. The eastern city of Jalalabad, the country's second largest, was captured on September 11, whereupon Taliban forces pursued retreating government troops to Kabul and mounted a new onslaught on the capital. After heavy fighting on the eastern side of the city, resistance crumbled, and the government fled. By September 25, Taliban units were in complete control of Kabul, where on September 27 a six-member Provisional Council was installed under the leadership of Mullah Mohammad RABBANI (not related to the ousted president). Meanwhile, Mullah Mohammad OMAR (the spiritual leader of the Taliban) assumed the status of de facto head of state. Among the first acts of the new rulers was to seize Najibullah, the former president, from the UN compound in which he had lived since April 1992 and to execute him in summary fashion, together with his brother Shahpur AHMADZAY (who had served as his security chief) and two aides. Mullah Rabbani justified the executions on the grounds that the former president had been "against Islam, a criminal, and a Communist."

After a period of disorganization, the ousted government of Burhanuddin Rabbani relocated to northern Afghanistan, where a military alliance of the regrouped government troops under Masoud's command, the forces loyal to General Dostam, and Hazara fighters served to block the Taliban offensive. The military situation remained effectively stalemated until May 1997, when Gen. Abdul Malik PAHLAWAN, who had apparently ousted General Dostam as leader of the National Front forces, invited the Taliban troops into the alliance's stronghold in Mazar-i-Sharif. However, just as the Taliban takeover of the entire country seemed imminent, General Pahlawan's forces suddenly turned on the Taliban, killing, according to subsequent reports, some 2,000–3,000 Taliban fighters. Anti-Taliban groups, including, significantly, Hekmatyar's Islamic Party, subsequently coalesced as the United National Islamic Front for the Salvation of Afghanistan (UNIFSA) and retained effective control of the north for the rest of the year. Collaterally, General Dostam, who had fled the country in June after General Pahlawan's "coup," returned to Afghanistan in late October to wrest control of the Uzbek forces from Pahlawan, who apparently fled to Turkmenistan. Meanwhile, Mullah Omar was named emir of the Islamic Emirate of Afghanistan that was proclaimed by the Taliban on October 26, 1997.

In early 1998 the Taliban and UNIFSA appeared willing to consider a negotiated settlement, agreeing in principle to establish a joint council of religious scholars to assist in the process. However, the Taliban olive branch did not extend to the Hazara Shiite community in central Afghanistan, where the regime was enforcing an economic blockade that was said to be threatening famine. Consequently, despite UN, U.S., and OIC mediation efforts, the peace talks quickly broke down, and heavy fighting resumed. The Taliban launched what its supporters hoped would be a final offensive to secure total control of the country in mid-July, and Mazar-i-Sharif fell from UNIFSA hands in mid-August. However, as Taliban forces approached the northern borders, neighboring countries sent troops to defend their own territory from possible Taliban incursions and also provided assistance to the beleaguered UNIFSA fighters. In addition, Iran, angered over the killing of eight of its diplomats during the recent fighting and concerned over the threat to the Afghan Shiite community, amassed some 250,000 soldiers along its border with Afghanistan, raising fears of a full-blown regional war. Further complicating matters, on August 20 U.S. cruise missiles struck camps in Afghanistan believed to be part of the alleged terrorist network run by Osama BIN LADEN. (The attack was ordered as retaliation for the bombing of U.S. embassies in Kenya and Tanzania earlier in the month, in which Washington suspected bin Laden's followers to have been involved.) Bin Laden's presence in Afghanistan subsequently proved to be a barrier to Taliban attempts to gain additional international recognition. However, after the government rejected Western calls for bin Laden's extradition, an Afghan court in November ruled that the United States had not produced evidence of his complicity in the embassy bombings and permitted him to remain in the country as long as he or his followers did not use it as a base for terrorist activity.

In July 1999 U.S. president Bill Clinton imposed economic sanctions on Afghanistan as the result of the Taliban's unwillingness to turn over bin Laden. Four months later, at Washington's urging, the UN Security Council directed UN members to freeze overseas assets of the Taliban government and to halt all flights to Afghanistan to pressure Kabul regarding bin Laden as well as to protest the perceived mistreatment of women, other human rights abuses, and ongoing opium production. (One correspondent for the *Christian Science Monitor* described the Taliban as having achieved the "rare feat of provoking the hostility of all five permanent members of the Security Council." China, for example, reportedly expressed concern about Taliban influence on Islamic unrest within its borders, while Russia went so far as to threaten to bomb Afghanistan if Kabul provided support to Chechen rebels or Islamist insurgents in neighboring Central Asian countries.) For their part, Taliban leaders appeared to remain preoccupied with attempting to secure control of the approximately 10 percent of the country in the northeast still in the hands of opposition forces. Major Taliban offenses were launched in the summers of 1999 and 2000, each being repulsed (after heavy fighting and large-scale civilian dislocation) by fighters, now referenced as the Northern Alliance, led by Ahmed Shah Masoud. Consequently, in September 2000 discussion was reported on yet another peace plan, under which Masoud would have been given special administrative powers in an autonomous northeastern region.

Negotiations between the Northern Alliance and the Taliban continued for the rest of 2000; however, they ultimately failed, and sporadic heavy fighting ensued in the first part of 2001. Meanwhile, the UN rejected a suggestion from the Taliban that bin Laden be tried in an Islamic country by Islamic religious leaders. Further complicating matters for the Taliban, Mullah Mohammad Rabbani, by then routinely referred to as chair of the Taliban's "council of ministers," died on April 15 of natural causes. Although he had been the architect of many of the harsh strictures imposed on the population by the Taliban, Rabbani had been viewed by the international community as more approachable than most of the other Taliban leaders. He was also generally well respected within Afghanistan for the prominent role he had played while a member of the Islamic Party in the mujahidin war against the Soviets. Most of Rabbani's duties were assumed by the vice chair of the ministerial council, Mohammed Hassan AKHUND, but no formal appointment to the chair was announced.

The Taliban launched a major attack against the Northern Alliance in June 2001 and once again appeared dedicated to the pursuit of a final, complete military victory. However, such hopes were irrevocably compromised by the terrorist attacks on September 11 in the United States, which the George W. Bush administration quickly determined to be the work of bin Laden's al-Qaida. Washington immediately demanded that bin Laden be turned over for prosecution or else military action would be initiated to remove him by force from Afghanistan. Intense debate was reported within the Taliban leadership on the issue, and efforts were made to forge a compromise under which, for example, bin Laden might be tried in a third country. However, President Bush declared the U.S. terms to be "nonnegotiable," and Mullah Omar finally decided that the Taliban would take a stand in defense of its "guest." Consequently, after having secured broad coalition support for the action, the United States launched Operation Enduring Freedom on October 7 against al-Qaida and Taliban targets.

Heavy bombing by U.S. aircraft and cruise missiles quickly shattered the minimal infrastructure available to the Taliban military, while Omar's call on October 10 to the rest of the Muslim world for assistance in countering the U.S. invasion elicited little response. The attention of the military campaign shifted later in the month to bombing al-Qaida and Taliban troops in the north to support a ground assault by the Northern Alliance. After a disorganized start, the anti-Taliban forces, substantially rearmed and resupplied by the United States and its allies, assumed an offensive posture at the end of October and drove toward the capital with few setbacks, as many warlords previously aligned with the Taliban defected to the Northern Alliance. The first big prize, Mazar-i-Sharif, fell on November 9, and Kabul was surrounded by November 11. The swiftness of the Taliban collapse apparently surprised coalition military planners, and confusion reigned over how control of the capital would be achieved, U.S. policymakers being aware of the complicated political overtones involved in the establishment of a new Afghan government. Despite apparent U.S. wishes to the contrary, the Northern Alliance moved into Kabul November 12–13, and the administration of Burhanuddin Rabbani announced it was reassuming authority, at least over the territory now controlled by the Northern Alliance.

Formal definition of the status of the Rabbani administration and governmental responsibility throughout the country overall remained ill-defined following the fall of Kabul, pending the results of a UN-sponsored conference that convened in Bonn, Germany, on November 27, 2001, to negotiate a power-sharing, post-Taliban government that would bridge the nation's myriad cleavages. In addition to UNIFSA/Northern Alliance officials, attendees at the conference included representatives from the so-called Rome Group (supporters of Afghanistan's former king, Mohammad Zahir Shah), the Peshawar Group (Afghan exiles who had been living in Pakistan), and a delegation of pro-Iranian refugees and exiles who had been centered in Cyprus. No Taliban officials were invited to participate.

Initial negotiations at the Bonn Conference proved difficult regarding the issues of proposed international peacekeepers for Afghanistan (opposed by the Northern Alliance) and the selection of the head of the planned interim government. A collapse of the talks appeared possible over the latter when it became apparent that the choice would not be Rabbani or the 84-year-old ex-king. However, the conference on December 3, 2001, agreed upon Hamid KARZAI, an obscure former deputy minister with U.S. backing. Karzai was formally appointed on December 5 as chair of an interim administration that would eventually include a 29-member cabinet that had been carefully crafted to include as broad an ethnic base as possible. The Bonn Declaration that concluded the conference on December 5 authorized the interim government for only six months, by which time an emergency *Loya Jirga* was to have established a new transitional government to prepare for free elections of a permanent government. The conference participants also agreed that a UN peacekeeping force would be stationed in Kabul, although details on its mandate and size were left for further negotiation.

Meanwhile, as plans for the installation of the interim administration proceeded, the military campaign against the remaining Taliban and al-Qaida forces continued unabated. After a sustained U.S. bombing campaign, the Taliban surrendered its last remaining stronghold in Kandahar to the UNIFSA/Northern Alliance on December 7, 2001, although Mullah Omar and a number of Taliban ministers escaped capture, perhaps as part of controversial secret negotiations. The air assault subsequently focused on the cave complexes in Tora Bora, southwest of Jalalabad, where it was estimated that as many as 1,700 al-Qaida and Taliban fighters may have died before the complex was overrun. However, bin Laden escaped, fleeing, apparently, to the remote tribal areas across the border in Pakistan.

Karzai and his interim cabinet were inaugurated on December 22, 2001, in a ceremony in Kabul that featured a role for Rabbani as "outgoing president." Notable attendees included General Dostam, who had earlier threatened to boycott the proceedings because he did not believe the Uzbek community was sufficiently represented in the government. On December 26 Dostam accepted a post as vice chair of the interim administration and deputy defense minister.

On January 10, 2002, final agreement was reached on the deployment of an International Security Assistance Force (ISAF), directed by the UN to assist in providing security in Kabul and surrounding areas but not to become involved outside that region. In May the mandate of the ISAF (comprising some 4,500 troops from 19 countries at that point) was extended for another six months, some Western leaders reportedly pressing for its eventual extension to other areas of the country. Meanwhile, U.S. ground forces (upward of 7,000 strong) remained in Afghanistan to conduct mopping-up activities against remnants of the Taliban and al-Qaida.

Former king Zahir Shah, who had returned to Afghanistan in April, was given the honor of opening the emergency *Loya Jirga* in Kabul on June 12, 2002. On June 13 Karzai received about 80 percent of the votes against two minor candidates in the balloting for president of the new transitional government, all potential major opponents (including Zahir Shah) having removed themselves from contention. On its final day (June 19) the *Loya Jirga* also endorsed, by a show of hands, the partial cabinet announced by Karzai. However, the council adjourned without having made a decision on the makeup of a proposed transitional legislature. The transitional government was authorized to hold power for up to two years, with a constitutional *Loya Jirga* to be convened in approximately 18 months to adopt a new constitution that would provide the framework for new elections by June 2004.

In April 2003 President Karzai appointed a 33-member constitutional commission that in November drafted a new basic law calling for a multiparty system headed by a president with broad powers and a mostly elected bicameral legislature. A *Loya Jirga* approved the constitution, with modifications, on January 4, 2004 (see Constitution and government, below, for details). Although both presidential and legislative elections were initially scheduled for June 2004, they were postponed due to difficulties in completing voter registration and other electoral arrangements. Presidential balloting was finally held on October 9, with Karzai winning in the first round of balloting with 55.4 percent of the vote. Authority was formally transferred from the transitional administration upon Karzai's inauguration on December 7; Karzai appointed a new "reconstruction" cabinet on December 23. Karzai pledged to combat the "mortal threat" of drug production and trafficking, to fight systemic poverty, and to promote "governmental accountability." Toward those ends, his new cabinet appeared to rely more heavily on technocrats than had his previous administration, although critics noted that most "power portfolios" remained in the hands of Pushtuns.

Meanwhile, a resurgence in the second half of the year of Taliban guerrilla attacks on U.S. and government forces killed hundreds. Karzai also had to contend with outbreaks of fighting between various warlords' militias, many of whom were resisting the new UN/Afghan demobilization and disarmament campaign. When Karzai dropped Vice President Mohammad Qasim FAHIM (a northern commander) as a running mate for the 2004 presidential campaign, many of the northern tribal leaders threw their support to Mohammad Yunos QANUNI, who finished second in the balloting with 16.3 percent of the vote. As a result, the election revealed a continued north/south divide that still threatened national unity.

Balloting for the new National Assembly was held in the last quarter of 2005. The successful candidates to the House of the People (*Wolesi Jirga*) represented a broad spectrum of the population, from mujahidin (including deeply conservative tribal leaders) to communists to reformists to former members of the Taliban. Most of the proposed members of the new cabinet were installed on May 2, 2006. However, five positions remained unfilled until August 7 due to objections within the *Wolesi Jirga* (dominated by conservatives) to the initial appointees. Friction between the legislative and executive branches intensified in May 2007 when the *Wolesi Jirga* attempted to impeach two of Karzai's ministers in the wake of the forced repatriation to Afghanistan of Afghan refugees in Iran. The Supreme Court subsequently ruled that the impeachments were invalid.

In the August 20, 2009, presidential balloting, President Hamid Karzai was initially credited with a first-round victory with 54.6 percent of the vote. However, runner-up Abdullah ABDULLAH of the United National Front (UNF) alleged that massive fraud had occurred, and most international observers concluded that the poll had at least been significantly flawed. An audit reduced Karzai's total to 49.67 percent, and a runoff with Abdullah was scheduled for November 7. However, declaring that fraud was again inevitable, Abdullah withdrew from the runoff (see Current issues, below). Karzai was declared the winner and inaugurated for another five-year term on November 19, along with First Vice President Mohammad Qasim FAHIM and Vice President Mohammad Karim KHALILI. Karzai subsequently proposed a new cabinet on January 2, 2010, although only 14 of his choices were initially approved by the legislature. The rest were appointed on an acting basis. Reportedly, many of those who were rejected had connections with warlords who had been supportive of Karzai's reelection.

In March 2010 the legislature defeated a proposal by Karzai that would have granted the president the power to appoint all members of the election commission. Legislative elections were held on September 18. Disputed balloting led to the disqualification of a number of candidates. In August 2011, the Independent Electoral Commission (IEC) reinstated 9 of the 21 members of the lower house whose victories had been suspended.

In September 2012 Karzai announced the replacement or reassignment of 10 of the nation's governors. Meanwhile, in October, the IEC announced that presidential elections would be held on April 5, 2014, along with concurrent balloting for provisional councils.

Constitution and government. Following their takeover of power in Kabul in September 1996, the Taliban quickly installed a six-member Provisional Council in Kabul that subsequently grew in stages into a full-fledged Council of Ministers. However, government decision-making authority appeared to remain in the hands of a small Taliban consultative council in Kandahar, the headquarters of the movement's spiritual leader (and emir of the Islamic Emirate of Afghanistan proclaimed in October 1997), Mullah Mohammad Omar, who served, among other things, as de facto head of state and commander in chief of the armed forces.

The constitution approved in January 2004 provided for a Western-style democracy with a strong central government headed by a popularly elected president (limited to two five-year terms) and a National Assembly (see Legislature, below, for details). The *Loya Jirga* (comprising the current members of the assembly and the chairs of the proposed elected provincial and district councils) was institutionalized as the "highest manifestation of the people of Afghanistan" and given full responsibility to amend the constitution, prosecute the president if necessary, and "make decisions relating to independence, national sovereignty, territorial integrity, and other supreme interests of the country." The new basic law enshrined Islam as the state religion but guaranteed freedom for other religions. Equal rights were guaranteed for men and women, as were freedoms of expression and association (see the introductory text under Political Parties and Groups, below, for details). Provisions were also made for an independent human rights commission and an independent judiciary headed by a Supreme Court comprising presidential appointees subject to confirmation by the lower house of the assembly. (The constitution called for a committee to be established to oversee the "implementation" of a Constitutional Court, but no action had been taken in that regard as of early 2009, despite regular confrontation between the legislature and the government on constitutional issues.)

The new constitution authorized the establishment of the Islamic Transitional State of Afghanistan pending what were expected to be simultaneous presidential and legislative elections. However, in view of the subsequent delay in holding assembly balloting, the transitional state was declared to have concluded with the inauguration in December 2004 of President Karzai to head the administration of the newly renamed Islamic Republic of Afghanistan. The process of "institution-creating" culminated in the election of provincial councils and the lower house of the new National Assembly on September 18, 2005 (see Legislature, below, for details).

Critics have become increasingly vocal recently in challenging the basic law, with its enshrinement of a strong presidential system, as "inappropriate" for dealing with the country's myriad ethnic and regional divisions. Northern groups that spearheaded the overthrow of the Taliban in particular have called for decentralization and reduction of presidential authority in favor of a parliamentary system.

Reporters Without Borders initially described the development of a degree of press freedom as one of the "few achievements" of the Afghan government following the fall of the Taliban in 2001. However, the journalism watchdog described the situation in Afghanistan as "fragile" in view of the deteriorating security situation and pressure from conservative elements inside and outside the government. In 2013 the group rated Afghanistan as 128th out of 179 countries in terms of freedom of the press.

In mid-2007, President Karzai declined to sign a new media law that was viewed in some circles as presenting curbs on journalists. A revised media law was adopted by the legislature in 2008, and press advocates indicated a greater degree of support for the new version than for the previous one. However, Karzai did not sign that measure either. Critics suggested that the administration was interested in instituting stronger governmental control of the media than the legislation would permit. In 2009, the government commission that oversees the media reportedly filed charges against several newspaper journalists and television stations for "anti-Islamic" reporting or broadcasting.

Foreign relations. Afghan foreign policy historically reflected neutrality and nonalignment, but by the mid-1970s Soviet economic and military aid had become paramount. After the April 1978 coup, the Taraki government, while formally committed to a posture of "positive nonalignment," solidified relations with the Soviet Union. Following what was, for all practical purposes, Soviet occupation of the country in late 1979, the Karmal regime asserted that Soviet troops had been "invited" because of the "present aggressive actions of the enemies of Afghanistan" (apparently an allusion to the United States, China, Pakistan, and Iran, among others)—a statement that proved unconvincing to most of the international community. The UN General Assembly called for the immediate and unconditional withdrawal of the Soviet forces, and many other international bodies supported the UN position. Most nations refused to recognize the Kabul regime; exceptions included India, which participated in a joint Indo-Afghan communiqué in early 1985 expressing concern about "the militarization of Pakistan."

In early 1986, following the accession to power in the Soviet Union of economy-conscious Mikhail Gorbachev, Moscow indicated a willingness to consider a timetable for withdrawal of its troops, conditioned on withdrawal of international support for the mujahidin. The signature of an Afghan-Pakistani agreement (guaranteed by the Soviet Union and the United States) called for mutual noninterference and nonintervention. Accompanying accords provided for the voluntary return of refugees and took note of a time frame established by Afghanistan and the Soviet Union for a "phased withdrawal of foreign troops" over a nine-month period commencing May 15. However, the agreements did not provide for a cease-fire, with both the United States and Pakistan reserving the right to provide additional military supplies to the Afghan guerrillas if Moscow continued to provide arms to Kabul.

In late 1990 the United States and the Soviet Union agreed on a policy of "negative symmetry," whereby both would cease supplying aid to their respective Afghan allies in expectation that the aid suspension would necessitate a cease-fire between the government and the rebels. Upon implementation of the mutual suspension in September 1991, even fundamentalist rebel leaders reportedly declared that they welcomed the end of foreign "interference." However, by early 1995 it was apparent that involvement by external powers had by no means ceased. Former students from Islamic seminaries in Pakistan launched the Taliban movement, with one observer initially characterizing the seminarians as "cannon fodder" in a Pakistani effort to reopen vital highway shipping routes to Tajikistan and beyond. Countering Pakistan's support of the Taliban was Indian aid to Rabbani and Masoud, particularly the provision of military aircraft that were crucial to the defense of Herat. For his part, General Dostam, the northern Uzbek warlord, had long been backed by Russia and Uzbekistan.

Washington initially exhibited a somewhat surprisingly warm stance toward the Taliban takeover in late 1996, reportedly out of the hope that it offered Afghanistan a chance for "stability" after 17 years of civil war. However, the U.S. posture cooled significantly during 1997 because of the Taliban's human rights record and harsh religious strictures, with U.S. secretary of state Madeleine Albright strongly criticizing the Taliban policies toward women. Meanwhile, Russia and members of the Commonwealth of Independent States (CIS), including Tajikistan and Uzbekistan, issued a stern warning to the Taliban in early 1997 not to attempt to spread militant fundamentalist influence beyond the Afghan borders. Collaterally, Iran displayed its support for the Shiite population in the Hazara region, which was aligned with the anti-Taliban forces.

After the fall of the Taliban in 2001, the Karzai government endeavored to restore relations with Western powers, including the United States, and to woo international organizations. As part of the Afghanistan Compact, negotiated with international donors, the Karzai administration in early 2006 agreed to improve human rights, combat corruption, eliminate illegal militias, counter the booming trade in narcotics, and "restore a functioning economy." Pledges were also made to triple the size of the Afghan army (from 24,000 in 2006 to 70,000 in 2009) and to establish a judiciary appointed on merit rather than tribal or religious status. In August 2003 the North Atlantic Treaty Organization (NATO) assumed command of the ISAF.

The Taliban continued a bloody and aggressive guerilla campaign into 2006, particularly in the south. (More than 1,600 people, including 60 Americans, died from conflict-related violence in 2005.) In early 2006 the NATO announced plans to increase the coalition force in Afghanistan from 8,500 to 16,000. Many of the new troops were to be deployed in the "volatile" south, a departure from the ISAF's previous primary role as a peacekeeping and security mission around Kabul and in the stable northern regions. The U.S.-led Combined Forces Command Afghanistan formally transferred control of six southern provinces to NATO/ISAF at the end of July, and in October NATO assumed responsibility for security throughout the country. By that time the ISAF forces had grown to 31,000, including many U.S. soldiers previously under direct U.S. command. However, the United States retained control over some 8,000 of its troops for counterterrorism activities and for training Afghan soldiers and the Afghan police.

In one of the bloodiest periods since the fall of the Taliban in 2001, Taliban guerrillas regained control of a number of southern villages in the second half of 2006, and the rate of suicide attacks escalated throughout the country. Some observers suggested that the Taliban movement was conducting an at least partially successful battle for the "hearts and minds" of southerners, who had reportedly been angered by the loss of civilian lives during NATO and U.S. military operations. Disagreement was reported within NATO over the degree of effort to be allocated toward the anti-insurgency campaign versus reconstruction, much of the population having reportedly grown pessimistic as a result of the lack of progress in the latter.

During a regional tour in March 2006, U.S. president George W. Bush consulted with President Karzai and President Musharraf of Pakistan on the delicate issue of the perceived use of Pakistani border areas by remnants of al-Qaida and the Taliban. Karzai later in the year claimed that Pakistan was not doing enough to curb the insurgents, who had made significant advances in southern Afghanistan.

In April 2007 U.S. officials noted what they described as the "unhealthy" involvement by Iran in Afghanistan, asserting that Iranian weapons were finding their way into the hands of Taliban insurgents. Iran denied providing the weapons, and independent analysts questioned whether Iran, which had been strongly anti-Taliban in 2001, would now be supplying the Taliban. For his part, Iranian president Mahmoud Ahmedinejad visited Afghanistan for the first time in August, at which time he signed a number of cooperation agreements with the Afghan government and pledged significant reconstruction aid.

In October 2007 Jaap de Hoop Scheffer, the secretary general of the NATO, urged NATO members to increase their troop commitments in order to combat the strengthening insurgency in Afghanistan. U.S. officials subsequently echoed that sentiment, suggesting that some European NATO members were underestimating the magnitude of the threat that a "destabilized" Afghanistan would present to them. However, disagreement continued within the alliance, as several leading European governments maintained their stance that resources should be earmarked primarily for political and economic reconstruction rather than counterinsurgency. In addition, several countries, including Germany, pressed for talks with moderate Taliban leaders to develop a negotiated settlement.

The situation in Afghanistan remained a primary focus of NATO's attention into the first half of 2009, with the new Obama administration in the United States describing conditions as "extremely perilous." Although President Barack Obama received pledges for only a minor number of new troops, the European NATO members strongly supported his call for a regional strategy to contain disruptions in Afghanistan and Pakistan. In that vein, it was reported that President Karzai had established a good relationship with new Pakistani president Asif Ali Zardari, who had campaigned on an anti-Taliban platform.

In September 2009 German forces called in a U.S. airstrike that killed 137 Afghan civilians. The incident led to the resignation of the German defense minister and further increased tensions between the Afghan government and foreign military forces. Meanwhile, Obama announced on December 1 the deployment of an additional 30,000 U.S. troops and other allied nations agreed to provide 9,000 more soldiers, bringing the total of coalition forces to about 130,000, including 100,000 U.S. soldiers.

Prior to a January 2010 conference in London hosted by British prime minister Gordon Brown, UN Secretary General Ban Ki Moon, and Karzai, confidential memos from the U.S. ambassador to Afghanistan, Karl Eikenberry, were leaked that voiced concern over Karzai and the level of corruption in the Afghan government. Nonetheless, attendees at the conference agreed to create a $130 million fund to support efforts to end the insurgency. In June the U.S. commander in Afghanistan, General Stanley McChrystal, was dismissed after a magazine article appeared which described McChrystal and his staff as critical of Obama and members of his cabinet. Meanwhile, Obama announced in June 2011 his intent to withdraw 33,000 U.S. forces from Afghanistan by the end of 2012, with a complete withdrawal by 2014.

Relations between Afghanistan and Pakistan worsened through 2011. In January 2011 Pakistani forces fired more than 400 rockets into Afghanistan at suspected Taliban bases. The attacks killed 36 Afghan civilians and injured dozens more. Afghan forces retaliated with artillery fire. Meanwhile, after the May raid that killed Osama bin Laden, Afghan leaders accused Pakistani officials of knowingly hiding the al-Qaida leader. One consequence was increased military ties between Afghanistan and India, including a June agreement to bolster cooperation between the air forces of the two countries.

In February 2012, the United States announced that its troops would end combat missions in Afghanistan in mid-2013. In May, NATO leaders met in Chicago and agreed to provide training and logistical support to the Afghan security forces through 2014. The Alliance also agreed to maintain a training mission in the country after 2014. Meanwhile, in September, New Zealand announced it would end its military mission in Afghanistan by April 2013, while the United Kingdom reduced its 9,000-member force in the country by 3,800 soldiers.

Following a meeting between Karzai and Obama in Washington, D.C., in January 2013, reports indicated that up to 20,000 U.S. troops would remain in Afghanistan after 2014. However, speculation emerged that the two leaders had discussed a "zero-option" whereby no U.S. soldiers would be permanently stationed there. Meanwhile, the two leaders agreed that all U.S. detention facilities in Afghanistan would be turned over to Afghan security forces within a six month period. Karzai and Obama also both endorsed the opening of a Taliban office in Qatar (see Political parties, below).

In March 2013 Afghanistan, Tajikistan, and Turkmenistan signed an agreement to construct a railway connecting the three nations. In May the United States announced that it would not maintain any permanent military bases in Afghanistan after 2014 but would rely on Afghan facilities. A number of states agreed to increase aid to Afghanistan in 2013, including Sweden ($690 million), India ($199 million), and Japan ($117 million).

Current issues. The Taliban insurgency intensified in 2007–2008, particularly in the south and east, despite several major anti-Taliban campaigns by the ISAF and Afghan troops. The UN estimated that 5,000 people (including 2,100 civilians) had died in 2008 as a result of the conflict, which was marked by numerous suicide attacks and roadside bombings. Some analysts suggested that half of the country was under Taliban "influence," although others said a more accurate figure would be 10 percent, with 30 percent under government control and the remainder ruled by warlords or other local leaders. Not surprisingly, the Karzai administration faced increasing criticism for its inability to restore order, curb corruption, slow opium production, or protect local officials and public servants from the insurgents' assassination campaign. In November 2008, in what was considered another overture to the Taliban, President Karzai again offered to conduct peace talks with any group that "accepts the constitution."

The Taliban continued to exercise substantial control over the southern provinces in early 2009, while a spate of suicide bombings spread to Kabul and other cities throughout the country. With the level of violence at its highest since 2001, international pressure grew for negotiations toward a peace settlement with "moderate" elements within the Taliban. President Obama ordered more than 20,000 additional U.S. troops to be deployed to Afghanistan, in part to provide additional security for presidential elections scheduled for August 20. The August presidential balloting was marred by allegations of widespread voter fraud and intimidation. Although Karzai was declared the winner, his credibility was undermined domestically and internationally. Reports indicated that the United States attempted to convince Karzai to create a coalition government with second-place finisher Abdullah Abdullah.

On January 18, 2010, while Karzai was in the midst of swearing in the new cabinet, the Taliban launched a series of attacks in Kabul, killing 15 and wounding more than 60. In February 15,000 coalition forces launched Operation Moshtarak directed at the Marjah area of Helmand Province. Although the offensive achieved military success, a number of civilians were killed, alienating many inhabitants of the region. A larger operation, involving 25,000 coalition troops, was launched to reassert control over Kandahar during the summer. On June 2–4 Karzai convened an assembly of some 1,600 Afghan political, religious, and social leaders and officials in an effort to develop solutions to end the conflict. The conference highlighted continuing political and ethnic differences, but attendees endorsed a proposal to create a national peace commission and initiate negotiations with moderate Taliban figures. The Taliban launched a suicide attack on the conference, prompting Karzai to replace the interior minister and the head of internal security. In June 60 U.S. service members were killed in Afghanistan, a monthly record, which was eclipsed the following month with 66.

In an effort to ensure stability during the 2010 legislative elections, NATO and Afghan forces undertook a major offensive against the Taliban during the summer and fall of 2010. Operation Hamkari sought to gain control of Kandahar. By November more than 1,200 Taliban had been killed in the fighting. In response, the Taliban increased suicide bombings and targeted assassinations of government officials and security forces.

Balloting for the *Wolesi Jirga* on September 18, 2010, was marred by violence, particularly in areas of Taliban influence, and—according to most observers—widespread fraud and other irregularities. The election commission ultimately threw out more than 20 percent of the votes and disqualified 21 candidates who initially appeared victorious, drawing harsh criticism from many sectors, including the Karzai administration. Observers concluded that the Karzai and opposition camps could count on approximately equal support (somewhere in the range of 90–100 legislators each among the 249 members). This marked an increase in the number of opposition members from the previous legislature.

Following the elections, a political crisis emerged after Karzai initially postponed the inauguration of the new legislation. The president argued that he wanted the electoral commission to have the time to investigate allegations of fraud, but critics charged that the administration sought to replace winning opposition candidates with proregime figures. Negotiations resolved the issue, and the *Wolesi Jirga* was sworn in on January 26, 2011. Efforts to elect a speaker for the new legislature were frustrated by disputes between the Pushtuns and Tajiks, and no candidate was able to gain more than the required 50 percent of the vote. On February 27, 2011, Abdul Rahoof IBRAHIMI, an Uzbek, was elected as a compromise candidate. Friction between the Karzai government and the NATO-led forces increased following two coalition airstrikes in March 2011 that left 74 civilians dead and prompted public apologies from President Obama and senior U.S. military commanders.

On July 12, 2011, Ahmed Wali KARZAI, the president's half brother and one of the most powerful figures in southern Afghanistan, was killed by one of his bodyguards. The assassination led to a power struggle among regional warlords to gain ascendancy in the volatile area. In October, six people, including one of Karzai's bodyguards, were arrested for allegedly planning to assassinate the president. On September 20 former president Rabbani was assassinated. He was the lead envoy in negotiations with the Taliban. Security officials blamed his death on the Haqqani network, a criminal and smuggling group linked to the Taliban (see Political parties and groups, below).

Karzai convened a *Loya Jirga* in Kabul from November 15–18, 2011. The meeting endorsed a proposal to maintain a long-term U.S. security presence after the planned 2014 withdrawal of combat troops. The outcome of the meeting led to protests in Jalalabad and other cities.

A report by the United Nations in 2012 found that civilian casualties in Afghanistan increased by 8 percent over the previous year, rising to 3,021 killed. The majority of the casualties were caused by insurgents, while coalition and government forces were responsible for approximately 9 percent of the deaths and injuries.

Anti-Western violence spread throughout Afghanistan after revelations emerged in February 2012 that U.S. forces had mistakenly burned copies of the Koran. At least 40 people, mainly civilians, were killed. Attacks on Western coalition forces by Afghan security troops (labeled as "green-on-blue" attacks) increased dramatically in 2012, peaking in August when 15 coalition soldiers were killed by Afghan forces. In response NATO-led forces ceased joint operations with Afghan troops in September and suspended training of the 16,000-member Afghan Local Police (ALP) force.

In August 2012 the legislature voted to dismiss Defense Minister Abdul Rahim WARDAK and Interior Minister Gen. Bismillah MOHAMMADI following rising violence along the border with Pakistan. Both were widely seen as pro-Western and their potential departures prompted concerns by the United States over the future stability of Afghan security forces. Karzai attempted to keep both in office as acting ministers, but Wardak subsequently resigned. The president then appointed Mohammadi as defense minister and Gen. Ghulam Mushtaba PATANG as interior minister. Both were approved by parliament on September 16. However, in July 2013, the parliament passed a no confidence vote against Patang, creating a new crisis between the president and the legislature.

Violence continued through 2012. For instance, a suicide bomber killed 41 and injured 56 at a mosque in Maimana on October 26. Nonetheless, a UN report found that for the first time in six years, the overall number of civilian deaths in Afghanistan declined by 12 percent, falling from 3,131 in 2011 to 2,754 in 2012.

On March 5, 2013, 21 Afghans were convicted of theft and corruption for their involvement in the 2010 collapse of the Bank of Kabul in which the institution lost $825 million. Karzai's brother Mahmood KARZAI had been widely seen as linked to the scandal but was not charged with any wrongdoing.

POLITICAL PARTIES AND GROUPS

Resistance to the Taliban was coordinated at first by the Supreme Defense Council, formed in October 1996 by the Islamic Afghan Society, the National Front, and the Islamic Unity Party. The umbrella organization's name was changed to the United National Islamic Front for the Salvation of Afghanistan (UNIFSA) in mid-1997 to reflect the addition of new members (including the National Islamic Front) as well as expansion of the alliance's mandate to cover political as well as military initiatives. UNIFSA, with heavy U.S. military and financial support, spearheaded the overthrow of the Taliban in late 2001.

The new constitution approved in January 2004 provided for freedom of association, with political parties being authorized if they had no military or paramilitary structures and their platforms were not "contrary to the principles of Islam." Parties based on ethnicity, language, religious sects, or regions were also prohibited. More than 80 parties have been registered. However, party influence remained minimal, particularly in the *Wolesi Jirga,* where all candidates in the 2005 and 2010 elections ran as independents.

In December 2011 a new opposition alliance, the **National Coalition,** was formed with former presidential candidate Abdullah Abdullah as its chair. The coalition endeavored to draw together opposition groups to unite behind a single presidential candidate in the 2014 elections. In August 2013 another coalition, the **Electoral Union of Afghanistan,** was announced.

New Afghanistan Party (*Hizb-i-Afghanistan-i-Nawin*). Formed by Mohammad Yunos Qanuni in advance of his 2004 presidential campaign, this party was among the core components at the formation of the **National Understanding Front**—NUF (*Jabha-i-Tafahon-i-Milli*), a defunct coalition of opposition parties. Qanuni, an ethnic Tajik, was considered the most formidable political rival to President Karzai. Nonetheless, Qanuni worked with Karzai in the effort to secure confirmations of the president's proposed cabinet. In 2010 Qanuni endorsed Karzai's effort to reach out to moderate Taliban in order to end the ongoing conflict. Qanuni declined to seek reelection as speaker in 2011. Reports in 2012 indicated that Qanuni brought the party into the opposition National Coalition. In 2013 Qanuni called for opposition parties to rally behind a single candidate ahead of the 2014 presidential balloting.

Leader: Mohammad Yunos QANUNI (2004 presidential candidate).

Islamic Unity Party of the People of Afghanistan (*Hizb-i-Wahdat-i-Islami Mardom-i-Afghanistan*). A primarily Shiite offshoot of the Islamic Unity Party, this organization is led by Mohammad Mohaqeq, a former member of the Karzai administration who left the government in 2004 in a dispute of unclear origin with President Karzai. Mohaqeq, an ethnic Hazara, finished third (as an independent) in the 2004 presidential election, with 11.7 percent of the vote. He was elected to the *Wolesi Jirga* in 2005. Mohaqeq and the party opposed Karzai's efforts at reconciliation with the Taliban moderates. Reports in 2012 were that Mohaqeq had joined the National Front. Reports in 2013 indicated that the party had joined the **Electoral Union of Afghanistan** (EUA).

Leader: Mohammad MOHAQEQ.

National Islamic Empowerment Party (*Hizb-i Iqtedar-i-Milli-Islami*). The formation of this party was reported in early 2006 under the leadership of Ahmad Shah Ahmadzay, previously referenced as leader of the Islamic Power Party. Ahmadzay, a religious conservative, ran as an independent in the 2004 presidential election on a platform of opposition to the presence of U.S. forces in Afghanistan. The party reportedly was a founding member of the EUA in 2013.

Leaders: Ahmad Shah AHMADZAY, Mustapha KAZEMI.

Islamic Afghan Society (*Jamaat-i-Islami Afghanistan*). The Islamic Afghan Society draws most of its support from Tajiks in the northern part of the country. It was long the most effective rebel force in the Panjsher Valley, and it engaged in heavy combat with Soviet forces in 1985, including sporadic invasions of Soviet Tajikistan.

Internal disagreement over relations with the Islamic Party threatened to splinter *Jamaat* in 1990, when military commander Ahmed Shah Masoud temporarily parted company with political leader

Burhanuddin Rabbani in rejecting an appeal to aid the Islamic Party's offensive against Kabul. In October, Masoud, long a leading military figure, gained additional prominence when he chaired a *shura* (assembly) of Afghan military chiefs.

Forces loyal to Rabbani fled from the Taliban offensive against Kabul in September 1996, subsequently coalescing under Masoud's command in the north, where, in conjunction with other anti-Taliban militias, they fought the Taliban to a stalemate. Masoud's forces were estimated to number 12,000–15,000 in the fall of 2001, having weathered heavy Taliban offensives during the summers of the past three years.

Masoud was killed in an attack by suicide bombers disguised as journalists on September 10, 2001. The assassination was widely attributed to al-Qaida as a prelude to the terrorist attacks in the United States the following day. Mohammad Qasim FAHIM, who became one of the top leaders in the subsequent expulsion of the Taliban, succeeded Masoud as military commander of the Northern Alliance.

Rabbani, whose government had maintained the recognition of many countries throughout the Taliban regime, returned to Kabul in mid-November 2001 to resume the exercise of presidential authority. He reportedly hoped that the subsequent Bonn Conference would appoint him as president of the proposed new interim administration, and he only reluctantly accepted the appointment of Hamid Karzai after holding up the conference for several days in apparent protest to being sidelined. Any remaining short-term political aspirations on Rabbani's part were also put on hold at the *Loya Jirga* in July 2002, where Rabbani endorsed Karzai's election as president of the new transitional government. Fahim, however, was named vice president and minister of defense, establishing himself as one of the administration's dominant figures. Rabbani supported Karzai in the 2004 presidential election even though Fahim was dropped from the Karzai ticket. Rabbani was elected to the *Wolesi Jirga* in 2005 and briefly campaigned for election as the speaker of that body before deferring to Yunos Qanuni. In 2007 Rabbani helped form the **United National Front** (UNF), a loose coalition of opposition groupings. The UNF brought together mujahidin, former communists, members of the royal family, and other diverse elements in pursuit of national unity, reconstruction, and establishment of a federal system under which governors and provincial councils would be directly elected and the national government would operate on a parliamentary rather than a presidential system. Members of the UNF reportedly included *Wolesi Jirga* speaker Qanuni, first vice president of the republic, Ahmad Zia MASOUD, Gen. Abdul Rashid Dostam (leader of the National Front [below] and a top military adviser to President Karzai), Mustapha Kazemi (a leader of the National Islamic Empowerment Party), representatives of the National Congress Party of Afghanistan, Mustapha ZAHIR (grandson of the former king), several cabinet members, and a number of legislators. The new grouping, primarily representing non-Pushtun northerners, was immediately perceived as the dominant political force in the *Wolesi Jirga*. It strongly supported a proposed national amnesty bill, not surprisingly considering the number of warlords and others with major roles in past conflicts involved in its formation. Saying that military defeat of the Taliban was impossible, Rabbani invited the Taliban and other antigovernment forces to lay down their arms and join the UNF in pursuit of national unity. Although the UNF remained formally supportive of President Karzai in early 2008, it subsequently instigated a legislative confrontation with the administration.

In 2009 Dr. Abdullah Abdullah, a former minister of foreign affairs, became the UNF nominee for the 2010 presidential elections. Meanwhile, President Karzai selected Fahim as a running mate. Fahim was subsequently elected first vice president of Afghanistan. Abdullah placed second in the balloting, and he then withdrew before a scheduled runoff, citing concerns over electoral fraud. After withdrawing, Abdullah called on his supporters to remain peaceful and was generally credited with helping prevent violence during the election crisis. Nonetheless, following the 2010 elections, the UNF emerged as the main opposition party to the Karzai regime. After Rabbani was assassinated, his son, Salahoddin RABBANI, was elected to lead the national peace council. Reports in 2012 indicated that Abdullah Abdullah was the leader of the new opposition grouping, the **National Coalition.** In 2013 the grouping reportedly became part of the EUA.

Leaders: Mohammad Qasim FAHIM (First Vice President of the Republic), Abdullah ABDULLAH (2012 presidential candidate), Abdul Hafez MANSUR, Munawar HASAN (Secretary General).

National Front (*Jumbish-i-Milli*). The *Jumbish-i-Milli* is a primarily Uzbek grouping formed by Gen. Abdul Rashid Dostam, who had been a military commander in the Najibullah government before aligning himself with Ahmed Shah Masoud in 1992. In early 1994 Dostam broke with Masoud to join forces with Gulbuddin Hekmatyar's *Hizb-i-Islami* and Abdul Ali Mazari's *Hizb-i-Wahdat* in an anti-Rabbani alliance. He did not, however, support those groups in decisive encounters in March 1995, thereby contributing to their defeat. Following the Taliban takeover of Kabul in 1996, General Dostam initially played an important role in the anti-Taliban alliance (see Political background, above). However, it was reported that he and his remaining forces had retreated to Uzbekistan following the Taliban offensive of the second half of 1998, and his influence had declined significantly by mid-2000.

Dostam returned to Afghanistan in March 2001 and rejoined the Northern Alliance. The general subsequently remained closely aligned with Burhanuddin Rabbani during the overthrow of the Taliban and strongly objected to the selection at the Bonn Conference of Hamid Karzai over Rabbani as president of the new interim government in December. Initially, it appeared that Dostam's disgruntlement would prove a threat to stability, but he accepted positions as vice chair of the interim administration and deputy minister of defense in late December, thereby calming the situation. General Dostam, burdened with a reputation for military ruthlessness and political shiftiness, was not included in the July 2002 cabinet.

Running as an independent, Dostam finished fourth in the 2004 presidential poll, with 10 percent of the vote. In April 2005 he became the chief of staff of the high command of the armed forces in Karzai's administration, seen as a largely symbolic post. Dostam's supporters subsequently had a number of confrontations with government officials, and several Tajik ministers were removed from the cabinet in 2008. Dostam was forced to resign as military chief in 2008 but was reappointed in June 2009 after he promised to support Karzai in that year's presidential elections. In 2012 Dostam pledged to support a consensus opposition candidate in the 2014 presidential election, and the National Front joined the EUA in 2013.

Leaders: Gen. Abdul Rashid DOSTAM, Azizullah KARQAR, Sayyed NUROLLAH, Faysollah ZAKI, Abdul Majid ROZI.

Islamic Unity Party of Afghanistan (*Hizb-i-Wahdat-i-Islami Afghanistan*). The *Hizb-i-Wahdat* was launched in mid-1987 by eight Iran-based groups. (See the list in the 2008 *Handbook.*) Also known as the Tehran Eight, the group claimed at its inception to represent an estimated 2 million Shiite Afghan refugees in Iran. During 1992 and early 1993 it joined with Hekmatyar's *Hizb-i-Islami* in a number of clashes with Rabbani's *Jamaat-i-Islami* and the Saudi-backed *Ittihad-i-Islami. Hizb-i-Wahdat*'s principal leader, Abdul Ali MAZARI, was killed on March 13, 1995, reportedly in a helicopter crash south of Kabul after having been captured by the Taliban militia.

Hizb-i-Wahdat was an important component of UNIFSA in that it represented the Hazara Shiite community in central Afghanistan. As of early 1998 the Hazaras were reportedly exercising autonomous government control in the Hazarajat region while contributing substantially to the anti-Taliban military alliance in the north. However, Taliban forces pushed *Hizb-i-Wahdat* out of most of the populated areas in the region (including the important city of Bamiyan) in September 1998. In consonance with the ouster of the Taliban by the UNIFSA/Northern Alliance in late 2001, *Hizb-i-Wahdat* regained control of much of central Afghanistan, and party leader Karim Khalili was named as a vice president in the transitional government installed in June 2002. He was elected as second vice president of the republic in 2004, and again in 2009. The party joined the EUA in 2013.

Leaders: Karim KHALILI (Second Vice President of the Republic), Ayatollah FAZL.

National Islamic Front (*Mahaz-i-Milli-i-Islami*). The most left-leaning of the moderate groups, the National Islamic Front had refused to join the Supreme Council in 1981 because not all of the participants had agreed to the election of people's representatives to a provisional government. In November 1990 party leader Pir Sayed Ahmad Gailani endorsed a reported U.S.-Soviet peace plan that would have left the Najibullah regime in power after the two countries withdrew their support for the combatants. Thereafter, at a meeting in Geneva, Switzerland, Gailani allegedly turned down an offer by Najibullah to assume control of the government, suggesting instead the return of Mohammad Zahir Shah, the former monarch.

Gailani, the spiritual leader of the Sufi Muslims, served in the Rabbani cabinet from 1992 to 1996, he and his supporters relocating to Cyprus following the Taliban takeover. They subsequently served as the core component of the so-called Cyprus Group at the 2001 Bonn Conference, where the front continued to display a proroyalist orientation. Gailani was elected chair of a prominent faction in the *Meshrano Jirga* in 2007. In the 2009 presidential balloting, Gailani supported former finance minister Ashraf Ghani AHMADZAI, who placed fourth in the first round of balloting. In April 2012 Gailani rejected the post of chair of the Afghan High Peace Council.

Leader: Pir Sayed Ahmad GAILANI.

Islamic Party (*Hizb-i-Islami*). Drawing most of its support from Pushtuns in the southeastern part of the country, the Islamic Party was one of the largest and most radical of the mujahidin groups and often engaged in internecine clashes with former allies including, most notably, the *Jamaat-i-Islami.* Its principal leader, Gulbuddin Hekmatyar, was known to have ties to both Iran and Libya in the 1970s and early 1980s, although they subsequently were believed to have weakened.

Hekmatyar was named prime minister following an all-party accord in March 1993 but was at that stage deeply opposed to the Rabbani presidency; Hekmatyar's appointment lapsed in mid-1994. Thereafter, his supporters maintained a partial siege of Kabul until forced to withdraw after a decisive defeat in March 1995. This experience eventually impelled Hekmatyar to break ranks with other mujahidin leaders by reaching his own accommodation with the government in May 1996, enabling him to resume the premiership from June until the overthrow of the government in September. Hekmatyar's decision to align his forces with those of Ahmed Shah Masoud and General Dostam was considered an important factor in their subsequent ability to stall the Taliban offensive in the north in 1997. However, Hekmatyar and the Islamic Party were described in 1998 as only nominally associated with UNIFSA and apparently not playing a major role in the remaining military opposition to the Taliban. Interviewed in Iran in mid-2000, Hekmatyar called on the Taliban to establish a provisional government including opposition representatives pending national elections, describing the civil war as benefiting only "foreign forces."

In the fall of 2001 Hekmatyar adopted a strongly anti–Northern Alliance stance and urged support for the Taliban against a U.S. invasion. Hekmatyar returned to Afghanistan in early 2002 but remained noticeably outside the negotiations toward a government of national unity. Considered a threat to the stability of the interim administration, Hekmatyar was reportedly the target of an unsuccessful assassination attempt in May on the part of the United States through the use of an unmanned, aerial drone. Hekmatyar subsequently reportedly fled to Iran, but he was eventually expelled from that country. Upon his return to Afghanistan, he was labeled a terrorist because of attacks on U.S. and Afghan forces. In early 2005 it appeared that some Islamic Party adherents had begun peace negotiations with the Karzai administration, although Hekmatyar (who rejected an apparent amnesty offer) and others remained committed to jihad (holy war) until U.S. forces were removed from Afghanistan and an "Islamic system" was installed.

Party members opposed to Hekmatyar's hard line participated (with some success) in the 2005 legislative balloting. Meanwhile, an arrest warrant reportedly remained in effect for Hekmatyar, while his supporters, now considered allied with the Taliban (and possibly al-Qaida) and reportedly sometimes operating out of Pakistan, participated in attacks on government and NATO forces in the north in 2006–2007. There were reports in 2008 of negotiations between the Karzai administration and Hekmatyar regarding a possible cessation of hostilities. In March 2010 Karzai met with senior leaders of the group but reportedly no progress was made in the talks, which were described as preliminary. Reports in 2010 indicated a split in the group, with one faction supporting Hekmatyar (**Islamic Party—Gulbuddin**), and a second, more moderate faction backing Abdul Hadi ARGHANDIWAL, the current economics minister (**Islamic Party—Afghanistan**). It was estimated that Arghandiwal had 50 supporters in the legislature following legislative balloting in 2010. In 2012 reports indicated that Hekmatyar was in negotiations with regional governors on a comprehensive peace agreement. Reports in 2013 indicated that members of the two factions of the party met in Kabul in an effort to reunify the factions.

Leaders: Gulbuddin HEKMATYAR (Former Prime Minister), Abdul Hadi ARGHANDIWAL (Minister of Economy).

Islamic Unity (*Ittihad-i-Islami*). Ultra-orthodox Sunni Muslims backed by Saudi Arabia formed the *Ittihad-i-Islami.* Like the other fundamentalist formations, it long opposed Westernizing influences in pursuing what it viewed largely as an Islamic holy war against Soviet-backed forces. One of its leaders, Abdul Rasul Sayaf, headed the Islamic Alliance of Afghan Holy Warriors at its inception in 1985.

The party endorsed President Karzai in the 2004 presidential campaign. Subsequently, Sayaf, described as an "archconservative," was elected to the *Wolesi Jirga* in 2005 and was only narrowly defeated for the speaker's position. He supported Karzai in the 2009 presidential balloting. In November 2009, Sayaf survived an assassination attempt that killed 16 persons. Reports in 2013 indicated that Karzai had endorsed Sayaf as his successor.

Leader: Abdul Rasul SAYAF (Former Prime Minister of Government-in-Exile).

National Liberation Front (*Jabh-i-Nijat-i-Milli*). The National Liberation Front was formed to support Afghan self-determination and the establishment of a freely elected government. Its leader, Sibghatullah Mojadedi, was chair of the moderate opposition bloc in the late 1980s. Subsequently, Mojadedi served as interim president from April to June 1992, before becoming a prominent opponent of the Rabbani government. Immediately following the Taliban takeover of Kabul in September 1996, it was reported that Mojadedi had announced his support for the new government. However, he was subsequently described as having moved to Egypt, from where he was "abstaining" from the conflict between the Taliban and its opponents. Mojadedi supported Hamid Karzai in the 2004 presidential campaign and was later named chair of the fledgling national reconciliation commission. He was also elected as speaker of the *Meshrano Jirga* in late 2005 but resigned in 2010. He was reappointed as a member of the chamber in 2011.

Leaders: Imam Sibghatullah MOJADEDI (Former President of Government-in-Exile and Former Speaker of the *Meshrano Jirga*), Dr. Hashimatullah MOJADEDI.

National Solidarity Movement of Afghanistan (*Nahzat-i Hambastagi-i Milli Afghanistan*). This party is led by Ishaq Gailani, who was a candidate for president in 2004 prior to withdrawing in support of Hamid Karzai. Gailani also supported Karzai in the 2009 balloting.

Leader: Ishaq GAILANI.

Afghan Nation (*Afghan Mellat*). Established during the reign of King Zahir Shah in support of Pushtun nationalism, this grouping (also referenced as the Social Democratic Party of Afghanistan) reportedly factionalized in the early 2000s. One faction, which supported Hamid Karzai in the 2004 presidential campaign, is led by Anwar al-Haq Ahadi, who was named minister of finance in the December 2004 cabinet and subsequently appointed minister of commerce and industry following Karzai's reelection in 2009. In 2012 a group of party dissidents accused Ahadi of embezzlement and called for his resignation. Reports in 2013 indicated that the party was in negotiations to join the EUA.

Leader: Anwar al-Haq AHADI (President).

National Congress Party of Afghanistan (*Hizb-i Kongra-i Milli-i Afghanistan*). This party was launched in April 2004 in support of the presidential candidacy of moderate Abdul Latif Pedram, who finished fifth in the October poll with 1.37 percent of the vote. Pedram, a former journalist and professor, proposed the establishment of a federal system in Afghanistan.

Leaders: Abdul Latif PEDRAM, Nasir OJABER.

National Movement of Afghanistan (*Hizb-i Nahzat-i Milli-i Afghanistan*). Primarily supported by Tajiks, *Nahzat* was launched by Ahmad Wali Masoud following the death of his brother, Ahmed Shah Masoud, the legendary mujahidin military leader. The party factionalized in 2004 when *Nahzat* member Yunos Qanuni ran against Hamid Karzai in the 2004 presidential campaign, while another Masoud brother, Ahmad Zia Masoud, was one of Karzai's vice presidential running mates. Karzai replaced Masoud as his running mate prior to the 2009 presidential elections.

Leaders: Ahmad Wali MASOUD (Party Leader), Ahmad Zia MASOUD (Former Vice President of the Republic).

Other recently launched parties include the **Afghanistan Independence Party** (*Hizb-i-Istiqlal-i Afghanistan*), led by Ghulam Faruq NEJRABI, who won 0.3 percent of the vote in the 2004 presidential poll on a platform that rejected all "direct or indirect influence" on the part of "foreigners," including aid organizations; the **Democracy and Progress Movement of Afghanistan** (*Nahzat-i-Faragir-i Democracy wa Taraqi-i-Afghanistan*), led by Mohammad BUZGAR;

the **Freedom Party** (*Hizb-i Azadi*), led by Gen. Abdul MALEK, a former leader of the National Front; the **Islamic Justice Party of Afghanistan** (*Hizb-i Adalat-i Islami-i Afghanistan*), which, under the leadership of Mohammad Kabir MARZBAN, also supported President Karzai in the 2004 campaign; the **National Awareness and Deliverance Movement of Afghanistan** (*Hizb-i Nahzet-i Bedari Milli Falah-i Afghanistan*), launched in late 2007 by a group of national legislators and government officials under the leadership of Mohammad Yasin HABIB; the **National Freedom Seekers Party** (*Hizb-i Azadi Khwahan-i Maihan*), led by Abdul Hadi DABIR, an independent presidential candidate in 2004; the **National Movement for Peace** (*Jumbish-i Milli-i Solk*), led by Shahnawaz TANAY, a former defense minister in the Communist regime; **National Need,** formed in February 2008 to focus on women's rights under the leadership of legislator Fatima NAZARI; the **National Party** (*Hizb-i Milli*), led by Abdul Rashid ARYAN, a former member of the PDPA and member of the cabinet during Communist rule; the **National Unity Movement** (*Tabrik-i-Wahdat-i Milli*), led by Mahmud GHAZI and Homayun Shah ASEFI; the **People's Islamic Movement of Afghanistan** (*Harakat-i Islami-i Mardon-i Afghanistan*), led by Hosayn ANWARI, the minister of agriculture in the transitional government; the **Republican Party** (*Hizb-i Jamhuri Khwahan*), led by Sebghatullah SANJAR, who supported Hamid Karzai in the 2004 presidential election; and the **Youth Solidarity Party of Afghanistan** (*Hizb-i-Hambastagi-i Milli-i Jawanan-i Afghanistan*), which, under the leadership of Mohammed Jamil KARZAI, supported President Karzai in the 2004 election.

Other minor opposition parties or groupings included the **Afghanistan Ethnic Unity Party** (*Hizb-i-Wahdat-i-Aqwam-i-Afghanistan*), led by Nasrullah BARAKZAI; the **Afghanistan National Independence Party** (*Hizb-i-Istiqlal-i-Milli Afghanistan*), led by Taj Mohammad WARDAK; the **Afghanistan Islamic Peace and Brotherhood Party** (*Hizb-i-Sulh wa Ukhwat-i-Islami Afghanistan*), led by Qadir Imami GHORI; a faction of the **Islamic Movement Party of Afghanistan** (*Hizb-i-Harakat-i-Islami-i-Afghanistan*), led by Mohammad Ali JAWID; a faction of the **Islamic Revolutionary Movement Party** (*Hizb-i-Harakat-i-Inqilah-i-Islami*), led by Ahmad NABI; the **National Islamic Party of Afghanistan** (*Hizb-i-Milli-Islami-i-Afghanistan*), led by Ustad Mohammad AKBARI and Rohullah LOUDIN; and the **New Islamic Party of Afghanistan** (*Hizb-i-Islami-i-Afghanistan Jawan*), led by the journalist Sayed Jawad HUSSEINI.

For more information on the **Homeland Party** (*Hizb-i-Watan*) and the **National Understanding Front**—NUF (*Jabha-i-Tafahon-i-Milli*), see the 2010 *Handbook.*

Movement Formerly in Power:

Taliban. Translated as "seekers" or "students," the Persian *taliban* was applied to a group of Islamic fundamentalist theology students from Pakistan who swept through southern Afghanistan during late 1994 in a campaign pledged to rid the country of its contending warlords and introduce "genuine" Islamic rule. In a statement issued in connection with U.S. congressional hearings on Afghanistan in June 1996, the Taliban movement listed its basic demands as including the resignation of President Rabbani, the demilitarization of Kabul, the formation of a national security force, and the convening of an elected assembly of the Afghan people charged with forming "a national Islamic government." The group's seizure of power in Kabul three months later gave it the opportunity to implement this program. Previous assessment of the Taliban as espousing a less ferocious brand of fundamentalism than the ousted regime was speedily revised in light of its imposition of strict Islamic law (sharia) and summary execution of opponents.

The Taliban militia launched several offensives in late 1996 and 1997 designed to win complete control of the country but was unable to defeat opposition forces in the north or maintain command of the Hazara region west of Kabul. In part, resistance to the Taliban was based on ethnicity or religion: in the north the opposition militias comprised Uzbeks and Tajiks, who had long been wary of domination by Pushtuns (the core Taliban ethnic group), while the Hazara-Taliban split pitted Shiite against Sunni Muslims. Despite international criticism, the Taliban leaders in 1997 exhibited little moderation in their harsh interpretation of sharia, described as "medieval" by some observers, particularly regarding strictures on women. Meanwhile, the Taliban's spiritual guide, Mullah Mohammad Omar, was described as a reclusive leader who rarely left Kandahar (where the movement was launched) and who, following Taliban interpretation of religious law, never permitted himself to be photographed. A small consultative council located in Kandahar reportedly advised Omar.

Although the Taliban nearly succeeded in the first half of 2001 in efforts to push opposition forces completely out of Afghanistan, the regime's fortunes reversed dramatically as the result of the terrorist attacks in the United States in September. Washington quickly blamed the al-Qaida network of Osama bin Laden (see below) for the hijackings and demanded that the Taliban turn their "guest" over for prosecution or face U.S. military intervention. Although some Taliban leaders reportedly argued that the U.S. demand should be met, Omar and other hard-liners refused and thereby sealed the movement's fate. Following the Taliban's final military defeat at the hands of the Northern Alliance in late December, Omar and a number of Taliban ministers were reported to have fled to Pakistan.

Although many observers predicted the total collapse of the Taliban in the wake of its fall from power, the movement subsequently regrouped and launched a series of deadly guerrilla attacks against U.S. troops and the new Afghan army. Mullah Omar, believed at that point to be operating as the head of a ten-man Taliban leadership council, called for a jihad against all foreign forces and vowed to "punish" Afghans who supported the Karzai administration. The Taliban failed in an announced plan to disrupt the October 2004 presidential election but intensified attacks in mid-2005 to disrupt upcoming legislative balloting. Although some former Taliban leaders by that time reportedly had entered into negotiations with the government toward a possible peace settlement, Mullah Omar maintained his hard line, rejecting an apparent amnesty offer from administration representatives. Some reports attributed the 2005 attacks to a "Neo-Taliban," while it was also clear that several Taliban splinter groups were operating, raising questions about the cohesiveness and precise leadership of the movement. Meanwhile, the United States, convinced of Mullah Omar's ties to al-Qaida, continued to offer a $10 million reward for his capture.

Several former Taliban commanders were reportedly elected to the *Wolesi Jirga* in September 2005, while a number of other former members of the movement had reportedly been released from custody in return for their commitment to "peace." Nevertheless, attacks attributed to the Taliban grew in number in late 2005 and early 2006, most of them emulating the roadside bombings and suicide attacks so prevalent in Iraq at that time. By then the Taliban movement was described as having significant ties to drug smuggling and was characterized as still representing a significant "menace" in parts of southern Afghanistan.

The Taliban insurgency, fueled by the use of sophisticated new weaponry, escalated steadily for the remainder of 2006 and the first half of 2007, resulting in the takeover (sometimes temporarily) by the Taliban of a number of villages and other rural areas in the south. Afghan, NATO, and U.S. officials alleged that Taliban forces were operating with impunity out of remote border areas in Pakistan. Western analysts estimated the Taliban's strength in 2006 at 6,000 fighters (up from 2,000 only a year earlier), while the Taliban claimed control of 12,000 fighters. In early 2007 Omar said he had not seen bin Laden since 2001 and indicated the Taliban had no direct alliance with al-Qaida, other than the shared goal of the expulsion of foreign forces from Afghanistan. The Taliban leader again refused an invitation to peace talks with the Karzai administration.

Mullah DADULLAH, described as the Taliban's senior military commander in Afghanistan, was killed in a NATO/government attack in May 2007. He was apparently succeeded by his brother, Mansur DADULLAH, who was reported in December to have been removed from his post by Mullah Omar in a policy dispute.

President Karzai reportedly offered cabinet posts to Taliban leaders in late 2007 in return for a cease-fire, prompting mixed responses from the insurgents. Meanwhile, the Taliban, responsible for the kidnapping of a group of South Korean missionaries in mid-2007, continued the campaign of suicide bombing into early 2008. In March Taliban leaders clearly indicated that their single goal was the exit of U.S.-led forces from Afghanistan and that the movement sought "positive relations" with neighboring countries, including Iran, and would consider negotiations with the Karzai administration. The announcement appeared to underscore a schism between at least some of the Taliban and al-Qaida, supporters of the latter having criticized the Taliban for a perceived lack of fervor in regard to "global jihad." The Taliban faction led by Jalaluddin Haqqani and his son, Sirajuddin HAQQANI, subsequently announced its "brotherly ties" with al-Qaida (in September 2013 the Haqqani network was designated by the United States as a terrorist organization). Supporters of the Haqqanis reportedly were responsible for much of the insurgency in southeastern Afghanistan, apparently benefiting from the use of bases in Pakistan, where several Taliban branches were operating, including one led by Baitullah Mehsud. (For additional information on Taliban activities in Pakistan, see the section on the *Tehrik-e Taliban Pakistan* under Political Parties and Groups in the article on Pakistan.) Meanwhile, Taliban attacks continued in Afghanistan into early 2009, the movement's success apparently prompting the Karzai administration to offer more olive branches to "moderate" Taliban supporters. At that point, some analysts concluded that a significant percentage of the Taliban rank and file might be interested in a negotiated peace settlement. In addition, it was reported that areas recently placed under Taliban control were not being subjected to social constraints as strict as those imposed by the earlier Taliban administration. However, Omar rejected Karzai's overtures in November 2009, although reports indicated that discussions continued between the government and moderate Taliban leaders.

In March 2010 Mullah Abdul Ghani BARADAR was captured by Pakistani security forces. Baradar was described as the number two Taliban leader in Afghanistan, second only to Mullah Omar. In July the Web site WikiLeaks released a large trove of classified U.S. documents. The Taliban reportedly used the documents to identify Afghans who had been working with coalition forces and the Afghan government.

Reports surfaced in 2011 of growing friction between the Taliban and al-Qaida, especially after the death of Osama bin Laden in May. In January 2012, the Taliban announced it had been granted permission to open a "political office" in Qatar, following intervention by the United States. It was reported that the office served as a site for ongoing peace negotiations.

In September 2013 Pakistan bowed to Afghan demands to release Baradar and six other militant leaders in an effort to reinvigorate negotiations on a ceasefire between the Taliban and Afghan government. However, Mullah Omar declared that the Taliban would not negotiate until NATO withdrew from the country.

Leaders: Mullah Mohammad OMAR (Spiritual Leader and Former Emir of the Self-proclaimed Islamic Emirate of Afghanistan), Laftullah HAKIMI (Self-proclaimed Spokesperson for the "Neo-Taliban"), Qari Mohammad Yousuf AHMADI, Muhammad HANIF, Jalaluddin HAQQANI (Military Commander).

Terrorist Group:

Al-Qaida (The Base). Al-Qaida was established in the 1990s by Osama bin Laden to force U.S. forces out of Saudi Arabia. Bin Laden, a member of one of the wealthiest Saudi families, had participated personally and financially in the mujahidin guerrilla campaign against Soviet forces in Afghanistan. He returned to his native land following the Soviet withdrawal from Afghanistan in 1989 and focused his fundamentalist fervor on the buildup of U.S. forces in Saudi Arabia following the invasion of Kuwait by Iraqi forces. Bin Laden adopted an antimonarchical stance when his call for the withdrawal of U.S. troops was rebuffed.

In 1991 bin Laden relocated to Sudan. He was stripped of his Saudi citizenship in 1995 for funding militant Islamic causes in a number of countries. Under heavy pressure from the United States, the Sudanese government expelled bin Laden in 1996, and he established a base in Afghanistan, where he reportedly helped to finance the Taliban takeover. U.S. officials subsequently accused bin Laden's "terrorist network" of masterminding the embassy bombings in Kenya and Tanzania on August 7, 1998, and American cruise missiles attacked suspected bin Laden camps in Afghanistan two weeks later. Several alleged supporters of bin Laden were arrested in the United States on conspiracy and terrorism charges later in the year, while bin Laden was indicted in absentia.

In March 2000 Jordan announced the arrest of some 28 alleged bin Laden followers on charges of conspiring to conduct a terrorist campaign in the kingdom. Arrests were subsequently also made in the United Kingdom and Germany in what officials described as an international crackdown on groups affiliated with the bin Laden network. Four of his alleged associates were charged in connection with the 1998 embassy bombings (they were subsequently sentenced to life in prison), and al-Qaida was also considered the main suspect in the bombing of the USS *Cole* in Yemen in October 2000 (see article on Yemen for details).

Immediately following the terrorist attacks in the United States on September 11, 2001, Washington described bin Laden as the mastermind of the conspiracy. The U.S. government unsuccessfully pressed the Taliban government to turn over bin Laden and his associates for prosecution before launching Operation Enduring Freedom in Afghanistan and its "war on terrorism" throughout the world. A reward of $25 million was offered for bin Laden, U.S. president George W. Bush declaring the al-Qaida leader would be brought to justice "dead or alive."

Al-Qaida forces fought alongside the Taliban army against advances by the Northern Alliance from October to December 2001, most analysts concluding that al-Qaida had become the main financial backer of the Taliban and its strongest military component. Mohammed ATEF, an al-Qaida military commander, was killed in a November 14 U.S. air strike, and many al-Qaida fighters died during heavy bombing of their cave complex in Tora Bora in the second half of December. Most analysts subsequently concluded that bin Laden had escaped to western Pakistan along with a number of other al-Qaida leaders, one of whom—Abu ZUBAYDAH—was captured in Pakistan in March 2002 and turned over to the United States.

In March 2003 U.S. officials announced that more than half of al-Qaida's "senior operatives" had been killed or captured, including Khalid Shaikh MOHAMMAD (considered one of the masterminds of the September 11, 2001, attacks on the United States), who was arrested in Pakistan. (In March 2007 Mohammad confessed to his role in the U.S. attacks and some 30 other terrorist operations around the world, although skeptics wondered if the confession had been unduly affected by his treatment in U.S. custody.) U.S. forces continued their assault on al-Qaida along the border with Pakistan in mid-2003, Pakistan having also sent soldiers to its side of the border to apply similar pressure. In response, in September Ayman al-Zawahiri (reportedly bin Laden's top lieutenant—see Holy War under Illegal Groups in the article on Egypt for additional information) urged Pakistanis to overthrow President Pervez Musharraf.

In April 2004 a bin Laden tape suggested that al-Qaida would no longer support terrorist attacks in Europe if European governments agreed to remove their military forces from Iraq and Afghanistan. (Many observers had suggested a possible link between al-Qaida and the train bombing in Madrid, Spain, the previous month.) The European leaders immediately rejected the "offer," although political events in Spain were dramatically affected by the train attacks (see article on Spain).

In June 2004, in response to the killing of a kidnapped American, Saudi Arabian security forces killed several leaders of a group calling itself "al-Qaida in the Arabian Peninsula," including Abdelaziz Issa Abdul-Mohson al-MUQRIN. At the same time, followers of Abu Musab al-ZARQAWI, a Jordanian militant heading a group called Tawhid, were reportedly conducting many of the insurgent attacks against U.S. and Iraqi targets in Iraq. Consequently, questions were raised concerning the extent to which bin Laden exercised control over al-Qaida adherents in particular and militant Islamists in general. However, in October al-Zarqawi declared his allegiance to bin Laden, who subsequently endorsed al-Zarqawi as the al-Qaida leader in Iraq (see article on Iraq).

Bombings in Egypt and London in July 2005 were considered by some observers to have links to al-Qaida. Subsequently, al-Zarqawi claimed direct responsibility for a series of bombings in Jordan in November as part of an apparent campaign to broaden his campaign beyond Iraq. (Some reports referred to al-Zarqawi's group as "al-Qaida in Mesopotamia.") However, a degree of friction was reported between al-Zarqawi and al-Zawahiri over al-Zarqawi's apparent endorsement of attacks on Shiites in Iraq and the beheading of hostages. For most of 2005 al-Zawahiri served as the primary al-Qaida spokesperson outside of Iraq, conducting what was described as a "political" campaign to gain greater support throughout the Muslim world. Among other things, al-Zawahiri was the target of a U.S. missile attack on a Pakistani village in January 2006. Meanwhile, Pakistani authorities insisted that Abu Hamza RABIA, described as "number three" in the al-Qaida hierarchy, had been killed in December by Pakistani security forces.

An audiotape released in December 2005 represented the first apparent public message from bin Laden in a year. The tape reportedly offered a vague truce to the United States if all U.S. troops were withdrawn from Afghanistan and Iraq. Washington immediately dismissed the proposal, announcing it would never "negotiate" with al-Qaida. The United States continued to proclaim that al-Qaida was in complete disarray, despite bin Laden's pledge that additional major attacks were being planned. Most analysts concluded that bin Laden and al-Zawahiri remained "deeply hidden" in the Pakistani border area as of spring 2006. Al-Zarqawi was killed in a U.S. air strike in Iraq in June.

Bin Laden subsequently accused the United States of "waging war against Islam," and al-Zawahiri in mid-2006 urged Afghans to "rise up" against the "infidel invaders," i.e., U.S. and NATO forces. It was widely accepted that al-Qaida subsequently continued to operate out of the "lawless tribal areas" of Pakistan. However, al-Qaida also intensified its efforts to serve as an umbrella organization for Islamic militants in other countries in the Middle East, East Africa, North Africa, and other regions. Among other things, a "merger" was announced in September between al-Qaida and the Salafist Group for Preaching and Combat in Algeria, which was later renamed the al-Qaida Organization in the Islamic Maghreb (see Illegal Groups in article on Algeria for details). Al-Qaida later was believed to be seeking affiliation with "franchises" in Kashmir, Lebanon, Libya, Somalia, Syria, and other places. Some analysts suggested that al-Qaida was moving away from an emphasis on direct action of its own and toward pursuing broader ideological influence on small local movements, supported by increasingly effective use of media technology and the Internet. However, in early 2007 UK terrorism experts warned that al-Qaida was still capable of "devastating attacks" and that its networks, now apparently "radiating" from "secure hideouts" in Pakistan, remained "incredibly resilient." Al-Zawahiri pledged that anti-U.S. attacks would increase unless U.S. forces ceased military action in Muslim countries. He also criticized the leaders of Egypt for "collaborating" with the United States and Israel.

U.S. forces attacked suspected al-Qaida targets in Somalia in early 2007 in conjunction with the entry of Ethiopian forces into that country to support the Somali government against Islamic militants. Over the next year arrests related to al-Qaida conspiracies were reported in Morocco, Kenya, Jordan, Italy, the United Kingdom, Yemen, Germany, Austria, Denmark, Azerbaijan, Turkey, and Belgium, while several attacks in Algeria, Yemen, and Mauritania were attributed to al-Qaida sympathizers. Al-Qaida was also described at the end of the year as "fortifying" its connections with antigovernment militants in Pakistan, bin Laden having called for the overthrow of the "infidel" President Musharraf.

In early 2008 analysts pointed out the "robust media and propaganda capability" of al-Qaida, which was increasingly relying on audio- and videotape recordings for recruitment. Much of that campaign was aimed at young people in Iraq, although al-Qaida supporters in that country had come under significant pressure from former Sunni insurgent groups who had realigned themselves with U.S. forces.

Shortly after being inaugurated in early 2009, U.S. president Barack Obama declared that his administration would give priority to efforts to "disrupt, dismantle, and defeat al-Qaida in Pakistan and Afghanistan," and in April U.S. drone missiles attacked suspected al-Qaida sites in Pakistan. Meanwhile, al-Qaida reiterated its support for militant groups in Sudan, Somalia, and other parts of the Horn of Africa.

By the summer of 2010, U.S. officials reported that there were only about 100 al-Qaida operatives left in Afghanistan as the organization increasingly shifted resources to Africa. Through 2010 the use of unmanned aerial drones to attack al-Qaida and Taliban targets in Afghanistan and Pakistan had doubled over the previous year. Meanwhile, reports continued to indicate that the Taliban was distancing itself from al-Qaida, especially from the terrorist group's use of attacks on civilians in Pakistan and Afghanistan.

On May 1, 2011, U.S. special operations forces killed bin Laden during a clandestine raid on the al-Qaida leader's secret compound in Abbottabad, Pakistan. Bin Laden's death was a major victory for the United States, but most observers did not expect his death to significantly change the structure or operations of the organization. On June 16 al-Qaida announced that al-Zawahiri had succeeded bin Laden as the group's new leader. In May 2012 al-Qaida's number two figure in Afghanistan, Sakhr al-Taifi, was killed in a U.S. airstrike. In December Abu Zaid, another senior al-Qaeda figure, and ten others were killed in a U.S. drone strike.

U.S. intelligence reports in 2013 estimated that there were only 50–100 al-Qaeda fighters left in Afghanistan. Other reports indicated a growing "fusion" between al-Qaeda, the Taliban, and other militant groups along the Afghan-Pakistani border. Meanwhile, al-Qaeda continued to be active around the world, including in Mali where the group led a rebellion following a 2012 military coup (see entry on Mali).

Leader: Ayman al-ZAWAHIRI.

LEGISLATURE

Following the overthrow of the Taliban in late 2001, an "emergency" *Loya Jirga* (Grand National Council) was held June 12–19, 2002, as authorized by the Bonn Conference of November–December 2001, to establish a transitional government. The *Loya Jirga* comprised more than 1,500 delegates, about two-thirds of whom were indirectly elected to represent various civic, business, academic, and religious organizations. The remaining delegates were selected by a special commission (appointed as part of the Bonn agreement) to represent minority groups and women.

A new *Loya Jirga* convened in December 2003 to consider a new proposed constitution drafted by a constitutional commission appointed by President Karzai in April. The *Loya Jirga* comprised 500 delegates—450 elected by representatives of the previous *Loya Jirga* and 50 appointed by the president. As approved on January 4, 2004, the new constitution provided for a bicameral **National Assembly** (*Shoray-i-Milli*).

House of Elders (*Meshrano Jirga*). The upper house comprises 102 members: 34 indirectly elected for three-year terms by provincial councils; 34 appointed by the president for five-year terms; and 34 indirectly elected by district councils for four-year terms. The first elections to the 34 provincial councils were held on September 18, 2005, and those councils subsequently each elected one permanent member of the *Meshrano Jirga* from among its ranks. The upper house convened for the first time on December 19, following the announcement of President Karzai's appointments (the president is required to ensure that there are at least 17 women in the *Meshrano Jirga,* as well as 2 Kuchi representatives and 2 representatives of the disabled population). The most recent elections for one-third of the house were held on January 22, 2011.

Speaker: Fazal Hadi MUSLIMYAR.

House of the People (*Wolesi Jirga*). The lower house of the assembly comprises 249 members who are directly elected for a five-year term in single-round balloting. Each of the country's 34 provinces has 2 or more *Wolesi Jirga* representatives, based on population. Voters cast a single vote for one candidate in their province. However, the constitution requires that at least 68 members of the lower house be women and 10 seats are reserved for Kuchi nomads, which can also alter the regular distribution of seats. The most recent election was held on September 18, 2010. Candidates (approximately 2,584) ran as independents, although a number of them appeared easily identifiable as members of various political parties.

Speaker: Abdul Rahoof IBRAHIMI.

CABINET

[as of September 1, 2013]

President	Hamid Karzai (Pushtun)
First Vice President	Mohammad Qasim Fahim (Tajik)
Second Vice President	Karim Khalili (Hazara)
Ministers	
Agriculture, Irrigation, and Livestock	Mohammad Asif Rahimi
Borders and Tribal Affairs	(Vacant)
Commerce and Industry	Anwarul Haq Ahadi
Communications and Information Technology (Acting)	Amir Zai Sangin
Counter-Narcotics	Zarar Ahmed Moqbel
Defense	Gen. Bismillah Mohammadi
Economy	Abdul Hadi Arghandiwal
Education	Farooq Wardak
Energy and Water (Acting)	Mohammad Ishmael Khan
Finance	Omar Zakhilwal
Foreign Affairs	Zalmai Rassoul
Haj and Islamic Affairs	Mohammad Yousef Neyazi
Higher Education (Acting)	Gholam Sarwar Danesh
Information, Culture, and Tourism	Sayed Makhdum Rahin
Interior	Gen. Ghulam Mushtaba Patang
Justice	Habibullah Ghaleb
Martyrs, Disabled, Social Affairs, and Labor	Amina Afzali [f]
Mines	Wahidollah Shahrani
Parliamentary Affairs	Hamyoon Azizi
Public Health (Acting)	Dr. Suraya Dalil [f]
Public Works	Abdul Qudus Hameedi
Refugees	Jamahir Anwari
Rural Rehabilitation and Development	Jarullah Mansoori

Transportation and Civil Aviation (Acting)	Daud Ali Najafi
Urban Affairs (Acting)	Sultan Hussain Hissary
Water and Energy (Acting)	Gen. Mohammad Ismael Khan
Women's Affairs (Acting)	Husn Banu Ghazanfar [f]

[f] = female

INTERGOVERNMENTAL REPRESENTATION

Ambassador to the U.S.: Eklil Ahmad HAKIMI.

U.S. Ambassador to Afghanistan: James B. CUNNINGHAM.

Permanent Representative to the UN: Zahir TANIN.

IGO Memberships (non-UN): ADB, ICC, IOM, NAM, OIC.

ALBANIA

Republic of Albania
Republika e Shqipëri

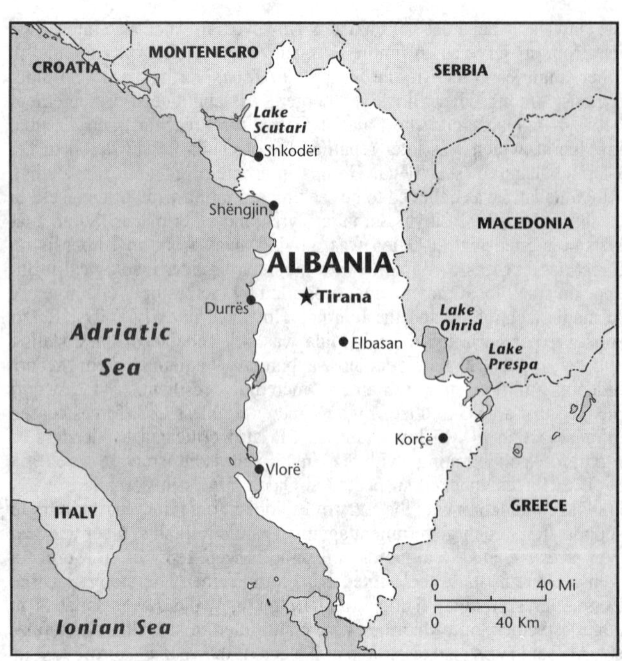

Political Status: Independent state since 1912; Communist regime established in 1946; interim democratic constitution adopted April 29, 1991; permanent constitution approved by national referendum on November 22, 1998, and signed into law by the president on November 28.

Area: 11,100 sq. mi. (28,748 sq. km).

Population: 3,282,246 (2012E—UN); 3,011,405 (2013E—U.S. Census).

Major Urban Centers (2011): TIRANË (TIRANA, 421,000), Elbasan (130,000), Durrës (116,000), Shkodër (96,000), Vlorë (80,000), Korçë (52,000).

Official Language: Albanian.

Monetary Unit: Lek (market rate November 1, 2013: 103.76 lekë = $1US).

President: Bujar NISHANI (formerly Democratic Party of Albania [PDS]); elected in the fourth round of voting by the People's Assembly on June 11, 2012, and sworn in for a five-year term on July 24, succeeding Bamir TOPI (formerly PDS). (Upon election the president is constitutionally required to discard formal party affiliations.)

Prime Minister: Edi RAMA (Socialist Party of Albania); nominated by the president on September 10, 2013 (following the legislative elections of June 23), approved by the People's Assembly on September 15 and inaugurated on September 14 to succeed Sali BERISHA (Democratic Party of Albania).

THE COUNTRY

The Republic of Albania, one of the smallest and least advanced of European nations, is located at the mouth of the Adriatic, where it is flanked by Kosovo and Montenegro on the north, Macedonia on the east, and Greece on the southeast. A mountainous topography has served to isolate the population and retard both national unity and development. The two main ethnic-linguistic groups—the Ghegs north of the Shkumbin River and the Tosks south of that river—together embrace 97 percent of the population. Albanian (*shqip*) is an independent member of the Indo-European language group. There are two dialects corresponding to the ethnic division, the Tosk dialect being in official use. A majority of the population has traditionally been Muslim, but in 1967 Albania was proclaimed an atheist state and religious observances were proscribed until April 1991. (Recent estimates describe 70 percent of the population as "nominally" Muslim, 20 percent Orthodox Christian, and 10 percent Roman Catholic.) More than 20 percent of the successful candidates in the 1991 balloting for the People's Assembly were women, but only 8 women were elected in 2001, 10 in 2005, and 22 in 2009.

Throughout the Communist era, agriculture was dominated by state farms and collectives. In mid-1991, however, the new government adopted a policy of gradually returning the land to peasant ownership or control, yielding a pattern of excessively small holdings with overall productivity one-tenth that of the European Union (EU). Nearly all farmland is now privately owned, and agriculture, primarily at the subsistence level, accounts for roughly a fifth of GDP, although a significant percentage of food and other basic goods is imported. Chrome, nickel, and copper are mined. Industry accounts for about 20 percent of GDP; textiles are a significant export, while the fledgling fishing sector has been targeted for government support. Remittances from workers abroad (an estimated 800,000 in Italy, Greece, and other Western European countries) continue to underpin the Albanian economy, equal to 9 percent of GDP in 2009. The leading trading partners are Italy and Greece, with whom traditional links were revived in the wake of the Communist collapse.

With per capita income estimated at no more than $340 in 1993, Albania was classified as Europe's only "least developed" country. The demise of the socialist system had yielded soaring inflation, paralysis in the industrial sector, massive unemployment, and a huge state budget deficit. Subsequently, however, Albania became one of Europe's fastest-growing economies, achieving an average annual GDP growth of more than 6.5 percent from 1993 to 2001 and more than 5.5 percent from 2002 to 2008. (See the entry in the 2010 *Handbook* for details.)

Despite political discord in Albania in the late 1990s and first half of the 2000s, international lenders such as the International Monetary Fund (IMF) and the World Bank continued to support the government's recovery programs. The IMF praised the government for "steadfast pursuit of sound macroeconomic policies" while urging focus on what was generally conceded to be widespread fraud and corruption, particularly in the customs service and judiciary. Albania's hopes for eventual EU accession also appeared to depend on, among other things, establishment of sufficient border controls to combat trafficking in drugs and arms, successful completion of bank reform currently underway under international supervision, further privatization of inefficient state-run enterprises, and "good governance" on the national and local levels. Other government priorities included modernization of the port in Durrës (as part of the "Corridor VIII" project, a transportation route running from the Black Sea through Bulgaria and Macedonia to Albania's Adriatic coastline), additional infrastructure improvements, and development of the energy sector. The government also pledged to promote the fledgling tourist industry and otherwise attract foreign investment by encouraging "more modern business practices." However, the IMF in 2006 described the business climate as still "relatively uninviting" and called for better enforcement of property rights. Meanwhile, heavy migration from the poor mountainous regions to urban areas compromised basic services and complicated an already unsatisfactory (by Western standards) electoral process. The announced discovery in 2008 of significant new oil and natural gas reserves offered a new spur to economic growth, but exploitation remained years in the future.

GDP growth slowed to an average 2.8 percent over 2009–2011. It was reported in 2009 that annual per capita income had risen to $6,300, although significant disparities remained in regard to the distribution of wealth. Despite having fallen steadily since 2000, unemployment remained high in 2012 at 15 percent. GDP growth slowed further to 1.3 percent in 2012 and is projected by the IMF to grow by 1.8 percent in 2013.

GOVERNMENT AND POLITICS

Political background. Following almost 450 years of Ottoman suzerainty, Albania was declared independent in 1912, but its central government remained weak, despite the proclamation of a monarchy in 1928 by President Ahmet Bey ZOGU, who ruled as King Zog until Italian invasion and annexation in 1939. During the later stages of World War II, the Communist-led National Liberation Front under Gen. Enver HOXHA assumed control of the country, proclaiming its liberation from the Axis powers on November 29, 1944. Hoxha's provisional government obtained Allied recognition in November 1945 on the condition that free national elections be held. On December 21 a Communist-controlled assembly was elected, and the new body proclaimed Albania a republic on January 11, 1946. The Albanian Communist Party, founded in 1941, became the only authorized political organization in a system closely patterned on other communist models. Renamed the Albanian Party of Labor (*Partia e Punës e Shqipërisë*—PPS) in 1948, its Politburo and Secretariat wielded decisive control. Mehmet SHEHU, chair of the Council of Ministers, was purged and killed in 1981 as part of a reorganization that would see Ramiz ALIA succeed as head of state and, after Hoxha's death in 1985, become the second PPS first secretary since World War II. (See the entry in the 2010 *Handbook* for details.)

As late as January 1990 President Alia displayed a hard-line posture in regard to the pace of change in Eastern Europe. In April, however, he proclaimed an end to Albania's policy of diplomatic isolation, and in early May the People's Assembly approved a number of major reforms, including an end to the ban on religious activity, liberalization of the penal code, increased autonomy in enterprise decision making, and the right to passports for all Albanians over the age of six. On December 11, following widespread popular demonstrations, liberalization was further advanced by a declaration that other parties would be recognized, with the Democratic Party of Albania (*Partia Demokratike e Shqipërisë*—PDS), the country's first opposition formation in 46 years, being launched the following day.

Student-led demonstrations in the capital on February, 20, 1991, prompted Alia to declare presidential rule and, two days later, to appoint a provisional government headed by the politically moderate Fatos Thanos NANO. At multiparty balloting on March 31 and April 17 the Communists secured 168 of 250 legislative seats, largely on the basis of their strength in rural areas, while the opposition PDS won 75. The restructured assembly fell into discord at its opening session because of a PDS boycott prompted by the killing of four party members on April 2. On May 9 the president nonetheless appointed Nano to head a new all-PPS government. A fresh wave of street violence ensued, and on June 5 a respected economist, Ylli BUFI, was named to head an interim coalition that was installed on June 12, coincident with redesignation of the PPS as the Socialist Party of Albania (*Partia Socialiste e Shqipërisë*—PSS). The new administration contained 12 representatives from the PSS, 7 from the PDS, and 5 from smaller groups that had failed to win assembly seats.

On December 4, 1991, the PDS announced that it was withdrawing from the government coalition because of foot dragging by the PSS in regard to political reform. Two days later Prime Minister Bufi resigned in favor of Vilson AHMETI, the first non-Marxist government head since World War II. On December 22, ten days after a rally of 20,000 people called for his resignation, President Alia agreed to the scheduling of a new general election.

At two-stage balloting on March 22 and 29, 1992, the PDS won close to a two-thirds majority in a reduced assembly of 140 seats, and on April 3 Alia resigned. Elected by the assembly as Albania's new head of state on April 9, PDS leader Sali BERISHA immediately named Aleksander MEKSI to succeed Ahmeti as prime minister of a tripartite administration that included representatives of the smaller Social Democratic Party of Albania (*Partia Socialdemokrat e Shqipërisë*—PSDS) and Albanian Republican Party (*Partia Republikane Shqiptare*—PRS), in addition to three independents.

President Berisha suffered an unexpected rebuff on November 6, 1994, when a referendum on a post-Communist constitution yielded a 53.9 percent majority against the proposed draft (which in October had failed to secure the required two-thirds legislative majority). The president responded by carrying out a major ministerial reshuffle on December 4. Although the PRS and the PSDS announced their withdrawal from the government, the two PSDS cabinet members promptly formed the breakaway Social Democratic Union of Albania (*Bashkimi i Social Demokratiket i Shqipërisë*—BSDS) and remained in their posts. The reshaped administration retained a comfortable parliamentary majority and derived some benefit from an economic upturn in 1994 and 1995.

A controversial Genocide Law enacted in September 1995 authorized the barring from public life until 2002 of Communist-era officials found to have committed crimes against humanity for political, ideological, or religious motives. Under these measures, some 70 opposition candidates (notably of the ex-Communist PSS) were barred from standing in the legislative elections held May–June 1996.

The first-round balloting on May 26, 1996, was so riddled with malpractice and fraud (as confirmed by international observers) that the main opposition parties boycotted the second round on June 2, as protest demonstrations in Tirana and elsewhere were broken up with considerable police brutality. The official results of the balloting gave the PDS 122 of the 140 seats, with 10 going to the PSS and the other 8 being shared by three parties. The PDS thus acquired substantially better than the two-thirds majority required for passage of constitutional amendments, one of its campaign pledges having been to draw up a fully democratic post-Communist constitution. The substantially changed government sworn in on July 12, under the continued premiership of Meksi, contained 22 PDS representatives, with two posts going to the reinstated PRS and one to the BSDS.

The collapse in early 1997 of the so-called pyramid financial schemes pushed the country to the brink of anarchy, and pressure mounted on President Berisha to resign and call new elections. On February 11 the PRS withdrew from the government, and, with dissent growing even within his own PDS, Berisha on March 1 conceded and ordered the resignation of the government. However, on March 2 the government declared a state of emergency, and, as "rebels" seized control of about one-third of the nation (primarily in the south), Berisha turned to security forces and "northern vigilantes" to defend the regime. Berisha was reelected president (unopposed) by the assembly on March 3, and he soon offered amnesty to the southern rebels and began negotiations with the opposition, which included the ad hoc Forum for Democracy, led by a number of former political prisoners. The opposition demanded Berisha's resignation, early elections, and installation of a government of technocrats to deal with economic problems. Berisha, also under pressure from the EU and the Organization for Security and Cooperation in Europe (OSCE), on March 12 announced the formation of an interim "government of reconciliation." The cabinet, led by the PSS's Bashkim FINO as the new prime minister, included all the major parties. However, Berisha refused to resign as president unless he was repudiated in an election, and the southern rebels declined to lay down their arms until he resigned.

In the face of that impasse, the UN Security Council on March 29, 1997, endorsed a proposal by the OSCE that affirmed the right of self-selected nations to accept the Albanian government's call for foreign military intervention. Fearing that refugees, disorder, and a torrent of smuggled weapons would spill into adjoining states unless the Albanian conflict was resolved, eight nations in mid-April sent a total of about 5,900 troops to Albania under "Operation Alba," designed to help provide humanitarian aid and keep the peace pending new elections.

New legislative elections were conducted on June 29, 1997, after a compromise was reached on enlargement of the assembly to include additional proportional representation. In balloting that was marred by violence but was ultimately deemed "reasonably free and fair" by the OSCE, the PSS overwhelmed the PDS by better than a three-to-one margin (101 seats to 28, including the results of runoff balloting in July). After a period of uncertainty as to his intentions, President Berisha resigned on July 23, and the assembly elected Rexhep MEJDANI (of the PSS) to succeed him the next day. PSS chair Fatos Nano (freed from jail during the recent domestic unrest and subsequently officially pardoned by Berisha) was again sworn in as prime minister on July 25, heading a coalition government of the PSS, the PSDS, the Party of the

Democratic Alliance (*Partia e Alenca Demokratike*—AD), the Albanian Agrarian Party (*Partia Agrare e Shqipërisë*—PAS), and the Union for Human Rights Party (*Partia e Bashkimi për te Drejtat e Njeriut*—PBDNj). Former prime minister Fino of the PSS was named deputy prime minister. Meanwhile, Operation Alba was concluded.

Although the southern rebellion subsided following the installation of the new PSS-led government in 1997, conflict erupted again in August 1998 when six members of the PDS were arrested on charges relating to the repression of the domestic unrest the previous year. In addition, the killing of a prominent PDS activist, Azem HAJDARI, on September 12 outside PDS headquarters prompted thousands of PDS-led protesters to march on government buildings in Tirana the following day. Gunfire was exchanged, and Nano and his cabinet were forced to flee their offices and go into hiding. Demonstrations continued for several days (some 7 people died and nearly 80 were injured) as Berisha called for the resignation of Nano, who in turn accused his PDS adversary of attempting a coup. However, the international community, fearful that Albania was about to repeat the civil strife of 1997, strongly pressured both camps to negotiate a settlement. Order was consequently restored, in part due to Berisha's plea for calm.

Prime Minister Nano resigned on September 28, 1998, and was succeeded by Pandeli MAJKO, who was sworn in on October 2 after receiving the endorsement of the PSS as well as President Mejdani. Majko's cabinet, as approved by the assembly on October 8, comprised the same five parties as the previous government. In keeping with one of Majko's declared priorities, a long-delayed constitutional referendum was held on November 22, the new basic law (see Constitution and government, below) receiving a reported 93.5 percent approval level in a turnout of just above 50 percent of the voters.

The appointment of Majko (at 30 years old, then the youngest prime minister in Europe) was initially perceived as a potentially stabilizing influence, particularly since he had no association with previous Communist governments. However, conflict with the "old guard" quickly surfaced, and Majko stepped down in late October 1999 after losing a PSS leadership battle with Nano. He was succeeded by Deputy Prime Minister Ilir META, whose revamped cabinet easily secured assembly endorsement despite a boycott of the vote by most legislators from the PDS-led Union for Democracy and the United Albanian Right.

The legislative election of June 24 and July 8, 2001, saw the PSS retain a majority, but with fewer seats. Despite PDS complaints of ballot-rigging and other irregularities, international observers regarded the campaign and balloting as fundamentally free and fair. Prime Minister Meta, having renegotiated a coalition agreement with the PSDS, AD, PAS, and PBDNj, won a parliamentary endorsement for his new cabinet on September 12.

Following sustained friction between him and Nano, Prime Minister Meta resigned on January 29, 2002. On February 7 the president invited former prime minister Majko to form a cabinet, which, as endorsed by the assembly on February 22, comprised the same five parties as the outgoing government.

Extensive squabbling over the nomination of the next president of the republic resulted in the selection of a compromise candidate—Gen. (Ret.) Alfred MOISIU—who was endorsed by both the PSS and the PDS. Moisiu took office on July 24, 2002, and the following day Prime Minister Majko retired to make way for Nano, after the PSS had voted to make Nano its parliamentary leader. Nano's new cabinet was sworn in on August 1; it included the PSS, PAS, and PBDNj, but not the PSDS, which objected to losing the post of deputy prime minister. In late December 2003 Nano appointed a new cabinet that included the PSDS and the PBDNj and was also supported by several small parliamentary parties.

The PDS and its allies in the new Alliance for Freedom, Justice, and Welfare (*Aleanca për Liri, Drejtësi, dhe Mirëqenie*—ALDM) secured 74 seats in the July 3, 2005, legislative balloting. Despite initial protests from the PSS over the conduct of the poll, PDS leader Sali Berisha was approved as the new prime minister by an 84–53 vote in the assembly on September 10. Berisha was inaugurated the following day as head of a center-right coalition government that comprised the PDS, Agrarian Environmental Party (*Partia Agrare Ambientaliste*—PAA), PBDNj, and members of two ALDM components (the PRS and the New Democrat Party [*Partia Demokrate e Re*—PDr]).

Local elections were initially planned for mid-2006, but the PSS, led by new chair Edi RAMA, and other opposition parties threatened to boycott the balloting unless broad electoral changes were implemented. An agreement was finally reached to hold the elections in February 2007, but during the crisis leading international organizations (including the EU, North Atlantic Treaty Organization [NATO], OSCE, and the Council of Europe) had warned that Albania's "political maturity" was in question. The PSS-led opposition won a majority of municipal elections, including eight of the nine largest cities (the PDS winning Shkodër). Prime Minister Berisha, acknowledging the need for additional reform, reshuffled his cabinet in March.

Divisions between the left and right continued in the 2007 presidential election. No suitable consensus candidate could be found, and the opposition boycotted the first two rounds of voting, preventing any candidate from achieving the 84 votes necessary for victory. Bamir TOPI of the PDS and Fatos Nano (standing as an independent) dominated the first rounds. In the third round some opposition lawmakers attended the proceedings for the first time, and Neritan ÇEKA of the DPA was added as a candidate. Since the constitution requires that new elections for the assembly must be called if five rounds of voting in the assembly fail to elect a president, additional members of the opposition attended the fourth round on July 20 in order to prevent such a development. Five voted in favor of Topi, who was elected with the support of 85 out of the 90 members present.

The PDS and its allies in the Alliance for Changes (*Aleanca për Ndryshim*—AN) won a plurality of 70 seats in the June 28, 2009, assembly election. On September 17 Prime Minister Berisha formed a new coalition government that included AN parties and the small Socialist Alliance for Integration (*Aleanca Socialiste për Integrim*—ASI).

The 2012 presidential election proved as divisive as that of 2007. The PDS, PSS, and several smaller parties submitted a combined list of 18 candidates. The PDS proposal of Xhezair ZAGANJORI as a compromise candidate was rejected by the PSS, a conflict that dominated the first three rounds, none of which proceeded to a vote. Zaganjori withdrew his candidacy after the third round. Bujar NISHANI of the PDS was elected on the fourth round with 73 votes, with the PSS boycotting the vote.

In early April 2013 the Socialist Movement for Integration (*Lëvizja Socialiste për Integrim*—LSI) announced it would join the PSS in an electoral coalition for the upcoming June 2013 election. The LSI withdrew from the coalition government on April 3, leading to a minor cabinet shake-up.

In the June 23, 2013, assembly election, the PSS and its allies in the Alliance for a European Albania (*Aleanca për Shqipërinë Europiane*—ASHE) won a majority with 84 seats. Edi Rama began the formation of a coalition government between the PSS and LSI, which was formally approved on September 14, 2013.

Constitution and government. A constitution adopted in December 1976 did not significantly alter the system of government introduced three decades earlier. Under its provisions, the former People's Republic of Albania was redesignated as the Socialist People's Republic of Albania and the PPS was identified as "the sole directing political power in state and society." Private property was declared to be abolished, as were the "bases of religious obscurantism"; financial dealings with "capitalist or revisionist monopolies or states" were also outlawed. Under the interim basic law of April 1991, all of these stipulations were abandoned, with the country's name being foreshortened to "Republic of Albania."

The constitution that was approved in a national referendum on November 22, 1998, and signed into law by the president on November 28 codified many of the changes implemented in 1991. The new basic law was described as a "Western-style" document modeled most directly on the German and Italian examples. It describes Albania as a "democratic republic" in which individual human rights (including religious freedom) are guaranteed, as are those of ethnic minorities. Private property rights are also protected, and emphasis is given to a "market-oriented" economy.

The supreme organ of government is the unicameral People's Assembly, none of whose members can be nominated by groups representing ethnic minorities. The assembly elects the republic's president, who is precluded from holding party office and is limited to two 5-year terms. The powers of the president, particularly those regarding the authority to govern by decree in times of emergency, were substantially diluted in the 1998 constitution. Responsibility for day-to-day governmental administration rests with the Council of Ministers, whose head serves as prime minister. The prime minister is appointed by the president, who, upon the proposal of the prime minister, also nominates the Council of Ministers for approval by the assembly. Should the assembly endorse a nonconfidence motion in the Council of Ministers, the president is directed to appoint a new prime minister in an effort to nominate an acceptable council.

The judiciary includes a Supreme Court and district and local courts. For purposes of local administration, Albania is divided into 36 districts (*rrethët*), the municipality of Tirana, over 200 localities, and

2,500 villages. Local councils, elected by direct suffrage for three-year terms, are the governing bodies in each subdivision.

Albanian newspapers tend to be highly politicized in their reporting, whether they are independent or represent a political party. Reporters without Borders has ranked Albania in 102nd place in its 2012 press freedom index.

Foreign relations. Prior to the democratic liberalization of the early 1990s, Albania's pursuit of an antirevisionist and anti-imperialist foreign policy was long conditioned by geography and shifting relationships among external Communist powers. (For a description of the country's four principal phases in dealings with the outside world from the end of World War II to the late 1980s, see the 2007 *Handbook.*)

Albania's transition to multiparty democracy in 1990 and 1991 brought about a transformation in its external relations. Relations with the Soviet Union, United States, Britain, and the Vatican were restored, and Albania became a full member of the OSCE in June 1991. (For details, see the 2012 *Handbook.*)

In the wake of perceived Western indifference to the growing threat to ethnic Albanians and other Muslims in former Yugoslavia, particularly in Kosovo and Macedonia, Albania was reportedly admitted to the Organization of the Islamic Conference (OIC) in December 1992. The OIC membership subsequently became controversial; Prime Minister Nano by 1998 apparently had a preference for orienting Albania toward Europe rather than the Islamic world. In that context, his government launched a crackdown on Islamic fundamentalists in 1998. Following Nano's resignation in September, government officials indicated that Albania was prepared to "reactivate" relations with the OIC.

Relations with Greece worsened in the post-Communist era due to a mass exodus of ethnic Greeks from Albania, attendant border incidents, and renewed Albanian fears of Greek territorial designs. Despite the signature of a series of cooperation agreements by the Albanian and Greek prime ministers in May 1993, tensions flared again in April 1994 as a result of the killing of two Albanian border guards during a raid by activists of the Greek-based Northern Epirus Liberation Front (NELF). Further deterioration caused by an Albanian crackdown on alleged ethnic Greek subversives was partially reversed by a visit to Tirana by the Greek foreign minister in March 1995 and by collateral Greek action against NELF militants. The improvement in bilateral relations yielded a Greek-Albanian friendship treaty in March 1996 that called for cooperation in various fields, as well as mutual respect for the rights of minorities. (Although the question of illegal Albanian immigration subsequently became a significant domestic political issue in Greece, it did not emerge as a significant issue in bilateral relations.)

Albania became a signatory of NATO's Partnership for Peace in February 1994, and Council of Europe membership was conferred in June 1995. A U.S.-Albanian military cooperation agreement was signed in October 1995, following an official visit to Washington by President Berisha a month earlier, and a U.S. military aid package worth over $100 million was approved in April 1996. Meanwhile, Albania's relations with Italy and other EU countries continued to be complicated by the role of Albanian Adriatic ports as staging areas for illegal immigrants of various origins seeking to reach Western Europe. In addition, the presence of significant ethnic Albanian populations in neighboring countries prompted discussions in some circles over the possibility of a "Greater Albania," particularly with respect to Kosovo and the western regions of Macedonia. In late 1998 and early 1999 Prime Minister Majko carefully endorsed Western policy regarding Kosovo, agreeing that the province should seek autonomy within Yugoslavia, not independence, despite significant sentiment within the Albanian populace for the latter.

Not surprisingly, the government strongly endorsed the military campaign that NATO launched against Serbia in late March 1999, although the initiative produced an influx of some 450,000 refugees from Kosovo. A NATO force of more than 5,000 personnel was stationed in Albania until September 1999 in connection with the anti-Serbian operation, Albania subsequently expressing the hope that support for NATO in the campaign would facilitate Albania's eventual accession to that alliance. During the ethnic fighting in neighboring Macedonia in 2001, Prime Minister Meta also made his intentions clear: although supportive of the cause of ethnic Albanian rights, he condemned violent acts, rejected militant calls for border changes, and disavowed any interest in formation of a "Greater Albania."

Albania supported the U.S./UK-led invasion of Iraq in 2003 and contributed a small contingent of troops to the NATO mission in Afghanistan, with 216 in place in June 2013.

The Nano government, keenly focused on potential accession to the EU, maintained its distance from the independence movement among ethnic Albanians in Kosovo. In early 2006 new Prime Minister Berisha referred to the "will for independence" among the population in Kosovo, perhaps thereby signaling a shift in attitude from the previous administration regarding that delicate issue. On February 18, 2008, Albania was one of the first states to formally recognize the independence of Kosovo.

Albania signed a Stabilization and Association Agreement with the EU in June 2006, and at the April 2008 Bucharest Conference NATO formally tendered an accession invitation to Albania. Meanwhile, in 2007 Albania became the first country under the Chemical Weapons Convention of 1997 to completely destroy its stockpiles of chemical weapons. On April 1, 2009, Albania formally became a member of NATO.

Albania's Stabilization and Accession Agreement with the EU entered into force on the same day, prompting its formal application on April 28, 2009, for full EU membership. The European Commission recommended in October 2012 that Albania be granted candidate status subject to key reforms in the judiciary, public administration, and parliamentary rules of procedures.

Current issues. Although domestic political differences are less volatile than in 1997–1998, the political divide—particularly between the PSS and PDS—remains a critical aspect of domestic affairs. Domestic nongovernmental organizations and foreign observers questioned whether the adoption of a new electoral code in 2009 would impair the ability of smaller parties to compete with the PDS and PSS (see the 2013 *Handbook*). Not surprisingly, the June 28 assembly elections produced a broad decline in the fortunes of smaller parties, despite the involvement of nearly every such party in large electoral coalitions. The election proved unusually close, however, and the PSS refused to recognize the validity of the results and requested recounts in selected districts, thereby delaying the announcement of a new PDS-led government until September.

Requesting a parliamentary inquiry into the 2009 election process, the PSS boycotted parliamentary sessions from September 2009 to May 2010, after which PSS deputies went on a 21-day hunger strike. Representatives of EU political groups met with Berisha and Rama in an attempt to mediate the political deadlock, warning that Albania's accession talks with the EU were in jeopardy over the issue. Despite this, the PSS continued to organize protests. Significant demonstrations in January 2011 followed the release of a videotape that appears to show Deputy Prime Minister Meta requesting preferential consideration for his associations regarding government contracts. Meta resigned amid allegations of corruption, but the resulting demonstrations organized by the PSS led to violence and four dead on January 21.

The OSCE described the May 2011 elections as "competitive and transparent but took place in an environment of high polarization and mistrust between parties in government and opposition" and expressed concern about outbreaks of violence, including a car bomb attack against a PSS candidate. Although the PDS and PSS each accused the other of misconduct, the most significant dispute emerged over the extremely close results for the mayoral race in Tirana. An initial victory by Rama by ten ballots was contested by the PDS, whose own candidate, Lulzim BASHA, was subsequently found to be the victor by 93 ballots in a recount conducted by the Central Electoral Commission. The PSS disputed the results, alleging voting irregularities, and had organized a new wave of antigovernment protests in mid-2011.

Nationalist ethnic Albanian parties criticized the October 2011 census for introducing questions on ethnicity and native language, fearing that this would encourage Greece to press territorial claims. The Greek minority parties *Omonia* and PBDNj in turn criticized the census' requirement that expressed ethnic identity must correlate with that on a respondent's birth certificate, and argued that Communist-era certificates often did not accurately reflect ethnicity. In May 2012, *Omonia* announced it would conduct its own census of the Greek population.

In November 2011, in an agreement widely reported to have been motivated by the desire to accelerate EU candidate status, the government and opposition agreed to work together for election reform. Subsequent progress, however, has been slow and marred by continued tension between the PDS and PSS.

In January 2012, Prosecutor General Ina RAMA ordered the arrest of the commander of the Republican Guard for murder in connection to the January 2011 demonstrations. In February, parliamentary immunity was removed from three PSS deputies accused of inciting violence in the demonstrations. Both the government and the opposition have attacked the ongoing investigation as politically motivated.

In advance of June 2013 parliamentary elections, the Central Election Committee (CEC) had deadlocked over proposals to reallocate parliamentary seats between districts in light of demographic changes. The CEC is comprised of four members nominated by the ruling government and three by the opposition, and the LSI's departure from government led to the PDS initiating parliamentary procedures to replace an LSI-nominated member. Two PSS-nominated members subsequently resigned in protest, leading to domestic and international expressions of concern as the political conflict continued into May.

The OSCE has characterized the June 2013 election as "competitive with … genuine respect for fundamental freedoms." But it also noted that political tensions continued to be a factor and that procedural irregularities took place. The EU has condemned an exchange of gunfire between PDS and PSS members near a polling station in the city of Lac on election day that left one dead and one wounded. Although the DPS initially contested the results, Sali Berisha conceded defeat for the PDS on June 26. However, both the PSS and DPS requested recounts in two regions, a request granted by the CEC in July.

POLITICAL PARTIES

Until December 1990, when the first opposition party was recognized, Albania accorded a monopoly position to the Albanian Party of Labor (*Partia e Punës e Shqipërisë*—PPS), which served as the core of the Democratic Front of Albania (*Fronti Demokratik ë Shqipërisë*—FDS), a mass organization to which all adult Albanians theoretically belonged. Although numerous parties were registered in 1991 and the first half of 1992, the People's Assembly in July 1992 banned all parties identifiable as "fascist, antinational, chauvinistic, racist, totalitarian, communist, Marxist-Leninist, Stalinist, or Enverist," the last in reference to former Communist leader Enver Hoxha. The 1992 law was revised in 1998 to repeal the ban against communist parties (among other things), although proscription was maintained against "antinational, anti-Albanian, antidemocratic, and totalitarian" groups. There are no current restrictions on parties based on ethnicity, religion, or regional status, as long as such parties do not denigrate other groups.

Government Parties:

Alliance for a European Albania (*Aleanca për Shqipërinë Europiane*—ASHE). This PSS-led coalition is a continuation of the 2009 **Unification for Changes** (*Bashkimi për Ndryshim*—BN) alliance, which had evolved from the "Union for the Future" formed for the 2007 municipal balloting. In addition to the PSS, the BN included the PSDS, PBDNj, G99, and PDSSh. The BN won 45.3 percent of the vote in the 2009 assembly elections and secured 66 seats. The PSS announced the formation of the ASHE on April 24, 2013, as a coalition of 37 opposition parties. The ASHE won 57.7 percent of the vote in the June 2013 assembly elections and secured 84 seats.

Socialist Party of Albania (*Partia Socialiste e Shqipërisë*—PSS). The PSS is a successor to the Communist Party of Albania (*Partia Komuniste e Shqipërisë*—PKSH), which was launched in November 1941 under the supervision of Yugoslav emissaries and became the ruling single party following World War II. The PKS was renamed the Albanian Party of Labor (*Partia e Punës e Shqipërisë*—PPS) in 1948.

In April 1991 at the conclusion of the country's first multiparty balloting since World War II, the PPS had won a better than two-thirds majority in the new People's Assembly. However, due to subsequent popular unrest, it was forced to participate in a "nonpartisan" governing coalition on June 12, at which time it adopted its current name. In light of these developments, a rump group organized the new Albanian Communist Party (see PKSH, below).

In the March 1992 general election the PSS won only 38 of 140 seats with 25 percent of the vote. As a result, Alia resigned as president of the republic, and the party, for the first time, moved into opposition. Alia and his successor as party leader, Fatos Thanos Nano, were both arrested in mid-1993, Nano being convicted in April 1994 of having mishandled $8 million in Italian aid funds during his 1991 incumbency as prime minister. Alia and nine former colleagues also received prison sentences. Alia was released in July 1995, but he was imprisoned in February 1996 on charges of "genocide" and "crimes against humanity" in connection with the alleged killing or internment of Albanians who had attempted to flee the country during his tenure. Nano also remained in prison during the May–June 1996 election, from which many PSS candidates were barred because of their Communist affiliations. Opposition protests over the conduct of the balloting were headed by the PSS, which was officially credited with 10 seats despite boycotting the second round.

In a communication from his prison cell in July 1996, Nano proposed that the PSS should drop all references to Marxism in its constitution. In the rebellion of early 1997 (see Political background, above), Nano and Alia escaped from prison along with hundreds of others. Nano was subsequently pardoned by President Berisha, who was under pressure to include the PSS in an interim "government of reconciliation." Meanwhile, Alia fled the country, returning in December after having been declared innocent of all outstanding charges by the Albanian courts in October.

The PSS, showing its greatest strength in the south, swept to victory in the 1997 elections, taking 101 seats, which, with 18 seats secured by five allies (the PSDS, AD, PBDNj, PUK, and PAS [see below]) in an Alliance of State coalition, gave the party a secure margin for amending the constitution. Following severe political turmoil in 1998, Nano resigned his PSS leadership in early 1999 but made a comeback at the October PSS Congress, defeating Majko for the chair by a vote of 291–261. PSS Deputy Chair Ilir Meta was subsequently selected to be the new prime minister.

In the 2001 national election the PSS barely retained its majority, winning 73 seats in a downsized People's Assembly. However, Nano was reelected chair of the PSS at a December 2003 congress that also demanded that PSS legislators toe the party line on major votes or else quit the party. Meta and a number of PSS legislators subsequently left the PSS to form the LSI (below).

The PSS in early 2005 reportedly announced plans to contest the July legislative poll under informal cooperative arrangements with the PSDS, PAS, PBDNj, and a faction of the AD. While the PSS called upon its supporters to vote for the smaller parties in the nationwide proportional balloting, the initiative failed to gain the kind of cohesion exhibited by the PDS-aligned ALDM (below). In addition, the PSS presented its own candidate in each single-member constituency, sometimes in direct competition with candidates from its "allies." The PSS secured 42 seats and moved to the opposition.

Following the defeat of the PSS in the July 2005 balloting, Nano resigned as the PSS chair in September. He was succeeded by Edi Rama (the mayor of Tirana), who defeated former president Mejdani for the post.

The PSS in 2006 led the opposition in demanding broad electoral changes for the scheduled municipal elections. In forming a left-wing coalition for the February 2007 municipal balloting, the PSS reportedly agreed to give its smaller partners greater representation among joint candidates than had been offered in the ill-fated 2005 negotiations.

Tensions between pro-Rama and pro-Nano factions increased in 2007 when Rama denied political backing for Nano's bid for the presidency. In September 2007 Nano announced his resignation from the party and the establishment of a new party, the **Movement for Solidarity,** although it subsequently failed to emerge as a significant political force.

Although initially supportive of the new electoral code approved in 2008, the PSS subsequently accused the ruling PDS of failing to implement some aspects of electoral reform. Domestic analysts suggested that Rama's support for electoral reform was intended to weaken the LSI as a rival on the left. Following the release of preliminary results of the June 2009 assembly elections (in which the PSS secured 65 of the BN's 66 seats), the PSS condemned the results as fraudulent. Rama continued to reject the results into August, calling for early elections for a new assembly. This position, combined with criticism that his refusal to cooperate with the LSI led to the defeat in the 2009 elections, led to calls within the party for Rama's resignation. However, he was reelected as leader of the PSS at an extraordinary party congress in September. The PSS organized frequent antigovernment rallies following the 2009 election, with notable protest waves in November 2009, May 2010, January–February 2011, and May 2011. In the May 2011 local elections, the PSS led the broad **Coalition for the Future** (*Aleanca për të Ardhmen*—ApA) of 25 parties.

On April 23, 2013, the PSS absorbed the **Real Socialist Party 91** (*Partia Socialiste e Vertete '91*—PSV '99), although the party remained on the electoral rolls as a member of ASHE.

In the 2013 assembly balloting, the PSS won 66 seats with 41.4 percent of the vote.

Leaders: Edi RAMA (Chair), Gramoz RUÇI (Parliamentary Leader).

Socialist Movement for Integration (*Lëvizja Socialiste për Integrim*—LSI). A left-of-center splinter from the PSS, the LSI was launched under the leadership of former prime minister Ilir Meta, who had been feuding with PSS leader Nano for several years. Nine PSS legislators reportedly joined the LSI, which ran separately from all other parties in the 2005 legislative poll, securing five seats (four on a vote share of 8.4 percent in the proportional balloting). The LSI agreed to join the PSS-led opposition coalition for the February 2007 local balloting but broke with the PSS in 2008 and led the formation of the ASI. In late 2008 the LSI formed the **Socialist Alliance for Integration** (*Aleanca Socialiste për Integrim*—ASI), an effort to build a left-leaning "third force" in Albanian politics. In addition to the LSI, the coalition included the LDLNj, PSV '91, PGj, PMDE, and PTR. In the 2009 assembly balloting the LSI garnered 5 percent of the nationwide vote (the ASI as a whole securing 5.5 percent) and secured all of the coalition's four seats. The LSI subsequently joined the new PDS-led AN government, which exacerbated the LSI's already acrimonious relations with the PSS. In early 2013 negotiations between the two parties led to an agreement in March to pursue an electoral alliance in the upcoming parliamentary elections.

In the 2013 assembly elections, the LSI won 16 seats with 10.4 percent of the vote.

Leaders: Ilir META (Party Chair, Chair of the Presidency of the People's Assembly, and Former Prime Minister), Pellumb XHUFI (Deputy Chair), Ndre LEGISI.

Union for Human Rights Party (*Partia e Bashkimi për te Drejtat e Njeriut*—PBDNj). The PBDNj was established in February 1992 following the enactment of legislation banning parties based on "ethnic principles." The new law was aimed in particular at the **Democratic Union of the Greek Minority** (*Bashkimia Demokratik i Minoritet Grek*), referenced as *Omonia,* the transliteration of the Greek word for "harmony." The PBDNj became the electoral successor of *Omonia,* winning two assembly seats in March 1992 against *Omonia*'s five seats in 1991.

Representing the southern ethnic Greek community, *Omonia* had been formed by clandestine opponents of the former regime in December 1989 but contended that any territorial change between Albania and Greece should come only from negotiation and agreement. Six prominent *Omonia* members were among many ethnic Greeks detained in May 1994 in a government crackdown on suspected subversion. A further crackdown against Greek separatists was mounted in March 1995.

The PBDNj was credited with winning three assembly seats in 1996 and four in 1997. It joined the PSS-led coalition in July 1997, a decision reportedly opposed by some members of *Omonia,* which had maintained a separate identity as a cultural organization despite usually close ties with the PBDNj. Vasil MELO, then leader of the PBDNj, defended the 1998 constitution as providing sufficient protection for minorities, although *Omonia* leaders in January 2000 called for greater attention to minority issues, particularly the provision of educational services in Greek where appropriate.

The PBDNj won three proportional seats, with 2.6 percent of the vote, in the 2001 election. Vangjel DULE was elected chair of the PBDNj at a party congress in February 2002 that Melo derided as "illegitimate and manipulated." The PBDNj was given one portfolio in the December 2003 cabinet led by the PSS.

After securing two proportional seats (on a vote share of 4.1 percent), the PBDNj was given the ministry of labor, social affairs, and equal opportunities in the new PDS-led cabinet. In the 2009 elections it won over 1 percent of the vote and secured a single seat in the assembly.

In March 2010 members of *Omonia* and the PBDNj founded a new party, the **Greek Minority for the Future** (*Minoriteti Etnik Grek për të Ardhmen*—MEGA), led by Kristo KICO. In late 2010 the PBDNJ reportedly absorbed the **Human Rights League Party** (*Partia Lëvizja për te Drejtat dhe Lirite e Njeriut*—LDLNj), a group led by Ligoraq Karamelo.

In the June 2013 assembly election, the PBDNj secured a single seat with 0.9 percent of the vote.

Leaders: Vangjel DULE (President), Leonard SOLIS (Deputy Chair), Ligoraq KARAMELO, Vasilis BOLLANO.

Christian-Democratic Party (*Partia Kristian Demokrate e Shqipërisë*—PKDSH). Registered prior to the 2011 local elections, the PKDSH was obscured by its participation in an electoral alliance with the Christian Democratic Alliance. The party gained notoriety after a member of the party was accused of the February murder of a local police chief; media attention increased when his brother, Mark Frroku, was registered as a parliamentary candidate.

In the June 2013 assembly election, the PKDSH secured a single seat with 0.5 percent of the ballot. In July Dhimiter Muslia was replaced as chair by Frroku (who held the party's lone assembly seat).

Leaders: Mark FRROKU (Chair), Dhimiter MUSLIA.

Party of National Unity (*Partia e Unitetit Kombëtar*—PUK). Organized in June 1991 by former Communists, the PUK forged links with Kosovo's Albanian community. Its posture of extreme nationalism was said to be supported, in part, by Albanian "Mafia" groups in Turkey and elsewhere. PUK leader Idajet Beqiri was sentenced to a six-month prison term in July 1993 for asserting that President Berisha sought to create a fascist dictatorship. In January 1996 Beqiri was again arrested, this time charged with crimes against humanity as a communist-era prosecutor. However, he was subsequently pardoned along with members of the PSS. (Beqiri has subsequently also been referenced as a leader of the underground AKSh, below.)

The PUK earned one seat in the 1997 election as a member of the PSS-led Alliance of State. It won only 0.2 percent of the vote and no seats in 2001.

The PUK participated in the 2005 assembly elections with several other small parties in a coalition called the **Albanian Social Parties and National Unity Party** (*Partite e Spektrit dhe Partia e Unitetit Kombëtar*—PSS + PUK). Other components of the coalition included the PA, the PPS, and the **Party for the Defense of Workers' Rights** (*Partia për Mbrojtjen e te Drejtave te Punëtorëve*—PMDP).

Beqiri was arrested in May 2012 in Kosovo, reportedly on an international arrest warrant for "inciting ethnic hatred," but was subsequently released.

Leader: Idajet BEQIRI (Chair).

G99 (*Grupim 99*—G99). Formed in 2008 by members of the Mjaft! ("Enough!") nongovernmental organization, the G99 is predominantly a party of younger Albanians who grew to adulthood after 1991. The party's platform is broadly social democratic, advocating both reform within Albania and youth participation in politics. Although polling well in late 2008 and early 2009, the party took less than 1 percent of the nationwide vote in the June 2009 elections.

Leader: Ervin METE (Chair).

Albanian Communist Party (Partia Komuniste Shqiptare—PKSH). The PKSH was organized in 1991 by a rump of the PPS after the parent group adopted the PSS rubric. Although accorded legal recognition in November 1991, the PKSH was subsequently outlawed by the mid-1992 ban on "extremist" organizations. When the 1992 law was repealed in April 1998, the PKSH was in effect reregistered. It won about 0.9 percent of the vote in 2001 and 0.7 percent in 2005.

Leader: Qemal CICOLLARI.

Albanian Homeland Party (*Partia Shqiptare Atdheu*—PShA). Initially denied legal status in 2004 on the grounds that it was a religion-based (Muslim) grouping, the PShA was subsequently permitted by the Court of Appeals to register for the 2005 assembly balloting. The founding leader of the PShA, Artan SHAQIRI, a prominent young religious leader, called, among other things, for the introduction of religious education into the Albanian school system.

Leader: Kreshnik OSMANI.

Law and Justice Party (*Partia Ligj dhe Drejtësi*—PLiDr). Founded in February 2009 by defectors from the PDS, the PLiDR is a center-right party with an anticorruption and "law and order" agenda. Running without coalition partners, it secured less than 1 percent of the vote in the 2009 assembly elections.

Leaders: Spartak NGJELA (Chair).

Social Democratic Party of Albania (*Partia Socialdemokrate e Shqipërisë*—PSDS). The PSDS was launched in 1991 on a platform of moderate socialism; it finished third in the 1992 poll, winning seven assembly seats, and became a junior partner in the new government headed by the PDS. Following the president's

November 1994 referendum defeat, the PSDS officially withdrew from the coalition, although the two cabinet representatives previously associated with the party opted to retain their portfolios as members of the breakaway BSDS.

The PSDS formed an alliance, called the Pole of the Center (*Poli i Quendres*—PQ), with the AD for the 1996 legislative poll as a centrist alternative to the ruling PDS on the right and the PSS on the left; the PQ secured no seats in that election. However, the PSDS offered some joint candidates with the PSS for the June 1997 balloting, in which nine PSDS members were elected, and the PSDS joined the subsequent coalition government. After winning four seats at the 2001 election, it again joined the government. The PSDS declined to join the July 2002 cabinet because it was not offered the post of deputy prime minister that it had previously held. However, the PSDS returned to the cabinet in December 2003, and, despite his steady criticism of perceived administration failures, PSDS chair Skënder Gjinushi said the party would support the PSS-led government in the run-up to the July 2005 legislative poll and beyond. The PSDS secured seven seats (on a vote share of 13 percent) in the proportional component of the 2005 balloting.

Leaders: Dr. Skënder GJINUSHI (Chair and Former Deputy Prime Minister), Engjell BEJTJA (General Secretary).

Social Democracy Party of Albania (*Partia Demokracia Sociale e Shqipërisë*—PDSSh). Formed in April 2003 by several disgruntled members of the PSDS (including Paskal Milo, a former member of the PSDS presidency), the PDSSh described itself as a center and center-left grouping devoted to the concerns of a populace that was "tired of the left's unkept promises." The PDSSh subsequently appeared to move in and out of the PSS-led Coalition for Integration, although it was reportedly supportive of the coalition during the run-up to the July 2005 legislative balloting. The PDSSh secured two proportional seats (on a vote share of 4.3 percent) in the 2005 assembly balloting. In the 2009 assembly elections it polled approximately 2 percent of the nationwide vote but failed to secure any seats.

Leader: Paskal MILO (Chair).

Minor parties within the coalition include the **Alliance for Equality and European Justice** (*Aleanca për Barazi dhe Drejtësi Europiane*—ABDE), led by Valentin MUSTAKA; **Environmentalist Party** (*Partia Ambjentaliste*—PA), led by Nasi BOZHEKU; **Albanian Future Party** (*Partia Ardhmërija Shqiptare*—PASH), led by Emin SUBASHI; **Albanian Republican Union** (*Partia Bashkimi Republikan Shqiptar*—PBR), led by Zane LLAZI; **Democratic Party for Integration and Prosperity** (*Partia Demokrate për Integrim e Prosperitet*—PDIP), led by Halil SEITAJ; **Party of Albanian Issues** (*Partia e Çështjeve Shqiptare*—PÇSH), led by Bujar SHURDI; **Green Party** (*Partia e Gjelber*—PGJ), led by Edlir PETANAJ; **Albanian Party of Labor** (*Partia e Punës Shqiptërisë*—PPSh), led by Muharrem XHAFAJ; **Democratic Reform Party** (*Partia e Reformave Demokratike Shqiptare*—PRDSh), led by Skender HALILI; **Albanian Communist Party of 8 November** (*Partia Komuniste e Shqipërisë 8 Nëntori*—PKSH-8 Nëntori), led by Preng CUNI; **Democratic Movement for Change** (*Partia Levizja Demokratike per Ndryshim*—PLDN), led by Nikolin STAKA; **Albanian Movement for Justice** (*Partia Lëvizja për Drejtësi e Shqiptarëve*—LDSH), led by Astrit KOSTURI; **Right Liberal Thought Party** (*Partia Mendimi i Djathte Liberal*—MDL), led by Mustafa LICI; **Party for Migrant's Rights** (*Partia për Mbrojtjen e të Drejtave të Emigrantëve*—PMDE), led by Ymer KURTI; **People with Disabilities Party** (*Partia Personat me Aftësi të Kufizuar*—PPAK), led by Afrim JESHILI; **Path of Freedom Party** (*Partia Rruga e Lirisë*—PRrL), led by Kurt KOLA; **Social Labor Party of Albania** (*Partia Socialpuntore Shqiptare*—PSP), led by Ramadan NDREKA; **Moderate Socialist Party** (*Partia Socialiste e Moderuar*—PSM), led by Gjergj KOJA; **New Tolerance of Albania Party** (*Partia Toleranca e Re e Shqipërisë*—PTReSh), led by Avdi KECI; **Albanian Labor Movement** (*Partia Lëvizja Punëtore Shqiptare*—PLPSH), led by Shefqet MUSARAJ; **National Arbnore Alliance** (*Aleanca Arbnore Kombetare*—AAK), led by Gjet NDOJ; **Christian Democratic Alliance** (*Partia Aleanca Demokristiane e Shqiperise*—ADK), led by Zef BUSHATI; **Party for National Reconciliation** (*Partia Pajtimit Kombëtar*—PPK), led by Spartak DOBI; **People's Alliance Party** (*Partia Aleanca Popullore*—AP), led by Artur DOJAKA; and **Reformed Albanian Labor Party** (*Partia e Punes e Shqiperise e Rioganizuar*—PPSHR), led by Marko DAJTI.

Opposition Parties:

Alliance for Employment, Prosperity and Inegration (*Aleanca për Punësim Mirëqenie dhe Integrim*—APMI). The APMI is an outgrowth of previous right-wing political alliances. In the 2005 assembly elections, the BLD, PBK, PRS, PDK, PBD, PLDLNj, and PDr had formed the PDS-supportive Alliance for Freedom, Justice, and Welfare (*Aleanca për Liri, Drejtësi, dhe Mirëqenie*—ALDM). Due to the PDS support, the ALDM received 33 percent of the proportional vote in the 2005 poll and was accorded 18 assembly seats (PRS, 11; PDr, 4; PDK, 2; and BLD, 1), subsequently joining the PSD in forming a government. This expanded into a rightist "grand alliance" for the February 2007 municipal elections, including the PDS, PRS, PDK, PAA, PBD, PLL, BLD, and other small groups. In the 2009 assembly elections, the PDS led the **Alliance for Changes** (*Aleanca për Ndryshim*—AN), which included the PBK, PRS, AD, PLL, AMIE, PAA, and six smaller parties. The AN secured 46.9 percent of the nationwide vote in the 2009 assembly elections and won 70 seats. A similar grouping, the **Coalition for the Citizen** (*Aleanca për Qytetarin*—ApQ), was formed for the May 2011 local elections.

The formation of the APMI was announced on April 24, 2013, and included 25 parties in all. The APMI took 39.4 percent of the vote and secured 56 assembly seats.

Democratic Party of Albania (*Partia Demokratike e Shqipërisë*—PDS). The PDS, launched in December 1990, sought protection of human rights, a free-market economy, and improved relations with neighboring states. Serious tensions in the PDS following the 1992 elections were highlighted by the departure of six moderate leftists in July 1992 to form the AD (below), after which the PDS-led government was accused of authoritarian leanings. The party leadership responded by expelling several rightists, who later formed the ultranationalist PDDS (see PDr, below).

In March 1995 Eduard SELAMI was dismissed as PDS chair for criticizing President Berisha,, then ousted from the PDS national council later that month along with seven other members. Although the party's landslide victory in the May–June balloting was tarnished by evidence of widespread voting irregularities, a new PDS-dominated government took office in July. However, the PDS was crushed in the legislative elections of June–July 1997, dropping from 122 to 28 seats. (The PDS participated in the 1997 balloting in a Union for Democracy [*Bashkimi për Demokraci*—BD] coalition that also included the PLL, BSDS, PDK, PBD and a number of other small parties. The BD won only 31 seats, including the 28 PDS seats. Meanwhile, another smaller conservative grouping—the United Albanian Right [*Djatha e Bashkuar e Shqipërisë*—DBS]—won 4 seats. Members of the DBS included the PBK, PRS, PDDS, and LD [see under PDr below].)

PSS/PDS friction continued following the 1997 balloting, reportedly fueled by animosity between Berisha and the PSS's Fatos Nano. Consequently, the PDS boycotted most legislative activity. Six high-ranking PDS members were arrested in August 1998 on charges related to suppression of the 1997 domestic unrest, and the tension between the two leading parties almost erupted into civil war in September after Azem Hajdari, a controversial PDS legislator, was assassinated outside PDS headquarters in Tirana. Although Hajdari's murder remained unsolved, an extraordinary PDS congress voted in July 1999 to end the party's ten-month assembly boycott. Subsequently, Berisha was able to beat back a challenge from Genc Pollo, leader of the PDS reform wing, for the party's chair at the October 1999 regular congress. In January 2001 Pollo broke from the PDS and established the Democrat Party (see PD, below).

Prior to the 2001 legislative balloting, the PDS organized the Union for Victory (*Bashkimi për Fitore*) coalition with the PLL, BLD, PBK, and PRS. The coalition was largely a successor to the Union for Democracy of 1997. The Union for Victory secured 46 seats, although Berisha claimed that massive irregularities had cost the PDS and its allies many other seats.

The PDS signed electoral cooperation agreements for the July 2005 legislative balloting with seven small groupings that had coalesced as the ALDM (above). Under the unique arrangements, the PDS presented 1 candidate in each of the 100 single-member constituencies, although 15 of those candidates reportedly were in fact members of various ALDM components. Collaterally, the PDS urged its supporters to vote for the ALDM in the national proportional balloting.

In 2007 PDS candidate Bamir Topi was elected president of Albania. Topi accordingly resigned his party membership in a show of impartiality, although for a time he maintained close political relations with Prime Minister Berisha.

In October 2008 the New Democrat Party (*Partia Demokrate e Re*—PDr) merged into the PDS. Also referenced simply as the Democrat Party (*Partia Demokrate*—PD), the PDr, originating in the reform wing of the PDS, was organized in January 2001 by former PDS leader Genc Pollo. The new formation also incorporated the former Movement for Democracy (*Lëvizja për Demokraci*—LD) and the Democratic Party of the Right of Albania (*Partia Demokratike e Djatha e Shqipërisë*—PDDS), both of which were participants in 1997's United Albanian Right. The PDr won six seats in the 2001 assembly balloting. In 2002 former LD leader Dashamir Shehi (then the PDr secretary general) and several other PDr legislators attempted unsuccessfully to push Pollo out of the PDr leadership. Shehi and the others subsequently formed a new party (see PDRn, under PLL, below). As part of the ALDM, the PDr secured four seats in the proportional component of the July 2005 assembly balloting.

In 2009 the PDS campaigned on a platform of further integration with Europe, citing the government's success in achieving admission into NATO early that year. The party won 68 of the AN's 70 seats in the June assembly balloting and 40 percent of the vote nationwide.

Berisha and President Bamir Topi clashed in February 2012 after Topi refused to sign PDS-backed legislation previously ruled unconstitutional by the country's Constitutional Court. Topi, accusing Berisha of corruption, brought a faction of the PDS out into a new party founded in April, the **New Democratic Spirit** (*Fryma e Re Demokratike*—FRD), led by Gazmend OKETA.

In the June 2013 election, the PDS won 49 and 30.5 percent of the vote. Following the electoral defeat, Berisha has renounced his position as party chair on June 26, to take effect in a party congress in September.

Leaders: Sali BERISHA (Outgoing Chair), Genc POLLO (Former Chair of the PDr), Jozefina TOPALLI (Vice President), Astrit PATOZI (Vice Chair and Parliamentary Leader), Ridvan BODE (Secretary General).

Albanian Republican Party (*Partia Republikane Shqiptare*—PRS). Third-ranked in the 1991 balloting, the PRS is an urban formation with links to the Italian Republican Party, from which it appears to have drawn financial support. The first PRS congress in June 1992 was marred by a major split, resulting in the creation of distinct centrist and right-wing groups.

The PRS withdrew from the ruling coalition in December 1994, criticizing the government's "shortcomings" but pledging itself to "constructive" opposition. It was reinstated with two posts in the government appointed in July 1996, despite winning only three seats in the preceding assembly election. The PRS again exited the government in February 1997 and, amid growing public disorder, called for it to resign. The party secured one of the United Albanian Right's four seats in the 1997 balloting for the assembly.

Early in November 1997, PRS Chair Sabri Godo denounced the PDS at a PRS party congress and said conservatives should rally around the PRS, which could become a "third force" against communism. Saying his legislative duties kept him too busy to lead his party, Godo relinquished the chair to Fatmir Mediu. However, Godo continued to serve as chair of the parliamentary constitutional commission that drafted the new basic law implemented in November 1998. Mediu was appointed to the PDS-led cabinet in September 2005, the PRS having secured 11 seats in the July legislative balloting as part of the ALDM. In March 2008 Mediu resigned as defense minister following the Gërdec disaster, the explosion of 400 tons of propellant at a site for the demilitarization of aging ammunition stockpiles from the Communist era, killing 26 and wounding more than 3,000.

In the 2009 assembly election the PRS won 1 seat and 2 percent of the nationwide vote. Mediu's election as a parliamentary deputy in September 2009 granted him immunity from prosecution over his role in the Gerdac explosion, prompting new calls for reform of the judiciary.

In the June 2013 assembly election, the PRS secured 3 seats with 3 percent of the vote.

Leaders: Fatmir MEDIU (Chair), Sabri GODO (Former Chair), Çerçiz MINGOMATAJ, Arian MADHI.

Party for Justice, Integration, and Unity (*Partia Drejtësi, Integrim dhe Unitet*—PDIU). This group was formed in 2005 as the **Party for Justice and Integration** (*Partia për Drejtësi dhe Integrim*—PDI) to represent the interests of the Cham (*Çamë*) minority. Ethnically Albanian, the group possesses a distinct regional identity; many of its members are expatriates from Greece, which expelled much of its Cham population during the Greek Civil War. The party is concentrated in a small number of districts, and benefiting from the new regional electoral arrangements, it won a seat in the 2009 assembly elections, although it secured less than 1 percent of the nationwide vote. In September 2009 elements of the PDI left to form the **Party for Justice and Unity** (*Partia për Drejtësi dhe Unitet*—PDU). The two parties reconciled and merged in February 2011.

In the June 2013 assembly election, the PDIU won 4 seats with 2.6 percent of the vote.

Leaders: Shpëtim IDRIZI (Chair), Tahir MUHEDINI (Honorary President).

Agrarian Environmental Party (*Partia Agrare Ambientaliste*—PAA). The PAA is a successor rubric for the PAS, which upon its formation in 1991 called for the privatization of all previously collectivized property, credit arrangements for farmers, and job stimulation for those thrown out of work by the collapse of collectivization. The PAS won one seat in the 1997 assembly election and three in 2001. The PAA was given a deputy ministerial post in the December 2003 PSS-led cabinet.

Although the PAA continued to cooperate with the PSS for the July 2005 assembly poll (at which the PAA secured four seats in the proportional balloting [on a vote share of 6.6 percent]), Lufter Xhuveli accepted a post in the new PDS-led government formed in September.

Leader: Lufter XHUVELI (Chair).

Christian Democratic Party of Albania (*Partia Demokristiane e Shqipërisë*—PDK). A member of the 1977 Union for Democracy coalition, the PDK drew support mainly from Shkodër and other northern Catholic towns. It won 1 percent of the vote in the 2001 legislative poll. The then chair of the PDK, Zef BUSHATI, was appointed Albania's ambassador to the Vatican in 2002 and was succeeded as PDK leader by Nikolle LESI, a well-known editor. The PDK secured two seats in the 2005 assembly who had recently left the New Democratic Party (PDr). In November 2007 Lesi split with the party and founded the **Albanian Christian Democratic Movement**, stating his intention to draw from PDK supporters and compete in the 2009 parliamentary elections.

For the 2009 legislative elections, the PDK founded the **Pole of Freedom** (*Poli i Lirisë*—PL), a coalition intended to become a center-right "third force" in domestic politics in opposition to both the PDS and PSS. The PDK was joined by the PDB, as well as several smaller parties: the LZhK, PKons, PRDSh, and PRrL. The PL overall won less than 2 percent of the nationwide vote in the 2009 assembly balloting, with the PDK and LZhK obtaining most of this support.

A local PDK party head was assassinated by a bomb attack in June 2009, although it was not confirmed that the attack was politically motivated.

In January 2011 members of the PDK took part in the protests against the PDS-led government, indicating a shift to open opposition to the government from a previously more ambiguous position.

Leader: Nard NDOKA (Chair).

Movement of Legality Party (*Partia Lëvizja e Legalitetit*—PLL). The PLL was founded in 1991 as the political wing of the monarchist movement, which has marginal support in Albania but some following among Albanians living abroad. Leka Zogu, son of the late King Zog (who fled the country in 1939) briefly attended the movement's 50th anniversary celebrations in Tirana in November 1993. Zogu, having returned to Albania to rally support for a referendum on the monarchy (held simultaneously with the 1997 assembly election), subsequently went back to South Africa and was later threatened with arrest, should he return to Albania, for leading an armed rally in Tirana at which there was a fatal shoot-out. Reporting on the early balloting, Prime Minister Fino initially estimated that 53 percent favored a monarchy, but official results subsequently put the figure at 33 percent, which the PLL insisted was a fraudulent count. The PLL won three seats in the collateral assembly election.

Zogu was permitted by invitation of the assembly to return to Albania in mid-2002 as a "common citizen." Although he initially indicated he would not pursue a political career, in mid-2004 he launched a Movement for National Development (*Lëvizja për Zhvillim Kombëtar*—LZhK) that comprised the PLL, the Conservative Party, and the small **Renewal Democratic Party** (*Partia Demokratika e Rinovor*—PDRn), led by Dashamir Shehi, who had recently split from the PDr. The LZhK's "law and order" platform for the 2005 legislative balloting called for anticorruption measures (including judicial reform) and pursuit of integration with the EU and NATO.

In early 2007 Zogu announced that he was formally withdrawing his affiliations with the PLL and LZhK on the grounds that a king should "stand above politics." The LZhK, which had emerged as a minor political party in its own right, joined the PL (above) for the 2009 assembly poll, in which the PLL took less than 1 percent of the nationwide vote.

Leader: Ekrem SPAHIA (Chair).

National Front Party (*Partia Balli Kombëtare*—PBK). The PBK is descended from the anticommunist wing of the National Front created in 1942 to oppose Axis occupation. The then PBK leader, Abaz Ermenji, returned to Albania in October 1995 after 49 years in exile. The party won three of the United Albanian Right's four seats to the assembly in the 1997 election.

Reports surrounding the July 2005 legislative poll referenced electoral cooperation between the PBK (under Adriatík Alimadhi's leadership) and the PDS. However, other reports also referenced PDS cooperation with the **Democratic National Front Party** (*Partia Balli Kombëtar Demokrat*—PBKD), founded by former PBK members in 1998. Negotiations toward a merger were conducted in 2005 between the PBK and PBKD but ultimately failed. The relationship between the two parties subsequently remained unclear, and even regional media reports frequently conflated or confused the two groups.

Leaders: Adriatík ALIMADHI (Chair), Arben HOXHA (Secretary).

Liberal Democratic Union (*Bashkimi Liberal Demokrat*—BLD). The BLD was launched as the Social Democratic Union of Albania (*Bashkimi i Social Demokratikët i Shqipërisë*—BSDS) in January 1995 by Teodor Laço and Vullnet ADEMI, formerly of the PSDS, who had opted to remain in the government in the December 1994 reshuffle, notwithstanding the decision of the parent party to go into opposition. Laço retained his post in the government appointed in July 1996, even though the BSDS had won no seats in the May–June election. His moderating influence was also apparent in late 1998 and early 1999, when he encouraged the Union for Democracy to end its legislative boycott, arguing it could serve more effectively as a genuine opposition party via full parliamentary participation. By then, the party had been transformed into the BLD.

Leaders: Arjan STAROVA (Chair), Shaqir REXHVELAJ (Deputy Chair).

Democratic Alliance (*Partia Aleanca Demokratike*—AD). Also abbreviated as the PAD, the AD was launched in October 1992 by a number of parliamentarians, including PDS cofounder Gramoz PASHKO, in opposition to what was termed the "autocratic rule" of President Berisha. Several prominent AD candidates were barred (because of their allegedly Communist past) from the 1996 legislative balloting, which the AD contested unsuccessfully as part of the PQ (above) alliance with the PSDS. The party won two assembly seats in the 1997 election and joined the new PSS-led government. It remained in the government after the 2001 election, in which it took three seats. However, a split in the party left its status in the government in limbo in 2002. One faction, led by Arben Imani and including at least one legislator, announced in May that it was taking the AD out of the Alliance of State on the grounds that effective governance was being compromised by PSS infighting. However, another faction, led by Neritan Çeka, reaffirmed its support for the government and named new members to fill the party vacancies created by the "defection" of Imani and his supporters. The factionalization continued into 2005 with Çeka and his supporters cooperating informally with the PSS while Imani's group aligned with the PDS. Competing, at least partially, as an ally of the PSS, the AD secured three proportional seats (on a vote share of 4.8 percent) in the July 2005 legislative poll.

Gramoz Pashko died in a helicopter crash in July 2006. In 2008 the AD began talks with the LSI to join a new left-leaning coalition as a "third force" in domestic politics, following a cited rift with the leadership of the PSS. In 2009, however, the AD joined the AN. Çeka was appointed ambassador to Italy in December 2012 and stood down as chair of the party, Arben Demiti being appointed until a planned party congress in October 2013.

Leaders: Arben DEMETI (Chair), Arben IMANI.

Democratic Union Party (*Partia Bashkimi Demokrat Shqiptar*—PBDSh). Another member of the 1977 Union for Democracy coalition, the PBDSh captured 0.6 percent of the vote in the 2001 general election and 0.5 percent in 2005. In 2009 it declined further, taking less than a tenth of a percent of the nationwide vote.

Leader: Ylber VALTERI.

Macedonian Alliance for European Integration (*Aleanca e Maqedonasve për Integrim Evropian*—AMIE; in Macedonian, *Makedonska Alijansa za Evropska Integracija*). Launched in mid-2005 and described as the first "ethnically-based" party to be registered, it pledged to support the interests of the Macedonian minority in Albania. In 2007 the group claimed that the government had exerted pressure on its supporters in municipal elections. In the 2009 elections the AMIE took less than a tenth of a percent of the nationwide vote. In the 2011 local elections, the party joined the coalition led by the PDS and won pluralities in two municipalities near the Albanian-Macedonian border.

Leader: Edmond THEMELKO.

Smaller parties in the APMI included the **Movement for National Development** (*Lëvizja për Zhvillim Kombëtar*—LZHK), led by Dashamir SHEHI; **Democratic National Front** (*Partia Balli Kombëtar Demokrat*—PBKD), led by Artur ROSHI; **New Party of Denied Rights** (*Partia e të Drejtave të Mohuara e Re*—PDM e Re), led by Fatmir HOXHA; **Greek Minority for the Future** (*Minoriteti Etnik Grek për të Ardhmen*—MEGA), led by Kristo KICO; **Conservative Party** (*Partia Konservatore*—PKons), led by Armando RUCO; **Time of Albania** (*Partia Ora e Shqipërisë*—POSh), led by Zef SHTJEFNI; **Christian-Democratic League of Albania** (*Partija Lidhja Demokristiane e Shqiperise*—LDK), led by Nikolle LESI; **Citizen's Party of Albania** (*Partia Civile e Shqipërisë*—PCSH), led by Dritan BROKA; **Movement for New Albania** (*Partia Lëvizja Shqipëria e Re*—LSHR), led by Emond Vlashaj; **Party of Denied Rights** (*Partia e te Drejtave te Mohuara*—PDM), led by Ilir VATA; **Party of the People's Union of Albanian Pensioners** (*Partia Bashkimi Popullor i Pensionistëve Shqiptarë*—PBPPSH), led by Selami JENISHERI; **Alliance for Democracy and Solidarity** (*Partia Aleanca per Demokraci dhe Solidaritet*—ADS), led by GAQO APOSTOLI; **Party of the Real Albanian Path** (*Partia Rruga e Vërtetë Shqiptare*—PRrVSh), led by Muharrem DODA; and the **New European Democracy Party** (*Partia Demokracia e Re Europiane*—PDRE), led by Koci TAHIRI.

New Democratic Spirit (*Fryma e Re Demokratike*—FRD). Founded on April 30, 2012 by former members of the DPS as a center-right party representing the interests of the middle class. Bamir TOPI became party leader after the end of his term as president.

In the June 2013 assembly elections, the FRD won 1.7 percent of the vote, failing to secure a seat in parliament.

Leaders: Bamir TOPI (Chair, Former President of the Republic), Gazmend OKETA.

Red and Black Alliance (*Aleanca Kuq e Zi*—AK). Founded as a civil initiative in March 2011, the AK was registered as a political party on March 20, 2012. The party characterizes itself as defending the rights of ethnic Albanians within and outside of Albania's borders. There were reports in 2012 that small groups formerly affiliated with the Albanian National Army (see below) had merged with or were now affiliated with the AK. The AK received attention for its use of social media and European media have reported expectations it would become a third force in the June 2013 assembly elections, but it received 0.6 percent of the vote and failed to secure a seat.

Leader: Kreshnik SPAHIU (Chair).

Also participating in the 2013 elections were the **League for Justice and Progress** (*Lidhja Per Drejtesi Dhe Progres*—LDP), led by Elmaz SHERIFI, and the **Christian Democratic People's Party of Albania** (*Partia Popullore Kristiandemokrate e Shqipërisë*—PPKDSH), led by Pal SHKAMBI.

Underground Group:

Albanian National Army (*Armata Kombëtare Shqiptare*—AKSh). Described as a "loosely organized criminal extremist group" by the U.S. government, the AKSh promotes establishment of a "Greater Albania" to include the current Albania, Kosovo, and portions of western Macedonia, southern Serbia, and southern Montenegro. It is reportedly a major component of the cross-national Albanian National Unification Front (*Frontit për Bashkimin Kombëtare Shqiptar*—FBKSh). The UN Mission in Kosovo has declared the AKSh to be a terrorist organization. Macedonian courts have also sentenced several purported AKSh members to prison for alleged participation in bomb attacks in Macedonia in 2003. After being active in Kosovo, Macedonia, and Serbia in the first years of the current decade, the AKSh was reported in 2004 to have gone "completely underground" following the arrest by NATO of several AKSh leaders.

In December 2004 one AKSh leader, Gafur Adili, was placed under house arrest in Tirana for his alleged encouragement of AKSh members to "intervene" in Macedonia. Meanwhile, another reported AKSh leader, Idajet Beqiri, was released from prison in Tirana after the Court of Appeals overturned his conviction for "inciting interethnic hatred."

In late 2005 Serbian representatives claimed that the FBKSh/AKSh had perpetrated a number of attacks on Serbs in Kosovo. For his part, Adili reportedly said that he believed an ethnic war would be "inevitable" in Kosovo if that province was granted independence. In November 2007 Macedonian security forces engaged an "armed criminal" group reportedly linked to the AKSh, killing eight and seizing several truckloads of weapons. Weapons caches attributed to the AKSh were reportedly uncovered in Macedonia in April and May 2010.

Leaders: Gafur ADILI, Idajet BEQIRI, Arber KASTRIOTI (FBKSh Chair).

LEGISLATURE

The unicameral **Assembly of Albania** (*Kuvendi i Shqipërisë*), named the People's Assembly (*Kuvënd Popullore*) until 2006, comprises 140 deputies serving four-year terms. Prior to 2009, 100 members were directly elected from single-member constituencies in single-round plurality balloting. The remaining 40 members were selected by proportional representation from party or coalition lists in a single nationwide constituency, assuming a minimum vote share of 2.5 percent for individual parties and 4 percent for coalitions. However, under constitutional amendments approved in April 2008, all 140 seats are now allocated via a regional proportional system. The country is divided into 12 electoral regions (corresponding to the country's administrative regions) with varying numbers of assembly seats depending on population (e.g., the Kukes region elects only 4 seats, while the Tirane region elects 32).

All parties, including those in coalitions, present their own candidate lists, and voters cast a single vote for an individual party in their district. Most parties also register as members of coalitions, and the total votes received by the individual parties in a coalition are added together to produce that coalition's vote percentage in a region. (Although the normal electoral threshold is 3 percent for parties and 5 percent for coalitions, regions with small numbers of assembly seats may have a higher "natural threshold" [the percentage of votes required to gain one seat]). A coalition's seats within a region are distributed to the individual parties within the coalition in proportion to the votes garnered by the individual parties in that region.

Following the election of June 23, 2013, the seats were distributed as follows: the Alliance for a European Albania, 84 seats (the Socialist Party of Albania, 66; the Socialist Movement for Integration, 16; the Union for Human Rights Party, 1; the Christian Democratic Party, 1) and the Alliance for Employment, Prosperity and Integration, 56 (the Democratic Party of Albania, 49; the Albanian Republican Party, 3; the Party for Justice and Integration, 4).

Chair of Presidency: Ilir Meta.

CABINET

[as of September 15, 2013]

Prime Minister	Edi Rama (PSS)
Deputy Prime Minister	Niko Peleshi (PSS)
Ministers	
Agriculture, Rural Development and Water Management	Edmond Panariti (LSI)
Culture	Mirela Kumbaro (Ind.) [f]
Defense	Mimi Kodheli (PSS) [f]
Economic Development, Trade and Entrepreneurship	Arben Ahmetaj (PSS)
Education and Sports	Lindita Nikolli (PSS) [f]
Energy and Industry	Damian Gjiknuri (PSS)
Environment	Lefter Koka (LSI)
European Integration	Klajda Gjosha (LSI) [f]
Finance	Shkelqim Cani (PSS)
Foreign Affairs	Ditmir Bushati (PSS)
Health	Ilir Beqja (PSS)
Interior	Samir Tahiri (PSS)
Justice	Nasip Naco (LSI)
Social Welfare and Youth	Erion Veliaj (PSS)
Transport and Infrastructure	Edmond Haxhinasto (LSI)
Without Portfolio	Milena Harito (PSS) [f]
	Ilirijan Celibashi (PSS)
	Bled Çuçi (PSS)

[f] = female

INTERGOVERNMENTAL REPRESENTATION

Ambassador to the U.S.: Gilbert GALANXHI.

U.S. Ambassador to Albania: Donald LU (nominated).

Permanent Representative to the UN: Ferit HOXHA.

IGO Memberships (Non-UN): CEUR, EBRD, ICC, OIC, OSCE, NATO, WTO.

ALGERIA

Democratic and Popular Republic of Algeria

al-Jumhuriyah al-Jazairiyah

al-Dimuqratiyah al-Shabiyah

Political Status: Independent republic since July 3, 1962; one-party rule established by military coup July 5, 1965, and confirmed by constitution adopted November 19, 1976; multiparty system adopted through constitutional revision approved by national referendum on February 23, 1989; state of emergency declared for 12 months by military-backed High Council of State on February 9, 1992, and extended indefinitely on February 9, 1993; three-year transitional period declared by High Security Council effective January 31, 1994, as previously endorsed by National Dialogue Conference; constitutional amendments approved by national referendum on November 28, 1996, in advance of return to elected civilian government via multiparty local and national legislative elections in 1997; state of emergency lifted February 24, 2011.

Area: 919,590 sq. mi. (2,381,741 sq. km).

Population: 36,756,986 (2012E—UN); 38,087,812 (2013E—U.S. Census).

Major Urban Centers (2005E): ALGIERS (El Djazair, 1,532,000), Oran (Wahran, 724,000), Constantine (Qacentina, 475,000). In May 1981 the government ordered the "Arabizing" of certain place names that did not conform to "Algerian translations."

Official Language: Arabic. French and Berber are also widely spoken. However, in 1996 the National Transitional Council adopted legislation banning the use of French in the public sector as of July 1998, with the

exception that universities were given until July 2000 to switch to the use of Arabic only. In the wake of unrest in Berber areas, the government announced in October 2001 that the Berber language—Tamazight—had been elevated to a "national" language.

Monetary Unit: Algerian Dinar (market rate November 1, 2013: 82.03 dinars = $1US).

President: Abdelaziz BOUTEFLIKA (National Liberation Front—FLN); declared winner of controversial election of April 15, 1999, and sworn in for a five-year term on April 27 to succeed Maj. Gen. (Ret.) Liamine ZEROUAL (nonparty), who in September 1998 had announced his intention to resign prior to the scheduled completion of his term in November 2000; reelected (due to internal FLN disputes, as the candidate of the National Democratic Rally [RND] and the Movement for a Peaceful Society [MSP]) on April 8, 2004, and sworn in for a second five-year term on April 19; reelected (officially as an independent but with the endorsement of the FLN, RND, and MSP) for a third five-year term on April 9, 2009.

Prime Minister: Abdelmalek SELLAL (nonparty); appointed by the president on September 3, 2012, and inaugurated (along with his new government) on September 4 to succeed Ahmed OUYAHIA (National Democratic Rally); reappointed on September 11, 2013.

THE COUNTRY

Located midway along the North African littoral and extending southward into the heart of the Sahara, Algeria is a Muslim country of Arab and Berber population and Islamic and French cultural traditions. The importance of agriculture in the economy has been replaced by reliance on hydrocarbons, with petroleum and natural gas now accounting for more than 95 percent of exchange earnings. Women currently make up approximately 20 percent of the workforce, although, in sharp contrast with much of the rest of the Arab world, they constitute more than half of the nation's lawyers, judges, and university students. Moreover, 146 women were elected to the 462-member National Assembly in 2012.

For nearly two decades following independence Algeria was perceived by many as a model for Third World liberation movements: the socialist government attended to social welfare needs, while the economy grew rapidly as oil prices rose in the 1970s. However, declining oil revenues and poor economic management subsequently led to major setbacks. Once nearly self-sufficient in food, the country became highly dependent on foreign imports. Other problems included 25 percent unemployment, high population growth (more than one-half of the population is under 20 years old), an external debt estimated at more than $26 billion, a severe shortage of adequate housing, a widespread perception of corruption among government officials, and a spreading black market.

In the mid-1980s the government began to impose budget austerity while attempting to reduce state control of large industries and agricultural collectives, boost nonhydrocarbon production, and cultivate a free-market orientation. The pace of economic reform accelerated following an outbreak of domestic unrest in late 1988, which also prompted the launching of what was initially considered one of the continent's "boldest democratic experiments." Although political liberalization was seriously compromised during the 1990s by confrontation with the Islamic fundamentalist movement, the government persevered with its new economic policies, thereby gaining partial rescheduling of the external debt and additional credits from the International Monetary Fund (IMF) and the World Bank. Meanwhile, as mandated by the IMF, privatization accelerated, the collateral loss of some 400,000 jobs in the public sector contributing to growing popular discontent with fiscal policy. Burgeoning terrorist activity in the second half of the 1990s impaired foreign investment in a number of sectors, but it did not affect activity in the oil and gas fields in the southern desert, where oil reserves were estimated at about 16 billion barrels.

The nonhydrocarbon sector grew by more than 6 percent annually in 2007–2011 and helped insulate Algeria from the effects of the international economic crisis. However, unemployment remained high at 10 percent (much greater among young people), contributing to public protests that began in early 2011 (see Current issues, below). In response, the government pledged major spending increases designed to create jobs and relieve the nation's severe housing shortage. Growth in 2012 was estimated at 2.5 percent.

GOVERNMENT AND POLITICS

Political background. Conquered by France in the 1830s and formally annexed by that country in 1842, Algeria achieved independence as the result of a nationalist guerrilla struggle that broke out in 1954 and yielded eventual French withdrawal on July 3, 1962. (The eight-year war of liberation, led by the indigenous National Liberation Front [*Front de Libération Nationale*—FLN], caused the death of some 250,000 Algerians, the wounding of 500,000, the uprooting of nearly 2 million others, and the emigration of some 1 million French settlers.) The new Algerian regime was handicapped by deep divisions within the victorious FLN, particularly between commanders of the revolutionary army and a predominantly civilian political leadership headed by Ahmed BEN BELLA, who formed Algeria's first regular government and was elected to a five-year presidential term in September 1963. Despite his national popularity, Ben Bella's extravagant and flamboyant style antagonized the army leadership, and he was deposed (and imprisoned) in June 1965 by a military coup under Col. Houari BOUMEDIENNE, who assumed power as president of the National Council of the Algerian Revolution.

During 1976 the Algerian people participated in three major referenda. The first, on June 27, yielded overwhelming approval of a National Charter that committed the nation to the building of a socialist society, designated Islam as the state religion, defined basic rights of citizenship, singled out the FLN as the "leading force in society," and stipulated that party and government cadres could not engage in "lucrative activities" other than those afforded by their primary employment. The second referendum, on November 17, approved a new constitution that, while recognizing the National Charter as "the fundamental source of the nation's policies and of its laws," assigned sweeping powers to the presidency. The third referendum, on December 10, reconfirmed Colonel Boumedienne as the nation's president by an official majority of 99.38 percent. Two months later, in the first legislative election since 1964, a unicameral National People's Assembly was established on the basis of a candidate list presented by the FLN.

President Boumedienne died on December 27, 1978, and he was immediately succeeded by assembly president Rabah BITAT, who was legally proscribed from serving as chief executive for more than a 45-day period. Following a national election on February 7, 1979, Bitat yielded the office to Col. Chadli BENDJEDID, who had emerged in January as the FLN presidential designee during an unprecedented six-day meeting of a sharply divided party congress.

At a June 1980 FLN congress, President Bendjedid was given authority to select members of the party's Political Bureau, and on July 15 he revived the military General Staff, which had been suppressed by his predecessor after a 1967 coup attempt by Col. Tahir ZBIRI. As a further indication that he had consolidated his control of state and party, Bendjedid on October 30 pardoned the exiled Zbiri and freed former president Ben Bella from house detention. (The latter had been released from 14 years' imprisonment in July 1979.)

President Bendjedid was unopposed in his reelection bid of January 12, 1984, and on January 22 he appointed Abdelhamid BRAHIMI to succeed Col. Mohamed Ben Ahmed ABDELGHANI as prime minister. Thereafter, the regime was buffeted by deteriorating economic conditions, growing militancy among Islamic fundamentalists and students, and tension within the government, the FLN, and the army over proposed economic and political liberalization. The political infighting limited the effectiveness of reform efforts, critics charging that many of those entrenched in positions of power were reluctant to surrender economic and social privileges.

The pent-up discontent erupted into rioting in Algiers in early October 1988 and quickly spread to other cities, shattering Algeria's reputation as an "oasis of stability" in an otherwise turbulent region. Upwards of 500 persons died when the armed forces opened fire on demonstrators in the capital, while more than 3,000 were arrested. President Bendjedid thereupon adopted a conciliatory attitude, converting what could have been a challenge to his authority into a mandate for sweeping economic and political change. In a referendum on November 3, voters overwhelmingly approved a constitutional amendment reducing the FLN's political dominance by assigning greater responsibility to the prime minister and making him accountable to the assembly. Two days later, Bendjedid appointed Kasdi MERBAH, described as a "determined" proponent of economic liberalization, as the new ministerial leader, and on November 9 Merbah announced a cabinet from which a majority of the previous incumbents were excluded. Collaterally, the president instituted leadership changes in the military and the FLN, the latter agreeing late in the month to open future legislative elections to non-FLN candidates. On December 22 Bendjedid was reelected to a third five-year term, securing a reported 81 percent endorsement as the sole presidential candidate.

The FLN's status was eroded further by additional constitutional changes in February 1989 that provided, among other things, for multiparty activity. Seven months later, arguing that economic reforms were not being implemented quickly enough, Bendjedid named Mouloud HAMROUCHE, a longtime political ally, to succeed Merbah as prime minister.

A multiparty format was introduced for the first time in elections for municipal and provincial councils on June 12, 1990. Contrary to expectations, the Islamic Salvation Front (*Front Islamique du Salut*—FIS), the country's leading Islamic fundamentalist organization, obtained 53 percent of the popular vote and a majority of the 15,000 seats being contested. Responding to demands from the FIS and other opposition parties, President Bendjedid announced in April 1991 that two-stage national legislative elections, originally scheduled for 1992, would be advanced to June 27 and July 18, 1991. However, the FIS called a general strike on May 25 to demand additional electoral law changes, the immediate application of sharia (Islamic religious law), the resignation of Bendjedid, and the scheduling of new presidential elections. Clashes in the capital between fundamentalists and police intensified in early June, leaving at least seven dead, and on June 5 Bendjedid declared a state of emergency, ordered the army to restore order, and postponed the legislative poll. He also called upon the foreign minister, Sid Ahmed GHOZALI, to form a new government.

On June 18, 1991, Prime Minister Ghozali, described as a "technocrat" committed to economic and political reform, announced his cabinet (the first since independence not to be dominated by FLN leaders) and pledged "free and clean" parliamentary elections by the end of the year. The schism between the government and the fundamentalists remained unbridged, however, and top FIS leaders and hundreds of their followers were arrested when new violence broke out in Algiers in early July.

Following a period of relative calm, the state of emergency was lifted on September 29, 1991, and two-round elections to a 430-seat assembly were scheduled for December 26, 1991, and January 16, 1992. Again testifying to the remarkable surge in fundamentalist influence, FIS candidates won 188 seats outright in the first round (compared to 25 for the Berber-based Socialist Forces Front [*Front des Forces Socialistes*—FFS] and only 15 for the FLN). With the FIS poised to achieve a substantial majority (possibly even the two-thirds majority needed for constitutional revision), Bendjedid initiated talks with the fundamentalists regarding a power-sharing arrangement. However, Bendjedid subsequently faced pressure from military leaders upset with his accommodation of the FIS, and he submitted his resignation on January 11, 1992. The High Security Council (*Haute Conseil de Securité*—HCS), composed of Prime Minister Ghozali and other top officials, including three senior military leaders, announced that it had assumed control to preserve public order and protect national security. (See the 2010 *Handbook* for information on the constitutional issues that surrounded the lack of clear presidential succession.)

On January 12, 1992, the HCS canceled the second stage of the national legislative election and nullified the results of the first stage. Two days later it announced that it had appointed a five-man High Council of State (*Haute Conseil d'État*—HCE) to serve as an interim collegial presidency. Mohamed BOUDIAF, vice president of the country's wartime provisional government, was invited to return from 28 years of exile in Morocco to assume the chair of the new body.

Following its "soft-gloved coup" in early 1992, the military launched what was described as an "all-out war" against the fundamentalist movement, arresting numerous FIS leaders (including moderates who had been counseling against violent confrontation) in addition to some 500 other FIS members. Bloody demonstrations throughout Algeria erupted shortly thereafter, and on February 9 the HCE declared a new 12-month state of emergency. With most constitutional rights effectively suspended by the declaration, the government intensified its anti-FIS campaign, while militant fundamentalists initiated guerrilla activity against police and security forces. The unrest continued following Ghozali's reappointment on February 23, even relatively moderate fundamentalists being driven underground by a March decision of the Algerian courts, acting on an HCE petition, to ban the FIS as a legal party. Meanwhile, the nonfundamentalist population, apparently fearing political, legal, and social constraints should the FIS come to power, reportedly accepted the military intervention with relief.

HCE Chair Boudiaf was assassinated on June 29, 1992, while addressing a rally in the eastern city of Annaba. Official investigators subsequently concluded there was a broad conspiracy behind the attack without being able to identify those involved. Suspects ranged from militant fundamentalists to members of the "power elite" who may have felt threatened by Boudiaf's anticorruption efforts. (Only one person was arrested in connection with the incident—a member of the presidential guard who was convicted in June 1995 following a trial that shed little light on his motives or possible coconspirators.) On July 2 the HCS named Ali KAFI, the secretary general of the National Organization of Holy Warriors (a group of veterans from the war of independence) as Boudiaf's successor. Prime Minister Ghozali, blaming corrupt government officials and radical fundamentalists equally for the country's disorder, resigned on July 8. He was replaced on the same day by Belaid ABDESSELAM, longtime industry and energy minister under former president Boumedienne.

On February 9, 1993, the HCE extended the state of emergency indefinitely, declaring that steps toward restoration of an elected civilian government would be taken only after successful completion of the "antiterrorist" crackdown. Four months later the HCE presented a blueprint for constitutional change, promising a democratic Muslim state and a free-market economy. In keeping with the new economic thrust, Prime Minister Abdesselam, viewed as strongly oriented toward state control of heavy industry, was replaced on August 21 by Redha MALEK, an advocate of privatization and other forms of liberalization geared to winning debt rescheduling from international creditors.

In October 1993 the HCE appointed an eight-member Committee for National Dialogue to negotiate an agreement on the nation's political future among the legal political parties, labor organizations, and trade and professional groups. However, talks were constrained by a mounting conviction among party leaders that full-scale civil war loomed unless the FIS was brought into the negotiations, a step the regime refused to accept. Consequently, the National Dialogue Conference held in Algiers in January 1994 was boycotted by nearly all the political parties, and its influence was extremely limited. The conference had been expected to name a president to succeed the HCE but failed to do so, reportedly because the military would not grant sufficient authority to a civilian leader. Therefore, on January 27 the HCS announced the appointment of Maj. Gen. (Ret.) Liamine ZEROUAL as president, his inauguration four days later coinciding with the dissolution of the HCE. Zeroual, who retained his former position as defense minister, was authorized to govern (in conjunction with the HCS) for a three-year transitional period, initial reports indicating he would seek a settlement with the FIS.

With debt rescheduling negotiations at a critical juncture, President Zeroual reappointed Prime Minister Malek on January 31, 1994, despite Malek's hard line regarding the FIS. Malek resigned on April 11, following the announcement of preliminary agreement with the IMF; he was replaced by Mokdad SIFI, who had held a number of ministerial posts recently. One month later the military-dominated regime set up an appointive National Transitional Council to act in a quasi-legislative capacity prior to elections tentatively scheduled for 1997. However, most of the leading parties boycotted the body, severely undercutting its claim to legitimacy.

A number of groups (including, significantly, the FIS, FLN, and FFS) drafted a proposed national reconciliation pact in Rome in late 1994 and early 1995. The plan called for cessation of antigovernment violence, release of fundamentalist detainees, recognition of the FIS, and inauguration of a national conference to establish a transitional government pending new national elections. Despite strong international endorsement of the proposal, the government quickly rejected it on the ground that no "credible" truce could be achieved. Further illustrating the sway held by the military's hard-liners, security forces subsequently launched a massive campaign against the Armed Islamic Group (*Groupe Islamique Armé*—GIA) and other militant factions that had claimed responsibility for a series of bombings and assassinations. At the same time, the Zeroual administration reportedly continued negotiations with the FIS in the hope that the front's supporters could be reintegrated into normal political processes. However, the talks collapsed in mid-1995, and the regime subsequently began to implement its own schedule for a gradual return to civilian government.

The first stage of the transition was a presidential election conducted on November 16, 1995, in which Zeroual, running as an independent but with the support of the military, was elected to a five-year term with 61 percent of the vote. His closest competitor, Sheikh Mahfoud NAHNAH of the moderate fundamentalist Hamas Party, secured 25 percent of the vote, followed by Saïd SAADI of the Berber Rally for Culture and Democracy (*Rassemblement pour la Culture et la Démocratie*—RCD), with 9 percent, and Nourreddine BOUKROUH of the Algerian Renewal Party (*Parti pour le Renouveau de l'Algérie*—PRA), with 4 percent. President Zeroual's resounding first-round victory was initially seen as easing the "sense of crisis" somewhat, much of the electorate having apparently endorsed his continued hard line toward the militants. Zeroual, whose platform contained strong anticorruption language, was also reportedly perceived as a buffer, to a certain extent, against complete domination of political affairs by military leaders. As anticipated, Prime Minister Sifi submitted his resignation following the successful completion of the election, and on December 31 President Zeroual appointed Ahmed OUYAHIA, former director of the president's office, to succeed Sifi. The government that was announced on January 5, 1996, included several members from Hamas and the PRA, seemingly as a "reward" for their participation in the presidential poll, which had been boycotted by several major legal parties (including the FLN and the FFS) in protest over the lack of an agreement with the FIS.

In mid-1996 President Zeroual proposed a number of constitutional amendments granting sweeping new powers to the president and banning political parties based on religion. Some 38 parties and organizations endorsed the proposals, although the absence of several major legal groupings (including the FFS and RCD) and, of course, the FIS (which would have been precluded from any eventual legalization under the revisions) undercut the impact of the accord. The government subsequently reported that 85 percent of those voting in a national referendum on November 28 had supported the changes in the basic law. However, opposition leaders and some international observers questioned those results and described the government's claim of an 80 percent vote turnout as vastly inflated.

A new wave of antiregime attacks broke out shortly after the constitutional referendum of November 1996 and reached an unprecedented scale in July–August, despite (or perhaps because of) the recent national legislative balloting and other progress toward full return to elected civilian government. Nevertheless, the administration proceeded with its timetable in 1997. New assembly elections were held on June 5, the balloting being dominated by the recently established, progovernment National Democratic Rally (*Rassemblement National et Démocratique*—RND), with 156 seats, followed by the Movement for a Peaceful Society (*Mouvement pour une Société Paisible*—MSP, as Hamas had been renamed) with 69 seats, and the FLN with 62. The MSP and the FLN subsequently agreed to join a new RND-led coalition government, which was announced on June 25 under the continued direction of Prime Minister Ouyahia. The RND also secured most of the seats in municipal elections conducted on October 23, although some were allocated to other parties after a judicial review of allegations from a number of groups (including the MSP and the FLN) of widespread fraud. The political transition was completed on December 25, 1997, with indirect elections to the Council of the Nation (the new upper house in the legislature), the RND winning 80 of the 96 contested seats. By that time, however, despite the progress on the institutional front, the wave of domestic violence had reached an unprecedented level.

As of early 1998 the government reported that about 26,000 people had died during the six-year insurgency, although other observers estimated the figure to be as high as 80,000. A special UN commission that visited Algeria at midyear placed the blame for the violence squarely on "Islamic terrorists" and argued that the Zeroual regime deserved international and domestic support. However, human rights organizations strongly criticized the UN report for inadequately addressing the harsh retaliatory measures employed by government security forces. In that context, it appeared that differences of opinion had emerged within the military and political elite over how to proceed vis-à-vis the fundamentalists. Hard-liners subsequently appeared to continue to dominate the debate, possibly contributing to the surprise announcement in September by Zeroual (seen as having come to favor a dialogue with moderate Islamist leaders) that he would leave office prior to the completion of his term.

The April 15, 1999, presidential election proved to be highly controversial, as six of the seven candidates quit the race shortly before the balloting out of conviction that the poll had been rigged in favor of the military's preferred candidate, Abdelaziz BOUTEFLIKA, who had served as foreign minister in the 1960s and 1970s but had been on the political sidelines for 20 years. Despite the opposition's demand for a postponement, the election proceeded as scheduled, Bouteflika being credited with 74 percent of the vote. He subsequently moved quickly to establish his leadership credentials by, among other things, announcing plans for a "civil concord," which proposed amnesty for most fundamentalist militants in return for their permanent renunciation of violence and surrender of arms. The pact easily secured legislative approval in the summer and was endorsed by 98 percent of those voting in a national referendum on September 16.

Following surprisingly long negotiations, President Bouteflika named Ahmed BENBITOUR, a former foreign minister who was described as a close friend of the president's, as prime minister on December 23, 1999. On the following day, Benbitour formed a new government that included seven parties, all of whom remained in the cabinet named by Ali BENFLIS after he replaced Benbitour in late August 2000.

Despite the partial success of President Bouteflika's civil concord, some 2,700 additional deaths were reported in 2000 from the ongoing conflict. In the face of a recent upsurge of antigovernment violence, the president in early 2001 promised an "iron fist" in dealing with the remaining militants. Subsequently, the government faced a new, unrelated crisis in April when riots broke out within the Berber population in the Kabylie region after a young man died under inadequately explained circumstances while in police custody. Government forces responded with a harsh crackdown, and some 1 million demonstrators reportedly participated in the antiregime protests that ensued in the Kabylie region and other areas, including Algiers. More than 60 people were killed and 2,000 injured in the clashes, and, in protest, the RCD left the government coalition in May.

Fueled by economic malaise and long-standing concern over the authoritarian rule of what one journalist described as the "overwhelming power of an opaque military leadership," turmoil continued into 2002, prompting the leading Berber parties (the FFS and the RCD) to boycott the national legislative poll on May 30.The FLN dominated the balloting, securing 199 seats, while the RND declined to 47. Prime Minister Benflis was reappointed on June 1, and on June 17 he formed a new government comprising FLN, RND, and MSP ministers.

Further successes by the FLN in the October 2002 assembly elections appeared to kindle presidential aspirations in Prime Minister Benflis, who was dismissed by President Bouteflika on May 5, 2003; Ahmed Ouyahia returned to the prime ministerial post he had held from 1995 to 1998. In September 2003 Bouteflika also dismissed several pro-Benflis cabinet ministers, exacerbating tensions that subsequently split the FLN into two camps.

Deadly bomb attacks continued in 2003, mostly the work of the GIA offshoot called the Salafist Group for Preaching and Combat (*Groupe Salafiste pour la Prédication et le Combat*—GSPC). However, the level of violence was greatly reduced from its height earlier in the decade.

The factionalization of the FLN resulted in confusing circumstances under which Bouteflika was reelected (with 85 percent of the vote) on April 8, 2004, as the candidate of the RND and MSP, while Benflis secured only 6.4 percent of the vote as the nominal FLN candidate. Most observers credited President Bouteflika's resounding reelection to popular appreciation of the improved security situation, along with recent economic advances and Algeria's renewed international status in connection with the U.S.-led war on terrorism.

A January 2005 accord between the government and Berber representatives called for enhanced economic support for Berber areas and appeared to reduce unrest within the Berber community. Even more significant was a national referendum on September 29 that overwhelmingly endorsed the government's proposed national charter for peace and reconciliation. The charter called for amnesty for most of the Islamic militants involved in the civil war that had started in 1991, although leaders of the "insurrection" were barred from future political activity. Collaterally, the charter praised the role of the army in the conflict, effectively eliminating any possibility that excesses on the part of the security forces would be investigated. (It was estimated that 6,000–20,000 Algerians had "disappeared" as the result of the army's anti-insurgency measures.) Most major political parties supported the charter, and President Bouteflika staked his political future on its passage. The government reported a 97 percent "yes" vote and an 80 percent turnout, although the latter figure was broadly discounted by opponents of the initiative as well as some independent analysts. (It was noted that turnout in Berber regions appeared to be less than 20 percent.) Despite protests over the perceived heavy-handedness of the government in stifling effective opposition to the charter, most analysts concluded that the vote was a clear indication that the majority of Algerians were prepared to put the matter behind them. (It was estimated that the conflict had cost more than $30 billion and left 150,000–200,000 people dead.) However, the state of emergency remained in effect "until terrorism is completely defeated."

After several months of debate, the legislature approved the details of the peace and reconciliation charter in February 2006, and in March several thousand "Islamist" prisoners were released. A $400 million fund was established to provide compensation to the civil war's victims, although they were precluded from filing other legal claims against the government. Critics of the plan denounced it for "sheltering" the military and security forces and demanded a more intensive, "South African–style" truth and reconciliation approach under which the facts of individual cases would be revealed prior to the issuance of pardons.

The president dismissed Prime Minister Ouyahia on May 24, 2006, and replaced him with Abdelaziz BELKHADEM, the secretary general of the FLN. The cabinet appointed by Belkhadem the next day was largely unchanged.

Although the government had offered remaining militants six months to accept the recent amnesty offer, the GSPC, now formally aligned with al-Qaida (as Al-Qaida in the Islamic Maghreb [AQIM]), stepped up its attacks in late 2006–early 2007, targeting Western business interests as well as Algerian police. The spate of bombings appeared to undercut the turnout (35 percent) for the May 17, 2007, assembly balloting, as did what was widely perceived to be popular discontent with the political process as a whole. Nearly 1 million ballots were spoiled by voters, apparently to protest the entrenched status of the ruling coalition. Although the FLN's representation declined to 136 seats, the FLN/RND/MSP coalition retained a strong legislative majority. The three parties formed a new government on June 4, again under Belkhadem's leadership.

On June 23, 2008, President Bouteflika appointed former prime minister Ouyahia to again head the government. Ouyahia announced a reshuffled cabinet that included former prime minister Belkhadem as a minister of state and personal representative of the president.

Parliament approved the elimination of presidential term limits by a vote of 500–21 in November 2008, thereby clearing the way for President Bouteflika to seek a third term. His reelection (with 90.2 percent of the vote) in the April 9, 2009, balloting was a foregone conclusion, especially since a boycott led by the RCD and FFS left him with only five minor challengers. As he started his third term, the president again pledged that his priorities would be national reconciliation and job creation. However, sporadic AQIM attacks subsequently dictated the continued heavy allocation of resources to security matters, and ongoing poor living conditions prompted a wave of protests in early 2010. Ouyahia remained at the head of a reshuffled cabinet announced on May 26, 2010.

The FLN easily outpaced all other parties in the May 10, 2012, assembly balloting and, with the addition of the RND (the second-place finisher), provided the administration with a solid legislative majority. In September Bouteflika named Abdelmalek SELLAL, theretofore the minister of water resources, to succeed Ouyahia as prime minister. Sellal appointed a new cabinet that included members from the FLN and RND, but not the MSP, which had decided to move into opposition.

Constitution and government. The 1976 constitution established a single-party state with the FLN as its "vanguard force." Executive powers were concentrated in the president, who was designated president of the High Security Council and of the Supreme Court, as well as commander in chief of the armed forces. He was empowered to appoint one or more vice presidents and, under a 1979 constitutional amendment that reduced his term of office from six to five years, was obligated to name a prime minister. In addition, he was authorized to appoint an 11-member High Islamic Council selected from among the country's "religious personalities." The 1976 document also stipulated that members of the National People's Assembly would be nominated by the FLN and established a judicial system headed by a Supreme Court, to which all lower magistrates were answerable.

In late 1983, as part of a decentralization move, the number of administrative departments (*wilayaat*) was increased from 31 to 48, each continuing to be subdivided into districts (*dairaat*) and communes. At both the *wilaya* and communal (town) levels there were provisions for popular assemblies, with an appointed governor (*wali*) assigned to each *wilaya*. The various administrative units were linked vertically to the minister of the interior, with party organization paralleling the administrative hierarchy.

On January 16, 1986, a referendum approved a new National Charter that, while maintaining allegiance to socialism and Islam, accorded President Bendjedid greater leeway in his approach to social and economic problems, particularly in regard to partial privatization of the "inefficient" public sector. Additional constitutional changes were approved by referendum on November 3, 1988. The revisions upgraded the prime minister's position, declaring him to be the "head of government" and making him directly responsible to the assembly. In effect, the change transferred some of the power previously exercised by the FLN to the assembly, particularly in light of a decision later in the month to permit non-FLN candidates in future elections. The role of the FLN was further attenuated by reference to the president as the "embodiment of the unity of the nation" rather than "of the unity of the party and the state."

Another national referendum on February 23, 1989, provided for even more drastic reform. It eliminated all mention of socialism, guaranteed the fundamental rights "of man and of the citizen" as opposed to the rights of "the people," excised reference to the military's political role, and imposed stricter separation of executive, legislative, and judicial powers. In addition, the FLN lost its "vanguard" status with the authorization of additional "associations of a political nature." Continuing the transfer to a multiparty system, the assembly on July 2 established criteria for legal party status, and on July 19 it adopted a new electoral law governing political campaigns. The new code established multimember districts for local and national elections, with any party receiving more than 50 percent of the votes to be awarded all the seats in each. However, reacting to complaints from newly formed opposition parties, the government in March 1990 approved a system of proportional representation for the June municipal elections. After intense debate, the electoral law was further changed in 1991 to provide for two-round balloting in single-member districts in future assembly elections.

In announcing a one-year state of emergency in February 1992, the newly formed High Council of State suspended a number of key constitutional provisions, and over the next ten months it ordered the dissolution of nearly 800 municipal assemblies controlled by the FIS since the 1990 elections. In furtherance of its antifundamentalist campaign, the High Council of State in October also created three secret courts in which persons over 16 years of age charged with "subversion" or "terrorism" could be sentenced without the right of appeal. The state of emergency was extended indefinitely in February 1993, a transitional government being named a year later for a three-year period leading to proposed multiparty elections and a return to civilian leadership.

The electoral code was amended in 1995 to provide for multicandidate presidential elections, in two rounds if no candidate received a majority in the first round. Potential candidates were required to obtain the signatures of 75,000 voters to be placed on the ballot, and anyone married to a foreigner was precluded from running.

In connection with the planned transition to civilian government, the Zeroual administration in the spring of 1996 proposed a number of constitutional amendments, which were approved by national referendum on November 28. Among other things, the amendments banned political parties from referencing religious or ethnic "identities," while codifying Islam as the state religion and Arabic as the official national language. The president was given authority to govern by decree in certain circumstances and to appoint one-third of the members of the Council of Nations, a new upper house in the Parliament. That second provision was viewed as one of the most significant aspects of the new charter because it gave the president effective blocking power on legislation. (New laws require the approval of three-quarters of the Council of Nations.) A Constitutional Council was established in April 1998, while a juridical State Council was installed two months later. In November 2008 Parliament eliminated the previous two-term presidential limit and formally reinstalled the position of prime minister (as opposed to "head of government"). The long-standing state of emergency was lifted in February 2011.

After a long period of strict control of national and foreign media activities, the government introduced a new Information Code in mid-1989 that formally ended the state monopoly on the print media and accorded journalists greater freedom of expression. It was succeeded in March 1990 by a more stringent code that mandated imprisonment for journalists who "offended" Islam or any other religion; the new regulations also stipulated that all new periodicals be printed in Arabic. However, those strictures were not rigorously implemented, and an information "explosion" subsequently took place in the increasingly independent press. Significant restrictions, largely directed at the Islamic fundamentalist press, were imposed following the declaration of a state of emergency in early 1992. In addition, journalists were permitted to report on "security matters" only with government authorization and only using information released by the state, stories on antigovernment activity consequently becoming quite limited. In part because they were often perceived as "apologists" for the government, journalists were subsequently targeted by fundamentalist radicals. New restrictions, including harsh penalties in a revised penal code, have been imposed on the press in recent years, prompting protests from both domestic and international journalism organizations. In late 2011 the Council of Ministers introduced new regulations designed to, among other things, allow private radio and television companies to operate in a sector previously dominated by state broadcasters.

Foreign relations. Algerian foreign relations have gone through a series of changes that date back to the preindependence period, formal contacts with many countries having been initiated by a provisional government created in September 1958. Foreign policy in the immediate postindependence period was dominated by President Ben Bella's anti-imperialist ideology. The period immediately following the 1965 coup was essentially an interregnum, with President Boumedienne concentrating his efforts on internal affairs. Following the Arab-Israeli War of 1967, Boumedienne became much more active in foreign policy, with a shift in interest from Africa and the Third World to a more concentrated focus on Arab affairs. After the 1973 Arab-Israeli conflict, the theme of "Third World liberation" reemerged, reflecting a conviction that Algeria should be in the forefront of the Nonaligned Movement. Subsequently, Algeria joined with Libya, Syria, the People's Democratic Republic of Yemen, and the Palestine Liberation Organization to form the so-called "Steadfastness Front" in opposition to Egyptian-Israeli rapprochement. (In conjunction with a softening Arab posture toward Egypt, Algiers resumed full diplomatic relations with Cairo in November 1988.)

A major controversy erupted following division of the former Spanish Sahara between Morocco and Mauritania in early 1976. In February the Algerian-supported Polisario Front (see under Morocco: Disputed Territory) announced the formation of a Saharan Arab Democratic Republic (SADR) in the Western Sahara that was formally recognized by Algeria on March 6; subsequently, a majority of other nonaligned states accorded the SADR similar recognition. However, the issue split the Organization of African Unity (OAU), with Morocco withdrawing from the grouping in 1984 in protest over the seating of an SADR delegation. Concurrently, relations between Algeria and Morocco deteriorated further, with President Bendjedid pledging full support for Mauritania's "territorial integrity" and Morocco referring to the Polisarios as "Algerian mercenaries." Relations improved significantly in late 1987, however, and in May 1988 Rabat and Algiers announced the restoration of formal ties, jointly expressing support for settlement of the Western Saharan problem through a self-determination referendum. Subsequent progress in Morocco-Polisario negotiations permitted Algiers to concentrate on a long-standing foreign policy goal: the promotion of economic, social, and political unity among Maghrebian states (see separate section on Arab Maghreb Union in the 2010 *Handbook*).

The victories of the Islamic fundamentalist movement in Algeria's 1990 and 1991 elections were characterized as generating "shock waves throughout northern Africa." The governments of Egypt, Libya, Morocco, and Tunisia (all struggling to contain fundamentalist influence) were reported to be greatly relieved by the military takeover in Algeria in January 1992 and supportive of Algiers' anti-FIS campaign. The government/fundamentalist schism also led in March 1993 to the severing of Algerian ties with Iran, which the administration accused of supporting local terrorist activity. France, concerned over the possible influx of refugees should a fundamentalist government be established in Algiers, also supported the military regime.

President Bouteflika in late 2001 pledged Algeria's support for Washington's recently launched war on terrorism. Among other things, the aftermath of the September 11, 2001, attacks in the United States appeared to shine a more positive light, in the minds of many international observers, on the hard line adopted by the Algerian regime toward militant fundamentalism since 1992.

In March 2003 French President Jacques Chirac made the first formal state visit by a French leader to Algeria since the war of independence. The Algerian population warmly greeted Chirac, who pledged further "reconciliation" initiatives. However, relations with France deteriorated in early 2005 when the French parliament endorsed a bill that recognized the "positive role" that colonization had played in Algeria. President Bouteflika subsequently demanded that France formally apologize for its actions in Algeria, and a proposed French/Algerian "friendship treaty" remained unsigned. Visiting Algeria in 2007, French president Nicolas Sarkozy described the colonial past as "profoundly unjust" but declined to apologize. Meanwhile, a number of French-Algerian business contracts were reportedly negotiated as Sarkozy promoted his vision for an economic "Mediterranean Union."

Severe tension reportedly developed between the Algerian and Egyptian governments in late 2009 following disturbances in both countries surrounding their national soccer teams. However, despite the specter raised by some observers of a "football war," officials of both governments subsequently downplayed the matter.

In 2010 Algeria, Mali, Mauritania, and Niger launched a joint military command as part of their effort to combat terrorism in the Saharan and sub-Saharan regions.

The Algerian administration initially adopted an ambiguous stance in 2011 toward the rebel action against Muammar Qadhafi in Libya, in part due to concern that the Libyan unrest might tangentially strengthen Algerian militants. Following Qadhafi's death, Algerian officials reached an agreement with the new Libyan government in April 2012 regarding security issues. Algeria's relationship with the new government in Tunisia also appeared satisfactory as the two countries at midyear agreed to negotiate the demarcation of their maritime border. Regional concerns for Algeria subsequently focused on the effects of the coup in Mali and civil war in the north of that country, which, among other things, prompted the influx of refugees and weapons to Algeria.

New French president François Hollande visited Algeria in November 2012 and referenced the "profoundly unjust and brutal" nature of colonial rule, further improving relations between the two countries. Algeria, which had previously opposed military action against the Islamist forces in Mali, ultimately supported the French-led multilateral intervention in January 2013 by permitting French planes to use Algerian airspace. Meanwhile, the United States reportedly provided Algeria with access to top-level U.S. intelligence in order to assist in preventing terrorist strikes in the region.

Although Morocco had previously been reported to be seeking improved ties with Algeria, the border between the two countries stayed closed in 2013 as the Algerian government remained committed to a self-determination referendum in the Western Sahara.

Current issues. Significant demonstrations broke out in January 2011 to protest, among other things, unemployment and escalating commodity prices, and the fervor of the antigovernment movement subsequently gained momentum in consonance with the Arab Spring developments in Tunisia and Egypt. Led by the newly formed National Coordination for Change and Democracy (*Coordination Nationale pour le Changement et la Démocratie*—CNCD), the emboldened opposition demanded the resignation of the Bouteflika administration and extensive constitutional revision. Police harshly suppressed several protests in February and March, but it was widely believed that the majority of Algerians, mindful of the violence of the 1990s, did not support overthrow of the government. Promising to "strengthen democracy," Bouteflika lifted the long-standing state of emergency and invited opposition parties to present proposals for constitutional reform (the CNCD ultimately boycotted those discussions). The administration also announced a massive increase in government spending, designed to relieve the current housing crunch and combat unemployment among young people (who dominated the antigovernment demonstrations).

Attacks by the AQIM intensified in frequency throughout the second half of 2011 and into 2012, as did counter-measures on the part of

Algerian security forces. Meanwhile, much of the electorate either abstained from the May 2012 assembly poll or purposely spoiled ballots. The country's independent elections commission described the balloting as "neither credible nor fair," although EU observers were kinder in their assessment, characterizing the elections as a positive "first step in the reform process." The balloting was perhaps most noteworthy for the relative lack of success (third place with 50 seats) of the MSP-led alliance, which had hoped to capitalize on rising Islamist support generated throughout the region by the Arab Spring. For his part, new prime minister Sellah, who had managed Bouteflika's 2004 and 2009 presidential campaigns, pledged in September that he would continue to pursue the reforms initiated by the president and the previous government, although that task was being taken over by a "new generation." The two major government parties (the FLN and RND) were the top vote-getters in the local elections in late November and the replenishment of the Council of the Nation in late December.

Islamist militants overran a major natural gas facility in the Algerian desert in January 2013. After Algerian special forces retook the facility, it was reported that nearly 40 workers (nearly all from foreign countries) had died, along with 29 militants. The government subsequently launched several anti-AQIM strikes and beefed up security forces at the borders with Mali and Tunisia.

President Bouteflika suffered what the administration characterized as a mini-stroke in late April 2013 and was not prominent on the political scene until he announced the September cabinet reshuffle, in which he appeared to transfer significant powers from the essentially independent intelligence services to his ministers. Attention subsequently focused on the presidential election scheduled for April 2014, many observers predicting that the infirm Bouteflika would attempt to handpick a successor.

POLITICAL PARTIES AND GROUPS

From independence until 1989 the National Liberation Front was the only authorized political grouping, Algeria having been formally designated as a one-party state. Under constitutional changes approved in 1989, however, Algerians were permitted to form "associations of a political nature" as long as they did not "threaten the basic interests of the state" and were not "created exclusively on the basis of religion, language, region, sex, race, or profession." To operate legally, parties were also required to obtain government permits. Subsequently, constitutional amendment of November 1996 and electoral law revision of February 1997 further restricted parties from referencing religion, ethnicity, or race. A number of existing groups were deregistered for failure to adapt to the changes by the deadline of April 1997. In addition, other parties were told to disband in May 1998, either for failing to have the minimum of 2,500 members or for violating other new regulations. Twenty-four parties participated in the 2007 legislative balloting.

In January 2011 a number of leftist opposition parties (including the RCD and the MDS) formed the National Coordination for Change and Democracy (*Coordination Nationale pour le Changement et la Démocratie*—CNCD) in conjunction with several trade unions to campaign for the "departure of the regime." In March the CNCD called for establishment of a national transitional council to oversee the installation of a transitional government pending constitutional revision and new elections. The CNCD promoted antigovernment demonstrations throughout the first half of 2011, but the protests failed to attract major popular support.

Several nationalist and Islamist groups (including the MRN) have launched the National Alliance for Change (*Alliance Nationale pour le Changement*—ANC) to promote constitutional reforms under the leadership of former prime minister Ahmed Benbitour, who in 2013 indicated he would run for president in 2014.

The government introduced new legislation regarding parties in December 2011, describing it as a liberalizing initiative. However, the opposition criticized the fact that the minister of the interior and local collectivities (rather than the judiciary, as demanded by critics of the administration) retained the power to legalize potential parties.

Government and Government-Supportive Parties:

National Liberation Front (*Front de Libération Nationale*—FLN). Founded in November 1954 and dedicated to socialism, nonalignment, and pan-Arabism, the FLN led the eight-year war of independence against France and subsequently assumed complete control of Algerian political and governmental affairs. By the late 1980s a cleavage was apparent within the FLN between an "old guard," dedicated to the maintenance of strict socialist policies, and a group, led by President Bendjedid, favoring political and economic liberalization. The reformers subsequently gained ascendancy (see the 2012 *Handbook* for details). In late June 1991 Bendjedid resigned as FLN president, and several other members of his administration relinquished their party posts as part of the government's effort to distance itself from FLN control.

Continuing a rapid decline in its electoral potency, the FLN won only 15 seats on the basis of a 24 percent vote share in the December 1991 first-round legislative poll. The party was subsequently reported to be divided over Bendjedid's resignation as president of the republic and the assumption of power by the High Security Council. However, the FLN Central Committee announced it would support the High Council of State, assuming adherence to that council's pledge to return the nation to a democratic process.

By late 1994 the FLN was firmly in the opposition camp, its leaders joining with those of the FIS, FFS, and other parties in negotiating a proposed plan for a return to civilian government. The FLN formally endorsed a boycott of the 1995 presidential election, although it appeared that many party members voted anyway, a large percentage of their support reportedly going to President Zeroual.

The 1995 electoral boycott having been widely acknowledged as a mistake, the FLN participated full force in the three 1997 elections and accepted junior partner status in the RND-led coalition government formed in June. The 1998 FLN congress reelected Secretary General Boualen BENHAMOUDA, thereby underlining the party's return to a "conservative tendency." The FLN also nominated military-backed Abdelaziz Bouteflika as its official candidate for the April 1999 presidential election. Benhamouda, viewed as a longstanding "rival" to Bouteflika, resigned as secretary general in September 2001; the post was later filled by Prime Minister Ali Benflis.

Following a resurgence of the FLN in the May 2002 assembly balloting and the October 2002 municipal elections, Benflis was reelected as FLN secretary general at a July 2003 congress, which also installed a pro-Benflis Central Committee. By that time it was clear that Benflis (who had been dismissed as prime minister in April 2003) planned to run for president in 2004, thereby causing a rupture in the FLN between his supporters and those of President Bouteflika. The FLN convention in December 2003 selected Benflis as the party's standard-bearer, but an Algerian court (apparently under pressure from the Bouteflika administration) "annulled" that nomination and ordered FLN funds frozen. After Benflis secured only 8 percent of the vote in the April 2004 presidential balloting, he resigned as FLN secretary general. At a party congress in February 2005, Bouteflika was named "honorary president" of the party, his supporters having clearly regained party control. In addition, Abdelaziz BELKHADEM, described as close to Bouteflika and a potential link to the moderate Islamic movement, was reelected as secretary general; he was named prime minister in May 2006. The FLN fell to 136 seats in the 2007 legislative poll (on a vote share of 35 percent), losing its majority but retaining government control with its coalition partners—the RND and MSP.

President Bouteflika was reelected for a third term in 2009 with 90.2 percent of the vote, officially as an independent but with the endorsement of the Presidential Alliance (*Alliance Présidentielle*—AP), which included the FLN, RND, and MSP. Belkhadem was reelected as FLN secretary general at a congress in March 2010 and declared there was no ideological opposition within the party despite reports of calls for "greater democratization." Nevertheless, FLN dissidents reportedly objected to what was described as Belkhadem's "Islamising" of the party. Facing growing opposition within the FLN Central committee, Belkhadem resigned from his party post in early 2013. He was succeeded later in the year by Amar Saadani, described as an ally of President Bouteflika.

Leaders: Abdelaziz BOUTEFLIKA (President of the Republic and Honorary President of the Party), Saïd BOUHADJA, Amar SAADANI (Secretary General).

National Democratic Rally (*Rassemblement National et Démocratique*—RND). Launched in February 1997 in support of the policies of President Zeroual, the RND dominated the subsequent assembly, municipal, and Council of the Nation balloting, in part due to substantial financing and other assistance from sitting government officials, many of whom ran for office under the RND banner. Formally committed to pluralism, a "modern" economy (including emphasis on privatization), and "social justice," the RND was widely viewed primarily as a vehicle for entrenched authority to participate in an expanding democratic process without facing a genuine threat to its hold on power.

A serious split developed in the RND over whom to support in the April 1999 presidential balloting. Consequently, Tahar BENBAIBECHE, who had complained that military leaders had been inappropriately pressuring the party to back Abdelaziz Bouteflika, was dismissed as secretary general in January 1999 and replaced by Ahmed Ouyahia, who had recently resigned as prime minister. Ouyahia quickly announced that Bouteflika, the official candidate of the FLN, enjoyed the support of most of the RND.

By early 2002 the RND was described as having failed to attract as much popular support as originally expected, apparently because of the party's ongoing ties to the military. The RND's representation in the assembly fell from 156 to 47 in the October balloting.

Ouyahia returned to the prime ministership in April 2003, and the RND supported President Bouteflika's reelection in 2004. However, Ouyahia was dismissed as prime minister in May 2006, apparently because he was considered a potential rival to Bouteflika. Although the RND subsequently remained in the FLN-led cabinet, Ouyahia, a hard-liner in regard to proposed reconciliation with Islamist militants, continued to challenge Bouteflika on several issues. The RND's legislative representation increased to 61 in the 2007 balloting on a vote share of 15.7 percent.

Ouyahia was again named prime minister in June 2008, having reportedly spent the previous two years concentrating on strengthening the RND. The RND supported President Bouteflika in his 2009 reelection campaign, and Ouyahia remained at the head of the new reshuffled cabinet named in May 2010. However, he was replaced as prime minister following the May 2012 assembly elections, at which the RND finished second with 68 seats. Fractionalization was subsequently reported within the RND, and Ouyahia resigned as secretary general in January 2013.

Leaders: Abdelkader BENSALAH (Acting Chair of the Party and Speaker of the Council of the Nation), Ahmed OUYAHIA (Former Prime Minister and Former Secretary General), Mouloud CHORFI.

Republican National Alliance (*Alliance Nationale Républicaine*—ANR). The ANR was formed in early 1995 by several former government officials, including Redha Malek, prime minister in 1993–1994, and Ali Haroun, a member of the 1992–1994 collective presidency. Formally opposed to any compromise with the Islamic fundamentalist movement, the ANR was considered a vehicle for a presidential bid by Malek. However, Malek was prevented from contesting the 1995 election because he failed to obtain the required 75,000 signatures of support. Malek was reelected chair of the ANR by the June 1996 congress in Algiers, which also elected a new 145-member National Council.

Despite retaining a seat in the cabinet, the ANR in early 2002 was described as "steering clear" of the upcoming legislative poll. However, it won four seats in the 2007 poll on a vote share of 1.0 percent. The ANR secured two seats in the May 2012 assembly balloting, and the party's secretary general, Belkacem Sahli, was named a secretary of the state in the government appointed in September.

Leaders: Redha MALEK (Chair), Ali HAROUN, Belkacem SAHLI (Secretary General).

Popular Algerian Movement (*Mouvement Populair Algérien*—MPA). The recently legalized MPA won seven seats in the May 2012 assembly poll, and its leader, Amara Benyounes, joined the new cabinet named in September.

Leader: Amara BENYOUNES.

Algeria Hope Alliance (*Tajamoud Amal el Djazair*—TAD). Described as an amalgam of moderate Islamist, nationalistic, and technocratic tendencies, the TAD held its founding congress in September 2012 under the leadership of Amar Ghoul, who had been named minister of public works as a member of the MSP in the cabinet named in 2010. When the MSP moved into opposition in September 2012, Ghoul remained in the cabinet and left the MSP. He was named transportation minister in the September 2013 cabinet.

Leader: Amar GHOUL.

Other Legislative Parties:

Movement for a Peaceful Society (*Mouvement pour une Société Paisible/Harakat Mujitamas al-Silm*—MSP/Hamas). Formerly known as the Movement for an Islamic Society (*Mouvement pour une Société Islamique*—MSI) or Hamas (an acronym from that grouping's name in Arabic), the MSP adopted its current rubric in 1997 in light of new national restrictions on party references to religion. The MSP is a moderate Islamic fundamentalist organization distinct from the more militant Palestinian formation also known as Hamas. It advocates "coexistence" with groups of opposing views in a democratic political structure and the introduction "by stages" of an Islamic state that would maintain "respect for individual liberties." Although it was reported in early 1992 that some Hamas members had been arrested in the sweeping antifundamentalist campaign, the government subsequently returned to its position that the grouping represented an acceptable moderate alternative to the FIS. Subsequently, Sheikh Mohamed BOUSLIMANI, a founder of Hamas, was killed in late 1993, while another leader, Aly AYEB, was assassinated in September 1994, the attacks being attributed to radicals opposed to Hamas's ongoing dialogue with the government.

Hamas leader Sheikh Mahfoud NAHNAH, who had announced his support for the regime's "antiterrorist" campaign but had described the nation as stuck "in a political dead end" in view of the "lack of trust between people and authority," received 25 percent of the vote in the 1995 presidential election. After finishing second in the June 1997 legislative balloting, the MSP joined the subsequent RND-led coalition government, a decision that was described as putting the party's "credibility on the line" vis-à-vis the more hard-line grouping, the MR (or *Nahda,* see below), which was competing for Islamic support.

Nahnah attempted to run in the April 1999 presidential balloting, but his candidacy was disallowed, ostensibly on the ground that he had not provided proof he had participated in the country's "war of independence" as required of all presidential contenders under the 1996 constitutional revision. Nahnah died in July 2003 after a long illness.

The MSP, which had seen its assembly representation fall from 69 to 38 in the 2002 balloting, supported President Bouteflika in the 2004 presidential campaign. Not surprisingly, MSP leader Bouguerra SOLTANI also strongly endorsed the 2005 national charter on peace and reconciliation. The MSP, whose campaign focused on economic diversification, increased its legislative representation to 52 in the 2007 balloting on a vote share of 13.4 percent. Soltani served in the cabinet until April 2009, when he left the government to focus on MSP affairs. By that time, a group of MSP members who opposed Soltani's strong support for the Bouteflika administration had announced formation of a splinter group named the Call and Change Movement.

The MSP announced in January 2012 that it was withdrawing its "political support" for President Bouteflika, but the MSP ministers kept their posts in the cabinet. For the May assembly poll the MSP formed an electoral coalition called the **Green Algeria Alliance** (*Alliance Algérie Verte*—AAV) with *Nahda* and *El Islah* (the two parties immediately below), hoping to emulate the recent successes of Islamist parties in Morocco and Tunisia. Although the AAV apparently expected to win at least a plurality, it finished third with 50 seats. Soltani and other MSP leaders expressed surprise at the results, characterizing the poll as rigged in favor of the FLN and RND. The MSP subsequently officially moved into opposition, a position that was solidified by the selection at the May 2013 MSP congress of Abderrazak Mokri to succeed Soltani as party leader. In 2013 the AAV parties reportedly agreed to present a joint presidential candidate in 2014, possibly in alignment with smaller Islamist groups.

Leaders: Abderrazak MOKRI (President), Abderrahmane SAIDI, Ahmed ISSAAD, Djemaa NACER.

Renaissance Movement (*Mouvement de la Renaissance/Harakat al-Nahda*—MR/*Nahda*). Previously called the Islamic Renaissance Movement (*Mouvement de la Renaissance Islamique/Harakat al-Nahda al-Islamiyya*—MRI/*Nahda*), the party dropped the "Islamic" portion of its rubric in early 1997 to conform to new national regulations. Initially a small, moderate fundamentalist grouping, *Nahda* was promoted in the mid-1990s by the government as a legal alternative to the banned FIS. The grouping performed "surprisingly well" in the June 1997 legislative balloting, finishing fourth with 34 seats. By that time *Nahda* had adopted a tougher stance than the other main legal Islamic party (the MSP), and its leaders ultimately declined to participate in the new RND-led coalition government.

A *Nahda* congress in early 1998 reportedly directed that some authority previously exercised by long-standing leader Sheikh Abdallah Djaballah be turned over to Secretary General Lahbib Adami. The apparent rivalry between the two came to a head late in the year when Adami announced that the party had agreed to support Abdelaziz Bouteflika, the military-backed FLN candidate, in the upcoming presidential balloting. Djaballah consequently left *Nahda* in January 1999 and formed the MRN (below), taking nearly half of the 34 *Nahda* assembly representatives with him. *Nahda* fell to only one seat in the 2002 assembly poll before rebounding to five seats in 2007 on a vote share of 1.3 percent. The party boycotted the 2009 presidential poll. It joined the AAV electoral coalition (see MSP, above) for the 2012 assembly poll.

Leaders: Fatah REBAI (President), Lahbib ADAMI (Secretary General).

Movement for National Reform (*Mouvement pour la Réforme Nationale*—MRN). The MRN, also known as *El Islah* (Arabic for "reform"), was launched in early 1999 to promote the presidential campaign of Sheikh Abdallah DJABALLAH, who had recently split from *Nahda.* The MRN, supportive of eventual establishment of an "Islamic State" but considered a member of the moderate Islamic camp, won 43 seats in the 2002 assembly balloting, thereby becoming the largest opposition grouping. Djaballah won 4.9 percent of the vote in the 2004 presidential poll.

Dissent within the MRN over Djaballah's reported "autocratic" style subsequently led to his ouster from the party, which fell dramatically to only three seats in the 2007 legislative poll on a vote share of 0.8 percent. New MRN leader Mohamed Djahid Younsi, described as lacking the popular appeal of Djaballah, secured only 1.4 percent of the vote in the 2009 presidential balloting. The MRN participated in the MSP-led AAV electoral front for the May 2012 assembly elections.

Leader: Mohamed Djahid YOUNSI (Secretary General).

Socialist Forces Front (*Front des Forces Socialistes*—FFS). Long a clandestine group, the predominantly Berber FFS was legalized in November 1989. Having earned the enmity of the government in 1985 when he briefly formed a "united front" with former president Ben Bella to oppose the FLN, FFS leader Hocine Aït-Ahmed, a revolutionary hero, remained in Swiss exile until December 1989. The FFS boycotted the 1990 municipal elections but, after failing to create a multiparty coalition to "block" the FIS, presented over 300 candidates in the December 1991 legislative balloting on a platform that endorsed a "mixed economy," greater regional autonomy, and official recognition of the Berber language. The FFS won 25 seats (second to the FIS) on a 15 percent vote share in the first election round, Aït-Ahmed strongly criticizing cancellation of the second prior to returning to self-imposed exile in Switzerland. The FFS subsequently joined the FIS and the FLN as the leading proponents of the unsuccessful January 1995 peace plan and boycotted the 1995 presidential balloting.

Aït-Ahmed, hitherto FFS general secretary, was elected to the newly created post of party president at the March 1996 FFS congress in Algiers. Dueling with the RCD for support within the Berber community, the FFS secured 20 seats in the June 1997 assembly balloting but was not invited to participate in the new RND-led government because of the FFS's insistence that negotiations should proceed with the goal of incorporating the FIS into the legal political process. A special congress in February 1999 nominated Aït-Ahmed, who had recently returned from exile, as the FFS candidate for the upcoming presidential balloting. A May 2000 congress reelected Aït-Ahmed as FFS president amid reports of deepening divisions within the party.

In the wake of severe unrest in Berber areas, the FFS boycotted the 2002 assembly balloting. The FFS also called for a boycott of the 2005 referendum on the national charter for peace and reconciliation, arguing that the charter would "consecrate impunity" for perpetrators of violent crimes on both sides of the recent conflict.

The FFS boycotted the 2007 assembly poll, although some members, opposed to Aït-Ahmed's hard line in the matter, reportedly ran as independents. The party also boycotted the 2009 presidential election, which it subsequently characterized as subject to widespread fraud.

In May 2011 the FFS was described as promoting "reengagement" with the public through meetings held peacefully "away from the street." After two decades of boycotting elections, the FFS participated in the May 2012 assembly balloting as part of its evolving efforts to present a "peaceful, democratic alternative to this despotic regime." The party finished fourth with 27 seats.

Aït-Ahmed, continuing to live in Switzerland, stepped down as FFS leader in December 2012 at the age of 86. The May 2013 congress named a five-member directorate to run the party, in conjunction with a first secretary.

Leaders: Ahmed BETATACHE (First Secretary); Hocine AÏT-AHMED (1999 presidential candidate [in Switzerland]); Aziz BALOUL, Mohand Amokrane CHERIFI, Rachid HALLET, Saida ICHLAMENE, Ali LASKRI (members of leadership council).

Workers' Party (*Parti des Travailleurs*—PT). The Trotskyist PT was one of the groups that signed the proposed national reconciliation pact in early 1995. It secured four seats in the June 1997 assembly balloting and subsequently continued to urge the government to negotiate with the FIS. The PT improved dramatically to 21 seats in the 2002 assembly balloting on a vote share of 4.8 percent. PT leader and women's rights activist Louisa Hannoun, described as the first woman to run for president in the Arab world, won 1.2 percent in the vote in the 2004 poll. The PT secured 26 seats in the 2007 legislative poll on a vote share of 6.7 percent, while Hannoun finished second in the 2009 presidential balloting with 4.2 percent of the vote. (She claimed the results were fraudulent.)

Leaders: Louisa HANNOUN, Djelloul DJOUDI.

Algerian National Front (*Front National Algérien*—FNA/*Jabhah al-Wataniyah al-Jazairiyah*). Organized in June 1999 in support of the "downtrodden," the FNA, describing itself as "republican and democratic," received official recognition the following November. It won 8 seats in the 2002 legislative poll on a 3.2 percent vote share. However, the proposed presidential bid in 2004 of FNA leader Moussa Touati was rejected by the Constitutional Council for a lack of sufficient voter signatures with his application. The FNA won 3.3 percent of the vote in the 2007 legislative poll, securing 13 seats. Touati, characterized during the campaign as a nationalist, won 2.3 percent of the vote in the 2009 presidential election. Touati described the 2012 legislative elections, in which the FNA was credited with 9 seats, as a "blatant fraud."

Leader: Moussa TOUATI.

Algerian Renewal Party (*Parti pour le Renouveau de l'Algérie*—PRA). A moderate Islamic group that first surfaced during the October 1988 demonstrations, the PRA announced in 1989 that it would concentrate on economic issues, particularly a fight to end "state capitalism and interventionism." PRA leader Noureddine Boukrouh, described as a "liberal businessman," won 4 percent of the votes in the 1995 presidential election. Although the government disallowed Boukrouh's candidacy for the 1999 presidential election, citing insufficient signatures of support, Boukrouh joined the coalition government announced in December 1999. The PRA secured 2.2 percent of the vote in the 2002 assembly balloting and 1.0 percent in 2007 (securing four seats).

Leaders: Noureddine BOUKROUH, Yacine TORKMANE.

***Ahd* 54.** A small, nationalist party, *Ahd* 54 (*Ahd* is Arabic for "oath," reportedly a reference to principles espoused at the beginning of the war of independence) secured 0.9 percent of the vote in the 2002 assembly balloting. Its leader, human rights activist Mohamed Ali Fawzi Rebaine, won 0.7 percent of the vote in the 2004 presidential poll. The party secured two seats in the 2007 assembly poll on a vote share of 0.5 percent, and Rebaine, reportedly facing internal party criticism, won 0.9 percent of the vote in the 2009 presidential election.

Leaders: Mohamed Ali Fawzi REBAINE, Toufik CHELLAL.

National Party for Solidarity and Development (*Parti National pour la Solidarité et le Développement*—PNSD). The center-right PNSD won a reported 1.6 percent of the popular vote in the June 1990 municipal elections. It secured 1.8 percent of the vote in the 2002 assembly poll and 0.5 percent in 2007 (good for two seats).

Leader: Mohamed Cherif TALEB (President).

Patriotic Republican Rally (*Rassemblement Patriotique Républicain*—RPR). The RPR is a successor to the Algerian Movement for Justice and Development (*Mouvement Algérien pour la Justice et le Développement*—MAJD), a reformist group launched in November 1990 by former prime minister Kasdi Merbah, who had resigned in October from the FLN Central Committee. Merbah, a staunch antifundamentalist, was assassinated in August 1993, the government accusing Islamic militants of the act. However, no group claimed responsibility for the killing, and observers pointed out that Merbah had a broad spectrum of enemies. In 1999 the government listed the RPR as the successor to the MAJD. The RPR secured two seats in the 2007 assembly poll on a vote share of 0.5 percent.

Leader: Abd al-Kader MERBAH (President).

Other small parties that won seats in the 2012 legislative balloting that had also won seats in 2007 included the **Algerian Rally** (*Rassemblement Algérien*—RA); the **Democratic National Front** (*Front National Démocratique*—FND), led by Sassi MABROUK; the ***Infitah* Movement** (*Mouvement El Intifah*); the **National Front of Independents for Concord** (*Front National des Indépendants pour la Concorde*—FNIC); and the **National Movement of Hope** (*Mouvement National d'Esperance*—MNE), led by Mohamed HADEF.

New parties that won seats in the 2012 poll included the **Algerian Light Party** (*Parti Ennour El Djazairi*), led by Badredine BELBAZ; the **Change Front** (*Front du Changement*—FC), led by Abdelmajid MENASARA, a prominent Islamist who accused the army of "manipulating" the assembly elections; the **Dignity Party** (*Parti El Karama*—PK), led by Mohamed BENHAMOU; the **Future Front** (*Front El Moustakbal*—FM), led by Abdelaziz BELAID; the **Justice and Development Front** (*Front pour la Justice et le Développement*—FJD/*El Addala*), an Islamist party led by former *Nahda* and *El Islah* leader Sheikh Abdallah DJABALLAH (the FJD deputies joined the AAV legislators and others in temporarily boycotting the new assembly to protect perceived fraud in the balloting); the **Movement of Free Citizens** (*Mouvement des Citoyens Libres*—MCL), led by Mustapha BOUDINA; the **National Front for Social Justice** (*Front National pour la Justice Sociale*—FNJS), led by Khaled BOUNEDJEMA; the **New Generation Party** (*Parti El Fedjr El Jadid*—PFJ), led by Sofiane DJILALI, who in 2013 called upon President Bouteflika to resign; the **Union of Democratic and Social Forces** (*Union des Forces Démocratiques et Sociales*—UFDS), led by former prime minister and presidential candidate (1999) Mokdad SIFI; and the **Youth Party** (*Parti des Jeunes*), launched in August 2011 under the leadership of Hamana BOUCHERMA to combat the "failure, mediocrity, and corruption" of those holding power.

Other Parties:

Rally for Culture and Democracy (*Rassemblement pour la Culture et la Démocratie*—RCD). Formed in February 1989 to represent Berber interests, the RCD proclaimed its commitment to "economic centralism," linguistic pluralism, and separation of the state and Islamic religion. It won 2 percent of the votes in the June 1990 municipal balloting.

In early 1994 Mohamed Ouramadane TIGZIRI, the RCD's national secretary, was assassinated, apparently as part of the militant fundamentalist campaign against groups such as the RCD that advocated a secular, Western-style political system. The RCD's strongly antifundamentalist leader, Saïd Saadi, was also subsequently prominent in the Berber Cultural Movement, described by the *New York Times* as having evolved into an influential political group in its campaign to have the Berber language sanctioned for use in schools and other public forums. Saadi captured 9 percent of the votes in the 1995 presidential poll, having been assured of the lion's share of Berber votes because of the boycott by the FFS, the RCD's primary competitor for support within that ethnic group. The RCD secured 19 seats in the June 1997 assembly elections but boycotted the December balloting for the new Council of the Nation. The RCD also announced in early 1999 that it was boycotting the upcoming presidential election. However, surprising many observers, the RCD subsequently joined the government coalition of December 1999, the party reportedly having become "increasingly closer" to President Bouteflika. The RCD left the coalition in May 2001 in the wake of severe government/Berber friction, and it boycotted the 2002 national and local elections. Saadi won 1.9 percent of the vote in the 2004 presidential poll.

The RCD strongly condemned the national charter for peace and reconciliation that was approved in 2005. The party also charged the government with fraud in regard to the official vote turnout for the related referendum. Meanwhile, another Berber grouping (the **Movement for the Autonomy of Kabylie** [MAK], led by singer Ferhat MEHENNI), also rejected the charter as an exercise in "self-amnesty" by the Algerian authorities.

The RCD rejoined the electoral process for the 2007 legislative balloting, winning 19 seats on a vote share of 4.9 percent. However, it boycotted the 2009 presidential poll (as did the MAK), Saadi describing the current political situation as a "pitiable and dangerous circus." The RCD claimed there were massive irregularities in the presidential balloting.

Under Saadi's direction, the RCD was one of the most vocal opposition groups calling for constitutional overhaul and the ouster of the Bouteflika government in concert with the Arab Spring in the first half of 2011. In February 2012 the RCD announced it would boycott the May assembly poll, Saadi arguing that the new legislature would be "one of political prostitution." Saadi in March resigned his party leadership post. The RCD dominated the balloting in the Kabylie region in the November 2012 local elections.

Leaders: Mohcene BELABES, (President), Saïd SAADI (Former President).

Movement of National Harmony (*Mouvement de l'Entente Nationale*—MEN). The MEN secured 1.9 percent of the vote in the 2002 assembly balloting and 1.0 percent in 2007 (good for four seats).

Leaders: Ali BOUKHAZNA, Amar LASSOUED.

Fidelity (*Wafa*). Organized by former foreign affairs minister Ahmed Taleb Ibrahimi following his 1999 presidential campaign in the hope of coordinating nationalist and Islamist opposition groups, *Wafa* was subsequently denied recognition by the government on the grounds that it was essentially an FIS "clone." Former *Wafa* leader Mohamed Said, described as a moderate Islamist, finished last in the 2009 presidential balloting with 0.9 percent of the vote as the candidate of the unrecognized Party of Liberty and Justice, which was legalized prior to the 2012 assembly poll.

Democratic Front (*Front Démocratique*—FD). An anti-Bouteflika grouping, the FD elected former prime minister Sid Ahmed Ghozali as its chair during the May 2000 inaugural congress. Ghozali was not permitted by the Constitutional Council to run in the 2004 presidential election, and he subsequently announced he was supporting Ali Benflis in that campaign. Ghozali, by then referenced as the leader of a Social Front, called for a boycott of the 2012 assembly poll.

A number of new small parties were legalized in advance of the May 2012 assembly elections. They included the **Algerian National Party,** led by Youcef HAMIDI; the **Equity and Proclamation Party,** led by Naima SALHI; the **Free National Party** (*Parti National Libre*), led by Liafa OUYAHIA, brother of (then) Prime Minister Ouyahiya; the **Free Patriotic Party,** led by Tarek YAHYAOUI; the **Good Governance Front,** led by Aissa BELHADJ; the **Movement of Free Nationalists,** led by Gharmoul ABDELAZIA; the **National Front for Freedoms** (*Front National pour les Libertés*—FNL), led by Mohammed ZERROUKI; the **New Algeria Front** (*Front de l'Algérie Nouvelle*—FAN), led by Djamel BENABDESLAM; the **Party of Democratic Youth,** led by Salim KHELFA; and the **Party of Liberty and Justice** (*Parti de la Liberté et de la Justice*—PLJ), led by Mohand Oussaid BELAID and former diplomat Mohammed SAID.

Illegal Groups:

Islamic Salvation Front (*Front Islamique du Salut*—FIS). The FIS was organized in early 1989 to represent the surging Islamic fundamentalist movement. Capitalizing upon strong antigovernment sentiment, it won control of a majority of town and departmental councils in the June 1990 municipal elections. Apparently to permit the broadest possible support for its effort to win national legislative control, the FIS leadership was subsequently reluctant to define its goals in specific terms. However, a significant proportion of the front's supporters appeared committed to the adoption and enforcement of sharia throughout Algeria's theretofore relatively secular society and the imposition of measures such as the segregation of the sexes in schools and the workplace, a ban on alcohol consumption, and obligatory veils for women. FIS leaders also made it clear that a national fundamentalist government, even one that came to power through a multiparty election, would not feel bound to maintain a "Western-style" democracy.

In June 1991 FIS leader Dr. Abassi Madani, Ali Belhadj (his deputy), other members of the party's Constitutional Council, and hundreds of FIS followers were arrested on charges of fomenting an "armed conspiracy against the security of the state" in connection with violent demonstrations in Algiers and other cities. Although hard-line FIS factions reportedly called for continued protest and an election boycott unless the detainees were released, the FIS ultimately participated in the December 26 legislative balloting under the leadership of the moderate Abdelkader HACHANI.

After winning 188 seats in the first round of the 1991 assembly poll, the FIS prepared to assume national political leadership, Hachani attempting to reassure the nonfundamentalist population that the FIS would "persuade, not oblige people into doing what we say." However, the party's plan to mount the world's first Islamic state established via the ballot box was thwarted by the military takeover of the Algerian government in early January 1992. Nearly all of the remaining FIS national leaders, including Hachani, were subsequently arrested, as were hundreds of its local and provincial officials, with upwards of 30,000 FIS followers reportedly being placed in desert detention camps. In addition, Algerian courts in March formally banned the FIS as a political party upon petition of the High Council of State, which also ordered the dissolution of many municipal councils under FIS control and their replacement by appointed bodies. The front was subsequently reported to be sharply divided between members remaining faithful to the group's official commitment to nonviolence and more radical adherents prepared to "move from words to rifles." It was generally believed that the latter were responsible for a number of attacks on Algerian security personnel during the rest of the year and for the subsequent emergence of armed groups such as the Islamic Salvation Army (*Armée Islamique du Salut*—AIS). (For comprehensive information on the AIS, which agreed to a cease-fire in 1999 and subsequently endorsed the country's civic concord, see the 2012 *Handbook.*)

In July 1992 Madani and Belhadj were sentenced to 12 years in prison for conspiring against the authority of the state, five other leaders receiving shorter terms. In the wake of Liamine Zeroual's appointment as president in early 1994, sporadic negotiations were reported between the government and the FIS, many reports suggesting that a breakthrough was imminent in mid-1995. However, the government finally declared the talks deadlocked, allegedly over the failure of the FIS leaders to renounce antiregime violence unequivocally. Consequently, no FIS participation was permitted in the 1995 presidential balloting, the front calling upon supporters to boycott the election as a way of embarrassing the government. That strategy backfired, however, as heavy voter turnout and Zeroual's strong showing served to undercut the front's insistence that it still held majority popular support.

The government released Madani on July 15, 1997, one week after Hachani had been freed when a court found him guilty of "inciting rebellion" in 1992 but sentenced him to time served. However, the nature of subsequent FIS-government talks was unclear, and Madani was placed under house arrest in September after he had called for UN mediation of the Algerian political impasse. Not surprisingly, the FIS urged its supporters to boycott the October local elections.

FIS leaders expressed the hope that President Bouteflika's civil concord of the second half of 1999 would lead to legalization of the party (perhaps under a different name). Meanwhile, the circumstances surrounding the assassination of Hachani in Algiers in November 1999 were unclear.

FIS leaders Madani and Belhadj were released from house arrest and prison, respectively, in July 2003, the former subsequently settling in Qatar. Both men were barred from political activity.

Rabeh Kebir, a longstanding FIS leader, returned to Algeria in September 2006 after 14 years in exile in Germany. He announced his support for the nation's current reconciliation program and indicated a desire to become involved in legal political affairs, thereby divorcing himself from other "historic" FIS figures such as Madani and Belhadj. Anwar Haddam, another former FIS leader, in early 2007 expressed similar sentiments, although he remained in the United States. Meanwhile, Belhadj described the national reconciliation program as a "trick" that was designed primarily to protect the military from further investigation regarding its activities in the antifundamentalist campaign. (Belhadj had earlier urged Muslims to join the jihad against U.S.-led forces in Iraq.)

The FIS called for a boycott of the May 2007 assembly elections as well as, after failing to get some of its members on the lists of legal parties, the November local elections. Belhadj was detained briefly by security forces in March 2010 after he issued a statement that was strongly critical of President Bouteflika. The FIS leader subsequently criticized the "approved" Islamic movement for failing to genuinely defend "Islam and its values." Belhadj was again detained in January 2011 in connection with charges of "harming state security" emanating from the antigovernment protest demonstrations triggered by similar events in Tunisia and Egypt. The new parties law introduced by the government in December maintained the ban on the FIS, which called for a boycott of the May 2012 assembly poll.

Leaders: Dr. Abassi MADANI (in Qatar), Ali BELHADJ, Abdelkader BOUKHAMKHAM, Sheikh Abdelkader OMAR, Abdelkrim Ould ADDA (Foreign Spokesperson), Rabeh KEBIR, Anwar HADDAM (in the United States).

Al-Qaida in the Islamic Maghreb (AQIM). The AQIM is a successor to the Salafist Group for Preaching and Combat (*Groupe Salafiste pour la Prédication et le Combat*—GSPC), which was established in 1999 by members of the Armed Islamic Group (*Groupe Islamique Armé*—GIA) who were opposed to the parent group's targeting of civilians but remained committed to attacks on military sites and personnel. (For comprehensive information on the GIA, apparently inactive since 2005, see the 2012 *Handbook.*) The GSPC was included on the list of proscribed organizations published by the United States following the September 11, 2001, terrorist attacks.

By 2003 the GSPC was one of the few Islamist groups "still fighting," hard-liner Nabil SAHRAOUI having supplanted GSPC founder Hassan HATAB as leader of the group. In October 2003 Sahraoui said that the GSPC supported Osama bin Laden's jihad against "the American heretics," and the GSPC was held responsible for several attacks on Algerian forces in 2003–2004. However, Sahraoui was killed by the Algerian army in June 2004, analysts suggesting that GSPC forces had dwindled to 400–450 guerrillas by that time. Another GSPC leader, Amari SAIFI, was taken into custody in late 2004 and subsequently sentenced to life imprisonment.

In late 2005 Hassan Hattab, one of the founders of the GSPC, said he believed most GSPC supporters were now willing to consider an amnesty agreement. However, he later withdrew his support for the nation's new reconciliation charter. In September 2006 Ayman al-Zawahiri, bin Laden's deputy, announced a "blessed union" between al-Qaida and the GSPC, indicating that French and U.S. supporters of the Algerian regime would be targeted. Although the government announced that several hundred GSPC fighters had been killed recently, the GSPC claimed responsibility for a series of attacks in late 2006–early 2007. Prompting even greater concern among Western leaders over the possible expansion of GSPC activity to Europe, the GSPC announced in early 2007 that it was adopting the AQIM rubric in support of an eventual Islamic state across North Africa.

The "rebranding" of the GSPC as the AQIM was perceived as a rejuvenation effort, and the AQIM subsequently became the "most active" militant group in North Africa. After claiming responsibility for attacks in April 2007 that killed more than 30 people, the AQIM warned voters not to participate in the May legislative poll.

AQIM leader Abdelmalek Droukdel was sentenced in absentia in June 2007 by an Algerian court to 20 years in prison, while Hattab was also convicted in absentia of terrorist activity. However, Hattab in September reportedly surrendered to pursue amnesty, the government describing him at that time as "repentant." (Hattab issued appeals in 2008 and 2009 for his former GSPC comrades to cease their attacks.)

Apparently bolstered by recruits (some from neighboring countries) enflamed by anti-Western sentiment regarding Iraq, the AQIM claimed responsibility for a number of attacks throughout the rest of 2007 (including double suicide bombings in December that killed 17 UN personnel and more than 20 others) and early 2008. The group, relying on tactics (notably suicide bombings) similar to those used by insurgents in Iraq, also vowed to target multinational companies in Algeria. Most analysts concluded that the AQIM suffered heavy losses in the intensified government campaign of late 2008–early 2009, although it remained a potent force not only in Algeria but also in neighboring countries, having called for attacks on Westerners throughout the world.

Droukdel was sentenced in absentia to death in November 2009, while eight other members of the AQIM were also sentenced to life imprisonment. Prompting another government offensive, the AQIM (also referenced in some news reports as Al-Qaida in the Land of the Islamic Maghreb [AQLIM] or the Al-Qaida Organization in the Islamic Maghreb [AQOIM]) claimed responsibility for several ambushes against Algerian security forces in 2009–2010 and was involved in several high-profile hostage situations, one of which prompted a failed French/Mauritanian raid in mid-2010 against an AQIM hideout.

Sporadic battles continued in 2011 between government security forces and the AQIM, said to be strongest at that time in the southern border areas. A number of AQIM attacks (including suicide bombings) were reported in 2012, analysts concluding that the AQIM's arsenal had been expanded by an influx of weapons facilitated by the civil war in Libya.

The January 2013 terrorist attack on an Algerian gas plant (see Current issues, below) was attributed in many circles to an AQIM offshoot called "Signatories in Blood," led by Mokhtar BELMOKHTAR, a longtime jihadist who reportedly had been pushed out of an AQIM leadership post in northern Mali, where the AQIM had contributed to the recent takeover by Islamist militants.

Several major offensives by Algerian security forces in 2013 reportedly significantly weakened the AQIM, although occasional antigovernment attacks continued.

Leader: Abdelmalek DROUKDEL (Abu Musab ABDULWAHOOD).

Defenders of the Salafi Call (*Dhanat Houmet Daawa Salafia*). One of the few Islamist militant groups active in Algeria as of 2005, this "Taliban-trained" grouping, another offshoot of the GIA, was reported to comprise about 150–250 fighters in western Algeria. Like the GSPC, it has been declared a terrorist organization by the United States. Three members of the Defenders of the Salafi Call went on trial in Algeria in mid-2012 for alleged terrorist attacks dating back to the early 1990s.

Leader: Mohammed BENSLIM.

LEGISLATURE

The 1996 constitution provided for a bicameral **Parliament** (*Barlaman*), consisting of a restructured National People's Assembly and a new upper house, the Council of the Nation. The first round of multiparty balloting for a new 430-member assembly was held December 26, 1991, with the Islamic Salvation Front winning 188 seats, the Socialist Forces Front, 25; the National Liberation Front, 15; and independents, 3. A runoff round involving the top two vote-getters in the remaining districts was scheduled for January 16, 1992. However, the second poll was canceled on January 12 by the High Security Council, which also declared the results of the first round invalid.

In April 1992 the High Council of State announced the appointment of a 60-member National Consultative Council (*Majlis al-Shoura al-Watani*) to serve in an advisory capacity to the government pending new assembly elections. The National Dialogue Conference of early 1994, in turn, authorized the appointment of a three-year National Transitional Council (*Conseil National de Transition*—CNT), which at its initial sitting in May encompassed 63 seats filled by parties, 85 by professional associations and trade unions, and 30 by government nominees, with 22 reserved for nonparticipating secular parties. The CNT was dissolved on May 18, 1997, in preparation for the elections to the bodies authorized by the new constitution.

Council of the Nation (*Majlis al-Umma/Conseil de la Nation*). The upper house has 144 members, 96 (2 from each *wilaya*) elected in secret ballot by an electoral college of the members of local councils and communal and *wilayaat* assemblies and 48 appointed by the president. The term of office is six years, although one-half of the initial members (elected on December 25, 1997) served only three years to permit 50 percent replenishment of the council every three years from that point. In the most recent balloting for half of the elected seats on December 29, 2012, the National Democratic Rally was credited with winning 24 seats (for a total of 44 elected seats); the National Liberation Front, 17 (40); the Socialist Forces Front, 2 (2); the Popular Algerian Movement, 1 (1); *Ahd* 54, 1(1); and the Future Front, 1 (1). The remaining elected seats were held by the Movement for a Peaceful Society, 2; the Algerian National Front, 1; the Rally for Culture and Democracy, 1; and independents, 3.

Speaker: Abdelkader BENSALAH.

National People's Assembly (*Majlis Ech Chaabi al-Watani, Assemblée Popularie Nationale*). The lower house has 462 members (raised in 2012 from 389), 454 representing the 48 *wilayaats* (each of which has at least 4 representatives) according to population, and 8 (4 in Europe and 4 in other Arab nations) elected by Algerians living abroad. Members are elected for a five-year term on a proportional basis from lists presented by parties or independents. Following the election of May 10, 2012, the distribution of seats was as follows: National Liberation Front, 208; National Democratic Rally, 68; Green Algeria Alliance, 50; Socialist Forces Front, 27; Workers' Party, 26; Algerian National Front, 9; Justice and Development Front, 8; Popular Algerian Movement, 7; New Generation Party, 5; National Party for Solidarity and Development, 4; Front for Change, 4; *Ahd* 54, 3; Republican National Alliance, 3; National Front for Social Justice, 3; Union of Democratic and Social Forces, 3; Algerian Rally, 2; Patriotic Republican Rally, 2; National Movement of Hope, 2; Future Front, 2; Dignity Party, 2; Movement of Free Citizens, 1; Youth Party, 2; Algerian Light Party, 2; Algerian Renewal Party, 1; National Democratic Front, 1; National Front of Independents for Concord, 1; *Infitah* Movement, 1; and independents, 18.

President: Mohamed Larbi OULD KHELIFA.

CABINET

[as of September 15, 2013]

President	Abdelaziz Bouteflika (FLN)
Prime Minister	Abdelmalek Sellal (ind.)
Minister of State	Tayeb Balaiz
Ministers	
Agriculture and Rural Development	Abdelwahab Nouri
Commerce	Mustapha Benbada
Communication	Abdelkader Messahel
Culture	Khalida Toumi [f]
Energy and Mining	Youcef Yousfi (ind.)
Finance	Karim Djoubi
Fishing and Marine Resources	Sid Ahmed Ferroukhi
Foreign Affairs	Ramtame Lamamra
Health, Population, and Hospital Reform	Abdelmalek Boudiaf
Higher Education and Scientific Research	Mohamed Mebarki
Housing and Urban Affairs	Abdelmajid Tebboune
Industrial Development and Promotion of Investment	Amara Benyounes (MPA)
Interior and Local Collectives	Tayeb Belaiz
Justice, Keeper of the Seals	Tayeb Louh (FLN)
Labor, Employment, and Social Security	Mohamed Benmeradi
National Defense	Abdelaziz Bouteflicka (FLN)
National Defense (Deputy) and Chief of Staff of the People's National Army	Ahmed Gaid Salah
National Education	Abdelatif Baba Ahmed
National Solidarity, Family, and Women's Affairs	Souad Bendjaballah [f]
Posts and Information and Communications Technologies	Zohra Derdouri [f]
Prime Minister's Office (In charge of Public Service Reform)	Mohamed El Ghazi
Public Works	Farouk Chiali
Relations With Parliament	Mahmoud Khedri (FLN)
Religious Affairs and Endowments	Bouabdallah Ghlamallah (RND)
Territorial Management and Environment	Dalila Boudjemaa [f]
Tourism and Handicrafts	Mohamed Amine Hadj Said
Training and Professional Education	Nouredine Bedoui
Transportation	Amar Ghoul (TAD)
War Veterans	Mohamed Cherif Abbes (RND)
Water Resources	Hocine Necib
Youth and Sports	Mohamed Tahmi
Ministers Delegate	
Budget	Mohamed Djellab
Maghreb and African Affairs	Abdelmadjid Bouguerra
National Defense	Gen. (Ret.) Abdelmalek Guenaïzia
Secretary General of the Government	Ahmed Noui

[f] = female

INTERGOVERNMENTAL REPRESENTATION

Ambassador to the U.S.: Abdallah BAALI.

U.S. Ambassador to Algeria: Henry S. ENSHER.

Permanent Representative to the UN: Mourad BENMEHIDI.

IGO Memberships (Non-UN): AfDB, AU, IOM, LAS, NAM, OIC, OPEC.

ANDORRA

Principality of Andorra
Principat d'Andorra (Catalan)
Principalité d'Andorre (French)
Principado de Andorra (Spanish)

Political Status: Sovereign "parliamentary co-principality," with the president of the French Republic and the Spanish Bishop of Urgell possessing certain powers as joint heads of state under constitution approved March 14, 1993, with effect from May 4.

Area: 180 sq. mi. (467 sq. km).

Population: 79,280 (2010E—UN); 85,293 (2013E—U.S. Census).

Major Urban Center (2013E): ANDORRA LA VELLA (22,400).

Official Language: Catalan (French, Spanish, and Portuguese are also used).

Monetary Units: There is no local currency. The French franc and the Spanish peseta both circulated until 2002, when Andorra adopted the euro (market rate November 1, 2013: 0.74 euro = $1US).

French Co-Prince: François HOLLANDE; became co-prince May 15, 2012, upon inauguration as president of the French Republic.
Permanent French Delegate: Christian FRÉMONT.

Spanish Episcopal Co-Prince: Mgr. Joan Enric VIVES Sicilia; became co-prince May 12, 2003, upon induction as Bishop of See of Urgell.
Permanent Episcopal Delegate: Nemesi MARQUES Oste.

Head of Government (*Cap del Govern*): Antoni MARTÍ Petit (Democrats for Andorra); elected for a four-year term by the General Council on May 11, 2011, following the legislative balloting of April 3 and sworn in on May 12 to succeed Jaume BARTUMEU Cassany (Social Democratic Party). Seven members of Martí's cabinet took their oath of office on May 16 and an eighth on August 1.

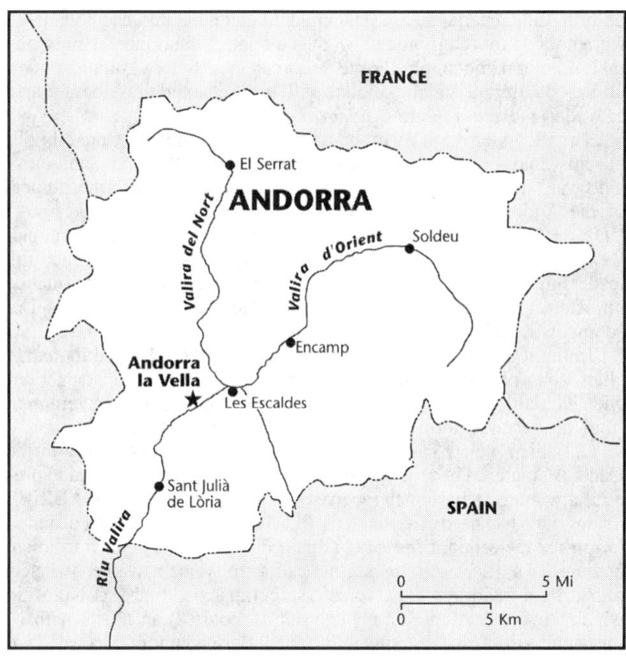

THE COUNTRY

A rough, mountainous country of limited dimensions, Andorra is set in a large drainage area of the Pyrenees between France and Spain. The main stream is the Riu Valira, which has two branches and six open basins. The indigenous residents are of Catalan stock and represent about one-third of the population; foreign residents include Spaniards (about 43 percent of the total population), Portuguese (11 percent), and French (7 percent). Virtually all of the inhabitants are Roman Catholic. The mainstays of Andorra's economy are tourism, which accounts for 80 percent of gross domestic product (GDP), and banking. Tourists come to the country for skiing, hiking, and duty-free shopping, while financiers have long been attracted to its reputation as a tax haven.

Other Andorran industries include sheep raising, timber, tobacco, handicrafts, and furniture. Only 2 percent of the land is arable, meaning that most food products must be imported. The main trading partners are Spain (70 percent) and France (20 percent). A hydroelectric plant at Les Escaldes produces 40 percent of the country's electricity; the rest is provided by Spain.

Andorra experienced steady economic growth for decades, comfortably living off modest import tariffs. Visitors came for goods that generally bear high tariffs in other countries, such as cigarettes, alcohol, perfume, and pharmaceuticals. GDP grew by an annual average of more than 3.5 percent between 2005 and 2008, and the influx of tourists sparked a construction boom. The economy suffered in 2007, when a warm winter and the global economic crisis kept tourists away. Andorra's economy contracted 12 percent over the next four years, as the annual number of tourists dropped from 12 million to 8 million. GDP fell 1.8 percent in 2011 and 1.6 percent in 2012. After reporting zero unemployment for years, the government acknowledged a 7 percent unemployment rate for 2010. The jobs situation improved with 1.9 percent unemployment in 2011 and 2.9 percent in 2012, but some of that apparent decline was from workers leaving the country.

The Andorran government, in an effort to offset some effects of the worldwide recession, opened the country to foreign investors in an unprecedented manner. The 2008 Foreign Investment Law raised the limit of one-third ownership for foreign investors to 49 percent for main industries and 100 percent for new industries in 200 sectors the government hoped to nurture, such as e-commerce and plastic surgery. Furthermore, in response to years of intense international pressure concerning the country's "tax haven" status, the government agreed to increase financial transparency, especially on foreign-owned bank accounts.

GOVERNMENT AND POLITICS

Political background. Andorra is the last independent survivor of the *Marca Hispanica* (or March states), a series of several former Spanish countries that served as buffer states and were established by Charlemagne around 800 A.D. to keep the Muslim Moors from advancing into Christian France. Charlemagne, who granted a charter to the Andorran people in return for their fighting the Moors, is credited as the founder of the country. The unique political structure of Andorra dates from 1278, when an agreement on joint suzerainty (a *paréage*) was reached between the French count of Foix, whose right ultimately passed to the president of the French Republic, and the Spanish bishop of the nearby See of Urgell. Andorra has no army of its own; Spain and France are jointly responsible for its defense.

Andorra's legislature, the General Council, traces its roots to the Land Council of 1419. Under a Political Reform Law approved after a stormy legislative debate in November 1981, a head of government (*cap del govern*) was created for the first time. The law also specified that the council as a whole would meet for concurrent four-year terms, designating the head of government (who appoints a seven-member cabinet) for a like term.

Following the December 9, 1981, legislative election, the General Council, on January 8, 1982, named Oscar RIBAS Reig to a four-year term as Andorra's first head of government. Ribas Reig resigned on April 30, 1984, following a lengthy dispute over tax policy. On May 21 the council elected Josep PINTAT Solans, who was re-appointed following a general election in December 1985.

Ribas Reig returned to power after balloting on December 10, 1989, and in 1990 Andorra obtained its first penal code, providing, among other things, for the abolition of the death penalty. Ribas Reig again resigned in January 1992 after conservatives had blocked his effort to introduce a constitution that would legalize parties and trade unions and guarantee civil rights. Retaining office as the result of legislative balloting on April 5 and 12, he announced that the new council's principal task would be to draft a basic law clarifying the division of powers. The process was completed in a referendum on March 14, 1993, when, in a turnout of 76 percent of the 9,123 eligible voters, 74.2 percent approved what was in effect Andorra's first written constitution. The adoption of the new basic law represented a conscious attempt by progressive elements led by Ribas Reig to bring Andorra into line with other European states in terms of prescribed civil and social rights.

In Andorra's first multiparty elections, held on December 12, 1993, Ribas Reig's National Democratic Grouping (*Agrupament Nacional Democràtic*—AND) emerged as the strongest party in the General Council, with Ribas Reig elected head of government on January 19, 1994. These victories confirmed the ascendancy of the modernizing political forces led by Ribas Reig, who said that his new government would give priority to fiscal and tax reforms and to the development of tourism. Nevertheless, in the emerging new party structure, conservative elements retained considerable influence in the General Council, and on November 25, following rejection of his 1995 budget, Ribas Reig again resigned and was succeeded on December 21 by Marc FORNÉ Molné of the Liberal Union (*Unió Liberal*—UL), the second-largest party in the General Council. Communal elections in December 1995 were notable for returning two women mayors, who broke the previous male mayoral monopoly. Forné was reelected twice, holding power until 2005, during which period the UL was renamed the Liberal Party of Andorra (*Partit Liberal d'Andorra*—PLA).

The PLA won 14 seats in the April 24, 2005, General Council poll, but this time it was under the leadership of Albert PINTAT Santolària, who was subsequently elected as head of government with the support of the Andorran Democratic Center (*Centre Demòcrata Andorrà*—CDA). However, the victory was tempered by the success of the Social Democratic Party (*Partit Socialdemòcrata*—PS), which, under the leadership of Jaume BARTUMEU Cassany (who had served as finance minister in the early 1990s), increased its seat total from 6 to 11. The cabinet was reshuffled on May 2.

In the legislative elections on April 26, 2009, the PS and its parish allies won a plurality of 14 seats with 45 percent of the vote in the nationwide balloting. After failing to gain formal support for a new government from the recently formed Andorra for Change (*Andorra pel Canvi*—APC), which won 3 seats, the PS was left without a major ally in the General Council. The first balloting for head of government failed to produce a winner, as Bartumeu received 14 votes to 11 for Joan GABRIEL Estany, who had been selected as the PLA candidate when Pintat declined to run for reelection. (The APC abstained from the voting.) Bartumeu, however, was elected in the second ballot (in which a winner is determined by a majority of the votes cast, compared to the first ballot, in which a majority of the full membership is required) on June 3 with 14 votes, the APC again abstaining. On June 9 Bartumeu formed a new cabinet comprising members of the PS and several independents.

In the legislative elections of April 3, 2011, Democrats for Andorra (*Demòcrates per Andorra*—DA), a new party, won an overwhelming majority, capturing 55.15 percent of the vote and 20 of the 28 seats on the General Council. The PS was a distant second and garnered only six votes. A regional party, the Lauredian Union (*Unió Laurediana*—UL), won both seats in its parish of Sant Julià de Lòria.

Constitution and government. The 1993 document defines Andorra as an independent "parliamentary co-principality" in which sovereignty is vested in the people (i.e., Andorran citizens), although the Spanish and French co-princes remain joint heads of state, with defined and largely symbolic powers. The text provides for an independent judiciary, civil rights, and elections by universal suffrage (of citizens) to the legislative General Council. For the first time, membership in political parties and trade unions is permitted, and the government is empowered to raise revenue by taxation and other means. As joint suzerains, the French president and the Bishop of Urgell are represented respectively by the prefect of the French department of Pyrenees-Orientales and the vicar general of the Urgell diocese. Their resident representatives in Andorra bear the titles of *viguier de France* and *veguer Episcopal.*

Women were enfranchised in 1970 and in 1973 were permitted to stand for public office. Second-generation Andorrans were allowed to vote in 1971, and first-generation Andorrans over the age of 28 were accorded a similar right in 1977.

The judicial structure is relatively simple. Each of the *viguiers* appoints two civil judges (*battles*), while an appeals judge is appointed alternately by each co-prince. Final appeal is either to the Supreme Court in Perpignan, France, or to the Ecclesiastical Court of the Bishop of La Seu de Urgell, Spain. Criminal law is administered by the *Tribunal de Corts,* consisting of the *battles,* the appeals judge, the *viguiers,* and two members of the General Council (*parladors*).

Local government functions at the district level through parish councils, whose members are selected by universal suffrage. At the lower levels there are *communs* and *corts.* The former are ten-member bodies elected by universal suffrage; the latter are submunicipal advisory bodies that function primarily as administrators of communal property.

Freedom of the press is fully guaranteed under Andorran law. In 2013, its first appearance on the Reporters Without Borders Press Freedom Index, Andorra ranked 5th out of 179 countries.

Foreign relations. The country concluded a customs union with the European Community (EC) in September 1989. Approval of the agreement by the General Council in March 1990 yielded the country's first international treaty in more than 700 years. Andorra was admitted to the UN on July 28, 1993, and established relations with the United States in 2005. It currently has diplomatic representation for 40 countries and international organizations.

On June 3, 1993, Andorra signed friendship and cooperation treaties with France and Spain. One year later, on November 10, 1994, Andorra became the 33rd full member of the Council of Europe. Andorra signed a double-taxation treaty with France on April 4, 2012, and is actively pursuing similar agreements with other countries.

In 2005 Andorra expanded its cooperation with the EU in a variety of areas, including the environment, public health, transportation, and communications. Also in 2005 China promised cooperation with Andorra on trade and tourism and praised Andorra for its support of the "one-China" policy. Relations with China were strengthened even further in 2007 when Andorra, endorsing China's position, opposed Taiwan's entry into the UN under the name Taiwan. Closer to home, Andorra signed an agreement with Portugal to allow free movement of citizens between the two countries, similar to agreements Andorra has with Spain and France. Andorra also signed an agreement with Luxembourg to avoid double taxation of their citizens, a partnership similar to Andorra's arrangements with Spain, Portugal, and France. The country is considering acceding to the European Economic Area.

After strained relations with French President Nicolas Sarkozy, who believed tax evasion and bank secrecy had fed the global economic crisis and sought a ban on such activities, the May 2012 victory by Socialist François Hollande may benefit Andorra. Hollande has threatened to impose a 75 percent tax on French citizens earning over €1 million per year (up from 41 percent), which may trigger an exodus to Andorra.

Current issues. In 2000 the Organization for Economic Cooperation and Development (OECD) included Andorra in its list of 35 "tax havens" that could face sanctions unless new standards were established regarding greater transparency in the financial sector and the exchange of information with other countries.

The changes necessary to bring Andorra into alignment with EU practices required an overhaul of banking regulations. Following the 2005 General Council, the PLA-led government reached a degree of accommodation on tax issues in a mid-2005 accord with the EU under which Andorran banks agreed to charge a withholding tax on foreign deposits rather than reveal secret information about the accounts.

By 2009 the global economic crisis pushed banking reform to the forefront, as leaders of EU member states wanted to find and tax money their citizens had hidden overseas. In March, Prime Minister Pintat promised to make the requested changes to bank secrecy laws by September 1, 2009. His pledge to meet OECD standards regarding the exchange of financial information was enough to have the OECD move Andorra from its "black list" of "uncooperative" states to the "grey list" (those countries that have committed to the global rules but not yet enacted the necessary legislation).

As Andorra becomes less attractive for tax dodgers, the country must develop other income streams. In 2008 the Pintat government announced an "Andorra 2020" strategy to attract foreign investment, raise financial regulation to international standards, and diversify the local economy.

But as the April 2009 legislative election approached, voters seemed frustrated with the PLA's pace for making necessary change to the banking laws, which was perceived as contributing, in part, to the country's economic slump. Possibly sensing an impending defeat, Pintat chose not to seek reelection, though he was eligible for a second term.

In a stunning electoral shift, liberal forces lost control over the government for the first time since the 1993 constitution came into force. The PS won 14 of the 28 General Council seats, just one seat shy of a majority. The opposition APC (which ran as a free-market, centrist party and won 3 seats in the General Council) declined the PS's invitation to form a coalition government. The PLA, running as part of the Reformist Coalition (*Coalició Reformista*—CR) won only 11 seats.

In February 2010 Andorra was taken off the OECD's "grey list" after the country reached accords to provide 17 European countries with the fiscal information necessary to monitor their citizens who do business in Andorra. On February 10, 2011, Bartumeu announced the conclusion of a monetary agreement with the EU. He also argued that Andorra should impose a new corporate tax, a 4.5 percent value-added tax (VAT), and an income tax on citizens making above $57,000 a year. Opposition parties criticized the agreement, saying Bartumeu had caved to EU pressure and blocked Bartumeu's draft budget for 2011, which included the new taxes, triggering the dissolution of parliament on February 15 and new elections.

Opponents of the proposed PS fiscal reforms, including the Liberals (PLA), New Centre, and some disillusioned members of the PS, consolidated into a new party, Democrats for Andorra (*Democrates per Andorra*—DA). Fear of new taxes and the economic malaise that gripped the country was fatal to the incumbent party, and the newly formed DA won 20 of the 28 seats, the largest mandate in the country's history. The PS mustered only 6 seats, while the Lauredian Union captured the remaining 2 slots. The DA made Antoni MARTÍ Petit the new head of government.

With tourism no longer generating substantial income, Martí and the DA realized there were few alternatives to taxing Andorra's own citizens. A business tax came online in January 2012 and will be followed by a sales tax in 2013, as well as a personal income tax. Prime Minister Martí has also called for the legalization of gambling, to revive tourism.

Observers have called for Andorra to improve its citizenship and migration regulations. Fiscal planners need an accurate population count in order to estimate how much revenue could be generated from individual income taxes. The Andorran government readily admits that it lacks this basic data. Thanks to stringent citizenship laws (requiring 20 years of legal residency; persons born in Andorra do not automatically get citizenship), only 43 percent of the population is comprised of citizens. Thus almost two-thirds of residents cannot vote. The International Service for Human Rights (ISHR) encouraged Andorra to reduce the residency requirement from 20 years to 15.

Migrants receive far different treatments depending on their economic level. Some obtain residency—and avoid taxes—by buying property in the country. Property is extremely expensive in Andorra, in part due to a housing shortage created by the difficult, mountainous terrain. Others come for work, and even legal labor migrants are often only issued temporary work permits. The construction boom in the 1990s attracted thousands of migrant workers, and between 1986 and 2008 the population almost doubled. But as the Andorran economy entered recession, migrant workers moved on to more affordable countries or returned home. The annual population growth rate plunged from 0.33 percent in 2010 to -8.1 percent in 2011, followed by a 0.27 percent increase in 2012. While migrants in Andorra now have access to unemployment benefits, they still lack equal access to health care.

In 2013 the Martí government introduced controversial measures to stabilize the economy and bring regulations in line with EU standards. Public sector wages were cut, and a 4.5 percent value-added tax was introduced. The country's first income tax will take effect in 2016. New, less stringent residency categories were introduced, including residency without a work permit (no Andorran income tax) and residency with a work permit (10 percent income tax). Individuals can gain tax residency status by investing a minimum of €400,000 in the country, such as purchasing property. The annual residency requirement was reduced from 180 days to 90 days.

POLITICAL PARTIES

Although political parties were technically illegal until March 1993, various unofficial groupings had contested elections in the 1970s and 1980s. The December 1993 balloting was the first held under multiparty auspices, with 18 associations of various kinds presenting or endorsing candidates. While parties have aligned, combined, and split ahead of elections, the political spectrum remains defined by a center-left element versus a center-right element, and national versus regional parties. Political parties generally agree on the broad outlines of policy, and voters tend to focus more on personalities than policies.

Government and Government-Supportive Parties:

Democrats for Andorra (*Democrates per Andorra*—DA). The DA was established on February 25, 2011, and immediately claimed it had "serious aspirations to govern." It is a center-right party that is the heir of the Reformist Coalition (*Coalició Reformista*—CR), an alliance of parties that joined together to battle the PS in the 2009 election. (See Defunct and Inactive Parties, below.) The DA consists of the PLA, the New Centre (*Nou Centre*—NC), the Parochial Union of Independents Group (*Grup d'Unió Parroquial Independents*—GUPI), and elements of the PS. It also received support from the Lauredian Union (*Unió Laurediana*—UL) and Andorra for Change. It was formed in reaction to the perceived failures of the PS and in the hope of creating a coalition broad enough to break the political stalemate that had paralyzed the nation in 2010.

Leaders: Antoni MARTÍ Petit (Head of Government, Party chair), Jordi CINCA Mateos (Minister of Finance and Civil Service).

Lauredian Union (*Unió Laurediana*—UL). This group is a local conservative party from the parish of Sant Julià de Lória, where it won the two parish seats in 2001. Those successful candidates subsequently joined the PLA parliamentary group in the General Council. The two successful candidates in the parish balloting in 2009 in Sant Julià de Lòria, however, were elected on a CR—Lauredian Union ticket. In 2011 the UL did not join the DA, but it supported all its candidates on the national list.

Leader: Montserrat Gil i ROSER (Head of Party).

Other Parliamentary Parties:

Social Democratic Party (*Partit Socialdemòcrata*—PS). The PS was established by Jaume BARTUMEU Cessany in 2000 when the National Democratic Grouping (*Agrupament Nacional Democràtic*—AND) split into two new parties. Bartumeu has steered the left-of-center party since its inception, increasing its representation in consecutive elections. The PS won 6 seats in the March 2001 legislative balloting, 4 of them on a 28 percent vote share in the national polling. In 2005 the party improved significantly to 12 seats, largely owing to voter dissatisfaction with Andorra's reputation as a tax haven and the seeming reluctance of the PLA to deal effectively with the problem.

In 2009 the PS campaigned (in alliance with the GUPI in Ordino parish and with independents in other parishes) as "PS, The Alternative," capturing 45.8 percent of the national vote and 14 seats (6 on the national level and the 2 seats from each of the parishes of Encamp, Ordino, Andorra la Vella, and Escaldes-Engordany). The sound defeat in the 2011 elections, where the party won only 6 national seats and 34.8 percent of the vote, has put it in disarray. In a stormy, poorly attended party congress that was held on June 18, Victor Naudi was elected president, but he garnered only 39 percent of the total possible voters and 61 percent of those attending the congress. He maintained that his election reflected a change in strategy, not substance, and that Bartumeu, who was reelected to the General Council, remained the leader of the party. Naudi and Bartumeu resigned from the party in January 2013, and Bartumeau reformed a new faction in the National Council: the Joint Parliamentary Group. The PS elected a completely new governing board at its April 2013 congress.

Leaders: Vicenç ALAY (President), Pedro LÓPEZ (First Secretary), David RIOS (Leader of Party Caucus in the General Council).

Other Parties That Contested the 2009 Parliamentary Elections:

Andorra for Change (*Andorra pel Canvi*—APC). The APC was formed in 2008 under the leadership of Juan Eusebio Nomen Calvert, a Spanish businessman, in reaction to international pressure for Andorra to reform its tax code and discourage the country's status as a tax haven. Despite its name, the party is committed to retaining the country's tax haven structure and also believes that the nation's current tax system should not be altered.

In the 2009 elections the APC secured three seats on a vote share of 18.9 percent nationwide, a significant showing for its first electoral foray. (The APC ran in alliance with the UNP in the parish of Encamp and with the RD in the parish of Escaldes-Engordany.) The APC subsequently declined an invitation from the PS to participate in a coalition government and abstained from voting for the head of government in the General Council, Nomen announcing that his party's stance would be neither progovernment nor opposition, but "bipartisan." However, in 2010 its conservative economic policy clashed with the goals of the socialist government. Nomen was supportive of the newly formed DA, and he did not run any candidates for parish seats in the 2011 election, a move that helped the DA since it did not divide the conservative vote. The APC, however, did run a national slate of candidates, but it won only 1,040 votes, 68 short of the minimum necessary (1,108) to have a seat in the General Council.

Leaders: Juan Eusebi NOMEN Calvert (President), Josep Maria BRINGUÉ (Vice President).

Greens of Andorra (*Verds D'Andorra*—VA). The VA is a left-leaning party that emphasizes a commitment to both social justice and environmentalism, which it sees as linked and necessary to a decent social order. The party ran for the first time in the 2005 legislative poll and secured 3.5 percent of the vote (no seats). The results were similar in 2009, when it obtained 3.8 percent of the vote and no seats in the legislature. VA President Isabel LOZANO Muñoz resigned after the election and was replaced by Anontia Escoda. The party subsequently expressed dissatisfaction with the lack of social reform. Their list in the 2011 election, however, was headed by the ex-president Isabel Lozano, and the party saw a modest improvement in their total votes (520) in comparison with the 2009 election (466), but the VA still won less than half the total needed to have a representative on the General Council. Escoda suddenly resigned in late 2012, citing personal reasons.

Leader: Isabel LOZANO Muñoz (President).

Parochial Union of Independents Group (*Grup d'Unió Parroquial Independents*—GUPI). The progressive GUPI is active only in the parish of Ordino. It contested the Ordino parish seats unsuccessfully in alliance with the PS in 2005, but won the seats in 2009 (again in alliance with the PS) on a vote share of 41 percent in the parish. Their leader, Esteve Lopez Montanya, became the subspeaker of the General Council. In a March 2010 interview, one of the GUPI representatives in parliament (Peter BABI) expressed frustration with the PS's leadership, maintaining, "There are things we do not share with the PS" and regretting the slow pace of change. Nevertheless in the 2011 elections the GUPI again joined with the PS, but it lost its two seats in the 2011 elections to the DA.

Leader: Esteve LOPEZ Montanya.

Defunct and Inactive Parties:

Reformist Coalition (*Coalició Reformista*—CR). The PLA-led CR was formed for the 2009 elections, in which it won 32.3 percent of the vote and 11 seats (5 national seats and the 2 seats from each of the parishes of Canillo, La Mariana, and Sant Julià de Lòria). The coalition subsequently dissolved, but many of its elements are present in the DA, which was established and took power in 2011.

Leader: Joan GABRIEL Estany (President).

Liberal Party of Andorra (*Partit Liberal d'Andorra*—PLA). The PLA was initially launched as the Liberal Union (*Unió Liberal*—UL) prior to the December 1993 legislative poll, in which the UL won five seats and 22 percent of the vote. After a year of opposition, the right-of-center formation came to power in December 1994. Its constituent, the Liberal Party (*Partit Liberal*—PL), joined the Liberal International in 1994.

The UL and its parish allies won 16 seats (6 national and 10 parish seats) in the February 1997 legislative elections. (The parish seats were won by groups that campaigned under their unique local party rubrics.) The working majority for the head of government, Marc Forné Molné, was subsequently improved when councilors representing the Union of the People of Ordino (*Unió del Poble d'Ordino*—UPd'O) joined the UL in forming a parliamentary faction in the General Council. (The now defunct UPd'O had won the 2 parish seats from Ordino in the 1997 poll.)

The UL adopted the PLA rubric prior to the March 2001 legislative balloting, in which it won 15 seats. The PLA secured 41.2 percent of the national vote in the 2005 legislative poll and 14 seats (6 national and 8 parish seats). After ten years as head of government, the PLA's Forné was not allowed to seek a second term. He was succeeded by Albert Pintat Santolària, whose new government was supported in the legislature by the CDA (see NC, below). Surprisingly, Pintat opted not to seek reelection in 2009, and he was succeeded as party leader by Joan GABRIEL Estany. After the 2009 election Gabriel became the opposition leader in parliament and president of the CR, but he was succeeded in the PLA by Enric Pujal Areny. The party merged with the NC and IO to form Democrats for Andorra in 2011.

Leaders: Enric PUJAL Areny (President), Josep Anton BARDINA Pau (Secretary General).

New Centre (*Nou Centre*—NC). The Christian-democratic NC was recently formed through the merger of the Andorran Democratic Centre (*Centre Demòcrata Andorrà*—CDA) and the conservative Century 21 (*Segle 21*). The CDA was established in 2000 as the Democratic Party (*Partit Demòcrata*—PD), the second party to spin off from the fragmentation of the AND. The PD won five seats in the 2001 legislative poll, three of them on a 22.4 percent vote share in the national constituency. The CDA secured two seats in the national poll of 2005 on an 11 percent vote share; it participated in that balloting in coalition with Century 21. The CDA subsequently agreed to support the new PLA government in the legislature. In 2009 it was part of the CR, but its former leader Enric TARRADO Vives served only as a supplementary candidate on the CR's electoral list. It united with the PLA to form the Democrats for Andorra in 2011.

National Democratic Grouping (*Agrupament Nacional Democràtic*—AND). The center-left AND, formed in 1979, emerged as the strongest party in the December 1993 elections, winning eight seats and 26.4 percent of the vote on a platform of modernization. Its leader, Oscar Ribas Reig, therefore remained head of government (having first attained the post in 1982) with the support of New Democracy (*Nova Democràcia*—ND), which won five seats in the 1993 balloting on a 19.1 percent vote share. However, Ribas Reig was forced to resign in November 1994 when the coalition collapsed. AND was definitively relegated to second-party status in the February 1997 General Council balloting, when it won four national seats (based on 28 percent of the vote) and the two seats from the parish of Encamp. The strength of the party, which appeared to have subsumed the ND, fell to two seats on a 17 percent share of national balloting in 1997.

Independents of Ordino (*Independents d'Ordino*—IO). This group is active only in the parish of Ordino, in which it unsuccessfully contested the parish seats in the 2009 election in what appeared to be an at least informal electoral arrangement within the CR. (The CR presented formal CR candidates in balloting in all parishes except Ordino.) The party merged with the Democrats for Andorra in 2011.

National Union of Progress (*Unió Nacional de Progrés*—UNP). The UNP, concerned with issues of social justice, emerged in 2007. It garnered only 0.8 percent of the nationwide vote in the 2009 elections, in which it contested the balloting in the parish of Encamp in alliance with the APC. In 2011 it suspended operations.

Democratic Renovation (*Renovació Democràtica*—RD). The RD describes itself as a social liberal party. It won 6.2 percent of the vote (no seats) in the 2005 legislative balloting. It apparently participated in a joint list with the PS called the PS/RD Alternative (*L'Alternativa PS/RD*) in four parishes in the 2005 poll, and several reports indicated that one of the parish seats nominally won by the PS in fact was won by a member of the RD. In the 2009 elections the RD backed the AFC, with which it joined in an alliance to contest (unsuccessfully) the balloting in the parish of Escaldes-Engordany. On February 23, 2011, its president Ricard de Haro issued a statement that the party did not have the finances to participate in the upcoming elections and the RD did not feel strongly enough about any of the candidates to endorse them, although it did share some goals with the PS.

Leader: Ricard de HARO Jiménez.

LEGISLATURE

The **General Council** (*El Consell General*) is a unicameral body consisting of 28 members. Fourteen councilors are elected from national party lists in proportion to the percent of votes received by the parties participating in nationwide balloting. The country is divided into seven administrative districts called parishes, and the remaining 14 councilors are elected in separate parish voting. The party with a plurality in each of the parishes wins that parish's 2 seats. Although all major parties run candidates for the national seats, not all compete in the parish elections, while others compete in the parish elections in alliance (formal or informal) with local parish parties.

In the most recent election of April 3, 2011, the distribution of seats was as follows: Democrats for Andorra, 20 (8 national seats and 12 parish seats); Social Democratic Party, 6 national seats; and Lauredian Union, 2 parish seats. Fifteen new councilors are women, who constituted 54 percent of the new legislature.

Speaker: Vicenç MATEU Zamora.

CABINET

[as of August 25, 2013]

Head of Government	Antoni Martí Petit (DA)
Executive Council	
Culture	Albert Esteve Garcia (ind.)
Economy and Planning	Jordi Alcobé Font (DA)
Education, Youth and Sports	Roser Suñé Pascuet (ind.) [f]
Finance and Civil Service	Jordi Cinca Mateos (DA)
Foreign Affairs	Gilbert Saboya Sunyé (DA)
Head of the Executive Council	Antoni Martí Petit (DA)
Health and Welfare	Cristina Rodríguez Galan (ind.) [f]
Justice and the Interior	Marc Vila Amigó (ind.)
Secretary General	Valenti Martí Castanyer (DA)
Tourism and the Environment	Francesc Camp Torres (ind.)

[f] = female

INTERGOVERNMENTAL REPRESENTATION

Andorra's quite limited foreign relations are largely conducted through the French co-prince, although it maintains a number of embassies, particularly in Europe.

Ambassador to the U.S. and Permanent Representative to the UN: Narcís CASAL DE FONSDEVIELA.

U.S. Ambassador to Andorra: James COSTOS (resident in Spain).

IGO Memberships (Non-UN): CEUR, ICC, OSCE.

ANGOLA

Republic of Angola
República de Angola

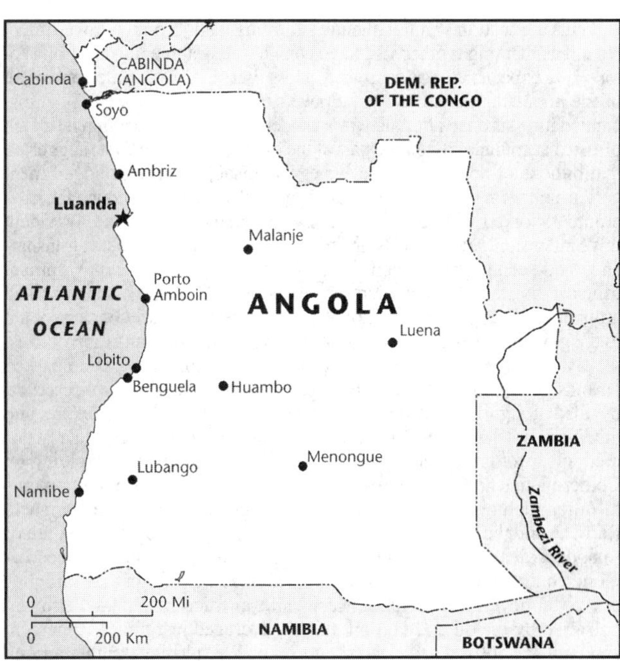

Political Status: Formally independent upon departure of the Portuguese High Commissioner on November 10, 1975; government of the Popular Movement for the Liberation of Angola (MPLA) recognized by the Organization of African Unity on February 11, 1976; peace accord signed with rebel National Union for the Total Independence of Angola on June 1, 1991; multiparty democratic system approved by constitutional amendment on August 26, 1992; new constitution promulgated on February 2010 provides for mixed presidential-parliamentary system.

Area: 481,351 sq. mi. (1,246,700 sq. km).

Population: 20,216,872 (2012E—UN); 18,565,269 (2013E—U.S. Census).

Major Urban Center (2011E—UN): LUANDA (urban area, 1,822,407).

Official Language: Portuguese (although most Angolans speak tribal languages).

Monetary Unit: Kwanza (market rate November 1, 2013: 97.45 kwanzas = $1US).

President: José Eduardo DOS SANTOS (Popular Movement for the Liberation of Angola); designated by the Central Committee of the Popular Movement for the Liberation of Angola—Labor Party (MPLA-PT) and sworn in September 21, 1979, following the death of Dr. António Agostinho NETO on September 10; confirmed by an extraordinary congress of the MPLA-PT on December 17, 1980; reconfirmed in 1985 and 1990; mandate extended following popular election on September 29–30, 1992, and extended indefinitely by presidential order on January 29, 1999; mandate extended to 2012 following adoption of new constitution by the National Assembly on January 21, 2010; reelected on August 31, 2012, and sworn in for a five-year term on September 26.

Vice President: Manuel Domingos VICENTE (Popular Movement for the Liberation of Angola); elected along with the president on August 31, 2012, and sworn in as vice president for a term concurrent with that of the president on September 26, succeeding Fernando Da Piedade Dias DOS SANTOS (Popular Movement for the Liberation of Angola).

THE COUNTRY

The largest of Portugal's former African possessions, Angola is located on the Atlantic Ocean, south of the Congo River. The greater part of its territory is bounded on the north and east by the Democratic Republic of the Congo (DRC, formerly Zaire), on the southeast by Zambia, and on the south by Namibia. It also includes the small enclave of Cabinda in the northwest (bordered by the Republic of the Congo and the DRC), where important offshore oil deposits are being exploited (see Separatist Groups under Political Parties, below). The overwhelming proportion of Angola's people is Bantus, who comprise four distinct tribal groups: the Bakongo in the northwest, the Kimbundu in the north-central region inland from Luanda, the Ovimbundu in the south-central region, and the Chokwe in eastern Angola. No native language is universally spoken, Portuguese being the only tongue not confined to a specific tribal area. Women have traditionally experienced equality with men in subsistence activities, and they were estimated to constitute 45 percent of the workforce in 2011. In the 2012 balloting, women secured 75 seats (34.1 percent) in the national legislature, a slight decline from the 2004 balloting in which women gained 84 seats (38.2 percent).

Because of its rail links with Zaire, Zambia, Zimbabwe, Mozambique, and South Africa, the port of Lobito served as a leading outlet for much of Central Africa's mineral wealth until independence in 1975. Thereafter, civil war crippled the Benguela Railway and devastated much of the formerly prosperous economy, including the export of diamonds and coffee. Guerrilla activity resulted in massive migration of peasant farmers to cities or neighboring countries, and, despite its potential as a breadbasket for southern Africa, Angola became dependent on food imports to stave off widespread famine. In addition, black market activity flourished, contributing to a substantial degradation of the local currency. Although the government attempted to stimulate the economy by reducing state control over industry and agriculture, its efforts were hampered by corruption, bureaucratic inefficiency, and the allocation of more than half of its income to military expenditure. Only oil kept the economy afloat, generating more than 85 percent of revenue and attracting private foreign investment. Vowing to promote a "mixed economy" with additional free-market influence, Angola became a member of the International Monetary Fund (IMF) and the World Bank in 1989, although assistance from those institutions was constrained prior to initial accommodation with leading rebel forces in June 1991. (For an overview of the economy between 1991 and 2000, please see the 2012 *Handbook.*)

In early 2000 the United Nations estimated that 4 million Angolans (approximately one-third of the population) had been directly affected by the conflict and that half of those individuals were "internally displaced." (Angola's massive repatriation program was reported to have officially ended in March 2007 with the return of some 400,000 refugees.) On a more positive note, the dos Santos government reported that GDP was growing, largely due to oil-related production. However, inflation remained out of control at 3,000 percent annually before declining to 305 percent in 2000 and 125 percent in 2001. New French investment pushed oil production to nearly 900,000 barrels per day in late 2001. Angola, a major oil exporter to the United States, was estimated to have reserves of more than 12.5 billion barrels.

Despite its oil wealth, Angola remained in severe economic and social distress in 2002, when the long-standing civil war finally concluded, leaving the nation's infrastructure in ruins and sapping government resources that might otherwise have gone to the health and education sectors. Life expectancy was estimated at less than 40 years, while 65 percent of the population lived below the poverty line. In addition, the IMF suspended its assistance after the war's end, citing, among other things, a lack of fiscal accountability on the part of the government. (Analysts suggested that billions of dollars in oil revenues had disappeared from government coffers and were hidden in secret offshore bank accounts.) Though the government worked with the IMF in 2004 on a plan to restore aid, President dos Santos continued to resist meeting IMF conditions for fiscal transparency and accountability. Nonetheless, the IMF commended government officials for their commitment to lowering inflation, which averaged around 10 percent annually in 2005 and 2006, and the World Bank gave aid to the government to reduce the spread of AIDS, malaria, and tuberculosis.

By 2007 the government and transnational companies had embarked on massive initiatives to further exploit not only Angola's oil reserves, but also its significant deposits of diamonds, gold, uranium, iron ore, and other minerals and ores. China, in particular, was one of Angola's major creditors, prompting criticism from the West that Angola was relying on Chinese loans as an alternative to the World Bank. Major improvements to infrastructure were planned, including an overhaul of the Benguela Railway and the construction of a new airport and a "mega-city" south of Luanda—all backed by Chinese financing. Also, the state-owned diamond company formed a partnership with leading foreign diamond producers for development rights. Meanwhile, average annual GDP growth, bolstered by the oil and non-oil sectors, averaged just under 19 percent annually for 2007–2008, according to the IMF, placing Angola among the fastest-growing economies in Africa. However, falling oil prices and a decline of 30 percent in exports due to the global economic recession led to a contraction of annual growth to 0.3 percent in 2009. Following an agreement with the government to adhere to regular, public reviews of its finances, the IMF loaned Angola $1.4 billion in November 2009. To further strengthen the economy, the government undertook a $42 billion spending plan aimed primarily at improving housing, health, and education. Annual GDP growth rebounded to 6.7 percent in 2010, owing in large part to increased spending by the private sector. Meanwhile, Angola surpassed Nigeria as Africa's largest oil producer and become the continent's third largest economy. In an effort to counterbalance the country's dependence on oil, however, Angola approved a wide-ranging biofuel law in 2010.

In January 2011 the IMF approved a $178 million loan, citing the government's "significant progress" toward economic stability as the result of restrained spending, a reduction in public payment arrears, and rebounding oil prices. Fund managers urged increased transparency in the public sector as "a critical goal" and advocated for further economic reforms. In its 2013 report on Doing Business, the World Bank ranked Angola 172 out of 185 countries. Meanwhile, the IMF estimated that GDP grew by 8.4 percent in 2012, while inflation was 10.2 percent. GDP per capita was $5,318, however, this masked significant disparities in wealth. An estimated two-thirds of Angolans lived on about $2 per day, and the 2013 UN Human Development Report ranked the country 148 out of 186 states.

GOVERNMENT AND POLITICS

Political background. Portuguese settlements were established in eastern Angola in the late 15th century by navigators seeking trade routes to India, but the territory's present boundaries were not formally established until the Berlin Conference of 1884–1885. In 1951 the colony of Angola became an Overseas Province of Portugal and was thus construed as being an integral part of the Portuguese state.

Guerrilla opposition to colonial rule broke out in 1961 and continued for 13 years, despite a sizable Portuguese military presence. At the time of the 1974 coup in Lisbon, there were three principal independence movements operating in different parts of Angola. The National Front for the Liberation of Angola (*Frente Nacional para a Libertação de Angola*—FNLA), which had established a government-in-exile in Zaire in 1963 under the leadership of Holden ROBERTO, controlled much of the north; the Soviet-backed Popular Movement for the Liberation of Angola (*Movimento Popular de Libertação de Angola*—MPLA), led by Dr. Agostinho NETO, controlled much of the central region plus Cabinda; the third group, the National Union for the Total Independence of Angola (*União Nacional para a Indepêndencia Total de Angola*—UNITA), operated in eastern and southern Angola under the leadership of Dr. Jonas SAVIMBI. On January 15, 1975, the three leaders signed an agreement with Portuguese representatives calling for the independence of Angola on November 11 (the 400th anniversary of the founding of Luanda). The pact provided for interim rule by a Portuguese high commissioner and a Presidential Collegiate consisting of one representative from each of the three liberation movements. During succeeding months, however, the FNLA and UNITA formed a tacit alliance against the MPLA, whose forces at the time of independence controlled the capital. On November 10 the Portuguese high commissioner departed after a brief ceremony in Luanda, and at midnight Neto proclaimed the establishment, under MPLA auspices, of the People's Republic of Angola. On November 23 the FNLA-UNITA announced the formation of a rival Democratic People's Republic of Angola, with the central highlands city of Huambo (formerly *Nova Lisboa*) as its capital.

Within a month of independence, some two dozen nations had recognized the MPLA government, although the Organization of African Unity (OAU, subsequently the African Union—AU) had urged all countries to withhold recognition until formation of a coalition government. Meanwhile, Cuba had dispatched upwards of 18,000 troops in support of the MPLA. The revelation that American money and equipment were being channeled to FNLA forces through Zaire posed the additional risk of a U.S.-Soviet confrontation. By late December the Cuban troops, equipped with Soviet armored vehicles and rocket launchers, had helped turn the tide in favor of the MPLA, and some 4,000–5,000 South African troops operating in support of the Huambo regime were substantially withdrawn a month later. In early February 1976 the MPLA launched a southern offensive that resulted in the capture of Huambo and other key cities, prompting declarations by the FNLA and UNITA that their forces would thenceforth resort to guerrilla warfare. On February 11 the OAU announced that the MPLA government had been admitted to membership, following formal recognition of the Neto regime by a majority of OAU member states.

The FNLA and UNITA continued to resist government and Cuban units from 1976 to 1978, and in early 1979 they announced the formation of a joint military force. Nevertheless, it subsequently appeared that Roberto's FNLA had been virtually annihilated in the north and that only UNITA was offering organized opposition to the Luanda regime.

On September 10, 1979, President Neto died in Moscow, where he had been undergoing medical treatment. He was succeeded on September 21 by José Eduardo DOS SANTOS (the minister of planning) as chief of state, head of government, and chair of the ruling party, which had been renamed the MPLA—Labor Party (*MPLA–Partido Trabalhista*—MPLA-PT).

In September 1984 the remaining 1,500 guerrillas and 20,000 civilian members of *Conselho Militar para a Resistência de Angola* (COMIRA), which had been founded by former FNLA members, surrendered to the Luanda government under a 1979 amnesty provision; its military members were integrated into the MPLA-PT forces. However, the confrontation with UNITA settled into an intractable civil war: the U.S.-backed rebels, charged with brutal intimidation of the peasantry, continued to dominate much of the countryside, while the government, supported by 50,000 Cuban troops and extensive Soviet aid, retained control of most urban areas.

With more than 300,000 people dead, an estimated 1.5 million dislocated, and the country's economy and social infrastructure in shambles, attention in the late 1980s turned to negotiation of a political settlement to the military stalemate. One major breakthrough was an agreement in late 1988 on curtailment of foreign military involvement in Angola. Domestic reconciliation proved more difficult, however, as a much-publicized cease-fire brokered by Zairean president Mobutu at a meeting attended by the leaders of 16 African nations in mid-1989 lasted only a few weeks. Despite further fighting, government-UNITA talks continued, yielding, with the involvement of both U.S. Secretary of State James Baker and Soviet Foreign Minister Aleksandr Bessmertnykh, a peace settlement signed in Washington on June 1, 1991, that provided for multiparty presidential and parliamentary elections in late 1992. Responsibility for monitoring the accord and organizing elections was assigned to the Joint Political and Military Commission (*Comissão Comun Política e Militar*—CCPM), consisting of Portuguese, U.S., USSR, MPLA-PT, and UNITA representatives, which was bolstered in June by the arrival of a 600-member United Nations Angola Verification Mission (UNAVEM).

In July 1992 dos Santos named former planning minister Fernando José França Dias VAN-DÚNEM to the recently restored prime ministerial post, without, however, relinquishing his powers of executive leadership. Thereafter, despite clashes between MPLA-PT and UNITA supporters, preelectoral activity continued, including the emergence of a number of opposition political parties and the return to Luanda of former MPLA-PT adversaries Holden Roberto and Jonas Savimbi.

On August 26, 1992, the MPLA-PT endorsed constitutional revisions formalizing the government's dedication to a democratic system. Subsequently, the party also dropped "Labor Party" from its name. On September 8 dos Santos and Savimbi agreed to form a postelection unity government based on voting percentages derived from the balloting later that month. On September 28 the Angolan Armed Forces (FAA), drawn from the MPLA's Popular Armed Forces for the Liberation of Angola (FAPLA) and UNITA's Armed Forces for the Liberation of Angola (FALA), was inaugurated. However, at 8,000 troops, the FAA was far below its projected troop strength, a shortfall consistent with reports that entire UNITA units remained intact outside the capital.

Although 11 presidential candidates and 18 political parties participated in balloting on September 29–30, 1992, the polling was dominated by dos Santos, Savimbi, and their respective parties. On September 30 Savimbi, facing certain defeat, rejected the conclusions of international observers by declaring the balloting "rigged" and stated that he would "not accept defeat." By mid-October widespread violence was reported in the countryside, while for the first time UNITA and MPLA units clashed in the capital. Election results released on October 17 confirmed the MPLA's near 2-to-1 legislative victory, although dos Santos's 49.57 percent share of the presidential vote was constitutionally insufficient to avoid a second round against Savimbi, whose 40.07 percent vote share eclipsed nine other candidates by a wide margin. No presidential repolling occurred, as Savimbi's forces returned to military confrontation.

By October 1992 the MPLA-UNITA struggle had reached a previously unmatched intensity. On November 26 UNITA legislators boycotted the inaugural convention of the National Assembly, and, despite a new cease-fire agreement the following day, the fighting continued. On December 2 a transitional government was named, headed by Marcelino José Carlos MOCO, who had been appointed by dos Santos on November 27. Although dominated by MPLA members, the "unity" government provided for the participation of five opposition parties, featuring most prominently UNITA, which was assigned one full ministry and four deputy posts. Five days later UNITA agreed to join the government, and on December 20 the rebels reportedly accepted yet another peace plan, which was again ignored.

By mid-January 1993 tens of thousands of people had been reported killed, with Savimbi's forces on the defensive. On January 26 UN Secretary General Boutros Boutros-Ghali warned that if fighting continued, the remaining UN peacekeepers would be removed upon expiration of their mandate on April 30. The following day peace talks in Addis Ababa, Ethiopia, were abandoned. On March 6 UNITA recaptured its headquarters in Huambo after a pitched, 55-day battle that left over 12,000 dead, including 5,000 civilians. In addition to leaving the insurgents in control of over 70 percent of Angolan territory, the victory was described as pivotal to UNITA's transformation from a guerrilla force to a conventional army. Furthermore, UNITA's military advantage was evidenced by the government's subsequent willingness to make concessions at peace talks that opened on April 13 in Côte d'Ivoire. In mid-May the government agreed to a peace plan brokered by the UN, the United States, Russia, and Portugal that incorporated UNITA's demand for decentralized power sharing under a national unity government. However, days later, UNITA rejected the agreement.

In response to UNITA's continued intransigence, the United States on May 18, 1993, announced its intention to recognize the dos Santos government, formally signaling an end to its support for UNITA. Subsequently, UNITA intensified its military activities, capturing oil rich Soyo on May 26. On June 2 the UN Security Council unanimously declared UNITA responsible for the breakdown of peace negotiations and extended the UNAVEM mandate until July 15, albeit with a sharply reduced staff. In mid-July the UN continued the UNAVEM mandate until September 15 and threatened to impose an embargo on UNITA unless the rebels agreed to honor the 1991 accord, respect the 1992 elections, and enact a verifiable cease-fire. Heavy fighting nonetheless continued, and on August 20 the World Food Program agreed to a six-month emergency food operation to help alleviate the suffering from what one observer described as the "world's worst war." On September 20 UNITA announced a unilateral cease-fire; nevertheless, its military activities escalated, and on September 26 the UN imposed an embargo on oil and arms sales to the rebels. On October 30 and 31 UNITA agreed to withdraw from territory it had seized after the 1992 elections. However, the MPLA dismissed UNITA demands that "thousands of military prisoners" be released, UN forces be encamped in all towns it vacated, and UNITA fighters be integrated on an equal basis with government troops into an Angolan army.

In November 1993 a fresh round of peace talks opened in Lusaka, Zambia, and were reportedly going well until government negotiators insisted that UNITA civilian supporters be disarmed. Although the demand precipitated a temporary suspension of the talks, another cease-fire agreement was reported on December 10 to be near completion. However, three days later, the negotiations were again suspended after UNITA accused the government of attempting to kill Savimbi in a bombing raid.

"Lusaka-2" negotiations were launched on January 5, 1994, with negotiators concluding an agreement on fundamental principles of national reconciliation on February 17. In March the government was reported to have offered four secondary ministerial posts to UNITA, which countered with a demand for the key portfolios of defense, interior, and finance. In late April agreement was reached on second-round conclusion of the presidential balloting that had been repudiated by UNITA in September 1992, although a deadlock ensued at midyear over UNITA's insistence that it be awarded the governorship of Huambo province. On September 5 the two sides agreed to a renewal of UNAVEM, whose existing mandate was scheduled to expire on September 30, and on October 31 they initialed a new peace agreement under which UNITA would be awarded 11 government portfolios and three provincial governorships. Nonetheless, heavy fighting continued, and on November 8 the rebel stronghold of Huambo again fell to government troops. Despite the absence of Savimbi, who was reported to have been wounded in an incident involving his own bodyguard, the latest peace accord was formally signed in Lusaka on November 20. On February 8, 1995, the UNAVEM mandate was extended for another six months amid evidence of tensions within UNITA because of hard-line opposition to Lusaka-2.

It was not until May 6, 1995, that a long-awaited meeting between dos Santos and Savimbi took place in Lusaka, at the conclusion of which the UNITA leader accepted his opponent as "president of my country." While there was no public mention at the meeting of demobilization of UNITA's guerrilla army, Savimbi later declared in talks with South African President Mandela that his group's revival of hostilities in late 1992 had been "stupid," and on May 31 the advance units of a projected 7,460-member UNAVEM peacekeeping force arrived in Angola.

On June 17, 1995, it was confirmed that Savimbi had been offered a vice presidency. While there was no immediate response from the UNITA leader, he was reported during a second meeting with dos Santos in Gabon, on August 10, to have accepted, subject to a number of "understandings" that included a role in defining economic policy. On the other hand, Radio Angola announced prior to a joint appearance by the two rivals at the Brussels donor conference in September that Savimbi would not assume office until the demobilization or integration of UNITA military units had been completed in early 1996. The latter process was halted in December after government troops launched a new offensive in northern Angola but was resumed on the basis of a new timetable negotiated with Luanda on January 9, 1996. However, only about 8,000 of whose 62,000-strong army had reported to UN-supervised confinement camps by mid-February 1996. Direct talks between dos Santos and Savimbi were held in Libreville, Gabon, on March 1, and the two leaders agreed that a government of national unity would be formed within four months and that a 90,000-member national army would be created from existing guerrilla forces. A further agreement on May 24 specified an immediate start to the integration of UNITA soldiers into a national force and the disarming of all civilians. Meanwhile, the UNAVEM mandate was renewed on May 8, this time for only a two-month period.

The new agreements produced no greater urgency on UNITA's part, so that by the end of May 1996 only some 23,000 UNITA forces had been confined. Losing patience with the slow rate of compliance, President dos Santos on June 8 appointed a new government in which Van-Dúnem (then assembly speaker) returned to the premiership. Charged in particular with launching an urgent assault on corruption and government inefficiency, the new ministerial list contained no UNITA representatives, although government spokespersons stressed that UNITA would be included as soon as it had honored its undertakings under the 1994 Lusaka agreement. The UN Security Council renewed the UNAVEM mandate in July and again in October, the second extension including a warning to UNITA that sanctions would be imposed on the group if it failed to comply with the Lusaka agreement promptly. On November 13, 1996, the National Assembly, citing a lack of electoral preparations, adopted a constitutional revision that extended its mandate for a period of two to four years. On December 12 the UNAVEM mandate was extended to February 28, 1997, and the following day UNAVEM officials declared that UNITA had fulfilled its obligations as delineated by the Lusaka accord; however, the desertion of approximately 15,000 UNITA members from confinement centers coupled with reports of UNITA's involvement in the fighting in Zaire rekindled concerns regarding Savimbi's dedication to the peace process. Subsequently, implementation of the peace accord stalled in the first quarter of 1997, as Savimbi formally rejected the offer of a vice presidential appointment and demanded instead a role as "principal adviser" and the establishment of a "joint basic government." Both requests were promptly dismissed by the dos Santos government, which further asserted that Savimbi remained unwilling to relinquish rebel-held territory and completely disarm his forces.

On a more positive note, on April 9, 1997, the National Assembly met for the first time with its full complement of UNITA legislators and approved legislation naming Savimbi the "Leader of the Largest Opposition Party." On the same day, dos Santos took the first formal step toward the establishment of a unity government, naming Van-Dúnem as prime minister of the Unity and National Reconciliation Government (*Governa da Unidade e da Reconciliação Nacional*—GURN), which included 11 UNITA members.

On August 31, 1998, the dos Santos administration announced that UNITA's legislators and cabinet members had been suspended because of UNITA's failure to adhere to the dictates of the Lusaka accord. However, most of the UNITA representatives were reported to have resumed their duties in September, some now apparently operating under the rubric of the new UNITA-Renewal faction (see UNITA under Political Parties). With relations between the government and the Savimbi faction of UNITA having deteriorated into full-scale war, dos Santos formed a new government on January 30, 1999, in which he left the prime minister's post unfilled and assumed the responsibilities of head of the government pending the "return of constitutional normality." The new cabinet included several UNITA-Renewal representatives but no Savimbi supporters. Dos Santos also announced he had taken over direct control of the armed forces as the government pursued what it hoped would be a final offensive against Savimbi's fighters.

In early 1999 the UN condemned the two combatants, asserting that their desire for a military conclusion to the strife had caused a humanitarian disaster. Following the expiration of the mandate of the UN Observer Mission at Angola (UNOMA) on February 26, the peacekeepers were withdrawn. Meanwhile, heavy fighting continued, and by May approximately 10,000 people had been killed and 1 million dislocated.

By mid-1999 UNITA forces had reportedly closed to within 40 miles of Luanda; however, the government unleashed a fierce offensive. Reportedly aided by Western intelligence, government forces captured Bailundo in October, and in December UNITA forces fled from Jamba in the face of a government attack that originated, in part, from Namibia. For its open support of Luanda, Namibia suffered a wave of UNITA attacks. On the political front, President dos Santos continued to reach out to opposition party leaders in Luanda while at the same time remaining adamantly opposed to suggestions that he reopen negotiations with Savimbi.

In March 2000 the Angolan conflict once again captured international attention when the UN Sanctions Committee on Angola issued a report accusing individuals and institutions in nearly a dozen countries of ignoring sanctions against supplying or trading with the UNITA rebels. The document underscored the UN's efforts to tighten the application of sanctions, with the ultimate goal of derailing UNITA's war-making capabilities. (UNITA earlier had suffered another blow to its already severely tarnished image when the Southern African Development Community [SADC] had formally branded Savimbi as a "war criminal.")

Significant pressure on the government to resume peace negotiations was reported in 2001 from civic and religious groups as well as small opposition parties, and a growing number of critics suggested that the MPLA was using Savimbi and UNITA to distract attention from the administration's long-standing inability to effectively confront the nation's social woes. Savimbi declared himself available for new power-sharing talks, but dos Santos, apparently buoyed by recent military successes, adopted a hard line, demanding that UNITA forces lay down their arms as a precondition to negotiations. By the end of the year, government forces were reportedly in control of more than 90 percent of the country, UNITA having once again been reduced to waging a guerrilla campaign.

Savimbi was killed in a government ambush on February 22, 2002. On April 4, two days after the National Assembly had approved an amnesty for all participants in the long-standing civil war who accepted a negotiated settlement, the government and UNITA signed a cease-fire that provided for disarmament of UNITA, integration of UNITA fighters into the Angolan military, and UNITA's return to normal political party activity.

In August 2002 the UN Security Council authorized the creation of the UN Mission in Angola (UNMA) to assist the government and UNITA in implementing the peace plan. An August 2 ceremony in Luanda formally marked the integration of 5,000 UNITA soldiers into the Angolan army. Declaring an end to the "exceptional period" that had existed since 1999, President dos Santos on December 6 appointed Fernando Da Piedade Dias DOS SANTOS as prime minister. The end of the civil war did not result in an immediate resolution concerning elections, and President dos Santos postponed balloting in December 2006 and December 2007. With some 8 million people reportedly having been registered to vote, a new National Assembly poll, the first since 1992, was finally held on September 5–6, 2008. Of 34 parties that sought to contest the elections, only 10 parties and 4 coalitions were approved by the Constitutional Court in July, just five days before the start of the official month-long campaign. UNITA, in particular, and other opposition parties were highly critical of the government's actions, including the transfer of oversight authority from the National Electoral Commission to a government commission that did not include any opposition members; delayed state funding for the political parties contesting the elections; government dominance of the media to convey pro-MPLA messages; and the arrests of and attacks against numerous UNITA supporters at rallies in mid-August. The election was allegedly fraught with irregularities, including intimidation, bribes, and other problems. A formal complaint about the voting process filed by UNITA was rejected by the elections commission. Ultimately, the elections were generally assessed by the international community as a major step toward democracy and stability in the country. The MPLA won 81.64 percent of the vote, while UNITA received 10.36 percent, with a small number of seats going to the FNLA and minor parties. President dos Santos's new prime minister, Antonio Paulo KASSOMA, named an enlarged cabinet comprised almost entirely of MPLA members, dismissing the few UNITA ministers from the previous government. One notable appointment outside of the party was that of António Bento BEMBE, former leader of the separatist group Front for the Liberation of the Cabinda Enclave (*Frente de Libertação do Enclave de Cabinda*—FLEC), as minister without portfolio. (FLEC disbanded in 2007 following the signing of a peace agreement between Cabinda and the government; see Separatist Groups, below.)

In December 2008 parliament approved a new Constitutional Commission, made up primarily of MPLA members, to rework a draft constitution drawn up by the previous legislature. Of greatest concern to opposition parties was the commission's consideration of options that would adopt a parliamentary system of governance, with a prime minister as head of state and a president indirectly elected; versus a system in which parliament elects the president, who would effectively operate as a prime minister. The opposition argued that either option would be unconstitutional and would virtually ensure dos Santos's reelection. The Constitutional Committee, in a move described by observers as "a rare process," invited proposals from citizens, civil societies, and other nonstate groups. President dos Santos, for his part, announced that presidential and (the first) municipal elections, widely anticipated in 2009, would not take place until a new constitution was promulgated. Meanwhile, in 2009 the registration process began for Angolans living abroad in anticipation of their participation in the next elections (see Legislature, below).

Following three months of unprecedented public review, a new constitution was promulgated in February 2010 that abolished direct presidential election in favor of a presidential-parliamentary system in which parliamentary balloting determines who will be president (see Constitution and government, below). President dos Santos's mandate was extended until 2012. The MPLA, which held 82 percent of the parliamentary seats, and the same percentage on the committee formed to draft the constitution, backed the new charter, which was approved by 186 of 220 legislators, with 2 abstentions. The opposition boycotted the vote, with 14 UNITA members walking out, asserting that the new charter's electoral provision was detrimental to a democratic system. On February 2, 2010, President dos Santos named assembly speaker Fernando Da Piedade Dias dos Santos, a former prime minister, to the newly created position of vice president, replacing Prime Minister Kassoma. Dos Santos's new, expanded government, composed predominantly of MPLA members and retaining many members of the previous cabinet, was sworn in on February 5.

Dos Santos created two new ministers of state, one for economic cooperation and one for energy, on January 31, 2012.

The MPLA won a commanding majority in legislative balloting on August 31, and Dos Santos was reelected president under the new electoral system. Minister of state Manuel Domingos VICENTE (MPLA) was named vice president. The president announced a reshuffled cabinet on October 1, that included 14 new members. Meanwhile, former vice president dos Santos was elected speaker of the Assembly. A minor cabinet reshuffle occurred on May 13, 2013.

Constitution and government. Under the 1975 constitution as amended, the government was headed by a president who also served as chair of the MPLA. In the event of presidential disability, the MPLA Central Committee was authorized to designate an interim successor, thus reinforcing the role of the party as the people's "legitimate representative." In December 1978 the positions of prime minister and deputy prime minister were abolished, while in November 1980 the legislative Council of the Revolution was replaced as the "supreme organ of state power" by the National People's Assembly, whose members were indirectly designated at meetings of locally elected provincial delegates. (The Council of the Revolution, subsequently renamed the Council of the Republic, continued to function as an advisory body.)

In late 1990 the government committed itself to a new constitution that would permit multiparty presidential and legislative elections. UNITA representatives were invited to help draft the document under the peace accord of June 1, 1991. Thus, on February 1, 1992, UNITA representatives (who boycotted a multiparty conference held January 14–26) agreed with the government that the September election would be held on the basis of proportional representation and that the post-electoral executive would be elected for a five-year term, while the assembly would serve for four years.

On August 26, 1992, the MPLA approved a revised constitution that, in addition to the February 1 stipulations, provided for a presidentially appointed prime minister to head a transitional government; the abolition of the death penalty; and, in keeping with the removal of "People's" from the Republic's formal name, the deletion of all constitutional references to "popular" and "people" as reflecting former Marxist tendencies. Negotiations between the government and the UNITA-led opposition on a new constitution began following the peace accord of 2002. By the end of 2004, the National Assembly had abolished the Constitutional Commission (the object of a boycott by the opposition), announcing that constitutional revision would henceforth be handled by a government-dominated assembly committee. On December 15, 2008, the assembly voted to form a new Constitutional Commission, comprising 45 members—35 from the MPLA, 6 from UNITA, and the remainder from smaller parties.

The National Assembly approved a new constitution on January 21, 2010, that establishes three tiers of government: executive, legislative, and judiciary, concentrating executive control with the president as head of state, head of the government, and commander in chief of the armed forces. The new charter, promulgated by President dos Santos on February 4, after the assembly adopted amendments required by the Constitutional Court, provides for the presidency to be filled by the person at the top of the winning party's list in a parliamentary election. The charter limits the president to two five-year terms and replaces the post of prime minister with that of a vice president, who, along with the cabinet, is appointed by the president. Parliament has the authority to call for the president's removal from office, but the matter must be referred to the Supreme Court, whose members are appointed by the president. The president also appoints the judges of the Constitutional Court and the Audit Court. Also set forth in the charter are the provisions that all land belongs to the state, which may transfer it to individuals or corporations; a ban on the death penalty; and a guarantee of freedom of the press, although in 2013 Reporters Without Borders ranked Angola 130th out of 179 countries in freedom of the press. Journalists continue to face harassment and the Ministry of Communications has threatened to suspend the media outlets that are critical of the government.

The country is divided into 18 provinces (*províncias*) administered by centrally appointed governors, with legislative authority vested in provincial assemblies. The provinces are further divided into councils (*concelhos*), communes (*comunas*), circles (*círculos*), neighborhoods (*bairros*), and villages (*povoações*).

Foreign relations. On June 23, 1976, the United States exercised its right of veto in the Security Council to block Angolan admission to the United Nations because of the continued presence of a sizable Cuban military force in the country. On November 19, however, the United States reversed itself, citing "the appeals of its African friends," and Angola was admitted on December 1. Senegal, the last black African state to withhold recognition of the MPLA-PT government, announced the establishment of diplomatic relations in February 1982, while the People's Republic of China, long an opponent of the Soviet-supportive regime, established relations in late 1983.

Relations with Portugal were suspended briefly in late 1976 and remained relatively cool prior to a June 1978 agreement providing for the mutual repatriation of Angolan and Portuguese nationals. Subsequently, relations were again strained by allegations of Portuguese-based exile support for UNITA rebels, although efforts were made to restore previously substantial trade links between the two countries.

Relations have fluctuated with neighboring Zaire (restyled the Democratic Republic of the Congo in 1997), which charged the Neto government with providing support for rebel incursions into Shaba (formerly Katanga) Province in March 1977 and May 1978. Shortly thereafter, President Mobutu agreed to end his support for anti-MPLA forces based in Zaire, in return for a similar pledge from President Neto regarding Zairean dissidents sited in Angola. In October 1979 the presidents of Angola, Zaire, and Zambia signed a more extensive trilateral nonaggression pact in Ndola, Zambia. Despite these agreements and a Kinshasa-Luanda security pact signed in early 1985, periodic accusations of Zairean support for Angolan insurgents continued to issue from Luanda.

In the south, Luanda's support for the South West African People's Organization (SWAPO), which began operating from Angolan bases in the mid-1970s, resulted in numerous cross-border raids by South African defense forces deployed in Namibia. On the other hand, despite periodic encouragement of UNITA and an unwillingness to establish formal relations prior to the withdrawal of Cuban troops, both the Carter and Reagan administrations in the United States made overtures to Luanda, citing the need for Angolan involvement in the Namibian independence process. In early 1985 statements by dos Santos indicating a willingness to negotiate on Cuban troop withdrawal were offered by Washington as evidence of its "constructive engagement" policy in southern Africa. All contacts, however, were suspended by Angola later in the year following U.S. congressional repeal of the "Clark Amendment" banning military aid to the insurgents, with repeated military activity by Pretoria having already reduced Luanda's willingness to negotiate.

A series of meetings in 1988 concluded with the signing of two accords (one a tripartite agreement among Angola, Cuba, and South Africa, and the other a bilateral agreement between Angola and Cuba) for the phased withdrawal of Cuban forces, coupled with South African acceptance of a 1978 Security Council resolution calling for UN-supervised elections for an independent Namibia. Under the withdrawal provisions, to be monitored by UNAVEM, half of the Cubans were to leave by November 1989, with the remainder to depart by July 1991. For its part, Pretoria agreed to end military assistance to the UNITA rebels, while insisting that Luanda would be in violation of the accord if it permitted African National Congress (ANC) guerrillas to use its territory as a staging area for infiltration into Botswana, Namibia, or South Africa. (For the Namibia portion of the settlement, see entries on Namibia and South Africa.) In January 1989, three months ahead of schedule, Cuban troops began their withdrawal, although South Africa's apparent adherence to the accord was offset by a reported doubling of U.S. aid to the rebels.

In the wake of the June 1991 peace settlement, Washington pledged $30 million to assist UNITA in its transformation from a military organization into a political party, and, following a September summit meeting between presidents dos Santos and George H. W. Bush, the United States reiterated its intent to restrict trade and investment until after multiparty elections. Nevertheless, dos Santos, citing a U.S. offer of humanitarian aid, electoral assistance, and the potential for postelection aid, stated that relations had reached a "turning point."

Resurgence of the Angolan civil war in late 1992 revived allegations by both combatants of military and financial intervention by neighboring states. Progovernment officials accused South Africa and Zaire of supporting UNITA efforts, while Namibia challenged UNITA to prove its allegation that Namibian forces were fighting alongside government troops.

Angola's foreign relations in 1993 were dominated by international efforts to thwart UNITA's widely condemned aggression and aid those adversely affected by the civil war. Most dramatically, on May 18 the United States announced its intention to recognize the Luanda government. The U.S. decision came after much exhortation by South Africa and Mozambique, both of whom feared that UNITA's refusal to accept the 1992 poll results might undermine their own election plans. Thereafter, France, Russia, and the United Kingdom announced that they were negotiating arms sales with the government.

Although both the MPLA and UNITA denied involvement in the fighting in Zaire in early 1997, observers there reported that MPLA units had provided at least rearguard and logistical assistance to Laurent Kabila's fighters, while UNITA forces had suffered heavy casualties fighting alongside the Mobutu regime's ultimately unsuccessful defenders. Meanwhile, in Luanda, government officials announced a reordering of their diplomatic priorities, with major emphasis being placed, in order of importance, on relations with the United States, France, and Angola's Asian economic partners. In late October President dos Santos hosted a summit of the leaders of the Republic of the Congo, Democratic Republic of the Congo (DRC), and Gabon during which the four presidents agreed to isolate UNITA as well as the Cabindan guerrillas.

In 1998 Luanda alleged that Burkina Faso, Rwanda, Togo, Uganda, and Zambia were either supplying the UNITA rebels or offering them safe haven. Meanwhile, international attention focused on Angola's prominent role in the civil wars in the DRC and the Republic of the Congo. President dos Santos sought to justify Angola's involvement there as an attempt to help prevent a "bloodbath" and expansion of the fighting. In September, Angola, the DRC, and the Republic of the Congo signed a border security agreement. Meanwhile, Namibia's willingness to let anti-UNITA troops operate from within its borders proved pivotal to Luanda's military successes in late 1999.

In December 1999 the Portuguese legislature approved a "vote of protest" against Angola's ongoing fighting, thus prompting Luanda to register its own complaint that Lisbon was attempting to interfere in its affairs. Thereafter, international attention turned to a UN investigation into alleged efforts by UNITA supporters to circumvent sanctions against supplying or trading with UNITA.

Following the mid-2002 peace accord in Angola, U.S. President George W. Bush welcomed President dos Santos at the White House, underscoring, among other things, the importance of Angolan oil to the United States. At the same time, ties between Angola and China intensified, resulting in major Chinese investment in Angolan oil production, and in 2006 dos Santos agreed to work with Venezuelan President Hugo Chávez on oil and natural gas exploration in Angola. (In the midst of the oil boom, the Organization of Petroleum Exporting Countries [OPEC] admitted Angola as a new member in 2007.)

Meanwhile, tensions increased on the border between Angola and the DRC in 2006 and early 2007, partially resulting from an incident in which Angolan security forces allegedly crossed into DRC villages and killed 11 Congolese diamond prospectors.

In 2008 the United States strengthened relations with Angola, providing ships and radar in an effort to stem the growing problem of piracy. Angola's relations with Cuba warmed in 2009 following talks between President dos Santos and Raúl Castro in Luanda.

The expulsion of hundreds of thousands of each other's nationals by Angola and the DRC prompted a request for UN intervention by Angola in early 2010. According to *Africa Confidential*, the "spree of mutual expulsions" masked long-standing economic disputes over oil, diamonds, and electric power to be generated by a dam on the Congo River. Many were deported from Cabinda, reportedly because of government fears that they might get on the voter registry after being recruited by the opposition. Another rift with the DRC evolved regarding maritime rights to oil drilling. In March parliament approved a measure authorizing the government to negotiate with the DRC regarding the maritime borders, which legislators recommended be in alignment with the former border agreement among colonial Angola, the DRC, Portugal, and Belgium. Late in 2010 the UN urged authorities in Angola and the DRC to investigate reports that some 700 women were raped along the border as 7,000 illegal immigrants were expelled from Angola. In 2011, Zambia formally apologized for supporting UNITA during the 1990s.

The worsening Portuguese economy led to increased emigration to Angola. By 2012 the number of Portuguese expatriates in the country had increased by 400 percent over the past decade to 100,000. In February Angola announced it would open an embassy in East Timor. In June Angola and São Tomé announced new bilateral cooperation in agriculture and port management.

In April 2012 Angola and Zambia finalized a defense cooperation accord which was designed to reduce border tensions between the neighboring states. In June Angola and South Africa signed a new economic agreement to improve infrastructure and industrial development between the two countries. The following month, the EU and Angola agreed to a new cooperation blueprint that covered aid and cooperation over a five-year period.

Current issues. President dos Santos's hold on the helm of state was virtually ensured with the approval on January 21, 2010, of the new constitution, a vote that was boycotted by the opposition, as UNITA members walked out of the assembly session. Though the new constitution limits a president to two five-year terms, President dos Santos's mandate was extended to 2012, when the next parliamentary elections are scheduled, which observers, in an early analysis, widely believed the MPLA would win. The constitution provides for the person at the top of the party list or coalition of parties' list, who wins the most votes in a parliamentary election, to be named president, rather than the winning party appointing any party member to be president, as first proposed. (The Constitutional Court required this amendment before the new charter was promulgated by President dos Santos.) The president's power was further consolidated by his control over the military (as commander in chief), the judiciary (as he appoints all judges and the head of the audit court that oversees public expenditures), and the government (as his appointed vice president replaces the post of prime minister and the president appoints the cabinet). Additionally, the charter states that all land belongs to the state, and only the state has the right to grant concessions. These concessions are limited to Angolan nationals or companies; thus any foreign investors must have an Angolan partner. Freedom of the press and freedom of religion are protected, and the death penalty remains banned. The charter also maintains the status of the Cabinda enclave. President dos Santos called the adoption of the new constitution "a significant advance in the consolidation of our democratic process and the creation of conditions for a harmonious and sustainable country." Critics, in response, said the new charter was "a recipe for long-term political instability."

Having been effectively shut out of the constitutional revision process, UNITA claimed the new charter creates "a state of tyranny" in Angola, calling it a "coup against democracy and the sovereignty of the Angolan people." The party also opposed the provision granting ownership of all land to the state. Further criticism was aimed at the governing party for taking up the new constitution at the same time the country was consumed with hosting the Africa Cup of Nations football tournament, January 10–31. Following an attack on January 8 on the team from Togo by separatists known as the Front for the Liberation of the Cabinda Enclave—Military Position (FLEC-PM) that killed three, the MPLA organized a rally to protest the shootings, and police arrested two men in connection with the violence. FLEC-PM faction leader Rodrigues MINGAS, exiled in France, claimed responsibility, but a few days later, the FLEC-Armed Forces of Cabinda (FLEC-FAC) said the army had been the intended target, not the Togo team. Still other reports accused Angolan security forces of organizing the attacks in a move to discredit FLEC.

In October 2010 President dos Santos gave a State of the Nation address—the first in his more than three decades as head of state. He acknowledged the challenges of hunger and poverty in the country and vowed to improve the quality of life and reform the judiciary and other institutions. Critics, including UNITA, dismissed his remarks as "blatant electioneering" ahead of polls scheduled for 2012. Months later, the government denied knowledge of the expulsion of illegal immigrants, despite international human rights groups' reports of mass rapes along the border with the DCR as thousands were forced to leave and reports by the BBC that state media had aired a campaign against illegal immigration. The interior minister reportedly had called on all foreign nationals to leave the country, and he was quoted as saying, "We will be ruthless with those who choose Angola to carry out activities which are harmful to our economy and society and which create embarrassment to the internal state security." Meanwhile, parliament passed a revised law on crimes against the security of the state, granting the government broader authority to restrict the rights to free speech and assembly.

Early in 2011 the government was accused of using intimidation to thwart an antigovernment demonstration planned for March 7. On March 5 thousands of people, described mostly as MPLA backers, participated in what was billed as the Patriotic March for Peace in Luanda, in a show of support ahead of the protest. According to Human Rights Watch, in the weeks leading up to the protest, said to be inspired by demonstrations in Tunisia and Egypt, the government warned that anyone who took part would be punished for inciting violence and attempting to return the country to civil war. Several people who had planned to protest were arrested; however, the rally did not take place. On the scheduled day, police arrested four journalists from a private newspaper, as well as 17 rap musicians who were reading poems and distributing pamphlets in the city center. The musicians were released the following day. Leaders of three unidentified opposition parties reportedly received death threats. UNITA, for its part, had announced that it would not participate in any demonstration but later issued a statement in support of "all forms of democratic struggle." The government issued a statement in March citing the progress over the past few years "toward stabilization, reconstruction, and development" while also noting the "acts of subversion and terrorism by FLEC that still occur." More than 30 demonstrators were arrested in Luanda on September 2 during anti-regime protests.

On May 17, 2012, the Supreme Court rejected the reappointment of Suzanna INGLÊS as head of the country's electoral commission because of her ties to the MPLA. The decision was hailed by opposition groups. In legislative balloting on August 31, the MPLA won 175 seats, followed by UNITA with 32, and the newly formed Broad Convergence for the Salvation of Angola (*Convergência Ampla de Salvação de Angola*—CASA) with 8. Opposition parties challenged the results, but the constitutional court rejected their complaints. Meanwhile, international observers generally assessed the balloting as fair and "credible," but noted instances of violence, voter intimidation, and irregularities in vote tallying. In October the government announced the creation of a $5 billion sovereign wealth fund designed to spur economic development and diversify Angola's petroleum-dominated economy. Opposition groups criticized the fund as a means to award contracts and business to MPLA leaders.

A *Forbes* report in January 2013 listed Isabel DOS SANTOS, the daughter of the president, as the first African woman billionaire. The story created considerable controversy in Angola and reignited allegations that the president and first family had diverted state funds into their personal holdings. In June the government announced that local elections would be postponed until 2015.

POLITICAL PARTIES

Angola was a one-party state for the first 16 years of its independence; however, in 1990 the government agreed to institute a multiparty electoral system, and, under legislation of March 26, 1991, more than 30 groups expressed interest in achieving formal party status. Thereafter, the imposition of strict registration guidelines limited participation in the September 1992 legislative balloting to 18 parties. (For information on several subsequent pro- and antigovernment coalitions, see the 2000–2002 *Handbook*.) In May 2013 the constitutional court deregistered 67 parties that had failed to receive at least a minimum of 0.5 percent of the vote in Assembly balloting in 2012 or had not campaigned in the two previous electoral cycles.

Government Party:

Popular Movement for the Liberation of Angola (*Movimento Popular de Libertação de Angola*—MPLA). Organized in 1956, the Soviet-backed MPLA provided the primary resistance to Portuguese colonial rule in central Angola prior to independence. During its first national congress December 4–11, 1977, the party was formally restructured along Marxist-Leninist lines and redesignated as the MPLA–Labor Party (*MPLA–Partido Trabalhista*—MPLA-PT).

Reflecting the dos Santos administration's increasingly pragmatic approach to economic problems, the party's second congress in 1985 adopted a resolution promoting several "Western-style" reforms, without, however, altering its alliance with Cuba and the Soviet Union or its hostility to the United States and South Africa regarding the UNITA insurgency (below). At its third congress, held December 4–10, 1990, the MPLA-PT abandoned Marxism-Leninism in favor of "democratic socialism" and endorsed multiparty elections in the wake of a peace settlement with UNITA. In consonance with those decisions, the party decided to drop "Labor Party" from its name prior to the 1992 elections.

Dos Santos was reelected as MPLA president at the 1998 and 2003 congresses, apparently positioning himself at the latter for a run in the presidential election (reportedly postponed until 2009). In 2006 and 2007 the MPLA held a series of meetings with opposition groups to discuss its National Consensus Agenda for the country's long-term development.

The 2008 legislative elections proved to be something of a turning point for the MPLA, which, according to observers, benefited from the public's fear that the economic boom days would end if the MPLA was not reelected. The party pledged to strengthen parliament's authority while still ensuring an "active role" for the president. With its overwhelming victory in the elections, on which it reportedly spent an estimated $8.7 million—more than seven times the total spent by the 13 other parties and coalitions—the MPLA no longer needed to include UNITA in the government, the latter's members being replaced when a new government was installed in October. The party's greater dominance also underscored its potential role in rewriting the constitution, as in 2009 parliament formed a committee, comprising largely MPLA members, to begin considering proposed changes. In December President dos Santos was reelected party president. In January 2010 the party led the assembly vote to approve the country's new constitution.

Following dos Santos's pronouncements to fight corruption, the party in March 2010 called for efforts to prevent the misuse of public funds. As expected, dos Santos was chosen to head the MPLA electoral list in 2012, assuring his reelection as president after the party won legislative balloting on August 31. Minister of state for economic cooperation Manuel Domingos VICENTE was number two on the electoral list, leading to speculation that he was being groomed as the successor to dos Santos. Subsequent reports indicated that dos Santos would not run for party president at the next MPLA congress in 2016.

Leaders: José Eduardo DOS SANTOS (President of the Republic and President of the Party), Manuel Domingos VICENTE (Vice President of the Republic), Roberto de Antonio Victor de ALMEIDA (Vice President of the Party), Fernando Da Piedade Dias DOS SANTOS (National Assembly President), Kwata KANAWA (Spokesperson), Julião Mateus PAULO (Secretary General).

Other Legislative Parties:

National Union for the Total Independence of Angola (*União Nacional para a Indepêndencia Total de Angola*—UNITA). Active primarily in southern Angola prior to the Portuguese withdrawal, UNITA, whose support is centered within the Ovimbundu ethnic group, joined with the FNLA in establishing an abortive rival government in Huambo in November 1975 and subsequently engaged in guerrilla operations against Luanda. Although its ideology was of Maoist derivation, the party's image within black Africa suffered because of U.S. and South African military assistance. In late 1982 UNITA leader Jonas Savimbi asserted that no basic ideological differences separated UNITA and the MPLA-PT and that the removal of all Cuban troops would lead to negotiations with the government. Although his subsequent avowals of "anti-communism" and increased solicitation of aid from Pretoria and Washington reportedly generated internal dissent, Savimbi remained in control.

In the peace accord of June 1, 1991, UNITA agreed to recognize the legitimacy of the dos Santos government until the holding of multiparty elections in September 1992. In March 1992 two of UNITA's most senior officials, Secretary General Miguel NZAU PUNA and Gen. Tony da Costa FERNANDES, left the party, ostensibly to focus on problems involving their native enclave of Cabinda. Late in the month, however, the two issued a statement in Paris charging UNITA with political killings and other human rights abuses. At midyear the party's election hopes were dealt another blow when Savimbi reportedly announced that a UNITA-led government would be composed of only black members, thus exacerbating the fear already existing in the mixed-race and Portuguese communities. Following the September election, Savimbi's rejection of the results and reports of UNITA military activities generated domestic and international condemnation. UNITA officials, however, blamed MPLA supporters for initiating the violence that broke out in Luanda in mid-October. In May 1993 UNITA's rejection of a peace plan that reportedly addressed most of Savimbi's demands appeared to reflect a split within the group between pro-negotiation moderates and fight-to-the-end hard-liners.

Meanwhile, on the diplomatic front, UNITA negotiators rejected demands in 1993 that its troops be withdrawn to their May 1991 positions, claiming that it feared MPLA reprisals against its supporters in the contested areas. In September the rebel leadership agreed to recognize the 1992 election results. Thereafter, in late 1993 and into 1994, UNITA, propelled by Savimbi's apparently undiminished desire to rule Angola, continued its pattern of simultaneous diplomatic negotiations and military offensives.

On November 15, 1994, UNITA's Secretary General Eugénio Manuvakola signed a truce on behalf of the rebels with the government. However, in February 1995 UNITA hard-liners were reported to be dissatisfied with the peace agreement, which was to have come into effect on November 22, and Manuvakola was replaced as secretary general by Gen. Paulo Lukamba Gato.

In addition to the four senior cabinet posts awarded the group in April 1997, UNITA representatives were also named to seven deputy ministerial positions. Amid speculation that UNITA was preparing to return to war, reports circulated at midyear that the group's military high command was planning on moving to the panhandle region along the Zambian border. Subsequently, General Manuvakola broke with the group, denouncing its hostile intentions.

Meanwhile, observers reported that a gap had developed between UNITA officials participating in the government in Luanda and those in Savimbi's inner circle, with the former attempting to distance themselves from the latter's confrontational stances. Evidence of the group's factionalization became apparent in February 1998 when the Luanda-based members ignored a Savimbi dictate to vote against a budget proposal. Thereafter, with the country once more poised for civil war, pro-Savimbi UNITA members fled Luanda in July, and, on August 31, the government announced the temporary suspension of UNITA representatives from the government and the assembly. In September, Jorge Alicerces VALENTIM, a UNITA cabinet minister, announced that he and a number of other UNITA ministers and parliamentarians had aligned with General Manuvakola. Furthermore, the dissidents announced the suspension of Savimbi and, under the banner of UNITA-Renewal (UNITA-*Renavado*), appointed an interim group to lead the party until the convening of its next congress. Thereafter, a third UNITA strain emerged under the leadership of Abel Chivukuvuku, the party's parliamentary leader, and Armindo KASSESSA, both of whom had rejected UNITA-Renewal's entreaties. Chivukuvuku, reportedly popular with both UNITA military leaders and international mediators, was reelected to his legislative post in late October in what observers described as a direct "slap" at Valentim.

In January 1999, delegates aligned with UNITA-Renewal elected General Manuvakola president of the party. Meanwhile, Savimbi dismissed the Luanda-based factions as "irrelevant." Thereafter, the government intensified its efforts to persuade UNITA militants to disarm and play a role in the political process.

Following Savimbi's death in February 2002, UNITA quickly negotiated an accord with the government that ended the long civil war and provided for the integration of about 5,000 UNITA fighters into the Angolan armed forces. The peace agreement also permitted reunification of the various UNITA factions, General Manuvakola suspending his UNITA-Renewal leadership to facilitate that initiative.

Again acting as a regular political party, UNITA elected its former representative in Paris, Isaias Samakuva, as its new president in June 2003. (Samakuva defeated General Gato, who had served as interim leader since Savimbi's death.) In 2004 UNITA announced it was forming the Campaign for a Democratic Angola with some seven small parties in preparation for the next elections. In 2005 Samakuva announced his intention to run for the presidency. Meanwhile, a rift developed in the party after Valentim was removed from his ministry post in 2005 and briefly suspended after publicly criticizing party leaders. He claimed party leaders were delaying his appointment to the assembly, though he was subsequently seated in April 2005. The following year he and three other UNITA members of parliament were expelled from the party for again speaking out against the party leadership. At the same time, General Manuvakola was suspended from the party for 12 months. In March 2007 the party claimed that Samakuva was the target of an assassination attempt by police when he was visiting a province east of the capital; the police who reportedly fired shots at the local party headquarters were arrested. In July Samakuva was reelected party president, handily defeating Chivukuvuku.

By the end of 2007, UNITA was becoming more vocal in its criticism of the long-delayed elections, claiming that the government had stepped up its brutal crackdown on political opponents in the countryside as "deliberate acts to postpone democracy."

In the run-up to the 2008 legislative elections, UNITA claimed intimidation, including suspension of the party-line radio station, and attacks against its supporters. Meanwhile, rifts developed within the party, resulting in Jorge Valentim's reported defection to the MPLA. Following the elections, in which UNITA received only 10.39 percent of the vote and 16 seats—a distant second to the MPLA—*Africa Confidential* said the party was put "on a level with other, previously insignificant opposition parties." However, unlike in the 1990s, UNITA accepted the results (after a complaint it had lodged about the balloting was rejected by the court), helping, observers said, to pave the way toward establishment of a peaceful democratic state after years of civil war. Subsequently, the three UNITA members of the cabinet were removed by Prime Minister Kassoma in October 2008, when he named a new government almost entirely comprised of MPLA members.

In early 2010 UNITA boycotted the assembly vote on the proposed new constitution, claiming that the MPLA was using its majority "to destroy democracy." All 14 lawmakers, dressed symbolically in black, walked out in protest, specifically, of the provision that abolished direct election of the president. UNITA leaders also said that the constitutional committee, comprising largely MPLA members, disregarded proposals from other political parties and members of the public, despite invitations to hear their recommendations. The party denounced the strengthening of presidential powers under the new constitution.

In April 2010 party secretary general, Camalata Numa, claimed someone tried to kill him after shots were reportedly fired at him near Lunge. At a party congress in December 2011 Samakuva was reelected president of UNITA with 85.6 percent of the vote. In March 2012 Chivukuvuku formed a new political grouping, the **Broad Convergence for the Salvation of Angola** (*Convergência Ampla de Salvação de Angola*—CASA), and negotiated with smaller parties to form an electoral coalition for the upcoming elections. CASA won 8 seats in the August assembly balloting.

On March 5, 2013, Samakuva survived a car accident that UNITA officials claimed was an assassination attempt. In June UNITA accused security forces of killing two party officials in Luanda, a charge the government denied.

Leaders: Isaias SAMAKUVA (President), Ernesto MULATO (Vice President), Abel CHIVUKUVUKU, Gen. Paulo Lukamba GATO, Gen. Eugénio MANUVAKOLA, Alcides SAKALA (Spokesperson), Camalata NUMA (Secretary General).

National Front for the Liberation of Angola (*Frente Nacional para a Libertação de Angola*—FNLA). Organized as a resistance group in 1962 in northern Angola, the FNLA was consistently the most anti-communist of the three major groups until the collapse of its forces in the late 1970s.

The FNLA was inactive throughout most of the 1980s; however, in 1991 longtime leader Holden Roberto announced his intention to seek the presidency and stated that the FNLA deserved to be accorded its earlier de facto parity with the MPLA-PT and UNITA. Nevertheless, in presidential and legislative balloting in September 1992 the FNLA fared poorly, with Roberto being held to 2.11 percent of the presidential vote and the party securing only five assembly seats.

In February 1999 Lucas Ngonda was elected party president. In addition, the party held balloting to fill its Central Committee and declared its willingness to participate in the government. The October 2004 congress reportedly agreed to have Roberto lead the party for the next ten months in an effort to reduce lingering friction between the FNLA's old guard and younger members. However, friction increased in 2005 with division over Roberto's suspension of Secretary General Francisco MENDES in September, and the majority's discontent with Roberto's failure to hold another congress to elect new leadership. While Roberto was out of the country in June 2006, reportedly for medical treatment, a party congress was convened by dissidents who elected Ngonda as the faction's president. Supporters of Roberto, under the leadership of Ngola Kabango in Roberto's absence, contended that only the legitimate president—Roberto—could convene a party congress. In March 2007, while the two factions were still awaiting a ruling on the status of the congress from Angola's high court, Roberto, 83, announced he was stepping down from an active role in politics and would not run for party chair at the next congress. He died in August 2007. Despite continuing rifts with the Ngonda faction, Kabango, who had been named interim chair following Roberto's death, was elected party chair in November 2007. Meanwhile, the Supreme Court had ruled Ngonda's presidency illegal. In July 2008 the Constitutional Court further solidified Kabango's leadership by accepting his faction's list of candidates for the upcoming legislative elections and rejecting the list of the Ngonda faction. The FNLA placed fourth with 1.1 percent of the vote.

In July 2009 the Constitutional Court, citing "serious irregularities" following Roberto's death, struck down Kabango's presidency. Subsequently, Ngonda was reappointed to the leadership position and called on Kabango for cooperation. In the months ahead of the party congress in July 2010, Ngonda said the factions within the party no longer existed, though in May the party's Central Committee had recommended that Kabango be replaced as parliamentary seat leader. Ngonda was subsequently elected president; Kabango did not attend the congress and later rejected the election. In February 2012 the Constitutional Court recognized the Ngonda faction as the legitimate FNLA ahead of elections scheduled for that year. In Assembly balloting in August, the FNLA received 1.1 percent of the vote and two seats.

Leaders: Lucas NGONDA (President), Ngola KABANGO, Paulo JOAQUIM (Secretary General).

Social Renewal Party (*Partido Renovador Social*—PRS). The PRS finished third in the legislative balloting of September 1992 by winning six assembly seats. At a congress in 1999 Eduardo Kwangana was reportedly elected to lead the PRS; however, the incumbent party chief, António João Machicungo, rejected the polling, arguing that Kwangana's supporters had ignored party statutes in an effort to gain control of the grouping. In 2006, Machicungo again rejected the December congress of the Kwangana faction as "illegal and undemocratic" and appealed for a ruling from the high court.

In July 2008 the Constitutional Court ruled in favor of Kwangana over the Machicungo faction. In the September elections, the PRS won 3.2 percent of the vote, and Kwangana was among eight party members to secure a seat in parliament.

In 2010 the PRS, two of whose members served on the Constitutional Commission, supported the country's new constitution. In June 2012 Kwangana was reelected party president at a PRS congress. The PRS secured three seats with 1.7 percent of the votes in the August legislative balloting

Leaders: Eduardo KWANGANA (Party President), Lindo Bernardo TITO, António João MACHICUNGO, João Baptista NGANDAGINA (Secretary General).

Other Parties and Groups That Contested the 2012 Legislative Elections:

Note: All of the parties in this section were deregistered by the Constitutional Court for failing to achieve the threshold required for continued recognition (0.5 percent of the national vote in the August 2012 Assembly elections).

New Democracy Electoral Union (*Nova Democracia União Eleitoral*—ND). Most of the six small parties comprising the ND, legally registered in July 2008, formerly were among the 14 parties that made up a coalition called the **Civil Opposition Parties** (*Partidos de Oposição Civis*—POC). The parties comprising ND are the **Movement for Angolan Democracy;** the **Independent Social Party of Angola** (*Movimento para Democracia de Angola*—MPDA); the **National Union for Democracy;** the **Liberal Socialist Party;** the **Angolan Union for Peace, Democracy, and Development;** and the **National Independent Alliance of Angola.**

The ND won 1.2 percent of the vote to secure two National Assembly seats in the 2008 legislative elections, and it supported the new constitution in 2010. Quintino MOREIRA of the MPDA was chosen in June 2012 as the union's presidential contender. The ND secured 0.23 percent of the vote in the 2012 Assembly balloting, and no seats.

Leader: Quintino MOREIRA (President of MPDA).

Other minor parties or coalitions that participated in the 2012 balloting included the **People's Party for Development** (*Partido Popular Para o Desenvolvimento*—Papod), led by Maria de LOURDES; the **United Front for Change in Angola** (*Frente Unida Para Mudanca de Angola*—Fuma), led by Antonio MUACHICUNGO; and the **Political Council of the Opposition** (*Conselho Politico da Oposicao*—CPO), led by João Mateus JORGE.

Other Parties and Groupings:

Democratic Party for Progress–Angolan National Alliance (*Partido Democrático para Progresso—Aliança Nacional Angolano*—PDP-ANA). The PDP-ANA is a right-of-center humanist grouping previously led by a prominent university professor, Mfulumpinga Lando VICTOR, who was formerly affiliated with the FNLA. In mid-1992 Victor was named as a presidential candidate; however, there were no reports of his having received any votes in the September balloting in which the party secured one assembly seat. Victor, a prominent opposition leader, was killed by unidentified gunmen during an attack in Luanda in July 2004. Sediangani Mbimbi, who had been acting president, was elected president of the party in April 2005, defeating Malungo Belo Honoré.

The PDP-ANA received 0.51 percent of the vote in the 2008 legislative elections, narrowly reaching the threshold required to maintain its legal party status. In 2009 the party suspended secretary general Malungo Belo Honoré for allegedly mismanaging campaign funds. A number of PDP-ANA activists were arrested at the September 2011 antigovernment protests in Luanda. The PDP-ANA was barred from competing in the 2012 Assembly balloting.

Leaders: Sediangani MBIMBI (President), Malungo Belo HONORÉ (Secretary General).

Party of the Alliance of the Youth, Workers, and Farmers of Angola (*Partido da Aliança da Juventude, Operários e Camponeses de Angola*—PAJOCA). The PAJOCA earned one seat in the legislative poll of September 1992 but received 0.24 percent of the vote, and thereby no seats, in 2008. Former party president Alexandre Sebastião ANDRÉ was reported to have been active in the formation of the CASA coalition in 2012 (see UNITA, above). PAJOCA was subsequently reported to be defunct.

Leaders: David MENDES, Alexandre Sebastião ANDRÉ.

Democratic Angola–Coalition (*Angola Democrática Coligação* [AD—*Coligação*]). This coalition, led by Kengele JORGE, has been described as a group of young activists who promote democracy and ecology. In 2008 it included the **Angolan National Ecological Party,** the **Angola National Democratic Convention,** and **Angola's Democratic Unification;** the coalition won 0.29 percent of the 2008 legislative vote.

Angolan Fraternal Forum Coalition (*Fórum Fraternal Angolano Coligação*—FOFAC). This electoral group, formed in 1997, was led in 2008 by Artur Quixona FINDA with the goals of promoting economic equality and reforming political and public institutions. It included the **Angolan People's Conservative Party,** the **Workers Democratic Party,** the **Social Democracy Juvenile Party,** and the **National Front for the Democratic Development of Angola.** The coalition received 0.17 percent of the vote in 2008.

Electoral Political Platform (*Plataforma Politica Eleitoral*—PPE). The PPE coalition, which included nine small parties, was chaired by José João MANUEL. Its platform focused on industrial development and government reforms. It received 0.19 percent of the vote in 2008.

For information on the defunct parties, the **Angola Democratic and Progress Support Party** (*Partido de Apoio Democrático e Progresso de Angola*—PADEPA), the **Democratic Renewal Party** (*Partido Renovador Democrático*—PRD), the **Liberal Democratic Party** (*Partido Liberal Democrático*—PLD), and the **Front for Democracy** (*Frente para a Democracia*—FpD), please see the 2012 *Handbook.* For information on other smaller parties, some of which are defunct, please see earlier editions of the *Handbook.*

Former Separatist Groups:

Since the early 1960s a number of groups have been active under the banner of the **Front for the Liberation of the Cabinda Enclave** (*Frente de Libertação do Enclave de Cabinda*—FLEC) in the oil-rich province of Cabinda, a sliver (7,300 sq. km; 2,819 sq. mi.) of land between the Republic of the Congo and what is now the Democratic Republic of the Congo (formerly Zaire). The original FLEC was founded in August 1963 by Luis Ranque FRANQUE, who, encouraged by Portuguese authorities to continue separatist activities, refused to join other Angolan independence movements. In 1974 the Front's attempts to gain military control of the enclave were rebuffed by the MPLA and, in 1975, the movement broke into three factions: FLEC–Ranque Franque; FLEC-Nzita, led by Henrique Tiaho NZITA; and FLEC-Lubota, led by Francisco Xavier LUBOTA.

In the early 1990s two other groups, the National Union for the Liberation of Cabinda (*União Nacional de Libertação de Cabinda*—UNLC), led by Lumingu Luís Caneiro GIMBY, and the Communist Committee of Cabinda (*Comité Comunista de Cabinda*—CCC), led by Kaya Mohamed YAY, were linked to separatist activities.

Anxious to create ties to the economically important region, both the government and UNITA named Cabindans to leadership positions in their parties. Nevertheless, in July 1991 a joint MPLA-PT/UNITA offensive was launched in Cabinda to eradicate the terrorists. Meanwhile, although past attempts to unify the numerous FLEC factions had proved short-lived, it was reported that four of the identifiable groups (FLEC-Lubota, the UNLC, CCC, and FLEC-R [*Renovada*]) were attempting to form a united front, FLEC-Nzita reportedly refusing to participate.

In mid-May 1993 FLEC responded to the U.S. recognition of Luanda by declaring that it did not extend to Cabinda and warning that "all those people with companies in Cabinda must choose between supporting the extermination of the Cabindan people or leaving the territory." Following UNITA's capture of Soyo in northwestern Angola in late May, the government, fearing a pact between the separatists and rebels, was alleged to be attempting to form an alliance with a FLEC-R opponent, the **FLEC-Armed Forces of Cabinda** (*Forcas Armadas de Cabinda*—FLEC-FAC), which was reportedly being led by Henrique Tiaho Nzita; his son, Emmanuel NZITA; and José Liberal NUNO. However, after a new guerrilla offensive in Cabinda from mid-1995, government and FLEC-R representatives meeting in Windhoek, Namibia, in April 1996 concluded a cease-fire agreement that was thought likely to be observed by the other FLEC factions. However, such optimism proved ungrounded as the government subsequently was unable to reach an agreement with the FLEC-FAC or Francisco Xavier Lubota's **Democratic Front of Cabinda** (*Frente Democrática de Cabinda*—FDC).

In September 1996 FLEC-R's Central Council advised its president, Jose Tiburcio LUEMBA, and a second party leader, Jorge Victor GOMES, not to attend a meeting in Brazzaville, Congo, with government officials. Their decision to ignore the committee led to their ouster on January 24, 1997. Subsequently, António Bento Bembe, theretofore party secretary general, and Arture TCHIBASSA, described by *Africa Confidential* as the group's "founder and most powerful leader," were named party president and secretary general, respectively.

Meanwhile, in early 1997 heightened military and political activity was reported in the enclave as the government launched an offensive aimed at dismantling the military capabilities of the separatists. With FLEC-R's cease-fire having formally lapsed in January, its newly installed, more militant leadership also acknowledged having increased its military operations. In 1998 skirmishes between the militants and government forces reportedly intensified as the latter sought to neutralize its opponents (both FLEC and UNITA) in the region. In the early 2000s, analysts suggested that the proliferation of FLEC-related groupings had resulted in confusion among Cabinda's 400,000 inhabitants, most of whom apparently would opt for independence or at least autonomy if offered a choice.

The Angolan government launched what was reportedly considered a successful campaign against the Cabindan fighters in late 2002, following conclusion of the peace accord with the much larger UNITA forces. However, tension regarding "the forgotten war" continued into 2005. By that time FLEC-R and FLEC-FAC had reportedly agreed to operate together as FLEC, with Tiaho Nzita as the group's leader and Bembe as secretary general. Although FLEC apparently indicated a willingness to negotiate with the government, no cease-fire had been achieved by February 2005, when a mass rally in Cabinda again underscored popular support for "self-rule." Meanwhile, an unprecedented strike by Catholic clergy fueled further unrest in 2005 after the Vatican sought to replace a retiring bishop with a non-Cabindan.

In a setback to FLEC, Bembe was arrested in mid-2005 in the Netherlands, where he had been invited by the Dutch foreign ministry to participate in peace negotiations regarding the situation in Cabinda. Bembe, who had been arrested for his alleged role in the kidnapping of an American oil company employee several years earlier, was released on bail but disappeared near the end of 2005. Meanwhile, Tchibassa was serving a 24-year sentence in the United States on the same charge. A few months later Bembe surfaced in the Republic of the Congo as Angola's negotiator, representing FLEC and a coalition referenced as the **Cabinda Forum for Dialogue**, on behalf of peace in Cabinda.

On August 1, 2006, a peace agreement was signed by the Angolan government and the Forum, representing some members of FLEC, the Catholic church, and civic groups. The agreement, approved by the assembly on August 10, officially ended 31 years of war in Cabinda and accorded it special status under the constitution. The Memorandum of Understanding, as the agreement was called, also provided amnesty for the rebels who disarmed, and in January 2007, FLEC was officially disbanded, with many of its members drafted by the national police and the FAA. The U.S. government was reported to have "strongly supported" the agreement. On the other hand, Nzita, who was in exile in Paris, and other FLEC and Forum members who had demanded independence for Cabinda, claimed that Bembe had no authority to negotiate on behalf of FLEC.

In late 2008 reports surfaced of cross-border "incursions" by Angolan troops into the Democratic Republic of the Congo (DRC) and by former FLEC fighters into Cabinda from the DRC. A former FLEC fighter was killed and several Cabindan refugees were wounded, allegedly by Angolan troops in a village in the DRC. Reportedly, several hundred Cabindans were forced from camps inside their territory due to the incursions by Angolan soldiers and by small groups of FLEC fighters from the Republic of the Congo and the DRC. The Angolan forces were said to be countering attempts by FLEC-Nzita fighters to "create havoc" in Cabinda.

Following the 2008 legislative elections and the appointment of a new prime minister, former FLEC leader António Bento Bembe was named to the new government installed on October 1.

In 2010 a group styled as the **Front for the Liberation of the Cabinda Enclave—Military Position** (FLEC—PM), led by Rodrigues Mingas, claimed responsibility for a deadly attack on the Togo football team when it arrived for the Africa Cup of Nations tournament in Angola in January (see Current issues, above).

In August 2010, following a reported "mass exodus" from its senior ranks, FLEC named new leaders, including Pastor Kitembo Antonio DA SILVA as vice president, Joel BETILA as secretary general, and Barros MANGGA and Alfonso MASSANGA.

In November 2010 and February 2011 Angolan armed forces were reportedly attacked in the Buco Zau area. In early March 2011 the army and the national police launched a counterattack against FLEC-FAC forces along the border.

In March 2012 FLEC's two senior military commanders, João Alberto GOMES and David NZAU, were killed by Angolan operatives in the Republic of the Congo. In April Henrique Tiaho Nzita formally requested peace negotiations with the government. Following a January 2013 deadline, some 40,000 Angolans who had fled to the DRC lost refugee status. Reports indicated that the groups included former FLEC fighters and their supporters who feared persecution if they returned to Angola.

LEGISLATURE

In accordance with the 1975 constitution, as amended, a 223-member National People's Assembly (*Assembleia Nacional Popular*) with a three-year term of office was elected in 1980 as successor to the Council of the Revolution, which had served as a legislature since formation of the republic. Subsequent balloting was deferred until late 1986, when the legislative term was extended to five years and the number of deputies increased to 289. The list of candidates, all members of the Popular Movement for the Liberation of Angola—Labor Party (MPLA-PT), was drawn up by the assembly's Permanent Commission.

In late 1990 the MPLA-PT approved liberalization measures providing for election of a restyled **National Assembly** (*Assembleia Nacional*) on a multiparty basis. The size of the assembly was reduced to 223 seats; 3 of those seats were reserved for overseas Angolans, but by mutual agreement of the parties, they were not filled in the balloting of September 29–30, 1992, in which the MPLA (which had dropped "Labor Party" from its name) secured 129 seats, followed by the National Union for the Total Independence of Angola (UNITA) with 70 seats and a number of smaller parties.

On November 13, 1996, the assembly overwhelmingly approved a constitutional revision extending the legislature's mandate (due to expire on November 26) for a minimum of two and a maximum of four years. On April 9, 1997, the assembly met for the first time with the full complement of UNITA representatives in attendance. However, the status of the UNITA contingent became clouded in 1998 as relations between UNITA and the government deteriorated. The government announced on August 31, 1998, that the UNITA legislators had been suspended, although many were subsequently permitted to reassume their seats under an agreement between the government and UNITA-Renewal, the new UNITA faction opposed to longtime UNITA leader Jonas Savimbi. At the same time, some of the UNITA legislators restated their allegiance to Savimbi. Following Savimbi's death in February 2002, the UNITA factions reunified as part of the broad peace accord with the government.

Legislative elections were subsequently postponed until September 5–6, 2008, when 220 members were elected for four-year terms, and the 3 seats for overseas Angolans were again left vacant due to difficulties in conducting balloting. Following legislative balloting on August 31, 2012, the seat distribution was as follows: MPLA, 175; UNITA, 32; Broad Convergence for the Salvation of Angola, 8; the Social Renewal Party, 3; and the National Front for the Liberation of Angola, 2.

President: Fernando Da Piedade Dias DOS SANTOS.

CABINET

[as of November 10, 2013]

President	José Eduardo dos Santos (MPLA)
Vice President	Manuel Domingos Vicente (MPLA)
Ministers	
Agriculture, Rural Development, and Fisheries	Alfonso Canga
Commerce	Rosa Escórcio Pacavira de Matos (MPLA) [f]
Construction	Waldemar Piers Alexandre
Culture	Rosa Maria Martins da Cruz e Silva [f]
Defense	Cândido Pereira dos Santos Van-Dúnem
Economy	Abraao Pio dos Santos Gourgel
Education	Mpinda Simão
Energy and Water	João Baptista Borge
Environment	Maria de Fátima Monteiro Jardim (MPLA) [f]
External Relations	Georges Rebello Chikoti (MPLA)
Family and the Promotion of Women	Maria Filomena de Fátima Lobäo Telo Delgado (MPLA) [f]
Finance	Armando Manuel
Fisheries	Vitória Francisco Lopes Cristovão de Barros Neto [f]
Former Combatants and Veterans Affairs	Kundy Paihama
Geology, Mines, and Industry	Francisco Manuel Monteiro de Queiróz (MPLA)
Health	José Viera Dias Van-Dúnem (MPLA)
Higher Education	Adão Ferreira do Nascimento
Hotels and Tourism	Pedro Mutinde
Industry	Bernarda Gonçalves Martins Henriques Da Silva (MPLA) [f]
Interior	Ângelo de Barros Veiga Tavares
Justice and Human Rights	Rui Jorge Carneiro Mangueira
Parliamentary Affairs	Rosa Luis de Sousa Micolo [f]
Petroleum	José Maria Botelho de Vasconcelos (MPLA)
Planning	Job Graça
Public Administration, Employment, and Social Welfare	António Domingos da Costa Pitra Neto (MPLA)
Science and Technology	Maria de Cândida Teixeira (MPLA) [f]
Social Assistance and Reintegration	João Baptista Kussumua (MPLA)
Social Communications	José Luís de Matos
Telecommunications and Information Technology	José Carvalho da Rocha
Territorial Administration	Bornito de Sousa Baltazar Diogo
Town Planning and Construction	José Antonio de Conceicao de Silva
Transport	Augusto da Silva Tomás (MPLA)
Youth and Sport	Manuel Gonçalves Muandumba (MPLA)
Ministers of State	
Head of Civilian House, Office of the President	Edeltrudes Mauricio Gaspar da Costa
Head of Military House, Office of the President	Gen. Manuel Helder Vieira Dias, Jr.
Secretaries of State	
Agriculture	José Amaro Tati
Budget	Alcides Safeca
Construction	António Teixeira Flor
Cooperation	Exalgina Renée Vicente Olavo Gamboa [f]
Defense	Gaspar Santos Rufino
Economy	Laura Alcântara Montiero [f]
External Relations	Manuel Domingos Augusto
Finance	Valentina Matias de Sousa Filipe [f]
Forestry	André de Jesus Moda
Geology and Mines	Miguel Bondo Júnior
Human Rights	António Bento Bembe
Interior	Eugénio César Laborinho
Local Government	Cremildo Félix Paca
Prison Services	José Bamukina Zau
Rural Development	Maria Filomena de Fátima Lobão Telo Delgado (MPLA) [f]
Science and Technology	João Sebastião Teta
Social Security	Sebastião Constantino Lukinda
Town Planning and Housing	Joaquim Silvestre António
Treasury	Manuel Neto Costa

[f] = female

INTERGOVERNMENTAL REPRESENTATION

Ambassador to the U.S.: Alberto do Carmo Bento RIBEIRO.

U.S. Ambassador to Angola: Helen M. LA LIME.

Permanent Representative to the UN: Ismael A. Gaspar MARTINS.

IGO Memberships (Non-UN): AfDB, AU, IOM, NAM, OPEC, SADC, WTO.

ANTARCTICA

Political Status: Normally uninhabited territory, subject to overlapping claims of national sovereignty that remain in suspense under provisions of the Antarctic Treaty signed December 1, 1959.

Area: 4,826,000 sq. mi. (12,500,000 sq. km).

Population: Various nations operating research stations under terms of the Antarctic Treaty maintain a transient population of about 3,000 (during the Antarctic summer); in addition, a limited number of treaty signatories (including the United States) maintain year-round stations populated by limited personnel.

Political Institution: In 2004 an Antarctic Treaty Secretariat was established in Buenos Aires, Argentina (see Posttreaty developments, below).

Executive Secretary: Manfred REINKE (Germany).

Political background. The most isolated and inhospitable of the world's continents, Antarctica remained outside the mainstream of exploration and colonial exploitation until the early 20th century. British explorer Capt. James Cook first sailed south of the Antarctic Circle in 1773, and in the following century ships from such countries as the United Kingdom, France, Russia, and the United States visited the coastal areas. Between 1900 and 1914 explorers Roald Amundsen of Norway (the first, in 1911, to reach the South Pole), Robert F. Scott and Ernest H. Shackleton of the United Kingdom, Douglas Mawson of Australia, and others penetrated the interior of the continent. This era saw the first territorial claims and the start of commercial Antarctic whaling. Competition for Antarctic territory increased in the interwar decades, while scientific exploration was aided by new technology, chiefly the airplane. Contention over territorial claims further intensified during and after World War II, but the coming of the International

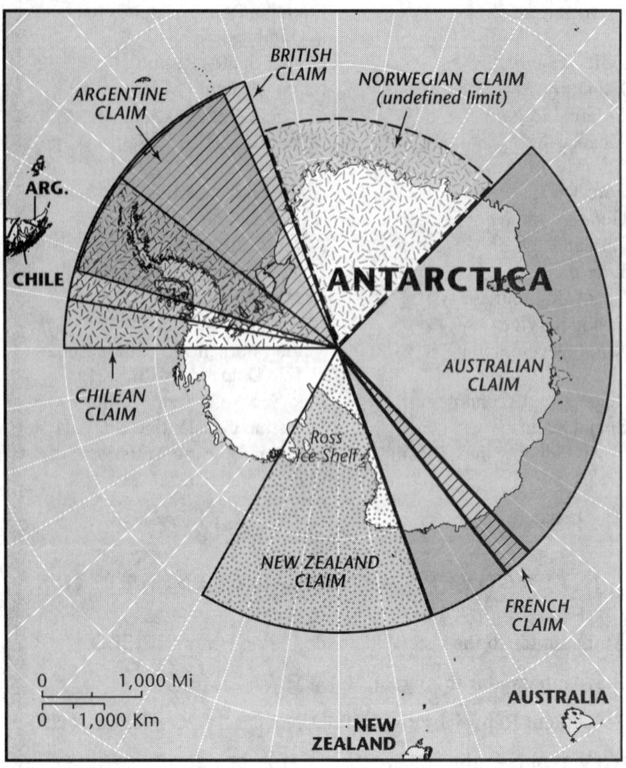

Geophysical Year (IGY) (July 1, 1957–December 31, 1958) brought the beginnings of a new, cooperative, nonpolitical approach to Antarctic problems.

Territorial claims. Prior to the conclusion of the Antarctic Treaty of 1959, the political geography of Antarctica followed the conventional 19th-century pattern of national claims to sovereignty over areas largely unexplored and unsettled. Such claims, advanced by seven governments, took the form of wedge-shaped sectors extending inward from the coast to the South Pole.

The overlapping claims of the United Kingdom, Argentina, and Chile in the area of the Antarctic Peninsula, the most northerly and accessible area of the continent, have been in dispute since the 1940s. The British claim is based on its early discovery and occupation, while those of Chile and Argentina are based on the "contiguity" principle, involving a southward extension of their national territories. The two latter claims overlap, but Argentina and Chile have consistently presented a united front in opposition to the British claim.

The remaining sector claims have occasioned no serious disputes. Norway's claim is based on coastal reconnaissance in the 1930s, France's on the 1840 expedition of Jules d'Urville. The Australian claim, assigned by the United Kingdom in 1936, is based on both exploration and "contiguity," while the "contiguous" area claimed by New Zealand resulted from conveyance by the United Kingdom in 1923. This sector provides the best access to the interior of the continent by way of the Ross Ice Shelf.

The unclaimed "Pacific Sector" (sometimes called Marie Byrd Land) has the most inaccessible coastline of the entire continent and was tacitly awarded to the United States because of Adm. Richard Byrd's work in that area. U.S. personnel are located primarily in the vicinity of the Palmer Peninsula in the northwest, at McMurdo Station near the Ross Ice Shelf, and at the Amundsen-Scott South Pole facility. As originally enunciated by Secretary of State Charles Evans Hughes in 1924, however, U.S. Antarctic policy has consistently denied the principle of valid sovereignty without actual settlement. While reserving all rights accruing from its discoveries and exploration, the United States has made no territorial claims and has refused to recognize those of any other nation.

The Soviet Union, which returned to the area during the IGY, established seven year-round scientific bases, including those in the Australian and Norwegian areas and in the Antarctic Peninsula; in 1993, however, the successor Russian Federation withdrew from Vostok Station, theretofore the only non-U.S. permanent installation on the Polar Plateau, which was subsequently maintained as an international research base. Russia, like the United States, has rejected all claims to territorial sovereignty, which are tabulated (roughly clockwise from the Greenwich meridian) below:

Queen Maud Land (Norway)	20°W	To	45°E
Australian Antarctic Territory (Australia)	45°E	To	136°E
Adélie Land (France)	136°E	To	142°E
Australian Antarctic Territory (Australia)	142°E	To	160°E
Ross Dependency (New Zealand)	160°E	To	150°W
"Pacific Sector" (unclaimed)	150°W	To	90°W
Antártida Chilena (Chile)	90°W	To	53°W
British Antarctic Territory (UK)	80°W	To	20°W
Antártida Argentina (Argentina)	74°W	To	25°W

The Antarctic Treaty. The IGY shifted the emphasis in Antarctic development to international cooperative scientific research. Under the IGY program 11 nations operated research stations: Argentina, Australia, Belgium, Chile, France, Japan, New Zealand, Norway, the Soviet Union, the United Kingdom, and the United States. Between 200 and 300 scientists and technical personnel participated in Antarctic projects in the fields of geology, terrestrial and upper atmospheric physics, biology, glaciology, oceanography, meteorology, and cartography. Following this effort, a conference of the same 11 nations and South Africa was held in Washington, D.C., on U.S. initiative in October 1959 to formalize continued scientific cooperation in Antarctica and to prohibit military use of the area. The resulting treaty, which was signed December 1, 1959, and entered into force June 23, 1961, set forth the following major principles applicable to the area south of 60 degrees south latitude:

1. *Peaceful purposes.* Article I of the treaty specifies that "Antarctica shall be used for peaceful purposes only" and specifically prohibits such measures as establishing military bases, carrying out military maneuvers, and testing weapons. Other articles prohibit nuclear explosions and the disposal of radioactive waste material (Article V) and confer on each contracting party a right to have duly designated observers inspect Antarctic stations, installations and equipment, and ships and aircraft (Article VII).

2. *Freedom of scientific investigation.* Articles II and III provide for continued freedom of scientific investigation and for cooperation toward that end, including the exchange of information, personnel, and scientific findings, and the encouragement of working relations with United Nations Specialized Agencies and other interested international organizations. There are also provisions for periodic consultations among the signatory powers.

3. *"Freezing" of territorial claims.* Article IV stipulates (1) that the treaty does not affect the contracting parties' prior rights or claims to territorial sovereignty in Antarctica, nor their positions relative to the recognition or nonrecognition of such rights or claims by others; and (2) that activities taking place while the treaty is in force are not to affect such claims, and no new claims may be asserted (or existing claims enlarged) during the same period.

The treaty is open to accession by any UN member state or any other state acceptable to the signatory powers, although the treaty makes a distinction between "consultative parties" (signatories that engage in Antarctic scientific activities and participate in consultative meetings) and "nonconsultative parties" (those that have only acceded to the treaty and do not attend the meetings). As of March 1, 2012, there were 28 consultative parties, including the original 12 signatories plus Poland (1977), the Federal Republic of Germany (1981 [absorbed the German Democratic Republic, 1987, in 1990]), Brazil (1983), India (1983), China (1985), Uruguay (1985), Italy (1987), Spain (1988), Sweden (1988), Finland (1989), the Republic of Korea (1989), Peru (1989), Ecuador (1990), the Netherlands (1990), Bulgaria (1998), and the Ukraine (2004), while the 22 acceding parties (apart from the 15 that subsequently moved into consultative status) included Austria, Belarus, Canada, Colombia, Cuba, the Czech Republic, Denmark, Estonia, Greece, Guatemala, Hungary, the Democratic People's Republic of Korea, Malaysia, Monaco, Pakistan, Papua New Guinea, Portugal, Romania, Slovakia, Switzerland, Turkey, and Venezuela.

The duration of the treaty is indefinite, but provision was made for modification by unanimous consent at any time and for a review of its operation at the call of any consultative member after 30 years (i.e., after June 23, 1991). The United States, among others, has carried out a number of inspections under Article VII and has declared itself satisfied that the provisions of the treaty are being faithfully observed.

Economic potential. It was long assumed that Antarctica's mineral resources (including coal, oil, gold, platinum, tin, silver, molybdenum, antimony, and uranium) would remain technologically unexploitable for an indefinite period, but the discovery of iron deposits in the Prince Charles Mountains bordering on the Indian Ocean, coupled with the possibility that similar deposits may lie in the Shackleton Range near the Weddell Sea, led to concern that political cooperation might yield to economic rivalry.

A number of governments and private corporations have expressed interest in pressing the search for petroleum, although the per-barrel cost of tapping any reserves is estimated at almost twice the current sales value. Attention has also been focused on potential offshore oil and natural gas deposits and on the harvesting of krill, a small crustacean that is the major living marine resource of the region and a potentially important source of protein. Those states currently fishing for krill include Germany, Japan, Poland, Russia, and Taiwan.

Posttreaty developments. At a meeting held May 7–20, 1980, in Canberra, Australia, 15 treaty members (the original 12 plus Poland and East and West Germany at that time) approved the final draft of the Convention on the Conservation of Antarctic Marine Living Resources, which was signed September 11 and, having been ratified by a majority of the participating governments, came into force April 7, 1982. The accord called for the establishment in Hobart, Tasmania, of both a scientific committee to set quotas for the harvesting of krill and an international commission responsible for conducting studies of Antarctic species and the food chain, recommending conservation measures, and supervising adherence to the convention. The area covered by the document extends beyond that specified in the 1959 treaty to roughly the "Antarctic Convergence"—where warm and cold waters meet and thus form a natural boundary between marine communities.

The establishment of an International Minerals Regime was discussed at the 11th Consultative Meeting in Buenos Aires, June 23–July 7, 1981; at the 12th Consultative Meeting in Canberra, September 13–27, 1983; and at a series of special consultative sessions between 1981 and 1987. The talks yielded approval of a convention on the Regulation of Antarctic Mineral Resource Activities at a meeting of 33 Antarctic Treaty members held May 2–June 2, 1988. The convention, which required ratification by 16 signatories (including the Soviet Union and the United States and all countries having territorial claims) to come into effect, was bitterly attacked by environmental groups, including the Cousteau Society and Greenpeace, which called for the designation of Antarctica as a "World Heritage Park"; by late 1990 the convention was effectively doomed because of the declared unwillingness of Australia, France, and New Zealand to become ratifying states.

The 13th Consultative Meeting in Brussels, Belgium, October 4–18, 1985, focused primarily on the growing environmental impact of scientific activity in the region. Specifically, the group decided to limit access to 13 special scientific zones and 3 environmental areas—a 75 percent increase in such restricted areas. Subsequently, a report of the World Commission on Environment and Development, chaired by Norway's Gro Harlem Brundtland, called in 1987 for more joint scientific activities in the area, stringent safeguards to protect the continent's environment, and closer working relations among parties to the Antarctic Treaty and other groups within and outside the UN system with responsibilities for science and technology, conservation, and environmental management.

The 15th Consultative Meeting in Paris, France, October 9–21, 1989, was dominated by the opponents of the minerals treaty and their efforts to have the continent declared a global "wilderness reserve." Because of a deadlock on the issue, it was agreed that special consultative meetings would be convened in 1990 to create a "comprehensive protection system in Antarctica." Concurrently, crew members of the Greenpeace vessel *Gondwana* issued a critical report on the waste disposal practices of scientific stations along the Antarctic Peninsula and indicated that Greenpeace would resume its environmental policing during the ensuing year.

Between November 16 and December 6, 1990, representatives of 34 signatory states met in Vina del Mar, Chile, to draft a protocol on environmental protection for the continent that would effectively supplant the 1988 convention. Unable to reach agreement on the duration of a moratorium on mining activity, the parties scheduled a further meeting in Madrid, Spain, in April 1991, at which a 50-year period was agreed upon after Japan had abandoned an appeal for limited mining. Subsequently, an apparent failure of communication within the U.S. administration precluded formal action as scheduled on June 23, although President George H. W. Bush, in response to an outcry from environmental groups, stated on July 4 that the United States would endorse the protocol. His only stipulation was that a two-thirds vote of full treaty members for lifting the ban after 50 years replace a unanimity requirement for such action. The change being made, the Environmental Protocol was signed on October 4 during ceremonies in Madrid. However, two problems remained: (1) the possibility that one or more signatories might not ratify the accord, and (2) the absence of a legal mechanism to prevent nonsignatories from initiating mining activity.

Four of nine former Soviet research stations were closed by late 1991, while Poland, which had been a leader in marine biology, cut its Antarctic staff by three-quarters. Subsequently, it appeared that the countries with the strongest commitments to Antarctica might be Argentina and Chile, both acting on the basis of nationalistic rather than scientific motivation.

The 17th Consultative Meeting in Venice, Italy, November 11–20, 1992, yielded a number of recommendations on environmental monitoring and data management, revised descriptions and proposed management plans for Specially Protected Areas, and established a new group of specialists on global change and international Antarctic programs.

Major topics of discussion during the 18th Consultative Meeting in Kyoto, Japan, April 11–22, 1994, centered on drafting an environmental protection protocol and creating an international mechanism for the certification of tourist groups. While only 50,625 tourists had visited Antarctica by late 1993, the number of summer voyages had surged from only a handful in the late 1950s to more than 50 in the 1992–1993 season, with the potential for a damaging impact on the natural habitat.

The 40-member International Whaling Commission voted May 26, 1994, to bar commercial whaling in a vast area around Antarctica. While largely symbolic in the short term because of an existing worldwide whaling moratorium, the ban would leave nearly a quarter of the world's oceans off-limits to whalers should the moratorium be rescinded.

During the 19th Consultative Meeting in Seoul, Korea, May 8–19, 1995, significant progress was reported on entry into force of the environmental protocol, with 16 of the 26 consultative parties having ratified the document. The meeting also continued examination of the impact of tourism and other nongovernmental activity on Antarctica. However, lack of consensus over its location continued to block establishment of an Antarctic Treaty Secretariat, which was described as a "high priority for most delegations." The principal difficulty was the British objection to Buenos Aires as the site, when Argentina's offer was the only one on the table.

The 20th Consultative Meeting in Utrecht, the Netherlands, April 29–May 10, 1996, focused largely on technical issues. The meeting did, however, endorse the desirability of information exchanges between Antarctic and Arctic groups, given the projected establishment of an Arctic Council. It was reported that 22 of the (then) 26 consultative parties had ratified the environmental protocol, while discussion continued on the impact of tourism on the Antarctic ecosystem and on what instruments might be necessary to establish a treaty secretariat.

In mid-1997 Russia announced further cuts in its Antarctic program: crews at its Bellingshausen and Myrny stations would be drastically reduced, while its Molodyozhnaya facility in eastern Antarctica would be closed in 2 to 3 years, leaving the Progress Station, some 800 miles away, as its main base in the region. Subsequently, in a ceremony held in Christchurch February 20, 1998, the U.S. Navy formally ended its 43-year role of moving people and supplies between Antarctica and the outer world. Air support of American stations was transferred to the 109th Air Wing of the New York National Guard, with on-site operations continuing under authority of the National Science Foundation.

The 22nd Consultative Meeting in Tromsø, Norway, May 25–June 5, 1998, yielded further discussion of the environmental protocol and establishment of a protocol committee. Also addressed was what action members would take in the event of oil spills in the region.

In their first gathering on the continent, 24 signatories of the Antarctic Treaty met January 27, 1999, at the U.S. McMurdo Station to reaffirm their commitment to preservation of the polar ecosystem, including both the land and surrounding seas.

The 24th Consultative Meeting, held in St. Petersburg, Russia, July 9–20, 2001, was most noteworthy for the United Kingdom's announcement that it was no longer opposed to locating the Antarctic Treaty's permanent secretariat in Buenos Aires, following a commitment from Argentina to transfer control of its Antarctic bases from military to civilian control. The United Kingdom had previously blocked the proposal, which required consensus, as a consequence of the 1982 Falklands War, and some analysts suggested that the UK decision was also facilitated by a secret agreement in which Argentina agreed to "demilitarize" its status in Antarctica by closing three of its six permanent bases there.

No major decisions were made at the 25th Consultative Meeting in Warsaw, Poland, September 10–20, 2002. The 26th Consultative Meeting in Madrid, Spain, June 9–20, 2003, however, dealt with a number of problems arising from tourism and illegal fishing in the region.

Final details on a secretariat, including the appointment of an executive secretary, were worked out during the 27th Consultative Meeting in Cape Town, South Africa, May 24–June 4, 2004, with the secretariat being launched shortly thereafter. The Cape Town participants also agreed to designate the McMurdo Dry Valleys (an ice-free zone sheltered by the Transantarctic Mountains) as an Antarctic Specially Managed Area (ASMA) within which human activity would be strictly limited.

The 28th Consultative Meeting in Stockholm, Sweden, June 6–17, 2005, featured, after 13 years of negotiation, a Liability Annex to the Environmental Protocol, under which those active in Antarctica who fail to take "prompt and effective response action to environmental emergencies arising from [their] activities" would be held liable for the cost of response actions taken by others. However, the agreement required approval by all of the contracting parties before it could come into effect.

A major focus of the 29th Consultative Meeting in Edinburgh, Scotland, June 12–23, 2006, was the International Polar Year 2007–2008. Hailed as the largest internationally coordinated scientific research effort in 50 years, its aim was to educate the public in polar issues, while paving the way for more than 200 projects by the next generation of Arctic and Antarctic scientists. Discussion of the International Polar Year continued at the 30th Consultative Meeting in New Delhi, India, April 30–May 11, 2007.The management of tourism, an issue discussed at the 2007 meeting, was continued at the 31st Consultative Meeting in Kiev, Ukraine, May 31–June 14, 2008, although most of the discussion focused on the impact of climate change on the Antarctic ecosystem.

The 32nd Consultative Meeting in Baltimore, Maryland, and Washington, D.C., on April 6–27, 2009, paved the way for an Antarctic Summit at Washington's Smithsonian Institution on November 30–December 1 that celebrated the 50th anniversary of the treaty's signing by issuing a Forever Declaration on Behalf of the Global Civil Society that reaffirmed the commitment to peaceful activity in Antarctica, while prohibiting the establishment of military bases and nuclear explosions or nuclear waste disposal. It also called for all states to accede to the treaty and take measures to eliminate climate change, pollution, and the like that take place outside the treaty area but might be harmful to the Antarctic environment.

Manfred Reinke, a scientist from the Alfred Wegener Institute for Polar and Marine Research in Bremen, Germany, was elected as the new executive secretary of the Antarctic Treaty system at the conclusion of the April 2009 Consultative Meeting.

The 33rd annual meeting held in Buenos Aires, Argentina in May 2010, continued previous discussions on environmental protection as a major theme of Antarctic progress. This theme carried over to the 34th annual meeting, which was held in Uruguay in June 2011. The 2011 meeting focused on major initiatives to reduce the impact to the environment. The CEP discussed and highlighted the importance of these initiatives through the plan for a new research station to be built by the Koreans. The meeting also addressed issues such as prevention of unauthorized access and the impacts of drilling into a subglacial lake.

Environmental protection was again a centerpiece at the 35th Consultative Meeting in Hobart, Australia, in June 2012. Parties identified areas of conservation importance and reaffirmed commitment to promoting scientific research of climate change on the continent. With the designation of Blood Falls as a Protected Area, the total number of protected areas rose to 72.

The 36th Consultative Meeting, held in May 2013 in Brussels, was designed to be a "green" event, meaning the gathering itself was designed to minimize environmental impact. In meetings attended by scientists and observers from 50 countries, environmentally responsible Antarctic tourism and search-and-rescue training exercises topped the discussion agenda. The 73rd Antarctic Specially Protected Area was established in the Ross Sea, encompassing a colony of about 20,000 breeding pairs of emperor penguins and a silverfish hatchery. The Czech Republic was approved as a consultant member and will be allowed to participate as full members at the 37th Consultative Meeting, scheduled for May 2014 in Brazil.

Current issues. Antarctica received widespread international attention in early 2002 when an ice shelf the size of the U.S. state of Rhode Island collapsed during a 35-day period, generating several thousand icebergs amid projections that continued shrinkage of the shelves could lead to a drastic increase in sea levels, with incalculable climatic change worldwide. Collaterally, the WMO reported that the hole in the ozone layer above Antarctica had grown to the largest level ever recorded. A subsequent survey in 2004 revealed that the Antarctic ice cap was one-tenth smaller and half the thickness as measured 30 years earlier, and in early 2008 British scientists reported that a massive fracture at the edge of the Wilkins Ice Shelf threatened collapse of the entire shelf, an area roughly the size of the U.S. state of Connecticut. The sobering reality was that global warming was proceeding at a much faster rate at the poles than elsewhere, a team of Australian scientists reporting in mid-2008 that the Antarctic oceans were warming 50 percent faster than previously estimated, with consequences that would entail widespread climate changes stemming from a catastrophic rise in sea levels.

In 2009, however, studies showed that the cause of the erosion was not just warming temperatures but also stronger ocean currents. The scientists noted that a 50 percent increase in the melting speed of the ice over a 15-year period was too dramatic to be from global warming alone.

The International Maritime Organization announced in April 2010 that large cruise ships would no longer be permitted to dump high-sulfur fuel in the Antarctic waters. The action effectively ended visits by cruise ships carrying more than 500 passengers, thereby reducing the number of passenger visits from over 15,000 a year to approximately 6,400.

India's Antarctic station became fully operational in June 2012. In 2013 scientists expressed concern about the Antarctic experiencing its warmest winter since 1957, when weather record-keeping in the South Pole first began.

ANTIGUA AND BARBUDA

Political Status: Former British dependency; joined West Indies Associated States in 1967; independent member of the Commonwealth since November 1, 1981.

Area: 171.5 sq. mi. (444 sq. km), encompassing the main island of Antigua (108 sq. mi.) and the dependent islands of Barbuda (62 sq. mi.) and Redonda (0.5 sq. mi.).

Population: 83,278 (2011—UN); 90,156 (2013E—U.S. Census).

Major Urban Center (2011E): ST. JOHN'S (22,193).

Official Language: English.

Monetary Unit: East Caribbean Dollar (market rate November 1, 2013: 2.70 EC dollars = $1US).

Sovereign: Queen ELIZABETH II.

Governor General: Dame Louise LAKE-TACK; inaugurated on July 17, 2007, to succeed Sir James B. CARLISLE.

Prime Minister: Winston Baldwin SPENCER (United Progressive Party); sworn in March 24, 2004, following election of March 23, succeeding Lester Bryant BIRD (Antigua Labour Party); reappointed following election of March 12, 2009.

THE COUNTRY

Located in the northern part of the Caribbean's Lesser Antilles, the islands of Antigua and Barbuda are populated largely by blacks whose ancestors were transported as slaves from western Africa in the 17th and 18th centuries. Minorities include descendants of British colonial settlers, Portuguese laborers, and Lebanese and Syrian traders.

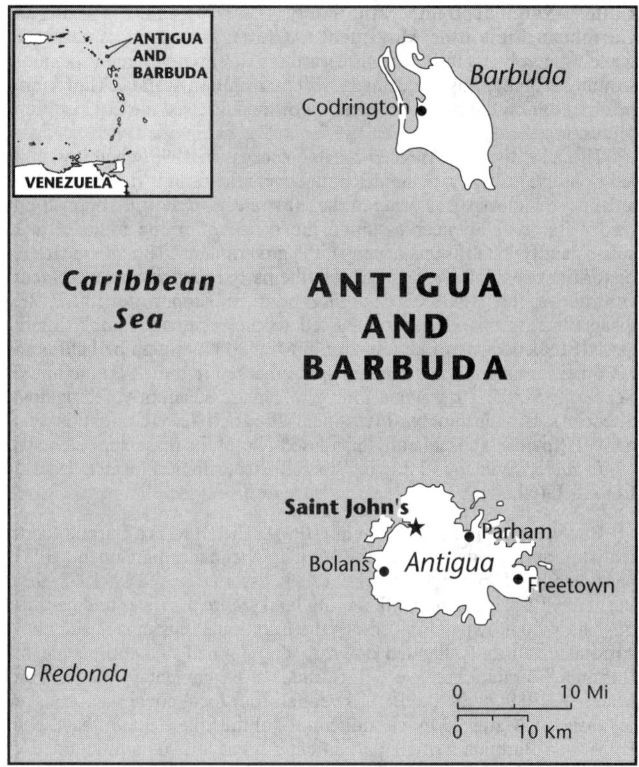

Anglican Protestantism and Roman Catholicism claim the largest number of adherents, although a wide variety of other denominations exist, and complete religious freedom prevails. Seven women hold seats in the current bicameral legislature.

Agriculture dominated the economy until the 1960s, when a pronounced decline in sugar prices led to the abandonment of most cane fields and increased reliance on tourism, which currently accounts for about 60 percent of GDP. The harbor at St. John's, long used as a dockyard for the British Navy, is a port of call for 11 major shipping lines, while a modern air facility, featuring a Canadian-financed terminal complex, is served by eight international carriers. Although real GDP rose by an average of 4.5 percent during 2000–2007, while inflation averaged less than 2.0 percent through the same period (the lowest in the region), the country has long faced a variety of economic problems, most notably high external debt. Economic woes further compounded when, in 2008, the GDP growth rate slowed to 1.8 percent, and the global economic downturn had a continued dramatic effect. In 2009 GDP contracted by more than 10 percent in GDP, the second highest decline of any country in the world, followed the next year by further decline of 9 percent. In 2010 the IMF approved a three-year stand-by arrangement for $128 million. The country undertook efforts to promote agriculture, particularly livestock and produce cultivation; expand the fishing industry; develop an Internet gambling industry; and increase tourism on the islands. Despite the efforts, GDP contracted by a further 3 percent in 2011, before rebounding to 1.6 percent the following year. GDP growth remained steady, though minimal, in 2013, at 1.7 percent, with inflation estimated at 3 percent.

GOVERNMENT AND POLITICS

Political background. Colonized by Great Britain in the early 17th century after unsuccessful efforts by Spain and France, Antigua became a founding member of the Federation of the West Indies in 1958, following the introduction of ministerial government two years earlier. Together with its northern dependency, Barbuda, it joined the West Indies Associated States in 1969 as an internally self-governing territory with a right of unilateral termination, which it exercised on November 1, 1981. At independence, Premier Vere C. BIRD Sr., whose Antigua Labour Party (ALP) had returned to power in 1976 and was victorious in the election of April 1980, became prime minister. In the election on April 17, 1984, the ALP swept all the Antiguan seats in the House of Representatives, with Bird forming a new government two days later.

From 1987 to 1992, the ALP government was plagued by intense party disagreements—even within Bird's own family—over his policies; charges of corruption and unethical behavior; and a series of resignations by top party leaders. Bird's leadership of the party was divisive, and many of his critics accused him of questionable and unethical practices. Despite calls for reform and change from within the party, Bird refused to enact any significant reforms. After 1992 allegations that Bird had received a government check for $25,000 prompted a general strike and widespread civil unrest (including arson attacks on public and private buildings), the prime minister announced he would not seek reelection in 1994. His son, Lester BIRD, assumed party leadership.

The ALP won its fifth consecutive general election in legislative balloting on March 8, 1994, albeit with a reduced majority of 11 of 17 seats. Two days later, Lester Bird announced a new government that included John ST. LUCE, his most recent challenger for the party leadership, but, to some surprise, excluded his brother Vere Bird Jr. The ALP majority in the House of Representatives increased to 12 seats in the election of March 9, 1999.

In the wake of long-standing charges of corruption involving senior ministers, the ALP was decisively defeated in the election of March 23, 2004, with Lester Bird among those losing their House seats. On March 24, Winston Baldwin SPENCER, leader of the United Progressive Party (UPP), took office as prime minister. Spencer remained in office after the election of March 12, 2009, though UPP parliamentary representation had plummeted to a bare majority of nine seats. Following the 2009 election, a District Court judge ordered three of the seats won by members of the UPP to be vacated, including the seat belonging to Prime Minister Spencer. After a yearlong appeals process, the decision was overturned and all three members retained their seats. The UPP has since been plagued by charges of governmental corruption that have led to the resignation of top officials and strife within the party. Government officials have attracted criticism for mismanagement of economic problems, and some of their practices have been questionable, for example, the expropriation of private property to generate government revenue. These actions led many in the ALP and the Democratic Progressive Movement to call for the resignation of top UPP cabinet officials. The next general election is expected to take place in 2014.

Constitution and government. In 1981 the independence constitution retained the existing bicameral legislative structure, composed of an appointed Senate and a House of Representatives elected from single-member constituencies (16 on Antigua and 1 on Barbuda) for a 5-year term, subject to dissolution. Of the 17 senators, 11 are selected in consultation with the prime minister, 4 in consultation with the leader of the opposition, 1 on the advice of the smaller island's Barbuda Council, and 1 at the governor general's discretion. Executive power is exercised by a Council of Ministers headed by a prime minister, all of whom are responsible to Parliament. The constitutional independence of the judiciary is reinforced by Antigua and five neighboring states (Dominica, Grenada, St. Kitts-Nevis, St. Lucia, and St. Vincent) participating equally in a Supreme Court, which encompasses a Court of Appeal with a High Court, one of whose judges is resident in Antigua and presides over a Court of Summary Jurisdiction. District courts deal with minor offenses and civil actions involving not more than EC$500.

While Antigua and Barbuda constitute a nominally unitary state, secessionist sentiment has long been pronounced on the smaller island. Premier Bird initiated, before independence, a limited devolution of powers to the Barbuda Council, which contains nine directly elected members in addition to a government nominee and the Barbuda parliamentary representative. However, in early 2000 Barbudans complained of the government's handling of their affairs through a single ministry (Home Affairs), and in March the Commonwealth appointed two members to review relations between the council and the government. Among other things, the council had called for establishment of a federal system under which Barbuda would have a legislative assembly with full authority over its internal affairs. In late 2000 the Commonwealth review commission rejected that proposal, although officials from Barbuda pledged to pursue the issue. Meanwhile, St. John's endorsed the creation of a new joint consultative committee of representatives from both islands to oversee a proposed five-year development plan for Barbuda, and in 2004 the Spencer administration established a separate Barbuda Affairs ministry, which, however, was abandoned in 2009.

Freedom of the press is constitutionally guaranteed. In May 2013 Prime Minister Baldwin indicated his intention to repeal the country's criminal defamation laws, a remnant of British colonial law.

Foreign relations. In 1965 Chief Minister Bird, a strong believer in regional cooperation, played a leading role in organizing the Caribbean Free Trade Association (Carifta), predecessor of the Caribbean Community and Common Market (Caricom). Upon independence, Antigua became a member of the Commonwealth and, shortly thereafter, the 157th member of the United Nations. Antigua is also an active member of the Organization of Eastern Caribbean States (OECS), which provided troops in support of the U.S. invasion of Grenada in October 1983. The swing to the right continued in 1985, with St. John's agreeing to the establishment of a U.S.-backed regional military training base on the main island and the use of existing U.S. bases for regional security exercises.

In mid-2003 an appeal was filed with the World Trade Organization (WTO) against restrictions on U.S. consumers regarding Internet gambling. In a landmark decision, the WTO ruled in favor of Antigua and ordered the United States to either lift its ban or remove a "discriminatory exemption" for horse-race betting. The U.S. ban, Antigua reported, caused the gambling industry to shrink to fewer than 500 employees, down from more than 4,000. The United States refused to comply with the WTO's order on the ground that to do so would violate a number of U.S. state laws. As a result, the WTO took the unusual action of awarding Antigua and Barbuda the right to violate U.S. copyright restrictions on goods such as films and music up to a value of $21 million a year (far less than the $3.4 billion in damages requested). In January 2013 the WTO approved Antigua's plan to seek repayment of $21 million from the United States by offering downloads of copyrighted American intellectual property. The United States responded that the move would only serve to further damage relations between the two countries. In early March, talks between the two countries resumed.

In June 2010 Antigua and Barbuda joined with the five other OECS members in an agreement to create an Economic Union. The accord also provided a framework for an OECS Commission, an executive body with decision-making capability. The OECS Economic Union was officially created on January 21, 2011, with Antigua and Barbuda the first to ratify the treaty. Antigua and Barbuda lead the push for integration of the OECS states by allowing free movement of people and goods among member states, a multilateral decision that was finalized at the January summit and went into effect on August 1. The OECS also voted at the January meeting to establish a legislative body with binding authority over all OECS states, structured similarly to European parliamentary systems and located in Antigua and Barbuda.

The People's Republic of China has strengthened ties with St. John since April 2011, providing funds for several public works projects including a new school and power plant.

During Prime Minister Spencer's May 2013 trip to the Doha Forum on Peace and Development, Qatar expressed plans for major investment in Antigua.

Current issues. In February 2009 the U.S. Securities and Exchange Commission filed charges that Antigua's leading private investor, R. Allen Stanford, committed fraud of a "shocking magnitude." Official Stanford Investor's Committee filed a lawsuit against Antigua in February 2013 for repayment of $90 million of documented loans and accused the country's elected officials of being "Stanford's partners in crime."

In March the East Caribbean High Court ordered the government to pay $70 million to Half Moon Bay Holdings following the 2005 acquisition of a 108-acre property, sparking financial concerns after public worker wages were overdue several times in early 2013. The tenth and final disbursement of the 2010 IMF stand-by arrangement was awarded in June 2013, bringing the total to $76.2 million.

After more than six months of debate, the legislature approved the Citizenship by Investment program in March 2013, qualifying major investors in the islands for citizenship. The bill, expected to alleviate some of the country's financial woes, divided the UPP, resulting in the dismissal of two government party senators (see the UPP entry in Political Parties, below).

In March 2013 elections for the local government on Barbuda (see Constitution and government, above), the Barbuda faction of the ALP ended the BPM's 32-year control of the Barbuda Council, winning four of five available seats and taking majority control with six seats to the BPM's five.

POLITICAL PARTIES

Government Party:

United Progressive Party (UPP). The UPP was launched in March 1992 by merger of the **Progressive Labour Movement** (PLM), the **United National Democratic Party** (UNDP), and the **Antigua Caribbean Liberation Movement** (ACLM). The action came in the wake of involvement by the three groups in antigovernment demonstrations triggered by the January 1992 corruption scandal. (For more information on the historical makeup of the UPP, see the 2011 edition of the *Handbook*.)

The UPP first experienced notable success in 1999 when it won 4 lower house seats. Growing discontent with the ruling ALP resulted in a decisive victory of 13 seats in the 2004 election. Former opposition leader Baldwin Spencer assumed the office of prime minister and subsequently established a new UPP government. Though the UPP majority declined to 9 seats in 2009, the party maintained government control. In the wake of declining political support for the UPP, disagreements on internal policy led to the resignation of Wilmoth DANIEL as deputy prime minister in May 2009, though he held onto his other ministerial portfolios. A split emerged in the UPP bloc in the Senate in March 2013 when four government senators voted against Spencer's Citizenship by Investment Program (see Current issues, above). Spencer subsequently dismissed two of the dissenters.

Leaders: Winston Baldwin SPENCER (Prime Minister), Harold LOVELL (Chair).

Barbuda People's Movement (BPM). The BPM is a Barbuda separatist party. Having rejected the 1981 independence agreement, BPM party leader Thomas Hilbourne Frank asserted in early 1982 that Parliament's passage of a bill altering land tenure practices and permitting individual ownership "erodes the traditional, customary and constitutional authority handed down to the Council and the people of Barbuda." Frank was elected Barbuda's parliamentary deputy on March 9, 1989, while the BPM swept all four local council contests at balloting on March 23 to win full control of the nine elective seats. The BPM won Barbuda's single parliamentary seat in 2004 and retained it in 2009. In March 2013 elections, the BPM lost its 32-year-long majority on the Barbuda Council, winning just one of five contested seats, bringing its total to five, against the ALP's six.

Leader: Trevor WALKER (Chair and Member of Parliament).

Opposition Party:

Antigua Labour Party (ALP). In power from 1967 to 1971 and a decisive victor in subsequent balloting in 1976, 1980, 1984, and 1989, the ALP has long been affiliated with the Antigua Trades & Labor Union. By the early 1980s, however, questions had arisen regarding its grassroots links. In accepting designation as party chair in June 1984, Lester Bird made an effort to reach out to women, youth, and other groups for "modern approaches" and "a proper philosophical base" for party activity.

In response to the corruption controversy that engulfed his administration in 1992, Vere Bird announced that he would not seek reelection as prime minister in 1994. Subsequently, balloting in a special ALP convention on May 24 to elect a new party leader ended inconclusively with an even split between party chair Lester Bird and (then) information minister John St. Luce. In a second poll at the party's annual convention on September 5–6, Bird defeated St. Luce and subsequently became prime minister in March 1994. He remained in office after the 1999 election but led the ALP to defeat in 2004. The party recovered in 2009, winning seven seats in the House, but failed by two seats to win a majority. Amid mounting concern over Bird's age and health, Gaston BROWNE was elected party leader at a convention in November 2012, marking the first time in ALP history that the leader is not a member of the Bird family. Gail CHRISTIAN became the first woman chair of the ALP.

In March 2013 the party's Barbuda faction won four of five available seats in the Barbuda Council elections, securing the council majority (see Current issues, above).

Leaders: Gaston BROWNE (Party Leader and Leader of the Opposition), Gail CHRISTIAN (Chair).

Other Parties Contesting the 2009 Election:

First Christian Democratic Movement (FCDM). The FCDM was launched in 2003.

Leader: Egbert JOSEPH

Barbuda People's Movement for Change (BPMC). Launched in 2004 as the successor to the former Organization for National Reconstruction (ONR), the BPMC favors self-government for Barbuda and is affiliated with the ALP.

Leader: Arthur SHABAZZ-NIBBS.

Organization for National Development (OND). The OND is a breakaway faction of the UPP organized in 2003. As of March 2012, the OND is in the process of merging with the ALP.
Leader: Melford NICHOLAS.

Other Parties:

Democratic Progressive Movement (DPM). The DPM was organized in 2011 as a "better alternative" to the UPP and ALP. The DPM focuses largely on youth involvement and champions the call for a better Antigua and Barbuda.
Leader: Steve WILLIAMS.

LEGISLATURE

The **Parliament** is a bicameral body consisting of an appointed Senate and a directly elected House of Representatives. One unique element of the Antigua and Barbuda parliamentary structure is the selection process for the speaker of the House of Representatives. The members of the House of Representatives are responsible for electing its speaker. The speaker of the house may or may not be a member of the House of Representatives when chosen. If the speaker is not a representative when selected, he or she will become a member by virtue of the office, bringing the total number of members of the house to 19.

Senate. The upper house has 17 members named by the governor general: 11 (including at least 1 from Barbuda) appointed on advice of the prime minister, 4 named after consultation with the leader of the opposition, 1 recommended by the Barbuda Council, and 1 chosen at the governor general's discretion.
President: Hazelyn MASON-FRANCIS.

House of Representatives. The lower house has 17 members chosen every 5 years (subject to dissolution) from single-member constituencies, a speaker, and the attorney general, ex officio. In the most recent election of March 12, 2009, the UPP won 9 seats; the ALP, 7; and the BPM, 1.
Speaker: Giselle ISAAC-ARRINDELL.

CABINET

[as of November 11, 2013]

Prime Minister	Winston Baldwin Spencer (UPP)
Ministers	
Agriculture, Lands, Housing, and the Environment	Hilson Baptiste (UPP)
Education, Gender, Sports, and Youth Affairs	Dr. Jacqui Quinn-Leandro (UPP) [f]
Finance, Economy, and Public Administration	Harold E. E. Lovell (UPP)
Foreign Affairs	Winston Baldwin Spencer (UPP)
Health, Social Transformation, and Consumer Affairs	Willmoth Daniel (UPP)
Legal Affairs and Attorney General	Justin L. Simon (UPP)
National Security	Dr. Leon Errol Cort (UPP)
Tourism, Civil Aviation, and Culture	John Herbert Maginley (UPP)
Works and Transportation	Trevor Myke Walker (BPM)
Ministers of State	
Agriculture, Lands, Housing and the Environment	Chanlah Codrington (UPP)
Education, Gender, Sports, and Youth Affairs	Winston Vincent Williams (UPP)
Legal Affairs	Joanne Maureen Massiah (UPP) [f]
Office of the Prime Minister	Dr. Edmond Mansoor (UPP)
Tourism, Civil Aviation and Culture	Eleston Montgomery Adams (UPP)
Works and Transportation	Elmore Charles (UPP)

[f] = female

INTERGOVERNMENTAL REPRESENTATION

Ambassador to the U.S.: Deborah Mae LOVELL.

U.S. Ambassador to Antigua and Barbuda: Larry Leon PALMER.

Permanent Representative to the UN: John William ASHE.

IGO Memberships (Non-UN): Caricom, CWTH, ICC, NAM, OAS, OECS, WTO.

ARGENTINA

Argentine Republic
República Argentina

Note: The ruling PJ-Victory Front and its allies won the parliamentary elections on October 27, 2013, and will control 132 of 257 seats in the National Assembly. The Radical Civic Union and its allies are the second-largest bloc in the Assembly, with 54 deputies, followed by the new Renewal Front with 19 deputies. The PJ-Victory Front and its allies also control 40 of the 70 Senate seats. President Fernández resumed her duties on November 19 and immediately shuffled her cabinet.

Political Status: Independent republic proclaimed 1816; under military regimes 1966–1973 and 1976–1983; current constitution adopted August 22, 1994.

Area: 1,068,013 sq. mi. (2,766,889 sq. km), excluding territory claimed in Antarctica and the South Atlantic.

Population: 41,281,631 (2013E—UN); 42,610,981 (2013E—U.S. Census).

Major Urban Centers (2010E): BUENOS AIRES (13,361,000), Córdoba (1,445,000), Rosario (1,240,000), La Plata (786,000).

Official Language: Spanish.

Monetary Unit: Argentine Peso (market rate November 1, 2013: 5.91 pesos = $1US).

President: Cristina FERNÁNDEZ de Kirchner (Justicialist Party-Victory Front); elected on October 28, 2007, and inaugurated for a four-year term on December 10, 2007, succeeding her husband, Néstor Carlos KIRCHNER (Justicialist Party). Reelected for a second four-year term on October 23, 2011, and inaugurated on December 10.

Vice President: Amado BOUDOU (Justicialist Party-Victory Front); elected on October 23, 2011, and inaugurated for a term concurrent with that of the president on December 10, succeeding Julio César Cleto COBOS (Radical Civic Union for Kirchner—Victory Front).

THE COUNTRY

Second in size among the countries of South America, the Argentine Republic includes the national territory of Tierra del Fuego and claims certain South Atlantic islands (including the Falklands, known to Argentines as the Malvinas) as well as portions of Antarctica. The country extends 2,300 miles from north to south and exhibits a varied climate and topography, including the renowned pampas, the fertile central plains. The population is largely Caucasian but of diverse national origin. Spaniards and Italians predominate, but there are also large groups from other Western and Eastern European countries, as well as Middle Easterners of both Arab and Jewish descent. Although Spanish is the official language, English, Italian, German, and French are also spoken. More than 90 percent of the population is Roman Catholic. Literacy is near universal, although the high-school dropout rate is nearly 57 percent.

Women pursue professional careers in great numbers. With the exception of both wives of former president Juan Perón, women have historically been minimally represented in government, although a women's group called *Las Madres de la Plaza de Mayo* was at the forefront of opposition to the former military regime. In 2007 the country elected its first female president.

Argentina has enjoyed one of the highest per capita incomes in South America but has often been subject to rampant inflation. Inflation rose to more than 1,000 percent in early 1985, then necessitating a drastic currency revision as part of a series of "war economy" measures, fell to an annualized rate of 50 percent the following year, only to escalate to an unprecedented rate of nearly 5,000 percent in 1989. A March 1991 currency convertibility plan pegged the peso to the U.S. dollar and subsequently eliminated hyperinflation. The peso was devalued in January 2002 and allowed to float in February in an effort to spur growth.

In March 2005 Argentina reached agreement with three-quarters of its private creditors on a write-down of approximately $100 billion, and in late December the country paid off its outstanding debt of $9.8 billion to the International Monetary Fund (IMF), with the Kirchner administration concurrently declaring that it was severing relations with the IMF. Growth averaged 8.8 percent in 2003–2007, and unemployment fell to 8.5 percent. In response to the global economic crisis in late 2008, a stimulus package provided $21 billion in public works spending, backed by the nationalization of ten private pension funds. GDP growth slowed to 0.9 percent in 2009, while unemployment of 8.7 percent was recorded.

In 2010 annual GDP soared to 9.2 percent, making Argentina's economy among the fastest growing in the region. A significant increase in soy exports and a surge in the auto industry helped fuel economic growth, while inflation of about 10 percent was recorded. Annual growth remained robust at 8.9 percent in 2011, owing in large part to consumer spending, the demand by Brazil for manufactured goods, and China's growing demand for soy and grain, but plunged to 1.9 percent in 2012 due to a poor harvest, inflation, and currency controls (see Current issues, below). Unemployment stood at 7.2 percent in 2011 and 2012, its lowest level in 20 years.

GOVERNMENT AND POLITICS

Political background. Following the struggle for independence from Spain in 1810–1816, Argentina experienced a period of conflict over its form of government. The provinces advocated a federal system to guarantee their autonomy, while Buenos Aires favored a unitary state in which it would play a dominant role. A federal constitution was drafted in 1853, but Buenos Aires refused to ratify the document until its 1859 defeat in a brief war. Following a second military reversal in 1880, the territory was politically neutralized by being designated a federal district.

The Conservative Party (*Partido Conservador*—PC) dominated the early years of the 20th century. However, the reformist Radical Civic Union (*Unión Cívica Radical*—UCR) successfully pressed in 1912 for a liberal electoral law that resulted in the election of UCR leader Hipólito IRIGOYEN as president in 1916. Faced with mounting economic problems, the Irigoyen government was overthrown and replaced by the nation's first military regime in 1930.

The election of Augustín P. JUSTO to the presidency in 1932 launched a second period of Conservative rule that lasted until 1943, when the military again intervened. Gen. Juan Domingo PERÓN Sosa was elected chief executive in 1946, inaugurating a populist dictatorship that was eventually overthrown in 1955. His second wife, María Eva Duarte de PERÓN (better known as Eva Perón or Evita) was an active participant. She initiated the Eva Perón Foundation with donations and funds coerced from the private sector, which helped to improve the lives of the poor. Juan Perón's influence over the political arena can hardly be exaggerated, as it was during his government and through his leadership that unions were recognized as legitimate political actors and that the "masses" (known as the *descamisados* or "shirtless ones") were incorporated into political strategies. Women's suffrage was introduced in 1951 after a strong campaign by Evita, who died of cancer in 1952. In the following years Juan Perón relied more on cooptation and coercion than on democratic representation, and he struggled when economic growth slowed and the politicized masses had minimal institutional channels to accommodate them. During his term in office, a divorce law was promulgated with Perón's approval, an act that put him at odds with the Catholic Church, which actively campaigned for his removal. Peron's loss of control was noted by elites, who supported the military coup that removed him in 1955. Subsequent military and democratic governments attempted to "ban" Peronism, but it remained the country's most powerful ideological influence.

In the March 1973 general election, which ended seven years of military rule, the Peronist Dr. Héctor J. CÁMPORA emerged victorious. Four months later Cámpora resigned to force a new election in which Perón would be eligible as a candidate. The new round of balloting, held in September, returned the former president to power with an overwhelming majority after 18 years of exile. Following his inauguration, Perón was plagued by factionalism within his movement and by increasingly widespread opposition from guerrilla groups. After his death on July 1, 1974, he was succeeded by his second wife, Isabel (born María Estela) Martínez de PERÓN, who had been elected vice president the preceding September. Isabel Perón's turbulent presidency was terminated on March 24, 1976, by a three-man military junta, which on March 26 designated Lt. Gen. Jorge Rafael VIDELA as her replacement.

In December 1976 General Videla stated that his government was "very close to final victory" over left-wing terrorists, most prominently the so-called *Montonero* guerrillas and the People's Revolutionary Army. The military government embarked on a campaign of repression, described as the "dirty war," that killed or "disappeared" as many as 30,000 people, the vast majority of whom were not involved with guerrilla groups.

Earlier, in an apparent consolidation of power by Videla, a number of rightist officers were forced to retire and replaced by moderates. On May 2, 1978, the government announced that while Videla had again been designated as president for a three-year term retroactive to March 29, he would cease to serve as a member of the junta following his military retirement on August 1. The pattern was repeated with the retirement of Lt. Gen. Roberto Eduardo VIOLA as army commander and junta member as of December 31, 1979, and his designation to succeed Videla in March 1981. Buffeted by health problems and an inability to deal with a rapidly deteriorating economy, Viola stepped down as chief executive on December 11, and he was succeeded 11 days later by the army commander, Lt. Gen. Leopoldo Fortunato GALTIERI, who continued as a member of the junta, along with Adm. Jorge Isaac ANAYA and Lt. Gen. Basilio Arturo LAMI DOZO, commanders of the navy and air force, respectively.

The country was shaken by a brief but intense conflict with Great Britain that erupted in 1982 as the result of a 149-year dispute over ownership of the Falkland Islands (*Islas Malvinas*), located in the South Atlantic about 400 miles northeast of Tierra del Fuego. Argentina invaded the islands on April 2, prompting the dispatch of a British armada that succeeded in regaining control with the surrender of about 15,000 Argentine troops in the capital, Stanley, on July 15 (see Contested Territory, below). Branded as having sold out the country by his conduct of the war, Galtieri resigned on June 17 and was succeeded immediately as army commander by Maj. Gen. Cristino NICOLAIDES and on July 1 as president by Gen. Reynaldo Benito Antonio BIGNONE. In the face of an economic crisis and mounting pressure from the nation's political parties, Bignone announced in February 1983 that elections for a civilian government would be advanced to the following October.

A ban on political activity, imposed by the military on its return to power in March 1976, was lifted by President Bignone at his inauguration on July 1, 1982, and more than 300 national and regional groups participated in the general election of October 30, 1983. However, two formations, the UCR and the Justicialist Liberation Front (Peronist) shared 92 percent of the vote. In balloting for national, provincial, and municipal authorities on October 30, 1983, the UCR, under the leadership of Raúl ALFONSÍN Foulkes, scored a decisive victory, winning not only the presidency but also a majority in the Chamber of Deputies. Following pro forma designation by the electoral college, Alfonsín and his vice-presidential running mate, Víctor MARTINEZ, were sworn in for six-year terms on December 10.

On November 3, 1985, at the first renewal of the lower house in 20 years, the UCR marginally increased its majority, largely at the expense of the *oficialista* wing of the Peronist party (see Justicialist Party [*Partido Justicialista*—PJ], under Political Parties, below). The combined vote share of the UCR and Peronists dropped to 77 percent, with "orthodox" and "renewing" factions of the latter (alone or in alliance with smaller parties) presenting separate lists in most districts. On September 6, 1987, on the other hand, the Radicals were reduced to plurality status, with most of the Peronist gains again being registered by the movement's *renovadores* faction, whose principal leaders, Buenos Aires governor Antonio CAFIERO and La Rioja governor Carlos Saúl MENEM, emerged as the leading Peronist contenders for presidential nomination. During lower house poll, the two major groups drew more than 79 percent of the vote, although the UCR slipped from majority to plurality status by retaining only 117 of 254 seats. In primary balloting in July 1988, Menem and the UCR's Eduardo César ANGELOZ were formally selected as their parties' standard-bearers for the presidential poll, which yielded a Peronist victory on May 14, 1989. The combined vote of the two parties in the presidential balloting was a little more than 84 percent, with the Peronists outpolling the UCR in 23 of 24 electoral districts.

Although they were not scheduled to be inaugurated until December 10, Menem and his running mate, Eduardo Alberto DUHALDE, were sworn in on July 8, following congressional acceptance of their predecessors' early resignations. The unprecedented early transfer resulted from suddenly escalating commodity prices in late May that necessitated the declaration of a state of siege to contain widespread food riots. However, Menem's standing in the opinion polls, which had reached a peak of 74 percent in September, plunged to a low of 31 percent by the end of the year because of his inability to halt the downward economic spiral.

In early December 1990 the army responded to the country's economic problems, as well as to the imprisonment of officers associated with the "dirty war" of 1976–1983, with its fourth revolt in three years. The government moved quickly, however, to counter the dissidents, who had seized the army headquarters in central Buenos Aires immediately prior to a state visit by U.S. President George H. W. Bush. A nationalist military faction headed by (former) Colonel Mohamed Alí SEINELDIN, who was under arrest at the time, reportedly staged the uprising. Thereafter, despite widespread popular opposition, Menem issued pardons for a number of former presidents and military leaders convicted of criminal acts during the period of military rule, as well as for former *Montonero* guerrilla leader Mario FIRMENICH and several others.

Largely because of continued implementation of stringent economic reforms, including the introduction of full currency convertibility in March, inflation plunged in 1991, yielding an unexpectedly strong Peronist showing in provincial and federal legislative elections between August and October. One of the victors was Vice President Duhalde, who resigned his federal post on December 5 to assume the governorship of Buenos Aires province.

In mid-1993 President Menem indicated that, subsequent to forthcoming congressional balloting, he might call a national referendum on constitutional reform, the most important component of which would permit him to seek reelection. However, as the Peronists secured an unprecedented victory at the poll of October 3, on November 14 Menem and opposition leader Alfonsín concluded a "Democratic Pact" (Olivos Pact) (see Constitution and government, below) that made the referendum unnecessary.

At Constituent Assembly balloting on April 10, 1994, both of the leading formations experienced setbacks. The Peronists were held to a plurality of 136 seats on a 37.7 percent share of the vote, while the UCR won 75 seats on a 19.9 percent vote share. The most striking gain was registered by the left-of-center Broad Front (*Frente Grande*—FG) coalition, which captured 31 seats as contrasted with only 3 chamber seats in 1993.

In the general election of May 14, 1995, Menem surpassed poll projections by easily winning direct election to a new four-year mandate on a 49.8 percent vote share—20.6 percent more than that of his nearest competitor, José Octavio BORDON, who headed a recently formed leftist coalition (the Front for a Country in Solidarity [*Frente del País Solidario*—Frepaso]), that included the FG. By contrast, the UCR candidate, Horatio MASSACCESI, came in third with 17.1 percent of the vote. The PJ, as the Peronists were formally known, also won control of a majority of lower house seats and 9 of 14 contested provincial governorships. Further rounds of regional balloting later in the year gave the PJ control of 14 of the country's 23 provinces; the UCR won 5 of the remainder while provincial parties won the other 4. However, in a dramatic reversal in Buenos Aires' first-ever mayoral election on June 30, 1996, the UCR candidate, Fernando DE LA RÚA, swept to victory with a 39.8 percent vote share, while the incumbent, Jorge DOMINGUEZ, placed third in the four-candidate field with 18.8 percent.

In nationwide balloting on October 26, 1997, the Peronists lost control of the Chamber of Deputies by winning only 51 of 127 contested seats; the opposition UCR and Frepaso secured 46 seats in coalition and an additional 17 seats on separate lists.

On October 24, 1999, opposition presidential candidate de la Rúa defeated the PJ's Duhalde with a 48.5 percent vote share. In simultaneous balloting for 130 of 257 Chamber of Deputies' seats, representation of the president-elect's Alliance for Work, Justice and Education (*Alianza por Trabajo, Justicia y Educación*—ATJE) rose to 127, which, with the support of third-party allies, gave it a working majority.

The de la Rúa administration was shaken by a bribery scandal in September 2000 that prompted a cabinet reshuffle on October 5. Protesting the retention of two ministers who had been implicated in the affair, Vice President Carlos Alberto ALVAREZ resigned the following day, his Senate presidency being assumed by the president pro tempore, Mario Aníbal LOSADA.

In congressional balloting on October 14, 2001, the Peronists regained control of both houses, the ATJE winning only 88 of 257 Chamber and 25 of 72 Senate seats. Two months later, on December 20, President de la Rúa resigned in the face of widespread public protests and generalized disorder sparked by a sharp and severe economic decline, and Senate President Ramón PUERTA became his temporary successor. On December 23 a special joint session of legislators and provincial governors elected the Peronist governor of San Luis, Adolfo RODRÍGUEZ Saá, as interim chief executive. Rodríguez Saá was popularly applauded when he immediately declared a moratorium on the payment of Argentina's international debt, but many established politicians did not back him on the measure. Rodríguez Saá resigned on December 30, his office devolving briefly on the president of the Chamber of Deputies, Eduardo CAMAÑO, before passing by another joint election to former vice president Eduardo Duhalde on January 1, 2002. Duhalde quickly ended the convertibility regime and allowed the peso to float. He chose Néstor Carlos KIRCHNER, a governor from the remote province of Santa Cruz, as his preferred successor, rejecting Menem. In first-round presidential balloting on April 27, 2003, former president Menem narrowly outpolled Kirchner, a fellow Peronist, with a plurality of 24.3 percent. On May 14, however, Menem withdrew from a runoff after it became apparent that the other minor candidates would support Kirchner. Kirchner and his running mate, Daniel SCIOLI, were subsequently inaugurated on May 25.

Before the legislative poll of October 23, 2005, Kirchner waged a bitter struggle with his immediate predecessor, Duhalde, over control of the PJ, while launching on August 24 a Victory Front grouping to contest constituencies where his supporters did not possess majorities. The strategy yielded a substantial victory for the *kirchneristas,* who won 69 of 127 contested seats in the Chamber of Deputies and 17 of 24 in the Senate.

In 2005 the Supreme Court annulled several amnesty laws that had protected low-ranking officers during the "dirty war," who argued that they had acted in due obedience.

In August 2006 congress voted to give President Kirchner expanded powers, including the ability to make alterations to the budget without congressional approval and to issue executive decrees. Concurrently,

Kirchner agreed to make Supreme Court judicial nominations more transparent and to reduce the size of the court from 9 to 5 (reversing the Menem expansion in 1990). He also reduced the size of the Magistrates' Council from 20 to 13 members, 5 of whom he appointed.

President Kirchner was widely credited with challenging the impunity granted by the Menem administration to those involved in the authoritarian excesses during the 1976–1983 junta rule. The president called for the prosecution of numerous officials who had been covered by the previous amnesty agreement. The challenge to impunity most prominently led to the overturning of pardons of Jorge VIDELA, the first leader of the military junta, and Albano HARGUINDEGUY and José Martínez de HOZ, former interior and economic ministers, respectively.

President Kirchner declined to stand in the 2007 election, announcing on July 1 that his wife, Senator Cristina FERNÁNDEZ de Kirchner, would be a candidate to succeed him, fueling speculation that the presidential couple aimed to circumvent constitutional convention by holding rotating presidencies the maximum number of terms. Other presidential candidates included former finance minister Roberto LAVAGNA, who enjoyed the backing of some more conservative PJ dissidents, including the Duhalde family, and some UCR members. Anti-Kirchner Peronists, including former presidents Menem and Puerta, supported Alberto Rodríguez Saá, representing the Union and Liberty Party (*Alianza Frente Justicia Union y Libertad*—JUL).

In presidential balloting on October 28, 2007, Cristina Fernández de Kirchner secured 44.9 percent of votes, precluding a recount by exceeding the 40 percent threshold to become Argentina's first elected woman president. Her nearest rival, Elisa María Avelina CARRIÓ of the Alternative for a Republic of Equals (*Alternativa para una República de Iguales*—ARI), represented the Civic Coalition (*Coalición Cívica*—CC) with a 23 percent vote share, followed by Roberto Lavagna of the Concertation Alliance (*Alianza Concertación UNA*—AC) with 16.9 percent. In concurrent legislative elections for half of the Chamber of Deputies and one-third of the Senate, the Victory Front (*Frente para la Victoria*—FPV) secured a plurality. Progovernment parties gained seats in both houses, while the center-left CC was the only opposition party to make any gains. Others, particularly the UCR and the Republican Proposal (*Propuesta Republicana*—PRO), lost ground.

In the 2009 midterm elections, which the president insisted be moved up to June 28, the PJ lost its majority in both houses of congress, and former president Kirchner was defeated in his congressional bid for Buenos Aires Province. Candidates from Civic and Social Accord (*Acuerdo Civico y Social*—ACS), a grouping of the UCR, the Socialist Party, CC, and others increased their seats in the lower chamber by 19 and in the Senate by 5. The center-right Union-Pro added 31 seats to become the third most powerful group. The FPV and its allies lost 25 seats in the lower house; its control of the Senate also slipped, but the party held onto a plurality in both houses. Ahead of the voting, the government was criticized for its handling of the outbreaks of dengue fever and the flu that killed hundreds. The administration's health minister, who later resigned, had recommended postponing the elections to help prevent the spread of the flu.

Observers said the election was a referendum on the president's two years in office and that the results reflected public discontent with her policies and style of governing. Following a report in July by President Fernández and her husband that their personal wealth had increased by 571 percent since 2003, CC opposition deputies demanded an investigation into the source of their wealth, alleging that the couple had engaged in illegal land speculation while holding office. The Kirchners were subsequently acquitted of the charges.

President Fernández reshuffled the cabinet on July 6, 2009, and won a major congressional victory with an extension of presidential powers that included the right to fix agricultural export taxes. In minor cabinet reshuffles, the minister of education was replaced on July 23, and on October 1 a ministry of agriculture, livestock, and fisheries was created.

In October the administration unveiled a sweeping electoral reform bill, subsequently approved by the legislature, that required parties to have open primaries, banned private campaign financing, reduced the length of political campaigns, and effectively removed some of the many tiny political parties by instituting minimum membership requirements and requiring that parties obtain at least 2 percent of the vote in two consecutive general elections to remain viable.

In early 2010 President Fernández sacked the country's central bank chief after he had blocked her attempt to use $6.6 billion to service the country's debt. He was later reinstated by a judge. In March, a court upheld the president's plan to use the bank's reserves to pay down international debt. In June the foreign minister quit, reportedly as a result of disagreements with the president over foreign policy.

Meanwhile, the sudden death in October of Néstor Kirchner cast a large measure of uncertainty on the political landscape, as Kirchner had been expected by many to again seek the presidency in 2011, with the two of them possibly alternating in power for years to come. He had continued to play a powerful role behind the scenes of government; the media regarded him as a de facto co-president and referred to the first couple as "Los K." In the wake of his death, analysts speculated there would be a scramble for power since Kirchner would not be there to control the various actors.

Attention in December turned to the sentencing of former dictator Jorge Videla for the torture and murders of 31 political prisoners during the "dirty war." He received a life sentence while already serving another life sentence for other human rights violations. A new security ministry was created that same month following fears of increasing crime after some 6,000 homeless people occupied public and private property to protest the government's housing policies.

Protests occurred in January 2011 when members of four farmers' unions, opposing export taxes, stopped grain sales for four days. Judicial cases continued against high-ranking officials involved in the "dirty war," and in April former president Bignone received a life sentence for crimes committed during that period. He was already serving a 25-year sentence for crimes against humanity. Eight former military officers received life sentences in May for the torture and murder of 11 political prisoners, and in July two former top-level officers from the "dirty war" era were sentenced to life imprisonment for human rights violations.

Cristina Fernández formally announced that she would seek reelection on June 23, 2011, two days before the deadline. She chose as her running mate Economy Minister Amado BOUDOU. Six challengers were on the ballot. On August 14, 2011, she won Argentina's first national, open primary election with 50 percent of the votes. Voting was compulsory in the poll, which was designed to screen out minor presidential candidates. Entrants had to receive more than 1.5 percent of the vote to advance to the October ballot. The president's strong showing was the result of a combination of factors, including public sympathy following the death of her husband, the weak and fragmented opposition, and the country's dynamic economic growth, higher wages, and increased public spending on social welfare programs. In the year since her husband's death, Fernández had proven able to govern in her own right.

Fernández was reelected for a second four-year term with 54 percent of the vote in multiparty presidential elections on October 23, 2011. Her 37 percent margin of victory was the largest in the country's history. In concurrent legislative elections for 130 seats in the Chamber of Deputies and 24 seats in the Senate, the Victory Front won enough seats to regain control of both houses. The PJ-FPV also won eight of the nine governors elected the same day.

In her acceptance speech, President Fernández promised to "continue the [national] project" begun by her husband, but their unorthodox economic strategy was becoming more difficult to manage. True to their populist roots, the two presidents focused on stimulating the domestic market through numerous social welfare programs to benefit the poor, ranging from fuel subsidies to payments for parents who send their children to school. Buenos Aires could not fund these programs with international loans, as the government's default on $100 billion of sovereign debt in 2001 had blacklisted it with international lenders. Instead, they financed these programs with high taxes on commodities exports, as well as trade with Brazil. The $30 billion gained from nationalizing private pension funds in 2010 helped fill the gap.

Soon after being sworn in for her second term, the president underwent surgery for thyroid cancer. She temporarily stepped down as president, and Vice President Boudou assumed her responsibilities from January 4–24, 2012. The cancer diagnosis later proved incorrect.

Constitution and government. After Argentina returned to civilian rule in 1983, most of the constitutional structure of 1853 was reintroduced. The president and vice president were again designated for nonrenewable six-year terms by an electoral college chosen on the basis of proportional representation, with each electoral district having twice as many electors as the combined number of senators and deputies. The National Congress consisted of a 46-member Senate, one-third being replenished every three years, and a 254-member Chamber of Deputies, one-half being elected every two years. The judicial system encompassed a Supreme Court, federal appeals courts, and provincial structures including supreme and subsidiary judicial bodies.

In 1993 President Carlos Menem negotiated an agreement (in what became known as the Olivos Pact [Democratic Pact]) on constitutional change that would allow reelection of the president in exchange for reducing the presidential mandate from six to four years. The pact also reduced some of the powers of the president over other branches.

The constitution of August 1994 provided for direct election of the president and vice president for four-year terms, with the possibility of one consecutive renewal. (First-round election requires a 45 percent majority [40 percent in the event of a gap greater than 10 percent between the two leading contenders].) Newly created was the post of cabinet chief (*jefe de gabinete*), a coordinating position filled by presidential appointment, subject to recall by an absolute majority of each of the legislative chambers.

The number of senators from each province was increased from two to three under the 1994 basic law revisions, the added member to represent the leading opposition party or group. The senatorial mandate, on the other hand, was shortened from nine years to six, with replenishment of one-third by direct election every two years commencing in the year 2001. The Chamber of Deputies continued to be renewed by halves every two years.

The 1994 basic law provided for an auditor general nominated by the largest opposition party and for a people's defender (ombudsman) appointed for a once-renewable five-year term by a two-thirds vote of each legislative chamber. It also affirmed Argentina's sovereignty over the Malvinas, South Georgia, and South Sandwich islands.

There are 23 provinces (Tierra del Fuego having been upgraded from the status of a National Territory in 1991), plus the Federal District of Buenos Aires. The provinces elect their own governors and legislatures and retain those powers not specifically delegated to the federal government; in practice, however, there has been a history of substantial federal intervention in provincial affairs. Included in the current constitution is a provision that the mayor of Buenos Aires (formerly a presidential appointee) also be directly elected.

Province and Capital	*Area (sq. mi.)*	*Population (2010E)*
Buenos Aires (La Plata)	118,843	15,625,000
Catamarca (Catamarca)	38,540	368,000
Chaco (Resistencia)	38,468	1,055,000
Chubut (Rawson)	86,751	509,000
Córdoba (Córdoba)	65,161	3,309,000
Corrientes (Corrientes)	34,054	993,000
Entre Ríos (Paraná)	29,427	1,236,000
Formosa (Formosa)	27,825	530,000
Jujuy (San Salvador de Jujuy)	20,548	673,000
La Pampa (Santa Rosa)	55,382	319,000
La Rioja (La Rioja)	35,649	334,000
Mendoza (Mendoza)	58,239	1,739,000
Misiones (Posadas)	11,506	1,102,000
Neuquén (Neuquén)	36,324	551,000
Río Negro (Viedma)	78,383	639,000
Salta (Salta)	59,759	1,214,000
San Juan (San Juan)	33,257	681,000
San Luis (San Luis)	29,632	432,000
Santa Cruz (Río Gallegos)	94,186	274,000
Santa Fé (Santa Fé)	51,354	3,195,000
Santiago del Estero (Santiago del Estero)	52,222	874,000
Tierra del Fuego (Ushuaia)	8,074	127,000
Tucumán (San Miguel de Tucumán)	8,697	1,448,000
Federal District		
Distrito Federal (Buenos Aires)	77	2,890,000

Reporters Without Borders ranked Argentina 54th out of 179 countries in its 2013 Index of Press Freedom. The country slipped seven places due to ongoing tension between the government and the Clarin media group.

Foreign relations. Argentina has traditionally maintained an independent foreign policy and has been reluctant to follow U.S. leadership in hemispheric and world affairs. Argentina claims territory in the Antarctic (see entry on Antarctica) and, despite the outcome of the 1982 war with Britain, continues to assert its long-standing claim to sovereignty over the Falklands (*Islas Malvinas*). The latter has won support at the UN General Assembly, which, since the cessation of hostilities, has repeatedly called on the claimants to initiate negotiations on a peaceful resolution of the dispute.

Relations with Chile became tense following the announcement in May 1977 that a panel of international arbitrators had awarded Chile the ownership of three disputed islands in the Beagle Channel, just north of Cape Horn. As in the case of the Falklands, there is evidence of petroleum in the area. Argentina repudiated the decision in January 1978. A 19-month mediation effort by Pope John Paul II resulted in a proposal that endorsed the awarding of the three islands to Chile while limiting the assignment of offshore rights on the Atlantic side of the Cape Horn meridian. The proposal was rejected by the Argentine junta but accepted by Raúl Alfonsín before his election as president of Argentina, and a treaty ending the century-old dispute was narrowly ratified by the Argentine Senate in March 1985. Additional border issues were ostensibly resolved by an agreement between presidents Menem of Argentina and Frei of Chile in 1991, but its terms drew opposition in both countries because of an "additional protocol" concluded by the two chief executives in late 1996. It was not until June 1999 that ratifications were completed on the Continental Glaciers Treaty that resolved the last remaining border dispute between the two countries.

For nearly a decade Argentina was embroiled in a dispute with Brazil over water rights on the Paraná River. In October 1979, however, both countries joined Paraguay in signing an agreement that not only resolved differences over Brazil's Itaipú Dam, the world's largest, but also freed the way for cooperative exploitation of the Uruguay River. Economic linkage between the continent's two largest states was further enhanced on December 10, 1986, with the signing by presidents Alfonsín and Sarney of 20 accords launching an ambitious economic integration effort. Under the plan, a customs union was established for most capital goods as of January 1, 1987, with cooperation in the exchange of food products, the promotion of bilateral industrial ventures, the establishment of a $200 million joint investment fund, and joint energy development (including a new $2 billion hydroelectric facility) to follow. President Sanguinetti of Uruguay, who was at the meeting, pledged his "determined support" for the move and agreed to a series of ministerial-level talks designed to pave the way for his country's participation in the integration process. The result was the signing in Asunción, Paraguay, on March 26, 1991, of a four-nation treaty (including the host country) providing for the formation of the Southern Cone Common Market (*Mercado Común del Cono Sur*—Mercosur).

In 1988 Argentina and Brazil agreed to cooperate in the nuclear power industry. While neither was a signatory of the Nuclear Non-Proliferation Treaty (see entry on the International Atomic Energy Agency), the two countries formally rejected the development of nuclear weaponry in a July 1991 accord that also banned the introduction of such arms from external sources. In addition, the Argentine Chamber of Deputies, after a lengthy delay, voted in November 1993 to ratify the 1967 Treaty of Tlatelolco (see entry on the Agency for the Prohibition of Nuclear Weapons in Latin America and the Caribbean), which bans nuclear weapons from the continent.

Although insisting during the 1989 presidential campaign that Argentina would recover the Falklands "even if blood has to be spilled," Menem subsequently indicated that he was prepared to engage in a "civilized dialogue" with Britain, particularly if the latter were to abandon its economic zone around the islands. At the conclusion of a second round of talks in Spain on February 15, 1990, an agreement was reached to restore full diplomatic relations.

Tensions with Britain heightened in August 1993 as the result of a suggestion that the Falkland Islanders be given cash awards by Buenos Aires to lift their opposition to Argentine sovereignty claims, coupled with the introduction by Britain of a new fishing licensing regime for the waters around South Georgia and the South Sandwich Islands. Soon after that issue was settled, a British geological survey suggested that the undersea oil potential in the Falklands area appeared to be substantially greater than in Britain's North Sea fields. The result was a major agreement signed in New York in September 1995 for joint oil and gas exploration in a 7,000-square-mile area southwest of the disputed islands (see Contested Territory).

In October 1998 President Menem traveled to Britain for the first such visit by an Argentine chief executive in four decades. Although he insisted during his stay that the question of sovereignty over the Falklands remained nonnegotiable, tension between the former combatants manifestly eased, and in mid-December the administration of Prime Minister Tony Blair announced that the British arms embargo would be relaxed. In mid-1999 an agreement was reached on the restoration of air traffic with the mainland and a resumption of visits to the territory by Argentina. However, Blair did not discuss the issue of sovereignty in August 2001 during a visit (the first by a British prime minister). The Argentinean hard line continued under President Kirchner, who, in April 2005, emphasized his government's commitment to "full recovery" of the islands.

With growth in Argentine exports to Brazil in 2003–2004 scarcely more than 10 percent of Brazil's to Argentina, Buenos Aires complained of Mercosur's "economic asymmetries." Argentina also objected to Brazil's posture as regional leader in its bid for a seat on the UN Security Council. Brazilian-Argentine relations continued to decline as Argentina turned much of its trade attention toward Venezuela, with which President Kirchner, as a "progressive Peronist," desired closer ties. Venezuela agreed to supply lower-priced oil to Argentina, and trade with Venezuela grew from $140 million in 204 to over $2 billion in 2013.

Relations with Iran became strained on November 18, 2006, when an Argentine judge issued warrants for former Iranian president Akbar Rafsanjani and eight other former Iranian officials for allegedly backing the bombing of a Jewish community center in Buenos Aires on July 18, 1994, that killed 85 people. The judge argued that the Lebanese group Hezbollah had been implicated in the bombing and that the Iranian officials were potentially liable because of their financial support of Hezbollah.

The warm ties between Argentina and Venezuela negatively affected U.S.-Argentine relations, especially after the Argentine government hosted Venezuelan president Chávez in Buenos Aires in March 2007 for a counter rally to the simultaneous visit of U.S. President George W. Bush to Uruguay.

Relations with Uruguay deteriorated as a result of Argentine opposition to the decision of a Finnish company, Botnia, to invest in a pulp mill along the Uruguay River, which forms the border between the two countries. Argentine protesters claimed that the mill would bring pollution and that Argentina should have been consulted on the project. The Spanish company Ence subsequently decided to move a related project to a less controversial section of Uruguay. President Néstor Kirchner, President-elect Cristina Fernández de Kirchner, President Tabaré Vazquez of Uruguay, and the king of Spain met in Chile in November 2007 to discuss the pulp mill. The following week, while negotiations continued in Chile, Vazquez closed the Uruguayan border with Argentina and gave the green light for the inauguration of the mill.

President Fernández sought to expand ties with Venezuela and Cuba in 2009, signing energy, agricultural, and industrial agreements with the former and bilateral agreements with the latter. She also visited the former Cuban leader Fidel Castro.

The long-standing dispute over pulp mills on the Uruguay River was resolved in April 2010 by an order of the International Court of Justice (ICJ), which ruled that though Uruguay had failed to inform Argentina about the mills, they did not pollute the river, negating the reason advanced to shut them down. Cordial relations were resumed between the two countries, and in August 2011 Argentina and Uruguay signed several bilateral agreements.

Argentina summoned the UK ambassador in December 2012 to express its dismay over London's naming 437,000 square miles of territory in Antarctica "Queen Elizabeth Land." Buenos Aires has claimed the same area for Argentina.

Fernández complicated efforts to prosecute Iranians in the 1994 attack on an Argentine Jewish community center in January 2013, announcing that she and the Iranian government had agreed to establish a "truth commission" to re-examine evidence in the case. However, many suspects are now high-ranking government officials in Iran, including Defense Minister Ahmad Vahidi, and would not be subject to the commission's authority.

President Fernández was not invited to the April 2013 funeral of Margaret Thatcher, who had been prime minister during the 1982 UK-Argentina war over the Falkland Islands. Foreign Minister Héctor TIMERMAN branded the snub "yet another provocation."

Current issues. Kirchner's second term concentrated on economic issues, including the nationalization of key sectors, controversy over economic indicators, and placing controls on foreign currency holdings. Two days after winning reelection, the president changed a 2002 decree so that oil, gas, and mining companies would now have to repatriate 100 percent of their export revenue, instead of the original 30 percent. The change was made to staunch capital flight, estimated at the time as $3 billion per month. On April 16 President Fernández announced plans to nationalize 51 percent (estimated value of $5 billion) of Spanish-owned Yacimientos Petrolíferos Fiscales (YPF), the largest oil company operating in Argentina. She maintained that the company was not adequately investing and producing in the Argentinian market, so it had become necessary to re-nationalize YPF from Repsol. After all, it had been a state-owned business for 70 years before being privatized in the 1990s. The move was popular with voters, if not with other potential investors. Experts pointed to a lack of capital investment in the oil sector as the real cause of Argentina's 2011 shift to becoming a net importer of gas.

Much less popular, the government has begun to cancel many of its subsidy programs. In January, ticket prices for the Buenos Aires subway rose 127 percent, with similar price hikes for electricity, gas, and water.

In March, the president reconfigured the relationship between the government and the Central Bank. Specifically, she secured unlimited use of the Central Bank's funds to pay government debts. Critics decried the end of bank independence.

Experts have accused the government of regularly underestimating the inflation rate in official publications since 2007. When economists and journalists became aware of the situation, they began publishing alternative inflation rates, usually 25–30 percent per year, only to be fined $125,000 and then sued by the government for deliberately "misleading" the public. The manipulated data has helped the government save $6.8 billion in interest payments since 2007. In addition, experts suspect the government has raised GDP figures by two percentage points each year. On February 1, 2013, the IMF officially reprimanded Argentina and ordered it to correct its statistical calculations or face sanctions.

Uneasy about currency values, many Argentinians sought to convert their pesos into more stable U.S. dollars, triggering cash flow problems. The government responded by limiting individual foreign currency holdings and banned dollar-denominated savings accounts. In February 2012 the government imposed daily limits on cash transactions (1,000 pesos) and ruled that individuals and firms must receive approval before importing any foreign goods. As a result of the new rules, capital flight dropped from $21.5 billion in 2011 to $3.4 billion in 2012. At the same time, a black market in dollars has emerged, the government has had to dip into reserve funds, and 2012 brought the first budget deficit since 1996. In February 2013 the government took the unusual step of asking supermarkets to freeze their prices for 60 days.

Vice President Boudou—along with his girlfriend, Augustina Kampfer, business partner, José María Nuñez, and business associate, Alejandro Vandenbroele—was accused of influence-peddling related to Ciccone Calcográfica, a printing company facing bankruptcy while he was minister of the economy. Attempts to impeach Boudou failed, given the PJ-FPV majorities in both houses of parliament. Instead, in March 2012 the Central Bank of Argentina awarded Ciccone Calcográfica a lucrative contract to print currency, and in August the Chamber of Deputies voted to nationalize the printing company, now known as South American Values Company.

Anti-government protests grew in size and frequency in 2012 and 2013, as citizens took to the streets to protest the government's belt-tightening policies and alleged corruption. For the first time since Fernandez's election, a one-day, nation-wide strike took place on November 21. The president's approval rating fell from 54 percent in October 2011 to 33.5 percent in October 2013.

Argentina continued to prosecute cases involving genocide and crimes against humanity during the "dirty war" era. Three former army officers were sentenced to life in prison in October 2012, as were another 23 former officials in December. Former president Bignone was convicted in March for ordering the kidnapping, torture, and rape of 23 women at the Campo de Mayo detention center from 1978 to 1983.

On October 31, 2012, the government lowered the voting age from 18 to 16, although 16- and 17-year-olds were exempted from mandatory voting regulations.

Former President Menem, former defense minister Oscar Camilión, and 11 other former officials on March 8 were convicted of smuggling illegal arms to Croatia and Ecuador in the 1990s. On March 13 the archbishop of Buenos Aires, Cardinal Jorge Mario MERGOGLIO, was elected to head the Roman Catholic Church. President Fernández flew to Rome to witness his installation as Pope Francis and asked him to intervene in the Falkland Islands dispute.

Congress passed legislation on April 25 to increase the Council of Magistrates, which controls lower-court appointments, from 13 members to 19. Twelve of the members would now be elected by popular vote and must have a political party affiliation. The judicial workers union condemned the change for politicizing the courts and staged a three-day strike that brought out over 1 million protestors across the country. The Supreme Court later struck down the election provision.

Fernández shuffled her cabinet in May, moving Arturo PURICELLI from Defense to Security, shifting Agustin ROSSI from the Chamber of Deputies to Defense, and Nilda GARRE from Security to the Organization of American States. The president also announced $3.2 billion in new social spending, mainly for families and pregnant women.

The legislative primary election took place on August 11. Designed by the president to weed out small parties by imposing a 1.5 percent minimum vote, instead her FPV suffered its worst showing in its existence. The FPV won a plurality of 26 percent, but lost in 14 of 23 provinces and the capital. Turnout was 75 percent.

Three weeks before the October 27 legislative elections, President Fernández disappeared from public view. Her office first reported that she had been ordered to rest for a month following a head injury, but later that she had emergency surgery on October 8 to drain a blood clot in her brain. Little information was released to the public, and it was not clear if power had been formally transferred to Vice President Boudou, who has been discredited by corruption charges. In any case, Fernández was absent from the last days of the campaign, under doctor's orders to rest.

The FPV was the top vote-getter on October 27, with 33 percent, but it did not secure the two-thirds majority needed to amend the constitution to allow a third term for Fernández. The Renewal Front, led by FPV defector Sergio MASSA, defeated the FPV in Buenos Aires province by 12 percentage points. The FPV remains the only party viable in every state, but political momentum appears to be shifting from the populist regions to the large cities. The FPV placed third in the four largest districts.

Candidates thus immediately began to look ahead toward the 2015 presidential election and the post-Kirchner era.

POLITICAL PARTIES

Since 1999, the Peronists have been dominant, particularly the Victory Front (FPV), the *kirchenismo* wing founded in 2003 to sustain the presidential candidacy of Néstor Kirchner, which also attracted the support of the "K Radicals"—those UCR members who supported Fernández in the 2007 presidential elections. In June 2013 Sergei MASSA left the FPV to found the rival Renewal Front (*Frente Renovador*).

Political parties formed five loose coalitions ahead of the 2013 legislative election.

Federal Parties with Legislative Seats:

Justicialist Party (*Partido Justicialista*—PJ). What was formerly the Justicialist Nationalist Movement (*Movimiento Nacionalista Justicialista*—MNJ) grew out of the extreme nationalist Peronist (also known as *laborista*) movement led by General Juan Perón from 1946 to 1955. Formally dissolved after its leader went into exile, the Peronists regrouped, in alliance with a number of smaller parties, as the Justicialist Liberation Front (*Frente Justicialista de Liberación*—Frejuli) before the 1973 election. Frejuli's victorious candidate, Héctor Cámpora, subsequently resigned to permit the reelection of Perón, who had returned in 1972. The movement's nominal leader, Isabel Perón, who was ousted as her husband's successor in 1976 and confined to prison and house arrest for five years thereafter, was permitted to go into exile in July 1981.

The Peronists (as they are still popularly known) have experienced a number of internal cleavages, including one occasioned by the *corrientes renovadoras* ("current of renewal"), which was initially launched by a group of moderate trade unionists and students calling for a more democratic party structure.

Senator Vicente SAADI resigned as the first PJ vice president following the 1985 legislative election, reportedly because of the movement's poor showing. In December 1985 the *renovadores* appointed a leadership of their own, headed by Antonio CAFIERO, Carlos GROSSO, and Carlos Saúl Menem. However, a cleavage subsequently developed within the dissident troika, Cafiero boycotting a *renovador* congress in Tucumán, while Grosso withdrew from the meeting because of a dispute over the timing of internal party elections.

Following the party's relatively poor showing in the 1987 election, Senator Saadi resigned as PJ president, paving the way for a "unity slate" that awarded the group's presidency and vice presidency to Cafiero and Menem, respectively. Menem defeated Cafiero as the party's 1989 standard-bearer at a PJ presidential primary on July 9, 1988, and led the party, campaigning with minor party allies as the Justicialist Front of Popular Unity (*Frente Justicialista de Unidad Popular*—Frejupo), to a conclusive victory in the nationwide balloting of May 14, 1989.

The party contested the partial legislative elections of 1991, 1993, and 1995 under the *Partido Justicialista* rubric, although the total number of "*Justicialista*" seats resulting from each poll included seats held by affiliated Peronist groups. In 1995 President Menem secured reelection to a foreshortened term of four years on a 49.8 percent vote share while the PJ won its first absolute majority in the Chamber of Deputies. In 1997 the party's lower house representation was reduced to 118 of 257 seats. With Menem ineligible to run for a third term, the party lost the presidency in 1999 and was reduced to second place in the Chamber of Deputies with 110 seats. It recovered its majority in both houses on October 14, 2001, despite its leader's arrest, four months earlier, on charges of UN arms embargo violations.

Menem secured a plurality in the 2003 presidential poll, but he withdrew from a runoff when it became apparent that he could not defeat Néstor Kirchner in a two-man race. Late in the year, after taking up residence in Chile, Menem was charged with tax fraud; however, the case was dismissed in May 2004. Menem returned to Argentina in December 2004, secured election to the Senate on a "best loser" basis in October 2005, and vowed to contest the 2007 presidential election.

Before the 2005 congressional balloting, the PJ split into two principal factions, a **Victory Front** (*Frente para la Victoria*—FPV), launched by President Kirchner, and a **Federal Peronist** (*Peronismo Federal*—PF) grouping headed by former president Duhalde. In addition, former presidents Menem and Rodríguez Saá campaigned as leaders of a distinctly minor **Justicialist Loyalty and Dignity** (*Lealtad y Dignidad Justicialista*—LDJ) faction. Several members of the UCR formed a coalition with the FPV for the 2007 elections. As part of the FPV electoral ballot, the PJ secured 42 Senate and 129 Chamber seats after the election, a decisive majority in both houses. The president received 44.9 percent of the votes. The anti-Fernández/Kirchner groups were grouped under the **Federal Peronism** umbrella for the 2011 elections.

Former president Néstor Kirchner, Buenos Aires governor Daniel Sciolo, and cabinet chief Sergio Massa, the leaders of the PJ list of candidates in the June 2009 legislative elections, were widely accused of developing a strategy in which they would use their popularity and name recognition to win seats for the party, then step down and assume their former positions, allowing lesser-known replacements to succeed them and maintain a strong Peronist presence in the legislature. The FPV was dealt a significant blow in June 2009 legislative elections, when it lost seats in both chambers of congress and could no longer be certain of mustering the votes for a quorum. It lost 42 seats in the lower chamber and held 87. In the Senate it lost 11 seats to hold a total of 31. Also Kirchner, who was up for reelection and headed the party's list of candidates in the Buenos Aires voting district, unexpectedly came in second behind Union PRO with 32.1 percent of the vote. The FPV suffered losses in eight provinces and the federal district but fared better in more rural parts of the country.

However, the party recouped those losses in October 2011, adding one more Senate seat for a total of 32, and jumping from 87 in the lower house to 116. President Fernández was reelected with nearly 54 percent of the vote, but she was sidelined in October 2013 with significant health problems. In legislative elections on October 27, 2013, the FPV retained its majority in both houses, winning 47 seats in the lower house and 14 seats in the Senate.

Leaders: Cristina Fernández de KIRCHNER (President of the Republic, PJ-FPV), Eduardo Alberto DUHALDE (Former President of the Republic, PF, and 2011 PJ presidential candidate), Carlos Saúl MENEM (Former President of the Republic, LDJ), Adolfo RODRÍGUEZ Saá (Former President of the Republic, LDJ, and Federal Commitment–PJ 2011 presidential candidate).

Renewal Front (*Frente Renovador*—FR). Founded in June 2013 by Sergio MASSA, FR is an anti-Kirchnerist branch of the Peronist movement. Massa, previously chief of cabinet for President Fernández, is mayor of Tigre. Massa's campaign focused on the country's rising crime and falling economy. Based in Buenos Aires province, which is home to 37 percent of voters, FR won 43.9 percent of the votes cast in the October elections, winning 16 of 35 seats. FR beat the FPV by nearly 12 percentage points, making Massa the front-runner for the 2015 presidential race.

Leader: Sergio MASSA (Founder).

Progressive, Civic, and Social Front (*Frente Progresista Civico y Social*—FPCyS). Former Santa Fe Governor Hermes Binner created a new national center-left alliance to succeed the **Broad Progressive Front** (*Frente Amplio Progresista*—FAP) that he organized for the 2011 elections. Members included the **Radical Civic Union** (*Unión Cívica Radical*—UCR), the **Civic Coalition–ARI** (*Coalición Cívica*—CC), and the **Socialist Party** (*Partido Socialista*—PS). While the FPCyS was the largest alliance, the same cluster of parties made similar alliances in specific provinces, such as the **Union for Chaco** (*Union de Chaco*), the **Jujuyan Front** (*Frente Jujeño*), the Catamarca-based **Civic and Social Front** (*Frente Cívico y Social*—FCS), the **Union for a Better Life** (*Union Para Vivir Mejor*) in Santa Cruz, **Meeting for Corrientes** (*Encuentro por Corrientes*), **Formosan Broad Front** (*Frente Amplio Formoseno*), and the **Riojana Civic Force** (*Fuerza Civica Riojana*). The UCR ran separately in Córdoba, Mendoza, and Entre Rios. FPCyS and its allies secured 36 seats in the Chamber and 3 in the Senate.

Leaders: Hermes BINNER (Chair), Mario BARLETTA (UCR President), Paul Javkin (CC-ARI), Margarita STOLBIZER.

Together They Unite (*Juntos UNEN*—UNITE). After the poor showing of their founder, Elisa Carrió, in the 2011 presidential election, **Civic Coalition–ARI** (*Coalición Cívica*—CC) formed a new centrist alliance for the 2013 legislative elections in Buenos Aires. Joining CC-ARI were the **Radical Civic Union** (*Unión Cívica Radical*—UCR), **South Project Movement** (*Movimiento Proyecto Sur*), and the **Freemen of the South Movement** (*Movimiento Libres del Sur),* led by Victoria DONDA and Carrió. The alliance won 5 deputy seats and 1 senate seat.

Leaders: Pino SOLANAS (South Project Movement), Ricardo Gil LAVEDRA (Parliamentary chair, UCR), Elisa CARRIÓ.

Civic Coalition–ARI (*Coalición Cívica*—CC). Elisa Carrió created the CC, which was founded as a coalition of political parties, nongovernmental organizations, and public personalities, on April 11, 2007. It was re-created as a party in 2009, including the **Alternative for a Republic of Equals** (*Alternativa por una República de Iguales*—ARI, see the 2013 *Handbook*), Union for Everybody (*Unión por Todos*—UPT), and some members of the Socialist Party and the UCR. The CC secured 2 seats in the upper house and 18 in the lower house. In advance of June 2009 legislative balloting the group formed an alliance called the Civic and Social Accord (*Acuerdo Civico y Social*—ACS; see Political Background, above) with the UCR, the PS, and other center-left candidates. It gained 1 seat in the lower house for a total of 19 and maintained 2 seats in the Senate. The party performed dismally in the 2011 elections, dropping to six deputies and one senator. Carrió again ran for the presidency in 2011 but finished with less than 2 percent of the vote.

Leaders: Paul JAVKIN (Secretary General), Hector Horacio PIEMONTE.

Union for Everyone (*Unión por Todos*—UPT). The UPT was founded in 2002 by Patricia Bullrich, a former minister who held the social security portfolio in 2000 and the labor portfolio in 2001. The party joined the CC for the 2007 election. It picked up one Chamber seat in 2009 legislative balloting. In 2013 UPT allied with PRO.

Leaders: Patricia BULLRICH (Founder), Juan Pablo ARENAZA (President).

Radical Civic Union (*Unión Cívica Radical*—UCR). The UCR, whose history dates from the late 19th century, represents the moderate left in Argentine politics. In the period following the deposition of Juan Perón, the party split into two factions, the People's Radical Party (*Unión Cívica Radical del Pueblo*—UCRP) and the Intransigent Radical Party (*Unión Cívica Radical Intransigente*—UCRI), led by former presidents Arturo ILLÍA and Arturo FRONDIZI, respectively. The UCR reemerged following the legalization of parties in 1971 and remained relatively unified during the 1973 presidential candidacy of Dr. Ricardo BALBÍN but suffered a number of internal cleavages thereafter. Balbín was instrumental in organizing the 1981 five-party alignment to press for a return to civilian rule but died in September, leaving the party without a unified leadership. Largely because of the personal popularity of its presidential candidate, Raúl Alfonsín, the party led the 1983 balloting with 51.8 percent of the vote, winning, in addition to the presidency, a majority in the Chamber of Deputies. Subsequently, internal dissention diminished, the *balbinista* faction concluding a late 1984 alliance with left-leaning elements, while the long-standing policy of incompatibility between government and party roles was abandoned with the designation of President Alfonsín as ex officio party leader. In early 1986, as the issue of presidential succession loomed, a new rivalry emerged between former labor minister Juan Manuel Casella, the apparent *alfonsinista* front-runner, and the influential governor of Córdoba province, Eduardo Angeloz, with the latter being designated the UCR candidate at internal party balloting in July 1988 but losing to the MNJ's Carlos Menem in May 1989.

In October 1991, following the poor showing of candidates he had endorsed for recent provincial elections, Alfonsín submitted his resignation as party president, while announcing the formation of an internal faction, the Movement for Social Democracy (*Movimiento por la Democracia Social*—MDS), devoted to defending traditional UCR "social-democratic" principles. He was reelected party leader by an overwhelming margin in November 1993.

In the 1995 presidential poll, UCR nominee Horatio MASSACESSI placed a distant third, with a 17.1 percent vote share; in the legislative balloting the party retained second rank, though its representation fell from 83 to 69 seats. Alfonsín again resigned on September 27, 1995, and was replaced on November 17 by Rodolfo TERRANGO.

For the legislative election of October 26, 1997, an alliance with a left-of-center electoral coalition styled the Front for a Country in Solidarity (*Frente del País Solidario*—Frepaso) yielded 46 of 127 contested seats, while the UCR secured 12 seats running separately. The alliance candidate, Fernando De La Rúa, won the presidency in 1999, but he resigned in December 2001 because of the economic crisis. The UCR's share of the presidential vote plummeted to 2.3 percent in 2003. It remained the second-ranked congressional party after the 2005 balloting, albeit with only 39 of 257 lower house seats.

The centralization of power in the hands of President Kirchner and his increased ability to control governors made him very popular among so-called "K Radicals" in the UCR. Others in the party preferred either supporting Roberto Lavagna (apparently still formally a member of the PJ) in the 2007 presidential balloting or presenting a candidate from the UCR ranks. After considerable negotiation, it was determined that Lavagna would run as a candidate of the UCR in an alliance with Just Society Peronists (Duhalde). Within the UCR, Lavagna had strong support from former president Alfonsín. The UCR decided not to run a candidate for president and ultimately coalesced behind Roberto Lavagna, who received 16.9 percent of the votes. The party lost 5 seats in the Senate and 16 in the Chamber of Deputies, leaving it with 8 senators and 24 deputies in the lower house.

The UCR expelled former governor and newly inaugurated vice president Cobos and four other governors who supported Kirchner in the elections. On March 15, 2008, under the banner of "K Radicals" Cobos urged like-minded politicians to join an Official National Concertation (*Concertación Nacional Oficial*) and to persuade the UCR leadership not to expel them but to support formation of a new Radicals for Concertation grouping. Cobos was reinstated by the UCR in early 2009, reportedly in response to a dying wish from former president Raúl Alfonsín.

The UCR, CC, PS, and other center left candidates struck an agreement in late April to form the ACS alliance, presenting a unified list of candidates for the June 2009 legislative elections in 11 provinces. The UCR improved its representation in the congress during the election, increasing to 14 Senate seats and 43 deputy seats. The ACS alliance ended in May 2011. The party kept its 14 Senate seats in the 2011 elections, but lost 5 seats in the lower house, dropping to 38. UCR presidential candidate Ricardo ALFONSIN placed third, with 11.14 percent of the vote.

Leaders: Mario BARLETTA (President of the Party), Ricardo ALFONSIN (2011 presidential candidate), Angel ROZAS, Leopoldo Raúl Guido MOREAU (2003 presidential candidate), Juan Manuel CASELLA (Secretary General).

Socialist Party (*Partido Socialista*—PS). The PS was launched in 2003 by merger of the Democratic Socialist Party (*Partido*

Socialista Democrático—PSD) and the Popular Socialist Party (*Partido Socialista Popular*—PSP), which had been reorganized as the Argentine affiliate of Socialist International. Rubén Héctor Giustiniani ran in the ticket with Elisa Carrió in 2007, while the PS presented a separate, independent ballot for the legislative polls that year, securing ten seats in the Chamber of Deputies. In Buenos Aires province only, the PS agreed to participate in an opposition coalition called the ACS, along with CC and UCR, to present candidates for the June 2009 legislative elections. The PS won one Senate seat and held on to six deputy seats in 2009 and kept them in 2011. Party leader Hermes Juan BINNER placed second in the 2011 presidential elections.

Leader: Hermes Juan BINNER (2011 presidential candidate).

Republican Proposal (*Propuesta Republicana*—PRO). Businessman Mauricio Macri launched the center-right Buenos Aires–based PRO before the 2005 election. It was able to capitalize on a center-left cleavage between the FPV and ARI to win 34 percent of the vote in the federal capital. In the 2007 balloting, Macri was elected mayor of Buenos Aires.

Ricardo López Murphy, the party's candidate for president in the 2007 election, received less than a 2 percent vote share, while the party lost 2 of its 11 Chamber seats in that year's legislative balloting.

The party was mounting a well-funded campaign to gain seats in the June 2009 legislative elections, with millionaire businessman Francisco De Narváez, a dissident Peronist, leading the list of candidates for the Chamber of Deputies in a loose alliance called the Union-PRO (see Political Background, above) between the PRO and several dissident Peronist groups. During the June 2009 legislative election the PRO regained 11 Chamber seats. De Narváez won a bruising battle in the Buenos Aires election, beating FPV's Kirchner with 34.6 percent of the vote. Pressure coming from between Union-PRO leadership threatened the alliance between PRO and dissident Peronists in August 2009, when several members suggested they would run for president. In March 2010 Macri was reelected mayor of Buenos Aires in runoff balloting on July 31, defeating the candidate backed by the president. PRO picked up 3 more seats in the Chamber in 2011, bringing its total representation to 11.

Leaders: Mauricio MACRI, Francisco de NARVÁEZ.

Minor and Regional Parties with Legislative Seats:

New Encounter (*Nuevo Encuentro*), 7; **Córdoba Civic Front** (*Frente Civico por Córdoba*), 5; **Neuquén People's Movement** (*Movimiento Popular Neuquino*—MPN), 4; **Democratic Mendoza** (*Demócrata Mendoza*—DM), 2; **Salta Renewal** (*Renovador de Salta*—SR), 1; **Civic Front for Santiago** (*Frente Civico por Santiago*), 1; **Progressive Democrats** (*Democrata Progresista*), 1; Federal Party of Tierra del Fuego, 1; **We Are All Salta** (*Salta Somos Todos*), 1; **Union for Everybody** (*Unión por Todos*), 1.

Other Parties:

A number of additional parties have been active in recent years, but the current status of most is unclear. See earlier editions of the *Handbook* for listings.

LEGISLATURE

Argentina's bicameral **National Congress** (*Congreso Nacional*) was dissolved in March 1976 and reconstituted after the election of October 30, 1983.

Senate (*Senado*). Before adoption of the 1994 constitution, the upper house consisted of 2 senators elected for nine-year terms by each of the 23 provincial legislatures, plus 2 from the federal district named by an electoral college, the body being replenished by thirds every three years. The 1994 basic law increased the membership to 72 (3 from each of the 23 provinces and 3 from the federal district of Buenos Aires). Since 2001, one-third of the seats have been renewed every two years for six-year terms.

President: Amado BOUDOU.

Chamber of Deputies (*Cámara de Diputados*). The lower house currently consists of 257 deputies, directly elected for four years, with approximately one-half reelected every two years.

President: Julián Andrés DOMÍNGUEZ.

CABINET

[as of October 28, 2013] (*See headnote.*)

President	Cristina Fernández de Kirchner [f]
Vice President	Amado Boudou
Ministers	
Agriculture, Livestock, and Fisheries	Norberto Yahuar
Chief of Cabinet	Juan Manuel Abal Medina
Defense	Agustin Rossi
Economy and Public Finance	Hernan Lorenzino
Education	Alberto Sileoni
Federal Planning, Public Investment, and Services	Julio Miguel de Vido
Foreign Relations, International Trade, and Worship	Héctor Timerman
Industry	Débora Giorgi [f]
Interior	Aníbal Florencio Randazzo
Justice and Human Rights	Julio Alak
Labor, Employment, and Human Resources	Carlos Alfonso Tomada
Public Health	Juan Luis Manzur
Science, Technology, and Productive Innovation	Lino Barañao
Security	Arturo Puricelli
Social Development and Environment	Alicia Kirchner [f]
Tourism	Carlos Enrique Meyer
Secretaries	
Presidency, Legal and Technical	Carlos Alberto Zannini
Presidency, Secretary General	Oscar Parrilli
Presidency, State Intelligence	Hector Icazuriaga

[f] = female

INTERGOVERNMENTAL REPRESENTATION

Ambassador to the U.S.: Maria Cecilia NAHON.

U.S. Ambassador to Argentina: Vilma S. MARTÍNEZ.

Permanent Representative to the UN: María Cristina PERCEVAL.

IGO Memberships (Non-UN): IADB, ICC, IOM, Mercosur, OAS, WTO.

CONTESTED TERRITORY

Falkland Islands (*Islas Malvinas*). First sighted by an English vessel in the late 17th century and named after the incumbent treasurer of the Royal Navy, the Falkland Islands were later styled Les Malouines (from which the Spanish *Las Malvinas* is derived) by a group of French settlers who transferred their rights to Spain in 1766. A British settlement, recognized by Spain in 1771, was withdrawn in 1774, the islands being uninhabited at the time of Argentine independence in 1816. The new government in Buenos Aires claimed the territory by right of colonial succession in 1820, although a group of its nationals were forcibly expelled in 1832, before a reaffirmation of British sovereignty in 1833. Argentine claims to the smaller South Georgia and South Sandwich islands, several hundred miles to the southeast, were not formally advanced until 1927 and 1948, respectively. The question of the legal status of the territories, collectively encompassing about 6,000 square miles (16,058 sq. km), became the subject of extensive negotiations initiated under UN auspices in 1966 and extending to early 1982. The British claim is based on continuous occupation since 1833 and the manifest sentiment of the 2,900 inhabitants (primarily sheepherders domiciled on East and West Falkland) to remain British subjects.

ARGENTINA

The immediate precipitant of the 1982 conflict was the arrival in South Georgia on March 19 of a group of workers to dismantle an old

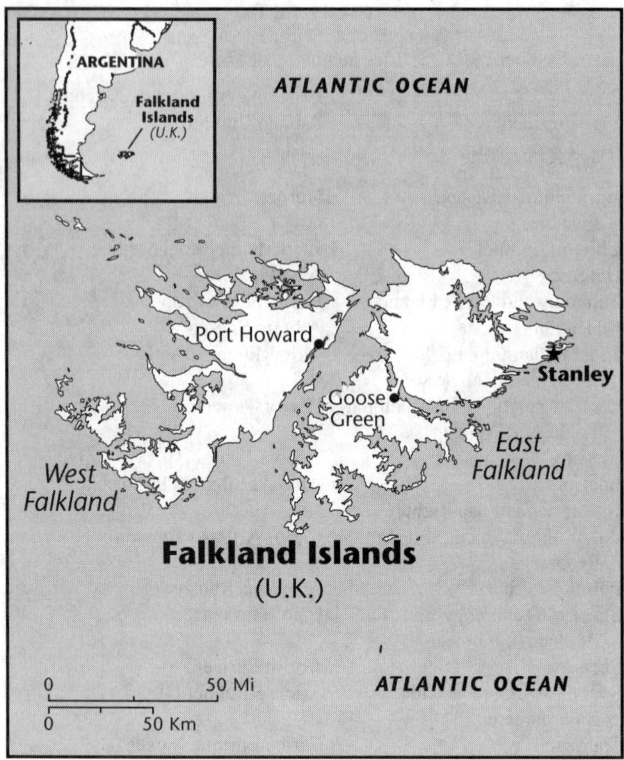

whaling station, in the course of which the Argentine flag was raised. Following a British protest to the UN Security Council, Argentinean troops landed on the Falklands on April 2 and quickly overcame resistance by a token force of Royal Marines. South Georgia and South Sandwich were seized on April 3. Two days later the lead ships of a British armada sailed from Portsmouth, England, participating in the recovery of South Georgia on April 25 and 26. On May 21 about 5,000 British troops began landing at San Carlos Bay on the northwestern coast of East Falkland, initiating an operation that culminated in the surrender of the main Argentine force in Stanley on June 14. Overall, the campaign cost 254 British and 750 Argentinean lives and heavy material losses, including that of Argentina's only heavy cruiser, the *General Belgrano,* and, on the British side, of two destroyers and two frigates. Subsequently, Argentina and 19 other Latin American countries submitted the Falkland issue to the UN General Assembly, although no de jure resolution of the sovereignty issue has yet been forthcoming.

During 1985 President Alfonsín repeatedly expressed alarm at the construction of an airport (approximately the size of that at Point Salines in Grenada) on Mount Pleasant and named as his government's priority "the demilitarization of the South Atlantic." A more serious problem arose in 1986 with a British announcement in late October that it would establish a 200-mile "exclusive economic zone," measured from the shore of the islands, as of February 1, 1987, thereby overlapping a 200-mile zone previously claimed by Argentina off its continental mainland. However, the effect of the action was subsequently diluted by a British foreign ministry declaration that it would police the new zone (impinging largely on fishing) only up to the limit of the previously established 150-mile Falkland Islands Interim Conservation and Management Zone, measured from the center of the islands. As part of the agreement concluded in Madrid in February 1990, Britain also yielded (save for fishing) on the 150-mile zone, allowing Argentine ships and planes to approach within 50 and 75 miles, respectively, of the islands without prior permission. (For additional details, see United Kingdom: Related Territories.)

In April 1990 the Argentine Congress, in what was termed a "purely symbolic act," approved the inclusion of the Falklands in the (then) national territory of Tierra del Fuego. Subsequently, a series of "technical" discussions were held between Argentine and British representatives to prevent overfishing in the waters surrounding the islands. The Falklanders protested their exclusion from the talks, which yielded an agreement in December on a third-party fishing ban in the portion of the 200-mile economic zone that did not overlap the corresponding Argentine limit.

Argentina and Britain in September 1991 reached new accords that liberalized military restrictions imposed by Britain in the aftermath of the 1982 conflict; Argentine authorities insisted, however, that the action should not be construed as implying relinquishment of their country's claim to the islands. Thus in early January 1992 President Menem proposed that the jurisdictional conflict be settled through international arbitration, in much the same manner as for the earlier border dispute with Chile, despite an assertion in May 1993 that recovery of the islands remained a "strategic" part of Argentina's foreign policy, he appeared unwilling to press the matter, lest it reverse the recent improvement in relations with London.

Following the Argentine reaffirmation of sovereignty over the Falklands in its 1994 constitution, Britain began patrolling the nonoverlapping portion of the "gap" between the 150- and 200-mile zones. British authorities responded to Argentine complaints that the new policy was an act of "reprisal" for the constitutional claim by insisting that they were simply attempting to deny unlicensed fishing vessels a staging area for intrusion into British- and Argentine-controlled areas.

During 1995 the question of oil rights supplanted that of fishing. On September 27, following a meeting between Argentine and British representatives in Madrid, the two countries signed an agreement in New York on the extraction of oil in waters surrounding the archipelago. Under the accord, Britain will earn two-thirds and Argentina one-third of the royalties from drilling east of the islands, while the two will share equally in the yield from extraction off the Argentine coast in the west. UCR legislators immediately charged that the Menem government had "ceded a measure of sovereignty" by agreeing to the lower share in the east, while the government insisted that its participation implied recognition of the Argentinean claim.

In May 1996 Foreign Minister Guido DI TELLA announced that Argentina would "never consent" to the Falklands becoming an independent state. The declaration came after Britain and the Falkland Island Council had urged the UN Special Committee on Decolonization to adopt a resolution on self-determination for the territory (an action that the UN body has been unwilling to pursue). In mid-1997 the committee cited its long-standing opposition to the "colonial situation" in the islands by reissuing an appeal to the two governments to resolve the dispute by peaceful negotiations.

In July 1999 Britain agreed to lift restrictions on travel by Argentine citizens to the islands and to reestablish Chilean flights to the mainland, which had been suspended by Santiago following the March detention in London of its former president Augusto Pinochet. In a further sign of improved relations, the British and Argentine navies conducted in November their first joint naval exercise since the 1982 war.

On July 19, 2000, the European Court of Human Rights in Strasbourg, France, dismissed as too late a lawsuit by Argentineans seeking compensation from Britain for the deaths of relatives killed when British forces sank the cruiser *General Belgrano.* Lawyers for the plaintiffs stated that they would pursue the matter at the World Court in The Hague, The Netherlands. As part of the suit, the plaintiffs had sought the extradition of former British prime minister Margaret Thatcher to stand trial for "aggravated homicide and war crimes." Subsequently, in a mark of improved relations, Argentina and Britain signed an agreement in early 2001 that permitted Argentinean planes to fly to the islands for the first time in nearly two decades.

In April 2004 Argentinean president Kirchner reaffirmed his government's commitment to regaining sovereignty over the islands through "dialogue and peace." The administration in 2005 also criticized the inclusion of the islands in the proposed new European Union constitution, arguing that the sovereignty question remained unsettled.

During events in 2007 commemorating the 25th anniversary of the 1982 war, Argentinean officials again accused the UK of "illegitimate occupation" of the islands. Perhaps in view of upcoming elections, President Kirchner appeared to adopt a hard line, unilaterally canceling some previous oil exploration agreements with the UK and revoking charter flights from the islands to the mainland. Meanwhile, although the issue of sovereignty remained nonnegotiable, the UK administration called for "constructive ties" in the hope of resolving lingering hostility. Popular opinion in Argentina remained highly supportive of Kirchner's position, although the inhabitants of the islands reportedly continued to support their UK status. (One recent report estimated that the islanders enjoyed annual per capita GDP of approximately $50,000, based largely on the sale of licenses for fishing and oil exploration.)

A new UK-Argentina dispute arose in February 2010 when UK-based Rockhopper oil company announced the discovery of a field, Sea Lion, believed to hold 320 million barrels of oil near the Falklands.

The Argentinean government subsequently announced it would require permits for ships travelling through its waters. On February 22, 32 Latin American and Caribbean countries renewed their support for Argentina's sovereign claim on the islands during a Rio Group summit. A few days later, Argentina lodged a protest at the United Nations on the renewed drilling. Britain subsequently rejected the offer, reiterating its position that it is up to the islanders to determine sovereignty. As U.S. and UK-based firms announced plans to buy stakes in Sea Lion, Argentina vowed to sue to prevent them from developing the field, and the capital city passed a law barring ships flying the British flag from using any of its ports.

In April 2012 both sides marked the 30th anniversary of the war, as Prince William arrived for a six-week deployment in the Falklands. While Buenos Aires called the heir to the throne's presence a provocation, London downplayed it as merely a training opportunity for the search-and-rescue pilot.

In a referendum on the political status of the islands held on March 10–11, 2013, 99.7 percent of voters indicated they preferred to remain an Overseas Territory of the United Kingdom. With a 92 percent turnout, only three valid "no" votes were recorded.

ARMENIA

Republic of Armenia
Hayastani Hanrapetoutioun

Political Status: Armenian Republic established on November 29, 1920; joined the Union of Soviet Socialist Republics (USSR) as part of the Transcaucasian Soviet Socialist Republic on December 30, 1922; became a constituent republic of the USSR on December 5, 1936; independence declared by the Armenian Supreme Soviet September 23, 1991, following national referendum of September 21.

Area: 11,506 sq. mi. (29,800 sq. km).

Population: 3,198,806 (2012E—UN); 2,974,184 (2013E—U.S. Census).

Major Urban Centers (2009E): YEREVAN (1,116,648), Gyumri (formerly Leninakan, 146,355).

Official Language: Armenian.

Monetary Unit: Dram (market rate November 1, 2013: 405.26 drams = $1US).

President: Serzh SARKISIAN (SARGSYAN; Republican Party of Armenia); directly elected in first-round balloting on February 19, 2008, and inaugurated for a five-year term on April 9 in succession to Robert KOCHARIAN (nonparty); reelected on February 18, 2013, and inaugurated for a second five-year term on April 9.

Prime Minister: Tigran SARKISIAN (SARGSYAN; Republican Party of Armenia); appointed (as an independent) by President Serzh Sarkisian on April 9, 2008, following Serzh Sarkisian's inauguration as president the same day; formed new government on April 21, 2008; formed new government on June 16, 2012; reappointed by the president on April 19, 2013.

THE COUNTRY

The eastern portion of what became (c. 301 AD) the world's earliest Christian state, contemporary Armenia has Georgia, Azerbaijan, Iran, and Turkey as its northern, eastern, southern, and western neighbors, respectively. Its population is more than 93 percent ethnic Armenian, the principal minorities (less than 3 percent each) being Azerbaijanis, Kurds, and Russians. Although more than a third of Armenians reside in the capital, Yerevan, agriculture remains a leading economic activity (approximately 20 percent of GDP). Crops include grain, potatoes, sugar beets, grapes, and a variety of other fruits and vegetables. Refined diamonds, crayfish, and brandy are among the major exports, while the technology sector has grown rapidly under the influence of Western investment. Remittances from abroad (particularly from the Armenian populations in Russia and the United States) contribute significantly to the economy.

Output declined substantially as a result of a massive earthquake in 1988, the onset of conflict with Azerbaijan the following year, and the effects of post–Communist economic restructuring. GDP underwent a 67 percent contraction between 1992 and 1993, and industry was reported to have virtually ceased by early 1993, with an estimated two-thirds of the country's workforce being unemployed. A partial recovery yielded GDP growth of 5 percent in 1994 and 1995, albeit with little tangible improvement in general economic and social conditions. Growth surpassed 6 percent in 1996 and 1997, earning Armenia continued assistance from financial institutions such as the International Monetary Fund (IMF), which had approved its first loan in 1996 to support Armenia's economic reform program, including massive privatization of state enterprises. However, the long-standing dispute with Azerbaijan over Nagorno-Karabakh continued to cause difficulties. (Armenia has controlled that enclave in Azerbaijan since 1994. See Political background and Foreign relations, below, and the entry on Azerbaijan for details.) In addition, widespread poverty, rising unemployment, and a huge trade deficit reportedly fueled discontent over the effects of shifting to a free-market economy, particularly the uneven distribution of wealth. Hope for improvement in part focused on the U.S. plan for an oil pipeline from the Caspian Sea through Armenia to a Turkish port on the Mediterranean, which, if constructed, would have meant a windfall in transit fees to Armenia. However, oil pipelines in the region subsequently skirted Armenia, reportedly at Azerbaijan's request.

GDP grew by an average of 12 percent annually from 2001 to 2005, fueled by an export boom, expanding foreign investment in the food-processing sector, and Armenia's admission to the World Trade Organization (WTO) in 2003. However, concern continued over poverty (33 percent of the population reportedly lived below the poverty line in 2006) and unemployment (officially 10 percent but possibly double that figure in the estimation of some independent observers). In addition, the IMF argued that Armenia would not reach its "full potential" until a resolution was achieved in the dispute over Nagorno-Karabakh, which, among other things, had led Azerbaijan and Turkey to close their borders with Armenia, thereby costing landlocked Armenia much-needed market access. A settlement of that conflict was also considered crucial for Armenia to achieve its long-term goal of membership in the

European Union (EU), which as of 2005 was additionally demanding immediate and substantial political reform in the face of what was widely judged to be Armenia's poor record regarding genuine democratization, protection of human rights, and press freedom. Meanwhile, Armenia made little progress in reducing its energy dependency on Russia, while Russian businesses also continued to dominate the non-energy sector in Armenia, having secured complete or partial ownership of many recently privatized entities.

GDP growth fell to 6.8 percent in 2008 (coming to a complete halt in the fourth quarter) under the influence of the global economic crisis, which, among other things, adversely affected the mining industry and other export sectors.

After approving a regular three-year lending agreement in November 2008, the IMF in March 2009 announced additional "anticrisis" lending to assist the government in restoring confidence in the currency and financial system while also increasing social spending. Nevertheless, GDP contracted by an estimated 14 percent in 2009 as remittances from abroad and foreign investment remained depressed. Although growth resumed in 2010, at only 2.1 percent it was lower than anticipated, primarily due to a severe agricultural downturn exacerbated by adverse weather. Increased exports (minerals and manufactured goods) contributed to growth of 4.6 percent in 2011, while inflation declined to approximately 4 percent. The IMF praised the government for its "sound monetary policies" but continued to call for policy reforms to strengthen the rule of law, improve tax administration, and promote business competition. Growth improved to 7.2 percent in 2012 as the agriculture and mining sectors performed well.

GOVERNMENT AND POLITICS

Political background. Ruled at various times by Macedonians, Romans, Persians, Byzantines, Mongols, Turks, and Russians, the territory of the present republic was obtained by Russia from Persia in 1828. A western region was controlled (prior to their defeat in World War I) by the Ottoman Turks, who engaged in what Armenians have called a systematic campaign of genocide between 1894 and 1922. (Armenians estimate that 1.5 million people died during the period in question, and they continue to press for international acknowledgment that genocide had indeed taken place. For its part, Turkey has strongly resisted the genocide label, claiming that the loss of life was much less than estimated by Armenians. The issue has received renewed international attention in recent years.)

As provided for in the 1918 Treaty of Brest-Litovsk, Russian Armenia became an independent republic under German auspices before emerging as the core of a revived Greater Armenia under the 1920 Treaty of Sèvres. The Russian component came under Communist control shortly thereafter and was designated a Soviet Socialist Republic in December 1922, western Armenia having been returned to Turkey.

In 1988 ethnic turmoil erupted in the form of protests by Armenians over the status of their compatriots in the Azerbaijani autonomous *oblast* (region) of Nagorno-Karabakh, and in February 1988 the *oblast* council requested that the territory be transferred to Armenian administration. The ensuing year was punctuated by ethnic violence, and in November 1989 the Armenian Pan-National Movement (*Hayots Hamazgain Sharzhum*—HHSh) was organized in support of "genuine sovereignty" for the Armenian people and resolution of the Nagorno-Karabakh dispute.

In early 1990 the Armenian Supreme Soviet proclaimed its right to veto legislation approved by Moscow after the Presidium of the USSR Supreme Soviet had ruled as unconstitutional a late 1989 declaration by Armenia of a "unified Armenian republic" that included the Azerbaijani-held region. The Armenian stance prompted demonstrations by Azerbaijani nationalists in Baku, and communal violence ensued, leading Moscow to dispatch military units in an attempt to restore order. Fighting nonetheless intensified along the border of the two republics during the following months. In July 1990 a newly elected Armenian Supreme Soviet refused to comply with a directive from USSR President Mikhail Gorbachev banning local "armed formations," and on August 23 it issued a declaration of Armenian "independent statehood," which did not, however, call for immediate secession from the Soviet Union.

In mid-April 1991 the Armenian government moved to nationalize the property of the Armenian Communist Party (*Hayastani Komunistakan Kusaktsutiun*—HKK), whose first secretary, Stepan POGOSIAN, resigned in favor of Aram SARKISIAN on May 14. At a congress on September 7, following the failure of the hard-line coup in Moscow and coincident with a vote by the Armenian Supreme Soviet to establish a directly elected presidency, the HKK voted to disband. In a referendum two weeks later, 94.39 percent of those participating voted for full independence, which was declared by the Armenian Supreme Soviet on September 23. Subsequently, on October 16, the incumbent Supreme Soviet chair, Levon TER-PETROSIAN, was elected president of the republic, with Gagik HAROUTIUNIAN becoming vice president and, additionally, acting prime minister, succeeding Vazgen MANUKIAN, who had resigned on September 25. On July 30, 1992, the vice president yielded the prime ministerial post to Khosrov HAROUTIUNIAN (no relation).

On February 2, 1993, President Ter-Petrosian dismissed Prime Minister Haroutiunian for having criticized government economic policies, and a successor administration under Hrand BAGRATIAN was inducted on February 16. The opposition parties thereupon pressed for new elections, mounting large antigovernment demonstrations in the capital in 1993 and 1994; however, the Ter-Petrosian administration remained firmly in control, despite a deteriorating economic situation and no progress in resolving the Nagorno-Karabakh dispute.

In Armenia's first postindependence election on July 5, 1995 (with reruns being held for some 40 seats on July 29), a six-party Republic bloc headed by Ter-Petrosian's HHSh won a substantial legislative majority, while a constitutional referendum the same day gave 68 percent endorsement to a new post-Soviet text conferring enhanced powers on the president. However, the fairness of the electoral process was questioned by international observers, partly because the government had suspended the opposition Armenian Revolutionary Federation (*Hai Heghapokhakan Dashnaktsutyun*—HHD/*Dashnak*) in December 1994, thereby preventing it from contesting the election as a party.

President Ter-Petrosian was reelected outright in first-round balloting on September 22, 1996, with the official results giving him 51.75 percent of the vote. His nearest challenger was former prime minister Vazgen Manukian of the National Democratic Union of Armenia (*Azgayin Zhoghovrdavarakan Miutiun*—AZhM), who was credited with 41.29 percent. Claims by Manukian and other opposition leaders of widespread electoral fraud in the incumbent's favor triggered several days of protests in Yerevan, during which demonstrators clashed violently with security forces. After the incidents, many opposition party members, including Manukian, were arrested. Although those prisoners were amnestied in mid-1997, various appeals filed by opposition leaders asking for annulment of the presidential elections were rejected. Meanwhile, observers from the Organization for Security and Cooperation in Europe (OSCE) confirmed that "very serious breaches" of Armenian electoral law had occurred. (The European parliament subsequently passed a resolution challenging the legitimacy of the elections and called for a new round of voting.)

On November 4, 1996, the president appointed Armen SARKISIAN, the former ambassador to the United Kingdom, to succeed

Bagratian as prime minister. The latter had resigned his post, ostensibly for personal reasons but perhaps under the influence of growing popular discontent over the effects of the government's economic reforms, which, although underpinning solid GDP growth, had also produced lower wages and higher unemployment. Sarkisian himself resigned on March 6, 1997; ill health was given as the cause of the resignation, although conflict between the popular prime minister and President Ter-Petrosian was widely believed to have been an underlying factor. Sarkisian was replaced on March 20 by Robert KOCHARIAN, the president of the self-proclaimed Republic of Nagorno-Karabakh.

President Ter-Petrosian appeared to step in political quicksand in September 1997 when he suggested that he would consider an arrangement in which an autonomous Nagorno-Karabakh would remain a part of Azerbaijan. The president's perceived willingness to compromise, based on his belief that Armenia's economic potential was being held hostage to the conflict, put him at increasingly greater odds with Prime Minister Kocharian. Ter-Petrosian resigned on February 3, 1998, apparently under pressure from hard-line military leaders, who by that time were widely believed to wield the strongest authority in Armenia. Although the constitution provided for the speaker of the National Assembly to assume the presidency temporarily under such circumstances, the speaker, Babken ARARKTSIAN, also resigned his post, leaving Kocharian, as prime minister, to serve as acting president pending new elections.

Twelve candidates contested the first round of presidential balloting on March 16, 1998, with Kocharian and Karen DEMIRCHIAN, who had led Armenia under Communist rule for 14 years (1974–1988), finishing in the top two spots. In the runoff poll on March 30, Kocharian was elected with 60 percent of the vote, although Demirchian challenged the accuracy of the count. On April 10 Kocharian named Economy and Finance Minister Armen DARBINIAN, a young (age 33) and reform-minded economist, as prime minister.

Having been embroiled in a series of conflicts with the assembly, President Kocharian called for early legislative elections to be held on May 30, 1999. Some 21 parties and blocs registered for the balloting, many of them bearing little resemblance to previous formations. The most prominent coalition was the Unity bloc, comprising Demirchian's People's Party of Armenia (*Hayastani Zhoghovrdakan Kusaktsutiun*—HZhK) and Vazgen SARKISIAN's Republican Party of Armenia (*Hayastani Hanrapetakan Kusaktsutiun*—HHK). The Unity bloc secured 42 percent of the nationwide proportional vote and a total of 55 seats in the new assembly. Demirchian was elected speaker of the assembly on June 10, and the following day Kocharian announced the appointment of Vazgen Sarkisian, a former defense minister widely believed to have been involved in the "ouster" of President Ter-Petrosian, as prime minister. Many incumbents were retained in Sarkisian's Unity-led government (formed June 15), which also included representatives from *Dashnak* and a number of independents.

Hope subsequently grew that Armenia was set for a period of much-needed political stability, but such optimism was dashed on October 27, 1999, when gunmen seized the assembly and killed Prime Minister Sarkisian, Speaker Demirchian, and five other government officials. Some observers suggested there was a link between a perceived softening on Kocharian's part in regard to Nagorno-Karabakh and the assassinations, the gunmen being described in some quarters as hard-line nationalists. Others theorized that the killings were part of a "delusional" coup attempt, whereas statements from the attackers, who said Sarkisian was the primary target, condemned "corruption" and "poor leadership" within the government. On November 3 President Kocharian named Aram SARKISIAN, Vazgen Sarkisian's brother, as the new prime minister.

A new cabinet (including members of Unity, *Dashnak,* the AZhM, and the reconstituted HKK [which had finished second in the May 1999 legislative balloting]) was announced on February 28, 2000, with significant friction in determining the structure and membership of the government being reported between Prime Minister Sarkisian and President Kocharian. Sarkisian also continued to criticize the president regarding the prosecution of the assassination case, and tension rose even higher in March when Kocharian issued several decrees asserting his right to appoint senior military officers. Impeachment proceedings against Kocharian were considered in the assembly in April but were not pursued, in part, apparently, because the president had appointed members of the Yerkrapah Union of Karabakh War Veterans, an important HHK power base, to top army posts. The infighting culminated in Kocharian's dismissal of Sarkisian on May 2 and his appointment of the HHK's Andranik MARKARIAN as prime minister on May 12. On May 20 Markarian announced a new cabinet, although many incumbents were retained. Kocharian said he hoped the changes would eliminate the "intrigues" that he described as barring government effectiveness. However, news reports throughout the summer and early fall focused on the perceived deterioration of relations between the two parties in the Unity coalition, which finally collapsed in mid-2001 (see Political Parties, below).

Tensions persisted throughout the second half of 2001, and mass demonstrations in the fall called for President Kocharian's resignation, while opposition parties again attempted (unsuccessfully) to have the assembly consider an impeachment motion. Kocharian's critics accused him of adopting a "Russian-style" authoritarian approach designed, among other things, to harass his opponents and muzzle the press.

Amid continuing political and public discord, Kocharian was credited with 49.48 percent of the vote against eight other candidates in the first round of presidential balloting on February 19, 2003. He defeated HZhK leader Stepan DEMIRCHIAN with 67.5 percent of the vote in the runoff poll on March 5. However, those results were strongly contested by opposition parties, as were the official results of the May 25 assembly elections that were again dominated by propresidential parties. Prime Minister Markarian formed a new cabinet (comprising members of the HHK and the Country of Law [*Orinats Yerkir*—OY] party) in June.

Widespread demonstrations organized by the opposition in April 2004 were suppressed, sparking condemnation from the Council of Europe, the U.S. State Department, and international human rights organizations. The domestic campaign to force President Kocharian's resignation ultimately failed, in part, apparently, because of new legislation passed in May that placed substantial restrictions on the right to demonstrate.

The United States and the Council of Europe supported constitutional amendments presented by the government for a national referendum on November 27, 2005, on the grounds that the revisions represented a significant first step on the road to democratic reform, most importantly through the dilution of presidential authority. However, most opposition parties called for a boycott of the balloting, and street protests were organized during the prereferendum campaign, although they did not reach the organizers' hopes regarding size or intensity. (Some leaders of the opposition concluded that Armenians were not yet ready for the kind of mass movements that had recently toppled strong-arm governments in Georgia, Kyrgyzstan, and Ukraine.)

The government announced a 65 percent turnout and a 93 percent "yes" vote in the 2005 referendum, claiming that voters had clearly indicated their support of the Kocharian administration's policies. Unfortunately for the government, however, international observers quickly concluded that the balloting had been rigged, primarily through ballot stuffing. The OY withdrew from the governing coalition in May 2006 (see section on the OY in Political Parties for details).

Prime Minister Markarian died on March 25, 2007, and on April 5 President Kocharian appointed Defense Minister Serzh SARKISIAN (who had joined the HHK the previous year) as the new prime minister pending assembly balloting already scheduled for May 12. Following that balloting (in which the HHK and its allies won a substantial majority), Kocharian reappointed Sarkisian, who formed a new government that included ministers from the HHK, HHD-*Dashnak,* OY, and the new Prosperous Armenia (*Bargavach Hayastan*—BH) party.

Former president Ter-Petrosian, who had spent the previous decade in "academic seclusion," dramatically altered the political landscape in September 2007 when he announced plans to compete in the 2008 presidential election. Ter-Petrosian adopted a populist platform (apparently to attract support from those who had benefited little from the recent economic advances) and attracted large crowds to his rallies. When preliminary results of the February 19, 2008, balloting indicated that Prime Minister Sarkisian had secured a first-round victory with 52.8 percent of the vote (compared to 21.5 percent for Ter-Petrosian, who ran as an independent, and 16.7 percent for the OY's Arthur BAGHDASARIAN), protesters filled the streets on the capital demanding an annulment of the poll. The antigovernment demonstrations intensified after the Constitutional Court validated the election results, and violent street battles erupted on March 1 when police used force against the protesters. Ten people died in the conflict, and more than 130 were injured, prompting President Kocharian to declare a 20-day state of emergency and direct the army to restore order. The crackdown also included the detention of many opposition leaders and heavy restrictions on the media, further blackening the country's image internationally. For their part, most Western capitals adopted a muted stance regarding the government's approach, apparently out of concern that instability in Armenia might exacerbate tensions in an already tumultuous region.

President Sarkisian, calling for national reconciliation, on April 9, 2008, named Tigran SARKISIAN, previously the head of the central bank, as the new prime minister. Tigran Sarkisian on April 21 formed a new government that included several other independents as well as ministers from the HHK, HHD-*Dashnak,* BH, and OY.

Restrictions were finally lifted on public demonstrations in June 2008, but the opposition remained highly skeptical of the government's intentions, and more protests continued on a regular basis until October, when Ter-Petrosian called for a moratorium. Among the developments upon which the opposition hoped to capitalize were the nation's recent economic decline (marked by, among other things, a major currency devaluation in March that prompted widespread panic buying of consumer staples) and reported friction within the government coalition. Subsequently, *Dashnak* left the governing coalition on April 27, 2009, in protest over what it perceived to be an "unacceptable" framework agreement moving toward improved relations with Turkey (see Foreign relations, below).

Domestic tensions declined in May 2009 when the assembly authorized a general amnesty for many of the opposition activists who had been arrested the year before. However, several clashes broke out in late May 2010 between Ter-Petrosian's supporters and riot police.

Facing intensified international pressure for reform, President Sarkisian in December 2010 pledged to pursue "European standards" of democracy and to combat the economic power of the nation's oligarchs. He also called for a "civilized dialogue" among all political parties. However, Ter-Petrosian's Armenian National Congress (*Hay Azgayin Kongress*—HAK) dismissed that initiative as insincere and organized numerous protest demonstrations in 2011, demanding the resignation of the "illegitimate, incompetent, and corrupt" government and the scheduling of early elections.

The HHK secured a majority (69 seats) on its own in the May 6, 2012, assembly elections (the legislative term of office having been extended from four to five years), followed by the BH (37 seats) and the HAK (7 seats). Prime Minister Sarkisian's new cabinet (formed June 16) included members from the HHK and OY but, significantly, not the BH. President Sarkisian was reelected to a second term in February 2013, and he reappointed Prime Minister Sarkisian in April to head a cabinet that again included the HHK, OY, and independents.

Constitution and government. A new constitution approved by referendum on July 5, 1995, replaced the existing Soviet-era text by providing for a strong presidential system of government balanced by separation of powers, strengthened independence of the judiciary, and the creation of a Constitutional Court. Directly elected for a maximum of two five-year terms, the president has the right to appoint the prime minister and other government ministers, subject to approval by the National Assembly. The president can also dissolve the assembly and call new elections, although a veto on legislation can now be overridden by simple majority in the assembly (instead of the two-thirds majority required previously).

Administratively, Armenia is divided into ten centrally controlled provinces or regions (*marzes*) plus the capital of Yerevan. The legal system is headed by the Court of Cassation and the Constitutional Court.

A national referendum on November 27, 2005, approved a number of constitutional amendments designed to reduce the powers of the president and strengthen the legislature and the judiciary. Among other things, the changes were intended to curb the president's previously essentially unchecked power to appoint and dismiss judges.

After a sustained period of relative tolerance of dissent on the part of the government, media were subjected to increasing governmental pressure in the early 2000s, prompting criticism from domestic journalists and international watchdog organizations. Reporters Without Borders has recently described the situation as "stabilized," although "arbitrary lawsuits" continue to constrain media pluralism.

Foreign relations. Armenia was a founding member of the Commonwealth of Independent States (CIS) in December 1991. By early 1992 diplomatic relations were established with a number of Western countries, including the United States, as well as with China and Japan. Armenia also became a member of the Conference on Security and Cooperation in Europe (CSCE, subsequently the OSCE). On March 2, 1992, Armenia was admitted to the United Nations, with membership in the IMF and World Bank following soon thereafter.

Armenia's major international issue since independence has been the status of Nagorno-Karabakh in Azerbaijan, a dispute that extends back to the early 20th century (see Political background in entry on Azerbaijan for additional information) and that played an important role in the Armenian independence movement in the late 1980s and early 1990s (see Political background, above). In May 1992 Armenian forces captured Azerbaijan's last major urban stronghold in the region and proceeded to open a corridor to Armenia proper. Concurrently, an attack was launched on the Azerbaijani enclave of Nakhichevan near Armenia's border with Turkey. Azerbaijan subsequently counterattacked in Nagorno-Karabakh and by early July had recaptured most of its northern sector, which, however, returned to Armenian control in ensuing months. Meanwhile, under a May 1992 agreement among Russia and five other CIS members (Azerbaijan not included), the signatories had pledged to provide assistance in the event of threats to each other's security. Armenia appealed to the pact after an Azerbaijani attack on one of its border villages in early August, receiving a manifestly cool response from Moscow, where there was little support for the proposed transfer of Armenian-populated Nagorno-Karabakh from Azerbaijan to Armenia. At the same time, Armenian forays into Nakhichevan raised the possibility of Turkish involvement, despite a pledge by Ankara to refrain from action that might lead to a wider conflict between the region's Christians and Muslims.

In May 1993 Armenia and Azerbaijan agreed to a cease-fire brokered by the United States, Russia, and Turkey that called for Armenian withdrawal from recently conquered Azerbaijani territory and the launching of peace talks in Geneva, Switzerland, under the auspices of the CSCE. However, the agreement was repudiated by the Nagorno-Karabakh leadership, and by mid-June Armenian forces had resumed military activity that left them in effective control of much of southwestern Azerbaijan.

On May 5, 1994, talks sponsored by the CIS Inter-Parliamentary Union in Bishkek, Kyrgyzstan, yielded a cease-fire protocol, which Azerbaijan signed three days later. A follow-up agreement was concluded in Moscow on May 11, although the Azerbaijani opposition criticized the pact as implying de facto recognition of the self-proclaimed Republic of Nagorno-Karabakh. Yet another accord on May 16 called for the deployment to the disputed territory of some 1,800 CIS peacekeepers under a Russian commander, but the placement of the troops was deferred because of an Azerbaijani objection to the size of the Russian component. Subsequently, whereas the military advantage had appeared to lie with Azerbaijan in early 1994, a CIS-brokered cease-fire in July left the Armenians in control of much of the disputed territory.

In late 1994 both sides accepted (in principle) a Budapest summit conference decision that 3,000 CSCE peacekeeping troops be deployed in Nagorno-Karabakh, subject to approval by the UN Security Council and formal cessation of hostilities by the contending parties. The Budapest decision represented the first potential peacekeeping venture by the CSCE/OSCE; it was further agreed that the force would be multinational, with no one country contributing more than 30 percent of the total. However, although the Russian government had endorsed the Budapest agreement, it reportedly was reluctant to accept the deployment of a genuinely multinational force in one of the former Soviet republics, and no OSCE peacekeeping troops were subsequently dispatched. Meanwhile, the Russian defense ministry estimated that some 18,000 people had died in the Armenia-Azerbaijan conflict since its inception.

Efforts to establish a lasting cease-fire on the basis of the December 1994 accord were set back in May 1995 when Armenia withdrew from the negotiating process, charging Azerbaijani involvement in a bomb attack by Georgian Azerbaijanis that severed a pipeline carrying vital gas supplies to Armenia from Turkmenistan. Talks resumed in September but made little progress, complicated by Nagorno-Karabakh's unilateral declaration of independence in March 1996. Despite calls by the Armenian opposition for the new entity to be recognized, the Ter-Petrosian government reacted cautiously, saying that recognition would not be extended by Yerevan until at least one other country had done so.

The appointment of Robert Kocharian, the president of the self-declared Republic of Nagorno-Karabakh, as the new prime minister of Armenia on March 20, 1997, seriously increased the tension between Armenia and Azerbaijan. Although some observers expressed the hope that the maneuver might provide renewed energy to negotiations, Azerbaijan quickly accused Armenian president Ter-Petrosian of "provocation" in the matter, and in mid-April fighting between Armenian and Azerbaijani forces broke out in two locations along the frontier. In late May the OSCE submitted a draft peace plan that proposed giving Nagorno-Karabakh autonomous status within Azerbaijan. The plan also called for the withdrawal of Armenian forces from five districts in Azerbaijan. Meanwhile, Prime Minister Kocharian announced that his government did not rule out the possibility of annexing Nagorno-Karabakh.

Following Armenia's 1999 legislative poll, international pressure continued to mount for a permanent resolution of the situation in Nagorno-Karabakh, one U.S. plan calling for the region to attain the status of an autonomous republic (with its own army and currency) within Azerbaijan. Washington reportedly offered financial incentives to both sides of the dispute, since a resolution would have facilitated construction of a pipeline to transport the anticipated flow of Caspian Sea oil from Azerbaijan through Armenia to a Turkish port on the Mediterranean Sea, thereby avoiding other routes preferred by Moscow. Such discussions also touched on the ongoing question of Armenia's international orientation; a number of Armenians reportedly supported the HKK's call for participation in the fledgling Union of Belarus and Russia (see entry on Belarus for details), while others urged a more "multifaceted" approach that would provide additional ties with the West. As a result, Armenia announced it did not intend to pursue full NATO membership, although it had joined NATO's Partnership for Peace Program in 1994.

Armenia's relations with Russia subsequently remained strong. A 1997 treaty permitted Russia to maintain military bases in Armenia for up to 25 years and to continue to "guarantee" Armenia's security. In addition, in 2001 the two countries signed a ten-year economic agreement, while in September 2003 Armenia transferred control of its sole remaining nuclear power plant to Russia.

In January 2004 the United States agreed to provide some $75 million in aid to Armenia, including $5 million for humanitarian assistance in Nagorno-Karabakh and $2.5 million in military aid. (Perhaps in response to the U.S. assistance, Armenia deployed 46 noncombat troops to Iraq in January 2005 to support the U.S.-led coalition. The Armenian troops were withdrawn in late 2008.)

In August 2004 Armenia and China initiated a series of military cooperation discussions that included the expansion of Chinese training of Armenian military personnel. On another front, plans were announced in December 2004 for construction of a gas pipeline from Iran to Armenia. (In 2006 Armenia announced that Russia would be a joint owner of the proposed pipeline, which was completed in 2007.) Meanwhile, relations between Armenia and Turkey remained strained. Turkey refused efforts to finalize the border between the two states because of the continuing presence of Russian troops along the border areas. In addition, Armenia continued to press for Turkish recognition that the Ottoman killing of Armenians in the late 19th and early 20th centuries had been a genocide. Turkey also demanded that Armenia renounce any claims to territory in eastern Turkey.

In mid-2007 President Kocharian stated that Armenia still had no intention of pursuing NATO membership, stressing instead Armenia's ties to Russia, for whom NATO expansion remained an anathema, and to Iran, an important trading partner. Kocharian also indicated that the government was "realistic" regarding Armenia's poor prospects for receiving an EU accession invitation in the foreseeable future.

Relations with Turkey began to improve significantly in the second half of 2008 as new Armenian president Serzh Sarkisian met several times with his Turkish counterpart, Abdullah Gül. Their discussions culminated in a Russian-mediated declaration in November pledging intensified negotiations toward a political resolution that would lead Turkey to reopen the border and, among other things, possibly permit Armenia to participate in the lucrative oil and gas pipelines from the Caspian to the West. (Analysts suggested that the recent war between Russian and Georgian forces in South Ossetia had underscored the vulnerability of such pipelines and had revealed the need for "diversification.") In April 2009 Sarkisian and Gül announced a framework agreement that outlined a "road map" toward a final settlement. Meanwhile, Armenia was one of six countries targeted by the EU's new "Eastern Partnership" (formally launched in May 2009), which hoped to draw the countries into deeper ties with the West without implying that full membership was in the offing. At the same time, Armenia concluded several joint infrastructure agreements with Iran and received a $500-million emergency loan from Russia.

In October 2009 the governments of Armenia and Turkey signed an agreement calling for the reopening of their border (closed since 1993) and establishment of normal diplomatic relations. The accord also called for an international commission to be established to review archives relating to the deaths of Armenians in 1915. However, the planned agreement subsequently remained in limbo (as of July 2013), the required ratification by the national legislatures having been postponed as each side accused the other of attaching new conditions to the proposal. (Armenia said Turkey was now seeking resolution of the Nagorno-Karabakh as a precondition, while Turkey said that Armenia was reinserting discussion regarding the "genocide" debate.) Meanwhile, regional attention also focused on the recently concluded agreement between Armenia and Russia under which Russia was permitted to maintain its military base (currently housing 4,000–5,000 troops) in Armenia until 2044. The accord, ratified by the Armenian assembly in April 2011, also provided expanded Russian security guarantees to Armenia under the CIS framework, while Armenia endorsed the right of Russian forces stationed in Armenia to operate outside Armenia if deemed necessary.

Current issues. Opposition parties alleged that the May 2012 assembly elections were marred by large-scale fraud and vote buying. Observers from the OSCE were less critical in their analysis but nevertheless questioned the accuracy of voter lists and concluded that "shortcomings" had "undermined confidence" in the electoral process. Meanwhile, the subsequent decision by the BH to opt out of the new government was attributed to friction between BH leader Gagik TSARUKIAN and prime minister Sarkisian. Apparently in part to bolster his 2013 reelection effort, President Sarkisian in September 2012 criticized the cabinet for its failure to combat perceived widespread corruption in the state procurement process. Improved economic conditions seemingly contributed to the HKK's success in the September 2012 municipal elections, although public attention by that time had been strongly refocused on the conflict in Nazorno-Karabakh, where at least eight soldiers had died in recent fighting at the border.

The two men (Tsarukian and former president Ter-Petrosian) considered the strongest possible challengers opted not to compete in the 2013 presidential election, leaving Raffi HOVANNISIAN, the mercurial leader of the Heritage party, as President Sarkisian's main opponent in a field of seven (including three independents). Apparently receiving popular credit for recent economic advances, Sarkisian easily won reelection in the first round with 58.6 percent of the vote. Hovannisian and his supporters challenged the results and organized a number of protest demonstrations. However, OSCE observers concluded the election had been "generally well-administered." Meanwhile, tensions over Nagorno-Karabakh continued at a "low simmer" into the summer.

POLITICAL PARTIES

The Unity (*Miasnutiun*) coalition was launched in early April 1999 by the People's Party of Armenia (HZhK) and the Republican Party of Armenia (HHK) in preparation for the upcoming legislative poll. Unity was described as a "marriage of convenience" that hoped to capitalize on the resurgent popularity of the HZhK's Karen Demirchian and the "political machine" of the HHK's Vazgen Sarkisian. The coalition of the left-leaning HZhK and the center-right HHK necessitated a "vague" campaign platform, although Unity broadly pledged to use government economic intervention to offset some of the problems associated with the free-market transition of the 1990s.

Unity won nearly 42 percent of the proportional vote in the May 1999 legislative balloting and, with support from independent legislators providing a comfortable parliamentary majority, formed a new government under Sarkisian's leadership, while Demirchian was elected speaker of the assembly. However, following the assassination of both leaders in October 1999 (see Political background, above) tension between the two Unity partners bubbled to the surface. Meanwhile, Unity's parliamentary strength had been eroded by the defection of a group of legislators opposed to the majority's willingness to cooperate with President Kocharian. HZhK leaders described Unity as defunct in mid-2001, and the HHK ran on its own in the 2003 elections.

The HZhK subsequently was at the center of a new opposition coalition, the Justice (*Artarutiun*) bloc, formed in early 2003 by opposition groups and parties to oppose the propresidential parties in the legislative elections. Other parties in the bloc included the AZhM, HDK, Republic, the **National Democratic Party**, the **Social-Democratic Hnchakian Party**, the **National Democratic Alliance**, and the **Union for Constitutional Rights**, then led by Hrant KHACHATARIAN. The Justice bloc gained 14 seats in the May 2003 legislative balloting, and it subsequently represented one of the two main opposition parties to Kocharian and led a series of demonstrations and protests against the government. The bloc called for a boycott of the November 2005 constitutional referendum and accused the government of massive fraud regarding the official results of the vote. The Justice bloc was subsequently plagued by infighting, and it disintegrated prior to the 2007 legislative poll.

An important opposition bloc called the **Armenian National Congress** (*Hay Azgayin Kongress*—HAK) was formed by supporters of former Armenian president Levon Ter-Petrosian in August 2008. Ter-Petrosian, whose defeat in the February presidential election had prompted widespread antiadministration protests, announced that the HAK did not intend to try to topple the government by force but planned a "civilized" electoral struggle, beginning with the municipal elections due in May 2009, in which Ter-Petrosian was an unsuccessful candidate for mayor of Yerevan. Some 22 parties and civic organizations reportedly participated in the launching of the HAK, including the HHSh; the HZhK; the Republic, Democratic Fatherland, Democratic Way, and Christian-Democratic Revival parties; the Social-Democratic Hnchakian Party, led by Lyudmila SARGSYAN; the **Liberty** (*Azatutyan*) party, led by Hrant BAGRATYAN; National Revival; Fatherland and Honor; the **Armenian Alliance of Volunteers**; the Liberal Party of Armenia; and the **Armenian Fatherland Party,** led by Arshak BAKLACHYAN.

In 2010 Ter-Petrosian argued that security and prosperity were unachievable without "peace" with Azerbaijan and Turkey. He also called for "radical transformation" of economic policy through higher taxes on "oligarchs" to support greater government spending on education and public service. A number of HAK supporters were arrested during an antigovernment protest in late May 2010. The HAK also promoted numerous antigovernment rallies in the first half of 2011. In October the HAK announced the formation of a Civic Forum to forge a "development plan" for the country.

Surprising many observers, Ter-Petrosian reportedly approached leaders of the BH (then a component of the government coalition) concerning possible cooperation in the 2012 legislative poll, an outreach that apparently upset some HAK components, who were also angered by the fact that Ter-Petrosian singlehandedly established the HAK list for the proportional part of the elections. (National Revival, Fatherland and Honor, the Christian-Democratic Revival party, and the Armenian Alliance of Volunteers reportedly boycotted the balloting due to their displeasure over the proportional list.)

The HAK was credited with winning 7 seats in the May 2012 assembly poll on the strength of 7.1 percent of the vote in the proportional balloting. (Majoritarian seats were contested under the rubrics of individual parties.) Three of the successful HAK candidates (including Levon ZURABIAN, who became the HAK's parliamentary leader) were officially listed as "non-party," while one seat each went to members of the HHSh, HZhK, Liberty, and the Social-Democratic Hnchakian Party.

After reportedly discussing the possibility of backing a single candidate with BH leader Gagik Tsarukian, Ter-Petrosian opted not to run in the February 2013 presidential election, citing, unconvincingly, his age (66) as an impediment. The HAK ultimately called for a boycott of the presidential poll. (Liberty party candidate Hrant Bagratyan finished third in the presidential balloting with 2.2 percent of the vote, the party having left the HAK to protest Ter-Petrosian's dalliance with the BH.)

Government Parties:

Republican Party of Armenia (*Hayastani Hanrapetakan Kusaktsutiun*—HHK). The HHK was launched in November 1998 as a merger of the small Republican Party (a founding member of the Republic bloc, see HHSh, below) and the Yerkrapah Union of Karabakh War Veterans, which had recently become influential in the National Assembly as well as in the national cabinet and a number of local administrations. Vazgen Sarkisian, the leader of Yerkrapah and a defense minister in the cabinet of former prime minister Armen Darbinian, was selected to lead the HHK, which he said would be dedicated to free economic competition, a stance that appeared somewhat at odds with the HZhK, its subsequent partner in the Unity coalition. Sarkisian also indicated he believed the HHK would serve as the future core of political support for President Kocharian, although ten Yerkrapah hard-liners subsequently dissociated themselves from the president in reaction to what they perceived as a softening in his position regarding Nagorno-Karabakh. A degree of appeasement appeared to develop in March 2000 when Kocharian appointed Yerkrapah leaders to a number of important military posts. Meanwhile, Kocharian had accepted the HHK's nomination of Andranik Markarian as prime minister in May 2000 after nearly six months of political instability precipitated by the October 1999 assembly shootings in which Vazgen Sarkisian was among those killed.

The HHK supported incumbent president Kocharian in the 2003 presidential balloting, and the party became the largest party in the assembly by gaining 33 seats in the 2003 legislative poll. In mid-2006 Serzh Sarkisian, the influential defense minister, announced his official alignment with the HHK, positioning himself as the leading candidate for the party's 2008 presidential nomination. Meanwhile, Yerkrapah leaders announced they would not endorse any parties for the 2007 legislative balloting.

The HHK secured 65 seats in the 2007 assembly poll. The **Powerful Homeland** (*Hzor Hayrenik*—HH) party, formed in 1997 under the leadership of Varden VARAPETIAN, was credited with 1 of the seats from the HHK's proportional list, as was the **Democracy and Labor** party, led by Spartak MELIKYAN. The HHK's Serzh Sarkisian, who had been named prime minister in April 2007, was elected president of the republic in February 2008, being credited (controversially) with 52.8 percent of the first-round votes.

The HHK's Tigran TOROSIAN resigned as speaker of the assembly in September 2008 in the wake of party and policy disputes. He also left the HHK, declaring that he would subsequently serve in the assembly as an independent. Prime Minister Tigran Sarkisian, previously an independent, joined the HHK in November 2009.

Despite recent reports of friction between President Sarkisian and BH leader Gagik Tsarukian, those two parties and the OY (the third member of the governing coalition) announced in March 2012 that they would not compete against each other in the legislative balloting scheduled for 2012. The three parties also agreed to support Sarkisian for a second term in the presidential balloting scheduled for 2013. However, that electoral pact collapsed later in the year, and the three parties presented their own candidates in the May 2012 balloting. The HHK improved to 69 seats, including 40 in the proportional balloting on a vote share of 44 percent. (The successful HHK candidates in the proportional elections included nine candidates formally listed as "non-party," two members of the **United Liberal National Party,** and one member each of Powerful Homeland, the **Constitutional Law Union,** the National Unity Party, and the **Christian-Democratic Union of Armenia**.) Even though it controlled a solid majority of assembly seats, the HHK subsequently negotiated a coalition agreement with the OY, the BH having declined an HHK invitation to remain in the government.

The HHK followed up on President Sarkisian's reelection in February 2013 with a victory in the May balloting for the Yerevan city council.

Leaders: Serzh SARKISIAN (Chair and President of the Republic), Tigran SARKISIAN (Deputy Chair and Prime Minister), Armen ASHOTYAN (Deputy Chair), Taron MARKARIAN (Mayor of Yerevan), Hovik ABRAHAMYAN (Speaker of the National Assembly), Galust SAHAKYAN (Parliamentary Leader), Eduard SHARMAZANOV (Spokesperson).

Country of Law (*Orinats Yerkir*—OY). Formed in 1998, the Country of Law party was subsequently reported to enjoy the support of influential interior minister Serzh Sarkisian, a native of Nagorno-Karabakh believed to have been instrumental in pressuring President Ter-Petrosian to resign earlier in the year. Describing itself as a centrist grouping, the OY won 5.28 percent of the votes in the proportional component of the May 1999 legislative poll. The party supported President Kocharian in the 2003 presidential balloting and secured 19 seats in the subsequent legislative elections.

Artur Baghdasarian, the OY's leader, resigned as speaker of the assembly in May 2006 and announced that the party was withdrawing from the cabinet over an apparent foreign policy dispute with President Kocharian. (Baghdasarian was reportedly viewed as too pro-NATO by the president.) A number of OY legislators reportedly later quit the party, while Sarkisian soon thereafter joined the HHK.

The OY won nine seats in the 2007 assembly poll, and the charismatic Baghdasarian, running on a populist platform, was credited with 16.7 percent of the vote in the 2008 presidential balloting, having reportedly angered some government critics by not supporting the candidacy of former president Ter-Petrosian. Despite its former differences with the HHK, the OY joined the new HHK-led government in June 2008, and Baghdasarian was later described as firmly planted in the camp of President Sarkisian. The OY declined to six seats in the 2012 assembly poll, including five seats on a 5.5 percent vote share in the proportional balloting. It subsequently served as the junior partner in the new two-party government coalition headed by the HHK, retaining that status in the April 2013 cabinet.

Leaders: Artur BAGHDASARIAN (Chair and Former Speaker of the Assembly), Heghine BISHARYAN (Deputy Chair and Parliamentary Leader).

Other Parliamentary Parties:

Prosperous Armenia (*Bargavach Hayastan*—BH). Formed in 2006 by wealthy businessman Gagik Tsarukian, the pro-Kocharian BH claimed a membership of more than 200,000. The new party called for greater cooperation with the United States and NATO as well as the promotion of "political pluralism" within Armenia. The BH became the second-largest party in the 2007 assembly balloting, with 25 seats. (The chair of the Social-Democratic Hnchakian Party, Ernest SOGHOMONYAN, was elected on the BH's proportional list. However, his party was subsequently reported to be one of the founders of the opposition ANC in 2008.)

Friction was reported in 2009–2010 between the BH and governing coalition partner HHK, as Tsarukian and Kocharian criticized the administration's economic policies. The BH subsequently continued to be seen as a potential vehicle for Kocharian's eventual return to political life, although the party in 2011 initially endorsed President Sarkisian's expected campaign for a second term in 2013 before the electoral pact among the governing parties (the HHK, BH, and OY) collapsed late in the year (reportedly due to lack of support from Tsarukian).

Running on a platform calling for greater support for small and medium-sized businesses, the BH improved to 37 seats in the May 2012 assembly poll, including 28 seats on a vote share of 30.2 percent in the proportional component of the poll. Two of the successful candidates on the BH's proportional list were described as "non-party," while a seat was secured by wealthy businessman Gurgen ARSENIAN, the leader of the **United Labor Party** (*Miavorvats Ashkhatankayin Kusaksutiun*—MIAK). (MIAK had won six assembly seats running on its own in 2003 but had narrowly missed reaching the 5 percent threshold in the 2007 proportional poll.)

When the BH decided not to continue in the governing coalition following the 2012 elections, one member quit the party in order to accept the post of minister for sport and youth affairs. Although the BH subsequently called for the resignation of Prime Minister Tigran Sarkisian, it pledged to be a "constructive" force. The BH did not present a candidate in the 2013 presidential election nor did it endorse any other candidates.

Leaders: Gagik TSARUKIAN (President and Parliamentary Leader), Samvel BALASANYAN (Mayor of Gyumri).

Armenian Revolutionary Federation (*Hai Heghapokhakan Dashnaktsutyun*—HHD/*Dashnak*). Originally founded in 1891, the HHD was the ruling party in pre-Soviet Armenia and retained a substantial following in the Armenian diaspora after it was outlawed by the Bolsheviks in 1920. Reestablished in 1991 as a nationalist and socialist opposition party, the HHD (popularly known as *Dashnak*) nominated the actor Sos SARKISIAN in the October 1991 presidential election, but he received only 4 percent of the vote. In 1992 the party struck a public chord with its criticism of the government's conduct of the war in Nagorno-Karabakh. The government responded by alleging that the HHD leaders then in exile had for many years cooperated with Soviet security authorities.

In late December 1994 the HHD was suspended by presidential decree on the grounds that it had engaged in terrorism, political assassination, and drug trafficking. It was therefore unable to contest the July 1995 election as a party. Although more than 100 *Dashnak* candidates stood as individuals in the majoritarian component of the balloting, only 1 candidate was elected. In March 1996, 31 party members were put on trial in Yerevan, charged with involvement in an abortive coup attempt at the time of the 1995 poll. However, the imprisoned HHD leaders were released in February 1998, and *Dashnak* was subsequently permitted to reregister as a legal party, several *Dashnak* members being named to the April cabinet.

Dashnak secured 7.83 percent of the vote in the proportional component of the May 1999 legislative poll, and the party accepted two cabinet posts in 2001. It gained 11 seats in the May 2003 legislative elections and joined the subsequent Unity government.

In 2006 *Dashnak* announced its "dissatisfaction" with the current "state of affairs" and indicated it would not back the HHK's presumptive nominee, Serzh Sarkisian, in the 2008 presidential campaign. However, the party remained in the HHK-led coalition government. *Dashnak* secured 16 seats in the 2007 assembly poll, all in the proportional component of the balloting. Vakan Hovkannisian, the HHD's presidential candidate in 2008, received 6.2 percent of the votes.

Dashnak subsequently remained what one analyst described as "the most opposition-minded of the progovernment forces," and in late April 2009 it withdrew from the government in opposition to, among other things, the recent rapprochement with Turkey (see Foreign relations, above). *Dashnak* leaders announced plans to cooperate with Heritage as opposition forces in the assembly but said *Dashnak* would not align with the recently formed HAK. (Although the three *Dashnak* cabinet ministers resigned from the government, *Dashnak* committee chairs in the assembly decided to retain their posts.)

Running on a platform calling for "comprehensive regime change" (including establishment of a true parliamentary system), *Dashnak* declined to six seats in the 2012 assembly poll, including five seats on a vote share of 5.7 percent in the proportional component. The party decided not to present a candidate in the 2013 presidential poll on the premise that the election "would not be democratic."

Leaders: Hrant MARKARIAN (Chair), Armen RUSTAMIAN (Parliamentary Leader), Vahan HOVKANNISIAN (2008 presidential candidate), Levon MKRTCHYAN.

Heritage (*Zharangutiun*). Led by outspoken former foreign minister Raffi Hovannisian, an Armenian from the United States who was precluded from pursuing his goal of campaigning for the Armenian presidency in 2003 because of citizenship issues, Heritage won seven seats in the 2007 assembly poll. It campaigned on a pro-Western platform that called for greater integration by Armenia into European institutions.

Heritage supported former president Levon Ter-Petrosian in his controversial 2008 presidential race and called for support of the "opposition" in the May 2009 municipal elections. However, Heritage did not specifically endorse Ter-Petrosian's new HAK, and relations between the two groups were described as having badly deteriorated in 2011. Meanwhile, Heritage legislators boycotted the assembly for much of the first half of 2011 to protest what the party argued were President Sarkisian's efforts to extend his grip on power.

Having been unsuccessful in its efforts to convince the other major opposition parties to present common candidates in the majoritarian component of the 2012 assembly poll, Heritage reached an electoral agreement with the **Free Democrats Party,** led by Alexander ARZOUMANIAN, who had served as foreign minister under President Ter-Petrosian. In order to avoid the 7 percent threshold required for blocs, the Free Democrats (who had broken away from the HAK in 2010) ran on the Heritage list for the proportional component. The list secured five seats (three for Heritage and two for the Free Democrats) on a vote share of 5.8 percent. Heritage leader Hovannisian resigned from his parliamentary seat in September 2012 in advance of his 2013 presidential bid, in which he finished second in the first round of balloting with 36.7 percent of vote. Hovannisian alleged that the poll had been subjected to fraud, and he led several protest demonstrations calling for new elections or a power-sharing agreement. Nevertheless, the BH reportedly rebuffed subsequent overtures from the governing HHK to join the April 2013 cabinet.

Leaders: Raffi HOVANNISIAN (Chair), Rubik HAGOBYAN (Parliamentary Leader).

People's Party of Armenia (*Hayastani Zhoghovrdakan Kusaktsutiun*—HZhK). The HZhK was formed in 1998 by former Communist leader Karen Demirchian following his defeat in the March presidential election, which he described as fraudulent. Demirchian had served as first secretary of the Armenian Communist Party from 1974 until 1988, when he was dismissed by Mikhail Gorbachev for his perceived failure to combat the nationalist movement in Armenia. Although Demirchian was subsequently considered a "political has-been," he made a remarkable comeback with his 1998 presidential campaign, which apparently struck a chord with those elements of the populace who yearned for the security of the Soviet era.

Demirchian campaigned for the May 1999 legislative poll on a pledge to slow down liberalization in order to protect the populace from economic dislocation, his popularity being deemed the primary reason for the success of the Unity bloc (see introductory text, above). Following his assassination in October, Demirchian was succeeded as party leader by his son, Stepan, and as speaker of the assembly by Armen KHACHATRIAN, himself a subject of controversy within the fragile Unity coalition.

Stepan Demirchian subsequently displayed increasingly anti-Kocharian sentiment, and the HZhK in 2001 announced the end of Unity, calling the HHK a "stooge" for President Kocharian. Demirchian was the HZhK's candidate in the 2003 presidential election; he finished second with 32.5 percent of the vote in the second round. The HZhK subsequently led the Justice bloc in the 2003 assembly poll (see introductory text, above), but Demirchian failed in his efforts to convince other parties to form a new antigovernment electoral alliance for the 2007 balloting after the Justice bloc collapsed. Demirchian was reelected chair of the HZhK in December 2010, and he was elected to the assembly in May 2012 on the HAK's proportional list. (*Note:* The HZhK should not be confused with the similarly named People's Party [below].)

Leaders: Stepan DEMIRCHIAN (Chair), Hmayak HOVANISSIAN.

Armenian Pan-National Movement (*Hayots Hamazgain Sharzhum*—HHSh). The HHSh was founded in November 1989 by proindependence leaders of the then-ruling Communist Party, including Levon Ter-Petrosian, who had been a key member of the unofficial Karabakh Committee seeking the transfer of the Armenian-populated enclave of Nagorno-Karabakh from Azerbaijan to Armenia. Advocating Armenia's withdrawal from the USSR, the HHSh swept the May 1990 legislative elections and subsequently led Armenia to full independence. Following dissolution of the Communist Party, Ter-Petrosian in October 1991 secured a presidential mandate through direct election by an 83 percent majority. As the governing party, the HHSh insisted that the conflict with Azerbaijan be pursued to a successful conclusion, including the transfer of Nagorno-Karabakh, with territorial adjustments to make it contiguous with Armenia proper.

The HHSh was the driving force in 1995 in the formation of the Republic (*Hanrapetutiun*) bloc, an electoral coalition that also included the Liberal Democratic Party; the Republican Party, led by A. NAVASARDIAN; the Social-Democratic Hnchakian Party; and the **Armenian Christian Democratic Union,** led by Azat ARSHAKIAN. The Republic bloc took a 42.7 percent vote share in the 1995 proportional balloting and won some two-thirds of the assembly seats by virtue of its dominance of the contests in the single-member districts.

During 1996 and 1997 the HHSh suffered serious internal problems and splits. Discord also permeated the party in regard to Ter-Petrosian's resignation as president of the republic in February 1998. Among those facing criticism was Vano SIRADEGHYAN, accused of ordering politically motivated killings while he was interior minister from 1992 to 1996. Following an effort by reformist legislators to remove his parliamentary immunity, Siradeghyan left the country in January 1999. Nevertheless, he was reelected HHSh chair in absentia in March.

The HHSh won only 1.17 percent of the vote in the proportional component of the May 1999 legislative balloting, although Siradeghyan was easily elected in his race for the seat in a single-member district. Siradeghyan's parliamentary immunity was subsequently lifted, and he was reported to have again gone into exile. In 2002 the HHSh absorbed the small National Democratic Party–21st Century, which was led by former national security minister Davit SHAHNAZARIAN, who had campaigned for the presidency in 1998.

Although he retained a low public profile in the early 2000s, Ter-Petrosian, running as an independent, finished second (with 21.5 percent of the vote), in the 2008 presidential election, although he and his supporters claimed victory. Those supporters reportedly included a dissident HHSh faction called **Armat** (Root), which, under the leadership of Babken ARARKTISIAN and Aleksandr ARZUMANIUM, was reportedly attempting to reduce the influence of Siradeghyan and bring the HHSh back from the "political wilderness." In 2008 Ter-Petrosian and his supporters launched the new HAK opposition grouping (see introductory text, above). HHSh chair Aram Manukian was elected to the assembly in 2012 as a candidate on the HAK proportional list. The HHSh also presented candidates on its own (unsuccessfully) in the majoritarian component.

Leaders: Aram MANUKIAN (Chair), Samvel ABRAHAMYAN (Deputy Chair), Vahagn HAYOTSYAN (Secretary).

National Unity Party (*Azgayin Miabanutiun*). A nationalist grouping formed in 1997 under the leadership of former Yerevan mayor Artashes Geghamian, the National Unity Party supported continued close ties with Russia as well as further integration into the institutions of Europe. Geghamian placed third in the first round of the 2003 presidential balloting with 16.9 percent of the vote. In the subsequent legislative elections, the party secured 8.8 percent of the vote and nine seats in the assembly, but the party boycotted the assembly from February 2004 to September 2005. After the party failed to secure representation in the 2007 assembly poll, Geghamian was credited with only 0.46 percent of the votes in the 2008 presidential balloting. Geghamian was elected to the assembly in May 2012 as a candidate on the HHK proportional list.

Leaders: Artashes GEGHAMIAN (Chair and 2003 and 2008 presidential candidate), Aleksan KARAPETIAN (Deputy Chair).

Other Parties Participating in the 2012 Legislative Elections:

Democratic Party of Armenia (*Hayastani Demokratakan Kusaktsutiun*—HDK). The HDK was founded in late 1991 as the self-proclaimed successor to the once-dominant HKK following the latter's suspension in September 1991, after which many of the HKK's senior members had switched allegiance to the ruling HHSh (see above). Weakened by the revival of the HKK for the 1995 legislative balloting, the HDK managed only a 1.8 percent vote share and no seats.

In 1996 the HDK was prominent in opposition calls for the government to recognize the self-declared independence of Nagorno-Karabakh. It was a strong supporter of Robert Kocharian in the 1998 presidential election, HDK leader Aram G. Sarkisian (not to be confused with former prime minister Aram Sarkisian [see Republic, below]), subsequently becoming an influential foreign policy adviser to the new president. The HDK secured 0.4 percent of the vote in the proportional component of the 2012 assembly balloting.

Leader: Aram G. SARKISIAN (Chair).

Republic (*Hanrapetutiun*). This party was formed in 2001 by former members of the HHK, including Albert Bazeyan (the former mayor of Yerevan) and Aram Sarkisian (prime minister for six months in 1999–2000 following the assassination of his brother, Prime Minister Vazgen Sarkisian). Republic was subsequently referred to as one of the most strongly anti-Kocharian parties, calling for, among other things, a more pro-Western orientation for the government, including support for Armenia's eventual accession to the EU and NATO. The party vehemently opposed the 2005 constitutional referendum and in early 2006 continued to press for "regime change" prior to the legislative elections of 2007. Meanwhile, Bazeyan had left Republic in late 2005 (see National Revival, below) in opposition to what he reportedly perceived to be Aram Sarkisian's "radical" antigovernment stance. In late 2006 Sarkisian claimed there would be a "revolution" if opposition parties were not successful in the 2007 legislative elections. However, Republic, which had won a seat in the 2003 assembly poll, failed to secure representation in 2007.

Aram Sarkisian, the leader of Republic, was included on the HAK proportional list in the 2012 assembly elections, and Republic also presented one unsuccessful candidate in the majoritarian component. Republic was subsequently described as having separated from the HAK. Aram Sarkisian, who had run in every presidential election since 1996, opted not to participate in the 2013 poll due to "popular apathy."

Leaders: Aram SARKISIAN (Chair and Former Prime Minister), Suren ABRAKAMIAN (Former Mayor of Yerevan).

Armenian Communist Party (*Hayastani Komunistakan Kusaktsutiun*—HKK). Having secured the second-largest number of legislative seats in the 1990 election, the Soviet-era HKK voted to disband in September 1991 under heavy government pressure, some of its remaining adherents regrouping in the HDK (above). Permitted to resume activities in 1994, the HKK took a 12.1 percent vote share in the July 1995 legislative balloting, winning seven seats, while HKK leader Sergey BADALIAN secured 6.3 percent of the votes in the September 1996 presidential election and 11 percent in the first round of the 1998 balloting.

Calling for Armenian reintegration with Russia and Belarus for security and economic reasons, the HKK secured 12.1 percent of the vote in the proportional component of the May 1999 legislative poll. Following Badalian's death from a heart attack in November 1999, Vladimir Darbinian was elected as the HKK's new first secretary, and the party reportedly accepted several portfolios in the February 2000 cabinet reshuffle.

Several members were expelled from the HKK in 2001 for suggesting greater cooperation with the government; they reportedly later announced the launching of a "renewed" HKK. In the 2003 legislative elections, the HKK received 2 percent of the vote and, therefore, no seats in the assembly, having supported some candidates from other parties in the balloting and, according to one self-assessment, having "disoriented" its "electorate." Several communist splinters, including the **United Communist Party** (led by Yuri MANUKIAN), announced plans to present candidates in the 2007 legislative poll, while Ruben Tovmasian, described as the HKK's leader as of 2006, announced the HHK would run on its own. The HKK secured 1.5 percent of the vote in the proportional component of the 2012 assembly elections. It boycotted what it perceived as the "corrupt" 2013 presidential poll.

Leaders: Ruben TOVMASIAN, Vladimir DARBINIAN, Sanatruk SAHAKIAN.

People's Party (*Zhoghovrdakan Kusaktsutium*—ZhK). Not to be confused with the HZhK (above), the ZhK, formed in 1995, is currently led by Tigran Karapetyan, the owner of an independent television station that was denied permission by the government to continue broadcasting in December 2010, ostensibly over licensing issues. Karapetyan was a strident critic of the administration in 2011 and, arguing that much of the population was "disappointed" in the HAK, ran unsuccessfully for a single-mandate seat in the 2012 assembly poll.

Leader: Tigran KARAPETYAN.

United Armenians Party. Led by Ruben Avakian, a 2003 presidential candidate, this party secured 0.2 percent of the vote in the proportional component of the 2012 assembly elections.

Leader: Ruben AVAKIAN.

Other parties that presented candidates in the majoritarian component of the 2012 assembly elections included the **Democratic Fatherland** party, led by Petros MAKEYAN, described at that time as a "dissident" HAK member (Makeyan unsuccessfully called for the opposition to unite behind a single candidate for the 2013 presidential election); the **Democratic Way** party, led by Manouk GASPARYAN; and the **Marxist Party of Armenia.** (All three had also participated in the 2007 elections.)

Other Parties and Groups:

Alliance (*Dashink*). Formed in November 2005 by former Nagorno-Karabakh strongman Gen. Samvel Babayan, Alliance described itself as a "neutral" party that favored decentralization and judicial reform. (Babayan, who had led the army in Nagorno-Karabakh in 1993–1999, was released from prison in September 2004 after having been given a 14-year sentence in 2000 for alleged participation in an assassination plot against Arkady Ghukasian, the prime minister of Nagorno-Karabakh.) Babayan joined the Republic party in 2001 but left that group in 2005 to launch Alliance, which won one seat in the 2007 assembly poll on a platform perceived as anti-Kocharian. There was no reference to Alliance in the 2012 legislative balloting.

Leaders: Gen. Samvel BABAYAN, Martun GRIGORYAN.

National Revival. Formed in November 2005 by dissenters from the Republic party, National Revival announced it would oppose the Kocharian administration but without the "radical antigovernment discourse" and strongly pro-Western tilt of Republic.

Leaders: Albert BAZEYAN (Former Mayor of Yerevan), Vagharshak HARUTIUNIAN (Former Defense Minister).

New Times (*Nor Zhamanakner*). The recently formed New Times party in early 2006 was described as a member of the "radical opposition" calling for regime change and early elections. Its leader, Aram Karapetian, backed former president Ter-Petrosian in the February 2008 presidential election, and Karapetian was one of the opposition leaders arrested following the subsequent disturbances.

Leader: Aram KARAPETIAN.

National Democratic Union of Armenia (*Azgayin Zhoghovrdavarakan Miutiun*—AZhM). The AZhM was formed by Vazgen Manukian following his resignation as prime minister and withdrawal from the HHSh in September 1991. In mid-1994 the AZhM organized large-scale demonstrations against the Yerevan government. It took 7.5 percent of the vote in the 1995 assembly election, securing five seats.

In 1996 Manukian challenged the official results of presidential balloting, in which he was runner-up to the incumbent with 41 percent of the vote. The AZhM leader won 12.2 percent of the vote in the first round of the 1998 presidential poll, while the party, described as displaying a center-right orientation, secured 5.17 percent of the vote in the proportional component of the May 1999 legislative balloting, just barely surpassing the threshold required to gain representation. The AZhM accepted a cabinet post in 2000, although significant opposition to that decision was reported within the party's rank-and-file. In the 2003 presidential elections, Manukian received less than 1 percent of the vote. In 2006 he indicated that the AZhM would boycott the 2007 legislative balloting unless additional political reform was enacted. Manukian garnered 1.3 percent of the vote in the 2008 presidential poll.

Leaders: Vazgen MANUKIAN (Chair), Arshak SADOYIAN.

National Self-Determination Union (NSDU). Formed in 1987 as a clandestine proindependence grouping by anti-Soviet dissident Paryur Hayrikyan, the NSDU won three seats in the 1995 legislative balloting. The party participated unsuccessfully in subsequent polls as a member of several electoral blocs (see the 2012 *Handbook* for details). Hairikian, a survivor of 17 years in a Soviet labor camp, finished second in the 1991 presidential balloting. He received 1.23 percent of the vote in the 2013 poll, having been shot in the shoulder during an apparent assassination attempt several weeks before election day.

Leader: Paruyr HAYRIKYAN.

LEGISLATURE

The 1995 constitution provided for a unicameral **National Assembly** (*Azgayin Zhoghov*) elected by direct vote for a five-year term (increased from four years following the 2007 elections). Following several revisions of its composition, the assembly currently comprises 131 members, 41 elected on a first-past-the-post system from single-member districts and 90 on a proportional basis from a national constituency. Parties must secure 5 percent of the vote and coalitions 7 percent to gain representation in the proportional component of the balloting. The most recent election, held May 6, 2012, yielded the following distribution of seats: Republican Party of Armenia (HHK), 69 (40 in the proportional vote, 29 in the single-member districts); Prosperous Armenia (BH), 37 (28, 9); the Armenian National Congress, 7 (7, 0); the Armenian Revolutionary Federation, 6 (5, 1); Country of Law, 6 (5, 1); Heritage 5 (5, 0); and independent, 1 (0, 1). (Several members from small parties secured seats as candidates on the HHK proportional list, as did one member from a small party on the BH proportional list. In addition, some of the parties that successfully contested the proportional balloting included elected candidates who were not formal members of the parties.)

Speaker: Hovik ABRAHAMYAN.

CABINET

[as of July 1, 2013]

Prime Minister	Tigran Sarkisian (HHK)
Deputy Prime Minister	Armen Gevorgyan (ind.)
Ministers	
Agriculture	Sergo Karapetyan (OY)
Culture	Hasmik Poghosyan (ind.) [f]
Defense	Gen. Seyran Ohanyan (ind.)
Diaspora	Hranush Hakobyan (HHK) [f]
Economy	Vahram Avanesyan (HHK)
Education and Science	Armen Ashotyan (HHK)
Emergency Situations	Armen Yeritzyan (OY)
Energy and Natural Resources	Armen Movsissyan (HHK)
Environmental Protection	Aram Harutyunian (HHK)
Finance	David Sargsyan (HHK)
Foreign Affairs	Edward Nalbandian (ind.)
Health	Dr. Derenik Dumanyan (HHK)
Justice	Hrair Tovmasyan (HHK)
Labor and Social Affairs	Artem Asatryan (HHK)
Sport and Youth Affairs	Yuri Vardanyan (HHK)
Territorial Administration	Armen Gevorgyan (ind.)
Transport and Communication	Gadik Beglaryan (HHK)
Urban Development	Samuel Tadevosyan (OY)
Chief of Government Staff	Vache Gabrielyan

[f] = female

INTERGOVERNMENTAL REPRESENTATION

Ambassador to the U.S.: Tatoul MARKARIAN.

U.S. Ambassador to Armenia: John A. HEFFERN.

Permanent Representative to the UN: Garen NAZARIAN.

IGO Memberships (Non-UN): ADB, CEUR, CIS, EBRD, IOM, OSCE, WTO.

AUSTRALIA

Commonwealth of Australia

Political Status: Established as a federal state under democratic parliamentary regime in 1901.

Area: 2,966,136 sq. mi. (7,682,300 sq. km).

Population: 23,454,989 (2013E UN); 22,263,300 (2013E U.S. Census).

Major Urban Centers (including suburbs, 2011E): CANBERRA (367,800), Sydney (4,610,000), Melbourne (4,170,000), Brisbane (2,150,000), Adelaide (1,260,000), Perth (1,830,000), Hobart (217,525), Darwin (129,100).

Official Language: English.

Monetary Unit: Australian Dollar (market rate November 1, 2013: 1.06 dollar = $1US).

Sovereign: Queen ELIZABETH II.

Governor General: Quentin BRYCE; formerly governor of Queensland; sworn into office September 5, 2008, replacing Maj. Gen. Michael JEFFERY.

Prime Minister: Anthony John (Tony) ABBOTT (Liberal Party of Australia), sworn in on September 18, 2013, succeeding Kevin Michael RUDD (Australian Labor Party) who was sworn in on June 27, replacing Julia Eileen GILLARD (Australian Labor Party), who was sworn in June 24, 2010.

THE COUNTRY

Lying in the Southern Hemisphere between the Pacific and Indian oceans, Australia derives its name from the Latin *australis* (southern). A country of continental size, with an area slightly less than that of the contiguous United States, Australia includes the separate island of Tasmania in the southeast and small outlying islands in the Tasman Sea and Indian Ocean. It is the driest of the inhabited continents, with the inner third of its territory a desert ringed by another third of marginal agricultural lands. The population is concentrated in the coastal areas, particularly in the southeastern states of New South Wales and Victoria. Persons of British extraction now comprise less than half of the total population; the majority includes a sizable group of immigrants of predominantly Western and Southern European origins, a substantial proportion of East and South Asians, and a growing number from the Middle East, Africa, and the Pacific islands. There are also an estimated 300,000 Aboriginal people. In 2008 women constituted 45 percent of the labor force, concentrated mainly in retail sales, health care, real estate, and education. In 2008 a woman was appointed governor general of Australia, and in 2011–2013 women served as the federal prime minister, state governors of New South Wales and Queensland, and elected premier of Queensland.

Traditionally dependent on exports of wool and wheat, the Australian economy industrialized rapidly after World War II, with subsequent expansion based on extensive mineral resources, including iron ore, bauxite, coal, nickel, gold, silver, copper, uranium (the world's largest deposits), oil, and natural gas. Agriculture employs 3.6 percent of the labor force and contributes 44 percent of GDP, whereas the industrial sector as a whole employs about 21 percent of workers and accounts for about 27 percent of GDP, with the service sector comprising the balance. The mining sector alone comprises 20 percent of GDP. Leading exports include minerals, fuels, manufactures, and foods. Principal export destinations in 2013 were China (30 percent), Japan (19 percent), South Korea (8 percent), and India (5 percent); main sources of imports were China (18 percent), United States (12 percent), Japan (8 percent), and Singapore (6 percent). Australia's trade balance was in deficit by A$47 billion in 2013.

Despite the 2008–2012 U.S. and European recessions, Australia has enjoyed steady economic growth. Unemployment was 5.7 percent as of July 2013 but is expected to rise to over 6 percent in 2014. The International Monetary Fund (IMF) forecast a GDP growth rate of 3 percent in 2013 and 3.3 percent in 2014, but federal treasurer Chris BOWEN reduced growth estimates to 2.5 percent in 2013–2014 as China's purchases of Australia's minerals slowed.

GOVERNMENT AND POLITICS

Political background. The Commonwealth of Australia was formed on January 1, 1901, by federation of the former British colonies of New South Wales, Queensland, South Australia, Tasmania, Victoria, and Western Australia, all of which became federal states. Two territorial units were added in 1911: the vast, underpopulated, and undeveloped area of the Northern Territory and the Australian Capital Territory, an enclave created within New South Wales around the capital city of Canberra. The small Jervis Bay Territory was added to the latter in 1915 to afford the capital direct sea access.

Political power since World War II has been exercised largely by three leading parties: the Australian Labor Party (ALP) on the one side and the Liberal Party of Australia (LPA), in alliance with the National Party (formerly the National Country Party), on the other. The Liberal–National Country coalition ruled from 1949 to 1972 and again from 1975 to 1983. Under Robert James Lee (Bob) HAWKE, former head of the Australian Council of Trade Unions, Labor won elections in 1983, 1984, 1987, 1990, and 1993. In December 1991 Paul KEATING supplanted Hawke as ALP party chief and prime minister; he lost to John HOWARD's Liberals and their National Party allies in March 1996 and was replaced in turn by Kim BEAZLEY, Simon CREAN, Mark LATHAM, and finally by Kevin RUDD, who led the party's return to government in 2007.

A fiery September 1996 speech by Queensland representative Pauline HANSON condemning Asian immigration set off an escalating debate not only over immigration by non-Europeans but also of affirmative action and funding for Aboriginal social programs. (For more on these policies in the 1990s, see the 2010 *Handbook.*) Howard's Liberal-National coalition rode a tide of popular support for its recently tightened Aboriginal and immigration policies, coupled with a strong economy and public backing for the United States following the September 11, 2001, al-Qaida attacks in New York and Washington, and won a third term in the election of November 10. Despite popular disapproval of the Howard government's participation in the March 2003 U.S.-led invasion of Iraq, Howard led his coalition to a third electoral victory in October 2004.

For two decades illegal immigration to Australia has been controversial. The issue flared up in 2001 when the Howard government, facing reelection, hardened its position on illegal immigrants and instructed the navy to intercept refugee-laden boats attempting to land on Australia's northern islands of Christmas Island and Ashmore Reef. The intercepted asylum-seekers, many of whom had fled Afghanistan or Iraq, were placed in detention centers in the Australian outback or were transported to Australian-funded facilities in Nauru and Manus Island, Papua New Guinea, pending resolution of their cases. Australia met all costs for this offshore internment in a policy labeled the "Pacific solution."

In the run-up to the 2007 election the opposition criticized the Howard government for its support of unpopular U.S. policies in Iraq, controversial workplace legislation that had been adamantly opposed by trade unions, and economic uncertainties related to competition from Asia, weaknesses in the U.S. economy, and the high value of the Australian dollar. Despite growing public concern about the environment and global warming, Howard refused to sign the Kyoto Protocol, instead joining with the United States, China, Japan, South Korea, and India in the less-ambitious Asia-Pacific Partnership on Clean Development and Climate.

The electorate on November 24, 2007, delivered a clear verdict, voting out the incumbent coalition in favor of the Labor Party. Howard lost not only his cabinet post but also his House seat after 11 years as prime minister, and Labor leader Kevin Rudd was sworn as prime minister on December 3.

The incoming Rudd government introduced a series of new policies, including signing the Kyoto Protocol in December 2007. This was followed by legislation to set up a carbon emissions trading scheme and to require industrial emitters to bid for permits. In August 2009 and again in December the Senate rejected the legislation, which was unpopular among those who would bear the higher costs of energy.

Further, in February 2008 Rudd closed the Australian-sponsored camps on Nauru and Manus islands and terminated the "Pacific solution" but also raised the quota for legal immigration to 300,000 and provided for a guest worker scheme for Pacific islanders. Other initiatives included refusing to sell uranium ore to India until it signed the Nuclear Non-Proliferation Treaty (NPT), allowing unions more latitude in workplace bargaining, and initiating a comprehensive review of environmental and water resource policy. On February 15, 2008, Rudd offered a formal apology in Parliament to Aborigines for the injustices of past governments and in April 2009 endorsed the UN-sponsored Declaration on the Rights of Indigenous Peoples. He also appointed as governor general Quentin BRYCE, the first woman to hold the nation's highest post.

Prime Minister Rudd's popularity sank rapidly in 2010, reaching a low of 39 percent in May 2010. Conservative critics charged that his immigration policies were too liberal, his border protection against asylum-seekers too soft, his climate change initiatives too costly, his stance toward unions too lenient, and his government's spending and debt policies too fiscally unsustainable. His erstwhile Labor supporters criticized his stillborn climate change initiatives and accommodating posture toward China's aggressive purchasing of Australian mineral assets. His ability to lead Labor to a second-term victory against a resurgent Liberal Party led by Tony ABBOTT was questioned, and the popularity of Rudd's deputy, Julia Gillard, particularly among the Labor Party faithful, rose accordingly. On June 24, 2010, as Labor ministers and parliamentary faction chiefs withdrew their support, Rudd resigned the Labor Party leadership and the prime ministership, and Julia Gillard was sworn in as Australia's first woman prime minister.

Upon taking power the Gillard government immediately postponed the mining profits tax, delayed proposals for an emissions trading scheme, and pledged a firm approach to immigration and border protection. Gillard's moderation earned her party an initial lead of 10 percent in the polls which led her to call an early election for August 21. However, her lead vanished, and by polling day Labor and the Liberal-National coalition were virtually equal in votes won, with Labor at 50.12 percent to the Coalition's 49.88 percent of the two-party preferred votes. This translated into 72 seats for each of the two principal contenders, who began urgent negotiations with the four independent, one Green, and one Country Liberal members-elect. Gillard was obliged to enter into agreements with three independents and one Green member for support in budget and confidence votes in order to form a minority government. The new Gillard cabinet retained previous cabinet ministers but with altered portfolios and featured Kevin Rudd as the new foreign minister. The influence of the independents, now holding the balance of power in the house, was manifested by Gillard's pledge of A$10 billion for regional development, the creation of a new cabinet portfolio titled Regional Australia, renewed consideration of a carbon tax on greenhouse gas emitters, and the scheduling of a parliamentary debate on Australia's troop deployment to Afghanistan.

Constitution and government. The Federal Constitution of July 9, 1900, coupled a bicameral legislative system patterned after that of the United States with the British system of executive responsibility to Parliament. The governor general, with limited prerogatives and few powers, represents the crown and is advised by a Federal Executive Council that includes all federal ministers. Most other links to the monarchy were severed by 1986. However, in November 1999, 55 percent of voters rejected adopting a republican form of government to be headed by a president chosen by a two-thirds majority of Parliament. Also, 61 percent of voters rejected a proposed constitutional preamble that would have recognized the Aboriginal population as "the nation's first people."

Responsibility for defense, external affairs, foreign trade, and certain other matters is entrusted to the federal government, residual powers being reserved to the states. The federal prime minister, who is the leader of the majority party or coalition in the House of Representatives (comprised of 150 elected members), is assisted by a cabinet selected from the membership of the House and Senate. The Senate is composed of 12 senators elected for 6 years from each of the six states, with 2 additional senators each from the Australian Capital Territory (ACT) and the Northern Territory. Approximately half of the Senate is renewed every three years. The House of Representatives is organized so as to have approximately twice as many members as the Senate. House membership is proportional to population, although no state can be allotted fewer than five representatives. Save in cases of early dissolution, the House is elected for a period of three years and must initiate all measures dealing with revenue and taxation. The entire House and Senate may be elected at once in the event of a "double dissolution," normally on the advice of the prime minister triggered by Senate intransigence in regard to government measures, as occurred in both 1983 and 1987.

The judicial system is comprised of the High Court of Australia, the Federal Court of Australia, state and territorial courts, and lower (magistrates') courts. Under legislation enacted in 1976, the High Court remains responsible for interpreting the Constitution while also maintaining original and appellate jurisdiction in certain areas. Established in 1977, the Federal Court has jurisdiction in a number of matters previously under the purview of the High Court in addition to replacing the Australian Industrial Court and the Federal Court of Bankruptcy.

State governments are patterned after the federal government, each state with an elected premier, an appointed governor, a bicameral legislature (with the exception of Queensland), and prerogatives in the areas of health, public safety, transportation, education, and public utilities. In 1974 the advisory councils of the Northern and Capital territories became fully elected legislative assemblies, and in 1978 a wide range of internal authority was transferred to the Northern Territory government. The ACT became self-governing in 1988, at which time the previously incorporated Jervis Bay Territory reverted to a separate status. The governor general is empowered to make ordinances governing Jervis Bay, 90 percent of which has been granted to the Wreck Bay Aboriginal Community Council which, in 1995, was granted limited authority to enact by-laws. In a 1998 referendum 53 percent of voters in the Northern Territory, concerned over possible loss of federal funding and higher taxation, rejected full statehood.

In April 2008, as a result of a ruling by the UN Commission on the Limits of the Continental Shelf, Australia gained control of an additional 2.5 million square kilometers of seabed, including rights to exploit oil, gas, and minerals. Parts of the new jurisdiction were designated as protected maritime areas.

State and Capital	*Area (sq. mi.)*	*Population (2011C)*
New South Wales (Sydney)	309,498	7,247,700
Queensland (Brisbane)	666,872	4,513,000
South Australia (Adelaide)	379,922	1,645,000
Tasmania (Hobart)	26,177	511,700
Victoria (Melbourne)	87,876	5,574,500
Western Australia (Perth)	975,096	2,387,200
Territory and Capital		
Australian Capital Territory (Canberra)	899	370,700
Northern Territory (Darwin)	519,768	232,400
Jervis Bay Territory	28	499

Foreign relations. Australia's long-standing internationalism is expressed by active membership in the United Nations, in such regional security organizations as ANZUS (in partnership with the United States and New Zealand), the Five Power Defence Arrangements (with Britain, Singapore, Malaysia, and New Zealand), and the ASEAN Regional Forum, and in such economic cooperation institutions as the IMF, the World Bank, the Asian Development Bank, the Organization for Economic Cooperation and Development (OECD), and the World Trade Organization (WTO), and the Asia Pacific Economic Cooperation (APEC) whose establishment Australia mentored in 1989.

In the 1960s Australia's foreign policy, traditionally based on loyalty to Great Britain and the Commonwealth, began adjusting to declining British power and the rising importance of Asia. During the 1970s Australia sought a foreign policy more independent of Britain and the United States. Labor Prime Minister E. Gough WHITLAM, an outspoken critic of U.S. policy in Vietnam, in 1972 established diplomatic relations with the People's Republic of China, East Germany, and North Vietnam. His successor, Liberal Prime Minister Malcolm FRASER, sought better relations with Washington. Following the refusal by New Zealand in 1985 to allow a U.S. Navy warship to visit without an affirmation that no nuclear weapons were on board, the ANZUS Treaty became "inoperative." Australia reinforced its security cooperation with the United States by initiating annual AUSMIN (Australia-U.S. ministerial) talks and enhancing military exercises and exchanges. John Howard formed a close personal relationship with U.S. President George W. Bush, committed Australian troops to the invasion of Iraq in 2003, joined the U.S.-led Proliferation Security Initiative, and negotiated a free trade agreement with Washington. Kevin Rudd came to office pledging to withdraw Australian combat troops from Iraq, which he did by December 2008. Following a March 2009 meeting with President Barack Obama, Rudd committed to a troop increase in Afghanistan of 450 to bring the total deployment to 1,550. A further 830 Australian troops were serving in the Middle East Area of Operations.

Although allowing visits by U.S. Navy vessels without requesting declarations of their nuclear weapons status, the Australian government in late 1986 responded to widespread antinuclear sentiment by ratifying the South Pacific Forum's Treaty of Rarotonga, which declared a nuclear-weapons-free zone in the region. In addition, the government's vocal opposition to French nuclear testing in the South Pacific, despite Australia's export of uranium to France and elsewhere, generated a diplomatic dispute between the two countries. Relations with Paris subsequently warmed when the French terminated nuclear-arms testing in the Pacific in 1996 and the two governments agreed on policies to protect Antarctic and South Pacific island resources.

In the 1990s China and Japan emerged as Australia's two most valuable trade partners. Despite a security cooperation declaration in 2007, relations were troubled by Canberra's outspoken opposition to Japan's "scientific" whaling and appeal to the International Court of Justice in 2013 for an injunction.

The Howard government initiated trade and investment facilitation negotiations with China, South Korea, Thailand, Singapore, Malaysia, and Indonesia aimed at eventual conclusion of free trade agreements. In November 2007 Australia and China signed a Nuclear Material Transfer Agreement and a Nuclear Cooperation Agreement regulating export of uranium. In April 2008 the new prime minister, Kevin Rudd, reiterated Australia's commitment to the ongoing free trade negotiations, and announced an agreement with Beijing on cooperation on climate change and environmental policy. In August Rudd attended the Beijing Olympics despite calls for a boycott over China's controversial policies in Tibet. The Australian Defence White Paper of May 2009, reportedly responding to China's ongoing arms buildup by foreshadowing Australia's acquisition of new long-range warships, planes, and missiles, drew a public response from a Chinese admiral who characterized Australia's plans as "dangerous" and risking a regional arms race. China's vigorous portfolio and direct investments in the resources sector by state enterprises made a visible contribution to Western Australian growth and employment but also stirred public unease, according to a June 2011 poll. While Australia welcomed the U.S. "rebalancing" in Asia, officials avoided taking sides against China, their most valuable export market.

In December 1995 Australia and Indonesia signed a security cooperation agreement providing for consultation in the event of "adverse challenges." In January 1999, however, the Howard administration stated that it would back an "act of self-determination" for East Timor (now Timor-Leste), a former Portuguese colony that Indonesia had annexed in 1976. When an independence referendum passed in Timor-Leste in August, precipitating widespread violence by pro-Indonesia militia, Australia negotiated the formation of an 8,000-person peacekeeping force (International Force for East Timor, INTERFET) and committed 5,000 Australian troops. The peacekeeping deployment, approved by the United Nations Security Council, restored order and supervised the emergence of an independent Timor-Leste in 2002. Affronted, Indonesia's president annulled the 1995 security agreement. By mid-2001 Jakarta appeared ready to restore relations, and the President Abdurrahman Wahid travelled to Canberra, the first visit by an Indonesian head of state to Australia in a quarter century, which was followed by Prime Minister Howard's reciprocal visit. Subsequently relations were strained by Jakarta's inability (or unwillingness) to stem the flow of asylum seekers embarking by boat from Indonesia to Australia's outer territories. Relations were further complicated by terrorism, particularly the actions of *Jemaah Islamiah,* an Indonesian-based militant Muslim group responsible for the October 12, 2002, bombing of a Bali tourist resort that cost 88 Australians their lives.

Relations warmed in the wake of the tsunami disaster of December 2004, for which Canberra mobilized an aid package worth A$1 billion over five years, the largest in Australia's history. In November 2006 Australia and Indonesia signed a new agreement on security cooperation despite Jakarta's displeasure, earlier in the year, at Canberra's decision to grant temporary visas to 43 Papuan separatists. Relations were further improved by visits to Jakarta by the new prime minister, Kevin Rudd, and two of his senior ministers in June 2008 and the hosting in Canberra of the Ninth Australia-Indonesia Ministerial Forum in November, at which time a five-year, A$2.5 billion aid package was announced. The two countries now have cooperative programs in trade, economic development, counterterrorism and security, illegal fishing, avian influenza, climate change, and interfaith dialogue, and work closely in intercepting boat-borne illegal migrants.

Relations with Timor-Leste have been positive since the resolution of a dispute over the maritime border in the Timor Sea. In January 2006 the disputants signed an agreement to share revenue, estimated at A$50 billion annually, on a 50–50 basis. Australia and Timor-Leste have also negotiated agreements on trade, development, illegal migration, people smuggling, counterterrorism, and security. In response to an assassination attempt against Timor-Leste's president, Australia in early 2008 dispatched 270 troops and police to shore up the International Stabilization Force (ISF), which underpinned the UN Mission in Timor-Leste (UNMIT). Order was restored and the deployment was terminated in March 2013. Australian aid is to be increased to A$126 million in 2013–2014.

Relations with Papua New Guinea, a former Australian-administered territory, improved significantly following the approval in 1985 of a treaty demarcating the maritime border in the Torres Strait. In 1998 Australia, upon the conclusion of a peace agreement brokered by New Zealand between the Papua New Guinea government and rebels on Bougainville, deployed troops to monitor the agreement and aid to rebuild the province. In 2003 Australia sent 200 police and civil servants to help Papua New Guinea combat crime, but objections by politicians alleging interference in the local affairs of another country obliged their departure in 2006. Australia's request in July 2011 to reopen the refugee processing center on Manus Island generated criticism in Port Moresby but was accepted by the PNG government in July 2013. Australia continued to be its former colony's most valuable trade partner, investor, and aid donor, with A$500 million in economic aid and A$27 million in defence assistance allocated for 2013–2014. Political turmoil in nearby Pacific islands led Australia in 2003 to initiate the Regional Assistance Mission to Solomon Islands (RAMSI) and to dispatch troops, police, and civilian experts to restore order and support the elected government after a flare-up of interisland ethnic hostility and lawlessness. The Australian presence in 2012 numbered approximately 85 defense force personnel with supporting contingents of police and civilian specialists; improved security led to the withdrawal of ADF troops in August 2013. Australia budgeted A$187 million for development aid to the Solomon Islands in the period 2013–2014, guided by the terms of the April 2009 Australia-Solomon Islands Partnership for Development, plus over A$100 million annually to support the Regional Assistance Mission.

Fiji's December 2006 coup triggered an Australian cutoff of military links, imposition of travel restrictions on the interim government's leaders, and a redirction aid to international and non-governmental agencies. Rudd supported suspension of Fiji from the Pacific Island Forum and the Commonwealth until it advanced plans for a return to civilian constitutional democracy by means of an election. Junta leader Commodore Frank Bainimarama blamed Australia's sanctions for imposing economic hardship on Fiji and in June 2010 expelled Canberra's high commissioner. But as China appeared to be gaining influence in Fiji, Canberra reassessed its policy. When Fiji's interim prime minister announced preparation for elections in 2014, the new foreign minister Bob CARR in July 2012 indicated that Australian sanctions would be eased, and Australlian aid would be boosted to A$58 million in 2013–2014 for health, education, economic development, and support of election institutions.

Australians remained well disposed toward the United States, with a June 2011 poll indicating that 82 percent believed the alliance with the United States was important and a majority supporting U.S. bases in the country and favoring joining forces with America in the event of hostilities with North Korea. In November President Barack Obama visited Australia and announced closer defense cooperation, including training deployments of up to 2,500 U.S. Marines, an initiative that attracted adverse comments by leaders in Beijing and Jakarta. Nevertheless, defense minister Stephen SMITH in April 2012 clarified that no American bases, only facilities to accommodate training and transit of U.S. forces, would be allowed on Australian soil.

Current issues. Despite Labor losses in New South Wales and Northern Territory and sagging polls, Gillard in 2011–2012 was able to lead the passage of a carbon tax and a mining tax, compel tobacco companies to adopt plain-paper packaging, and undertake successful consultations with the leaders of China, South Korea, the United States, and New Zealand. She instructed her officials to explore free trade negotiations with a widening circle of partners, including China, Japan, South Korea, Malaysia, Indonesia, Vietnam, India, Gulf Cooperation Council members, and Latin American states. In the wake of rising costs (A$8.3 billion since 2001) and combat casualties (40 dead by mid-2013), a majority of Australians opposed the continued involvement of troops in Afghanistan, and Gillard in April 2012 announced that most troops would be withdrawn by the end of 2013. The May 2013 defense white paper muted previous hints of a threat from "rising China" and advocated instead cooperation with both China and the United States, introduced a new strategic orientation to the "Indo-Pacific," and foreshadowed more attention to Australia's Southeast Asian neighbors. Gillard's treasurer Wayne SWAN in May 2013 announced a budget that increased taxes and defense and aid spending, provided more for schools, families and disabled people, and reduced expenditure on the public service; he also projected a budget surplus by the end of 2015.

On June 27, 2013, Kevin Rudd won a Labor leadership challenge to become prime minister again. After an initial surge of popularity brought Labor equal to the Coalition, Labor, and Rudd, sagged in the polls as the campaign descended into negative rhetoric and personal attacks.

Criticism of the government's handling of illegal migrants emerged as the most prominent issue of 2013. A failed rebellion in late 2009 in Sri Lanka had generated a wave of Tamil refugee-filled smuggler boats; these were intercepted by the navy, and their passengers were transferred to the detention facility on Christmas Island and other facilities on the mainland. Gillard devised a scheme for Malaysia to take 800 asylum seekers in exchange for 4,000 refugees authenticated by the *UN High Commissioner for Refugees* but this was rejected by the courts, refugee rights advocates, and the opposition parties and stalled in parliament in July 2012 as boat people numbers, and drownings, increased. From January to June 2013 over 13,000 asylum seekers arrived by boat, double the previous peak in 2010. As the election approached, the government and the opposition vied to propose more decisive action. In May the House passed legislation authorizing the removal of all persons entering Australia illegally to Manus or Nauru for processing and in July prime minister Rudd decreed that intercepted asylum seekers, even if found to be genuine refugees, would not be settled in Australia but in another safe country. In July and August Australia secured formal approval from the host governments to reopen the Manus and Nauru processing centers, to be financed by Australia, returning to the "Pacific solution" of the Howard government. The opposition leader of the day, Tony Abbott, publicly criticized Indonesia for not doing enough to curb people smugglers. New Zealand offered to accept up to 150 genuine refugees in return for assurance that Australia would prevent people-smuggling boats from proceeding to New Zealand.

On September 7, 2013, the Liberal-National Coalition won a clear majority of seats in the House and on September 18 Abbott was sworn in as prime minister. His new cabinet of 19 contained only one woman, Julie BISHOP, as foreign minister. The new government set about abolishing the carbon and mining taxes and agencies such as the Climate Commission and appointed an army general to head a new campaign "Operation Sovereign Borders" to stop illegal migration by boat. Abbott's proposal to turn people-smuggler boats back to Indonesia, followed by revelations of Canberra's electronic eavesdropping, precipitated temporary non-cooperation by Jakarta despite Abbott's consultation with President Yudhoyono on September 30.

POLITICAL PARTIES

Government Parties: The Coalition

Liberal Party of Australia (LPA or The Liberals). The LPA, a successor to the United Australia Party, was founded in 1944 by Sir Robert MENZIES, who served as prime minister in 1939–1941 and 1949–1966. It represents an amalgamation of traditional liberals and conservatives with strong ties to the business community. The Liberals have a record of conservative financial policies, economic stability, counterinflationary measures, and cooperation with Britain, the Commonwealth, and the United States. They are skeptical about welfare, affirmative action, immigration, conservation, and the Third World.

After governing for eight years under Prime Minister Malcolm Fraser, the LPA lost to Labor in 1983 and remained in opposition until 1996, led successively by Andrew PEACOCK, John Howard, Peacock again, John HEWSON, Alexander DOWNER (an economic centrist and progressive on such social issues as race relations, immigration, and homosexuality), and finally Howard again. A declared monarchist and "Thatcherite," Howard moved to a more centrist stance for the March 1996 federal election and led the Liberals to a landslide lower house victory, forming a government that again included the National Party. The LPA won the 1998 and 2001 elections and in 2004 the LPA-NPA coalition secured a Senate majority. In June 2005 the Liberals elected their first woman party president, Chris McDIVEN.

In the 2007 general election the Liberals lost, suffered a negative swing of 4.2 percent of the two-party vote, winning only 36.6 percent and 55 seats in the House of Representatives. John Howard lost his House seat and announced his retirement. He was replaced by former minister of defense Brendon NELSON, whose leadership proved lackluster. In September 2008 Malcolm Turnbull, former minister for environment and water resources, was selected as party leader. Also in September the Liberals in coalition with the Nationals broke Labor's monopoly of all federal and state governments by winning elections in Western Australia and in 2011, New South Wales.Party leader Turnbull was replaced on December 1, 2009, by Tony Abbott, who had served in ministerial posts in the Howard governments. Abbott led a revived Liberal Party to a near-victory in the August 21, 2010, election, securing, with his coalition partners, 49.88 percent of the two party preference votes and 72 seats, thus cementing his position as party leader. Abbott, in forming his new shadow cabinet, awarded Turnbull the post of shadow minister of communications and broadband. The election of September 7, 2013, brought the party into government with 3.5 percent swing and Abbott into the primeministership.

Leaders: Tony ABBOTT (Federal Liberal Party Leader and Prime Minister), Julie BISHOP (Deputy Party Leader and Foreign Minister), Eric ABETZ (Liberal Party Leader in the Senate and Minister for Employment), Helen COONAN (Deputy Party Leader in the Senate), Alan STOCKDALE (Federal President), Philip HIGGINSON (Federal Treasurer), Brian LOUGHNANE (Federal Director).

National Party of Australia (NPA or The Nationals). Founded in 1920 as the Country Party and then known as the National Country Party from 1975 until 1982, the NPA changed its name in 1983 to broaden its appeal beyond its rural roots. Conservative in outlook, the party's policies traditionally reflected rural and farming interests such as guaranteed farm prices, tax rebates for capital investment and conversion to electricity, and soil conservation. Precluded by its limited constituency from winning a majority in the House, it has a long history of alliance with the Liberal Party (previously the United Australia Party), and its leaders have served in Liberal-led coalition cabinets.

The Nationals lost seats in the 1998, 2001, and 2004 House elections but in 2004 gained two Senate seats, thereby helping the Liberal-National bloc retain a slim majority in the upper house.

In June 2005 party leader John ANDERSON was succeeded by the party's deputy leader, Mark VAILE. After the 2007 general election, in which the NPA held on to 10 seats in the House, Vaile retired and Warren TRUSS was chosen to succeed him. In the August 2010 election, the NPA won seven House seats, but on July 1, 2011, lost a seat in the Senate with the expiration of Warren TRUSS's term, lowering their Senate total to five. The party rebounded in the 2013 election, winning nine House seats.

Leaders: Warren TRUSS (Party Leader and Deputy Prime Minister), Nigel SCULLION (Deputy Party Leader and Minister of Indigenous Affairs), Barnaby JOYCE (Deputy Party Leader and Minister of Agriculture), Christine FERGUSON (Federal Party President), Dexter DAVIES (Senior Vice President), Scott MITCHELL (Federal Party Director), Pam STALLMAN (Federal Party Secretary), John SHARP (Federal Party Treasurer).

Liberal National Party (Queensland) (LNP). The LNP is a merger of the Liberal and National Parties in Queensland, effected in July 2008. The party won increasing numbers of seats in the Queenland Assembly culminating in a 78 seat (out of 89) landslide in 2012, and former Brisbane mayor Campbell NEWMAN was named state premier. In the 2013 general election, the LNP won 22 House seats.

Leaders: Campbell NEWMAN (President), Jeff SEENEY (Deputy President), Brad HENDERSON (Registered Officer).

Country Liberals (Northern Territory) (CLP). Established in the Northern Territory in 1974 as the Country Liberal Party (CLP), the conservative CLP constituted an amalgamation of the Country Party of Sam CALDER and supporters of the Northern Territory's Liberal Party branch. In the territory's first Legislative Assembly election, in 1974, the CLP won 17 of 19 seats. In 1979 it established close official ties to both the LPA and the NPA. At various times CLP members of Parliament have chosen to sit with both those federal parties.

Following the October 2004 election, the CLP continued to hold one seat in the federal House of Representatives and one seat in the Senate and between four and 11 seats in the territorial legislature. The party won no federal House seats in the 2007 general election. In December 2008 the party voted to change its name to Country Liberals. In the August 2010 election the party returned to the House, winning one seat. Country Liberal member Nigel SCULLION assumed the deputy leadership of the National Party, reflecting a coalition agreement between the two parties. The party triumphed over Labor in the Northern Territory election in August 2012 and following the September 2013 Liberal election victory Scullion was appointed Deputy Prime Minister in the Abbott government.

Leaders: Terry MILLS (Party Leader), Kezia PURICK (Deputy Party Leader), Sue FRASER-ADAMS (Party President), Peter ALLEN (Party Director), John ELFERINK (Party Treasurer).

Main Opposition Party:

Australian Labor Party (ALP). The oldest of the existing political parties, with a continuous history since the 1890s and first winning office in 1904, the ALP began as the political arm of the trade union movement, to which it still has close ties. Present policies include support for extensive social services, racial and gender equality, and a more independent foreign policy. It is ambivalent about expanded immigration. It has long been divided between a moderate, pragmatic wing, which commands a majority in terms of parliamentary representation, and a dogmatically socialist, trade union–oriented left wing, which tends to be more strongly entrenched in the party organization.

From 1941 to 1949 the ALP formed governments, then languished in opposition until E. Gough Whitlam led the party to victory in 1972. The governor general's dismissal of Whitlam's administration in 1975, triggered by Senate rejection of the proposed national budget, was followed by electoral defeat, but the ALP returned to power in 1983 under the leadership of Robert (Bob) Hawke, who also won the three succeeding elections in 1984, 1987, and 1990.

On December 1991 Hawke was replaced by his treasurer, Paul Keating. Despite economic recession, record unemployment, and a series of financial scandals, the ALP won a fifth term in March 1993. The ALP failed to win the March 1996 election, however, following which Keating resigned as party leader and was succeeded by former deputy prime minister Kim BEAZLEY. Losses in 1998 and 2001 obliged Beazley to step aside for Simon CREAN, who in turn resigned in November 2001 to be succeeded by Mark LATHAM. Following the party's electoral loss in 2004, Latham resigned his party and legislative posts and Beazley was chosen to lead the party again. In December 2006, however, Kevin Rudd mounted a successful challenge to become party leader and leader of the opposition. Beazley retired from politics and later was named ambassador to the United States.

Despite lack of success at the national level, the ALP in the period 2002–2008 controlled all six state governments and both self-governing territories. In the March 2009 Queensland state election Labor prevailed over the Liberal-National coalition by 50 seats to 35 in the 89-seat Parliament, and Anna BLIGH became the state's first elected woman premier.

In the general elections of 2007 Labor won 52.7 percent of the consolidated party vote and 83 seats in the House of Representatives and was able to form a government. Labor also won 40.5 percent in the election for half of the Senate, bringing its total seats to 32, equal to that of the Liberal Party. The new Rudd government undertook ambitious reforms that did not find favor with the state leaders and the union rank and file. In June 2010 state and federal party leaders, discontented with Kevin Rudd, who was perceived as a party outsider and newcomer and not able to galvanize the party faithful to mobilize for the coming election campaign, threw their support to deputy leader Julia Gillard, who had risen through party ranks in Victoria and was judged able to mobilize the female vote. On June 24 Kevin Rudd resigned and Gillard became party leader and prime minister, naming Wayne Swan, then serving as federal treasurer, as her deputy. In the August 21 election Labor won only 40 percent of the first-preference votes, and the second-preference count gave Labor only 72 of the 76 seats needed to govern. But Labor was able to secure from the Green member Adam BANDT and the other three independent members, Andrew WILKIE, Tony WINDSOR, and Rob OAKESHOTT, a commitment to back a Labor-led minority government in budget and confidence votes, thus allowing Gillard to remain prime minister.

Gillard survived a leadership challenge in February 2012 but was displaced by Kevin Rudd in June 2013, whereupon she and six Labor ministers retired to the back benches. Prime Minister Rudd appointed Anthony ALBANESE as his deputy and Chris Bowen as his treasurer and set September 7 for the general election. In that election Labor suffered a negative 3.6 percent swing and lost 17 seats in the House, whereupon Rudd and six other former Labor ministers retired. The ensuing leadership contest was won by Bill SHORTEN; former minister for health in the Gillard government Tanya PILBERSEK was named his deputy.

Leaders: Bill SHORTEN (Leader and Leader of the Opposition), Tanya PILBERSEK (Deputy Leader), Chris EVANS (Leader in the Senate), Jenny MCALLISTER (National President), Tony SHELDON (National Vice President), Jane GARRETT (National Vice President), George WRIGHT (National Secretary).

Other Parliamentary Parties:

Australian Greens. Preferring not to be called a "party," the Australian Greens is a confederation of the following autonomous environmental groups: **ACT Greens** (Australian Capital Territory), **The Greens NSW** (New South Wales), **Queensland Greens, Greens SA** (South Australia)**, Tasmanian Greens, NT Greens** (Northern Territory), the **Victorian Greens,** and the **Greens (WA)** (Western Australia). From its founding in 1990 until October 2003, the Greens (WA) was organizationally separate from the federal Greens, although closely allied. It had held a federal Senate seat from 1993 until 1998. In a September 2003 ballot 80 percent of Western Australia Greens voted to join the federal Australian Greens.

Although the Greens had not won election to the House of Representatives until a by-election victory by Michael ORGAN in 2002, they have had a presence in the Senate since 1996, when party leader Bob BROWN was elected from Tasmania. A second seat was added in 2001, and total representation was doubled in the 2004 election, when the Greens captured 7.5 percent of the first-preference vote, for third place behind the Liberal-National coalition and Labor. In the 2007 general election the Greens attracted 7.8 percent of the vote but won no seats in the House of Representatives. In the Senate election they garnered 9.0 percent of the vote and won two seats, for a total of five seats. In the 2010 election the party increased its first-preference vote to 11.76 percent and leader Adam BANDT won the Greens' first ever House seat in a general election. His subsequent support for Labor allowed Julia Gillard to form a Labor-led minority government. The Greens also increased their presence in the Senate from five to nine seats, giving them the balance of power in that chamber. In 2013 election Bandt kept his House seat and the Greens increased their total to 10 seats in the Senate, giving them the balance of power between the Coalition and Labor.

Leaders: Christine MILNE (Party Leader), Adam BANDT (Deputy Leader), Andrea MILSOM (National Convenor), Emma YOUNG (National Secretary), Andrew BARTLETT (Registered Officer).

Democratic Labor Party (DLP). With roots in the split of the Australian Labor Party in 1955, the DLP is a moderate social-conservative and antiliberal party of Catholic inclination. Its strength lies at the state level in Victoria. On July 1, 2011, the DLP's first federal senator since 1974 was sworn in. In the 2013 election the party won a Senate seat.

Leaders: Paul FUNNELL (Federal President), Mark FARRELL (Federal Secretary and Registered Officer), John MADIGAN (Senator for Victoria). Peter WHELAN (Party President), Peter LEYONHJELM (Treasurer).

Palmer United Party (PUP). Claiming origins in the United Australia Party of 1931 formed by moderate dissidents from the Labor Party and National Party, PUP was founded in 2013 by wealthy philanthropist Professor Clive Palmer. It opposes big government, the carbon tax, refugee processing camps, and sale of minerals to foreign processors and supports maximum freedom for Australia's states, businesses, and individuals. It won two Senate seats and one House seat in the 2013 election.

Leader: Clive PALMER (President).

Other parties.

Australian Democrats (AD or The Democrats). The social democratic AD was organized in 1977 by former Liberal cabinet minister Donald L. CHIPP and some members of the Australia Party, a small reformist group. By increasing its Senate representation from two seats to five in the October 1980 national election, it secured the balance of power in the upper house, a position that it maintained until the 2004 elections.

Sharp divisions over the 10 percent goods and services tax (GST) and other issues roiled the party from 1999 to 2001 and led to party leader Meg LEES's displacement in April 2001 by GST opponent Natasha STOTT DESPOJA, who in turn proved controversial and resigned her party post in August, to be succeeded on an interim basis by Sen. Brian GREIG. In October Sen. Andrew BARTLETT was named parliamentary leader, but he stepped down in December 2003 after an altercation with another senator. He was replaced by Sen. Lyn ALLISON. Meanwhile, in April 2003 Lees had formed the Australian Progressive Alliance (APA), but she failed to win reelection in 2004 and the APA was deregistered at the end of her senatorial term.

Although Stott Despoja won a Senate seat in the October 2004 federal election, the Democrats saw their senatorial delegation halved and their percentage of the first-preference vote drop to 2.1 percent.

In the 2007 general election the Democrats attracted only 0.7 percent of votes and won no seats in the House of Representatives or the Senate. When the terms of four senators who took their seats in 2004 expired on June 30, 2008, the Democrats were left with no federal parliamentary seats. They won no seats in the 2010 and 2013 general elections.

Leaders: Derren CHURCHILL (National President), Roger HOWE (Senior Deputy President and National Secretary), Ian URQUHART (National Treasurer), John Charles BELL (Registered Officer).

Family First Party (FFP). Initially organized in South Australia, where Andrew Evans, an Assemblies of God pastor, was elected to the upper house of the legislature in early 2002, the FFP quickly attracted wider support based on its family values orientation. In August 2004, soon after organizing at the federal level, it named Andrea MASON as leader, the first indigenous woman to head an Australian party.

Despite its Christian roots, the party seeks to cross religious as well as social and ethnic lines. The party supports ecologically sustainable development, the war on terrorism (although it opposed involvement in the war in Iraq), mandatory filtering of the Internet by service providers, and requiring women who seek publicly funded abortions to first receive counseling. In 2004 both the Liberals and Labor sought its support.

In the 2007 general election an FFP candidate, Steve FIELDING, won a Senate seat, but the party attracted only 2.0 percent support in the House election and won no seat. The party won 2.3 percent of the first-preference votes in the 2010 election but no House or Senate seat, and the term of its sole senator expired on June 30, 2011. In 2013 party leader Bob DAY won a Senate seat in Western Australia.

Leaders: Bob DAY (Federal Chair), Steve FIELDING (Leader of Family First Federal Party), Dennis HOOD (South Australia State Leader).

Liberal Democratic Party (LDP). Founded by John HUMPHRIES in 2001 on classical liberal, libertarian, individualism, and small government principles, the LDP contested only Australian Federal Territory elections until 2007 when it entered, without success, the federal House and Senate races. It registered as the Liberty and Democracy Party in 2007 and resumed its present name in 2008, subsequently setting up branches in Queensland, South Australia, Western Australia, and Tasmania. In 2010 it garnered 1.81 percent of votes for the Senate but no seats. In September 2013 the LDP's Peter LEYONHJELM captured a seat in the Senate in Western Australia.

One Nation (ON). Formed in April 1997 by Pauline Hanson, One Nation quickly became the rallying point for Australians skeptical of non-European immigration, Aboriginal welfare programs, and trade liberalization. It captured 11 of 89 seats in Queensland's legislature in the 1998 state election, but in the October 1998 national election it won only 8.4 percent of the vote and a single Senate seat, and Hanson herself lost her House seat.

Although Hanson was reelected party leader in 1999, dissatisfaction with the party's alleged autocratic and undemocratic structure led the majority of its Queensland state representatives to bolt or be dismissed from the party. In early October 2000 Hanson forced the expulsion of a party cofounder, David OLDFIELD, over his participation in forming a new No GST Party with David ETTRIDGE, another One Nation cofounder. The party's disintegration accelerated after that, and in the November 2001 federal election it took only 4.3 percent of the House votes. In January 2002 Hanson resigned as leader. In August 2003 both she and Ettridge were convicted of electoral fraud in connection with the party's registration in Queensland in 1997, but the convictions were quashed by the Queensland Court of Appeals.

Hanson's breakaway party, Pauline Hanson's One Nation, was deregistered in February 2005. By then, most One Nation members of various state legislatures had been defeated or had left the party, although in September 2006 it retained its one seat in the Queensland legislature. From that time the One Nation party has had no national leadership organization, only state leaders.

In the 2007 general election One Nation gained 0.3 percent of votes for the House and 0.4 percent for the Senate but won no seats. Pauline Hanson stood in the Queensland Senate election at the head of her new Pauline's United Australia Party, which she had launched in May, but with only 4 percent of the vote she failed to gain a seat, and the party was deregistered in March 2010. In the March 2009 Queensland state election the last sitting member of One Nation, Rosa Lee LONG, lost her House seat, marking the end of One Nation representation in any national or state legislature. Pauline Hanson, standing as an independent, was also unsuccessful. One Nation was equally unsuccessful in the 2010 general election, attracting only 0.22 percent of the first-preference votes, and Hanson attracted only 2.41 percent of the New South Wales Legislative Council election vote. In June 2013 Hanson rejoined One Nation and ran for a seat on the Senate but no One Nation candidate was successful in the September general election.

Leaders: Pat LOY (National Secretary), Ian NELSON (National Party Agent), Stan BATTEN, Jim SAVAGE, Dale TOWNSEND, Andrew WEBBER (State Party Presidents), Rodney Andrew Evans (National Registered Officer), Brian BURSTON (Campaign Manager).

Australia has many smaller parties, some operating at the state level and others focusing on single issues. Candidates from five new parties were successful in winning federal House or Senate seats in the 2013 election (subject to the re-run of the election in Western Australia): the **Australian Motoring Enthusiasts Party,** the **Australian Sports Party, Katter's Australian Party, Nick Xenophone Group,** and **Palmer United Party.**

Other minor parties that registered for the 2010 or 2013 general election but won no federal seats included the **Animal Justice Party, Australia First Party of New South Wales, Australian Christians, Australian First Nations Political Party, Australian Fishing and Lifestyle Party, Australian Independents, Australian Protectionist Party, Australian Sex Party, Australian Sovereignty Party, Australian Stable Population Party, Australian Voice Party, Bank Reform Party, Building Australia Party, Bullet Train for Australia, Carers Alliance, Christian Democratic Party (Fred Nile Group), Citizens Electoral Council, Coke in the Bubblers Party, Country Alliance, Drug Law Reform Party, Future Party, Help End Marijuana Prohibition (HEMP) Party, No Carbon Tax Climate Sceptics, Non-Custodial Parents Party (Equal Parenting), Nuclear Disarmament Party, Outdoor Recreation Party, Pirate Party Australia, Republican Party of Australia, Rise Up Australia Party, Secular Party of Australia, Senator-On-Line, Shooters and Fishers Party, Smokers Rights Party, Socialist Equality Party, Stop CSG Party, The 23 Million, The Wikileaks Party, Uniting Australia Party,** and **Voluntary Euthanasia Party.**

Of the small leftist parties that did not contest the 2004, 2007, 2010, or 2013 federal elections, the best known is the **Communist Party of Australia** (CPA), which in 1996 changed its name from the Socialist Party of Australia (a 1971 splinter from the original, defunct CPA). The CPA is currently led by longtime activist Hannah MIDDLETON (General Secretary) and Vinnie MOLINA (President). In 2009 it joined with several small communist groups to form the **Communist Alliance** to support Denis DOHERTY for a seat in the House in the 2010 election, without success, the Alliance attracting only 0.01 percent of the vote. The Victorian branch secretary was Andrew IRVING. Renamed **The**

Communists in 2011, the party was deregistered on May 22, 2012. The Socialist Alliance, set up in 2001, is an amalgam of eight Marxist factions and is distinct from the Socialist Equality Party, which enlists Trotskyites advocating global revolution and expropriate of all private enterprises for worker control.

LEGISLATURE

The Australian **Federal Parliament** is a bicameral legislature with an upper chamber (Senate) and a lower chamber (House of Representatives), both elected by direct universal suffrage.

Senate. The Senate consists of 76 members (12 from each state plus 2 each from the Australian Capital Territory and the Northern Territory), who are elected from state or territorial lists by proportional representation for staggered six-year terms. Balloting is normally conducted every three years for one-half of the Senate, at the same time as the elections for the House of Representatives. When the last term began on July 1, 2011, the party distribution was Liberal-National Coalition, 34; Labor Party, 31; Greens, 9; Democratic Labor Party, 1; independent, 1. The provisional party distribution when the new senators take office on July 1, 2014, is Liberal-National Coalition, 33; Labor Party, 25; Greens, 10; Palmer United Party, 2; Democratic Labor Party, 1; Liberal Democratic Party, 1; Family First Party, 1; Australian Motor Enthusiasts Party,1; Australian Sports Party, 1; and Nick Xenophone Group, 1. The Australian Electoral Commission has recommended a re-run of the Western Australia election affecting 12 seats.

President: John HOGG.

House of Representatives. The House consists of 150 representatives elected from single-member constituencies by preferential balloting (progressive elimination of lowest-ranked candidates with redistribution of preferences until one candidate secures a majority). Members are elected for three-year terms, subject to dissolution. The election of September 7, 2013, produced the following distribution of seats (2010 election results are shown in parentheses): Australian Labor Party, 55 (72); Liberal Party, 58 (44); Liberal National Party, 22 (21); The Nationals 9 (7); Country Liberals 1 (1); Greens 1 (1); Katter's Australian Party 1 (0); Palmer United Party 1 (0); independents, 2 (4).

Speaker: Bronwyn BISHOP.

CABINET

[as of October 1, 2013]

Prime Minister	Tony Abbott (LPA)
Deputy Prime Minister	Warren Truss (NPA)
Cabinet Ministers	
Agriculture	Barnaby Joyce (NPA)
Arts	George Brandis (LPA)
Attorney General	George Brandis (LPA)
Communications	Malcolm Turnbull (LPA)
Defense	David Johnston (LPA)
Education	Christopher Payne (LPA)
Employment	Eric Abetz (LPA)
Environment	Greg Hunt (LPA)
Finance	Mathias Cormann (LPA)
Foreign Affairs	Julie Bishop (LPA) [f]
Health	Peter Dutton (LPA)
Immigration and Border Protection	Scott Morrison (LPA)
Indigenous Affairs	Nigel Scullion (NPA)
Industry	Ian Macfarlane (LPA)
Infrastructure and Regional Development	Warren Truss (NPA)
Small Business	Bruce Billson (LPA)
Social Services	Kevin Andrews (LPA)
Sport	Peter Dutton (LPA)
Trade and Investment	Andrew Robb (NPA)
Treasurer	Joe Hockey (LPA)

[f] = female

INTERGOVERNMENTAL REPRESENTATION

Ambassador to the U.S.: Kim C. BEAZLEY.

U.S. Ambassador to Australia: Jeffrey L. BLEICH.

Permanent Representative to the UN: Gary F. QUINLAN.

IGO Memberships (Non-UN): ADB, CWTH, EBRD, G-20, ICC, IEA, IOM, OECD, PIF, WTO.

RELATED TERRITORIES

Ashmore and Cartier Islands Territory. The Ashmore Islands (comprising Middle, East, and West islands) and Cartier Island, totaling about 0.36 square miles, are situated in the Indian Ocean about 200 miles off the northwestern coast of Australia. All are uninhabited save for a seasonal presence. Under the Ashmore and Cartier Islands Acceptance Act (effective May 10, 1934), it was intended that the territory be administered by Western Australia, but by a 1938 amendment to the act it was formally annexed to the Northern Territory. Since July 1978 Ashmore and Cartier have been under the direct administration of the Australian government, with oversight currently falling under the Attorney General's Department. Two oilfields, Challis and Jabiru, are located near the islands, and in April 2005 the Australian government included an area near Ashmore and Cartier among 29 new offshore exploration sites open for bidding by the petroleum industry.

In May 1996 officials from Australia and Indonesia visited the territory during discussions on the maritime boundary. International attention has since been drawn to Ashmore by "people smuggling" of refugees seeking Australian residency. To counter the flow, in 2001 Parliament passed legislation that excised the territory from the country's migration zone, thereby removing the right of refugees who land there to apply for asylum.

Australian Antarctic Territory. A legacy of British claims, the Australian Antarctic Territory encompasses two sectors of Antarctica extending from 45 to 136 degrees east longitude and from 142 to 160 degrees east longitude. Together these sectors comprise almost 2.5 million square miles, or nearly 50 percent of the continent. The provisions of the Antarctic Treaty of 1959 have placed the area in a state of suspended sovereignty, although nominally the laws of the Australian Capital Territory are in effect. Australian activities in the territory are administered by the Australian Antarctic Division of the Department of the Environment, Water Resources, Heritage, and the Arts.

In 1991 an international treaty banned all mining in the Antarctic, including the Australian Antarctic Territory and the adjacent continental shelf.

A more recent concern has been whaling by Japanese ships within the EEZ, particularly in the Australian Whale Sanctuary, which was established in 2000 under the Environment Protection and Biodiversity Conservation Act of 1999. As part of the International Polar Year 2007–2008 Australian scientists participated in over 60 projects, including a Census of Antarctic Marine Life.

Christmas Island. Named by a British captain on December 25, 1643, Christmas Island, with an area of about 52 square miles, is located in the Indian Ocean about 230 miles south of Java, Indonesia. It was annexed as a crown colony by the United Kingdom in 1888, and in the late 1890s Chinese workers were brought in to mine phosphate. Administered from Singapore, the colony was occupied by Japan during World War II. A 2001 census recorded 1,508 persons, 70 percent of whom were Chinese and 10 percent Malays, with the balance comprising persons of European descent. Inhabitants in July 2010 were estimated at 1,402.

Britain transferred Christmas Island to Australian jurisdiction in 1958. The Christmas Island Act of 1958–1959 and the Territories Law Reform Act of 1992 prescribe Australian law and place authority in the hands of an administrator responsible to the federal Attorney General's Department. The nine-member Christmas Island Shire Council, established in 1992 as successor to the Christmas Island Services Corporation, provides municipal services and economic management. Independence referenda in 1994 and 1999 failed to gain majorities, although they did highlight local frustrations, for example, of a housing shortage.

The only nonservice industry on the island, the extraction of nearly exhausted phosphate deposits, was previously under management of the British Phosphate Commission, the shareholders being Australia, New Zealand, and the United Kingdom. However, in 1991 a new corporation, Phosphate Resources Ltd., was formed by mine workers to exploit existing sites. In 2006 controversy arose over the company's plan to extend mining into a previously untouched rainforest.

The Australian government has encouraged commercial diversification, mainly tourism, to broaden the economic base. But private projects such as the Christmas Island Resort failed, and public projects including a satellite launching facility and an airport and infrastructure upgrade have lagged.

Just over half of the revenue in the 2009/2010 budget was derived from grants, subsidies, contributions, and donations from the mainland, supplemented by local fees and charges; there is no income tax. Salaries of officials and transportation were the major expenditures.

Beginning in early 1999 Christmas Island witnessed a wave of illegal immigrants smuggled by boat from nearby Indonesia attempting to enter Australia. In November 1999 alone, nearly 1,000 people landed, while hundreds drowned attempting the passage. A decision by Canberra not to allow some 430 mainly Afghan refugees rescued by the freighter *Tampa* to land in August 2001, and Parliament's subsequent removal of Christmas Island from Australia's immigration zone, led to wide international criticism of the Howard government's increasingly tough anti-immigration policies. In 2007 construction commenced on a new Christmas Island Immigration Reception and Processing Center, designed to accommodate up to 1,500 persons. Local residents, including the president of the Shire Council, opposed the expanded facility, fearing that it might be used to hold suspected terrorists and would deter tourists. The center was closed in February 2008 when the Rudd government terminated the "Pacific solution" of offshore detention but reopened in September to accommodate a surge of unauthorized persons entering Australian waters. In March 2011 detainees rioted and torched buildings in the center. The drowning of 200 asylum seekers off Christmas Island cliffs in December 2011, and dozens subsequently, inflamed debate but did not deter others; by May 2013 the Christmas Island facility had exceeded its capacity of 2,078 (about the same number as that of the island's permanent residents) and the island's morgue was filled with 50 bodies of unidentified drowned asylum seekers.

The value of Christmas Island as a strategic outpost was brought into focus by the Defence Force Posture Review announced by minister of defense Stephen Smith in July 2011, which foreshadowed strengthening Australia's presence in the Indian Ocean region, and further announcements made by Smith in March 2012.

Administrator: Jon STANHOPE.

President of the Shire Council: Kee Heng FOO.

Chief Executive Officer: Kelvin MATTHEWS.

Cocos (Keeling) Islands. Located in the Indian Ocean about 580 miles southwest of Java, the Cocos Islands consist of two atolls of 27 islands with a total area of about 5.5 square miles. They were discovered in 1609 by Capt. William Keeling of the British East India Company and were transferred from Singapore to Australia in 1955. In 1978 John Clunies-Ross, the descendant of a Scottish sea captain who was granted authority over the islands by Queen Victoria in 1886, yielded his claim after agreeing to financial compensation of A$7 million.

The population of the islands at the 2001 census was 618: some 500 on Home Island, where virtually all the inhabitants are Muslims of Malay extraction, and the balance on West Island, where mainly federal government employees and their families reside. By 2006, the total had dropped to an estimated 587. The islands have no significant industry apart from the production of coconuts and copra. In early 2000 plans to open a casino were scrapped.

In a referendum conducted in 1984 an overwhelming majority of the inhabitants voted for integration with Australia rather than free association or independence. While Australia's administrator of the Indian Ocean Territories remains the chief executive officer of the islands, a seven-member Cocos (Keeling) Islands Shire Council with municipal-level powers was established in 1993 under the Territories Law Reform Act of 1992. For voting purposes, the islands are treated as part of Australia's Northern Territory.

In 2001 the territory was removed from Australia's migration zone to deter asylum seekers, a number of whom were being held at a former quarantine facility. The asylum seekers were later moved to the Christmas Island Immigration Reception and Processing Center, as were subsequent illegal arrivals, most recently in April 2009.The Defence Force Posture Review announced in July 2011 by the minister of defense, emphasizing the protection of Australia's growing interests in the Indian Ocean, drew attention to the strategic value of Cocos' airfield and protected anchorage, not least to U.S. forces. In March 2012 ministerial talks explored the potential for stationing of U.S. surveillance drones at the Cocos facility.

Administrator: Brian James LACY.

President of the Shire Council: Balmut PIRUS.

Chief Administrator: Peter CLARKE.

Coral Sea Islands Territory. The Coral Sea Territory was created in 1969 as a means of administering a number of very small islands and reefs east of Queensland. Except at a weather station on Willis Island, there are no inhabitants. In 1997 the Coral Sea Islands Act of 1969 was amended to include Elizabeth and Middleton reefs, in the Tasman Sea. The widely scattered islands and reefs of the territory are under the jurisdiction of the Attorney General's Department.

Heard Island and McDonald Islands. Heard and the McDonalds, totaling about 150 square miles and located about 2,500 miles southwest of Fremantle in Western Australia, serve primarily as scientific stations. There are no permanent inhabitants, and the islands are administered by the Australian Antarctic Division of the Department of the Environment, Water, Heritage, and the Arts.

In recent years poaching of Patagonian toothfish in the vicinity has led to increased patrolling of nearby waters. In August 2003 a Uruguayan-registered trawler was apprehended with an illegal toothfish cargo and three crewmen were convicted, fined, and deported. A year earlier, Australia had established around the islands a fully protected marine reserve second in size only to the Great Barrier Reef Marine Park.

Norfolk Island. Located about 1,000 miles east of Queensland, Norfolk Island was discovered by Captain James Cook in 1774 and served as a penal colony after the founding of Sydney in 1788. The island has an area of 14 square miles. Many of its present inhabitants descended from *Bounty* mutineers who moved from Pitcairn in 1856. In 2010 the population was estimated at just over 2000 but by 2013 it had declined to below 1500. Tourism, the principal industry, has declined from some 40,000 visitors a year to half that number.

The island is supported by grants and personnel secondments from Canberra, but the Norfolk Island Act 1979 obliged expenses increasingly to be met from local sources, particularly tourism. Under the act, a nine-member Norfolk Island Legislative Assembly is elected for a three-year term; the assembly's leaders constitute an Executive Council with cabinetlike functions. An administrator is named by the governor general of Australia and is responsible to the federal government. Norfolk has no formal parties, the principal division being between "Islanders" (of Pitcairn descent) and "Mainlanders" (Australians and New Zealanders).

The main political issue has long been whether Norfolk is an integral part of Australia, as argued by Canberra, or whether the Pitcairners are an indigenous people and have a right of self-determination. Legislation in 1999 intended to further integrate the island with the mainland prompted Islanders to accuse Canberra of "bloodless ethnic cleansing" and the local assembly to demand immediate and full internal self-government, which Canberra ignored. In March 2003 mounting pressure from Canberra for electoral reform induced the Legislative Assembly to reduce the residency requirement from 900 days to one year and to extend suffrage to all Australian, New Zealand, or British citizens.

In a December 2005 report, "Norfolk Island Financial Stability: The Challenge—Sink or Swim," a parliamentary committee recommended that Norfolk's taxation and welfare systems be brought into the commonwealth's systems. This unpopular issue precipitated the ouster of Chief Minster Geoffrey GARDNER by the Legislative Assembly in June 2006.

In October 2008 federal interior minister Bob DEBUS, indicting the Norfolk Island government for falling behind in provision of basic services and risking financial insolvency, warned that it could become a "failed state." The Norfolk Island government responded on December 29, with its *Submission to the Commonwealth on Governance Issues,* building on its *Submission to the Senate Select Committee on State Government Financial Management* of August 28, 2008, both of which pledged reforms but argued for continued autonomy and exemption from personal income taxes. In March 2009, the Legislative Assembly approved an administrative complaints system and tabled a proposal to accept the jurisdiction of the Australian ombudsman. In June the assembly introduced a budget incorporating further tax reforms but not a personal income tax regime.

On March 17, 2010, Norfolk Island chose a new assembly and on 24 March a new cabinet, promising reforms, was sworn in, with David BUFFETT taking the post of chief minister and André NOBBS becoming minister for tourism, industry, and development. Nevertheless the Australian Parliament's National Capital and Territories Committee reported in May 2010 that Norfolk Island still required reforms in the areas of privacy protection, freedom of information, ombudsman jurisdiction, administration, and financial management. The Australian government was reported to have disbursed A$35 million in the period 2010–2013 to subsidize Norfolk Island.

Amid reports of declining population and tourist arrivals and a growing budget deficit, requiring a federal subsidy of A$35 million since 2010, Catherine KING, federal minister of territories, visited in April 2013 to discuss the Norfolk Island Road Map. This plan, negotiated by Canberra officials with the island's Legislative Assembly in 2011, foreshadowed the island's closer integration with the Australian fiscal institutions but was opposed by most islanders, who want greater political autonomy and freedom from federal taxes.

Administrator: Neil POPE.

Chief Minister: Lesle SNELL.

Speaker of the Legislative Assembly: David BUFFETT.

AUSTRIA

Republic of Austria
Republik Österreich

Political Status: Federal republic established in 1918; reestablished in 1945 under Allied occupation; independence restored under the Four-Power Treaty of July 27, 1955.

Area: 32,376 sq. mi. (83,853 sq. km).

Population: 8,423,136 (2013E—UN); 8,221,646 (2013E—U.S. Census).

Major Urban Centers (2013E): VIENNA (1,731,236), Graz (265,318), Linz (191,107), Salzburg (148,528), Innsbruck (121,329).

Official Languages: German, Croatian (in Burgenland), Slovene (in Carinthia).

Monetary Unit: Euro (market rate November 1, 2013: 0.74 euro = $1US).

Federal President: Heinz FISCHER (Social Democratic Party of Austria); elected on April 25, 2004, and sworn in for a six-year term on July 8 to succeed Thomas KLESTIL (independent), who had been constitutionally precluded from running for a third term and who had died on July 6; reelected as independent candidate on April 25, 2010, and sworn in on July 8 for a second six-year term.

Federal Chancellor: Werner FAYMANN (Social Democratic Party of Austria); invited by the president on October 8, 2008, to form a new government following the legislative election of September 28 and sworn in on December 2, 2008, to succeed Alfred GUSENBAUER (Social Democratic Party of Austria).

THE COUNTRY

Situated at the crossroads of Central Europe, Austria is topographically dominated in the south and west by the Alps, while its eastern provinces lie within the Danube river basin. The vast majority of the population is of Germanic stock, but important ethnic enclaves exist, including a Slovene minority in the province of Carinthia, which borders Slovenia to the south, and a Croatian minority in Burgenland, a province bordering Hungary. Approximately 66 percent of the population is Catholic, although religious freedom is guaranteed. An influx of immigrants from southeastern Europe and Turkey over the last 20 years has created a small (4 percent) but growing Muslim minority, mostly concentrated in Vienna and Vorarlberg.

Austria has a mixed economy with highly organized and powerful national-level business and labor associations that have worked with the government to preserve economic growth and a social safety net in a "social partnership." Despite recent privatizations, the state still owns or holds major shares in several large industries. Although limited in scope by the mountainous terrain, agriculture continues to provide much of the domestic food requirements, with an emphasis on grains, livestock, and dairy products. About 12 percent of all farms follow organic principles. Agriculture accounts for about 2 percent of GDP, the industrial sector accounts for 30 percent, and tourism and other services account for more than 69 percent.

Austria weathered the global financial crisis relatively well: GDP grew by 2.3 percent in 2010 and 3.0 percent in 2011, but only 0.8 percent in 2012 and 0.6 percent is predicted for 2013. The downturn slowed inflation (1.7 percent in 2010, 3.6 percent in 2011, and 2.2 percent in 2012) but had little impact on Austria's unemployment, which at 4.4 percent was the lowest level in Europe for 2012. The coalition governments that took office in January 2007 and late 2008 bickered about how to mitigate the impact of the global financial crisis but by 2012 had successfully reduced the public budget deficit to 2.5 percent, below the EU-mandated threshold of 3 percent of GDP by 2013.

EU expansion boosted the Austrian banking sector and presented promising trade opportunities. Building on the success of the 1990s, much of Austria's recent economic growth was fueled by expanded investment and trade with Eastern and Central European states beyond its immediate neighbors. The severe contraction in world markets in late 2008 hobbled the Austrian finance sector, due to the substantial loan portfolios held by their subsidiaries in EU countries at the greatest risk of credit default. Moody's Investors Service downgraded the credit rating of Austria's three largest banks in June 2012.

GOVERNMENT AND POLITICS

Political background. Austria was part of the Habsburg-ruled Austro-Hungarian Empire until the close of World War I, the Austrian republic being established in November 1918. Unstable economic and political conditions led in 1933 to the imposition of a dictatorship under Engelbert DOLLFUSS, while civil war in 1934 resulted in suppression of the Social Democratic Party and Dollfuss's assassination by National Socialists. Hitler invaded Austria in March 1938 and formally incorporated its territory into the German Reich.

With the occupation of Austria by the Allies in 1945, a provisional government was established under the Social Democrat Karl RENNER. Following a general election in November 1945, Leopold FIGL formed a "grand coalition" government based on the Austrian People's Party (*Österreichische Volkspartei*—ÖVP) and the Social Democratic Party of Austria (*Sozialdemokratische Partei Österreichs*—SPÖ). The coalition endured under a succession of chancellors until 1966, when the ÖVP won a legislative majority and Josef KLAUS organized a single-party government. In 1970 the SPÖ came to power as a minority government under Bruno KREISKY. Subsequent elections in 1971, 1975, and 1979 yielded majority mandates for Chancellor Kreisky.

Following legislative balloting on April 24, 1983, in which the SPÖ failed to retain clear parliamentary control, Kreisky resigned in favor of Vice Chancellor Fred SINOWATZ, who formed a coalition government on May 24 that included three members of the third-ranked Freedom Party of Austria (*Freiheitliche Partei Österreichs*—FPÖ).

In a runoff election on June 8, 1986, that attracted world attention because of allegations concerning his service in a German unit guilty of demonstrable atrocities in the Balkans during World War II, former UN secretary general Kurt WALDHEIM, an independent supported by the ÖVP, defeated the SPÖ candidate, Kurt STEYRER, for the Austrian presidency. In protest, Chancellor Sinowatz and three other cabinet members resigned, and a new SPÖ-FPÖ government was formed under the former finance minister Franz VRANITZKY on June 16.

The government collapsed in mid-September 1986 after the FPÖ elected Jörg HAIDER, a far-right nationalist, as its chair, thereby rendering it unacceptable as a coalition partner for the SPÖ. In the ensuing lower house election of November 23, the SPÖ lost ten seats but retained a slim plurality, and on January 14 Vranitzky formed a new grand coalition with the ÖVP. The coalition continued with a somewhat restructured cabinet following the legislative balloting on October 7, 1990, which yielded a substantial gain for the nationalist FPÖ opposition. The FPÖ continued to gain strength in the 1991 provincial elections, and its 16.4 percent support in the first round of presidential elections on April 26, 1992, was assumed to have provided the margin that enabled the ÖVP candidate, Thomas KLESTIL, to defeat the SPÖ's Rudolf STREICHER in a runoff vote on May 24.

Austria became an EU member on January 1, 1995; however, the SPÖ-ÖVP government collapsed on October 12 due to a major dispute between the coalition parties over budget deficit reduction measures. An early election held on December 17 yielded unexpected gains for both the SPÖ and the ÖVP at the expense of the FPÖ. After lengthy negotiations, the SPÖ and ÖVP succeeded in resolving their differences, enabling Vranitzky to enter his fifth term as chancellor on March 12, 1996.

In the first direct election for the European Parliament in October 1996, the SPÖ (with 29.1 percent of the vote) unexpectedly finished second to the ÖVP (29.6 percent), while the FPÖ secured a surprisingly high 27.6 percent. Chancellor Vranitzky resigned on January 18, 1997, in favor of Finance Minister Viktor KLIMA, who made substantial changes in the SPÖ ministerial contingent in the government formed on January 29.

On April 19, 1998, President Klestil, running as an independent with the support of the ÖVP and the FPÖ, was easily reelected with 63.4 percent of the vote.

The federal election of October 3, 1999, ended the grand coalition of the SPÖ and ÖVP when the FPÖ placed second, with 27 percent of the vote, virtually tied with the ÖVP. After three months of fruitless budget negotiations with its former coalition partners, the ÖVP turned to the FPÖ, notwithstanding the threat of sanctions by the EU, which was alarmed by the anti-immigration and anti-EU rhetoric of FPÖ populist Haider, who resigned as party leader amid a storm of international criticism. A center-right/far-right coalition of the ÖVP and FPÖ was subsequently sworn in on February 4, 2000, with the ÖVP's Wolfgang SCHÜSSEL as chancellor.

In early September 2002, Susanne RIESS-PASSER, the vice chancellor and leader of the FPÖ, resigned both posts following a rebellion within the FPÖ led by Haider, who opposed the government's decision to forestall planned tax cuts in the wake of severe flooding in August. Announcing that the ÖVP could no longer work with the FPÖ, Chancellor Schüssel dissolved the National Council, and new elections were held on November 24. The ÖVP won a plurality of 79 seats, and Schüssel failed to form a coalition government with either the SPÖ or The Greens, and a new ÖVP-FPÖ government was installed on February 23, 2003.

In presidential elections on April 25, 2004, Heinz FISCHER of the SPÖ defeated the ÖVP's Benita FERRARO-WALDNER by 52.4 percent to 47.6 percent. Outgoing President Klestil, who was constitutionally precluded from seeking a third term, died on July 6, and Schüssel temporarily assumed the duties of president until Fischer was inaugurated on July 8.

In April 2005 the FPÖ was replaced as the junior coalition partner by the new Alliance for the Future of Austria (*Bündnis Zukunft Österreich*—BZÖ), formed by former FPÖ members, including Haider, who had recently been marginalized in the FPÖ.

The SPÖ won a slim plurality over the ÖVP in the legislative balloting of October 1, 2006, with 35.3 percent of the vote versus 33.5 percent for the ÖVP. The SPÖ's Alfred GUSENBAUER was sworn in as chancellor on January 11, 2007, to head another SPÖ-ÖVP coalition government. The government partners reached a consensus on policies emphasizing development of a high-technology and knowledge-centered economy via increased public funding for research and development, but they fought publicly over the nature and timing of tax reforms and budget priorities. The final blow came when Chancellor Gusenbauer and transport minister Werner FAYMANN called for public referenda on any future decisions relating to the EU constitution. ÖVP Vice Chancellor Wilhelm MOLTERER pulled his party's ministers out of the coalition on July 7, 2008. The snap elections that followed set off a chain reaction that almost overnight remade the top leadership of nearly all of Austria's political parties, as Chancellor Gusenbauer announced that he would not seek another term, and Molterer eventually stepped down as ÖVP leader.

In the legislative balloting on September 28, 2008, the SPÖ won a slim plurality with 29.3 percent of the national vote. Taking 26 percent, the ÖVP lost ground to the far-right FPÖ and BZÖ, which won 17.5 percent and 10.7 percent, respectively. Turnout was just over 78 percent of registered voters. The election occurred just as global financial markets were sliding into crisis, prompting the rival parties to form a government quickly in order to deal with the fallout in the banking and securities markets. Snubbing the resurgent right-wing parties, a new SPÖ-ÖVP coalition government was sworn in on December 2 with FAYMANN, now SPÖ leader, as the new chancellor. (See the 2013 PHW for details of the coalition agreement.)

In the June 7, 2009, European Parliament elections, the SPÖ posted its worst percentage in the postwar era with just 23.8 percent of the votes cast with 42 percent turnout, nearly 10 percentage points below the party's 2004 results. The ÖVP won a plurality with 30.6 percent, securing six seats to the SPÖ's four seats. Hans-Peter Martin's List won 18.1 percent with three seats. The FPÖ doubled its percentage from 2004 with 12.7 percent of the vote and two seats. The Greens secured 9.7 percent of the vote for two seats, while the BZÖ fell below the 5 percent threshold.

Running as an independent, President Fischer won reelection on April 25, 2010, with 79 percent of the national vote, handily defeating two challengers with turnout at 53.6 percent. The FPÖ nominated Barbara ROSENKRANZ, who ran on the party's anti-immigrant and anti-Muslim platform but garnered only 15 percent of the vote. The ÖVP and the Greens supported Fischer and did not put forward candidates.

By 2012 the FPÖ had moved ahead of the ÖVP in national polls and was rapidly closing in on the first-place SPÖ, after modifying its traditional anti-foreign rhetoric to capitalize on public frustration over EU bailouts.

Constitution and government. Austria's constitution, adopted in 1920 and amended in 1929, provides for a federal democratic republic embracing nine provinces (*Bundesländer*), including Vienna. Although most effective power is at the federal level, the provinces have considerable latitude in local administration. The national government consists of a president whose functions are largely ceremonial, a cabinet headed by a chancellor, and a bicameral Federal Assembly (*Bundesversammlung*). The chancellor is appointed by the president from the party with the strongest representation in the lower house, the National Council (*Nationalrat*). The upper house, the Federal Council (*Bundesrat*), which represents the provinces, is restricted to a review of legislation passed by the National Council and, for the most part, has only delaying powers, although approval of the assembly in full sitting is required in certain situations.

Each province has an elected legislature (*Landtag*) and an administration headed by a governor (*Landeshauptmann*) designated by the legislature. The judicial system is headed by the Supreme Judicial Court (*Oberster Gerichtshof*) for civil and criminal cases and includes two other high courts, the Constitutional Court (*Verfassungsgerichtshof*), which decides constitutional issues, and the Administrative Court (*Verwaltungsgerichtshof*), which reviews disputes involving actions of government ministries. The judges who serve on these courts are appointed by the president for specified terms. There are also four higher provincial courts (*Oberlandesgerichte*), 18 regional courts (*Landesgerichte und Kreisgerichte*), and numerous district courts (*Bezirksgerichte*).

Province and Capital	*Area (sq. mi.)*	*Population (2012E)*
Burgenland (Eisenstadt)	1,531	286,215
Carinthia (Klagenfurt)	3,681	557,773
Lower Austria (administered from Vienna)	7,402	1,617,455
Salzburg (Salzburg)	2,762	534,122
Styria (Graz)	6,327	1,213,255
Tirol (Innsbruck)	4,883	714,449
Upper Austria (Linz)	4,625	1,416,772
Vorarlberg (Bregenz)	1,004	371,741
Vienna	160	1,731,236

A two-year commission studying constitutional reform known as the Austria Convention submitted a report to the National Council in January 2005. Any further action on its recommendations is subject to legislation by the National Council. Changes to the constitution require a two-thirds majority in that chamber; if the proposed changes affect the competencies of the provinces, the Federal Council must also approve the changes with a two-thirds majority. In May 2007 the government lowered the voting age to 16 years, set the minimum age to stand for election at 18 years old (35 for presidential candidates), and changed the terms of office for members of the *Nationalrat* to five years instead of the previous four years.

Austria's press freedom fell slightly, with the country dropping from fifth place in 2012 to 12th in 2013, according to the annual list issued by Reporters Without Borders. The International Press Institute expressed concern over a proposed law that would compromise the confidentiality of media sources.

Foreign relations. The Austrian State Treaty of 1955 ended the four-power occupation of Austria; reestablished the country as an independent, sovereign nation; and forbade any future political or economic union with Germany. In October 1955 the Federal Assembly approved a constitutional amendment by which the nation declared its permanent neutrality, rejected participation in any military alliances, and prohibited the establishment of any foreign military bases on its territory.

The European Community (EC, subsequently the EU) opened a bilateral mission in Vienna in April 1988, and, despite manifest Soviet displeasure, Austria formally submitted an application to join the EC in July 1989. While EC membership remained the priority, Austria also cultivated relations with post-communist Central and Eastern Europe, taking a lead in the Central European Initiative (CEI) established in March 1992 on the basis of earlier regional cooperation. Intended to counter the economic power of the reunited Germany, the CEI grouping corresponded in part with the old Habsburg domains and was thus seen by some as the embryo of a resurgent Austrian economic empire.

On the basis of terms agreed upon in March 1994 and strongly recommended by the government, accession to the EU was endorsed by Austrian voters in a referendum on June 12 by a convincing margin of 66.4 to 33.6 percent. On January 1, 1995, Austria (together with Finland and Sweden) ceased to be on the European Free Trade Association side of the European Economic Area table, where it had sat for just a year, and instead became a full EU member.

On February 10, 1995, Austria joined the Partnership for Peace program of the North Atlantic Treaty Organization (NATO). It also obtained observer status at the Western European Union, while stressing that it would retain its long-standing neutrality. In April 1995 Austria became a signatory of the Schengen Accord, which provided for free movement among a number of EU states, and in November it agreed to contribute 300 soldiers to the NATO-commanded Implementation Force in Bosnia-Herzegovina.

In March 1998 Austria was 1 of 11 states recommended for inclusion in the EU's Economic and Monetary Union, which became effective on January 1, 1999. Although Austria's role in the new Europe did not include full membership in an expanding NATO, Austria expanded its cooperation with NATO via participation in the International Security Assistance Force peacekeeping mission to Afghanistan beginning in late 2001. Austria currently has peacekeepers in Afghanistan, Bosnia and Herzegovina, and Kosovo, but pulled out of the Golan Heights, Lebanon in June 2013, due to the conflict in Syria.

In the late 1990s, an influx of migrants and refugees from Eastern Europe and the former Yugoslavia prompted the Austrian government to tighten restrictions on immigration. In addition, the success of the radical FPÖ in Austria's 1999 elections prompted renewed questions about Austria's commitment to European integration and created image problems for Vienna reminiscent of the Kurt Waldheim years. Following the formation of a governing coalition that included the anti-immigrant FPÖ in 2000, the EU imposed diplomatic sanctions against Austria. France and Belgium were among the strongest backers of the sanctions, but by May 2000 at least six EU members reportedly were looking for a face-saving way to end them, especially as Vienna threatened to block EU reforms and EU enlargement. On September 12 the EU lifted the sanctions but pledged to monitor the activities of the FPÖ. Subsequently, the National Council approved the EU's Treaty of Nice in November 2001.

The Austrian legislature in May 2005 ratified the proposed EU constitution (although a majority of the Austrian public appeared to be against the measure). Popular support for the EU continued to decline in Austria with the rapid expansion of EU membership, rejection of the EU constitutional referenda in France and the Netherlands in 2005, high-profile squabbling over EU budgets, and high domestic unemployment attributed to the influx of foreign workers. In January 2006 the ÖVP-BZÖ government announced that it would extend until 2009 labor restrictions on citizens from new EU members. During the 2006 elections the campaign rhetoric of the right-wing parties focused on opposition to continued immigration (with a pronounced anti-Muslim overtone), continued opposition to Turkey's membership in the EU, and a backlash against further EU expansion or integration. Citing a shortage of skilled laborers, which hurt Austrian firms, the SPÖ-ÖVP government began lifting restrictions on skilled workers in 2008 and removed all restrictions on both skilled and unskilled workers on May 1, 2011.

The Austrian Parliament ratified the Treaty of Lisbon in April 2008. Public discontent with the Lisbon treaty was on the rise, however, after Irish voters rejected it in a referendum. Vienna supported the creation of the European Stability Mechanism to help member states facing bankruptcy, and Chancellor Faymann endorsed a banking union and financial transaction tax. On September 30, 2011, after a heated debate amid heckling by right-wing members, legislators approved a measure to expand the European Financial Stability Facility, the EU bailout fund intended to prevent the collapse of Greece and other indebted EU countries.

In May 2013 the government agreed to share information on foreigners with bank accounts in Austria.

Austria's relationship with its northern, eastern, and southern neighbors is influenced by its strong commercial ties to their economies and by environmental issues posed by the energy and environmental policy legacies of the communist era. Austrians have long been concerned about the safety of the Temelin nuclear power plant in the Czech Republic (only 40 miles from the Austrian border) and the Mochovce and Bohunice nuclear plants in Slovakia. Plans to expand these facilities sparked protests in Austria. In 2011 Chancellor Faymann sued Slovakia at the European Court of Justice to halt construction.

Current issues. After a shaky 2011, the SPÖ-ÖVP government successfully reduced spending. The budget deficit for 2012 was 2.5 percent of GDP—lower than the EU's 3 percent threshold and lower than the 3.1 percent predicted in late 2012. Finance Minister Maria FEKTER praised regional governments for their "impressive budget discipline." Standard & Poor's restored Austria's AAA credit rating in January 2013, after downgrading it to AA+ a year earlier.

In January 2013 voters rejected a SPÖ proposal to end military conscription in favor of a smaller, professional army. While Chancellor Faymann portrayed the move as a cost-cutting measure, the ÖVP insisted conscripts were needed to maintain Austria's security. The public also wanted to maintain alternative service programs that provide cheap labor for social services and disaster relief. The SPÖ Defense Minister, Norbert DARABOS, subsequently resigned to lead the SPÖ election campaign.

Popular faith in the traditional political parties has crumbled as more parties and politicians have been swept up in a continuous series of corruption scandals. Numerous members of the 2003–2007 ÖVP-BZÖ government, including former chancellor Schüssel, have been accused of taking kickbacks from Telekom Austria contracts. Chancellor Faymann stands accused of embezzlement and pressuring newspapers for favorable coverage and refused to appear before the parliamentary investigatory committee. Top figures at the Austrian National Bank are under investigation for bribery. Salzburg had a snap election on May 5, 2013, due to a financial scandal. The SPÖ-led government had allowed civil servant Monika RATHGEBER invest state tax receipts for years, then discovered she had hidden losses of €340 million. Some €400 million earmarked for residential development was missing. The state turned out to be in debt €1.8 million more than it realized. The SPÖ placed second in the snap election.

Likewise, the early election in Carinthia came as the Hypo Alpe Adria bank scandal widened. While governor of Carinthia, Jörg Haider borrowed €500 million from Hypo Alpe Adria ahead of a bond offering that never happened. Subsequent revelations about Haider's financial mismanagement damaged his party's reputation. The government nationalized the Carinthia-based bank in December 2009 and injected $2.6 billion to save the country's sixth-largest bank. Bavaria's Bayerische Landesbank injected an additional €4 billion. The Austrian government planned to sell the bank in 2013, but the European Commission is investigating legality of the state aid. Vienna has refused to repay Bayerische Landesbank, triggering a growing dispute between Austria and Germany.

The Greens are the only major party that has not been tainted by scandal, and they have headed the parliamentary investigation committee. According to a 398-page review of the various cases issued in January 2013, corruption consumed 5 percent of the national economy in 2012, some €17 billion. Austria slipped nine slots in the 2012 Transparency International Corruption Perception Index, from 16 to 25. New disclosure regulations on political donations and politicians' incomes were adopted in 2012, at the request of the Council of Europe's Group of States Against Corruption body.

POLITICAL PARTIES

Government Coalition:

Social Democratic Party of Austria (*Sozialdemokratische Partei Österreichs*—SPÖ). Formed in 1889 as the Social Democratic Workers' Party and subsequently redesignated the Socialist Party of Austria (*Sozialistische Partei Österreichs*) before assuming its current name in 1991, the center-left SPÖ represents the overwhelming majority of workers and part of the lower middle class; as such, it advocates progressive taxation, high social expenditure, and economic planning. However, the SPÖ renounced state ownership as a necessary element of a democratic socialist economy in 1978. After serving as junior coalition partner to the ÖVP from 1947 to 1966, the SPÖ returned to office as a minority government in 1970 under Bruno Kreisky, who won an absolute majority in 1971 and retained it in the 1975 and 1979 elections. Losing its overall majority in 1983, the SPÖ formed a coalition with the FPÖ, with Kreisky yielding the chancellorship and party leadership to Fred Sinowatz, who resigned in June 1986 over the Waldheim affair and was replaced by Franz Vranitzky.

In September 1986, in light of the FPÖ's sharp swing to the right, the SPÖ terminated the government SPÖ-FPÖ coalition but lost ground in the resultant elections, opting in January 1987 to re-form a "grand coalition" with the ÖVP. This provoked the resignation of Kreisky as SPÖ honorary chair, on the grounds that Vranitzky had turned his back on socialism in favor of the "banks and bourgeoisie." Nonetheless, a party congress in October gave qualified support to the government's privatization program.

The grand coalition was maintained after the 1990 election, with the SPÖ remaining the largest party; it was also preserved after the October 1994 balloting, when the SPÖ vote slipped to a postwar low of 34.9 percent, and after the December 1995 election, when the SPÖ recovered to 38.1 percent.

Following the SPÖ's relatively poor performance in the October 1996 balloting for the European Parliament, Vranitzky in January 1997 resigned as chancellor and was succeeded by Viktor Klima, who was also elected to replace Vranitzky as SPÖ chair at a special party congress in April.

In the parliamentary elections of October 1999, the SPÖ representation fell from 71 to 65 seats on a vote share of 33 percent, although the SPÖ retained a legislative plurality. After months of negotiations with the ÖVP, the grand coalition collapsed, reportedly over the unwillingness of the labor wing of the SPÖ to agree to budget cuts necessary to keep deficit spending within bounds. In February 2000 Klima resigned as party chair.

The SPÖ improved to 36.5 percent of the vote and 69 seats in the November 2002 elections, although it lost its legislative plurality to the ÖVP. In 2004 Heinz Fischer became the first member of the SPÖ in 30 years to be elected to the nation's largely ceremonial presidency, while the SPÖ's Gabi BURGSTALLER was elected governor of Salzburg after decades of conservative control of that province. The provincial turnover continued in late 2005 with the election of Franz VOVES as governor of Styria province, leaving the SPÖ with four of the nine provincial governorships, and costing the ÖVP its majority in the Federal Council in 2006.

Following its success in the October 2005 provincial elections, the SPÖ enjoyed a slight lead over the ÖVP in national opinion polls, but the surge in popular opinion shrunk to a virtual tie in early 2006 amid a deepening banking fraud scandal associated with the BAWAG bank owned by the Austrian Trade Union Federation, which has close ties to the SPÖ. A government investigation revealed in March 2006 that the bank had averted failure via a massive loan guarantee from the trade union federation's strike fund. A subsequent poll revealed that most Austrians believed that SPÖ Chair Alfred Gusenbauer had knowledge of the events surrounding the bailout.

The SPÖ won a narrow plurality in the October 1, 2006, balloting, securing 68 seats in the lower house with 35.3 percent of the vote. Gusenbauer's handling of the subsequent negotiations for the new SPÖ-ÖVP coalition drew significant criticism from within SPÖ ranks, specifically his concession of strategic cabinet posts to the ÖVP, as well as his abandonment of campaign promises regarding the Eurofighter contract and other social democratic goals. Gusenbauer also was criticized from within and outside the party for his mild response to the release of photos of FPÖ leader Heinz-Christian STRACHE taking part in paramilitary exercises and allegedly using a neo-Nazi greeting, which Gusenbauer characterized as "youthful pranks."

Dissatisfaction with Gusenbauer's handling of the coalition relationship with the ÖVP continued to grow in party ranks during 2007; it grew louder when the coalition infighting increased in 2008, hurting the SPÖ's standing in public opinion polls. After the SPÖ suffered setbacks in the provincial elections in Lower Austria (down 8 percent from the 2003 election) and Tirol (down 10 percent from 2003) in the first half of 2008, Gusenbauer agreed to step down as party chair in June. He ceded control to a new party leader, Werner Faymann, the minister for transport. When the coalition government collapsed in July, Gusenbauer announced that he would not seek reelection. Faymann was officially approved as leader by the party with over 98 percent support on August 8.

Faymann delivered a plurality of 29.3 percent for the SPÖ in the September 2008 election, but the percentage was the lowest postwar tally ever for the party, with the right-wing parties receiving the biggest percentage increases, making the victory somewhat hollow. After successfully brokering a new coalition government with the ÖVP, installed in December, Faymann called on party loyalists to close ranks and support him at a meeting commemorating the party's founding in Hainfeld.

The SPÖ retained Hannes Swoboda as its top candidate for the June 2009 European parliamentary elections, where it ceded its leadership position to the ÖVP, winning four seats to the ÖVP's six.

In provincial elections in Salzburg and Carinthia on March 1, 2009, the SPÖ lost more ground to right-wing parties. In Salzburg the SPÖ won a slim plurality but lost 2 seats to the FPÖ. In Carinthia the party had a nearly 10 percent drop in support. These poor results came on the heels of the 2008 loss in Lower Austria, where 4 seats were lost to the FPÖ, and in Tirol, where the party also lost 4 seats but remained in the governing coalition with the ÖVP. Provincial elections in Vorarlberg and Upper Austria held in September continued the poor poll results. In Vorarlberg the SPÖ slid from second to fourth place (while the FPÖ doubled its share of the vote and moved into second place). In Upper Austria the party suffered its worst defeat ever with 25 percent of the vote, a full 13 percentage points below the vote percentage in the previous election and a loss of 14 seats, its worst defeat ever in the province. The stinging defeats in the 2009 provincial elections undermined Faymann's position as party leader as criticism from the SPÖ ranks over the losses, especially to the benefit of the FPÖ, grew louder.

In the May 30, 2010, Burgenland election the party lost its majority, with 48 percent of the vote and one seat lost. The setbacks in provincial elections continued in the fall, with the SPÖ winning smaller pluralities in Styria (38 percent, down 4 percent from the previous election) and Vienna (44 percent, down 4 percent and a loss of six seats).

Norbert DARABOS resigned as minister of defense in March 2013 to guide the SPÖ into the September general election, in which the party dropped from 57 to 52 seats on a 26.86 percent share.

Leaders: Werner FAYMANN (Federal Chancellor and Chair of the Party), Heinz FISCHER (President of the Republic), Laura RUDAS, Norbert DARABOS (Federal Directors), Reinhard BUCHINGER (General Secretary).

Austrian People's Party (*Österreichische Volkspartei*—ÖVP). Catholic in origin, the ÖVP developed out of the prewar Christian Social Party. Dominated by farmers and businesspeople, it advocated a conservative economic policy and strongly supported EU accession. The dominant government party from 1946 to 1970, the ÖVP was thereafter in opposition for 16 years, with longtime party chair Aloïs Mock standing down in 1980 following provincial election reverses. Damaged by its support of Kurt Waldheim at the 1986 presidential poll, the party lost ground in the November legislative balloting and opted to return to a grand coalition as junior partner to the SPÖ. The coalition was maintained despite further losses in 1990 and 1994 (the overall decline being only partially disguised by the easy victory of ÖVP nominee Thomas Klestil in the 1992 presidential poll).

The ÖVP's 1994 vote share of 27.7 percent was a postwar low, with the party close to being overtaken on the right by the radical FPÖ (see below). The setback led to the ouster of Vice Chancellor Erhard BUSEK as party chair in April 1995 and the appointment of Wolfgang Schüssel as his successor, although the coalition with the SPÖ was maintained. ÖVP ministers precipitated the collapse of the coalition in October and an early election in December, in which the ÖVP vote unexpectedly improved to 28.3 percent. The grand coalition with the SPÖ was resumed in March 1996. However, the party slipped in the October 1999 parliamentary election to less than 27 percent, tied for second place with the FPÖ at 52 seats each. Schüssel, favoring reforms that a divided SPÖ would not accept, became a reluctant partner with the FPÖ and was sworn in as chancellor on February 4, 2000 (see Political background section for subsequent developments).

The ÖVP's results in the provincial elections in October 2005 were mixed. The party increased its share in Vienna to 49 percent but lost control over the provincial assembly and governorship to the SPÖ in Styria. Its national coalition partner, the BZÖ (see below), fared badly, however, undermining confidence that the ÖVP-BZÖ coalition could survive the next parliamentary election. In the October 1, 2006, balloting, the ÖVP received 33.5 percent of the national vote, a loss of more than 8 percentage points off its 2002 results. The party's poor showing in the 2006 balloting spurred a leadership shift, and Schüssel resigned as party leader in January 2007 after declining a position in the new cabinet. However, Schüssel took control of the ÖVP parliamentary group, a position previously held by Wilhelm Molterer, who succeeded Schüssel as party leader.

Molterer became vice chancellor in the SPÖ-ÖVP coalition government with the finance portfolio. The ÖVP also secured the foreign affairs, economics, and interior ministries, giving the junior member of the coalition the most prestigious cabinet posts, and leverage in cabinet negotiations with the SPÖ. Molterer, with Schüssel maintaining party discipline in the lower house, pushed Gusenbauer and the SPÖ hard in negotiations over government policy, raising tensions within the grand coalition, but generally winning the battle for public support in opinion polls.

In the 2008 provincial elections the ÖVP managed a slight increase in its share of the vote in Lower Austria but lost 9.5 percent in Tirol from the 2003 election results, largely due to the challenge posed by an ex-ÖVP partisan, Fritz Dinkhauser (see below). In April former minister and EU commissioner Franz FISCHLER called for Schüssel to step down as leader of the parliamentary group, claiming that Schüssel was interfering with Molterer's ability to operate effectively as vice chancellor in negotiations with the SPÖ, but the ÖVP cabinet ministers closed ranks and defended Schüssel's role.

The ÖVP received only 26 percent of the national vote in the September 2008 legislative election, which was scheduled after Molterer's withdrawal of the ÖVP ministers from the cabinet in July. A lackluster campaign and disappointment over the party's poor results (in the face of major gains by the right-wing FPÖ and BZÖ), however, led Molterer to step down as party leader immediately after the balloting, ceding control to Josef Pröll. Pröll was confirmed as party leader with nearly 90 percent of the votes cast at a party conference in Wels on November 28. Pröll's ascension to the leadership swept away the cadre of party leaders closely allied with Schüssel and Molterer. His good personal relations with SPÖ chancellor-designate Faymann helped propel the ÖVP's negotiations with the SPÖ to form the new coalition government. Three ÖVP executive committee members, however, voted against participating in a new coalition.

In March 2009 Pröll announced that Ernst STRASSER, a former cabinet minister, would head the party's list for the June European parliamentary elections, with the previous top ÖVP choice, MEP Othmar KARAS now listed second. Winning 30 percent of the vote, the ÖVP retained its six seats and displaced the SPÖ as the leading party in the Austrian delegation. Strasser was sentenced to four years in jail in January 2013 for corruption.

In the 2009 and 2010 provincial elections, the ÖVP either held onto its seats or lost little ground to right-wing parties, avoiding the large drop in support experienced by the SPÖ. The lone exception was the Vienna provincial election, where the party lost 5.5 percent of its previous support and five seats.

Citing health reasons, Pröll resigned his party and government posts in April 2011, and was replaced by European and International Affairs Minister Michael Spindelegger. Former chancellor Schüssel resigned from parliament on September 5, 2011, when he was implicated in the Telekom Austria kickback scheme. In 2012 the ÖVP launched a campaign to create a leaner, more efficient, more transparent government. One component was the introduction of "direct democracy"; that is, abandoning proportional representation in favor of direct elections, either through a national referendum or an act of parliament. Spindelegger also called for a code of conduct for party members, an idea that former chancellor Busek labeled "a joke."

The ÖVP placed second in the 2013 national election, dropping from 51 seats to 47 on a 24 percent share.

Leaders: Michael SPINDELEGGER (Vice Chancellor and Chair of the Party), Aloïs MOCK (Honorary Chair of the Party), Karlheinz KOPF (Vice Chair and Leader of the Parliamentary Group), Nikolaus BERLAKOVICH, Maria FEKTER, Andrea KAUFMANN, Reinhold MITTERLEHNER (Vice Chairs), Hannes RAUCH (General Secretary).

Opposition Parties:

Freedom Party of Austria (*Freiheitliche Partei Österreichs*—FPÖ). Formed in 1956 as successor to the League of Independents, which drew much of its support from former National Socialists, the FPÖ in the early 1970s moderated its extreme right-wing tendencies in favor of an essentially liberal posture. Its coalition with the SPÖ after the 1983 election, the first time that it had participated in a federal administration, collapsed as the result of the election of rightist Jörg Haider as party chair in 1986. Nonetheless, the FPÖ made substantial gains at the expense of both the SPÖ and the ÖVP in the National Council balloting of November 1986 and in provincial elections in March 1989. On the basis of a platform stressing opposition to immigration from Eastern Europe, it nearly doubled its lower house representation in 1990, almost entirely at the expense of the ÖVP.

In November 1992 the FPÖ launched an Austria First campaign for a referendum on the immigration issue, which was rejected in September 1993 by a large majority in the legislature. Three months later, moderate elements broke away to form the Liberal Forum (see below), which subsequently replaced the FPÖ as the Austrian affiliate of the Liberal International. Haider's anti-EU stance failed to prevent a decisive referendum vote in favor of entry in June 1994; in the October federal election, however, the FPÖ advanced further, its 22.5 percent vote share enabling Haider to claim that he was on course to win the chancellorship.

Although the FPÖ unexpectedly fell back to 21.9 percent in the December 1995 federal balloting and remained in opposition, it rebounded to capture nearly 28 percent of the vote in the October 1996 elections to the European Parliament. In March 1999 the party won the regional election in Carinthia, Haider's home province, with 42 percent of the vote. It was the first time the party had won a provincial election. Haider's victory was capped in April by his election as governor by the Carinthian legislature, which had been dominated by the SPÖ for about 50 years.

The FPÖ tied for second with the ÖVP in the October 1999 parliamentary election, picking up 12 seats to bring its total to 52. The disintegration of the grand coalition allowed the FPÖ to join the government, but only after agreeing with the ÖVP to end its opposition to EU membership and EU enlargement. When this failed to satisfy the FPÖ's critics abroad, Haider resigned as party leader, effective May 1, 2000, in favor of a Haider loyalist. Political analysts viewed this as a purely tactical move.

The party lost significant ground in provincial elections in Styria, Burgenland, and Vienna in late 2000 and early 2001. It also performed poorly in the November 2002 legislative balloting (18 seats on a 10.2 percent vote share), the June 2004 poll for the European Parliament (6.3 percent of the vote), and the March 2005 municipal elections in Lower Austria. In the ensuing internal struggle, Haider and his supporters (who advocated maintaining the coalition government with the ÖVP) lost the battle and immediately quit the FPÖ to form the BZÖ (see below), the FPÖ thereby losing most of its legislative representation and all its cabinet ministries.

Now led by the new party chair Heinz-Christian Strache (elected on April 23, 2005, at the party congress in Salzburg), the FPÖ contested the provincial elections in October 2005 on an anti-immigration and anti-EU platform in a bid to recapture the support of its right-wing populist base. This strategy moved the FPÖ to the right of the BZÖ, which had a more pragmatic approach because of its membership in the government. In the Vienna provincial election the FPÖ won 15 percent of the vote, but in Styria, a traditional FPÖ stronghold, the party failed to win any representation in the provincial assembly.

Strache's strategy for the FPÖ 2006 national election campaign emphasized anti-immigrant and anti-Muslim themes, as well as continued opposition to Turkish entry into the EU. The results of the balloting left the party tied with The Greens as the third largest block in the lower house with 21 seats and 11 percent of the national vote share, slightly improved from 2002, and well ahead of the BZÖ in the competition for right-wing populist support in every province except Carinthia, home province of former FPÖ and BZÖ party chair Jörg Haider.

The FPÖ opposed the ratification of the Lisbon Treaty in 2008 and advocated that the decision be put before the electorate in a referendum. In the provincial elections the FPÖ saw gains over its 2003 results of 6 percent in Lower Austria and nearly 5 percent in Tirol. This was consistent with national opinion poll results showing some voters turning to the FPÖ as an alternative to the ÖVP or BZÖ.

The FPÖ, which along with the BZÖ was the main beneficiary of voter frustration over infighting within the grand coalition and voter backlash against immigration and the Lisbon Treaty, won 17.5 percent of the national vote in the September 2008 legislative election. The strong national results for the FPÖ and BZÖ (when combined, the parties drew 28.2 percent of the vote, a full point more than the ÖVP) led to speculation that the two parties might reunite. Strache made several overtures to this effect, first after the death of BZÖ leader Jörg Haider in October 2008, and again following the provincial elections in Carinthia and Salzburg in March 2009 (in the Salzburg provincial election the FPÖ won 13 percent of the vote and gained two additional seats for a total of five). The new BZÖ leadership, reluctant to lose its identity after the death of party leader Haider, rebuffed Strache each time.

Strache was reelected party leader for the third time with 97 percent of the ballots cast at a party conference on May 16, 2009. In February Strache announced that Andreas MÖLZER would head the party's ticket for the European parliamentary elections.

The tone of the FPÖ campaign rhetoric drew intense criticism in the run-up to the European parliamentary elections. The party's campaign advertisements declared that the FPÖ would veto Turkey and Israel for EU membership, and its posters declared that the party would keep "The West in Christian Hands." Muslim and Christian leaders condemned the introduction of religious symbols and rhetoric into the campaign, as did President Heinz Fischer. SPÖ leader Chancellor Werner Faymann accused the FPÖ of anti-Semitism (since Israel was not a candidate for EU membership), and the head of the ÖVP European Parliament list said the words were "on the border of Nazism." Strache countered that it was insulting to accuse the FPÖ of anti-Semitism; party secretary Herbert Kickl dismissed the criticism as anxiety over the SPÖ's recent setbacks.

Following the FPÖ's gains in the June European parliamentary elections, when it gained one seat for a total of two, the party scored impressive results in the September provincial elections in Vorarlberg and Upper Austria. In both instances the FPÖ nearly doubled its share of the vote and gained seats, largely at the expense of the SPÖ. The gains did not carry over to the 2010 federal presidential election, however, as the FPÖ's nominee, Barbara Rosenkranz, was beaten soundly by the incumbent.

In 2010 provincial elections the FPÖ picked up one seat in Burgenland after nearly tripling its previous vote share. In the run-up to the Styrian elections the party stirred up more controversy for its anti-Muslim rhetoric after the release on its regional party Web site of an online game, Bye Bye Mosque, that encouraged players to block the construction of mosques and target muezzin. Following complaints by left-wing parties and religious leaders, the game was taken down. Despite the controversy, the anti-immigration and anti-Muslim campaign rhetoric garnered the party larger shares of the vote in the autumn provincial elections. In Styria, the FPÖ won nearly 11 percent of the vote and secured one seat in the nine-member government. In Vienna's regional provincial election the party won nearly 27 percent of the vote, more than a 10 percent gain over the previous election, making the FPÖ the second largest bloc in the provincial legislature.

While the FPÖ scored impressive victories in regional elections in 2012, the trend did not continue into 2013. While the FPÖ gained slightly in Salzburg (May 5), rising from 13 percent to 16 percent, it took only 8.2 percent in Lower Austria (March 3), and fell from 44.9 percent to 17.1 percent in Carinthia (March 3).

The FPÖ received 20.55 percent of the vote in the September 2013 national elections, good for 40 seats, six more than in 2008.

Leaders: Heinz-Christian STRACHE (Chair of the Party), Johann GUDENUS, Manfred HAIMBUCHNER, Norbert HOFER, Barbara ROSENKRANZ, Harald STEFAN (Vice Chairs), Hans WEIXELBAUM (Federal Manager), Herbert KICKL, Harald VILIMSKY (General Secretaries).

The Greens (*Die Grünen*). Austria's principal ecology-oriented party, *Die Grünen* was organized as The Green Alternative (*Die Grüne Alternative*—GAL) during a congress in Klagenfurt on February 14 and 15, 1987, of two groups that had jointly contested the 1986 election: the **Alternative List of Austria** (*Alternative Liste Österreichs*—ALÖ), a left-wing formation with links to the West German Greens, and the **United Greens of Austria** (*Vereinte Grünen Österreichs*—VGÖ). After failing in a bid to retain its organizational identity, the VGÖ withdrew, leaving the GAL with seven National Council deputies, one seat short of the minimum needed to qualify as a parliamentary group. The party overcame the difficulty in 1990 by winning ten seats, with three more being added in 1994 on a 7 percent vote share before declining to 4.8 percent and nine seats in December 1995. In 1993 it adopted its present name but continued to offer national candidate lists as The Greens—The Green Alternative. A July 2001 party congress passed a new platform based on core principles of ecology, solidarity, autonomy, grassroots democracy, nonviolence, and feminism.

Die Grünen became the fourth-largest parliamentary party following the October 1999 election when it gained 5 additional seats, for a total of 14, with 7.4 percent of the vote. It improved to 9.5 percent of the vote and 17 seats in 2002.

In the run-up to the October 2006 national balloting, The Greens' platform emphasized an energy policy that moved away from oil and nuclear power; investment in "green jobs" and education; priority for women's rights, social justice, and organic foods; and a global foreign policy that repudiated the "xenophobic" stance on the EU and the status of immigrants.

Die Grünen polled 11 percent of the national vote, securing 21 seats, the same number as the FPÖ and a high-water mark for the party. Twelve of The Greens' delegates to the lower house were women, giving them the only party bloc where women outnumber men. In 2008 The Greens joined the two right-wing parties in calling for a parliamentary inquiry into the allegations of misconduct in the Interior Ministry during the ÖVP-led governments. In the provincial elections The Greens generally lost ground over their showing in 2003, despite signs in public opinion polls that the party was benefiting from public frustration with the infighting between the grand coalition parties at the national level. However, in the Graz municipal election in January, The Greens nearly doubled their share of the vote from the 2003 balloting.

Long-time party leader Alexander VAN DER BELLEN stepped down as party chair after The Greens' poor results in the September 2008 balloting. The Greens finished with the lowest margin of all the parliamentary parties with 10.4 percent. Eva Glawischnig replaced Van der Bellen as chair.

Ulrike Lunacek won the party's top spot in the candidate list for the European Parliament, where The Greens retained their two seats.

The Greens lost some ground in the early 2009 provincial elections in terms of the percentage of votes won, but the slide had little effect on the seats secured in the provincial legislatures. In the September provincial elections, The Greens held their vote percentages steady and retained their seats. In 2010, however, The Greens lost one seat in Burgenland. In the autumn elections, The Greens lost vote share in Vienna but posted modest gains in Styria.

The Greens picked up four seats in the 2013 national elections, securing 24 seats with 12.34 percent of votes cast.

Leaders: Eva GLAWISCHNIG (Chair), Stefan WALLNER (National Manager), Maria VASSILAKOU (Deputy Federal Speaker), Werner KOGLER (Leader of Parliamentary Group).

Team Stronach for Austria (*Team Stronach für Österreich*). Frank Stronach, an 80-year old Austro-Canadian and self-made billionaire in the auto parts industry, created his own party in 2012. The party has attracted protest voters for its anti-euro, pro-business stance. The party was recognized as a parliamentary bloc in October, thanks to defections by two BZÖ, one SPÖ, and two independent MPs. Team Stronach won seats in the provincial parliaments of Carinthia and Lower Austria in March 2013 and joined the governing coalition in Salzburg after winning 8.3 percent of the vote on May 5, 2013.

The party placed sixth in the September 2013 National Council election, securing 5.74 percent of the vote and 11 seats.

Leader: Frank Stronach (Founder).

New Austria (*Das Neue Österreich—Neos*) was created in October 2012 and is aimed at dissatisfied members of the Greens and ÖVP. Its leader, Matthias Strolz, previously was a member of ÖVP. The group calls for an end to conscription, opposes any new property tax, and wants to increase direct democracy through referenda and ending federal party financing. The Neos ran a joint list with the Liberal Forum, Young Liberals, and online Party of Austria for the 2013 federal elections. The party entered the National Council on its first try, winning 9 seats with 4.93 percent of the vote.

Leader: Matthias Strolz.

Other Parties or Groups That Contested the 2013 Election:

Alliance for the Future of Austria (*Bündnis Zukunft Österreich—* BZÖ). Disgruntled FPÖ members, including all of the FPÖ cabinet ministers and most of the FPÖ legislators, launched the BZÖ in April 2005. The BZÖ, which elected prominent right-winger Jörg Haider as its chair, therefore became the junior partner in an ÖVP-BZÖ coalition government and averted a fall of the coalition government that would have triggered early national elections. In the same month Siegfried KAMPL, a BZÖ member from Carinthia who was scheduled to assume the rotating presidency of the Federal Council in July 2005, tarred the new party's image by denouncing deserters from the Nazi-era Austrian armed forces. Amid a storm of protest Kampl pledged to resign his seat but reneged on the promise in May 2005, and he subsequently resigned his membership in the BZÖ.

In the October 2005 provincial elections the BZÖ secured less than 2 percent of the vote in Vienna (and thus no representatives) and also failed to win any seats in the Styrian provincial assembly. The poor results immediately cast doubt on the BZÖ's potential fortune in the October 2006 national polls, specifically its ability to win the 4 percent needed to retain seats in the parliament. Following the provincial elections Haider made overtures to reunite with the FPÖ but was rebuffed.

Haider announced his intent to resign as national party chair in late 2005 and finally stepped down in May 2006. Acting Chair Peter Westenthaler was formally elected chair at a party congress in Salzburg on June 23, 2006. Westenthaler reiterated the party's call for enforcement of immigration restrictions and deportation of long-term unemployed immigrants as well as opposition to EU expansion to include Turkey. In the October 2006 balloting the BZÖ polled just over the 4 percent threshold, with 4.1 percent of the national vote.

The BZÖ, like the FPÖ, opposed the ratification of the Lisbon Treaty in 2008 and supported calls for putting the decision before the voters in a national referendum. The BZÖ made overtures to the SPÖ in 2008 with a promise to support an SPÖ minority government or perhaps form an alliance in government, but with so few seats in the lower house, deep distrust and disdain from the other opposition parties (The Greens and the FPÖ), and no momentum to get past 4 percent support in national polls or recent provincial elections, there was little chance that such an alliance would succeed.

Party leader Peter Westenthaler was convicted of perjury in July 2008 and forced to step down. In a bid to revive the party's electoral fortunes in the run-up to the September 28 snap election, the BZÖ brought back Jörg Haider to replace Westenthaler as party leader. The move produced the best national election result to date for the party, with a 10.7 percent margin. Immediately thereafter Haider and FPÖ leader Heinz-Christian Strache worked out an agreement on draft economic measures to spur growth for submission to the five parliamentary parties, but Haider subsequently died in a car accident on October 11. Stefan Petzner, a protégé of Haider, was named acting party leader. In April 2009 Josef Bucher, a leader of the parliamentary group in the National Council, was elected leader with over 99 percent of the votes cast. Ewald Stadler was chosen to lead the party's list for the European parliamentary election, but the party failed to win enough votes to claim a seat.

The BZÖ won a huge victory in the Carinthian provincial elections in March 2009 by securing nearly 45 percent of the vote. Its vote share in the September provincial elections in Vorarlberg and Upper Austria, however, failed to crest the 5 percent threshold for securing seats in the provincial legislatures. The BZÖ's dominance in Carinthia was undermined, however, by a factional split later in 2009 which resulted in the formation of a new regional party, the **Freedom Party in Carinthia** (FPK), and the defection of key regional party leaders. The FPK may turn out to be short-lived, as it fell from 45 percent to 17.1 percent in the March 2013 provincial election, amid mounting corruption scandals.

In 2010 party leader Bucher continued to try to steer the party toward a more centrist position focusing on economic issues and made overtures toward the reorganized Liberal Forum (LiF). Despite the shift in platform, the BZÖ continued to lose support outside of its Carinthian regional base, weathering another internal revolt in Vienna, where local party leaders rebelled and formed a new party, the **Free Alliance for the Future** (FBZ). The BZÖ failed to post any measurable gains in the 2010 provincial elections.

Nine BZÖ MPs defected to other parties during the 2009–2013 National Council session.

Polling only 3.53 percent support in the 2013 national election, the BZÖ lost all representation in the National Council.

Leaders: Josef BUCHER (Chair of the Party), Ursula HAUBNER (Vice Chair), Hubert SCHEIBNER (Secretary General), Michael A. RICHTER (Federal Director).

Communist Party of Austria (*Kommunistische Partei Österreichs—* KPÖ). The KPÖ, founded in 1918, supports nationalization, land reform, and a neutralist foreign policy. Its strength lies mainly in the industrial centers and in trade unions, but it has not been represented in the legislature since 1959 and obtained only 0.3 percent of the vote in 1994, 0.5 percent in 1999, and 0.6 percent in 2002. The KPÖ did, however, surpass the BZÖ vote total in the October 2005 provincial election in Vienna, finishing in fifth place to the BZÖ's sixth place, but well short of the 5 percent necessary to win representation in the provincial assembly.

In the October 2006 national election the KPÖ won just over 1 percent of the national vote. Results in the September 2008 election were slightly worse, with the party capturing only 0.76 percent of the national vote and just over 1 percent of the vote in Vienna and Styria provinces.

The KPÖ was part of the European Left grouping for the European parliamentary elections, with Günther Hopfgartner as the party's candidate for the June balloting.

In the fall 2010 provincial elections, the party posted losses in the vote share in both Vienna and Styria, losing two of its previous four seats in the Styrian assembly and polling barely more than 1 percent of the votes in Vienna.

The KPÖ finished a surprising second in the Graz city election in November 2012 with 20.1 percent of the vote, an 8.9 percent gain. That success did not carry into the 2013 federal election, where it received 1.02 percent of the vote.

Leaders: Melina KLAUS and Mirko MESSNER (Cochairs), Michael GRABER, Walter BAIER, Melina KLAUS, Günther HOPFGARTNER.

Pirate Party of Austria (*Piratenpartei Österreich—PPÖ*) was founded in 2006 and attracts young men with computer and information-technology skills. Part of the international Pirate Parties movement, it opposes the international Anti-Counterfeiting Trade Agreement and other forms of copyright enforcement. The PPÖ also favors direct democracy, free day care, and a federal Europe. The party won seats in the Innsbruck city council in April 2012 and the Graz city council in November 2012. However, party unity is shaky; Alexander OFER, the Innsbruck winner, broke from the national party to create a Tyrolean Pirate party. Party leaders have ruled out joining any governing coalition, further eroding its potential impact. The young voters, who were attracted to the PPÖ in 2012, moved toward the SPÖ and Stronach in 2013. The Pirates received 0.77 percent of the votes for the National Assembly.

Leaders: Christopher CLAY, Luke Daniel KLAUSNER, André IGLER, Andreas CZAK, Walter BONHARDI (Board Members).

Other Parties:

Liberal Forum (*Liberales Forum*—LiF). The LiF was founded in February 1993 by five FPÖ deputies opposed to the party's nationalist agitation, among them the FPÖ presidential candidate in 1992, Heide SCHMIDT. In the October 1994 federal balloting, the LiF limited the gain for its parent party by winning 11 seats on a 6.0 percent vote share, although it slipped to 5.5 percent and 10 seats in December 1995. Party Leader Schmidt ran in the presidential election of April 1998 and came in a distant third (with 11.1 percent of the vote) in a field of five. She resigned her leadership position when the party lost all 10 seats in 1999 on a vote share of 3.65 percent, less than the 4 percent threshold required for representation. The LiF managed to secure only 0.1 percent of the vote in 2002.

The LiF did not contest the October 2006 national poll under its own banner, but Alexander ZACH, the party chair, was elected to the National Council on the SPÖ list and caucused with SPÖ delegates.

In the September 2008 election the LiF drew more than 1 percent of the vote in every province for a total of 2.1 percent of the national vote.

On October 25, 2008, the LiF reorganized under new leadership selected at a meeting held in Vienna. The party announced in 2009 that it would not run any candidates in the European parliamentary election. In June 2009, a new slate of leaders were selected at a conference in Vienna, and a new party program was put in place that emphasized human rights, freedom, and the benefits of an open society where the state is in a subordinate role, as well as a pro-EU orientation. The LiF fielded a joint list with the Neos (see below) for the 2013 parliamentary election.

Leaders: Angelika MLINAR (Chair), Michael POCK (Secretary).

Citizens' Forum Austria Fritz Dinkhauser's List (*Bürgerforum Österreich Liste Fritz Dinkhauser*—FRITZ). Led by its namesake, a former ÖVP partisan unhappy about the ÖVP's close ties with farm interests, FRITZ scored a major victory in the 2008 provincial election in Tirol by garnering 18 percent of the vote and winning seven seats in the provincial assembly, two more than the SPÖ. In the September 2008 national election FRITZ received 1.76 percent of the national vote, drawing votes from every province, with strong support in Tirol and Vorarlberg, but well below the 4 percent threshold for securing seats in the National Council. In January 2009 Dinkhauser announced that the forum would focus exclusively on Tirol. It did not field candidates for the June 2009 European parliamentary election, and its name has been shortened to Civil Forum Tyrol List Fritz. Dinkhauser sat out the April 2013 election in Tirol, and the party's share plummeted to 5.6 percent.

Leaders: Fritz DINKHAUSER (Chair), Andreas BRUGGER (Vice Chair), Bernhard ERNST (Parliamentary Group Leader).

Independent Citizens' Initiative Save Austria (*Unabhängige Bürgerinitiative Rettet Österreich*—RETTÖ). The RETTÖ group, founded by Wilfried Auerbach, claimed not to be a party but instead an independent movement of citizens skeptical of the established Austrian political parties and of EU-imposed policies not subject to approval by Austrian citizens. The group's manifesto opposed extremism, fanaticism, and violence, including Austrian participation in foreign military operations. The group drew a small fraction of votes in every province in the 2008 legislative elections but ultimately polled only 0.74 percent of the total national vote. The movement is no longer active.

Leaders: Karl Walter NOWAK, Wilfried AUERBACH.

Christian Party of Austria (*Christliche Partei Österreichs*—CPÖ). A conservative religious party founded in October 2005 as **The Christians** (*Die Christen*—DC) and registered in January 2006, the party's platform reflected conservative Christian social values centered on the sanctity of family, religious faith, and a limited role for the government. DC contested the provincial elections in Lower Austria and Tirol in 2008 but failed to win any seats. In the September 2008 national election DC secured 0.6 percent of the national vote and over 1 percent in Vorarlberg province.

In 2009 the party relaunched under its new name and chose a new leader, Rudolf Gehring. Gerhring ran for the federal presidency in April 2010 and secured 5.4 percent of the vote.

Leaders: Rudolf GEHRING (Chair), Gernot STEIER (Secretary General).

Hans-Peter Martin's List (*Liste Hans-Peter Martin*). In the 2004 balloting for the European Parliament, two Austrian seats (on a 14 percent vote share) were won by an independent list headed by Hans-Peter Martin, a member of the European Parliament since 1999 who had gained significant attention for his campaign against the perceived exorbitant financial allowances accorded some of his peers.

In the 2006 legislative balloting the List won 2.8 percent of the vote, short of the 4 percent necessary to secure seats in the assembly. The List won three seats in the European Parliament in 2009, reduced to two in 2010, after Angelika WERTHMANN, a member of Martin's faction, left over Martin's failure to publicly disclose the disbursement of EU campaign subsidies.

Leader: Hans-Peter MARTIN.

LEGISLATURE

The bicameral **Federal Assembly** (*Bundesversammlung*) consists of a Federal Council (upper house) and a National Council (lower house).

Federal Council (*Bundesrat*). The upper chamber consists of 62 members representing each of the provinces on the basis of population, but with each province having at least three representatives. Chosen by provincial assemblies in proportion to party representation, members serve for terms ranging from five to six years, depending on the life of the particular assembly. The presidency of the council rotates among the nine provinces for a six-month term. In the council as of August 2012, the Austrian People's Party held 27 seats; the Social Democratic Party of Austria, 22; the Freedom Party of Austria, 8; The Greens, 3; the Citizens' Forum Austria Fritz Dinkhauser's List, 1; and The Alliance for the Future of Austria, 1.

President: Edgar MAYER (through December 2013).

National Council (*Nationalrat*). The lower chamber consists of 183 members elected by universal suffrage from 43 electoral districts for maximum terms of five years. In the most recent election of September 28, 2013, the Social Democratic Party of Austria won 52 seats; Austrian People's Party, 47; the Freedom Party of Austria, 40; The Greens, 24, Team Stronach for Austria, 11, and New Austria, 9.

President: Barbara PRAMMER.

CABINET

[as of November 15, 2013]

Chancellor	Werner Faymann (SPÖ)
Vice Chancellor	Michael Spindelegger (ÖVP)
Ministers	
Agriculture, Forestry, Environment, and Water Management	Nikolaus Berlakovich (ÖVP)
Defense and Sports	Gerald Klug (SPÖ)
Economic Affairs, Family, and Youth	Reinhold Mitterlehner (ÖVP)
Education, Arts, and Culture	Claudia Schmied (SPÖ) [f]
Finance	Maria Fekter (ÖVP) [f]
European and International Affairs	Michael Spindelegger (ÖVP)
Health	Alois Stöger (SPÖ)
Interior	Johanna Mikl-Leitner (ÖVP) [f]
Justice	Beatrix Karl (ÖVP) [f]
Labor, Social Affairs, and Consumer Protection	Rudolf Hundstorfer (SPÖ)
Science and Research	Karlheinz Töchterle (ÖVP)
Transportation, Innovation, and Technology	Doris Bures (SPÖ) [f]
Women and Civil Service	Gabriele Heinisch-Hosek (SPÖ) [f]

[f] = female

INTERGOVERNMENTAL REPRESENTATION

Ambassador to the U.S.: Hans Peter MANZ.

U.S. Ambassador to Austria: Aleksa WESNER.

Permanent Representative to the UN: Martin SAJDIK.

IGO Memberships (Non-UN): ADB, AfDB, EIB, EU, IADB, ICC, IEA, IOM, OECD, OSCE, WTO.

AZERBAIJAN

Azerbaijan Republic
Azerbaycan Respublikasy

Political Status: Azerbaijan Republic established under Turkish auspices in May 1918; joined the Union of Soviet Socialist Republics as part of the Transcaucasian Soviet Federated Republic on December 30, 1922;

became separate Soviet Socialist Republic on December 5, 1936; independence declared August 30, 1991, by the Azerbaijani Supreme Soviet and confirmed by that body on October 18; new constitution providing for a strong presidential system adopted by national referendum on November 12, 1995, and entered into force November 27.

Area: 33,436 sq. mi. (86,600 sq. km).

Population: 9,540,584 (2012E—UN); 9,590,159 (2013E—U.S. Census).

Major Urban Center (2010E): BAKU (2,078,485).

Official Language: Azeri (Azerbaijani).

Monetary Unit: Azerbaijani New Manat (official rate November 1, 2013: 0.78 manat = $1US). The new manat, equivalent to 5,000 old manats, was introduced in January 2006.

President: Ilham ALIYEV (New Azerbaijan Party); elected by popular vote on October 15, 2003, and sworn in for a five-year term on October 31 to succeed Heydar ALIYEV (New Azerbaijan Party); reelected on October 15, 2008, and October 9, 2013.

Prime Minister: Artur RASIZADE (New Azerbaijan Party); appointed acting prime minister by the president on July 20, 1996, to succeed Fuad KULIYEV (New Azerbaijan Party), who had resigned July 19; confirmed as prime minister by the president on November 26, 1996; reappointed by the president on October 23, 1998; resigned on August 4, 2003, but reappointed on an acting basis on August 6; reappointed in full capacity by the president on November 4, 2003; reappointed by the president and confirmed by the National Assembly on October 28, 2008, following the presidential election of October 15; reappointed by the president on October 22, 2013, following the presidential election of October 9.

THE COUNTRY

Home to a largely Turkic-speaking population, Azerbaijan is bordered by Georgia on the northwest, Russia on the north, the Caspian Sea on the east, Iran on the south, and Armenia on the west. Within its territory is the predominantly Armenian enclave of Nagorno-Karabakh (see map in article on Armenia), which has been the focus of intense conflict since independence. Azerbaijan also controls the noncontiguous, but largely Azeri, autonomous region of Nakhichevan on the southwestern border of Armenia. Shiite Muslims constitute the majority of the country's population, although the percentage of Sunnis (located primarily in the north) has risen recently. Ethnic Azeris make up an estimated 90 percent of the population. Minorities include Avars, Tsakhurs, and Lezgins in the north, among whom a degree of support is reported for a possible alignment with similar populations in Russia's southern Dagestan. Women are generally underrepresented in government. Twenty women were elected to the National Assembly in 2010, but there are no women in the current cabinet.

Baku, the capital of Azerbaijan, is located on the Caspian's Apsheron Peninsula, one of the world's oldest oil-producing regions, the proceeds from which made Baku one of Europe's richest cities in the years before World War I. Agriculture employs 40 percent of the labor force but accounts for only 6.0 percent of GDP, with crops including wheat, barley, potatoes, cotton, tobacco, rice, and tea. The country's mineral resources, which, in addition to petroleum (7 billion barrels of proven reserves) include natural gas, iron, zinc, copper, lead, and cobalt, support a number of manufacturing industries. Oil and gas account for 50 percent of GDP and 90 percent of exports.

The war with Armenia over Nagorno-Karabakh absorbed 25 percent of the state budget in the early 1990s, amid GDP contraction of some 60 percent between 1990 and 1994 and attendant widespread impoverishment. Since 1994 Nagorno-Karabakh, which represents some 14 percent of Azerbaijan's territory, and several contiguous provinces (constituting an additional 8 percent of Azerbaijani territory) have been under Armenian control. Meanwhile, Azeri refugees from Nagorno-Karabakh and surrounding regions (estimated at more than 750,000) reside in camps throughout the rest of the country awaiting a permanent settlement of the conflict and possible return to their former homes. Azerbaijan is also home to an estimated 220,000 Azeri refugees from Armenia proper.

Little immediate progress was made toward a market economy following the 1994 cease-fire in Nagorno-Karabakh, although in 1995 Azerbaijan obtained its first loans from the International Monetary Fund (IMF) to support economic transition amid hopes that Western exploitation of the country's oil reserves would yield major financial benefits. Meanwhile, the non-oil sector essentially stagnated in the late 1990s, with widespread corruption reported at all levels of government.

In April 1999 a 515-mile oil pipeline from Baku to the Black Sea port of Supsa, Georgia, was opened amid great fanfare. Attention subsequently focused on a Western-backed oil pipeline of even greater capacity from Baku through Georgia to the Mediterranean port of Ceyhan, Turkey (see below).

The second phase of the country's privatization program, launched in mid-2000, was directed toward major state enterprises in the energy, telecommunications, and transportation sectors. However, relations with the IMF subsequently remained mixed, the fund suspending some of its support in 2002 and 2003 because of the government's failure to implement several promised reforms. Meanwhile, Transparency International ranked Azerbaijan as one of the most corrupt countries in the world (95th out of 102 countries). As did many other international institutions, the IMF also subsequently criticized the dearth of "good governance" on the part of Azerbaijan's Aliyev regime.

The $4 billion, 1,000-mile oil pipeline from the Caspian to Turkey was completed in May 2005 by a consortium that included British Petroleum as the largest shareholder. The pipeline, which began operating in June 2006, was ultimately expected to pump 1 million barrels per day, with some experts predicting it could eventually be extended under the Caspian to Kazakhstan, providing the West with even greater access to Caspian oil without dealing with Russia or Iran.

Fueled by the booming oil sector, GDP rose by 24.3 percent in 2005, 31 percent in 2006, and more than 20 percent in 2007, making Azerbaijan's economy the fastest growing in the world. Moreover, the economy was further augmented by the opening of gas export lines from large deposits recently discovered in the Caspian Sea region. (After many years of gas dependency on Russia, Azerbaijan is now considered a potential gas supplier for Europe, also trying to reduce its reliance on Russia. Shipments to Europe from Azerbaijan's vast offshore *Shah Deniz* gasfield were expected to begin in 2017, assuming completion of extensive new pipelines.) In response to higher revenues, the government has dramatically increased expenditures since 2005 in an effort to combat poverty (which still afflicts one-third of the population), reinvigorate agriculture (the country had been known as the "vegetable garden" of the Union of Soviet Socialist Republics [USSR]), and rehabilitate dilapidated railways, roads, and water distribution networks. Meanwhile, the IMF has called for additional structural reform to support the non-oil sector and other liberalization to facilitate Azerbaijan's proposed accession to the World Trade Organization. (Negotiations with the WTO continued as of late 2013.) Some analysts have described Azerbaijan as a prime candidate to suffer the "oil curse" under which similarly positioned nations have failed to capitalize effectively on economic potential because of a lack of transparency in governmental activities and systemic corruption.

Azerbaijan weathered the international economic storm of 2009 better than many countries, as GDP grew by 9.3 percent in 2009 and 5.0 percent in 2010. A temporary reduction in oil production (attributed in part to maintenance and repairs) contributed to GDP stagnation in 2011–2012, although the non-oil sector grew by more than 9 percent in each year.

GOVERNMENT AND POLITICS

Political background. Historic Azerbaijan spanned the area of the present republic plus a somewhat larger region located in northern Iran. Persia and the Ottoman Empire competed for the territory in the 16th century, with the former gaining control in 1603. The northern sector, ceded to Russia in the early 19th century, joined Armenia and Georgia in a short-lived Transcaucasian Federation after the 1917 Bolshevik Revolution. Azerbaijan proclaimed its independence the following year but was subdued by Red Army forces in 1920. In 1922 it entered the USSR as part of the Transcaucasian Soviet Federal Republic, becoming a separate Soviet Socialist Republic (SSR) in 1936. Whereas the largely Armenian-populated enclave of Nagorno-Karabakh had been ceded to the new Armenian SSR in 1920, three years later, at Joseph Stalin's direction, it was returned to the Azerbaijan SSR. In 1924 the western enclave of Nakhichevan was also placed under Azerbaijan's jurisdiction (this step was approved by Turkey in its capacity as a regional guarantor power under the 1921 Treaty of Kars).

In 1989, as the Communist monolith began to crumble, a secessionist Azerbaijan Popular Front (*Azerbaycan Xalq Cebhesi*—AXC) emerged and became the object of intense repression by Soviet troops. Meanwhile, conflict had erupted with neighboring Armenia regarding the status of Nagorno-Karabakh (see entry on Armenia for additional information), and the Azerbaijan Communist Party (*Azerbaycan Kommunist Partiyasi*—AKP) was able to deflect support from the nationalists by strongly opposing any compromise involving the enclave. As a result, the Communists were clear victors in elections to the Azerbaijani Supreme Soviet on September 30 and October 14, 1990.

In March 1991 it was reported that 93 percent of those voting in a national referendum in Azerbaijan had approved the draft "Union Treaty" proposed by Mikhail Gorbachev for the continuation of a Union of Soviet Republics with additional rights being extended to the constituent republics. (Armenia declined to conduct a referendum on the matter for fear the new treaty would compromise its claim to Nagorno-Karabakh.) However, the chair of the Azerbaijani Supreme Soviet, Ayaz Niyaz Ogly MUTALIBOV, subsequently appeared to side with hard-liners who in mid-August in Moscow attempted a coup aimed at stopping Gorbachev's reforms. When the coup failed, Mutalibov denied having supported the initiative and resigned his post as first secretary of the AKP, apparently to show his solidarity with demonstrators clamoring for independence and separation from Communist rule.

On August 30, 1991, the Azerbaijani Supreme Soviet voted to "restore the independent status of Azerbaijan." Opposition groups called for a delay in the presidential election scheduled for September 8, but Mutalibov insisted the balloting be held. As a result of an opposition boycott, Mutalibov, describing himself as a "new Communist," was elected as the sole candidate. On October 10 the Azerbaijan Supreme Soviet passed legislation providing for the formation of a national defense force, and on October 18 it unanimously approved the Constitutional Act on the State Independence of the Republic of Azerbaijan, which reaffirmed the independence announcement of August 30. However, the administration flatly rejected the opposition's demands for new legislative elections.

President Mutalibov resigned on March 6, 1992, because of his government's inability to protect the Azeri minority in Nagorno-Karabakh from Armenian guerrilla attacks; Yagub MAMEDOV was named his interim successor. However, following a major reversal for Azerbaijani forces in Nagorno-Karabakh, a quorumless legislature voted on May 14, 1992, to restore Mutalibov to the presidency. The action triggered a clash between ex-Communists and AXC supporters that resulted in Mutalibov again being toppled on May 15. Four days later the Supreme Soviet voted to disband in favor of an AXC-dominated National Assembly, and on June 7 the AXC candidate, Abulfaz Ali ELCHIBEY, easily defeated four competitors in a new round of presidential balloting.

In 1993 President Elchibey came under increasing pressure for his government's failure to evict Armenian forces from Nagorno-Karabakh, and in early June a domestic insurrection was launched by the garrison in the country's second-largest city, Gyandzha. On June 16 the president left Baku for Nakhichevan as the rebel units, commanded by Col. Surat GUSEINOV, approached the capital. On June 18 former AKP first secretary Heydar ALIYEV, who as leader of the New Azerbaijan Party (*Yeni Azerbaycan Partiyasi*—YAP) had been installed as parliamentary chair on June 15, declared that, because of Elchibey's "inexplicable and unwarranted absence," he (Aliyev) had assumed "the duties and responsibilities of the presidency of Azerbaijan." On June 30 Aliyev named Colonel Guseinov to head a new government, and in popular balloting on October 3, YAP candidate Aliyev was confirmed as president, officially winning 98.8 percent of the vote.

Following a power struggle, President Aliyev on October 6, 1994, dismissed Guseinov as prime minister, in favor of Fuad KULIYEV (theretofore a deputy premier), while stressing that he (Aliyev) was head of the government. The president described the outgoing cabinet as "a den of criminals" and indicated that treason charges would be leveled against Guseinov, who had fled to Russia. (Guseinov was extradited to Azerbaijan in 1996 and was sentenced to life imprisonment in early 1999 following his conviction on more than 40 charges. He was pardoned by President Aliyev in 2004.)

A new crisis erupted in March 1995 when rebel interior ministry forces led by Deputy Interior Minister Ravshan JAVADOV staged an attempted coup, which was put down with numerous fatalities, including that of Javadov. Amid the turbulence, President Aliyev accused Russia of plotting to destabilize his government in concert with hard-line exiles, notably Mutalibov. According to Baku authorities, the effort reflected Moscow's anger at a Caspian Sea oil-exploitation agreement that Azerbaijan had signed in September 1994 with a consortium of oil companies led by British Petroleum, a charge that the Russian foreign ministry rejected as groundless.

Internal instability and stringent registration requirements resulted in only eight parties contesting the first round of legislative balloting on November 12, 1995; the exclusion of a dozen opposition parties and other factors led a monitoring mission from the United Nations and the Organization for Security and Cooperation in Europe (OSCE) to conclude that the election had been less than fair. The official results (including runoff contests for 15 seats in February 1996) gave the ruling YAP and its allies a massive majority in the new 125-member assembly. In a referendum held simultaneously with the initial assembly balloting, a new constitution establishing a presidential republic officially secured 91.9 percent approval.

The legislative balloting of November 1995 and February 1996 served to entrench the Aliyev regime, which became noticeably more vigorous in its actions against those seeking to challenge its hold on power. It was assisted in this endeavor by traditionally compliant courts, which handed down a series of harsh sentences, including the death penalty, for opposition activists convicted of subversion. The government also received unprecedented support from Russia, which Aliyev had previously castigated for harboring Azerbaijanis plotting to overthrow his government. In April 1996 ex-president Mutalibov and former defense minister Rakhim GAZIYEV were both arrested in Moscow, the latter being quickly extradited to Baku (where two months earlier a military court had sentenced him to death for high treason), while the former escaped extradition only on a legal ruling by the Russian procurator general. (Gaziyev's sentence was reduced to life in prison, and he was pardoned in 2005.)

The shift in Russian policy reflected a partial resolution in October 1995 of the dispute between Russia and Azerbaijan about the exploitation of Caspian oil reserves, in particular, the route by which the oil would be piped to Western markets. As ratified by the Azerbaijani National Assembly in November 1994, the $7.5 billion agreement signed with a Western-led consortium in September 1994 had included Lukoil of Russia (with a 10 percent stake). Nevertheless, Moscow had rejected the accord's legitimacy, arguing that the Caspian Sea was the joint possession of the sea's five littoral states (Azerbaijan, Iran, Kazakhstan, Russia, and Turkmenistan) and that each should share in its exploitation. Further complications had ensued from Azerbaijan's granting an increased stake in the venture to Turkey in April 1995, much to the chagrin of Iran. In the October 1995 announcement, however, Russian concerns were substantially met, the consortium agreeing that two pipelines from the Caspian Sea would be used, one an upgrade of the existing pipeline running through Russian territory to the Black Sea and the other a new pipeline through Georgia and thence potentially to Turkey. The U.S. government was reported to have played a significant role in the pipeline-route decision and in securing the exclusion of Iran from the consortium. In the latter regard, Azerbaijan was later able to make partial amends by allocating the Iranians a 10 percent stake in the next phase of Caspian oil development.

Internal instability subsequently continued to complicate President Aliyev's efforts to steer Azerbaijan to a negotiated settlement of the Nagorno-Karabakh conflict under the auspices of the OSCE. (Several cease-fire agreements in 1993 and 1994 had proved abortive, not least because the opposition AXC had assailed associated provisions as amounting to de facto recognition of Nagorno-Karabakh as a separate entity. Subsequent efforts to establish a permanent cease-fire had made little progress by May 1995, when Armenia withdrew from negotiations, alleging Azerbaijani involvement in a Georgian Azeri bombing that severed a pipeline carrying vital gas supplies to Armenia from Turkmenistan.) Talks resumed under OSCE auspices in September 1995 but were complicated by the issuance of a unilateral declaration of independence by the Karabakh Armenians in March 1996, an action that drew predictably fierce condemnation from Azerbaijan.

Prime Minister Kuliyev and his government came under increasing criticism in 1996, not least from President Aliyev, for the slow pace of economic reform, particularly the privatization program. Matters came to a head with an announcement on July 19 that the president had accepted the prime minister's resignation "on health grounds" and had also dismissed several senior economic ministers and state managers. The following day Artur RASIZADE was appointed to the premiership.

In January 1997 Azerbaijani officials claimed that a coup attempt against President Aliyev, allegedly involving a number of foreign intelligence officers and supporters of former president Mutalibov and former prime minister Guseinov, had been prevented in October 1996. Subsequently, after fighting had broken out in April–May 1997 in Nagorno-Karabakh, the OSCE submitted a draft peace plan for the region, proposing that the enclave be given autonomous status within Azerbaijan. However, the appointment of Robert Kocharian (the president of the self-declared Republic of Nagorno-Karabakh) as the prime minister of Armenia and the election of Arkady GHUKASIAN to replace him as the president of the disputed republic on September 1 were rejected by Azerbaijani officials as "intolerable provocations." On October 16 President Aliyev claimed that an agreement had been reached to settle the conflict on the basis of the proposals put forward by the OSCE, and on November 17 Ghukasian indicated that his government might agree to a step-by-step settlement of the conflict provided that the status of the region was determined in advance. However, no progress was achieved during the remainder of the year, and the ascendancy of hard-liner Kocharian to the presidency of Armenia in early 1998 (see entry on Armenia) seemed to place further impediments in the way of a final negotiated settlement.

Aliyev was reelected to another five-year term on October 11, 1998, although many prominent politicians and opposition parties boycotted the balloting to protest the government's stranglehold on the national election commission. The opposition also alleged fraud in the counting of ballots, which officially showed Aliyev (with 76 percent of the vote against four other candidates) surpassing the two-thirds threshold required to eliminate the need for a second round of balloting. Although the cabinet resigned on October 20 (as constitutionally required following a presidential election), Aliyev reappointed Prime Minister Rasizade on October 23. Many incumbents were also subsequently returned to the cabinet, although the process dragged on for several months.

Western leaders, hopeful that political liberalization in Azerbaijan would facilitate the exploitation of oil and gas, pressured the government to revamp its electoral code so that the municipal elections in December 1999 would be fully contested by opposition parties. However, many parties ultimately boycotted the polling, while those opposition groups that participated cited massive irregularities, which exacerbated antigovernment discontent that culminated in April 2000 in mass demonstrations calling for Aliyev to resign. The government's initial response was a crackdown that included a number of arrests. However, in June the president announced the release of some 87 political prisoners, a decision that was apparently designed to facilitate Azerbaijan's accession to the Council of Europe. (The membership was formally approved in January 2001; similar concurrent action regarding Armenia led some analysts to suggest that a military "solution" in Nagorno-Karabakh had thereby become even less likely.)

Controversy again surrounded the November 2000 assembly elections, as the government initially barred some parties and blocs from contesting the proportional component of the poll. International pressure influenced the administration to relent at the last minute, but the parties involved argued that their prospects had already been irrevocably compromised. (The YAP dominated the election by winning 75 seats.) Many observers also described the balloting as seriously flawed, and the election commission significantly revised the results of the proportional balloting.

The Constitutional Court ruled in 2002 that President Aliyev was eligible to run for a third term in 2003 on the grounds that his first term should not count toward the two-term limit because he had been elected to it prior to the constitutional revision of 1995. Campaign issues included the growing influence of Islamist groups in Azerbaijan (which had prompted the government to institute more extensive oversight of religious organizations) as well as continued accusations against the administration of human rights violations, such as harassment of opposition parties and torture and other mistreatment of political prisoners.

In April 2003 President Aliyev collapsed twice during a televised speech, and he later announced he would not run for reelection in October. On August 4 Prime Minister Rasizade announced his resignation, purportedly for health reasons. President Aliyev's son, Ilham ALIYEV, was appointed as the new prime minister, but on August 6 he announced he was taking an unpaid leave of absence to participate in the presidential campaign. Rasizade returned to the prime minister's post in an acting capacity. The brief elevation of Ilham Aliyev to the premiership was widely perceived as a heavy-handed measure designed to ensure that he would succeed his father as president. Large-scale demonstrations broke out to protest the action, prompting what critics called brutal suppression by security forces.

Ilham Aliyev won the presidency in first-round balloting on October 15, 2003, securing 79.5 percent of the votes. Second place went to Isa GAMBAR, leader of the New Equality Party (*Yeni Musavat Partiyasi*—YMP), with 12 percent of the vote. (Opposition groups and a number of international observers decried the election as neither free nor fair.) Rasizade returned to the premiership in a permanent capacity as head of a reshuffled cabinet on November 4.

Despite ongoing negative reaction in Western capitals, Ilham Aliyev's administration subsequently maintained his father's hard line, quashing political protests and imposing restrictions on the media. Human rights groups estimated that more than 1,000 people were arrested, including a number of prominent officials from opposition parties. Numerous violations, including voter intimidation and ballot-box tampering, were also alleged in the December 2004 local elections, which were boycotted by most opposition groups, including the YMP. Subsequently, the government condemned as illegal the June 2005 legislative balloting in Nagorno-Karabakh in which the ruling pro-Armenian government secured a majority.

Most international observers and numerous domestic analysts (including some associated with the government) strongly condemned the way the November 2005 assembly poll, at which the YAP and its supporters again gained an overwhelming majority, was conducted. The opposition Freedom (*Azadliq*) coalition charged that ballot stuffing, vote buying, intimidation of voters by the government, and fraudulent tallying had cost it many assembly seats. *Azadliq* organized mass demonstrations in Baku throughout November, its supporters wearing orange in an apparent attempt to duplicate the so-called Orange Revolution that had toppled the government of Ukraine a year earlier. However, support for regime change did not nearly reach critical mass, despite Azerbaijan's ongoing reputation as what one *Financial Times* contributor described as a "highly corrupt post-Soviet state." The OSCE bluntly reported that the assembly elections had failed to meet international standards, while other observers used stronger language such as "electoral crime" and "rigged elections." The United States and the EU also criticized the government over its handling of the balloting, although, as one journalist put it, "not too loudly." (The opposition suggested that criticism has been toned down in recognition of Western military and energy interests in Azerbaijan.)

The November 2006 municipal elections did little to improve Azerbaijan's dismal reputation regarding genuine democratization, as government repression of the press and opposition parties appeared, if anything, to intensify. Meanwhile, human rights activists expressed increasing concern about conditions in Azerbaijan, while Western capitals, including Washington, pressed for reforms in the judiciary and relaxation of curbs on the media and opposition activity. Some analysts argued that strong-arm tactics by the Aliyev administration and widespread corruption might create fertile conditions for militant Islamic fundamentalists. In that regard, Azerbaijani security forces announced a number of arrests in 2007 (see Political Parties and Groups, below, for details).

On October 15, 2008, President Aliyev was reelected for a second five-year term, being credited with 88.7 percent of the vote against six other minor candidates, none of whom received more than 3 percent of the vote. The major opposition parties boycotted the election, which international observers characterized as not fully democratic. On October 28 the assembly approved Prime Minister Rasizade's reappointment by a vote of 101–2; all but one of the incumbent ministers were also reappointed to the cabinet.

Aliyev's critics appeared increasingly impotent in March 2009 when the government reported a 92 percent "yes" vote in a national referendum on constitutional amendments that, among other things, eliminated the two-term presidential limit, thereby appearing to pave the way for Aliyev's potential "life presidency."

The YAP and allied independents again dominated the balloting for the assembly on November 7, 2010, and President Aliyev was reelected for another five-year term on October 9, 2013 (see Current issues, below, for details). On October 22 Aliyev reappointed Prime Minister Rasizade to head a slightly reshuffled cabinet.

Nagorno-Karabakh. Little progress was achieved in 2005–2007 toward a permanent resolution of the dispute regarding Nagorno-Karabakh despite numerous bilateral meetings and ongoing involvement by international mediators, most of whom appeared to support the withdrawal of Armenian troops from the enclave in favor of international peacekeeping forces pending an eventual self-determination vote. (In December 2006 a referendum among the Armenian population in Nagorno-Karabakh had given a reported 99 percent approval to a "constitution" designating the territory as a sovereign state, as proposed by Arkady GHUKASIAN, then the "president" of Nagorno-Karabakh. The legitimacy of the referendum was rejected by all the leading international organizations involved in the search for a political settlement.)

On July 19, 2007, Bako SAHAKIAN (a former national security chief for the de facto Armenian government in the region) was elected president of Nagorno-Karabakh with the support of the Democratic *Artsakh* Party (led by Ghukasian). Following Sahakian's inauguration on September 7, the legislature of Nagorno-Karabakh unanimously approved the appointment of Arayik HARUTIUNIAN as prime minister in succession to Anushavan DANIELIAN.

Following several informal meetings in the second half of 2008, the Armenian and Azerbaijani presidents signed a declaration (the first such document in 15 years) in support of a peaceful resolution of the so-called frozen conflict in Nagorno-Karabakh. For their part, Azerbaijani officials called for the immediate withdrawal of Armenian forces from the buffer zone around Nagorno-Karabakh while negotiations continued regarding Nagorno-Karabakh proper.

Sahakian welcomed the resumption of talks but asked that his administration be accorded full negotiating status (denied to date) in future discussions. In 2010 Sahakian pledged that Nagorno-Karabakh would never submit to Azerbaijani control.

Boosted by the region's recent economic improvement, Sahakian (supported by the three parties in the legislature [the Democratic *Artsakh* Party, the Free Homeland Party, and the regional branch of *Dashnak*], the Communist Party, and numerous trade unions) was reelected in the presidential poll on July 19, 2012, with 66 percent of the vote. Gen. (Ret.) Vitaly BALASANIAN, a former Sahakian advisor backed by the reformist "Movement 88" finished second with 32 percent of the vote. As has been the case in past such elections, the Azerbaijani government decried the 2012 poll as illegitimate. The next legislative election in Nagorno-Karabakh was scheduled for 2014.

Constitution and government. After nearly four years under a modified Soviet-era constitution (an interim 50-member legislature replacing the former 360-seat Supreme Soviet in May 1992), Azerbaijan adopted a new basic law on November 12, 1995, that provided for a strong presidency. Executive power is vested in a popularly elected head of state who appoints the prime minister and other cabinet members, subject to approval by the National Assembly, the 125-member legislative authority. Presidents were previously limited to two five-year terms, but a national referendum in March 2009 approved constitutional amendments that, among other things, eliminated presidential term limits. In other respects, preindependence administrative structures remain largely intact. The judicial system includes a Constitutional Court, Supreme Court, and High Economic Court.

The country includes two autonomous regions: Nagorno-Karabakh, an Armenian-populated enclave that has been the object of military contention with Armenia since 1990; and Nakhichevan, a largely Azeri-populated enclave within Armenia that has also been a source of military confrontation. The Azerbaijani assembly approved a new constitution for Nakhichevan in late 1998, formalizing its autonomous status despite objection from some legislators concerned that such action was setting a troublesome precedent.

A national referendum on controversial constitutional revisions was approved by a reported 84 percent "yes" vote on August 24, 2002. Opposition groups strongly objected to a provision designating the presidentially appointed prime minister as the presidential successor in case of the incapacitation or death of the president. The constitutional successor previously had been the speaker of the assembly, and critics of President Aliyev argued that the change had been implemented to permit him to handpick his successor. They also strongly protested the elimination of partial proportional representation beginning with the 2005 assembly elections.

A new media law entered into force in early 2000, its restrictions drawing significant domestic and international criticism, and journalism watchdogs subsequently expressed growing concern over the treatment of reporters in Azerbaijan. Only a small percentage of the media can be considered independent, and the government controls the main national broadcasting network, described as having "a distinctly Soviet-era" approach. In 2009 the government announced that foreign organizations (such as Radio Free Europe/Radio Liberty, Voice of America, and the British Broadcasting Corporation) would no longer be able to broadcast over national frequencies, which government critics described as yet another effort to suppress divergent views. Bloggers and users of social media have also been arrested for criticizing the government during recent protest demonstrations.

Foreign relations. Although Azerbaijan participated in the formal launching of the Commonwealth of Independent States (CIS) in December 1991, its legislature voted against ratification of the CIS foundation documents on October 7, 1992. In late 1991 Azerbaijan was admitted to the Organization of the Islamic Conference, and by early 1992 it had established diplomatic relations with a number of foreign countries, including the United States. On March 2 it was admitted to the UN, with membership in the IMF and the International Bank for Reconstruction and Development following on September 18. Azerbaijan's closest emerging links, however, were with Iran (because of a shared Shiite faith) and Turkey (because of a common Turkic ancestry). During a regional summit in Tehran in February 1992, Azerbaijan joined with the four Central Asian republics of Kyrgyzstan, Tajikistan, Turkmenistan, and Uzbekistan in gaining admission to the long-dormant Economic Cooperation Organization that had been founded by Iran, Pakistan, and Turkey in 1963.

Meanwhile, an additional threat to regional stability had been posed by the emergence of conflict in Nakhichevan. While troops of the former Soviet army remained stationed along the border with Turkey and Iran, an increasing number of clashes between Armenian and Azerbaijani militias were erupting in the northern portion of the region. Following Heydar Aliyev's assumption of the Azerbaijani presidency in mid-1993, direct talks were initiated with Karen BABURYAN, the president of the Karabakh parliament. Subsequently, after a meeting between Aliyev and Russian President Boris Yeltsin in Moscow on September 6, the Azerbaijani assembly endorsed CIS membership, although the government steadfastly distanced itself from Russian-led CIS security plans.

Azerbaijan concluded a ten-year friendship and cooperation treaty with Turkey in February 1994 and became a signatory of NATO's Partnership for Peace in May. In the latter month it also became an observer member of the Nonaligned Movement. In May 1997 Turkey and Azerbaijan issued a joint declaration condemning "Armenian aggression" in Nagorno-Karabakh and asking Armenia to withdraw its troops from the region.

In January 2001 Russian President Vladimir Putin visited Azerbaijan, the two countries agreeing in principle on demarcation of the Caspian seabed border and signing numerous other cooperation protocols. Azerbaijan's relations with the West also subsequently improved, particularly after Baku agreed to support Washington's antiterrorism initiatives following the attacks in the United States on September 11, 2001. In January 2002 a grateful U.S. president George W. Bush lifted the partial economic sanctions that had been imposed on Azerbaijan as the result of Azerbaijan's blockade of Armenia in connection with the Nagorno-Karabakh dispute. The United States also provided humanitarian aid and granted Azerbaijan most-favored-nation trade status.

Subsequently, Azerbaijan lent troops to the U.S.-led occupying forces in Iraq in 2003.

In February 2004 Azerbaijan and Russia signed the Moscow Declaration, which confirmed earlier agreements and pledged further bilateral cooperation regarding security, economic development, and other issues. Washington, seen as interested in using improved ties with Azerbaijan as a counter to potential Russian dominance in the region, also signed a security cooperation agreement with Baku. Meanwhile, the Aliyev administration reportedly remained strongly interested in cooperation with the European Union (EU), in part because it considered the Armenian force in Nagorno-Karabakh to be essentially a Russian proxy.

In May 2005 the defense ministers of Azerbaijan and Iran signed a security cooperation agreement, the two countries having previously (in 2002) agreed to build a joint natural gas pipeline and to facilitate the transport of goods. However, strains developed in the relationship between the two countries in 2007 when Azerbaijani security forces arrested a group of men who were allegedly plotting to overthrow the government with support from members of Iran's Revolutionary Guards Corps. Meanwhile, attempting to maintain its delicate position as a bridge between East and West, Azerbaijan as of early 2008 indicated it had no plans to seek full NATO membership (so as not to offend Russia). Concurrently, Russia continued to offer its radar base in Azerbaijan for potential United States use as part of a possible compromise regarding the Bush administration's controversial missile-defense initiative. For its part, Washington praised Azerbaijan for its assistance in combating Islamic militancy and promoted Azerbaijan as a key transit route for the rapidly increasing delivery of oil and gas to the West from the Caspian region. However, Azerbaijan diverged significantly from U.S. policy by refusing to accept the recent independence declaration by Kosovo, declaring the separatist initiative "illegal," apparently out of concern that Kosovo's independence would influence the situation in Nagorno-Karabakh.

Azerbaijan's East-West balancing act became even more difficult as a result of the Georgian-Russian conflict in South Ossetia in mid-2008, which to many analysts indicated that increased Russian pressure could be expected throughout the Caucusus region. In a perhaps related vein, it was reported in early 2009 that talks were underway for delivery of natural gas, highly coveted by the EU, from Azerbaijan to Russia. Meanwhile, Azerbaijan was one of six former Soviet republics invited to participate in the EU's "Eastern Partnership." Azerbaijan's other international focus at that time was the recent improvement in relations between Armenia and Turkey. Azerbaijani officials insisted that no final agreement should be reached for the reopening of the Armenian-Turkish border without a resolution of the situation in Nagorno-Karabakh, which had triggered the border's closure 15 years earlier, and they were highly critical of the accord signed by Armenia and Turkey in August (see entry on Armenia for details). Perhaps as a means of reassuring Azerbaijan, Russia subsequently agreed to sell surface-to-air missiles to Azerbaijan. Many analysts concluded that Russian ties to both countries by that time had made the possibility of unilateral action by Azerbaijan in Nagorno-Karabakh extremely remote.

Tension between Azerbaijan and Iran intensified in early 2012 when the Aliyev regime arrested a group of "Iranian spies" allegedly planning to commit terrorist attacks against the Israeli and U.S. embassies in Baku. Complicating matters was Azerbaijan's subsequent purchase of $1.6 billion in Israeli weapons and rumors (strongly denied by Azerbaijan) that Israel had been granted access to military bases in Azerbaijan.

In mid-2012 Azerbaijan announced that it would not accept Russia's invitation to join the Eurasian Economic Community, and the Russian radar base in Azerbaijan was closed late in the year after a new lease agreement could not be negotiated. Those strains notwithstanding, Russian president Putin visited Baku in August 2013, and the two countries signed new agreements regarding oil and gas projects and pledged additional economic cooperation. Meanwhile, Azerbaijan continued to negotiate an association agreement with the EU, although such an accord would not cover trade or be considered a precursor to EU accession, which Azerbaijan is not seeking.

Current issues. Again displaying the heavy-handedness for which it has been regularly known, the government unexpectedly shortened the official campaign period for the November 2010 assembly poll and reinforced constraints regarding the freedom of assembly and the press. The "marginalized and demoralized" opposition also charged that many candidates were barred without an appropriate explanation. The overwhelming victory by the YAR and its allies prompted domestic claims of fraud and gross irregularities, and the OSCE, while less virulent, concluded that the conduct of the election had not been "sufficient to constitute meaningful progress." The recently formed Public Chamber, led by the AXC and *Musavat*, led protest demonstrations in 2011–early 2013, with the government's harsh responses (including the arrest of bloggers and other activists) eliciting strong criticism from the European Parliament. Other groups conducted rallies protesting the government's ban on Islamic headscarfs in public schools, also prompting arrests. Subsequently, the assembly adopted tougher penalties for unauthorized demonstrations and declared it a crime to use the Internet to present defamatory or "insulting" views.

In the run-up to the October 2013 presidential elections, the EU expressed concern over the "continued pressure" being exerted by the government on its critics, calling for significantly greater attention to the protection of human rights. Meanwhile, most of the opposition coalesced as the National Council of Democratic Forces (NCDF) to challenge President Aliyev, citing widespread corruption (particularly between business and government leaders), the nation's growing income disparity, and the administration's "dictatorial" policies. Although observers suggested that disaffection was growing in some segments of the population (particularly the educated young), the official results of the presidential balloting accorded Aliyev 84.5 percent of the vote against nine challengers. NCDF candidate Camil HASANLI, who finished second in the balloting, called for an annulment of the results, while the OSCE characterized the conduct of the election as seriously flawed, particularly in regard to ballot stuffing and the counting of votes (assessed in "overwhelmingly negative terms" by monitors).

POLITICAL PARTIES AND GROUPS

Following independence in 1991, Azerbaijan moved to a limited multiparty system, qualified by the exigencies of the ongoing war with Armenia, internal political conflict, and the continuing dominance of the state bureaucracy by former functionaries of the long-dominant Azerbaijan Communist Party (*Azerbaycan Kommunist Partiyasi*—AKP). (For information on several opposition groups, now apparently defunct, from the late 1990s and early 2000s, see the 2007 *Handbook.*)

In preparation for the upcoming presidential election, in May 2013 most opposition parties (including the AXC and *Musavat* [the leading opposition groupings], and the VHP, LPA, Intellectuals Party, Open Society Party, Classical Popular Front Party, National Unity Party, and Great Azerbaijan Party) participated in the launching of the National Council for Democratic Forces (NCDF) with the goal of presenting a single candidate to challenge President Aliyev. Founders of the new coalition also included representatives of civic organizations, professional societies, and groups representing, among others, youth and human rights activists. The idea for such a "pragmatic" coalition had emanated from the *El* (People) Movement that had been launched in March by Eldar NAMAZOV, a former advisor to President Heydar Aliyev who had joined the opposition in 2008, and Rustan IBRAHIMBAYOV (Ibraqimbekov), an internationally known screenwriter. Among other things, *El* vowed to combat the "swamp of corruption" surrounding national and local governments.

The NCDF initially nominated Ibrahimbayov as its 2013 presidential candidate, but he was rejected by the elections commission because he held dual Russian-Azerbaijani citizenship. Consequently, Camil (Jamil) HASANLI, a noted historian and former national legislator, served as the NCDF standard-bearer. The NCDF pledged to pursue constitutional revision that would reduce presidential authority in favor of a true parliamentary system and establish an independent judiciary that would uphold basic human rights. Hasanli, described as the only truly antiregime presidential candidate, was credited with 5.5 percent of the vote (second place) in the disputed October balloting.

Government and Government-Supportive Parties:

New Azerbaijan Party (*Yeni Azerbaycan Partiyasi*—YAP). The YAP was founded by Heydar Aliyev in September 1992 as an alternative to the then-ruling AXC (see below) following his exclusion from the June 1992 presidential election because he was over a newly decreed age limit of 65. At that time, Aliyev held the presidency of the Azerbaijani enclave of Nakhichevan, previously having been a politburo member of the Soviet Communist Party and first secretary of the party in Azerbaijan (from 1969). He had also served as a Soviet deputy premier until he was dismissed by Mikhail Gorbachev in 1987 for alleged corruption. Aliyev used the YAP to rally opposition against the AXC government of Abulfaz Ali Elchibey, who was deposed in June 1993 with assistance from Nakhichevan military forces. Elected interim head of state, Aliyev won a presidential election in October 1993 (for which the 65-year age limit had been rescinded), being credited with 98.8 percent of the vote.

Amid a fragile internal security situation and with the major opposition parties barred from participation, the YAP and its allies secured an overwhelming parliamentary majority in legislative balloting in November 1995 and February 1996, and Aliyev was reelected president on October 11, 1998. Aliyev was also reelected YAP chair at the December 1999 party congress, while his son Ilham was chosen as a deputy chair in what was viewed as the first step in establishing himself as his father's successor. Ilham Aliyev was elevated to first deputy chair at the YAP's November 2001 congress, which also unanimously reelected Heydar Aliyev as party chair and 2003 presidential candidate.

Following the decline of his father's health in early 2003, Ilham Aliyev assumed control of the YAP, and he was elected president of the republic in the controversial October 2003 presidential poll. Heydar Aliyev died in December.

The YAP retained overwhelming control (with the support of many so-called independents) in the 2005 and 2010 assembly elections, being credited with 45.8 percent of the vote in the latter poll. When Ilham Aliyev was reelected chair of the YAP in June 2013, his wife (Mehriban Aliyeva) was elected as a deputy chair, underscoring her growing political influence.

Leaders: Ilham ALIYEV (President of the Republic and Party Chair), Artur RASIZADE (Prime Minister), Oqtay ASADOV (Speaker of the National Assembly), Mehriban ALIYEVA (Deputy Chair), Ali AHMADOV (Deputy Chair and Executive Secretary), Mubariz GURBANLI (Deputy Executive Secretary).

Motherland Party (*Anatavan Partiyasi*—AP). Strongly allied with the YAP, the Motherland Party is modeled on the Turkish party of the same name. It secured two seats in the 2005 and 2010 assembly elections.

Leaders: Fazail AGAMLEY, Yusef CUNAYDIN.

Other small parties allied with the YAP for National Assembly elections have included the **Azerbaijan Independent Democratic Party** (*Azerbaycan Müstaqil Demokrat Partiyasi*—AMDP), led by Leyla YUNUSOVA; the **Independent Azerbaijan Party** (*Müstaqil Azerbaycan Partiyasi*—MAP), led by Nizami SULEYMANOV, who contested the 1992 and 1998 presidential elections, coming in third in the latter with 8.6 percent of the votes; and **United Azerbaijan** (*Azerbaycan Vahid*—AV), whose leader, Kerrar ABILOV, had received a 0.3 percent presidential vote share in 1993.

Other Parties and Blocs That Contested the 2010 Legislative Elections:

Civil Solidarity Party (*Vatandasş Hamrayliyi Partiyasi*—VHP). Founded in 1992 to support "progress toward a democratic society," the VHP was credited with securing one seat in the 1995–1996 legislative balloting. It subsequently was routinely referenced as a participant in various opposition groupings and activities, and it won three legislative seats in 2000 and 2005. The VHP chair secured 1 percent of the vote in the 2003 presidential balloting.

For the 2010 legislative poll, the VHP formed an electoral bloc called "Democracy" (*Demokratiya*) with the **Azerbaijan Democratic Reforms Party,** led by Asim MOLLAZADE, which had secured one seat in 2005.

Leaders: Sabir RUSTAMKHANLY (Chair), Fazael IBRAHIMLI (Deputy Chair), Rafiz MANAFLI (Parliamentary Leader).

Justice (*Adalat*). Formed in November 2000 under the leadership of former ADP (see below) chair Ilyas Ismayilov, *Adalat* was reportedly supported mainly by judges and law enforcement officials. (Ismayilov had been a minister of justice in the early 1990s.) For the 2010 legislative poll, *Adalat,* which had secured one seat in the 2005 assembly poll, formed an electoral bloc called Reform (*Islahat*) with the **Great Creation Party,** founded in 2003 under the leadership of Fazil MUSTAFAYEV, who received 2.5 percent of the vote in the 2008 presidential election; the **United Azerbaijan Popular Front Party,** founded under the leadership of Gudrat HANSANGULIYEV, who was credited with 2.3 percent of the vote in the 2008 presidential poll; and the **Azerbaijani Evolution Party,** founded in 1996 under the leadership of Teyub GANIEV. The leaders of the Reform bloc called for other opposition groups to eschew "radicalism" in favor of "responsible opposition," part of an apparent attempt to undercut support for the AXC/*Musavat* alliance. Ismayilov, who reportedly received support from some members of the banned IPA, secured 1.1 percent of the vote as the Justice presidential candidate in 2013, while Hansanguliyev won 2.0 percent as the candidate of his party (described as progovernment at that point).

Leaders: Ilyas ISMAYILOV (Chair and Member of the Assembly), Isa MIRZEYEV.

Civic Unity Party (*Ventendash Birliyi Partiyasi*—VBP). At the launching of the VBP in May 2000, its chair was announced as Iqbal AGAZADE. However, at a congress in December the VBP elected ex-Azerbaijani president Ayaz Mutalibov, in exile in Russia, as its chair. As of May 2001 the party had reportedly split into two factions, one headed by Agazade, who accused the other, headed by Mutalibov, of pursuing "Russian interests" to the detriment of Azerbaijan. (Agazade had been elected to the assembly in November 2000, having been referenced variously as an independent, as a member of the "non-Mutalibov faction of the VBP," or as a member of a VBP splinter called the **National Unity Party,** whose chair in 2012 was reported to be Hajibaba AZIMOV.)

In July 2002 the government accused Mutalibov and a group of supporters of plotting a coup attempt in late 2001. The VBP derided the charges and demanded that the government permit the safe return of Mutalibov to Azerbaijan. In 2005 Mutalibov ran (from exile) as an assembly candidate in the YeS electoral bloc (see AMİP, below), while Agazade was elected as a candidate of the Hope Party (see ADP, below). (Mutalibov reportedly was serving at that time as chair of the **Social Democratic Party.**) Running on its own, the VBP in 2010 retained the one assembly seat it had secured in 2005.

In August 2011 Mutalibov, against whom criminal charges were still pending, temporarily returned from 19 years of exile to attend his son's funeral in Azerbaijan. At that time he was referenced as cochair (along with Araz ALIZADEH) of the Social Democratic Party. After the assembly subsequently adopted legislation granting immunity to past presidents for any crimes they may have committed before or during their terms of office, Mutalibov moved back to Azerbaijan permanently in 2012. Concurrently, he announced his resignation as cochair of the Social Democratic Party, which presented Alizadeh as its 2013 presidential candidate (he received 0.9 percent of the vote).

Leader: Sabir HAJIYEV.

Democratic Party of Azerbaijan (*Azerbaycan Demokrat Partiyasi*—ADP). An opposition grouping launched in February 2000, the ADP included among its leaders Rasul GULIEV, who lived in the United States following his resignation as speaker of the assembly in 1996. The new party issued a joint statement in April 2000 with the AMİP (below) strongly criticizing the Aliyev regime. Subsequently, the government accused ADP supporters of having planned a coup on behalf of Guliev and issued a warrant for his arrest.

The ADP was initially declared ineligible for the November 2000 legislative balloting, but the ban was lifted shortly before the election. In 2004 Nuraddin MAMMADLI (the chair of the party's Supreme Council) and several other ADP members defected to the AXC.

Guliev attempted to return to Azerbaijan in 2005 to run as a candidate in the November assembly elections, but his plane was denied landing rights. Subsequently, ADP deputy chair Sardar Calaloglu reportedly appeared headed for victory in the assembly poll, but the results in his district were annulled. An ADP leadership struggle was subsequently reported between Calaloglu and close associates of Guliev, prompting the defection of some party members to other opposition groups. Internal friction continued into 2007 within the ADP, with Calaloglu's faction, which called for "constructive dialogue" with the YAP, subsequently appearing to gain control of the party and Guliev announcing plans to launch a new grouping called the **Open Society Party**.

The ADP, which had been a founding member of the Freedom (*Azadliq*) opposition bloc in 2005, split from that umbrella organization in 2008. For the 2010 assembly poll, the ADP formed the Karabakh coalition with the **Hope Party** (*Ümid Partiyasi*—UP) and the **Intellectuals (Aydinlar) Party,** led by Gulamhuseyn ALIBAYLI, a former close associate of former president Elchibey.

Ümid chair Iqbal Agazade had previously been involved in a leadership struggle in the VBP (see above). Having served as head of the assembly's human rights committee, he secured 2.9 percent of the vote in the 2008 presidential poll as the *Ümid* candidate. *Ümid* was credited with the one seat won by the Karabakh bloc in 2010. ADP chair Calaloglu subsequently became one of the most vocal critics of the Aliyev administration in 2011.

In December 2011 Rasul Guliyev announced the formation of a new opposition grouping called the Resistance Movement for Democracy (RMD). In addition to Guliyev's Open Society (chaired by Sulhaddin AKBAR), other RMD components reportedly included *Aydinlar;* the Classical Popular Front Party; the **Azerbaijani Liberal Democratic Party** (ALDP), led by Fuad ALIYEV (the ALDP had run unsuccessfully in the 2010 assembly poll; Aliyev, who had won 0.8 percent of the vote in the 2008 presidential poll, was disqualified as a candidate in 2013 because of insufficient signatures of support); and the small *Azadliq* party (not to be confused with the defunct *Azadliq* bloc that participated in the 2005 elections), led by Ahmad ORUC.

In August 2012 ADP chair Calaloglu called upon all opposition parties to coalesce behind a single candidate for the 2013 presidential balloting. However, the ADP did not participate in the launching of the NCDF in mid-2013, and Calaloglu ran as the ADP candidate in the October presidential poll, finishing last with 0.6 percent of the vote. Meanwhile, Iqbal Agazade, calling for the return of Nagorno-Karabakh to Azerbaijani control, won 2.4 percent as the *Ümid* candidate, and Guliyev's Open Society Party (chaired by Sulhaddin AKBAR) participated in the NCDF.

Leaders: Sardar CALALOGLU (Chair), Zakir HUSEYNOV (Deputy Chair), Sharvarsh KOCHARYAN.

Azerbaijan Popular Front Party (*Azerbaycan Xalq Cebhesi*—AXC). The AXC was launched in 1989 as an opposition movement urging reform by the Communist regime. Spanning a range of political currents and led by philosophy teacher Abulfaz Ali Elchibey, the movement evinced a broadly pan-Turkic orientation, supporting irredentist calls for the acquisition of Azerbaijani-populated areas of Iran.

In January 1990 some 150 AXC activists and others were killed by security forces in Baku and elsewhere in disturbances arising from AXC-led anti-Armenian demonstrations. Allowed to contest the Supreme Soviet elections of September–October 1990, the AXC-led opposition won 45 of the 360 seats. Together with other opposition parties, the AXC boycotted the direct presidential poll of September 1991, but it subsequently forced the resignation of President Mutalibov in March 1992. In a further presidential election in June 1992, Elchibey was elected with 59 percent of the vote against four other candidates.

Replaced as head of state by Heydar Aliyev of the YAP in June 1993, Elchibey fled to Nakhichevan, and the AXC boycotted the September presidential election won by Aliyev. The authorities subsequently launched a crackdown against the AXC, raiding its headquarters in Baku in February 1994 and arresting a large number of its supporters. In May 1995 Elchibey repeated his call for a "greater Azerbaijan" to include Azerbaijani-populated northern Iran.

In January 1995 some 20 AXC members received jail sentences for antistate offenses, and in February former AXC defense minister Rakhim Gaziyev was sentenced to death in absentia for alleged high treason. Two months later, he was extradited to Baku from Moscow, and he was subsequently jailed, his sentence having been changed to life imprisonment. (Gaziyev was pardoned in 2005.)

In the November 1995 assembly election, the AXC was credited with winning three proportional seats on a national vote share of 10 percent, its tally increasing to four in the runoff balloting in February 1996. (The official name of the grouping was apparently changed prior to the 1995 balloting to the Azerbaijan Popular Front Party [AXCP or APFP]; subsequent reports have regularly referenced both the original and new names.) Elchibey returned to Azerbaijan from exile in October 1997, but he and the AXC boycotted the 1998 presidential poll.

Internal division between Elchibey's conservative or "traditionalist" wing and a faction of young reformers continued despite Elchibey's death in late August 2000. Deputy Chair Mirmahmud FATTEYEV reportedly signed a cooperation agreement with the YMP (below) on behalf of the conservative faction for the November legislative balloting, an initiative that was criticized by the reformist wing, led by Deputy Chair Ali Kerimli and Asim MOLLAZADE, which preferred cooperation with the Civil Solidarity Party (above).

The AXC presidential candidate in 2003, Qudrat Muzaffar HASANQULIYEV, won only 0.4 percent of the vote. The AXC was a major component, along with *Musavat* and the ADP, of the Freedom (*Azadliq*) opposition bloc formed prior to the 2005 assembly balloting. *Azadliq* called for regime change in the apparent hope of igniting antigovernment sentiment similar to the kind that had peacefully toppled strong-arm regimes in several other former Soviet states recently. However, *Azadliq*'s results (five seats for *Musavat* and one for the AXC) in the elections were disappointing, leaders claiming that their campaign efforts had been repressed by the government and that massive fraud had occurred in counting the votes. (Several reformists, including Kerimli, were reportedly leading in districts for which the voting was annulled.) The AXC and ADP consequently decided to boycott the May 2006 reballoting in ten districts, although the YMP agreed to participate, putting the future effectiveness of the coalition in doubt, as did the fractionalization of the ADP (see above). The AXC subsequently boycotted assembly activity, while the YMP and the ADP reportedly separated from *Azadliq*.

As of the spring of 2008 the active members of *Azadliq* reportedly comprised the AXC, LPA, and the CDP. In mid-2008 Kerimli, criticizing President Aliyev's "fully-fledged authoritarian regime," announced the AXC would boycott the October presidential balloting so as not to be part of the "illusion" of democracy. (The government had refused for two years to permit Kerimli to leave Baku.)

Former components of *Azadliq* participated in the formation of several electoral blocs for the 2010 legislative poll. The AXC formed a bloc with *Musavat* for the November 2010 legislative poll, but the bloc secured no seats. Decrying the results as fraudulent, the AXC and *Musavat* subsequently spearheaded the formation of a Public Chamber, which also reportedly included the AMİP (at least initially), ADP, CDP, LPA, other small parties, nongovernmental organizations, and civic groups. The new umbrella grouping organized a number of protest demonstrations in 2011–2013 calling for broad constitutional reforms and new elections. A number of activists associated with the protests were arrested, including members of the AXC, who were later sentenced to jail terms. Meanwhile, AXC leader Kerimli accused President Aliyev of establishing a "neo-monarchy."

Leaders: Ali KERIMLI (Leader), Ibrahim IBRAHIMLI (Chair), Hasan KERIMOV (Deputy Chair), Gozel BAYRAMLI (Deputy Chair).

New Equality Party (*Yeni Musavat Partiyasi*—YMP). Indirectly descended from the pre-Soviet *Musavat* nationalists, the pan-Turkic and Islamist YMP (often referenced as *Musavat*) was founded in June 1992 and was closely allied with the 1992–1993 AXC government. In sharp conflict with the succeeding Aliyev regime, the party was barred from the first round of legislative elections in November 1995, although YMP chair Isa Gambar, a former speaker of the assembly, won a constituency seat in the February 1996 runoff balloting. The YMP boycotted the 1998 presidential balloting, and although it participated in the 2000 legislative poll (winning two seats), the YMP subsequently called for a boycott of the assembly. (According to some reports, the successful YMP candidates refused to follow the decree and were expelled from the party.)

Gambar placed second in the 2003 presidential balloting with 12.1 percent of the vote, with *Musavat* reportedly being perceived as significantly weakened by the government crackdown that followed that election. Following the November 2005 assembly poll, Gambar announced that the YMP would participate in the May 2006 reballoting, indicating that the YMP would withdraw from *Azadliq* over the issue. Significant leadership infighting was subsequently reported within *Musavat,* with Gambar alleging that government repression had left the populace afraid to support opposition parties. In calling for a boycott of the 2008 presidential balloting, Gambar charged the Aliyev regime with not even bothering "to imitate democratic elections."

Musavat formed an electoral bloc with the AXC for the 2010 legislative poll, Gambar describing the alliance as the country's most effective opposition force. Gambar's son, Turgent GAMBAR, was among those arrested in regard to the antigovernment protests sponsored, in part, by the Public Chamber (see AXC, above) in 2011. Other *Musavat* members received jail sentences for their involvement in subsequent protest demonstrations.

In January 2013 *Musavat* nominated Gambar for the October presidential elections, but Gambar subsequently endorsed Camil Hasanli (the NCDF candidate).

Leaders: Isa GAMBAR (Chair), Arif GACILI (Deputy Chair), Gulaga ASLANLI (Deputy Chair), Tofiq YAQUBLU (Deputy Chair), Arif HACIYEV, Rauf ARIFOGLU, Niyazi IBRAHIMOV (General Secretary).

Azerbaijan National Independence Party (*Azerbaycan Milli İstiqlal Partiyasi*—AMİP). The AMİP was founded in July 1992 by Etibar Mamedov, who had been a prominent leader of the then-ruling AXC but had defected in light of resistance to his hard-line nationalist approach to the conflict with Armenia over Nagorno-Karabakh.

Mamedov backed Heydar Aliyev's accession to power in June 1993 but declined to join the new cabinet. Thereafter, the AMİP vigorously opposed the government's support for deployment of Russian troops in Azerbaijan to help guarantee a Nagorno-Karabakh settlement. The party was officially credited with winning three seats in the 1995–1996 assembly elections on the basis of a national vote share of 9 percent. Theretofore regarded as part of the "loyal opposition," the party became strongly critical of the Aliyev regime in 1996. Mamedov finished second in the presidential election of October 1998 with 11.6 percent of the votes.

A number of AMİP supporters were given prison sentences in early 1999 for their role in demonstrations in Baku in November 1998 protesting the government's handling of the recent presidential election.

Mamedov finished fourth in the 2003 presidential balloting. In February 2005 an AMİP congress elected Ali Nader Aliev as the new party chair, Mamedov being named honorary chair.

The AMİP subsequently served as a core component of the New Policy (*Yeni Siyasat*—YeS) electoral bloc, which also reportedly included several civic and professional groups; the Social Democratic Party (see VBP, above); the **Azerbaijan National Movement Party,** led by Samir JAFAROV; the **Union of Free Democrats,** launched in March 2004 by former deputy prime minister Ali MASIMOV; and supporters of Nazim IMANOV, who had left the AMİP following the 2003 presidential election. The YeS declared itself to be a "third force" in politics, supporting "evolutionary" rather than "revolutionary" change. Ayaz Mutalibov, the former president of Azerbaijan who was living in Russia, was permitted to run as a YeS candidate in the 2005 assembly poll, even though he reportedly faced possible arrest if he returned to Azerbaijan. (See VBP, above, for subsequent information on Mutalibov.) Friction was reported within the AMİP in early 2006 as Mamedov and Aliev held rival congresses, and the YeS suspended its activities in the summer.

The AMIP boycotted the 2008 presidential election. It presented its own candidates (without success) in the 2010 assembly poll under the leadership of Yusif Bagirzade.

Leaders: Yusif BAGIRZADE, Ayaz RUSTAMOV, Ali Nader ALIEV (Former Chair), Etibar MAMEDOV (Honorary Chair).

Liberal Party of Azerbaijan (LPA). Formed in 1995, the LPA was initially reported to have been involved in the formation of the New Policy bloc (see AMİP, above) for the 2005 assembly poll. However, subsequent reports indicated that the party had decided to cooperate (as the leader of a National Unity Movement) with *Azadliq* for the election. Lala Shovket Haciyeva, an LPA leader, was described in some reports as having won an assembly seat, which she reportedly refused to accept as an antigovernment protest. The LPA called for a boycott of the 2008 presidential poll. For the November 2010 legislative balloting, it formed a For Human bloc with the **Citizens and Development Party** (CDP), formed in 2006 by Ali ALIYEV and other former members of the AMİP; and the **Green Party**, led by Mayis GULALIYEV.

Leaders: Lala SHOVKET HACIYEVA, Avaz TEMIRKHAN (Chair).

Other parties that participated on their own in the 2010 assembly poll included the **Classical Popular Front Party,** headed by Mirmahmud MIRALIOGLU, who had led the "traditionalist" wing of the AXC in a struggle with reformists led by Ali Kerimli for control of that party; the **People's Party,** led by Panah HUSEYN; the **Azerbaijan National Democrat Party,** led by Iskander HAMIDOU; the **National Revival Movement,** led by Faraj GULIYEV (one of the officially independent candidates elected to the assembly in 2010 may have been a member of this party; Guliyev received 0.9 percent of the vote in the 2013 presidential poll); the **Modern *Musavat* Party,** whose chair, Hafiz HACIYEV, was credited with 0.7 percent of the vote in the 2008 and 2013 presidential elections (the party is described as generally supporting the policies of the Aliyev administration despite its self-declared orientation as a member of the "constructive opposition"); the **Democratic Azerbaijan World Party** (*Demokratik Azerbaycan Dünyasi Partiyasa*), led by Mammad ALIZADE; the **Progress Party**, founded in 2001 under the leadership of Cingiz DAMIROGLU; the **Azerbaijan National Statehood Party,** whose chair, Nemat PANAKHLY, was sentenced to six years in jail in connection with antigovernment protests in early 2011; and the **Social Welfare Party,** led by Khanhuseyn KAZYMLY, who received 0.2 percent of the vote in the 2008 presidential poll (the Social Welfare Party secured one seat in the 2005 assembly poll, and some reports reported it as winning a seat in 2010, although that successful candidate probably officially ran as an independent).

Other Parties and Groups:

Azerbaijan United Communist Party (*Azerbaycan Vahid Kommunist Partiyasi*—AVKP). The AVKP was founded in November 1993 as the successor to the AKP, which had governed the republic during the Soviet era, latterly under the hard-line rule of Ayaz Mutalibov. In elections to the 360-member Azerbaijan Supreme Soviet in 1990, the AKP won 280 of the 340 contested seats, and Mutalibov was reelected president in September 1991 in direct balloting that was boycotted by the opposition. As a result of military setbacks in Nagorno-Karabakh, Mutalibov was forced to resign in March 1992, and he fled to Russia after a brief return to power in May. The AKP was effectively suspended under the subsequent AXC government; nevertheless, party members remained preponderant in the state bureaucracy, and AKP deputies continued to regard the 1990 Supreme Soviet as the legitimate legislative body. The relaunching of the party in November 1993 under the AVKP rubric was aimed at rallying these elements in opposition to the YAP government.

In September 1995 the Supreme Court banned the AVKP for alleged antistate activities (such as advocating the restoration of the Soviet Union), but the decision was reversed later in the month. As a result, the party was able to contest the November election, albeit unsuccessfully.

The Communists were subsequently described as severely factionalized. The **Azerbaijan Communist Party-2** (AKP-2) was recognized as a legal party, and it put forward Firudin HASONOV as a presidential candidate in 1998, although he received less than 1 percent of the vote. Meanwhile, Sayad SAYADOV led a hard-line faction, and Ramiz AHMEDOV led a pro-Russian group reportedly allied with the Communist Party of the Russian Federation. Sayadov's faction was generally identified with the AVKP, while Ahmedov's faction was routinely referenced under the old AKP rubric. Another group of AVKP members reportedly left the party in 2000 to form a small Stalinist party (led by Telman NURULLAYEV) called the **Communist Party of Azerbaijan.**

Ahmedov died in September 2007, prompting additional turmoil within the Communist ranks. Despite self-acknowledged "weak finances," the AKP announced plans to contest some 60 seats in the November 2010 legislative poll, although it ultimately did not appear on the official list of parties registered for that balloting.

Leader: Rauf GURBANOV (Chair).

Other parties referenced recently include **Free Azerbaijan,** led by Hasan HASANOV, and the **Republican Alternative** (REAL), whose cochair, Ilgar MAMMADOV, was detained at midyear with several other REAL members in connection with an opposition protest demonstration. Mammadov was arrested again in early 2013 and remained in detention through the fall. Nevertheless, he attempted to run for the presidency in October, REAL having not participated in the formation of the NCDF. His candidacy was rejected after a number of his support signatures were ruled invalid.

A grouping called **Azerbaijan's Path** was launched in the early 2002 under the leadership of former prosecutor Ilgar GASYMOV with the aim of promoting a "favorable" solution to the conflict in Nagorno-Karabakh that would rectify conditions for the Azerbaijanis who had been forced from that enclave. A number of ADP defectors reportedly joined the grouping in 2006.

In mid-2000 the **Karabakh Liberation Organization,** which claimed a membership of 10,000 under the leadership of Akif NAGIYEV, was denied party status in view of its military orientation. Meanwhile, several members of **Allah's Army** (*Jeyshullah*), a Wahhabi opposition guerrilla movement that has operated in Azerbaijan since 1996 under the leadership of Mubariz ALIYEV, were convicted on terrorism charges in October 2000. Aliyev received a life sentence.

In early 2007 security forces arrested some 15 men accused of fomenting antigovernment activity through a militant Islamist group identified by the government as the **Northern Madhi Army** under the leadership of Said DADASBEYLI, a young cleric. The Azerbaijani and U.S. governments alleged that the group had ties to the Quds Force of Iran's Revolutionary Corps and was plotting to install a religious regime in Azerbaijan. However, Dadasbeyli's attorneys described the allegations as groundless, adding that Dadasbeyli and his supporters were devoted entirely to charity work. All of the detainees received prison sentences upon their conviction on various charges in December.

Banned Party:

Islamic Party of Azerbaijan (IPA). The IPA, described as a pro-Iranian Shiite group, was officially reorganized in 1992 but was denied further legal status in 1995. Following protests in the outskirts of Baku in 2002, members of the IPA were briefly imprisoned. Movsum Samedov succeeded Gadjiaga NURI as chair of the IPA in 2007. The party strongly condemned the government's decision in late 2010 to ban female students from wearing Islamic headscarfs in state educational institutions. Samadov was arrested in early 2011 after accusing President Aliyev of leading a "despotic regime," and a number of party members were also arrested in connection with various protest demonstrations.

Samadov was sentenced in October to 12 years in prison, while deputy chair Arif Ganiev was given an 18-month term in early 2012 on a charge of illegal possession of weapons. Five other IPA members were also handed prison terms. One faction of the IPA reportedly supported Justice candidate Ilyas Ismayilov in the 2013 presidential poll, while another endorsed NCDF candidate Camil Hasanli.

Leaders: Movsum SAMADOV (in prison), Elchin MANAFOV (Interim Chair), Arif GANIEV (Deputy Chair, in prison).

LEGISLATURE

The unicameral **National Assembly** (*Milli Majlis*) created under the 1995 constitution is elected for a five-year term and has 125 members elected in single-member districts in one-round balloting. (Prior to 2005, 25 of the 125 members were elected from party lists by proportional representation [6 percent threshold] in a single, nationwide constituency.) In the most recent balloting of November 7, 2010, the seat distribution was as follows: the New Azerbaijan Party (YAP), 71; the Democracy bloc, 4 (Civil Solidarity Party, 3; Azerbaijan Democratic Reforms Party, 1); the Reform bloc, 3 (Justice, 1; the Great Creation Party, 1; the United Azerbaijan Popular Front Party, 1); the Civic Unity Party, 1; the Karabakh bloc, 1 (the Hope Party, 1); and independents, 45. (Many of the independents were considered to have allied with the YAP. Also, reports differed on the precise allocation of seats with regard to the small parties, several officially independent candidates apparently self-identifying with a party following election.)

Speaker: Oqtay ASADOV.

CABINET

[as of November 1, 2013]

Prime Minister	Artur Rasizade
First Deputy Prime Minister	Yagub Eyyubov
Deputy Prime Ministers	Ismet Abbasov
	Ali Ahmadov
	Elchin Efendiyev
	Ali Hasanov
	Abid Sharifov
Ministers	
Agriculture	Heydar Asadov
Communications and Information Technology	Ali Mohammed Abbasov
Culture and Tourism	Abulfaz Garayev
Defense	Zakir Hasanov
Defense Industries	Yaver Jamalov
Ecology and Natural Resources	Huseyn Bagirov
Economic Development	Sahin Mustafayev
Education	Mikayil Cabbarov
Emergencies	Kyamaleddin Heydarov
Finance	Samir Sharifov
Foreign Affairs	Elmar Mammadyarov
Industry and Energy	Natiq Aliyev
Internal Affairs	Lt. Gen. Ramil Idris Usubov
Justice	Fikrat F. Mammadov
Labor and Social Security	Salim Muslumov
National Security	Eldar Makhmudov
Public Health	Oqtay Siraliyev
Taxation	Fazil Asad Mammadov
Transportation	Ziya Arzuman Mammadov
Youth and Sports	Azad Rahimov

INTERGOVERNMENTAL REPRESENTATION

Ambassador to the U.S.: Elin SULEYMANOV.

U.S. Ambassador to Azerbaijan: Richard MORNINGSTAR.

Permanent Representative to the UN: Agshin MEHDIYEV.

IGO Memberships (Non-UN): ADB, CEUR, CIS, EBRD, IOM, NAM, OIC, OSCE.

BAHAMAS

Commonwealth of the Bahamas

Political Status: Independent member of the Commonwealth since July 10, 1973.

Area: 5,380 sq. mi. (13,935 sq. km).

Population: 355,406 (2012E—UN); 319,031 (2013E—U.S. Census).

Major Urban Center (2005E): NASSAU (227,000).

Official Language: English.

Monetary Unit: Bahamian Dollar (market rate November 1, 2013: 1.00 dollar = $1US).

Sovereign: Queen ELIZABETH II.

Governor General: Sir Arthur FOULKES; appointed on April 13, 2010, following the resignation of Arthur Dion HANNA.

Prime Minister: Perry G. CHRISTIE (Progressive Liberal Party); served as prime minister 2002–2007; returned to office on May 8, 2012, as a successor to Hubert A. INGRAHAM (Free National Movement), following election of May 7.

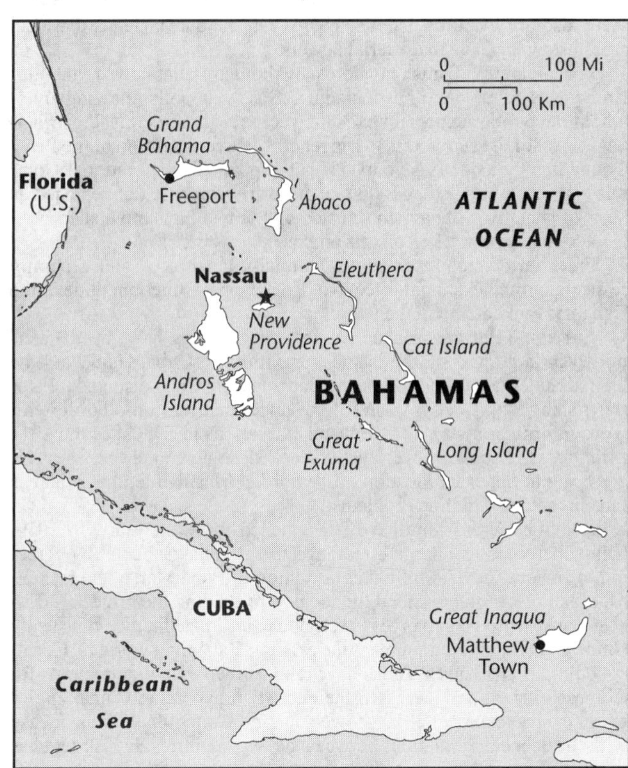

THE COUNTRY

The Commonwealth of the Bahamas encompasses a group of about 700 flat, coral islands stretching from the western Atlantic near Florida to the Caribbean Sea. Geomorphically an extension of the Little and Great Bahama banks, the archipelago features as its principal components New Providence and Grand Bahama. The islands have a temperate climate with modest rainfall but lack sufficient fresh water, much of which must be imported. An estimated 85 percent of Bahamians are descendants of former slaves. The most important religious denominations are Anglican, Baptist, Methodist, and Roman Catholic.

Tourism and banking have long been mainstays of the Bahamian economy, making up a combined more than 60 percent of the GDP. The country's extensive resort facilities typically attract in excess of 4 million tourists annually. Similarly, being one of the first—and largest—of the offshore tax havens, the country has more than 400 financial institutions, including nearly 100 Eurocurrency branches of foreign banks; there are currently no corporate, capital gains, or personal income taxes in the Bahamas. The Bahamas concluded Tax Information Exchange Agreements with a sufficient number of countries by mid-2010 to meet the requirements of the Organization for Economic Cooperation and Development (OECD) regarding international financial standards, thereby reducing its appeal as a tax haven.

From 1990 to 2008, the Bahamian economy experienced periods of inconsistent rise and fall as tourism experienced both increase and decline during this almost 20-year period. After experiencing several years of growth, another severe decline hit the Caribbean islands in 2009, yielding a reduction of 5.4 percent GDP, thus reflecting the impact of the global recession, at which time unemployment jumped from 8.7 percent to 14.2 percent. Subsequently, the country has experienced minimal growth of 1.8 percent since 2009 and is expected to continue to see growth of 2.7 percent in 2013. According to the IMF, unemployment rates declined from a peak of 15.9 percent in 2011 to an estimated 9 percent in 2014, and inflation is 2 percent.

GOVERNMENT AND POLITICS

Political background. A landfall of Columbus in 1492 and subsequently inhabited by a variety of private settlers, the Bahamas suffered harassment by the Spanish and by pirates until becoming a British Crown Colony in 1717. During the U.S. Civil War the islands enjoyed a degree of prosperity as a base for blockade runners. Similar periods of prosperity occurred during the U.S. prohibition era and following World War II.

After more than two centuries of colonial rule, constitutional changes were negotiated in 1964 that called for the establishment of an internal self-government with a bicameral legislature and prime minister. These changes were implemented following an election in 1967 that resulted in a victory for the Progressive Liberal Party (PLP) under the leadership of Lynden O. PINDLING. Local government authority was broadened in 1969, and independence, which was not supported by the opposition Free National Movement (FNM), was formally granted on July 10, 1973. In the parliamentary elections of 1982 and 1987, the PLP retained control of the House of Assembly, although falling short of the three-fourths majority it had previously enjoyed. The quarter-century Pindling era came to an end in the balloting of August 19, 1992, with the FNM, led by Hubert A. INGRAHAM, winning 33 of 49 lower house seats. The FNM retained control for a decade until suffering a decisive reversal in the elections of May 2, 2002, winning only 7 seats compared with 29 won by the PLP, led by Perry G. CHRISTIE.

The PLP was ousted after only one 5-year term when the FNM returned to power in the election of May 2, 2007. Prime Minister Hubert Ingraham orchestrated a major cabinet reorganization in 2008. In 2010 an FNM minister of state, Branville McCARTNEY, resigned his post in the cabinet to create a new political party, the Democratic National Alliance (DNA). (For more on the DNA, see Political Parties below.) Contrary to expectations that the 2012 general election would be a close contest, the PLP won decisively with 29 seats while the FNM won 8. The dramatic shift of power reflected national concerns over rising crime rates and high unemployment, which reached nearly 15 percent under the Ingraham government. Prime Minister Perry Christie, serving his second term as prime minister, took office May 8.

Constitution and government. Under the 1973 constitution, executive authority is vested in the queen (represented by a governor general with largely ceremonial powers) and the prime minister, who serves at the pleasure of the elective House of Assembly, in which legislative authority is concentrated; the appointive upper house (Senate) of the bicameral Parliament has limited functions.

Internal administration is based on the natural division into island groupings. Islands other than New Providence and Grand Bahama are administered by centrally appointed commissioners, despite a program that was launched in early 2000 to transfer authority over the smaller entities to elected local officials. The judicial system is headed by a Supreme Court and a Court of Appeal, although certain cases may be appealed to the Judicial Committee of the Privy Council in London;

there also are local magistrates' courts. On the outer islands the local commissioners have magisterial powers.

In March 2006 British law lords invalidated Bahamian capital punishment as inhumane and degrading. But with polls showing overwhelming public support for executing convicted murderers, the principal impact of the action was to trigger debate over retention of the Privy Council as the country's court of final appeal. A Constitutional Commission recommended in 2006 that the British monarch be replaced as head of state by a Bahamian selected by the two legislative chambers. No action has been taken on this proposal, however.

Freedom of the press is constitutionally guaranteed and generally respected. In the annual Freedom House press freedom index, the Bahamas ranked 20th in the world.

Foreign relations. Bahamian foreign relations have been determined in large part by the islands' proximity to Cuba, Haiti, and the United States. Since the 1980s, the Bahamas and Cuba disputed territorial fishing rights, a symptom of the undefined maritime border (for more information on Cuban-Bahamian relations in 1980, see the 2011 *Handbook*). The two governments reached an agreement on May 11, 2011, about the exact location of the border. Meanwhile, the Bahamas face illegal immigration problems.

Relations with China have strengthened in recent years. In 2010, China increased its foreign direct investment in the Bahamas by agreeing to finance the $3.4 billion construction of Baha Mar, a luxury metropolitan resort on the island. In addition to funding the project, a Chinese construction company was selected to build the facility, thus using Chinese workers to supplement the existing Bahamian workers. Corresponding to this, the Bahamas have relaxed their visa requirements for Chinese citizens and increased their crawfish exports to China. Diplomatic cables leaked in 2010 showed that the United States was uneasy with the deepening relations between the two countries. Investment has continued, with a $35 million stadium, a gift from the Chinese government, opening in February 2012.

Affairs with the United States have been generally cordial, although periodically strained by U.S. accusations of high-level Bahamian participation in drug trafficking. In April 2012 formal negotiations began to settle the long-disputed northern maritime border between the two countries, which will settle law enforcement and resource management confusion. A second round of negotiations took place in December, and the United States also agreed to provide the Bahamas with more than $2 million to support the fight against the transnational drug trade. In May 2013 the U.S. embassy issued a warning to citizens traveling in the Bahamas after an American man was killed during an armed robbery.

The Bahamas is a member of the United Nations, the Commonwealth, and the Organization of American States (OAS). An OAS electoral observation team invited by the government monitored the 2012 election and found no significant issues. The country participates in the Caribbean Community and Common Market (Caricom) as a member of the Community but not the Common Market. Thus, it elected not to join the more integrated Caricom Single Market (CSM) at the latter's launching on January 30, 2006.

Current issues. Offshore drilling became a central issue for the island nation during the 2012 general election, when former FNM prime minister Ingraham alleged that the PLP is strongly in favor of the industry. The PLP government in 2006 approved exploration permits for the Isle of Man–based company, Bahamas Petroleum (BPC). In April 2012, BPC announced plans to drill the country's first offshore well between December 2012 and April 2013. Under the FNM government, a moratorium was placed on offshore drilling in September 2010, which remains in place. The PLP announced it would hold a referendum on offshore drilling in May 2013, but the referendum was postponed until 2015. In March 2013 the government approved plans for an exploratory offshore oil well to gauge extent of resources. Bahamas Petroleum Company anticipated a 25–30 percent chance of finding oil.

The 2009 financial crisis and its aftermath had a large impact on tourism in the Bahamas, the country's largest sector. In 2011, tourism was down 2 percent on 2010. With improving markets, however, tourism increased by 6 percent in 2012 and was projected to do the same in 2013. Meanwhile, the financial situation has remained grim. In February the Finance Ministry asked government departments to cut their budgets by 25 percent for the 2014–2015 fiscal year. Under recommendations by the IMF, a value-added tax of 15 percent is expected to be implemented in July 2014.

Sparked by an increase in web shop gambling, a referendum was held on January 28 to legalize gambling for Bahamians and to introduce a national lottery. Despite the support of the majority PLP for both measures, the proposal to legalize web shop gambling was rejected 39.3 percent to 60.7 percent, and the national lottery, 59.6 percent to 40.4 percent. Voter turnout was less than 50 percent.

POLITICAL PARTIES

Government Party:

Progressive Liberal Party (PLP). A predominantly black-supported party, the PLP was formed in 1953 in opposition to the policies of business interests that controlled the government at the time. The party was a leading supporter of the independence movement and endorsed policies promoting tourism and foreign investment while at the same time preventing land speculation and providing more opportunity for indigenous Bahamians. Despite some internal dissent, the PLP secured commanding parliamentary majorities from 1972 through 1987, but lost by a better than two-to-one margin in 1992. Following the further loss of all but six seats on March 14, 1997, Lynden PINDLING resigned as party leader and on July 7 announced his retirement from parliamentary politics. Perry G. Christie led the party to victory in the election of May 3, 2002, but lost again to the FNM in 2007. In the May 7, 2012, election, Christie and the PLP returned to power with a decisive victory.

Leaders: Perry G. CHRISTIE (Prime Minister and Leader of the Party), Philip Edward DAVIS (Deputy Prime Minister), Bradley B. ROBERTS (Chair).

Opposition Party:

Free National Movement (FNM). The FNM was founded in 1972 by amalgamation of the **United Bahamian Party** (UBP) and a number of anti-independence dissidents from the PLP. In 1979 it was reconstituted as the **Free National Democratic Movement** (FNDM) by merger with the **Bahamian Democratic Party** (BDP), which had been organized in late 1976 when five FNM parliamentary deputies withdrew from the parent group. Before the 1982 election, which the party contested under its original name, it was joined by the two remaining representatives of the **Social Democratic Party** (SDP), which had been founded by BDP dissidents in late 1979 and had been recognized thereafter as the official opposition. Following the 1987 balloting, Kendal G. L. ISAACS resigned as parliamentary leader, the party's chair (and founder), Sir Cecil Wallace-Whitfield, being designated his successor; Sir Cecil, who died in May 1990, was in turn succeeded by Hubert A. INGRAHAM, a former independent MP who had joined the party only a month before. Isaacs died in May 1996.

Hubert Ingraham, who had retired from politics following the 2002 general election, returned in mid-2005 and was designated opposition leader in the House of Assembly before returning as prime minister in May 2007. After the defeat of the FNM in the 2012 general election, Ingraham again retired, stepping down from party leadership. Former Minister of Health Hubert MINNIS became party leader on May 26, 2012.

Leaders: Hubert MINNIS (Party Leader), Loretta BUTLER-TURNER (Deputy Party Leader), Darron CASH (Party Chair).

Other Parties:

Democratic National Alliance (DNA). The DNA is a people-centered party founded in mid-2011 by former FNM minister of state Branville McCartney. Although the DNA did not win any seats in the 2012 election, party candidates contested in each of the 38 races, making it the first third party in Bahamian history to do so.

Leader: Branville McCARTNEY (Founder and Party Chair).

Bahamas Constitution Party (BCP). The BCP, founded in 1999, is a conservative party rooted in Christianity. A BCP candidate ran in one district in the 2002 election but did not contest in 2007. In 2012, BCP candidates ran in five constituencies.

Leaders: S. Ali McINTOSH (Party Leader), Samuel J. THOMPSON (Party Chair).

For more information on Coalition Plus Labour alliance, please see the 2012 *Handbook*.

LEGISLATURE

The **Parliament** consists of an appointed Senate with limited powers and a directly elected House of Assembly.

Senate. The upper house consists of 16 members, 9 of whom are appointed on the advice of the prime minister, 4 on the advice of the leader of the opposition, and 3 on the advice of the prime minister after consulting the leader of the opposition.
President: Sharon WILSON.

House of Assembly. The lower house presently consists of 38 members directly elected on the basis of universal suffrage for five-year terms (subject to dissolution). The membership was reduced from 41 to 38 as recommended by the Boundary Commission, effective as of the May 7, 2012, general elections. In that election, the Progressive Liberal Party won decisively with 29 seats while the Free National Movement won 9.
Speaker: Kendal MAJOR.

CABINET

[as of November 8, 2013]

Prime Minister	Perry Christie (PLP)
Deputy Prime Minister	Philip B. Davies (PLP)
Ministers	
Agriculture, Marine Resources and Local Government	Alfred Gray (PLP)
Education, Science and Technology	Jerome Fitzgerald (PLP)
Environment and Housing	Kendred Dorsett (PLP)
Finance	Perry Christie (PLP)
Financial Services	Ryan Pinder (PLP)
Foreign Affairs and Immigration	Frederick A. Mitchell (PLP)
Grand Bahama	Michael Darville (PLP)
Health	Perry Gomez (PLP)
Labor and National Insurance	Shane Gibson (PLP)
Legal Affairs and Attorney General	Allyson Maynard (PLP) [f]
National Security	Bernard J. Nottage (PLP)
Social Services	Melanie Griffin (PLP) [f]
Tourism	Obediah Wilchcombe (PLP)
Transport and Aviation	Glenys Hanna Martin (PLP) [f]
Works and Urban Development	Philip B. Davies (PLP)
Youth, Sports, and Culture	Daniel Johnson (PLP)
Ministers of State	
Finance	Michael Halkitis (PLP)
Investments	Khaalis Rolle (PLP)
Legal Affairs	Damien Gomez (PLP)
National Security	Keith Bell (PLP)
Transport and Aviation	Hope Strachan (PLP) [f]

[f] = female

INTERGOVERNMENTAL REPRESENTATION

Ambassador to the U.S.: Cornelius A. SMITH.

U.S. Ambassador to the Bahamas: John DINKLEMAN.

Permanent Representative to the UN: Paulette BETHEL.

IGO Memberships (Non-UN): Caricom, CWTH, IADB, IOM, NAM, OAS.

BAHRAIN

Kingdom of Bahrain
al-Mamlakah al-Bahrayn

Political Status: Independent emirate proclaimed August 15, 1971; constitution adopted December 6, 1973; constitutional monarchy established on February 14, 2002, under constitutional amendment decreed by the emir in purported accordance with National Action Charter endorsed by national referendum on February 14–15, 2001.

Area: 258 sq. mi. (668 sq. km).

Population: 1,363,523 (2012E—UN); 1,281,332 (2012E—U.S. Census).

Major Urban Centers (2011E—UN): MANAMA (262,000).

Official Language: Arabic.

Monetary Unit: Bahraini Dinar (official rate November 1, 2013: 0.38 dinar = $1US).

Sovereign: King Sheikh Hamad bin Isa Al KHALIFA, descendant of a ruling dynasty that dates from 1782; succeeded to the throne as emir on March 6, 1999, upon the death of his father, Sheikh Isa bin Salman Al KHALIFA; proclaimed himself king under constitutional amendment adopted on February 14, 2002.
Heir to the Throne: Crown Prince Sheikh Salman ibn Hamad Al KHALIFA.

Prime Minister: Sheikh Khalifa bin Salman Al KHALIFA, uncle of the emir; appointed January 19, 1970, by his brother, then-emir Sheikh Isa bin Salman Al KHALIFA; continued in office upon independence.

THE COUNTRY

An archipelago of some 33 largely desert islands situated between the Qatar peninsula and Saudi Arabia, the Kingdom of Bahrain consists primarily of the main island of Bahrain plus the smaller islands of Muharraq, Sitra, and Umm-Nassan. Summer temperatures often exceed 100 degrees (F), and annual rainfall averages only about four inches; however, natural springs provide sufficient water. The predominantly Arab population is about two-thirds indigenous Bahraini, with small groups of Saudi Arabians, Omanis, Iranians, Asians, and Europeans. An estimated 65 percent are Shiite Muslims, while 30 percent, including the royal family, adheres to the Sunni sect. Women constitute 39 percent of the labor force, though their representation in the government is low, with just four elected in the 2010 legislative elections.

Oil, produced commercially since 1936, and natural gas account for some 65 percent of the government's income, although recoverable petroleum reserves may be exhausted in 15 years. Additional revenue is derived from operation of the Aluminum Bahrain smelter, one of the largest nonextractive enterprises in the Gulf area, and from one of the Middle East's largest oil refineries, devoted largely to processing crude (about 150,000 barrels per day) from Saudi Arabia. Bahrain also has been a prominent financial center for many years; its more than 50 offshore banks handle much of the region's oil-related wealth.

Aided by financial support from Saudi Arabia, Kuwait, and the United Arab Emirates, the government upon independence began to establish an extensive network of social services, including free education and medical care, and in 1982 mounted an ambitious program for infrastructure development and improvements in agriculture and education. An economic downturn in the mid-1980s, caused by declining foreign aid, appeared to have been reversed by the end of the decade; however, the Gulf crisis precipitated by the August 1990 Iraqi invasion of Kuwait generated additional economic problems for the emirate as aid from Gulf neighbors was severely constrained and offshore banking activity fell sharply. The economy rebounded in the mid-1990s under the influence of steady oil revenue. Subsequently, falling oil prices in 1998 led to a 3 percent decline in GDP for the year and intensified concern over the government's budget deficit. However, the economy rebounded strongly in 1999 as the result of the sharp turnaround in oil prices and the subsequent positive response from foreign investors. GDP growth subsequently remained strong, averaging more than 5 percent annually in 2000–2006, with increased nonoil revenue and continued low inflation.

Annual GDP declined from 7 percent in 2007 to 4.7 percent through 2010, owing in large part to a drop in global oil prices. The government focused on diversification, particularly toward the service sector, and improved subsidies and incentives in the agriculture sector. Transparency and regulatory practices of the Central Bank have reportedly made it among the most progressive in the region. As a result of domestic unrest, the country's economy slowed to an annual growth rate of 2.1 percent in 2011, though has since rebounded to 4.5 percent in 2013. Inflation was 2.7 percent, and unemployment, 3.8 percent.

GOVERNMENT AND POLITICS

Political background. Long ruled as a traditional monarchy, Bahrain became a British protectorate in 1861 when Britain concluded a treaty of friendship with the emir as part of a larger effort to secure communication lines with its Asian colonies. The treaty was modified in 1892, but little evolution in domestic politics occurred prior to the interwar period. In 1926 Sir Charles BELGRAVE was appointed adviser to the emir, providing guidance in reform of the administrative system—an especially important step in light of accelerated social change following the discovery of oil in 1932. Belgrave continued to have a direct and personal effect on Bahraini policy until his departure in 1957, the result of Arab nationalist agitation that began in 1954 and reached a peak during the 1956 Anglo-French action in Egypt. Incipient nationalists also provoked disturbances in 1965 and in 1967, following the second Arab-Israeli conflict.

In 1968 Britain announced that it would withdraw most of its forces east of Suez by 1971, and steps were taken to prepare for the independence of all of the British-protected emirates in the Persian Gulf. Initially, a federation composed of Bahrain, Qatar, and the seven components of the present United Arab Emirates was envisaged. Bahrain, however, failed to secure what it considered an appropriate allocation of seats in the proposed federation's ruling body and declared separate independence on August 15, 1971.

Despite nominal efforts at modernization, such as the creation of an Administrative Council following the 1956 disturbances and a quasi-ministerial Council of State as its successor in 1970, virtually absolute power remained in the hands of the emir until the adoption in 1973 of the country's first constitution, which provided for a partially elected National Assembly. However, total control returned to the royal family when the emir, describing the new legislative body as "obstructionist," ordered its dissolution in August 1975.

Although initially less intense than in other regional countries, rebellious sentiments among some of the majority Shiites, resentful of Sunni rule, precipitated conflict following the Iranian revolution of 1979 and the accompanying spread of Islamic fundamentalism. In December 1981 the government declared that it had thwarted a conspiracy involving the Iranian-backed Islamic Front for the Liberation of Bahrain (IFLB). That plot and the discovery in February 1984 of a rebel arms cache resulted in the banning of a Shiite religious organization (the Islamic Enlightenment Society) and the issuance of compulsory identity cards to nationals and resident aliens. The government subsequently maintained a tight rein on the activity of fundamentalists. Several arrests occurred in 1992 for participation in illegal organizations. In January 1993, apparently in response to Western calls for political liberalization, the emir established a Consultative Council of 30 "elite and loyal men," including some former National Assembly members.

A wave of clashes with security forces erupted during the summit of the Gulf Cooperation Council (GCC) in Manama in December 1994, following the arrest of Sheikh Ali SALMAN, a religious leader who had demanded more jobs for Shiites. In January 1995 Salman and two followers were deported to Dubai and thereafter granted temporary asylum in Britain. However, after the emir complained of "meddling by foreign countries in our internal affairs," in an implicit reference to Iran, further disturbances occurred in March in which a police officer was killed. In April two people were killed and dozens injured during a raid on the home of another opposition cleric, Sheikh Abd al-Amir al-JAMRI, and on May 2 ten Shiites, including Jamri, received jail terms for property damage resulting from the December and January outbreaks.

Sheikh Jamri was released on September 25, 1995, following the initiation of reconciliation talks between the government and the Shiite opposition. However, a new outbreak of violence in early 1996 prompted the rearrest of Jamri and seven followers. Following several bombings in early 1996, the government announced on June 3 that it had foiled an allegedly Iranian-backed plot to seize power and that more than 80 participants had been arrested. Recalling its ambassador from Tehran, Bahrain accused Iranian authorities of conspiring with a Bahraini branch of the Lebanon-based Hezbollah (Party of God), whose members had been trained in Iran and had been the principal instigators of the recent unrest among Bahraini Shiites. Denying the Bahraini charges, Iran withdrew its ambassador from Manama, though offered to mediate between the government and the Shiite opposition. Meanwhile, apparently responding to international pressure for political liberalization throughout the Gulf, the emir in September appointed an expanded 40-member Consultative Council.

Sheikh Isa ibn Salman Al KHALIFA, the emir of Bahrain since 1961, died of a heart attack on March 6, 1999. He was immediately succeeded by his son and longtime heir apparent, Sheikh Hamad ibn Isa Al KHALIFA, reputedly more reform-minded than his father. The new cabinet appointed on May 31 comprised most members of the previous government, including the emir's uncle, Prime Minister Sheikh Khalifa ibn Salman Al KHALIFA. In November 2000 the emir appointed a 46-member Supreme National Committee to draft a National Action Charter that would serve as a blueprint for political development and democratization. Although some members reportedly resigned over alleged "interference" by the emir, the draft charter was endorsed by a reported 98.4 percent in a national referendum on February 14–15, 2001. A year later the emir decreed constitutional amendments that incorporated the charter's provisions, including the establishment of a constitutional monarchy in which authority was to be shared by a bicameral National Assembly and the former emir (now to bear the title "king"). As the first step in the progressive (by regional standards) democratization process, local elections were held in May 2002, with a number of opposition political "associations" or "societies" participating. However, several such groups boycotted the October balloting for the Chamber of Deputies to protest the king's decision that the assembly's upper house, the Consultative Council, would continue to be appointed rather than elected.

Tensions escalated between Shiites and Sunnis in advance of the 2006 parliamentary elections, with reports of confrontations between Shiite villagers and government security forces early in the year. (For more information on the 2006 elections, see the 2011 *Handbook.*)

Attention in mid-2007 turned to the government's imposition of an annual income tax, with Bahrain becoming the first country in the region to institute such a levy. Despite the objections of trade unions, religious leaders, and some political groups, the tax went into effect in June, with a deduction of 1 percent from the paychecks of some 100,000 workers, with part of the revenue intended for a program to help relieve unemployment. Religious officials said the tax was unfair because exemptions were granted to the military and to elected officials, and they argued it was against Islamic precepts to take the money without workers' permission.

In December 2007, 39 people were arrested following a week of antigovernment demonstrations in villages near the capital, reportedly prompted in part by increasing economic disparity between Shiites and the Sunni ruling family.

In January 2008 the king consolidated the royal family's control of the military by appointing his eldest son, Crown Prince Sheikh Salman ibn Hamad Al KHALIFA, as deputy commander in chief of the army.

Sectarian tensions heightened again in 2009 following the arrests of some 35 Shiite activists, including Abduljalil ALSINGACE and Husayn MUSHAYMA of the Movement of Liberties and Democracy–Bahrain (*Haq*) and a Shiite cleric, who were accused of planning terror attacks and attempting to overthrow the government. Their arrests prompted three days of protests in the capital in advance of their trial. The government alleged that the defendants had received military training in Syria in 2008. Alsingace accused the government of quashing dissent, thus marginalizing Shiites. Alsingace and Mushayma were pardoned by the king in April 2009, along with 175 other detainees, following pressure from international and local groups, including the Islamic National Accord Society (INAS), the Shiite opposition. Sectarian divisions came to the forefront in October when thousands of demonstrators protested the government's refusal to review the naturalization law that eases the way for Sunnis to become citizens, claiming it was an effort to change the demographics of the largely Shiite country ahead of the 2010 elections.

Also in 2009, the king approved a new family law protecting the rights of Sunni women in Islamic courts. Shiites were excluded from the law after conservative scholars, clerics, and legislators—including INAS members—criticized it for not upholding sharia principles.

In February 2010 the Bahrain Center for Human Rights (BCHR) continued to press for government reforms regarding freedom of expression, specifically citing threats against the INAS. The Human Rights Commission issued a set of demands to Bahraini authorities, including abolishing the political parties law and guaranteeing "the rights of citizens in choosing their government and equal access to public office." Shortly thereafter, the INAS parliamentary bloc demanded that the cabinet be named by the elected parliament rather than appointed by the king. A subsequent meeting between the British ambassador and the INAS parliamentarians prompted harsh criticism by the Shiites, particularly members of the National Islamic Society (*al-Minbar*), and provoked protests, including a minor bomb explosion at the British embassy, over Britain's perceived interference in Bahrain's internal affairs. A crackdown in August on Shiite protesters rallying against torture and discrimination resulted in the arrest of some 250 activists and clerics and led to weeks-long clashes between the Shiites and the Sunni-led security forces. The government claimed the protests were stirred by foreign insurgents and said the arrests were made in accordance with the country's antiterrorism laws, though observers largely agreed with an assessment in *The New York Times* that Bahrain "appears to be reconsidering its decade-long flirtation with reform."

The state prosecutor banned the media from reporting on Shiite activist Abduljalil, who remained in custody with dozens of others who were arrested. A month ahead of parliamentary elections, the government announced it would try 23 Shiites for allegedly plotting to overthrow the monarchy and charged them with having formed a "terror network" led by Alsingace (despite his having been pardoned a year earlier on similar charges). Shortly thereafter, the government suspended the board of the BCHR, claiming it was too sympathetic to the Shiite majority, and declared it would appoint a new temporary director. As the crackdown continued, the government on September 20 revoked the citizenship of Ayatollah Hussein al-NAJATI, described as Bahrain's most influential Shiite cleric and the representative of Iran's Grand Ayatollah.

Increased numbers of security forces were visible ahead of parliamentary balloting on October 23 and October 30, 2010, in which 127 candidates participated. Balloting was peaceful as an estimated 67 percent of voters went to the polls. Opposition Shiites retained their strength in parliament by winning all the 18 seats they contested; independents were second with 17. Following the second round in nine constituencies, Sunni Islamist groups added 3 seats, increasing their representation to 5 (for an overall loss of 12 seats compared with 2006). The secular National Democratic Action Society (*Waad*) failed to secure the two seats it contested in the second round. On November 2, the king appointed an additional deputy prime minister, Sheikh Khalid ibn Abdullah Al KHALIFA, and made only a few changes to the cabinet. Two days before the second balloting, the trial of 25 Shiites accused of terrorism progressed amid heightened security in Manama. The defendants recounted torture and other abuses they had endured in prison.

On February 16, all 18 members of the INAS suspended their participation in parliament, in a show of support for antigovernment protesters (see Current issues, below). In a cabinet reshuffle on February 26, 2011, five ministers, including the health minister, were replaced. On March 16, the minister of health resigned, and the minister of housing announced that he was "boycotting," both in protest against the government. A new housing minister was appointed on March 24, and the health portfolio was given to the minister for social development.

In March 2013 Crown Prince Al Khalifa was appointed first deputy prime minister (see Current issues, below).

Constitution and government. In December 1972 the emir convened a Constituent Council to consider a draft constitution that provided for a National Assembly composed of a cabinet (which had replaced the Council of State in 1971) and 30 members elected by popular vote. The constitution was approved in June 1973 and became effective December 6, 1973, and an election was held the following day. However, the assembly was dissolved in August 1975, with the emir suspending the constitutional provision for an elected legislative body. The Consultative Council named in January 1993 was established by the emir's decree, observers predicting it would operate on a "trial basis" before provision for it or some other such body was incorporated into the constitution. At the time of the appointment of the council in September 2000, the government announced plans to conduct elections in 2004 for the next council. Meanwhile, the emir in April had decreed the establishment of a new Supreme Council for Economic Development to oversee the privatization of some state-owned industries.

The constitutional amendments of February 2002 proclaimed the country a "constitutional monarchy" based on separation of powers, the rule of law, respect for human rights, and freedom of association. In addition, the changes in the basic law provided for formation of a bicameral legislature; women were empowered not only to vote but also to run for office. However, critics accused King Hamad of reserving too much authority for himself. (The king was designated head of state and commander in chief of the armed forces and was given uncontested power to appoint cabinet ministers, judges, and members of the upper house in the new National Assembly.)

The legal system is based on sharia (canonical Muslim law); the judiciary includes separate courts for members of the Sunni and Shiite sects. A constitutional court was established in July 2002.

The six main towns serve as bases of administrative divisions that are governed by municipal councils.

Though the constitution guarantees freedom of expression, the media is severely restricted by a 2002 press law that allows for five years imprisonment for criticizing the king or undermining state security. The constitution allows for censorship. In 2013, Reporters Without Borders ranked Bahrain 165th for press freedom.

Foreign relations. Since independence, Bahrain has followed Saudi Arabia's lead in foreign policy. However, it was more moderate than most other Arab states in its support of the Palestine Liberation Organization and in condemning the Israeli–Egyptian peace treaty of 1979.

Generally regarded as the most vulnerable of the Gulf sheikhdoms, Bahrain was a target of Iranian agitation and territorial claims following the overthrow of the shah. Although Manama adopted a posture of noncommitment at the outbreak in 1980 of the Iran–Iraq war, it subsequently joined the other five members of the GCC in voicing support for Iraq. A security treaty with Saudi Arabia was concluded in December 1981, and in February 1982 the foreign ministers of the GCC states announced that they would actively oppose "Iranian sabotage acts aimed at wrecking the stability of the Gulf region." Bahrain joined with the other GCC states in annual joint military maneuvers. In April 1986 tensions emerged with Qatar over an uninhabited island, Fasht al-Dibal, that had been reclaimed from an underlying coral reef for use as a Bahraini coast guard station. Following a brief takeover by Qatari armed forces, an agreement was reached to return the site to its original condition. In January 1989 the two countries agreed to mediation by Saudi Arabia to resolve other territorial problems, including Bahrain's claim to Zubara, the ancestral home of the Al Khalifa family on the Qatari mainland. Nonetheless, in mid-1991 Qatar instituted a suit at the International Court of Justice (ICJ), claiming sovereignty not only over Fasht al-Dibal, but another reef, Qitat Jaradah, and the larger Hawar Island. Following the ICJ's March 2001 ruling on the dispute (wherein Zubara was awarded to Qatar and Fasht al-Dibal, Qitat Jaradah, and Hawar Island to Bahrain), relations between the two countries improved.

Relations with Washington have long been cordial. In October 1991, following UN action against Iraq, Bahrain and the United States signed a defense cooperation agreement, similar to one concluded between the United States and Kuwait, which provided for joint military exercises and authorized the storage of equipment and the use of port facilities by U.S. forces. The Gulf crisis was seen as having provided the government with a powerful means of surmounting Sunni Arab fears that an ongoing U.S. presence would promote unrest among the country's numerically predominant Shiite population, and in October 1995 Manama announced it had granted the United States permission to base 30 military aircraft in Bahrain. Meanwhile, the emirate and its GCC associates continued to seek regional security arrangements that would dilute domestic political pressure on individual members regarding military ties with the West. However, upon ascending to power in March 1999, Sheikh Hamad quickly pledged to maintain the close ties that his father had established with the Western powers. Subsequently, Bahrain signed a free trade agreement with the United States, whose naval base in Bahrain remained an important component of U.S. military force in the Gulf. Anti-American sentiment has remained relatively low in Bahrain, although protests broke out in May 2004 against attacks by U.S. forces on Shiite "holy cities" in Iraq. Though Bahrain reportedly lifted its ban on imports of Israeli products in late 2005 under terms of the U.S. free trade agreement, conflicting reports emerged. While U.S. officials contended it had been closed in advance of implementation of the free trade agreement in 2006, others stated that Bahrain's boycott was still in effect, in compliance with Arab League dictates. In November 2007, Bahrain participated in the Middle East peace summit aimed at helping to resolve the Israeli-Palestinian conflict, hosted by the United States in Annapolis, Maryland.

Iran's president, Mahmoud Ahmadinejad, visited Bahrain in November 2007 to ease tensions following verbal confrontations between Iran and the United States that had prompted fears of a military buildup in the Gulf region. In 2008, Bahrain announced that it would join other Arab countries in a plan to develop nuclear energy for civilian purposes.

In February 2009 tensions again flared with Iran following an Iranian official's comment about Bahrain's sovereignty that was perceived as an insult by a delegation from Bahrain, prompting the suspension of a gas import deal with Tehran. Though President Ahmadinejad subsequently reiterated Iran's respect for Bahrain's sovereignty in a letter to the king, the situation was exacerbated when Iran announced its naval vessels were ready to move beyond the Gulf into the Indian Ocean. Observers said hostile moves by Iran were meant as a deterrent to keep the Gulf states from participating in possible direct negotiations with the United States over Iran's nuclear program. Tensions eased by late 2009, however, as the prime minister underscored Bahrain's support for Iran's "inalienable right to use civilian nuclear energy."

In an unprecedented move, Bahrain in 2008 named a Jewish ambassador to the United States, Huda Ezra Ebrahim NONOO. She is a member of the legislature and secretary general of the Bahrain Human Rights Watch Society. Though Bahrain has no official relations with Israel, the Israeli government expressed concern in 2009 over legislation drafted by the lower house of parliament prohibiting any contact with Israelis.

In May 2011 Crown Prince Al Khalifa met with Prime Minister David Cameron on an official visit to the United Kingdom. Though the United Kingdom had signaled its concern over Bahrain's crackdown on human rights, both men asserted the importance of continued bilateral economic and security relations. On May 29 it was reported that the UK had continued to train Bahraini army officers within its borders after the start of the Shia revolt in February.

In May 2012 the United States resumed arms sales to Bahrain, which had been halted in 2011 over human rights concerns. The shipment was intended to help Bahrain "maintain its external defense systems" and did not include crowd control equipment.

In the midst of ongoing domestic unrest, Bahrain in April 2013 became the first Arab country to brand Hezbollah as a terrorist organization. The following month, as part of an effort to restrict foreign influence in domestic politics (see Current issues, below), political groups were banned from any contact with the Lebanese Shiite movement, a move condemned by Iran.

Current issues. In early 2011 antigovernment protests broke out as civil unrest swept through other Middle Eastern and North African countries in the so-called Arab Spring. Some 31 deaths were reported, hundreds were detained, and more than 1,000 workers were dismissed from their jobs during the turmoil, as a result of demonstrations in Manama and across the country. What began as a prodemocracy rally in early February soon turned into a Shiite protest against the Sunni monarchy and the minority sect in particular. The government, long regarded as moderate in the region, responded in an "uncompromisingly repressive" way, according to *Keesing's Record of World Events.* Violence escalated when police opened fire on demonstrators on February 18, but calmed down to a standoff the following day as protesters were allowed to occupy one of the main squares in the capital. Protesters' demands ranged from constitutional reform to abolition of the monarchy. The king, for his part, announced that every family in the country would receive a gift of about $2,600. However, protests worsened after one demonstrator was killed during a mourners' procession for a protester who had been killed a day earlier by police. All 18 members of the opposition INAS (*al-Wifaq*) bloc in parliament resigned in protest of the regime's actions.

Meanwhile, the government reported that some 300,000 supporters of the monarchy rallied on February 21, matched, reportedly, by a 100,000-strong antigovernment rally the next day. Tensions continued to escalate after protesters surrounded the National Assembly building. In response, on March 14 some 1,500 troops arrived from Saudi Arabia and the United Arab Emirates to help maintain order, and the GCC agreed to deploy its military arm to guard key facilities. The following day the king declared a three-month period of martial law. Bolstered by these moves, observers said, the police carried out an early-morning assault on the protesters' camp, destroying it on March 16, a move that drew sharp criticism from U.S. Secretary of State Hillary Clinton. Several opposition leaders were arrested shortly thereafter, the king having declared the existence of "an external plot" to destabilize the country, a veiled reference to Iran.

Despite calls for restraint from Western countries, the regime's crackdown continued into April, marked by the arrest of human rights activists, an announcement by the Justice and Islamic Affairs Ministry that it would seek court approval to outlaw *al-Wifaq,* and the dismissal of 100 civil servants who had participated in protests. (In the wake of harsh criticism by the United States, however, Bahrain backed off from its plan to ban *al-Wifaq.*) The opposition, meanwhile, claimed that troops supported by the Saudis had destroyed or desecrated seven Shiite mosques and 50 prayer centers or shrines. On April 25 the Committee to Protect Journalists reported that Karim FAKHRAWI, founder of the independent daily newspaper *al-Wasat,* died a week after he was taken into state custody. He had gone to a police station on April 5 to complain that his house was about to be bulldozed by authorities. Earlier in the month the government had accused the newspaper of "deliberate news fabrication and falsification." The government said that around 400 people had been detained in the aftermath of the protests and that all would face prosecution.

The king announced in early May 2011 that the state of emergency would be lifted by June 1, which was met with approval from President Obama. The king called for talks on reform, inviting all parties to participate "without preconditions." On June 1, army troops withdrew from Manama and groups of police officers entered, clashing with Shia demonstrators. On June 29, the king addressed the troubled nation, announcing that he was establishing a five-member Bahrain Independent Commission of Inquiry (BICI) to investigate the unrest and report its findings by October 30. On June 30 the military courts set up under the martial law regime were disbanded.

On July 2 a "national dialogue" was launched, initially with the participation of *al-Wifaq,* but further violence erupted in Manama, with protestors chanting "dialogue is suicide" as police unleashed rubber bullets and tear gas. The dialogue lasted until July 25 and included members of more than 300 civil society groups and political concerns, including both houses of the National Assembly. On July 28 the king announced that measures agreed upon in the dialogue process would be implemented, such as cabinet member approval by the House of Representatives. *Al-Wifaq* dismissed these developments as "theater," and continued to call for the resignation of the king's government.

Al-Wifaq boycotted the September 24 by-elections, scheduled to fill the 18 seats the party had vacated in February. The elections were preceded by violent clashes between security forces and Shia youth, and the boycott led to the election of mostly progovernment independents. In the second round of voting on October 1, Sawsan Taqawi, a member of the first group in Bahrain to consist of both Shias and Sunnis, became the first woman to hold a leadership position in the House.

The BICI report, published on November 23, asserted that the government had used "excessive force"—including systematic torture—in suppressing the uprising and that at least five detainees had died under the torture regime. The king largely accepted the commission's findings and pledged that officials would be held accountable, though he rejected the BICI's conclusion that there was no evidence for Iran's role in stirring up unrest among Shias. *Al-Wifaq* refused to participate in the BICI process, saying the commission had no real power.

December was marked by further violence, and by the middle of the month, media estimated that 35 people had died since the start of the unrest. Street protests continued on an almost daily basis in January, despite the king's announcement of plans to amend the constitution to bestow additional powers on the National Assembly. As the year anniversary of the beginning of the unrest approached, increasing numbers of Bahrainis were reported to be leaving the country to escape the increasing violence. On February 6, a group calling itself the Patriotic Independent Gathering, led by a former health and education minister, was launched with a stated aim of promoting reconciliation. Nevertheless, on February 13 and 14 Shia demonstrators once again violently clashed with police on the first anniversary of the uprising. The government blamed the violence on *al-Wifaq,* saying the group failed to control the demonstrators. The largest antigovernment demonstrations since December took place on March 9, and it was largely peaceful.

The Bahrain leg of the 2012 Formula One motor racing championship went ahead as planned on April 22, with the government bracing for attempted disruptions of the route with troops, tanks, and armored cars. Daily clashes between Shias and security forces erupted, and by the end of April the death toll had risen to over 50. The demonstrations continued in May and were forcefully repelled by security police.

On June 26 the government announced it would compensate families of 17 people who had been killed in the unrest and would pay out $2.6 million from a fund established in November 2011 on BICI's recommendation. Protests continued through the summer in areas outside the capital, but in September Shiite protesters brought rallies back into Manama, leading to violent clashes with security forces. In September the government announced it would implement most of the recommendations from the UN report on the country's human rights record, including toleration of dissent, a crackdown on torture, and fair trials. At the opening of parliament in October, the king called for renewed dialogue with the opposition. That month, the interior ministry announced that all rallies and gatherings were outlawed because they "have been associated with violence, rioting, and attacks on public and private property."

Encouraged by Washington and other allies, the Bahraini government pressed for negotiations between pro- and antigovernment groups. Opposition groups, chiefly *al-Wifaq*, were reluctant, wary that the talks would not lead to meaningful change. They caved to pressure in late January 2013, and negotiations between opposition and progovernment groups began on February 10. Four days later, on the second anniversary of the beginning of the protests in 2011, protests erupted, and security forces were deployed to halt demonstrators in Manama, with clashes resulting in the death of a teenager. Subsequently, eight nationals were arrested for alleged links with overseas militant groups. Reconciliation talks faltered later in the month when the negotiations reached a stalemate, reportedly over opposition groups' demand to have an official representative of the king involved.

Sparking speculation about reform, the king appointed Crown Prince Al Khalifa to first deputy prime minister in March 2013. The heir to the throne is seen as a reformer and is favored by the West.

In May, opposition leaders announced a two-week boycott of the dialogue, citing the slow pace of the talks and a recent raid on a prominent Shiite cleric's home. Opposition groups indefinitely suspended their participation in negotiations in September after *al-Wifaq* leader Khalil al-MAZOOQ was detained for 30 days over alleged links with a terror group.

Meanwhile, 2013 brought fresh efforts to limit foreign influence on domestic politics. In May parliament passed legislation to halt "interference" of the U.S. ambassador, banning his meetings with opposition groups. In September a new law was passed requiring political organizations to inform the government of all overseas communication.

POLITICAL GROUPS

Political parties are proscribed in Bahrain. At the first National Assembly election in 1973, however, voters elected ten candidates of a loosely organized Popular Bloc of the Left, while such small clandestine groups as a Bahraini branch of the Popular Front for the Liberation of Oman and the Arabian Gulf (PFLOAG), apparently consisting mainly of leftist students, subsequently continued to engage in limited activity. During the 1994 disturbances, a Shiite opposition group, the Islamic Front for the Liberation of Bahrain (IFLB), insisted that security forces were arresting its followers "at random" and condemned deportations of regime opponents.

Reports in the first half of the 1990s concerning activity on behalf of Shiites focused on Hezbollah, based in Lebanon and believed to be financed by Iran. The government charged that a Hezbollah-Bahrain was formed in Iran in 1993 and contributed to anti-regime activity, including the alleged coup attempt of 1996.

Although the constitutional amendment of February 2002 did not lift the ban on political parties, several "groups" and "societies" were subsequently legalized in line with the democratic reforms. Staffed largely by formerly exiled opposition figures who had returned to Bahrain following the amnesty issued by the king in February 2002, those groups and associations "unofficially" endorsed candidates in local elections in May. In 2005 some groups registered under the new political associations law (see Political background, above) and entered candidates in the 2006 parliamentary elections. The political associations appeared to be functioning as de facto political parties, although parties remain formally banned.

In June 2011 the progovernment National Unity Gathering (NUG) voted to register as a political group. Headed by Sheikh Abdullatif al-MAHMUD, its members—numbering in the hundreds of thousands—demonstrated in support of the government months earlier. Group leaders said the NUG promoted national dialogue and reforms. A splinter group led by Yaqub al-SLAISE, Al Fateh Youth Coalition, broke off from the NUG in June 2013.

Islamic National Accord Society (INAS). Referenced as *"al-Wifaq"* ("accord"), this Shiite grouping is led by cleric Sheikh Ali Salman, a former prominent member of the Bahrain Freedom Movement. *Al-Wifaq,* reported to be the country's largest opposition group, was credited with winning upward of 70 percent of the seats in the municipal elections of May 2002. However, the INAS boycotted the October 2002 national balloting to protest some of the king's constitutional amendments that *al-Wifaq* leaders considered inimical to genuine power-sharing. In 2004 it was reported that a number of INAS members split off to form a new **Justice and Development Society,** which INAS loyalists said would divide and weaken the Shiites. (The Justice and Development Society pledged to participate in the 2006 national poll, though was apparently dissolved sometime before the election.) In 2005 INAS decided to register, as called for under the new political associations law, though a number of members, including Vice President Husayn Mushayma and Abduljalil appointed the group's first secretary general. The group greatly increased the Shiite representation (to 42.5 percent) in the 2006 Chamber of Deputies elections. Though favored to become speaker of the chamber, Salman lost to the incumbent.

In 2007 Salman tried to intervene in the imposition of the annual income tax despite the group's initial support for such a levy. In 2009 the group called for an ad hoc national committee to address the turmoil surrounding the arrest of several Shiite leaders (see Political background, above).

During the unrest that began in early 2011, the party urged antigovernment protesters to refrain from using violence. Following the walkout of all 18 *al-Wifaq* members of parliament in February in support of the protesters, 11 resigned from the Chamber of Deputies in March. The remainder were prohibited from seeking reelection in a by-election scheduled for September to replace those who had resigned. In April the government took steps to ban the party but backed off under pressure from the United States. In June, hours before the government announced an end to martial law, several senior party leaders, including Sheikh Ali Salman and Khalil al-Mazooq, were hauled in for questioning. Shortly thereafter, protesters again gathered to demonstrate in various towns around the country, though *al-Wifaq* was not among the groups calling for the rallies. *Al-Wifaq* has remained deeply skeptical of the government's reform declarations, boycotting the by-elections in November 2011 and refusing to participate in the BICI process.

Beginning in February 2013, *al-Wifaq* participated in reconciliatory talks with progovernment groups, though remained reluctant as demands for involvement of a representative of the king went unheeded. The talks faltered several times through the course of the year, most significantly in September, when the group announced an indefinite suspension of participation due to the month-long detention of Khalil al-Mazooq for his alleged ties to a terrorist group.

Leaders: Khalil al-MAZOOQ, Husayn al-DAIHI (Deputy Secretary General), Sheikh Ali SALMAN (Secretary General).

Progressive Democratic Forum (PDF). This group was launched by former members of the Marxist **National Liberation Front of Bahrain** (NLFB)—active mainly in exile since the 1950s—upon their return to Bahrain in 2002 following reforms by King Hamad. The PDF subsequently registered as an official group. In 2005 the group was one of nine that urged the king to suspend the new political associations law and to institute more democratic reforms. The PDF unofficially supported candidates in the 2002 and 2006 balloting for the Chamber of Deputies.

Following the government's deployment of police and the use of force against antigovernment protesters in February, the party called for "a demonstration of solidarity" in front of Bahrain's embassies or the UN offices. Party leaders called for reform, social justice, and negotiations with the country's leaders.

Leaders: Hassan MADAN, Hussein UREYBI.

National Islamic Society (*al-Minbar*). This Sunni group, reported to be part of the political wing of the Muslim Brotherhood, won representation in the 2006 parliamentary election.

In 2007 the group pressed for reinstituting censorship in advance of publication and prison sentences for journalists who allegedly disparaged Islam. In 2009 *al-Minbar* called for a national dialogue in connection with the arrest of several Shiite leaders.

Al-Minbar warned the British embassy in Manama against "meddling" in the country's internal affairs in 2010, following the British ambassador's meeting with *al-Wifaq* parliamentarians who had proposed that the cabinet be chosen by elected legislators rather than appointed.

The progovernment group won two seats in the 2010 parliamentary elections. Former party leader Salah ALI was second deputy chair of parliament in 2011.

Leader: Ali Ahmed Abdulla al AMIN (Secretary General).

Al-Asala. A progovernment Sunni Salafi society of some 240 members, *al-Asala* was the first political society to register under the new political associations law. Ghanim al-Buaneen replaced former leader Sheikh Adel MOUWDA after the latter was accused of Shia leanings in 2005. It secured five seats in the 2006 parliamentary elections and reportedly formed an alliance with the National Islamic Society to offset gains by Shiite groups in the Chamber of Deputies.

In 2010 *al-Asala* was highly critical of *al-Wifaq*'s proposed changes to the government, accusing it of orchestrating "a constitutional and political coup." The group won three seats in the October parliamentary elections.

The group expelled Abdel al-MOUAWDA, one of its senior leaders, in March 2011 for "noncompliance" with *al-Asala*'s stance on the resignation from parliament of 18 *al-Wifaq* members in protest of the government crackdown on prodemocracy demonstrators. Al-Mouawda had been elected to parliament in 2002, 2006, and 2010.

In June 2013, amid ongoing civil unrest, *al-Asala* called for the deportation of pro-Hezbollah Lebanese nationals.

Leaders: Ghanim al-BUANEEN, Abdul Halim MURAD.

Al-Mithaq. Established in 2005, *al-Mithaq* ("covenant") backed the National Action Charter and the government's decision to offer financial support to political groups since the new political associations law banned them from receiving money from foreign sources. Other societies criticized *al-Mithaq*'s position, saying its support for the government hindered other groups' attempts to expand democracy. *Al-Mithaq*'s only candidate for the 2006 parliamentary election withdrew before the poll.

Leaders: Ahmad JUMA (President), Muhammad JANAHI (Secretary General).

National Democratic Action Society (*Waad*). This leftist, nationalist group boycotted the October 2002 balloting for the Chamber of Deputies. However, in 2005 its members voted in favor of registering under the new political associations law despite having vowed months earlier to challenge some aspects of the law. The group failed to win seats in the 2006 parliamentary election.

Group leader Ibrahim Sharif, who took over in 2005 after party founder Abdul Rahman al-NUAIMI lapsed into a coma, was injured in clashes with the police at an opposition rally in May 2007.

In 2010 the group protested against changes to ease naturalization of foreigners, claiming that granting citizenship to Sunni Muslims would affect the elections in the Shia-majority country. The group lost the two seats it contested in the second round of parliamentary elections in 2010.

Sharif, a Sunni, described by observers as among the most moderate of the opposition, was arrested at his home in the middle of the night in March 2011 in the wake of his calling for democratic reforms. The first word of his case came in May, when his wife was allowed a brief visit with him in prison. On April 8 it was reported that the party had been suspended, as military prosecutors said all of its offices and its Website had been shut down "until further notice." Following Sharif's May 11 preliminary court hearing, along with that of 13 other dissidents—all of whom denied the charges—Amnesty International issued an urgent call for action, saying the defendants were prisoners of conscience.

Leaders: Ibrahim Kamal al-DEEN, Abdulnabi al-EKRI, Ibrahim SHARIF (Secretary General).

Islamic Arab Democratic Society (*Wasat*). A Pan-Arab opposition group, *Wasat* ("center") fielded candidates in the 2002 parliamentary election. In 2005 the group participated in protests aimed at the political associations law and continued to press for amendments to the law through the legislature.

Leader: Ahmad Sanad Al BINALI (Secretary General).

National Justice Movement (*Adalah*). This Sunni opposition group announced its formation in March 2006 to offset the influence of the INAS and to give more weight to secular groups. The group, whose focus was naturalization and constitutional issues, was highly critical of government actions against Islamists alleged to be jihadists. The group, which is reportedly pro al-Qaida, supported candidates who ran as independents in the 2006 parliamentary election.

Leader: Abdullah HASHIM (Secretary General).

Islamic Action Society. This grouping was formed by followers of Shiite religious scholar Muhammad Mahdi al-SHIRAZI. It was initially led by Sheikh Muhammad Ali Mahfuz, a former leader of the IFLB. The Islamic Action Society, which supported political reforms and was seen as furthering the aims of the IFLB, boycotted the 2002 elections but supported candidates who ran as independents in the 2006 parliamentary election.

After the group's leader Sheikh Muhammad Al Mahfud participated in a demonstration against Bahrain's increasing poverty in 2007, a court dissolved the IAS in July 2007 on the grounds that it answered to a religious authority that is hostile and that calls for violence.

The group later reactivated and participated in the demonstrations of 2011. However, a court ruled in July to disband the grouping, citing financial irregularities.

Leader: Sheikh Muhammad Al MAHFUD.

Bahrain Freedom Movement (BFM). Based in London in the 1990s under the leadership of Mansur al-JAMRI (the son of popular Shiite leader Sheikh Abd al-Amir al-Jamri), the BFM called for "passive resistance" on the part of the Bahraini populace to pressure the government into adopting "democratic reforms."

Some members of the London-based BFM returned to Bahrain in 2002, including former BFM leader Majid al-AWALI, who was named to the new cabinet in November. However, other BFM members remained in exile in London, criticizing King Hamad for orchestrating a "constitutional putsch." The group continued to be active in its criticism of the government in early 2006, with one senior member calling for a boycott of the next elections. In 2007 group members participated in demonstrations, which became violent, protesting the detention of a Shiite cleric who had been detained at the Manama airport following his visit to Iran. In 2010 the BFM posted on its Websites accounts of alleged arrests and, in some cases, torture of prodemocracy protesters who took to the streets during the Formula 1 race week.

Leader: Said Al SHEHABI (in London).

Movement of Liberties and Democracy–Bahrain (*Haq*). This mostly Shiite separatist group, which was formed in 2005 after its members broke away from the INAS, does not recognize the country's constitution. In 2006 the group participated in several protest rallies and boycotted the Chamber of Deputies elections.

In February 2007 group leader Husayn Mushayma and two other political activists, including the head of the Bahrain Center for Human Rights, were arrested. They faced trial on charges that included plotting to overthrow the government, but the king subsequently pardoned them. Mushayma, Abduljalil Alsingace, and other Shiites faced trial again in 2009. The group has continued to protest "deterioration" of human rights and freedom of expression.

In March 2011 the group's secretary general, Husayn Mushayma, was detained during the government's crackdown on protests by Shiites and others who demonstrated for reforms. In 2011 both Mushayma and Alsingace were sentenced to life imprisonment by a military court for conspiring against the monarchy with a foreign terrorist group. On April 30, 2012, a Bahraini court ordered a civilian retrial.

Leaders: Abduljalil ALSINGACE, Husayn MUSHAYMA (Secretary General).

Other political societies active in 2006 included the Baathist **Democratic National Rally**, the leftist **Progressive Democratic Society**, **Constitutional Rally**, and **National Free Thought**.

LEGISLATURE

The first election to fill 30 non-nominated seats in the **National Assembly** was held December 7, 1973. In addition to the elected members, who were to serve four-year terms, the assembly contained 14 cabinet members (including 2 ministers of state). The assembly was dissolved on August 26, 1975, on the grounds that it had indulged in debates "dominated by ideas alien to the society and values of Bahrain."

In January 1993 the emir appointed a 30-member Consultative Council to contribute "advice and opinion" on legislation proposed by the cabinet and, in certain cases, suggest new laws on its own. In accordance with reforms announced in April 1996, the emir appointed new 40-member councils on September 28, 1996, and September 27, 2000. (The council appointed in 2000 included women for the first time.)

The king dissolved the Consultative Council on February 14, 2002, in anticipation of the establishment of the new bicameral National Assembly (*Majlis al-Watani*) provided for in the constitutional revision of the same day.

Consultative Council (*Majlis al-Shura*). The upper house comprises 40 members appointed by the king for a four-year term. The first appointments, including six women as well as representatives of the Christian and Jewish communities, were made by King Hamad on November 16, 2002. The king appointed 40 new members on December 5, 2006. In renewing council the on November 24, 2010, 30 appointees maintained their seats and 10 new members joined the council, bringing the number of women to 11 and marking the first appointment of a Christian and a Jew.

Speaker: Abdul Jalil Ebrahim al-TARIF.

Chamber of Deputies (*Majlis al-Nuwwab*). The lower house comprises 40 members directly elected on a majoritarian basis for a four-year term. In the most recent elections on October 23 and October 30, 2010, the seat distribution was as follows: Islamic National Accord Society, 18 seats; independents, 17; *al-Asala,* 3; and National Islamic Society, 2.

Speaker: Khalifa al-DHAHRANI.

CABINET

[as of September 15, 2013]

Prime Minister	Sheikh Khalifa bin Salman Al Khalifa
Deputy Prime Ministers	Sheikh Ali bin Khalifa Al Khalifa
	Sheikh Muhammad bin Mubarak Al Khalifa
	Jawad bin Salim al-Urayid
	Sheikh Khalid bin Abdullah Al Khalifa
Ministers	
Cabinet Affairs	Khalid bin Ahmed bin Muhammad Al Khalifa
Commerce and Industry	Hassan bin Abdullah Fakhro
Culture	Sheikha Mai bint Muhammad Al Khalifa [f]
Education	Majid bin Ali al-Nuaimi
Energy, Oil, Electricity, and Water	Abdullahussain bin Ali Mirza
Finance	Sheikh Ahmed bin Muhammad Al Khalifa
Foreign Affairs	Sheikh Khalid bin Ahmad bin Muhammad Al Khalifa
Health	Sadiq bin Abdul Karim Al Shehabi
Housing	Bassem bin Yacoub Al Hamer
Human Rights and Social Development	Fatima al-Balushi [f]
Industry and Commerce	Hassan Abdullah Fakhro
Interior	Sheikh Rashid bin Abdullah bin Ahmed Al Khalifa
Justice and Islamic Affairs	Sheikh Khalid bin Ali Al Khalifa
Labor	Jameel bin Muhammad Hmaidan
Municipal Affairs and Urban Planning	Juma Ahmad Al Ka'abi
Public Works	Esam bin Abdullah Khalaf
Transport and Communications	Kamal bin Ahmed Mohammed
Ministers of State	
Defense	Sheikh Muhammad bin Abdullah Al Khalifa
Follow-up Affairs	Muhammad Al Mutawa
Foreign Affairs	Ganem bin Fadel al-Buainain
Human Rights Affairs	Salah Ali
Information Affairs	Sameera Rajab [f]
Interior Affairs	Adel bin Khalifa al-Fadhel
Shura Council and Parliamentary Affairs	Abdulaziz Muhammad al-Fadel

[f] = female

INTERGOVERNMENTAL REPRESENTATION

Ambassador to the U.S.: Huda Azra NONOO.

U.S. Ambassador to Bahrain: Thomas C. KRAJESKI.

Permanent Representative to the UN: Jamal Fares ALROWAIEI.

IGO Memberships (Non-UN): GCC, LAS, NAM, OIC, WTO.

BANGLADESH

People's Republic of Bangladesh
Ganaprojatantri Bangladesh

Political Status: Independent state proclaimed March 26, 1971; de facto independence achieved December 16, 1971; republican constitution of December 16, 1972, suspended following coup of March 24, 1982, but restored on November 10, 1986; parliamentary system (abandoned in favor of presidential system in January 1975) restored by referendum of September 15, 1991.

Area: 55,598 sq. mi. (143,999 sq. km).

Population: 153,501,050 (2012E—UN); 163,654,860 (2013E—U.S. Census).

Major Urban Centers (2005E): DHAKA (Dacca, 6,788,000), Chittagong (2,640,000), Khulna (881,000).

Official Language: Bangla (Bengali).

Monetary Unit: Taka (official rate November 1, 2013: 77.75 takas = $1US).

President: Abdul HAMID (Awami League); as the only candidate, declared president-elect by the Election Commission on April 22, 2013, and sworn in on April 24, 2013, following the March 20, 2013, death of Mohammad Zillur RAHMAN (Awami League).

Prime Minister: Sheikh HASINA Wajed (Awami League); sworn in on January 6, 2009, following the general election of December 29, 2008, succeeding Chief Adviser (head of caretaker government) Fakhruddin AHMED, who had served in that capacity from January 12, 2007.

THE COUNTRY

Located in the east of the Indian subcontinent, Bangladesh comprises a portion of the historic province of Bengal (including Chittagong) in addition to the Sylhet district of Assam. Except for a short boundary with Myanmar in the extreme southeast, the country's land frontier borders on India. Endowed with a tropical monsoon climate that produces devastating cyclones—one in 1991 killed an estimated 150,000 people—as well as annual floods, Bangladesh possesses rich alluvial plains dominated by the Ganges and Brahmaputra rivers. One

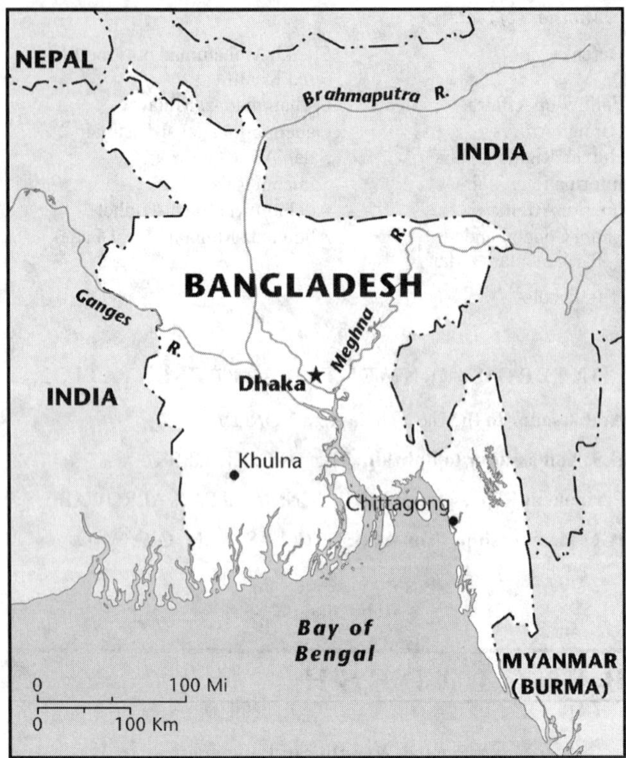

of the world's most densely populated independent countries, with over 1,000 people per square kilometer of land, it is ethnically homogeneous: 98 percent of the people are Bengali and speak a common language. Urdu-speaking, non-Bengali Muslim immigrants from India, largely Bihari, comprise 1 percent; the remaining 1 percent includes assorted tribal groups, of which one of the most important is the Chakma of the Chittagong Hill Tracts. Bangladesh has more Muslim inhabitants than any other country except Indonesia and Pakistan; nearly 90 percent of its people profess Islam. Most of the remainder are Hindu. Women constitute about 40 percent of the economically active population, more than half in the agricultural sector. Although women remain underrepresented in politics, since 1991 two women have alternated as prime minister, and women constitute 19.7 percent of the members of Parliament.

Bangladesh continues to rank as one of the world's poorest countries. About 45 percent of the labor force is engaged in agriculture, which now accounts for about 19 percent of the GDP. Rice, sugarcane, pulses, and oilseeds are among the leading food crops. Industry contributes about 29 percent of GDP and employs 30 percent of the paid labor force. Textiles and related articles, especially ready-made garments, account for two-thirds of merchandise export earnings. Exported jute and jute goods, once mainstays of the economy, are now surpassed in value by sales of frozen fish and shrimp.

GDP growth consistently registered between 6.0 and 6.6 percent in fiscal years (July–June) 2004–2008, largely fueled by exports, remittances, and domestic activity. In 2006 Bangladeshi economist Mohammad YUNUS and his Grameen Bank were awarded the Nobel Peace Prize for innovative work in extending microcredits, primarily to poor women. After slipping to 5.9 percent in 2009, GDP growth rebounded to 6.4 the following year and has remained fairly steady since. In 2013 GDP growth was 6.0 percent, and inflation, 6.5 percent.

GOVERNMENT AND POLITICS

Political background. When British India was partitioned into independent India and Pakistan in August 1947, Bengal was divided along communal lines. Predominantly Hindu West Bengal was incorporated into India, while predominantly Muslim East Bengal was joined with the Sylhet district of Assam as the Eastern Province of Pakistan.

During the 1960s Bengali resentment over major disparities in development expenditure and representation in the public services intensified, and in 1966 Sheikh Mujibur RAHMAN (Mujib), president of the East Pakistan branch of the Awami League (AL), called for a constitutional reallocation of powers. The sheikh's subsequent arrest helped coalesce Bengali opinion against the Pakistani president, Ayub Khan, who was forced from office in March 1969.

Ayub's successor, Gen. Yahya Khan, endorsed a return to democratic rule, and during the 1970 electoral campaign Sheikh Mujib and his party won 167 of 169 seats allotted to East Pakistan in a proposed National Assembly of 313 members. The issue of power distribution remained unresolved, however, and postponement of the National Assembly session on March 1, 1971, led to massive civil strife in East Pakistan. Three weeks later, Sheikh Mujib was again arrested and his party banned. Martial law was imposed following disturbances in Dhaka, and civil war ensued. India, having protested against suppression of the eastern rebellion and the resultant influx of millions of refugees, declared war on Pakistan on December 3, 1971, and the allied forces of India and Bangladesh defeated Pakistani forces in the East on December 16. The new, war-ravaged nation of Bangladesh emerged on the same day.

Sheikh Mujib assumed command of the provisional government and began restructuring the new state along socialist lines that featured a limitation on large landholdings and the nationalization of banks, insurance companies, and major industries. On January 25, 1975, the Constituent Assembly revised the constitution to provide for a presidential form of government and the adoption of a one-party system under the rubric of the *Bangladesh Krishak Sramik Awami League* (Baksal), a socialist political platform.

On August 15, 1975, a group of pro-Pakistan, Islamic right-wing army officers mounted a coup, killing Sheikh Mujib, his wife, and five of their children. The former minister of trade and commerce Khandakar Moshtaque AHMED was sworn in as president. On November 3 the new president was himself confronted with a rebellion led by Brig. Khalid MUSHARAF, the pro-Indian commander of the Dhaka garrison. Three days later President Ahmed vacated his office in favor of the chief justice of the Supreme Court, Abu Sadat Mohammad SAYEM, and on November 7 Musharaf was killed during a left-wing mutiny led by Col. Abu TAHER. As a result, President Sayem announced that he would assume the additional post of chief martial law administrator, with the army chief of staff, Maj. Gen. Ziaur RAHMAN (Zia), and the heads of the air force and navy as deputies. Vigorous action was taken against those implicated in the November 7 mutiny, and Colonel Taher was hanged.

Although President Sayem announced in mid-1976 that his government would honor former president Ahmed's pledge to hold a general election by the end of February 1977, he reversed himself in November. Shortly thereafter, he transferred the office of chief martial law administrator to Ziaur Rahman, who assumed the presidency in April 1977. President Zia was confirmed in office by a nationwide referendum in May.

President Zia announced in April 1978 that a presidential election would be held in June, to be followed by a parliamentary election. Opposition allegations of polling irregularities notwithstanding, Zia was credited with a near three-to-one margin of victory over his closest rival in the presidential balloting and was sworn in for a five-year term. A new Parliament dominated by Zia's Bangladesh Nationalist Party (BNP) was elected in February 1979, and in April a civilian cabinet with Shah Azizur RAHMAN as prime minister was announced.

The Zia government encountered continuing unrest, including several coup attempts and a major uprising by tribal guerrillas in the southeastern Chittagong Hill Tracts in early 1980. On May 30, 1981, longstanding differences within the army precipitated the assassination of President Zia in the course of an attempted coup in Chittagong. The former vice president was elected to a five-year term as Zia's successor in November. Azizur Rahman stayed on as prime minister.

The armed forces again intervened on March 24, 1982, suspending the constitution, ousting the Sattar government, and installing military chief of staff Hossain Mohammed ERSHAD as chief martial law administrator. Three days later, on Ershad's nomination, Abul Fazal Mohammad Ahsanuddin CHOWDHURY, a retired Supreme Court judge, was sworn in as the nation's eighth president.

In September 1983, in an effort to bring an end to martial law, two broad opposition alliances—one headed by the Awami League under President Mujib's daughter, Sheikh Hasina WAJED, and the other led by the BNP under former president Sattar and President Zia's widow, Begum Khaleda ZIA—formed the 22-party Movement for the Restoration of Democracy (MRD). In November a regime-supportive People's Party (*Jana Dal*) was formed under President Chowdhury, who resigned his office in December in favor of Ershad. General Ershad was reconfirmed as president by referendum in March 1985. The promotion of a "transition to democracy" was announced by a *Jana Dal*-centered National Front in August.

On January 1, 1986, coincident with revocation of a ban on political activity, it was announced that the National Front had been converted into a proregime National Party (*Jatiya Dal*), and in early March President Ershad scheduled parliamentary balloting for late April. Both the Awami League alliance and the fundamentalist Bangladesh Islamic Assembly (*Jamaat-i-Islami Bangladesh*), but not the BNP, agreed to compete in an election rescheduled for May despite continuing martial law.

Despite widespread unrest, the *Jatiya Dal* won a narrow majority of legislative seats, and a new government took office in July 1986 that included as prime minister Mizanur Rahman CHOWDHURY, then leader of a minority conservative faction of the Awami League. Subsequently, General Ershad formally joined the government party to permit his nomination as its presidential candidate, and in October he was credited with winning 84 percent of the vote. In November Ershad announced the lifting of martial law and restoration of the amended 1972 constitution.

In January 1987 the Awami League, which was now under the undisputed "Mujibist" leadership of Sheikh Hasina, withdrew from parliamentary proceedings in response to President Ershad's projection of an enhanced political role for the military. In December the president dissolved Parliament after declaring a state of emergency in November. None of the leading opposition parties presented candidates for the legislative election of March 1988, in which the government officially swept more than 80 percent of the seats.

Antiregime demonstrations by the student wings of the BNP and the Awami League in October 1990 mushroomed into nationwide strikes and riots. President Ershad's declaration of a state of emergency in November was generally ignored by increasingly violent mass protests, and in early December, 19 MPs from the president's own party resigned their seats. With army officers having indicated that they were unwilling to take control of the country, Ershad announced his intention to resign. On December 5 the principal opposition formations nominated Shahabuddin AHMED, theretofore chief justice of the Supreme Court, as successor to the beleaguered head of state, who named Ahmed vice president (hence next in line to the presidency) prior to withdrawing from office.

At the legislative election of February 1991, the BNP won a sizable plurality of seats, enabling it, with the support of the *Jamaat-i-Islami,* to claim a majority when the 30 additional seats reserved for women were distributed by the newly elected Parliament. In March the BNP's Khaleda Zia was sworn in as prime minister, although her political mandate was constitutionally limited to offering "advice" to the president. Voters approved the return to a Westminster-style parliamentary system in a referendum on September 15, and Khaleda Zia became, effectively, the executive through her reappointment as prime minister four days later. A month later the legislature filled the substantially weakened presidency by electing the BNP's Abdur Rahman BISWAS.

Beginning in May 1994 with a legislative boycott, the Awami League and other opposition parties began demanding new elections. In November President Biswas, acting on the prime minister's advice, dissolved Parliament and asked Zia to continue in an interim capacity pending an early general election, though opposition parties boycotted, calling for a neutral caretaker government.

Their decision to boycott the February 1996 election enabled the BNP to win all but 2 of the 214 seats declared by the end of February, amid further violent clashes and the temporary arrest of half a dozen prominent opposition figures. By late February, after more than two years of continuous political unrest, more than 100 people had been killed and at least 1,000 injured.

At the opening of the new Parliament in March 1996, protesters attempted to storm the building as Prime Minister Zia was sworn in for a second term. However, near-paralysis of the civil service machine induced Zia to resign as prime minister at the end of March, whereupon the president again dissolved Parliament and named former chief justice Mohammad Habibur RAHMAN as chief adviser of a neutral caretaker government, in accordance with a recently instituted constitutional amendment. The election of June 1996 saw some 2,500 candidates from over 80 parties (including Ershad of the *Jatiya* Party, campaigning from prison) contest the 300 seats. In a record turnout, the Awami League obtained a decisive plurality of 146 seats (against 116 for the BNP and 32 for the *Jatiya Dal*) and thus returned to power after 21 years in opposition.

Sheikh Hasina was sworn in as the head of a government that also included representatives of the *Jatiya* Party and the small National Socialist Party (Rab). Their support gave the new administration an immediate parliamentary majority, which was consolidated in July when the Awami League took 27 of the 30 additional seats reserved for women and the *Jatiya* Party claimed the other 3. In a unanimous parliamentary vote in July, Shahabuddin Ahmed (nonparty) was elected president of Bangladesh in succession to Biswas, thus returning to the post he had previously held on a transitional basis following the demise of the Ershad regime in December 1990.

In its first year in office, the Hasina government moved to resolve a major disagreement with India over water rights to the Ganges (see Foreign relations, below) and, as it had also pledged in the 1996 campaign, to settle the rebellion led by the Chakma tribal group in the Chittagong Hill Tracts. An accord with the Chittagong insurgents was finally reached in December 1997, bringing to a close a conflict that may have cost 20,000 lives.

In March 1998 the *Jatiya* Party left the coalition, in part over objections to the Chittagong peace agreement. In May, amid opposition resistance, the Awami League majority passed four Chittagong implementation bills.

Beginning in December 1998, opposition efforts to force Sheikh Hasina's government to step down escalated. The four-party alliance of the BNP, the *Jamaat-i-Islami,* the *Jatiya* Party, and the Islamic Unity Front (*Islami Oikya Jote*—IOJ) boycotted parliamentary sessions and conducted a campaign of demonstrations and *hartals* (organized disruptions). The opposition also protested the nationwide municipal council elections of February 1999, which went ahead as scheduled, but not without violent altercations that injured over 1,000 people.

On July 13, 2001, in accordance with the constitution, Parliament was dissolved, having completed its five-year term—the first to do so in 30 years. Collaterally, Sheikh Hasina and her cabinet stepped down, and a caretaker government headed by Chief Adviser Latifur RAHMAN, a retired chief justice, was named on July 16. With many observers citing national concern over civil violence as a primary factor, in the balloting on October 1 Khaleda Zia's BNP won a massive victory, capturing 191 of 300 seats. Sheikh Hasina's Awami League took only 62 seats. On October 10 Khaleda Zia was sworn in as the head of a BNP cabinet that also included two members of the *Jamaat-i-Islami.*

On September 6, 2002, Iajuddin AHMED, a nonpartisan with close ties to the BNP, assumed office as Bangladesh's largely ceremonial president, having been declared elected by the Election Commission the previous day upon the technical disqualification of the two other candidates. Ahmed's predecessor, A. Q. M. Badruddoza CHOWDHURY, who assumed office in November 2001, resigned in June 2002 under BNP pressure because he had not marked the May 30 anniversary of Ziaur Rahman's death with an obligatory visit to the slain president's grave.

The Zia government stepped down at the end of the parliamentary term on October 27, 2006, but with the government and the opposition having failed to agree on the makeup of a caretaker government that would hold office until the election scheduled for January 22, 2007, President Ahmed took on the additional role of chief adviser. Accusing Ahmed and the Election Commission of favoring the BNP, and questioning the validity of the existing inflated election roll, a "Grand Alliance" of the Awami League, its allies, and most other opposition parties announced in early January that it would boycott the election, while exerting pressure with a series of demonstrations and strikes. In response, on January 11, with the tacit support of Army Chief of Staff Lt. Gen. Moin AHMED and the rest of the military leadership, President Ahmed instituted a state of emergency, indefinitely postponed the election, and announced his resignation as chief adviser. The next day, he named economist and former central bank governor Fakhruddin AHMED to head a new caretaker administration.

By mid-2007 some 190,000 people had been arrested during the state of emergency, and the national Anti-Corruption Commission (ACC) and other authorities, operating under emergency power rules (EPRs), continued to file corruption cases against prominent politicians, businessmen, and former government ministers—some 170 in all—many of whom were held without bail into mid-2008. Allegations of extortion, graft, illegally amassing wealth, and concealing financial information were the most common charges. The military-backed government arrested former prime ministers Sheikh Hasina and Khaleda Zia on July 16 and September 3, 2007, respectively, and charged each with corruption and other offenses allegedly committed during their terms in office. Other prominent detainees included the Awami League secretary general, Abdul JALIL, and Khaleda Zia's elder son and heir-apparent, Tarique RAHMAN. In addition, Sheikh Hasina and other Awami leaders faced a murder charge in connection with the October 2006 deaths of *Jamaat-i-Islami* members during rioting in the capital.

In July 2008 the Election Commission announced that the new voter roll, numbering some 80 million registrants (down by 13 million from the previous listing), had been completed. Less than a month later, elections were held in four cities and nine municipalities, and although all candidates were required to run as independents under the EPRs, AL members reportedly won in all but one of the localities.

With a national election scheduled for December, Khaleda Zia was released on bail on September 9, 2008, after the caretaker government determined that, given wide popular support for both her and Sheikh Hasina, no legitimate election could be conducted without their presence. Sheikh Hasina, who had been released on June 12 to undergo medical treatment in the United States, returned to Bangladesh on November 6.

Sheikh Hasina's Awami League and its allies won an overwhelming victory in the election of December 29, 2008, taking 263 seats to 33 for the BNP-led four-party alliance. Hasina selected almost entirely new cabinet ministers, reducing ties to past corruption allegations; the new government took office on January 6, 2009. For the first time, women held the majority of key portfolios, including defense and foreign affairs.

A month later, the Election Commission named the Awami League's unopposed presidential candidate, 79-year-old Mohammad Zillur RAHMAN, to succeed Iajuddin Ahmed as head of state. In July 2009 Sheikh Hasina expanded the cabinet and conducted a minor reshuffle of portfolios. In June 2011, Parliament passed a constitutional amendment that abolished the practice of appointing a caretaker government after elections. This decision was highly controversial among members of the opposition and resulted in violent protests and the expansion of the opposition from 4 parties to 18 (see Current issues, below).

In December 2011, there was a minor reshuffle of cabinet officials within the administration. Allegations of corruption led to the resignation of two ministers in 2012. President Rahman died on March 20, 2013. Parliamentary speaker Abdul HAMID acceded the position on an acting basis on March 14; subsequently, he was elected permanently on April 22.

Constitution and government. The constitution of December 1972 has been subjected to numerous revisions, the most important being the adoption of a presidential system in January 1975 and a return to the earlier parliamentary form in September 1991. At present, the essentially titular president is elected for a once-renewable five-year term by the Parliament (*Jatiya Sangsad*), from which the prime minister and all but one-tenth of the other ministers must be drawn. The president appoints as prime minister the individual who commands a legislative majority. Under the 13th Constitutional Amendment, adopted unanimously by the Parliament in 1996, the president has authority to create a nonparty caretaker government for a three-month interim period beginning with a dissolution of Parliament and concluding after a general election.

The unicameral legislature, which has a five-year mandate, contains 300 seats filled by direct election from single-member constituencies. Legislators lose their seats if they defect from their parties. A 2004 constitutional amendment reserves an additional 45 seats for women, who are chosen by the directly elected members. The 45 seats are proportionally distributed among the parliamentary parties.

The Supreme Court is divided into a High Court, with both original and appellate jurisdiction, and an Appellate Division that hears appeals from the High Court. Other courts are established by law. Under an ordinance approved in February 2007 by the interim Council of Advisers, authority over lower judges and magistrates was removed from the executive branch and delegated to higher courts.

Bangladesh comprises six administrative divisions (Barisal, Chittagong, Dhaka, Khulna, Rajshahi, and Sylhet), 64 districts (*zillas*), over 500 towns (*thanas*), over 4,400 unions, and some 87,000 villages. In addition, there are four metropolitan cities and over 100 other municipalities.

In March 2010, the Bangladesh Supreme Court threw out the fifth amendment of the constitution, which had legitimized dictatorships of the 1970s, as unconstitutional. By nullifying the amendment, the Supreme Court made religious and military dictatorships unconstitutional and gave the government the authority to outlaw religion-based political parties.

Upon resumption of civilian rule in 2009, press freedom improved considerably. However, the constitutional guarantee of freedom of expression with "reasonable restrictions" constrains the press, as do criminal libel laws and national security provisions. In 2013, the media watchdog Reporters Without Borders ranked Bangladesh 144th out of 179 on its annual press freedom index.

Foreign relations. Bangladesh joined the United Nations in 1974, when the People's Republic of China, an ally of Pakistan, withdrew its objections. Bangladesh acknowledged the natural ties of geography, culture, and commerce with India, and in March 1972 the two countries signed a 25-year treaty of friendship, cooperation, and peace. Relations with Pakistan, initially characterized by mutual hatred and suspicion, slowly improved, with Islamabad according Bangladesh diplomatic recognition in 1974.

A lingering source of tension between Bangladesh and Pakistan involves the status of what now totals 300,000 Biharis, many of whom supported Pakistan during the independence struggle in 1971 and whom Pakistan agreed to "repatriate" from Bangladesh but did not. In August 1992 the 21-year stalemate appeared broken, but a repatriation program was suspended after Pakistan's prime minister Benazir Bhutto took office in 2003, effectively stranding the Biharis in over 100 refugee camps. A May 2003 High Court ruling paved the way for Biharis to become citizens. In September 2007 the interim government announced that those Biharis who were born in Bangladesh or who were minors when independence occurred, and who willingly chose to remain in Bangladesh, would be entered on the voter lists for the upcoming parliamentary elections. In May 2008 the High Court ruled that some 150,000 Biharis were entitled to citizenship. In 2010 Dhaka began constructing a housing project for 39,000 Biharis.

Dhaka also has been burdened, to a lesser extent, by Rohingya Muslims who fled Myanmar's western Rakhine (Arakan) State in the 1990s. At its peak in 1992, the Rohingya flight numbered over 250,000. An agreement between Dhaka and Yangon led to repatriation by mid-1997 of all but about 21,000 Rohingyas. Repatriation resumed in November 1998, but Myanmar again suspended the operation a month later. In April 2004 Yangon once again agreed to accept the remaining Rohingyas, but most refused to leave, or Myanmar officials have not authorized their return. (At least one estimate has placed the number of unregistered Rohingya refugees in Bangladesh at over 200,000.) The 2006–2007 interim government in Dhaka called for the United Nations to join Bangladesh and Myanmar in a tripartite initiative to resolve the issue.

In 1976 Bangladesh lodged a formal complaint at the United Nations alleging excessive Indian diversion of water from the Ganges at the Farakka barrage. India's 1980 unilateral seizure of two newly formed islands in the Bay of Bengal further complicated relations. The Hasina government and India finally concluded a Ganges pact in December 1996. An Indo-Bangla Joint Rivers Commission now meets regularly. In October 2003 they signed a water-sharing agreement for the Teesta and six other rivers.

Meeting in April 2003, representatives of India and Bangladesh agreed to move forward on delineating the final five kilometers of their mutual border and to discuss exchange of enclaves. (There are over 100 Indian enclaves in Bangladesh and 50 Bangladeshi enclaves in India.) Meanwhile, competing claims to a 50-hectare shoal in Parshuram. Border security has also been a persistent irritant. (For more on territorial disputes before 2005, see the 2013 *Handbook*.)

In 1999 Bangladesh hosted the second summit of the fledgling D-8 (Developing Eight) group of Islamic nations, organized in 1997 by Bangladesh, Egypt, Indonesia, Iran, Malaysia, Nigeria, Pakistan, and Turkey.

During U.S. president Bill Clinton's March 2000 visit to Dhaka, Sheikh Hasina urged that Lawful Permanent Resident status be given to some 50,000 undocumented Bangladeshis living in the United States.

In October 2009 the Bangladeshi government filed a suit against Myanmar with the International Tribunal for the Law of the Seas to settle a long-standing dispute between the two nations about the appropriate maritime borders in the Bay of Bengal. The suit was filed in light of increasing competition for fishing and exploration of oil reserves in the disputed territory. In March 2012 the tribunal ruled in favor of Bangladesh, granting it a 200-mile nautical zone with exclusive rights to all economic activity.

Following the April 2013 collapse of a garment factory that killed more than 1,000 workers, Bangladesh received pressure from the international community to improve domestic labor conditions. The European Union, which receives 60 percent of Bangladeshi garment exports, threatened to cut trade benefits if workers' rights issues went unaddressed. In June Bangladesh approved a Trade and Investment Cooperation Forum Agreement with the United States after a decade of negotiations. However, later that month, U.S. president Barack Obama moved to suspend long-standing trade privileges for Bangladesh because of labor violations.

Current issues. The newly elected Awami League government faced its first challenge on February 25–26, 2009, when paramilitary troops belonging to the BDR, the country's border guards, mutinied against their regular-army officers. The complaints involved pay, corruption, and mistreatment. Following a February 26 televised warning from the prime minister, some 900 mutineers surrendered, although at least that many escaped. Afterward, government forces began recovering 74 bodies, 57 of them slain officers, within the BDR headquarters complex. By June 2011 more than 2,600 soldiers had been convicted of involvement in the mutiny, with prison sentences ranging from four months to seven years. The BDR, meanwhile, was restructured and renamed the Border Guards Bangladesh.

In May 2011 the Supreme Court ruled that religious decrees issued by Islamic clerics do not carry the force of law. On May 12 Mohammad Yunus resigned as head of the Grameen Bank following legal efforts by AL officials to force his ouster. Sheikh Hasina publicly accused the Nobel Prize–winning economist of diverting aid funds to other economic development projects. In June Parliament passed a constitutional amendment that abolished the practice of appointing a caretaker government after elections. The BNP and other opposition parties boycotted the vote, protesting that the change to the basic law was designed to allow the AL-led government to secure power for another term.

In April 2012 the BNP announced the creation of a new alliance of 18 parties, accordingly dubbed the 18-Party Alliance, which BNP officials stated indicates growing opposition to the Awami League government. Some analysts countered that the move was just an attempt to draft people for the BNP-led street protests against the abolishment of electoral caretaker governments, which the BNP claimed would result in unfair elections designed to favor the Awami League. During the protests of late April and May, more than 100 people were injured and more than 20 killed. The violence escalated with the use of several small bombs, but no injuries resulted. At least 30 opposition party officials were arrested and charged with arson in relation to the protests.

In June, a large strike by 500,000 workers in clothing factories near Dhaka resulted in 300 factories being forced to close due to lack of workers. Workers demanding an increase in the minimum wage led this strike, which lasted for a week. In December at least four protesters were killed and two more protesters were killed and 600 injured in clashes with police, as activists called for early elections under a caretaker government, which intensified following the arrest of BNP acting secretary general Mirza Fakhrul Islam ALAMGIR for instigating violence. Protests continued to erupt through 2013, driven largely by *Jamaat-i-Islami*, with activists protesting the caretaker government abolishment, the war crimes tribunal verdicts, and in April, the lack of antiblasphemy legislation.

In March 2012 the Bangladesh government established a tribunal comprising three judges to try the human rights violation cases from the war of independence in 1971. Two BNP and ten *Jamaat-i-Islami* leaders faced charges. As of September 2013, the Bangladesh International Crimes Tribunal-2 (ICT-2) has sentenced three key *Jamaat-i-Islami* figures to death—Delwar Hossain SAYEEDE, current secretary general Ali Ahsan Mohammad MUJAHID, and assistant secretary general Muhammad KAMARUZZAMAN—and awarded a fourth, former party leader Golam AZAM, a 90-year prison sentence.

President Rahman died on March 20, 2013. Parliamentary speaker Abdul Hamid became acting president on March 14, a week before President Rahman died. Hamid was elected, unopposed, by the Election Commission on April 22 and took office on April 24.

On August 1 a high court invalidated the *Jamaat-i-Islami*'s party registration, barring it from participating in the upcoming election. The case, filed in 2009 by the Bangladesh Tariqat Federation, hinged on the party charter's failure to recognize the sovereign power of parliament and the Bangladeshi people.

POLITICAL PARTIES

The current election law states that to be registered, a party (1) must have won, in any election since independence, at least one parliamentary seat or at least 5 percent of the vote in at least one election, or (2) must maintain central officers and a central committee as well as a presence in at least 10 administrative districts and 50 localities. In addition, the party constitution must disavow discrimination on the basis of religion, race, caste, language, or gender, and provisions must be in place for women to hold at least one-third of committee positions by 2020.

A total of 107 parties sought recognition for the December 2008 general election, but the Election Commission registered only 39. (Many Islamic parties refused to open their ranks to non-Muslims and to women, resulting in their disqualification.) The poor electoral showing of most registered parties—the 25 at the bottom of the results collectively accounted for under 2.5 percent of the vote—led to proposals for tightening registration requirements before the next general election.

Government and Progovernment Parties:

Awami League (AL). A predominantly middle-class party organized in East Pakistan in 1948 under Sheikh Mujibur Rahman (Mujib), the Awami (People's) League was, with Indian support, a major force in the drive for independence. Although formally disbanded by President Moshtaque Ahmed in 1975, it remained the best-organized political group in the country and served as the nucleus of a Democratic United Front that supported the presidential candidacy of Gen. Mohammad Ataul Ghani Osmani (National People's Party) in 1978.

During 1980–1981 a cleavage developed between a majority faction, which elected Mujib's daughter, Sheikh Hasina Wajed, as its leader in February 1981, and a right-wing minority faction led by Mizanur Rahman Chowdhury, who accepted appointment as prime minister of the Ershad government in July 1986 and later joined Ershad's *Jatiya Dal.* Committed to socialism, secularism, and a "Westminster-style" parliamentary system, Sheikh Hasina's AL participated in the legislative election of May 1986 but boycotted most parliamentary proceedings and the March 1988 poll. It contested the election of February 1991 but was runner-up to the Khaleda Zia's BNP. In 1991 the *Bangladesh Krishak Sramik Awami* League (Baksal), a left-wing faction that had broken away in 1984 under the leadership of Abdur RAZZAQ, returned to the parent organization. (In 1997 Baksal was reestablished by new leaders.)

Following the ultimately successful campaign for the resignation of the BNP government, the League dominated the June 1996 election and thus took office for the first time since 1975. In the October 2001 election, however, the party suffered a devastating defeat, winning only 62 legislative seats. Sheikh Hasina nevertheless maintained firm control of the party apparatus. At a party rally in August 2004 she was among the 200 injured by a grenade attack that killed some two dozen people.

After the 2001 election the AL headed a 14-party opposition "combine" that also included an 11-party leftist alliance, the National Socialist Party (Inu), and the National Awami Party (NAP). In January 2007 the 14-party grouping's decision to boycott the upcoming parliamentary election caused President Ahmed's resignation as chief adviser of the caretaker government and postponement of the poll. Subsequently, a group of reformers emerged in opposition to the continued dominance of Sheikh Hasina.

On June 12, 2008, after 11 months in detention while facing corruption charges, Sheikh Hasina was paroled to receive medical treatment in the United States. She returned to Bangladesh on November 6 to lead the AL alliance into the December legislative election, at which the AL won 49 percent of the vote and 230 of 300 seats. Hasina returned as prime minister, but in choosing her cabinet she bypassed nearly all members of her previous administration in favor of younger ministers to distance the administration from past corruption charges. In July 2009 she was elected to a sixth term as party president.

In December 2013 Sheikh Hasina, running unopposed, was unanimously elected party leader for the seventh consecutive term. Following President Rahman's death on March 20, 2013, parliamentary speaker Abdul Hamid acceded the post on April 24 (see Current issues, above). In the first half of the year, the BNP defeated AL incumbents in nearly a half dozen mayoral elections, including the AL stronghold of Gazipur, representing the widespread opposition for the ruling party, stemming largely from the controversial abolishment of the pre-electoral government.

Leaders: Sheikh HASINA Wajed (Prime Minister and Party President), Abdul HAMID (President of Bangladesh), Syed Ashraful ISLAM (General Secretary).

Jatiya Party (JP). The current *Jatiya* (National) Party traces its origin to the *Jatiya Dal,* which was initially launched in August 1985 as the National Front, a somewhat eclectic grouping of right-wing Muslims and Beijing-oriented Marxists who rejected the confrontational politics of their former alliance partners in favor of cooperation with President Ershad. The Front embraced the People's Party (*Jana Dal*), founded in 1983 by President Chowdhury; the United People's Party (UPP), then led by Kazi Zafar Ahmed; the Democratic Party (*Ganatantrik Dal*), led by Sirajul Hossain KHAN and Nasrullah KHAN; the Bangladesh Muslim League (BML), led by Tofazzal ALI; and a dissident faction of the Bangladesh Nationalist Party (BNP) led by former prime minister Azizur Rahman. It was declared to have been converted into a unified party on January 1, 1986, although the BML and the UPP subsequently functioned as independent parties.

Following the May 1986 election, the *Jatiya Dal* held 178 of 300 directly elective legislative seats, plus all 30 indirectly elected women's seats. In 1988, as both leading opposition parties abstained, it won 250 elective seats. The party participated in the February 1991 election, despite corruption charges that had been brought against most of its top leadership, including General Ershad, who was detained in December 1990 and convicted of a variety of offenses during 1991–1993.

In September 1993 several party dissidents formed a *Jatiya* Party (National) under the nominal chairpersonship of Ershad (from his prison cell). Ershad's wife, Raushan, became a presiding member. Having participated in the opposition boycott of the February 1996 election, the party won 32 elective seats in the June balloting and joined a coalition government headed by the AL, in part on the understanding that Ershad would be released on parole. In January 1997 Ershad was released from detention, but conflict continued within the party. In June a dissident group led by Kazi Zafar Ahmed and Shah Moazzem HOSSAIN formed the *Jatiya* Party–Zafar-Moazzem.

In March 1998 the *Jatiya* Party left the government, although its lone minister, Anwar Hossein MANJU, decided to stay in the cabinet. Collaterally, Ershad removed him as the party's secretary general. At a "unity conference" in December Ershad and the Zafar-Moazzem splinter mended their rift, but in April 1999 a meeting of party dissidents led by Manju and Vice Chair Mizanur Rahman Chowdhury "expelled" Ershad and formed their own *Jatiya* Party—see JP(M), below.

Before the October 2001 election, Ershad distanced the party from opposition partners, intending to campaign independently even though he himself was barred from running. His decision led to yet another rift, with the party's ousted secretary general, Naziur Rahman Manjur, forming another *Jatiya* offshoot in April (see BJP, below). The now-titled *Jatiya* Party (Ershad) won 14 seats in the October election.

In June 2002 the right-wing *Jatiya Ganatantrik* Party (Jagpa), led by Shafiul Alam Prodhan, and the Progressive Nationalist Party (*Progatishil Jatiyabadi Dal*—PJD), created in 1986 by BNP dissidents and led by Shawkat Hossain Nilu, merged into the *Jatiya* Party (Ershad). Both later joined the Islamic National Unity Front (*Islami Jatiya Oikya* Front), which Ershad and Pir Fazlul KARIM established to contest the 2001 elections. Also identified with the Front were the Islamic Constitution Movement (see under the BKA, below) and the Alhaj Zamir ALI faction of the **Bangladesh Muslim League** (BML), both of which ran a few parliamentary candidates under their own banners.

Ershad tried to reunite the various *Jatiya* parties and forge a coalition substantial enough to challenge the BNP and the Awami League for the 2007 election. However, Shafiul Alam Prodhan left to establish a new Jagpa (below), and subsequently, Nilu also departed and formed the current National People's Party (NPP, below). Meanwhile, Ershad confronted a well-publicized rupture with his second wife, Bidisha, whom he had promoted within the party. (Ershad's first wife, Raushan, to whom he has remained married, continues to play a significant role in the party.)

Turmoil erupted in mid-2007 when, in late June Raushan Ershad announced that she was assuming the chair in an acting capacity. Former president Ershad announced his intention to retire as party leader and named as acting chair former foreign minister Anisul Islam Mahmud. In September eight reform-minded presidium members, including former party adviser Kazi Firoz RASHID, were dropped from the leadership for undermining party discipline and violating its constitution.

In late 2008 the JP (Ershad) was formally registered simply as the *Jatiya* Party. Speculation over whether Ershad would join the Awami-led Grand Alliance persisted nearly until voting day. In the end, the JP ran with the AL, winning 7 percent of the vote and 27 seats and then joining the government. In July 2009, at the party's seventh National Council, Ershad declared himself chair for life.

Though Ershad has been a vocal supporter of the 2011 abolishment of a pre-electoral caretaker government, he has been critical of the Election Commission ahead of the elections expected by early 2014. In August 2013 he called for all parties to participate in the next election and noted that the *Jatiya* Party would not participate unless the current electoral commission is impartial and strengthened.

Leaders: Lt. Gen. (Ret.) Mohammad ERSHAD (Chair), Begum Raushan ERSHAD, Ruhul Amin HAWLADER (Secretary General).

National Socialist Party (*Jatiya Samajtantrik Dal*—Jasad). Jasad, which is sometimes referenced as the JSD (Inu), is one of the two principal splinters from the JSD that originated as a Scientific Socialists (*Boigyanik Samajtantrabadi*) faction within the Awami League in the early postindependence period. The largely student group, led by Abdur Rab and Shajahan SIRAJ, defected from the AL in 1972. Many of its leaders were arrested following President Zia's assumption of power. It was reinstated as a legal entity in 1978, although several leaders were not released from detention until March 1980.

Differences within the JSD over participation in a loosely formed 10-party opposition alliance contributed to a November 1980 split that produced the Bangladesh Socialist Party (BSD, below). In 1983–1985 the party was a prominent member of the 15-party anti-Ershad coalition led by the AL.

In May 1986 Rab and Siraj presented separate electoral lists. The JSD (Rab) remained an autonomous party, winning one seat in June 1996 (and joining the government), by which time the Siraj faction had become part of the *Gano* Forum (below). A third faction led by Hasanul Haq Inu joined the Left Democratic Front (LDF; see under the Communist Party of Bangladesh, below). Siraj later joined the BNP; after negotiations, the Rab and Inu factions reunited.

The party failed to win any parliamentary seats in October 2001, after which the Inu and Rab factions reestablished separate identities as the JSD (Inu) and the JSD (Rab)—for a discussion of the latter, see below. In the 2008 general election Jasad won three seats (despite obtaining only 0.6 percent of the vote) as part of the Awami-led Grand Alliance. Party leader Inu led the opposition within the governing coalition against the 2011 constitutional amendment abolishing caretaker governments following elections.

Leaders: Hasanul Haq INU (Chair), Mainuddin Khan BADAL (Executive President), Sharif Nurul AMBIA (General Secretary).

Bangladesh Workers' Party (BWP). The BWP began as a pro-Soviet offshoot of the United People's Party (UPP). Having opposed formation of a front with Ziaur Rahman, the BWP left the UPP in the late 1970s and in 1983 joined the anti-Ershad movement. It was a founding member of the Left Democratic Front (LDF) in 1994.

As a member of the Grand Alliance in 2008, the BWP won two parliamentary seats.

Leaders: Rashed Khan MENON (Chair), Bimal BISWAS.

Communist Party of Bangladesh (Marxist-Leninist)—CPB-ML (*Bangladesher Samyabadi Dal [Marxbadi-Leninbadi]*). Dating from 1971 and frequently referred to as simply the *Samyabadi Dal,* the branch of the CPB-ML led by Dilip Barua began as a Maoist formation, but in 1983, adopted a pro-Soviet posture. It supported the 15-party AL alliance in the anti-Ershad Movement for the Restoration of Democracy (MRD) and later participated in the LDF and the 11-party leftist opposition to the Zia government of 2001–2006.

Though the CPB-ML won no seats as a member of the Awami-led alliance in 2008, longtime party leader Dilip Barua was awarded a cabinet post.

Leader: Dilip BARUA (Chair and Minister of Industry).

Eighteen-Party Opposition Alliance:

Bangladesh Nationalist Party—BNP (*Bangladesh Jatiyabadi Dal*). The BNP was formally launched in September 1978 by various groups that had supported President Zia in his election campaign. During 1978–1980 a number of defectors from other parties joined the government formation. In 1983 a BNP-led seven-party coalition helped form the anti-Ershad MRD.

The party, led by Zia's widow, Begum Khaleda Zia, refused to participate in the parliamentary poll of May 1986, the presidential balloting of October 1986, or the legislative election of March 1988. In 1989, a dissident bloc led by former BNP secretary general A. K. M. Obaidur RAHMAN formed against a majority group led by Khaleda Zia, who was installed as prime minister following the 1991 elections.

The BNP won only 116 seats in the June 1996 election, Khaleda Zia becoming leader of an opposition "combine" that also included as principal participants the *Jamaat-i-Islami* and the Islamic Unity Front (IOJ). Following its March 1998 departure from the government, the *Jatiya* Party joined the alliance.

The BNP's October 2001 election victory returned Khaleda Zia to the prime minister's office on the strength of a 191-seat parliamentary majority, plus an additional 23 seats won by its three allied parties, the JI, BJP, and IOJ (all below). In June 2002 Zia appointed her son, Tarique Rahman, joint secretary general of the BNP.

Facing imminent arrest by the interim government, on September 2, 2007, Khaleda Zia named Khander Delwar HOSSAIN as acting secretary general, replacing Abdul Mannan BHUIYAN, whom she expelled for "antiparty" activities with Joint Secretary General Ashraf HOSSAIN. On October 29 a majority of the party's Standing Committee named M. Saifur Rahman as acting chair and Hafizuddin Ahmed as acting secretary general, both "reformers" who joined Bhuiyan and Ashraf Hossain in demanding greater democracy within the party. An adviser to former prime minister Hannan Shah led the pro-Zia faction. The Election Commission invited the reform faction to represent the BNP in the commission's planned dialogue with leading parties; subsequently, the issue of party leadership was brought before the High Court, which in April 2008, ruled that the Election Commission invitation to the reformers was not illegal.

May 2008 reports that the party would reunite proved incorrect when differences surfaced between Zia loyalists Hannan Shah and Delwar Hossain. Though Zia's September release on bail calmed internal disputes, reformers were mostly passed over in selecting candidates for the December election. Zia again led the party into the parliamentary voting, but the BNP won just 30 seats on a 33 percent vote share.

At the party's fifth National Council, held in December 2009, Khaleda Zia was reelected chair. Following Secretary General Khandaker Delwar Hossain's death in May 2011, Mirza Fakhrul Islam Alamgir has served as acting secretary general. In April 2012, the BNP announced the formation of the opposition 18-Party Alliance ahead of the next presidential election. That month, Organizing Secretary Mohammed Ilias Ali went missing (one of several BNP disappearances in 2012), drawing accusations that the government abducted him.

Since the abolishment of an election caretaker government, the BNP has campaigned for its reinstatement and led the 18-Party Alliance in violent street protests that have erupted frequently in late 2012 and early 2013 (see Current issues, above). Two BNP leaders, including current parliamentarian Salahuddin Quader Chowdhury, faced charges from the ICT-2 (see Current issues, above).

Leaders: Begum Khaleda ZIA (Former Prime Minister and Chair of the Party), Tarique RAHMAN (Senior Vice Chair), Mirza Fakhrul Islam ALAMGIR (Acting Secretary General).

Jamaat-i-Islami (JI). Tracing its origins to prepartition India, where the *Jamaat-i-Islami* (Islamic Assembly) was established in 1941 under Syed Abul Ala MAUDUDI, the Bangladeshi JI also descends from the East Pakistan wing of the postpartition Pakistani party. Banned after the 1971 war of independence for its alleged pro-Pakistani leanings, the *Jamaat-i-Islami* Bangladesh was permitted to resume political activities later in the decade. Leader Golam Azam returned from self-imposed exile.

JI Bangladesh won 18 parliamentary seats in 1991. After winning just 3 seats in 1996, the party actively opposed the Awami League government. In October 2001 it captured 17 seats and joined the new Khaleda Zia government.

Seeking registration for the December 2008 parliamentary election, the JI dropped the word "Bangladesh" from its name and reformed its constitution to comply with the electoral law.

Party President Matiur Rahman Nizami and Secretary General Ali Ahsan Muhammad Mujahid were jailed in November 2008 in connection with corruption charges, but both were released on bail a week later. At the election the JI won only 2 seats.

Ten JI leaders faced war crimes charges before the ICT-2 in 2013 (see Current issues, above). As of September, six have been convicted, including Golam Azam and current secretary general Mujahid, who were sentenced to 90 years in prison and to death, respectively. After the JI was the target of a sit-in protest in April organized by bloggers demanding the banning of the party, the JI and other Islamist groups retaliated with violent street protests calling for blasphemy laws, culminating in a violent clash in May that left 29 people dead. On August 1 a high court issued a verdict banning the JI from participating in the next elections on the grounds that the party charter violates electoral law in several ways, most significantly by failing to acknowledge the absolute sovereignty of the people of Bangladesh.

Leaders: Matiur Rahman NIZAMI (Party President), Abul Katam Muhammad YUSUF (Senior Vice President), Maulana Rafiqul Islam KHAN (Acting Party Secretary General).

Bangladesh Jatiya Party (BJP). Initially identified at its formation in April 2001 as the *Jatiya* Party (M-N) in honor of its initial president, M.A. Matin, and its prime mover, Naziur Rahman MANJUR, the party was often referenced leading up to the October 2001 parliamentary election as the *Jatiya* Party (Naziur). Since that election, in which it won four seats, it has most often been identified as the BJP. (For a history of the parent *Jatiya* Party's formation and complicated history, see the JP, above.)

In March–April 2005 differences between Manjur and Matin erupted. The warring leaders tried to expel each other following what Matin characterized as an "anticoalition" speech by Manjur, who had attacked the BNP's deference to *Jamaat-i-Islami* and the latter's alleged contacts with Islamic extremists. Manjur, in turn, accused Matin of "antiorganizational activities." In early March the BJP's secretary general, Kazi Firoz Rashid, and other party leaders had defected to the JP. After that, Matin and Manjur headed separate wings.

In April 2008 Manjur died at age 59. He was succeeded as leader by Andalib Rahman. For the December 2008 election the two wings were registered as separate parties. The Naziur-Rahman branch won one seat as the **Bangladesh Jatiya Party–BJP;** the Matin branch, running simply as the **Bangladesh Jatiya Party,** won none. In October 2010 Nasim OSMAN, a prominent party member, accused the party leader of killing Bangladesh's former president, stirring controversy. In June 2012 Matin died, but the faction continued.

Bangladesh Jatiya Party–BJP Leader: Andalib RAHMAN (Chair of the Party and Member of Parliament).

BJP (Matin) Leader: Abu Naser Mohammad NASER (Secretary General).

Islamic Unity Front (*Islami Oikya Jote*—IOJ). A fundamentalist organization that has urged the adoption of Islamic law, the IOJ was highly critical of Sheikh Hasina's secularist policies during her first term in office. After the June 1996 election, it participated in the BNP-led opposition, although its sole member of Parliament, Golam Sarwar HIRU, was threatened with expulsion by the IOJ leadership for breaking party discipline. In October 2001 it won two seats but was offered no cabinet posts. Afterward, as in the BJP, some elements of the IOJ were increasingly dissatisfied with the BNP's alleged deference to *Jamaat-i-Islami.*

Already divided into two principal factions, the party split further in 2005. In May 2006 the third faction, led by Misbahur Rahman Chowdhury and Mufti Izharul Islam, attacked the governing alliance for corruption, nepotism, and misrule and announced formation of a separate noncommunal *Bangladesh Islami Oikya Jote* (BIOJ) that subsequently aligned with the Awami League. In the December 2008 election the IOJ won no seats. Abdul Latif Nizami assumed party leadership following the death of party chair Fazlul Huq AMINI

Leader: Abdul Latif NIZAMI (Chair).

Liberal Democratic Party (LDP). In late October 2006 former president A.Q.M. Chowdhury, joined by BNP dissident Oli Ahmed, announced formation of the LDP, which, in most respects, was a continuation of Chowdhury's previous party, the Alternative Stream Bangladesh (BDB, below). By June 2007 differences over the leadership had led to a rupture between Chowdhury and Ahmed factions, resulting in Chowdhury's reviving the BDB.

In February 2008 the LDP and the *Samyabadi Dal* of Dilip Barua (see CPB-ML, below) announced their intention to present identical proposals on electing a new parliament when participating in the ongoing "dialogue" with the Elections Commission. Both ultimately joined the Awami alliance. The LDP won one parliamentary seat in the December election.

In October 2009 the Anti-Corruption Commission accused the party's secretary general, Jahanara Begum, of corruption. In April 2012 the LDP joined the 18-Party Alliance led by the BNP.

Leaders: Oli AHMED (Chair), Redwan AHMED (Secretary General).

Jatiya Ganatantrik Party (Jagpa). The current right-wing Jagpa was reestablished by Shafiul Alam Prodhan upon his departure from General Ershad's JP. The preceding Jagpa, dating from the 1990s, had merged into the Ershad's party in 2002. For the 2008 parliamentary election Jagpa ran in alliance with the BNP. In April 2012 Jagpa joined the 18-Party Alliance led by the BNP.

Leader: Shafiul Alam PRODHAN (President).

Bangladesh National Awami Party (NAP). Founded by the late Maulana Abdul Hamid Khan BHASANI, the original NAP was the principal opposition party prior to the 1975 coup. Thereafter it underwent numerous cleavages, the main splinters being the NAP-Bhasani (NAP-B) and the NAP-Muzaffar (NAP-M), the later named for Muzaffar AHMED.

The NAP-B began as a pro-Beijing grouping that participated in a five-party left-wing Democratic Front (*Ganatantrik Jote*), which was organized in 1979. The NAP-M began as a pro-Moscow splinter. Both NAP factions later joined the Awami League alliance within the anti-Ershad MRD.

In 2008 the Election Commission registered the Muzaffar branch as the **Bangladesh National Awami Party** (BNAP) and the Bhasani branch as the **Bangladesh National Awami Party–Bangladesh NAP**, the former of which was allied with the Awami League. In April 2012, both groups joined the 18-Party Alliance led by the BNP.

BNAP Leaders: Zebel Rahman GANI (President), Gulam Mustafa BHUIYAN (Secretary General).

Bangladesh NAP Leaders: Sheikh Anwarul HAQUE (President), Mohammad Abdul MATIN (Secretary General).

Other parties in the 18-Party Alliance include the **Bangladesh Kalyan Party**, led by Syed Muhammad IBRAHIM; the unregistered **Bangladesh Labor Party**, led by Sekander ALI; **Khelafat Majlish;** the **Bangladesh Muslim League** (BML), led by Tofazzal ALI; the **Bangladesh People's Party**; the **National Democratic Party**; the **Bangladesh Islamic Party**; the **Democratic League**; the **Jamiat-e-Ulama-e-Islam Bangladesh**; and the **Bangladesh People's League**. Not all of the parties in the alliance are registered with the government.

Other Parties and Alliances:

Alternative Stream Bangladesh (*Bikalpa Dhara Bangladesh*—BDB). The BDB was launched in May 2004 by former president and BNP leader A. Q. M. Badruddoza Chowdhury. In 2005, the BDB reached a "strategic understanding" with the Awami League. In October 2006, however, Chowdhury dissolved the BDB and replaced it with a new Liberal Democratic Party (LDP, above). By June 2007, however, the LDP had split, leading Chowdhury to revive the BDB.

In October 2007 Chowdhury proposed that resolution of the country's political crisis required a "government of national consensus" that would include all major parties and govern for ten years. For the December 2008 election, he instead proposed organizing a "third force" of parties to oppose both the AL and the BNP. The resultant **Jatiya Jukta Front** (JJF), announced in November, was the latest in a series of similar groupings (including the *Jatiya Oikya* Front, which the BDB had helped organize in preparation for the canceled January 2007 election). Parties associated with the JJF, none of which won more than 0.03 percent of the vote, also included the Gano Forum (below); the **Peasants' and Workers' People's League** (*Krishak Sramik Janata League*—KSJL), which had been established in December 1999 by Kader SIDDIQUI, a former AL stalwart who won the KSJL's only parliamentary seat in October 2001; and the **Progressive Democratic Party** (*Progotishil Ganatantrik Dal*—PGD), founded in July 2007 by Ferdous Ahmed QURESHI. The JJF identified itself as an "alliance for change" and campaigned for reform, an end to corruption, and an end to poverty. Ahead of the 2014 election, BDB President Chowdhury again emphasized the necessity of a third political force. In July 2013 he spoke out against the abolishment of the nonpartisan caretaker government.

Leader: A. Q. M. Badruddoza CHOWDHURY (Chair).

Gano Forum. Launched in August 1993 by a breakaway Awami League faction, the leftist *Gano* (People's) Forum declared as its objectives "violence-free politics, economic progress at the grassroots, and basic amenities for all." It initially absorbed the faction of the National Socialist Party (JSD; see Jasad, above) led by Shajahan Siraj. In 1997 a JSD (Siraj) emerged from the Forum as a separate organization, but Siraj subsequently joined the BNP. The Forum's secretary general, Saifuddin Ahmed MANIK, died in February 2008.

In 2008, although initially allied with the Awami League, the Forum's president, Kamal Hossain, was critical of Sheikh Hasina's alleged corruption. The parties' relationship withered as a result. In November the Forum joined the BDB in forming the "third force" *Jatiya Jukta* Front. In December, the Forum won only 0.01 percent of the vote. In February 2013 a presidium Forum member defected to join the AL.

Leader: Dr. Kamal HOSSAIN (President).

Jatiya Party (Manju)—JP(M). The JP(M) began as the JP (Mizan-Manju), which was formed in April 1999 when a "special council" held by rebellious members of General Ershad's *Jatiya* Party broke from his leadership, charging him with undemocratic tendencies and with corruption during his years as the country's president. Among those condemning Ershad was former prime minister (and party vice chair) Mizanur Rahman Chowdhury. Another factor in the break was Ershad's removal from all party offices of Anwar Hossain Manju, who had stayed in the Hasina cabinet despite the JP's departure from the government in March 1998. The new grouping included 11 members of Parliament, all of whom objected to Ershad's recent alliance with the BNP. Shortly before the October 2001 election, Chowdhury, the party chair, left to join the Awami League, and the JP(M) won only one seat. In April 2004 Manju denied participating in reunification efforts by Ershad.

In December 2008 the JP(M) ran as an ally of the Awami League but won no seats. Manju has appealed four recent convictions for offenses including possessing foreign liquor and amassing wealth illegally. In May 2013, ahead of the 2014 polls, Manju and Ershad met to discuss mending party divisions. Subsequent meetings sparked speculation that a merge was imminent.

Leaders: Anwar Hossain MANJU (Chair), Sheikh Shahidul ISLAM (Secretary General).

National People's Party—NPP (*Jatiya Janata Party*). A social democratic party organized in 1978, the NPP supported the candidacy of its founder, Gen. Mohammad Ataul Ghani OSMANI, in the 1978 and 1981 presidential elections. Following Osmani's death in 1985, the group split into a number of factions. In the October 2001 election three personalist factions ran a total of six candidates, none successfully.

In July 2007 former leader of the JP(Nilu) faction, Shawkat Hossain Nilu, launched a new NPP, but the party won only 0.02 percent at the polls in December.

Leader: Shawkat Hossain NILU (Chair).

National Socialist Party–Rab (*Jatiya Samajtantrik Dal*—JSD or JSD [Rab]). The JSD (Rab) began as the Abdur Rab faction of the JSD (for details, see Jasad, above). More recently, with Rab having formed a new political forum, the Unity for Political Reforms (UPR), the JSD (Rab) was usually referenced as the JSD (Ziku), after the party's then-president, Nur Alam ZIKU. Ziku died in February 2010.

In September 2006 the JSD (Rab) and the UPR joined two other parties in announcing formation of the *Sangskarbadi Jukta Front* (SJF) to contest the anticipated January 2007 parliamentary election. Based on the nationalist Bengali *Jukta Front* of the 1950s, the SJF called for national unity, adoption of a bicameral legislature, governmental decentralization, people's participation, and economic policies based on the people's welfare.

In the December 2008 election the JSD (Ziku) won only 0.04 percent of the vote. In July 2013 the JSD (Rab) participated in talks about forming a political alliance led by the BDB ahead of the 2014 elections.

Leaders: Abdur RAB, Abdul Malek RATAN (General Secretary).

Among the other parties belonging to or supporting the AL-led "Grand Alliance" in 2008 were the **Bangladesh Islami Oikya Jote** (BIOJ; see the IOJ, above), led by Misbahur Rahman CHOWDHURY and Mufti Izharul ISLAM; the **Communist Center** (*Communist Kendra*), led by Ajoy ROY; the **Ganatantri Party,** led by Mohammad Afzal HOSSAIN since the December 2008 death of Mohammad Nural ISLAM; the moderate **Islamic Front Bangladesh;** the **People's Freedom League** (*Gano Azadi* League), led by Abdus SAMAD, and the moderate Islamic **Zaker Party** of Mustafa Amir FAISAL.

The **United Citizens Movement** (*Oikyaboddho Nagorik Andolon*—ONA), led by Quazi Faruque AHMED, was organized in October 2008 on the basis of a nongovernmental organization, *Proshika,* dedicated to serving the poor and ensuring democratic rights. It won 0.01 percent of the December parliamentary vote.

Left and Far-Left Parties:

Communist Party of Bangladesh (CPB). Originally the Communist Party of East Pakistan, the pro-Moscow CPB was often banned, following independence, during periods of military and rightist rule. The party held its first congress since 1974 in February 1980 and participated in the opposition alliance of the same year.

The CPB was a leading component of the Patriotic Democratic Front from 1991 until formation of the Left Democratic Front (LDF) in 1994 by the CPB, CPB-ML, BWP, BSD, JSD (Inu), the Unifying

Process (*Oikya Prokria*), and the Workers' and Peasants' Socialist Party (*Sramik Krishak Samajbadi Dal*—SKSD). The LDF served as the core of an 11-party leftist opposition alliance after the 2001 election.

In the 2008 parliamentary election the CPB ran about 40 candidates but won only 0.06 percent of the vote. Amid violent protests in Dhaka in May 2013, a homemade bomb was detonated at CPB headquarters.

Leader: Mujahidul Islam SELIM (President).

Bangladesh Socialist Party (*Bangladesh Samajtantrik Dal*—BSD). The BSD, formed following a 1980 split in the JSD (see Jasad, above), itself subsequently split into factions. In October 2004 one of the faction leaders, A. F. M. Mahbubul Haq, was seriously injured by unidentified assailants.

In September 2007 BSD leader Khalequzzaman announced formation of an 11-member **Democratic Left Alliance** (DLA) that, intending to engage in "bold politics based on ideology," included many of Bangladesh's more radical leftist parties. Most participants were not previous members of the LDF, and only the BSD was registered for the December 2008 election. Among the other DLA participants are a branch of the CPB-ML, the **Communist Party of Bangladesh (Marxist-Leninist-Maoist)**—CPB-MLM (*Bangladesher Samyabadi Dal [Marxbadi-Leninbadi-Maobadi]*); the **Democratic Workers' Party** (*Ganotantrik Majdur Party*), led by Abdus SALAM and Zakir HOSSAIN; the **National People's Front** (*Jatiya Gano Front*), led by Tipu BISWAS; the **People's Solidarity Movement** (*Gano Sanghati Andolon*), led by Julhasnain BABU; and the **Revolutionary Unity Front** (*Biplobi Oikya Front*), led by Mushrefa MISHU. Khalequzzaman agreed to serve as DLA convener.

Leaders: KHALEQUZZAMAN Bhuiyan (Central Convener), Bazlur Rashid FIROZ, A. F. M. Mahbubul HAQ (Convener, BSD Mahbub), Abdul Matin TAKUKDER (BSD Mahbub).

Revolutionary Workers Party of Bangladesh (*Bangladesher Biplobi Workers Party*—BBWP). The BBWP was formed in 1994 as a splinter from the BWP (above). Frequently allied with the CPB, it ran in a handful of constituencies in the December 2008 election, winning under 0.01 percent of the vote. In addition to calling for equal rights for minorities and women, an end to poverty, food security, and employment opportunity, its election manifesto targeted corruption, "black money holders," terrorists, and "mafias." The party's most recent congress was held in April 2010.

Leaders: Khandaker Ali ABBAS (President), Saiful HUQ (General Secretary).

Other Right and Center-Right Parties:

Bangladesh Caliphate Movement (*Bangladesh Khelafat Andolon*—BKA). The Caliphate Movement was founded in 1981 to support the unsuccessful campaign for the presidency of its leader, Maulana Mohammed Ullah Hafezji HUZUR, who ran again in 1986. In 1993 it participated in formation of the National Democratic Alliance (NDA), which included nearly a dozen conservative Islamic parties. The BKA staunchly opposed the U.S. invasions of Afghanistan in 2001 and Iraq in 2003.

In November 2006, looking toward the parliamentary election scheduled for early 2007, the BKA joined a Three-Party Islamic Movement that was intended to counter *Jamaat-i-Islami.* Other participants were the Islamic Constitution Movement (*Islami Shashantantra Andolon*) of Syed Fazlul KARIM, which was registered in 2008 as the **Islami Andolon Bangladesh,** and the **Jamiat-e-Ulama-e-Islam Bangladesh.** In July 2008 the BKA called for prohibiting women from serving as head of state or government. In the December election it won only 0.02 percent of the vote.

Leader: Maulana Zafrullah Mohammad KHAN (Secretary General).

Bangladesh Tariqat Federation (BTF). Formation of the BTF was announced in October 2005 by Najibul Bashar MAIZBHANDARI. Formerly an official of the BNP, he resigned in September 2005 over the party's alliance with *Jamaat-i-Islami* and the latter's alleged involvement in recent bombings of shrines. In 2006 it joined in forming the *Jatiya Oikya Front.*

In the 2008 general election the BTF won 0.03 percent of the vote. The BTF submitted a petition in 2009 challenging the party status of *Jamaat-i-Islami*, resulting in the August 2013 court ruling banning the Islamist party (see Current issues, above.)

Leader: Maulana Syed Rezaul Haque CHANDPURI (Secretary General).

Islamic Democratic Party (IDP). In November 2008 the Election Commission refused to register the new IDP, which had been established by individuals previously associated with the banned militant organization *Harkat-ul-Jihad Islami* (HuJI; see below). In April 2009 the government included the IDP as well as the HuJI on a watch list of suspected militant organizations.

Leaders: Sheikh Abdus SALAM, Kazi AZIZUL HUQ.

Chittagong Groups:

Chittagong Hill Tracts People's Solidarity Association (*Parbattya Chattagram Jana Sanghati Samity*—PCJSS). Formed in 1972 under the leadership of Manabendra Narayan LARMA, a former member of Parliament, the PCJSS long opposed the influx of Bengali settlers into the Chittagong Hill Tracts. Consisting mainly of Chakma tribesmen, the organization formed a military wing, the *Shanti Bahini* (Army of Peace), under Larma's brother Jytrindriyo (also known as Shantu Larma) in 1973. In 1982 a PCJSS faction led by Priti Kumar CHAKMA left the parent grouping; many of its supporters, but not Chakma, surrendered to the government in 1985.

M.N. Larma was killed in November 1983 by a rival group, with his brother leading subsequent negotiations with Dhaka and concluding a peace agreement in December 1997. The accord included amnesty for all members of the PCJSS, including the *Shanti Bahini,* and granted the Hill Tracts limited autonomy over regional affairs. Some of the more militant Chakma guerrillas objected, however, demanding full autonomy and stating that they would continue the insurgency. Subsequent clashes with the PCJSS occurred.

In February 1999 it was announced that Larma would assume a status equal to that of a minister of state in the Hasina government, effective upon his formally taking office as chair of the interim Chittagong Hill Tracts Regional Council. The 21-member Council was installed on May 2, 1999, and the PCJSS held its first party congress in November. Subsequently, Larma demanded that the Khaleda Zia government fully implement the 1997 accord, including ending discrimination, distributing development money, and permitting greater local control. In December 2006 he threatened to take up arms again if the next government failed to do so.

In July 2007 the party's secretary general, Satyabir DEWAN, was sentenced to 17 years in prison for possession of an unlicensed weapon and ammunition. In mid-March 2009 Shantu Larma and 13 others were accused of attempted murder by Chandra Shekhar CHAKMA, a reformist, who had been shot in January. Chakma died of natural causes the following August.

At a national conference held March 29–31, 2010, Shantu Larma expelled seven senior members (including the late Chandra Shekhar Chakma) for breaking party discipline. Led by former vice president Rupayan DEWAN and Sudhasindhu KHISA, on April 10 dissident members attacked Sharma's "autocratic and deviant leadership" and established a convening committee for a separate organization.

Leaders: Jytrindriyo Bodhipriyo (Shantu) LARMA (President), Ushatan TALUKDER (Vice President), Pranati Bikash CHAKMA (Secretary General).

United People's Democratic Front (UPDF). The UPDF was formally organized in late 1998 by opponents of the 1997 Chittagong settlement who demanded full regional autonomy. Some of those claiming allegiance to the UPDF have since been responsible for killings, kidnappings, and other criminal acts and have repeatedly clashed with central government officials and the PCJSS. The party held its first congress in November 2006.

Leaders: Prasit Bikash KHISHA (President), Rabi Shankar CHAKMA (General Secretary).

Militant Islamic Groups:

The country's first militant Islamic groups were apparently organized as part of the anti-Soviet war effort in Afghanistan. Chief among these was the Bangladesh branch of the international **Harkat-ul-Jihad Islami** (HuJI), the existence of which was long denied by Dhaka authorities. As a consequence, the HuJI was not banned until October 2005 despite its links to al-Qaida. Many of its members had branched out and helped found other militant organizations, including the **Shahadat al-Hikma,** which was banned in 2003. In August 2006, under the name **Sachetan Islami Janata** (Enlightened Islamic People), members of the HuJI held a meeting at Dhaka's largest mosque. Efforts were reportedly made to convince the government that the new group was not a terrorist organization.

On December 23, 2008, the HuJI's Mufti Abdul HANNAN and 2 others were sentenced to hang for their involvement in a May 2004 grenade attack on a former British high commissioner. Hannan and 13 others have also been charged in connection with a grenade attack on an Awami League rally that left 24 dead in August 2004. In April 2009 Hannan was also indicted in connection with a 2001 bombing that killed 10, and in May 2010 he was charged with involvement in a 2000 bombing at a meeting attended by Sheikh Hasina.

Two closely linked banned organizations, the **Jamaat-ul-Mujahidin Bangladesh** (JMB) and the **Jagrata Muslim Janata Bangladesh** (JMJB), which reportedly merged in October 2005, have attracted considerable recent attention, especially following the coordinated explosion of some 460 crude bombs on August 17, 2005. Leaflets apparently left by the JMB at bomb sites demanded the adoption of strict Islamic law. Among those sought by authorities in the aftermath were JMB leader Maulana Abdur RAHMAN and JMJB operations chief Siddiqul ISLAM (alias Bangla BHIA). Both also were implicated by the government in two courthouse bombings in November 2005 that killed two judges. Abdur Rahman and Siddiqul Islam were both captured in March 2006 and sentenced to death in May. They and four other JMB members were executed in 2007.

In October 2009 the government banned the London-based **Hizb-ut-Tahrir.** The organization's goal is to establish a caliphate comprising all Muslim countries.

At present, there may be as many as 30 groups, although some may be using alternate names and may have overlapping memberships.

LEGISLATURE

The **Parliament** (*Jatiya Sangsad,* or House of the Nation) is a unicameral body of 345 seats: 300 filled by direct election for a five-year term, subject to dissolution, and 45 indirectly elected seats reserved for women and filled on a proportional basis among represented parties. In the election of December 29, 2008 (including a January 12, 2009, vote in one district), the Awami League and its "Grand Alliance" allies won 263 seats (Awami League, 230; *Jatiya* Party [JP], 27; National Socialist Party, 3; Workers Party of Bangladesh, 2; Liberal Democratic Party, 1); the Four-Party Alliance, 33 (Bangladesh Nationalist Party [BNP], 30; *Jamaat-i-Islami,* 2; Bangladesh *Jatiya* Party, 1); and independents, 4. The 45 seats reserved for women were filled as follows on March 19, 2009: Awami League, 36; BNP, 5; JP, 4.

Speaker: Shirin Sharmin CHAUDHURY.

CABINET

[as of August 1, 2013]

Prime Minister	Sheikh Hasina Wajed [f]
Ministers	
Agriculture	Matia Chowdhury [f]
Civil Aviation and Tourism	Lt. Col. (Ret.) Faruq Khan
Commerce	G. M. Kader (JP)
Communications, Roads, and Bridges	Obaidul Quader
Cultural Affairs	Abul Kalam Azad
Defense	Sheikh Hasina Wajed [f]
Disaster Management and Relief	Abdul Hasan Mahmud Ali
Education	Nurul Islam Nahid
Expatriates' Welfare and Overseas Employment	Khandker Mosharraf Hossain
Finance	Abul Maal Abdul Muhith
Fisheries and Livestock	Abdul Latif Biswash
Food	Abdur Razzak
Foreign Affairs	Dipu Moni [f]
Health and Family Welfare	A. F. M. Ruhul Haque
Home Affairs	Mohiuddin Khan Alamgir
Housing and Public Works	Abdul Mannan Khan
Industry	Dilip Barua (CPB-ML)
Information	Hasanul Haq Inu
Information and Communication Technology	Mostafa Faruque Mohammad
Jute and Textiles	Abdul Latif Siddique
Labor and Employment	Rajiuddin Ahmed Raju
Land	Rezaul Karim Hira
Law, Justice, and Parliamentary Affairs	Shafique Ahmed
Local Government, Rural Development, and Cooperatives	Syed Ashraful Islam
Planning	Air Vice Mar. (Ret.) A.K. Khandker
Posts and Telecommunications	Shahara Khatun [f]
Power, Energy, and Mineral Resources	Sheikh Hasina Wajed [f]
Primary and Mass Education	Dr. Mohammad Afsarul Amin
Public Administration	Sheikh Hasina Wajed [f]
Religious Affairs	Shahjahan Miah
Railways	Mujibul Hoque
Shipping	Mohammad Shajahan Khan
Social Welfare	Enamul Huq Mustafa Shahid
Water Resources	Ramesh Chandra Sen
Without Portfolio	Suranjit Sen Gupta
Ministers of State (Independent Charge)	
Chittagong Hill Tracts Affairs	Dipanker Talukdar
Environment and Forests	Hasan Mahmud
Liberation War Affairs	Capt. (Ret.) A.B.M. Tajul Islam
Science and Technology	Yeafesh Osman
Women and Children	Meher Afroze [f]
Youth and Sports	Ahad Ali Sarkar

[f] = female

Note: Unless otherwise indicated, ministers belong to the Awami League.

INTERGOVERNMENTAL REPRESENTATION

Ambassador to the U.S.: Akramul QADER.

U.S. Ambassador to Bangladesh: Dan MOZENA.

Permanent Representative to the UN: Abulkalam Abdul MOMEN.

IGO Memberships (Non-UN): ADB, CWTH, ICC, IOM, NAM, OIC, SAARC, WTO.

BARBADOS

Political Status: Independent member of the Commonwealth since November 30, 1966.

Area: 166 sq. mi. (431 sq. km).

Population: 282,746 (2012E—UN); 288,725 (2013E—U.S. Census).

Major Urban Center (2005E): BRIDGETOWN (urban area, 142,000).

Official Language: English.

Monetary Unit: Barbadian Dollar (official rate November 1, 2013: 2.00 dollars = $1US).

Sovereign: Queen ELIZABETH II.

Governor General: Elliott BELGRAVE; succeeded Sir Clifford HUSBANDS, who resigned on October 31, 2011.

Prime Minister: Freundel STUART (Democratic Labour Party); succeeded David THOMPSON (Democratic Labour Party), who died October 23, 2010.

THE COUNTRY

Geographically part of the Lesser Antilles, Barbados is also the most easterly of the Caribbean nations. The island enjoys an equable climate and fertile soil. Approximately 85 percent of the land being arable. Population density is among the world's highest, although the birth rate has declined in recent years. Approximately 80 percent of the population is of African origin, and another 15 percent is of mixed blood, with Europeans representing only 5 percent of the total; nonetheless, there is a strong and pervasive sense of British tradition and culture. The Anglican Church enjoys official status, but other Protestant, Roman Catholic, and Jewish groups are active. The island historically was dependent on sugar exports, but it was announced in September 2012 that it will no longer produce for the European market. Tourism is the leading source of foreign exchange, while manufacturing, especially that geared toward fellow members of the Caribbean Community, also is an important source of income.

From 1988 to 2008 Barbados experienced periods of major economic fluctuations between growth and decline in GDP. With the global financial crisis of 2009, the economy contracted by 4.2 percent. The economy has remained largely stagnant since, averaging GDP growth of less than 1 percent through 2013. The IMF projects growth of 1 percent in 2014. Meanwhile, inflation, which peaked at 11.2 percent in September 2008, has since recovered marginally and is estimated to be 4.5 percent in 2013. According to the 2010 UN World Development Report, Barbados was recognized as having "very high human development," but despite its Human Development Index rating, it is not a member of the Organization of Economic Cooperation and Development (OECD) or considered an "advanced economy" by the IMF. Unemployment in 2014 was projected at 9.5 percent. (For more on the economy, see Current issues, below.)

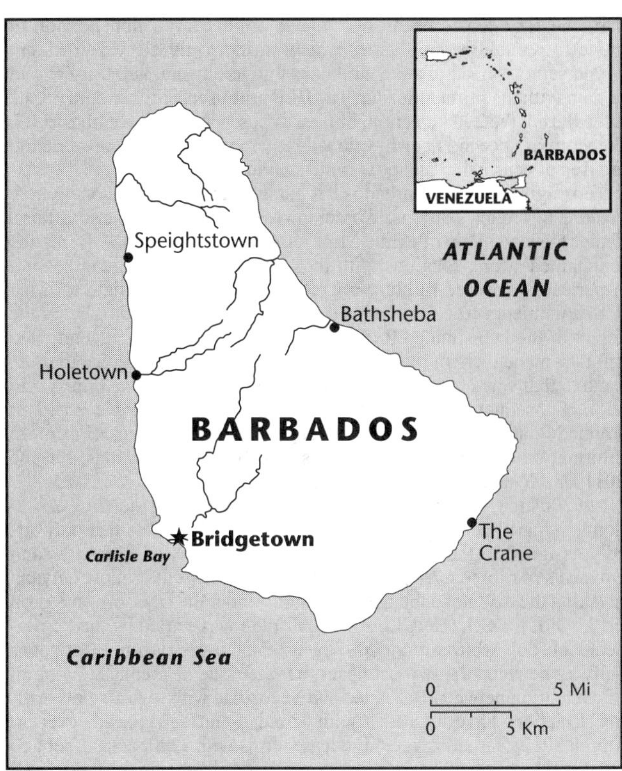

GOVERNMENT AND POLITICS

Political background. Historically a planter-dominated island, and often called the "Little England" of the Caribbean, Barbados has been molded by a British tradition extending back to 1639. In 1937 economic problems caused by the fluctuating price of sugar led to demonstrations in Bridgetown, which resulted in the establishment of a British Royal Commission to the West Indies. The commission proved instrumental in bringing about social and political reform, including the introduction of universal adult suffrage in 1951. The island was granted full internal sovereignty ten years later.

Barbados played a leading role in the short-lived West Indies Federation (1958–1962) and supplied its only prime minister, Sir Grantley ADAMS. The collapse of the federation and the inability of Barbadian leaders to secure the establishment of an Eastern Caribbean Federation as a substitute left independence within the Commonwealth, which was achieved on November 30, 1966, as the only viable alternative. An election held November 3, 1966, confirmed the dominant position of the Democratic Labour Party (DLP), whose leader, Errol Walton BARROW, had been named premier in 1961 and was reappointed prime minister in 1971.

In an election held September 2, 1976, the opposition Barbados Labour Party (BLP) upset the DLP, and Barrow's 15-year rule ended the following day with the designation of Sir Grantley's son, J.M.G.M. ("Tom") ADAMS, as prime minister. In voting that was extremely close in many constituencies, the BLP retained its majority on June 18, 1981. Adams died in March 1985 and was succeeded by his deputy, H. Bernard ST. JOHN, who was unable to contain deepening fissures within the party. As a result, the DLP won a decisive legislative majority of 24–3 in balloting on May 28, 1986, with a second Barrow administration being installed the following day. Barrow died suddenly on June 1, 1987, and was succeeded the following day by Lloyd Erskine SANDIFORD, who led the party to victory on January 22, 1991, with a reduced margin of ten seats in the lower House of Assembly.

After losing a legislative confidence vote on June 7, 1994, over his appointment of a new chief executive of the Barbados Tourism Authority (BTA), Sandiford dissolved the House of Assembly and called for a premature general election on September 6. The result was an overwhelming defeat for the DLP, with the newly installed BLP leader, Owen S. ARTHUR, being named to head a government that was sworn in on September 12. The BLP inflicted a shattering 26–2 defeat on its opponent in the election of January 20, 1999, with analysts crediting the victory to a buoyant economy. Riding a wave of favorable public opinion, Arthur was elected to a third term at an early vote on May 21, 2003.

In balloting on January 15, 2008, the DLP returned to power under the leadership of David THOMPSON, winning 20 of 30 lower house seats. Thompson died of pancreatic cancer on October 23, 2010, and was succeeded by Deputy Prime Minister Freundel STUART, who conducted a major cabinet reshuffle in June 2011. The DLP narrowly retained power in the most recent polling held on February 21, 2013, winning 16 seats to the BLP's 14. (For more on the 2013 general election, see Current issues, below.) Stuart formed a reshuffled government on February 28.

Constitution and government. The Barbados governmental structure is modeled after the British parliamentary system. The queen remains titular head of state and is represented by a governor general with quite limited functions. Executive authority is vested in the prime minister and his cabinet, who collectively report to a bicameral legislature. The upper house of the legislature, the Senate, is appointed by the governor general after consultation with the government, the opposition, and other relevant social and political interests. The lower house, the House of Assembly, sits for a maximum term of five years. The franchise is held by all persons 18 years of age and older, and voting is by secret ballot.

The judicial system comprises lower magistrates, who are appointed by the governor general with the advice of the Judicial and Legal Service Commission, and a Supreme Court, encompassing a High Court and a Court of Appeal. The chief justice is appointed by the governor general on the recommendation of the prime minister after consultation with the leader of the opposition.

Previously elected local government bodies were abolished in 1969 in favor of a division into 11 parishes, all of which (in addition to the municipality of Bridgetown) are now administered by the central government.

In 1996 Prime Minister Owen Arthur established a Constitutional Committee to examine the nation's governmental structure. In 2000, parliamentary debate began over the committee's recommendation to move to republic status, under which an indirectly elected president would serve as head of state while most governmental authority would remain with the prime minister. The BLP promised a referendum on the issue during the 2008 election, but it was postponed in December 2007. Freedom of speech is constitutionally guaranteed, and all news media are free of censorship and government control.

Foreign relations. Barbados has pursued an active, but nonaligned, posture in United Nations, Commonwealth, and hemispheric affairs. Under the leadership of Prime Minister Adams (1976–1986), Barbados maintained strong relations with the United States by joining several American-sponsored military operations and defense initiatives. This U.S. alignment earned Barbados the position in early 1985 of being the center of the U.S.-funded Regional Security System, which conducted military maneuvers in the eastern Caribbean the following September, a move that was opposed by the newly elected DLP prime minister in 1986. Subsequently, Barbadian ties to the United States resulted in strained relations with the UK and other Caribbean nations. (For more information on the role of Barbados in U.S. military actions, see the 2011 *Handbook.*)

In 2004 the Arthur administration reiterated its long-standing objection to a maritime treaty between Trinidad and Venezuela that purportedly assigned to the signatories "an enormous part of Barbados' and Guyana's maritime territory" and declared that it would follow Guyana in taking the dispute to the United Nations under the UN Convention on the Law of the Sea (UNCLOS). The dispute was settled by the Permanent Court of Arbitration in 2007 by establishing a maritime boundary halfway between the two countries, but the issue has remained a point of contention between Barbados and Venezuela with regard to oil drilling. Relations have improved with Trinidad and Tobago, however. In March 2012, Barbados agreed to lease terms with Trinidad and Tobago for the construction of an underwater natural gas pipeline that will eventually be extended to 725 kilometers, serving islands around the region. In April 2013, it was announced that construction of the first 330-kilometer segment stretching from Trinidad to Barbados will begin in 2014. The US$300 million line will come into operation in 2016.

Asserting in late 2009 that Barbados had been "tardy" in not progressing beyond diplomatic relations with emerging economic and political powers, Prime Minister Thompson said his government would open new overseas missions in China and Brazil, in addition, because of "its generosity to Barbados," in Cuba. (For more on Barbados-Cuba relations, see the 2012 *Handbook.*) Formal embassies officially opened in Beijing and Brasília in February 2010. Relations with China further grew in June 2011, when Prime Minister Stuart traveled to China at the request of Chinese premier Wen Jiabao, when the two leaders signed an economic and technical cooperation agreement.

Barbados has struggled to implement immigration laws to stem a perceived heightened influx of immigrants. Claiming that the number of nonnationals was unacceptably high, Prime Minister Thompson severely tightened laws in May 2009. Immigration has become an increasingly important issue as the Organization of Eastern Caribbean States (OECS) moves toward approving the free movement of citizens through other OECS nations. The Barbadian government has been the leading critic of integration, arguing that immigration problems must be solved before integration can occur.

In January 2011 the OECD's Global Forum on Transparency and Exchange of Information for Tax Purposes issued a report stating that Barbados does not meet international standards concerning transparency and tax information exchange with other countries. The OECD encouraged the island nation to review its existing laws and make revisions to bring the laws up to the global standards. Barbados revised its 2011 Income Tax Regulations in an attempt to increase transparency.

Barbados assumed a leading role in regional efforts to oppose the U.S. "cover-over" program, under which the U.S. Virgin Islands and Puerto Rico are exempt from 98 percent of excise duties on rum sold in the United States. Prime Minister Stuart indicated in December 2012 that Caricom and the Dominican Republic would be prepared to take the matter to the WTO, arguing that the United States subsidizes multinational drink companies that produce in territories.

Current issues. In late January 2013 Prime Minister Stuart called the next general election for February 21. The election took place against a dismal economic backdrop of zero growth. The BLP campaigned to lower cost of living by reducing the VAT to 15 percent from 17.5 percent. The DLP promised economic development, environmental practices, and socially balanced policies. Despite opinion polls predicting a strong victory for the BLP, the DLP retained power with a narrow victory in the assembly, and Stuart formed a new government.

In March BLP leader Mia MOTTLEY condemned a recent spate of crime targeting tourists as "economic terrorism." A UK couple was hospitalized after being shot, just two months after another couple was stabbed in their rented vacation home. In December 2012 local law enforcement came under fire for the handling of an investigation of a 2010 rape case when the man who had been wrongly charged with the rape of two British tourists was released.

POLITICAL PARTIES

Government Party:

Democratic Labour Party (DLP). A moderate party founded in 1955 by dissident members of the BLP, the DLP has, for most of its existence, been closely allied with the country's principal labor group, the Barbados Workers' Union. From 1970 to 1985 the DLP experienced a period of ups and downs characterized by frequent reversals in government. These role reversals resulted in several leadership changes, most notably the resignation of former prime minister Errol Barrow as party president in 1976 and again in 1981 following a short term as party president from 1980 to 1981. Through a successful legislative campaign, the DLP regained control of the house in 1985.

Barrow returned as prime minister in 1986, but he died the following year; his deputy, Erskine Sandiford, assumed leadership of the government and the party. Former finance minister David Thompson was named to succeed Sandiford after the party's electoral loss in September 1994. After a failed attempt to regain control of Parliament in 1999 and further challenges within the party, Thompson resigned as party president in September 2001; he was succeeded by Clyde MASCOLL. The party continued in the opposition after the 2003 poll, with a net gain of five house seats and Mascoll assuming the opposition leadership in the lower house, thus resulting in the election of Freundel Stuart as party president.

In August 2005 Thompson returned to the party presidency, defeating Stuart by an Annual Conference vote of 345–164. Thompson consequently became opposition leader and succeeded Owen Arthur as prime minister following the DLP's electoral victory in January 2008. On October 4, 2010, Prime Minister Thompson, suffering from pancreatic cancer, announced a cabinet reshuffle in which his ministerial responsibilities were reduced. Thompson died on October 23, and he was succeeded by Deputy Prime Minister Freundel Stuart. With the DLP's victory in the February 21, 2013, general election, Stuart retained his position.

Leader: Freundel STUART (Prime Minister and Party President).

Opposition Party:

Barbados Labour Party (BLP). Founded in 1938, the BLP is the oldest of the leading parties. After dominating Barbadian politics in the 1950s under the leadership of Sir Grantley Adams, it went into opposition, winning nine seats in 1966, three of which were lost in 1971. It returned to power in 1976 under Sir Grantley's son, J.M.G.M. ("Tom") Adams, and retained its majority in the election of June 18, 1981. The party split into a number of factions after the death of the younger Adams in 1985, thereby contributing to the defeat of the St. John government a year later. Former foreign minister Henry FORDE, named to succeed St. John as parliamentary leader in October 1986, declared that the party would have to be rebuilt as a "highly decentralized" organization featuring "mass democracy in the formation of policy." Forde was succeeded in July 1993 by Owen Arthur, who led the party to victory 14 months later. The BLP retained power in an electoral landslide on January 20, 1999, winning 26 of 28 lower house seats, 3 of which were lost in 2003.

Although Arthur remained personally popular, the BLP was decisively defeated at the early election of January 15, 2008. Arthur retained his legislative seat but announced his retirement from active politics. He returned to the political scene in September 2009 and regained the leadership of the BLP in October 2010.

In February 2013 Mia Mottley replaced Arthur as Party Leader. The party was projected to win the general election, but lost 14–16. Mottley previously served as Opposition Leader from February 2008 through October 2010 but was succeeded by Arthur after she was removed from her position by a vote of no confidence.

Leaders: Mia MOTTLEY (Party Leader and Leader of the Opposition), Dale Dermot MARSHALL (Deputy Leader), Jerome WALCOTT (Chair).

Parties Contesting the 2013 Election:

Coalition of United Parties (CUP). The CUP was formed by the **People's Democratic Congress (PDC)** and the **Bajan Free Party (BFP)** for the 2013 elections. The PDC was founded in 2005 as an outgrowth of the Society for Mass Freedom and Democracy and unsuccessfully campaigned in the 2008 elections. Four candidates ran, but failed to win any seats.

Leaders: Mark Adamson (PDC President), Alex Mitchel (BFP President).

New Barbados Kingdom Alliance (NBKA). The NBKA formed in January 2012, advocating an apostolic Kingdom society. One candidate contested and lost in the 2013 elections.

Leader: Lynroy SCANTLEBURY (Party founder and leader).

Other Parties:

People's Empowerment Party (PEP). Launched in 2006 by Robert Clark, the PEP is a leftist political party founded on democratic, socialist ideologies. The PEP is committed to creating a new government in Barbados that embodies equality for all and encourages cooperation between community organizations and the government. Four PEP candidates campaigned in the 2008 election but did not win. No PEP candidates ran in the 2013 elections.

Leaders: David COMMISIONG (Chair), Robert CLARK (Founder).

LEGISLATURE

The bicameral **Parliament** consists of an appointed Senate and an elected House of Assembly.

Senate. The Senate consists of 21 members appointed by the governor general; 12 are appointed on advice of the prime minister, 2 on advice of the leader of the opposition, and 7 to represent social, religious, and economic interests.

President: Kerryann F. IFILL.

House of Assembly. The House currently consists of 30 members elected for five-year terms by direct popular vote. In the most recent election of February 21, 2013, the Democratic Labour Party won 16 seats, and the Barbados Labour Party, 14.

Speaker: Michael CARRINGTON.

CABINET

[as of November 8, 2013]

Prime Minister	Freundel Stuart
Ministers	
Agriculture, Food, Fisheries, Industry, and Water Resource Management	Dr. David C. Estwick
Commerce and Trade	Sen. Haynesley L. Benn
Culture, Sports, and Youth	Stephen A. Lashley
Education, Science, Technology, and Innovation Development	Ronald D. Jones
Environment and Drainage	Dr. Denis S. Lowe
Finance and Economic Affairs	Christopher P. Sinckler
Foreign Affairs and Foreign Trade	Sen. Maxine P. O. McClean [f]
Health	John D. E. Boyce
Home Affairs and Attorney General	Adriel D. Brathwaite
Housing, Lands, and Rural Development	Denis Kellman
Industry, International Business, Commerce, and Small Business Development	Donville Inniss
Labor, Social Security, and Human Resource Development	Dr. Esther Byer-Suckoo [f]
National Security	Freundel Stuart
Social Care, Constituency Empowerment, and Community Development	Steven D. Blackett
Tourism and International Transport	Richard L. Sealy
Transport and Works	Michael Lashley
Ministers of State	
Parliamentary Secretary in Finance and Economic Affairs	Sen. Jepter Ince
Parliamentary Secretary in Education, Science, Technology, and Innovation	Sen. Harry Husbands
Parliamentary Secretary in the Ministry of Tourism and International Transport	Sen. Virginia Irene Sandiford-Garner [f]
Minister of State for the Office of the Prime Minister	Patrick Todd
Parliamentary Secretary in the Office of the Prime Minister	Sen. Darcy Boyce

[f] = female

Note: All ministers are members of the Democratic Labour Party.

INTERGOVERNMENTAL REPRESENTATION

Ambassador to the U.S.: John E. BEALE.

U.S. Ambassador to Barbados: Larry Leon PALMER.

Permanent Representative to the UN: Joseph E. GODDARD.

IGO Memberships (Non-UN): Caricom, CWTH, IADB, ICC, NAM, OAS, WTO.

BELARUS

Republic of Belarus
Respublika Belarus

Note: The transliteration of Belarusan names into Latin script is complicated by language politics within Belarus. Individuals and groups may self-identify with a Belarusan or Russian form of their name; the Belarusan government, however, generally uses Russian forms, as does much of the international media. Belarusan forms are used here, with Russian forms given in parentheses (if different) for key figures.

Political Status: Formerly the Byelorussian Soviet Socialist Republic, a constituent republic of the Union of Soviet Socialist Republics (USSR); declared independence on August 25, 1991; postindependence constitution entered into force on March 30, 1994; amended constitution declared to be in force by the government on November 27, 1996, following approval by national referendum on November 24.

Area: 80,155 sq. mi. (207,600 sq. km).

Population: 9,841,253 (2012E—UN); 9,625,888 (2013E—U.S. Census).

Major Urban Center (2013E): MINSK (Miensk, 1,906,000), HOMEL (Gomel, 516,000).

Official Languages: Belarusan and Russian (the latter being the first language of most inhabitants).

Monetary Unit: Belarusan Ruble (official rate November 1, 2013: 9259.26 rubles = $1US). On January 2, 2009, the ruble was devalued by 20.5 percent against the dollar and pegged to a basket comprising, in equal weight, the euro, the dollar, and the Russian ruble.

President: Alyaksandr LUKASHENKA (Alexander LUKASHENKO); elected in popular runoff balloting on July 10, 1994, and inaugurated for a five-year term on July 20, succeeding Mechyslaw HRYB (Mechislav GRIB), who, as chair of the Supreme Council, had theretofore served as head of state; term extended to 2001 by constitutional referendum of November 1996; reelected on September 4–9, 2001;

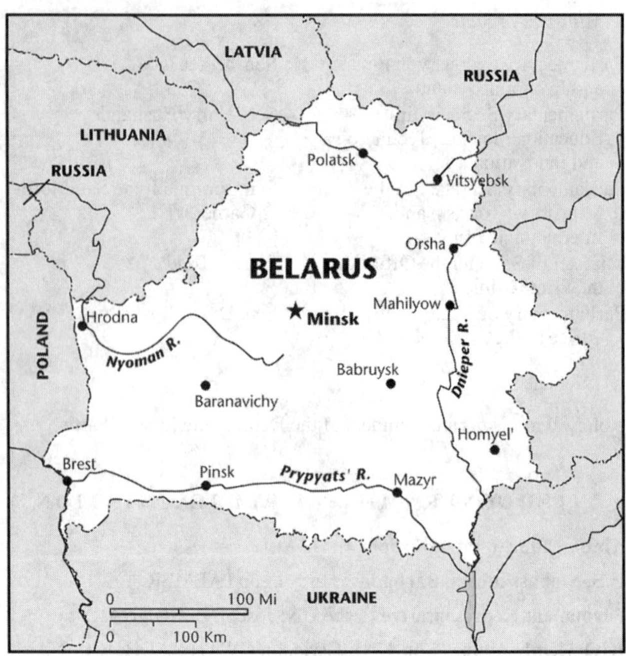

reelected for a third term on March 19, 2006, and sworn in on April 8; reelected to a fourth term on December 19, 2010, and sworn in on January 11, 2011.

Prime Minister: Mikhail MYASNIKOVICH; appointed on December 28, 2010, to succeed Syarhey SIDORSKY (Sergei SIDORSKY).

THE COUNTRY

Located east of Poland in the western region of the former Soviet Union, Belarus is bordered on the north by Latvia, on the northwest by Lithuania, on the east by the Russian Federation, and on the south by Ukraine. The 2009 Belarus census had accounted that 84 percent of its population is Belarusan, 8 percent Russian, 3 percent Polish, and 2 percent Ukrainian. The predominant religion is Eastern Orthodox, with another 7 percent of the population professing Roman Catholicism. A 2002 law prohibits publication and missionary work by churches that have not been registered for at least 20 years. Women make up 53 percent of the labor force. Following the September–October 2012 legislative elections, women held 27 percent of the seats in the lower house and 36 percent of the seats in the upper house.

Agriculture, which continues to be dominated by state and collective farms, and forestry account for about 9 percent of employment and 9 percent of GDP, overall output having declined significantly during the 1990s. The leading crops include grains (rye, oats, wheat), potatoes, and sugar beets, while extensive forests support a major timber industry. Industrial output includes machinery, chemicals, processed foods, and wood and paper products, with industry as a whole employing 46 percent of the workforce and contributing about 46 percent of GDP. Belarus is generally considered "the most unreformed" of the former European Soviet republics, and the state continues to control most assets and economic activity. The private-sector share of GDP stands at about 25 percent.

The postindependence economy suffered a significant contraction that averaged nearly 14 percent of GDP annually in 1993–1995, and GDP growth in the second half of the 1990s was sporadic. From 2004 through 2008 growth averaged about 10 percent annually, but inflation remained a problem, partly because of dramatically increased costs for hydrocarbons shipped from Russia. In 2009 the GDP experienced a sharp downturn, to a rate of 1.2 percent, as the ongoing international financial crisis took hold. Meanwhile, inflation rose to 13 percent.

According to the International Monetary Fund (IMF), the GDP of Belarus grew at a vigorous rate of 7.6 percent in 2010, spurred by economic policies that the organization called "unsustainable." The country had to borrow extensively in foreign currencies rather than the ruble. In May 2011 the Belarusan central bank weakened the ruble by 36 percent against the dollar. By December the ruble had depreciated by 64 percent against the dollar, contributing to an annual inflation rate of 109 percent in 2011 and 59 percent in 2012. GDP growth was 5.3 percent in 2011, slowing to 1.5 percent in 2012. The IMF estimates 2.1 percent growth in 2013, and a lowered inflation rate of 16.8 percent.

GOVERNMENT AND POLITICS

Political background. Merged with Poland in the 16th century after a lengthy period of Lithuanian rule, Byelorussia became part of the Russian Empire as a result of the Polish partitions of 1772, 1793, and 1795. A major battlefield during World War I, the region was reconquered by Red Army troops following a declaration of independence in 1918 and became a constituent republic of the USSR in 1922. In 1939 a western area that had been awarded to Poland in 1921 was reclaimed and incorporated into the Byelorussian SSR.

On July 27, 1990, Byelorussia emulated a number of its sister republics by issuing a declaration of sovereignty. On August 25, 1991, following the abortive Moscow coup against USSR President Mikhail Gorbachev, the Byelorussian Communist Party was suspended, and the Supreme Soviet proclaimed the republic's "political and economic independence." On September 18 its name was changed to Belarus, and Stanislau SHUSHKEVICH was designated chair of the Supreme Soviet (head of state), succeeding Nicholai DEMENTEI, who had been obliged to resign after displaying support for the Moscow hard-liners. Belarus hosted the December 8 tripartite meeting with Russia and Ukraine that proclaimed the demise of the Soviet Union.

Belarus became fully independent with virtually all of its Soviet-era power structure and personnel still in place, but in 1992 disputes between the government and the non-Communist opposition became more heated. While the Supreme Soviet voted to lift the suspension of the Communist Party, its property remained under state ownership. Strains then intensified between Shushkevich, a free-market nationalist, and the chair of the Council of Ministers, Vyacheslau KEBICH, a veteran Communist who favored state control of the economy and close ties with Moscow. In January 1994 Shushkevich's opponents won legislative approval of a censure motion that accused him of "personal immodesty" (i.e., corruption). Shushkevich resigned and was succeeded by Mechyslaw HRYB (Mechislav GRIB), a former Communist apparatchik who supported closer economic and military cooperation with Russia.

In the first round of voting for the newly created office of president on June 23, 1994, Alyaksandr LUKASHENKA, a pro-Russian anticorruption campaigner, topped a six-man field with 44.8 percent of the vote. Lukashenka, running as an independent, went on to defeat Kebich by a near 6–1 margin in a two-way second-round poll on July 10. Lukashenka's nomination of Mikhail CHYHIR (CHIGIR) as prime minister secured legislative approval on July 21. In the first postindependence legislative election, held May 14 and 28, 1995, only 119 of the 260 seats were filled, well short of the two-thirds constitutionally required for a quorum. The victors included contingents of Communists, Agrarians, and conservative independents, almost all supportive of the government's pro-Russian line and unenthusiastic about market reform. Further elections in November and December increased the number of seats properly filled to 198. Together, Communists and Agrarians ended up with a substantial majority of party-based seats, although 95 went to technically unaffiliated candidates, most of whom were thought to support the president.

In the context of an ongoing dispute with the Constitutional Court and his opponents in the Supreme Council over what they charged were his efforts to "rule by decree," in mid-1996 President Lukashenka proposed sweeping constitutional revisions. Prime Minister Chyhir resigned on November 18 to protest Lukashenka's plans, the president naming Deputy Prime Minister Syarhey LING to serve as acting prime minister. Six days later, over 70 percent of the voters approved an amended constitution in a highly controversial referendum that strengthened the presidency and extended Lukashenka's term from five to seven years, until 2001. On November 27, rejecting assertions that the referendum results were undemocratic and fraudulent, the government declared the amended constitution in force.

Among other things, the changes provided for a new, bicameral National Assembly, although more than 40 members of the Supreme Council refused to recognize the referendum's legitimacy and continued to meet in rump sessions as the former legislature's "13th convocation." In January 1997 the defiant legislators initiated a shadow cabinet, the Public Coalition Government–National Economic Council (subsequently the National Executive Council—NEC).

In January 1999, 43 members of the rump Supreme Council announced a "presidential" election for May, in conformance with the 1994 constitution. Organizations supporting the move included the three largest opposition parties. By March exiled opposition leader Zyanon PAZNYAK (POZNIAK) and former prime minister Chyhir had been certified as presidential candidates by the opposition's Central Electoral Commission (CEC). Ultimately, however, the CEC declared the results of the May election invalid because of official harassment, resultant organizational difficulties, and Paznyak's decision to withdraw over procedural objections.

On February 18, 2000, President Lukashenka replaced Prime Minister Ling with Uladzimir IARMOSHYN (Vladimir YERMOSHIN), the chair of the Minsk Executive Committee (mayor). He was confirmed on March 14 by the House of Representatives.

Controversial elections to the House took place on October 15, 2000, although much of the opposition, linked through a Coordinating Council of Democratic Forces, called for a boycott. Only about 50 of the 562 official candidates for office represented the opposition, many others having been disqualified on technicalities or intimidated into withdrawing. Following a second round on October 29, the election results were declared valid in 97 of 110 constituencies, with the remaining seats being filled in March–April 2001.

Although most of the opposition united behind Uladzimir HANCHARYK (Vladimir GONCHARIK) of the Belarusan Federation of Trade Unions for the presidential election of September 4–9, 2001, President Lukashenka claimed some 76 percent of the disputed vote. Inaugurated on September 20, he nominated a new prime minister, Henadz NAVITSKI (Gennady NOVITSKY), on October 1. Formation of a new Council of Ministers was concluded by mid-December.

On July 10, 2003, President Lukashenka dismissed Prime Minister Navitski and several agricultural officials and named a deputy prime minister, Syarhey SIDORSKY, to head the cabinet in an acting capacity. Sidorsky's elevation to prime minister was completed on December 19, following endorsement by a 111–9 vote of the House of Representatives earlier in the day.

During the second half of 2003 opposition forces began organizing for the 2004 legislative election. The principal alliances to emerge from the process were the Popular Coalition "Five-Plus" and the European Coalition "Free Belarus." In September 2004 Lukashenka announced that the October 17 election also would include a referendum on ending the two-term limit for presidents. Although the opposition united in an effort to defeat the constitutional change, the referendum easily passed, according to the official results, thereby permitting Lukashenka to seek a third term in 2006. The simultaneous election for the House of Representatives saw the opposition parties shut out: Of the 110 contested seats, only 12 were won by party candidates, all of them government supportive.

Although President Lukashenka's term was not due to expire until September 2006, on December 16, 2005, the legislature unanimously endorsed holding the next presidential election six months early. At a National Congress of Democratic Forces, held October 1–2, 2005, the leading opposition parties, including those in the Five-Plus and European Coalition alliances, had selected as their joint candidate Alyaksandr MILINKEVICH, a nonpartisan academic and experienced nongovernmental organization leader. To no one's surprise, Lukashenka emerged the victor at the March 19, 2006, election, winning 82.6 percent of the vote. Milinkevich finished second, officially with 6.1 percent of the vote, in the four-way contest, the conduct of which was uniformly condemned by Western monitors.

May 2007 saw the release of jailed opposition figures Mikalay STATKEVICH, head of the unregistered Belarusan Social Democratic Party "People's Assembly" (*Belaruskaya Satsyal-Demakratychnaya Partya "Narodnaya Hramada"*—BSDP-NH), and youth organizer Pavel SEVYARYNETS, both of whom had been convicted in 2005 of spearheading protests against the conduct of the 2004 parliamentary elections. Dzmitryy DASHKEVICH, leader of the Young Front (*Malady Front*) nongovernmental youth organization, serving an 18-month sentence for belonging to an unregistered organization, was freed in January 2008. Another Young Front leader, Artur FINKEVICH, had his sentence commuted in early February. The most prominent incarcerated politician remained 2006 presidential candidate Alyaksandr KAZULIN (Aleksandr KOZULIN), who in July 2006 had been sentenced to serve more than five years for his activities during the campaign and for disturbing the peace at a postelection rally. Kazulin was freed by presidential pardon on August 16, 2008.

In the September 28, 2008, election for the House of Representatives the opposition once again failed to win any seats. Monitors from the Organization for Security and Cooperation in Europe (OSCE) noted "minor improvements" in the conduct of the election but continued to criticize Belarus for its failure to meet democratic commitments. On December 19, 2010 Lukashenka was reelected president in balloting marred by fraud (see Current issues, below). Following the election, Mikhail MYASNIKOVICH was appointed prime minister on December 28.

Eight parties participated in the September 23, 2012, elections, although two opposition parties withdrew before the balloting. Opposition parties again failed to secure any seats, with all but five seats won by independent but pro-Lukashenka candidates. Monitors from the OSCE characterized the elections as marred by unequal coverage on state media, nontransparent vote counting, and administrative processes that excluded a quarter of nominated candidates.

Constitution and government. After a two-year gestation period, a new constitution secured legislative approval on March 15, 1994, and entered into force on March 30. It provided for an executive president to be directly elected for a once-renewable five-year term, and assigned him powers that included serving as commander in chief; declaring a state of emergency; and appointing the prime minister, cabinet, and judges. The powers of the presidency were vastly expanded by referendum on November 24, 1996. Revisions to the constitution extended the current president's term of office and gave him the authority to nullify decisions of local councils, set election dates, and call parliament into session as well as dissolve it. The president also was empowered to appoint half the members of the Constitutional Court, as well as the chief justice, and officials of the Central Electoral Commission. The unicameral Supreme Council was replaced by a two-chamber body comprising an upper Council of the Republic and a lower House of Representatives. A referendum on October 17, 2004, eliminated a two-term limitation on the presidency.

Although media independence and the freedom to disseminate information are protected by the constitution and in law, the government continues to control electronic news transmission and newspaper distribution. The government is also the only legal Internet service provider. Independent, opposition publications have been subjected to a variety of threats and pressures, including confiscation of printing equipment by tax authorities and allegations of libeling or defaming President Lukashenka and other officials. Journalists have been jailed and publications fined, leading the international Committee to Protect Journalists to rank Belarus among the ten "worst places to be a journalist." In 2012, Reporters Without Borders designated Belarus as one of its "Enemies of the Internet" for government crackdowns on opposition Websites and blogs, attributed to be an effort to prevent "revolution by social media."

Local government is based in the country's 6 regions (*voblasti*), 118 administrative districts (*rayons*), and the municipality (*horad*) of Minsk.

Foreign relations. Although not then an independent country, Byelorussia was accorded founding membership in the United Nations in a move by the Western Allies to reconcile the USSR's Joseph Stalin to the creation of a world organization that would appear to have a built-in anti-Soviet majority. In contrast, it did not join the IMF and World Bank until July 1992. By then, independent Belarus had been recognized by a wide variety of foreign governments and had become a founding member of the Commonwealth of Independent States (CIS).

After protracted diplomatic exchanges, Belarus ratified a series of agreements by which it renounced its inherited nuclear weapons. Under one of the accords, signed in Washington on July 22, 1992, the U.S. government pledged $59 million to assist in dismantling about 80 Belarus-based SS-25 missiles. In November 1996 Russia reported that it had removed the last nuclear missiles from Belarus.

Under a December 1993 agreement Russia obtained the right to guide seven CIS members, including Belarus, in defense policy. Belarus nevertheless joined the Partnership for Peace program of the North Atlantic Treaty Organization (NATO) in January 1995, although it proceeded more slowly than many other countries in negotiating the specifics of its participation in the program.

Belarus and Russia have negotiated several treaties providing for bilateral reintegration, including economic and monetary union. These included a February 1995 friendship and cooperation treaty; the April 1996 Treaty on the Formation of the Community of Sovereign Republics (CSR); the May 1997 signing of the Charter of the Union; and the December 1999 Treaty on the Creation of a Union State. Efforts at integration remained largely symbolic, although a joint CSR budget for military cooperation, anticrime efforts, and customs measures was created in 1997, and a Council of Ministers of the Union began meeting in April 2000. (For details on the individual treaties, see the article in the 2013 *Handbook*.)

A monetary union was to have been established by January 2005, but adoption of a single currency was repeatedly postponed, in part because of a failure to agree on what compensation Belarus would receive to offset the consequent economic damage.

Relations have also been clouded by persistent differences related to Belarus's purchase of hydrocarbons from Russia and transit fees imposed by Minsk on Russian oil headed to other European countries. The Russian natural gas monopoly, Gazprom, successfully demanded an end to a generous energy subsidy enjoyed by Belarus, but annual supply and pricing agreements have typically been rancorous. On numerous occasions, including in June 2010, westbound transit shipments of hydrocarbons have been delayed.

Relations with Western European countries and institutions long suffered because of their objections to the Lukashenka regime's political practices. In October 2002 the last foreign member of the OSCE Advisory and Monitoring Group (AMG) in Belarus was obliged to leave the country due to the expiration of her visa. The Lukashenka regime, alleging that the AMG had repeatedly interfered in the country's internal affairs, demanded revision of the mission's mandate. In late December the OSCE and Belarus agreed to scrap the AMG and establish in its place a new OSCE Office in Minsk to assist "in further promoting institution building," to help with economic and environmental activities, and to monitor events.

In February 2003 the OSCE Parliamentary Assembly restored Belarus's membership, but in the same month the European Parliament adopted a resolution that criticized the Lukashenka regime for an adverse human rights climate and "indiscriminate attacks" on opponents, journalists, human rights activists, and others. In March 2005 the European Parliament labeled the government a dictatorship. In October 2006 it awarded Alyaksandr Milinkevich its Sakharov Prize for Freedom of Thought, the most prestigious human rights award in the European Union (EU). Two months later, the outgoing EU president, Finnish Prime Minister Matti Vanhanen, described Belarus as "a black hole on the face of European democracy." In 2006 the United States imposed tightened sanctions directed primarily against Belarus's state-owned petrochemical company. The dispute escalated into a diplomatic spat in March 2008, when Washington and Minsk recalled their respective ambassadors and Lukashenka ordered the downsizing of U.S. embassy staff. On April 30 the government labeled ten U.S. diplomats personae non gratae and ordered them to leave Belarus. Accusations were also made that the United States had set up a spy ring in Belarus.

In April 2009, commenting on his country's relations with Russia, President Lukashenka said that no one in his government opposed closer integration but that he wanted "more clarity and transparency" from Moscow. Lukashenka and Russian president Dmitri Medvedev conferred that August, but little progress was made in resolving any of their differences. For instance, Russia's markets remained closed to Belarusan dairy exports. Tensions remained over Minsk's refusal to recognize the self-declared independence of the Russian-backed Georgian breakaway regions of South Ossetia and Abkhazia, and Belarus remained aloof from participation in a Joint Rapid Reaction Force advocated by the Moscow-led Collective Security Treaty Organization. In 2010 what has become a perennial battle over the pricing and taxation of oil imports from Russia—Moscow has lately insisted that Belarus pay full duties on petroleum intended for resale—contributed to Lukashenka's efforts to establish closer economic ties with China and to reach an oil deal with Venezuela.

Meanwhile, from the mid-2000s onward, the Lukashenka regime endeavored to improve relations with the EU, which in turn has been more willing to reduce Belarus's isolation despite continuing concerns over human rights issues and an absence of economic reform. In February 2009 Javier Solana, EU high commissioner for foreign policy and security, became the highest-ranking EU official to visit Belarus. In March the EU subsequently added Belarus to its proposed Eastern Partnership program, which included Armenia, Azerbaijan, Georgia, Moldova, and Ukraine. A month later, the European Parliament endorsed a resolution that was described as representing "pragmatic engagement" with Minsk, which was in turn expected to introduce electoral reforms and relax restrictions on associations, the right of assembly, and the media. On April 26–28 Lukashenka visited Italy, taking advantage of a moratorium on travel bans that had been put in place by the EU against several dozen individuals after the 2006 presidential election. He met with Prime Minister Silvio Berlusconi and Pope Benedict XVI in his first visit to Western Europe in a decade. In November Berlusconi became the first Western European leader to enter Belarus in more than ten years.

In 2010 EU member Poland expressed its outrage when Belarusan officials issued warrants to members of an unrecognized branch of the Union of Poles who had participated in unsanctioned gatherings. Warsaw insisted not only that the rights of Belarus's ethnic Poles be protected but also that further EU economic aid be tied to improved minority rights and economic liberalization.

Meanwhile, the fallout from the corrupt presidential elections of December 2010 was a diplomatic disaster for Belarus. Poland unilaterally issued a visa ban on around 100 Belarusian officials in January 2011. The EU and the United States also coordinated a new round of financial and travel sanctions against Belarus. The EU imposed a visa ban on 158 top-ranking officials, including Lukashenka, who also had his international assets frozen. Meanwhile, the United States, forbade U.S. companies and individuals from conducting business with several key Belarusan state-owned companies. In response to the continued harassment of its citizens, the United States extended its ban to four other businesses that were linked to Lukashenka in August. Belarus retaliated by suspending an agreement to surrender its enriched uranium.

Although Moscow has also been critical of Lukashenka, in June 2011 Russia agreed to a $3 billion loan over three years. In return Belarus will privatize $7.5 billion of state property, which critics charged meant selling the assets to the Russians. In July customs barriers between Russia and Belarus were removed, and Belarus joined the Eurasian Economic Union, formed to integrate the economies of Russia, Belarus, and Kazakhstan by 2013.

In February 2012 renewed tensions over Belarus' human rights record led Belarus to expel the Polish ambassador and the head of the EU representative office; the EU retaliated by recalling all ambassadors of member states and imposed a new series of visa bans in March, but ambassadors returned in April.

Current issues. President Lukashenka again won reelection on December 19, 2010, capturing 79.6 percent of the vote, according to the official count, against nine challengers. The failure of the fractured opposition to decide on a single candidate as well as blatant electoral fraud made the outcome a foregone conclusion. On election day and immediately afterward police and security personnel arrested an estimated 600 protesters, who condemned the vote count as corrupt. Many of the protesters and several of the candidates were beaten. Seven of Lukashenka's nine challengers were detained, including his closest competitor, Andrei SANNIKAU (Andrei SANNIKOV), who won 2.4 percent of the vote, as well as Sannikau's wife. The second-place finisher was sentenced to five years in prison in May 2011 (later presidentially pardoned in April 2012), while his wife was sentenced to two years. Western observers, including monitors from the OSCE, widely condemned the postelection developments. In response, OSCE monitors were banned from the country. Lukashenka, responding to the protests, announced that "there will be no more mindless democracy in this country." Yet he did shuffle his cabinet and appoint a new prime minister on December 28, in an effort to mollify his critics.

Growing economic distress led to mass demonstrations through 2011. In June of that year another dramatic rise in the price of gasoline precipitated protests, which forced the government to rescind the increase. The following month several hundred protesters were arrested. In order to avoid arrest, citizens resorted to silent protests, during which large numbers of them stood in sullen silence in a public place. The government subsequently banned those demonstrations as well. At the end of August Lukashenka agreed to release all political prisoners by early October in order, he maintained, to have better relations with the EU.

Parliamentary elections were held on September 23, 2012. Leading opposition groups called for a boycott, although they failed to unify their efforts in this regard. In August and September Belarusan human rights groups reported arrests of journalists and administrators of opposition Web sites. In August, election officials denied Milinkevich's registration as a candidate, ruling that he had provided invalid signatures and incorrect personal information. On September 6, the offices of the **United Civic Party of Belarus** (*Abyadnanaya Hramadzyanskaya Partya Belarusi*—AHPB) were reportedly raided by police and internal security officers.

POLITICAL PARTIES

As in post-Soviet Russia, top Belarusan officials have generally avoided direct involvement in political party activity while in office, despite (or because of) their earlier associations with the Soviet-era Communist Party. Unlike in Russia, however, where party politics has often dominated proceedings in the powerful State Duma, the less powerful Belarusan legislature has been controlled by Lukashenka loyalists rather than by party caucuses. Political and personal support for the head of state has often coalesced in broad alliances of assorted parties, nongovernmental organizations, and interest groups.

Under a presidential decree issued in January 1999, all 27 officially registered political parties, all public associations, and all trade unions were required to reregister under stricter standards regarding, for example, national membership. Only 17 parties met the new criteria when the reregistration period expired in August; most of the others had not applied, and 2 were denied official recognition for technical reasons. In 1998 half a dozen other small parties had already been disbanded by order of the Supreme Court. At present, parties must have offices in Minsk and at least four regional capitals. In addition, official party offices are prohibited from being located in residences or residential complexes, placing a considerable burden on some of the cash-strapped opposition groups.

Opposition policy coordination has often been lacking despite unifying efforts spearheaded by the largest parties, including the Belarusan Popular Front "Revival" (NFB-A), the United Civic Party of Belarus (AHPB), and the Belarusan Social Democratic Party "People's Assembly" (BSDP-NH). In mid-2003, looking toward the parliamentary balloting scheduled for October 2004, opposition elements began organizing alliances. The largest of these, encompassing the AHPB, the Belarusan Social Democratic Assembly (BSDH), the NFB-A, the Party of Communists of Belarus (PKB), and the Belarusan Labor Party (*Belaruskaya Partya Pratsy*—BPP), as well as a number of smaller parties and nongovernmental organizations, adopted the name Popular Coalition "Five-Plus" (*Piaciorka Plus*) in November. Despite ideological and other differences, the participating organizations endorsed a uniform "Five Steps to a Better Life" platform that emphasized economic and social dignity for everyone, job creation and worker protection, self-governance and equality before the law, budget transparency and an end to official corruption, and "mutually beneficial friendly relations with all neighboring and EU countries." At the same time, a European Coalition "Free Belarus" (*"Svabodnaya Belarus"*) was taking shape under the leadership of the BSDP-NH, the Belarusan Women's Party "Hope" (*Belaruskaya Partya Zhanchyn "Nadzeya"*—BPZ-N), the Charter-97 (*Khartita-97*) human rights group, a number of youth groups, and assorted public associations, but none of the opposition parties won seats.

In November 2004 most opposition leaders agreed that they would select a single candidate for the 2006 presidential contest. Late in the same month they organized a Permanent Council of Democratic Forces that included the original Five-Plus members (technically minus the BPP, which had been deregistered by the government), the Free Belarus parties, the Belarusan Green Party (BPZ), the Public Youth Organization "Civil Forum," the Young Front, and various nongovernmental organizations. At a National Congress of Democratic Forces, held October 1–2, 2005, in Minsk, this "unified opposition" endorsed the unaffiliated Alyaksandr Milinkevich as their 2006 presidential candidate by a narrow margin over the AHPB's Anatol Lyabedzka. Shortly after the congress the PKB's chair, Syarhey Kalyakin, assumed leadership of the Political Council of the **United Democratic Forces** (UDF), which was later led by Milinkevich. At a second national congress, held May 26–27, 2007, however, the opposition voted to replace Milinkevich with a four-person rotating leadership from the AHPB, NFB-A, PKB, and Alyaksey Kazulin's Belarusan Social Democratic Party "Assembly" (BSDP-H). The following August, those four parties, the BPZ, the BPZ-N (liquidated by the government in September 2007), a founding committee for a new Labor Party, and Pavel Sevyarynets's as-yet-unregistered Belarusan Christian Democracy agreed to work together in preparation for contesting the next legislative election. Milinkevich, heading the then-unregistered Movement for Freedom, and several other leaders declined to participate. They argued that the opposition should press the government for democratic reforms before agreeing to take part in the vote. According to the Central Election Commission, 56 of 263 candidates for the September 2008 election were UDF members, but none won.

Opposition parties attempted to negotiate a boycott of the September 2012 elections but were unable to negotiate a common approach.

Leading Progovernment Parties in Parliament:

Agrarian Party of Belarus (*Agrarnaya Partya Belarusi*—APB). The APB was founded in 1994 in opposition to the restoration of peasant land ownership in Belarus, as advocated by the Belarusan Peasants' Party (*Belaruskaya Syalarskaya Partya*—BSP), which was deregistered in 1999. The APB returned 33 candidates in the 1995 legislative balloting and later attracted 13 "unaffiliated" deputies to its group in the Supreme Council, of which party chief Semyon SHARETSKY was elected chair.

The party ruptured in 1996, with Sharetsky and his supporters disavowing the results of the November constitutional referendum. Sharetsky continued as the chair of the opposition's reconstituted Supreme Council but, fearing for his safety, ultimately fled to Lithuania in 2000. A congress of the APB had pledged its loyalty to President Lukashenka earlier in the year. In 2004 the APB won three House seats but in 2008 it held only one.

In March 2008, at the party's fifth convention, Mikhail Rusy (Mikhail Rusyi), a member of the House of Representatives and a former minister of agriculture, was unanimously elected chair. His predecessor, Mikhail SHYMANSKI, chose not to seek reelection. In May 2010 Rusy was again named minister of agriculture and food. The APB did not run an independent candidate in the balloting. In the September 2012 elections, the APB won a single House seat.

Leader: Mikhail RUSY (Chair).

Communist Party of Belarus (*Kommunisticheskaya Partya Belarusi*—KPB). The Soviet-era Communist Party had originated as a regional committee of the Russian Social Democratic Labor Party (formed in 1904). Established as the ruling party of the Soviet Socialist Republic of Byelorussia in 1920, the party suffered heavily during the terror of the 1930s and thereafter remained wholly subservient to Moscow. The conservative Minsk leadership miscalculated, however, when it backed the abortive coup by hard-liners in Moscow in August 1991. In the immediate aftermath, many party officials were ousted, the party was suspended, and its property was nationalized. The party was subsequently legalized as the Party of Communists of Belarus (PKB; see under Belarusan Party of United Leftists, below) and backed the ouster of reformist head of state Stanislau Shushkevich in January 1994. Embracing the concept of multipartyism, the PKB contested the mid-1994 presidential elections in its own right by supporting Vasil NOVIKAU, who placed last of six candidates. Nevertheless, the Communists' strong organization enabled them to win 42 seats in the 1995 Assembly election, a plurality that later rose to 44 because of accessions by independents.

Tensions in the party were revealed in September 1996 when First Secretary Syarhey Kalyakin was publicly criticized by several other party leaders for aligning with opponents of President Lukashenka. The factionalization culminated with a pro-Lukashenka group headed by Viktar CHYKIN readopting the KPB designation at a congress in November, while Kalyakin's supporters continued to operate as the PKB. The KPB subsequently endorsed the president's push for reintegration with Russia, and in 1998 Chykin was chosen as leader of the BPPU. Nevertheless, at its August 2000 congress the party paradoxically claimed to be part of the opposition. At the October 2004 general election the KPB won eight seats in the House of Representatives.

In March 2005 Tatsyana Holubeva was named chair, the previous party chief, Valery ZAKHARCHENKA, having died in July 2004. In the 2008 election for the House of Representatives, the KPB won six seats, which was more than any other party's tally. The party supported Lukashenka in the 2010 presidential election. In the 2012 parliamentary elections, the KPB won three seats in the House.

Leaders: Tatsyana HOLUBEVA (Tatyana GOLUBEVA, First Secretary), Aleksandr KAMAY.

Republican Party of Labor and Justice (*Respublikanskaya Partya Pratsy i Spravyadlivasti*—RPPS). Founded in 1993 as a self-described center-left party. It won a single seat in the 1995 legislative elections and two seats in the 2000 elections, but failed to win any seats in 2004 or 2008. In the September 2012 elections, it won a single seat in the House.

Leader: Vasil' ZADNYAPRYANY (Vasily ZADNEPRYANY, Chair).

Other Progovernment Parties:

Liberal Democratic Party of Belarus (*Liberalna-Demakratychnaya Partya Belarusi*—LDPB). Registered in 1994 under the leadership of Vasil KRYVENKA, the LDPB views itself as the Belarusan counterpart of Russia's ultranationalist Liberal Democratic Party and therefore advocates close links with Russia. It subsequently allied with pro-Lukashenka forces as a founding member of the BPPU. By March 1999, however, responding in part to what it considered unfair official tactics against its candidates for local soviets, the party distanced itself from other presidential supporters, claiming that democratic elections were impossible.

The LDPB initially refused to participate in the opposition boycott of the October 2000 House of Representatives election, but it withdrew from the voting before the second round because of alleged electoral violations. It subsequently announced that it would rejoin the opposition Coordinating Council. Reelected chair of the party at a congress in August 2000, Syarhey Haydukevich described himself as Lukashenka's "very decent rival" for the presidency in 2001, but he won only 2.5 percent of the vote.

At an extraordinary convention in September 2003, supporters of the party's deputy chair, Aleh MARKEVICH, voted their opposition to Haydukevich's leadership, but the Ministry of Justice subsequently ruled in the chair's favor. Other efforts to wrest the party from Haydukevich in 2005 and 2006 also failed.

The LDPB won one House seat in 2004. In 2006 Haydukevich again sought the presidency and finished third, with 3.5 percent of the vote. In September 2008 none of the party's eight candidates for the House won. Haydukevich ran for president in 2010, campaigning on a platform that advocated union with Russia, but he withdrew from the race in October. It participated in the September 2012 elections but failed to win any seats.

Leader: Syarhey HAYDUKEVICH (Sergei GAIDUKEVICH, Chair).

Leading Opposition Parties:

Belarusan Popular Front "Revival" (*Narodni Front Belarusi "Adradzhennie"*—NFB-A). The NFB-A was launched in June 1989 at a conference in Vilnius, Lithuania, of pro-independence groups. They chose as their leader Zyanon Paznyak (Zenon Poznyak), an archaeologist who in 1988 had published evidence of mass graves found at Kurapaty, near Minsk, on the site of a detention/execution camp established on Stalin's orders in 1937. In the 1990 Supreme Soviet elections in Belarus, the NFB-A won only 34 of 360 seats against an entrenched Communist hierarchy. The NFB-A defines itself as a broad popular movement with a "closely integrated" political party, the **Party of the BPF** (*Partyja BPF*), which was established in 1993.

The issuance of a warrant for his arrest after an antigovernment demonstration in 1996 caused Paznyak to flee abroad. Granted asylum by the United States, he was reelected chair in absentia at the party congress in 1997 and later agreed to serve as the NFB-A standard-bearer in the controversial symbolic presidential election in May 1999. (In 1994 he had won 13.9 percent of the first-round presidential vote.)

A major split in the party occurred following a 1999 congress at which neither Paznyak nor his principal challenger, Deputy Chair Vintsuk Vyachorka, received sufficient votes to resolve a leadership dispute occasioned by Paznyak's continuing exile and his alleged authoritarianism. With another leadership vote expected in October, the party ruptured; at a congress on September 26, 1999, the Paznyak supporters "renamed" the party the Conservative-Christian Party of the BNF (KKhP-NFB, below). A month later the rump NFB-A elected Vyachorka as its new chair.

In 2005 Vyachorka was one of the early supporters behind Alyaksandr Milinkevich's quest for the presidency in 2006. A party congress in December 2007 elected Lyavon Barshcheusky as successor to Vyachorka when neither the sitting chair nor his principal opponent, Ales MIKHALEVICH, managed to obtain a majority of votes. Barshcheusky, who had already announced his intentions to seek the presidency in 2010, was in turn replaced in September 2009 by Alyaksey Yanukevich, who called for greater cooperation with other opposition organizations. Mikhalevich, who had been expelled from the party in 2008 for factionalism, ran as an independent presidential candidate in 2010. He was subsequently imprisoned and tortured. Ryhor Kastusyov, the vice chair of the party, was selected as its presidential candidate. He too was arrested after the election, although he was subsequently released.

The NFB-A nominated candidates in the September 2012 elections but withdrew before the balloting in protest at the detention of opposition political activists.

Leaders: Alyaksey YANUKEVICH (Chair), Ryhor KASTUSYOV (Deputy Chair and 2010 presidential candidate).

Belarusan Social Democratic Assembly (*Belaruskaya Satsyal-Demakratychnaya Hramada*—BSDH). The BSDH held its founding congress in 1998 under the leadership of former Supreme Council chair Stanislau Shushkevich, who called for restoration of the 1994 constitution. The new formation attracted many members of the Belarusan National Party (*Belaruskaya Natsyanalnaya Partya*—BNP), including its chair, Anatol ASTAPENKA. (The BNP was not reregistered in 1999.)

In 2003 the United Social Democratic Party (USDP), led by Alyaksey KAROL, merged into the BSDH. Karol's party had been denied registration following its August 2002 formation through merger of a faction of the now-defunct Belarusan Women's Party "Hope" (BPZ-N) and the unregistered Belarusan Social Democratic Party (*Belaruskaya Satsyal-Demakratychnaya Partya*—BSDP). The BSDP, dating from December 2001, had been formed by Karol and other defectors from the BSDP-NH (below).

In April 2005, over Shushkevich's objection, elements of the BSDH voted to merge with the BSDP-NH but instead ended up helping establish the BSDP-H (below) when Shushkevich's supporters ultimately retained control of the party. One of four candidates selected to vie for the 2006 presidential endorsement of the unified opposition, Shushkevich withdrew before the secret balloting by the National Congress of Democratic Forces in October 2005.

First Deputy Leader Syarhey Skrabets announced in March 2009 that he was leaving the party because of differences involving the next national presidential election and "international issues." After unsuccessful efforts to establish the Social Democratic Party *"Svaboda"* (Freedom), he joined the BSDP-NH.

The BSDH participated in the September 2012 legislative elections but failed to win any seats.

Leader: Stanislau SHUSHKEVICH (Chair).

Belarusan Social Democratic Party "People's Assembly" (*Belaruskaya Satsyal-Demakratychnaya Partya "Narodnaya Hramada"*—BSDP-NH). The original BSDP was founded in 1991 as a latter-day revival of the Revolutionary *Hramada* Party (founded in 1902), which spearheaded the early movement for the creation of a Belarusan state but was outlawed following declaration of the Soviet Socialist Republic in 1919. The revived party contested the 1995 legislative election, winning 2 seats and later increasing its parliamentary group to 15 members. In 1996 it absorbed the Party of Popular Accord (PPA), which dated from 1992, although some members of the latter rejected the merger and went on to form the Social Democratic Party of Popular Accord (see Other Parties, below).

The party organized unsanctioned anti-Lukashenka rallies in 1996–1999, for which party leader Mikalay Statkevich was jailed repeatedly. Tactical differences with other opposition parties emerged in 2000, with Statkevich opposing the boycott of the October legislative election and advocating nomination of a single opposition candidate—one acceptable to Communists and nationalists alike—to run against Lukashenka in 2001.

In December 2004, seeking to bring together the country's moderately leftist parties, Statkevich led formation of an organizational committee for a "United Social Democratic Party of Belarus." At the same time, opposition was growing within the BSDP-NH to his allegedly autocratic style and his strong support for Belarusan EU membership. Dissident elements led by Anatol Lyawkovich attempted to expel Statkevich and key supporters, who responded in kind. In January 2005 the Ministry of Justice ruled in favor of the dissidents, who formally retained title to the party, but Statkevich's supporters claimed control of the party at a February 2005 congress. In April the anti-Statkevich elements of the BSDP-NH, having been joined by elements of the BSDH, voted to drop "People's" from their party's name, as demanded by the Justice Ministry, and become the Belarusan Social Democratic Party "Assembly" (BSDP-H, below). Statkevich's BSDP-NH remained unregistered.

In May 2005 Statkevich was convicted of participating in illegal protests against the conduct of the October 2004 election and was sentenced to three years' detention and community service. He was transferred to house arrest in November 2005, but the conviction meant that he was ineligible to run for president in 2006. He was released in May 2007. The party held a founding conference in November 2007, but as of July 2010 the government had not permitted it to register.

Into early 2008 Statkevich remained aloof from the decision of other UDF participants to present a joint candidate list for the September 2008 parliamentary election, arguing that the opposition should pressure the government for democratic reforms before agreeing to participate in the poll. Statkevich himself was not permitted to contest the election, in part because of his criminal record.

Statkevich was the party's presidential candidate in 2010, eligible since sufficient time had passed since completion of his sentence. He was arrested after the balloting. In May 2011 he was sentenced to six years in prison, and his family has been forbidden to visit him. Commentators speculated that his criticism of Lukashenka during the campaign was responsible for the harsh sentence. Among other things, he urged the dictator to "give back what he stole."

The party continues to participate in an informal pro-EU "European Coalition."

Leaders: Mikalay (Mikola) STATKEVICH (Party Chair and Coordinator of the European Coalition); Alyaksandr ARASTOVICH, Alaksey HAWRUTSIKAW, and Syarhey KULINICH (Deputy Chairs).

Belarusan Social Democratic Party "Assembly" (*Belaruskaya Satsyal-Demakratychnaya Party "Hramada"*—BSDP-H). Formation of the BSDP-H, by factions of the BSDH and the BSDP-NH, was announced in early 2005. Led at that time by Anatol Lyawkovich, the party initially retained "People's" as part of its title but soon dropped it to comply with a Justice Ministry decision. Alyaksandr Kazulin, former rector of Belarusan State University, assumed leadership of the party in April 2005. He had hoped to accomplish a full merger of the BSDP-NH and BSDH but was ultimately opposed by BSDH leader Stanislau Shushkevich as well as by BSDP-NH leader Mikalay Statkevich, who had originally supported the idea. Kazulin's supporters included former BSDH deputy chair Mechyslaw Hryb. In September 2005 the Permanent Council of Democratic Forces rejected Kazulin and his party's participation in the October National Congress of Democratic Forces, the BSDH having accused him of playing a divisive role.

Kazulin was officially registered as a presidential candidate in February 2006. He finished last in the four-way contest, with only 2.2 percent of the vote. In July he was convicted of disturbing the peace and other charges and sentenced to five and a half years in prison. In October, hoping to draw international attention to Belarus and demanding that the results of the presidential election be declared invalid, he began a hunger strike that lasted more than seven weeks.

Meeting in December 2006 in Ukraine, the leaders of the BSDP-H, the BPZ-N, and the PKB agreed to form the Union of Left Parties (ULP) with Kazulin as honorary chair. Named as his deputies were the chairs of the three founding parties plus Alyaksandr BUKHVOSTAU of the liquidated Belarusan Labor Party. The Justice Ministry has refused to register the ULP. Having mended fences with most of the other leading opposition parties, which had made Kazulin's release from prison a key demand, the BSDP-H became active in the United Democratic Forces.

In April 2008 Mechyslaw Hryb was elected secretary general of the party. In early August, however, a party congress replaced Kazulin as chair by the former acting chair, Anatol Lyawkovich. Kazulin's supporters, including former deputy chair Ihar RYNKEVICH and members of the For In-Party Democratization faction, described the move as a "staff coup," while Kazulin, shortly after his release from prison on August 16, described it as a "pure betrayal." In June 2010 Mechyslaw Hryb announced that he would run as the party's candidate for president in December.

Leader: Irina VESHTARD (Chair).

Movement for Freedom (*Rukh "Za Svabodu"*). Organized by former opposition presidential candidate Alyaksandr Milinkevich, the anti-Lukashenka Movement for Freedom is a Western-oriented association, not a political party per se. In December 2007 the Supreme Court upheld the decision of the Justice Ministry to deny registration to the organization on the grounds that its most recent founding conference had failed to obtain a permit from local authorities and had therefore violated the Mass Events Law. The government had previously rejected the movement's application in July, citing an inadequate charter. In August 2008 the Supreme Court backed the decision of the Ministry of Justice not to register Milinkevich's movement, but registration was finally granted in December 2008. Milinkevich had already stated that he planned to seek the presidency again at the next election, but he withdrew from consideration in September 2010 on the grounds that a free and fair election would not be held.

In October 2009 Milinkevich announced formation of the **Belarusan Pro-Independence Bloc** (*Belaruski Nezalezhnitski Blok*), a pro-EU coalition that also included among its participants the Party of the BPF. Milinkevich was the party's candidate in the 2010 presidential election. In June and July 2011 he met with leaders of five other opposition parties to form a common platform to promote democracy in Belarus.

The Movement for Freedom did not register for the September 2012 elections but did support a slate of independent candidates.

Leaders: Alyaksandr MILINKEVICH (Chair and 2010 presidential candidate); Viktar KARNYAYENKA, Yury HUBAREVICH (Deputy Chairs).

Belarusan United Left Party "A Fair World" (*"Spravadlivy Mir"*). Until October 2009 Fair World was called the Party of Communists of Belarus (*Partya Kamunistau Belaruskaya*—PKB), which had originated as the refashioned Soviet-era Communist Party. In November 1996 a major split occurred over whether to support President Lukashenka. As a result, the Lukashenka supporters became the Communist Party of Belarus (KPB, above), with the opposition faction retaining the PKB designation.

While not opposed to closer ties with Russia, the PKB rejects Soviet-style rule and loss of Belarusan sovereignty. It has called for democratic reforms, including reduction of presidential powers and transfer of authority to soviets. It condemned the 2000 House of Representatives election as a "farce," despite polling better than expected. Party leader Syarhey Kalyakin was initially a presidential candidate in 2001 but withdrew in a show of unity behind Vladimir Goncharik.

Looking toward the 2006 presidential race, Kalyakin was again named as the party's preferred candidate. Following the October 2005 decision of the unified opposition to support Alyaksandr Milinkevich, Kalyakin became a leading figure in the Milinkevich campaign.

In July 2006 a Communist congress was held ostensibly to reunite the PKB and KPB, but Kalyakin described the effort as a government-backed attempt to liquidate his party. Two months later the Justice Department asked the Supreme Court to deregister the PKB because it no longer met membership requirements. In September 2007 the Supreme Court ordered the party to suspend its activities for six months because of registration violations.

Over the objections of some members who wished to retain "Communist" in the party's title, the PKB was renamed at a congress in October 2009. Supporters of the change argued that the previous name carried with it "negative overtones." In May 2011 Kalyakin was reelected as party chair. He was critical of the opposition's failure to present a single candidate in the December 2010 election, and he took part in the meeting of six opposition parties in June and July to form a common opposition party.

Fair World participated in the September 2012 legislative elections but failed to win any seats.

Leaders: Syarhey KALYAKIN (Chair), Alena SKRYHAN (Central Committee Secretary).

United Civic Party of Belarus (*Abyadnanaya Hramadzyanskaya Partya Belarusi*—AHPB). The promarket AHPB was founded in October 1995 as a merger of several organizations—most notably the professional/technocratic United Democratic Party of Belarus (*Abyadnanaya Demakratychnaya Partya Belarusi*—ADPB), which had been formed in 1990 as a merger of three prodemocracy groups—that had contested the first round of that year's legislative election in an alliance called the Civic Accord Bloc. The leader of the merged party, Stanislau BAHDANKEVICH, had recently been dismissed as president of the National Bank after disagreeing with President Lukashenka's pro-Russian policies. In the 1995 legislative balloting the AHPB won nine seats in its own right, forming the Civic Action parliamentary group, which rose to 18 members with the adhesion of previously unaffiliated deputies. It subsequently continued its anti-Lukashenka stance, organizing demonstrations against the government and boycotting the 2000 legislative election.

Anatol Lyabedzka was endorsed as the party's 2006 presidential candidate. At the opposition's National Congress in October 2005, he finished second to Alyaksandr Milinkevich, 391 votes to 399, in balloting to select the unified opposition's candidate.

A party activist, Andrey KLIMAW, was sentenced to two years in prison in August 2007 for using the party's Web site to promote the overthrow of the government. His sentence was commuted in February 2008. Klimaw had been imprisoned in 1998–2002 for embezzlement and forgery—politically motivated charges, according to his supporters—and had been detained from June 2005 until December 2006 for organizing an antigovernment march in March 2005.

One of the party's deputy chairs, Yaraslau Ramanchuk, an economist, ran as the party's candidate for the presidency in 2010.

The AHBP nominated candidates for the September 2012 elections but withdrew before the balloting in protest at the detention of opposition political activists.

Leaders: Anatol LYABEDZKA (Anatoly LEBEDKO, Chair), Stanislaw BAHDANKEVICH (Honorary Chair), Lev MARGOLIN, Antonina KOVALEVA, Lyudmila PETINA (Deputy Chairs).

Conservative-Christian Party of the Belarusan Popular Front (*Konservativnaya Khrystsiyanska Partiya–Narodni Front Belarusi*—KKhP-NFB). The strongly nationalist KKhP emerged from a congress held in September 1999 by supporters of Zyanon Paznyak within the NFB-A. It was registered as a party in February 2000. The party staunchly opposed the Lukashenka regime and union with Russia and has attacked OSCE efforts to mediate between the opposition and the government as lending legitimacy to the present regime. The KKhP was a principal organizer of an "All-Belarusan Congress" that met on July 29, 2000, in Minsk and condemned any agreements that would result in a loss of Belarusan independence and sovereignty. Paznyak was reelected party leader in December 2003.

The KKhP-NFB was the only major party to boycott the October 2004 election. As expected, Paznyak later stated that he would run for president in 2006, but in January 2006, from exile in the United States, he endorsed conducting a "people's vote." The plan called for anti-Lukashenka voters to cast fake ballots, leave with the real ballots, and submit the latter to an independent commission as evidence of opposition to the incumbent. The party's seventh congress, held in May 2006, overwhelmingly endorsed Paznyak's reelection as chair, and he was reelected in December 2008.

Leaders: Zyanon PAZNYAK (Zenon POZNYAK, Chair, in exile), Yury BIELENKI (Acting Chair), Syarhey PAPKOV (Vice Chair).

Belarusan Green Party (*Belaruskaya Partya "Zyaleny"*—BPZ). The BPZ was established in 1994 by ecological activists. It supported the Five-Plus alliance in 2004 and the presidential candidacy of Alyaksandr Milinkevich in 2006. Both the BPZ and another environmental party, the **Belarusan Ecological Party of the Greens,** were subsequently threatened with liquidation by the Justice Department for failing to meet all requirements of the political party law.

In 2008 the BPZ participated in the UDF's selection of a joint candidate list for that year's parliamentary election. Deputy Chair Yury Hlushakow was expected to run for president in December 2010, but he withdrew in October, citing the failure of the opposition to decide on a single candidate.

Leaders: Aleh NOVIKAU (Oleg Novikov, Chair), Yury HLUSHAKOW (Deputy Chair).

Belarusan Christian Democracy (*Belaruskaja Hhristsijanskaja Demakratija*—BHD). In September 2007 youth leader Pavel Sevyarynets was named one of five coleaders at a founding conference for the BHD association, which intended ultimately to organize a political party of the same name. (The BHD mirrors the name of a pre–World War II party.) Meanwhile, the BHD was included among the opposition organizations supporting a joint UDF candidate list for the October 2008 lower house election. The government has not yet registered the BHD.

A party cochair, Vital Rymasheuski, was the party's 2010 presidential candidate. He was arrested after the election and was given a two-year suspended sentence. He participated in a meeting in July 2011 with six opposition parties to form a united front against the government.

Leaders: Pavel SEVYARYNETS (Pavel SEVERINETS), Heorhi DMITRUK, Vital RYMASHEUSKI (Cochairs).

Party of Freedom and Progress (*Partya Svabody i Pragrzsu*—PSP). The government has repeatedly denied registration to the PSP, which held its initial congress in November 2003 under the leadership of Uladzimir Navasyad, who at that time was a member of the House of Representatives. Following its fourth "founding congress" in April 2009, the party was again denied registration by the Ministry of Justice.

Leader: Uladzimir NAVASYAD (Vladimir Novisyad, Chair).

Other Registered Parties:

Other recently active parties include the pro-Lukashenka **Belarusan Patriotic Party** (*Belaruskaya Patryatychny Partya*—BPP); the pro-Lukashenka **Belarusan Social-Sporting Party** (*Belaruskaya Satsyalna-Sportyunaya Partya*—BSSP), which lost its one House seat in 2004; the **Republican Party** (*Respublikanskaya Partya*—RP), founded in 1994; and the **Social Democratic Party of Popular Accord** (*Satsyal Demakratychnaya Partya Narodnay Zgody*—SDPNZ), formed in 1997 by former members of the Party of Popular Accord who had opposed the latter party's 1996 absorption by the BSDP-NH.

LEGISLATURE

The controversial amended constitution of November 1996 provided for abolishing the unicameral Supreme Council and establishing a two-chamber **National Assembly** (*Natsionalnoye Sobrani*) consisting of a House of Representatives and a Council of the Republic. Although the referendum approving the constitution was declared "nonbinding" by the Constitutional Court and denounced as illegitimate by some opposition parties, a majority of the Supreme Council members on November 28 voted to abolish the Council and appointed themselves to the new House of Representatives. For a time, an anti-Lukashenka rump continued to meet as the Supreme Council, arguing that it remained the legitimate legislature.

Council of the Republic (*Soviet Respubliki*). The upper house has up to 64 members: 8 elected by local soviets from each of the country's 6 regions and the municipality of Minsk, plus 8 appointed by the president. The most recent elections took place on October 19, 2012, with the 56 elective seats being filled. Two additional seats were filled by presidential appointment. As of July 2012 the membership was 58, including the Council president and deputy president.

President: Anatoly RUBINOV.

House of Representatives (*Palata Predstaviteley*). The constitutional revisions of November 1996 provided for direct election of a 110-member lower house for a four-year term. More than 100 members of the former Supreme Council met for the first time as the new House shortly after voting to abolish the Supreme Council on November 28, 1996.

The most recent election took place on September 23, 2012. The vast majority of the winning candidates were Lukashenka loyalists who had run without party affiliation. The Central Electoral Commission described 5 of the winners as party candidates: Communist Party of Belarus, 3; Agrarian Party of Belarus, 1; Republican Party of Labor and Justice, 1. One constituency required a by-election, which returned an independent candidate.

Speaker: Uladzimir ANDREYCHANKA (Vladimir ANDREICHENKO).

CABINET

[as of November 15, 2013]

Prime Minister	Mikhail Myasnikovich
First Deputy Prime Minister	Uladzimir Syamashka (Vladimir Semashko)
Deputy Prime Ministers	Mikhail Rusy (Mikhail Rusyi)
	Anatoliy Kalinin (Anatoly Kalinin)
	Piotr Prokopovich
	Anatoliy Tozik
Ministers	
Agriculture and Food	Leanid Zayats (Leonid Zaitsev)
Architecture and Construction	Anatol' Chorny (Anatoly Cherny)
Communications and Information Technology	Mikalay Pantsyaley (Nikolai Pantelei)
Culture	Barys Sviatlou (Boris Svetlov)
Defense	Yury Zhadabin (Yuri Zhadobin)
Economy	Mikalay Snapkou (Nikolai Snopkov)
Education	Syarhey Maskevich (Sergei Maskevich)
Emergency Situations	Vladimir Vaschenko (Vladimir Vashchenko)
Energy	Uladzimir Patupchyk (Vladimir Potupchik)
Finance	Andrei Kharkavets (Andrei Kharkovets)
Foreign Affairs	Uladzimir Makey (Vladimir Makey)
Forestry	Mikhail Amelyanovich (Mikhail Amelianovich)
Health	Vasil' Zharko (Vasily Zharko)

Housing and Municipal Services	Andrey Shorats (Andrey Shorets)
Industry	Dzmitry Katsyarynich (Dmitry Katerinich)
Information	Aleh Pralyaskouski (Oleg Prolekovsky)
Interior	Ihar Shunevich (Igor Shunevich)
Justice	Aleh Slizhewski (Oleg Slizhevsky)
Labor and Social Security	Mariana Shchotkina (Marianna Shchetkina) [f]
Natural Resources and Environmental Protection	Uladzimir Tsalka (Vladimir Tsalko)
Revenue and Taxes	Uladzimir Paluyan (Vladimir Poluyan)
Sport and Tourism	Alyaksandr Shamko (Alexander Shamko)
Trade	Valyantsin Chekanaw (Valentin Chekanov)
Transportation and Communications	Anatol' Sivak (Anatoly Sivak)

[f] = female

INTERGOVERNMENTAL REPRESENTATION

Ambassador to the U.S.: Oleg I. KRAVCHENKO (interim since 2009).

U.S. Ambassador to Belarus: Ethan A. GOLDRICH.

Permanent Representative to the UN: Andrei DAPKIUNAS.

IGO Memberships (Non-UN): CIS, IOM, NAM, OSCE.

BELGIUM

Kingdom of Belgium
Koninkrijk België (Dutch)
Royaume de Belgique (French)
Königreich Belgien (German)

Political Status: Independence proclaimed October 4, 1830; monarchical constitution of 1831 most recently revised in 1970.

Area: 11,781 sq. mi. (30,513 sq. km).

Population: 11,139,100 (2013E—UN); 10,444,268 (2013E—U.S. Census).

Major Urban Centers (2013E): BRUSSELS (urban area, 1,139,000), Antwerp (urban area, 502,000), Ghent (248,000), Charleroi (204,000), Liège (196,000), Bruges (117,000), Namur (110,000).

Official Languages: Dutch, French, German.

Monetary Unit: Euro (market rate November 1, 2013: 0.74 euro = $1US).

Sovereign: King PHILLIPPE; ascended the throne on July 21, 2013, following the abdication of his father, King ALBERT II.
Heir to the Throne: Princess ELISABETH, daughter of the king.

Prime Minister: Elio Di RUPO (Socialist); appointed by the king on December 5, 2011, and sworn in on December 6, 2011, to succeed Yves LETERME (Christian Democratic and Flemish), after prolonged negotiations to form a government following the federal elections on June 13, 2010.

THE COUNTRY

Wedged between France, Germany, and the Netherlands, densely populated Belgium lies at the crossroads of Western Europe. Its location has contributed to a history of ethnic diversity, as manifested by linguistic and cultural dualism between Flanders in the north and Wallonia to the south. Dutch-speaking Flanders has 58 percent of the total population; Francophone Wallonia has 31 percent, while Brussels, with 11 percent, officially bilingual. There is also a small German-speaking minority located along the eastern border. In contrast to the linguistic division, 75 percent of the population is Roman Catholic, with small minorities of Jews, Protestants, and Muslims.

The economy is largely dominated by the service sector, which provides 74 percent of GDP and employs 75 percent of the nation's labor force. Belgium's industry, responsible for less than 24 percent of GDP, has shifted from textiles, steel, and glass to production of machinery, fabricated metals, food, and chemicals. Agriculture occupies less than 2 percent of the labor force and accounts for less than 1 percent of GDP, although it supplies most food requirements. Unemployment has hovered around 8 percent since 2000.

Labor force participation rates have grown from 50 to 60 percent in recent decades but remain among the lowest in the industrialized world, with participation rates below one-third for those under the age of 25 and over the age of 55. Women constitute approximately 44 percent of the labor force. In government, women currently occupy 39.3 percent of the seats in the Chamber of Representatives and 38 percent of the seats in the Senate (42.5 percent of the elected seats). Women hold the portfolios of 6 of 15 cabinet ministries (plus 2 of 6 deputy prime ministers) and 1 of the 6 secretary of state positions.

A substantial regional imbalance exists between the more modern, industrialized Flanders and the French-speaking Wallonia, home to older, declining enterprises. This disparity was accentuated by the move to a federal governmental structure in the early 1990s, despite government efforts to reduce the imbalance.

Moderate but steady economic growth prevailed during most of the two decades after World War II, but the annual increase in GDP fell to an average of less than 2 percent following the OPEC-induced "oil shock" of 1973–1974. Higher growth in the late 1980s was accompanied by a persistent 10 percent unemployment rate and was followed by recession, although growth resumed in 1994–1995 and continued at a solid rate through 2007.

Spiking oil prices, turmoil in global financial markets, and political stalemates over forming governments contributed to a slowdown in growth beginning in 2008. GDP fell by 2.8 percent in 2009, but steadily recovered at 2.3 percent in 2010, 1.9 percent in 2011, but –0.2 percent in 2012.

The regional cultural and economic disparities have contributed to a growing separatist movement, with the wealthier Flemish community in the north considering independence. Leaders in the Francophone southern region have raised the possibility of becoming a region of France if Flanders exits Belgium. The regional standoff prolonged efforts to form a government following the 2007 and 2010 national elections.

GOVERNMENT AND POLITICS

Political background. After centuries of Spanish and Austrian rule and briefer periods of French administration, Belgium was incorporated into the Kingdom of the Netherlands by the Congress of Vienna in 1815. Independence was proclaimed on October 4, 1830, and Prince LEOPOLD of Saxe-Coburg was elected king in 1831, although Belgian autonomy was not formally recognized by the Netherlands until 1839. In the 20th century the country was subjected to German invasion and occupation during the two world wars.

Since World War II, Belgium has been governed by a series of administrations based on one or more of its three major political groups: Christian Democratic, Socialist, and Liberal. Beginning in the early 1960s, however, the traditional system was threatened by ethnic and linguistic antagonism between the Dutch- and French-speaking regions. By a series of constitutional amendments in 1970–1971, substantial central government powers were to be devolved to regional councils for Flanders, Wallonia, and Brussels (nominally bilingual but in fact largely French speaking), while German speakers also were recognized as forming a distinct cultural community.

Following up on the earlier constitutional revision, Belgium's major parties, after years of discord, agreed under the Egmont Pact of 1977 to establish a federal system based on Flanders, Wallonia, and Brussels. However, in August 1978 the Supreme Court ruled that certain aspects of the plan were unconstitutional, and on October 11 the government of Prime Minister Léo TINDEMANS was forced to resign. The ensuing general election produced a new center-left government under Dr. Wilfried MARTENS of the Christian People's Party (*Christelijke Volkspartij*—CVP) that included five of the six participating parties in the outgoing government.

In early 1980 Prime Minister Martens, bowing to militant Flemish pressure, announced the postponement of self-government for Brussels while committing his government to the establishment of regional bodies for Flanders and Wallonia. In response, representatives of the Democratic Front of French Speakers (*Front Démocratique des Francophones*—FDF) withdrew on January 16, leaving the government without the two-thirds majority needed for constitutional revision and forcing its resignation on April 9. Nonetheless, Martens succeeded in forming a "grand coalition" on May 18 that included representatives of the two Liberal parties—the Flemish Liberals and Democrats (*Vlaamse Liberalen en Demokraten*—VLD) and the Liberal Reformation Party (*Parti Réformateur Libéral*—PRL)—as well as the CVP; the Christian Social Party (*Parti Social Chrétien*—PSC); and two Socialist formations, the *Parti Socialiste* (PS) and the *Socialistische Partij* (SP). Requisite constitutional majorities thus having been restored, the government was able to secure parliamentary approval during July and August 1980 to establish councils for the Dutch- and French-speaking regions.

Alleviation of the constitutional crisis brought to the fore a number of long-simmering differences on economic and defense policies. As a result, the government resigned on October 4, 1980, and 12 days later Martens announced the formation of a center-left coalition (CVP, PSC, SP, and PS). On April 8, 1981, Martens stepped down as prime minister in favor of the CVP's Mark EYSKENS, but a general election on November 8 yielded little in the way of party realignment in either legislative house. Eventually, on December 17, Martens secured approval for a center-right administration that included both Liberal parties (the VLD and PRL) while excluding the Socialists. Having introduced an economic austerity program, the coalition marginally increased its majority in parliamentary balloting on October 13, 1985, a new government (Martens's sixth) being sworn in on November 28.

In the late 1980s linguistic controversy erupted again over specifics of regionalization. Particularly controversial was the status of a group of villages in southeastern Flanders (Les Fourons/Voeren) whose French-speaking majority doggedly resisted the authority of the surrounding Dutch-speaking region. Amid fierce interparty discord, Martens was again forced to resign on October 15, 1987. In the ensuing election of December 13 the Christian parties lost ground, and the Socialists achieved a plurality for the first time since 1936. A 144-day impasse followed, with Martens responding on May 6, 1988, to the king's request to form a new five-party government that encompassed the Christian parties, the Socialists, and the Flemish nationalist People's Union (*Volksunie*—VU), while again excluding the Liberals.

In September 1991 the VU ministers withdrew over an arms export controversy. As a result, Prime Minister Martens stepped down for the seventh time, precipitating a general election on November 24, at which the four remaining coalition parties all lost seats without collateral gains by the opposition Liberal parties. Against a groundswell of anti-immigration sentiment, the main victor was the militant Flemish Bloc (*Vlaams Blok*—VB), which overtook the less extreme VU; two environmental parties also registered substantial gains. Another lengthy interregnum ensued before the CVP's Jean-Luc DEHAENE succeeded in forming a four-party Christian-Socialist administration (Belgium's 35th since World War II) on March 7, 1992.

Although the Dehaene government lacked the two-thirds parliamentary majority required to enact constitutional amendments, the St. Michael Accords of September 29, 1992, enabled it to win a historic vote on February 6, 1993; by dint of support from the VU and the Ecologists, the government mustered the necessary Chamber majority for a constitutional amendment transforming Belgium from a unitary state into a federation of its linguistic communities. The decision was formally confirmed by the Chamber on July 14.

On July 31, 1993, a reign that had spanned more than four decades came to an end with the death of King BAUDOUIN. His brother, Prince ALBERT of Liège, was crowned on August 9.

Belgium was saved from having to find a new prime minister when the Franco-German nomination of Dehaene as European Union (EU) Commission president was vetoed by Britain in June 1994 on the grounds that he was too federalist. Meanwhile, the ruling coalition had been weakened by the Agusta-Dassault scandal, involving the PS's alleged receipt of some $3.2 million in kickbacks for expediting the award of military contracts to Italian and French firms in 1988–1989. The allegations later extended to the Flemish socialists (SP), notably to former prime minister Guy SPITAELS and to Willy CLAES, who had been economics minister in 1988 and who was appointed North American Treaty Organization (NATO) secretary general in September 1994. The Agusta affair figured prominently in the campaign for early general elections held on May 21, 1995, the first under the new federal constitution. The government parties again secured about 50 percent of the vote among them, and Dehaene was reappointed prime minister on June 23 at the head of the same four-party coalition (CVP, PSC, PS, and SP). The government subsequently faced severe difficulties in attempting to meet the criteria for participation in the EU's Economic and Monetary Union (EMU), and related job and spending cuts precipitated widespread public-sector protest strikes in 1995 and 1996.

In October 1995 the Belgian lower house voted to lift the parliamentary immunity of Claes, so that he could be brought to trial on Agusta-Dassault affair charges. As a consequence, he resigned as NATO secretary general, and in December 1998 he and a dozen other individuals were convicted of corruption, with Claes receiving a suspended three-year sentence.

Not surprisingly, the 1999 national electoral campaign largely focused on high-level corruption and law enforcement concerns. (For more on the 1999 campaign, see the 2012 *Handbook.*) In balloting on June 13, Prime Minister Dehaene's CVP lost plurality status, permitting the VLD to fashion a 94-seat, six-party majority coalition with the PS, SP, PRL, and two environmental parties, the Ecologists (*Ecologistes Confédérés pour l'Organisation de Luttes Originales*—ECOLO) and Live Differently (*Anders Gaan Leven*—Agalev). The new prime minister, VLD leader Guy VERHOFSTADT, became Belgium's first Liberal prime minister in more than a century. His "blue-red-green" coalition cut broadly across ideological lines, bringing together the rightist Liberals, the Socialists, and the Greens, while excluding the Christian Democrats from the national government for the first time in 40 years. He and his cabinet were sworn in on July 12.

At the October 2000 local elections most of the government parties fared well, but the far-right VB captured the headlines by achieving larger gains, including winning one-third of the votes in Antwerp, the country's second-largest city. Often compared ideologically to Austria's Freedom Party, the VB had campaigned on a separatist and anti-immigrant platform.

Prime Minister Verhofstadt's refusal to send troops to support U.S.-UK actions in Iraq apparently contributed to the success of the VLD and its coalition partners in the May 18, 2003, general elections. Unemployment, national security, and taxes also played prominent roles in the campaign, although the leading parties differed only slightly in their approach to those issues. Following the elections, Verhofstadt remained in office as head of another coalition government that comprised the VLD, PS, the Socialist Party–Different (*Socialistische Parti—Anders*—SP.A), the Reformist Movement (*Mouvement Reformateur*—MR), and SPIRIT (*Sociaal, Progressief, International, Regionalistisch, Integraal-democratisch en Toekomstgericht*—SPIRIT).

To address the aging workforce and rising pension costs, in 2005 the government proposed raising the minimum retirement age from 58 to 60, starting in 2008, and limiting certain long-standing retirement benefits. In response, hundreds of thousands of workers initiated the first general strike in 12 years.

The campaign for the June 2007 legislative elections raised divisive questions about constitutional reform, including proposed continued devolution of economic policy, which Walloon interests feared would mean a diminution of subsidies from the federal level. Other matters receiving attention included employment and retirement policies, energy supplies, health care reform, and the generosity of state welfare system.

Prime Minister Verhofstadt's party, running under the banner of "Open VLD," fell to third place in Flanders in the June 10, 2007, legislative balloting and finished in fourth place overall in the Chamber of Representatives. Verhofstadt accepted responsibility for the poor showing and resigned his premiership. However, he agreed to stay on in a caretaker capacity while negotiations for a new government got underway. Initially, the Flemish Christian Democrats (CD&V) leader Yves LETERME was expected to form a cross-language, Christian-Liberal Coalition of the CD&V/New Flemish Alliance (*Nieuw-Vlaamse Alliantie*—N-VA), CDH, Open VLD, and MR. But by mid-August the negotiations had collapsed over cross-community disagreement on constitutional reform, including increased economic policy control for regional governments. Leterme had campaigned on a platform of greater regional autonomy on tax and employment policies.

Leterme began another series of exploratory discussions in September, but in December he once again declared failure. Since the caretaker administration held no effective power to make or change policy, Verhofstadt formed an emergency interim government of limited powers, which received a vote of confidence in the legislature on December 23.

The protracted negotiations on a permanent government in the second half of 2007 and early 2008 represented a major crisis, some analysts wondering whether Belgium might dissolve as a single country over the matter. The five-party (CD&V, MR, PS, Open VLD, CDH) coalition of March 2008 appeared to at least temporarily prevent such a development, the new Leterme government agreeing to greater regional autonomy over industrial policy, housing, and agriculture. However, other contentious matters, such as proposed regional self-rule on tax and employment matters, were left for subsequent discussion.

Prime Minister Leterme offered his resignation on July 14, 2008, when he described the disagreement in his government over proposed additional devolution of power to Flanders as "irreconcilable." The king declined to accept Leterme's resignation, asking the government to concentrate on other matters while a new three-member mediation committee attempted to come up with fresh proposals regarding devolution.

However, the king did accept when Leterme submitted his resignation on December 19. The prime minister had been accused of interfering in the sale of Fortis Belgium, a financial services group. On December 18 a letter from the head of the Court of Cassation to the president of the Chamber of Representatives alleged that Leterme's office had tried to influence the Court of Appeals' decision. Calls for Leterme's resignation were swift. The king tapped the CD&V's Herman VAN ROMPUY to lead a government comprised of the same five parties as Leterme's administration. Van Rompuy was inaugurated on December 30, 2008.

In a sign of political change to come, the N-VA gave up its electoral coalition arrangement with the CD&V and contested the June 7, 2009, EU parliamentary and Flemish regional elections on its own. In the EU balloting there were no signs of major realignment of political support as the major parties held onto the seats they previously occupied. However, elections in the Flemish region showed a marked shift away from the more hard-line separatist VB to the N-VA, a party committed to Flemish secession but through a more patient approach than that of the VB. The newly formed List Dedecker party gained one seat at the expense of the Flemish Interest.

The new government lasted until November 2009, when Van Rompuy was elected president of the European Council and resigned the Belgian premiership on November 25. The same day the king appointed Leterme as prime minister for a third time, with the Chamber of Representatives voting, 82–52, two days later to approve his appointment as head of the same five-party government as Van Rompuy's.

Leterme's tenure was once again short-lived. In April 2010 the Open VLD resigned from government when negotiations over the Brussels-Halle-Vilvoorde electoral district broke down. The king accepted Leterme's resignation on April 26 and early elections were set for June 13.

The June 2010 balloting for the 40 elected Senate seats and all 150 seats in the Chamber of Representatives saw surges in support for the N-VA, which won vote and seat pluralities in both houses (19.6 percent in the Senate and 17.4 percent in the Chamber). The N-VA's former coalition partner and theretofore government leader CD&V fell to a distant second position in votes among Flemish parties, winning 10.0 percent in Senate contests and 10.9 percent in Chamber contests. In Wallonia the PS was the leading francophone party, receiving 13.7 percent of the Chamber vote and 13.6 of the Senate vote. (The MR had been the leading francophone party in 2007 balloting.)

The king initially appointed N-VA president Bart DE WEVER to explore government coalition possibilities, and De Wever sought negotiations with Elio DI RUPO, leader of the Walloon PS, with the intention of Di Rupo becoming prime minister because the Flemish-plus-Walloon Socialist parties commanded the largest number of seats of any of three cross-region major party groupings (Christian Democrats, Liberals, and Socialists). (The N-VA has no counterpart in the Wallonia.) In early July the king relieved De Wever of his duties and appointed Di Rupo to try and forge a coalition. Di Rupo was unable to garner enough support to forge a working coalition, and in September the king accepted Di Rupo's resignation as prospective prime minister. A second attempt by De Wever at forming a coalition failed in mid-October, leading the king to appoint Johan VANDE LANOTTE—a former leader of the SP.A/Spirit—with the task of rebuilding trust between the potential coalition parties.

Belgium's political crisis took a financial toll in late 2010 and early 2011 in response to growing concern over the country's ability to repay its debt and implement austerity measures. After several spikes in bond yields that reached ten-year highs and a downgrading of the country's credit rating by Standard & Poor's in December, King Albert II pushed for resumed coalition negotiations and strong cuts in the 2011 budget. In February 2011 Belgium set the new world record for the number of consecutive days without a government (249), and on April 26 it reached the one-year mark without a government. In response to the continuing crisis, Leterme's government was granted an unusually high degree of power for a caretaker government in order to pursue spending cuts and a new budget. After Vande Lanotte, the king turned to Didier Reynders (MR) in February 2011, Wouter Beke (CD&V) in March, and Di Rupo again in May.

In August 2011 the CD&V reversed its position on including the N-VA in any coalition talks and announced that it would be willing to consider a coalition that did not include the N-VA. Viewed as a politically risky maneuver, the move by the CD&V opened up new possibilities for the coalition formation process. Belgium's continued lack of a federal government has typically been seen as a political victory for De Wever, whose popularity has increased in Flanders.

Constitution and government. Belgium's constitution of 1831 (as amended) provides for a constitutional monarchy with a parliamentary form of government (voting being compulsory). Executive power is theoretically exercised by the monarch, who is head of state, but actual power rests with the prime minister and the cabinet, both responsible to a bicameral legislature. There are 15 members in the cabinet, 7 from each of the two language communities plus the prime minister. Formally, the cabinet is called the Council of Ministers, and the cabinet plus the secretaries of state form the executive branch, termed the Council of Government. The judicial system, based on the French model, is headed by the Court of Cassation, which has the power to review any judicial decision; it may not, however, pass on the constitutionality of legislation. That power resides with the Constitutional Court (on a limited range of federalism and nondiscrimination conflicts arising under the constitution), with the proviso that advisory opinions may be sought from a technically nonjudicial special legal body, the Council of State. There also are assize courts, courts of appeal, and numerous courts of first instance and justices of the peace.

Male primogeniture was eliminated from the law of succession in 1991. Princess Elisabeth, daughter of King Phillippe, will be Belgium's first sovereign queen when she assumes the throne.

The ethnic-linguistic reorganization finally enacted in 1993 involved the creation of three self-governing regions—Dutch-speaking Flanders, French-speaking Wallonia, and bilingual Brussels—each with directly elected assemblies of 124 (including 6 from Brussels), 75, and 75 members, respectively. There also are cultural councils for the Dutch-speaking and French-speaking communities (the former being identical with the Flanders assembly and the latter being indirectly constituted by the Wallonia assembly members and 19 members of the Brussels assembly), as well as a 25-member directly elected cultural council for the small German-speaking minority in eastern Belgium. The regional governments of Flanders, Wallonia, and Brussels are responsible to the respective assemblies, exercising broad social and economic powers; only defense, foreign relations, and monetary policy are reserved to the federal government, the size of which has been reduced as responsibilities have been devolved to the regions. Also reduced, as of the 1995 election, was the size of the central legislature (see Legislature, below). Local administration is based on ten regions and nearly 600 communes.

Belgium ranked 21st out of 179 countries in the 2013 Reporters Without Borders Index of Press Freedom.

Foreign relations. Originally one of Europe's neutral powers, Belgium has been a leader in international cooperation since World War II. It was a founding member of the United Nations (UN), NATO, the Benelux Union, and all of the major West European regional organizations. Its only overseas possession, the former Belgian Congo, became independent in 1960, while the Belgian-administered UN Trust Territory of Ruanda-Urundi became independent in 1962 as the two states of Rwanda and Burundi.

Belgium contributed to the U.S.-led multinational coalition that liberated Kuwait in early 1991. In September 1991 Belgian troops were sent to Zaire (now the Democratic Republic of the Congo) to oversee the evacuation of Belgian nationals from that strife-torn state, the action marking an effective end to Belgium's close relationship with its former colony. Belgian nationals also came under serious threat when Rwanda descended into bloody anarchy in April 1994. (In 2007 a former Rwandan army major was convicted for the killing of 10 Belgian peacekeepers in 1994.)

The cornerstone of Belgium's external policy remains active participation in the EU. Belgium was a prime proponent of the Schengen accord, providing for the abolition of border controls between certain EU members, as inaugurated in March 1995, although in November 2000 the Verhofstadt government, responding to anti-immigrant sentiment and a rising number of asylum cases, announced that it favored tighter restrictions. (In the spring of 2005 the Belgian Parliament approved the proposed new EU constitution.)

In late 2001 the Verhofstadt government hailed a 35-country agreement on international diamond certification as a necessary step toward ending the illegal trafficking in so-called conflict, or "blood," diamonds. A UN report had criticized the Antwerp diamond market, the largest in the world, for "lax controls and regulations" that permitted gem transactions to finance wars in Africa. By the time of the 2001 agreement, Belgium had already signed certification agreements with Angola, Botswana, the Democratic Republic of the Congo, Guinea, and Sierra Leone.

The Verhofstadt administration sided with many other European governments in opposing the U.S./UK-led invasion of Iraq in 2003. However, relations with Washington subsequently improved when Belgium agreed to send fighter planes to Afghanistan to help provide security for elections. Brussels later sent 585 troops to help train the Afghan army. Foreign Minister Didier REYNDERS visited Afghanistan in May 2012 and committed to signing a long-term strategic cooperation pact.

Belgium irritated both the United States and Israel with its laws that allowed individuals to file cases in Belgian courts for crimes against humanity by individuals outside of Belgian jurisdiction. Palestinians and Lebanese living in Belgium brought a case against Israeli Prime Minister Ariel Sharon in 2001, and cases were brought against U.S. President George W. Bush and British Prime Minister Tony Blair in 2003 in connection with the war in Iraq. The cases were all ultimately dismissed, and the law was amended in 2004 to make such charges more difficult to bring.

In 2006 Belgium agreed to help NATO financially but not with more troops as worldwide requests for more peacekeepers increased. Belgium dispatched peacekeepers to Kosovo in 2000, Lebanon in 2006, Afghanistan in 2009, and Libya in 2011. The government provided noncombat advisors for the conflict in Mali in 2013, as well as €31.5 million in economic aid.

In 2013 Belgium participated in the UN Security Council sessions about violent insurgent groups in the Democratic Republic of the Congo and the African Great Lakes region.

Current issues. After a record 541 days with a caretaker government in place, on December 6, 2011, Elio Di Rupo of the Socialist Party was sworn in as prime minister of a six-party coalition government. Di Rupo is the first Francophone prime minister since 1974. He speaks Dutch very poorly, which critics say will not help bridge the country's regional and cultural divide. The conservative New Flemish Alliance, the largest single party in parliament, refused to join the government and became the main opposition party.

Arguments over federalism and the redistribution of power led to the collapse of the government in 2010 and remained an obstacle throughout the months of negotiations. The main sticking point was the status of the country's largest constituency, Brussels-Halle-Vilvoorde. Unlike other voting districts, French speakers living in the predominantly Dutch-speaking Halle-Vilvoorde could vote for French parties in addition to Dutch parties, but Dutch-speakers in Brussels did not have a similar choice. On July 13, 2012, parliament voted 106 to 42 to divide the district in half—a bilingual portion inside the city and a Dutch-speaking area outside. The N-VA, which wants to abolish the capital district, criticized the decision, saying it was too costly and did not go far enough. Another regional cleavage is emerging between Brussels, where young, mostly Muslim immigrants have gravitated, and the rest of the country.

Di Rupo spearheaded negotiations over the 2012 budget, which gained additional urgency when Standard & Poor's downgraded Belgium's credit rating from AA+ to AA. He concluded a pact that included €11.3 billion in spending cuts that would result in a 2.8 percent deficit. Taking some of the most rigorous economic steps in 70 years, he predicted that Belgium would have a balanced budget by 2015.

While the budget appeared to satisfy European financial markets, government workers went on strike on December 22, idling trains and stranding holiday travelers. In particular, they objected to plans to raise the retirement age in order to defer pension costs. The king weighed in on the austerity package in January, announcing that he would personally pay many of the property management costs usually borne by the government. Di Rupo froze €1 billion in planned railway maintenance and defense procurement expenses, while the three largest trade unions staged a general strike that closed shops, schools, airports, and train stations as foreign officials were to arrive for an EU summit at the end of January 2012. The prime minister subsequently agreed to keep the current retirement age and inflation-indexed pensions. The government passed a €78 million supplemental stimulus package in July.

Provincial and municipal elections were held on October 14, 2012, across all three regions. The big winner was the nationalist New Flemish Alliance, whose leader, Bart De Wever, became mayor of Antwerp, the economic hub of northern Belgium and a Socialist stronghold for 90 years. Overall, the party won 20 out of 35 districts in Flanders. The right-wing Flemish Interest party was nearly wiped out, losing half of its voters. The new Islam Party of Belgium won two seats in Brussels, alarming right-wing politicians with its call to implement Islamic law.

Belgium and France injected €2.9 billion and €2.6 billion, respectively, into the trouble-plagued Dexia bank in early November, giving the countries almost complete ownership of the bank. The unexpected expense, the third bailout for Dexia, put further strain on Belgium's finances. The 2013 budget, released by the government on November 20, included higher taxes worth €3.4 billion to reach a budget deficit of 2.15 percent of GDP. Revenue would come from repatriated bank accounts, higher levies on alcohol, tobacco, and life insurance; pensions, health care, and sales tax were spared. The figures relied on growth of at least 0.7 percent. The actual budget deficit grew from 3.7 percent of GDP in 2011 to 3.9 percent in 2012.

The national economy stagnated in 2013, forcing the government to seek additional spending cuts. In January, Queen Fabiola, widow of King Baudouin, acknowledged plans to set up a fund to benefit her Spanish relatives—and avoid Belgium's 70 percent inheritance tax. Prime Minister Di Rupo, prompted by complaints raised by the N-VA, admonished the queen's plan and slashed her annual stipend from €1.4 million to €900,000, effective immediately.

A supplemental budget deal was passed in March, to cover the revenue gap caused by flat growth and the late 2012 Dexia bailout. New taxes were offered to help small- and medium-sized businesses, and the budget deficit prediction revised to 2.46 percent of GDP.

Tensions between Muslim immigrants and the European population increased in April, when a nationwide police raid arrested six men for allegedly recruiting young men for the Syrian insurgency. The raids were part on an ongoing official investigation into whether the group Sharia4Belgium is a terrorist organization.

Leaders of eight political parties reached agreement on the sixth state reform in July whereby healthcare, employment, and other responsibilities will shift to the regions. The new responsibilities will be funded through a one-time transfer of €20 billion. The N-VA denounced the deal as insufficient but pledged to accept the new authority and funds.

On July 3, 2013, King Albert II stunned his subjects by announcing that he would abdicate in favor of his son, Prince Phillippe, on July 21, a national holiday. "My age and health no longer allow me to carry out my duties as I would like to," he explained. As one of the few unifying forces in Belgium, Albert was instrumental in bringing forces together throughout the prolonged effort to form a government following the 2010 elections, and Phillippe may not have the same mediation skills should another intervention be needed following the June 2014 parliamentary elections. The abdication also provided an opportunity for the country to reevaluate the role of the monarchy, with many political parties calling for an end to state subsidies for members of the extended royal family. N-VA called for removing the king as the head of the armed forces and slashing of stipends to the same level as cabinet salaries. Phillippe was crowned on July 21 in a low-key, relatively low-cost ceremony.

The N-VA will likely continue to be the most popular political party, and by refusing to participate in Di Rupo's grand coalition, De Wever can easily criticize government policies. Additional constitutional reforms are under discussion, including redistributing fiscal policies, and likely will be as contentious as the Brussels-Halle-Vilvoorde issue.

POLITICAL PARTIES

Belgium's leading parties were long divided into French- and Dutch-speaking sections, which tended to subscribe to common programs for general elections. Beginning in the late 1960s the cleavages became more pronounced, leading eventually to formal separation as the country moved to a federal structure. Collaterally, the dominance of the three principal groupings (Christian Democratic, Socialist, and Liberal) has been eroded somewhat by an increase in the strength of numerous smaller ethnic and special interest groups.

Government Parties:

Socialist Party (*Parti Socialiste*—PS). Until formal separation in October 1978 the PS was the dominant French-speaking wing of the historic Belgian Socialist Party (*Parti Socialiste Belge*—PSB), an evolutionary Marxist grouping organized in 1885 as the *Parti Ouvrier Belge*. Both the PS and the SP had trade union roots and are essentially pragmatic in outlook, concentrating on social welfare and industrial democracy issues within a free-enterprise context.

Becoming the largest lower house bloc in the 1987 elections (for the first time since 1936), the two Socialist parties joined a center-left coalition but lost ground in the 1991 balloting, the PS vote slipping to 15.6 percent. It remained in the federal government and also headed the regional governments of Wallonia and Brussels, but from 1993 it was badly compromised by defense-related bribery scandals, which necessitated the resignations of several senior PS figures. It won a lower house vote share of 11.9 percent (for 21 seats) in 1995. Despite retaining only 19 seats on 10.2 percent of the vote in 1999, it remained in the new VLD-led government. The PS won 11 seats in the upper house and 25 seats in the lower house in the 2003 elections and secured the largest vote and seat shares in Wallonia in the 2004 provincial elections. By 2005, however, corruption scandals touched the party again, forcing the resignation of Jean-Claude VAN CAUWENBERGHE as minister president of the Walloon Region. In the 2006 municipal elections the PS lost ground but held its first-place standing in the Walloon region. Still suffering from the scandals, the PS vote share fell by more than 2 points, to 10.9 percent, and its seats by 5, to 20, in the 2007 Chamber balloting. The party rebounded in the 2010 balloting, and, together with its Flemish counterpart, the PS became the largest cross-region grouping in Parliament. Because the largest single party (the N-VA) had no francophone partner, PS leader Elio Di Rupo became prime minister when a government was finally agreed on December 6, 2011. The PS immediately designated Thierry GIET as acting party president.

Leaders: Elio DI RUPO (Prime Minister); Laurette ONKELINX (Deputy Prime Minister); Paul MAGNETTE (Acting President); Willy DEMEYER, Olga ZRIHEN (Vice Presidents); Rudi VERVOORT (Minister-President Brussels Capital Region); Rudy DEMOTTE (Minister-President French Community and Walloon Region); Karl-Heinz LAMBERTZ (Minister-President German Community).

Reformist Movement (*Mouvement Reformateur*—MR). The MR was formed in March 2002 through the merger of the Liberal Reformation Party (*Parti Réformateur Libéral*—PRL), the Democratic Front of French Speakers (*Front Démocratique des Francophones*—FDF), and the Citizens' Movement for Change (*Mouvement des Citoyens pour le Changement*—MCC). The Party of Freedom and Progress (*Partei für Freiheit und Fortschritt*—PFF), the German branch of the PRL, allied with the MR but remained a separate party.

The PRL had been formed in May 1979 under the leadership of Jean GOL by merger of the Party of Walloon Reform and Liberty (*Parti des Réformes et de la Liberté en Wallonie*—PRLW) and the Brussels-based Liberal Party (*Parti Libéral*—PL). Electorally weaker than its Flemish counterpart, the PRL was in government in 1981–1988 but slipped to a vote share of 8.2 percent in the 1991 Chamber elections. In 1995 it campaigned with the FDF on a joint list that captured 10.3 percent of the Chamber vote.

The FDF, a formation of French-speaking Brussels interest groups founded in 1964, sought to preserve the French character of the Belgian capital. It participated in a center-left coalition in 1977–1980 to help enact the Egmont Pact on devolution, under which Brussels became a separate (bilingual) region, but it made little progress in the 1980s. The FDF won only a 1.5 percent vote share in the 1991 balloting.

Disavowing the role of a traditional party, the MCC was organized by Gérard Deprez in March 1998, after his January expulsion from the PSC (below). The MCC was formally constituted the following October.

At the 1999 general election the PRL again joined with the FDF as well as with the recently formed MCC. The joint federation list won 18 lower house seats on a 10.1 percent vote share and joined the Verhofstadt government. PRL president, Daniel DUCARME launched the MR in December 2000, and in 2002 the MR became the country's second largest Liberal party. The MR had a respectable showing in the 2003 balloting (24 seats and an 11.4 percent vote share) and ran second to the PS in the 2004 provincial and 2006 local elections. In the 2007 Chamber balloting the MR won the second largest number of seats, 23, with a 12.5 percent vote share. In the 2010 election its vote share fell to 9.3 percent, resulting in 18 seats. The FDF quit the MR on September 25, 2011, to protest the Brussels-Halle-Vilvoorde agreement. The MR campaign for local and regional elections in October 2012 focused on job creation, school choice, and increasing public safety.

Leaders: Charles MICHEL (President); Willy BORSUS, Gérard DEPREZ, Kattrin JADIN (Vice Presidents).

Christian Democratic and Flemish (*Christen-Democratisch en Vlaams*—CD&V). The CD&V was called the Christian People's Party (*Christelijke Volkspartij*—CVP) until September 2001. The CVP and the PSC (see CDH, below) were joint heirs to the former Catholic Party (*Parti Catholique Belge*—PCB), which traced its origins to 1830 and traditionally upheld the position of the Catholic Church in Belgium. The PCB included representatives of commercial and manufacturing interests as well as of the working classes. Following World War II the PCB was reshaped into two wings, the CVP and PSC, which remained closely linked until the 1960s. Both Christian parties are now nondenominational and, with substantial representation from the Catholic Trade Union Federation (the country's largest labor organization), favor a variety of social and economic reforms. Consistently the plurality parliamentary party until 1999, the CVP provided the prime minister in a long series of coalitions, with Wilfried Martens serving for 13 years until 1992. Following its 1993 congress, the CVP committed itself to "refocus on renewal." Its lower house vote share of 17.2 percent and its 29 seats gave it plurality status in May 1995, but it fell to 22 seats and a 14.1 percent share in June 1999, as a consequence of which Prime Minister Jean-Luc Dehaene resigned. The party's current designation was formally adopted at a party congress on September 29, 2001.

The CD&V defined itself as a moderate alternative to the Verhofstadt government in the 2003 general elections. However, the party's very public stance favoring Turkey's accession to the EU apparently cost it some vote share. Following the 2003 losses, Yves Leterme was named party chair, succeeding Stefaan DE CLERCK. In the June 2004 balloting for the European Parliament, the CD&V allied itself with the N-VA (below).

The CD&V did very well in the 2004 regional Flemish elections, reestablishing itself as the largest party in Flanders. Following the election, Leterme resigned as party chair to become the Flemish prime minister. The CD&V repeated its performance in the 2006 local elections, once again in alliance with the N-VA.

In the June 2007 parliamentary elections the CD&V/N-VA alliance won the largest vote share, 18.5 percent, and the most seats, 30. In the nine months of protracted negotiations to form a new government, party leader and prospective prime minister Leterme twice resigned his formateur duties, being unable to bridge the gulf between Flemish and Francophone parties over constitutional changes that would bolster Flemish regional governmental authority. Successful negotiations concluded in February 2008, and Leterme was sworn in as prime minister on March 20 as head of a five-party government. However, he resigned the following December and was succeeded as prime minister by the CD&V's Herman Van Rompuy.

When Van Rompuy resigned in November 2009 to become president of the European Council, Leterme was reinstated as prime minister. His new government collapsed five months later, and Leterme asked Marianne Thyssen to lead the party for the June 13, 2010, election campaign. With the CD&V and N-VA running on separate and distinct lines, the CD&V and N-VA alliance lost its plurality standing in Parliament. Leterme continued to head a caretaker administration after the election. Deputy Prime Minister Steven VANACKERE resigned abruptly in March 2013 over allegations he arranged a low-interest-rate loan to a labor union linked with the party.

Leaders: Wouter BEKE (Chair), Raf TERWINGEN (Party leader, Chamber of Representatives), Kris PEETERS (Minister-President Flemish Community and Flanders Region).

Open Flemish Liberals and Democrats (*Open Vlaamse Liberalen en Demokraten*—Open VLD). In 1961 Belgium's traditional Liberal Party changed its name to the Party for Freedom and Progress (*Partij voor Vrijheid en Vooruitgang*—PVV), its Flemish wing becoming autonomous in 1970. Having participated in various coalitions in the 1970s, both the PVV and its Walloon counterpart were in government with the CVP and PSC in 1981–1988. They were regarded as occupying the coalition's right wing, in part because of their reluctance to accept federalization. In the 1991 Chamber balloting the PVV increased its vote share to 11.9 percent but remained in opposition. In November 1992 it opted for the designation of the Flemish Liberals and Democrats (*Vlaamse Liberalen en Demokraten*—VLD), to which it appended "Citizens' Party" (*Partij van de Burger*).

A smaller-than-anticipated rise to 13.1 percent of the Chamber vote (for 21 seats) in 1995 prompted the resignation of Guy Verhofstadt as party president. However, in June 1997 he was reelected as party president after only one round of voting, and he completed his comeback by being named prime minister after the June 1999 election, at which the VLD led all parties with 14.3 percent of the Chamber vote and 23 seats.

During the 2003 election campaign, the VLD continued to emphasize deregulation and tax reduction, while arguing that new EU legislation should demonstrate it would not diminish the purchasing power of European citizens or have a negative impact on employment.

In 2006 tensions within the VLD resulted in the expulsion of conservative member Jean-Marie Dedecker, who vowed to form a new right-wing party before the next federal elections and founded List Dedecker (see below). In local elections of October 8, 2006, the VLD had a weaker showing than expected, particularly in Flemish areas. Gains made by the right-wing Flemish Interest (VB) cost the VLD some representation. In an effort to stem the loss of support, the VLD contested the June 2007 parliamentary elections under the banner of Open VLD after absorbing two smaller parties—Alive (see the 2010 *Handbook*) and Liberal Appeal. The alliance failed to prevent losses as the Open VLD received only 11.8 percent of the vote. After the Open VLD lost votes and seats in the 2009 Flemish regional elections, Bart SOMERS resigned as party leader. In December 2009, Alexander De Croo, son of former leader Herman DE CROO, was elected party president. The party's electoral performance in the 2010 Chamber balloting left it in fourth position among Flemish parties with only 8.6 percent of the vote, as right-wing voters abandon it for the N-VA. Going into the 2012 election, the party called for pension reform and stricter citizenship laws. Gwendolyn Rutten defeated Egbert LACHAERT to become party president in December 2012.

Leaders: Gwendolyn RUTTEN (President); Guy VERHOFSTADT (Former Prime Minister); Alexander DE CROO (Deputy Prime Minister); Maggie DE BLOCK (Vice Chair).

Socialist Party–Different (*Socialistische Parti–Anders*—SP.A). Originally known as the Socialist Party (*Socialistische Partij*—SP), this grouping was until October 1978 the Dutch-speaking wing of the historic Belgian Socialist Party. Until 2008 it had participated in all coalitions involving its French-speaking counterpart while becoming markedly less supportive of state ownership than the PS. It slipped to a 12 percent vote share in the 1991 national balloting and won 12.6 percent (for 20 lower house seats) in May 1995. The SP also was heavily implicated in the Agusta bribery scandal, its former chair, Frank VANDENBROUCKE, becoming the most senior ministerial casualty when he was obliged to resign as deputy prime minister and foreign minister in March 1995. Party Chair Louis TOBBACK, who had been named deputy prime minister and interior minister in April 1998, resigned in September after a Nigerian was killed in custody while resisting forcible deportation.

At the June 1999 balloting SP vote support slipped further, to 9.6 percent, but it was able to negotiate a role in the VLD-led coalition government that was formed in July. The SP appended the term Anders to its name in August 2001 and then also adopted the additional alternative designation "Social Progressive Alternative" (*Sociaal Progressief Alternatief*).

Positioning itself as a prolabor and environmentally friendly party, the SP.A (which also vigorously opposed the U.S.-led invasion of Iraq) ran in coalition with SPIRIT (see Flemish Progressives, below) in the 2003 general election. The SP.A did well, increasing its share of the national vote from 9.4 to 14.9 percent and its seats from 14 to 23. As a result, the SP.A continued as part of the VLD-led government.

Although the SP.A gained votes and seats in the 2004 regional elections for the Flemish Parliament, the party performed below expectations. In 2005 party president Steve STEVAERT resigned to become governor of Limburg; he was succeeded for a brief period by Caroline Gennez until the election of Johan Vande Lanotte in October, 2005. Vande Lanotte led the party into the June 2007 federal elections and stirred controversy when he raised doubts about whether the 1915 killing of Armenians by the Turks was genocide, as the Belgian Parliament had declared, with the support of the SP.A forerunner SP, in a 1998 resolution. The SP.A again aligned with SPIRIT for the 2007 federal election, the alliance losing much of what had been gained in the 2003 federal balloting by securing only 10.3 percent of the vote and 14 seats. On June 11, 2007, the day after the balloting, Vande Lanotte resigned as party president and was replaced by Gennez. The SP.A held almost steady, in the 2010 balloting, returning 13 members to the Chamber on 9.2 percent of the vote. Bruno TOBBACK, a former minister of the environment and son of Louis Tobback, ran unopposed for party president on September 18, 2011.

Leader: Bruno TOBBACK (President).

Democratic Humanist Center (*Centre Démocrate Humaniste*—CDH). This party was originally called the Christian Social Party (*Parti Social Chrétien*—PSC), the French-speaking (Walloon) counterpart of the CVP. (The PSC and the CVP established autonomy in the late 1960s and formally separated in 1972.) The substantially smaller PSC was subsequently a junior partner in coalitions headed by the CVP, its vote share falling below 8 percent in 1991 and 1995. At the 1999 election the PSC saw its vote share drop below 6 percent despite efforts to redefine itself as a "party-movement" with a broader focus on mediating between civil society and the state. In May 2002 a PSC congress agreed to adopt the CDH rubric. The name change apparently reflected a desire to emphasize the party's support for social welfare and high levels of government intervention in the economy as well as a "Christian ethic" to guide public and private actions. It won 10 seats in the 2007 balloting for the Chamber of Representatives on a vote share of 6.1 percent and performed almost as well in 2010, winning 9 seats on a 5.5 percent vote share.

Leaders: Benoît LUTGEN (President of the Party), Joëlle MILQUET (Deputy Prime Minister, Minister of the Interior), André ANTOINE (First Vice President), Melchior WATHELET Jr. (Secretary of State for Environment, Energy, and Mobility, Second Vice President), Eric PONCIN (General Secretary).

Opposition Parties:

New Flemish Alliance (*Nieuw-Vlaamse Alliantie*—N-VA). The N-VA was established in mid-October 2001 by the largest, most conservative faction of the recently defunct People's Union (*Volksunie*—VU). Also known as the Flemish Free Democrats (*Vlaamse Vrije Democraten*), the nationalist VU had been founded in 1954 and had championed an autonomous Flanders within a federal state. After steady electoral advance on a "socially progressive, tolerant, modern, and forward-looking platform," the VU first entered the government in 1977–1978 in a center-left coalition that enacted key stages of regional devolution under the Egmont Pact. This was regarded as insufficient by its militant wing, which later joined the Flemish Bloc (VB). The VU was again in government in 1988–1991 but was overtaken by the VB in the 1991 elections, when it slipped to 5.9 percent of the lower house vote. The VU secured 4.7 percent of the vote in 1995 and claimed five seats, but advanced to 5.6 percent and eight seats in a 1999 coalition with the ID21 (see Flemish Progressives, below). Intraparty ideological differences led to the VU's demise in the summer of 2001, shortly after it had been embarrassed by the forced resignation of Johan SAUWENS, interior minister of the Flemish regional government, because of his association with a pro-Nazi organization.

The N-VA's principal goal is formation of an independent Flanders republic. Regarded as the heir of the VU (but having rejected Nieuwe Volksunie as its name), the N-VA also attracted members of the VU's middle wing, while the more liberal "Future" wing subsequently joined the ID21 in establishing SPIRIT. Like its predecessor, the N-VA adamantly rejects the far-right posture of Flemish Interest and frames its argument for Flemish independence on the basis of international law and the principle of self-determination.

In the federal elections in 2003 the N-VA won only 5 percent of the vote and a single seat in the Chamber. In February 2004 the party formed an alliance with the CD&V and won six seats in the Flemish Parliament. In the 2006 local elections and the 2007 legislative elections, the N-VA joined forces with the CD&V. Although the N-VA declined to join the cabinet formed in March 2008 because the government program did not go far enough on questions of economic policy autonomy for Flanders, the party initially pledged to support the Leterme government. (The N-VA at that point claimed six members in the lower house and one senator.) However, frustrated over the lack of progress on the further devolution of powers to the regions, the N-VA withdrew its pledge of support for the government in September. The break with its coalition partner paid political dividends as the party won 16 seats in the Flemish regional elections in June 2009, mostly at the apparent expense of the VB, and a plurality of 27 Chamber seats in the federal Parliament in the 2010 poll. However, N-VA leader Bart De Wever was unable to form a new government. The party won 20 of Flanders' 35 districts in October 2012, with De Wever becoming mayor of Antwerp.

Leaders: Bart DE WEVER (Chair), Ben WEYTS (Vice Chair), Andries GRYFFROY (General Secretary).

Flemish Interest (*Vlaams Belang*—VB). Previously known as the Flemish Bloc (*Vlaams Blok*—VB), this grouping contested the election of December 1978 as an alliance of the National Flemish Party (*Vlaamse Nationale Partij*—VNP) and the Flemish People's Party (*Vlaamse Volkspartij*—VVP). The right-wing VB was formally constituted as a unified party in May 1979. Capitalizing on an upsurge in anti-immigrant sentiment, it increased its lower house representation sixfold (to 12) in 1991, with a 6.6 percent vote share, ahead of the more moderate People's Union (VU; see N-VA, below). In the 1994 local elections the VB won a 29 percent plurality in Antwerp but was excluded from the mayorship by the other parties. Its share of the Chamber vote in 1995 was 7.8 percent, for 11 seats, rising to 9.9 percent and 15 seats in 1999. In the October 2000 local elections the VB made additional gains, prompting the Flemish *De Morgen* paper to comment, "One in three Antwerp citizens believes in fear, intolerance, unadulterated racism, and law and order."

The party became increasingly nationalistic in the 2003 election campaign, decrying the "Islamization of Europe" and calling for independence for the Flemish part of Belgium. After the Flemish Bloc won 18 seats in the Chamber vote, the Supreme Court upheld a lower court's decision that the bloc's policies violated antiracist laws. Consequently, the bloc disbanded in November and reformed as Flemish Interest, but only after running a vigorous campaign in the June 2004 balloting for the European Parliament and winning the second highest vote share among all Belgian parties. Under the Flemish Interest banner, the VB held its position in the 2006 municipal elections and again in the 2007 parliamentary balloting, recording a 12 percent vote share. However, other parties continued to exclude Flemish Interest from government as an extension of the "*cordon sanitaire*" that had been applied to the Flemish Bloc. The VB lost electoral ground to the N-VA in the 2010 balloting, winning only 7.8 percent of the vote and 12 seats. In 2012 the party set up a hotline for citizens to report "problems and nuisances" caused by illegal immigrants.

Leaders: Bruno VALKENIERS (President), Marijke DILLEN (Vice President).

Ecologists (*Ecologistes Confédérés pour l'Organisation de Luttes Originales*—ECOLO). Formed in 1978, the Walloon-based ECOLO, which takes a libertarian approach to environmentalism, won 5 Chamber seats in 1985, 2 of which were lost in 1987. It recovered strongly in 1991, capturing 10 lower house seats and a 5.1 percent vote share, which slipped to 4 percent and 6 seats in 1995. In June 1999 the party advanced to 7.4 percent and 11 seats, thereafter joining the new VLD-led government. However, it was dropped from the government following its disappointing performance in the 2003 general election. ECOLO suffered a small setback in the 2006 local elections but rebounded in the 2007 federal balloting, winning a 5.1 percent vote share, up 2 points over 2003, and 8 seats. It faired nearly as well in 2010, retaining its 8 seats on 4.8 percent of the vote. Emily HOYOS and Olivier DELEUZE were elected to four-year terms as co-presidents on March 4, 2012. The party had its best showing to date in the 2012 municipal elections.

Leaders: Emily HOYOS, Olivier DELEUZE (Co-Presidents).

Green! (*Groen!*). ECOLO's Flemish counterpart, this party was formally known as Live Differently (*Anders Gaan Leven*—Agalev), which obtained 4 lower house seats in the 1985 balloting, 6 in 1987, and 7 in 1991, when its vote share was 4.9 percent. Agalev fell back to 4.4 percent of the Chamber vote (for 5 seats) in 1995. Loosely allied with the VLD and ECOLO, Agalev won 7 percent of the vote in 1999 and then joined the governing coalition. The new party name was adopted in November 2003, Agalev having won no seats in the May general election.

In 2003 the party also gave permission to local divisions to form alliances with other parties. In November 2003 the party replaced Dirk HOLEMANS as party leader with Vera Dua. In the 2006 local elections Green! fared well in Brussels. The party also improved in the 2007 parliamentary election, winning 4.0 percent of the vote and four Chamber seats. Despite vote and seat levels holding steady in the 2009 Flemish regional parliamentary election, former leader Mieke VOGELS considered the results below expectation and resigned her position. The 2010 federal election saw a slight increase in votes to 4.4 percent, which resulted in five seats. The party absorbed the Social Liberal Party (*Sociaal-Liberale Partij*—SLP), in late 2009. (For more on the SLP, see the 2013 *Handbook*.) In January 2012, the party dropped the exclamation point from its name, as part of an effort to appear more moderate and mature.

Leaders: Wouter VAN BESIEN (Chair), Elke VAN DEN BRANDT (Vice Chair).

Libertarian, Direct, Democratic (*Libertair, Direct, Democratisch*—LDD). Libertarian, Direct, Democratic was established in January 2007 by Jean-Marie Dedecker after he was expelled from the VLD in 2006. (Dedecker had fiercely campaigned against SP.A candidates in the recent municipal elections and had strongly [and very publicly] criticized the VLD's subsequent decision to form a coalition with the SP.A in the municipality of Ostend.) Originally known as The List Dedecker, Dedecker initially sought a place in the pro-Flemish independence N-VA, but this threatened the N-VA alliance with the CD&V because the CD&V objected to Dedecker's membership. By early spring 2007 two Flemish Interest members of Parliament had joined List Dedecker, and in May an SP.A senator joined the new party. List Dedecker contested the 2007 federal elections on a market-liberal platform of lower tax rates and reduced unemployment benefits along with a pro-Flemish independence stand favoring self-determination for the province and an end to the *cordon sanitaire* that excludes Flemish Interest from government. The 2007 federal elections proved a success for List Dedecker as the party won a 4.0 percent vote share and five Chamber seats, as well as one Senate seat. That success was short-lived as the party fell to no Senate seats and only one chamber seat (on a vote share of just 2.3 percent) in the 2010 parliamentary elections. The party adopted its new name on January 22, 2011, and focused on reducing taxes and traffic in its 2012 campaign.

Leaders: Jean-Marie DEDECKER (Chair), Steven EVERAERT (National Party Secretary).

Other Parties That Contested the 2010 Elections:

National Front (*Front National*—FN). Inspired by the French party of the same name and based in the Walloon community, the right extremist FN was founded in 1983 on a platform of opposition to non-European immigration. It won one Chamber seat in 1991 with 1.1 percent of the vote and took two seats on 2.3 percent of the lower house vote in 1995. In 1999 it fell back to one seat and 1.5 percent of the vote. After the 2003 elections it held one Chamber seat and two senate seats. Party leader Daniel Féret was sentenced in 2006 to 250 hours of community service (helping immigrants) after he was found guilty of inciting racial hatred. The court also ruled he could not stand in elections for 10 years, and he lost his seat in Parliament. Féret said he would consider seeking asylum in Russia. Despite these setbacks, the FN held its 2.0 percent vote share in the 2007 Chamber balloting, securing one seat. It fell to 0.5 percent of the vote and no seats in 2010. In late 2011 the FN changed its name to National Democracy (*Démocratie Nationale*), rallying the francophone population to prevent the Islamization of Belgium.

Leader: Marco SANTI (President).

People's Party (*Parti populaire*—PP). A principally francophone party founded by Rudy AERNOUDT and Mischaël MODRIKAMEN in November 2009, the PP modeled itself on right-leaning Spanish and French popular parties, though with a moderate stance on immigration and cultural assimilation issues and with a decidedly pro-federal emphasis. The PP contested its first election in the June 13, 2010, national balloting and returned one member to the lower house on a vote of 1.3 percent. Its continued existence was subsequently called into doubt as the two founders parted ways in August over Mondrikamen's implicit endorsement of France's Roma deportation policy and his less than full-throated support for the party's federal principles. Aernoudt's public disapproval ultimately led to his expulsion from the party. Modrikamen announced he was resuming his law practice in 2012 but planned to enter the 2014 federal election.

Leaders: Mischaël MODRIKAMEN (President), Sophie COLIGNON (Vice President).

Other parties that participated unsuccessfully in the 2010 elections included the **Rally Wallonia-France** (*Rassemblement Wallonie-France*—RWF), which was founded in November 1999 by the merger of three small parties supporting unification with France: the Walloon Rally (*Rassemblement Wallon*—RW); the Walloon Democratic Alliance (*Alliance Démocratique Wallonne*—ADW), a 1985 splinter from the RW; and the Walloon Movement for the Return to France (*Mouvement Wallon pour le Retour à la France*—MWRF). The RWF Brussels branch is the *Rassemblement Bruxelles-France* (RBF). The party leadership includes Laurent BROGNIET (Co-President) with Paul-Henri GENDEBIEN (Founding and Co-President).

The Maoist **Belgian Party of Labor** (*Partij van de Arbeid van België/Parti du Travail de Belgique*—PvdA/PTB), led by Peter MERTENS was established in 1979 in opposition to the Eurocommunist line of the PCB/KPB. It lost the races it contested in 2010 but won 52 local seats in 2012.

Other Parties:

Belgium's smaller political parties include the nationalist **New Belgian Front** (*Front Nouveau de Belgique/Front Nieuw België*—FNB), established in 1997 by former FN member Marguerite BASTIEN and currently led by François-Xavier ROBERT. Other small Walloon formations include the leftist **Walloon Party** (*Parti Wallon*—PW), which was founded by merger in 1985 and which won 0.2 percent of the lower house vote in 1999.

Parties representing the German-speaking community include the **Party of Belgian German-Speakers** (*Partei der Deutschsprächigen Belgier*—PDB), founded in 1971, renamed **Pro-DG** in 2008, and currently led by Oliver PAASCH. Parties of the left include the Wallonia-based **Communist Party** (*Parti Communiste*—PC), led by Pierre BEAUVOIS, and the Flanders-based **Communist Party** (*Kommunistische Partij Vlaanderen*—KP), led by Jaak PERQUY. Both trace their origins to the historic Belgian Communist Party (*Parti Communiste de Belgique/Kommunistische Partij van België*—PCB/KPB) founded in 1921.

LEGISLATURE

The bicameral **Parliament** (*Federale Parlament/Parlement Fédérale*) consists of a Senate and a Chamber of Representatives, both elected for four-year terms and endowed with virtually equal powers. The king may dissolve either or both chambers on the advice of the prime minister.

Senate (*Senaat/Sénat*). The upper house consists of 71 members, of which 40 are directly elected (25 from Flanders, 15 from Wallonia), 21 are indirectly elected (10 each by the Flemish Council and the French Council, and 1 by the German Council), and 10 are appointed by the elected senators (6 Flemish and 4 Walloon). At least six of the Walloon senators must be legally resident in Brussels, as must at least one of the Flemish senators. In addition, the reigning monarch's children or Belgian heirs are senators by right from the age of 18, with voting rights from the age of 21. Following the election of June 13, 2010, the distribution of elected seats (with directly elected seats in parentheses) was as follows: New Flemish Alliance, 14 (9); Socialist Party (Walloon), 13 (7); Christian Democratic and Flemish 7 (4); Reformist Movement, 8 (4); Socialist Party-Different, 7 (4); Open Flemish Liberals and Democrats, 6 (4); Flemish Interest, 5 (3); Ecologists, 5 (2); Democratic Humanist Center, 4 (2); and Green!, 2 (1).

President: Sabine de BETHUNE.

Chamber of Representatives (*Kamer van Volksvertegenwoordigers/Chambre des Représentants*). The lower house consists of 150 deputies directly elected by proportional representation and compulsory adult suffrage from multimember electoral districts. Each district's complement of deputies is in proportion to population. The election of June 13, 2010, yielded the following distribution of seats: New Flemish Alliance, 27; Socialist Party (Walloon), 26; Reformist Movement, 18; Christian Democratic and Flemish, 17; Open Flemish Liberals and Democrats, 13; Socialist Party-Different, 13; Flemish Interest, 12; Democratic Humanist Center, 9; Ecologists, 8; Green!, 5; List Dedecker, 1; Popular Party, 1.

President: André FLAHAUT.

CABINET

[as of September 12, 2013]

Prime Minister	Elio Di Rupo (PS)
Deputy Prime Ministers	Koen Geens (CD&V)
	Laurette Onkelinx (PS) [f]
	Alexander de Croo (Open VLD)
	Johan Vande Lanotte (MR)
	Didier Reynders (MR)
	Joëlle Milquet (CDH) [f]
Ministers	
Budget and Administration Simplification	Olivier Chastel (MR)
Civil Service and Public Enterprises	Inge Vervotte (CD&V) [f]
Climate and Energy	Paul Magnette (PS)
Defence	Pieter De Crem (CD&V)
Economy, Consumers, and the North Sea	Johan Vande Lanotte (MR)
Employment	Monica De Coninck (SP.A) [f]
Finance and Sustainable Development	Koen Geens (CD&V)
Foreign Affairs, Foreign Trade and European Affairs	Didier Reynders (MR)
Interior	Joëlle Milquet (CDH) [f]
Justice	Annemie Turtelboom (Open VLD) [f]
Middle Classes, Small and Medium Enterprises, the Self-Employed and Agriculture	Sabine Laruelle (MR) [f]
Pensions	Alexander de Croo (Open VLD)
Public Enterprises, Science Policy, and Development Cooperation	Jean-Pascal Labille (PS)
Social Affairs and Public Health	Laurette Onkelinx (PS) [f]
Secretaries of State	
Environment, Energy, and Mobility	Melchior Wathelet Jr. (CDH)
Social Affairs, Family Policy, and the Disabled	Philippe Courard (PS)
Institutional Reforms	Servais Verherstraeten (CD&V)
Asylum and Migration Policy, Social Integration, and Fight against Poverty	Maggie De Block (Open VLD) [f]
Civil Service and Modernization of Public Services	Hendrik Bogaert (CD&V)
Fight against Social and Tax Fraud	John Crombez (PS)

[f] = female

INTERGOVERNMENTAL REPRESENTATION

Ambassador to the U.S.: Jan MATTHYSEN.

U.S. Ambassador to Belgium: Howard G. GUTMAN.

Permanent Representative to the UN: Bénédicte FRANKINET.

IGO Memberships (Non-UN): ADB, AfDB, CEUR, EBRD, EIB, EU, IADB, ICC, IEA, IOM, NATO, OECD, OSCE, WTO.

BELIZE

Political Status: Former British dependency; became independent member of the Commonwealth on September 21, 1981.

Area: 8,867 sq. mi. (22,965 sq. km).

Population: 327,264 (2012E—UN); 334,297 (2013E—U.S. Census).

Major Urban Centers (2010E): BELMOPAN (13,600), Belize City (53,500).

Official Language: English. Spanish is the country's second language, and a form of English creole is widely spoken.

Monetary Unit: Belizean Dollar (market rate November 1, 2013: 1.99 dollars = $1US).

Sovereign: Queen ELIZABETH II.

Governor General: Sir Colville YOUNG; sworn in November 17, 1993, following the resignation of Dame Minita Elvira GORDON.

Prime Minister: Dean BARROW (United Democratic Party); sworn in on February 8, 2008, succeeding Said MUSA (People's United Party), following legislative election of February 7; reelected as part of legislative election of March 7, 2012, and sworn in on March 21.

THE COUNTRY

Located on the Caribbean coast of Central America, bordered by Mexico's Yucatan Peninsula on the north and by Guatemala on the west and south, Belize is slightly larger than El Salvador but with less than 3 percent of the latter's population. Most of the inhabitants are of mixed ancestry. Mestizos of Spanish and Mayan Indian derivation comprise the largest part of the population (48.7 percent), while Creole descendants of African slaves and English settlers form the second largest group (24.9 percent). Other smaller ethnic groups include Amerindians (mainly Mayans), African Caribbeans (*Garifunas*), Asians, German Mennonites, and others of European descent. Roman Catholics constitute the largest religious group (40 percent).

Approximately three-quarters of the country is forested, but the quality of its timber has been depleted by more than two centuries of exploitation by British firms. Less than a fifth of the country's arable land, located primarily in the south, is under cultivation. The economy suffers from chronic trade deficits. Nearly one-quarter of the country's population lives in Belize City, where living conditions are poor. Despite the poor living conditions, however, school attendance is high, and adult literacy is nearly 80 percent.

The principal export commodities are agricultural, particularly bananas, sugar, and citrus. Tourism is an increasingly important economic sector, with the total contribution of travel and tourism to GDP standing at over 30 percent. Revenues have also been bolstered by the discovery of an oil field in Spanish Lookout in western Belize, although output remains low. In 2009 the economy recorded no growth, mostly due to the effects of the worldwide recession, including a drop in consumer spending and tourism, and flooding that occurred in 2008, which caused a significant drop in agricultural output. Also in 2009 the government reported a significant increase in poverty from a 2002 assessment; it increased from 34 percent to 41 percent, with indigence rising by 50 percent. GDP growth has resumed, with 5.3 percent for 2012, and with 4.05 percent growth forecast for 2013. Unemployment dropped from 12.7 percent in 2009 to 10.5 percent in 2012.

GOVERNMENT AND POLITICS

Political background. Initially colonized in the early 17th century by English woodcutters and shipwrecked sailors, the territory long known as British Honduras became a Crown dependency governed from Jamaica in 1862 and a separate colony in 1884. The country's western boundary was delineated in an 1859 convention that was repudiated by Guatemala in 1940 (see Foreign relations, below). Internal self-government was granted under a constitution effective January 1, 1964, and the official name was changed to Belize in June 1973. Although the dispute with Guatemala remained unresolved, independence was granted on September 21, 1981, with Great Britain agreeing to provide for the country's defense "for an appropriate period." At independence, George Cadle PRICE, who had served continuously in an executive capacity since his designation as first minister in 1961, was named prime minister.

In the country's first postindependence election on December 14, 1984, the electorate rejected three decades of rule by Price's People's United Party (PUP), turning by a substantial margin to the more conservative United Democratic Party (UDP) led by Manuel A. ESQUIVEL. However, in balloting on September 4, 1989, the PUP returned to power, in a narrow electoral victory (50.3 to 48.4 percent) over the incumbent UDP.

Buoyed by sweeping victories in a 1993 parliamentary by-election in January and local government balloting in April, Prime Minister Price called a snap lower house election for June 30. This proved a mistake, as the opposition UDP captured 16 of 29 seats, returning Esquivel to government leadership. However, PUP swept municipal balloting on March 11, 1997, winning all seven town boards, and went on to a conclusive victory in the lower house poll of August 27, 1998, winning 26 of 29 seats. Shortly thereafter Said Musa was named to succeed Esquivel as prime minister, and he remained in office following the PUP victory in the election on March 5, 2003.

After the 2003 elections, public support for PUP declined substantially amid a weakening economy and allegations of financial mismanagement and corruption. Among other accusations, the PUP administration lost large sums of social security funds in risky investments, some of which were run by party supporters. In May 2009, the Supreme Court of Belize ruled that the loan note signed by Musa with the Belize Bank for $17.2 million on behalf of the United Health Service was unlawful because any loan agreement of that size had to be approved by the National Assembly. The Belize government demanded the Belize Bank return the money paid to satisfy the voided loan. In June, the Court ruled that there was insufficient evidence to put Musa on trial.

The UDP won 64 of 67 seats in the municipal elections on March 1, 2006. This landslide foreshadowed the UDP victory in the February 2008 general elections, in which the party secured 25 seats in the House of Representatives. UDP party leader Dean BARROW was sworn in as prime minister on February 8 and named a UDP cabinet four days later. The UDP's electoral success continued in 2009 when it again swept municipal elections, retaining all 64 seats.

The UDP narrowly won a snap parliamentary election in March 2012, and Barrow remained prime minister.

Constitution and government. With modifications appropriate to Britain's yielding of responsibility in the areas of defense, foreign affairs, and the judiciary, Belize's 1981 constitution is structured after its 1964 predecessor. The British Crown is represented by a governor general of Belizean citizenship who must act, in most matters, on the advice of a cabinet headed by a prime minister. The National Assembly, with a normal term of five years, is a bicameral body currently encompassing a 31-member House of Representatives elected by universal adult suffrage, plus the speaker, if not an elected member, and an appointed Senate of 13 members. Cabinet members may be drawn from either house, except that the finance minister must sit in the House of Representatives, where all money bills originate. Freedom of the press is constitutionally guaranteed, and there are few restrictions on the media. However, in September 2009 the government took control of Belize Telemedia Limited, the nation's largest telecommunications firm.

The governor general is empowered to appoint a 5-member Elections and Boundaries Commission and, on the advice of the prime minister, 8 members of a 13-member Public Services Commission (the remaining members serving ex officio). The judicial system includes a Supreme Court as superior court of record, whose chief justice is appointed on the advice of the prime minister after consultation with the leader of the opposition, and a Court of Appeal. There also are courts of summary jurisdiction and civil courts in each of the six districts into which the country is divided for administrative purposes.

In the nation's first-ever referendum on February 7, 2008, voters were also asked whether they thought the Senate should be directly elected. While 61.5 percent of voters supported the measure, the prime minister rejected the results, preventing the implementation of the proposed reform.

Following a constitutional amendment in February 2010, Belize announced that it would join the Caribbean Court of Justice (CCJ). The CCJ would replace the British Privy Council as the nation's highest appellate court.

Foreign relations. Belize became a full member of the Commonwealth upon independence and was admitted to the United Nations in September 1981, despite a Guatemalan protest that the "unilateral creation" of an independent state in disputed territory constituted "an invitation to third powers to become protectors of Belize" and thus make Central America "an area for ambitions and confrontation." Guatemala had long contended that its dispute was with Britain, not with Belize, citing Britain's failure to fulfill certain treaty obligations of the 1859 Convention as the reason for not accepting the Belizean boundary. Thus, under its 1945 constitution, Guatemala claimed British Honduras, as Belize was first known, as part of its national territory.

After several failed attempts in 1981, 1983, and 1987, a Joint Permanent Commission was established in May 1988, with Guatemala appearing to yield in its demand for a land corridor across Belize in return for the right of free transit and guaranteed access to Belizean waters. Collaterally, British aid for road improvements on the Guatemalan side of the border was seen as a means of securing token compliance with the 1859 treaty, which lay at the heart of the dispute. The commission subsequently held a number of "positive and cordial" meetings, including a session in Miami in February 1989, which concluded with a call for talks "at a higher level" to settle on the details of a draft treaty.

In May 1990 tension again flared in the form of a clash between residents of Belize's Toledo district and Guatemalan agricultural workers who had unknowingly planted crops on the Belizean side of the border. The incident prompted a meeting between Guatemalan president Vinicio Cerezo Arévalo and Prime Minister Price on the Honduran island of Roatán on July 9, at the conclusion of which "significant progress" was reported in reaching a solution to the lengthy impasse.

In January 1991 Belize was admitted to the Organization of American States after the Guatemalan president-elect, Jorge Serrano ELÍAS, indicated that his administration would continue talks aimed at settling the controversy. Despite the statements of Guatemalan foreign minister Alvaro ARZÚ that Guatemala claimed the territory of Belize, Serrano reasserted that his administration recognized "the right of the Belizean people to self-determination" and on September 5 extended diplomatic recognition to Belmopan. Termination of the lengthy dispute was reinforced in November 1992 by the Guatemalan Constitutional Court, which upheld Serrano's action in a 4–3 vote, and on April 16, 1993, the two countries reached agreement on a nonaggression pact during a meeting in Miami. On May 13 the United Kingdom announced that its army garrison and jet aircraft would be withdrawn by August 1994.

The rapprochement with Guatemala came after Belize had agreed to reduce its southern territorial limit by three miles and to grant its neighbor access to the sea from the northern department of Petén. Belize also ceded the use of port facilities in Stann Creek and the right to participate in offshore ventures, such as oil exploration, in Belize's 12-mile economic zone. Criticism of the accord ensued in both countries: Guatemalan foreign minister Arzú resigned after insisting that Serrano's action was unconstitutional, while a faction of the Belizean UDP, the National Alliance for Belizean Rights, argued that the maritime provisions would have adverse consequences, particularly for fishermen. During another round of territorial negotiations in Miami on November 20, 1998, the Belizean delegation rejected a Guatemalan proposal that the underlying dispute be resolved by an international court, but the two governments did agree to establish a mixed commission to deal with a variety of issues concerning the rights of their respective citizens.

Following a number of border incidents, agreement was reached in September 2002 to deploy OAS observers to the disputed area pending the holding of a referendum on the issue in both countries. However, the accord was repudiated by Guatemala in August 2003, and in May 2004 new discussions were launched at OAS headquarters in Washington, D.C., to find an "equitable and permanent solution" to the controversy.

After lengthy negotiations, an Agreement on a Framework of Negotiations and Confidence Building Measures between Belize and Guatemala was signed on September 8, 2005. The document provided for a bilateral commission to undertake cooperative projects and develop a solution to the territorial dispute. Evidence of the thaw in relations was provided in October 2005 by the conclusion of the first bilateral trade accord between the two countries and again in July 2006 when they endorsed a preliminary trade agreement that would allow 150 products to be traded duty-free. Despite these positive steps a final resolution to the territorial dispute could not be reached, and on November 19, 2007, the OAS recommended that the dispute be settled by the International Court of Justice (ICJ).

In December 2008, officials from Belize and Guatemala signed an agreement to allow the ICJ to rule on the territorial dispute, pending referendums in both countries to ratify the agreement. The referendum date, October 6, 2013, was announced in May 2012. In October Guatemala approved the 2006 bilateral trade agreement. That same month, Belize and Mexico signed a trade accord to improve cooperation in agriculture.

In its 2011 Trafficking in Persons report, the U.S. State Department upgraded Belize to a Tier 2 country after it showed progress in developing legislation to fight the trade in people. Belize was still considered a major source, destination, and transit country for men, women, and children engaged in forced labor and prostitution.

Guatemala canceled the border referendum in April 2013, saying it would be too expensive.

Current issues. Out of power for the first time in a decade, the PUP began to fragment after 2008. Top members, including former prime minister and party leader Musa and Ralph Fonseca, were accused of corruption, while party leadership changed hands in 2008 and again in 2010. With the main opposition party in disarray Prime Minister Barrow called snap elections for March 7, 2012, in conjunction with already scheduled municipal elections. Crime, the economy, and energy dominated the campaign.

Violent crime has increased in Belize in recent years, and the country is ranked the sixth most-dangerous country in the world. Police blamed much of the violence on the expansion of gangs, including territorial consolidation in Belize by the Mexican Golfo Cartel, and organized crime in urban areas, especially the capital. Barrow negotiated a truce among the major criminal gangs in September 2011, and the homicide rate subsequently dropped slightly. In addition, the House of Representatives in May 2011 passed a raft of anticrime laws, including a constitutional amendment bill that provides for anonymity of witnesses, preventive detention, stronger legislation governing the use of the death penalty, and trial without a jury.

In June 2011 the government passed legislation to nationalize Belize Electricity Limited, the principal distributor and generator of power in the country. The Barrow administration also announced plans to amend existing laws to allow for the 2009 government takeover of Belize Telemedia Limited, the nation's largest telecommunications company, a move that was ruled unconstitutional by an appeals court on June 24 but did not dissuade Barrow. Both nationalization projects created budget holes that the government has been unable to plug. The government still owes shareholders $269 million.

Barrow centered his 2012 campaign on the need to restructure the debt accumulated under the most recent PUP government. In 2007 the debts had been aggregated into one "superbond," whose interest rate began at 4.5 percent, then increased to 6 percent, and up to 8.5 percent in 2012. Just the interest on the $550 million superbond would be 12 percent of government revenue. PUP candidate Francis FONSECA vowed to raise additional funds by expanding the economy, primarily through tourism. The candidates also differed on energy policy, with Barrow promising a referendum on expanding offshore oil drilling, while Fonseca pledged to institute a moratorium on that type of exploration.

Voters seemed unpersuaded by either party, giving the UDP a margin of victory of barely 3,600 votes. A group of smaller parties formed the Belize Unity Alliance, but the coalition did not win any national or local seats. The UDP won just 17 seats in the House, giving it a slim 1-seat majority. The PUP added 8 seats, rising from 6 to 14. The UDP also won six municipal elections to the PUP's three.

On August 20, 2012, Belize missed a scheduled $23 million interest payment on its superbond and threatened to default. Creditors were upset, saying they had received no warning from the government. Standard & Poor's downgraded the country's sovereign debt rating to junk status.

Street gang activity and other violence continued unabated, with a record 145 murders recorded in 2012. In November the government invoked a law to designate "crime-infested areas," allowing law enforcement to conduct warrantless searches of people and property.

In December the government reached an agreement with its creditors to restructure the debt into a superbond that was then exchanged for U.S.-denominated bonds. The deal brought a much-needed cash injection of $130 million over five years and saved $247 million in interest payments.

Government plans to drill for oil along the Mesoamerican Reef were dashed in April 2013, when the Supreme Government nullified contracts awarded between 2004 and 2007 to Princess Petroleum. The case had been filed by Oceana, Citizens Organized for Liberty through Action, COLA, and the Belize Coalition to Save Our Natural Heritage, environmental groups concerned that the winning company did not have the expertise or capital to safeguard the reef. Princess originally was a hotel and casino company. The civic groups had successfully staged a "people's referendum" on the contract on February 29, 2012. About 10 percent of the population had participated in the grassroots referendum.

POLITICAL PARTIES

Government Party:

United Democratic Party (UDP). The UDP was formed in 1974 by merger of the People's Democratic Movement, the Liberal Party, and the National Independence Party. A largely Creole grouping, the party boycotted the preindependence constitutional discussions and the independence ceremonies on the grounds that assurances of continued support by Britain were vague and uncertain. In January 1983 Manuel Esquivel was named party leader in succession to Theodore ARANDA, who withdrew from the UDP while retaining his parliamentary seat. Aranda later formed the center-right Christian Democratic Party before joining PUP in mid-1987.

After securing an unexpectedly lopsided victory in the balloting of December 14, 1984, Esquivel became head of the first non-PUP government since independence. In December 1986 the UDP triumphed again, winning all nine seats on the Belize City Council. Hampered by opposition criticism of its economic policies, the UDP lost its legislative majority in the September 1989 balloting and failed to retain a single council seat the following December.

The UDP won only 3 of 29 seats in the election of August 27, 1998, and lost all 7 seats in Belmopan's first municipal poll on March 1, 2000, while retaining control in only one of seven other municipalities. Although the party lost to the PUP by a wide margin in March 2003, it secured an overwhelming victory in the municipal poll of March 2006 when it won 64 of 67 seats. This overwhelming victory was a precursor to the UDP's huge victory in the February 2008 general elections, when it won 25 of the available 31 lower house seats after campaigning on an anticorruption platform. The UDP statement of philosophy affirms the party's commitment to social justice. Barrow promised in his inaugural address to combat the corruption of the previous administration, reduce the cost of living and unemployment, distribute land to the poor, and expand free public education.

The UDP's political dominance continued in March 2009 when it again won the majority of seats in the municipal elections. In municipal voting through May 2010, the UDP secured majorities in 24 of 39 villages. The UDP expelled Zenaida Moya-Flowers, the mayor of Belize City, from the party after she was arrested on corruption charges in October. In November the UDP's Edmund CASTRO, the minister of state in the ministry of works and a member of the House of Representatives, was stripped of his portfolio after allegations of corruption.

By 2011 the UDP's perceived inability to tackle the simmering crime and unemployment problems was viewed as the main issue the opposition would try to exploit in future elections. The UDP lost 8 seats in the snap parliamentary election of March 7, 2012, leaving it with 17, a one-vote majority.

Leaders: Dean BARROW (Prime Minister and Party Leader), Gaspar VEGA (Deputy Party Leader), Alberto AUGUST (Chair), Fern GUTIERREZ (Deputy Chair).

Opposition Party:

People's United Party (PUP). Founded in 1950 as a Christian Democratic group, PUP was dominant for most of the period after the achievement of internal self-government in 1964. After 34 years in office (largely under colonial administration), PUP was decisively defeated in the December 1984 election. Following the election, the (then current) PUP chair and right-wing faction leader Louis SYLVESTRE resigned from the party. At a January 1986 "Unity Congress," the leader of the left-wing faction, Said Musa, was elected party chair, while the leader of the rump right-wing faction, Florencio MARÍN, was elected deputy chair.

Promising a liberalized media policy and an expanded state role in the economy, PUP regained legislative control in the September 1989 election, before again losing it in the early vote of June 1993.

In May 1996 deputy chair Marín resigned, prompting speculation that he was positioning himself for a power struggle with Musa for the party leadership post. In balloting at the party's national convention on November 10, Musa outpolled Marín, 358 to 214, to capture the top PUP slot. Musa became prime minister following the party's landslide victory on August 27, 1998. Musa remained prime minister when the PUP won a comfortable victory in the general election five years later, on March 5, 2003.

The PUP's overwhelming loss in municipal elections in 2006 indicated that the PUP might lose power in the upcoming 2008 general elections. Prime Minister Musa called early elections, which were held on February 7, 2008. After the PUP won only 6 of the 31 seats in that election, Musa resigned his position as PUP party leader on February 13, 2008. On March 30 the PUP held a convention to elect a new leader. After bitter infighting within the party, John Briceño, who had been deputy leader of the party since 2006, defeated the PUP leadership's candidate, Francis FONESCA. The party won only 3 out of 67 seats in the municipal elections of March 2009. However, the PUP gained majorities in seven councils in village elections in April and May 2010.

PUP politicians in 2011 opposed elements of the anticrime legislation that was passed in the National Assembly in May on the grounds that the laws violated civil rights. The PUP also raised concerns over the nationalization of public utilities, but the highly splintered party's national prospects were not expected to improve until it could develop a strategy to counter Belize's burgeoning crime and unemployment problems. The party picked up 8 seats in the March 7, 2012, parliamentary election, giving it 14.

Leaders: Francis FONSECA (Party Leader), Henry USHER (Party Chairman).

Other Parties Contesting the 2012 Elections:

The People's National Party, Vision Inspired by the People, and a handful of independents combined forces into the **Belize Unity Alliance** to field candidates in nine constituencies in the March 2012 elections. They did not win representation at any level.

People's National Party (PNP). The PNP was organized in February 2007 and launched on February 18 in San Antonio, a village populated almost exclusively by indigenous Maya. PNP campaigned in the 2008 general elections under the banner of the National Belizean Alliance (NBA). The NBA was an alliance between the PNP, the We the People Reform Movement, and Christians Pursuing Reform. Both the PNP and the NBA were headed by Wil Maheia. The PNP stands for the elimination of government corruption and sustainable development. The PNP ran three candidates in the 2008 general elections but won no seats. The PNP held their town council convention, open to all residents of Punta Gorda Town, on November 29, 2008, and selected seven candidates to run in the March 2009 municipal elections. All candidates were defeated.

Leader: Wil MAHEIA (Party Leader).

Vision Inspired by the People (VIP). The VIP first fielded candidates in the 2003 Belmopan City Council Elections, capturing 20 percent of the vote. Encouraged by those results, the VIP decided to field candidates in the 2008 general elections. Ten VIP candidates ran for seats in the legislature, campaigning on the need to attain what they called the "five pillars of nationhood": national unity, a culture of productivity, a family life environment, social justice, and fair representation in government. VIP favored giving the electorate more political power, endorsing an elected Senate, proportional representation in the House of Representatives, and stronger referendum powers and recall power. The VIP failed to win any seats in the 2008 election. In the municipal elections in Belmopan in 2009, three of the seven VIP candidates earned more votes than the PUP candidates; the slate of candidates there won 23 percent of the cast ballots. Despite the strong showing, the VIP failed to win any municipal seats in 2009, 2010, or 2012. The party elected new leaders at its June 2013 congress.

Leaders: Hubert ENRIQUEX (Chair), Jennifer ARZU-WILLIAMS (Deputy Chair), Paul MORGAN, Sr. (Secretary General).

Other Parties:

Congress of the Punta Gorda People (CPGP). The CPGP ran three candidates in the 2009 municipal elections in Punta Gorda, winning no seats. It again failed to gain seats in 2010 and did not run in 2012.

Leader: Herman Marion LEWIS (Party Leader).

National Reality Truth Creation Party (NRTCP). The NRTCP was created in 1997 by Jorge Ernesto Baab as an outgrowth of a religious movement that challenged the ideas of racial supremacy. Baab uses his church as a vehicle for advancing the NRTCP, and vice versa. The NRTCP contested both the 1998 and the 2008 elections but with no success.

Leader: Jorge Ernesto BAAB (Founder and Party Leader).

National Reform Party (NRP). The NRP, a Christian conservative party, was founded in 2006. In 2007 it announced it would run a full slate of 31 candidates for the general elections in 2008. However, on January 19, 2008, NRP presented only 11 candidates for election. The party platform emphasized the supremacy of God, the family as the cornerstone of society, zero tolerance for governmental corruption, and the need to substantially raise the minimum wage. The NRP secured no seats in the 2008 balloting and fielded no candidates in the 2009 or 2010 municipal elections.

Leader: Cornelius DUECK (Party Leader).

LEGISLATURE

The Belize **National Assembly** is a bicameral body consisting of an appointed Senate and a directly elected House of Representatives, both serving five-year terms, subject to dissolution.

Senate. The upper house currently has 12 members, plus the Senate president. The governor general appoints 6 members on the advice of the prime minister, 3 on the advice of the leader of the opposition, and 3 on the advice of various sectors of society.

President: Marco PECH.

House of Representatives. In 2005 a reorganization of electoral districts increased the number of districts from 29 to 31. The 31 members of the lower house, one representing each district, are elected by universal adult suffrage for five-year terms. In the election of March 7, 2012, the United Democratic Party won 17 seats, while the People's United Party won 14.

Speaker: Michael PEYREFITTE.

CABINET

[as of September 30, 2013]

Prime Minister	Dean Barrow (UDP)
Deputy Prime Minister	Gaspar Vega (UDP)
Ministers	
Education, Youth, and Sport	Patrick Faber (UDP)
Energy, Science and Technology, and Public Utilities	Joy Grant (UDP) [f]
Finance and Economic Development	Dean Barrow (UDP)
Foreign Affairs	Wilfred Elrington (UDP)
Forestry, Fisheries, Sustainable Development, and Indigenous Peoples	Liselle Alamilla (UDP) [f]
Health	Pablo Marin (PUP)
Housing and Urban Development	Michael Finnegan (UDP)
Human Development, and Social Transformation, and Poverty Alleviation	Anthony "Boots" Martinez (UDP)
Labour, Local Government, Rural Development, and National Emergency Management	Godwin Hulse (UDP)
Natural Resources and Agriculture	Gaspar Vega (UDP)
National Security, Police, and Belize Defense Force	John Saldivar (UDP)
Public Service and Elections and Boundaries	Charles Gibson (UDP)
Tourism and Culture	Manuel Heredia Jr. (UDP)
Trade, Investment, Private Sector Development, and Consumer Protection	Erwin Contreras (UDP)
Works and Transport	Rene Montero (UDP)
Attorney General	Wilfred Elrington (UDP)
Ministers of State	
Conscious Youth Development Program and Gang Truce Program	Mark King (UDP)

[f] = female

INTERGOVERNMENTAL REPRESENTATION

Ambassador to the U.S.: Nestor MENDEZ.

U.S. Ambassador to Belize: Margaret HAWTHORNE (chargé d'affaires).

Permanent Representative to the UN: Lois Michele YOUNG.

IGO Memberships (Non-UN): Caricom, CWTH, IADB, ICC, IOM, NAM, OAS, WTO.

BENIN

Republic of Benin
République du Bénin

Note: Following a year of political infighting and allegations of several coup plots (see Current issues, below), on August 8, 2013, President Boni Yayi dismissed Prime Minister Pascal Koupaki and the entire cabinet. On August 11 the president appointed a new cabinet, which excluded half of the incumbent ministers and did not include a prime minister. Yayi described the changes as designed to "inject a new team dynamic" into the government, while his critics noted that the absence of a prime minister automatically enhanced presidential authority.

Political Status: Independent Republic of Dahomey established August 1, 1960; military regime established October 26, 1972, becoming Marxist one-party system 1972–1975; name changed to People's Republic of Benin on November 30, 1975; name changed to Republic of Benin on February 28, 1990, by National Conference of Active Forces of the Nation, which also revoked constitution of August 1977; multiparty constitution approved by popular referendum on December 2, 1990.

Area: 43,483 sq. mi. (112,622 sq. km).

Population: 6,769,914 (2002C); 9,385,608 (2012E—UN).

Major Urban Centers (2010E): PORTO NOVO (289,880), Cotonou (862,445).

Official Language: French.

Monetary Unit: CFA franc (official rate November 1, 2013: 486.52 CFA francs = $1US). The CFA franc is permanently pegged to the euro at 655.957 CFA francs = 1 euro.

President: Boni YAYI (nonparty); elected in second-round balloting on March 19, 2006, and inaugurated for a five-year term on April 6 to succeed Brig. Gen. (Ret.) Mathieu KÉRÉKOU; reelected to another five-year term in first-round balloting on March 13, 2011.

Prime Minister: (*See headnote.*) Pascal Irénée KOUPAKI; appointed by the president on May 28, 2011. (The post had been vacant since May 8, 1998, when Adrien HOUNGBÉDJI [Party of Democratic Renewal] resigned and President Kérékou did not name a successor, the post not being constitutionally required. President Yayi also did not include a prime minister in the cabinets he named in April 2006, June 2007, October 2008, and June 2010.)

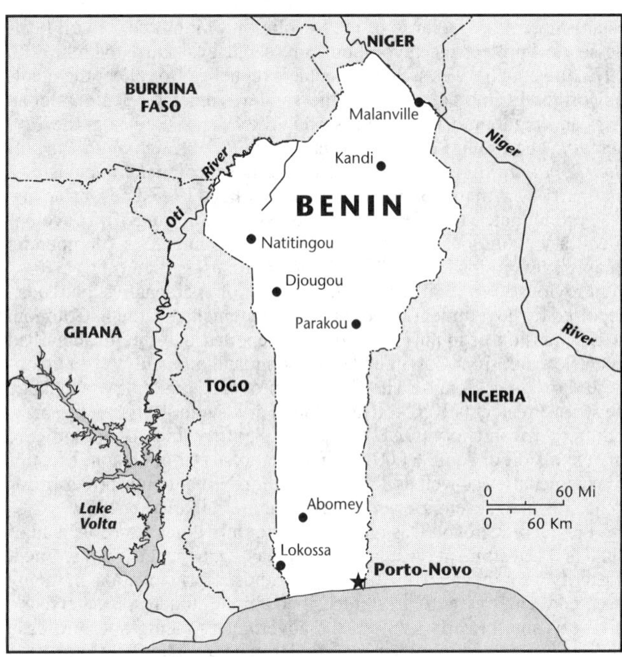

THE COUNTRY

The elongated West African state of Benin (formerly Dahomey) lies between Togo and Nigeria, with a southern frontage on the South Atlantic and a northerly bulge contiguous with Burkina Faso and Niger. The country's population exhibits a highly complex ethnolinguistic structure, the majority falling within four major tribal divisions: Adja, Bariba, Fon, and Yoruba. The principal tribal languages are Fon and Yoruba in the south and Bariba and Fulani in the north. Approximately 70 percent of the people are animists, the remainder being almost equally divided between Christians (concentrated in the south) and Muslims (concentrated in the north). The labor force includes nearly three-quarters of the adult female population, which is concentrated primarily in the cultivation of subsistence crops. Although female participation in government was previously minimal (the first female cabinet member was named in 1989), there are seven women in the current cabinet, and seven women were elected to the National Assembly in 2011.

Benin is one of the world's poorest countries, with an average per capita wage of only $3 per day. It has been reported recently that 60 percent of adults are illiterate, while only 50 percent of school-age children attend school. The country also ranks near the bottom in other "quality of life" measures, a high rate of population growth having hindered recent antipoverty initiatives. The economy is based primarily on agriculture, with cotton accounting for 40 percent of GDP and more than 75 percent of export volume. Other exports include textiles, cocoa, and various oilseeds. Benin's major trading partner, France, subsidizes current expenses as well as basic development. Black-market activity is widespread, and contraband trade, especially with Nigeria, is a significant source of income for many Beninese. Small deposits of oil and gas have been located, although exploitation has been minimal and significant impact from that sector on the economy is not currently anticipated.

The government adopted a strongly Marxist orientation in the mid-1970s but thereafter moved to privatize a number of state-run companies in an effort to counter high external debt, corruption, and severe economic stagnation. In addition, wide-ranging austerity measures were adopted, facilitating international aid agreements but also contributing to social unrest. In 1998 the International Monetary Fund (IMF) reported that Benin's implementation of a structural adjustment program in the mid-1990s had resulted in "real income growth, a decline in inflation, and a reduction in internal and external imbalances." Additional debt relief was announced in 2000 and 2003, although concern was expressed in some quarters that the nation's poor were not benefiting from economic advancement.

The IMF has described the government's economic policies as "broadly satisfactory" but has continued to press for reform in the cotton sector and banking system. Growth was subdued in 2010, compromised by the effects of the global recession and by flooding (the worst in 50 years) in September–October, which destroyed more than 50,000 homes and heavily damaged farmlands. GDP grew by approximately 3.5 percent in both 2011 and 2012, while higher prices on gasoline imported from Nigeria contributed to a spike in inflation in the latter year to more than 6 percent. The IMF characterized the medium-term outlook as favorable, although it called for additional infrastructure development, emphasis on policies designed to promote the private sector, and implementation of poverty-reduction programs.

GOVERNMENT AND POLITICS

Political background. Under French influence since the mid-19th century, the territory then known as Dahomey became self-governing within the French Community in December 1958. However, Dahomey permitted its community status to lapse upon achieving full independence on August 1, 1960. During the next 12 years, personal and regional animosities generated five military coups d'état, most of them interspersed with short-lived civilian regimes.

The country's first president, Hubert MAGA, was overthrown in October 1963 by Col. Christophe SOGLO, who served as interim head of state until the election in January 1964 of Sourou-Migan APITHY. In December 1965, after a series of political crises and a general disruption of civilian government, Soglo again assumed power as president of a military-backed regime. Another military coup, led by Maj. Maurice KOUANDÉTÉ on December 17, 1967, ousted Soglo and established an interim regime under Lt. Col. Alphonse ALLEY. Following an abortive attempt at a new election in May 1968, the former foreign minister, Dr. Émile-Derlin ZINSOU, was appointed president of a civilian administration. In December 1969 the Zinsou government was overthrown by Kouandété, and military rule was reinstituted. After another failed election in March 1970, the military established a civilian regime based on the collective leadership (Presidential Council) of the country's three leading politicians: Justin AHOMADEGBE, Apithy, and Maga. On October 26, 1972, following an unsuccessful coup attempt by Kouandété in February, the triumvirate was overthrown by (then) Maj. Mathieu KÉRÉKOU. The new president abolished the Presidential Council and Consultative Assembly and established a Military Council of the Revolution committed to a division of posts on the basis of regional equality.

On December 3, 1974, President Kérékou declared that Dahomey was to become a "Marxist-Leninist state," and two days later he announced that the nation's banks, insurance companies, and oil distribution facilities would be nationalized. Subsequently, he ordered the establishment of "Defense of the Revolution Committees" in all businesses to "protect the revolution from sabotage." On November 30, 1975, the country was styled a "people's republic" (to reflect the ideology officially embraced a year earlier) and was renamed Benin, after an African kingdom that had flourished in the Gulf of Guinea in the 17th century. The Benin People's Revolutionary Party (*Parti de la Révolution Populaire du Bénin*—PRPB) was established as the nucleus of a one-party system the following month. In August 1977 a new basic law was promulgated to reflect a commitment to three stages of development: a "revolutionary national liberation movement," a "democratic people's revolution," and a "socialist revolution."

Previously, in January 1977, a group of mercenaries had been repulsed by government forces in a brief but pitched battle in Cotonou. A UN mission of inquiry subsequently reported that the invaders had been flown in from Gabon under the command of an adviser to Gabonese President Bongo. The incident provoked an angry exchange between Presidents Kérékou and Bongo at a summit of the Organization for African Unity (OAU) in July 1978, after which Bongo ordered the expulsion of some 6,000 Beninese nationals from Gabon. Most of the mercenaries as well as 11 Benin "traitors" (including former president Zinsou in absentia) were condemned to death in May 1979.

President Kérékou was redesignated for a five-year term as head of state and government on July 31, 1984, having launched a government austerity program that included the proposed privatization of many parastatal enterprises. Unrest intensified among students, teachers, and civil servants in early 1989 as the government, facing a severe cash shortage, withheld scholarship and salary checks. The PRPB nonetheless maintained complete control of legislative balloting on June 18, the single list that was advanced being credited with 89.6 percent voter approval. Subsequently, on August 2, Kérékou, the sole candidate, was reelected to another five-year presidential term by a reported 192–2 vote in the National Assembly.

In response to continued difficulties that included damaging charges of official corruption and widespread public opposition to an IMF-mandated structural adjustment program, the government convened an unprecedented joint session of the PRPB Central Committee, the National Revolutionary Assembly Standing Committee, and the National Executive Council (cabinet) in late 1989. That meeting followed the lead of Eastern-bloc countries by abandoning formal adherence to Marxism-Leninism. It also called for a national conference in early 1990 to consider constitutional reforms. The resultant National Conference of Active Forces of the Nation met on February 19–28, 1990. Unexpectedly assuming the posture of a "sovereign" body, the conference revoked the 1977 basic law, dropped the word "People's" from the country's official name, dissolved the existing legislature, and named Nicéphore SOGLO, a former World Bank official, as interim prime minister pending the formation of a "transitional government." President Kérékou, after initially terming the proceedings a "civilian coup d'état," endorsed the conference's decisions and was designated to remain head of state with the defense portfolio (but not command of the armed forces) removed from his jurisdiction.

A 50-member High Council of the Republic (*Haut Conseil de la République*—HCR) was installed on March 9, 1990, to replace the former National Revolutionary Assembly. Three days later a new government, containing no carryovers from the previous administration, was announced. In April the preliminary text of a new constitution providing for a multiparty system was submitted to the HCR. After being presented for public comment and revision, the new basic law was approved by a reported 80 percent of those participating in a December 2 referendum.

Two dozen parties competed in balloting for the National Assembly on February 17, 1991, with the leading party winning only 11 of 64 seats. Subsequently, in a second-round presidential poll on March 24, Prime Minister Soglo was elected president, defeating Kérékou, who became the first incumbent chief executive in mainland Africa to fail in a reelection bid. In an unusual appeal during the campaign, Kérékou asked "forgiveness" from those who had suffered from "deplorable and regrettable incidents" during his 17 years of military-Marxist rule. The transitional government, in one of its concluding actions, responded to the mea culpa by granting immunity to Kérékou for any crimes committed while he was in office.

Opposition parties secured a 16-seat advantage in the 1995 legislative poll, and in January 1996 the assembly rejected the administration's 1996 budget. In response, President Soglo issued an edict enacting the budget, insisting that failure to implement his plan would imperil approximately $500 million of international assistance. Shortly thereafter, former president Kérékou announced his intention to contest the presidential elections scheduled for March, alleging that the incumbent's economic policies had devastated Benin's poor. Kérékou joined a field of seven other contenders, including Soglo, former assembly president Adrien HOUNGBÉDJI of the Party of Democratic Renewal (*Parti du Renouveau Démocratique*—PRD), and Bruno AMOUSSOU, Houngbédji's assembly successor and leader of the Social Democratic Party (*Parti Social-Démocrate*—PSD).

Soglo secured a slim lead over Kérékou (35.69 percent to 33.94) in the first round of presidential balloting on March 3, 1996. However, Houngbédji and Amoussou, the third- and fourth-place finishers, respectively, subsequently urged their parties to support Kérékou, and in second-round balloting on March 18 Kérékou was returned to power with a vote share of 52.49 percent. On April 1 the Constitutional Court rejected Soglo's claim that he had been the victim of polling fraud and a "vast international plot," and on April 6 Kérékou was officially inaugurated. On April 8 the new president named an 18-member government headed by Houngbédji in the reestablished post of prime minister. Houngbédji's PRD controlled the most cabinet portfolios, with four, while Amoussou's PSD was second, with three.

On May 8, 1998, Prime Minister Houngbédji and his PRD colleagues quit the government amid speculation that they were about to be demoted in a cabinet reshuffling. Six days later the president named a new government that did not include a prime minister.

In legislative balloting on March 30, 1999, opponents of the president, led by Soglo's Renaissance Party (*Renaissance du Bénin*—RB) and the PRD, captured a one-seat majority (42 to 41) in the assembly. (The RB, PRD, and their allies performed well in the pivotal capital region, while supporters of President Kérékou dominated balloting in the north.) On June 22 Kérékou named a new government that included representatives from ten presidential-supportive parties. The PSD controlled the most posts (four), followed by the Action Front for Renewal and Development-Alafia (*Front Action pour la Renouvellement et le Développement-Alafia*—FARD-Alafia), which assumed two. No opposition members were included in the cabinet.

Seventeen candidates contested the first round of presidential balloting on March 4, 2001, with Kérékou finishing first with 45 percent of the vote, followed by Soglo (27 percent), Houngbédji (13 percent), and Amoussou (8 percent). However, Soglo challenged the results of the first round and refused to participate in the runoff, as did Houngbédji. Consequently, the balloting on March 22 pitted Kérékou against Amoussou, with the president easily winning another term by an 84–16 percent vote.

The country's continuing north-south split was apparent in the December 2002–January 2003 municipal elections, in which the president's supporters won about 50 percent of the seats while the opposition secured the mayorships in Cotonou and Porto Novo. However, significant economic growth and increased political stability appeared to solidify Kérékou's popularity prior to the March 30, 2003, National Assembly balloting, in which propresidential parties won 52 of 83 seats, marking the first time since 1990 that a president could count on a solid legislative victory. Kérékou replaced about half the ministers in a June reshuffle, but he again declined to appoint a prime minister.

Some observers worried that President Kérékou (constitutionally precluded from seeking a third term) might attempt to extend his tenure in 2006, particularly when he announced that the government did not have sufficient funds to conduct the March balloting. However, Kérékou ultimately accepted a peaceful democratic transition, resisting (apparently under heavy European pressure) the "temptation" to which a number of West African leaders had recently succumbed to remain in power through heavy-handed measures. With both Kérékou (Benin's leader for 28 of the last 33 years) and former president Soglo (precluded from another presidential bid because of his age) out of the picture, the campaign drew 26 hopefuls, including a number of independents who apparently believed that the electorate was ready to move beyond old-time politics and concentrate on the troubled economy.

In the first round of presidential balloting on March 5, 2006, Boni YAYI, a prominent economist and political newcomer, led 26 candidates with 35.6 percent of the vote. He was followed by Houngbédji (24 percent), Amoussou (15.3 percent), and Léhady SOGLO (the son of former president Soglo), who secured 8.5 percent of the vote. Yayi scored a landslide victory over Houngbédji in the runoff on March 19 with 75 percent of the vote. The new cabinet, appointed on April 8, was comprised of a number of technocrats, although the PSD and RB also were reportedly represented.

Yayi, an independent who had recently resigned after 12 years as head of the West African Development Bank, pledged to combat corruption, promote small and medium-sized businesses (particularly in the food-processing sector), and increase budget allocations for education and youth employment programs. His landslide victory also was attributed in part to the fact that he was of mixed tribal descent, had been born in the country's "middle belt," and was a Christian from a predominantly Muslim family, which helped him bridge the ethnic, geographic, and religious divides so prevalent in previous elections. In addition, Yayi, an economic advisor in the Soglo administration in the early 1990s, was viewed as a "modernizer" whose regional contacts would prove useful in helping Benin to deal with its "economically aggressive" neighbors (most notably Nigeria). Among other things, the third peaceful transfer of power in 15 years contributed to Benin's status as a regional leader in regard to democratization.

In balloting for the National Assembly on March 31, 2007, the pro-presidential Cauri Forces for an Emerging Benin (*Force Cauris pour un Bénin Émergent*—FCBE) secured 35 of 83 seats, followed by the Alliance for a Democratic Dynamic (*Alliance pour une Dynamique Démocratique*—ADD) with 20 seats and the PRD with 10 seats. Legislators from a number of smaller parties subsequently announced they would support President Yayi in the assembly, thereby giving him a working legislative majority. Yayi announced a reshuffled cabinet on June 17, most of the ministers being described as nonparty technocrats.

In the wake of declining support for his administration, President Yayi announced a major cabinet reshuffle on October 23, 2008. However, several important opposition groups declined to participate, thereby compromising Yayi's hope for a government of national unity. The new cabinet appointed on June 18, 2010, was similarly constrained.

President Yayi secured a second term in the controversial first-round balloting on March 13, 2011 (see Current issues, below). Subsequently, the FCBE and other propresidential parties gained enough seats in assembly balloting on April 30 to provide Yayi with a comfortable legislative majority. Yayi named a new cabinet on May 28, including, for the first time since 1998, a prime minister (Pascal Irénée KOUPAKI). Koupaki remained at the head of the cabinet in an April 2012 reshuffle, at which time Yayi assumed the defense portfolio.

Constitution and government. The Marxist-inspired *Loi Fondamentale* of 1977 was rescinded in February 1990 by the National Conference, which authorized the formation of the High Council of the Republic to exercise legislative power during the transition to a new regime. The constitution approved by referendum on December 2, 1990, instituted a multiparty presidential system headed by an executive elected for a five-year, once-renewable term. (Presidential candidates must be between 40 and 70 years of age and have been a citizen for 10 years.) The new basic law also provided for a Constitutional Court, a Supreme Court, a High Court of Justice, an Economic and Social Council, and an Audiovisual Authority.

The country is divided into 12 provinces (6 prior to 1997), which are subdivided into 86 districts and 510 communes. (Legislation is currently under consideration to increase the number of provinces [or "departments"] to 21.) Local administration is assigned to elected provincial, district, town, and village councils.

Censorship was extensive prior to the liberalization that was codified in the 1990 constitution. Press freedoms are currently considered among the most liberal in Africa, although several suspensions of media outlets and arrests of journalists have been reported recently.

Foreign relations. Throughout the Cold War era Benin adhered to a nonaligned posture, maintaining relations with a variety of both Communist and Western governments. Traditionally strong military and economic ties with France were reaffirmed during meetings in 1981 and 1983 between Presidents Kérékou and Mitterrand, following a revision of treaty relations in 1975.

Although its early regional links were primarily with other francophone states, Benin later sought to consolidate its interests with the broader African community. Relations with Nigeria, initially strained by Nigeria's expulsion of foreign workers in the mid-1980s, subsequently improved to the point that Kérékou felt obliged in July 1990 to deny rumors that Benin was to become Nigeria's 22nd state. Subsequent trade between the two countries allegedly occurred primarily in the "informal sector dominated by smuggling and unrecorded business."

Benin has been a strong supporter of multilateral development through the Economic Community of West African States, while bilateral ventures have been initiated with Ghana, Mauritania, and Togo. However, a confrontation developed between Benin and Niger in mid-2000 over Lété and some 25 other islands in the Niger River, where sovereignty had been disputed for four decades. In April 2002 Benin and Niger agreed to submit the case to the International Court of Justice (ICJ), although the two countries in June had reached a tentative agreement to redraw the border to settle other disputes. Improved relations also were apparent in the initiation of joint border patrols and an agreement among Benin, Ghana, Nigeria, and Togo to build an oil pipeline through their countries.

Relations between Benin and the United States underwent a dramatic improvement in 2003 when the two countries agreed to cooperate on security and military issues. (The United States also announced more than $300 million in aid in early 2006 for port rehabilitation and the promotion of small businesses.) Benin also became more involved in regional security, participating in several regional peacekeeping missions, including those in the Democratic Republic of the Congo, Liberia, and Côte d'Ivoire.

In July 2005 the ICJ allocated Lété (the most important of the disputed islands) to Niger, along with 15 of the other 25 islands. Also in 2005, Nigeria agreed to cede seven villages along its disputed border with Benin to Benin; collaterally, Benin ceded three villages to Nigeria. Meanwhile, a border dispute resurfaced between Benin and Burkina Faso, with Benin claiming sovereignty over territory beyond the Pendjari River and Burkina Faso contending the river constituted the border. In early 2008 the two countries decided to establish a joint commission to oversee infrastructure development in the region. Collaterally, each agreed to withhold any "visible sovereignty act" (such as deployment of police or military forces) in the disputed territory, while residents were authorized to vote in the country of their choice.

In late 2008 Benin signed several cooperation agreements with China involving, among other things, a proposed new bridge in Cotonou. Bilateral agreements with India were also announced in 2009, President Yayi collaterally indicating Benin would support India's bid for a permanent seat on the UN Security Council.

As the (then) president of the African Union, Yayi in the first half of 2012 strongly condemned the coups in Guinea-Bissau and Mali, analysts noting his continuing reputation for providing stability in an increasingly tumultuous region. His image was also burnished by his participation (along with three other African leaders) in discussions about food security issues at the G-8 summit in May. Another recent focus of regional attention has been the rapid rise in piracy in the Gulf of Guinea (more than 20 attacks were reported off the coast of Benin in 2011).

Current issues. Voter registration issues marred the run-up to the March 2011 presidential election, and Yayi's first-round victory (53.1 percent of the vote compared with 35.6 percent for the second-place finisher [former prime minister Adrien Houngbédji, behind whom most of the major opposition parties had coalesced]) was challenged as fraudulent by several of the defeated candidates and prompted street protests. However, after the Constitutional Court endorsed the declared results, the FCBE secured a strengthened plurality in the April assembly balloting. Consequently, Yayi, with the additional support of smaller legislative parties, became well positioned to pursue the reforms requested by the IMF and otherwise address the nation's economic difficulties and to continue his anticorruption initiatives.

As promised in the 2011 election campaign, Yayi and his legislative supporters lobbied for significant constitutional revision in early 2012. Although their proposals called for some seemingly popular changes (such as the creation of an autonomous central election commission), other aspects faced opposition from lawmakers who worried that the groundwork was being established for a possible third term for the president (currently precluded by the constitution). In face of the impasse in the assembly, Yayi, declaring no interest in a third term, withdrew all the constitutional proposals from formal legislative debate and called for renewed popular discussion on the issues involved.

The government announced in November 2012 that it had arrested four people (some previously close to the president) in connection with an alleged plot to poison Yayi. Several other prominent businessmen were also charged in March 2013 with fomenting a military takeover. Yayi's supporters attributed the alleged plots to a backlash from anticorruption measures, while his critics accused him of a "smear campaign" against perceived "enemies," including several broadcasters. Much of the political intrigue focused on the cotton sector and port development, the administration having assumed greater control in both areas recently due to "governance problems."

POLITICAL PARTIES AND GROUPS

On April 30, 1990, at the conclusion of a closed-door congress in Cotonou, the ruling Benin People's Revolutionary Party (*Parti de la Révolution Populaire du Bénin*—PRPB) voted to dissolve itself. The

PRPB had been the country's only authorized political formation from its December 1975 founding until installation of the Soglo government in March 1990. Delegates to the congress approved the launching of a new grouping, the Union of the Forces of Progress, to replace the PRPB.

By 2002 there were reportedly more than 160 registered parties, a total that, according to a number of Benin's political observers, presented a hindrance to political development. A number of parties and civic organizations that supported President Kérékou formed the Union for the Benin of the Future (*Union pour le Bénin du Futur*—UBF), which served as the core component of the Presidential Movement (*Mouvement Présidential*—MP) that dominated the 2003 legislative balloting. Included in the UBF were the PSD, RDL-Vivoten, the Action Front for Renewal and Development-Alafia (*Front Action pour la Renouvellement et le Développement—Alafia*—FARD-Alafia), and Our Common Cause (*Notre Cause Commune*—NCC). (For information on the FARD-Alafia and NCC, see the 2012 *Handbook.*) Meanwhile, it was reported that some 120 groups supported the MP. Subsequently, the UBF, under the leadership of Joseph GANAHO, reported in late 2004 that a number of small parties had disbanded and merged into the UBF. References to the UBF diminished in 2005 as it became clear that the Kérékou government was coming to an end. However, Modeste KÉRÉKOU (the son of the former president) was listed as a member of the UBF when he was appointed to the cabinet in June 2010.

The formation of the Coordination of Political Forces for 2006 was announced in early 2005 by some ten "propresidential" parties and groups. The leader of the alliance, Idrissou IBRAHIMA, secured less than 1 percent of the vote in the first round of the 2006 presidential balloting.

A number of small parties that supported President Yayi launched an umbrella electoral grouping called the Cauri Forces for an Emerging Benin (FCBE, see below) in advance of the 2007 legislative poll. Meanwhile, the major opposition parties (the PRD, PSD, RB, and MADEP) aligned as the so-called Group of Four (G4), which subsequently became the core of the Build the Nation Union (see below) for the 2011 elections. Nineteen electoral lists from parties or coalitions were authorized for that balloting.

Legislative Parties and Groups:

Cauri Forces for an Emerging Benin (*Forces Cauris pour un Bénin Émergent*—FCBE). The FCBE coalition was formed in January 2007 by some 20 small parties (some referenced below) that supported President Yayi, who officially remained an independent. The FCBE secured 35 seats in the March assembly poll (on a vote share of 23 percent) and joined with a number of small parties to give Yayi a working legislative majority. However, the FCBE did more poorly than expected in the April 2008 local elections, and several FCBE legislators reportedly defected to the new G13 (see under UPR, below). Although additional division was reported within the FCBE in the first half of 2009, the party won a plurality of 41 seats in the 2011 assembly poll.

Leaders: Mathurin NAGO (President of the National Assembly), Sacca LAFIA.

Build the Nation Union (*Union fait la Nation*—UN). Formed by the following parties as an opposition coalition committed to toppling the Yayi administration, the UN presented the PRD's Adrien Houngbédji as its 2011 presidential candidate and finished second in the 2011 assembly poll with 30 seats. However, some defections to the government camp were subsequently reported. A proposal for the UN component to formally coalesce as a single "grand party" was subsequently discussed, although Houngbédji was described as cool to the idea.

Leaders: Adrien HOUNGBÉDJI (2011 presidential candidate), Bruno AMOUSSOU, Léhady SOGLO, Emmanuel GOLOU, Lazare SÉHOUÉTO.

Party of Democratic Renewal (*Parti du Renouveau Démocratique*—PRD). Led by (then) National Assembly president Adrien Houngbédji, the PRD won nine legislative seats in 1991 and 19 in 1995, its support centering in the south around Porto Novo. Houngbédji finished third in the first round of presidential balloting in March 1996 with 18.72 percent of the vote. Subsequently, the PRD's support proved pivotal to Mathieu Kérékou in the second round of balloting, and the new president rewarded the party by appointing Houngbédji as prime minister and naming four other PRD members to his new cabinet.

In May 1998 Houngbédji and his PRD colleagues resigned from the government amid reports that the president was preparing to demote them in a cabinet reshuffling. The PRD was subsequently allied with a number of other parties in an anti-Kérékou coalition in mid-2000. However, the groups were unable to agree on a joint presidential candidate for 2001.

In February 2003 Houngbédji was elected mayor of Porto Nova, but he lost the assembly president's position in April 2003. He finished second to Boni Yayi in the 2006 presidential runoff with 25 percent of the vote. The PRD was considered "neutral" (i.e., in neither the presidential nor the opposition camps) in the 2007 legislative elections, in which it secured ten seats. However, Houngbédji subsequently became increasingly critical of President Yayi's administration, and the PRD reportedly made significant gains in the April 2008 municipal balloting.

In light of rumors that the PRD was planning to rally to the government, Houngbédji in April 2012 reaffirmed his commitment to the opposition and called upon other groups to oppose what he called the "opportunistic" constitutional revisions proposed by supporters of President Yayi.

Leader: Adrien HOUNGBÉDJI (Former President of the National Assembly, Former Prime Minister, 2006 presidential candidate, and Mayor of Porto Novo).

Social Democratic Party (*Parti Social-Démocrate*—PSD). In June 1995 the PSD's leader and former presidential candidate, Bruno Amoussou, captured the assembly presidency. Thereafter, in March 1996, Amoussou failed to advance beyond the first round of presidential balloting; however, for rallying behind Mathieu Kérékou, the PSD was awarded cabinet posts in April. Amoussou, described by *Africa Confidential* as a "kingmaker" for his role in the 1996 election and strongly positioned in the cabinet, enjoyed solid backing in portions of southern Benin.

Amoussou finished third in the first round of the 2006 presidential election with 15.3 percent of the vote as a candidate of an alliance of parties. The alliance supported Boni Yayi in the second round and reportedly secured four seats (two for the PSD) in Yayi's new cabinet. However, Amoussou soon drifted toward the opposition camp, and the PSD joined the RB, MADEP, and other southern-based opposition parties in forming the Alliance for a Democratic Dynamic (*Alliance pour une Dynamique Démocratique*—ADD), which finished second in the March 2007 assembly poll with 20 seats.

Leaders: Bruno AMOUSSOU (Coordinator and 2006 presidential candidate), Felix ADIMI (First Vice Chair of the National Executive Committee), Emmanuel GOLOU (Parliamentary Leader).

Renaissance Party (*Renaissance du Bénin*—RB). The RB was founded in March 1992 by Rosine Soglo, the wife of (then) President Nicéphore Soglo. In July 1993 President Soglo announced his intention to "come down into the arena" to help the RB serve as a "catalyst" for Benin's democracy movement, and in July 1994 he assumed leadership of the party. On October 1, 1994, the RB absorbed the small Pan-African Union of Democracy and Solidarity (*Union Panafricaine de la Démocratie et la Solidarité*—UPDS), but the enlarged party managed to gain only 20 of 83 legislative seats in two rounds of balloting in March and May 1995.

Among the reasons cited for President Soglo's electoral defeat in his 1996 reelection bid was his increasing reliance on a small circle of family members and the exclusion of the supporters who had helped him capture the presidency. In August 1998 RB dissidents led by Nicolas TCHOTCHONE left the party and formed the **African Movement for Development and Integration** (*Mouvement Africain pour le Développement et l'Intégration*—MADI), with Tchotchone calling for the establishment of a "new economic and political order."

In February 2003 Nicéphore Soglo was elected mayor of Cotonou. After the March 2003 assembly elections, the RB became the largest opposition party, with 15 seats.

With Nicéphore Soglo unable to run because of his age (over 70), the RB presented his son, Léhady Soglo, as its 2006 presidential candidate. Léhady Soglo finished fourth in the first round of balloting with 8.5 percent of the vote. The RB was reportedly given one seat in the new cabinet formed by President Boni Yayi following the election.

In early 2008 Nicéphore Soglo criticized President Bayi for a perceived lack of commitment to "genuine democracy." The RB, promising improved living conditions, secured a majority of the council seats in Cotonou in the April 2008 municipal balloting.

Léhady Soglo ultimately supported the PRD's Adrien Houngbédji in the 2011 presidential race, but friction was reported between the two leaders. A member of the RB accepted the environmental, housing, and urban affairs portfolio in the May 2011 cabinet, although it did not appear that the party as a whole or the UN had endorsed that decision.

Leaders: Nicéphore SOGLO (President of the Party, Former President of the Republic, 2001 presidential candidate, and Mayor of Cotonou), Léhady SOGLO (Deputy Mayor of Cotonou and 2006 presidential candidate), Rosine SOGLO (Chair).

African Movement for Democracy and Progress (*Mouvement Africain pour la Démocratie et le Progrès*—MADEP). Led by Séfou Fagbohoun, a wealthy businessman, the MADEP captured six seats in the 1999 legislative elections and in 2003 became the second-largest propresidential party, after the UBF. The MADEP's Antoine Kolawolé Idji finished fifth in the first round of the 2006 presidential poll with 3.25 percent of the vote. The MADEP was subsequently described as highly factionalized as several members accepted portfolios in the new Yayi cabinet in October.

Leaders: Séfou FAGBOHOUN (Chair), Antoine Idji Kolawolé IDJI (Former Speaker of the National Assembly and 2006 presidential candidate), Christophe Kint AGUIAR (Secretary General).

Key Force (*Force Clé*—FC). Having won four seats on its own in the 2007 assembly poll, the FC, led by Lazare Séhouéto (who had been credited with 2.1 percent of the vote and a sixth-place finish in the 2006 presidential poll as the candidate of the Movement for an Alternative for the People), joined the other major opposition forces in the UN for the 2011 elections.

Leaders: Lazare SÉHOUÉTO, Eric HOUNDATE.

Union for Relief (*Union pour la Relève*—UPR). Salifou Issa, the leader of the UPR, finished fourth in the March 2011 presidential poll with 1.3 percent of the vote. For the April legislative balloting, the UPR formed an electoral coalition with the **Hope Force** (*Force Espoir*—FE), which won two seats. (Antoine DAYORI, the leader of the FE, had won 0.3 percent of the vote in the 2011 presidential balloting.) The UPR had secured three seats in the 2007 assembly election, while the FE, identified at that time as supportive of President Yayi, had won two.

In 2008 it was reported that a number of legislators had formed, under Issa's leadership, an influential **Group of 13** (G13), which was a focus of President Yayi's national unity discussions in September. After declining the invitation to join Yayi's new cabinet, the G13, which primarily represented business interests, joined the G4, FC, and other small parties in initially pledging to cooperate in the campaign to unseat Yayi in 2011. Many analysts at first concluded that the G13's favored candidate would be Abdoulaye BIO TCHANÉ (the president of the West African Development Bank), who reportedly enjoyed the support of Benin's former president Mathieu Kérékou. However, Bio Tchané ultimately ran officially as an independent, although apparently with the support of at least some non-UPR elements of the G13. Bio Tchané finished third in the poll with 6.1 percent of the vote, having campaigned on a platform pledging economic competence and anticorruption efforts. Subsequently, in the April assembly election, a **G13 Baobab Alliance**, led by Valentin Aditi HOUDÉ, won two seats.

Leader: Salifou ISSA.

Four small propresidential parties also won two seats each in the April 2011 assembly balloting. They were the **Amana Alliance,** led by Nassirou BAKI ARIFARI and Zimé KORA GOUNOU; the **Cauris 2 Alliance,** led by Léon Bani BIO BIGOU and Étienne KOSSI; the **Strength in Unity Alliance** (*Alliance Force dans l'Unité*—AFU), led by André Okounlola; and the **Union for Benin** (*Union pour Bénin*—UB), led by Barnabé DASSIGLI.

Other Parties and Groups That Contested the 2011 Assembly Elections:

Rally of Liberal Democrats for National Reconstruction (*Rassemblement des Démocrates Libéraux pour la Reconstruction Nationale*—RDL-Vivoten). Led by Sévérin Adjovi, an advocate for the reelection of former president Kérékou, the RDL-Vivoten secured three seats in the 1993 legislative balloting. Adjovi served as minister of defense from 1996 to May 1998, at which time he was named minister of communications, culture, and information.

In the 1999 legislative balloting the RDL-Vivoten reportedly campaigned along with four other groups under the banner of the **Movement for Citizens' Commitment and Awakening** (*Mouvement pour l'Engagement et le Réveil des Citoyens*—MERCI).

Adjovi secured 1.8 percent of the vote in the first round of presidential balloting in 2006.

Leader: Sévérin ADJOVI (2006 presidential candidate).

Other parties and coalitions presenting legislative candidates in 2011 included the following: the **Common Action Front for the Emergence of a New Ethic in Benin** (*Front d'Action Common pour l'Émergence d'une Éthique Nouvelle en Bénin*'Faceen-Bénin), led by Tossa CYRIAQUE; the **Movement of Benin–Fight Against Poverty** (*Movement du Bénin—Lutte Contre la Pauvreté*—MB-LCP), led by Georges GANSI; the **Movement for Renewal, Democracy, and Development** (*Movement pour le Réveil, la Démocratie, et le Développement*—MRDD), led by Zoumènou DOSSA; the **New Courage Alliance** (*Alliance Nouveau Courage*—ANC 2011), led by Pascal Irénée Koupaki (named prime minister in May 2011) and Bossou LUC; the **New Force Alliance-2011** (*Alliance Nouvelle Force*—ANF-2011); the **New Forces for Democracy and Development** (*Forces Nouvelles pour la Démocratie et le Développement*—FNDD), led by Irani SANIGUI; **Our Common Destiny** (*Notre Destin Commien*—NDC), led by Romuald YAMONGBÈ; **Patriotic Revival** (*Réveil Patriotique*—RP), led by Janvier YAHOUÉDÉOU, who received 0.6 percent of the vote in the 2011 presidential poll (Yahouedeou had reportedly led the **National Union for Democracy and Progress** [*Union National pour la Démocratie et le Progrès*—UNDP] when that party secured two seats in the 2007 assembly balloting; at that time the UNDP was described as propresidential, but Yahouedeou reportedly became disenchanted with the Yayi administration in 2009); the **Republican Union Party** (*Parti pour l'Union Républicaine*—PUR), whose candidate, Victor TOPANU, secured 0.4 percent of the vote in the 2011 presidential election; and the **Sacred Union of Awakening for Development** (*Union Sacrée d'Eveil pour le Développement*—USED), led by Abel Cocou ATOU.

Other Parties and Groups:

Alliance (*Alliance*). The Alliance was a grouping of three propresidential parties formed prior to the 2003 legislative elections. The component parties were the **Congress of the People for Progress** (*Congrès du Peuple pour le Progrès*—CPP), led by Sédégnon ADANDE-KINTI; the **Movement for Development Through Culture** (*Mouvement pour le Développement par Culture*—MDC), led by Codjo ACHODE; and the **Party of the Beginning** (*Parti du Salut*—PS), led by Damien Alahassa. The CPP ran on its own in the 2007 legislative elections.

Leader: Damien ALAHASSA.

Star Alliance (*Alliance Etoile*—AE). A platform for northern political figures, the AE includes **The Greens** (*Les Verts*) and the **Union for Democracy and National Solidarity** (*Union pour la Démocratie et la Solidarité Nationale*—UDSN), led by Sacca Lafia and Adamou N'DIAYE. The AE secured four seats in the March 1999 poll, and thereafter an AE representative was named to the cabinet. The AE backed an opponent of the PSD's Amoussou in a contest for the assembly presidency and was subsequently excluded from the government named in June 1999. In the 2003 elections, the AE won three seats. AE and UDSN leader Sacca Lafia was subsequently referenced as a leader of the propresidential FCBE.

Leader: Sacca LAFIA (Chair).

New Alliance (*Nouvelle Alliance*—NA). Led by Soulé Dankoro, the NA won two seats in the 2003 legislative elections. Dankoro won less than 1 percent of the vote in the first round of the 2006 presidential balloting.

Leader: Soulé DANKORO.

Communist Party of Benin (*Parti Communiste du Bénin*—PCB). Founded in 1977 as the Communist Party of Dahomey (*Parti Communiste du Dahomey*—PCD) and informally functioning for the next 12 years as the sole opposition grouping, the PCB filed for legal recognition in early June 1993. In 1990 the party had boycotted the National Conference, labeling it a "plot between French imperialism and its Beninese lackeys."

Theretofore in opposition, the PCB allied itself with propresidential forces in May 1995, and in first-round presidential balloting in March 1996 PCB First Secretary Pascal Fatondji secured 1.3 percent of the vote. The PCB called for a boycott of the 2001 presidential balloting.

Leader: Pascal FATONDJI (First Secretary and 1996 presidential candidate).

Eleven legislators from small parties agreed to support President Yayi in the assembly following the March 2007 legislative elections. Their parties (which had also supported Yayi in the 2006 presidential poll) included the FE, UNDP, **Coalition for an Emerging Benin** (*Coalition pour un Bénin Émergent*—CBE), **Party for Democracy and Social Progress** (*Parti pour la Démocratie et le Progrès Social*—PDPS), **Renewal Alliance** (*Alliance du Renouveau*—AR), and **Restore Hope** (*Restaurer l'Espoir*—RE), led by Candida AZANAI, who had recently left the RB.

Other successful small parties in the 2007 legislative poll included the **Alliance of the Forces of Progress** (*Alliance des Forces du Progrès*—AFP), led by Valentin Aditi Houdé, who led the G13 Baobab Alliance in 2011.

Other groups (in addition to the AFP and FC) allied with President Kérékou prior to his retirement in 2006 included the **Alliance for Democracy and Progress** (*Alliance pour la Démocratie et le Progrès*—ADP), led by Sylvain Adekpedjou AKINDES; the **Chameleon Alliance** (*Alliance Caméléon*—AC); the **Impulse for Progress and Democracy** (*Impulsion pour le Progrès et la Démocratie*—IPD), led by Théophile NATA; the **Movement for Development and Solidarity** (*Mouvement pour le Développement et la Solidarité*—MDS); the **Rally for Democracy and Progress** (*Rassemblement pour la Démocratie et le Progrès*—RDP); the **Rally for the Nation** (*Rassemblement pour la Nation*—RPN), led by De Sodji Zanclan ABEO; and the **Together Party.** In the 2003 legislative balloting, the AFP, FC, IPD, MDS, and RDP all captured seats. The IPD presented candidates in the 2007 legislative elections, as did a number of new small parties, including the **Belier Social Democratic Party** (*Parti Social Démocrate Le Belier*—PSD–Belier); and the **Union of Citizen Forces** (*Union des Forces Citoyennes*—UFC). New alliances presenting candidates in 2007 included the **Awakening Alliance** (*Alliance Le Réveil*—AR), led by Martin Dohou AZONHIHO; the **Cauri Alliance for Change** (*Alliance Cauris pour le Changement*—ACC), led by Codjo ACHODE, a participant in the former MP; the **National Alliance for Change** (*Alliance Nationale pour le Changement*—ANC), founded by Philippe ABOUMON and other former MP supporters; and the **Alliance for the Defense of Change** (*Alliance pour la Défense du Changement*—ADC), led by former Kérékou supporter Touré MERE.

The **African Congress for Democracy** (*Congrès Africain pour la Démocratie*—CAD) presented Lionel Jacques AGBO as its presidential candidate in 2006. The candidate of the **Rally of Liberal Democrats–Heviosso** (*Rassemblement des Démocrats Libéraux–Heviosso*) was Leandre DJAGOUE. Agbo and Djagoue each received less than 1 percent of the vote in the first round.

LEGISLATURE

National Assembly (*Assemblée National*). Benin's unicameral legislature currently includes 83 deputies serving four-year terms and elected by party-list proportional representation in 24 constituencies. At the most recent election of April 30, 2011, the propresidential Cauri Forces for an Emerging Benin won 41 seats; the opposition Build the Nation Union, 30; the Amana Alliance, 2; the G13 Baobab Alliance, 2; the alliance of the Hope Force and the Union for Relief, 2; the Strength in Unity Alliance, 2; the Cauris Alliance, 2; and the Union for Benin, 2.

President: Mathurin NAGO.

CABINET

[as of July 1, 2013] (*See headnote.*)

President	Boni Yayi
Prime Minister	Pascal Irénée Koupaki
Minister of State	
Presidential Affairs	Issifou Kogui N'Douro
Ministers	
Administrative and Institutional Reform	Martial Sounton
Agriculture, Husbandry, and Fisheries	Katé Sadaï
Communications and Information Technology	Max Barthélémy Ahouèkè
Culture, Literacy, Handicrafts, and Tourism	Babalola Jean-Michel Hervé Abimbola
Decentralization, Local Governance, and Territorial Administration and Management	Raphaël Edou
Economic Analysis, Development, and Planning	Marcel Alain de Souza
Economy and Finance	Jonas Gbian
Energy, Water, Mineral and Petroleum Research, and Development of Renewable Energy	Barthélémy Kassa
Environment, Housing, and Urban Affairs	Glélé Ahanhanzo
Family, National Solidarity, Social Affairs, Elderly, and the Handicapped	Fatouma Amadou Djibril [f]
Foreign Affairs, African Integration, Francophony, and Beninese Abroad	Nassirou Bako Arifari
Health	Dorothée Akoko Kindé Gazard [f]
Higher Education and Scientific Research	François Adebayo Abiola
Industry, Commerce, and Small- and Medium-Sized Enterprises	Akuavi Marie-Elise Christiana Gbèdo [f]
Interior and Public Security	Benoît Assouan Comlan Dègla
Justice, Legislation, Human Rights, and Keeper of the Seals, and Government Spokesperson	Reckya Madougou [f]
Labor and Civil Service	Maïmouna Kora Zaki Leadi [f]
National Defense	Boni Yayi
Primary and Prekindergarten Education	Eric Kouagu N'Da
Public Works and Transportation	Lambert Koty
Secondary Education, Professional and Technical Training, and Youth Retraining and Integration	Alassane Soumanou
Sports, Leisure, and Youth	Didier Aplogan-Djibode
Ministers Delegate	
Maritime Economy, Port Infrastructure, and Maritime Transportation	Valentin Djenontin-Agossou
Microfinance and the Employment of Youth and Women	Sofiatou Onifadé Babamoussa [f]
Relations With Institutions	Safiatou Bassibi Issifou Morou [f]

[f] = female

INTERGOVERNMENTAL REPRESENTATION

Ambassador to the U.S.: Segbe Cyrille OGUIN.

U.S. Ambassador to Benin: Michael RAYNOR.

Permanent Representative to the UN: Jean-Francis Régis ZINSOU.

IGO Memberships (Non-UN): AfDB, AU, ECOWAS, ICC, IOM, NAM, OIC, WTO.

BHUTAN

Kingdom of Bhutan
Druk-yul

Political Status: Independent parliamentary monarchy; first formal constitution adopted June 2, 2008.

Area: 18,147 sq. mi. (47,000 sq. km).

Population: 755,919 (2012E—UN); 725,296 (2013E—U.S. Census).

Major Urban Center (2011E): THIMPHU (99,000, district).

Official Language: Dzongkha.

Monetary Unit: Ngultrum (official rate November 1, 2013: 62.33 ngultrum = $1US). The ngultrum is at par with the Indian rupee, which circulates freely within the country.

Monarch: Dasho Jigme Khesar Namgyel WANGCHUK; proclaimed king (*Druk Gyalpo*) on December 14, 2006, upon the voluntary abdication of his father, Jigme Singye WANGCHUK; crowned as constitutional monarch on November 6, 2008.

Prime Minister: Tshering TOBGAY (People's Democratic Party); elected by his party on July 19, 2013, following the National Assembly election of July 13; assumed office on July 25, succeeding Jigme Yoser THINLEY (Bhutan Peace and Prosperity Party).

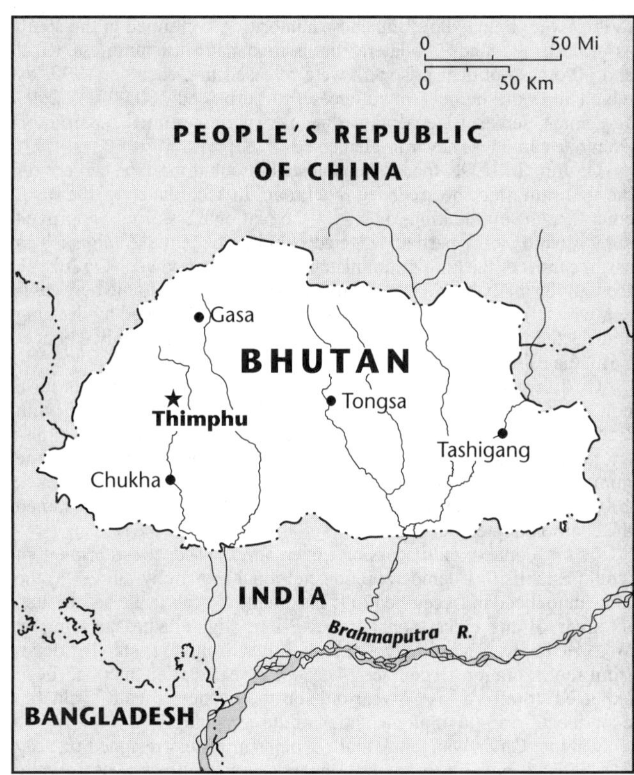

THE COUNTRY

The Kingdom of Bhutan is situated in the eastern Himalayas between Tibet and India. Mountainous in the north and heavily forested in the south, the country's terrain long served to isolate it from the rest of the world. In recent decades official census results have been challenged, particularly by people of Nepalese extraction (Lhotshampas), who appear to constitute 40 percent or more of the population. The principal Bhutanese communities are the Sarchops (an estimated 30 percent) and the ruling Ngalung Drukpas of West Bhutan (15 percent). Four main languages are spoken: Dzongkha (the official language) in the north and west, Bumthangkha in the central section, Sarachapkha in the east, and Nepali in the west and south. The *Druk Kargue* sect of Mahayana Buddhism is the official state religion, and Buddhist priests (lamas) exert considerable political influence. The lamas, numbering about 3,500, are distributed in 8 major monasteries (*dzongs*) and 200 smaller shrines (*gompas*). Most of the Nepalese are Hindu. Women, who constitute about 41.5 percent of the economically active population, play a minimal role in governance. They hold 3 of 47 seats (6.4 percent) in the Assembly, and 2 of 25 seats in the National Council (8 percent).

The economy remains largely agrarian. About 44 percent of the paid labor force engages in agriculture and animal husbandry, which account for about 22 percent of the GDP. The main crops are maize, rice, and other cereals; potatoes and other tubers and roots; and apples and other fruits. Industry, contributing about 39 percent of GDP and employing 17 percent of the workforce (mostly in construction), is led by production of hydroelectric power and by food and distillery operations. Electricity is now the leading source of nonservice export earnings; in 2011 nearly five times as much electricity was exported as was consumed domestically (see Foreign relations, below). India remains Bhutan's principal trading partner.

With support from international donors, transportation, power, and communications have improved dramatically since the 1960s. The Tenth Five-Year Plan (July 2008–June 2013) included among its goals poverty alleviation, reduced unemployment, road construction, and rural electrification. (Bhutan's development philosophy's overall goal is improving "Gross National Happiness.") GDP growth has been uneven, peaking at 13.2 percent in fiscal year 2006–2007 but falling to 8.5 percent in 2011. That year inflation was 8.9 percent, but unemployment was only 3.1 percent. The kingdom remained heavily dependent on foreign grants, which accounted for one-third of government revenue. The economy continued to decline, with growth falling to 6.3 in 2013. That year inflation reached 10.2 percent, though unemployment stayed low at 3.2 percent.

GOVERNMENT AND POLITICS

Political background. A consolidated kingdom since the mid-16th century, Bhutan is presently governed by a hereditary monarch, the *Druk Gyalpo* (Dragon King). Historically, the country was ruled by a dyarchy of temporal and spiritual rajas, but in 1907 Ugyan WANGCHUK was established on the throne with British assistance. British guidance of Bhutan's external affairs, which began in 1865 in exchange for a financial subsidy, was confirmed by treaty in 1910. India succeeded to the British role by a treaty concluded August 8, 1949, in which India pledged not to interfere in Bhutanese internal affairs. Bhutan agreed to be "guided" by Indian advice in its external relations.

The post–World War II era witnessed increased social and political change, primarily at the initiative of King Jigme Dorji WANGCHUK, who ascended the throne in 1952. In 1964 Prime Minister Jigme Polden DORJI was assassinated amid unrest over reforms. Nonetheless, the king pursued his policy of modernization. Western-educated Jigme Singye WANGCHUK succeeded his father as monarch on July 24, 1972.

From the late 1980s there was increased restiveness among Bhutan's large Nepalese immigrant community, particularly after the monarch's launching of a national integration (*Driglam Namzha*) drive that mandated the wearing of traditional Bhutanese dress and proscribed the teaching of Nepali. Based in the southern regions, the Nepalese agitation spawned a number of political groups, including the Bhutan People's Party (BPP). Violent outbreaks accelerated what had initially been a small refugee problem, and by 1993 some 80,000 or more ethnic Nepalese had relocated to seven camps in eastern Nepal run by the Office of the United Nations High Commissioner for Refugees (UNHCR).

In October 1993 representatives of Bhutan and Nepal held the first in a series of ministerial-level meetings to work toward resolution of the problem. Further rounds of talks in 1994 yielded agreement that a Joint Verification Team would categorize the refugees according to whether they were bona fide Bhutanese nationals, non-Bhutanese refugees from elsewhere, Bhutanese emigrants who had forfeited citizenship, or criminals. Meanwhile, a number of ethnic Nepalese leaders, most prominently Tek Nath RIZAL of the BPP, had been sentenced by Bhutan's High Court to life imprisonment or other lengthy terms for terrorist activities. Intermittent violence by "antinationals" (*ngolops*), as they were branded by Bhutanese authorities, continued in the south as succeeding rounds of bilateral discussions made little progress. Rizal and 40 other political prisoners were released in December 1999, by which time the number of refugees had surpassed 100,000. A 2003 agreement between Nepal and Bhutan to permit limited repatriation from one camp was never implemented.

On June 16, 1998, the king announced dissolution of the cabinet for the first time since he ascended the throne. In accordance with a royal edict (*kasho*) by the king, on July 1 the National Assembly approved the formation of a partially elected cabinet (*Lhengye Zhungtsho*) to assume most of the king's administrative duties and powers. On July 20 the king formally handed governmental authority over to the new cabinet, which included six ministers who had been nominated by the king and elected for five-year terms by secret ballot of the assembly. Thenceforth, the cabinet chair rotated annually among ministers.

On July 10, 2003, the king announced portfolio assignments for a new ten-member cabinet, which assumed office on August 30 with Jigme THINLEY as chair. Yeshey ZIMBA, minister of trade and industry, took over as chair on August 18, 2004, and he was succeeded by the minister of health and education, Sangay NGEDUP, on September 5, 2005. The minister of foreign affairs, Khandu WANGCHUK, assumed the chair on September 7, 2006.

In the context of discussions over a proposed constitution that would establish a "democratic constitutional monarchy" in 2008, the king announced in December 2005 his intention to abdicate before then in favor of his eldest son, Crown Prince Jigme Khesar Namgyel WANGCHUK. Accordingly, the king, himself only 51, stepped down from the throne on December 14, 2006, a year earlier than had been expected, to afford his 26-year-old son the chance to gain "valuable experience" prior to implementation of the constitution.

Cabinet Chair Wangchuk and six other ministers resigned on July 31, 2007, to prepare to contest Bhutan's first multiparty, democratic legislative elections. Kinzang DORJI, minister for works and human settlements, was named by the king to head a small caretaker cabinet.

Following a lengthy preparatory process that included the registration in 2007 of Bhutan's first political parties, voters on March 24, 2008, elected the 47 members of a new National Assembly. The Bhutan Peace and Prosperity Party (*Druk Phuensum Tshogpa*—DPT), led by former cabinet chair Jigme Thinley, took 45 seats, with the other 2 being won by the People's Democratic Party (PDP) of Sangay Ngedup. On December 31, 2007, and January 28, 2008, voters cast ballots for the 20 elective, nonpartisan members of the new Parliament's upper house, the National Council. Thinley took office as prime minister on April 9.

Beginning in January 2011 local elections were held for 1,109 posts at the village, county, and district levels. The government attracted accusations of disenfranchisement for requiring all candidates pass a literacy test and security check. On October 13 the King married Jetsun PEMA.

In 2013 the government saw a major turnover with National Council elections in April. Two-rounds of National Assembly elections culminated in July with the opposition PDP, led by Tshering TOBGAY, winning a decisive victory of 32 to 15 seats over the DPT (see Current issues, below).

Constitution and government. Work on the country's first formal constitution began in 2001, with the first draft completed in 2005. Following an extended period of national consultation, a slightly revised, 35-article third draft was presented in August 2007. Meanwhile, the electoral process, authorized by royal decree, began in 2007 and concluded in March 2008. Formal adoption of the constitution occurred early in the parliamentary term.

The most controversial provisions of Bhutan's constitution concern citizenship. To be a citizen an individual must be the child of two Bhutanese parents or must have been officially registered as a resident on or before December 31, 1958. To be eligible for naturalization an individual must have resided in Bhutan for at least 15 years; have committed no criminal offenses; be able to speak and write Dzongkha; have a "good knowledge" of the country's culture and history; and "have no record of having spoken or acted against the King, the Country, and the People of Bhutan." Most of the ethnic Nepalese community are thereby excluded from citizenship.

Bhutan is a constitutional monarchy with executive, legislative, and judicial branches. The *Druk Gyalpo* remains head of state but must step down upon reaching the age of 65; females are included in the line of succession, although a male heir, even if younger, takes precedence. The bicameral Parliament has a 25-member National Council as an upper house and a new National Assembly as the lower. Members of the National Assembly (a maximum of 55) are elected through single-member constituencies. Both houses serve five-year terms, although the National Assembly is subject to early dissolution in the event of a political impasse and concurrence by two-thirds of the National Assembly's members and the monarch. The monarch is empowered to declare a state of emergency for up to 21 days, with a two-thirds vote of Parliament, sitting in joint session, then needed to extend it.

The leader or nominee of the majority party in the National Assembly becomes prime minister (subject to a two-term limit), with the monarch naming other ministers on the recommendation of the prime minister. The National Assembly and National Council, sitting in joint session, may override a monarchical veto by a two-thirds vote. By a three-fourths vote and with popular concurrence in a national referendum, they may force the king to abdicate. The judicial system comprises a Supreme Court, a High Court, district courts, and other lower courts.

The constitution describes Buddhism as "the spiritual heritage" of the country but guarantees freedom of religion as well as freedom of speech, press, and assembly. A media bill passed in 2006 restricts cross-ownership of media and requires equitable treatment of parties and candidates during election campaigns. In 2012 the group Reporters Without Borders ranked Bhutan 82nd out of 179 nations in terms of freedom of the press.

The country is divided into 20 administrative districts (*dzongkhags*). Villages (*chiwogs*) are grouped into counties (*gewogs*). The constitution specifies the election of assemblies at all levels of government. Local elections were first held in 2011 (see Current issues, below).

Foreign relations. Historically, Bhutan's external relations were conducted largely through the Indian government, although the 1949 treaty that required Thimphu to seek "advice" from New Delhi in foreign affairs came under periodic criticism. Bhutan's establishment of diplomatic relations with Bangladesh in 1980 was Thimphu's first effort to deal directly with a third country, although it had acted independently of India in several international forums, including the UN General Assembly. On February 8, 2007, during a visit by the king to New Delhi, Bhutan and India signed a revised India-Bhutan Friendship Treaty that eliminated the reference to Indian guidance in foreign affairs. The treaty entered into force on March 5. In May 2008 Manmohan Singh became the first Indian prime minister to visit Bhutan in 25 years. In April 2010 Thimphu hosted negotiations between India and Pakistan on Kashmir.

Since 1980 Bhutan has joined a number of multilateral bodies, including the World Bank, the International Monetary Fund, and the Asian Development Bank. Bhutan, along with Bangladesh, India, the Maldives, Nepal, Pakistan, and Sri Lanka, formed the South Asian Association for Regional Cooperation (SAARC) in 1985. In 2005 the seven reached agreement on establishing a South Asia Free Trade Area, which became operational in 2006. Thimphu hosted the 16th SAARC summit on April 28–29, 2010, and endorsed the group's Charter of Democracy in February 2011.

In late 2003 Bhutan moved to resolve a decade-old problem involving Indian separatists who were using bases in southeastern Bhutan to mount cross-border raids. In mid-December, the Royal Bhutanese Army attacked some 30 camps occupied by an estimated 3,000 Assamese and Bodo separatists associated with three militant Indian movements: the United Liberation Front of Assam, the National Liberation Front of Bodoland, and the more recently organized Kamatapur Liberation Organization. In February 2004 India reported that over 400 insurgents had been killed in the successful offensive.

Since the 1980s Bhutan and China have held discussions to resolve a border controversy linked to the Chinese–Indian dispute over portions of Arunachal. Chinese territorial claims include some 270 square kilometers in the western sector and somewhat more in the northern sector. In June 2012 Bhutan and China announced they would establish full relations and begin talks to resolve their remaining border disputes.

In November 2011 India announced plans to develop a 10,000-megawatt hydropower plant in Bhutan. In January 2012 Bhutan and Vietnam established diplomatic relations, followed in November by the establishment of formal ties with Bulgaria. In January 2013 Bhutan and Tajikistan made plans to establish formal relations.

Regular border dispute meetings with China continued in 2013. In January India expressed urgency for Bhutan to resolve the issue, concerned about the implications the settlement will have on its own security. During talks in August, representatives agreed to dispatch a joint Sino-Bhutan technical survey team. The survey was completed in September.

Current issues. The long-standing issue of refugees in UNHCR camps has yet to find a political resolution. Thimphu refused to talk directly to refugee groups, insisting that most of the refugees are not legitimately Bhutanese and arguing that the refugee camps have been infiltrated by Maoists and others who wish to overthrow the government. In 2006 the UNHCR asked Nepal to grant refugees permission to leave the camps for third countries. In October 2006 the United States offered to admit 60,000 of the Nepalese. Despite opposition to the program by many leaders, the first 120 refugees left for the United States in March 2008. Other countries including Australia, Canada, Denmark, the Netherlands, New Zealand, and Norway, agreed to accept smaller numbers of refugees. As of September 2009 more than 20,000 had been relocated. In April 2011 Prime Minister Thinley agreed to restart bilateral negotiations with Nepal over the estimated 70,000 Bhutanese refugees remaining in that country.

By royal decree issued in March 2013, the second National Council elections took place on April 23. Sixty-seven candidates contested for the 20 available seats in the nonpartisan higher chamber. At 45 percent, voter turnout was 11 points lower than the June 2011 local elections.

On April 29 the National Assembly primary election was set for May 31, with a runoff between the two leading parties on July 13. Five parties registered to contest the May polls, though the Electoral Commission disqualified the Bhutan Kuen-Nyam Party (BKNP) in May citing shortcomings in the party's application. In the first round of balloting, the ruling DPT emerged victorious with 44.5 percent of the vote, while the opposition PDP placed second with 32.5 percent. The recently formed parties Druk Nyamrup Tshogpa (DNT) and Druk Chirwang Tshogpa (DCT) secured 17 and 5.9 percent of the vote, respectively. Subsequently, campaigns focused on economic issues and relations with India, following the mid-June announcement of significant reductions in energy subsidies from India. (The subsidy was restored by the end of July.) The PDP scored an unexpected upset on July 13, winning 32 seats, a comfortable margin over the DPT's 15. PDP president Tshering Tobgay, a skeptic of Bhutan's oft-touted "Gross National Happiness" development approach, was installed as prime minister by the king on July 25.

POLITICAL PARTIES

Until 2007, Bhutan had no legal parties. Under the 2008 constitution political parties are permitted as long as their membership is not based on "region, sex, language, religion, or social origin." Members of the royal family, appointed government officials, members of the police force and the military, members of the clergy, and civil servants are prohibited from participation in parties. Only members may contribute money to a party. The two parties contesting the March 2008 election, the *Druk Phuensum Tshogpa* (DPT) and the People's Democratic Party (PDP), had no significant ideological differences. Ethnic Nepalese parties support a limited constitutional monarchy, a parliamentary system, and equal rights for all ethnic groups, but there are differences regarding the issue of repatriation of displaced Nepalese versus resettlement of those refugees in third countries. Reports in 2010 and 2011 indicated that exiled Nepalese groups had formed a new umbrella organization under the leadership of Rongthong Kinley DORJI of the Druk National Congress (see below). Ahead of the 2013 election a new formation, the **Bhutan Kuen-Nyam Party** (BKNP), was disqualified by the Electoral Commission, reportedly on the grounds that criteria were absent from the application.

Registered Parties:

People's Democratic Party (PDP). The PDP was established in March 2007 under the leadership of former chair of the Council of Ministers Sangay Ngedup and became the country's first registered party in September. Promoting "well being for everyone" through economic development, expansion of basic infrastructure, and improved access to health care, the PDP secured two seats in the March 2008 National Assembly election.

After Ngedup resigned at the annual PDP meeting in March 2009, PDP parliamentary and opposition leader Tshering Tobgay assumed party leadership. In June 2012 it was reported that the PDP had failed a financial audit but pledged to have its books in order prior to the 2013 balloting.

After placing second in the first round of balloting in May 2013, the PDP merged with the DNT (below). On July 13 the PDP secured 32 seats and 54.9 percent of the vote. Insisting upon an internal secret ballot, Tobgay was unanimously elected prime minister by his party on July 19.

Leaders: Tshering TOBGAY (Prime Minister and Party President), Damcho DORJI (Vice President and Home and Cultural Affairs Minister), Sanjay NGEDUP, Ritu Raj CHHETRI, Sonam JATSHO (General Secretary).

Druk Nyamrup Tshogpa (DNT). Registered in January 2013, the DNT promoted a social democratic platform. After coming in third with 17 percent of the vote in May 2013 balloting, the DNT merged in mid-June with the PDP.

Leader: Dorji OM (Party President).

Bhutan Peace and Prosperity Party (*Druk Phuensum Tshogpa*—DPT). Formation of the DPT by merger of the Bhutan People's United Party (BPUP) and an offshoot, the All People's Party (APP), was announced in late July 2007, following the decision of a handful of cabinet ministers to resign their posts and unite for the multiparty assembly election of 2008. Personality differences led a faction headed by Sigay DORJI and Penjore DORJI to reestablish the BPUP, but in November the Election Commission rejected the registration application, citing a lack of clear ideology and "credible leadership."

Hallmarks of the DPT platform included fighting poverty and fostering equitable development. In the March 2008 election the DPT won 67 percent of the vote and 45 National Assembly seats. In 2012 DPT vice president Chang UGYEN was accused of complicity in a fraudulent land scheme.

In July 2013 elections the DPT lost its majority, winning 15 seats with 45 percent of the vote. Former prime minister Thinley resigned his seat in August, offering no explanation.

Leaders: Jigme Yoser THINLEY (President of the Party and former primer minister), Thinley GYAMTSHO (Secretary).

Druk Chirwang Tshogpa (DCT). The DCT launched in 2013, and campaigned on a platform of economic self-sufficiency. The DCT secured 5.9 percent of the vote in May balloting—a fourth-place finish that precluded it from participating in the July runoff.

Leader: Lily WANGCHHUK.

Ethnic Nepalese Formations:

Bhutan People's Party (BPP). With backing from the Nepali Congress and the Communist Party of Nepal (Marxist-Leninist), the BPP evolved in 1990 from the still-extant People's Forum for Human Rights. After being banned in September 1990, the BPP became a leading component of the Appeal Movement Coordination Council (AMCC), which organized a number of refugee marches and protests.

The party's founder, Tek Nath Rizal, having been imprisoned since 1989 and sentenced to life in 1993 for "masterminding" antinational activities, was released by the king in December 1999 but barred from political activity. BPP president R. K. BUDHATHOKI was assassinated in Nepal in September 2001. Repeated requests by the BPP to be registered as an official party were declined. SK PRADHAN, the leader of the Nepalese group, the People's Forum for Human Rights and Development, was arrested in April 2012 for the murder of Budhathoki.

Leader: Balaram POUDEL (President).

Druk National Congress–Democratic (DNC-Democratic). Founded in 1994 by Rongthong Kinley Dorji, leader of the Sarchop community in Bhutan, the **Druk National Congress** (DNC) operated in Bhutan until 1995, when the regime began to limit its activities. A split in the party was reported in 2001, with one faction remaining loyal to Dorji and another naming Chheku DUKPA as leader. Although Dorji remains leader of the DNC, a splinter, the DNC-Democratic appears to be more prominent.

Leaders: Thinley PENJORE (President), Narad ADHIKARI (General Secretary).

Bhutan Gorkha National Liberation Front (BGNLF). Organized in 1994, the BGNLF called for constitutional protection of ethnic Nepalese, immediate repatriation of refugees, greater representation in the National Assembly, and establishment of an independent judiciary.

Leaders: D. B. Rana SAMPANG, Aaiman RAI.

Communist Party of Bhutan (Marxist-Leninist-Maoist)—CPB (MLM). The Communist Party was reportedly formed in 2003 in the Bhutanese refugee camps in Nepal. It has close links to the Communist Party of Nepal (Maoist). In December 2007 30 alleged members were sentenced to between five and nine years in prison for subversive activities, including recruiting members. A group called the **Bhutan Tiger Force** (BTF) has sometimes been identified as the party's military wing, as has the **United Revolutionary Front of Bhutan** (URFB). All have claimed responsibility for various minor bombings.

Reports have suggested that the CPB (MLM) may have links to various militant separatist groups in India's Assam, particularly the United Liberation Front of Assam (ULFA). The CPB (MLM) has reportedly split into two factions because of ideological differences. In 2010 the BTF and the URFB were estimated to number approximately 600 combined.

Faction Leaders: VIKALPA, BIRAT.

Liberation Army of Bhutan (LAB). Expelled URFB member Tara Mukarung founded the LAB in 2009. In February 2010 some leaders of the repatriation movement accused the LAB of murdering the reputed underground leader of the URFB, Ramesh SUBBA (aka Kaila FAGU).

Leader: Tara MUKARUNG.

In addition, various expatriate human rights organizations—all of which the Bhutanese government classifies as political and therefore bans—have been operating abroad. In July 2003 seven of them banded together to organize the **Human Rights Council of Bhutan** (HRCB) under the chairmanship of Tek Nath Rizal, whose status as leader of the human rights community was further solidified in March 2006, when he was selected to head a new **Bhutanese Movement Steering Committee.** Founding groups in the HRCB were the **Bhutanese Refugees Representative Repatriation Committee** (BRRRC), chaired by Rizal; the **Bhutanese Refugee Women Forum** (BRWF), led by Garima ADHIKARI (Coordinator); the **Center for Protection of Minorities and Against Racism and Discrimination** (CEMARD Bhutan), led by Rakesh CHHETRI (Executive Director); the **Association of Human Rights Activists of Bhutan** (AHURA Bhutan), led by Ratan GAZMERE (Chief Coordinator); the **Human Rights Organization of Bhutan** (HUROB), led by S. B. SUBBA; the **People's Forum for Human Rights in Bhutan** (PFHRB), formed in 1989 by Rizal and later led by D. P. KAFLE; and the **Students Union of Bhutan** (SUB), represented by Mukti GURUNNG.

For more information on the **Bhutan National Democratic Party** (BNDP), see the 2011 *Handbook.* For information on the **National Front for Democracy in Bhutan** (NFDB), please see the 2012 *Handbook.*

LEGISLATURE

Until 2008 the National Assembly was a unicameral legislature of 150 members, including 100 elected district representatives, the 6 indirectly elected members of the Royal Advisory Council (formally abolished under the 2008 constitution), 10 members chosen by religious bodies, the 10 members of the Council of Ministers, and 24 senior civil servants designated by the king. Under a June 30, 2007, electoral law instituted by royal decree, Bhutan set about instituting a bicameral **Parliament** (*Chitshog*) in accordance with the constitution that was formally adopted in 2008. Candidates for both houses must have a university degree.

National Council (*Gyalyong Tshogde*). The upper house of Parliament comprises 25 members, 20 elected on a nonpartisan basis (1 from each district) and 5 appointed by the king, all for five-year terms. The first elections took place in December 2007 and January 2008. All members serve five-year terms. In addition to its regular legislative duties, the National Council is regarded as a "house of review" on security and sovereignty matters. It is not subject to early dissolution. The most recent balloting took place on April 23, 2013.

Chair: Sonam KINGA.

National Assembly (*Gyalyong Tshogdu*). The lower house may have up to 55 members, all elected on a partisan basis from single-member constituencies (a minimum of 2 and a maximum of 7 per *dzongkhag*). All candidates must belong to political parties. Members serve five-year terms, subject to early dissolution. Defection to another party is prohibited.

Elections are to be held in two stages. If there are more than two registered parties, all participate in a "primary round," with the two parties winning the most votes then entering the general election. Four parties contested the first round of the 2013 National Assembly elections in May. Following a runoff election on July 2013, distribution was as follows: People's Democratic Party, 32; Bhutan Peace and Prosperity Party, 15.

Speaker: Jigme ZANGPO.

CABINET

[as of September 15, 2013]

Prime Minister	Tshering Tobgay
Council of Ministers	
Agriculture and Forests	Yeshey Dorji
Economic Affairs	Norbu Wangchuk
Education	Mingbo Dukpa
Finance	Namgay Dorji
Foreign Affairs	Rinzin Dorji
Health	Tandin Wangchuk
Home and Cultural Affairs	Damcho Dorji
Information and Communications	D. N. Dhungyel
Labor and Human Resources	Ngeema Sangay Chenpo
Works and Human Settlements	Dorji Choden [f]

[f] = female

INTERGOVERNMENTAL REPRESENTATION

Diplomatic relations between Bhutan and the United States are conducted through the government of India.

Permanent Representative to the UN: Lhatu WANGCHUK.

IGO Memberships (Non-UN): ADB, NAM, SAARC.

BOLIVIA

Plurinational State of Bolivia
Estado Plurinacional de Bolivia

Political Status: Independent republic proclaimed 1825; civilian government reestablished in October 1982 after virtually constant military rule since September 1969; present constitution promulgated on February 7, 2009.

Area: 424,162 sq. mi. (1,098,581 sq. km).

Population: 10,624,495 (2012E—UN); 10,461,053 (2012E—U.S. Census).

Major Urban Centers (2005E): LA PAZ (administrative capital, 835,400), Sucre (judicial capital, 284,000), Santa Cruz (1,616,100), Cochabamba (618,400), Oruro (216,700).

Official Languages: Spanish, Aymará, Quechua (Aymará and Quechua were adopted as official languages in 1977).

Monetary Unit: Boliviano (market rate November 1, 2013: 6.91 bolivianos = $1US).

President: Juan Evo MORALES Ayma (Movement to Socialism); elected December 18, 2005, and inaugurated January 22, 2006, for a five-year term, succeeding Interim President Eduardo RODRÍGUEZ Veltsé (Nonparty); reelected December 6, 2009, in early elections after a constitutional change that allowed a second five-year term and inaugurated on January 22, 2010.

Vice President: Álvaro Marcelo GARCÍA Linera (Movement to Socialism); elected December 18, 2005, and inaugurated January 22, 2006, for a term concurrent with that of the president, succeeding an empty office after the assumption of the presidency by Carlos Diego MESA Gisbert on October 17, 2003; reelected December 6, 2009, and inaugurated on January 22, 2010, for a term concurrent with that of the president.

THE COUNTRY

A country of tropical lowlands and *pampas* flanked by high mountains in the west, landlocked Bolivia is noted for a high proportion of Indians (predominantly Aymará and Quechua), who constitute more than 60 percent of the population, although their integration into the country's political and economic life progressed slowly until recently. Women constitute approximately 44 percent of the labor force, with roughly equal numbers in agricultural, manufacturing, clerical, and service activities. Spanish, the sole official language until 1977, is the mother tongue of less than 40 percent of the people, while Roman Catholicism is the predominant religion.

Although providing only 9.27 percent of Bolivia's gross national product, agriculture employs about one-third of the population, mostly on a subsistence level. The main crops are soybeans, corn, sunflowers, rice, potatoes, and wheat. Land ownership has long been uneven, with the vast majority of arable land held by a small number of families, a situation the current administration has tried to alter through a controversial land distribution plan. Tin mining has been a traditional mainstay of the economy, although the state-owned mines have long been wracked by labor difficulties. The country holds an estimated 50 percent of the world's lithium reserves and exports silver, zinc, and tungsten. Bolivia also reportedly controls one of the world's largest unexploited reserves of iron ore. A limited number of large-scale gold mines have operated around the country since 2002, with the largest to date beginning production in 2008.

Natural gas is the leading export commodity. Gas reserves (estimated as the second largest in Latin America) are located primarily in the eastern lowlands, exacerbating a long-standing divide between the poorer western highlands (populated mainly by Indians) and the richer east (populated mainly by people of European descent and mestizos). With their rapidly growing gas and agricultural sectors, Santa Cruz and other lowland departments have served as the country's "economic engine" for several decades. Petroleum production peaked in 1974. A leading contributor to the underground economy has long been coca leaf production, with the overwhelming proportion of annual output entering the cocaine trade. In 2013 Bolivia was the third-largest cocaine producer in the world.

The International Monetary Fund (IMF) noted in a 2013 report that "prudent macroeconomic policies, accompanied by strong terms of trade, have allowed Bolivia to achieve impressive economic outcomes in recent years." Real GDP growth averaged 4.7 percent in 2006–2011. GDP per capita grew from $1,200 in 2006 to $2,530 in 2012. While 60.6 percent of all Bolivians lived below the poverty line in 2005, only 48.5 were in 2011. Similarly, extreme poverty has dropped from 38.2 percent to 24.3 percent in the same time period, thanks to cash transfer programs, subsidies, and infrastructure improvements.

Economic growth in 2009 fell to 3.4 percent, and unemployment stood at 7.9 percent due to slowing private investment and consumption in the wake of the global economic downturn. The Morales administration announced stimulus measures to counter the slowdown, including $1.9 billion to improve infrastructure and services and another $1 billion in the hydrocarbons sector. The administration rebuffed an IMF recommendation to increase privatization and instead embarked on a controversial program of nationalization of the energy and mining sectors (see Current issues, below). The World Bank upgraded the country from low to middle income in August 2010, citing a strong and sustained economic performance that raised per capita income. The economy grew by 5.1 percent in 2011 and 5.2 percent in 2012, fueled by mining and hydrocarbon sales, and unemployment reached record lows of 5.5 percent in 2011 and 5.4 percent in 2012. The country raised $500 million in an October 2012 bond sale, the first international credit auction held since the 1920s.

GOVERNMENT AND POLITICS

Political background. Bolivia's history since its liberation from Spanish rule in 1825 has been marked by recurrent domestic instability and frequent conflicts with neighboring states, especially Chile, Peru, and Paraguay. Few countries have matched Bolivia's unhappy record of political instability, which yielded nearly 200 chief executives in its first century and a half of independence. There were 13 presidents from 1969 to 1982, the most durable incumbency being that of General Bánzer (1971–1978). Eight more presidents held office between 1983 and 2006.

Increased unrest in the mid-20th century prompted a seizure of power in April 1952 by the reform-minded Nationalist Revolutionary Movement (*Movimiento Nacionalista Revolucionario*—MNR), which proceeded to carry out a thoroughgoing social and political revolution under the leadership of presidents Víctor PAZ Estenssoro and Hernán SILES Zuazo, who alternately dominated the political scene in four-year terms from 1952 to 1964. MNR rule was cut short in November 1964, when the vice president, Gen. René BARRIENTOS Ortuño, acting in the midst of widespread disorder, assumed power by a military coup. After serving with Gen. Alfredo OVANDO Candía as copresident under a military junta, Barrientos resigned to run for the presidency and was elected in July 1966. Supported by the armed forces and a strong coalition in Congress, his regime encountered intense opposition from the tin miners, who charged repression of workers' unions. A southeastern-rainforest uprising led by Castroite revolutionary Ernesto "Ché" GUEVARA in 1967 resulted in Guevara's death at the hands of government troops and the capture of guerrilla ideologist Régis DEBRAY.

In August 1971 the armed forces, in alliance with the MNR and the Bolivian Socialist Falange (*Falange Socialista Boliviana*—FSB), appointed a government under Col. Hugo BÁNZER Suárez. (For more on the numerous coups of the early 1970s, see earlier *Handbooks.*) Two years later the MNR withdrew from the coalition, and, after an abortive revolt the following November, Bánzer rescinded an earlier pledge to return the nation to civilian rule in 1975.

In November 1977 President Bánzer again reversed himself, announcing that a national election would be held on July 9, 1978. After balloting marked by evidence of massive fraud, the military candidate, Gen. Juan PEREDA Asbún, was declared the winner over his closest competitor, former president Siles Zuazo. However, faced with a suddenly unified opposition, Pereda was forced to call for an annulment. President Bánzer then declared that he would not remain in office beyond August 6, and on July 21 Pereda was installed as Bolivia's 188th head of state. Pereda was himself ousted on November 24 by Brig. Gen. David PADILLA Arancibia, who promised to withdraw following an election on July 1, 1979.

At the 1979 election, Siles Zuazo, the nominee of a center-left coalition, obtained a bare plurality (36.0 percent to 35.9 percent) over former president Paz Estenssoro, who headed a new MNR coalition that included a number of leftist groups. Called on to decide the outcome because of the lack of a majority, the Congress was unable to choose between the front-runners and on August 6 designated Senate President Walter GUEVARA Arce to serve as interim executive pending a new presidential election in May 1980.

Guevara was ousted on November 1, 1979, in a military coup led by Col. Alberto NATUSCH Busch, who was himself forced to resign 15 days later in the face of widespread civil disorder, including a paralyzing general strike in La Paz. On November 16 the Congress unanimously elected the president of the Chamber of Deputies, Lidia GUEILER Tejada, to serve as the country's first female executive for an interim term expiring August 6, 1980.

In the national election on June 29, 1980, Siles Zuazo again secured the largest number of votes while failing to win an absolute majority. As a result, before the new Congress could meet to settle on a winner from among the three leading candidates, the military, on July 17, once more intervened, forcing the resignation of Gueiler the following day in favor of a "junta of national reconstruction" that included Maj. Gen. Luis GARCIA MEZA Tejada (sworn in as president on July 18), Maj. Gen. Waldo BERNAL Pereira, and Vice Adm. Ramiro TERRAZAS Rodríguez.

On May 26 García Meza resigned as army commander and as junta member, naming Gen. Humberto CAYOJA Riart as his successor in both posts; three days later Admiral Terrazas resigned as navy commander and junta member in favor of Capt. Oscar PAMMO Rodríguez. On June 27 General Cayoja was arrested for involvement in a plot to remove García Meza from the presidency, Brig. Gen. Celso TORRELIO Villa being designated his successor. On August 4, following a rebellion in Santa Cruz, the president resigned in favor of General Bernal, who, in turn, yielded the office of chief executive to General Torrelio on September 4.

Amid growing economic difficulty, labor unrest, pressure from the parties, and lack of unity within the military, President Torrelio announced that a constituent assembly election would be held in 1984. The increasingly beleaguered government issued a political amnesty in late May 1982 and authorized the parties and trade unions to resume normal activity. On July 19 General Torrelio was ousted in favor of Gen. Guido VILDOSO Calderón, who announced, following a meeting of armed forces commanders on September 17, that the Congress elected in 1980 would be reconvened to name a civilian president. The lengthy period of military rule formally ended on October 10 with the return to office of Siles Zuazo and the concurrent installation of Jaime PAZ Zamora as vice president.

During the ensuing two years, numerous government changes proved incapable of reversing steadily worsening economic conditions, and in November 1984 Siles Zuazo announced that he would retire from the presidency following a general election in mid-1985. In the balloting on July 14, 1985, former president Bánzer of the right-wing Nationalist Democratic Action (*Acción Democrática Nacionalista*—ADN) obtained a narrow plurality (28.6 percent) of the votes cast, while the MNR of runner-up Paz Estenssoro won a plurality of congressional seats. In a second-round poll in Congress on August 5, Paz Estenssoro secured a clear majority over his ADN competitor. He was inaugurated for his fourth presidential term on August 6 in the country's first peaceful transfer of power since his succession of Siles Zuazo exactly 25 years earlier.

While successful in virtually eliminating one of history's highest rates of inflation, the new administration proved unable to resolve a wide range of other economic difficulties that included massive unemployment (generated, in part, by a crippling decline in world tin prices) and an illegal cocaine trade that provided half the country's export income. The public responded on December 6, 1987, by rejecting most government candidates in municipal balloting that yielded impressive gains for both the rightist ADN and the Movement of the Revolutionary Left (*Movimiento de la Izquierda Revolucionaria*—MIR).

As in 1985 the results of the nationwide balloting of May 7, 1989, were inconclusive. MNR candidate Gonzalo ("Goni") SANCHEZ DE LOZADA Bustamente obtained a slim plurality (23.1 percent) in the presidential poll over the ADN's Bánzer (22.7 percent) and the MIR's Paz Zamora (19.6 percent). A period of intense negotiation ensued that yielded a somewhat improbable pact of "national unity" between the right-wing ADN and the left-of-center MIR on August 2 and the congressional selection four days later of Paz Zamora to head an administration in which 10 of 18 cabinet posts were awarded to the ADN. The unusual accord (which excluded the MNR) was seen, in part, as a continuation of long-standing personal animosity between former president Bánzer and MNR leader Sánchez de Lozada. Bánzer claimed as his reward the chair of an interparty Political Council of Convergence and National Unity (*Consejo Superior de Unidad y Convergencia*), which some interpreted as the effective locus of power within the MIR-ADN coalition.

In the nationwide poll of June 6, 1993, Sánchez de Lozada again defeated Bánzer, this time by a sufficiently impressive margin to ensure designation by Congress under a new procedure that confined its options to the two front-runners. In the legislative balloting, the MNR obtained an equally improved plurality (69 of 157 seats overall) that yielded a pre-inaugural governing pact between the MNR, the rightist Civic Solidarity Union (*Unión Cívica Solidaridad*—UCS), and the leftist Free Bolivia Movement (*Movimiento Bolivia Libre*—MBL). The UCS withdrew from the coalition in September 1994, apparently because of government concessions to labor in furtherance of its antidrug campaign; however, the party rejoined the coalition in June 1995.

The 1997 candidacy of the ADN's Bánzer was aided by the withdrawal of the highly respected René BLATTMANN Bauer, in favor of the relatively colorless Juan Carlos DURAN. Despite his advanced age of 71 and former role as a military dictator, Bánzer led the June 1 poll with 22.3 percent of the vote and ensured his congressional designation by entering into a post-election coalition with the MIR, the UCS, and the fourth-ranked Conscience of the Fatherland (*Conciencia de Patria*—Condepa). Overall, the group controlled 96 of 130 seats in the Chamber of Deputies and 24 of 27 in the Senate. Following a leadership dispute within Condepa in mid-1998, its two cabinet members resigned, and Bánzer dropped the party from the ruling coalition. An ailing Bánzer resigned on August 7, 2001, and was succeeded by Vice President Jorge Fernándo QUIROGA Ramírez to serve for the balance of the presidential term to August 2002.

In the election of June 30, 2002, the MNR, in alliance with the MBL, won pluralities of 11 Senate and 36 Chamber seats, while Sánchez de Lozada outpolled Movement to Socialism (*Movimiento al Socialismo*—MAS) leader Evo MORALES by a bare 1.5 percent margin in presidential balloting and was reappointed by Congress on August 4. The ensuing year was marked by turmoil on a number of fronts, including opposition to the U.S.-backed coca eradication program, anger at the plight of the landless, objections to the export of natural gas to Chile, and discontent with tax increases and a number of recent privatizations. On October 13, 2003, Vice President Carlos MESA Gisbert withdrew his support for the president, and on October 17, amid widespread clashes between security forces and demonstrators, Sánchez de Lozada was forced to resign and flee the country. Mesa assumed the presidency, naming a new and formally nonpartisan cabinet.

President Mesa won the approval of a somewhat ambiguous five-part hydrocarbons referendum in July 2004 that called for "using gas as a strategic resource to recover sovereign and viable access to the sea" (a reference to the dispute with Chile; see Foreign relations, below). Also approved were the recovery of "all hydrocarbons at the wellhead" and the levying of taxes of up to 50 percent on oil and gas production.

The referendum, as presented, had been opposed by the eastern, natural gas–producing department of Santa Cruz. The *cruceños,* who included most of the country's European descendants, contrasted their region of "productive Bolivia" with the Inca-dominated "conflictive Bolivia" of the western highlands; by mid-2004 they were calling for regional autonomy, if not secession. In January 2005 Santa Cruz announced the formation of an autonomous regional government. President Mesa responded by terming the unconstitutional action as "one of the gravest and most difficult situations that Bolivia has ever had to face."

President Mesa resigned on June 6, 2005, in the wake of widespread unrest over the hydrocarbon policies and related autonomy pressure in several regions. The Congress named Supreme Court Justice Eduardo RODRÍGUEZ Veltsé the interim president after the presidents of Congress and the Chamber of Deputies removed themselves from the official line of succession to permit a compromise with the MAS, the party most directly involved in the protests. Rodríguez promptly announced an interim cabinet and launched negotiations for new elections, which were complicated by a constitutionally mandated redistribution of seats to reflect demographic changes recorded by the 2001 census.

On September 22, 2005, the Constitutional Court voided a congressional effort to sidestep the redistricting issue by decreeing that elections called for December 4 would be based on the 1992 census. On November 1, Rodríguez issued a constitutionally questionable decree redistricting the legislative seats, and on December 18 MAS leader Morales won the presidency, securing 53.7 percent of the vote. (Morales was the first presidential contender since the end of military rule in 1982 to gain a majority in the national poll and thereby secure victory without congressional action.) MAS also won control of the lower house with a 72-seat majority, while running a close second to former president Quiroga's Social Democratic Power (*Poder Democrático Social*—Podemos) in the Senate. However, the MAS won the governorships in only three of the nine departments in concurrent balloting.

Beginning in 2006, Morales announced a plan for wide-scale land reform and redistribution to the country's indigenous rural workers. Under the plan, 12 million state-owned acres would be redistributed initially, followed by the seizure and redistribution of privately owned land deemed "unproductive" because it was not used for farm production. The government contended that the legal ownership of much of the eastern lowlands under consideration was dubious because wealthy landowners under the Bánzer dictatorship had acquired it illegally. Vice President Alvaro Garcia Linera attempted to assuage fears among Santa Cruz landowners by giving them the opportunity to legalize their deeds and retain property that was under cultivation. Ultimately, the government's plan called for about 48 million acres to be redistributed by 2011, with limits to be placed on the size of private holdings.

At the president's request, Congress in March 2006 authorized the election of a Constituent Assembly to rewrite the constitution. In balloting on July 2, the MAS secured 137 of 255 seats in the assembly, while in concurrent balloting on a referendum regarding proposed greater regional autonomy, the five western departments (La Paz, Oruro, Potosi, Chuquisaca, and Cochabamba) voted no and the four eastern departments (Santa Cruz, Tarija, Beni, and Pando) voted yes. Autonomy was thereby not granted to any of the departments, the National Elections Court (*Corte Nacional Electoral*—CNE) having previously ruled (much to the consternation of the easterners) that a majority of voters nationwide needed to approve the measure for it to be adopted in any department. The national no vote totaled 57 percent.

The Constituent Assembly discussed a number of complicated issues, including the president's land redistribution policy and demands for greater regional autonomy. Much of the population in the eastern departments appeared to support increased autonomy, particularly because it would mean greater local control of resource revenues. The movement for more autonomy burst out into large-scale anti-Morales demonstrations in several cities earlier in the year. Due to the contentiousness of the issues, the assembly was unable to meet its August deadline and its mandate was extended until December. Tensions resulting from the polarization of the country were heightened throughout the latter part of the year as the homes of politicians aligned with Morales, trade unions, and other public offices were the targets of bomb attacks.

On December 9, 2007, the Constituent Assembly approved a new charter that did not include the provision defining "unproductive land holdings" that were key to the president's controversial redistribution plan. That article was postponed so that it could be subject to the 2008 constitutional referendum. Thousands of supporters and opponents of the new charter demonstrated in the streets.

In March 2008 the National Electoral Court postponed indefinitely the May 4 constitutional referendum. As tensions continued to mount, the prosperous department of Santa Cruz voted for autonomy—seen as a largely symbolic move—by over 85 percent on May 5, prompting violent protests between groups on either side of the issue. In June two of the poorer departments, Beni and Pando, also voted for greater autonomy; a subsequent referendum in Tarija, a region that contains 85 percent of the country's natural gas reserves, also supported greater autonomy. While President Morales declared all of the votes to be illegal, they underscored the seemingly intractable differences between the eastern lowland regions, which opposed Morales's redistribution plans, and the poverty-stricken western regions, where most of the indigenous population resides.

Faced with a political stalemate, Morales announced an August 10 referendum on his own government and on eight of the nine provincial governors. (The ninth governor had been recently elected.) Morales received the support of 67 percent of voters, but two of the governors who had been critics of the Morales administration lost their posts. The four most powerful opposition governors kept their seats. On September 20 a group of 20 indigenous political workers were killed in the northern province of Pando. The province's opposition governor, Leopoldo FERNANDEZ, was accused of orchestrating the killings and was arrested. Morales named a military leader to restore order in the province and to try to control drug traffickers working in the region.

In February 2009 the Morales government seized 36,000 hectares from several large landowners in the Alto Parapeti region as its first move to redistribute land. A month later, the president held a ceremony on one of the confiscated ranches and handed out titles to 34 indigenous people and poor farmers. Bolivia's constitution limits land ownership to 5,000 acres and permits reclamation by the government if it deems the land is not being used to its full potential or for other social reasons, a measure that drew strong opposition from eastern landowners. As of April 2011 the government had redistributed 4.1 million hectares since 2005, but critics complained the pace was too slow, and that pace slowed further between 2011 and 2013.

Following the installation of a new government in February 2009, leftist groups that supported the president criticized the new cabinet, saying that the changes amounted to name-swapping and continued to leave poor people without representation in the government. On April 7 Morales sent a bill to Congress that sought, among other things, to change electoral law based on the new constitution by redrawing voting districts and assigning more seats to the rural and majority indigenous areas. The lower house, with an MAS majority, quickly approved the legislation, while the opposition Podemos-controlled Senate blocked it from moving forward, saying it would give MAS complete control over both houses. To protest the Senate's refusal to cooperate, Morales went on a hunger strike beginning April 9. That public move, combined with negotiations that ultimately reduced the number of seats in the lower chamber, thus giving indigenous politicians a voting advantage, garnered enough support for the measure to be approved by the Senate. The new law, signed by Morales on April 14, set the next general elections for December 6 and gave Bolivians living outside the country the right to vote.

During legislative elections on December 6, 2009, Morales' MAS took two-thirds of ballots in the opposition's eastern provinces, earned 64 percent of the national vote, and won majorities in both chambers of the assembly. The nascent rightist Progress Plan for Bolivia-National Convergence (*Plan Progreso para Bolivia–Convergencia Nacional*—PPB-CN) came in second place with 26 percent of ballots. The sweep by MAS meant that 95 percent of new Plurinational Assembly (the congress's name after the new constitution's fundamental changes took effect) members were serving for the first time.

On February 12, 2010, the new legislature passed a bill that gave Morales the power to name five Supreme Court judges, ten Constitutional Court magistrates, and three members of the Judiciary Council (*Consejo de la Judicatura*)—effectively giving him control of all three branches of government. The opposition and the country's lawyers' association called the appointments "political," though Morales gave only one seat on the Supreme Court to an MAS affiliate.

The MAS also won regional and local elections on April 4, 2010. The ruling party took 6 of 9 gubernatorial seats and two-thirds of the 337 municipalities and increased its presence in the restive eastern departments. Morales replaced two ministers during the annual reshuffle of his cabinet on February 15, 2011, and created a new communications ministry.

In early 2010 the government continued to seize private land, and the Senate approved a bill to nationalize the state pension system. Legislators separately approved an independent justice system for indigenous communities, lowered the retirement age to 58, and extended pensions to the informal sector, where 67 percent of the population works.

But the administration's rhetoric concerning nationalization, coupled with a mining sector that remained as much as 89 percent owned by foreign interests and extreme poverty that reached 67 percent in the mining region of Potosi, led to protests and simmering frustration in mid-2010. Around 100,000 protestors took to the streets in the area, including some politicians aligned with MAS.

A drug-related shootout on May 15, 2010, in Santa Cruz prompted the Morales government to deploy troops to 17 outposts along the country's borders with Brazil and Paraguay in an effort to combat the rise of international drug gangs, who were entering the country to process and traffic cocaine. The administration played down the deployment in light of its "coca, yes—cocaine, no" policy. Previous legislation allowed the legal cultivation of 12,000 hectares of coca annually and promoted consumption of coca leaves, long a part of Bolivian culture. Morales raised the cultivation to 20,000 hectares annually, and a 2010 UN report said the crop accounted for 2 percent of the total GDP in 2009. But the abiding connection between coca cultivation and processed drug trafficking was put into the spotlight on February 24, 2011, when Gen. René SANABRIA, an intelligence official and the former head of Bolivia's antinarcotics police agency, was arrested in Panama with 60 kg of cocaine on him and extradited to the United States on smuggling charges. Sanabria pleaded guilty in a U.S. federal court in June. Bolivian authorities arrested three other police officers for their connection to the same smuggling ring. Several weeks later, Morales dismissed the head of the national police force after giving him an ultimatum to purge the agency of drug traffickers.

In December 2010 the opposition governor of the eastern Tarija department, Mario COSSÍO, was suspended from his post on corruption charges. He was replaced with a politician allied with MAS. Cossío was later granted asylum in Paraguay on the grounds that he was subject to political prosecution, and he joined a number of other municipal and regional politicians and judges who observers said were targeted for their political opposition. Governors in the last two regions held by the opposition, Beni and Santa Cruz, also came under legal scrutiny. Some 125 opposition figures and their relatives were said to have fled the country since 2007.

On April 18, 2011, Morales reached an agreement with the country's largest trade union after two weeks of protests—some leading to injuries during clashes with the police—over the wages of public sector employees. The government agreed to give the workers an 11 percent pay raise. The Morales administration faced growing public anger over a number of issues besides the rift over public salaries, the greatest being over a failed plan to remove fuel subsidies and over the spike in food prices in early 2011.

Constitution and government. The constitution of February 1967 was Bolivia's 16th since independence. It vested executive power in a popularly elected president and legislative authority in a bicameral Congress. Suspended in 1969, it was reinstated in 1979, the country having been ruled during the intervening decade by presidential decree; the constitution remained technically in effect following the 1980 coup subject to military contravention of its terms and was restored to full force upon the return to civilian rule in October 1982.

Under the 1967 basic law the president was directly elected for a four-year term if the recipient won an absolute majority of votes; otherwise, Congress made the selection from among the three leading candidates. However, given the selection in 1989 of the third-ranked contender, congressional leaders in mid-1990 agreed on a revision that limited Congress to choosing between the plurality candidate and the runner-up. In 1997 the term of office was extended to five years, with a limit of only one term.

The bicameral legislature consists of a 27-member Senate and a 130-member Chamber of Deputies, both directly elected for five-year terms. The judicial system is headed by a Supreme Court whose 12 members divide into four chambers: two for civil cases, one for criminal cases, and one for administrative cases. There is a District Court in each territorial department as well as provincial and local courts to try minor offenses.

There are nine territorial departments, each administered by a prefect (governor), who was appointed by the central government until first-ever direct elections were held for the posts in December 2005. Although the 1967 constitution called for the biennial election of municipal councils (empowered to supplant the president in the designation of mayors), implementing legislation was deferred until 1986, with local balloting being conducted in December 1987 for the first time in 39 years.

In July 1996 the government secured approval from the Chamber of Deputies for a constitutional amendment on redistribution of seats in the chamber, giving added representation to the more populous and powerful departments of La Paz and Santa Cruz at the expense of the peripheral departments of Chuquisaca, Pando, and Potosi. Agreement also was reached on the first-ever introduction of single-member constituencies.

Congress, under pressure from the Morales administration, passed a resolution in March 2006 calling for a 255-member elected Constituent Assembly to rewrite the Bolivian constitution beginning August 6, 2006, following direct elections on July 2, 2006, for the assembly delegates. The assembly was given a one-year mandate, after which its proposals were to be presented for a national referendum. Little progress was reported within the assembly throughout most of 2007, as government and opposition members argued over procedures. The Morales administration was pursuing, among other things, revisions to basic law that would permit presidents to serve more than one term as well as codification of the government's plans to redistribute land to the benefit of the Indian population and to give indigenous populations the power to conduct political and economic affairs according to their traditions. Meanwhile, opposition parties (dominant in the resource-rich eastern lowlands) called for greater regional autonomy, the establishment of elected regional legislatures, and other decentralization measures that would weaken the power of the president.

On December 9, 2007, the Constituent Assembly approved a new charter, subject to a 2008 national referendum that was postponed to 2009. A new constitution was approved by 61.4 percent of voters in a national referendum on January 25, 2009, and was promulgated on February 7. The changes allowed the president to seek election for a second term, conferred new legal rights on 36 indigenous groups, and gave the government greater control over Bolivia's natural resources by allowing nationalization of resource-dependent industries. Later, more than 80 percent of voters approved a ceiling of 5,000 hectares on an individual's landholdings. But in a sign that divisions remained between the wealthy eastern and poorer western regions, the four eastern departments voted against the constitutional changes.

Constitutional amendments also led to establishment of four tiers of local autonomy—departmental, regional, municipal and indigenous. Decision making was redistributed, away from the capital, and in the case of indigenous communities, local leaders were allowed to practice traditional communal forms of governance and justice. The national government's role was altered to set policies on foreign relations, energy, economics, and security. The Senate was increased from 3 to 4 senators from each of the 9 departments for a total of 36. New provisions mandated that Supreme Court judges be popularly elected, instead of appointed by Congress, and serve nonrenewable six-year terms, instead of lifetime tenure. In addition, constitutional amendments required a two-thirds majority of Congress.

Reporters Without Borders ranked Bolivia 109th of 179 countries in its 2013 Index of Press Freedom.

Foreign relations. Throughout most of the modern era, Bolivia's relations with its immediate neighbors have been significantly influenced by a desire to regain at least a portion of the maritime littoral that was lost to Chile in the War of the Pacific (1879–1884). In February 1975 relations with Chile were resumed after a 12-year lapse, Chile announcing that an "agreement in principle" had been negotiated between the two countries whereby Bolivia would be granted an outlet to the sea (*salida al mar*) along the Chilean-Peruvian border in exchange for territory elsewhere. However, definitive resolution of the issue was complicated in late 1976 by a Peruvian proposal that the corridor from Bolivia be linked to an area north of the city of Arica (obtained by Chile as a consequence of the war) that would be under the three nations' joint sovereignty. The proposal was based on a 1929 treaty that provided that any cession of former Peruvian territory must be approved by Peru. (For developments from 1976 to 1994, see the 2007 *Handbook.*) In 2006, Evo Morales became the first president-elect in more than half a century to invite Chile's president to attend his inauguration, while insisting that restoration of full diplomatic relations would be contingent on Chile's acceding to Bolivia's demand for a sovereign corridor to the sea. During July of that year, Morales and Chilean President Bachelet reached agreement on an "agenda" for resolving the territorial issue, and by early 2007 it was reported that the "cold war" between the two countries had clearly been replaced by a period of confidence building.

Under the Bánzer dictatorship, Bolivia pursued an anti-communist and pro-U.S. line in inter-American affairs, although links with the United States were tenuous during most of the period of military rule because of the alleged involvement of senior officials in the cocaine trade. Relations with Colombia, Ecuador, Peru, and Venezuela were severed after the 1980 coup.

In July 1992 Bolivia applied for membership in the recently launched Southern Cone Common Market (Mercosur), while indicating that it wished to retain the membership in the Andean Pact. Subsequently, the Sánchez de Lozada administration endorsed a proposal to construct a 1,360-mile natural gas pipeline from Santa Cruz to São Paulo, Brazil, as well as a joint venture with Paraguay to develop a waterway for oceangoing ships from Bolivia to the Atlantic. While flow through the gas line following its inauguration in mid-1999 was far less than anticipated, talk of a second line arose in the wake of additional gas discoveries in Bolivia and a substantial increase in projected Brazilian demand. Meanwhile, the route of a pipeline to the coast to permit gas exports to Mexico and the United States became a major factor in domestic politics.

In an elaborate demonstration of reconciliation that included an exchange of trophies between former opponents in the bloody Chaco War of 1932–1935, President Wasmosy of Paraguay visited La Paz in August 1994. Subsequently, at the conclusion of a Rio Group meeting on September 10, Sánchez de Lozada signed a free-trade agreement with Mexican President Salinas de Gortari.

In 1996 Bolivia and the United States issued seemingly divergent assessments of the coca eradication campaign, the former insisting that a targeted reduction of 5,000–8,000 hectares for the year would be reached, and the latter claiming that the area under cultivation had remained constant during an eight-year period. (The statements were not incompatible, as land taken out of production could have been offset by new plantings elsewhere.) A revised U.S. estimate in mid-1997 contended that the total area under cultivation had increased by 27 percent during the preceding decade, and under a new cooperation agreement signed in late August the United States cut its farmer compensation funding by half. In September 2001 Bolivia conceded that claims by former president Bánzer that most illegal plantations had been eradicated were in error and that about 6,000 hectares (rather than 600) remained under cultivation. In late 2002, amid reports that new plantings were far outstripping eradication, U.S. satellite imagery placed the figure at 24,400 hectares. By 2007, estimates indicated Bolivia's coca production had increased to around 29,000 hectares, 5 percent more than the year before, though still significantly lower than production in the 1990s. The country's potential for cocaine production amounted to 104–120 metric tons the same year, ranking Bolivia as the world's third largest cocaine producer and coca cultivator. Total area under coca cultivation and cocaine refinement increased steadily beginning in 2000. By 2009 potential production capacity had grown to 195 tons/year.

In early 2006 (then) U.S. secretary of defense Donald Rumsfeld described the election of Morales, whose campaign had showcased anti–United States rhetoric, as "clearly worrisome," and the United States quickly announced plans to reduce military aid to Bolivia. However, any potential gap from that decision was apparently resolved by Bolivia's conclusion of a military agreement with Venezuela, which was reportedly greeted with concern in neighboring Peru and Paraguay. Venezuelan President Hugo Chávez also pledged massive aid to Bolivia for the construction of hospitals and other social needs. In addition, Morales and Chávez negotiated a "people's trade area" with Cuba. (The pact, the Bolivarian Alternative for the Americas [ALBA], was signed on April 29, 2006, as a counter to the U.S. Free Trade Agreement of the Americas and focused on enhancing social programs and economic cooperation between the signatories.) On the other hand, Morales, revealing a pragmatic approach that his critics had not anticipated, declined to follow Chávez's decision to withdraw from the Andean Community of Nations. He also toned down his criticism of the United States, and met with U.S. officials to mend relations following protests on the U.S. embassy that turned violent on June 9, 2008. The Bolivian government expelled the U.S. ambassador on September 10 after declaring him persona non grata for fomenting opposition to the Morales administration. The U.S. government responded the next day by expelling the Bolivian ambassador. Both offices remained vacant through 2012.

On May 23, 2008, Bolivia became a member of the Union of South American Nations (UNASUR). In November the U.S. government suspended Bolivia from participating in the Andean Trade Promotion and Drug Eradication Act (ATPDEA), a U.S. trade preference program that gives countries incentives to develop economic alternatives to drug production. Bolivia was suspended for alleged noncompliance with law enforcement efforts.

In April 2009 officials from Chile and Bolivia reached an initial agreement to resolve disputed rights to the Silala River. The deal was meant to compensate Bolivia for Chile's use of the water. In what was hailed as a historic event, Bolivia and Paraguay signed an agreement on April 27 that officially ended their long-standing border dispute over the Chaco region, which had triggered a war in the 1930s. The agreement reconfirmed the border as it had been designated in a 1938 treaty, giving a larger portion of the area to Paraguay. Improved bilateral relations followed the resolution, before foundering again in March 2011, when President Morales said his government would press Bolivia's claims for access to the sea through Chile in international courts. Bolivia filed a claim against Chile with the International Court of Justice in April 2013.

On June 30, 2009, the U.S. government made permanent Bolivia's exclusion from ATPDEA due to the country's nationalization of the hydrocarbons sector, weak enforcement of intellectual property rights, increasing export tariffs, and, most important, lack of cooperation in counter-narcotics operations as reasons for exclusion.

On October 19, 2010, Morales signed an agreement with Peruvian president Alan García Pérez that granted Bolivia access to the Pacific Ocean. The agreement expanded a 1993 accord that ceded a plot of land to the landlocked country and granted Bolivia the right to build a free trade zone, docks, buildings, a Bolivian navy school, and export facilities. Observers pointed to the ongoing maritime disputes between each country and Chile to explain the warmth between the two ideologically antipodal leaders.

After three years of diplomatic silence, Bolivia and the United States agreed to resume diplomatic relations in November 2011. Two months later, leaders of the two countries and of Brazil signed a new antidrug cooperation agreement to develop better technology to discover illegal coca fields. As of September 2013, however, no new ambassadors had been appointed.

Tensions with Washington flared in 2013, beginning in May, when Morales ordered USAID to cease operations in Bolivia. He accused the organization of conspiring against the state through its democracy-promotion activities. In particular, Morales was angered by an "imperialist" statement by U.S. Secretary of State John Kerry, namely that "the Western Hemisphere is our backyard. . . . It's critical to us." However, USAID had already significantly scaled back its programs in Bolivia.

While attending a conference in Russia in July, Morales commented that Bolivia might offer asylum to Edward Snowden, who was then living at Moscow's international airport to avoid arrest for leaking U.S. national security secrets. Morales boarded his presidential airplane to return home, only to be denied access to French, Italian, Portuguese, and Spanish airspace. The plane had to detour to Vienna, where it sat on the ground for 14 hours while Washington tried to determine whether Snowden was on board. Morales was livid, and other Latin American leaders rallied to his defense, denouncing U.S. imperialism.

Current issues. A government plan, announced in June 2011, to build a 300-kilometer highway through the Isiboro Sécure (TIPNIS) national park in the Amazonian rainforest sparked widespread protests and halved the president's approval ratings. Environmental groups warned of deforestation while the indigenous people of the area worried that the road would be used by cocaine traffickers and complained they had not been consulted, as specified in the new constitution. The government insisted the project was vital to future economic growth, as it would link the country to the Pacific Ocean via Chile and Atlantic Ocean via Brazil. Beginning on August 15, more than 1,500 protestors participated in a planned 40-day, 500-kilometer march from the region to La Paz to make their case. The dispute escalated on September 25, 2011, when police attacked protestors at their campsite, firing tear gas, brandishing clubs, and arresting hundreds. Defense Minister Cecilia Chacón, Interior Minister Sacha Llorenti, and Migration Minister María René Quiroga subsequently resigned to protest the brutality. Morales suspended the highway project on October 21, pending further consultations with local communities. Ultimately 55 of 69 communities voted for the project, 3 opposed it, and 11 boycotted the process.

As required by the 2009 constitution, Bolivians voted for members of the Supreme Tribunal of Justice, the Plurinational Constitutional Tribunal, the Agro-Environmental Tribunal, and the Council of the Judiciary on October 16, 2011. Designed to open access to the judiciary and resolve case backlogs, the format was criticized by opposition political groups, which argued that the MAS would play too great a role in the vote, since the candidate list must be approved by a two-thirds majority of the lower house, which was controlled by the government party. When the ballots were counted, officials discovered that nearly 60 percent were spoiled or blank. Voters had apparently heeded the opposition's call to lodge protest votes.

The ruling MAS lost its two-thirds legislative majority in the Chamber of Deputies on January 18, 2012, when five indigenous legislators announced they were forming an independent voting bloc, following conflict with Morales over the proposed highway. On January 31 hundreds of pro-highway citizens assembled in La Paz to try to revive the project. The national legislature passed a bill allowing for residents of the region to hold a nonbinding referendum on the project. In March the government announced a revised, 300-kilometer road with aqueducts and viaducts for animals to traverse safely. The referendum process began in July, but was plagued by boycotts, poor weather, and remote locations. Morales ordered an extension of the deadline to complete the consultation process and in the interim created a "green brigade" unit within the army. The president said the green brigade was to protect against deforestation and drug trafficking, but opposition groups feared it was a first step in militarizing the region in case it rejects the highway.

Delegates to the MAS national conference on March 26–28 announced that Morales would be their candidates for the 2014 presidential election. Technically this would be Morales' third term, and the 2009 constitution specifies a two-term limit. MAS officials explained that this would not be the case, as Morales' first term predates the current constitution. The Constitutional Court ruled in Morales' favor in April 2013.

President Morales continued his nationalization of resources program on May 1, seizing Transportadora de Electricidad, the Bolivian branch of Spain's Red Eléctrica de España, which provided about 74 percent of the country's electricity. The government next seized a silver, tin, and zinc mine belonging to Swiss-owned Glencore in June, followed by a South American Silver mine for silver, indium, and gallium in July. Two more Spanish-owned electrical companies, Electropaz and Elfeo, were appropriated in December.

Police in La Paz mutinied in June, as indigenous protestors approached the capital city. Long underpaid, the police demanded raises so that their income would be equal to that of the military. The government agreed and granted a 20 percent increase.

Morales has implemented a coca-licensing regime that balances cultural and criminal uses. The president, who has been head of the Bolivia coca growers union since 1996, successfully appealed to the UN to legalize coca-leaf chewing, calling it a Bolivian tradition. The government is funding programs to find alternative uses for coca and keep it out of the hands of drug dealers, including turning the leaves into fertilizer—a stimulant for plants. A September 2012 report by the United Nation Office on Drugs and Crime praised Bolivia for achieving a 12 percent drop in the total number of acres planed with coca in 2011, the first verified reduction since Morales took office. However, the potential yield increased by 25 percent due to more efficient cultivation methods. The UN also reports that as much as half of the legally grown coca winds up in the illegal cocaine market.

In February 2013 Morales nationalized the country's three largest airports, seizing more Spanish-owned assets. His government continued to emphasize infrastructure and urbanization projects, with \$3.8 billion—13 percent of GDP—budgeted for 2013, although many regional governments have not spent their allocations. Civic unrest increased throughout 2013, as unions protested the nationalization of the pension system, while employees alleged mismanagement at the newly nationalized enterprises.

Morales put the TIPNIS highway project on hold in April, declaring that it would not be built until the region's extreme poverty had been eradicated. His announcement came as several indigenous people's organizations and the main trade union federation, groups that had supported Morales through the Unity Pact since 2006, informed MAS that they would create their own political groups in time for the 2014 elections.

The official results of the 2012 census were announced in July 2013, but the total population figure was 362,649 people fewer than indicated in the preliminary results released in January. The discrepancy sparked controversy, especially as legislative districts were redrawn to reflect population shifts. The census also revealed a dramatic decrease in the number of Bolivians who identify themselves as indigenous—from 66.4 percent in 2001 to 48 percent.

In October, Bolivia passed landmark law granting legal rights to Bolivia's natural world, including freedom from genetic modification or damage from infrastructure projects.

POLITICAL PARTIES

Opposition groups began to prepare for the December 2014 national elections more than a year in advance. Over a dozen parties were registered by September 2013, with the opposition clustering into three fluid coalitions of national and regional civic groups. While long-time Morales opponent Samuel DORIA Medina has argued that the three groups should have a primary election and unite behind a single candidate, the other two alliances have rejected the proposal.

Broad Front (*Frente Amplio*) draws from four of Bolivia's nine departments. Its core is **Unity for Democracy** (*Unidad po la Democracia*—UN) led by Samuel Doria Medina. Other members include **New Citizen Power** (*Nuevo Poder Ciudado*), led by Senator Germán Antelo of Santa Cruz and **New Alliance Bolivia** (*Nueva Alianaza Bolivia*—AB), led by Amilcar BARRAL. Loyola GUZMAN, a former member of the National Liberation Army, also joined the alliance.

A second opposition alliance, the **Social Democratic Movement** (*Movimiento Demócrata Social*—MDS) emerged in April as an alliance of regional parties: *All for Cochabamba* (*Todos por Cochabamba*—TPC); the **Unit New Hope** (*Unidad Nueva Esperanza*—UNE) citizens group; **Greens of Santa Cruz** (*Los Verdes de Santa Cruz*); and **Beni First** (*Primero el Beni*), among other. Santa Cruz governor Ruben COSTAS will be the MDS presidential candidate.

The third group is **Movement Without Fear** (*Movimiento Sin Miedo*—MSM), a center-left party established in La Paz in 1999. The MSM joined the MAS in an alliance for national elections between 2005 and 2009, securing four seats in the Chamber of Deputies but went its separate way in 2010. It has since gained considerable attention as a national rival to the MAS. Founder Juan de GRANADO Cosio has been mayor of La Paz since 2000.

Government:

Movement to Socialism—Political Instrument for the Sovereignty of the People (*Movimiento al Socialismo-Instrumento Político por la Soberanía de los Pueblos*—MAS). Traditionally a minor leftist grouping, the MAS contested the 1997 election as a component of the United Left. In 2002 it emerged as the leading opposition group with 8 Senate and 27 Chamber seats. Militant coca-grower leader Evo Morales, an Aymara Indian, was "adopted" by the MAS for the 2002 presidential campaign, placing second to the MNR's Sánchez de Lozado. The party led all others in the 2004 municipal elections, winning 13 departmental capitals.

Morales won the presidency with 53.7 percent of the vote in 2005, and the MAS secured a comfortable majority in the Chamber of Deputies. The party also won the prefectures of the departments of Chuquisaca, Oruro, and Potosi.

The MAS won a majority in the July 2006 balloting for the Constituent Assembly established to propose constitutional revision and subsequently established ties with the MBL (below) and other small parties to extend its influence in that assembly.

With the promulgation of a new constitution in 2009, Morales ran for a second term, winning with a decisive 64.22 percent of the vote. The party increased its representation to 88 deputies and 26 senators, giving it a majority in both chambers. In 2012 he announced he would run again in 2014, insisting it would not violate the two-term limit in the 2009 constitution because would only be his second term under that document.

Over the course of his administration, rifts emerged within MAS as Morales reallocated seats to his indigenous Indian support base and as the constituents that had supported the party saw disparities between rhetoric and action. He came under increasing fire for allegedly favoring the coca industry over the environment and the indigenous communities. In July 2010 a group of 100 MAS dissidents said they would break away to form the **Coordinadora Indianista Katarista** (CIK), named after the 18th-century Aymara rebel Túpac KATARI. Morales instigated unrest in other camps of MAS too, including the powerful trade unionists, who revolted over public employee salaries and the plan to remove fuel subsidies.

Leaders: Juan Evo MORALES Ayma (President of the Republic), Álvaro GARCÍA Linera (Vice President of the Republic).

Opposition Parties:

Progress Plan for Bolivia-National Convergence (*Plan Progreso para Bolivia-Convergencia Nacional*—PPB-CN). The Progress Plan for Bolivia (*Plan Progreso para Bolivia*—PPB) was founded on July 31, 2007, by former La Paz prefect José Luis Paredes Muñoz. On September 4, 2009, party leaders announced the merger of PPB with **Autonomy for Bolivia** (*Autonomía para Bolivia*—APB) and the **Nationalist Revolutionary Movement** (*Movimiento Nacionalista Revolucionario*—MNR). The alliance drew together the most conservative of the country's traditional landowners, eastern opposition governors, and former Podemos legislators. The rightwing alliance, with former Cochabamba department prefect Manfred Reyes Villa on the ticket as presidential candidate and imprisoned former Pando prefect Leopoldo FERNANDEZ as vice-presidential candidate, won 26.46 percent of the vote during national elections in 2009. Its distant second-place showing earned 37 Chamber and 10 Senate seats. It became the single opposition voice in the Senate. Amid separate corruption charges brought by the government, Villa and Paredes fled the country after the election. Their exile led to a power struggle within the alliance and suggestions by members of the parties that a split could not be ruled out due to deep differences in ideology. Roger PINTO, CN faction leader in the Senate and a vocal critic of Morales, fled the country 2012. The alliance's surviving members have sought new partners for 2014.

Nationalist Revolutionary Movement (*Movimiento Nacionalista Revolucionario*—MNR). Founded in 1942 by Víctor Paz Estenssoro, the original MNR ruled from 1952 until 1964 but was outlawed for a time after the 1964 coup. It joined with the FSB and others in a National Popular Front in support of the Bánzer coup in 1971 but withdrew two years later. The MNR spawned a number of other parties as a result of leadership disputes and contested the 1978 election as the leading component of an electoral coalition styled the Historic Nationalist Revolutionary Movement (*Movimiento Nacionalista Revolucionario Histórico*—MNRH), after failing to negotiate an accord with the moderately leftist Democratic and Popular Union (UDP, under MNRI, below). The MNRH in turn contested the 1979 and 1980 elections as the core party of the Alliance of the Nationalist Revolutionary Movement (*Alianza de Movimiento Nacionalista Revolucionario*—A-MNR). Although tendered left-wing congressional support in defeating General Bánzer for the presidency in August 1985, Paz Estenssoro subsequently concluded a political accord with the ADN to facilitate implementation of a hard-line economic stabilization program. The MNR was decisively defeated in most of the municipal contests of December 6, 1987, and was unable to retain the presidency despite recovery to marginal front-runner status at the general election of May 7, 1989. Three months later Paz Estenssoro, who had been living in the United States since the inauguration of his nephew as president of the republic, announced that he was resigning the party leadership. The decision was formalized at a party congress in mid-1990 by the election of Gonzalo Sánchez de Lozada as his successor. During the congress the 84-year-old MNR founder attempted to heal a breach between a group of "renewalists" headed by Sánchez de Lozada and a "traditionalist" faction led by former vice president Julio GARRET. (Paz Estenssoro died on June 7, 2001.)

On October 27, 1992, Sánchez de Lozada resigned as MNR president and withdrew from the 1993 presidential election campaign after reportedly receiving a death threat from an MNR congressional deputy. However, he resumed both activities on November 20 and subsequently served as chief executive from 1993 to 1997. Reelected in 2002, he was forced to resign in October 2003. The party was virtually annihilated in the 2004 municipal balloting. In the December 2005 poll it secured one Senate and seven Chamber seats, while its presidential candidate secured 6.5 percent of the vote. The MNR, currently described as a "traditionalist" and right-wing grouping, won eight seats on its own in the 2006 balloting for the Constituent Assembly and apparently shared ten other seats in alliance with other parties. The 2009 alliance with PPB marked the first time since 1951 that the MNR did not run its own presidential candidate in an election.

Leader: Guillermo Bedregal GUTIERREZ (Chair).

Alliance for Consensus and National Unity (*Alianza por el Consenso y la Unidad Nacional*—UN-CP). An electoral alliance formed between the UN and the CP in August 2009. The UN-CP aligned behind the UN's Samuel Doria Medina for the 2009 presidential election and remained partners for the 2010 regional and local elections. Medina came in third place with 5.65 percent of the vote. The alliance secured three seats in the Chamber of Deputies.

The UN-CP, along with the PPB-CN, lobbied the government to bring back the U.S. Drug Enforcement Administration in March 2011 after its expulsion in 2008 from the country on the grounds that the Morales administration was failing to prevent drug trafficking in Bolivia. Alliance members in the assembly claimed in July that their allegations against candidates on the list for judicial elections in October were not properly answered.

Leaders: Samuel DORIA Medina Arana (2009 presidential candidate), Óscar ORTIZ Antelo (Former President of the Senate).

National Unity Front (*Frente Unidad Nacional*—UN). The UN was launched in late 2003 by cement magnate Samuel Doria Medina, a defector from the MIR (below), who called for equal representation of men and women in the new group and economic policies favoring "those entrepreneurs who generate employment and are absent from national decision-making." Doria Medina ran third in the 2005 presidential poll with 7.8 percent of the vote. The UN won eight seats in the 2005 balloting for the Chamber of Deputies and the same number in the 2006 poll for the Constituent Assembly.

As the global financial crisis worsened, the UN called for an end to political struggles to focus on shoring up the flagging economy and creating jobs. Doria Medina invited former presidents Carlos Mesa Gisbert and Eduardo Rodríguez Veltzé, former vice president Víctor Hugo Cárdenas, and Potosi mayor René Joaquino to unify their efforts to defeat the president.

Leaders: Samuel DORIA Medina Arana (2005 and 2009 presidential candidate), José VILLAVICENCIO (Former President of the Senate), Ricardo POL.

People's Consensus (*Consenso Popular*—CP). In March 2009 Senate president Óscar Ortiz Antelo threatened to leave Podemos after rifts developed in the party when a majority agreed to a compromise with the governing MAS party. Thirteen of the party's members of parliament said they would join Ortiz in a new party. Ortiz and his supporters, all from the opposition stronghold Santa Cruz area, strongly disapproved of the administration's agenda. On May 22, 2009, the group began to organize a party under the CP name. The group made public its bid for the presidency in June, but Ortiz put his weight behind the UN's Doria in August. The CP narrowly lost to the MAS in Pando Province during the 2010 regional elections.

Leader: Óscar ORTIZ Antelo (Former President of the Senate).

Social Alliance (*Alianza Social*—AS). AS is a Potosi-based grouping that was founded on October 9, 2005. It won six seats in the same year's balloting for the Constituent Assembly. The party won 2.31 percent of the vote during the 2009 elections and secured two seats in the Chamber of Deputies on a third-way platform that espoused reforming the Bolivian government as a meritocracy. In August 2010 former presidential candidate and then Potosi mayor Réne Joaquino, a highly popular opposition figure, was removed from office, convicted, and sentenced to three years in jail for financial irregularities. His conviction was overturned in 2013.

Leader: René JOAQUINO Cabrera (Founder and 2009 presidential candidate).

Other Parties That Contested Recent Elections:

Other parties that contested the 2009 elections but did not win legislative representation include the **Social Patriotic Unity Movement** (*Movimiento de Unidad Social Patriótica*—MUSPA), led by Juan Gabriel BAUTISTA; **People** (*Gente*), a group led by trade union leader Román LOAYZA Caero that won 0.34 percent of the vote; **People for Freedom and Sovereignty** (*Pueblos por la Libertad y la Soberanía*—PULSO), led by Alejandro VELIZ Lazo; and the **Bolivian Social Democrats** (*Bolivia Social Democrata*—BSD).

Túpac Katari Revolutionary Movement–Liberation (*Movimiento Revolucionario Túpaj Katari–Liberación*–MRTK-L). The MRTK-L outpolled its parent party in 1985, winning two congressional seats, both of which were lost in 1989. In late 1992 the MNR sought to "balance" its 1993 presidential ticket by selecting the MRTK-L's Víctor Hugo Cárdenas as Gonzalo Sánchez de Lozada's running mate.

On the eve of the government's first redistribution of land to indigenous people in February 2009, Morales's supporters attacked Cardenas's family and seized his property. Later, Cardenas, an Aymara Indian and outspoken critic of the socialist elements in the new constitution, said he would challenge President Evo Morales in the December 2009 presidential election. Cardenas was thought to have one of the best chances against Morales as his campaign got underway, but by early September 2009 the probability of the incumbent's massive support forced the former vice president to end his candidacy.

Leaders: Víctor Hugo CÁRDENAS Conde (Former Vice President of the Republic), Norberto PÉREZ Hidalgo (Secretary General).

Free Bolivia Movement (*Movimiento Bolivia Libre*—MBL). A breakaway faction of the MIR, sometimes styled the Leftist Revolutionary Movement–Free Bolivia (*Movimiento de Izquierda Revolucionaria–Bolivia Libre*—MIR-BL), the MBL was formed in January 1985. It was a member of the IU before the municipal elections of December 1989. The party secured four lower house seats in 1997. In 2002 it entered into an electoral alliance with the MNR.

The MBL, centered in the department of Cochabamba, cooperated with the MAS in the 2006 balloting for the Constituent Assembly, securing eight seats, but failed to gain any seats in the 2009 legislative balloting.

Leaders: Franz BARRIOS, Orlando CEVALLOS.

Social and Democratic Power (*Poder Democrático Social–*Podemos). The right-wing Podemos was launched in 2005 under the leadership of former president and former ADN leader Jorge Quiroga before the December 2005 balloting, at which it won a plurality of Senate seats and placed second to the MAS in the Chamber of Deputies. Quiroga, who enjoyed strong support within the business community, also finished second in the concurrent presidential race with 28.6 percent of the vote, while Podemos won the prefectures of the departments of La Paz, Beni, and Pando. Podemos, in many respects considered an "extension" of the ADN, won 60 seats in the 2006 balloting for the Constituent Assembly, calling for constitutional change that would strengthen the legislature at the expense of the president and provide for the direct election of more officials. In 2007 Quiroga accused the Morales administration of "undemocratic behavior." A group of the party's representatives in Congress, including the then president of the Senate, who began to disagree with Podemos's political agenda, split with the group to form the new CP (see above).

A La Paz court on September 8, 2010, sentenced Quiroga in absentia to 32 months in prison for slander and defamation related to unsubstantiated claims he had made in 2009 that a major bank had become corrupt after being seized by the government. Quiroga, living in the United States, said he would appeal the verdict.

Other parties and groups active in recent elections include the **21st Century Alliance** (*Alianza Siglo XXI*), led by Pablo Mauricio IPIÑA Nagel; the **Agrarian Patriotic Front of Bolivia** (*Frente Patriótico Agropecuario de Bolivia*—FrePAB), led by Eliceo RODRÍGUEZ Pari; the **Social Union of the Workers of Bolivia** (*Unión Social de Trabajadores de Bolivia*—USTB); and the **Revolutionary Left Front** (*Frente Revolucionario de Izquierda*—FRI) led by Oscar Zamora MEDIANACELLI.

LEGISLATURE

The bicameral Bolivian **Plurinational Legislative Assembly** (*Asamblea Legislativa Plurinacional*) currently sits for five years. The most recent election was held on December 6, 2009.

Senate (*Senado*). The upper house consists of 36 members, 4 directly elected by each of the country's nine departments for five-year terms concurrent with the Chamber of Deputies. Seats are divided based on the share of the vote received by each party. The Senate had 27 members until the constitution was changed in 2009. As a result of the December 6, 2009, election, Movement to Socialism secured 26 seats and Plan Progress for Bolivia—National Convergence, 10.

President: Gabriela MONTAÑO.

Chamber of Deputies (*Camara de Diputados*). The lower house currently has 130 members, including 70 uninominal members, directly elected from geographic districts; 53 plurinominal seats, awarded via proportional representation; and 7 indigenous deputies, elected from noncontiguous indigenous districts. Members serve five-year terms, and suffrage is universal and compulsory. After the 2009 election, seats were distributed in the following way: Movement to Socialism, 88 seats; Progress Plan for Bolivia—National Convergence, 37; the National Unity Front, 3; and Social Alliance, 2.

President: Betty TEJADA Soruco.

CABINET

[as of October 3, 2013]

President	Juan Evo Morales Ayma (MAS)
Vice President	Álvaro Marcelo García Linera (MAS)
Ministers	
Autonomy	Carlos Romero Bonifaz
Communications	Amanda Davila Torrez [f]
Cultures	Pablo Cesar Groux Canedo
Economy and Public Finance	Luis Alberto Arce Catacora
Education	Roberto Iván Aguilar Gomez
Environment and Water	Jose Zamora
Foreign Affairs	David Choquehuanca Céspedes
Health and Sport	Juan Carlos Calvimontes Camargo
Hydrocarbons and Energy	Juan José Hernando Sosa Soruco
Interior	Carlos Romero
Justice	Cecilia Luisa Ayllón Quinteros [f]
Labor, Employment, and Social Security	Daniel Santalla Tórrez
Legal Defense of the State	Hugo Montero Lara
Mining and Metallurgy	Mario Virreyra Iporre
National Defense	Ruben Saavedra Soto
Planning and Sustainable Development	Elba Viviana Caro Hinojosa [f]
Presidency	Juan Ramon Quintana Taborga
Production Development and Plural Economy	Ana Teresa Morales Olivera [f]
Public Works, Public Services, and Housing	Arturo Vladimir Sánchez Escóbar
Rural Development and Land	Nemecia Achacollo Tola [f]
Transparency and the Fight against Corruption	Nardy Suxo Iturri [f]

[f] = female

INTERGOVERNMENTAL REPRESENTATION

Ambassador to the U.S.: Freddy BERSATTI Tudela.

U.S. Ambassador to Bolivia: Larry L. MEMMOTT.

Permanent Representative to the UN: Sacha Sergio LLORENTTY SOLÍZ.

IGO Memberships (Non-UN): IADB, ICC, IOM, Mercosur, NAM, OAS, WTO.

BOSNIA AND HERZEGOVINA

Republic of Bosnia and Herzegovina
Republika Bosna i Hercegovina (BiH)

Constituent "Entities":

Federation of Bosnia and Herzegovina
Federacija Bosne i Hercegovine (FBiH)

Serb Republic of Bosnia and Herzegovina
Republika Srpska Bosne i Hercegovine (RS)

Political Status of the Republic of Bosnia and Herzegovina (BiH): Former constituent republic of the Socialist Federal Republic of Yugoslavia; declared independence on March 3, 1992. (The Dayton agreement of November 21, 1995, specified that the institutions of the existing republic's government were to function until the holding of countrywide elections, after which a new central government would be formed with joint FBiH-RS participation and retention of purely internal functions by each of the two constituent "entities." The existence of a single state of Bosnia and Herzegovina and other provisions of the Dayton accords were confirmed by an international treaty signed in Paris, France, on December 14. Elections were held on September 14, 1996, and the central and entity governments were subsequently established in stages.)

Political Status of the Federation of Bosnia and Herzegovina (FBiH): Federation of the areas of the BiH containing majority Bosniac (Muslim) and Croat populations authorized by framework agreement of March 18, 1994, which envisaged the federation as a sovereign nation that would pursue a loose political confederation with Croatia; federation agreement "reinforced" by the Dayton accord of November 10, 1995, with permanent territorial boundaries established by the Dayton accord of November 21, under which, in revision of the 1994 agreement, it was decided that the FBiH would be an entity within the BiH.

Political Status of the Serb Republic (RS): Proclaimed by leaders of Serbian-held areas of the republic on March 27, 1992; established (under revised territorial boundaries) as an entity of the BiH under the Dayton accord of November 21, 1995.

Area (BiH): 19,741 sq. mi. (51,129 sq. km). At the launching of the FBiH in 1994 the area under its control totaled some 30 percent of the former area of the BiH, the balance being under Serb control. Under the Dayton accord of November 21, 1995, approximately 51 percent of the country's total area was assigned to the FBiH and the remaining 49 percent to the RS.

Population (BiH): 4,622,292 (2012E—U.S. Census).

Major Urban Centers (2005E): SARAJEVO (380,000), Banja Luka (165,000).

Official Languages: Serbian, Croat, Bosnian.

Monetary Unit: Convertible Mark (market rate November 1, 2013: 1.45 convertible marks = $1US).

Presidency of the BiH: Željko KOMŠIĆ (Croat Member, Social Democratic Party of Bosnia and Herzegovina), elected on October 1, 2006, to succeed Ivo Miro JOVIĆ (Croatian Democratic Union of Bosnia and Herzegovina); reelected on October 3, 2010, and sworn in on November 10; Nebojša RADMANOVIĆ (Serb Member, Alliance of Independent Social Democrats), elected on October 1, 2006, to succeed Borislav PARAVAC (Serbian Democratic Party of Bosnia and Herzegovina); reelected on October 3, 2010, and sworn in on November 10; and Bakir IZETBEGOVIĆ (Bosniac Member, Party of Democratic Action), elected on October 3, 2010, and sworn in on November 10 to succeed Haris SILAJDŽIĆ (Party for Bosnia and Herzegovina). The chair of the presidency rotates among them every eight months.

President of the FBiH: Živko BUDIMIR (Croatian Party of Rights), a Croat; confirmed for a four-year term by the FBiH House of Peoples on March 17, 2011; succeeding Borjana KRIŠTO (Croatian Democratic Union), a Croat.

Vice Presidents of the FBiH: Mirsad KEBO (Party of Democratic Action), a Bosniac, and Svetozar PUDARIĆ (Party for Bosnia and Herzegovina), a Serb; confirmed by the FBiH House of Peoples on March 17, 2011, for terms concurrent with that of the president; succeeding Desnica RADIVOJEVIĆ (Party of Democratic Action) and Spomenka MIČIĆ (Party for Bosnia and Herzegovina), respectively.

President of the RS: Milorad DODIK (Alliance of Independent Social Democrats), a Serb; elected on October 3, 2010, and sworn in on November 15 to succeed Rajko KUZMANOVIĆ (Alliance of Independent Social Democrats), a Serb.

Vice Presidents of the RS: Emil VLAJKI (independent), a Croat, and Enes SULJKANOVIC (Social Democratic Party of Bosnia and Herzegovina), a Bosniac; elected on October 3, 2010, for terms concurrent with that of the president of the RS; succeeding Davor ČORDAŠ (Croatian Democratic Union), a Croat, and Adil OSMANOVIĆ (Party of Democratic Action), a Bosniac, respectively.

Prime Minister of the BiH (Chair of the BiH Council of Ministers): Vjekoslav BEVANDA (Croatian Democratic Union of Bosnia and Herzegovina) endorsed by the BiH presidency on January 5, 2012, and elected by the BiH House of Representatives on January 12, succeeding Nikola ŠPIRIĆ (Alliance of Independent Social Democrats) who had served as interim prime minister during negotiations over a successor following the October 3, 2010, elections.

Prime Minister of the FBiH: Nermin NIKŠIĆ (Social Democratic Party of Bosnia and Herzegovina); nominated and confirmed by the FBiH House of Representatives on March 17, 2011; succeeding Mustafa MUJEZINOVIĆ (Party of Democratic Action).

Prime Minister of the RS: Željka CVIJANOVIĆ (Alliance of Independent Social Democrats); nominated by the president of the RS and confirmed by the National Assembly on March 12, 2013; succeeding Aleksandar DŽOMBIĆ (Alliance of Independent Social Democrats).

THE COUNTRY

A virtually landlocked Balkan country with approximately 12 miles of Adriatic coastline, Bosnia and Herzegovina is bordered on the west and north by Croatia, and on the east by Serbia and Montenegro (see map). Serbo-Croat is the principal language of a population encompassing approximately 1.9 million Muslim Slavs (Bosniacs), 1.4 million Eastern Orthodox Serbs, and 820,000 Roman Catholic Croats. Women make up about 37 percent of the active labor force and 21.4 percent of the national House of Representatives. In 2011 the UN Human Development Index ranked Bosnia 74th out of 187 nations based on quality-of-life measurements including education, life expectancy, literacy, and standard of living.

In 2011 the agricultural sector accounted for about 10.1 percent of GDP, compared with 28.4 percent for industry and 64.1 percent for services. Timber is an important product in the north, in addition to maize, wheat, and potatoes, while the largely deforested south yields tobacco and various fruits and vegetables. Natural resources include fairly extensive deposits of lignite, iron ore, bauxite, manganese, and copper, as well as considerable hydroelectric capacity. Industrial output is low, however, and the economy overall compares unfavorably with those of most other regional republics. Leading industrial exports include base metals and related products, machinery and mechanical appliances, mineral products, textiles and footwear, and wood and wood products.

The GDP contracted by some 80 percent as a result of the internal conflict of 1991–1995, which destroyed much of the infrastructure and displaced several million people (see the 2011 *Handbook* for more information on the economy prior to the 2000s). Annual GDP growth averaged 5.1 percent from 2000 to 2008 before contracting by 2.9 percent in 2009 due to the global economic crisis. It rose slightly by 0.7 percent in 2010, and 1.7 percent in 2011. Unemployment remained high at 27.6 percent in 2011 and 2012, with inflation dipping from 3.7 percent in 2011 to 2.2 percent in 2012. GDP per capita that year was $8,200.

GOVERNMENT AND POLITICS

Political background. Settled by Slavs in the 7th century, Bosnia annexed Herzegovina in the mid-15th century, with both subsequently being conquered by the Turks. At the 1878 Congress of Berlin the territories were placed under the administration of Austria-Hungary, which continued to recognize Turkish sovereignty until formal annexation in 1908. The June 1914 assassination of the Austrian imperial heir in Sarajevo by a Serbian nationalist led directly to the outbreak of World War I. In 1918 the country became part of the Kingdom of the Serbs, Croats, and Slovenes, which was officially renamed Yugoslavia in October 1929. In November 1945 Bosnia and Herzegovina became one of the six constituent republics (along with Croatia, Macedonia,

Montenegro, Serbia, and Slovenia) of the Communist-ruled Federal People's Republic of Yugoslavia.

During November–December 1990, in the constituent republic's first multiparty balloting since World War II, the three leading nationalist parties (appealing to Bosniacs, Serbs, and Croats) won an overwhelming collective majority in the restructured 240-member bicameral assembly, limiting the previously dominant League of Communists to only 19 seats. In a separate poll on November 18, the three groups also captured all 7 seats in the republican presidency. A month later the three announced that Alija IZETBEGOVIĆ, a Bosniac, would become president of the state presidency; Jure PELIVAN, a Croat, would become prime minister; and Momčilo KRAJIŠNIK, a Serb, would become president (speaker) of the assembly.

Declarations of independence by Croatia and Slovenia on June 25, 1991, precipitated incursions into both by the Serb-dominated Yugoslav army, and by early September fighting had spread to Bosnia and Herzegovina. On September 12 a Serbian "autonomous province" was proclaimed on the border with Montenegro, with a number of interior "autonomous regions" being announced by Serb militants later in the month.

At a referendum on February 29–March 1, 1992, in Bosnia and Herzegovina, 99.4 percent of the participants endorsed secession from Yugoslavia, although most Serbs boycotted the poll; on March 3 President Izetbegović issued a proclamation of independence. Subsequently, on March 18, leaders of the country's three main ethnic groups concluded an agreement in Sarajevo that called for division of Bosnia and Herzegovina into three autonomous units based on the "national absolute or relative majority" in each locality. However, most Serbs continued to insist that Bosnia and Herzegovina be included in Yugoslavia, while many Bosniacs, despite the Sarajevo accord, also called for rejection of the division along ethnic lines.

On March 27, 1992, Bosnian Serbs proclaimed a "Serb Republic of Bosnia and Herzegovina" with Dr. Radovan KARADŽIĆ as its president. As ethnic conflict mounted, the UN Security Council in April authorized the deployment of a sizable UN Protection Force (UNPROFOR), although its mandate was to facilitate the distribution of humanitarian aid rather than to engage in active peacekeeping. Subsequently, the Serbs tightened their grip on eastern Bosnia and stepped up their attack on Sarajevo. By mid-May the siege of the capital had created severe shortages of food and medical supplies, with Foreign Minister Haris SILAJDŽIĆ appealing to the Security Council for the creation of "security zones" similar to those used to protect Kurds in Iraq after the 1991 Gulf war. On June 26 the Security Council issued an ultimatum to the Serbs to place their heavy weapons under UN control or face international military action to open Sarajevo's airport to relief supplies.

By late 1992 Serbian nationalists controlled approximately 70 percent of Bosnia and Herzegovina, with Croatian forces holding much of the remainder. In March 1993 agreement appeared to have been reached among President Izetbegović, Bosnian Serb leader Karadžić, and Bosnian Croat leader Mate BOBAN on a peace plan advanced by former U.S. secretary of state Cyrus R. Vance (on behalf of the UN) and Britain's Lord Owen (on behalf of the European Community) to create a new decentralized state divided into ten semiautonomous provinces. The plan was repudiated, however, by the self-styled Bosnian Serb parliament on April 2. On June 7 the Bosnian government felt obliged to cooperate with a UN Security Council resolution that would recognize Bosniac "safe areas" in the six enclaves of Bihać, Goražde, Sarajevo, Srebrenica, Tuzla, and Žepa.

Shortly thereafter, in negotiations chaired by Lord Owen and former Norwegian foreign minister Thorvald Stoltenberg (the new UN mediator), a provisional agreement was reached in Geneva that envisaged the division of Bosnia and Herzegovina into three ethnically based states under a federal or confederal constitution. By November, however, the viability of the Owen-Stoltenberg plan for a "Union of Three Republics" had evaporated, with Bosnia Serb leader Karadžić calling for a currency union between the Bosnian Serb Republic and Serbia proper, Izetbegović insisting that the Croats guarantee Bosniac access to the Adriatic, and intra-Muslim conflict in the northwestern enclave of Bihać yielding the proclamation of an "Autonomous Province of Western Bosnia" under the leadership of dissident Bosnia presidency member Fikret ABDIĆ. In addition, Serbian forces had renewed their bombardment of Sarajevo, while fighting between Croats and Bosniacs continued in Mostar.

On February 8, 1994, hard-line Bosnian Croat leader Boban resigned as president of the separatist "Croatian Republic of Herceg-Bosna," which had been proclaimed in August 1993, and on February 24 Bosnian government and Croat forces agreed to a general cease-fire. On February 28, in the first offensive action by the North Atlantic Treaty Organization (NATO) in its 44-year history, allied aircraft enforcing a "no-fly zone" over Bosnia and Herzegovina shot down four Serbian attack aircraft. At a Washington ceremony hosted by U.S. President Bill Clinton on March 18, Bosnian and Croatian representatives signed a framework agreement for a federation of the Bosnian Muslim and Croat populations, together with a preliminary accord on establishment of a loose confederation involving the proposed federation and Croatia. On March 24 the Assembly of the Bosnian Serb Republic declined to endorse the plan.

On May 30, 1994, Krešimir ZUBAK, a Bosnian Croat, was elected to a six-month term as president of the new Federation of Bosnia and Herzegovina (FBiH), with Haris Silajdžić, who had been named prime minister of Bosnia and Herzegovina in October 1993, being designated the FBiH's prime minister. However, at the expiration of his term on November 30, Zubak refused to step down, arguing that if the presidency passed to the Bosniac vice president, Ejup GANIĆ, no major office would then be held by an ethnic Croat. Despite the impasse, both Croat and Bosniac leaders reaffirmed their support for the FBiH on February 5, 1995.

An international "Contact Group" (France, Germany, Russia, the United Kingdom, and the United States) on July 6, 1994, presented a package of peace proposals that called for awarding 51 percent of Bosnian territory to the Muslim-Croat FBiH, with key areas placed under protection of either the UN or the European Union (EU). While the plan would have permitted the Serbs to retain a number of "ethnically cleansed" areas, they would have been obliged to cede about a third of their currently held territory to the FBiH. Although branded as "seriously flawed," the plan was accepted by the Bosnian government, but, as in the case of the Vance-Owen and Owen-Stoltenberg plans, it was rejected by the Serbs, who continued to insist on Serb access to the Adriatic, control of Sarajevo, and the right to confederate areas under their control with Serbia and Montenegro.

A four-month cease-fire began at the end of 1994, but it failed to break the political logjam. New fighting in May 1995 led to further Bosnian Serb advances and renewed heavy shelling of Sarajevo, to which the external powers responded by calling a UN/NATO air strike on an ammunition dump near Pale (the Bosnian Serb capital) on May 25. The Bosnian Serb military reacted by taking some 400 UN peacekeepers as hostages to deter additional strikes, thereby creating a major international crisis. Intensive negotiations led to the phased release of all the UN hostages by early July 1995.

By then, a Bosnian government offensive around Sarajevo had petered out, and Bosnian Serb forces were on the advance in eastern Bosnia, threatening the three Muslim-populated safe areas close to the Serbian border (Srebrenica, Žepa, and Goražde). The Bosnian Serbs overran Srebrenica on July 11, with most of its Muslim population fleeing or disappearing, despite the presence of 200 inadequately armed UNPROFOR troops in the town. (The world subsequently learned that more than 8,000 Muslim men and boys had been massacred in Srebrenica—the worst such incident in Europe since the end of World War II.) On July 25, with Žepa also having fallen to the Bosnian Serbs, NATO announced detailed plans for the protection of Goražde, the largest eastern safe area.

The killing of 37 people in a Sarajevo market on August 28, 1995, provoked NATO to launch "Operation Deliberate Force," involving heavy air strikes against Serb positions. A U.S. initiative secured the signature of a 60-day cease-fire agreement on October 5. This was followed on November 1 by the launching of new talks at a Dayton, Ohio, air base. The negotiations produced several historic accords among Presidents Franjo Tudjman of Croatia, Slobodan Milošević of Serbia, and Izetbegović of the Republic of Bosnia and Herzegovina, the last of which had continued to function in tandem with the FBiH's new government. On November 10 Tudjman and Izetbegović agreed to "reinforce" the provisions of the 1994 federation agreement, the resultant government having exercised little real authority. In addition, the Croatian and Bosnian leaders accepted the "reunification" of Mostar to serve as the capital of the FBiH. Finally, on November 21 a comprehensive settlement was reached regarding the permanent political status of Bosnia and Herzegovina, and the agreement was formally signed in Paris on December 14.

The Dayton accords specified that Bosnia and Herzegovina would remain a single state under international law but would be partitioned into Bosniac-Croat and Serb "entities" that would enjoy substantial autonomy. The FBiH was awarded 51 percent of the country's territory, including all of Sarajevo, while the Serb Republic (RS) obtained 49 percent, including several areas once inhabited by Bosniacs. All the parties undertook to cooperate with the International Criminal Tribunal for the former Yugoslavia (ICTY), which had been established in The Hague by decision of the UN Security Council in 1993. Those indicted by the tribunal were to relinquish public office. Final authority to interpret the nonmilitary terms of the agreement in Bosnia and Herzegovina was granted to the Office of the High Representative of the International Community, whose head would be endorsed by the Security Council after nomination by a Peace Implementation Council of 55 governments and multilateral organizations.

Compliance with the agreement was to be assured by the speedy deployment of a 60,000-strong Implementation Force (IFOR), which would operate under NATO command but would draw contingents from non-NATO countries and be subject to UN authorization. Including some 20,000 U.S. troops (the first American ground involvement in Bosnia and Herzegovina), IFOR began to arrive at the end of 1995, replacing the ill-starred UNPROFOR contingent. A quick cessation of open hostilities and the withdrawal of opposing forces to the designated cease-fire lines were achieved by the end of January 1996, although interethnic clashes and altercations with IFOR occurred throughout the year. The tensest situations involved the ethnically mixed cities of Brčko and Mostar, the latter split between Bosniacs and Croats in the FBiH.

In late January 1996 Hasan MURATOVIĆ (nonparty) was installed as prime minister of the Republic of Bosnia and Herzegovina in succession to Silajdžić, while Izudin KAPETANOVIĆ became prime minister of the FBiH. The previous month Rajko KASAGIĆ had been elected the new prime minister of the RS; however, as a moderate favored by Western governments, Kasagić quickly came into conflict with the RS president, Radovan Karadžić, who in May 1996 announced Kasagić's dismissal and replacement by Gojko KLIČKOVIĆ, a hard-liner. This controversial action served to intensify international pressure for the ouster of Karadžić, one of several prominent Bosnian Serbs indicted for alleged war crimes by the ICTY and therefore disqualified from public office under the Dayton agreement. After failed efforts by the first high representative, Carl Bildt, U.S. negotiators stepped in and, with Belgrade's backing, secured the formal resignation of Karadžić from all his offices on July 19, with Vice President Biljana PLAVŠIĆ taking over as acting president of the RS.

At the same time, evidence began to mount that atrocities had been committed during the recent hostilities. The discoveries served to intensify calls for those responsible to be brought before the UN tribunal, which began its first actual trial of a suspect in May 1996. In addition to Karadžić, the 75 persons indicted by the tribunal by mid-1996 included Gen. Ratko MLADIĆ, the Bosnian Serb military commander; Mico STANŠIĆ, the Serbian secret police chief; and a number of prominent Bosnian Croats.

Karadžić's departure from office (although not from dominant influence in the RS) unblocked the political obstacles to presidential and legislative elections supervised by the Organization for Security and Cooperation in Europe (OSCE). Within the FBiH, former prime minister Silajdžić mounted a challenge to President Izetbegović, seeking to rally moderate nonsectarian opinion to his new Party for Bosnia and Herzegovina (*Stranka za Bosnu i Hercegovinu*—SBiH). In the RS, the new acting president, Biljana Plavšić, also succeeded Karadžić as presidential candidate of the Serbian Democratic Party of Bosnia and Herzegovina (*Srpska Demokratska Stranka Bosne i Hercegovine*—SDS).

Despite last-minute controversies and much confusion, the elections went ahead on September 14, 1996, involving what OSCE officials described as the most complex popular consultation in the history of democracy. The official results confirmed the dominance of the main nationalist parties of the three ethnic groups, namely the Bosniac Party of Democratic Action (*Stranka Demokratske Akcije*—SDA), the Serb SDS, and the Croatian Democratic Union of Bosnia and Herzegovina (*Hrvatska Demokratska Zajednica Bosne i Hercegovine*—HDZ). In the contests for the three-member presidency of the state, President Izetbegović of the SDA took 80 percent of the Bosniac vote, Momčilo Krajišnik of the SDS took 67 percent of the Serb vote, and Krešimir Zubak of the HDZ took 89 percent of the Croat vote. In the legislative contests, the SDA achieved a plurality in the national House of Representatives and a majority in the lower house of the FBiH, while the SDS won a majority in the Serb Assembly. In the RS's presidential election, Plavšić was confirmed in office with 59 percent of the vote.

The worst fighting since the signature of the Dayton agreement erupted in mid-November 1996, on the eastern line of separation, as Bosnian Serbs mounted armed resistance to Bosniacs who were attempting to return to their former homes. In early December NATO authorized a new Stabilization Force (SFOR) to take over when the IFOR mandate expired on December 20. The SFOR was given an 18-month mandate, with 17 non-NATO countries also agreeing to contribute to its total of 31,000 personnel.

On December 12, 1996, the collective presidency appointed the SBiH's Silajdžić and Boro BOSIĆ of the SDS to co-chair the new six-member Council of Ministers of the Republic of Bosnia and Herzegovina. Five days later the leaders of the previous Bosnian Republic formally transferred authority to the new FBiH, while Bosnian Croats collaterally announced that the Croatian Republic of Herceg-Bosna had ceased to exist. On December 18 the House of Representatives of the FBiH elected Edhem BIČAKČIĆ of the SDA as prime minister of the FBiH's Council of Ministers; also during December, the National Assembly of the RS reconfirmed the SDS's Kličković as prime minister of the RS. The national House of Representatives formally approved the central government on January 3, 1997.

An indirect presidential election in the FBiH was held on March 18, 1997, Krešimir Zubak having continued to hold the office until then, despite his elevation to the central presidency the previous fall. Vladimir ŠOLJIĆ of the HDZ, representing Croats, was elected as the new FBiH president, while Ejup Ganić of the Bosniac SDA was elected vice president. Under the power-sharing arrangement in the FBiH constitution, the two men would exchange positions on January 1, 1998, with Ganić serving out the remaining year of the presidential term.

Meanwhile, political affairs in the RS had been complicated by a power struggle between President Plavšić's Banja Luka faction and the Karadžić-led Pale faction of the SDS. Plavšić and Krajišnik signed a peace accord mediated by Serbian President Milošević in Belgrade in September 1997. As part of their agreement, new elections were held for the RS's National Assembly in late November. The SDS and its coalition allies from the Serb Radical Party of the Serb Republic (*Srpska Radikalna Stranka Republike Srpske*—SRS) fell three seats short of a majority, and initial parliamentary sessions were unable to agree upon a government. When a coalition of all other parties in the assembly finally selected a pro-Western moderate, Milorad DODIK of the Party of Independent Social Democrats (*Stranka Nezavisnih Socijaldemokrata*—SNSD), as the new prime minister on January 18, 1998, the SDS and SRS deputies temporarily walked out and vowed to ignore all new legislation.

A new cabinet for the RS was sworn in on January 31, 1998, but there were neither Muslims among the ministers nor any representatives from Karadžić's stronghold in Pale. The assembly further underscored its majority stance against Karadžić by voting to transfer the RS's seat of government from Pale to Banja Luka, where Plavšić supporters dominated. In June the assembly also endorsed a no-confidence motion against Assembly Speaker Dragan KALINIĆ and Deputy Speaker Nikola POPLAŠEN, both hard-liners, and elected moderates to replace them.

Another full round of state and entity elections took place on September 12–13, 1998, nationalist candidates performing well in most executive races despite a moderate decline in support for nationalist parties in the three legislatures. Izetbegović easily won reelection to the Bosniac seat on the central presidency as the candidate of the SDA-backed Coalition for a Unified and Democratic Bosnia and Herzegovina (*Koalicija za Cjevolitu Demokratsku Bosnu i Hercegovinu*—KCD), while hard-liner Ante JELAVIĆ of the HDZ secured the Croat seat. However, in a result that was widely applauded in the West, Momčilo Krajišnik was defeated for the Serb seat by Živko RADIŠIĆ of the new *Sloga* (Accord) coalition, which comprised Plavšić's recently established Serbian People's Alliance (*Srpski Narodni Savez*—SNS), Radišić's Socialist Party of the Serb Republic (*Socijalisticka Partija Republike Srpske*—SPRS), and Dodik's SNSD.

At the same time, Western officials were dismayed by Poplašen's victory over Plavšić in the race for president of the RS. Following the election, the assembly rejected Poplašen's first two nominees to replace Prime Minister Dodik. On March 5, 1999, Carlos Westendorp, who had succeeded Bildt as high representative, announced the "dismissal" of Poplašen as president for "abuse of power" in his attempt to oust Dodik. Poplašen refused to accept the directive, his position having been strengthened by Serb anger (even among moderates) over the ruling by an international arbitration panel that the city of Brčko, which had been under de facto Serbian control, should be designated as a "neutral" (multiethnic) city under the central presidency.

On December 28, 1998, the central presidency named Silajdžić to continue as a cochair of the central Council of Ministers and nominated

Svetozar MIHAJLOVIĆ of *Sloga* and the SNS to succeed hard-liner Bosić as the Serb cochair. However, Mihajlović's appointment was strongly criticized by the SDS and Poplašen, and the central House of Representatives did not confirm the appointments until February 3, 1999.

In August 1999 Wolfgang Petritsch, the Austrian ambassador to Yugoslavia and EU special envoy for Kosovo, was named to succeed High Representative Westendorp, and in October he prohibited Poplašen and two other SRS officials from competing in local and general elections scheduled for 2000. At the same time, he rejected the application of Serb Vice President Mirko SAROVIĆ of the SDS to become the RS's president, and the office therefore remained vacant for another 14 months. In the FBiH, Vice President Ejup Ganić rotated to the presidency on January 1, 2000, exchanging offices with Ivo ANDRIĆ-LUŽANSKI (HDZ); the two had been elected to the rotating offices by the FBiH Parliament on December 11, 1998.

On April 12–13, 2000, the Republic of Bosnia and Herzegovina's Parliamentary Assembly voted to abandon the practice of having two chairs head the Council of Ministers. Instead, as with the collective presidency, the leadership would rotate among the three ethnic constituencies every eight months. The decision was partly a response to acrimonious differences between Cochairs Mihajlović and Silajdžić, the former having accused the latter of, among other things, "war-mongering" and attempting to undermine ethnic parity. In May the presidency nominated independent economist Spasoje TUŠEVLJAK, a Serb, as prime minister, and he was confirmed on June 6, succeeding Silajdžić and Mihajlović.

Meanwhile, the SPRS's differences with Dodik had led it to announce its withdrawal from the RS's *Sloga* government in February 2000. Despite losing a September 7 no-confidence vote, 43–1, in the 83-member National Assembly, Dodik stated that he would remain in office until the November 11 election, at which he was challenging Sarović for the presidency of the RS.

On October 14, 2000, Minister of Human Rights and Refugees Martin RAGUŽ of the HDZ was nominated to succeed national Prime Minister Tuševljak, collateral with Živko Radišić's rotation to the chair of the collective presidency in succession to Alija Izetbegović, who had decided to retire from office. (Tuševljak and Radišić, both Serbs, were prohibited from filling the two positions simultaneously.) The House of Representatives confirmed Raguž on October 18.

The parliamentary elections of November 11, 2000, saw many voters move away from hard-line nationalist parties at the central level and in the FBiH, the principal beneficiary being the new multiethnic Social Democratic Party of Bosnia and Herzegovina (*Socijaldemokratska Partija Bosne i Hercegovine*—SDP), which pulled even with the Bosniac SDA and surpassed both the Serb SDS and the Croat HDZ. In the RS, however, the SDS continued its dominance, easily winning a plurality in the legislature and seeing its candidate for president, Vice President Sarović, defeat Prime Minister Dodik 2–1. Sarović took office on December 16, and a week later he nominated a centrist, Mladen IVANIĆ of the year-old Party for Democratic Progress of the Serb Republic (*Partija Demoktatskog Progresa Republika Srpska*—PDP), as Serb prime minister. Confirmed on January 12, 2001, the multiparty Ivanić government included at least one member of the SDS, Trade Minister Goran POPOVIĆ. Less than a week later, however, in response to wide international criticism and, more specifically, U.S. threats to cut off aid if the SDS remained in the government, Popović resigned. Although refusing to identify his other ministers' party affiliations, Ivanić announced that they would not participate in partisan activity while in office.

With the 42 seats in the central House of Representatives distributed among 13 parties after the November 2000 election, the SDP, with 9 seats, had announced that it was prepared to open negotiations on forming a government with all but the main nationalist parties—the SDA (8 seats), the SDS (6 seats), and the HDZ (5 seats). Led by the SDP chair, Zlatko LAGUMDŽIJA, an Alliance for Change (*Alijanse za Promene*) was established on January 13, 2001, encompassing the SDP, the SBiH, and eight other parties. Together, they controlled 17 seats in the House, and on February 22, with the support of several moderate Serb parties, the SDP's Božidar MATIĆ won parliamentary approval of a multiparty Council of Ministers. Prime Minister Matić, a Bosniac, had been nominated by a majority of the collective presidency—over the objections of the HDZ's Ante Jelavić—after the House of Representatives rejected the redesignation of the Croat Raguž on February 7.

On July 1, 2000, a sharply divided central Constitutional Court had ruled that the country's constitution extended the constituent status of all three major ethnic communities throughout the entire country and required that the separate constitutions of the FBiH and the RS be brought into line with the central document. The plurality Bosniac constituency praised the decision, whereas the smaller Serb and Croat constituencies feared a loss of concessions that had been recognized in Dayton.

Under the leadership of copresident Jelavić, on October 28, 2000, some nine Croat parties formed an unofficial Croatian National Assembly (*Hrvatskih Narodnog Sabora*—HNS), which on March 3, 2001, declared a boycott of the FBiH government as well as establishment of a "Croatian self-administration" for cantons having Croat majorities. Jelavić stated that the HNS would consider revoking the self-administration edict if the government met a list of demands, including rescindment of recent changes that had been made by the OSCE to electoral rules. Those changes allowed all members of the FBiH's ten cantonal assemblies, whatever their ethnicity, to elect the Croat members of the central government's upper parliamentary chamber, the House of Peoples, thereby increasing the prospects of multiethnic parties and potentially diminishing the power of the HDZ. On March 7 High Representative Petritsch removed Jelavić from the central presidency because of his involvement in the autonomy movement, which violated the Dayton agreement.

Confronted by nearly universal condemnation, including that of the government in Zagreb, on March 16, 2001, the HNS announced a two-month postponement in self-rule, and on March 20 the new House of Peoples was constituted as scheduled. A week later the central House of Representatives elected Jozo KRIŽANOVIĆ (SDP) to Jelavić's former seat in the collective presidency, and Beriz BELKIĆ (SBiH) to the Bosniac seat, replacing Halid GENJAC (SDA), who for five months had served as Alija Izetbegović's interim replacement.

Meanwhile, on February 27–28, 2001, the FBiH Parliament had elected two members of the Alliance for Change, Karlo FILIPOVIĆ of the SDP and Safet HALILOVIĆ of the SBiH, to the FBiH's rotating presidency/vice presidency. The previously announced departure from office on January 11, 2001, of Prime Minister Bičakčić had also opened the way for the Alliance (with some 70 seats in the 140-seat House of Representatives) to forge the FBiH's first nonnationalist government, which won lower-house approval on March 12. Headed by Prime Minister Alija BEHMEN of the SDP, the cabinet was dominated by the SDP and the SBiH but also included several independents.

On June 22, 2001, central Prime Minister Matić resigned following the failure of the Parliamentary Assembly to pass an elections bill designed to address the Constitutional Court's concerns about ethnic constituencies. Passage also would have opened the way for Bosnia and Herzegovina's admission to the Council of Europe. On July 10 the central presidency nominated as Matić's replacement the SDP's Lagumdžija, who had been serving as foreign minister. Legislative confirmation followed on July 18. Dragan MIKEREVIĆ of the PDP succeeded Lagumdžija in the rotating post on March 15, 2002.

On April 19, 2002, a month before being succeeded as high representative by Lord Paddy Ashdown of the United Kingdom, Wolfgang Petritsch promulgated constitutional amendments and electoral law changes for the FBiH and the RS, neither of which, in his assessment, had mustered sufficient legislative support for achieving the ends outlined in the July 2000 Constitutional Court decision. With the overarching goal of instituting political equality among Serbs, Croats, and Bosniacs, Petritsch's revisions mandated significant changes to the structure of the entities' legislatures as well as requirements that all ethnic groups be represented at all levels of government.

Overall, in the general election of October 5, 2002, the three principal nationalist parties—the Bosniac SDA, the Serb SDS, and the Croat HDZ (in coalition with other, smaller Croat parties)—had the greatest success in the national and entity legislative contests in addition to sharing the tripartite presidency. On October 28 Dragan ČOVIĆ (HDZ), Mirko Sarović (SDS), and Sulejman TIHIĆ (SDA) were inaugurated as the triumvirate, although Sarović's tenure was brief: he resigned on April 2, 2003, after being implicated in the sale of armaments to Iraq, despite a UN embargo, and in efforts by Bosnian military intelligence agents to spy on NATO and EU personnel. Sarović was succeeded a week later by Borislav PARAVAC (SDS).

Dragan ČAVIĆ (SDS) was inaugurated as president of the RS on November 28, 2002. Niko LOZANČIĆ (HDZ) was sworn in on January 27, 2003, as president of the FBiH, following his election (despite a lack of Serb support in the House of Peoples) by the new FBiH Parliament. Also in January, new national and RS prime ministers—Adnan TERZIĆ (SDA) and Dragan Mikerević (PDP), respectively—won legislative approval. A new FBiH prime minister, Ahmet HADŽIPAŠIĆ (SDA), was confirmed in February.

Objecting to High Representative Ashdown's recent dismissals of Serb officials for non-cooperation with the ICTY, Serb Prime Minister Mikerević resigned in December 2004 and was succeeded in February 2005 by Pero BUKEJLOVIĆ (SDS). Less than two months later, on March 29, Ashdown dismissed the Croat member of the national presidency, Dragan Čović, who had refused to step down voluntarily in response to corruption allegations dating back to his 2000–2003 tenure as FBiH deputy prime minister. His replacement, Ivo Miro JOVIĆ (HDZ), was confirmed by the national Parliamentary Assembly in early May.

Meeting in Washington on November 22, 2005, to mark the tenth anniversary of the Dayton accords, leaders from Bosnia's three principal ethnic groups, pressured by the EU as well as the United States, agreed that they would take "first steps" toward comprehensive institutional reforms, including the abandonment of the tripartite republican presidency. Signatories to the "Washington declaration" included the three co-presidents and leaders from eight parties: the Serbian SDS, SNSD, and PDP; the Bosniac SDA, SBiH, and SDP; and the Croat HDZ and an ally, the Croatian National Union (*Hrvatska Narodna Zajednica*—HNZ). Nevertheless, on April 26, 2006, the constitutional reform package fell two votes short of the required two-thirds majority in the national House of Representatives, primarily because of opposition from most Croatian members and the SBiH.

Led by the SNSD, on January 26, 2006, opposition forces in the Serb National Assembly ousted the Bukejlović government by passing a no-confidence motion 44–29. Crucial support for the motion came from the PDP, which had withdrawn from the SDS-led administration in late November 2005, citing the slow pace of reform. The SDS subsequently indicated that it would join the opposition at both the national and RS levels. On February 4 Serb President Čavić designated a former prime minister, the SNSD's Milorad Dodik, to form a new government, which was endorsed by the National Assembly on February 28.

The general election of October 1, 2006, at the national, entity, and cantonal levels concluded with significant changes in executive leadership. Former prime minister Haris Silajdžić (SBiH) returned to power by handily defeating the incumbent Bosniac member of the presidency, Sulejman Tihić, with 62 percent of the vote. In addition, Nebojša RADMANOVIĆ (SNSD) captured the Serb seat from the SDS, while the Croat seat was won by the multiethnic SDP's Željko KOMŠIĆ, who defeated incumbent Ivo Miro Jović of the HDZ and Božo LJUBIĆ of the new Croat splinter party HDZ 1990. Another incumbent, the SDS's Dragan Čavić, lost his post as RS president to the SNSD's Milan JELIĆ, who, in a crowded field, took 49 percent of the vote to Čavić's 29 percent.

In legislative contests, the clearest victor was the SNSD, which came within a single seat of capturing a majority in the RS National Assembly—an accomplishment that solidified the preeminence of its leader, RS Prime Minister Dodik, among Serb politicians. In the 42-seat national House of Representatives, no party dominated: the SDA won 9; the SBiH, 8; and the SNSD, 7. In the FBiH, the SDA retained its plurality, but the SBiH made significant gains and the Croat vote split between alliances led by the HDZ and the HDZ 1990.

In early 2007 the tripartite national presidency nominated the SNSD's Nikola ŠPIRIĆ as prime minister of the republic, and the House of Representatives concurred on January 11. The Špirić government encompassed a total of seven parties: the SDA, SBiH, SNSD, HDZ, HDZ 1990, PDP, and People's Party "Working for Prosperity" (*Narodna Stranka "Radom za Boljitak"*—NS-RzB). In the FBiH, it wasn't until February 21, 2007, that the FBiH House of Representatives elected Borjana KRIŠTO (HDZ) as FBiH president, and achieving lower-house approval of a new FBiH government took even longer. On March 23 the latest high representative, Christian Schwarz-Schilling of Germany, nullified the previous day's confirmation of a new cabinet and reinstated Hadžipašić's caretaker administration because the vetting process for five ministerial nominees had not been formally completed. Following replacement of the initial candidate for interior minister, the new FBiH cabinet, headed by Prime Minister Nedžad BRANKOVIĆ (SDA), won approval by the legislature on March 30.

On November 1, 2007, Nikola Špirić resigned as central prime minister over his objections to governmental reforms announced in October by High Representative Miroslav Lajčák. The principal procedural change involved a new method of calculating a quorum in governmental sessions and in the legislature so that ministers and legislators who objected to policies and proposed legislation could no longer obstruct consideration "through pure absence." Lajčák's change was meant to expedite consideration of reform proposals—especially those related to the police. On November 12 the collective presidency of the republic accepted Špirić's resignation. Following lengthy negotiations, however, the principal national parties agreed to accept Lajčák's reforms. Crucially, a sufficient number of Serb representatives agreed to eliminate the separate Serb police force. The BiH House of Representatives reconfirmed Špirić as prime minister on December 28.

The president of the Serb Republic, Milan Jelić, died on September 30, 2007. The SNSD's Rajko KUZMANOVIĆ won an early presidential election with 42 percent of the vote on December 9, which was contested by ten candidates. He assumed office on December 28.

On April 10, 2008, by a vote of 22–19–1, the BiH House of Representatives passed the Law on Independent and Supervisory Bodies of the Police Structure and the Law on the Directorate for the Coordination of Police Bodies and Agencies for Support to the Police Structure. The upper house concurred on April 16, removing the last major obstacle to concluding an EU Stabilization and Association Agreement (SAA).

At nationwide local elections held October 5, 2008, the major ethnic parties continued their dominance: Milorad Dodik's SNSD more than doubled the number of mayoralties it held in the RS, while Sulejman Tihić's SDA and Dragan Čović's HDZ dominated in the FBiH.

On May 27, 2009, the FBiH prime minister, Nedžad Branković, resigned, having been indicted in April for abuse of office. He allegedly used government funds to purchase an apartment but resisted resigning until the SDA chair, Tihić, who had called for him to step down, won reelection to the party's top post. The nomination of Branković's replacement, Mustafa MUJEZINOVIĆ (SDA), was endorsed by the legislature on June 25.

On July 22, 2009, by a vote of 28–7, the BiH House of Representatives (reportedly under pressure from the United States and others) voted to remove the SDA's Tarik SADOVIĆ from his position as BiH deputy prime minister and minister for security. He had been accused of failing to deport foreign Islamic elements who had entered Bosnia to fight in the 1992–1995 civil war. The SDA then nominated its new deputy chair, Sadik AHMETOVIĆ, as Sadović's successor, but Prime Minister Špirić delayed the appointment, insisting that filling vacancies in the leadership of various government agencies should have priority. SDA chair Tihić responded by accusing Špirić of obstructionism and deliberately weakening state institutions in an effort to demonstrate that they cannot function.

The International Criminal Tribunal in The Hague began its war crimes trial against the "most wanted" Bosnian, Radovan Karadžić, on October 26, 2009. He was charged with 11 counts of war crimes and crimes against humanity, including 2 counts of genocide. The accused refused to show up for the trial until November 3, saying he had not had enough time to prepare his defense. The prosecution took two years to present its case, and the defendant will have an equal amount of time. Karadžić began to present his defense, acting as his own lawyer, on October 16, 2012. (For additional war crimes trials, see the 2013 *Handbook*.)

On February 10, 2010, the RS parliament adopted a controversial law that would allow a plebiscite in the RS on whether the international community's representatives should be afforded power within the entity. Observers viewed the new law as a possible first step to a referendum on secession, though RS prime minister Milorad Dodik said he had no intention of calling for a vote for independence. The Constitutional Court of the RS later upheld the law.

Also in February 2010 Bosnian and international law-enforcement officers conducted a high-profile raid in the remote northern town of Gornja Maoča, where Islamic fundamentalists were believed to have established a base. Authorities confiscated a cache of weapons, ammunition, and military uniforms along with fundamentalist Wahhabi propaganda. Seven people were arrested. A number of death threats sent to high-level politicians and a June explosion at a police station were attributed to Wahhabists retaliating for the raid.

Presidential, parliamentary, and cantonal elections were held on October 3, 2010. The SDP and the SNSD tied for the most number of seats in the 42-member BiH House of Representatives, with 8 each. Incumbents Komšić and Radmanović were reelected to the three-member presidency, while the third seat was won by Bakir IZETBEGOVIĆ of the SDA. The close race made it difficult to form a government.

Winning 37 seats, the SNSD maintained its majority in the RS assembly, and incumbent prime minister Dodik was elected RS president with 50.5 percent of the vote. Alexsandar DŽOMBIĆ of the SNSD was sworn in as prime minister of a new coalition government in the RS on December 29.

In balloting for the FBiH, the SDP won the most number of seats in the House (28) but remained short of the 50 needed for an absolute majority. Nermin NIKŠIĆ (SDP) was nominated as prime minister, but Bosniacs in the Council of Peoples vetoed the cabinet until February 1, 2011, because of dissatisfaction over the distribution of portfolios. After five months of negotiations, Nikšić was confirmed by the FBiH House of Representatives on March 17, 2011, as prime minister of a four-party coalition government that included the SDP, SDA, NS-RzB, and HSP (Croatian Party of Rights; see below). Živko BUDIMIR (HSP) was elected president on the same day.

Voters also elected 289 representatives in the ten cantonal assemblies; top parties included the SDP with 61 seats; SDA, 55; HDZ, 48; SBB, 29; and SBiH, 23.

Negotiations over a BiH government continued into the fall of 2011 while Špirić remained prime minister of a caretaker government. Finally on December 28, the SDA and SDP parties agreed to nominate Vjekoslav BEVANDA of the HDZ as prime minister. He was approved by the House on January 12 and formed a new cabinet that was sworn in on February 10. Disputes among ethnic groups in the BiH House of Representatives prevented the election of a speaker for the chamber until May 2011.

Constitution and government. The Dayton peace agreement of November 1995 laid down a new constitutional structure under which the Republic of Bosnia and Herzegovina, while having a single sovereignty, was to consist of two "entities," namely the (Bosniac-Croat) Federation of Bosnia and Herzegovina, and the Serb Republic (*Republika Srpska*) of Bosnia and Herzegovina. Responsibilities accorded to the central republican government include foreign relations, trade and customs, monetary policy, international and interentity law enforcement, immigration, international and interentity communications and transportation, interentity policy coordination, and air traffic control. The institutions of the central republic include a three-person presidency (one Bosniac, one Croat, and one Serb), a Council of Ministers, a bicameral legislature, a judicial system, and a central bank. The presidency has exclusive control over foreign affairs and the armed forces, while the chair of the Council of Ministers (prime minister), who is appointed by the presidency and confirmed by the House of Representatives, is the head of government.

The judicial branch is headed by a State Court (with criminal, administrative, and appellate divisions), which began functioning in January 2003. A nine-member Constitutional Court (four judges nominated by the FBiH House of Representatives, two by the Serb National Assembly, and three non-citizens nominated by the president of the European Court of Human Rights in consultation with the presidency) also functions at the national level, while both entities have their own court systems. A High Judicial Council, with participation by international jurists, screens candidates for judicial and prosecutorial positions.

Government functions not specifically vested in the Republic of Bosnia and Herzegovina are regarded as the responsibility of the entities, although some of these may eventually revert to the central administration by agreement of the parties. The Dayton agreement provides for the protection of human rights and the free movement of people, goods, capital, and services throughout the country. It also commits the entities to cooperate with the orders of the UN International Criminal Tribunal in The Hague and to accept binding arbitration in the event of their being unable to resolve disputes. Any person indicted by the tribunal or the Bosnian justice system may not hold appointed or elected office.

In 2000 the Constitutional Court ruled that all citizens should have equal standing throughout the country, which resulted in an April 2002 decision by the high representative to amend the FBiH and RS constitutions. As a consequence, proportional ethnic representation was mandated at all levels of government and the judiciary. In addition, with effect from the October 2002 election, the FBiH's bicameral parliament was reconfigured, and a new Council of Peoples, with limited powers, was established in the RS. (See the discussion of the various legislative bodies in the Legislatures section, below.)

The Muslim-Croat federation agreement of March 18, 1994, provided that indirectly elected representatives of the two ethnic communities would serve alternate one-year terms as president and vice president, although no change in the initial appointments of May 1994 were made prior to the September 1996 legislative elections. From 2002, however, the president serves a four-year term, supported by two vice presidents from the other two communities. The president nominates a government headed by a prime minister for legislative endorsement. Ministers must have deputies who are not from their own constituent group. Local government is based on ten cantons, each with its own elected assembly, and municipalities, each with an elected council and mayor. The judiciary includes both Constitutional and Supreme courts as well as cantonal and municipal courts. There is also provision for a Human Rights Court.

The government of the Serb Republic of Bosnia and Herzegovina, declared in March 1992 and recognized under the 1995 Dayton accords, is headed by a directly elected president. Since 2002 he has been assisted by two vice presidents, instead of one, representing the other ethnic communities. The National Assembly, directly elected by proportional representation, elects the prime minister upon the nomination of the president. The separate Council of Peoples, elected by the ethnic caucuses of the National Assembly, was first constituted in 2003. At the local level, administration is based on municipalities, each with an elected assembly and a mayor. The judiciary is headed by a Supreme Court and a Constitutional Court and also includes district and basic courts.

At present, the entire executive, legislative, and judicial structure, at both the central and entity levels, is subject to decisions by the Office of the High Representative of the International Community, a position established to oversee implementation of the Dayton accords. The high representative, who is nominated by an international Peace Implementation Council and confirmed by the UN Security Council, has broad powers to issue decrees, dismiss officials who violate the accords, and establish civilian commissions. As of late 2007, high representatives had imposed over 800 laws and decrees.

In 2013 the media watchdog group Reporters Without Borders ranked Bosnia 68th out of 179 countries in terms of freedom of the press. Reports from the 2012 municipal elections mentioned obviously biased media coverage of candidates, including reports from journalists who were themselves seeking office.

Foreign relations. On December 24, 1991, prior to its declaration of independence, Bosnia and Herzegovina joined Croatia, Macedonia, and Slovenia in requesting diplomatic recognition from the European Community (EC, later the EU). However, the first foreign power to recognize its sovereignty was Bulgaria on January 16, 1992, with the EC according recognition on April 6 and the United States taking similar action the following day. On May 22 Bosnia and Herzegovina was admitted to the UN, thereby qualifying for immediate membership in the Conference on Security and Cooperation in Europe (CSCE, subsequently the OSCE).

Bosnia and Herzegovina became a member of the Central European Initiative (CEI), originally formed in 1989 as a "Pentagonal" group of Central European states committed to mutual and bilateral economic cooperation; however, development of relations with the Council of Europe and other bodies was stalled by the unresolved internal conflict. (Membership in the Council of Europe was achieved in April 2002.) In the wider international arena, the Sarajevo government obtained some diplomatic backing from the Nonaligned Movement, and, as an observer at the Organization of the Islamic Conference (OIC) summit in December 1994, President Izetbegović received numerous pledges of financial and other support from member states. On December 14, 1995, the Bosnian and rump Yugoslav governments accorded one another formal recognition.

Both the RS and the FBiH signed "special relations" treaties with their ethnic confreres in Yugoslavia and Croatia, respectively, even though such treaties were considered by some to be in conflict with both the Dayton accords and the Bosnian constitution. In addition, an agreement was negotiated between the Republic of Bosnia and Herzegovina and Croatia in 1998 providing each country with trade advantages. The FBiH also concluded an agreement (despite some opposition from Bosniac leaders) establishing extensive cooperation with Croatia. Formal diplomatic relations were established with Yugoslavia in December 2000. The first summit of the presidents of Yugoslavia, Croatia, and Bosnia and Herzegovina (including the two entity presidents) convened in Sarajevo on June 15, 2002, although a number of difficult issues, including dual citizenship for ethnic Croats and Serbs, were not addressed. A dual citizenship agreement with Yugoslavia (now the separate republics of Montenegro and Serbia) was concluded in October 2002, and one with Croatia dates from August 2005.

In June 2004 NATO reduced its troop level from 12,000 to 7,000, and six months later, on December 4, the SFOR mission concluded. At that time the EU's newly established EUFOR assumed the peacekeeping mandate, utilizing basically the same troops. (Two years earlier an EU Police Mission had replaced the UN Mission in Bosnia and Herzegovina [UNMIBH], which the UN had described as "the most extensive police reform and restructuring mandate ever undertaken by the United Nations.") A total of 22 EU member states and 11 other countries pledged personnel for EUFOR's "Operation Althea." On February 28, 2007, in view of the improved security situation, the EU confirmed that it would reduce its troop level to 2,500. The U.S. military presence in Bosnia, once numbering 700, was reduced to about 250 personnel in late 2004. Following the handover to Bosnia of NATO's base in Tuzla in July 2007, the U.S. military presence has amounted to a few intelligence officers who work with NATO.

Given strong objections within the RS and the Serbian community at large, as of mid-2009 Bosnia and Herzegovina had declined to recognize the independence of Kosovo, which had declared its separation from Serbia on February 17.

In October 2009 the BiH took a step toward accession into NATO when it submitted a membership action plan to the organization. The application was initially denied in December but was then granted in April 2010, with the stipulation that the two entities' defense-related properties be transferred to BiH federal ownership.

On December 22, 2009, the European Court of Human Rights ruled that the 1995 Bosnian constitution illegally discriminated against minority groups by calling for power sharing only among the three majority ethnic groups. In its ruling, known as the Sejdić-Finci decision, the court said the constitution limited the right of Jews, Roma, and other minorities to run for political office and required that the constitution be amended to include equal access to the political process.

At a meeting in Turkey in April 2010, the presidents of the BiH and Serbia signed a joint declaration pledging to settle longstanding disputes over borders, property, and debt. The two agreed to work on some major disagreements to advance their mutual goal of acceding to the EU and attracting foreign investment. Turkish president Abdullah Gül helped soften relations between the two countries over the course of six months. The Serbian legislature supported his efforts and on March 31 adopted a resolution apologizing for not doing enough to prevent the 1995 massacre in Srebrenica.

In January 2010 the chief prosecutors of Albania, the BiH, Croatia, Macedonia, and Serbia signed a pact that formalized their joint fight against organized crime in the Balkans. In addition to creating channels for direct cooperation, the pact laid out several judicial reforms, which all five of the countries needed to undertake to accede to the EU.

On May 27, 2010, the European Commission voted to allow BiH passport holders visa-free travel throughout the EU, a major step toward the country's goal of integration into the EU. However, before final approval, the Commission declared that BiH needed to improve its law enforcement and prosecutorial capabilities and harmonize criminal codes throughout the country.

In June 2010 the U.S. State Department released its annual worldwide human-trafficking report in which the BiH was commended for a "sea change" in its fight against the problem. The country attained Tier-1 classification for imposing stronger sentences, partnering with NGOs on victim protection, and reducing its use of suspended sentences. The country had long been at the bottom of the list.

On May 26, 2011, the accused war criminal Ratko MLADIC was arrested in Serbia. Mladić was the most wanted of the remaining Bosnian Serb war criminals. He was extradited to the Hague at the end of May, and his trial began in June. In July leaders of Serbia, Croatia, and the BiH agreed to cooperate in broad efforts to gain EU membership, including efforts to resolve the remaining border issues. On October 28, Mevlid JASAREVIĆ, an Islamic extremist, attacked the U.S. embassy in Sarajevo. Jasarević and three others were subsequently arrested for their role in the terrorist strike that injured a Bosnian police officer. Meanwhile, the inability to form a BiH government led the IMF to temporarily suspend aid until a new government was chosen in January 2012.

The RS and Russia signed an agreement in April 2012 for a Russian company to build three hydroelectric plants in the republic. Russia also initiated negotiations over constructing gas pipelines to other areas of Bosnia. The expansion of Russian commercial interests in Bosnia coincided with better relations with ethnic Croat political leaders who were eager for external investments.

Croatia, Bosnia's neighbor and significant trade partner, joined the EU on July 1, 2013. The changed relationship necessitated new border checkpoints and trade regimes, but the Bosnian government has thus far proved too dysfunctional to implement them.

Current issues. Bosnia and Herzegovina completed a Stabilization and Association Agreement (SAA) with the European Union on December 4, 2007, but it has made little progress toward joining the EU. Intransigence and political deadlock have prevented action on key stipulations. The Serbian population, for its part, has pushed for more autonomy from federal institutions; Croats have looked for greater division along ethnic lines; and Bosniacs and the international community have advocated more centralization of power at the federal level. Meanwhile, the Office of the High Representative, due to close in 2007 if the country became more stable, remained open indefinitely because of the deadlock in negotiations over reforms.

In a November 8, 2008, meeting in the Prud district of Odžak, Milorad Dodik (SNSD), Dragan Čović (HDZ), and Sulejman Tihić (SDA) agreed on a set of principles (the Prud Agreement) for altering the BiH constitution, conducting a population census, dividing state property, and determining the legal status of Brčko. All three ethnic leaders acknowledged that further movement toward EU membership depends on resolving constitutional issues, especially strengthening central structures and bringing the constitution into line with the European convention on human rights. Strengthening central institutions will necessitate changes at the entity level, the principal proposal being reorganization into four territorial divisions, although ethnic Serbians have made it clear that they will not accept any redefinition of RS boundaries. On March 27, 2009, the newest high representative, Valentin INZKO of Austria, took office, pledging to help the country "pick up the pace" toward "EU integration," although no one viewed rapid progress on the constitutional issues as an easy undertaking.

On August 24, 2009, High Representative Inzko repealed the ban on entering politics that his office had issued against Dragan Kalinić, Savo KRUNIĆ, Jovo KOSMAJAC, and Nemanja VASIĆ, who were accused of obstructing implementation of the Dayton accords. Observers said Inzko lifted the ban to inject another voice into the highest levels of Bosnian Serb politics, which had been turning increasingly nationalistic. In September Inzko told the EU's Foreign and Security Policy Committee that the political situation in the country was deteriorating and that needed reforms had either stalled or were being ignored as a result of ethnic intransigence. Little was accomplished over the next four years, further highlighting the political standoff that had taken hold of the BiH.

The state government adopted two EU-mandated laws in February 2012. The State Aid Law created a new pool of development funding available to both entities, while the Census Law provided for the first national population count since 1991. An accurate census is needed to fully implement the Sejdić-Finci ruling (see Foreign relations, above).

Serb-nationalist parties continue efforts to undermine federal institutions, introducing bills in February to abolish the State Court of BiH and the BiH Prosecutor's Office. The SNSD also called for the abolition of the country's armed forces because, according to the party president, the country is about to collapse.

SDA members of the BiH parliament voted against the government's proposed 2012 budget in May 2012, as it cut salaries for civil servants. As a result, the SDP–SDA alliance collapsed at all levels of governance. At the state level, the SDP formed a six-way pact comprised of two Bosniak parties (SDP, SDA), two Serb parties (SNSD, SBB), and two Croat parties (HDZ, HDZ 1990). The SDP also formed a four-party government for the FBiH, consisting of the SDP, SDA, NS-RzB, and HSP. However, the SDP could not command enough votes to remove FBiH President Budimir or the FBiH government at the time.

Political leaders reached agreement in June to amend the constitution and create a "roadmap" with key policy changes and firm deadlines to satisfy the remaining requirements for EU accession. Little substantive action was taken, however, and they missed their August 31 deadline to submit constitutional changes to parliament in line with Sejdić-Finci. Komšić, the Croat member of the state presidency, quit the SDP in July 2012 when he was excluded from negotiations on Sejdić-Finci. He planned to launch his own political movement, the Democratic Front.

The RS and FBiH were also at odds over the disposition of military property leftover from the former Yugoslav state. According to the Constitution, any military installations and equipment on the territory of Bosnia and Herzegovina belong to all of the people of Bosnia and Herzegovina and should be turned over to the state ministry of defense. RS leaders, however, insist that any property located on RS territory should belong to the RS and refused to comply. The issue is the final barrier to NATO membership.

By mid-2012 the FBiH government had become paralyzed by infighting. Budimir tried to fire Minister of Urban Planning Desnica RADIVOJEVIĆ (SDA) over the latter's plans to sack the leadership of six public companies. Radivojević refused and went to the FBiH Constitutional Court, which ordered his reinstatement. Budimir stalled for six months before complying.

In September the state government received a €405.3 million stand-by loan from the IMF to cover, among other things, "domestic structural weaknesses."

In October, long-time rivals RS President and SNSD leader Dodik and SDP leader and BiH minister of foreign affairs Zlatko Lagumdžija announced a new political partnership to last through elections in 2014. They planned to collaborate at all levels of government, with special emphasis on EU accession and judicial reform. Meanwhile, the parliament voted to shuffle the state cabinet in October 2012, removing two SDA ministers. SBB leader Fahrudin RADONČIĆ was subsequently appointed minister of security and Zekerjah OSMIĆ (SDP) became minister of defense.

National issues and political bickering dominated the October municipal elections. Over 30,000 candidates, from 190 political parties, participated. The SDA—now out of power at the state level—took the most mayor's races (37) and city council seats (516). The SDP picked up 10 more mayors than in 2008. The SNSD suffered considerable losses, as opposition parties in the RS jointly nominated candidates to run against the party. The SDS benefitted from the anti-SNSD campaigns, also picking up 10 more mayors than in 2008. In Croat-dominant areas, the HDZ and HDZ 1990 took a combined 16 mayoralties.

New regulations marred the voting in Srebrenica. Previously, any person listed on the city census in 1991 could vote, a provision resulting from the large numbers of people who fled Srebrenica when Bosnian Serb soldiers overran the city in July 1995. The refugee ballots had ensured that the mayor was a Bosniak. Locals worried that a Serb victory might lead to the local government denying the fact that Bosnian Serbs massacred 8,000 residents. To lessen that chance, three Bosniak parties (SDP, SDA, and SBiH) agreed to field a joint candidate for mayor, Ćamil Duraković, who ultimately won.

The refugee issue continues to be salient nearly 20 years after the Dayton Accords. The Office of the UN High Commissioner for Refugees (UNHCR) has estimated that of the 2.2 million who fled the strife of the early 1990s, about 1.03 million have returned. Of those, fewer than half have "accessed their property rights" or otherwise returned to their place of origin in Bosnia and Herzegovina. This suggests that many have relocated to communities where they are in the ethnic majority. At the end of 2012, some 113,000 individuals remained internally displaced.

In December, FBiH Prime Minister Nikšić asked Budimir to fire eight ministers from SDA, HSP, and NS-RzB who were allegedly "hindering" the work of the government. The eight ministers, in turn, accused Nikšić of violating procedure by sending the 2013 FBiH budget directly to parliament, without government approval.

The state and entity legislatures passed the 2013 budget in December, paving the way for the IMF to release the next tranche of its standby agreement. The budget featured a deficit under 2.5 percent of GDP, but the wage cuts prompted public-sector employees to strike on January 21.

RS Prime Minister Aleksandar Džombić resigned on February 27 because, according to President Dodik, the government needed "new energy." Dodik nominated Željka CVIJANOVIĆ, SNSD minister of economic relations and regional cooperation, to the post. She was confirmed by the National Assembly on March 12, becoming the first female RS prime minister. A minor cabinet reshuffle followed.

On April 26, members of the State Information and Protection Agency arrested Živko Budimir, the Croat president of the FBiH, while another team searched the home of FBiH Deputy Prime Minister Jerko IVANKOVIĆ-LIJANOVIĆ. The raid was part of a sweep that took 19 federation officials into custody on a range of corruption charges. Budimir was released in late May, when the state Constitutional Court ruled that his detention was illegal. By then the SBB was threatening to leave the coalition because it had not received any cabinet appointments.

The law on personal identification numbers lapsed in February, while lawmakers were unable to agree on a new one. As a result, babies born after February were not issued the personal ID numbers needed for medical care and foreign travel. The sticking point was the RS's insistence on a special code within the 13-number series that would indicate region of birth. Public outrage at the government impasse erupted when a three-month old baby was prevented from traveling abroad for a stem-cell transplant because he did not have the proper paperwork. On June 6, more than 3,000 citizens formed a human chain around the state parliament building for 14 hours, preventing 1,500 legislators, staff, and guests from going home until they had passed the appropriate legislation. High Commissioner Inzko persuaded the crowd to disburse by promising to work on the issue. MPs from the RS then refused to return to work, citing concerns for their safety. The six-party state government effectively collapsed after seven months.

POLITICAL PARTIES

For four and a half decades after World War II, the only authorized political party in Yugoslavia was the Communist Party, which was redesignated in 1952 as the League of Communists of Yugoslavia (*Savez Komunista Jugoslavija*—SKJ). In 1989 noncommunist groups began to emerge in the republics, and in early 1990 the SKJ approved the introduction of a multiparty system, thereby effectively triggering its own demise. In Bosnia and Herzegovina the League of Communists of Bosnia and Herzegovina–Party of Democratic Changes succeeded the party's local branch (SK BiH-SDP; see SDP, below). Since then, political parties have flourished.

During the 1990s a number of coalitions emerged to contest elections at the central and entity levels. Please see the 2011 *Handbook* for more information on the following defunct coalitions: the Coalition for a Unified and Democratic Bosnia and Herzegovina (*Koalicija za Cjevolitu i Demokratsku Bosnu i Hercegovinu*—KCD); Accord (*Sloga;* also translated as Unity); and the Alliance for Change (*Alijanse za Promene*). The BiH's central electoral commission reported 48 parties, and 15 independent candidates had successfully registered for the October 3, 2010, general election.

Parties Represented in the Central House of Representatives:

Party of Democratic Action (*Stranka Demokratske Akcije*—SDA). Organized in May 1990 by Alija Izetbegović, Fikret Abdić (later of the DNZ, below), and others, the SDA is a nationalist grouping representing Bosniacs. Favoring both decentralization and a unitary state, it obtained substantial pluralities in the 1990 legislative and presidency elections, thereafter dominating the republican government (in coalition with other parties) despite being weakened in April 1996 by formation of the breakaway Party for Bosnia and Herzegovina (SBiH, below).

With the party having performed poorly at local elections, in April 2000 it registered a vote of no confidence in the leadership of its deputy chairs, Halid Genjac and Ejup Ganić, who were replaced in May by Edhem Bičakčić, the FBiH prime minister, and Sulejman Tihić. At virtually the same time the party expelled Ganić for refusing to resign as president of the FBiH, a position he had assumed on a rotational basis at the end of 1999 after having served a year as vice president. In October 2000 the SDA's dominant figure, Alija Izetbegović, left the collective presidency, citing age and ill health, with Genjac assuming the Bosniac seat on an interim basis. Izetbegović died in 2003.

In the November 2000 election the SDA remained the strongest party in the FBiH, winning 38 seats in the House of Representatives on a 27 percent vote share. In the simultaneous balloting for the central House of Representatives, it finished second, with about 20 percent of the vote and 8 seats, while in the RS it captured 6 National Assembly seats. In January 2001 Prime Minister Bičakčić left the office he had held for four years to resume his position as general manager of the state electricity company, but shortly thereafter High Representative Wolfgang Petritsch dismissed him because of corruption allegations.

The SDA emerged from the 2002 elections as the dominant Bosniac party, winning a leading 10 seats in the national House of Representatives, capturing twice as many seats as any other party and 33 percent of the vote in the downsized FBiH House of Representatives, and retaining its status as the leading Bosniac party in the RS. In addition, Party Chair Tihić won the Bosniac seat in the national presidency. New national and FBiH coalition governments were then formed under the SDA's Adnan Terzić and Ahmet Hadžipašić, respectively.

The SDA lost ground in the October 2006 elections, when the SBiH's Haris Silajdžić easily foiled Copresident Tihić's reelection bid and its delegation in the FBiH lower house fell to 28 (based on a 25 percent vote share)—still a plurality, but only 4 seats more than the SBiH. It retained 9 seats in the national House of Representatives and remained in the central government, but lost the prime ministership. In 2008 an intraparty leadership dispute involved supporters of Tihić and Vice Chair Bakir Izetbegović, son of the party's founder. Both sought to head the party at a congress in May 2009, as did Deputy Chair Adnan Terzić. The moderate Tihić won a third four-year term, taking 57 percent of the vote. There had been considerable speculation that should Izetbegović's bid fail, he would establish his own party, but he instead indicated that he planned to remain in his father's party. Bakir Izetbegović, the party's candidate, won the Bosniac seat of the BiH collective presidency during the 2010 election. However, the SDA lost its majority in the FBiH legislature, and an SDP-led government was appointed. In 2012 the SDA's opposition to the government's proposed budget led to the replacement of the party within the governing coalition of the BiH. The February 2013 party congress expanded the number of vice presidents from five to eight and created a power-sharing arrangement between Izetbegović and Tihić. The party won the October 2012 municipal elections, with 37 mayors and 516 city council seats.

Leaders: Bakir IZETBEGOVIĆ (Copresident of the Republic and Deputy Chair of the Party); Sulejman TIHIĆ (Former Copresident of the Republic and Chair of the Party); Adil OSMANOVIĆ, Sadik AHMETOVIĆ, Sanjin HALIMOVIĆ, Šefik DŽAFEROVIĆ, Asim SARAJLIĆ, Senad ŠEPIĆ, Safet SOFTIĆ, Salko SELMAN (Vice Chairs); Ramiz SALKIĆ (RS Vice President); Amir ZUKIĆ (Secretary General).

Party for Bosnia and Herzegovina (*Stranka za Bosnu i Hercegovinu*—SBiH). The SBiH was launched in April 1996 by Haris Silajdžić, who had resigned as prime minister of the central government in January after disagreeing with fundamentalist elements of the ruling SDA. The new party aimed to appeal to all ethnic communities and had some success in the September 1996 balloting, winning 10 seats in the FBiH House of Representatives and two in the central House of Representatives, while Silajdžić polled 14 percent in the presidential contest.

Silajdžić returned to the copremiership of the central government in January 1997 and continued in that office until the April 2000 passage of a new Council of Ministers law and the resultant appointment of a single prime minister, Spasoje Tuševljak, two months later. In the November 2000 elections, the SBiH captured 5 seats in the central House of Representatives (on a 12 percent vote share) and 21 seats in the FBiH's lower house (with a 15 percent vote share). It also won 4 seats in the RS's National Assembly. In January 2001 it joined the SDP as a leading force behind formation of the antinationalist Alliance for Change, and in late February the FBiH House of Representatives confirmed the party's secretary general, Safet Halilović, as vice president for a year in the FBiH's rotating presidency/vice presidency.

Silajdžić announced his retirement from politics in September 2001 but in 2002 ran for the Bosniac seat in the state presidency, finishing a close second with 35 percent support. The SBiH won 6 seats in the national House of Representatives, second to the SDA, and 15 seats in the FBiH lower house, while retaining its 4 seats in the Serb National Assembly. Following the elections, the SBiH joined in the governing coalitions at the national and entity levels.

Silajdžić, who was reelected head of the SBiH in May 2006, completed a return to power with his victory in the October 2006 contest for the Bosniac seat in the central presidency. At the same time, the SBiH saw its electoral support rise to 8 seats in the national House and 24 seats in the FBiH lower house, posing a direct challenge to the SDA's continuing leadership. Unlike the SDA, the SBiH supported the police reforms passed in April 2008. Silajdžić ran as the party's incumbent candidate for the Bosniac seat in the BiH collective presidency during the 2010 election but was placed third in the polling. The SBiH lost six seats in the BiH house in the concurrent balloting, leaving it with only two seats in the chamber. Silajdžić nominated Amer Jerlagić, head of the national power utility, to replace him as party chair in March 2012.

Leaders: Amer JERLAGIĆ (Party Chair); Haris SILAJDŽIĆ (Former Copresident of the Republic); Gradimir GOJER, Besim IMAMOVIĆ, Snežana MILAVIĆ, Dževad OSMANČEVIĆ (Vice Chairs); Salem HALILOVIĆ (Secretary General).

Alliance of Independent Social Democrats (*Savez Nezavisnih Socijaldemokrata*—SNSD). The SNSD was formally established in 1996 as the Party (*Stranka*) of Independent Social Democrats and adopted its present name in May 2002, upon completion of a merger with the Democratic Socialist Party (*Demokratska Socijalistička Partija*—DSP), a dissident offshoot of the Socialist Party of the Serb Republic (SPRS, below).

After participating in the NSSM-SMP electoral alliance in 1996 (see the SPRS), the SNSD ran its own candidates in the November 1997 balloting for the RS National Assembly, winning two seats. The SNSD's leader, Milorad Dodik, was subsequently elected prime minister of the RS, pledging to conduct governmental affairs on a nonpartisan basis. The SNSD improved to 6 seats in the 1998 election for the National Assembly. In December 1999 the Social Liberal Party (*Socijalno-Liberalna Stranka*—SLS) merged with the SNSD, with its former leader, Rade DUJAKOVIĆ, named an SNSD deputy chair.

Prime Minister Dodik finished second in the RS's presidential contest in November 2000. At the central level, the SNSD competed in alliance with the DSP, but the coalition managed to win only a single seat in the House of Representatives. In the RS, running on its own, the SNSD tied for second with the Party for Democratic Progress of the Serb Republic (PDP, below), taking 11 seats in the National Assembly.

In October 2002 Nebojša Radmanović, who had been expelled from the SPRS and then helped form the DSP before the latter's merger with the SNSD, finished second in the balloting for the Serb seat in the national presidency, winning 20 percent of the vote. The party finished second in the balloting for the Serb National Assembly, winning 19 seats, while its candidate for president of the RS, Milan Jelić, likewise came in second. The SNSD also won 3 seats in the national House of Representatives and 1 in the FBiH House.

In January 2006 the SNSD, as the leading opposition party in the Serb National Assembly, introduced a no-confidence motion against the SDS-led government of the RS. With the support of the PDP (below), the motion passed and the government fell. In early February the SNSD's Dodik was designated prime minister.

In the October 2006 elections the SNSD's performance overshadowed those of the other Serb parties, thereby confirming Dodik's rise to prominence. The party picked up 4 more seats in the central House of Representatives and won a near-majority of 41 seats in the RS National Assembly, taking 43 percent of the vote and far outdistancing the second-place SDS. In addition, Radmanović captured the Serb seat in the central presidency from the SDS, while Jelić defeated the incumbent, the SDS's Dragan Čavić, for the RS presidency. Jelić died in September 2007 and was succeeded by Rajko Kuzmanović.

In the lead-up to the 2010 elections Prime Minister Dodik began increasing nationalist and secessionist rhetoric in what observers said was an attempt to bring more votes to his party. The incumbent, Radmanović, was the party's candidate for the Serb seat in the BiH collective presidency during the 2010 elections and was reelected with 48.9 percent of the vote. Meanwhile, Dodik was elected president of the RS.

In 2012 the SNSD was expelled from the Socialist International because of the party's nationalism. Reports in 2012 indicated a power struggle within the SNSD between Dodik and Radmanović. The party suffered in the October 2012 local elections, as opposition parties ran joint candidates. SNSD won only 19 mayor seats, down from 40 in 2008.

Leaders: Milorad DODIK (President of the RS and Chair of the Party); Nebojša RADMANOVIĆ (Copresident of the Republic and Executive Board President); Nikola ŠPIRIĆ, Nada TEŠANOVIĆ, Velimir KUNIĆ, Radovan VIŠKOVIĆ (Party Vice Chairs); Igor RADOJIČIĆ (Speaker of the RS National Assembly and Party Vice Chair), Rajko VASIĆ (General Secretary).

Social Democratic Party of Bosnia and Herzegovina (*Socijaldemokratska Partija Bosne i Hercegovine*—SDP, or *Socijaldemokrati*). The multiethnic SDP was formed in February 1999 as a merger of the Democratic Party of Socialists (*Demokratska Stranka Socijalista*—DSS) and the Social Democrats of Bosnia and Herzegovina (*Socijaldemokrati Bosne i Hercegovine*). The two had reportedly been pressured by social democratic parties in Western European countries to coalesce in order to better oppose the nationalist parties dominating affairs in Bosnia and Herzegovina.

Also styled the Socialist Democratic Party (*Socijalistička Demokratska Partija*—SDP), the DSS had been formed in June 1990, initially as the Democratic Socialist League of Bosnia and Herzegovina (*Demokratski Socijalistički Savez Bosne i Hercegovine*—DSS-BiH). As such, it was the successor to the local branch of the former ruling "popular front" grouping, the Socialist League of the Working People of Yugoslavia (*Socijalistički Savez Radnog Narodna Jugoslavija*—SSRNJ). Later, it absorbed the League of Communists of Bosnia and Herzegovina–Party of Democratic Changes (*Savez Komunista Bosne i Hercegovine–Stranka Demokratskih Promjena*—SK BiH-SDP), which had resulted from reorganization of the republican branch of the SKJ after its withdrawal from the federal party in March 1990. Subsequently, the DSS was a member of the United List (ZL; see HSS, below) but left after the September 1996 elections.

The Social Democrats of Bosnia and Herzegovina was the new name adopted in May 1998 by the former Union of Bosnian Social Democrats (*Zajednica Socijalistička Demokratska Bosna*—ZSDB), led by Selim BESLAGIĆ. The ZSDB was originally established in September 1990 as the Alliance of Reform Forces of Yugoslavia (*Savez Reformskik Snaga Jugoslaviji za Bosnu i Hercegovinu*—SRS-BiH), the local affiliate of the postcommunist Alliance of Reform Forces that had been launched by the federal prime minister, Ante Marković, several months earlier. Beslagić, a Muslim, subsequently emerged as one of the country's leading proponents of a multiethnic approach to government and culture.

With firm support from most of the international community, the SDP made major inroads against the nationalists in the local elections of April 2000 and then at the balloting for the central and FBiH legislatures in November 2000. Nationally, the SDP won a slim plurality (9 of the 42 lower house seats) in November, while it finished second, with 37 seats, in the FBiH's House of Representatives. With the party president, Zlatko Lagumdžija, having spearheaded formation of the Alliance for Change in January 2001, SDP leaders quickly assumed leading positions at both governmental levels. By late March they held the Croat seat in the central presidency, the presidency of the FBiH, and both prime ministerships.

By 2002, however, the SDP had lost considerable ground to the more nationalist parties. Following the October 2002 election, the SDP held only 4 seats in the national House of Representatives, 15 seats in the downsized FBiH House, and no major executive office (except for Vice President Ivan TOMLJENOVIĆ in the RS). A former FBiH prime minister, Alija Behmen, had finished third among Bosniac candidates for the state presidency.

Partly as a consequence of the poor showing at the polls, the party split over the issue of whether to join nationalist-led coalition governments. Opponents retained control of the party, which led a dissident group to establish the Social Democratic Union (SDU, below) in December 2002. At its third congress, held in February 2005, the SDP reelected President Lagumdžija.

In October 2006 a party vice chair, Željko Komšić, won the Croat seat of the state presidency with 40 percent of the vote, defeating the HDZ incumbent, Ivo Miro Jović. Legislatively, the party made only marginal gains, winning 5 seats in the national House and 17 in the FBiH House. It then chose to remain outside the national and entity governments. The SDP's Slobodan Popović finished fourth in the December 2007 election to replace the deceased RS President Jelić, winning 2.1 percent of the vote.

At the party's fifth congress, held March 14–15, 2009, Lagumdžija was reelected party president. During the 2010 election, Komšić was again elected to the Croat seat in the BiH collective presidency. The party gained three seats in the balloting for the BiH House of Representatives, tying with the SDA with eight seats. The SDP gained the largest number of seats in the FBiH House. Former SDP general secretary Nermin Nikšić was appointed prime minister of a coalition government. Komšić quit the SDP in July 2012 to form his own political movement. The SDP won 26 mayoralties in the October 2012 local elections, but lost in Bihać and Novi Grad Sarajevo, previous strongholds.

Leaders: Zlatko LAGUMDŽIJA (Former Prime Minister of the Republic of Bosnia and Herzegovina and President of the Party); Nermin NIKŠIĆ (FBiH Prime Minister, General Secretary of Party); Denis BEĆIROCIĆ, Mirsad DJAPO, Damir HADŽIĆ, Mira LUJBLJANKIĆ (Vice Presidents).

Croatian Democratic Union of Bosnia and Herzegovina (*Hrvatska Demokratska Zajednica Bosne i Hercegovine*—HDZ). The HDZ was launched in August 1990, reportedly on the initiative of its counterpart in Croatia. It ran third in the 1990 balloting and joined the postelection government. Serious strains developed when the party spearheaded the declaration of the ethnic Croat Republic of Herceg-Bosna in 1993, headed by HDZ leader Mate Boban. Under pressure from Zagreb, the party participated in the creation of the FBiH in March 1994, following which Boban was replaced as HDZ leader. In the September 1996 post-Dayton legislative balloting, the HDZ had no serious challengers where the voters were Croats.

Prior to the September 1998 elections a number of HDZ candidates were banned from competing by the OSCE for what was perceived as "blatant support" from Croatian television. Nevertheless, the party emerged as the second largest grouping (behind the KCD) in the Houses of Representatives of the state and the FBiH, and its chair, Ante Jelavić, a former defense minister of the FBiH, was elected to the Croat seat on the central presidency, with nearly 53 percent of the Croat vote.

On March 7, 2001, the Office of the High Representative dismissed Jelavić from the presidency because of the support he had voiced, in violation of the Dayton agreement, for the unofficial Croatian National Assembly's declaration of "Croatian self-administration." He had been reelected party chair at a congress in July 2000, by which time the party had drafted a new statute severing its connection to Croatia's HDZ. (The latter party, following the death of Croatian President Tudjman in December 1999, had already discontinued its ideological and financial support of the Bosnian HDZ.)

At the November 2000 general election the party remained the leading Croat formation despite winning only 5 seats in the central House of Representatives. It fared better in the FBiH election, finishing third, with 25 seats in the lower house, but it was excluded from the new Alliance for Change government. On February 7, 2001, the Alliance and other parties in the state-level House of Representatives also rejected the collective presidency's nomination of the HDZ's Martin Raguž to be sole prime minister of Bosnia and Herzegovina. Raguž, who had been serving as prime minister under a rotation system since October 18, 2000, subsequently served as coordinator of the "Croatian self-administration."

In the October 2002 elections the HDZ's Dragan Čović easily won the Croat seat in the collective presidency, capturing 62 percent of the Croat vote as the candidate of the Coalition (*Koalicija*) formed by the HDZ and the small Croatian Demo-Christians (HD; see HDZ 1990, below). At the FBiH level the Coalition also included the **Croatian National Union** (*Hrvatska Narodna Zajednica*—HNZ, also translated as the Croatian People's Community), now led by Milenko BRKIĆ, with a fourth partner, the Croatian Christian Democratic Union (HKDU; see HDZ 1990), joining in the RS. The Coalition won 4 seats in the national House of Representatives and finished second, with 16 seats, to the SDA in the FBiH House. In January 2003 the FBiH Parliament elected the HDZ's Niko Lozančić as the FBiH president. In 2004 a number of HDZ hard-liners left the party and formed the more militant Croatian Bloc (HB, below).

In October 2004 Jelavić, former FBiH president Ivo Andrić-Lužanski, and five other Croats pleaded not guilty to charges stemming from the 2001 declaration of Croat self-administration. A year later Jelavić fled to Croatia to avoid incarceration for embezzlement of aid funds in the 1990s. Because of his dual citizenship, Croatia would not extradite him.

A party session in June 2005 elected ousted national copresident Dragan Čović party president by a vote of 283–258 over Božo Ljubić. (Čović's predecessor, Bariša ČOLAK, had withdrawn from the contest following criticism of his leadership.) The contest did not settle the differences between the Čović and Ljubić factions, however, and in April 2006 the party split in half, with supporters of Ljubić and Martin Raguž forming the HDZ 1990. The immediate consequence was evident in the results of the October 2006 election, when the HDZ 1990, in coalition with several other Croat parties, siphoned off nearly half of the HDZ-HNZ's support, costing Ivo Miro Jović his position as national copresident and resulting in the HDZ's winning only 3 seats in the national House of Representatives. In the FBiH House of Representatives the coalition of the HDZ, HNZ, and HSP won only 8 seats. In the RS, the HDZ participated, without success, in the Croat Coalition for Equality along with the HNZ, the New Croatian Initiative (NHI; see HSS-NHI, below), and the HSP (below).

Dragan Čović's corruption trial concluded in November 2006 with his sentencing to five years in prison for corruption and abuse of power. A month later he was released on bail, and in September 2007 an appellate court ordered a retrial.

Efforts by some Croats to promote reunification of the HDZ and the HDZ 1990 have not yet succeeded in large part because of animosity between the two parties' leaders. The party nominated FBiH incumbent president Borjana Krišto as its candidate for the Croat member of the BiH collective presidency. As the 2010 election drew near, the party combined efforts with HDZ 1990 in an unsuccessful bid to remove incumbent BiH copresident Željko Komšić. Krišto placed second with 19.7 percent of the vote. In March 2012 the HDZ and the SDA finalized an accord to increase cooperation between the two parties.

Leaders: Dragan ČOVIĆ (Former National Copresident and President of the Party); Niko LOZANČIĆ (Former FBiH President and Party Deputy President); Borjana KRIŠTO (Former FBiH President and Party Vice President); Marinko ČAVAR, Mladen BOŠKOVIĆ, Anto DOMIĆ (Vice Presidents).

Serbian Democratic Party of Bosnia and Herzegovina (*Srpska Demokratska Stranka Bosne i Hercegovine*—SDS). Formed in July 1990, the SDS quickly established itself as the main political organ of the Serbian population. Almost from the birth of the party, hard-line nationalists began purging more moderate factions. The party was technically banned in 1992, after its electoral victories in 1990, due to the role of party leader Radovan Karadžić in the war. In August 1995 Karadžić was indicted for war crimes and thus became, under the later Dayton accords, ineligible to hold office. Nevertheless, he was reelected as party president in June 1996 and named as its nominee for president of the RS. Bowing to joint U.S.-Serbian pressure, however, he soon stepped down from his party office and relinquished the party's presidential nomination to the new acting RS president, Biljana Plavšić. Those changes notwithstanding, the SDS remained essentially under the control of Karadžić.

A split subsequently opened up between the more moderate Banja Luka faction of the SDS, led by Plavšić, and the hard-line Pale faction of Karadžić and Momčilo Krajišnik (then the Serb member of the copresidency). The fissure caused a constitutional crisis and resulted in the expulsion of Plavšić from the SDS and the formation of her own party, the Serbian People's Alliance (SNS; see discussion under the DNS, below). Once the conflict was resolved, the SDS saw its representation drop precipitously (from 45 to 24 out of 83) in the November 1997 balloting for the RS National Assembly, allowing the opposition to exclude the SDS from government for the first time.

Dragan Kalinić was named chair of the SDS in June 1998, shortly after his controversial dismissal as speaker of the National Assembly. Kalinić subsequently accused Plavšić and her supporters of conducting an anti-SDS "witch hunt" in the media. In the September 1998 election the party's representation fell even further in the National Assembly (to 19). Krajišnik, who also had the support of the Serb Radical Party (SRS, below), was defeated in his campaign for reelection to the central presidency, securing 45 percent of the votes within the Serb population. However, the SDS supported the successful candidate in the race for president of the RS—Nikola Poplašen of the SRS.

In the November 2000 elections the SDS again easily finished first in Serb National Assembly balloting, capturing 31 seats on a 38 percent vote share, and its candidate for president of the RS, Serb Vice President Mirko Sarović, also proved successful, winning 50 percent of the vote and narrowly avoiding a runoff. When the new National Assembly convened, Kalinić was again chosen as speaker. At the central level, the SDS won 6 seats in the House of Representatives on a 15 percent vote share.

Although Sarović attempted to distance himself and the party from the extreme nationalism of the past and from Karadžić, many observers remained skeptical of statements from the SDS leadership that Karadžić no longer held sway behind the scenes. On April 3, 2000, former member of the presidency Krajišnik was arrested by the SFOR and quickly transported to The Hague, where he pleaded not guilty to charges that included crimes against humanity and violations of the Geneva Convention. (His trial opened in February 2004 and concluded with a guilty verdict in September 2006, when he was sentenced to 27 years in prison. The sentence was reduced to 20 years in 2009.)

In the October 2002 general election the SDS remained the leading Serbian party at the national level, winning five seats in the House of Representatives and the Serb seat in the collective presidency, and retained both the presidency of the RS and a plurality in the Serb National Assembly. In April 2003, however, Mirko Sarović stepped down from the tripartite national presidency over allegations related to a spying scandal and violations of a UN embargo against arms sales to Iraq. He was arrested in November 2005 on corruption charges but was acquitted in October 2006.

In July 2008 Radovan Karadžić was captured by Serbian security forces in a Belgrade suburb, but a number of other internationally indicted Bosnian Serbs remained at large. Noncooperation had prompted the Office of the High Representative to dismiss dozens of Serb officials, including then party chair Dragan Kalinić, for noncompliance with the ICTY. Kalinić's successor, Dragan Čavić, was formally elected to the chair in March 2005. In January 2006, as a consequence of the Serbian National Assembly's vote of no confidence in the Pero Bukejlović government, the SDS moved into the role of what Čavić termed "constructive opposition" at both the national and entity levels.

In October 2006 Čavić, winning only 29 percent of the vote, lost his bid for reelection as RS president, while the party's candidate for the Serb seat on the national copresidency, Mladen Bosić, also finished second. The SDS won only 3 seats in the national House of Representatives and dropped to 17 seats in the RS National Assembly, as a consequence of which Čavić lost an intraparty confidence vote in November and resigned as chair. On December 16 Bosić was elected to the chair, pledging to introduce reforms before a full party assembly in 2007. In late June Bosić was overwhelmingly reelected.

In March 2007, with the Constitutional Court having ruled that Dragan Kalinić's rights had been violated by former high representative Ashdown, speculation increased that the former SDS leader, who had been living in Belgrade, Serbia, would attempt a return to power. The SDS was widely viewed as split between factions loyal to Kalinić and Čavić. That conflict led to the formation in 2008 of the **Social Democratic Party of Bosnia and Herzegovina 1990** (SDS 1990) by a group of Kalinić supporters under Miladin NEDIĆ. They felt that Čavić and Bosić had led the SDS away from the party's "original principles" and were contributing to the "disappearance" of the RS. A more serious rupture occurred in December 2008, when Čavić left to form the Democratic Party (DP, below). A month earlier, Bosić had been reelected party chair.

In February 2010, the SDS voted to expel former leader Kalinić on the grounds that he was damaging party unity because of his radical positions. With that decision, the party moved to position itself as a more positive alternative to the SNSD's increasing nationalism. The SDS gained one additional seat in the BiH house in the 2010 balloting, bringing its total to five. The party won 26 mayoralties in 2012, 10 more than in 2008.

Leaders: Mladen BOSIĆ (Chair), Predrag KOVAĆ (Vice Chair), Ognjen TADIĆ (2007 RS presidential candidate), Dragan ĆUZULAN (Secretary General).

Croatian Democratic Union 1990 (*Hrvatska Demokratska Zajednica 1990*—HDZ 1990). The HDZ 1990 was organized on April 8, 2006, by disaffected members of the HDZ who wished to return to the democratic, conservative, and Christian principles that underlay the foundation of the parent party. The leadership also wished to restore a closer relationship with Croatia's HDZ and rejected proposed constitutional changes, which the Bosnia HDZ had endorsed, that were designed to strengthen the central government.

The HDZ 1990 contested the October 2006 election at the head of the **Croat Unity** (*Hrvatsko Zajedništvo*—HZ) coalition, which also included the Croatian Peasants' Party of Bosnia and Herzegovina (HSS, below); the Croat Democratic Union of Bosnia and Herzegovina (HDU, below); the **Croatian Christian Democratic Union** (*Hrvatska Kršćanska Demokratska Unija*—HKDU), led by Ivan MUSA, a vocal advocate of separation from the FBiH; and the **Croatian Demo-Christians** (*Hrvatski Demokršćani*—HD), led by Ivan MILIĆ. (In 2002 the HD had been allied with the HDZ, as had the HKDU in the Serb Republic; running independently, the right-wing, nationalist HKDU had won one seat in the FBiH lower house, as it had in 2000.) Ljubić finished third in the race for the Croat seat in the copresidency, but his presence may have been the principal factor in defeating the incumbent, the HDZ's Ivo Miro Jović. The coalition won two seats in the national House of Representatives and seven in the FBiH House. Martin Raguž stood as the unified candidate of the HDZ 1990 and the Croatian Party of Rights of Bosnia and Herzegovina (HSP, below) for the Croat seat in the BiH collective presidency during the 2010 election. He placed third in the balloting. The two parties also ran a joint candidate list and won two seats in balloting for the BiH House of Representatives. Raguž was elected to replace Ljubić at the June 2013 party congress; members hope he will better differentiate the party from the HDZ.

Leaders: Božo LJUBIĆ (Founder), Martin RAGUŽ (President), Rudo VIDOVIĆ (Vice President), Stjepan KREŠIĆ (Former Chair of the FBiH House of Representatives).

Croatian Party of Rights of Bosnia and Herzegovina (*Hrvatska Stranka Prava Bosne i Hercegovine*—HSP). Closely linked to Anto Djapić's HSP in Croatia, the rightist, nationalist HSP won two seats in both the 1996 and the 1998 balloting for the FBiH's House of Representatives. In 2000 it dropped to one seat, which it retained in 2002 as part of a coalition with the **United Croatian Party of Rights** (*Ujedinjena Hrvatska Stranka Prava*—UHSP). By then, however, differences had already emerged among the various Croatian "parties of rights," which led, in part, to the formation, prior to the October 2002 elections, of a Croatian Rights Bloc (*Hrvatska Pravaški Blok*—HPB). The latter, led by Željko KOROMAN, won one FBiH seat.

A further split developed between the HSP factions loyal to Zdravko HRSTIĆ and Zvonko Jurišić, which led to the formation of the separate HSP–Djapić-Dr. Jurišić. During the October 2006 elections, a coalition with the NHI (see HSS–NHI, below), the **Croat Coalition for Equality** (*Hrvatska Koalicija za Jednakopravnost*), won one seat in the

FBiH House of Representatives. Jurišić finished fifth in the balloting for the Croat seat on the tripartite presidency, with 7 percent support.

A **Posavina Croatian Party of Rights** (Posavina HSP) was established under the leadership of Andrija MENDES in June 2008, which then aligned with the HSS–NHI (below) in Brčko.

In 2010 the HSP and the HSP–Djapić-Dr. Jurišić agreed to campaign under the unified HSP banner. In 2011 Živko BUDIMIR of the HSP was elected president of the FBiH. In 2012, Budimir called for the creation of a separate Croatian republic within the federation.

Leaders: Živko BUDIMIR (President of the FBiH), Zvonko JURIŠIĆ (Chair), Zarko PAVLOVIĆ (Vice President), Matija IVANČIĆ (Secretary General).

Democratic People's Alliance of the Serb Republic (*Demokratski Narodni Savez Republike Srpske*—DNS). The DNS (also translated as the Democratic National Alliance or the Democratic People's Union) was established on June 16, 2000, by anti-Plavšić members of the Serbian People's Alliance of the Serb Republic (*Srpski Narodni Savez Republike Srpske*—SNS) following their failed attempt to oust her as party leader. Ideologically moderate, the DNS parted ways with the SNS primarily for reasons of personality. In the November 2000 elections it failed to win a seat in the central House of Representatives but took three in the Serb National Assembly, one more than the SNS.

In 2002 the DNS won three seats in the Serb legislature but none nationally. (The SNS won only one seat and became defunct following Plavšić's sentencing by the ICTY in 2003.) The DNS candidate for the Serb seat in the national presidency, Milorad COKIĆ, finished far down the list, with only 3 percent support. The party chair, Dragan KOSTIĆ, was equally unsuccessful in his bid for president of the RS.

Following the October 2006 general election, at which the DNS won one seat in the central House of Representatives and four in the RS National Assembly, the party's current chair, Marko Pavić, agreed that the DNS would continue in the SNSD-led RS government of Milorad Dodik. The DNS has consistently rejected any constitutional change that would reduce the authority of the RS. It voted against the 2008 police reforms.

In the 2010 balloting the DNS secured one seat in the BiH lower chamber and six in the RS house. Nedeljko Čubrilović was reappointed minister of transport and communications in the postelection coalition government, while Lejla Resić became minister of administration and local government.

Leaders: Marko PAVIĆ (Chair), Nedeljko ČUBRILOVIĆ (RS Minister of Transport and Communications).

Democratic People's Union of Bosnia and Herzegovina (*Demokratska Narodna Zajednica Bosne i Hercegovine*—DNZ). A Muslim party, the DNZ was launched in April 1996 by Fikret Abdić as the successor to his Muslim Democratic Party (*Muslimanska Demokratska Stranka*—MDS), which had been founded in 1993 in the Muslim-populated northern town of Bihać. A former chicken farmer, Abdić had been a member of the state presidency for the ruling SDA but later cooperated with the Bosnian Serbs in the defense of Bihać, until its capture by government forces in August 1994. Earlier, he had attempted to proclaim an "Autonomous Province of Western Bosnia."

Abdić won 6.2 percent of the vote in the 1998 balloting for the Bosniac seat on the central presidency. The party also captured one seat in the national House of Representatives and three in the FBiH House, retaining all four in 2000. In July 2001 Abdić went on trial in Croatia, where he had resided since 1995, charged with war crimes dating back to 1992–1995. Found guilty in July 2002 and sentenced to 20 years in prison, Abdić chose to run for the national presidency from his prison cell while appealing the conviction; he finished fourth, with 4 percent of the Bosniac vote. At the same time, the DNZ won one seat in the state House of Representatives and two in the FBiH's lower house (as it also did in October 2006). Abdić's sentence was reduced to 15 years by the Croatian Supreme Court in March 2005, but with the verdict having been confirmed, he resigned as DNZ president in May. The party nominated Ibrahim Djedović to run in 2010 for the Bosniac seat in the collective presidency of the BiH. He was placed fourth in the balloting with 2.9 percent of the vote. Meanwhile, the DNZ retained its one seat in the BiH House of Representatives. In 2012 the DNZ called for the replacement of the three-member BiH presidency with a single, popularly elected head of state.

Leaders: Rifet DOLIĆ (President); Hafeza SABLJAKOVIĆ, Muhamed ŠKRGIĆ (Vice Presidents); Ibrahim DJEDOVIĆ (Chair).

Party for Democratic Progress of the Serb Republic (*Partija Demoktatskog Progresa Republika Srpska*—PDP). The founding congress of the PDP was held on September 26, 1999, under the leadership of prominent economist Mladen Ivanić, a centrist. After having registered a modest success in the April 2000 local elections, the PDP finished in a tie for second in the November balloting for the Serb National Assembly, winning 11 seats. In the election for the central House of Representatives, the party won 2 seats. A month later RS President Mirko Sarović nominated Ivanić as prime minister of the Serb entity. In 2001 the PDP joined the Alliance for Change.

In October 2002 the PDP won two seats in the national House of Representatives and finished third in the RS lower house, with nine seats. Its candidate for president of the RS, Dragan Mikerević, also finished third, with 8 percent of the vote, but he was subsequently named prime minister of the entity. He resigned in December 2004 to protest recent dismissals by the Office of the High Representative and related "threats and ultimatums" by the West. In November 2005 the PDP withdrew its support from the SDS-led Bukejlović government, which fell in January 2006. A month later, the PDP joined Milorad Dodik's new multiparty cabinet.

In October 2006 the PDP won one seat in the national House of Representatives and eight in the RS Assembly. In addition to participating in Dodik's reshuffled RS cabinet, it was one of seven parties forming a coalition government at the national level. In December 2007 Ivanić ran third, with 17 percent of the vote, in the RS presidential contest. Two months earlier, he and 12 others had been charged with corruption during his tenure as RS prime minister. The trial concluded in June 2008 with Ivanić's conviction for negligence, although he was acquitted of all other charges. Sentenced to a year and a half in prison, he launched an appeal.

In February 2009 the PDP withdrew from the RS government and joined the opposition, largely because of objections to domination by the SNSD. Ivanić ran as the party's nominee for the Serb seat in the BiH collective presidency during the 2010 election. Observers said that Ivanić was courting the 50,000 Bosniac citizens in the RS to win against incumbent SNSD candidate Nebojša Radmanović. Ivanić was placed second in the balloting with 47.3 percent, losing by only 1.6 percent of the vote.

Leaders: Mladen IVANIĆ (Former Prime Minister of the RS and Chair of the Party); Dragan MIKEREVIĆ (Former Prime Minister of the RS); Branislav BORENOVIĆ, Zoran DJERIĆ (Deputy Chairs); Nevenka TRIFKOVIĆ (General Secretary).

People's Party "Working for Prosperity" (*Narodna Stranka "Radom za Boljitak"*—NS-RzB). A Croat party established in mid-2002, the NS-RzB joined with the HDU (below) to form the Economic Bloc "Croat Democratic Union for Prosperity" (*Ekonomski Blok HDU–Za Boljitak*) prior to the October elections; the bloc's sole successful candidate was the NS-RzB's Mladen Potočnik, who subsequently became leader of the Republican Party (below). The Economic Bloc's candidate for the Croat seat in the presidency, NS-RzB leader Mladen Ivanković-Lijanović, finished second, with 17 percent support. In March 2005 he was charged in the scandal that led to the dismissal of the Croatian member of the state presidency, Dragan Čović, but he was acquitted in 2006 for lack of evidence.

In the October 2006 elections Ivanković-Lijanović ran for the Croat seat on the national Presidency, finishing fourth. The party's candidate for the Bosniac seat, Muhamed ČENGIĆ, also finished fourth, while the nominee for the Serb seat, Ranko BAKIĆ, came in sixth. The NS-RzB won one seat in the national House of Representatives and three in the FBiH lower house. It then joined in forming the seven-party national coalition government.

Ivanković-Lijanović was placed fourth in the 2010 presidential balloting, while the party kept its single seat in the BiH House of Representatives. Jerko Ivanković-Lijanović, the brother of the NS-RzB leader, was appointed minister of agriculture, water management, and forestry for the FBiH.

Leaders: Mladen IVANKOVIĆ-LIJANOVIĆ (2010 BiH presidential candidate), Anton JOSIPOVIĆ (2007 RS presidential candidate).

Union for a Better Future for the BiH (*Savez za Bolju Budućnost BiH*—SBB). The SBB was founded in September 2009 by businessman, former journalist, and owner of the Sarajevo newspaper *Dnevni Avaz*, Fahrudin Radončić. Radončić ran unsuccessfully as the party's nominee for the Bosniac seat in the BiH collective presidency during the 2010 election. The party platform focused on strong economic development and the fight against poverty to alleviate ethnic tension and radicalism. The SBB secured four seats in the BiH House of Representatives in the 2010 balloting. In June 2012 the SBB signed a coalition agreement with the SDP to join the governing coalition of the BiH, but it threatened to pull out of the coalition in 2013.

Leaders: Fahrudin RADONČIĆ (2010 presidential candidate and Party Founder), Fehim ŠKALJIĆ (Chair), Aleksandar REMETIĆ (Vice Chair).

Other Parties Represented in the FBiH House of Representatives:

Bosnian Party (*Bosanska Stranka*—BOSS). BOSS won one seat in the FBiH's House of Representatives in the September 1998 balloting. In 2000 it won two seats in the FBiH's lower house and then added one more in 2002, when it also won one seat in the state-level lower house. Its candidate for the state presidency, Faruk BALIJAGIĆ, won only 2 percent of the Bosniac vote.

In October 2006 BOSS and the Social Democratic Union (SDU, below) ran in coalition as the **Patriotic Bloc BOSS-SDU BiH** (*Patriotski Blok BOSS-SDU BiH*), which won three FBiH seats but failed to win at the national level. Its candidate for the Bosniac seat on the central presidency, Mirnes Ajanović, finished third, with 8 percent of the vote. Its candidate for the Serb seat, Slavko DRAGIČEVIĆ, won only 2 percent.

BOSS candidate Izudin Kešetović was placed eighth in the BiH presidential balloting, and the party secured one seat in the FBiH House of Peoples.

Leaders: Mirnes AJANOVIĆ (Chair), Izudin KEŠETOVIĆ (2010 presidential candidate).

Other Parties Represented in the RS National Assembly:

Serb Radical Party of the Serb Republic (*Srpska Radikalna Stranka Republike Srpske*—SRS). Related to the Serbian Radical Party in Serbia, the SRS is widely seen as an extension of the Pale faction of the SDS. It increased its electoral performance in the November 1997 National Assembly election, gaining 8 seats, for a total of 15, before declining to 11 in 1998. The SRS supported the SDS's Momčilo Krajišnik in the 1998 campaign for the Serb seat on the central presidency, with the SDS in turn supporting the SRS's Nikola Poplašen in his successful run for president of the RS.

On March 5, 1999, the Office of the High Representative removed Poplašen from the presidency for abuse of power, which included efforts to dismiss Prime Minister Dodik. Poplašen refused to step down, however, and the office remained vacant until December 2000. Moreover, in November 1999 the high representative prohibited the SRS from participating in the April 2000 local elections and the November 2000 general election, citing obstruction of the Dayton accords by party leaders. As a consequence, a number of party members ran for office under the banners of other Serb parties.

Reelected president of the party in May 2002, Poplašen stepped down less than a month later so that the SRS could compete in the October election. (Earlier, the high representative had announced that parties would be ineligible if their official leadership included individuals who had been banned from holding office.) In the general election the SRS won one seat in the national House of Representatives and four seats in the Serb National Assembly. Ognjen Tadić, the SRS candidate for the Serb seat in the national presidency, finished third, while Radislav Kanjerić finished fifth in the election for president of the RS.

In December 2002 the party split, primarily over the issue of support for inclusion of the Bosniac SDA in the Serb government. The more nationalist group, which included Kanjerić and Tadić, ultimately established the SRS "Dr. Vojislav Šešelj" (SRS-VŠ, below). The other faction, based in Banja Luca, elected a new leadership and retained three of the four SRS deputies in the National Assembly.

In the October 2006 elections, the SRS won only two seats in the RS National Assembly. In the lead-up to the 2010 general election, the SRS supported Mladen Ivanić, the PDP's BiH collective-presidency candidate. In the polling the SRS secured two seats in the RS assembly.

Leader: Milanko MIHAJLICA (Chair).

Socialist Party of the Serb Republic (*Socijalistička Partija Republike Srpske*—SPRS). Founded in June 1993, the SPRS was affiliated with Slobodan Milošević of Yugoslavia and his Socialist Party, although one wing of the party was very close to other social democratic parties in Europe. The SPRS was the driving force behind the Peoples' Union for Peace–Union for Peace and Progress (*Narodni Savez za Mir–Savez za Mir i Progres*—NSSM-SMP), an alliance of five parties that competed in the 1996 elections for the central and RS legislatures, winning two seats in the former and ten in the latter. However, the NSSM-SMP did not subsequently compete as an alliance. Running on its own, the SPRS secured nine seats in the National Assembly of the RS in 1997, improving to ten in 1998, at which time its president, Živko Radišić, was elected to the presidency of the Republic of Bosnia and Herzegovina as the *Sloga* candidate.

In February 2000 the party leadership decided to withdraw from the governing coalition in the RS. Observers attributed the move in part to Prime Minister Dodik's dismissal of his deputy prime minister, Tihomir GLIGORIĆ of the SPRS, in January. A number of opponents of the withdrawal were soon expelled from or left the party voluntarily to form the DSP (see SNSD, above). In late April the country's collective presidency nominated Gligorić for the post of central prime minister, but the nomination was withdrawn in early May without a vote in the House of Representatives, support being insufficient for confirmation. In the November 2000 elections the SPRS won one seat at the central level and four in the RS's National Assembly.

In February 2002 Živko Radišić was ousted as party president and replaced by Petar Djokić. In May Radišić formally resigned from the SPRS and subsequently joined the newly organized People's Party of Socialists (*Narodna Partija Socijalista*—NPS), which prompted the SPRS to request that he step down as the Serb member of the national presidency.

In the October 2002 elections the SPRS won one seat in the national House of Representatives and three in the Serb National Assembly. Its candidate for the national presidency, Dargutin ILIĆ, won under 4 percent of the Serb vote, while Djokić, its candidate for president of the RS, won 5 percent.

In January 2006, contrary to a directive from the party leadership, National Assembly members Nedjo DJURIĆ and Dragutin ŠKREBIĆ voted against the no-confidence motion that ousted the Bukejlović government in the RS. The party then expelled them. Shortly before the October 2006 elections, in which the SPRS won three seats in the RS lower house, Gligorić defected to the SNSD. Following the balloting, the party remained in the SNSD-led Dodik government.

In the 2010 balloting the SPRS secured three seats in the RS assembly and was given two cabinet posts in the RS government.

Leaders: Petar DJOKIĆ (President), Živko MARJANAC (Secretary General).

Additional Parties:

Bosnian-Herzegovinian Patriotic Party (*Bosanskohercegovačka Patriotska Stranka*—BPS). The BPS won two seats in the FBiH's House of Representatives in 1998, while its candidate for the Bosniac seat in the central presidency, Sefer Halilović, a former commander of the Bosnia and Herzegovina army, finished third with 5.7 percent of the vote. In the November 2000 elections, the BPS won one seat in the national House of Representatives and two in the FBiH's lower house. It subsequently joined the Alliance for Change, and Halilović was named to the Behmen cabinet in the FBiH.

In October 2002 the BPS won only one seat in the FBiH's lower house. Its candidate for the Bosniac seat in the state presidency, Emir ZLATAR, won less than 2 percent of the vote.

On November 15, 2005, the ICTY acquitted Halilović of charges related to the killing of Croatian civilians by troops under his command. He had surrendered to the ICTY in September 2001. He has since argued for membership in both the EU and the NATO.

In the October 2006 election, running as the **Bosnian-Herzegovinian Patriotic Party–Sefer Halilović,** the party won one seat at the national level and four in the FBiH lower house. Mujo DEMIROVIĆ ran as the party's BiH presidential candidate in 2010 but received only 1.9 percent of the vote.

Leader: Sefer HALILOVIĆ.

Democratic Party (*Demokratska Partija*—DP). The formation of the center-right DP was announced by Dragan Čavić in December 2008 upon his departure from the SDS. He described the new party as an effort to reinvigorate the opposition to Prime Minister Dodik. Strongly pro-Dayton, the party was registered in January 2009.

Momčilo Novaković, theretofore the head of the SDS deputy group in the national House of Representatives, left the SDS in January 2009 because of disagreements with party leader Mladen Bosić. Soon after, he joined the DP, which also initially attracted two members of the RS lower house.

The DP failed to secure any seats in the BiH, FBiH, and RS legislatures in the 2010 balloting.

Leaders: Dragan ČAVIĆ (Former President of the RS), Momčilo NOVAKOVIĆ.

Croat Democratic Union of Bosnia and Herzegovina (*Hrvatska Demokratska Unija Bosne i Herzegovine*—HDU). The HDU was organized in May 2002 by Miro Grabovac Titan and other former members of the HDZ who sought a less nationalist posture. For the October 2002 elections, the HDU joined forces with the NS-RzB (above) in forming the Economic Bloc "Croat Democratic Union for Prosperity," which won one seat in the national legislature and two in the FBiH lower house. In the RS the Croatian Peasants' Party (HSS, below) also participated in the Economic Bloc.

In 2006 the HDU ran as part of the Croat Unity coalition (see HDZ 1990, above), which won seven FBiH lower house seats. In the lead-up to the 2008 elections, Grabovac asked Croats to boycott the contests in order to call the international community's attention to the problems plaguing the BiH. The HDU failed to secure representation in the BiH, FBiH, and RS assemblies in the 2010 balloting.

Leader: Miro GRABOVAC TITAN (President).

Croatian Peasants' Party of Bosnia and Herzegovina–New Croatian Initiative (*Hrvatska Seljačka Stranka Bosne i Hercegovine–Nova Hrvatska Inicijativa*—HSS-NHI). The HSS-NHI was established in late September 2007 by the merger of the HSS and the NHI. At the time, the party claimed to be second in membership to the HDZ among Croat parties.

Affiliated with a similar party in Croatia, the HSS had been formed in the early 1990s by the moderate Croat leader Ivo KOMŠIĆ, who was named for the collective presidency in November 1993. Komšić subsequently played a significant role in negotiations leading up to the 1995 Dayton accords, and in 1996 he was the candidate for the Croat seat in the new central presidency from the United List (*Združema Lista*—ZL), a coalition of five parties devoted to a multiethnic approach to affairs in Bosnia and Herzegovina. (Otherwise, the parties in the ZL—the HSS, the Muslim Bosniac Organization [*Muslimanska Bošnjačka Organizacija*—MBO], the Republican Party [below], and the two predecessors of the SDP, the Democratic Party of Socialists [DSS] and the Union of Bosnian Social Democrats [ZSDB]—spanned the political spectrum in orientation.) Komšić finished second in the race, while the ZL's candidate for the Bosniac seat in the central presidency, Sead AVDIĆ (later of the SDP, SDU, and BHSD [Free Democrats; see below]), finished fourth. Meanwhile, the ZL secured seats in all three legislatures. Komšić later joined the SDU.

The HSS won one seat in the FBiH's House of Representatives in both 1998 and 2000. In January 2000 it participated in forming the Alliance for Change. In October 2002 it retained its FBiH seat, as it did in 2006, running as part of the Croat Unity coalition (see HDZ 1990, above). In March 2005, looking toward the 2006 elections, the HSS and four other small, moderate opposition parties—the NHI, the Liberal Democratic Party (LDS), the Civic Democratic Party (GDS), and a pensioners' party—had signed a cooperation statement, but no coalition resulted.

The NHI had been founded in June 1998 by Krešimir Zubak, a former Croat member of the central presidency, and a group of supporters who had recently left the HDZ. Zubak described the NHI as "Christian Democratic" in orientation and committed to peaceful political existence with Muslims and Serbs, in contrast to the HDZ, which he described as still in pursuit of political separation. Zubak finished third in the race for the Croat seat of the central presidency in the September balloting, while the NHI secured representation in all three legislatures.

In the November 2000 elections the NHI held its single seats at the national and RS levels but fell from four to two seats in the FBiH's House of Representatives. The NHI joined the Alliance for Change in early 2001 and accepted ministerial posts in the resultant national and FBiH governments. In the October 2002 election, the NHI won one seat in the national House of Representatives, two in the FBiH lower house (one representative was dismissed in March 2003 by the Office of the High Representative because of corruption allegations), and one in the Serb National Assembly. Its candidate for the Croat seat in the state presidency, Mijo ATIĆ, finished a distant third. In March 2004 Atić and a number of other NHI leaders attempted to remove Zubak from the party leadership, but Zubak was reelected at a party assembly, prevailing 173–31 over Drago VRBIĆ. In 2006 the NHI ran in coalition with the HSP (above) but failed to retain any seats at the national or entity levels.

Shortly before the announcement of the HSS–NHI merger, the HSS had joined the HDZ, HDZ 1990, HKDU, HSP–Djapić-Dr. Jurišić, and NS-RzB in crafting the Kresevo Declaration in an effort to present a united Croat front. The declaration called for abolishing the entities, establishing minimum ethnic quotas in Bosnia's legislatures, and maintaining ethnic parity in executive and judicial offices.

In late March 2008 Marko Tadić unexpectedly stepped down as HSS-NHI president. The HSS-NHI did not secure any seats in the 2010 balloting in the BiH, FBiH, or RS assemblies.

Leaders: Ivan KRNDELJ (President), Krešimir ZUBAK (Chair), Marko TADIĆ.

Social Democratic Union of Bosnia and Herzegovina (*Socijaldemokratska Unije Bosne i Hercegovine*—SDU). The SDU was organized in December 2002 by former members of the SDP who, following losses at the polls in October, had failed to change the party's policy of nonparticipation in nationalist-dominated governing coalitions. Among those forming the SDU was Sead Avdić, who was named the new party's president but in late 2003 announced his decision to sit in the national House of Representatives as an independent. He subsequently formed the Free Democrats (below).

In the October 2006 elections the SDU ran in partnership with the BOSS (above) as the Patriotic Bloc, which won three seats in the FBiH House of Representatives. In October 2007 a dispute over party leadership erupted. Sejfudin TOKIĆ, who refused to recognize his dismissal by the party board and his replacement by Ivo Komšić, retained control. In the 2010 balloting the SDU failed to gain any seats in the BiH or FBiH legislatures.

Leaders: Nermin PEĆANAC (President), Esad MEDOŠEVIĆ (Secretary General).

Liberal Democratic Party (*Liberalno Demokratska Stranka*—LDS). Formation of the centrist LDS was announced in May 2000 by the Liberal Party of Bosnia and Herzegovina (*Liberalna Stranka Bosne i Hercegovine*—LS-BiH) and the Liberal Bosniac Organization (*Liberalna Bošnjačka Organizacija*—LBO). A formal unification congress was held a month later. The new party won one seat in the FBiH's House of Representatives in November 2000 and subsequently joined in formation of the Alliance for Change. It again won one FBiH seat in 2002, while the party's chair took 1 percent of the Bosniac vote for the state presidency. In 2006 the party fared poorly, losing its seat amid indications that the chair, Rasim KADIĆ, intended to step down.

Leaders: Bojan Zec FILIPOVIĆ (President), Enida HRBAT (Vice President).

Republican Party (*Republikanska Stranka*—RS). The Republican Party was formed in 1993 by Stjepan KLJUIĆ, who had been elected to Bosnia-Herzegovina's collegial presidency in 1990 as a representative of the HDZ but had become unhappy at the parent party's identification with ethnic Croat aims. Thus, the present party strongly favors a multiethnic state.

In 1998 the Republicans and the Liberal Bosniac Organization, campaigning as the Center Coalition (*Koalicija Centra*—KC), won one seat in the FBiH House of Representatives. Human rights activist Senka NOŽICA won 3.1 percent of the vote as the Republican candidate for the Croat seat on the central presidency.

In August 2000 the Republicans and the Liberal Social Party (*Liberalno Socijalna Partija*—LSP) agreed to run jointly in the November elections, in which the Republicans again won one seat in the FBiH's lower house. The party then joined the Alliance for Change in January 2001. In October 2002 the party failed to hold its FBiH seat; Kljuić won 5 percent of the Croat vote for the central presidency. In 2003 he became a foreign policy adviser to the HDZ's winning candidate, Dragan Čović. Party President Mladen Potočnik was elected in 2002 to the national House of Representatives from the Economic Bloc "Croat Democratic Union for Prosperity."

In January 2006 the Republican Party joined four other small organizations in forming the **Alliance of Parties of the Political Center** (*Savez Stranaka Političkog Centra*—SSPC), which voiced support for a new constitution and rapid integration into NATO and, in the next decade, the EU. Partners in the SSPC included the **Bosnian Podrinje People's Party** (*Bosansko Podrinjska Narodna Stranka*—BPNS), led by Seid KARIĆ, and the **Bosnia-Herzegovina Party of Rights** (*Bošanskohercegovačka Stranka Prava*—BHSP), led by Besim ŠARIĆ. None won national or entity-level legislative seats in October 2006 or October 2010.

Leader: Mladen POTOČNIK (President).

Serb Radical Party "Dr. Vojislav Šešelj" (*Srpska Radikalna Strana "Dr. Vojislav Šešelj"*—SRS-VŠ). The SRS-VŠ resulted from a split in the SRS (above) following the October 2002 elections. The more nationalist Bijeljina-based SRS faction, led by national presidency candidate Radislav Kanjerić and Serb presidential candidate Ognjen TADIĆ, opposed inclusion of the Bosniac SDA in the new Serb entity government.

In November 2003 the Kanjerić wing held a founding assembly for the new party. Named in honor of the ultranationalist Serb leader Vojislav Šešelj, who had been indicted as a war criminal by the ICTY, the party was initially known as the Serb Radical Alliance "Dr. Vojislav Šešelj" (*Srpski Radikalni Savez "Dr. Vojislav Šešelj"*). One of the four SRS members elected to the Serb National Assembly in 2002 chose to join the SRS-VŠ.

In 2006 Kanjerić finished fifth in voting for the Serb seat on the collective presidency. In December 2007 the party's candidate for the RS presidency, Mirko BLAGOJEVIĆ, finished fifth, winning 1.8 percent of the vote.

Leader: Radislav KANJERIĆ (President).

For information on the **Civic Democratic Party of Bosnia and Herzegovina** (*Gradjanska Demokratska Stranka Bosne i Hercegovine*—GDS), the **Croatian Bloc of Bosnia and Herzegovina** (*Hrvatski Blok Bosne i Hercegovina*—HB), and the **Free Democrats** (*BH Slobodni Demokrati*—BHSD), please see the 2011 *Handbook*.

LEGISLATURES

The 1995 Dayton accords provided for a bicameral Parliamentary Assembly (*Parlamentarna Skupština*) of the Republic of Bosnia and Herzegovina, a bicameral Federation Parliament (*Parliamenta Federacije*) of the Federation of Bosnia and Herzegovina, and a unicameral National Assembly of the Serb Republic of Bosnia and Herzegovina. A second legislative body for the RS was created by constitutional amendment in 2002.

In addition to competing in multimember constituencies, parties may submit separate lists of candidates for compensatory seats that are awarded as needed to ensure proportionality of representation in the central and entity lower houses.

Parliamentary Assembly of the Republic of Bosnia and Herzegovina:

House of Peoples (*Dom Naroda*). The upper chamber has 15 members: 5 Bosniacs and 5 Croats elected by their respective ethnic caucuses in the House of Peoples of the FBiH, and 5 Serbs elected by the National Assembly of the RS. All members serve four-year terms. The office of speaker rotates every eight months among three members, one from each ethnic community. The upper house was most recently constituted on June 9, 2011, with the following party breakdown:

Bosniacs: Party of Democratic Action, 3 seats; Social Democratic Party of Bosnia and Herzegovina, 2.

Croats: Croatian Democratic Union of Bosnia and Herzegovina, 2; Croatian Democratic Union 1990, 1; Social Democratic Party of Bosnia and Herzegovina, 1; Croatian Party of Rights–Djapić-Jurišić, 1.

Serbs: Alliance of Independent Social Democrats, 2; Party for Democratic Progress of the Serb Republic, 1; Serbian Democratic Party of Bosnia and Herzegovina, 1; Democratic People's Union of Bosnia and Herzegovina, 1.

Speakers: Dragan ČOVIĆ (Croat), Ognjen TADIĆ (Serb), Sulejman TIHIĆ (Bosniac).

House of Representatives (*Zastupnički Dom/Predstavnički Dom*). The lower chamber consists of 42 directly elected members (28 from the FBiH and 14 from the RS), who serve four-year terms. The office of speaker rotates every eight months among three members, one from each ethnic community. The balloting of October 3, 2010, yielded the following results: Social Democratic Party of Bosnia and Herzegovina, 8 seats; Alliance of Independent Social Democrats, 8; Party of Democratic Action, 7; Serbian Democratic Party of Bosnia and Herzegovina, 4; Union for a Better Future, 4; Croatian Democratic Union of Bosnia and Herzegovina, 3; Party for Bosnia and Herzegovina, 2; Croatian Democratic Union 1990, 2; Party for Democratic Progress of the Serb Republic, 1; People's Party "Working for Prosperity," 1; Democratic People's Union of Bosnia and Herzegovina, 1; Democratic People's Alliance of the Serb Republic, 1.

Speakers: Denis BECIREVIĆ (Bosniac), Bozo LJUBIĆ (Croat), Milorad ŽIVKOVIĆ (Serb).

Federation Parliament:

House of Peoples of the Federation (*Dom Naroda Federacije*). The upper chamber comprises 58 members (17 Bosniacs, 17 Croats, 17 Serbs, and 7 others) indirectly elected by the entity's ten cantonal assemblies. The current House began its constituting session on May 26, 2011. The following party breakdown reflects the full complement of 58 seats: Social Democratic Party of Bosnia and Herzegovina, 21; Croatian Democratic Union of Bosnia and Herzegovina, 10; Party of Democratic Action, 9; People's Party "Working for Prosperity," 4; Union for a Better Future for the BiH, 3; Alliance of Independent Social Democrats, 2; Bosnian Party, 1; Croatian Party of Rights–Djapić-Jurišić, 1; Democratic People's Union of Bosnia and Herzegovina, 1; Croatian Democratic Union 1990, 1; Liberal Democratic Party, 1; Democratic People's Alliance, 1; Our Party, 1; independents, 2.

Speakers: Karolina PAVLOVIĆ (Croat), Slavko MATIĆ (Serb), Jasmin SMAILBEGOVIĆ (Bosniac).

House of Representatives of the Federation (*Predstavnički/Zastupnički Dom Federacije*). The lower chamber has 98 directly elected members. The balloting of October 3, 2010, resulted in the following distribution of seats: Social Democratic Party of Bosnia and Herzegovina, 28; Party of Democratic Action, 23; Union for a Better Future, 13; Croatian Democratic Union of Bosnia and Herzegovina, 12; Party for Bosnia and Herzegovina, 9; People's Party "Working for Prosperity," 5; Croatian Democratic Union 1990, 5; Democratic People's Union of Bosnia and Herzegovina, 2; Party of Democratic Action, 1.

Speakers: Denis ŽVIŽDIĆ (Bosniac), Stanko PRIMORAĆ (Croat), Svetozar PUDARIĆ (Serb).

Legislative Bodies of the RS:

Council of Peoples (*Vijeće Naroda*). The Council of Peoples, which was established as part of the constitutional amendments implemented in 2002, has limited powers on "issues of vital national interest," its primary mandate being to ensure that no ethnic group is disadvantaged by legislative acts of the National Assembly. Its 28 members (8 Serbs, 8 Bosniacs, 8 Croatians, and 4 others) are elected by the respective ethnic caucuses in the National Assembly. The first Council was constituted on March 20, 2003, after a delay caused by difficulties related to selection of Bosniac delegates. Party representation was as follows after the third constituting session, convened on December 11, 2010: Alliance of Independent Social Democrats, 13; Party of Democratic Action, 4; Party for Bosnia and Herzegovina, 3; New Croatian Initiative, 2; Party for Democratic Progress of the Serb Republic, 2; Democratic People's Alliance of the Serb Republic, Serbian Democratic Party of Bosnia and Herzegovina, Social Democratic Party of Bosnia and Herzegovina, and Socialist Party of the Serb Republic, 1 each.

Chair: Momir MALIĆ.

National Assembly of the Serb Republic (*Narodna Skupština Republike Srpske*). The lower house consists of 83 directly elected members. The election of October 3, 2010, yielded the following distribution of seats: Alliance of Independent Social Democrats, 37; Serbian Democratic Party of Bosnia and Herzegovina, 18; Party for Democratic Progress of the Serb Republic, 7; Democratic People's Alliance of the Serb Republic, 6; Party for Bosnia and Herzegovina, 4; Party of Democratic Action, 3; Socialist Party of the Serb Republic, 3; Serb Radical Party of the Serb Republic, 2; Social Democratic Party of Bosnia and Herzegovina, 1; independents, 2.

Speaker: Igor RADOJIČIĆ.

CABINETS

Republic of Bosnia and Herzegovina

[as of August 15, 2013]

Prime Minister	Vjekoslav Bevanda (HDZ)
Ministers	
Civil Affairs	Sredoje Nović (SNSD)

Defense	Zekerijah Osmić (SDP)
European Integration	Vjekoslav Bevanda (HDZ)
Finance and Treasury	Nikola Špirić (SNSD)
Foreign Affairs	Zlatko Lagumdžija (SDP)
Foreign Trade and Economic Relations	Mirko Šarović (SDS)
Human Rights and Refugees	Damir Ljubić (HDZ 1990)
Justice	Bariša Čolak (HDZ)
Security	Fahrudin Radončić (SBB)
Transport and Communications	Damir Hadžić (SDP)

Federation of Bosnia and Herzegovina

[as of August 15, 2013]

Prime Minister	Nermin Nikšić (SDP)
Deputy Prime Ministers	Jerko Ivanović-Lijanović (NS-RzB)
	Desnica Radivojević (SDA)

Ministers

Agriculture, Water Management, and Forestry	Jerko Ivanović-Lijanović (NS-RzB)
Culture and Sports	Salmar Kaplan (SDA)
Development, Entrepreneurship, and Crafts	Sanjin Halimić (SDA)
Displaced Persons and Refugees	Adil Osmanović (SDA)
Education and Science	Damir Mašić (SDP)
Energy, Mining, and Industry	Erdal Trhulj (SDP)
Environment and Tourism	Branka Đurić (SDP)
Finance	Ante Krajina (HSP)
Health	Rusmir Mesihović (SDP)
Interior	Predrag Kurteš (SBiH)
Issues of Veterans and Disabled Veterans	Zukan Helez (SDP)
Justice	Zoran Mikulić (SDP)
Trade	Milorad Bahilj (NS-RzB)
Transport and Communications	Enver Bijedić (SDP)
Urban Planning	Desnica Radivojević (SDA)
War Veterans and Disabled Veterans	Zukan Helez (SDP)
Work and Social Welfare	Vjekoslav Čamber (HSP)

Serb Republic of Bosnia and Herzegovina

[as of August 15, 2013]

Prime Minister	Željka Cvijanović (SNSD) [f]

Ministers

Administration and Local Government	Lejla Resić (DNS) [f]
Agriculture, Water Management, and Forestry	Stevo Mirjaniić (SNSD)
Economic Affairs and Coordination	Igor Vidović (SNSD)
Education and Culture	Goran Mutabdžija (SNSD)
Energy, Industry and Mining	Željko Kovačević (SNSD)
Family, Youth, and Sports	Nada Tesanović (SNSD) [f]
Finance	Zoran Tegeltija (SNSD)
Health and Social Welfare	Slobodan Stanić (SNSD)
Interior	Radislav Jovičić (SNSD)
Justice	Gorana Zlatković (SP) [f]
Labor and Veterans	Petar Djokić (SPRS)
Refugees and Displaced Persons	Davor Cordaš (SDA)
Science and Technology	Jasmin Komić (Ind.)
Spatial Planning, Construction, and Environment	Srebenka Golić (SNSD) [f]
Trade and Tourism	Maida Ibrišagić-Hrstić (SNSD) [f]
Transport and Communications	Nedeljko Čubrilović (DNS)

[f] = female

INTERGOVERNMENTAL REPRESENTATION

Ambassador to the U.S.: Jadranka NEGODIC.

U.S. Ambassador to Bosnia and Herzegovina: Patrick S. MOON.

Permanent Representative to the UN: Mirsada ČOLAKOVIĆ.

IGO Memberships (Non-UN): EBRD, ICC, IOM, OSCE.

BOTSWANA

Republic of Botswana

Political Status: Independent republic within the Commonwealth since September 30, 1966.

Area: 231,804 sq. mi. (600,372 sq. km).

Population: 2,024,904 (2011C); 2,063,370 (2012E—UN).

Major Urban Centers (2005E): GABORONE (213,000), Francistown (91,000), Molepolole (64,000), Selebi-Pikwe (54,000).

Official Language: English (SeTswana is widely spoken).

Monetary Unit: Pula (official rate November 1, 2013: 8.61 pula = $1US).

President: Lt. Gen. (Ret.) Seretse Ian KHAMA (Botswana Democratic Party); elevated (as constitutionally ordained) from the vice presidency to the presidency on April 1, 2008, to succeed President Festus MOGAE (Botswana Democratic Party), who had retired the same day; sworn in for a five-year term on October 20, 2009, after his mandate was renewed by the National Assembly following the legislative elections on October 16.

Vice President: Ponatshego H. K. KEDIKILWE (Botswana Democratic Party); appointed in an acting capacity by the president on February 1, 2011, in the wake of the hospitalization of Vice President Lt. Gen. (Ret.) Mompati MERAFHE (Botswana Democratic Party); appointed by the president and inaugurated, following endorsement by the National Assembly, on August 1, 2012, to formally succeed Merafhe, who had resigned effective that day.

THE COUNTRY

Landlocked Botswana, the former British protectorate of Bechuanaland, covers areas of desert, swamp, and scrubland situated on a high plateau in the heart of southern Africa. The country is bordered on the west by Namibia, on the south by South Africa, and on the northeast by Zimbabwe, with a narrow strip adjacent to Zambia in the north. The population is divided into eight main tribal groups, the largest of which is the Bamangwato (including an estimated 39,000 "San," or "bushmen," some 3,000 of whom continue to live in traditional nomadic fashion in the Kalahari desert). A majority of the people follow ancestral religious practices, but about 15 percent are Christian. Due in part to the large-scale employment of males in neighboring South African mines, 80 percent of households are headed by women. Female representation among senior officials has traditionally been limited, although two women were elected to the National Assembly in 2009, a presidentially appointed legislator was elected speaker of the assembly, and there are two females in the current cabinet.

At independence in 1966 Botswana was one of the world's poorest countries, dependent on stock-raising for much of its income because of an extremely dry climate that made large-scale farming difficult.

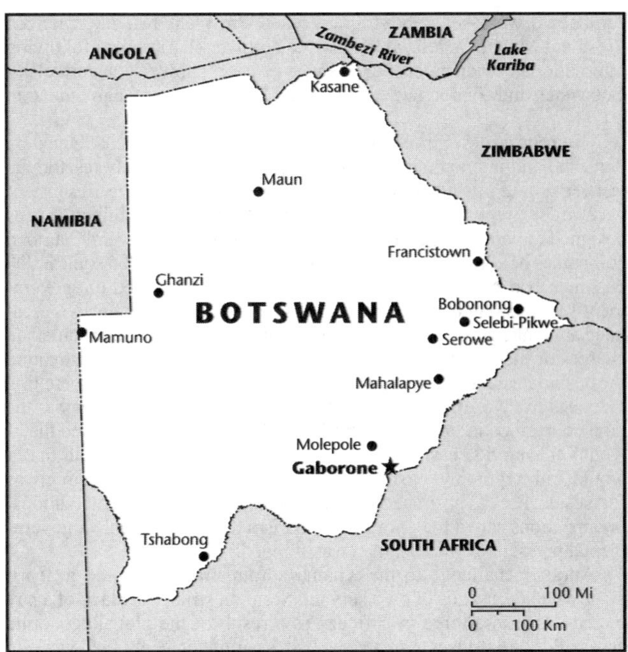

Subsequent mineral discoveries raised real GDP growth to an annual average of more than 8 percent from the 1970s through the first few years of the 21st century.

Botswana is one of the world's largest producers of diamonds, which provide 80 percent of exports, 50 percent of government revenue, and 30–40 percent of gross domestic product. While extractive activity (also involving copper, nickel, and coal) has yielded infrastructural gains, food production has remained a problem. Although a large majority of the workforce is involved in subsistence agriculture, the largely barren soil has led to a dependence on imported food that is only slowly being overcome.

The government's free-enterprise orientation and conservative monetary policies have attracted substantial foreign aid. Meanwhile, the lucrative diamond industry has enabled the government to amass large financial reserves, although international advisers have urged diversification in order to insulate the economy from fluctuations in global demand for diamonds. Recent government programs have focused on agricultural improvements, educational expansion, the promotion of tourism, revitalization of the public sector, efforts to promote investment in the private sector in order to combat unemployment among unskilled workers, and an anti-HIV/AIDS campaign. (Botswana suffers from one of the highest HIV infection rates in the world, but officials reported in 2013 that the infection rate had been cut by 70 percent since its peak, thanks in part to heavy international aid for prevention programs.)

Annual GDP growth averaged 4.5 percent from 2004 to 2008, but the global demand for diamonds subsequently decreased as the result of the global economic crisis, causing GDP to decline by 4.7 percent in 2009. The economy subsequently rebounded sharply, with real GDP growing by 7 percent in 2010 and 5.1 percent in 2011, partly as the result of increased exports of diamonds (facilitated by the government's launching of a joint mining company with diamond giant De Beers) and other minerals, textiles, and plastic products. Meanwhile, the government issued new exploration licenses for what was hoped would be major expansion of the coal sector. GDP grew by 4 percent in 2012.

GOVERNMENT AND POLITICS

Political background. A British protectorate from 1885, Botswana achieved independence within the Commonwealth on September 30, 1966, under the leadership of Sir Seretse KHAMA and has subsequently been regarded as a showplace of democracy in Africa. Following the National Assembly election of October 20, 1979, in which his Botswana Democratic Party (BDP) won 29 of 32 elective seats, President Khama was given a fourth five-year mandate. His death on July 13, 1980, led to the selection of Ketumile Joni MASIRE, theretofore vice president and minister of finance and development planning, to fill the remainder of the presidential term. Both Masire and Vice President Peter S. MMUSI were reappointed following the legislative election of September 8, 1984. However, the opposition Botswana National Front (BNF) showed surprising strength (20.2 percent) in that election and in concurrent municipal balloting. In the election of October 7, 1989, the BNF vote share increased to 26.9 percent (as contrasted with 64.8 percent for the BDP). Presenting himself as the sole candidate, President Masire was reconfirmed by the assembly and sworn in for a third term on October 10. On March 8, 1992, Mmusi resigned the vice presidency in favor of Festus MOGAE, who retained his position as finance minister.

In May 1993 representatives of the BDP, BNF, and four other parties met in Francistown to debate a recently released BNF proposal for electoral reform that included calls for the establishment of a multipartisan electoral commission to replace the existing presidentially appointed body and a lowering of the voting age from 21 to 18. Rebuffed by the government, the BNF declared six months later that it had tentatively decided to boycott the next election. Subsequently, however, it reversed itself, winning 13 legislative seats in the balloting of October 15, 1994, compared to 26 for the BDP, whose vote share of 53.1 percent was its lowest in its 28 years of rule.

The unexpected electoral gains of the BNF in 1994 were achieved despite rejection by the High Court of an opposition demand that the poll be canceled because of electoral roll deficiencies that allegedly favored the BDP. Contributing to the reduction in the BDP's majority were a series of corruption scandals and economic difficulties, including rising unemployment within a rapidly expanding urban population. Social tensions erupted into serious antigovernment rioting in Gaborone in February 1995.

In late 1997 President Masire announced his intention to resign as head of state, and he endorsed the succession of Vice President Mogae. Masire resigned on March 31, 1998, at an official ceremony that coincided with the conclusion of U.S. President Bill Clinton's visit to Botswana. On April 1 Mogae was inaugurated, and he announced the formation of a new cabinet on the same day. Two days later the new president nominated Lt. Gen. (Ret.) Seretse Ian KHAMA, son of Botswana's first president, to be his vice president. Khama, who had resigned from the military on March 31 to accept an appointment as minister of presidential affairs and public administration, captured a legislative by-election victory on July 6 (assembly membership being a prerequisite for the vice presidential slot) and, following assembly approval, assumed his new post on July 13. In regular legislative balloting on October 16, 1999, the BDP secured 33 of 40 elective seats, and Mogae was consequently sworn in for a five-year presidential term. Mogae announced a new cabinet on October 21, retaining Khama as vice president (and thereby the heir apparent as the next BDP presidential contender).

The BDP maintained its legislative dominance in the October 2004 assembly balloting, and President Mogae was sworn in for another five-year term on November 1. However, he stepped down from his post on April 1, 2008, and handed over authority to Vice President Khama, who was inaugurated the same day. Khama, a former army commander and son of the country's founding father, immediately appointed Foreign Minister Mompati MERAFHE, also of the BDP, as vice president and named a new government. (The BDP had rejected opposition demands for constitutional revision that would have provided for popular election of the president.)

In 2009 as attention turned to the upcoming legislative elections, President Khama came under increasing public criticism about rising poverty and unemployment, as well as for the government's cozy relationship with mining companies. Meanwhile, a major rift was developing within Khama's BDP over his reportedly authoritarian leadership style (see BDP, under Political Parties, below). However, the BDP won 45 of 57 seats in the October 16 assembly poll on turnout of 77 percent. President Khama and Vice President Merafhe were subsequently elected for another five-year term, and a new all-BDP government was named on October 22.

On February 1, 2011, the president named Mines, Energy, and Water Resources Minister Ponatshego KEDIKILWE as acting vice president "until further notice" following Vice President Merafhe's hospitalization in South Africa. Ponatshego was formally appointed to the vice presidency on August 1, 2012, following the resignation of Merafhe, whose continued ill health had prevented him from reassuming vice presidential responsibilities.

Constitution and government. The 1966 constitution provides for a president who serves as head of state and government, a Parliament consisting of a National Assembly and a consultative House of Chiefs, and a judicial structure embracing a High Court, a Court of Appeal, and a Magistrate's Court in each district. Sitting as an electoral college, the assembly elects the president for a term coincident with its own. (In August 1997 the assembly approved by two-thirds majority a bill limiting the president to two five-year terms.) The House of Chiefs acts as a consultative body on matters of native law, customs, and land, and also deliberates on constitutional amendments. The president can delay for up to six months, but not veto, legislation.

In June 1996 the government accepted opposition demands for an independent electoral commission and agreed to consider lowering the voting age from 21 to 18 and granting proxy votes to Botswanans living abroad. The latter two measures, in addition to a bill designating the vice president as the president's successor, were approved by popular referendum in October 1997.

At the local level, Botswana is divided into nine districts and five towns, all governed by councils. Chiefs head five of the district councils, elected leaders the remaining four. The districts impose personal income taxes to generate revenue, the local funding being supplemented by central government grants.

The situation as far as freedom of the press is concerned is generally described as satisfactory, although the state-run newspaper and broadcasting facilities dominate the field, usually, according to critics, with a progovernment bias.

Foreign relations. Although generally pro-Western in outlook, Botswana belongs to the Nonaligned Movement and has consistently maintained diplomatic relations with members of the former Soviet bloc as well as with the People's Republic of China. Botswana's major trading partner and the employer of over half its nonagricultural workforce is South Africa, but relations between the two countries have been problematic. Although Botswana attempted to maintain peaceful coexistence with its neighbor, it participated as one of the six Front-Line States (also including Angola, Mozambique, Tanzania, Zambia, and Zimbabwe) opposing minority rule in southern Africa. Tensions heightened in 1985 when South African Defense Forces (SADF) mounted a cross-border attack on alleged havens for the African National Congress (ANC), killing 15 people. Botswana subsequently vowed not to condone any "terrorist activity" from its territory and forced numerous ANC adherents to leave the country. Following another SADF raid near Gaborone in May 1986, the Masire government informed the other Front-Line States that it "would not stand in the way" of those who might wish to initiate economic sanctions against South Africa. Despite its denunciation of three more SADF raids, Gaborone announced a joint Botswanan/South African resource development project in 1988, further underlining what critics termed Botswana's contradictory position as a member of both the South African Customs Union (SACU) and the anti-apartheid South African Development Coordination Conference (SADCC, subsequently the Southern African Development Community—SADC), whose headquarters were in Gaborone.

In 1992 the Namibian government, under pressure from opposition politicians to clearly demarcate its borders, claimed a small island in the Chobe River that had previously been assumed to be part of Botswana. The two sides signed an agreement in 1996 providing for the dispute to be submitted to the International Court of Justice (ICJ). Subsequently, in the wake of tension generated by Botswana's buildup of sophisticated weaponry, both countries, under the aegis of the Namibian and Botswanan Joint Commission on Defense and Security, agreed in 1998 to resolve border disputes through diplomatic solutions. In late 1999 the territorial dispute was resolved when the ICJ ruled in favor of Botswana. In 2002 Botswana and Namibia agreed to the repatriation of some 2,000 Namibian refugees in Botswana, while in 2003 the two countries established an eight-member commission to begin final demarcation of the border.

The reported influx of some 100,000 refugees from Zimbabwe led the Botswanan government in 2004 to enact a number of measures, including the erection of an electric fence in some areas, designed to increase border security. By 2006 it was estimated that nearly a half-million Zimbabwean immigrants were living in Botswana.

In 2007 a new border crossing linking Botswana, South Africa, and Namibia was opened at a wildlife park, easing access for travelers. In a move cited by observers as further bolstering cooperation between Botswana and Namibia, the two countries signed a Walvis Bay port agreement in February 2008. Later that year, Botswana's relations with Zimbabwe were severely strained when President Khama criticized President Mugabe's refusal to agree to a power-sharing deal following internationally disputed elections in Zimbabwe. Nevertheless, Botswana and Zimbabwe signed a $74 million trade agreement in 2011.

Current issues. Since 2001 the government has been challenged by domestic and international critics for its decision to forcibly resettle the last remaining bushmen out of the Central Kalahari Game Reserve. It was widely reported that the government's relocation initiative was designed to permit expanded mining in the tribal lands, several diamond companies holding prospecting rights in the reserve. By 2005 some 3,000 bushmen had been relocated, although others had resisted the government's financial inducements and pressure tactics. In 2006 tensions escalated amid allegations of police brutality and arrests of some bushmen on charges of illegal hunting practices. The government denied mistreating the bushmen and said that those arrested had given up traditional hunting practices in favor of using modern guns and vehicles. In December the high court ruled in favor of the bushmen, but the government said that it would not provide basic services, such as water, in the park and that it would still require the bushmen to provide proof that their hunting was for sustenance. (The issue continued into 2013 as some international organizations called for a boycott of tourism in Botswana unless governmental pressure on the bushmen was stopped.)

Another challenge to the Khama administration erupted in April 2011 when thousands of civil servants went on strike over lack of a pay increase due to a three-year freeze as a result of the global economic crisis. Public services came to a halt as more than 90,000 workers stayed away from their jobs in what was, at first, announced as a short-term protest. However, after the president refused to consider their demand of a 16 percent pay raise, the protesters extended their strike "indefinitely" and called for the finance minister to resign. Tensions heightened in late May following the government's firing of some 1,500 workers, including teachers, medical personnel, and border officials, as the president said the government could not afford to meet their demands. The courts subsequently ruled that at least some of the dismissals had been illegal, and the strike was officially concluded by mid-year, although many grievances remained unresolved. Consequently, trade unions subsequently strongly endorsed the creation of an opposition coalition called the Umbrella for Democratic Change (UDC) in 2013 to oppose President Khama and the BDP in the October 2014 elections. However, Khama and his administration reportedly remained popular for having implemented programs to assist the poor and unemployed and for having fostered general economic advances.

POLITICAL PARTIES

Government Party:

Botswana Democratic Party (BDP). Founded in 1962 as the Bechuanaland Democratic Party, the BDP has been the majority party since independence. It advocates self-development on a Western-style democratic basis, cooperation with all states, and multiracialism. In June 1984 BDP president Sir Ketumile Joni Masire (who had become president of the republic in 1980) announced measures to "democratize" party nominations through a revamped primary system. However, all candidates remained subject to approval by a central committee dominated by government ministers.

During a BDP congress in 1993 divisions within the party widened when Peter Mmusi and Daniel K. Kwelagobe, both of whom had been forced to resign from the government in 1992 in the wake of a land transaction scandal, were elected chair and secretary general, respectively, while traditional southern leaders failed to secure leadership positions. Immediately thereafter, the Mmusi/Kwelagobe faction was reported to be in conflict with the party's "Big Five" cabinet members, led by Lt. Gen. Mompati S. Merafhe, who represented the BDP's cattle-raising wing. Mmusi died in October 1994 and was eventually succeeded as BDP chair by Ponatshego Kedikilwe, the minister of presidential affairs and public administration. The government reshuffling in late 1997 was reportedly hailed by party officials for balancing the number of northern and southern ministers.

On March 31, 1998, Masire resigned from both his national and party presidency posts, and on April 1 Festus Mogae assumed both positions. The BDP maintained its dominance in the 1999 assembly poll by securing 57 percent of the vote.

With President Mogae's nomination of Lt. Gen. Seretse Ian Khama as the vice president of the republic, and thus the possible "heir," the factionalized structure of the BDP became more apparent. In June 2000 Kedikilwe resigned as minister of education, observers noting that Kedikilwe and BDP Secretary General Kwelagobe were uneasy with Khama, who had publicly called them the "old guard." However, at the party congress in 2001 a compromise averted a possible crisis, and Khama was elected vice chair of the party, while Kedikilwe and Kwelagobe both kept their positions.

Kedikilwe was replaced by Khama as chair of the BDP at the 2003 congress, following which the party remained divided into two camps. One, seen as supportive of Khama, was led by Merafhe (then the minister of foreign affairs) and Jacob NKATE (the minister of education). The other faction was led by Kedikilwe and Kwelagobe. Discord between the factions was renewed at the July 2005 congress, but Secretary General Kwelagobe managed to fend off a challenge for his post from Local Government Minister Margaret NASHA after Khama intervened on Kwelagobe's behalf in an effort to keep peace in the party. All remaining top party positions went to the pro-Khama faction, with Nkate being retained as deputy secretary general.

Strife continued to increase to the point that in early December 2005 the BDP High Command ordered the dissolution of party factions. The so-called K-K faction (Kedikilwe-Kwelagobe) refused to disband, maintaining its demand for cabinet posts and insisting on a meeting with President Mogae to push for power sharing at all levels of government. With the prospect looming of Khama's ascendance to the presidency of the republic, the party was still divided in the run-up to its 2007 congress, at which Kwelagobe resigned as secretary general. In the balloting to succeed Kwelagobe, Nkate defeated Gomolemo Motswaledi, a youthful BDP activist aligned with the K-K faction. Although the K-K faction was subsequently considered to be in decline, Kwelagobe was elected to succeed Khama as chair in 2008 after Khama ascended to the presidency of the republic and Merafke was named vice president.

Both Kwelogobe and Kedikilwe were subsequently named to the cabinet, but Khama in mid-2009 decreed that party officials could not also serve in the government, prompting Kwelogobe's resignation from the cabinet. Despite fierce opposition from Khama and his followers in the BDP, Kwelogobe, whose supporters were now referred to as the Barata-Phathi faction, was reelected as party chair at the June 2009 congress, while Motswaledi was elected secretary general.

Secretary General Motswaledi was initially suspended in September 2009 for 60 days after he criticized attorneys who defended Khama's single-handed appointments to the Central Committee (considered a counter move to the Barata-Phathi's dominance on the panel); the suspension was later extended to five years. Tensions heightened further following the successful showing of the BDP in the October elections (45 seats [on a vote share of 53 percent] in the assembly and 68 percent of local council seats) when Khama bypassed faction members in his four nominations to Parliament and his cabinet appointments. The latter, in particular, prompted the defection of several faction members, including Secretary General Motswaledi, who broke away to form the new BMD (see below). Although Kwelagobe was initially expected to face a challenge for the secretary generalship at the July 2011 BDP congress, he was reelected in what was perceived as a relatively harmonious session, several of the legislators who had defected to the BMD having reportedly returned to the BDP fold. Subsequently, Kedikileve was appointed vice president of the republic in view of Merafhe's poor health.

As of the fall of 2013 the BDP, continuing to receive heavy financial support from the business community, was deemed to have survived its recent internal turmoil and was expected to maintain its control in the October 2014 legislative elections, which would propel Khama to another five-year presidential term.

Leaders: Lt. Gen. (Ret.) Seretse Ian KHAMA (President of the Republic), Ponatshego H. K. KEDIKILWE (Vice President of the Republic), Sir Ketumile Joni MASIRE (Former President of the Republic), Daniel K. KWELAGOBE (Chair), Thabo Fanu MASALILA (Executive Secretary), Satar DADA (Treasurer), Malebogo KRUGER (Deputy Secretary General), Mpho BALOPI (Secretary General).

Other Legislative Parties:

Botswana National Front (BNF). The BNF is a leftist party organized after the 1965 election. Its principal leader, Dr. Kenneth KOMA, initially announced his intention to oppose Seretse Khama for the presidency in 1979, but Koma failed to retain his assembly seat and thereby became ineligible for the presidency. The party's share of the vote increased to 20 percent in the 1984 election, with its legislative representation growing from two to four; it also won control of the Gaborone city council.

In the late 1980s a number of right-wing members of the BNF defected to the BDP in response to the BNF's left-wing, procommunist orientation. In the wake of the October 1989 election, in which BNF assembly representation was reduced to three, Koma characterized party members as "social democrats" who are "not Marxists." In the 1989 poll the BNF gained control of two local councils, including the capital, despite a loss of membership to two new splinter groups.

In August 1990 the BNF joined with the Botswana Progressive Union (BPU) and BPP (below) in forming a joint "Unity in Diversity" committee, which was formalized as a Botswana People's Progressive Front (BPPF) in October 1991. In 1993, however, Front members could not agree on whether they should boycott the next election if their demands for electoral reform were not met. As a result, the BNF contested the October 1994 poll on its own, substantially increasing its vote share to 37.7 percent and winning 13 elective seats, including all 4 in Gaborone.

In mid-1998 the BNF was severely weakened by the withdrawal of a faction (reportedly including 11 legislators) led by Michael Kitso DINGAKE, who subsequently helped to form the Botswana Congress Party (BCP, below). The BNF was initially described in early 1999 as negotiating participation in the new Botswana Alliance Movement (BAM, see BCP). However, delivering a blow to opposition legislative hopes of cutting into the BDP majority, the BNF ultimately decided to run its own candidates in all districts, securing six seats on 26 percent of the vote in the October balloting.

Although he did not take responsibility for the BNF's poor electoral showing in 1999, Koma announced in January 2000 that he would step down as the party's president. At a November 2001 congress, Otsweletse MOUPO beat Peter WOKO, who was supported by Koma, and became the new BNF leader. Koma was expelled from the party in 2002 for reportedly encouraging factionalism, and he moved on to help form the New Democratic Front (NDF, below) with other BNF dissidents in 2003.

In the 2004 elections the BNF secured 12 seats. Following the election, a rift emerged within the party between supporters of Moupo and those of BNF Vice President Kopano LEKOMA, who unsuccessfully challenged Moupo at the party conference in July 2005. In 2008 Moupo expelled the party's national chair, Nehemiah MODUBULE, and several other members for starting a faction within the BNF called the United Socialist Party, and he suspended the faction for six months. In June the suspension was lifted, but BNF leaders did not change their stance on Modubule's status. The expelled members sought reconciliation with the party in 2009, but Moupo refused.

Despite the BNF's poor showing in the 2009 elections, at which its assembly seat total fell from 12 to 6 on a vote share of 22 percent, Moupo refused to resign, attributing the "humiliating" defeat to longtime rifts within the party. Meanwhile, the expelled Modubule became the first independent candidate to be elected to the assembly. Moupo eventually declined to seek reelection as party president, and he was succeeded at a July 2010 congress by human rights lawyer Duma Boko, who subsequently was described as having moved the party to the center (or even the center-right), to the reported consternation of party veterans who continued to support heavy state control of economic affairs.

Severe factionalization was reported within the BNF in the first half of 2012 in regard to the extent of the party president's authority (long an issue within the BNF) as well as Boko's strong support for a proposed electoral umbrella with the BCP and BMB for the 2014 elections. (Boko's critics reportedly supported alignment with only the BCP, not the BMB.) Boko's stance was endorsed by a BDP special congress in May, and Boko was named president of the Umbrella for Democratic Change (UDC) that was subsequently formed by the BNF, BMD, and BPP, but not, significantly, the BCP. A number of labor unions and student associations also announced support for the UCD, although the coalition's chances in the 2014 balloting appeared severely compromised by the BCP's absence.

Leaders: Duma BOKO (President of the BNF and the UDC), Isaac MABILETSA (Vice President), Harry MOTHEI (Chair), Moeti MOHWASA (Spokesperson), Akanyang MAGAMA (Secretary General).

Botswana Congress Party (BCP). The BCP was formally registered in June 1998 by a group of BNF legislators interested in pursuing more centrist policies than the left-leaning parent grouping (personal animosity between BNF leader Kenneth Koma and dissident leader Michael Dingake also reportedly contributed to the rupture). The

BCP secured 12 percent of the vote in the 1999 legislative poll but only one seat, Dingake theorizing the party had been punished by the voters for splitting the opposition ranks. The party retained its seat in the 2004 balloting.

In advance of the 2009 elections, the BCP entered into an electoral alliance with the Botswana Alliance Movement (BAM), with whom it had been conducting unity talks for much of the decade. The BAM had been formed for the 1999 legislative elections by the BPP (below); the Botswana Progressive Union (BPU), founded in 1982; the Independent Freedom Party (IFP), founded in 1994 by a merger of the Botswana Independence Party (BIP) and the Botswana Freedom Party (BFP); and the United Action Party (UAP, also referenced as the Bosele Action Party [BAP]), launched in 1997 by a group of BDP dissidents. The BAM secured only 5 percent of the vote (and no seats) in the 1999 poll after having failed to convince other anti-BDP parties, most notably the BNF, to join in a single opposition coalition. The BAM again failed to secure representation in the 2004 elections, the BPP having left the grouping prior to the balloting.

Under a recently negotiated electoral agreement, the BCP and BAM did not present competing candidates in any legislative constituency in 2009 and jointly supported the presidential candidacy of the BCP's Gilson SALESHANDO, one of the BCP's founders. The BCP, which presented a candidate in 42 constituencies, improved to four seats on a vote share of 19.2 percent, while the BAM, which presented candidates in 4 constituencies, secured one seat on a vote share of 2.3 percent. The BCP and BAM formally merged in May 2010, maintaining the BCP rubric. Also reportedly included in the merger was the New Democratic Front (NDF), which had been formed in 2003 by dissidents from the BNF, including former BNF leader Kenneth Koma. The NDF, a center-left, social-democratic party, secured less than 1 percent of the vote in the 2004 assembly poll. In 2009 it was reported that the NDF, now led by Dick BAYFORD, had agreed to participate in the electoral accord with the BCP and BAM, but no formal NDF candidates were presented for the October poll.

Although the BCP initially expressed interest in joining the BNF, BMD, and BPP in an alliance for the October 2014 elections, the BCP ultimately declined to participate in the new UDC (see BNF). Issues reportedly included disagreement over the proposed distribution of seats on a coalition list as well as anti-BMD sentiment among some senior BCP officials.

Leaders: Dumalong SALESHANDO (President and Leader of the Opposition), Ephraim SETSHWAELO (Vice President), Batisani MASWIBILILI (Chair), Kesitegile GOBOTSWANG (Secretary General).

Botswana Movement for Democracy (BMD). The BMD was formed in early 2010 by a group of dissident BDP legislators who, among other things, opposed President Khama's unilateral approach to the four assembly appointees. The disaffected legislators, led by Sidney PILANE, Botsalo Ntuane, and Kabo MORWAENG, set forth the party platform as supporting democratization, civil liberties, and the rule of law. The leaders pledged to curb executive authority, strengthen civil society, and empower youth and women. Shortly after its official launch, the party called on President Khama to resign, dissolve the assembly, and call for new elections. That demand came in response to remarks by the president that any members of the assembly aligned with the BMD should step down. Subsequently, ousted BDP secretary general Gomolemo Motswaledi joined the BMD as did other dissidents from the BDP's Barata-Phathi faction (see BDP, above).

The BMD was cited in news reports for its use of social networking to attract young members, who turned up in significant numbers at the party's inaugural convention on May 29, 2010. Those who did not attend were able watch the event live on the Internet.

Motswaledi, who had been BMD interim chair, was elected to head the party at its first congress in May 2011, defeating Pilane. The BMD subsequently endorsed (in principle, at least) alignment with the BNF and BCP for the 2014 elections. However, animosity was reported between Motswaledi and BCP President Dumalong Saleshando, apparently contributing to the BCP's decision not to join the opposition's new Umbrella for Democratic Change. Meanwhile, a number of BMD members by that time had reportedly returned to the BDP fold.

Leaders: Gomolemo MOTSWALEDI (President of the BMD and Secretary General of the UDC), Wynter MMOLOTSI (Secretary General).

Other Parties That Contested the 2009 Legislative Elections:

Botswana People's Party (BPP). Founded in 1960 and for some years the principal minority party, the northern-based BPP advocates social democracy and takes a pan-Africanist line. After winning no assembly seats on a vote share of 4.6 percent in the 1994 assembly poll, the BPP contested the 1999 elections as part of the BAM (see BCP, above) and was subsequently described as in disarray. According to the *Africa News*, ten members of the party's National Executive Council, including former chair Kenneth MKHWA and former secretary general Matlhomola MODISE, were expelled in November 2000 for "having failed to carry out a resolution which directed the party to withdraw from the BAM." The party officially left the BAM prior to the 2004 legislative elections, at which the BPP gained only 1.9 percent of the vote and therefore no seats. The BPP in October 2005 signed on to a memorandum of agreement with the BCP, BAM, and BNF to cooperate in ousting the BDP in 2009. However, such cooperation failed to materialize, and the BPP ran on its own in the 2009 poll, securing none of the six seats for which it competed on a vote share of 1.4 percent. Party chair Bernard BALIKANI resigned after the elections. The BPP joined the UDC (the opposition's electoral coalition, see BNF) in advance of the 2014 legislative balloting.

Leaders: Whyte MAROBELA (President), Motlatsi MOLAPISI (Vice President), Richard GUDU (Chair), Shathiso B. TAMBULA (Secretary General).

Marx, Engels, Lenin, Stalin Movement of Botswana (MELS). Also reportedly referenced as the Mars Movement of Botswana, the MELS received only 0.1 percent of the vote in the 1999 and 2004 legislative balloting. The MELS fielded four candidates in the 2009 parliamentary election but failed to win any seats on a vote share of 0.05 percent.

Leaders: Mogae TAWANANA, Themba JOINA (President).

The **Botswana Tihoko Tiro Organization** (BTTO) presented a single candidate in the 2009 assembly poll.

Other Parties:

Other registered parties in 2004 included the **Social Democratic Party** (SDP), led by Rodgers SEABUENG, and the **Botswana Workers Front** (BWF), led by Mothusi AKANYANG. In 2009 the **Green Party of Botswana,** headed by Benjamin SEGOBAETSO, lent its support to several members who were expelled from the BNF in 2008, including its national chair, Nehemiah Modubule. The Green Party called for a boycott of the 2009 general elections.

LEGISLATURE

The **Parliament** consists of an elective National Assembly with legislative powers and a consultative House of Chiefs.

House of Chiefs. The House of Chiefs (*Ntlo ya Dikgosi*) is an advisory body of 35 members (increased from 15 in 2007): the hereditary chiefs from the 8 principal tribes; 4 members elected by and from the subchiefs of Chobe, North East, Ghanzi, and Kgalagadi districts (1 from each district); 18 additional members elected by the chiefs and subchiefs; and 5 presidential appointees. It is an eligibility requirement for elected members that they must not have been "active in politics" for five years prior to their election.

Chair: Kgosi Puso GABORONE.

National Assembly. The National Assembly, which sits for a five-year term, currently consists of 57 (raised from 40 in 2002) members directly elected from single-member constituencies in one-round voting; 4 members nominated by the president (subject to approval by the elected members of the assembly); the president (serving ex officio but with full voting rights); and the attorney general (ex officio, nonvoting). The speaker may be elected from inside or outside the assembly membership and becomes a full voting member upon election if elected from outside the assembly. (The current speaker was one of the presidential appointees to the assembly.) In the most recent general election on October 16, 2009, the seat distribution of the elected seats was as follows: Botswana Democratic Party, 45; Botswana National Front, 6; Botswana Congress Party, 4; Botswana Alliance Movement, 1; and independent, 1. (Defections subsequently altered the distribution of seats significantly. See individual party sections under Political Parties for details.) The next elections were scheduled for October 2014.

Speaker: Margaret Nnananyana NASHA.

CABINET

[as of October 1, 2013]

President	Lt. Gen. (Ret.) Seretse Ian Khama
Vice President	Ponatshego H. K. Kedikilwe
Ministers	
Agriculture	Christian De Graaf
Conservation, Wildlife, and Tourism	Kitso Mokaila
Defense, Justice, and Security	Dikgakgamatso Seretse
Education and Skills Development	Pelonomi Venson-Moiti [f]
Environment, Wildlife, and Tourism	Tshekedi Khama
Finance and Development Planning	Ontefetse Kenneth Matambo
Foreign Affairs and International Cooperation	Phandu Skelemani
Health	Dr. John Seakgosing
Infrastructure, Science, and Technology	Johnnie Swartz
Labor and Home Affairs	Edwin Batshu
Lands and Housing	Lebonamang Mokalake
Local Government	Peter Siele
Mines, Energy, and Water Resources	Kitso Mokaila
Presidential Affairs and Public Administration	Mokgweetsi Masisi
Trade and Industry	Dorcas Makgato-Malesu [f]
Transport and Communication	Nonofo Molefi
Youth, Sports, and Culture	Shaw Kgathi

[f] = female

Note: All ministers are BDP members.

INTERGOVERNMENTAL REPRESENTATION

Ambassador to the U.S.: Tebelelo Mazile SERETSE.

U.S. Ambassador to Botswana: Michelle D. GAVIN.

Permanent Representative to the UN: Charles Thembani NTWAAGAE.

IGO Memberships (Non-UN): ADB, AU, CWTH, IOM, NAM, SADC, WTO.

BRAZIL

Federative Republic of Brazil
República Federativa do Brasil

Political Status: Independent monarchy proclaimed 1822; republic established 1889; current constitution promulgated October 5, 1988.

Area: 3,286,470 sq. mi. (8,511,965 sq. km).

Population: 201,492,154 (2012E—UN); 205,716,890 (2012E—U.S. Census).

Major Urban Centers (2011): BRASILIA (federal district, 2,609,997), São Paulo (11,316,149), Rio de Janeiro (6,355,949), Salvador (2,693,605), Belo Horizonte (2,385,000), Manaus (1,832,423), Curtiba (1,764,540), Recife (1,546,516), Pôrto Alegre (1,413,094), Belém (1,402,056).

Official Language: Portuguese.

Monetary Unit: Real (market rate November 1, 2013: 2.26 reals = $1US).

President: Dilma Vana ROUSSEFF (Workers' Party); elected in runoff balloting on October 31, 2010, and inaugurated on January 1, 2011, for a four-year term, succeeding Luiz Inacio DA SILVA (Workers' Party).

Vice President: Michel TEMER Lulia (Party of the Brazilian Democratic Movement); elected in runoff balloting on October 31, 2010, as the running mate of Dilma ROUSSEFF, and inaugurated on January 1, 2011, for a term concurrent with that of the president, succeeding Jose ALENCAR Gomes de Silva (Liberal Party).

THE COUNTRY

The population of South America's largest country, which occupies nearly half the continent, is approximately 50 percent Caucasian, 43 percent biracial, 7 percent Afro-Brazilian, and less than 0.5 percent Indigenous and Asian, according to the 2006 census. The Caucasians are mainly of Portuguese descent but include substantial numbers of Belgian, Dutch, German, Italian, and Spanish immigrants. There are also small Arab, Japanese, and Chinese minorities. In general, Brazilian identity is based on economic and not racial status. Roman Catholicism is by far the predominant religion (73 percent), with evangelical Protestantism making substantial gains (around 15 percent). Women are about 30 percent less likely to be in employment than men, a gender differential that is considerably higher than the OECD average of 18 percent. Female representation in political life is relatively low. As of 2013 women held just 8.6 percent of the seats in the Chamber of Deputies (the lower house) and 16 percent in the Senate (upper house), which ranked Brazil 120th in the world for female parliamentary representation. The country's most powerful political office, however, that of president, has been occupied by a woman since January 2011.

The Brazilian economy was traditionally based on one-crop agriculture under the control of a landed aristocracy. In recent years, however, substantial diversification has occurred, with coffee, which once accounted for 50 percent of the nation's exports, now competing with other agricultural products like soybeans, corn, sugar, orange juice, poultry, and beef to be Brazil's leading commodities. Part of the surge seen in farm production and exports since the 1990s has been due to Brazil planting more genetically modified crops, especially soy and corn. As of 2010 it was the third largest exporter of agricultural products in the world, after the European Union (first) and the United States (second) with exports of $69 billion. Exports to emerging economies like China and India have been particularly buoyant as demand for food in those countries has risen in light of rising living standards. In industry, stiff competition from China and other emerging Asian economies, in particular since 2000, has put traditional Brazilian industries such as textiles manufacturing under pressure. However, Brazil's sugar-cane-based ethanol and petroleum industries are growing rapidly, while the country has become one of the world's leading producers of civilian aircraft and exporters of iron ore. Numerous minerals are mined commercially, including quartz, chromium, manganese, gold, and silver. In 2012 Brazil registered a trade surplus of $19.4 billion in its goods sector. Exports of goods have increased from $137.8 billion in 2006 to $242.6 billion in 2012, while goods imports increased even more dramatically, from $91.4 billion in 2006 to $223.2 billion in 2012.

After suffering crippling, triple-digit levels of inflation in the 1980s, Brazil implemented radical fiscal reforms in the 1990s that succeeded in stabilizing its economy. By the 2000s the government had more or less gotten inflation down to a manageable level. The architect of these fiscal reforms—which were called the "Real Plan"—was Finance Minister Fernando Henrique CARDOSO, who served two terms as president (1995–2002), largely as a result of his success in stabilizing the economy by linking the real's value to that of the dollar. However, a sudden sharp depreciation of the real against the U.S. dollar in 2013—it lost 15 percent of its value in just a few months—pushed up prices significantly, renewing fears of inflation. On the positive side, the market-generated depreciation of 2013 has helped Brazil's agricultural exports and consequently has been a boost for its economic growth.

GDP growth has slowed since 2011, partly in response to weaknesses in the global economy, but by autumn of 2013, the economy was clearly getting some wind back in its sails.

Historically, Brazil has had one of the largest gaps between rich and poor in the world. However, price stability and the direct transfer of government resources to the poor through income support programs like Bolsa Familia (Family Fund) are widely considered to have significantly alleviated the uneven distribution of wealth. Trade diversification, combined with an already reformed and well-supervised banking sector, helped Brazil avoid the devastating effects of the global financial crisis of 2008–2009, and the Great Recession of 2009 was thus experienced by Brazil as a relatively small bump in the road. Unemployment, at 5.6 percent as of June 2013, is less than half of its historical high of 13 percent set in 2004. The country's economy is forecast to grow by 4 percent in 2014.

GOVERNMENT AND POLITICS

Political background. Ruled as a Portuguese colony from 1500 to 1815, Brazil retained its monarchical institutions as an independent state from 1822 until the declaration of a republic in 1889. The constitution was suspended in 1930 as the result of a military coup d'état led by Getúlio VARGAS, whose dictatorship lasted until 1945. Enrico DUTRA, Vargas, Juscelino KUBITSCHEK, and Jânio QUADROS subsequently served as elected presidents. During the 1950s Brazil decided to move its capital from Rio de Janeiro to Brasília, a modernistic city it constructed especially to be the new capital, 650 miles northwest of Rio de Janeiro. In 1961 Quadros resigned and was succeeded by Vice President João GOULART. Goulart's leftist administration, after being widely criticized for inflationary policies, governmental corruption, and pro-labor and alleged procommunist tendencies, was overturned by the military in March 1964. Marshal Humberto de Alencar CASTELLO BRANCO, who served as president from 1964 to 1967, vigorously repressed subversive and leftist tendencies, instituted a strongly anti-inflationary economic policy, and reestablished governmental authority on a strictly centralized basis. Brazil's 13 political parties were dissolved in 1965, and political freedom was drastically curtailed by an "institutional act" whose main provisions were later incorporated into a constitution adopted under presidential pressure in 1967. Direct presidential elections were abolished, the president was given sweeping powers to regulate the press, and formal political activity was limited to two newly authorized parties—the progovernment National Renewal Alliance (Aliança Renovadora Nacional—Arena) and the opposition Brazilian Democratic Movement (Movimento Democrático Brasileiro—MDB).

The policies of Castello Branco were continued under Artur da COSTA E SILVA (1967–1969) and Emílio Garrastazú MEDICI (1969–1974). Despite periodic disturbances, the ease with which power was passed to President Ernesto GEISEL in early 1974 suggested that the military and its allies were still firmly in control. In 1978 the opposition MDB won a clear majority of votes cast but failed to capture either the Chamber of Deputies or the Senate because of electoral arrangements favoring the government party.

On March 15, 1979, João Baptista FIGUEIREDO was sworn in for a six-year term as Geisel's hand-picked successor. In the electoral college balloting of January 15, 1985, Tancredo NEVES of the Party of the Brazilian Democratic Movement (*Partido do Movimento Democrático Social*—PMDB) defeated Paulo MALUF, candidate of the newly established Social Democratic Party (PDS), but was unable to assume office because of illness. His vice-presidential running mate, José SARNEY Costa of the Liberal Front Party (*Partido dâ Frente Liberal*—PFL), became acting president on March 15 and succeeded to the presidency at Neves's death on April 21. During the ensuing three years, despite promulgation of a new, substantially liberalized constitution in October 1988, Sarney's popularity eroded sharply, with leftist parties registering significant gains in November municipal elections.

In early 1989 Fernando COLLOR de Mello, the young and relatively obscure governor of Alagoas, the country's second-smallest state, presented himself as presidential candidate of the newly launched National Reconstruction Party (*Partido da Reconstrução Nacional*—PRN). Running on a free enterprise platform, Collor won in a runoff against Luiz Inácio ("Lula") da SILVA, leader of the socialist Workers' Party (*Partido dos Trabalhadores*—PT).

In 1992 President Collor came under fire as the result of charges that his former campaign manager had operated a vast extortion network, part of the proceeds of which were intended to finance a reelection bid. As a result, the Chamber of Deputies on September 29 voted 441–38 to impeach Collor, and they installed Vice President Itamar Augusto Cautiero FRANCO as acting successor on November 2. Collor was indicted on criminal charges, and on December 29 he resigned in favor of Franco, who was immediately invested for the remaining two years of the presidential term.

On October 3, 1994, presidential candidate and former finance minister Fernando Henrique Cardoso, who had gained credit for a decline in inflation, beat his principal opponent, Lula da Silva, winning an absolute majority of 54.3 percent.

Following his inauguration on January 1, 1995, President Cardoso presided over the breakup of the state's oil and telecommunications monopolies, civil service and land reform, and a series of fiscal measures that included deindexation of wages and revision of the tax system.

Despite substantial opposition, Cardoso secured legislative approval for a constitutional amendment that permitted him to seek reelection in 1998. On October 4, 1998, Cardoso became the first Brazilian president to win a second term. In 2000 the country was threatened by a wave of political scandals and an energy crisis in early 2001 that necessitated power rationing. Cardoso's chosen PSDB successor, José SERRA, lost during second-round presidential balloting on October 27, 2002, to the PT's Lula da Silva, who took 61.4 percent of the vote. In 2005 PTB leader Roberto JEFFERSON accused the PT of making monthly payments to its allies in Congress in return for passing legislation. Those accused, many of them allies of President Lula da Silva, included former PT president José GENOINO and eight ministers. Despite the PT's alleged links to the corruption scandal, Lula da Silva was reelected in runoff balloting on October 29, 2006, when he took 60.8 percent of the vote against the PSDB's Geraldo ALCKMIN.

President Lula da Silva's overwhelming reelection victory was attributed in large part to his administration's having reduced inflation, maintained economic stability, and fostered the direct transfer of government resources to some 11 million of Brazil's poorest families.

However, new corruption and bribery charges prompted thousands to demonstrate against the president in August 2007, leading to the dismissal of several government ministers and more than 2,000 officials. In October 2007, in what was hailed as a landmark decision, the Supreme Court effectively banned lawmakers from changing party affiliation once elected, excepting specific, limited circumstances (e.g., if a party changed its ideology), thus ending lawmakers' propensity to change affiliation with some frequency. Additionally, the ruling required parties to maintain identical coalitions at both the national and regional levels, making it more difficult for governments to build coalitions.

Despite the corruption scandals, Lula da Silva left office on December 31, 2010, with a historically high popularity rating, due largely to him gaining credit for Brazil's strong economic performance during his tenure. In balloting on October 3, 2010, for the Chamber of Deputies, For Brazil to Keep on Changing (a propresidential coalition led by the PT and PMDB) secured 311 seats; Brazil Can Do More (an alliance led by the PSDB), 136; Progressive Party, 41; Green Party, 15; and others, 11. Following concurrent balloting for two-thirds of the Federal Senate, For Brazil to Keep on Changing controlled 50 seats and Brazil Can Do More, 25. Meanwhile, Dilma Rousseff of the PT was elected president on October 31, defeating José Serra of the PSDB in the runoff ballot with 56 percent of the vote. Rousseff, the country's first female president, was sworn in on January 1, 2011, along with a new cabinet comprising the PT, PMDB, Brazilian Socialist Party, Democratic Labor Party, Communist Party of Brazil, Progressive Party, and Brazilian Republican Party. Michel Miguel TEMER Lulia of the PMBD was elected vice president.

Rousseff's first priority was to stimulate the sluggish Brazilian economy. She announced in September 2012 that the government was reducing electricity charges for industry and consumers by 28 percent and 16 percent, respectively, in a bid to enhance the country's competitiveness. Other reforms that her government put in place caused Brazil's interest rates to fall to historic lows. However, Rousseff has also had to contend with a surge in industrial action, with about half of the public workforce either going on strike or protesting in 2012, riding a wave that was launched when teachers went on strike in May 2012. The country was rocked by popular demonstrations on an even bigger scale in June 2013, when more than a million people took to the streets in 52 cities to protest against the government. The immediate trigger for the protests was an increase in fares on public buses. However, the protests were also motivated by more underlying frustration toward the ruling political class, which has yet to use Brazil's impressive economic performance to give the country's public infrastructures—roads, public transportation, and ports—an urgently needed upgrade.

Constitution and government. Brazil's current constitution was adopted on September 2, 1988, by the Congress. The text encompassed 246 articles covering a wide range of social and economic issues, including a 40-hour work week, minimum wages, health and pension benefits, access to education, maternity and paternity leaves, labor autonomy and the right to strike, Indian rights, and protection of the environment.

The 1988 document provided for a president to be directly elected for a nonrenewable five-year term (reduced to four years in May 1994), with Brazilians in an April 1993 plebiscite decisively rejecting a return to either a parliamentary or monarchical form of government. In addition, provisions for referenda and "popular vetoes" on proposed and enacted legislation, respectively, were introduced, as well as provisions for "popular initiative" of draft bills for congressional consideration. An amendment ratified on June 5, 1997, authorized reelection of the president, as well as of state governors and mayors.

In May 2009 the Supreme Court struck down a 1967 censorship law enacted by the military regime that threatened journalists with prison time for publishing stories that jeopardized national security. In November 2011 a truth commission was established to investigate allegations of human rights crimes committed by the government between 1946 and 1988. Due to complete its investigations by the end of 2013, the commission made news in August 2013 when it announced it was exhuming the body of ousted president Goulart to determine if we was assassinated while in exile in Argentina in 1976. Brazil's ranking in Reporters Without Borders' World Press Freedom Index for 2013 was 108th place out of 179 countries. It has slipped down 50 places since 2011. Five journalists were killed in 2012. There are persistent problems with media pluralism, and regional media is subjected to frequent attacks, physical violence, and court censorship orders.

Brazil's legislature is called the National Congress, and it consists of a Senate and Chamber of Deputies. Its judiciary is headed by a Supreme Court whose members must be approved by the Senate. There are also federal courts in the state capitals, a Federal Court of Appeals, and special courts for dealing with military, labor, and electoral issues.

Brazil is divided into 26 states and the Federal District of Brasília. The states, which have their own constitutions, legislatures, and judicial systems, may divide or join with others to form new states. Thus, the former state of Guanabara merged with Rio de Janeiro in 1975, the new state of Mato Grosso do Sul was formed out of the southern part of Mato Grosso in 1979, and the former territory of Fernando de Noronha was included in Pernambuco under the 1988 constitution.

State and Capital	*Area (sq. mi.)*	*Population (2013E)*
Acre (Rio Branco)	59,343	776,463
Alagoas (Maceió)	11,238	3,300,935
Amapa (Macapá)	54,965	734,996
Amazonas (Manaus)	605,390	3,807,921
Bahia (Salvador)	218,912	15,044,137
Ceará (Fortaleza)	56,253	8,778,576
Espírito Santo (Vitória)	17,658	3,839,366
Goiás (Goiânia)	131,339	6,434,048
Maranhão (São Luís)	127,242	6,794,301
Mato Grosso (Cuiabá)	348,040	3,182,113
Mato Grosso do Sul (Campo Grande)	138,021	2,587,269
Minas Gerais (Belo Horizonte)	226,496	20,593,356
Pará (Belém)	481,404	7,969,654
Paraíba (João Pessôa)	20,833	3,914,421
Paraná (Curitiba)	76,959	10,997,465
Pernambuco (Recife)	39,005	9,208,550
Piauí (Teresina)	97,017	3,184,166
Rio de Janeiro (Rio de Janeiro)	16,855	16,369,179
Rio Grande do Norte (Natal)	20,528	3,373,959
Rio Grande do Sul (Pôrto Alegre)	108,369	11,164,043
Rondônia (Pôrto Velho)	92,039	1,728,214
Roraima (Boa Vista)	86,880	488,072
Santa Catarina (Florianópolis)	36,802	6,634,254
São Paulo (São Paulo)	95,852	43,663,669
Sergipe (Aracajú)	8,441	2,195,662
Tocantins (Miracema do Tocantins)	107,075	1,478,164
Distrito Federal (Brasília)	2,237	2,789,761

Foreign relations. For long a leader in the inter-American community, Brazil has traditionally been aligned in international affairs with the United States, a major trading partner. Brazil had strained relations with the United States during the 1970s too, when the military held sway in the government. For example, there was some estrangement due to the Geisel government's refusal to sign the 1968 UN Treaty on the Non-Proliferation of Nuclear Weapons (NPT), while rising coffee prices and the strong stand on human rights taken by U.S. President Jimmy Carter also caused tensions. This led to a shift in trade flows, as Brazil increasingly sold arms to other countries, including Iran, Libya, and Saudi Arabia, resulting in it becoming one of the largest arms dealers in the world. Since the late 1970s Brazil has become more integrated with its neighbors in Latin America. On July 3, 1978, a Treaty of Amazon Cooperation (Amazon Pact) was signed with Bolivia, Colombia, Ecuador, Guyana, Peru, Suriname, and Venezuela. During the 1982 Falkland Islands war, Brazil joined with its regional neighbors in supporting Argentina, while the Brazilian embassy in London represented Argentine interests in the British capital. However, Brazil's posture throughout was distinctly muted, partly because of traditional rivalry between the continent's two largest countries and partly because of an unwillingness to offend British financial interests, which were viewed as critical to resolution of Brazil's foreign debt problems.

On December 10, 1986, the Brazilian and Argentine presidents signed 20 accords, marking the launch of an ambitious integration effort whose ultimate goal was a Latin American common market. In 1988 Brazil and Argentina agreed to cooperate in the nuclear power industry, although (without endorsing the NPT) they formally rejected the development of nuclear weaponry in a July 1991 accord that also banned the introduction of such arms from external sources. Diplomatic relations with Cuba were restored in June 1986, after a 22-year rupture.

In June 1992 Brazil drew international attention by hosting the largest gathering of world leaders in history for the United Nations Earth Summit in Rio de Janeiro (see United Nations Conference on Environment and Development under UN General Assembly, Special Bodies).

In 1995 Brazil joined with Argentina, Paraguay, and Uruguay in creating a regional free trade zone called the Southern Cone Common Market (Mercado Común do Cono Sur—Mercosur). U.S. President Bill Clinton hailed Mercosur as a stepping-stone to a Free Trade Area for the Americas (FTAA) during a visit to Brazil in October 1997. In 1999 Brazil and Argentina agreed to adopt mutually compatible mechanisms of fiscal restraint, with a view to moving toward a common currency within Mercosur.

At the 2005 Summit of the Americas, Brazil, along with four other Latin American nations, rejected the U.S.-backed FTAA, reflecting the change in Brazil's leadership and the regional shift to more leftist politics. President Lula da Silva made expanding Brazil's trade and diplomatic ties throughout Africa and with China more of a priority than it had previously been. For example, whereas in 2000 Brazil's trade with China amounted to $2 billion, by 2010 this had skyrocketed to almost $60 billion. Brazil's relations with Venezuela were mixed. While their mutual coolness toward the U.S. administration in the 2000s served as a bond of unity, there were concurrent tensions in trade relations as they competed with one another for preeminence in the region's petroleum market. But Venezuelan president Hugo Chávez and Lula da Silva cooperated on the construction of various large projects, such as a $1.2 billion bridge over the Orinoco River to facilitate the transport of Brazilian goods to Venezuelan ports. In cooperation with Venezuela, Brazil led efforts to found the South American Defense Council in May 2008 under the umbrella Union of South American Nations (Unasur), which was also established that year.

From the late 1980s, environmental groups—and later on international agencies—started stepping up pressure on Brazil to halt the deforestation of its Amazon rainforests as climate experts concluded this was a major cause of global warming. By the mid-2000s Brazil was finally making progress in slowing the rate of deforestation, partly due to a very active environment minister, the Green Party's Marina SILVA, who came from an Amazonian rubber tapper family. Meanwhile, the country began asserting itself as a regional power—in January 2009 it stepped into a joint antidrug program with Bolivia, taking up the position vacated by the expulsion of the U.S. Drug Enforcement Administration. In its trade relations with the United States, Brazil in the late 2000s stepped up its calls for U.S tariffs on Brazilian ethanol exports to be reduced. The Brazilian government also refused to budge from its decision to impose $560 million of retaliatory trade tariffs on U.S. consumer goods because of U.S. domestic cotton subsidies. On the diplomatic front, the relationship faced some stresses too as, for example, when the United States in 2010 rebuffed a Turkish-Brazilian effort to mediate an international deal with Iran aimed at resolving a decade-long dispute over Iran's nuclear program. At the heart of Brazil's strained relationship with the United States was Lula da Silva's belief that the United States was failing to pay sufficient attention to Latin America.

The current president, Dilma Rousseff, made a concerted effort to rejuvenate relations with the United States after being elected, with U.S. president Barack Obama being warmly received on a high-profile official visit in March 2011. These improved relations had been expected to culminate in a state visit to Washington in October 2013. However, the revelations in the summer of 2013 of U.S. government spying activities in Brazil, including allegations that Rousseff's personal e-mails were intercepted, caused a sudden deterioration in the relationship, and in September 2013 the Brazilian president cancelled the state visit.

Current issues. In recent years, the spotlight has increasingly shone on Brazil's responsibility to conserve the Amazon. The current flash points are the government's ongoing plans to construct a hydroelectric dam and a power plant in the Amazon, the Belo Monte project, which has upset many environmentalists and indigenous groups and led to violent protests. The structure is expected to be the world's third largest dam and to power 23 million Brazilian homes. The dam is supposed to start producing electricity in 2015. Oil and gas production in Brazil is set to increase substantially in the coming years with the recent discovery of large quantities of both about 12 miles off Brazil's easy coast, lying under a thick layer of submarine salt. If that happens, it is likely to further increase Brazil's rivalry with Latin America's largest oil producer, Venezuela. Since taking office, President Rousseff has sought to repair the relationship with Washington. In April 2011, Rousseff visited China on a largely trade-oriented visit, China having overtaken the United States in 2009 to become Brazil's largest trade partner. Brazil has been investing more in Africa too, including through generous development aid projects, and is contributing more and more to UN peacekeeping missions—for example, taking the lead in a UN peace-enforcing mission in Haiti. Given this increased global engagement, coupled with its strong economy, Brazil has been making a case for itself to be given a permanent seat at the UN Security Council, although this campaign has failed to gain major traction thus far.

Brazil and the United States remain major trading partners, with recent surges in trade in energy products, such as oil, gas, and ethanol, although the two do not yet have a bilateral Free Trade Agreement. The revelations in summer of 2013 that the U.S. National Security Agency (NSA) has been monitoring e-mails and phone records of millions of Brazilians have made the conclusion of such a free trade pact a more distant prospect. The spy programs were disclosed by former NSA contractor Edward Snowden. In the case of Brazil, the allegations included both political espionage—notably of Rousseff's personal communications—and industrial espionage, with Brazil's state-run oil company Petrobras also allegedly targeted. Responding to widespread public anger over the allegations, Rousseff's decision to cancel her state visit to Washington was a strong diplomatic step to take given that such visits are rare, the previous one from a Brazilian head of state having taken place in 1995. Rousseff later explained that she felt obliged to cancel the visit as the U.S. refused to offer an apology over the spying activities. Bolivian-Brazilian relations suffered a shock in August 2013 after a Bolivian opposition leader, Roger Pinto, wanted by Bolivian authorities to face trial on corruption charges, was smuggled over the border and into Brazil by Brazilian diplomats and marines. Pinto had been living at Brazil's embassy in La Paz since 2012 after being granted asylum. The episode claimed a major political scalp, with Brazil's foreign minister Antonio PATRIOTA resigning over it.

At the close of 2013, Brazil was in the midst of preparing to host two major world sporting events: the 2014 World Cup in soccer, to take place in stadiums in 12 cities, and the 2016 Olympics in Rio de Janeiro. The government pumped billions of dollars into projects aimed at improving the country's shaky infrastructure, with a strong emphasis on roads and airports. As the events drew nearer, pressure mounted, because the country was acutely aware that the world will view its performance as a barometer of how far Brazil has advanced. The channeling of so much public funds into organizing these two events has also attracted criticism and was another underlying factor behind the June 2013 public protests.

Tackling organized crime—in particular by regaining control over many of the country's vast urban slums from entrenched drug-trafficking gangs—is another top priority for the government. A core part of the administration's strategy is the introduction of "police pacification units," small teams of law enforcement officers embedded in the community that aim to build up residents' trust. Murder rates in major cities like Rio de Janeiro and São Paulo have been decreasing from their epidemic levels of the 1990s and early 2000s.

POLITICAL PARTIES

Brazil has, for more than two decades, been consolidating itself as a multiparty democracy with free and fair elections, having emerged from a difficult period from the 1960s to the mid-1980s, when political freedoms were severely curtailed. Following the 1964 military coup, all of Brazil's parties were dissolved by decree, clearing the way for establishment of a single government party, Arena, and a single opposition party, MDB, which began organizing in 1969. Both groups were formally dissolved on November 22, 1979, after enactment of legislation sanctioning a more liberal party system. On May 9, 1985, Congress enacted a bill that restored direct presidential elections and legalized all political parties. On the other hand, a law passed before the 1990 balloting required that a party have at least 300,000 members to qualify for formal registration. A 2007 court ruling restricted officials' ability to change party affiliations and parties' ability to form coalitions (see Political Background above). By 2013, however, Brazil still had more than 20 registered political parties, most of which were involved in loosely defined and frequently changing coalitions at the regional and local levels. Indeed, the fragmented political party system of Brazil compels parties to form coalition pacts with various other parties if they wish to secure parliamentary majorities or win the presidency in elections.

Government Parties:

Workers' Party (*Partido dos Trabalhadores*—PT). Founded in 1981 under the slogan "a pure form of socialism" that rejected orthodox Marxism, the PT has since 2003 been serving in government at the federal level, as part of a coalition. As of September 2012, it held 88 seats in the Chamber of Deputies and 14 in the Senate, making it one of Brazil's leading political parties. Brazil's current and previous presidents, Dilma Rousseff and Luiz Inacio Lula de Silva, have both emerged from within the PT's ranks.

The party has been increasing its support steadily since being founded. For example, the PT made important gains in the 1985 municipal balloting, electing Maria Luisa FONTONELLE as one of the country's first two women mayors in Ceará's capital, Fortaleza, and winning 20 percent of the vote in São Paulo. It registered significant gains in the November 1988 municipal balloting, securing, most notably, the election of Luiza ERUNDINA as São Paulo's first woman mayor. In late 1991, at the party's first congress since its founding a decade earlier, the Lula da Silva–led majority voted to abandon its former advocacy of "democratic socialism" and the "dictatorship of the proletariat" in favor of coexistence (not excluding cooperation) with other groups, both socialist and nonsocialist. Lula da Silva was runner-up to Collor de Mello in the 1989 presidential poll and placed second behind Fernando Henrique Cardoso in 1994. Failing again in 1998, he was victorious in 2002.

Following Lula da Silva's inauguration in 2003, the party shifted from a leftist-socialist to a more center-left social democratic orientation, which spurred internal debate and the expulsion of four dissident legislators, including Heloísa HELENA, who subsequently founded the PSOL (see below). Further turmoil within the party occurred during a corruption scandal in 2005, which resulted in the replacement of several high-ranking party officials. Nevertheless, Lula da Silva was reelected with an overwhelming mandate in 2006, and PT deputies under investigation were reelected in concurrent legislative elections. However, the PT trailed the PMDB in number of legislative seats.

On February 20, 2010, the party nominated Dilma Rousseff, Lula da Silva's former chief of staff as its candidate in the upcoming October election. Rousseff emerged as the winner of the presidential ballot, in both the first and the second rounds of voting, and became Brazil's first female president on January 1, 2011.

Leaders: Dilma Vana ROUSSEFF Linhares (President of the Republic); Rui FALCÃO (President of the party); José GUIMARES (Leader of the party in the Chamber of Deputies); Wellington DIAS (Leader of the party in the Senate); Humberto Sergio Costa Lima, Alberto Lopes Cantalice, Maria De Fátima BEZERRA (Vice Presidents). **Party of the Brazilian Democratic Movement** (*Partido do Movimento Democrático Brasiliero*—PMDB). The PMDB is currently sparring with the PT to be the top political party of Brazil. As of 2011 it had 79 seats in the Chamber of Deputies and 19 Senate seats. Its membership is large and very diverse, with various wings espousing different ideologies.

Rejecting government strictures against the adoption of names implying continuity with earlier party groups, the PMDB was launched in 1979 by about 100 federal deputies and 20 senators representing the more moderate elements of the former MDB. In late 1981 it was enlarged by a merger with the Popular Party (*Partido Popular*—PP), a center-right grouping, most of whom had also been affiliated with the MDB. In March 1991 the 20-year party leadership of Ulysses GUIMARÃES came to an end with the election of Orestes QUÉRCIA to succeed him as president. Quércia resigned on April 26, 1993, in response to allegations of corruption during his recent term as governor of the state of São Paulo, although subsequently he presented himself as a candidate for the federal presidency in 1994.

The largest single contributor to the Franco coalition, the PMDB in 1994 won 9 of 26 gubernatorial contests and secured a plurality of seats in both houses of Congress. Retaining its preeminence in the Senate, it fell to third place in the chamber in 2002. It participated in the Lula da Silva government until the party officially withdrew its support in late 2004, although its cabinet representatives chose to remain in office. Opting not to field a presidential candidate in 2006, the party joined coalitions at the state and national levels. It held a plurality in the chamber following the 2006 election and was brought back into the government in 2007, its members having been appointed to several ministry posts. Considerable opposition to these appointments was reported within the party, but overall the party's "amorphous" ideology and preference for office led to its continued support for the Lula da Silva government and its position as the government's main ally. In the 2010 presidential campaign the PMDB backed PT candidate Dilma Rousseff for a number of concessions, and the two parties worked to develop joint tickets in 15 states. The Chamber of Deputies' president Michel Miguel Elias Temer Lulia was offered the vice-presidential candidate slot by Rousseff.

Leaders: Michel Miguel Elias TEMER Lulia (Vice President of the Republic), Valdir RAUPP (First Vice President), Iris ARAUJO (Second Vice President), Romero Juca (Third Vice President), Mauro LOPES (Secretary General).

Government-Supporting Parties:

Democratic Labor Party (*Partido Democrático Trabalhista*—PDT). The PDT is a left-wing party, which has 25 Chamber of Deputies and 5 Senate seats. It was founded in 1979 by Leonel da Moira BRIZOLA, who had previously served as governor of Rio Grande do Sul and leader of the pre-1965 Brazilian Labor Party, before spending 15 years in exile. After some success in municipal and state elections in the 1980s, Brizola ran unsuccessfully for president in 1989 and 1994. He was Lula da Silva's running mate in the 1998 contest. The party supported the PT's Dilma Rousseff in the October 2010 presidential election.

Leaders: Carlos LUPI (President), Andre FIGUEIREDO (Vice President), Carlos Eduardo VIEIRA da Cunha (First Vice President), Micheline VECCHIO (Second Vice President), Manoel DIAS (General Secretary).

Christian Social Party (*Partido Social Cristão*—PSC). The PSC was launched in 1970 as the Democratic Republican Party (*Partido Democrático Republicano*—PDR); it adopted the PSC rubric in 1985. In the 1990s the party formed a secret coalition with President Durán BALLÉN in support of market reforms aimed at modernizing the Brazilian economy. It competed in the 2010 elections as part of the victorious PT-led "For Brazil to Keep on Changing" coalition and emerged with 17 seats in the Chamber of Deputies and 1 in the Senate.

Leaders: Vítor Jorge Abdala NOSSIES (President), Antonio OLIBONI (General Secretary).

Brazilian Republican Party (*Partido Republicano Brasileiro*—PRB). The PRB was formed in 2005 as a successor to the Municipal Renewal Party (*Partido Municipalista Renovador*—PMR), which was established following the 2005 corruption scandals by Brazil's leading evangelical group, the Universal Church of the Kingdom of God (Igreja Universal do Reino de Deus—IURD). The IURD is a well-known Pentecostal group, with branches in 172 countries, headed by an entrepreneurial "bishop," Edir MACEDO. The PRB, however, has been described as being more driven by pragmatism than by ideology, though a party that defends the interests of the church. The PRB has supported the Lula da Silva and Rousseff presidencies on the basis of their concern for social democracy and for eliminating inequality. It currently has eight seats in the Chamber and one in the Senate.

Leaders: Marcos Antônio PEREIRA (President), Evandro GARLA (General Secretary).

Opposition Parties:

Brazilian Social Democratic Party (Partido da Social Democracia Brasileira—PSDB). The PSDB emerged as the leading opposition party following the October 2010 election, heading up the Brazil Can Do More coalition, with 53 seats in the Chamber and 11 seats in the Senate.

The PSDB was launched in June 1988 by a number of center-left congressional deputies who issued a manifesto calling for social justice, economic development, land reform, and environmental protection. In addition, it pledged to call for a plebiscite on the establishment of a parliamentary system within the next four years. In 1994 and 1998 it supported the successful presidential bids of Fernando Henrique Cardoso.

The PSDB has struggled since the Cardoso administration to find a presidential candidate who could unify the party. In the 2010 presidential elections, the party chose former São Paulo state governor José Serra as its candidate. His candidacy was backed by the PPS and the DEM25. Serra's was defeated by PT candidate Dilma Rousseff in the runoff ballot, after winning 44 percent of the vote, compared with Rousseff's 56 percent.

Leaders: Aécio NEVES (President), Alberto GOLDMAN (First Vice President); Alvaro DIAS, Bruno ARAÚJO, Cássio CUNHA LIMA, Ciro MIRANDA, Tasso JEREISSATI (Vice Presidents); Antônio Carlos MENDES Thame (General Secretary).

Democrats 25 (*Democratas 25*—DEM25). The Democrats is the name adopted in 2007 by the **Liberal Front Party** (*Partido da Frente Liberal*—PFL). Following the October 2010 parliamentary elections, DEM25 have 43 seats in the Chamber of Deputies and 6 in the Senate.

The PFL was formed in 1984 as a faction that opposed the presidential candidacy of Paulo Maluf. The PFL was a supporter of Brazilian president José Sarney, who had been a cofounder of the party. The "25" in the party name refers to the party's electoral code. By 1992 it was the largest progovernment formation in the Chamber of Deputies and subsequently became the largest component of the Cardoso coalition. The PFL withdrew from the coalition government in March 2002 to protest an official investigation into the business dealings of Roseana SARNEY, the PFL's 2002 presidential candidate. Sarney withdrew from the race in April, and the PFL subsequently threw its support behind Ciro GOMES, then of the PPS (see below). In the 2010 presidential election, the party allied with the PSDB, whose presidential candidate, José Serra, chose lawyer and first-term DEM25 deputy Indio DA COSTA as his vice-presidential running mate.

Leaders: Jose Agripino MAIA (President), Onyx LORENZONI (General Secretary), Rosalba CIARLINI (Governor of Rio Grande do Norte), Romero AZEVEDO (Treasurer).

Brazilian Labor Party (*Partido Trabalhista Brasileiro*—PTB). The PTB was founded in 1980 by Ivete VARGAS, a niece of the country's former president Getúlio Vargas. It was part of the losing Brazil Can Do More coalition in the 2010 parliamentary elections and currently has 21 seats in the Chamber plus 6 in the Senate. The PTB was a member of the Cardoso coalition government installed in 1994 but withdrew from the cabinet in March 1999. It withdrew from the Lula da Silva administration in June 2005 when its leader, Roberto Jefferson Monteiro Francisco, initiated charges of high-level corruption.

Leaders: Roberto JEFFERSON Monteiro Francisco (President), Benito GAMA (Vice President), Fernando COLLOR de Mello (Former President of the Republic), Antônio Carlos De Campos MACHADO (General Secretary).

Other Legislative Parties:

Republic Party (*Partido da República*—PR). The center-right PR attained 41 Chamber of Deputies seats and 4 Senate seats, following the October 2010 elections.

The party was formed under the leadership of Sergio TAMER in December 2006, when the **Liberal Party** (*Partido Liberal*—PL) merged with the **Party for the Rebuilding of the National Order** (*Partido de Reedificação da Ordem Nacional*—PRONA). The PL had been founded in 1985 as a tradesmen's party committed to free enterprise and a more just wages policy. PRONA was a far-right grouping founded in 1989 by a São Paulo cardiologist, Enéas Ferreira CARNEIRO, who was the party's candidate in the country's first presidential election that year. He ran for various offices over the years and in 2006 was elected as a deputy, securing one of his party's two seats. He died in May 2007.

Leader: Alfredo Pereira do NASCIMENTO (President).

Brazilian Socialist Party (*Partido Socialista Brasileiro*—PSB). One of Brazil's older political parties, founded in 1947, the PSB has been described by observers as more pragmatic than other socialist parties in the country. In 1994 it was part of a broad coalition that supported Lula da Silva's presidential bid. The party nominated former PPS president and federal deputy Ciro Gomes as its presidential candidate for the October 2010 election. However, Gomes pulled out in late April 2010 because the government-friendly party decided to continue its alliance with the PT. The PSB emerged from the October 2010 legislative elections with 34 seats in the Chamber and 3 seats in the Senate.

Leaders: Fernando Bezerra COELHO (Federal Minister for National Integration), José Leônidas CRISTINO (Federal Minister for Ports), Eduardo CAMPOS (President), Ariano VILAR Suassuna (Honorary President), Roberto AMARAL (First Vice President), Beto ALBUQUERQUE (Second Vice President), Joao Alberto CAPIBERIBE (Third Vice President).

Progressive Party (*Partido Progressista*—PP). The PP designation was adopted in 2003 by the former Brazilian Progressive Party (*Partido Progressista Brasiliero*—PPB), which was launched in 1995 as a merger of three other Progressive parties. The party is considered a center-right one ideologically and has aligned itself at the national level with the PT in recent years. The PP has been damaged by numerous scandals in the 2000s, with several high-level party officials accused of corruption. In the 2010 parliamentary elections, the PP secured 41 seats in the Chamber of Deputies and was left with four Senators.

Leaders: Ciro NOGUEIRA (President), Francisco DORNELLES (Honorary President), Mário NEGROMONTE (First Vice President), Ângela AMIN (Second Vice President).

Green Party (*Partido Verde*—PV). The PV was established in 1988, largely by a group of PMDB deputies. Following the October 2010 elections, the party had 15 seats in the Chamber of Deputies but no senator.

Its first president was Fernando Gabeira, a former guerrilla who campaigned for mayor of Rio de Janeiro in 1986 under the PT banner. He left the PV in 2002 to join the PT but returned in 2006. In 2008 party cofounder Carlos MINC defected to the PT and was appointed minister of environment. In August 2009 the former environment minister Marina Silva resigned from PT and joined PV on the grounds that the government was not ambitious enough in the fight against global warming. Silva, a well-known figure on the international environmental stage, ran for president as the PV's candidate in the October 2010 election and finished in third place, winning 19 percent of votes in the first-round ballot. In 2011, Silva left the party and in February 2013 launched her own new party, called **Sustainability Network** (*Rede Sustentabilidade*).

Leaders: José Luiz de França PENNA (President), Paulo DAVIM (Senator).

Communist Party of Brazil (*Partido Comunista do Brasil*—PCdoB). An offshoot of the PCB, which was founded in 1922, the PCdoB was formed in 1961 as a Maoist group in support of rural guerrilla operations against the military. In August 1978 it publicly expressed its support for the Albanian Communist Party in its break with the post-Maoist Chinese leadership. In the mid-1980s, the party was instrumental in promoting huge demonstrations against the military regime. The party was a strong supporter of Lula da Silva in the 1990s and 2000s. The party, whose platform calls for a socialist Brazil that is "truly democratic and sovereign," won 15 chamber seats in the 2010 elections.

Leaders: Renato REBELO (President), Luciana SANTOS (Vice President).

Socialist Peoples Party (*Partido Popular Socialista*—PPS). The PPS was launched in January 1992 as a successor to the Brazilian Communist Party (*Partido Comunista Brasileiro*—PCB), which had been formed in 1922 but enjoyed only nine years of legal existence thereafter. In June 1991 the PCB elected a "renewalist" leadership and argued that it was "no longer necessary [for] a Marxist to be a Communist." In furtherance of this posture, the party voted to confine Marxism-Leninism to the status of "historic relevance" and authorized the pursuit of socialism by democratic means. In 2004 the party withdrew from the governing coalition and subsequently expelled party leader Ciro Gomes, who had decided to remain in his cabinet post. Gomes then joined the PSB. The PPS won 12 Chamber and 1 Senate seat in the 2010 legislative elections.

Leaders: Roberto João Pereira FREIRE (President), Antonio Ribeiro GRANJA (Honorary President).

Socialist and Liberty Party (*Partido do Socialismo e da Libertade*—PSOL). A far-left formation, the PSOL was launched in June 2004 by Heloísa Helena, who had been expelled from the PT in late 2003 for voting against the government. She was subsequently joined by a number of other PT defectors.

The PSOL follows an ideology similar to that of the PCdoB. It has benefited from the public perception that its members have been considered "honest politicians." Helena secured 6.8 percent of the vote in the first round of the 2006 presidential balloting. However, the party's candidate in the 2010 presidential election, Plinio de Arruda SAMPAIO, won less than 1 percent.

Leaders: Ivan VALENTA (President), Edilson SILVA (First General Secretary). Other parties represented in the legislature are the **National Mobilization Party** (*Partido da Mobilização Nacional*—PMN), led by Oscar NORONHA; the **Christian Labor Party** (*Partido Trabalhista Cristão*—PTC) led by Daniel TOURINHO; the **Humanist Party of Solidarity** (*Partido Humanista da Solidariedade*—PHS), led by Eduardo MACHADO; the **Labor Party of Brazil** (*Partido Trabalhista do Brasil*—PtdoB), led by Luis TIBÉ; the **Renewed Brazilian Workers Party** (*Partido Renovador Trabalhista Brasileiro*—PRTB), led by 2010 presidential candidate Levy FIDELIX; the **Progressive Republican Party** (*Partido Republicano Progressista*—PRP), led by Ovasco RESENDE; and the **Social Liberal Party** (*Partido Social Liberal*—PSL), led by Luciano Caldas BIVAR.

LEGISLATURE

The bicameral **National Congress** (*Congresso Nacional*) consists of a Federal Senate and a Chamber of Deputies, both of which are directly elected by universal suffrage. The two houses, sitting together, form a Constituent Assembly for purposes of constitutional revision. The most recent elections took place in October 2010.

Federal Senate (*Senado Federal*). The upper house consists of 81 members (3 for each state, plus 3 for the Federal District) elected for eight-year terms, with one-third and two-thirds, respectively, elected every four years. Senators are elected in single-round plurality voting. Voters vote for one candidate when one-third of the membership is renewed and two candidates when two-thirds of the membership is renewed.

Following the balloting of October 3, 2010, for two-thirds of the seats, the distribution of seats in the full senate was as follows: PMDB 19; PT, 15; PSDB, 11; PTB, 6; DEM25, 6; PR, 4; PDT, 4; PP, 4; PSB, 3; PCdoB, 2; PSOL, 2; PSC, 1; PRB, 1; PPS, 1; PMN, 1.

President: José SARNEY.

Chamber of Deputies (*Câmara dos Deputados*). Seats in the lower house are allocated on a population basis, their 513 current occupants serving four-year terms. Members are directly elected via party-list proportional balloting from 27 multimember constituencies (1 for each state and 1 for the Federal District).

In the most recent balloting on October 3, 2010, the seat distribution was as follows: PT, 88 seats; PMDB, 79; PSDB, 53; DEM25, 43; PP, 41; PSB, 34; PDT, 28; PSC, 17; PCdoB, 15; Verde, 15; PPS, 12; PRB, 8; PMN, PTdoB, 3; PSOL, 3; PHS, 2; PRTB, 2; PRP, 2; PTC, 1; PSL, 1.

President: Henrique Eduardo ALVES.

CABINET

[as of September 1, 2013]

President	Dilma Rousseff [f]
Vice President	Michel Temer (PMDB)
Chief of Staff	Gleisi Helena Hoffmann (PT) [f]
Secretary General of the Presidency	Gilberto Carvalho (PT)
Ministers	
Agrarian Development	Jose "Pepe" Vargas (PT)
Agriculture, Livestock, and Food Supply	Antonio Andrade (PMDB)
Aquaculture and Fisheries	Marcelo Crivella (PRB)
Cities	Aguinaldo Ribeiro (PP)
Communications	Paulo Bernardo Silva (PT)
Culture	Marta Suplicy (PT)[f]
Defense	Celso Amorim (PT)
Development, Industry, and Foreign Trade	Fernando Pimentel (PT)
Education	Aloizio Mercadante (PT)
Environment	Izabella Teixeira [f]
Finance	Guido Mantega (PT)
Foreign Affairs	Luiz Alberto Figueiredo
Health	Alexandre Padilha (PT)
Justice	Jose Eduardo Cardozo (PT)
Labor and Employment	Manoel Dias (PDT)
Mines and Energy	Edison Lobão (PMDB)
National Integration	Fernando Bezerra Coelho (PSB)
Planning, Budget, and Management	Miriam Belchior (PT) [f]
Science and Technology	Marco Antonio Raupp
Social Development and the Fight against Hunger	Tereza Campello (PT) [f]
Social Security	Garibaldi Alves Filho (PMDB)
Sport	Aldo Rebelo (PCdoB)
Tourism	Gastao Dias Vieira (PMDB)
Transport	César Borges (PR)
Secretaries with Ministerial Status	
Central Bank	Alexandre Tombini
Comptroller General	Jorge Hage Sobrinho
AttorneyGeneral	Luis Inacio Lucena Adams
Human Rights	Maria do Rosário Nunes [f]
Institutional Relations	Ideli Salvatti (PT) [f]
Institutional Security in the Office of the President	Gen. Jose Elito Carvalho Siqueira
Policies to Promote Racial Equality	Luiza Helena de Bairros [f]
Ports	José Leonidas Cristino (PSB)
Social Communication	Helena Chagas [f]
Strategic Affairs in the Office of the President	vacant
Women's Policies	Eleonora Menicucci de Oliveira (PR) [f]

[f] = female

INTERGOVERNMENTAL REPRESENTATION

Ambassador to the U.S.: Mauro VIEIRA.

U.S. Ambassador to Brazil: Thomas A. SHANNON Jr.

Permanent Representative to the UN: Antonio PATRIOTA.

IGO Memberships (Non-UN): AfDB, G-20, IADB, ICC, IOM, Mercosur, OAS, WTO.

BRUNEI

State of Brunei Darussalam
Negara Brunei Darussalam

Political Status: Formerly a constitutional monarchy in treaty relationship with the United Kingdom; independent sultanate proclaimed January 1, 1984.

Area: 2,226 sq. mi. (5,765 sq. km).

Population: 416,125 (2012E—UN); 415,717 (2013E—U.S. Census).

Major Urban Center (2005E): BANDAR SERI BEGAWAN (30,000).

Official Language: Malay (English is widely used).

Monetary Unit: Bruneian Dollar (market rate November 1, 2013: 1.24 dollars = $1US). The Bruneian dollar is at par with the Singapore dollar.

Head of State and Prime Minister: Sultan Sir Haji HASSANAL BOLKIAH Muizzaddin Waddaulah; ascended the throne October 5, 1967, upon the abdication of his father, Sultan Sir Haji Omar ALI SAIFUDDIN; crowned August 1, 1968; assumed office of prime minister at independence, succeeding former chief minister ABDUL AZIZ bin Umar.

Heir Apparent: Crown Prince Haji al-Muhtadee BILLAH, eldest son of the sultan; installed as crown prince August 10, 1998.

THE COUNTRY

Brunei consists of two jungle enclaves on the north coast of Borneo. About 56.3 percent of its population is Malay, 11.2 percent is Chinese, and the remainder belongs to indigenous tribes. Malay is the official language, but the use of English is widespread. A majority, 67 percent, of the population follows Islam, which is the official state religion; smaller groups are Buddhist, Confucian, Christian, and pagan.

Brunei's per capita income, at $44,000 in 2012, is third highest in East Asia. The same year, Forbes ranked Brunei the fifth wealthiest country in the world. Its wealth is derived from royalties on oil produced by Brunei Shell Petroleum and Brunei Shell Marketing, in both of which the government now holds a 50 percent interest, and on liquefied natural gas (LNG) produced primarily by Brunei LNG, in which the government holds a 50 percent interest and Shell and Mitsubishi of

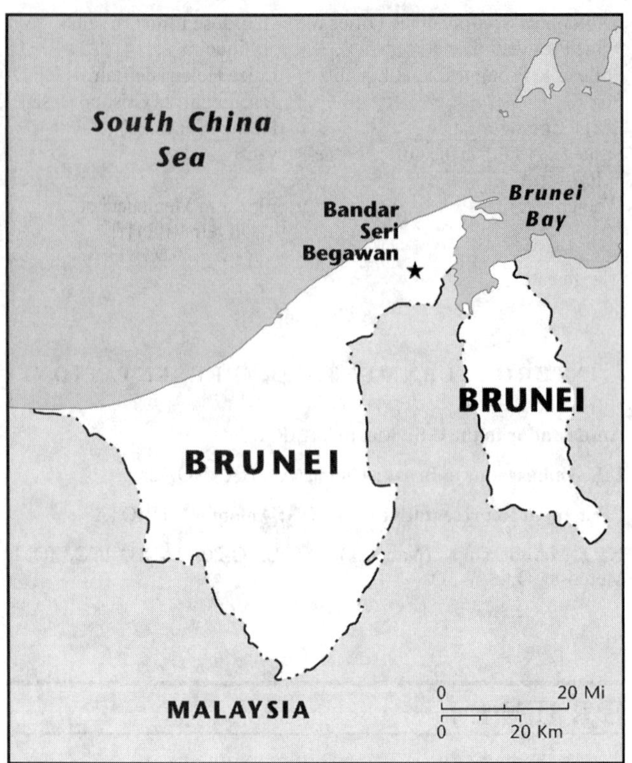

Japan each hold 25 percent. Oil and gas account for 70 percent of nominal GDP, over 90 percent of government tax revenues, 70 percent of nontax revenue, and 96 percent of exports, the principal market being Japan.

Concern over declining oil reserves has led the government to accelerate diversification in such areas as tourism, fishing, and trade and to initiate privatization of government services including electricity, water, and telecommunications. As yet, government service remains the second largest contributor to GDP. Private sector growth has been slowed not only by restrictions on foreign investment but also by an inability to equal the high remuneration paid to public sector workers

Agriculture and fishing contribute less than 1 percent of GDP but account for over 4 percent of employment, while the largest nonpetroleum component of the industrial sector is construction (under 3 percent of GDP, 25 percent of employment). Manufactures include food and beverages, garments and textiles, wood products, and building materials. Nongovernment employment is dominated by temporary residents, who account for about 70 percent of all private sector employment. With the impact of the global recession, GDP fell by 1.9 percent in 2008, prompting the government to cut corporate tax rates and pursue public-private investment partnerships in telecommunications, the energy sector, and infrastructure projects. After further decline in 2009, GDP rebounded to 2.5 percent in 2010. Steady growth has continued since. In 2013, GDP increased by 1.2 percent. Inflation was 1.5 percent, and unemployment, 2.7 percent.

GOVERNMENT AND POLITICS

Political background. Brunei became a British protectorate in 1888 and was administered from 1906 to 1959 by a British resident. Sultan Sir Haji Omar ALI SAIFUDDIN, 28th in a line of hereditary rulers dating from the 15th century, promulgated Brunei's first written constitution in 1959, creating a framework for internal self-government while retaining British responsibility for defense and external affairs.

At voting in August–September 1962, all 10 elective seats in a 21-member Legislative Council were won by the left-wing Brunei People's Party (*Parti Rakyat Brunei*—PRB), led by A. M. N. AZAHARI, which sought a unitary state that would include the adjacent British territories of North Borneo (subsequently Sabah) and Sarawak. In December a rebellion was launched by the PRB-backed North Borneo Liberation Army, which, with Indonesian support, proclaimed a "revolutionary State of North Kalimantan." The revolt was quickly suppressed, however, and Azahari was granted political asylum by Indonesia.

A plan to join the Federation of Malaysia was accepted by the sultan in 1963 but later rejected because of disagreements regarding Brunei's position within the federation and the division of its oil royalties. Following talks with the British Commonwealth secretary in 1964, the sultan introduced constitutional reforms to allow a limited form of ministerial government, and a new general election was held in March 1965. Britain continued to press for a more representative government, however, and on October 4, 1967, the sultan, personally unwilling to accept further change, abdicated in favor of his 22-year-old son, Crown Prince HASSANAL BOLKIAH, who was crowned on August 1, 1968.

In early 1970 the constitution was suspended and the Legislative Council was reconstituted as an entirely appointive body, the sultan subsequently ruling primarily by decree. In 1971, renegotiated arrangements with Great Britain gave the sultan full responsibility for internal order but left the British with responsibility for external affairs. An agreement on formal independence, concluded in London on June 30, 1978, specified that Britain's responsibilities for Brunei's defense and foreign affairs would terminate at the end of 1983. Formal treaty signing on January 7, 1979, came only after Indonesia and Malaysia gave assurances that Brunei's sovereignty would be respected and that the sultan's opponents would not be allowed to maintain guerrilla bases in either country.

On January 1, 1984, after proclaiming independence, the sultan assumed the office of prime minister and announced a cabinet dominated by the royal family. In the early 1990s he attempted to shed his earlier "playboy" image in support of a new and demonstrably conservative ideology that blended elements of Bruneian Malay culture with the role of the monarch as defender of Islam (*Melayu Islam Beraja*).

In 1998 Sultan Hassanal Bolkiah removed his younger brother, Prince Muda Haji JEFRI BOLKIAH, as chair of the Brunei Investment Agency (BIA) and as head of the Amedeo Development Corporation, an investment and construction company that Jefri had started in 1994. Brunei's largest nonpetroleum company, Amedeo collapsed at an estimated cost of $16 billion, and the ensuing scandal, compounded by Jefri's notoriously lavish lifestyle, caused a major rift in the royal family.

On July 15, 2004, the sultan announced that the Legislative Council would soon reconvene. On September 25 the newly appointed members met to consider constitutional amendments, including provisions for a partially elected council, which were approved by Hassanal Bolkiah on September 29. A major cabinet reshuffle on May 30, 2005—the first in 17 years—included the elevation of Crown Prince Haji al-Muhtadee BILLAH to the new post of senior minister in the Prime Minister's Office. On September 2 the sultan appointed a new, 29-member Legislative Council. To date, the provisions for restoring elected members to the council have not been pursued.

In November 2007 the United Kingdom Privy Council ruled in favor of Hassanal Bolkiah in his decade-long effort to force Prince Jefri to return assets valued at $6–8 billion. In 2008 a London High Court judge issued a bench warrant for Jefri's arrest when he failed to appear in court to answer charges that he concealed bank accounts and accessed frozen funds. Jefri fled England to avoid a possible two-year jail term and ultimately took up residence in Singapore. In September 2009, however, he returned to Brunei as a consequence of what some international media outlets described as a "truce" with the sultan.

In a nationwide address on May 29, 2010, the sultan announced a cabinet shuffle in which most of the posts changed hands. He retained for himself the defense and finance portfolios. Sworn in on June 9, ostensibly for five-year terms, the ministers were all royalists. The most notable appointment was that of Adina binti OSMAN, Brunei's first female deputy minister, who assumed responsibilities in the Ministry of Culture, Youth, and Sports.

In June 2011 the sultan increased the size of the Legislative Council from 29 to 33 members.

Constitution and government. Many provisions of the 1959 constitution have been suspended since 1962; others were effectively superseded upon independence. The sultan, as head of state, presides over a Council of Cabinet Ministers and is advised by a Legislative Council, a Privy Council to deal in part with constitutional issues, and a Religious Council; the basic law also provides for a Council of Succession. The Legislative Council is currently wholly appointive, but the amendments approved in September 2004 authorize the future election of 15 members to a 45-member body. The judicial system includes the Supreme Court, which encompasses the High Court and the Court of Appeal, and magistrates' courts; there are also religious courts that apply Islamic law (sharia) to such matters as marriage and divorce. Final appeal in civil actions may advance to the UK Privy Council if all parties to the case agree.

For administrative purposes Brunei is divided into four districts, each headed by a district officer responsible to the sultan. District councils with a minority of elected members advise the district officers on local affairs. Subdivisions include some three dozen *mukims,* each headed by a *penghulu* (chieftain), and villages, each led by a *ketua* (headman).

Press freedom is limited. Media are dominated by the royal family, self-censorship is uniformly practiced, and publishing "false news" is punishable by up to three years in prison. Outspoken critics of the regime continue to face the prospect of prosecution under the country's Internal Security Act. In 2013 Reporters Without Borders ranked Brunei 122nd in the world in its annual press freedom index.

Foreign relations. Upon independence, Brunei became a member of the Commonwealth and in January 1984 joined the Association of Southeast Asian Nations (ASEAN) as its sixth member. Soon after, it was admitted to the Organization of the Islamic Conference (OIC). In 1984 it became a member of the United Nations and in 1985 joined the International Monetary Fund and World Bank. In 1989 it became a founding member of the Asia-Pacific Economic Cooperation (APEC) group. Brunei also participates in the Nonaligned Movement and the World Trade Organization.

At independence, the sultan transferred the bulk of Brunei's substantial investment portfolio from British management to the newly established BIA. In the defense sphere, however, a 1983 agreement provided for British Army Gurkhas to be stationed in Brunei under British command, on the understanding that their sole function was to protect the country's oil and gas installations (i.e., they could not be used by the sultan for internal security purposes). Originally concluded for a five-year term, the agreement has been periodically extended.

Brunei's relations with Indonesia and Malaysia were long marred by territorial claims and support offered to the sultan's political opponents, but in the 1970s relations improved. In 1997, in the midst of a regional economic crisis, Brunei attempted to support its neighbors by pledging over $1 billion in loans to Jakarta and by buying Malaysia's ringgit and the Singapore dollar on foreign-exchange markets. More recently, the government participated in formation of the Brunei-Indonesia-Malaysia-Philippines–East ASEAN Growth Area (BIMP-EAGA). The group's subregional development roadmap for 2006–2010 emphasizes improved air and sea links as well as trade and investment. Brunei is also a member of the Trans-Pacific Partnership, with Chile, New Zealand, and Singapore—prospective members include Australia, Peru, the United States, and Vietnam—and a participant in the Gas Exporting Countries Forum (GECF), which, at a December 2008 meeting in Moscow, Russia, formalized its structure and membership. Effective January 1, 2010, Brunei and five other ASEAN members—Indonesia, Malaysia, Philippines, Singapore, and Thailand—established a free trade area with China that provides for tariff-free trade in 90 percent of goods.

An ongoing foreign policy concern has been the status of the reputedly oil-rich Spratly Islands, portions of which Brunei, China, Malaysia, Philippines, Taiwan, and Vietnam all claim. Meanwhile, Brunei undertook an increasingly active role in endeavoring to mediate the Mindanao conflict in the Philippines, including participation in a September 2010 summit that included representatives from Indonesia, Malaysia, and the Moro National Liberation Front (see entry on the Philippines).

Through 2010 and 2011 Brunei continued to expand its foreign ties around the world, establishing diplomatic relations with a range of countries, including the Dominican Republic, Fiji, and Jamaica. Brunei and Pakistan solidified their existing naval collaboration in April 2012.

In November 2012 Brunei assumed the chairmanship of the Association of South East Asian Nations (ASEAN), marking an opportunity for the small sultanate to increase its influence over regional economic development. Brunei hosted several high profile summits in 2013, leading discussions about ongoing territorial disputes in the South China Sea and regional calls for the denuclearization of North Korea.

Brunei ratified the Comprehensive-Nuclear-Test-Ban Treaty in January 2013, 16 years after becoming a signatory.

Current issues. In 2011 Brunei was placed on a human trafficking watch list by the United States for the second consecutive year, because of reports of abuse toward foreign domestic workers.

Brunei was included in a piracy watch list by the United States in 2012. Although the report condemned Brunei's "high piracy and counterfeiting rates," it acknowledged that the Sultanate was making progress to reduce violations.

At the Second Asian Pacific Water Summit held in Thailand in May, Hassanal Bolkiah took a leading role, calling for countries in the region to pursue the approximately $380 billion projects to upgrade water and sanitation systems to realize full water security. Along with eight other country leaders, the sultan signed the Chiang Mai Declaration, reaffirming commitment to preventing water-related disasters.

POLITICAL PARTIES

Political parties were essentially moribund for most of the quarter-century after the failed 1962 rebellion. A Brunei People's Independence Front (*Barisan Kemerdekaan Rakyat*—Baker), formed in 1966 by amalgamation of a number of earlier groups, was deregistered because of inactivity in early 1985. A Brunei People's National United Party (*Parti Perpaduan Kebangsaan Rakyat Brunei*—Perkera), founded in 1968, had also stopped functioning. The moderate Islamist Brunei National Democratic Party (*Parti Kebangsaan Demokratik Brunei*—PKDB), led by Abdul LATIF Hamid and Abdul LATIF Chuchu, and offshoot, the Brunei National United Party (PPKB), led by Mohamed Hatha ZAINAL ABIDIN, were accorded legal recognition in 1985 and 1986, respectively. In 1988, however, the government confirmed that it had dissolved the PKDB, while the PPKB disappeared from view until permitted to hold a general assembly in 1995. After that, two additional parties, the National Development Party (PPK, below) and the People's Awareness Party (*Parti Kesedaran Rakyat*—Pakar), were registered, but neither challenged the government. In 2007 Pakar was deregistered because of a leadership dispute, as was the PPKB because of its failure to submit required reports to the government. That left the PPK as the only officially recognized party.

Party membership and activities are strictly regulated by the Registrar of Societies. Civil servants are banned from political activity, and members of deregistered parties are prohibited from joining other parties for three years.

Registered Party:

National Development Party (*Parti Pembangunan Kebangsaan*—PPK). The PPK was registered on August 31, 2005, under the leadership of Muhammad Yassin AFFANDI, former leader of the Brunei People's Party (PRB, below) who had been imprisoned from 1962 to 1973 and again in 1997–1999. The PPK quickly established branches in the country's four districts and announced its intention to work as a government "partner." Its objectives include inculcating a "sense of undivided loyalty" to the sultan.

The party held its third congress in June 2008, at which time Affandi proposed that Brunei replace Malaysia as coordinator of the International Monitoring Team that has been overseeing a temporary peace between the Philippine government and the Mindanao-based Moro Islamic Liberation Front (MILF). The MILF politely replied that it preferred that Malaysia continue in that role.

In February 2011 Affandi resigned as PPK leader, citing ill health. He was replaced by deputy party president Mahmud Morshidi Othman.

Leaders: Mahmud Morshidi OTHMAN (Acting President), Aminorrashid GHAZALI (Secretary General).

Exile Formation:

Brunei People's Party (*Parti Rakyat Brunei*—PRB). Formerly a legal party that was deeply involved in the 1962 insurgency, the PRB has since been supported by a somewhat shadowy membership of about 100 individuals, most of them living as exiles in Indonesia or Malaysia. News reports from the June 2006 general session of Malaysia's Pan-Malaysian Islamic Party noted the attendance of PRB representatives.

Over the years, the sultan has pardoned a number of participants in the 1962 rebellion, including former PRB leader Muhammad Yassin Affandi, who was released in August 1999 and formed the PPK in 2005. Party founder A. M. N. Azahari died in exile in May 2002.

LEGISLATURE

At present, legislation is enacted by proclamation. A 21-member advisory **Legislative Council** (*Majlis Mesyuarat Negara*), a wholly nonelective body that incorporates all cabinet members, met in September 2004, two decades after last convening. It quickly approved constitutional amendments, including a provision for the future election of 15 representatives to an expanded 45-member body. On September 1, 2005, the sultan dissolved the Legislative Council, and on September 2 he appointed a new 29-member council, which has subsequently met regularly and was expanded in 2011 to 33 members.

Speaker: Awang Isa Awang Ibrahim.

CABINET

[as of November 12, 2013]

Prime Minister	Sultan Sir Hassanal Bolkiah
Senior Minister in the Prime Minister's Office	Prince Al-Muhtadee Billah
Ministers	
Communications	Abdullah bin Begawan Bakar
Culture, Youth, and Sports	Hazair bin Abdullah
Defense	Sultan Sir Hassanal Bolkiah
Development	Suyoi bin Osman
Education	Awang Abu Bakar bin Apong
Energy	Mohammad Yasmin bin Umar
Finance	Sultan Sir Hassanal Bolkiah
Finance II	Abdul Rahman bin Ibrahim
Foreign Affairs and Trade	Prince Muda Mohamed Bolkiah
Foreign Affairs and Trade II	Lim Jock Seng
Health	Adanan bin Begawan Mohamed Yusof
Home Affairs	Badaruddin bin Othman
Industry and Primary Resources	Yahya bin Begawan Bakar
Religious Affairs	Mohammad bin Abdul Rahman
State Mufti	Ustaz Awang Abdul Aziz
Attorney General	Hajah Hayati

INTERGOVERNMENTAL REPRESENTATION

Ambassador to the U.S.: YUSOFF bin Abdul Hamid.

U.S. Ambassador to Brunei Darussalam: Daniel SHIELDS.

Permanent Representative to the UN: Dato Abdul Ghafar ISMAIL.

IGO Memberships (Non-UN): APEC, ASEAN, CWTH, NAM, OIC, WTO.

BULGARIA

Republic of Bulgaria
Republika Balgariya

Political Status: Communist constitution of May 18, 1971, substantially modified on April 3, 1990; present name adopted November 15, 1990; current democratic constitution adopted July 12, 1991.

Area: 42,823 sq. mi. (110,912 sq. km).

Population: 7,694,576 (2012E—UN); 7,364,570 (2011C). More than 900,000 Bulgarians have emigrated since 1989.

Major Urban Centers (2012E): SOFIA (1,241,000), Plovdiv (339,000), Varna (335,000), Bourgas (211,000), Ruse (150,000).

Official Language: Bulgarian.

Monetary Unit: Lev (market rate November 1, 2013: 1.45 leva = $1US). The lev is pegged to the euro, which Bulgaria hopes to adopt as its official currency, at the rate of 1.95583 leva = 1 euro.

President: Rosen PLEVNELIEV (elected as the candidate of the Citizens for European Development of Bulgaria [GERB], from which he resigned following his election); sworn in for a five-year term on January 19, 2012, and assumed office on January 22, having been popularly elected in the second round of presidential balloting on October 30, 2011, succeeding Georgi PARVANOV (originally Bulgarian Socialist Party [BSP], later independent).

Vice President: Margarita POPOVA (Citizens for European Development of Bulgaria); sworn in January 19, 2012, and assumed office on January 22 for a term concurrent with that of the president, succeeding Angel MARIN (Bulgarian Socialist Party).

Chair of the Council of Ministers (Prime Minister): Plamen ORESHARSKI (Bulgarian Socialist Party); nominated by the president on May 23, 2013, following the inability of the Citizens for European Development of Bulgaria (GERB) to negotiate a coalition government (GERB received a plurality in the legislative elections of May 12, 2013, and was first nominated to form a government), and inaugurated on May 29 (following approval that day of his proposed cabinet by the National Assembly) in succession to Boiko BORISOV (Citizens for European Development of Bulgaria).

THE COUNTRY

Extending southward from the Danube and westward from the Black Sea, Bulgaria occupies a key position in the eastern Balkans adjacent to Macedonia, Romania, Serbia, Greece, and Turkey. Like Greece and Macedonia, the country includes portions of historic Macedonia, and tensions with neighboring states long existed because of the commonly held position in Bulgaria that all Slavic-speaking inhabitants of Macedonia are ethnic Bulgarians. More than 85 percent of Bulgaria's population is considered ethnically Bulgarian, while there are sizable minorities of Turks (8.8 percent) and Roma (officially 325,000 but unofficially estimated at 500,000–800,000). The predominant language is Bulgarian, a component of the southern Slavic language group. The principal faith is that of the Bulgarian Orthodox Church; there is also a substantial Muslim minority (officially 577,000 but estimated at 800,000), in addition to small numbers of Catholics, Protestants, and Jews. Following the 2013 legislative elections, women held 59 seats, or 24.6 percent of the total, in the assembly.

Traditionally an agricultural country, Bulgaria achieved a measure of industrialization after World War II under a series of five-year plans. As a result, machine building, ferrous and nonferrous metallurgy, textile manufacturing, and agricultural processing grew in importance, with agriculture accounting for only 14 percent of GDP by the end of communist rule in 1990. Despite a variety of reforms, the economy in the 1990s was disrupted by the loss of the Soviet market for Bulgarian exports, creating high rates of inflation, unemployment, and a severe contraction of the Bulgarian GDP. Growth resumed in 1998 under tight fiscal policies that received praise from international institutions but generated domestic unrest as social benefits were constrained. (See the 2011 *Handbook* for more details on the economy prior to 2004.)

Aided by expanding industrial and tourism sectors, annual GDP growth averaged more than 5.6 percent in 2004–2007. However, the IMF and other Western institutions called for additional reform in the health and educational sectors and for more effective antipoverty policies on the part of the administration. Foreign investors also complained of inordinate bureaucratic delays in getting permits for new businesses. Despite substantial questions in those areas as well as the lack of progress in combating corruption and organized crime, Bulgaria was admitted to the European Union (EU) on January 1, 2007. With a per capita income ($7,311 in 2012) of less than one-third that of Western European nations Bulgaria, thereupon, became the poorest EU member. Critics of its EU accession also described Bulgaria as a "hub" for trafficking in drugs and weapons.

GDP growth reached 6 percent in 2008, while unemployment dropped below 7 percent, the lowest rate since 1990. Inflation, however, registered 9.8 percent in 2007 and 7.8 percent in 2008, fueling populist sentiment that blamed the increases on EU accession. The global economic crisis contributed heavily to GDP contraction of 5.5 percent in 2009. GDP grew by a modest annual 1.1 percent average in 2010–2011, and by 0.78 percent in 2012. Unemployment was 12.4 percent in 2012. The IMF forecasts 1.2 percent GDP growth in 2013.

GOVERNMENT AND POLITICS

Political background. Bulgarian kingdoms existed in the Balkan Peninsula during the Middle Ages, but the Ottoman Empire ruled the area for 500 years prior to the Russo-Turkish War of 1877–1878; full independence was not achieved until 1908. Long-standing territorial ambitions led to Bulgarian participation in both Balkan Wars (1912 and 1913) and in both world wars. Talks aimed at the country's withdrawal from World War II were interrupted on September 5, 1944, by a Soviet declaration of war, followed by the establishment four days later of a communist-inspired "Fatherland Front" government.

The monarchy was rejected by a 92 percent majority in a disputed referendum held September 8, 1946, after which King SIMEON II, who had come to the throne at age six in 1943, went into exile. A "People's Republic" was formally established on December 4, 1947, under the premiership of Georgi DIMITROV, who died in 1949. Communist rule was consolidated under the successive regimes of Vulko CHERVENKOV and Anton YUGOV. From 1954 until his ouster in November 1989, Todor ZHIVKOV, occupying various positions within the government and party hierarchies, maintained his status as Bulgaria's leader while continuing the pro-Soviet policies instituted by his predecessors.

On November 3, 1989, more than 9,000 demonstrators marched in Sofia in the first prodemocracy rally in the country's postwar history. One week later a number of key Politburo changes were announced, including the replacement of Zhivkov as party general secretary by the reformist foreign minister, Petur MLADENOV. On November 17 the National Assembly named Mladenov to succeed Zhivkov as head of state, and the following day 50,000 persons assembled in the capital to applaud the new government. On December 13 Zhivkov was formally expelled from the party. Subsequently, the former leader was indicted on a variety of charges that included misappropriating state property, inciting ethnic hostility, and abusing his powers of office. (He was convicted of embezzlement and sentenced to seven years imprisonment on September 1, 1992. He died in 1998, having been released from house arrest the previous year.)

In multiparty elections held on June 10 and 17, 1990, the Bulgarian Socialist (formerly Communist) Party (*Balgarska Sotsialisticheska Partiya*—BSP) captured a majority of National Assembly seats, with the recently launched Union of Democratic Forces (*Sayuzna Demokratichni Sili*—SDS) trailing by nearly 100 seats. Subsequently, President Mladenov was obliged to resign on July 6 in the wake of evidence that he had endorsed the use of tanks to crush an antigovernment demonstration in late 1989. After nearly a month of political stalemate, the assembly elected SDS chair Zhelyu ZHELEV as Mladenov's successor on August 1. On September 19, after efforts to form a coalition had failed, a new all-Socialist cabinet was announced under the continued premiership of Andrei LUKANOV (first appointed in February 1990). However, Lukanov resigned on November 29 after two weeks of street protests and a four-day general strike. On December 7 a politically independent judge, Dimitur POPOV, was named premier designate, and on December 20 he succeeded in forming a coalition administration that included eight Socialists, four representatives of the SDS, and three Agrarians.

Despite a boycott by many opposition parliamentarians, who demanded a referendum in the matter, a democratic constitution was adopted on July 12, 1991, followed by a new legislative poll on October 13. Emerging with a narrow four-seat plurality, the SDS, with support from the ethnically Turkish Movement for Rights and Freedoms (*Dvizhenie za Prava i Svobodi*—DPS), installed Filip DIMITROV on November 8 as head of the country's first wholly non-communist government since World War II.

On January 19, 1992, in the second round of Bulgaria's first popular presidential poll, Zhelev was reelected to a five-year term. The SDS depended on parliamentary support from the DPS, and, not surprisingly, confirmation of the new Dimitrov administration was accompanied by reversal of a ban, introduced by the communists, on optional Turkish-language instruction in the secondary schools.

In March 1992 the National Assembly completed work, initiated a year earlier, on land privatization, providing for all agricultural cooperatives to be phased out and permitting foreign investors to participate, as minority members, in joint land ventures with Bulgarians. However, other promised reforms remained stalled, including a decommunization bill, amid serious labor unrest and a growing conflict between President Zhelev and the Dimitrov government over their respective responsibilities. The SDS tried to respond by organizing pro-Dimitrov rallies, but a DPS decision on September 23 to withdraw its support from the government proved fatal. On October 28 the government was defeated 121–111 on a nonconfidence motion and was obliged to resign. An interregnum ensued, during which the BSP wasted its constitutional opportunity to nominate a successor premier. The initiative passed to the DPS, which nominated the president's economic adviser, Lyuben BEROV, to form a nonparty administration of "national responsibility." Somewhat unexpectedly, with the backing of BSP and SDS dissidents, Berov obtained parliamentary approval on December 30 by 124 votes to 25, with the bulk of the SDS deputies abstaining.

Prime Minister Berov was incapacitated by a heart attack on March 8, 1994, and President Zhelev announced on April 2 that he was withdrawing political support from the government because of the slow pace of privatization and a failure to attract foreign investment. The ailing Berov sought to regain the initiative on June 28 by launching a much-delayed mass privatization scheme for some 500 state-owned companies; finance officials also successfully concluded a rescheduling of Bulgaria's $10 billion external debt, enabling IMF and World Bank credit lines to be reactivated. Political pressure nevertheless mounted on the government, which resigned on September 2. Attempts by the president to find an alternative were thwarted by the preference of the BSP and the SDS for early elections, pending which a caretaker cabinet was installed on October 18 under Bulgaria's first woman prime minister, Reneta INDZHOVA.

In the legislative poll of December 18, 1994, Bulgarian voters continued the East European trend of restoring ex-communist parties to power, according the BSP and two minor party (Agrarian and Ecoglasnost Political Club [*Politicheskiklub Ekoglasnost*—PKE]) allies an overall majority of 125 of the 240 seats. By contrast, the SDS obtained only 69, its electoral appeal having been eroded by the decision of several of its factions to stand independently. As a result, 35-year-old BSP leader Zhan VIDENOV was sworn in on January 26, 1995, as prime minister of a government that included two members of the Bulgarian Agrarian National Union–People's Union (*Balgarski Zemedelski Naroden Sayuz–Naroden Sayuz*—BZNS-NS), one PKE member, and several nonparty technocrats reputed to favor market reforms. At that stage less than 40 percent of state-owned land had been restored to private ownership, and only 35 of the country's 3,000 large- and medium-sized industrial enterprises had been privatized.

Party politics in 1996 focused on the presidential election in November, for which incumbent Zhelyu Zhelev declared his candidacy. Because Zhelev had fallen out with the SDS since his 1992 election, the opposition held a primary to find a joint candidate, with Zhelev running as the nominee of the People's Union (*Naroden Sayuz*—NS) coalition and the SDS endorsing Petar STOYANOV, a little-known lawyer. The outcome of the primary balloting on June 1 was a decisive 65.7 percent majority for Stoyanov, who thereupon received Zhelev's endorsement. The ruling coalition parties supported the BSP foreign minister, Georgi PIRINSKI, but his candidacy was effectively blocked by a controversial Constitutional Court ruling on July 23 that, having been born in the United States of Bulgarian émigré parents, he did not meet the constitutional requirement of being Bulgarian by birth. On September 2 the Supreme Court rejected the BSP's appeal, and the BSP culture minister, Ivan MARAZOV, was drafted as a replacement. Stoyanov was subsequently the easy victor, heading the first-round balloting on October 27, 1996, with 44.1 percent of the vote and then obtaining 60 percent in a two-way runoff against Marazov on November 3.

In the wake of Stoyanov's victory, Videnov resigned as prime minister and leader of the BSP on December 21, 1996, the assembly accepting his resignation on December 28. The SDS immediately called for the installation of a caretaker government pending proposed early assembly elections. However, the BSP, ignoring massive public demonstrations in support of the SDS proposal, insisted upon its right (as leading parliamentary party) to name a new prime minister, and on January 7, 1997, it tapped Interior Minister Nikolai DOBREV to succeed Videnov. Public opposition again quickly erupted, and on January 11 President Zhelev announced he would not invite Dobrev to form a new government, arguing that such a government would not be viable. Consequently, the government was stalemated when Stoyanov took office on January 22, 1997. After weeks without a prime minister and a siege of the assembly by SDS supporters, the BSP in early February finally agreed to allow Stoyanov to appoint an interim government, which, as announced on February 12, was led by Stefan SOFIANSKI, the mayor of Sofia. In the April 19 assembly, the SDS-led United Democratic Forces (*Obedineni Demokratichni Sili*—ODS) scored a massive victory, securing 137 seats to 58 for the BSP-led Democratic Left (*Demokratichna Levitsa*—DL). ODS leader Ivan KOSTOV, an economist and former finance minister, was named prime minister on May 21, pledging that his new cabinet would steadfastly pursue the economic reforms launched by Sofianski.

On April 6, 2001, the political landscape shifted when the former king, Simeon SAXE-COBURG-GOTHA, after 55 years in exile, announced formation of a National Movement Simeon II (*Natsionalno Dvizhenie Simeon Tvori*—NDST) that would contest the upcoming National Assembly election. Although the party was refused registration on technical grounds, two small parties agreed to register for the election as a coalition under the NDST designation, thereby providing visibility to a slate of candidates loyal to Simeon. In the June 17 balloting the NDST secured 120 of the assembly's 240 seats, while Kostov's ODS and the BSP-led Coalition for Bulgaria (*Koalitsiya za Balgariya*—KzB) trailed with 51 and 48 seats, respectively. Picked by President Stoyanov to form a cabinet, the former king, under the name Simeon SAKSKOBURGGOTSKI, received legislative endorsement on July 24. The first former Eastern European monarch to assume a republican office, he was sworn in as the head of an NDST-dominated Council of Ministers that included two DPS and two BSP members. (Despite the participation of the BSP members in the cabinet, the BSP said it had made no political commitment to the government and would in fact remain in "constructive opposition.")

In presidential balloting on November 11, 2001, President Stoyanov, running as an independent but with NDST support, won only 35 percent of the vote on a low voter turnout of 39 percent. His chief rival, BSP Chair Georgi PARVANOV, took 36 percent and in second-round balloting on November 18 won with 54 percent.

On July 16, 2003, Prime Minister Sakskoburggotski announced a cabinet reshuffle and expansion designed, among other things, to facilitate Bulgaria's planned accession to the EU and the North Atlantic Treaty Organization (NATO). However, in March 2004 the NDST/DPS coalition became a minority government when a group of NDST legislators left that grouping to launch a new party called New Time (*Novoto Vreme*). New Time joined the cabinet in a February 21 reshuffle after offering support in several no-confidence votes (see the 2013 *Handbook* for details).

The NDST had fallen sharply in public opinion polls leading up to the 2005 assembly elections. Despite having scored significant successes with the country's accession to NATO in 2004 and progress toward EU membership, among other things, the NDST-led government was apparently widely perceived as having been ineffective in combating corruption and organized crime. In addition, average Bulgarians reportedly were disappointed that the "prosperity" promised through the implementation of IMF reforms had failed to trickle down to needy segments of the population such as pensioners. Consequently, the assembly campaign was tumultuous, particularly after the emergence of the National Union Attack (*Natsionalno Obedinenie Ataka*), an extreme right-wing grouping with populist overtones. (*Ataka* campaigned on an antiminority/anti-immigrant platform that also proposed severing ties with NATO, the EU, and the IMF.)

The BSP-led KzB led all parties by winning 82 seats in the assembly balloting on June 25, 2005. Seven coalitions or parties (including *Ataka*) secured seats in the poll, making for the "most fragmented" legislature in history. The NDST eventually agreed to join the KzB and DPS in a cabinet led by the BSP's young (38 years old), "reform-minded" leader, Sergei STANISHEV, who was inaugurated on August 16. The new administration immediately announced that maintaining the EU accession schedule was its top priority.

President Parvanov received 64 percent of the vote against six opponents in the first round of presidential balloting on October 22, 2006. However, since the turnout was less than 50 percent, a second round was held on October 29, with Parvanov being reelected (the first post-communist president to achieve that feat) with 76 percent of the vote over Volen SIDEROV of *Ataka*. Parvanov's reelection was considered a triumph for pro-EU forces, but EU officials subsequently criticized Bulgaria for myriad problems, including unacceptable farm and food-processing standards, poor aviation controls, inadequate money-laundering policies, and ineffective governmental administration in general. Nevertheless, noting the country's recent economic progress and announcing it did not want to discourage reformers by delaying accession, the EU in September declared that Bulgaria, as well as Romania, which was facing similar problems, would be admitted as scheduled on January 1, 2007, even though some members of the European Parliament bluntly described Bulgaria as "not ready."

The recently formed Citizens for European Development of Bulgaria (*Grazhdani za Evropejsko Razvitie Balgarija*—GERB) achieved a spectacular victory in the July 5, 2009, assembly balloting by winning a plurality of 116 of 240 seats. (The nearest competitor was the KzB, with 40 seats.) After two weeks of negotiations failed to produce agreement on a formal coalition government, GERB founder Boiko BORISOV was sworn in as prime minister on July 27 after his all-GERB cabinet had been approved by a vote of 162–78 in the assembly. Although technically a minority government, Borisov's cabinet enjoyed the pledged legislative support (for the time being, at least) of *Ataka*, the SDS-led Blue Coalition (*Sinyata Koalitsiya*—SK), and the new Order, Law, and Justice party (*Red, Zakonnost, i Spravedlivost*—RZS), all of whose members voted in favor of the new government. The Borisov government survived a BSP-sponsored no-confidence vote on June 17, 2011, by 124–70.

The first round of presidential balloting was held on October 23. Eighteen candidates competed in the polling, including 12 party candidates and 6 independents. Rosen PLEVNELIEV (GERB) received 40.1 percent of the vote and Ivailo KALFIN (BSP) 29 percent, and both advanced to runoff balloting on October 30. In the second round, Plevneliev was elected with 52.6 percent of the vote over Kalfin, who secured 47.4 percent.

In January 2013 protests over utility prices (see Current issues, below) escalated into the largest nationwide protests since 1997. Borisov and his cabinet resigned on February 20 (effective on March 13, as successive parties declined President Plevneliev's offers to form a government). A caretaker government under Marin NIKOLOV was appointed on March 13, and early elections were announced for May.

GERB led all parties to win a plurality of 97 seats in the legislative elections of May 12, 2013. Only three other parties (the BSP, the MRF, and *Ataka*) secured seats. Voter turnout was low, at 51.3 percent, and the four parties that secured representation in parliament only accounted for 75.8 percent of the national vote with the rest fragmented between minor parties. GERB was unable to form a government, while the BSP and MRF were unable to form a majority (together, the two parties held 120 seats: exactly 50 percent). Some *Ataka* deputies subsequently did not attend the assembly session on May 29, giving the BSP and MRF a temporary majority (the remaining *Ataka* deputies abstained from the vote).

Constitution and government. The constitution of July 1991 describes Bulgaria as a parliamentary republic. It guarantees freedom of association, religion, and opinion, while supporting an economy based on "market forces" and a respect for private property. It provides for a president and vice president, elected jointly for no more than two 5-year terms by majority vote of at least 50 percent of those eligible to cast ballots (a second ballot, if necessary, is confined to the top two tickets from the first round). The president nominates the chair of the Council of Ministers (prime minister), who must be confirmed (and can ultimately be dismissed) by the National Assembly. The assembly, popularly elected for a four-year term, is a unicameral body of 240 members, who may not concurrently hold ministerial office. The highest judicial organs are a Supreme Court of Cassation, which oversees application of the law by lower courts, and a Supreme Administrative Court, which rules on the legality of acts by government organs. There is also a Constitutional Court that interprets the basic law and rules on the constitutionality of legislation and decrees. At the local level Bulgaria encompasses 28 administrative regions, each headed by a governor appointed by the Council of Ministers. There are nearly 300 elected municipal councils, each of which appoints a mayor as chief administrative officer for the duration of its four-year term.

The National Assembly may amend the constitution by the casting of majorities of 75 percent on three separate days. On September 24, 2003, the assembly passed the first constitutional amendments to the 1991 constitution, giving life tenure to magistrates and granting them immunity against charges except in cases of criminal misconduct or abuse of office. (The changes were part of a broader effort to harmonize the legal system with EU standards.)

In 2013 Freedom House described the press as only "partially free" in Bulgaria because of political leaders' "intolerance for media criticism," the failure of the state to take action against threats and pressure directed against reporters, and the concentrated ownership of most newspapers by two companies. In 2013 the organization ranked Bulgaria 87th out of 179 countries in freedom of the press.

Foreign relations. A longtime Bulgarian alignment with the Soviet Union in foreign policy reflected not only the two countries' economic and ideological ties, but also traditional ties stemming from Russian assistance in Bulgarian independence struggles.

Bulgarian-Turkish relations have fluctuated. Following the establishment of the communist regime in 1947, 150,000 ethnic Turks emigrated in 1950–1951 and 100,000 more in 1968–1978. Subsequent efforts toward assimilation of those that remained (including the forced adoption of Bulgarian names) generated pronounced tension with Ankara. Bulgaria emphatically rejected all "Turkish accusations" in the matter, calling the Bulgarian Turks "a fictitious minority" and claiming that the name changes were merely those of Bulgarians voluntarily reversing a process mandated during Ottoman rule.

In May 1989, following a series of clashes between ethnic protestors and security police in the Islamic border region, a large number of Bulgarian Muslims took advantage of newly issued passports to cross into Turkey. However, in August Ankara closed the border to stem an influx that had exceeded 310,000. In late December, following the downfall of the Zhivkov regime, National Assembly Chair Stenko TODOROV told a group of Turkish demonstrators in Sofia that henceforth "everybody in Bulgaria [would] be able to choose his name, religion, and language freely."

In October 1991 the Bulgarian and Greek prime ministers signed a 20-year friendship treaty, with Greece offering support for its neighbor's application to join the European Community (EC, subsequently the EU). However, relations with Greece cooled in January 1992, following the inclusion of Macedonia in the former Yugoslav republics to which Bulgaria accorded recognition. Greece, which had long refused to acknowledge a separate Macedonian nationality (whereas Bulgaria had traditionally contended that all Macedonians were ethnically Bulgarians), responded by appealing to its EC partners to limit or halt aid to Bulgaria.

In March 1993 Bulgaria completed negotiations on an association agreement with the EU and the same month signed a free trade agreement with the European Free Trade Association (EFTA). In February 1994 it became a signatory of NATO's Partnership for Peace, and in May it was one of nine East European states to become an "associate partner" of the Western European Union (WEU). Meanwhile, an exchange of high-level visits with Russia in September 1995 confirmed the stability of bilateral relations.

In February 1997 the caretaker government of Stefan Sofianski announced its intention to seek full membership for Bulgaria in NATO. That position was reaffirmed by incoming Prime Minister Kostov in April, when he said Bulgaria would also seek EU membership. Although NATO did not include Bulgaria in the "first wave" of new members approved in June, the alliance subsequently indicated that Bulgaria was a "strong contender" for the next round of expansion. Meanwhile, Bulgaria was also left off the EU's "fast track" membership list approved in 1997; however, EU officials said it was only a matter of "when" and not "if" Bulgaria would eventually join, assuming continued economic reform on the part of the government. In January 1999 Bulgaria became a member of the Central European Free Trade Agreement (CEFTA).

In February 1999 Bulgaria appeared to have resolved its last major outstanding regional dispute when it reached agreement with Macedonia concerning the language to be used in bilateral accords. A number of agreements had been held up for six years because of Bulgaria's insistence that Macedonian was a dialect of Bulgarian and not a language in its own right. (The issue reflected deeper concerns regarding the status of self-described Macedonians in Bulgaria as well as the two countries' concern over each other's possible territorial claims.) In an apparent easing of Bulgaria's stance, the 1999 accord authorized the use of the languages recognized by each country's constitution. Several bilateral accords were subsequently concluded, including one providing for military cooperation. Relations with Turkey were also described in early 1999 as greatly improved, border demarcation issues having been resolved and the Turkish business sector having found significant investment opportunities in the vastly improved Bulgarian economy.

Early in 2000 Bulgaria began formal accession talks with the EU, but it remained a "second tier" prospect. In May the National Assembly approved a resolution, 189–3, to pursue membership in the EU as well as NATO.

At NATO's Prague Summit in November 2002, Bulgaria was one of seven Central and Eastern European states invited to join the alliance. As part of its pre-accession protocols (signed in May 2003), Bulgaria subsequently enacted a series of military reforms. The National Assembly formally endorsed NATO accession by a vote of 226–4 on March 18, 2004, and Bulgaria joined the alliance on March 29.

Perhaps in consonance with the NATO developments, the Saksko-burggotski government supported the U.S.-led invasion of Iraq in 2003. In return, the United States provided guarantees on the repayment of Iraq's foreign debt to Bulgaria (these payments had been suspended since 1990). After the fall of the regime of Saddam Hussein, Bulgaria deployed one of the largest contingents in the U.S.-led coalition (some 500 troops, the last elements withdrawn in December 2008).

On the other major international front, Bulgaria completed the final "chapters" in negotiations toward EU accession in late 2004, and in April 2005 a treaty was signed whereby it was envisioned that Bulgaria would become a member of the EU as of January 1, 2007. However, that date was contingent on Bulgaria making promised reforms. EU accession at the beginning of 2007 was reportedly met with "relief" on the part of the Bulgarian government and was broadly welcomed by the populace. However, the EU imposed stringent safeguards in connection with the accession, announcing that EU assistance to Bulgaria (estimated at nearly $900 million for the first year) might be withheld unless quick progress was made in combating corruption and organized crime. The EU also warned that Bulgarian court rulings might not be accepted throughout the union unless Bulgaria adopted wide-ranging police and judicial reforms. In addition, some EU countries quickly imposed restrictions on the number of immigrant workers they would accept from Bulgaria. Although Prime Minister Stanishev announced that the "modernization" of Bulgaria in various areas would be his administration's priority, in May 2008 the EU froze funds allocated for infrastructure projects in Bulgaria.

In March 2009 Bulgaria's contribution to the NATO mission in Afghanistan reached a high point of 820 soldiers, reduced to 383 by June 2013.

Current issues. Frustration with the existing political parties (perceived as ineffective in combating corruption and organized crime) was a major issue in the dramatic July 2009 assembly balloting, in which the BSP produced its worst performance since 1989, the NDSV (as the NDST had been renamed) collapsed completely by failing to win any seats, and the SDS continued to decline. Meanwhile, the new GERB, a center-right anticorruption party led by the popular mayor of Sofia, Boiko Borisov, soared to a near legislative majority. Other contributing factors in the GERB's ascendance were the recent economic contraction (after several years of high growth) and scandals involving Ahmed DOGAN, the leader of the DPS (see DPS, below under Political Parties, for details). Analysts concluded that anger over Dogan influenced a higher than expected turnout (60 percent) as non-Turkish voters punished the parties (the BSP and NDSV) that had granted the DPS key roles in recent governments.

Upon assuming the premiership, Borisov announced that his administration's priorities would be to make Bulgaria "worthy" of its EU status, expand cooperation with NATO, pursue judicial reform, and initiate intensified anticorruption measures. However, skeptics warned that the "gentlemen's agreement" for legislative support for the GERB from the SK, RZS, and *Ataka* (whose major bond appeared to be dislike of the BSP) could prove fragile if the new government failed to produce quick results.

In the wake of the financial crisis in Greece, a comprehensive investigation by the EU's official statistics agency, Eurostat, in April 2010 revealed that the Bulgarian government had significantly under-reported the country's annual budget deficit for 2009. Eurostat estimated the actual figure at 3.9 percent of GDP, as opposed to the government's stated figure of 1.9 percent. The actual level exceeded the 3 percent limit required for countries seeking to adopt the euro, and the discrepancy triggered an infringement procedure by the European Commission. The government responded with a new wave of budget cuts and tax increases, some of the initiatives being criticized by the GERB's informal allies on the right and by opposition parties.

Political tensions have increased slightly due to recent populist appeals by nationalist parties. In May 2010 the Internal Macedonian Revolutionary Organization (*Vatreshna Makedonska Revolutsionerna Organizatsiya*—VMRO) attempted to take the issue of whether or not Bulgaria should support Turkey's proposed EU membership directly to the people by calling for a public referendum. It subsequently claimed to have collected 300,000 signatures opposing Turkey's entrance into the EU. In July 2010 *Ataka* called for the "purge" of all BSP and DPS-affiliated journalists in the state television and radio stations.

Interparty tensions were exemplified by the attempt in March 2010 to impeach President Parvanov. Following an interview in which Finance Minister Simeon DYANKOV made allegedly disparaging remarks regarding Parvanov and his family, the president and finance minister traded a series of acrimonious public statements. The GERB initiated impeachment procedures with the support of the SK, *Ataka,* and RZS on the basis that Parvanov secretly recorded Dyankov during a private conversation. The BSP and DPS emerged in opposition to the motion, which saw heated debate in parliament before it was moved to a vote. Ultimately, the RZS abstained from the vote (despite having previously supported the motion), and the motion to impeach failed with only 155 of the 161 votes needed.

The revelation in December 2010 that 35 senior Bulgarian diplomats and half of the diplomatic service overall (as well as the Minister for Bulgarians Abroad Bozhidar DIMITROV) had been agents or collaborators with the Communist-era State Security service led to renewed attention to lustration laws. In May 2011 the National Assembly amended government policies to forbid former security collaborators from working in the diplomatic services.

The European Commission's July 2011 report praised the Bulgarian government's dedication to reform but criticized efforts to eliminate "high-level" corruption that "have not yet led to convincing results." Concern by other EU members over whether corruption undermines Bulgaria's border controls was a factor in the June and September 2011 decisions to delay Bulgaria's entry to the Schengen Area, which waives border controls between members.

The European Commission's February 2012 report stressed that while a legal framework to combat corruption and organized crime is in place, implementation by the police and judiciary continues to lag. Citing these concerns, the Netherlands again vetoed Bulgaria's Schengen entry in April 2012. Schengen membership was postponed again in March 2013, over German concerns that not all criteria have been met. Entry will be delayed until 2014 at the earliest, which raised concerns that the 2014 deadline to open the EU labor market to Romanians could be similarly postponed.

On January 28, 2013, protests over electrical prices broke out in 2 towns in southwest Bulgaria. These protests had spread to the 10 largest cities in the country by February 10 and evolved into protests against the GERB-led government, accusations of collusion between political leaders and organized crime, and public anger over the economy. On February 17 protest organizers claimed that 100,000 protesters demonstrated in more than 35 cities and towns across the country, with some protesters blocking a major highway. Borisov had attempted to respond by lowering power prices and withdrawing the license of the Czech firm ČEZ (České Energetické Závody) that held a prominent place in the Bulgarian electrical utilities market. The protests were punctuated, however, by four separate incidents over the course of a month where protesters self-immolated, with that of Plamen GORANOV on February 20 receiving particular attention. Borisov and his cabinet resigned on February 20, stating concern over violent clashes between police and protesters on February 20. No political party was willing to form a government, so President Plevneliev had appointed a caretaker government while major protests continued on February 24, March 3, and March 6.

Elections were held on May 12, leading to a BSP-led government. On May 10, 350,000 illegally printed ballots had been seized in Sofia at the printing house commissioned for the May 12 legislative elections. Following the election, GERB asked the Constitutional Court to cancel the election results, but the Court denied the petition on July 9.

On June 14 parliament voted to appoint Delian PEEVSKI to head the National Security Agency. Although small protests had been staged through May and June, the appointment of Peevski, whose mother owns a major media firm that reportedly owns 40 percent of the print media in the country, was seized as a symbol of the corruption of the "political system" and reignited anger with the government. The evening after his appointment 10,000 protesters gathered in Sofia, with significant protests continuing through June and into July. On the night of July 23–24, protesters clashed with police in an attempt to blockade parliament, preventing members of parliament from exiting the building. Eight protesters and two police were reportedly injured. Protests continued into August, when the National Assembly went into a holiday recess.

POLITICAL PARTIES

Prior to the political upheaval of late 1989, Bulgaria's only authorized political parties were the Bulgarian Communist Party (BKP) and the Bulgarian Agrarian National Union (*Balgarski Zemedelski Naroden Sayuz*—BZNS), which formed the core of the Fatherland Front (*Otechestven Front*), a communist-controlled mass organization that also included the trade unions, the communist youth movement, and individual citizens. In the wake of the ouster of longtime BKP leader Todor Zhivkov in 1989, a large number of opposition groups surfaced, while the BKP changed its name to the Bulgarian Socialist Party (BSP). Since then, parties and coalitions have proliferated. By 2004 there were some 80 registered parties, and a new electoral law was approved prior to the 2005 assembly poll with the intent of reducing the number of small parties. Among other things, parties were required to provide signatures of support from at least 5,000 people. Financial deposits were also required of any party presenting legislative candidates, with the deposits being returned only if the party secured more than 1 percent of the national vote. As a result, although 42 parties or coalitions had participated in the 2001 assembly balloting, their number had fallen to 20 in 2009. In 2013, however, 7 coalitions and 38 parties participated in the legislative election.

Government and Government-Supportive Parties:

Coalition for Bulgaria (*Koalitsiya za Balgariya*—KzB). Established in preparation for the 2001 legislative election, the KzB was the descendant of the BSP-led but less inclusive Democratic Left (*Demokratichna Levitsa*—DL). The DL had been formed prior to the 1996 presidential election by the BSP, the Ecoglasnost Political Club (PKE), and the BZNS-AS, which had contested the 1994 legislative election in alliance and had then formed the subsequent government under the BSP's Videnov. The three-party coalition saw its representation fall from 125 seats in 1994 to 58 in 1998. In May 2000 the PKE left the DL.

In November 2000 the parliamentary delegations of the BSP, the BSDP, the OBT, and the PDSD announced a cooperative agreement that led in January 2001 to formal establishment of a New Left political program. On January 25 the KzB was announced, which won 48 seats in the 2001 assembly balloting. At that time its membership comprised the BSP, at least one faction of the BZNS-AS, the BSDP, PDSD, KPB, the United Labor Bloc (OBT), and the Alliance for Social Liberal Progress (*Alians za Sotsialliberalen Progres*—ASLP). The KzB (then comprising the BSP, BZNS-AS, BSDP, PDSD, KPB, ZPB, DSH, and the Roma Party) won 82 seats in the 2005 assembly elections on a 31 percent vote share, having campaigned on a platform pledging, among other things, to promote higher wages and additional jobs for Bulgarian workers.

In the 2009 assembly balloting, the KzB (now minus the PDSD and ZPB, but having added the NZ) won 40 seats (on a nationwide vote share of 19 percent), losing more than half of the seats it had won in 2005. The KzB subsequently announced it would serve as "strong opposition" to the new GERB government.

In the May 2013 legislative election, the KzB (including all its 2009 participants, and adding the party **European Security and Integration** [*Evropoiska Signarnost i Integratsiya*—ESI]) won 84 seats with 26.6 percent of the vote.

Bulgarian Socialist Party (*Balgarska Sotsialisticheska Partiya*—BSP). The BSP resulted from a change of name by the Bulgarian Communist Party (*Balgarska Komunisticheska Partiya*—BKP) on April 3, 1990. The BKP traced its origins to an ideological split in the old Social Democratic Party, the dissidents withdrawing in 1903 to form the Bulgarian Workers' Social Democratic Party, which became the Communist Party in 1919. Banned in 1924, the party came to power in 1944 in the wake of the Red Army's military success and, in coalition with other "progressive" forces, took full control from 1946. The BKP's "leading role" in state and society was terminated on January 1990, when an extraordinary party congress renounced "democratic centralism," restructured its leadership bodies, and endorsed "human and democratic socialism" in the context of a "socially oriented market economy."

As the BSP, the party retained a legislative majority at multiparty elections in June 1990, but in December it accepted a coalition under the premiership of the opposition SDS. At a new poll in October 1991 a BSP-led alliance was narrowly defeated by the SDS, the BSP thus going into opposition for the first time since 1944. In a leadership contest at a BSP congress in December, Zhan Videnov, advocate of a "modern left-socialist party," easily defeated a reformist social democratic opponent. In December 1992 most BSP deputies backed the formation of the nonparty Berov government, under which the party reasserted its influence. In further elections in December 1994, the BSP, joined by the PKE and the BZNS-AS, won an overall assembly majority, with 43.5 percent of the vote.

A powerful conservative wing in the BSP attached the blame for a 1996 financial crisis to the Videnov modernizers and to over-hasty economic liberalization, whereas the Videnov supporters cited entrenched Soviet-era personnel and attitudes.

When Videnov resigned from the premiership in December 1996, he also relinquished his role as party chair, an extraordinary BSP congress subsequently selecting Deputy Chair Georgi Parvanov as his successor. Although new elections were also held for the BSP Supreme Council and its 15-member Executive Board, hard-liners continued to dominate both bodies. They insisted on trying to exercise the BSP's right to choose a new prime minister, despite massive public demonstrations in support of installation of an interim government pending early elections (see Political background, above). However, the prime minister-designate, Interior Minister Nikolai Dobrev, finally capitulated in early February 1997 to pressure for the BSP to relinquish its mandate, his decision to go against the party hard-liners being widely praised domestically and internationally as preventing further severe political conflict and possibly even civil war.

Following the Democratic Left's poor showing in the April 1998 legislative balloting, the BSP leadership announced it would support the new ODS government's economic reform policies but would oppose the Bulgarian bid for NATO membership. Continued friction was subsequently reported between Parvanov's moderate camp and party hard-liners, the latter enjoying the support of the large number of pensioners and veterans in the BSP. In May 2000 Parvanov, now backing integration into NATO, was easily reelected chair, although the party's electoral defeat in June 2001 led a faction headed by the former parliamentary chair, Krasimir PREMYANOV, to call for Parvanov's resignation. The Sakskoburggotski cabinet of July 2001 included two members of the BSP (later reduced to one), but the party itself remained outside the government, choosing to abstain during the July 24 confirmation vote in the National Assembly.

Designated on September 30, 2001, as the BSP presidential candidate, Parvanov won in second-round balloting in November, after which he resigned from the party in the interest of national unity. He was succeeded as BSP leader by Sergei Stanishev, who was named prime minister following the 2005 assembly poll, the BSP having embraced "Euro-style socialism" and having for the most part removed hard-line communists from influential party positions.

Ivaylo KALFIN was the BSP candidate in the 2011 presidential balloting, receiving 29 percent of the vote in the first round and 47.4 percent in the second round.

Leaders: Sergei STANISHEV (Chair and Former Prime Minister), Georgi PIRINSKI, Rumen Stoyanov OVCHAROV.

Bulgarian Agrarian National Union "Aleksandar Stamboliyski" (*Balgarski Zemedelski Naroden Sayuz "Aleksandar Stamboliyski"*—BZNS-AS). The BZNS-AS is one of several current groups claiming direct descent from the historic BZNS that had been founded in 1899. The BZNS's most prominent leader, Aleksandar Stamboliyski, was an Agrarian prime minister killed in a right-wing coup in 1923. After World War II, a pro-communist rump BZNS was allowed pro forma assembly and government representation as part of the Fatherland Front, usually holding the agriculture portfolio. Asserting its independence as communism began to crumble, the BZNS replaced longtime leader Petur TANCHEV in November 1989 and refused to join the Lukanov government of February 1990. Nevertheless, the anti-Communist BZNS-Nikola Petkov faction broke away to join the opposition SDS.

The rump BZNS won 16 assembly seats in June 1990 but lost them all in October 1991. A complex sequence of abortive unity schemes and further splits ensued in Agrarian ranks, one outcome being the creation of the BZNS-AS, which contested the 1994 elections in alliance with the victorious BSP. The BZNS-AS also participated in the Democratic Left for the 1996 presidential balloting.

It was reported that an "1899" faction of the BZNS-AS, led by Dragmir SHOPOV, participated in the KzB for the 2001 assembly elections. However, reports about the 2005 assembly balloting indicated no participation by the 1899 faction, with the KzB apparently claiming the support of the BZNS-AS faction.

Leader: Spas PANCHEV (President).

Euroroma (*Evroroma*). A "sociopolitical" organization formed to support the interests of the Roma minority, Euroroma competed as a political party in the 2005 assembly balloting in Bulgaria, securing slightly more than 1 percent of the vote.

Leader: Tsvetelin KANCHEV (President).

Smaller parties within the KzB include the **Party of Bulgarian Social Democrats** (*Partiya Balgarski Sotsialdemokrati*—PBS), led by Georgi ANASTASOV; the **Communist Party of Bulgaria** (*Komunisticheska Partiyana Balgariya*—KPB), led by Aleksandar PAUNOV; **New Dawn** (*Nova Zora*—NZ), led by Rumen BODENICHAROV; and the **Movement for Social Humanism** (*Dvizhenie za Sotsialen Humanizam*—DSH), led by Aleksandur RADOSLAVOV.

Movement for Rights and Freedoms (*Dvizhenie za Prava i Svobodi*—DPS). Representing the Turkish minority, the DPS won 23 assembly seats in June 1990. It became the swing party in October 1991 by winning 24 seats and in late 1992 played a crucial role in the ouster of the SDS government and the advent of the nonparty Berov administration. The DPS was weakened in 1993 by defections and splits as well as by the emigration to Turkey of many of its supporters, and its representation fell to 15 seats on a 5.4 percent vote share in December 1994. In 1996 the DPS participated in the ODS in support of the presidential candidacy of Petar Stoyanov.

A split was reported in the DPS in early 1997 over the decision by Ahmed Dogan not to remain aligned with the ODS for the April legislative balloting and instead to form a broad Alliance for National Salvation (*Obedinenie za Natsionalno Spasenie*—ONS). As configured for the 1997 legislative balloting, the ONS also included an ideologically incongruous mix of small liberal centrist, environmental, and monarchist parties. The ONS nevertheless secured 19 seats in the 1997 balloting, as compared to 15 for the DPS in 1994. The ONS broadly supported the ODS government for most of the rest of the year before the DPS in December charged Prime Minister Kostov with pursuing "populist measures, rather than reforms."

In preparation for the 1999 local elections the DPS helped establish the Liberal Democratic Union (see Liberal Union in the 2007 *Handbook*). Following the 2001 legislative election, a dispute between Dogan and former deputy chair Osman Oktay over party direction threatened a split in the DPS, which had been invited to join the Sakskoburggotski government as a junior partner. In July 2003 several members of the DPS (including Oktay) who were reportedly disillusioned with the party's leadership helped to launch a new party, the Democratic Wing Movement (see Coalition of the Rose, below).

For the 2001 assembly elections, the DPS led a coalition that also included the Liberal Union (Liberalen Sayuz—LS; see the 2007 *Handbook*) and Euroroma (see above); the coalition won 21 seats. In 2005 the DPS, running on its own, secured 34 seats on a vote share of 13 percent.

In 2009 statements by Dogan ignited controversy and populist anger among ethnic Bulgarian voters. Among other things, Dogan had allegedly described himself as a "king-maker" in past coalition governments and alluded to his extensive authority in the dispersal of government funds. He also reportedly said that he had possessed the power in the past to stir ethnic conflict in Bulgaria but had held his hand. The DPS also suffered from perception that the party was involved in government corruption scandals, many circulating around the ministry of agriculture. Some domestic analysts accordingly suggested that "anti-Doganism" was an important factor in the decline of its government partners (the KzB and the NDSV) in the 2009 assembly elections, although the DPS, maintaining its base within the Turkish population, itself placed third, winning 38 seats (up from 34 in 2005) with a vote share of 14.5 percent nationwide. In January 2011 Kasim DAL, long considered to be Dogan's political heir apparent, was expelled from the party. It is reported that he subsequently drew away a faction of the DPS to union with the **United People's Party** (*Edinna Narodna Partiya*—ENP), led by Maria KAPON.

During the January 2013 party congress, Dogan was assaulted by an attacker in what was widely reported as an assassination attempt.

In the May 2013 legislative elections, the MRF secured 36 seats with 11.3 percent of the vote.

Leaders: Lufti MESTAN (Chair), Ahmed DOGAN (Honorary Chair).

Opposition Parties:

Citizens for European Development of Bulgaria (*Grazhdani za Evropeisko Razvitie Balgariya*—GERB). Initially formed as a nonprofit association in early 2006, the GERB officially registered as a party in December with the intention of uniting other center-right parties and organizations. Boiko Borisov, the popular mayor of Sofia, was one of the group's founders. The party's platform focused on combating corruption and organized crime while supporting "civil liberties" and business-friendly economic policies. The GERB showed significant strength by winning over 21 percent and 24 percent of the vote in the 2007 and 2009 European Parliament elections, respectively. The party's success in casting itself as an alternative to the political establishment culminated in its plurality victory (116 seats and 43 percent of the national vote) in the July 2009 assembly balloting, following which Borisov formed a GERB government. Rosen Plevneliev was the GERB candidate in the 2011 presidential balloting, receiving 40.1 percent of the vote in the first round and 52.6 percent in the second round.

In the May 2013 legislative election GERB won 97 seats with 30.5 percent of the vote. Although placing first in the election and being offered a mandate to form a government, it was unable to secure support from other parties.

Leaders: Boiko BORISOV (Party Chair and Former Prime Minister), Tsvetan TSVETANOV (Vice Chair).

National Union Attack (*Natsionalno Obedinenie Ataka*). The "ultra-nationalistic" *Ataka* was formed under the leadership of controversial television journalist Volen Siderov in April 2005 by several movements and parties that opposed NATO, EU, and IMF membership for Bulgaria. *Ataka* also demanded the abolition of the DPS (the leading ethnic Turkish party) for being "unconstitutional." This, along with Siderov's controversial writings on alleged conspiracies within Freemasonry and Judaism, contributed to the broad perception of *Ataka* as a right-wing, antiminority formation. (One of the group's slogans was "Bulgaria for the Bulgarians.") *Ataka* also opposed the participation of Bulgarian troops in the U.S.-led operation in Iraq and demanded that the sale of Bulgarian lands to foreigners be banned. Surprising most observers (many of whom condemned *Ataka*'s leadership for engaging in "hate speech"), *Ataka* finished fourth in the June 2005 assembly poll, securing 21 seats on an 8 percent vote share. *Ataka*'s surge continued in the 2006 presidential race, in which Siderov garnered 21 percent and 24 percent of the vote in the first and second rounds, respectively. Siderov's campaign again targeted the Muslim and Roma minorities, earning him a "racist" label. However, he also reportedly attracted support for "populist" rhetoric that criticized recent government cutbacks and economic reform, notably the privatization of state-run enterprises. *Ataka* won 2 seats in the 2009 European Parliament balloting and finished fourth in the 2009 assembly poll with 21 seats (10 percent of the votes nationwide). Siderov subsequently announced that *Ataka* would support the new GERB government, at least temporarily.

On May 20, 2011, *Ataka* supporters protesting the use of loudspeakers at the Banya Bashi mosque in Sofia clashed with Muslims gathered there for prayer.

Siderov, as the party's presidential candidate, received 3.6 percent of the vote in the first round of the 2011 presidential election.

Rifts within the party emerged in November when Dimitar STOYANOV, Siderov's stepson, called for the latter's resignation. The Bulgarian media widely reported that this was linked to family issues after Siderov separated from his wife (Stoyanov's mother). Several members of the party's parliamentary group defected, while Stoyanov was expelled from the party and formed his own nationalist formation, the NDP (below).

In the May 2013 legislative balloting, *Ataka* won 23 seats with 7.3 percent of the vote.

Leader: Volen SIDEROV (President and 2011 presidential candidate).

Other Parties and Coalitions Contesting the 2012 Legislative Elections:

National Front for the Salvation of Bulgaria (*Natsionalen Front za Spasenie na Balgariya*—NFSB). Founded on May 17, 2011, the party's founding platform pledged to resist "foreign interests" and revive the nation. Its presidential candidate in the 2011 elections, Stefan SOLAKOV, took 2.5 percent of the first round. In the May 2013 legislative election, the NFSB won 3.7 percent of the national vote, falling short of the 4 percent threshold.

Leaders: Valeri SIMEONOV, Valentin KASABOV, Dancho HADZHIEV (Cochairs).

Movement Bulgaria for Citizens (*Dvizhenie Balgariya na grazhdanite*—DBG). The DBG was formed in December 2011 as a "civic movement" by Meglena Kuneva, a former member of the European Commission and independent candidate in the October 2011 presidential elections, in which she received 14 percent of the vote in the first round. Kuneva was a founding member of the NDSV and reportedly drew active support from elements of that party. On July 1, 2012, the DBG was officially re-founded as a political party.

In the May 2013 assembly balloting, the DBG won 3.25 percent of the vote, failing to pass the threshold.

Leaders: Meglena KUNEVA (Chair), Nayden ZELENOGORSKI (former mayor of Pleven).

Democrats for a Strong Bulgaria and Bulgarian Democratic Forum. This electoral coalition included the DSB and BDF. In the May 2013 election, it won 2.93 percent of the vote and failed to pass the threshold.

Democrats for a Strong Bulgaria (*Demokrati za Silna Balgariya*—DSB). Dissatisfaction with the leadership of the SDS prompted party leader and former prime minister, Ivan Kostov, and SDS Deputy Chair Ekaterina Mikhailova to quit the SDS and form the DSB in February 2004. Twenty-six deputies left the SDS to help launch the DSB. Campaigning on a strongly "anti-communist" (and thereby anti-BSP) platform, the center-right DSB won 17 seats on a 6.4 percent vote share in the 2005 assembly elections. Facing a drop in the polls following the 2005 assembly elections, the DSB joined the SDS and others in the SK for the 2009 assembly elections. Kostov subsequently emerged as an outspoken critic of the GERB's handling of the Bulgarian economy, predicting a continued economic crisis through 2011. Following the poor showing of the DSB-BDF coalition in May 2013, Kostov resigned as party leader.

Leaders: Raden KANEV (Chair), Ivan KOSTOV (Former Party Chair and Former Prime Minister).

Bulgarian Democratic Forum (*Balgarski Demokraticheski Forum*—BDF). Founded in 1990, the BDF considers itself a continuation of interwar conservative patriotic youth movements banned during the Communist period.

Leader: Zhalkin TOLEVA (Chair).

Internal Macedonian Revolutionary Organization (*Vatreshna Makedonska Revolutsionerna Organizatsiya*—VMRO). Founded in 1996, the VMRO drew on the heritage of the 19th-century Macedonian revolutionary organization to emerge as the most successful nationalist political party until *Ataka.* The VMRO participated in an electoral coalition with the DG (below) in the 2001 assembly elections before helping to launch the BNS in 2005. Krassimir Karakachanov, VMRO's 2011 presidential candidate, received 1 percent of the vote in the first round. In the May 2013 assembly elections, VMRO won 1.89 percent of the vote.

Leader: Krassimir KARAKACHANOV.

Liberal Initiative for Democratic European Development (*Liberalna Initsiativa za Demokratichno Evropeisko Razvitie*—LIDER).

A conservative, probusiness party, LIDER, roughly translated as "Leader," was founded in 2007 by energy magnate Hristo Kovachki. (The short form of the party's name is universally used by the Bulgarian media and election officials.) After nearly winning a European Parliament seat in the June 2009 elections with almost 6 percent of the vote, LIDER joined with the NV in an electoral coalition (named LIDER) for the July assembly balloting. The coalition, however, won only 3 percent of the vote nationwide and therefore no seats.

In the May 2013 assembly elections, LIDER won 1.74 percent of the vote.

Leader: Kancho FILIPOV (Chair).

Order, Law and Justice (*Red, Zakonnost, i Spravedlivost*—RZS). The center-right RZS was founded in opposition to the BSP-led government in December 2005 by dissidents from the BZNS-NS (see ZNS, below). Among other things, the new party called for intensified anticorruption measures. In the first round of the 2006 presidential balloting, RZS candidate (and former constitutional judge) Georgi MARKOV received 2.7 percent of the vote.

The RZS won ten seats (on a vote share of 4.8 percent nationwide) in the July 2009 assembly elections and subsequently pledged at least six months of "unconditional" support for the new GERB government. In December 2009, however, the party officially stated that it would move to become a "right-wing conservative opposition."

RZS candidate Atanas SEMOV received 1.8 percent of the vote in the first round of the 2011 presidential balloting.

In the May 2013 legislative balloting, the RZS won 1.67 percent of the vote.

Leaders: Yane YANEV (Chair), Georgi MARKOV.

Center-Freedom and Dignity (*Centar-Svoboda i dostoinstvo*—CSD). A 2013 electoral coalition between the NDSV and the **Freedom and Dignity People's Party** (*Narodna Partiya "Svoboda i dostoinstvo"*—NPSD), led by Korman ISMAILOV. In the May 2013 assembly election, the CSD won 1.63 percent of the vote.

National Movement for Stability and Progress (*Natsionalno Dvizhenie za Stabilnosti Vazhod*—NDSV). Originally formed in April 2001 as the National Movement Simeon II (*Natsionalno Dvizhenie Simeon Tvori*—NDST) by the former king, Simeon Saxe-Coburg-Gotha (an English translation of the family's original German name), a month after he had returned from exile in Spain. On April 28, however, the Supreme Court upheld an April 23 ruling by the Sofia City Court denying registration to the NDST party because it failed to meet legal requirements. In order to get on the ballot for the June National Assembly election, the former monarch's supporters quickly negotiated an arrangement with two small, officially sanctioned parties, the **Party of Bulgarian Women** (PBZh) and the **Movement for National Revival "Oborishte"** (which refers to the site of a 19th-century uprising against the Ottomans), whereby they agreed to contest the election as the NDST. Thus, the NDST was registered as a coalition by the Central Election Commission on May 2. In the June balloting, the formation won 120 seats and a 42.7 percent vote share, far outdistancing its opponents. Simeon II, who was not himself a parliamentary candidate, subsequently accepted the nomination as prime minister. (It was announced that the former king had adopted the common name Sakskoburggotski for the premiership.)

The NDST was formally registered as a political party in April 2002, and the prime minister was elected as party leader after initially indicating he would not pursue that post in the interest of party unity.

Five NDST legislators had left the party in March 2002 to protest their leader's perceived failure to follow up on his campaign promises, while 11 others formed New Time (above) in 2004. The NDST fell to 53 seats (on a vote share of 20 percent) in the 2005 assembly elections. In June 2007, although Sakskoburggotski was reelected as party leader to deemphasize his role in the movement and broaden its appeal, the group formally changed its name to the NDSV, replacing "Simeon II" with "Stability and Progress." However, factionalization continued within the party, and 17 NDSV MPs quit the party in May 2008 to form a parliamentary faction called Bulgarian New Democracy (BND) under the leadership of former defense minister Nikolay SVINAROV and Borislav RALCHEV. The BND registered as a party and participated (unsuccessfully) on its own in the June 2009 European Parliament elections.

The rump NDSV continued its precipitous decline by garnering only slightly more than 3 percent of the assembly vote nationwide in the June balloting, thereby failing to win any seats. Sakskoburggotski subsequently resigned as party leader.

Although the NDSV did not offer a candidate for the October 2011 presidential elections, it played an active role in the simultaneous local elections, winning eight municipal mayorships.

Leaders: Hristina HRISTOVA (President), Milen VELCHEV, Plamen MOLLOV.

Union of Democratic Forces Coalition. The latest successor of a line of center-right coalitions formed by the SDS. The first, the SDS-led United Democratic Forces (*Obedineni Demokratichni Sili*—ODS), was an "anti-Communist," primarily center-right formation that was launched by a number of groups opposed to the BSP-led government elected in 1994. In an unusual procedure, the ODS conducted a primary in June 1996 to determine its presidential candidate, the two contenders being Petar Stoyanov of the SDS and incumbent President Zhelyu Zhelev, the nominee of the People's Union (*Naroden Sayuz*—NS), an alliance of the BZNS-NS and the DP. (The NS had secured 18 seats on a vote share of 6.5 percent in the 1994 assembly elections.) Stoyanov easily defeated Zhelev and went on to victory in the November national election. As configured for the presidential balloting, the ODS included not only the SDS and the NS but also the Movement for Rights and Freedom (DPS, below). The DPS, however, opted out of the coalition for the April 1997 legislative balloting, in which the ODS won a majority of 137 assembly seats and presented Ivan Kostov of the SDS as the next prime minister. The reconfigured ODS won only 51 seats on an 18.2 percent vote share in the June 2001 election, prompting Kostov's resignation. For the November 2001 presidential election, Stoyanov chose to run as an independent, although he received the ODS's endorsement.

The ODS subsequently suffered severe factionalization. In addition, the NS left the ODS in March 2004 to form its own legislative grouping, claiming 11 seats. The ODS fell to 20 seats on a 7.7 percent vote share in the 2005 assembly poll, when its components were the SDS, DP, DG, and the small National Democratic Party (*Natsional na Demokraicheska Partiya*—NDP).

The ODS was transformed into the **Blue Coalition** (*Sinyata Koalitsiya*—SK) prior to the 2009 European Parliament and national parliamentary elections, the most important change being the inclusion of the DSB. Campaigning on an anticorruption, progrowth platform, the SK won 15 seats (on a nationwide vote share of 7.2 percent) in the July balloting and subsequently pledged to support (at least temporarily) the new GERB government, based on what SK leaders called "coinciding goals" and antipathy toward the BSP. While the SK continued to support the GERB as an informal partner, SK leaders criticized the government's approach to the recession and pushed for a greater voice in determining economic policies.

A rift within the SK was reported in August 2011, with the SDS and DSB reportedly in conflict over the allocation of candidacies and over potential electoral alliances with smaller conservative parties. In the first round of the 2011 presidential balloting SK candidate Rumen HRISTOV received 2 percent of the vote. In May 2012 the national council of the SDS announced it would complete on its own in the 2013 legislative elections, breaking the SK coalition. Subsequently, however, the SDS was able to create a coalition with the BSDP, RP, OZ, DG, and **Patriot** (*Patriot*), a civic association created by former *Ataka* members.

In the May 2013 elections, the SDS-led coalition won 1.38 percent of the vote, failing to pass the threshold.

Union of Democratic Forces (*Sayuzna Demokratichnite Sili*—SDS). The SDS was launched in late 1989 as a loose opposition coalition of intellectual, environmental, trade union, and other groups. Chaired by Zhelyu Zhelev (a dissident philosophy professor of the Zhivkov era), the SDS entered into talks with the government and negotiated arrangements for multiparty elections in June 1990, which were won by the BSP. Nevertheless, the new assembly elected Zhelev as president of Bulgaria in August 1990, while SDS opposition forced the resignation of the BSP government in November and its replacement by a coalition that included SDS members.

Dissension between moderate and radical elements resulted in the presentation of three distinct SDS lists in the election of October 1991: the main SDS-Movement, the SDS-Centre, and the SDS-Liberals. The outcome was a narrow plurality for the main SDS, which won 110 of the 240 seats and 34.4 percent of the vote, with neither of the other SDS lists gaining representation. The main SDS proceeded to form Bulgaria's first wholly noncommunist government since World War II, headed by Filip Dimitrov, with the external support of the ethnic Turkish DPS. In direct presidential elections in January 1992, Zhelev secured a popular mandate, winning 53 percent of the second-round vote. However, serious strains quickly developed between the president and Prime Minister Dimitrov, while the SDS assembly group became racked with dissent. The government fell in October 1992 and was replaced by a nonparty administration under Lyuben Berov, with the support of some 20 SDS dissidents.

Seen as increasingly conservative, the anti-Berov SDS in mid-1993 mounted demonstrations against President Zhelev for his alleged backing of "recommunization," but defections of left-inclined deputies reduced SDS assembly strength to below that of the BSP by early 1994. In June the remaining SDS deputies launched a boycott of the assembly, prompting the resignation of the Berov government in September. However, an assembly poll in December resulted in defeat for the grouping, which moved quickly to install Ivan Kostov (a former finance minister) as its new leader on December 29, 1994. With 69 of the 240 assembly seats, it formed the principal opposition to the BSP-led government.

The SDS led the protests against the BSP in early 1997, finally forcing the calling of early elections. In preparation for the April balloting, an SDS conference in February 1997 approved the reformation of the coalition into a political party. (For a list of the members of the SDS prior to its establishment as a single party, see the 1997 *Handbook.*) Following the electoral loss of June 2001, Ivan Kostov resigned as party chair and was replaced by a former chief secretary, Ekaterina MIKHAILOVA. Although regarded as a "natural partner" by the NDST, the SDS declined to join the Sakskoburggotski government, at least in part because it objected to inclusion of an ethnic formation, the DPS.

At a January 2004 meeting, Mikhailova was reelected as party leader, prompting Kostov and a group of 26 SDS legislators to leave the SDS on February 23 (see DSB, above). Internal tensions and successive poor electoral results led to frequent changes in party leadership after 2005 (see the 2013 *Handbook* for details).

Leaders: Bozhidar LUKARSKI (Chair), Yordan BAKALOV.

Bulgarian Social Democratic Party (*Balgarska Sotsialdemokraticheska Partiya*—BSDP). The BSDP traces its descent from the historic party founded in 1891 and more especially from the secession of its nonrevolutionary wing in 1903. Left-wing Social Democrats participated in the Communist-led Fatherland Front that came to power in 1944, the BSDP being merged with the Communist Party in 1948. Over the next four decades exiles kept the party alive as the Socialist Party, which was reestablished in Bulgaria in 1989 under the leadership of Petar DERTLIEV, a veteran of the pre-1948 era. In March 1990 the party reinstated the BSDP title in view of the imminent decision of the Communist Party to rename itself the BSP. As a component of the SDS, the BSDP took 29 seats in the June 1990 assembly election.

The BSDP supported the decision of some SDS elements to enter a BSP-dominated coalition government in December 1990 but thereafter came into conflict with the promarket policies of the SDS leadership, arguing that privatized industries should become cooperatives where possible. In the October 1991 assembly election the BSDP headed a separate SDS-Centre list, which failed to surmount the 4 percent barrier. The BSDP backed Zhelev's successful candidacy in the January 1992 direct presidential balloting and thereafter sided with the president against the SDS minority government. From March 1993, seeking to establish a credible third force between the BSP and an SDS seen as moving to the right, the BSD launched a series of center-left alliances, culminating in the **Democratic Alternative for the Republic** (*Demokratichna Alternativa za Republikata*—DAR).The BSDP, however, joined the SDS-led ODS for the April 1997 legislative balloting, although only 1 of the 137 successful ODS candidates belonged to the BSDP.

Late in 1998 the BSDP split, and Petar Dertliev led a wing of the party into the opposition. That group joined the United Labor Bloc (OBT) in establishing a Social Democratic Union (*Balgarska Sotsialdemokraticheska Sayuz*—BSDS) in preparation for the 1999 local elections. Dertliev died in November 2000.

In the 2001 legislative election the Social Democrats remained fractured. One of the principal branches renegotiated its standing within the ODS, the former Dertliev wing joined the KzB, and another "united group" participated in the coalition led by the BEL (below). The claim to status as the "legitimate" BSDP remained contentious prior to the 2005 assembly balloting, with a faction led by Petar AGOV running as part of the KzB and a faction led by Yordan NIHRIZOV reportedly participating in the ODS. (Some reports indicated that Nihrizov's supporters had earned the "official" right to the BSDP rubric in 1997, with Agov's supporters subsequently sometimes being referred to as the Party of the Bulgarian Social Democrats (PBS, see above) Both Agov and Nihrizov won seats in the 2005 assembly elections.

Leader: Iordan NIHRIZOV (President).

Radical Democratic Party (*Radikaldemokraticheska Partiya*—RP). A historic Bulgarian liberal party of the early 20th century, the RP was reestablished in 1989.

Leader: Zahari PETROV (Chair).

United Agrarians (*Obedineni Zemedeltsi*—OZ). The OZ was founded in 2008 after a split within the BZNS-NS (see ZNS, below).

Leaders: Petya STAVREVA (Chair), Anastasia DIMITROVA-MOSER (Honorary Chair).

Saint George Day Movement (*Dvizhenie Gergyovden*—DG). The DG participated in the 2001 assembly poll in a coalition with the VMRO that secured 3.6 percent of the vote, reportedly appealing to young liberal voters. After joining the ODS for the 2005 assembly balloting, the DG returned to its affiliation with the VMRO for the 2005 polls.

Leader: Lyuben DILOV Jr.

People's Voice (*Glas Naroden*—GN). A new party founded in 2013 by Svetoslav Vitkov, the lead singer for the former 1990s Bulgarian rock band Hipodil. Vitkov had previously run as an independent candidate in the 2011 presidential elections, placing eighth with 1.6 percent of the nationwide vote. In the May 2013 legislative election, the GN won 1.34 percent of the vote.

Leader: Svetoslav VITKOV (Chair).

The Greens (*Zelenite*). Founded in May 2008, the Greens was established by a group of NGOs as a rival to the existing ZPB in support of "moral and ethical principles" relating to the environment, human rights, democracy, and economic life. The party won 0.5 percent of the vote in the 2009 assembly elections and 0.75 percent in the May 2013 elections.

Leaders: Georg TUPAREV, Borislav SANDOV, Stoyan YOTOV (Cochairs).

Democratic Party (*Demokraticheska Partiya*—DP). Descended from the conservative Christian party of the same name founded in 1896, the DP was revived in 1989 and joined the opposition SDS. The DP formed the NS with the BZNS-NS in 1994 and participated in that grouping as part of the ODS in the 1997 and 2001 assembly balloting. However, following the apparent collapse of the NS, the DP served as a single component of the ODS for the 2005 poll, though leaving the ODS parliamentary group later that year. It did not compete in the 2009 elections; in the May 2013 elections, it won less than 0.1 percent of the vote.

Leader: Aleksandar PRAMATARSKI (Chair).

Bulgarian Spring (*Balgarska Prolet*). This coalition included the **Party of the Greens** (*Partiya na Zelenite*), led by Valentin SIMOV and **Bulgarian Social Democracy** (*Bulgarska Sotsialdemokratsiya*—BSD), led by Aleksandar TOMOV. It won slightly more than 0.1 percent of the vote in the May 2013 legislative elections.

Other parties and coalitions that competed unsuccessfully in the 2013 assembly elections included the **New Alternative** (*Nova Alternativa*); the coalition **Proud Bulgaria** (*Gorda Balgariya*), between the **Civil Union for Real Democracy** (*Grazhdansko Obedinenie za realna demokratsiya*), the **Union of the Patriotic Forces "Defense"** (*Sayuz na Patriotichnite Sili "Zashtita"*—SPSZ), the **United Labor Bloc** (*Obedinen Blok na Truda*—OBT), and the **Free Nation** (*Svoboden Narod*); the **Democratic Civil Initiative** (*Demokratichna Grazhdanska Initsiativa*—DGI); the coalition **Civil List-Modern Bulgaria** (*Grazhdanska Lista-Moderna Balgariya*), comprising the **Bulgarian Party of Liberals** (*Balgarska Partiya Liberali*) and **Burgas;** the **Liberal Alliance** (*Liberalen Alians*); the

Bulgarian Agrarian National Union (*Balgarski Zemedelski Naroden Sayuz–Naroden Sayuz*—BZNS); the **Party of Bulgarian Women** (*Partiya na balgarskite zheni*—PBZh); the **Union of Communists in Bulgaria** (*Sayuz na komunistite v Balgariya*); the **Bulgarian Left** (*Balgarskata Levitsa*); the **Unified People's Party** (*Edinna Narodna Partiya*—ENP); the **Christian Democratic Party of Bulgaria** (*Hristiyandemokraticheska Partiya na Balgariya*); the party **Middle European Class** (*Sredna Evropaiska Klasa*); the **National-Democratic Party** (*Natsional-Demokratichna Partiya*); the **Democratic Alternative for National Unification** (*Demokratichna Alternativa za Natsionalno Obedinenie*); the **National Patriotic Unity** (*Natsionalno Patriotichno Obedinenie*); the **Other Bulgaria** (*Drugata Balgariya*); the **Cause Bulgaria** (*Kauza Balgariya*); the **National Unity Movement** (*Natsionalno Dvizhenie Edinstvo*); the **Christian Social Union** (*Hristiyan-Sotsialen Sayuz*); and the **Social Democratic Party** (*Sotsialdemokraticheska Partiya*).

Other Parties:

Agrarian People's Union (*Zemedelski Naroden Sayuz*—ZNS). The ZNS was formed in 2006 as an offshoot of the Bulgarian Agrarian National Union–People's Union (*Balgarski Zemedelski Naroden Sayuz–Naroden Sayuz*—BZNS-NS). The BZNS-NS was one of several factions claiming descent from the BZNS, a major Bulgarian political party in the beginning of the 20th century that was subsequently co-opted into the Communist-led Fatherland Front, with much of its prewar leadership emigrating abroad.

Among the figures contesting for leadership of the BZNS after 1989 was Anastasia DIMITROVA-MOSER, the daughter of G. M. DIMITROV, a prewar Agrarian leader who had emigrated to the United States after World War II. Dimitrova-Moser became leader of the BZNS-Nikola Petkov (named after an Agrarian leader who was executed in 1947) in February 1992. The Petkov group was then a member of the SDS, but the latter became increasingly divided after it lost power in December 1992, with the result that Dimitrova-Moser led a section of the BZNS-NS into a separate alliance with the DP. The BZNS-NS launched the NS coalition with the DP in 1994 and participated in the ODS in the 1997 and 2001 assembly polls before serving as the core component of the Bulgarian People's Union (*Balgarski Naroden Sayuz*—BNS) for the 2005 legislative elections. The BNS, a center-right grouping that also included the VMRO (above) and the Union of Free Democrats (*Sayuzna Svobodnite Demokrati*—SSD), won 13 assembly seats on a 5.2 percent vote share. (The SSD's leader, former prime minister Stefan Sofianski, was among those elected on the BNS ticket.)

Following a leadership struggle at the May 2006 party congress, the BZNS-NS fragmented into two wings. Former party leader Dimitrova-Moser led one wing to found the new United Agrarians (OZ, above), while Stefan Lichev led other factions in formation (or renaming) of the ZNS. In 2009 the ZNS joined other BZNS-derived parties to form the Koalitsiya BZNS, but its registration to participate in the 2009 assembly elections was ruled invalid by the Central Electoral Commission because of problems with the required number of signatures. In 2013 it was able to register for elections but internal divisions within the party had resulted in a failure to submit candidate lists.

Leader: Stefan LICHEV (President).

Political Movement "Social Democrats" (*Politichesko Dvizhenie "Sotsialdemokrati"*—PDSD). The PDSD was established in 2000 following a split within the **Euroleft** (see BSD, below) over the parent group's direction and leadership. The new formation pledged to advance social democratic interests as well as openness and accountability in government. It participated in the 2005 assembly elections as a member of the KzB.

In January 2013 the PDSD announced an agreement with the PBS (see KzB, above) and OBT (above) to create a unified social democratic party through a future merger.

Leaders: Lachezar SHIKOV (President); Bozhidar MITEV, Vladimir MATEV (Vice Presidents).

Bulgarian Social Democracy (*Balgarska Sotsialdemokratsia*—BSD). The BSD was formed in early 2003 by a merger of the **Bulgarian Euroleft** (*Balgarska Evrolevitsa*—BEL), the Bulgarian United Social Democrats, and others. The new formation reportedly did well in the 2003 municipal elections.

The BEL was organized prior to the 1997 legislative elections under the leadership of former deputy prime minister Aleksandar Tomov, who had broken from the BSP in 1994. The ranks of the KEL were enlarged by more BSP defectors in the wake of the collapse of the Videnov government, as well as by recruits from other leftist organizations. The KEL won 14 seats in the 1997 poll, subsequently solidly aligning itself with the ODS in support of economic reform as well as EU and NATO membership for Bulgaria.

In January 2011 Tomov was sentenced to nine years in prison for embezzlement while chief of the Kremikovtsi steel plant.

Leader: Aleksandar TOMOV.

United Macedonian Organization—Party for Economic Development and Integration. Founded in February 1998 and based in the Pirin region, near the border with Macedonia, this party is generally referred to as **OMO "Ilinden"** (*Obedineta Makedonska Organizatsiya "Ilinden,"* the fourth word being a reference to a failed 1903 Macedonian uprising begun on the feast day of St. Elijah, August 2). The party won three seats in the 1999 municipal elections before being banned by the Constitutional Court in February 2000 as a group "directed against Bulgaria's sovereignty." In 2006 the organization's right to register as a political party was upheld by the European Court of Human Rights, and in 2008 the European Commission requested to review the government's current steps on adhering to the ECHR's ruling. However, the Bulgarian government had not recognized the party as of September 2010.

Leader: Ivan SINGARIYSKI.

Green Party in Bulgaria (*Zelena Partiyana Balgariya*—ZPB). Established in 1989, the environmentalist ZPB participated in the 1990 elections in coalition with the SDS. The ZPB was split in 1991 by the formation of the now-defunct Ecoglasnost Political Club (*Politicheskiklub Ekoglasnost*—PKE) and subsequently participated in several widely varied electoral alliances, including the KzB in the 2005 assembly elections.

Leader: Marina DRAGOMIRETSKAYA (President).

LEGISLATURE

The **National Assembly** (*Narodno Sabranie*) is a unicameral body of 240 members elected for four-year terms. Prior to 2009, all members were proportionally elected from party lists on a district basis. However, changes to the electoral law in April 2009 provided for election of 31 of the 240 members through first-past-the post voting in 31 single-member districts. The remaining 209 members continued to be elected on a proportional basis from 31 districts. In January 2011 a new law eliminated the single-member districts, with all 240 members again proportionally elected. There is 1 district for each of the country's 28 administrative regions (including the cities of Sofia and Plovdiv) and 2 additional districts for Sofia and 1 additional seat for Plovdiv. The number of proportional seats in districts ranges from 4 to 12, depending on population. Independents may contest the single-mandate voting, but the proportional voting is limited to lists from parties or coalitions. Although the proportional seats are distributed according to the results within each district, a party or coalition must receive at least 4 percent of the nationwide vote to be eligible for proportional seats from any district.

In the most recent balloting of May 12, 2013, the Citizens for European Development of Bulgaria won 97 seats; the Bulgarian Socialist Party, 84; the Movement for Rights and Freedoms, 36; and the National Union Attack, 23 (all proportional).

Chair: Mihail MIKOV.

CABINET

[as of August 15, 2013]

Prime Minister	Plamen Oresharski (Ind.)
Deputy Prime Minister for EU Funds	Zinaida Zlatanova (BSP) [f]
Deputy Prime Minister for Security and Intelligence	Tsvetlin Yovchev (BSP)
Deputy Prime Minister in charge of the Economy, Foreign Investments, e-Government, and Administrative Services	Daniela Bobeva (Ind.) [f]
Ministers	
Agriculture and Food	Dimitar Grekov (BSP)
Culture	Petar Stojanovic (Ind.)

Defense	Angel Naydenov (BSP)
Economy and Energy	Dragomir Stoynev (BSP)
Education and Science	Aneliya Klisarova (BSP) [f]
Environment and Water	Iskra Mihaylova-Koparova (MRF) [f]
Finance	Peter Tchobanov (BSP)
Foreign Affairs	Kristian Vigenin (BSP)
Health	Tanya Lyubomirova-Ryanova (BSP) [f]
Interior	Tsvetlin Yovchev (BSP)
Investment Design	Ivan Danov (Ind.)
Justice	Zinaida Zlatanova (BSP) [f]
Labor and Social Policy	Hassan Ademov (MRF)
Regional Development	Desislava Terzieva (Ind.) [f]
Transport, Information Technology, and Communications	Daniel Papazoff (BSP)
Youth and Sports	Mariana Georgieva (MRF) [f]

[f] = female

Note: All of the above are members of the Citizens for Economic Development of Bulgaria.

INTERGOVERNMENTAL REPRESENTATION

Ambassador to the U.S.: Elena POPTODOROVA.

U.S. Ambassador to Bulgaria: Marcie B. RIES.

Permanent Representative to the UN: Stephan TAFROV.

IGO Memberships (Non-UN): EBRD, EIB, EU, ICC, IOM, NATO, OSCE, WTO.

BURKINA FASO

Political Status: Became independent as the Republic of Upper Volta on August 5, 1960; under largely military rule 1966–1978; constitution of November 27, 1977, suspended upon military coup of November 25, 1980; present name adopted August 4, 1984; multiparty constitution adopted by popular referendum on June 2, 1991.

Area: 105,869 sq. mi. (274,200 sq. km).

Population: 14,196,259 (2006C); 17,511,878 (2012E—UN).

Major Urban Center (2006E): OUAGADOUGOU (1,485,223).

Official Language: French.

Monetary Unit: CFA franc (official rate November 1, 2013: 486.52 CFA francs = $1US). The CFA franc is permanently pegged to the euro at 655.957 CFA francs = 1 euro.

President: Capt. Blaise COMPAORÉ (Congress of Democracy and Progress); leader of military coup that overthrew Cdr. Thomas SANKARA on October 15, 1987; popularly elected (as leader of the Popular Front) to a seven-year term on December 1, 1991; reelected to another seven-year term on November 15, 1998; reelected to five-year terms on November 13, 2005, and November 21, 2010.

Prime Minister: Luc Adolphe TIAO (Congress of Democracy and Progress): appointed by the president on April 15, 2011, to succeed Tertius ZONGO (Congress of Democracy and Progress), who had been dismissed the same day; formed a new government on April 22, 2011; reappointed December 21, 2012, following legislative elections of December 2; formed new government on January 2, 2013.

THE COUNTRY

A land of arid savannas drained by the Mouhoun (Black), Nazinon (Red), and Nakambe (White) Volta rivers, Burkina Faso occupies a bufferlike position between the other landlocked states of Mali and Niger on the west, north, and east, and the coastal countries of Côte d'Ivoire, Ghana, Togo, and Benin on the south. The most prominent of its numerous African population groups is the Mossi, which encompasses an estimated 50 percent of the population and has dominated much of the country for centuries. Other tribal groups include the Bobo, located near the western city of Bobo-Dioulasso, and the Samo. It is currently estimated that 60 percent of the population adheres to Islam, 25 percent to Christianity (primarily Catholicism), and 15 percent to traditional tribal religions. Women have traditionally constituted over half the labor force, producing most of the food crops, with men responsible for cash crops. Captain Compaoré's 1987 dismissal of a number of women appointed by his predecessor to politically influential posts was consistent with customary law that was described as "unfavorable" to female property and political rights. However, subsequent cabinets have usually included several female ministers, and 20 women were elected to the national legislature in 2012.

The former Upper Volta is one of the poorest and least developed countries in Africa, with a GNP per capita estimated at $300 and an average life expectancy of less than 50 years. In addition, its illiteracy rate (more than 70 percent) is among the highest in the world. Nearly 80 percent of the population is engaged in subsistence agriculture; cotton, karité nuts, shea nuts, livestock, and peanuts are exported. (Cotton reportedly accounts for some 20 percent of exports, and Burkina Faso is one of the largest cotton producers in sub-Saharan Africa.) Although mineral deposits (including gold, uranium, manganese, phosphate, and zinc) remained largely unexploited for many years due to a lack of transportation facilities, a number of gold mines have been opened recently, and gold is currently the leading export. In addition to mining, industry (about 25 percent of GDP) includes the production of textiles and processed agricultural goods. Remittances from Burkinabè working in nearby countries contribute significantly to the economy.

In 1991 the government began to implement a structural adjustment plan dictated by the International Monetary Fund (IMF) focusing on redirecting the economy from a "centralized to market-oriented one." In mid-2000 the IMF and the World Bank announced a $700 million debt relief package for Burkina Faso, contingent in part on further privatization and implementation of poverty-reduction policies. Development programs continued to emphasize the construction of rural roads and the expansion of irrigation systems, while the IMF called for strengthening of the government's fiscal management (including improved tax administration) and intensification of policies designed to promote the private sector. Social spending by the government also increased significantly, although an estimated 42 percent of the population continued to live in poverty.

The IMF in 2012 noted that the government had enhanced revenue collections, rehabilitated the cotton sector, and pledged additional banking reforms designed to improve the overall business environment. Expanded gold mining (seven mines were operating) and a good harvest contributed to GDP growth of 9 percent in 2012.

GOVERNMENT AND POLITICS

Political background. Under French control since 1896, what was then known as Upper Volta gained separate identity in March 1959 when it became an autonomous state of the French Community under Maurice YAMÉOGO, leader of the Voltaic Democratic Union (*Union Démocratique Voltaïque*—UDV) and a political disciple of President Félix Houphouët-Boigny of Côte d'Ivoire. Under Yaméogo's leadership, Upper Volta became fully independent on August 5, 1960. Though reelected for a second term by an overwhelming majority in 1965, Yaméogo was unable to cope with mounting student and labor dissatisfaction, and he resigned in January 1966. Lt. Col. Sangoulé LAMIZANA, the army chief of staff, immediately assumed the presidency and instituted a military regime.

Faithful to his promise to restore constitutional government within four years, President Lamizana submitted a new constitution for popular approval in December 1970 and sponsored a legislative election in which the UDV regained its pre-1966 majority. Gérard Kango OUÉDRAOGO was invested as prime minister by the National Assembly in February 1971, while Lamizana was retained as chief executive for a four-year transitional period, after which the president was to be

popularly elected. However, on February 8, 1974, the army, under General Lamizana, again seized control to prevent the political rehabilitation of ex-president Yaméogo. Declaring that the takeover was aimed at saving the country from the threat of squabbling politicians, Lamizana suspended the 1970 constitution, dissolved the National Assembly, and dismissed the cabinet. A new government was formed on February 11, with Lamizana continuing as president and assuming the office of prime minister.

In the wake of a ministerial reorganization in January 1977, the president announced that a constitutional referendum would take place by midyear, followed by legislative and presidential elections at which he would not stand as a candidate. The referendum was held November 27, with a reported 97.75 percent of the voters endorsing a return to democratic rule. Lamizana reversed himself, however, and announced his candidacy for the presidency in 1978. Rejecting an appeal by opponents that he abandon his military rank and campaign as a civilian, Lamizana retained the presidency in a runoff on May 29 after having obtained a plurality in first-round balloting on May 14. Earlier, on April 30, the regime-supportive UDV–African Democratic Assembly (UDV–*Rassemblement Démocratique Africain*—UDV-RDA) obtained a near-majority in a reconstituted National Assembly, which on July 7 designated Dr. Joseph Issoufou CONOMBO as prime minister.

Despite restrictions imposed on all but the leading political groups, Upper Volta remained one of only two multiparty democracies (the other being Senegal) in former French Africa until November 25, 1980, when the Lamizana regime was overthrown in a military coup led by former foreign minister Col. Sayé ZERBO. Officials of the ousted government, including the president and the prime minister, were placed under arrest, while a Military Committee of Recovery for National Progress (*Comité Militaire de Redressement pour le Progrès National*—CMRPN) suspended the constitution, dissolved the legislature, and banned political activity. A 17-member Council of Ministers headed by Colonel Zerbo as both president and prime minister was announced on December 7.

Accusing Zerbo of having "made the paramilitary forces an agent of terror," a group of noncommissioned officers on November 7, 1982, mounted a coup that installed Maj. Jean-Baptiste OUÉDRAOGO, a former army medical officer, as head of what was termed the People's Salvation Council (*Conseil de Salut du Peuple*—CSP). On August 4, 1983, Ouédraogo was in turn overthrown in a brief rebellion led by Capt. Thomas SANKARA, who had been named prime minister in January, only to be arrested, along with other allegedly pro-Libyan members of the CSP, in late May. Immediately after the August coup, Sankara announced the formation of a National Revolutionary Council (*Conseil National de la Révolution*—CNR) with himself as chair. A year later, following two failed counter-coup attempts, the name of the country was changed to Burkina Faso, a vernacular blend meaning "democratic and republican land of upright men."

In the wake of a state visit by Libya's Col. Muammar al-Qadhafi in December 1985, Commander Sankara declared that Burkina Faso had "gone beyond the era of republics." He therefore proclaimed the establishment of a Libyan-style "Jamahiriya" system aimed at linking national government policy to the wishes of the population as expressed through local people's committees.

Sankara was killed in a coup led by his second-in-command, Capt. Blaise COMPAORÉ, on October 15, 1987. Following the execution of a number of former government officials, Compaoré and his "brothers-in-arms," Maj. Jean-Baptiste LINGANI and Capt. Henri ZONGO, charged that Sankara had been a "madman" who had planned to consolidate power under a one-party system. Faced with substantial domestic hostility, Compaoré pledged to continue the "people's revolution," naming himself head of a Popular Front (*Front Populaire*—FP) administration. In March 1988 Compaoré announced a major government reorganization (see Constitution and government, below), and, vowing to carry on the "rectification program" begun with the October coup, he appealed to elements that Sankara had labeled "entrenched interest groups"—labor unions, tribal chieftaincies, conservative civilians, and the military elite. However, Compaoré's efforts, hailed by some as welcome relief from Sankara's chaotic governing style, lacked his predecessor's wide popular appeal.

In September 1989 Lingani and Zongo, who had been named first and second deputy chairs, respectively, of the FP three months earlier, were arrested and summarily executed on charges of "betraying" the regime by attempting to blow up the plane on which Compaoré was returning from a state visit to the Far East. Three months later, another alleged coup attempt was reportedly foiled by the president's personal guard, with the government subsequently denying press reports that several persons had been executed for involvement in the plot.

The first FP congress, held in early 1990, included representatives of a variety of unions and political groups and drafted a democratic constitution. On June 11 Compaoré dissolved the government and announced the opening of a 24-party consultative assembly to discuss implementation of the new basic law. The following day, however, 13 opposition parties walked out of the assembly when the government rejected their demands that the body be granted sovereign status and be expanded to include trade unionists, traditional leaders, and human rights organizations. Consequently, on June 16 Compaoré named a 34-member transitional government consisting of 28 ministers and 6 secretaries of state, 21 of whom were members of the FP's core formation, the Organization for People's Democracy–Labor Movement (*Organisation pour la Démocratie Populaire—Mouvement Travailliste*—ODP-MT). However, three opposition members withdrew prior to the first cabinet meeting, and they were followed on August 17 by three more, including Herman YAMÉOGO (son of Upper Volta's first president), who had been assigned the agriculture portfolio only three weeks earlier.

In September 1990 Compaoré, who had resigned from the military as required by the new constitution, announced his presidential candidacy. Thereafter, in the run-up to the presidential balloting, clashes intensified between the FP and opposition forces. On September 25 much of the opposition, loosely allied in a Coalition of Democratic Forces (*Coalition des Forces Démocratiques*—CFD), threatened to boycott elections if a national conference was not held. Compaoré responded by offering to hold a referendum on Burkina's transitional institutions. However, at the urging of government supporters, the proposal was quickly withdrawn. Thus, all four opposition presidential nominees boycotted the December 1 balloting, in which Compaoré, running unopposed, won a renewed seven-year mandate. Subsequently, the proposed new constitution was approved by an assembly of 2,000 provincial delegates on December 15 and adopted by popular referendum on June 2, 1991.

Prospects for a representative legislature were dampened when only a quarter of the known parties indicated a willingness to participate in the upcoming legislative poll. At the core of the complaint of the other parties was the government's refusal to convene a national conference endowed with plenary powers to oversee the transition to a wholly democratic system. In mid-December 1991 opposition leaders rejected an overture by President Compaoré to participate in a less authoritative National Reconciliation Forum, and the assemblage that was ultimately convened on February 11, 1992, was suspended nine days later because of a disagreement over live radio coverage of its deliberations. Therefore, only 27 of 62 registered parties participated in the balloting that was eventually conducted on May 24, the ruling ODP-MT winning an overwhelming majority of seats.

On June 15, 1992, Compaoré dissolved the transitional government, and the following day he named economist Youssouf OUÉDRAOGO as prime minister. The cabinet named by Ouédraogo on June 20 included representatives from seven parties, although 13 of the 22 portfolios were awarded to the ODP-MT.

Prime Minister Ouédraogo resigned on March 17, 1994, after the mid-January devaluation of the CFA franc and subsequent collapse of a wage agreement with the trade unions. Three days later President Compaoré appointed Roch Marc Christian KABORÉ, theretofore minister of state in charge of relations with institutions, as Ouédraogo's successor.

On February 6, 1996, Prime Minister Kaboré resigned to assume the vice presidency of the Congress of Democracy and Progress (*Congrès pour la Démocratie et le Progrès*—CDP), a newly formed government grouping created by the ODP-MT and a number of other groups. Kaboré, who was also named special advisor to the president, was replaced as prime minister by Kadré Désiré OUÉDRAOGO, theretofore deputy governor of the Central Bank of West African States.

In January 1997 the assembly approved constitutional amendments that abolished provisions limiting the number of presidential terms (previously two). The opposition strongly protested the change, arguing it was designed to insure Compaoré the presidency for as long as he desired.

In legislative balloting on May 11, 1997, the dominance of the pro-Compaoré groupings was underlined by the CDP's capture of 97 of 111 seats, a majority that swelled to 101 in June following elections in four constituencies where earlier results had been invalidated. On June 11 the president reappointed Ouédraogo prime minister and named a cabinet that was largely unchanged.

In April 1998 the Compaoré government announced the establishment of an independent electoral commission and charged it with organizing the presidential polling scheduled for late 1998. The government asserted that the creation of the commission was a sign of a willingness to install transparent electoral procedures. However, that assessment was rejected by many of the leading opposition groups, which, under the banner of the February 14 Group (*Groupe du 14 Février*—G14), subsequently vowed to boycott the balloting unless further reforms were implemented. In September President Compaoré met with opposition leaders in an effort to break the impasse. That initiative failed, and consequently, in presidential polling on November 15, the incumbent easily secured a second term, overwhelming several candidates from minor parties.

Violent antigovernment protests broke out throughout the country in mid-December 1998 following the discovery of the bodies of Norbert ZONGO (a prominent independent journalist) and two colleagues in a burned vehicle outside of Ouagadougou. Zongo, a vocal critic of the administration, had reportedly been investigating the role the president's brother, François COMPAORÉ, had allegedly played in the death of one of Zongo's assistants. Subsequently, the president appointed an independent judicial commission to investigate the journalists' deaths; nevertheless, demonstrations continued through the first part of 1999.

In May 1999 the judicial commission issued a report that implicated the Presidential Guard in the Zongo killings. Antigovernment unrest subsequently intensified, and the leaders of a number of opposition groups were detained. The CDP dismissed the commission's findings as reflecting "partisan" concerns; nevertheless, President Compaoré created a 16-member Council of Elders on May 21 and asked its members (including three former heads of government) to help create an environment for "reconciliation and social peace." In August the council called for the establishment of a national unity government. Two months later, Prime Minister Ouédraogo reshuffled the cabinet, bringing into its ranks members of two theretofore opposition groups. However, members of the so-called radical opposition refused to participate, dismissing the government's entreaties as disingenuous and asserting that the political crisis would continue until those responsible for political killings were brought to justice.

In November 1999 Compaoré established two new bodies, the Consultative Commission on Political Reforms and the National Reconciliation Commission, which he charged with drafting "concrete proposals" for resolving the continuing imbroglio. However, opposition members refused to assume the seats set aside for them in the Consultative Commission, complaining that the president had reneged on a pledge to make the commission's findings binding.

Antigovernment demonstrations continued through the end of 1999, and in the first days of 2000 the opposition criticized the administration's call for early legislative elections and condemned the "culture of impunity" engendered by the president. The government subsequently announced plans for municipal elections to be held in late July, but the balloting was later delayed in view of opposition complaints about voter registration and electoral procedures.

In August 2000 three soldiers from the Presidential Guard were given prison sentences for having tortured one of Zongo's assistants to death in 1998. Subsequently, in October, the university in Ouagadougou was shut down by the government in response to several months of protests by students, teachers, and unions. After the government agreed to most of the protesters' demands, the university was reopened in December.

The municipal elections of September 2000 underscored the division between the moderate and radical opposition parties, as some of the latter refused to participate. On November 6, 2000, Prime Minister Ouédraogo resigned, and on November 7 the president appointed one of the ministers from the CDP, Ernest Paramanga YONLI, as the new prime minister. The CDP subsequently signed a "Protocol of Agreement" with a number of parties that consequently accepted posts in the new cabinet formed on November 12, their inclusion being seen by some analysts as evidence of a new atmosphere of compromise and easing of tensions, as well as the split structure of the opposition.

In February 2001, in a further development on the prosecution of the political killings, a warrant officer was charged with the murder of Zongo. Implying that the investigations of the political killings had produced tangible results, the government organized a "National Day of Forgiveness" in March with the hopes of reconciling with the more radical opposition parties. However, the Party for Democracy and Progress (*Parti pour la Démocratie et le Progrès*—PDP), the Social Forces Front (*Front des Forces Sociales*—FFS), and several other parties refused to take part in the event. Charges in the Zongo case were subsequently dismissed.

Facing increased domestic and international criticism, the government authorized several significant electoral reforms prior to the 2002 assembly balloting, including a revision of the proportional voting system that had previously favored the CDP (it had won 69 percent of the vote in the 1997 balloting but had been awarded 97 of 111 seats). The measures appeared to produce the desired effect, as the CDP majority fell to 57 seats in the May 5 elections. The leading opposition parties were the Alliance for Democracy and Federation/African Democratic Rally (*Alliance pour la Démocratie et la Fédération/Rassemblement Démocratique Africaine*—ADF/RDA) with 17 seats and the PDP/Socialist Party (PDP/*Parti Socialiste*—PDP/PS) with 10 seats. However, unlike the November 2000 cabinet, the new cabinet named by Prime Minister Yonli on June 11 did not include members of the opposition.

In early 2005 President Compaoré announced he would be a candidate for reelection despite the two-term limit implemented in 2000. (Compaoré's position was that the term limits could not be applied retroactively, meaning that, in theory, he was eligible for two more terms.) Not surprisingly, opposition leaders (already angered by the May 2004 reversal of election rules that had favored anti-CDP forces in the 2002 assembly poll) demanded that the Constitutional Court reject Compaoré's candidacy. However, the court quickly dismissed their suit, thereby permitting Compaoré to seek another term. He was reelected with 80 percent of the vote against 12 other candidates in balloting on November 13, 2005. He subsequently reappointed Prime Minister Yonli to head a new government which, as formed on January 7, 2006, was again dominated by the CDP, although several small parties that had supported Compaoré in the presidential poll were also included.

Opposition parties had hoped that the April 2006 municipal balloting would offer them a better chance for success than previous elections, but the CDP continued its dominance, securing about two-thirds of the seats. In balloting for the Assembly of People's Deputies on May 6, 2007, the CDP won 73 of 111 seats, followed by the ADF/RDA with 14 seats and some 11 small parties with 1–5 seats each. The international community appeared to welcome the results (described by observers from the African Union as generally "free and transparent") as offering the best hope for continued "stability" and continued market-oriented economic growth. Prime Minister Yonli resigned on June 3, and the following day President Compaoré named Tertius ZONGO, the country's ambassador to the United States, to the post. The cabinet was reshuffled on June 10; it remained dominated by the CDP.

Compaoré easily secured a fourth term by winning 80.2 percent of the vote against six challengers in the first round of presidential balloting on November 21, 2010. He subsequently reappointed Prime Minister Zongo in a cabinet reshuffle on January 16, 2011. However, in the wake of significant public unrest (see Current issues, below), Compaoré on April 15 replaced Zongo with Luc Adolphe TIAO (theretofore the ambassador to France), who announced a new cabinet on April 22. Following the December 2, 2012, assembly balloting, which was again dominated by the CDP, Tiao was reappointed to head a new government comprising the CDP and three small parties.

Constitution and government. After the 1977 constitution was suspended in November 1980, a period of uncertain military rule followed, yielding, in August 1985, a revised government structure intended to promote "the Burkinabè identity." (See the 2007 *Handbook* for details.)

A new government was formed on October 31, 1987, two weeks after Thomas Sankara's overthrow. However, it was not until March 1988 that Captain Compaoré's Popular Front (FP) announced that Sankara's Revolutionary Defense Committees (which had assumed power at the local level) had been abolished and replaced by Revolutionary Committees. Described as "mass socio-professional organizations," the new committees were mandated to meet every two years to modify FP programs, define the country's political orientation, and oversee admission into the FP. Although mimicking Sankara's call for extensive citizen involvement in government, the new regime ordered the banning of all political parties that did not align with the FP. Subsequently, the ban was relaxed for all but the most virulent opposition formations, and in August 1990 a commission was charged with drafting a new constitution. The multiparty document approved by popular referendum on June 2, 1991, provided for a separation of powers, a president and legislature elected by universal suffrage for seven- and five-year terms, respectively, and the establishment of an independent judiciary. The president has the right to name a prime minister, who must, however, be acceptable to the legislature. In April 2000 the Assembly of People's Deputies passed a law reducing the president's term from seven to five years, with a maximum of two terms. The new law did not affect the length of President Compaoré's current term. It also did not address the issue of "retroactivity," which led supporters of Compaoré to declare that he was eligible to run for a third term in 2005 and a fourth term in 2010. The country's Supreme Court is split into four separate courts, namely, the Constitutional Court, the Court of Appeals, the Council of State, and the government audit office.

Administratively, the country is divided into 13 regions and 45 provinces, which are subdivided into departments, arrondissements, and villages. Local elections were held in April 2006 for 49 "urban communes" and 302 "rural communes."

In December 2011 a government-sponsored national conference (boycotted by a number of opposition parties) endorsed constitutional revisions proposed by a Consultative Council on Political Reforms (*Conseil Consultatil sur les Réformes Politiques*—CCRP), which had been established the previous spring in the wake of major domestic unrest. The proposed reforms included the creation of a consultative Senate, the establishment of the post of vice president, the codification of gender equality, and an increase in the membership in the assembly as part of an overall effort to shift some presidential authority to the legislature. In June 2012 the assembly approved amendments granting immunity from prosecution for all presidents since independence and requiring that presidential candidates be 35–75 years of age.

A Press Code adopted in 1993 ostensibly provided for a "free and transparent press" following decades of near-total state domination of the media. However, although a number of independent media outlets have since been established and the press is described as "generally free," controversial provisions in the Press Code (providing penalties for journalists deemed guilty of publishing "false information") have been used by the government to close radio stations and arrest journalists. Consequently, "self-censorship" is considered to be widespread. International and domestic observers also strongly criticized the government's handling of the investigation into the death of journalist Norbert Zongo in 1998 (see Political background, above), which remained unsolved as of mid-2013.

Foreign relations. Upper Volta had consistently adhered to a moderately pro-French and pro-Western foreign policy, while stressing the importance of good relations with neighboring countries. However, after the 1983 coup, relations between Burkina Faso and France cooled, a result primarily of France's unease over Commander Sankara's vigorous attempts to rid the country of all vestiges of its colonial past (made manifest by the 1984 change in country name, the adoption of radical policies modeled on those of Ghana and Libya, and the widely publicized arrests of allegedly pro-French former government officials and trade unionists accused of plotting against the Sankara regime). Subsequent relations with francophone neighbors remained less than uniformly cordial, in part because of Sankara's blunt style in attacking perceived government corruption throughout the region and his strong ideological opinions.

In December 1985 a 20-year-long controversy involving the so-called Agacher Strip at Burkina's northern border with Mali yielded four days of fighting with approximately 300 dead on both sides. However, a ruling from the International Court of Justice (IGJ) on December 22, 1986, which awarded the two countries roughly equal portions of the disputed territory, largely terminated the unrest. Relations with another neighbor, Togo, were strained in 1987 over allegations of Burkinabè complicity (heatedly denied) in a September 1986 coup attempt against Togolese President Eyadema.

The October 1987 coup in Burkina Faso was manifestly welcomed by the region's most respected elder statesman, President Houphouët-Boigny of Côte d'Ivoire, with whom Captain Compaoré had long enjoyed close personal relations. Subsequently, in an attempt to gain recognition of his government and to repair strained ties with "Western-leaning" neighbors, Compaoré traveled to 13 countries during his first year in power.

The long-standing border dispute with Mali was formally resolved in early 1988, followed by a resumption in relations with Togo and a border agreement with Ghana. Nevertheless, Compaoré also continued to maintain communist ties: in September 1988 he signed cooperation agreements with North Korea, and in September 1989 he was the first head of state to visit China following the crushing of that country's prodemocracy movement.

In September 1992 Malian president Alpha Oumar Konaré met in Ouagadougou with Compaoré to reactivate bilateral cooperation and to address Burkina Faso's policy of allowing Tuaregs from Mali and Niger refuge in northern Burkina Faso. In November the United States recalled its ambassador to Burkina Faso, accusing the Compaoré government of continuing to supply arms to Charles Taylor's Liberian rebel forces despite Washington's earlier warnings about Ouagadougou's "destabilizing" involvement with Taylor.

In February 1994 Ouagadougou reestablished relations with Taiwan after a 20-year lapse, thus prompting China's suspension of relations with Burkina Faso one week later. Meanwhile, regional relations continued to be dominated by the Tuareg dilemma, and in October Ouagadougou was the host site for successful negotiations between the Niger government and its Tuareg rebels. On a far less positive note, the refugee crisis along Burkina Faso's border with Mali was exacerbated by intensified fighting between Tuaregs and Malian government forces. In January 1995 the United Nations reported that the number of Malian Tuareg refugees in Burkina Faso had risen to 50,000, up from 9,000 in 1993. In October Ouagadougou announced plans to send troops to join ECOMOG forces in Liberia, saying it had changed its policy because the peacemaking effort there appeared "more credible than previous ones."

Regional cooperation efforts topped Burkina's foreign policy agenda in 1996, Ouagadougou reaching agreement with Niger in March on the repatriation of that country's refugees. In March 1997 Burkina Faso was the site for joint military exercises with Benin, Togo, and France, while in 1998 President Compaoré hosted summits for representatives of combatants in the Eritrean and Ethiopian border conflict as well as participants in the civil war in the Democratic Republic of the Congo. Burkinabè troops also participated in the UN-sponsored peacekeeping mission in the Central African Republic from 1997 to 2000.

In November 1999 a violent land dispute erupted in Côte d'Ivoire between Ivorians and Burkinabè, and by the end of the year approximately 12,000 of the Burkinabè had crossed back into Burkina Faso in search of refuge. Following a coup attempt in Côte d'Ivoire in January 2001, the two countries' relations were strained even further, as some Ivorian authorities unofficially implied that Burkina Faso may have been behind the overthrow effort. The Ivorian government subsequently began forced deportations of Burkinabè who lived or were working in Côte d'Ivoire. Estimates were that 20,000 Burkinabè expatriates were expelled by 2002. Throughout 2002 and into 2003, the Ivorian government continued to blame its neighbor for promoting unrest, and there was another massive wave of Burkinabè refugees. The Compaoré government officially closed the border in September 2002 but reopened it a year later. By 2003 some 350,000

Burkinabè had fled Côte d'Ivoire. In 2003 Compaoré hosted a summit with his Ivorian counterpart and representatives of the main rebel groups in Côte d'Ivoire in an effort to improve bilateral relations. The government also banned several Ivorian rebel groups from using Burkina Faso to undertake political activities in Côte d'Ivoire. However, in October it was reported that the alleged leader of a coup plot in Burkina Faso had been in contact with officials in Togo and Côte d'Ivoire, further straining relations between the Compaoré administration and those two nations. In 2004 Burkinabè opposition leaders called for an investigation into the possibility that Compaoré had provided support for antigovernment activity in Côte d'Ivoire, Mauritania, and other places.

One topic of discussion during the 2005 presidential campaign in Burkina Faso was the possibility that President Compaoré might be investigated by the UN court preparing to prosecute former Liberian president Charles Taylor for his alleged war crimes in Sierra Leone. (Critics alleged that Compaoré may have assisted Taylor in arming and training rebels in Sierra Leone.) However, Compaoré's regional reputation improved significantly when he played a prominent role in facilitating the negotiated settlements in Togo in 2006 and Côte d'Ivoire in March 2007. At the same time, however, tension was reported along Burkina Faso's border with Niger, both countries agreeing in mid-2010 to ask the ICJ to demarcate the most contentious part of the border as part of a broader effort to resolve a dispute that had "simmered" since 2000. (The ICJ formally demarcated the border in April 2013, both sides appearing satisfied with the result.) Additionally, a border dispute with Benin appeared headed toward a peaceful compromise (see Foreign affairs in the entry on Benin for details).

Supporters of Alassane Ouattara reportedly used bases in Burkina Faso to launch their campaign against the forces aligned with Laurent Gbagbo in the wake of the disputed presidential election in Côte d'Ivoire in late 2010.

Current issues. President Compaoré, only 59 years old and having been in control for 23 years, won a landslide reelection in 2010, partly because of the continued weakness of the opposition, which focused on allegations of continued widespread corruption and human rights abuses.

The death of a college student while under police detention in February 2011 sparked a series of protest demonstrations that were joined by members of the general public distressed by rising fuel and food prices (exacerbated by unsettled conditions in neighboring Côte d'Ivoire). Presenting an even more serious threat to the government, soldiers rioted in the capital and other towns in April out of anger over the administration's failure to deliver the promised housing and other allowances. Compaoré weathered the storm by, among other things, dismissing Prime Minister Zongo, whose home had been burned in the unrest, and providing bonuses for the troops. The government also established the CCRP (see Constitution and government, above) to consider overhaul of the constitution, while at midyear Compaoré announced that hundreds of the mutinous soldiers had been dismissed and that many could face criminal charges. In addition, the president replaced or reassigned all 13 regional governors and imposed a temporary freeze on the prices of basic foods. Meanwhile, new prime minister Tiao called upon the country to focus upon alleviating widespread social problems rather than pressuring Compaoré to leave office. In that vein, the CCRP's recommendations at midyear did not address the issue of presidential term limits, although the opposition parties that boycotted the council and the December national conference continued to argue that the proposed constitutional reforms would eventually authorize a "life presidency" for Compaoré.

Conflicts in Mali and Guinea-Bissau dominated Burkina Faso's regional concerns in the first half of 2012, as Compaoré expanded his reputation as a valuable mediator in an increasingly volatile area. More than 60,000 refugees from Mali had relocated by May 2013 to Burkina Faso, which received emergency international aid to address humanitarian issues at the camps. Meanwhile, Burkina Faso's support was considered vital in the success of the French-led military operation in Mali. Compaoré's international stature also continued to be bolstered by Burkino Faso's participation in U.S.-based antiterrorism efforts. Domestically, Compaoré's critics voiced the suspicion that he would still pursue options to permit him (or at least his clan) to retain the presidency past 2015, the CDP having extended its dominance in the December 2012 assembly elections. Among other things, demonstrators in June 2013 protested the proposed make-up of the new Senate, arguing that the provision for one-third of the members to be appointed by the president would give Compaoré additional prerogative.

POLITICAL PARTIES

Prior to the 1980 coup the governing party was the Voltaic Democratic Union–African Democratic Assembly (*Union Démocratique Voltaïque—Rassemblement Démocratique Africain*—UDV-RDA), an outgrowth of the Ivorian RDA. In opposition were the National Union for the Defense of Democracy (*Union Nationale pour la Défense de la Démocratie*), organized by Herman Yaméogo and the Voltaic Progressive Front, a socialist grouping led by Joseph KI-ZERBO that contained a number of UDV-RDA dissidents. Most such individuals subsequently left the country, Ki-Zerbo having been accused of planning a coup against Thomas Sankara in May 1984.

Political party activity was suspended in the immediate wake of Sankara's overthrow in 1987, although several groups maintained a highly visible identity, most importantly the Patriotic League for Development (*Ligue Patriotique pour le Développement*—Lipad), a Marxist organization that had been founded in 1973. In March 1988 Captain Compaoré declared that while his recently created Popular Front should not be construed as a political party, separate parties would be permitted to operate within it. A year later an apparent attempt was made to create a single government party (ODP-MT, below). In a return pendulum swing, the Popular Front was described on the eve of its first congress in March 1990 as consisting of "four national unions and seven political groups," although details regarding some of the components were sparse. In addition, it was reported that a number of nonlegalized (but otherwise unidentified) opposition groups had been invited to send representatives to the congress.

The June 1991 constitution provided for multiparty activity, and 44 parties had been recognized by November. References to the Popular Front were dropped following the formation of the CDP (below) in February 1996. Subsequently, the opposition mantle appeared to have been assumed in 1998 by the February 14 Group (*Groupe du 14 Février*—G14), a coalition that included the ADF/RDA, PAI, PDP, and FFS. (For additional information on the G14 and several other opposition coalitions in 1998–2005, see the 2007 *Handbook.*) The government reported that 74 parties participated in the December 2012 assembly elections.

Government Parties:

Congress of Democracy and Progress (*Congrès pour la Démocratie et le Progrès*—CDP). The CDP was formed in 1996 as a result of an agreement between the ODP-MT and a number of other parties, including the CNPP-PSD, the Rally of Independent Social Democrats (*Rassemblement des Social-Démocrates Indépendants*—RSI), the Group of Revolutionary Democrats (*Groupement des Démocrates Révolutionnaires*—GDR), and the Movement for Socialist Democracy (*Mouvement pour la Démocratie Socialiste*—MDS). The Compaoré government's commitment to the new grouping was highlighted by the assignment of ODP-MT Executive Committee Chair Arsène Bongnessan Yé and Prime Minister Roch Marc Christian Kaboré to the CDP's presidency and vice presidency, respectively. (Some news reports described the CDP as a "merger" of the various parties, indicating that they might not retain autonomous identities within the Congress. Following is information on the OPD-MT and the CNPP-PSD as they existed immediately prior to the formation of the CDP. For information on the history of the RSI, GDR, MDS, and a number of other small parties reported to have joined the CDP, see the 2000–2002 *Handbook.*)

At a CDP congress on August 1, 1999, party delegates elected Kaboré to the newly created post of national executive secretary, a position that superseded both the party presidency and secretary generalship. Kaboré's ascendancy to the CDP's top post was described by some observers as evidence of a triumph for party moderates over hard-liners. Kaboré and the moderates appeared to extend their influence even further when he was elected as the new assembly president following the May 2002 legislative balloting, at which the CDP won 57 seats. The CDP improved to 73 seats in the 2007 assembly poll.

In 2008 President Compaoré's brother, François Compaoré, was named head of a new Associative Federation for Peace and Progress with Blaise Compaoré (*Fédération Associative pour la Paix et le Progrès avec Blaise Compaoré*—FEDAP-BC), which was reportedly organized as a fund-raising vehicle for the president and, eventually, his brother, who was considered a strong candidate to become the next president of Burkina Faso. Friction was reported in the CDP in 2009 between the FEDAP-BC and a party faction led by Simon COMPAORÉ (the mayor of Ouagadougou [no relation to the president]) and Salif DIALLO, who was recently dismissed from the cabinet.

Blaise Compaoré was nominated by a CDP convention in August 2010 to seek a fourth presidential term. Marc Kaboré relinquished the CDP leadership at the party congress in March 2012. He was succeeded by Assimi Kouanda (an assistant to President Compaoré), who called for renewed dynamism among CDP followers.

Leaders: Capt. Blaise COMPAORÉ (President of Burkina Faso); Luc Adolphe TIAO (Prime Minister); Assimi KOUANDA (Secretary of the National Executive Secretariat); Kanidoua NABOHO, Alain YODA, Pascaline TAMINI/BIHOUN (Assistant Secretaries of the National Executive Secretariat); François COMPAORÉ; Ollo Anicet POODA (Secretary); Soungalo Apollinaire OUATTARA (President of the National Assembly).

Organization for People's Democracy–Labor Movement (*Organisation pour la Démocratie Populaire—Mouvement Travailliste*—ODP-MT). The leftist ODP-MT was launched on April 15, 1989, as a means of unifying "all political tendencies in the country." Most prominently associated with the new formation were the Union of Burkinabè Communists (*Union des Communistes Burkinabè*—UCB) and a number of dissidents from the former Union of Communist Struggles from which the UCB had earlier split.

During a congress in Ouagadougou in March 1991, the ODP-MT endorsed Blaise Compaoré's candidacy in the forthcoming presidential balloting and formally abandoned Marxism-Leninism in favor of free enterprise and a market economy. Meanwhile, in anticipation of multiparty elections, the ODP-MT moved to position itself as an independent grouping within the Popular Front, thus abandoning efforts to present the image of a nonhierarchical coalition.

In early 1996 the ODP-MT renounced its status as a "revolutionary party of the democratic masses" to become a "social democratic" party, shortly thereafter spearheading the formation of the CDP.

National Convention of Progressive Patriots–Social Democratic Party (*Convention Nationale des Patriotes Progressistes–Parti* Social-*Démocrate*—CNPP-PSD). The CNPP-PSD was expelled from the Popular Front in March 1991 for criticizing ODP-MT policies and calling for a national conference. The party subsequently emerged as the opposition's most powerful force, winning 12 assembly seats as runner-up to the ODP-MT in May 1992.

The CNPP-PSD's decision to join its former Popular Front allies in the formation of the CDP in early 1996 was considered a major political victory for the Compaoré administration.

National Union for Democracy and Development (*Union Nationale pour la Démocratie et le Développement*—UNDD). The UNDD was launched in mid-2003 by Herman Yaméogo, one of the country's leading opposition figures, following a leadership squabble within the ADF/RDA. Among other things, Yaméogo had been accused by other ADF/RDA members of acting "too independently." The UNDD selected Yaméogo as its 2005 presidential candidate, but Yaméogo and the party formally withdrew the candidacy to protest the decision by the Constitutional Court to permit President Compaoré to run for another term. The UNDD called for "civil disobedience" in view of the court's ruling. The UNDD was described in late 2006 as controlling six assembly seats, although it failed to gain representation in the 2007 assembly balloting. The UNDD did not present a presidential candidate in 2010 after Yaméogo opted out. After winning a seat in the December 2012 assembly poll, the UNDD was one of two opposition parties to accept portfolios in the January 2013 cabinet.

Leaders: Herman YAMÉOGO (Chair), Amadou DABO, Adama OUÉDRAOGO, Salif OUÉDRAOGO (Minister of Environment and Sustainable Development), Mathieu N'DO.

Convention of the Democratic Forces of Burkina (*Convention des Forces Démocratiques du Burkina*—CFD-B). The CFD-B was formed as an electoral coalition in advance of the 2007 assembly elections by the **Convention for Democracy and Federation** (*Convention pour la Démocratie et la Fédération*—CDF), led by Amadou Diemdioda Dicko; the **Convention for Democracy and Liberty** (*Convention pour la Démocratie et la Liberté*—CDL), led by Kiello Célestin Dabiré; the **Rally for Independent Forces/Party of the Youth of Burkina** (*Rassemblement des Forces Indépendantes/Parti des Jeunes du Burkina*—RFI/PJB), led by Ali Diaby KASSAMBA; and the Greens of Burkina.

The CDF had been one of the parties that had formed the Coalition of Democratic Forces (*Coalition des Forces Démocratiques*—CFD) prior to the 2002 legislative poll. Other members of the CFD included the UVDB (see Greens of Burkina, below), the **Movement for Tolerance and Progress** (*Mouvement pour la Tolérance et le Progrès*—MTP; see the 2013 *Handbook*), and a number of smaller parties, including the **Refuser's Front/African Democratic Rally** (*Front de Refus/ Rassemblement Démocratique Africain*—FR/RDA), a breakaway faction of the RDA whose leader, Frederic Fernand GUIMA, had finished third in the 1998 presidential balloting. The CFD secured five seats in the 2002 assembly balloting, and it was reported that the primary education and literacy cabinet post was awarded to a CFD member in June.

The CFD-B secured three seats in the May 2007 legislative balloting, some news reports indicating a degree of cooperation between it and the ruling CDP. The CFD-B coalition was credited with winning three seats again in the December 2012 assembly poll, for which the CDL and RFI/PJB also presented their own individual candidates. Dicko was named a minister delegate in the January 2013 cabinet, the CFD-B being routinely described as a member of the "presidential movement."

Leaders: Amadou Diemdioda DICKO (President), Kiello Célestin DABIRÉ (Vice President).

The Other Burkina/Party for Socialism and Reorganization (*L'Autre Burkina/Parti pour le Socialisme et la Refondation*—*L'Autre Burkina*/PSR). A small opposition party devoted to political and institutional reform, *L'Autre Burkina*/PSR failed to secure representation in the December 2012 assembly poll. However, party leader Alain Zoubga, who had served as health minister in 1987–1989, accepted the post of minister of social action and national solidarity in the January 2013 government.

Leader: Alain ZOUBGA.

Other Legislative Parties:

Union for Progress and Change (*Union pour le Progrès et le Changement*—UPC). Recently formed by Zépherin Diabré, a businessman from the energy sector and a former member of the CDP, the opposition UPC made a dramatic entrance onto the political stage by finishing second in the December 2012 assembly balloting with 19 seats. Diabré, considered a possible candidate for president in 2015, alleged that the legislative poll had been marred by fraud. In June 2013 he helped organize protest demonstrations against the government's plans for the proposed Senate.

Leaders: Zépherin DIABRÉ, Louis Armand OUALI.

Alliance for Democracy and Federation/African Democratic Rally (*Alliance pour la Démocratie et la Fédération/Rassemblement Démocratique Africain*—ADF/RDA). The ADF and RDA announced their merger in May 1998. The ADF had been formed in December 1990 by Herman Yaméogo, whose previous party had been expelled from the Popular Front in July 1990, largely because of criticism from intraparty critics of Yaméogo. In February 1991 the ADF called for an immediate amnesty for all political prisoners, the appointment of a transitional government, and "democratization" of the press. By midyear Yaméogo had emerged as the opposition's most prominent government critic. Subsequently, Yaméogo announced his presidential candidacy; however, he and the other opposition candidates eventually withdrew from the December 1 balloting. Somewhat inexplicably, Yaméogo joined the cabinet as a minister of state in February 1992.

The ADF participated in the May 1992 legislative poll, capturing four seats, and in June Yaméogo was redesignated minister of state. In legislative balloting in May 1997 the party captured only two seats, and Yaméogo was not included in the cabinet named in June. A leading component of the February 14 Group, the ADF boycotted the 1998 presidential elections.

Formed in 1946 as an outgrowth of the Ivorian RDA, the RDA was a partner in the ruling UDV-RDA grouping that was unseated by the 1980 coup. The party captured six seats in the May 1992 balloting, and an RDA member, Clement SANOU, was included in the government named in June. Compaoré's appointment of Sanou was greeted with suspicion, however, with *Africa Confidential* suggesting that the president was attempting to create friction within the RDA. The RDA presented candidates in slightly more than half of the polling districts in 1997, retaining only two seats.

The Party of the Convergence of Liberties and Integration (*Parti de la Convergence pour les Libertés et l'Integration*—PCLI) joined the ADF/RDA subsequent to the 1998 merger. The ADF/RDA signed a protocol with the CDP and others and was given cabinet posts in November 2000, although it returned to formal opposition status following the May 2002 legislative poll, in which it finished second to the CDP. Leadership disagreements within the ADF/RDA in 2003 led Yaméoga to quit the party and form the UNDD (below). Subsequently, the ADF/RDA supported President Compaoré in his reelection bid in 2005, and ADF/RDA leader Gilbert Ouédraogo was appointed to the new cabinet in January 2006. The ADF/RDA finished second to the CDP in the April 2006 municipal elections as well as in the May 2007 legislative poll (14 seats), having endorsed Compaoré's economic policies. The ADF/RDA also supported Compaoré's successful 2010 reelection bid. The party improved to 18 seats in the December 2012 assembly poll and was initially expected to remain in a new CDP-led government. However, apparently dismayed at the small number of portfolios it had been offered, the ADF/RDA declined to join the cabinet formed in January 2013.

Leaders: Gilbert Noël OUÉDRAOGO (President), Gérard Kango OUÉDRAOGO (Honorary President), Dabo HAMADOU (Vice President).

Union for the Republic (*Union pour le République*—UPR). The recently formed UPR finished third in the April 2006 municipal balloting, having campaigned on a platform that pledged to address the needs of rural areas. As of the end of 2006 it was reported that six members of the assembly had joined the UPR, which subsequently finished third in the May 2007 assembly balloting with five seats.

Leader: Toussaint Abel COULIBALY.

Union for Rebirth/Sankarist Party (*Union pour la Renaissance/Parti Sankariste*—UNIR/PS). The UNIR/PS was launched in March 2009 by the Union for Rebirth/Sankarist Movement (*Union pour la Renaissance/Mouvement Sankariste*—UNIR/MS) in conjunction with the Convention of Sankarist Parties (*Convention des Partis Sankaristes*—CPS), and some members of the FFS (below).

Formed in 2000 under the leadership of Bénéwendé Sankara, the UNIR/MS won three seats in the 2002 assembly elections. In addition, Sankara, a lawyer and prominent human rights activist, finished second in the 2005 presidential poll with 4.95 percent of the vote. He subsequently chaired the assembly's opposition faction, which claimed 11 members as of early 2009.

Also referenced as the Sankarist Panafrican Convention (*Convention Panafricaine Sankariste*), the CPS was formed in mid-1999 by the Burkinabè Socialist Bloc (*Bloc Socialiste Burkinabè*—BSB), the United Social Democracy Party (*Parti de la Démocratie Sociale Unifié*—PDSU), a breakaway faction of the FFS, and other small groups. The CPS signed a protocol with the CDP and others and was given cabinet posts in November 2000, a decision that reportedly caused internal CPS tensions. (For additional information on the anti-Compaoré BSB, see the 2013 *Handbook*.)

Bénéwendé Sankara was named president of the UNIR/PS national executive secretariat, while the FFS's Nestor BASSIERE was named vice president. Sankara was also chosen by a party congress as the UNIR/PS candidate for the 2010 presidential poll. He subsequently announced the formation of a new bloc called the Consultation of the Parties of the Opposition (*Concertation des Parties de l'Opposition*—(CPO), which initially reportedly included most of the members of the G14, all of the opposition parliamentarians, and the MPS/PF. The UNDD, RDEB, and other small parties were also invited to join the CPO in backing a single presidential candidate. However, CPO adhesion proved elusive, and some of its prospective members supported candidates other than Sankara, who finished third in the balloting with 6.3 percent of the vote as the UNIR/PS nominee. Sankara subsequently opened an office under the rubric of Leader of the Ranks of the Political Opposition (*Chef de File de l'Opposition Politique*—CFOP), claiming the support of more than 40 parties.

In May 2011 Sankara called upon President Compaoré to resign, describing him as an "obstacle to reform." Sankara and CFOP supporters subsequently refused to participate in the CCRP in view of the perceived "lack of transparency" in that government-sponsored constitutional review.

In 2012 dissident members of the UNIR/PS announced the formation of the **Union for Democratic Revival/Sankarist Movement** (*Union pour la Renaissance Démocratique/Mouvement Sankariste*—URD/MS) under the leadership of Alphose Marie OUÉDRAOGO.

Leader: Bénéwendé Stanislas SANKARA (2005 and 2010 presidential candidate).

Party for Democracy and Socialism/Builders Party (*Parti pour la Démocratie et le Socialism/Parti des Bâtisseurs*—PDS/*Metba*). The formation of the leftist PDS/*Metba* was announced in March 2012 by the Party for Democracy and Socialism (*Parti pour la Démocratie et la Socialisme*—PDS); the Builders of Faso (*Faso Metba*), led by (then) legislator Étienne TRAORÉ; other small parties and civic groups; and the faction of the PAI (below) loyal to Philippe Ouédraogo. After gaining representation in the 2002 assembly balloting, the PDS had presented Ouédraogo as its 2005 presidential candidate. He finished fourth with 2.28 percent of the vote.

The PDS nominated Hama Arba DIALLO, a former UN official and diplomat, as its 2010 presidential candidate. Enjoying the support of the PAI, FFS, UDPS, and other small parties, Diallo, the mayor of the northern town of Dori, finished second in the poll with 8.2 percent of the vote. The PDS won two seats in the 2007 assembly poll, the PDS/Metba matching that number in 2012.

Rally for the Development of Burkina (*Rassemblement pour le Développement du Burkina*—RDB). The recently launched RDB finished fourth in the April 2006 municipal balloting and won two seats in the 2007 assembly poll and one in the 2012 balloting.

Leader: Saidou Célestin COMPAORÉ.

Other parties winning single seats in the December 2012 legislative included the **National Convention for the Progress of Burkina** (*Convention Nationale pour le Progrès du Burkina*—CNPD), led by Kouroubondou René LOMPO; **The Other Faso** (*Le Faso Autrement*), led by Ablassé OUÉDRAOGO; the **Organization for Democracy and Work** (*Organization pour la Démocratie et le Travail*—ODT); and the **Rally for Democracy and Socialism** (*Rassemblement pour la Démocratic et le Socialism*—RDS), led by Salfo Théodore OUÉDRAOGO.

Other Parties Contesting the 2012 Legislative Elections:

Party for Democracy and Progress/Socialist Party (*Parti pour la Démocratie et le Progrès/Parti Socialiste*—PDP/PS). The PDP was launched in May 1993 by Joseph KI-ZERBO in the aftermath of a struggle that erupted when a parliamentary coalition between Ki-Zerbo's Union of Independent Social Democrats (*Union des Sociaux-Démocrates Indépendants*—USDI) and the CNPP-PSD splintered following the retirement of the latter's leader. Ki-Zerbo had previously been linked to the Voltaic Progressive Front (*Front Progressiste Voltaïque*—FPV), which he and a group of UDV-RDA dissidents had formed prior to the 1980 coup. The socialist-oriented FPV was proscribed until early 1991, when its longtime leader was given amnesty; he returned from eight years in exile the following September.

The PDP, operating under the umbrella of the February 14 Group, boycotted the 1998 presidential elections. In May 2001 the PDP merged with the Burkinabè Socialist Party (*Parti Socialiste Burkinabè*—PSB), and the present name was adopted. Led by François Ouédraogo, the PSB was a breakaway formation from the PAI.

Under the leadership of Ki-Zerbo, described as one of the fiercest critics of the Compaoré administration, the PDP/PS boycotted the 2000 municipal elections. However, the party presented candidates in the May 2002 assembly balloting, increasing its representation from six to ten. Ali Lankoandé finished sixth (with 1.74 percent of the vote) as the candidate of the PDP/PS in the 2005 presidential election. Ki-Zerbo died in December 2006. The PDP/PS won two seats in the 2007 assembly poll. Its 2010 presidential candidate, the hydrogeologist François O. Kaboré, finished last with 0.64 percent of the vote.

Decrying a perceived "total lack of democracy" in the country, Kaboré in 2012 announced that the PDP/PS would attempt to align with other opposition parties for the upcoming legislative poll. However, that initiative proved fruitless.

Leaders: François O. KABORÉ (Chair and 2010 presidential candidate), Sébastien ZABSONRE (General Secretary), François OUÉDRAOGO, Ali LANKOANDÉ (2005 presidential candidate).

Party for National Renaissance (*Parti pour la Renaissance Nationale*—PAREN). This party was launched in 1989 by Laurent Bado, who claimed that PAREN was neither socialist nor capitalist, but rather "Africanist." In August 2003 PAREN and the MPS/PF (below) announced they had formed an electoral coalition called the United Opposition of Burkina (*Opposition Burkinabè Uni*—OBU). However, Bado was described as the PAREN candidate when he finished third in the 2005 presidential poll with 2.61 percent of the vote. The party won a single seat in the 2007 assembly poll. PAREN did not present a presidential candidate in 2010, calling the balloting "an electoral charade." It competed unsuccessfully in the 2013 assembly balloting.

Leaders: Laurent BADO (2005 presidential candidate), Tahirou BARRY (President).

Movement for the People and Socialism/Federal Party (*Movement pour le Peuple et le Socialisme/Parti Féderal*—MPS/PF). The MPS/PF was formed in 2002 by disaffected members of the PDP/PS under the leadership of Parqui Emile Paré. The party presented candidates in the 2003 assembly poll in cooperation with PAREN (above), while Paré was credited with 0.87 percent of the vote in 2005 as the presidential candidate of a **Socialist Alliance** (*Alliance Socialiste*—AS), which comprised the MPS-PF and the PSU. Paré secured 0.85 percent of the presidential vote in 2010 as the MPS-PF candidate.

Leader: Parqui Emile PARÉ.

Rally of the Ecologists of Burkina (*Rassemblement des Ecologistes du Burkina*—RDEB). A moderate green party, the RDEB was formed by former UVDB leader Ram Ouédraogo in October 2002. Ouédraogo was subsequently referenced as the national coordinator of the CFD. He finished fifth in the 2005 presidential balloting with 2.03 percent of the vote. The RDEB presented candidates on its own (unsuccessfully) for the 2007 and 2012 legislative polls.

Leader: Ram OUÉDRAOGO (President and 2005 presidential candidate).

Social Forces Front (Front des Forces Sociales—FFS). A purported "Sankarist" group, the FFS was launched in October 1996. In 1998 it gained national attention for its vocal role in the February 14 Group. The government accused FFS leader Norbert Tiendrébéogo of being involved in a coup plot in 2003, but Tiendrébéogo was subsequently exonerated. Tiendrébéogo finished seventh in the 2005 presidential poll with 1.6 percent of the vote. Although Tiendrébéogo initially indicated interest in running again in 2010, the FFS ultimately endorsed Hama Arba Diallo of the PDS for that poll. In 2011 Tiendrébéogo blamed the "deep crisis" in the country on President Compaoré.

Leaders: Norbert Michel TIENDRÉBÉOGO (President and 2005 presidential candidate), Drissa KOMO (Vice President).

Other parties that competed unsuccessfully in the 2007 and 2012 assembly elections included the **Patriotic Front for Change** (*Front Patriogique pour le Changement*—FPC), a Sankarist party led by Tahirou Ibrahim ZON; the **Alliance for Democracy of Faso** (*Alliance pour la Démocratie du Faso*—ADEFA), led by Boureima OUÉDRAOGO; the **Union of Patriots for Development** (*Union des Patriotes pour le Développement*—UPD), which had been credited with holding a legislative seat as of late 2006; and the **Independent Party of Burkina** (*Parti Indépendant du Burkina*—PID), led by Maxime KABORÉ.

Other Parties and Groups:

Union of Sankarist Parties (*Union des Parties Sankaristes*—UPS). The UPS was formed prior to the 2007 assembly poll by the CPS (see UNIR/PS, above), FFS (above), and the **Convergence of Hope** (*Convergence de l'Espoir*), led by Jean Hubert BAZIÉ; the **Movement of Diverse Sankarists** (*Mouvement des Sankaristes Divers*—MSD), led by Joseph OUÉDRAOGO; and the **Party for National Unity and Development** (*Parti pour l'Unité Nationale et le Développement*—PUND). Ouédraoga, described as the president of the UPS, opposed participation in the formation of the UNIR/PS in 2009 by the CPS and members of the FFS. The UPS and FFS rumps subsequently indicated they would continue to operate outside the UNIR/PS despite having lost many members to the new party. Ouédraogo was subsequently referenced as president of the **UPS/ Progressive Movement** (UPS/*Movement Progressiste*—UPS/MP), whose candidate, former army commander Boukary KABORÉ, finished fourth in the 2010 presidential poll with 2.3 percent of the vote. Kaboré was endorsed by the PUND and other groups, but some reports indicated that Ouédraogo and other UPS/MP "militants" withdrew their support for Kaboré prior to the poll, while it was also unclear where the other fractionalized Sankarist groups stood in regard to the election. The UPS/MP and PUND each presented candidates in the 2012 assembly balloting.

African Party for Independence (*Parti Africain pour l'Indépendance*—PAI). Prior to Sankara's overthrow, the PAI's leader, Soumane Touré, was reportedly targeted for execution by the UCB. Despite Touré's reported allegiance to the Compaoré regime, the PAI joined the opposition February 14 Group in early 1998. However, in August the PAI withdrew from the coalition, a schism having emerged in the party between factions led by Touré, who favored participating in the November presidential polling, and Philippe Ouédraogo, who agreed with boycott plans. At a September 13 meeting, Touré was ousted by Ouédraogo, and the group subsequently announced plans to observe the boycott. Rejecting this decision, Touré claimed that he and his followers represented the "true PAI" and continued to use the rubric. In November 2000 Touré's wing signed a protocol with the CDP and others and was given cabinet posts. Ouédraogo's wing stayed in opposition, however. The two factions subsequently fought over the right to use the PAI rubric.

The PAI won five seats in the 2002 assembly balloting, and it was reported that a PAI member was named to the June 2002 cabinet as minister of animal resources. However, apparently underscoring continued PAI disputes, Philippe Ouédraogo was subsequently described as the leader of a strongly anti-Compaoré faction in the assembly known as the Justice and Democracy Parliamentary Group.

Two PAI ministers were reportedly dismissed from the cabinet in September 2005 in an apparent response by Compaoré to Touré's announcement that he intended to oppose Compaoré in the upcoming presidential election. (Touré finished eighth in that poll with 1.12 percent, while Ouédraogo ran as the candidate of the PDS [above]). The PAI supported the PDS presidential candidate in 2010. In 2012 Ouédraogo's faction of the PAI reportedly joined the new PDS Metba (above), and the PAI did not participate in the 2012 elections.

Leaders: Soumane TOURÉ (2005 presidential candidate), Zegouma SAMOU.

Greens of Burkina (*Les Verts du Burkina*). This party is a partial successor to the Union of Greens for the Development of Burkina (*Union des Verts pour le Développement du Burkina*—UVDB), launched in 1991. UVDB leader Ram Ouédraogo had the distinction of being the first opposition member to announce his presidential candidacy in 1991. However, prior to the December balloting, he withdrew at the same time as the other opposition candidates.

In 1998 Ouédraogo campaigned for the presidency on a UVDB platform highlighted by a call for the elevation of water management issues to the forefront of national policymaking concerns. He finished second in the November presidential balloting, garnering just 6.61 percent of the vote. In October 1999 Ouédraogo was named a minister of state in the Kadré Ouédraogo government. He kept his position after the formation of the new government in November 2000 but was not retained in June 2002.

Following the 2002 legislative balloting, disagreements broke out over the scope of cooperation between the UVDB and other opposition parties, and Ouédraogo left the UVDB to form the RDEB (above). The rump UVDB subsequently adopted the party's current rubric, although leadership of the group remained unclear and a UVDB was listed as presenting candidates on its own in the 2007 assembly balloting. A **Greens of Faso** was listed as participating in the 2012 assembly elections.

Other parties that won seats in the 2007 assembly balloting included the **Popular Rally of Citizens** (*Rassemblement Populaire des Citoyens*—RPC), led by Antoine OUARE; and the **Union for Democracy and Social Progress** (*Union pour la Démocratie et le Progrès Social*—UDPS), led by Fidèle AIEN and Baba OUATTARA.

LEGISLATURE

The former National Assembly was dissolved following the 1980 coup, and no successor body was established under the Sankara regime. The 1991 constitution provided for an Assembly of People's Deputies (*Assemblée des Députés*) with a five-year mandate, balloting for which was initially scheduled for January 12, 1992, but was subsequently postponed until May 24. Although the new constitution envisioned the eventual creation of a second, consultative legislative chamber, basic law revision in 2002 provided for a unicameral legislature, with the National Assembly title being readopted for that body. In 2011 the Consultative Council on Political Reforms endorsed the eventual formation of a consultative Senate comprising tribal leaders, representatives of civil society, and presidential appointees. The National Assembly in

May 2013 approved legislation calling for the creation of a 91-member Senate; one-third of the members were to be appointed by the president. Despite protest demonstrations against the plan (see Current issues, above), the government announced that the new upper house would be installed in the fall.

National Assembly (*Assemblée Nationale*). In January 1997 the Assembly of People's Deputies approved a constitutional amendment increasing its seat total from 97 to 111. The party-list proportional system that was revised in advance of the 2002 balloting with the goal of greater opposition representation. Ninety deputies were elected in 2002 from 15 electoral districts (reduced from the previous 45 districts), and 21 deputies were elected from a national list. Fifteen legislators were elected from the national constituency in 2007, while 96 were elected from 13 multimember constituencies corresponding to the country's 13 regions. The membership was expanded for the 2012 election to 127, 16 from the nation-wide constituency and the remainder from 45 multimember constituencies corresponding to the country's provinces. The term of office is five years.

At the most recent balloting on December 2, 2012, the Congress of Democracy and Progress was credited with 70 seats (62 from the multimember constituencies and 8 from the national constituency); the Union for Progress and Change, 19 (17, 2); the Alliance for Democracy and Federation/African Democratic Rally, 18 (16, 2); the Union for the Republic, 5 (4, 1); the Union for Rebirth–Sankarist Party, 4 (3, 1); the Convention of the Democratic Forces of Burkina, 3 (2, 1); the Party for Democracy and Socialism–Builders Party, 2 (1, 1); the National Union for Democracy and Development, 1 (1, 0); the Rally for the Development of Burkina, 1 (1, 0); the Organization for Democracy and Work, 1 (1, 0); the National Convention for the Progress of Burkina, 1 (1, 0); the Rally for Democracy and Socialism, 1 (1, 0); and The Other Burkina/Party for Socialism and Reorganization, 1 (1, 0).

Chair: Soungalo Apollinaire OUATTARA.

CABINET

[as of October 1, 2013]

President	Blaise Compaoré
Prime Minister	Luc Adolphe Tiao
Ministers of State	
Foreign Affairs and Regional Cooperation	Yipèné Djibril Bassole
Presidential Office	Assimi Kouanda
Relations with Institutions and Political Reforms	Bongnessan Arsène Ye
Ministers	
Agriculture and Food Security	Mahama Zoungrana
Animal Resources and Fisheries	Jérémie Tinga Ouédraoga
Civil Service, Labor, and Social Security	Vincent Zakane
Commerce, Industry, and Handicrafts	Patiendé Arthur Kafando
Communications and Government Spokesperson	Alain Edouard Traoré
Culture and Tourism	Baba Hama
Defense	Blaise Compaoré
Development, Digital Economy, and Posts	Jean Koulidiati
Economy and Finance	Lucien Marie Noël Bembamba
Environment and Sustainable Development	Salif Ouédraogo
Health	Léne Sebgo
Housing and Urban Planning	Yacouba Barry
Human Rights and Civic Promotion	Prudence Julie M.N.K. Nigna/Somda [f]
Infrastructure, Access, and Transportation	Jean Bertin Ouédraogo
Justice and Keeper of the Seals	Dramane Yameogo
Mines and Energy	Lamoussa Salif Kaboré
National Education and Literacy	Koumba Boly/Barry [f]
Promotion of Women and Gender	Nestorine Sangaré/Compaoré [f]
Scientific Research and Innovation	Gnissa Isaïe Konaté
Secondary and Higher Education	Moussa Ouattara
Social Action and National Solidarity	Alain Zoubga
Sports and Leisure	Yacouba Ouédraogo
Territorial Administration and Security	Jèrôme Bougouma
Territorial Management and Decentralization	Toussaint Abel Coulibaly
Water, Hydraulic Infrastructure, and Sanitation	Mamounata Belem/Ouédraogo [f]
Youth, Employment, and Training	Basga Émile Dialla
Ministers Delegate	
Budget	Clotilde Ki/Nikiema [f]
Literacy	Amadou Diemdioda Dicko
Local Collectives	Toussaint Abel Coulibaly
Regional Cooperation	Thomas Palé
Transportation	Baba Dieme

[f] = female

INTERGOVERNMENTAL REPRESENTATION

Ambassador to the U.S.: Seydou BOUDA.

U.S. Ambassador to Burkina Faso: J. Thomas DOUGHERTY.

Permanent Representative to the UN: Der KOGDA.

IGO Memberships (Non-UN): AfDB, AU, ECOWAS, IOM, NAM, OIC, WTO.

BURUNDI

Republic of Burundi
Republika y'u Burundi (Kirundi)
République du Burundi (French)

Political Status: Independent state since July 1, 1962; military control imposed November 28, 1966; one-party constitution adopted by referendum of November 18, 1981; military control reimposed following coup of September 3, 1987; multiparty constitution adopted March 13, 1992, following referendum of March 9; military rule reimposed following coup of July 25, 1996; transitional constitution signed into law June 6, 1998; new transitional constitution providing for a three-year transitional period adopted October 27, 2001; new constitution (institutionalizing Hutu/Tutsi power sharing) approved by national referendum on February 28, 2005; transitional period concluded with local and national elections in June–September 2005.

Area: 10,747 sq. mi. (27,834 sq. km).

Population: 8,780,879 (2012E—UN); 10,888,321 (2013E—U.S. Census).

Major Urban Center (2005E): BUJUMBURA (407,000).

Official Languages: Kirundi, French (Swahili is also spoken).

Monetary Unit: Burundi Franc (official rate November 1, 2013: 1,548.99 francs = $1US).

President: Pierre NKURUNZIZA (Hutu from the National Council for the Defense of Democracy–Forces for the Defense of Democracy); elected by the Parliament on August 19, 2005, and inaugurated for a five-year term on August 26 in succession to Domitien NDAYIZEYE (Front for Democracy in Burundi); reelected in direct balloting for a five-year term on June 28, 2010.

First Vice President (In Charge of Political and Administrative Affairs): Therence SINUNGURUZA (Tutsi from the Union for National Progress); inaugurated on August 29, 2010, following appointment by the president and approval by Parliament to succeed Yves SAHINGUVU (Tutsi from the Union for National Progress).

Second Vice President (In Charge of Social and Economic Affairs): Gervais RUFYIKIRI (Hutu from the National Council for the Defense of Democracy–Forces for the Defense of Democracy); inaugurated on August 29, 2010, following appointment by the president and approval by Parliament to succeed Gabriel NTISEZERANA (Hutu from the National Council for the Defense of Democracy–Forces for the Defense of Democracy).

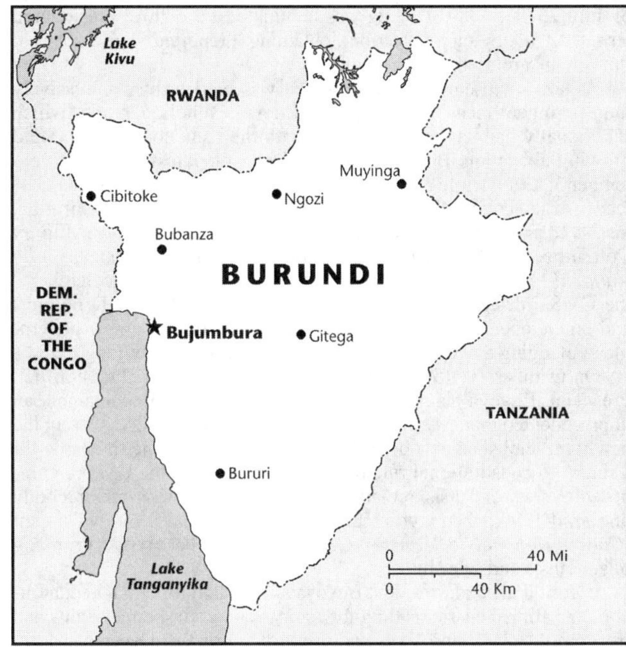

THE COUNTRY

Situated in east-central Africa (bordered by Rwanda, Tanzania, and the Democratic Republic of the Congo), Burundi, one of Africa's smallest nations, is a country of grassy uplands and high plateaus. It is one of the most densely populated countries on the continent, with over 400 persons per square mile. There are three main ethnic groups: the Hutu (Bahutu), who constitute 84 percent of the population; the Tutsi (Batutsi, Watutsi), who are numerically a minority (15 percent) but have long dominated the country politically, socially, and economically; and the Twa, or pygmies (1 percent). A majority of the population is nominally Christian (67 percent), primarily Roman Catholic (62 percent of the total population), while 10 percent is Muslim, and the remainder practice a variety of traditional beliefs. Women account for almost half of the labor force, although they are concentrated in subsistence activities, with men predominant in paid labor. Female representation in politics and government was traditionally minimal, although the prime minister from July 1993 to February 1994 was a woman. Under the constitution adopted in 2005 significant female representation is guaranteed in the Parliament and in the cabinet. Women constitute 32 percent of the current legislature.

Burundi remains dependent on agriculture. In 2012, Burundi ranked 178th of 186 countries on the UN human development index. More than 80 percent of its inhabitants are farmers, primarily at the subsistence level, and coffee accounts for more than 70 percent of export earnings. The small industrial sector consists for the most part of agricultural processing. Small quantities of cassiterite, gold, columbite-tantalite, and wolframite are extracted, while major deposits of nickel and potentially significant reserves of phosphate, petroleum, and uranium await exploitation.

It was estimated that 300,000 people had lost their lives in a 12-year civil war, between 1993 and 2005. GDP declined by more than a third, and per capita annual income plummeted to $100. Nearly 60 percent of the country's children suffered from stunted growth due to poor nutrition, according to one relief agency.

Since the 1990s, there have been advances in education and health care, although corruption and a small but "persistent" insurgency (see Current issues, below) continued to compromise efforts to combat the growing HIV/AIDS infection rate, spur economic development, and improve the power grid (reportedly, only 1 percent of the population had regular access to electricity).

GDP growth between 2006 and 2009 averaged approximately 4 percent, although annual inflation rose sharply to 26 percent in 2008 and 2009, mostly due to dramatic hikes in food and fuel prices. In February 2009 the IMF, describing the government's economic efforts as "broadly satisfactory," joined the World Bank in canceling $1.4 billion of Burundi's debt and called upon the government to invest the "savings" in social programs and infrastructure improvements. Meanwhile, the African Development Bank announced a $5.8 billion, 20-year program to improve the nation's communications, transport, and utility infrastructure. The country's economy continues to improve with assistance from international organizations. The IMF announced in January 2012 that it would provide a three-year, 30 million special drawing rates (SDR) contract in order to further economic gains and reduce poverty. This move, coupled with further economic progress from the government, resulted in a GDP growth of 4.0 percent in 2012, which increased to 4.5 percent in 2013, according to the IMF. Inflation decreased to 9.0 percent in 2013.

GOVERNMENT AND POLITICS

Political background. Established in the 16th century as a feudal monarchy ruled by the Tutsi, Burundi (formerly Urundi) was incorporated into German East Africa in 1895 and came under Belgian administration as a result of World War I. From 1919 to 1962 it formed the southern half of the Belgian-administered League of Nations mandate (later The United Nations Trust Territory) of Ruanda-Urundi. Retaining its monarchical form of government under indigenous Tutsi rulers (*mwami*), Urundi was granted limited self-government in 1961 and achieved full independence as the Kingdom of Burundi on July 1, 1962.

Rivalry between Tutsi factions and between Tutsis and Hutus resulted in the assassination of Prime Minister Pierre NGENDANDUMWE in January 1965 and an abortive Hutu coup the following October. The uprising led to repressive action by government troops under the command of Capt. Michel MICOMBERO. Named prime minister as the result of military intervention in July 1966, Micombero suspended the constitution, dissolved the National Assembly, and on November 28 deposed King NATARE V. In addition to naming himself president of the newly proclaimed Republic of Burundi, Micombero took over the presidency of the Union and National Progress (*Union et Progrès National*—Uprona), the Tutsi-dominated political party that was accorded monopoly status.

Despite antigovernment plots in 1969 and 1971, the Micombero regime was generally able to contain conflict in the immediate postcoup era. In 1972, however, the mysterious death of the former king and another attempted Hutu uprising provoked renewed reprisals by Micombero's Tutsi supporters. At least 100,000 deaths (largely of Hutus) ensued, with countless thousands fleeing to neighboring countries.

On November 1, 1976, Micombero was overthrown in a bloodless coup led by Lt. Col. Jean-Baptiste BAGAZA, who suspended the constitution and announced that a 30-member Supreme Council of the Revolution would assume formal power under the "Second Republic" with himself as head of state. At an Uprona congress in December 1979 the Supreme Council was abolished, effective January 1980, and its functions were transferred to a party Central Committee headed by the president. On October 22, 1982, elections were held for a new National Assembly and for pro forma reconfirmation of Bagaza as chief executive. Following his redesignation as party leader at the Uprona congress of July 25–27, 1984, Bagaza was nominated for a third presidential term (the first by direct election), obtaining a reported 99.6 percent of the vote in a referendum on August 31.

Bagaza's subsequent administration was marked by progressively more stringent measures against the Roman Catholic Church, which traditionally maintained strong links with the Hutu community. Amid growing alienation, Bagaza was ousted in a bloodless revolt on September 3, 1987, while attending a francophone summit in Canada. The leader of the coup, Maj. Pierre BUYOYA, suspended the constitution, dissolved the National Assembly, and named a 31-member Military Committee for National Salvation (*Comité Militaire pour le Salut National*—CMSN) to exercise provisional authority. On September 9 the CMSN designated Buyoya as president of the "Third Republic," and on October 1 Buyoya announced the formation of a new government, pledging that the "military will not remain in power long."

On October 19, 1988, following a renewal of Tutsi-Hutu conflict, President Buyoya named a 23-member cabinet that contained an unprecedented majority of Hutus, including Adrien SIBOMANA in the newly reestablished post of prime minister. However, the timetable for a return to constitutional rule remained unclear, and the CMSN, composed entirely of Tutsis, remained the dominant decision-making body until mid-1990, when it was replaced by the National Security Council (*Conseil National de Sécurité*—CSN), an 11-member civilian grouping of six Tutsis and five Hutus.

In furtherance of President Buyoya's campaign for ethnic reconciliation, a national charter calling for "unity, respect for human rights and freedom of expression" was endorsed by Uprona in December 1990 and adopted by popular referendum on February 5, 1991. In accordance with charter provisions calling for an end to military rule, Buyoya on March 22 empowered a 35-member constitutional commission to outline the framework of a multiparty system. The commission's report, released on September 10, served as the basis of a pluralist constitution that was approved in a referendum on March 9, 1992.

In the June 1993 elections Hutu opposition candidate Melchior NDADAYE defeated President Buyoya, and Ndadaye's Front for Democracy in Burundi (*Front pour la Démocratie au Burundi*—Frodebu) won 65 of 81 seats. (For more on the 1993 elections, see earlier editions of the *Handbook.*)

On July 10, 1993, Ndadaye reached out to the previously dominant Tutsis and included seven Uprona members in a new cabinet that was also headed by a Tutsi, Sylvie KINIGI, as prime minister. Pledging continuance of his predecessor's reconciliation program, Ndadaye in September amnestied 5,000 prisoners (earlier he had granted clemency to Bagaza, allowing the former president to return from six years in exile). In early October Ndadaye announced plans to begin the repatriation of the approximately 300,000 Burundians displaced by earlier conflicts.

Optimism engendered by the reconciliation effort was dashed on October 21, 1993, when Ndadaye, the National Assembly president, and a number of senior Hutu government officials were slain during a military coup attempt spearheaded by Tutsi paratroopers. The rebellion ended within two days as senior military personnel, some of whom had been implicated in the plot, sought to disassociate themselves from the frenzy unleashed by the president's assassination. In addition to a number of senior Tutsi officers from the Burore region, the coup plotters allegedly included Bagaza; the recently appointed army chief-of-staff, Col. Jean BIKOMAGU; and François NGEZE, a former interior minister and vocal critic of the new administration, who on October 21 was named president of the rebels' short-lived National Committee of Public Salvation (an appointment he later claimed was forced on him). Denying involvement in the uprising, Bikomagu on October 24 offered to aid in reestablishing the government in exchange for amnesty. However, the offer was rejected by Prime Minister Kinigi, who said, from her refuge in the French embassy, that she would remain underground until the military had returned to its barracks and an international protective force had been established for the government.

By October 24, 1993, most of the rebel soldiers had fled Bujumbura in the face of a massing of progovernment troops and revenge-minded Ndadaye supporters. On November 2, following the arrest of at least ten of the plotters, including Ngeze, Kinigi emerged from her embassy sanctuary to retake control of the government. Six days later she met with 15 cabinet ministers under the protection of a French special forces unit to discuss ways of ending the tribal bloodbath that had left 10,000 dead and hundreds of thousands exiled in Rwanda, Tanzania, and Zaire.

On January 13, 1994, the National Assembly elected a Hutu moderate, Agriculture Minister Cyprien NTARYAMIRE, to the presidency. However, Ntaryamire and Rwandan President Juvénal Habyarimana were killed in an airplane bombing over Kigali, Rwanda, on April 6, 1994. On April 8 Sylvestre NTIBANTUNGANYA, who had been elected assembly president on December 23, 1993, became Ntaryamire's acting successor.

Amid escalating violence, opposition leaders boycotted talks on the selection of a new president in June 1994. However, on July 13 a power-sharing agreement was concluded, under which Frodebu was to be awarded control of 9 provinces and 74 communes, with opposition groups being given 7 provinces and 48 communes. A follow-up "Convention on Government" was signed on September 10, under which 45 percent of cabinet posts, including the prime ministership and interior ministry, were to be allocated to the Uprona-led opposition, with the defense and justice portfolios reserved for "neutral persons." Subsequently, the National Assembly ratified the convention's nomination of the acting president for a regular term, with swearing-in ceremonies on October 1. Instability nonetheless continued, with the controversial election on December 3 of Frodebu's Jean MINANI as National Assembly speaker being defended by the Uprona prime minister, Anatole KANYENKIKO, who had succeeded Kinigi in February. Opposition to Minani led to his replacement by Léonce NGENDAKUMANA on January 12, 1995, while Kanyenkiko was, in turn, obliged to resign on February 15 after being expelled from Uprona for indiscipline in regard to the Minani affair. With the appointment of the Uprona-nominated Antoine NDUWAYO as Kanyenkiko's successor as prime minister on February 20, the political crisis appeared to ease, although Tanzania reported that some 25,000 refugees had crossed its border with Burundi since the first of the month.

A new cycle of fighting erupted following the murder on March 11, 1995, of a prominent Hutu leader, Ernest KABUSHEMEYE, prompting another wave of refugees into Zaire and Tanzania. Meanwhile, President Ntibantunganya rejected proposals (apparently advanced by U.S. officials) that the problems of Burundi and Rwanda be addressed by the creation of two ethnically based countries, in effect a "Hutuland" and a "Tutsiland." In July the UN announced the formation of a commission of inquiry into the October 1993 coup attempt and urged the feuding political groups to begin peace negotiations, warning that the UN could play only a minor role in ending the conflict.

Following the killing of at least 58 Tutsis at a displaced persons camp in early August 1995, Prime Minister Nduwayo claimed that former Rwandan soldiers and militiamen (both Hutu-dominated) were responsible for at least "two-thirds of the recent violence." Nduwayo's assertion worsened the already incendiary debate within the cabinet over which ethnic group was responsible for the latest round of violence, and on October 12 President Ntibantunganya reshuffled the government, ousting the most vocal combatants and replacing them with less "partisan" ministers. The violence nonetheless continued, and in December three of the ten parties participating in the government withdrew.

With ethnic fighting intensifying, the United States and the European Union (EU) suspended aid payments to Burundi, citing the government's failure to end the violence. President Ntibantunganya and Prime Minister Nduwayo agreed in principle in early July 1996 to the deployment of foreign peacekeeping forces to quell ethnic violence and protect Burundi's infrastructure, borders, and political leaders. That plan was denounced by militants in both the Tutsi and Hutu camps, however, and, following the massacre by Hutu rebels of over 300 Tutsis in a camp on July 20, antigovernment demonstrations broke out in Bujumbura and other cities. After being stoned by Tutsi mourners at funeral services for the massacre victims, President Ntibantunganya sought refuge in the U.S. embassy on July 23. The next day Uprona announced it was withdrawing from the coalition government. On July 25 the military declared that it had taken power, dismissed the government, suspended the constitution and the National Assembly, and appointed former president Buyoya head of state. (Prime Minister Nduwayo accepted his dismissal, but President Ntibantunganya subsequently insisted that he remained the nation's lawful head of state.) On July 31 Buyoya announced the appointment of Pascal Firmin NDIMIRA, a Hutu member of Uprona, as prime minister, and a new 25-member Uprona-based government was formed on August 2. Despite Buyoya's reputation as a "moderate" among Tutsi military leaders and the credit he had received for the orderly transfer of power three years earlier, the July 1996 coup was broadly denounced by the United Nations, Western capitals, and, most strongly, by neighboring states, who immediately imposed severe economic sanctions against Burundi. For his part, asserting that the military had taken over only to "stop the bloodshed," Buyoya called for a three-year transitional period prior to a return to civilian government and pledged to clamp down on military abuses.

On September 12, 1996, in the face of the strong international condemnation of the recent coup, Buyoya lifted the assembly suspension and declared that political party activity could resume. However, less than half of the legislators participated in the reopening of the assembly on October 7, contributing factors including the recent murder of a number of legislators, an opposition boycott, and apathy resulting from the fact that the suspension of the constitution had left the body virtually powerless. In October regional leaders decided to maintain the economic sanctions against Bujumbura despite the regime's announcement that it intended to hold unconditional peace talks with the dominant rebel group—the National Council for the Defense of Democracy (*Conseil National pour la Défense de Démocratie*—CNDD). Moreover, in late 1996 both the UN and Amnesty International charged the regime with responsibility for massacres that had taken place since July.

Despite continued violence, in mid-April regional leaders agreed to loosen sanctions on humanitarian supplies. On June 7 former president Ntibantunganya left the U.S. embassy, declaring his intention to resume his political life and calling for the opening of peace talks. One week later Buyoya asked for international assistance in establishing a genocide tribunal to punish those responsible for the recent ethnic violence; the UN Security Council rejected his request, citing continued high levels of instability.

Following intense negotiations on a power-sharing agreement between Buyoya and Hutu remnants in the assembly (led by Speaker Léonce Ngendakumana), Buyoya signed a transitional constitution into law on June 6, 1998. Provisions included enlargement of the assembly, the formal recognition of established political parties, and formation of a transitional government. Consequently, Buyoya was officially sworn in as president on June 11, and the following day he appointed two vice presidents, including Frodebu leader Frederic BAMVUGINYUMVIRA, to assume responsibilities formerly held by the prime minister, whose post was abolished. On June 13 the president appointed a new cabinet, 13 of whose 22 members were Hutus, while the Transitional National Assembly was inaugurated on July 18, new members representing small parties as well as social and professional groups.

Regional leaders meeting in Tanzania in early September 1997 agreed to maintain economic sanctions against the Burundian regime, warning President Buyoya that "additional measures" would be considered unless progress was made toward restoration of civilian government. Buyoya had declined to participate in the summit's proposed peace talks, in part, reportedly, out of conviction that Tanzania was "pro-Hutu." (It was estimated that as many as 300,000 Hutu refugees were encamped inside the Tanzanian border.) Buyoya appeared to be attempting to follow a difficult middle course between the militant Hutu guerrilla groups, who had been fighting since 1993 to take over the government, and predominately Tutsi hard-liners in the government and military, who opposed negotiations of any sort with the "rebels." At the same time, Western capitals remained concerned over the Buyoya regime's refusal to permit the resumption of normal political party activity as well as its highly controversial "resettlement" program in which perhaps as many as 600,000 people were confined to "refugee" camps. Although the government argued that the measures were designed to protect people displaced by guerrilla activity, critics argued that Hutus were being placed in the camps so that they could not offer support to the rebels.

Perhaps in part to improve his "battered image" in the West, President Buyoya in March 1998 agreed to participate in talks with representatives of Frodebu, the CNDD, and other factions. During the fourth round of negotiations in January 1999, the sanctions were lifted. In October 1999 former South African president Nelson Mandela assumed the task of facilitating the negotiations, which had reached an impasse. He announced in May 2000 that an agreement in principle had been reached, and a partial, preliminary agreement was signed on August 28. Highly contentious negotiations dragged on for months, as did efforts by the government to negotiate a cease-fire with the Hutu rebel groups that had rejected the accord—the Forces for the Defense of Democracy (*Forces pour la Défense de Démocratie*—FDD) and the National Forces of Liberation (*Forces Nationales de la Libération*—FNL). Finally, following mediation by the Organization of African Unity (OAU, subsequently the African Union—AU) and further efforts by Mandela, a power-sharing agreement was accepted on July 23, 2001, during a meeting in Arusha of 19 groups (representatives from the government, Transitional National Assembly, and all members of the pro-Hutu Group of Seven and pro-Tutsi Group of Ten—see listings in Political Parties and Groups, below).

On October 28, 2001, the assembly adopted a transitional constitution to implement the Arusha accords, and the following day the assembly confirmed Buyoya as president of the new transitional government and Domitien NDAYIZEYE, secretary general of Frodebu, as vice president. Buyoya was sworn in on November 1 for an 18-month term, after which he was to be replaced, according to the agreement, by Ndayizeye for the remaining 18 months of the transition period. (A Tutsi was scheduled to replace Ndayizeye as vice president following his elevation to president, although Buyoya announced he would not be a candidate for that post.) A new cabinet, comprising 15 political parties, was also installed on November 1, while on November 27 the assembly adopted legislation providing for a new transitional legislature. However, the two main rebel groups (the FDD and FNL) remained adamantly opposed to the accord and, in fact, intensified their military activity. (Other rebel forces had accepted the Arusha provisions for their gradual integration into what would ultimately become ethnically balanced national defense and security forces.) Moreover, even within the political parties that had signed the power-sharing agreement, Tutsi and Hutu hard-liners scoffed at the prospects for a permanent negotiated settlement and the potential for cohesiveness within the coalition government, which contained highly disparate elements. Nevertheless, President Buyoya and Vice President Ndayizeye pledged to promote national unity. Meanwhile, South Africa deployed peacekeeping troops in Burundi to protect the hundreds of thousands of Hutu refugees (including numerous prominent politicians) who had been invited to return to Burundi. The UN endorsed the South African initiative, which was soon augmented by forces from other neighboring countries. However, no official UN peacekeeping mission was authorized at that point in view of the lack of a cease-fire agreement from the rebels.

Fighting between government forces and both the FDD and FNL continued into autumn 2002, followed by the declaration of a cease-fire with the FDD in December and the subsequent deployment of an AU peacekeeping force. Under the terms of the transitional constitution, at the end of his 18-month term Buyoya turned the presidency over to Ndayizeye, who was inaugurated on April 30, 2003. That same day, Alphonse-Marie KADEGE of Uprona was appointed vice president.

Renewed fighting in July 2003 between the government and the FNL led the UN to withdraw its nonessential personnel from the country and by September had left 170 dead and created some 50,000 additional internal refugees. In October peace negotiations under the leadership of South African President Thabo Mbeki led to an agreement that granted five cabinet posts to the primary CNDD faction, now known as the CNDD-FDD. Three provincial gubernatorial posts and the vice presidency of the assembly were also accorded to the CNDD-FDD. In return, the CNDD-FDD pledged to begin disarmament. To oversee that process, the AU peacekeeping force was increased to more than 3,000 troops. On November 16 the government and the CNDD-FDD signed a comprehensive peace agreement to implement the Arusha accords, and on November 23 Ndayizeye reshuffled the cabinet to form a government of national unity that included the CNDD-FDD and most other major parties. In December Pierre NKURUNZIZA, the leader of the CNDD-FDD, returned to Burundi for the first time since 1993, and 6,000 CNDD-FDD fighters began demobilization. However, at least one faction of the FNL continued its armed struggle. In May 2004 the UN authorized its own peacekeeping mission (the United Nations Operation in Burundi [*Opération des Nations Unies au Burundi*—ONUB]) to succeed the AU forces and supervise the disarmament of an estimated 40,000 "rebels."

On October 20, 2004, Ndayizeye signed a new draft constitution that had been approved by a special joint session of the legislature. The document called for permanent power sharing between the Tutsis and Hutus through a system of proportional representation (see Constitution and government, below). National legislative elections were subsequently scheduled for July 2005, and Ndayizeye's term was extended until the new elections, at which time a new president would be chosen by the legislature. (Subsequent presidents would be popularly elected.) Ndayizeye announced that he intended to retire from politics at the end of his current term.

On November 10, 2004, Vice President Kadege resigned following continued disagreements with the president over power-sharing arrangements and Kadege's opposition to the new constitution. Frederic NGENZEBUHORO of Uprona replaced Kadege the following day.

In December 2004 President Ndayizeye signed legislation creating a new national army and police force incorporating the former FDD fighters. At that point sporadic, albeit intense, fighting between government forces and the FNL still presented a serious barrier to successful conclusion of the transitional government.

The CNDD-FDD completed a remarkable transition in 2005 from a former rebel group to the country's dominant political force. Observers attributed the CNDD-FDD's success to appreciation among the Hutu population for the past willingness of the CNDD-FDD to back up its political stance with guns. In contrast, Hutu support for Frodebu had declined as the perception had apparently grown that its engagement with Uprona since the mid-1990s had been largely ineffective.

Voters approved the proposed new constitution by a 92 percent margin in a national referendum on February 28, 2005, and in May most elements of the FNL finally agreed to a truce. Consequently, communal elections were held on June 3, with the CNDD-FDD (now a legal party) securing more than 55 percent of votes and more than 1,780 of the 3,325 seats up for election. The CNDD-FDD also dominated the July 4 assembly balloting, and CNDD-FDD leader Nkurunziza was elected president (as the sole candidate) with 91 percent of the votes cast during a joint session of the assembly and the Senate on August 19. In keeping with constitutional requirements, Nkurunziza appointed a Tutsi (Martin NDUWIMANA, from Uprona) as first vice president. Nkurunziza subsequently formed a new national unity government that included members from the CNDD-FDD, Uprona, Frodebu, Parena, and several small parties. However, Frodebu in March 2006 announced its withdrawal from the government (see Frodebu under Political Parties and Groups, below). Underscoring the complexity of political affairs as well as friction within the CNDD-FDD, Second Vice President Alice NZOMUKUNDA resigned in September 2006, accusing CNDD-FDD leader Hussein RADJABU of strong-arm interference in the administration and of being largely responsible for a perceived high level of cronyism and corruption. Marina BARAMPAMA, a previously little-known member of the CNDD-FDD, succeeded Nzomukunda.

President Nkurunziza effectively lost his legislative majority in early 2007 as a result of severe CNDD-FDD fractionalization (see CNDD-FDD under Political Parties and Groups for details). He attempted to form a new cabinet in June but could not achieve legislative approval when Uprona, Frodebu, and the CNDD-FDD dissidents refused to participate. After reaching agreement with Frodebu (in late October) and Uprona (in early November), Nkurunziza on November 14 announced a new national unity cabinet that included four Frodebu and two Uprona ministers, although the CNDD-FDD retained control of the major ministries. The new government also included a new first vice president—Dr. Yves SAHINGUVU of Uprona. The cabinet was reshuffled on January 29, 2009, although the constitutionally prescribed ethnic and party distribution of positions was again carefully followed.

In the May 2010 communal balloting, the CNDD-FDD secured 65.5 percent of the vote, followed by the FNL with 14.5 percent. Opposition groups, led by the FNL, rejected the results as fraudulent. International observers described the elections as generally free and fair, but monitors were critical of the lack of competition. Most opposition groups decided to boycott subsequent elections scheduled for 2010. Consequently, Nkurunziza was the sole candidate in the June 28 presidential polling. He won with 91.6 percent of the vote. Only the CNDD-FDD, Uprona, and a faction of Frodebu, the Real Frodebu (*Sahwanya Frodebu Nyakuri*), participated in the Senate and assembly elections. The CNDD-FDD won commanding majorities in both chambers. On August 30 Nkurunziza appointed a new, smaller, ethnically mixed cabinet that included 21 ministers. The new government was dominated by the CNDD-FDD but included representatives from Uprona and Real Frodebu. Meanwhile, the president named Therence SINUNGURUZA (Uprona) as first vice president and Gervais RUFYIKIRI (CNDD-FDD) as second vice president.

In November 2011, Nkurunziza announced a major cabinet reshuffle of the posts held by the members of his CNDD-FDD party. Nkurunziza replaced seven cabinet ministers within his party. Following the major reshuffle of November, two additional cabinet ministers were replaced in February 2012. Nkurunziza orchestrated a cabinet reshuffle in February 2013, replacing seven ministers. The president explained that the reshuffle was based on an evaluation of the cabinet minister's performances while in office.

Constitution and government. (For details on the March 1992 constitution and subsequent constitutional developments until 2001, see the 2007 *Handbook.*) Following the signing of the Arusha power-sharing accord in July 2001, the assembly adopted a "Constitution of Transition" on October 28 providing for a three-year transitional government. Power was concentrated in the presidency and vice presidency, with a Tutsi (President Buyoya) to serve as president for 18 months before being replaced for the next 18 months by a Hutu. Provision was also made for a new Transitional Parliament to include a National Assembly and a Senate. Elections were scheduled to be held, under undetermined electoral arrangements, at the communal level by the end of the first 18 months of the transition and at the national level (for a new assembly and senate) by the end of the second 18-month period.

The new constitution approved via national referendum on February 28, 2005, was most noteworthy for its efforts to institutionalize Hutu/Tutsi power sharing. The new basic law provided for the new legislature to elect the next president, but subsequent chief executives were popularly elected, beginning in 2010.

The president is elected for a five-year term, renewable once. There are two vice presidents; if the president is a Hutu, then the first vice president must be a Tutsi, and vice versa. The first vice president must also be from a different party than the president. It is mandated by the constitution that maximum cabinet membership be 60 percent for Hutus and 40 percent for Tutsis. In addition, all parties that secure more than 5 percent in an assembly election must be represented in the subsequent cabinet in proportion to the number of seats won. The defense minister must also be from a different ethnic group than the minister responsible for internal security, and no single ethnic group can make up more than 50 percent of military and security forces.

For administrative purposes the country is divided into 17 provinces, each headed by an appointed governor. The provinces are subdivided into 129 communes as well as smaller districts, with elected communal and district councils directing local affairs.

A new media law in 2003 provided for broad journalistic freedom. However, the CNDD-FDD government installed in 2005 regularly represses and intimidates print and radio journalists, who have reportedly been subjected to arrest and attack by security forces. The passage in June 2013 of a restrictive media law, which eliminates source protection, mandates university qualifications, and restricts coverage of matters deemed to undermine national security, drew harsh criticism from international rights groups. Supporters of the law argue it will professionalize the media and discourage sensationalism, but opponents fear that it will further suppress the country's opposition voices in the lead-up to the 2015 elections. In 2013, the media watchdog group Reporters Without Borders ranked Burundi 132nd out of 179 countries.

Foreign relations. Internal conflicts have significantly influenced Burundi's relations with its neighbors. During the turmoil of the Micombero era, relations with Rwanda (where the Hutu were dominant), as well as with Tanzania and Zaire, were strained. Under President Bagaza, however, a new spirit of regional cooperation led to the formation in 1977 of a joint Economic Community of the Great Lakes Countries (*Communauté Économique des Pays des Grande Lacs*—CEPGL), within which Burundi, Rwanda, and Zaire agreed to organize a development bank, exploit gas deposits under Lake Kivu, and establish a fishing industry on Lake Tanganyika. In 1984 Burundi (along with the rest of CEPGL) entered the Economic Community of Central African states, signaling greater regional economic cooperation.

An August 1991 meeting of Burundian, Rwandan, and Ugandan representatives yielded agreement on efforts to contain ethnic destabilization movements operating near border areas. However, observers reported mounting grassroots tensions stemming from persistent rumors of Tutsi "empire-building" ambitions. Although punctuated by cross-border rebel activities, negotiations continued in 1992 between Burundi and Rwanda on establishing cooperative security arrangements.

The October 1993 presidential assassination and coup attempt in Burundi were immediately and unanimously condemned by international observers, with initial calls for economic and political isolation of the rebels giving way to plans to establish a regional peacekeeping force to bolster the government and stem the ethnic violence. However, with the Tutsi military and Uprona leadership openly hostile to intervention, UN and OAU officials resisted the Kinigi government's call for a large-scale intervention.

International efforts to contain ethnic violence were frustrated throughout 1995 by the intransigence of the combatants as well as by the Tutsi military leadership's adamant opposition to a foreign military presence. Burundi expressed wariness over Tanzanian and Ugandan mediation in the first half of 1996, suggesting that its East African neighbors were interested in expanding their territories. Burundi's relations with its neighboring countries subsequently remained tense, and Burundian troops were sent into the Democratic Republic of the Congo (DRC, formerly Zaire) in 1999 in an attempt to dislodge staging areas of the rebel FDD.

Burundi's troops in the DRC reached 3,000 prior to a withdrawal in January 2002. Meanwhile, continued fighting between the DRC government and its own rebels in the DRC prompted the flight of some

35,000 refugees to Burundi. In addition, more than 300,000 refugees from fighting in Burundi reportedly continued to reside in Tanzania. Progress in the repatriation of refugees was reported in 2004–2005. Moreover, following the installation of the newly elected power-sharing government in Burundi in 2005, Burundi concluded an agreement with Uganda, Rwanda, and the DRC for establishment of a regional intelligence gathering unit.

ONUB (the UN's peacekeeping mission) disbanded on December 31, 2006, although it left behind neither war nor peace, with an ongoing stalemate between the government and Palipehutu-FNL rebels (see Current issues, below). ONUB's role was partially assumed by a new AU peacekeeping force, which once again relied heavily on South African troops, as had ONUB. Meanwhile, a new mission, the UN Integrated Office in Burundi (BINUB), was launched to support disarmament and political reconciliation.

Even though Burundi itself remained unsettled, the government announced in March 2007 that it would contribute 1,700 troops to the proposed AU peacekeeping mission in Somalia. Analysts suggested that, in addition to trying to promote regional stability in general, the CNDD-FDD government had a vested interest in preventing an Islamist takeover of Somalian affairs. The other major regional initiative in 2007 involved Burundi's accession in June to the East African Community (EAC), which became the focus for proposed infrastructure development and other initiatives (such as a planned trade deal with the EU) considered critical by the Burundian government to the nation's economic advancement. On a less positive note, however, violence in Kenya and renewed conflict in the DRC underscored the region's fragile status, as did tension over the proposed return of the estimated 280,000 Burundian refugees in Tanzania. (Although some of those refugees were slated to return to Burundi following the cease-fire there in 2008, a majority, many of whom had been in Tanzania for some 35 years, reportedly opted to be formally integrated into the Tanzanian population.) In April 2010 Tanzania announced that it would grant citizenship to 162,000 Burundians. The UNHCR initiated a program in October to facilitate the return of some 15,000 refugees from the DRC to Burundi. Concurrently, the UN began returning 2,000 of an estimated 40,000 DRC refugees from Burundi back to their home country.

In December 2010 BINUB was superseded by a much reduced UN mission, the UN Office in Burundi (BNUB). BNUB was tasked by the UN to help Burundi create an independent human rights commission. Meanwhile, Burundian participation in the AU mission in Somalia continued to grow, and by the summer of 2011, there were about 4,500 Burundian troops in the AU force, about half the total strength of the operation.

In February 2013 the UN Security Council passed a resolution extending BNUB until 2014. The Council indicated concerns over ongoing extrajudicial and political killings, as well as corruption and political and economic instability.

Current issues. After a renewed outbreak of violence in 2008, the civil war officially came to an end in April 2009 when FNL leader Rwasa ceremoniously turned over his rifle and declared that the FNL, which was formally registered as a political party, was now "a part of society." (For more on the FNL's activities from 2006 to 2009, see the 2013 *Handbook.*) An estimated 3,500 FNL fighters were scheduled for integration into the police or army, while some 5,000 more were given modest financial incentives to demobilize and return to civilian life.

In January 2010, 16 soldiers were arrested and charged with plotting a coup. Opposition parties bitterly disputed the communal elections in May, but their complaints were rejected by the electoral commission. The FNL led a boycott of presidential and legislative balloting amid escalating violence, which left 3 dead and more than 100 injured. Much of the violence was directed at polling places and officials, as well as CNDD-FDD candidates and party installations. Media outlets reported that more than 250 opposition figures were arrested during the series of elections. Nkurunziza was reelected, and the CNDD-FDD gained absolute majorities in both chambers of the Parliament in voting in June and July. Following the balloting, former second vice president of the republic Gabriel NTISEZERANA of the CNDD-FDD was elected speaker of the Senate. Opposition parties also boycotted the local elections held on September 7. In November Richard CIRAMUNDA announced the formation of a new rebel group, the Patriotic Front for Liberation (*Front Patriotique de Liberation*—FPL) (see Political Parties and Groups).

From late 2010 and early 2011, more than 500 people were killed in interethnic and political strife in Burundi. Opposition groups blamed the increasing violence. Reports in May indicated that forces from both Burundi and the DRC were increasingly undertaking cross-border raids. Further violence continued throughout 2011, with claims that an additional 300 people were killed in the latter half of the year. Some opponents blamed the killings on the CNDD-FDD, claiming that it was an attempt to silence those opposition parties that had contested the 2010 election. The violence reached its height in the post-election period in September 2012. FNL forces, which many believe are in hiding in the DRC, declared a war against Nkurunziza and his CNDD-FDD government. Rwasa, the leader of the FNL, claimed that the administration was guilty of "graft and economic mismanagement" that had not improved over the last few years. He charged that the CNDD-FDD had persecuted, tortured, and murdered FNL members. Rwasa urged the president to step down before the government was toppled by the FNL military. In January 2013 a document signed by FNL chief of staff Aloys NZABAMPEMA announced that Rwasa had been replaced as party leader by diplomat Isidore NIVISI. Although Rwasa has made no comment to confirm the change in power, his relatives have strongly denied it.

Nkurunziza orchestrated a cabinet reshuffle in February 2013, replacing seven ministers. The president explained that the reshuffle was based on an evaluation of the cabinet ministers' performances while in office.

Fears of looming widespread civil unrest continued into 2013. In March, 6 people were killed and 35 injured after police clashed with worshippers of a Catholic cult in a northern district. In May, the Forum for the Strengthening of Civil Society, a coalition of 200 rights groups in Burundi, spoke out over concerns about instances of violence by the Imbonerakure, the youth branch of the CNDD-FDD. The Imbonerakure is suspected to be behind a recent spate of murders, beatings of opposition party members, and disruption of opposition party meetings. UN representatives in Burundi welcomed the statement and urged the government to act on extrajudicial killings and violence.

The passage of a restrictive media law in June drew harsh criticism from international rights groups. The law forces journalists to reveal their sources, requires them to have university qualifications, and restricts reporting on matters that could undermine national security, the economy, or public order. The bill passed the legislature with a significant majority, winning 82 to 16 in the national assembly, and 32 to 6 in the senate. Supporters of the law argue it will professionalize the media and discourage sensationalism, but opponents fear that it will further suppress the country's opposition voices in the lead-up to the 2015 elections.

POLITICAL PARTIES AND GROUPS

Of the 24 political parties that contested Burundi's pre-independence elections in 1961, only the Union for National Progress (Uprona) survived, serving as the political base of the Micombero and Bagaza regimes. On April 16, 1992, a month after the constitutional revival of pluralism, President Buyoya signed a bill guaranteeing that the next election would be conducted on a multiparty basis. By mid-1993, 11 parties, including Uprona, had been legally registered. Political party activity was suspended following the coup of July 1996 but was reactivated in 1998.

Government and Government-Supportive Parties:

National Council for the Defense of Democracy–Forces for the Defense of Democracy (*Conseil National pour la Défense de Démocratie–Forces pour la Défense de Démocratie*—CNDD-FDD). The CNDD-FDD is one of the successors to the CNDD that was formed in 1994 in Zaire following the assassination of President Ndadaye and the flight into exile of many Hutu political figures. Leonard Nyangoma, a former member of Frodebu and former cabinet minister who was branded a "warlord" by the Ntibantunganya government, led the CNDD from exile in Kenya. Nyangoma, who charged Frodebu with being terrorized by the "mono-ethnic Tutsi army," called in early 1995 for the deployment of a 5,000-man "international intervention force to protect the country's democratic institutions." If such intervention was not forthcoming, he asserted that the CNDD's armed wing—the Forces for the Defense of Democracy (*Forces pour la Défense de Démocratie*—FDD)—would have "no other choice but to step up popular resistance."

In March 1996 the CNDD issued a list of conditions for a cease-fire, including the release of 5,000 Frodebu political prisoners; the return of government troops to their barracks; and the withdrawal of international arrest warrants for Nyangoma and his second-in-command, Christian

SENDEGEYA. Although some observers cited the CNDD's willingness to negotiate as cause for optimism about scheduled peace talks, within weeks the rebels had reversed their stance, vowing to keep fighting until the Tutsis gave "power back to the people." Rebel leader Nyangoma was excluded from peace talks in June, prompting a surge in FDD military activity. In March 1997 the regime blamed CNDD operatives for deadly bomb attacks in Bujumbura, and the following month the government asserted that former Rwandan "Interhamwe" fighters (see article on Rwanda) and Zairean Hutus were supporting the rebels.

In April 1997 the CNDD criticized regional leaders for easing sanctions on the regime in Burundi, and in June the rebels turned down an invitation to attend a peace conference in Switzerland. However, the group subsequently agreed to participate in peace talks sponsored by regional leaders, earning the enmity of Palipehutu (below), with whose forces the FDD clashed repeatedly in late 1997 and early 1998. In March 1998 the CNDD began a purge that ousted at least seven leading figures, including Sendegeya. Relations between the CNDD, which attended the June 1998 peace talks, and the FDD, which was not invited (reportedly at the insistence of the mediation leader, President Nyerere of Tanzania), came to a breaking point in May when CNDD leader Nyangoma sacked Jean-Bosco NDAYIKENGURUKIYE, head of the FDD, as well as Hussein Radjabu, a CNDD party official. However, CNDD spokesperson Jerome NDIHO claimed that the party had, in fact, suspended Nyangoma and replaced him with Ndayikengurukiye. Nonetheless, Nyangoma attended the talks as CNDD president, and the CNDD joined the G-7. Observers in Bujumbura saw the split between the political and military wings of the rebel movement as the result of jockeying for positions of power in advance of a possible near-term settlement.

The Nyangoma faction subsequently became increasingly marginalized within the CNDD in favor of supporters of Ndayikengurukiye, who strongly criticized the finalization of the 2001 power-sharing accord with the government. However, it was reported that a faction led by Pierre Nkurunziza and Radjabu had ousted Ndayikengurukiye in September 2001. The anti-Ndayikengurukiye wing was described as "pro-Frodebu" and inclined to pursue further negotiations with the government, and it participated in a regional summit on Burundi's future in Pretoria in October. However, with both factions still claiming legitimacy, fierce fighting was reported in FDD strongholds in the east and south between the FDD and government troops in the last two months of the year following the installation of the new transitional government.

Elements of the FDD entered into negotiations with the government in 2002, with the Ndayikengurukiye faction signing a cease-fire in December and the Nkurunziza faction in October 2003. (By that time the Nkurunziza faction was referencing itself as the CNDD-FDD.) The CNDD-FDD was given four portfolios in the November 2003 cabinet, while one ministry was accorded to the Ndayikengurukiye faction of the CNDD.

In May 2004 Ndayikengurukiye announced that his group would thenceforth be known as *Kaza* (Welcome)-FDD. In early 2005 the interior ministry announced the formal registration of *Kaza*-FDD, the CNDD-FDD, and the CNDD (still under Nyangoma's leadership) as separate parties for the upcoming legislative elections. (See section on Nyangoma's CNDD, below.)

The CNDD-FDD dominated the communal elections in June 2005 as well as the National Assembly and Senate balloting in July. Nkurunziza resigned as leader of the CNDD-FDD shortly before he was elected president of the republic in August. Radjabu succeeded him in the CNDD-FDD post. By early 2006, the CNDD-FDD claimed to have made significant strides toward its goal of becoming a truly "national party" by having Tutsis fill a number of leadership posts.

Relations between Nkurunziza and Radjabu subsequently deteriorated, in part due to perceptions that Radjabu (a Muslim) was pursuing the "Islamization" of the party and, by extension, the government. (Among other things, Radjaba had reportedly organized an armed youth wing of the party with 30,000 members.) Radjabu was also strongly criticized by Alice Nzomukunda when she resigned as second vice president of the republic in September 2006. Radjabu eventually lost the ensuing power struggle within the CNDD-FDD when Jeremy Ngendakumana, a former ambassador to Kenya, replaced him as party chair at a special congress in early February 2007. However, more than 20 of the CNDD-FDD's 59 members of the assembly remained loyal to Radjabu and boycotted subsequent assembly sessions, thereby costing the party its legislative majority and prompting a political stalemate. The CNDD-FDD dissidents, many of whom had joined other parties, were dismissed from the assembly in May 2008, while Radjabu was sentenced to 13 years in prison following his conviction on charges of plotting a rebellion and "insulting the president." Meanwhile, an extraordinary CNDD-FDD congress in January had also expelled Nzomukunda from the party.

In the May 2010 communal balloting, the CNDD-FDD secured 64 percent of the total vote. Nkurunziza was reelected president of the republic in June, and the CNDD-FDD secured majorities in both the Senate and Assembly in subsequent balloting. The CNDD-FDD dominated the subsequent coalition government, with 14 of the 21 cabinet posts.

The CNDD-FDD has found itself on the end of increasing criticism and accusation from opposition groups throughout the country since the 2010 election. Many claim that the CNDD-FDD is behind the killings of its political opponents throughout the country. These accusations are further compounded by the September 2012 announcement of the FNL (see below) to declare war against the CNDD-FDD and its government.

Leaders: Pierre NKURUNZIZA (President of the Republic); Gabriel NTISEZERANA (Speaker of the Senate and Former Second Vice President of the Republic); Gervais RUFYIKIRI (Second Vice President of the Republic); Pascal NYABENDA (Party President); Victor BURIKUKIYE, Joseph NTAKARUTIMANA (Party Vice Presidents).

Union for National Progress (*Union pour le Progrès National*—Uprona). Founded in 1958 as the *Union et Progrès National,* Uprona was dissolved after the 1976 coup but subsequently reemerged as the country's only authorized party. In December 1979 the party pledged to return the country to civilian rule under President Bagaza's leadership. Following the 1987 coup and designation of Maj. Pierre Buyoya, previously a little-known Uprona Central Committee member, as president of the republic, all Uprona leaders were dismissed, and formal party activity ceased. By early 1988 the party was again functioning, a Buyoya supporter having been selected as its new secretary general. Thereafter, with Tutsis comprising 90 percent of Uprona's membership, party leaders attempted to recruit more Hutus and implement additional "democratization" measures. The March 1992 Uprona congress approved a new Central Committee with a Hutu majority.

Uprona won only 16 of 81 legislative seats at the June 1993 nationwide balloting. Subsequently, party president Nicolas MAYUGI decried Frodebu's "antidemocratic" electoral victories, claiming they were based on "ethnic manipulation." Although observers described Mayugi's sentiments as pervasive in the Tutsi community, seven members of the government named in July, including the prime minister, were Uprona members. Similar concessions were made in the government arrangements of 1994–1995.

In 1995 and the first half of 1996, Uprona militants called for the ousting of President Ntibantunganya and repudiation of the power-sharing arrangements with Frodebu. Uprona also refused to negotiate with representatives from the CNDD, despite otherwise broad consensus that the latter's participation was imperative for any peace initiative. In addition, Uprona remained steadfastly opposed to foreign military intervention. Thus, in June 1996 Tanzanian President Nyerere labeled Uprona as one of the "main obstacles" to peace. It was therefore not surprising that Uprona was heavily represented in the new government formed following the July coup.

A split occurred in Uprona between those who supported President Buyoya's efforts to reach a negotiated settlement with opposition groups in 1997–1998 and those opposed to any concessions to the "rebels." Uprona President Charles MUKASI, a member of the latter camp, was reportedly briefly detained in late 1997 for conducting a press conference in September 1997 in which he criticized the government for dealing with "genocidal" Hutu rebels. Ironically, Mukasi was one of the few high-ranking Hutus in the predominately Tutsi Uprona. The dispute over how to deal with the rebels came to a head in October 1998 when Mukasi expelled three members from the party, including Luc RUKINGAMA, a cabinet minister. Buyoya immediately reasserted his authority, and the Central Committee suspended Mukasi and replaced him with Rukingama as interim chair. While divisions remained with the party, the Mukasi wing was subsequently largely marginalized.

New Uprona President Jean-Baptiste MANWANGARI opposed the constitution approved in February 2005 on the grounds that it provided insufficient guarantees for Tutsis. Uprona won only 6.3 percent of the vote in local elections in June 2005 and 7.3 percent in assembly balloting in July, *Africa Confidential* subsequently describing the party as having "quietly accepted its defeat." Manwangari was defeated in his bid for reelection to the Uprona presidency at a congress in January 2006. Uprona subsequently split into two factions, one (led by Uprona President Aloys Rubeka) inclined to participate in the government headed by the CNDD-FDD and the other (led by Bonaventure GASUTWA) firmly entrenched in the opposition camp. The internal dissension came to a head in July 2007 when Uprona's Martin NDUWIMANA was suspended from the party for remaining in the government as first vice president despite Uprona's formal refusal to participate in the recently announced cabinet. Following Uprona's decision to join the national unity cabinet in November (at which time Dr. Yves Sahinguvu replaced Nduwimana as first vice president), the party in May 2008 launched an internal "reunification" drive.

Uprona received 6.4 percent of the vote in the communal elections in May 2010. Sahinguvu was selected as the party's presidential candidate but withdrew before the balloting. Uprona secured 2 seats in the Senate, and 17 in the assembly. Uprona subsequently joined the CNDD-FDD-led government.

Leaders: Charles NDITIJE (President of the Party), Felix MBONEKO (Vice President of the Party), Maj. Pierre BUYOYA (Former President of the Republic), Therence SINUNGURUZA (First Vice President of the Republic).

Real Frodebu (*Sahwanya Frodebu Nyakuri*). The Real Frodebu was formed from dissident members of the **Front for Democracy in Burundi** (*Front pour la Démocratie au Burundi*—Frodebu) (see Frodebu, below) by former party president Jean MINANI. Real Frodebu received 1.39 percent of the vote in the 2010 communal elections, placing sixth overall. The party gained no seats in the Senate but secured five in the assembly in the July elections and was part of the CNDD-FDD-led postelection government.

Leader: Jean MINANI.

Other Parties:

Front for Democracy in Burundi (*Front pour la Démocratie au Burundi*—Frodebu). Frodebu was launched in support of a "no" vote at the referendum of March 1992, arguing that the government's failure to convene a national conference meant that there had been no opposition input to the constitutional draft. However, following the vote, the group's leadership announced, "We are ready to play the game."

Party leader Melchior Ndadaye won the presidency of the republic on June 1, 1993, with Frodebu securing 65 of 81 assembly seats on the basis of a 71.4 percent vote share. However, the October 21 assassination of President Ndadaye and a number of other prominent party members eviscerated Frodebu. Furthermore, a number of Frodebu leaders were tainted by their involvement in subsequent revenge attacks on Tutsis.

On December 23, 1993, Sylvestre Ntibantunganya, foreign minister and Ndadaye confidante, was elected party president and president of the National Assembly. Ntibantunganya became acting president of the republic on April 8, 1994, and president five months later.

Despite the emergence of militant anti-Tutsi emotions within Frodebu, a number of prominent leaders, including party president Jean Minani, called in 1995 for continued dialogue with their Tutsi counterparts. However, following the coup of July 1996, some Frodebu leaders urged supporters to join forces with the CNDD in attempting to topple the Buyoya regime.

In early 1997 Minani called on the international community to pressure the UN to send troops into Burundi and to observe the sanctions imposed on the regime in July 1996. In addition, he decried Bujumbura's "villagization" efforts for having created "concentration camps." The following week, party Secretary General Augustin NOJIBWAMI was jailed for "sabotaging the government's efforts to establish peace" after he echoed Minani's statements. In early 1998 Frodebu leaders reaffirmed their support for all-party talks toward a negotiated settlement of the conflict in Burundi, although the party was splitting into differing factions. For example, Minani remained in exile in Tanzania and attended the peace talks as the party's representative, while certain CNDD elements argued that they, not he, represented the genuine Frodebu leadership.

In the wake of the power-sharing agreement of June 1998, Frodebu was authorized to keep the 65 legislative seats in the new Transitional National Assembly that it had obtained in 1993. However, the party had to appoint new legislators to more than 20 of the seats, the incumbents having either fled into exile or fallen victim to the recent violence. Concurrently, Nojibwami took over leadership of the Frodebu faction functioning in Burundi.

In July 1999 reports indicated that Minani had entered into an alliance with former president Bagaza and Parena in opposition to President Buyoya and Uprona, an initiative that was condemned by Nojibwami and others. This split was accommodated within the Arusha negotiations through the presence of the "internal" Nojibwani Frodebu wing in the National Assembly delegation to the talks. Minani led the main "external" Frodebu delegation. Following the installation of the new transitional government on November 1, 2001, Minani, who had recently returned to Burundi after more than five years in exile, was elected president of the new Transitional National Assembly.

After Frodebu's Domitien Ndayizeye became president of the republic in April 2003, Frodebu campaigned in support of the new constitution approved in February 2005. However, Frodebu secured only about 23 percent of the vote in the June 2005 local elections and July assembly poll. Many Frodebu supporters by that time had reportedly defected to the CNDD-FDD. Internal party leadership struggles continued, and late in the year Minani was voted out of the party presidency in favor of Léonce Ngendakumana, although a number of Frodebu stalwarts reportedly remained outside the new president's sphere of influence.

Frodebu joined the national unity government installed in September 2005, although sharp dissatisfaction was voiced because the party had received neither the vice-presidential post nor the number of ministerial positions it believed it deserved based on its standing as the second largest group in the assembly. Tensions culminated in a March 2006 decision by Frodebu to withdraw from the government. When three Frodebu ministers opted to stay in the cabinet, they were expelled from the party.

Frodebu agreed to join the national unity cabinet in November 2007, receiving four ministerial and two vice-ministerial posts, although friction reportedly continued within the party regarding the degree of cooperation with CNDD-FDD initiatives. In June 2008 Minani announced that he and some 12 legislators had formed a new faction called Real Frodebu (Frodebu-*Nyakuri*) (see above), which was seen as more closely aligned with the CNDD-FDD. (Ngendakumana had strongly criticized the recent dismissal [requested by the CNDD-FDD] of 22 members of the assembly who had left the CNDD-FDD following an internal dispute within that party.)

Former Burundian president Ndayizeye was chosen in 2009 as Frodebu's candidate for the 2010 presidential election but withdrew his candidacy as part of the opposition boycott. Frodebu secured 5.55 percent of the vote in communal elections in 2010, but the party boycotted the legislative elections that year. Frodebu subsequently led the creation of a broad opposition coalition, the Democratic Alliance for Change (*Alliance des Democrates pour le Changement*—ADC).

Leaders: Léonce NGENDAKUMANA (President of the Party), Domitien NDAYIZEYE (Former President of the Republic), Frederic BAMVUGINYUMVIRA (Vice President of the Party), Euphrasie BIGIRIMANA (Secretary General).

Guarantor of Freedom of Speech in Burundi (*Inkinzo y Ijambo Ryabarundi*). Founded in 1993, *Inkinzo* (also referenced then as the Shield of Freedom of Speech) joined the PRP and Raddes in their December 1995 withdrawal from the government. However, *Inkinzo* subsequently participated in the first cabinet led by the CNDD-FDD.

At a March 2009 congress, Tite Bucumi defeated incumbent Alphonse RUGAMBARARA for the leadership of the party, now referenced as the **Pan-Africanist Socialist Movement–*Inkinzo*** (*Mouvement Socialiste Panafricain–Inkinzo*—MSP-*Inkinzo*).

Leader: Tite BUCUMI.

Movement for the Rehabilitation of the Citizen (*Mouvement pour la Réhabilitation du Citoyen*—MRC). After securing 2 seats in the 2005 assembly elections, the MRC (also referenced as the National Resistance Movement for the Rehabilitation of the Citizen) accepted the public service and social security portfolio in the new cabinet led by the CNDD-FDD. The MRC secured less than 1 percent of the vote in communal elections and boycotted legislative balloting in 2010.

Leaders: Epitace BAYA-GANAKANDI (Party President), Laurent NZEYIMANA, Col. (Ret.) (Spokesperson).

Party for National Recovery (*Parti pour le Recouvrement National*—PRN or Parena). Launched in August 1994 by former head of state Col. Jean-Baptiste Bagaza, Parena was allegedly linked with a number of Tutsi militias. Bagaza, who had dismissed the 1993 elections as an "ethnic referendum," refused to sign the 1994 power-sharing agreement, saying there could be no solution that included Frodebu. He also accused the president's party of planning a Tutsi genocide. In 1995 Bagaza reportedly concurred with calls for the establishment of a "Tutsiland" and a "Hutuland" as separate entities.

On January 18, 1997, the Buyoya regime's security forces placed Bagaza under house arrest, and on March 17 five senior Parena members were imprisoned for their alleged roles in a coup plot against the president. However, Bagaza was subsequently released and permitted to travel to neighboring countries to participate in discussions regarding a possible permanent solution to the instability in Burundi. (The others were convicted in January 2000 of plotting to kill Buyoya, but they were released in August 2000.) Parena was frequently critical of the Arusha negotiations, accusing Buyoya of selling out Tutsi interests. Although it eventually signed the accord, Parena subsequently declined to ratify various implementation measures. In November 2002 the government banned Parena and placed Bagaza under house arrest. However, the ban and arrest were suspended in May 2003. In February 2005 there were reports that a new rebel group, the **Justice and Liberty United Front,** had been formed to support Bagaza. However, Parena accepted a ministerial position in the new coalition government installed in September 2005. At a December 2009 party conference, Bagaza was elected as Parena's 2010 presidential candidate. He subsequently withdrew as part of the opposition boycott of presidential and legislative elections. Parena secured less than 1 percent of the vote in communal elections. As a former head of state, Bagaza received a lifetime appointment in the Senate, where he led the opposition to the CNDD-FDD.

Leaders: Col. Jean-Baptiste BAGAZA, Cyrille BARANCIRA (Secretary General).

African-Burundi Salvation Alliance (*Alliance Burundaise-Africaine pour le Salut*—Abasa). Abasa is a small Tutsi-dominated opposition group that in 1997 called for new national leadership, criticizing the Buyoya regime for lacking a "clear strategy." Abasa gained less than 1 percent of the vote in communal polling in 2010.

Leaders: Terrence NSANZE (Former Permanent Representative to the UN), Serge MUKAMARAKIZA (in exile).

National Council for the Defense of Democracy (*Conseil National pour la Défense de Démocratie*—CNDD). This grouping was reorganized under the CNDD rubric in early 2005 after sustained factionalization within the original CNDD (see CNDD-FDD, above, for details). The CNDD won four seats in the 2005 assembly poll and dominated balloting in local elections in Bururi Province, home of the CNDD leader, Leonard Nyangoma, who filled one of the assembly seats. However, Nyangoma went into exile in 2006 (after his parliamentary immunity was lifted) because of what he claimed was systematic suppression of opposition parties by the CNDD-FDD. Nyangoma returned to Burundi in July 2007 and, following the formation of a national unity cabinet in November, became the de facto leader of the opposition. The CNDD secured 1.28 percent of the vote in the 2010 communal elections. Nyangoma went into exile after the national elections but announced in February 2013 that he plans to return to Burundi before the 2015 elections.

Leaders: Leonard NYANGOMA (Party President, in exile), François BIZIMANA.

National Forces of Liberation (*Forces Nationales de la Libération*—FNL). Founded in the mid-1990s by Palipehutu military leader Cossan KABURA, the FNL (often referenced at that time as the Palipehutu-FNL) subsequently conducted guerrilla actions against government forces, primarily in and around Bujumbura. The hard-line Palipehutu-FNL appeared to separate from the main Palipehutu grouping when the latter agreed in 1999 to participate in the Arusha peace talks.

In late February 2001 it was reported that Kabura had been "ejected" from the FNL by a faction led by Agathon Rwasa, said by that time to command some 90 percent of the FNL's fighters. Rwasa and his supporters criticized Kabura for failing to convene a national congress to discuss strategy. Apparently to underscore its militancy, the Rwasa faction invaded Bujumbura in early March in an apparent takeover attempt that was eventually repulsed by government forces. Both FNL factions condemned the July power-sharing accord, and more intense FNL attacks were reported late in the year.

In December 2002 dissident members of the FNL formed the **FNL-Icanzo** under the leadership of Alain MUGABARABONA. (In 2007 Mugabarabona was sentenced to 20 years in prison following his conviction on charges relating to the alleged coup plot of 2006. Mugabarabona claimed that his confession had been elicited through torture and subsequently denied that any plot had been undertaken.) Following the cease-fire between the government and the FDD, the FNL subsequently remained the only major rebel group still fighting the transitional government. The group became increasingly marginalized and lost much of its foreign support following an attack in August of 2004 on a UN refugee camp in Gatumba, Burundi. The government and several neighboring states subsequently designated the FNL a terrorist organization. FNL forces were repulsed in a December 2004 attack but managed to assassinate the governor of Bubanza Province in January 2005.

In May 2005 the government and the FNL reportedly signed a peace deal whereby both sides agreed to cease fighting. Additional agreements to allow the FNL to participate in upcoming elections or future governments remained elusive, however.

In October 2005 reports surfaced that Rwasa had been ousted as chair of "Palipehutu-FNL" in favor of a "pronegotiation" leadership including Jean-Bosco SINADAYIGAYA as chair. In January 2006 Sinadayigaya announced that his faction had ceased hostilities. However, Rwasa's faction continued antigovernment activity in the hills around Bujumbura into May 2006, having reportedly forged an alliance with rebels in the DRC. Rwasa signed a temporary cease-fire agreement in September 2006, but a permanent resolution remained elusive. Outstanding issues included the proposed integration of the estimated 3,000 FNL fighters into the national army and civil service, the future political role of the FNL, and the release of imprisoned FNL supporters.

FNL negotiators disengaged from talks with the government in July 2007, and fighting was reported in September between Rwasa's supporters and FNL dissidents, who accused Rwasa of "insincerity" in pursuing a final agreement and were pursuing demobilization (which included a financial incentive) on their own. The FNL accused the government of failing to follow through on its promises of jobs for FNL supporters, including integration of FNL fighters into a new national army that would more accurately reflect the Hutu majority. The FNL also launched attacks against government forces near Bujumbura in April and May 2008, prompting President Nkurunziza to call for international help in resolving the rebellion. For its part, the FNL accused the government of prolonging the hostilities by "chasing" FNL fighters and trying to "eliminate" them rather than dealing with issues surrounding demobilization.

Regional leaders subsequently reportedly told Rwasa and his fighters that they faced expulsion from Tanzania unless they laid down their arms. Consequently, Rwasa in May 2008 signed yet another tentative peace agreement with the Burundian government and returned to Bujumbura after nearly two decades of guerrilla activity. Under intense pressure from regional leaders, the government and the FNL appeared to resolve most of their outstanding issues at a meeting in December 2008. Among other things, the government reportedly agreed to release FNL detainees and appoint FNL members to positions of authority in various state institutions.

In January 2009 Rwasa announced that the Palipehutu-FNL was formally dropping Palipehutu from its name to conform with the constitutional injunction against ethnically based political parties. The civil war officially came to an end in April 2009 when Rwasa ceremoniously turned over his rifle and declared that the FNL, which was formally registered as a political party, was now "a part of society." In August 2010 a dissident FNL congress voted to replace Rwasa with Emmanuel MIBURO, a former advisor to Nkurunziza. However, most FNL members continued to accept Rwasa as the legitimate party president. The FNL placed second in communal balloting in 2010 with about 14 percent of the vote. The grouping led the subsequent boycott of legislative polling. Rwasa briefly went into hiding after the June presidential elections, claiming that the government sought his arrest. As political violence rose in late 2010 and early 2011, reports indicated that the FNL had begun to rearm. These claims of rearmament were realized in September 2012, when the FNL declared war against the Burundi government led by the CNDD-FDD. Rwasa called for president Nkurunziza to step down before the government was toppled. In January 2013 FNL chief of staff Aloys Nzabampema issued a statement that Rwasa had been replaced as party leader by Isidore Nivisi (see Current issues, above).

Leaders: Isidore NIVISI, Agathon RWASA, Jean-Berchmans NDAYISHIMIYE, Pasteur HABIMANA.

Movement for Security and Democracy (*Mouvement pour la Sécurité and la Démocratie*—MSD). The MSD was formed in December 2007 by Alexis Sinduhije, who had gained prominence since the early 2000s as the operator of a radio station devoted to reconciliation between Hutus and Tutsis, a theme the MSD hoped to pursue for the 2010 legislative elections. However, the government refused to register the MSD, and Sinduhije and nearly 40 of his supporters were arrested in early November 2008 on charges of "conducting an illegal political meeting." Although the other MSD members were released shortly thereafter, Sinduhije remained in jail until his March 2009 acquittal on a charge of insulting the president, the case having prompted widespread criticism from the international community of the government's apparent heavy-handed tactics. The MSD placed fifth in the 2010 communal elections, with 3.84 percent of the vote. Sinduhije fled into exile in September 2010, after party spokesperson François NYAMOYA was arrested for criticizing the military (Nyamoya was released in October). In March 2013 Sinduhije returned to Burundi ahead of the 2013 elections.

Leader: Alexis SINDUHIJE (Party President).

People's Reconciliation Party (*Parti pour la Réconciliation du Peuple*—PRP). The promonarchist PRP was founded in September 1991 on a platform calling for a parliamentary monarchy with a prime minister and an ethnically mixed council of nobles. The group was officially recognized on July 1, 1992, and in November it called for the government to open negotiations with the opposition.

PRP candidate Pierre-Claver Sendegeya finished a distant third in the June 1, 1993, presidential balloting, and the party failed to secure representation in the subsequent legislative elections. Considered an extremist by the government, PRP leader Mathias Hitimana was arrested in August 1994, provoking a series of deadly street clashes by his followers that shut down the capital for three days.

The PRP was awarded a post in the government named in March 1995; however, nine months later it quit the cabinet, and in January 1996 Hitimana was again arrested. In July party militants took part in the anti-Ntibantunganya demonstrations that sought to vilify the president for agreeing to foreign intervention. Although the PRP was given a ministerial post in the transitional cabinet of November 2001, its minister left the government in July 2002. However, the party accepted a new post in 2003.

Déo Niyonzima, the president of the PRP, was among those arrested in mid-2006 in connection with an alleged coup plot. However, he was acquitted in January 2007.

Leaders: Déo NIYONZIMA (President), Mathias HITIMANA (Former President), François MBESHERUBUSA, Jean Bosco YAMUREMYE.

Hutu People's Liberation Party (*Parti Libération du Peuple Hutu*—Palipehutu). Palipehutu was formed by Hutu exiles in Rwanda and Tanzania who opposed the long-standing political and economic dominance of Burundi's Tutsis. The government attributed the Hutu-Tutsi conflict of August 1988, as well as the attempted coup of November 1991, to Palipehutu activism, although there was no outside confirmation of either allegation. In 1990 Palipehutu founder Rémy GAHUTU died in a Tanzanian prison. (His successor, Etienne Karatasi, remained exiled in Denmark.)

In 1993 the party was split by the defection of its military leader, Cossan Kabura, who "declared war on the Ndadaye government." He subsequently founded the National Forces of Liberation (FNL, below). In early 1997 *Africa Confidential* reported that Palipehutu and the FNL had agreed to form a military alliance with a group from the DRC styled the **National Council of Kivu Resistance** (*Conseil Nationale de Résistance du Kivu*—CNRK). Led by Arema Bin AMISI, the ethnic Bembe CNRK reportedly opposed the government of Laurent Kabila in the DRC.

In the second half of 1997 Palipehutu leaders accused the CNDD of "collaborating" with the Buyoya regime by agreeing to join peace talks. Severe intra-Hutu fighting was subsequently reported between Palipehutu forces and the CNDD's armed wing, the FDD. In early 2000 it was reported that FNL fighters had clashed in Burundi with Rwandan Hutu guerrilla groups with which the FNL had previously been allied. Palipehutu eventually joined the G-7 grouping at the Arusha talks and was a signatory to the August 28, 2000, accord, although the FNL did not accept the agreement. Palipehutu reportedly joined the national unity government installed in 2003. However, Palipehutu-FNL continued military action against the government (see FNL, for details). Palipehutu reportedly altered its name to the **Burundi People's Liberation Party** (*Parti Libération du Peuple Burundais*—Palipe—Agakiza) in an effort to broaden its appeal. The party secured less than 1 percent of the vote in the 2010 communal elections. Reports in 2011 indicated that Palipehutu members had carried out a series of attacks on the local CNDD-FDD party headquarters.

Leaders: Etienne KARATASI, Antoine SEZOYA-NGABO.

National Liberation Front (*Front de Libération Nationale*—Frolina). A small movement composed primarily of militant Hutu refugees, Frolina (previously referenced as *Umbumwé* [Solidarity]) was organized in the mid-1980s. It reportedly conducted a guerrilla attack on a Burundi military installation in Mabandal on August 13, 1990. Four days later the group's leader, former Palipehutu member Joseph Karumba, was arrested in Tanzania.

In June 1992 Karumba was linked to militant refugees in Mpanda, Tanzania. In announcing their intent to arrest the group, Tanzanian officials reported that Karumba had recently sought their assistance in "liberating" Burundi. However, Karumba was subsequently granted asylum in Tanzania, from which he conducted Frolina's political affairs while Frolina fighters, referenced as the People's Armed Forces, engaged in sporadic guerrilla action in Burundi through 1998. In signing the Arusha accord of August 2000, Karumba agreed that Frolina forces would eventually be incorporated into the national forces of Burundi, although a militant Frolina wing reportedly remained opposed to that measure and other Arusha "concessions." Frolina named four of its members to the new Transitional National Assembly in late 2001; however, no ministers in the new cabinet were identified as belonging to Frolina. Karumba was among the former rebels who were "demobilized" in mid-2005. Frolina gained less than 1 percent of the vote in the 2010 communal elections. Karumba was initially the Frolina candidate in the 2010 elections, but he withdrew along with other opposition figures.

Leader: Joseph KARUMBA.

Other past government parties include the **Independent Workers' Party** (*Parti Indépendent de Travailleurs*—PIT), which is led by Nicéphore NDIMURUKUNDO and Etienne NTAHONZA and which held portfolios in the cabinets of 1994, 1995, 2001, and 2003, and the **People's Party** (*Parti Populaire*—PP), a pro-Frodebu grouping led by Shadrack NIYONKURU, which was allocated one cabinet ministry in 1995, 2001, and 2003.

Other minor political parties and groups include the **Democratic Forum** (*Forum Démocratique*—FODE), formed in 1999 and led by Deogratias BABURIFATO; the **New Alliance for Democracy and the Development of Burundi** (*Alliance Nouvelle Pour la Démocratie et le Développement au Burundi*), formed in 2002 by Jean-Paul BURAFUTA; the **Party for Democracy and Reconciliation** (*Parti pour la Démocratie et la Réconciliation*—PDR), formed in 2002 and led by Augustin NZOJIBWAMI; the **Patriots' Council,** formed in early 2009 under the leadership of Anicet NIYONGABO; the **Union for Peace and Development** (*Union pour la Paix et le Développement*—UPD), established in 2002 and led by Freddy FERUVI; and the **Patriotic Front for Liberation** (*Front Patriotique de Liberation*—FPL), an armed, exile group formed by Richard Ciramunda in November 2010.

For more information on the **Social Democratic Party** (*Parti Social-Démocrate*—PSD), the **Liberal Alliance for Development** (*Alliance Libérale Pour la Développement—Imboneza*), and the **Alliance of the Brave** (AV-*Intwari*), see the 2011 *Handbook.*

LEGISLATURE

The new constitution approved in February 2005 codified the bicameral **Parliament** (*Parlement*) consisting of a Senate and a National Assembly elected for five-year terms. (For extensive information on parliamentary developments from 1987 to 2002, see the 2007 *Handbook.*)

Senate (*Sénat*). The upper house comprises 34 indirectly elected members (1 Hutu and 1 Tutsi from each province as selected by electoral colleges comprised of members of the local councils within each province), all former presidents (currently 4), 3 members of the Twa ethnic group, and enough women to make the number of female senators at least 30 percent of the total. (There are currently 41 members, including 17 women.) The provincial electoral colleges' balloting took place on July 28, 2010. Of the 34 seats filled, 32 were reportedly secured by the National Council for the Defense of Democracy—Forces for the Defense of Democracy, and 2 by the Union for National Progress.

Speaker: Gabriel NTISEZERANA.

National Assembly (*Assemblée Nationale*). The lower house is comprised of 100 members directly elected by party-list proportional representation, enough additional members (currently 3) to fulfill the constitutional mandates that 60 percent of the regular seats be filled by Hutus and 40 percent by Tutsis and that 30 percent of the regular seats be filled by women, and three members of the Twa ethnic group. In the balloting of July 23, 2010, the National Council for the Defense of Democracy—Forces for the Defense of Democracy (CNDD-FDD) won 80 seats; the Union for National Progress (Uprona), 16; and the Real Frodebu, 4. Of the 3 additional seats subsequently allocated to meet the constitutional mandates, 1 each was given to the CNDD-FDD, Uprona, and the Real Frodebu.

Speaker: Pie NTAVYOHANYUMA.

CABINET

[as of October 1, 2013]

President	Pierre Nkurunziza (CNDD-FDD)
First Vice President (in Charge of Political and Administrative Affairs)	Therence Sinunguruza (Uprona)
Second Vice President (in Charge of Social and Economic Affairs)	Gervais Rufyikiri (CNDD-FDD)

Ministers

Agriculture and Livestock	Odette Kaytesi (CNDD-FDD) [f]
Civil Service, Labor, and Social Security	Annonciata Sendazirasa (Real Frodebu) [f]
Communications, Telecommunications, Information, and Relations with Parliament	Leocadi Nihazi (Uprona) [f]
Communal Development	Jean-Claude Ndihokubwayo (Uprona)
Energy and Mines	Come Manirakiza (CNDD-FDD)
External Relations and International Cooperation	Laurent Kavakure (CNDD-FDD)
Finance and Economic Development Planning	Tabu Abdallah Manirakiza (CNDD-FDD) [f]
Higher Education and Scientific Research	Joseph Butore (CNDD-FDD)
Interior	Edouard Nduwimana (CNDD-FDD)
Justice, Keeper of the Seals, and Attorney General	Pascal Barandagiye (CNDD-FDD)
National Defense and War Veterans	Maj. Gen. Pontien Gaciyubwenge (ind.)
National Solidarity, Repatriation of Refugees, and Social Reintegration	Clotilde Niragira (CNDD-FDD) [f]
Office of the President (Good Governance and Privatization)	Isse Ngendakumana (Real Frodebu)
Office of the President (East African Community Affairs)	Hafsa Mossi (CNDD-FDD) [f]
Primary and Secondary Education	Rose Gahiru (CNDD-FDD) [f]
Public Health	Dr. Sabine Ntakarutimana (CNDD-FDD) [f]
Public Security and Police Commissioner	Gabriel Nizigama (CNDD-FDD)
Trade, Industry, Postal Services and Tourism	Victoire Ndikumana (Uprona) [f]
Transport, Public Works, and Equipment	Deogratias Rurimunzu (CNDD-FDD)
Water, Environment, Territorial Management, and Urban Planning	Jean-Claude Nduwayo (CNDD-FDD)
Youth, Sports, and Culture	Adolphe Rukenkanya (ind.)
Secretary General of the Government and Governmental Spokesperson	Philippe Nzobonariba

[f] = female

INTERGOVERNMENTAL REPRESENTATION

Ambassador to the U.S.: Angele NIYUHIRE.

U.S. Ambassador to Burundi: Dawn M. LIBERI.

Permanent Representative to the UN: Herménégilde NIYONZIMA.

IGO Memberships (Non-UN): AU, AfDB, Comesa, ICC, NAM, WTO.

CAMBODIA

Kingdom of Cambodia
Preahreachanachak Kampuchea

Political Status: Became independent as the Kingdom of Cambodia on November 9, 1953; Khmer Republic proclaimed October 9, 1970; renamed Democratic Kampuchea by constitution of January 5, 1976, following Communist (*Khmer Rouge*) takeover on April 17, 1975; de jure authority contested by the Coalition Government of Democratic Kampuchea (CGDK) and the People's Republic of Kampuchea (PRK, formed January 8, 1979) following the Vietnamese invasion of December 1978; PRK redesignated as State of Cambodia on April 30, 1989; CGDK redesignated as National Government of Cambodia on February 3, 1990, collateral with reversion of Democratic Kampuchea to Cambodia; transitional Supreme National Council formally endorsed by all-party peace agreement signed in Paris, France, on October 23, 1991; interim coalition regime (without *Khmer Rouge* participation) authorized on June 16, 1993, following multiparty legislative election of May 23–28; current constitution ratified on September 21 and promulgated on September 24, 1993.

Area: 69,898 sq. mi. (181,035 sq. km).

Population: 14,542,566 (2012E—UN); 15,205,539 (2013E—U.S. Census)

Major Urban Center (2011E—UN): PHNOM PENH (1,570,791). Following the 1975 Communist takeover, virtually the entire population of the capital, some 1.8 million, was evacuated. In early 1979 substantial reverse migration began, with the population again in excess of 1 million by 2003. Bat DAMBANG (1,126,345), Seam REAB (999,703).

Official Language: Khmer; in addition, French is widely spoken.

Monetary Unit: Riel (official rate November 1, 2013: 4,026.90 riels = $1US).

Monarch: King NORODOM Sihamoni; elected by the Royal Throne Council on October 14, 2004, and crowned on October 29, succeeding NORODOM Sihanouk, who had announced his wish to abdicate, for reasons of health, on October 6.

Prime Minister: HUN Sen (Cambodian People's Party); former cochair of the Council of Ministers of the Provisional National Government; named second prime minister of government formed on October 23, 1993; named prime minister on November 26, 1998, in succession to First Prime Minister UNG Huot (formerly Funcinpec Party) under formal coalition agreement of November 23; continued in office as a caretaker following the legislative election of July 27, 2003; renominated as prime minister by the king on July 14, 2004, confirmed by the National Assembly on July 15, and sworn in on July 16 as the head of a renewed coalition government; reelected by the National Assembly on September 25, 2008, following the legislative election on July 27; reelected on September 23, 2013, following legislative elections on July 28.

THE COUNTRY

The smallest of the French Indochinese states to which independence was restored in 1953, Cambodia is bounded by Thailand on the west and northwest, Laos on the north, and Vietnam on the east and southeast. The southwestern border of the country is an irregular coastline on the Gulf of Thailand. It is a basically homogeneous nation, with Khmers (Cambodians) constituting approximately 85 percent of the total population. Ethnic minorities were estimated in 1970 to include 450,000 Chinese, 400,000 Vietnamese, 80,000 Cham-Malays (Muslims descended from the people of the ancient kingdom of Champa), 50,000 Khmer Loeus (tribals), and 20,000 Thais and Laotians. Many of the Chinese and most of the Cham-Malays and Vietnamese were reported to have been massacred during the period of *Khmer Rouge* rule, from 1975 to 1979.

Social cohesion and stability traditionally derived from a common language (Khmer), a shared sense of national identity, and the pervading influence of Theravada Buddhism, the state religion. Only a handful of Muslims and Christians were said to have survived the 1975–1979 holocaust. Women have long played a major economic role as agricultural laborers and have also been prominent as local traders; they constitute about half of the economically active population. In 2012 women accounted for 20.3 percent of the National Assembly and 13.56 percent of the Senate.

Cambodia's economy was traditionally based on the agricultural sector (including forestry and fishing), which continues to employ about 60 percent of the active labor force and to account for 33 percent of GDP. The chief agricultural crop is rice. It accounts for approximately 80 percent of cultivated land and the largest agricultural export, doubling in the first half of 2012 over 2011. Since 1997 a rapidly expanding garment industry and tourism have become the state's most valuable industries. Total visitor arrivals have nearly doubled since 2004 and in 2007 surpassed 2 million for the first time. In 2010, tourist arrivals were up 16 percent from the preceding year at over 2.5 million. The garment industry has expanded except for a moderate decline during the world recession and represents approximately 90 percent of exports mostly to the United States and EU. The discovery of oil in commercially viable quantities in 2010 has the potential to radically change the Cambodian economy with production expected in late 2012. About 10 percent of the workforce is employed in manufacturing, with the industrial sector as a whole contributing about 22 percent of GDP.

In 2007 the Asian Development Bank cited a "pressing need" for Cambodia to diversify its economy, although it commended the government for its fiscal prudence and progress in structural reforms. External debt, comprising about a third of Cambodia's GDP, and payments arrears have also been an issue of ongoing concern. GDP growth averaged 10.5 percent annually in 2006–2007 but dropped to 6.7 percent in 2008, owing to a slowdown in garment export, and then grew only by 0.1 percent in 2009. GDP growth rebounded in 2010 and 2011, rising to 6 percent and 6.1 percent, respectively, with a moderate increase in GDP per capita from $703 in 2009 to $851 in 2011. Inflation grew –0.7 percent in 2009 and 5.48 percent in 2011. In March 2011 the government enacted a sweeping anticorruption law, while in July the nation's first stock market opened in Phnom Penh. The following month, the World Bank suspended loans to Cambodia in response to forced evictions for economic development (see Current issues, below). In 2012, GDP rose by 6.5 percent, while inflation remained low at 2.9 percent, and GDP per capita was 1,017. In 2013 the World Bank ranked Cambodia 133rd in its annual Doing Business index, highlighting the need for economic reforms.

GOVERNMENT AND POLITICS

Political background. Increasing pressure from Siam (Thailand) and Vietnam had almost extinguished Khmer independence prior to the establishment of a French protectorate at the request of King ANG Duong in 1863. In the early 1940s Japan, in furtherance of its "Greater East Asia Co-prosperity Sphere," seized de facto control of Cambodia. A Thai claim to the western portion of the region had been resisted by the French, but Japan permitted Thailand to annex the provinces of Battambang and Siem Reap, with the French retaining nominal control in the rest of the country. After the surrender of Japan in World War II, Cambodia was recognized as an autonomous kingdom within the French Union, and the two northwestern provinces were returned by Thailand. In 1949 Cambodia signed an accord with France that brought it into the French Union as an Associated State.

Political feuds within the governing Democratic Party having hampered negotiations with the French, King Norodom Sihanouk dissolved the National Assembly in January 1953 and personally negotiated his country's full independence, which was formally announced on November 9. Independence was reinforced by the Geneva Agreement of 1954, which called for the withdrawal from Cambodia of all foreign troops, including *Vietminh* elements that had entered from North Vietnam as a "liberation" force. To enhance his status as national leader, Sihanouk abdicated in 1955 in favor of his father, NORODOM Suramarit. Reverting to the title of prince, Sihanouk organized his own mass political movement, the People's Socialist Community (*Sangkum Reastr Niyum*), which dominated the government for the next decade.

Opposed only by the People's Party (*Kanakpak Pracheachon*), a pro-Communist formation, the *Sangkum* captured all 82 National Assembly seats in an election held in 1966. Unlike in the past, however, the candidates were not handpicked by Sihanouk, and the conservative tendencies of the resultant government, headed by Lt. Gen. LON Nol, prompted Sihanouk to set up a countergovernment of moderates and leftists to act as an extraparliamentary opposition. Subsequent rivalry between the conservative and radical groups, coupled with an April 1967 revolt in Battambang Province in which Communists played a leading role, led Sihanouk to assume special powers as head of a provisional government in May. The new cabinet resigned in January 1968, and Sihanouk appointed another headed by PENN Nouth. Penn Nouth resigned in July 1969, and Gen. Lon Nol returned to the premiership. In March 1970 Prince Sihanouk was deposed as head of state, and on October 9 the monarchy was abolished and Cambodia was proclaimed the Khmer Republic. An election initially scheduled for the same year was postponed because of a military confrontation with North Vietnam.

Under a new constitution adopted on May 4, 1972, the Lon Nol government allowed political parties to organize and then held a presidential election in June. The final tally gave Lon Nol 55 percent of the vote. Opposition parties then boycotted the September legislative election, and all seats in the Senate and National Assembly fell to the progovernment Social-Republican Party.

During 1974 a four-year war between government forces and insurgent communists, the *Khmers Rouges* (Red Khmers), gained in intensity. At midyear Lon Nol offered to engage in peace negotiations with the Communist-affiliated National United Front of Cambodia (*Front Uni National du Cambodge*—FUNC), nominally headed by Prince Sihanouk, who rejected the offer in a statement issued from exile. Following *Khmer Rouge* advances to the vicinity of the capital in early 1975, Prime Minister LONG BORET presented the president with a request that he leave the country. On April 10 Lon Nol departed, and the president of the Senate, Maj. Gen. SAUKHAM Khoy, was named interim president. Two days later, U.S. embassy personnel evacuated Phnom Penh, accompanied by Saukham Khoy, and a temporary Supreme Committee of the Republic surrendered to the FUNC on April 17. The Communist-controlled government that followed included Prince Sihanouk, who was reinstated as head of state, and Penn Nouth, who returned as prime minister.

In December 1975 the National United Front of Kampuchea (FUNK, formerly the FUNC) approved a new constitution for what was to be Democratic Kampuchea, effective from January 5, 1976. An election of delegates to a new People's Representative Assembly was held in March, and in April Prince Sihanouk resigned as head of state, receiving a pension and honorary title of "Great Patriot." At its opening session on April 11 the assembly designated KHIEU Samphan as chair of the State Presidium and Pol POT as prime minister. During its ensuing period of rule, the Pol Pot regime launched a massive effort at imposing a communist agrarian ideology, killing 2 million people or 20 percent of the population.

Hostility between the Khmer and Vietnam reached a climax in late 1978 after months of border conflict resulting in a full-scale invasion by the Vietnamese, supported by a small force of dissident Khmers calling themselves the Kampuchean National United Front for National Salvation (KNUFNS). On January 7, 1979, Phnom Penh fell to the invaders, who proclaimed a People's Republic of Kampuchea (PRK) the following day and installed HENG Samrin, a former assistant chief of the Kampuchean General Staff, as president of a People's Revolutionary Council. Remnants of the defending forces withdrew to the west, where guerrilla-type operations against the Vietnamese-supported regime were maintained by *Khmer Rouge* and right-wing *Khmer Serei* (Free Cambodian) forces, in alliance with a smaller unit claiming allegiance to Prince Sihanouk.

In June 1982 the three anti-Vietnamese groups concluded an agreement on a Coalition Government of Democratic Kampuchea (CGDK). Under the agreement, Prince Sihanouk would serve as president; Khieu Samphan as vice president in charge of foreign affairs; and SON Sann, the leader of the *Khmer Serei*'s Khmer People's National Liberation Front (KPNLF), as prime minister. In January 1985 HUN Sen, a former *Khmer Rouge* official who had defected to the Vietnamese in 1977, became chair of the PRK Council of Ministers.

Sihanouk and Hun Sen, meeting in July 1988 (the first "Jakarta Informal Meeting"—JIM), brought together, for the first time, representatives of all four Cambodian factions as well as those of Vietnam, Laos, and the members of the Association of Southeast Asian Nations (ASEAN). Sihanouk met again with Hun Sen in France in November and resumed the CGDK presidency in February 1989, immediately prior to a second round of all-party discussions in Jakarta (JIM-II). In April 1989 Hun Sen announced that his government was changing the country's official name to State of Cambodia (SOC). Although further multiparty talks proved unproductive, as did a July 30–August 30 Paris International Conference on Cambodia (PICC), Vietnam announced the withdrawal of its troops from Cambodia on September 20, honoring a pledge made the previous May. In February 1990, in an effort to dissociate the resistance movement from the *Khmers Rouges,* Sihanouk announced that the CGDK would henceforth be known as the National Government of Cambodia (NGC).

On June 6, 1990, Sihanouk and Phnom Penh representatives signed an accord that called for the establishment of a Supreme National Council (SNC) of rebel and government members to pave the way for a cease-fire by the end of July, but the *Khmer Rouge* guerrillas refused to participate unless they were granted representation equal to that of Phnom Penh. During an informal meeting in September 1990, all four Cambodian groups approved a "framework document" that had been drafted by the permanent members (P-5) of the UN Security Council assigning most SNC powers to the UN pending the election of a new government. A 12-member SNC convened, accepting "most of the fundamental points" of a November P-5 proposal that provided for a UN Transitional Authority in Cambodia (UNTAC) charged with overseeing a cease-fire, a nationwide election, and the drafting of a new constitution. In January 1991, however, hard-line elements of the SOC effectively repudiated the agreement.

On May 1, 1991, the first cease-fire in the history of the 12-year struggle took effect. Subsequently, Prince Sihanouk won agreement on a permanent truce and acceptance of the council as a supergovernment superior to both the SOC and NGC. In mid-July Sihanouk resigned as NGC president and was named SNC chair. On August 23 a 12-member UN truce-monitoring team arrived in Cambodia.

SNC negotiations in August and September 1991 resolved most remaining issues, and a peace agreement was signed on October 23. On November 19 Sihanouk announced a "treaty of cooperation" between the Hun Sen regime and his own political formation, known since 1989 as the United National Front for an Independent, Neutral, Peaceful, and Cooperative Cambodia (*Front Uni National pour un Cambodge Indépendant, Neutre, Pacifique et Coopératif*—Funcinpec). However, the November 19 alliance, which had been widely construed as an attempt to limit *Khmer Rouge* influence, was terminated on December 5, reportedly at Chinese insistence.

The *Khmers Rouges* boycotted the election of a constituent National Assembly held May 23–28, 1993, at which the Funcinpec Party (FP) won a plurality of 58 seats to 51 for the SOC's Cambodian People's Party (CPP). On June 16 the FP and the CPP agreed that Hun Sen and Prince NORODOM Ranariddh, Sihanouk's eldest son and FP chair, would share powers equally as cochairs of the Council of Ministers, with Sihanouk as head of state. The two parties also agreed that each would hold 45 percent of cabinet posts, with 10 percent allocated to Son Sann's Buddhist Liberal Democratic Party (BLDP, successor to the KPNLF), which had run a distant third in the legislative election.

Cambodia's new constitution was approved on September 21, 1993, and promulgated three days later, at which time Sihanouk was recrowned king. On October 23 a new royal government was formed, with Prince Ranariddh as first prime minister and Hun Sen as second prime minister. Most UNTAC units withdrew in November 1993, at which time the UN General Assembly established a human rights center in Phnom Penh. A major government offensive on remaining *Khmer Rouge* strongholds in the first half of 1996 yielded a split in which a group led by IENG Sary opted to negotiate with the government. The fracturing of the *Khmers Rouges* served to intensify the power struggle between Second Prime Minister Hun Sen and First Prime Minister Prince Ranariddh, both camps reportedly seeking alliances with *Khmer Rouge* factions. In February 1997 Ranariddh rankled Hun Sen further by announcing the formation of a National United Front (NUF) electoral alliance that included opposition leader SAM Rainsy, then of the Khmer Nation Party (KNP). In a further complication, *Khmer Rouge* leader Khieu Samphan indicated his support for the alliance and led to fighting between FP and CPP loyalists.

In April 1997 Hun Sen announced the defection of several legislators from the FP, which had split into pro- and anti-Ranariddh factions and accused the prince of *Khmer Rouge* collaboration. By June the government was split, as were the *Khmers Rouges:* Pol Pot apparently ordered the execution of *Khmer Rouge* military leader SON Sen for negotiating with the government, while several days later *Khmer Rouge* radio announced that Pol Pot himself had been "arrested." The *Khmers Rouges* subsequently convicted Pol Pot of treason and sentenced him to house arrest.

With the threat of *Khmer Rouge* and KNP support for Prince Ranariddh growing steadily, Hun Sen's followers went on the offensive. Civil war broke out near Phnom Penh in July 1997, and Prince Ranariddh left the country. The National Assembly on August 6 confirmed Hun Sen's choice of Foreign Minister UNG Huot, a leader of the anti-Ranariddh FP camp, to replace Ranariddh as first prime minister. At the same time, the legislature stripped Ranariddh of his immunity and charged him with treason for conspiring with the *Khmers Rouges* and with illegally importing weapons. Nevertheless, in September the assembly refused to approve a new cabinet devoid of all FP members. After initially resisting any compromise, Hun Sen in February 1998 accepted a Japanese-brokered agreement under which Ranariddh briefly returned to Cambodia on March 30, having received a prearranged pardon from King Sihanouk. Meanwhile, government operations against the *Khmers Rouges* continued in the north, with reports surfacing in March 1998 that forces had driven hard-line commander TA Mok (UNG Choeun) from his base in Anlong Veng. Accompanying Ta Mok were Khieu Samphan and former second-in-command NUON Chea as well as Pol Pot, who died on April 15, reportedly of a heart attack. By the end of May, Ta Mok's final stronghold, Ta Tum, had fallen, and on June 15 five additional senior *Khmer Rouge* officials defected.

In the run-up to the July 26, 1998, legislative election, the opposition repeatedly accused the CPP of campaign violations, leading Sam Rainsy, now the head of his own Sam Rainsy Party (SRP), to threaten an election boycott. In the end, however, 39 parties contested the election, in which the CPP received 41.4 percent of the votes, followed by the FP with 31.7 percent and the SRP with 14.3 percent. While the formula for allocating the assembly's 122 seats awarded the CPP a majority of 64, compared to 43 for the FP and 15 for the SRP, the distribution left Hun Sen far short of the two-thirds needed to form a new government. Neither Ranariddh nor Rainsy accepted the results, which led to public demonstrations and provoked reprisals by CPP supporters.

With King Sihanouk presiding, Hen Sen, Prince Ranariddh, and Sam Rainsy met in Siem Reap in September 1998. On November 14 Ranariddh concluded a coalition agreement with Hun Sen that had been brokered by King Sihanouk. The pact, formally signed on November 23, provided for Hun Sen to serve as sole prime minister, Ranariddh to assume the presidency of the National Assembly, and CPP chief CHEA Sim, theretofore presiding officer of the assembly, to become chair of a newly created, largely advisory Senate. The CPP and the FP agreed to control 12 and 11 ministries, respectively, while continuing to share the defense and interior portfolios. On November 30 the National Assembly approved the new cabinet.

On December 24–25, 1998, Khieu Samphan and Nuon Chea surrendered to the government. They soon relocated to Pailin, in the northwest, where their former colleague, Ieng Sary, supported by 25,000 or more former *Khmers Rouges,* had established a semiautonomous enclave. Ta Mok was captured on March 6, 2001 (he died in 2006), bringing the insurgency to an end.

In the National Assembly election of July 27, 2003, the CPP won 73 of 123 seats, 9 fewer than the two-thirds needed to form a government on its own. Initially, both FP and the SRP, the only other parties to win representation, refused to join any coalition headed by Hun Sen, who refused to step aside as prime minister. His refusal produced an 11-month impasse, during which the existing CPP-Funcinpec government continued on as caretaker. On June 2, 2004, Hun Sen and Prince Ranariddh announced that they had resolved remaining differences and would again share power. The resultant accord, formally signed on June 30, gave the CPP 60 percent of the cabinet posts and excluded SRP. On July 14 King Sihanouk nominated Hun Sen as prime minister and asked him to form a cabinet, which the National Assembly approved 96–0 on July 15. (The SRP boycotted the vote.)

On October 6, 2004, King Sihanouk, citing his age (81) and health concerns, expressed his desire to abdicate, and on October 14 the Royal Throne Council endorsed his preferred successor, Prince NORODOM SIHAMONI. The new king was crowned on October 29.

On March 2, 2006, the National Assembly passed a constitutional amendment requiring that a new government be backed by a simple majority of lower house members rather than by a two-thirds majority. Although Hun Sen stated after the vote that the CPP did not intend to force FP from Cambodia's governing coalition, he quickly dismissed the Funcinpec co-ministers of defense and interior. On March 3 Prince Ranariddh resigned as president of the National Assembly.

In regular elections for the National Assembly on July 27, 2008, the CPP won 90 of the legislature's 123 seats; the SRP, with 26 seats, was the only other party in double digits as FP, damaged by Prince Ranariddh's departure and subsequent formation of the Norodom Ranariddh Party (NRP), won only 2. On September 24 the National Assembly, despite a boycott by opposition members, voted to reelect Hun Sen as prime minister. He immediately formed a new Council of Ministers that, except for one position, consisted of CPP members.

In Senate elections held on January 29, 2012, the CPP won 46 seats, while the SRP secured 11 seats in the 61-member chamber. The election was largely denounced by monitoring groups because of a lack of transparency. In controversial balloting on July 28, 2013, the CPP won a reduced majority of 68 seats, while the Cambodian National Rescue Party (formed as a merger of the HRP and the SRP, see Current issues, below) won an additional 26 seats for a total of 55. Hun Sen was reelected prime minister on September 23.

Constitution and government. Under the 1993 basic law, Cambodia's head of state is a monarch who enjoys considerable latitude, including the power to dissolve the legislature during a national emergency. Selection of the monarch is the responsibility of the Royal Throne Council, which can choose from among several royal lines. The prime minister, chosen from the leading parliamentary party, is appointed by the monarch upon recommendation by the president of the National Assembly.

The November 1998 CPP-FP pact included provision for establishing a Senate as the upper house of a bicameral Parliament, and in March 1999 the constitution was amended to that effect by the National Assembly. Although the initial Senate comprised 61 appointees, since January 2006 it has been indirectly elected, except for two appointees named by the monarch and two chosen by the National Assembly. The Senate's role is largely advisory; principally, it may recommend changes to legislation passed by the lower chamber, which, however, is under no obligation to enact them. The president of the Senate serves as acting head of state when the king is abroad.

A nine-member Constitutional Council is empowered to resolve election disputes as well as to interpret the constitution and legislation. The independent judiciary is headed by a Supreme Court. In 2004 the National Assembly approved a law establishing an Extraordinary Chambers in the Courts of Cambodia (ECCC) to handle prosecution of *Khmer Rouge* leaders accused of war crimes between 1975 and 1979. The ECCC's trial chamber has three Cambodian and two international judges; the Supreme Court Chamber has four Cambodian and three international judges. Trial Chamber decisions require concurrence by at least four judges; Supreme Court Chamber decisions, five. The first trial began in 2009 (see Current issues, below).

Although the Cambodian constitution grants freedom of expression, press, and publication, "no one shall exercise this right to infringe upon the rights of others, to affect the good traditions of the society, or violate public law and order and national security." In practice, the government has often acted to restrict publication of information it considers false or defamatory, and defamation suits have frequently been filed against opposition figures. In 2013 Reporters Without Borders ranked Cambodia 143rd out of 179 countries in terms of freedom of the press, a decline from 117th the year before. The group cited a ban on reporting on local elections for the June 2012 Councilor/Sangkat elections as example of continued issues.

Local administration encompasses 24 provinces and municipalities, the former subdivided into districts (*srok*) and communes (*khum*), and the latter into sectors (*khan*) and urban communes (*sangkat*). Local council elections were held for the first time in February 2002. Indirect voting (by communal councilors) for provincial, municipal, and district councils were first conducted in May 2009. Commune Councils/Sangkats serve as the lowest level of governance and are directly elected for five years. Elections are held in a proportional system with parties of at least 4,000 members allowed to submit potential candidates. The national parties, and specifically the party in power, control the institutions that approve which parties are registered and voter registration efforts.

Foreign relations. The collapse of the Soviet Union and the subsequent loss to Phnom Penh and its Vietnamese backers of both financial and political aid contributed significantly to the domestic events of 1993. At the same time, the United States began supporting the new coalition government's military efforts to eliminate the remaining *Khmer Rouge* strongholds.

Cambodia's relations with other countries were dramatically affected by the political turmoil in 1997–1998. Following Prince Ranariddh's ouster, the UN refused to allow the Hun Sen/Ung Huot government to occupy the Cambodian seat in the General Assembly, while many Western countries suspended foreign aid. Japan, however, refused U.S. pressure to cut off aid and signaled its growing interest in Cambodian affairs by brokering the cease-fire of January 1998 between Prince Ranariddh and Hun Sen.

Following formation of the November 1998 coalition government, Cambodia was permitted to reclaim its UN General Assembly seat, and in April 1999 the country was formally admitted to ASEAN. The formation of a coalition government also reopened the pockets of Western donors, who continue to offer substantial support.

Cambodia enjoys good relations with China, with the Chinese government providing millions in development loans and heavily investing in the kingdom's infrastructure. China has invested over $8.8 billion since 1994 making them Cambodia's largest contributor. The United States ranks 10th in investments as of 2011. Prime Minister Hun Sen has praised China for its assistance, which he said has been offered without the criticism that has accompanied Western aid.

The neighboring country most directly affected by the quarter-century of strife in Cambodia—and the one most deeply opposed to recognition of the Vietnamese-backed Heng Samrin government in 1979—was Thailand, whose eastern region provided sanctuary for some 250,000 *Khmer Rouge* refugees. It was not until June 2000 that Thai and Cambodian officials signed a memorandum of understanding regarding demarcation of land boundaries. The two governments also agreed to work jointly toward elimination of smuggling, drug trafficking, and illegal entry.

In October 2004 Cambodia became a member of the World Trade Organization (WTO). Cambodia signed a bilateral Trade and Investment Framework Agreement (TIFA) with its largest trading partner, the United States, in 2006.

In February 2006 Cambodia and Thailand announced that they intended to complete their land border demarcation before the end of the year, with the maritime demarcation to follow in 2007, but the process was slowed by the September 2006 coup in Thailand. The most recent border conflict has concerned the Hindu temple of Preah Vihear, an 11th-century site that was awarded to Cambodia by the International Court of Justice (ICJ) in 1962. The disputed area, about 1.8 square miles (4.6 square kilometers), was recently added to the list of world heritage sites by UNESCO.

Relations were further soured in November 2009 when Hun Sen named THAKSIN Shinawatra as an economic adviser. Thaksin, a former Thai prime minister, was convicted of corruption by a Thai court in 2008. The appointment resulted in a series of tit-for-tat diplomatic recalls and expulsions by the two countries and also led Thailand to announce that it was withdrawing from maritime border talks. In August 2010 Thailand and Cambodia appeared to be working toward resuming diplomatic relations as the two countries began the process of reinstating the ousted diplomats. Trade between the two countries increased 54 percent between 2009 and 2010 despite tension along the border.

In February 2011 skirmishes between Cambodian and Thai forces around the Preah Vihear temple killed 10, wounded more than 20, and displaced approximately 21,000 locals. The clash escalated and widened in April, but a cease-fire was instituted on May 4. In July the ICJ ordered Cambodia and Thailand to withdraw their forces. Both nations pledged to comply with the order, while the ICJ considered a Cambodian petition to reexamine its 1962 ruling. Hostilities over border demarcation continue to simmer, culminating in a minor exchange of fire in December 2011 despite efforts by the ICJ to implement a provisional demilitarized zone. Cambodia announced in July 2012 its willingness to withdraw troops from the region without indicating a date to "honor the Court's order."

The Cambodian-Chinese relationship was further solidified by the visit of Chinese President Hu Jintao on March 31, 2012, as well as the continued development of a comprehensive strategic partnership between the two nations and the signing of a military cooperation pact.

In July 2012 the United States signaled increased interest in Cambodia by the visit of Secretary of State Hillary Rodham Clinton for the 2012 East Asia Summit. President Barack Obama visited Cambodia in mid-November as part of the 2012 ASEAN-U.S. summit, marking the first time a U.S. president had set foot in Cambodia in more than 30 years. In a private meeting with Prime Minister Sen that was described by U.S. officials as "tense," Obama pushed Sen to do more for human rights and to hold free and fair elections. In September, Sweden pledged $59.4 million in development funding for Cambodia.

In January 2013, Japan announced it would provide $2.5 million to allow the ECCC to continue functioning.

Current issues. The much delayed first formal indictment by the ECCC against a *Khmer Rouge* figure was issued on August 13, 2008, the target being KANG KEK IEU (KAING GUEK EAV, a.k.a. Comrade DUCH), who ran Phnom Penh's brutal Tuol Sleng (S-21) prison. During his March–November 2009 trial for war crimes, he accepted responsibility for 12,380 deaths but stated in his defense that he was a "cog" in the *Khmer Rouge* machinery. On July 26, 2010, the ECCC rendered a guilty verdict on charges of crimes against humanity, torture, and murder, but the sentence of 19 years in prison was widely condemned as too lenient. At age 67 when his trial concluded, Kang was the youngest of the five defendants.

In December 2009 additional charges were brought against Nuon Chea, Ieng Sary, and Khieu Samphan for genocide in the deaths of thousands of ethnic Vietnamese and Cham-Malays, but the Hun Sen government and the Cambodian co-prosecutor have strongly opposed efforts by international members of the ECCC to investigate five other possible defendants. The president of the Senate, Chea Sim, and the speaker of the lower house, Heng Samrin, are among the officials who have refused to appear before the international investigating judge. In June 2011 the ECCC began the trials for the four remaining *Khmer Rouge* leaders in custody. The long-delayed trials are accused of being politically tainted. In August 2011 the World Bank suspended $70 million in additional development loans to Cambodia in response to the forced relocation of approximately 15,000 people who were evicted in order to develop an area near Phnom Penh as a Chinese industrial park. In response, Prime Minister Sen ordered the creation of a housing area for the homeless and pledged compensation for those who were displaced.

In August through November 2011, heavy storms caused severe flooding in 18 of 24 provinces and affected an estimated 1.7 million Cambodians, killing 234. Experts expect the disaster to impact the economy through 2012.

In March 2012, ICJ Judge Siegfried Blunk and Judge Laurent Kasper-Anserment resigned from the war crimes tribunal; this was followed in December by resignations of three lawyers, who cited excessive government interference in the proceedings. The exodus raised doubt to the validity of the *Khmer Rouge* trial and doubt over the possibility of reaching a successful conclusion to the trials before the aged former leaders die.

Senate elections on January 29, 2012, and Commune/Sangkat elections on June 3, 2012, continued to demonstrate the grasp of CCP on party politics and the decline of FP. The SRP, however, secured nine seats. In 2012 the SRP merged with the small Human Rights Party (HRP) to form the Cambodia National Rescue Party (CNRP) in an effort to increase opposition potential in the 2013 Assembly balloting. On October 15, former king Norodom Sihanouk died in Beijing at age 89 of natural causes. More than 500,000 turned out to view the popular monarch's funeral march in Phnom Penh on October 17.

In July, Rainsy was granted a pardon by the king and returned to Cambodia. However, election officials ruled he was ineligible to run for office. In the July 28 balloting, the CPP secured 68 seats to 55 for the CNRP. No other party gained representation in the Assembly. Opposition parties denounced the balloting and accused the government of widespread fraud. The United States and other international donors threatened to withhold aid over the conduct of the balloting. There were demonstrations throughout the country and clashes between security forces and opposition protesters. The CNRP boycotted the opening of the Assembly to protest the results. As of November 2013, CPP and CNRP, amid widespread public demonstrations, continue to negotiate for a solution to the political deadlock resulting from the July elections.

POLITICAL PARTIES

No current party claims a *Khmer Rouge* heritage, although various leaders of the Cambodian People's Party (CPP), including Prime Minister Hun Sen, were at one time *Khmers Rouges*. From a historical perspective, the Democratic National United Movement (DNUM), formed in 1996 by *Khmer Rouge* defector Ieng Sary, would appear to have been the last successor to a series of *Khmer Rouge* parties, the most important being the Pol Pot wing of the Communist Party of Kampuchea (PCK; see under CPP), which ruled the country from 1975 to 1979 but was declared dissolved in December 1981. Ieng Sary, a former Democratic Kampuchea deputy premier and the brother-in-law of Pol Pot, having received a pardon from King Sihanouk, set up DNUM but it did not compete in the 1998 national election. The DNUM is no longer active.

Of Cambodia's 57 registered parties, only 8 were eligible to contest the July 28, 2013, National Assembly elections. Under the election law, parties had to present at least 41 candidates to qualify.

Government Party:

Cambodian People's Party—CPP (*Kanakpak Pracheachon Kampuchea*). The CPP was launched as a non-Communist successor to the Kampuchean People's Revolutionary Party (KPRP) during an extraordinary party congress in Phnom Penh held October 17–18, 1991.

The KPRP had been founded in early 1951, when the Indo-Chinese Communist Party, led by Ho Chi Minh, was divided into separate entities for Cambodia, Laos, and Vietnam. Following the 1954 Geneva Agreement, it encompassed three factions: the *Khmer Vietminh,* controlled largely by the North Vietnamese; an underground force that served as the ideological core of the *Khmers Rouges;* and adherents of the legal People's Party (*Kanakpak Pracheachon*). At its Second Congress the organization changed its name to the Communist Party of Kampuchea (*Parti Communiste du Kampuchea—PCK/Kanakpak Kumunist Kampuchea*) but continued to be divided, largely between supporters of the North Vietnamese and a Maoist contingent led by Pol Pot (then known as Saloth Sar). In 1962 the incumbent PCK general secretary was assassinated, allegedly on order of Pol Pot, who assumed the office the following year.

The two factions were nominally reunited during 1970–1975, although most pro-Vietnamese went into exile in the wake of a purge that commenced in 1974. Following the overthrow of the *Khmer Rouge* government in 1979, the Hanoi-supported exiles staged a "reorganization Congress" at which PEN SOVAN was elected secretary general (he also served briefly as chair of the PRK Council of Ministers in 1981), and the KPRP label was readopted to distinguish the Phnom Penh group from the *Khmer Rouge* faction that continued to be led by Pol Pot until its dissolution on December 6, 1981. Two days earlier, the KPRP Central Committee, following a power struggle, had elected Heng Samrin as its secretary general.

Later that month, a congress of the Kampuchean National United Front for National Salvation (KNUFNS), a mass organization established in 1978 by Khmer opponents of the Democratic Kampuchean regime, recognized the KPRP as its "leading nucleus." At the same congress the front changed its name to the Kampuchean United Front for National Construction and Defense (KUFNCD). Another change, to the United Front for the Construction and Defense of the Kampuchean Fatherland (UFCDKF), occurred in 1989. The most recent renaming, to the **Solidarity Front for Development of the Cambodian Motherland** (SFDCM), occurred at the Front's fifth congress, held in May 2006.

After abandoning Marxism-Leninism, the CPP at its 1991 founding congress supported the adoption of a multiparty system, endorsed a free-market economy, called for the designation of Buddhism as the state religion, and announced a number of structural and leadership changes. The former KPRP Politburo and Secretariat were merged into a single CPP Standing Committee; Heng Samrin was named CPP honorary president; and Chea Sim and Hun Sen, the second- and third-ranked members of the KPRP Politburo, were designated chair and vice chair, respectively, of the CPP Central Committee. The party was runner-up in the balloting of May 1993, winning 51 assembly seats on a vote share of 38 percent.

Amid charges of irregularities, in the July 1998 election the CPP took 41 percent of the vote and 64 seats, making it the leading legislative party. It retained that standing in the July 2003 election, winning 47 percent of the vote and 73 seats—a majority, but shy of the two-thirds needed to govern. A year later, following the conclusion of protracted coalition negotiations with FP, the CPP's two main factions—the hard-liners led by Chea Sim and the more moderate faction of Hun Sen—apparently collided over the issue of cabinet-level appointments, which may have been a factor in Chea Sim's departure for Thailand. In October 2007 the party nominated Hun Sen as its candidate for prime minister in 2008. In the run-up to the election, several members of FP left what was described as an "ailing" party to join the CPP (see Funcinpec, below). In June 2008 the CPP won 58 percent of the vote and a commanding 90 seats, after which Hun Sen was reelected prime minister. The CPP won 77.81 percent of the vote in Senate balloting on January 29, 2012, securing 46 seats.

The party won 48.8 percent of the vote in the 2013 assembly balloting, securing 68 seats, its lowest total since 1998.

Leaders: HENG Samrin (President of the National Assembly, Chair of the SFDCM National Council, and Honorary Chair of the CPP), CHEA Sim (Chair of the CPP Permanent Committee and President of the Senate), HUN Sen (Prime Minister and Vice Chair, CPP Central Committee), SAY Chhum (Chair of the Standing Committee).

Parliamentary Opposition:

Cambodian National Rescue Party—CNRP (*Kanakpak Songkruos Cheat Kampuchea*). The CNRP was formed in 2012 by a merger of the **Sam Rainsy Party**—SRP (*Pak Sam Rainsy*) and the Human Rights Party (HRP). The HRP was created in July 2007 by Kem Sokha, a human rights campaigner and former member of the Buddhist Liberal Party (see Funcinpec, above).

In March 1998 the faction of the Khmer Nation Party (KNP) led by labor activist and former finance minister Sam Rainsy changed its name to the SRP, following the government's earlier decision to officially recognize the KNP faction led by KONG Moni. Rainsy had established the KNP in 1995, having been expelled from the FP in May and the National Assembly in June after complaining of corruption in the awarding of government contracts. (Kong Moni's faction, renamed the Khmer Angkor Party in 1998, had no electoral success.)

In the 1998 election the SRP won 14 percent of the vote and 15 seats in the National Assembly. In 2003 the SRP won 24 seats, only 2 less than the FP. Although the SRP strongly opposed Hun Sen's continuation as prime minister, in 2004 it considered joining the CPP and the FP in a three-way coalition government. That possibility ended, however, when the CPP and the FP agreed to constitutional amendments that would permit the election of the prime minister and National Assembly president by a single show of hands. From Thailand, where he and all the other SRP legislators were ensconced during the July 15 confirmation vote, Rainsy declared the process unconstitutional and the resultant government illegal.

In February 2005 Rainsy fled to France after the National Assembly revoked his parliamentary immunity, leaving him open to criminal lawsuits alleging defamation. He had accused Hun Sen of ordering a grenade attack at a 1997 party rally that killed 16 people. He had also accused Prince Ranariddh of accepting bribes to cement Funcinpec's alliance with the CPP. Convicted in absentia in December and sentenced to prison, Rainsy was pardoned by the king in early February 2006 after offering apologies. Another SRP legislator, CHEAM Channy, was also pardoned. In August 2005 a military court had sentenced Cheam to seven years in prison for involvement in "an illegal rebel group"—an opposition committee formed to examine the government's defense-related decisions. On February 10 Rainsy returned to Cambodia, and on February 28 the National Assembly reinstated him, Cheam Channy, and a third SRP legislator, CHEA Poch, who had also fled into exile a year earlier to avoid defamation charges.

After having lost more than 85 percent of its seats in the April 2007 local council elections, many SRP members began defecting to the CPP. By March 2008, some 12,000 SRP members reportedly had been accepted into the CPP. Also in March, a member of the SRP and two others were arrested for allegedly intimidating party members who sought to defect. The SRP claimed the arrests were orchestrated by the CPP. In the 2008 National Assembly election the SRP won 22 percent of the vote and 26 seats.

In January 2009 the SRP and the Human Rights Party (below) announced formation of a **Democratic Movement for Change.** The parties' leaders stated that they intended to run jointly in the next national election.

In February 2009 Sam Rainsy once again briefly lost his parliamentary immunity for allegedly defaming CPP leaders. His immunity was restored in March, after he had agreed to pay a fine of 10 million riels ($2,450), but his actions in opposition to a border agreement with Vietnam led to yet another loss of immunity in November. In January 2010 he was convicted in absentia of racial incitement and removing border markers and the court imposed a two-year prison sentence and an additional fine. Rainsy, in exile, also faced charges of propagating false information and fake documents about the border agreement.

In June 2010 the Supreme Court rejected an appeal by another prominent SRP leader, MU Sochua, who had been convicted of defaming Hun Sen. The case had originated in a defamation lawsuit brought by Mu Sochua against the prime minister, who countersued. Mu Sochua indicated that she intended to serve a six-month jail term rather than pay the specified fine.

In March 2011 Rainsy was again stripped of his parliamentary immunity by the National Assembly. Despite Rainsy's continued exile, the SRP won 11 of 61 seats in the Senate in January 2012 and 22 of 1,633 commune/sangkat seats in June 2012. The party secured 55 seats in the 2013 Assembly elections. The party led a series of protests against the results, claiming electoral fraud.

Leaders: SAM Rainsy (President), KEM Sokha (Vice President).

Other Parties:

Funcinpec Party (FP). Funcinpec, the acronym for *Front Uni National pour un Cambodge Indépendant, Neutre, Pacifique et Coopératif* (United National Front for an Independent, Neutral, Peaceful, and Cooperative Cambodia), was proclaimed in 1989 as the political counterpart of the **National Army of Independent Cambodia,** formerly the Sihanoukist National Army (*Armée Nationale Sihanoukiste*—ANS). At a congress held February 27–28, 1992, the group was redesignated as the Funcinpec Party, with Prince Norodom Ranariddh, who had theretofore served as general secretary, being named chair. The FP secured a plurality of 58 National Assembly seats in May 1993 on a vote share of 46 percent. In June, Prince Ranariddh was named cochair of the interim government's Council of Ministers and then, in October, first prime minister under the new constitution.

The FP was split in 1997 between supporters of Prince Ranariddh (and his courting of *Khmer Rouge* defector factions) and those more in consonance with the policies of Hun Sen's CPP. A number of FP legislators defected to the CPP parliamentary camp in April, establishing a dissident faction under the leadership of TOAN Chhay, who then formed the unsuccessful National Union Party (*Kanakpak Ruop Ruom Cheat*) to contest the 1998 election. Following the ouster of Prince Ranariddh from the government as the result of the midyear civil war, anti-Ranariddh FP dissident Ung Huot was named first prime minister; he subsequently campaigned under the banner of the Populism Party (*Reastr Niyum Party*—RNP), while former Funcinpec secretary general LOY Sim CHHEANG formed the New Society Party (*Sangkum Thmei Party*—STP). Neither the RNP nor the STP took seats at the election. (Ung Huot returned to FP; the STP eventually dissolved.)

Prior to the July 1998 election, Funcinpec formed the **National United Front** (NUF) alliance with SRP, the **Son Sann Party** (SSP), and the small **Khmer Neutral Party** (*Kanakpak Kampuchea Appyeakroet*), which had disappeared after an unsuccessful 1993 election campaign but reemerged in 1996. In 1998 the FP was runner-up to the CPP, claiming 32 percent of the vote and 43 seats in the National Assembly. The November 1998 coalition agreement with the CPP specified that the FP would control 11 of 25 ministries and would share the defense and interior portfolios.

In mid-January 1999, the SSP merged with the FP. The SSP had originated in a faction of the Buddhist Liberal Democratic Party (BLDP) that was loyal to the former BLDP president, Son Sann. (Both factions claimed legal right to the BLDP name but agreed to adopt alternate designations: the SSP and the Buddhist Liberal Party.) Despite participation in the NUF alliance, the SSP won no seats in the July 1998 election. With Son Sann having retired from politics, SSP leadership passed to his son, SON Soubert, who was subsequently named to the Constitutional Court and therefore resigned from his party post. The party's de facto leader, Kem Sokha, negotiated the merger with the FP.

At the FP National Congress held March 19 through 21, 2000, Prince Ranariddh urged the party to readmit former members who wished to rejoin, particularly the RNP contingent. In May and June 2002, however, Funcinpec saw two new parties formed by departing leaders Prince NORODOM Chakrapong and Hang Dara.

In the July 2003 general election, the FP lost 17 seats, and its vote share fell to 21 percent. A month later it formed the Alliance of Democrats with the SRP. After protracted negotiations, Ranariddh signed a new coalition agreement with the CPP in late June 2004.

On March 3, 2006, a day after Hun Sen had dismissed the Funcinpec coministers of defense and interior, Ranariddh resigned as National Assembly president. Within days, he announced a party reorganization that included naming former party dissident Norodom Chakrapong (who had led the eponymous Norodom Chakrapong Soul Khmer Party at the time of the 2003 election) as secretary general. On October 18, however, Ranariddh lost control of the party when an extraordinary congress chose the country's ambassador to Germany, Keo Puth Rasmey, as his successor. A week later, the National Assembly confirmed Keo as a deputy prime minister. Ranariddh's ouster was attributed to corruption: He allegedly had kept $3.6 million for himself from the sale of party headquarters. He subsequently was sentenced to 18 months in jail, but from exile in 2007 he claimed that the charge was politically motivated. Ranariddh earlier had refused the party title of historic president and established the Norodom Ranariddh Party (NRP).

In October 2007 the party nominated as its 2008 candidate for prime minister Princess NORODOM Arun Rasmey, the youngest daughter of Norodom Sihanouk, wife of party president Keo Puth Rasmey, and Cambodia's ambassador to Malaysia. In the 2008 National Assembly election, Funcinpec won 5.1 percent of the vote and two seats. Nevertheless, it was retained in the government by Prime Minister Hun Sen, who offered it one cabinet-level position and a number of junior appointments.

In June 2010 the FP and the NRP signed an agreement to contest the 2013 legislative election in a coalition to be called the Funcinpec-Nationalist Alliance and, in May 2012, agreed to a full merger after the June 3 commune/sangkat elections. The merger fell apart by mid-June because of disagreements between party leaders, the FP's Bun Chhay and the NRP's Norodom Ranariddh.

In January 2012, Funcinpec lost its remaining 10 Senate seats in uncontested elections. In June, Funcinpec won 151 commune/sangkrat seats, down from its 2007 election total of 274. In 2013, the party received 3.6 percent of the vote in the assembly balloting and no seats.

Leaders: KEO Puth Rasmey (President), NHIEK Bun Chhay (Secretary General of the Party).

Norodom Ranariddh Party (NRP). Following Prince Ranariddh's ouster from the leadership of the FP in October 2006, he announced his intention to form the NRP. In mid-November, however, having accused the Interior Ministry of delaying his new party's registration, he was elected president of the small Khmer Front Party—KFP (*Ronakse Chuncheat Khmer*). The KFP then revised its bylaws and changed its name to the NRP, which quickly established itself as a royalist challenger to the FP.

In 2006, Ranariddh was living in exile when the party nominated him as its candidate for prime minister in the 2008 elections. The NRP won 5.6 percent of the vote (slightly better than FP) and two seats. The following October, shortly after returning from Malaysia, Ranariddh resigned from the party and, having been pardoned by the king, accepted an appointment as president of the Supreme Privy Advisory Council.

With Ranariddh's departure, a leadership dispute broke out between CHHIM Seak Leang, who was Ranariddh's successor, and SUTH Dina, who had been serving as party spokesperson, but Leang was elected leader in late January 2009. The following June, the party renamed itself the Nationalist Party (NP).

In June 2010 the NP and the FP agreed to establish a Funcinpec-Nationalist Alliance to contest the next legislative election, due in 2013.

After Ranariddh announced his intention to return to politics in late 2010, the party reinstated its original name and elected Ranariddh its president. In December, Prime Minister Hun Sen proposed that Ranariddh be removed from the Supreme Privy Advisory Council. In May 2012 the FP and the NRP agreed to a merger following the June 3 commune elections, however the agreement broke down. The NRP won 52 seats in commune/sangkat elections held June 3, a decline from the 425 seats won in the 2007 election. Reports in 2013 indicated that the party had merged with the FP.

Leaders: NORODOM Ranariddh (President), PEN Sangha (Spokesperson).

Other parties that contested the 2008 or 2013 National Assembly elections include the following: The **Khmer Democratic Party** (*Kanakpak Pracheathipatei Khmer*), led by UK Phourik, had claimed 1.8 percent of the 2003 vote but in 2008 won only 0.5 percent. The **Hang Dara Democratic Movement Party** (*Hang Dara Cholana Pracheathipatei*), an FP splinter led by HANG Dara, won 0.4 percent in 2008, slightly better than it had in 2003. The **Khmer Anti-Poverty Party,** founded in 2007 by DARAN Kravanh, finished last in 2008, with under 0.2 percent of the vote, and fifth in 2013, with 0.7 percent of the vote. The **Khmer Republican Party,** established in 2006 and led by LON Rith, son of Lon Nol, won 0.2 percent in 2008. The **League for Democracy Party,** established in 2006 by KHEM Veasna, won 1.2 percent in 2008 and 1 percent in 2013. The **Society of Justice Party** (*Sangkum Yutethor*), established in 2006 by BAN Sophal, won 0.2 percent in 2008. In 2008, the Election Commission had ruled that the **United People of Cambodia Party,** led by SARSATH Oeurn, could not compete because several of its proposed candidates were ineligible and not registered voters, leaving the party with fewer than the minimum number of eligible candidates. In the 2013 balloting, three new groupings all received less than 1 percent of the vote: the **Cambodian Nationality Party**, led by SENG Sokheng; the **Khmer Economic Development Party**, led by HUON Chamroeun; and the **Democratic Republican Party,** led by SOVAN Paphchaksella.

LEGISLATURE

Constitutional amendments passed by the National Assembly in March 1998 reestablished a bicameral **Parliament** (*Sepiacheat*) by creating an upper house, the Senate.

Senate (*Pritsepia*). As constituted on March 25, 1999, the upper house comprised 61 appointed senators: 59 named by parties, in proportion to representation in the lower house, and 2 named by the king. All were to serve five-year terms. In January 2003 the government announced that the first senatorial election, slated for 2004, would be shelved for budgetary reasons, and the Senate term was later extended twice. Senators now serve six-year terms.

Indirect election of January 29, 2012, for 57 seats produced the following distribution: Cambodian People's Party, 46; Sam Rainsy Party, 11. Members were elected by 11,470 eligible electors—the 119 members of the National Assembly plus the 11,351 commune/sangkat members. The king and the National Assembly each appointed 2 additional members for a total of 61 seats.

President: CHEA SIM.

National Assembly (*Radhsphea Ney Preah Recheanachakr*). The 123 members of the National Assembly were most recently elected to five-year terms on July 28, 2013. Preliminary results gave the Cambodian People's Party 68 seats; and the Cambodian National Rescue Party, 55.

President: HENG Samrin.

CABINET

[as of September 20, 2013]

Prime Minister	Hun Sen
Deputy Prime Ministers	Sar Kheng
	Bin Chhin
	Hor Namhong
	Keat Chhon
	Ke Kimyan
	Men Sam An [f]
	Nhiek Bun Chhay (FP)
	Sok An
	Gen. Tea Banh

Senior Ministers

Commerce	Cham Prasidh
Environment	Mok Mareth
Land Management, Urban Planning, and Construction	Im Chhun Lim
Planning	Chhay Than
Special Envoys	Serei Kosal

Ministers

Agriculture, Forestry, and Fisheries	Chan Sarun
Culture and Fine Arts	Him Chhem
Economy and Finance	Keat Chhon
Education, Youth, and Sports	Im Sethy
Foreign Affairs and International Cooperation	Hor Namhong
Health	Mam Bun Heng
Industry, Mines, and Energy	Suy Sem
Information	Khieu Kanharith
Interior	Sar Kheng
Justice	Ang Vong Vathana
Labor and Vocational Training	Vorng Soth
National Defense	Gen. Tea Banh
Office of the Council of Ministers	Sok An
Office of the Prime Minister	Chheang Yanara
Parliamentary Affairs and Inspection	Som Kimsuor [f]
Post and Telecommunication	So Khun
Public Works and Transport	Tram Iv Tek
Religious Affairs	Min Khin
Royal Palace	Kong Sam Ol
Rural Development	Chea Sophara
Social Affairs, Veterans, and Youth Rehabilitation	Ith Sam Heng
Tourism	Thong Khon
Water Resources and Meteorology	Lim Kean Hor
Women's Affairs	Ing Kantha Phavi [f]

[f] = female

Note: Except as indicated, all cabinet members belong to the CPP.

INTERGOVERNMENTAL REPRESENTATION

Ambassador to the U.S.: Hem HENG.

U.S. Ambassador to Cambodia: William (Bill) E. TODD.

Permanent Representative to the UN: Sea KOSAL.

IGO Memberships (Non-UN): ADB, ASEAN, ICC, IOM, NAM, WTO.

CAMEROON

Republic of Cameroon
République du Cameroun

Political Status: Independence proclaimed 1960; federation established 1961; one-party unitary republic declared June 2, 1972; multiparty system introduced under legislation approved December 6, 1990.

Area: 183,568 sq. mi. (475,442 sq. km).

Population: 20,559,861 (2012E—UN); 20,549,221 (2013E—U.S. Census).

Major Urban Centers (2011E—UN): YAOUNDÉ; (1,817,524), Douala (1,907,479).

Official Languages: French, English.

Monetary Unit: CFA Franc (official rate November 1, 2013: 486.52 CFA francs = $1US). The CFA franc, previously pegged to the French franc, is now permanently pegged to the euro at 655.957 CFA francs = 1 euro.

President: Paul BIYA (Democratic Rally of the Cameroon People); served as prime minister 1975–1982; installed as president on November 6, 1982, to complete the term of Ahmadou Babatoura AHIDJO, who had resigned on November 4; reelected without opposition on January 14, 1984, and April 24, 1988; reelected for a five-year term in multicandidate balloting on October 11, 1992, for a seven-year term on October 12, 1997; reelected for another seven-year term on October 11, 2004; formed new government on June 30, 2009; reelected for another seven-year term on October 9, 2011.

Prime Minister: Philémon Yungi YANG (Democratic Rally of the Cameroon People), appointed by the president on June 30, 2009, following the dismissal the same day of Ephraim INONI (Democratic Rally of the Cameroon People).

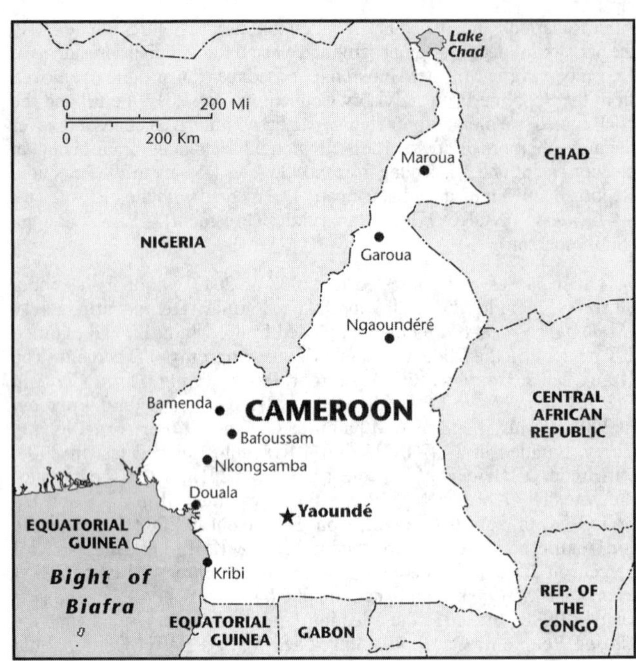

THE COUNTRY

Situated just north of the equator on the Gulf of Guinea and rising from a coastal plain to a high interior plateau, Cameroon is the product of a merger in 1961 between the former French and British Cameroon trust territories. Its more than 100 ethnic groups speak 24 major languages and represent a diversity of Christian (53 percent), traditional African (25 percent), and Muslim (22 percent) religious beliefs. Reflecting its dual colonial heritage (the source of lingering political cleavage), Cameroon is the only country in Africa in which both French and English are official languages. In 1996 women were reported to constitute 38 percent of the official labor force.

Cameroon's economy has long been primarily rural, and despite the discovery of major oil deposits in 1973, agriculture has provided a large share of the country's export earnings. Coffee, cocoa, and timber are among the most important agricultural products, but bananas, cotton, rubber, and palm oil also are produced commercially. Oil production has declined since 1985, but the government has adopted laws meant to encourage investors. Industrial development has focused on aluminum smelting from both domestic and imported bauxite. More recent initiatives have been aimed at hydroelectric expansion, the resolution of long-standing transportation problems, and the development of medium-sized farms to halt the exodus of rural youth to urban areas. The economy faltered during the mid-1980s and early 1990s under the influence of depressed oil and other commodity prices, sustained capital flight, rising external debt, and widespread corruption and inefficiency in state-run enterprises. The government, which initially shunned involvement with the International Monetary Fund (IMF), since 1988 has negotiated agreements with it and other international lenders in a context of budget austerity and a commitment to privatization.

In order to increase public transparency, in late 1999 the IMF asked the government to set up a system whereby oil revenues would be directly deposited in a monitorable state budget. In addition, the IMF counseled Yaoundé to continue its efforts to raise the "non-oil revenue-to-GDP ratio." While the IMF and the World Bank subsequently praised the government's efforts regarding structural reforms and anti-corruption measures, concerns were raised over the pace of privatization and poverty reduction.

The opening of the Chad-Cameroon pipeline in 2003 further supported the overall improvement in the economy. In 2006 the IMF and the World Bank approved debt relief of $1.3 billion, and in an agreement with significant long-term economic implications, the country gained sovereignty over the oil-rich Bakassi Peninsula (see Foreign relations, below). GDP growth remained steady at 4 percent in 2007, but dipped to a more modest 2.3 percent annually in 2009, due to declining oil prices and commodities exports as a consequence of the global economic recession. Annual growth averaged 3.6 percent in 2010–2011, and on the back of increased public investment and measures to boost agricultural production, the economy continued its recovery in 2011, reaching 4.2 percent. At the same time, the fiscal situation deteriorated under pressure to meet past payment obligations, high current expenditures, and an increase in the cost of fuel subsidies. However, the IMF projected a gradual increase to 5.5% annual growth by 2016, owing to a planned increase in oil production and efforts to improve the economy and business climate. The IMF also advised the restructuring of weak banks and steps to promote higher and more inclusive growth. In 2012, GDP grew by 4.7 percent, while inflation was 3 percent, and GDP per capita was $1,165.

GOVERNMENT AND POLITICS

Political background. A German protectorate before World War I, Cameroon was divided at the close of that conflict into French and British mandates, which became United Nations trust territories after World War II. French Cameroons, comprising the eastern four-fifths of the territory, achieved autonomous status within the French Community in 1957 and, under the leadership of Ahmadou Babatoura AHIDJO, became the independent Republic of Cameroon on January 1, 1960. The disposition of British Cameroons was settled in February 1961 by a UN-sponsored plebiscite in which the northern and southern sections voted to merge with Nigeria and the former French territory, respectively. On October 1, 1961, the Federal Republic of Cameroon was formed, with Ahidjo as president and John Ngu FONCHA, prime minister of the former British region, as vice president.

The federal structure was designed to meet the challenge posed by Cameroon's racial, tribal, religious, and political diversity. It provided for separate regional governments and political organizations, joined at the federal level. A transition to unitary government began with the 1965–1966 merger of the regional political parties to form the Cameroon National Union (UNC) under the leadership of President Ahidjo and was completed on June 2, 1972, following a referendum on May 20 that indicated overwhelming support for the adoption of a new constitution. Subsequently, President Ahidjo faced no organized opposition, and on April 5, 1980, he was reelected to a fifth successive term. However, in an unanticipated move on November 4, 1982, Ahidjo announced his retirement in favor of his longtime associate, Prime Minister Paul BIYA. Immediately following his installation as president, Biya, a southerner, named a northern Muslim, Maigari Bello BOUBA, to head a new government designed to retain the somewhat tenuous regional and cultural balance that had been established by the former head of state. Bouba was dismissed in August 1983, following a coup attempt that allegedly involved Ahidjo, then resident in France. (Ahidjo died in Senegal in 1989.)

President Biya was unopposed for reelection on January 14, 1984, and immediately following his inauguration on January 21 the National

Assembly voted to abolish the post of prime minister and to abandon "United Republic of Cameroon" as the country's official name in favor of the pre-merger "Republic of Cameroon." The following April Biya survived a coup attempt by elements of the presidential guard. While reportedly dealing harshly with the rebels, the administration nevertheless initiated steps toward democratization. Elections for local and regional bodies within the government party, which had been renamed the Democratic Rally of the Cameroon People (RDPC), also referenced in English as the Cameroon People's Democratic Movement (CPDM) in 1985, were held in 1986, followed by local government elections in 1987 that, for the first time, featured competitive balloting, albeit within an RDPC/CPDM framework. Alternative candidates also were presented for National Assembly balloting on April 24, 1988; however, each of the two lists was restricted to ruling party nominees, with opponents attacking the "snail's pace" of liberalization, continued repression of dissent, and barriers to any genuine political challenge to Biya, who was unopposed in the presidential poll.

In emulation of trends elsewhere in Africa and beyond, democratization advocates intensified their pressure in late 1989 and early 1990. Initially, the government responded harshly: 11 opposition leaders were arrested in February 1990, and a massive prodemocracy demonstration in the western town of Bamenda was violently broken up by security forces, leaving at least six people dead. However, in the wake of growing domestic and international criticism, President Biya announced in June that a multiparty system would be introduced and other reforms implemented. Consequently, on December 6 the National Assembly enacted legislation restricting the government's authority to deny legal status to opposition groups, and the formal recognition of new parties began in early 1991. On the other hand, Biya's refusal to call a national conference (similar to those convened in other regional countries) to determine the nation's political future provoked continued antigovernment demonstrations.

In an effort to force the government's hand regarding a national conference, opposition parties in June 1991 launched a *villes mortes* ("dead cities") campaign during which shops were closed on weekdays to undercut tax revenue. In response, the government put seven provinces under military administration and temporarily banned several of the parties responsible for the general strike. However, faced with ongoing unrest, Biya announced in October that new legislative elections would be moved up by a year to early 1992. He also convened a meeting of government and opposition leaders that in November established a ten-member committee to oversee constitutional reform. In addition, the government promised to release detainees from earlier protests in return for discontinuation of the *villes mortes* campaign.

In the March 1, 1992, assembly balloting the RDPC/CPDM won 88 seats, enough to ensure its continued government control in coalition with the small Movement for the Defense of the Republic (MDR). However, the results were tainted somewhat by the refusal of some groups, most importantly the anglophone Social Democratic Front (SDF) and a faction of the Cameroonian People's Union (UPC), to participate in the election. Boycott leaders insisted that a ban on coalition or independent candidates favored the government formation and that the early balloting made it impossible for fledgling opposition parties to organize effectively. On April 9 President Biya announced the appointment of Simon ACHIDI ACHU, an anglophone, as prime minister. However, Achidi Achu's designation failed to stem ongoing ethnic and political violence, while the regime's efforts to quell the unrest were described as "repressive."

In September 1992 Biya announced that presidential elections scheduled for March 1993 would be advanced to October 11 and, following a widely criticized run-up to the poll, Biya subsequently claimed a narrow victory over SDF leader John FRU NDI and four other candidates. On October 15 the Supreme Court rejected a petition by Fru Ndi and the third-placed Maigari Bello Bouba, now leader of the National Union for Democracy and Progress (UNDP), to annul the balloting on the basis of prepoll and election day irregularities. The polling process was also denounced by international observers, who charged that inspectors were denied access to some balloting sites. On October 23 the official election results confirmed Biya's victory, with 39.98 percent of the vote, over Fru Ndi (35.97 percent) and Bouba (19.22 percent). Subsequently, nationwide antigovernment rioting was reported, the most serious incidents occurring in Bamenda in Fru Ndi's home province. Six days later Fru Ndi was placed under house arrest as violent street protests continued despite the declaration of a state of emergency in Bamenda.

On November 25, 1992, Biya reappointed Achidi Achu, and two days later a new government, including a number of opposition members, was named. Further efforts by the regime to ease postelection tensions included the release of Fru Ndi in early December, termination of the state of emergency in Bamenda on December 29, and the freeing of some 175 political prisoners in January 1993. However, renewed violence was reported in March as the opposition increased pressure on Yaoundé to hold a national conference.

In November 1994 President Biya announced that a "debate" on the constitution, in addition to scheduling of municipal elections, would be forthcoming; however, he refused to agree to a sovereign conference and gave no date for the local balloting, which had already been postponed several times. In early April 1995 Biya pledged that elections would be held by the end of the year, and on April 24, 64 new local districts were created by presidential decree. In November, buoyed by the IMF's endorsement of his administration's 1995–1996 economic and financial reform plan, the president ordered that local elections be held in January 1996.

Propelled by a candidate list nearly twice the size of its closest competitor, the RDPC/CPDM captured 57 percent of the posts in municipal balloting on January 21, 1996. The SDF followed with 27 percent, while the UNDP and Cameroonian Democratic Union (UDC) garnered the remainder. The administration's decision to place presidential appointees in 20 municipalities that the opposition claimed to have captured in the local balloting drew immediate condemnation and calls for civil disobedience from opposition leaders. In March at least five people were killed when antigovernment demonstrators clashed with security forces. Subsequent antigovernment initiatives were undermined, however, by the opposition's intraparty factionalization and their mutual distrust. On September 19 the president announced that he had appointed businessman Peter Mafany MUSONGE to replace Achidi Achu as prime minister. The new government formed the following day was generally described as being of the "technocrat" variety.

In the run-up to the May 17, 1997, legislative elections, the opposition criticized the administration's allegedly fraudulent handling of electoral preparations. Subsequently, both domestic and international observers charged that the ruling party's capture of 109 seats had been severely tarnished by blatant irregularities and the violent intimidation of opposition candidates and supporters. In second-round polling in early August the RDPC/CPDM captured all of the undecided seats (raising its total to 116), and at mid-month the Supreme Court dismissed opposition appeals for fresh elections. Meanwhile, the administration rejected widespread calls for it to establish an independent electoral commission prior to presidential balloting and refused to meet with opposition leaders, whose preelection demands also included a shortening of the presidential term from seven to five years, equal distribution of state campaign funds, and access to the state-run media. In September the leading opposition legislative parties (the SDF, UNDP, and UDC) announced that they would not take part in the presidential elections and called on voters to observe another *villes mortes* boycott to undermine the polling.

At balloting on October 12, 1997, Biya easily recaptured the presidency, reportedly securing 92 percent of the vote; meanwhile, the nearest of the six minor party candidates to compete garnered less than 3 percent. However, administration claims that 84 percent of eligible voters had participated in the polling were disputed by the opposition, which labeled the elections a "farce" and asserted that a boycott by over 80 percent of the electorate had made them the "victors." On December 7 Biya reappointed Musonge as prime minister; three UNDP representatives, including former prime minister Bouba, were included in the reshuffled government announced the same day. Reshuffles were announced on March 18, 2000, and April 27, 2001. The most recent cabinet included members from the RDPC/CPDM, the UNDP, the UPC, and independents.

Municipal elections originally scheduled for January 2001 were postponed first to January 2002 and then to June 30. Although the government gave technical reasons for the postponements, opposition parties claimed that the government was stalling the operation of the democratic process. In any event, the RDPC/CPDM dominated the local balloting as well as the National Assembly poll conducted the same day. President Biya also was easily reelected on October 11, 2004, securing a reported 70.8 percent of the vote against 15 rivals. On December 8 Biya appointed Ephraim INONI to head a new cabinet that included members of the RDPC, UNDP, UPC, and the MDR. (The SDF and UDC reportedly declined cabinet representation.) President Biya reshuffled the cabinet on September 22, 2006, retaining Ephraim Inoni as prime minister and maintaining the dominance of the RPDC/CPDM. Near the end of 2006, the government created a new electoral commission, Elections Cameroon (ELECAM), to replace the controversial National Electoral Observatory (NEO).

In the July 22, 2007, assembly elections, the RDPC/CPDM increased its significant majority by four seats. Despite claims of vote-rigging and fraud by a number of political parties that petitioned the Supreme Court, the court upheld the results in all but five districts. (Elections were repeated in those districts on September 30, with the RDPC/CPDM securing most of the seats.) The cabinet was reshuffled on September 7, 2007, the vast majority of posts still held by the RPDC/CPDM, and Prime Minister Ephraim Inoni retained his post.

On June 30, 2009, the president dismissed Inoni, naming a member of his inner circle, magistrate Philémon Yungi YANG of the RPDC/CPDM, as the new prime minister. The president reshuffled the cabinet—still dominated by the RPDC/CPDM—the same day.

Parliamentary elections were held on September 30, 2013, after having been postponed July 2012, February 2013, and July 2013. The elections resulted in the expected continued hold of CDPM on the government winning 148 of the 180 seats of the National Assembly.

Constitution and government. The 1972 constitution provided for a unitary state headed by a strong executive directly elected by universal suffrage for a five-year term. In November 1983 independents were authorized to seek the presidency upon securing the endorsement of at least 50 prominent figures from each of the country's provinces, although the incumbent presented himself as the sole, party-backed candidate in both 1984 and 1988 (the 1988 poll being advanced by one year to coincide with legislative balloting). The president is assisted by a cabinet drawn from the civil service rather than the legislature. Members may return to their former positions upon termination of their ministerial duties. Under a constitutional revision of January 1984, the president of the assembly becomes, in the event of a vacancy, chief executive, pending the outcome, within 40 days, of a presidential election at which he cannot stand as a candidate. Legislative authority is vested in the National Assembly, whose normal five-year term may be lengthened or shortened at the discretion of the president. An upper chamber, the Senate, was approved in 1996 but not constituted until 2013 (see Current issues, below). The judicial system is headed by a Supreme Court and a High Court of Justice; there also are provincial magistrates and a court of appeal.

Under a constitutional amendment of December 23, 1995, the presidential term was extended to seven years and the maximum number of terms reduced to two. In addition, provision was made for the establishment of a bicameral legislature. A constitutional amendment of April 10, 2008, removes presidential term limits and grants the president immunity from prosecution for any offenses committed during his term of office. An additional amendment adopted the same day centralizes more authority in the head of state.

Cameroon is administratively divided into ten provinces, each headed by a provincial governor appointed by the president. The provinces are subdivided into regions and local districts, the latter totaling 340 (307 rural, 22 urban, and 11 special regime districts) following the creation of 64 new jurisdictions in April 1995. On November 12, 2008, President Biya replaced the provinces with regions, each headed by a governor appointed by the president.

Official censorship of the press was abolished in Cameroon in 1999. However, laws remain in place that provide harsh penalties for media infractions, including libel. On the eve of elections in September 2013, 11 media outlets were temporarily closed, accused of violating "journalistic ethics." Reporters Without Borders ranked Cameroon 120th out of 179 countries in 2013.

Foreign relations. Cameroon's ties with France remain especially strong, with Yaoundé becoming a full participant in francophone affairs during the May 1989 summit in Dakar, Senegal.

Dominating foreign policy concerns for many years was the civil war in neighboring Chad, which resulted in an influx of some 100,000 refugees into the country's northern provinces. Thus the Ahidjo government took part in several regional efforts to mediate the dispute prior to the ouster of the Libyan-backed Queddei regime in Chad in mid-1982; later Cameroon served as a staging ground for France's support of the Habré government.

Relations with other neighboring states have been uneven. Border incidents with Nigeria, resulting in a seven-month suspension of diplomatic relations in May 1981, continued into early 1987, with Lagos threatening "to take military reprisals" against alleged incursions by Cameroonian *gendarmes* into Borno State. However, relations improved thereafter.

In October 1992 the Biya regime's alleged manipulation of presidential balloting drew widespread criticism from Western observers, including the European Community, Germany, and the United States, with the latter two announcing the suspension of aid payments in mid-November. On the other hand, Paris's continued support of the regime drew outcries from Cameroonian opposition leaders.

In late 1993 conflict again erupted with Nigeria in the form of an alleged Cameroonian troop raid into Nigeria's Cross River State and the reported dispatch of Nigerian soldiers to two islands off the Bakassi Peninsula that were claimed by Cameroon. Underlying the dispute was the presence of substantial oil reserves along an ill-defined border between the two countries. In 1994 Cameroon filed a suit in the International Court of Justice (ICJ). The conflict reignited in September with a Nigerian attack that left ten Cameroonian soldiers dead. In October Nigeria claimed to have indisputable proof of its claim to the Bakassi region in that a 1913 agreement transferring the area to German Kameroun had never been ratified because of the outbreak of World War I. Two months later the Organization of African Unity (OAU, subsequently the African Union—AU) formally agreed to mediate the dispute.

On November 1, 1995, Cameroon was officially granted membership in the Commonwealth. Although a full participant in francophone affairs, Yaoundé had campaigned for membership as part of an effort to appease secessionist leaders in the former British Cameroons region.

The border conflict remained unresolved, with skirmishes reported between Cameroonian and Nigerian forces in the late 1990s, and the two countries trading charges that the other was attempting to influence the ICJ's decision. At a June 1999 summit, Biya and his Nigerian counterpart, Gen. Abdulsalam Abubakar, reportedly held "breakthrough" talks regarding the Bakassi region. However, in early 2000 the Nigerian military was placed on "maximum alert" following Lagos's discovery that France was constructing a military base near the peninsula in Cameroon. Furthermore, Nigerian officials accused Cameroonian forces of regularly firing on its forces. Although minor skirmishes continued in 2000 and 2001, the Nigerian Cross River state opened its Cameroonian border in June 2000.

In 2002 the ICJ ruled in favor of Cameroon in its boundary dispute with Nigeria, but Lagos initially refused to accept the decision. However, after UN-brokered mediation talks in Geneva in August 2003, the two countries agreed to settle the dispute, and a three-year demarcation project was initiated. By December 2003 Nigeria had turned control of 32 villages over to Cameroon, while Cameroon had turned one village over to Nigeria. In January 2004 the two countries agreed to reopen diplomatic ties and to establish joint patrols in the region until final demarcation was completed. In July a second round of territorial exchange occurred. However, Nigeria failed to meet the next round of transfer requirements on September 15, leading to renewed UN efforts to finalize a settlement. In June 2006 President Biya and Nigerian President Olusegun Obasanjo signed an agreement that called for Nigeria to withdraw all of its troops from the Bakassi Peninsula within two months and for Cameroon to assume full authority over the region in two years. While thousands of Nigerians protested turning over what they referred to as their ancestral land, some 3,000 Nigerian troops withdrew by the August deadline. By October the border situation was reported to be "calm" with steady progress being made on demarcation.

Tensions resumed in the region in November 2007 when gunmen killed 21 Cameroonian soldiers, with a Cameroon separatist group claiming responsibility (see Regional Groups in Political Parties, below). The Nigerian senate subsequently declared the Bakassi agreement with Cameroon unconstitutional and thus "illegal," but the federal government declined to reopen the issue. Attacks occurred again in mid-2008, when two soldiers were among 12 people killed, and rebels, under the rubric Niger Delta Defense and Security Council (NDDSC), threatened more fighting if Cameroon did not renegotiate its claim to the territory. Though Nigeria formally handed over control of the Bakassi Peninsula to Cameroon on August 14, another major attack occurred several months later when pirates in the Gulf of Guinea exchanged gunfire with Cameroonian soldiers. The NDDSC, which claimed responsibility, took 10 hostages and threatened to kill them unless their demand for autonomy was met. The group finally released the hostages in November in a prisoner exchange with Cameroon. The piracy prompted the United States and France to consider military aid to Cameroon, despite allegations of corruption in the armed forces.

Relations with neighboring Equatorial Guinea were strained in late 2008 following the kidnapping of a former colonel in the Equatorial Guinean army (and a nephew of Equatorial Guinea's president, Gen. Teodoro Obiang Nguema Mbasogo), who had been granted refugee status in Cameroon in 2003. Two Cameroonian police officers reportedly received $30,000 in the plot. Meanwhile, the Equatorial Guinea embassy denied claims that it was involved in the abduction.

In addition to strengthening economic relations with China in 2009, Cameroon embraced the Chinese government's donation in March of a malaria research center in Yaoundé, the first of 14 it planned to open throughout Africa.

Tensions again flared in the Bakassi region in 2010 when at least 17 Nigerians were reportedly killed by Cameroonian police in the wake of allegations of harassment and torture of several thousand Nigerians still living on the peninsula. Though the first boundary markers were laid in early January, and though the ICJ agreement protected the rights of Nigerians, abuses continued to be reported. Meanwhile, human rights groups urged the UN to deploy peacekeepers to the region. In April 2013, reports indicated that 5 Nigerians were killed, 17 injured, and more than 1,900 forced to flee following a new round of fighting.

In July 2013, the *Fédération Internationale de Football Association* (FIFA), the worldwide governing body for soccer, lifted a ban on Cameroon that would allow the country's team to compete in World Cup qualifying matches. Cameroon's national team had been disqualified over accusations of "government interference" in the country's football program. In September, Cameroon arrested Abdoulaye MISKANE, a leader of the Democratic Front of the Central African Republic People (see entry on the Central African Republic).

Current issues. In April parliament approved the controversial amendment removing restrictions on the number of presidential terms, thus allowing Biya to stand for reelection in 2011, among other revisions (see Constitution and government, above). Described as a setback to democracy, the term-limits revision drew sustained criticism from not only the opposition, but also the MDR, which had been generally supportive of the government. Fifteen SDF members of parliament boycotted the vote. Subsequently, Cameroonians in Switzerland called for freezing President Biya's Swiss bank accounts because of his "manipulation" of the constitution "to remain president for life."

The arrests of numerous senior government officials allegedly involved in corruption scandals in 2008 were seen by observers as paving the way for Biya's reelection in 2011, "based on his anti-corruption crusades." Meanwhile, the president also increased government salaries by 15 percent, ordered price cuts for food staples, and reduced fuel costs. However, in 2009 it was unclear whether the aging president, reportedly ailing, would, in fact, stand for reelection. With no apparent successor and the president spending more and more time out of the country, observers speculated about a potential power vacuum. After a delay of two years, President Biya finally nominated members of the electoral commission, ELECAM, all connected to the governing party, in December 2008. The swearing in of the members on January 29, 2009, seemingly served to energize the opposition, which decried the commission's lack of independent civil society, or opposition members. One governing RDPC/CPDM member of parliament even said the appointments were "inconsistent with the law," according to published reports. Subsequently, the SDF challenged the move by filing a petition with the Supreme Court. The ELECAM appointments also drew criticism from the European Union. ELECAM members, responding to the criticism, pledged to conduct free, fair, and transparent elections. However, in March 2010 Biya was sharply criticized by the opposition, which accused him of "preparing to steal the 2011 election" after parliament passed a law giving oversight of poll preparations to the government, an authority that had belonged to the electoral board. The move was seen as a setback to transparent elections, and assailed by the Foundation for Human Rights and Development as "the worst law we've ever had" because of the alleged potential for electoral abuse by the administration and the judiciary. In April ELECAM nevertheless began organizing plans for voter registration. Meanwhile, the opposition UDC said it would participate in the polling despite what it described as the "colossal weaknesses" of the electoral board. Earlier, a well-known opposition figure associated with the *villes mortes* campaign, Mboua MASSOCK, was arrested during a walk across the country to protest the country's electoral system. Massock had also announced he would contest the 2011 presidential election.

In October 2010 President Biya dismissed a police chief and the head of internal security in the wake of rumors of a coup plot in the preceding month. No reason was given for the dismissals.

Attention in 2011 turned to the presidential elections scheduled for October, with Biya widely expected to defeat all challengers, despite his remarks early in the year that he would not run. In February, the SDF leader urged the president to ensure peace during the elections and transparency in the process. Meanwhile, challengers began to emerge from within the president's own party, as one of his close allies, Ester DANG, an economist, resigned from the RDPC/CPDM and announced her intention to run. Member of parliament Ayah Paul ABINE also quit the party to contest the presidential election, as did Mila ASSOUTE, who declared he would run as an independent. The resignations were indicative not only of mounting rifts within the party but also of dissatisfaction with Biya, observers said. In the months ahead of the election, the high rate of unemployment, particularly among young adults, loomed over Biya and his administration. News reports of a newspaper editor who had allegedly been tortured and who died during his imprisonment in 2010 also surfaced. President Biya, for his part, ordered a judicial inquiry into the matter by France, the United States, and the United Nations Educational, Scientific and Cultural Organization (UNESCO).

By midyear, despite what had been described as unprecedented talks in late 2010 between Biya and the SDF's Fru Ndi—for the first time in 20 years—the SDF leader was not swayed. He challenged the makeup of ELECAM, alleged irregularities in voter registration, and declared the party would boycott the presidential election. Meanwhile, speculation regarding a successor to the 78-year-old Biya began to gain momentum since there was no clear heir apparent. Questions arose about the process, or lack thereof, of naming a successor. The constitution provides for the president of the senate, or upper house of parliament, to be the successor in the event of a midterm presidential vacancy. However, the country has no senate, as that provision of the charter has never been implemented.

On September 29 vague reports emerged that, earlier that morning, soldiers had fired into the air from a bridge outside central Douala, unfurling a banner that called for the end of Biya's rule. The timing and location of the incident—at dawn in a neighborhood where the opposition has historically done well—prompted suspicions the event was orchestrated by authorities to justify the heavy security crackdown that followed, cutting off the possibility of real preelection protests. Nonetheless, observers described the general political mood as one of apathy and resignation to the likelihood of another seven-year term for the president, amid an uninspiring campaign by a divided opposition. Although it went off peacefully, and with a turnout of 68.4 percent, the October 9 election was described as "deeply flawed" by U.S. Ambassador Robert P. Jackson, who pointed out irregularities, opportunities for multiple voting, as well as incompetence and lack of training among the staff of the new electoral commission ELECAM. (French officials had earlier declared the voting fair, but subsequently condemned the election following Jackson's criticism.) Amid complaints of multiple voting by RDPC supporters, ballot box stuffing, and the disenfranchisement of opposition supporters, several candidates requested an annulment of the vote, which the Supreme Court rejected on October 20. The court ratified the official results the next day, showing Biya with 77.99 percent and Fru Ndi, his chief contender, with 10.71 percent. On December 10 Biya announced a cabinet reshuffle.

In response to complaints about fraud, the legislative elections scheduled for July were postponed to February 2013 in order to incorporate biometric voter identification measures. July 23 marked the beginning of a trial against MARAFA Hamidou Yaya, a former cabinet minister, and other former officials for the embezzlement of $29 million that was supposed to be used for the purchase of a new presidential jet. (The "new" jet was later discovered to be an old jet with mechanical problems.) Marafa was arrested in April over the scandal, along with former Prime Minister Ephraim Inoni. Many reportedly viewed the trial as political, as Marafa was said to harbor ambitions to succeed Biya. From jail, he wrote open letters to the president offering information about past scandals. Nevertheless, Marafa and three co-defendants were convicted in mid-September and sentenced to 25 years in prison. Marafa continued to assert he is the victim of "slander."

In March 2013, a report by Human Rights Watch and three other organizations found that Cameroon "aggressively" prosecuted more people for homosexuality than almost any other country, with at least 28 people prosecuted since 2010. On April 14, indirect elections were held for the Senate, the upper legislative chamber that had been approved 17 years earlier but never constituted. Local and regional councilors formed an electoral college that elected 70 members of the chamber, while the president appointed 30. The RDPC/CDPM won 56 of the elected seats. A 2013 UN report found that between 2004 and 2011, the percentage of HIV/AIDS prevalence declined from 5.4 percent to 4.3 percent.

POLITICAL PARTIES

Cameroon had only one legal party (the Cameroon National Union [UNC], later the Democratic Rally of the Cameroon People [RDPC]/ Cameroon People's Democratic Movement [CPDM], below) from 1966 until early 1991 despite the fact that the 1972 constitution guaranteed the right of political parties to organize and participate in elections. In June 1990 President Biya announced that the government, which had theretofore refused to legalize opposition parties, would no longer stand in the way of a multiparty system. In December the National Assembly passed new legislation covering the registration of parties, and as of November 2000, nearly 170 parties had been legalized.

Prior to the 2004 presidential balloting, nine opposition parties (including the SDF, UDC, UPC, MDP, and MLDC, below) formed a National Coalition for Reconciliation and Reconstruction (NCRR) with the goal of coalescing behind a single candidate. However, the SDF (the leading party in the coalition) subsequently withdrew following a dispute over the selection of the NCRR standard-bearer. The NCRR candidate, Adamon Ndam Njoua of the UDC, finished third in the balloting with 4.4 percent of the vote.

Government and Government-Supportive Parties:

Democratic Rally of the Cameroon People (*Rassemblement Démocratique du Peuple Camerounais*—RDPC). Formerly the Cameroon National Union (*Union Nationale Camerounaise*—UNC), the RDPC was until early 1991 the only officially recognized party. The RDPC is also referenced in English as the Cameroon People's Democratic Movement (CPDM). The UNC was formed in 1966 by merger of the Cameroon Union (*Union Camerounaise*); the former majority party of East (French) Cameroons; and of several former West (British) Cameroons parties, including the governing Kamerun National Democratic Party (KNDP), the Kamerun United National Congress (KUNC), and the Kamerun People's Party (KPP). The present name was adopted, over significant anglophone resistance, at a 1985 congress that also established a National Council as the party's second-highest body. The latter, at its first meeting held November 24–26, 1988, urged that Cameroon maintain its nonaligned foreign policy, called for the imposition of stiff anti-embezzlement measures, and asked citizens to accept the "necessary compromise between freedom and order."

At the party congress in June 1990, President Biya called for a loosening of subversion laws and told party members to expect political "competition," the way for which was cleared by the National Assembly's approval of a pluralism law in December. The RDPC/CPDM won 88 seats in the March 1992 legislative elections, subsequently forming a coalition with the MDR (below) to create a working majority in the assembly. At an extraordinary RDPC/CPDM congress on October 7, 1995, Biya secured a new five-year term as party president.

Beginning with the resignation of Ayissi NVODO in October 1996, the RDPC/CPDM and Biya were stung by the defection of three prominent party statesmen and their declarations of presidential candidacy. Following Nvodo in that regard were Albert NDZONGANG and the minister of health and Biya's personal physician, Titus EDZOA, who accused the administration of "permanent attempts to humiliate him." Edzoa was subsequently arrested on fraud charges, and in mid-1997 Nvodo, who had been ill, died. On the other hand, the party's success in legislative balloting in May was attributable, in part, to its recruitment of prominent UNDP and SDF leaders. In addition, observers credited the party's legislative gains to the adoption of a preelection primary process and the support of Prime Minister Musonge's ethnic Sawa constituency in the South-West and Littoral provinces.

The government named in December 1997 reflected, in part, a shift of power within the RDPC/CPDM from those sympathetic to Edzoa, who had been sentenced to 15 years in prison in October, and more senior members to a youthful cadre with "technocratic" tendencies in line with the prime minister's. In April 2001 and September 2006 Biya reshuffled the cabinet, both times strengthening control over his faction-ridden party. In July 2006 Biya was reelected to another five-year term as president of the party.

Following the party's resounding success in the 2007 assembly elections, its leaders began to press for the constitutional revision that would lift presidential term limits, paving the way for Biya's reelection and fulfillment of his modernization program for Cameroon. Meanwhile, rifts reportedly developed in the party with those who wanted to leave Biya's name out of the constitutional revision process so as not to link his tenure to the amendment. Observers said the party's desire to have Biya as "president for life" could result in the opposition's rallying greater support against the proposed revision. In February 2008 Biya called for an extraordinary congress to delineate strategies for organizing grassroots support for the proposed amendment, which subsequently was adopted by parliament and promulgated in April. The party's dominance in the legislature also enabled Biya to follow up with a decree that further enhanced his executive power over government agencies.

In the run-up to the 2011 presidential election, three key party members resigned (see Current issues, above) to challenge Biya, though the president had not officially declared his candidacy by midyear. René Emmanuel SADI was mentioned as a possible successor to Biya, but the 78-year-old president eventually decided to run again himself, winning 77.99 percent of the official vote. RDPC senator Marcel Niat Njifenji was elected president of the upper chamber in June 2013.

Leaders: Paul BIYA (President of the Republic and President of the Party), Grégoire OWONA (Deputy Secretary General), René Emmanuel SADI (Secretary General).

National Union for Democracy and Progress (*Union Nationale pour la Démocratie et le Progrès*—UNDP). Seen primarily as a vehicle for supporters of former president Ahidjo, the UNDP was formed in 1991 under the leadership of Samuel Eboua. In early 1992, however, it was reported that Eboua had been "squeezed out" of his position by former prime minister Maigari Bello Bouba, who had recently returned from exile. After a last-minute reversal of a proposed electoral boycott, the UNDP won 68 seats in the March legislative balloting, running most strongly in the predominately Muslim northern provinces. Bouba was subsequently described as the "strongman of the opposition."

In the immediate aftermath of the October 1992 presidential election the UNDP leader, who had finished third, joined SDF leader Fru Ndi in petitioning the Supreme Court to annul the controversial poll. Nevertheless, in late November two party members, Hamadou MOUSTAPHA and Issa Tchiroma BAKARY, accepted cabinet ministries, and in early 1993 Fru Ndi denounced Bouba for negotiating with President Biya on the formation of a unity government.

On November 8, 1994, the UNDP announced a boycott of the National Assembly, pending the release of 30 party activists who had been arrested in July. While the walkout was abandoned four weeks later, the UNDP Central Committee confirmed in late December that Moustapha and Bakary had been expelled from the party (the latter proclaiming the formation of a rival UNDP). Although advancing the second-highest number of candidates (180) in the 1996 local elections, the UNDP finished third in the balloting. Highlighting the UNDP's electoral showing was the victory of former president Ahidjo's son, Mohamed AHIDJO, who had returned from exile two years earlier. Subsequently, the party was buffeted by a power struggle between Bouba and the virulently anti-Biya Mohamed Ahidjo.

Still reeling from the loss of Moustapha and Bakary in 1994, the UNDP fared poorly in legislative balloting in May 1997, its representation dropping to 13 seats. Having reached an impasse in its dialogue with the administration concerning a possible unity government, the UNDP helped spearhead a boycott of the October presidential elections, after which Bouba disputed the government's claims to a high voter turnout. Nevertheless, in December Bouba announced that he had accepted a cabinet post, asserting that Biya was seeking to incorporate opposition leaders in his government and admitting that his appointment was part of an apparent presidential effort to isolate Fru Ndi. Bouba remained in the cabinet following the March 2000 reshuffling, although substantial criticism was reported at the UNDP congress in June over his decision to stay in the government despite what delegates charged was a distinct lack of progress regarding the political liberalization promised by the Biya administration in the 1997 compact. (The dissent to Bouba became more apparent with the resignation of UNDP vice president Nicole OKALA in July.) The congress formally criticized the government's human rights record and demanded broad changes in the electoral code and establishment of an independent election commission prior to the 2002 balloting.

In the 2007 assembly elections, the UNDP increased its number of seats by five, though the party was among those leveling fraud charges against the government after the results were announced. Bouba, nevertheless, retained his post following a cabinet reshuffle in September. Though some "militant" members of the party wanted to speak out against President Biya's appointments to the electoral commission in 2009 (see Current issues, above), Bouba refrained from making any public statement on the matter.

In the June 2009 cabinet reshuffle, Bouba was named to a minister of state post.

Reports in 2013 indicated that a number of party members had defected to the RDPC/CPDM.

Leaders: Maigari Bello BOUBA (Chair and Former Prime Minister), Youmegne Manuel PAPIN, Peter Kuma KOMBAIN, Pierre Flambeau NGAYAP (Secretary General).

Cameroon People's Union (*Union des Populations Camerounaises*—UPC). The Marxist–Leninist UPC was formed in 1948 and, although outlawed in 1955, continued to operate clandestinely in Cameroon, its membership fragmenting into pro-Soviet and Maoist factions in the 1960s. Sporadic UPC guerrilla activity presented no serious challenge to the Ahidjo regime, and by 1971 most UPC adherents had been forced into exile. Headquartered in Paris, the UPC subsequently served as the most prominent of the groups opposing Cameroon's one-party regime, claiming thousands of "militants" in both France and Cameroon.

In October 1990 UPC secretary general Ngouo WOUNGLY-MASSAGA, having been accused by colleagues of "anti-social behavior and embezzlement," broke with the party and returned to Cameroon, where he eventually organized the People's Solidarity Party (*Parti de la Solidarité du Peuple*—PSP). Upon legalization of the UPC in 1991 most former exiles returned, including Ndeh Ntumazah, the "last surviving founder of the UPC," who reportedly enjoyed a "larger-than-life" reputation in Cameroon despite his 20-year absence. The party subsequently split regarding the March 1992 legislative elections, Ntumazah leading a partial boycott of the balloting despite Secretary General Augustin Frederick Kodock's decision that the UPC should participate. Presenting candidates in about half of the 180 districts, the UPC won 18 seats, thereby becoming the third-leading parliamentary party.

In May 1992 the party was a founding member of the National Convention of the Cameroonian Opposition (see under PDC, below), and in September Henri Hogbe Nlend was described as a UPC presidential candidate. However, there were no reports of his having garnered any votes or of the UPC having taken part in the elections. In February 1995 Woungly-Massaga returned to the UPC, which absorbed his PSP.

Intraparty tension mounted following the UPC's poor showing in the January 1996 municipal elections, in which it won only 3 of 336 contests, and in April the party announced a number of dismissals and reportedly sought closer ties with the RDPC/CPDM. In May the UPC's parliamentary leader, Charles Oma BETOW, and three other senior leaders announced the removal of Secretary General Kodock, labeling his party management "disastrous." Kodock argued that his detractors had met illegally, thus invalidating their motion. Kodock was named minister of state for agriculture in the government announced on September 20, a UPC conference earlier in the month reportedly revealing at least four factions in the grouping.

At legislative balloting in May 1997 Kodock's "pro-Biya" wing forwarded 35 candidates, while Ntumazah and his followers supported an additional 17; subsequently, the group's representation plummeted from 16 posts to 1 as Kodock alone secured a seat. In presidential polling in October the party once again forwarded Henri Hogbe Nlend, who secured only 2.8 percent of the vote. In December Nlend was named minister of scientific and technical research in the new cabinet. In 2001 the UPC was reportedly split into two factions, out of which Kodock's became increasingly "anti-Biya," while Nlend's wing represented the "pro-Biya" orientation.

In the 2002 legislative elections the national election board treated the two factions as a single party, although candidates identified themselves as UPC (N) for the Nlend supporters and UPC (K) for the Kodock supporters. Kodock accepted a cabinet post after the balloting and continued to serve in the reshuffled cabinet after the presidential elections in 2004. The UPC (N) participated in the anti-Biya presidential electoral coalition in 2004. In 2006 Kodock reiterated his support for Biya, but in September 2007 he was dismissed from his cabinet post in the wake of allegations of embezzlement within his ministry. He then denounced Biya for "assassination of democracy" by dropping the UPC from his cabinet (though ultimately another UPC member received a cabinet post.

The leaders of the two factions reconciled in 2008, and a subsequent ministerial ruling backed Kodock's leadership. However, new divisions subsequently emerged.

In July 2013, reports emerged that the various party factions had reunited for the September assembly balloting.

Leaders: Henri Hogbe NLEND (1997 presidential candidate and UPC [N] Leader), Augustin Frederick KODOCK (UPC [K] Secretary General).

Front for the National Salvation of Cameroon (*Front pour le Salut National du Cameroun*—FSNC). Founded by Issa Tchiroma Bakary in the mid-2000s after a rift with UNDP leaders, the FSNC was registered as a party in 2007. Bakary had been critical of the decision by the UDC's Adamou Ndam Njoya and the SDF's John Fru Ndi to contest the 2004 presidential poll, in circumvention of a plan for a coalition candidate to avoid splitting the opposition vote.

The party promotes a prodemocracy, anticorruption platform, and in 2008 it supported the government's proposed constitutional amendments, with Bakary particularly favoring a provision that would extend the 45-day period for organizing a new election in the event of a vacancy in office. Despite having been a member of the vocal opposition in the past, Bakary in recent years has criticized opposition leaders while denying their claims that he was bribed to support the constitutional amendments and the Biya government. In the June 2009 cabinet reshuffle Bakary was appointed minister of communications and subsequently initiated some harsh actions against journalists. One member of the FSNC was appointed by the president as a senator in 2013.

Leaders: Issa Tchiroma BAKARY (Chair), Morto OUMAROU (Secretary General).

Movement for the Defense of the Republic (*Mouvement pour la Défense de la République*—MDR). The northern-based MDR, supported primarily by the small Kirdi ethnic group, was organized shortly before the March 1992 legislative balloting in an apparent effort to dilute the electoral strength of the UNDP (above), the region's dominant party. Six of the MDR's 32 candidates won assembly seats, enough to make the party a crucial element in formation of the subsequent government. Five MDR members were appointed to the cabinet in April, including party leader Dakolé Daïssala, who had been placed in detention following the 1984 coup attempt. Although never formally charged or tried, Daïssala had remained in jail until 1991, when he began what was viewed as an extraordinary ascent to governmental prominence.

At legislative balloting in May 1997 the MDR managed to recapture only one of its legislative posts. Subsequently, the party was not included in the government named in December. The MDR failed to gain any seats in the 2002 elections, but Daïssala joined the government in 2004 as minister of transport. He was dismissed in the cabinet reshuffle of September 2007, reportedly as a result of alleged ineptitude and also in part because President Biya considered him to be "politically baseless" since the MDR did not win any seats in the 2007 assembly. The party supported the government's proposed constitutional amendments in 2008.

Leader: Dakolé DAÏSSALA (President).

Opposition Parties:

Social Democratic Front (SDF). The SDF was launched in early 1990 in the English-speaking town of Bamenda in western Cameroon. Shortly thereafter a number of its leaders were arrested for belonging to an illegal organization, and an SDF rally in May was broken up by security forces, leaving several people dead. However, following the government's endorsement of political liberalization in June, the SDF detainees were released, and the party (legalized in 1991) became one of the most active opposition groups. Although it would probably have secured substantial representation, particularly in the anglophone western provinces, the SDF boycotted the March 1992 legislative election on grounds that there was insufficient time for opposition parties to organize effectively and that the electoral code favored the RDPC/CPDM.

Party president John Fru Ndi's strong showing in the October 1992 presidential balloting was heralded by the SDF as evidence that its appeal was not limited to the anglophone community. Hence, the party continued to distance itself from the Cameroon Anglophone Movement, the self-described "socio-cultural association" headquartered in Buea in the South-West province, which advocated a return to the 1972-style federal government system. In November the SDF rejected calls for a unity government headed by Biya, insisting that his handling of the presidential balloting and Fru Ndi's arrest proved that he could not be trusted. Instead it called for a two-year transitional program to be highlighted by the establishment of a new electoral code and the convening of a constitutional conference to draw up a new basic charter.

In May 1994 Secretary General Siga ASSANGA was dismissed by the party's disciplinary council for making approaches to the government on possible SDF participation in a government of national unity. Five months later Fru Ndi spearheaded the launching of the Allies' Front for Change (FAC, below), prior to yielding the office under a revolving presidency system to Samuel Eboua (then of the UNDP) in January 1995.

In early 1995 the SDF experienced a deep crisis that resulted in the departure or exclusion from its executive committee of a dozen influential members. One of those excluded, party treasurer Jean DJOKOU, accused Fru Ndi of "secret management and swindling the party finances," while others complained of the lack of attention to francophones within the party, most of whom strongly supported a unitary state.

During the run-up to balloting in January 1996 the SDF suspended its membership in the FAC and issued a list of 105 candidates. In the January 21 polling the party secured victories primarily in large towns and "traditional fiefdoms." Subsequently, the party's performance in legislative balloting in May 1997 (43 seats captured) fell shy of analysts' predictions. Thereafter, SDF militants took to the streets to protest the government's alleged fraudulent administration of the polling, and on June 12 a number of party members were arrested. Nevertheless, on June 17 Fru Ndi called on the party's legislators to assume their seats. Fru Ndi's "statesman-like" decision to distance himself and the SDF from violent dissention had its roots, according to some analysts, in his ambitions for the presidential elections scheduled for October. Subsequently, Fru Ndi and other senior SDF members traveled to African and Western capitals to gain allies in their efforts to pressure the recalcitrant Biya administration into addressing the opposition's preelectoral demands. While such visits reportedly improved Fru Ndi's standing with the international community, Biya's stance remained unchanged. Consequently, on September 12 in Paris Fru Ndi announced the SDF's decision to boycott the presidential polling.

The SDF's (then) secretary general, Tazoacha ASONGANY, led the party's negotiating team in talks with the government, which opened in December 1997. The talks collapsed in early 1998, and in mid-February the SDF formed a "common front" with the UDC (below). In July the SDF suffered its most traumatic infighting since 1995, as 10 of the party's 43 legislators resigned from the party to protest Fru Ndi's leadership, which they reportedly characterized as "authoritarian." Subsequently, Fru Ndi ousted SDF vice chair Souleimane MAHAMAD after Mahamad convened an extraordinary party congress that served as an anti–Fru Ndi forum. In lopsided balloting at the SDF's annual congress in April 1999, Fru Ndi retained the party's top post.

The SDF protested that the 2002 legislative elections were flawed because of government interference, and Fru Ndi launched a boycott of the assembly and municipal councils. However, in July Fru Ndi announced an end to the boycott, prompting a group of SDF dissidents to form a new party (see AFP, below).

The SDF was instrumental in the formation of the anti-Biya electoral coalition, the NCRR, in April 2004. However, Fru Ndi withdrew the SDF from the NCRR in September after a dispute over the manner in which the coalition's presidential candidate would be chosen. Fru Ndi instead ran as the SDF's candidate and received 17.4 percent of the vote.

Rifts in the party developed in late 2005 after Asonganyi criticized party leadership for being ineffectual as a catalyst for change in Cameroon. Asonganyi was subsequently suspended, prompting protest by some members, who walked out. He was then replaced as secretary general by Michael NDOBEGANG. Asonganyi was dismissed from the party in early 2006 after the party found him guilty of six "charges," including questioning or criticizing party policies, ideals, and hierarchy. Shortly thereafter, Ndobegang resigned over Asonganyi's expulsion. In May 2006, with tensions again on the rise and reports of some 300 members having defected to the RDPC/CPDM, the SDF split into two factions, with Fru Ndi elected chair of one and Ben MUNA chosen as leader of the rival wing at separate congresses. Precipitating the dispute was Muna's challenge to Fru Ndi's party leadership and an attempt by Fru Ndi to amend the party constitution in a way critics said was meant to enhance his control. In November, however, the high court confirmed Fru Ndi as the legitimate SDF chair. Muna subsequently joined the AFP.

Following assembly elections in 2007, Fru Ndi led the way in the opposition's claims of fraud and "gross irregularities," unsuccessfully petitioning the Supreme Court to have the elections annulled. The SDF lost six seats in the balloting, its only stronghold being in Fru Ndi's North-West region.

In early 2008 two people were killed when police broke up an SDF demonstration against the government's ban on a private television station. The SDF also was vocal in its continuing opposition to the 2008 constitutional amendment that lifted presidential term limits, Fru Ndi supporting revision only if it were done through a constitutional conference. In August Fru Ndi's murder trial got under way on charges that he beat to death Gregoire DIBOULE, secretary of the Muna faction, in 2006. Fru Ndi, for his part, said the charges were politically motivated and meant to keep him from standing in the 2011 presidential election. Meanwhile, another SDF militant, Pierre Roger LAMBO, was on trial for allegedly inciting violence during the February 2008 protests.

In the wake of its protests against the Biya-appointed members of the electoral commission in 2008, the SDF said it would try to prevent any election from taking place. Fru Ndi called the appointment of RDPC/CPDM members "an electoral coup d'état" by Biya.

In 2009 two SDF members of parliament reportedly defected to the RDPC/CPDM. About the same time, a member of the RDPC/CPDM defected to the SDF.

A women's movement within the SDF was initiated by party secretary general Elizabeth Tamanjong in 2010 to promote leadership roles for women not only in the party, but also in the country. Also in 2010 the party criticized President Biya's approval of a measure that grants electoral oversight to the Ministry of Territorial Administration, accusing him of stealing that authority from the independent electoral board (see Current issues, above). "Paul Biya doesn't want change. He wants to die in power," Tamanjong said. A key party member, Kah WALLA, resigned in November to run for the presidency as an independent in 2011. *Africa Confidential* noted that in the run-up to elections a younger generation of leaders was eager to take the reins, a possibility the traditional leadership rejected.

Fru Ndi's insistence that the party would boycott the election reportedly caused deep rifts within the SDF. But Fru Ndi subsequently surprised many when he changed his mind and contested. After the election, he claimed that ballots had been cast in the names of dead people and joined other opposition leaders in rejecting the vote. Fru Ndi faced calls to resign after the SDF was heavily defeated in indirect Senate balloting in April 2013. The SDF announced in July that it would not boycott elections scheduled for September.

Leaders: John FRU NDI (Chair), Pierre KWEMO, Joshua OSIH (Second Vice President), Bernard TABALI, Elizabeth TAMANJONG (Secretary General).

Cameroonian Democratic Union (*Union Démocratique du Cameroun*—UDC). The UDC was formed in 1991 under the leadership of Adamou Ndam Njoya, who held several senior posts in the Ahidjo administration. Although the party boycotted the March 1992 legislative election, Ndam Njoya subsequently competed in the October 1992 presidential elections, gaining 3.62 percent of the vote.

In 1997 Ndam Njoya was a leading advocate of the opposition's boycott of the October presidential polling, although the party had secured five seats in the May legislative balloting. Following the 2002 elections the UDC became the third-largest party in the assembly with five seats. Ndam Njoya helped form the anti-Biya coalition in the 2004 presidential election and was the coalition's candidate for the presidency. He placed third with 4.4 percent of the vote. In late 2006, Njoya claimed the government tried to assassinate him during a reported military operation at his residence in which one person was killed.

The UDC lost one seat in the 2007 assembly elections, the party leader subsequently alleging that President Biya was leading the country into "civil war" in the wake of violent incidents in several regions. In 2009 Njoya denounced Biya's electoral commission appointments, saying the move turned over the electoral process to the governing party "on a platter of gold."

In January 2011 party veteran Theophile Yimgaing MOYO resigned to form a new party, the Citizens Movement (below). In April the party again nominated Njoya as its presidential flag bearer. In the 2011 elections Njoya won 1.26 percent of the official vote. In 2013, the president appointed one member of the UDC as a senator.

Leader: Adamou NDAM NJOYA (1992, 2004, and 2011 presidential candidate).

Progressive Movement (*Mouvement Progressif*—MP). The opposition MP, led by Jean-Jacques Ekindi, was formed in 1991 after

Ekindi split from the CPDM. Following a government crackdown on protest marches in August 2004, in advance of the October presidential elections, Ekindi was placed under house arrest. He was among 16 registered presidential candidates, winning just 0.27 percent of the vote. Subsequently, Ekindi challenged the results of the election, claiming vote rigging.

In 2007, Ekindi was elected to a seat in the assembly.

Leader: Jean-Jacques EKINDI (President of the Party and 2004 and 2011 presidential candidate).

Other Parties and Groups:

Citizens Movement (*Mouvement Citoyen*—MOCI). Founded in January 2011 by disaffected UDC member Theophile Yimgaing Moyo, the party was launched to promote peace, dialogue, and social justice.

Leaders: Theophile Yimgaing MOYO (Chair), Elie MBPOAFOURI, Florent NAYO, Valentin ATEB ABENG.

Movement for the Liberation and Development of Cameroon (*Mouvement pour la Libération et le Développement du Cameroun*—MLDC). The MLDC was formed by dissident members of the Movement for the Liberation of Cameroonian Youth (*Mouvement pour la Libération de la Jeunesse Camerounaise*—MLJC) in 2002. Led by Dieudonné TINA, the MLJC secured one seat in legislative balloting in May 1997 and none in the 2002 balloting. A subsequent leadership dispute led members to leave the party and establish a new political group. The MLDC participated in the anti-Biya electoral coalition in 2004.

Leaders: Marcel YONDO, Jean PAHAI.

Alliance of Progressive Forces (*Alliance des Forces Progressistes*—AFP). Created in 2002, the AFP was formed by former members of the SDF who opposed Fru Ndi's leadership and willingness to compromise with President Biya. The party's 2004 presidential candidate reportedly was rejected by the high court. One of the party's founders, Évariste Fopoussi Fotso, returned to the party in 2005 after having resigned in 2002.

In 2008 party leader Ben Muna, formerly of the SDF, spoke out against the constitutional amendment backed by President Biya and his governing party. Further, the AFP claimed that Biya's appointments to the electoral commission were unconstitutional. In 2010 the party opposed the government's move to assume authority over poll preparations, which the AFP believes rightly belongs with the independent electoral board.

The AFP nominated Muna as its presidential candidate in the 2011 election. Prior to the 2013 assembly balloting, the AFP agreed to join an electoral alliance with the three other small parties.

Leaders: Ben MUNA (Chair), Saidou MAIDADI (Secretary General).

Liberal Democratic Party (*Parti Libéral Démocrate*—PLD). The PLD was formed in 1991 under the leadership of Njoh Litumbe, who subsequently visited the United States as a spokesperson for the opposition groups in Cameroon. Dormant for many years, the group called in 2005 for President Biya to negotiate with the SCNC (below).

Leader: Njoh LITUMBE.

Union of Democratic Forces of Cameroon (*Union des Forces Démocratiques du Cameroun*—UFDC). The UFDC was considered one of the more important groups to boycott the March 1992 legislative election, its leader, Victorin Hameni Bieleu, having served as president of an opposition coordinating committee in 1991. On November 3, 1992, Bieleu was arrested for his involvement in antigovernment protests. Bieleu ran for the presidency in 2004 but received less than 1 percent of the vote.

Leader: Victorin Hameni BIELEU (2004 and 2011 presidential candidate).

Movement for Democracy and Progress (*Mouvement pour la Démocratie et le Progrès*—MDP). The MDP was headed by former UNDP leader Samuel Eboua, who was elected to a FAC leadership post in 1996. Eboua's 1997 presidential campaign yielded just 2.4 percent of the vote in October balloting. Eboua, who had been a state minister in the 1970s and 1980s, died in 2000 after a lengthy illness. In 2008 the party made an appearance at an anniversary celebration in Matomb. Reports in 2013 indicated that the party was defunct.

Social Liberal Congress (SLC). The SLC, based in Buea in southern Cameroon, was founded in 2000 by George Dobgima Nyamndi, formerly of the UDC and the LDA. Nyamndi, who promoted electoral and education reforms, secured 0.18 percent of the vote in the 2004 presidential election.

Leader: George Dobgima NYAMNDI (2004 and 2011 presidential candidate).

Action for Meritocracy and Equal Opportunity (AMEC). In presidential balloting in October 1997 the anglophone AMEC's candidate, Joachim Tabi Owono, secured less than 1 percent of the vote. In 2007 the party fielded candidates in the legislative elections but did not win any seats. In 2008 the AMEC was among the parties challenging the legality of the constitutional amendments adopted by parliament. The Supreme Court rejected the claims. The party ran a limited number of candidates in the 2013 assembly elections.

Leader: Joachim Tabi OWONO (President of the Party and 1997 presidential candidate).

Other parties that contested the 2002 legislative or the 2004 or 2011 presidential elections included the **Alliance for Development and Democracy** (*Alliance pour la Démocratie et le Développement*—ADD), led by 2004 and 2011 presidential candidate Garga Haman ADJI; the **Justice and Development Party** (JDP), which promotes the rights of English-speaking Cameroonians under the leadership of publisher Boniface FORBIN, who was the JDP's 2004 presidential candidate; the **African Movement for New Independence and Democracy** (*Mouvement Africain pour la Nouvelle Indépendance et la Démocratie*—MANIDEM), led by Pierre Abanda KPAMA and comprised of former members of the UPC; and the **People's Action Party,** led by the 2011 presidential candidate Ayah Paul ABINE.

(For a list of some 40 other small parties and groups, see the 1999 *Handbook.*) For more information on the **Social Movement for the New Democracy** (*Mouvement Social pour la Nouvelle Démocratie*—MSND), the **Cameroonian Party of Democrats** (*Parti des Démocrates Camerounais*—PDC), and the **Allies' Front for Change** (*Front des Alliés pour le Changement*—FAC), please see the 2013 *Handbook.*

Regional Groups:

Southern Cameroon National Council (SCNC). The leading vehicle for expression of secessionist sentiment in the former British Cameroons region, the SCNC originally served as the elected executive organ of the Southern Cameroon People's Conference (SCPC), an umbrella organization for a number of professional and trade associations, political parties, youth groups, and other grassroots bodies opposed to the domination of francophone influence in the country. The SCPC was the successor to the All Anglophone Conference (AAC), which first met in 1993 in an effort to persuade the nation's francophone leadership to return to the federal structure of the 1960s in which the anglophone region enjoyed broad autonomy. The SCPC rubric was subsequently adopted in part because the term *anglophone* was deemed too "colonial" and "limiting" and in part to reflect the region's shift in favor of independence based on a perceived lack of interest in dialogue regarding autonomy on the part of the Biya administration. Most observers subsequently referred to the SCNC when discussing affairs in the Southern Cameroons, prompting the SCPC, for the sake of clarity, to formally adopt the SCNC name. (For more on the leadership struggles of the SCNC before 2005, please see an earlier *Handbook*).

In late 2005 several party members, including Henry Fossung, the chair of one of the factions, were arrested after illegal demonstrations. Party official Chief Ayamba Ette Otun was released but soon rearrested for his role in launching Radio Free Southern Cameroons which aired programs highly critical of the administration. In early 2006 one of the detainees died, his supporters alleging his death was the result of torture. In April 65 people were arrested during a meeting at the residence of one of the members.

In November 2007 a faction referred to as the Southern Cameroon Peoples Organization (SCAPO), also known as the Ambazonians, led by Kevin Ngwang GUMNE, claimed responsibility for the killing of 21 Cameroonian soldiers in the Bakassi region, declaring that region and other areas of the country as the independent Republic of Ambazonia.

In February 2008 some 20 SCNC members were arrested and 10 jailed following the group's preparations for a Youth Day celebration. A year later party leaders Ayamba Ette Otun and Nfor Nfor, along with 22 other activists, were arrested at the residence of party secretary general James Sabum. After the court adjourned the case until April

6, 2009, the group returned to Sabum's home, whereupon soldiers arrived and allegedly attacked and beat some of them. Meanwhile, the new "president" of the so-called Southern Cameroons Restoration Government said that a proposed constitution had been written and would be circulated via the Internet for debate and discussion.

The SCNC gained new hope for its push for autonomy under the auspices of Libya's leader, Col. Muammar Abu Minyar al-QADHAFI. As president of the AU, Qadhafi invited SCNC leaders to Addis Ababa, Ethiopia, in February 2009 in connection with the SCNC's request to the African Commission for Human and People's Rights for a ruling on the SCNC's independence. Seen as another boost to the SCNC cause was the AU's deletion from the agenda of an item that had been pressed by the Biya administration regarding the Bakassi Peninsula. SCNC officials claimed it was because of them that the item was removed from the agenda, according to *Africa News*. The published report said such a move might cause Biya some concern since he was aware of Qadhafi's "track record as far as liberation movements are concerned." (Qadhafi had helped other "outlaw" groups such as the Irish Republican Army and the Palestine Liberation Organization.)

In late 2009 secession was dealt another blow, however, when the African Commission on Human and People's Rights rejected the SCNC's demand. In August 2010 the government refused to confirm or deny claims that 50 SCNC members were being held in jail with no provisions for a trial. Authorities said they refused to negotiate with the group as long as it advocated secession. Ahead of the 2013 elections, reports emerged of widespread arrests of SCNC members and supporters.

Leaders: Henry FOSSUNG (Chair of the SCAPO/Ambazonia faction), Augustine NDANGAM (Deputy Chair of the SCAPO/Ambazonia faction), Chief AYAMBA Ette Otun (SCNC Chair), Frederick EBONG Alobwede (National Chair of the SCNC and President of the Federal Republic of the Southern Cameroons), Nfor NFOR (Vice Chair of the SCNC), Hitler MBINGLO (Chair of the Northern Zone), James SABUM (Secretary General).

South West Elite Association (SWELA). The reactivation of SWELA was announced in March 2000, apparently at the urging of Prime Minister Musonge in the hope of countering the secessionist movement in South-West province led by the SCNC. SWELA leaders subsequently voiced support for a "united Cameroon." In July 2006 Enow Orock was elected to a two-year term as the party's new leader.

The group elected new officers at a general assembly in February 2010, attended by several ministers and other government officials.

Leaders: Juliet BECKE (Treasurer), Bake ITOE (Financial Secretary), Shadrack Epie EKALLE (Secretary General).

Guerrilla Group:

National Liberation Front of Cameroon (*Fronte de la Libération Nationale du Cameroun*—FLNC). The anti-Biya FLNC is led by Mbara Guerandi, who reportedly fled from Cameroon in 1984 following his indictment for participating in an alleged coup attempt. In late 1997 it was reported that Guerandi, now based in Burkina Faso, had reached agreement with antigovernment rebels in Chad to coordinate guerrilla activities. There have been few reports of recent activity by the FLNC.

Leader: Mbara GUERANDI (in exile in Burkina Faso).

LEGISLATURE

Senate (*Sénat*). The Senate has 100 members, 10 from each of the country's 10 provinces. Seven of each province's senators are indirectly elected by an electoral college that includes local and regional councilors. The remaining three senators for each region are appointed by the president. Although approved in 1996, the Senate was not constituted until 2013. In indirect balloting on April 14, 2013, the RDPC/CPDM secured 56 seats, and the SDF secured 14. The president subsequently appointed 30 RDPC/CPDM members or allies to the chamber.

President: Marcel Niat NJIFENJI.

National Assembly (*Assemblée Nationale*). The assembly currently consists of 180 members elected for five-year terms. In the April 1988 election voters in most districts were permitted to choose between two lists (in the case of single-member constituencies, between two candidates) presented by the Cameroon People's Democratic Movement. Multiparty balloting was introduced in the March 1, 1992, election, which was brought forward one year in response to pressure from the nation's burgeoning prodemocracy movement. However, no independent or coalition candidates were permitted, contributing to the decision by some opposition groups to boycott the poll. The number of parties participating in legislative balloting increased from 32 in 1992 to 40 in 1997, and the number of parties securing seats rose from 4 to 7, respectively.

Legislative elections were held on September 30, 2013, after having been postponed three times since originally scheduled in July 2012. With the Cameroon Supreme Court rejecting all cases claiming irregularity, the CPDM continued its hold on power winning 148 of the 180 seats available. The Social Democratic Front carried 18 seats. The National Union for Democracy and Progress carried 5 seats. The Cameroon Democratic Union carries 4 seats. The Union of the Peoples of Cameroon carried 3 seats. The Cameroon Renaissance Movement and the Movement for the Defense of the Republic each carried 1 seat.

President: Djibril Cayavé YEGUIE.

CABINET

[as of September 15, 2013]

Prime Minister	Philemon Yang (RDPC/CPDM)
Deputy Prime Minister	Amadou Ali (RDPC/CPDM)
Ministers of State	
Justice; Keeper of the Seals	Laurent Esso (RDPC/CPDM)
Territorial Administration and Decentralization	René Emmanuel Sadi
Tourism and Leisure	Maigari Bello Bouba Maigari (UNDP)
Ministers	
Agriculture and Rural Development	Menye Lazare Essimi
Civil Service and Administrative Reform	Michel Ange Angouin
Communication	Issa Tchiroma Bakari (FSNC)
Culture and Arts	Ama Tutu Muna [f]
Defense	Edgar Alain Mebe Ngo'o
Economy, Planning, and Regional Development	Emmanuel Nganou Djoumessi
Education	Alim Youssouf née Adjidja (RDPC/CPDM) [f]
Employment and Vocational Training	Zacharie Perevet (RDPC/CPDM)
Environment	Pierre Hélé (RDPC/CPDM)
Finance	Ousmane Mey ALAMINE
Foreign Affairs	Pierre Moukoko Mbonjo
Forests and Wild Animals	Philip Ngwese Ngole
Higher Education	Jacques Fame Ndongo (RDPC/CPDM)
Labor and Social Insurance	Grégroire Owona
Livestock, Fisheries, and Animal Industries	Dr Taiga (RDPC/CPDM)
Mines, Industry, and Technological Development	Emmanuel Bonde (RDPC/CPDM)
Posts and Telecommunications	Jean Pierre Biyiti Bi Essam
Public Health	André Mama Fouda
Public Works	Patrice Amba Salla
Relations with Assemblies	Amadou Ali (RDPC/CPDM)
Scientific and Technical Research	Madeleine Tchuenté (ind.) [f]
Secondary Education	Louis Bapes Bapes (RDPC)
Small and Medium Enterprises	Laurent Etoundi Ngoa (RDPC/CPDM)
Social Affairs	Cathérine Bakang Mbock (RDPC/CPDM) [f]

Sports and Physical Education	Adoum Garoua (RDPC/CPDM)
State Property and Land Affairs	Jacqueline Koung Abissike [f]
Tourism	Baba Amadou (RDPC/CPDM)
Trade	Luc Magloire Mbarga Atangana (ind.)
Transport	Robert Nkili (RDPC/CPDM)
Urban Development and Housing	Jean Claude Mbwentchou
Water and Power	Basile Atangana Kouna
Women and the Family	Marie Thérèse Abena Ondoa [f]
Youth	Kpwatt Ismaël Bidoung

[f] = female

INTERGOVERNMENTAL REPRESENTATION

Ambassador to the U.S.: Joseph B. C. FOE-ATANGANA.

U.S. Ambassador to Cameroon: Robert P. JACKSON.

Permanent Representative to the UN: Michel Tommo MONTHE.

IGO Memberships (Non-UN): AfDB, AU, CWTH, IOM, NAM, OIC, WTO.

CANADA

Political Status: Granted Dominion status under the British North America Act of 1867; recognized as autonomous state within the Commonwealth in 1931; constitution "patriated" as of April 17, 1982.

Area: 3,855,081 sq. mi. (9,984,670 sq. km), including inland water.

Population: 34,880,491 (2013E—UN); 34,568,211 (2013E—U.S. Census).

Major Urban Centers (urban areas, 2011C): OTTAWA (1,236,324), Toronto (5,583,064), Montreal (3,824,221), Vancouver (2,313,328), Calgary (1,215,839), Edmonton (1,159,869), Quebec (766,706), Winnipeg (703,018), Hamilton (721,053).

Official Languages: English, French.

Monetary Unit: Canadian Dollar (market rate November 1, 2013: 1.04 dollar = $1US).

Sovereign: Queen ELIZABETH II.

Governor General: David JOHNSTON; appointed by Queen Elizabeth II on the advice of the prime minister and installed for a traditional five-year term on October 1, 2010, succeeding Michaëlle JEAN, who assumed a UNESCO post at the conclusion of her term.

Prime Minister: Stephen HARPER (Conservative Party of Canada); asked by the governor general on January 24, 2006, to form a new government following the general elections of January 23; appointed a new government on February 6 in succession to Paul Martin (Liberal Party of Canada); returned to office for a second term following early elections on October 14, 2008, and for a third term following elections on May 2, 2011.

THE COUNTRY

Canada, the largest country in the Western Hemisphere and the second largest in the world (after Russia), extends from the Atlantic to the Pacific and from the Arctic to a southern limit near Detroit, Michigan. Because of its northerly location, severe climate, and unfavorable geographic conditions, only one-third of its total area has been developed, and more than two-thirds of its people inhabit a 100-mile-wide strip of territory along the U.S. border. Colonized by both English and French settlers, it retained throughout a long period of British rule a distinctive cultural and linguistic duality. Of the more than 6.7 million Canadians who claim French as their mother tongue, approximately 86 percent are concentrated in the province of Quebec, where demands for political and economic equality (or even separation from the rest of Canada) persist. A major step toward linguistic equality was taken in 1969 with the enactment of an official-languages bill that provided for bilingual districts throughout the country. Nevertheless, Quebec enacted legislation establishing French as its sole official language in 1977, although a series of court rulings from 1984 to 1988 voided some provisions of the act.

In early 1987 the *Inuit,* an Eskimo people accounting for about 17,000 of the sparse overall population of 51,000, won tentative agreement to the formation of their own territory (Nunavut) in the larger, eastern portion of the vast Northwest Territories; the smaller western region is home to a more varied population that includes Western Arctic (*Inuvialuit*) Eskimos, Yukon Indians, Athapaskan-speaking *Déné* Indians, and *Métis* (mixed Indian and European), but with a narrow white majority. The creation of Nunavut was eventually approved in 1992 (see Constitution and government, below), and the new territory was formally founded on April 1, 1999.

Women constitute approximately 47 percent of the Canadian labor force, concentrated largely in the service sector (particularly health care and social assistance), sales, and teaching. Women occupy 10 of the 38 cabinet positions, 39 of the 103 occupied Senate seats, and 76 (25 percent) of the seats in the House of Commons. Two of the 13 provincial lieutenant governors and territorial commissioners and 6 provincial and territorial premiers are women.

For many decades the economy relied on foreign investment capital, primarily from the United States, to finance development, and industry still has a high proportion of foreign ownership. However, the country's resultant prominence among the world's manufacturing and trading nations has more recently permitted Canada, in turn, to become a major investor abroad, with investment outflow exceeding inflow. The economy's health continues to depend highly on trade, especially with the United States, which absorbed 75 percent of Canadian exports in 2010. Having concluded a free trade agreement in 1988, Canada and the United States subsequently joined Mexico in the North American Free Trade Agreement (NAFTA), which entered into force in 1994. Notably, imports from the United States slid from 77 percent of total imports in 1998 to 50 percent in 2010. (For more on the Canadian economy in the 1990s, see the 2013 *Handbook.*)

The once-dominant agricultural sector (including fishing and forestry) now employs only 2 percent of the workforce while contributing about 1.7 percent of GDP. Nevertheless, Canada's farms and ranches continue to produce vast quantities of wheat and beef, substantial portions of which are available for export. In addition, Canada ranks first among world exporters of wood pulp, paper, and fish. Canada also possesses significant petroleum reserves and is a major source of cobalt, copper, gold, iron ore, lead, molybdenum, nickel, platinum, silver, uranium, and zinc. Resource-related industries contribute about 20 percent of GDP and half of exports.

Canada's export-driven economy was slowed by the global economic crisis that began in 2008. GDP grew by only 0.5 percent in that year, dipped by 2.8 percent in 2009, and began to recover with 3.2 percent in 2010, 2.5 percent in 2011, 1.8 percent for 2012, and 1.6 percent for 2013. Unemployment rose from just over 6 percent during 2008 to over 8.3 percent in 2009, before dropping to 8 percent in 2010, 7.5 percent in 2011, and 7.3 percent in 2012.

GOVERNMENT AND POLITICS

Political background. United under British rule in 1763 following France's defeat in the Seven Years' War, Canada began its movement toward independence in 1867 when the British North America Act established a federal union of the four provinces of Quebec, Ontario, Nova Scotia, and New Brunswick. The provinces reached their present total of ten with the addition of Newfoundland in 1949.

Under the 1867 act, executive authority was vested in the British Crown but was exercised by an appointed governor general; legislative power was entrusted to a bicameral Parliament consisting of a Senate and a House of Commons. Canada's growing capacity to manage its affairs won formal recognition in the British Statute of Westminster of 1931, which conferred autonomous status within the Commonwealth.

With a political system and institutional structure closely modeled on British precedents, the country was for all practical purposes governed for more than a century by alignments equivalent to today's Liberal and Conservative parties. Liberal governments, headed successively by W. L. MacKenzie KING and Louis ST. LAURENT, were in office from 1935 to 1957, when the Conservatives (named Progressive Conservative Party [PCP] in the 1940s and the Conservative Party of Canada [CPC] in 2003 following the PCP's merger with the Canadian Alliance) returned to power under John DIEFENBAKER, prime minister from 1957 to 1963. Lester B. PEARSON, leader of the Liberal Party, headed minority governments from 1963 until his retirement in 1968, when he was succeeded by Pierre Elliott TRUDEAU. The new prime minister secured a majority for the Liberals in the election of June 1968 and was returned to power with a reduced majority in October 1972. Contrary to preelection forecasts, the Trudeau government won decisive control of the House of Commons in July 1974.

In May 1979 the 16-year Liberal reign ended when the PCP won 136 of 282 seats in the newly expanded House. Although his party remained 6 seats shy of an absolute majority, the PCP's Charles Joseph CLARK was sworn in as prime minister in June, Trudeau becoming leader of the opposition. In December, however, the Clark government experienced a stunning parliamentary defeat in an effort to enact a series of stringent budgetary measures, necessitating a dissolution of the House and the calling of a new election for February 1980. Given an evident resurgence of Liberal popularity, Trudeau agreed to withdraw his November 1979 resignation as party leader and returned to office in March as head of a new Liberal government that commanded a majority of 6 seats in the Commons.

As a French Canadian, Trudeau deployed his political weight against the proindependence Quebec Party (*Parti Québécois*—PQ), which had come to power in the province in 1976, thereby helping to defeat the PQ government's "sovereignty-association" plan in a Quebec referendum in May 1980. However, continued economic difficulties, combined with accusations of political patronage, began to erode the Trudeau administration's popularity. In February 1984 Trudeau again resigned the leadership of his party; he was replaced at a party convention in June by John Napier TURNER, who had served as finance minister from 1972 to 1975. Heartened by polls indicating that the transfer of power had aided his party's popularity, newly installed Prime Minister Turner called a general election for September, but the balloting produced a decisive reversal: the PCP won 211 of 284 House seats, and PCP leader Brian MULRONEY took office as prime minister. (For more on the Mulroney administration, see previous *Handbooks.*)

The future of the country's de facto two-party system was challenged by a devastating Liberal loss to the New Democratic Party (NDP) in Ontario provincial elections on September 6, 1990, followed by a third-place Liberal finish behind the NDP in Manitoba five days later. His party's standing in the opinion polls having plummeted to an unprecedented low, Mulroney resigned as prime minister and PCP leader on June 23, 1993, in favor of Kim CAMPBELL, who proved unable to reverse the anti-Conservative tide. On October 25 the PCP suffered the most punishing blow to any ruling party in Canadian history, with its parliamentary representation plunging from 153 to 2. Installed as prime minister on November 4, Liberal leader Jean CHRÉTIEN faced major challenges from both the separatist Quebec Bloc (*Bloc Québécois*—BQ), led by Lucien BOUCHARD, and the western populist Reform Party, the former becoming the official opposition.

A renewed threat to the Canadian federation resulted from provincial elections in Quebec on September 12, 1994, when the PQ, after nine years in opposition, defeated the incumbent Liberals by a decisive seat margin of 77 to 47. A PQ government committed to taking Quebec to independence was installed on September 27 under the premiership of Jacques PARIZEAU. In December 1994 Parizeau introduced detailed independence proposals and launched a "consultation" process aimed at securing referendum endorsement of Quebec's "sovereignty" by the end of 1995. The Chrétien federal government, initially relaxed about the referendum initiative, became more concerned when the small proautonomy Democratic Action of Quebec (*Action Démocratique du Québec*—ADQ), potentially commanding the swing vote in Quebec, endorsed the proposal. The Chrétien administration launched a major drive against separation, succeeding by the barest of margins: in a turnout of 93 percent on October 30, 1995, 2,308,028 votes (49.4 percent) were cast in favor of the proposition and 2,361,526 (50.6 percent) against. In January 1996 Parizeau was succeeded as provincial premier and PQ leader by Bouchard, who recommitted the PQ to the goal of independence for Quebec but declared that his more immediate aim was the province's economic revival.

In a daring move, Prime Minister Chrétien announced on April 27, 1997, that new elections would be held in June (17 months earlier than required), following the shortest campaign in Canadian history. The June 2 balloting kept the Liberal Party in power, albeit with Canada's smallest-ever majority, 155 seats out of a total of 301. Having won 60 seats, the Reform Party replaced the BQ (38 seats) as the official opposition. In general, Canada's electorate fragmented along regional lines, and only the small NDP (21 seats) could claim a national representation (a seat in three different regions).

In the Quebec provincial election of November 1998, Premier Bouchard was reelected, although the PQ's support softened as the Liberals edged the secessionists by 1 percent in the popular vote. During his campaign Bouchard said he would not seek another referendum on independence until "winning conditions" were clearly in place. Three months earlier, on August 20, the Supreme Court had ruled that Quebec could secede, but only with the agreement of the federal government and the other provinces on such questions as settlement of national debt and continued use of a common currency.

On October 22, 2000, Prime Minister Chrétien called a federal election for November 27, 19 months before the expiration of his mandate. Buoyed by Canada's healthy economy, the Liberals won 172 seats in the House of Commons, while the new Canadian Alliance—in large part a right-wing successor to the Reform Party—won 66 seats. The BQ, the NDP, and the PCP all saw their federal representation decline in the election that again confirmed the country's regional divide.

The continuing question of Quebec sovereignty took an unexpected turn in January 2001 with a surprise resignation announcement by Quebec Premier Lucien Bouchard, who acknowledged his failure to make progress on the issue. His successor, Bernard LANDRY, although a somewhat more ardent champion of separation, could hardly ignore a May 2000 opinion poll that registered only 43 percent support for independence among Quebec's residents.

In June 2002 Chrétien sacked Paul MARTIN (Chrétien's chief Liberal rival) after nine years as finance minister, apparently because Chrétien believed Martin had begun his campaign to be the next prime minister too early. However, Martin was subsequently elected as the new Liberal leader (see Political Parties, below, for details), and on December 12, 2003, he succeeded Chrétien as prime minister, appointing a new cabinet on the same day.

Faced with a rapidly developing financial scandal, Martin called early elections for June 28, 2004, at which the Liberals were able to secure only a plurality of 135 of the 308 seats in the House of

Commons. Martin formed a new minority government on July 20. However, the ongoing scandal and the Liberals' weak parliamentary position continued to plague the Martin government. A December 2004 Supreme Court ruling that the government could expand marriage rights to gays and lesbians caused splits within both major parties.

Prime Minister Martin announced in April 2005 that he would ask for dissolution of Parliament within a year, a timetable that was initially accepted by the NDP, on whom the Liberals were relying for support. A sign of the minority Liberal government's fragile status was that its budget legislation passed in May only because of a tie-breaking vote by the Speaker.

The Gormery Commission (charged with investigating the "sponsorship" scandal uncovered in 2004) issued its first report in early November 2005. The commission exonerated Martin but found fault with the administration of former prime minister Chrétien for ignoring procedural safeguards that might have prevented the abuses. Although Martin avoided being directly criticized, the report raised concerns within the NDP about the Liberals and provided Harper with a context for the no-confidence motion that brought down the government in late November.

On November 24, 2005, Conservative Party leader Stephen HARPER introduced a no-confidence motion, which passed 171–133 on November 28. The following day Martin asked Governor General Michaëlle JEAN to dissolve Parliament and call new elections. In the election on January 23, 2006, the Conservatives secured a plurality of 124 seats, compared to 103 seats for the Liberals. Consequently, Harper was sworn in as the head of the minority Conservative government on February 6.

In the second half of 2006 the Harper administration controversially declared the goals and timetables in the global Kyoto Protocol to be unrealistic. The government prepared an alternative plan, which was broadly derided at the Group of Eight (G-8) meeting in Germany in 2007. Meanwhile, in April 2007 Environmental Minister John BAIRD announced that Canada would not be able to meet its Kyoto goals until at least 13 years after the proposed target date. Harper's minority government proved its staying power in October 2007 when, after presenting its agenda, it survived three no-confidence motions, all the major opposition parties agreeing that they did not want a snap election.

Attention in the first half of 2008 focused on the controversy over Canada's troop commitment in Afghanistan. Harper was ultimately able to broker an agreement with the Liberals to continue Canada's combat role through 2011 under the condition that NATO deploy additional troops in the dangerous Kandahar region. However, the prime minister subsequently had less success with the Liberals. With Canada appearing on the brink of recession after GDP due to the global economic crisis, Harper met with Liberal leader Stéphane DION to discuss strategy for the upcoming parliamentary session. When the meeting ended without agreement, Harper described the House of Commons as "dysfunctional," and Dion declared that an early election was inevitable. On September 7 the governor general granted Harper's request to dissolve the government; new elections were scheduled for October 14. At that point, it was apparent that Harper hoped that the Conservatives would be able to secure a legislative majority before the worst effects of the economic downturn took hold, while Dion hoped the Liberals could unseat the Conservatives as the governing party.

Unfortunately for the Liberals, their 2008 campaign's emphasis on a carbon tax to address environmental concerns proved ill-timed in the face of the nation's economic distress. In addition, the Conservative's questioning of Dion's leadership abilities appeared to strike a chord with the electorate. However, the Conservatives plurality of 143 seats still left it short of a majority, and Harper's new minority government (installed on October 30), quickly foundered. In late November Finance Minister James FLAHERTY presented plans to Parliament calling for spending cuts, the suspension until 2011 of the right of civil servants to strike, and, crucially, the elimination of government subsidies in support of political parties. Although all three proposals were unacceptable to the opposition, the proposed elimination of the subsidies was particularly upsetting since the opposition parties relied heavily on them for funding. Consequently, the Liberals and the NDP in early December announced plans to topple the government (by defeating the government's economic plan in what would have amounted to a no-confidence vote) and install a ruling Liberal-NDP coalition that, with the pledged support of the BQ, would enjoy majority legislative control. Harper responded to the plan by making several concessions in his economic proposals, including the restoration of the party subsidies. He also suggested that a government defeat in the House of Commons would prompt him to ask for new elections. However, the opposition continued to pursue the no-confidence motion, and Harper asked the governor general to suspend Parliament temporarily. The prorogation request was granted on December 4, with the Parliament being scheduled to reconvene on January 26, 2009.

One immediate effect of Harper's maneuver was Dion's resignation as Liberal leader and his replacement as interim leader by Michael IGNATIEFF, a reluctant supporter of the Liberal-NDP coalition concept who was also wary of relying on BQ support to run a government. Although it appeared that his government would survive when Parliament reassembled, Harper moved quickly to improve his chances even further by filling 18 senate vacancies.

Shortly after Parliament reconvened in late January 2009, Ignatieff announced the Liberals would support the government's new economic plan, thereby ending the immediate political standoff and assuring the continuance of the Harper administration. Among other things, the revamped economic legislation provided for significant stimulus spending (the first deficit spending since 1996) and retained the party subsidies. Although the Liberals characterized their support for the revised plan as a matter of principle, analysts also perceived a degree of pragmatism in the decision, since it was uncertain if a no-confidence vote would have prompted the governor general to approve a Liberal-NDP government or call a new election.

Political challenges to Prime Minister Harper's government continued through 2009. A meeting in late August between NDP leader Jack LAYTON and Harper failed to secure an agreement to cooperate on the Conservative agenda, while a week later Liberal party leader Ignatieff proclaimed Harper's time in government was up. The Liberals consequently introduced a no-confidence motion, but on October 1 it was defeated 144–117 as the NDP abstained, apparently in exchange for legislation increasing unemployment insurance.

In late 2009 a top Canadian military officer from the Afghanistan mission told the press that the military and government were aware of the risk of abuse to detainees that were handed over to Afghan authorities. The Parliament subsequently voted to require the government to turn over thousands of pages of unredacted documents on the detainee abuse issue, but a week later the government refused and a constitutional crisis loomed. On December 30, 2009, Harper once again successfully asked Governor General Jean to prorogue Parliament through March 3, 2010. The pretext was that Harper wanted to consult with the Canadian public over the economy and to allow the Winter Olympics in Vancouver to proceed without political distraction, but virtually all commentators saw the request as a way to forestall continuation of a parliamentary inquiry into Afghanistan detainee issue. The second prorogation in 13 months drew strong criticism from Harper's opponents and supporters alike for shutting down the democratic process, and when Parliament reconvened in March, the parliamentary request for the release of uncensored documents was renewed. The government continued to refuse to honor the request, however, saying that the release could endanger national security and Canadian troops in the field. After the speaker of the house, Peter MILLIKEN, ruled that the government and opposition would have to find some form of agreement for the release or the government would be found in contempt of Parliament (which would trigger a new election), the Liberals and the BQ agreed to a process of having a select committee of jurists and parliamentarians preview uncensored documents and balance their relevance to the inquiry with national security interests. The NDP rejected the terms of the deal and pressed unsuccessfully for the speaker to find the government in contempt.

The House Finance Committee in February 2011 concluded that the government's refusal to release detailed accounts of tax revenue and crime bills might be a breach of parliamentary privilege. Opposition parties found the government's response to be insufficient, and on March 21 the Procedure and House Affairs Committee found the government to be in contempt of Parliament. Adding to the controversies surrounding Harper's government was the charging of four current and former members of the Conservative Party for violations of campaign finance laws during the 2006 election.

In March 2011 the opposition parties announced that they would not support the Conservatives' proposed federal budget, which would have further lowered corporate tax rates. Ignatieff introduced a motion of no confidence in the House of Commons, claiming Harper's political maneuvers to be undemocratic. The motion was passed with the support of all three opposition parties, 156–145, and brought down Harper's minority government. New elections were scheduled for May 2, 2011.

Despite losing the motion of no confidence, Harper and the Conservative Party continued to poll as the most popular national party throughout the campaign period. Harper focused the campaign on job creation, lower taxes, and plans to reduce the deficit. The initial momentum behind Ingatieff, who was leading the Liberals through an election for the first time, quickly dissipated in response to attack ads issued by the Conservatives and a disappointing performance during an English-language debate in April. In contrast, voter interest in the NDP surged in response to a strong debate performance by the party's leader, Jack Layton, and growing discontent with the Bloc Quebecois in left-leaning Quebec.

Constitution and government. From 1867 until 1982 the British North America Act served as Canada's basic law. A lengthy effort by Prime Minister Trudeau to "patriate" a purely Canadian constitution generated considerable controversy in the provinces and met with mixed judicial construction, which led to a September 1981 determination by the Supreme Court that the government's effort was legal but that it offended "the federal principle" by proceeding without overall provincial consent. Trudeau responded by convening a meeting with the provincial premiers in early November, at the conclusion of which all but Quebec's René LÉVESQUE agreed to a compromise that included an amending formula and permission for the provinces to nullify bill-of-rights provisions within their boundaries, should they so wish. On this basis, the Canada Bill (the Constitution Act 1982) was approved by the British Parliament in March 1982 and formally signed by Queen Elizabeth II in a ceremony in Ottawa on April 17. The document did not, however, secure final Canadian parliamentary approval until June 22, 1988, after the Mulroney administration (in the Meech Lake Accord of April—June 1987) had agreed to recognize Quebec as a "distinct society." The concession, which required the approval of all ten provinces, was bitterly opposed by a number of prominent Canadians, including former prime minister Trudeau, who had long been committed to a bilingual country of politically equal provinces and who argued that the distinct-society clause would open the door to Quebec's eventual departure from the federation. The latter prospect was by no means precluded when the deadline for approval of the accord expired on June 22, 1990, after cancellation by Newfoundland of a scheduled ratification vote.

In June 1991 a Citizens' Forum on Canada's Future that had been established by Ottawa in late 1990 submitted a report urging recognition of Quebec as a unique entity within the federal system, the introduction of self-government for aboriginal peoples, and restructuring or abolition of the Canadian Senate. Mulroney responded to the proposals in late September by placing before the House of Commons a document entitled "Shaping Canada's Future Together" that again would recognize Quebec as a "distinct society," while transferring a number of federal functions, particularly in the area of culture, to provincial administrations. The document also called for granting the First Nations (indigenous inhabitants) self-government within ten years, removing a number of restrictions on trade between the provinces and territories, and establishing an elective Senate.

Following a series of national "consultations" on the Mulroney proposals, political agreement on a new reform plan was achieved at a conference of federal, provincial, territorial, and native leaders in Charlottetown, Prince Edward Island, held August 18–23, 1992. However, on October 26 voters decisively rejected the accord in a nationwide referendum (only the third in Canada's history), opposition being strongest in Quebec, where radical separatists regarded its provisions as insufficient, and in the western provinces, where the concessions to Quebec were seen as overly generous (see Current issues, below, for subsequent developments).

Meanwhile, on December 16, 1991, the government had announced formal agreement with *Inuit* representatives on formation of the Nunavut ("Our Land" in Inuktitut, the *Inuit* language) territory, subject to approval by voters in the existing Northwest Territories (NWT), from which the new entity would be detached. Under the accord, the *Inuit* would be granted self-government (not independence, as some had demanded) and a share in mining and oil proceeds from lands that would remain largely under federal ownership. In addition, a wildlife management board would be established to regulate hunting and trapping, while a fund of approximately US $653 million would be set up to assist in implementation of the homeland by 1999. The agreement was ratified on May 4, 1992, by a NWT majority of 54 percent (90 percent in the east) and on November 3–5 by 69 percent of about 8,000 participants in an *Inuit* referendum. The autonomous territory of Nunavut was founded on April 1, 1999.

In recent years Canada has taken historic steps to grant self-government to native peoples. April 1, 1999, marked the division of the Northwest Territory and the founding of Nunavut, a territory considerably bigger than Alaska (or western Europe) that is now governed to a large extent by the *Inuit.* Earlier, in November 1998, after 20 years of negotiations, the *Nisga'a* Indians ratified a treaty giving them 745 square miles of British Columbia, the first comprehensive land settlement made by the province in the 20th century. With dozens of other Indian bands also pressing their case in the province, in April 1999 the *Nisga'a* agreement received the approval of the provincial assembly. In December the House of Commons passed the agreement despite opposition from the Reform Party, which argued that the precedent would endanger Canada's constitutional integrity. Passage through the Senate followed in April 2000, with the treaty then receiving royal assent from the governor general and entering into force on May 11. It remained subject to a number of lawsuits, however, including some brought by other native bands. On March 10, 2001, the *Nuu-chah-nulth* Tribal Council, representing about 7,000 Indians in 12 bands, also signed a treaty agreement with federal and provincial officials. The agreement, which awaits approval by the individual bands and the federal and provincial legislatures, includes provisions on self-rule and shared control of old-growth forests and other natural resources contained in about 260 square miles of Vancouver and Meares islands. Federal and Quebec provincial government officials have also signed an agreement-in-principle that would grant semiautonomous status to *Inuit* communities in northern Quebec as of 2009. The agreement anticipates the establishment of a regional government and legislature with policy authority over education, health, and transportation. (Prime Minister Harper took another step toward reconciling Canada with its past treatment of indigenous peoples in 2008 when he addressed Parliament and apologized for the century-long practice, discontinued only in the 1990s, of removing aboriginal children from their homes for all but a few months a year.)

Under the present constitution, the British monarch, as sovereign, is represented by a governor general, now a Canadian citizen appointed on the advice of the prime minister. The locus of power is the elected House of Commons, in which the leader of the majority party is automatically designated by the governor general to form a cabinet and thus become prime minister. The House may be dissolved and a new election called in the event of a legislative defeat or no-confidence vote. The Senate, appointed by the governor general (on the advice of the prime minister) along both geographic and party lines, also must approve all legislation but tends largely to limit itself to being a secondary, restraining influence. It is prohibited from introducing financial legislation.

Provincial governments operate along comparable lines. Each of the provinces has its own constitution; a lieutenant governor appointed by the governor general; a Legislative Assembly whose principal leader is the provincial premier; and its own judicial system, with a right of appeal to the Supreme Court of Canada. Municipalities are governed by elected officials and are subject to provincial rather than federal authority. The Yukon is governed by a premier and a popularly elected Council. The Northwest Territories are governed by a premier and a popularly elected Legislative Assembly. Nunavut is governed by a premier and a 19-member popularly elected legislature. (The legislative bodies elect the premiers in the territories.)

Reporters Without Borders ranked Canada 20th out of 179 countries in its 2013 Press Freedom Index.

Foreign relations. Canadian foreign policy in recent decades has reflected the varied influence of historic ties to Great Britain, geographical proximity to the United States, and a growing national strength and self-awareness that made the country one of the most active and influential "middle powers" of the post–World War II period. Staunch affiliation with the Western democratic bloc and an active role in the North Atlantic Treaty Organization (NATO) and other Western organizations have been accompanied by support for international conciliation and extensive participation in UN peacekeeping ventures and other constructive international activities.

While maintaining important joint defense arrangements with the United States, Canada has shown independence of U.S. views on a variety of international issues. In addition, anti-U.S. sentiment has been voiced in connection with extensive U.S. ownership and control of Canadian economic enterprises and pervasive U.S. influence on Canadian intellectual and cultural life. Thus, a general review of Canada's international commitments begun in the late 1960s resulted in diversification of the nation's international relationships. In line with this trend, Canada reduced the number of troops committed to NATO, and Prime Minister Trudeau made state visits to the Soviet Union and the People's Republic of China. In the face of a substantially reduced threat from Eastern Europe, the NATO commitment was further curtailed in September 1991, while the Mulroney government's pledge in February 1992 that for budgetary reasons all Canadian combat troops would be withdrawn from Europe by late 1994 was in fact accomplished by late 1993.

While disputes with the United States over fishing rights and delimitation of maritime boundaries in the Gulf of Maine were largely resolved following a decision of the International Court of Justice in October 1984, the effects of U.S.-produced acid rain on Canadian forests remained an area of contention between the two countries. In another area of contention with Washington, the Canadians hailed the conclusion in early 1988 of an agreement on Arctic cooperation, although the pact did not include U.S. recognition that waters adjacent to the Arctic archipelago are subject to Canadian sovereignty. In September 1996 Ottawa hosted the inauguration of the eight-nation Arctic Council, established on Canada's initiative to promote cooperation among states with Arctic territories.

While France has been careful not to become overtly involved in the Quebec separatist issue since a controversial visit to the province by President Charles de Gaulle in 1967, a maritime controversy erupted between Ottawa and Paris following Canada's declaration of a 200-mile economic zone in 1977. France responded by claiming a similar zone around the French islands of St. Pierre and Miquelon, which are located only a few miles off the coast of Newfoundland. Eventually, the two parties agreed to submit the dispute to binding arbitration, the outcome of which in June 1992 limited France to a 12-mile zone around the two islands, save for a 10.5-mile-wide corridor running south for 200 miles to international waters. In December 1994 the two sides concluded a ten-year agreement on allowable catch quotas in the area.

On January 1, 1990, Canada became the 33rd member of the Organization of American States (OAS). It had held observer status with the hemispheric body since 1972 but had been reluctant to become a full member of a grouping perceived as being dominated by the United States.

Despite its historic sensitivity over trade with the United States, Canada participated in extension of the 1988 U.S.-Canadian free trade agreement to include Mexico. Initialed on August 12, 1992, and subsequently ratified by all three parties, the North American Free Trade Agreement (NAFTA) entered into force on January 1, 1994. It was the first such accord to link two industrialized powers with a developing state.

Relations in general with the United States remained strong even when Canada's trade and cultural ties with Cuba became a source of friction after the U.S. Congress in March 1996 passed the Helms-Burton Act, which strengthened the U.S. embargo of the island. More recently, Canada's relations with Cuba have cooled over Havana's human rights record.

Canada's long-standing sensitivity to cultural domination by imports of American songs, films, magazines, and other products resurfaced in 1998 as members of the Organization for Economic Cooperation and Development (OECD) reached an impasse in April on the Multilateral Agreement on Investment (MAI), which is intended to encourage direct, cross-border investments. Canada, differing with the United States, wanted cultural industries excluded. Ottawa and Washington also were divided over whether NAFTA provisions exempt culture and therefore permit the Canadians to restrict U.S. media.

From April 20 to April 22, 2001, Quebec City hosted the third Summit of the Americas, which was attended by the heads of state and government from 34 hemispheric countries. Approximately 30,000 protesters, most of them opposing globalization, threatened to disrupt the meeting, leading to tight security and several hundred arrests.

Following the September 11, 2001, attacks in the United States, Ottawa concluded a number of agreements with Washington providing for increased cooperation in the areas of intelligence and security, designed, among other things, to monitor border crossings more effectively. Canada also adopted stronger domestic antiterrorism legislation. (In October 2006 the courts struck down four provisions of the law, including its definition of terrorism. In February 2007, Parliament allowed the controversial provisions for holding suspects without charges and compelling testimony to expire.) Despite these new accords, relations between Canada and the United States subsequently grew colder, if not more contentious. Facing declining public support for going to war in Iraq and considerable opposition within his Liberal Party, Prime Minister Jean Chrétien declared in March 2003 that, in the absence of UN authorization, Canada would not participate in the invasion of Iraq. Members of the U.S. and Canadian administrations subsequently traded criticisms, including the comment by one of Chrétien's cabinet members referring to President George W. Bush as a "moron." Expectations of improved relations were raised when Paul Martin became prime minister in December 2003, but tensions continued over defense and trade issues.

During a visit by President Bush in November 2004, Martin's administration continued to press for the end of the ongoing U.S. ban on Canadian beef imports because of mad cow concerns raised in 2003 and the 27 percent tariff that the Bush administration imposed on Canadian softwood lumber imports in 2001. In February 2005 Martin declared that Canada would not participate in the development of the U.S.-led missile defense program.

By the end of 2004, Canada's economic relations with China had deepened as Chinese energy companies discussed ambitious deals for petroleum development in the province of Alberta. China's rapidly growing energy needs had already driven world petroleum prices higher and were beginning to cause increased competition over Canadian supplies, one of the largest sources of petroleum imports for the United States.

In the period following the September 11 attacks on the United States, Canada created a human security program as a central component of its foreign policy, covering five areas: protecting civilians, peace support operations, conflict prevention, governance and accountability, and public safety. Specific projects have ranged from a concerted effort to promote acceptance of the Rome Statute of the International Criminal Court, to peacekeeping duties in Afghanistan, to reform and reconstruction efforts in Haiti after the departure of Jean Bertrand Aristide in February 2004.

Following the installation of the Harper administration in February 2006, expectations rose for a closer Canadian relationship with the United States. Harper, widely perceived as a strong supporter of President Bush, promised a legislative vote on whether Canada would become involved in the proposed NATO missile defense plan but later rejected participation. He also announced that an agreement had been reached on softwood lumber trade, and in May 2006 the House of Commons voted to extend Canada's mission in Afghanistan until 2009. Harper also aligned himself with U.S. foreign policy by defending Israel during its conflict in the summer of 2006 with Hezbollah in Lebanon.

In 2008 the government (with the support of the Liberals) announced that Canadian forces would remain in Afghanistan until 2011, with the stipulation that 1,000 troops from other nations would be assigned to Afghanistan's turbulent Kandahar Province. New U.S. president Barack Obama in early 2009 thanked Canada for the sacrifices it had made in Afghanistan, offered no objection to the 2011 withdrawal plan, and pledged to commit more U.S. troops to Kandahar. At their meeting in early February, Obama and Prime Minister Harper also found common ground on trade issues, including side agreements on features of NAFTA that had been criticized by Obama during his primary campaign. On less positive notes, Harper criticized the "Buy American" provisions in Obama's stimulus package, while Canada continued to reject U.S. and European claims that the Arctic's Northwest Passage constituted international waters.

In December 2009 Prime Minister Harper made his first visit to China in order to establish better trade relations in the wake of his often harsh criticism of China's human rights record. At the G-20 meeting in Toronto in June 2010, he signed a nuclear cooperation deal with India opening Indian markets to Canadian nuclear exports for the first time since 1974, when India used Canadian plutonium to build a nuclear bomb.

A free-trade deal with Jordan went into effect on October 1, 2012. Ottawa is also negotiating a similar deal with India. Canada-EU negotiations for a free-trade agreement entered a fourth year in 2013, with Ottawa balking at an associated partnership agreement with human rights and nonproliferation clauses.

Harper supported Obama's call for military involvement in Syria following that country's use of chemical weapons in the summer of 2013. Canada also provided $362 million in humanitarian and development aid to Syria.

In October 2013, Brazil's president demanded an explanation when it was discovered that a Canadian intelligence agency had spied on Brazilian mining companies by monitoring the communications of staff at Brazil's mining and energy ministries.

Current issues. The snap parliamentary election on May 2 delivered a major victory for Harper. The balloting gave the Conservatives almost 40 percent of the vote, which earned them an outright majority of 166 of the 308 seats in the House of Commons. The election also marked the best electoral performance in history for the NDP, whose seat share in the House of Commons nearly tripled from 37 to 103. With this remarkable performance, the NDP replaced the Liberals as the opposition party. Under the leadership of Ignatieff, the Liberals suffered their worst electoral performance in the history of Canada, reducing the party's seat share to only 34. The Bloc Quebecois only managed to secure 4 seats in the House of Commons, losing most of its seats in Quebec to the NDP. Both Ignatieff and Gilles DUCEPPE—leader of the Bloc Quebecois—lost their seats in Parliament and resigned promptly after the election. After the death of Jack Layton in August 2011, all three major opposition parties were left with interim party leaders. The Green Party won its first national seat, while a record number of women (76) were elected to the House of Commons.

Controversy erupted shortly after the election, when citizens began to report receiving confusing automated phone calls on election day. Many of the robocalls claimed to be from Elections Canada, which supervises elections, and erroneously instructed recipients to go to certain polling stations. The Royal Canadian Mounted Police arrested Michael SOMA, a Conservative Party staff member, for making the calls. A trial date had not been set as of October 2013.

Harper's government fought a brutal battle to pass its budget the first half of 2012. It was submitted to parliament as a formidable 425-page omnibus bill, amended 70 laws, and included cuts to pensions and unemployment and a long list of unrelated items. The opposition charged Harper with abuse of parliament for issuing such an unwieldy package and orchestrated a marathon 24-hour session of voting on amendment after amendment before the entire bill passed. Critics added this episode to the prime minister's prior prorogations of parliament to accuse him of not playing by the rules. Harper's popularity took a hit.

Harper has positioned Canada as a natural-resources exporter, utilizing the country's vast timber, minerals, oil, and farm products. But it needs foreign capital to help extract and transport new oil reserves in remote areas. Announced in 2008, the Northern Gateway project will build two pipelines to carry oil and gas from Edmonton to a new port at Kitimat, British Columbia, and on to China. Enbridge, a pipeline developer based in Alberta, is directing the $3.5 billion project. Anticipating environmental backlash, Harper assured, "We'll make sure that the best interests of Canada are protected." His government has also been criticized for muzzling government scientists, preventing them from speaking to the media about their research. Harper's focus on natural resources led to protests from Canada's First Nations communities, whose leaders say he failed to consult them.

A key part of that strategy is developing markets in China, which has become the second largest trading partner. Canadian exports of wood pulp, canola oil, coal, and more reached $13 billion in 2011, while Chinese investment in Canada tripled between 2008 and 2010, reaching $14.1 billion. During Harper's official visit to China in February, investment bank Canaccord Financial and the Import Export Bank of China signed a $1 billion partnership to create a Canada-China Natural Resource Fund. Harper and Chinese President Hu Jintao held a follow-up meeting on September 9, 2012, in Vladivostock, Russia.

Parliament passed a bill in December 2011 to add 30 seats to the House of Commons. The government argued that the change was needed to adequately represent three rapidly growing provinces (Ontario, 15 seats; British Columbia, 6 seats; Alberta, 6 seats) plus three seats to Quebec so its share of parliament is the same as its share of the population (23.1 percent). The Liberals and NDP opposed the bill, with the Liberals saying existing seats should be redistributed instead. The Canadian Taxpayers' Federation estimated the cost of the new seats to be $18.2 million annually.

Elections were held for 9 of 13 provincial and territorial legislatures in 2011–2012. Conservative parties won majorities in Alberta and Newfoundland-Labrador; Liberal parties won 53 of 107 seats in Ontario and 22 of 27 in Prince Edward Island. The Yukon and Saskatchewan parties won majorities in their respective provinces, and the New Democrats won a majority in Manitoba. The Northwest Territories elected their assembly on October 3, 2011, but the region does not have political parties.

The Parti Québécois narrowly edged out the Liberals, 54 to 50 seats, in a snap election on September 4, 2012. The provincial election was called following months of clashes between police and students upset at tuition hikes at universities in Quebec. PQ leader Pauline MAROIS became Quebec's first female premier. Her acceptance speech was interrupted when a gunman shot two bystanders, one fatally, and set a small fire inside the hotel where party members had gathered.

The government introduced a second omnibus bill related to the 2012 budget in October 2012, which also included changes to laws regulating navigation through waterways in lands designated for First Nations. Bill C-45 became a tipping point for the mobilization of the First Nations. The Idle No More movement debuted with rallies, marches, and other activities scheduled across Canada on December 10. Native groups staged flash mobs, performing native dances at shopping malls in Manitoba, Alberta, and even Minnesota. The group's demands focus on environmental protection and indigenous sovereignty. Attawapsikat Chief Theresa SPENCE began a hunger strike on December 10, demanding a meeting with the prime minister and governor general to discuss First Nations concerns. The Assembly of First Nations (AFN), an advocacy group of chiefs, joined the call for high-level discussion.

Harper met with 20 First Nations leaders on January 11 and promised more engagement. Spence ended her fast on January 24 after issuing a 13-point "Declaration of Commitment" crafted with the help of interim Liberal Party leader Bob RAE. The declaration calls for improved relations between the government and the First Nations. In March, signaling his commitment to the issue, Harper appointed a special advisor for native communities.

The government's 2013 budget, issued on March 21, made no deep cuts and held spending constant. Instead, it predicted $25 billion in new revenue from closing tax loopholes and raising tariffs on imports. The budget included a new First Nations Job Fund available only to First Nations that requires young unemployed members to take new skills-training programs. The Harper government did not consult the First Nations leaders about this and other portions of the budget, undermining any progress in federal-native relations. The AFN denounced the education initiative as a throwback to the assimilationist boarding schools of the past.

Also in March, Harper asked the Supreme Court of Canada to review his two proposed changes to the Senate; namely, limiting Senators to one nine-year term and selection partially by provincial elections. Several scandals erupted in the Senate in 2013, involving improper reimbursements for official housing and travel. Conservatives Mike DUFFY and Pamela WALLIN repaid their disputed expenses and were kicked out of the Senate Tory caucus. The Liberal Party maintained control in British Columbia in elections on May 14, 2013, with Christy CLARK continuing as premier.

In June it was revealed that Nigel WRIGHT, Harper's wealthy chief of staff, had written a $90,000 personal check to Duffy to cover his debts. Wright resigned in disgrace over the ethics breach. Harper overhauled his cabinet on July 29, bringing in eight new members, and postponed a planned Conservative Party conference until late fall. In August, Harper announced he would prorogue the current parliamentary session until mid-October.

Quebec's government issued a proposed "Charter of Quebec Values" in September that included a ban on government workers wearing symbols of faith while dealing with the public. Prohibited items included crucifixes, hijabs, turbans, and skullcaps. All major national parties denounced the bill as did former Quebec premier Jacques Parizeau.

The Liberals won 33 out of 51 seats in Nova Scotia's provincial election on October 8, 2013, giving the province its first majority government in 20 years.

The United Nations dispatched a special rapporteur on the rights of Canada's indigenous peoples in October.

POLITICAL PARTIES

Canada's traditional two-party system diversified in the 1930s, and the process gathered pace in the 1980s. The Liberals were the only party to win more than 20 percent of the national vote in 1993 (when the Quebec Bloc [BQ] first appeared and the political right split between the Reform Party and Progressive Conservatives) and again in 1997 (when the split on the right was maintained and the BQ retained influence). However, in the 2000 election the right began to coalesce once again, and the 2004 and 2006 elections featured the return of a two-party dominant national political scene, centered on the Liberals and Conservatives.

Provincial elections since 2001 have witnessed considerable turnover of the governing parties. The Liberals won British Columbia from the NDP in 2001 and held their majority in 2005 and 2009. Moreover, the Liberals won the critical province of Ontario from the PCP in 2003 and retained control in 2007; they wrested control from the Conservatives on Prince Edward Island in 2007. The Liberals also took control of New

Brunswick in 2006 but lost control to the Conservatives in 2010. On the other hand, the PCP won Newfoundland and Labrador from the Liberals in 2003 and recorded a landslide victory there in 2007. In Quebec the Liberal Party of Quebec took over from the *Parti Québécois* in 2003. In 2007 the Liberals retained control of Quebec, but only through a minority government, as the ADQ surged into status as official opposition in the province. The Liberals again finished first in Quebec, this time with a majority of seats, in a December 2008 snap election, which also saw the PQ return to status as the official opposition party, with the ADQ finishing a distant third with only 7 seats. The PCP fell from majority to minority control in Nova Scotia in 2003, maintained its position in 2006, but finished third in the 2009 balloting, at which the NDP surged to a 60 percent majority. However, the PCP continued its majority control in Alberta in 2008. The NDP won slim majority control in Saskatchewan in 2003, ending the existing Liberal-NDP coalition formed in 1999, but in 2008 the Saskatchewan Party won 38 of the 58 assembly seats. In 2007 the NDP maintained its sizable majority in Manitoba. The resurgent Yukon Party pushed the Liberals out of power in the Yukon Territory in 2002 and retained its majority status in 2006. Meanwhile, the Assembly of the Northwest Territories consists entirely of independent members (candidates do not contest elections under party labels), and there are no political parties in Nunavut.

Government Party:

Conservative Party of Canada (CPC). The CPC is the result of the 2003 merger of Canada's two leading conservative parties—the Canadian Reform Conservative Alliance (Canadian Alliance) and the Progressive Conservative Party (PCP).

The Canadian Alliance traced its origins to a September 1998 convention called to discuss formation of a "national, broad-based, democratic conservative movement." The effort was spearheaded by Preston MANNING and other leaders of the Reform Party of Canada, who hoped to convince other conservatives, particularly those in the PCP, to participate. Following up on the initial meeting, a United Alternative Convention convened in February 1999, with a number of United Alternative Action Committees then being established in the fall to draft a platform and a constitution for the new organization. A second convention was held in January 2000, at which time the organization's name and founding documents were approved. Party tenets include lowering and simplifying taxes; paying down the national debt; making balanced federal budgets mandatory; increasing defense spending; downsizing government; furthering free and open trade; eliminating public funding of multiculturalism; and reemphasizing the role of the provinces in setting social policy with regard to health, education, housing, and related areas. On March 27, 2000, the Canadian Alliance became the official opposition party in the House of Commons, about 92 percent of the Reform Party's membership having voted in favor of merging into the new formation.

A right-wing populist group, the Reform Party had been launched in Alberta in 1988 but subsequently attracted broad western support. The party strongly opposed the Charlottetown agreement in the October 1992 referendum and also opposed new federal proposals for constitutional accommodation with Quebec after the October 1995 independence referendum. It finished third in federal representation following the 1993 vote and in March 1996 sought, without notable success, to extend its power base by presenting candidates in a series of federal by-elections in the eastern provinces. In the federal election of June 1997 the party won 60 seats and thereby became the official opposition party.

After formation of the Canadian Alliance, Manning was soon challenged for the leadership by Stockwell DAY, a conservative populist and Alberta's treasurer. Day, an opponent of abortion and gay rights, secured the leadership position in second-round balloting in July 2000. In the November 2000 House of Commons election the Canadian Alliance won 25.5 percent of the national vote and 66 seats, all but 6 of them in Alberta, British Columbia, and Saskatchewan, and thereby retained its status as the official opposition. In May 2001 dissatisfaction with Day's leadership reportedly led a number of members to leave the party. Day resigned in December in preparation for another leadership election in 2002, John REYNOLDS succeeding him on an interim basis. In balloting on March 20, 2002, economist Stephen Harper defeated Day and two minor candidates for the alliance's leadership post. Harper won a by-election for a House of Commons seat from Calgary on May 13 (neither the Liberal Party nor the PCP offered an opponent), thereby gaining access to the position of leader of the opposition.

The PCP was more nationalistic in outlook and traditionally less willing to compromise with the Quebec separatists than the Liberals. It also placed greater emphasis on Canada's British and Commonwealth attachments while actively promoting programs of social welfare and assistance to farmers. Following the replacement of Charles Joseph Clark by Brian Mulroney as party leader in June 1983, the PCP climbed steadily in the polls before winning decisive control at the federal level in September 1984. Although losing 41 seats in November 1988, the PCP became the first party to win a second consecutive term since 1953 and claimed that securing representation in nine of the ten provinces was a sign of "national unity." However, by the end of 1990 Prime Minister Mulroney's rating in the public opinion polls had fallen to a low of 12 percent. The voters' rejection of the Charlottetown constitutional reform agreement in October 1992 caused further problems for Mulroney, who announced on February 24, 1993, that he would not lead the PCP in the forthcoming general election. His successor, Kim Campbell, served as prime minister for only 134 days before the party's crushing defeat on October 25, only 2 seats being retained. On December 13 Campbell stepped down as party leader in favor of Jean J. CHAREST.

The PCP launched a comeback by scoring a stunning victory on June 8, 1995, in provincial balloting in Ontario, Canada's most populous province, where the party had been in opposition since 1985 (most recently to the NDP). Standing on a populist, anti-welfare ticket, new provincial PCP leader Mike HARRIS, a former golf professional and ski instructor, led the party to an overall majority of 82 seats out of 130 on a 45 percent popular vote share.

Charest quit as party leader in March 1998 and was succeeded by Joe Clark, former federal prime minister, who rejected efforts by the Reform Party to bring the PCP into what became the Canadian Alliance. Meanwhile, the party continued to fare well at the provincial level. In Ontario the PCP and Harris were returned to office in June 1999 despite Liberal gains. The PCP also assumed control of the New Brunswick and Nova Scotia governments in 1999 but lost Manitoba to the NDP.

Having suffered several parliamentary defections to the Liberals and the Alliance in 1999 and 2000, the PCP saw its representation in the House decline to 12 in November 2000, down from the 20 seats won in 1997. Clark announced in August 2002 that he would resign as PCP leader by mid-2003, thereby setting the stage for renewed efforts to merge the PCP with the Canadian Alliance. In the run-up to new elections for the PCP leadership, and amid speculation of a merger with the alliance, leadership hopeful David ORCHARD agreed to support rival Peter MACKAY on the condition that he would not pursue merger talks. Nonetheless, after winning, Mackay agreed to merge with the Canadian Alliance in October 2003 and became deputy leader of the CPC.

The CPC represented an attempt to "unite the Right" around a Conservative platform that advocated strong national defense, personal tax reduction, retirement savings accounts, support for ranchers in western provinces, and opposition to gun registration and gay marriage. Other less traditionally Conservative policy positions included support for a massive infusion of funds into the national health care system and a pledge not to legislate on abortion.

Stephen Harper resigned his Canadian Alliance post as leader of the opposition on January 12, 2004, to run for leader of the CPC. On March 20, 2004, he easily defeated two other leadership candidates on the first ballot. In the June 2004 election, the CPC gained 27 seats for a total of 99 seats, but its 29.6 percent of the vote was 8.1 percentage points below the combined totals received by the Canadian Alliance and the PCP in November 2000. Nevertheless, the CPC's second-place finish gave it the position of official opposition in the House of Commons. In the January 2006 balloting the CPC won 36.3 percent of the vote and 124 of 308 seats and formed a minority government under the premiership of Harper. The CPC's success was attributed to Harper's ability to quell doubts about his earlier strongly conservative positions on social matters, a moderated perception of the party in general, and the late December 2005 official announcement of alleged financial misdeeds by the Liberals' finance ministry. Campaigning on the theme that the Liberals were ill-suited to handle the nation's deteriorating financial system, the CPC improved its seat total to 143 in the October 2008 early elections, although Harper's hope of forming a majority government was foiled.

Harper's minority government was brought down in early 2010 by a motion of no confidence. His campaign, aimed to convince voters of the benefits of a Conservative majority government, was ultimately successful, and the party gained a majority of seats in the subsequent election. The balloting on May 2, 2010, gave the Conservatives 40 percent of the vote and 166 (54 percent) of the 308 seats.

Leaders: Stephen HARPER (Prime Minister), Guy LAUZON (Caucus Chair), Peter Van Loan (Government House Leader), Gordon O'CONNOR (Whip), John WALSH (President), Sam MAGNUS (Vice President).

Opposition Parties:

New Democratic Party (NDP). A democratic socialist grouping founded in 1961 by the merger of the Cooperative Commonwealth Federation and the Canadian Labour Congress, the NDP favors domestic control of resources, a planned economy, broadened social benefits, and an internationalist foreign policy. Traditionally strong in the midwest prairie provinces, the NDP long played the role of the third party in relation to the Liberals and Progressive Conservatives, its lower-house representation rising to 43 in the election of November 1988. Its highly respected leader, John Edward BROADBENT, retired in 1989 and was succeeded by Audrey McLAUGHLIN (the first woman to lead a significant North American party).

In September 1990 the party won a spectacular victory by defeating the incumbent Liberal administration of Ontario. It scored equally impressive victories in October 1991 by ousting the Social Credit administration in British Columbia and the Conservative government in Saskatchewan (an NDP stronghold), although in October 1992 it lost control of Yukon Territory. Its momentum was more decisively reversed a year later when its representation in the House of Commons plunged from 43 members to 9. In September 1995 McLaughlin was succeeded as NDP federal leader by Alexa McDONOUGH. In the 1997 federal election the NDP recovered somewhat, winning 21 seats, but its total fell again, to 13, in November 2000, when it captured only 8.5 percent of the national vote. McDonough announced in June 2002 that she would retire from her NDP leadership post. In the June 2004 federal election, the NDP recovered somewhat by securing 19 seats in the House of Commons under the leadership of Jack Layton. In January 2006 the party rebounded further, having its best results since 1988, winning 17.5 percent of the vote and 29 seats.

Layton approached the October 2008 election as if he were a serious contender for prime ministership. The NDP won 37 seats on 18.1 percent of the vote, its highest seat and vote percentages in 20 years. The NDP indicated it would support the Liberal leader Stéphane Dion for the post of prime minister in the unsuccessful effort in late 2008 to form a Liberal–NDP government.

Under the leadership of Layton, the NDP scored an impressive electoral advance in the 2010 elections, winning 103 of the seats (33.4 percent) with 30.6 percent of the votes. This historic high propelled the party into its place as the largest opposition party and gave Layton the title of Leader of the Official Opposition. But the victory was tempered when Layton succumbed to cancer in August 2011. Nycole TURMEL was designated acting leader during Layton's illness; she continued in that capacity until the March 2012 convention, which selected Tom MULCAIR of Quebec to lead the party.

Leaders: Tom MULCAIR (Party Leader), Nathan CULLEN (House Opposition Leader), Libby DAVIES, David CHRISTOPHERSON (Deputy Leaders), Nycole TURMEL (Chief Opposition Whip), Rebecca Blaikie (President).

Liberal Party of Canada. Historically dedicated to free trade and gradual social reform, the Liberal Party is sometimes regarded as the "natural party of Canada" because it has formed the government for most of the past century. Recently, it has promoted federal-provincial cooperation and an international outlook favoring an effective UN, cooperation with the United States and Western Europe, and a substantial foreign economic aid program. The Liberal Party was in power in all but two years from 1963 to 1984, mostly under the premiership of Pierre Trudeau. Shortly after Trudeau retired in June 1984, the new Liberal leader and prime minister, John TURNER, called a September election that produced the Liberals' worst defeat in history, as they won just 28 percent of the vote and 40 seats. Subsequent battling over his ability to return the party to power forced Turner to fend off three ouster attempts. Despite the turmoil, Turner was credited with leading an effective albeit losing campaign in November 1988 that yielded a doubling of Liberal parliamentary representation. In February 1990 Turner resigned as opposition leader, with Jean Chrétien, a former Trudeau aide, being elected his successor on June 23 and steering the party to victory in October 1993. The Liberals won again, with a smaller majority of 155 seats (22 less than in 1993), in June 1997. In the November 2000 election the party won 40.9 percent of the vote and 172 seats, making Chrétien the first prime minister since 1945 to win parliamentary majorities in three consecutive elections. Nevertheless the party entered a period of turmoil when increasing competition for party leadership from Finance Minister Paul Martin caused Chrétien to sack him from the cabinet in June 2002. Martin's dismissal apparently involved his perceived unofficial campaign to succeed Chrétien, the prime minister having directed that no campaigning or fund-raising be conducted until a party convention scheduled for February 2003.

In August 2002 Chrétien announced that he would not seek another term as prime minister, and a party convention in November 2003 overwhelmingly elected Martin as the new party leader. Chrétien then moved his retirement (scheduled for February 2004) up to December 12, 2003, on which date he was succeeded by Martin as prime minister.

Martin led the party in the June 28, 2004, election when it lost its majority status but won a plurality of votes and seats. It subsequently formed a minority government. In May 2005 the Liberals barely survived a budget battle that could have turned into a vote of no confidence only to lose a similar vote six months later. The January 2006 election saw the Liberals' vote fall by 6.5 points, to 30.2 percent, and its seats reduced to 103. Following the defeat, Martin resigned as leader on February 1. Bill GRAHAM replaced him as interim leader of the party and leader of the opposition.

Michael Ignatieff, a well-known academic who had lived in the United Kingdom and the United States for several decades until 2005, was considered the early favorite among eight candidates in December 2006 balloting for the party leader's post. Although he led the first two ballots, Ignatieff lost the fourth and final ballot to Stéphane Dion. Dion subsequently became a foil for the Conservatives, whose campaign for the October 2008 election focused on his on-air fumbling of questions on what he would do about the upheaval in financial markets, his proposed environmental tax policies, his difficulties in expressing himself clearly and forcefully in English (his second language), and his perceived lack of overall leadership abilities.

The Liberals' seat total fell to 77 in the October 2008 balloting, and Dion shortly thereafter announced he would resign his leadership post in May 2009. However, the subsequent short-lived attempt by the Liberals, NDP, and BQ to form a new government (see Current issues, above, for details) proposed that Dion be installed as prime minister. When the proposed no-confidence motion against the Harper government was forestalled by the prorogation of Parliament in early December 2008, Dion, under heavy pressure from all quarters of the party, announced he would step down as party leader as soon as a replacement was selected. Ignatieff, who had earlier signaled his reluctance to join forces in government with the NDP, was named interim party leader on December 10. A party convention in May 2009 affirmed Ignatieff's permanent position, no challenger having surfaced.

The Liberals suffered their worst electoral result in history in the 2011 elections, receiving only 34 seats on 18.9 percent of the vote and losing their status as the largest opposition party in Parliament. Ignatieff was unable to retain his own seat in Parliament and resigned on May 3.

The January 2012 party conference produced a sweeping overhaul of party structure—and voted to legalize marijuana. Leadership selection will be open to any interested person so long as they register online; they do not have to pay dues. On April 14, 2013, Justin Trudeau was elected party leader with over 80 percent of the vote. The 41-year-old is the charismatic son of former premier Pierre Trudeau. The younger Trudeau's admission that he had used marijuana while an MP did little to damage his popularity.

Leaders: Justin TRUDEAU (Leader), Mike CRAWLEY (President), Jeremy BROADHURST (National Director), Judy FOOTE (Whip).

Quebec Bloc (*Bloc Québécois*—BQ). The BQ is a francophone grouping organized by former Liberal environment minister Lucien Bouchard and six defectors from other parties after the collapse of the Meech Lake Accord in mid-1990. Although presenting candidates only in Quebec Province, it became the second-ranked federal party in October 1993, Bouchard thereby becoming leader of the opposition. Operating as the Ottawa representative of Quebec separatism, the BQ backed the provincial Quebec Party (PQ, below) in its declared aim of independence for Quebec following the September 1994 balloting, subject to the creation of a two-state institutional framework covering political and economic relations.

Bouchard's popular standing increased by late 1994 as he led the separatist movement in the national capital. A year later, after the failure of the sovereignty referendum in 1995 and the subsequent resignation of Quebec's premier Jacques Parizeau, Bouchard left federal politics to become premier of Quebec and leader of the PQ. The BQ was the third-ranked party, with 44 seats, after the 1997 federal election and retained that position in November 2000 despite dropping to 38 seats in the House of Commons, based on a provincial vote share of 39.9 percent. In the 2004 elections the BQ retained its third-place ranking, but it increased its seat total to 54 in the House of Commons. In 2006 its seat total fell slightly, to 51, again making it the third-largest parliamentary party. The October 2008 balloting led to a further slight decline, but its 49 seats maintained the BQ as the third largest parliamentary party. While it pledged to support the planned November 2008 vote of no-confidence and thereafter support a proposed Liberal-NDP government, it declared it would not join a federal government as a matter of party principle.

In the 2010 elections the party retained only 4 of its seats in Parliament. This caused it to lose official status as a political party, which requires 12 seats. Following the party's poor performance and the loss of his own seat in the house, Gilles Duceppe resigned as party leader. In February 2012 the BQ was accused of illegally using parliamentary funds to pay director general Gilbert GARDNER's salary for seven years.

Leaders: Daniel PAILLÉ (Leader), Jean-Claude ROCHELEAU (General Director), Louis PLAMONDON (Caucus Chair).

The Green Party. The Green Party was founded in 1983 and contested its first election in 1984 under the leadership of Trevor HANCOCK. Its platform rests on issues of environmental and economic sustainability, peace and international cooperation, and participatory government. Under the leadership of Elizabeth May, the party received 3.9 percent of the vote in the 2010 election and its first parliamentary seat.

Leaders: Elizabeth MAY (Party Leader), Adriane CARR, Georges LARAQUE (Deputy Leaders).

Other Parties:

The following parties participated in the 2011 election and received 0.1 percent or less of the national vote: The **Animal Alliance Environment Voters Party of Canada,** led by Liz WHITE (0.01 percent of the vote); the **Canadian Action Party,** currently led by Jason CHASE (0.01 percent); the **Christian Heritage Party of Canada,** led by James HNATIUK (0.1 percent); the **Communist Party of Canada,** led by Miguel FIGUEROA (0.02 percent); the Libertarian Party of Canada, led by Katrina CHOWNE (0.04 percent); the **Marijuana Party,** led by Blair T. LONGLEY (0.01percent); the **Marxist-Leninist Party of Canada,** led by Anna Di CARLO (0.07 percent); the **Pirate Party of Canada,** currently led by Travis McCREA (0.02 percent); the **Progressive Canadian Party,** led by Sinclair M. STEVENS (0.04 percent); the **Rhinoceros Party,** led by François Yo GOURD (0.03 percent); the **United Party of Canada,** led by Robert KESIC (293 votes); the **Western Block Party,** currently led by Paul St. LAURENT (751 votes).

Perhaps of greatest historical significance is the **Social Credit Party** (Socred), which controlled Alberta from its founding in 1935 until 1971 and which governed British Columbia from 1975 until 1991. It has not been represented at the federal level since 1980.

Regional Parties:

Quebec Party (*Parti Québécois*—PQ). The PQ was founded in 1968 by the journalist René LEVESQUE. Running on a platform of French separatism, it won control of the provincial assembly from the Liberals in the election of November 1976, Lévesque becoming premier. In a referendum held in May 1980, however, it failed to obtain a mandate to enter into "sovereignty-association" talks with the federal government. In April 1981 it increased its majority in the 122-member assembly to 80. In 1985 the party was weakened by the defection of a militant group to form the Democratic Rally for Independence (*Rassemblement Démocratique pour l'Indépendance*—RDI).

In October 1985 Pierre-Marc JOHNSON was sworn in as provincial premier in succession to Lévesque, who was in poor health and whose influence had waned because of divisiveness over the sovereignty issue. However, neither Johnson's conciliatory posture on federalism nor an emerging conservatism on economic issues averted a crushing defeat in provincial balloting in December, when the PQ obtained only 23 seats to the Liberals' 99.

Lévesque died in November 1987. Ten days later, amid a resurgence of proindependence sentiment, Johnson stepped down as party president. His successor, Jacques Parizeau, promised a return to the PQ's separatist origins, and in provincial elections on September 12, 1994, the PQ won a commanding majority of 77 of the 125 legislative seats. On being inducted as premier, Parizeau pledged that a referendum on the independence question would be held in 1995. The vote on October 30 yielded a margin of less than 1 percent against separation and the resignation of Parizeau as PQ leader and Quebec premier. He was succeeded in January 1996 by Lucien Bouchard, theretofore leader of the federal BQ.

The PQ won 75 seats in the provincial election of November 30, 1998, although observers attributed the victory more to the moderate Bouchard's successes in the economic sphere than to his gradualist approach toward the sovereignty issue. At a party convention in May 2000, 91 percent of the delegates endorsed his leadership. In January 2001, however, a series of developments, including continuing pressure from adamant separatists (many of whom want more stringent French-language laws and less attention to minority rights), led Bouchard to announce his surprise resignation from party and government offices, effective upon designation of a successor. In February Quebec finance minister Bernard Landry assumed the party leadership, promising to reinvigorate the separatist cause upon becoming premier in early March. Despite Landry's pledge, the PQ lost control of the provincial government to the rival Liberal Party of Quebec (*Parti Libéral du Quebec*—PLQ) in the 2003 balloting, securing only 45 of 125 seats.

Landry announced in late summer 2004 that he would stay on as leader. However, after a vote on his leadership in June 2005 fell short of the endorsement he was seeking, he was replaced on an interim basis by Louise HAREL and then, in the November leadership election, by Andre BOISCLAIR. Harel stayed on as leader of the opposition in Quebec, because Boisclair did not hold an assembly seat.

The PQ's electoral fortunes declined further in the March 2007 provincial balloting, at which it finished third with only 36 seats on a vote share of 28.3 percent and lost its position as official opposition in the province to the ADQ (see below). (The PLQ led all parties with 48 seats to retain control of the provincial government.) Boisclair announced his resignation in May, and he was succeeded in late June by Pauline Marois, the only announced candidate for the post. When Premier Jean Charest (PLQ) called a snap election for December 8, 2008, the PQ electoral fortunes rebounded, as it won 35 percent of the vote and 51 seats. These increases came mostly at the expense of the ADQ, allowing the PQ to regain its position as the official opposition party in the province. The PQ edged out PLQ 54 seat to 50 in the September 4, 2012, provincial election, with Marois becoming premier with a minority government.

Leaders: Pauline MAROIS (Premier, Leader), Raymond ARCHAMBAULT (President).

Coalition for the Future of Quebec (*Coalition Avenir Québec—CAQ*). Founded on November 14, 2011, by François Legault, the party calls for a 10-year moratorium on any sovereignty referendum and advocates improving education and health care in the province. The party has drawn members of the PQ, and in January 2012 the Democratic Action of Quebec, led by Christian LÉVESQUE, voted to merge with CAQ. The CAQ placed third in the September 4, 2012, provincial election with 19 seats. (For more on Democratic Action of Quebec, please see the 2013 *Handbook.*)

Leaders: François LEGAULT (Leader), Dominique ANGLADE (President).

Quebec Solidarity (*Québec Solidaire*—QS) is a left-wing, pro-independence party that has two seats in the provincial assembly. The party emerged in 2006 as an umbrella for environmentalists, feminists, globalists, anticapitalists and other left-wing affiliates. Unlike other pro-independence parties, QS seeks a sovereign, secular Quebec that exhibits social justice. The party operates with a collective leadership, with both male and female cospokespeople.

Leaders: Andrés FONTECILLA (President), Régent SÉGUIN.

Saskatchewan Party (SP). The SP was established in August 1997 and held a leadership election in April 1998 that was won by a former Reform Party MP, Elwin HERMANSON. Contesting the provincial election of September 1999 on a platform that called for lower taxes, better health care, and improved highways, the SP finished a surprising second, capturing 26 of the 58 seats in the Legislative Assembly. In the November 2003 provincial balloting the SP improved to 28 seats on a 39 percent vote share. In the November 7, 2007, provincial balloting the

SP won 38 seats on a vote share of 51 percent, the first absolute vote majority in the province since the NDP won 51 percent in 1991. The SP won 49 seats on 64.21 percent of the vote in the 2011 provincial election.

Leaders: Brad WALL (Premier of Saskatchewan), Gary MESCHISHNICK (President).

Wildrose Alliance Party (WP). Formed in 2008 through a merger of the Wildrose Party and the Alberta Alliance Party, the WP took 17 seats in the 2012 elections for Alberta's provincial legislature. The center-right party draws support from rural communities and opposed Conservative Party spending. Conservative members of the legislature, angry at the perceived lack of democracy in the local branch, defected to Wildrose in 2010. The party name comes from Alberta's official flower, which is the wild rose.

Leaders: Danielle SMITH (Party Leader), David YAGER (President).

Yukon Party (YP). A newly formed group, the YP won a plurality in Yukon territorial elections on October 19, 1992, thus ousting the NDP from the territorial government. Holding 7 of the 17 seats, it subsequently formed a minority administration under John OSTASHEK. In the 1996 election the party retreated to 3 seats as the NDP surged, while in April 2000 the YP captured only 1 seat in the territorial legislature as the Liberal Party won control. When early elections were called in 2002, voters, reportedly angry at having to vote after only two years, gave the YP an overwhelming victory with 12 of the 18 legislative seats. Resignations reduced the YP majority to 10 seats as of May 2006. The YP retained its 10-seat majority in the October 2006 territorial elections, followed by the Yukon Liberal Party (5 seats) and the Yukon New Democratic Party (3 seats). The YP prevailed again in the October 11, 2011, provincial election, taking 40.5 percent of the vote (11 seats), followed by Yukon New Democratic Party (6 seats), Yukon Liberal Party (1), and independent (1).

Leaders: Darrell PASLOSKI (Premier and Party Leader), Pat McINROY (President).

Dozens of additional provincial parties exist, but none currently holds seats in any provincial or territorial legislature.

LEGISLATURE

Influenced by British precedent (although without its own peerage), Canada's bicameral **Parliament** consists of an appointed Senate and an elected House of Commons.

Senate. The upper house consists of individuals appointed to serve until 75 years of age by the governor general and selected, on the advice of the prime minister, along party and geographic lines. Its current and normal size is 105 senators, although under a controversial constitutional provision successfully invoked for the first time by Prime Minister Mulroney in 1990, it can, with the queen's assent, be increased to no more than 112. Senate reforms remain under consideration. As of October 2013, the distribution of seats was as follows: Conservative Party of Canada, 60; Liberal Party of Canada, 33; Independents, 5; Progressive Conservatives, 1; Vacant, 6.

Speaker: Noël KINSELLA.

House of Commons. The lower house currently consists of 308 members elected for five-year terms (subject to dissolution) by universal suffrage on the basis of direct representation. In the elections of May 2, 2011, the Conservative Party of Canada won 166 seats, the New Democratic Party, 103; the Liberal Party, 34; the Bloc Quebecois, 4; and the Green Party of Canada, 1.

Speaker: Andrew SCHEER.

CABINET

[as of October 8, 2013]

Prime Minister	Stephen Harper
Ministers	
Aboriginal Affairs and Northern Development	Bernard Valcourt
Agriculture and Agri-Food	Gerry Ritz
Asia-Pacific Gateway	Edward Fast
Atlantic Canada Opportunities Agency	Rob Moore
Atlantic Gateway	Keith Ashfield
Canadian Heritage and Official Languages	Shelly Glover
Canadian Northern Economic Development Agency	Leona Aglukkaq [f]
Canadian Wheat Board	Gerry Ritz
Citizenship and Immigration	Jason Kenney
Democratic Reform	Pierre Poilievre
Economic Development Agency of Canada for the Regions of Quebec	Denis Lebel
Economic Development Initiative for Northern Ontario	Greg Rickford
Employment and Social Development	Jason Kenney
Environment	Leona Aglukkao [f]
Finance	James Michael Flaherty
Fisheries and Oceans	Gail Shea [f]
Foreign Affairs	John Baird
Health	Rona Ambrose [f]
Industry	James Moore
Infrastructure, Communities, and Intergovernmental Affairs	Dennis Lebel
International Trade	Edward Fast
Justice and Attorney General	Peter Gordon MacKay
Labor	Kellie Leitch [f]
Multiculturalism	Tim Uppal
National Defense	Robert Douglas Nicholson
National Revenue	Kerry-Lynne Findlay [f]
Natural Resources	Joe Oliver
Public Safety	Steven Blaney
Public Works and Government Services	Diane Finley [f]
Science and Technology	Greg Rickford
Seniors	Alice Wong [f]
Sport	Bal Gosal
Status of Women	Kellie Leitch [f]
Transport	Lisa Raitt [f]
Veterans Affairs	Julian Fantino
Government Leader in the House	Peter Van Loan
Government Leader in the Senate	Claude Carignan
President, Queen's Privy Council for Canada	Denis Lebel
President, Treasury Board	Tony Clement

[f] = female

Notes: All of the above are members of the Conservative Party of Canada. The Government Leader in the Senate is no longer a cabinet level position; the position has been downgraded.

INTERGOVERNMENTAL REPRESENTATION

Ambassador to the U.S.: Gary Albert DOER.

U.S. Ambassador to Canada: (Vacant).

Permanent Representative to the UN: Guillermo RISHCHYNSKI.

IGO Memberships (Non-UN): ADB, AfDB, APEC, CWTH, EBRD, G-8, G-20, IADB, ICC, IEA, IOM, NATO, OAS, OECD, OSCE, WTO.

CAPE VERDE

Republic of Cape Verde
República de Cabo Verde

Political Status: Former Portuguese dependency; became independent July 5, 1975; present constitution adopted September 25, 1992.

Area: 1,557 sq. mi. (4,033 sq. km).

Population: 512,012 (2012E—UN); 531,046 (2013E—U.S. Census).

Major Urban Centers (2011E): CIDADE DE PRAIA (133,863).

Official Language: Portuguese.

Monetary Unit: Cape Verde Escudo (market rate November 1, 2013: 80.58 escudos = $1US). When Portugal adopted the euro as its official currency in 2002, the Cape Verde escudo, which had been pegged to the Portuguese escudo since 1998, was pegged to the euro at the rate of 110.265 Cape Verde escudos = 1 euro.

President: Jorge Carlos FONSECA (Movement for Democracy); elected by popular vote on August 21, 2011, and inaugurated on September 9 for a five-year term, succeeding Gen. (Ret.) Pedro Verona Rodrigues PIRES (African Party for the Independence of Cape Verde).

Prime Minister: José Maria Pereira NEVES (African Party for the Independence of Cape Verde); appointed by the president on February 1, 2001, and sworn in with the new cabinet on the same day in succession to António Gualberto DO ROSARIO (Movement for Democracy) following the legislative election of January 14; reappointed by the president and sworn in on March 8, 2006, following the legislative election of January 22; reappointed by the president on March 10, 2011, following the legislative election of February 6 and sworn in with the new cabinet on March 21.

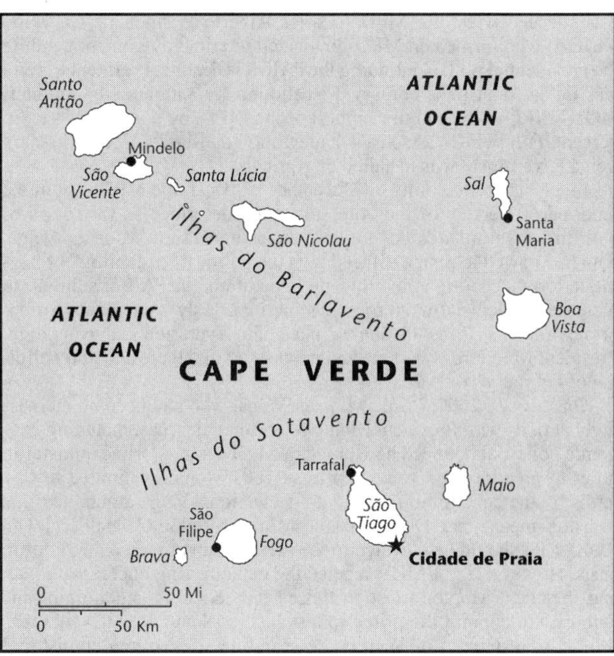

THE COUNTRY

Cape Verde embraces ten islands and five islets situated in the Atlantic Ocean some 400 miles west of Senegal. The islands are divided into a northern windward group (Santo Antão, São Vicente, Santa Lúcia, São Nicolau, Sal, and Boa Vista) and a southern leeward group (Brava, Fogo, São Tiago, and Maio). About 60 percent of the population is composed of *mestiços* (of mixed Portuguese and African extraction), who predominate on all of the islands except São Tiago, where black Africans outnumber them; Europeans constitute less than 2 percent of the total. Most Cape Verdeans are Roman Catholics and speak a Creole version of Portuguese that varies from one island to another. Partly because of religious influence, women have traditionally been counted as less than 25 percent of the labor force, despite evidence of greater participation as unpaid agricultural laborers; female representation in party and government affairs has been increasing slowly, and the legislature currently includes 15 women.

The islands' economy has historically depended on São Vicente's importance as a refueling and resting stop for shipping between Europe and Latin America. The airfield on Sal has long served a similar function for aircraft. Corn is the major subsistence crop, but persistent drought since the late 1960s has forced the importation of it and other foods. Support from the World Bank and the African Development Fund bolstered infrastructure rehabilitation in the 1990s.

Cape Verde in 1998 adopted a structural reform program prescribed by the International Monetary Fund (IMF) in an effort to restore financial stability in the wake of a dismal economic performance in the first half of the decade. Debt reduction and private sector growth topped the government's goals. Though increased tourism and exportation of manufactures goods buoyed the GDP in the late 1990s, unemployment increased, and by 2002 some 36 percent of the population was reportedly living in poverty. The IMF, World Bank, and African Development Bank subsequently provided significant additional assistance to support the government's economic restructuring.

Through the early 2000s, the GDP growth fluctuated, reaching a peak of 11 percent in 2006, while unemployment and poverty rates dropped. As a result of a decline in tourism and construction due largely to the global economic crisis, growth in 2009–2011 slowed to an annual average of 5.3 percent. The IMF praised the government for its "prudent economic management" and for its plans to accelerate spending on infrastructure, including $375 million in port improvements. The Africa Development Bank also took note of Cape Verde's economic progress and updated its status with the bank from low-income to middle-income country—a milestone on the continent and a reflection of good governance and sound economic policy—qualifying Cape Verde for additional funding resources. The IMF approved a 15-month policy support program for economic diversification and increased social spending. Fund managers cited an increase in tourism and construction for Cape Verde's rebound from the global economic downturn and praised the authorities for their efforts toward reducing unemployment.

By the end of 2011 growth eased to 5 percent, while inflation had reached 4.5 percent. The IMF credited Cape Verde for meeting or making substantial progress toward benchmarks, but noted that it responded slowly to a weakening balance of payments in the face of external shocks from high fuel and food prices and the economic disarray in Europe, which remained a persistent risk. A loan from the International Fund for Agricultural Development in January 2013 was designated to combat poverty, targeting less-developed rural areas. In 2013, the GDP increased by 4.1 percent, with inflation at 4.0 percent. The unemployment rate stayed at 10 percent.

GOVERNMENT AND POLITICS

Political background. Cape Verde was uninhabited when the Portuguese first occupied and began settling the islands in the mid-15th century; a Portuguese governor was appointed as early as 1462. During the 1970s several independence movements emerged, the most important being the mainland-based African Party for the Independence of Guinea-Bissau and Cape Verde (*Partido Africano da Independência do Guiné-Bissau e Cabo Verde*—PAIGC), which urged the union of Cape Verde and Guinea-Bissau, and the Democratic Union of Cape Verde (*União Democratica de Cabo Verde*—UDCV), which was led by João Baptista MONTEIRO and rejected the idea of a merger.

An agreement signed with Portuguese authorities on December 30, 1974, provided for a transitional government prior to independence on July 5, 1975. A 56-member National People's Assembly was elected on June 30, 1975, but only the PAIGC participated; the results indicated that about 92 percent of the voters favored the PAIGC proposal of ultimate union with Guinea-Bissau. Upon independence, the assembly elected Aristides PEREIRA, the secretary general of the PAIGC, as president of Cape Verde. On July 15 Maj. Pedro PIRES, who had negotiated the independence agreements for both Cape Verde and Guinea-Bissau, was named prime minister of Cape Verde. However, the question of eventual unification with Guinea-Bissau remained unresolved. For more on how the 1980 coup in Guinea-Bissau led to the abandonment of unification plans, see the 2012 *Handbook.*

In keeping with currents elsewhere on the continent, the National Council of the African Party for the Independence of Cape Verde (PAICV, as the PAIGC had been restyled in 1981) announced in April 1990 that the president would henceforth be popularly elected and that other parties would be permitted to advance candidates for the assembly. On July 26 Pereira stepped down as PAICV party leader, declaring that the head of state should be "above party politics."

In the country's first multiparty balloting on January 13, 1991, the recently formed Movement for Democracy (*Movimento para Democracia*—MPD) won 56 legislative seats on the strength of a 68 percent vote share, compared to the PAICV's 23 seats. Prime Minister Pires announced his resignation on January 15, and on January 28 he was succeeded by the MPD's Carlos Alberto Wahnon de Carvalho VEIGA, who formed an MPD-dominated interim government pending the presidential poll. Continuing the PAICV's decline, President Pereira was defeated in the February 17 balloting by António Mascarenhas MONTEIRO, who had the support of the MPD, by a vote of 74 to 26 percent. Following Monteiro's inauguration on March 22, a permanent Veiga government was installed on April 4.

In legislative balloting on December 17, 1995, the MPD captured a reported 60 percent of the vote, a triumph described as validation of both the government's economic policies and Prime Minister Veiga, who had vowed to resign if faced with the political "instability" of having to form a coalition government. In addition, the PAICV's failure to increase its legislative representation reportedly convinced former prime minister Pires to shelve plans for a presidential campaign. President Monteiro was reelected unopposed in the presidential balloting of February 18, 1996.

On July 29, 2000, Prime Minister Veiga, who had become increasingly at odds with President Monteiro on several issues, including economic policy, announced he would no longer serve as prime minister in order to prepare for a campaign to succeed Monteiro (limited to two terms by the constitution) in the 2001 elections. Veiga argued that his decision meant that Deputy Prime Minister António Gualberto DO ROSARIO should be elevated to the premiership at least on an interim basis. However, the PAICV labeled the maneuvering unconstitutional, and President Monteiro also criticized the action as undermining his authority to appoint the prime minister. (It was not clear if Veiga was officially resigning or merely "suspending" his prime ministerial responsibilities.) An institutional crisis was finally averted when Veiga subsequently submitted a formal resignation letter. On October 6 President Monteiro invited do Rosario to form a new government that, as constituted on October 9, comprised all but one of the incumbent ministers.

In legislative balloting on January 14, 2001, the PAICV won 47 percent of the vote and 40 seats. On January 26 President Monteiro invited PAICV leader José Maria Pereira NEVES to form a new government, which was sworn in on February 1. Subsequently, former prime minister Pires of the PAICV was elected after two rounds of presidential balloting on February 11 and February 25, defeating Veiga and two independent candidates. Pires again defeated Veiga in the presidential balloting of February 12, 2006, securing 50.9 percent of the vote versus Veiga's 49 percent, following the PAICV's winning 41 seats in legislative balloting on January 22. Neves was reappointed to head another PAICV government and was sworn in along with the new (mostly PAICV) government on March 8. The cabinet was reshuffled on June 27, 2008.

Prime Minister Neves reshuffled the cabinet in February 2010, most notably abolishing the ministry of the economy, growth, and competitiveness.

The PAICV hung on to its majority with 38 seats in National Assembly elections on February 6, 2011, while the MPD picked up three seats on turnout of more than 71 percent. Prime Minister Neves, who was reappointed by the president on March 10, named a new government on March 18 that included six independents and eight women. In the presidential election of August 21, MPD candidate Jorge Carlos FONSECA won with 54.3 percent of the vote, edging out the PAICV's Manuel Inocêncio SOUSA, who won 45.7 percent.

Constitution and government. The constitution of September 7, 1980, declared Cape Verde to be a "sovereign, democratic, unitary, anti-colonialist, and anti-imperialist republic" under single-party auspices. Legislative authority was vested in the National People's Assembly, which elected the president of the republic for a five-year term. The prime minister was nominated by the assembly and responsible to it. The basic law was amended in February 1981 to revoke provisions designed to facilitate union with Guinea-Bissau, thus overriding, inter alia, a 1976 judiciary protocol calling for the merger of legal procedures and personnel. The likelihood of a merger was virtually eliminated by adoption of the mainland constitution of May 1984, which emulated its Cape Verdean counterpart by lack of reference to the sister state.

On September 28, 1990, the National People's Assembly approved constitutional and electoral law revisions, forwarded in early 1990 by the PAICV National Council, which deleted references to the party as the "ruling force of society and of state," authorized balloting on the basis of direct universal suffrage, and sanctioned the participation of opposition candidates in multiparty elections that were subsequently held in January and February 1991.

A new constitution that came into force in September 1992 provided for direct presidential election to a five-year term, with provision for a run-off if no candidate secures a majority in the first round. Legislative authority is vested in a popularly elected national assembly of between 66 and 72 deputies. The assembly's normal term is also five years, although the president may, in certain circumstances, dissolve it. The prime minister continues to be nominated by and responsible to the assembly, although appointed by the president. On the prime minister's recommendation the president appoints the Council of Ministers, whose members must be assembly deputies. The court system features a Supreme Court of Justice, beneath which are courts of first and second resort. There also are administrative courts, courts of accounts, military courts, and tax and customs courts. In July 2004 the government proposed the creation a Constitutional Court, but the PAICV rejected the idea, and no further progress has been reported.

Press freedom is guaranteed by law in Cape Verde. Cape Verde ranked 25th of 179 countries in the Reporters Without Borders, making it the second highest rated African country.

At present there are 17 local government councils, which are popularly elected for five-year terms.

Foreign relations. Cape Verde has established diplomatic relations with some 50 countries, including most members of the European Union (EU), with which it is associated under the Lomé Convention. Formally nonaligned, it rejected a 1980 Soviet overture for the use of naval facilities at the port of São Vicente as a replacement for facilities previously available in Conakry, Guinea. The Pereira government subsequently reaffirmed its opposition to any foreign military accommodation within its jurisdiction. In March 1984 Cape Verde became one of the few non-Communist countries to establish relations with the Heng Samrin government of Cambodia and, following a visit by Yasir Arafat in August 1986, it exchanged ambassadors with the Palestine Liberation Organization.

The country's closest regional links are with Guinea-Bissau (despite a 20-month rupture following the ouster of the Cabral government in November 1980) and the other three Lusophone African states: Angola, Mozambique, and São Tomé and Príncipe. Relations with Bissau were formally reestablished in July 1982 prior to a summit meeting of the five Portuguese-speaking heads of state in Praia held September 21–22, during which a joint committee was set up to promote economic and diplomatic cooperation.

Following the MPD legislative victory in January 1991, Prime Minister Veiga moved quickly to strengthen relations with anti-Marxist groups in Guinea-Bissau, Angola, and Mozambique, despite declaring he expected no major foreign policy changes.

In August 1998 international attention focused on Praia as the recently launched Community of Portuguese Speaking Countries (CPLP), under Monteiro's leadership, and the Economic Community of West African States (ECOWAS) forged a cease-fire agreement between the combatants in Guinea-Bissau.

The government established diplomatic and trade relations with China in 2001, while in 2002 it launched a broad initiative to gain preferential trade relations with the EU. Subsequently, a seaborder agreement with Mauritania in December 2003 offered the hope for additional oil and mineral exploitation.

In 2007 the EU approved a "special partnership" agreement with Cape Verde, aimed at strengthening the relationship between the entities. In 2009 Cape Verde announced plans to negotiate its own economic partnership with the EU, abandoning a similar agreement established through ECOWAS.

In an August 2009 visit U.S. secretary of state Hillary Clinton called Cape Verde "a model of democracy and economic progress in Africa." A visit to Cape Verde by Cuban vice president José Ramón MACHADO Ventura in 2009 strengthened bilateral relations. In September, Cape Verde signed an energy agreement with Venezuela and established diplomatic relations with Australia.

Cape Verde's economic partnership with the EU was formalized in April 2010, allowing Cape Verde to benefit from EU funding.

In September 2012, Singapore and Cape Verde signed an open skies agreement, easing travel between the two countries and paving the way for increased economic cooperation.

At a summit in Cape Verde in March 2013, finance ministers from the 15 member states of ECOWAS agreed to establish a common external tariff regulating region-wide taxes on goods. In June 2013, Cape Verde joined 21 other states in signing a code of conduct to prevent piracy and armed robbery against ships in waters around Africa.

Current issues. For organizational reasons, the 2011 parliamentary polls were postponed from January until February, and presidential balloting was rescheduled from February to August. The MPD conceded defeat before the final results of the February 6 assembly election were announced, a move observers said underscored the strength of democracy in Cape Verde. Though the MPD picked up three seats, the PAICV held on to its majority. Also in March, the PAICV nominated party vice president Manuel Inocêncio Sousa as its flag bearer over the hopeful, David Hopffer ALMADA, who stepped aside. The MPD officially endorsed Jorge Carlos Fonseca, a founder of the party who had defected a decade earlier to start the Democratic Convergence Party (*Partido da Convergência Democrática*—PCD), which folded in 2007. The third party legislative party, the Cape Verdean Independent and Democratic Union (*União Caboverdeana Independente e Democrática*—UCID), endorsed attorney Gerald ALMEIDA for president.

The two main contenders, Sousa and Fonseca, campaigned on policies to modernize the country's tourism-based economy and reduce unemployment. A rift emerged within the PAICV after Aristides LIMA, a former speaker of the National Assembly, lost the PAICV nomination to Sousa and then decided to run as an independent. The resulting split in the vote opened the way for centrist Fonseca to eventually win. In balloting on August 7 Fonseca won 37.8 percent of the vote; Sousa won 32.7 percent; Lima won 27.7 percent; Joaquim MONTEIRO (independent) won 1.8 percent. Because neither of the top vote-getters won an absolute majority, the constitution required a runoff. In August 21 balloting Fonseca won 54.3 percent of the vote and Sousa won 45.7 percent. The election marked the first time in Cape Verde's history that the president and the government are from different parties.

Partisan tensions emerged in July 2012 when the PAICV-dominant parliament passed an environmental tax law to reduce pollution that Fonseca vetoed, declaring it an unconstitutional infringement on municipalities' authority. PAICV legislators ignored the president's veto and passed the bill a second time, forcing Fonseca to promulgate it.

In May 2013, President Fonseca and Angolan Vice President Manuel VICENTE discussed launching a joint commission to reinforce and diversify existing cooperation between the two countries. The meeting came several weeks after parliamentary leaders from the two countries discussed deepening relations between the two legislative bodies.

POLITICAL PARTIES

Although a number of parties existed prior to independence, the only party that was recognized for 15 years thereafter was the African Party for the Independence of Guinea-Bissau and Cape Verde (PAIGC). The reference to Guinea-Bissau was dropped and the party restyled the African Party for the Independence of Cape Verde (PAICV), insofar as the islands' branch was concerned, on January 20, 1981, in reaction to the mainland coup of the previous November.

Government Party:

African Party for the Independence of Cape Verde (*Partido Africano da Independência de Cabo Verde*—PAICV). The PAIGV's predecessor, the PAIGC was formed in 1956 by Amílcar Cabral and others to resist Portuguese rule in both Cape Verde and Guinea-Bissau. Initially headquartered in Conakry, Guinea, the PAIGC began military operations in Guinea-Bissau in 1963 and was instrumental in negotiating independence for that country. Following the assassination of Cabral on January 20, 1973, his brother Luís, and Aristides Maria Pereira assumed control of the movement, Luís Cabral serving as president of Guinea-Bissau until being overthrown in the 1980 coup.

In February 1990 the National Council endorsed constitutional changes that would permit the introduction of a multiparty system, and in April the council recommended that further reforms be adopted in preparation for legislative and presidential elections. In August Maj. Pedro Pires was elected PAICV secretary general, replacing Pereira, who was defeated for reelection as president of the republic on February 17, 1991, and promptly announced his retirement from politics.

At a party congress on August 29, 1993, Pires was appointed to the newly created post of party president to exercise "moral authority." Pires won reelection to the PAICV's top post at a party congress in September 1997, staving off a challenge by newcomer José Neves.

Apparently bolstered by his party's success in local balloting in February 2000, Pires announced in March that he was stepping down from his PAICV post to prepare for presidential balloting scheduled for 2001. A June PAICV congress elected Neves to succeed Pires over PAICV vice president Felisberto Viera. In the legislative elections in January 2001, the PAICV won 47 percent of the vote, and Pires secured 46 percent of the votes in the first round of presidential voting in February and was elected in a close race in the second round with 49.43 percent of the vote. In local elections in March 2004, the PAICV suffered a major defeat by losing control of the council on Sal Island, the country's major tourist destination. In response to the losses, Neves reshuffled the cabinet in April. Pires was reelected in 2006, and the PAICV won a majority of seats in the 2006 assembly elections.

The PAICV lost three seats in the 2011 National Assembly elections but retained its majority. The party chose its vice president, Manuel Inocêncio Sousa, as its 2011 presidential candidate. After losing the nomination, Aristides Lima opened a division within the party by running as an independent. Taking a centrist position, Lima drew votes from both the PAICV and the MPD. Neves threw his support heavily behind Sousa, publicly chastising Lima and carving deep divisions within the party. The resulting split in the vote opened the way for Fonseca's win. As a consequence, Minister for Social Development and Family Felisberto Alves Viera, a Lima supporter who had publicly threatened to call for a vote of no confidence in Neves's government, stepped down from his cabinet post after Lima was eliminated in the first round of voting. Fonseca subsequently transferred his responsibilities to another minister.

Sousa's defeat was seen as a personal blow to Neves and his image as a strong party leader. Trying to paper over the divisions, the PAICV National Council met on September 11, 2011, at a tense meeting in which Neves called for party cohesion. The meeting reportedly concluded with the decision that the leadership should strictly support candidates on the basis of party policies, not personal preference, underscoring the leadership's fears about losing elections if the party fails to show a unified front.

Neves was reelected party chairman in March 2013. By 2030, he hopes to quadruple per capita income from $3,000 to $12,000.

Leaders: José Maria Pereira NEVES (Prime Minister and President of the Party), Cristina Fontes LIMA, Manuel Inocêncio SOUSA, Felisberto Alves VIEIRA (Vice Presidents of the Party), José Manuel ANDRADE (Parliamentary Faction Leader), Julio CORREIA (Secretary General), Basílio Mosso RAMOS (Speaker of the National Assembly).

Other Legislative Parties:

Movement for Democracy (*Movimento para Democracia*—MPD). Then a Lisbon-based opposition grouping, the MPD issued a "manifesto" in early 1990 calling for dismantling of the PAICV regime, thereby prompting the ruling party to schedule multiparty elections. In June the MPD held its first official meeting in Praia, and in September it met with the PAICV to discuss a timetable for the balloting that culminated in MPD legislative and presidential victories of January and February 1991.

The MPD retained legislative control in 1995, although its seat total dropped from 56 to 50. In addition, President António Monteiro, an independent who enjoyed the support of the MPD, was reelected unopposed to a second term as president of the republic in February 1996. However, in the wake of estrangement between Monteiro and the MPD's Carlos Veiga, prime minister from March 1991 to October 2000 (see Political background, above), the party secured only 39 percent of the vote in the January 2001 legislative poll, losing control to the PAICV. Meanwhile, Veiga finished second in the first round of presidential balloting in February with 45 percent of the vote before losing an exceedingly close race in the second round. The MPD gained control of 9 municipal councils, up from 6, in the March 2004 elections, reversing the dissatisfaction in leader Agostinho LOPES since the 2001 national elections. However, in 2006 the MPD's power showed signs of decline as Veiga again lost a presidential bid and the party won only 29 seats in the legislative election. Jorge Santos was elected party president in late 2006.

Veiga was returned to the party's helm at the MPD convention in October 2009. The party gained three seats in the 2011 National Assembly elections, winning 42 percent of the vote to the PAICV's 51.4 percent. Jorge Carlos Fonseca was chosen as the flag bearer for the 2011 presidential election (see Current issues, above).

Praia mayor Ulisses Correia e Silva, running unopposed, succeeded Veiga in internal elections on June 16, 2013. Despite winning with 97.5 percent of the vote, his first proposal, to restructure the party, sparked controversy.

Leaders: Ulisses CORREIA E SILVA (Party Chair), Jorge Carlos FONSECA (President), José MOREIRA (Secretary General), Carlos Alberto Wahnon de Carvalho VEIGA (Former Prime Minister and 2001 and 2006 presidential candidate).

Cape Verdean Independent and Democratic Union (*União Caboverdeana Independente e Democrática*—UCID). The UCID is a right-wing group long active among the 500,000 Cape Verdean emigrants in Portugal and elsewhere. In mid-1990 the UCID, whose local influence appeared to be limited to one or two islands, signed a cooperation agreement with the MPD.

In legislative balloting in December 1995, the UCID received 5 percent of the vote, the third-largest tally, but failed to secure representation. With the Democratic Convergence Party (PCD) and the Labor and Solidarity Party (PTS), the UCID formed the Democratic Alliance for Change (*Aliança Democrática para a Mudança*—ADM) in the 2001 legislative election. (The ADM won 6 percent of the vote and two assembly seats [one each for the PCD and the PTS] in 2001.) There was no reference to the ADM in the 2006 elections; the UCID placed a distant third in legislative balloting with 2.64 percent of the vote and promised to fight for political ethics in parliament.

The UCID retained its two seats on a 4.5 percent vote share in the 2011 legislative election. The party endorsed Geraldo Almeida in the 2011 presidential election.

On July 28, 2013, party president Antonio Monteiro was reelected.

Leaders: Antonio Mascarenhas MONTEIRO (President of the Party and Former President of the Republic), Geraldo Almeida (2011 presidential candidate), Celso CELESTINO.

Other Parties That Contested Recent Elections:

Democratic Socialist Party (*Partido Socialista Democrático*—PSD). Launched in 1992, the PSD was legalized on July 14, 1995. The party's platform calls for greater governmental support for development programs and the elimination of "injustices." The PSD secured less than 1 percent of the vote in the 1995, 2001, 2006, and 2011 legislative balloting.

Leader: João ALÉM.

Labor and Solidarity Party (*Partido de Trabalho e da Solidariedade*—PTS). This grouping is a socialist-oriented party that was launched by the mayor of São Vicente, Onésimo SILVEIRA, in May 1998. In a confusing series of events following the formation of the ADM, Silveira announced his plans to run for president in 2001 as an independent before withdrawing from the race several days prior to the balloting. (He had previously been listed as the successful ADM/PTS candidate in the January 2001 assembly poll.) In 2006, when he was elected to parliament, Silveira was reported to be a member of the PAICV.

The party won 0.5 percent of the vote in the 2011 assembly election.

Democratic Renewal Party (*Partido da Renovação Democrática*—PRD). Established in July 2000, the PRD is an offshoot of the MPD. The party won 3.2 percent of the vote in the 2001 legislative balloting but failed to secure any seats. The PRD won less than 1 percent of the vote in legislative balloting in 2006.

Leader: Simao MONTEIRO.

LEGISLATURE

The unicameral **National People's Assembly** (*Assembleia Nacional Popular*) became a 79-member bipartisan body in the election of January 14, 1991; in 1995 the membership was reduced to 72. The normal term is five years, although the body is subject to presidential dissolution. Following the most recent balloting on February 6, 2011, the African Party for the Independence of Cape Verde won 38 seats; Movement for Democracy, 32; and Cape Verdean Independent and Democratic Union, 2.

Speaker: Basílio Mosso RAMOS.

CABINET

[as of November 11, 2013]

Prime Minister	José Maria Pereira Nevesx
Deputy Prime Minister	Maria Cristina Lopes Almeida Fontes Lima [f]
Ministers	
Culture	Mário Lúcio Matias de Sousa Mendes
Communities	Maria Fernanda Tavares Fernandes [f]
Defense	Jorge Homero Tolentino
Education and Sport	Fernanda Maria de Brito Marques [f]
Environment, Housing, and Territorial Management	Sara Maria Duarte Lopes [f]
Finance and Planning	Cristina Duarte [f]
Foreign Affairs	Jorge Alberto da Silva Borges
Health	Maria Cristina Lopes Almeida Fontes Lima [f]
Higher Education, Science, and Innovation	Antonio Leão de Aguiar Correia e Silva
Infrastructure and Maritime Resources	José Maria Veiga
Internal Administration	Marisa Helena do Nascimento Morais [f]
Justice	José Carlos Lopes Correia
Parliamentary Affairs	Rui Mendes Semedo
Rural Development	Eva Verona Teixeira Ortet [f]
State Reform	José Maria Pereira Neves
Tourism, Industry, and Energy	Humberto Santos de Brito
Youth, Employment, and Human Resources Development	Janira Isabel Fonseca Hopffer Almada [f]
Secretaries of State	
Foreign Affairs	José Luis Rocha
Marine Resources	Adalberto Filomeno Carvalho Santos Vieira
Public Administration	Romeu Fonseca Modesto

[f] = female

INTERGOVERNMENTAL REPRESENTATION

Ambassador to the U.S.: Maria de Fatima LIMA DE VEIGA.

U.S. Ambassador to Cape Verde: Adrienne O'NEAL.

Permanent Representative to the UN: Antonio Pedro Monteiro LIMA.

IGO Memberships (Non-UN): AfDB, AU, ECOWAS, ICC, IOM, NAM, WTO.

CENTRAL AFRICAN REPUBLIC

Central African Republic
République Centrafricaine

Political Status: Became independent August 13, 1960; one-party military regime established January 1, 1966; Central African Empire proclaimed December 4, 1976; republic reestablished September 21, 1979; military rule reimposed September 1, 1981; constitution of November 21, 1986, amended on August 30, 1992, to provide for multiparty system; present constitution adopted January 7, 1995, following acceptance in referendum of December 28, 1994; civilian government suspended following military coup on March 15, 2003; new constitution adopted by national referendum on December 5, 2004, providing for a return to civilian government via national elections that were held March–May 2005; constitution suspended on March 25, following overthrow of government.

Area: 240,534 sq. mi. (622,984 sq. km).

Population: 4,598,447 (2012E—UN); 5,166,510 (2013E—U.S. Census).

Major Urban Center (2005E): BANGUI (783,000).

Official Language: French. The national language is Sango.

Monetary Unit: CFA Franc (official rate November 1, 2013: 486.52 francs = $1US). The CFA franc, previously pegged to the French franc, is now permanently pegged to the euro at 655.957 CFA francs = 1 euro.

President: Michel DJOTODIA (*Séléka*); proclaimed president on March 24, 2013, following rebellion which displaced Gen. François BOZIZÉ Yangouvonda (nonparty); formally elected president by transitional legislature on April 13, for an 18-month term.

Prime Minister: Nicolas TIANGAYE (nonparty); appointed by the president on January 17, 2013, to succeed Faustin-Archange TOUADERA (nonparty), who was dismissed on January 12, under the terms of a ceasefire agreement; reappointed on March 27 to lead unity government; reappointed on June 12.

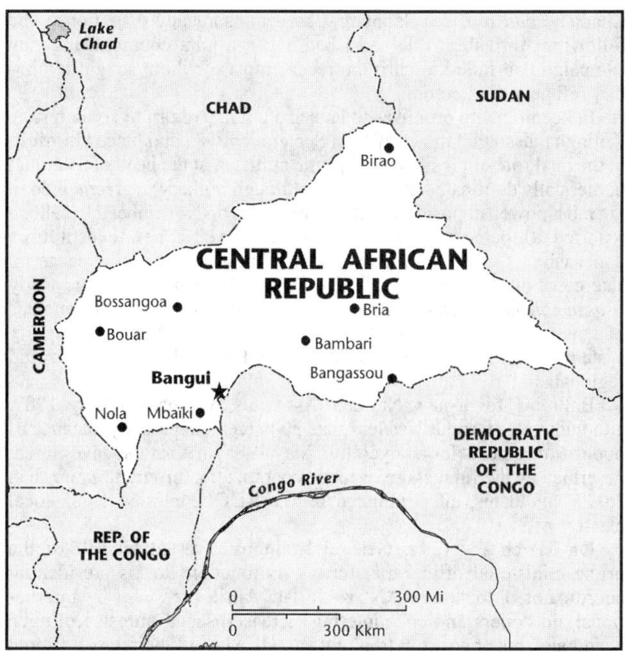

THE COUNTRY

The Central African Republic (CAR) is a landlocked, well-watered plateau country in the heart of Africa. Its inhabitants are of varied ethnic, linguistic, and religious affiliations. In addition to French and many tribal dialects, Sango is used as a lingua franca. A majority of the population is Christian, and there also are sizable animist and Muslim sectors.

About four-fifths of the inhabitants are employed in farming and animal husbandry, primarily at a subsistence level. Leading exports include diamonds, coffee, timber, and cotton. Most of the small industrial sector is engaged in food processing, while uranium resources have been developed with French and Swiss partners. Economic diversification, long impeded by a lack of adequate transportation facilities, was further constrained by the personal aggrandizement in 1976–1979 of self-styled Emperor Bokassa, a virtually empty national treasury at the time of his ouster in September 1979 only partially mitigated by marginal increases in commodity exports in ensuing years. France is the country's main source of imports, chief market for exports, and principal aid donor.

In the mid-1990s political turmoil significantly diverted attention from economic development; however, following the restoration of stability in the CAR, the republic recorded average annual GDP growth of 3.9 percent from the late 1990s to 2000.

By 2006 GDP growth had increased to 4.1 percent, the highest in a decade, and at year's end the republic qualified for $54.5 million in aid over three years under the IMF's poverty reduction program. In addition, the World Bank approved $6.8 million to help the government provide such basic services as water, health care, and education. Growth contracted to 1.7 percent in 2009, due in large part to the global economic crisis, but recovery in the agriculture sector helped boost GDP to 3.5 percent in 2010.

In 2011, real GDP growth averaged 3.2 percent, mostly due to a rebound in agricultural production, which helped to bring down inflation to less than 1 percent by the end of 2011. On June 25, 2012, the IMF approved a three-year credit facility for $63.2 million to support the CAR's economy. In 2012, GDP grew by 4.1 percent, while inflation was 5.2 percent and GDP per capita was $447. In 2013, the World Bank ranked the CAR last, 185th out of 185 countries, in ease of conducting business. Fighting in 2012 and 2013 severely constrained the economy and damaged the already fragile infrastructure (see Current issues, below). In July 2013, the United Kingdom pledged $7.6 million in humanitarian assistance to the CAR.

GOVERNMENT AND POLITICS

Political background. Formerly known as Ubangi-Shari in French Equatorial Africa, the Central African Republic achieved independence on August 13, 1960, after two years of self-government under Barthélemy BOGANDA, founder of the Social Evolution Movement of Black Africa (*Mouvement de l'Évolution Sociale de l'Afrique Noir*—MESAN), and his nephew David DACKO, the republic's first president. As leader of MESAN, President Dacko rapidly established a political monopoly, dissolving the principal opposition party in December 1960 and banning all others in 1962. Dacko was ousted on January 1, 1966, in a military coup led by Col. Jean-Bédel BOKASSA, who declared himself president. Bokassa abrogated the constitution, dissolved the assembly, assumed power to rule by decree, took over the leadership of MESAN, and became chief of staff and commander in chief of the armed forces.

Following his assumption of power, Bokassa survived a number of coup attempts, often relying on French military intervention. Designated president for life by MESAN in 1972, he assumed the additional office of prime minister in April 1976 but relinquished it to Ange-Félix PATASSÉ the following September, when a new Council of the Central African Revolution (*Conseil de la Révolution Centrafricaine*—CRC) was established. In the context of widespread government and party changes, Bokassa further enhanced his image as one of Africa's most unpredictable leaders by appointing former president Dacko to be his personal adviser.

On December 4 he announced that the republic had been replaced by a parliamentary monarchy and that he had assumed the title of Emperor Bokassa I. In the wake of a lavish coronation ceremony in Bangui on December 4, 1977, the Bokassa regime became increasingly brutal and corrupt. In mid-1979 Amnesty International reported that scores of schoolchildren had been tortured and killed after protesting against compulsory school uniforms manufactured by the Bokassa family. In August an African judicial commission confirmed the report, the emperor responding with a series of arrests and executions of those who had testified before the commission.

On the night of September 20–21, 1979, while on a visit to Libya, the emperor was deposed, with French military assistance, by former president Dacko. While several prominent members of the Bokassa regime were arrested, the "government of national safety" that was announced on September 24 drew widespread criticism for including a number of individuals who had held high-ranking posts in the previous administration. (Bokassa lived in exile until he returned in 1987 to face trial on charges of murder, torture, and cannibalism. Following conviction on the murder charge he was imprisoned until his sentence was commuted in 1993. Prolonged ill health precluded any subsequent extensive political activity on his part, and Bokassa died in November 1996.)

In a presidential election on March 15, 1981, Dacko was credited with 50.23 percent of the votes cast, as contrasted with 38.11 percent for his closest competitor, former prime minister Patassé. Alleged balloting irregularities triggered widespread violence in the capital prior to Dacko's inauguration and the naming of Simon Narcisse BOZANGA as prime minister on April 4. In mid-July opposition parties were temporarily banned after a bomb explosion at a Bangui theater, and on July 21 the army, led by Gen. André-Dieudonné KOLINGBA, was asked to restore order. On September 1, it was announced that Dacko, known to be in failing health, had resigned in favor of a Military Committee for National Recovery (*Comité Militaire pour le Redressement National*—CMRN), headed by General Kolingba, which suspended the constitution, proscribed political party activity, and issued a stern injunction against public disorder.

Patassé and a number of senior army officers were charged with an attempted coup against the Kolingba regime on March 3, 1982, after which the former prime minister took refuge in the French Embassy in Bangui. He was flown out of the country a month later.

Internal security merged with regional concerns in late 1984 after an opposition group led by Alphonse MBAIKOUA, who had reportedly been involved in the alleged 1982 coup attempt, joined with

Chadian *codo* rebels in launching border insurgency operations. The following April the CAR and Chad began a joint counterinsurgency campaign that failed to curb the rebels, most of whom sought temporary refuge in Cameroon.

In keeping with promises to launch a gradual return to civilian rule, Kolingba dissolved the CMRN in September 1985 and placed himself, in the dual role of president and prime minister, at the head of a cabinet numerically dominated by civilians, although military men remained in the most powerful positions. At a referendum on November 21, 1986, a reported 91 percent of the electorate approved a new constitution, under which General Kolingba continued in office for a six-year term. The constitution also designated a Central African Democratic Rally (*Rassemblement Démocratique Centrafricain*—RDC) as the nucleus of a one-party state, General Kolingba having asserted that a multiparty system would invite "division and hatred as well as tribalism and regionalism."

Balloting for a new National Assembly was held in July 1987, although voter turnout was less than 50 percent, apparently because of opposition appeals for a boycott. In May 1988, in what the government described as the final stage of its democratization program, more than 3,000 candidates, all nominated by the RDC, contested 1,085 local elective offices.

On March 15, 1991, General Kolingba divested himself of the prime ministerial office, transferring its functions to his presidential coordinator, Edouard FRANCK. In late April, pressured by international aid donors and encountering increased social unrest, Kolingba abandoned his opposition to pluralism. On May 18 the regime offered to accelerate political reform in exchange for an end to civil strife, and on June 7 a national commission was established to revise the constitution and prepare for the introduction of multipartyism. In July the government announced that political parties were free to apply for legal status. Subsequently, a broad-based committee was named to prepare for the convening of a national conference on February 19, 1992.

Because of its lack of plenary power, the conference that convened on August 1, 1992, was boycotted by most opposition groups and was accompanied by street demonstrations and antigovernment strikes.

On February 26, 1993, following what observers described as three months of political paralysis in Bangui, Kolingba dismissed prime minister Timothée MALENDOMA of the Civic Forum (*Forum Civique*—FC), whom he had appointed in December, and his transitional government for "blocking the democratic process" and named Enoch Dérant LAKOUÉ, leader of the Social Democratic Party (*Parti Social-Démocrate*—PSD), as the new prime minister. In late April the president overrode an electoral commission recommendation and further postponed elections until October, prompting an outcry by Dr. Abel GOUMBA of the Guéne of the Concertation of Democratic Forces (*Concertation des Forces Démocratiques*—CFD), who accused Kolingba and Lakoué of conspiring to use the delay to revive their flagging presidential campaigns.

On June 11, 1993, Prime Minister Lakoué announced that elections would be brought forward to August. The policy reversal came only six days after the French minister of cooperation, Michel Roussin, reportedly told Kolingba that continued aid was directly linked to the speed of reform. At the August 22 poll eight candidates, including Africa's first female contender, Ruth ROLLAND, vied for the presidency, while 496 candidates contested 85 legislative seats. Although the election was conducted in the presence of international observers, Kolingba, faced with unofficial tallies showing that he had finished in fourth place, attempted to halt release of the official results; however, he was obliged to reverse himself upon domestic and international condemnation of what Goumba described as the "last convulsion of his regime."

In second-round presidential balloting on September 19, first-round plurality winner Patassé defeated Goumba 53.49 to 46.51 percent. In concurrent rounds of legislative balloting, Patassé's Central African People's Liberation Movement (*Mouvement de Libération du Peuple Centrafricaine*—MLPC) won 34 seats, followed by the CFD, whose members collectively won 17. Meanwhile, on September 1 Kolingba had released thousands of convicted criminals, the most prominent of whom was former emperor Bokassa.

On October 25, 1993, Patassé named an MLPC colleague, Jean-Luc MANDABA, as prime minister. Five days later Mandaba announced the formation of a coalition government that drew from the MLPC, the Liberal Democratic Party (*Parti Liberal-Démocratic*—PLD), the CFD-affiliated Alliance for Democracy and Progress (*Alliance pour la Démocratic et le Progrès*—ADP), supporters of former president Dacko, and members of the outgoing Kolingba administration.

Prime Minister Mandaba was forced to resign on April 11, 1995, upon the filing of a nonconfidence motion signed by a majority of National Assembly members, who charged him with corruption, mal-administration, and a lack of communication between the executive and legislative branches. President Patassé promptly named as his successor Gabriel KOYAMBOUNOU, a senior civil servant who announced that combating financial irregularities would be one of his principal objectives.

In early April 1996 a newly formed opposition umbrella group, the Democratic Council of the Opposition Parties (*Conseil Démocratique des Partis de l'Opposition*—CODEPO), organized an anti-Patassé rally in Bangui. An even more serious challenge developed on April 18 when several hundred soldiers, angered over payment arrears, left their barracks in the Kasai suburb of Bangui and took control of important locations in the capital. The rebels went back to their barracks several days later, after French troops were deployed in support of the government, but they returned to the streets on May 18. The rebellion finally ended on May 26 after French forces, supported by helicopter gunships, engaged the mutinous soldiers in fierce street battles. Patassé, describing the nation as "shattered" by the near civil war, replaced Koyambounu on June 6 with Jean-Paul NGOUPANDÉ, a former ambassador to France. Thereafter, in a further attempt to stabilize the political situation, Patassé's MLPC and the major opposition parties signed a pact under which, among other things, the authority of the prime minister was to be extended so as to dilute presidential control. Moreover, on June 19 Ngoupande announced the formation of what was optimistically described as a "government of national unity."

On November 16, 1996, another mutiny erupted in Kasai (see an earlier *Handbook* for more details). On January 25, 1997, in Bangui, Patassé and the leader of the mutineers signed a peace accord that had been brokered by a group comprising representatives of Burkina Faso, Chad, Gabon, and Mali. The agreement included provisions for a general amnesty for the mutinous soldiers, the reintegration of the rebels into their old units, and the deployment of a regional peacekeeping force styled the Inter-African Mission to Monitor the Bangui Accords (*Mission Internationale du Suivi des Accords de Bangui*—MISAB). On January 30 Patassé appointed Foreign Minister Michel GBEZERA-BRIA to replace Prime Minister Ngoupandé, and on February 18 a new 28-member cabinet, the Government of Action for the Defense of Democracy (*Gouvernement pour l'Action et la Défense de la Démocratie*—GADD), was installed. Although the MLPC retained all the key posts, the GADD included representatives from ten parties, including nine members from four "opposition" groups. On March 15 the National Assembly voted to extend amnesty to those remaining rebels who agreed to be disarmed by the peacekeepers within 15 days; however, clashes broke out later in the month when a number of the rebels resisted the peacekeeping forces.

On May 5, 1997, the nine opposition cabinet ministers announced the "suspension" of their postings and called for nationwide strikes to protest the deaths two days earlier of three alleged mutinous soldiers being held in police custody. Amid mounting tension, on May 20 the rebels' two cabinet representatives (they had been appointed in April as part of the Bangui agreement) also quit the government. Subsequently, more than 100 people, primarily civilians, were killed in Bangui and the Kasai camp during clashes between rebel and government troops, the latter again supported by French troops, before another cease-fire was signed on July 2.

MISAB, which had the endorsement of the UN Security Council, began disarming the army mutineers in mid-July, and in late August the government released the last of more than 110 detainees connected to the "revolt." Consequently, the nine cabinet members who had walked out in May formally rejoined the government of September 1. Tension continued at a somewhat reduced level into 1998, prompting the convening of a national conference in late February. On March 3 the conference's participants, including the opposition parties coalesced under the banner of the influential Group of 11 (G-11), signed a reconciliation pact aimed at improving interparty relations and reducing the lawlessness gripping the country.

A new UN peacekeeping force took over MISAB and French responsibilities on April 15, 1998, with a mandate that included assisting in preparations for legislative elections.

Approximately 30 parties forwarded candidates for the 109 seats (enlarged from 85) available at first-round legislative balloting on November 22, 1998, the MLPC emerging with a small lead after that round. However, opposition groups signed an electoral pact under the banner of the Union of Forces Supporting Peace and Change (*Union des Forces Acquises à la Paix et au Changement*—UFAPC), whereby they agreed to back the leading opposition candidates in the undecided contests. As a result, following second-round balloting on December 13, the UFAPC-affiliated parties controlled 55 seats (led by the RDC with 20) and the MLPC 47. However, the small PLD (2 seats) and five independents subsequently confirmed their allegiance to the MLPC, and Patassé supporters were ultimately able to gain legislative control when, under highly controversial circumstances, a legislator-elect from the PSD defected to the MLPC. Most opposition legislators boycotted the convening of the new assembly in early January 1999, and ten opposition cabinet members resigned from the government in protest against the MLPC's actions. On January 4 Patassé named Finance and Budget Minister Anicet Georges DOLOGUÉLÉ to replace Gbezera-Bria as prime minister. However, the UFAPC rejected Patassé's authority in the matter, arguing that it should have control over the appointment as holder of the true legislative majority.

On January 15, 1999, Prime Minister Dologuélé announced a new cabinet comprising eight ministers from the MLPC, four from the PLD, four from the opposition Movement for Democracy and Development (*Mouvement pour la Démocratic et la Développement*—MDD), one from the MLPC-allied National Convention (*Convention National*—CN), and eight independents. However, three of the MDD members resigned several days later, party leaders reiterating their support for the UFAPC.

The opposition ended its assembly boycott in early March 1999, apparently in part due to the government's agreement to let UFAPC members sit on a new election commission charged with overseeing the upcoming presidential poll. On September 19, Patassé secured another six-year term by winning 51.6 percent of the vote in the first-round balloting, defeating nine other candidates, including Kolingba, Dacko, and Goumba. Dologuélé was subsequently reappointed to head another MLPC-led government, the UFAPC having declined overtures to join the cabinet. In January 2000 the administration issued several decrees designed to restructure the armed forces so as to reduce the likelihood of a repeat of the 1996–1997 mutinies. Subsequently, the UN peacekeepers formally withdrew on February 15, while Paris announced an increase in aid to Bangui for military training. The Patassé/Dologuélé administration announced that its new top priority was to attract international economic assistance. However, the image-building campaign stalled in April when a series of scandals involving alleged money-laundering and other corrupt practices precipitated a cabinet reshuffle amid opposition complaints that economic reforms contained in the 1997 peace accord were being ignored.

Because of increasing economic difficulties, the government was unable to pay the salaries of state employees and military personnel for most of 2000. The government's handling of the situation cost Dologuélé his post, as he was replaced by the president in April 2001 by the MLPC's Martin ZIGUÉLÉ. On April 6 Ziguélé announced a new cabinet that included the MLPC, the PLD, the CN, the African Development Party (*Parti Africain du Développement*—PAD), the Democratic Union for Renewal/Fini Kodro (*Union Démocratique pour le Renouveau/Fini Kodro*—UDR/FK), one independent, and others.

In May 2001 the government managed to suppress a coup attempt reportedly masterminded by the former president and de facto leader of the RDC, André-Dieudonné Kolingba, who nevertheless remained at large. (It was subsequently reported that Kolingba had traveled to Uganda and then, in September 2002, to France. By that time he had been sentenced in absentia to death for his role in the coup attempt. Sentences in absentia also were handed down against more than 500 other participants.) Human rights activists voiced concern over the alleged acts of retaliation against Kolingba's Yakoma ethnic group. Reportedly, more than 200 people were killed and 50,000 displaced in the fighting following the coup attempt. Some cabinet members, as well as Gen. François BOZIZÉ, the chief of staff and close associate of Patassé, were also implicated in the conspiracy. Following a reshuffle in August that replaced those ministers allegedly supportive of the coup, Patassé dismissed Bozizé in late October. Government troops subsequently fought Bozizé loyalists who offered armed resistance to an effort to arrest the general. After Bozizé fled to Chad in November, the situation got increasingly "internationalized" (see Foreign relations, below), as many neighboring countries worked to arrange negotiations among Patassé, Kolingba, and Bozizé. The Central African Republic's courts dropped legal proceedings against Bozizé in December. However, sporadic skirmishes broke out along the Chadian border in the first half of 2002, the CAR government accusing Chad of supporting rebellious CAR soldiers. The Organization of African Unity (OAU, subsequently the African Union—AU), called upon the UN to send peacekeepers to the CAR, but no such action ensued. Among other things, Western capitals objected to the continued presence in the CAR of Libyan troops and tanks, which had rushed to Patassé's aid in May 2001. For his part, Bozizé in September 2002 announced his intentions of ousting Patassé by force.

In October 2002 government forces supported by Libyan troops turned back pro-Bozizé rebels who were advancing on Bangui. However, after the Libyan troops withdrew in January 2003 in favor of a 350-member peacekeeping force from the Central African Economic and Monetary Community (*Communauté Économique et Monétaire de l'Afrique Centrale*—CEMAC), Bozizé's forces entered Bangui on March 15 while Patassé was out of the country on a diplomatic mission. The following day Bozizé declared himself president, suspended the constitution, and disbanded the National Assembly. On March 23 Bozizé appointed what was termed a government of national unity (comprising five major parties) under the leadership of Abel Goumba of the Patriotic Front for Progress. At the end of May, Bozizé established a 98-member National Transitional Council (*Conseil National de Transition*—CNT) to oversee the planned return to civilian government under a revised constitution within 18—30 months. Goumba was dismissed in favor of Célestin-Leroy GAOMBALET on December 12.

The revised constitution was approved by a reported 90.4 percent of voters in a national referendum on December 5, 2004. In accordance with the provisions of the new constitution, the first parliamentary and presidential elections were held in two rounds of balloting on March 13 and May 8, 2005. Bozizé lacked a majority with 43 percent of the vote in the first round, with MLPC leader Ziguélé receiving 24 percent, and the RDC-backed Kolingba, 16 percent. In the two-way runoff, Bozizé, with the support of some of the other presidential candidates who had received only a small percentage of votes, defeated Ziguélé with 64.6 percent of the vote. Ziguélé called for the election to be invalidated, claiming soldiers intimidated voters, but the constitutional court dismissed the allegations as unfounded. Meanwhile, a coalition of business groups and small political parties that had formed under the name National Convergence (*Kwa na Kwa*—KNK) to support Bozizé won 42 legislative seats, while the former ruling party (the MLPC) won only 11 seats, and independents won 34.

A new government, composed largely of members of the KNK, was sworn in on June 19. The cabinet reshuffle on January 31, 2006, included a number of other groups in addition to the dominant KNK. The cabinet was reshuffled again on September 2.

On January 18, 2008, Prime Minister Elie Doté and his government resigned as parliament was considering a no-confidence vote against Doté in the wake of a weeks-long civil service strike. On January 22 the president appointed Faustin-Archange TOUADERA, a math professor, as prime minister. Touadera named a new cabinet on January 28 that included five women and President Bozizé as defense minister.

Following national reconciliation talks that began in early 2008, parliament in October approved an amnesty, paving the way for a final round of peace talks. The talks culminated in a peace accord negotiated December 8–20, 2008, among the government, former president Patassé, political parties, rebel and opposition groups, and civil societies. Subsequently, President Bozizé dissolved the Touadera government on January 18, 2009, and the following day he reappointed the prime minister and named a new "consensus" government that included one representative from each of the two main rebel groups—the Popular Army for the Restoration of the Republic and Democracy (*Armée Populaire pour la Restauration de la Republique et la Démocratie*—APRD) and the Union of Democratic Forces for the Rally (*Union des Forces Démocratique pour le Rassemblement*—UFDR)—and at least five political parties.

Meanwhile, in early 2009 the Democratic Front for the Central African People (*Front Démocratique du Peuple Centraficaines*—FDPC), claimed that the government had failed to adhere to the terms of the December accord. Clashes between new rebel groups and government forces intensified from January to March. Further, an association of army officers in March called for Bozizé's ouster. The new government, for its part, followed through with its efforts toward peace and stability as outlined in the accord by establishing a committee to oversee disarmament, demobilization, and reintegration (DDR). Meanwhile, the UN approved deployment of 5,000 peacekeepers to replace EU troops in the northern CAR–Chad border area. By midyear the UN and the AU became increasingly concerned about the growing violence in the north, where at least 3 government soldiers and 15 rebels were killed in attacks by the rebel group Convention of Patriots for Peace and Justice (*Convention des Parties pour la Paix et de la Justice*—CPJP), led by Charles MASSI.

In October 2009, the government granted Patassé amnesty after six years in exile, and the former leader announced he would seek the presidency in the next election. Meanwhile, he was expelled by the MLPC, whose leader Martin Ziguélé (who was married to Patassé's niece) was tapped as its presidential candidate. Violence resumed in December, and UN peacekeepers increased their presence in the northeast.

Two ministers were replaced on April 20, 2010, resulting in the National Party for a New Central Africa (*Partie Nationale pour la Nouvelle Afrique Centrale*—PNCN) losing its representation in government. The president accused the PNCN minister of embezzling money earmarked for the disarmament campaign. In May the parliament passed legislation extending the president's term beyond its expiry on June 11, 2010, until the next election (for more information on the extension, please see the 2013 *Handbook*).

Following several delays, presidential and parliamentary elections were held on January 23, 2011, President Bozizé easily won reelection with 64.4 percent of the vote, thus avoiding a runoff. Patassé came in a distant second with 21.4 percent of the vote, followed by the MLPC's Ziguélé, the RDC's Emile Gros Raymond NAKOMBO, and the NAP's Jean-Jacques DEMAFOUTH, each with less than 7 percent of the vote. The results were immediately disputed by all challengers except Patassé (who died in April) on grounds of fraud and irregularities. The dispute spilled over into the concurrent first round of National Assembly elections, in which the KNK won 26 seats. The opposition boycotted second-round voting on March 27, when 68 seats were to be decided. New votes were also scheduled for two constituencies on that date. The KNK and the presidential majority grouping won an overwhelming majority of assembly seats. Fourteen seats were invalidated, for which no reason was given. On April 18, the president reappointed Prime Minister Touadera, who named a new government dominated by the KNK on April 22. Some former opposition members were included in the cabinet, though senior posts were assigned to presidential allies. The president's son, Col. Jean-Francis Bozizé, was given the defense portfolio. Following the disputed presidential election, an opposition coalition formed a grouping styled as the Front for Annulment and the Rerun of the Elections (FARE 2011), seeking the dissolution of the electoral commission.

In September 2012, opposition militias united in a new coalition, the Alliance (*Séléka*). *Séléka* included, among other groups, the UFDR, FDPC, and the Convention of Patriots for Peace and Justice (*Convention des Parties pour la Paix et de la Justice*—CPJP). *Séléka* advanced rapidly to the outskirts of Bangui in December, prompting Bozizé to agree to unity government, under a new prime minister, following negotiations in January 2013 in Libreville, Gabon (see Current issues, below). On January 17, political independent Nicolas Tiangaye was appointed prime minister, and he formed a cabinet that included members of the opposition and militia groups on February 4. However, *Séléka* accused Bozizé of not following through on the conditions of the peace accord, and renewed fighting forced the president from office on March 24 (he subsequently went into exile). *Séléka* leader Michel DJOTODIA was installed as president, although Tiangaye was reappointed prime minister (see Current issues, below). The constitution and legislature were suspended and a new CNT selected. The cabinet was reshuffled on June 13.

Constitution and government. The imperial constitution of December 1976 was abrogated upon Bokassa's ouster, the country reverting to republican status. A successor constitution, approved by referendum on February 1, 1981, provided for a multiparty system and a directly elected president with authority to nominate the prime minister and cabinet. The new basic law was itself suspended on September 1, 1981, both executive and legislative functions being assumed by a Military Committee for National Recovery, which was dissolved on September 21, 1985. The constitution approved in November 1986 was a revised version of the 1981 document, one of the most important modifications being confirmation of the RDC as the country's sole political party. The 1986 basic law also provided for a congress consisting of an elected National Assembly and a nominated Economic and Regional Council.

In June 1991 General Kolingba appointed a national commission to draft constitutional amendments providing for political pluralism, and in July the government announced that parties could apply for legal status. Other amendments approved at the "grand national debate" of August 1992 included creation of a semipresidential regime with executive authority vested in a prime minister and stricter separation of executive, legislative, and judicial powers. The basic law that was ratified in a referendum in December 1994 retained those provisions while expanding the permissible mandate of the head of state to two six-year terms and specifying that the prime minister will implement policies proposed by the president, who is to "embody and symbolize national unity." In addition, the new charter (formally adopted on January 14, 1995) expanded the judicial system by adding a Constitutional Court to the existing Supreme Court and High Court of Justice and provided for an eventual substantial devolution of state power to directly elected regional assemblies.

The constitution was suspended following the coup of March 2003, although the 1995 basic law served as a model in many areas for the new constitution that was approved by national referendum on December 5, 2004, and entered into effect on December 27. The new constitution reduced the presidential term from six to five years (renewable once), while the prime minister (to be appointed by a majority within the new 105-member National Assembly) was given expanded powers.

In May 2010 the National Assembly adopted legislation that extended the president's mandate beyond its June 11, 2010, expiration, allowing him to remain in office until the next election in 2011.

The constitution was suspended on March 25, 2013, and a transitional government and legislature appointed (see Legislature, below).

Foreign relations. As a member of the French Community, the country has retained close ties with France throughout its changes of name and regime. A defense pact between the two states permits French intervention in times of "invasion" or outbreaks of "anarchy," and French troops, in the context of what was termed "Operation Barracuda," were prominently involved in the ouster of Bokassa. By contrast, in what appeared to be a deliberate policy shift by the Mitterrand government, some 1,100 French troops remained in their barracks during General Kolingba's assumption of power and, despite debate over alleged French involvement in the Patassé coup attempt, the French head of state declared his support for the regime in October 1982. French troops remained permanently stationed at the Bouar military base and were instrumental in propping up the Patassé administration during the army revolt of April–May 1996.

The civil war in neighboring Chad long preoccupied the CAR leadership, partly because of the influx of refugees into the country's northern region. In addition, trepidation about foreign intrusion not only from Chad but also from throughout Central Africa prompted the CAR in 1980 to sever diplomatic ties with Libya and the Soviet Union, both of which had been accused of fomenting internal unrest. Relations with the former, although subsequently restored, remained tenuous, with two Libyan diplomats declared *persona non grata* in April 1986. Formal ties were reestablished with the Soviet Union in 1988 and with Israel in January 1989. In July 1991 China severed diplomatic relations with the CAR after the Kolingba regime reestablished links with Taiwan.

In the run-up to the August 1993 balloting, Abel Goumba emerged as France's "consensus candidate" while his primary competitor, Ange-Felix Patassé, was reportedly viewed with trepidation by Paris because of commercial links to Washington and other Western capitals. On August 28 Paris condemned Kolingba's efforts to stall the release of election results, suspended all aid payments, and stated that French troops and materials were no longer at the president's disposal.

Tension with the CAR's "new" neighbor, the Democratic Republic of the Congo (DRC), developed in 1997, and in February 1998 fighting was reported along their shared border. However, in May the two signed a defense pact, and thereafter CAR troops were reported to be assisting the forces of DRC President Kabila. The CAR was subsequently described as trying to maintain a neutral position in regard to the intertwined conflicts that produced what one reporter called a "ring of fire" in the region into mid-2000.

Relations between the CAR and the DRC soured, with the increasingly close ties between President Patassé and the DRC rebels, most prominently the forces loyal to Jean-Pierre Bemba (see entry on the DRC). Patassé employed Bemba's troops and Libyan military detachments to suppress the coup attempt in May 2001. The CAR's relations with Chad also became strained in late 2001 after Gen. François Bozizé, who was accused by Patassé of having been involved with the coup attempt, fled to Chad in November. In December Patassé and Chadian president Idriss Déby met in Libreville, Gabon, for talks under the auspices of CEMAC, which deployed an ultimately ineffective peacekeeping force to the CAR after Bozizé's successful coup in 2003. In the years following the coup, the peacekeeping forces spread out beyond the capital to the troubled northern and eastern regions as violence increased. In early 2006, CAR leaders met with the leaders of six other African countries in their continuing efforts to defuse the escalating tensions at the border of Chad and Sudan. For its part, the CAR extended its relations with Sudan by signing an agreement with the latter and the United Nations High Commissioner for Refugees (UNHCR) providing for the return of the first group of 10,000 Sudanese refugees who had lived in the CAR for 16 years. Tensions reignited in 2006 when the CAR dismissed its ambassador in Sudan over alleged ongoing contact with Patassé, and government officials accused Patassé loyalists of training rebels in Sudan. (For more developments in the region, see Current issues, below.)

In 2007 the government signed economic cooperation agreements with Egypt and China to assist in developing the republic's oil and mineral resources.

Adding to the CAR's cross-border conflicts, in 2008 the Lord's Resistance Army (LRA), a Ugandan rebel group, targeted villages in southeast CAR, abducting civilians and looting. In response to the attacks, the government sent troops to its border with the Republic of the Congo in January 2009. The abduction of two French aid workers near the border with Sudan in November increased security concerns, coming in the wake of the killing of 12 government soldiers in September in the northern region.

In March 2010 the LRA was reported as having begun operations in the CAR after having been driven out of Uganda and southern Sudan and then into the neighboring Democratic Republic of the Congo. Following more killings in June, the UN reported a dramatic rise in both the frequency and the brutality of the LRA's attacks against civilians. The attacks escalated throughout 2010, the CAR army blaming dissidents from the Movement of Central Africa Liberators for Justice (*Mouvement des Libérateurs de l'Afrique Centrale pour la Justice*—MLCJ) (see Rebel Groups under Political Parties and Groups, below). In October several countries in the region pledged to form a military force to combat the rebels, who were reported to have also staged attacks in the south. In November 2010 the CAR and the UNHCR began relocating another 3,500 Sudanese refugees from northeast CAR to a safer position farther south.

Following the outbreak of fighting between *Séléka* and government forces, in November 2012, Bozizé appealed for military assistance from regional allies. Chad deployed 2,000 troops, and South Africa, 200, in addition to the existing 500-member Economic Community of Central African States (*Communauté Economique des Etats d'Afrique Centrale*—CEEAC) peacekeeping force, *Mission de Consolidation de la Paix en République Centralafricaine*—Micropax). France dispatched additional soldiers, raising its garrison to about 600, but Paris pledged the soldiers were there only to protect French citizens and interests. Meanwhile, reports indicated that *Séléka* received support, including men and material, from Sudan and factions in Chad. As the rebels advanced on Bangui in December, the United States and other Western governments evacuated their citizens and closed their embassies.

On January 2, 2013, *Séléka* agreed to negotiations hosted by the CEEAC in Libreville, Gabon. The result was the Libreville Accords called for an immediate ceasefire and a transitional government (see Current issues, below). *Séléka* launched a new offensive in March and captured the capital on March 24. Twelve South African soldiers were killed in the fighting, and 26 were injured. Bozizé fled to the Democratic Republic of the Congo, then Cameroon, before finally being given asylum in Benin. The UN and the AU condemned the overthrow, and the CAR was suspended from both the AU and the *Organisation Internationale de la Francophonie* (OIF).

By April 2013, most foreign troops had withdrawn from the CAR, although South African President Jacob Zuma called for the deployment of an international peacekeeping force at a CEEAC meeting on April 4. In May, there were reports that Sudanese allies of *Séléka* had raided villages in the northern areas of the CAR.

Current issues. With donors reportedly concerned about Bozizé's consolidation of power, including draft changes to the constitution that would allow him to remain in office, the president took steps to reassure international supporters in 2011. In June Bozizé revived the DDR program, under pressure from Chad's President Idriss Déby Itno. But in December the process was halted for lack of funding. On August 2, police arrested a French citizen working for the local telecom company as part of an ongoing investigation into corruption allegations involving former ministers Fidèle NGOUANDJIKA and Thierry Savanarole MALÉYOMBO. On direct orders from Bozizé, police also raided Maléyombo's home.

Throughout much of 2012, the security situation outside the capital continued to deteriorate. The government launched an offensive against Baba LADDÉ's (aka Omar Abdul Kader) Patriotic Front for Unity (FPR). But many fighters escaped and were roaming the countryside as highway bandits while their leader called for new negotiations. The leader of the APRD, Jean-Jacques Demafouth MAFOUTAPA, was arrested in January and then released in April. The next month he announced that the APRD had been dissolved, which analysts considered unlikely, and the government announced it was resuming the stalled DDR program for the group. On May 12, Ugandan troops, part of an AU force deployed in March to hunt down Joseph KONY, ambushed and captured a senior LRA commander in the country.

In June 2012, Bozizé fired his nephew, finance minister Sylvain NDOUTINGAÏ. Once a key member of the president's inner circle, Ndoutingaï gave Bozizé plenty of reasons to dismiss him: In addition to not inspiring trust with IMF, World Bank, and U.S. officials, Ndoutingaï had reportedly been discouraging KNK legislators from endorsing a constitutional change that would allow Bozizé a third term; he was also said to be storing weapons in his home and meeting in secret with military leaders. Amid rumors of a possible coup, Bozizé began a purge of his nephew's supporters in the security services.

Following Ndoutingaï's dismissal, the IMF announced a three-year, $62 million arrangement with the CAR. Some analysts said the ensuing political crisis pushed Bozizé to rely more on his extended family network, despite questions about their competence to tackle challenges like implementing the IMF program, which would require budgetary discipline.

In a visit to the capital, President Déby of Chad brought 30 Chadian soldiers to bolster Bozizé's bodyguard. In a sign of his influence over Bozizé, Déby pressured him to negotiate with the armed groups in the country's north and went so far as to meet with the opposition and call for the formation of a national unity government. In late June it was announced that Chad would train the CAR's Army.

In late August the CPJP, the largest rebel group still active in the country, signed onto the global peace agreement the government had reached with other major rebel groups in 2008. In late August, Baba Laddé turned himself in to authorities in the capital, along with a reported 100 FPR fighters. Meanwhile, the government began the reparation of some 3,000 Chadian FPR fighters.

After its formation in September 2012, the *Séléka* quickly captured a series of towns and advanced on Bangui, prompting Bozizé to agree to CEEAC-sponsored peace talks in Libreville, Gabon. The resultant Libreville agreement called for the president to appoint a new prime minister, chosen by the opposition, and install a government of national unity. New parliamentary elections were to be held within a year. In addition, Bozizé agreed to not seek reelection in 2016.

Touadera was dismissed as prime minister on January 12, 2013, and replaced by Nicolas Tiangaye, who had been president of the CNT from 2003–2005. A new government was appointed on February 4, including representatives from *Séléka*, pro-Bozizé groups, the political opposition, and civil society. However, *Séléka* asserted that the president sought to undermine the accords and withdrew its ministers from the government on March 17. Renewed fighting commenced, and *Séléka* quickly overran the capital. Widespread looting was reported after the fall of Bangui.

Séléka leader Djotodia was proclaimed president on March 24, 2013. The next day Djotodia suspended the constitution and the Assembly. Tiangaye was reappointed prime minister, along with a new unity cabinet and new transitional legislature (see Legislature, below). Djotodia was formally elected president by the CNT on April 13.

In April 2013, the Ugandan government suspended its search for Kony in the CAR as a result of the civil war. Meanwhile, the strife created an estimated 170,000 internally displaced persons within the CAR. Renewed fighting erupted in June 2013 as rebels claimed the new government failed to provide payments to reintegrate the soldiers into civil society.

POLITICAL PARTIES AND GROUPS

Following the formation of an MLPC-led "unity" government in June 1996, 11 opposition parties, most of whom were theretofore aligned under the banner of the Democratic Council of the Opposition Parties (*Conseil Démocratique des Partis de l'Opposition*—CODEPO), formed the **Group of Eleven** (G-11), under the leadership of former CODEPO president Dr. Abel GOUMBA Guéne (for more information, please see the 2013 *Handbook*). During the run-up to legislative balloting in 1998 the G-11 appeared to have been superseded by the **Union of Forces Committed to Peace and Change** (*Union des Forces Acquises Ã la Paix et au Changement*—UFAPC), which comprised a number of parties (including the RDC, PSD, FPP, MDD, FODEM, and FC), labor unions, and human rights organizations. The UFAPC, also routinely referenced as the UFAP, proved unable to coalesce behind a single candidate for the first round of presidential balloting in September 1999, although an accord was reported if a second round had been required. Despite apparent objections from some components, the UFAPC rejected overtures from President Patassé to join the new cabinet in early November, and the grouping was subsequently described as in disarray following the withdrawal of the PSD and FPP and was reduced to limited membership as of late 1999.

After General Bozizé in 2004 announced his intention to seek the presidency in 2005, a coalition called the National Convergence was formed to support his candidacy, although Bozizé ran as an independent. A coalition of groups opposed to Bozizé, styled the Union of the Active Forces of the Nation (*Union des Forces d'Active de la Nation*—UFVN), was unsuccessful in its bid to have the 2005 legislative elections declared invalid due to alleged fraud.

In September 2012, a new opposition coalition, the **Alliance** (*Séléka*), was formed, and it led the overthrow of the Bozizé regime (see below).

Unity Government and Government-Supportive Parties:

Alliance (*Séléka*). *Séléka* was formed in September 2012, as a coalition of mainly northern, anti-Bozizé militias, including the UFDR, FDPC, CPJP, along with the **Patriotic Convention for Saving the Country** (*Convention Patriotique pour le Salut du Kodro*—CPSK), formed in June 2012 and led by Mohamed-Moussa Dhaffane and the lesser-known **Alliance for Revival and Rebuilding** (A2R), comprised of disaffected military officers. Chaired by Michel Djotodia of the UFDR, *Séléka* launched an offensive against the Bozizé government and forced the president to negotiate a ceasefire in January 2013. In the subsequent unity government, Djotodia was appointed deputy prime minister and defense minister. *Séléka* resumed fighting in March and captured Bangui on March 24, ending the Bozizé regime. Djotodia was named president of a transitional government.

Leaders: Michel DJOTODIA (President of the Central African Republic and Coalition Chair), Noureddine ADAM (CPJP), Mohamed-Moussa DHAFFANE (CPSK).

Union of Democratic Forces for the Rally (*Union des Forces Démocratique pour le Rassemblement*—UFDR). The UFDR, also referenced as the Union of Democratic Forces for Unity, formed in October 2006, demanding that Bozizé step down or share power. The group, dominated by the Muslim Gula ethnic group, claimed responsibility for numerous attacks in northern regions of the Central African Republic. After numerous clashes with government forces, the UFDR agreed to reconciliation. A peace accord was signed in February 2007 by Abdoulaye Miskine, leader of the UFDR faction referenced as the FDPC (below); Andre Ringui Le Gaillard, associated with the APRD (below); and the CAR. Meanwhile, UFDR leader Michel Djotodia, who lived in exile in Benin, was arrested by Benin authorities. The CAR, in the aftermath of the February accord, asked Benin to release Djotodia and another rebel faction leader, Abacar Sabone. Meanwhile, fighting was reported in the northeast, particularly in Birao, between the UFDR and government forces in March 2007. A renewed peace accord was signed on April 13, granting amnesty to rebels and establishing a cease-fire.

Djotodia and Sabone were still imprisoned as of December 2007, and a rival, Zacharia Damane, was the titular head of the party. Damane was reported to have signed a separate peace deal with the government in April 2007 and was subsequently named a presidential adviser. Miskine reportedly refused an offer of the post of presidential adviser in August on the grounds that the government had not implemented the peace agreement. According to the *Africa Research Bulletin,* the group allegedly has bases in the Darfur region of Sudan.

In December 2008, the UFDR participated in extensive peace talks with the government and other groups and signed on to a peace accord designed to end years of guerrilla warfare. Subsequently, a member of the group was named to a ministry in the new unity government installed in January 2009. In February Djotodia and Sabone were released from prison in Benin, both men saying they wanted to return to the CAR and participate in the national reconciliation effort. Sabone, who returned to the CAR in June 2009, headed the splinter rebel group MLCJ (see Rebel Groups, below).

The UFDR was instrumental in the formation of *Séléka* in September 2012.

Leaders: Michel DJOTODIA (President of the Central African Republic), Zacharia DAMANE, Selemane ALCHIMENE, Djarnib GREBAYE.

Convention of Patriots for Peace and Justice (*Convention des Parties pour la Paix et de la Justice*—CPJP). Established in January 2009, the CPJP called for the end of the inclusive government established on January 19. Its fighters were reported to have clashed with government soldiers in northern CAR in February. CPJP founder, Charles Massi, was a former minister and former leader of FODEM, which expelled him in 2008 because of his ties to the rebel group.

In November 2009 nine rebels and two soldiers were killed when several hundred CPJP rebels attacked a military post in the northern part of the country. The CPJP, which had not signed a peace accord with the government, was reported to have led several attacks against government forces in 2009–2010. In January 2010, after Massi was widely reported to have died in prison, his family claimed he had been tortured to death by government forces, an allegation the government denied. The CPJP asked for an investigation but then withdrew the request and signed a cease-fire. CPJP joined *Séléka* in September 2012.

Leaders: Noureddine, ADAM (Chair and Minister of Public Security, Immigration, Emigration, and Public Order), Abdoulaye HISSENE, Bevarrah LALA (Spokesperson), Assan Mbringa TOGBO (Secretary General).

Democratic Front for the Central African People (*Front Démocratique du Peuple Centraficaines*—FDPC). A former faction within the UFDR, the FDPC is headed by Abdoulaye Miskine, a former Chadian and bodyguard for former President Patassé. In 2003 Miskine was charged with war crimes by the International Criminal Court, and in 2005 he joined the armed resistance against the Bozizé government. The FDPC faction split off from the UFDR in 2007 when Miskine signed a peace accord with the government. Throughout most of 2008, the FDPC balked at participating in further accords, however, and FDPC rebels were blamed in attacks that took place in November near the border with Chad. Subsequently, Miskine signed on to the inclusive peace accord that evolved from a December meeting between the government and opposition and rebel groups.

FDPC rebels again took up arms and attacked a northern town in February 2009, reports saying they were displeased with the government's efforts toward disarmament, demobilization, and reintegration. The FDPC joined Séléka in September 2012. Reports in January 2013 indicated that Miskine withdrew from *Séléka* over the group's willingness to negotiate with Bozizé. However, other factions of the FDPC continued their alliance with *Séléka.* In June 2013, reports indicated fighting between government troops and FDPC militias led by Miskine near the Cameroonian border.

Leaders: Abdoulaye MISKINE, Ringui Le GAILLARD.

National Convergence (*Kwa na Kwa*—KNK). The *Kwan a Kwa* (literally Work, Nothing But Work) is coalition of business groups and small political parties was formed in 2004 to support Gen. François Bozizé's presidential bid in 2005. The KNK also entered candidates in the 2005 legislative balloting and secured by far the most seats (42). The KNK retained positions in the new unity government named in 2009, backed Bozizé in his 2011 reelection bid, and dominated the National Assembly after controversial parliamentary polling in 2011. The KNK joined the unity government appointed in January 2013, and continued in the successive *Séléka*-led governments. However, the KNK criticized those cabinets as not being inclusive.

Leader: Jean-Eudes TÉYA.

Central African Democratic Rally (*Rassemblement Démocratique Centrafricain*—RDC). The RDC was launched in May 1986 as the country's sole legal party, General Kolingba declaring that the formation would represent "all the various tendencies of the whole nation" but would deny representation to those who "seek to impose a totalitarian doctrine." At an extraordinary party congress on August 17, 1991, one month after the official endorsement of multipartyism, President Kolingba resigned as party president, saying he wanted to operate "above politics." Kolingba nonetheless ran as the RDC's 1993 presidential candidate, failing to make the second-round ballot because of a fourth-place finish on the first.

In mid-1995 party militants organized antigovernment demonstrations to protest the imprisonment of party leader and *Le Rassemblement* editor Mathias Gonevo Reapogo, who had been convicted of publishing an "insulting" article about President Patassé. However, following the aborted army mutiny of April–May 1996, the RDC (unlike most other opposition groupings) signed the national unity agreement and was given four ministries in the government announced on June 19. The RDC cabinet members resigned in early 1999. The party remained part of the UFAPC (see above) as of late 1999. The RDC and Kolingba were reportedly involved in the failed coup attempt in May 2001. Subsequently, numerous party officials and members were arrested, although Kolingba remained at large. The RDC's activities were suspended for three months in June, with the government threatening to shut down the party permanently in late 2001. In late 2004, however, Kolingba announced his intention to return to the CAR and run for the presidency in 2005. He received 16.36 percent of the vote, while his party won 8 assembly seats. Days after the balloting, Kolingba's camp claimed that a shooting incident outside his residence between his guards and soldiers had been an assassination attempt, but the government dismissed the matter as "confusion" in communications between the two sides. Subsequently, one of Kolingba's sons was appointed to the new cabinet announced in early 2006.

In 2009 the RPC was reported to be among several parties in the grouping known as the UFVN that opposed the reappointment of Prime Minister Touadera. Meanwhile, Kolingba was named to serve on a committee, along with President Bozizé, to implement provisions of the 2008 peace accords. Kolingba died in 2010. The RDC held a cabinet position in 2009.

Emile Gros Raymond Nakombo placed a distant fourth in the 2011 presidential election with 4.6 percent of the vote, and the party secured one seat in the second round of parliamentary polling. Party member Marguérite PÉTRO-KONI-ZEZÉ was appointed social affairs minister in the new government named in April 2011. RDC member Alexandre-Ferdinand NGUENDET was elected president of the CNT in April 15, 2013.

Leaders: Emile Gros Raymond NAKOMBO (2011 presidential candidate), Louis-Pierre GAMBA (Deputy President), Honoré NZASSIWE, Mathias Gonevo REAPOGO (imprisoned), Daniel LAGANDI (Secretary General).

Popular Army for the Restoration of the Republic and Democracy (*Armée Populaire pour la Restauration de la Republique et la Démocratie*—APRD). The APRD, formed in April 2006 with reported ties to Patassé, was allegedly responsible for burning homes and seizing several northern towns in early 2007. The group, led by Jean-Jacques Demafouth, a former defense minister who lives in exile in France, claimed that little has been done on behalf of people in the northwest region; its armed members reportedly include Chadians, Nigerians, and Cameroonians. In December 2007 the APRD did not participate in preparations for a national dialogue for reconciliation among political groups that was being organized by President Bozizé. According to *Africa Research Bulletin*, the APRD had earlier in the year established ties with Lord's Resistance Army (LRA) rebels in Uganda in 2007.

However, in February 2008 the APRD agreed to participate under certain conditions, including the return of former president Patassé and other political exiles. Subsequently, Demafouth said he hoped the peace agreement he signed in May would improve the lives of the people who had suffered for so long in northwestern CAR. In August, when the group was allowed to form a political party, it established a political wing, also headed by Demafouth, called the New Alliance for Progress (*Nouvelle Alliance pour le Progrès*—NAP). In December the APRD signed on to the inclusive peace accord, and was subsequently given a cabinet post in the unity government formed in 2009. Party member François NAOYAMA, who had been appointed to the unity government, retained his ministerial post after the cabinet reshuffle in 2011. Demafouth was arrested in January 2012 on spurious charges of plotting a coup, but he was released without charge in April. The APRD was reportedly disbanded in 2012. Demafouth went into exile into Chad under threat of arrest by the post-Bozizé government in March 2013.

Leaders: Jacques DEMAFOUTH, Bedaya NDJADDER, Laurent NDIGNOUE, Henri Tchebo WAFIO.

Central African People's Liberation Movement (*Mouvement de Libération du Peuple Centrafricaine*—MLPC). The MLPC was organized in Paris in mid-1979 by Ange-Félix Patassé, who had served as prime minister from September 1976 to July 1978 and was runner-up to Dacko in the presidential balloting of March 1981. At an extraordinary congress held September 14—18, 1983, Patassé was accorded a vote of no confidence and replaced with a nine-member directorate as part of a move from "nationalism" to "democratic socialism." In July 1986 it was announced that the MLPC had joined forces with the FPP (see below) to present a united front against the Kolingba government, with subsequent news stories again referring to Patassé, then living in Togo, as the MLPC's leader. The party was granted legal status in September 1991.

In early 1993 Patassé, who had reportedly been running second when presidential balloting was suspended in October 1992, accepted an appointment to the CNPPR, despite allegations that Kolingba was using the council to co-opt the most prominent opposition figures. In March, on the other hand, the party refused to enter the Lakoué government.

Patassé was elected president of the republic in 1993, while MLPC candidates secured a plurality of 34 legislative seats. The MLPC, whose strength was concentrated in the north, advanced to 47 legislative seats in 1998. Following his appointment as prime minister in January 1999, former MLPC stalwart Anicet Georges Dologuélé reportedly asserted that he wanted to be regarded as an independent. Patassé replaced him as the prime minister on April 1, 2001, with his close associate and leading party member Martin Ziguélé, who then formed another MLPC-dominated cabinet on April 6. Following his ouster in March 2003, Patassé went into exile in Togo. The MLPC subsequently endorsed General Bozizé's schedule for a return to civilian government. After Patassé's proposed candidacy was rejected by the transitional constitutional court, Ziguélé was named as the MLPC standard bearer for the 2005 elections, but he ultimately lost to Bozizé in the second round of presidential balloting.

One member of the MLPC was appointed to the cabinet in early 2006, although Patassé clearly remained at odds with the government. In April the Bozizé administration asked the International Criminal Court at The Hague to investigate alleged war crimes on Patassé's part during the 2002–2003 turmoil. In August 2006 Patassé was tried in the CAR and found guilty of fraud in connection with misuse of public funds during his term in office. He was sentenced to 20 years' imprisonment. A month earlier Patassé had been suspended from the party and replaced as president by Ziguélé.

In 2009 the MLPC was critical of the peace process steered by President Bozizé and denounced the reappointment of Prime Minister Touadera. In December, Patassé, who had returned to the CAR two months earlier under a government amnesty, lost his bid to overtake the party leadership when a court ruling confirmed Ziguélé's place at the helm after the party had expelled Patassé. However, a wing of the party led by Luc Apollinaire Dondon was said to support Patassé.

In 2010 the party named Ziguélé as its presidential candidate; he finished a distant third in the 2011 presidential election with 6.8 percent of the vote. Former president Patassé, who ran as an independent in the 2011 presidential poll and finished second, died in April 2011 from complications of an illness. His funeral in May turned into a protest, supporters claiming that the government had not allowed him to leave the country for medical treatment.

The party won one seat in the 2011 parliamentary election. Following the appointment of Jean-Michel MANDABA as public health minister in the new government, he was expelled from the party. The MLPC joined the succession of post-Bozizé governments in 2013.

Leaders: Martin ZIGUÉLÉ (President of the Party and Former Prime Minister; 2005 and 2011 presidential candidate), Luc Apollinaire DONDON (Vice President of the Party), Gabriel Jean Edouard KOYAMBOUNOU, Francis Albert OUKANGA (Secretary General).

Other Parties That Contested Recent Elections:

National Unity Party (*Parti de l'Unité Nationale*—PUN). Led by former prime minister Jean-Paul Ngoupandé, the PUN won three seats in the late-1998 legislative balloting. Following the 1999 presidential balloting, in which Ngoupandé won 3.1 percent of the vote, a PUN member was named to the new cabinet, albeit reportedly without the endorsement of the party leadership, and was not reappointed in the new cabinet formed in April 2001. In the 2005 presidential balloting, Ngoupandé won 5.08 percent of the vote in the first round and backed Bozizé in the second round. Subsequently, he was appointed to the cabinet as one of the ministers of state, but justice minister Lea Koyassoum Doumta, the party's secretary general, was dismissed. Subsequently, Ngoupandé was replaced in a cabinet reshuffle of September 2, 2006, and the party was no longer represented in the government until the formation of a new cabinet of January 28, 2008, and the appointment of Gaston MACKOUZANGBA. He was retained in the government named in 2009 but replaced in the 2011 cabinet reorganization.

Leaders: Jean-Paul NGOUPANDÉ (Former Prime Minister and 2005 presidential candidate), Lea Koyassoum DOUMTA (Secretary General).

Alliance for Democracy and Progress (*Alliance pour la Démocratie et le Progrès*—ADP). A founding member of the CFD (see Political background, above), the ADP applied for legal status in late 1991. In October 1992 (then) party leader Jean-Claude CONJUGO was killed by government forces during a union-organized demonstration. However, the party was one of five groups represented in the government named on October 30, 1993, thereby breaking with the CFD. One of the party's leaders, Olivier Gabirault, ran for president in 2005, finishing last with less than 1 percent of the vote. The ADP was reportedly defunct by 2012.

Leaders: Jacques MBOITEDAS, Olivier GABIRAULT (2005 presidential candidate), Tchapka BREDE (National Secretary).

Patriotic Front for Progress (*Front Patriotique pour le Progrès*—FPP). Launched initially by Abel Goumba Guéne as the Congo-based Ubangi Patriotic Front—Labor Party (*Front Patriotique Oubanguien–Parti Travailliste*—FPO-PT), the FPP repudiated the Dacko government in 1981, called for the withdrawal of French troops, and forged links with the French Socialist Party and other European socialist groups. Linkage with the MLPC was announced in 1986, the two groups calling for a boycott of the 1987 legislative balloting and the creation of a multiparty system as envisioned by the 1981 constitution. Between September 1990 and March 1991 Goumba was imprisoned for his involvement with the CCCCN. Leader of the core party of the opposition's Concertation of Democratic Forces (*Concertation des Forces Démocratiques*—CFD), Goumba was reported to be outpolling his four competitors at the abortive presidential balloting of October 1992 but fell to second place in 1993 and fourth place in 1999 (with 6.6 percent of the vote).

Goumba was appointed prime minister in the transitional government named following the March 2003 coup, but he was replaced in that post in December and named "honorary vice president." After receiving less than 3 percent of the vote in the first round of the 2005 presidential balloting, Goumba claimed widespread fraud. He was subsequently dismissed as honorary vice president on March 16. The official government explanation for his removal was that the new constitution did not provide for a vice president, but observers said his refusal to join those backing Bozizé cost him the post. However, in mid-2005, Goumba was appointed as "mediator of the republic" to improve relations between citizens and the government. The party won two seats in the 2005 legislative elections. In 2006 rifts were reported, as an unspecified splinter group held a separate congress.

Abel Goumba died in May 2010 at age 83.

Leader: Patrice ENDJIMOUNGOU (Secretary General).

Social Democratic Party (*Parti Social-Démocrate*—PSD). For the October 1992 balloting the PSD offered as a presidential candidate its leader, Enoch Dérant Lakoué, who was reportedly running in last place when the poll was aborted. In February 1993 Lakoué accepted appointment as Prime Minister Malendoma's successor.

During the first half of 1993 the PSD suffered numerous defections, while Lakoué's own popularity continued to plummet. Thus, by the June 11 opening of a party congress, the PSD was, according to *Africa Confidential*, "run almost entirely by [Lakoué] family and friends."

At legislative balloting in 1998 the PSD captured six seats; however, one successful candidate, Dieudonné KOUDOUFARA, immediately defected to the MLPC, giving that party and its allies a disputed one-vote legislative majority. Two other PSD legislators reportedly followed Koudoufara's example in March 1999. Lakoué finished seventh in the 1999 presidential balloting with only 1.3 percent of the vote. The cabinet announced in November 1999 included a PSD member, but he was not reappointed in the new cabinet formed in April 2001. In 2005, the party won four seats in the assembly.

Lakoué was appointed minister of Economic Planning and Cooperation in the January 2013 unity government but lost his post in the subsequent cabinet reshuffle.

Leader: Enoch Dérant LAKOUÉ (Former Prime Minister).

Democratic Forum for Modernity (*Forum Démocratique pour la Modernité*—FODEM). FODEM was launched in the summer of 1997 by Agriculture Minister Charles Massi, who had recently been held hostage by rebellious soldiers and reportedly had been persuaded of the merits of their case. Massi was dismissed from the government in December, ostensibly because of his dealings in the diamond sector.

FODEM was officially recognized in May 1998, and in September Massi was cleared of the charges that had led to his removal from government in 1997. Massi won 1.3 percent of the vote in the 1999 presidential balloting and 3.2 percent in the 2005 presidential elections. He backed Bozizé in the 2005 runoff and was appointed a minister of state in 2006.

In May 2008 Massi was suspended from the party due to his links with the rebel group CPJP (see Rebel Groups, below).

Leader: Nicaide SALLE (Secretary General).

Other Parties:

Movement for Democracy and Development (*Mouvement pour la Démocratie et le Développement*—MDD). The MDD was launched in January 1994 by former president David Dacko. MDD members were given four posts in the Dologuélé cabinet announced on January 15, 1999. However, party leaders, denying any interest in participating in an MLPC-led government, pressured three of the appointees to quit several days later. (The fourth member, who remained in government reportedly against the wishes of the grassroots, was not reappointed in the new cabinet formed in April 2001.) Dacko, who had won 20 percent of the presidential vote in 1993, finished third with 11.2 percent in 1999, his strength being the greatest in the capital region in the south. Dacko died in 2003.

There was no reference to the MDD in the 2005 election, although leader Auguste Boukanga reportedly ran as a presidential candidate under the banner of the Union for Renewal and Development. In the new government installed in 2009, the MDD retained one cabinet position.

Leaders: Ruffin MOLONMADON, Louis PAPENIAH, Auguste BOUKANGA, Ambroise ZAWA.

National Party for a New Central Africa (*Partie Nationale pour la Nouvelle Afrique Centrale*—PNCN). Little has been reported about this hitherto unreferenced party, which was reported to have backed Gen. François Bozizé's presidential bid in 2005. Cyriaque Gonda, who was named minister of communication and national reconciliation, was deputy speaker of parliament in 2005 and was a spokesperson for President Bozizé in 2006 and 2007. Gonda was named a minister of state in the 2009 cabinet, but he was replaced in April 2010. Reports in 2012 indicated that the PNCN had joined the KNK.

Leader: Cyriaque GONDA (Chair).

Democratic Movement for the Renaissance and Evolution of Central Africa (*Mouvement Démocratique pour la Renaissance et l'Evolution en Centrafrique*—MDREC). In mid-1992, MDREC party leader Joseph Bendounga, a prodemocracy advocate, was arrested and sentenced to six months' imprisonment for criticizing the president. The group secured one legislative seat in 1993. Bendounga, the mayor of Bangui, supported incumbent President Patassé in the 1999 presidential poll. Through 2001 the MDREC remained supportive of the MLPC and Patassé. The party named Bendounga as its candidate for the 2005 presidential election, but his name did not appear in the list of results. The MDREC supported *Séléka* in the 2013 overthrow of Bozizé.

Leaders: Joseph BENDOUNGA, Léon SEBOU (Secretary General).

Social Evolution Movement of Black Africa (*Mouvement de l'Évolution Sociale de l'Afrique Noire*—MESAN). The present MESAN is a faction-torn remnant of the group founded in 1949 and once headed by former president Dacko. The party won one assembly seat in 1993 balloting, and a MESAN member was appointed minister of communication in June 1996.

In 2006 MESAN leader Dieudonne Stanislas Mbangot was among three ministers removed from the cabinet for alleged financial irregularities.

Leader: Dieudonne Stanislas MBANGOT (Chair).

Justin WILITE of the small opposition party **Congress for the African Renaissance** was rejected as a presidential candidate in the 2011 election because of lack of funds.

For more information on the **Union for Renewal and Development** (*Union pour la Renaissance et le Développement*—URD), the **Forces for the Unification of the Central African Republic** (*Forces pour l'Unification de la République Centraficaine*—FIRCA), the **Movement for Democracy, Independence, and Social Progress** (*Mouvement pour la Démocratie, l'Indépendance, et le Progrès Social*—MDI-PS), **Civic Forum** (*Forum Civique*—FC), the **Patriotic Front for the Liberation of Central Africa** (*Front Patriotique pour La Libération du Centrafrique*—FPLC), and the **Republic Convention for Social Progress** (CRPS), please see the 2013 *Handbook*.

Rebel Groups:

Movement of Central Africa Liberators for Justice (*Mouvement des Libérateurs de l'Afrique Centrale pour la Justice*—MLCJ). Once part of an alliance formed by the UFDR in 2006, the MLCJ in December 2008 signed the peace accord with the government and other opposition and rebel groups. Subsequently, in actions similar to those of the FDPC, the MLCJ accused the government of failing to adhere to terms of the accord, including a cease fire, and in February 2009 the group launched attacks in northern CAR. In April the group sought the release of prisoners and the dismissal of Jacques Demafouth as head of the APRD (above). In June Sabone returned to the CAR, claiming he had made a deal with the government and was prepared to disarm his troops.

In July 2010 the army reported that it had regained control of Birao in the north, following a raid on a military base by dissident MLCJ rebels. Attacks in the north intensified through the remaining months of 2010, with CAR authorities blaming MLCJ dissidents (see Foreign relations, above).

Sabone was appointee minister for tourism in the 2013 unity government but lost his portfolio in a subsequent cabinet reshuffle.

Leader: Abacar SABONE.

Patriotic Front for Unity (*Front Patriotique pour le Rassemblement*—FPR). Led by Omar Abdul Kader (aka Baba Laddé, or Bush Daddy), the FPR runs a sort of protection racket for ethnic Peulh (Mbororo) herders against bandits, other militias, the national army, and the Gendarmerie. A Peulh from Chad, Ladde was a gendarme until his arrest in 1998 for "his activities in support of other Peulh," as *Africa Confidential* describes. He escaped jail the next year and went to Cameroon and Nigeria before briefly joining Chadian rebels in Darfur, then leaving because of the contempt with which rebel leaders from other ethnic groups treated Peulhs. As of September 2012 he had turned himself over to authorities in the CAR, hoping to secure assurances that would allow him to return to Chad. Peulh traders in the diaspora have reportedly helped fund the group and frame a political message, and the militia has built a permanent base in the countryside with up to 800 families. It was believed to comprise 2,000 well-armed fighters.

Kader surrendered to CAR security forces on September 2012 and subsequently signed a peace accord with the government. The following month, the FPR was disarmed and the CAR began to repatriate the fighters to Chad.

LEGISLATURE

The 1986 constitution provided for a bicameral Congress (*Congrès*) encompassing a largely advisory Economic and Regional Council composed of nominated members and an elective National Assembly with a five-year mandate.

The assembly was suspended following the March 2003 coup, and self-declared President Bozizé on March 30 established a 98-member National Transitional Council (*Conseil National de Transition*—CNT). The members were chosen by the president to represent the military, clergy, trade unions, political parties, human rights groups, and other sectors. The December 2004 constitutional revision provided for the creation of a new 105-member National Assembly.

The National Assembly was suspended on March 24, 2013, and a new 105-member CNT was appointed on April 11. The CNT consisted of 38 representatives from political parties, 50 non-political deputies, including clergy and civic leaders, and one representative from each of the 16 regions and the capital.

Speaker: Alexandre-Ferdinand NGUENDET.

CABINET

[as of August 1, 2013]

Prime Minister	Nicolas Tiangaye
Ministers	
Arts and Culture	Bruno Yapande
Basic, Secondary, and Technical Education	Marcel Loudegue
Civil Service and Administrative Reform	Gaston Mackouzangba
Development Industries	Georges Bozanga
Environment and Ecology	Paul Doko
Economy, Planning, and International Cooperation	Abdallah Hassan Kadre
Finance and the Budget	Christophe Bremaïdou
Foreign Affairs and the Diaspora	Léonie Banga-Bothy [f]
Higher Education and Scientific Research	Rainaldy Sioke
Human Rights	Claude Lenga
Justice and Moral Standards and Keeper of the Seals	Arsene Sendé
Labor, Employment, Professional Training, and Social Security	Jérémie Tchimanguere
Livestock and Animal Industries	Joseph Bendounga
National Defense	Michel Djotodia
Posts and Telecommunications	Henry Pouzer
Program for Disarmament, Demobilization, and Reintegration	Zéphirin Mamadou
Promotion of Small and Medium-Size Enterprises	Guy Simplice Adouma-Issa
Public Health and AIDS Prevention	Aguinde Sounk
Rural Development	Marie Noëlle Koyara [f]
Secretary General of the Government and Relations with Institutions	Ahamat Arol Teya
Social Affairs, National Solidarity, and Gender Promotion	Lucile Mazangue Blay-Eureka [f]
Social Economy and Microfinance	Mathieu Ngoubou
Territorial Administration and Decentralization	Aristide Sokambi
Tourism and Handicrafts	Mahamat Abdel Yacoub
Town Planning, Property, and Land Reform	Rizigala Ramadan
Trade and Industry	Amalas Amias Haroun
Transport and Civil Aviation	Arnaud Djoubaye Abazen
Youth, Sports, Arts, and Culture	Abdoulaye Hissen
Ministers of State	
Communications, Civil Education, and National Reconciliation	Christophe Gazam-Betty
Equipment, Public Works, and Access	Crépin Mboli-Goumbase
Mines, Oil, Energy, and Hydraulics	Herbert Gontran Djono-Ahaba
Public Security, Immigration, Emigration, and Public Order	Nourredine Adam
Water Resources, Forestry, Hunting, Fisheries, and the Environment	(Vacant)

[f] = female

INTERGOVERNMENTAL REPRESENTATION

Ambassador to the U.S.: Stanislas MOUSSA-KEMBE.

U.S. Ambassador to the Central African Republic: Laurence D. WOHLERS.

Permanent Representative to the UN: Charles-Armel DOUBANE.

IGO Memberships (Non-UN): AfDB, AU, IOM, NAM, WTO.

CHAD

Republic of Chad
République du Tchad

Political Status: Independent since August 11, 1960; military regime instituted in 1975, giving way to widespread insurgency and ouster of Transitional Government of National Unity in 1982; one-party system established by presidential decree in 1984; constitution of December 10, 1989, suspended on December 3, 1990, following military coup; interim national charter announced February 28, 1991; transitional national charter adopted by Sovereign National Conference effective April 9, 1993; present constitution approved by national referendum on March 31, 1996, and revised by national referendum on June 6, 2005.

Area: 495,752 sq. mi. (1,284,000 sq. km).

Population: 11,863,179 (2012E—UN); 11,193,452 (2013E—U.S. Census).

Major Urban Center (2005E): N'DJAMENA (864,000).

Official Languages: French and Arabic. In addition, some 25 indigenous languages are spoken.

Monetary Unit: CFA Franc (market rate November 1, 2013: 88.51 francs = $1US). The CFA franc is permanently pegged to the euro at 655.957 CFA francs = 1 euro.

President: Col. Idriss DÉBY Itno (Patriotic Salvation Movement); self-appointed as president on December 4, 1990, following overthrow of the government of Hissène HABRÉ on December 2; confirmed by national charter adopted February 28, 1991; reconfirmed by the Sovereign National Conference on April 6, 1993; popularly elected to a five-year term in two-stage multiparty balloting on June 2 and July 3, 1996, and sworn in on August 8; reelected on May 20, 2001, and sworn in for another five-year term on August 8; reelected for another five-year term on May 3, 2006; reelected for another five-year term on April 25, 2011.

Prime Minister: Joseph Djimrangar DADNADJI; appointed by the president on January 22, 2013, to succeed Emmanuel NADINGAR, who had resigned the same day; formed new government on January 26, 2013.

THE COUNTRY

Landlocked Chad, the largest in area and population among the countries of former French Equatorial Africa, extends from the borders of the equatorial forest in the south to the Sahara in the north. Its unevenly distributed population is characterized by overlapping ethnic, religious, and regional cleavages. The primarily black population in the south is largely animist or Christian, while the north is overwhelmingly Sudanic and Muslim. Of the country's 12 major ethnic groups, the largest are the Saras in the south and Arabs in the center, north, and east. However, the Zaghawa clan (an estimated 5 percent of the population) has dominated political affairs since the installation of the Déby regime in 1990. French is an official language, but Chadian Arabic has recognized status in the school system, and the major black ethnic groups have their own languages. Women constitute roughly one-fifth of the official labor force and more than 65 percent of unpaid family workers. Female participation in government and politics, traditionally close to nonexistent, has increased slightly in recent years. The government also has introduced new legislation designed to protect certain rights of women, reportedly generating criticism from conservative elements of the population.

Until significant oil production began recently (see below), the economy was almost exclusively agricultural, nearly one-half of the gross national product being derived from subsistence farming, livestock raising, and fishing. Cotton, grown primarily on the rich farmland in the south, accounted for more than 70 percent of export earnings, with cotton-ginning being the most important industry. Uranium and other mineral deposits are believed to be located in the northern Aozou Strip, long the source of a territorial dispute with Libya (see Foreign relations, below), while gold and diamonds also are mined.

Chad remains one of the poorest nations in the world, with a per capita annual income of less than $300. An estimated 80 percent of the population lives below the poverty level, nearly one-third of that number existing in near-starvation conditions. Meanwhile, the illiteracy rate is estimated at 75 percent, and infant mortality is extremely high. Chad is also widely considered to be one of the world's most corrupt nations, with a "culture of clans and warlordism" dominating much of everyday existence and contributing to numerous insurgencies that have compromised development efforts.

Despite aid from such sources as the UN Development Program, the World Bank, and the African Development Fund, widespread civil war through much of the 1970s, 1980s, and early 1990s precluded measurable economic development. In the mid-1990s the government began to privatize many state-run enterprises and to adopt other measures designed to promote free-market activity, earning support from the International Monetary Fund (IMF) for its efforts. However, the IMF urged Chadian leaders to move beyond "crisis management" and "fiscal stabilization" to long-term policies designed to combat poverty.

Prospects for economic advancement subsequently focused almost exclusively on exploitation of the southern oil fields, which are estimated to contain at least 1.5 billion barrels of oil. A 665-mile pipeline to carry the oil through Cameroon to the Atlantic Ocean was opened in October 2003, a consortium led by the Exxon Mobil Corporation having earmarked more than $4 billion for the extraction and piping processes. Significant financing was also provided by the World Bank, which was given control of an escrow fund containing Chad's portion of the oil revenue. As part of the arrangements with the World Bank, the Chadian government agreed to direct two-thirds of that revenue toward improving living standards and to deposit 10 percent into a special fund to be reserved for use after the oil reserves were exhausted. However, internal unrest and political discord subsequently prompted serious friction between the government and the World Bank. In late December 2005 the Chadian National Assembly approved new legislation permitting the administration to allocate additional oil revenue toward the general budget, which critics argued President Idriss Déby would use almost exclusively to purchase armaments. The World Bank, which had been charged with allocating the oil revenues, decried the change as a violation of the prior agreement and in January 2006 suspended the disbursement of $125 million in accumulated revenues. The Bank also halted its own lending program to Chad. The Déby administration responded with a threat to halt oil production altogether if the Bank did not reverse its course, sending a shiver through the world's oil markets.

Realpolitik appeared to play a role in the World Bank's decision to resume lending to Chad in May 2006 and to agree to begin releasing oil revenue gradually upon the anticipated adoption of more transparent accounting practices by the Chadian administration. The accord also permitted the government to close the fund that had been established for the "post-oil" years and, apparently, to direct additional resources to security matters.

In September 2008 the World Bank announced it was withdrawing from the Chad-Cameroon pipeline project because the Chadian government had failed to allocate oil revenues to social programs and development projects as originally promised. At that point, Chad was exporting approximately 170,000 barrels of oil per day, providing an estimated three-quarters of the government's revenue.

GDP contracted by 0.4 percent in 2008 in the aftermath of a rebel incursion in February. Growth fell further to –2 percent in 2009 as the result of declining oil prices (influenced by the global economic recession) and insufficient rainfall, which severely depressed agricultural output and raised the specter of a food crisis for large segments of the population. Growth was estimated at 3 percent in 2011, one of the most noteworthy developments during the year being the opening of the first domestic oil refinery. Meanwhile, the government hoped for significant economic benefits from a major public investment program that included ongoing modernization of N'Djamena, the capital city. On the negative side, human rights advocates characterized abuses in the country as systemic, particularly in prisons.

GDP grew by 5.5 percent in 2012, in part due to a strong performance by the agricultural sector and a rise in oil prices. However, analysts pointed out that oil production had declined to about 105,000

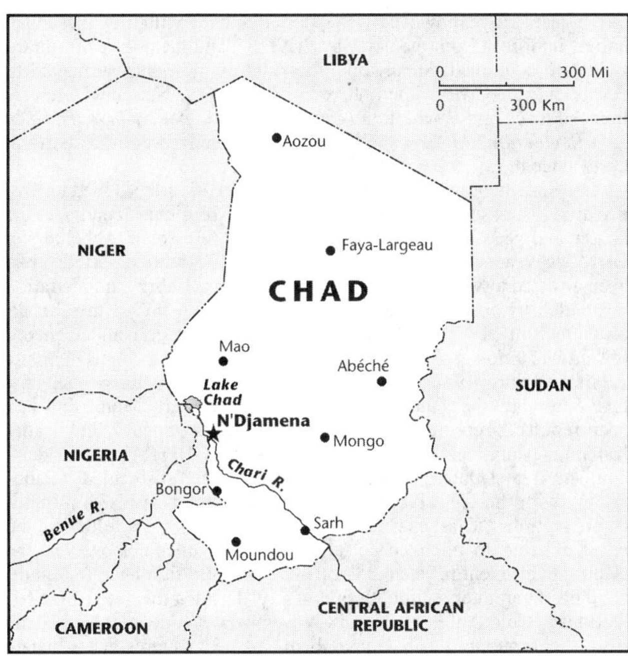

barrels per day and that known reserves could be exhausted in 20 years. In 2013 the IMF described Chad's business climate as weak and criticized the government for insufficient financial transparency.

GOVERNMENT AND POLITICS

Political background. Brought under French control in 1900, Chad became part of French Equatorial Africa in 1910 and served as an important Allied base in World War II. It was designated an autonomous member state of the French Community in 1959, achieving full independence under the presidency of François (subsequently N'Garta) TOMBALBAYE one year later. Tombalbaye, a southerner and leader of the majority Chad Progressive Party (*Parti Progressiste Tchadien*—PPT), secured the elimination of other parties prior to the adoption of a new constitution in 1962.

The northern (Saharan) territories—historically focal points of resistance and virtually impossible to govern—remained under French military administration until 1965, when disagreements led Chad to request the withdrawal of French troops. Dissatisfaction with Tombalbaye's policies generated progressively more violent opposition and the formation in 1966 of the Chad National Liberation Front (*Front de Libération Nationale du Tchad*—Frolinat), led by Aibrahim ABATCHA until his death in 1969, and then by Dr. Abba SIDDICK. French troops returned in 1968 at the request of President Tombalbaye, but the disturbances continued, culminating in an attempted coup by Frolinat in 1971 (allegedly with Libyan backing). In a further effort to consolidate his regime, Tombalbaye created the National Movement for Cultural and Social Revolution (*Mouvement National pour la Révolution Culturelle et Sociale*—MNRCS) in 1973 to replace the PPT.

On April 13, 1975, President Tombalbaye was fatally wounded in an uprising by army and police units. Two days later, Brig. Gen. Félix MALLOUM, who had been in detention since 1973 for plotting against the government, was designated chair of a ruling Supreme Military Council. The new regime, which banned the MNRCS, was immediately endorsed by a number of former opposition groups, although Frolinat remained aloof.

Following a major encounter between Libyan and Frolinat forces in the Tibesti Mountains in June 1976, Frolinat military leader Hissène HABRÉ attempted to negotiate a settlement with the Malloum regime but was rebuffed. In September Habré lost control of the main wing of Frolinat to Goukhouni OUEDDEI, who elected to cooperate with the Libyans, and in early 1978 Oueddei's Frolinat launched a major offensive against government forces in Faya-Largeau, about 500 miles northeast of the capital. Subsequently, on February 5, the government announced that it had concluded a cease-fire agreement with a rebel group, the Armed Forces of the North (*Forces Armées du Nord*—FAN), that was loyal to Habré. A truce also was reached with Oueddei's People's Armed Forces (*Forces Armées du Peuple*—FAP), the largest Frolinat faction, in late March. However, the FAP resumed military operations in April, its advance being repulsed only with major French assistance to the Chadian government. As of midyear the northern two-thirds of the country remained in the effective control of one or the other of the competing Frolinat factions.

On August 29, 1978, President Malloum announced the appointment of Habré as prime minister under a "basic charter of national reconciliation" pending the adoption of a permanent constitution. However, a serious rift developed between Malloum and Habré later in the year, and an abortive coup on February 12, 1979, by forces loyal to Habré was followed by a month of bloody, but inconclusive, confrontation between the rival factions. On March 16 a four-party agreement was concluded in Kano, Nigeria, involving Malloum, Habré, Oueddei, and Aboubakar Mahamat ABDERAMAN, leader of the Popular Movement for the Liberation of Chad (*Mouvement Populaire de la Libération du Tchad*—MPLT). Under the Kano accord, Oueddei on March 23 became president of an eight-member Provisional State Council, which was composed of two representatives from each of the factions and was to serve until a new government could be constituted. French troops were to be withdrawn under a truce guaranteed by Cameroon, the Central African Empire, Libya, Niger, Nigeria, and Sudan. At a second Kano conference on April 3–11, however, the pact broke down, primarily because agreement could not be reached with five other rebel groups, one of which, the "New Volcano," headed by the Revolutionary Democratic Council (*Conseil Démocratique Révolutionnaire*—CDR) of Ahmat ACYL, had apparently become a leading beneficiary of Libyan support in the north. Meanwhile, former Malloum supporter Lt. Col. Wadal Abdelkader KAMOUGUÉ, commander of the Chadian Armed Forces (*Forces Armées Tchadiennes*—FAT), had launched a secessionist uprising in the south, also with Libyan backing.

On April 29, 1979, a second provisional government was announced under Lol Mahamat CHOUA of the MPLT, with Gen. Djibril Negue DJOGO, former army commander under President Malloum, as his deputy. However, the Choua government was repudiated by the six "guarantor" states during a meeting held May 26–27 in Lagos, Nigeria, with no Chadian representatives being present. In early June fighting erupted in N'Djamena between Frolinat and MPLT contingents, while other altercations occurred in the east, south, and north (where an invasion by a 2,500-man Libyan force, launched on June 26, met stiff resistance). In another effort to end the turmoil, a fourth conference convened August 20–21 in Lagos, attended by representatives of 11 Chadian groups and 9 external states (the original 6, plus Benin, Côte d'Ivoire, and Senegal). The August meeting resulted in the designation of Oueddei and Kamougué as president and vice president, respectively, of a Transitional Government of National Unity (*Gouvernement d'Union Nationale de Transition*—GUNT), whose full membership, announced on November 10, included 12 northerners and 10 southerners.

Although the August 1979 Lagos accord had called for demilitarization of N'Djamena by February 1980, fighting resumed in the capital in March 1980 between Defense Minister Habré's FAN and President Oueddei's FAP, the latter subsequently being reinforced by Kamougué's FAT and elements of the post-Lagos Front for Joint Action, of which Ahmat ACYL was a leader. The coalescence of all other major forces against the FAN occurred primarily because of the perception that Habré, contrary to the intent of the Lagos agreement, had sought to expand his sphere of influence. While the FAN, clearly the best organized of the military units, continued to maintain control of at least half the city, the Organization of African Unity (OAU, subsequently the African Union—AU) and such regional leaders as Togo's President EYADÉMA arranged several short-lived cease-fires in late March and April.

Moving into a vacuum created by the removal of the last French military contingent on May 17, Libya on June 15 concluded a military defense treaty with the Oueddei government. By early November, 3,000–4,000 Libyan troops had moved into northern Chad and also had established a staging area within 40 miles of N'Djamena. Habré's position in the capital subsequently came under attack by Libyan aircraft, and fighting in the countryside spread as the government attempted to sever the FAN's link to its main base at Abéché, near the Sudanese border. An assault against FAN-controlled sectors of the capital was launched by government and Libyan forces on December 6, after Habré had rejected an OAU-sponsored cease-fire. Five days later the FAN withdrew from the city, some elements retreating toward Abéché and others crossing into Cameroon.

On January 6, 1981, the governments of Chad and Libya announced a decision to achieve "full unity" between their two countries. The action prompted OAU Chair Siaka Stevens of Sierra Leone to convene an extraordinary meeting of the OAU's Ad Hoc Committee on Chad in the Togolese capital of Lomé, where, on January 14, representatives of 12 governments repudiated the proposed merger, reaffirmed the validity of the 1979 Lagos accord, called on Libya to withdraw from Chad and authorized the formation of an OAU peacekeeping force. Subsequently, it was reported that President Oueddei had been opposed to unification and had signed the agreement in Tripoli under duress, the Libyans expressing their disenchantment with his lack of "Islamic fervor" and calling for his replacement by Acyl. Both Vice President Kamougué and Frolinat's Dr. Siddick vehemently opposed the proposed merger, the former terming it an "impossible marriage" and the latter fleeing to Sudan in April after resigning as health minister.

In late May 1981 the transitional government announced that several faction leaders had agreed to disarm and join in the formation of a "national integrated army" in anticipation of a Libyan withdrawal. Nonetheless, factional conflict continued, while at midyear a revitalized FAN mounted an offensive against Libyan and Libyan-backed government troops in the east. In mid-September, during a two-day meeting in Paris with Oueddei, French authorities agreed to provide logistical support to an OAU force to supplant the Libyans, and in November most of the latter were withdrawn after Benin, Gabon, Nigeria, Senegal, Togo, and Zaire had undertaken to form a 5,000-man contingent to maintain order, supervise elections, and assist in establishing a unified Chadian army.

During early 1982, FAN forces regained control of most of the eastern region and began advancing on N'Djamena, which fell on June 7. GUNT president Oueddei fled to Cameroon before establishing himself at the northern settlement of Bardai on the border of the Libyan-controlled Aozou Strip. Upon entering the capital, the Council of the Commander in Chief of the FAN (*Conseil du Commandement en Chef des FAN*—CCFAN) assumed political control, and on June 19 it named Habré to head a 30-member Council of State. Earlier, on June 11, OAU Chair Daniel arap Moi had ordered the withdrawal of the OAU force, which, at maximum strength, had reached only 3,000 troops, two-thirds from Nigeria. During the ensuing months, the FAN, with assistance from FAT units, succeeded in gaining control of the south.

On September 29, 1982, the CCFAN promulgated a Fundamental Act (*Acte Fondamental*), based on the August 1978 charter (which had been effectively abrogated in 1979), to "govern Chad until the adoption of a new constitution." In accordance with the new act, Habré was sworn in as president of the republic on October 21. Following his investiture, the new chief executive dissolved the Council of State in favor of a 31-member government that included Dr. Siddick; DJIDINGAR Dono Ngardoum, who had served briefly as prime minister under Oueddei in May; and Capt. Routouane YOMA, a former aide of Colonel Kamougué. As stipulated in the Fundamental Act, Habré also announced the formation of a 30-member National Consultative Council (*Conseil National Consultatif*—CNC) to serve as the state's "highest advisory organ." Two months later N'Djamena announced that the FAN and FAT would be consolidated as the Chadian National Armed Forces (*Forces Armées Nationales Tchadiennes*—FANT).

After the declaration in Algiers in October 1982 of a "National Peace Government" by 8 of the 11 signatories of the 1979 Lagos accord, Oueddei forces regrouped in Bardai with renewed support from Tripoli. By May 1983 GUNT units were advancing south, and, with the aid of 2,000 troops and several MIG fighters supplied by Libya, they captured the "northern capital" of Faya-Largeau on June 24. Habré immediately called for international assistance and received aid from Egypt, Sudan, and the United States, with France avoiding direct involvement despite a 1976 defense agreement. FANT troops recaptured Faya-Largeau on June 30, only to lose it again on August 10, while France, under mounting pressure from the United States and a number of francophone African countries, began deploying troops along a defensive "red line" just north of Abéché on August 14. The French—who eventually numbered some 3,000, supported by 2,000 Zairean troops—imposed a tenuous cease-fire for the remainder of the year while calling for a negotiated solution between the two factions. While Habré continued to urge France to aid him in a full-scale offensive against Oueddei, the Mitterrand government refused, at one point urging "a federation of Chad" as a means of ending the conflict. Meanwhile, in the wake of renewed fighting, the "red line" was moved 60 miles north.

In April 1984 Libyan leader Muammar al-Qadhafi proposed a mutual withdrawal of "Libyan support elements" and French forces, with talks thereupon initiated between France and Libya that yielded an accord on September 17. The French pullout was completed by the end of the year; Libya, however, was reported to have withdrawn less than half of its forces from the north by that time, and the political-military stalemate continued. Meanwhile, the Habré regime had attempted to consolidate its power with the June formation of the National Union for Independence and Revolution (*Union Nationale pour l'Indépendence et la Révolution*—UNIR), the first legally recognized political party in Chad since the 1975 banning of the MNRCS.

In a statement issued in Tripoli on October 15, 1985, Oueddei was declared dismissed as FAP leader. The GUNT president repudiated the action and on November 5 announced the release of Acheikh ibn OUMAR, leader of the GUNT-affiliated CDR, who reportedly had been arrested a year earlier. On November 11 the Habré administration responded by concluding a "reconciliation agreement" with a breakaway faction of the CDR, the Committee for Action and Concord (*Comité d'Action et de Concord*—CAC).

In February 1986 GUNT forces mounted an offensive against FANT troops at the center of the "red line," but by early March they had been repulsed, reportedly with heavy losses. On June 19 FAT leader Kamougué announced his resignation as the GUNT vice president, while in August Oumar declared that the CDR had "suspended collaboration" with the GUNT but would "maintain solidarity with all anti-Habré factions." Clashes between CDR and GUNT units followed, the latter offering to open peace talks with N'Djamena. However, the Habré government insisted that the GUNT would first have to repudiate the Libyan intervention. Subsequently, during a meeting of GUNT factions in Cotonou, Benin, in mid-November, Oueddei was "expelled" from the grouping, with Oumar being named its president. In late December, as FANT forces were reported to be moving north, fighting broke out between FAP units loyal to Oueddei and what Libyan sources characterized as Oumar's "legitimate" GUNT.

On March 22, 1987, in what was seen as a major turning point in the lengthy Chadian conflict, FANT troops captured the Libyan air facility in Ouadi Doum, 100 miles northeast of Faya-Largeau. Deprived of air cover, the Libyans withdrew from Faya-Largeau, their most important military base in northern Chad, abandoning an estimated $1 billion worth of sophisticated weaponry. On August 8 Chadian government troops captured the town of Aozou, administrative capital of the northern strip; however, it was retaken by Libyan forces three weeks later. Chad thereupon entered southern Libya in an unsuccessful effort to deprive Libyan forces of air support in the continued struggle for the disputed territory. Subsequent international and regional criticism of the Chadian "invasion" led Habré to accept a September 11 cease-fire negotiated by OAU chair Kenneth Kaunda of Zambia; however, by late November the government reported FANT clashes with Libyan troops crossing into eastern Chad from Sudan.

In early 1988 Habré charged that Libya was still violating Chadian air space and backing antigovernment rebels despite Qadhafi's pledge of support for OAU peace-treaty negotiations. Nonetheless, Chad and Libya agreed in mid-October to restore diplomatic relations and "resolve peacefully their territorial dispute" by presenting their respective Aozou strip claims to a special OAU committee (see Foreign relations, below, for subsequent developments).

In April 1989 Habré survived a coup attempt that allegedly involved a number of senior government officials, including former FANT commander Idriss DÉBY, who subsequently mounted a series of cross-border attacks from sanctuary in Sudan. Eight months later, Chadian voters approved a constitution to replace the Fundamental Act. One of its provisions extended Habré's incumbency for another seven years; others formalized the UNIR's supremacy and authorized an elected National Assembly, balloting for which was conducted in June 1990.

In November 1990 a variety of antigovernmental forces, allied under Déby's leadership in the Patriotic Salvation Movement (*Mouvement Patriotique du Salut*—MPS), mounted a decisive offensive against FANT troops in eastern Chad. The rebels captured Abéché on November 30, reportedly prompting large-scale desertion by government troops. With France having announced that it would not intervene in what was characterized as an "internal Chadian power struggle," the MPS was left with a virtually unimpeded path to N'Djamena; consequently, Habré and other government leaders fled to Cameroon. (Habré was indicted in February 2000 in Senegal and charged with torture during his term in power. In June, however, the court ruled that Senegal did not have jurisdiction over the case, a decision that was heavily criticized as being politically motivated; human rights groups, which had filed the initial complaint against Habré, appealed to a higher Senegalese court. In March 2001 the appeals court upheld the lower court's ruling, President Wade of Senegal stating that he was prepared to send Habré to a third country to face trial. However, Habré remained in Senegal, although there had been attempts to extradite him to Belgium by victims of the regime who were Belgian citizens. In July 2006 an AU panel declared that Habré should be tried in Senegal on genocide charges. Although a commission was subsequently established in Senegal to gather evidence in the case, little progress toward prosecution was achieved. For its part, the Belgian government asked the International Court of Justice [ICJ] to force Senegal to either try Habré or extradite him to Belgium. However, the Senegalese government continued to delay prosecution, suggesting that international financial assistance was required to offset the cost of the trial. Meanwhile, a magistrate's court in Chad sentenced Habré to death in absentia. In July 2012 the ICJ ruled that Senegal, as a signatory of the Convention Against Torture, was required to organize a trial for Habré quickly or make plans for his extradition. The new government in Senegal subsequently proved more amenable to proceeding with the case and established a special tribunal of AU-appointed judges in February 2013 to consider charges against Habré, who was arrested in June. The tribunal, financed in part by Western aid, was not expected to conclude for at least a year.)

On December 3, 1990, one day after having occupied the capital, Déby suspended the constitution and dissolved the assembly. On December 4 he announced that a provisional Council of State had assumed power with himself as president and a fellow commander, Maldoum BADA ABBAS, as vice president. On February 28, 1991, an interim National Charter was adopted, and on March 5 the Council of State was dissolved in favor of a new Council of Ministers and an appointed Provisional Council of the Republic. The vice presidency was abandoned upon formation of the new government, Bada Abbas being named minister of state for the interior and former National Assembly president Jean Bawoyeu ALINGUÉ being appointed to the revived post of prime minister.

The overthrow of the Habré regime generated minimal international concern or domestic protest, in part because of reports that the deposed government had engaged in widespread human rights abuses. For his part, President Déby pledged to work toward implementation of a multiparty democracy in which "fundamental rights" would be guaranteed. However, the new regime also insisted that "security issues" took precedence over political liberalization.

In response to opposition demands for the convening of a Sovereign National Conference (*Conférence Nationale Souveraine*—CNS) to chart the nation's political future, Déby tentatively scheduled such a body for May 1992. Meanwhile, the Council of Ministers adopted guidelines for registering parties.

The regime faced a serious challenge in late 1991 when Habré loyalists, organized as the Movement for Development and Democracy (*Mouvement pour le Développement et la Démocratie*—MDD), launched an invasion from the Lake Chad border region. The campaign enjoyed some initial success, and, as the rebels advanced on N'Djamena in early January 1992, French paratroopers reinforced the brigade of 1,110 French soldiers permanently stationed near the capital. In addition to its symbolic significance, the French reinforcement permitted the release of additional Chadian troops to confront the rebels, and within days the government reported that the MDD forces were in full retreat. In the wake of the insurgency, security forces arrested a number of prominent opposition leaders and launched what was perceived as a reprisal campaign against suspected MDD supporters, former officials in the Habré administration, and members of the fledgling Rally for Democracy and Progress (*Rassemblement pour la Démocratie et le Progrès*—RDP). Shortly thereafter, in response to pressure from Paris, the government announced an amnesty for those recently detained as well as those implicated in an alleged October 1991 coup attempt. Reaffirming its commitment to democratization, the regime began legalizing opposition parties, including the RDP, in March. However, the CNS opening scheduled for May was postponed indefinitely because of ongoing security concerns, the government having reported another coup attempt in April.

On May 19, 1992, the National Charter was modified to strengthen the authority of the prime minister, and the following day Alingué was replaced by Joseph YODEYMAN. On May 22 a new Council of Ministers was announced that included representatives of newly organized parties, although a number of them subsequently resigned from the "coalition" government as the result of policy disputes. Following a minor reshuffle in October, the government announced that the CNS would convene on January 15, 1993, with a mandate to appoint a new prime minister, select a transitional legislature, and draw up constitutional revisions that would lead, following a national referendum on the proposals, to multiparty presidential and legislative balloting. Significantly, the CNS was not empowered to replace Déby, who was viewed as having the best chance to maintain a semblance of stability in an increasingly divided society. Thus, Déby remained as president and commander in chief of the armed forces under the transitional national charter adopted at the conclusion of the CNS on April 6, 1993. Quasi-legislative authority was extended to a Higher Transitional Council (*Conseil Supérieur de Transition*—CST), whose members were elected by the CNS. In addition, broad responsibility for economic and social policies was conferred on the new prime minister, Dr. Fidèle MOUNGAR, a southerner named by the CNS to form the first transitional government. The CNS, supported by some 40 political parties (recognized and unrecognized), several rebel movements, and numerous trade and professional associations, approved a transitional period of up to 12 months pending the drafting of a permanent constitution and the holding of national elections. However, the CST was authorized to extend the transitional charter's authority for an additional year, if necessary.

Despite the prime minister's expression of confidence that he and the president could work together, friction between the two leaders quickly surfaced, Déby being particularly critical of the new government's "amateurish" economic program. The dispute culminated with the CST forcing Prime Minister Moungar's resignation via a nonconfidence motion on October 28, 1993. After three rounds of voting, the CST on November 6 elected Delwa Kassiré KOUMAKOYE, the outgoing justice minister, to succeed Dr. Moungar. A new cabinet was named one week later, followed by a minor reshuffle in January 1994 in which MPS dominance was maintained despite the continued presence of ministers from anti-Déby parties. Subsequently, on April 4, the CST voted to extend the transitional period for 12 more months in view of the nation's seeming inability to reverse political fragmentation, with a major cabinet reshuffle following on May 17.

The CST approved a new electoral code and a draft constitution in January 1995; however, the subsequent registration of voters was strongly criticized by opposition leaders, who claimed the process was skewed in favor of the MPS. Acknowledging that the validity of the new voter lists was questionable, the CST postponed a constitutional referendum indefinitely, and in early April it extended the transitional period for another 12 months. Collaterally, the CST dismissed Prime Minister Koumakoye on April 8 for failing to "create the proper conditions" for elections, replacing him with Djimasta KOIBLA, who suspended his activity within the Union for Democracy and the Republic (*Union pour la Démocratie et la République*—UDR) upon assuming national office.

The extension of the nation's transitional political status in 1995 was controversial, opponents noting that a National Reconciliation Committee appointed in 1994 had negotiated peace accords with several rebel groups and thereby reduced security concerns. Consequently, with the Déby regime reportedly facing international pressure to proceed with democratization, the constitutional referendum was finally conducted on March 31, 1996. The new basic law (see Constitution and government, below) was approved by 63.5 percent of the voters in what officials reported to be a 69 percent turnout. (Not surprisingly, the "no" vote was heaviest in the south, where sentiment had long preferred a federal structure that would accord substantial autonomy to the region.) As approved by the referendum, Déby remained in office pending new presidential balloting, while the CST continued to operate until the election of a new legislature. In addition, although the cabinet submitted an essentially pro forma resignation on April 18, Déby reappointed Koibla the next day to head an interim government that included all but one of the incumbent ministers.

Fifteen candidates contested the first round of presidential balloting on June 2, 1996, Déby being credited with 43.9 percent of the votes. His closest rival was former southern military leader and GUNT vice president Kamougué, running under the banner of the Union for Renewal and Democracy (*Union pour le Renouveau et la Démocratie*—URD), who secured 12.4 percent of the votes. Déby was subsequently elected to a five-year term on July 3 in the second-round balloting, defeating Kamougué 69.1 percent to 30.9 percent. Déby again named Prime Minister Koibla to head the significantly revamped government announced on August 12.

Although opposition parties charged that "massive fraud" had occurred in the first round of the presidential election in June 1996, international observers reportedly expressed satisfaction with the conduct of the balloting. The vote shares garnered by President Déby and Colonel Kamougué appeared to reflect the long-standing cultural, religious, and ethnic divide between southern Chad and the rest of the country. Meanwhile, Western capitals (most importantly Paris) signaled their support for President Déby as Chad's best hope for ongoing stability, despite concern over his administration's human rights record and its ties with Sudan and collateral support for the Islamic fundamentalist movement.

Elections to the new National Assembly were held on January 5 and February 23, 1997, with MPS candidates ultimately securing 65 of 125 seats following a redistribution ordered by the national electoral commission upon appeal by the governing party (which was initially credited with only 55 seats). Election monitors described the balloting as "relatively free and fair." On the other hand, there was widespread domestic and international condemnation of the allegedly progovernment bias of the national electoral commission, especially regarding perceived irregularities in the initial tallies. However, Western leaders appeared willing to overlook such heavy-handed tactics, perhaps out of appreciation for the relative stability of the Déby regime in a region of recent intense political and military turbulence. For its part, the government continued to pursue cease-fire agreements with various rebel groups, as observers warned that tribal influences remained the most serious threat to the regime and the fledgling democratic process.

On May 16, 1997, President Déby appointed Nassour OUAÏDOU Guelendouksia to succeed Koibla as prime minister, a number of incumbents retaining their posts in the new cabinet announced on May 21. Ouaïdou also headed the reshuffled cabinet appointed on January 1, 1998. However, on December 13, 1999, in the wake of economic turbulence, President Déby appointed a "technocrat," Negoum YAMASSOUM, as prime minister. Yamassoum's new cabinet, announced December 14, included ministers from the MPS, URD, and the National Union for Development and Renewal (*Union Nationale pour le Développement et le Renouvellement*—UNDR).

President Déby was reelected to another term with 68 percent of the vote in controversial balloting on May 20, 2001. The opposition objected to de facto control by the MPS over the electoral commission as well as perceived bias in the votes registration process. (The European Union [EU] "regretted" the many shortcomings in the poll and expressed concern about the restriction of political liberties by the government.) Following his inauguration on August 8, Déby reappointed Yamassoum as prime minister.

The MPS maintained its dominance in the April 21, 2002, National Assembly balloting (postponed from 2001 on the grounds that the government lacked sufficient funds to conduct the poll), the opposition charging that the balloting was fraudulent. On June 11 President Déby appointed Haroun KABADI as prime minister. Kabadi was succeeded by Moussa FAKI on June 24, 2003, and Pascal YOADIMNADJI on February 3, 2005.

A national referendum was held on June 6, 2005, on constitutional changes proposed by the assembly, the most contentious being elimination of the two-term presidential limit, which thereby permitted Déby to seek another term. Most opposition parties, many of which had served in Déby governments, strongly condemned the revisions and urged a boycott of the referendum. However, the government announced that 58 percent of voters participated in the referendum and that the changes were approved by a 66 percent "yes" vote. (The opposition dismissed the results as "imaginary.") Subsequently, Déby reshuffled the cabinet on August 7; the most significant change involved his consolidation of control of the armed forces through the transfer of the defense ministry to the office of the president. Following the outbreak late in the year of renewed rebel activity (some on the part of military deserters incensed over the constitutional changes), the assembly in January 2006 voted 129–0 (with opposition legislators boycotting the vote) to postpone the assembly elections scheduled for April 2006 until at least April 2007, citing security and budget concerns.

Mass military defections to the newly formed United Front for Change (*Front Uni pour le Changement*—FUC) were reported in February 2006, and more than 100 soldiers were arrested in March in relation to an alleged attempt to shoot down Déby's plane. The unrest culminated in a rapid incursion by FUC forces from the Sudanese border that reached the outskirts of N'Djamena on April 13 before encountering significant resistance. The rebels were finally repulsed at the steps of the assembly building. More than 300 people were killed in the fighting, which also severely damaged eastern portions of N'Djamena. Déby accused the Sudanese government of backing the FUC, announcing that a "state of hostility" existed between Chad and Sudan. (Most analysts agreed with Déby's assertions, suggesting that Sudan, which had supported Déby's takeover in 1990, was now convinced that the Chadian government was providing assistance to the largely Zaghawa rebel groups fighting the *Janjaweed* militias in Darfur [see entry on Sudan for details].)

Significantly, France sent an additional 150 troops to its garrison in Chad during the April 2006 FUC incursion, and a French jet fired warning shots over the rebel forces in an apparent indication that France would not tolerate any attacks on French citizens. Although the French forces did not assist government troops in repulsing the rebels, their presence underscored the widespread perception that France preferred that Déby remain in power. Other Western countries also appeared to consider Déby the most likely leader to prevent Chad from descending further into ethnic/regional/political fragmentation that might threaten oil flows or lead to installation of a "pro-Sudan" administration.

In controversial balloting on May 3, 2006, Déby was reelected to another five-year presidential term, officially securing 77.5 percent of the votes against only four other candidates. Nearly all opposition parties had called for a boycott of the election in view of the recent failed rebel takeover attempt. Western criticism was moderate concerning the presidential election, which Chadian opposition parties characterized as Déby simply "installing himself for life." (Déby's only opponents were "three cronies" and one candidate from a minor opposition party.)

Rebels operating out of Sudan launched a series of attacks in eastern Chad in September 2006, prompting the government to declare a state of emergency in the east in November to, among other things, deal with an estimated 50,000 internal refugees. Subsequently, under Libyan mediation, the Chadian government and the major rebel groups in the east initiated peace negotiations in June.

Prime Minister Yoadimnadji died on February 22, 2007, and five days later Déby reappointed former prime minister Koumakoye to the position. A major cabinet reshuffle in March was most notable for the inclusion of several former rebels—including Mahamat NOUR Abdelkerim of the FUC. (Nour was dismissed from the cabinet in December 2007 [see FUC under Political Parties and Groups for details].)

In late January 2008 the Union of Forces for Democracy and Development (*Union des Forces pour la Démocratie et le Développement*—UFDD) and other eastern rebels launched an offensive that reached N'Djamena in several days. By February 2 the 3,000 well-armed rebels had surrounded the presidential palace and appeared poised to oust Déby. However, French forces protected the capital's airport from a rebel takeover, permitting government helicopters to attack the rebels, who were forced to withdraw after three days of fierce fighting that left more than 700 people dead and 10,000 displaced. (France had initially adopted a neutral stance in regard to the conflict but became "pro-Déby" after the UN Security Council condemned the rebel incursion and called upon member states to support the government. An AU summit also condemned the rebel initiative, as did the United States, with whom Déby had been cooperating recently regarding the U.S. antiterror campaign.)

President Déby in mid-February 2008 announced a state of emergency under which strong press restrictions were adopted and a number of opposition leaders were arrested. He also described the rebels as "Sudanese mercenaries." Faced with an international backlash against his crackdown on the opposition, Déby dismissed Prime Minister Koumakoye on April 16 and immediately named Youssouf SALEH ABBAS, theretofore Déby's diplomatic adviser, to the post. Five days later Abbas announced a new cabinet, which, although still dominated by the MPS, included four members of the opposition's Coordination of Parties for the Defense of the Constitution (*Coordination des Partis pour la Défense de la Constitution*—CPDC).

However, the rebels in the east vowed to continue their anti-Déby campaign, describing him as a "corrupt and autocratic ruler" who had "plundered" recent oil revenues. Rebel activity intensified in June on the part of a newly formed National Alliance (*Alliance Nationale*—AN), and although the government subsequently claimed a "decisive victory," attacks were also reported later in the year.

Chadian government troops in May 2009 repulsed another rebel offensive that had been launched by the recently formed Union of Resistance Forces (*Union des Forces du Resistance*—UFR), which most analysts described as enjoying Sudanese backing. Tensions with Sudan became even more inflamed when Chadian warplanes crossed the border to attack rebel bases in Sudan.

A new electoral commission that included a number of opposition members was established in June 2009 to prepare for legislative and presidential balloting rescheduled for 2010 and 2011, respectively. Meanwhile, the government continued to negotiate cease-fire agreements with small rebel groups and to encourage its former opponents to participate in the electoral process. Although tension remained high at the Sudanese border for the remainder of 2009 and major fighting with the UFR erupted in December, Chad and Sudan reached a surprising rapprochement in early 2010 that appeared to provide a foundation for a permanent resolution of their conflict. Déby and President al-Bashir of Sudan agreed to establish a joint military force to monitor the border, to cooperate in rebuilding the areas damaged by the fighting, and most importantly, to end support for rebel groups conducting the "proxy war."

After months of reported friction between the president and the prime minister, Saleh Abbas resigned on March 5, 2010, and was immediately succeeded by Emmanuel NADINGAR, a former oil minister who was described as a close ally of Déby. On March 10 Nadingar announced a 40-member cabinet, which again included members of the CPDC.

The MPS and its allies dominated the long-delayed balloting for the National Assembly in February 2011, and Déby was reelected to a fourth presidential term in April by securing 88.7 percent of the vote in the first round of voting against two minor candidates, the major opposition parties having called for a boycott of that poll. As required, Nadingar and his cabinet resigned following Déby's inauguration on August 8, but on August 13 the president reappointed Nadingar, who announced his new cabinet on August 17. In return for having formed a coalition with the MPS for the legislative and presidential elections, the RDP and former prime minister Koumakoye's National Rally for Democracy and Progress (*Rassemblement National pour la Démocratie et le Progrès*—RNDP) were given positions in the new cabinet.

Prime Minister Nadingar resigned on January 21, 2013, and was succeeded by Joseph Djimrangar Dadnadji, theretofore President Déby's chief of staff.

Constitution and government. A 17-member Constitutional Committee, established in December 1993, drafted a new basic law in 1994 calling for establishment of a bicameral legislature and a strong presidential system based on the French model. The changes were endorsed by the Higher Transitional Council in January 1995, but a national referendum on the matter was postponed until March 31, 1996, when the proposed constitution was endorsed by 63.5 percent of the voters.

The new basic law provided for direct popular election (in two-round balloting, if necessary) of the president for a maximum of two five-year terms. The prime minister is appointed by the president, although he is also held "responsible" to the legislature. The constitution also authorized the creation of a Constitutional Council and a Supreme Court, both of which were installed in April 1999.

Although the 1996 constitution provided for a new Senate, that body was never constituted, and a constitutional revision approved by national referendum on June 6, 2005, eliminated references to the Senate in favor of an advisory body called the Economic, Social, and Cultural Council, whose members are appointed by the president, subject to approval by the assembly. In a more controversial area, the amendments also permitted President Déby to seek a third term and removed an age restriction of 70 for the president.

In early 2000 the government doubled the number of prefectures (previously 14) and subprefectures, which are administered by government appointees. The cited reason was to promote decentralization of government functions. However, critics claimed that the reforms also had the effect of further cementing the ruling party's hold on power. Mayors, previously appointed by the central government, were popularly elected (along with local councils) for the first time in February 2012.

The Ministry of Information controls much of the media, while independent newspapers and radio stations are subjected to what watchdog organizations have described as constant intimidation.

Foreign relations. Chad's internal unrest was exacerbated for many years by conflict with Libya over delineation of their common border. The dispute was intensified in 1975 by Libya's annexation of an area of some 27,000 square miles in northern Chad (the Aozou Strip) that was said to contain substantial iron ore and uranium deposits. (For information regarding developments in this matter from 1977 to 1994, see the 2007 *Handbook.*)

Relations with France became complicated in the mid-1970s, when French involvement in the Chadian civil war was intensified by rebel kidnapping of a French national. In March 1976 a new cooperation pact was concluded, France agreeing to come to Chad's defense in the event of external, but not domestic, attack. Despite this assertion, French forces aided government troops throughout the late 1970s in stemming rebel, most notably Frolinat, offensives.

Chadian affairs also were of particular interest to a number of other Western nations in the 1980s, especially in relation to the Habré government's dispute with Libya. Thus, U.S. surveillance photographs and anti-aircraft weapons were allegedly used by Habré forces during the 1987 struggle in southern Libya.

France's decision not to intervene in the fighting that broke out in November 1990 was considered critical to the success of the MPS campaign. Not surprisingly, the new Chadian president in early 1991 invited the approximately 1,100 French troops to remain in the country for security purposes, and their presence was considered a psychological factor in the Déby regime's ability to withstand several subsequent overthrow attempts. Meanwhile, U.S. protests over the events of late 1990 were relatively moderate, despite apparent Libyan support for the victorious rebel forces.

In February 1994 the ICJ ruled in favor of Chad in its territorial dispute with Libya by a vote of 16–1. After initially appearing to hesitate, Libya formally accepted the ICJ ruling in April, and the withdrawal of Libyan troops from the territory was completed by the end of May. Shortly thereafter President Déby met with Libya's Colonel Qadhafi in Tripoli to sign a treaty of friendship and cooperation.

In September 1998 Chad sent more than 2,000 troops to support the Kabila regime in the civil war in the Democratic Republic of the Congo (DRC, formerly Zaire). In April 1999 the Déby administration announced that the soldiers (some 200 of whom had been killed) would be withdrawn soon, as regional mediators attempted to broker a settlement to that intractable dispute, which had drawn in some half-dozen of the DRC's neighbors (see entry on the DRC for details). Meanwhile, troops from Nigeria and Niger continued to assist in flushing out Chadian rebels in the Lake Chad region. (Fighting had broken out between Nigerian and Chadian troops in April 1998 over possession of an island in the lake; however, the conflict had settled down quickly, the two countries agreeing to leave formal demarcation of the boundary to the Lake Chad Basin Commission.) Chad's relations with Sudan and Libya also continued to improve, some observers suggesting that the Déby regime was hoping to dilute the country's long-standing dependence on French support or at least increase its negotiating leverage with Paris.

Tension intensified with the Central African Republic (CAR) in 2001 when Chad provided refuge for Gen. François Bozizé, one of the main protagonists in the CAR's infighting (see entry on the CAR for details). However, relations improved when Bozizé assumed control in the CAR, and Chad sent troops to help maintain order in the CAR following the takeover.

In 2002 Chad joined Algeria, Mauritania, and Niger in signing the "Pan Sahel Initiative" with the United States under which U.S. forces were to be deployed to the region to help combat terrorism, drug trafficking, and arms smuggling. (As part of that project, Chadian and U.S. troops reportedly broke up an Algerian rebel operation in Chad in 2004.) Meanwhile, President Jacques Chirac in 2002 became the first French head of state to visit Chad. (In February 2006 the two countries signed a declaration calling for full normalization of relations.)

The intense fighting that broke out in the Darfur region of Sudan in early 2003 had major repercussions for Chad. Some 200,000 refugees from the non-Arab population of Darfur fled across the border into Chad, populated by many of the same ethnic groups as those in Darfur (including President Déby's Zaghawa group). Sudan subsequently accused Chad of permitting Sudanese rebels to operate out of Chad, while Chad made similar accusations about Chadian rebels in Sudan. President Déby was prominent in subsequent efforts to mediate a settlement to the Darfur violence.

In August 2006 Chad broke off ties with Taiwan and restored relations with China, apparently seeking increased investment from China and also hoping that Chinese influence might help resolve the crisis in Darfur.

Following the surprising negotiation of a reconciliation agreement between Chad and Sudan in early 2010 (see Political background, above), the two countries began to expel the leaders of each other's rebel groups. Joint border monitoring intensified in 2011, with the CAR joining the initiative. Sudanese president al-Bashir attended President Déby's inauguration in August 2011, prompting heavy criticism from the EU and others over the failure of Déby to arrest al-Bashir on the outstanding warrant from the International Criminal Court. Meanwhile, the refugee situation in Chad had become even more complicated because of Libyans fleeing across the border to Chad to avoid the fighting between Qadhafi's forces and rebels.

Chad contributed significantly to the successful French-led offensive against militant Islamists and jihadists in northern Mali in early 2013, further bolstering Déby's regional reputation. Déby also sent troops to assist the CAR government in March in an ultimately unsuccessful effort to thwart the rebel takeover in that beleaguered country.

Current issues. In late October 2010 the CPDC and other opposition parties approved a new electoral calendar calling for legislative and presidential balloting in February and April 2011, respectively. However, although the assembly balloting proceeded smoothly, the CPDC condemned the official results as fraudulent. (EU observers noted irregularities but said they were not the result of "bad intentions.") In any event the continued legislative dominance of the MPS was considered inevitable in view of fragmentation among the opposition parties, who, among other things, argued that the government was inappropriately spending all the oil revenue on the military rather than on improving social conditions. Déby's first-round victory in the April presidential poll was also assured when the candidates from the CPDC withdrew, citing "influence peddling" on the part of the authorities and concern over ballot security.

The CPDC ultimately agreed to participate in the first-ever local elections in February 2012, but again alleged fraud when the MPS dominated the balloting. Overall, the region's Arab Spring did not appear to resonate strongly with the Chadian population, save for a student clash with police (in November 2011) that resulted in some 150 arrests.

Security forces in May 2013 arrested at least 15 people (including members of the military, journalists, and several legislators) in connection with what the government described as a coup plot. However, neutral observers were unable to determine if the case against the alleged plotters was legitimate.

POLITICAL PARTIES AND GROUPS

Prior to the collapse of the Habré regime and the suspension of the constitution on December 3, 1990, by Idriss Déby, single-party government control had been exercised by the National Union for Independence and Revolution (*Union Nationale pour l'Indépendence et la Révolution*—UNIR). President Déby, governing in the name of the Patriotic Salvation Movement (MPS, see below), declared himself to be a supporter of multipartyism, and on October 1, 1991, the Council of Ministers authorized the legalization of parties provided they "shun intolerance, tribalism, regionalism, religious discrimination, and recourse to violence." The first parties were recognized in March 1992, and there are currently more than 100 active parties (most of them minor).

Legislative Parties:

Patriotic Salvation Movement (*Mouvement Patriotique du Salut*—MPS). The MPS was formed in Libya in March 1990 by a number of groups opposed to the regime of President Hisséne Habré. The movement was headed by Idriss Déby, a former Chadian military leader and presidential adviser, who had participated in an April 1989 coup attempt. (For a list of groups that participated in the launching of the MPS, see the 2007 *Handbook*.)

The MPS endorsed a prodemocracy platform, while "preaching neither capitalism nor socialism." After ousting the Habré government in late 1990, it gained the allegiance of a number of other groups. Déby subsequently governed in the name of the MPS, remaining as president of the republic and commander in chief of the armed forces. An extraordinary MPS congress held April 10–11, 1996, "unanimously" selected Déby as the party's presidential nominee, the MPS leader later receiving the endorsement of a number of minor parties grouped as a Republican Front during his successful campaign. The MPS initially was credited with winning 55 seats in the assembly elections of early 1997 but was subsequently given additional seats following a controversial review by the national electoral commission. Its final total was placed at 65, which gave the MPS a working majority in the 125-member legislature. The MPS was credited with 108 seats in an expanded 155-member assembly in the 2002 balloting.

The MPS formed an Alliance for the Renaissance of Chad (*Alliance pour la Renaissance du Tchad*—ART) for the February 2011 assembly poll with two former opposition parties—the RDP and RNDP (see below). Presenting joint candidates in some districts, the ART was credited with winning 132 seats on a reported vote share of 53 percent, enjoying its strongest support in the north. According to the national electoral commission, the MPS won 83 of the ART's seats on its own. MPS members were also elected on the joint tickets, and some reports indicated that as many as 117 of the ART's successful candidates were in fact MPS members. Subsequently, Déby was credited with 88.7 percent of the vote when reelected for a fourth presidential term in April as the ART candidate. The MPS extended its political dominance in the February 2012 local elections by securing six of ten council seats in N'Djamena and majorities or pluralities in many other constituencies, including control of all northern towns.

Leaders: Idriss DÉBY Itno (President of the Republic and Chair of the Party), Haroun KABADI (Secretary General and President of the National Assembly).

Rally for Democracy and Progress (*Rassemblement pour la Démocratie et le Progrès*—RDP). The RDP held its organizational congress in December 1991, its leadership including the mayor of N'Djamena, Lol Mahamat Choua, who had been proposed as president of an eventually aborted provisional national government in 1979. A number of RDP members were reportedly among those killed or arrested by Chadian security forces during the crackdown that followed the coup attempt of January 1992. (It was believed that the RDP was subjected to reprisal because of the support it enjoyed among the Kanem ethnic group, centered in the Lake Chad area, where the rebels had apparently received popular assistance.) Nevertheless, in early March the RDP was one of the first political parties to be legalized and was considered one of the leading components of the opposition coalition prior to the designation of Choua as chair of the Higher Transitional Council (CST) in April 1993.

In October 1994 Choua was replaced as CST chair, with the RDP leader subsequently accusing the Déby regime of human rights violations, including the harassment of many RDP members. Choua was credited with 5.9 percent of the vote in the first round of the 1996 presidential election. In a surprise development, Choua supported President Déby in the 2001 presidential election.

The RDP secured 14 seats in the 2002 assembly balloting and subsequently served in the cabinet until November 2003, when it withdrew from the government to protest Déby's announced plans to seek a third term. Choua subsequently served as a prominent figure in the anti-Déby CPDC (below), and he was briefly detained by security forces following the rebel attack on N'Djamena in early 2008. However, Choua signed an electoral accord with the MPS and the RNDP for the February 2011 assembly poll, arguing that President Déby "had changed." Twenty-seven of the successful candidates from the MPS-led ART were reportedly elected on joint MPS-RDP tickets, while four others were elected as joint MPS-RDP-RNDP candidates. However, subsequent reports indicated that only eight or nine of those elected were formal RDP members. (The RDP had secured 14 seats as part of the CPDC in 2002.) In an apparent reward for its participation in the ART, the RDP was allocated five portfolios in the cabinet announced in August.

Leaders: Lol Mahamat CHOUA (Parliamentary Leader and Former Chair of the Higher Transitional Council), Chetti Ali ABBAS.

National Assembly for Democracy and Progress (*Rassemblement National pour la Démocratie et le Progrès*—RNDP). Formed in the spring of 1992, the RNDP (also regularly referenced as VIVA-RNDP) was subsequently described as a prominent exponent of the formation of opposition coalitions; its leader, Delwa Kassiré Koumakoye, served as a spokesperson for a number of such groups. Koumakoye was named justice minister in the reshuffled transitional government announced in June 1993 and was elected prime minister in November. Following his dismissal in April 1995, Koumakoye charged that he had been made a scapegoat by President Déby and the Higher Transitional Council, which he described as bearing true responsibility for the delay in national elections.

In March 1996 Koumakoye was sentenced to three months in prison for the illegal possession of weapons, the RNDP leader accusing the Déby regime of manufacturing the charge in order to thwart his presidential ambitions. The following September it was announced that Koumakoye had been named spokesperson for a new opposition alliance called the Democratic Opposition Convention, which claimed the allegiance of more than 20 parties. The RNDP was initially credited with having secured four seats in the 1997 legislative poll, but all were given to other parties following the review by the national electoral commission. Koumakoye won 2 percent of the votes in the 2001 presidential poll.

The RNDP served in various cabinets following the 2002 assembly balloting, in which it won five seats. Koumakoye, by then considered to be aligned with Déby, was one of five candidates in the 2006 presidential election; he finished second with 8.8 percent of the vote. Following the death of Prime Minister Pascal Yoadimnadji in February 2007, Koumakoye was again appointed as prime minister. Although Koumakoye was dismissed from the premiership in April 2008 after his relations with Déby had again become strained, he aligned the RNDP with the MPS and the RDP in the ART for the February 2011 assembly poll. Fifteen of the ART's successful candidates were reportedly elected on joint MPS/RNDP tickets, while four others were elected as joint MPS/RDP/RNDP candidates. However, subsequent reports indicated that only five of the successful candidates were formal members of the RNDP. The RNDP was accorded four positions in the August 2011 cabinet, Koumakoye announcing that the party wanted to "consolidate democracy" by joining the government.

Leader: Delwa Kassiré KOUMAKOYE (Former Prime Minister, President of the Party, and 2001 and 2006 presidential candidate).

Coordination of Parties for the Defense of the Constitution (*Coordination des Partis pour la Défense de la Constitution*—CPDC). In 2004 some 20–30 opposition parties (including a number formerly aligned with the MPS) formed the CPDC to protest, among other things, the MPS plan to revise the constitution to permit another presidential term for Déby. The CPDC also demanded revision of the electoral code, appointment of a truly independent election commission, and the use of international election observers at future balloting. Having failed to affect the plans of the MPS, the CPDC (whose components were considered to be in agreement on the constitutional issues "but little else") called for a boycott of the 2005 national referendum and the 2006 presidential election. Following the rebel attack on N'Djamena in April 2006, CPDC spokesperson Ibni Oumar Mahamat SALEH (see PLD, below) said the CPDC was neither prorebel nor progovernment, although it opposed violent overthrow of the administration. Rebel leaders insisted that CPDC representatives be included in the peace talks launched in June 2007, but the government rejected that request. However, the government and the CPDC concluded an agreement in August 2007 under which new legislative elections were tentatively scheduled for December 2009 under the auspices of a new independent election commission.

Following the rebel attack on N'Djamena in January–February 2008, several CPDC leaders were temporarily detained by security forces, and Saleh's whereabouts subsequently remained unknown. However, in April four representatives from CPDC parties were named to the new cabinet, CPDC leaders urging President Déby to enter into peace negotiations with the rebels. As of late 2008 it was widely assumed (although not officially confirmed) that Saleh,who was widely respected in international socialist circles, had died while in the custody of Chadian security forces. Although members of some CPDC components subsequently continued to serve in the cabinet, other members strongly criticized the government for perceived repressive policies.

The CPDC was embroiled in numerous disputes with the administration prior to the 2011 assembly poll, particularly with regard to the impartiality of the national electoral commission and voter cards. Although the components of the CPDC (diminished by the defection of the RDP) participated in the legislative poll, they dismissed the results as fraudulent and ultimately called for a boycott of the April presidential balloting, describing it as "a great electoral charade." After reportedly receiving a pledge from the government for greater transparency, the CPDC participated in the February 2012 local elections, although some analysts questioned the wisdom of that decision, particularly after CPDC leaders complained of "fraud everywhere." The most noteworthy success for the CPDC in the local polls was in the economically important southern city of Moundou.

Union for Renewal and Democracy (*Union pour le Renouveau et la Démocratie*—URD). The URD was legalized in May 1992 under the leadership of Lt. Col. Wadal Abdelkader Kamougué, a former commander of the forces of the Chadian Armed Forces (Forces Armées Tchadiennes—FAT) in southern Chad who had served as a GUNT vice president (see Political background, above) and was subsequently a member of the Provisional Council of the Republic.

Kamougué was the runner-up to President Déby in the June 1996 presidential election, his strong performance establishing the URD as the nation's leading opposition force, particularly in view of its strong southern support. The URD finished second to the MPS in the 1997 legislative balloting with 29 seats. Kamougué was elected president of the new assembly, and the URD subsequently participated in MPS-led cabinets. In the 2001 presidential election Kamougué received 6 percent of the vote. The URD, which won 3 seats in the 2002 assembly poll, subsequently moved into the opposition camp to protest various constitutional changes engineered by the MPS. However, Kamougué was named minister of national defense as one of the CPDC members of the new cabinet named in April 2008.

The URD was credited with winning eight seats in the February 2011 assembly poll on a vote share of 5.4 percent. Kamougué initially intended to be a candidate in the April presidential election, but he ultimately joined the other potential CPDC candidates in calling for a boycott of that balloting, claiming irregularities in the assembly poll. Kamougué died of natural causes in May.

Leader: Sangde NGARNOUDJIBE (Secretary General).

National Union for Democracy and Renewal (*Union Nationale pour le Développement et le Renouvellement*—UNDR). The UNDR is led by Saleh Kebzabo, who was a minister of public works and transportation in the Moungar government and ran third in the first round of the June 1996 presidential election with 8.6 percent of the vote. He subsequently announced the UNDR's alliance with the MPS and threw his support to President Déby for the second round, thereby earning appointment to the cabinet formed in August. The party won 15 seats in the 1997 legislative poll, reportedly participating in an electoral alliance with the MPS. News reports surrounding subsequent political activity described the UNDR as primarily representing the interests of Muslims in the southwest of Chad.

Kebzabo was named minister of mines, energy, and oil in January 1998, but he and two UNDR secretaries of state left the government four months later. However, Kebzabo and four UNDR colleagues were named ministers in the December 1999 cabinet reshuffle. Kebzabo ran for president in 2001, receiving 7 percent of the vote. The UNDR won six seats in the 2002 assembly poll and was subsequently referenced as being firmly in the opposition camp.

Kebzabo was reportedly targeted for arrest following the rebel offensive of early 2008, but he fled the country. He subsequently returned after a security guarantee from the government and served as the primary spokesperson for the CPDC, initially arguing that dialogue with President Déby had broken down and that little progress had been achieved in implementing the August 2007 accord on electoral reform. However, in mid-2010 Kebzabo said "considerable advances" had been made and urged voters to participate in the upcoming legislative elections, at which the UNDR hoped to present common candidates with the other CPDC parties.

The UNDR, described as the nation's principal opposition party, was credited with winning ten seats (on a vote share of 5.5 percent) on its own in the February 2011 assembly poll; two candidates were also reportedly elected as joint UNDR/PLD candidates. Kebzabo ultimately called for a boycott of the April presidential poll after initially expressing a desire to run.

Leader: Saleh KEBZABO (President, Parliamentary Leader, and 2001 presidential candidate).

National Alliance for Development (*Alliance Nationale pour le Développement*—AND). Nabia NDALI, a member of the AND, was named minister of civil service and labor in the May 1992 cabinet. However, he resigned two months later following a dispute between AND leaders and Prime Minister Yodeyman, who was initially described as "close" to the AND but was subsequently reported to have been formally expelled from the group.

The AND was initially reported to have won no seats in the 1997 assembly balloting but, following a review by the national electoral commission, it was subsequently awarded two. AND president Salibou Garba was a member of the cabinet from May 1994 to April 2002, although he was subsequently referenced as a leader of the opposition's CPDC.

Garba, who reportedly narrowly avoided arrest following the rebel offensive in early 2008, reportedly objected to the inclusion of CPDC members in the April 2008 cabinet, arguing that President Déby was trying to "divide" the CPDC. The AND retained its single seat in the 2011 assembly poll.

Leader: Salibou GARBA (President).

Union for Democracy and the Republic (*Union pour la Démocratie et la République*—UDR). The UDR was launched by Jean Bawoyeu Alingué in March 1992 and was formally recognized a month later. Although Alingué was replaced as prime minister in May, the new cabinet included Djimasta Koibla, another UDR member. However, after being named prime minister in April 1995, Koibla was subsequently described as having taken a leave of absence from the party. Meanwhile, the UDR moved into position as one of the main opposition parties, Alingué receiving 8.3 percent of the vote in the first round of the 1996 presidential election. He also was one of the main critics of the government's involvement in the Democratic Republic of the Congo in 1998 and 1999. Alingué ran for president again in 2001, receiving only 2 percent of the ballots cast. The UDR boycotted the 2002 legislative elections, and Alingué subsequently remained a vocal critic of the government and proponent of the formation of opposition coalitions. However, he was named to the cabinet announced in April 2008. The UDR secured two seats in the 2011 assembly poll.

Leader: Dr. Jean Bawoyey ALINGUÉ (President of the Party and 2001 presidential candidate).

Party for Freedom and Development (*Parti pour la Liberté et le Développement*—PLD). Formed in late 1993 to promote the "rehabilitation" of Chad, the PLD captured three seats in the 1997 legislative elections. The PLD's candidate, Ibni Oumar Mahamat Saleh, secured 3 percent of the vote in the 2001 presidential election. The PLD boycotted the 2002 legislative elections. Saleh subsequently was described as the leader of the CPDC (see above). Following the rebel offensive against N'Djamena in January–February 2008 Saleh was reportedly arrested by security forces. Although CPDC members joined the cabinet named in April, Saleh's whereabouts subsequently remained unknown, and his followers announced they would not support the new government. The PLD reportedly secured two seats in the 2011 assembly poll on joint tickets with the UNDR.

Rally of Nationalists for the Development of Chad/Awakening (*Rassemblement des Nationalistes pour le Développement du Chad/Le Réveil*—RNDT/Awakening). After the RNDT won a seat in the 2002 assembly balloting, its leader, Albert Pahimi Padacké, was named agriculture minister in 2005 and was a presidential candidate in 2006, securing 5.4 percent of the vote. He subsequently served as justice minister and was also named to the cabinet announced in April 2008.

The RNDT/Awakening, described as a moderate party, secured eight seats in the February 2011 assembly poll (six were officially credited to the RNDT and two to the RNDT/Awakening). Padacké finished second in the April presidential poll with 6.0 percent of the vote, the major opposition parties having withdrawn from that balloting.

Leader: Albert Pahimi PADACKÉ.

Front of Action Forces for the Republic (*Front des Forces d'Action pour la République*—FFAR). Described as a "separatist" grouping, the FFAR won one seat in the 1997 legislative balloting. Its legislator, Ngarledjy Yorongar, subsequently became a prominent critic of government policy regarding the development of oil fields in southern Chad. He received a surprising 14 percent of the vote while finishing second in the 2001 presidential election. The FFAR was also credited with winning ten seats in the 2002 assembly poll.

Although Yorongar called for a boycott of the 2005 constitutional referendum and the 2006 presidential poll, he and the FFAR did not participate in the CPDC. Yorongar also described the August 2007 electoral agreement between the CPDC and the government as a "waste of time." He was briefly detained by security forces following the rebel offensive of early 2008 and reportedly left the country briefly for France in March.

The "profederalist" FFAR won four seats in the February 2011 assembly poll. Yorongar accused the government of fraud in that balloting and ultimately called for a boycott of the April presidential election.

Leaders: Yorongar LEMOHIBAN, Ngarledjy YORONGAR (Parliamentary Leader and 2001 presidential candidate).

National Convention for Social Democracy (*Convention National pour la Démocratie Sociale*—CNDS). The leader of the CNDS, former Habré minister Adoum Moussa SEIF, won 4.9 percent of the vote in the first round of the 1996 presidential election, and the party won one seat in the 1997 legislative balloting. In 1998, however, Seif was described in news reports as heading a rebel group (the Armed Resistance Against Anti-Democratic Forces) in the Lake Chad region. The rump CNDS, under the leadership of Adoum Daye Zere, supported President Déby in his 2001 reelection campaign. Some reports credited the CNDS with winning one seat in the 2002 assembly poll, and it appeared that the seat credited to Action for the Renewal of Chad in 2011 was won on a joint ticket with the CNDS. The CNDS was also apparently involved in two other joint tickets for which the successful candidates were formally members of other small parties.

Leaders: Adoum Daye ZERE, Assane Amath PATCHA.

Other minor parties that gained seats in the 2011 legislative elections included the following: the **Socialist Movement for Democracy in Chad** (*Mouvement Socialiste pour la Démocratie au Tchad*—MSDT), led by Albert Mbainaido DJOMIA; the **Party for Democracy and Integral Independence** (*Parti pour la Démocratie et l'Indépendance Intégrale*—PDI), which secured its seat in coalition with the **Rally of the Chadian People** (*Rassemblement du Peuple du Tchad*—RDT); **Action for the Renewal of Chad,** which, under the leadership of Oumar BOUCHAR, won its seat in coalition with the CNDS; and the **People's Movement for Democracy in Chad** (*Mouvement Populaire pour la Démocratie au Tchad*—MPDT), whose leader, Mahamat ABDOULAYE, was appointed to the cabinet in 2005 and was a presidential candidate in 2006. The seat credited to the MPDT was apparently won on a joint ticket with the CNDS and an offshoot of the RDP called the RDR/Renovated. (The PDI and Action for the Renewal of Chad had each won a single seat in the 2002 poll.)

A number of other previously unreferenced parties (about which little information was available) also secured legislative seats in 2011. See Legislature, below, for their names.

Other Parties:

Action for Unity and Socialism (*Action pour l'Unité et le Socialisme*—Actus). Actus is a former GUNT tendency led by Fidéle Moungar, who briefly served as prime minister in 1993. (See the 2013 *Handbook* for additional information on Actus.)

Some reports credited Actus with winning one seat in the 2002 assembly poll. Moungar has reportedly been living in exile recently.

Also active have been the **New African Socialist** (*Socialiste Africain Rénové*—SAR), which fielded a candidate, Ibrahim KOULAMALLAH, in the 2006 presidential election; the **Rally for Progress and Social Justice** (*Rassemblement pour le Progrès et la Justice Sociale*—RPJS), registered in January 1996 and the first Chadian party to be led by a woman (Leopoldine Adoun NDARADOUNRY); and the **Rally of Chadian Nationalists** (*Rassemblement des Nationalistes Tchadiennes*—RNT). The previously unreferenced **Socialist Alliance for Integral Renewal** (*Alliance Socialiste pour le Renouvellement Intégral*—ASRI) presented Nadji MADOU as its 2011 presidential candidate. She secured 5.3 percent of the vote.

Other Groups:

Union of Forces for Democracy and Development (*Union des Forces pour la Démocratie et le Développement*—UFDD). The UFDD, based in eastern Chad and perceived to be supported by Sudan, was formed in mid-2006 under the leadership of Mahamat Nouri, a northerner who had been considered the second in command (as leader of the UNIR) during the Habré regime but had also served as a cabinet minister and diplomat in the Déby administration. The UFDD was prominent (along with the FUC, SCUD [see RFC, below], and the Revolutionary Democratic Council [*Conseil Démocratique Révolutionnaire*—CDR; see Political background, above]) in the rebel coalition that invaded eastern Chad from Sudan in September 2006 (see Current issues, above, for additional information). The UFDD, whose members come mainly from the Goran ethnic group, in December announced military cooperation with the RFC and CNT and continued antigovernment activity throughout the first half of 2007, the UFDD at that point being considered the leading rebel organization in view of the FUC's Mahamat Nour Abdelkerim having joined the Déby cabinet.

In October 2007 the UFDD joined the RFC, CNT, and UFDD Fundamental (see below) in signing a Libyan-brokered cease-fire agreement that called for a permanent peace settlement under which the rebels would be integrated into the national army. However, a month later Nouri accused Déby of reneging on the agreement, and fighting broke out again between government forces and the UFDD, RFC, UFDD Fundamental, and other rebel groups, who in late January 2008 launched an offensive against the capital that almost deposed Déby (see Political background, above, for details). Following their retreat, the UFDD, UFDD Fundamental, RFC, and other small groups announced the formation of a **National Alliance** (*Alliance Nationale*—AN) to continue the anti-Déby campaign under the "single leadership" of Nouri. (Some members of the component groups reportedly objected to Sudan's apparent insistence that the post be given to Nouri, and some news reports subsequently referred to Ali GADAYE as the leader of the AN.) The AN, urging French or other foreign troops not to "prop up" the Déby government, vowed further efforts to take over the capital unless all-inclusive negotiations toward a unity government were launched.

In May 2010 Nouri was described as the leader of a new rebel coalition called the **National Alliance for Democratic Change** (*Alliance Nationale pour le Changement Démocratique*—ANCD), which included the UFDD, CDR, the **Front for the Salvation of the Republic** (*Front pour la Salvation de la République*—FSR), and the **Democratic Movement for Chadian Redevelopement** (*Movement Démocratique pour le Rédéveloppement Tchadien*—MDRT). The ANCD declared committed itself to the overthrow of Déby "by any means." (Some members of the above groups may have participated in a cease-fire agreement with the government that was announced in mid-2009.)

Nouri, then resident in Qatar after being expelled from Sudan, reportedly expressed an interest in late 2010 in dialogue with the Déby administration, but in 2011 he again called on France to abandon its support for Déby. Meanwhile, four prominent UFDD members were amnestied by Déby in 2011 after they had turned themselves over to the authorities, although some UFDD adherents reportedly remained armed.

The ANCD claimed in 2012 that Djilbrine AZENE, an ANCD military commander who had been released from prison in 2011, had died as the result of the effects of having been tortured while in jail. Meanwhile, there was a report in March 2012 that the FSR had opened an office in Tunis under the leadership of Capt. Ismael MOUSSA, who called for an uprising in Chad in consonance with the region's Arab Spring.

Nouri subsequently was reported to be living in France, from where he was fighting an international arrest warrant issued by Chad.

Leaders: Mahamat NOURI (in France), Hassane BOULMAYU, Abakar TOLLIMI (Secretary General).

Union of Forces for Democracy and Development Fundamental (*Union des Forces pour la Démocratie et le Développement Fondamentel*—UFDD Fundamental). The Arab-led UFDD Fundamental broke from the UFDD in 2007 in a leadership dispute with UFDD leader Mahamat Nouri. However, the UFDD Fundamental joined the UFDD and other rebel groups in the attack on N'Djamena in early 2008.

Leaders: Abdelwahid Aboud MAKAYE, Acheickh ibn OUMAR.

Rally of Forces for Change (*Rassemblement des Forces pour le Changement*—RFC). A new rebel faction, the RFC was organized in December 2006 by brothers Tom and Timan Erdimi, relatives of President Déby who stopped supporting the president after the controversial constitutional revision in 2004 to permit Déby to run for another term. The Erdimis had previously participated in the Platform for Change, Unity, and Democracy (*Socle pour le Changement, l'Unité, et la Démocratie*—SCUD), which had been formed in October 2005 by some 300 former members of the Presidential Guard and other government forces. The SCUD, which reportedly attracted members of President Déby's Zaghawa clan, subsequently engaged government troops in eastern Chad but did not participate in the failed April 2006 attack on N'Djamena by the FUC. Major rebel activity for the rest of 2006 was conducted by an umbrella group called the Rally of Democratic Forces (*Rassemblement des Forces Démocratiques*—RAFD), which included the SCUD and the CNT. The RFC appeared to serve as a partial successor to the RAFD in 2007. (See UFDD, above, for information on the RFC's participation in subsequent antigovernment activity.)

In January 2009 the RFC served as a core founder of the **Union of Resistance Forces** (*Union des Forces du Résistance*—UFR), an umbrella for some eight rebel groups dedicated to the overthrow of President Déby. Timan Erdimi was named chair of the grouping, whose estimated 2,000 fighters launched an unsuccessful offensive against government forces in May 2009. The UFR was subsequently described as factionalized, with some components reportedly endorsing, along with other rebel groups, a midyear peace accord. Members of several UFR factions participated in the formation of the ANCD in 2010 (see UFDD, above, for details.

Abderaman Koulamallah, a former member of the FUC and in recent years referenced as a leader of the UFR, was arrested in mid-2011 when he returned to Chad from exile. Koulamallah had been under indictment in regard to the 2008 rebel offensive against N'Djamena. He was also referenced as a former spokesperson for the ANCD, which condemned his arrest. UFR remnants who had not accepted the 2009 demobilization agreement announced in May 2013 from Qatar that they intended to resume armed struggle, although they were not considered a serious threat.

Leaders: Tom ERDIMI, Timan ERDIMI (in Qatar), Abderaman KOULAMALLAH.

Union of Forces for Change and Democracy (*Union des Forces pour le Changement et la Démocratie*—UFCD). The UFCD was formed in March 2008 by UFDD and RFC dissidents who opposed the designation (apparently at Sudan's insistence) of the UFDD's Mahamat Nouri as the leader of the new National Alliance of rebel groups. However, a degree of reconciliation with the National Alliance was subsequently reported.

Leaders: Adouma HASSABALLAH, Karim Bory ISSA.

Chadian National Concord (*Concorde Nationale Tchadienne*—CNT). The largely Arab CNT was one of the most active rebel groups in eastern Chad in 2006, often in alliance with the RAFD. The CNT joined other rebel groups in signing a much-heralded peace agreement with the government in October 2007. However, when the other three signatories resumed antigovernment activity a month later, CNT leader Hassan Al Djinedi, other CNT officials, and their followers remained supportive of the government and the cease-fire. Al Djinedi was named a secretary of state in a February 2008 cabinet reshuffle, although some CNT members continued their rebel activity, having announced the "expulsion" of Al Djinedi and his supporters.

Leaders: Hassan Al DJINEDI, Ismail MOUSSA (leader of militant faction).

United Front for Change (*Front Uni pour le Changement*—FUC). The FUC was formed in December 2005 by the Rally for Democracy and Liberty (*Rassemblement pour la Démocratie et la Liberté*—RDL) and a number of other groups, some of which comprised deserters from the Chadian army as well as Chadian exiles in Sudan opposed to the recent constitutional changes and the "dictatorial rule" of President Déby. The RDL had been formed earlier in the year in the Darfur region of Sudan and had launched an unsuccessful attack on the Chadian city of Adré near the Sudanese border on December 18. The RDL was led by Mahamat Nour Abdelkerim, who had branched out of the National Alliance of Resistance (*Alliance Nationale de la Résistance*—ANR), which had been formed in the mid-1990s by five rebel groups and had grown to include eight antigovernment groups operating in the eastern part of the country. The ANR signed a peace agreement with the government in January 2003 with a long-term plan to transition to a formal political party, and Col. Mahamat GARFA (an ANR founder) joined the MPS-led cabinet later in the year. However, one faction of the ANR refused to accept the cease-fire and continued fighting under the leadership of Nour Abdelkerim, who was instrumental in the organization of the FUC, which demanded the convening of a national forum to address the country's political future, the installation of a transitional government, and new elections. (Nour Abdelkerim is a member of the Tama ethnic group, which reportedly led to leadership tension within the FUC, a predominantly Zaghawa grouping.) The FUC, also referenced as the United Front for Democratic Change, attempted a military takeover of the government in April 2006, the Déby government alleging that the Sudanese government was supporting the FUC. On December 24, 2006, Nour Abdelkerim signed a peace agreement with the government, and he was appointed minister of defense in March 2007. Among other things, the accord called for the integration of FUC fighters (estimated at 6,000) into the national army. However, reports indicated that disaffected members of the FUC had established a rival rebel grouping, still called the FUC, but with a new leadership, led by Abderman Koulamallah, who was subsequently referenced as a spokesperson for the UFR.

Nour Abdelkerim was dismissed as defense minister in December 2007, in part, apparently, because he had been reluctant to direct FUC fighters to join the government's battle against the UFDD and other rebel groups. President Déby had also ordered government forces to forcibly disarm the FUC, which led to FUC/government fighting. It was subsequently reported that a number of Nour Abdelkerim's Tama supporters had been arrested, while Nour Abdelkerim, apparently in poor health, took refuge in the Libyan embassy. Some FUC fighters reportedly joined the rebel offensive against N'Djamena in early 2008, and Nour Abdelkerim was subsequently sentenced to death in absentia by a Chadian magistrate's court.

Leaders: Mahamat NOUR Abdelkerim, Col. Regis BECHIR.

United Front for Democracy and Peace (*Front Uni pour la Démocratie et la Paix*—FUDP). Formed in 2005 by dissidents from the MDJT as well as members of rebel groups (based in Benin) seeking a negotiated peace settlement, the FUDP subsequently was joined by a number of other parties and rebel groups, including the MDD.

Movement for Development and Democracy (*Mouvement pour le Développement et la Démocratie*—MDD). The MDD was formed in 1991 as the political arm of pro-Habré rebel forces, which in late December launched an attempted overthrow of the Déby regime from the western border, where they had been camped since Habré's ouster a year earlier. Although the government at first estimated the MDD strength at more than 3,000, it was subsequently reported that only about 500 had participated in the attempted coup.

Despite the highly publicized announcement of several peace agreements during 1992, fighting continued between government troops and MDD followers, who sometimes referred to themselves as the Western Armed Forces (*Forces Armées Occidentales*—FAO). In early 1993 the MDD was reportedly split into a pro-Habré faction known as the National Armed Forces of Chad (*Forces Armées Nationales Tchadiennes*—FANT), led by Mahamat Saleh FADIL, and an anti-Habré faction loyal to Goukhouni Guët (reportedly in prison). Members of the latter faction were reportedly invited to the Sovereign National Conference that began in January, but the FANT, described by *Africa Confidential* as "much feared in N'Djamena by both government and opposition," remained outside the national reconciliation process.

In January 1994 the MDD announced an alliance with another guerrilla group, the **National Union for Democracy and Socialism** (*Union National pour la Démocratie et le Socialisme*—UNDS), and called upon other anti-Déby rebels to join them in united military activity. A year later, however, the MDD was described as still split into two factions "fighting each other, not Déby." Meanwhile, Habré remained in exile in Senegal, the general amnesty of December 1994 having specifically excluded him.

The apparent reunification of the MDD factions was reported in April 1995, and an extraordinary congress in August elected a new 16-member executive bureau headed by Mahamat Seïd Moussa MEDELLA. In November, an agreement was announced between the government and the MDD calling for the cessation of hostilities, exchange of prisoners, and the integration of MDD guerrillas into the national army. Some MDD fighters subsequently remained in conflict with government forces, however, and factionalization on that issue surfaced within the grouping again in 1998. The MDD joined the FUDP in 2003. By that time there were two main factions of the MDD: one led by Ibrahim Malla Mahamet, the other led by Issa Faki Mahamet.

Leaders: Goukhouni GUËT (in detention), Abouharkaye HAROUN (Representative in Paris), Ibrahim Malla MAHAMET (Chair of the Executive Bureau).

National Liberation Front of Chad (*Front de Libération National du Tchad*—Frolinat). Frolinat was established in 1966 by northerners opposed to the administration of President Tombalbaye, a southerner. The organization eventually suffered such severe factionalization that Frolinat became little more than a generic name for various groups originally based in the north, including splinters loyal to subsequent Chadian presidents Goukhouni Oueddei and Hissène Habré.

Following Habré's capture of N'Djamena in 1982, most of the factions opposed to his Frolinat/FAN coalesced under a reconstituted GUNT. During 1983 and 1984, dissent among GUNT factions over the extent of Libyan involvement led to reported dissolution of the coalition, although pronouncements continued to be issued in its name. During a meeting in Sebha, Libya, on August 7, 1984, most of the pro-Libyan military components of GUNT joined in forming the National Council of Liberation (*Conseil National de la Libération*—CNL), which was succeeded by a more inclusive Supreme Revolutionary Council (*Conseil Suprême de la Révolution*—CSR) a year later. By 1986, however, anti-Libyan sentiment appeared to have gained the ascendancy, with Oueddei being removed as CSR chair (and president of GUNT) in November. Thereafter, the CSR declined in importance, many of its component groups having announced their dissolution and acceptance of integration into the UNIR. Although Oueddei announced a cabinet reshuffle in May 1988 in an attempt to consolidate his position among remaining GUNT factions, he was described in mid-1990 as "essentially marginalized" as an antigovernment influence.

Continuing to position himself as the leader of Frolinat, Oueddei made a highly publicized return from exile to meet with President Déby in May 1991 and suggested that cooperation with the new regime was possible if opposition political parties were permitted. Subsequently, however, Oueddei returned to Algiers and, following the abortive October coup, was reportedly informed that he was again not welcome in his homeland. During an interview in mid-1992 Oueddei described Frolinat as "still an armed liberation movement" but one that was "currently not fighting" and dedicated, for the time being, to "resolving problems through dialogue." Oueddei, described as remaining widely respected by the public and considered a potential mediator among Chad's many ethnic and political adversaries, participated in the Sovereign National Conference in early 1993. Although he was reported in 1995 to be still harboring presidential ambitions, there was little evidence of his influence in the nation's 1996 democratization process. In December 1998 Oueddei issued a statement in Algiers calling for an "uprising" against the Déby government, and in early 1999 Frolinat announced its support for the Toubou rebels in northern Chad.

Oueddei, who had lived primarily in Algeria and Libya since leaving Chad in the early 1990s, said in late 2005 that he supported the rebels in eastern Chad who were attempting to overthrow the Déby regime. However, in mid-2007 he offered to serve as a mediator between the remaining rebels and the government, and in mid-2008 he called for a "national dialogue" among all Chadian groups. Oueddei returned from exile in August 2009 and announced his intention to assist in the pursuit of national reconciliation.

Leaders: Goukhouni OUEDDEI (Former President of the Republic), Mahmoud Ali MAHMOUD.

Movement for Democracy and Justice in Chad (*Mouvement pour la Démocratie et la Justice en Tchad*—MDJT). Led then by Youssef TOGOIMI, a former minister in the Déby administration, the MDJT launched guerrilla activity against government troops in late 1998 in northern Chad and by April 1999 was claiming control of substantial territory. It was still active in mid-2001, although there was little independently verifiable information on the breadth and scope of its activities. The government was sufficiently concerned about the MDJT to periodically issue communiqués minimizing the extent of the rebellion. The grouping reportedly drew its support from the Toubou ethnic group, described as a "traditional warrior community" in the Tibesti mountain region along the border with Niger.

In 2002 Togoimi was killed by a land mine, and one faction of the MDJT left the group to participate in the formation of the FUDP (see above). The government subsequently was reported to have negotiated a cease-fire with a number of local MDJT commanders, and a broader accord was brokered in January 2003, many MDJT elements reportedly accepting amnesty for an end to attacks. In August 2005 the government signed a final agreement with the MDJT that provided for the eventual integration of remaining MDJT fighters into the national army. At an extraordinary congress in November 2006, MDJT members still opposed to conciliation with the government reportedly voted to disband the MDJT and merge with Frolinat. However, it was reported in late 2008 that a rump MDJT had aligned with the recently formed National Alliance rebel grouping. The rump MDJT, led by Chouhai DAZI, reportedly signed a peace agreement with the government in April 2010 calling for the integration of the remaining MDJT fighters into the national army.

Other rebel groups have included the **Movement for Peace, Reconstruction, and Development** (*Mouvement pour la Paix, la Reconstruction, et le Développement*—MPRD), led by Djibrine DASSERT from the Central African Republic. Dassert, who had fought alongside Déby in the 1990 takeover but had initiated antigovernment rebel activity in the south in 2005, was arrested in January 2010 along with some 20 MPRD fighters. However, Dassert was subsequently amnestied by President Déby. As of mid-2010 the **Popular Front for National Resistance** (*Front Populair pour la Résistance Nationale*—PFNR), a small eastern group led by Adoum YACOUB, was described as one of the last rebel movements still operating inside Chad. The **Popular Front for Reconstruction** (FPR), led by Gen. Abdel Kader BABA LADDE, reportedly signed a peace accord with the government in mid-2011 that allowed its fighters to return to Chad from their base in the CAR. However, renewed conflict broke out in the CAR in early 2012 between FPR fighters and a joint security force from Chad and the CAR. UN negotiators subsequently facilitated another peace agreement between the FPR (primarily composed of members of the Fula ethnic group from several countries) and the Chadian government. Baba Ladde returned to N'Djamena and, in early 2013, was named a special advisor to the government. Meanwhile, the repatriation to Chad of an estimated 3,000 FPR fighters continued, analysts suggesting that prospects for peace in northeast CAR depended on the success of that demobilization.

LEGISLATURE

As provided for in the constitution approved by national referendum in December 1989, a 123-member unicameral **National Assembly** (*Assemblée Nationale*) was elected by direct universal suffrage for a five-year term on July 8, 1990. However, the assembly was dissolved on December 3 upon the overthrow of the Habré regime. Subsequently, President Déby appointed a Provisional Council of the Republic (*Conseil Provisoire de la Républic*) to serve as an interim consultative body, which in turn was replaced by a 57-member Higher Transitional Council (*Conseil Supérieur de Transition*—CST) elected by the Sovereign National Conference (CNS) in April 1993. The national constitutional referendum in March 1996 authorized the CST to continue to function pending the installation of the new bicameral legislature. Elections (for a four-year term) to the new 125-member National Assembly were held on January 5 and February 23, 1997. In February 2001 the assembly extended its mandate until April 2002, at which time elections were held to an expanded 155-member assembly slated to serve a four-year term. However, in January 2006 the assembly voted to postpone new elections (scheduled for April 2006) until at least April 2007. New balloting was subsequently again postponed due to security problems in the east and the government's related imposition of a state of emergency. Elections were finally held on February 13, 2011, to an expanded assembly of 188 members, directly elected for four-year terms in a mixed majoritarian-proportional system. (Majority voting determines the winner in the 25 single-member constituencies. Voters choose from party lists in the 34 multimember constituencies. If a party wins a majority of votes in a constituency, it is awarded all of that constituency's seats. Otherwise, the seats are distributed on a proportional basis.) Following revoting for 13 seats on May 9, the distribution of seats was as follows (reports differed slightly on the distribution): the Alliance for the Renaissance of Chad, 132; the National Union for Democracy and Renewal, 10; the Union for Renewal and Democracy, 8; the Rally of Nationalists for the Development of Chad/Awakening, 8; the Front of Action Forces for the Republic, 4; the Union for Democracy and the Republic, 2; the Social Democratic Party for a Changeover of Power, 2; the Chadian Convention for Peace and Development, 2; the Party for Freedom and Development, 2; the Chadian Democratic Union, 1; the Socialist Movement for Democracy in Chad, 1; the National Alliance for Development, 1; the Party for Democracy and Integral Independence, 1; the African Party for Peace and Social Justice, 1; the New Breath of Air for the Republic, 1; the Union of Democratic Forces–Republican Party, 1; the Union of Chadian Environmentalists/The Greens, 1; Action for the Renewal of Chad, 1; the Movement of Chadian Patriots for the Republic, 1; the People's Movement for the Development of Chad, 1; the Party for Unity and Reconstruction, 1; and others, 6.

President: Haroun KABADI.

CABINET

[as of November 5, 2013]

Prime Minister	Joseph Djimrangar Dadnadji
Ministers	
Advisor to the President	Beyom Malo Adrien
Agriculture and Irrigation	Ngariera Rimadjita
Basic Education and Literacy	Albatoul Zakaria [f]
Civil Aviation and Meteorology	Haqua Acyl [f]
Civil Service, Labor, and Employment	Abdoulaye Abakar
Communication and Government Spokesperson	Hassan Silla Bakari
Culture, Arts, and Conservation of Heritage	Dayang Menwa Enock
Economy, Planning, and International Cooperation	Mariam Mahamat Nour [f]
Environment and Marine Resources	Mahamat Issa Halikimi
Finance and Budget	Bédoumra Kordjé
Foreign Relations and African Integration	Moussa Faki Mahamat
Higher Education and Scientific Research	Lamine Moustapha
Human Rights and Promotion of Fundamental Liberties	Laona Gong Raol
Infrastructure and Public Equipment	Adoum Younousmi
Interior and Public Security	Abderagun Bireme Hamid
Justice and Guardian of the Seals	Jean Bernard Padaré
Micro-Finance and the Promotion of Women and Youth	Banata Tchalet Sow [f]
Mines and Geology	Oumar Adoum Sini
Minister Delegate to the President (National Defense, Veterans, and War Veterans)	Benaindo Tatola
Oil and Energy	Djérassem Le Bémadjiel
Pastoral Development and Animal Production	Issa Ali Taher
Posts and New Information Technologies	Daoussa Deby Itno
Public Health	Ahmed Djidda Mahamat
Public Morality and Promotion of Good Government	Abderaman Sallah
Secondary Education and Vocational Training	Adelkerim Bakhit Amadaye
Social Action, Family, and National Solidarity	Baiwong Djibergui Amane Rosine [f]
Territorial Administration, Decentralization, and Local Freedoms	Mahamat Yaya Oky Dagache
Tourism and Promotion of Handicrafts	Abderahim Younous Ali
Transport and Civil Aviation	Adoum Younousmi
Urban Affairs, Housing, and Property and Landowner Affairs	Gata Ngoulou
Water Resources	Youssouf Hamat Moussa
Youth and Sports	Adoum Forteye
Secretary General to the Government, in Charge of Relations with the National Assembly	Abdoulaye Sabre Fadoul

[f] = female

INTERGOVERNMENTAL REPRESENTATION

Ambassador to the U.S.: Maitine DJOUMBE.

U.S. Ambassador to Chad: Mark BOULWARE.

Permanent Representative to the UN: Ahmad ALLAM-MI.

IGO Memberships (Non-UN): AfDB, AU, ICC, NAM, OIC, WTO.

CHILE

Republic of Chile

República de Chile

Note: In parliamentary elections held on November 17, the New Majority (*Nueva Mayoria*) coalition of former president Michelle Bachelet secured majorities in both chambers. New Majority, composed of the same parties in Bachelet's previous *Concertación* coalition, won 67 of the 120 seats in the Chamber of Deputies and holds 21 of the 38 Senate seats. In simultaneous presidential elections, Bachelet won 46.67 percent of the vote, necessitating a run-off with Evelyn Matthei (UDI), who placed second with 25.01 percent. Bachelet won a decisive 62.2 percent in the December 15 runoff, but the low turnout of only 42 percent may weaken her mandate.

Political Status: Independent republic since 1818; present constitution approved September 11, 1980 (in effect from March 11, 1981), partially superseding military regime instituted in 1973; fully effective as of March 11, 1990.

Area: 292,256 sq. mi. (756,945 sq. km).

Population: 17,402,630 (2013E—UN); 17,216,945 (2013E—U.S. Census).

Major Urban Centers (2012E): SANTIAGO (4,963,000), Puente Alto (583,000), Antofagasta (330,000), Viña del Mar (331,000), Valparaíso (280,000), Concepción (207,000).

Official Language: Spanish.

Monetary Unit: Peso (market rate November 1, 2013: 509.50 pesos = $1US).

President: (*See headnote.*) Sebastián PIÑERA Echenique (Coalition for Change—National Renovation); elected in runoff balloting on January 17, 2010, and inaugurated on March 11 for a four-year term, succeeding Michelle BACHELET (Socialist Party of Chile).

THE COUNTRY

Occupying a narrow strip along about 2,700 miles of South America's west coast, the Chilean national territory also includes Easter Island, the Juan Fernández Islands, and other smaller Pacific territories. The population is predominantly mestizo (mixed Spanish and Indian) but also includes German, Italian, and other foreign groups. Roman Catholicism, which was disestablished in 1925, is the religion of 70 percent of the people. Women constitute about 40 percent of the paid labor force.

Chile, the fifth-largest economy in Latin America, is the world's leading copper producer, the commodity accounting for more than two-fifths of export earnings and a third of all government revenue, although reserves are expected to be exhausted within 20 years. Other commercially mined minerals include gold, silver, coal, and iron. In addition, there are extensive nitrate deposits in the north and some oil reserves in the south.

The global recession and falling copper prices caused the country's economy to contract by 1.7 percent in 2009 while unemployment rose to 9.6 percent. More than 15 percent of Chileans lived in poverty in 2009. Chile used $4 billion—a fifth of the country's rainy-day sovereign wealth funds, which it had accumulated as a result of its countercyclical fiscal policy—to stimulate GDP growth, which rebounded to 6.1 percent in 2010 and 5.9 percent in 2011, while unemployment fell to 8.2 percent and 7.1 percent, respectively. GDP grew 5.5 percent in 2012, with unemployment dropping to 6.5 percent. Chile has the highest per capital GDP in Latin America at $16,273 in 2013.

GOVERNMENT AND POLITICS

Political background. After winning its independence from Spain from 1810 to 1818 under the leadership of Bernardo O'HIGGINS, Chile experienced a period of alternating centralized and federal constitutions. The political struggles between conservative and liberal elements culminated in the civil war of 1829–1830, the conservatives emerging victorious. Conflicts with Peru and Bolivia from 1836 to 1839 and 1879 to 1884 (the War of the Pacific) resulted in Chile's territorial expansion at the expense of both.

The election of Arturo ALESSANDRI Palma in 1920 was a victory for the middle classes, but the reforms he advocated were never implemented because of parliamentary intransigence. Left-right antagonism after World War II occasioned widespread fears for the future of the democratic regime, but the election in 1964 of Eduardo FREI Montalva initially appeared to open the way to fundamental economic and social reforms. The failure of the Frei regime to accomplish these goals led to the election of Salvador ALLENDE Gossens in 1970. Chile thus became the first republic in North or South America to choose an avowedly Marxist president by constitutional means. Allende immediately began to implement his openly revolutionary "Popular Unity" program, which included the nationalization of Chile's principal foreign-owned enterprises, a far-reaching redistribution of social benefits, and the pursuit of a more independent foreign policy. Despite the very real benefits that began to accrue to the lower classes as a result of these and other policies, Allende gradually alienated the middle class, a sizable portion of the legislature, the judiciary, and finally the military. He died (subsequent evidence indicating suicide) during a right-wing coup on September 11, 1973, which resulted initially in rule by a four-man junta. On June 26, 1974, Maj. Gen. Augusto José Ramón PINOCHET Ugarte was designated head of state, the other junta members assuming subordinate roles.

Proclaimed president on December 17, 1974, Pinochet governed on the basis of unwavering army support, despite widespread domestic and foreign criticism centering on human rights abuses, including the "disappearance," arbitrary arrest and detention, torture, and exiling of opponents. Citing the need for harsh measures to combat communism, the Pinochet regime typically operated under either a state of siege or a somewhat less restrictive state of emergency.

In a national referendum on January 4, 1978, a 3-to-1 majority of Chileans endorsed the policies of the Pinochet government. However, the significance of the poll was lessened by the inability of opposition groups to mount an effective antireferendum campaign.

On September 11, 1980, the electorate, by a 2-to-1 margin, approved a new constitution designed over a nine-year period that commenced March 11, 1981, to serve as the framework for "slow and gradual evolution" toward a democratic order. At a plebiscite of October 5, 1988, 54.7 percent of the participants rejected a further eight-year term for General Pinochet. As a result, he continued in office only until March 11, 1990, when Patricio AYLWIN Azócar, a Christian Democrat who had led a Coalition of Parties for Democracy (*Concertatión de los Partidos por la Democracia*—CPD) to a 53.8 percent vote share at presidential balloting on December 14, 1989, was sworn in as his successor.

In the general election of December 11, 1993, Eduardo FREI Ruiz-Tagle (Frei Montalva's son) secured a remarkable 58 percent majority in a field of seven presidential contenders. The CPD was equally successful, retaining its majorities of elected Senate and Chamber members. However, the coalition failed to gain control of the upper house because of unelected senators named to eight-year terms by the Pinochet administration in 1989.

The legislative balance was essentially unchanged after the election of December 11, 1997, with rightist forces continuing to control the Senate, and the Chamber limited to passage of a nonbinding motion "rejecting and repudiating" Pinochet's scheduled congressional seating. Pinochet subsequently secured the title of senator-for-life, a position granted by the 1980 constitution to any president serving more than six years. While this position afforded him immunity from prosecution in his own country, he was arrested while visiting England for medical treatment in 1998, on a warrant issued by a Spanish court. He was placed under house arrest until 2000, when he was allowed to return to Chile.

In the first round of presidential balloting on December 12, 1999, CPD candidate Ricardo LAGOS bested his right-wing opponent, Joaquín LAVÍN Infante, by less than 1 percentage point, necessitating the first runoff in Chilean history. Despite a marginally improved victory in the second round on January 16, Lagos, a former Socialist, faced formidable opposition from the Senate controlled by a right-leaning majority.

At the time of Pinochet's return to Chile in 2000, more than 100 actions had been filed against him, most on behalf of the more than 3,000 people who had died or disappeared during his tenure. A major hurdle to legal action was Pinochet's senatorial immunity, which the Chilean Court of Appeals revoked in May. Then, in a complicated scenario, the appeals court suspended proceedings against Pinochet in July 2001 on the grounds that he was suffering from "moderate dementia."

Meanwhile, in the legislative election of December 16, 2001, the CPD retained its lower house majority by a greatly reduced margin, while the right-wing Independent Democratic Union (*Union Demócrata Independiente*—UDI) supplanted National Renovation (*Renovación Nacional*—RN) as the dominant component of the opposition alliance.

The decision to suspend the Pinochet trial for medical reasons was upheld by the Supreme Court on July 1, 2002, which appeared to void further prosecution by ruling that the former president's dementia was irreversible. On July 4 Pinochet resigned as senator-for-life. Subsequently, in May 2004 the appeals court removed Pinochet's immunity from prosecution, and on December 13 Pinochet was indicted on charges of kidnapping and murder, an action that was upheld by the Supreme Court on January 4, 2005. Further legal proceedings culminated in a Supreme Court ruling on December 26 that Pinochet was mentally fit to stand trial.

Except for the elimination of nonelective senators, the legislative distribution was relatively unchanged after the election of December 11, 2005. The CPD displayed marginal improvement in the Chamber of Deputies, winning 65 of 120 seats, while retention of its existing 20 seats yielded a majority in the now wholly elective Senate. In the presidential race on December 11, 2005, and runoff balloting on January 15, 2006, Michelle BACHELET of the CPD's Socialist component outpolled her competitors but failed to win an absolute majority. In runoff balloting on January 15, however, she defeated Sebastián PIÑERA Echenique of the right-wing Alliance for Chile 53.5 percent to 46.5 percent to become the country's first elected woman president.

General Pinochet died on December 10, 2006, and his legacy became the dominant topic of discussion. Though he had always been a polarizing figure, his support waned as investigations turned up evidence of torture and foreign bank accounts. Particularly galling for many was the discovery that Pinochet held some $27 million in foreign accounts under different names.

Michelle Bachelet's presidential victory in January 2006 was attributed to the continued popularity of her CPD predecessor, her success in retaining the support of most of the PDC's conservative faction, and a rightist split between runner-up Piñera and former contender Joaquín Lavín. Earlier, Lavín's UDI had split with Piñera's RN by refusing to accept constitutional rights for Chile's indigenous communities.

Having campaigned on a pledge that she would govern differently from previous politicians, President Bachelet chose a cabinet equally divided between men and women, raised pensions, increased the number of state-run nurseries, and adopted other progressive policies.

After a PDC member was expelled in late 2007 for voting against the government on a serious transportation issue hurting Bachelet's government, five PDC members resigned in protest in January 2008, leaving the governing coalition with only 57 of 120 seats and forcing it to relinquish control of the Chamber of Deputies for the first time since Chile's return to democracy. President Bachelet subsequently reshuffled the cabinet on January 8, maintaining a balance among the four parties in the coalition. The Bachelet administration maintained high public approval ratings despite criticisms and protest over issues of transportation, labor, and increasing unemployment, as well as unrest among indigenous Mapuche residents in the Araucania region.

The December 13, 2009, legislative elections awarded Piñera's new center-right Coalition for Change (*Coalición por el Cambio*—CC) 58 seats in the Chamber of Deputies, giving it a plurality in the lower body and signaling a resurgence of the more conservative coalition. Meanwhile, Piñera outpolled his opponents in the first round of presidential balloting but failed to win a majority, triggering a January 17, 2010, runoff at which Piñera captured 51.6 percent of the vote versus 48.4 percent for his CPD opponent, former president Eduardo Frei Ruiz-Tagle. The elections marked the first time a right-of-center government was handed power since the fall of the Pinochet regime.

A powerful 8.8-magnitude earthquake struck offshore of southern-central Chile on February 27, 2010. More than 500 people were killed in the disaster, and 200,000 homes were destroyed. Officials estimated that reconstruction could cost $30 billion—18 percent of GDP. Piñera's government's prioritized rebuilding schools, roads, and other infrastructure, leaving hundreds of thousands of Chileans still homeless one year later. The new president also annoyed the opposition by frequently blaming Bachelet's response to the disaster. His government received criticism for not including the CPD in any of the negotiations over reconstruction plans and from more conservative members of his own coalition, who flinched at the raft of taxes Piñera proposed to help pay costs.

Layoffs of at least 1,000 civil servants, public transit rate hikes, and other concerns triggered union- and student-led mass protests in Santiago in May 2010 that continued for weeks. On July 1, Piñera won a political victory in his push to significantly raise the minimum wage, which analysts said was a move to woo working- and middle-class CPD voters. Piñera's popularity also rose with the dramatic rescue of 33 Chilean miners in October after they had been trapped underground for more than two months. At the same time, Piñera worked out a deal with the CPD to increase mining royalties to help pay for earthquake reconstruction.

Government negotiations with public sector unions collapsed in November 2010, leading some 400,000 workers to go on strike. Thirteen unions supported the strike after the government countered their demand for an 8.9 percent pay raise, with one totaling 3.7 percent for the fiscal year 2011.

Long-simmering tensions over Easter Island escalated in late 2010, when the president of the assembly of Easter Island threatened to take the possession out of Chile's jurisdiction and into that of Polynesia. In December, a bloody clash ensued when Chilean police tried to evict islanders squatting on government land that they claimed as ancestral territory.

Constitution and government. The basic law drafted by the former Council of State and adopted by popular vote in September 1980 provided for a directly elected president serving a nonrenewable eight-year term, in the course of which he or she would be permitted one legislative dissolution. It also called for a bicameral National Congress encompassing a Senate of 26 elected and 9 designated members (exclusive of former presidents) and a 120-member Chamber of Deputies sitting eight and four years, respectively, subject to dissolution. In an unusual electoral requirement, political lists or coalitions must double their rivals' votes to secure both parliamentary seats in any district.

At a plebiscite on July 30, 1989, the term of the next president (but not those of the president's successors) was reduced to four years, and the number of directly elected senators was increased to 38; in addition, the congressional majority needed for constitutional amendment was reduced from three-quarters to two-thirds, and the ban on Marxist parties was replaced by a clause calling for "true and responsible political pluralism." By constitutional amendment in January 1994 Congress approved a new presidential term of six years. In November 2004 the presidential term was again reduced, to four years, with simultaneous presidential and congressional elections. The 2004 changes also eliminated lifetime seats and restored the president's authority to remove military commanders. The double-your-rival provision was retained, but a provision calling for the Congress to elect a presidential successor should the incumbent die or become incompetent failed to pass.

In 1975 the country's 25 historic provinces were grouped into 12 regions plus the metropolitan region of Santiago, each headed by a governor (*governador*), and were further subdivided into 40 new provinces and more than 300 municipalities, headed by intendents (*intendentes*) and mayors (*alcaldes*), respectively.

Foreign relations. Chile has traditionally adhered to a pro-Western foreign policy, save for the Allende era, when contacts with Communist states were strengthened, including the establishment of diplomatic relations with Cuba. Concomitantly, Chilean relations with the United States cooled, primarily as a result of the nationalization of U.S. business interests. Following the 1973 coup, U.S. relations improved, diplomatic ties with Cuba were severed, and links with other Communist-bloc nations were curtailed. However, the assassination in Washington, D.C., on September 21, 1976, of Orlando LETELIER del Solar, a prominent government official under the Allende regime, became a festering bilateral issue. In May 1979 the Chilean Supreme Court refused a U.S. Justice Department request for the extradition of three army officers who had been charged in the case, including the former chief of the Chilean secret police, and Washington moved to curtail diplomatic, economic, and military relations with Santiago after the Court-ordered closure of investigations into possible criminal charges against the three in Chile. A Chilean court reopened the case in mid-1991, only weeks before expiration of a statute of limitations, and indictments were subsequently handed down for two of the three men (the third having confessed his involvement after voluntarily surrendering to U.S. authorities in 1987). In January 1992 an international tribunal awarded noncontestable damages of $1.2 million to the Letelier family, plus damages of $815,000 to the family of an aide who had also been killed, while the two officers indicted in Santiago—Gens. Manuel CONTRERAS Sepúlveda and Pedro ESPINOZA Bravo—were found guilty and sentenced to prison terms of seven and six years, respectively, in November 1993. In June 1994 Chile's Supreme Court ruled that a 1978 amnesty law did not apply to the convicted Letelier killers, and on May 30, 1995, the Court upheld the convictions. Contreras was later convicted of other crimes, including a 1974 car bombing in Argentina that killed the then commander in chief of the Chilean armed forces.

In March 1978 Bolivia severed diplomatic relations with Chile because of its alleged inflexibility in negotiations in regard to Bolivia's long-sought outlet to the Pacific. Further inflaming tensions were two Bolivian military incursions into Chile in May 2004 and Peru's claim in October 2005 to about 70,000 square miles of ocean controlled by Chile under treaties concluded in 1952 and 1954, which Lima insisted referenced only fishing rights. (In 2008 Peru sued Chile in the International Court of Justice over the unresolved water rights. Resolution of the legal issues was expected to take at least seven years.) A lengthy dispute with Argentina over the ownership of three islands in the Beagle Channel north of Cape Horn was technically resolved in May 1977, when a panel of international arbitrators awarded all three islands to Chile. However, the award was repudiated by Argentina, as it permitted Chile to extend its territorial limits into the Atlantic, thereby strengthening its claims to contested territory in the Antarctic. Mediation initiated by Pope John Paul II in 1981 yielded an agreement in 1984 under which Chile still received the islands but claimed only Pacific Ocean territory, conceding all Atlantic rights to Argentina.

In August 1991, Presidents Aylwin of Chile and Carlos Menem of Argentina reached accord on all but one of 23 other boundary disputes that had long plagued relations between their countries, but it was not until June 1999 that ratifications were completed on the Continental Glacier Treaty that resolved the last remaining border controversy. At the conclusion of the 1991 state visit to Argentina (the first by a Chilean president in 38 years), Aylwin and Menem also signed a number of accords dealing with investment and transportation, including access to Pacific port facilities for Argentine exporters.

During the Summit of the Americas in Miami, Florida, in December 1994, Chile was invited to become the fourth nation to join the North American Free Trade Agreement (NAFTA). The action came six months after Santiago had announced that Chile intended to join Mercosur, Latin America's biggest trading bloc, as an associate member, an agreement that was signed on June 25, 1996. Five months later, Chile responded to the effective U.S. obstruction of Chilean membership in NAFTA—the Clinton administration had failed to persuade the U.S. Congress to pursue "fast track" approval—by concluding a bilateral free-trade agreement with NAFTA member Canada, complementing an earlier commercial accord with Mexico. It was not until late 2002 that the pact with the United States was finalized.

Tension with Britain arose in October 1998 over the arrest of General Pinochet at a London medical clinic on a Spanish warrant alleging "crimes of genocide and terrorism" against Spanish nationals during his presidency. On October 28 the British High Court quashed the warrant on the grounds that Pinochet was entitled to sovereign immunity while serving as head of state. The House of Lords reversed the decision on November 25, and on December 9 Chile recalled its ambassador to London. In March 1999 a panel of law lords upheld the legality of Pinochet's detention, although it ruled that 27 of the 30 charges filed by the Spanish prosecutor were invalid because they involved events before 1988, the year the International Convention Against Torture was implemented in the United Kingdom. After 16 months of house arrest, Pinochet was released on grounds of mental and physical infirmity, and on March 3, 2000, he returned to Santiago to face a variety of domestic charges.

Relations with Venezuelan president Hugo Chávez posed a problem for the CPD government. In 2006, when Venezuela and Guatemala competed for a seat on the UN Security Council, President Bachelet initially indicated solidarity with Chávez, prompting protests from her own foreign minister, Christian Democrat Alejandro FOXLEY Rioseco. Over time, the Chilean government became less sympathetic to Chávez's "Bolivarianism" and firmer in its defense of market-based, social-democratic policies.

On May 23, 2008, Chile joined the Union of South American Nations (UNASUR) as a founding member. While the union still only existed on paper in 2009, Bachelet was picked to serve as UNASUR's first president pro tempore. The Senate passed a bill in September 2010 ratifying Chile's participation in the organization.

In April 2009 Chilean and Bolivian officials announced they were nearing a deal to compensate Bolivia for the use of Silala River water by Chilean companies. Chile was expected to pay for using 50 percent of the river's water, which is needed by the country's mining companies. Officials said the deal would eliminate a long-standing area of conflict and would also clear the way to confront larger water resource issues between the two nations. However, the Bolivian government suspended the agreement in February 2010, concerned about the pro-business credentials of president-elect Piñera and foreign minister–designate Alfredo MORENO Charme.

Peruvian and Chilean leaders signaled a new level of détente between the two nations was in the offing in May 2010, when they agreed to reestablish full diplomatic relations, harmonize military spending, and, in the future, collaborate militarily. The agreement appeared to indicate that the two sides were trying to move past the long contentious issue of water rights along their shared coastal frontier.

In early 2011 Chile recognized Palestine as a free, independent, and sovereign state but said the borders it shares with Israel need to be renegotiated. In March Piñera visited Palestine and met with the head of the Palestinian Authority, Mahmoud Abbas.

Relations with Bolivia deteriorated in early 2013, when Chilean police arrested and tried three Bolivian soldiers who had crossed into Chilean territory in pursuit of a group of smugglers. On April 24, Bolivia filed suit against Chile at the International Court of Justice, reasserting its demand for access to the Pacific Ocean.

Current issues. The national unity on display when the 33 miners were rescued in late 2010 was replaced by violent street protests, occupied schools, and plummeting faith in the country's political leadership. President Piñera's popularity sunk from 63 percent in October 2010 to 29 percent in April 2012.

In January 2012, Piñera secured passage of a new law that automatically made all citizens over the age of 18 registered voters, instantly expanding the pool of registered voters by 50 percent, from 8.1 million to 12.6 million.

Chile has a strong economy, but wealth is unevenly distributed, creating resentment among youth and indigenous peoples, in particular. The economy needs skilled workers, but the higher education system is not meeting the demand. Students complained that the state had allowed for-profit diploma mills to flourish, leaving students with few marketable skills and high student loan debts.

Frustrated by their perceived lack of representation in the political system, students across the country had held near-constant, often violent, street protests since April 2011, calling for free, quality higher education. Many college and high school students have boycotted classes for more than a year. The protests often brought out huge crowds; a May 16, 2012, event in the capital had more than 100,000 participants, and police used tear gas and water cannons to disperse the demonstrators. Their disruptions have the support of 70 percent of the population and have turned Camila VALLEJO, the 25-year-old leader of the student movement, into a popular national leader.

Unhappy Chileans have adopted the student protest model for other issues. Residents of Aysén, in Patagonia, blocked roads to protest new fishing regulations and gasoline prices the spring, while farmers clashed violently with police while protesting increased demands on Lake Maul for hydropower generation.

The Piñera administration took a hardline toward the Mapuche indigenous community and its demands for autonomy and restitution of ancestral lands. In January 2012 Piñera invoked Pinochet-era counter-terrorism laws to track down the source of forest fires in Araucanía region. The fires spread to neighboring Biobío region, and seven firefighters were killed while trying to contain the blaze. Interior Minister Rodrigo HINZPETER suggested that the Mapuche group *Coordinadora Arauco Malleco* might be responsible, as the group is based nearby. Government-Mapuche relations worsened even further during 2012, with police forcibly evicting 60 Mapuche from ancestral territory on July 23. A brawl later erupted between police and Mapuche gathered outside a hospital where the wounded had been taken; several children were injured in the incident, prompting calls for investigation by UNICEF and Amnesty International. On July 30, a group of Mapuche set fire to barricades blocking a highway south of Santiago to protest the lack of road construction in their area. Police responded with a water cannon and rubber bullets, leaving tribal chief Felicindo HUAQUINAO Huaiquimil in a coma. Mapuche arrested in these incidents began a hunger strike in August. Later that month, Piñera announced a comprehensive plan to improve security and stimulate economic growth in Araucanía, including new schools and hospitals..

Chile enacted a landmark law against hate crimes and discrimination on the basis of race, gender, sexual orientation, religion, or appearance in July 2012. The bill had languished in parliament for seven years but was fast-tracked following a brutal attack that killed Daniel Zamundo. The 24-year-old gay man was found beaten and mutilated in a park in Santiago on March 3, 2012.

On September 4 President Piñera announced a new 20 percent corporate tax rate that would raise $1.23 billion for education spending. Criticizing the tax as insufficient, students responded by seizing the headquarters of the DC, UDI, PPD, and PS parties. Police were called in to evict them from the premises.

In municipal elections on October 28, 2012, the left-wing *Concertación* coalition won 168 mayoral seats and 43.1 percent of the vote, compared to 121 mayors and 37.5 percent for Piñera's alliance. The election was the first since mandatory voting was abolished, and turnout was barely 40 percent.

Police clashed with Mapuche activists outside a courtroom in Araucanía in February where Fernando MILLACHEO was charged with murder, robbery, and arson. Millacheo denied the charges and went on a hunger strike. Police also arrested Emilio Berkhoff JÉREZ, leader of the militant Mapuche group *Coordinadora Arauco-Malleco* (CAM).

On March 15 former president Bachelet resigned her post as executive director of UN Women and returned to Chile to prepare to run for president in November.

Street protests continued in April, with 100,000 students marching in Santiago and a 24-hour strike against Codelco, the state-owned copper producer. The government again came under fire in May amid allegations that Piñera had underreported inflation by 1.0–1.5 percent since 2009 and added an extra 800,000 people to the census.

Bachelet easily won the *Concertación* presidential primary on June 30, beating three opponents with 73 percent of the vote. The UDI had difficulty settling on a candidate. Its charismatic first candidate, Laurence GOLBORNE, was implicated in a credit card fee scheme when he was CEO of retailer Cencosud and dropped out on April 30. Golborne had directed the rescue of the trapped miners in 2010. Its second candidate, Minister of Economy Pablo LONGUEIRA won the center-right primary against Andrés ALLAMAND Zavala (RN) but dropped out on July 17 after being diagnosed with depression. Instead of turning to Allamand, the UDI selected Minister of Labor Evelyn MATTHEI. Interestingly, Bachelet and Matthei were childhood friends. Their fathers were generals in the Chilean air force, but General Bachelet opposed the Pinochet coup in 1973 and was arrested and tortured to death.

Matthei's campaign emphasized continuity of Piñera's policies and the prosperity enjoyed during his presidency. Bachelet's platform addressed the many disaffected social groups, offering constitutional amendments, free university tuition, same-sex marriage, and environmental protection. She brought the communists into her alliance, saying they shared an interesting in creasing "a more inclusive and fair country."

Piñera shuffled his cabinet on July 25 in the wake of Matthei's resignation. This was the 30th cabinet change for Piñera and the 6th of 2013.

A UN Special Rapporteur visited Chile in July 2013 to examine the situation of the Mapuche people. Ben EMMERSON warned the government to stop using the Pinochet-era anti-terrorism laws or risk "widespread disorder and violence."

POLITICAL PARTIES AND GROUPS

For details on electoral alliances formed before the most recent electoral campaign, see the 2013 *Handbook*. Four electoral coalitions formed or continued their electoral agreements in advance of the 2013 legislative and presidential elections. The right-wing **Coalition for Change** from 2010 was renamed **Alliance**, while the centrist **Coalition of Parties for Democracy** became the **New Majority** (*Nueva Mayoría*), comprised of the Socialist Party of Chile, the Party for Democracy, the Broad Social Movement, the Communist Party, Citizen Left, the Christian Democratic Party, and the Social Democratic Radical Party. The left-leaning **Everybody to La Moneda Movement** (*Movimento Todos a la Moneda con Marcel Claude*) combined the Humanist Party and the United Left, while **Chile Changes, If You Want It** (*Si Tú Quieres Chile Cambia*) brought together the Progressive Party, the Liberal Party, and the Allendist Socialism Movement.

Governing Coalition:

Alliance (*Alianza*), previously known as the Coalition for Change (*Coalición por el Cambio*—CC) is comprised of Chile's leading center-rightist groups. It was launched in April 2009 by Chile First and the MHC and was expanded dramatically by the subsequent addition of the Alliance for Chile (*Alianza por Chile*—AC). The name reverted to Alliance following the 2012 municipal elections.

The AC had been launched before the 1997 election as the Union for Chile (*Unión por Chile*) in emulation of its 1993 predecessor, the Union for the Progress of Chile (*Unión por el Progreso de Chile*—UPC). In 2006 AC candidate Sebastián Piñera came in second place in a runoff election for president with 46.51 percent of the vote against CPD winner Michelle Bachelet. After local elections in 2008, the AC for the first time held more mayors' seats than center-left groups, signaling improving conditions for their more conservative message.

The center-right AC secured power in both houses of congress on March 18, 2009, for the first time since 1990 after the CPD expelled a coalition party, which left it without a majority in either legislative body. UDI and AC member Rodrigo ÁLVAREZ was elected president of the Chamber of Deputies president a week after UDI senator Jovino NOVOA was appointed Senate president.

Piñera, relying upon a conservative platform that featured job creation, economic progress, family values, and improved education, never relinquished a strong lead going into the 2009 presidential election, when he won 44.1 percent of the vote in the first round. He secured the presidency during the second round of votes with 51.6 percent of ballots cast. It was the first win for a right-wing candidate since the 1958 election of Jorge Alessandri Rodríguez. The CC subsequently developed a cooperation agreement with newcomer PRI to take weak de facto control of the Chamber of Deputies.

Cracks began forming within the CC as soon as it took power in 2010. UDI members, who leaned more heavily to the right, ridiculed Piñera's centrist approach, especially on the decision to raise taxes to help pay for reconstruction from the 2010 earthquake and the installation of technocrats in the cabinet instead of rightist ideologues. But Piñera attempted to leverage a surge in popularity following the rescue of 33 miners in October 2010 to launch an ambitious legislative agenda that included education, health, crime, poverty, the environment, and reforming the political system. However, his plan—and his popularity—were jeopardized in 2011 by public perception that he had failed to hit his presidential stride. As his approval ratings sagged, he also came under mounting pressure from the UDI to make good on his inaugural promise to unify the country or be marginalized during jockeying for his replacement.

Leader: Sebastián PIÑERA Echenique (President of the Republic).

National Renovation (*Renovación Nacional*—RN). The RN, then most commonly referenced as the National Renovation Party (PRN or Parena), was formed in 1987 by merger of the Movement for National Union (*Movimiento de Unión Nacional*—MUN), led by Andrés Allamand Zavala; the National Labor Front (*Frente Nacional del Trabajo*—FNT), led by Sergio Onofre JARPA Reyes; and the UDI (see below), with whom it split over the 1988 plebiscite. Jarpa withdrew as a presidential candidate in August 1989, and the coalition subsequently joined the UDI in supporting the candidacy of Hernán Büchi.

The RN's long-standing support of the military eroded in late 1992 when two of its leaders, Evelyn MATTHEI and Sebastián

Piñera, were forced to withdraw as presidential hopefuls in the wake of a wiretapping incident involving the army's telecommunications battalion. Piñera subsequently ran in 1993 as an independent, and in 1999 as the candidate of the alliance. Recently the RN has been perceived as separating itself from the legacy of General Pinochet and adopting a more centrist position.

In 2005, Piñera, one of the wealthiest men in Chile, lost his presidential bid by a narrow margin in a runoff election with Michelle Bachelet. The RN gained some popular support in the October 2008 local elections, when the party won a significant number of mayoral and council races. During the 2009 legislative elections, the RN won 8 Senate seats and 18 in the Chamber. Piñera won the presidency in the concurrent 2009 presidential elections. Piñera's troubles in rallying public approval during his presidency threatened to weaken the RN's future prospects both within the CC and in prospective ballots.

Andrés Allamand Zavala was the RN nominee in the 2013 presidential primary.

Leaders: Carlos LARRAIN Pena (President), Sebastián PIÑERA Echenique (1999, 2005, and 2009 presidential candidate and President of the Republic), Francisco CHAHUÁN Chahuán, Claudio EGUILUZ Rodriguez, Baldo PROKURICA (Vice President), Mario DESBORDES (Secretary General).

Independent Democratic Union (*Unión Demócrata Independiente*—UDI). The UDI joined in the formation of Parena but withdrew following the expulsion in April 1988 of its founder, Jaime GUZMAN Errázuriz, from the coalition leadership. Previously a legal adviser to General Pinochet, Guzman organized a "*UDI pour el Sí*" campaign on Pinochet's behalf in October 1988. He was assassinated, with the Manuel Rodriguez Patriotic Front (FPMR) claiming responsibility, on April 1, 1991.

The UDI won pluralities of 33 Chamber and 9 Senate seats in the 2005 election, making it the single party holding the most legislative seats. The conspicuous absence of the UDI's Jaoquín Lavín from Pinochet's funeral in 2006, and his earlier offer to assist President Bachelet with the student strike, appeared to reveal an effort by Lávin to move from the right toward the center, possibly with the goal of appealing to Christian Democrats, according to observers. The party made further strides during the 2009 legislative elections, when it won 37 of the CC's 58 Chamber seats, a gain of 3. It received more than 1.5 million votes for Chamber of Deputies, far more than any other party.

With Piñera's political trajectory stumbling in early 2011, observers and CC constituents began looking to Lavín. His name became part of the conversation about successors to Piñera's presidency based on his successful shepherding of an education reform package through the congress as the government's education minister.

The UDI selected Laurence Golborne as its 2013 presidential candidate, but he withdrew in the face of financial improprieties. Its second candidate, Pablo Longueira, won the center-right primary against Andrés Allamand Zavala (RN) but dropped out after being diagnosed with depression. Ultimately, Labor Evelyn Matthei became the center-right candidate.

Leaders: Patricio MELERO (President), Evelyn MATTHEI (2013 presidential candidate), Joaquín LAVÍN Infante (1999 and 2005 presidential candidate), José Antonio KAST (Secretary General).

Chile First (*Chile Primero*). *Chile Primero* is a splinter centrist group launched in 2007 by PPD dissidents, including Sen. Fernando Flores, in advance of the 2009 presidential election. The party ran its leader, Vlado Mirosevic, for president, criticizing the approach of the leading parties as populist, ineffective, and overly encumbered by Chile's history. Its manifesto emphasized the need to pragmatically address income inequality, access to technology, and Chile's global competitiveness. It focused specifically on disenfranchised young voters. The executive committee was reconstituted in March 2009 with young professionals with an average age of 30. The party withdrew from the CC coalition in early 2012 due to policy differences with UDI. The party renamed itself the **Liberal Party of Chile** (*Partido Liberal de Chile*) in 2013.

Leaders: Vlado Mirosevic (President), Iván MORAN Morán (Secretary General).

Christian Humanist Movement (Movimiento Humanista Cristiano—*MHC)*. Formed in 2007, the MHC claims a broad-based, non-ideological, and nondenominational approach to politics. The MHC's major objectives are to improve the economy and to provide for the welfare of all Chileans.

Leaders: Ricardo MACCIONI (President), Carlos PEREZ (Secretary General).

Main Opposition Coalition:

Coalition of Parties for Democracy (*Concertación de los Partidos por la Democracia*—CPD). The CPD had its origins in the anti-Pinochet *Multipartidaria,* which was formed in early 1983 and months later became the Democratic Alliance (*Alianza Democrática*—AD). In 1987 the Christian Democratic core of the AD endorsed "single-party" opposition to the regime that would include right-centrist and moderate-leftist formations, while excluding groups advocating the use of violence. The result was the formation of the CPD, which successfully supported Aylwin Azócar's bid for the presidency in 1989 and was equally successful in backing the 1993 candidacy of Frei Ruiz-Tagle.

The Democratic Left Participation (*Participación Democrática de Izquierda*—PDI), a coalition member formed in 1991 by a group of former Communist Party of Chile human rights activists, was dissolved in November 1994, after having failed to gain the required minimum vote share of 5 percent in the 1993 election. PDI leader Fanny POLLAROLLO joined the Socialist Party of Chile, while PDI secretary general Antonio LEAL joined the Party for Democracy.

The CPD won 70 Chamber seats in 1993 and a similar number in 1997, fell to 62 in 2001, and recovered marginally in 2005.

Michelle Bachelet, the former defense minister and Socialist Party member, won the presidency in 2006 with 53.5 percent of votes in a run-off election against Alliance for Chile candidate Sebastián Piñera. Bachelet maintained soaring popularity throughout her term, mainly due to the popular belief that she had competently navigated the country through the global economic downturn. However, term limits prevented her from running again in 2009. Former president Eduardo Frei became the coalition's presidential candidate for the December 2009 elections. Meanwhile in April, the CPD had formed an electoral alliance with the JPM (below) in an effort to defeat the favored CC in the December legislative elections. The negotiations followed the defections of several leftist CPD members over their disillusionment with what they perceived to be the coalition's drift to the center.

With 29.6 percent of the vote, Frei came in a distant second to CC candidate Sebastián Piñera in the first round of presidential balloting in December 2009. Frei secured 48.4 percent of the ballots cast in the January 2010 runoff. It was the first time the CPD lost control of the government in 20 years.

The future of the coalition came into question in December 2010 as it became known that leaders of the PPD (Party for Democracy) and the PRSD (Social Democratic Radical Party) had been courting other parties to either expand or change the composition of the CPD without the backing of other member parties. At issue in the debate between leaders on how to regain power was whether the CPD should jettison some of the current member parties to form the coalition anew or expand it. Without leadership as of mid-2011, public support for CPD hit a low as observers said primary elections scheduled for mid-2012 would be the point of reckoning for the coalition.

Leader: Ignacio WALKER Prieto (Spokesperson).

Christian Democratic Party (*Partido Demócrata Cristiano*—PDC). Founded in 1957, the PDC is currently Chile's third-strongest party, although long divided into right-, center-, and left-wing factions. It obtained 39 lower house seats in 1997, 24 in 2001, and 20 in 2005.

The PDC reportedly considered leaving the CPD in late 2006 to protest apparent corruption in government ministries. In 2007 party rifts developed, and in January 2008, five PDC deputies resigned their Chamber posts in protest over the party's dismissal in December 2007 of Sen. Adolfo ZALDIVAR, who had refused to support financing for the administration's transportation initiative. Zaldivar also had clashed with other party leaders, most notably Soledad ALVEAR, who replaced him as party president. With Chamber representation reduced to 57 seats following the resignations, coupled with resignations from the PPD (below), the CPD was seen as losing significant political influence.

On April 5, 2009, the PDC's Frei Ruiz-Tagle, a senator and Chile's former president, defeated PRSD senator *José Antonio* GÓMEZ to secure the CPD nod to represent the coalition in the December presidential elections. Frei Ruiz-Tagle's platform focused on continuing the programs begun in the Bachelet administration and enhancing social protections. But the nation's slowing economy and protests over public education and transportation issues found Frei Ruiz-Tagle's falling behind in polls in the run-up to the election.

The December 2009 legislative elections saw the PDC recoup most of its losses from the Zaldivar affair and secure 19 of the CPD's 57 Chamber seats. As the CPD faced a schism in late 2010, PDC leaders looked to keep the coalition together and add new member parties. They were opposed to a more aggressive plan to scrub away membership and re-form the coalition.

Leaders: Ignacio WALKER Prieto (President of the Party), Laura ALBOMOZ Pollmann (National Vice President), Eduardo FREI Ruiz-Tagle (Former President of the Republic, Former President of the Senate, and 2009 presidential candidate), Patricio AYLWIN Azócar (Former President of the Republic), Andrés ZALDIVAR Larraín (Former President of the Senate), Victor MALDONADO Roldan (National Secretary).

Socialist Party of Chile (*Partido Socialista de Chile*—PS or PSCh). Founded in 1933, the PSCh was long split into a number of factions that reunited in late 1989 under the presidency of Clodomiro ALMEYDA Medina, with Jorge ARRATE MacNiven as general secretary. Subsequently, Arrate succeeded Almeyda as president, and yielded the position in November 1991 to Ricardo NUÑEZ. Almeyda died on September 25, 1997.

In the run-up to the 2001 congressional poll, the PSCh split with the PDC in asserting that it would support Communist candidates in two constituencies; however, it subsequently reversed itself and agreed to support CPD nominees. In recent years, the party has been described as becoming more centrist.

PS dissident Marco Antonio Enriquez-Ominami Gumucio was nominated as the PS candidate in the 2009 presidential election but eventually broke from the party and ran as an independent. He came in third place during December's first round of voting and reluctantly supported CPD candidate Eduardo Frei during the January 2010 runoff. Meanwhile, analysts attributed the decline of the PS in the December 2009 legislative balloting to its having shed Enríquez-Ominami and leftist Jorge Arrate from its ranks.

In July 2013, former president Bachelet won the center-left primary with 73 percent of the vote and became the New Majority candidate for president.

Leaders: Osvaldo ANDRADE Lara (President), Álvaro ELIZALDE Soto (Secretary General), Michelle BACHELET (Former President of the Republic).

Party for Democracy (*Partido por la Democracia*—PPD). The PPD was organized in 1987 by a group of Socialist Party dissidents under Ricardo Lagos Escobar, who was succeeded as president by Eric SCHNAKE in mid-1990. The PPD and the PSCh formed a subpact for the June 1992 municipal poll, and both endorsed Lagos Escobar for the presidency in 1993.

The PPD was rattled in 2006 by a corruption scandal involving allegations dating back to the Lagos administration. Several prominent leaders subsequently left the party, including former PPD president Jorge SCHAULSOHN, who said there was an "ideology of corruption" within the CPD. The dissidents launched a splinter centrist group, Chile First (*Chile Primero*), in advance of the 2009 presidential election to promote education and combat poverty (see above). The PPD won 18 of the CPD's 57 Chamber seats in 2009.

Party President Carolina Tohá said during the late-2010 negotiations over the future of the CPD coalition that the PPD would be in favor of innovation and change, at the same time calming concerns by other member parties by saying that no group would be expelled.

Leaders: Daniel Jaime QUINTANA Leal (President), Ricardo LAGOS Escobar (Former President of the Republic), Pepe AUTH Stewart (First Vice President), Luis Gonzalo NAVARRETE Muñoz (Secretary General).

Social Democratic Radical Party (*Partido Radical Social Demócrata*—PRSD). The oldest of Chile's extant parties, the Radical Party (*Partido Radical*—PR) was founded in 1863, but appeared, according to the *Latin American Weekly Report,* to be "headed for extinction" as the result of its extremely poor showing in the 1993 balloting. In an effort to revamp its image, the party adopted its present name in 1994. It increased its Chamber representation from two seats to seven in 2005 but fell back to five in 2009.

Leaders: José Antonio GÓMEZ Urrutia (President), Ricardo NAVARRETE Betanzo (First Vice President), Ernesto VELASCO Rodriguez (Secretary General).

Communist Party of Chile (*Partido Comunista de Chile*—PCC or PCCh). Founded in 1922 and a participant in the Allende government of 1970–1973, the PCCh was proscribed during the Pinochet era. In January 1990 the party renounced its policy of "armed popular rebellion" and secured legal recognition the following October. Ten months later its president at the time, Volodia TEITELBOIM, declared that Marxism-Leninism was a "narrow formula" and that the dictatorship of the proletariat was "reductionist."

In 1991 the PCCh was the core party in formation of the Movement of the Allendist Democratic Left (*Movimiento de Izquierda Democrática Allendista*—MIDA). MIDA leader Andrés Pascal ALLENDE, a nephew of the former president, had led the Movement of the Revolutionary Left (*Movimiento de Izquierda Revolucionaria*—MIR), a quasi-guerrilla organization formed by PCCh elements in the 1960s, before returning secretly from exile in August 1986. MIDA secured a vote share of 6.6 percent in the June 1992 municipal balloting, with its presidential candidate securing only 4.7 percent in 1993.

The PCCh ran on its own in 1997, winning three Senate seats. The party secured no congressional representation thereafter until joining the CPD in 2009, when it won three seats in the Chamber of Deputies. The PCCh joined the New Majority alliance for the 2013 elections.

Leaders: Guillermo TEILLIER del Valle (President), Lautaro CARMONA (Secretary General).

Groupings affiliated with the PCCh following the demise of the MIDA included the **Chilean Christian Left Party** (*Partido Izquierda Cristiana de Chile*); the **Socialist Alternative Party** (*Partido Alternativa Socialista*); and the **New Popular Alliance Party** (*Partido Nueva Alianza Popular*).

Other Legislative Parties:

Regionalist Party of Independents (*Partido Regionalista de los Independientes*—PRI). The PRI is a democratic centrist group formed in July 2006 that claims more than 50,000 members. Its leader, Adolfo Zaldivar, was expelled from the PDC for voting with the right-wing opposition against giving more money to a government transport plan in December 2007. The PRI joined the MAS in a voting alliance called For a Clean Chile (*Chile Limpio Vote Feliz*) for the 2009 legislative elections. The alliance won 5.4 percent of the votes cast for the Chamber of Deputies, with the PRI securing 4 percent, the MAS winning 0.4 percent, and allied independents garnering 1 percent. The PRI subsequently weakly aligned with the CC, and PRI member Alejandro Sepúlveda Orbenes was elected president of the Senate. The PRI nominated Ricardo ISRAEL for the 2013 presidential election.

Leaders: Humberto DE LA MANZA (President), Eduardo Edmundo SALAS Cerda (Secretary General).

Broad Social Movement (*Movimiento Amplio Social*—MAS). The MAS was recently established as a left-wing and progressive alternative to the two parties that had dominated Chile's politics. It focused on improving the living conditions and prosperity of Chileans. The MAS called for more home rule and decentralization of power away from the two major parties, which it said had become divorced from the country's workers.

Among the PS dissidents who helped to found the MAS was Alejandro Navarro, who in March 2009 announced plans for a new left-wing electoral coalition called the Progressive Left Pole (*Polo Progresista de Izquierda*—PPI), which, in addition to the MAS, initially attracted the attention of the FSD and G80. Navarro hoped that the PPI would serve as a vehicle for his planned presidential candidacy, but the PPI subsequently failed to coalesce. Navarro dropped out of the presidential race in September, and the MAS supported the candidacy of independent socialist Marco Enriquez-Ominami. Meanwhile, the MAS joined the PRI (above) in an alliance called For a Clean Chile (*Chile Limpio Vote Feliz*) for the 2009 legislative balloting, at which Navarro was elected to the Senate.

In 2010 and 2011 MAS moved closer to the CPD, and both were part of the New Majority alliance for the 2013 elections.. However, 17 MAS members left to form their own party, the **United Left** (*Izquierdo Unida*), which allied with the Humanist Party.

Leaders: Alejandro NAVARRO Brain (President), Alejandro CARPINTERO (Vice President), Fernando ZAMORANO Fernandez (Secretary General).

Other Parties:

Progressive Party of Chile (*Partido Progresista de Chile*—PRO). The PRO was founded in 2010 by Marco Enriquez-Ominami, a socialist who ran as an independent in the 2009 presidential election and won 20.14 percent of the vote. MEO, as he is known, sought to unify the many small groups outside the two dominant blocs and held an online vote to select the new party's name. The PRO won three mayoral races in the October 2012 municipal elections, running with the Green Party. The PRO joined the Chile Changes, If You Want It for the 2013 elections, nominating MEO for president.

Leaders: Marco ENRIQUEZ-OMINAMI (President), Camilo Ernesto LAGOS Miranda (Secretary General).

Wallmapuwen. *Wallmapuwen* was launched in February 2006 to represent the indigenous Mapuche people located largely in the Araucanía region of southern Chile. The group supports Mapuche autonomy and calls itself democratic, progressive, and pluralistic. It has not qualified as a party yet, so *Wallmapuwen* partnered with the PRO to run candidates in the October 2012 municipal elections.

Leaders: Luis MORALES Penchuleo, Rodrigo MARILAF, Millalen ALVARO Gutierrez.

Humanist Party (*Partido Humanista*—PH). Formerly a member of the CPD, the PH joined with the Greens (below) in a Humanist-Green Alliance (*Alianz Humanista–Verde*—AHV) for the 1993 presidential campaign in support of Cristián REITZE. It campaigned as an ally of the PCCh in 2005 but secured no congressional representation. The PH renewed its alliance with the Green Party for the 2009 presidential and legislative elections, calling the coalition the NMC. The PH received 1.4 percent of votes cast for Chamber seats, the Greens won 0.1 percent, and allied independents took 4.6 percent.

Leaders: Danilo MONTEVERDE Reyes (President), Mercedes BRAVO Valenzuela (Secretary General).

Green Party (*Partido Ecologista*). The Greens's stated goal was to be a "distinct alternative," focusing on environmental issues, social justice, diversity and peace. The party formed a coalition with the PH for the 2009 elections (see above) but entered its own slate for 2013, including Alfredo SFEIR for president.

Leaders: Alejandro SAN MARTÍN Bravo (President), Sara LARRAIN Ruiz-Tangle (1999 presidential candidate), Manuel Pablo PEÑALOZA Torres (Secretary General).

Other minor and regional parties registered for the 2013 elections include the leftist **Equality Party** (*Partido Igualdad*) of Roxana Miranda; the **North Green Ecologist Party** (*Partido Ecologista Verde Del Norte*) led by Maria Josefina Barros Aroca, the center-left **North Force** (*Fuerza Del Norte*), led by Mandiza Rosa Barbaric Sciaraffia; and the **Citizen Left Party** (*Partido de Izquierda Ciudadana de Chile*), led by Victor Hugo Osorio Reyes.

For information on **Together We Can Do More for Chile** (*Juntos Podemos Más*—JPM), the **Social and Democratic Force** (*Fuerza Social y Democrática*—FSD) and the **Generation 80 Movement** (*Movimiento Generación 80*—G80), please see the 2013 *Handbook*.

LEGISLATURE

The bicameral **National Congress** (*Congreso Nacional*) established under the 1980 constitution encompasses a Senate and a Chamber of Deputies, elected for terms of eight and four years, respectively, subject to a one-time presidential right of dissolution.

Senate (*Senado*). The upper house currently consists of 38 directly elected members, with half of the members renewed every four years. The alliance/party distribution of seats following the December 13, 2009, election was as follows: Coalition of Parties for Democracy, 19 (Christian Democratic Party, 9; Party for Democracy, 4; Socialist Party of Chile, 5; Social Democratic Radical Party, 1); Coalition for Change, 16 (National Renovation, 8; Independent Democratic Union, 8); Broad Social Movement, 1; independent, 2.

President: Jorge PIZARRO Soto.

Chamber of Deputies (*Cámara de Diputados*). The lower house consists of 120 directly elected members. In the most recent election on December 13, 2009, the Coalition for Change won 58 seats (Independent Democratic Union, 37; National Renovation, 18; allied independents, 3); the Coalition of Parties for Democracy 57 (Christian Democratic Party, 19; Party for Democracy, 18; Socialist Party of Chile, 11; Social Democratic Radical Party, 5; Communist Party of Chile, 3; allied independents, 1); Regionalist Party of Independents, 3; independents; 2.

President: Edmundo ELUCHANS Urenda.

CABINET

[as of October 14, 2013] (*See headnote.*)

President	Sebastian Piñera Echenique (RN)
Ministers	
Agriculture	Luis Mayol Bouchon (ind.)
Culture and the Arts	Ampuero Roberto Espinoza (ind.)
Defense	Rodrigo Hinzpeter Kirberg (RN)
Economy, Development, and Tourism	Félix de Vicente Mingo (ind.)
Education	Carolina Schmidt Zaldivar (ind.) [f]
Energy	Jorge Bunster Betteley (ind.)
Environment	María Ignacia Benítez Pereira (UDI) [f]
Finance	Felipe Larraín Bascuñán (ind.)
Foreign Relations	Alfredo Moreno Charme (ind.)
Health	Jaime Mañalich Muxi (ind.)
Housing and Urban Development/National Assets	Rodrigo Pérez Mackenna (ind.)
Interior	Andrés Chadwick Piñera (UDI)
Justice	Patricia Perez Goldberg (RN) [f]
Labor and Social Welfare	Juan Carlos Jobet Eluchans (RN)
Mining	Hernán de Solminihac Tampier (ind.)
Planning and Social Development	Bruno Baranda Ferran (RN)
Secretary General of Presidency	Cristián Larroulet Vignau (ind.)
Public Works	Maria Loreto Silva (RN) [f]
Secretary General of Government	Cecilia Perez Jara (RN) [f]
Transport and Communications	Pedro Pablo Errázuriz Domínguez (ind.)
Women's Affairs	Loreto Seguel King (ind.) [f]

[f] = female

INTERGOVERNMENTAL REPRESENTATION

Ambassador to the U.S.: Felipe BULNES Serrano.

U.S. Ambassador to Chile: Alejandro D. WOLFF.

Permanent Representative to the UN: Octavio ERRÁZURIZ Guilisasi.

IGO Memberships (Non-UN): APEC, IADB, ICC, IOM, Mercosur, NAM, OAS, OECD, WTO.

CHINA

Zhongguo (Chung-hua)

Note: As of January 1, 1979, the People's Republic of China officially adopted the Hanyu version of a system known as Pinyin for rendering Chinese names into languages utilizing the Roman alphabet. The system was not concurrently adopted in Taiwan, where the Wade-Giles form of transliteration, introduced by the British in the 19th century, was, for the most part, retained. In August 2002 Taiwan adopted as its official romanization system Tongyong Pinyin, which was designed to accommodate island dialects. In the material that follows, personal and place names—such as Mao Zedong (Mao Tse-tung) and Beijing (Peking)—are rendered in Hanyu or Tongyong Pinyin, as appropriate, with occasional parenthetical reference to Wade-Giles or other English equivalents for purposes of clarification. For Taiwan and the Special Administrative Regions of Hong Kong and Macao, some anomalies will be evident, particularly for individuals who have adopted English given names.

Political Status: Politically divided since 1949; mainland under (Communist) People's Republic of China; Taiwan under (Nationalist) Republic of China.

Area: 3,705,805 sq. mi. (9,598,045 sq. km), including Taiwan.

Population: 1,379,071,849 (2013E—UN); 1,372,885,554 (2013E—U.S. Census), mainland (including Hong Kong and Macao) plus Taiwan.

THE COUNTRY

The most populous and one of the largest countries in the world, China dominates the entire East Asian landmass but since 1949 has been divided between two governments. The Communist-ruled People's Republic of China (PRC) controls the Chinese mainland, including Manchuria, Inner Mongolia, Sinkiang (Chinese Turkestan), Tibet, Hong Kong, and Macao. The anti-Communist government of the Republic of China on Taiwan (Nationalist China) administers the island province of Taiwan and some smaller islands, including Kinmen (Quemoy), Matsu, and the Pescadores.

Climatically and geographically, the vast and varied expanse of mainland China ranges from tropical to far-northern temperate, from desert to extremely wet-humid, from river plains to high mountains. Population density varies from fewer than 1 to more than 200 per square kilometer. Of the mainland population, 93 percent is ethnically Han Chinese, but there are 18 minority groups totaling over 1 million, including Manchus, Mongols, Tibetans, and Uighurs (Uygurs). In 2013, 46 percent of the active labor force was female, with approximately 90 percent of adult women employed full time outside the home. In 2013, women comprised 23.4 percent of the deputies in the PRC's National People's Assembly (699 seats out of 2,987).

With the majority of the population still living in the countryside, agriculture remains a major rural occupation, although agriculture currently contributes only 11 percent of GDP. In comparison, industry accounts for 49 percent and services for 40 percent of GDP. Over the last two decades China's "socialist market economic system" has expanded at an annual average of 9.6 percent, and from 2003 through 2007 it grew by 10 percent or better annually (13.0 percent in 2007), making China one of the fastest growing economies in the world and surpassing Germany as the world's third largest economy. The financial crisis and recession that threatened to strangle the world economy in the final quarter of 2008 dramatically altered Beijing's economic outlook. By December 2008, the government faced rising unemployment as overseas markets retracted, deflation had replaced inflation as a potential threat, the central bank had introduced the largest interest rate cut in a decade, and Beijing had hurriedly introduced a $586 billion economic stimulus package, emphasizing infrastructure projects.

Since 2007 Chinese industry has repeatedly come under fire for having shipped a host of substandard products around the world, including contaminated pet food, toothpaste, fish, and toys. The biggest domestic scandal of 2008 concerned the deliberate adulteration of infant formula and milk with the chemical melamine. Over 300,000 Chinese may have been sickened by the tainted products. Dozens of individuals were tried for the contamination, and in November 2009, two of the convicted were executed.

In 2008 the PRC's record trade surplus of $296 billion reinforced accusations that the value of the yuan was still being artificially manipulated despite China's decision in July 2005 to permit its narrow fluctuation against a basket of foreign currencies. The U.S. trade deficit with China reached a record $266 billion in 2008 (including reexports from Hong Kong). For 2009, the deficit fell to $229 billion. In June 2010 the Chinese central bank announced that it would permit greater flexibility in the value of the yuan, but as of mid-July it had dropped only marginally in value, to 6.78 yuan per dollar versus 6.83 a month earlier. Thereafter, international pressure continued to mount for a more dramatic change in exchange rate policy.

It was announced in August 2010 that China had surpassed Japan to become the world's second largest economy, behind the United States. Estimates from the International Monetary Fund (IMF) indicate that unemployment averaged 5 percent between 2008 and 2011 (it was 4.1 percent in 2012). GDP grew by 10.4 percent in 2010, 9.3 percent in 2011, and 7.8 percent the next year. In 2012 inflation was 2.7 percent. GDP per capita reached $6,091 in 2012. In 2013, the World Bank ranked China 91st among 185 countries in its annual Doing Business index, between Jamaica and the Solomon Islands.

Taiwan, a semitropical island 100 miles off China's southeastern coast, has small plains suitable for agriculture in the west and towering mountains along its east-central spine. About 98 percent of the population is ethnically Chinese; the remainder comes from 13 aboriginal tribes of Malayo-Polynesian stock. The Chinese are divided into three groups: numerically predominant Amoy Fukienese, whose ancestors arrived before the Japanese occupation of Taiwan in 1895; a minority of Hakkas, whose ancestors likewise arrived before 1895; and "mainlanders," who arrived after 1945 from various parts of China. Population density, at more than 1,500 persons per square mile, is exceeded only by Singapore and Bangladesh among independent eastern Asian jurisdictions.

The major occupations in Taiwan are commerce and other services, with the service sector as a whole contributing 72 percent of GDP according to the government. Light and high-tech manufacturing leads the industrial sector, which constitutes 26 percent of GDP and employs 37 percent of the workforce. Taiwan's leading export is electronics. The economy's traditional mainstays, farming and fishing, now account for only 5 percent of employment and less than 2 percent of GDP. In the second half of 2008, the economy fell into recession, and 2009 saw a 1.87 percent contraction despite a rapid recovery in the second half of the year. GDP rebounded in 2010, growing by 10.3 percent. GDP grew by 4 percent in 2011, and 1.25 percent the next year. Inflation was 2.3 percent in 2012. Unemployment fell slightly in 2010 to 5.2 percent, compared with 5.9 percent in 2009, fell again in 2011 to 4.9 percent, and was 4.2 percent in 2012. The standard of living is one of the highest in East Asia, with per capita gross national income of about $20,328 in 2012. In 2013 the World Bank ranked Taiwan 16th out of 185 countries in the annual Doing Business index, placing it between Ireland and Canada. Female representation in government has increased in recent years. In 2013, women held 40 of 113 seats (33.6 percent) in the legislative branch, while women concurrently held 33 percent of all local elected offices.

POLITICAL HISTORY

China's history as a political entity is less ancient than its cultural tradition but extends back to at least 221 B.C., when northern China was unified under the Ch'in dynasty. In succeeding centuries of alternating unity and disunity, the domain of Chinese culture spread southward until it covered what is today considered China proper. After the fall of the Manchu dynasty in 1912, a republic was established under the leadership of Sun Yat-sen, who abdicated the presidency in favor of the northerner Yuan Shih-kai but subsequently formed a rival regime in the south following Yuan's attempt to establish a new dynasty. During the Northern Expedition of 1926–1928 (an attempt by the southern government, after Sun's death, to reunify China), Chiang Kai-shek defeated his rivals, gained control of the Nationalist Party (*Chung-kuo Kuo-min Tang* or Kuomintang—KMT), and expelled the Communists from participation in its activities. With the capture of Beijing (Peking) in June 1928, the Kuomintang regime gained international recognition as the government of China. Many warlord regimes continued to exist, however, while the Communists set up local governments in Jiangxi Province (Kiangsi) and later, after the Long March of 1934–1935, in Yan'an, Shaanxi Province (Yenan, Shensi). In a display of Chinese unity following the Japanese invasion of July 1937, most groups, including the Communists, accepted the leadership of the central government.

Communist strength increased during World War II, and the failure of postwar negotiations on establishing a coalition government was followed by full-scale civil war, in which the Communists rapidly won control of the entire mainland. In December 1949 the Nationalists moved their capital to Taipei on the island of Taiwan, but they continued to claim legal authority over the whole of China. The Chinese Communist Party (CCP) established its own government, the People's Republic of China (PRC), in Beijing on October 1, 1949, and have since maintained a parallel claim to sovereignty over all of China, including Taiwan.

On October 25, 1971, the UN General Assembly voted to recognize the PRC delegation as comprising "the only legitimate representatives of China" to the world body. This action also encouraged increased acceptance of the PRC by individual governments, an overwhelming majority of which now recognize the PRC.

In 1989 Taipei began inching toward direct, but limited, relations with the mainland. In April 1991, an extraordinary session of the National Assembly approved constitutional measures permitting Lee to terminate the "Period of National Mobilization for the Suppression of the Communist Rebellion." From April 28 to May 5, 1991, members of the private, but officially recognized, Straits Exchange Foundation (SEF) of Taiwan held a series of meetings with the Chinese State Council's Taiwan Affairs Office in the first such officially approved contact. The SEF acted on the basis of a mandate from Taipei's Mainland Affairs Council (MAC) to seek resolution of "cross-strait" disputes in such areas as trade, travel, piracy, and illegal immigration.

In April 1993 a Taiwanese group led by the chair of the SEF met unofficially in Singapore with a group headed by the mainland's nongovernmental Association for Relations Across the Taiwan Strait (ARATS). In June 1997, through the offices of the two organizations, the PRC and Taiwan reached agreement on the repatriation of airplane hijackers and other illegal entrants.

During 1998 relations with the PRC eased further. In July the ARATS deputy secretary general visited Taiwan as a guest of the SEF, and two months later the SEF vice chair paid an official visit to China. The SEF chair made a similar visit in October, during which a four-part agreement was concluded between SEF and ARATS representatives on both political and economic issues.

In 2000 the PRC bitterly opposed Chen Shui-bian's quest for Taiwan's presidency because his Democratic Progressive Party supported independence. In the wake of his March election, however, Chen adopted what became known as his "four no's plus one" policy, giving assurances that Taiwan would not declare independence, alter its official name, amend the constitution in a way that could be interpreted as acknowledging the existence of two states, or hold a referendum on the independence question. Furthermore, late in 2000 Chen's administration announced its intention to complete work on a "three links" plan for direct trade, transport, and postal services between the two regimes. As a step toward that goal, in January 2001 three ships completed the first direct transit between the mainland and nearby Kinmen and Matsu since 1949, thereby opening what was dubbed the "mini-three-links."

In September 2003 Taiwan's Legislative Branch amended the island's Statute Governing Relations Between People of the Taiwan Area and the Mainland Area by giving the MAC and SEF authority to approve links to the mainland by local government bodies and private groups. On January 29, 2005, shortly before the Chinese New Year holiday, a charter jet left Beijing airport for a nonstop flight to Taipei, restoring after 56 years direct, albeit strictly limited, civil aviation links.

In March 2005 the PRC passed an antisecession law amid continued assertions by the PRC leadership that the use of force would "become unavoidable" if Taiwan openly defied the "one China" principle. Although the law caused a furor in Taiwan, on April 26, 2005, the KMT chair, Lien Chan, began an eight-day visit to the PRC. The first KMT chair to travel to the mainland since 1949, he signed a joint communiqué with PRC president Hu Jintao calling for an end to the "hostile situation," establishment of economic links, and discussion of the island's international status.

In early 2006 President Chen clearly hardened his public stance toward reunification, suggesting, for example, that UN membership might be sought for "Taiwan" instead of the "Republic of China" and that a new constitution should be drafted. A year later, Chen further roiled relations with Beijing. In a March 4, 2007, speech he outlined "four wants and one without": independence for Taiwan, a change in the jurisdiction's official designation, a new constitution, and new economic development, all without reference to left/right politics.

In January 2008 the MAC complained that Beijing, in an effort to influence the outcome of Taiwan's March 22 presidential election, had "set up obstacles" to concluding arrangements for passenger and cargo flights. Meanwhile, KMT presidential candidate Ma Ying-jeou had pledged to resume SEF-ARATS negotiations, which had been stalled under President Chen, and to press for establishment by mid-2008 of weekend charter flights to the mainland. In a controversial move following his election victory, Ma named a proindependence politician to head the MAC, but he also pledged not to pursue de jure independence during his term in office.

The thaw that accompanied Ma's election was immediately evident. In the highest-level meeting of executives since 1949, on April 13, 2008, Vice President-elect Vincent Siew met informally with PRC president Hu Jintao on the sidelines of a regional forum in Hainan, China. On May 27–31 the KMT chair, Wu Poh-hsiung, visited the mainland, where he conferred with Hu (the CCP general secretary as well as PRC president). Less than a month later, on June 12–14, the first formal SEF-ARATS session in 9 years concluded with an agreement to set up liaison offices and to establish direct weekend charter flights between Taiwan and the mainland. The first such flights took place on July 4. On November 3–7 Chen Yunlin, the ARATS chair, made the most senior official visit to Taiwan in 60 years, during which the number of weekly roundtrip flights was expanded to over 100, approval was given for 60 direct cargo flights per month, improved postal links were authorized, and 11 Taiwanese ports and 63 PRC ports (expanded to 68 in May 2009) were designated to handle freight shipments. These "three direct links" were officially inaugurated on December 15.

In April 2009 Chen and the chair of the SEF, Chiang Pin-kung, signed additional economic agreements, in part to make it easier for PRC companies to invest in Taiwan. In May Jia Qinglin, the chair of the Chinese People's Political Consultative Conference (CPPCC), an umbrella grouping of various mainland political, social, cultural, and other groups, called for broad-based exchanges and cooperation between the PRC and Taiwan. In July, in an unprecedented gesture, Hu Jintao, in his capacity as CCP general secretary, congratulated Taiwanese president Ma Ying-jeou on his election as KMT chair. Late in the year, the ARATS and SEF chiefs signed three trade agreements concerning fishing, industrial standards, and agricultural quarantines.

In what was generally described as the most significant pact between the PRC and Taiwan since the civil war, on June 29, 2010, Chen and Chiang, meeting in Chongqing, signed an Economic Cooperation Framework Agreement (ECFA) designed to cut or eliminate tariffs on hundreds of products and to open a number of service industries, including banking and insurance. In September 2012 China announced it would provide "assistance" to Taiwanese fishing vessels operating in disputed waters around the Senkaku Islands that are controlled by Japan, but claimed by both China and Taiwan. There were anti-Japanese protests and boycotts of Japanese products over the islands though the summer of 2012 in both China and Taiwan. Tensions were exacerbated following the purchase of three of the Senkaku islands by the Japanese government, triggering a new wave of anti-Japanese demonstrations in September in more than 100 cities and the cancellation of a series of social and cultural events. In April 2013, Taiwan and Japan signed an accord that allowed Taiwanese vessels to fish in the waters around the Senkaku Islands. The PRC condemned the accord since Japan had negotiated it directly with Taiwan.

CHINA: PEOPLE'S REPUBLIC OF

Zhongguo Renmin Gongheguo
(Chung-hua Jen-min Kung-ho Kuo)

Political Status: Communist People's Republic established October 1, 1949; government controls mainland China, Hong Kong (since 1997), and Macao (since 1999); present constitution adopted December 4, 1982.

Area: 3,692,213 sq. mi. (9,562,842 sq. km), excluding Taiwan.

Population: 1,349,585,838 (2013E—U.S. Census), excluding Taiwan.

Major Urban Centers (urban areas, 2005E): BEIJING (Peking, 12,100,000), Shanghai (18,150,000), Guangzhou (Canton, 9,550,000), Wuhan (9,100,000), Tianjin (Tientsin, 6,350,000), Shenyang (4,550,000), Nanjing (Nanking, 3,500,000), Harbin (3,400,000), Dalian (Dairen, 2,900,000). Most of these figures are substantially less than previous estimates.

Official Language: Northern (Mandarin) Chinese (*Putunghua* is the officially promoted Beijing dialect).

Monetary Unit: Yuan (official rate November 1, 2013: 6.10 yuan = $1US). The overall currency is known as renminbi (RMB, people's currency). On June 19, 2010, the People's Bank stated that China would permit increased exchange rate flexibility but added that the "basis for large-scale appreciation of the RMB exchange rate does not exist." China's trading partners, especially the United States, have long argued that Beijing keeps the value of the RMB artificially low to encourage exports. On April 14, 2012, the People's Bank announced that the renminbi would be allowed to fluctuate up to 1 percent against the dollar.

President of the People's Republic and General Secretary of the Chinese Communist Party: XI Jinping; named to succeed HU Jintao as general secretary on November 13, 2012; elected president for a five-year term by the National People's Congress on March 15, 2013.

Vice President: LI Yuanchao; elected by the National People's Congress on March 15, 2013, for a term concurrent with that of the president, succeeding XI Jinping, who was elected president.

Premier of the State Council: LI Keqiang; elected to a five-year term by the National People's Congress on March 16, 2013, succeeding WEN Jiabao.

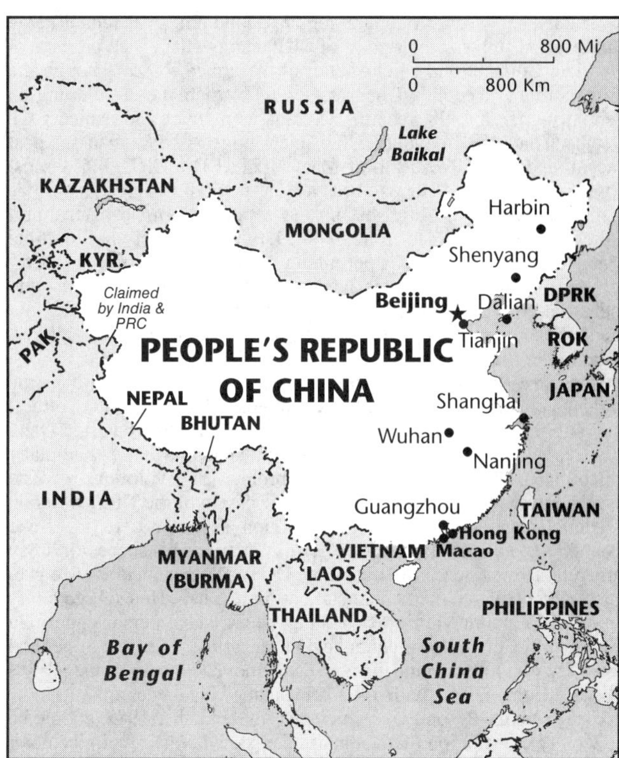

GOVERNMENT AND POLITICS

Political background. Following its establishment in 1949, the government of the People's Republic of China (PRC) devoted major attention to the consolidation of its rule and to socialization of the Chinese economy. Within China proper, Communist rule was firmly established by the early 1950s. Xizang (Tibet), over which China historically claimed suzerainty, was brought under military and political control in 1950–1951 and then, after a nationalist revolt and the flight of the DALAI LAMA (TENZIN Gyalso) to India in 1959, was incorporated as an autonomous region of the PRC in 1965. In contrast, occupation of Taiwan was prevented by the protective role assumed by the United States in 1950.

The internal policy and economic planning of the PRC, originally modeled on Soviet experience and supported by Soviet technical aid and loans, began to deviate markedly from Soviet models with the proclamation in 1958 of the Great Leap Forward, a new system of economic development based on organization of the peasant population into rural communes and the use of labor-intensive, as opposed to capital-intensive, methods of production. The failure of the Great Leap Forward was followed by a period of pragmatic recovery from 1961 to 1965 that coincided with growing ideological differences between the Chinese and Soviet Communist parties.

Apparently believing that the revolutionary ardor of the Chinese Communist Party (CCP) had succumbed to bureaucratization, Chairperson MAO Zedong (MAO Tse-tung) launched the Great Proletarian Cultural Revolution in 1965–1966 to reassert the primacy of Marxist-Leninist doctrine against "revisionist" tendencies within the CCP. A period of internal turmoil and civil strife from 1966 to 1968 found Mao, Defense Minister LIN Biao (LIN Piao), and others denouncing the influence of PRC Chair LIU Shaoqi (LIU Shao-ch'i), whose ouster was announced in October 1968, and other alleged revisionists, some of whom—including former CCP secretary general DENG Xiaoping (TENG Hsiao-p'ing)—were subsequently "rehabilitated." After causing vast internal turbulence that reached a peak in 1967, the Cultural Revolution diminished in intensity amid indications that one of its main results had been an increase in the power of the military.

At the CCP's Ninth Congress, held in April 1969, Lin Biao was hailed as the "close comrade in arms and successor" of Chairperson Mao. Two years later, however, Lin disappeared from public view and was subsequently branded as an inveterate anti-Maoist who had been largely responsible for the excesses of the Cultural Revolution. He was later reported to have perished in a plane crash in Mongolia in September 1971 while en route to the Soviet Union after failing in an attempt to seize power. In early 1974 "counter-revolutionary revisionism" of the Lin variety was indirectly, but vigorously, attacked by means of a campaign directed against China's ancient sage Confucius, with some arguing that the true target was Premier ZHOU Enlai (CHOU En-lai). By the end of the year, however, increasing numbers of senior officials had reappeared, including many who had been purged during the Cultural Revolution.

A subsequent period of relative quiescence was shattered by the deaths of Premier Zhou on January 8, 1976, and of Chairperson Mao on September 9. Shortly after Zhou's death, Vice Premier HUA Guofeng (HUA Kuo-feng) was named acting premier. The appointment came as a surprise to foreign observers, who had anticipated the elevation of the rehabilitated Deng Xiaoping. As first vice premier, Deng had performed many of Zhou's functions during the latter's long illness, but in April, following demonstrations in Beijing and elsewhere in support of Deng, it was announced that he had again been dismissed from all government and party posts and that Hua had been confirmed as premier. A widespread propaganda campaign was subsequently launched against Deng and other "unrepentant capitalist-roaders."

Mao's death precipitated a renewed power struggle that resulted in a victory for the "moderate," or "pragmatic," faction within the Political Bureau (Politburo) over the "radical" faction composed of Vice Premier ZHANG Chunqiao (CHANG Ch'un-ch'iao); JIANG Qing (CHIANG Ch'ing), Mao's widow; WANG Hongwen (WANG Hung-wen); and YAO Wenyuan (YAO Wen-yüan), who had called for a return to the principles of the Cultural Revolution. Stigmatized as the "Gang of Four," the radicals were arrested in October 1976, a day before Hua's designation as chair of the CCP Central Committee. Having been indicted on charges that included plotting to overthrow the government. all four, plus six associates of Lin Biao, were convicted in January 1981, with Jiang and Zhang receiving deferred death sentences. (The ailing Jiang was released to house arrest in 1984 and committed suicide in 1991; Zhang, released in 1998 for medical reasons, died in 2005.)

In July 1977 Deng Xiaoping, for the second time, was rehabilitated and restored to his former posts of CCP deputy chair, vice premier of the State Council, and chief of staff of the armed forces. Though the Fifth National People's Congress (NPC), which met in Beijing in February–March 1978, reconfirmed Hua as premier and named CCP Deputy Chair YE Jianying (YEH Chien-ying) as NPC chair—a post vacant since the 1976 death of Marshal ZHU De (CHU Teh)—most observers considered Deng to be at least as powerful as Hua.

Subsequently, the PRC began a sweeping reform in agricultural policy that, as implemented in 1979–1980, progressively nullified the Maoist commune system by permitting a return in many areas to farming on a family basis. Some land was later converted to cash- and industrial-crop production, while state farms were transformed into integrated enterprises operating on the basis of long-term, low-interest loans rather than state subsidies.

During a February 1980 plenum of the CCP Central Committee, the party Secretariat, which had been abolished during the Cultural Revolution, was reinstated with HU Yaobang (HU Yao-pang), a Deng ally, named general secretary, while Liu Shaoqi was posthumously rehabilitated as "a great Marxist and proletarian revolutionary." The trend continued in an August–September session of the NPC, which at its conclusion accepted Hua's resignation as premier of the State Council and named Vice Premier ZHAO Ziyang as his successor. In an apparent effort to ease the transition, Deng also resigned as vice premier, while Hua retained titular status as party chair. Hua subsequently retired from public view after yielding the CCP chairpersonship to Hu at a Central Committee plenum held in June 1981. The post of general secretary was left vacant. Hua was also removed as chair of the party's Military Commission, with Deng being named his successor.

The 12th CCP Congress, which met in September 1982, adopted a new party constitution that abolished the posts of chair and vice chair while reinstating that of general secretary, to which Hu was again named. The restructuring of the upper CCP echelon was accompanied by a program of widespread personnel "rectification" at the provincial and municipal levels in late 1982 and early 1983. The following October, a three-year consolidation campaign was announced to eliminate vestiges of "leftist factionalism" among party cadres. One year later, the party's Central Committee unanimously approved an unprecedented program for Reform of the Economic Structure that urged reliance "on the world's advanced methods of management, including those of developed capitalist countries."

The "rectification" campaign continued into 1985, with General Secretary Hu Yaobang announcing in April that some 70 percent of the leaders in 107 party and State Council departments, as well as in 29 regional, provincial, and municipal governments, were to be replaced. The most dramatic implementation of the policy came in September, when an extraordinary National CCP Conference of Party Delegates (less amenable to local influence than a congress) was convened for the first time since 1955 and proceeded to abolish de facto lifelong tenure by retiring nearly one-fifth of the Central Committee; the latter body then met to accept the resignation of approximately 40 percent of the ruling Politburo. Although further consolidating the position of Deng Xiaoping, the shake-up at the senior level fell short of purging all those with misgivings about his policies, including Hua Guofeng.

Earlier, in December 1982, the NPC had approved a new PRC constitution that reinstated the post of head of state (abolished under the 1975 constitution), with the incumbent to bear the title of president rather than that of chair. Following elections to the Sixth NPC in March–April 1983, LI Xiannian was named to fill the new position, with a prominent Inner Mongolian leader, General ULANHU, being named vice president. In the course of an extensive government reorganization at the opening session of the Seventh NPC in March–April 1988, the two leaders were replaced by YANG Shangkun and WANG Zhen, respectively.

Political relaxation had reached its peak during 1986. Early in the year, General Secretary Hu endorsed open criticism of party pronouncements and subsequently revived a short-lived 1957 appeal by Chairperson Mao to "Let a hundred flowers bloom." In December student demonstrations broke out in at least a dozen cities, including Beijing, calling for the election of more genuinely representative people's congresses. The situation generated bitter resentment among conservatives, and in January 1987 Hu was forced to resign as party leader. Named as his successor, on an acting basis, was Zhao, who stepped down as premier coincident with confirmation of his status as CCP general secretary in November. LI Peng was designated to fill Zhao's vacated post.

The death of Hu Yaobang in April 1989, in the course of an attempted political comeback, prompted student demonstrations in Beijing that precipitated a split within the government and party leadership. By mid-May the protest had led to student occupation of Tiananmen Square, which proved an embarrassment to the government by severely disrupting a visit by Soviet general secretary Mikhail Gorbachev (the first such event in three decades). Immediately after the Soviet leader's departure, martial law was declared in the capital, although it was not until the early morning of June 4, with hard-liners having assumed control of the CCP Politburo, that the military was ordered to disburse the demonstrators in an action that reportedly resulted in several thousand deaths. On June 24 General Secretary Zhao Ziyang was formally purged and replaced by the Shanghai party chief, JIANG Zemin. On November 9 Deng Xiaoping turned over his last party post, the chair of the Central Military Commission, to Jiang.

The most important domestic event of 1992, the 14th CCP Congress, held in October, saw an unusually large number of Politburo and Central Committee members replaced. Subsequently, at the first session of the Eighth NPC in March 1993, General Secretary Jiang was named to succeed Yang Shangkun as PRC president. Li Peng was reconfirmed as premier, although he received an unprecedented 330 negative ballots. Jiang's elevation meant that he held the three key posts of PRC president, party general secretary, and chair of the CCP Central Military Commission—a consolidation unequaled since Hua Guofeng had held them in the immediate post-Mao era.

Deng Xiaoping, who had not appeared in public since early 1994, died in February 1997. No major policy changes ensued, in large part because the succession issue had long been settled with the accession of Jiang Zemin at the head of a third generation of leaders. In the other major event of the year, Hong Kong returned to Chinese sovereignty on July 1 (see Special Administrative Regions, below). Jiang was reelected PRC president by the first session of the Ninth NPC in March 1998, while ZHU Rongji was named to succeed the outgoing premier, Li Peng, who was elected NPC chair.

Sweeping leadership changes marked the first session of the Tenth NPC, held March 5–18, 2003. HU Jintao, who had been named CCP secretary general in November 2002, was designated state president. On March 17, a new State Council was announced, only a handful of whose members were carryovers from the previous body. The second session of the Tenth NPC, held March 5–14, 2004, approved a number of constitutional amendments, including formal guarantees of private property and human rights. Six months later, on September 19, a CCP Central Committee plenum relieved former president Jiang as chair of the Central Military Commission, Hu Jintao thereby becoming, like his predecessor, holder of the three most powerful positions in state and party.

What apparently began on March 10, 2008, as a demonstration in the Tibetan capital, Lhasa, marking the 49th anniversary of a failed uprising quickly escalated into rioting by Tibetans. During the next several weeks protests and rioting were also reported outside the region, in localities with large Tibetan communities. On May 4, representatives of the Dalai Lama and the PRC government met in Shenzhen, with both sides agreeing to resume formal talks.

Hu was reelected to a second presidential term on March 15, 2008, at the first session of the newly elected Eleventh NPC. The following day, Wen was returned as premier, heading a restructured cabinet that included five new "superministries": Environmental Protection, Housing and Urban-Rural Construction, Human Resources and Social Security, Industry and Information, and Transport.

The 20th anniversary of the Tiananmen Square crackdown of June 1989 was marked by heightened security measures, the arrest of dissidents, and tight media restrictions through 2009. Alongside Tibet, the most restive area of China is the Xinjiang Uygur Autonomous Region, where a Muslim separatist movement has long opposed the central government (see the discussion of Dissident and Separatist Groups, below). About 45 percent of the population are ethnic Uighurs; about 40 percent are Han Chinese. In July 2009 a protest in the regional capital, Urumqi, descended into rioting directed against Han Chinese, and that in turn produced retaliatory assaults on Uighurs. The toll included some 200 deaths and 1,700 injuries, mainly of Han Chinese.

On November 15, 2012, Xi Jinping was chosen as the general secretary of the CCP and as chair of the Central Military Commission. Xi was then elected president at the Twelfth NPC, March 5–17, 2013, to replace the retiring Hu. Concurrently, Li Yuanchao was elected vice president and Li Keqiang was voted in as premier (see Current issues, below). The cabinet was reduced from 27 portfolios to 25, and the superministries were eliminated.

Constitution and government. The constitution adopted by the First NPC on September 20, 1954, defined the PRC, without reference to the Communist Party, as "a people's democratic state led by the working class and based on the alliance of workers and peasants"; by contrast, both the 1975 and 1978 constitutions identified the PRC as "a socialist state of the dictatorship of the proletariat" and specifically recognized the CCP as "the core of leadership of the whole Chinese people."

Article One of the most recent (1982) constitution defines the PRC as "a socialist state under the people's democratic dictatorship led by the working class and based on the alliance of workers and peasants." The document defines minority rights, mandates equal pay for equal work, and specifies that deputies may be recalled at all legislative levels. Enumerated responsibilities include observing "labor discipline," paying taxes, and exercising family planning. Rights to a defense and to a public trial are retained, save in cases "involving special circumstances as prescribed by law."

The National People's Congress, "the highest organ of state power," convenes once a year. Deputies, who serve five-year terms, are elected by lower-level legislative bodies and by units of the armed forces. Among the NPC's functions are constitutional amendment and the election of most leading government officials, including the president and vice president of the PRC, whose terms are concurrent with that of the legislature; state councilors (including the premier and vice premiers); and ministers. Judicial authority is exercised by a hierarchy of people's courts under the supervision of the Supreme People's Court. A Supreme People's Procuratorate supervises a parallel hierarchy of people's procuratorates, with both the courts and the procuratorates accountable to legislative bodies at relevant levels. The principal regional and local organs are provincial and municipal people's congresses (elected for five-year terms); prefecture, city, and county congresses (elected for three-year terms); and town congresses (elected for two-year terms).

In 1999 the NPC approved two constitutional amendments, one of which declared private enterprise to be "an important component of the socialist economy." The impact of a surging economy and China's heightened presence on the world stage was reflected in 2003 amendments concerning property rights and human rights, although a loophole was attached to the former by confining its scope to "legal private property" as defined, presumably, by the regime.

Although the constitution guarantees freedom of speech and of the press, the exercise of all freedoms and rights "may not infringe upon the interests of the state, of society, and of the collective, or upon the lawful freedoms and rights of other citizens." Mainland media and Internet sites are under rigid government control, and numerous journalists have been jailed for failing to follow government prescripts. To protect "national cultural identity," the government maintains tight controls over access to foreign news sources and foreign-owned satellite broadcasts. In 2013 Reporters Without Borders ranked China 173rd of 179 countries. In Hong Kong, however, media have retained considerable editorial independence since reversion.

Administratively, the PRC is divided into 22 provinces (excluding Taiwan); the 5 autonomous regions of Guangxi Zhuang, Nei Monggol (Inner Mongolia), Ningxia Hui, Xinjiang Uygur (Sinkiang Uighur), and Xizang (Tibet); 2 special administrative regions, namely, Hong Kong and Macao; and the 4 centrally governed municipalities of Beijing (Peking), Chongqing (Chungking), Shanghai (Shanghai), and Tianjin (Tientsin).

Foreign relations. Historically a regional hegemon periodically weakened by dynastic and other internal difficulties, China suffered its most extensive modern occupation following the Japanese invasion of Manchuria in 1931–1932, after nearly a century of coastal penetration by Britain and other Western powers. Technically a victor at the conclusion of World War II, China received substantial Soviet assistance after the Maoist takeover in 1949 but was progressively estranged from Moscow in the wake of Stalin's death in 1953.

From the Soviet cancellation of its technical aid program in 1960 to the lapse of a 30-year friendship treaty in 1980, the ideological hostility persisted. It was aggravated by conflicting territorial claims, Moscow's invasion of Afghanistan in 1979, the presence of Soviet-backed Vietnamese troops in Cambodia, and what Beijing viewed as a threatening Soviet military presence in Mongolia. Subsequently, in the context of leadership changes in both countries, tensions subsided, and low-level normalization talks were initiated in 1982.

In May 1989, three months after completion of the Soviet withdrawal from Afghanistan, Soviet general secretary Gorbachev traveled to Beijing for a summit with Chinese leaders. Li Peng reciprocated in April 1990, becoming the first Chinese premier since 1964 to travel to Moscow. Shortly after the demise of the Soviet Union in late 1991, China established diplomatic relations with Russia and the other 14 former Soviet republics. In July 2001 President Jiang and Russian President Vladimir Putin signed a 20-year friendship and cooperation treaty. In October 2004 President Putin again visited Beijing, the most important result of which was agreement on delineation of the full 2,700-mile Sino-Russian border.

In June 2001 China and Russia had joined their three "Shanghai Five" partners (Kazakhstan, Kyrgyzstan, and Tajikistan) in establishing a new Shanghai Cooperation Organization (SCO). The original Shanghai forum had emerged from a 1994 meeting in Shanghai directed toward resolving border disputes and addressing security issues in Central Asia. It had subsequently developed a more encompassing posture toward regional stability, a principal focus being mutual opposition to Islamic militancy. Joining the Shanghai Five as a founding member of the SCO was Uzbekistan.

An ally of Hanoi during the Vietnam War, China denounced Vietnam as Moscow's "Asian Cuba" in mid-1978 and continued its support for Kampuchea (Cambodia) in the border dispute that culminated in the Vietnamese invasion of its western neighbor at the end of the year. A Chinese incursion into northern Vietnam in February 1979, triggered by the Vietnamese action in Cambodia but rooted in a series of border disputes going back to the mid-19th century, proved to be an embarrassment for the comparatively inexperienced Chinese military. The Chinese withdrew in mid-March, claiming that they had succeeded in their objective of "teaching Hanoi a lesson," but sporadic border clashes continued thereafter into the mid-1980s. In 1991, upon completion of a peace agreement that ended 13 years of conflict in Cambodia, China and Vietnam began normalizing relations. In 1994, however, long-smoldering tension over the Spratly Islands erupted, with Beijing denouncing Vietnam for violating its "indisputable sovereignty" over the islands, which are also claimed by Brunei, Malaysia, Philippines, and Taiwan. At the same time, Vietnam charged Chinese fishermen with "systematic and unacceptable" intrusion into its exclusive economic zone in the Gulf of Tonkin. Relations fluctuated for several years thereafter, but the two neighbors signed a land border agreement on December 30, 1999, and in 2000 pledged to resolve the sea disputes. In December 2000 the two settled the Tonkin issue, but the conflicting claims in the South China Sea remain open. In February 2007 Chinese, Vietnamese, and Philippine oil companies agreed to conduct joint seismic studies in a wide area that includes the Spratlys. However, in 2010 and 2011 a number of incidents between Chinese and both Vietnamese and Filipino vessels reignited tension over the Spratlys. In July 2011 a delegation of ASEAN (Association of Southeast Asian Nations) states and China finalized a framework agreement on negotiations aimed at resolving the status of the disputed region. In October China and Vietnam signed an agreement to ease tensions over the Paracel and Spratleys that included biannual bilateral meetings. A naval stand-off between China and Philippines began on April 10, 2012, over fishing rights around the Scarborough Shoal, near the Spratley Islands. The dispute was resolved when both nations withdrew national forces from the area in June (see entry on the Philippines).

For more than a quarter-century, relations with India were strained by a territorial dispute that resulted in full-scale fighting between the two countries in October 1962. China occupied some 14,500 square miles of territory adjacent to Kashmir in the west and also claimed some 36,000 square miles bordering Bhutan in the east, south of the so-called McMahon Line drawn by the British in 1915. The first direct negotiations on the issue were held in Beijing in 1981. Periodic discussions thereafter culminated in a visit to Beijing by Indian prime minister Rajiv Gandhi in December 1988—the first such meeting in 34 years—during which it was agreed that a joint working group of technical experts would be established to facilitate settlement "through peaceful and friendly consultation." Renewed border talks began in March 1999. In 2003 India acknowledged Chinese sovereignty over Tibet, while China indicated de facto recognition of India's sovereignty over Sikkim. In April 2005, following meetings between Premier Wen Jiabao and Indian prime minister Manmohan Singh, the two countries announced plans for a "strategic and cooperative partnership for peace and prosperity." They also set out an 11-point framework for settling the border issue. In July 2006 the Nathu Lu pass, a trade route between Tibet and Sikkim, was opened for the first time in 44 years.

Japan, long China's leading trading partner, recognized the PRC as the "sole legal government of China" in 1972, and in 1978 the two signed a treaty of peace and friendship, culminating six years of intermittent talks. In November 1998 President Jiang became the first

Chinese head of state to visit Japan. While the event was considered a breakthrough in Sino-Japanese relations, Jiang was unable to secure concessions from Tokyo in regard to Taiwan or to obtain a long-sought formal apology for the suffering inflicted by Japan's occupation of China from 1937 to 1945. Since then, relations have remained cool, in part because U.S.-Japanese security guidelines have implications regarding the defense of Taiwan.

A lengthy process of rapprochement between China and South Korea concluded in August 1992 with the normalization of diplomatic relations. While the reaction from North Korea was muted, Taiwan, which immediately severed relations with Seoul, branded the action as a "violation of international justice." More recently, Seoul has acknowledged China's importance in regional affairs, particularly its influence with North Korea. Since the opening in August 2003 of six-party talks (also involving Japan, Russia, South Korea, and the United States) on Pyongyang's nuclear ambitions, Beijing has played a crucial role in repeatedly bringing the Kim Jong Il regime back to the bargaining table.

Beginning in the early 1970s, relations with the West improved dramatically, highlighted initially by U.S. president Richard Nixon's visit to China in February 1972, at which time a joint communiqué included acknowledgment that "all Chinese on either side of the Taiwan Strait maintain that Taiwan is part of China." The United States and the PRC established de facto diplomatic relations in 1973 by agreeing to set up liaison offices in each other's capitals and subsequently completed the exchange, on a de jure basis, on January 1, 1979.

In 1993 the United States imposed a number of economic sanctions against China, claiming that it had breached the 1968 UN Treaty on the Non-Proliferation of Nuclear Weapons, which China had ratified in 1992, by selling missile technology to Pakistan. The action came two months after Washington had agreed to a one-year renewal of China's most-favored-nation (MFN) trading status, despite continued criticism of Beijing's human rights record. That record was believed to be at least partially responsible for a late September decision by the International Olympic Committee to reject China's bid to host the 2000 Summer Games, although it was subsequently named host for the 2008 Games. In May 1994 Beijing agreed to cease jamming Voice of America broadcasts and to end the export to the United States of prison-made products. In return, U.S. president Bill Clinton again renewed China's MFN status, implicitly severing its linkage to the human rights issue. A new trade issue promptly surfaced over U.S. charges of intellectual copyright infringement. The trade dispute was momentarily resolved during "last-ditch" talks in February 1995, but other highly divisive Sino-U.S. issues persisted.

In mid-1998 Clinton paid the first presidential visit to China since the 1989 Tiananmen massacre. In April 1999 Premier Zhu Rongji reciprocated with a nine-day visit to the United States, but he was unable to secure Washington's backing for entry into the World Trade Organization (WTO). It was not until September 19, 2000, that the way was paved for WTO accession by U.S. Senate approval of a landmark bill that granted China permanent trading status. (Formal WTO admission came in December 2001.) Since then, the most persistent principal conflict between Washington and Beijing has involved a massive trade imbalance. The launch of the PRC's first aircraft carrier in August 2011 was seen as a threat to U.S. military superiority in the region.

In June 2012 the WTO ruled that China had violated trade rules by imposing tariffs on $200 million in U.S. steel products that Beijing claimed were subsidized. Meanwhile, the United States, the EU, and Japan filed a complaint on Chinese restrictions on the export of rare earth elements.

In April 1998 representatives of China and the European Union (EU) met in London for the first in a projected annual series of talks, with the participants pledging greater mutual cooperation in trade and other economic relations. Politically, the EU aggravated Beijing in October 2008 when it awarded its Sakharov Prize for Freedom of Thought to Chinese dissident HU Jia, who was recognized for his commitment to human rights, environmental causes, and the HIV/AIDS crisis. In March 2008 the Chinese courts had sentenced Hu to three and a half years in prison for subversion.

In the 2000s, international human rights activists and many governments have urged China to exert more pressure on Sudan to end the humanitarian crisis in Darfur. Beijing, the leading market for Sudanese oil and the principal arms supplier to the government, has blocked UN Security Council action against Khartoum.

In the 1990s an indeterminate number of Uighurs had received weapons and other forms of military training in the Afghanistan-Pakistan border region. In the aftermath of the 2001 U.S. invasion, a number of Uighurs were captured by U.S. forces. Classified as "enemy combatants," approximately two dozen were ultimately shipped to the U.S. detention facility in Guantánamo Bay, Cuba. In late May 2009, the U.S. Department of Justice began releasing Uighurs to countries including Albania, Bermuda, and Palau (see Entry on Palau). As of July 2013, three remained in custody at Guantánamo Bay.

China severely criticized U.S. president Barack Obama for conferring with the Dalai Lama on February 18, 2010. (Earlier, Obama had been chastised by U.S. critics and others for not meeting with the Tibetan leader prior to undertaking a November 15–18, 2009, state visit to China.)

In October 2011, during a state visit by Russian president Putin, $7 billion in economic agreements were signed between Russia and China. In December China began joint maritime patrols with Laos, Myanmar, and Thailand, following an incident on October 5 when 13 Chinese sailors were killed by Thai security forces.

In 2012 China joined Russia in blocking UN action against the Syrian regime of Bashar al-Assad during that country's civil war (see entry on Syria), including vetoing a February 2012 UN Security Council resolution calling on Damascus to accept an Arab League peace plan. China and Canada signed a sweeping financial agreement on September 8, which removed restrictions on foreign investments. In December, Vietnam deployed naval vessels to protect its fishing fleet in disputed waters in the Gulf of Tonkin. Also in December, China announced it would provide free military equipment and training to the Maldives.

In January 2013, the Philippines submitted its maritime dispute with China over the Spratly Islands to arbitration through the UN Convention on the Law of the Sea. In response, Beijing reasserted its claim over the territory. Following North Korea's third nuclear weapons test in February, China supported a March UN Security Resolution imposing new sanctions on North Korea (see entry on North Korea) in a move that indicated growing strains with Pyongyang. On April 15, Chinese troops occupied an area of the disputed region of Ladakh, prompting emergency talks between China and India. No resolution to the incursion had been achieved by July 2013. Also in July, China and Switzerland signed a free trade agreement.

Current issues. In January 2010 the government released the last individual imprisoned as a consequence of the 1989 Tiananmen Square protests. On October 8, 2010, Chinese officials vehemently attacked the announcement from Norway that the "criminal" Liu Xiaobo had been awarded the Nobel Peace Prize. The Nobel committee cited Liu's "long and nonviolent struggle for fundamental human rights in China."

The government has undertaken a broad campaign to install Internet filtering software on all personal computers as part of an effort to create a so-called Great Fire Wall between computer users and pornographic and politically sensitive Internet sites. Access to social network and messaging sites is also being restricted. In 2006 Google admitted that it had censored its Chinese-language search engine to produce results deemed acceptable by the government. In March 2010 Google began automatically rerouting users from its mainland site to its uncensored Hong Kong site, but in July Google and the mainland government reached a new license agreement under which Google agreed to cut access on its mainland site to what the PRC termed "lawbreaking content." Mainland users may, however, continue to access the Hong Kong site.

Following the Arab Spring in the Middle East, opposition groups in the PRC endeavored to organize a series of antigovernment protests in what was dubbed the "Jasmine Resolution." The government reacted by imposing additional restrictions on electronic media and preemptively arresting more than 100 dissident leaders. A number of foreign journalists were arrested or abused by security forces, prompting a protest by the EU.

The worst drought since the 1960s severely constrained Chinese agricultural production and prompted the government to release a record amount of water from the Three Gorges Dam beginning in May 2011. The drought was estimated to have affected more than 12.6 million people. Meanwhile, also in May, the PRC banned smoking in public places.

On September 29, 2011, China launched its first space laboratory with plans to expand the unmanned craft with additional modules. In June 2012 LIU Yang became the first Chinese woman astronaut to enter space.

Following a rebellion against local party officials in Wukan over land seizures, the village was permitted to elect its seven-member council on March 3, 2012, without interference from the Communist Party. Meanwhile, in March there were ten separate incidents of self-immolation in protest against Chinese rule. Repression of concurrent pro-independence demonstrations left two dead and more than 100 injured. In April 2012 human rights activist CHEN Guangcheng escaped house arrest and sought refuge at the U.S. embassy in Beijing. A deal was subsequently reached that allowed the blind Chen and his immediate family to travel to the United States, where he received a fellowship at New York University. In response to slowing economic growth, China's central bank cut interest rates in June 2012 for the first time since 2008.

On October 11, 2012, noted author MO Yan became the first Chinese citizen to win the Nobel Prize for Literature. Meanwhile, domestic and international media reports revealed that Premier Wen Jiabao and his family had amassed a fortune estimated at $2.7 billion. The revelations were an apparent embarrassment to the government, which blocked news and Internet stories about Jiabao. After he was selected CCP general secretary in November, Xi Jingping ordered new rules against excessive displays of wealth or extravagance at party meetings or functions. He also pledged an anti-corruption campaign. Meanwhile, the government ordered all Internet users to register using their real names in November. On December 14, 22 students were wounded when a mentally disturbed man attacked a primary school.

Massive pollution in Beijing in January 2013 led the government to suspend more than 30 construction projects, along with implementing limitations on industrial production and travel restrictions on vehicles. Smog even forced Beijing's airport to halt operations. In March, more than 16,000 pig carcasses were discovered in the Huangpu River, near Shanhai, raising renewed concerns over public health and sanitation. The following month, a new form of the avian flu virus (H7N9) spread through Eastern China, killing 43. The disease prompted the closure of poultry markets and the culling of wild and domesticated birds. On April 20, a magnitude 7 earthquake left 196 dead and more than 21,000 injured in Sichuan. Eager to avoid criticism that the central government was slow to respond, Beijing quickly deployed troops to the region but banned non-governmental organizations and private volunteer groups. In June 2013, Chen Guangcheng announced that New York University (NYU) had ended his fellowship, reportedly under pressure from China, which threatened to withdrew permission for NYU to establish an overseas campus in Shanghai. In July, the central bank removed controls on interest rates set by banks and other financial institutions in an effort to loosen credit and increase economic growth.

POLITICAL PARTIES AND GROUPS

Although established essentially as a one-party Communist state, the PRC has preserved some of the characteristics of a "united front" regime by permitting the continued existence of eight small minority parties, some of whose leaders hold high government office along with Communists and nonparty personnel. In addition, the **Chinese People's Political Consultative Conference** (CPPCC), which originally included representatives of all bodies adopting the 1949 constitution, reemerged in 1978, its last previous meeting having been held in 1965. Among the groups represented were political parties; minority nationalities; the All-China Federation of Trade Unions, the All-China Women's Federation, and the Communist Youth League, all three of which had been denounced during the Cultural Revolution; religious groups; and an assortment of other social, scientific, artistic, and cultural interests. The current chair of the CPPCC is YU Zhengsheng.

Leading Party:

Chinese Communist Party—CCP (Zhongguo Gongchan Dang). The CCP, founded in 1921 in Shanghai, has exerted unquestioned political dominance since 1949 despite being weakened in the mid-1960s as a result of the Cultural Revolution and the disruptive activities of Red Guard forces. Reconstruction of the party organization, begun in late 1969, was largely completed by late 1973, with the revolutionary committees created during the Cultural Revolution being made subordinate to party committees. The CCP's resurgence was formalized in 1975, when, for the first time, it was constitutionally recognized as the "vanguard" of state and society; by contrast, in the 1982 constitution the party is mentioned only in the preamble, where, at several points, its leadership role is acknowledged.

The party's highest organ is the National Party Congress, whose Central Committee elects a Political Bureau (Politburo) as well as other top figures. In theory, party congresses are elected every five years and hold annual sessions; however, the 8th Congress held only two sessions (in 1956 and 1958), while the 9th Congress did not convene until 1969. At the 13th Congress, held in 1987, most of the remaining "founding generation" CCP leaders retired, including Deng Xiaoping, who continued, however, as chair of the party's Central Military Commission until November 1989. For information on the 15th, 16th, and 17th Congresses, please see the 2012 *Handbook.*

On November 14, 2011, British businessmen Neil HEYWOOD was found dead in his hotel room in Chongqing. His death was reportedly linked to alcohol, however, on February 6, 2012, regional police chief WANG Lijun attempted to defect to the United States and charged that Heywood had been murdered by GU Kailai, the wife of Politburo member BO Xilai and a rising political figure. On March 15 Bo was removed from his posts and his wife and an associate were charged with murdering Heywood. She was convicted and sentenced to life in prison on August 20. Wang was subsequently convicted of bribery and abuse of power and given a 15-year jail term. On September 28, Bo was expelled from the party, convicted of bribery and corruption in September 2013, and sentenced to life in prison.

As of late 2012, the CCP claimed to have more than 85 million members, making it the world's largest political party. At the 18th Congress, in November 2012, XI Jinping was selected as the new party leader and chair of the CCP central military commission, thereby ensuring his selection as PRC president. Meanwhile, Politburo member LI Yuanchao was reportedly blocked from being selected to the standing committee by opposition from former president JIANG Zemin. Li's selection as PRC vice president in March 2013 was as a rebuff to Jiang.

General Secretary: XI Jinping (PRC President and Chair, Central Military Commission).

Other Members of Politburo Standing Committee: LI Keqiang (Premier), YU Zhengsheng (Party Secretary of the Standing Committee of the National People's Congress), ZHANG Dejiang (Chair, Chinese People's Political Consultative Conference), LIU Yunshan (Chair, Central Guidance Commission for Building Spiritual Civilization), WANG Qishan (Secretary, Central Commission for Discipline Inspection), ZHANG Gaoli (Deputy Party Secretary, State Council of the People's Republic of China).

Other Members of Politburo: FAN Changlong (Vice Chair, Central Military Commission), GUO Jinlong (Party Secretary, Beijing), HAN Zheng (Party Secretary, Shanghai), HU Chunhua (Party Secretary, Guangdong), LI Yuanchao (PRC Vice President), LI Jianguo (Vice Chair), LI Keqiang (Premier), LIU Yangdong (Vice Premier) [f], LI Zhanshu (Chief, General Office of the CCP), LIU Yunshan (Chair, Guidance Commission for Building Spiritual Civilization), LIU Qibao (Secretary, Central Secretariat), MA Kai (Vice Premier), MENG JIanzhu (Chair, Central Politics and Law Commission), SUN Chunlan (Party Secretary, Tianjin) [f], SUN Zhengcal (Party Secretary, Chongqing), WANG Yang (Vice Premier), WANG Huning (Director, Policy Research Office), WANG Qishan (Secretary, Central Commission for Discipline Inspection), XU Qiliang (Vice Chair, Central Military Commission), YU Zhangsheng (Chair, Chinese People's Political Consultative Conference), ZHANG Gaoli (Vice Premier), ZHANG Chunxian (Party Secretary, Xinjiang), ZHANG Dejiang (Chair, Standing Committee of the NPC), ZHAO Leji (Chief, CCP Organization Department).

Secretariat: LI Zhanshu, LIU Qibao, LIU Yunshan, ZHAO Leji, DU Qinglin, ZHAO Hongzhu, YANG Jing.

Regime-Supportive Minority Parties:

While expected "to work under the leadership of the Communist Party," in 1979 the following groups, largely middle-class and/or intellectual, were permitted to recruit new members and to hold national congresses for the first time in two decades: the **China Association for Promoting Democracy** (*Zhongguo Minzhu Cujin Hui*), a Shanghai cultural and educational group founded in 1945; the **China Democratic League** (*Zhongguo Minzhu Tongmeng*), founded in 1941 by a group of intellectuals opposed to Chiang Kai-shek's Nationalist Party (*Chung-kuo Kuo-min Tang* or Kuomintang—KMT); the **China Democratic National Construction Association** (*Zhongguo Minzhu Jianguo Hui*), a business-oriented group founded in 1945; the **China Party for Public Interests** (*Zhongguo Zhi Gong Dang*), an outgrowth of a 19th-century secret society organized by overseas Chinese; the **Chinese Peasants and Workers' Democratic Party** (*Zhongguo Nong Gong Minzhu Dang*), founded in 1947 as an outgrowth of a prewar movement that had joined forces with the CCP in 1935; the **Revolutionary Committee of the Kuomintang** (*Zhongguo Guomin Dang Geming Weiyuanhui*), founded in 1948 by a group of Hong Kong–based KMT dissidents opposed to Chiang Kai-shek's leadership; the **September 3, 1945 (V-J Day) Society** (*Jiu San*

Xuehui); and the **Taiwan Democratic Self-Government League** (*Taiwan Minzhu Zizhi Tongmen*), founded in 1947 by a group of pro-PRC Taiwanese.

Dissident and Separatist Groups:

During 1998 a number of dissidents sought to organize legal parties, notably WANG Youcai, QIN Yongmin, and XU Wenli on behalf of the **China Democratic Party** (CDP). In November Wang, Qin, and Xu were arrested for "subversion of the state process" and sentenced to 11, 12, and 13 years imprisonment, respectively. The sentencing of 15 other CDP leaders during the ensuing year virtually destroyed the party. (Xu and Wang were released for medical reasons in December 2002 and March 2004, respectively, and left for the United States.) In February 2012 ZHU Yufu of the CDP was sentenced to seven years in prison for subversion. In early 1999 the regime also cracked down on the China Labor Party, although in March it released two leaders of the China Democratic United Front–Liberal Democratic Party, LI Li and WANG Ce, after four months' incarceration. In August 2008 the government released HU Shigen, cofounder of the China Freedom and Democracy Party, from prison after he had served 16 years of a 20-year sentence.

A clandestine **East Turkestan Islamic Movement** (ETIM) operates primarily in Xinjiang Uygur Autonomous Region, where elements of the Uighur minority have long sought separation. Small-scale antigovernment attacks have become more frequent in recent years, but foreign journalists have had only restricted access to the region and incidents are not uniformly reported. In 2003 the Chinese government branded the ETIM and three other groups—the **East Turkestan Information Center,** the **East Turkestan Liberation Organization,** and the **World Uighur Youth Congress**—as terrorist organizations. The UN and the United States have also identified the ETIM as a terrorist group. In January 2007 police reported destroying a camp in southern Xinjiang run by the ETIM, killing 18 and arresting 17 others. In the most deadly recent attack attributed to the ETIM, 17 paramilitary troops were killed in August 2008 in Kashgar. In May 2012 Pakistan condemned the ETIM and pledged to suppress the group. In July 2013, Chinese authorities blamed the ETIM for riots in Xinjiang that killed 24.

In July 2010 the arrest of three alleged terrorists in Norway and Germany focused attention on the **Turkestan Islamic Party** (TIP), which, with assistance from al-Qaeda, was apparently planning a bomb attack in the West. The TIP's founder, Hasan MAHSUM, was killed by Pakistani forces in 2003, after which leadership apparently passed to Abdul HAQ, who has also been identified as an al-Qaeda leader. In January 2010 a missile fired from a drone in Afghanistan reportedly killed 15 TIP members, one of whom may have been Haq. The 2010 arrests in Europe were noteworthy in part because they may be an indication that the TIP has decided to expand its campaign beyond Xinjiang Uygur and its surroundings. On September 7, 2011, the TIP claimed responsibility for attacks in July on two southern Xinjiang cities, Hotan and Kashgar. The TIP also claimed responsibility for a suicide bombing that killed 47 in Xiamen. Chinese authorities refuted the claim.

LEGISLATURE

National People's Congress—NPC (*Quanguo Renmin Daibiao Dahui*). A unicameral body indirectly elected for a five-year term, the NPC holds one session annually, although the Second Congress (1959–1963) did not meet in 1961 and the Third Congress met only once. No subsequent election was held until 1974, after which the Fourth Congress convened in complete secrecy in Beijing in January 1975.

Meetings became regularized with the 5th Congress, elected at a series of municipal and provincial congresses held between November 1977 and February 1978. A total of 2,987 newly elected deputies from 34 electoral units plus the People's Liberation Army attended the first session of the 12th Congress, which was held in Beijing, March 5–17, 2013. At the session, Wu Bangguo was elected chair of the NPC.

Chair of the Standing Committee: WU Bangguo.

CABINET

[as of November 5, 2013]

Premier	Li Keqaing
Vice Premiers	Zhang Gaoli
	Liu Yandong [f]
	Wang Yang
	Ma Kai
State Councilors	Yang Jing
	Chang Wanquan
	Yang Jiechi
	Guo Shengkun
	Wang Yong
Ministers	
Agriculture	Han Changfu
Civil Affairs	Li Liguo
Commerce	Gao Hucheng
Communications and Transport	Yang Chuantang
Culture	Cai Wu
Education	Yuan Guiren
Environmental Protection	Zhou Shengxian
Finance	Lou Jiwei
Foreign Affairs	Wang Yi
Health	Li Bin
Housing and Urban-Rural Construction	Jiang Weixin
Human Resources and Social Security	Yin Weimin
Industry and Information Technology	Miao Wei
Justice	Wu Aiying [f]
Land and Natural Resources	Jiang Daming
National Defense	Chang Wanquan
Public Security	Guo Shengkun
Science and Technology	Wan Gang
State Commission for Ethnic Affairs	Wang Zhengwei
State Commission for National Development and Reform	Xu Shaoshi
State Commission for Population and Family Planning	Li Bin [f]
State Security	Geng Huichang
Supervision	Huang Shuxian
Water Resources	Chen Lei
Auditor General	Liu Jiayi
Chair, Central Military Commission	Xi Jinping
Governor, People's Bank of China	Zhou Xiaochuan
Secretary General, State Council	Yang Jing

[f] = female

Note: All members of the cabinet belong to the CCP except the minister of science and technology, who is a member of the China Party for Public Interests.

INTERGOVERNMENTAL REPRESENTATION

Ambassador to the U.S.: ZHANG Yesui.

U.S. Ambassador to China: Gary LOCKE.

Permanent Representative to the UN: LI Baodong.

IGO Memberships (Non-UN): ADB, AfDB, APEC, G-20, IADB, WTO.

SPECIAL ADMINISTRATIVE REGIONS

Hong Kong (*Xianggang*). The former Crown Colony of Hong Kong, situated on China's southeastern coast, consists of Hong Kong Island and Kowloon Peninsula, as well as the mainland area of the New Territories. Its total area is 423 square miles (1,095 sq. km), the New Territories alone occupying 365 square miles. The inhabitants, concentrated on Hong Kong Island and Kowloon, total some 7,130,000 (2010C), 7,067,800 (2011E—U.S. Census). The population is 98 percent Chinese, nearly one-quarter from the PRC. The capital is Victoria, on Hong Kong Island.

The economy was formerly based on exported industrial products, especially cotton textiles, but the services sector now accounts for 93 percent of GDP, in the wake of Hong Kong's emergence as one of the world's premier banking and financial centers. The GDP grew by an annual average of 7.2 percent from 2004–2011 but slowed to 2.8 percent growth in 2012. GDP per capita was $35,156 in 2012, while inflation increased by 4.1 percent.

Hong Kong Island and Kowloon Peninsula were both ceded by China to Great Britain "in perpetuity" in the mid-19th century, and the New Territories was leased for 99 years in 1898. In October 1982 British and Chinese diplomats began discussing a transition to full Chinese sovereignty. The talks culminated in the signature on December 19, 1984, in Beijing of a Sino-British Joint Declaration of the Question of Hong Kong, which took effect in May 1985. Under the slogan "one country and two systems," China would regain title to the entire area on July 1, 1997, when the lease of the New Territories expired, but agreed to maintain the enclave as a capitalist Special Administrative Region (SAR) for at least 50 years thereafter.

On April 4, 1990, the PRC's National People's Congress (NPC) approved a postreversion "mini-constitution" that included a complicated formula for Legislative Council (LegCo) representation: one-third of its members were to be elected at the first postreversion balloting, with the proportion rising to two-fifths in 1999 and to one-half in 2003. The law made no reference to the future status of a Bill of Rights that had been approved by the colony's Executive Council a month earlier. In late April 1990 the UK House of Commons approved a bill permitting the issuance of British passports to some 300,000 Hong Kong Chinese (out of some 3.5 million who were entitled to restricted British national overseas passports), but fewer than 60,000 applied for passports prior to the end of February 1991.

In April 1992 UK prime minister John Major named Chris Patten, the Conservative Party chair, to the post of Hong Kong governor. The new governor quickly became embroiled in an acrimonious dispute with Beijing over plans for reform of Hong Kong's system in the period before its reversion to China, which claimed that his plan breached signed Sino-UK agreements. Patten, backed by liberal members of LegCo, published his proposals in March 1993. At the same time, Beijing continued to create alternative bodies to handle the transfer, including a Preparatory Committee (PC) for the Hong Kong Special Administrative Region (HKSAR). Amid growing strains in UK-Chinese relations, the director of the Hong Kong and Macao Affairs Office of the Chinese State Council, LU Ping, visited the colony in May but refused to meet with Patten.

In 1994 Hong Kong prepared for its first fully democratic elections. In April the United Democrats of Hong Kong (UDHK), led by Martin LEE Chu-ming, announced a merger with the prounification Meeting Point group to form the **Democratic Party** (DP), which advocated autonomy for Hong Kong following the reversion to Chinese sovereignty. Also launched in April, the business-oriented Hong Kong Progressive Alliance (HKPA), with Ambrose LAU Hon-chuen as its spokesperson, favored close relations with China. In addition, the **Association for Democracy and People's Livelihood** (ADPL), led by Frederick FUNG Kin-kee, attracted considerable support in the run-up to the election, which took place in September for a total of 346 seats on 18 district boards. Independents won 167 seats; the DP, 75; the ADPL, 29; four pro-Chinese parties, a total of 68; and other parties, 7. The prodemocracy DP and ADPL also polled strongly in elections to urban and regional councils held in March 1995.

Two months earlier, new strains had developed over China's demand for access to the personal files of Hong Kong civil servants. Tensions eased somewhat with the signature in June of an accord on maintaining elements of an independent legal system after reversion. Prodemocracy parties fiercely criticized concessions made to the PRC, but LegCo passed the agreement by a two-to-one margin in July. Earlier in the month, the Hong Kong chief secretary, Anson CHAN (CHAN Fang On-sang), confirmed that she had paid an unprecedented visit to Beijing for talks with Chinese leaders.

Elections to the 60-seat LegCo in September 1995 gave the DP 12 of the 20 directly elected seats plus 7 indirectly elected seats, although China had indicated that no DP members would be permitted to serve in the future legislature of the HKSAR. The **Liberal Party** (LP), a business group favoring accommodation with Beijing, won 10; the strongly pro-Chinese Democratic Alliance for the Betterment of Hong Kong (DAB), 6; and the ADPL, 4, with independents claiming most of the balance.

In December 1995 China published the names of the 150 members of the PC, including 94 Hong Kong residents but no DP supporters. Tasks assumed by the PC included establishing a 400-member selection committee to appoint a chief executive for the HKSAR, and in March 1996 it voted 149 to 1 to constitute a Provisional Legislative Council (PLC) that, over British objections, would replace the existing LegCo after reversion.

Shipping magnate TUNG Chee-hwa (generally known as "C.H."), China's favored candidate for the position of HKSAR chief executive, resigned from the Executive Council in June 1996 while remaining vice chair of the PC. The first round of balloting by the selection committee in November was contested by 8 candidates, after China had rejected 23 other nominees. Tung was formally designated chief executive after securing 320 votes in a runoff in December against former chief justice Sir TI-LIANG Yang and Peter WOO. In late December the PC went on to nominate the 60 members of the PLC, thereby generating a series of DP-led demonstrations as well as strong protests from Patten, who nevertheless pledged to cooperate with Tung in the transition period.

At midnight on June 30, 1997, in a ceremony attended by Britain's Prince Charles, Chinese President Jiang Zemin, and UK Prime Minister Tony Blair, Hong Kong was returned to Chinese sovereignty. Immediately thereafter Chief Executive Tung formally named an administrative team that included Anson Chan as chief secretary and, somewhat surprisingly, Sir Donald Tsang (Tsang Yam-kuen), the incumbent financial secretary, who had earlier expressed opposition to Tung's economic policies. Most of the remaining members of the Executive Council were newcomers.

In April 1998 approximately 5 percent of Hong Kong's 2.6 million voters, representing professional, labor, and religious groups, were permitted to vote for 588 members of an 800-seat Election Committee that was, in turn, to name 10 members of the first postreversion LegCo. Another 30 LegCo members were to be selected by professional and business groups. In the LegCo election in May, prodemocracy candidates won 14 of the 20 directly elected seats but constituted a minority because pro-China groups dominated the remaining 40 seats. The DP once again led the prodemocracy forces, taking 9 directly elective seats, while a new party, **The Frontier,** led by Emily LAU Wai-hing, took 3; Christine LOH Kung-wai's Citizens' Party, 1; and an independent, 1. The DAB, led by TSANG Yok-sing, won 5 seats in the direct balloting. The LP won only 1; its leader, Allen LEE Peng-fei, was among the defeated.

Largely because of widespread frustration with the convoluted electoral system, the turnout was only 43.6 percent in the LegCo election of September 10, 2000, after which the prodemocracy DP held only 12 of 60 seats on a declining vote share, while the pro-Beijing DAB total rose to 11. The overall balance of power on the LegCo remained with the pro-Beijing forces following the election, which also saw the LP, the HKPA, the Frontier, and the **New Century Forum,** led by MA Fung-kwok, winning seats.

Although denying that she was reacting to pressure from Beijing, the enclave's popular civil rights advocate, Anson Chan, resigned as chief secretary on January 12, 2001. Financial Secretary Tsang was named as her successor on February 15, amid speculation that Chan might challenge Tung's reelection bid in early 2002.

Passage of the Chief Executive Election Bill by the LegCo on July 11, 2001, generated considerable controversy and precipitated a walkout by opponents, principally because of a provision permitting Beijing to remove a chief executive considered "incapable of serving." Opposition deputies branded the provision as a fundamental betrayal of Hong Kong's autonomy.

The voting for chief executive on February 28, 2002, was conducted by a committee containing a minority of pro-Beijing appointees, with three-fourths of the 800 delegates representing various functional and other constituency groups. The result was a fait accompli, however, since Tung, who retained solid support from President Jiang, had collected more than 700 nominating signatures, thereby preventing any prospective opponent from obtaining the minimum 100 signatures needed for consideration. On June 24 Tung announced the formation of a new Executive Council, which was approved by a 36–21 LegCo vote despite strenuous opposition from prodemocracy forces.

In the September 12, 2004, LegCo election, in which 30 seats were directly elected from geographic constituencies and the other 30 chosen by functional groups, prodemocracy advocates came away with 25 seats, but the DP, led by Martin Lee and YEUNG Sum, saw its total drop to 9. Most of the other prodemocracy seats being claimed by unaffiliated candidates. The DAB and the resurgent LP, the latter now led by James TIEN Pei-chun, won 12 and 10 seats, respectively, to lead the pro-Beijing contingent, which won an overwhelming majority of functional constituency seats and thereby ended up with 35 seats overall.

A new centrist organization of barristers, the Article 45 Concern Group, led by Alan LEONG Kah-kit, won four prodemocracy seats in the September 2004 election on a platform that called for direct election of the chief executive (as advocated in Article 45 of Hong Kong's Basic Law). Leong's group had originally been formed as the Article 23 Concern Group, which had mounted a successful campaign against adoption of a stringent national security law despite its being mandated by Article 23 of the Basic Law.

After weathering numerous demonstrations, triggered in part by Beijing's assertion in April 2004 that it would not tolerate a direct election in 2007, Chief Executive Tung resigned on March 10, 2005, citing health reasons, and was succeeded on an interim basis by his deputy, Donald Tsang. Having declared himself a candidate to fill the two-year balance of Tung's term, Tsang resigned on May 25 and was replaced by the financial secretary, Henry Tang Ying-yan. The DP's LEE Wing-tat also declared his candidacy, but Tsang was confirmed on June 16 after obtaining over 700 signatures of support from members of the Election Committee. He was sworn in on June 24 in Beijing.

In March 2006 the Article 45 Concern Group announced formation of a new **Civic Party** (CP), led by Leong and Audrey EU. Leong subsequently indicated his intention to run for chief executive as the candidate of the CP and DP. (Martin Lee and Anson Chan both declined to run.) Although Leong secured sufficient supporting signatures to contest the March 25, 2007, election, Tsang won another term easily, by a 649–123 vote of the 796-member Election Committee. Leong, who had not expected to win, stated that he intended to run again in 2012 and would continue to advocate universal suffrage and full democracy.

Earlier, in August 2006, LegCo voted 32–0 in favor of granting police wide powers to conduct covert surveillance, including wiretapping, bugging homes and businesses, and monitoring e-mail. Prodemocracy legislators boycotted the vote after failing to add a prohibition against political surveillance.

On December 29, 2007, the Standing Committee of the NPC stated that it would actively consider electing Hong Kong's chief executive by universal suffrage in 2017, but not in 2012. It also ruled out direct election of the full LegCo until at least 2020.

The district council elections of November 18, 2007, were marked by a surge in support for the DAB, which had absorbed the HKPA in 2005 and was now called the **Democratic Alliance for the Betterment and Progress of Hong Kong**. The DAB nearly doubled its 2003 representation, to 115 seats. The DP, in contrast, saw its representation drop from 95 to 59 seats. The CP won 8; the **League of Social Democrats** (LSD), a prodemocracy party formed in October 2006 and led by Raymond WONG Yuk-man, 6; and the LP, 1.

In the LegCo election of September 7, 2008, the pro-Beijing faction retained a majority by virtue of its strength among functional constituencies, among which it won 24 of 30 seats. Overall, the pro-Beijing DAB, now led by TAM Yiu-chung, won a leading 13 seats. The prodemocracy group's 23 total seats were sufficient to deny the pro-Beijing faction, with 34 seats, a controlling two-thirds majority (for more information on the 2008 balloting, please see the 2013 *Handbook*).

The relatively poor electoral performance of the LP, which won a disappointing 7 seats, led James Tien, who had lost his LegCo seat, to resign as chair, leaving acting chair Miriam LAU Kin-yee in charge. At the same time, three of the LP's recently elected legislators announced their resignations from the party. In other party developments after the 2008 election, the Alliance changed its name to the **Professional Forum,** and the Frontier announced in November that it would cooperate with the DP while retaining its separate identity. The overall balance of power remained unchanged following by-elections held for five seats on May 16, 2010. The by-elections had been forced by the January resignations of five prodemocracy legislators—three from the LSD and two from the CP—who wished to turn the voting into a referendum on universal suffrage and democracy. All five were reelected.

In April 2010 the government introduced a reform package that called for increasing the Election Committee to 1,200 members and expanding the LegCo to 70 seats, including 35 directly elected seats and 35 indirectly elected posts. On June 24–25 the LegCo passed the changes, which included adding 5 geographical constituency seats and 5 functional seats to the legislature. On March 25, 2012, Chun-ying Leung was elected chief executive. In legislative balloting on September 9, pro-Beijing groups, including independents, secured 43 seats, led by the DAB with 13; the **Hong Kong Federation of Trade Unions**, 6; the LP, 5; **Economic Synergy** (*Jingi Dongli*), formed in 2008, 3; the **New People's Party**—NPP, formed in 2011, 2; the **Kowloon West New Dynamic**—KWND, 1; the **Federation of Hong Kong and Kowloon Labour Unions**—FLU, 1; and the **New Century Forum**, 1. Pro-Beijing independents won 11 seats. Prodemocracy parties won 27 seats, led by the DP with 6; Civic, 6; the **Labour Party**, formed in 2011, 4; **People Power**—PP (*Renmin Liliang*), formed in 2011, 3; the LSD, 1; the ADPL, 1; the **Neighborhood and Workers Service Center**—NWSC, 1; the **Neo-Democrats**, formed in 2010, 1; and the **Hong Kong Professional Teachers' Union**—PTU, 1. Prodemocracy independents won 3 seats. The prodemocracy group's total seats were again sufficient to deny the pro-Beijing faction a controlling two-thirds majority. After the balloting, Albert HO, chair of the DP, resigned and accepting blame for the inability of the prodemocracy groups to create a united opposition coalition.

In June 2013, Edward Snowden, a U.S. intelligence contractor, fled to Hong Kong following revelations about U.S. security programs (see entry on the United States). Although the United States requested Snowden's extradition, he was allowed to leave Hong Kong for Russia after authorities determined that the U.S. request needed further "clarification."

Chief Executive: Chun-ying LEUNG.
Secretary for Finance: John TSANG Chun-wah.
Secretary for Security: LAI Tung-kwok.

Macao (*Aomen*). Macao comprises a peninsula and two small islets in the mouth of the Canton River, about 40 miles west of Hong Kong. Its area of 6 square miles (15.5 sq. km) contains some 557,000 inhabitants (2010C), 558,100 (2011E—U.S. Census). The population is predominantly Chinese, with a Portuguese minority of 2,000–3,000. Its economy shrank by 4.6 percent in 1998 and by 2.9 percent in 1999, but increased substantially thereafter as the former Portuguese colony became an Asian center of casino gambling. Recently, growth has exceeded even the mainland's accelerated pace, reaching 16.5 percent in 2006 and then 25.3 percent in 2007. In 2008 GDP growth fell to 13.2 percent, reflecting a steady rate decline as Macao felt the impact of the international financial crisis. GDP grew dramatically at 26.2 percent in 2010, and 20.7 percent in 2011, before slowing to 9.9 percent in 2012. Inflation that year was 5.4 percent, and unemployment 2.7 percent.

In 1557 Macao became the first European enclave on the China coast. In 1974 Western diplomats in Beijing reported that the governor of Macao, Col. José Eduardo Martinho García Leandro, had been directed to communicate to Chinese representatives the Lisbon government's willingness to withdraw from the enclave. China had no desire, however, to alter the status of the territory, which was flourishing, partly because of legalized casino gambling—the source of nearly half of its revenue—and partly because of its status as an entrepôt for trade with China. (It had long been alleged that the port also exported opium into the international market.) The trade relationship had been enhanced by creation of a Special Economic Zone in the nearby province of Zhuhai.

The establishment of diplomatic relations between Portugal and the PRC in February 1979 did not alter the status of Macao, Portuguese prime minister Carlos Mota Pinto declaring that it would remain "Chinese territory under Portuguese administration." Following conclusion of the agreement on Hong Kong's future in December 1984, China changed course, however, and initiated discussions on Macao's status.

In May 1985, following the designation of Joaquim Pinto Machado as Macao's latest governor, Portuguese president António Eanes announced that Sino-Portuguese talks on reversion would begin in 1986. On May 26, 1987, the two countries initialed an agreement for the return of the territory to Chinese sovereignty on December 20, 1999, under a plan similar to the "one country and two systems" approach approved for Hong Kong. China agreed to grant Macao 50 years of noninterference with its capitalist economy, and residents holding or entitled to hold Portuguese passports were given the right to continue doing so after reversion.

In January 1993 the ninth and final session of the Macao Special Administrative Region (MSAR) Basic Law Drafting Committee, meeting in Beijing, approved the text of the document that would serve as the MSAR constitution following reversion. In late March the text was approved by the Chinese legislature. In the last assembly election before the reversion to Chinese rule, a record 64.4 percent turnout in September 1996 delivered a majority for pro-Chinese groupings.

A Chinese-appointed MSAR Preparatory Committee was launched in Beijing in May 1998. Charged with defining the procedure for the election of Macao's first postreversion government, the committee consisted of 100 members, 40 of whom were from China. In its fourth plenary session held in November, the group authorized its chair, Chinese vice premier Qian Qichen, and his vice chairs to designate candidates for a 200-member Nominating Committee, which, following election by the Preparatory Committee, would be responsible for electing members of the new government. In December Beijing announced a new nationality law for the enclave: Upon reversion, all residents of Chinese descent would become Chinese citizens, while those of mixed Chinese and Portuguese descent would be allowed to choose either Chinese or Portuguese allegiance.

Immediately following its formation in April 1999, the Chinese Nominating Committee winnowed the list of potential chief executives from nine to two, with HO Hau Wah (Edmund HO), a banker, appearing to hold a decided preelection advantage over AU Chong Kit (Stanley AU), another banker. On May 15 the committee elected Ho by a landslide of 163 votes to 34. The territory's inhabitants looked to the widely popular Ho to reverse a languishing economy and take decisive action against long-standing violence by underworld groups, known as triads. Because of the turmoil, which had severely damaged the economy by inhibiting tourism, Chinese troops were widely applauded by Macanese at reversion in December 1999.

In its first postreversion parliamentary election, held September 23, 2001, Macao saw the 10 popularly elected seats filled by 4 pro-Beijing, 4 probusiness, and 2 prodemocracy representatives, including NG Nuok Cheong, leader of the **New Democratic Macao Association** (*Associação de Novo Macau Democrático*—ANMD). An additional 10 Legislative Assembly members were indirectly elected by four functional groups: labor; employers; professionals; and welfare, cultural, educational, and sports constituencies. The final seven assembly members were subsequently appointed by Chief Executive Ho.

The election of September 25, 2005, saw 58 percent of Macao's voters turn out to fill 12 seats on the 29-seat Legislative Assembly. A dozen associations offered candidates, with 8 of them winning at least 1 seat, including 2 each by the ANMD, the **Union for Development** (*União para o Desenvolvimento*—UD), the **United Citizens' Association of Macao** (*Associaçãdos Cidadão Unidos de Macau*—ACUM), and the **Union for Promoting Progress** (*União Promotora para o Progresso*—UPP). As in the past, functional groups indirectly elected ten members, and Chief Executive Ho appointed the balance.

In March 2007 the troubled Macao-based Banco Delta Asia (BDA) returned to the headlines when the U.S. Treasury Department ruled, in confirmation of allegations made in 2005, that the bank had aided North Korea in laundering money. In the context of ongoing six-party talks in Beijing aimed at ending North Korea's nuclear weapons program, the United States agreed to the transfer to Pyongyang of $25 million frozen in a BDA account, although it took until June to complete the transaction.

On January 30, 2008, former secretary of transport and public works AO Man-long was sentenced to 27 years in prison for having accepted some $100 million in bribes from companies seeking approvals for casino and hotel projects. Ao was the highest-ranking public official to face corruption charges since the reversion to China in 1999.

In May 2009 the government announced the names of the 300 members of the Chief Executive Election Committee (254 representatives of socioeconomic sectors, the 12 Macanese deputies to the National People's Congress, 16 representatives from Macao's Legislative Assembly, 12 members of the Chinese People's Political Consultative Conference, and 6 religious representatives). With Edmund Ho ineligible for a third term, the front-runner for the July 26 contest was generally regarded to be Fernando Chui Sai-on, who resigned his post as secretary for social affairs and culture to stand for election. Other expected candidates were Prosecutor General HO Chio-meng and Secretary for Economy and Finance Francis TAM Pak-yuen, but in the end Chui proved to be the only candidate. Declared the winner on July 26, he won the approval of the PRC's cabinet on August 10.

Sixteen groups contested the 12 directly elected Legislative Assembly seats at polling held September 20, 2009. An unusual number of potentially spoiled ballots delayed the release of final results. Nine different groups won at least one seat, with only the ACUM, the UD, and the **Association for Prosperous Democratic Macao** (*Associação de Próspero Macau Democrático*—APMD) claiming 2 each. The APMD had been established by prodemocracy supporters with the expectation that having a second list, in addition to the ANMD, would garner additional seats. In the end, the ANMD won one seat, with the **New Hope** (*Nova Esperança*—NE) adding a fourth prodemocracy seat. In 2011, in response to a dramatic rise in inflation, the government initiated a series of measures, including a series of five payments of $875 to all Macao residents. Also in 2011, Macao surpassed Las Vegas as the largest gaming center in the world with gambling revenue of $33.5 billion.

In August 2012, security forces arrested more than 150 people connected with organized crime in Macao in response to rising crime, including three gang-related murders.

Chief Executive: CHUI Sai-on (Fernando CHUI Sai-on).

Secretary for Administration and Justice: Florida Rosa Silva CHAN.

Secretary for Economy and Finance: Francis TAM Pak Yuen.

CHINA: TAIWAN

Republic of China
Chung-hua Min-kuo

Political Status: Chinese province; controlled by the government of the Republic of China (established 1912), whose authority since 1949 has been limited to the island of Taiwan (Formosa), Penghu (the Pescadores), and certain offshore islands, including Kinmen (Quemoy) and Matsu; present constitution adopted December 25, 1946, effective from December 25, 1947.

Area: 13,592 sq. mi. (35,203 sq. km).

Population: 23,176,000 (2010C); 23,299,716 (2011E—U.S.).

Major Urban Centers (2005E): TAIPEI (2,619,000), Kaohsiung (1,522,000), Taichung (1,039,000), Tainan (761,000), Keelung (394,000).

Official Language: Mandarin Chinese.

Monetary Unit: New Taiwan Dollar (market rate November 1, 2013: 29.43 dollars = $1US).

President: MA Ying-jeou (Nationalist Party); elected March 22, 2008, and sworn in May 20 for a four-year term, succeeding CHEN Shui-bian (Democratic Progressive Party); reelected on January 14, 2012, and sworn in on May 20.

Vice President: WU Den-yih (Nationalist Party); elected January 14, 2012, and sworn in May 20 for a term concurrent with that of the president; succeeding Vincent SIEW (Nationalist Party).

President of Executive Branch (Premier): JIANG Yi-huah (Nationalist Party); designated by the president on February 1, 2013, and sworn in on February 18, succeeding Sean CHEN-Chun (Nationalist Party) who resigned on February 1, 2013.

GOVERNMENT AND POLITICS

Political background. Following its move to Taiwan in 1949, the Chinese Nationalist regime continued to insist that it represented all of China and vowed to return eventually to the mainland. The danger of Communist conquest, which appeared very real in 1949–1950, was averted primarily by the decision of U.S. president Harry Truman to interpose the protection of the American Seventh Fleet upon the outbreak of the Korean War in 1950. Thereafter, the Nationalist government continued under the domination of the Nationalist Party, or Kuomintang (*Chung-kuo Kuo-min Tang*—KMT), led by CHIANG Kai-shek until his death in 1975.

As part of a major reorganization in 1969, the post of vice premier was awarded to President Chiang's son, CHIANG Ching-kuo, who was subsequently named premier in 1972. The younger Chiang was selected by the National Assembly in 1978 to succeed C.K. YEN as president. Vice President LEE Teng-hui, an islander who had served earlier as governor of Taiwan, succeeded to the presidency following Chiang's death in 1988 and was then elected to the post in 1990.

In 1991, a year after Lee's implicit recognition of the People's Republic of China (PRC) on the mainland, the National Assembly rescinded the "Temporary Provisions" that, since 1948, had conferred emergency powers on the president and frozen the tenure of mainland-elected officials. In addition, a number of constitutional amendments were promulgated, including a stipulation that all mainland parliamentarians would be obliged to retire prior to the election of a new National Assembly. In May 1991 the Legislative Branch repealed the Statute of Punishment for Sedition that for more than four decades had served as the principal weapon against the KMT's opponents. Nevertheless, the KMT secured a resounding victory in the December 1991 National Assembly election, winning 254 of 325 seats, while its principal competitor, the Democratic Progressive Party (DPP), won 66.

The KMT suffered a serious reversal in the election for a new 161-member Legislative Branch in December 1992. While it retained control with nearly 60 percent of the seats, KMT candidates garnered only 53 percent of the vote. In January 1993, after losing a tumultuous intraparty struggle with liberal opponents, the conservative HAU Pei-tsun, who had served as premier since June 1990, signaled his wish to resign, and in February the ethnic Taiwanese provincial governor, LIEN Chan, was approved by the KMT's Central Standing Committee as his successor.

At the Legislative Branch election of December 1995, the KMT retained a narrow majority (85 of 164 seats), although its vote share was a worst-ever 46 percent. Earlier, in July 1994, the National Assembly, over the objections of the DPP, had passed constitutional reforms that included direct presidential elections. In the first such presidential balloting, held in March 1996, Lee Teng-hui secured a second term by winning 54 percent of the vote. In simultaneous election of a third National Assembly, the KMT won 183 of the 334 seats with 55 percent of the votes, while the DPP advanced to 99 seats and 30 percent.

Lien Chan had resigned as premier in January 1996 to pursue the vice presidency as Lee's running mate, but he had then been sworn in as head of a caretaker government at the end of February. Despite some resistance in the new National Assembly, in June Vice President Lien was reappointed premier.

In the months that followed, President Lee encountered rising popular discontent over the issue of corruption, efforts to downsize provincial government, and a deterioration in law and order. Undaunted, Lee moved ahead in 1997 with a series of reform proposals that had been broached at a National Development Conference in December 1996. In the end, a consensus was reached on a number of key elements in the Lee agenda, but only after the prounification New Party (NP) had withdrawn from the deliberations to protest a "tacit coalition" between the KMT and the DPP.

Under the package as approved by the National Assembly in July 1997, the president would have sole discretion in the selection of a premier, while the legislature, with the support of one-third of its members, would be able to propose a no-confidence motion. It was also agreed that the number of Legislative Branch members would be increased from 164 to 225 and that elections for Taiwan's provincial governor and legislators would be suspended upon expiration of the incumbents' terms in late 1998, pending the adoption of legislation to reduce the scale of the provincial administration. In late July Vice President Lien announced that he intended to resign as premier, and on September 1 Vincent SIEW was installed as his successor.

At the large-city mayoral and county magistrate elections in November 1997, the KMT was, for the first time, outpolled by the DPP, 43 to 42 percent, raising what some Taiwanese considered to be the once-unthinkable prospect that the DPP might become Taiwan's next ruling party. In elections in January 1998, however, the KMT rebounded to win 59 percent of the contests for county and city councilors, small-city mayors, and township chiefs, and in December it again won a majority in Legislative Branch balloting.

In a stunning development, in the presidential poll of March 18, 2000, the KMT's nominee, Lien Chan, finished third, with 23 percent of the vote, behind the DPP's CHEN Shui-bian (39 percent) and James SOONG (37 percent), a KMT dissident who ran as an independent. Shortly after the election, the DPP and KMT agreed to abolish the National Assembly; however, the move was superseded on April 24 by the assembly's own decision to transfer significant powers to the Legislative Branch (see Constitution and government, below).

At his inauguration on May 20, 2000, President Chen distanced himself somewhat from the position of his own party. He declared, in what became known as his "four no's plus one" policy, that, in the

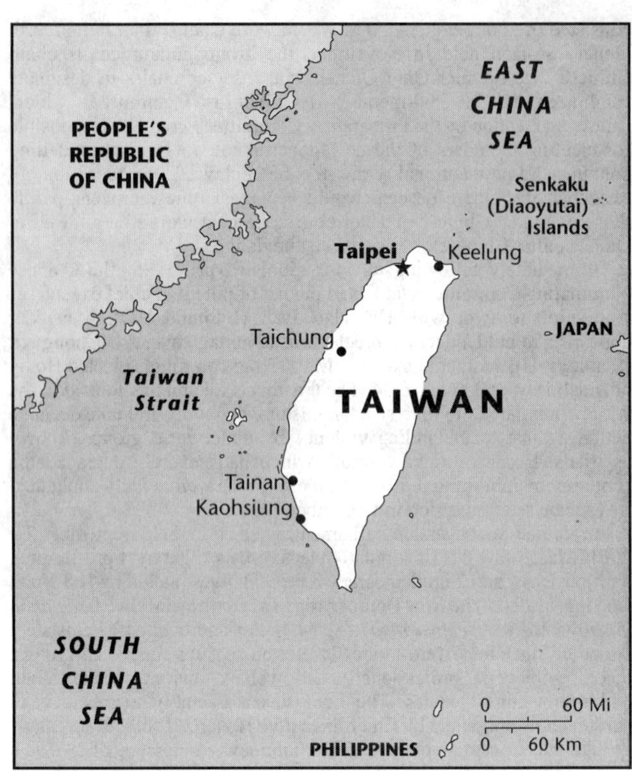

absence of aggressive action by the PRC, Taiwan would not declare independence, alter its official name, amend the constitution to suggest the existence of two Chinas, or hold an independence referendum. He added that his predecessor's National Unification Council (NUC) and its phased Guidelines for National Unification, drafted in 1991, would remain in place. Earlier, on May 1, he had announced a cabinet headed by his KMT predecessor's defense minister, Gen. TANG Fei, but Tang resigned five months later, ostensibly for health reasons, although most analysts considered the precipitating factor to be his opposition to a presidential decision terminating work on the country's fourth nuclear power plant. On October 4 Chen's former campaign manager, Vice Premier CHANG Chun-hsiung, stepped in as Tang's successor.

At the general election of December 1, 2001, the KMT lost its legislative majority for the first time, capturing only 68 seats in the 225-member Legislative Branch. It nevertheless retained control of the legislature by virtue of the 46 seats won by James Soong's new People First Party (PFP), the KMT's principal partner in an informal "pan-blue" alliance (a reference to the KMT's party color) that also included the NP. The DPP achieved a plurality of 87 seats, while its allies, the Taiwan Solidarity Union (TSU) and the small Taiwan Independence Party (TAIP), won 13 and none, respectively, as part of the DPP-led "pan-green" alliance (a reference to the DPP's color). Although President Chen had proposed during the election campaign that the leading parties establish a "National Stabilization Alliance," both the KMT and the PFP dismissed the idea after the polling.

Premier Chang and the entire cabinet resigned on January 21, 2002, prior to the opening of the new legislative session. President Chen immediately named YU Shyi-kun, a former vice premier, as Chang's replacement, and a substantially new cabinet, which included four KMT members despite the objections of their party, assumed office on February 1. In the meantime, township, county, and provincial elections of January 26, 2002, confirmed the KMT's relative strength at the local level.

The presidential election of March 20, 2004, concluded with President Chen and his "pan-green" running mate, Vice President LU Hsiu-lien (Annette LU), also of the DPP, winning 50.1 percent of the vote, but the "pan-blue" ticket (49.9 percent) of the KMT's Lien and the PFP's Soong immediately challenged the results. In the end, the Supreme Court dismissed KMT allegations of electoral fraud and other irregularities. Chen's razor-thin success at the polls did not, however, carry over to the Legislative Branch election of December 11, after which the KMT and its allies continued to hold a slim majority, 114 seats, compared to 101 for the DPP and the TSU. On January 25, 2005,

President Chen named the mayor of Kaohsiung, Frank Chang-ting HSIEH, to succeed Premier Yu, who, along with the rest of the cabinet, had resigned the previous day. Most of the departing ministers were, however, reappointed on January 31.

With the backing of both the DPP and the KMT, on August 23, 2004, the Legislative Branch had approved a constitutional reform package that included halving its own membership, to 113 seats, and abolishing the National Assembly. Following an ad hoc election on May 14, 2005, to fill its 300 seats, a final National Assembly convened and on June 7 voted 249–48 in favor of the constitutional amendments, which the president promulgated on June 10.

Premier Hsieh resigned on January 17, 2006, following DPP losses in the local elections of December 2005, and was replaced by SU Tseng-chang (DPP). Sworn in on January 25, Premier Su conducted an immediate cabinet shuffle. Meanwhile, President Chen was arguing for further constitutional reform. He also announced that he intended to abolish the NUC and abandon the Guidelines for National Unification, a proposal attacked by the opposition and viewed by the administration of U.S. president George W. Bush as potentially destabilizing. On February 27 Chen confirmed that the NUC would "cease to function"—a considered change in language that Washington had reportedly encouraged but that failed to placate Beijing. Under increasing pressure to resign over corruption allegations, charges of mismanagement, and dissatisfaction with his hard-line stance toward cross-strait relations, Chen stated on May 31 that he would transfer many of his powers to Prime Minister Su, retaining authority only in defense matters and foreign policy, and that he would disengage from party politics.

Premier Su resigned on May 12, 2007, less than a week after he was defeated by former premier Hsieh in an intraparty contest for the DPP's 2008 presidential nomination. On May 14 President Chen returned Chang Chun-hsiung to the premiership. A reshuffled cabinet took office under Chang on May 21.

As opinion polls had predicted, the election on January 12, 2008, to a downsized Legislative Branch concluded with a resounding victory for the KMT, which, with its allies, won 85 of 113 seats and 55.9 percent of the party-list vote. The DPP took 27 seats and 40.7 percent of the proportional vote. Two months later, on March 22, the KMT's MA Ying-jeou defeated the DPP's Frank HSIEH for the presidency, winning 58.5 percent of the vote. He was sworn in on May 20, as was a new cabinet headed by former vice premier and university president LIU Chao-shiuan.

Once in office, President Ma moved toward thawing relations with Beijing. On April 14 Vice President–elect (and former premier) Vincent Siew met Chinese President Hu Jintao, and it was subsequently announced that the KMT chair, WU Poh-hsiung, had accepted an invitation from the Chinese Community Party to visit the mainland in late May, thereby becoming the first head of a Taiwanese ruling party to do so. Instead, the government pursued a middle course some described as "one China, two interpretations."

On September 7, 2009, accepting responsibility for the government's inadequate initial response to a deadly typhoon that struck Taiwan on August 7–8, Premier Liu announced that he and his cabinet would resign on September 10. President Ma, who had already issued his own apology for the government's failure, immediately named WU Den-yih, the KMT secretary general, as Liu's replacement. Premier Wu and members of a substantially new cabinet were sworn in on September 10. Additional changes to the Executive Branch were made later in the month.

On September 11, 2009, former president Chen was convicted of embezzlement, accepting bribes, and other offenses during his terms in office. He and his wife, WU Shu-chen, who was also convicted on corruption charges, received life sentences.

On May 17, 2010, Sean Chun CHEN was appointed vice premier after his predecessor resigned to campaign in local polling. Chen's appointment was accompanied by a minor reorganization of the cabinet. Another cabinet reshuffle was conducted in February 2011.

The KMT-led Pan Blue Coalition won legislative balloting on January 14, 2012, with 67 seats, to the 43 of the DPP-led "pan-green" coalition. Meanwhile, President Ma was reelected president in concurrent balloting (see Current issues, below). Premier Wu was Ma's vice-presidential running mate, and the president appointed vice premier Chen to replace Wu on January 31. Chen was sworn in along with a reshuffled cabinet on February 6. As was customary, the cabinet resigned on the eve of Wu's inauguration, but was reappointed with one exception on May 20. The president conducted a minor cabinet reshuffle on September 20.

Chen resigned on February 1, 2013 (see Current issues, below). He was replaced by vice premier JIANG Yi-huah, who named a reshuffled cabinet, which was sworn in on February 18.

Constitution and government. The government of the Republic of China (ROC), launched in 1912 under the leadership of SUN Yat-sen, drew on both Western and traditional Chinese elements in a constitution promulgated January 1, 1947, effective from December 25, 1947. At the apex of the complex system was the 3,045-member National Assembly, which was popularly elected on an all-China basis for a six-year term. The term was extended, however, following the government's exodus to Taiwan, and for more than four decades its surviving members periodically reconvened either as an electoral college to select the president and vice president (as in March 1990) or as a constituent body (as in April 1991). Although downsized to fewer than 350 members in a December 1991 election, it continued to hold powers of recall and impeachment, of constitutional amendment, and of nomination to three of the government's five specialized branches, or *yuans* (Judicial, Examination, and Control).

An election for a third, 334-member National Assembly took place in March 1996, but an election scheduled for March 2000 was canceled, after which the assembly was reduced, by constitutional amendment, to a nonstanding body of 300 members empowered to consider a limited range of matters—constitutional amendments, presidential or vice presidential impeachment, national boundaries—referred to it by the Legislative Branch.

Following passage of a constitutional reform bill by the Legislative Branch on August 23, 2004, an ad hoc National Assembly election was called for May 14, 2005. Voter turnout was only 23 percent. On June 7 this final National Assembly passed the reform package, which included its abolition as an institution. Upon promulgation of the reforms by the president on June 10, the National Assembly's impeachment powers were transferred to the Judicial Branch. Constitutional amendments and boundary changes now require not only approval by at least three-fourths of a Legislative Branch quorum but also concurrence by at least half of those eligible to vote in a referendum.

The unicameral Legislative Branch, the formal lawmaking organ of the ROC, first convened in 1948. Its 760 members were popularly elected on a regional and occupational basis for three-year terms. In December 1992, in the first election for a full house since 1948 (all mainland members had retired by late 1991), a total of 125 directly elected and 36 proportionally allocated seats were filled. Currently a 113-member body popularly elected for a four-year term, the Legislative Branch enacts laws but cannot increase the budget. Its powers include initiating impeachment of the president or vice president, which requires a two-thirds vote of the full membership for the charges to be forwarded to the Judicial Branch.

The president, elected for a once-renewable four-year term since 1996, can declare war and peace and issue emergency decrees that must, however, secure legislative confirmation within ten days. The president also has wide powers of appointment, acts as mediator in disputes between two or more *yuans,* and may dissolve the Legislative Branch if it passes a vote of no confidence in the government. The president of the Executive Branch (premier) is appointed by the state president but is subject to a legislative no-confidence vote. The president's authority with regard to cross-strait relations is also extensive. A cabinet-level Mainland Affairs Council (MAC) oversees cross-strait policy implementation. With the imprimatur of the MAC, a private Straits Exchange Foundation (SEF) has served as a semiofficial vehicle for contact with the mainland government (see the China entry for details).

The 15-member Court of Grand Justices sits at the apex of the Judicial Branch. Nominated by the president and confirmed by the legislature, the grand justices serve terms of four or eight years. Their duties include constitutional interpretation and administrative oversight of the entire court system. They sit as the Constitutional Court in impeachment matters. Within the Judicial Branch are district courts, high courts, and the Supreme Court.

The Examination Branch deals with personnel, legal, and other matters affecting civil servants. Its 21 members are presidentially appointed, subject to Legislative Branch confirmation.

The Control Branch, comprising 29 members serving six-year terms, is responsible for auditing and general administrative surveillance and can impeach or censure public officials. Filled by presidential nomination, subject to legislative confirmation, it did not function from January 31, 2005, until the end of President Chen's term because of opposition objections to his nominees. Newly elected President Ma presented a new slate of nominees in June 2008, but it was mid-November before the balance of the *yuan* membership was filled.)

The territorial jurisdiction of the ROC currently extends to one Chinese province (Taiwan) and part of a second (Fujian's offshore islands). In April 2009 the Local Government Act was amended so that counties and provincial municipalities could merge or become special municipalities, a status already held by Taipei City and Kaohsiung City. Effective December 20, 2010, the number of special municipalities increased to 5 (Taipei City, Taipei County, and the newly merged Kaohsiung City and County, Tainan City and County, and Taichung City and County), with a corresponding drop in the number of counties and provincial municipalities to 17. In January 2013, the cabinet approved the elevation of Taoyuan County to become a special municipality, effective 2014. Below the county level are county municipalities and townships.

On December 31, 1998, the Legislative Branch formally declared the uninhabited Tiaoyutai Islands northeast of Taiwan and the Spratly Islands in the South China Sea to be within Taiwan's territorial jurisdiction. The former are also claimed by both China and Japan, while the latter have long been subject to rival claims by Brunei, China, Malaysia, the Philippines, and Vietnam.

Taiwan has a free and open media. In 2013 Reporters Without Borders ranked Taiwan 47th out of 179 countries in media freedom.

Foreign relations. The most important factor in the foreign policy of the Taiwan government has been the existence on the mainland of the Communist regime, which was awarded the Chinese seat at the United Nations (UN) on October 25, 1971. Reflecting its diminished political status, the ROC is today recognized by none of the major powers, though its trade relations are extensive. Relations with the United States, once extremely close, cooled after President Richard Nixon's visit to the mainland in February 1972. The communiqué issued at the conclusion of the Nixon visit acknowledged "that all Chinese on either side of the Taiwan Strait maintain that there is but one China" and advocated "a peaceful settlement of the Taiwan question by the Chinese themselves."

Concurrent with the announcement in December 1978 that the United States and the PRC would establish diplomatic relations on January 1, 1979, Washington issued a statement saying that both diplomatic relations and, upon expiration of a required one-year's notice, the Mutual Defense Treaty with the ROC would be terminated. Although all U.S. military personnel were withdrawn from Taiwan, arms shipments have continued in the interest of maintaining a balance of power with the mainland.

Taipei initially shunned relations with states or intergovernmental organizations linked to Beijing, but it now applies "pragmatic diplomacy," aimed particularly at ministates capable of being wooed by development assistance. On such a basis it broadened its international contacts, including diplomatic relations with 31 countries as of early 1996. The diplomatic network shrank marginally thereafter, most significantly by the severance of relations with South Africa. As of July 2010, the Holy See plus 22 countries in Africa, the Pacific, Latin America, and the Caribbean maintained full diplomatic relations with Taiwan. In May 2008 the outgoing foreign minister, a vice premier, and a deputy defense minister resigned in connection with the loss of some $30 million to two private individuals who had been hired as part of an effort to establish diplomatic ties with Papua New Guinea. In March 2010 President Ma toured the six Pacific states—Kiribati, Marshall Islands, Nauru, Palau, Solomon Islands, and Tuvalu—that have diplomatic relations with Taiwan. Collaterally, he announced that future aid to the region would be offered in cooperation with the Pacific Island Forum (PIF) and other regional organizations.

For years the government has sought to secure ROC readmission to the United Nations, but the UN General Committee has repeatedly refused to act, citing a lack of consensus in the matter. In 2007, for the first time, the government applied for admission as "Taiwan" but was again rebuffed. Two referenda held on March 22, 2007, in conjunction with the presidential election, asked the Taiwanese voters if they wished to pursue readmission to the UN under the name Taiwan or the Republic of China. Although both received a majority of "yes" votes, neither achieved the necessary threshold for passage (50 percent of registered voters).

Washington has not actively supported Taiwan's UN bid, but during the 1990s it moved to enhance the ROC's official presence in the United States by allowing what had been known as the Coordinating Council for North American Affairs to restyle itself in a number of locations as the Taipei Economic and Cultural Office. In addition, in December 1994 President Bill Clinton permitted U.S. Transportation Secretary Federico Peña to become the first American cabinet official to visit Taiwan in more than 15 years. The action, which caused Beijing "strong displeasure," heightened pressure from Taipei for a long-sought visit by President Lee to the United States, and in early May 1995 the U.S. Senate and House of Representatives, by votes of 97–1 and 360–0, respectively, approved resolutions calling upon President Clinton to permit Lee to enter the country in a "private capacity." After some hesitation, the White House agreed, and in June, in what Beijing termed a "wanton wound inflicted upon China," the Taiwanese leader arrived to attend an alumni reunion at Cornell University. The mainland regime responded by suspending all contacts with Taiwan; further protests were issued by Beijing following issuance of a visa to Vice President Li Yuan-zu for a 1996 stopover in Los Angeles while en route to Guatemala. A similar courtesy was extended to Vice President Lien Chan in 1998 and President Chen in 2001.

On January 1, 2002, Taiwan became the 144th member of the World Trade Organization under the listing of Separate Customs Territory of Taiwan, Penghu, Kinmen, and Matsu.

In September 2011 the United States announced a $5.9 billion arms agreement to upgrade Taiwan's fleet of F-16 fighter aircraft. In retaliation, the PRC suspended military exchanges with the United States.

In March 2012 Taiwan announced it would end a ban on certain genetically modified beef imports from the United States. The action led to the resumption of trade talks between the two countries in September. Also in September, Vietnam protested after Taiwanese officials planted a flag on Ban Than Shoal in the disputed Spratley Islands. In October, former premier Hsieh became the highest-ranking DPP official to visit the PRC.

In June 2013, Taiwan formally requested Japanese assistance in joining regional economic forums, including the Trans-Pacific Partnership and the Regional Comprehensive Economic Partnership. Meanwhile, the United States Congress approved a resolution endorsing Taiwan's bid to join the International Civil Aviation Organization.

Current issues. On June 29, 2010, Taiwan and the PRC concluded the Economic Cooperation Framework Agreement (ECFA). Although some Taiwanese remain wary of increasing economic dependence on the PRC, reductions in tariffs and the opening of various service industries would appear to benefit Taiwan more than the mainland. Cross-strait relations did, however, have a low point earlier in the year, when in January the U.S. Department of Defense, as part of a $6.5 billion defense package, approved shipment of Patriot air defense missiles, mine hunters, and helicopters to Taiwan.

With former president Chen having lost his presidential immunity, the Supreme Prosecutor's Office quickly announced that it would investigate corruption allegations that had already seen his wife, Wu Shu-chen, and several presidential aides indicted for misuse of a discretionary state affairs fund controlled by the president. In the decades since the KMT introduced the accounts, informal understandings largely determined how the funds were used. Although intended for work-related expenses, officials long used part of the funds as personal allowances, without repercussion.

In November 2008 former president Chen was arrested for suspicion of forgery and money laundering, and a month later he and a dozen other individuals, including close relatives, were indicted for embezzlement and taking bribes. The life sentences imposed on Chen and his wife were seen by many as too severe and tainted by political considerations. In June 2010 the Supreme Court reduced the sentences to 20 years. A son, a daughter, and their spouses have also been convicted of corruption.

The resignation of Liu and his cabinet in September 2009 was in response to a public outcry over the government's lack of disaster preparedness and its slow response to Typhoon Morakot, the worst storm to strike the island in half a century and, in terms of rainfall, by far the heaviest ever recorded there. Over 700 people were killed or declared missing, as flooding and severe mudslides caused more than $3 billion in damage.

In local elections on November 27, 2010, the KMT won three mayoral posts, including Taipei, while the DPP won two. The DPP did actually receive a higher overall vote total, 49.9 percent, than did the KMT, 44.5 percent. Each party secured 130 seats on the local councils.

On May 20, 2011, Maj. Gen. LO Hsein-che was indicted for spying for the PRC. Lo was the most senior military figure to be accused of espionage in Taiwan's history. Meanwhile, former president Chen was convicted of money laundering (the verdict was overturned on appeal in August 2012).

TSAI Ing-wen of the DPP was the nation's first woman presidential candidate. She was defeated by Ma, who secured 51.6 percent of the vote to Tsai's 45.6 percent in the January 2012 balloting. The PFP's Soong placed a distant third with 2.8 percent. In September 2012 opposition parties held a no-confidence vote against premier Chen. The measure, only the second no-confidence vote in Taiwan's history, failed on a vote of 66–46.

Typhoon Saola struck Taiwan on August 2, 2012, killing 5 and leaving more than 8,000 homeless. On August 24, Typhoon Temblin caused the heaviest rainfall reported in more than a century.

On February 1, 2013, premier Chen resigned, ostensibly for "family and health" concerns. However, reports indicated the resignation was prompted by falling opinion polls. As was customary, the cabinet subsequently resigned, although most ministers were reappointed to their posts under new premier Jiang Yi-huah. In April, Taiwanese military forces conducted their first major, live fire exercises since 2008. The exercises were condemned by Beijing, as was the visit to Taiwan by Chinese dissident CHEN Guangcheng in June 2013.

POLITICAL PARTIES

Prior to 1986, two non-KMT (*tang-wai*) political groups were occasionally successful in Taiwanese elections, although their representatives were obliged to run as independents since opposition parties were not allowed to compete for public office. In a major concession to opposition sentiment, the government in May 1986 permitted an umbrella Tangwai Public Policy Association to open offices in Taipei and elsewhere; four months later, two new dissident groups were formed, one of which, the Democratic Progressive Party (DPP), was permitted to participate in the December 1986 election, even though it did not achieve legal status until 1989. By August 1993 some 74 parties were reported to have been formed, but only the KMT, the DPP, and the New Party (NP) had significant standing.

In the run-up to the December 2001 legislative election, two informal alliances began to be commonly labeled, with reference to the dominant parties' respective colors, as the "pan-blue" camp (the KMT, the People First Party [PFP], and the NP) and the "pan-green" camp (the DPP, the Taiwan Solidarity Union, and the now-defunct Taiwan Independence Party). Neither alliance subsequently evolved formal structures. There are well over 100 registered parties, although fewer than a dozen typically present candidates for election.

Governing "Pan-Blue" Alliance:

Nationalist Party (*Chung-kuo Kuo-min Tang* or Kuomintang—KMT). Founded in 1912 by the Republic of China's first president, Sun Yat-sen, the KMT dominated Taiwanese politics until March 2000 at all levels of government. In November 1976, at its first party congress since 1969, it elected Premier Chiang Ching-kuo to succeed his father, Chiang Kai-shek, as chair. In 1984, as the result of a party "rejuvenation" campaign, it was reported that 70 percent of an estimated 2 million party members were native Taiwanese.

Contrary to expectations in the early 1990s that newly legalized groups might undercut the party's longtime political dominance, the KMT continued to retain a majority in the Legislative Branch for another decade. After the 1992 election, however, many younger and reform-minded members formed an alternative New KMT Alliance within the party. Most withdrew to launch the New Party (NP, below) in August 1993. In the same month, at its 14th congress, the previously "revolutionary democratic" KMT redefined itself as a "democratic party" and provided for election of its chair by secret ballot.

The KMT won only 45 percent of the seats in local council balloting in June 1998; however, it recovered to win 57 percent (123 of 225 seats) at the Legislative Branch poll in December. It ran third in the presidential contest of March 2000, winning only 23 percent of the vote and surrendering the Taiwanese presidency for the first time.

In late 2000 the KMT announced that it would hold its first direct election for party chair in early 2001. The March 24 election of unsuccessful presidential candidate Lien Chan ended up being uncontested, however, as his only announced opponent, TUAN Hong-chun, failed to collect the necessary 100,000 nominating signatures. In September 2001 the KMT formally expelled former president Lee Teng-hui, who had emerged as a supporter of the new Taiwan Solidarity Union (TSU, below).

In the December 2001 Legislative Branch election the KMT lost considerable support to the PFP and the TSU, contributing to the first loss of its majority in the Legislative Branch. Four members of the KMT, including Minister of National Defense TANG Yian-min, were named to the new DPP-led cabinet in January 2002, which led to the suspension of their party rights.

In December 2004 the party gained 11 Legislative Branch seats over its 2001 tally, for a total of 79—sufficient, in coalition with its "pan-blue" allies, the PFP and NP, to control the body. Largely as a result of subsequent defections from the PFP, by the end of 2006 the KMT's legislative delegation had risen to 89, surpassing that of the DPP.

In late April 2005 Lien Chan had become the first KMT chair to visit the PRC. After Lien declined to run again for the chairship, Taipei's mayor, Ma Ying-jeou was elected party leader in July 2005. At the party's 12th congress, held in July 2006, it adopted reforms that included a collective leadership and abolition of internal factions.

In February 2007, immediately after being indicted for corruption involving some $330,000 in expenditures from a special discretionary allowance fund during his years as mayor, Ma resigned the chair. He indicated, however, that he would seek the KMT's nomination for president in 2008, as did Legislative Branch president Wang Jin-pyng, representing the indigenous Taiwanese wing of the party. On May 2 Ma received the party's nod for the 2008 presidential race and later named former premier Vincent Siew as his running mate. In August a district court acquitted Ma of the corruption allegations, and the decision was affirmed by the Supreme Court in April 2008.

In January 2007 the KMT and its principal ally, the PFP, had agreed to field joint candidates in the next Legislative Branch election. The possibility of bringing the Non-Partisan Solidarity Union (NPSU, below) into the alliance was also raised, although, in the end, the KMT instead endorsed the three successful NPSU candidates, who ran separately. In contrast, the NP directed its incumbents to join the KMT and ran only a slate of party-list candidates. In January 2008 the "pan-blue" alliance won 85 seats, including 8 for the PFP. In the March presidential contest, Ma won handily, garnering 58.5 percent of the vote.

In July 2009 the party overwhelmingly endorsed President Ma's bid to resume the party chair at its 18th national congress, held in September. The outgoing chair, Wu Poh-hsiung, was made an honorary chair.

Upon the resignation of Premier Liu Chao-shuian in September 2009, President Ma selected as his successor the KMT's secretary general, Wu Den-yih. Wu's replacement, Chan Chuen-po, had been serving as secretary general of the Presidential Office.

The KMT won 64 seats in the January 2012 legislative balloting, and Ma was reelected president. Wu was elected vice president and Sean CHEN-Chun appointed premier. In September TSENG Yung-chuan was appointed secretary general of the party. Chen resigned in February 2013 and was replaced by Jiang Yi-huah. In July, Ma was reelected KMT chair.

Leaders: MA Ying-jeou (President of the Republic and Chair of the Party), WU Poh-hsiung (Honorary Chair), LIEN Chan (Honorary Chair), WU Den-yih (Vice President of the Republic), JIANG Yi-huah (Premier), WANG Jin-pyng (President, Legislative Branch), CHAN Chuen-po (Vice Chair), TSENG Yung-chuan (Secretary General).

People First Party (PFP). The PFP is a prounification formation launched by KMT dissident James Soong following the 2000 presidential election, in which he placed second with a 36.8 percent vote share. The PFP performed well in the December 2001 Legislative Branch election, winning 46 seats, primarily at the expense of the KMT and NP.

Prior to the December 2004 legislative election the PFP and its "pan-blue" partners, the KMT and the NP, agreed to coordinate their campaigns to avoid vote-splitting. Largely as a consequence, the PFP lost 12 seats and the KMT gained 11 more than in 2001, which created considerable resentment within the PFP. Subsequent defections to the KMT further soured PFP hard-liners.

Talks in December 2005 with the KMT leadership were widely expected to lead to a long-anticipated merger, but differences could not be resolved. In February 2006 Soong announced that the PFP would "walk its own path" in future relations with the KMT. Following a third-place finish, with only 4 percent of the vote, in the December 2006 contest for mayor of Taipei, Soong announced his intention to retire from politics, although he did not immediately resign as party chair.

For the January 2008 Legislative Branch election the PFP again ran in conjunction with the KMT. It won six constituency seats (five under the KMT banner plus one aboriginal seat) and three proportional seats from a joint KMT-PFP list. In April 2010 Soong was among the Taiwanese political leaders who met with Hu Jintao during the Shanghai World Exposition.

Soong was the PFP candidate in the 2012 balloting. He placed third. The PFP secured three seats in the concurrent legislative polling. In July 2013, one of the PFP's three legislators lost his seat following a conviction on bribery charges.

Leader: James SOONG Chu-yu (Chair).

"Pan-Blue" Ally:

Non-Partisan Solidarity Union (NPSU). The centrist NPSU was established in June 2004 by ten independent members of the Legislative Branch, led by former interior minister CHANG Po-ya. Advocating a "middle way" between the "pan-blue" and "pan-green" camps, the party won six seats in the December 2004 Legislative Branch election.

Following the December 2006 municipal elections the NPSU proposed setting up a joint think tank with the PFP and increasing their cooperation in legislative matters. Although not a member of the "pan-blue" alliance, in January 2008 its three successful constituency candidates ran with KMT endorsement. The NPSU won only 0.7 percent of the party-list vote. The NPSU secured two seats in the 2012 legislative elections.

Leader: LIN Ping-kuan (Chair).

"Pan-Green" Alliance:

Democratic Progressive Party—DPP (*Min-chu Chin-pu Tang*). Despite the ban on organization of new parties, a group of dissidents, advocating trade, tourism, and communications links with the mainland, met in Taipei in September 1986 to form the DPP (sometimes rendered as Democratic Progress Party). Although unrecognized, the group won 11 National Assembly and 12 Legislative Branch seats in December 1986.

Delegates to the party's second annual congress in 1987 approved a resolution stating that "the people have the freedom to advocate Taiwan independence"; however, its leaders agreed to abandon the position during a meeting with KMT representatives in February 1988, and the party was legalized in April 1989. As a former political prisoner, DPP Chair HUANG Hsin-chieh continued to be barred from election to public office in the December 1989 election, in which the party nearly doubled its representation, to 21 legislative seats.

Having captured the presidency in March 2000 on a 39.3 vote share, the DPP went on to claim a plurality of 87 Legislative Branch seats in the December 2001 election. Nevertheless, the DPP and its allies in the "pan-green" camp fell short of a majority. (For information on the DPP in 1990–2000, see the 2010 *Handbook.*)

President Chen Shui-bian and his running mate, Annette Lu, won reelection by a minuscule 0.2 percent margin in March 2004. When the DPP's seat total fell by two in the December Legislative Branch election, Chen resigned as chair of the party, which in January 2005 elected Su Tseng-chang as his replacement. The following December, the party suffered a major defeat in local elections, winning only 42 percent of the vote to the KMT's 51 percent, prompting Su to step down. In mid-January 2006 a Chen ally, former premier Yu Shyi-kun, won election as Su's successor despite dissatisfaction within the party over Chen's leadership. One of the leading critics, former chair LIN Yihsiung, resigned his membership on January 24, a day before Su was sworn in as premier in succession to Frank Hsieh. Former chairs Hsu Hsin-liang and SHIH Ming-teh had already departed, and in August 2006 the latter launched a public movement to oust President Chen.

In 2007, four party leaders—Hsieh, Premier Su, Vice President Lu, and DPP Chair Yu—sought the party's 2008 presidential nomination. On May 7 Hsieh unexpectedly took 45 percent of the intraparty vote, after which Su (33 percent) and the other candidates withdrew. Five days later Su resigned as premier, although he later agreed to be Hsieh's running mate.

In September 2007 Vice President Lu and DPP Chair Yu were among several DPP members charged with corruption involving alleged misappropriations from expense accounts. All proclaimed their innocence, although Yu resigned his party post. President Chen later announced that he would accede to the chair, but he resigned the position following the party's defeat in the January 2008 Legislative Branch election, in which the DPP won only 27 seats, 14 of them on the basis of 40.7 percent of the party-list vote. Presidential candidate Hsieh thereupon assumed the party presidency but stepped aside after his March defeat.

On May 18, 2008, the DPP elected its first female chair, former vice premier Tsai Ing-wen, who, with 57 percent of the vote, defeated proindependence traditionalist KOO Kuan-min despite the latter's late endorsement by TRONG Chai, the third candidate for the top party post. In December 2008 Chen Shui-bian became the first former president to be indicted for corruption, and thus, in September 2009, the first to be convicted.

The DPP won 40 seats in the 2012 legislative elections, an increase of 13 seats from the previous balloting. Tsai Ing-wen was the DPP candidate in the concurrent presidential balloting. After she lost the election, she resigned as party leader. In May 2012 former premier SU Tseng-Chang was elected party chair.

Divisions within the party emerged in 2013 over the "One China" policy, with a faction, led by Hsieh, advocating closer relations with the PRC.

Leaders: SU Tseng-Chang (Chair), KER Chien-ming (Legislative Whip), Frank HSIEH (2008 presidential candidate), CHEN Chu (Mayor of Kaohsiung), SU Chia-chuan (Secretary General).

Taiwan Solidarity Union (TSU). Formation of the TSU was announced in July 2001 by former KMT leader and interior minister HUANG Chu-wen. Declaring Taiwan to be a sovereign state, the TSU attracted defectors from both the KMT and the DPP, its most senior supporter being former president Lee Teng-hui. (Lee, having accused the KMT of aligning with Beijing, was subsequently expelled by the KMT, but he never officially joined the TSU.) The TSU finished fourth, with 13 seats, in the December 2001 election, a ranking that was retained with 12 seats in 2004.

Huang resigned after the party's disappointing performance in the 2004 election. His successor, SU Chin-Chiang, likewise resigned following the December 2006 municipal elections. Huang Kun-huei, who was named chair in January 2007, has stated his intention to transform the TSU into a center-left party oriented toward meeting the needs of the Taiwanese people. In October–November 2007 four of the TSU's Legislative Branch members joined the DPP, and in the January 2008 legislative election the TSU lost its remaining seats. It won only 3.5 percent of the party-list vote.

In May 2008 Huang asked all TSU members to reregister and announced that the party would put aside the independence issue and focus its attention on serving the "medium- and low-echelon sectors of society." On October 27, 2011, Huang filed a lawsuit against President Ma for violating Article 104 of the Criminal Law code, alleging that while secretary general of the National Security Council Su Chi, Ma forged a consensus in 1992 that provided the basis for future cross-strait agreements, which Huang declared an act of "treason."

The TSU won three seats in the 2012 legislative balloting. However, in July 2013, lawmaker LIN Shih-Chia was expelled from the TSU for "defying" party leadership and lost her seat in the legislature. She was replaced by YEH Chin-ling.

Leaders: HUANG Kun-huei (Chair), LIN Chih-chia (Secretary General).

Other Parties:

New Party—NP (*Hsin Tang*). The prounification NP was formally launched in August 1993 by a group of KMT dissidents theretofore associated with the New KMT Alliance. Seeking support from second-generation mainlanders, the new formation advocated more energetic reform than the KMT leadership. The NP placed a distant third in the urban and provincial elections of November 1993, however, winning only 3.1 percent of the vote. A week prior to the election it reportedly absorbed the Chinese Social Democratic Party (CSDP), formed in 1991 by a group of DPP dissidents, although the CSDP chair, JU Gau-jeng, did not pledge to withdraw the party's registration until 1994, when he was campaigning for the Taiwan governorship under the NP banner.

The NP tripled its legislative representation in December 1995, from 7 to 21. However, NP leader WANG Chien-shien withdrew from the 1996 presidential race after the legislative poll in an effort to consolidate a "third force" in Taiwanese politics. Its Legislative Branch representation fell to 11 in 1998.

With much of the NP leadership supporting independent presidential contender James Soong, the party's official nominee, LI Ao, won only 0.1 percent of the 2000 presidential vote. Further injured by defections to Soong's PFP, the party secured only one Legislative Branch seat in 2001. For the 2004 election most of the party's legislative candidates ran under the banner of its principal "pan-blue" ally, the KMT, although the NP again won one seat under its own name. In 2005 it parted ways with the KMT on the issue of constitutional reform, which it opposed.

Prior to the December 2006 municipal elections, the NP chair, Yok Mu-ming, speculated that the NP might disband if it failed to carry all 4 of the seats it was contesting in the 52-seat Taipei city council. It won the seats, however, after which Yok pledged to work toward "pan-blue" unity. In an unusual move, the NP directed its sitting legislators to join the KMT prior to the January 2008 Legislative Branch election, in which its constituency candidates ran as KMT members and won seats. In the party-list contest the NP won just under 4 percent of the vote and thus no additional seats.

The NP endorsed incumbent president Ma of the KMT in the 2012 presidential balloting. It only secured 1.5 percent of the vote in legislative balloting, and therefore no seats, as part of the Pan Blue Coalition. In August 2012, the NP announced it was endeavoring to purchase one or more of the disputed Senkaku islands to secure them for Taiwan.

Leader: YOK Mu-ming (Chair).

Green Party Taiwan (GPT). The GPT dates from 1996, when it was organized by members of the Taiwan Environmental Protection Union to contest the March National Assembly election, in which the GPT's KAO Ming-ting unexpectedly won a seat. The party's platform is based on such traditional green party concerns as ecological balance, opposition to nuclear power, antimilitarism, and social equality. It won one seat in the Legislative Branch poll in December 2001 but lost it in 2004. In 2008 the party won only 0.6 percent of the party-list vote. It ran in conjunction with the small **Raging Citizens Act Now!** alliance, led by WANG Fang-ping. In 2012 the GPT secured 1.7 percent of the vote and no seats.

Leaders: CHANG Hong-lin, CHUNG Bau-Ju (Cochairs), Calvin WEN, PAN Han-shen (Secretary General).

Please see the 2012 *Handbook* for information on the **Taiwan Constitution Association** (TCA), the **Citizens' Party,** the **Hakka Party,** the **Home Party,** the **Taiwan Farmers' Party,** and the **Third Society Party.**

LEGISLATURE

Under the unusual post–World War II constitutional system of the ROC, parliamentary functions were performed by the National Assembly (*Kuo-min Ta-hui*), the Legislative Branch, and even the Control Branch before its 1992 transformation into a more supervisory agency. The National Assembly, whose powers included selecting the president (until 1996) and approving constitutional amendments, was abolished in June 2005.

Legislative Branch (*Li-fa Yuan*). Constitutional reforms ratified by the National Assembly in May 2005 halved the Legislative Branch to 113 members, effective from the next election, which was held on January 12, 2008. Under a new single constituency, two ballot electoral system, 73 members were directly elected from redrawn single-member constituencies, 6 seats were filled by aboriginal communities, and 34 at-large and overseas expatriate seats were proportionally allocated to political parties that won at least 5 percent of the votes on a separate ballot. In addition, the legislative term was lengthened from three to four years.

Results for the January 14, 2012, balloting were as follows for the Pan Blue Coalition: Nationalist Party (KMT), 64 (48 constituency seats and 16 party-list seats); the People First Party (PFP), 3 (1 constituency, 2 party list); and the Non-Partisan Solidarity Union (NPSU), 2 (2 constituency seats won with the endorsement of the KMT). The "pan-green" coalition: the Democratic Progressive Party (DPP) won 40 seats (27 constituency, 13 party list); and the Taiwan Solidarity Union (TSU), 3 (all party list). The final constituency seat was won by an independent.

President: WANG Jin-pyng.

CABINET

The cabinet is known as the Executive Branch Council (*Hsing-cheng Yuan Hu-yi*). The premier is currently chosen by the president (subject to a legislative no confidence vote), whereas the vice premier and other cabinet members are appointed by the president upon recommendation of the premier. Cabinet officials are chosen individually; the cabinet is not responsible collectively.

[as of November 5, 2013]

President, Executive Branch (Premier)	Jiang Yi-huah
Vice President, Executive Branch (Vice Premier)	Mao Chi-kuo
Ministers	
Culture	Lung Ying-tai [f]
Economic Affairs	Chang Chia-juch
Education	Chiang Wei-ling
Finance	Chang Sheng-ford
Foreign Affairs	David Lin Yung-lo
Health	Chiu Wen-ta
Interior	Lee Hong-yuan
Justice	Lou Ying-shay [f]
National Defense	Gen. Yen Ming
Transportation and Communications	Yeh Kuang-Shih
Without Portfolio	Schive Chi
	Kuan Chung-ming
	Yang Chiu-hsing
	Huang Kuang-nan
	Lin Junq-tzer
	Joyce Feng Yen [f]
	Chang San-cheng
	Chern Jenn-chuan
Commission Ministers	
Central Election	Chang Po-ya [f]
Financial Supervisory	William Tseng Ming-chung
Mongolian and Tibetan Affairs (acting)	Chen Ming-jen
National Communications	Shyr Shyr-hau
National Youth	Chen Yi-chen
Overseas Compatriot Affairs	Steven Chen Shyh-Kwei
Public Construction (acting)	Yan Jeou-rong
Research, Development, and Evaluation	Chu Chin-peng
Veterans' Affairs	Tung Hsaing-lung
Council Ministers	
Agriculture	Chen Bao-ji
Atomic Energy	Tsai Chuen-horng
Aviation Safety	Chang Yu-hern
Economic Planning and Development	Yiin Chii-ming
Hakka Affairs	Lin Chiang-i
Indigenous Peoples	Sun Ta-chuan
Labor Affairs	Pan Shih-wei
Mainland Affairs	Wang Yu-chi
National Science	Cyrus Chu
Research, Development and Evaluation	Sung Yu-hsieh
Sports Affairs	Tai Hsia-ling [f]
Other Ministers	
Coast Guard Administration	Wang Ginn-wang
Directorate General of Budget, Accounting, and Statistics	Shih Su-mei [f]
Environmental Protection Administration	Stephen Shu-hung Shen
Chair, Fair Trade Commission	Wu Shiow-ming
Chief, Government Information Office	Hu Yu-wei
Director, National Palace Museum	Fung Ming-chu [f]
Chair, Central Personnel Administration	Huang Fu-yuan
Governor, Central Bank	Perng Fai-nan

Secretary General, Executive Branch	Chen Wei-zen
Deputy Secretary General, Executive Branch	Chen Ching-tsai

[f] = female

INTERGOVERNMENTAL REPRESENTATION

A founding member of the United Nations, the Republic of China lost its right of representation in that body's major organs on October 25, 1971. The United States terminated formal diplomatic relations on January 1, 1979. Informal relations continue to be maintained through the American Institute in Taiwan and its Nationalist Chinese counterpart in Washington (and other U.S. cities), the Taipei Economic and Cultural Office.

IGO Membership (Non-UN): ADB (listed as Taipei, China), APEC, WTO (listed as Separate Customs Territory of Taiwan, Penghu, Kinmen, and Matsu).

COLOMBIA

Republic of Colombia
República de Colombia

Political Status: Independent Gran Colombia proclaimed 1819; separate state of New Granada established 1831; republican constitution adopted 1886; bipartisan National Front regime instituted in 1958 but substantially terminated in 1974; current constitution promulgated July 5, 1991.

Area: 439,734 sq. mi. (1,138,914 sq. km).

Population: 46,581,823 (2013E—UN); 45,745,783 (2013E—U.S. Census).

Major Urban Centers (urban areas, 2011E): SANTAFÉ DE BOGOTÁ (formerly Bogotá, 8,759,000), Medellín (3,592,000), Cali (2,783,000), Barranquilla (1,886,000), Cartagena (911,000).

Official Language: Spanish.

Monetary Unit: Peso (principal rate November 1, 2013: 1902.80 pesos = $1US).

President: Juan Manuel SANTOS Calderón (Social Party of National Unity); elected in runoff balloting on June 20, 2010, and inaugurated on August 7 for a four-year term, succeeding Álvaro URIBE Vélez (independent).

Vice President: Angelino GARZÓN (Social Party of National Unity); elected in runoff balloting on June 20, 2010, and inaugurated on August 7 for a term concurrent with that of the president, succeeding Francisco SANTOS Calderón (independent).

THE COUNTRY

Situated at the base of the Isthmus of Panama, with frontage on both the Caribbean and the Pacific, Colombia is divided geographically into three main regions defined by ranges of the Andes Mountains: a flat coastal area, a highland area, and an area of sparsely settled eastern plains drained by tributaries of the Orinoco and Amazon rivers. In terms of population, Colombia is more diverse than most other Latin American countries. About 75 percent of Colombians are of mixed blood, including both mestizos and people who claim dual European and African heritage. Groups claiming a single ethnicity (Spanish, Indian, or African) are quite small. Spanish is the language of most people, except for isolated Indian tribes. More than 80 percent of the population identifies itself as Roman Catholic, while the remainder is either Protestant or evangelical Christian. Women constitute approximately 40 percent of the official labor force, with a substantial additional proportion engaged in unpaid agricultural labor; in the urban sector, women are concentrated in domestic service and informal trading. Overall, female participation in government is minor, although five women currently hold cabinet posts.

Colombia's economy is diverse and includes large manufacturing, agriculture, and mineral sectors, as well as sizable public and private-service sectors. Petroleum and petroleum products rank first among official exports. Coffee, cut flowers, and bananas are the most important agricultural exports, while efforts to develop agricultural alternatives—cotton, palm oil, and sugar, in particular—have been partially successful. Colombia has a reputation for prudent economic management, with a tradition of modest debt and independent monetary policy. The country did not record a single year of negative GDP growth between the 1930s depression and the late 1990s, when a severe economic crisis, caused chiefly by a worsening armed conflict, caused the economy to contract. The country's debt increased during the 1990s, as a new constitution added a number of social obligations, and more than one-third of the population lives below the poverty line.

GDP growth averaged 4.2 percent a year in 2000–2008, with corresponding declines in inflation and unemployment. Inflation, which had been as high as 30 percent a year in the previous decade, dropped into the single digits in 2000 and settled at 3.2 percent in 2013, while the unemployment rate over the same period fell from 16 percent in 2002 to 12 percent in 2010, 10.8 percent in 2011, and 10.4 percent in 2012. Annual growth dropped precipitously in 2009 to 1.5 percent, owing to the global economic crisis, but rebounded to the decade's average of 4.3 percent in 2010. The economy expanded by 5.9 percent in 2011 and 4.0 percent in 2012.

GOVERNMENT AND POLITICS

Political background. Colombia gained its independence from Spain in 1819 as part of the Republic of Gran Colombia, which also included what are now Ecuador, Panama, and Venezuela. In 1830 Ecuador and Venezuela separated. The remaining territory, New Granada, was designated the Granadan Confederation in 1858, the United States of Colombia under a federal constitution promulgated in 1863, and the Republic of Colombia under a unitary constitution adopted in 1886. Bogotá did not recognize Panamanian independence, proclaimed in 1903, until 1909.

The critical 19th-century issues of centralism versus federalism and the role of the Catholic Church gave rise to the Liberal (*Partido Liberal Colombiano*—PL) and Conservative (*Partido Conservador Colombiano*—PC) parties, which remain critical, if no longer exclusive, determinants of Colombian politics. Relative calm extended from 1903 to the early 1940s, when domestic instability emerged, culminating in a decade (1948–1958) of internal violence (*la Violencia*) that may have taken as many as 300,000 lives. This period included a coup d'état in 1953 that yielded a four-year dictatorship under Gen. Gustavo ROJAS Pinilla. To avert a resumption of full-scale interparty warfare after the fall of Rojas, the two major parties agreed in the so-called Pact of Sitges, concluded in July 1957, to establish a National Front (*Frente Nacional*) under which they would participate equally in government, to the exclusion of other parties. The National Front lasted until 1974, with Conservative Misael PASTRANA Borrero in 1970 being the last president to have won under this framework. The 1970 elections were also noteworthy for allegations of electoral fraud from supporters of former dictator Rojas, who ran as a third-party candidate.

Electoral competition for the presidency resumed, in 1974, with Liberal Alfonso LÓPEZ Michelsen capturing 56 percent of the vote over Conservative candidate Álvaro GÓMEZ Hurtado. Together, the Liberals and Conservatives secured 90 percent of the legislative seats. The presidential election of June 4, 1978, was much closer, with the Liberal candidate, Dr. Julio César TURBAY Ayala, defeating his Conservative opponent, Dr. Belisario BETANCUR Cuartas, by a paper-thin margin.

In a March 1982 legislative election the Liberals captured a majority of lower house seats; however, an intraparty dispute between orthodox and New Liberalism (*Nuevo Liberalismo*—NL) factions resulted in the nomination of ex-president López by the former and of Dr. Luis Carlos GALÁN Sarmiento by the latter for the presidential balloting on May 30. As a result of the Liberal split, Betancur, who had been renominated by the Conservatives, emerged as the victor with 46.8 percent of the valid votes and took office on August 7.

The orthodox Liberal camp secured a majority in both houses in the March 7, 1986, legislative elections. Galán then withdrew from the presidential election of May 25, paving the way for Virgilio BARCO Vargas to decisively defeat the Conservatives' 1974 nominee, Gómez.

Galán, an unswerving critic of the Medellín and Cali drug cartels (the powerful and violent organizations that controlled much of the world's cocaine trade), resurfaced in 1989 as the Liberals' leading presidential candidate but was assassinated on August 18. His equally outspoken successor, César GAVIRIA Trujillo, easily defeated Gómez (now running as a candidate of his party, the National Salvation Movement [*Movimiento de Salvación Nacional*—MSN]) in the May 1990 presidential election, with the official Conservative candidate, Rodrigo LLOREDA Caicedo running fourth behind Antonio NAVARRO Wolff, of the recently legalized Democratic Alliance/April 19 Movement (*Alianza Democrática/ Movimiento 19 de Abril*—AD/M-19) following the assassination of Carlos PIZARRO León-Gómez on April 26.

While M-19 secured only one seat in the legislative poll of March 11, 1990, it captured second place (only five seats behind the Liberals) in constituent assembly balloting on December 9, suggesting that the traditional bipartisan era might have run its course. After six months of debate, a new constitution (see below) was adopted in 1991. Meanwhile, the drug problem increasingly drained government resources, as the Revolutionary Armed Forces of Colombia (*Fuerzas Armadas Revolucionarias de Colombia*—FARC) and the National Liberation Army (*Ejército de Liberación*—ELN) guerrilla groups (see below) began to fund their operations with cocaine proceeds.

The Liberals retained control in legislative and gubernatorial balloting on October 27, 1991, winning majorities in both houses of Congress and capturing 15 of 27 governorships. Leftist parties suffered a major defeat in the legislative poll of March 13, 1994, when voters endorsed a return to the historic dominance of Liberals and Conservatives. Subsequently, the narrow victory of the Liberal candidate, Ernesto SAMPER Pizano, in the second-round presidential balloting on June 19, accompanied by a remarkably low voter turnout of only 35 percent, was attributed to the basic similarity of the leading parties' programs.

On December 2, 1993, security forces killed the head of the Medellín drug cartel, Pablo ESCOBAR, who had escaped from confinement in mid-1992 after having surrendered to authorities a year earlier. President Gaviria immediately proclaimed the "dismemberment" of the Medellín group, while indicating that the drug problem would remain until authorities were able to destroy the more sophisticated cartel in the southwestern city of Cali. The latter effort yielded significant results during the first half of 1995, with the arrests of several top Cali cartel figures.

Four months before Escobar's capture, the ruling PL had plunged into crisis over alleged links between nine of its legislators and the cartel. On July 27 Santiago MEDINA, President Samper's 1994 campaign treasurer, was arrested on charges of having accepted contributions from the Cali drug lords. Medina alleged that Defense Minister Fernando BOTERO Zea was also involved in the affair. Botero resigned on August 8 and was arrested a week later amid allegations that Samper himself was aware of the funding source. While public opinion had initially supported the president against his accusers, public sentiment appeared to have turned decisively against him by 1996. Nonetheless, Samper, benefiting in part from an upsurge in anti-U.S. sentiment over the drug issue—Washington had revoked the president's U.S. visa—succeeded in rallying a majority of the lower house to his side in late May, thus averting a threat of impeachment.

Army estimates indicated that the strength of guerrilla groups, particularly that of the FARC, had risen by 1998 to control two-fifths of the country's municipalities. The rapidly growing force alarmed U.S. and Colombian observers with a string of overwhelming victories against outmatched Colombian forces in remote rural zones.

In the 1998 presidential election the Liberals split between pro- and anti-Samper factions, many of the latter supporting the PC nominee, Andrés PASTRANA Arango, who defeated his Liberal opponent, Horacio SERPA Uribe, by half a million votes in the second-round of balloting on June 21. The Liberals, however, retained decisive majorities in the Senate and Chamber of Representatives.

Pastrana launched peace talks with the FARC in late 1998, but negotiations faltered quickly, and the talks' credibility subsequently eroded. Along with a badly slumping economy, the collapse of the FARC talks in February 2002 fundamentally undermined Pastrana's presidency.

Despite introducing an ambitious "Plan Colombia," designed to defeat drug traffickers (primarily with $1.3 billion in military aid from the United States), President Pastrana's popularity plummeted to a low of 20 percent by September 2000. The Conservatives were punished in the October 29 municipal balloting, winning only 2 of 30 gubernatorial races and an equal number of mayoralties in departmental capitals.

On March 10, 2002, both of the traditional parties were outpolled in legislative balloting by an unprecedented aggregate of minor candidates. In the presidential election of May 26, 2002, independent Álvaro URIBE Vélez, a longtime Liberal running with Conservative support, easily defeated the PL's official candidate, Serpa. A hard-liner and outspoken opponent of Pastrana's peace effort, Uribe benefited from his predecessor's inability to conclude a successful negotiation. Most minor parties threw their support to Uribe.

Following his inauguration on August 7, 2002, President Uribe adopted what he called a "democratic security" strategy of increased troop deployments, defense spending, and integration of the population in intelligence gathering against the insurgencies. Uribe also offered to negotiate with any armed group that first declared a cease-fire, an offer that was only accepted by the rightist paramilitaries. In December the main components of the paramilitary umbrella organization, the United Self-Defense Groups of Colombia (*Autodefensas Unidas de Colombia*—AUC, see Rebel and Clandestine Groups, below) agreed to demobilize, although the process was not completed until mid-2006.

The paramilitaries' demobilization took place within the framework of a 2005 "Justice and Peace" law, which granted light (maximum eight years) prison terms in exchange for a commitment to tell the truth about past crimes, compensate victims, and help dismantle the paramilitaries' powerful drug trafficking and political networks. A 2006 Constitutional Court decision strengthened the law's provisions, addressing criticism that the law failed to provide the legal tools necessary to dismantle the paramilitary warlords' sources of wealth and political control. The Uribe government held that paramilitary leaders who cooperated with Justice and Peace investigators would not be extradited to the United States to face drug-trafficking charges.

In 2006 the two leading left-of-center parties announced that they would merge to form an Alternative Democratic Pole (*Polo Democrático Alternativo*—PDA; see Political Parties, below) to contest the legislative and presidential elections. The March 12, 2006, legislative elections gave the pro-Uribe parties a majority of seats in the Congress, and in peaceful first-round presidential balloting on May 28, Uribe won convincingly with 62 percent of the vote. Sen. Carlos GAVIRIA Díaz of the PDA placed second with 22 percent, while PL candidate Serpa was third with 11.8 percent.

Small opposition parties and pro-Uribe candidates continued to perform well in October 28, 2007, municipal and departmental elections. Left-of-center parties and movements, including the PDA in Bogotá, won the mayorships of Colombia's three largest cities (Bogotá, Medellín, and Cali).

The most significant challenge during Uribe's second term was the "parapolitics" scandal, in which 38 congressmen and 5 governors were eventually convicted of colluding with the AUC paramilitary group. While there had been similar allegations in the past, information collected from a computer owned by a former paramilitary leader, combined with the public confessions of paramilitary leaders as part of the Justice and Peace investigation, led to dramatic evidence of electoral manipulation and intimidation in Colombian departments where the right-wing paramilitaries, with their drug trafficking and death squad activities apparent to all Colombians, had long operated freely. Meanwhile, the FARC, though weakened, remained a security threat, especially in the southern jungle lowlands.

In August 2007 President Uribe accepted Venezuelan president Hugo Chávez's offer to mediate talks between the government and the FARC, and Uribe further extended the invitation to include renewed negotiations with the ELN. However, the efforts failed to yield quick results, and Uribe dismissed Chávez as mediator. Chávez later infuriated Colombians when he made a speech calling on the nations of the world to offer political recognition to the FARC and ELN and to remove the groups from their lists of terrorist organizations. The remarks spurred a massive demonstration on February 4 by some 10 million Colombians protesting against the FARC and its tactics.

In May 2008, as criminal evidence mounted against paramilitary leaders and speculation grew about how many politicians might be involved in the scandal, the government extradited 14 former AUC leaders to the United States to face drug charges. Two more people were extradited in the next 12 months, along with all the captured leaders of the defunct North Valle cartel that had dominated cocaine transshipments during the late 1990s and early 2000s. Violence by the FARC continued to escalate, however. In a crackdown on July 2, the army carried out "*Operación Jaque*" (Operation Check), in which soldiers posing as humanitarian workers rescued 14 hostages, including three Americans and former presidential candidate Íngrid Betancourt. Following the attack the guerrillas retreated to more remote areas, including border zones, and began to rely more heavily on landmines, improvised explosive devices, and sneak attacks on small military targets.

The military came under severe criticism in September and October 2008, when it was alleged that members of the army had deliberately killed nearly 3,000 civilians and presented their bodies as those of members of armed groups killed in combat in order to reap rewards for high body counts. The so-called false-positives scandal forced the resignation of the army chief, General Montoya, and prompted increased criticism of the president, whose demands that the military produce more results were seen as creating a climate for such abuse.

In February 2009 the Administrative Department of Security (DAS), the nation's leading intelligence agency, was accused of conducting telephonic surveillance and smear campaigns against opposition politicians, reporters, human rights defenders, and Supreme Court justices, specifically those justices investigating parapolitics cases.

The same month, FARC guerrillas released their two remaining civilian hostages, along with four police officers and soldiers, to a citizens' group, Colombians for Peace, which had been negotiating with the guerrilla leaders. On December 21 FARC guerrillas kidnapped and murdered the governor of Caquetá department. In retaliation, the Colombian military killed 25 guerrillas and captured 13 more in Meta department on January 1, 2010. At the end of March the FARC unilaterally released two soldiers, one who had been held for 12 years. On June 13, 300 Colombian Special Forces soldiers conducted a raid on an FARC camp and freed four army and police hostages.

In second-round presidential balloting on June 20, 2010, Juan Manuel SANTOS Calderón, a former defense minister and the candidate of the Social Party of National Unity (*Partido Social de Unidad Nacional*—PSUN) defeated Aurelijus Rutenis Antanas MOCKUS Šivickas of the Colombian Green Party (*Partido Verde Colombiano*—VC) with more than 69 percent of the vote. During the runoff, the FARC and the ELN launched three attacks that killed ten security force members and wounded two more, depressing voter turnout to 45 percent. (For more on 2010 terrorist attacks, please refer to the 2013 edition of the *Handbook*.) On August 7 Santos formed a new government comprising members of the PSUN, PC, and Radical Change, as well as independents. He reorganized the executive branch, establishing ministries of justice, labor, and environment.

The judicial system continued to investigate the false positives, illegal surveillance, and parapolitics scandals through 2011, and on October 12, 2010, a legislative committee opened an investigation into wiretapping after former president Uribe accepted responsibility for it. Maria del Pilar HURTADO, Uribe's former DAS chief in 2007–2008, was granted asylum in Panama in November. Hurtado was wanted in Colombia in connection with the illegal surveillance campaign. In December a former DAS intelligence director was sentenced to eight years in prison for his role in the wiretapping scandal.

The Supreme Court in February 2011 found Mario URIBE Escobar, former president Uribe's second cousin and longtime political ally, guilty of conspiracy related to the parapolitics scandal and sentenced him to more than seven years in prison and imposed a fine of $1.86 million. The court said that he had entered into a pact with senior AUC leaders in exchange for supporting his candidacy. Meanwhile, the former president's aides, including his former chief of staff and agriculture minister, were incarcerated in 2011 for wiretapping and corruption, respectively.

Constitution and government. The 1886 constitution, one of the world's oldest, had been extensively revised before its replacement in 1991. The most notable amendment had been that of 1957, which instituted the *Frente Nacional,* under which the presidency alternated between Liberals and Conservatives, with equal numbers of offices held by members of the two parties. The parity rule also applied to the legislative and judicial branches until 1974, when a new president and all legislative bodies were elected on a nonrestrictive basis.

Under the 1991 constitution, the Senate was reduced from 114 seats to 102 (including 2 for indigenous communities), with senators elected nationally rather than by department. The Chamber of Representatives was reduced from 199 members to 161, each department or territory electing at least 2 representatives, with additional seats allotted on a population basis. In addition, up to 5 special seats could be assigned to minority groups or citizens living abroad.

The earlier Napoleonic judicial system was supplanted by an essentially adversarial U.S. system. An office of general prosecutor (*fiscalía general*) was established to investigate and charge offenders; an inspector-general (*procuraduría*) was created to investigate and mete out administrative sanctions for offenses committed by state representatives; in addition, a people's defender (*defensor del pueblo*) was installed to oversee the *fiscalía* and ensure the protection of human rights, while a judicial council (*consejo superior de la judicatura*) was convened to review the professional qualifications of the judiciary. Finally, a *corte constitucional* was created to interpret the constitution, leaving to the Supreme Court the sole responsibility of serving as the highest court of appeal.

In October 2003 a referendum on a number of constitutional reforms sought by President Uribe (including a further reduction in the number of legislative seats) failed because the electoral turnout fell short of a mandated 25 percent. In December 2004, however, Congress gave formal approval to an amendment permitting presidential reelection, which was affirmed by the Constitutional Court in late 2005.

Another constitutional amendment promulgated in 2003 and implemented in the 2006 elections, requires political parties to offer only one list of candidates per office. The new rules established a 2 percent electoral threshold requirement in legislative elections for a party to maintain its legal status (exempting indigenous and Afro-Colombian parties).

Colombia is divided into 32 departments plus the Federal District of Santafé de Bogotá. The governors of the departments have been popularly elected since 1991. (The president had appointed the governors under the 1886 constitution.) Reform in 1988 allowed for the popular election of mayors (akin to county administrators in all but large urban areas).

Reporters Without Borders ranked Colombia 129th out of 179 countries in its 2013 Index of Press Freedom, up from 143rd place in 2012. Paramilitary groups continue to target journalists working in Colombia, but the murder rate has dropped.

Foreign relations. Apart from cooperation with the United States in attempts to limit the drug trade, Colombia's international activities center on regional affairs. Relations with Nicaragua, already strained because of deportations of Colombian migrant workers, were further exacerbated in late 1979 by Managua's decision to revive a series of long-standing claims to the Caribbean islands of San Andrés and Providencia, both acquired by Colombia under a 1928 treaty, and the uninhabited cays of Quita Sueño, Roncador, Serrana, and Serranilla, which were assigned to Colombia under a 1972 agreement with the United States. In February 1980 Nicaragua formally denounced the 1928 accord as having been concluded under U.S. military occupation, while arguing that the cays were located on its continental shelf and thus constituted part of its national territory. On December 13, 2007, the International Court of Justice (ICJ) ruled in Colombia's favor in the case of San Andrés, Providencia, and Santa Catalina islands, citing Nicaragua's failure to mount a challenge in the first 50 years after the 1928 treaty. The ICJ also determined that it could adjudicate any future disputes over the three cays and the two countries' maritime border.

Since 1979, relations with Venezuela, the country's northeastern neighbor, have been strained because of a dispute involving the maritime boundary through the Gulf of Venezuela. Tensions over contraband trade and containment of cross-border guerrilla activity intensified in February 1995 as the result of a National Liberation Army (*Ejército de Liberación Nacional*—ELN) guerrilla raid that resulted in the death of eight Venezuelan marines. President Samper then proposed that a joint force be created to patrol the area while rejecting Venezuela's claim to a right of "hot pursuit" of intruders. In November, following an incursion of Venezuelan troops into Colombia, the two countries announced the appointment of a bilateral commission to delineate the border more accurately as a means of preventing the recurrence of such incidents.

In mid-1996 Washington announced the cancellation of President Samper's U.S. visa as the result of accusations of linkages between Samper and the Cali cartel; four months earlier the administration of U.S. president Bill Clinton had "decertified" Colombia for insufficient antidrug efforts, an action that was repeated in February 1997, despite ongoing cooperation between the two countries' military establishments. The United States was displeased by the Colombian Congress's vote in November 1997 to revoke its ban on extradition; while the change was approved, it was made nonretroactive, thus precluding the extradition of Cali cartel kingpins for trial in U.S. courts (after several years in Colombian prisons, however, the Cali cartel's senior leaders were extradited to the United States in 2004). Extraditions—the first in nearly a decade—were resumed in late 1999 as the U.S. Congress moved to approve a $1.36 billion antidrug package. U.S. president George W. Bush visited Colombia on November 22, 2004, where he praised President Uribe's anti-insurgent efforts.

A serious row with Venezuela erupted in late 2004 with the kidnapping in Caracas of the FARC "foreign minister" Rodrigo GRANDA (a.k.a. Ricardo GONZALEZ), who was transported to the border and handed over to Colombian agents. In mid-January 2005, after Venezuela had threatened to break relations, Colombia admitted that it had paid bounty hunters for the abduction. Relations with Venezuela remain strained, as Venezuela withdrew from the Andean Community over, among other things, a free trade pact negotiated between Colombia and the United States.

Relations improved in mid-2007 when Venezuelan president Hugo Chávez visited President Uribe in Bogotá on August 31, 2007, to accept Uribe's short-lived offer to allow Chávez to mediate negotiations with the FARC for a release of hostages. In mid-2008 the bilateral relationship worsened, as captured guerrilla computers indicated that the Venezuelan government may have provided material support to the FARC.

Colombia's relations with Ecuador also deteriorated, as disagreements with the government of Rafael Correa arose regarding aerial herbicide fumigation of coca plants in border zones, border security cooperation, and, most crucially, on March 1, 2008, when government forces killed a FARC leader about a mile inside Ecuadorian territory. Subsequently, Ecuador withdrew its ambassador, and Venezuelan president Chávez ordered the deployment of troops to the Colombian border to prevent a similar incursion into Venezuela. Ultimately, negotiations were brokered by several neighboring states. Despite public declarations that the crisis was over, tensions between Colombia and its neighbors remained strained over Colombia's allegations that Venezuela and Ecuador had provided the guerrillas with weapons and equipment.

In June 2008 relations with Nicaragua were strained after Managua granted asylum to three Colombian citizens who survived the Colombian Army's March raid on a FARC guerrilla camp in Ecuador. Nicaraguan President Daniel Ortega accused President Uribe of "state terrorism" and wanting to "murder" the three citizens. The Colombian government denounced Nicaragua before the Organization of American States (OAS) for "supporting terrorism." Meanwhile, Chávez surprised observers by calling on the FARC and ELN to release all of their kidnap victims and disband. Uribe and Chávez held cordial meetings in January and April 2009, during which they discussed infrastructure projects and economic cooperation. Security and defense cooperation remained nonexistent in the border zone, however, and Colombian defense officials alleged that key FARC leaders were operating freely on the Venezuelan side of the border.

President Bush visited Colombia again on March 11, 2007, and indicated that he would ask the U.S. Congress to augment the more than $5.4 billion spent from 2000 to 2007 and to approve a bilateral free trade agreement signed in November 2006 (the United States is Colombia's largest trading partner). The U.S. Congress, despite an intense lobbying effort that included two visits to Washington by President Uribe in 2007, did not embrace the trade pact. U.S. Democratic congressional leaders, along with labor and human rights groups, opposed the proposal, citing the large number of Colombian labor union members killed with impunity. The U.S. congressional leadership resisted calling a vote to ratify the agreement. When the Bush administration sought to force a vote by introducing the agreement in the U.S. House of Representatives in April 2008, the House Democratic leadership employed an unusual legislative maneuver to postpone consideration of the agreement indefinitely.

President Bush, further underscoring his administration's support for Uribe, awarded the Colombian president the Medal of Freedom, the highest U.S. civilian honor, in January 2009. Uribe's relations with U.S. president Barack Obama cooled but remained cordial in the wake of the Obama administration's reversals on key issues: it refrained from promoting the free trade agreement in Congress; proposed a 5 percent cut in military aid to Colombia; and was more vocal about human rights concerns than the Bush administration. Colombia, however, remained the world's seventh-largest recipient of U.S. government aid. During a two-day visit to Washington in June 2009 to promote the free trade agreement, President Uribe met with President Obama. In July, negotiations to allow the United States to increase its number of troops in Colombia in an expanded anti-drug effort angered President Hugo Chávez, who subsequently withdrew Venezuela's ambassador from Bogotá following accusations by Colombia that Venezuela had assisted the FARC. The proposed troop increase also angered other states in the region and analysts described Colombia as becoming "increasingly isolated" from its neighbors.

On March 14, 2010, in an election run concurrently with Colombia's legislative races, voters for the first time selected five representatives to take seats in the Andean Parliament, the legislative arm of the Andean Community of Nations.

Tensions between Colombia, Venezuela, and Ecuador flared in April 2010, with Chávez and Correa taking the unusual step of strongly rejecting the candidacy of Colombian presidential contender Juan Manuel Santos. Their statements came after Santos said he was proud of authorizing a raid against the FARC within Ecuadorian territory. But concerns eased again toward the end of the year, and on November 26 the presidents of Ecuador and Colombia announced that full diplomatic relations had been restored between the two countries.

Colombian cooperation with U.S. Justice Department investigations touching Colombia continued through 2010–2011. In October 2010 a U.S. grand jury indicted 18 FARC rebels for kidnapping American defense contractors working in Colombia in 2003, and Colombian authorities extradited five Colombians (including a former DAS agent) to the United States on drug-smuggling charges.

Arriving in Bogotá in January 2011, Ecuador's new ambassador to Colombia, Raul VALLEJO, said he wanted to see the border area between the two countries, which often served as a respite for rebel groups, turned into a peace zone. He went on to say that the Ecuadorian forces had destroyed almost 450 FARC camps in the region since 2008.

The United States–Colombia Trade Promotion Agreement (CTPA) entered into force on May 15, 2012, after being stalled in the U.S. Senate since 2006 over human rights concerns. Colombia also concluded a free trade agreement with the European Union in June.

The International Court of Justice ruled in November 2012 that a disputed group of seven western Caribbean islands belonged to Colombia but also drew a line of demarcation that gave Nicaragua some 30,000 square miles of what had been Colombian territorial waters around the islands. Law-enforcement officials worried that the zone could attract drug smugglers, as Nicaragua did not have the capacity to properly patrol the waters.

Tensions with Venezuela were not eased by the death of President Chávez in March. Two months later, his successor Nicolas MADURO accused former president Uribe of conspiring with the Venezuelan opposition to assassinate him.

Colombia assumed the rotating presidency of the Pacific Alliance in June 2013. Comprised of Colombia, Chile, Peru, and Mexico, the free trade group was responsible for 50 percent of the continent's exports in 2012.

Current issues. President Santos's landmark Victims and Land Restitution Law was approved on June 10, 2011, and implemented in January 2012. The plan will compensate the estimated 4 million people forced off their land by rebel groups, paramilitaries, and drug traffickers over the course of Colombia's long internal conflict. The law sought to return some 7 million hectares of land that had been illegally taken by armed groups or abandoned by owners due to fear of violence. Land ownership is highly skewed, with 1.15 percent of landowners controlling 52 percent of farms. The presence of foreign landowners and agribusiness companies is also a source of resentment among local farm workers.

The Santos plan diverged significantly from the tack taken against lawlessness by former president Uribe and angered the more conservative elements of his coalition by including the wording "internal armed conflict" to describe the Colombian government's fight against rebel groups. Supporters of Uribe's previous plan said that such a designation improved the position of groups like the FARC and ELN by giving them legal recognition as belligerent combatants instead of illegally armed terrorist organizations.

Uribe's crackdown on insurgents had several bloody consequences that only fully emerged once he left office. FARC regrouped as a terrorist organization, relying on high-profile attacks led by small guerrilla units. Demobilized paramilitary groups fractured in numerous small groupings dubbed "BACRIM" (*bandas criminals emergentes*—emerging criminal bands), led by former members of the AUC and other paramilitary formations. While the rate of kidnappings dropped 90.63 percent between 2002 and 2009, kidnappings jumped by 25 percent in just the first six months of 2011. FARC attacks grew 10 percent in 2011.

On September 14, 2011, former intelligence chief Jorge NOGUERA was sentenced to 24 years in prison for passing information to the AUC that led to the murder of three persons. Noguera headed DAS from 2002 to 2005 and was a close ally of President Uribe. President Santos replaced the scandal-plagued DAS with a new organization, the National Intelligence Agency (ANI), as of January 1, 2012.

Regional and municipal elections were held on October 30, 2011. FARC attacks surged in the weeks leading to the vote, and at least 41 candidates were killed. Gustavo PETRO, a former M-19 member, defeated Enrique PENALOSA (PV) to become mayor of Bogotá. Five leftist candidates won mayoral races in seven of the country's largest cities.

The Santos government has focused on eliminating high-value targets in its anti-insurgency campaign. The strategy has brought considerable success, with three of the FARC's seven-man secretariat now dead. Guerrillas killed in military raids include Vargas Jorge BRICENO Suárez (a.k.a. Mono JOJOY) and FARC supreme commander Guillermo León SAENZ Vargas (a.k.a. Alfonso CANO). Saenz was killed when the military attacked a rebel camp on November 4. Within hours, FARC announced the selection of a new leader, Rodrigo Londoño ECHEVERRI (a.k.a. Timoleón JIMENEZ or Timochenko). The president's approval rating jumped from 79 percent to 83 percent at the news of Cano's death.

Santos has also set clear terms for negotiations with the insurgents: release hostages, stop violence and lawlessness, and stop pursuing political goals through violence. In a move seen as a peace overture, FARC announced in February 2012 that it would "abandon the practice" of kidnapping for ransom.

The Senate passed (61–3) the "Legal Framework for Peace" bill on June 14, paving the way for the government to negotiate with the FARC and ELN. The law suspends previously imposed prison sentences for members of "illegal armed groups" and allowed other insurgents to escape punishment in return for confessions and restitution. Opponents denounced the bill as "an amnesty in disguise," but the Constitutional Court upheld the law in August 2013.

Unlike his predecessors, former president Uribe has remained a presence on the political scene, frequently criticizing his successor. Uribe has been especially vocal in his criticism of the Santos administration approach to insurgent groups, taking to Twitter with daily posts about FARC activities. Following a formal accusation from Congressman Ivan CEPEDA in April 2012, the prosecutor-general reopened an investigation into Uribe's involvement in the parapolitics scandal that had been dismissed in 2000. Constitutionally barred from another term as president, Uribe formed his own party, the Pure Democratic Center (*Puro Centro Democrático*), in July 2012, which has been plagued by infighting. He planned to run for a senate seat in 2014.

On August 22 the entire cabinet submitted its resignation. The move coincided with the halfway point in Santos's presidency and a new poll showing his approval rating had fallen to 48 percent, down from 64 percent in April. Analysts suggested a link between the developments, noting that the president could rid himself of dissenting voices in the cabinet.

In a stunning televised address, President Santos on August 27, 2012, announced that his government had been secretly meeting with the FARC in Havana for several months and that the two sides had agreed to begin peace negotiations. Formal negotiations began in October, and the FARC announced a two-month cease-fire in November, calling it a good-will gesture for Christmas. Former vice president Humberto de la CALLE LOMBANA was the chief negotiator for the government, while Luciano Marín ARANGO (a.k.a. Iván MARQUEZ) had that position for the FARC.

The ELN was not included in the negotiations in Havana, although the government has offered to create a similar, parallel forum. Germany voiced opposition to including the ELN, after the insurgents kidnapped two German nationals in November 2012. The two hostages were released on March 8, 2013.

In May, the peace negotiations produced a draft document on rural development and land reform. Specifically, the government agreed to expand the creation of special "peasant reserve zones" protected from potential land grabs. When the Havana talks reconvened in June, Arango urged the government to postpone the March 2014 parliamentary elections and November 2014 presidential elections and instead create a popular assembly "to find a true solution to the conflict." Santos declined. The FARC continued to press the issue, later calling for the creation of a regions-based house of parliament.

Peasant protests erupted in in July in Catatumbo region, on the border with Venezuela, as locals demanded their region be designated a peasant reserve zone. They also denounced recent free trade agreements for falling crop prices. On July 22, the FARC openly offered to send weapons and troops to the peasants, prompting accusations that the FARC was behind the protests.

On July 24, an independent commission issued a report on the costs of Colombia's insurgencies and called on all parties to accept responsibility for violations of human rights. The next day, Santos complied [in translation]: "The Colombian state has been responsible . . . in serious violations of human rights and infractions to international humanitarian law during these 50 years of conflict." FARC made a similar admission on August 19.

The farmers' protests grew in size and blocked major roads. Miners, indigenous peoples, and other groups joined in, including 30,000 university students in the capital on August 29. When fighting erupted between protestors and police, Santos imposed martial law in Bogotá. The entire cabinet resigned on September 3, but Santos only changed the ministers of interior, justice, agriculture, mines and energy, and environment. Santos concluded a framework for negotiations with the national agriculture union on September 20, and the protestors retreated. By October, Santos's approval rating had dropped to 20 percent.

POLITICAL PARTIES

The Liberal and Conservative parties traditionally dominated Colombian politics and from 1958 to 1974 shared power under the National Front system, with the leading minority group remaining entitled to representation in the executive branch until adoption of the 1991 constitution. The major parties in the past were forced to deal with as many as 70 minor parties who vied for votes during legislative elections, but political reform in 2003 that mandated that every party meet a 2 percent electoral threshold requirement reduced the number of viable parties and forced several minor parties into coalitions with each other.

Prior to the 2010 legislative elections, the PSUN, PC, and CR negotiated a cooperation agreement under which the PSUN, expected to gain at least a plurality in both legislative houses, looked to cement its power in Congress by agreeing to adopt some of the smaller parties' campaign pledges and to include some of their members in the cabinet of presumed incoming president Juan Manuel Santos. In return, the PL pledged support for the incoming president's agenda. Meanwhile, the PIN members of Congress were expected to vote often with the new center-right alliance, giving it a majority of up to 85 percent of legislators. In addition, the VC said it would not start from a position of opposition, making the PDA the only true opposition party.

Government Parties:

Social Party of National Unity (*Partido Social de Unidad Nacional*—PSUN). More commonly referenced as the Party of the U

(*Partido de la U*), the PSUN was established in 2005 by former members of the PL and miscellaneous small parties. Its most prominent founder, journalist and former government minister Juan Manuel Santos, served as defense minister from 2006 until May 2009.

The balance of power in Congress shifted after the 2006 elections as the PSUN candidates won 30 seats in the Chamber on a national vote share of 16.7 percent (making the party the second-largest voting bloc in the lower house and the largest bloc of votes supporting the Uribe government) and won a plurality in the Senate (20 seats and 17.5 percent of the vote).

The PSUN won 26 percent of the total votes cast in the Chamber of Representatives race in 2010 and secured 47 seats, gaining 18 from the previous elections. The party also won 28 Senate seats, amassing almost 26 percent of the overall vote in that race, and increased its representation in the upper house by 7 seats.

With 47 percent of the vote, Santos finished nearly 25 percentage points ahead of his closest competitor in the first round of presidential voting on May 30, 2010. He handily beat his VC competitor in the June runoff with 69 percent of the vote. Along with backing from allies in the PC and the CR, Santos, a former member of the PL, also secured the support of a majority of Liberal members of Congress.

In June 2011 former Senate president and prominent PSUN member Armando BENEDETTI Villaneda said the party was in crisis and could face defeat in October's regional elections. He pointed to a lack of leadership from party executives and an ideological divide between supporters of the former president Uribe and the current president Santos. The party further fragmented in 2013, as Santos waited until November to decide whether he would seek reelection in 2014. In December 2012 Sen. Aurelio Irragorri Hormanza and Congressman Jaime Buenahora Febres were named party cochairs.

Leaders: Juan Manuel SANTOS Calderon (President of the Republic), Angelino GARZÓN (Vice President of the Republic), Aurelio IRRAGORRI Hormanza, Jaime BUENAHORA Febres (Party Cochairs).

Colombian Conservative Party (*Partido Conservador Colombiano*—PC). A traditional party formerly based in the agrarian aristocracy, the *Partido Conservador* was long divided between National Front conservatives and an independent faction composed of followers of the late president Laureano Gómez. The split continued until November 1981, when the more moderate *ospina-pastranistas,* led by Dr. Misael Pastrana Borrero (president, 1970–1974), concluded an agreement with the rightist *alvaristas,* led by Dr. Álvaro Gómez Hurtado (an unsuccessful 1974 candidate who was later murdered in 1995). In 1986 Gómez Hurtado was the Conservative nominee but was decisively beaten by the PL's Barco, in part because of the association with his dictatorial father, Laureano, during the period of *la Violencia.*

For the 1990 campaign the party was again split, the official candidate, Rodrigo LLOREDA Caicedo, being outpaced by Gómez Hurtado, who, as candidate of a dissident **National Salvation Movement** (*Movimiento de Salvación Nacional*—MSN), was decisively defeated by the PL's Gaviria Trujillo in the May balloting. (From 1987 to 1992 the party operated under the name Social Conservative Party [*Partido Social Conservador*—PSC], although it then reverted back to the PC rubric.) In 1994 Andrés Pastrana Arango (running as an independent with PC endorsement) lost to the PL's Samper Pizano by a mere 0.8 percent of the second-round vote. Before accepting the PC nomination, Pastrana Arango, a former mayor of Bogotá, headed a dissident conservative group, the **New Democratic Force** (*Nueva Fuerza Democrática*—NFD), which secured eight Senate seats in 1991 (only one less than the mainline PC) but only one upper house seat in 1998. Pastrana defeated the PL's Horacio Serpa Uribe in second-round presidential balloting on June 21, 1998. For the 2002 campaign a largely disoriented PC endorsed the former Liberal and current president, Álvaro Uribe (after its candidate withdrew from the contest). Carlos HOLGUIN Sardi resigned as PC president following his party's poor showing in the March legislative poll. President Uribe later named Holguín to the post of interior minister. The party supported Uribe in the May 2006 presidential election rather than fielding its own candidate.

In 2010 the PC picked up more than 21 percent of the votes cast in the Chamber of Representatives race, which meant 37 seats, an increase of 7 seats over the previous legislative election. It took 22 Senate seats, a gain of 4 from 2006. The party selected former ambassador and ministry head Noemí Sanin Posada as its presidential candidate for the May 30 election, ending the PC's eight-year support of the PSUN. She came in fifth place with just over 6 percent of the ballot.

In March 2011 PC leaders said the party's coalition with PSUN had become strained over what they saw as the Santos administration's attempt to purge several agencies of PC members. New party leaders were elected at the November 2011 party congress.

Leaders: Efrain CEPEDA Sarabia (President), Eduardo ENRIQUEZ Caicedo (Vice President), Noemi SANÍN Posada (2010 presidential candidate), Jorge Humberto MANTILLA (Secretary General).

Radical Change (*Partido Cambio Radical*—CR). Founded in 1998 by a group primarily made up of dissident Liberals, the center-right party supported Uribe in the 2002 election and in 2006 became one of several medium-sized parties to form a pro-Uribe legislative bloc. The CR's electoral strength was concentrated around Bogotá and the departments of Antioquia, Cundinamarca, Valle, Boyacá, and Tolima.

The CR won 16 Chamber seats and 8 Senate seats in 2010, declining by 4 Chamber seats and 7 Senate seats compared to the previous legislative elections. The party nominated Germán VARGAS Lleras as its 2010 presidential candidate. He ran on a platform of continuing the Uribe administration's policies. He came in third place with just over 10 percent of the vote during first-round balloting on May 30. Many party members were caught up in the parapolitics scandal, and Vargas decided to step down as leader following his 2010 loss.

The party operated with a rotating leadership until Carlos Fernando Galán was elected president in September 2013.

Leader: Carlos Fernando GALÁN (President).

Other Legislative Parties:

Colombian Liberal Party (*Partido Liberal Colombiano*—PL). A traditional party that tends to reflect the interests of the more commercialized and industrialized sector of the electorate, the PL (not abbreviated as PLC) has endorsed moderately paced economic and social reform and has observer status in the Socialist International.

At a party convention in September 1981, former chief executive López Michelsen was designated Liberal candidate for the presidency in 1982, leading his archrival, Lleras Restrepo, and another former president, Alfonso Lleras Camargo, to support an independent center-left campaign launched by Dr. Luis Carlos GALÁN Sarmiento of the then newly organized **New Liberalism** (*Nuevo Liberalismo*—NL). Galán drew enough Liberal votes from López Michelsen to throw the May presidential election to the Conservative candidate, Belisario Betancur.

For the 1986 campaign the mainstream leadership, including the still-influential Lleras Camargo, joined in supporting the former mayor of Bogotá, Virgilio Barco Vargas, a political centrist, whose capture of the presidency on May 25 was preceded by a PL victory in the legislative poll of March 9.

Having fared poorly in the 1986 legislative balloting, the NL reentered the parent party in mid-1988 to bolster support for President Virgilio Barco. Galán Sarmiento, who had emerged as the leading Liberal candidate for the presidency in 1990, was assassinated on August 18, 1989. Subsequently, in an unprecedented primary poll conducted in conjunction with legislative and municipal balloting on March 11, 1990, César Gaviria Trujillo was formally selected as the new PL nominee and went on to defeat his closest competitor, Conservative dissident Gómez Hurtado, by a near two-to-one margin.

The PL's presidential candidate in 1994, Ernesto Samper Pizano, was from the *Nuevo Liberalismo,* while his running mate was drawn from the party's right wing. Although outpolling the Conservatives by a more than two-to-one margin in first-round balloting on March 8, 1998, the PL's Horacio Serpa Uribe lost the presidency to the independent (and PC-endorsed) candidate Andrés Pastrana in second-round balloting on June 21. Returning as his party's nominee in 2002, Serpa Uribe ran second to Álvaro Uribe Vélez, a former PL conservative who ran as an independent.

In 2006 Serpa was again the PL presidential nominee, placing third behind President Uribe and the PDA candidate, Carlos Gaviria Díaz. Serpa polled less than 12 percent in the election—widely described as the worst showing by a Liberal candidate in the modern era. In the parapolitics scandals that surfaced after the elections, Juan Manuel López, a Liberal senator from Córdoba, was identified as one of the politicians who had signed the "Pact of Ralito," a declaration of common political purpose, with leaders of the AUC.

The PL selected Rafael Pardo Rueda to be its presidential candidate for the 2010 election. He came in sixth place with 4.4 percent of the vote during the May 30 first round of balloting. During legislative elections held the same year, the PL dropped 1 seat in the Chamber of Representatives from the 2006 election for a total of 35, and dropped 1 Senate seat for a total of 17.

In March 2011 two PL politicians were expelled from the party for their involvement in a scandal involving improperly awarded city contracts in Bogotá. The same month PL politicians went on the offensive against former president Uribe, saying that the flowering of new criminal gangs throughout the country was a direct result of his administration's efforts to demobilize the AUC.

In October 2013, the party elected Simon Gaviria Muñoz, as national director, after his serving as party leader in the Chamber of Representatives.

Leaders: Simon GAVIRIA Muñoz (Director), César GAVIRIA Trujillo (Former President of the Republic), Horacio SERPA Uribe (1998, 2002, and 2006 presidential candidate), Hector EXPINOSA Olympus (Secretary General).

Colombian Green Party (*Partido Verde Colombiano*—VC). This moderate left party was formed in June 2007 as the Green Party Center Option (*Partido Verde Opción Centro*), a spin-off of the 2005 creation of the Center Option Party (*Partido Opción Centro*). The VC stands for sustainable development, government transparency, and responsible cultural and environmental stewardship. Members of the party competed in 2007's departmental and local elections, winning 2 governorships, 27 mayoral races, and 10 deputy and 307 council seats. The party's 2010 presidential candidate, Antanas Mockus, a mathematician turned politician, came in second place during first-round voting on May 30, 2010, with 21.5 percent of the vote. He lost to PSUN candidate Juan Manuel Santos during the second round on June 20, receiving 27.5 percent of the vote. The VC won 5 Senate and 3 Chamber seats in its first appearance during 2010 legislative elections.

Mockus quit the party in June 2011 after the VC accepted an endorsement by former president Uribe for party copresident Enrique Peñalosa's bid to become mayor of Bogotá in the October regional elections. Mockus said that the backing of the scandal-touched former president betrayed everything for which the party stood. Peñalosa finished second, with 25 percent of the vote, to the Progressive Movement's Gustavo Gustavo PETRO Urrego.

The VC and the **Progressive Movement** (*Movimiento Progresistas*—MP) of Gustavo Petro Urrego merged into a new party, the **Green Alliance** (*Alianza Verde*—AV) in September 2013, ahead of the 2014 elections. They hope more parties will join their effort to field a strong candidate for president. AV is jointly led by Peñalosa and Petro.

National Integration Party (*Partido de Integración Nacional*—PIN). Founded in November 2009, the PIN was a right-wing group that sought to defend national sovereignty and human dignity. The party created a storm of controversy when it became known that many of its members had family or other ties to jailed right-wing paramilitary operators. The group's founder, Luis Alberto Gil Castillo (former teacher's union leader and M-19 member), was said to lead the PIN from a Bogotá prison cell, where he was serving time for his connections with the AUC paramilitary group (see below). The PIN's roots lay in the Citizens' Convergence Party (*Partido Convergencia Ciudadana*—CC), which was formed in 1997 by Gil and Jairo CÉSPEDES Camacho and was one of a handful of pro-Uribe parties whose membership was disproportionately implicated in the parapolitics scandal. The PIN won 9 Senate and 11 Chamber seats during the 2010 legislative elections, making it the fourth most powerful party in the upper chamber. Gil stepped down during the party's June 2013 congress, which saw a complete overhaul to improve the party's image. The party was renamed **Citizens Option** (*Opción Ciudadana*).

Leaders: Doris Vega CLEMENCIA Quiroz (Chair), Bioscar Edison RUIZ Valencia (General Secretary).

Alternative Democratic Pole (*Polo Democrático Alternativo*—PDA). The left-of-center PDA was launched in late 2005 by merger of the **Independent Democratic Pole** (*Polo Democrático Independiente*—PDI) and the **Democratic Alternative** (*Alternativa Democrática*—AD) and contains elements of a number of far-left parties like the **Communist Party of Colombia** (*Partido Comunista de Colombia*—PCC) and the **Independent and Revolutionary Labor Movement** (*Movimiento Obrero Independente y Revolucionario*—MOIR).

With a significant representation of demobilized M-19 members, the PDI had been formed in July 2003 by former labor leader Luis Eduardo ("Lucho") GARZON, who argued that President Uribe's policy of "democratic security" had emphasized security to the detriment of democracy, and in 2004 was elected as the first leftist mayor of Bogotá. The AD had been organized in November 2003 by a group of minor left-wing parties equally opposed to the president's policies.

In 2006 PDA flagbearer Carlos Gaviria Díaz lost to President Uribe, having secured only 22 percent of the vote in the presidential run-off balloting. The party won ten Senate seats and eight Chamber seats in the legislative elections.

As the parapolitics scandal reached its zenith in March and April of 2007, PDA senator (and former M-19 member, see Other Parties and Non-Rebel groups, below) Gustavo PETRO claimed President Uribe was linked to the paramilitaries in his activities as governor and later as president, and he criticized the PDA leadership for not being more openly critical of the FARC. Petro's remarks drew the ire of the party's leadership, who considered sanctioning Petro and abstained from any public defense of his remarks.

The party threw all of its resources behind Samuel MORENO in the October 2007 municipal and gubernatorial elections, securing his victory and thus maintaining control of the mayorship of Bogotá. Its only other significant victory was in the Nariño department, where former M-19 leader Antonio NAVARRO Wolff was elected as the party's only governor.

The PDA began to fragment in 2009, as more moderate and electorally successful members like Garzón feuded with more leftist members, who generally led more effective political operations. Garzón officially abandoned the party in May.

Petro, the party's presidential candidate for the May 2010 election, came in fourth place with 9.2 percent. The PDA lost two Senate seats during the 2010 legislative elections and held eight total, while it lost five Chamber seats and held onto four. It became the only true opposition party after others in the Congress threw their qualified support behind President Santos. On March 23, 2011, Petro, claiming to be tired of the pyramid structure of the PDA, split the party and formed the **Progressive Movement** (*Movimiento Progresistas*—MP).

The party's prospects for the 2011 regional elections were thrown into question in May, when the PDA's star mayor of Bogotá, Samuel Gustavo MORENO Rojas, was arrested for rigging city contracts, but Gustavo PETRO Urrego, who switched from the PDA to MP in 2011, won the post with 32 percent of the vote.

Leaders: Clara LÓPEZ Obregón (President), Germán ÁVILA (Secretary General).

Smaller parties that received 3 percent or less of the vote but nonetheless gained legislative representation in 2010 included: the **Independent Movement of Absolute Renovation** (*Movimiento Independente de Renovación Absoluta*—MIRA) led by Carlos Alberto BAENA; the **Indigenous Social Alliance** (*Alianza Social Indigena*), led by Marco AVIRAMA; the **Indigenous Authorities of Colombia Movement** (*Movimiento Autoridades Indígenas de Colombia*—AICO), led by Alberto CUACES Inguilan; the **Liberal Alternative of Social Advance** (*Alternativa Liberal de Avanzada Social*); the **Liberal Opening Movement** (*Movimiento Apertura Liberal*), led by Miguel Angel FLOREZ Rivera; **Civic Compromise for Colombia** (*Compromiso Ciudadano por Colombia*); the **Afrovides Political Movement** (*Movimiento Político Afrovides*), led by Sixto Manuel GARCIA Mejia; and the **Regional Integration Movement** (*Movimiento Integracion Regional*).

Other Parties and Non-Rebel Groups:

Democratic Colombia (*Colombia Democrática*—CD). The CD was founded by Alvaro Uribe Velez and Mario Uribe, the Senate president in 2000–2001, who was later arrested for his alleged involvement with paramilitaries and is also former president Uribe's cousin. It won three Senate seats and two Chamber seats in 2006. All three senators chose to step down in favor of alternates as they faced parapolitics accusations.

In February 2011 the Supreme Court found Uribe Escobar guilty of charges related to the parapolitics scandal (see Current issues, above). He was sentenced to 90 months in prison but released in November 2012. The party collapsed while he was in prison.

Living Colombia Movement (*Movimiento Colombia Viva*—CV). The CV, a small right-of-center party, was created by a coalition of legislators from Colombia's Caribbean coastal region and protestant evangelical leaders. It won two Senate seats in 2006 and no seats in the Chamber. The CV was criticized during that campaign for accepting candidates expelled from other parties on suspicion of paramilitary ties.

The party had difficulty keeping its two Senate seats, as the replacements of those forced to resign by parapolitics scandals were also forced to resign.

Party president Sen. Dieb MALOOF was arrested in February 2007 for his ties with the paramilitaries. In 2010 the CV attempted to reorganize under the name **Democratic National Alliance** (*Alianza Democrática Nacional*—ADN) from within Bogotá's La Picota Prison, but the national electoral council banned it for violating election rules.

Rebel and Clandestine Groups:

In 1985 the ELN and FARC joined with M-19, **Hope, Peace and Liberty** (*Esperanza, Paz y Libertad*—EPL), the **Quintín Lame Commando** (*Comando Quintín Lame*) and **Free Homeland** (*Patria Libre*) formations operating in Cauca and Sucre departments, respectively, and the **Workers' Revolutionary Party** (*Partido Revolucionario de los Trabajadores*—PRT) in forming a National Guerrilla Coordination (*Coordinadora Guerrillera Nacional*—CGN). The name was changed to **National Guerrilla Coordination Simón Bolívar** (*Coordinadora Nacional Guerrillera Simón Bolívar*—CNGSB). Quintín Lame and the PRT laid down their weapons in 1991, with the CNGSB becoming defunct after a breakdown in talks on demobilizing the remaining rebel units. The EPL was dealt a near fatal blow when the faction led by Oscar William Calvo that operated in the Antioquia, Caldas, and Risaralda departments surrendered to government forces in July 2006. By 2008 the FARC and ELN no longer coordinated their efforts but were instead rivals. A report released at the end of 2009 stated that the FARC had increased attacks on civilians and the military by up to 25 percent from the year before. Meanwhile, the ELN had increased its territory and made successful alliances with other rebel groups and drug traffickers. In December 2009 ELN and FARC leaders announced they had agreed to a cease-fire and that the two parties would unite. The proposed unification was thrown into serious doubt in May 2010 when fighting broke out between the two groups in the eastern Arauca department. A June radio transmission from the FARC leader called for an all-out war on ELN after the FARC claimed the ELN had assassinated one of its leaders.

The Santos government opened peace talks with FARC in November 2012 in Havana and offered a similar framework for negotiations with the ELN (see Current issues, above).

National Liberation Army (*Ejército de Liberación Nacional*—ELN). Once the largest and most militant of the insurgent organizations, the Cuban-line ELN was founded by radical students and priests in 1964. Less involved in the drug trade, it has supported itself by pioneering the practice of kidnapping for ransom, as well as extortion, particularly of businesses in the energy sector. It has mounted more than 400 attacks on the country's oil pipelines, causing losses estimated at more than $1 billion.

A "moderate" breakaway group, the **Socialist Renovation Current** (*Corriente de Renovación Socialista*—CRS), agreed to sign a final peace agreement in April 1994. Longtime ELN leader Gregorio Manuel PEREZ Martínez, a priest born and raised in Spain, died on February 14, 1998. It is now commanded by a five-member Central Command led by Nicolás RODRIGUEZ Bautista, alias "Gabino."

Peace talks with ELN representatives and the Pastrana government were opened at an undisclosed northern location in late December 1999 but proved unproductive and were ultimately called off in May 2002.

ELN leader and spokesperson Gerardo Bermudez, known as Francisco Galán, was released conditionally from prison in January 2007 after serving 15 years of a 30-year sentence. Galán's release was intended to further progress in peace talks between the government and the ELN in Havana, Cuba. In mid-2008, these talks ended in a standstill, with ELN leaders refusing to respond to the government after President Uribe's November 2007 termination of Venezuelan president Hugo Chávez's mediating role. Bermudez announced his departure from the ELN in early 2008.

The ELN's top command structure has been weakened by the government's military campaigns, and ELN forces have been on the short end of armed confrontations with the FARC in Arauca and Nariño departments over oil profits and drug smuggling routes. The ELN refused to demobilize under the terms of the justice and peace law, however, and reiterated the demand for a constituent assembly for formulating social and economic reforms as a precondition. The group refused a government demand that an ELN cease-fire include the guerrillas' concentration in specific zones, which the ELN viewed as tantamount to surrender.

One small splinter group of the ELN known as the *Ejército Revolucionario del Pueblo*—ERP, operating in Bolívar department, demobilized in April 2007.

In 2008 ELN activity diminished, and 18 rebels and 45 breakaway group members surrendered to the government. Violence increased in 2009, particularly in the departments of Arauca, Bolívar, and Nariño, owing largely to the group's increased involvement in drug trafficking. In July the government seized explosives from ELN rebels in the department of Boyaca, preventing an attack on Colombian Independence Day. In November 2010 and again in April 2011, José Nicolás Rodriguez Bautista, the ELN's leader, released statements announcing interest in a peaceful resolution to the conflict. The government did not respond to either statement because of firm preconditions that any insurgent group hoping to negotiate with the authorities must stop taking hostages, conducting attacks, and trafficking in drugs.

ELN documents captured during a jungle raid in July 2011 showed that the group was strategizing an attitude of dialogue with the FARC and indicated that relations between the two had improved. In August the group, estimated to total 1,500 guerrillas, announced that it would change its tactics to counter a new offensive announced by President Santos.

Leaders: José Nicolás RODRIGUEZ Bautista (a.k.a. Gabino) (Political Commander), Antonio GARCIA (Military Commander), Pablo BELTRAN, Juan Carlos CUELLAR, Oscar SANTOS.

Revolutionary Armed Forces of Colombia (*Fuerzas Armadas Revolucionarias de Colombia*—FARC). Founded in 1964 by radicalized peasants, the FARC was long a Moscow-line guerrilla group affiliated with the now moribund **Communist Party of Colombia** (*Partido Comunista de Colombia*—PCC). In late 1983 it indicated a willingness to conclude a cease-fire agreement, which was formalized in March 1984. The agreement was renewed on March 2, 1986, in return for which the Betancur government guaranteed (without conspicuous fulfillment) the safety of electoral candidates advanced by the FARC's alleged political wing, the Patriotic Union. Inconclusive peace talks with the government were resumed in late 1989, with the group formally joining the CNGSB a year later, shortly after the death of its cofounder, Luis Alberto MORANTES (a.k.a. Jacobo Arenas). FARC's urban wing is known as the **Bolivarian Militias** (*Milicias Bolivarianas*), which was significantly weakened by the Uribe government's urban-focused security policies.

In July 1998 President-elect Pastrana held an unprecedented jungle meeting with FARC commander Manuel MARULANDA Vélez, after which Pastrana declared that he would comply with the rebels' demands for withdrawal of government forces from five southern municipalities as a precondition for peace talks that would commence subsequent to his August inauguration. On January 7, 1999, Pastrana participated in a ceremonial launching of the talks in San Vincente del Caguán. Although Marulanda failed to appear because of alleged threats against his life, Pastrana insisted that his absence would not derail the peace process. However, the FARC withdrew from the peace negotiations temporarily later in the month in the wake of increased activity by the AUC. The FARC would go on to suspend the talks on numerous occasions. The demilitarized zone was extended eleven times between 1999 and 2002, while the negotiators failed to move from procedural issues to more substantive topics. After the FARC hijacked an aircraft and kidnapped a senator on February 20, 2002, President Pastrana declared the FARC peace talks over.

Fueled by proceeds from its drug trade, the FARC grew rapidly during the 1990s, reaching approximately 18,000 members by the early 2000s. The guerrilla group, which is unpopular in Colombia because of its human rights record, has suffered reversals during the years of the Uribe and Santos presidencies.

In May 2008 it was reported that the FARC's paramount leader and cofounder, Pedro Antonio MARIN (a.k.a. Manuel MARULANDA), had died. He was replaced by FARC Secretariat member Guillermo León Saenz Vargas (a.k.a. Alfonso CANO).

In June 2009, in what was reported as "a heavy blow" to FARC, the military killed three associates of a key FARC commander, Jorge Torres Victoria (a.k.a. Pablo Catatumbo), who allegedly controlled cocaine distribution policies. The U.S. State Department was reported to be offering a $2.5 million reward for the capture of Torres.

In January 2011 FARC supreme commander Saenz released a statement promising to redouble activities throughout the year. Soon after, FARC rebels attacked the home of the mayor of Puerto Asis and killed his grandson. The attack was suspected to be retribution for the killing of five FARC rebels by government forces in a gunfight a few days earlier. The group was blamed the next month for two roadside bombs that injured 29 soldiers in Aracua department and for a failed attack in March on a military base in Puerto Asis. By midyear the FARC had executed several more bombing raids that killed a number of civilians and kidnapped three Chinese oil workers. The group also started operations to influence the coming October regional elections.

After the Santos administration successfully shepherded a new Victims Law to promulgation in June 2011, a newspaper interview with FARC commander Saenz was published in which he called for a negotiated solution to the protracted conflict with the government. Santos quickly rejected the proposition until the FARC met government demands to release hostages and minors serving in its ranks and completely demobilize itself. Observers said the group had lost momentum under pressure from the Santos administration, with membership falling to 8,000 by early 2012. Following Saenz's death in a military attack in November 2011, FARC announced the selection of a new leader, Rodrigo Londoño ECHEVERRI (a.k.a. Timoleón JIMENEZ or Timochenko). In 2012 FARC launched **Patriotic March** (*Marcha Patriotica*), a civic movement that could become the basis of a political party.

Leaders: Rodrigo Londoño ECHEVERRI (a.k.a. Timoleón JIMENEZ or Timochenko) (Supreme Commander), Luciano Marín ARANGO (a.k.a. Iván MARQUEZ), Milton de Jesús TONCEL (a.k.a. Joaquín GOMEZ), Jaime Alberto PARRA (a.k.a. Mauricio JARAMILLO or "The Doctor"), Jorge TORRES Victoria.

The **United Self-Defense Groups of Colombia** (*Autodefensas Unidas de Colombia*—AUC) was the most prominent right-wing paramilitary grouping. It was organized in 1996 to coordinate the activity of about 20 smaller organizations. Many of these groups had been founded by drug traffickers, large landowners, businessmen, conservative politicians, and military factions as counterinsurgent militias, with the goal of reducing the influence of guerrillas and leftist political activists.

Until 2003, the leader of the AUC was Carlos CASTAÑO, who had earlier formed the Cordoba and Uraba Self-Defense Union (*Autodefensas Unidas de Córdoba y Urabá*—ACCU) following the death of his father, a wealthy landowner, reportedly at the hands of leftist guerrillas. At its zenith in the late 1990s and early 2000s, the AUC was responsible for the majority of human rights abuses in Colombia, and Colombia's security forces faced widespread accusations of collusion with the rightist militias.

In mid-2001 the AUC claimed that 5,000 new recruits had joined its ranks, bringing their total to 13,000. During the early 2000s, the group became more divided over the question of drug trafficking, an important source of its income. Castaño, who opposed the increasing influence of drug lords in the group, was later murdered by his own men in 2004.

In 2002 the AUC entered into peace talks with the Colombian government; beginning in November 2003, 27 of the AUC's component blocs—32,000 people in all—participated in demobilization ceremonies, turning in about 15,000 weapons. However, there have been reports that some within the junior leadership refused to participate in the demobilization process and were still heavily involved in drug trafficking. Moreover, demobilized members who soured on the peace process were joining the holdouts and resuming paramilitary activities.

In May 2008 14 of the AUC's leaders were extradited to the United States, where they faced narcotrafficking charges. The state of the groups' leadership, and its dominion over criminal activity in Colombia, remained unclear, and the AUC entity began to be viewed by outside observers as being disbanded. By mid-2009 estimates of new groups, at least partly led by former mid-level AUC leaders, reportedly claimed between 4,000 and 10,000 members. Some of the most commonly named paramilitary groups were the **Black Eagles, *Rastrojos,* New Generation, Office of Envigado,** and ***Cuchillos.*** Many were engaged principally in drug trafficking and claimed to do drug business with guerrillas, rather than identifying themselves as counterinsurgency groups. A former paramilitary believed to have been a principal sponsor of some of the new groups, Daniel RENDÓN Herrera (or "Don Mario") was arrested in April 2009. A Colombian NGO report at the end of 2009 stated that new paramilitary groups were being formed throughout the country by demobilized former members of AUC. The groups were said to have as many as 11,000 guerrillas.

In December 2010 a former AUC commander, Jorge Ivan LAVERDE Zapata (or El Iguana), was sentenced to eight years in prison for the murders of at least 28 people. Laverde confessed during his trial that he had ordered the killing of more than 4,000 people. AUC commanders Hector GERMAN Buitrago (Martin Llanos) and his brother, Nelson BUITRAGO Parada, were arrested in Venezuela and extradited to Colombia in February 2012 on murder, kidnapping, and other charges. Justice officials began investigating diamond dealer Victor CARRANZA on suspicion of financing the AUC in the 1990s.

LEGISLATURE

The Colombian **Congress** (*Congreso*) is a bicameral legislature consisting of a Senate and a Chamber of Representatives, each elected for a four-year term. From 1958 to 1974 both houses were theoretically divided equally between Liberals and Conservatives, although members of other groups could run as nominal candidates of one of the two major parties and thus gain representation.

Since 2006 numerous lawmakers have resigned from Congress, most of them forced to do so to confront allegations related to the parapolitics scandals. The party of any legislator who resigns remains in control of the seat, with the party naming as replacement the runner-up candidate on the party list. (Some seats have been occupied by as many as five lawmakers since 2006.)

Senate (*Senado de la República*). The upper house is composed of 102 members, including 2 elected to represent indigenous communities.

In the most recent election of March 14, 2010, the seat distribution was as follows: the Social Party of National Unity, 27; Colombian Conservative Party, 23; Colombian Liberal Party, 17; National Integration Party, 9; Radical Change, 8; Alternative Democratic Pole, 8; Colombian Green Party, 5; Independent Movement of Absolute Renovation, 3; Indigenous Social Alliance, 1; Indigenous Authorities of Colombia Movement, 1.

President: Juan Fernando CRISTO Bustos.

Chamber of Representatives (*Cámara de Representantes*). The lower house has 166 members, with each department being entitled to at least 2 representatives and 5 seats being set aside for special representation (2 for Afro-Colombians, 1 for indigenous persons, 1 for Colombians living abroad, and 1 for other political minorities).

The seat distribution for the most recent election, March 14, 2010, was as follows: Social Party of National Unity, 48; Colombian Liberal Party, 38; Colombian Conservative Party, 36; Radical Change, 16; National Integration Party, 11; Alternative Democratic Pole, 5; Colombian Green Party, 3; Liberal Opening Movement, 2; Independent Movement of Absolute Renovation, 1; Indigenous Social Alliance, 1; Liberal Alternative of Social Advance, 1; Civic Compromise for Colombia, 1; Afro Vides, 1; and Regional Integration Movement, 1.

President: Hernán PENAGOS Giraldo.

CABINET

[as of October 11, 2013]

President	Juan Manuel Santos Calderon (PSUN)
Vice President	Angelino Garzón (PSUN)
Ministers	
Agriculture and Rural Development	Ruben Dario Lizarralde (PSUN)
Culture	Mariana Garcés Córdoba (ind.) [f]
Education	María Fernanda Campo Saavedra (ind.) [f]
Environment	Luz Helena Sarmiento (PSUN) [f]
Finance and Public Credit	Mauricio Cardenas Santa Maria (PC)
Foreign Affairs	María Ángela Holguín Cuéllar (ind.) [f]

Foreign Trade, Industry, and Tourism	Sergio Díaz Granados (PSUN)
Housing, Urban Affairs, and Territorial Development	Luis Felipe Henao (ind.)
Information and Communication Technologies	Diego Molano Vega (PL)
Interior	Aurelio Iragorri Valencia (PSUN)
Justice	Alfonso Gomez Mendez (PSUN)
Labor	Rafael Pardo Rueda (PL)
Mines and Energy	Amylkar Acosta (PSUN)
National Defense	Juan Carlos Pinzon Bueno (PSUN)
Transport	Cecilia Orozco (ind.) [f]

[f] = female

INTERGOVERNMENTAL REPRESENTATION

Ambassador to the U.S.: Carlos URRUTIA Valenzuela.

U.S. Ambassador to Colombia: P. Michael McKINLEY.

Permanent Representative to the UN: Néstor OSORIO.

IGO Memberships (Non-UN): IADB, ICC, IOM, Mercosur, NAM, OAS, WTO.

COMOROS

Union of the Comoros
Union des Comores (French)

Political Status: Former French dependency; proclaimed independent July 6, 1975; Federal Islamic Republic of the Comoros proclaimed in constitution approved by national referendum on October 1, 1978; constitution of October 20, 1996, suspended following military coup of April 30, 1999; new constitution providing for the Union of the Comoros adopted by national referendum on December 23, 2001.

Area: 718 sq. mi. (1,860 sq. km), excluding the island of Mahoré (Mayotte), which voted in 1976 to retain its affiliation with France as a "Territorial Collectivity," subsequently became classified as a French "Overseas Collectivity," and in 2009 voted to extend its relationship further by becoming an "Overseas Department" (achieved in March 2011).

Population: 775,870 (2012E—UN); 752,288 (2013E—U.S. Census). Excludes residents of Mayotte (see section on Related Territories in the entry on France).

Major Urban Centers (2005E): MORONI (Ngazidja [Grande Comore], 43,000), Mutsamudu (Nzwani [Anjouan], 24,000), Fomboni (Mwali [Mohéli], 13,000).

Official Languages: Arabic, French, Comorian (Skikomor, a Bantu language that is primarily a mixture of Arabic and Swahili; variants are spoken on each island).

Monetary Unit: Comoros Franc (official rate November 1, 2013: 364.89 francs = $1US). The Comoros franc is permanently pegged to the euro at 491.968 francs = 1 euro.

President of the Union: Ikililou DHOININE (Mwali); elected in Union-wide runoff balloting on December 26, 2010, and sworn in for a five-year term on May 26, 2011, in succession to Ahmed Abdallah Mohamed SAMBI (Nzwani).

President (Governor) of Mwali (Mohéli): Mohamed Ali SAÏD; directly elected in runoff balloting on June 24, 2007, and sworn in for a five-year term on July 1 in succession to Mohamed Saïd FAZUL; term shortened by one year in 2009; reelected in runoff balloting on December 26, 2010, and sworn in for a five-year term on May 23, 2011.

President (Governor) of Ngazidja (Grande Comore): Mouigni BARAKA Said Soilihi; elected in runoff balloting on December 26, 2010, and sworn in for a five-year term on May 23, 2011, in succession to Mohamed ABDOULOIHABI.

President (Governor) of Nzwani (Anjouan): Anissi CHAMSIDINE; elected in runoff balloting on December 26, 2010, and inaugurated for a five-year term on May 23, 2011, in succession to Moussa TOYBOU.

THE COUNTRY

Located in the Indian Ocean between Madagascar and the eastern coast of Africa, the Union of the Comoros consists of three main islands: Mwali (Mohéli); Ngazidja (Grande Comore), site of the capital, Moroni; and Nzwani (Anjouan). A fourth component of the archipelago, Mahoré (Mayotte), is claimed as national territory but remains under French administration (see France: Related Territories). The indigenous inhabitants in the Comoros derive from a mixture of Arab, Malagasy, and African strains. Islam is the state religion (as codified in the May 2009 constitutional revision); most Muslims are Sunnis. Leaders of the small Shiite community (primarily on Nzwani) have objected recently to anti-Shiite rhetoric on the part of Sunni clerics and government officials.

Volcanic in origin, the islands are mountainous, with a climate that is tropical during the rainy season and more temperate during the dry season. There has been no significant mineral exploitation to date, and soil conditions are poor on the more populous islands of Nzwani and Ngazidja. Economically, the islands have long suffered from an overemphasis on the production of a few export crops, such as vanilla, cloves, olives, and perfume essences—the latter shipped primarily to France—and an insufficient cultivation of food, particularly rice, needed for local consumption. Most of the population is engaged in subsistence agriculture, and manufacturing is practically nonexistent. (Industry accounts for only 4 percent of GDP.) The government remains highly dependent on foreign assistance to cover administrative and developmental expenses as well as trade deficits. Annual per capita income is currently estimated at less than $900, and more than half of the people live below the poverty line. Remittances from Comorians living abroad (particularly on Mayotte) contribute significantly to the economy.

Development has been severely hampered since independence in 1975 by some 20 coups or coup attempts, sustained interisland conflict, and widespread corruption. Per capita annual income declined in the 1990s, while real GDP growth was marginal throughout most of the decade before falling by 1.1 percent in 2000 in the wake of severe political uncertainty following a bloodless military coup in April 1999. The turmoil also depressed tourism, impeded government economic plans, and precipitated a sharp decline in donor support. However, the international community pledged substantial aid in 2002 in response to negotiations that had led to the establishment of the Union of the Comoros (see Political background, below), which proponents hoped would, among other things, resolve separatist pressures on Nzwani. However, the International Monetary Fund (IMF) rejected a request from the Comoros for additional assistance, citing continued power-sharing contention between the island governments and the Union government.

After nearly a year of political conflict between the Union government and the self-proclaimed government on Nzwani ended with a Union military victory in March 2008, the Union government, IMF, and development banks expressed hope that focus could return to negotiations regarding badly needed debt cancellation or rescheduling. The Union government also pledged to combat deep-rooted poverty and other social problems. The IMF in 2009 described the government's fiscal efforts as "broadly satisfactory" and approved lending for poverty alleviation. In April 2010 the Fund and the World Bank also deemed the Comoros eligible for debt relief, based on ongoing structural reform. The new government installed in 2011 pledged to continue the pursuit of structural reform, while analysts subsequently noted an uptick in interest from foreign investors in light of the apparent easing of political tensions in the Comoros and the granting of the country's first offshore exploration contract.

In December 2012 the IMF and the World Bank announced a debt-relief package for the Comoros valued at approximately $176 million. The Paris Club followed that lead in March 2013 by canceling $8 million

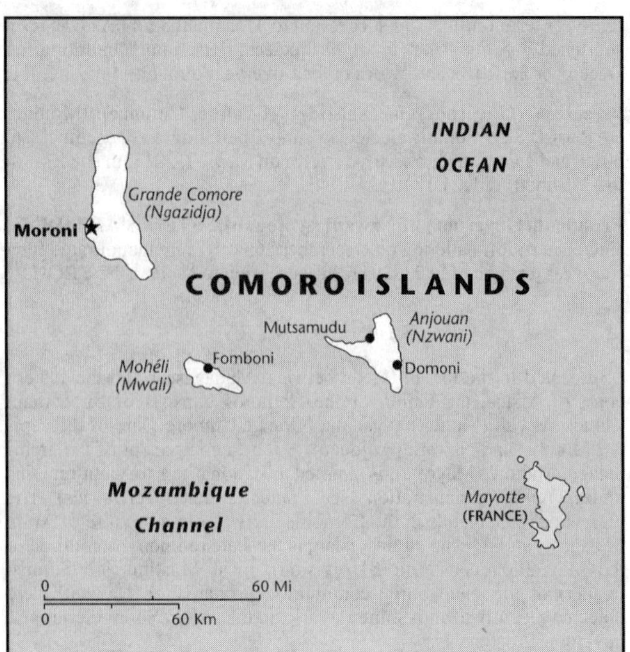

of the Comoros' $12 million in debt from private and/or bilateral creditors. Meanwhile, GDP grew by 3 percent in 2012 under the influence of stronger domestic demand and government investment in infrastructure.

GOVERNMENT AND POLITICS

Political background. Ruled for centuries by Arab sultans and first visited by Europeans in the 16th century, the Comoro archipelago came under French rule in the 19th century. Mayotte became a French protectorate in 1843, while Anjouan, Grande Comore, and Mohéli were added to the protectorate in 1886. In 1912 the islands were joined administratively with Madagascar, from which they were governed until after World War II. Because of the lengthy period of indirect rule, the Comoros suffered comparative neglect, as contrasted with the nearby island of Réunion, which became an overseas French department in 1946.

In the wake of a 1968 student strike in the Comoros that was suppressed by French police and troops, France agreed to permit the formation of legal political parties in the archipelago. In December 1972, 34 of the 39 seats in the Comorian Chamber of Deputies were claimed by a coalition of proindependence parties: the Democratic Rally of the Comorian People, led by Prince Saïd Mohamed JAFFAR; the Party for the Evolution of the Comoros, which was linked to the Tanzanian-based National Liberation Movement of the Comoros; and the Democratic Union of the Comoros, led by Ahmed ABDALLAH Abderemane. The other 5 seats were won by the anti-independence Popular Movement of Mahoré, headed by Marcel HENRY. As a result of the election, the chamber named Abdallah president of the government, succeeding Prince Saïd IBRAHIM, who had served as coleader with Ali SOILIH of the People's Party (*Umma-Mranda*), which had campaigned for a more gradual movement toward independence. The new government immediately began negotiations with France, and an agreement was reached in July 1973 providing for a five-year transition period during which France would retain responsibility for defense, foreign affairs, and currency. The only unresolved issue was the status of Mayotte, whose inhabitants remained strongly opposed to separation from France.

In a Comorian referendum held December 22, 1974, 95 percent of participating voters favored independence, despite a negative vote from Mayotte, where 25 percent of the registered electorate abstained. On July 6, 1975, a unilateral declaration of independence was approved by the territorial Chamber of Deputies, which designated Abdallah as head of state and prime minister. The action was timed to preempt the passage of legislation by the French National Assembly calling for an island-by-island referendum on a Comorian constitution—a procedure designed to allow Mayotte to remain under French jurisdiction. Having announced his intention to sever economic as well as political ties with France, the increasingly dictatorial Abdallah (who was visiting Anjouan at the time) was ousted on August 3 in a coup led by Ali Soilih and supported by a National United Front of several parties. On August 10 governmental power was vested in a 12-member National Executive Council headed by Prince Jaffar, who was appointed president and prime minister. In September, following an armed invasion of Anjouan by forces under Soilih, Abdallah surrendered. He was subsequently exiled.

At a joint meeting of the National Executive Council and the National Council of the Revolution on January 2, 1976, Soilih was named to replace Jaffar as head of state, and the National Council of the Revolution was redesignated as the National Institutional Council. The presidency was also divorced from the premiership, and on January 6 Abdellahi MOHAMED was named to the latter post.

As president, Soilih encountered substantial resistance in attempting to mount a Chinese-style program designed to "abolish feudalism." During a month-long *"Période Noire"* in 1977, he dismissed civil servants, temporarily dismantled the regular governmental machinery, and vested the "people's power" in a 16-member National People's Committee of recent secondary-school graduates. The "revolution" also included establishment of people's committees at island, district, and local levels, despite numerous skirmishes between people's militia forces and Islamic traditionalists. Between April 1976 and January 1978, at least three unsuccessful countercoups against the regime were mounted.

During the night of May 12–13, 1978, President Soilih was ousted by a group of about 50 mercenaries under the command of Col. Bob DENARD (the alias of Gilbert BOURGEAUD), a Frenchman previously involved in rebellions elsewhere in Africa and southern Arabia. The successful coup resulted in the return of Ahmed Abdallah, who joined Mohamed AHMED as copresidents of a Political-Military Directorate that also included Denard. It was subsequently reported that Soilih had been killed on May 29 in an attempt to escape from house arrest. An exclusive "political directorate" was announced on July 22 in view of the "calm" that had resulted from a decision to return to traditional Islamic principles.

Copresident Ahmed resigned on October 3, 1978, following the approval by referendum two days earlier of a new constitution that had proclaimed the establishment of the Federal Islamic Republic of the Comoros. Abdallah was thus enabled to stand as the sole candidate in presidential balloting held October 22. Following a legislative election that concluded on December 15, Salim Ben ALI was designated prime minister, a post he continued to hold until he was dismissed by the president on January 25, 1982. Ali's successor, Foreign Minister Ali MROUDJAE, was appointed on February 8, with the rest of the cabinet being named a week later. President Abdallah was unopposed in his bid for reelection to a second six-year term on September 30, 1984.

Amid evidence of serious dissent within the government, President Abdallah subsequently secured a number of constitutional amendments that, among other things, abolished the position of prime minister and reduced the powers of the Federal Assembly, prompting an unsuccessful coup attempt by junior members of the presidential guard on March 8, 1985, while the chief executive was on a private visit to Paris. Subsequently, the Democratic Front, a Paris-based opposition group, was charged with complicity in the revolt. Many of the front's domestic supporters were sentenced to life imprisonment in early November, although some were granted presidential amnesty at the end of the year.

At legislative balloting on March 22, 1987 (denounced as manifestly fraudulent by regime opponents), the entire slate of 42 candidates presented by President Abdallah was declared elected. Ostensibly open to any citizen wishing to compete as an independent, polls on two of the islands (Anjouan and Mohéli) involved only presidential nominees. By contrast, opposition candidates were advanced in 20 constituencies on Grande Comore. In November the president survived another coup attempt with the assistance of Colonel Denard who, although officially retired, had remained in control of the country's small security force.

On November 4, 1989, an ostensible 92 percent of the participants in a national referendum approved a constitutional amendment permitting Abdallah to seek a third term. However, on November 27 Abdallah was assassinated in a reported clash between the Presidential Guard and forces loyal to a former army commander, Ahmed MOHAMED. (Subsequent evidence suggested that Abdallah had been killed by his own troops on the order of Colonel Denard.) Abdallah was succeeded on an interim basis by the president of the Supreme Court, Saïd Mohamed DJOHAR, who was elected to a regular six-year term on March 4 and 11, 1990, in the country's first contested presidential balloting since independence. Three months earlier, Denard, who denied complicity in the Abdallah assassination, was deported (in the company of some 30 other mercenaries) to South Africa, with the Presidential Guard being supplanted by a contingent of French paratroopers. The latter were credited with thwarting a coup attempt by four mercenaries allegedly linked to Mohamed TAKI Abdoulkarim, the runner-up in the March presidential poll, on the weekend of August 18–19.

On August 3, 1991, the new president of the Supreme Court, Ibrahim Ahmed HALIDI, failed in an attempt to oust President Djohar by judicial impeachment and was arrested, along with a number of colleagues. Ten days later, amid mounting social unrest, public demonstrations were banned, and on August 27 a major cabinet shakeup was announced, from which the president's own party, the Comorian Union for Progress (*Union Comorienne pour le Progrès*—UCP/*Udzima*), dissociated itself.

In October 1991 five domestic participants in an Opposition Union accepted an invitation from the exiled Mohamed Taki to meet in Paris to discuss the formation of an interim government of national union and the scheduling of a National Conference. Subsequently, Taki and his associates met with President Djohar in Paris, and on November 25 Taki and Djohar returned together to Moroni. Halidi and the other detainees from the failed impeachment effort in August were released on December 2, and on December 17 President Djohar announced his willingness to enter into a pact of reconciliation with his opponents, on condition that they not challenge the legitimacy of his incumbency or attempt to destabilize the regime. On December 31, upon endorsement of the pact by all of the recognized parties, Djohar dissolved the existing government. On January 6, 1992, he appointed a broadly based nine-member successor, with Taki described vaguely as "coordinator of government action."

A long-sought National Conference, encompassing nearly two dozen parties, met January 24–April 8, 1992, and approved the draft of a new constitution. On May 8 President Djohar announced the formation of a new cabinet headed by Taki, and the new constitution was endorsed by a 74 percent majority in a national referendum on June 7. Although Taki's cabinet had been scheduled to serve until the next election, the president dismissed the government on July 4 following Taki's designation of a former mercenary as the country's international investment adviser. A new transitional administration was named with no ministerial head.

On September 26, 1992, while President Djohar was visiting Paris, a group of some 30 officers from the Defense Forces mounted a coup attempt, which was put down the following day. Additional clashes occurred on October 13 and 21, with the president, at opposition insistence, announcing a third postponement of the next legislative poll to November 8. In first-round balloting that had been further deferred until November 22, only 4 of 42 seats were filled outright. A second round on November 29 was scarcely more conclusive, with none of the 22 participating groups winning a majority of seats.

The vacant post of prime minister was filled on January 1, 1993, with the appointment of Ibrahim Abderemane HALIDI (not related to Ibrahim Ahmed Halidi), who announced the appointment of a 12-member cabinet five days later. A period of extreme instability ensued. On February 25 the president ordered an extensive cabinet reshuffle, and on May 19 Prime Minister Halidi was himself ousted by a parliamentary vote of no confidence for his "manifest inability to rally support" and the "inability of the government to cope with social problems." On May 25 the president called upon Saïd Ali MOHAMED to form a new government, which, however, drew support from only 13 of the 42 legislators. Thus, to forestall another no-confidence vote, the president on June 18 dissolved the assembly. Despite a declaration of support for Mohamed at the time of dissolution, President Djohar dismissed Mohamed the following day, naming a former adviser, Ahmed Ben Cheikh ATTOUMANE, as the new prime minister.

Although the constitution called for legislative balloting within 40 days of the assembly's dissolution, a series of postponements delayed the poll until mid-December 1993. In the wake of the first cancellation, the president issued a decree ousting Electoral Commission members deemed hostile to the administration. A second decree established new constituency boundaries and revoked a requirement that ministers resign before standing for election. Both were branded as unconstitutional, and in early November, President Djohar, in a concession to the opposition, removed the incumbent chair of the Electoral Commission.

Despite the blatant gerrymandering and other irregularities, all four individuals elected in first-round legislative balloting on December 12, 1993, were from the opposition, with the second round on December 20 characterized in one report as a "veritable masquerade." Thus, after the opposition had appeared to have swept the entire island of Anjouan, the voting was declared "null and void." The interior ministry then pronounced that government candidates had triumphed on Anjouan, while on Mohéli the secretary general of the presidency, whose candidacy had been formally invalidated in the first round, was permitted to contest the second. Understandably, the opposition called for cancellation of the second-round results, failing which it announced that it would participate in no further electoral activity and would take up no seats in the Federal Assembly.

On January 2, 1994, President Djohar named Mohamed Abdou MADI, secretary general of the recently launched Rally for Democracy and Renewal (*Rassemblement pour la Démocratie et le Renouveau*—RDR), to head a new government of regime supporters. In the wake of a scandal following attempted privatization of the national air carrier (*Air Comores*), coupled with a prolonged strike by schoolteachers and hospital workers, Prime Minister Madi was dismissed on October 13 and replaced by a relatively obscure education official, Halifa HOUMADI. In the ninth government change in 40 months, Houmadi was himself replaced on April 29, 1995, by former finance minister Mohamed Caabi El YACHROUTU.

The last four months of 1995 were marked by a degree of instability that was remarkable even by Comorian standards. On the night of September 27–28, Colonel Denard reappeared as the leader of some 30 mercenaries who, with local support, seized President Djohar and established a "military committee of transition" headed by a little-known army captain, Ayouba COMBO. Meanwhile, Prime Minister Yachroutu, who had sought refuge in the French embassy, called on France to intervene. On October 3 Combo announced that he was withdrawing in favor of Mohamed Taki Abdoulkarim and Prince Saïd Ali KEMAL as civilian joint presidents. The next day 900 French troops landed and quickly rounded up the mercenaries. (Paris courts in 2006 and 2007 found Denard and others guilty of various charges in connection with the 1995 coup attempt, although all received suspended sentences, fueling speculation that some French intelligence sectors may have been aware of Denard's plans in advance. Denard died in October 2007.) The French troops did not, however, reinstate the 80-year-old Djohar, who was flown to the nearby French island of Réunion, with Yachroutu proclaiming himself "interim president in accordance with the constitution." Yachroutu thereupon named a new Government of National Unity, which Djohar repudiated from Réunion by announcing a rival government headed by former prime minister Saïd Ali Mohamed.

On December 3, 1995, a somewhat diverse group of Comorian political leaders assembled in Paris in an effort to persuade Yachroutu to cancel a snap presidential election that he had scheduled for January 21, 1996. Yachroutu responded by calling for two-stage balloting on January 28 and February 7, arguing that although the dates fell within the month-long Muslim feast of Ramadan, postponement would mean loss of Comorian consideration in the current cycle of World Bank/IMF structural-adjustment programming. Subsequently, however, he relented and postponed the voting to March 6 and 16. He also agreed to send representatives to a conference sponsored by the Organization of African Unity (OAU, subsequently the African Union—AU) in Madagascar concerning Djohar's status. The gathering yielded agreement on January 23, 1996, that Djohar would return to Moroni as president but would cease to have any executive authority forthwith and would accept a new electoral code that effectively barred him from seeking reelection by specifying an obligatory 40–70 age range for a presidential candidate. With some 50 French troops remaining on station to guarantee order, presidential balloting accordingly went ahead on March 6 and 16, with 15 candidates contesting the first round. Of these, Mohamed Taki Abdulkarim of the National Union for Democracy in the Comoros (*Union National pour la Démocratie aux Comores*—UNDC) headed the first round with 21.3 percent of the vote. He secured a 64.3 percent second-round victory over Abbas DJOUSSOUF, leader of the Movement for Democracy and Progress, standing as candidate of the Forum for National Recovery (*Forum pour le Redressement National*—FRN).

Sworn in on March 25, 1996, President Taki assigned the premiership to Tadjidine Ben Saïd MASSONDE (UCP/*Udzima*), who named a government on March 28 that included several of the candidates eliminated in the recent first round of presidential balloting. On April 11 President Taki dissolved the assembly and announced that new balloting would take place on October 6 (notwithstanding the constitutional requirement of elections within 40 days of dissolution), adding that a referendum on a new constitution would be held before the end of June (later rescheduled to October). In August, Taki formally proposed the establishment of a single "presidential" party, with opposition forces grouped into two parties. Among the critics of the proposal were two government parties, both of whom subsequently lost their cabinet postings. On October 6 the propresidential National Rally for Development (*Rassemblement National pour le Développement*—RND) was formed, Taki confidante Ali Bazi SELIM being named to head the group.

On October 20, 1996, 85 percent of those voting in a national referendum approved a new constitution that increased presidential powers and restricted political party formations. The new charter had been championed by Taki and the RND, but its controversial amendments had elicited opposition condemnation and calls for a boycott of the referendum. Thereafter, relations between the administration and opposition continued to deteriorate, and on November 10, 1996, the opposition announced that it would boycott the upcoming legislative elections after the government refused to establish an independent electoral commission. Consequently, in balloting on December 1 and 8, RND candidates faced little competition, capturing an overwhelming majority of the assembly seats being contested, with the remaining seats being secured by the Islamic National Front for Justice (*Front National pour la Justice*—FNJ) and an independent candidate. On December 27 Ahmed ABDOU, a former assistant to ex-president Abdallah, was named prime minister, replacing Massonde, who had resigned on December 11.

Antigovernment strikes and violent demonstrations erupted in early 1997, sparked by the Taki administration's failure to fulfill an earlier pledge to pay civil-servant salary arrears. On Anjouan, where the government's increasing inability to provide basic services had already fueled simmering secessionist emotions, the unrest quickly gained intensity. In mid-March deadly clashes erupted between strikers and government security forces following the arrest of Abdou ZAKARIA, the leader of the Democratic Front Party (*Parti du Front Démocratique*—PFD). Subsequently, amid reports that the demonstrators were in open rebellion, the government dismissed the Anjouan governor.

Following the arrest of secessionist leader Abdallah IBRAHIM and the banning of antigovernment parties in late July 1997, full-scale rioting broke out in the Anjouan capital of Mutsamudu. Thereafter, separatist militants affiliated with the Anjouan People's Movement (*Mouvement du Peuple d'Anjouan*—MPA) gained control over key island facilities. On August 3 the MPA declared independence from the Comoros government and announced its intention to petition France for a return to overseas territory status. On August 5 the MPA named Ibrahim, who had been released from detention, president of the breakaway state and head of a 12-member cabinet. Meanwhile, separatists on Mohéli also declared their independence. For its part, France rebuffed the entreaties from the secessionists and urged them to respect Comoros' "territorial integrity." Subsequently, under pressure from the OAU, which had also refused to recognize the declaration of independence, the MPA agreed to participate in reconciliation talks with the Taki administration in September.

On September 3, 1997, seaborne government forces attempting to regain control of Anjouan suffered heavy casualties while being repelled by separatist fighters, who also took dozens of the "invaders" captive. The government's ill-fated offensive, which it had at first declared a success, drew sharp OAU criticism, and reconciliation talks were indefinitely postponed. On September 8 Ibrahim announced the creation of the "State of Anjouan" and declared that he would rule by decree. Meanwhile, amid rumors in Moroni of an impending military coup, President Taki dissolved the Abdou government and assumed absolute power on September 9. On September 13 Taki formed a State Transition Committee, an advisory body that included three representatives from Anjouan and two from Mohéli.

On October 26, 1997, secessionist officials in Anjouan organized a referendum on independence that reportedly received a 99 percent affirmative vote. Two days later Ibrahim was formally appointed head of the provisional government of Nzwani (the island's traditional name having been readopted by the secessionists) and was charged with drafting a constitution and preparing for elections. Such efforts were delayed, however, when in mid-November Ibrahim's provisional government again succumbed to OAU pressure and agreed to attend talks with the Taki administration in December. On December 7 Taki appointed Nourdine BOURHANE, a former cabinet official with ties to Nzwani, to head a government that included a number of members of the State Transition Committee.

From December 10 to 14, 1997, representatives of the Taki government and secessionist representatives from Nzwani and Mwali met in Ethiopia for OAU-sponsored "reconciliation" talks, which failed to yield any major breakthroughs. In mid-February 1998 fighting erupted on Nzwani between Ibrahim's forces and a dissident faction led by former prime minister Mohamed Abdou Madi, who, Ibrahim claimed, had the backing of the OAU. Unable to dislodge Ibrahim, Madi was forced to flee, and a number of his fighters were arrested.

At a constitutional referendum on February 25, 1998, voters on Nzwani reportedly approved a basic document that called for the revocation of all Comorian laws. Thereafter, despite OAU calls for the secessionists to delay further provocations, Ibrahim named CHAMASSI Ben Saïd Omar as prime minister of Nzwani in March. However, Ibrahim and his new prime minister subsequently clashed, and in July Chamassi and his supporters reportedly attempted to oust Ibrahim. Fighting among the various factions on Nzwani, including Madi's reorganized militants, continued through the end of 1998.

Following violent antigovernment rioting by civil servants in Moroni in mid-May 1998, Taki dismissed the Bourhane government on May 29. The following day he named a cabinet that did not include a prime minister.

On November 5, 1998, President Taki died of a heart attack. The following day former prime minister Tadjidine Ben Saïd Massonde assumed the presidency as constitutionally mandated because of his position as president of the High Council of the Republic (the country's constitutional court). On November 22 Massonde named the FRN's Abbas Djoussouf to head an interim government. Djoussouf's appointment and subsequent formation of an FRN-dominated (with six ministers) cabinet was denounced by the RND, whose governmental representation had fallen to four posts. Meanwhile, Massonde called for a loosening of economic sanctions against the secessionists on Nzwani and appealed to their leaders to participate in an internationally sponsored, interisland conference. However, plans for the meeting were derailed by the outbreak of fierce fighting on Nzwani in December 1998. Subsequently, Massonde announced that presidential elections would be postponed until the secessionist crisis was resolved, and in February 1999 the High Court approved the extension of his mandate.

At an OAU-mediated conference in Madagascar on April 19–25, 1999, representatives from Ngazidja, Nzwani, and Mwali tentatively reached agreement on a pact that would have granted the latter two increased autonomy within the republic (to be restyled the Union of Comorian Islands). General elections consequently were scheduled for April 2000. The delegation from Nzwani departed, however, without signing the accord, and violent demonstrations subsequently erupted on Ngazidja, where protesters reportedly chanted anti-Nzwani slogans and attacked people who had been born on Nzwani. On April 30, Armed Forces Chief of Staff Col. Assoumani AZALI announced that, in an effort to stem the unrest, the military had assumed control of the country, ousted the president and government, and suspended the constitution, legislature, and judiciary.

Among Colonel Azali's first acts upon seizing power was to announce his intention to honor the 1999 Madagascar accord, including its provisions for presidential and legislative elections in 2000. Nevertheless, the coup was widely condemned by the international community, with the criticism from the OAU and France being among the more strident.

Facing continued international isolation, Colonel Azali on December 7, 1999, announced the appointment of Bianrifi TARMIDI as prime minister to head a new government, which Azali hoped would be viewed more positively because of the inclusion of several political parties. Meanwhile, events continued to percolate on Nzwani, where yet another referendum on January 23, 2000, endorsed independence by a reported vote of 95 percent. In response, the OAU on February 1 imposed economic sanctions on the separatists.

In April 2000 several demonstrations protested the passing without action on the one-year deadline for Azali's promised withdrawal from power. Also to protest the delay, Hachim Saïd HACHIM resigned his post as chair of the National Salvation Coordination (*Coordination de Salut National*—CSN), a grouping of former party figures and civic leaders that had been formed to support Azali. For his part, Azali claimed he had been unable to act as expected due to the intransigence of the leaders of Nzwani. In August, however, Azali and Lt. Col. Saïd ABEID Abdéréman reached agreement on a preliminary plan for a new federal entity that would provide each island with substantially expanded autonomy. Although the OAU lambasted the accord as contrary to the guidelines established in Madagascar in 1999, the agreement appeared to represent the best hope for a negotiated settlement to date, despite the at times violent opposition of hard-line separatists on Nzwani.

On May 6, 2000, Colonel Azali was sworn in as president, and he appointed a cabinet-like state council with six ministers from Ngazidja, four from Mwali, and two from Nzwani, promising to turn over the reins of authority to a civilian government within one year. He also introduced a new "constitutional charter" authorizing himself to rule by decree (in conjunction with a "state committee") while negotiations continued toward the adoption of a new constitution. Meanwhile, Abeid, the former French officer who had "elbowed out" Ibrahim for dominance on Nzwani, announced the formation of a government on that island and indicated that Nzwani would not adhere to the Madagascar agreement, prompting the OAU to threaten sanctions and even military intervention.

On November 29, 2000, President Azali named Hamada Madi BOLERO, one of his chief negotiators with Nzwani, to replace Prime Minister Tamadi. Bolero formed a new government on December 10, although he was unable to persuade opposition parties to join.

On February 17, 2001, a potentially historic agreement was reached in Fomboni, the capital of Mwali, by members of the military junta, the former separatists on Nzwani (led by Colonel Abeid), delegates from Mwali, and representatives from political parties and civic organizations. Although Colonel Abeid was overthrown in a bloodless coup in Nzwani in August, his successor, Maj. Mohamed BACAR, quickly signaled his support for the proposed new federal system. A national referendum on a new constitution establishing a Union of the Comoros was held on December 23, voters responding with a reported 76 percent "yes" vote.

On January 17, 2002, President Azali nominated Prime Minister Bolero to head a new transitional government (installed on January 20) to prepare for presidential elections for the Union as well as for each island. Azali on January 21 resigned as president, as he was constitutionally required to do to compete in the upcoming balloting for the presidency of the Union. The primary was held March 17 on Ngazidja, with Azali finishing first with 39.8 percent of the vote, followed by Mahamoud MRADABI with 15.7 percent. Also on March 17, voters on Mwali and Nzwani approved the requisite new local constitutions. However, the constitutional referendum on Ngazidja failed, prompting a rerun (this time successful) on April 9.

Although the top three finishers in the March 17, 2002, primary on Ngazidja were authorized to compete in the Union-wide balloting for president of the Union on April 14, Azali ultimately ran unopposed when the other two candidates boycotted the poll to protest what they considered to be "anomalies" in the first round and ongoing questions about the integrity of electoral rolls. The national election commission ruled the results of April 14 to be void in view of the boycott, but the commission was dissolved for "incompetence" on April 23 by the follow-up committee charged with overseeing implementation of the 2001 Fomboni Agreement. A special commission was subsequently established to review the matter, and Azali's victory was confirmed on May 8. Azali was sworn in as president of the Union on May 26, and on June 5 he announced his Union cabinet, which comprised his two vice presidents and only three other members. Meanwhile, separate balloting on each of the islands had resulted in Bacar's election as president of Nzwani, the selection of Mohamed Saïd FAZUL as president of Mwali, and a presidential victory on Ngazidja for Abdou Soule ELBAK, an outspoken critic of Azali.

Elections for the proposed island and Union assemblies were postponed indefinitely in March 2003 in the wake of an apparent coup plot against Azali (emanating from Ngazidja) and ongoing conflict over the delineation of power between the federal and island authorities. However, at an August meeting sponsored by the AU in Pretoria, South Africa, representatives of the island and Union governments appeared to settle several contentious issues, including how tax revenues would be shared. The accord also provided for each island to have its own police force, while the army would remain under Union control. Azali and the three island presidents ratified the agreement on December 20 and established a national committee to oversee its implementation.

Balloting for the three island assemblies was held on March 14 and 21, 2004. The Azali, pro-Union camp fared poorly in the face of coordinated opposition efforts. Pro-Bacar candidates won 20 of 25 seats on Nzwani, pro-Elbak candidates won 14 of 20 seats on Ngazidja, and pro-Fazul candidates won 9 of 10 seats on Mwali. The opposition (by then formally coalesced as the Camp of the Autonomous Islands [*Camp des Îles Autonomes*—CdIA]) also dominated the April 18 and 25 balloting for the Assembly of the Union, securing 12 directly elected seats compared to 6 for the pro-Azali Convention for the Renewal of the Comoros (*Convention pour le Renouveau des Comores*—CRC). Because of its control of the island assemblies, the CdIA also gained all 15 of the indirectly elected seats in the Assembly of the Union.

On July 13, 2004, President Azali formed a new Union cabinet in which CRC members held a majority of the portfolios. However, the "opposition" was given three seats—one from Nzwani, one from Mwali, and one from the Islands Fraternity and Unity Party. Elbak declined an invitation to appoint a cabinet member from Ngazidja, citing Azali's perceived foot-dragging in devolving power to the islands. Azali announced another cabinet reshuffle in early July 2005.

Political tensions intensified when the pro-Azali camp introduced legislation that would have permitted Azali to run for president of the Union again in 2006. (According to the rotating mechanism codified in the constitution, the next Union president was scheduled to be elected from Nzwani.) Although the proposed revision was withdrawn in the face of public protests, uncertainty continued to pose a threat to the April 2006 primary election on Nzwani, prompting the AU to send a contingent of peacekeepers and police officers to help ensure peaceful balloting. (Local forces were confined to their barracks.)

In the primary balloting on Nzwani on April 16, 2006, moderate Islamist leader Ahmed Abdallah Mohamed SAMBI of the FNJ led 13 candidates with 23.7 percent of the vote, followed by two "secular" rivals—Mohamed DJAANFARI (a retired French air force officer) with 13.1 percent and former prime minister Ibrahim Halidi (who had Azali's endorsement) with 10.4 percent. In the nationwide runoff balloting among the three on May 14, Sambi was declared the winner with 58 percent of the vote. Surprising those analysts who predicted that the Comoros was not yet ready for a peaceful transfer of power, the April primary and May nationwide balloting proceeded in a generally orderly fashion, the AU characterizing the voting as "free, transparent, and credible." New president Sambi, who formed a new cabinet on May 27, presented himself as a political newcomer devoted to combating corruption, by, among other things, developing an independent judiciary and investigating the perceived widespread "embezzlement" of government funds in recent years. Some observers suggested that Sambi, a Muslim theologian educated in Iran, might promote the installation of an Islamic regime, but he declared that Comorians were currently opposed to such a change and that he would accept public opinion on the matter. A successful businessman, Sambi pledged that his administration's activities would involve "more economics and less politics."

Facing criticism over his perceived foot-dragging regarding power-sharing, President Sambi in September 2006 signed legislation designed to broadly define arrangements between the Union and island governments in regard to the judiciary, security, health care, and the ownership of public companies. However, negotiations on the implementing legislation broke down in December, and island authorities grew increasingly critical of Sambi, who argued that it was "absurd" for a country as small as the Comoro Islands to have four presidents, four legislatures, and four "armies." The latter element proved particularly troublesome in February and May 2007 when Union soldiers clashed with island armed forces on Nzwani, whose president, Mohamed Bacar, argued that each island required extensive armaments to preserve its "security." In light of the turmoil, the Union government, supported by the AU, ordered Bacar to postpone the upcoming presidential elections on Nzwani. However, Bacar snubbed his nose at the directive and declared himself reelected to a second term in balloting conducted on June 10. Meanwhile, in balloting on June 10 and 24, Mohamed ABDOULOIHABI, a judge described as "close" to Sambi, was elected president of Ngazidja, and Mohamed Ali SAÏD, a strong opponent of outgoing president Fazul, was elected president of Mwali.

Following nine months of acrimonious efforts to resolve the dispute on Nzwani, about 400 Union troops and 600 AU forces (primarily from Tanzania and Sudan) on March 15, 2008, launched a campaign that took control of Nzwani within hours in the face of minimal resistance that generated few casualties. (The public on Nzwani was generally perceived as unperturbed by the changeover.) Although France (like the United States) had supported the anti-Bacar initiative and provided logistical support to the Union forces, anti-French riots broke out in Moroni and elsewhere after Bacar fled to Mayotte and then to the French island of Réunion, where a court denied an extradition request from the Comoros. Union Vice President Ikililou Dhoinine was temporarily placed in charge of governmental affairs on Nzwani by President Sambi, but Sambi on March 31 named Lailizamine Abdou CHEIKH as Nzwani's interim president pending new elections. In second-round balloting on June 29, Sambi's preferred candidate, Moussa TOYBOU (a civil engineer described as new to politics), was elected president of Nzwani with 52.4 percent of the vote versus 47.6 percent for Mohamed

Djaanfari, who had led the first-round balloting. Djaanfari, who had been supported by the presidents of Ngazidja and Mwali, charged that the balloting had been rigged.

In April 2009 President Sambi announced that a Union-wide referendum would be held in May on a number of proposed constitutional revisions designed to strengthen the authority of the Union president and to harmonize Union and island election schedules. Opposition leaders strongly criticized the short notice of the proposal and called for a boycott of the vote, arguing that Sambi was primarily concerned with remaining in power by extending his term for at least one year (until 2011). The presidents of Ngazidja and Mwali also joined in the protest, expressing concern over the proposed downgrading of their offices from presidencies to governorships and the reduction of their current terms to permit simultaneous Union and island balloting in 2011.

The government reported a 51.8 percent turnout and a 94 percent "yes" vote in the May 17, 2009, referendum on Sambi's proposed constitutional changes, although the opposition (supported by some independent analysts) argued that turnout had been only 15–20 percent. Most Western capitals appeared "cautious" in their reaction to the rapid political developments, although there appeared to be broad agreement that simplification of some kind was needed in the Comoros' complex system of governance. Upon installing the new cabinet in June, the president said he was stressing "competence," not regional or "insular" preferences in his administration.

President Sambi's supporters secured a strong majority in the December 2009 election for the Assembly of the Union, Sambi describing the results as validation of his policies and the electorate's preference for stability. Although the Constitutional Court in May 2010 ruled that Sambi's term should end that month (despite the assembly's endorsement in March of the one-year extension), it declared that Sambi could continue to govern "with limited authority" until new presidential elections were held. Sambi consequently announced a new interim cabinet in June.

Facing heavy international criticism, Sambi, whose security forces on Mwali had been joined by Libyan troops, accepted an AU-sponsored compromise in August under which the new elections were scheduled for November–December 2010, with Mwali slated to assume the Union presidency.

Ten candidates contested the first round of presidential balloting on Mwali on November 7, 2010, with Vice President Ikililou Dhoinine, endorsed by Sambi, securing a plurality of 27 percent of the vote. Ikililou Dhoinine was elected with 61 percent of the vote in the three-person runoff on December 26, although the opposition candidate, Mohamed Saïd Fazul (the runner-up with 33 percent of the vote), alleged fraud and called for protest demonstrations. International observers cited irregularities in the balloting, but they concluded that it had been "generally free and fair." In concurrent balloting for the island presidents (governors), Mouigni BARAKA and Anissi CHAMSIDINE (both pro-Sambi candidates) were declared victors over the incumbents on Ngazidja and Nzwani, respectively, while the incumbent Mohamed Ali Saïd was reelected from Mwali. Upon his swearing in on May 26, 2011, President Ikililou Dhoinine appointed a new cabinet.

Constitution and government. The 1996 constitution was suspended by the military junta that assumed power on April 30, 1999, and all state institutions were dissolved. On May 6, 1999, Col. Assoumani Azali, the leader of the junta, proclaimed a new "constitutional charter" with himself as president and head of a State Committee empowered to govern pending the return to civilian government. A progovernment "national congress" in Moroni on August 7, 2000, adopted a "national charter" that extended the authority of the president (as chosen by the military) even further. Among other things, the new document called for the president to appoint a prime minister and envisioned the eventual establishment of a vaguely defined "legislative council."

Following extensive and difficult negotiations among government officials, opposition parties, and representatives of Mwali and Nzwani, a national referendum on December 23, 2001, approved a new federal structure for the renamed Union of the Comoros. (The complete official name of the country had previously been the Federal Islamic Republic of the Comoros.) Autonomy was granted to the three island components of the Union to a much greater degree than in previous constitutions, especially in regard to finances. Meanwhile, the Union government was given responsibility for religion, currency, external relations, defense, nationality issues, and national symbols. New constitutions were also subsequently adopted by referendums on each island, although the division of authority between the island governments and the Union government was insufficiently delineated to prevent the immediate outbreak of confusion, especially on Ngazidja.

Under the 2001 constitution the president of the Union served a four-year term, with the office rotating among the islands each term. Two vice presidents, one from each of the islands not holding the presidency, also serve. The president and vice presidents constitute a Council of the Union. A primary election is held on the island scheduled to assume the presidency (Ngazidja was chosen as first in the rotation, followed in order by Nzwani and Mwali). The top three vote-getters in the primary earn a place on the ballot in subsequent Union-wide balloting. Each presidential candidate must select two vice-presidential running mates, one from each of the islands that the presidential candidate does not represent, prior to the Union-wide poll. The president is authorized to appoint a prime minister and cabinet, with the new basic law requiring that all the islands be represented in the federal government. Legislative power is vested in an elected Assembly of the Union (see Legislature, below, for details). The new constitutions for the islands also provide for direct election of their presidents and island assemblies.

Several major constitutional revisions were approved in a controversial referendum on May 17, 2009 (see Political background, above, for additional information). The presidential term of office was extended from four to five years (ostensibly to permit simultaneous Union and island voting in 2011), while island presidencies were reclassified as governorships. In an additional effort to strengthen the authority of the Union president, he was empowered to dissolve the Assembly of the Union if the legislators were deemed to be "an impediment to national development."

The Union's other prominent institution is the High Council, which serves as a constitutional court and is responsible for validating election results as well as ruling on questions regarding the division of authority between the federal and island governments. Members of the High Council are appointed for six-year terms by the president and vice presidents of the Union, the president of the Assembly of the Union, and the presidents of the island governments. The judiciary is headed by a Supreme Court.

The constitution provides for freedom of the press, and, for the most part, that principle has been upheld by the government. However, there have been several reports of the harassment of journalists, and journalistic watchdog organizations have reported a decline in press freedom, underscored by the temporary suspension in 2012 of a state-run newspaper that reported on alleged corruption and waste in the public sector.

Foreign relations. Following the declaration of independence in July 1975, Comorian foreign relations were dominated by the Mayotte (Mahoré) issue. On November 21, French military personnel on Mayotte resisted an "invasion" by Ali Soilih and an unarmed contingent that attempted to counter the Mahori "secession." At the end of the year, France recognized the sovereignty of the other three islands, but referendums held on Mayotte in February and April 1976 demonstrated a clear preference for designation as a French department. On December 16 the French Senate ratified a measure according the island special standing as a *collectivité territoriale,* with that status being extended on December 6, 1979, for another five years. In October 1981 President Abdallah pressed for French withdrawal from Mayotte during a Paris meeting with President Mitterrand, who, he noted, had in 1975 opposed detachment of Mayotte from the rest of the archipelago. Abdallah repeated the argument during a visit to France in June 1984, the French government responding that a further referendum on the issue would be deferred because the inhabitants of Mayotte were not sufficiently "well informed" on the options open to them.

On January 20, 1995, a mass demonstration was mounted outside the French embassy in Moroni to protest a decision by French Prime Minister Edouard Balladur to reimpose a requirement that citizens of the Comoros obtain entry visas for travel to Mayotte. Thereafter, Mohamed Taki contested the March 1996 presidential election on a public platform of Islamic traditionalism and moderate nationalism, depicting his main rival as the candidate preferred by the French government. However, once in office Taki confirmed that the existing defense agreement with France not only would be maintained but also would be expanded to cover the external defense of the Comoros and to allow a French military presence on the islands.

In early 1997 French financial aid to the Comoros was suspended pending Moroni's restarting discussions with the IMF and World Bank on the establishment of a structural adjustment program. In 1998 international attention focused on the crisis on Nzwani, France in March rejecting the secessionists' call for the reestablishment of a link between France and Nzwani as "unrealistic." Meanwhile, the OAU, whose mediation efforts were rebuffed by the separatists, also adopted an increasingly hard-line stance against the breakaway movement. (In early December the OAU urged its members to comply with Moroni's call for military intervention to end the violence.)

The OAU and most of the rest of the international community strongly criticized the coup of April 1999, while the OAU continued to pressure the separatists on Nzwani into early 2001 (see Political background, above, for further information). However, most capitals and the OAU/AU ultimately endorsed the political settlement subsequently reached regarding the new constitutional structure for the Comoros. France restored full ties with the Comoros in September 2002 and signed several economic agreements in 2005.

In 2006 and 2007 Iran agreed to assist the Sambi government on several fronts, including security matters, agricultural development, and the payment of salary arrears to civil servants. Concurrently, conservative Pakistanis reportedly established religious schools on several islands in the Comoros, although most analysts agreed that the Comorian population in general did not embrace the highly doctrinaire Islamic schools. Subsequently, Sambi was described as having made the Comoros an "enthusiastic member" of the Arab League.

Tension continued in 2007–2008 between the Comoros and France over the question of illegal immigration from the Comoros to Mayotte. Among other things, the government of the Comoros urged that its citizens should be free to travel to Mayotte without visas. Meanwhile, China's initiative to expand its influence throughout Africa extended to Comoros in the form of financing for a new airport at Moroni and several commercial agreements.

The Sambi administration condemned the March 2009 referendum on Mayotte (in which 95 percent of the voters endorsed the island's eventual upgrade in status to a French Overseas Department) as an "unfriendly act" on the part of France and said it would not recognize the results. In a similar vein, Iranian president Mahmoud Ahmadinejad, who visited the Comoros in February, to, among other things, underscore cooperative efforts in defense, trade, and other sectors, criticized France's "colonialist aims" in Mayotte. Visa issues in regard to Mayotte subsequently further strained relations between the Comoros and France, although an agreement calling for normalization of relations was reached in April 2010. Meanwhile, the Comoros had renewed its defense cooperation pact with France in 2010. (For additional information on events in Mayotte, see the entry on France: Related Territories.)

New president Ikililou Dhoinine was described in 2011 as "more conciliatory" toward France than his predecessor, and he called for "tripartite" negotiations to resolve the Mayotte visa issue. However, he also subsequently strongly supported greater ties with Iran, particularly in regard to investment.

In late 2011 the Comoros signed an agreement (under negotiation for many years) for delineation of its maritime borders with Mozambique and Tanzania. The accord was considered significant because of the recent discovery of offshore gas reserves and growing interest in oil exploration.

President Ikililou Dhoinine made a state visit to France in June 2013, concluding a two-year cooperation agreement with French president Hollande.

Current issues. Upon taking office in May 2011, President Ikililou Dhoinine, the first president from Mwali, emphasized his links with the previous administration as an important element in fostering stability. He pledged to combat corruption (he signed long-dormant anticorruption legislation in June) and to pursue structural reforms that would promote private foreign investment and, thereby, create jobs. He also promised to pursue "national unity," although the Union government subsequently continued to face sporadic unrest on Nzwani, as evidenced by allegations of an unsuccessful coup attempt there in November.

Cabinet infighting was reported in 2012 regarding several issues, including the awarding of offshore oil exploration contracts. In the spring of 2013 former president Sambi criticized the administration for dismissing a number of his appointees, and analysts suggested Sambi was considering a return to national politics, possibly as a vice-presidential candidate in the next elections.

In April–May 2013 the government announced that some 25 people (including foreign nationals) had been charged with fomenting a coup plot. One of those reportedly held was Mahamoud Ahmed ABDALLAH, the son of former president Abdallah.

POLITICAL PARTIES

In 1979 the Federal Assembly effectively voided an endorsement of pluralism in the 1978 constitution by calling for the establishment of a single-party system, which prevailed until the resanctioning of multiparty activity in December 1989. Under the Djohar presidency, Comorian parties were mostly aligned into progovernment and opposition camps.

The October 1996 constitution included a number of restrictive regulations for political party activity that the Taki administration had been advocating since assuming power the previous March. However, the December 2001 constitution permitted parties to operate without hindrance, provided they respect "national sovereignty, democracy, and territorial integrity."

Some 20 political parties, led by, among others, Houmed Msaidie of the CRC (below) and Saïd Ali Kemal of Chuma, announced plans in late May 2009 to formulate a manifesto based on their opposition to the recent constitutional referendum and the government's decision to delay national legislative balloting. Several of the successful opposition candidates in the December 2009 assembly elections were reportedly affiliated with the fledgling bloc, which subsequently became known as the National Convergence for May 2010. However, party structures and affiliations subsequently remained largely informal and fluid, and references to some of the groups included below have been scarce or nonexistent recently, information on them being provided here primarily to supply historical perspective.

A number of propresidential parties and groups in February 2013 announced the formation of the Rally for Democracy in the Comoros (*Rassemblement pour la Démocratie aux Comores*—Radeco), although the coalition apparently was later renamed the Union for the Development of the Comoros (*Union pour le Développement des Comores*—UDC). Meanwhile, another propresidential alliance called the Movement for the Presidential Majority (*Mouvement pour la Majorité Presidentielle*—MMP) was also formed in April, adding to the already considerable confusion regarding party affairs. Groups associated with the MMP (led by Ben Massoud RACHID [president] and Djaé Ahamada CHANFI [secretary general]) reportedly included the MPU (see FNJ, below), the **Party for Harmony of Comorians** (*Parti de l'Entente des Comoriens*—PEC), led by Fahmi Said IBRAHIM; the **Alliance for Revival and Progress** (*Alliance pour le Renouveau et le Progrès*—ARP); and the **Movement for Revival** (*Mouvement pour le Renouveau*—MR), a recently formed grouping led by Boucief Ould Sid AHMED. Surprisingly, the **Alliance for Justice and Development** (*Alliance pour la Justice et le Développement*—AJD), which comprises supporters of former president Sambi, joined neither new coalition, instead announcing it was moving into the opposition camp.

National Front for Justice (*Front National pour la Justice*—FNJ). A moderate Islamic party, the FNJ was founded by Ahmed Abdallah Mohamed Sambi (nicknamed "Ayatollah" because of his theological training in Iran). In December 1996 legislative balloting the FNJ captured its first-ever seats, including one by Sambi.

FNJ members were not immediately linked to the unrest on Anjouan in 1997, and at midyear the group issued a statement saying that it was not a separatist body. However, the FNJ expressed sympathy for critics of government "negligence" and called for establishment of a "proper federal state."

The FNJ eventually joined the government following the coup of April 1999 but withdrew in October 2001 to protest the decision to remove "Islamic" from the name of the country in the constitution being readied for a national referendum in December. Sambi, a prominent businessman in addition to being a popular cleric, was elected president of the Union in 2006, running formally as an independent.

Mohamed ABDOULOIHABI, elected president of Ngazidja in 2007 with 57 percent of the vote in the second round of balloting, was identified in some reports as the candidate of a pro-Sambi **Unified Presidential Affiliation** (*Mouvance Presidentielle Unie*—MPU). In the June 2008 balloting for the president of Nzwani, Sambi actively supported the candidacy of Moussa Toybou, although the FNJ's Bastoine SOULAIMANE was also a candidate.

President Sambi's subsequent formal relationship to the FNJ was unclear. In 2009 several sources referenced a **Movement of Citizens for Justice and Progress** (led by former prime minister Ahmed Abdou) as "Sambi's party." For the December 2009 assembly poll, the numerous parties that supported Sambi were grouped as the ***Baobab* Coalition,** which endorsed Ikililou Dhoinine, a close ally of Sambi, in the 2010 presidential poll.

Leaders: Ahamda RACHID, Miftahou Ali BAMBA.

Convention for the Renewal of the Comoros (*Convention pour le Renouveau des Comores*—CRC). The CRC was launched in September 2002 by members of the Movement for Socialism and Democracy (*Mouvement pour le Socialisme et la Démocratie*—MSD), which had been formed in July 2000 by Abdou SOEFOU after he and his supporters were expelled from the FDC (below) for supporting President Azali following the April 1999 coup. Described as an extension of the National Salvation Coordination that had been formed following the coup, the CRC was established to provide Azali with a party prior to the elections for island and Union assemblies.

The CRC fractionalized in its efforts to present a candidate for the 2006 Union presidential elections. One group, led by former prime minister Mohamed Abdou Madi (who had sought the CRC nomination), reportedly backed Union Vice President Mohamed Caabi El Yachroutu (another former prime minister), while Soefou and Azali supported Ibrahim Halidi of the MPC (below). Yachroutu secured 9.56 percent of the vote in the presidential primary. Soefou was replaced as the CRC secretary general in early 2007 in the wake of a financial scandal. CRC Secretary General Houmed Msaidie won 7.2 percent of the vote in the June 2007 presidential balloting on Ngazidja and subsequently became a leading spokesperson for the opposition.

In September 2011 the CRC filed a court complaint alleging that former president Sambi had misused government funds while in office.

Leaders: Col. Assoumani AZALI (Former President of the Union of the Comoros), Houmed MSAIDIE (Secretary General).

Movement for the Comoros (*Mouvement pour les Comores*—MPC). Formed in 1997 by Saïd Hilali, an adviser to President Mohamed Taki Abdoulkarim, the MPC stressed "national unity" under a federal government. Ibrahim Halidi, the MPC's secretary general, finished third in the Union's April 2006 presidential primary, having secured the endorsement of President Azali's faction of the CRC as well as the Chuma and *Djawabu* parties (see below). Among other things, Halidi, who had served briefly as prime minister in 1993, promised greater "friendship" with France if elected. After several years of absence from the political scene, Halidi in 2012 indicated that the MPC, centered on Nzwani, might seek formal party status in support of Comorian "cohesion."

Leaders: Ibrahim Abderemane HALIDI (Secretary General and 2006 candidate for president of the Union), Saïd HILALI.

Rally for a Development Initiative with an Enlightened Youth (*Rassemblement pour une Initiative de Développement avec une Jeunesse Avertie*—RIDJA). Launched in April 2005 by Saïd Larifou, a prominent lawyer who had led antigovernment protests in 2003, RIDJA was a vocal opponent of efforts to rewrite the constitution to permit President Azali to run for another term. The RIDJA candidate, Chadhouli Abdou, finished seventh in the Union's 2006 presidential primary with 3.12 percent of the vote. Larifou finished second in the second round of presidential balloting on Ngazidja in 2007 with 43 percent of the vote.

Larifou urged a boycott of the May 2009 constitutional referendum and subsequently accused the government of using threats and intimidation to influence the voting and of releasing "false results." He was briefly detained by police in November 2009 and February 2010 for "insulting the head of state," having been selected as the national secretary of the National Convergence for May 2010.

Leaders: Saïd LARIFOU (Chair), Chadhouli ABDOU (2006 candidate for president of the Union), Abdou SOIMADOU.

***Djawabu* Party.** This grouping promotes the policies espoused by the administration of former president Soilih (see Political background, above). Its candidate, Youssouf Saïd Soilih, won 6.7 percent of the vote in the 2002 primary for president of the Union. In 2006 the party supported Ibrahim Halidi of the MPC in his campaign for president of the Union. Saïd won only 1.8 percent of the vote in the first round of presidential balloting on Ngazidja in June 2007.

Leader: Youssouf SAÏD Soilih.

Camp of the Autonomous Islands (*Camp des Îles Autonomes*—CdIA). Launched by the five parties below and other smaller groups, the CdIA campaigned for the island and Union elections in 2004 on a platform calling for greater autonomy for the islands and support for the three island presidents. On the island of Ngazidja, the coalition was commonly referenced as Autonomy (*Mdjidjengo*).

The CdIA dominated the 2004 balloting for the Assembly of the Union, capturing 12 of the 18 directly elected seats and all of the 15 indirectly elected seats. However, references to the CdIA subsequently declined significantly, suggesting that its mission had been purely electoral. Components of the CdIA endorsed various candidates in the April 2006 primary election for president of the Union, although the three island presidents endorsed Ahmed Abdallah Mohamed Sambi in the May final balloting. There was no reference to the CdIA in the December 2009 assembly poll.

Movement for Democracy and Progress (*Mouvement pour la Démocratie et le Progrès*—MDP). The MDP, also styled the Popular Democratic Movement (*Mouvement Démocratique Populaire*), is a Moroni-based formation that campaigned in favor of the 1992 constitution. It later became the leading element of an anti-Djohar alliance called the Forum for National Recovery (*Forum pour le Redressement National*—FRN), of which MDP leader Abbas DJOUSSOUF was the principal spokesperson.

The FRN was launched in January 1994 by opposition parties that had presented joint lists in the December 1993 elections. President Djohar's eventual agreement to a transfer of power served to relax FRN discipline, in that a majority of its components put up candidates for the March 1996 presidential contest in their own right. Following the 1996 election, parties that had supported the failed candidacy of Djoussouf reorganized under the FRN rubric. In October the group was bolstered by the addition of Chuma (below) and the Forces for Republican Action (*Forces pour l'Action Républicaine*—FAR), which had rejected President Taki's call for the establishment of a single presidential party. Subsequently, the FRN organized boycotts of both the October 20 constitutional referendum and the December legislative balloting.

On January 18, 1997, Djoussouf and the FDC's Mustapha Saïd Cheikh were detained and questioned about their roles in the unrest that had erupted at the beginning of the year. On March 1 senior French government officials met with FRN leaders in an effort to persuade them to establish a dialogue with the Taki administration. However, the opposition's relations with the government subsequently worsened when security officials accused the FRN of financing student disturbances in Moroni. Ironically, observers cited the FRN's financial difficulties as the main reason the group failed to secure a more prominent negotiating role in the late 1997 reconciliation talks.

Djoussouf was appointed prime minister in November 1998, and he subsequently formed an FRN-dominated cabinet. Not surprisingly, he strongly protested the April 1999 coup, announcing the withdrawal of the MDP from the FRN when it appeared that some FRN components had acquiesced to the government of self-proclaimed President Azali. Djoussouf subsequently became the dominant figure in the opposition camp as it participated in negotiations on the creation of a new federal structure. He signed the Fomboni Agreement of February 2001 in that capacity and urged his supporters to vote "yes" in the December constitutional referendum. Djoussouf finished fourth in the 2002 primary election for president of the Union by securing 7.9 percent of the vote, analysts suggesting he probably would have made the top three and thereby qualified for the runoff if the FRN had been preserved. Djoussouf died in 2010, and there have been few references to the MDP in recent years.

Democratic Front of the Comoros (*Front Démocratique des Comores*—FDC). The FDC was formerly an exile group led, within the Comoros, by its secretary general, Mustapha Saïd Cheikh, who was imprisoned for complicity in the 1985 coup attempt until President Abdallah's assassination. The front was one of the opposition groups invited to participate in the Djohar administration of August 1990. Subsequently, it campaigned in favor of the 1992 constitution and was a leading component of the FRN. Some FDC members supported the government of President Azali following the April 1999 coup and were expelled from the party.

Cheikh won 3.4 percent of the vote in the 2002 primary election for president of the Union and subsequently served as a major founding member of the CdIA.

In 2009 the FDC condemned what it characterized as the "colonial occupation" by France of Mayotte.

Leaders: Mustapha Saïd CHEIKH, Ahmed Saïd ALI, Abdou MHOUMADI (2002 candidate for president of Ngazidja).

Islands' Fraternity and Unity Party (*Chama cha Upvamodja na Mugnagna wa Massiwa*—Chuma). Chuma, a "patriotic alliance to fight the antidemocratic regime of Ahmed Abdallah," was formed in the 1980s by the Paris-based National Committee for Public

Salvation (*Comité National de Salut Public*—CNSP), an exile group led by Prince Saïd Ali Kemal, and two other exile groups—the Comorian National United Front (*Front National Uni des Komores*—FNUK) and the Union of Comorians (*Union des Komoriens*—Unikom). Kemal headed the economy and trade ministry in the first Djohar administration.

Chuma did not immediately adhere to the FRN, since Kemal was abroad at the time of the FRN's creation. Having stood unsuccessfully in the March 1996 presidential election, Kemal was appointed to the first post-Djohar government, but he was dismissed in August for opposing President Taki's proposal for a merger of government parties. Subsequently, Chuma announced that it was aligning with the FRN.

Kemal urged his supporters to vote "no" in the constitutional referendum of December 2001, arguing that the proposed federal structure would lead to the "Balkanization" of the Comoros. Kemal finished third in the primary election on Ngazidja for president of the Union in March 2002 with 10.8 percent of the vote; he called for a boycott of the runoff in April. Chuma supported Ibrahim Halidi of the MPC in the 2006 balloting for president of the Union, Kemal serving as one of Halidi's vice-presidential running mates. Kemal won 3.6 percent of the vote in the June 2007 presidential balloting on Ngazidja. Kemal supported Ikililou Dhoinine in the 2010 race for Union president.

Leader: Prince Saïd Ali KEMAL (1996 and 2002 presidential candidate).

National Rally for Development (*Rassemblement National pour le Développement*—RND). The RND was officially launched on October 6, 1996, as a merger of the National Union for Democracy in the Comoros (*Union National pour la Démocratie aux Comores*—UNDC) and a number of former FRN parties under the leadership of a confidante of Mohamed Taki, Ali Bazi SELIM. The formation of a single "presidential" party was first proposed by newly elected President Taki in August 1996 on the grounds that almost all of the eliminated first-round candidates had supported his candidacy in the runoff balloting.

Subsequent intraparty competition for the RND's 26 elected Central Committee seats was described as "fierce," and the results—14 seats for Selim's supporters and 12 for a "youth wing" led by Abdoul Hamid AFFRETANE—underlined reports of deep divisions in the fledgling grouping. Additional seats were set aside for the general secretaries of the parties joining the RND as well as for what was described as the Comorian "diaspora." Thereafter, despite the RND's electoral success in December 1996 legislative balloting, observers reported that its members' support for Taki remained their only commonality.

In November 1998 the RND denounced the appointment of the FRN's Djoussouf to the top government post. Subsequently, the RND's cabinet representation fell to four posts, and in early 1999 two former RND members were appointed to the government (see Maecha Bora Party, below).

One faction of the RND reportedly backed the new administration of President Azali after the coup of 1999, while another, led by Omar TAMOU, lobbied for the reinstatement of former interim president Massonde. Ntara MAECHA, the former foreign minister who secured 7.86 percent of the vote in the 2002 primary election on Ngazidja for president of the Union, was identified as the candidate of the RND's "revival wing." Maecha reportedly supported Ahmed Abdallah Mohamed Sambi in the May 2006 balloting for president of the Union. Subsequently, Kamar EZAMANE Mohamed was regularly referenced as the secretary general of the UNDC, while Vice President Idi NADHORM was identified as a member of the UNDC executive body. Ezamane ran for the presidency of Ngazidja in 2007 as the candidate of the UNDC, finishing fourth with 8.4 percent of the vote, while Maecha ran for the post as the candidate of the RND-Revival, finishing ninth in the first round of balloting with 4.1 percent of the vote. In 2010 Maecha was referenced as one of the leaders of the anti-Sambi opposition coalition.

Comorian Party for Democracy and Progress (*Parti Comorien pour la Démocratie et le Progrès*—PCDP). The PCDP is led by Ali Mroudjae, who was an *Udzima* leader prior to President Abdallah's assassination and subsequently held the production and industry portfolio under President Djohar. The party joined *Udzima* in moving into opposition in November 1991. Mroudjae secured 4.2 percent of the vote in the 2002 primary election for president of the Union. Abdou Soule Elbak, the president of Ngazidja until 2007, is a former deputy in the PCDP and until recently was still referenced regularly as a member of the party. Meanwhile, several members of the PCDP served in Elbak's cabinet on Ngazidja.

Adinane was the candidate of the PCDP in the 2006 primary for Union president, but he received less than 3 percent of the vote and did not qualify for the general election.

Elbak failed in his bid to be reelected president of Ngazidja in 2007 when he finished third in the first round of balloting with 13 percent of the vote. In April 2008 it was reported that Elbak had founded the **Social Democratic Party of Comoros** (*Parti Social-Démocratique des Comoros*—PSDC-*Doudja*) to pursue "national reconciliation." In July 2010 Elbak indicated he might return to an active political role, while the *Doudja* candidate for the December Union presidential election was Mohamed Fazul, the former president of Mwali.

Leaders: Loufti ADINANE (Chair), Ali MROUDJAE (Secretary General).

Maecha Bora Party. Maecha Bora is led by two RND dissidents, Issoufi Saïd Ali and 1996 presidential candidate Ali Ben Ali, who were named to the Djoussouf government in early 1999. The party was described as a member of the "presidential majority" in 2011.

Leaders: Issoufi Saïd ALI, Ali Ben ALI (1996 presidential candidate).

Comorian Union for Progress (*Union Comorienne pour le Progrès*—UCP/*Udzima*). Launched as a regime-supportive group in 1982 by President Abdallah, *Udzima* was the sole legal party until 1989. *Udzima* presented Saïd Mohamed Djohar, interim president following Abdallah's assassination in November 1989, as its official candidate in the presidential balloting of March 1990. However, *Udzima* withdrew its support from Djohar in November 1991 and moved into opposition to protest the formation of a coalition administration three months earlier. It did not participate in the 1992 balloting after its principal leaders had been either imprisoned or driven into hiding because of alleged complicity in the September coup attempt.

A member of the opposition FRN beginning in January 1994, *Udzima* experienced internal divisions after President Djohar had agreed to a transfer of power, with the result that two candidates (Omar Tamou and Ntara Maecha) from *Udzima* stood in the March 1996 presidential election. Although both were eliminated in the first round, the *Udzima* leader, Tadjidine Ben Saïd Massonde, was appointed prime minister by the successful UNDC candidate. Massonde resigned as prime minister in December 1996, but he was named, due to his position as president of the High Council of the Republic, as interim president of the Republic following President Taki's death in November 1998. Confusion subsequently surrounded *Udzima*'s membership, as news reports referenced Massonde, Tamou, and Maecha as being members of the RND in 1999. In early 2002, Tamou, former *Udzima* secretary general, returned to the Comoros after two years in France.

Republican Party of the Comoros (*Parti Républicain des Comores*—PRC). The PRC was formed in the second half of the 1990s by Mohamed Saïd Abdallah Mchangama, then president of the Federal Assembly, and Hamada Madi Bolero, who served as PRC secretary general until rallying to the cause of President Azali following the coup of April 1999. Mchangama, the son-in-law of former president Djohar, had been instrumental in the launching of the Rally for Democracy and Renewal (*Rassemblement pour la Démocratie et le Renouveau*—RDR) in December 1993 by merger of the Dialogue Proposition Action (*Mwangaza*), led by Mchangama, and dissidents from other parties. Personal rivalries had resulted in three prominent RDR members, including Mchangama, contesting the March 1996 presidential election, all being eliminated in the first round.

Mchangama called for dialogue with the Azali administration following the coup of April 1999, but the PRC was described as a member of the opposition in early 2001. Mchangama won 3.5 percent of the vote in the first round of presidential balloting on Ngazidja in 2007.

Leader: Mohamed Saïd Abdallah MCHANGAMA.

Other parties referenced recently include the **Social Action Movement for Democracy and Alternation**, whose candidate, Abdou DJABIR, finished third in the first-round presidential balloting on Mwali in 2007; and the **Party for National Salvation** (*Parti pour le Salut National*—PSN) and the **Rally for Development and Democracy** (*Rassemblement pour le Développement et la Démocratie*—RDD), which in 2006 decided to cooperate as the PSN/RDD under the leadership of Saïd Ahmed MOUHYIDDINE (president) and Antoy ABDOU (secretary general). Abdou was replaced as general secretary of the Union government after he and the PSN/RDD supported (against the wishes of President Sambi) Mohamed Djaanfari in the June 2008 presidential balloting on Nzwani.

A new opposition party called the **National Alliance for the Comoros** (*Alliance Nationale pour les Comores*—ANC) was launched in September 2009 by Mahamoudou Ali MOHAMED and Ali RASHIDI. The ANC was subsequently referenced as an influential component of the National Convergence for May 2010.

Former Separatist Groups:

Anjouan People's Movement (*Mouvement du Peuple d'Anjouan*—MPA). The MPA emerged as the most prominent of the secessionist groups in Anjouan after the arrest of its leader, Abdallah IBRAHIM (a well-known businessman), on July 22, 1997, served as a rallying cry for antipresidential and separatist militants. Ibrahim was released days later, and on August 5 he was named president of the "State of Anjouan" (name later changed to Nzwani). The MPA lobbied against the Union constitution of December 2001. In February 2002 it named Col. Mohamed Bacar, then the military ruler of Nzwani, as MPA honorary chair. Following Bacar's election to the presidency of Nzwani in March, some elements of the MPA joined the island government, and two MPA members were appointed to the nine-member Nzwani cabinet. Bacar subsequently emerged as the most vocal proponent of greater autonomy for the islands. However, other members of the MPA remained staunch secessionists and denounced Bacar for even his limited cooperation with the Union government. Abdullah MOHAMED was subsequently identified as the leader of the hard-line secessionist wing of the party. In 2005 he and other members of the MPA were arrested for antigovernment activity, and there have been few reports of MPA activity since those developments.

Organization for the Independence of Anjouan (*Organization pour l'Indépendance d'Anjouan*—OPIA). Theretofore a propresidential grouping, the OPIA in late 1996 grew critical of the Taki administration and was subsequently linked to the growing number of antigovernment demonstrations in Anjouan. In mid-1997 leadership of the OPIA reportedly shifted from former armed forces chief of staff Col. Ahmed Mohamed HAZI to Mohamed Ahmed Abdou. Critics of Abdou, who has also been identified as a spokesperson for the **Coordination Committee of Anjouan,** accused him of placing his personal ambitions ahead of the movement's. The OPIA steadfastly maintained its separatist stance into mid-2002, although subsequent references to OPIA activity have been very limited.

Leader: Mohamed Ahmed ABDOU.

LEGISLATURE

The 1992 constitution provided for a bicameral legislature. However, the Senate, which was to have 15 members (5 from each island) indirectly elected to six-year terms, was never named and was abolished by the 1996 basic charter. Prior to the April 1999 coup, legislative authority was vested in a Federal Assembly (*Assemblée Fédérale*), which comprised 43 members directly elected for four-year terms (subject to dissolution).

Under the December 2001 constitution, an **Assembly of the Union** (*Assemblée de l'Union*) was established, as were assemblies for each of the three islands that comprise the Union. Until 2009, 18 of the assembly's 33 members, who serve five-year terms, were directly elected (9 from Ngazidja, 7 from Nzwani, and 2 from Mwali) and 15 were indirectly elected by the three island assemblies (5 each). Under constitutional revisions of May 2009, the number of directly elected members was increased to 24 (elected in 24 single-member districts in two rounds of voting if necessary to obtain a majority), and the number of indirectly elected members was decreased to 9 (3 selected by each of the island assemblies). In balloting held on December 6 and December 20, 2009 (with revoting in 3 constituencies on December 30), members of President Sambi's *Baobad* Coalition were credited with winning 16 of the 24 directly elected seats. Three seats were reportedly secured by other propresidential candidates, while the opposition was credited with 4 seats and an independent with 1.

Speaker: Bourhane HAMIDOU.

CABINET

[as of November 5, 2013]

President	Ikililou Dhoinine (Mwali)
Vice President (Territorial Management, Urban Development, and Housing)	Nourdine Bourhane (Nzwani)
Vice President (Production, Environment, Energy, Industry, and Handicrafts)	Fouad Mohadji (Mwali)
Vice President (Finance, Economy, Investment Budget, Foreign Trade, and Privatization)	Mohamed Ali Soilihi (Ngazidja)
Ministers	
Foreign Affairs and Cooperation (in Charge of the Diaspora, Francophone Affairs, and the Arab World)	Elarif Said Hassane
Health, Solidarity, Social Cohesion, and Promotion of Gender Equality	Fouad Mohadji (Mwali)
Interior, Information, Decentralization, and Relations with Institutions	Housseine Hassan Ibrahim
Justice, Islamic Affairs, Keeper of the Seals, Public Affairs, Administrative Reform, Human Rights, and Islamic Affairs	Abdou Housseni
Labor, Employment, Professional Training, Women's Enterprises, and Government Spokesperson	Siti Kassim (Mwali) [f]
National Education, Research, Arts, Culture, Youth, and Sports	Abdoulkarim Mohamed
Posts, Telecommunications, Promotion of New Technologies, Information, Communication, Transport, and Tourism	Bahiat Massound [f]

[f] = female

INTERGOVERNMENTAL REPRESENTATION

Ambassador to the U.S. and Permanent Representative to the UN: Roubani KAAMBI.

U.S. Ambassador to the Comoros: (Vacant).

IGO Memberships (Non-UN): AfDB, AU, Comesa, ICC, LAS, NAM, OIC.

DEMOCRATIC REPUBLIC OF THE CONGO

République Démocratique du Congo

Political Status: Independent republic established June 30, 1960; one-party constitution of February 1978 modified in June 1990 to accommodate multiparty system; all government institutions dissolved on May 17, 1997, following rebel takeover of the capital, and executive, legislative, and judicial authority assumed the same day by a self-appointed president backed by the military; interim constitution providing for a transitional national government approved April 2, 2003, by various groups participating in the Inter-Congolese National Dialogue; new constitution endorsed by national referendum on December 18, 2005, and promulgated on February 18, 2006, providing for new national elections later in the year.

Area: 905,562 sq. mi. (2,345,409 sq. km).

Population: 69,770,226 (2012E—UN); 75,507,308 (2013—U.S. Census).

Major Urban Centers (2005E): KINSHASA (7,000,000), Mbuji-Mayi (1,300,000), Lubumbashi (1,275,000).

Official Languages: French. Kikongo, Lingala, Swahili, and Tshiluba are classified as "national languages."

Monetary Unit: Congolese Franc (market rate November 1, 2013: 923.25 francs = $1US).

President: Joseph KABILA (nonparty); appointed by the Legislative and Constituent Assembly—Transitional Parliament on January 24, 2001, and inaugurated on January 26 to succeed his father, Laurent Désiré KABILA (Alliance of Democratic Forces for the Liberation of Congo-Zaire), who had died on January 18 of injuries suffered in an assassination attempt two days earlier; inaugurated as interim president on April 7, 2003, in accordance with a peace agreement signed on April 2; popularly elected in second-round balloting on October 29, 2006, and inaugurated for a five-year term on December 6; reelected on November 28, 2011.

Prime Minister: Augustin Matata PONYO Mapon (People's Party for Reconciliation and Development); appointed by the president on April 18, 2012, to succeed Louis Alphonse KOYAGIALO (Unified Lumumbist Party), who was appointed acting prime minister on March 6; announced new cabinet on April 30, 2012 (approved by Parliament on May 9).

THE COUNTRY

Known prior to independence as the Belgian Congo and variously thereafter as the Federal Republic of the Congo, the Democratic Republic of the Congo (for the first time), Congo-Kinshasa, and Zaire, the Democratic Republic of the Congo (DRC) is situated largely within the hydrographic unit of the Congo River basin, in west-central Africa. The second-largest of the sub-Saharan states, the equatorial country is an ethnic mosaic of some 200 different groups. Bantu tribes (Bakongo, Baluba, and others) represent the largest element in the population, about half of which is Christian. Among the rural population, women are responsible for most subsistence agriculture, with men being the primary cash-crop producers; in urban areas women constitute more than a third of wage earners, many of whom also engage in petty trade on the black market to supplement family income. In 2012 women comprised 8.9 percent of the members of the national assembly (44 of 492 seats) and 4.6 percent of the Senate (5 of 108 seats).

The DRC has major economic potential based on its vast mineral resources, agricultural productivity sufficient for both local consumption and export, and a system of inland waterways that provides access to the interior and is the foundation for almost half of the total hydroelectric potential of Africa. Mineral extraction dominates the economy: cobalt, copper, diamonds, tin, manganese, zinc, silver, cadmium, gold, and tungsten are among the valuable reserves. In addition, offshore oil began flowing in late 1975. Important agricultural products include coffee, rubber, palm oil, cocoa, and tea. Despite these assets, per capita income is one of the lowest in Africa at $236 per year (2012), and the economy has for many years hovered on the brink of disaster. Consequently, infant mortality is high, and primary and secondary education is poor. In addition, universities, once among the continent's finest, are currently neglected, while the country (nearly the size of Western Europe) remains largely devoid of roads outside the major cities.

Economic issues were relegated to the background when civil war broke out in August 1998 (see Political background, below). Real annual per capita GDP fell significantly over the next three years, reaching a low of $85 by the end of 2000 (down from $224 in 1990). (See the 2011 *Handbook* for more detail on the economy prior to 2000.) The alarming situation was also marked by hyperinflation (more than 550 percent in 2000), an estimated 2 million internally displaced persons, and some 350,000 refugees from other countries.

The IMF and World Bank approved a reduction of some 80 percent of the DRC's external debt in 2003, and continued economic improvement was expected in the wake of the partial conclusion of the five-year civil war in 2003 and the installation of a transitional national unity government. An estimated 3–4 million people had died as a result of the recent civil war, mostly from conflict-related disease, starvation, and lack of medicine. In addition, one-fifth of the country's children were dying by the age of five, contributing to "1,200 unnecessary deaths per day," while 1.6 million people remained internally displaced, mostly in the "lawless" east, where rebel groups continued to exploit mineral riches while often brutalizing civilians.

Presidential and legislative elections in 2006 offered hope that political conditions would stabilize and therefore permit the necessary emphasis on economic development. Consequently, the World Bank in May 2007 agreed to provide additional support for the transition. On a more negative note, however, an inquiry was launched in early 2007 into the perceived lack of transparency in mining deals concluded with several Western companies in 2005. For its part, the government announced in June that it would review mining contracts awarded from 1998 to 2003, indicating that it would attempt to renegotiate the contracts so that the DRC would have greater ownership of the assets under review.

In September 2007 China announced plans to invest $5–10 billion to rehabilitate mines and related infrastructure in the DRC. Although GDP grew by 6 percent in 2008, conditions deteriorated sharply in the final quarter of the year as the result of the global economic crisis. The mining sector was particularly hard hit due to a collapse in prices and a collateral decline in foreign investment. With unemployment soaring and annual inflation climbing to 50 percent in April 2009, the IMF approved $195 million in emergency lending to help offset the recent shocks (growth for the year fell to 2.8 percent). In mid-2010 the IMF, World Bank, and other international creditors approved a $12 billion debt relief program after changes were made in the controversial Sino-Congolese "mines for infrastructure" plan. (The IMF and other creditors had demanded that Chinese aid become more concessionary so as not to add to the DRC's external debt.) In 2011, GDP grew by 6.9 percent, and it grew by 7.2 percent the following year. Meanwhile, inflation moderated from 23.5 percent in 2010 to 15.5 percent in 2011 and 9.4 percent in 2012. In 2013, the World Bank ranked the DRC as 181st out of 185 countries in its annual Doing Business survey.

GOVERNMENT AND POLITICS

Political background. The priority given to economic rather than political development during Belgium's 75-year rule of the Belgian Congo contributed to an explosive power vacuum when independence was abruptly granted in June 1960. UN intervention, nominally at the request of the central government headed by President Joseph KASAVUBU, helped check the centrifugal effects of factionalism and tribalism and preserved the territorial integrity of the country during the troubled early years, which witnessed the removal and death of its first prime minister, Patrice LUMUMBA, and the gradual collapse of separatist regimes established by Albert KALONJI in Kasai, Moïse TSHOMBE in Katanga (now Shaba Region), and Antoine GIZENGA in Stanleyville (now Kisangani). The withdrawal of UN peacekeeping forces in 1964 did not mark the end of political struggle, however, with Tshombe, who was appointed interim prime minister in July, and Kasavubu subsequently vying for power of what became (for the first time) the Democratic Republic of the Congo in August. On November 24, 1965, the commander of the army, Maj. Gen. Joseph D. MOBUTU, who had previously held control of the government from September 1960 to February 1961, dissolved the civilian regime and proclaimed himself president of the "Second Republic."

During 1966 and 1967 President Mobutu put down two major challenges to his authority by white mercenaries and Katangan troops associated with the separatist activities of former prime minister Tshombe. (Tshombe died in captivity in Algeria in June 1969.) Other plots were reported in 1971, one of them involving former associates of Mobutu, who in 1970 had been directly elected (albeit as the sole candidate) to the presidency following establishment of the Popular Movement of the Revolution (*Mouvement Populaire de la Révolution*—MPR). Shortly thereafter, in an effort to reduce tension and solidify national unity, Mobutu embarked upon a policy of "authenticity," which included the general adoption of African names. The country was officially redesignated the Republic of Zaire in October 1971.

The country's Shaba Region was the scene of attempted invasions in March 1977 and May 1978 by rebel forces of the Congolese National Liberation Front (*Front de la Libération Nationale Congolaise*—FLNC) directed by a former Katangan police commander, Nathaniel MBUMBA. The first attack, repulsed with the aid of some 1,500 Moroccan troops airlifted to Zaire by France, was said to have failed because of Mbumba's inability to enlist the aid of other groups opposed to the Mobutu regime, particularly the Popular Revolutionary Party (*Parti de la Révolution Populaire*—PRP) in eastern Zaire, led by Laurent Désiré KABILA. Government forces were initially assisted in 1978 by French and Belgian paratroopers, whose presence was defended as necessary to ensure the orderly evacuation of Europeans,

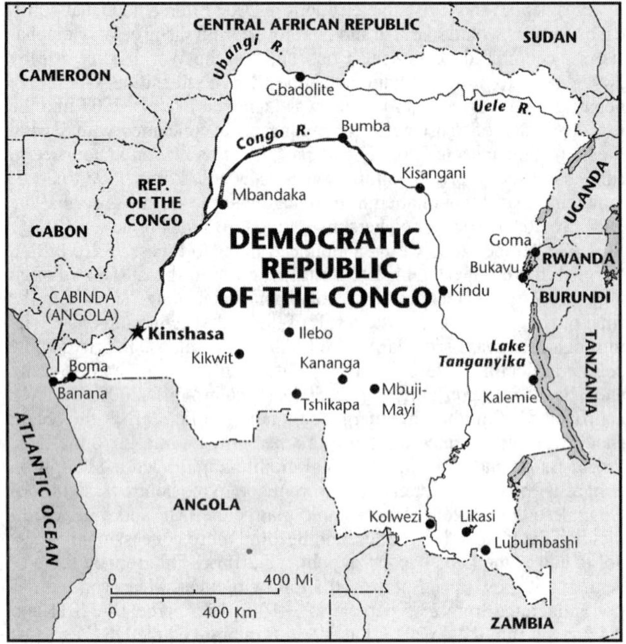

and later by a seven-nation African security force that was not withdrawn until July–August 1979.

The 1977 Shaba invasion was followed by a series of government reforms that included the naming in July of MPINGA Kasenda to the newly created post of first state commissioner (equivalent to prime minister) and the holding of direct elections in October to urban councils, to the National Legislative Council (*Conseil Législatif National*—CLN), and for 18 seats on the MPR Political Bureau. Having been reconfirmed by referendum as MPR president, Mobutu was invested for a second seven-year term as head of state on December 5.

In March 1979 the National Executive Council (cabinet) was reorganized, with André BO-BOLIKO Lok'onga being named to replace Mpinga, who became permanent secretary of the MPR. Jean NGUZA Karl-I-Bond was designated first state commissioner on August 27, and Bo-Boliko assumed the new position of party executive secretary. In April 1981 Nguza resigned while on a trip to Belgium, declaring that he would have been imprisoned had the announcement been made prior to his scheduled departure; N'SINGA Udjuu Ongwakebi Untube was named as his successor. N'singa was in turn replaced by Joseph Léon KENGO wa Dondo in a major government reorganization on November 5, 1982, following a single-party (but multiple-candidate) election to the CLN on September 18–19.

Again presenting himself as the sole candidate, President Mobutu was reelected for a third seven-year term on July 27, 1984. Fifteen months later, on October 31, 1986, he announced that the post of first state commissioner had been abolished. However, the office was restored in the course of a major ministerial reshuffling in January 1987, with former finance minister MABI Mulumba being designated its incumbent. Mabi was in turn succeeded on March 7, 1988, by SAMBWA Pida Nbagui. In the fourth cabinet reshuffling of the year, Sambwa was removed on November 26, and Kengo wa Dondo returned to the post he had held in 1982–1986.

On April 24, 1990, bowing to rising demands for social and political change, Mobutu announced an end to Zaire's one-party system, calling for the constitution to be revised to permit the formation of trade unions and at least two additional parties. One day later he named the secretary general of the Economic Community of Central African States, Vincent de Paul LUNDA Bululu, to succeed Kengo wa Dondo as head of a substantially restructured "transitional" government that was installed on May 4.

The euphoria generated by the prospect of a liberalized "Third Republic" quickly dissipated with continued repression of opposition activity and a presidential declaration that the launching of the limited multiparty system would not take place for at least two years. The result was a bloody confrontation at the University of Lubumbashi on May 11, 1990, during which more than 50 student protesters were reported to have been killed. The legislature responded in late June by altering the constitution to accommodate the regime's April promises and reduce Mobutu's powers. Domestic and international impatience with the government's economic and human rights policies nonetheless continued, and in late November the basic law was further amended in favor of "full" multiparty democracy. On December 31 the president pledged that both presidential and legislative elections, in addition to a referendum on yet another new constitution, would be held in 1991.

On March 3, 1991, most of the more than five dozen political parties issued a demand that the government call a National Conference to consider more extensive constitutional revision. The government acquiesced to the request, but on May 2 the National Conference was postponed following the massacre of 42 opposition supporters by security forces. Subsequently, on July 22, the regime announced that Étienne TSHISEKEDI wa Malumba, leader of the opposition Sacred Union (*Union Sacrée*) coalition, had agreed to become prime minister, and on July 25 MULUMBA Lukoji, who had been named on March 15 to succeed Lunda, was dismissed. However, under pressure from Sacred Union members, Tshisekedi denied that he had accepted the government's offer, and on July 27 Mulumba was returned to office.

The National Conference finally convened on August 7, 1991, but it was suspended a week later after opposition delegates had walked out, protesting that they had been harassed by the police and that the meeting had been illegally packed with regime supporters. The conference reconvened on September 16 after Mobutu agreed to grant it sovereign powers but was again suspended after a near-riotous first day. On September 29 Mobutu accepted a proposed reduction of presidential powers and formation of a cabinet dominated by the opposition. However, the next day Tshisekedi was elected prime minister, triggering a power struggle between the heads of state and government that prevented a scheduled resumption of the National Conference on October 2. On October 14 Tshisekedi secured acceptance of his cabinet nominees, but seven days later he was dismissed by Mobutu. Tshisekedi immediately challenged the legality of the action, and the Sacred Union refused the president's invitation to nominate a successor. Mobutu responded on October 23 by naming Bernadin MUNGUL Diaka, the leader of a small Sacred Union affiliate, to head a new government. Encountering an increasingly violence-prone public, the president on November 22 agreed to a Senegalese-mediated accord with the Sacred Union that stipulated that the next prime minister would be a mutual choice that would "of necessity, come from the ranks of the opposition." Thereupon, former prime minister Jean Nguza Karl-I-Bond, nominally an opposition leader but an opponent of Tshisekedi, presented himself as a candidate for the position and was immediately expelled from the Sacred Union. Apparently hoping to exploit the opposition's disarray, Mobutu disregarded the accord of three days before and designated Nguza as prime minister on November 25.

Mobutu's third seven-year term as president expired on December 4, 1991, but he refused to step down, insisting that he would remain in office until elections could be scheduled. On December 11 the National Conference reconvened, naming Laurent MONSENGWO Pasinya, the archbishop of Kisangani and an outspoken critic of Mobutu, as its president the following day.

On January 14, 1992, Prime Minister Nguza ordered suspension of the National Conference on the grounds that some of its decisions were "provoking a political crisis," and in early February he called for the convening of a smaller "national round table" to draft a new constitution and set a timetable for elections. However, the conference resumed on April 6, and 11 days later it disregarded a government order by asserting its sovereign status. On June 21 President Mobutu again suspended the conference after it had begun debate on the choice of a new prime minister, insisting that such an appointment was a presidential prerogative. That objection notwithstanding, a "global comprehensive policy on transition" was reached on July 30, whereby Mobutu would remain in office for the duration of the interregnum, with former prime minister Tshisekedi being redesignated as head of government.

On August 29, 1992, Tshisekedi named a 21-member cabinet, which, unlike his previous short-lived administration, included no Mobutu associates or MPR members. On September 4 the ban on political demonstrations was lifted, and on September 19 the National Conference revealed details of a draft multiparty, parliamentary-style constitution that it promised to present for a referendum prior to general elections. Meanwhile, Mobutu announced that the MPR would "take no part in the government of national union" and that he too would be presenting a draft constitution. On October 5 Mobutu, supported by the 20,000-strong Special Presidential Division (*Division Spéciale Présidentielle*—DSP), reconvened the CLN for constitutional debate, ignoring the National Conference's August dissolution of the CLN. However, with both Tshisekedi and National Conference president Monsengwo urging a boycott of the "rebellious" legislature, the proceedings were poorly attended and were quickly halted.

On December 1, 1992, Mobutu ordered the dissolution of the Tshisekedi government and the National Conference. Thereafter, faced with the prime minister's refusal to step aside, the president ordered DSP troops to be deployed throughout the capital and released new 5-million Zaïre notes, which he insisted were necessary to pay the army. Meanwhile, on December 6, the National Conference concluded its sitting, electing Monsengwo as head of a transitional legislature (the High Council of the Republic [*Haut Conseil de la République*—HCR]) and demanding that Mobutu abandon his efforts to dissolve the transitional government.

On January 7, 1993, Mobutu declared that he would ignore the HCR's "ultimatum" that he recognize the Tshisekedi government, describing the HCR as having been established "according to antidemocratic procedures." Consequently, the HCR authorized the government to seek foreign intervention to force Mobutu to comply with its dictates and, after accusing Mobutu of "high treason" for "blocking the functioning of the country's institutions at every level," declared its intent to begin impeachment proceedings. On January 20 Tshisekedi announced that he would include MPR members in a "reconciliation" cabinet, and the Sacred Union, announcing a unilateral truce, suspended its demonstrations in support of Mobutu's ouster. However, a new crisis erupted on January 28, when DSP troops attacked anti-Mobutu forces in the capital. On January 29 Belgium and France dispatched troops to protect their citizens, but within days more than 45 people were reported killed, including the French ambassador. On February 3 Belgium, France, and the United States issued a joint statement blaming Mobutu for the breakdown in public order and threatening to isolate the president unless he transferred his executive powers to the prime minister. Mobutu responded two days later by announcing the dismissal of Tshisekedi because of his "inability" to form a national unity government. The president also initiated legal proceedings against Tshisekedi for offenses against state security. On February 9 the HCR, while reportedly chastising Tshisekedi for failing to form a government more acceptable to the president, rejected the dismissal order.

The HCR's efforts to initiate a dialogue between Mobutu and Tshisekedi collapsed on February 24, 1993, when soldiers surrounded the HCR building and demanded that the council recognize the new zaïre note. The siege ended on February 26 following Western diplomatic intervention, and on March 5 Mobutu met with Monsengwo. Although the two failed to reach agreement, Mobutu on March 9 inaugurated a "conclave of the last chance," which, he claimed, had HCR support. On March 17 the conclave, which was ultimately boycotted by the HCR, named former Sacred Union spokesperson Faustin BIRINDWA as prime minister. Birindwa, who had been expelled from the Sacred Union on March 1 for "political truancy," was confirmed by Mobutu on March 29 at the opening of an extraordinary session of the CLN, which had been charged by the president with adopting a "Harmonized Constitutional Text" drafted by the mid-March conference.

On April 2, 1993, Mobutu, in an effort to bolster both his and the CLN's legitimacy, promulgated constitutional amendments establishing the CLN as a transitional institution equal in status to the HCR and confirming the president's right to appoint the prime minister. Concurrently, Birindwa announced a government highlighted by the appointment of Nguza as deputy prime minister for defense. On April 5 Sacred Union activists organized a general strike to protest Birindwa's action, and on April 9 Tshisekedi, who had rejected Birindwa's right to name a cabinet, presented his own reshuffled government, which was approved by the HCR on April 13. On May 7 the Birindwa government released an election timetable calling for a constitutional referendum on July 30, to be followed three months later by elections to choose among the competing governmental institutions. The HCR promptly disputed Birindwa's legal right to call a referendum and urged the opposition to boycott any such proceedings.

In mid-July 1993 the Mobutu regime announced that it had dispatched presidential guardsmen to Kasia, Kivu, and Shaba provinces to help quell ethnic violence that had reportedly claimed more than 3,000 lives. By August the number of casualties had reportedly doubled, eliciting charges by foreign observers that the president's forces were exacerbating the situation in an effort to slow the democratization process. Thereafter, negotiations in September between the regime-supportive Political Forces of the Conclave (*Forces Politiques du Conclave*—FPC) and the Sacred Union of Radical Opposition (*Union Sacrée de l'Opposition Radicale*—USOR), a successor to the Sacred Union, yielded a draft Constitutional Act of the Transition. However, efforts to finalize the accord stalled through the remainder of the year as the FPC continued to reject the USOR's demand that Tshisekedi's prime ministerial status be recognized, arguing that the National Conference's authority had been superseded by the HCR. Meanwhile, at a December 14 rally attended by former prime minister Nguza, Shaba governor Gabriel KUNGUA Kumwanza declared the province's "total autonomy" from Zaire and reversion to its former name of Katanga.

On January 4, 1994, Mobutu issued an ultimatum to the deadlocked FPC and USOR leaderships, ordering them to implement the September 1993 agreement by January 12. Consequently, the two sides agreed on January 11 to the formation of a national unity government that included members from both Birindwa's and Tshisekedi's cabinets, thus prompting Mobutu's January 14 dismissal of Birindwa and dissolution of the CLN and HCR. In addition, Mobutu directed the newly organized High Council of the Republic–Parliament of Transition (*Haut Conseil de la République—Parlement de Transition*—HCR-PT) to deliberate on the prime ministerial candidacies of Tshisekedi and Mulumba Lukoji, who was backed by moderate opposition parties. However, on January 17 Tshisekedi rejected Mobutu's right to dissolve the original HCR and called for a "dead city" general strike on January 19 (the date the new legislature was scheduled to convene).

On January 23, 1994, the HCR-PT held its inaugural meeting, and two days later it appointed Monsengwo as its president. Thereafter, on April 8, the HCR-PT endorsed a second transitional constitution act, inaugurating a 15-month transitional period to culminate in general elections. Following the HCR-PT's acceptance of the credentials of seven prime ministerial candidates (including Tshisekedi) on May 2, Tshisekedi's followers announced their intention to boycott the proceedings and rebuked their USOR coalition partners for nominating candidates to compete against Tshisekedi. Two weeks later, the split within the USOR was formalized when the Tshisekedi faction ousted a number of parties aligned with former prime minister Kengo wa Dondo's Union for the Republic and Democracy (*Union pour la République et la Démocratie*—URD). On May 13 the HCR-PT appointed a commission to define the criteria for choosing a prime minister, and on June 11 it ratified a list of seven individuals that did not include Tshisekedi because "he had not made a proper application to be a candidate." On June 14 the HCR-PT restored Kengo wa Dondo as prime minister, and on July 6 Kengo wa Dondo named a new government. For his part, Tshisekedi insisted that he remained Zaire's legitimate prime minister.

In August 1994 Kengo wa Dondo announced the formation of two electoral preparation commissions and pledged to adhere to a transitional schedule calling for prompt elections. Two months later the USOR rejoined the HCR-PT, and on November 16 Kengo wa Dondo reshuffled his cabinet to allow USOR members to assume posts that had been set aside for them in July. Subsequently, already strained relations between Kengo wa Dondo and Mobutu further deteriorated when Mobutu refused to endorse Kengo wa Dondo's nominee to head the Central Bank of Zaire. Meanwhile, Kengo wa Dondo in mid-December announced in mid-December that long overdue presidential and parliamentary elections, as well as a constitutional referendum, would be held in July 1995; however, in May 1995 the balloting was again postponed.

FPC interim president Mandungu BULA Nyati orchestrated a legislative alliance between his party and the USOR that on June 30, 1995, provided overwhelming support for a two-year extension of the political transition period and, on July 2, successfully forwarded a motion calling for the resignation of HCR-PT president Monsengwo. Thereafter, amid reports that the alliance was planning to force his ouster, Prime Minister Kengo wa Dondo invited the "whole spectrum of the political class" to hold a dialogue and reportedly sought opposition participation in the reshuffled government he named on July 23. However, his entreaties were rebuffed by the USOR, which described the new cabinet as "illegal."

In February 1996 Kengo wa Dondo ousted 23 cabinet ministers, including all remaining opposition sympathizers, and filled their slots with his supporters, thereby rejecting the FPC's call for a new division of cabinet portfolios. Underscoring the level of factionalization in Kinshasa, the prime minister's allies boycotted the inauguration of the National Elections Commission (*Commission des Élections Nationales*—CEN) on April 3, claiming that they had been excluded from leadership positions. Meanwhile, the CEN was charged with preparing for a constitutional referendum in December 1996, presidential and legislative elections in May 1997, and local balloting in June and July 1997.

In May 1996 fighting broke out between indigenous Banyamulenge Tutsis and Rwandan Hutu refugees in the eastern region of South Kivu. Tension had been escalating there since an estimated 700,000–1,000,000 Hutus had fled Rwanda to Zaire in 1994 following the takeover of Kigali by Tutsi military forces. Among the refugees were members of *Interahamwe,* the Hutu militia that had been implicated in the massacre of hundreds of thousands of Tutsis and Hutu "collaborators" in Rwanda in April 1994 (see article on Rwanda). The Hutu militants subsequently gained control of the camps in Zaire, providing a degree of security for the Hutu refugees, who feared reprisals from Tutsis on both sides of the border for the recent "genocide" in Rwanda. Conflict quickly developed between the refugees and the Banyamulenge Tutsis, who numbered an estimated 400,000 in eastern Zaire, where their ancestors had migrated 200 years earlier and where they had achieved a high level of unofficial governmental autonomy. For their parts, the Rwandan government accused the *Interahamwe* of cross-border attacks in western Rwanda, while the Zairean government claimed that Banyamulenge militants were being armed and trained in Rwanda.

On October 8, 1996, amid escalating hostilities in the region, the deputy governor of Kivu, citing a 1981 law stripping the Tutsis of their Zairean citizenship, ordered them to leave the country within a week or risk annihilation. Although the governor was immediately suspended for his comments, thousands of Tutsis fled the area. At the same time, the Banyamulenge fighters, now reportedly numbering 3,000, launched an offensive that resulted in the quick rout of the Hutu fighters from the refugee camps and the retreat of the Zairean troops.

On October 29, 1996, Kinshasa declared a state of emergency in North and South Kivu as theretofore sporadic firefights between Rwandan and Zairean regular forces escalated into intense cross-border shelling. Collaterally, Kinshasa accused the Rwandan and Ugandan governments of attempting to take advantage of the absence of President Mobutu, who continued to convalesce in France from the effects of cancer surgery in August. Meanwhile, the Tutsi rebels, now widely identified as associated with the Alliance of Democratic Forces for the Liberation of Congo-Zaire (*Alliance des Forces Démocratiques pour la Libération du Congo-Zaire*—AFDL) and led by longtime anti-Mobutu guerrilla Laurent Kabila, continued to gain territory along Zaire's eastern border. Their numbers having grown with the addition of militants from dissident ethnic groups, the AFDL fighters reportedly faced little resistance from fleeing Hutus and Zairean troops (many of whom were accused of pillaging the towns they were assigned to protect).

Earlier, in Kinshasa on October 6, 1996, the HCR-PT had adopted a draft constitution that it pledged to present for a referendum in December. The proposed charter was immediately denounced by the USOR's Tshisekedi, who argued that the constitution produced by the 1991–1992 National Conference should be presented unaltered for referendum.

Faced with continued AFDL advances, the HCR-PT on November 1, 1996, called for the expulsion of all Tutsis from Zaire. On November 2 the AFDL captured the city of Goma, and on November 4 Kabila announced a unilateral cease-fire to allow international aid groups to facilitate the repatriation of refugees, the bulk of whom (700,000) were reportedly massed near Mugunga. Amid international demands for the deployment of a military intervention force to stave off a humanitarian disaster, the AFDL on November 11 agreed to open a corridor for aid to reach the refugees and subsequently drove off the remaining Hutu militiamen in the area. Consequently, from November 15 to 19 more than 400,000 Hutu refugees, apparently convinced that it was now safer in Rwanda than in Zaire, flowed across the border, thus effectively dampening international support for the UN's military deployment plans.

On November 21, 1996, the AFDL declared an end to its cease-fire, and over the next several days it announced the appointment of its own officials to administrative positions in the Kivu regions. By early December the rebels had encircled Kisangani, Zaire's fifth-largest city, and reportedly controlled five large towns and a wide swath of territory. On December 17 a visibly ailing Mobutu returned to Kinshasa, and the following day he appointed a new chief of staff, Gen. Mahele Lioko BOKUNGU, and charged him with ending the rebellion. Mobutu met with a broad spectrum of political leaders on December 19 in an attempt to establish a government of national unity to confront the AFDL advance. However, Tshisekedi and his Union for Democracy and Social Progress (*Union pour la Démocratie et le Progrès Social*—UDPS) boycotted the meeting, effectively dooming its chances for success. Consequently, following a week of reportedly intense debate within the presidential circle, Mobutu on December 24 reappointed Kengo wa Dondo as prime minister.

The AFDL drive across Zaire proceeded quickly in early 1997, forcing a tide of Hutu refugees ahead of it, as demoralized Zairean troops offered little effective resistance to the rebels, who were substantially supported by Rwandan forces. (France, the last nation to drop a strong pro-Mobutu stance, described the AFDL as an "invading army.") On March 23 Prime Minister Kengo wa Dondo resigned, although he accepted caretaker status pending establishment of a new government. In what appeared to be a desperate final effort at a political settlement that would preclude a humiliating surrender, Mobutu on April 2 appointed longtime foe Tshisekedi as prime minister. A new cabinet, which included six spots reserved for the AFDL, was announced the following day. However, conflict between security forces and UDPS supporters subsequently broke out in Kinshasa, and Mobutu abruptly dismissed Tshisekedi on April 9, replacing him with Gen. Likulia BOLONGO, former defense minister, who named a cabinet dominated by the military on April 11.

With the international community calling for a negotiated settlement and establishment of a transitional government to avoid widespread bloodletting as the AFDL neared Kinshasa, Mobutu agreed to meet with Kabila and South African president Nelson Mandela on a boat moored off the Zairean coast on May 4. However, although Mobutu reportedly expressed a willingness to relinquish power to a transitional government, final arrangements for his departure were never settled. Mobutu ultimately fled Kinshasa for Togo (and eventually Morocco, where he died on September 7) at the last moment on May 16. Following a brief but murderous rampage by Mobutu loyalists against "traitors" in Kinshasa, AFDL forces entered the capital on May 17. Kabila, still located in the east, immediately declared himself president of the renamed Democratic Republic of the Congo (DRC) and ordered all governmental institutions dissolved.

Kabila arrived in Kinshasa on May 20, 1997, and, after conferring with leaders of various political groupings, made the first appointments to his new cabinet on May 22. However, to the great dismay of long-standing Mobutu opponents, the new regime announced there would be no role for Tshisekedi, whose supporters immediately organized a protest demonstration. In view of the unrest, Kabila on May 26 ordered the suspension of all political party activity and banned mass gatherings of any sort. Surrounded by the presidents of Angola, Burundi, Rwanda, Uganda, and Zambia, Kabila took the presidential oath of office on May 29, having promised a referendum on a new constitution by the end of 1998 and new legislative and presidential elections by April 1999.

After 32 years of Mobutu's dictatorial rule, the populace in May 1997 initially appeared, for the most part, to welcome the AFDL forces as "liberators." Regional leaders also strongly endorsed the regime of President Kabila, reflecting their long-standing complaint that Mobutu had permitted their opponents to conduct rebel activity against them from Zaire. The support from Western capitals was somewhat more cautious, particularly as reports surfaced of the alleged massacre of Hutus by the AFDL during its march across the country. Concern on that front deepened throughout the year and into early 1998 as the administration appeared to stonewall a UN investigation. In addition, widespread domestic disenchantment was reported by early 1998, particularly in regard to the stifling of political party activity and the dismissive treatment accorded to the UDPS and former prime minister Tshisekedi, described as the most popular political figure in the country. Ethnic tensions also continued to simmer, as evidenced by anti-AFDL rebel activity in several regions and reported growing concern over the heavy Tutsi influence at all levels of the AFDL administration. Kabila argued that "outsiders" did not appreciate the difficulties facing the DRC and that it was appropriate for his government to concentrate on reconstruction and the restoration of order while proceeding at a moderate pace toward general elections.

In April 1998 the UN withdrew its investigators, asserting that the Kabila government had purposely blocked their inquiry. Meanwhile, relations deteriorated between the president and the Rwandan-backed Banyamulenge Tutsis who had guided him to power; furthermore, increasing ethnic unrest was reported in the provinces bordering Rwanda and Uganda. In late July Kabila demanded that Rwanda withdraw all of its remaining forces (he had reportedly become convinced that Kigali was preparing to overthrow his government). On August 2 government soldiers stationed in the east were attacked by Banyamulenge rebel forces supported by Rwandan troops. Within days the rebels had opened a second front within striking distance of Kinshasa, and, at a mid-August summit in Goma, the anti-Kabila forces—now bolstered by the addition of "Mobutists" and other former Kabila supporters—formed the Congolese Rally for Democracy (*Rassemblement Congolais pour la Démocratie*—RCD). Meanwhile, the rebel forces continued to capture large swaths of territory and appeared prepared to launch a full-scale attack on Kinshasa. However, in late August Zimbabwean and Angolan troops fighting on behalf of Kabila launched a counteroffensive against the RCD, and soon thereafter Kabila's defenders (now including Namibia and Chad) had fought the rebels to a standstill.

Fierce clashes were reported throughout the end of 1998 and in early 1999, as the fighting spread beyond the DRC's borders. Peacemaking efforts were stymied, however, by Kabila's refusal to negotiate with the RCD, which he had described as a front for Rwandan and Ugandan invasion forces.

A cease-fire agreement was signed in July 1999 at a meeting in Lusaka, Zambia, of the six countries then involved in the fighting in the DRC (Angola, Namibia, and Zimbabwe on the government's side; and Rwanda and Uganda in support of differing RCD factions and increasingly in conflict with one another) as well as Jean-Pierre BEMBA, the "Mobutist" leader of an increasingly important rebel force backed by Uganda called the Movement for the Liberation of the Congo (*Mouvement pour la Libération du Congo*—MLC). The Lusaka accord envisioned the withdrawal of all foreign troops from the DRC, the disarming of local militias under the supervision of a Joint Military Commission, and the eventual deployment of UN peacekeepers. The ruptured RCD (see Political Parties and Groups, below) signed the agreement in August, but renewed fighting quickly broke out between the RCD factions, both of which had repudiated the agreement by the end of the year. (Among other things, the RCD infighting served as a surrogate for the conflict between the forces from Uganda and Rwanda, each of whom was viewed in many quarters as participating in the exploitation of the DRC's mineral wealth.) Nevertheless, in November the UN Security Council authorized the creation of the UN Organizational Mission in the Democratic Republic of the Congo (*Mission de l'Organisation des Nations Unies en République Démocratique du Congo*—MONUC) to assist in monitoring any eventual peace settlement. (In February 2001 the Security Council authorized up to 5,000 personnel for MONUC.)

President Kabila was shot by one of his bodyguards on January 16, 2001, and he was declared dead from the wounds two days later. (The motive for the attack and any possible related conspiracy remained unclear, the assailant having been shot to death immediately after the attack.) On January 24 Kabila's son, Maj. Gen. Joseph KABILA, theretofore his father's chief of staff, was selected by the transitional legislature (installed by Laurent Kabila in August 2000 [see Legislature, below]) to succeed his father. Joseph Kabila immediately called for an intensification of talks toward national reconciliation, and in February another tentative UN-brokered accord was reached. The following month the first MONUC forces arrived in the DRC, but the proposed withdrawal of other foreign troops was delayed, in large part due to Rwanda's insistence that the Hutu militias be disarmed as a precondition to withdrawal. In April, Kabila appointed a new cabinet from which antinegotiation ministers were purged. Fighting, often intense, among RCD factions and between government forces and the rebels continued throughout 2001 and into early 2002 as peace talks inched toward a settlement.

In July 2002 the DRC and Rwanda finally reached a conclusive agreement providing for the withdrawal of the 20,000 Rwandan troops in the DRC starting in mid-September. Two months later a similar accord was struck with Uganda, setting the stage for intensification of talks (known as the Inter-Congolese National Dialogue) involving the government, domestic opposition parties, and rebel groups. Under the weight of heavy international pressure, a potentially historic accord was signed in mid-December in Pretoria, South Africa, by Kabila, the RCD factions, the MLC, and representatives of opposition parties and civil society. The accord provided for a cease-fire and installation of a transitional government pending new national elections within 30 months. Power in the interim government was to be shared, with Kabila, as president, being assisted by four vice presidents and a transitional legislature, whose members would be selected, on a carefully allocated basis, by the signatories. An estimated 3–4 million people died during the 1998–2003 civil war.

The warring factions approved a new interim constitution providing for the installation of Kabila's national unity government in April 2003. Integral to the composition of the cabinet was the inclusion of the four vice presidents representing various constituencies (see Vice President, above). More than half of the cabinet members represented either opposition or rebel groups. In late June most of the former combatants agreed in principle to their integration into a unified national army in which power sharing was to be carefully delineated. That initiative began in August, with Kabila appointing several former rebel commanders to prominent military positions. Rebel groups, civil organizations, and opposition parties were also represented prominently in Kabila's appointments in May 2004 to new provisional governments for the country's ten regions and capital district.

On May 5, 2005, the transitional legislature approved the draft of a new constitution (see Constitution and government, below, for details) for consideration via national referendum, which on December 18 endorsed the new basic law with an 84 percent "yes" vote. President Kabila signed the new constitution into effect on February 18, 2006, setting the stage for national elections of a permanent civilian government.

In the first round of presidential balloting on July 30, 2006, President Kabila, running as an independent but supported by the People's Party for Reconciliation and Development (*Parti du Peuple pour la Réconciliation et le Développement*—PPRD) and some 30 other parties in the Alliance for a Presidential Majority (*Alliance pour la Majorité Présidentielle*—AMP), was credited with 45 percent of the vote. Second place (20 percent of the vote) went to Vice President Jean-Pierre Bemba, the candidate of the MLC and some 23 other parties aligned in the Rally of Congolese Nationalists (*Regroupement des Nationalistes Congolais*—RENACO). The announcement of the first-round results (characterized as fraudulent by Bemba and other candidates) triggered violent demonstrations in Kinshasa. Meanwhile, results from the July 30 voting for the 500-seat National Assembly indicated that the AMP and its allies had secured more than 300 seats, followed by RENACO, with approximately 100 seats, and the Unified Lumumbist Party (*Parti Lumumbiste Unifée*—PALU), with 34 seats.

Kabila was credited with 58 percent of the vote in the runoff presidential balloting against Bemba on October 29, 2006. Bemba immediately challenged the results as fraudulent, but the courts (supported by reports from international observers describing the balloting as generally free and fair) upheld the tally, and Kabila was inaugurated on December 6. On December 31 Kabila announced the appointment of Antoine Gizenga, the aged secretary general of PALU, as prime minister. Following Senate elections on January 19, 2007 (in which the AMP secured a majority of seats), Gizenga formed a new multiparty cabinet on February 5.

The administration hoped that the installation of a multiparty cabinet in February 2007 would signal a peaceful conclusion of the four-year transitional period. However, fighting again broke out in March when security forces attempted to disarm some of Bemba's militia. More than 60 people died, and the government issued an arrest warrant for Bemba, who took refuge in the South African embassy before leaving the country.

Security conditions in the east deteriorated sharply in the fall of 2007 when the National Congress for the Defense of the People (*Congrès National pour la Défense du Peuple*—CNDP) announced it was "going to war" with the DRC army and Hutu militias to protect the Tutsi population. (See section on the CNDP, under Political Parties and Groups, below, for additional information.) The government negotiated a cease-fire with the CNDP and some 20 other small rebel groups in January 2008, but multifaceted unrest continued. The security situation was complicated by the presence in the east of factions of the Democratic Forces for the Liberation of Rwanda (*Forces Démocratiques pour la Libération du Rwanda*—FDLR), which had not signed the earlier cease-fire. (See Political Parties in the article on Rwanda for information on the FDLR, which had been formed by Hutus who had fled to the DRC in the 1990s.)

Prime Minister Gizenga announced his resignation as prime minister on September 25, 2008, citing his advanced age and ill health as obstacles to the government's prospects for resolving the nation's economic crisis and the recent intensification of rebel activity in the east. President Kabila subsequently named PALU's Adolphe MUZITO, theretofore the budget minister, to head a new cabinet, which was approved by the Parliament on November 2. Muzito retained the premiership in a major cabinet reshuffle on February 19, 2010.

Government security forces defeated a coup attempt on February 27, 2011 (see Current issues, below). On March 20 Deputy Prime Minister François Joseph Nzanga MOBUTU (Udemo) was dismissed.

Following the dismissal or resignation of several other ministers, the cabinet was reshuffled in September. Elections scheduled for 2011 were repeatedly postponed.

In disputed balloting on November 28, 2011, Kabila was reelected president (see Current Issues, below). Kabila was sworn in for another term on December 20. Meanwhile, the PPRD secured a reduced plurality in Assembly balloting but was able to fashion a majority with other propresidential parties.

Muzito resigned on March 6, 2012. Louis Alphonse KOYAGIALO (PALU) was appointed acting prime minister the same day. On April 18, 2012, Finance Minister Augustin Matata PONYO Mapon (PPRD) was named prime minister, and he announced a new, smaller cabinet on April 30, which was approved by the legislature on May 9.

Constitution and government. A constitution drafted under President Mobutu's direction and approved by popular referendum in 1967 established a strong presidential system, certain features of which were drastically modified by amendments enacted in August 1974. (For lengthy information on constitutional changes and various proposals for revision from 1974 to 1997, see the 2007 *Handbook.*)

President Laurent Kabila appointed a constitutional commission in September 1997 to produce a new draft basic law by the end of March 1998. The commission was expected to endorse a strong presidential system based on the U.S. model. On March 30, 1998, the commission reportedly adopted a draft basic charter that included provisions for the creation of an elective vice-presidential post, the establishment of an enhanced judiciary system topped by a Supreme Court, and the dissolution of the prime minister's post. Subsequently, President Kabila issued a decree authorizing the formation of a 300-member Legislative and Constituent Assembly, which upon inauguration was to be charged with preparing for a constitutional referendum and legislative elections. Although the assembly was inaugurated in August 2000, no action was taken on the proposed constitution prior to Kabila's death in January 2001, after which the nature of the country's next constitutional arrangements was a primary focus of discussions between the government and rebel forces regarding a permanent peace settlement.

An interim constitution providing for a transitional government was adopted in April 2004 by most of the participants in the Inter-Congolese National Dialogue. The bicameral transitional legislature established by that accord (see Legislature, below, for details) subsequently (in May 2005) approved a draft of a new permanent constitution that was endorsed by national referendum in December. The new basic law provided for a "semipresidential" system in which the prime minister has greater authority than in the past. The president's term was set at five years, renewable once. The minimum age for presidential candidates was reduced to 30, a measure clearly inserted to permit current President Joseph Kabila (34) to run for the office. Presidential balloting is conducted by direct vote under a simple majoritarian system after the legislature abolished the need to gain an absolute majority (through two-round balloting if necessary) in January 2011. The president was mandated to appoint the prime ministerial candidate selected by the majority party (or coalition of parties needed to make a majority) in the National Assembly, the lower house of the new Parliament (see Legislature, below, for details on the Parliament).

The new constitution permitted the current transitional government to remain in place until new national elections were held. Other important aspects included provisions to protect freedom of religion, expression, and political pluralism and to strengthen the judiciary. Citizenship was extended to members of all ethnic groups that were residing in the country at the time of independence.

The new constitution also called for significant devolution of governmental authority to the provinces, the number of which was to be extended from 10 to 26 (including the capital "province" of Kinshasa). Provincial authority was to be shared by presidentially appointed governors and directly elected provincial assemblies. Provinces were to be further subdivided into communes and cities. The provinces were slated to receive 40 percent of all government revenues, but the new decentralization law (covering revenue distribution as well as final codification of provincial powers) remained under debate in the Parliament as of early 2010, reportedly causing consternation among local officials. Judicial authority at the national level was invested in a Supreme Court, a Constitutional Court, a Court of Cassation, and a High Military Court.

Opposition parties have accused state media of favoring the PPRD over other parties, and journalists have been arrested for reporting on demonstrations. Journalism watchdog organizations have reported that press freedom was "deteriorating" and described the media as "highly politicized," with reporters facing a bewildering array of legal restrictions as well as the threat of violence. In 2013 the media watchdog group Reporters Without Borders ranked the DRC 142nd out of 179 countries in terms of freedom of the press.

Foreign relations. The DRC has generally pursued a moderate line in foreign policy while avoiding involvement in non-African issues. Relations with Belgium, its former colonial ruler, were periodically strained following independence, partly because vocal anti-Mobutu factions were based in Brussels. However, Belgium remained a major aid donor. Development efforts following independence led to enhanced economic ties with Japan, the United States, and Western European countries, especially France, which Kinshasa in 1986 called its new European "fountainhead."

Relations with former French territories in central Africa have fluctuated. The Union of Central African States was formed with Chad in 1968, and more than 3,000 Zairean troops were sent to Chad in support of President Habré in 1983. In addition, Burundi and Rwanda joined Zaire in establishing the Economic Community of the Great Lakes Countries, the object being an eventual common market. Relations with Zambia remained cordial despite a Zairean claim (resolved in 1987) to part of that country's northern Kaputa and Lake Mweru districts. In the west, border incidents involving the Republic of the Congo periodically erupted in the 1980s, while in the east, Zairean troops were given permission by Kampala in July 1987 to cross into Ugandan territory to engage rebels associated with the Congolese National Movement (see Political Parties and Groups, below).

A lengthy cold war between Zaire and Angola was formally terminated as the result of a visit by Angolan President Neto to Zaire in August 1978 and a reciprocal visit by President Mobutu to Angola the following October. The latter concluded with the signing of a cooperation agreement between the two governments and a mutual pledge to proceed with the establishment of a commission under the Organization of African Unity (OAU, subsequently the African Union—AU) to guard against rebel violations from either side of the 1,250-mile common border. By 1987, however, it had become apparent that the United States was deeply involved in covert activities in the vicinity of the Belgian-built air base at Kamina in southern Zaire, with plans to remodel the facility for delivery of supplies to the Angolan rebel forces led by Jonas Savimbi. Such collusion notwithstanding, President Mobutu joined in April with the heads of state of Angola, Mozambique, and Zambia in concluding, in Luanda, a declaration of intent to reopen the Benguela railroad, which had effectively been closed by Angolan guerrilla operations since 1976.

In May 1982 Kinshasa announced that it was resuming diplomatic relations with Israel, reversing a rupture that had prevailed since the 1973 Arab-Israeli war. In response, a number of Arab governments severed relations with Zaire, while regional leaders expressed concern at the Israeli "reentry" into Africa. In November, Israel's defense minister, Ariel Sharon, flew to Zaire to conclude arrangements for the supply of arms and the training of Zairean forces, particularly a "presidential battalion" under Mobutu's direct command. Further military-aid commitments were secured by Mobutu during a May 1985 visit to Israel, the regional backlash being tempered in 1986 by Zaire's resumption of participation in the OAU after a two-year hiatus occasioned by the OAU's admission of the Saharan Arab Democratic Republic.

In January 1989 President Mobutu, who had been strongly criticized in the Belgian press for financial aggrandizement, announced that he was abrogating agreements defining his country's postcolonial relations with Belgium. In addition, he said Zaire would halt payments on its more than $1 billion Belgian debt and explore alternatives to shipping its minerals to Belgium for refining. However, the dispute was settled, and relations were normalized at midyear.

In May 1990 Mobutu, labeling Brussels the "capital of subversion," rejected appeals from Belgium and the European Community (EC, subsequently the European Union—EU) for an international inquiry into the slayings at Lubumbashi University. Consequently, on May 24 Belgium halted aid payments, and, following Kinshasa's decision to sever diplomatic links on June 22, Belgium withdrew a debt-cancellation pledge. In August the U.S. Lawyers' Commission for Human Rights released a report describing Zaire's human rights record as a "systematic pattern of abuses." Subsequently, on November 5 the U.S. Congress voted to suspend military aid and redirect humanitarian aid through nongovernmental agencies.

On September 24, 1991, France and Belgium ordered their troops to Zaire to protect foreign nationals threatened by widespread rioting and looting. One month later France and Belgium announced their disengagement from Kinshasa and called for regional intervention. Mobutu responded by vowing to stay in power and accusing international forces of "wanting my head at any price." In November, U.S. officials described Mobutu as having "lost the legitimacy to govern" and called for the regime to begin sharing power with the opposition.

In June 1992 the government announced that it was seizing the assets of all foreign oil companies as a means of alleviating chronic fuel shortages. While officials insisted that the measure was only temporary and promised reimbursement, the companies argued that the action was equivalent to confiscation, given Zaire's lack of currency reserves.

The appointment of the Tshisekedi government in August 1992 paved the way for an end in October to a ten-month-old aid embargo by the EC, although the EC stated its intention to continue to withhold funding until it received guarantees that it would be channeled to the appropriate recipients. Subsequently, in early December 1992 Prime Minister Tshisekedi's Western supporters criticized President Mobutu's attempts to dissolve the government, with Belgium reportedly preparing for a possible military role. The likelihood of such intervention increased dramatically in mid-January 1993 after the HCR had granted the government authorization to seek foreign assistance in ousting the president. Thereafter, following the outbreak of widespread military rioting in Kinshasa, Belgian and French troops were deployed in Kinshasa to protect their citizens.

On February 3, 1993, Belgium, France, and the United States issued a joint statement that described Mobutu as the architect of Zaire's ruin, called for the president's resignation, and threatened "total political and economic isolation" of his regime if he refused to capitulate. In late February, Western diplomats continued to pressure Mobutu, warning him that he would be held personally responsible for the lives of the HCR members then being held captive in Kinshasa. The siege ended the following day.

Following the establishment of the Birindwa government in early April 1993, Mobutu's relations with Zaire's three largest donors deteriorated even further. On April 7 the EC, which followed the lead of several of its members in repudiating the legal status of the new regime, reaffirmed its support for the Tshisekedi government, announced an embargo on arms sales to Zaire, and imposed visa restrictions on Mobutu and his allies. The Birindwa government responded by denouncing the "interference" in its internal affairs, expelling two Belgian diplomats, and, while rebuffing a CLN call to sever ties with the Europeans, warning against further Western action.

In February 1994 Amnesty International accused the regime of continued complicity in human rights violations, charging the Mobutu-controlled military with responsibility for "indiscriminate executions." Moreover, international observers reporting on the plight of Rwandan refugees encamped along the Zairean border in mid-1994 accused Zairean troops of attacking refugees and confiscating their property. However, the Mobutu regime's support for French peacekeeping efforts in Rwanda was apparently rewarded with an easing of international pressure on Mobutu's domestic policies, and in mid-1994 France, Belgium, and the United States recognized the Kengo wa Dondo government.

In early September 1994 Zaire announced that the approximately 1.2 million Rwandan refugees in Zaire would have to leave by the end of the month. Although observers described the demand as unrealistic, it provoked renewed dialogue on the refugees' plight, and on October 24, Rwanda, Zaire, and the United Nations High Commission for Refugees (UNHCR) signed an agreement designed to facilitate their repatriation. However, during the first half of 1995 no further diplomatic progress was reported and conditions in the approximately 40 camps continued to deteriorate. On August 18, 1995, Zaire again ordered the expulsion of the refugees, citing rumors that both Rwanda and Burundi were preparing to attack the camps to suppress rebel groups. Within five days, 15,000 people were forcibly repatriated, while more than 100,000 others fled into the countryside. Pressured by the international community to end the expulsions, Kinshasa halted the program on September 7 and signed an accord with the UNHCR that, echoing the events of 1994, provided for the repatriation of the refugees by December.

In February 1996 Zairean troops, under UNHCR supervision, began sealing off the camps (in an effort to isolate them from the local communities) and urging the refugees to return home. The program was quickly abandoned, however, when the troops, demanding payment of salary arrears, left their posts.

Reportedly concerned about who would actually benefit from a militarily backed humanitarian aid program, as well as fearing involvement in a Somalia-like imbroglio, a number of regional and international capitals, including Washington, reacted warily toward a French- and Spanish-led call for foreign intervention in eastern Zaire in 1996. However, faced with the onset of what aid agencies predicted would ultimately be mass starvation, Canada, South Africa, and the United Kingdom had agreed by November to participate. Further bolstered by a U.S. commitment of 1,000 troops on November 13, the UN-sponsored, Canadian-led multinational force of 15,000 troops began deployment preparations on November 14. The efforts were suspended, however, following the subsequent mass repatriation of hundreds of thousands of refugees to Rwanda between on November 15–19. Consequently, despite continued French lobbying for the dispatch of a military force, wide support for the plan dissipated, and at a meeting of the representatives of 29 countries and 6 aid agencies in Stuttgart, Germany, the operation was officially abandoned on November 22.

The DRC's foreign relations from 1998 to 2001 turned on the roles its neighbors played on both sides of the civil war that erupted in August 1998. Officially supporting the Kabila government with troops were Zimbabwe, Angola, Namibia, and Chad. In addition, Equatorial Guinea, Eritrea, Gabon, and Sudan expressed their sympathies with the DRC government but adopted far smaller roles in the dispute than did the aforementioned countries. On the side of the rebels, Rwanda and Uganda provided such large amounts of personnel and supplies that the Kabila administration accused them of invading DRC territory. To a lesser extent the insurgents were aided by Angolan rebels and supporters in Burundi. Noting the number of countries directly involved in the fighting, a Western official in late 1998 warned that the region was on the brink of the first "African world war."

Uganda withdrew its forces from the DRC by May 2003, and the two countries in 2004 agreed to cooperate in suppressing rebel groups on both sides of their border. However, relations with Rwanda remained strained, the DRC charging that Rwanda was still "stoking discontent" as of 2005.

In December 2005 the International Court of Justice (ICJ) ruled in favor of the DRC in regard to the case the DRC had filed charging Uganda with an "illegal incursion" into the DRC during the 1998–2003 conflict and the "plunder" of the DRC's natural resources. Uganda was ordered by the ICJ to pay reparations to the DRC, although a final amount was not determined. (The DRC was reportedly seeking $6–10 billion.) A similar DRC case was filed against Rwanda, but Rwanda refused to accept ICJ jurisdiction.

Tension resurfaced at the border with Uganda in mid-2007 over islands on Lake Albert, a major base for oil operations in the region. Uganda protested the DRC's establishment of a military presence on one of the islands, but the two countries subsequently agreed to form a joint commission to demarcate the border. (Little progress was reported in that context by mid-2011, while additional border questions had arisen in regard to Uganda's northwest frontier with the DRC, where significant oil deposits had recently been discovered.)

In the wake of extensive fighting in eastern DRC, the DRC and Rwanda in November 2007 announced an agreement to cooperate in disarming militias formed by Hutu rebels in the region. In addition, in April 2008 the DRC, Rwanda, Uganda, and Burundi signed an accord pledging not to harbor each other's dissidents. Meanwhile, the DRC's relations with Belgium deteriorated after a Belgian official criticized the human rights situation in the DRC, perceived ongoing corruption, and the DRC's growing ties with China (whose financial support did not come with the good-governance addendums favored by the EU and Belgium).

Ugandan and Rwandan forces were invited into the DRC in late 2008 and early 2009, respectively, as part of controversial new anti-rebel campaigns (see Current issues, below, for details). Rwanda reestablished diplomatic relations with the DRC in the spring, while the DRC established a joint commission with Angola to negotiate a settlement in regard to their poorly demarcated border, a recent source of friction. Following a meeting between the presidents of the DRC and Rwanda on September 6, 2010, security forces from the two nations conducted joint operations to suppress the FDLR (Democratic Forces for the Liberation of Rwanda).

In April and May 2011 Angola expelled more than 15,000 Congolese refugees. Reports indicated that Angola had also deployed additional troops along its border with the DRC to prevent further refugees.

In February 2012 three senior DRC diplomats in London resigned and sought asylum in the UK after participating in demonstrations in December 2011 against the disputed November balloting (see Current issues, below). Meanwhile international donor agencies threatened to withhold aid over the conduct of the elections.

As part of a regional effort to suppress the Ugandan-based Lord's Resistance Army (see Current issues, below), the United States provided the DRC $10 million to equip and train security forces.

In August 2012, Rwanda announced it would withdraw all its forces from the DRC. A new rebel grouping, the March 23 Movement (*Mouvemet du 23 Mars*—M23), conducted attacks in the eastern region of the DRC throughout the summer, culminating in the capture of Goma in November 2012. Under pressure from regional leaders, the M23 was persuaded to leave Goma in December and enter into talks with the DRC government. The fighting created an estimated 200,000 refugees. Government sources and UN experts accused both Rwanda and Uganda of supporting the militia (see entry on Uganda). The United Kingdom suspended aid to Rwanda over its alleged support for the M23 (see entry on Rwanda). Meanwhile, new reports emerged of rebel groups from Burundi launching attacks into the DRC.

On February 24, 2013, 11 African countries signed the UN-sponsored Peace and Security Cooperation Framework, which aimed to end conflict in the eastern DRC. To support the agreement, in April, the UN Security Council authorized the creation of a 3,000 member "special intervention brigade" to combat the M23. The new force was to operate under the auspices of MOMUSCO and consisted of troops from Tanzania, Malawi, and South Africa. However, the deployment reportedly led to a breakdown in ongoing cease-fire talks between the government and M23. Meanwhile, the mandate of MONUSCO was extended to March 2014. By June, the fighting had created more than 400,000 displaced persons.

Current issues. Periodic violations of the January 2008 cease-fire with the CNDP continued throughout the summer, and the accord collapsed completely in late August and early September when supporters of the CNDP's Laurent NKUNDA launched an intensive campaign against government troops in North Kivu. The fighting displaced more than 250,000 civilians, who also reportedly faced assaults by soldiers on both sides of the conflict as MONUC peacekeeping forces proved ineffective.

In late 2008 the DRC government accused Rwanda of backing the CNDP, a charge that was at least partially validated by a subsequent UN report. Facing intense international pressure, Rwanda in early 2009 agreed to send some 2,000 troops into the DRC for a joint campaign against the FDLR. At the same time dramatic changes within the CNDP significantly altered that group's status (see CNDP under Political Parties and Groups, below, for details). President Kabila was criticized in some domestic quarters for "inviting foreign forces" into the DRC in connection with the anti-FDLR campaign, and Rwanda withdrew its troops in March. DRC forces also continued to battle remnants of the Lord's Resistance Army (LRA) who had crossed over the border from Uganda, despite an anti-LRA campaign in the region involving some 3,000 Ugandan troops earlier in the year.

Instead of leading to the promised "eradication" of the FDLR, the government offensive in 2009 in the east produced what one journalist called "a self-perpetuating pattern of brutality," in which both rebel and army forces were accused of vicious abuses against civilians. Meanwhile, the illegal exploitation of minerals continued unabated, often with the collusion of corrupt government officials and, to at least some extent, the willingness of transnational corporations to turn a blind eye to the source of "conflict minerals." Human rights activists described conditions in North and South Kivu as disastrous and urged MONUS to reconsider its role in the fighting.

In May 2010 the UN operation was renamed the UN Organization Stabilization Mission in the Democratic Republic of the Congo (*Mission de l'Organization des Nations Unies pour le Stabilization de la République Démocratique du Congo*—MONUSCO) as DRC forces were supposed to assume full responsibility for security. Many analysts questioned whether the Kabila administration would be up to that task or be able to deal effectively with widespread corruption, discontent over the slow pace of decentralization, and several outbreaks of ethnic fighting throughout the country. In June, in recognition of continuing strife, the UN extended the mandate of MONUSCO through 2012.

In October 2010 UN officials reported that more than 15,000 rapes had occurred during the 2009 government offensive. UN peacekeepers were criticized for their inability to curb the violence, but officials responded that there were not enough international troops to effectively maintain order. On October 5 a militia commander allied with the FDLR, Lt. Col. Sadoke Kakunda MAYELE, was arrested for crimes against humanity for a raid on a village in North Kiva in which more than 300 rapes were committed. In an effort to address the crimes, a mobile gender court began travelling from area to area to adjudicate gender crimes.

On February 27, 2011, antigovernment forces attacked the presidential palace in a failed coup attempt. Six rebels were killed and more than 30 arrested in what reports described as an attack by disaffected soldiers unhappy over low pay and living conditions. On April 4 an aircraft carrying UN staff crashed, killing 32 of the 33 on board.

Amid widespread violence, Kabila secured 49 percent of the vote in the November 2011 presidential election and won the balloting. Tshisekedi of the UDPS placed second with 32.3 percent, followed by nine other candidates. International observers, opposition groups, and even the country's senior Catholic bishops rejected the results and called for new balloting. Nonetheless, on December 16, the country's high court affirmed Kabila's victory.

In March 2012 CNDP forces started a new round of fighting, and the LRA launched new attacks. In December, the IMF suspended $240 million in loans over mismanagement of natural resources, including mining, oil, and forestry.

In February 2013 a new Mai-Mai militia, the *Bakata Katanga*—(Cut Katanga Off [From Congo]), carried out a series of attacks in villages in the Katanga province, killing at least 65 and creating more than 300,000 displaced persons. In response, the army deployed about 2,500 soldiers, while UN troops were moved along the border with Zambia to prevent cross-border incursions.

In June 2013 the government held a conference on financing the $12 billion Inga III Dam on the Congo River. The project, when combined with the Inga I and Inga II dams, was expected to provide 39,000 megawatts of power, more than China's Three Gorges Dam. South Africa had already pledged $1.4 billion of the costs in exchange for 2,500 megawatts of power under the terms of a March 2013 accord. The African Development Bank and other international financial organizations also pledged funding. Construction is supposed to begin in 2015.

POLITICAL PARTIES AND GROUPS

All existing parties were outlawed in 1965. For the greater part of the next quarter century the only legal grouping was the Popular Movement of the Revolution (MPR). Established under General Mobutu's auspices in April 1967, the MPR progressively integrated itself with the governmental infrastructure. The formation in 1980 by a number of parliamentarians of the opposition Union for Democracy and Social Progress (UDPS) was countered by the MPR, which effectively co-opted most of the UDPS domestic leadership and severely repressed the remainder.

In April 1990 the president announced that the MPR, the UDPS, and one other party would be granted legal status during a "transitional period" culminating in a multiparty election in December 1991. Thereupon, more than 60 groups presented themselves for the remaining legal party position. However, in the face of manifest dissatisfaction with the pace and breadth of his reform program, President Mobutu reversed himself in October and lifted the numeric restriction. As a result, 28 parties were registered by January 1991, the applications of 94 others having been rejected as "incomplete." An additional 38 parties were registered by mid-February, a majority of which were reportedly sympathetic to the MPR, and by March 30 a total of 58 parties had accepted the government's terms for the National Conference scheduled to convene on April 29. Meanwhile, however, leaders of the Sacred Union (*Union Sacrée*), an opposition coalition that included the influential UDPS, UFERI, and the PDSC (see below), announced plans to boycott the conference, refused to recognize the recently named transitional government, and called for President Mobutu's resignation. Thereafter, while the 159 parties registered for the May 3–19 National Conference preparatory committee were described as largely proregime, Mobutu's continued reluctance to enact reforms had begun to alienate many groups, and by midyear the Sacred Union was credited with a membership of approximately 150 parties. The Sacred Union adopted the rubric of the Sacred Union of the Radical Opposition (*Union Sacrée de l'Opposition Radicale*—USOR) in 1993. (For an extensive history of the USOR, defunct as of 1998, see the 1999 *Handbook.*)

Governmental authority was taken over in May 1997 by the Alliance of Democratic Forces for the Liberation of Congo-Zaire (*Alliance des Forces Démocratiques pour la Libération du Congo-Zaire*—AFDL), a predominantly Tutsi grouping of three rebel factions and the ADP (see RCD, below) that had been formed in November 1996 under the leadership of Laurent Kabila, a non-Tutsi

"Lumumbist" who had been linked to anti-Mobutu militant groups since the 1960s. (For more information on the AFDL, which was dissolved by Kabila in 1999, see the 2005–2006 *Handbook.*) The AFDL immediately suspended all political party activity indefinitely, but President Kabila in late January 1999 lifted the ban on the formation of new political parties without, however, addressing the status of the previously existing parties. Moreover, the requirements for registering new parties demanded organizational and financial resources beyond most prospective groupings, while restrictions (such as a ban on any parties with connections to international organizations) also served to preclude participation.

Barriers to party activity were lifted in May 2001, and more than 150 parties had reportedly registered by the end of the year. During the negotiations for the Pretoria Accord of 2002, 15 of the largest opposition political parties formed an alliance called the Opposition General Assembly (OGA) to coordinate strategy and priorities. As a result of the discussions, one of the four vice-presidential posts was designated for Arthur Z'ahidi NGOMA (Forces of the Future), the president of the OGA. Ngoma's appointment was opposed by some opposition parties, while other groups later became dissatisfied with his performance and called for his resignation. The result was a fracturing of the OGA.

By 2005 more than 400 parties had reportedly registered with the Central Election Commission, with some 213 reportedly presenting candidates for the legislative balloting in 2006.

Parties supporting the presidential candidacy of Kabila (officially an independent) formed an Alliance of the Presidential Majority (*Alliance pour la Majorité Présidentielle*—AMP) in June 2006. Core components included the PPRD, UDEMO, PALU, MSR, CCU, PDC, UNAFEC, and more than 20 other small parties. Meanwhile, a number of small parties joined with the MLC to support the presidential candidacy of the MLC's Jean-Pierre Bemba in a coalition called the Rally of Congolese Nationalists (*Regroupement des Nationalistes Congolais*—RENACO). For the second round of presidential balloting, the pro-Bemba parties formed a new coalition called the Union for the Nation (*Union pour la Nation*—UpN). More than 100 parties contested the 2011 legislative balloting.

Government and Government-Supportive Parties:

People's Party for Reconciliation and Development (*Parti du Peuple pour la Réconciliation et le Développement*—PPRD). Formed in March 2002, the PPRD, composed mainly of former regime supporters and members of the government, was seen primarily as a political vehicle for President Joseph Kabila. Kabila initially asserted that he was not formally a member of the party, and even though press reports routinely referenced him as the PPRD presidential candidate in 2006, Kabila officially ran as an independent in order to be the candidate of "all the Congolese people." However, recent reports have routinely referenced the PPRD as "Kabila's party," and the president appeared to solidify his control in March 2009 when he orchestrated the resignation of the PPRD's Vital KAMERHE as speaker of the assembly. Kamerhe, who had criticized Kabila's recent anti-rebel compact with Rwanda, was succeeded by Kabila loyalist Evariste Boshab. Kamerhe subsequently formed a new party, the **Union for the Congolese Nation** (see below).

At a party congress in August 2011, the PPRD chose to endorse Kabila's presidential bid for the November 2011 elections. He won contested balloting as an independent backed by the PPRD and subsequently appointed Augustin Matata PONYO Mapon as prime minister. In June 2013, the PPRD denied reports that it sought to modify the constitution to allow Kabila a third term.

Leaders: Augstin Matata PONYO (Prime Minister), Evariste BOSHAB (Secretary General).

Unified Lumumbist Party (*Parti Lumumbiste Unifiée*—PALU). Another party claiming adherence to its namesake's teachings, PALU is headed by Antoine Gizenga, the former leader of one of the three separatist regimes that emerged in Zaire following Belgium's withdrawal in 1960. On July 29, 1995, at least ten party members were killed during a clash with government security forces outside the parliamentary building.

Gizenga finished third in the first round of presidential balloting in July 2006 with 13 percent of the vote and subsequently endorsed President Kabila in the second round. As the new prime minister, Gizenga formed a government of national unity in February 2007. Following Gizenga's resignation in September 2008, he was succeeded as prime minister by PALU stalwart Adolphe Muzito. PALU endorsed Kabila for the 2011 presidential elections. PALU member Daniel Mukoko SAMBA was appointed deputy prime minister in March 2012. In 2013, PALU member and Mines Minister Martin KABWELULU Labillo was widely criticized after the DRC was suspended from an international mining group after the discovery of an $88 million discrepancy in mine royalties.

Leaders: Antoine GIZENGA (Former Prime Minister and 2006 presidential candidate), Adolphe MUZITO (Former Prime Minister), Daniel Mukoko SAMBA (Deputy Prime Minister), Rémy MAYELE (Secretary).

Other parties that participated in the launching of the AMP included the **Social Movement for Renewal** (*Mouvement Social pour le Renouveau*—MSR); the **Convention of United Congolese** (*Convention des Congolais Unis*—CCU); the **Christian Democratic Party** (*Parti Démocrate Chrétien*—PDC); and the **Union of the Federalist Nationalists of the Congo** (*Union des Nationalistes Fédéralistes du Congo*—UNAFEC). Following the first round of presidential balloting, the **Union of Mobutuist Democrats** (*Union des Démocrates Mobuistes*—UDEMO), whose candidate (François Joseph Nzanga Mobutu, a son of former president Mobutu) had finished fourth with 4.8 percent of the vote, announced its support for President Kabila in the second round of the 2006 balloting. Mobutu subsequently ran as a candidate in the 2011 presidential balloting and secured 1.6 percent of the vote. In the 2011 legislative balloting, the propresidential **People's Party for Peace and Democracy** (*Parti Populaire pour la Paix et la Démocratie*—PPPD) placed third in the balloting with 27 seats.

Other Parties and Groups:

Union for Democracy and Social Progress (*Union pour la Démocratie et le Progrès Social*—UDPS). The UDPS was the outgrowth of an effort in late 1980 to establish an opposition party within Zaire dedicated to the end of President Mobutu's "arbitrary rule." Subsequently, the government arrested, sentenced, and eventually amnestied a number of its members. The leadership was thrown into disarray in late 1987 when UDPS President Frédéric KIBASSA Maliba and several other prominent party members joined the Central Committee of the MPR (see below) following a meeting with President Mobutu in which an agreement was reportedly reached to permit the UDPS to operate as a "tendency" within the governing formation. However, other leaders, including Secretary General Etienne Tshisekedi wa Malumba, vowed to remain in opposition and press for creation of a multiparty system, accusing government security forces of continuing to imprison and torture UDPS adherents.

During a visit to the United States in November 1990, Tshisekedi declared, "The people of Zaire are demanding that he [Mobutu] must go," and, following the UDPS's official registration on January 16, 1991, he announced his presidential candidacy. Thereafter, the party stated that it would boycott any national conference not granted sovereign status and would refuse to join in a transitional government as long as Mobutu remained president.

On September 30, 1991, Tshisekedi agreed to be named prime minister, but two weeks later, following a struggle with Mobutu for executive authority, he was dismissed. Refusing to accept the validity of the president's action, Tshisekedi on November 1 chaired the first meeting of a parallel cabinet. On August 14, 1992, the National Conference voted to return Tshisekedi to the post of prime minister, which he retained until his controversial ouster on December 1.

Tshisekedi served as prime minister for one week in April 1997 as Mobutu desperately attempted to find a political solution to his impending ouster by the AFDL. The UDPS supporters were subsequently described as welcoming to the AFDL and new president Laurent Kabila. However, the relationship deteriorated quickly when Kabila declined to name Tshisekedi to his new government. The UDPS leader was detained in June 1997, and in February 1998 he was sent to his home village under house arrest for violating the ban on party activity. In July, Tshisekedi was returned to Kinshasa and released.

Following Kabila's death in early 2001, Tshisekedi proved to be one of the few old-time party leaders able to retain significant influence. Among other things, he participated in peace and reconciliation negotiations in conjunction with rebel groups and other opposition figures. Nonetheless, the UDPS refused to participate in the 2003 transitional government, and in 2005 it organized a series of demonstrations and rallies to protest the postponement of elections.

Under Tshisekedi's direction (called "dictatorial" by some party dissidents), the UDPS called for a boycott of the December 2005 constitutional referendum. Although Tshisekedi in early 2006 appeared ready to rejoin the political process in preparation for a presidential bid, he ultimately called for a boycott of the presidential and legislative balloting to protest the government's refusal to conduct new voter registration. (Some UDPS dissidents registered for the assembly poll, prompting their expulsion from the party.) Tshisekedi had been considered President Kabila's potentially most serious rival, while the UDPS, which claimed support of some 30 percent of the electorate, had been expected to perform well (and perhaps lead) the legislative election.

The UDPS officially declined to endorse either candidate in the second round of presidential balloting in September 2006, although some local party cadres reportedly supported the MLC's Jean-Pierre Bemba. The UDPS also refused to participate in the February 2007 national unity government. Tshisekedi was the UDPS candidate in the 2011 presidential election and placed second in the balloting with 32.3 percent of the vote. He charged Kabila with electoral fraud and unsuccessfully challenged the results of the contest. The UDPS also led an opposition boycott of the legislature beginning in February 2012. In July 2013, the UDPS rejected a call by Kabila for a "national dialogue" that the party labeled a "sham" designed to legitimize his regime.

Leaders: Etienne TSHISEKEDI wa Malumba (President of the Party and 2011 presidential candidate), Rémy MASSAMBA Makiesse (Secretary General).

Union for the Congolese Nation (*Union pour la Nation Congolaise*—UNC). Formed by Vitale KAMERHE in 2010, the UNC drew defectors from the PPRD. Kamerhe placed third as that party's presidential candidate in 2011 with 7.7 percent of the vote. Meanwhile, the UNC placed sixth in the concurrent legislative balloting, with 16 seats. In November 2012, Kamerhe called on the government to negotiate with the M23.

Leader: Vitale KAMERHE (2011 presidential candidate).

Congolese Rally for Democracy (*Rassemblement Congolais pour la Démocratie*—RCD). The RCD was formed in mid-August 1998 in Goma by the leaders of the predominantly Banyamulenge Tutsi rebels who had launched a military offensive against the government of Laurent Kabila on August 2. Ernest WAMBA dia Wamba, a theretofore largely unknown academic, emerged from the Goma meeting as the leader of the anti-Kabila forces. In addition, the RCD's leadership committee included Arthur Z'ahidi Ngoma, the prominent founder of the anti-Mobutu and subsequently anti-Kabila Forces of the Future, as well as two former Kabila government ministers, Bizima KARABA and Déogratias BUGERA. Bugera had been the leader and founder of the People's Democratic Alliance (*Alliance Démocratique des Peuples*—ADP), a military grouping of Tutsis that had been described as the dominant component of the AFDL as it marched across Zaire to seize the capital in May 1997 but had been ordered out of Kinshasa by the president in late July 1998.

In early 1999 RCD dissidents led by Bugera broke away from the group and formed the Reformers' Movement (*Mouvement des Réformateurs*—MR), and in February Ngoma formed the Union of Congolese for Peace, which he asserted would seek a peaceful solution to the country's crisis. Further intraparty friction was reported in March between Wamba dia Wamba, who allegedly sought a "political" end to the civil war, and a promilitary faction led by Alexis TAMBWE and former prime minister Vincent de Paul Lunda Bululu. Meanwhile, a hard-liner, Emile ILUNGA, assumed command of the RCD's military operations amid reports that Wamba dia Wamba was losing control of the group. In May, Ilunga replaced Wamba dia Wamba as president of the RCD, and the group split into two warring factions, Ilunga's being backed by Rwanda and Wamba dia Wamba's by Uganda. In October the latter faction adopted the rubric **RCD–Liberation Movement** (*RCD—Mouvement de la Libération*—RCD-LM). Ilunga was succeeded as president of the main RCD faction (now referenced as RCD-Goma) in October 2000 by Adolphe Onusumba Yemba. Meanwhile, yet another faction (**RCD–National** [RCD-N]) had broken off in June 2000 under the leadership of Roger Lumbala Tshitenge. In May 2001 Antipas Mbusa Nyamwisi forcefully took control of the RCD-LM from Wamba dia Wamba.

The RCD groups participated in the Inter-Congolese National Dialogue and were signatories to the Pretoria Accord. Under the terms of the agreement, RCD-Goma secretary general Azarias Ruberwa Manywa was appointed one of four vice presidents of the republic in July 2003. The RCD factions agreed to disarm, and a portion of their troops were integrated into the national security forces. In addition, the RCD factions received seats in both the Senate and National Assembly and posts in the transitional cabinet. However, the RCD-Goma briefly suspended participation in the transitional government in 2004 to protest the massacre of Tutsis in neighboring Burundi and what it viewed as the failure of the DRC government to take stronger action to protect refugees.

For the 2006 presidential election Ruberwa was listed as the official candidate of the RCD, although press reports continued to reference him as the candidate of RCD-Goma, while Lumbala ran as a candidate of the RCD-N and Nyamwisi as the candidate of the **Forces of Renewal** (*Forces du Renouveau*—FR).

Ruberwa finished 6th in the first round of presidential balloting in July 2006 with 1.7 percent of the vote, while Nyamwisi finished 11th with 0.6 percent and Lumbala 17th with 0.45 percent. (Shortly before the election, Nyamwisi had announced his support for President Kabila, and Nyamwisi joined the cabinets installed in February and November 2007 and February 2010 as a representative of the FR.) Nyamwisi ran unsuccessfully as an independent in 2011 presidential balloting and won 1.7 percent of the vote. By 2013, Ruberwa had reportedly become focused on the Congo Family Restoration NGO, which placed orphans with families in the DRC.

Leaders: Antipas Mbusa NYAMWISI (RCD-LM and FR), Adolphe ONUSUMBA Yemba (RCD-Goma), Roger LUMBALA Tshitenge (RCD-N), Azarias RUBERWA Manywa (Former Vice President of the Republic and Secretary General of RCD-Goma).

Movement for the Liberation of the Congo (*Mouvement pour la Libération du Congo*—MLC). The MLC was launched in Equateur Province in November 1998 by Jean-Pierre Bemba, a "Mobutist" who was allegedly funded by Ugandan sources. Subsequently, bolstered by a series of military successes against government forces, the MLC agreed to coordinate its actions with the RCD, which was backed by Rwanda. That alliance proved short-lived, however, in view of the conflict that soon developed between Uganda and Rwanda.

Like the other major rebel groups, the MLC participated in the Inter-Congolese National Dialogue and signed the Pretoria Accord. MLC fighters were subsequently integrated into the national security forces, and the party became a member of the transitional government. MLC leader Bemba was sworn in as one of four vice presidents for the DRC on July 17, 2003, and the MLC was given equal representation with the RCD-Goma and the opposition alliance in the cabinet and the transitional legislature.

After finishing second in the 2006 presidential election, Bemba was accused by the government in early 2007 of fostering antigovernment "rebellion." He left the country for Portugal after a warrant for his arrest was issued in the DRC in March 2007. Bemba was arrested in May 2008 in Belgium on a warrant issued by the International Criminal Court (ICC) in The Hague, Netherlands, accusing him of war crimes in connection with MLC activity in the Central African Republic (CAR) in 2002–2003. (The MLC had intervened in the CAR in support of President Patassé, who was ultimately overthrown.) Bemba, a DRC senator who had recently been "elected" as the unofficial leader of the opposition, was arraigned at the ICC in July, and his assets were subsequently seized in Portugal. Meanwhile, friction was reported between MLC hard-liners and those party members inclined to cooperate with the new national unity government. Bemba's trial began on November 22, 2010, and he was not able to participate in campaigning for the DRC presidential poll scheduled for November 2011 since the ICC refused bail. Consequently, the MLC did not field a presidential candidate, although longtime party official Adam Bombole INTOLE ran as an independent and secured 0.7 percent of the vote. Bemba was scheduled to conclude his defense before the ICC in October 2013.

Leaders: Jean-Pierre BEMBA (2006 presidential candidate; currently on trial in the Netherlands), François MWAMBA (Secretary General).

Federalist Christian Democracy (*Démocratie Chrétienne Fédéraliste*). This party is led by Pierre Pay-Pay wa Syakassighe, a former central bank governor who, as the candidate of the 18-party **Coalition of Congolese Democrats** (*Coalition des Démocrates Congolais*—CODECO), finished seventh in the first round of presidential balloting in July 2006 with 1.6 percent of the votes. He endorsed Joseph Kabila in the second round, and CODECO joined the AMP, thereby earning participation in the 2007 national unity cabinet. However, Syakassighe did not participate in subsequent governments or the 2011 presidential election.

Leader: Pierre Pay-Pay wa SYAKASSIGHE (2006 presidential candidate).

Popular Movement for Renewal (*Mouvement Populaire Renouveau*—MPR). Founded in 1967 as the principal vehicle of the Mobutu regime and known until August 1990 as the Popular Movement of the Revolution (*Mouvement Populaire de la Révolution*), the MPR was long committed to a program of indigenous nationalism, or "authenticity." Prior to political liberalization in 1990 each Zairean was legally assumed to be a member of the party at birth.

The 1988 MPR Congress reaffirmed support for the country's single-party system. However, in May 1990 President Mobutu, after signaling the introduction of a multiparty system, stepped down as MPR chair, stating that he would henceforth serve "above parties"; he resumed the post in April 1991. During Mobutu's absence the party split into factions led by N'SINGA Udjuu Ongwakebei (the new chair) and Felix Vunduawe te Pemako, who termed the restructured entity "illegitimate" and presented himself as leader of a "group to renew the People's Revolution."

Faced with vigorous Western opposition to Mobutu's continuance in office, the party at an April 1993 general meeting called on the Birindwa government to sever diplomatic relations with Belgium, France, and the United States, all of which were accused of "stirring up hatred, division, and destruction" and engaging in "neo-colonialism, imperialism... and terrorism against Zaire."

Mobutu died of prostate cancer in September 1997, only months after his ouster from Kinshasa by the AFDL. Subsequently, the MPR (with the term "Revolution" once again being used routinely in its references rather than "Renewal") split into two factions, one led by Vunduawe and a second led by Catherine Nzuzi wa Mbombo. Nzuzi was subsequently jailed for 20 months before being released by Joseph Kabila. She was appointed minister for solidarity and humanitarian affairs in the 2003 transitional government, and she received 0.38 percent of the vote in the first round of presidential balloting in July 2006. By 2012 the party was reportedly defunct.

Leaders: Felix VUNDUAWE te Pemako, Catherine NZUZI wa Mbombo (2006 presidential candidate).

Innovating Forces of the Sacred Union (*Forces Innovatrices de la Union Sacrée*—FONUS). FONUS is led by Joseph Olenghankoy, a hard-line USOR member who was arrested in 1994 for declaring the government guilty of "unconstitutional" behavior and in 1998 for engaging in illegal party activity. Olenghankoy was appointed minister of transport and communication in the 2003 transitional government. He received 0.6 percent of the vote in the first round of presidential balloting in July 2006, and the party won one seat in the Assembly. FONUS opposed the deployment of UN peacekeepers along the border between the DRC and Rwanda.

Leader: Joseph OLENGHANKOY (2006 presidential candidate).

Congolese National Movement (*Mouvement National Congolais*—MNC). From the 1970s to the 1990s, the MNC was an exile group with at least two discernible factions, the Congolese National Movement–Lumumba (*Mouvement National Congolais–Lumumba*—MNC-L), whose military wing operated as the Lumumba Patriotic Army (*Armíe Patriotique Lumumba*—APL), and the Reformed Congolese National Movement (*Mouvement National Congolais Rénové*—MNCR). The MNC became visible in 1978 when its president was detained by Belgian authorities and expelled to France, with similar action taken against its secretary general in 1984 after the group claimed responsibility for a series of March bombings in Kinshasa. In 1985 the MNC emerged as the most active of the external groups; in April it issued a statement calling Mobutu "an element of instability in central Africa" and listing those allegedly killed by government troops during disturbances in eastern provinces in late 1984. In September 1985 leaders of both the MNC-L and the MNCR joined with the Swiss-based Congolese Democratic and Socialist Party (*Parti Démocratique et Socialiste Congolaise*), led by Allah FIOR Muyinda, in inviting other opposition groups to participate in a joint working commission to oversee "activities [to be launched] over the whole country in coming days." MNCR leader Paul-Roger MOKEDE was named president of the exile provisional government at a meeting in Switzerland in September 1987 but rejected the designation on the grounds that Zaire could not "afford the luxury" of a parallel regime.

In September 1994 a group identifying itself as the MNC-L was reportedly "formed" in Kinshasa by "nationalists" and Lumumbists under the leadership of Pascal TABU, Mbalo MEKA, and Otoko OKITASOMBO. The older, or original, MNC faction became known as the MNC–*Lumumba Originel* or Original Lumumba (MNC-LO).

In early 1998 François Lumumba, eldest son of the former prime minister, charged that the regime of Laurent Kabila was denying freedom of expression to him and other family members. Lumumba emerged as leader of the MNC-L. He was briefly detained by the government in 2000.

Leader: François Tolenga LUMUMBA (MNC-L).

Mai-Mai Ingilima. The Mai-Mai was an ethnic Bahunde militia whose members were described as "armed mystics" for their belief, among others, that the grass headgear they wore in battle possessed the power to turn their enemies' bullets into water (*mai-mai* is the Swahili word for water). Credited with disarming Hutu fighters and Zairean soldiers at the start of the 1996 rebellion, the Mai-Mai was expected to coordinate their actions with the AFDL as the fighting moved into northern Zaire. However, in December 1996 the Mai-Mai was accused of attempting to assassinate AFDL commander Andre Ngandu KISSASSE, who allegedly wanted the Mai-Mai to disarm and report for training. In early 1997 further clashes between the rebel groups were reported, and later in the year the Mai-Mai grouping was described as fully confrontational with the national army of the new Kabila regime in pursuit of regional autonomy for South Kivu. Thereafter, beginning in August 1998, the Mai-Mai was described as alternately cooperating with and clashing with elements of the RCD, in addition to continuing its antigovernment military activities. The Mai-Mai became formally allied with the Kabila government during the Inter-Congolese National Dialogue that culminated in the Pretoria Accord, and the Mai-Mai was subsequently given cabinet posts and seats in the transitional government. However, some Mai-Mai forces later turned hostile to the government under the leadership of a warlord identified as GÉDÉON and assumed control of regions of Katanga. After his forces were accused of attacks on civilians, Gédéon surrendered to MONUC in April 2006. The group presented candidates in the 2006 assembly balloting under the banner of the **Mai-Mai Movement** (*Mouvement Maï-Maï*—MMM).

Fighting was subsequently reported between members of the CNDP (below) and a Mai-Mai offshoot called the **Congolese Resistance Patriots** (*Patriotes Résistants du Congo*—Pareco), described as a "progovernment civil defense" grouping under the leadership of Sendugu MUSEVENI. Pareco was also believed to have aligned itself informally with the FDLR in eastern DRC, but in February 2009, following the DRC/Rwanda initiative against the FDLR, it was reported that Pareco for the most part had agreed to integrate into the DRC's military, while Pareco sought legal party status under Museveni's leadership. Subsequently, a faction called **The Alliance of Patriots for a Free and Sovereign Congo** (*Alliance des Patriotes pour un Congo Libre et Souverain*—APCLS) reportedly remained in conflict with the government, possibly in alliance with Rwandan rebels. In 2011 Human Rights Watch accused the APCLS of forcibly recruiting youth under the age of 18 to fight against government forces. In August 2012 the government reportedly requested assistance from the APCLS in fighting the M23 militia. A new militant force, the *Bakata Katanga*—(Cut Katanga Off [From Congo]), led by Ferdinand Tanda IMENA, emerged in 2013.

Union of Congolese Patriots (*Union des Patriotes Congolais*—UPC). The UPC was formed as an antigovernment militia by members of the Hema ethnic group in the Ituri region. Although the UPC was reportedly subsequently registered as a political party, its leader, Thomas LUBANGA, was turned over to the new International Criminal Court (ICC) in March 2006 to face charges of war crimes and human rights abuses. By that time, some remnants of the UPC had reportedly helped launch the MRC (see below). ICC judges ordered Lubanga released in July 2008 on the grounds that evidence had been mishandled by prosecutors, although Lubanga remained in custody pending an appeal of that decision. The case against Lubanga was reinstated in early 2009. He was convicted in March 2012 and sentenced to 14 years in prison in July. The ICC also ruled that his victims were entitled to compensation from the court's Trust Fund for Victims.

National Congress for the Defense of the People (*Congrès National pour la Défense du Peuple*—CNDP). The CNDP was formed in late 2006 by rebel leader Gen. Laurent Nkunda, a Congolese Tutsi whose followers had aligned with Rwanda in the rebellion against the government of Laurent Kabila in the late 1990s. Nkunda described the

CNDP as a "political-military movement" intended to protect the interests of Tutsis, who reportedly felt "marginalized" by the DRC government and threatened by Hutu rebels who had coalesced in eastern DRC as the Democratic Forces for the Liberation of Rwanda (*Forces Démocratiques pour la Libération du Rwanda*—FDLR). Fighting was reported later in the year between the CNDP and FDLR, with the CNDP accusing MONUC and the DRC government of "siding" with the FDLR.

In January 2007 Nkunda agreed to discuss a peace agreement with the government on the assumption that CNDP fighters would eventually be integrated into the national army and that the government would agree to protect the rights of Tutsis. However, in September Nkunda announced his forces would resume antigovernment military activity and intensify its anti-FDLR campaign. Heavy fighting throughout the rest of the year left as many as 500,000 people displaced in the conflict zone. Having achieved significant military success (despite the tacit endorsement by the United States and other western nations of the government's anti-CNDP initiative), Nkunda in January 2008 joined a number of other rebel leaders in signing a cease-fire agreement with the government providing for a buffer zone to be monitored by MONUC, amnesty for the "insurrectionists," and integration of rebel troops into the national army. However, the accord subsequently collapsed, the CNDP having been charged with numerous violations of the cease-fire as well as human rights abuses.

After a UN report in late 2008 catalogued the CNDP's Rwandan ties, the Rwanda government in early 2009 appeared to sever any relationship with Nkunda and other CNDP militants, apparently in return for the DRC's cooperation in an anti-FDLR campaign (see Current issues, above, for additional information). Jean-Bosco Ntaganda, theretofore the CNDP's chief of staff and, like Nkunda, wanted on war crimes charges by the ICC, announced that he had assumed leadership of the CNDP. In a dramatic reversal, the Rwandan authorities arrested Nkunda in late January in Rwanda, while Ntaganda announced a cease-fire with the DRC. The CNDP subsequently indicated it would seek legal party status in the DRC under the leadership of Désiré Kamandji.

The CNDP was not included in the new cabinet appointed in February 2010, and Kamandji charged the government with dragging its feet in regard to implementation of a March 2009 peace agreement. Meanwhile, Nkunda remained under house arrest as of midyear, although his trial was postponed. By 2011 an estimated 6,600 CNDP fighters had been integrated into the DRC army. In March 2012 Ntaganda led a revolt by CNDP fighters who broke away from government security forces. He later was instrumental in the formation of the M23.

Leaders: Gen. Laurent NKUNDA, (under house arrest in Rwanda), Philippe GAFISHI, Désiré KAMANDJI, Bertrand BISIMWA, Serge Kambatsu NGEVE (Secretary General).

Bundu Dia Kongo (BDK). The BDK is a political-religious movement dedicated to the restoration of the former Kingdom of Kongo in the DRC's southwestern province of Bas-Congo and surrounding regions, both inside and outside the DRC. Significant fighting was reported in March 2008 between BDK fighters and government security forces. A 2010 UN report was critical of government forces for human rights violations in their campaign against the BDK, including the massacre of more than 100 BDK members.

Leader: Ne Mwanda NSEMI.

Other groups include the **Congolese People's Movement for the Republic** (*Mouvement Populaire Congolais pour le République*—MPCR), led by Jean-Claude VUEMBA; the **Congolese Socialist Party** (*Congolais Parti Socialiste*), led by Christian BADIBANGI; the **Union of Forces of Change** (*Union des Forces du Changement*—UFC), led by 2011 presidential candidate Léon Kengo Wa DONDO; the **Alliance of Congolese Nationalist Believers** (*Alliance des Nationalistes Congolais Croyants*—ANCC), led by 2011 presidential candidate Jean Andeka DJAMBA; the **Union for the Revival and the Development of the Congo** (*Union pour le Renouveau et le Développement du Congo*—URDC), led by 2011 presidential contender François Nicéphore Kakese MALELA; the **Union for the Rebuilding of Congo** (Union pour la reconstruction du congo—UREC), led by the party's 2011 presidential candidate Oscar KASHALA LLUKUMUENA; the **Forces of the Future** (*Forces du Futur*—FDF), led by Arthur Z'ahidi NGOMA, who had been jailed from November 1997 to June 1998 and subsequently became an RCD leader before going into exile in France (see RCD, above) and then returning to serve as vice president of the republic from 2003 to 2006 (Ngoma ran for president in 2006 as the candidate of a party called **Camp of the Fatherland** [*Camp de la Patrie*]); the **Movement for Solidarity, Democracy, and Development** (*Mouvement pour la Solidarité, la Démocratie, et le Développement*—MSDD), whose leader, Christophe LUTUNDULA Apala, chaired the legislative committee that investigated alleged corruption in the issuance of government contracts during the 1998–2003 civil war; the **National Convention for Political Action**; the **Union of Republicans** (*Union des Républicains*), whose leader, Norbert LUYEYE, was arrested in May 2009 for criticizing the presence of Ugandan and Rwandan troops on DRC territory; the **Peasant Reconciliation and Development Party**, formed in April 2009 by a Mai-Mai faction led by Bita ZEBEDE; the **Congolese Democratic Party**, whose leader, Gabriel MOKIA, was sentenced to ten months in prison in April 2009 on a charge of "undermining the authority of the state" in connection with his criticism of government military policy; the **Union of Congolese Revolutionaries,** whose leader, Raymond Cheni ANDRIOZI, was reportedly arrested in Uganda in March 2010 along with Boston KASONGO, the leader of the **Popular Movement of Social Democracy,** on charges of planning an "invasion" of the DRC; the **Congolese National Liberation Front,** which, under the leadership of retired general Elie Kapend KANYIMBU, was reportedly involved in a demonstration in mid-2010 calling for the secession of Katanga; and the **Peasant Reconciliation and Development Party,** comprising former Mai-Mai warriors led by Pastor Bita ZEBEDE. For more information on the **Alliance for the Renaissance of Congo** (*Alliance pour la Renaissance du Congo*—ARC), please see the 2013 *Handbook.*

Other parties that won representation in the assembly in the 2006 balloting included the **Convention of the Christian Democrats** (*Convention des Démocrates Chrétiens*—CDC), whose presidential candidate, Florentin Mokonda BONZA, won 0.29 percent of the vote in 2006 and whose president is Gilbert KIAKWAMA; **Christian Democracy** (*Démocratie Chrétienne*—DC), which presented Eugene Ndougala DIOMI as its 2006 presidential candidate; the **Rally of Socialist Forces** (*Rassemblement des Forces Sociales et Fédéralistes*—RSF), whose presidential candidate, Vincent de Paul LUNDA Bululu (former prime minister), placed eighth in the first round of the 2006 poll with 1.4 percent of the vote; the **Convention for the Republic and Democracy** (*Convention pour la République et la Démocratie*—CRD), whose leader, Christophe N'KODIA Pwango Mboso, secured 0.47 percent of the vote in the first round of the 2006 presidential poll; the **Alliance of Congolese Democrats** (*Alliance des Démocrates Congolais*—ADECO), whose 2006 presidential candidate was Jonas Kadiata Nzemba MUKAMBA; and the **Union for the Defense of the Republic** (*Union pour la Défense de la République*—UDR), whose 2006 presidential candidate was Wivine N'Landu KAVIDI. (For a list of parties that participated unsuccessfully in 2006, see the 2010 *Handbook.*)

Rebel and Militia Groups:

March 23 Movement (*Mouvemet du 23 Mars*—M23). M23 was formed in April 2012. The eastern rebel group took its name from the March 23, 2009, peace accord between the government and the CNDP. The group was reportedly supported by Rwanda and had a series of military victories in 2012, including the capture of Goma, from which it later withdrew. By 2013, the group had split into two factions, after Jean-Marie RUNIGA Lugerero was ousted as M23 leader following internal strife over whether to negotiate with the DRC government. One group was led by Gen. Sultani Makenga, with about 1,300 fighters, the other by Gen. Bosco Ntaganda (who was allied with Runiga). Ntaganda and approximately 700 of his supporters fled to Rwanda in March 2013, where he surrendered to the International Criminal Court to face trial for war crimes against civilians.

Leaders: Sultani MAKENGA, Bosco NTAGANDA.

Other rebel and former rebel groups include the **Nationalist and Integrationist Front** (*Front Nationaliste Integrationiste*—FNI), an ethnic Lendu separatist group active in Ituri that was suspected of being responsible for attacks against MONUC forces and whose military leader, Etiene LONA, surrendered to the UN in March 2005 and another former FNI leader, Mathieu NGUDJOLO Chui, was arrested in February 2008 on an ICC warrant accusing him of war crimes in relation to ethnic fighting in Ituri in 2002–2003, although he and other FNI fighters had been integrated into the DRC's national army (Ngudjolo was acquitted of all charges in December 2012); the **Congolese Patriots Union–Kisembo** (UPC-Kisembo), a breakaway faction of the UPC, led by Floribert Kisembo BAHEMUKA; the **Patriotic Resistance Force in Ituri** (*Force de Résistance Patriotique en Ituri*—FRPI), a Lendu group linked to the FNI and led by Germain KATANGA, who was transferred to the control of the ICC in 2008 after being charged with war crimes; the **Popular Front for Justice in the Congo** (*Front Populair pour la Justice au Congo*—FPJC), an FRPI offshoot formed in October 2008 and subsequently reported to be conducting operations against government forces in the northeast under the leadership of Sheriff MANDA; the **Republican Resistance Forces** (FRF), a Tutsi group that signed a peace accord in 2008 but was reportedly still in conflict with the government at the end of 2009; and the **Front for the Liberation of Eastern Congo,** a group composed of former members of the RCD.

For more information on the **Democratic and Social Christian Party** (*Parti Démocrate et Social Chrétien*—PDSC), the **Nationalist Common Front** (*Front Commun Nationaliste*—FCN), and the **Planters' Solidarity Party** (*Parti du Solidarité du Planteurs*—PSP), see the 2011 *Handbook*. For information on the **Congolese Revolutionary Movement** (*Mouvement Révolutionnaire Congolais*—MRC) and the **Rwanda Democratic Liberation Front**, please see the 2012 *Handbook*.

LEGISLATURE

On August 21, 2000, a new Legislative and Constituent Assembly–Transitional Parliament was inaugurated. President Laurent Kabila directly appointed 60 of the 300 members, while the remaining members were selected in consultation with a presidentially appointed commission. (For information on quasi-legislative development from 1992 to 2000, see the 2007 *Handbook*.)

The December 2002 Pretoria Accord provided for the establishment of a bicameral legislature through an interim constitution. The representatives from both chambers were appointed from the major political parties, civic groups, and rebel factions. Both chambers of the Transitional Parliament were inaugurated on August 23, 2003.

The constitution promulgated in February 2006 provided for a new bicameral **Parliament** comprising a Senate and a National Assembly.

Senate (*Sénat*). The interim Senate appointed through negotiations following the Pretoria Accord of 2002 consisted of 120 members. Each of the 5 major political groups received 22 positions, including pro-presidential parties (led by the People's Party for Reconstruction and Development [PPRD]); the opposition alliance; the Congolese Rally for Democracy (RCD-Goma); the Movement for the Liberation of Congo (MLC); and civic groups. In addition, the Mai-Mai received 4 seats; the RCD-Liberation Movement, 4; and the RCD-National, 2.

The current Senate comprises 108 members elected indirectly by the provincial assemblies for five-year terms, as well as all former elected presidents of the republic, who serve as senators for life. Direct elections for the nation's 11 provincial assemblies were held on October 29, 2006, and those assemblies selected the members of the Senate on January 19, 2007, resulting in the following distribution of elected seats: the PPRD, 22; the MLC, 13; the RCD, 8; the Christian Democrat Party, 8; the Forces for Renewal, 6; the Convention of Christian Democrats, 1; the RCD-National, 1; the Democratic Social Christian Party, 1; the National Alliance Party for Unity, 1; the Union of Mobutuist Democrats, 1; the Democratic Convention for Development, 1; the Social Front of Independent Republicans, 1; the Coalition of Congolese Democrats, 1; the Alliance of Congolese Democrats, 1; the National Union of Christian Democrats, 1; the Rally of Social and Federalist Forces, 1; the Rally for Economic and Social Development, 1; the Federalist Christian Democracy, 1; the National Union of Federalist Democrats, 1; others, 4; and independents, 25. The next Senate elections were postponed until June 2013.

President: Joseph Léon KENGO wa Dondo.

National Assembly (*Assemblée Nationale*). The interim National Assembly comprised 500 deputies appointed from the major political groups in the DRC. The five main groups each received 94 seats, including propresidential parties (led by the People's Party for Reconstruction and Development [PPRD]); the opposition alliance; the Congolese Rally for Democracy (RCD-Goma); the Movement for the Liberation of Congo (MLC); and civic groups. The RCD–Liberation Movement was given 15 seats; the Mai-Mai, 10; and the RCD-National, 5.

The current assembly comprises 500 deputies—69 elected by one-round plurality voting in single-member constituencies and 431 elected by proportional representation in 109 multimember constituencies. In the most recent elections to the assembly on November 28, 2011, the most significant groupings to secure seats were the People's Party for Reconciliation and Development, which won 63 seats; the Union for Democracy and Social Progress, 41; the People's Party for Peace and Development, 27; the Movement for the Liberation of the Congo, 22; the Unified Lumumbist Party, 19; and the Union for the Congolese Nation, 17. The remaining 294 seats were divided among 98 other parties (17 seats remained vacant following the balloting).

Speaker: Timothée KOMBO Nkisi (acting).

CABINET

[as of November 5, 2013]

Prime Minister	Augustin Matata Ponyo Mapon (PPRD)
Deputy Prime Ministers	
	Daniel Mukoko Samba (PALU)
	Alexandre Luba Ntambo
Ministers	
Agriculture and Rural Development	Jean Chrysostome Vahamwiti Mukesyayira
Budget	Daniel Mukoko Samba (PALU)
Civil Service	Jean Claude Kibala
Commerce and Economy	Jean Paul Nemoyato Begepole
Employment, Labor and Social Welfare	Modeste Bahati Lukwebo
Environment, Conservation of Nature, and Tourism	Bayon N'sa Mputu Elima
Finance	Augustin Matata Ponyo Mapon (PPRD)
Foreign Affairs, International Cooperation, and Francophonie	Raymond Tshibanda N'Tunga Mulongo
Gender, Family, and Children	Géneviève Inagosi [f]
Higher Education and Scientific Research	Chelo Lotsima
Hydrocarbons	Crispin Atama Tabe
Hydropower and Energy	Bruno Kapanji Kalala
Industry	Rémy Musungayi Bampale
Interior, Security, Decentralization, and Customary Affairs	Richard Muyej Mangez (PPRD)
Justice and Human Rights	Wivine Mumba Matipa [f]
Land Affairs	Robert Mbwinga Bila
Media, in Charge of Relations with Parliament and Citizenship	Lambert Mende Omalanga
Mines	Martin Kabwelulu Labillo (PALU)
National Defense and Veterans	Alexandre Luba Ntambo
Planning and Modernization	Celestin Vunabandi Kanyamihigo
Posts, Telecommunications, New Information Technologies, and Communications	Tryphon Kin Kiey Mullumba
Primary, Secondary, and Professional Education	Maker Mwangu Famba
Public Health	Félix Kabange Numbi Mukwampa
Regional and Town Planning, Housing, Infrastructure, Public Works, and Reconstruction	Fridolin Kasweshi Musoka
Small- and Medium-Sized Enterprises	Rémy Musungayi Bampale
Social Affairs, Humanitarian Action, and National Solidarity	Charles Nawej Mundele
Transport and Communications	Justin Kalumba Mwana Ngongo (PANU)

Youth, Sports, Culture, and the Arts	Banza Mukalayi Nsungu
Without Portfolio	Louise Munga Mesozi [f]

[f] = female

INTERGOVERNMENTAL REPRESENTATION

Ambassador to the U.S.: Faida MITIFU.

U.S. Ambassador to the Democratic Republic of the Congo: James F. ENTWISTLE.

Permanent Representative to the UN: Ignace GATA MAVITA.

IGO Memberships (Non-UN): AfDB, AU, Comesa, ICC, IOM, NAM, SADC, WTO.

REPUBLIC OF THE CONGO

République du Congo

Political Status: Independent since August 15, 1960; one-party People's Republic proclaimed December 31, 1969; multiparty system authorized as of January 1, 1991; constitution approved in referendum of March 15, 1992, suspended in October 1997 following overthrow of the government; current constitution adopted by referendum of January 20, 2002.

Area: 132,046 sq. mi. (342,000 sq. km).

Population: 4,254,470 (2012E—UN); 4,492,689 (2013E—U.S. Census).

Major Urban Center (2007C): BRAZZAVILLE (1,373,382).

Official Language: French.

Monetary Unit: CFA Franc (official rate November 1, 2013: 486.52 francs = $1US). The CFA franc, previously pegged to the French franc, is now permanently pegged to the euro at 655.957 CFA francs = 1 euro.

President: Gen. Denis SASSOU-NGUESSO (Congolese Labor Party); sworn in on October 25, 1997, following the military overthrow of the government of Pascal LISSOUBA (Pan-African Union for Social Democracy) on October 23; elected for a seven-year term on March 10, 2002, and inaugurated on August 10; reelected on July 12, 2009, and sworn in for another seven-year term on August 14; formed a new government (abolishing the position of prime minister) on September 15.

THE COUNTRY

The Republic of the Congo is a narrow 800-mile-long strip of heavily forested territory extending inland from the Atlantic along the Congo and Ubangi rivers. It is bordered on the west by Gabon, on the north by Cameroon and the Central African Republic, and on the east and south by the Democratic Republic of the Congo (formerly Zaire). The members of the country's multitribal society belong mainly to the Bakongo, Matéké, Mbochi, and Vili tribal groups and include numerous pygmies, who are thought to be among the first inhabitants of the area. Linguistically, the tribes speak related Bantu languages. French, although the official language, is not in widespread use. However Monokutuba is widely employed in commerce. In recent decades there has been substantial rural-to-urban migration, with close to 50 percent of the population living in or near Brazzaville or Pointe Noir. Partly because of its level of urbanization, the Republic of the Congo has a literacy rate estimated at 70–85 percent, one of the highest in black Africa. About half of the population adheres to traditional religious beliefs, while Roman Catholics, Protestants, and Muslims comprise the remainder. Women remain underrepresented in politics. Following the 2011 elections, women held 10 of 72 seats in the Senate (13.9 percent). After the 2012 Assembly balloting, women held 10 of 136 seats (7.4 percent).

Although the country possesses deposits of manganese, copper, lead-zinc, and gold, its leading resources are oil and timber. The economy was severely compromised following the five-month civil war of mid-1997, which, among other things, heavily damaged the capital and reduced GDP growth from about 6.3 percent in 1996 to a negative rate in 1997.

The International Monetary Fund (IMF) and the World Bank suspended aid to the Republic of the Congo in 2000 because of the perceived failure of the government to enact economic reforms. Partial aid was restored in 2004, although the government by that time faced heavy international criticism on an important regional issue—diamond exporting. Meanwhile, the Republic of the Congo remained one of the poorest countries in the world, although increased revenue from high oil prices had at least permitted the government to pay off arrears in civil service salaries.

High oil prices, along with increased stability since the end of the civil war, helped bolster the economy in 2005–2006, with average GDP growth of about 6 percent recorded. However, a debt relief agreement with the IMF and the World Bank in early 2006 failed to come to fruition in October due to the government's reported failure to provide greater transparency in state finances, particularly in regard to oil revenues. The IMF was particularly concerned by a British court's confirmation that Sassou-Nguesso's government had channeled oil revenues into secret accounts.

A temporary setback in oil production, caused by an accident at an oil platform, contributed to a decline in overall economic activity in 2007, according to the IMF, but robustness resumed in 2008 in both the oil and non-oil sectors, with annual GDP growth of 8.5 percent. Fund managers also commended the government for its social reforms, a number of which had helped offset the impact of high food and fuel prices early in the year. Despite the global economic crisis, annual GDP averaged 9 percent in 2009–2010, owing to significant expansion of oil production, which peaked in 2011. Meanwhile, the IMF and the World Bank agreed to provide $1.9 billion in debt relief under the Heavily Indebted Poor Countries program. Growth slowed to 3.4 percent in 2011 and 3.8 percent in 2012, as oil production declined (an estimated 68 percent of the country's GDP was tied to petroleum production). In 2012, inflation was 5 percent, while GDP per capita was $4,426. Unemployment was estimated to be as high as 50 percent, with 50 percent of the population living in poverty. In 2013, the World Bank ranked Republic of the Congo as one of the worst countries in which to do business, rating it 183rd out of 185 nations.

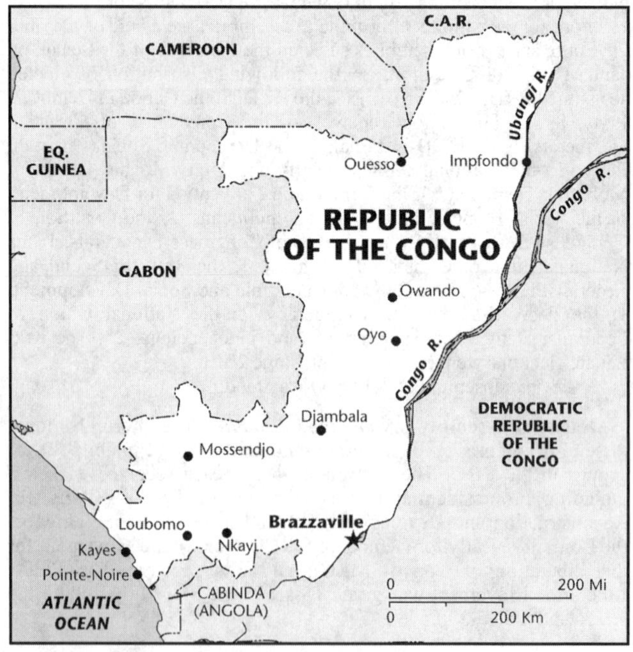

GOVERNMENT AND POLITICS

Political background. Occupied by France in the 1880s, the former colony of Middle Congo became the autonomous Republic of the Congo in 1958 and attained full independence within the French Community on August 15, 1960. The country's first president, Fulbert YOULOU, established a strong centralized administration but resigned in 1963 in the face of numerous strikes and labor demonstrations. His successor, Alphonse MASSAMBA-DÉBAT, was installed by the military and subsequently reelected for a five-year term. Under Massamba-Débat the regime embraced a Marxist-type doctrine of "scientific socialism," and the political system was reorganized on a one-party basis. In 1968, however, Massamba-Débat was stripped of authority as a result of differences with both left-wing and military elements. A military coup led by Capt. Marien NGOUABI on August 3 was followed by the establishment of a National Council of the Revolution to direct the government.

Formally designated as head of state in January 1969, Ngouabi proclaimed a "people's republic" the following December, while a constitution adopted in January 1970 legitimized a single political party, the Congolese Labor Party (*Parti Congolais du Travail*—PCT). Three years later, a new basic law established the post of prime minister and created a National Assembly to replace the one dissolved in 1968.

President Ngouabi was assassinated on March 18, 1977, and the PCT immediately transferred its powers to an 11-member Military Committee headed by Jacques-Joachim YHOMBI-OPANGO, which reinstituted rule by decree. Former president Massamba-Débat, who was accused of having plotted the assassination, was executed on March 25. On April 3 it was announced that Maj. Denis SASSOU-NGUESSO had been named first vice president of the Military Committee and that Maj. Louis-Sylvain GOMA, who retained his post as prime minister, had been named second vice president.

Responding to pressure from the Central Committee of the PCT after having made disparaging remarks about the condition of the country's economy, General Yhombi-Opango, as well as the Military Committee, resigned on February 5, 1979. The Central Committee thereupon established a ruling Provisional Committee and named Sassou-Nguesso as interim president. At a March congress the party confirmed Sassou-Nguesso as president, while on July 8 the voters approved a new constitution and elected a People's National Assembly in addition to district, regional, and local councils. On July 30, 1984, the president was elected for a second term, and on August 11, as part of a reshuffling aimed at "strengthening the revolutionary process," he named Ange-Edouard POUNGUI to succeed Goma as prime minister.

In July 1987, 20 military officers linked to a group of Paris-based exiles were arrested on charges of plotting a coup. Thereafter, an alleged co-conspirator, Lt. Pierre ANGA, who charged that Sassou-Nguesso had participated in the murder of former president Ngouabi, led a rebellion in the north. Reports of attacks by rebel forces continued until July 4, 1988, when the killing of Anga by government troops ended the uprising.

On July 30, 1989, Sassou-Nguesso was reelected for a third term at the fourth PCT party congress. However, continued debate over the foundering economy led to an extraordinary congress in August at which a moderate technocrat, Alphonse POATY-SOUCHLATY, was named to succeed Poungui as prime minister.

In October 1990, confronted with a general strike that had brought the country to a standstill and acting on a party decision reached three months earlier, General Sassou-Nguesso announced that a multiparty system would be introduced on January 1, 1991, followed by the convening of an all-party National Conference to chart the nation's political future. On January 14 he appointed a "transitional" government headed by former prime minister Goma, Poaty-Souchlaty having resigned on December 3 in protest over the president's call for the introduction of pluralism.

The National Conference, which encompassed representatives of 30 parties and 141 associations, convened for a three-month sitting on February 25, 1991, eventually approving the draft of a new democratic constitution; dropping "People's" from the country's name; transferring most presidential powers to the prime minister; scheduling a constitutional referendum for November; and calling for multiparty local, legislative, and presidential elections during the first half of 1992. On June 8, two days before its conclusion, the conference elected André MILONGO prime minister. Four days later, Milongo named a 25-member cabinet, which on September 15 was reduced to 15 ministers amid charges that members of the opposition coalition Forces of Change (*Forces de Changement*—FDC) were overrepresented.

After a series of postponements, the March 15, 1992, referendum on the new basic law was credited with securing 96 percent approval. Meanwhile, the Milongo government had barely survived a January 19 army mutiny triggered by allegations that transfers of senior officers had been politically motivated. Municipal elections, originally scheduled for March, were eventually held on May 3, while two-stage legislative balloting that was to have been held in April and May was also delayed, with numerous complaints of irregularities at the first stage on June 24.

At second-stage assembly balloting on July 24, 1992, the Pan-African Union for Social Democracy (*Union PanAfricaine pour la Démocratie Sociale*—UPADS) emerged as the clear winner, as it did in a senate poll two days later, albeit without securing a majority in either body. In first-round presidential balloting on August 2, the UPADS nominee, Pascal LISSOUBA, led a field of 17 candidates but secured only 35.9 percent of the vote, thus necessitating a second round against Bernard KOLÉLAS of the Congolese Movement for Democracy and Integral Development (*Mouvement Congolais pour la Démocratie et le Développement Intégral*—MCDDI), who had garnered 22.9 percent. Among those eliminated in the first round were Sassou-Nguesso and Milongo, with vote shares of 16 and 10 percent, respectively. On August 11 the UPADS and PCT announced a coalition, with the outgoing president urging his followers to support the UPADS leader. Thus reinforced, Lissouba outdistanced Kolélas in the second round on August 16 by a margin of 61.3 to 38.7 percent. In the wake of his victory, Lissouba promised a broadly representative government and indicated that he would petition the National Assembly to pardon Sassou-Nguesso and other top officials for crimes committed while in office. On September 1 Lissouba named Maurice-Stéphane BONGHO-NOUARRA of the National Alliance for Democracy (*Alliance Nationale pour la Démocratie*—AND) as prime minister. Six days later Bongho-Nouarra announced a cabinet that included a number of opposition leaders, although Kolélas declined to join them.

In late September 1992 the UPADS-PCT pact dissolved over the choice of a National Assembly president. Shortly thereafter, the PCT concluded an Opposition Coalition (*Coalition de l'Opposition*—CO) with Kolélas's recently formed Union for Democratic Renewal (*Union pour le Renouveau Démocratique*—URD), itself a seven-party antigovernment alliance that included the MCDDI. The CO moved quickly to assert itself and on October 31 successfully moved a no-confidence vote against the government. On November 11 the coalition called for a campaign of civil disobedience and strikes in an effort to force Lissouba to name a CO member as prime minister. On November 14 Bongho-Nouarra resigned, praising President Lissouba for attempting to "pull Congo out of the abyss." Subsequent negotiations between Lissouba and Kolélas led to an impasse, and on November 17 the president, accusing the coalition of "despicable and premeditated acts," dissolved the National Assembly and scheduled a new election for December 30. A wave of civil unrest promptly paralyzed the capital's commercial sector, and by the end of November opposition legislators and security forces were described as in "open confrontation." On December 2 the military occupied Brazzaville, dispersed demonstrators, ordered the government and opposition to form a unity government headed by a compromise prime minister, and suspended election preparations. Four days later, Lissouba appointed Claude-Antoine DACOSTA, an agronomist and former World Bank representative, as prime minister. The government named by Dacosta on December 25 included 12 members from the CO and 9 with links to the president.

At rescheduled assembly balloting on May 2 and June 6, 1993, President Lissouba's 60-party Presidential Tendency (*Tendance Présidentielle*) was credited with winning 69 of 125 seats. However, insisting that the first round had been "tarnished by monstrous irregularities," the opposition demanded a rerun in 12 constituencies and boycotted the second-round balloting. Furthermore, on June 8 Kolélas called for a campaign of civil disobedience to force new elections, thus igniting widespread violence. Subsequent negotiations to stem the unrest failed, as the Opposition Coalition rejected Lissouba's offer to rerun the second round. On June 22 the CO boycotted the National Assembly's inauguration, and the following day, concurrent with Lissouba's appointment of Yhombi-Opango as prime minister, it named Jean-Pierre THYSTERE-TCHICAYE of the Rally for Democracy and Social Progress (*Rassemblement pour la Démocratie et le Progrès Social*—RDPS) to head a parallel "national salvation" government.

On July 7, 1993, amid what Lissouba now labeled an "armed rebellion," a curfew was imposed in Brazzaville. Negotiations remained at an impasse until late July, when Gabonese and UN mediators brokered an unofficial disarmament pact, and on August 4 government and opposition negotiators in Libreville, Gabon, signed an agreement calling for an internationally supervised rerun of the second round of assembly elections and the establishment of an international arbitration committee to rule on first-round disputes. On August 16, with the violence abating, a month-old state of emergency in Brazzaville was rescinded, and on September 17 the curfew was lifted. Meanwhile, the Senate agreed to a rerun of the June voting, although it rejected establishment of the arbitration committee on the grounds that the August accord had been a "private deal among political parties."

At the second-round rerun in October 1993, the Opposition Coalition won 7 of the 11 contests, increasing its representation to 56 seats, while the Presidential Tendency's majority fell to 65. However, in early November the cease-fire collapsed, with dozens of people reported killed in the capital when government forces responded to the kidnapping of two government officials and a sniper attack with a fierce assault on opposition strongholds, particularly in the Bacongo District. Despite bilateral calls in late November for a cease-fire and disarmament, fighting continued throughout 1994.

On January 23, 1995, CO unity was shattered by a URD agreement to participate in a restructured Yhombi-Opango government, a move that was flatly rejected by the PCT. Another coalition member, the National Union for Democracy and Progress (*Union Nationale pour la Démocratie et Progrès*—UNDP), echoed the PCT's sentiments, declaring that it would take no part in the government's "chaotic management of the country" and accusing President Lissouba of "a divide-and-rule strategy."

Regional divisions remained at the fore in 1995 as the Lissouba administration sought to end the northerners' dominance of the 25,000-member military as well as to disarm and integrate the numerous militias that were organized during the 1993 civil unrest and continued to cause widespread instability. In August Lissouba declared that the military would be restructured to reflect a "tribal and regional equilibrium"; however, the military leadership and opposition strenuously objected to the plan, particularly efforts to integrate Lissouba loyalists. In September government troops attempting to disarm militiamen loyal to Sassou-Nguesso met fierce resistance in Brazzaville. Consequently, on November 3 Lissouba proposed assimilating all militiamen into the armed forces. Nevertheless, two days later, National Defense Minister (and former prime minister) Maurice-Stéphane Bongho-Nouarra rejected an administration attempt to absorb 250 militiamen with alleged presidential loyalties, saying that he wanted to depoliticize the recruitment process.

On December 24, 1995, the leaders of the Congo's major propresidential and opposition tendencies signed a peace pact that included provisions for the disarmament and subsequent integration of the former combatants into the national army. However, efforts to implement the accord were dealt a setback on February 14, 1996, when more than 100 recently integrated former militiamen with ties to the UPADS led a violent mutiny in Mpila that left 5 people dead and 40 injured. The rebellion ended on February 19 after negotiations between the government and rebellious troops yielded another integration agreement favoring the latter. Consequently, the opposition United Democratic Forces (*Forces Démocratiques Unies*—FDU) boycotted the peace process for a month, denouncing the government's willingness to "reward" the mutineers and calling for equal representation in the armed forces.

On August 23, 1996, Prime Minister Yhombi-Opango resigned. (He went into exile in 1997.) His replacement, David Charles GANAO, leader of the Union of Democratic Forces (*Union des Forces Démocratiques*—UFD), on September 2 organized a new government that was nearly evenly split between old and new ministers.

Preparations for presidential elections (scheduled for July 27, 1997) had begun in earnest on May 4, 1996, when the National Census Commission (*Commission Nationale pour le Recensement*—CNR) was inaugurated. However, the CNR was immediately immersed in controversy when the opposition sharply criticized the appointment of President Lissouba as the commission's chair, arguing that it undermined the government's pledge to "ensure transparency" during the electoral run-up. Lissouba subsequently resigned as CNR chair; however, the appointment of Prime Minister Yhombi-Opango as his successor proved equally unsatisfying to the opposition, which called for establishment of an independent commission. In July MCDDI leader Kolélas announced his presidential candidacy, joining a field that already included Lissouba and Gen. Jean-Marie Michel MOKOKO of the Movement for Congolese Reconciliation (*Mouvement pour la Réconciliation Congolaise*—MRC).

Tensions between supporters of Sassou-Nguesso and Lissouba, the two leading presidential candidates, increased as the election approached. In May 1997 Sassou-Nguesso survived an assassination attempt while campaigning, and on June 5 the army surrounded his home, claiming it was part of an effort to disarm private militias. The showdown quickly escalated into civil war, and by mid-July about 4,000 were dead. President Lissouba successfully petitioned the Constitutional Court to postpone the election and extend the expiration date of his mandate, as of July 22. The action enraged Sassou-Nguesso's forces, and fighting spread north despite mediation efforts by the United Nations (UN) and the Organization of African Unity (OAU, subsequently the African Union—AU).

Lissouba appointed Kolélas, then mayor of Brazzaville, as prime minister on September 9, 1997, replacing Ganao, who had resigned on the same day. Kolélas formed a new unity government on September 13, but allies of Sassou-Nguesso declined the posts reserved for them. Kolélas was backed by a 40-party movement, the Republican Space for the Defense of Democracy and National Unity (*Espace Républicain pour la Défense de la Démocratie et Unité Nationale*—ERDDUN), though apparently it was identified too closely with Lissouba forces to have credibility with the rebels.

With the participation of a variety of mercenaries and regular troops from neighboring countries, the civil war continued into mid-October, with Sassou-Nguesso triumphantly entering the destroyed capital on October 23 and being sworn in as president two days later. On November 3 Sassou-Nguesso named a new, broadly representative transitional government but abolished the position of prime minister and initially reserved the defense portfolio for himself.

On January 5–14, 1998, the government hosted the National Forum for Reconciliation, Unity, Democracy, and the Reconstruction of the Congo, which was attended by more than 1,400 participants, most of them, however, from within parties or other organizations identified with the FDU. The forum endorsed a "flexible" three-year transition to democracy during which a new constitution would be drafted and a national constitutional referendum held. New presidential and legislative elections would follow. The forum elected a 75-member National Transition Council to oversee the process, but it also accused the ousted president, Lissouba, and his allies of a planned "genocide" and urged that they be brought before the appropriate judicial venue. Meanwhile, Lissouba and Kolélas proclaimed a government in exile, with the former prime minister calling for a campaign of civil disobedience in opposition to the Sassou-Nguesso regime.

Throughout 1998, militias loyal to Lissouba and Kolélas—the so-called Cocoyes (in the south) and Ninjas (in the central Pool region), respectively—continued to battle the Cobra militias, which supported Sassou-Nguesso, forcing tens of thousands of civilians to flee and causing thousands of deaths. In December a major battle for control of Brazzaville erupted, and it was not until mid-1999 that victories by the army and Cobra forces made the eventual outcome a near-certainty. In August Sassou-Nguesso offered amnesty to opposition militiamen who surrendered their arms, and on November 16 a peace plan, including the amnesty and a cessation of hostilities, was accepted by most of the opposition forces. Lissouba and Kolélas, still abroad, rejected the agreement. In late December, President Omar Bongo of Gabon, who had assumed the role of mediator between the interim government and the opposition militias, oversaw the signing of a second peace agreement, and by early 2000 the conflict appeared to have reached a conclusion. The 1990s had witnessed an estimated 20,000 deaths due to civil strife, with some 800,000 made homeless. On May 4, 2000, Kolélas and his nephew, former minister of the interior Col. Philippe BIKINKITA, having been tried in absentia, were sentenced to death for crimes committed against prisoners in 1997. Kolélas subsequently went into exile.

Although some areas of the country remained under militia control, in January 2001 the government announced that a "non-exclusive national dialogue" on a draft constitution, the peace plan, and national reconstruction would be held. Local sessions were conducted throughout the country in March and were followed by a convention in Brazzaville April 11–14. Although some representatives of former governments participated, Lissouba and Kolélas continued their opposition. The convention concluded by adopting the constitutional draft, which was approved in final form by the National Transition Council in September. The new basic law, which retained a strong presidency and a bicameral parliament, was endorsed by 84 percent of the voters in a public referendum on January 20, 2002, though much of the opposition leadership urged a boycott. A month earlier Lissouba had been convicted in absentia of treason and misappropriation of funds and sentenced to 30 years in prison.

Sassou-Nguesso, facing no significant opponent following the withdrawal of former prime minister Milongo from the race, was elected to a seven-year term in presidential balloting on March 10, 2002, with 89.4 percent of the vote. He was sworn in on August 14. In two-stage balloting for the new 137-seat National Assembly on May 26 and June 20, the president's PCT and the allied FDU won 83 seats, while indirect elections for the 66-seat Senate on July 11 produced an even greater majority for the government.

The PCT and FDU reportedly secured more than two-thirds of the seats in local balloting on June 30, 2002, a number of opposition parties having boycotted those elections to protest perceived mismanagement in the recent presidential poll. Consequently, the new Council of Ministers appointed on August 18 did not include any members of the opposition.

On January 7, 2005, President Sassou-Nguesso appointed Isidore MVOUBA of the PCT to what the president called the "honorary" post of prime minister and reshuffled the cabinet. In a partial senate election on October 2, 2005, the PCT won 23 of 30 contested seats, with 6 of the remaining seats reportedly going to members of government coalition parties and 1 to an independent.

In March 2007, ahead of National Assembly elections scheduled for June and July, President Sassou-Nguesso reshuffled the cabinet, and in a notable political move he offered former CNR rebel leader Frédéric BITSANGOU a nonministerial government position. (The CNR had registered as a political party in January 2007.) Another historically significant event occurred following Kolélas's return from exile, when the MCDDI agreed in April 2007 to an electoral alliance with the PCT for the 2007 legislative elections and the 2009 presidential poll. (Fighting in the Pool region, where the MCDDI has significant support, had restricted the MCDDI's participation in the 2002 assembly elections to only 8 of 24 areas in the region.) The unprecedented alliance with the PCT was seen as enhancing prospects for both parties for a "comfortable and stable majority" in the isolated Pool region. The two parties agreed to "rule together," according to the pact.

In balloting that the opposition claimed was marred by irregularities—charges that postponed second-round balloting by several weeks—the PCT and its allies reportedly secured 124 of the 137 National Assembly seats in the elections held on June 24 and August 5, 2007. While independents were recorded as having won 37 seats, most of those candidates were said to be aligned with the PCT. Eight of the independents elected were said to be affiliated with the Pole Young Republicans (PJR), a political association established by the president's son, Christel Denis SASSOU-NGUESSO. Meanwhile, Bitsangou's status in his newfound government position was unclear as of October 2007, following an outburst of violence in which at least two rebels were killed when former Ninjas traveled to the capital in advance of a ceremony in which Bitsangou was to have formally accepted his post.

The president reshuffled the cabinet on December 31, 2007. While the PCT retained its dominance in government posts, the cabinet also included two members of the MCDDI and at least one member each from five small parties (see Political Parties and Groups, below.) In addition, at least one independent minister was reportedly affiliated with the PJR.

President Sassou-Nguesso, as expected, was reelected on July 12, 2009, with 78.61 percent of the vote, the opposition again claiming massive irregularities. His closest challenger among 12, Joseph Kignoumbi Kia MBOUNGO of UPADS, who ran as an independent, received 7.46 percent of the vote. The main opposition candidate, Mathias DZON of the Alliance for the Republic and Democracy (*Alliance pour la République et Démocratie*—ARD), composed of 14 parties and groups, was fourth with 2.3 percent of the vote. Dzon subsequently sought to have the results voided on the grounds of fraud; however, on July 25 the Constitutional Court confirmed the outcome. Sassou-Nguesso named a new government on September 15, abolishing the post of prime minister (which he had restored with the appointment of Mvouba in 2005). The former prime minister was given a minister of state post in the new cabinet.

In legislative elections on July 15 and August 5, 2012, the PCT won a commanding 89 seats, followed by the MCDDI and UPADS, both with 7 seats (see Current issues, below). Sassou-Nguesso maintained the same cabinet after the balloting. The president conducted a cabinet reshuffle on September 25 (see Current issues, below).

Constitution and government. The 1979 constitution established the Congolese Labor Party (PCT) as the sole legal party, with the chair of its Central Committee serving as president of the republic. Under a constitutional revision adopted at the third PCT congress in July 1984, the president was named chief of government as well as head of state, with authority to name the prime minister and members of the Council of Ministers.

The 1979 document was abrogated and a number of existing national institutions dissolved by the National Conference in May 1991. President Sassou-Nguesso remained in office pending the election of a successor, while a 153-member Higher Council of the Republic (*Conseil Supérieur de la République*—CSR) was appointed to oversee the implementation of conference decisions.

The constitution endorsed by the CSR on December 22, 1991, and approved by popular referendum on May 3, 1992, provided for a president elected for a once-renewable five-year term. The head of state, authorized to rule by decree in social and economic matters, appointed a prime minister capable of commanding a legislative majority. The bicameral parliament consisted of an indirectly elected Senate sitting for a six-year term and a directly elected National Assembly with a five-year mandate, subject to dissolution. A Supreme Court headed the judicial system, with a High Court of Justice empowered to rule on crimes and misdemeanors, with which the president, members of parliament, and other government officials could be charged. A Constitutional Court interpreted the constitutionality of laws, treaties, and international agreements.

The 1992 constitution was suspended by the new Sassou-Nguesso regime following its military takeover in October 1997. During the subsequent transitional period, the republic was governed by Sassou-Nguesso as self-appointed president with the assistance of a National Transitional Council (see Legislature, below). In November 1998 the regime established a 26-member committee to rewrite the constitution, and in November 2000 the government approved a draft document that was then discussed in March and April 2001 as a key element in a "non-exclusive national dialogue." With the participation of many opposition groups (but not those closest to Bernard Kolélas and Pascal Lissouba), the draft was approved on April 14, and a final version was endorsed by referendum on January 20, 2002.

The current constitution retains a bicameral parliament and provides for a directly elected president, serving a once-renewable seven-year term, who functions as both head of state and head of government. The president has sole power to appoint and dismiss government ministers, but he does not have the power to dismiss parliament. Nor does the legislature have the power to remove the president. Members of parliament forfeit their seats if they switch parties during the legislative term.

The judicial branch is headed by a Supreme Court. There are also Courts of Appeal, a Court of Accounts and Budgetary Discipline, and a Constitutional Court. Local administration is based on ten regions (subdivided into 76 districts and 5 municipalities) and the capital district, each with an elected Regional Council.

The constitution guarantees freedom of the press. In 2013 the media watchdog group Reporters Without Borders ranked the Republic of the Congo 76th out of 179 countries, a significant rise from 90th the previous year.

Foreign relations. The People's Republic of the Congo withdrew from the French Community in November 1973 but remained economically linked to Paris. In June 1977 it was announced that diplomatic ties with the United States would be resumed after a 12-year lapse, although the U.S. embassy was not reopened until November 1978, and ambassadors were not exchanged until May 1979.

For many years Brazzaville maintained close relations with Communist nations, including the People's Republic of China, Cuba, and the Soviet Union, signing a 20-year Treaty of Friendship with the USSR in May 1981. While the Congo remained on relatively good terms with its other neighbors, recurrent border incidents strained relations with Zaire (now the Democratic Republic of the Congo) despite the conclusion of a number of cooperation agreements, the most notable being the economic and social "twinning" of the countries' capital cities in February 1988. Subsequent reports of mutual deportations and a mass exodus of Zaireans from the Congo were downplayed by Brazzaville and Kinshasa as an exaggeration of the international press.

As an active member of the then OAU, the Republic of the Congo hosted a number of meetings aimed at resolving the civil war in Chad, although it tacitly endorsed the claims of Chadian leader Hissein Habré by serving as a staging area in 1983 for Habré-supportive French troops. In 1986 President Sassou-Nguesso was selected the OAU's chief mediator in the Chadian negotiations. In early 1987 he embarked on a nine-nation European tour to emphasize the gravity of the economic situation facing sub-Saharan Africa and the need for effective sanctions against South Africa. Further enhancing the country's image as regional mediator was the choice of Brazzaville for international peace talks on the Angola-Namibia issue in 1988 and 1989. Because of his key role in the Namibian negotiations Sassou-Nguesso in mid-February 1990 was the first African leader to be welcomed to Washington, by U.S. President George H. W. Bush.

In early 1989 Brazzaville became the first francophone African capital to negotiate a debt swap, trading shares in agriculture, timber, and transport industries to a U.S.-based lender in return for debt reductions. Another financial "first" for the government was the signing of a comprehensive investment agreement with the United Kingdom in May 1989. Later Sassou-Nguesso met with Cameroon's Paul Biya and Gabon's Omar Bongo as part of an ongoing effort by the three to create a joint bargaining unit to negotiate with external creditors.

The 1997 overthrow of the Lissouba government reportedly involved a number of foreign powers. President Lissouba claimed that the Sassou-Nguesso forces included a coalition of Rwandan Hutu militiamen and elements of the defeated army of Zaire's Mobutu Sese Seko, though Lissouba's own fighters also were reported to include former Mobutu forces. The participation of the former Zairean elements on the rebel side was apparently enough to induce the new neighboring Kabila regime of the Democratic Republic of the Congo, whose capital of Kinshasa had been shelled from Brazzaville, to send troops in support of Lissouba, even though he had been one of Africa's last supporters of Mobutu. Meanwhile, the apparent entry into the fray by Angola on the side of the insurgents helped turn the tide with tanks and air power. Lissouba had reportedly hired mercenaries from the National Union for the Total Independence of Angola (UNITA), the rebel group whose participation gave Angola another reason to support Sassou-Nguesso. The Angolans were also keen to eliminate the separatist movement in Cabinda, an oil-rich Angolan province bordering the Republic of the Congo, where the separatists were suspected of having bases.

The insurrection of 1997, starting just three weeks after the Kabila victory in the neighboring Democratic Republic of the Congo, disturbed Western diplomats and African democrats, who suggested that both conflicts, ostensibly civil wars, were actually regional wars in which African armies crossed their borders to enforce political change in a neighboring country. In October the U.S. State Department protested Angola's involvement in the Republic of the Congo and threatened to cut off aid.

Following the outbreak of a rebellion in the Pool region of the Republic of the Congo in 2002, Angola sent troops to assist the Congolese forces in dealing with the insurrection. (Angola, the Democratic Republic of the Congo, and the Republic of the Congo had signed an agreement in 1999 to cooperate regarding border and refugee issues.) The Republic of the Congo was chosen over Sudan to head the AU in 2006 as a result of opposition to the situation in Darfur, where the AU had peacekeepers.

In 2009 relations between Brazzaville and the Democratic Republic of the Congo were strengthened by an agreement for a road and railway bridge to link the two capital cities by 2014.

The country signed economic, commercial, and technical agreements with Qatar in 2010. Also that year, the U.S. government paid nearly $2 million to destroy more than 878,000 weapons in the Republic of the Congo.

In February 2012 a French inquiry found that Sassou-Nguesso's family owned more than 24 properties in France and more than 100 bank accounts, leading to speculation that resources were being surreptitiously transferred out of the Republic of the Congo. In July, reports revealed that French authorities were considering bringing charges against Sassou-Nguesso and his family. Also, in July the Republic of the Congo and Sri Lanka established diplomatic relations. The following month, the Republic of the Congo and Rwanda finalized an economic agreement to lower tariffs and increase trade. Brazzaville and Beijing announced a $700 million hydroelectric project in October that, when complete, would allow the export of electricity to neighboring states.

The Republic deployed 500 troops to the DRC as part of the African Union's regional task force in February 2013. In March, President Xi Jinping became the first Chinese head of state to visit Brazzaville. Xi and Sassou-Nguesso agreed to enhance bilateral economic and cultural cooperation. The next month, Brazzaville and Luanda resumed negotiations to demarcate the Angolan-Congolese border and to improve the repatriation of refugees. In May, Brazil announced that it would cancel the Republic of the Congo's $352 million debt.

Current issues. In 2009, some 20 opposition parties and groups comprising the FUPO coalition, led by former National Assembly president Guy-Romain KINFOUSSIA of the Union for Democracy and the Republic–Mwinda (*Union pour la Démocratie et la République*—UDR-Mwinda), protested the government's revision of the voter registry, which the coalition said contained the names of dead and fictitious people. The FUPO also called for an independent electoral panel composed of members of the judiciary, claiming that the sitting commission was biased in favor of Sassou-Nguesso and his allies. In April the FUPO boycotted the government-sponsored "Republican Dialogue," a national forum for civic and political groups to prepare for the election; a subsequent rally planned by the opposition was banned by the government. On May 11 it was announced that the president had signed a decree setting July 12 as the election date. Though it was widely understood that Sassou-Nguesso would seek reelection, he did not announce his candidacy until June 6. Meanwhile, other coalitions had been forged ahead of the election, notable among them the Rally for the Presidential Majority (*Rassemblement pour la Majorité Présidentielle*—RMP). In that electoral alliance, former prime minister Jacques-Joachim Yhombi-Opango of the opposition Rally for Democracy and Development (*Rassemblement pour la Démocratie et le Développement*—RDD) agreed to present a single candidate (Sassou-Nguesso) and to join the government if Sassou-Nguesso were reelected. The opposition ARD, meanwhile, encompassed 14 small parties, including the Patriotic Union for National Reconstruction (*Union Patriotique pour la Réconstruction Nationale*—UPRN), whose leader, Mathias Dzon, received the bid as the ARD's presidential candidate. On June 19 the Constitutional Court disqualified four candidates, three of them for not having met the residency requirement, including former prime minister Ange-Edouard Pongui of UPADS. Christophe MOUKOUÉKÉ, described as a UPADS dissident, was rejected on the grounds that, at 70, he exceeded the age limit. Observers said the court's action left Dzon as the most viable opposition candidate in a field of 12 challengers, most of whom dropped their affiliation and were listed as independents. Two days before the poll, the FUPO and six opposition candidates—including Dzon—called for a boycott, claiming the electoral lists contained the names of ineligible voters and "ghost lists" of people who did not exist. (*Africa Confidential* reported that independent observers believed the lists contained 458,000 ghost voters.)

Provisional results on July 15, 2009, delayed for one day by the government, showed the president soundly defeated 12 challengers, including Joseph Kignoumbi Kia Mboungo of UPADS, who ran as an independent and won just 7.5 percent of the vote. Nicéphore Antoine FYLLA of the Liberal Republican Party finished third, with 7 percent. Dzon, who received 2.3 percent despite his boycott, and the five other candidates who had boycotted the balloting, disputed the government report of 66.4 percent turnout, claiming that less than 10 percent of voters had participated. Dzon appealed to the Constitutional Court to void the election, but on July 25, 2009, the court confirmed the results. The OCDH reported that the poll was marked by fraud and irregularities, and that the government's official rate of participation was "exaggerated." However, international monitors, including those from the AU and the Economic Community of Central African States, found the election to be free and transparent. The president's spokesperson subsequently said that Sassou-Nguesso was committed in his second term to peace and reconciliation and to "rebuilding the state and cleaning up the public finances." Meanwhile, a protest march in Brazzaville following the announcement of election results was blocked by police, and opposition leader August Pongui of the UPADS, among others, was arrested and banned from leaving the country. Authorities lifted the ban in November. In December President Sassou-Nguesso granted amnesty to former president Lissouba, who had been sentenced to death in 1999 for his role in a $150 million deal with the U.S. firm Occidental Petroleum "for personal gain." Lissouba, who was in exile in London, was pardoned for "humanitarian reasons," according to the president.

Though nearly 5,000 weapons had been collected from former militants in the Pool region, it was reported in late 2010 that very little had been done to reintegrate the youthful combatants into civilian life. Critics claimed the government had failed to honor its commitment to reintegration, despite the appointment of former rebel leader Frédéric Bitsangou to a post in the office of the president in charge of promoting peace and postwar reconstruction. Meanwhile, security forces moved into the Pool region to help ensure order during preparations for more than $1 billion in nationwide infrastructure projects, scheduled to begin in 2012.

On March 4, 2012, a series of explosions at an ammunition depot in Brazzaville killed more than 300 and injured more than 1,500. The military was widely criticized for improperly storing munitions at the site. Twenty-six soldiers and civilians were subsequently charged for negligence over the blasts. In heavily criticized balloting that began in July, the PCT won an absolute majority in the assembly. Observers claimed systemic fraud and other irregularities during the balloting. The results were rejected by opposition parties.

In September 2012, the president conducted a cabinet reshuffle after Defense Minister Charles Zacharie BOWAO refused to resign over the munitions explosions. Bowao was dismissed and charged with "criminal responsibility" for the incident. He was replaced by Maj. Gen. Charles Richard MONDJO. Twenty-three others were awaiting trial on charges related to the explosion.

In October 2012, the Republic of the Congo was praised by the UN Program on HIV/AIDS (UNAIDS) for its aggressive campaign to reduce the number of new HIV infections. UNAIDS reported that Brazzaville had cut the number of new infections by 22 percent and had made great strides in reducing the number of HIV transmissions from mother to child. Nonetheless, in 2012, there were an estimated 83,000 people infected with HIV/AIDS, including 7,900 new cases. Approximately 4,600 Congolese died from AIDS that year.

POLITICAL PARTIES

The Republic of the Congo became a one-party state in 1963 when the National Revolutionary Movement (*Mouvement National Révolutionnaire*—MNR) supplanted the two parties that had been politically dominant under the preceding administration: the Democratic Union for the Defense of African Interests (*Union Démocratique pour la Défense des Intérêts Africains*—UDDIA) and the African Socialist Movement (*Mouvement Socialiste Africain*—MSA). The MNR was in turn replaced by the Congolese Labor Party (PCT) in 1969, coincident with the declaration of the People's Republic. On July 4, 1990, the PCT agreed to abandon its monopoly of power, and nearly two dozen opposition groupings were legalized as of January 1, 1991. Thereafter, estimates of the number of parties ranged to upward of 100.

Following Denis Sassou-Nguesso's return to power in 1997, an already complex political party system, in which personal, tribal, and regional loyalties typically overpowered ideology, became further entangled. (See the 1999 *Handbook* for more detailed information about the period preceding the 1999 civil conflict.) In 2002 a reported 141 parties and alliances presented candidates for at least one of the 137 National Assembly seats. At that time the principal formations were Sassou-Nguesso's PCT and the allied United Democratic Forces; the Convention for Democracy and Salvation (*Convention pour la Démocratie et le Salut*—Codesa), a new multiparty alliance led by former prime minister André Milongo of the Union for Democracy and the Republic (UDR); the Pan-African Union for Social Democracy (UPADS), led from exile by former president Pascal Lissouba; and the Congolese Movement for Democracy and Integral Development (MCDDI), led from exile by former prime minister Bernard Kolélas.

In advance of the 2007 National Assembly elections, a grouping of seven small parties, formerly members of the United Democratic Forces (FDU) coalition (launched in 1994), aligned themselves as the New Democratic Forces (FDN) led by Léon Alfred OPIMBA and Jean-Marie TASSOU. The FDN included some 15 parties and groups, including the National Union for Democracy and Progress (UNDP), led by Pierre NZE, and the Union for National Renewal (URN), led by Gabriel BOKILO.

In early 2007 the PCT was reported to have retained its association with the FDU, though that association eventually dissolved after PCT hard-liners rejected a proposal by President Sassou-Nguesso that the PCT and the FDU merge. The URN subsequently withdrew after Gabriel Bokilo failed to secure the FDN presidency.

The FDN won three seats in the legislature in August 2007. In advance of the 2009 presidential election, the FDN joined the Rally for the Presidential Majority (RMP), which included the PCT, the MCDDI, and the Union of Democratic Forces (UFD). Subsequently, the heretofore opposition Rally for Democracy and Development (RDD) joined the RMP in an electoral alliance with the PCT, pledging its support to Sassou-Nguesso. Meanwhile, a coalition of 20 parties, the United Front of Opposition Parties (FUPO) led by led by Guy-Romain Kinfoussia of the UDR-Mwinda, and the Alliance for the Republic and Democracy (ARD) boycotted the balloting (for more information on FUPO, please see the 2013 *Handbook*).

Government and Government-Supportive Parties:

Rally for the Presidential Majority (*Rassemblement pour la Majorité Présidentieele*—RMP). Ahead of the 2009 presidential election, the PCT, as part of the larger RMP coalition, brought the opposition RDD on board in an electoral alliance following assurances that the RDD would back the PCT's Sassou-Nguesso and that the RDD would participate in the new government. The FDN (above), the MCDDI, and the Union of Democratic Forces (UFD) were also part of the broader coalition. In the 2012 assembly balloting, the individual parties of the RMP campaigned independently.

Leaders: Michel NGAKALA (Vice President of the Coalition), Isidore MVOUBA (Former Prime Minister and Secretary General).

Congolese Labor Party (*Parti Congolais du Travail*—PCT). The PCT monopolized Congolese political life from its launching in 1969 until its agreement in 1990 to allow the formation of opposition groups. In mid-1992 the PCT finished third in the National Assembly election (19 seats) and fifth in the senate poll (5 seats). On August 2 the party's fall from power was seemingly completed by Sassou-Nguesso's inability to proceed beyond the first round of presidential balloting; however, it allied itself with the UPADS for the second round and was included in the government named on September 1. The alliance broke down shortly thereafter, with the PCT entering into a new coalition with Bernard Kolélas's Union for Democratic Renewal (*Union pour la Renouveau Démocratique*—URD), a seven-party alliance that included the MCDDI and the RDPS (see below).

Although generally listed as a member of the FDU (see below), the PCT ran in its own right in the May–June 2002 National Assembly election, winning 53 seats. PCT candidates won 15 lower house seats in 1993. In the October 2, 2005, partial Senate elections, the PCT won most of the 30 contested seats, with 21 going to the party's "new direction" wing and 2 to an unidentified dissident faction.

Meanwhile, the PCT formed an alliance with the MCDDI meant to increase stability and governance in the southern Pool region (the PCT already having strong ties in the north linked to President Sassou-Nguesso's ethnic group). The alliance with the MCDDI was also seen as helping to ensure security in the southern area, which had been a stronghold of former militants of the CNR. Subsequently, in balloting that the opposition charged was marred by irregularities, the PCT and its allies won an overwhelming majority of seats in the 2007 legislative elections.

Ambroise Noumazalaye, who had been president of the Senate and secretary general of the PCT, died in 2007.

In the run-up to the 2009 elections, the PCT expanded the progovernment coalition to include the opposition RDD. Sassou-Nguesso, as widely expected, was reelected for a seven-year term. In July 2011 the **Party of Justice and the Republic** (PJR), formed in 2005 by Denis Christel Sassou-Nguesso, the president's son, and Bernard Caesar Serges BOUYA, merged with the PCT. Denis Christel Sassou-Nguesso was subsequently elected to the PCT's political bureau. The PCT won an absolute majority in the 2012 assembly balloting. Contrary to widespread speculation, Denis Christel Sassou-Nguesso was not given a post following the September 2012 cabinet reshuffle.

Leaders: Gen. Denis SASSOU-NGUESSO (President of the Republic), Pierre NGOLO (Secretary General).

Congolese Movement for Democracy and Integral Development (*Mouvement Congolais pour la Démocratie et le Développement Intégral*—MCDDI). A right-of-center group and former member of the Forces of Change (*Forces de Changement*—FDC) coalition, the MCDDI was formed in 1989 by Bernard Kolélas, who had served as an adviser to former prime minister Milongo. In 1990 Kolélas was a leader of the opposition movement that successfully campaigned for multipartyism. In the first local and municipal elections in 1992, the party ran second, while Kolélas was runner-up in the subsequent presidential poll, with 38.7 percent of the vote. The MCDDI and the RDPS (below) were the principal members of the Union for Democratic Renewal (*Union pour la Renouveau Démocratique*—URD) alliance that was launched in mid-1992 and shortly thereafter formed the Opposition Coalition with the PCT.

In legislative balloting in 1993, the MCDDI secured 28 seats, half of the opposition's total. Meanwhile, Kolélas's leadership role in what the Lissouba administration labeled an "armed rebellion," made him a target for progovernment forces, and in October his residence in Brazzaville was hit by artillery fire. In a demonstration of antigovernment sentiment, Kolélas was elected mayor of Brazzaville in July 1994.

Kolélas maintained an opposition stance against the Lissouba government as well as a complex relationship with Sassou-Nguesso, ostensibly an ally but also a rival when the two were 1997 presidential candidates. However, during the four-month insurrection of 1997, Kolélas attempted to mediate between the Lissouba government and the Sassou-Nguesso rebels before joining the government as prime minister in September. He fled the country when the government fell in October, and the party effectively split into two wings, one remaining loyal to Kolélas and the other, headed by Michel Mampouya, supporting the new interim regime. Mampouya himself accepted a cabinet post and assumed party leadership. In the 2002 legislative election, Kolélas called for a boycott, but Mampouya, despite contending that "there is only one MCDDI," headed a slate of unsuccessful candidates.

In late 2005 Kolélas was pardoned by the government and allowed to return from exile to bury his wife in Brazzaville. A subsequent reconciliation with the Sassou-Nguesso administration ensued, a move which led in early 2006 to the resignation of several MCDDI members, including Mampouya, who subsequently established a new group, the PSV (below). Observers widely believed that Kolélas's pardon paved the way for his renewed alliance with the Sassou Nguesso government.

In advance of the 2007 legislative balloting, the MCDDI and the PCT joined in an agreement called the Bedrock of National Unity to ensure peaceful elections in the war-torn Pool region and joined in an electoral alliance, the RMP, for the assembly elections, as well as for the 2009 presidential elections. With the divisive episode of the party apparently over, the president named two members of the MCDDI to his reshuffled cabinet in December 2007.

Party leader and former prime minister Kolélas died in Paris in November 2009 at age 76. His son Guy Brice Parfait Kolélas, who had been given a cabinet post in September, was subsequently named interim party chair. In 2012 the MCDDI won seven seats in the assembly. At a 2012 party convention, Kolélas was elected permanent party leader.

Leaders: Guy Brice Parfait KOLÉLAS (President), Jacques MAHOUKA.

Union of Democratic Forces (*Union des Forces Démocratiques*—UFD). Although close to President Lissouba, the UFD's leader, David Charles Ganao, was reportedly backed by the opposition to succeed André Milongo as National Assembly president because of his reputation for nonpartisanship. Ganao was replaced as prime minister in September 1997 when President Lissouba appointed the MCDDI's Bernard Kolélas in an effort to settle the civil war. In January 1998 the UFD broke with the opposition, urging its members to support the reconciliation and reconstruction efforts of the Sassou-Nguesso government, and in February Sebastien EBAO was elected chair. At the time Ganao was in exile, but by November 2001 he had resumed control of the party and, in a turnaround, concluded an electoral pact with Sassou-Nguesso's PCT. The party won one seat in the 2007 National Assembly elections but was not represented in the new government named in 2009. The UFD gained one seat in the 2012 legislative elections. Ganao died in Paris on July 6, 2012, at age 85. UFD Assembly deputy Josué Rodrigue Ngouonimba was appointed minister of tourism and the environment in the September 2012 cabinet reshuffle.

Leader: Josué Rodrigue NGOUONIMBA (Minister of Tourism and the Environment).

Other Legislative Parties:

Pan-African Union for Social Democracy (*Union PanAfricaine pour la Démocratie Sociale*—UPADS). Previously a member of the National Alliance for Democracy (*Alliance Nationale pour la Démocratie*—AND), a coalition of 40-plus parties that objected to the 1991 Milongo government, the UPADS ran alone in the 1992 municipal, legislative, and presidential elections. The party's preelectoral prospects were bolstered by attracting numerous dissidents from the RDPS (above) and the UNDP, which had been a leading component of the prodemocracy movement (and which later helped form the FDU). In legislative polling at midyear, the UPADS secured a plurality of seats in both houses. Following the first presidential round in August, the party concluded a pact with the PCT that ensured the second-round victory of the UPADS candidate Pascal Lissouba. The alliance, upon which a legislative majority had been forged, was dissolved soon after Lissouba's inauguration.

The UPADS was the key player in the Presidential Tendency (*Tendance Présidentielle*), formed prior to the National Assembly balloting of June 1993 by a large number of pro-Lissouba parties (including many that would establish Codesa in 2002). The formation controlled a majority of seats following the second-round repolling in October. The UPADS retained its legislative plurality in 1993 but was weakened on January 27, 1995, by the withdrawal of 12 of its MPs, who complained of being marginalized and subsequently formed a new grouping, the Union for the Republic (UR).

At a UPADS congress on December 30, 1995, Lissouba was reelected to the party's top post. In addition, a 220-member National Council was formed in an apparent attempt by party leaders to appease its largest internal tendency, the "Reforming Democrats Group," which complained of the lack of partywide deliberations. In the midst of the 1997 civil war, the UPADS was a principal member of the 40-party self-described peace movement called the **Republican Space for the Defense of Democracy and National Unity** (*Espace Républicain pour la Défense de la Démocratie et de l'Unité Nationale*—ERDDUN).

Following the overthrow of President Lissouba, the UPADS split into two wings, one headed by Lissouba from abroad and the other led by Martin Mberi, a member of the National Council who became a minister in the new government of Sassou-Nguesso. In 2001 Mberi left and formed the CNRS (see below), but UPADS remained divided over strategy. It presented a slate of candidates for the 2002 National Assembly election and won three seats, although Lissouba had urged his supporters to boycott the balloting. In March the UPADS presidential candidate, Joseph Kignoumbi Kia Mboungou, finished second with 2.8 percent of the vote.

In 2006 the government and UPADS remained at odds over what the government described as an "inadequate" apology from the party on behalf of Lissouba, whom authorities insist must acknowledge responsibility for his role in the country's civil war.

The UPADS was the only major opposition party contesting the 2007 National Assembly; it won 11 seats and subsequently claimed the polling was rigged.

The party's candidate for the July 2009 presidential election, former prime minister Ange-Edouard Pongui, whose wife is a cousin of Sassou-Nguesso, was disqualified in June by the Constitutional Court on the grounds that he had not continuously lived in the country for at least two years. Joseph Kignoumbi Kia Mboungou, who ran as an independent, finished a distant second behind Sassou-Nguesso. Following the elections, Pongui was placed under house arrest and barred from leaving the country for four months. In the 2012 assembly elections, UPADS secured seven seats.

In December 2012, in a reported bid to exacerbate divisions within UPADS, President Sassou-Nguesso nominated prominent UPADS moderate Martial de Paul IKOUNGA to be the AU's commissioner for human resources, science and technology (Ikounga was elected to the post in January 2013).

Leaders: Pascal LISSOUBA (in exile), Joseph Kignoumbi Kia MBOUNGOU (Vice President and 2009 presidential candidate), Jean ITADI (Vice President), Dominique Nimi MADINGOU (Deputy Vice President), Ange-Edouard PONGUI (Former Prime Minister), Alphonse Ongagou DATCHOU, Pascal TSATY-MABIALA (Secretary General).

Rally for Democracy and Social Progress (*Rassemblement pour la Démocratie et le Progrès Social*—RDPS). Despite dissident withdrawals, the RDPS secured both upper and lower house representation in the 1992 legislative balloting. The party's leader, Jean-Pierre Thystere-Tchicaye, a former PCT member, was eliminated from presidential contention after capturing only 5.8 percent of the first-round vote. In legislative balloting in 1993 the RDPS secured ten seats. Thystere-Tchicaye was named prime minister of a short-lived parallel government named by the Opposition Coalition, and then in mid-1994 was elected mayor of the country's second-largest city, Pointe-Noire.

In late 1996, in anticipation of the scheduled 1997 presidential election, the RDPS joined the Union for the Republic (*Union pour la République*—UR) of Benjamin BOUNKOULOU and the Movement for Democracy and Solidarity (*Mouvement pour la Démocratie et la Solidarité*—MDS) of Paul KAYA in forming a coalition called the Movement for Unity and Reconstruction (*Mouvement pour l'Unité et la Réconstruction*—MUR). After the civil war of 1997 the party was reportedly divided over the extent to which it should cooperate with the government. In 2002 the party's cofounder and former secretary general, Jean-Félix Demba TELO, ran for president as an independent, finishing fourth with 1.7 percent of the vote.

In 2001 the RDPS concluded a cooperation agreement with the PCT. In August 2002 Thystere-Tchicaye was selected to serve as speaker of the new lower house. The RDPS won two seats in the 2007 National Assembly elections. Thystere-Tchicaye died in 2008 and was succeeded as party leader by Bernard Batchi, and subsequently rifts within the party were reported. Subsequently, Mabio Mavoungou Zinga was elected president at a party congress. In the 2012 assembly elections, the RDPS won five seats.

Leader: Mabio Mavoungou ZINGA.

In the 2012 assembly elections, the **Action and Renewal Movement** (*Action et Mouvement de Renouvellement*—MAR), founded by Jean-Bâptiste TATI-LOUTARD, who died in 2009, won four seats; the **Citizens' Rally** (*Le Rassemblement des Citoyens*—RC), led by Claude Alphonse NSILOU, won three seats; and the newly formed **Movement for Unity, Solidarity and Work** won two seats. Other small parties that each won a single seat were the **Patriotic Union for Democracy and Progress** (*Union Patriotique pour la Démocratie et le Progrès*—UPDP), led by Ngongarad-Auguste Celestine NKOUA; the **Union for the Republic** (*Union pour la République*—UR), led by Benjamin BOUNKOULOU; the **Prospects and Realities Club;** the **Republican and Liberal Party;** and the **Club 2002–Party for the Unity of the Republic** (*Partie pour l'Unité de la République*—PUR).

Other Parties and Groups:

Rally for Democracy and Development (*Rassemblement pour la Démocratie et le Développement*—RDD). Led by former prime minister Jacques-Joachim Yhombi-Opango, who returned from exile, the RDD under his leadership pledged to support President Sasso-Nguesso in advance of the 2009 presidential election, abandoning the opposition ANR coalition (below). Reports in 2013 indicated that the RDD had joined the RMP.

Leaders: Jacques-Joachim YHOMBI-OPANGO (former Head of State and Former Prime Minister), Mathieu Martial KANI (Secretary General).

National Resistance Council (*Conseil National de Résistance*—CNR). Having emerged from militia groups loyal to former president Lissouba, the CNR's "combat wing" (known as "Ninjas") was led by Frédéric Bitsangou (alias Pastor Ntoumi). By 2002 the CNR had reportedly broken with Lissouba in pursuit of greater autonomy for the Pool region. Although some factions (including the MNLC, see above) broke from the CNR to form legal parties, the Ninjas launched attacks on government and security sites that forced the postponement of assembly balloting in Pool in 2002. The CNR and the government signed a cease-fire in March 2003 that called for the exchange of prisoners, demobilization of CNR fighters and their integration into national security forces, and a general amnesty. Nevertheless, some Ninja groups continued to conduct operations against government forces and international aid workers. Bitsangou subsequently called for CNR's inclusion in a proposed new government of national unity, but President Sassou-Nguesso refused. In 2005 Bitsangou reportedly began to disarm the rebels, and subsequently the CNR announced that it hoped to participate as a political party in future elections in Pool.

The CNR registered as a political party in January 2007 and subsequently entered an agreement with the government to reaffirm the peace accord of 2003 and the reinstitution of a cease-fire. President Sassou-Nguesso's offer in May of a government position to CNR leader Frédéric Bitsangou drew criticism from some party members, as the president had changed the position offered to Bitsangou, from head of humanitarian affairs to general delegate to the office of the president in charge of promoting peace and postwar reconstruction. After security issues marred Bitsangou's trip to Brazzaville to formally accept the position, the president called on him in October 2007 to return to the capital and to take up his new post "without conditions."

The CNR contested the 2007 legislative elections but did not win any seats. Bitsangou reportedly accepted a position in the government transition and reconciliation office in 2011.

Leaders: Frédéric BITSANGOU, Ane Philippe BIBI.

Alliance for the Republic and Democracy. Formed in October 2008 in advance of the 2009 presidential election, the Alliance for the Republic and Democracy (*Alliance pour la République et Démocratie*—ARD) was composed of 14 parties and groups.

The ARD's 2009 presidential candidate, Mathias Dzon of the **Patriotic Union for National Reconstruction** (*Union Patriotique pour la Réconstruction Nationale*—UPRN), had participated in the PCT government in the early 1990s and then went into exile in 1996 until Sassou-Nguesso was returned to power in 1997. Dzon later served as finance minister in the PCT government but ultimately was dismissed amid allegations of corruption. The UPRN, of which Dzon remained chair, joined the ARD in 2007. The alliance opposed the 2012 legislative elections.

Minor parties included in the ARD were: the UPRN, led by André GANFINA; **Congolese Social Democratic Party** (CSDP), led by Clement MIERASSA, who ran as an independent in the 2009 presidential election; **Movement for the General Construction of the Congo** (MGCC), led by Jean Michel BOKAMBA-YANGOUM; **Rally for the Democracy and the Republic** (RDR), led by Raymond Damase NGOLLO; **Citizens Convergence** (CC), led by Bonaventure MBAYA; **Republican Convention** (CR), led by Hervé MALONGA; **Republican Movement of the Congo** (MRC), led by Gérard BOUKAMBOU; **Green Movement of the Congo** (VMC), led by Christophe NGOKAKA; **Social Party for the Republic and Democracy** (PSDR), led by Gabriel NGOULOU; **People's Congress** (PC), led by Eugene DKAMONA; **National Convention for Alternance in 2009** (CNA), led by Aurélien MIANISSA; **Rally for the Congo** (Rapco), led by Ebate-Stanislas MONGO; **National Convention for Democracy and Development** (CNDD), led by André NGALIBAKI; and a group known by the initials **MJDAC**, led by Eustache BOMBOKO.

Union for Democracy and the Republic–Mwinda (*Union pour la Démocratie et la République*—UDR-Mwinda). This offshoot of the UDR (below) was originally established by André Milongo and affiliated with Codesa. The party won one seat in the 2007 legislative elections. Following Milongo's death in July 2007, Dominica Basseyla was named acting president. The UDR-Mwinda briefly participated, along with the RDD and UPADS, in a coalition known as the Alliance for the New Republic (ANR), but abandoned that grouping in 2008. Following his election as chair in 2008, Guy-Romain Kinfoussia formed the FUPO opposition coalition in advance of the 2009 presidential election. Kinfoussia, who had called for a boycott of the election, ran as an independent and finished sixth with 0.9 percent of the vote.

Leaders: Guy-Romain KINFOUSSIA (former National Assembly President and 2009 presidential candidate), Dominica BASSEYLA.

Convention for Democracy and Salvation (*Convention pour la Démocratie et le Salut*—Codesa). Formation of Codesa was announced in late March 2002 by a dozen parties. (See the 2003 edition of the *Handbook* for details.) An anti-PCT/FDU coalition, Codesa was the latest in a series of unwieldy opposition formations in which individual parties have historically failed to coalesce, thereby diminishing their effectiveness as an electoral force (for more information, please see the 2013 *Handbook*).

Union for Democracy and the Republic (*Union pour la Démocratie et la République*—UDR). Launched following a split in the MCDDI (see above) and subsequently characterized as "close to the Presidential Tendency," the UDR secured six assembly seats in the first two rounds of balloting in May and June 1993; however, as a result of the second-round rerun in October, its representation dropped to two seats. Its leader, André Milongo, ran for president in 1992 but was eliminated in the first round, securing only 10.2 percent of the vote. In July 1993 Milongo's selection as assembly president drew sharp criticism from the Opposition Coalition.

In 2002 Milongo withdrew from the presidential election shortly before the March balloting, which he characterized as a "masquerade." In the subsequent National Assembly election the UDR won six seats to lead the opposition. Milongo had also established the UDR-Mwinda (above), which participated in the 2007 National Assembly elections.

For more information on the **Congolese People's Party**; the **People's Congress and Sympathizers/Citizens Consensus**; and the **Party for Alternative Democracy**, please see the 2013 *Handbook*. For information on the **Take Action for Congo** (*Agir pour le Congo*—APC), the **Movement for Solidarity and Development** (*Mouvement* *de Solidaire et le Développement*—MSD), the **Youth Movement** (*Mouvement de la Jeunesse*—JEM), the **Life Party** (*La Vie*), the **Movement for Democracy and Progress** (*Mouvement pour la Démocratie et le Progrès*—MDP), the **Union for Progress** (*Union pour le Progrès*—UP), and the **Party of the Safeguard of Values** (*Parti de la Sauvegarde des Valeurs*—PSV), please see the 2012 *Handbook*. (See earlier editions of the *Handbook* for details on additional smaller parties, many of which have participated since the early 1990s in various alliances of shifting membership.)

LEGISLATURE

The constitution endorsed by the CSR in December 1991 and approved by popular referendum in May 1992 provided for a bicameral Parliament (*Parlement*) composed of a Senate and National Assembly. Following the civil war of mid-1997, the parliament was replaced by the National Transitional Council (*Conseil National de la Transition*—CNT), whose 75 members were elected in mid-January 1998 at a reconciliation forum attended by more than 1,400 delegates. The CNT candidate lists were put forward by political and legal commissions as well as the government. The forum recommended that the CNT exercise quasi-legislative authority pending the proposed election of a new bicameral assembly following a constitutional referendum. The constitution approved by referendum in January 2002 restored a bicameral system, with the **Parliament** comprising a Senate and a National Assembly.

Senate (*Sénat*). The upper house is a 66-member body—6 senators from each region and from the capital—indirectly elected by local and regional councils for a six-year term. Initial balloting was held on July 11, 2002, in all regions except Pool, where violence had forced cancellation of voting. In the future, one-third of the membership is to be renewed every two years. Of the 60 seats filled on July 11, 2002, the Congolese Labor Party (PCT) reportedly won 44 seats; the United Democratic Forces, 12; the Convention for Democracy and Salvation, 1; others (civic organizations and independents), 3. In partial elections held on October 2, 2005, for 30 seats, the PCT won 23, with 6 going to government coalition parties and 1 independent.

Following partial elections on August 5, 2008, 42 seats were filled, 33 by members of the Rally for the Presidential Majority (comprised of the PCT and the Rally for Democracy and Development), and the body was expanded to 72 to include members from the new department of Pointe-Noire. Also, for the first time, elections were held in the Poole region. Two members of the Pan-African Union for Social Democracy and seven independents also won seats.

President: André Obami ITOU.

National Assembly (*Assemblée Nationale*). The lower house has 139 members directly elected for five-year terms. Balloting is conducted in two rounds, with a majority needed for election. In the most recent balloting of July 15 and August 5, 2007, the seat distribution was as follows: the Congolese Labor Party won 89 seats; the Congolese Movement for Democracy and Integral Development, 7; the Pan-African Union for Social Democracy, 7; the Rally for Democracy and Social Progress, 5; the Action and Renewal Movement, 4; Citizens' Rally, 3; the Movement for Unity, Solidarity and Work, 2; Patriotic Union for Democracy and Progress, 2; Prospects and Realities Club, 1; Union of Democratic Forces, 1; Union for the Republic, 1; Club 2002–Party for Unity and the Republic, 1; Republican and Liberal Party, 1; and independents, 12. Voting in the three districts impacted by the March 2012 explosion was postponed.

Speaker: Justin KOUMBA.

CABINET

[as of November 5, 2013]

President	Denis Sassou-Nguesso
Ministers	
Agriculture and Livestock	Rigobert Maboundou (PCT)
Civic Education and Youth	Anatole Collinet Makosso
Civil Service, in Charge of State Reform	Guy Brice Parfait Kolélas (MCDDI)
Commerce	Claudine Munari [f]
Communications, in Charge of Relations with Parliament	Bienvenu Okiemy
Construction, Town Planning, and Housing	Claude Alphonse Ntsilou (RC)
Culture and Arts	Jean-Claude Gakosso (PCT)
Energy and Water	Henri Ossebi
Equipment and Public Works	Émile Ouosso (MAR)
Fisheries, in Charge of Aquaculture	Bernard Tchibambelela
Foreign Affairs and Francophone Affairs	Basile Ikouébé (PCT)
Forestry, Environment, and Sustainable Development	Henri Djombo (PCT)
Health and Population	François Ibovi
Higher Education	Georges Moyen
Hydrocarbons and Petroleum	André Raphaël Loemba
Interior and Decentralization	Raymond Mboulou
Land Affairs and Public Domain	Pierre Mabiala
Mines, Mineral Industries, and Geology	Gen. Pierre Oba (PCT)
Posts, Telecommunications, and New Technologies	Thierry Moungala (PCT)
Presidency, in Charge of National Defense	Maj. Gen. Charles Richard Mondjo
Presidency, in Charge of Planning and Major Projects	Jean Jacques Bouya
Presidency, in Charge of Special Economic Zones	Alain Akouala-Atipault
Primary and Secondary Education	Hellot Matson Mampouya [f]
Promotion of Women and the Integration of Women in Development	Catherine Embondza [f]
Scientific Research	Bruno Jean-Richard Itoua
Small and Medium Enterprises and Handicrafts	Yvonne-Adelaide Mougany (Club 2002–PUR) [f]
Social Affairs, Humanitarian Action, and Solidarity	Émilienne Raoul [f]
Sports and Sports Education	Léon Alfred Opimbat
Technical Education and Vocational Training	Serge Blaise Zoniaba
Tourism and Leisure	Josué Rodrigue Ngouonimba (UFD)
Ministers of State	
Economy, Planning, and Territorial Development	Gilbert Ondongo
Labor and Social Security	Gen. Florent Ntsiba
Justice and Human Rights	Aimé Emmanuel Yoka (PCT)
Industrial Development	Isidore Mvouba (PCT)
Transport, Civil Aviation, and Merchant Marine	Rodolphe Adada
Ministers Delegate	
Navigable Waterways	Gilbert Mokoki
Maritime Economy	Martin Parfait Aimé Coussoud-Mavoungou
Territorial Development	Raphaël Mokoko

[f] = female

INTERGOVERNMENTAL REPRESENTATION

Ambassador to the U.S.: Serge MOMBOULI.

U.S. Ambassador to the Republic of the Congo: Christopher W. MURRAY.

Permanent Representative to the UN: Basile IKOUEBE.

IGO Memberships (Non-UN): AfDB, AU, IOM, NAM, WTO.

COSTA RICA

Republic of Costa Rica
República de Costa Rica

Political Status: Part of the Captaincy General of Guatemala that declared independence from Spain in September 1821; member of the United Provinces of Central America that was launched in 1824; autonomy reestablished in 1839; republic declared in 1848; democratic constitutional system instituted in 1899.

Area: 19,575 sq. mi. (50,700 sq. km).

Population: 4,868,247 (2012E—UN); 4,95,942 (2013E—U.S. Census).

Major Urban Centers (2011E): SAN JOSÉ (288,054), Alajuela (254,886), Desamparados (208,411).

Principal Language: Spanish (there is no "official" language).

Monetary Unit: Colón (market rate November 1, 2013: 504.55 colónes = $1US).

President: Laura CHINCHILLA (National Liberation Party); elected on February 7, 2010, and inaugurated for a four-year term on May 8, succeeding Oscar ARIAS Sánchez (National Liberation Party).

First Vice President: Alfio PIVA Mesén (National Liberation Party); elected on February 7, 2010, and inaugurated for a four-year term on May 8, succeeding Laura CHINCHILLA (National Liberation Party), who resigned on October 8, 2008.

Second Vice President: Luis LIBERMAN Ginsburg (National Liberation Party); elected on February 7, 2010, and inaugurated for a four-year term on May 8, succeeding Kevin CASAS Zamora (National Liberation Party) who resigned on September 22, 2007.

THE COUNTRY

One of the smallest of the Central American countries, Costa Rica lies directly north of Panama and combines tropical lowland, high tableland, and rugged mountainous terrain. Its people, known as *Costarricenses,* are overwhelmingly (94 percent) of European (predominantly Spanish) descent. This unusual homogeneity is broken only by mestizo and African minorities, which are concentrated in the provinces of Guanacaste and Limón, respectively. More than 90 percent of the population is Roman Catholic, the state religion, but other faiths are permitted. The country's literacy rate, which was 95.9 in 2010, is among the highest in Central America. Women constituted 41.2 percent of the nonagricultural, paid workforce in 2010. They are employed mainly in administrative positions, human resources, and customer services. Additionally, 22 members of the current legislature are women.

In 1948 Costa Rica embarked on the establishment of what became one of the world's most progressive welfare states, providing a universal program of health care and education for its citizens that contrasted with less generous systems elsewhere in Latin America (see the 2011 *Handbook* for economic conditions prior to 1999). GDP growth averaged 5.5 percent from 1999 through 2008. Surging food and fuel prices, as well as rapid credit expansion, pushed the 2008 inflation rate to a record high 13.4 percent, driving up the cost of living and compounding poverty. In 2009, the IMF approved $735 million in stand-by funds to support Costa Rica's efforts to cope with the global recession. That year, GDP declined by 1 percent and unemployment grew to 8.4 percent, the highest level since 1985. Recovery began the following year, and the economy has seen steady growth at a rate of at least 4 percent since. According to the IMF, GDP increased by 4.2 percent in 2013. Inflation was 4.7 percent and unemployment was 6.5 percent.

GOVERNMENT AND POLITICS

Political background. Costa Rica declared its independence from Spain in 1821 but accepted inclusion in the Mexican Empire of 1822–1823. It was a member of the United Provinces of Central America from 1824 to 1839, when its autonomy was reestablished. A republic was formally declared in 1848 during a period characterized by alternating political conflict and rule by the leading families, who monopolized the indirect electoral system. In 1897 Costa Rica joined El Salvador, Honduras, and Nicaragua in the Greater Republic of Central America, but the federation was dissolved in 1898. A year later, President Bernardo SOTO sponsored what is considered to be Costa Rica's first free election, inaugurating a democratic process that has survived with only two major interruptions, one in 1917 and the other in 1948. Since the uprising led by José FIGUERES Ferrer, following annulment of the 1948 election by President Teodoro PICADO, transfer of power has been accomplished by constitutional means, further securing Costa Rica's reputation as what has been called "perhaps the most passionately democratic country in Latin America."

In the election of February 6, 1994, Figueres Ferrer's son, José María FIGUERES Olsen of the National Liberation Party (*Partido Liberación Nacional*—PLN), defeated Miguel Angel RODRÍGUEZ of the Social Christian Unity Party (*Partido Unidad Social Cristiana*—PUSC). In a close race with the PLN's José Miguel CORRALES, Rodríguez was elected president in balloting on February 1, 1998. In concurrent legislative balloting the PUSC reversed the tables on the PLN (the leading party in the previous Legislative Assembly) by securing 27 of the 57 seats.

Four years later, the PUSC lost 8 of its seats in the legislative balloting on February 3, 2002, although it retained a 2-seat plurality over the PLN. The PUSC's presidential candidate in that year—Abel PACHECO—led a field of 13 in the concurrent first round of presidential balloting, with Rolando ARAYA Monge finishing second with 31 percent. Pacheco won the second round over Araya by 58 to 42 percent. These 2002 elections marked the end of the two-party system in Costa Rica, as neither of the two historically dominant political parties—the PUSC and the PLN—won a majority of seats in the legislature. The new Citizens' Action Party (PAC), a faction that split from the PLN, won 13 seats. (See Political Parties, below.)

In 2003 the Supreme Court validated presidential reelection, overturning a 2000 ruling that the court lacked constitutional authority in the matter. The action generated intense debate, with the opposition PAC insisting that an issue of such importance should be decided by elected, rather than by nonelected, officials.

PLN candidate Oscar ARIAS Sánchez won by a thin margin of 40.9 percent over the PAC candidate in the 2006 election, and subsequently gained legislative support for his new government (installed on May 8) by reaching accommodation with the centrist Libertarian Movement Party (*Partido Movimiento Libertario*—PML), which held six legislative seats.

The primary goal of the Arias administration was to implement the Central American Free Trade Agreement (CAFTA). Arias pledged to maintain the PLN's social-democratic thrust, through drew unionist and student opponents. In April 2007 the Supreme Electoral Tribunal ruled that the opposition had the right to seek a national referendum on the matter, revising the assumption that CAFTA would be decided by assembly vote. The referendum was narrowly approved by 51.6 percent of voters on October 7. Twelve new laws, called "enabling legislation," were passed by the assembly near the end of 2008, and CAFTA was implemented on January 1, 2009.

In October 2008 First Vice President Laura CHINCHILLA resigned in order to run for president. She won the election on February 7, 2010, becoming the country's first female chief executive. She secured 46.8 percent of the vote, easily defeating Ottón SOLÍS Fallis (PAC), who received 25.2 percent, and five other candidates. Despite winning the most seats, the PLN again fell short of a majority and relied on the PML's support.

In May 2011 Chinchilla and the PLN lost control of the assembly after all of the other legislative parties agreed to a parliamentary alliance. The new majority coalition gained control over the parliamentary committees and the legislative agenda and elected Juan Carlos MENDOZA (PAC) as speaker.

Through 2012 the Chinchilla administration saw a large turnover of cabinet officials because of several unrelated incidents. The PLN regained control of the assembly with the election of Luis Fernando MENDOZA as speaker in May 2013, but several scandals rocked the party's public image in the run up to the February 2014 general elections (see Current issues, below).

Constitution and government. The 1949 constitution provides for three independent branches of government: legislative, executive, and judicial. The legislative branch enjoys genuinely coequal power, including the ability to override presidential vetoes. The president serves as chief executive and is assisted by two elected vice presidents in addition to a cabinet selected by the president. By Latin American standards the president's powers are limited, and a 1969 constitutional amendment prohibited the reelection of all previous incumbents. However, in an unexpected and controversial ruling in April 2003, the Supreme Court declared the amendment invalid.

The judicial branch is independent of the president, its members being elected for eight-year terms by the legislature. The judicial structure encompasses the Supreme Court of Justice, which may rule on the constitutionality of legislation; four courts of appeal; and numerous local courts distributed among the judicial districts. One unique feature of the Costa Rican governmental system is the Supreme Electoral Tribunal (*Tribunal Supremo de Elecciones*), an independent body of three magistrates and three alternate magistrates elected by the Supreme Court of Justice for staggered six-year terms. The Tribunal oversees the entire electoral process, including the interpretation of electoral statutes, the certification of parties, and the adjudication of alleged electoral irregularities. In December 2012, the Tribunal announced that Costa Rica would implement overseas voting for the first time for the 2014 general elections. An estimated 200,000 likely voters live abroad.

All news media are free of censorship, subject to limitations such as the abuse of public officials. The country's defamation laws place some limits on freedom of expression. In 2010, the Supreme Court removed prison sentences for defamation crimes. Costa Rica ranked 18th of 179 countries on the 2013 index by Reporters Without Borders, making it the highest rated Latin American country for press freedom.

For administrative purposes the country is divided into 7 provinces and 81 *municipios,* the former administered by governors appointed by the president. The latter are governed by councils that have both voting and nonvoting members and by executive officials appointed by the president. The executive officers may veto council acts, but all such vetoes are subject to judicial review.

Costa Rica is one of only a handful of countries that constitutionally prohibit the raising of a national army, except under strictly limited circumstances of public necessity. The proscription has, however, yielded a proliferation of legally sanctioned armed groups, including private auxiliary police units and separate police forces for virtually every government ministry, most of which are beyond the control of the ministry of public security.

Foreign relations. A founding member of the United Nations (UN) and of the Organization of American States (OAS), Costa Rica has typically been aligned with the liberal, democratic wing in Latin American politics and has opposed dictatorships of both the right and the left. In May 1981 it broke relations with Cuba after a protest regarding the treatment of Cuban political prisoners had elicited an "insulting" response by Cuba's representative to the UN. The principal external concern for the remainder of the decade was the Nicaraguan *sandinista-contra* conflict and the associated U.S. involvement in regional affairs. Although formally neutral on the issue, Costa Rica strongly criticized Nicaragua's post-Somoza Marxist orientation, while accepting more than $730 million in economic aid from the United States. In early 1987 President Arias introduced a peace plan that served as the basis of intensive effort to negotiate an end to fighting in Nicaragua, El Salvador, and Guatemala. The initiative earned him the 1987 Nobel Peace Prize, while his reputation was further enhanced by brokering the *sandinista-contra* cease-fire in March 1988.

In early 1991 President Rafael Angel CALDERÓN Fournier concluded a free trade agreement with Venezuelan President Carlos Pérez and subsequently became the first Central American chief executive to negotiate a similar agreement with Mexico. In June 1995, on the other hand, Costa Rica formally ratified the December 1991 Tegucigalpa Protocol establishing the Central American Integration System as a means of promoting regional economic integration. In March 2004 it also signed the CAFTA pact with the United States.

In a move that some viewed as an attempt to reduce unemployment among Costa Ricans, the government in late 1993 launched a campaign to deport an estimated 2,000 undocumented Nicaraguans. The action, which came in the wake of two highly publicized kidnappings by Nicaraguans, exacerbated a long-standing dispute over navigation rights and demarcation of the border along the San Juan River. While an 1858 treaty had granted Nicaragua sovereignty over the river, it guaranteed both parties "free navigation" for commercial purposes, which Nicaragua interpreted to exclude tourism. A further problem stemmed from Costa Rica's issuance in 1979 of land deeds to *campesino* settlers on a tract of land south of the river that later proved to be Nicaraguan territory. On June 26, 1995, despite a long-standing Costa Rican offer of relocation to its side of the border, the settlers proclaimed the independence of the "Republic of Airrecú" (a word meaning "friendship" in the local Maleku language), thereby provoking the dispatch of Nicaraguan troops to evict them. In July 1998 the two countries concluded an agreement to make the treaties governing navigation on the San Juan "more functional," including a provision that army vessels could accompany Nicaraguan police patrols along the river. The agreement was, however, rescinded by Nicaragua less than a month later.

Domestic insurrection followed by underemployment in Nicaragua led an estimated 300,000 to 500,000 migrants to cross the Costa Rican border by 1996. In October 1999 about 160,000 of the migrants were reported to have availed themselves of an amnesty declared by Costa Rica after Hurricane Mitch had devastated their homeland, although Nicaragua continued to insist that they were being mistreated. Tension over the river dispute was partially abated by an agreement in mid-2000 that restored Costa Rica's right to armed patrols as long as Nicaragua received prior notification of their movements.

The river controversy appeared to be further abated in September 2002 by an agreement on bilateral talks over a three-year period. However, soon thereafter Nicaraguan President Enrique Bolaños ordered the interdiction of Costa Rican police boats "under any circumstances," and in September 2005, after Costa Rica had submitted the dispute to the International Court of Justice (ICJ), he announced that henceforth all vessels navigating the river would be obliged to fly the Nicaraguan flag. Costa Rica responded in May 2006 by deploying police officers to patrol the border, raising concerns in Nicaragua. Three years later, the ICJ ruled that the river belonged to Nicaragua but that Costa Rica had navigation rights on the waterway.

In March 2009 Costa Rica and Cuba reestablished diplomatic relations. In early 2010 the Arias government signed free trade agreements with Singapore and China and established diplomatic ties with the United Arab Emirates. In July the assembly enacted legislation to allow the deployment of a United States military task force to conduct counternarcotics operations from July to December 2010, which was later extended. Increased drug trafficking saw homicide rates double since 2004, and Costa Rica was included among the top 20 drug-producing or trafficking countries in a U.S. State Department list released in September 2010. Costa Rican authorities seized more than 10 tons of narcotics in 2011, a record high.

In October 2010 the Chinchilla government accused Nicaragua of violating its sovereignty by dumping sediment from the San Juan River on Costa Rica's Calero Island. Costa Rica deployed a border patrol unit to the region, and Nicaragua strengthened its troop presence. The following month, the OAS adopted a resolution calling for both countries to withdraw security forces from the region, and the ICJ called for the removal of forces and for an assessment of the damage by environmental experts.

Tensions between Costa Rica and Nicaragua resurfaced in June 2012 when Nicaraguan president Daniel Ortega Saavedra proposed a bill to create a state body to plan construction of an inter-oceanic canal, an idea originating in the 19th century but stinted by lack of funds and the San Juan River controversy, prompting President Chinchilla to lodge a formal complaint with the Ortega administration. On June 13, 2013, the Nicaraguan Congress approved a $40 billion canal proposal, awarding the rights to a Chinese-owned company. Despite assurances that the route will not be near the disputed border zone, Costa Rican officials expressed concern that the canal would tap into the San Juan River headwaters of Lake Nicaragua, thus altering downstream flow.

On May 22, 2013, Costa Rica received approval to become a full member of the Pacific Alliance after fulfilling membership requirements by signing free trade agreements with Chile, Colombia, Mexico, and Peru—the four founding members of the trade bloc, which formed in June 2012.

Current issues. In the first half of 2012, six cabinet members resigned from their posts, two of them amid unrelated ethical and corruption issues. President Chinchilla announced a cabinet reshuffle in October 2012, replacing three ministers and creating a new post, Minister of Women's Affairs. The mishandling of protests over the deal with a Brazilian company to handle the renovation of a highway from San Ramón to San José further impacted the administration and led Chinchilla to annul the contract, further damaging the party.

In early May 2013, the PLN gained a small victory when Luis Fernando Mendoza was elected speaker of the National Assembly, which was secured with support from PASE, PRN, PRC, and some members of the PML. However, later in the month, the administration was rocked by revelations that a private plane Chinchilla had borrowed from Canadian oil company THX on at least two occasions belonged to Gabriel MORALES Fallón, a Colombian businessman under investigation for his links to drug cartels. Three government officials resigned over the incident, including Communications Minister Francisco CHACÓN. A poll conducted in July found that Chinchilla's approval rating was at a record low of 9 percent.

Despite the president's unpopularity, early polls found PLN presidential candidate Johnny ARAYA to have a significant lead over opposition candidates. Though there were early discussions among opposition parties to form a coalition for the 2014 general election, including a meeting in January 2013 to explore the possibility of uniting seven opposition parties behind a single presidential candidate, no alliances had been formalized by mid-2013.

POLITICAL PARTIES

Government Party:

National Liberation Party (*Partido Liberación Nacional*—PLN). Founded by former president José Figueres Ferrer in the aftermath of the 1948 revolution, the PLN has traditionally been the largest and best organized of the Costa Rican parties and is a classic example of the democratic left in Latin America. Affiliated with the Socialist International, it has consistently favored progressive programs.

In July 1976 President Figueres precipitated a crisis within the party leadership by calling for revocation of the constitutional requirement that a president may not serve more than one term, thereby contributing to the defeat of Luis Alberto Monge as PLN presidential candidate in 1978. Subsequently, the cultivation of a network of predominantly regional and local support, coupled with a "return to the land" (*volver a la tierre*) campaign slogan, enabled Monge to secure a decisive victory in 1982. Although Oscar Arias Sánchez won a primary election over the more conservative Carlos Manuel CASTILLO in early 1985 (subsequently serving as president from 1986 to 1990), disagreement between their supporters, largely abated during the 1986 campaign, continued in the assembly. Castillo was the party's nominee to succeed Arias in 1990 but fell short by obtaining only 48 percent of the vote. Longtime party leader Figueres Ferrer died on June 8, 1990.

The PLN's José María Figueres captured the presidency in 1994, but the party failed to retain either that office or a legislative plurality in 1998 or 2002. The membership of the party's 2002 presidential candidate, Rolando Araya Monge, was suspended for six months in March 2003 for dubious electoral financing.

Arias's second-term effort succeeded by a narrow margin. By seeking a second term in 2006, Arias appeared to flaunt the constitution but also, as a neoliberal, generated ideological controversy within the PLN. A number of displeased high-ranking members left the party, including its secretary general, Luis Guillermo SOLÍS, and former president Luis Alberto MONGE. In the December 2006 local elections, the PLN won control of nearly three-fourths of the municipalities, including the mayorship of San José.

The main objective of the Arias administration was to shepherd CAFTA through the implementation process. In November 2007 President Arias signed the CAFTA treaty and appealed to the opposition to help pass the 13 needed reforms. When Security Minister Fernando BERROCAL resigned in March 2008, some speculated that President Arias forced the resignation to avoid antagonizing the left, which could block implementation of CAFTA.

In 2009 former vice president and minister of justice Laura Chinchilla received Arias's backing to succeed him as president and defeated former San José mayor Johnny Araya to secure the party's nomination in the presidential primary on June 7, 2009. Chinchilla won the 2010 presidential election, while the PLN secured 23 seats in the assembly.

Running unopposed in the presidential primary of June 6, 2013, Araya secured the PLN's nomination for the 2014 presidential election.

Leaders: Laura CHINCHILLA (President of the Republic), Johnny ARAYA (2014 presidential candidate), Antonio CALDERÓN Castro (Secretary General), Alex SIBAJA Granados (Party Treasurer).

Other Legislative Parties:

Libertarian Movement Party (*Partido Movimiento Libertario*—PML). Launched in early 1995, the PML is a right-of-center group that opposes state interventionism and policies that constrain individual liberties and advocates privatization of all state monopolies. The PML sharply improved its legislative representation from one seat to seven seats in February 2002, winning 9.3 percent of the vote, although its candidate took only 1.7 percent in the first round of presidential balloting. The party fell to six legislative seats in 2006, its leader placing third in the presidential poll. The PML subsequently agreed to support the PLN government in the legislature in return for the PLN's pledge to pursue reforms designed to promote business competitiveness and to make it easier for people in border regions and marginal urban areas to gain property rights. In June 2008, the party announced a reorganized executive committee in preparation for the 2010 elections. On July 9, 2009, the PML National Assembly nominated Otto Guevara as the party's 2010 presidential candidate. Guevara placed third in the balloting with 20.8 percent of the vote, while the PML won nine seats in the legislature. After initially supporting the Chinchilla government, the PML joined the opposition in May 2011. Guevera announced in 2012 that he will run for president for the fourth time in the 2014 election.

Leaders: Otto GUEVARA Guth (President and 2002, 2006, and 2010 presidential candidate), Danilo CUBERO Corrales (Secretary General).

Citizens' Action Party (*Partido Acción Ciudadana*—PAC). Launched in early 2001 by, among others, PLN defector Ottón Solís Fallas and Epsy Cambell BARR, the PAC ran in the 2002 election on a populist platform promising to combat corruption and help farmers and traditional industries that had been weakened by recent market reforms. Solís finished a surprisingly strong third in the first round of presidential balloting in February 2002 with 26 percent of the vote, while the PAC garnered 13 seats in concurrent legislative balloting. A year later, six PAC members withdrew to form the Patriotic Bloc (*Bloque Patriotico*—BP).

In his 2006 campaign for the presidency, Solís lost to the PLN's Arias by 1.1 percent of the vote. The PAC won 17 seats in the concurrent legislative election.

Solis won the PAC's presidential primary on May 31, 2009, defeating Barr. He placed second in the general election, while the PAC lost 5 seats in the assembly balloting, securing just 12 positions in its worst electoral showing in more than a decade. PAC legislator Juan Carlos Mendoza was elected as speaker of the assembly for the term beginning in May 2011.

Four candidates contested in the presidential primary on July 21, 2014.

Leaders: Elizabeth Fonseca CORRALES (President), Ottón SOLÍS Fallas (2002, 2006, and 2010 presidential candidate), Olga Marta SÁNCHEZ (Secretary General).

Social Christian Unity Party (*Partido Unidad Social Cristiana*—PUSC). The party is a loose alliance of the essentially conservative parties, including the **Calderonist Republican Party** (*Partido Republicano Calderonista*—PRC), formed in 1976; the **Christian Democratic Party** (*Partido Demócrata Cristiano*—PDC), formed in 1962; the **Popular Union Party** (*Partido Unión Popular*—PUP); and the former Democratic Renovation Party (see National Union Party, below). The PUSC campaigned before the 1978 election as the *Partido Unidad Opositora* (PUO) and as the *Coalición Unidad* in 1978, adopting its present name in December 1983. Partly because of conflict within the PLN leadership, the party won the presidency in 1978 but was defeated in both 1982 and 1986. The PUSC returned to power with a 52 percent presidential mandate in 1990 before losing a close race in May 1994. It regained the presidency in 1998 and retained it in 2002. In the 2006 presidential election, PUSC candidate Ricardo Toledo came in fourth, and the party won five parliamentary seats in concurrent balloting, amid allegations of corruption against the administration of retiring president Abel Pacheco. In addition, corruption charges were filed against former presidents Miguel Angel Rodriguez, and Rafael Angel CALDERON Fournier. (For more information on the PDC, the PDC, and the PUP, see the 2008 *Handbook*.)

Despite being on trial for corruption, in April 2009 Calderon announced that he would run for the presidency. However, he was convicted in October and withdrew his candidacy. Party president Luis FISHMAN Zonzinsky was the PUSC candidate and placed fourth in the election. The PUSC gained one additional seat in the assembly polling, bringing its total to six. Fishman left the party bloc in the assembly in November 2012 when he disagreed with the PUSC lawmakers' decision to oppose the reelection of a Supreme Court judge.

In the presidential primary of May 19, 2013, Rodolfo Hernández Gómez secured the party's nomination.

Leaders: Gerardo VARGAS Rojas (President of the Party), Rodolfo HERNÁNDEZ Gómez (2014 presidential candidate), Rafael Angel CALDERÓN Fournier (Former President of the Republic).

Accessibility Without Exclusion Party (*Partido Accesibilidad Sin Exclusión*—PASE). This San José—based party was formed in 2005 as a voice against the free trade agreement and against discrimination toward the disabled, senior citizens, and their families. The new party won one seat in the 2006 assembly poll. Party leader Oscar Andrés LÓPEZ Arias was the PASE candidate in the 2010 presidential election. He came in fifth, while the PASE increased its representation in the assembly from one to four seats. In May 2012, Víctor Emilio GRANADOS Calvo became president of the Legislative Assembly, shortly after PASE formed a new alliance with the PLN.

Leaders: Oscar Andrés LÓPEZ Arias (President), Victor Emilio GRANADOS Calvo (Secretary).

Broad Front (*Frente Amplio*). This progressive group, which promotes "more participative and direct forms of democracy," is a provincial party based in San José with a platform advocating sustainability, equal rights, feminism, and human rights. It won one seat in the 2006 assembly elections and maintained that seat in the 2010 balloting. Eugenio TREJOS was the party's candidate in the 2010 presidential elections, but he received less than 1 percent of the vote.

In March 2013, José María Villalta won the party's nomination for the 2014 presidential elections.

Leaders: Patricia MORA Castellanos (Party President), José María VILLALTA (2014 presidential candidate), Eugenio TREJOS (2010 presidential candidate).

National Restoration Party (*Partido Restauración Nacional*—PRN). A San José—based provincial party based on a platform of "Christian ethics," the PRN won one seat in the 2006 assembly poll with 2 percent of the vote. It did not field a presidential candidate in 2006 or 2010. The PRN retained its seat in the 2010 assembly elections. In May 2013, the party announced that it would nominate a presidential candidate to contest the 2014 elections.

Leader: Carlos Luis AVENDAÑO Calvo (President).

Costa Rican Renewal Party (*Partido Renovación Costarricense*—PRC). A small conservative party, the PRC won no seats in the 2006 legislative polls. Its 2006 presidential candidate, Bolivar Serrano Hidalgo, secured less than 1 percent of the vote, as did its 2010 candidate, Mayra GONZALEZ. The PRC secured one seat in the 2010 legislative balloting.

Leaders: Justo OROZCO Alvarez (President and 2002 presidential candidate), Mayra GONZALEZ (2010 presidential candidate), Rafael Ángel MATAMOROS Mesén (Vice President), Jimmy SOTO Solano (Secretary).

Other Parties:

National Integration Party (*Partido Integración Nacional*—PIN). The PIN was launched in 1996 but won no representation in 2002, 2006 or 2010. Dr. Walter MUÑOZ Céspedes was the PIN candidate for the presidency in 2010, but he withdrew to support Solís of the PAC in the balloting.

Leaders: Dr. Walter MUÑOZ Céspedes (President and 2006 presidential candidate), Heiner Alberto LEMAITRE Zamora (Secretary General).

Other provincial parties that unsuccessfully contested the 2010 legislative balloting included the **Patriotic Alliance Party** (*Partido Alianza Patriótica*—PAP) of Alajuela, led by Esli Antonio VEGA Alvarado; the **Authentic Heredian Party** (*Partido Autentica Herediano*) of Heredia, led by José Francisco SALAS Ramos; the **Cartagen Agricultural Union Party** (*Partido Unión Agrícola Cartaginesa*—PUAC) of Cartago, led by Juan Guillermo BRENES Castillo; the **Movement of Workers and Peasants** (*Movimiento de Trabajadores y Campesinos*—MTC) of Limón, under Orlando BARRANTES Cartín; the **Alajuelan Restoration** (*Restauración Alajuelense*), led by Miguel Ángel QUESSADA Niño; the **Green Ecologist** (*Verde Ecologista*), led by Rodrigo José ARIAS Gutiérrez; the **Cartaginese Transparency** (*Transparencia Cartaginés*), led by Sandra María Hidalgo MARÍN; the **Greater Alliance** (*Alianza Mayor*), under José Miguel ABARCA Solano; and the **Alajuelan Familiar Force** (*Fuerza Familiar Alajuelense*), led by José Miranda BARAHONA.

See the article in the 2010 *Handbook* for details on these parties: the **National Union Party** (*Partido Unión Nacional*—PUN); **Popular Vanguard Party** (*Partido Vanguardia Popular*—PVP); the **Democratic Force Party** (*Partido Fuerza Democrática*—PFD); **National Democratic Alliance** (*Alianza Democrática Nacionalista*—ADN); **National Rescue Party** (*Partido Rescate Nacional*—PRN); **Patriotic Union Party** (*Partido Unión Patriótica*—PUP); **Union for Change** (*Unión Para el Cambio*—UPC); and the **Homeland First Party** (*Partido Patria Primero*—PPP).

LEGISLATURE

The **Legislative Assembly** (*Asamblea Legislativa*) is a unicameral body whose 57 members, representing the provinces in proportion to population, are elected under a proportional representation system for four-year terms by direct popular vote and may not be immediately reelected. In the most recent election of February 7, 2010, the National Liberation Party won 23 seats; the Citizens' Action Party, 12; the Libertarian Movement Party, 9; the Social Christian Unity Party, 6; the Accessibility Without Exclusion Party, 4; the Broad Front, 1; the National Restoration Party, 1; and the Costa Rican Renewal Party, 1.

President: Luis Fernando MENDOZA Jiménez.

CABINET

[as of July 1, 2013]

President	Laura Chinchilla [f]
First Vice President	Alfio Piva Mesén
Second Vice President	Luis Liberman Ginsburg
Ministers	
Agriculture and Livestock	Gloria Abraham [f]
Communications and Public Institutions	Carlos Roverssi
Culture and Youth	Manuel Obregon
Decentralization and Local Government	Juan Marin
Economy, Trade, and Industry	Mayi Antillon [f]
Environment, Energy, and Telecommunications	Rene Castro
Finance	Edgar Ayales
Foreign Affairs	Jose Enrique Castillo
Foreign Trade	Anabel Gonzalez [f]
Health	Dr. Daisy Maria Corrales [f]
Housing and Human Settlements	Guido Monge

Justice	Fernando Ferraro
Labor	Olman Segura
Planning	Roberto Gallardo
Presidency	Carlos Ricardo Benavides
Public Education	Leonardo Garnier
Public Security	Mario Zamora
Public Works and Transport	Pedro Castro
Science and Technology	Alejandro Cruz Molina
Social Welfare	Fernando Marin
Sport	Wiliam Corrales
Tourism	Allan Flores
Women's Affairs	Maureen Clark [f]

[f] = female

INTERGOVERNMENTAL REPRESENTATION

Ambassador to the U.S.: Meta Shanon Figueres BOGGS.

U.S. Ambassador to Costa Rica: Anne S. ANDREW.

Permanent Representative to the UN: Eduardo ULIBARRI.

IGO Memberships (Non-UN): IADB, ICC, IOM, OAS, PCA, WTO.

CÔTE D'IVOIRE

République de Côte d'Ivoire

Note: In November 1985 the United Nations responded affirmatively to a request from the Ivorian government that *Côte d'Ivoire* be recognized as the sole official version of what had previously been rendered in English as Ivory Coast and in Spanish a *Costa de Marfil*.

Political Status: Independent since August 7, 1960; present constitution adopted October 31, 1960; under de facto one-party regime prior to legalization of opposition parties on May 30, 1990; constitution suspended and governmental authority assumed by the military following a bloodless coup on December 24, 1999; new constitution providing for a return to civilian government approved by national referendum on June 23–24, 2000.

Area: 124,503 sq. mi. (322,463 sq. km).

Population: 20,683,319 (2012E—UN); 22,400,835 (2013E—U.S. Census).

Major Urban Center (2005E): Abidjan (4,100,000). In March 1983 the interior city of YAMOUSSOUKRO (484,000, 2005E) was designated as the nation's capital. However, as of mid-2013 most government offices remained in Abidjan (the former capital), and most foreign governments were also still maintaining their embassies there.

Official Language: French.

Monetary Unit: CFA Franc (official rate November 1, 2013: 486.52 francs = $1US). The CFA franc is permanently pegged to the euro at 655.957 CFA francs = 1 euro.

President: Alassane OUATTARA (Rally of Republicans); elected on November 28, 2010, in disputed second-round balloting and inaugurated for a five-year term on May 21, 2011, to succeed Laurent GBAGBO (Ivorian Popular Front). (Both Ouattara and Gbagbo claimed victory in the 2010 presidential poll and installed competing governments, prompting a civil war that culminated in Gbagbo's arrest by Ouattara's forces on April 11, 2011.)

Prime Minister: Daniel Kablan DUNCAN (Democratic Party of Côte d'Ivoire); appointed by the president on November 21, 2012, to succeed Jeannot Kouadio AHOUSSOU, whose government had been dismissed by the president on November 14; formed government on November 22, 2012.

THE COUNTRY

A land of forests and savannas, with a hot, humid climate, Côte d'Ivoire is one of the more resource-rich states of former French West Africa and potentially the most nearly self-sufficient. A substantial percentage of the population consists of migrant workers, mostly from Burkina Faso, Ghana, and Mali. There traditionally has also been a sizable non-African expatriate community consisting primarily of Lebanese and French. About 40 percent of the population is Muslim and 30 percent is Christian, with the balance adhering to traditional religious practices. Women constitute approximately 33 percent of the adult labor force, primarily in agriculture; female representation in government is minimal, although there have been several women in recent cabinets.

The economy experienced rapid growth following completion in 1950 of the Vridi Canal, which transformed Abidjan into a deepwater port. Although agriculture now accounts for only one-fourth of total GDP, Côte d'Ivoire is the world's leading producer of cocoa. (Cocoa was responsible for 20 percent of GDP and 40 percent of exports in 2006.) Côte d'Ivoire is also one of Africa's primary exporters of coffee, bananas, and tropical woods, and, despite a UN embargo, diamonds continue to be smuggled out of the country. In addition, the government has recently signed contracts with several foreign companies to develop new gold mines, the first of which began production in 2010.

The country's image as a model African economy was tarnished in the 1980s by debts attributed to extensive government borrowing in the 1970s. In the first half of the 1990s, sagging cocoa and coffee prices, the decimation of lumber-producing forests, and the government's inability to make debt payments prompted economic reform and diversification efforts. Such measures enabled Côte d'Ivoire to rebound quickly from the inflationary effects of the 1994 CFA franc devaluation. However, the International Monetary Fund (IMF) and the World Bank cited poor economic management and a multitude of governance problems as contributing to ongoing fiscal fragility. (The IMF temporarily suspended aid in 1999 because of perceived corruption within the administration.)

In light of the political uncertainty that followed a military coup in December 1999, the economy shrunk in 2000–2001. The resumption of civil war in 2002 strained the economy even further. The IMF and World Bank suspended some aid and debt-reduction programs because of the strife, which also compromised major trade routes through the north of the country to neighboring states and prompted a sharp decline in foreign investment.

The government launched a broad campaign in 2006 to meet the conditions necessary for the resumption of IMF and World Bank lending, while a peace agreement in March 2007 appeared to set the stage for full focus on much-needed economic development. (The recent civil war had left more than 3,000 people dead and more than 700,000 displaced.) The IMF quickly approved emergency support for the new transitional government's economic program.

Following up emergency credits in 2008 to help offset the effects of higher food prices, the IMF in March 2009 approved $565 million in new lending to support the government's economic program. The Fund and the World Bank shortly thereafter announced that Côte d'Ivoire had qualified for $3 billion in debt relief. The debt arrangements were contingent upon the government's intensification of structural reforms and poverty-reduction efforts. (Some estimates placed the poverty rate at more than 60 percent of the population.) Despite the global economic crisis, GDP grew by 3.9 percent in 2009 and 2.4 percent in 2010, thanks to rising cocoa prices, agricultural harvests improved by abundant rainfall, and increased oil production.

The civil war that followed the November 2010 presidential election severely disrupted economic activity, and GDP contracted by 4.7 percent in 2011. However, growth recovered more rapidly than expected (9.8 percent in 2012), and the IMF and World Bank at mid-year approved $4.4 billion in new debt relief. Late in the year international donors pledged $8 billion for 2012–2015 to assist the Ouattara administration, which had adopted a decidedly free-market stance.

GOVERNMENT AND POLITICS

Political background. Established as a French protectorate in 1842, Côte d'Ivoire became part of the Federation of French West Africa in 1904, an autonomous republic within the French Community in 1958, and a fully independent member of the French Community in August 1960. Membership in the French Community was abandoned

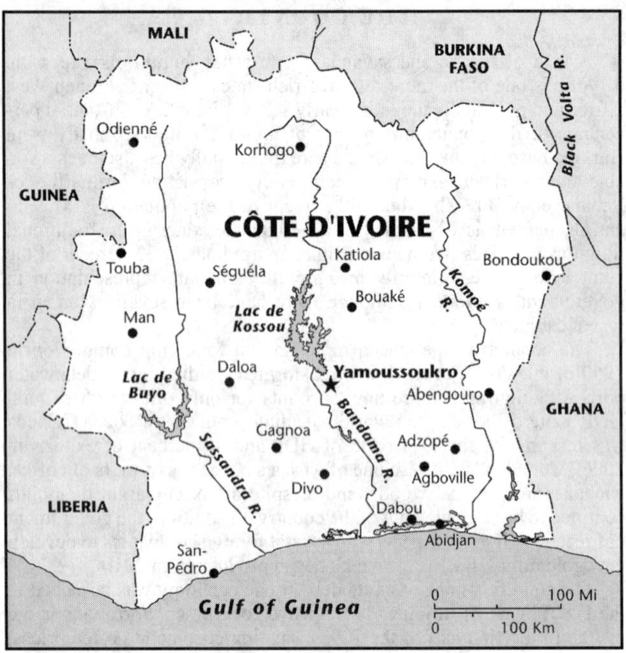

with the adoption of the country's present constitution in October 1960. The dominant political figure since the 1940s was Félix HOUPHOUËT-BOIGNY, who in 1944 organized the *Syndicat Agricole Africain* (an African farmers' union) and helped to found of the African Democratic Rally (*Rassemblement Démocratique Africain*—RDA), an international political party with branches in numerous French African territories. As leader of the RDA's Ivorian branch—the Democratic Party of the Ivory Coast (*Parti Démocratique de la Côte d'Ivoire*—PDCI)—Houphouët-Boigny served in the French National Assembly from 1946 to 1959, became prime minister of the autonomous republic in 1959, and served as president beginning in 1960.

The postcolonial era was relatively stable by African standards, although there were periodic student demonstrations and university closings. Another source of tension was the presence of many foreign workers, with whom indigenous Ivorians sporadically clashed in competition for jobs.

The election of an enlarged National Assembly on November 9 and 23, 1980, marked the first time since independence that nominees were not confined to a single PDCI list, although all of the candidates were members of the PDCI. In May 1990 the government was compelled by increasingly strident protests to authorize opposition party activity. On October 28 Houphouët-Boigny won a seventh term in office, capturing a reported 82 percent of the vote, while Laurent GBAGBO, leader of the opposition Ivorian Popular Front (*Front Populaire Ivoirien*—FPI), was credited with the remainder. On November 7, one day after the National Assembly approved creation of the post of prime minister, Alassane OUATTARA, the highly regarded governor of the Central Bank of West African States (*Banque Centrale des États de l'Afrique de l'Ouest*—BCEAO), was appointed to the position.

On December 7, 1993, President Houphouët-Boigny died in his Yamoussoukro palace of complications stemming from an operation earlier in the year. Prime Minister Ouattara held a cabinet meeting in the presidential offices later in the day. However, National Assembly president Henri Konan BÉDIÉ announced that evening that he had assumed presidential power in accord with a 1990 constitutional amendment. Two days later Ouattara resigned, apparently unwilling to cooperate with Bédié, his PDCI rival, and the Supreme Court immediately confirmed Bédié's succession. On December 10 Bédié appointed Daniel Kablan DUNCAN as prime minister. Duncan, a former economy minister described as a "technocrat" dedicated to economic reform, named a 24-member interim cabinet on December 15.

In preparation for presidential and legislative elections scheduled for late 1995, the PDCI-dominated National Assembly voted overwhelmingly in late 1994 to adopt a new electoral code that the opposition had strongly criticized as biased in favor of the government. The run-up to the 1995 poll was marked by violent protests against the code, its new provisions (requiring parents and grandparents of presidential candidates to have been of Ivorian birth) having thwarted the aspirations of Ouattara, Bédié's main challenger and the consensus leader of the new opposition Republican Front (*Front Républicain*—FR). Moreover, the government refused to appoint an independent electoral commission. Although the government in September banned all demonstrations for three months, the FR continued its antigovernment marches, and on October 2 at least five people were killed when government forces attempted to disperse protestors. Meanwhile, the field of presidential contestants (which had numbered 11) continued to dwindle as some candidates announced their intention to honor the FR's call for an electoral boycott. Consequently, at presidential balloting on October 22, President Bédié easily won reelection, capturing 96.25 percent of the tally while his sole adversary, Francis WODIÉ of the Ivorian Workers' Party (*Parti Ivoirien des Travailleurs*—PIT), secured a meager 3.75 percent. Although the government claimed a 62 percent voter participation rate, the opposition reported much lower figures.

Following a meeting with President Bédié in early November 1995, the FR announced its intention to participate in the upcoming legislative balloting. However, the FR proved unable to agree on a joint list of candidates; consequently, at assembly balloting on November 26 the PDCI retained all 148 of its seats while the FPI and the Rally of Republicans (*Rassemblement des Républicains*—RDR) managed only small gains.

In May 1996 the government confirmed rumors that a coup attempt led by senior military officers had been thwarted prior to the 1995 assembly balloting. (The administration had previously maintained that the clashes were between government security forces and opposition militants.) On August 10 the administration removed Minister of Sports Gen. Robert GUEÏ, who was the army chief of staff in 1995 and had subsequently been linked by junior military officials to the "conception and preparation" of the coup plot (a charge he denied). Moreover, between November 1996 and January 1997 the government dismissed eight senior officers, including Gueï, from the armed forces and penalized at least four others for their alleged roles in the 1995 coup attempt.

On June 30, 1998, the PDCI-dominated assembly approved constitutional amendments that dramatically increased the scope of the chief executive's powers and, two years after it was first proposed, provided for the creation of an upper legislative body, or Senate (never established, see Constitution and government, below). Opposition legislators (including those from the FPI) boycotted the assembly vote, asserting that the PDCI had ignored their legislative recommendations, including a call for the amendments to be submitted to a national referendum. Subsequently, antigovernment demonstrations erupted in Abidjan in September. However, the ruling party and the FPI began discussions that yielded a "good governance," prodemocracy pact on December 24. Four days later the National Assembly took action on a key element of the agreement, adopting a draft law that authorized the government to grant amnesty to opposition activists jailed during the 1995 unrest. Electoral reform was the focus of the accord's other major directives, most notably the financing of presidential election campaigns and the establishment of a national electoral commission. Subsequently, in March 1999, the PDCI launched talks with the RDR on establishing the conditions necessary for elections in 2000 and the drafting of a "consensus constitution." However, the discussions quickly stalled, and attention in Abidjan turned toward the potential for an electoral confrontation between Bédié and Alassane Ouattara, the latter having reportedly announced his intention to relinquish his position as IMF deputy secretary general to mount a presidential campaign as the RDR's standard-bearer.

Growing dissatisfaction with President Bédié's autocratic rule contributed to his overthrow in a bloodless military coup on December 24, 1999. General Gueï, the dominant figure in the junta, assumed the presidency of a transitional National Committee of Public Salvation (*Comité National de Salut Public*—CNSP), promising he would cede power within a year to a democratically elected president. In January 2000 membership in the CNSP was expanded to include the PDCI, FPI, and RDR, although ultimate control remained in the hands of the military. Gueï subsequently appeared to be maneuvering to consolidate his power in anticipation of a possible run for the presidency, despite his previous pledge that he would not be a candidate. The question of candidate eligibility was significant in the preparation of the new draft constitution, which originally required that a person needed only one parent of Ivorian nationality to be a legal candidate, a provision that would have permitted Ouattara to run. However, at Gueï's insistence, the draft basic law was redrawn to require that both parents of a presidential candidate had to be Ivorian citizens. In early October the Supreme Court, headed by Gueï's former legal adviser, confirmed that Ouattara's candidacy was invalid, as was that of Emile Constant BOMBET, the potential candidate of the PDCI.

The new constitution was approved in a national referendum July 23–24, 2000 (see Constitution and government, below, for details). Gueï and the FPI's Laurent Gbagbo were the primary contenders in the October 22 presidential balloting, a boycott by the PDCI and RDR having reduced the rest of the field to several candidates from minor parties. Voter turnout was low (only 35 percent), in large part due to the boycott. When initial results suggested a Gbagbo victory, Gueï attempted to dismiss the Independent Electoral Commission and declare himself victor. However, massive street demonstrations erupted to protest Gueï's actions, and more than 300 people died in the violence, much of it centered on conflict between the RDR and security forces as well as between the predominantly Muslim northern supporters of the RDR and the mainly Christian southern supporters of the FPI. Gueï was forced to abdicate power and accept the legitimacy of the victory by Gbagbo, who was sworn in as president on October 27. One day later Gbagbo named Pascal Affi N'GUESSAN of the FPI to head a new cabinet that was dominated by the FPI but also included members of the PDCI and PIT.

New assembly balloting was held on December 10, 2000, the RDR boycotting the poll because Ouattara was again declared ineligible to be a candidate. The FPI scored considerable gains, securing 96 seats to 77 for the PDCI. (Elections were not held for 28 northern seats due to violence related to the RDR boycott.)

The PDCI significantly improved its legislative standing in the January 14, 2001, balloting for 26 of the 28 seats that had not been filled the previous December, winning 17 of the contests. However, the FPI subsequently established a more comfortable plurality by negotiating a cooperation agreement with independent legislators who in February formed the new, pro-Gueï Union for Democracy and Peace in Côte d'Ivoire (*Union pour la Démocratie et la Paix de la Côte d'Ivoire*—UDPCI). On January 24 a new cabinet, again led by N'Guessan, was appointed, with the FPI, PDCI, and PIT accepting portfolios. Municipal elections in March 2001 were most noteworthy for the success of the RDR, which, among other things, shed some of its reputation as a "one man" or "one region" party by gaining control of local councils throughout the country.

Under heavy international pressure, President Gbagbo convened a Forum for National Reconciliation in October 2001, which upon its conclusion in January 2002 had heard from Gbagbo, Bédié, Gueï, and Ouattara. The "big four" attended negotiations together in late January to review the forum's proposals, which, among other things, provided for Ouattara to be issued a nationality certificate. Based on the success of those talks, the RDR joined the new government named on August 5.

In mid-September 2002 a group of soldiers about to be demobilized launched antigovernment attacks that soon left more than half of the country in the hands of a new rebel group called the Patriotic Movement of Côte d'Ivoire (*Mouvement Patriotique de la Côte d'Ivoire*—MPCI). France sent additional troops to augment its 500-member permanent garrison in case a quick evacuation was required but declined to assist the government militarily, calling the conflict a domestic issue. For its part, the Gbagbo administration blamed the insurrection on supporters of General Gueï, who was killed under murky circumstances in a seemingly nonmilitary situation on the first day of fighting.

With the predominantly Muslim MPCI holding significant portions of the northern and central regions, the government in late September 2002 reportedly instituted harsh countermeasures that led the RDR to withdraw its support for the administration. Meanwhile, two new rebel groups (the Movement for Justice and Peace [*Mouvement pour la Justice et la Paix*—MJP] and the Ivorian Popular Movement for the Greater West [*Mouvement Populaire Ivoirien du Grand Ouest*—MPIGO]) had emerged in the west. With the conflict having developed into a full-blown civil war, France deployed some 2,500 troops to Côte d'Ivoire to try to maintain order, while regional leaders initiated mediation efforts. In January 2003 an agreement was reached under the auspices of the Economic Community of West African States (ECOWAS), under which Gbagbo was to remain president while allowing security authority to be assumed by a new prime minister. For their part, the rebel groups agreed to end hostilities, with both sides being guaranteed amnesty for any human rights violations. ECOWAS peacekeepers joined French forces in an effort to patrol the cease-fire line.

President Gbagbo subsequently appointed Seydou DIARRA, a well-respected independent, as prime minister. After intense negotiations, it was announced that a new cabinet would be formed comprising ten members from the FPI, eight from the PDCI, seven from the RDR, seven from the MPCI, one from the MJP, one from the MPIGO, and additional ministers from small established parties. However, the unity cabinet essentially collapsed before it began work when antigovernment protests (asserting that Gbagbo had reneged on his pledge regarding the prime minister's authority) were met with violent suppression. Fighting resumed in several areas, and even international observers were unable to pinpoint which side was to blame.

In June 2003 the UN Security Council authorized the creation of UN peacekeeping for Côte d'Ivoire (the UN operation for Côte d'Ivoire [*Opération des Nations Unies pour Côte d'Ivoire*—ONUCI]), but fighting continued, the MPCI, MJP, and MPIGO coalescing in August under the banner of the New Forces (*Forces Nouvelles*—FN). Meanwhile, progovernment demonstrations for the most part appeared to be conducted by the Coordination of Young Patriots (*Coordination des Jeunes Patriotes*—CJP), which was strongly criticized for alleged responsibility for a campaign of violence against opposition leaders and foreigners. The CJP was banned in September, but its hallmark attacks continued. For his part, Guillaume SORO, the leader of the FN, announced his forces would not lay down their arms until Gbagbo surrendered his security power. In response, the UN imposed an arms embargo on the country in November 2004. However, subsequent reports indicated that the government and rebel groups were able to violate the embargo easily.

By the end of 2004 some 250,000 Ivorians had fled the civil war to neighboring countries, and 600,000 people had been displaced internally. In addition, tensions had grown between the government and French peacekeepers, French forces having "destroyed" the Ivorian air force after a government attack on a rebel base had accidentally left nine French soldiers dead.

President Gbagbo and FN leader Soro met at a summit in April 2005 sponsored by South African president Thabo Mbeki and reached yet another tentative peace agreement. The rebels began to disarm in late June, while rebel and government forces started to withdraw from conflict zones.

In July 2005 the assembly endorsed legislation required by the recent peace agreement that provided for public financing of political campaigns, a new voter registration campaign, reform of citizenship laws, and establishment of a new election commission in preparation for the presidential and legislative elections scheduled for October. However, the FN temporarily withdrew from the peace process in September, claiming that South African officials were exhibiting a bias toward the Gbagbo administration. Consequently, upon the recommendation of UN secretary general Kofi Annan that the elections be postponed, the UN Security Council on October 21 endorsed the extension of Gbagbo's presidential mandate for up to 12 months. The UN also called upon Gbagbo to appoint a new prime minister with enhanced powers to lead a new transitional government.

The African Union (AU) and ECOWAS endorsed the UN's decision, but the FN rejected the action and demanded that Soro be named as the nation's new prime minister. Collaterally, FN forces "remobilized," and President Gbagbo created new elite security forces to deal with the potential resumption of fighting. However, in November 2005 the FN returned to negotiations, which, after 16 other candidates were rejected, led to the appointment of Charles BANNY, a governor of the BCEAO, to the premiership. Banny's new transitional government comprised representatives of the FPI, PDCI, MPCI, PIT, RDR, UDPCI, and FN.

Prime Minister Banny, described as "pro-French," soon clashed with President Gbagbo over the extent of Banny's authority. Consequently, the UN established an International Working Group (IWG) to assist the new transitional government. In one of its first decisions, the IWG in early January 2006 announced that it would not endorse the proposed extension of the mandate of the current assembly (a primary source of support for Gbagbo). The president's supporters subsequently launched a series of protests that included the occupation of UN headquarters in Abidjan and attacks on foreign businesses. In response, the UN threatened to impose travel restrictions and financial sanctions on any Ivorian leaders perceived as encouraging the unrest, and general calm returned. On January 27 Gbagbo announced that the mandate of the assembly had in fact been extended for up to one year. The IWG described the extension as a violation of the spirit of the peace agreements but took no formal action. A number of parties boycotted the subsequent assembly activity.

Another round of peace talks was held by the main factions in February 2006, with tentative agreement being reached for new national elections in October. Collaterally, the UN bolstered its peacekeeping mission in Côte d'Ivoire by transferring troops to it from the successful UN initiative in Liberia. Voter registration began in May, along with an intensified campaign to disarm former rebel groups and progovernment militias.

In August 2006 a Greek freighter leased by a European energy firm unloaded a cargo of toxic waste in Côte d'Ivoire in an apparent attempt to avoid the high costs of processing the material in Europe. The toxins reportedly killed ten people in Côte d'Ivoire and caused health problems for thousands of others, prompting widespread protest demonstrations. Government corruption was suspected in the matter because of the unusual speed with which the ship was granted a license to unload its cargo. Prime Minister Banny and his cabinet resigned on September 6 in the wake of the toxic waste scandal, but the president reappointed Banny on September 16 to head a reshuffled cabinet, which included a new minister of environment, water, and forests. In February 2007 the European energy firm involved in the toxic dump agreed to pay the government $200 million to settle the matter.

On November 1, 2006, the UN Security Council (with the support of the AU and ECOWAS) extended President Gbagbo's term for another year, accepting his argument that new elections could not be held in light of continuing government/rebel conflict and organizational problems in arranging elections. However, the resolution also demanded the strengthening of the powers of the prime minister and the dilution of presidential authority. Among other things, the prime minister was granted the power to schedule and organize future elections, and the president was stripped of the ability to postpone balloting any further. The prime minister was also given authority over the security forces.

Another round of violence began in November 2006 when some 200 militia fighters abducted UN personnel in the town of Duejoue, in the west of the country, following clashes between pro- and antigovernment militias. In mid-December Gbagbo called for a new peace dialogue that he suggested could include a general amnesty for rebel fighters. Talks began in mid-January 2007 under the mediation efforts of Burkina Faso president Blaise Campaoré, and a comprehensive peace agreement was signed on March 4 between Gbagbo and Soro in Burkina Faso. The accord called for disarmament of rebel forces (estimated at more than 40,000), the integration of some of them into a new national army, the phased withdrawal of ONUCI peacekeeping forces, and comprehensive identification of voters in advance of new national elections. (A major impetus for the rebellion had been that as many as 3 million northerners had been denied Ivorian nationality papers, costing them, among other things, their voting rights.) The settlement also paved the way for Soro (Gbagbo's former archenemy) to replace Banny as prime minister in April as head of a new unity government that included members of the FPI, FN, PDCI, RDR, and other minor parties. (Banny objected to his ouster and led a protest rally in Yamoussoukro against the new accord.)

The 2007 peace accord called for elections to be held within ten months, but that schedule, clearly optimistic to begin with, was soon compromised by continuing security issues and delays in the massive proposed voter identification process. Meanwhile, FN officials reportedly continued to exercise de facto authority in much of the north even though government representatives had returned to many official posts. For their part, opposition parties alleged that they were being marginalized in the reunification initiative and strongly criticized the government for its perceived failure in battling corruption, crime, and high food prices. In December 2008 President Gbagbo and Prime Minister Soro signed another accord, which provided for some 5,000–9,000 former rebels to be integrated in national forces and authorized a "demobilization allowance" for the others.

Prime Minister Soro and his government were dismissed on February 12, 2010, but President Gbagbo immediately asked Soro to form a new cabinet, which was installed on March 4. Incumbent president Laurent Gbagbo and opposition candidate Alassane Ouattara of the RDR each claimed victory in the second round of presidential balloting on November 28, and they named competing prime ministers and cabinets. Most of the international community (including the UN, AU, ECOWAS, United States, and European Union) recognized Ouattara as the legitimate victor, but Gbagbo, supported by the army, remained in de facto control until he was overthrown on April 11, 2011, by fighters loyal to Ouattara, supported by international forces (see Current issues, below). Ouattara was subsequently sworn in as president on May 21. He reappointed Soro as prime minister of a reshuffled cabinet on June 1.

The RDR and its allies dominated the December 2011 elections, which were boycotted by the FPI. Soro resigned as prime minister on March 8 after being elected speaker of the new assembly. He was succeeded by the PDCI's Jeannot Kouadio AHOUSSOU, who named a cabinet that included many of the incumbent ministers. Ahoussou was in turn succeeded on November 21 by former prime minister Daniel Kablan Duncan, whose new government was again dominated by the PDCI and RDR.

Constitution and government. The 1960 constitution provided the framework for a one-party presidential system based on the preeminent position of President Houphouët-Boigny and the PDCI. Although other parties were not proscribed, no challenge to the PDCI was permitted until May 1990 when the government authorized the registration of opposition groups. (For constitutional developments from 1990 through 1998, see the 2007 *Handbook.*)

The military junta that assumed power in a bloodless coup on December 24, 1999, immediately suspended the constitution. However, a new basic law was presented for a national referendum July 23–24, 2000, with 87 percent of the voters, according to official reports, approving the document. Much of the language in the 1960 constitution was retained in the 2000 version. A strong presidential system was confirmed; among other things the president retained the authority to appoint the prime minister and, in consultation with the prime minister, the Council of Ministers. The president's term was reduced to five years, renewable once. The post is selected through direct universal suffrage in two-round (if necessary) majoritarian balloting. Restrictions were also placed on presidential candidates regarding their parentage and formal nationality, again prompting substantial controversy (see Political background, above). (The National Assembly in December 2004 passed legislation to allow citizens with only one Ivorian parent to run for office, although President Gbagbo insisted a national referendum would be required for the change to be implemented.) The National Assembly remained the sole legislative body, a proposed Senate, which had never been established, being formally abolished. For the first time, the new constitution included detailed protection for human rights. Other noteworthy provisions included one granting civil and penal immunity for people involved in the 1999 coup.

The judiciary is headed by a Constitutional Council comprising three members appointed by the president and three appointed by the president of the assembly. There are also a High Court of Justice (whose members are elected by the assembly), a Court of Cassation, and local appeals courts. In addition, the new constitution created the post of a presidentially appointed mediator of the republic to serve as a national ombudsman.

The country is divided for administrative purposes into 58 departments, each headed by a prefect appointed by the central government, but with an elected council. Municipalities (numbering nearly 200) have elected councilors and mayors.

Côte d'Ivoire has long been known for its "pluralistic" press, although Reporters Without Borders described the country as one of Africa's most dangerous for both local and foreign media during the 2002–2007 civil war. Complaints have also been registered of harassment and intimidation of journalists in the wake of the 2010–2011 post-election crisis.

Foreign relations. In line with its generally pro-French orientation, Côte d'Ivoire has adhered to a moderate policy in African affairs and a broadly pro-Western posture in general. Relations with neighboring states were periodically strained in the 1980s, particularly in the wake of growing xenophobic sentiment in Côte d'Ivoire, especially among the mainly Christian population in the south. Although ties with neighboring Burkina Faso had previously been weakened because of that country's links to Libya and Ghana, Burkinabè leader Capt. Blaise Compaoré, who led the 1987 overthrow of Col. Thomas Sankara's government, long enjoyed close personal relations with Ivorian president Houphouët-Boigny. Relations with the Central African Republic (CAR), cool upon the provision of sanctuary by Côte d'Ivoire to the CAR's former emperor Bokassa, improved once the ex-sovereign departed for Paris in late 1983. Relations with Israel, which had been broken off in 1973, were reestablished in December 1985.

In the early 1990s, France, the country's leading financial donor and cultural influence, appeared to lose interest in maintaining a high profile in its former protectorate. Among other things, France stunned Côte d'Ivoire in 1990 by refusing Houphouët-Boigny's request for troops to help quell an uprising of military conscripts.

Burdened by the presence of 200,000 refugees along its western border, Côte d'Ivoire continued diplomatic efforts to resolve the Liberian crisis through the first half of the 1990s. In September 1996 Abidjan, citing the need to stem attacks on its nationals as well as foreign refugees, established a military "operational zone" along its border with Liberia. In April 1997 the Bédié government and the United Nations Office of the High Commissioner for Refugees (UNHCR) reached agreement on a plan to repatriate the approximately 200,000 Liberians still living in Côte d'Ivoire.

The Organization of African Unity (OAU, subsequently the AU) and ECOWAS did not agree with General Gueï's successful efforts to bar the presidential candidacy of Alassane Ouattara in the summer of 2000, and they subsequently exerted considerable diplomatic pressure to undermine Gueï's legitimacy.

Following disputed presidential balloting in November 2010 (see Current issues, below), ECOWAS suspended Côte d'Ivoire's participation in most committees of the body, and the AU suspended the country's membership. After President Gbagbo ordered the withdrawal of international peacekeepers, the UN instead extended the mandate of its force and formally recognized Gbagbo's challenger in the balloting, former prime minister Ouattara, as the legitimate president of Côte d'Ivoire. The AU and individual countries, including France, also recognized Ouattara. ECOWAS issued an ultimatum on December 28 for Gbagbo to cede power or face military action.

AU mediation efforts in January and February 2011 failed as fighting within the country spread. The UN, AU, and other international organizations imposed sanctions on the government and froze the assets of Gbagbo and his main supporters. International troops, and in particular 1,000 French forces, assisted fighters loyal to Ouattara in the resultant civil war. After Gbagbo surrendered to the international forces in April, most of the international economic sanctions were subsequently lifted, except for a long-standing UN embargo on the export of diamonds.

Current issues. When President Gbagbo dismissed the cabinet in February 2010, he also dissolved the electoral commission, which was headed by a member of the opposition. (FPI hard-liners argued that the commission planned to include more than 500,000 "unqualified persons" on the voting rolls.) Violent protests subsequently broke out across the country, and opposition parties initially refused to join the proposed new government. However, a compromise was negotiated regarding a revamped electoral commission, and the opposition parties accepted 11 seats in the new 28-member cabinet appointed in March. Prime Minister Soro pledged greater intensity toward "unification," and the integration of FN fighters into the national defense forces began in earnest at midyear.

In the first round of presidential balloting on October 31, 2010, President Gbagbo secured 38 percent of the vote, while former prime minister Ouattara of the RDR, gained 32.1 percent. The Independent Election Commission initially declared Ouattara the winner of the November 28 runoff with 54.1 percent of the vote to Gbagbo's 45.9 percent. However, Gbagbo challenged the results, and the Constitutional Court nullified the ballots in seven northern provinces. On December 4 the court declared Gbagbo the winner with 51.5 percent of the vote to Ouattara's 48.5 percent. The new results were rejected by Ouattara as well as the international community, which subsequently recognized Ouattara as the legitimate president.

Through January and February 2011, international mediation efforts failed to resolve the standoff, as did economic and other sanctions on the Gbagbo regime. Fighting between supporters of Gbagbo and Ouattara (mainly FN fighters) spread throughout the country, and by March forces loyal to Ouatarra controlled most of the country, with the exception of Abidjan. On April 11 FN fighters backed by French and AU forces stormed Gbagbo's compound and captured the presidential claimant and his leading supporters. Ouattara was sworn in as the president of Côte d'Ivoire in May and the following month he reappointed Soro as prime minister. An estimated 3,000 people were killed in the postelection fighting, which also created more than 500,000 refugees.

Observers attributed much of the violence to reprisals against Gbagbo supporters, although pro-Gbagbo militias were also deemed responsible for killings and other abuses. In early December Gbagbo was extradited to The Hague, Netherlands, to face charges at the International Criminal Court of crimes against humanity allegedly committed during the civil war.

ECOWAS observers described the December 2011 assembly elections as "generally acceptable," although the FPI boycott clearly undercut the prospects for political reconciliation anytime soon. Relations between the government and the FPI deteriorated further by mid-2012 as FPI leaders argued that "atrocities" committed by Ouattara's supporters were going unpunished while many Gbagbo loyalists were under arrest.

Gbagbo supporters ("bent on destabilization," according to one UN report) were considered responsible for a number of attacks launched from Ghana and Liberia on Ivorian troops in August and September 2012, and the military responded with a fierce crackdown that, according to human rights organizations, involved widespread abuses. The government also established a new reconciliation commission with at least rhetorical commitment to dialogue with the FPI, but observers warned of potential "disintegration" as intense polarization continued. Meanwhile, new prime minister Duncan (who had served in that position in the 1990s) and a number of the ministers in his new cabinet came from the banking and business sectors, President Ouattara apparently hoping to emphasize "economic competence" in order to at least partially offset concerns in the minds of potential foreign investors about security issues and perceived widespread corruption.

The RDR and PDCI dominated the April 2013 local elections in light of a boycott by the FPI. Meanwhile, the government attempted (without much success) to convince Ghana to extradite additional Gragbo supporters to face charges in Côte d'Ivoire.

POLITICAL PARTIES AND GROUPS

On May 30, 1990, Côte d'Ivoire ceased to be a one-party state with the legalization of 9 opposition groups. By the first-round legislative balloting of November 25 the number of recognized parties exceeded two dozen, while in May 1991 the government legalized 14 more, some of which were alleged to be PDCI fronts created to dilute opposition cohesiveness. By July 1993, 40 of the reported 82 active political parties had been recognized. The July 2002 constitution provided for unrestricted party activity "within the law."

In advance of presidential elections originally scheduled for October 2005, opposition groups formed a loose electoral coalition known (in homage to former president Houphouët-Boigny) as the **Rally of Houphouëtists for Democracy and Peace** (*Rassemblement des Houphouëtistes pour la Démocratie et la Paix*—RHDP). The group subsequently became commonly known as the G7 after the FN agreed to work with the coalition. (G7 referred to the fact that it contained seven groups—the FN, PDCI, RDR, UDPCI, MFA, and two minor parties.) In July 2005 the RDR's Alassane Ouattara and the PDCI's Henri Bédié held discussions in Paris aimed at agreement on a single opposition candidate to challenge President Gbagbo in the planned presidential elections. Alphonse Djédjé Mady (the secretary general of the PDCI) was appointed as the nominal leader and spokesperson for the G7. After the presidential elections were postponed, the G7 organized mass protests against Gbagbo in Abidjan in November 2005. The G7 supported the proposed appointment of the FN's Guillaume Soro as prime minister in December 2005 but endorsed Charles Banny after his appointment to the post. The G7 also promoted a boycott of the assembly after it was announced that the mandate of the current assembly would be extended. The parties and groups within the G7 continued to operate as independent entities and use the coalition only as a coordinating body. The G7 endorsed the accession of the FN's Soro to the prime minister's post in April 2007, although friction was subsequently reported within the group over strategy for the upcoming presidential and legislative elections.

Subsequent reports for the most part referenced the RHDP (comprising the PDCI, RDR, UDPCI, and MFA) rather than the G7. The RHDP coordinated the nationwide protests in February 2010 (see Current issues, above) but subsequently joined the new cabinet and urged its supporters to participate in the upcoming presidential elections, at which RHDP components presented separate candidates in the first round but backed the RDR's Alassane Ouattara in the runoff with President Gbagbo. Although the RHDP parties forwarded their own candidates in the December 2011 assembly poll, preliminary results indicated that four legislators were elected under the RHDP rubric. Those four subsequently announced their formal affiliations with specific parties. Distinct RHDP candidates (as opposed to those presented individually by the RDR, PDCI, and UDPCI) were also credited with securing the leadership of nine regional councils and three municipal councils in the April 2012 local elections.

Government and Government-Supportive Parties:

Rally of Republicans (*Rassemblement des Républicains*—RDR). The essentially centrist RDR was launched in June 1994 by ex-PDCI members led by Djény KOBINA and a number of ministers from the government of former prime minister Alassane Ouattara, who had operated within the PDCI for the previous three years as a "reform" wing loyal to Ouattara. Kobina announced that the new grouping controlled 30 National Assembly seats and had a membership of 1.5 million. Initially, the RDR could only claim to have "excellent relations" with Ouattara, whose willingness to campaign under the RDR's banner was considered necessary to the party's electoral viability. However, in January 1995 Kobina announced that Ouattara had joined the party.

In July 1995 the RDR officially endorsed Ouattara as its presidential candidate; however, the government refused to rescind the electoral code, and on August 2 Ouattara, who was ineligible under the new provisions, abandoned his campaign plans, citing his respect for Ivorian laws, even those he considered "aberrant." Thereafter, on November 22 the constitutional court rejected Kobina's appeal against the nullification of his legislative candidacy, both of his parents reportedly being Ghanaian.

Meanwhile, the RDR had earlier helped to launch the Republican Front (*Front Républicain*—FR), an electoral alliance that also included the FPI and the UFD (see PPS, below). Although the FR called for a boycott of the October 1995 presidential elections, it agreed to participate in the subsequent legislative elections. However, beset by legal problems and unable to agree on a joint candidate list, coalition members fared poorly in the assembly balloting. Flagging coalition cohesiveness was underscored by the decision of the RDR and the FPI to forward competing candidates in more than 100 municipal electoral races in February 1996.

Djény Kobina died in October 1998, and he was succeeded as RDR secretary general by Henriette Dagbi Diabaté, who reportedly became the first woman to hold such a powerful post in an Ivorian political party.

In early 1999 Ouattara confirmed that he would be the RDR's standard bearer at the 2000 presidential elections. A number of party leaders were detained late in the year, prompting violent antigovernment demonstrations in RDR strongholds.

The RDR initially welcomed the December 1999 coup, since General Gueï was widely viewed as supportive of Ouattara, who returned from exile on December 29. A number of RDR members were appointed to Gueï's transitional cabinet, but relations between the RDR and military leaders subsequently deteriorated as Gueï began to retreat from his pledge not to run for presidency. Several RDR officials were detained in the wake of an aborted coup in early July 2000, while Ouattara's subsequent exclusion from the presidential campaign (see Political background, above) signaled a final rupture with Gueï. Following Gueï's failed attempt to manipulate the presidential balloting in October, RDR supporters fought with security forces as well as partisans of the FPI. The RDR's "outside" status continued into December, Ouattara being ruled ineligible to compete in the legislative balloting, which the RDR boycotted. However, some RDR members ignored the boycott and campaigned for the assembly under the rubric of the RDR–Movement of Moderate Activists and Candidates (*RDR–Mouvement des Militants et Candidates Modérés*—RDR-MMCM), securing five seats.

Secretary General Diabaté was briefly detained by the government following the unsuccessful coup attempt in January 2001, and a number of RDR members remained imprisoned throughout the summer in connection with the violence that had erupted in late 2000. Despite the government pressure, the RDR performed very well in the March 2001 local elections, securing victories in the south, west, and center of the country as well as the traditional RDR strongholds among the northern Muslim population.

Following the outbreak of civil war in 2002, Ouattara again went into exile, from where he reportedly became the opposition's leading presidential candidate. However, President Gbagbo continued to consider Ouattara ineligible to run due to his failure to meet residency and citizenship requirements, despite a National Assembly ruling to the contrary in December 2004. In December 2005 Gbagbo issued a decree allowing Ouattara to campaign in future presidential elections, and Ouattara returned from exile in January 2006. The RDR, which had received five seats in the December 2005 transitional government, was also given five portfolios in the April 2007 cabinet. Ouattara, still considered the most popular northern politician, was the RDR candidate in the October 2010 presidential balloting. He was recognized as the winner of the disputed balloting and was installed as president in May 2011 following the civil war over the issue. The RDR, described as "mainly Muslim," dominated the 2011–2012 assembly balloting and, following its absorption of independents, commanded a legislative majority of 138 seats. The RDR was credited with winning control of 10 of 31 regional councils and 65 of 195 municipal councils in the April 2013 local elections.

Leaders: Alassane Dramane OUATTARA (President of the Republic), Amadou Gon COULIBALY (Deputy Secretary General), Henriette Dagbi DIABATÉ (Secretary General).

Democratic Party of Côte d'Ivoire (*Parti Démocratique de la Côte d'Ivoire*—PDCI). Established in 1946 as a section of the African Democratic Rally (*Rassemblement Démocratique Africain*—RDA), the PDCI (often referenced as the PDCI-RDA) was the country's only authorized party for the ensuing 44 years, although other parties were never formally banned. Although the PDCI reportedly divided into fractious "old and new guards" in response to the country's mounting socioeconomic problems, the party's 1990 congress endorsed President Houphouët-Boigny's bid for a seventh term, proposed the naming of a prime minister, and revived the office of party secretary general.

Divisions within the party were underscored in mid-1992 when Djény Kobina, a spokesperson for the party's so-called progressive wing, called for the release of opposition leaders detained in February. Prime Minister Alassane Ouattara announced in early 1993 that he would seek the party's 1995 presidential nomination, thus highlighting the widening gulf between his northern, Muslim followers and the southern, predominantly Catholic supporters of the National Assembly president and presidential "heir apparent," Henri Konan Bédié. In the wake of Houphouët-Boigny's death in December 1993 and Bédié's subsequent succession, there were reports that Ouattara was planning to launch his own party and that the old-line "barons of *houphouëtisme*" had aligned with him and were demanding an extraordinary PDCI congress to reconsider succession policy. Nonetheless, Bédié was unanimously elected party chair in April 1994.

In June 1994 Kobina's wing, including a number of senior party officials, broke from the party to form the RDR (above), with a loss to the PDCI of nine assembly seats. Subsequently, Ouattara, who had accepted an IMF post in May, disavowed his PDCI membership. (He joined the RDR in 1995.)

Discouraged by the party's primary system, a number of PDCI legislative aspirants reportedly opted to compete as independents in the general elections in 1995; however, there was no indication that they secured seats. Delegates to the 1996 PDCI congress reportedly approved the establishment of a "high leadership," which included an executive branch and five commissions (political, economic, human resources, security, and environmental affairs). Furthermore, a 400-member deliberative body that had been created in 1990 was expanded into a 1,500-member parliament led by a "council of old ones" and charged with aiding the party president in charting "major political directions." In addition, Bédié and Laurent Dona-Fologo were reelected as party president and general secretary, respectively.

Following the overthrow of the PDCI government by the coup of December 1999, Bédié fled to Paris, from where he attempted to retain control of the party. Although disagreement existed regarding the extent to which the PDCI should cooperate with the coup leaders, several party members joined the transitional government of Gen. Robert Gueï, who subsequently tried to secure the PDCI nomination for president of the republic. However, the party rejected Gueï's plan, nominating instead former interior minister Emile Constant Bombet, whose candidacy was ultimately ruled invalid by the Supreme Court. The PDCI accepted three posts in the new cabinet appointed in October 2000 and has participated in all subsequent cabinets.

Bédié returned from France in October 2001 and was reelected as PDCI president at the April 2002 party congress. In 2003 the PDCI temporarily suspended participation in the government along with other parties. However, its ministers rejoined the cabinet in August 2004.

Bédié returned in September 2005 from another year of self-imposed exile to participate in the presidential election then scheduled for October. After those elections were postponed, Bédié was active in negotiations regarding the installation of a new transitional cabinet in which the PDCI, whose support was concentrated in the southern and central portions of the country, was accorded four seats. Announcing that his advanced age would force this campaign to be his last, Bédié was nominated as the PDCI candidate for the October 2010 presidential poll. He placed third in the first round of balloting with 25.2 percent of the vote. The PDCI supported Alassane Ouattara in the second round, and, after the party's second-place finish in the 2011–2012 assembly poll, the PDCI's Jeannot Kouadio Ahoussou was named prime minister in March 2012. He was succeeded in November by Daniel Kablan Duncan, also a PDCI member. The party's aging leadership was subsequently described as facing a growing challenge from its youth wing.

The PDCI was credited with gaining control of 5 regional councils and 49 municipal councils in the April 2013 local elections.

Leaders: Henri Konan BÉDIÉ (President of the Party and Former President of the Republic), Daniel Kablan DUNCAN (Prime Minister),

Eugène Aka Aouele (Vice President), Laurent DONA-FOLOGO (Former Secretary General), Charles BANNY (Former Prime Minister), Kovadio Konan BESTIN, Alphonse Djédjé MADY (Secretary General).

Union for Democracy and Peace in Côte d'Ivoire (*Union pour la Démocratie et la Paix de la Côte d'Ivoire*—UDPCI). The UDPCI was launched in February 2001 by former members of the PDCI who had left that party to support Gen. Robert Gueï in the 2000 presidential campaign. (As many as 14 of the successful "independent" candidates in the December 2000 assembly balloting were subsequently identified as belonging to the PDCI dissident group; most were believed to have participated in the formation of the UDPCI.) General Gueï was elected president of the UDPCI in May 2002. However, Gueï was killed in September when fighting erupted between government forces and rebels.

The UDPCI joined the national unity government in 2002 and also participated in the 2005 transitional government and the April 2007 government. Albert Toikeusse Mabri finished fourth as the UDPCI candidate in the first round of the 2010 presidential poll, and the UDPCI joined the cabinets subsequently appointed by Alassane Ouattara.

Leaders: Albert MABRI TOIKEUSSE (President of the Party and 2010 Presidential Candidate), Paul Akoto YAO, Alasane SALIF N'DIAYE (Secretary General).

Union for Côte d'Ivoire (*Union pour Côte d'Ivoire*—UPCI). Konan Gnamien, the leader of the recently formed UPCI, secured 0.4 percent of the vote in the first round of the 2010 presidential election, running on a platform that invited "all Ivorians" to join the party in pursuit of economic development. Gnamien was named to the new cabinet in 2011.

Leader: Konan GNAMIEN (2010 presidential candidate).

Movement of Forces for the Future (*Mouvement des Forces pour l'Avenir*—MFA). The MFA, formed in 1995, was credited with one seat in the December 2000 legislative balloting, although little other information concerning the grouping was available. In 2003 the MFA joined the national unity government, and it remained in the 2005 and 2007 transitional governments. Although MFA leader Kobenan Anaky announced in March 2009 that the party was leaving the cabinet to protest lack of electoral progress, the MFA rejoined the government at the formation of a new cabinet in March 2010. Anaky secured 0.2 percent of the vote in the first round of the presidential poll in 2010.

Leader: Kobenan ANAKY (Secretary General).

Other Parties That Contested the 2011 Legislative Elections:

Ivorian Workers' Party (*Parti Ivoirien des Travailleurs*—PIT). The PIT was formally recognized in May 1990, although a PIT rally three months later was dispersed by government forces. The party captured one seat in the November legislative balloting. Three PIT leaders were among those given prison terms in March 1992 for alleged involvement in the February rioting.

At presidential balloting in 1995 PIT leader Francis Wodié captured less than 4 percent of the vote. Wodié's candidacy had been sharply criticized by his opposition colleagues, who cited the PIT leader's own advocacy of a boycott in 1990. In August 1998 Wodié was appointed to the Bédié government, while party members also held posts in 2000 in the transitional governments of General Gueï. Wodié secured 5.7 percent of the vote in the October 2000 presidential balloting, and the PIT participated in all of the subsequent FPI-led cabinets, including the 2005 transitional government and the April 2007 national unity government. As of mid-2009 it appeared that the PIT would support President Gbagbo's reelection effort, but subsequent reports described the PIT as "allied" with the opposition RHDP. Wodié placed sixth with 0.29 percent of the vote in the first round of the 2010 balloting.

Leader: Francis WODIÉ (General Secretary and 2000 and 2010 presidential candidate).

Democratic Citizen's Union (*Union Démocratique Citoyenne*—UDCY). Launched in January 2000, the UDCY criticized the PDCI for failing to make the "necessary changes" to promote national "reconciliation and reconstruction." UDCY Chair Théodore Mel Eg, mayor of the Cocody District in Abidjan, was credited with 1.5 percent of the vote in the October 2000 presidential balloting, while the party secured one seat in the December legislative poll. The UDCY was given one cabinet post in 2003, and Mel Eg was appointed minister of culture and francophone affairs in the 2005 transitional government and minister of urban development and sanitation in the April 2007 cabinet. The UDCY supported Alassane Ouattara of the RDR following the disputed presidential balloting in 2010.

Leader: Théodore MEL EG (Chair).

Party for Social Progress (*Parti pour le Progrès Social*—PPS). The predominantly ethnic Djoula PPS is led by Bamba Morifére, reportedly one of the wealthiest opposition politicians. During the run-up to legislative balloting in November 1995 Morifére was jailed for alleged financial fraud and subsequently given a four-month suspended sentence, a verdict the FPI's Gbagbo decried as "shameful."

The PPS had been one of the members of the Union of Democratic Forces (*Union des Forces Démocratiques*—UFD), an opposition grouping launched in December 1992. Other UFD members had included the PIT, the UND, the **Social Democratic Movement** (*Mouvement Démocratique et Social*—MDS), and the **African Party for the Ivorian Renaissance** (*Parti Africain pour la Renaissance Ivoirienne*—PARI). PPS leader Morifére had served as president of the UFD. His proposed candidacy (presumably under the rubric of the Alliance for Democracy [*Alliance pour la Démocratie et le Socialisme*—ADS]) for the 2000 presidential election was rejected by the Supreme Court. (The left-wing ADS had been recently launched by the PPS, Renaissance, and two other small parties.) The PPS supported the RDR's Alassane Ouattara in the 2010–2011 civil war.

Leader: Bamba MORIFÉRE.

Renaissance. Initially known as FPI-Renaissance, this grouping was formed in 1996 under the leadership of Don Mello Ahoua, who claimed that his faction would remain within the FPI but would work independently to promote "democracy" within the larger body. However, in July 1997, following an alleged shooting attack on Ahoua's car and threats to faction members, the group withdrew from the FPI.

Leader: Don Mello AHOUA (Coordinator).

Freedom and Democracy for the Republic (*Liberté et Démocratie pour la République*—LIDER). Formed by former FPI leader Mamadou Koulibaly in mid-2011, the LIDER was described as a "liberal opposition party" during the campaign for the December assembly poll.

Leader: Mamadou KOULIBALY (Former Speaker of the National Assembly).

Some 24 other small parties also participated unsuccessfully in the 2011 assembly poll.

Other Parties and Groups:

Ivorian Popular Front (*Front Populaire Ivoirien*—FPI). The FPI was founded by history professor Laurent Gbagbo, who, upon his return to Côte d'Ivoire in September 1988, was granted a state pardon for previous dissident activity. At its founding congress in November 1989, the FPI adopted a platform calling for a mixed economy with a private sector emphasis. Legalized in May 1990 and becoming thereafter the unofficial leader of a coalition that included the PIT and USD, the party called for President Houphouët-Boigny's resignation, the appointment of a transitional government, and freedom of association.

Angered at apparent electoral irregularities and claiming fraudulent tallying, FPI supporters clashed with government forces during and after the October 1990 presidential balloting (in which Gbagbo finished second as the FPI candidate), with 120 reportedly being arrested. In mid-1991 the FPI refused to join in an opposition call for a national conference, insisting instead that Houphouët-Boigny's government resign.

Reportedly believing that the FPI would be offered the premiership in a transitional government, Gbagbo publicly backed Henri Konan Bédié of the PDCI in the months prior to Houphouët-Boigny's death in December 1993. However, when it became apparent that Bédié would not extend such an offer, Gbagbo broke off negotiations with the ruling party.

In February 1994 Gbagbo called for the establishment of a transitional government, the creation of a West African currency, the holding of "clean" elections, and repeal of the constitutional amendment detailing presidential succession procedures. In July 1995 he called the government's electoral code "legalized fraud," and he subsequently withdrew from the presidential campaign.

After Gbagbo was elected president of the republic in October 2000, he appointed the FPI's Pascal Affi N'Guessan to head a new FPI-dominated cabinet. N'Guessan, who had managed Gbagbo's presidential campaign, succeeded Gbagbo as FPI leader in mid-2001.

Following the renewed civil war in 2002, a number of propresidential groups affiliated with the FPI emerged. Foremost among them was the Coordination of Young Patriots (*Coordination des Jeunes Patriotes*—CJP), led by a close Gbagbo ally, Charles Blé GOUDÉ. The CJP organized a number of demonstrations in support of the president, but it was banned in September 2003 for the alleged use of violence and intimidation.

The FPI filled 7 posts (the most of any party) in the new transitional government installed in December 2005 and retained a plurality of 11 portfolios in April 2007 and 7 in March 2010. Following President Gbagbo's removal from office in April 2011, reports surfaced of factionalization within the FPI, with some members arguing for dialogue with the Ouattara government and others maintaining a harder line. The former included Mamadou Koulibaly, the speaker of the national assembly and interim leader of the FPI, who at midyear formed the LIDER (above).

The FPI declined to join the June 2011 cabinet and boycotted the December legislative elections, insisting it would not participate in the political process unless Gbagbo and his supporters were released. The government attributed some of the attacks on security forces in 2012 to FPI-affiliated "terrorists," and a number of FPI officials and adherents were subsequently arrested. Although Goudé was extradited from Ghana in January 2013 to face charges in Côte d'Ivoire, other FPI leaders remained in Ghana, to which thousands of Gbagbo loyalists had fled in 2011.

The FPI, accusing the government of a vendetta, formally boycotted the April 2013 local elections.

Leaders: Pascal Affi N'GUESSAN (President of the Party and Former Prime Minister), Laurent AKOUN (Spokesperson), Laurent GBAGBO (Former President of the Republic [awaiting trial at the International Criminal Court in The Hague, Netherlands]), Alphonse DOUATÉ (Former Secretary General), Richard KODJO (Interim Secretary General).

New Forces (*Forces Nouvelles*—FN). The FN was launched in August 2003 by the three main rebel groups opposing the Gbagbo government, including the **Patriotic Movement of the Côte d'Ivoire** (*Mouvement Patriotique de la Côte d'Ivoire*—MPCI), the predominately Muslim northern grouping that had initiated the 2002 civil war. The other FN components were the **Movement for Justice and Peace** (*Mouvement pour la Justice et la Paix*—MJP) and the **Ivorian Popular Movement for the Greater West** (*Mouvement Populaire Ivoirien du Grand Ouest*—MPIGO), both based in western regions of the country and formed after the 2002 strife had commenced. In April 2003 the leader of the MPIGO, Félix DOH, was killed by government forces.

Under the Marcoussis Accords of January 2003, the three FN components were allocated posts in the cabinet of March 2003. However, the FN representatives did not take their seats until August 2004.

After the FN's efforts to have Guillaume Soro (then the FN secretary general) named prime minister failed in October 2005, the FN was given six posts (including Soro as minister of state for reconstruction and reintegration) in the new transitional cabinet installed in December. However, the status of the MJP and MPIGO within the FN at that point was unclear, some reports indicating that the MJP and MPIGO had left the ranks of the umbrella organization.

Following Soro's appointment as prime minister, the FN was accorded seven portfolios in the new national unity government installed in April 2007. Soro, a northern Christian, officially stepped down as leader of the FN in July 2010, focusing instead on MPCI party activity. Meanwhile, dissent was reported within the FN on the part of hard-liners opposed to Soro's continued governmental cooperation with President Gbagbo.

The FN supported Ouattara following the disputed 2010 presidential balloting, and the group's fighters were instrumental in the overthrow of Gbagbo. Soro, who was reappointed prime minister in June 2011, ran successfully on the RDR ticket for the assembly in December, the FN having opted not to present its own candidates. Soro was subsequently elected speaker of the assembly and consequently stepped down as prime minister (a legislator is constitutionally proscribed from being prime minister). As of mid-2013, Soro was described as "still the controlling force" of the FN, whose members by that time made up much of the new national army.

Leaders: Guillaume Kigbafori SORO (Speaker of the Assembly and Former Prime Minister), Mamadou Kone (Secretary General), Louis-André Dakoury TABLEY (Deputy Secretary General), Alain LOBOGNAN.

Union of Social Democrats (*Union des Sociaux-Démocrates*—USD). The USD describes itself as a "compromise between capitalism and socialism." Longtime leader Bernard ZADI-ZAOUROU resigned as USD general secretary in July 2000. The presidential candidacy of his successor, Jerome Climanlo Coulibaly, was subsequently rejected by the Supreme Court. Following the outbreak of civil war in 2002, Coulibaly emerged as a major opposition figure to the Gbagbo regime. He also supported the RDR's Ouattara in the 2010–2011 civil war.

Leader: Jerome Climanlo COULIBALY (General Secretary).

LEGISLATURE

The **National Assembly** (*Assemblée Nationale*) is a unicameral body with 255 members (raised from 147 to 175 in 1985, to 225 in 2000, and to 255 in 2011) elected for five-year terms in single-round balloting in 205 constituencies. Balloting was held on December 10, 2000, for all but 28 seats, 26 of which were filled in elections on January 14, 2001. The next election was scheduled for December 2005 but was postponed repeatedly due to civil unrest. Elections were finally held on December 11, 2011, with the following preliminary distribution of seats being reported: the Rally of Republicans (RDR), 127; the Democratic Party of Côte d'Ivoire (PDCI), 77; the Union for Democracy and Peace in Côte d'Ivoire (UDPCI), 7; the Rally of Houphouëtists for Democracy and Peace (RHDP), 4; the Movement of Forces for the Future (MFA), 3; the Union for Côte d'Ivoire (UPCI), 1; independents, 35; and vacant, 1. Following reballoting for 12 seats on February 26, 2012, the Independent Electoral Commission reported the following distribution of seats, a number of independents and the RHDP legislators having apparently announced their formal affiliation with other parties: the RDR, 138; PDCI, 86; UDPCI, 8; MFA, 3; UPCI, 1; independents, 17; and vacant, 2.

President: Guillaume SORO.

CABINET

[as of September 1, 2013]

Prime Minister	Daniel Kablan Duncan (PDCI)
Ministers of State	
Development and Planning	Albert Toikeusse Mabri (UDPCI)
Employment, Social Affairs, and Professional Training	Moussa Dosso (RDR)
Foreign Affairs	Charles Koffi Diby (PDCI)
Interior and Security	Hamed Bakayoko (RDR)
Office of the President	Jeannot Kouadio Ahoussou (PDCI)
Ministers	
Agriculture	Mamadou Sangafowa Coulibaly (RDR)
African Integration and Ivorians Abroad	Ally Coulibaly
Civil Service and Administrative Reform	Konan Gnamien (UPCI)
Commerce, Handicrafts, and Promotion of Small- and Medium-Sized Enterprises	Jean-Louis Billon (RDR)
Communications	Affoussiata Bamba-Lamine (RDR) [f]
Construction, Housing, Sanitation and Urban Planning	Mamadou Sanogo (ind.)
Culture and Francophonie	Maurice Kouakou Bandama (RDR)
Economic Infrastructure	Patrick Achi (PDCI)
Environment, Sustainable Development, and Urban Healthfulness	Rémi Kouadio Allah (PDCI)
Family, Women, Children, and Solidarity	Anne Désirée Ouloto (RDR) [f]
Fight Against AIDS and Health	Raymonde Goudou Coffie (PDCI) [f]
Finance and Economy	Daniel Kablan Dunca (PDCI)
Forestry and Water	Mathieu Babaud Darret (RDR)
Higher Education and Scientific Research	Ibrahima Bacango Cisse (RDR)

Industry and Mines	Jean Claude Brou
Justice, Human Rights, and Public Liberties and Keeper of the Seals	Gnénéma Mamadou Coulibaly (ind.)
Livestock Resources and Fisheries	Kobena Kouassi Adjoumani (PDCI)
Minister to the President (Defense)	Paul Koffi Koffi (PDCI)
Minister to the Prime Minister (Finance and Economy)	Nialé Kaba (RDR) [f]
National Education and Technical Training	Kandia Kamissoko Camara (RDR) [f]
Petroleum and Energy	Adama Toungara (RDR)
Post and Information and Communication Technology	Bruno Nabagné Kone (ind.)
Promotion of Youth, Sports, and Leisure Activities	Alain Michel Lobognon
Tourism	Roger Kacou
Transport	Gaoussou Toure (RDR)

[f] = female

INTERGOVERNMENTAL REPRESENTATION

Ambassador to the U.S.: Daouda DIABATE.

U.S. Ambassador to Côte d'Ivoire: Phillip CARTER III.

Permanent Representative to the UN: Youssoufou BAMBA.

IGO Memberships (Non-UN): AfDB, AU, ECOWAS, IOM, NAM, OIC, WTO.

CROATIA

Republic of Croatia
Republika Hrvatska

Political Status: Former constituent republic of the Socialist Federal Republic of Yugoslavia; constitution proclaiming Croatian sovereignty promulgated December 21, 1990; independence declared June 25, 1991; dissociation from Yugoslavia approved by the Croatian Assembly effective October 8, 1991.

Area: 21,829 sq. mi. (56,538 sq. km).

Population: 4,398,150 (2013E—UN); 4,475,611 (2013E—U.S. Census).

Major Urban Centers (2011E): ZAGREB (688,000), Split (167,000), Rijeka (128,000).

Official Language: Croatian.

Monetary Unit: Kuna (market rate November 1, 2013: 5.66 kune = $1US).

President: Ivo JOSIPOVIĆ (Social Democratic Party of Croatia); elected in runoff balloting on January 10, 2010, and inaugurated on February 18 for a five-year term to succeed Stjepan MESIĆ (Croatian National Party).

Prime Minister: Zoran MILANOVIĆ (Social Democratic Party of Croatia); elected by the parliament and sworn in on December 23, 2011, to succeed Jadranka KOSOR (Croatian Democratic Union), following legislative elections on December 4.

THE COUNTRY

With a long western coastline on the Adriatic Sea, Croatia half encircles Bosnia and Herzegovina in an arc that extends north and eastward to the province of Vojvodina in Serbia; it also borders Hungary in the northeast and Slovenia in the northwest. At independence in 1991, Croats comprised 78 percent of the population, which also included a 12 percent ethnic Serb component, concentrated south of the capital, Zagreb, and along the western Bosnian border; however, an exodus from these areas in the 1995 hostilities reduced the Serb population to an estimated 2–3 percent. Forests covering more than a third of the country have supported a major timber industry, while agricultural activity in the eastern Pannonian plain is devoted to the growing of wheat, maize, and potatoes, in addition to the raising of cattle, sheep, pigs, and poultry. Extensive mineral resources, including hydrocarbons, bauxite, iron ore, and copper, helped make Croatia the most industrialized component of the former Yugoslav federation, with a GDP per capita substantially higher than that of Yugoslavia as a whole. However, the onset of regional conflict in the early 1990s resulted in the loss of about 30 percent of Croatian territory to the Serbs, inflicted substantial damage on Croatia's economy, and decimated the important tourist industry. National output declined by 50 percent in 1992, during which the annual inflation rate peaked at 662 percent. A partial recovery in 1993–1994 was offset by the high cost of supporting hundreds of thousands of refugees from strife-torn areas of former Yugoslavia. Croatia's recovery of most of its territory and the Dayton Accords of late 1995 stimulated the economy, which, despite continued high unemployment, subsequently exhibited relatively strong growth and low inflation (for more on the Croatian economy prior to 2000, please see the 2012 *Handbook*).

Foreign investment in Croatia subsequently expanded significantly from 2000 to 2007. Foreign banks also invested heavily in the Croatian financial sector, and 90 percent of private banks were foreign owned by 2006. Meanwhile, the government's deficit was reduced to 2.6 percent of GDP. The improving economy allowed the government to increase spending on a variety of social programs. The government also continued its privatization program. Tourism became an increasingly important part of the Croatian economy. GDP growth in Croatia averaged 4.3 percent between 2000 and 2008, while inflation averaged 3.2 percent.

The global economic crisis contributed to a slowdown in Croatia's economy. GDP declined by 5.4 percent in 2009, 1.2 percent in 2010, 0.04 percent in 2011, and 2.0 percent in 2012. Meanwhile, unemployment was 15 percent in 2012 and inflation was 3.4 percent. Per capita income that year was $12,971.

GOVERNMENT AND POLITICS

Political background. The greater part of historic Croatia was joined with Hungary in a personal union under the Hungarian monarch from the early 12th century until after World War I, except for a period of Ottoman Turkish rule from 1526 to the early 18th century. By the 19th century Serbo-Croat had evolved as the common language of Croats and Serbs (the two main South Slav groups), although the Catholic Croats use the Latin alphabet and the Orthodox Serbs use Cyrillic script. In December 1918 the country became part of the Kingdom of the Serbs, Croats, and Slovenes, which was officially renamed Yugoslavia in October 1929. When the Germans invaded Yugoslavia in April 1941, an "Independent State of Croatia" was proclaimed by the *Ustaše* movement, a fascist grouping whose brutality (including the massacre of tens of thousands of Serbs) induced much of the population to support the Communist-inspired partisan forces led by Josip Broz TITO. In November 1945 Croatia became one of the six constituent republics of the Federal People's Republic of Yugoslavia under the one-party rule of what became the League of Communists of Yugoslavia.

On April 22 and May 6–7, 1990, in the first multiparty balloting since World War II, the right-wing Croatian Democratic Union (*Hrvatska Demokratska Zajednica*—HDZ) won 208 of 349 seats in the constituent republic's tricameral legislature, which on May 30 named HDZ leader Franjo TUDJMAN state president and his associate, Stjepan MESIĆ, president of the Executive Council (prime minister). On July 22 the word "Socialist" was deleted from the constituent republic's official name, and the Executive Council was redesignated as the government. Three days later Serb leaders in Croatia issued a statement proclaiming their community's right to sovereignty. On October 1 the Serbs proclaimed three "autonomous regions" encompassing districts within Croatia where they were in a majority. Subsequently, on December 21, the assembly, in an action boycotted by Serb deputies, approved a new constitution that formally asserted the republic's sovereignty, including the right to secede from the Yugoslav federation.

On February 8, 1991, Croatia and Slovenia concluded a mutual defense pact. Three weeks later, Croatia's Serb enclaves announced the formation of a "Serbian Autonomous Region of Krajina," which promptly declared its intention to secede from Croatia and subsequently, on joining with adjacent Serb areas of Bosnia and Herzegovina, assumed the name "Republic of Serbian Krajina" (RSK).

In a May 19, 1991, referendum, 83.6 percent of Croatia's registered electorate voted for dissociation from Yugoslavia, and on June 25 the republic joined Slovenia in declaring independence. The Croatian government shortly thereafter accepted a three-month moratorium on the dissociation process, as urged by the European Community (EC, subsequently the EU) in an effort to prevent a military conflict. (Due to the presence of a significant Serbian population in Croatia, Serbian leaders had indicated a much stronger inclination to resist Croatia's secession, as opposed to Slovenia's.) As part of the EC-brokered negotiations, Mesić was named president of the Yugoslavian Collective State Presidency on July 1. The long-feared civil conflict immediately erupted, with the Serb-dominated Yugoslav National Army (*Yugoslavenska Narodna Armija*—JNA), openly allied with local Serb insurgents, winning control of nearly one-third of Croatia by early September. The Croatian government refused to extend the July dissociation moratorium beyond its three-month deadline and announced formal separation from Yugoslavia effective October 8. The fierce Serb-Croat conflict subsided following the declaration of a cease-fire on January 3, 1992, and the acceptance by both sides of a UN Security Council resolution of January 8 that provided for the deployment of a peacekeeping force in sensitive areas. Accordingly, advance units of the UN Protection Force (UNPROFOR) arrived on March 9.

On August 2, 1992, Croatia's first elections since independence involved balloting for both the House of Representatives and the presidency. The HDZ maintained its substantial overall majority in the legislative contest, and President Tudjman received a decisive 57 percent popular mandate to serve another term, with Hrvoje ŠARINIĆ taking office as prime minister on September 8. Subsequently, in polling for the new upper House of Counties in February 1993, the HDZ was again the victor, gaining majorities or pluralities in 20 of the 21 constituencies. The Šarinić government resigned on March 29, 1993, and was succeeded on April 3 by another HDZ-dominated administration, headed by Nikica VALENTIĆ.

In April 1994 concern that the government had authoritarian tendencies and that a distinct "cult of personality" was emerging around President Tudjman, prompted the defections of some 18 liberal HDZ deputies to form the Croatian Independent Democrats (*Hrvatski Nezavisni Demokrati*—HND), with the attendant acrimony provoking an opposition boycott of parliament until September.

Croatia launched a major military offensive on April 30, 1995, and its forces quickly overran Serb positions in western Slavonia. Serb forces in the RSK retaliated by shelling Zagreb on May 2–3, killing civilians and strengthening Croatia's post-1994 alliance with the Bosnian Muslim-Croat Federation. In a new offensive in late July and early August, Croatian forces overran Serb positions in western Krajina, capturing the capital, Knin, on August 4 and prompting the mass flight of ethnic Serbs from the area. As a result of the Croatian advances, the only part of Croatia still under Serb control in late 1995 was eastern Slavonia, on the border with Serbia proper (see Foreign relations, below, for subsequent developments regarding eastern Slavonia).

Buoyed by military success, the Tudjman government was confirmed in power in lower house elections on October 29, 1995, although the ruling HDZ failed to achieve its target of a two-thirds majority, which is required for constitutional amendments. A new HDZ government appointed on November 7 was headed by Zlatko MATEŠA, a close associate of the president. The HDZ consolidated its strength in the upper house balloting of April 13–15, 1997, securing 40 of 63 elective seats, while Tudjman was reelected to another five-year term by receiving 61 percent of the votes in the presidential election of June 15.

Early in 1998 the nation was rocked by a series of protests over a new 22 percent value-added tax. By the end of the year, the HDZ had been further weakened by a succession struggle between party moderates and hard-liners, with several of President Tudjman's leading advisers quitting the government over allegations that party right-wingers were using the intelligence service to spy on and smear the moderates.

Tudjman's deteriorating health in late 1999 prompted a constitutional crisis because no process had been put in place to deal with such a situation. On November 24 the legislature approved new legislation that permitted the Constitutional Court on November 26 to declare Tudjman "temporarily incapacitated"; presidential authority therefore devolved on an acting basis to Vlatko PAVLETIĆ, the chair of the House of Representatives and a longtime close associate of Tudjman's. Tudjman died on December 10, prompting new elections.

A coalition of four parties led by the Social Democratic Party of Croatia (*Socijaldemokratska Partija Hrvatshe*—SDP) and the Croatian Social-Liberal Party (*Hrvatska Socijalno-Liberalna Stranka*—HSLS) surprised most observers by winning a substantial plurality of 71 seats in the balloting for the House of Representatives on January 3, 2000, while the HDZ's representation fell to 46 seats. The SDP's Ivica RAČAN was inaugurated as prime minister on January 27 to lead a reformist government that included the HSLS as well as four smaller parties (the Croatian Peasant Party [*Hrvatska Selijačka Stranka*—HSS], the Croatian National Party [*Hrvatska Narodna Stranka*—HNS], the Istrian Democratic Assembly [*Istarki Demokratski Sabor*—IDS], and the Liberal Party [*Liberalna Stranka*—LS]) that had won 24 house seats as an electoral coalition.

The collapse of the HDZ following the death of President Tudjman in late 1999 was not a surprise. The economy was in the midst of a recession, unemployment was high, and the administration was perceived as riddled with corruption. In addition, Tudjman's decade of autocratic rule had kept Croatia largely outside the reformist movement so prevalent in many of the other former communist states. In particular, Western capitals criticized Tudjman's record on minority rights, the slow pace of democratic reform, and his lack of enthusiasm for full implementation of the provisions in the Dayton Accords, particularly the return of Serbian refugees to Croatia and the extradition of Croatian military leaders as requested by the UN International Criminal Tribunal for the Former Yugoslavia (ICTY).

Although the SDP/HSLS coalition was expected to dominate the first round of presidential balloting on January 24, 2000, its candidate, Dražen BUDIŠA of the HSLS, finished second to Stjepan Mesić, the candidate of the HNS/HSS/IDS/LS coalition. Mesić outdistanced Budiša by 56 percent to 44 percent in the runoff on February 7. Mesić immediately reversed his predecessor's positions on many issues that had been perceived as retrograde; he also pledged to eliminate covert support to Croatians in Bosnia and Herzegovina who were opposed to the current government. Prime Minister Račan strongly endorsed the reformist agenda, vowing to pursue Croatia's eventual full membership in the EU and NATO.

In June 2001 the IDS left the government because of the refusal by the other coalition members to support its request that Italian be made an official language in Istria, the peninsula near the head of the Adriatic Sea with many ties to Italy. A number of HSLS ministers also quit the cabinet in July to protest the government's decision to extradite several generals to the ICTY for possible prosecution regarding war crimes in the 1991–1995 fighting. The HSLS finally left the coalition completely in early July 2002 because of its opposition to the government's recent agreement with Slovenia over the operation of the Krsko nuclear power plant, located in Slovenia but paid for in part by Croatia during communist rule. (The HSLS opposed the provision that forced Croatia to handle radioactive waste from the plant.) Prime Minister Račan and his government resigned on July 5, but Račan retained the prime ministership in a new government (comprising the SDP, HSS, HNS, LS, and several HSLS dissidents) that was approved by the House of Representatives on July 30.

The HDZ regained a plurality in the November 23, 2003, balloting and formed a minority government that included a minister from the Democratic Center (*Demokratski Centar*—DC) and was supported in the legislature by the HSLS, HSS, and several independent deputies. Ivo SANADER of the HDZ was named prime minister.

Sanader promised economic, military, and judicial reforms, primarily aimed at entry into the EU. In 2004 the EU authorized the start of formal accession negotiations, in part because of Croatia's apparent willingness to cooperate more enthusiastically with the ICTY. Croatia indicated it hoped to gain EU membership by 2007, but progress stalled in April 2005 when the UN accused the Croatian government of poor faith in extraditing alleged war criminals to the ICTY. (The government argued that it had been unable to locate Ante GOTOVINA, one of the most prominent suspected war criminals. However, the ICTY alleged Gotovina was being shielded by supporters that included Croatian officials.)

Thirteen candidates vied for the presidency in elections in 2005, with most center-left parties supporting incumbent President Mesić. In the first round of balloting on January 2, 2005, Mesić received 48.9 percent of the vote, followed by Jadranka KOSOR, the vice president of the HDZ, with 20.3 percent of the vote. Mesić was reelected for a second five-year term by securing 65.9 percent of the vote in the runoff balloting.

In the May 2005 local elections, the far-right Croatian Party of Rights (*Hrvatska Stranka Prava*—HSP) saw its representation triple in consonance with growing popular antipathy toward the ICTY. Sanader subsequently strongly criticized the ICTY for expanding the list of Croatians it hoped to bring to trial. In October the ICTY's chief prosecutor issued a positive report on Croatia's cooperation with the tribunal, and as a result accession negotiations recommenced. Croatia's prospects for EU membership subsequently brightened considerably in December 2005, when Gotovina was arrested by Spanish authorities in the Canary Islands, partially as a result of intelligence provided by the Croatian government. Since the arrest and transfer of Gotovina to The Hague in late 2005, Croatia has continued to cooperate fully with the ICTY and was certified to be in full compliance, clearing the way for continued EU negotiations. In 2006 the EU granted Croatia €245 million to aid in preparations to join the organization, and formal accession talks were launched on June 12 in Luxembourg. In October 2006 Branimir GLAVAS, a member of the House of Representatives (see the Croatian Democratic Assembly of Slavonia and Baranja under Political Parties, below) and former military officer was stripped of his immunity and arrested on charges related to the massacre of ethnic Serbs in 1991. Glavas was the Croat with the highest profile to date to be tried for crimes against humanity by the national judiciary.

In February 2006 tensions between the prime minister and the justice minister, Vesna ŠKARE-OŽBOLT, the leader of the DC, led to her forced resignation. The DC subsequently withdrew its support for the government.

In March 2007 Prime Minister Sanader rebuffed opposition efforts to force a referendum on NATO membership, arguing that the constitution did not require such a vote. In the November House elections, no political party gained an absolute majority. Both the HDZ and the SPD endeavored to form a coalition government, but the president reappointed Sanader once the HDZ reached an agreement with the HSLS, the HSS, and the SDSS. In the legislative balloting, Nazif MEMEDI, a member of the Roma ethnic minority, was elected to the House for the first time. Despite his ongoing trial, Glavas was also elected to the legislature.

The HDZ won the most seats in the legislative elections on November 25, 2007, and formed a coalition government with the HSLS, the HSS, and the Independent Democratic Serbian Party (*Samostaina Demokratska Srpska Stranka*—SDSS). In addition, the government had the support of the Croatian Pensioners' Party (*Hrvatska Stranka Umirovljenika*—HSU) and four independent deputies, giving it 82 votes in the 153-member chamber. Sanader was again appointed prime minister.

In October 2008 in response to perceived government inaction against organized crime, the opposition SDP sponsored a no-confidence vote against the Sanader government. The motion failed on a vote of 75 opposed and 53 in favor.

Glavas was convicted of war crimes in 2009, but evaded arrest (see Political Parties, below).

In local elections on May 17 and 31, 2009, the HDZ won a resounding victory. The party secured majorities in ten prefects and formed coalitions with the HSS in three others. The HDZ also won control of 15 local councils (all with coalition governments). Meanwhile, the SDP secured seven prefects, including two coalition governments and six local councils, all in coalition governments. In October Damir POLANCEC resigned as deputy prime minister following revelations of his involvement in a financial scandal. In June the legislature passed a series of reforms needed to align Croatian law with EU requirements.

On July 1, 2009, Sanader abruptly announced that he intended to resign and leave politics. Deputy prime minister and HDZ vice president Kosor was elected by the party to replace Sanader three days later. She retained most of the Sanader cabinet, with only minor changes. Ivo JOSIPOVIĆ (SDP) was elected president in runoff elections on January 10, 2010, defeating independent candidate and mayor of Zagreb, Milan BANDIC.

The HSLS withdrew its support for the coalition government in July 2010, citing differences with the ruling HDZ (see Political Parties, below). The withdrawal led to the resignation of HSLS member and Deputy Prime Minister Durda ADLEŠIČ. The HSU also withdrew from the coalition over a new tax on pensions and retirement income that month. However, the HDZ-led coalition continued to maintain a slim majority in the House through the support of independents. The Kosor government survived a no-confidence vote in October. In December Kosor replaced four cabinet ministers who faced allegations of corruption.

Former generals Gotovina and Mladen MARKAC were convicted of war crimes on April 15, 2011. The convictions prompted widespread protests in Croatia, where the two are viewed as national heroes. The convictions were overturned on appeal on November 16, 2012, which most Croatians interpreted as a form of endorsement of their independence movement.

In legislative elections on December 4, 2011, a center-left coalition, led by the SDP, won a majority with 81 seats. SDP leader Zoran MILANOVIĆ formed a coalition government and was sworn in as prime minister on December 23. In a referendum on January 22, 2012, voters endorsed EU membership by a margin of 66.3 percent in favor to 33.1 percent against.

Constitution and government. The 1990 constitution defined the Republic of Croatia as a unitary (and indivisible), democratic, and social state, in which power "comes from and belongs to the people as a community of free and equal citizens." The highest values of the republic were stated to be freedom, equal rights, national equality, peace, social justice, respect for human rights, inviolability of ownership, respect for legal order, care for the environment, and a democratic multiparty system of government. Legislative power was vested in a bicameral assembly, both houses of which were directly elected and sat for four-year terms. The "supreme head of the executive power" was the president, who was directly elected for a five-year term and who, subject to parliamentary confirmation, appointed the prime minister and, on the proposal of the latter, other members of the government.

Significant changes to the constitution were approved by the House of Representatives on November 9, 2000, primarily to reduce the power of the president. According to those revisions, the prime minister and the cabinet are now appointed by the legislature, although the president remains commander in chief of the military. Another important change was made in March 2001 when the House of Representatives (by then controlled by reformist parties) voted to abolish the upper house (the House of Counties), which was still dominated by the HDZ.

The ordinary court system is headed by a Supreme Court, whose judges are appointed and relieved of duty by a 15-member Judicial Council of the Republic elected by the House of Representatives. There is also provision for a Constitutional Court, whose members are elected by the House of Representatives for eight-year terms. The main local self-government units are 21 counties (*Zupanije*) and more than 500 towns and other small municipalities.

On December 12, 1997, the legislature approved a constitutional amendment proposed by President Tudjman forbidding Croatia from joining a union with any Yugoslav or Balkan state.

Croatia generally has a free press, although intimidation and violence against reporters has increased in recent years. The media watchdog group Reporters Without Borders ranked Croatia 64th out of 179 nations in 2013.

In June 2010 the parliament approved a range of constitutional amendments required for admission into the EU (see Foreign relations, below). The measures enhanced the independence of the judiciary and central bank, and included a provision to allow Croatian citizens to be extradited to EU member states.

Foreign relations. Germany unilaterally recognized Croatia on December 23, 1991, with the EC following with recognition of both Croatia and Slovenia on January 15, 1992. Croatia and Slovenia established diplomatic relations with each other on February 17, 1992. On that same date, Russia accorded diplomatic recognition to Croatia. The United States followed suit on April 7. On May 22 Croatia, Slovenia, and Bosnia and Herzegovina became members of the UN. The mandate of the UNPROFOR forces deployed in Croatia from March 1992 was regularly renewed thereafter, although with increasing reluctance on Croatia's part.

Admitted to the Conference on Security and Cooperation in Europe (CSCE, subsequently the Organization for Security and Cooperation in Europe—OSCE) in March 1992 and to the IMF in January 1993, Croatia also developed its regional links, becoming a member of the Central European Initiative (CEI), originally formed in 1989.

In January 1993 Croatia launched an offensive to recover territory lost in 1991 to what had became the Serb-controlled RSK. However, despite some strategic successes on the part of the Croatian thrust, the RSK remained viable, and sporadic fighting continued, although not on the scale of the escalating conflict in Bosnia and Herzegovina. In May 1993 the Tudjman government signed the Vance-Owen peace plan for Bosnia and Herzegovina, albeit clearly without any expectation that it would be implemented in the form proposed. In June, Tudjman and Serbian President Slobodan Milošević reportedly reaffirmed their aim of bringing about the eventual partition of Bosnia and Herzegovina between Croatia and Serbia on the basis of an "orderly" transfer of population. In 1994, however, advocates of a resumption of the earlier Croat-Muslim alliance gained the ascendancy in Croatia. The result was the signing on March 18 of a U.S.-brokered agreement between Bosnian Croats and Muslims providing for a federal structure in the neighboring republic (see article on Bosnia and Herzegovina), accompanied by a preliminary accord envisaging the creation of a confederation between the new Bosnian federation and Croatia, with each remaining sovereign entities.

In October 1994 Croatia welcomed the creation of the so-called Zagreb Four (Z-4) mini-contact group (the UN, EU, United States, and Russia), which was charged with resolving the Croat-Serb deadlock. Speedy progress seemed to be made by the Z-4 under a December agreement reestablishing essential services between Croatia and the RSK and reopening major roads; however, the accord was suspended by the RSK in February 1995 after Croatia had given formal notice of terminating the UNPROFOR mandate. In the same month Croatia rejected a Z-4 peace plan as "unacceptable" in its "structure, basic provisions, title, and preamble." On March 6 the military commanders of Croatia, the Bosnian government, and the Bosnian Croats concluded a formal alliance in response to a military pact between Croatian Serb and Bosnian Serb forces announced on February 20. A week later President Tudjman bowed to U.S. and German pressure by agreeing to the renewal of the UNPROFOR mandate from March 31, on condition that most UN forces would be stationed on Croatia's international borders.

In the wake of Croatian military successes in 1995 and the restoration of government control over most of Croatia, President Tudjman was a key participant in the Dayton Accords talks that yielded a Bosnian peace agreement in November, and he was a signatory of the accord in Paris in December. On November 30 the UN Security Council voted to withdraw UN troops from Croatia by mid-January 1996. In a state of the nation address on January 15, Tudjman reported that, in what he called the "homeland war" of 1991–1995, Croatia proper had suffered some 13,500 deaths and nearly 40,000 people injured, as well as material damage estimated at $27 billion.

Although the status of Serb-held eastern Slavonia did not feature in the accords, Croatia's endorsement of the agreement was predicated on an international understanding that the area would be restored to Croatian rule. An agreement signed by Croatia and local Serb leaders on November 12, 1995, provided for the reintegration of eastern Slavonia into Croatia within two years, during which a UN-sponsored transitional administration would exercise authority. In January 1996 the UN Security Council approved the deployment of a 5,000-strong peacekeeping force (the UN Transitional Administration for Eastern Slavonia, Baranja, and Western Sirmium—UNTAES) to supervise the demilitarization of the area. The deployment began in May as the Serbs of the region elected a new leadership that appeared to be reconciled to the eventual restoration of Croatian rule. (Croatia formally reassumed authority over Slavonia on January 15, 1998, following the expiration of the UNTAES mandate. A small UN support group was collaterally assigned to remain in the region to monitor relations between the Croatian police and returning displaced persons.) The progress made on the Slavonian front in 1996 enabled Croatia, following talks between Presidents Tudjman and Milošević near Athens on August 7, to sign a formal accord with the Federal Republic of Yugoslavia on August 23 providing for the establishment of full diplomatic relations between the two countries. Collaterally, Croatia increased pressure on the Bosnian Croats to accept federation with the Bosnian Muslims, to which end Presidents Tudjman and Izetbegović of Bosnia, conferring in Geneva on August 14, reached agreement on detailed steps to inject substance into a federation structure theretofore existing only on paper. Croatia joined the Council of Europe on October 16, 1996, after the government issued assurances on a 21-point program on democracy and human rights previously negotiated with the council. After years of negotiations, Croatia tentatively accepted two agreements with Bosnia and Herzegovina on November 22, 1998. The Ploce-Neum accord gave Bosnia, which had very limited sea access, the right to use Croatia's large-vessel port of Ploce, while the Croatians gained transit rights through Bosnia's Neum region without border formalities. A second treaty called for a "special relationship" between Croatia and the Muslim-Croat Federation of Bosnia and Herzegovina.

Although Croatia continued to express an interest in joining the EU and NATO during the latter years of the Tudjman administration, Croatia satisfied neither group that it was committed to key prerequisites for inclusion, including press freedom, fair elections, civilian control of the military, and full implementation of the Dayton peace agreements (particularly the return of Serb refugees). As a result, NATO took no immediate action on Croatia's application to join the Partnership for Peace program. However, Croatia voiced support for NATO air strikes against Serbia in March 1999, and Foreign Minister Mate GRANIĆ claimed on April 1 that he had obtained a security guarantee from NATO in the event that the conflict in Kosovo spread.

Following Tudjman's death in late 1999 and the subsequent installation in early 2000 of a reformist government, Croatia's relations with the West improved with remarkable speed. In May membership in NATO's Partnership for Peace program was approved, in December Croatia joined the World Trade Organization, and in October 2001 Croatia signed an association agreement with the EU.

In April 2002 Croatia negotiated an agreement to delineate the border between Croatia and Montenegro, and President Mesić and the president of Serbia and Montenegro in 2003 exchanged mutual apologies for atrocities committed during the civil war.

President Mesić was outspoken in his opposition to the U.S./UK-led invasion of Iraq in early 2003, and Croatia rebuffed a request to contribute troops to that initiative. However, relations with Washington improved following the installation of the HDZ government in late 2003, and Croatia subsequently agreed to permit the United States to use Croatian airspace and waters in future military action. Croatia also deployed 150 troops to train Afghan security forces in 2003.

On May 2, 2003, Croatia signed an Adriatic Charter along with the United States, Albania, and Macedonia. Among other things, Croatia, Albania, and Macedonia agreed to work together to pursue NATO membership, while the United States pledged to promote the candidacy of all three for simultaneous membership. In May 2006 U.S. Vice President Dick Cheney made a visit to Croatia. Croatia concurrently began upgrading its military transport aircraft so they could further support missions in Afghanistan and other out-of-area operations. Croatia and Italy announced an agreement in 2006 that would allow Italians to own land in Croatia. (Italians had been forbidden from purchasing property in Croatia because of continuing disputes over property rights in Istria, which had been transferred to Yugoslavia from Italy at the end of World War II.) Also in 2006 Croatia announced plans to build a new gas and oil pipeline system that would allow the export of energy resources to neighboring states such as Hungary and Serbia.

In March 2007 Croatia signed a trade agreement with the People's Republic of China designed to remove barriers to Chinese investment in the country and to open Chinese markets to Croatian goods. (Croatia had imported about $1 billion in products from China in 2006 but had exported only $17 million.) Also, in 2007, Croatia joined the International Whaling Commission (IWC). Meanwhile, as of 2007 Croatia had contributed troops to ten UN peacekeeping missions, including operations in Ethiopia, Georgia, and Sierra Leone. Croatia also increased its deployment in Afghanistan to 300 soldiers in 2008.

In March 2008 Croatia offered diplomatic recognition to Kosovo. Recognition was strongly opposed by the Serb community in Croatia (see Current issues). Also, Serb protesters in Belgrade, Serbia, subsequently damaged the Croatian embassy on February 21. Croatia was invited to join NATO at the alliance's April summit in Bucharest, Romania.

Russian shipments of natural gas were cut off to Croatia in January 2009 during a dispute between Russia and Ukraine. Croatia, which imported 40 percent of its natural gas from Russia, launched a broad effort to reduce energy imports. In April Croatia and Albania signed an agreement to develop a joint nuclear power plant as part of that initiative.

Membership in NATO enjoyed broad public and political support, and had the unanimous endorsement of both government and opposition parties. Croatia formally joined NATO on April 1, 2009. Negotiations over Croatian entry into the EU were delayed over a lingering boundary dispute with Slovenia over maritime rights and the land border in and around the Bay of Piran. The Sanader government had sought to conclude talks with the EU and gain membership by the end of 2009, but the disagreement threatened to delay entry.

On October 2, 2009, Slovenia withdrew its veto of Croatian membership in the EU following an agreement between the two states to allow international arbitrators to fix the maritime boundary in the Adriatic. In June 2010 Slovenes approved the agreement in a national referendum. Negotiations over Croatian entry into the EU were subsequently restarted, with 2012 as a target date for admission.

Croatia agreed to participate in the Russian South Stream gas pipeline project designed to bring energy to Southeastern Europe in March 2010. In April the Croatian parliament voted to increase to 320 the country's contribution to the NATO-led Afghan security force. By June Croatia had met 20 of 35 policy requirements to join the EU. Also in June, Croatia and Serbia signed a bilateral military cooperation agreement.

Talks on EU membership for Croatia concluded in June 2011, and the EU accession treaty was signed on December 9. As part of the negotiations on membership, the EU and Croatia signed an agreement on December 15 for the training of Croatian judges and legal officials to ensure they would comply with EU jurisprudence.

Croatian voters endorsed EU membership in a January 2012 referendum. Also in January, Plinacro, a Croatia-based transmission firm, signed a €60 million deal with Russia's Gazprom to build a portion of the South Stream pipeline linking Croatia and Serbia. The agreement was overshadowed by Prime Minister Milanović's refusal to meet with Gazprom president Alexei Miller, a close ally of Russian president Vladimir Putin.

On July 1, 2013, Croatia became a member of the EU.

Current issues. Croatia's recognition of Kosovo independence in March 2008 led to protests by ethnic Serbs in the country. In addition, SDSS Deputy Prime Minister Slobodan UZELAC attempted to resign in protest; however, his resignation was not accepted by Sanader. In October 2008 the high-profile murder of two journalists by organized crime figures prompted a range of government efforts to reduce crime, including the replacement of the interior and justice ministers. The government created a new, specialized police unit that concentrated specifically on organized crime. Despite the rise in organized crime, overall crime rates continued to decline in Croatia. The worldwide economic crisis that began in 2008 prompted the government to cut spending and reduce wages for most public-sector employees by 6 percent.

The World Bank approved a $145 million loan to aid Croatia's economic recovery in 2009 and granted the country an additional $291 million in financial assistance in 2010.

In December 2010 former prime minister Sanadar fled to Austria to avoid prosecution on corruption charges. In May an Austrian court approved Sanadar's extradition, and he was transferred to Croatia in July. In September the legislature removed Sanadar's immunity from prosecution, clearing the way for his trial, which began on November 3.

High unemployment and continuing recession eroded the popularity of the Kosor government. Her cabinet also faced charges of corruption, prompting the replacement of several ministers. In March 2011 there were widespread protests against the government, coordinated by social media. The SDP, HNS, IDS, and the HSU formed an electoral coalition ahead of parliamentary balloting in 2011. The new grouping was dubbed *Kukuriku* ("Cock-a-Doodle-Doo") after the restaurant where the negotiations were finalized on the alliance.

In legislative balloting on December 4, 2011, *Kukuriku* won a majority with 81 seats. SDP leader Milanović became prime minister and brokered a coalition government that included the SDP, HNS, and the IDS. The new cabinet was sworn in on December 23. A center-right coalition, led by the then-ruling Croatian Democratic Union, and including the DC and the **Croatian Civic Party** (*Hrvatska građanska stranka*—HGS), placed second in the balloting with 47 seats.

The SDP government's 2012 budget contained measures to reduce the deficit from 5.5 percent of GDP in 2011 to 3.8 percent. Austerity measures included an increase in the value-added tax (VAT) rate from 23 percent to 25 percent and $700 million in spending cuts through layoffs. Government officials hoped the measures would boost the country's BBB–credit rating, but critics blasted the combination of job cuts and higher consumption taxes.

First Deputy Prime Minister Radimir ČAČIĆ resigned on November 14 after a Hungarian court sentenced him to almost two years in prison for killing two persons in a 2010 auto accident. He immediately resigned from the government. Milanović shuffled his cabinet, promoting Foreign Minister Vesna Pusić to first deputy prime minister and giving Čačić's economy portfolio to Minister of Construction Ivan VRDOLJAK. Pusić also replaced Čačić as head of the HNS. (Čačić reported to the Remetinec prison in Zagreb on June 17, 2013.)

On November 20, 2012, Sanader was convicted of accepting bribes of €5 million from Hungary's MOL energy and €545,000 from Hypo Alpe Adria Bank and sentenced to ten years in prison. He still faces trial on charges that he diverted funds from state companies and contracts to create a slush fund for the HDZ. The party was also to stand trial and faced bankruptcy if forced to repay the questionable $5.78 million. His conviction provided evidence that Croatia was serious about cracking down on corruption, a precondition for EU membership.

Croatia entered is fifth consecutive year in an economic recession in 2013. Unemployment remained high, especially for persons under age 25. Some 60,000–70,000 Croats had left the country to look for work since 2008. With state revenue not meeting projections, in February Milanović announced an across-the-board 3 percent salary cut for all state employees.

Citizens protested two new government policies affecting their daily lives. In February more than 20,000 people in Vukovar protested the introduction of signs with Cyrillic letters. With over 20 percent of Vukovar's population being ethnic Serbs, they were constitutionally entitled to use their own language and alphabet, but painful memories of a 1991 siege by Serbian forces remained. Alphabet-related clashes continued throughout the year, spreading to Zadar and Dubrovnik. Parents and the Catholic Church denounced a new sex education curriculum launched in February in the public schools. The Supreme Court suspended the lessons on grounds that the government had violated the constitution by not consulting parents first.

In nationwide elections on April 14, the HDZ won 6 of Croatia's 12 seats in the European Parliament. The SDP took 5 seats and HL 1. Turnout was only 20.75 percent, the lowest ever recorded. Opposition members blamed the low turnout on President Josipović, arguing that it should have been held concurrently with the local elections. The HDZ also came out on top in the May 19 local elections, winning 10 municipalities to the SDP's 5.

Croatia was admitted to the EU on July 1, but it did not adopt the euro. It was immediately slated for the Excess Deficit Procedure, as its budget deficit will likely remain above the 3.0 percent of GDP ceiling for several years.

POLITICAL PARTIES

For four and a half decades after World War II, the only authorized political party in Yugoslavia was the Communist Party, which was redesignated in 1952 as the League of Communists of Yugoslavia (*Savez Komunista Jugoslavija*—SKJ). In 1989 noncommunist groups began to emerge in the republics, and in early 1990 the SKJ approved the introduction of a multiparty system, thereby effectively triggering its own demise. In 2013 there were 123 registered political parties in Croatia, 13 of which are represented in parliament.

Government and Government-Supportive Parties:

Social Democratic Party of Croatia (*Socijaldemokratska Partija Hrvatske*—SDP). Founded in 1937 as the Communist Party of Croatia and redesignated in 1952 as the League of Communists of Croatia (*Savez Komunista Hrvatske*—SKH), the SDP was runner-up to the HDZ in the 1990 balloting, winning 75 of 349 legislative seats outright, in addition to 16 captured in joint lists with other parties. Then called the Party of Democratic Changes (*Stranka Demokratskih Promjena*—SDP) to signify its rejection of communism, it slumped to only 11 seats (out of 138) in the 1992 election. The party changed its name again in April 1993 when it became the Social Democratic Party of Croatia, angering another leftist party of the same name (*Socijaldemokratska Stranka Hrvatske*—SDSH), with which it would merge a year later. (The SDSH, launched in December 1989, had won one seat in 1990 and was a member of the ruling coalition until August 1992, when its leader, Antun VUJIĆ, finished last of eight presidential candidates.)

The sole successful SDP candidate in the 1993 upper house polling was returned by virtue of an alliance with the HSLS. The united SDP performed better in the October 1995 lower house election, winning 8.9 percent of the vote. In the April 1997 upper house elections the SDP showed further strength (in frequent alliance with the HNS), and in the June presidential campaign SDP candidate Zdravko TOMAC ran second (21 percent) in the three-way race. The SDP's gains in both races indicated to some observers that it had displaced the HSLS as the strongest opposition party.

The SDP participated in an electoral coalition in the 2000 legislative elections with the HSLS, PGS, and SBHS. The coalition secured 47 percent of the vote and 71 seats; SDP leader Ivica Račan subsequently formed a coalition government. However, the joint SDP/HSLS presidential candidate, Dražen Budiša of the HSLS, finished second in the 2000 presidential poll.

In the 2003 legislative elections the SDP formed a new coalition with the LS, IDS, and Libra (see under HNS below). The SDP developed a broader coalition in 2005 to support the candidacy of President Mesić.

In April 2007 Račan's health rapidly declined, and he resigned as SDP leader. Zeljka ANTUNOVIĆ became interim president, but she announced that she would not campaign to be prime minister or president, thereby opening a leadership race for the party ahead of the November 2007 legislative elections. Zoran MILANOVIĆ was elected SDP president at a party congress on June 2 to fill the remainder of Račan's term. In the 2007 legislative balloting the SPD placed second with 31.2 percent of the vote and 56 seats in the House. Milanović was reelected party leader on May 11, 2008. In 2009 the SDP joined the HSU in an electoral coalition for local balloting.

Ivo JOSIPOVIĆ of the SDP placed first in the initial round of presidential balloting on December 27, 2009, with 32.4 percent of the vote. He won the January 10, 2010, runoff polling with 60.3 percent of the vote. As required by law, Josipović resigned from his party after taking the oath of office as president. Party leader Milanović became the youngest prime minister in Croatian history after the party's coalition won the majority of seats in the 2011 balloting.

Leaders: Zoran MILANOVIĆ (Prime Minister and President of the Party), Neven MIMICA (Deputy Prime Minister), Milanka OPAČIĆ (Deputy Prime Minister and Party Vice President), Zlatko KOMADINA, Gordan MARAS, Rajko OSTOJIĆ (Party Vice Presidents).

Croatian National Party–Liberal Democrats (*Hrvatska Narodna Stranka–Liberalni Demokrati*—HNS). Formed in January 1991, the Croatian National Party (HNS) was also widely known as the Croatian People's Party. The party secured lower house representation by the co-option of five deputies elected in 1990 under other party labels. It was an antitraditionalist grouping committed to political pluralism and a free-market economy. The party won six seats in the 1992 legislative election, with its leader securing 6 percent of the presidential vote. It slipped to two seats in 1995 and ran joint candidates with the Social Democratic Party of Croatia (*Socijaldemokratska Partija Hrvatske*—SDP) in the 1997 House of Counties balloting.

The HNS participated in the 2000 legislative elections in a coalition with the HSS, IDS, and LS, gaining 2 of the coalition's 24 seats. Despite its modest status in the realm of Croatian parties, the HNS served as the springboard for the successful presidential campaign in 2000 of Stjepan Mesić, a founding member of the HDZ who had broken from President Tudjman in 1994 and joined the HNS in 1997. Mesić won 41.1 percent of the vote in the first round of the presidential poll and 56.0 percent in the runoff.

In the 2003 elections the HNS joined a coalition with the SBHS and the PGS. In 2005 Mesić was reelected president with support from an SDP-led coalition. In February 2005 a party convention voted to merge the HNS with the Party of Liberal Democrats (*Stranka Liberalni Demokrati*—Libra) and adopt the expanded party name, while apparently retaining the HNS abbreviation. Libra had been formed in 2002 by former members of the HSLS when the HSLS left the SDP-led coalition government over the handling of the Krsko nuclear power plant issue with Slovenia. Libra deputies continued to support the government after the departure of the HSLS. Libra sought to appeal to younger, more educated urban voters with a centrist, economically liberal platform. In the 2003 House of Representatives elections Libra joined the SDP-led electoral coalition and secured three seats. Libra also participated in the SDP-led coalition that supported President Mesić in the 2005 presidential election before merging with the HNS. Libra President Jozo Radoš became a vice president of the expanded HNS in 2005.

In the 2007 House elections the HNS secured six seats. In April 2008 Radimir Čačić was reelected as party president. Vesna PUSIĆ was the party's 2009 presidential candidate. She placed fifth in the first round of balloting and received 7.25 percent of the vote. The HNS reportedly joined an electoral alliance with the SDP ahead of the next national elections. In 2010 Dragutin LESAR defected from the party to form the **Croatian Labourists-Labour Party** (*Hrvatski Laburisti—Stranka Rada*—HL) (see below). In 2011 the HNS participated in the SDP-led electoral alliance, and secured 13 seats. It subsequently joined the SDP-led government and Čačić was appointed a deputy prime minister. Čačić resigned from both the government and party on November 14, 2012, after a Hungarian court sentenced him to 22 months in prison for killing two persons in a 2010 auto accident. Pusić was elected party president in March 2013, with the support of 577 of 603 delegates.

Leaders: Stjepan MESIĆ (Former President of the Republic), Vesna PUSIĆ (First Deputy Prime Minster, Foreign Minister, and President of the Party), Savka DABČEVIĆ-KUČAR (Honorary President), Mladen BELIICZA, Jozo RADOŠ, Ivan VRDOLJAK (Vice Presidents).

Istrian Democratic Assembly (*Istarski Demokratski Sabor*—IDS). Founded in February 1990, the IDS represents ethnic Italians and other minorities in Istria, advocating the creation of a "trans-border region" encompassing Croatian, Slovenian, and Italian areas. In the 1992 lower house balloting it formed a regional front with **Dalmatian Action** (*Dalmatinska Akcija*—DA), led by Mira LJUBIĆ-LORGER, and the Rijeka Democratic Alliance (see PGS, below), which won six seats, of which the IDS took four. In the 1993 upper house election the IDS took 66 percent of the vote in Istria, winning one elective seat and being allocated two more by presidential prerogative. In 1995 the IDS tally as part of the ZL was four seats. The party won two seats in the April 1997 elections for the House of Counties. In August the IDS called a meeting of several opposition parties to agitate for changes in electoral law that would reduce the power of the presidency and make referendums mandatory for all key issues.

The IDS won four seats in the 2000 balloting for the House of Representatives in coalition with the HSS, HNS, and LS. The IDS joined the January 2000 cabinet formed by the SDP's Ivica Račan but left the government in June 2001. The IDS again campaigned with the SDP coalition in the 2003 House election, and it also joined the SDP-led coalition that supported President Mesić in his 2005 reelection campaign. In the November 2007 legislative polling the IDS won three seats in the House. IDS vice president Damir KAJIN was the party's presidential candidate in the 2009 elections. He was eighth in the initial round of balloting with just 3.9 percent of the vote. The IDS joined the SDP-led electoral coalition in 2011 and subsequently secured one cabinet appointment, the ministry of tourism.

Leaders: Ivan JAKOVČIĆ (President), Tedi CHIAVALON (Secretary General), Damir KAJIN (2009 presidential candidate), Nevija POROPAT, Giovanni SPONZA, Marianna Jellcich BULĆ, Boris MILETIĆ (Vice Presidents).

Croatian Pensioners' Party (*Hrvatska Stranka Umirovljenika*—HSU). The HSU was a center-left party that was formed in 1991 to promote pensioners' rights. In the 2003 assembly elections the HSU won three seats, and the party supported the HDZ-led coalition government. In 2007 the party won 4.1 percent of the vote and 1 seat, and subsequently supported the new HDZ-led government. In 2008 Silvano Hrelja was elected to replace Vladimir Jordan as party leader. Ahead of the 2009 local elections, the HSU signed a coalition agreement with the SDP (see below). In July the HSU withdrew from the HDZ coalition government and subsequently joined the HNS and the IDS in an electoral alliance with the SDP. The HSU won three seats in the 2011 balloting but did not join the SDP-led government.

Leaders: Silvano HRELJA (President), Mijo PRGOMET (Vice President).

Other Parliamentary Parties:

Croatian Democratic Union (*Hrvatska Demokratska Zajednica*—HDZ). Founded in June 1989, the right-wing HDZ won a decisive majority of seats in the 1990 elections in each of the three assembly chambers in the Croatian constituent republic within Federal Yugoslavia. After leading Croatia to independence in 1991, the HDZ won a further overall parliamentary majority in the 1992 balloting, when the party's leader was popularly returned as head of state with 56.7 percent of the vote. Having previously headed a coalition government, the HDZ was the sole ruling party until, after winning a majority in upper house balloting in February 1993, it accepted the small Croatian Peasant Party (see below) as a ministerial partner. In September 1994 ideological conflict flared when extreme rightist Vladimir ŠEKS resigned as deputy prime minister but was speedily elected chair of the party's parliamentary group. Strengthened by Croatian military advances against the Serbs, the HDZ retained a comfortable lower house majority on a 45.2 percent vote share in October 1995. In the upper house elections of April 1997, the HDZ won 40 of 63 elected seats, while President Tudjman in June won a landslide victory in the presidential balloting. He was also unanimously reelected as party president in February 1998. Tudjman appeared to side with party hard-liners in a succession struggle leading to the resignation of two top presidential advisers in October 1998. The hard-liners, who reportedly shared with Tudjman a desire to carve Croatian territory from Bosnia and Herzegovina, were led by Ivić PAŠALIĆ, the president's special adviser for domestic affairs, who many observers believed was the likely successor to the president.

Following Tudjman's death in late 1999, Pašalić lost the HDZ leadership election to Mate Granić, who finished a disappointing third in the first round of the 2000 presidential poll with 22.4 percent of the vote. The party's fortunes also slid significantly in the January 2000 legislative balloting as it secured only 24 percent of the vote and 46 seats. Granić subsequently left the HDZ (along with three other HDZ legislators) to form the Democratic Center. Meanwhile, Ivo Sanader was selected as the new HDZ president in 2000, Pašalić being expelled from the party in July 2002 for characterizing Sanader's reelection as "illegal." (Pašalić subsequently formed the Croatian Bloc–Movement for a Modern Croatia.)

HDZ Vice President Jadranka Kosor placed second in the first round of presidential voting in 2005 and was defeated in the runoff balloting by the incumbent president. The HDZ expelled three legislators from the party in 2005 for advocating greater regional autonomy.

The HDZ won 43.1 percent of the vote in the 2007 legislative elections and 66 seats in the House, and Sanader formed a new HDZ-led government in January 2008. The following May Sanader was reelected HDZ leader for the fourth time, and in June Ivan Jarnjak was unanimously reelected as secretary general of the party for a second four-year term. However, Sanader resigned in July 2009 as prime minister and party leader. Jadranka KOSOR was elected to replace him as party and government leader. Andrija HEBRANG was the HDZ candidate in the 2009 presidential elections. He placed third in the balloting with 12 percent.

Sanader was expelled from the HDZ in January 2010 following public criticism of the current leadership of the party and its management of the 2009 presidential elections. Media reports in 2011 charged that under Sanadar, some HDZ leaders created a "black fund" to launder bribes and other illicit monies. The HDZ suffered its worst electoral defeat in 2011, securing only 29.1 percent of the vote and 44 seats. In May 2012 Tomislav KARAMARKO was elected HDZ president. Kosor was expelled from the party on March 1, 2013, on grounds that she had damaged the party by publicly criticizing Karamarko's leadership.

Leaders: Tomislav KARAMARKO (President), Drago PRGOMET (Vice President).

Croatian Peasant Party (*Hrvatska Seljačka Stranka*—HSS). Originally founded in 1904 as the Croatian Popular Peasant Party and influential in the interwar period, the HSS was relaunched in November 1989 as a party committed to pacifism, localism, and economic privatization. It won 3 lower house seats in August 1992 and 5 upper house seats in February 1993, thereafter accepting ministerial representation in coalition with the dominant HDZ. It switched to opposition status for the October 1995 election, winning 10 seats as a member of the Joint List Bloc (*Zajednica Lista*—ZL), which also included the HNS, HKDU, IDS, and SBHS. The ZL took second place on an 18.3 percent vote share, which yielded a total of 18 seats (10 for the HSS, 4 for the IDS, 2 for the HNS, and 1 each for the HKDU and SBHS). However, the ZL did not present candidates for the April 1997 House of Counties balloting, its members variously running their own candidates, collaborating with other Bloc components, or even aligning with parties outside the Bloc. The HSS presented a number of joint candidates with the HSLS in that balloting.

The HSS contested the 2000 legislative balloting in coalition with the IDS, HNS, and LS, the coalition securing 16 percent of the vote and 24 seats (16 for the HSS). The so-called Opposition Four also presented the successful 2000 presidential candidate—Stjepan Mesić of the HNS. In the 2003 legislative elections, the HSS ran outside of its previous coalition, winning 9 seats (just over half of its previous representation). The HSS subsequently supported the HDZ-led government, although it did not receive any cabinet posts. The HSS supported President Mesić in the 2005 presidential election.

In March 2007 the HSS signed a coalition agreement with the HSLS and the Primorian-Goranian Union (*Primorsko-Goranski Savez*—PGS) to cooperate ahead of the legislative elections scheduled for November. In the balloting, the HSS secured six seats. It joined the subsequent HDZ-led coalition government.

In 2008 party leader Josip Friščič was elected as a deputy speaker in Parliament. The HSS finalized a series of joint electoral agreements with its coalition partners ahead of local balloting in May 2009. The HSS did not field a candidate in the 2009 presidential election.

After legislative elections were scheduled for 2011, Friščič pledged to resign as party leader if the HSS did not secure at least six seats. After the party secured only one seat in the December balloting, Friščič did not campaign in the January 2012 leadership election which was won by Branko HRG.

Leaders: Branko HRG (Chair), Josip M. TOBAR (Honorary Chair), Stjepan RADIĆ (Honorary President), Marijana PETIR, Darko RUKAVINA, Vlasta HUBICIKI, Krešo BELJAK, Marina KOLAKOVIĆ (Vice Presidents).

Independent Democratic Serbian Party (*Samostaina Demokratska Srpska Stranka*—SDSS). Based in Vukovar, a major town in Slavonia, the SDSS was founded as the Independent Serbian Party in October 1995; the party adopted its current name in March 1997 in time for Serbs to contest the local elections in April. It quickly merged with the Party of Serbs (*Stranka Srpski*—SS) led by Milorad Pupovac. (The SS, advocating democratic and liberal principles, had been launched in 1993 and included the *Prosveta* ["Enlightenment"] movement.) The SDSS initially was formed to represent ethnic Serbs in Slavonia, but the merged party aimed to address the concerns of the 120,000 Serbs throughout Croatia. However, in its first outing, the party limited itself to contests for local and county assemblies and did not seek representation in the upper house in Zagreb. Ethnic Croatian parties won 16 of the 27 districts in eastern Slavonia, with 11 going to the SDSS. Following the April elections to the House of Counties, President Tudjman appointed SDSS party leader Vojislav Stanimirović and another ethnic Serbian leader, Jovan BAMBURAC, to the upper house, accounting for two of the five appointments the president made to that body. To the surprise of some analysts, the SDSS was unsuccessful in the 2000 balloting for the House of Representatives. However, in the 2003 legislative election, the SDSS gained the three seats reserved for the Serb minority. In exchange for support on key issues, the HDZ-led government agreed to advocate on behalf of SDSS priorities, including refugee return and increased minority rights. In the 2007 House elections the SDSS secured three seats and joined the HDZ governing coalition. The SDSS opposed the 2008 recognition of Kosovo by Croatia and threatened to leave the coalition; however, negotiations kept the party in the government. After the loss of the HDZ candidate in the first round of presidential balloting in 2009, the SDSS supported the SDP candidate, and eventual election winner, Ivo Josipović. In December 2010 Slobodan Uzelac of the SDSS was reappointed as deputy prime minister in the HDZ-led government. In the 2011 legislative balloting, the SDSS maintained its three seats.

Leader: Vojislav STANIMIROVIĆ (President).

Croatian Democratic Assembly of Slavonia and Baranja (*Hrvatski Demokratski Savez Slavonije i Baranje*—HDSSB). The HDSSB is a right-wing political party that was formed in May 2006 in Osijek under the leadership of Branimir Glavas, an independent member of the House of Representatives, and Kresimir Bubalo, the county prefect of Osijek-Baranja. Two other deputies in the House of Representatives joined the new party, and Glavas became the leader of the parliamentary faction. He was subsequently stripped of his parliamentary immunity and arrested in June 2006 following charges that he participated in crimes against humanity against ethnic Serbs in 1991. In the 2007 balloting, despite his trial, Glavas was elected to the House along with two other members of the HDSSB. The Glavas trial was suspended following his election, but the House again voted to strip his immunity in January 2008 and the trial resumed in November. Glavas was subsequently sentenced to 10 years imprisonment for war crimes. However, he fled into exile in Bosnia, where Croatian requests for extradition have been denied. In 2008 the **Croatian Party of Slavonia and Baranja** (*Slavonsko-Baranjska Hrvatska Stranka*—SBHS), which had been founded in 1992, merged with the HDSSB.

In 2011 the HDSSB rejected the conviction of Govotina and backed protests in support of the former general. The HDSSB secured six seats in the 2011 elections.

Leaders: Vladimir ŠIŠLJAGIĆ (President), Kresimir BUBALO (Vice Presidents), John DRUMIĆ (Secretary General).

Croatian Labourists-Labour Party (*Hrvatski Laburisti—Stranka Rada*—HL). This center-left party was formed in February 2010 by former HNS House member Dragutin LESAR, who was the HL's sole member of the parliament. The party gained six seats in the 2011 balloting.

Leader: Dragutin LESAR.

Croatian Civic Party (*Hrvatska Građanska Stranka*—HGS). The right-wing HGS was formed in 2009 and led by Željko KERUM, the mayor of Split from 2009 to 2013. It joined the HDZ-led coalition for the 2011 elections and won two seats in the polling.

Leader: Željko KERUM.

Democratic Center (*Demokratski Centar*—DC). The DC was founded in March 2000 by former foreign minister Mate Granić and several HDZ legislators. The new party advocated Croatia's accession to the EU and NATO and other efforts to improve "international integration." In the 2003 House of Representatives elections the DC joined the HSLS in a coalition. However, the DC subsequently joined the HDZ-led coalition government, although party leader Vesna Škare-Ožbolt was forced to resign her cabinet post in February 2006 following repeated disagreements with the prime minister and charges that she leaked confidential government materials. The DC subsequently withdrew from the government. The DC campaigned with the ZS, but neither party gained enough votes to secure representation in the House. Škare-Ožbolt was a presidential candidate in the 2009 elections, but she won less than 2 percent of the vote and was eliminated in the first round of voting. Škare-Ožbolt testified on behalf of former general Govotina during his trial at The Hague in 2011. In the 2011 parliamentary elections, the DC ran as part of the HDZ-led coalition and secured one seat.

Leaders: Vesna ŠKARE-OŽBOLT (Chair), Mato BRLETIĆ.

Croatian Party of Rights (*Hrvatska Stranka Prava*—HSP). A far-right formation established in 1990, the HSP is descended from a prewar nationalist party of the same name. Discord among party leaders during 1991 led a faction to form the **Croatian Democratic Party of Rights** (*Hrvatska Demokratska Stranka Prava*—HDSP) in June 1992. The HSP went on to win five seats in the August 1992 lower house election, its (then) president, Dobroslav PARAGA, taking 5.4 percent of the vote in the national presidential contest. Thereafter, the party came under pressure from the authorities, which in October asked the Constitutional Court to ban the HSP and instituted legal proceedings against three leading members. The HSP's military wing, called the Croatian Defense Association (*Hrvatska Obrambeni Savez*—HOS), was heavily involved in interethnic conflict; from mid-1993 steps were taken by the authorities to integrate the HOS into the official security forces. Paraga was ousted from the party leadership in September 1993, subsequently forming the breakaway HSP-1861. The HSP narrowly surmounted the 5 percent threshold in the October 1995 legislative balloting, securing four seats.

The HSP contested the 2000 legislative balloting in coalition with the HKDU, securing four of the five seats won by the coalition. Meanwhile, Anto Dapić, president of the HSP, won 1.8 percent of the votes in the first round of the 2000 presidential poll. In the 2003 House of Representatives elections the HSP formed a coalition with the Democratic Party of Zargorje (ZDS) and the Medimurian Party (MS). Only the HSP secured representation, with eight seats. Slaven Letica was the HSP candidate in the 2005 presidential polling. He placed fifth with 7.59 percent of the vote.

In August 2005 it was announced that the HSP would absorb the Croatian Democratic Republican Party (*Hrvatska Demokratska Republikanska Stranka*—HDRS). The HDRS had been launched in October 2000 via merger of Croatian Spring (*Hrvatska Proljeća*—HP) and two other small opposition parties. In the 2003 elections the HDRS had received less than 1 percent of the vote.

In March 2007 the HSP announced it would contest the November legislative elections without any coalition partners. In the balloting the HSP won one seat in the House. In January 2009 HSP national board member Ante TANFARA and about 20 other local leaders from Sibenik left the party and joined the HDZ. The defectors asserted that the HSP had become too conservative. In November Daniel SRB was elected party president. In 2011 Srb announced that the HSP would not participate with either the progovernment or the opposition groupings in the December elections. The party secured one seat in the balloting.

Leaders: Daniel SRB (President), Pejo TRGOVČEVIĆ (Vice President).

Other Parties That Contested the 2011 Elections:

Croatian Social-Liberal Party (*Hrvatska Socijalno-Liberalna Stranka*—HSLS). Founded in May 1989, the HSLS was characterized as a traditional European liberal grouping. Having performed modestly in the 1990 election, it became the second-strongest and main opposition party in August 1992, winning 14 lower house seats and, for its leader, a creditable 21.9 percent of the presidential vote. Securing 16 seats in the 1993 upper house balloting, the HSLS took part in an opposition boycott of Parliament in mid-1994. In the 1995 lower house balloting the HSLS took 11.6 percent of the vote, confirming its status as the single strongest opposition party. However, in April 1997 balloting for the House of Counties, the HSLS slipped from 16 to 6 seats of its own, although it had supported successful candidates from the HSS in some districts. In the June presidential race, HSLS candidate Vlado GOTOVAĆ, who was beaten up by an army officer at a rally and could not finish the campaign, came in third in the three-man race despite having the backing of a number of other opposition parties. The HSLS's showing in the 1997 elections apparently indicated it was declining in strength relative to the SDP, and divisions within the HSLS came to a head at the party's congress in November when a deadlock between Gotovać and his longtime rival Dražen Budiša prevented the election of a party president. Aside from the leadership issue, the party was also divided over whether to cooperate with the HDZ. On December 6, following his defeat by Budiša in the party's presidential election, Gotovać and his leading supporters resigned from the party to form a new grouping called the Liberal Party (see below).

Budiša, also endorsed by the SDP, finished second in the first round of presidential balloting in 2000 with 27.7 percent of the vote and lost the runoff with 44 percent. Meanwhile, the HSLS, now described as a "mildly nationalistic, socially conservative" party, won 24 seats in the 2000 elections to the House of Representatives as part of a coalition with the SDP, PGS, and SBHS. Although the HSLS joined the government following that balloting, Budiša's relationship with Prime Minister Račan of the SDP proved conflictual, and the HSLS officially left the cabinet in July 2002, although some HSLS members kept their posts and left the party. The HSLS ran with the Democratic Center in an electoral coalition in the 2003 elections.

The HSLS began merger negotiations with the smaller **Liberal Party** (*Liberalna Stranka*—LS) in 2005. The LS had been launched in January 1998 by defectors from the HSLS, including HSLS founders such as Vlado Gotovać, its presidential candidate in 1997, and a number of HSLS legislators. The LS saw itself as a guardian of the democratic principles on which the HSLS was founded, including staunch opposition to the HDZ. The LS was part of the "Opposition Four" coalition with the HSS, HNS, and IDS in the 2000 legislative balloting. Gotovać died in late 2000.

The LS participated in an electoral alliance for the 2003 legislative elections with the SDP, IDS, and Libra; the LS secured 2 of the alliance's 43 seats. After supporting President Mesić in the 2005 presidential polling, the LS was formally absorbed by the HSLS in 2006, and former

LS President Zlatko KRAMARIĆ became a vice president of the expanded HSLS. Opponents of the merger, led by Ante TEŠIJA, split from the LS and formed the **Dalmatian Liberal Party** (*Dalmatinska Liberalna Stranka*—DLS). In 2006 Durda Adlešić was reelected president of the HSLS with 80 percent of the vote at a party congress.

In March 2007 the HSLS joined the HSS and the PGS in an electoral coalition to contest the November House of Representatives elections. The HSLS won two seats in the balloting and joined the HDZ-led government. The HSLS continued its coalition with the HSS and the PGS in local elections in May 2009. In November party leader Adlešić announced her resignation. Darinko KOSOR was elected to replace her.

In July 2010 the HSLS withdrew its support of the HDZ-led government, leading its two members of the House to resign from the party and join an independent caucus. Kosor was highly critical of the conviction of former general Gotovina. The HSLS won 3 percent of the vote in the 2011 elections and failed to secure any parliamentary seats.

Leaders: Darinko KOSOR (Chair), Dorica NIKOLIĆ.

Party of Democratic Action of Croatia (*Stranka Demokratske Akcije Hrvatske*—SDAH). The SDAH was formed in 1990 to represent the interests of the Bosniak ethnic community in Croatia. The SDAH secured one seat in the House in the legislative elections in 2003 and 2007. Semso Tanković, the sole SDAH member of Parliament, was elected party leader in 2001. The SDAH failed to secure representation in the 2011 parliamentary elections.

Leaders: Semso TANKOVIĆ (President), Mirsad SREBRENIKOVIĆ (Secretary General).

Primorian-Goranian Union (*Primorsko-Goranski Savez*—PGS). Also known as the Alliance of Croatian Coast and Mountains Department, this party was initially established in March 1990 as the Rijeka Democratic Alliance (*Riječki Demokratski Savez*). The party changed its name in 1996 to reflect its activities beyond the Rijeka region. Its platform advocates respect for all ethnic groups, a free-market economy, and civil liberties. The PGS ran in coalition with the SDP and the HNS for the House of Counties in 1997; by virtue of the success of SDP candidates in some of those races, the PGS was referenced as a parliamentary party, although no PGS members were legislators in their own right. In the 2000 balloting for the House of Representatives the PGS secured two seats as part of an electoral coalition with the SDP, HSLS, and SBHS. The PGS campaigned in a coalition with the HNS and the SBHS in the 2003 legislative elections. In the 2005 presidential election the PGS joined the pro-Mesić coalition. In March 2007 the PGS signed a coalition agreement with the HSS and the HSLS for the November 2007 legislative elections; however, unlike its coalition partners, it failed to gain representation in the House. It also did not secure any seats in the 2011 balloting.

Leader: Darijo VASILIĆ (President).

Other Parties and Groups:

Croatian Christian Democratic Union (*Hrvatska Kršćanska Demokratska Unija*—HKDU). The HKDU was formed in December 1992 by the **Croatian Christian Democratic Party** (*Hrvatska Kršćanska Demokratska Stranka*—HKDS), led by Ivan CESAR, and a majority faction of the Croatian Democratic Party of Rights (HDSP), led by Marko Veselica, both constituents dating from 1989. (Veselica had spent 11 years in jail during communist rule.) The HKDS had participated in the ruling coalition from 1990 but lost its two lower house seats in August 1992, Cesar placing seventh in the concurrent presidential poll. As part of the ZL, the HKDU won one seat in the 1995 lower house balloting. The HKDU secured one seat in the 2000 balloting for the House of Representatives, which it contested in coalition with the HSP. The HKDU failed to gain representation in the House in the 2003 legislative elections. Anto KOVAČEVIĆ, the party's candidate in the 2005 presidential balloting, received less than 1 percent of the vote. The party did not win any seats in the 2007 or 2011 legislative balloting.

Leader: Željko NUĆ (President).

Serbian People's Party (*Srpska Narodna Stranka*—SNS). Founded in May 1991, the SNS (also known as the Serbian National Party) is an ethnic party that advocates a market economy, civil rights, and membership in the EU. Although much of Croatia's ethnic Serb population was not under Zagreb's jurisdiction at the time of the August 1992 election, the SNS returned three deputies on a platform of opposition to the Serb separatism represented by the self-proclaimed Republic of Serbian Krajina. Following Zagreb's recovery of Krajina in 1995 and the resultant exodus of many ethnic Serbs, the SNS won only two seats in the October election. Its representation fell to one in the 2000 balloting for the House of Representatives. The SNS did not secure any seats in the 2003 and 2007 House elections as the SDSS emerged as the dominant Serb party. In 2009 the SNS led an unsuccessful effort to force a national referendum on Croatian membership in NATO.

Leaders: Zmago JELINCIĆ (President), Josip MANOLIĆ (Honorary President).

For other minor parties active between 2000 and 2012, please see the 2013 *Handbook*.

LEGISLATURE

Under the 1990 constitution, the Croatian Assembly (*Sabor*) consisted of an upper House of Counties (*Županijski Dom*) and a lower House of Representatives, both popularly elected for four-year terms. The House of Counties was abolished by a vote in the House of Representatives in 2001.

House of Representatives (*Zastupnički Dom*). The present House comprises 140 members elected from ten regular constituencies (14 seats each) under a proportional system that requires a party to receive 5 percent of the vote in any constituency to gain representation from that constituency. An additional 5 members are elected (on a plurality basis) to represent ethnic minorities (1 each for Serbian, Hungarian, and Italian minorities; 1 shared by the Czech and Slovak minorities; and 1 shared by the Austrian, German, Ruthenian, Ukrainian, and Jewish minorities), while up to 15 are elected on a proportional basis by Croatians living abroad. (The number of seats from the diaspora is determined at each election via comparison of voter turnout relative to previous turnouts.)

The most recent balloting, held December 4, 2011, resulted in the election of 151 members (including 3 representing Croatians living abroad). The seat distribution was as follows: Social Democratic Party of Croatia,(SDP), 61; Croatian Democratic Union (HDZ), 44; Croatian National Party (HNS), 14; Croatian Labourists-Labour Party (HL), 6; Croatian Democratic Assembly of Slavonia and Baranja (HDSSB), 6; Istrian Democratic Assembly (IDS), 3; Croatian Pensioners' Party (HSU), 3; Independent Democratic Serbian Party (SDSS), 3; Croatian Civic Party (HGS), 2; Democratic Center (DC), 1; Croatian Peasant Party (HSS), 1; Croatian Party of Rights (HSP), 1; independents, 7.

Speaker: Josip LEKO.

CABINET

[as of October 11, 2013]

Prime Minister	Zoran Milanović (SDP)
First Deputy Prime Minister	Vesna Pusić (HNS) [f]
Deputy Prime Ministers	Milanka Opačić (SDP) SDP [f]
	Neven Mimica (SDP)
	Branko Grčić (SDP)
Ministers	
Agriculture, Fisheries and Rural Development	Tihomir Jakovina (SDP)
Construction and Spatial Planning	Anka Mrak-Taritas (HNS-LD) [f] (acting)
Culture	Anrea Zlatar Violić (HNS) [f]
Defense	Ante Kotromanović (SDP)
Economy, Labor, and Enterprise	Ivan Vrdoljak (HNS-LD)
Entrepreneurship and Crafts	Gordon Maras (SDP)
Environmental Protection and Nature	Mihael Zmajlović (SDP)
Finance	Slavko Linić (SDP)
Foreign and European Affairs	Vesna Pusić (HNS) [f]
Health and Social Welfare	Rajko Ostojić (SDP)
Interior	Ranko Ostojić (SDP)

Justice	Orsat Miljenić (Independent)
Labor and Pension System	Mirando Mrsić (SDP)
Maritime Affairs, Tourism, Transport, and Development	Siniša Hajdaš Dončić (SDP)
Public Administration	Arsen Bauk (SDP)
Regional Development and EU Funds	Branko Grčić (SDP)
Science, Education, and Sports	Željko Jovanović (SDP)
Social Welfare and Youth	Milanka Opačić (SDP) [f]
Tourism	Darko Lorencin (IDS)
War Veterans	Predrag Matić (Independent)

[f] = female

INTERGOVERNMENTAL REPRESENTATION

Ambassador to the U.S.: Josip PARO.

U.S. Ambassador to Croatia: Kenneth MERTEN.

Permanent Representative to the UN: Vladmir DROBNJAK.

IGO Memberships (Non-UN): CEUR, EBRD, IADB, ICC, IOM, NATO, OSCE, WTO.

CUBA

Republic of Cuba
República de Cuba

Political Status: Independent republic founded in 1902; Marxist-inspired regime established January 1, 1959; designated a Communist system in December 1961; present constitution adopted February 16, 1976.

Area: 42,803 sq. mi. (110,860 sq. km).

Population: 11,244,543 (2013E—UN); 11,061,886 (2013E—U.S. Census).

Major Urban Centers (2010E): HAVANA (2,135,000), Santiago de Cuba (426,000), Camagüey (306,000), Holguín (277,000), Santa Clara (206,000), Guantánamo (208,000).

Official Language: Spanish.

Monetary Unit: Peso (official rate November 1, 2013: 1 peso = $1US [a 10 percent Cuban tax is also added when converting directly from dollars to pesos]). There are two pesos used in Cuba. One, the "regular" peso, is used for state salaries and government goods and services. The "convertible peso" is used by visiting foreigners and by Cubans for most goods and services. It had been pegged at 1.00 convertible peso = $1US for many years until the government announced two revaluations in the first half of 2005 (2008 exchange rate quoted above). The regular peso in 2008 continued to trade at approximately 24 regular pesos = 1 convertible peso.

President of the Council of State and of the Council of Ministers, and First Secretary of the Communist Party of Cuba: Gen. Raúl CASTRO Ruz; elected February 24, 2008, and reelected February 24, 2013; designated first vice president of the Council of State and of the Council of Ministers by the National Assembly on December 2, 1976; reappointed in 1981, 1986, 1993, 1998, and on March 16, 2003; named acting president on July 31, 2006, following incapacitation of President Fidel CASTRO Ruz.

Vice Presidents of the Council of State: Miguel DÍAZ-CANEL Bermúdez (First Vice President), Gladys Maria BEJERANO Portela, Mercedes LOPEZ Acea, José Ramón MACHADO Ventura, Ramiro VALDÉS Menéndez, and Salvador VALDES Mesa. Díaz-Canel, Lopez, and Salvador Mesa were appointed on February 24, 2013. Bejerano and Ramior Valdes were reappointed on February 24, 2013.

THE COUNTRY

The largest of the Caribbean island nations, Cuba lies at the western end of the Greater Antilles, directly south of Florida. Its varied terrain, with abundant fertile land and a semitropical climate, led to early specialization in the production of sugar as well as tobacco, coffee, and other crops. Its demographic composition is a mixture of Caucasian and African ethnic groups. A plurality of the population is Roman Catholic though the church's mainstream religion is increasingly being challenged by *santería,* a hybrid religion characterized by components of Catholicism and African animism. In addition, there are more than 50 registered Protestant denominations, nearly half of which are joined in a largely regime-supportive Ecumenical Council of Cuba (*Consejo Ecuménico de Cuba*), and a notable Jewish community. Women constitute nearly 40 percent of the labor force and provide close to half of the country's administrators.

The Cuban economy faced great difficulty following the 1959 Communist revolution. Production lagged, dependence on foreign assistance (mainly from the Soviet Union) increased, and real per capita income declined. Despite sporadic attempts at industrialization, the Castro regime emphasized agricultural development, and sugar remained the principal export. Political developments within the Soviet Union and Eastern European "socialist camp" in 1989–1990 resulted in the effective loss of Cuba's leading trade partners and a need to place the domestic economy on a near-wartime footing, including an expansion of rationing to include virtually all consumer goods. In May 1991, following a five-month suspension in food shipments from the Soviet Union, it was agreed that subsequent shipments would be made only on a barter basis; concurrently, it was announced that as of 1992 hard currency valuation would be required for Russian oil. As a result, the government mounted a drive to achieve self-sufficiency in food production, coupled with an effort to augment foreign reserves by enhancing tourism and the export of pharmaceuticals. The opening of farmers' markets on October 1, 1994, led to a substantial decline in domestic prices and in the black market rate for U.S. dollars. By December 1 the government had opened markets for consumer goods at deregulated prices.

After suffering a contraction of 40 percent from 1989 to 1994, the GDP grew, according to government figures, by an average of 3.9 percent annually during the next ten years. Arguing that wages alone did not indicate "true purchasing power," Cuba in 2005 adopted a new measure of economic growth that included free services to its citizens. The result was a surge in reported GDP, which precluded meaningful comparison with other developing economies. Robust growth was interrupted in 2008, however, when three successive hurricanes caused more than $10 billion of damage. Since 2008, Cuba's annual GDP has averaged 2.0 percent.

The global economic crisis caused a 22 percent decline in exports and a 37 percent drop in imports for 2009. The government cancelled a party congress scheduled for 2010 and ended a popular free lunch program that provided daily meals for an estimated one-third of the country at a cost of $350 million annually.

The long-standing U.S. trade embargo against Cuba continues to constrain the nation's economy, and the government has gradually allowed private enterprise to develop in order to stimulate the economy. By 2013 15–20 percent of workers were employed in the private sector. The government plans to have near equal amounts of state and private economic activity by 2015.

GOVERNMENT AND POLITICS

Political background. Liberated from Spanish rule as a result of the Spanish-American War of 1898, Cuba was established as an independent republic on May 20, 1902, but remained subject to U.S. tutelage until abrogation of the so-called Platt Amendment in 1934. Subsequent political development was severely limited by the antidemocratic influence of Fulgencio BATISTA, who ruled the country directly or indirectly from 1933 to 1944 and maintained a repressive dictatorship from 1952 to 1959. On January 1, 1959, a revolutionary movement, *Movimiento 26 de Julio,* under Fidel CASTRO Ruz, who had commenced guerrilla operations in 1956, overthrew Batista's regime, which had been weakened by army and middle-class disaffection.

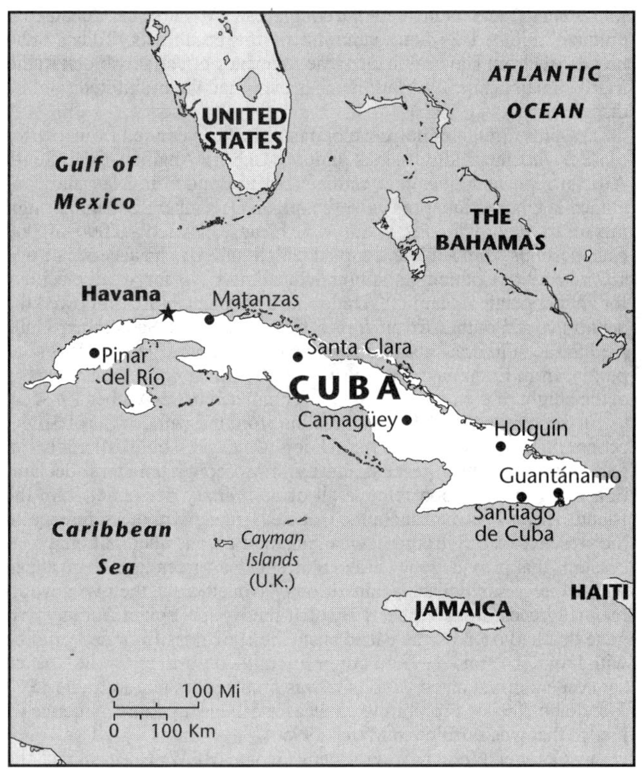

After a brief period of moderation, the Castro government embarked on increasingly radical internal policies, which gradually developed into a full-scale social revolution purportedly based on the adaptation of Marxist-Leninist ideas to Latin American conditions. Relations with the United States deteriorated rapidly, leading to the October 1960 expropriation of all U.S. business interests. The United States responded by severing diplomatic relations, imposing a trade embargo, and supporting an ill-fated invasion by anti-Castro Cuban exiles at the Bay of Pigs in April 1961.

Castro cultivated increasingly close ties with Communist countries, particularly the Soviet Union, whose emplacement of offensive missiles in Cuba precipitated the Cuban Missile Crisis of October 1962. Thereafter, the Castro government consolidated its internal authority, aided in part by the departure of thousands of disaffected Cubans, most of whom settled in the United States.

In the fifth general election on April 30 and May 7, 1989, 14,246 delegates were elected to local municipal bodies, with subsequent indirect election to provincial and national assemblies. Thereafter, a party Central Committee meeting in January 1990 decided that the responsibilities of the municipal and provincial assemblies would be strengthened and that the National Assembly would be converted from a largely ceremonial body into a genuine parliament. Thus, on February 24, 1993, the National Assembly was for the first time directly "elected" when candidates approved by the Communist Party of Cuba (PCC) faced a "yes or no" decision from the voters. The sole anti-regime option (exercised by 11.6 percent of the participants) was to vote against the solitary candidate in each race.

Heightened isolation and economic distress, brought about by the end of Soviet subsidies, prompted a series of major policy reforms in 1993. The government legalized the possession and spending of U.S. dollars and other convertible currencies, lifted restrictions on exile visitations and on self-employment in 117 occupations, including taxi drivers and sellers of farm products. In late October the new self-employed sector was declared subject to progressive taxation, based on income as part of a new revenue system designed to "re-establish order" in the state's finances. One indicator of such a need was a sharp decline in the sugar harvest (an estimated 4.2 million tons, as contrasted with 7.0 million tons in 1992).

The second election to the National Assembly was held on January 11, 1998, with the 601 candidates approved by the PCC again facing a "yes or no" decision from the voters. All of the candidates received the required 50 percent endorsement in what was officially reported as a 98 percent turnout. (President Castro hailed the election as a "vote of unity" by his country.) On February 24 the new assembly reappointed Castro to another five-year term as president of the Council of State. All six incumbent vice presidents were also reappointed (including Castro's brother, then First Vice President Raúl CASTRO Ruz, who had reportedly been exercising growing governmental influence), and some new members were included in the Council.

Subsequent direct elections of assembly deputies were held on January 19, 2003, with results identical to those of 1998, except that the number of members had been increased to 609. Following the poll, President Castro and all six incumbent vice presidents were again reappointed.

On July 31, 2006, President Castro was hospitalized for an undisclosed but obviously serious illness, and he ceded power, on a provisional basis, to his brother Raúl. In legislative balloting on January 20, 2008, Fidel Castro was reelected, despite an 18-month hiatus from public politics. On February 19, five days before the Council of State met to elect a new president, Fidel Castro announced that he would not consider another term. On February 24 Raúl Castro was unanimously elected president of the Council of State, and president of the Council of Ministers.

Municipal balloting was conducted in April and May 2010. All candidates were members of the PCC. Run-off elections were required in 2,121 districts where no candidate received more than 50 percent of the vote.

In March 2011 it was announced that Fidel Castro had resigned all official positions in the government. Between January and March 2011, Raúl Castro announced a series of minor reforms aimed at enhancing the individual Cuban's ability to make and spend money. He also signed two international human rights treaties that his brother had refused to sign, including one guaranteeing numerous political rights denied under his brother's regime. The new administration also encouraged unprecedented debate and moved to address some of the public's concerns, such as the substandard transportation system.

The power shift in Havana was not accompanied by political reform. A major cabinet reshuffle occurred on March 3, 2009, as ten members regarded as hard-line *Fidelistas* were replaced by Raúl loyalists. When rumors of a fraternal rift emerged, Fidel stated his support for the changes and claimed that he had, indeed, been consulted.

Remittances and travel from Cuban-Americans living in the United States increased dramatically in 2009 after U.S. president Barack Obama eased travel restrictions for Americans with family members in Cuba and promised to review U.S. policy toward the country. In response, Raúl Castro agreed that the two leaders should meet, stating that everything—including human rights and democracy—was open for discussion. Officials of the two countries began meeting informally in Washington soon after.

Meanwhile, the government reasserted that whatever steps were taken toward economic liberation should not be interpreted as political reform. The crackdown on dissidents continued, when in May police disrupted a meeting of about 30 dissidents, 17 of whom were briefly detained for allegedly maintaining connections to the U.S. embassy and planning a protest on the U.S. Independence Day, July 4. Among those arrested were three of the president's most vocal critics, including Martha Beatriz ROQUE Cabello (see Dissident Groups under Political Parties and Groups, below). In February 2010, Orlando ZAPATA Tamayo, a political prisoner, died in custody after an 80-day hunger strike undertaken to protest prison conditions.

In February 2011, 14 political prisoners were released. The next month, Marino Alberto MURILLO Jorge, the minister of economics and planning, was promoted to the post of vice president of the council of ministers and tasked to coordinate economic reform efforts. During the sixth PCC congress, the delegates approved more than 300 reforms, including a measure to allow Cubans to buy and sell residential property. A new, streamlined politburo was elected, but the committee was dominated by senior party officials, disappointing the reformists. The National Assembly approved the reforms in July.

Constitution and government. A revised basic law, which had been under preparation for nearly a decade, was approved at the first PCC congress in December 1975, adopted by popular referendum on February 16, 1976, and declared in effect eight days later, on the anniversary of the commencement of the 1898 war of Cuban independence. It provided for an indirectly elected National Assembly, which, under a 1991 amendment, was changed to a directly elected body. The assembly designates a Council of State from among its membership. The

Council of State appoints a Council of Ministers in consultation with its president, who serves as head of state and, in his role of president of the Council of Ministers, as chief of government. The judiciary consists of a People's Supreme Court in addition to intermediate and local courts. Members of the judiciary, as well as of the state council and cabinet, are subject to legislative recall.

Under the 1976 constitution, Cuba's 6 traditional provinces were abandoned in favor of a 14-province structure, with provincial assemblies designed to encourage greater popular involvement in government. Members of the provincial assemblies are drawn from 169 popularly elected municipal assemblies, an earlier provision for intraprovincial regional assemblies having been dropped following a "popular power" experiment in Matanzas Province in June 1975. Members of the municipal and provincial assemblies serve for terms of two-and-one-half years, while the National Assembly sits for five years. According to Cuban electoral law one deputy is elected to the assembly for every 20,000 inhabitants and each municipality is guaranteed at least two deputies regardless of size. Thus, with population growth the size of the assembly increases.

The 1991 adoption of direct and secret balloting did not authorize opposition formations, and "the final objective of building a Communist society" was reaffirmed. However, in calling for socialist ownership of the means of production, the wording was revised to "basic means of production," while (then) National Assembly president Juan ESCALONA Reguera subsequently declared that retention of the one-party system was necessary because of the U.S. economic blockade. In other changes, all references to the Soviet Union were deleted, the state's religious orientation was characterized as laical rather than atheistic, and the sanctioning of "mixed enterprises" opened the door to joint ventures with foreign investors. In September 1995 investment rules were further relaxed to permit 100 percent foreign ownership, equality of opportunity for émigré investors, and free remittance abroad of profits and capital. In 2002 the constitution was amended to state that socialism, the political system, and the revolutionary society established by the constitution are "irrevocable and Cuba will never return to capitalism."

The press is censored and all channels of communication are under state control. In its 2013 list, the media group Reporters Without Borders ranked Cuba 171st out of 179 countries in terms of freedom of the press.

Foreign relations. Partly because of its attempt to promote Castro-type revolutions throughout Latin America, Cuba was for a number of years ostracized by most other Latin American governments. It was excluded from participation in the Organization of American States (OAS) in 1962, and the OAS imposed diplomatic and commercial sanctions in 1964. However, following the 1967 death in Bolivia of the Argentine-born revolutionary Ernesto ("Ché") GUEVARA, the Castro regime scaled down its support of external guerrilla activity. Subsequently, Havana served as a conduit for the flow of military and other assistance to the *Sandinista* government of Nicaragua as early as 1967. By 1974 a number of OAS states had moved to reestablish relations.

Although Cuba no longer stands out as a self-proclaimed nemesis of other Latin American governments, its foreign relations were long shaped by an ingrained hostility toward the United States and other established governments in the Americas, and by a corresponding affinity for revolutionary movements around the world. In March 1969 it became the first country to accord formal recognition to the National Liberation Front of South Vietnam and during 1975 initiated a major program of military assistance to the Soviet-backed regime in Angola. As host of the Sixth Conference of Heads of State of the Nonaligned Movement in September 1979, it sought, with some success, to identify the "socialist camp" as the "natural ally" of the third world movement.

During 1981 Havana's international posture was dominated by an increasing emigration of Cuban citizens after President Castro had indicated that Cuban exiles in the United States would be permitted to pick up anyone who wished to leave from the port of Mariel. Subsequently, more than 114,000 Cubans departed by boat for Florida in what came to be known as the Mariel Boatlift.

In 1982 Cuba was placed on the U.S. "State Sponsors of Terrorism" list and in the wake of the Grenada crisis in October 1983, Cuban relations with the United States and the region at large fell to their lowest ebb in years. Although there were indications of a thaw in 1984, with formal talks on the status of the Mariel refugees leading to a December 1984 immigration agreement, the accord was suspended by Havana in May 1985 after Radio Martí, an "alternative" radio station directed at Cuba, had commenced transmissions from Florida. Five years later, following the U.S. launching of a companion TV Martí, the Cuban government initiated 24-hour jamming of the broadcasts. Today radio broadcasts from Havana on the same frequency effectively block Radio Martí signals while TV Martí reaches the island via prohibited satellite dishes.

A major foreign policy development in 1988 stemmed from a series of U.S.-mediated discussions among Cuban, Angolan, and South African representatives that commenced in London in May and concluded at UN headquarters in New York on December 22 with the signing of an accord for the withdrawal of an estimated 40,000–50,000 Cuban troops from Angola, coupled with South African acceptance of a 1978 Security Council resolution demanding UN-supervised elections for an independent Namibia. Under the agreement, which followed the departure of South African forces from Angola in September, Cuba pledged to withdraw its troops during a 30-month period. A similar pullout from Ethiopia (where nearly 15,000 Cubans had been deployed at the height of the Ogaden war) was completed in September 1989.

In September 1991 Havana, reeling from the withdrawal of Soviet economic support (the Soviet Union would dissolve officially on December 31, 1991), reacted angrily to Moscow's unilateral declaration that it would soon remove all of its military personnel from the island. Havana termed the announcement, made without reference to the presence of U.S. troops at Guantánamo Bay, an "unconditional concession" that provided the United States with a "green light to go ahead with its aggressive plans against Cuba." Nonetheless, the two governments agreed in September 1992 that the former Soviet military brigade that had been on the island since the 1962 missile crisis would be withdrawn by mid-1993. Earlier, in mid-August, a foreign office spokesperson indicated that Cuba was prepared to accede to the 1967 Tlatelolco Treaty prohibiting nuclear weapons in Latin America, a pledge that was fulfilled in March 1995.

In October 1992 U.S. President George H. W. Bush signed the Cuban Democracy Act (popularly known as the "Torricelli Law"), which tightened the U.S. economic embargo by making it illegal for overseas subsidiaries of U.S. firms to trade with Cuba. In an unusually strong response, the UN General Assembly voted 59 to 3, with 92 abstentions, to support repeal of the measure, reflecting a steady erosion of the U.S. position. In actions reflecting Washington's lack of political consensus, President Bill Clinton in October 1995 eased a number of constraints, including certain impediments to travel and communication, despite the approval, only days before, of a congressional bill to tighten the embargo.

Earlier, a crisis had arisen over Cuban boat people. Castro, in evident frustration with U.S. intransigence over the embargo, announced in August 1994 that Cubans would no longer be prevented from leaving. More than 13,000 promptly did so (more than the total for the preceding decade). President Clinton reacted by declaring that Cubans arriving in Florida would be accorded the same treatment as Haitians in being denied automatic refugee status. The crisis eased late in the month when Clinton endorsed bilateral talks on "legal, orderly, and safe migration," and on September 9 an agreement was concluded whereby Havana would reintroduce restrictions on "unsafe departures," while the United States would move toward compliance with a 1984 agreement to issue up to 20,000 entry visas a year. The status of about 22,000 Cubans being held at the U.S. naval base at Guantánamo Bay, Cuba, was eventually resolved in early May 1995, with Washington agreeing to admit them to the United States, while Havana agreed to accept the return of any further migrants attempting to reach the United States by sea.

During 1998 the Castro regime participated in a number of initiatives designed to end its diplomatic isolation. Pope John Paul II made a historic visit to the island in January, and in March Havana announced that it would launch negotiations to become the 16th member of Caricom (Caribbean Community) and expressed an interest in becoming a member of the African, Caribbean, and Pacific (ACP) organization affiliated with the European Union (EU). In early April Spain restored relations that had been severed 16 months earlier, and later in the month Jean Chrétien made the first visit to Cuba by a Canadian prime minister. That summer a repatriation agreement was concluded with the Bahamas, and President Castro embarked on state visits to Jamaica, Barbados, Grenada, and the Dominican Republic. Thereafter, in what was viewed as a harbinger of return to the regional community, Cuba was admitted to full membership in the Latin American Integration Association (ALADI) on November 6.

Relations with the United States in late 1999 and the first half of 2000 were dominated by a custody battle over Elián GONZALEZ, whose mother and stepfather were among 11 Cuban nationals who drowned in an attempt to reach Florida on November 25, 1999. Despite demands by his natural father, Juan Miguel GONZALEZ, that Elián be returned to Cuba, relatives in Miami obtained a temporary custody order. In March 2000 a federal court effectively upheld a decision by the U.S. Immigration and Naturalization Service (INS) to send the boy back to Cuba, and on April 6 Juan Miguel arrived to claim his son.

On April 12, 2000, President Castro called for abolition of the International Monetary Fund (IMF) in an attack on the global capitalistic system during a Group of 77 summit in Havana. Cuba withdrew its ACP application, 15 days later, after the EU had voted with the United States in favor of a UN resolution that criticized Cuba's record on human rights.

Russian President Vladimir Putin visited Havana in December 2000, the first such visit by a Russian leader since the collapse of the Soviet Union. Although several cooperation agreements were signed, little diplomatic reference was made to the estimated $20 billion Soviet-era debt still owed by Cuba.

At U.S. insistence, Cuba was excluded from the Summit of the Americas held in Quebec, Canada, in April 2001, which endorsed establishment of the Free Trade Agreement of the Americas (FTAA), in which Cuba was also not permitted to participate. When former U.S. president Jimmy Carter traveled to Cuba in May 2002, the U.S. administration of President George W. Bush criticized Carter for his suggestion that Washington consider ending the embargo. Among other things, Carter met with Cuban dissident Oswaldo PAYA, who had attracted international attention by submitting a petition to the National Assembly calling for a national referendum on the extension of political freedom.

Relations with the United States deteriorated in 2003, even though U.S. food sales to Cuba surged and, despite retention of the embargo for most commodities, the United States by early 2004 had become Cuba's seventh-largest trading partner. In June 2004 the Bush administration announced a series of measures drastically increasing restrictions on travel to the island. Under the new rules, Cuban Americans could visit only once every three years, instead of once a year, and more stringent limits were imposed on the amount of cash and baggage that could be carried.

In a slap at the United States, Cuba in early 2006 won a seat on the recently launched UN Human Rights Council, formed as successor to the discredited UN Commission on Human Rights, which in April 2004, by a margin of one vote, had approved a motion censuring Cuba for human rights abuses.

While Raúl Castro reportedly has not left the island since taking power in July 2006, an increasing number of foreign dignitaries have visited from China, Jamaica, Vietnam, Uruguay, Venezuela, and Brazil. At the same time an increasing number of Cuban officials are traveling abroad on official delegations. On June 19, 2008, the EU defied the United States and voted to conditionally lift sanctions on Cuba. In February 2008 Cuba signed both the International Covenant on Civil and Political Rights and the International Covenant on Economic, Social, and Cultural Rights. However, the government has not ratified either accord.

In 2008 the U.S. Congress voted to increase United States Agency for International Development (USAID) funding for democracy promotion in Cuba to $45.7 million for fiscal year 2009, five times the previous funding levels. Tensions between the United States and Cuba heightened in May 2008 after Cuba accused top U.S. embassy officials in Havana of passing money to dissidents on the island. The United States, for its part, said the money was for humanitarian purposes. Following the inauguration of U.S. president Barack Obama in 2009, a shift in U.S. policy began to occur, most notably the easing of some travel restrictions between the two countries (see Current issues, below).

In June 2009 the OAS voted to lift the ban on Cuba's membership imposed in 1962. Before full reintegration into the regional organization would be permitted, however, Cuba was required to comply with various stipulations for a democratic government and respect for human rights. Cuba, which had not sought to return to the OAS, issued a statement expressing its appreciation, but reiterated its accusations that the OAS played a role in U.S. hostility toward Cuba over many decades.

Cuba protested its inclusion on a U.S. list of state sponsors of terrorism in January 2010. The April Deep Water Horizon oil spill in the Gulf of Mexico prompted direct discussions between the United States and Cuba on how best to deal with the environmental impact of the disaster. In June Cuba released one political prisoner and transferred six more from prison to their homes as part of an arrangement with the Catholic Church. The following month, the government began to release an additional 47 political prisoners, including several who were expected to seek asylum with the United States.

In November 2010 Cuba and Venezuela extended a bilateral economic cooperation pact in which Caracas provided 53,000 barrels of oil per day in exchange for the deployment of Cuban medical personnel to Venezuela. By 2012, Cuba was receiving 100,000 barrels per day and was believed to be reselling up to 40 percent of that amount. The Cuba–Venezuela deal was worth nearly $7 billion annually.

On January 13, 2011, the United States lifted a range of travel restrictions to the island and increased the amount of remittances allowed to be sent to Cuba to $2,000 per year. In June 2011 the Cuban government confirmed that Venezuelan president Chávez had traveled to Havana for medical treatment. He returned to Cuba several times for additional treatments before succumbing to cancer on March 5, 2013 (see entry on Venezuela).

The Cuban government awarded a sugar production contract to a Brazilian firm in November 2013 and granted oil exploration permits to Angola in January 2013.

In February 2013 a delegation of seven U.S. senators and congressmen visited Cuba, where they met with President Castro for discussions about improving bilateral relations. The delegation unsuccessfully sought the release of Alan Gross, a U.S. contractor jailed for subversive activities. Bilateral migration talks between the U.S. and Cuba resumed in June after being suspended in 2011, when Gross was sentenced to 15 years in prison.

A Panama-registered ship detained in July was found to be carrying 529,000 pounds of missile parts en route from Cuba to North Korea, raising concerns about ties between the two countries.

Current issues. The PCC held its first-ever party conference on January 28–29, 2012. Raúl Castro used his closing speech to make clear that the one-party system would remain in place, but he raised the possibility of limiting Central Committee membership to two consecutive five-year terms. The party voted to begin replacing one-fifth of the Central Committee over the next four years as a way to bring in younger cadres.

Leadership succession is an increasingly urgent issue. Raúl Castro turned 82 in June 2013, and Fidel turned 87 in August. The Cuban population in general is aging; by 2030 some 30 percent of the population will be aged 60 or older, up from 18.1 percent today. The average age of the Politburo is 70, and many of the "next generation" party leaders have been sacked for corruption. The slowing birth rate means fewer workers supporting more and more pensioners. Venezuela has supplied Havana with two-thirds of its oil needs (plus over $5 billion annually) in return for doctors, sports coaches, and security experts, but regime change in Venezuela could cancel the Cuban deal. High hopes for energy security were dashed when Spain's Repsol oil exploration firm twice came up dry off the Cuban coast and pulled out in May. China is Cuba's largest creditor, at $4 billion, but so far Havana has ignored offers of economic advice from Beijing.

Iranian President Mahmoud Ahmadinejad made an official visit to Havana in January 2012, followed by Pope Benedict XVI in March. The pontiff disappointed anti-Castro groups by refusing to meet with dissident groups but finding time for an unscheduled meeting with Chavez, who was on the island for medical treatment. Activists allege that 150 "peaceful dissidents" were arrested ahead of the papal visit and many others placed under house arrest for the duration of his stay.

Cuba was again excluded from the Summit of the Americas, which met in Colombia in April 2012. Obama refused to sign a declaration by other members stating that Cuba should be invited to attend the next summit.

On September 11, 2012, the government granted more flexibility to co-op farms and businesses, allowing them to sell surplus goods and to directly purchase inputs from suppliers. The move was intended to boost domestic agriculture, as Cuba still must import 70 percent of its food needs. It follows an August 2012 vote by the National Assembly to gradually introduce an income tax. The state has also leased 70 percent of farmland to co-ops and individuals.

Hurricane Sandy struck Cuba in November 2012, damaging 115,000 houses and destroying 15,000. Nearly one-third of Cuba's coffee crop was destroyed. News of the storm and its impact spread quickly through text messages, which quickly outpaced official reports.

New passport regulations were introduced in October 2012, making it easier for Cubans to travel beyond the island. No longer required to get an exit visa, dissident blogger Yoani SANCHEZ was allowed to travel to Brazil in February 2013. Similarly, Berta SOLER, a leader of the Ladies in White, was allowed to travel to Europe to receive the European Union's Sakharov Prize for Freedom of Thought, which had been awarded to the Ladies in 2005. However, police detained several dozen members of Ladies in White who had planned to greet Soler upon her return in May.

Elections to the National Assembly were held on February 3. All 612 candidates ran unopposed and easily won their seats. The new assembly convened on February 24, 2013, and elected Raúl Castro to a second five-year presidential term. Castro announced that he would step down at the end of his term in 2018 and proposed a 10-year term limit for future presidents. While he promoted two veterans of the revolution to the Council of Ministers, he also promoted Miguel Díaz-Canel Bermúdez to the post of first vice president and heir apparent. Díaz-Canel, a 52-year-old former higher education minister, could become president sooner, given the advanced age of Castro.

The economy remains stagnant and in May Raúl Castro announced that the country should conserve its material resources, which are the main source of income.

POLITICAL PARTIES AND GROUPS

Communist Party of Cuba (*Partido Comunista Cubano*—PCC). The country's only authorized political party, the PCC, is a direct descendant of the Rebel Army and the 26th of July Movement (*Movimiento 26 de Julio*), which constituted Fidel Castro's personal political following during the anti-Batista period. The organizational revolution began in 1961 with the formation of the Integrated Revolutionary Organizations (*Organizaciones Revolucionarias Integradas*—ORI), which included the Popular Socialist Party (*Partido Socialista Popular*—PSP), the 26th of July Movement, and the Revolutionary Directorate (*Directorio Revolucionario*—DR). The ORI was transformed into the United Party of the Cuban Socialist Revolution (*Partido Unido de la Revolución Socialista Cubana*—PURSC) in 1963, the latter being redesignated as the PCC in 1965. The first PCC congress was held December 17–22, 1975, and the second December 17–20, 1980. The third congress, which held its first session February 4–7, 1986, reconvened November 30–December 2, primarily to discuss a campaign aimed at the "rectification of mistakes and negative tendencies." The rectification campaign received added emphasis at an extraordinary plenum on February 16, 1990, during which the Central Committee reiterated its commitment to one-party Marxism-Leninism, "adapted to Cuban mentality, history and traditions."

During its fourth congress, held in Santiago de Cuba October 10–14, 1991, the PCC endorsed direct election to the National Assembly, dropped a requirement that only atheists could become party members, abolished the party Secretariat and the appointment of alternates to other party organs, and approved a substantially restructured Politburo from which five existing members were excluded. In July 1994 numerous changes in provincial leaders were announced as part of a revamping of political cadres. The party's fifth congress was held in Havana October 8–10, 1997.

At a Plenary Party Meeting on July 1, 2006, a new 12-member Executive Committee was launched, seemingly as a resuscitation of the former Secretariat. In April 2010 officials of the party, including Raúl Castro, held a series of unprecedented meetings with Catholic leaders in an effort to gain church support in an anticorruption campaign.

More than 1,000 delegates attended the sixth party congress in April 2011. During the meeting, Raúl Castro was elected to succeed his brother as first secretary of the party, and a new, smaller, 15-member politburo was announced, including 3 new members. The Congress granted individuals the right to buy and sell property and to work for themselves, a decision Raúl described as a "defining event," necessary to secure the future of the socialist revolution in Cuba. The PCC announced during the congress that its membership exceeded 800,000.

The PCC held a Party Conference in January 2012, the first in its history.

First Secretary: Gen. Raúl CASTRO Ruz (President, Council of State and Council of Ministers).

Second Secretary: José Ramón MACHADO Ventura (First Vice President, Council of State).

Other Members of the Politburo: Miguel Mario DÍAZ-CANEL Bermúdez (First Vice President of the Council of Ministers), Gen. Leopoldo CINTRA Frías (Minister of the Revolutionary Armed Forces), Gen. Abelardo COLOMÉ Ibarra (Interior Minister), Gen. Ramon ESPINOSA Martín (Deputy Minister of the Revolutionary Armed Forces), Juan Estebán LAZO Hernández (President, National Assembly), Ramiro VALDÉS Menéndez (Vice President of the Council of Ministers), Salvador Antonio VALDÉS Mesa (Vice President of the Council of Ministers), Alvaro LÓPEZ Miera (First Vice Minister and Chief of the General Staff, Revolutionary Armed Forces), Marino Alberto MURILLO Jorge (Vice President of the Council of Ministers), Adel IZQUIERDO Rodriguez (Vice President of the Council of Ministers), Lazara Mercedes LÓPEZ Acea (First Secretary, Havana Provincial Committee), Bruno Eduardo RODRIGUEZ Parrilla (Foreign Minister).

Dissident Groups:

There are numerous dissident groups that tend to fluctuate, in part as their leaders are jailed or released. Many have appealed, without success, for official recognition. As of early 2007 about 365 such groups had joined an **Assembly to Promote Civil Society in Cuba** (*Asamblea para Promover la Sociedad Civil en Cuba*), led by Martha Beatriz Roque Cabello. The most visible dissident group is ***Las Damas de Blanco*** (The Ladies in White), also led by Roque. Rogue led nine activists in an unsuccessful, but highly publicized, hunger strike in 2009 to protest the lack of civil liberties in Cuba. The **Patriotic Union of Cuba** (*La Unión Patriótica de Cuba*) was established in August 2011 as an umbrella group of opposition groups. It works closely with The Ladies in White. The government uses frequent arrests and short-term detentions to harass members. Wilman VILLAR Mendoza died in January 2012 following a hunger strike to protest his imprisonment.

LEGISLATURE

A unicameral **National Assembly of People's Power** (*Asamblea Nacional del Poder Popular*) was convened, with a five-year term, on December 2, 1976, following elections (the first since 1958) to municipal assemblies, which in turn had elected delegates to both provincial and national legislative bodies. A similar procedure was used to elect assemblies that convened in December 1981 and December 1986. In July 1991 the assembly voted to extend its existing mandate by one year to consider reform proposals within the one-party context.

In the most recent balloting on February 3, 2013, all 621 candidates approved by the Communist Party of Cuba received the 50 percent favorable vote required for election.

President: Juan Esteban LAZO Hernández.

CABINET

[as of October 10, 2013]

President, Council of State and Council of Ministers	Raúl Castro Ruz
Ministers	
First Vice President, Council of Ministers	Miguel Díaz-Canel Bermúdez
Vice Presidents, Council of Ministers Executive Committee	José Ramón Machado Ventura
	Ricardo Cabrisas Ruíz
	Ulises Rosales del Toro
	Ramiro Valdés Menéndez
	Marino Alberto Murillo Jorge
	Antonio Enrique Lusson Batlle
Ministers	
Agriculture	Gustavo Rodriguez Rollero
Auditing and Control	Gladys Maria Bejarano Portera [f]
Construction	René Mesa Villafaña
Culture	Rafael Bernal Alemany
Domestic Trade	Mary Blanca Ortega Barredo [f]
Economy and Planning	Abel Izquierdo Rodriguez
Education	Ana Elsa Velázquez Cobiella [f]
Energy and Mines	Alfredo López Valdéz
Finance and Prices	Lina Olinda Pedraza Rodriguez [f]
Food and Fishing	María del Carmen Concepción Gonzalez [f]
Foreign Relations	Bruno Eduardo Rodriguez Parrilla

Foreign Trade and Economic Cooperation	Rodrigo Malmierca Díaz
Higher Education	Rodolfo Alarcón Ortiz
Information and Communications	Maimir Mesa Ramos
Interior	Gen. Abelardo Colomé Ibarra
Industries	Salvador Pardo Cruz
Justice	María Ester Reus González [f]
Labor and Social Security	Margarita Marlene González Fernandez [f]
Public Health	Roberto Morales Ojeda
Revolutionary Armed Forces	Gen. Leopoldo Cintra Frías
Science, Technology, and Environment	Elba Rosa Pérez Montoya [f]
Tourism	Col. Manuel Marrero Cruz
Transportation	Cesar Ignacio Arocha Masid
President, Central Bank of Cuba	Ernesto Medina Villaveirán

[f] = female

Note: All cabinet members are members of the PCC.

INTERGOVERNMENTAL REPRESENTATION

There are, at present, no diplomatic relations between Cuba and the United States. On September 1, 1977, however, a U.S. interest section was established in the Swiss Embassy in Havana; concurrently, a Cuban interest section was established in the Czech Embassy in Washington, D.C., which moved to the Swiss Embassy after the post–Communist Czech government announced in early 1990 that it no longer wished to serve as Havana's "protecting power" in the United States.

Permanent Representative to the UN: Rodolfo REYES Rodríguez.

IGO Memberships (Non-UN): NAM, OAS, WTO.

CYPRUS

Republic of Cyprus
Kypriaki Dimokratia (Greek)
Kıbrıs Cumhuriyeti (Turkish)

Political Status: Independent republic established August 16, 1960; member of the Commonwealth since March 13, 1961; under ethnic Greek majority regime until coup led by Greek army officers and subsequent Turkish invasion on July 20, 1974; Turkish Federated State proclaimed February 13, 1975, in Turkish-controlled (northern) sector; permanent constitutional status under negotiation (currently suspended) despite proclamation of independent Turkish Republic of Northern Cyprus (TRNC) on November 15, 1983.

Area: 3,572 sq. mi. (9,251 sq. km), embracing approximately 2,172 sq. mi. (5,625 sq. km) in Greek-controlled (southern) sector and 1,400 sq. mi. (3,626 sq. km) in Turkish-controlled (northern) sector.

Population: 1,159,317 (2012E—UN); 1,155,403 (2013E—U.S. Census). Includes the population of the Turkish Sector.

Major Urban Centers (Urban Areas, 2005E): NICOSIA/LEFKOSÍA (224,000, excluding Turkish sector), Limassol/Lemesós (175,000), Larnaca/Lárnax (77,000), Paphos/Néa Páfos (54,000). In 1995, city names were changed by the government as part of a campaign to standardize them in accordance with their Greek pronunciation; however, both names are accorded official status.

Official Languages: Greek, Turkish.

Monetary Unit: Euro (market rate November 1, 2013: 0.74 euro = $1US). In the wake of its accession to the European Union in May 2004, Cyprus on January 1, 2008, adopted the euro to replace the Cyprus pound as its official currency.

President: Nicos ANASTASIADES (Democratic Rally); elected in second-round popular balloting on February 24, 2013, and inaugurated for a five-year term on February 28, succeeding Dimitrios (Dimitris) CHRISTOFIAS (Progressive Party of the Working People); formed new government on March 1, 2013.

Vice President: Vacant. Rauf R. DENKTAŞ, then president of the Turkish Republic of Northern Cyprus (see entry on Cyprus Turkish Sector), was elected vice president by vote of the Turkish Community in February 1973, but there has been no subsequent vice-presidential balloting.

THE COUNTRY

Settled by Greeks and Phoenicians in antiquity, the island of Cyprus formed a part of the Roman and the Byzantine Empires. It was conquered by the Crusaders in 1191 and the Ottoman Empire in 1571, placed under British administration in 1878, and annexed by Britain in 1914. Cyprus has been independent since 1960 (although de facto partitioned since 1974). The largest island in the eastern Mediterranean, it supports diverse and often antagonistic ethnic groups and traditions. About 78 percent of the population speaks Greek and belongs to the Orthodox Church, while about 18 percent is Turkish-speaking Muslim; adherents of other religions account for approximately 4 percent.

Although Cyprus was historically an agricultural country, the Greek Cypriot rural sector presently employs only about 13 percent of the total labor force and contributes a small and decreasing percent of GDP (the corresponding Turkish Cypriot figures being 25 and 12 percent, respectively). Nonetheless, vegetables, fruits, nuts, and wine rank with clothing and footwear as leading exports. Following the de facto partition of the island into Greek and Turkish sectors in 1974, rebuilding in the south emphasized manufacturing of nondurable consumer goods, while the more severely damaged north has relied on its citrus groves, mines, and tourist facilities as well as on direct budgetary assistance from Turkey (estimated at around 20 percent of budgeted expenditure in recent years). Whereas 70 percent of predivision productive resources had been located in the north (including 80 percent of the island's citrus groves and 60 percent of tourist installations), the postdivision southern economy rapidly outdistanced that of the north, achieving consistently high annual growth rates and virtually full employment. In addition to developing tourism and agriculture, Greek Cyprus diversified into financial, shipping, and other services, becoming a major offshore banking center.

The country's economic focus was on efforts to harmonize policies in areas such as taxation, customs, and government spending with those of the European Union (EU), with which Cyprus began conducting formal accession negotiations in 1998. (For information on the economy prior to 1998, please see the 2013 *Handbook*.) Accession to the EU on May 1, 2004, spurred economic growth, although the unresolved political division of the island continued to be a significant complication.

GDP growth between 2001 and 2008 averaged 3.6 per year, while inflation averaged 2.6 percent and unemployment 3.8 percent for the same period. Growth in housing and tourism helped boost annual GDP growth, as did gains in the manufacturing, electricity, gas, and water sectors.

In the wake of the global financial crisis, tourism receipts on Cyprus declined by 16.7 percent in 2009. The country went into its worst recession in more than 40 years, with GDP declining by 1.7 percent that year. Unemployment rose to 5.3 percent. The government deficit increased to 6.1 percent of GDP, well above the EU's 3 percent cap on annual deficits, before falling to 5.5 percent in 2010 (see Current issues, below). GDP grew by 1 percent in 2010, and 0.5 percent in 2011. However, GDP contracted by 2 percent in 2012. Inflation that year was 3.1 percent, and unemployment 12.1 percent. GDP per capita that year was $26,389. The near collapse of the country's banking sector and the subsequent strict conditions of a Eurozone bailout package were expected to cause GDP to decline by 8.7 percent in 2013 (see Current issues, below).

The northern economy (for which reliable figures are scarce) appears to have made only limited progress since 1974, being hard hit by the collapse in 1990 of the Polly Peck International fruit-packaging and tourism conglomerate (which had accounted for a third of the Turkish Republic of Northern Cyprus's [TRNC] GDP and 60 percent of its exports) and by external rulings banning imports from the TRNC as an unrecognized entity. Meanwhile, the use of the Turkish lira as the TRNC currency has forced the country to deal with rapid inflation, unlike the Greek Cypriot sector. The TRNC's strong economic dependence on Turkey rendered its economy vulnerable to turmoil in the Turkish economy. Droughts and water shortages remain a major factor limiting economic growth in the TRNC and forcing water rationing (see Foreign relations, below). GDP grew by an average of 5.8 percent between 2001 and 2011, although GDP fell in 2008 and 2009. Declines in tourism as a result of the global economic slowdown constrained the economy from 2008 to 2012. As of 2012 annual aid from Turkey was approximately $600 million, one-third of the government's budget. GDP per capita in the TRNC was $16,590 in 2012.

GOVERNMENT AND POLITICS

Political background. The conflict between Greek and Turkish Cypriot aspirations shaped the political evolution of Cyprus both before and after the achievement of formal independence on August 16, 1960. Many Greek Cypriots had long agitated for *enosis,* or the union of Cyprus with Greece; most Turkish Cypriots, backed by the Turkish government, consistently rejected such demands, opposed the termination of British rule in 1960, and advocated division of the island into Greek and Turkish sectors. Increased communal and anti-British violence after 1955 culminated in the Zurich and London compromise agreements of 1959–1960, which provided for an independent Cyprus guaranteed by Greece, Turkey, and Britain and instituted stringent constitutional safeguards for the protection of the Turkish community. These agreements expressly prohibited either union with Greece or partition of the island between Greece and Turkey.

The government of Archbishop MAKARIOS proposed numerous constitutional changes in November 1963, including revision of articles considered inviolable by the Turkish Cypriots. The proposals led to the outbreak of communal conflict, the withdrawal of Turkish Cypriots from the government, Turkish air raids and invasion threats, and, in 1964, the establishment of the UN Force in Cyprus (UNFICYP), whose mandate was thereafter regularly extended for six-month periods by the Security Council. Most Turkish Cypriots were forced to move to UNFICYP-protected enclaves. Further conflict broke out in 1967, nearly precipitating war between Greece and Turkey.

Following the 1967 violence, Turkish Cypriots created the Turkish Cypriot Provisional Administration, a de facto government in the Turkish communities. The Turkish Cypriot withdrawal meant that from 1967 until the Turkish military intervention in July 1974 the prime conflicts were between the Makarios regime and radicals in the Greek community (led, until his death in January 1974, by Gen. Georgios GRIVAS).

On July 15, 1974, the Greek Cypriot National Guard, commanded by Greek army officers, launched a coup against the Makarios government and installed a Greek Cypriot newspaper publisher and former terrorist, Nikos Georgiades SAMPSON, as president following the archbishop's flight from the island. Five days later, Turkish troops were dispatched to northern Cyprus, bringing some 1,400 square miles (39 percent of the total area) under their control before agreeing to a cease-fire. On July 23 the Sampson government resigned and the more moderate presiding officer of the Cypriot House of Representatives, Glafcos CLERIDES, was sworn in as acting president. On the same day, the military government of Greece fell, and on July 25 representatives of Britain, Greece, and Turkey met in Geneva in an effort to resolve the Cyprus conflict. An agreement consolidating the cease-fire was concluded on July 30, but the broader issues were unresolved when the talks collapsed on August 14 and the Turkish invasion was resumed, before a final cease-fire was proclaimed on August 16. Upon his return to Cyprus and resumption of the presidency on December 7, Makarios rejected Turkish demands for geographical partition of the island, although he had earlier indicated a willingness to give the Turks increased administrative responsibilities in their own communities.

On February 13, 1975, Turkish leaders in the occupied northern sector proclaimed a Turkish Federated State of Cyprus (see map) with Rauf DENKTAŞ, the nominal vice president of the republic, as president. Although the action was immediately denounced by both President Makarios and Greek Prime Minister Karamanlis, the formation of a Turkish Cypriot Legislative Assembly was announced on February 24.

Extensive negotiations between Greek and Turkish representatives were held in Vienna in April 1977. The Makarios government insisted that only 20 percent of the island's area be reserved for Turkish administration, while the Turks countered with demands that would entail judicial parity and a presidency to rotate between Greek and Turkish chief executives.

Archbishop Makarios died on August 3, 1977, and was succeeded, as acting president, by Spyros KYPRIANOU, who was elected on August 31 to fill the remaining six months of the Makarios term. Following the kidnapping of Kyprianou's son on December 14 by right-wing extremists, Clerides withdrew as a contender for the presidency, and Kyprianou became the only candidate at the close of nominations on January 26, 1978. As a result, the election scheduled for February 5 was canceled, Kyprianou being installed for a five-year term on March 1. In April 1982 the two government parties, the Democratic Party (*Dimokratiko Komma*—DIKO) and the (Communist) Progressive Party of the Working People (*Anorthotiko Komma Ergazomenou Laou*—AKEL), agreed to support Kyprianou for reelection in February 1983.

In a three-way race that involved Clerides and Vassos LYSSARIDES, the leader of the United Democratic Union of Cyprus–Socialist Party (*Ethniki Dimokratiki Enosi Kyprou–Sosialistiko Komma*—EDEK-SK), who technically withdrew on January 4, Kyprianou won reelection on February 13, 1983, securing 57 percent of the vote. On November 15, the Turkish Cypriot Legislative Assembly unanimously approved the declaration of an independent TRNC.

President Kyprianou and Turkish Cypriot leader Denktaş met at UN headquarters January 17–20, 1985, for their first direct negotiations in five years after endorsing a draft proposal to establish a federal republic that entailed substantial territorial concessions by the Turkish Cypriots and the removal of foreign troops from the island. The talks collapsed after Kyprianou reportedly characterized the plan as no more than an "agenda." Subsequently, the government's coalition partner, AKEL, joined with the opposition Democratic Rally (*Dimokratikos Synagermos*—DISY) in blaming Kyprianou for the breakdown in the talks and calling for his resignation as president.

At the conclusion of a bitter debate on the president's negotiating posture, the House of Representatives voted unanimously on November 1, 1985, to dissolve itself. In the balloting on December 8, Kyprianou's DIKO gained marginally (though remaining a minority grouping), while the opposition failed to secure the two-thirds majority necessary to enact a constitutional revision that would require the chief executive to conform to the wishes of the House.

Deprived of the backing of AKEL, Kyprianou placed third in first-round presidential balloting on February 14, 1988. In a runoff election one week later, Georgios VASSILIOU, a millionaire businessman running with AKEL endorsement, defeated Clerides by securing a 51.5 percent majority.

On August 24, 1988, presidents Vassiliou and Denktaş met in Geneva for the first summit talks between the two communities in over three years, with formal negotiations being resumed in September. By June 1989 deadlock had again been reached, an acceptance in principle by both sides of the UN-proposed concept of a bicommunal, bizonal federation under one sovereignty being negated by fundamental differences on implementation. More positively, in May 1989 both sides began the withdrawal of forces from 24 military posts along the central Nicosia/Lefkosia sector dividing the island.

A new round of UN-sponsored talks in February 1990 ended prematurely the following month when a demand by Denktaş for a "right of self-determination" was construed by Vassiliou as a demand for separate sovereignty. Relations were further exacerbated by the Greek Cypriot government's application in July for entry into the European Community (EC, subsequently the EU). Benefiting from association with Vassiliou's high negotiating profile, AKEL registered the biggest advance in legislative balloting on May 19, 1991, but DISY retained a narrow plurality as DIKO representation plummeted.

In 1992 the UN suggested a demarcation of Greek and Turkish sectors under a federal structure that would entail the transfer of about 25 percent of TRNC territory to Greek Cypriot administration. The plan was described as "totally unacceptable" by Denktaş, who warded off growing criticism from TRNC hard-liners by reiterating his self-determination/sovereignty demand for Turkish Cypriots. Also divided were the Greek Cypriots, with AKEL and DISY broadly supporting

Vassiliou's acceptance of the UN plan, whereas DIKO and the EDEK-SK complained that the president was accepting effective partition. Because of the continuing deadlock, the UN Security Council in November proposed so-called confidence-building measures as the basis for an overall settlement, including troop reductions, small transfers of TRNC territory to UN administration, and the reopening of Nicosia international airport (closed since 1974). However, differences on these proposals proved to be intractable.

Veteran DISY leader Clerides emerged as the surprise victor in Greek Cypriot presidential balloting on February 7 and 14, 1993, when Vassiliou (again backed by AKEL) was narrowly defeated in the runoff contest (50.3 to 49.7 percent). During the campaign the DISY leader's previous support for the Vassiliou line had mutated into forceful criticism, thus enabling DIKO and the EDEK-SK (whose joint candidate was eliminated in the first round) to swing behind Clerides in the second round. A new government appointed by Clerides on February 25 contained six DISY and five DIKO ministers.

Hopes that Clerides would break the deadlock in the Cyprus negotiations were quickly disappointed. On the other hand, because of continuing economic progress in Greek Cyprus, the administration went into legislative balloting on May 26, 1996, in a buoyant mood. DISY retained its narrow plurality of 20 seats, DIKO lost 1 of its 11, and AKEL managed only a 1-seat advance, to 19; the remaining seats went to the EDEK-SK, 5; and the new Free Democrats Movement (*Kinima ton Eleftheron Dimokraton*—KED), 2.

The DISY-DIKO coalition collapsed when the DIKO central committee decided to break from the government on November 4, 1997, after Clerides revealed his intention to seek reelection in the February 1998 elections. The five DIKO cabinet members who consequently resigned were replaced by nonparty ministers. There were seven candidates in the February 1998 presidential balloting: President Clerides; Georgios IACOVOU, an independent backed by AKEL and DIKO; Georgios Vassiliou, former president and the leader of the KED; Nikos ROLANDIS, leader of the Liberal Party (KP); Vassos LYSSARIDES, president of EDEK-SK; Nikolaos KOUTSOU of New Horizons (NO); and independent candidate Alexis GALANOS, who had broken from DIKO over its endorsement of Iacovou.

Iacovou led Clerides by a very slight margin in the first-round balloting (40.61 to 40.06 percent) on February 8, with Lyssarides finishing third with 10.59 percent. The EDEK-SK took no position regarding the runoff, but the other first-round contenders endorsed Clerides, who secured a 50.8 to 49.2 percent victory in the second round on February 15 at which a 94 percent turnout was reported. On February 28 Clerides announced a new "national unity" government comprising, in addition to DISY, the KP, EDEK-SK, United Democrats, and several DIKO "rebels." Among other things, the multiparty cabinet was reportedly designed to present a unified stance regarding EU membership and proposed reunification talks. However, the EDEK-SK resigned from the government in late 1998 as the result of a dispute regarding the proposed deployment of Russian missiles on the island (see Current issues, below).

In legislative balloting on May 27, 2001, AKEL secured a plurality of 20 seats, followed by DISY with 19. In presidential elections on February 16, 2003, Tassos PAPADOPOULOS of DIKO, campaigning on domestic political issues, won a first-round election with 51.5 percent of the vote. His new coalition cabinet was sworn in on March 1, 2003.

On July 14, 2003, after the breakdown of negotiations over reunification, the Greek Cypriot House of Representatives unanimously approved EU entry. Greek Cypriots rejected the UN-brokered peace plan in a referendum on April 24, 2004. Consequently, the Republic of Cyprus joined the EU on May 1, 2004, without a resolution of its political problem (see Current issues, below).

In the parliamentary elections of May 21, 2006, DIKO received 17.9 percent of the vote, up from 14.8 percent in 2001, while support for both AKEL and DISY declined somewhat. The president reshuffled the cabinet on June 8, with members of DIKO, AKEL, and EDEK.

In the first round of presidential balloting on February 24, 2008, Ioannis Kassoulides won 33.51 percent of the vote and Dimitrios (Dimitris) CHRISTOFIAS, 33.29 percent. DIKO and EDEK subsequently endorsed Christofias in exchange for a place in the incoming coalition government. In the second poll on February 24, 2008, Christofias won 53.37 percent of the vote to Kassoulides's 46.63 percent, marking the first time an AKEL candidate was elected. Christofias formed a new government that included members of AKEL, DIKO, and EDEK on February 29, 2008.

The EDEK withdrew from the government in February 2010 over claims that Christofias did not sufficiently consult with the cabinet before making decisions. The two EDEK ministers resigned from the government and were replaced on March 1 by the president. The withdrawal of the EDEK left the Christofias government with a slim majority in the parliament.

The DISY placed first in legislative elections held on May 22, 2011, with 20 seats, followed by AKEL with 19 and DIKO with 9. On August 5 DIKO withdrew from the governing coalition after Christofias asked the cabinet to resign in order to conduct a major government reshuffle (see Current issues, below). The subsequent government, appointed on August 5, consisted of members of AKEL, EDEK, the nonparliamentary United Democrats (EDI), and independents, but it lacked a majority in parliament. Following the resignation of the finance minister on March 16, 2012, a minor cabinet reshuffle was conducted on March 19.

Nicos Anastasiades (DISY) won presidential run-off balloting on February 24, 2013 (see Current issues). On February 28, he named a cabinet that included members from DISY, DIKO and the European Party (*Evropaiko Komma*—EVROKO).

Constitution and government. The constitution of 1960, based on the Zürich and London agreements, provided for a carefully balanced system designed to protect both Greek Cypriot and Turkish Cypriot interests. A Greek president and a Turkish vice president, both elected for five-year terms, were to name a cabinet composed of representatives of both groups in specified proportions. Legislative authority was entrusted to a unicameral House of Representatives, with 35 Greek and 15 Turkish members to be elected by their respective communities. In addition, Greek and Turkish Communal Chambers were established to deal with internal community affairs. Collateral arrangements were made for judicial institutions, the army, and the police. Following the original outbreak of hostilities in 1963 and the consequent withdrawal of the Turkish Cypriots from the government, there were a number of changes, including merger of the police and gendarmerie, establishment of a National Guard, abolition of the Greek Communal Chamber, amendment of the electoral law, and modification of the judicial structure.

Subsequent to withdrawal, the Turkish community practiced a form of self-government under the Turkish Cypriot Provisional Administration, an extraconstitutional entity not recognized by the government. It formed a Turkish Cypriot Provisional Assembly composed of the 15 Turkish members of the national legislature and the 15 representatives to the Turkish Cypriot Communal Chamber. In early 1975 the Provisional Administration was reorganized as a Turkish Federated State in the northern sector of the island, followed by a unilateral declaration of independence in November 1983 (see entry on Cyprus Turkish Sector). From the December 1985 election the national membership of the House of Representatives was increased to 80 seats, although only the 56 Greek Cypriot seats were filled in that and subsequent contests.

Prior to the invasion by mainland Turkish forces, the island was divided into six administrative districts, each headed by an official appointed by the central government. Municipalities were governed by elected mayors.

Freedom of the press is protected under the constitution of Cyprus, and the media in the republic are independent. One significant issue, according to Reporters Without Borders, was the hindrance of the free flow of information between northern and southern sectors of the island. The example cited was the refusal of the Greek Cypriot government in 2006 to allow journalists from the Turkish Republic of Northern Cyprus to report on a sports event in the south. In 2012 the media group Reporters Without Borders ranked Cyprus 24th out of 179 countries in press freedom.

Foreign relations. Following independence in 1960, Cyprus became a member of the UN and a number of other intergovernmental organizations. Cyprus joined the Non-Aligned Movement. As a result of the events of 1974, the domestic situation became in large measure a function of relations with Greece and Turkey, two uneasy NATO partners whose range of disagreement has by no means been confined to Cyprus. Britain, because of its treaty responsibilities in the area and its sovereign bases on the island, has long played a major role in attempting to mediate the Cyprus dispute. The intercommunal talks, held intermittently since 1975, were initiated at the request of the UN Security Council, which has assumed the principal responsibility for truce supervision through the UNFICYP.

In October 1987 the government concluded an agreement with the EC to establish a customs union over a 15-year period commencing January 1, 1988; in July 1990 it submitted a formal application for full membership.

Amid a persistent deadlock in intercommunal negotiations, there were specific condemnations of Turkish Cypriot intractability that issued regularly from the UN secretary general and Security Council beginning in 1992.

In October 1993 the Council of Ministers of the EU called on the Brussels Commission to begin "substantive discussions" with Cyprus to prepare for accession negotiations. The result was agreement by the EU's Corfu summit in June 1994 that Cyprus would be included in the next round of enlargement negotiations. Turkish Cypriot hostility to Greek Cypriot EU aspirations was compounded when the European Court of Justice ruled on July 5 that all EU imports from Cyprus would require authorization from the Greek Cypriot government, in effect banning direct trade between the EU and the Turkish sector. President Denktaş informed the UN Security Council on July 26 that resumption of the peace talks was contingent on cancellation of the court's ruling, while TRNC Assembly resolutions called for defense and foreign policy coordination with Turkey and rejected a federal Cyprus solution as required by the UN, urging instead "political equality and sovereignty" for the Turkish sector.

Pursuant to an agreement on November 16, 1993, placing Cyprus within the "unified Greek defense space," joint Greek–Greek Cypriot military exercises were held for the first time in October 1994. Concurrently, closer relations were established between the Greek Cypriot government and Russia, which in March 1995 informed Turkey of its firm commitment to a federal solution to the Cyprus problem in accordance with UN resolutions.

While continuing to attach importance to U.S. and British mediation, the Greek Cypriot government gave increasing priority to the EU route to a settlement. Under this scenario, Turkish Cypriot would perceive the potential benefits of EU membership to the beleaguered northern economy and would accordingly be brought to accept a federal "one sovereignty" settlement as the Greek Cypriot application progressed. Besides, the EU would form an ideal anchor for the successful implementation of any settlement. However, such hopes were dashed in August 1996, when Greek Cypriot antipartition demonstrators clashed with Turkish soldiers and civilians after penetrating the UN buffer zone.

In response to a UN draft agreement for the establishment of a federal Cyprus in 1997, President Denktaş restated his demand that Cyprus suspend its application for EU membership before talks proceeded. In December the EU summit in Luxembourg included Cyprus among the six countries for which formal membership negotiations would begin in the spring of 1998 (Turkey being pointedly excluded from the list), and the TRNC subsequently suspended all bicommunal activities. The Greek Cypriot government invited the TRNC to appoint representatives to the Cypriot team being established to negotiate with the EU; however, the Denktaş administration rejected the overture, reportedly out of concern (in part, at least) that it would be in a "subservient" position under such arrangements.

Tension between the Greek Cypriot government and the TRNC escalated sharply in late December 1998 when Clerides announced the impending deployment of Russian S-300 antiaircraft missiles on Greek Cypriot soil. Turkey quickly threatened possible military intervention, and the EU said it would suspend accession talks with Cyprus if the plan was pursued. Consequently, Clerides agreed to have the missiles deployed instead on the Greek island of Crete, with Greece maintaining "operational control" of the weapons. Subsequently, the administration called upon the international community to bring greater pressure on Ankara and the TRNC to return to the bargaining table.

Apparently in consonance with Greek–Turkish rapprochement (see entries on Turkey and Greece), the tension between the Greek and Turkish Cypriots eased considerably after a major earthquake hit western Turkey in mid-August 1999 and the Greek Cypriot government sent monetary and humanitarian aid to Turkey. In what some saw as a compromise step, Denktaş in 2001 backed away from his insistence of Cypriot recognition of the TRNC as a precondition to resuming talks and proposed a "partnership republic" instead of a confederation.

For most of 2002 periodic negotiations between the Greek and Turkish sides failed to produce tangible results. In October the European Commission announced that Cyprus, among others, had fulfilled the political criteria for admission to the EU and was expected to sign an accession treaty in the spring of 2003 in anticipation of membership in 2004. Consequently, international pressure intensified for resolution of the Turkish/Cypriot dispute. (Although the EU made it clear that Cyprus's accession was not contingent on a political settlement and that the EU was prepared, if necessary, to admit only the Greek part of Cyprus.) In an effort to solve the deadlock, UN Secretary General Kofi Annan launched a comprehensive plan in early November proposing a reunification in which the two component states would have equal status and substantial autonomy. Central to Annan's plan was the return of property from the Turkish Cypriots to the Greek Cypriots, compensation for property losses in both communities, and a reduction of the TRNC from 36 percent of the island to 28.5 percent. The plan would displace 42,000 Turkish Cypriots and allow 85,000 Greek Cypriots to return to their former homes.

Following the February 2003 presidential election of Tassos Papadopoulos, the new president declared his commitment to the UN plan. While the partial reopening of the "Green Line" on April 23 helped defuse tension and allowed refugees from both sides to visit their homes, little progress was realized through the talks.

In early 2004 Papadopoulos agreed to authorize a referendum on a revised UN plan by Annan. A few days before the referendum, Papadopoulos surprisingly made a strong appeal against the plan, demanding more concessions from the TRNC. Consequently, the plan was defeated by Greek Cypriots by a 3–1 margin on April 24, and as a result, only the Greek Cypriot sector joined the EU on May 1. (Sixty-five percent of voters in the TRNC had supported the plan forwarded by UN Secretary General Annan.)

The UN-controlled border between the TRNC and the south opened to some trade and travel in 2004, although the TRNC government charged that the Greek Cypriot government restricted trade. Although bitterness continued on both sides, new reunification talks were launched in mid-2005, Papadopoulos arguing that the island was too small to remain divided.

In the May 2006 parliamentary elections, the mood of the voters reflected their rejection of the UN reunification plan. Papadopoulos's DIKO gained a small increase in vote share compared with the 2001 results, while parties that had backed the UN plan for reunification, most notably DISY, did not fare well. The elections included one Turkish Cypriot candidate, and for the first time since 1963, Turkish Cypriots living in the Greek-controlled part of the island were allowed to vote.

Meanwhile, Turkey's consideration for admission into the EU continued to influence politics and government activity in both Cyprus and the TRNC (see entry on Turkey for details on its negotiations with the EU). In July 2006, under a set of principles mediated by the UN, Greek Cypriot and TRNC officials traded lists of bicommunal issues for discussion, the new effort coming on the heels of a meeting between Presidents Papadopoulos and TALAT in Nicosia several days earlier. In the TRNC, friction within the ruling coalition over reunification led to the collapse of the government in September and the establishment of a new coalition government (see entry on Cyprus Turkish Sector for details).

In 2007 Cyprus and Turkey were engaged in a dispute over oil and gas exploration rights in the Mediterranean granted to Egypt and Lebanon. Turkey had warned the latter countries that any agreements with Greek Cyprus also required discussion with the Turkish north. Egypt subsequently halted its agreement with Cyprus; Lebanon did not succumb to pressure from Turkey.

In October 2009 Cyprus joined Spain and Romania in a lawsuit at the International Court of Justice arguing that Kosovar independence was illegal. The action was seen as an effort to forestall autonomy by the TRNC. In November Cyprus announced that it was prepared to block Turkey's bid for EU membership. Also in November relations between Cyprus and Israel grew tense after Israel seized a container ship carrying arms and munitions destined for Lebanon. Relations further deteriorated in May 2010 after Cyprus officially protested the well-publicized Israeli interdiction of a humanitarian flotilla traveling to Gaza (see entry on Israel). Nonetheless, Cyprus issued an order forbidding ships traveling to Gaza to break the Israeli blockade from departing out of Cypriot ports.

Cyprus joined a number of other EU states in February 2011 in opposing Franco-German proposals to reduce social welfare expenditures by establishing a uniform retirement age and cutting various benefits. On May 5 Cyprus and the TRNC reached an agreement through which international treaties would continue in force for a united Cyprus. Following credit downgrades in June, Cyprus was unable to borrow in international financial markets. In October Russia loaned Cyprus $3.1 billion, or about 10 percent of GDP, to provide credit reserves for a year.

On January 9, 2012, Cyprus and Israel signed two defense agreements that were described as manifestations of a new era in bilateral relations. The two countries also pledged to cooperate in the exploration of gas in the Mediterranean after a U.S. energy company discovered a massive natural gas field in Cypriot waters. In March Cyprus, Israel, and Greece signed an agreement for Israel to supply electricity to Cyprus and Crete through the construction of an underwater cable. On March 22 the Cypriot House enacted a resolution calling for the removal of UK military bases from the island. Meanwhile, in June Turkey announced it would not recognize Cyprus's six-month assumption of the EU presidency and would boycott official EU functions presided over by the Cypriot president.

Through 2012 and into 2013, Cyprus finalized a series of taxation treaties with countries ranging from Finland to Ukraine, in an effort to allay concerns that the island had become a tax haven and center for money laundering (see Current issues, below).

Current issues. Intercommunal negotiations were launched again on September 3, 2008, following a four-year hiatus, amid optimism fueled by what was viewed as the moderate approach of new Cypriot president Christofias. The negotiations were expected to draw increasing international attention as Turkey's EU accession process was scheduled for review by the European Council late in the year, and the expiration of a deadline neared for Turkey to lift its embargo on Cypriot vessels and aircraft. Because of the embargo, Cyprus blocked the opening of some of the issues in EU-Turkey accession negotiations. Meanwhile, relations between AKEL and the junior coalition members were at times strained because of DIKO's and EDEK's opposition to Christofias's alleged willingness to make concessions to the Turkish Cypriots in the course of intercommunal negotiations. That same month, the escape of the notorious criminal Antonios KITTAS from a private hospital caused a major domestic political crisis, as details about his extremely lax treatment by prison authorities at the hospital were leaked. The minister of justice and public order, Kypros CHRYSOSTOMIDES, resigned, along with the leadership of the police. Kittas was subsequently rearrested in January 2009.

In 2009 the European Court of Justice (ECJ) issued a ruling regarding a British couple who had bought and developed land in the town of Lapithos/Lapta. They were sued by the displaced owner of the property, who had not exercised effective control over it since 1974. In April the ECJ supported the earlier ruling of a Cypriot court that the British couple demolish their home, return the land, and pay damages, and further ruled that the order must be recognized and enforced by the EU even though the land in question is in the TRNC. This ruling strengthened Greek Cypriot positions on the property issues and was seen as the potential harbinger of similar cases and was upheld by a British appeals court in January 2010.

Meanwhile, the global financial crisis and government stimulus efforts caused the deficit to increase dramatically in 2009, and the government announced that it would cut more than $500 million from the budget through reductions in operating costs and civil service positions.

In January 2010 UN-backed negotiations between the Greek- and Turkish-Cypriot leaders were reenergized by a visit from UN secretary general Ban Ki-moon. Also in 2010 Cyprus implemented a nationwide smoking ban in public places.

In legislative elections on May 22, 2011, DISY overtook AKEL as the largest party in the house. The election was seen as a referendum on the ruling coalition's management of the economy and its conciliatory approach toward negotiations with the TRNC. The government announced plans for tax increases and deep cuts to social welfare programs on July 1. On July 11 confiscated Iranian explosives improperly stored at the Evangelos Florakis naval base exploded, killing 13 and injuring more than 60. The accident also damaged the main Cypriot power station, cutting power to more than half of the island and forcing the government to import electricity from the TRNC. Widespread public anger over the incident and the government's management of the crisis led the defense minister and the foreign minister to resign. Disagreement over austerity measures led opposition parties to refuse to join a new cabinet appointed by Christofias on August 5.

On January 24, 2012, the foreign minister and defense minister were arrested with six others for their roles in the July explosion. Meanwhile, a government report placed ultimate responsibility for the incident on Christofias for allowing the storage of the explosives. Also in January, the major credit agencies further downgraded Cyprus's debt. In June reports emerged that Cyprus would request a bailout from the Eurozone after losing an estimated $2.2 billion as a result of the Greek financial crisis. Although observers believe a bailout is inevitable, in December 2012 the IMF demanded a Greek-style restructuring take place before any bailout could proceed.

DISY's Nicos Anastasiades secured 45.5 percent of the vote in the first round of presidential elections on February 17, 2013. Stavros MALAS, supported by AKEL, placed second and advanced to run-off balloting with Anastasiades on February 24. Anastasiades won that polling with 57.5 percent of the vote to 42.5 percent for Malas.

On March 25, 2013, the EU and IMF approved an unprecedented €10 billion package of emergency loans for Cyprus to prevent a massive default within the country's banking sector, which initially required an estimated €17.2 billion to remain solvent. In exchange for the bail-out, Cyprus had to impose a complicated one-time charge of up to 60 percent on deposits of more than €100,000; 37.5 percent of those deposits would be exchanged for bank stocks that were essentially worthless; and 22.5 percent would go to a non-interest-bearing fund that could be used to support the bank. Creditors had initially sought more stringent requirements, including a one-time tax on all deposits (9.9 percent on accounts over €100,000 and 6.75 percent on accounts under €100,000). However, Anastasiades reportedly threatened to resign if the conditions were not modified.

The rescue plan marked the first occasion that a Eurozone bailout required individual bank depositors, including foreign nationals, to fund a rescue. The plan's announcement prompted the Cypriot government to announce a three-day bank holiday to prevent a run on deposits. When banks reopened, daily withdrawals were limited to €300, while travelers were only allowed to take €1,000 out of the country. Reports indicated that the harsh conditions of the rescue were the result of concerns by Germany and other EU members over money laundering among the banks, which held an estimated €20 billion in deposits from Russia, with reports that a portion of those funds were connected to organized crime. The measures were highly unpopular but were approved by the parliament on a 29–27 vote on April 30. Meanwhile, revelations emerged that the cost of the bailout had risen to €23 billion, forcing the government to cut salaries for civil servants and downsize the public sector, while also implementing a new property tax and reforming the pension system. Following the reforms, the IMF agreed to provide an additional €1 billion.

POLITICAL PARTIES

Throughout the 14 years preceding the Turkish intervention, the Cypriot party system was divided along communal lines. As a result of population displacement, the Greek parties now function exclusively in the south, while the Turkish parties function in the north. All are headquartered within the divided city of Nicosia. The Greek parties are listed below (see the entry on Cyprus Turkish Sector for Turkish parties).

Government Parties:

Democratic Rally (*Dimokratikos Synagermos*—DISY). The Democratic Rally was organized in May 1976 by Glafcos CLERIDES following his resignation as negotiator for the Greek Cypriots in the intercommunal talks in Vienna. The Rally has long favored a strongly pro-Western orientation as a means of maintaining sufficient pressure on the Turks to resolve the communal dispute. It secured 24.1 percent of the vote in 1976 but won no legislative seats. Its fortunes were dramatically reversed in the 1981 balloting, at which it obtained 12 seats, with 7 more being added in 1985. The party absorbed the small New Democratic Alignment (*Nea Dimokratiki Parataxi*—NEDIPA), led by Alekos MIHAILIDES, prior to the 1988 presidential balloting, at which Clerides was defeated in the second round. The party won a plurality of 19 seats at the legislative election of May 1991, with an additional seat going to its coalition partner, the Liberal Party (*Komma Phileleftheron*—KP).

Clerides withdrew from the party presidency upon being elected president of the republic in February 1993. A DISY-Liberal alliance won 20 seats in the May 1996 election, with a vote share of 34 percent, all seats going to DISY candidates. In February 1998 the KP officially merged with DISY. The KP had been organized in 1986 by Nikos ROLANDIS (formerly a close associate of President Kyprianou), who supported Georgios Vassiliou in 1988. It secured one legislative seat as an electoral partner of DISY in 1991 but failed to retain it in 1996. Rolandis won less than 1 percent of the vote in the first round of the 1998 presidential balloting and, after throwing his support behind Clerides in the second round, was subsequently named to the February 1998 cabinet. In the first round of the February 2003 presidential elections, Clerides received 38.8 percent of the vote. The party supported the UN reunification proposal in advance of the 2004 referendum, in which Cypriot voters overwhelmingly rejected the UN plan. In 2005 dissidents opposed to the party's support of the UN reunification plan left to form a new party, EVROKO (see below).

In the May 2006 parliamentary election, DISY secured 30.34 percent of the vote and lost 1 of its 19 seats. In the February 2008 presidential elections, DISY nominated Ioannis KASSOULIDES, former foreign minister of the Clerides administration and member of the European Parliament. In his electoral campaign, Kassoulides advocated a "European Cyprus," fully integrated into European institutions. In the first round of the elections, he surprisingly won the plurality of votes, leaving AKEL candidate Christofias second and disqualifying the incumbent president Papadopoulos. While the alliance between Christofias and Papadopoulos secured a rather comfortable victory for Christofias in the second round, Kassoulides's performance attested to the resilience of DISY, which recovered from the 2004 crisis to secure a central role in Cypriot politics. Following the formation of the AKEL-DIKO-KISOS government alliance, DISY remained the chief opposition party in parliament.

DISY secured the most seats (20) in the 2011 house balloting but declined to join with AKEL in a unity government. Party leader Nicos Anastasiades won the 2013 presidential polling. Deputy party president Averof Neophytou became acting DISY president after Anastasiades was inaugurated.

Leaders: Nicos ANASTASIADES (President of the Republic), Averof NEOPHYTOU (Acting President), Eleni VRAHIMI (Secretary General).

Democratic Party (*Dimokratiko Komma*—DIKO). The Democratic Party is a center-right grouping organized in 1976 as the Democratic Front to support President Makarios's policy of "long-term struggle" against the Turkish occupation of northern Cyprus. It won the most seats in the House of Representatives in the 1976 election, with 21 seats. Its representation fell to 8 seats in 1981. In December 1985 it obtained 16 seats in an enlarged house of 56 members, after its former coalition partner, AKEL, had supported a censure motion against the then president Kyprianou. DIKO absorbed the Center Union (*Enosi Kentrou*—EK), a minor formation led by former chief intercommunal negotiator Tassos Papadopoulos, in February 1989. It won 11 legislative seats in 1991 and endorsed Clerides for the presidency in 1993, then slipped to 10 seats (on a 16.5 percent vote share) in May 1996.

The run-up to the February 1998 presidential election produced a serious split in DIKO, whose leadership formally endorsed (along with AKEL) the candidacy of independent Georgios Iacovou. Many DIKO members reportedly objected to that endorsement, and DIKO vice president Alexis Galanos presented himself as a candidate, securing 4 percent of the vote in the first round of balloting. Galanos supported Clerides in the second round, and several DIKO rebels were appointed as independents to the new coalition government, with Galanos named presidential adviser. Galanos, a former president of the House of Representatives, was subsequently identified as the leader of the new Eurodemocratic Renewal Party.

DIKO's vote share fell to 14.8 percent in the May 2001 balloting, and the party's legislative representation slipped to nine seats.

Kyprianou, former president of the republic and a founder of DIKO, stepped down as president of the party in 2000 due to ill health; he died in March 2002. Kyprianou was replaced by Tassos Papadopoulos, who adroitly gained the support of AKEL and the Social Democrats' Movement (EDEK) in the February 2003 presidential election with a campaign that emphasized the need for more concessions from the TRNC in negotiations for a permanent peace plan. He won the election with 51.5 percent of the vote.

DIKO urged a "no" vote in the 2004 referendum on the proposed UN reunification plan. It garnered a vote share of 17.9 percent in the May 2006 parliamentary balloting. In October 2006 Papadopoulos stepped down from the DIKO presidency and was replaced by Marios Karogian. Following the failure of Papadopoulos to reach the second round in the February 2008 presidential elections, DIKO supported the candidacy of Dimitrios (Dimitris) Christofias in the second round. Following Christofias's election, DIKO president Marios Karogian was elected president of the House of Representatives in accordance with the terms of the pre-second-round agreement between DIKO and AKEL. Papadopoulos died in December 2008.

Following the formation of Christofias's coalition government, two factions formed within the party: those aligned with Karogian, favoring closer cooperation with AKEL and compromise in order to achieve a breakthrough in intercommunal negotiations, and those led by the elder son of the late Tassos Papadopoulos, Nikolaos (Nikolas) PAPADOPOULOS, who opposed any deviations from the stance that had been supported by the Papadopoulos administration. The divisions led Karogian to threaten the expulsion of DIKO members who were publicly critical of the party leadership.

The small **Fighting Democratic Movement** (*Agonistiko Dimokratiko Kinima*—ADIK) voted to combine with DIKO in 2011 (for more on ADIK, please see the 2012 *Handbook*). DIKO secured just nine seats in the house in the May 2011 elections. It subsequently withdrew from the ADEK-led government in July. Following the election of Anastasiades as president in 2013, DIKO joined the DISY-led cabinet.

Leaders: Marios KAROGIAN (Party President), Georgios KOLOKASIDES (Deputy President), Kyriakos KENEVEZOS (Secretary General).

European Party (*Evropaiko Komma*—EVROKO). The European Party was founded in July 2005 by dissidents from DISY who had opposed DISY's stance on the 2004 referendum. In 2005 EVROKO merged with the **New Horizons** (*Neoi Orizontes*—NO). NO had been launched in early 1996, backed by the Church and advocating that Cyprus should be a unitary rather than a federal state. NO leader Nikolaos (Nikos) Koutsou won less than 1 percent of the vote in the first round of the 1998 presidential balloting and 2.1 percent of the vote in 2003. In advance of the 2006 parliamentary elections, EVROKO also formed an alliance with the Fighting Democratic Movement. EVROKO garnered 5.75 percent of the vote and three seats, all credited to EVROKO. In the February 2008 presidential elections, EVROKO supported the candidacy of President Papadopoulos, while in the second round it abstained from endorsing a candidate.

Despite the opposition of its founding members to the UN plan of 2004, EVROKO states that it favors a reunification plan based on the resolution of EU issues with Turkey. In the view of the party leadership, this would be a "truly European" solution, which would respect the fundamental European freedoms for all Cypriot citizens and throughout the island. EVROKO secured two seats in the May 2011 house balloting. EVROKO supported Anastasiades in the 2013 presidential election and was given one post in the subsequently DISY-led government.

Leaders: Dimitrios SILLOURIS (President), Nikolaos (Nikos) KOUTSOU (Vice President).

Opposition Parties:

Progressive Party of the Working People (*Anorthotiko Komma Ergazomenou Laou*—AKEL). Organized in 1941 as the Communist Party of Cyprus, AKEL dominates the Greek Cypriot labor movement.

Its support for President Kyprianou, withdrawn for a period in 1980 because of the latter's handling of "the national issue," was renewed in September when the government agreed to a renewal of intercommunal talks; it was again withdrawn as a result of the breakdown in talks at UN headquarters in January 1985. The party won 12 legislative seats in 1981 and 15 in 1985; it endorsed the candidacy of Georgios Vassiliou in 1988.

In January 1990 a number of dissidents, including 4 of the Politburo's 15 members, were dismissed or resigned in a controversy over democratic reforms that led to the creation of ADISOK (see below, under the EDE) by 5 of the party's (then) 15 parliamentarians. In the May 1991 balloting, AKEL representation increased to 18 seats. A further advance, to 19 seats, was registered in May 1996. AKEL supported independent Georgios Iacovou in the February 1998 presidential poll. The party got a surprising victory in the May 2001 balloting with 34.7 percent of the vote and became the largest party in the legislature with 20 seats. AKEL, having supported DIKO candidate Papadopoulos in the 2003 presidential elections, received four posts in the new Council of Ministers.

In general, the party has supported a federal solution to the divided island, backing an independent, demilitarized Cyprus and rapprochement with Turkish Cypriots. However, it urged a "no" vote in the 2004 referendum on the proposed UN plan for reunification. AKEL's share of the vote dropped to 31.1 percent in the May 2006 parliamentary elections, resulting in a loss of 2 seats. Despite initial expectations that AKEL would support the reelection of President Papadopoulos, Secretary General Dimitrios (Dimitris) Christofias announced his own candidacy. On February 23, 2008, Christofias was elected president. In January 2009 Andros KYPRIANOU was elected general secretary of the party. The party secured 19 seats in the 2011 balloting. In May 2012 Christofias announced he would not seek reelection as president in 2013. Instead, the party backed independent candidate Stavros MALAS, who was defeated in the second round of balloting on February 24.

Leaders: Dimitrios (Dimitris) CHRISTOFIAS (Former President of the Republic), Andros KYPRIANOU (General Secretary).

Movement for Social Democracy (*Kinima Sosialdimokraton EDEK*—EDEK). This grouping was formed as the Unified Democratic Union of Cyprus–Socialist Party (*Ethniki Dimokratiki Enosi Kyprou–Sosialistiko Komma*—EDEK-SK), a moderately left-of-center grouping that supported a unified and independent Cyprus. The EDEK-SK had concluded an electoral alliance with the Democratic Front and AKEL in 1976 but campaigned separately in 1981, its three representatives refusing to support the government after the new house convened. Its chair (and founder of the EDEK-SK), Vassos Lyssarides, campaigned for the presidency in 1983 as leader of the National Salvation Front; although he announced his withdrawal prior to the actual balloting as a means of reducing polarization within the Greek Cypriot community, he was nonetheless credited with obtaining a third-place, 9.5 percent vote share. The party obtained six legislative seats in 1985. Lyssarides ran fourth in the first round of the 1988 presidential poll, after which EDEK-SK gave its support to Georgios Vassiliou. The party improved to seven seats in the 1991 house election but fell back to five in May 1996. Lyssarides secured 10.6 percent of the votes in the first round of the February 1998 presidential balloting. Although the EDEK-SK did not endorse President Clerides in the second round (encouraging members to vote for the candidate of their choice), the party was given the defense and education portfolios in the subsequent coalition government. However, the EDEK-SK withdrew from the government following Clerides's decision to cancel the proposed deployment of Russian missiles on the island in December.

The party adopted the name **Social Democrats' Movement** (*Kinima Sosial-dimokraton*—KISOS) in 1999. In the 2001 legislative balloting, the party's vote share fell to 6.5 percent. KISOS supported DIKO candidate Tassos Papadopoulos in the 2003 presidential elections and received two posts in the new coalition government. The party urged a "no" vote in the 2004 referendum on the proposed UN reunification plan. Meanwhile, the party adopted its current name, the **Movement for Social Democracy** (*Kinima Sosialdimokraton EDEK*—EDEK).

In the May 2006 parliamentary elections, EDEK's vote share was 8.9 percent, and it increased its number of seats to five. In the February 2008 presidential elections, EDEK supported the candidacy of President Tassos Papadopoulos. When he was disqualified from the second round, EDEK shifted its support to the AKEL candidate, Dimitrios (Dimitris) Christofias. Christofias's election secured EDEK's participation in the new government. Yet major differences persisted regarding the resolution of the Cyprus question, as EDEK opposed any compromise solution with a clear bizonal, bicommunal character. EDEK withdrew from the government in February 2010.

In the May 2011 elections EDEK maintained its five seats. It joined the ADEK-led government in August. In May 2012 EDEK led an unsuccessful effort to build an electoral coalition ahead of the 2013 presidential election. The party supported independent candidate Giorgos LILLIKAS in the 2013 presidential election (he placed third in the first round of balloting).

Leaders: Yiannakis OMIROU (President), Kyriakos MAVRONICOLAS (Deputy President), Vassos LYSSARIDES (Honorary President), Antonis KOUTALIANOS (General Secretary).

United Democrats (*Enomenoi Dimokrates*—EDI). The leftist EDI was formed in 1996 by members of the **Free Democrats Movement** (*Kinima ton Eleftheron Dimokraton*—KED) and the **Democratic Socialist Reform Movement** (*Ananeotiko Dimokratiko Sosialistiko Kinima*—ADISOK). The center-left KED had been launched in April 1993 by former president Georgios Vassiliou following his unexpected failure to win a second term in February. He pledged that the new group would "promote the admission of Cyprus into Europe." The party won two seats on a 3.6 percent vote share in the May 1996 election.

The ADISOK had been launched in early 1990 by a number of AKEL dissidents favoring settlement of the Cyprus issue on the basis of UN resolutions. It failed to retain legislative representation in the 1991 and 1996 elections.

Vassiliou, who won just 3 percent of the vote in the first round of the February 1998 presidential balloting, supported President Clerides in the second round. Vassiliou was subsequently named as the government's chief EU negotiator, while the EDI was also given a ministry in Clerides's new coalition government. The EDI won a single legislative seat in 2001.

The EDI, which supported the UN reunification proposal put forth in the 2004 referendum, subsequently lost its legislative seat in the May 2006 elections, securing only 1.6 percent of the vote. Party president Michalis PAPAPETROU subsequently resigned.

In 2007 former cabinet minister and party member Costas THEMISTOCLEOUS announced his bid for the presidency in the February 2008 elections, but the EDI ultimately decided to endorse the Christofias candidacy to reduce the reelection chances of President Papadopoulos.

Although the party failed to gain any seats in the 2011 house elections, it joined the ADEK-led coalition government in August 2011, and party leader Praxoula Antoniadou was appointed minister of commerce, industry, and tourism. Antoniadou was the EDI candidate in the 2013 election and placed fifth in the balloting.

Leaders: Praxoula ANTONIADOU (President), George VASSILIOU (Former President of the Republic and Honorary President of the Party), Mikis SHANIS (Secretary General).

Ecological Environmental Movement–Cyprus Green Party (*Kinima Oikologon Perivallontiston*). The Cyprus Green Party was established as a political party in February 1996 but failed to make much impact in the May 1996 election, winning only 1 percent of the vote. The party managed to gain legislative representation for the first time in the May 2001 balloting. It received 1.98 percent of the vote and won a single seat. The party retained its seat with 1.95 percent of the vote in the May 2006 elections. In 2007 the Green Party made a joint announcement with the Turkish Cypriot **New Cyprus Party,** calling for military withdrawal from Nicosia as a first step toward demilitarization of the entire island. The party opposed any division of the island based on geography, ethnicity, or religion. In the February 2008 presidential elections, the party supported the candidacy of President Papadopoulos, while in the second round it endorsed the Christofias candidacy. The party secured one seat in the 2011 house elections. The party supported independent candidate Malas in the 2013 balloting.

Leaders: Georgios PERDIKIS (Chair), Ioanna PANAYIOTOU (General Secretary).

Other Parties:

Other minor parties that contested the 2011 elections or the 2013 presidential balloting were the **National Popular Front** (*Ethniko Laiko Metopo*); the **Citizens's Rights Burea of the Popular Socialist Movement** (*Grapheio Dikaiomaton Tou Polite LASOK*); the **Balance—Independent Citizens Movement** (*Zygos—Kinima Anexartiton*); and the **Cypriot Progressive Cooperation** (*Kypriaki Proodevtiki Synergasia*). Minor parties that participated in the 2006 parliamentary elections were the **Free Citizens' Movement,** founded in 2004 and led by Timis EYTHIMIOU, and the **Hunters' Political**

Movement, led by Michalis PAFITANIS. In April 2013, a new grouping, the **Citizens' Alliance** was reportedly formed by former presidential candidate Giorgos LILLIKAS.

For information on the **European Democracy** (*Evropaiki Dimokratia*—EVRODI), please see the 2012 *Handbook.*

LEGISLATURE

The Cypriot **House of Representatives** (*Vouli Antiprosópon/ Temsilciler Meclisi*) is a unicameral body formerly encompassing 35 Greek and 15 Turkish members, although Turkish participation ceased in December 1963. By contrast, the balloting of December 8, 1985, was for an enlarged House of 56 Greek members. At the most recent election of May 22, 2011, the seat distribution was as follows: the Democratic Rally, 20; the Progressive Party of the Working People, 19; the Democratic Party, 9; the Movement for Social Democracy, 5; the European Party, 2; and the Ecological Environmental Movement–Cyprus Green Party, 1. There are also 24 seats nominally reserved for Turkish Cypriots.

President: Yiannakis OMIROU.

CABINET

[as of November 5, 2013]

President	Nikos Anastasiadis (DISY)
Ministers	
Agriculture, Natural Resources, and Environment	Nicos Kouyialis (EVROKO)
Commerce, Energy, Industry, and Tourism	Georgios Lakkotrypis (DIKO)
Communications and Works	Tasos Mitsopoulos (DISY)
Defense	Fotis Fotiou (DIKO)
Education and Culture	Kyriacos Kenevezos (DIKO)
Finance	Harris Georgiades (DISY)
Foreign Affairs	Ioannis Kasoulides (DISY)
Health	Petros Petrides (DIKO)
Interior	Socrates Hasikos (DISY)
Justice and Public Order	Ionas Nicolaou (DISY)
Labor and Social Insurance	Zeta Emilianidou (DISY) [f]

[f] = female

INTERGOVERNMENTAL REPRESENTATION

Ambassador to the U.S.: George CHACALLI.

U.S. Ambassador to Cyprus: John M. KOENIG.

Permanent Representative to the UN: Nicholas EMILIOU.

IGO Memberships (Non-UN): CEUR, CWTH, EIB, EU, ICC, IOM, OSCE, WTO.

CYPRUS: TURKISH SECTOR

Turkish Republic of Northern Cyprus
Kuzey Kıbrıs Türk Cumhuriyeti

Political Status: Autonomous federal state proclaimed February 13, 1975; independent republic (thus far recognized only by Turkey) declared November 15, 1983; TRNC constitution approved by referendum of May 6, 1985.

Area: Approximately 1,400 sq. mi. (3,626 sq. km).

Population: 294,906 (2011C), Turkish Cypriot census, which includes nonindigenous settlers (more than half of the total).

Major Urban Centers (2005E): LEFKOŞA (Turkish-occupied portion of Nicosia, 42,200), Gazi Mağusa (Famagusta, 37,100).

Principal Language: Turkish.

Monetary Unit: Turkish Lira (market rate November 1, 2013: 2.02 Turkish liras = $1US). Use of the Cyprus pound as an alternative unit of exchange was terminated on May 16, 1983.

President: Derviş EROĞLU (National Unity Party); elected in first round of popular balloting on April 18, 2010, and inaugurated April 23 for a five-year term in succession to Mehmet Ali TALAT (Republican Turkish Party).

Prime Minister: Özkan YORGANCIOĞLU (Republican Turkish Party–United Forces); appointed by the president on August 15, 2013, to succeed interim prime minister Sibel SIBER (Republican Turkish Party–United Forces), who had been appointed on June 6, following the resignation on the previous day of İrsen KÜÇÜK (National Unity Party).

GOVERNMENT AND POLITICS

Political background. The Turkish Cypriots withdrew from the government of the Republic of Cyprus in January 1964 in the wake of communal violence precipitated by Archbishop MAKARIOS's announcement of proposed constitutional changes in November 1963. In 1967 a Turkish Cypriot Provisional Administration was established in the Turkish areas, its representatives subsequently engaging in sporadic constitutional discussions with members of the Greek Cypriot administration. Meanwhile, an uneasy peace between the two communities was maintained by a UN peacekeeping force that had been dispatched in 1964, while most Turkish Cypriots were forced under Greek Cypriot pressure to move to UN-protected enclaves. The constitutional talks, which ran until 1974, failed to bridge the gap between Greek insistence on a unitary form of government and Turkish demands for a bicommunal federation.

A Turkish Federated State of Cyprus was established on February 13, 1975, following the Greek army coup of July 15, 1974, and the subsequent Turkish occupation of northern Cyprus. Rauf DENKTAŞ, nominal vice president of the Republic of Cyprus and leader of the National Unity Party (*Ulusal Birlik Partisi*—UBP), was designated president of the Federated State, retaining the office as the result of a presidential election on June 20, 1976, in which he defeated the Republican Turkish Party (*Cumhuriyetçi Türk Partisi*—CTP) nominee, Ahmet Mithat BERBEROĞLU, by a majority of nearly four to one. He was reelected for a five-year term in June 1981, remaining in office upon proclamation of the Turkish Republic of Northern Cyprus (TRNC) in November 1983.

Intercommunal discussions prior to the death of Archbishop Makarios on August 3, 1977, yielded apparent Greek Cypriot abandonment of the unitary government condition but left the two sides far apart on other issues, including Greek Cypriot efforts to secure a reduction of approximately 50 percent in the size of the Turkish Cypriot sector, in accordance to the population size of the Turkish Cypriot community, and Turkish Cypriot demands for virtual parity in such federal institutions as the presidency (to be effected on the basis of communal rotation) and the higher judiciary. In the meantime, an intensive settlement project was launched. Thousands of Turkish citizens were invited to settle on the properties of Greek Cypriots who were displaced during the events of 1974, in an apparent attempt to tilt the demographic balance on the island in favor of Turkish Cypriots.

Prior to the breakdown in discussions between Denktaş and the president of the Republic of Cyprus and Greek Cypriot leader Spyros KYPRIANOU at UN headquarters in January 1985, the Turkish Cypriots had agreed to make significant concessions, particularly with regard to power sharing and territorial demarcation of the projected federal units. Specifically, they had abandoned their earlier demand (revived in 1991) for presidential rotation and had agreed on a reduction of the area to be placed under Turkish local administration to approximately 29 percent of the island. However, the two sides disagreed on a specific timetable for Turkish troop withdrawal, the identification of Turkish Cypriot-held areas to be returned to Greek Cypriot control, and a mechanism for external guarantees that the pact would be observed. In announcing on January 25 that presidential and legislative elections would be held in June, President Denktaş insisted that neither the balloting nor the adoption of the TRNC constitution should be construed as efforts to "close the door to a federal solution."

The constitution was approved by 70 percent of those participating in a referendum on May 5, 1985. At the presidential poll on June 9, Denktaş was accorded a like margin, while the UBP fell two seats short of a majority at the legislative balloting of June 23. On July 30 a coalition government involving the UBP and the Communal Liberation Party (*Toplumcu Kurtuluş Partisi*—TKP), with Derviş EROĞLU as prime minister, was confirmed by the assembly.

The EROĞLU government fell on August 11, 1986, over differences between the UBP and TKP. However, the prime minister was able to form a new administration on September 2 that included the UBP and the center-right New Dawn Party (*Yeni Doğus Partisi*—YDP).

President Denktaş drew 67.5 percent of the vote in securing reelection to his fourth five-year term on April 22, 1990. Subsequently, a rift developed between Denktaş and Eroğlu over the conduct of negotiations with the south, the prime minister advocating a harder line on concessions to the Greek Cypriots than did the president. As a result, a group of dissidents withdrew from the UBP in July 1992 to form the Democratic Party (*Demokrat Parti*—DP), to which Denktaş transferred his allegiance in late October, thereby provoking a power struggle with UBP leader Eroğlu, who became highly critical of the president's "unacceptable concessions" in negotiations with the Greek Cypriots.

Denktaş eventually gained the upper hand by calling an early assembly election on December 12, 1993, in which the UBP, although retaining a narrow plurality, lost ground, while the DP and the CTP both registered gains. The outcome was the formation on January 1, 1994, of a center-left DP-CTP coalition headed by DP leader Hakki ATUN, which supported the Denktaş line in the intercommunal talks.

In the run-up to the 1995 presidential balloting, Atun resigned as prime minister on February 24 after the CTP had opposed President Denktaş's preelection offer to distribute to TRNC citizens the title deeds of Greek Cypriot property in the north. In the presidential contest on April 15 and 22, Denktaş for the first time failed to win an outright majority in the first round (taking only 40.4 percent of the vote), although he scored a comfortable 62.5 to 37.5 percent victory over Eroğlu in the second. Protracted interparty negotiations were needed to produce, on June 3, a new DP-CTP administration headed by Atun. The coalition again collapsed in November, following the resignation of the CTP deputy premier, Ösker ÖZGÜR, but it was reestablished the following month with Mehmet Ali TALAT of the CTP as Atun's deputy. The DP-CTP coalition government resigned on July 4, 1996, and the UBP's Eroğlu was again given, on August 1, 1996, the job of forming a new government. A UBP-DP coalition cabinet headed by Eroğlu was approved by the president on August 16, 1996.

In the legislative balloting of December 6, 1998, the UBP improved from 17 to 24 seats. On December 30 President Denktaş approved Eroğlu to head a new UBP-TKP coalition government, the DP having fallen into dispute with the UBP over economic policies and cabinet representation. The legislature approved the new cabinet on January 12, 1999, by a strict party-line vote of 31–18. Denktaş won 43.6 percent of the vote in the first round of presidential balloting on April 15, 2000, while UBP candidate Eroğlu received 30.1 percent; the TKP's Mustafa AKINCI, 11.7 percent; the CTP's Mehmet Ali Talat, 10 percent; and Arif Hasan TAHSIN of the Patriotic Unity Movement (*Yurtsever Birlik Hareketi*—YBH), 2.6 percent. Three other minor candidates each received less than 1 percent of the vote. The second round of balloting, scheduled for April 22, was canceled when Eroğlu withdrew on April 19 after the TKP decided to back neither of the candidates for the second round. Denktaş was sworn in on April 24.

After a series of disagreements between the coalition partners (mainly regarding the direction to be taken in foreign relations), the UBP-TKP government resigned on May 25, 2001. President Denktaş asked Eroğlu to form a new government, and a UBP-DP coalition was appointed on June 7.

The CTP returned to a plurality (19 seats) in the December 14, 2003, assembly balloting, and Talat formed a CTP-DP coalition government on January 13, 2004. However, only two days after the TRNC population had endorsed a UN plan for reunification (see Current issues, below), the coalition became a minority government when two DP legislators quit the party to protest the administration's pro-unification stance. After numerous attempts by Talat and the UBP's Eroğlu to form coalition governments failed, new assembly elections were held on February 20, 2005. The CTP increased its seat total to 24, and Talat was able to form a more secure CTP-DP coalition cabinet on March 16.

Talat secured 55.6 percent of the vote in the first round of presidential balloting on April 17, 2005, with Eroğlu finishing second with 22.7 percent. Talat resigned as prime minister on April 20 and was inaugurated as president on April 24. The following day, Ferdi Sabit SOYER, a close ally of Talat and CTP stalwart, formed another CTP-DP coalition government. The government collapsed in September 2006 over differences between the coalition partners. A new coalition government, again headed by Soyer, was established in October between the CTP and the newly formed Freedom and Reform Party (*Özgürlük ve Reform Partisi*—ÖRP), headed by former UBP leader Turgay AVCI. The new government enjoyed good relations with the Greek Cypriot government led by the Justice and Development Party (*Adalet ve Kalkınma Partisi*—AKP) and maintained a moderate stance on the Cyprus issue. Talat and Christofias have held several informal meetings, while expert committees representing both parties have met regularly since April to prepare the start of direct negotiations. Public foreign debt dropped from 14.9 percent of GDP in 2006 to 14.6 in 2007 and was projected to fall to 14 percent in 2008.

In the wake of rising popular discontent, the CTP-BG called for early parliamentary elections on April 19, 2009. The mandate turned out to be a clear defeat for the CTP-BG, as the right-wing nationalist opposition, the National Unity Party (*Ulusal Birlik Partisi*—UBP), won 44 percent of the vote and 26 seats, while the CTP-BG won 29 percent of the vote and 15 seats. UBP chair Eroğlu was named prime minister and formed a new, sıngle-party government on May 4.

Eroğlu was elected president in balloting on April 18, 2010, with 50.4 percent of the vote. He defeated incumbent president Talat, his closest rival, who received 42.9 percent of the vote, and five other candidates. Turnout was 76.4 percent. Although perceived as a hardliner, Eroğlu pledged to work for reunification and to work with his Greek Cypriot counterpart. He appointed İrsen KÜÇÜK of the UBP as prime minister on May 10. However, the election of Eroğlu and the defection of one deputy from the party left the UBP with only 24 seats (see Political parties, below). The new minority government survived a confidence vote by 31 to 16 on May 27.

A major cabinet reshuffle took place on April 6, 2011, when three ministers were replaced and two others were given different portfolios (see Current issues, below). On January 13, 2012, Dentaş died at age 83.

On June 5, 2013, the Küçük government lost a vote of no confidence (see Current issues, below). An interim government was appointed under Sibel SIBER of the CTP-BG, who became the first woman prime minister of the TRNC. New elections, held on July 28, were won by the CTP-BG, which formed a coalition government with the DP on August 15, led by Prime Minister Özkan YORGANCIOĞLU (CTP-BG).

Constitution and government. The constitution of the TRNC provides for a presidential-parliamentary system headed by a popularly elected chief executive, who cannot lead a party or be subject to its decisions. The president appoints a prime minister, who (unlike other ministers) must be a member of the legislature and whose government is subject to legislative recall. Like the president, the 50-member Assembly of the Republic is elected for a five-year term (subject to dissolution) and its presiding officer, who is chosen at the beginning of the first and fourth year of each term, becomes acting head of state in the event of presidential death, incapacity, or resignation. The members of the Supreme Court, composed of a president and seven additional judges, also form a Constitutional Court (five members) and a Court of Appeal and High Administrative Court (three members each). Lesser courts and local administrative units are established by legislative action.

The constitution of the TRNC guarantees freedom of the press, except for legislative restrictions intended to safeguard public order, national security, public morals, or the proper functioning of the judiciary. In 2013 Reporters Without Borders ranked the TRNC as 94th out of 179 countries in terms of freedom of the press.

Current issues. The European Council meeting held in late 1997 decided that Cyprus would be included in the first group of applicants to join the expanded European Union (EU), while determining that "political and economic conditions" required for the membership of Turkey were not satisfied. The EU also expressed a desire to see action taken on the Cyprus government's wish to include the Turkish Cypriots in the negotiating delegation. However, President Denktaş of the TRNC indicated his unwillingness to proceed with negotiations unless further international recognition of the TRNC was forthcoming, and new discussions were not launched as expected. In August Denktaş attempted to counter the UN push for reunification by formally proposing a confederation of "equal states," with the UN continuing to patrol the border. That proposal was quickly rejected by most of the international community.

Meanwhile, Greek Cypriot refugees filed suit against Turkey at the European Court of Human Rights (ECHR) over property rights. In its July 1998 verdict on the *Loizidou v. Turkey* case the ECHR confirmed the property rights of the applicant over her house in Kyrenia (Girne) and declared that Turkey, not the TRNC, had violated her property rights and was liable for compensation. The significance of this decision lay not only in the recognition of Greek Cypriot property rights in the TRNC, but also in the refusal to recognize the TRNC as the case defendant.

Approximately 1,400 displaced Greek Cypriots followed the Loizidou example and appealed to the ECHR. In the 2006 *Xenides-Arestis v. Turkey* case, the court, while confirming the property rights of displaced Greek Cypriots, indicated that Turkey should offer redress for the applicants' losses. Pending implementation of general measures, the court adjourned its consideration of all relevant individual applications. This provided Turkey and the TRNC with an opportunity to organize an "Immovable Properties Compensation Commission" as an "effective domestic remedy" to keep Greek Cypriots from directly appealing to the European Court by granting them legal recourse in Cyprus.

Tension between the TRNC government and opposition parties and groups became more severe with Denktaş's decision to withdraw from the talks with the Greek Cypriot side in late 2000. However, observers noted some easing after Denktaş decided to resume dialogue in 2002. Attention subsequently focused almost exclusively on the plan forwarded by UN Secretary General Kofi Annan under which the island would be reunified in a loose federation with the Greek Cypriot and Turkish Cypriot constituent states retaining broad autonomy in most domestic areas. (For complete details on the Annan plan, see Current issues in the entry on Cyprus.) In December 2002 the president of the Republic of Cyprus, Glafkos CLERIDES, declared his intention to sign the Annan Plan, if the Turkish Cypriot side was willing to do the same. Denktaş's refusal to sign the plan attested to the intransigence of the Turkish Cypriot side and facilitated the European Council's decision to approve Cyprus's EU membership without resolving the Cyprus issue. Denktaş later tried to defuse mounting domestic and international pressure by showing his commitment to a resolution. A major symbolic move was the opening on April 23, 2003, of the "Green Line" dividing the island. This allowed refugees from both sides to visit their homes for the first time in 29 years. However, the decoupling of Cyprus's EU accession from the resolution, combined with a change of government in the Republic of Cyprus in February 2003, reduced the incentive for Greek Cypriots to endorse the Annan Plan. Having secured EU membership without committing to the UN plan, the new Papadopoulos administration saw EU membership as an opportunity to gain more concessions against Turkish Cypriots.

With the encouragement of new prime minister Talat of the CTP (which had led all parties in the December 2003 assembly balloting), the voters in the TRNC endorsed the UN reunification plan by a 65 percent "yes" vote in a national referendum on April 24, 2004, despite Denktaş's opposition. The plan, however, was rejected by a three-to-one margin by the Greek Cypriot community. Consequently, the TRNC was excluded when Cyprus acceded to the EU with nine other new members on May 1. The EU immediately pledged substantial economic assistance to the TRNC as a reward for the "yes" vote regarding reunification. However, in October Cyprus vetoed an EU plan to establish trade relations with the TRNC. The government of Cyprus indicated that too much assistance to the TRNC might embolden Turkish Cypriots still hoping for additional recognition for the TRNC. The EU membership thus provided Greek Cypriots with additional leverage, as their veto power effectively meant that any EU initiatives in favor of Turkish Cypriots had to meet Greek Cypriot approval first.

The early legislative elections of February 2005 in the TRNC were widely viewed as a strong endorsement of reunification, the Turkish Cypriots clearly having suffered political and economic isolation since Cyprus's accession to the EU. Following Talat's election in April to succeed President Denktaş (who, at age 81, had decided to retire), those favoring unification again saw reason for hope. Negotiations, again centered on the Annan plan, subsequently resumed in an atmosphere that led one observer to conclude that nearly "everyone seems to want reunification." Included on that list were Russia (which had been unconvinced in early 2004), the United States (which sent economic development missions to the TRNC), Greece, and Turkey (for whom the stakes were arguably higher than for the others). Turkey, hoping to begin its own EU accession process, keenly desired an end to the island's split in view of the fact that the perpetuation of the conflict could pose an additional obstacle to its own EU membership. In July, Turkey signed a protocol that would extend its long-term customs union with the EU to the ten new EU members, including Cyprus. However, Turkey insisted its decision did not constitute recognition of the Republic of Cyprus. (Turkey was the only country to recognize the TRNC and the only European country yet to recognize the Republic of Cyprus.)

Despite continued heavy international pressure, no substantive negotiations toward reunification were conducted throughout the remainder of 2005. Further exacerbating the situation, Cyprus forced the EU to withhold $140 million in aid earmarked for the TRNC. On a more positive note, the TRNC assembly in December ratified legislation permitting Greek Cypriots to seek the return of property seized in the north following the 1974 partitioning of the island. (The commission established to adjudicate the property returns [or reparations] was described as fully operational as of May 2006.)

UK Foreign Secretary Jack Straw met with TRNC President Talat in the TRNC in January 2006, prompting strong criticism from Greek Cypriot leaders who accused some EU members of attempting to "legitimize" the northern government. In return, Straw described the current Greek Cypriot stance as "not conducive" to reunification. Complex EU issues subsequently continued to dominate TRNC affairs. Just a day after formally authorizing the start of EU accession talks with Turkey, the EU in February announced it would release $165 million to the TRNC for infrastructure development. Although the Republic of Cyprus accepted that decision, it continued to block the proposed easing of EU trade sanctions against the TRNC. For its part, Turkey pressed for a comprehensive settlement of the island's status rather than a "piecemeal" approach. As a result, even discussions on minor "technical" issues, such as immigration and environmental protection remained stalled in May 2006.

The legislative elections in the south in May 2006 (see entry on Cyprus for details) indicated growing popular support for President Papadopoulos's negative stance toward the UN reunification plan. Collaterally, TRNC President Talat acknowledged that Turkish Cypriots had become "greatly disheartened and pessimistic" over the lack of progress in talks with the Greek Cypriots and the ongoing economic "isolation" of the north. Nevertheless, Talat said his government had not yet reached the point of pursuing additional international recognition of the TRNC as an independent entity, preferring instead to retain its support for the UN plan. On July 8, Presidents Talat and Papadopoulos agreed to a "set of principles" mediated by the UN that recommitted both sides to discussions on the UN plan by, among other things, establishing the "right atmosphere" for such talks. By the end of the month both sides had submitted issues for discussion, but the effort was short-lived. A subsequent plan by Finland to host an emergency summit in November was canceled, the reason reported as "no progress would be forthcoming." Meanwhile, the EU, citing Turkey's lack of progress toward normalizing relations with Cyprus, halted the opening of relevant chapters in accession negotiations with Turkey until the latter agreed to open its ports and airports for use by Cyprus. Reunification was at the core of the dispute between the CTP and the DP that resulted in the collapse of the government in September and the establishment of a new coalition that received official approval in October. The CTP allied itself with the new ÖRP, which had been formed by dissident deputies from the DP and the UBP.

While progress on reunification had stalled in early 2007, the leading Muslim cleric from the TRNC for the first time crossed the demarcation line into Cyprus to meet with the head of the Greek Orthodox Church in an effort to promote the resumption of talks. During the February 2008 presidential elections in the Republic of Cyprus, the incumbent president Papadopoulos was defeated by the AKEL president Dimitrios (Dimitris) CHRISTOFIAS. As Papadopoulos was perceived as a "hard-liner" who had already recommended the rejection of the Annan Plan in the April, 23, 2004, referendum, it was hoped that Christofias's election provided a new opportunity to resolve the Cyprus question. This position was reinforced by the historic links of AKEL with the Turkish Cypriot community of the island and the personal links between Talat and Christofias. A few days after the opening of the Ledra Street (*Lokmacı Kapısı*) roadblock, Talat crossed the checkpoint on April, 11, 2008, and visited Greek Cypriot shops along Ledra Street. His unexpected move had a positive effect on Greek Cypriot public opinion.

The launch of intercommunal negotiations on September 3, 2008, for the first time since 2004 produced short-lived optimism over the possibility of a resolution, given the moderate stance of both Talat and Christofias. However, negotiations proceeded at a slow pace with no deadlines for the drafting of a comprehensive solution, and the issue of Turkey's EU accession negotiations became another stumbling block. The international trade and transport embargo against the TRNC further complicated matters.

A key property rights issue was the focus of attention in April 2009 when the European Court of Justice (ECJ) ruling regarding a case involving British property owners strengthened Greek Cypriot positions on the divisive Cyprus property issue and raised concerns about the viability of the TRNC vacation real estate sector (see entry on Cyprus for details.)

Relations between Nicosia and Ankara have always been a key parameter of TRNC politics, with cordial relations having been maintained between President Talat and the AKP government in Turkey. Their common agenda included the promotion of EU-Turkey relations and the incorporation of Turkish Cypriots in the European Union through a compromise solution of the Cyprus issue based on the UN initiatives. However, following the investigation and subsequent trials in the so-called Ergenekon conspiracy in Turkey in 2008, significant repercussions were felt in the TRNC. (Ergenekon was a clandestine terrorist organizations accused of plotting to overthrow the Turkish government; see the entry on Turkey for details.) Subsequently, speculation arose about the connections of former TRNC President Rauf Denktaş and UBP leader and Prime Minister Derviş Eroğlu to the Ergenekon plot, given their close ties to the key defendants in the case. (In 2009 Denktaş and Eroğlu were under investigation for their possible involvement in the case.)

Economic dependence on Turkey continued. Promised administrative and economic reform did not materialize, however. An oversized public sector increasingly controlled by the CTP-BG government became one of the major obstacles to any domestic reform. A government plan to tighten spending in the public sector met with the fierce opposition of civil servant unions and was eventually withdrawn. This and the fact that intercommunal negotiations were expected to reach a critical point in 2009 prompted the CTP-BG to call for early parliamentary elections in April in an effort to strengthen the standing of the TRNC in its talks with Cyprus. During the campaign, UBP leader Eroğlu called for a strong mandate for a single-party UBP government, arguing that "now it is time for national unity." Meanwhile, CTP leader, Prime Minister Ferdi Sabit Soyer, warned that the UBP campaign claims distorted the reality about the state of the TRNC economy and could threaten the TRNC's integration in the European Union.

Shortly before the April 19, 2009, election Soyer requested that Denktaş and Eroğlu be investigated based on the material uncovered by the Ergenekon investigation in Turkey. Yet no major development took place prior to the elections, which resulted in a majority victory for UBP, which won 26 seats to the CTP's 15, and Eroğlu being named prime minister. Having won a majority of seats, the UBP did not have to form a coalition government. Subsequently, Eroğlu said that "the continuation of Cyprus talks was one of the main policies of UBP" and added that his government would support President Talat to that end and act in unity with Turkey on any progress achieved at the negotiations.

The 2009 parliamentary election highlighted growing Turkish Cypriot discontent with the pro-solution forces in the TRNC, owing largely to the lack of any significant change regarding the trade and transport embargo against the TRNC, combined with the rise of anti-EU sentiment and nationalism in Turkey. While President Talat remained chief negotiator for the Turkish Cypriots, his political clout had been weakened by his "cohabitation" with Eroğlu, according to observers. In addition, the UBP's clear victory in the poll foreshadowed Talat's defeat in the TRNC presidential elections in 2010, in which he was defeated by Eroğlu of the UBP. In the local elections in June 2010 the UBP won 12 of 28 mayoral posts. The CTP won eight, the DP five, and the remaining three were won by independent candidates.

Under an agreement brokered by UN secretary general Ban in April 2011, Eroğlu and Christofias agreed to hold 19 bilateral meetings between July and October in an effort to achieve an agreement on power sharing. In July a new immigration measure was enacted that provided amnesty for illegal Turkish immigrants and made it easier for mainland Turks to immigrate to the island. The measure was expected to provide TRNC citizenship for an estimated 25,000 to 100,000 mainland Turks. Following the July 11 explosion at a Cypriot naval base (see entry on Cyprus), the TRNC supplied electricity and water to the Greek Cypriot community.

The discovery of a large natural gas field offshore of Cyprus led the Greek Cypriot government to authorize drilling by international energy companies in 2012. In response, Turkish companies began exploratory drilling in TRNC areas in April. Both communities called each other's explorations "illegal" and the race to secure energy resources further heightened tensions. Reports from Ankara indicated growing support in the Turkish government for annexation of the TRNC. On May 18 Turkish aircraft were dispatched after an Israeli military aircraft violated the airspace of the TRNC. The incident increased tensions between Israel and Turkey.

In April 2013, Eroğlu invited new Cypriot president Nicos ANASTASIADES to an informal dinner in an effort to restart stalled negotiations on a political settlement. Also in April, Turkey began construction on a $550 million underwater pipeline to supply up to 19.8 billion gallons of water annually to the TRNC.

In June 2013, 8 UBP members of parliament resigned from the party and joined the DP (see Political parties, below), prompting a no-confidence vote on June 5 against the Küçük government. The prime minister and government subsequently resigned and were replaced with a caretaker administration, pending the outcome of new elections. In balloting on July 28, 2013, the CTP-BG won 21 seats, followed by the UBP, 14; the DP, 12; and the Communal Democracy Party (*Toplumcu Demokrasi Partisi*—TDP), 3. Meanwhile tensions with Turkey increased after Ankara openly supported Küçük in the UBP intraparty dispute. The results of the balloting were widely seen as a snub for Turkey. CTP-BG chair Özkan YORGANCIOĞLU was appointed prime minister following the balloting and named a coalition government with the DP on August 30.

POLITICAL PARTIES

Most of the Turkish Cypriot parties share a common outlook regarding the present division of the island. Differences have surfaced, however, as to the degree of firmness to be displayed in negotiations with the Greek community.

Government Parties:

Republican Turkish Party–United Forces (*Cumhuriyetçi Türk Partisi–Birleşik Güçler*—CTP-BG). A Marxist formation at the time, the CTP campaigned against the 1985 constitution because of its repressive and militaristic content. For the 1990 election (at which it lost 5 of 12 seats won in 1985), the CTP joined with the TKP and YDP (see DP, below) in a coalition styled the Democratic Struggle Party (*Demokratik Mücadele Partisi*—DMP). It made a comeback to 13 seats in the 1993 balloting, entering a coalition with the DP that effectively collapsed in February 1995 on the issue of Greek Cypriot property rights but was later reconstituted in May. Two further coalition collapses and reconstitutions in 1995 led to the ouster of Ösker ÖZGÜR as CTP leader in January 1996. A DP-CTP coalition government under the leadership of Hakki ATUN resigned on July 4, 1996, and the CTP became the main opposition party. However, it was supplanted in that regard by the DP following the 1998 legislative balloting, in which CTP representation fell from 13 to 6 seats on a vote share of 13.4 percent. In part, the electoral decline was attributed to the CTP's stance that negotiations should be resumed with Greek Cypriot officials regarding a settlement of the political stalemate on the island. Chair Mehmet Ali Talat ran as the party's presidential candidate on April 15, 2000, and received 10 percent of the vote.

The CTP competed in the 2003 assembly elections under the rubric of the CTP–United Forces (*CTP–Birleşik Güçler*—CTP-BG) to reflect its attempt to broaden its base through extended cooperation with nongovernmental organizations and independent voters on an anti-Denktaş, pro-EU platform. The CTP-BG secured a plurality of 19 seats in the 2003 balloting on a vote share of 35 percent.

Talat subsequently formed a coalition government with the DP, which continued in office following the February 2005 assembly balloting in which the CTP-BG's vote share grew to 44 percent (good for 24 seats).

The coalition collapsed in September 2006 following a dispute with the DP over the CTP's demand for a reallocation of ministries based on the additional 2 seats the CTP gained in assembly by-elections in June, and more significantly, over reunification. Prime Minister Soyer criticized the DP for its hard-line positions in negotiations with Greek Cypriots, despite pressure from the EU, and for its increasing nationalism. The CTP subsequently formed a coalition with the newly formed ÖRP, the alliance being granted official approval by the president and, in October, by the assembly. However, the party appeared to have subsequently returned to the CTP-BG designation by 2008 in an effort to promote the appearance of a broader leftist grouping that extended beyond the party. The close historic links of the CTP with AKEL improved the outlook for relations when AKEL candidate Christofias was elected president of the Republic of Cyprus in February 2008. On June 30, the CTP became a consultative member of Socialist International. However, a decision on granting full membership was postponed due to the objection of the Greek Cypriot Movement of Social Democrats (EDEK).

Meanwhile, on July 9, 2008, the CTP-BG parliamentary group backed Mehmet Ali Talat's proposed solution on Cyprus based on a single sovereignty–single citizenship basis. In the run-up to the 2009 elections, the party stressed that its primary focus was EU membership. Yet lack of any progress in resolving the Cyprus issue, ending the economic embargo, and resolving long-standing economic and social problems led to the weakening of the party's popular appeal. In the April parliamentary elections, the party won 15 seats, down from 25 in the previous election, losing its stronghold to the UBP (below). In the 2010 presidential balloting, Talat was defeated by Eroğlu of the UBP. In June Özkan YORGANCIOĞLU was elected chair of the UBP. He became prime minister following the July 2013 legislative elections.

Leaders: Özkan YORGANCIOĞLU (Prime Minister and Party Chair), Ferdi Sabit SOYER (Former Prime Minister), Mehmet Ali TALAT (Former President of the TRNC).

Democrat Party (*Demokrat Parti*—DP). The DP was formed in 1992 by a group of pro-Denktaş UBP dissidents who advocated a more conciliatory position in the intercommunal talks than the party mainstream. The DP was runner-up in the 1993 legislative balloting, thereupon entering into a majority coalition with the CTP (see above). In 1993 the party accepted the **New Dawn Party** (*Yeni Doğus Partisi*—YDP), led by Ali Özkan ALTINIŞIK, into its ranks. The DP–CTP coalition government ended on July 4, 1996, and the UBP's Derviş Eroğlu formed a new coalition government with the DP as a partner on August 16, 1996. However, the DP moved into opposition status following the December 1998 legislative poll, in which it secured 22.6 percent of the vote. Meanwhile, in September 1998 the DP had reportedly accepted the Free Democratic Party (*Hür Demokrat Parti*—HDP) into its ranks. The HDP, led by İsmet KOTAK and Özel TAHSİN, was one of several parties launched following the 1990 election. Prior to the 1993 election the HDP had joined with two smaller groups, the Homeland Party (*Anavatan Partisi*—AP) and the Nationalist Justice Party (*Milliyetçi Adalet Partisi*—MAP), led by Zorlu TÖRE, in a coalition styled the National Struggle Party (*Milli Mücadele Partisi*—MMP). The DP extended support to Rauf Denktaş in the 2000 presidential election. The DP became the junior partner in the new coalition government announced with the UBP in June 2001. Following the December 2003 balloting, the DP joined an unsteady, CTP-led coalition. Two of the seven DP legislators resigned from the party in April 2004 to protest the government's pro-unification stance, forcing early elections in February 2005, in which the DP gained six seats on a 13.5 percent vote share. Mustafa ARABACIOĞLU won 13.2 percent of the vote in the first round of the April 2005 presidential poll.

The rift between the DP and the CTP increased, primarily over reunification of the island. DP leader Denktaş maintained that the reunification issue could not be resolved until the TRNC is recognized. He also blamed Turkey for allegedly influencing the DP and UBP deputies' decision to resign, a move he said was designed ultimately to further Turkey's bid to join the EU. Following the collapse of its coalition government with the CTP and the party's subsequent move into opposition status, the DP called for early elections, boycotted the initial meeting of the assembly under the new government, and held demonstrations. The DP then became increasingly alienated from Turkey's AKP government due to its alleged support for the coalition government of the CTP-BG (*Birleşik Güçler*) and the ÖRP. In domestic policy, Denktaş supported a "third-way" program that allegedly bridged social and ideological divisions to promote social justice and development. In the 2009 legislative campaign, Denktaş stressed the critical state of the Cyprus issue and focused on economic issues. In the April 19 elections, the party won five seats.

The DP supported UBP leader Eroğlu in the April 2010 presidential elections. However, negotiations to form a coalition government with the UBP were unsuccessful. The party did support the UBP minority government in the May confidence vote in the assembly. The DP subsequently joined the UBP-led government in April 2011. Following the July 2013 parliamentary elections, the DP joined the CTP-BG-led coalition government. Denktaş was appointed deputy prime minister in the new cabinet.

Leaders: Serdar DENKTAŞ (Chair and Deputy Prime Minister), Mustafa ARABACIOĞLU (2005 presidential candidate), Ertuğrul HASIPOGLU (Secretary General).

Other Legislative Parties:

National Unity Party (*Ulusal Birlik Partisi*—UBP). The right-wing UBP was established in 1975 as an outgrowth of the former **National Solidarity** (*Ulusal Dayanışma*) movement. Originally committed to the establishment of a bicommunal federal state, it captured three-quarters of the seats in the Turkish Cypriot Legislative Assembly at the 1976 election but was reduced to a plurality of 18 seats in 1981 and survived a confidence vote in the assembly on September 11, only because the motion failed to obtain an absolute majority. The UBP's former leader, Rauf Denktaş, was precluded by the constitution from serving as president of the party or from submitting to party discipline while president of the republic; nevertheless, he was instrumental in launching the breakaway DP in 1992 after clashing with party leader Derviş Eroğlu, who moved to an increasingly pro-partition stance. The UBP retained its plurality in the 1993 balloting but remained in opposition. Eroğlu took Denktaş to the second round in the 1995 presidential election, winning 37.5 percent of the vote. Staying in the opposition until a DP-CTP coalition government came to an end on July 4, 1996, the UBP rose to power as a member of a coalition government with the DP on August 16, 1996. The UBP increased its vote share to over 40 percent in the 1998 legislative balloting, Eroğlu subsequently forming a coalition with the TKP. Eroğlu ran as presidential candidate for the UBP on April 15, 2000, and won 30.1 percent of the vote at the first round. He withdrew from the race on April 19 prior to the scheduled second round between himself and Denktaş. The UBP-TKP coalition broke down in May 2001, and Eroğlu formed a new government with the DP in June. However, he was obliged to resign as prime minister following the December 2003 legislative balloting in which the UBP was outpolled by the CTP 35 percent to 33 percent. The UBP secured 19 seats on a vote share of 31.7 percent in the February 2005 assembly balloting, while Eroğlu finished second in the first round of presidential balloting in April with 22.7 percent of the vote. Citing the need for "fresh blood" in the party's leadership, Eroğlu resigned as UBP chair in late 2005. He was succeeded in February 2006 by Hüseyin ÖZGÜRGÜN. Three UBP deputies resigned in September 2006 to establish, with a former DP deputy, the ÖRP, which became the junior partner in a new coalition government with the CTP.

At a UBP Congress on December, 16, 2006, Özgürgün was replaced by Tahsin ERTUĞRULOĞLU. The party maintained a hard-line stance regarding the resolution of the Cyprus question and accused the Talat administration of being willing to compromise Turkish Cypriot sovereignty in favor of a solution of the Cyprus question. Despite this stance, official talks with a Greek Cypriot political party were held for the first time on May 27, 2007, when a delegation from the opposition **Democratic Rally** (*Dimokratikos Synagermos*—DISY) visited the UBP headquarters. In fall 2008, Ertuğruloğlu was replaced by Eroğlu, which gave the party a more centrist profile.

The UBP gained government control following the April 19, 2009, parliamentary elections, in which it won 44 percent of the vote and 26 seats, overtaking the CTP, which had won 25 seats in the previous election and only 15 in 2009.

In 2010 UBP deputy Tahsin Ertuğruloğu left the party to run unsuccessfully for the presidency. He remained in the assembly as an independent. In April Eroğlu was elected president of the TRNC. İrsen Küçük was elected party leader to replace him on May 9 and appointed prime minister the following day. In June, the **Politics for the People Party** (*Halk İçin Siyaset Partisi*—HİS), merged with the UBP. The HİS was an Islamist, nationalist, and populist party that was founded by Ahmet YÖNLÜER. Küçük was reappointed prime minister of a reshuffled cabinet on April 6, 2011.

In June 2012 presidential advisor Kudret ÖZERSAY resigned over his leadership of a social movement that reports indicated may emerge as a new political party. Following a no confidence vote in June 2013, Küçük resigned as prime minister. Reports indicated that party infighting between Eroğlu and Küçük contributed to the UBP's poor performance in the 2013 legislative balloting in which the party only won 14 seats, down from 26.

Leaders: Derviş EROĞLU (President of the TRNC), İrsen KÜÇÜK (Former Prime Minister and Chair), Nazım ÇAVUŞOĞLU (Secretary General).

Communal Democracy Party (*Toplumcu Demokrasi Partisi*—TDP). The TDP was formed in November 2007 by the merger of the **Communal Liberation Party** (Toplumcu Kurtuluş Partisi—TKP) and the **Peace and Democracy Movement** (Bariş ve Demokrasi Hareketi—BDH). The TKP was a left-of-center grouping organized in 1976. The six assembly seats won by the party in 1976 were doubled in 1981, two of which were lost in 1985. The TKP joined the Eroğlu government in July 1985 but withdrew in August 1986. In 1989 the TKP absorbed the **Progressive People's Party** (*Atılımcı Halk Partisi*—AHP), which itself had resulted from the merger in early 1986 of the **Democratic People's Party** (*Demokratik Halk Partisi*—DHP) and the **Communal Endeavor Party** (*Toplumsal Atılım Partisi*—TAP). The DHP, which advocated the establishment of an independent, nonaligned, and biregional Cypriot state, was organized in 1979 by former prime ministers Nejat KONUK and Osman ÖREK, both of whom had left the UBP because of dissension within the party. The TAP was a centrist party formed in 1984.

The TKP's legislative representation fell from ten seats to seven in 1990 and to five in 1993. It rebounded to seven seats (on a vote share of 15.4 percent) in December 1998 and became the junior partner in the subsequent coalition government with the UBP. Chair Mustafa Akıncı ran as the TKP's presidential candidate on April 15, 2000, and received 11.7 percent of the vote. Following the breakdown of the coalition government with the UBP in May 2001, the TKP joined the opposition. Chair Akıncı subsequently stepped down as the party leader, and the post was assumed by the former secretary general, Hüseyin Angolemli.

The BDH was a coalition of leftist parties that joined together to improve their electoral opportunities prior to the 2003 legislative elections. The grouping was formed under the leadership of Mustafa Akıncı, formerly the party leader of TKP, which provided the core of the BDH. Other constitutive parties of the BDH included the **Socialist Party of Cypress** (*Kıbrıs Sosyalist Partisi*—KSP) and the **United Cyprus Party** (*Birleşik Kıbrıs Partisi*—BKP). The BDH won six seats in the 2003 assembly balloting but only one in the 2005 poll (on a 5.8 percent vote share).

The TKP's performed poorly in the 2006 municipal and parliamentary by-elections, and the twentieth congress of the party approved a merger with the BDH in November 2007, forming the new **Communal Democracy Party** (*Toplumcu Demokrasi Partisi*-TDP) under Mehmet Çakıcı.

In the April 19, 2009, parliamentary elections, the party won two seats. The TDP voted against the UBP minority government in May 2010. The grouping won 3 seats in the 2013 parliamentary elections.

Leader: Mehmet ÇAKICI.

Other Parties That Contested the 2013 Legislative Elections:

United Cyprus Party (*Birleşik Kıbrıs Partisi*—BKP). The BKP, which was founded by İzzet İZCAN in 2002 and had joined the BDH coalition in previous elections, fielded candidates independently in the April, 19, 2009, parliamentary elections. It was supported by the liberal newspaper *Afrika*. The party did not win any seats in 2009. In 2011 the BKP announced its support for a federal solution for unification. The party won 3.2 percent of the vote in the 2013 parliamentary elections and no seats.

Leader: İzzet İZCAN (Chair).

Other Parties:

Freedom and Reform Party (*Özgürlük ve Reform Partisi*—ÖRP). The ÖRP was formed in September 2006 by Turgay Avcı, former secretary general of the UBP. He was joined by two other UBP deputies and one from the DP to promote a "reformist, democratic, and transparent" government. The four defectors blamed their parties for not working in harmony with Turkey. Observers said the ÖRP would help move the TRNC government toward averting "a major crisis" in Turkey's bid for EU membership (see entry on Cyprus for details). The new party became a junior partner in coalition with the CTP in September 2006, the alliance vowing to pursue political equality for the TRNC and a bizonal solution to reunification. Avcı said he left the UBP because he wanted a party that would promote policies similar to those of Turkey.

In 2006 the ÖRP was given four cabinet ministries when the new coalition government was formed. Strong tension has characterized the relations between the UBP and the ÖRP ever since. The party was also accused of developing ties with Turkey's incumbent AKP. Despite tension and polarization, however, the party won two seats in the April 19, 2009, parliamentary elections. In the May 2010 confidence vote in the assembly, the ÖRP supported the UBP minority government. The party did not participate in the 2013 balloting, and reports indicated that many of its members had joined the UBP.

Leaders: Turgay AVCI (Chair), Erdoğan SANLIDAĞ, Mustafa GÖKMEN.

New Cyprus Party (*Yeni Kıbrıs Partisi*—YKP). The left-wing YKP was formed as a result of a merger between the party, the **Patriotic Unity Movement** (*Yurtsever Birlik Hareketi*—YBH), and some former members of the CTP (see above) in 1998. The YKP had been founded in 1989 by Alpay Durduran, the TKP/AHP 1985 presidential candidate. In 1998 Durduran urged Turkish Cypriot leaders to return to the bargaining table with their Greek Cypriot counterparts.

The YBH favored the unification of the island and equal treatment for all Cypriots, Greek and Turkish. In 2003 the YBH filed suit with the European Court of Human Rights to challenge the electoral process of the TRNC. The party presented Arif Hasan Tahsin as its candidate in the first round of presidential balloting in 1999.

In 2006 the YKP had reemerged as a separate party with Rasih KESKINER as secretary general. The party held its ninth general congress in May 2007, inviting leftist political parties from Turkey, Greece, and the Republic of Cyprus. The YKP boycotted the 2013 parliamentary elections.

Leader: Alpay DURDURAN (Chair).

Reports on the 1998 legislative balloting indicated that a **National Resistance Party** (*Ulusal Direniş Partisi*—UDİP) had received 4.5 percent of the vote, and the recently formed **Our Party** (*Bizim Parti*—BP), led by Okyay SADIKOĞLU, had received 1.2 percent. The BP, described in 1998 as the first Islamist grouping to participate in a TRNC election, supported President Denktaş in his reelection bid.

On August 25, 2000, Arif Salih KIRDAĞ formed the **Freedom and Justice Party** (*Özgürlük ve Adalet Partisi*—ÖAP) to "safeguard bank victims' rights." In December a new centrist formation, the **New Democracy Party** (*Yeni Demokrasi Partisi*), was founded by Eşref DÜŞENKALKAR. In January 2001 the **Liberal Party** (*Liberal Parti*—LP) was launched by Kemal BOLAYIR and Ünal Aki AKİF. The small **Cyprus Socialist Party** (*Kibris Sosyalist Partisi*—KSP) boycotted the 2013 legislative elections.

For more details on the **New Party** (*Yeni Parti*—YP), the **Free Thought Party,** and the **Nationalist Justice Party** (*Milliyetçi Adalet Partisi*—MAP), see the 2010 *Handbook*. For information on the **Solution and EU Party** (*Çözüm ye AB Partisi*—ÇABP) and the **Nationalist Peace Party** (*Milliyetçi Bariş Partisi*—MBP), see the 2009 *Handbook*. For information on the **National Revival Party** (*Ulusal Diriliş Partisi*—UDP), see the 2008 *Handbook*.

LEGISLATURE

A Turkish Cypriot Legislative Assembly, formerly the Legislative Assembly of the Autonomous Turkish Cypriot Administration, was organized in February 1975. Styled the **Assembly of the Republic** (*Cumhuriyet Meclisi*) under the 1985 constitution, it currently consists of 50 members who are elected for five-year terms on a proportional basis in which parties must surpass a 5 percent threshold to gain representation. In the most recent elections on July 28, 2013, the seat distribution was as follows: the CTP-BG, 21 seats; UBP, 14; DP, 12; and Communal Liberation Party, 3.

President: Hasan BOZER.

CABINET

[as of November 5, 2013]

Prime Minister	Özkan Yorgancioğlu (CTP-BG)
Deputy Prime Minister	Serdar Denktaş (DP)
Ministers	
Agriculture	Önder Sennaroğlu (CTP-BG)
Economy, Tourism, Culture, and Sports	Serdar Denktaş (DP)
Education	Mustafa Arabacioğlu (DP)
Environment and Natural Resources	Hamit Bakirci (DP)
Finance	Zeren Mungan (CTP-BG)
Foreign Affairs	Ozdil Nami (DP)
Health	Ahmet Gulle (CTP-BG)
Interior and Local Administration	Teberrüken Uluçay (CTP-BG)
Labor and Social Security	Aziz Gürpinar (CTP-BG)
Public Works and Transportation	Ahmet Kaşif (DP)

INTERGOVERNMENTAL REPRESENTATION

The Turkish Federated State maintained no missions abroad, except for a representative in New York who was recognized by the UN as official spokesperson for the Turkish Cypriot community. The present Turkish Republic of Northern Cyprus has proclaimed itself independent but has been recognized as such only by Turkey, with whom it exchanged ambassadors on April 17, 1985.

IGO Memberships (Non-UN): OIC.

CZECH REPUBLIC

Česká Republika

Note: Early elections to the Chamber of Deputies were held October 25–26, 2013, following the resignation of Prime Minister Peter Nečas in June and the parliament's rejection of the cabinet assembled by interim Prime Minister Jiří Rusnok in August. The CSSD emerged with a plurality of 20 percent of the vote and 50 seats and must try to form a government from six other parties, including the new right-wing, populist Action of Dissatisfied Citizens, which placed second, with 18.66 percent of the vote and 47 seats.

Political Status: Independent Czechoslovak Republic proclaimed in 1918; People's Republic of Czechoslovakia established June 9, 1948; redesignated Czechoslovak Socialist Republic on July 11, 1960; renamed Czech and Slovak Federative Republic on April 21, 1990; present Czech Republic proclaimed upon separation of the constituent components of the federation on January 1, 1993.

Area: 30,450 sq. mi. (78,864 sq. km).

Population: 10,496, 672 (2013E—UN); 10,162, 921 (2013E—U.S. Census).

Major Urban Centers (2011E): PRAGUE (1,268,796), Brno (385,913), Ostrava (296,224), Plzeň (170,322).

Official Language: Czech.

Monetary Unit: Koruna (market rate November 1, 2013: 19.19 koruny = $1US).

President: Miloš ZEMAN (SPOZ); elected by the people in the second round of balloting on January 26, 2013, and sworn in for a five-year term on March 8 to replace Václav KLAUS (Civic Democratic Party), who had completed the maximum of two five-year terms.

Prime Minister: Jiří RUSNOK (ind.); appointed by the president on June 28, 2013, to succeed Peter NEČAS (Civic Democratic Party), who resigned on June 17 amid a scandal involving bribery and illegal surveillance. Rusnok and his cabinet were sworn in on July 10 but rejected by the Chamber of Deputies on August 13.

THE COUNTRY

Situated at the geographical heart of Europe, the Czech Republic consists of about 60 percent of the area of the former Czechoslovak federation. It is bounded by Slovakia on the east, Austria on the south, Germany on the west, and Poland on the north. Incorporating the old Czech "crown lands" of Bohemia and Moravia (plus part of Silesia), the country has a population that is 90.4 percent Czech; small ethnic minorities include Moravians, Slovaks, Poles, Germans, Roma (Gypsies), and Hungarians (Magyars). The inhabitants are to a large extent nominally Roman Catholic but encompass a sizable Protestant minority. Women comprise 44 percent of the paid workforce in the Czech Republic. Following the most recent legislative balloting, women held 44 seats (22 percent of the total) in the Chamber of Deputies, and 15 seats in the Senate (18.5 percent). One of the nation's two deputy prime ministers is a woman. In 2011, in its Gender Index, the UN ranked the Czech Republic 27th out of 187 countries in terms of women's equality.

Although much of the terrain has moderate soil quality, agriculture nonetheless features an extensive dairy sector, as well as traditional strength in the cultivation of grains, potatoes, and hops. The Czech industrial sector, centered in Ostrava and Prague, includes the manufacture of automobiles, steel, armaments, heavy machinery, glass, and footwear. Export of electrical and electronic goods has grown significantly in recent years, with record annual trade surpluses, led by exports of automobiles, computers, and advanced technologies. Tourism is another important source of foreign currency.

In postwar Eastern Europe, Czechoslovakia ranked second only to the German Democratic Republic in per capita income, although Slovakia had long been less affluent than Bohemia and Moravia. (For more information on the Czech economy prior to 2000, see the 2011 *Handbook*.) GDP growth averaged 4.2 percent between 2000 and 2008, while inflation averaged 2.9 percent and unemployment, 7.2 percent. The global economic crisis that began in 2008 caused the nation to slide into a recession in 2009, with GDP declining by 4.2 percent. Meanwhile, unemployment rose to 8.1 percent, though inflation remained low at 1 percent. In an effort to stimulate the economy, the government increased spending, causing the deficit to climb to a record level of 6.5 percent of GDP (see Current issues, below). In 2010 GDP growth resumed at 2.3 percent, while it was 1.7 the next year. In 2011, inflation remained low at 1.9 percent, while unemployment fell to 6.7 percent. GDP per capita was $27,060.

GOVERNMENT AND POLITICS

Political background. From its establishment in 1918 until its dismemberment following the Munich agreement of 1938, Czechoslovakia was the most politically mature and democratic of the new states of Eastern Europe. Backed by the Soviet Union, the Communists gained a leading position in the postwar politics and assumed full control of the country in February 1948.

The trial and execution of top Communist leaders such as Vladimír CLEMENTIS and Rudolf SLÁNSKÝ during the Stalinist purges in the early 1950s exemplified the country's posture as a docile Soviet satellite under the leadership of Antonín NOVOTNÝ, first secretary of the Communist Party and (from 1957) president of the republic. By 1967 growing unrest among intellectuals and students led in early 1968 to Novotný's ouster and his replacement by Alexander DUBČEK as party first secretary and by Gen. Ludvík SVOBODA as president. Dubček, a prominent Slovak Communist, rapidly emerged as the leader of a popular political and economic reform movement.

A reformist cabinet headed by Oldřich ČERNÍK took office in April 1968 with a program that included strict observance of legality, broader political discussion, fewer economic and cultural restrictions, and increased Slovak autonomy under new constitutional arrangements designed in part to provide for redress of economic disadvantages. Widely hailed within Czechoslovakia, the so-called Prague Spring was sharply criticized by the Soviet Union, which, on August 20–21, 1968, invaded and occupied the country in concert with the other Warsaw Pact nations except Romania.

The period after the 1968 invasion was characterized by the entrenchment of more conservative elements within the government and the party and by a series of pacts that specified Czechoslovakia's "international commitments," set limits on internal reforms, and allowed the stationing of Soviet troops on Czech soil. For a time, the pre-August leadership was left in power, but Dubček was replaced by Gustáv HUSÁK as party leader in 1969, removed from his position in the Presidium, and expelled from the party in 1970. Černík retained his post as chair of the government until 1970, when he was also expelled from the party. The actions against the "Prague Spring" leaders were paralleled by widespread purges of other reformers during 1969–1971, some 500,000 party members ultimately being affected. President Svoboda, although reelected by the Federal Assembly to a second five-year term in 1973, was replaced on May 29, 1975, by Husák, who retained his party posts. Husák was unanimously reelected president in 1980 and 1985.

The policies of reconstruction (*perestroika*) in the Soviet Union following Mikhail Gorbachev's assumption of power in 1985 proved particularly difficult for the Czech leadership to emulate, since it appeared the government was being called upon to implement reforms it had opposed since 1968. Thus, the designation in mid-December 1987 of Miloš JAKEš to succeed Husák as party leader seemed to represent a compromise between hard-line conservatives and Gorbachev-oriented liberals. Over the course of 1988, numerous members of Charter 77 (formed by prominent playwright Václav HAVEL and other dissidents to monitor compliance with both domestically and internationally mandated human rights obligations) were arrested, as were hundreds of Roman Catholics. There were notable dissident protests in August 1988 on the 20th anniversary of the Soviet-led invasion and again in October on the 70th anniversary of the country's independence.

As elsewhere in Eastern Europe, Communist power crumbled quickly in Czechoslovakia in late 1989. On November 20, one day after formation of the opposition Civic Forum under Havel's leadership, 250,000 antiregime demonstrators marched in Prague, and government leaders held initial discussions with Forum representatives the next day. On November 22 Dubček returned to the limelight with an address before an enthusiastic rally in Bratislava, and on November 24 Karel URBÁNEK was named to succeed Jakeš as party general secretary. In the course of a nationwide strike on November 28 (preceded by a three-day rally of 500,000 in Prague), the government agreed to power sharing, but an offer on December 3 to allocate a minority of portfolios to non-Communist ministers was rejected by opposition leaders. Two days later the regime accepted loss of its monopoly status, and on December 10 President Husák resigned after swearing in the first non-Communist-dominated government in 41 years, under the premiership of Marián ČALFA. On December 29 the assembly unanimously elected Havel as the new head of state.

The Civic Forum and its Slovak counterpart, Public Against Violence, won a substantial majority of federal legislative seats in nationwide balloting on June 8 and 9, 1990, with Čalfa (who had resigned from the Communist Party on January 18) forming a new government on June 27 and Havel being elected to a regular two-year term as president on July 5. However, during 1991 the anti-Communist coalition, its major objective achieved, crumbled into less inclusive party formations. In November negotiations between federal and republican leaders over the country's future political status collapsed, with the Federal Assembly becoming deadlocked over the issue of a referendum on separate Czech and Slovak states. With the legislature's presidium having called an election for June, a contest between Czech Finance Minister Václav KLAUS and former Slovak prime minister Vladimír MEČIAR emerged. Klaus favored a right-of-center liberal economic policy with rapid privatization; Mečiar preferred a slower transition to capitalism for the eastern republic, where unemployment, at 12 percent, was three times that of the Czech lands. The two retained firm control of their respective regions in federal and national balloting on June 5–6, after which Mečiar returned to the post of Slovak prime minister, with Klaus choosing to serve as prime minister of a Czech, rather than a federal, administration.

In postelection constitutional talks, the Czech side argued that there should be either a properly functioning federation with a strong central administration or a speedy separation. When the Slovak side rejected Prague's concept of a continued federation, Klaus moved quickly for a formal dissolution, which was endorsed by the two governments by late August 1992. Since majority public opinion in both republics opposed separation, the left-wing opposition parties mounted determined rearguard resistance to the governmental plan, which on October 1 failed to obtain the required three-fifths majority in the federal parliament. Amid growing constitutional confusion, Klaus and Mečiar on October 6 drew up virtually identical separation blueprints, to come into effect on January 1, 1993. On November 25 the plan secured the backing of 183 of the 300 federal deputies—3 more than the required minimum—during a historic vote in which several opposition members broke party discipline by voting in favor. Concurrently, a proposal by the left-wing parties that the separation issue should be submitted to a popular referendum was rebuffed.

Following the official birth of the new state on January 1, 1993, Klaus remained as the Czech Republic's prime minister, heading an ongoing coalition of his own Civic Democratic Party (*Občanská Demokratická Strana*—ODS), the Civic Democratic Alliance (*Občanská Demokratická Aliance*—ODA), and the Christian and Democratic Union–Czech People's Party (*Křest'anská a Demokratická Unie–Česká Strana Lidová*—KDU-ČSL). On January 26 the Czech Parliament endorsed the government's unopposed nomination of Havel as president for a five-year term. Other constitutional institutions were subsequently put in place, including a Constitutional Court. Legislation adopted in July 1993 declared the former Communist regime to have been illegal and lifted the statute of limitations on politically motivated crimes committed during the Communist era.

In October 1994 the government was shaken by the disclosure of alleged corruption in the much-vaunted privatization program. Klaus strove to calm public fears, but the left-wing opposition parties were boosted in their claim that overly hasty privatization was mainly benefiting profiteers and criminals. Nevertheless, the ODS took some 30 percent of the vote, well ahead of the other parties, in the November local elections.

Relative political stability and economic progress in 1995 appeared to confirm the Czech Republic as being the ex-Communist state closest to achieving Western European standards, although a substantial gap remained to be closed. In the campaign for legislative elections on May 31–June 1, 1996, the ruling coalition parties stressed the need for continuity, while the left-wing parties called for political change amid widespread public disquiet about the negative social consequences of rapid transition to a market economy. The results yielded an unexpected setback for the government, which was reduced to minority status (99 seats) in the new Chamber of Deputies, while the Czech Social Democratic Party (*Česká Strana Sociáln Demokratická*—ČSSD) quadrupled its support; the Communists also gained ground, although the left fell well short of an aggregate majority. The outcome was the formation on July 4 of a minority center-right coalition of the ODS, ODA, and KDU-ČSL under the continued premiership of Klaus, who also received a conditional promise of external support from the ČSSD. The ČSSD continued its electoral advance in November in the nation's first Senate balloting, securing 25 seats to the ODS's 32.

In the wake of an ODS campaign financing scandal and mounting evidence that the Czech economic "miracle" had been somewhat illusory, Klaus, under pressure from Havel, ODS dissidents, and his coalition partners, submitted his resignation on November 30, 1997, although he agreed to stay on in a caretaker capacity. On December 17 Havel invited Josef TOŠOVSKÝ, governor of the central bank, to form a government, which, as approved on January 2, 1998, included anti-Klaus representatives from the ODS, members of the ODA and the KDU-ČSL, and a number of unaffiliated "technocrats." Subsequently, on January 20, Havel was reelected to a second five-year term, albeit by only one vote in the second round of parliamentary balloting. Eight days later the government won a confidence motion by a vote of 123–71, thanks in part to the support of the ČSSD, which had agreed only upon the condition that early elections be held in the summer.

The ČSSD won a plurality of 74 seats in the legislative balloting of June 19–20, 1998, followed by the ODS with 63 seats. However, neither Miloš ZEMAN, the prime minister-designate of the ČSSD, nor the ODS's Klaus was able to form a majority coalition government following the balloting. Zeman was ultimately appointed on July 17 as a result of an "opposition contract" under which the ODS agreed to support the ČSSD in crucial legislative votes, if necessary, while remaining outside the government. On the following day he announced a ČSSD cabinet, in which many ministries went to former members of the Communist Party. President Havel formally appointed the new cabinet on July 22, and it received a 73–39 vote of confidence in the Chamber of Deputies on August 19, the ODS deputies, as agreed, not participating in the vote. The 24 deputies from the Communist Party of Bohemia and Moravia (*Komunistická Strana Čech a Moravy*—KSČM) also abstained.

The ČSSD won a plurality of 70 seats at the June 14–15, 2002, balloting for the Chamber of Deputies. On July 15 Vladimír ŠPIDLA of the ČSSD was sworn in to head a new cabinet comprising the ČSSD, the KDU-ČSL, and the Freedom Union–Democratic Union (*Unie Svobody Demokratická Unie*—US-DEU). Upon his installation as prime minister, Špidla made it clear that European Union (EU) accession was the top priority. To that end, the government initiated bank reforms, introduced new tax measures, and reduced public spending in order to bring the deficit down to EU standards. However, those initiatives caused a split within the ČSSD (whose left-wingers accused Špidla of caving in to the demands of the rightist elements of the KDU-ČSL and the US-DEU) and discord within sections of the population adversely affected by the cutbacks.

It took three rounds of contentious balloting to choose a new president in 2003, after incumbent President Václav Havel announced his intention to resign at the end of his term. As a result, following Havel's resignation on February 2, the duties of the president were temporarily divided between the prime minister and the speaker of the Chamber of Deputies. Finally, on February 28, Václav Klaus of the ODS was declared the victor over Jan SOKOL of the ČSSD.

President Klaus remained a vocal opponent of the Czech Republic's accession to the EU, but a national referendum on July 13–14, 2003, endorsed membership by a 77 percent "yes" vote. Consequently, the Czech Republic joined the EU with nine other new members on May 1, 2004. However, the cutbacks and other reforms required by the EU appeared to erode support for Prime Minister Špidla, who resigned on June 30 in the wake of the fifth-place performance by the ČSSD in the recent balloting for the European Parliament in June 2004 (the ČSSD won only 8.8 percent of the vote, compared to 30 percent for the ODS and 20 percent for the KSČM). He was succeeded by former deputy prime minister and interior minister Stanislav GROSS, who also assumed leadership of the ČSSD. Gross's new government (also comprising the ČSSD, KDU-ČSL, and US-DEU) won approval by a vote of 101–98 in the Chamber of Deputies on August 24. Gross raised public sector wages while also indicating his administration would attempt to improve the economic climate for the business community.

The KDU-ČSL members resigned from the cabinet in late March 2005 as the result of questions raised concerning Prime Minister Gross's financial affairs in his private property dealings. Gross resigned on April 25, and he was succeeded by the ČSSD's Jiří PAROUBEK, who immediately announced a cabinet comprising the same three parties and many of the ministers who had belonged to the previous government. Paroubek pledged to lower income taxes but also reduce the budget deficit, which to many observers sounded like a standard (but probably unattainable) campaign platform in advance of the legislative elections scheduled for June 2006. Paroubek also promised to push for Czech ratification of the proposed EU Constitution but was unable to secure enough support in parliament.

In a close election that divided the electorate almost evenly between the left and center-right, the ODS won a plurality of 81 seats in the legislative balloting of June 2–3, 2006, followed by the ČSSD with 74 seats. Neither party secured enough seats to form a majority government without including the other or the communist KSČM (with 26 seats) in a coalition. The close split between the two major parties led to a political stalemate over the next seven months and raised the prospect of early elections.

On August 16, 2006, President Klaus accepted the resignation of Prime Minister Paroubek's government and appointed ODS leader Mirek TOPOLÁNEK as prime minister. Topolánek's efforts to form a coalition government with the KDU-ČSL and the Green Party (*Strana Zelených*—SZ) fell apart on August 22. A subsequent bid to form an ODS minority government was nixed by the ČSSD. A ČSSD gambit to form a coalition government with the KDU-ČSL and the KSČM failed in late August.

On September 4, 2006, Topolánek formed a minority government comprising nine members of the ODS and six independents. The new government was rejected on October 3 in a 99–96 vote of no confidence in the Chamber of Deputies; the entire cabinet subsequently resigned on October 11. President Klaus reappointed Topolánek as prime minister on November 8 with instructions to form a majority government. After his negotiations with the ČSSD, KDU-ČSL, and SZ failed to yield an agreement into early December, Topolánek assembled a coalition with the KDU-ČSL and SZ later in the month. However, with the three parties controlling only 100 seats in the 200-seat chamber, the coalition's ability to secure a vote of confidence depended on tacit support from opposition deputies. The new government, with nine ODS, five KDU-ČSL, and four SZ ministers, was appointed by the president on January 10, 2007; it won approval from the Chamber of Deputies (by a 100–97 vote) on January 19, 2007, when two ČSSD deputies were deliberately absent from the vote of confidence and another deputy abstained. Soon after the vote of confidence, the new culture minister resigned to protest alleged pressure from Prime Minister Topolánek to appoint a deputy minister who had been instrumental in lobbying the renegade ČSSD deputies. In early February KDU-ČSL Chair and Deputy Prime Minister Jiří ČUNEK was accused of accepting a half-million-koruna bribe five years earlier while he was mayor of Vsetin, and he faced the prospect of prosecution despite his public denial of any wrongdoing. The opposition parties called for his immediate dismissal from the cabinet in February. Topolánek refused to seek Čunek's resignation, preferring to await action from the KDU-ČSL to remove Čunek, more concrete official charges, or a finding of guilt. But Green Party Chair and Deputy Prime Minister Martin BURSÍK called directly for Čunek's departure from the government. The KDU-ČSL refused to remove Čunek, however, and threatened to leave the coalition if Čunek were dismissed.

In 2007 President Klaus and Prime Minister Topolánek steered the coalition government away from adoption of the text of the EU Constitution rejected by French and Dutch voters in 2005. They argued instead for a renegotiated, stripped-down constitutional text, a position that prevailed at the June 2007 EU summit in Lisbon, where member states agreed to draw up a new "reform treaty" to replace the original text. The Lisbon Treaty had to be ratified by the Czech Parliament. After the first reading in parliament, ODS deputies moved to refer questions of whether the reform treaty was consistent with the Czech constitutional regime to the Czech Constitutional Court. The SZ and ČSSD MPs, however, pushed for approval without further delay.

After surviving the confidence vote in January 2007, Prime Minister Topolánek's three-party coalition government had little or no margin for error since it could only count on 100 votes, 1 vote short of a majority in the Chamber of Deputies. Popular support for the new ODS-led government in early 2007 gave Topolánek some leverage over his chief political rivals. This popular advantage gradually diminished as controversial government proposals, including the U.S. radar base treaty and unpopular health reforms, combined with numerous political scandals, eroded trust within the coalition government and shifted public sentiment toward the ČSSD. Topolánek compounded his precarious strategic situation with several high-profile personal gaffes, coarse treatment of political opponents, and highly publicized points of disagreement with President Klaus. (For details, see the 2013 *Handbook*.)

SZ Education Minister Dana KUCHTOVÁ resigned in October 2007 for failure to secure eligible EU funds in support of research and development for Czech educational programs. The SZ's Ondřej LIŠKA, was appointed to the post by President Klaus on December 4. Deputy Prime Minister Jiří Čunek was forced to resign from the cabinet on November 7, in the wake of renewed corruption charges. President Klaus reinstated Čunek to his previous cabinet positions on April 2, 2008, after Čunek was acquitted.

The ČSSD challenged Topolánek's finance reform legislation in the Constitutional Court, claiming that the measures had been adopted contrary to the procedural requirements of the constitution and that various provisions of the reform law violated the Charter of Fundamental Rights and Freedoms. The Constitutional Court ruled on January 31, 2008, that the passage of the reforms did not violate the fundamental law, but in a later ruling issued in April, the court overturned the unpaid sick leave provision because it failed to protect an employee's right to security during illness. In a third ruling issued in May, the court upheld the fees instituted for physician visits and hospital stays. The fees proved popular with Czech physicians, as they reduced the heavy demand for office visits and cut down on abuse of the health care system. But popular opposition to the health care fees and to new government proposals for reform, including measures aimed at charging tuition for university and raising the retirement age, grew over the course of 2008. Responding to the pressure to scale back, the government agreed to exempt children younger than six years old from the medical fees but declined to exempt older children and pensioners. Nonetheless, the opposition to the reforms culminated in a massive one-day work stoppage on June 24 during which more than 1 million Czechs joined strikes or slowdowns, including many workers from the transport and health care sectors.

In the third round of presidential balloting on February 15, 2008, President Václav Klaus was reelected, defeating challenger Jan ŠVEJNAR in a joint session of parliament by a vote of 141–111. Several rounds of balloting the previous week had failed to yield the required majority in each chamber for one candidate. Klaus was sworn in for a second five-year term on March 7, 2008. Švejnar, a university professor in the United States but a Czech citizen and former economic adviser to President Havel, agreed to run against Klaus with the support of the ČSSD and the SZ. He did not have the backing of the KSČM, however, whose votes were necessary to unseat Klaus. The first round of the election was held on February 8, 2008, in a joint session of parliament and by public ballot (the ODS had moved for a secret ballot, but that measure was defeated). After two inconclusive rounds in which Klaus prevailed in the Senate poll, but Švejnar won the Chamber of Deputies poll, a third round was scheduled for the following day, when the ballots of both houses would be pooled. The February 9 round proved inconclusive as Klaus fell 1 vote short of the 140 votes needed for victory (KSČM MPs declined to vote for either candidate). A new election was scheduled for the following week. On February 15 the election once again had two inconclusive rounds. In the third round Klaus prevailed with 141 votes to 111 for Švejnar.

The parliament passed antidiscrimination legislation in April 2008 that guaranteed equal access to health care, social welfare, and educational benefits without regard to race, ethnic origin, religion, age, gender, or sexual orientation. The Czech Republic was the last holdout in adopting the measures mandated by the EU's European Commission. Consistent with his euroskepticism, President Klaus vetoed the legislation on May 16 claiming it was "unnecessary, counterproductive, and of poor quality." The Chamber of Deputies overturned the veto in June 2009 with 118 votes.

An alarming, growing trend of anti-Roma marches, protests, and acts of violence inspired by far-right ultranationalist movements (and right-wing political parties allegedly affiliated with these groups) gripped the Czech Republic throughout 2008 and 2009. The marches sparked violent clashes between the far-right protestors and riot police as well as the protestors and counter-protestors. In response to the rise in racist rhetoric and a series of violent attacks on Romany families, Czech Roma advocates called for emigration of Romany to Canada to escape the persecution. An attempt by the ODS-led government in early 2009 to ban far-right parties was struck down by the administrative courts for lack of evidence of direct links to the ultranationalist groups. The interim government renewed the effort to suppress groups associated with racist appeals after a much-publicized, near-fatal arson attack in April 2009 on a Romany family in Moravia. In June the government cracked down on selected far-right groups with a series of police raids and by August had arrested four suspects in the arson case with ties to such groups. More raids followed in October as the interim government sought once more to ban the Workers' Party for its alleged links to these organizations.

Two hundred candidates registered to contest the October 2008 Senate elections, in which 27 of 81 seats were up for election, but only the ODS, ČSSD, and KSČM fielded a candidate in each of the districts. The ČSSD sweep in the Senate and regional elections set off a chain reaction of events that substantially altered the leadership structure and strength of the coalition parties.

The Constitutional Court ruled in late November 2008 that the Lisbon Treaty provisions under question did not violate the Czech constitution. The Chamber of Deputies ratified the treaty on February 18, 2009, and the Senate followed suit several months later. Nonetheless, President Klaus refused to sign it, asserting that the treaty was in conflict with the Czech constitution and that it was unnecessary to promulgate the treaty unless Irish voters, who had previously voted it down in a referendum, ratified it with new protocols in place addressing Irish objections. Klaus eventually signed the treaty in November 2009, after EU members agreed to allow Prague to opt-out of the treaty's provisions on fundamental rights.

Prime Minister Topolánek's survived four no-confidence votes in the midst of numerous cabinet-level scandals and public relations fiascos throughout 2007 and 2008. He responded to the coalition parties' poor showing in the Senate elections with a minor cabinet reshuffle in January 2009. Among those dismissed was Jiří Čunek, leader of the KDU-ČSL. Vlasta PARKANOVÁ, minister of defense and KDU-ČSL deputy chair, was named the new deputy prime minister. The ODS-led government finally lost its mandate following passage of a no-confidence vote sponsored by the ČSSD on March 24, 2009. Two ODS and two SZ deputies broke party ranks to vote with the ČSSD and KSČM deputies to pass the motion with 101 votes. The cabinet submitted its resignation immediately thereafter but was not dismissed until a new interim government of nonpartisan experts and civil servants, negotiated by the coalition parties with the opposition ČSSD, was appointed by President Klaus on May 8. Jan FISCHER, head of the Czech Statistical Office, was named interim prime minister on April 9. The interim government won a vote of confidence from the Chamber of Deputies on June 7.

All legislative parties expected new elections to be held in early October, based on an amendment to the Constitution passed in June and signed by President Klaus (see Constitution and government). One independent deputy filed an objection with the Constitutional Court to halt the premature expiration of his mandate, and the court ruled in his favor in September. Parliament immediately passed a new amendment providing for the early dissolution of the Chamber of Deputies by a three-fifths vote of that chamber as well as an amendment to the election law speeding up the permissible scheduling of polls in order to bring early elections in November. The ČSSD, however, refused to support the vote to dissolve the Chamber of Deputies, and the KSČM announced it would abstain from any votes on dissolution.

Elections to the Chamber of Deputies were thus held as scheduled, on May 28, 2010. The ODS and the ČSSD lost votes share and seats in the lower house to the new center-right parties, Tradition, Responsibility, and Prosperity 09 (*Tradice Odpovědnosti Prosperita*—TOP 09) and Public Affairs (*Věci Veřejné*—VV). Meanwhile, both the KDU-ČSL and the SZ failed to reach the 5 percent threshold required for representation in the legislature. Only the KSČM maintained its share of deputies in the new parliament. Although the ČSSD gained the largest number of seats, none of the center-right parties would join it in a coalition government and Klaus, instead, asked Nečas of the ODS to form a government, which assumed office in July.

Constitution and government. Adopted by the then Czech National Council on December 16, 1992, the constitution of the Czech Republic came into effect on January 1, 1993, upon the dissolution of Czechoslovakia. It defines the Czech Republic as a unitary state with legislative power vested in a bicameral parliament, in which three-fifths majorities are required for the passage of constitutional amendments. Considerable executive authority is exercised by the president, who is elected for a five-year term by parliament. The president appoints the prime minister and, in consultation with the prime minister, the Council of Ministers. A new Council of Ministers must pass a vote of confidence in the Chamber of Deputies within one month of the council's appointment.

The National Council decided that much Czechoslovak federal law would continue to apply in the Czech Republic; however, in cases of conflict between Czech and federal law, the former would apply. Following the deletion from the Czechoslovak Constitution in December 1989 of the guarantee of Communist power, a systematic revision of legal codes was initiated to reestablish "fundamental legal norms," including the appointment of judges for life. A revision of the criminal law included abolition of the death penalty and provision of a full guarantee of judicial review, while a law on judicial rehabilitation facilitated the quashing of almost all of the political trials of the Communist era. Commercial and civil law revisions established the supremacy of the courts in making decisions relating to rights. In July 2000 parliament passed electoral revisions that, for purposes of decentralization, established 14 regional assemblies.

On June 15, 2009, President Klaus signed into law a special constitutional bill limiting the term of the sitting parliament and paving the way for early elections in early October 2009. On September 10 the Constitutional Court overturned the law. Soon thereafter both chambers of parliament passed a new amendment providing for the Chamber of Deputies to dissolve before the end of term by a three-fifths vote of the Chamber. The amendment was promulgated by President Klaus on September 13.

In 2012 the Czech Parliament approved legislation for popular presidential elections in which the winning candidate would have to receive a majority of the vote in the first round of balloting or face a run-off election. Similar legislation failed in 2003, despite public sentiment that favored direct elections, given the difficulties associated with the past three presidential elections. President Klaus, after initially condemning the change as a "fatal error," signed the bill on August 1, 2012. The first direct presidential election took place in January 2013 (see Current issues, below).

The Czech Republic has a free press and was ranked 16th out of 179 countries in terms of media freedom by Reporters Without Borders in 2013.

Foreign relations. The collapse of Communist rule in late 1989 led to a transformation of Czechoslovakia's external relations. On December 14 the newly installed non-Communist foreign minister, Jiří DIENSTBIER, declared that the 1968 agreement under which Soviet troops were stationed in Czechoslovakia was invalid because it had been concluded under duress. Subsequently, during a visit by President Havel to Moscow on February 26–27, 1990, the Soviets agreed to withdraw most of their forces by May, with the remainder to leave by July 1991 (a pledge that was honored, amid considerable Czech fanfare, on June 25, 1991).

In September 1990 the Federative Republic signaled its return to the international financial community by rejoining the International Monetary Fund (IMF) and the World Bank; a founding member of both institutions, it had withdrawn from membership in 1954 after a dispute with the IMF over consultation on exchange restrictions. On January 21, 1991, Czechoslovakia joined with Hungary and Poland in withdrawing from the Warsaw Pact (disbanded soon thereafter), while in June of that year the (Soviet-bloc) Council for Mutual Economic Assistance (Comecon) was formally dissolved after the failure of half-hearted proposals for a successor body. (See the 1991 *Handbook* for articles on both groupings.) Meanwhile, Czechoslovakia had been admitted to the Council of Europe on February 21 and had publicly set membership of the European Community (EC, subsequently the EU) and the North Atlantic Treaty Organization (NATO) as key objectives. On December 16, 1991, an EC-Czechoslovak association agreement was signed.

EC membership was the joint aim of the "Visegrád" cooperation bloc formed on February 15, 1991, by Czechoslovakia, Hungary, and Poland. Czechoslovakia also participated in the Central European Initiative (CEI) created on January 28, 1992, and on March 18 became the first former Communist state to ratify the European Convention of Human Rights. President Havel signed a ten-year friendship treaty with the Russian Federation in Moscow on April 1, as well as a collateral agreement with the Commonwealth of Independent States (CIS), settling outstanding issues related to the withdrawal of Soviet troops.

On December 21, 1992, the Visegrád countries concluded a Central European Free Trade Agreement (CEFTA), to which the Czech and Slovak republics were deemed to have acceded at their attainment of separate sovereignty on January 1, 1993. (See Poland, Foreign relations, for additional information about CEFTA.)

On January 19, 1993, the UN General Assembly admitted the Czech and Slovak republics to membership, dividing between them the seats on various subsidiary organs that had been held by Czechoslovakia. The Czech Republic also became a member of the Conference on (later Organization for) Security and Cooperation in Europe (CSCE/OSCE), the European Bank for Reconstruction and Development (EBRD), and the Council of Europe. After some delay, revised association agreements were signed by the EC with the Czech Republic and Slovakia on October 4, 1993. Meanwhile, President Havel had signed a further friendship and cooperation treaty with Russia during a visit by President Boris Yeltsin in August. The treaty was finally ratified by parliament in September 1995.

A priority for the new Czech Republic was to normalize its relations with Slovakia. A temporary currency union between the two countries quickly broke down, while the notional existence of a customs union did not prevent a dramatic slump in bilateral trade in 1993. Progress was made in 1994 in implementing some 30 bilateral treaties and agreements, covering such matters as the division of federal property, debt settlement, and border arrangements. However, disputes persisted, notably over outstanding Slovak debts and the Czech rejection of a Slovak proposal for joint citizenship for the 300,000 Slovaks in the Czech Republic. At prime ministerial meetings on November 24, 1999, and May 22, 2000, the two republics resolved their remaining property and debt disputes.

It became clear in 1994 that neither NATO nor the EU envisaged the speedy accession of the former Communist states. In the case of NATO, the Czech government welcomed, though without great enthusiasm, the alternative Partnership for Peace program (becoming a signatory in March), while instituting major army reforms designed to bring about compatibility with NATO norms and to reduce the Czech military complement from 85,000 to 65,000. In July 1997 NATO invited the Czech Republic, Hungary, and Poland (but, notably, not Slovakia) to join the alliance, and formal entry occurred on March 12, 1999.

The Czech Republic joined with the other Visegrád states in a continuing effort to promote NATO expansion to other Central and East European states. The Czech Republic in particular sought the inclusion of Slovakia in NATO as a means to secure the state's eastern borders and to enhance Slovakia's democratic prospects. At NATO's 2002 Prague summit, seven states from the region, including Slovakia, were invited to join the alliance (formal accession occurred in March 2004).

On January 23, 1996, the Czech Republic formally applied for EU membership despite domestic opposition from the unreconstructed left and the ultra-nationalist right. In December 1997 the EU included the Czech Republic in the so-called first wave of potential new members (see EU article for details), and entry negotiations began in the spring of 1998 in anticipation of accession within five years.

Prague's quest for EU membership had been complicated by the issue of the property of the Sudeten Germans expelled from Czechoslovakia immediately after World War II. German government officials had warned that the Czechs would have to negotiate on this issue, whereas Prague insisted that it would accept liability only for property confiscated after the Communist takeover in 1948. In January 1994 the Czech government adopted a draft law providing for the restitution of certain Jewish properties expropriated after 1938; however, a preamble defined this measure as exceptional and as not providing a precedent for claims in respect to the Sudeten Germans. In March 1995, moreover, the Constitutional Court upheld the legality of the 1945 expulsion of the ethnic Germans and the confiscation of their property. The issue was prominent during the 1996 Czech election campaign, after the German finance minister called on the Prague government to apologize for the postwar treatment of the Sudeten Germans. His remark drew a public rebuke from Prime Minister Klaus and a request from the Czech foreign minister that German politicians stop "lecturing" Czechs about events surrounding World War II. Czech parliamentary debate on the issue was capped on March 5, 1997, when the Senate followed the lower chamber in approving (54 votes to 25) the Czech-German declaration already ratified by Germany. In that document Germany expressed its regret for its occupation of Czech territory, while Prague took a similar stance regarding excessive brutality in expelling ethnic Germans. Both sides agreed not to strain their relationship by pursuing further legal or political claims arising from the war.

At the EU Copenhagen summit in December 2002, the Czech Republic was one of ten states invited to join the EU. In a referendum held on June 13–14, 2003, Czechs approved EU entry on a vote of 77.3 percent in favor and 22.7 against. Differences between the government and the president were evident during the referendum's campaign, as Klaus declined to publicly campaign in support of accession. The Czech Republic joined the EU on May 1, 2004. Throughout 2005 the EU repeatedly warned the Czech Republic that it lagged far behind in adopting directives related to a wide range of economic activity, even initiating proceedings in some cases.

The Czech Republic achieved another milestone in EU integration when it joined the Schengen zone in December 2007; the Schengen treaty provided for the elimination of border controls for citizens of signatory countries, allowing Czech citizens unrestricted travel within the zone without the need for passports or identification cards.

(Tensions arose in 2008, however, when Czech motorists complained about excessive police stops by Austrian and German police beyond the border crossings.)

Belgium, Denmark, and France indicated in 2008 that they intended to open their labor markets to Czech citizens by 2009. In addition, the Czech Republic joined the European Space Agency on June 25, 2008. Currency integration remained the major obstacle to full integration, however, as Czech public deficits remained above the thresholds set for entering the eurozone. Even as the deficits came in line with EU criteria in 2008, the Czech government put off setting a target date for adoption of the euro. Some additional areas of diplomatic friction remained. After receiving a lower carbon emission quota than it requested in 2007, the Czech government sued the European Commission for the first time, citing its projected growth rate as its reason for requesting an emission quota that exceeded Czech yearly emissions. Czech and international human rights organizations criticized the government in 2007 for not ratifying the International Criminal Court (ICC) treaty (the Czech Republic was the last EU holdout, ratifying the treaty in 2009). The Czech government pushed for EU enlargement in 2008–2009 to include the Balkan states, despite the preference of Germany, France, and others for ratification of the Lisbon Treaty before accepting new members.

U.S. President George W. Bush visited President Klaus in Prague (before the June 2007 G8 summit in Germany) to advance the ongoing U.S. effort to secure a radar facility in the Czech Republic as part of a proposed U.S. antimissile defense system. (Washington announced that the system was designed to detect attacks from the Middle East, with the missile interceptor site to be located in Poland.) Bush pledged in return to eliminate visa requirements for Czech citizens visiting the United States. The Russian government had previously reacted negatively to the initiative, calling it a threat to Russian security and countering with threats to target the antimissile facilities with Russian weapons. The controversy surrounding the radar base dominated discussions between Russian President Putin and President Klaus in April on the first official state visit to Russia by a Czech head of state. During the June 2007 G8 summit, President Putin proposed that a Russian radar base in Azerbaijan be used jointly with the United States to detect missile attacks, instead of building the radar facility in the Czech Republic. Negotiations continued with the United States until the Czech government announced that a final agreement had been reached in early April 2008. The parties signed the treaty on July 8, 2008, pending ratification by the legislatures of the two governments. Several days later, amid protests and veiled threats of military countermeasures from its defense ministry, the Russian government announced that oil supplies to the Czech Republic would be reduced by several hundred thousand tons in July. The decline was attributed to technical difficulties, not retaliation for the radar agreement.

A regional dispute emerged in October 2000 over the Temelin nuclear power plant. Austria, in particular, objected to completion of the facility, and in September environmentalists blocked border crossings with Austria and Germany in protest. In December the Austrian and Czech governments reached a measure of accommodation, agreeing to a new EU-supervised environmental impact study (the Melk agreement). However, tension over the plant resurfaced in 2001, with Austria threatening to block the Czech Republic's proposed accession to the EU unless safety issues were resolved. Late in the year Prime Minister Zeman announced that some $27 million would be spent to alleviate the concerns. The controversy flared up again in early March 2007 after Prime Minister Topolánek met in late February in Prague with his Austrian counterpart, Chancellor Alfred Gusenbauer, to discuss Austrian concerns over the plant's safety and management within the terms of the Melk agreement. The two leaders agreed to establish a joint Czech-Austrian commission to oversee operation of the facility. A leak of radioactive water from the facility occurred on the same day as the bilateral meeting; news of the incident was not made public for several days. Reports of the incident sparked new protests from Austrian antinuclear demonstrators at the Czech border and complaints from Gusenbauer over Czech reluctance to share information. A second, smaller leak occurred during a test one week later. Subsequently, the Austrian government announced preliminary plans to file an international lawsuit to enforce the December 2000 Melk agreement or close the plant. In May 2007 the Austrian foreign ministry sent a diplomatic note on the issue to Prague. Continued antinuclear protests by Austrian activists at the Czech border disrupted travel and increased the pressure on the Austrian government to pursue the lawsuit. In response, a Czech ultranationalist party staged a counterprotest at the Austrian border. The Czech government complained that the border protests were disrupting travel and commerce in violation of EU rules.

Prime Minister Topolánek opened a new opportunity to resolve another minor regional dispute in a January 2007 visit to Warsaw, Poland, when he signaled a willingness to settle a disputed border between the two countries. At issue were 368 hectares of farmland across seven municipalities in Silesia.

About 500 Czech troops served in the NATO-led Kosovo Force (KFOR) after that operation began in 1999, and a much smaller contingent has served in Bosnia and Herzegovina. After the Kosovars declared independence from Serbia in 2008 the Czech government, despite internal divisions over the move, recognized Kosovo.

The Špidla administration declined a request to contribute troops to the U.S./UK-led invasion of Iraq in 2003, although the subsequent governments provided a small contingent of support staff to assist coalition efforts in that country. Czech troops have been participating in the NATO Multinational Force in Afghanistan since March 2005. The total Czech deployment to Afghanistan was approximately 720 in August 2011.

The Czech ambassador to Pakistan was killed in a terrorist bomb attack on a hotel in Islamabad on September 20, 2008.

In January 2009 the Czech Republic assumed the rotating presidency of the EU for the customary six-month term. The collapse of the governing coalition halfway into the EU presidency and the initial refusal of President Klaus to sign the Lisbon Treaty undermined the effectiveness of the Czech EU presidency and its initiatives. In August the Czech Republic and Liechtenstein established formal diplomatic relations, overcoming a rift concerning confiscation of property following World War II. Bhutan and the Marshall Islands are the only remaining nations without formal diplomatic relations with the Czech Republic.

Tensions between Russia and the Czech Republic over the proposed radar base continued into 2009. In September 2009 U.S. president Barack Obama cancelled plans to build the radar base, citing a reassessment of the missile capability of Iran, the principal potential threat the defense shield was intended to deter. After the cancellation, the Czech Republic announced in October that it would join a smaller U.S. initiative that included mobile antimissile systems based in Poland. Also in October the EU agreed to allow the Czech Republic to opt out of the Lisbon's Treaty's Charter of Fundamental Rights (see Current issues, below). The following month Klaus signed the Lisbon Treaty after a ruling by the Czech high court that the accord did not violate national law. The Czech Republic was the last country to approve the treaty, paving the way for its implementation on December 1.

In April 2011 the EU decreed that Austrian and German restrictions on the movement of workers from the Czech Republic and other Central and East European EU members had to be eliminated by May. In July the Czech government approved a strategic framework that maintained European integration and transatlantic cooperation as the cornerstone of the nation's foreign policy.

In January 2012 the Czech Republic announced that it would not sign a new EU fiscal compact (the UK also refused to join the accord). The agreement was negotiated in response to the eurozone crisis, and the Czech government asserted that it violated the country's constitution. However, in June the Czech legislature approved the European Stability Mechanism, a $630 billion rescue fund for EU states in the midst of credit crises.

Current Issues. In elections on May 28 and 29, 2010, the ČSSD gained the most seats in the Chambers of Deputies but failed to gain an overall majority. Instead, Peter NEČAS, leader of the ODS, negotiated a coalition agreement between his party and two new center-right groupings, Tradition, Responsibility, and Prosperity 09 (*Tradice Odpovědnosti Prosperita*—TOP 09) and Public Affairs (*Věci Veřejné*—VV). The new government was named on July 13 and had the support of 118 deputies. It included 6 ODS ministers, 5 from TOP 09 and 4 from VV.

Nečas campaigned on an anti-corruption platform that resonated with citizens fed up with a series of scandals. He sought to close the budget deficit, which was 5.9 percent in 2009, through an austerity program that included cuts in childcare subsidies, pension reform, and tax increases in order to meet the EU deficit limit of 3 percent by 2012. The deficit had ballooned under interim Prime Minister Fischer, leading many observers to fear that the Czech economy would collapse along the lines of the concurrent Greek financial meltdown. In September

Nečas offered a budget that would reduce the deficit to 4.6 percent of GDP in 2010, 3.5 percent in 2012, and 2.9 percent in 2013. The budget slashed government spending by 10 percent, prompting demonstrations and strikes by soldiers, police, and medical personnel. It also raised the minimum value-added tax (VAT) from 10 percent to 14 percent.

In the Senate election in October 2010, the ČSSD secured 12 seats and the ODS, 8. No other party gained more than 2 seats. The election gave the ČSSD a majority with 41 senators, with the ODS second with 25. Although the ČSSD attempted to block various government actions and legislation, the coalition maintained enough support in the lower house to override Senate vetoes.

In local balloting on October 15–16, the ODS gained 5,181 seats in the municipal councils, compared with the ČSSD with 4,633, the KDU-ČSL with 3,897, and the KSCM with 3,252.

Disputes within the government coalition following a minor cabinet reshuffle in April 2011 led the ODS, TOP 09, and the VV to renegotiate their governing agreement. Under the terms of the new framework, Nečas appointed Karolina PEAKE of the VV as a second deputy prime minister. In May 2011 opposition groups and labor unions organized massive demonstrations in Prague and other cities against the government's austerity plans. Trade Minister Martin KOCOUREK (ODS) resigned on November 9, following media revelations that he had hidden nearly $1 million in his mother's bank account to keep them from his estranged wife.

By early 2012, the economy had entered recession. Austerity had driven many Czech consumers to buy cheaper goods in neighboring states, driving down tax revenue. In April VV parliamentarians Vit BARTA and Jaroslav SKARKA were convicted of bribery. The convictions led to the break-up of the VV and the formation of a new coalition government under Nečas that included the ODS, TOP 09, and the newly formed *LIDEM* (see Political parties and groups, below). The VV subsequently joined the opposition. The resultant center-right government immediately announced new austerity measures, including a rise in the VAT. The new cabinet survived a no-confidence vote on May 2, but the National Assembly rejected additional tax increases in August.

The center-right government suffered more losses in Senate and regional elections in October 2012. In the Senate race, the ČSSD picked up 13 seats, giving it a strong majority with 48 seats, while the ODS lost 10 seats, reducing it to just 15. The ODS eked out only 12.3 percent of the votes in the local elections and lost 78 seats. The ČSSD took 23.6 percent of the vote, losing 75 seats, while the Communist Party of Bohemia and Moravia added 68 seats with a 20.4 percent share of the vote. Together the two parties won in 11 of the 13 regions and are one vote shy of a majority in the Senate. Analysts saw the outcome as a rejection of the government, corrupt politicians, and growing euroskepticism.

On October 23, 2012, members of the ODS deserted Nečas on a critical bill that would further raise the VAT and income tax rates. Following the ODS losses in that month's elections, Nečas reversed course, saying the government must "stop scaring" the public with austerity measures. In December, Nečas shuffled his cabinet for the second time in 2012, bringing in new ministers to head defense and transportation.

On New Year's Day 2013, President Klaus granted amnesty to 6,300 prisoners, including some convicted in recent corruption and fraud schemes. When Prime Minister Nečas endorsed the controversial farewell gesture, opposition parties called a vote of confidence on January 17. Nečas survived the vote, the fifth since he came to power in 2010.

In January 2013, left-leaning former prime minister Miloš Zeman became the first popularly elected president of the Czech Republic. Zeman campaigned on a populist platform that appealed to what he called the "bottom 10 million," the villagers, farmers, and blue-collar workers who had suffered most from the austerity measures taken to alleviate the 18-month-long recession. His blunt demeanor appealed to voters tired of the numerous political scandals, and he indicated a willingness to work with the EU that was a marked contrast with outgoing president Klaus.

As expected, Zeman finished first in the field of nine candidates on January 11–12, with 24.22 percent. The slate included two former prime ministers, three women, and Vladimir FRANZ, an artist completely covered in tattoos. Former prime minister Jan Fischer was expected to finish second, but instead it was the incumbent foreign minister, Karel SCHWARTZENBERG, with 23.41 percent. Zeman won the run-off on January 25–26 with 54.8 percent. He immediately clashed with Schwartzenberg, insisting that Livia KLAUSOVÁ, the Slovak-born outgoing first lady, be appointed ambassador to Slovakia and blocking other appointments until he got his way. The new president also regularly invoked his margin of victory, arguing that he has a stronger voter mandate than any political party. Zeman signed the European Stability Mechanism on April 8.

On June 11 Prime Minister Nečas announced that his wife of 25 years had agreed to an uncontested divorce. On June 12 and 13, over 400 police raided government offices, netting $8 million in cash, dozens of kilograms of gold, and reams of documents. Six people were arrested, including the prime minister's chief of staff, Jana NAGYOVÁ, the current head of military intelligence, and his predecessor. The extensive list of charges focused on two areas. First, Nagyová allegedly offered jobs in partially state-owned companies to three MPs who had opposed the VAT increase in return for their quitting parliament, thus allowing the tax hike to pass. Second, Nagyová allegedly ordered the national military intelligence service to spy on three individuals—including the prime minister's estranged wife. The latter news fueled long-standing rumors that Nečas and Nagyová had more than a professional relationship.

Within days, the junior coalition partner parties abandoned Nečas, and the ČSSD threatened a no confidence vote if Nečas did not resign. The prime minister submitted his resignation on June 17 and also stepped down as head of the ODS. He seemed to confirm the rumors about Nagyová, saying, "I am fully aware how the twists and turns of my personal life are burdening the Czech political scene and the Civic Democratic Party." The ODS put forward Miloslava NĚMCOVÁ, the president of the Chamber of Deputies, as their choice to replace Nečas.

President Zeman ignored both the nomination and the ČSSD's call for new elections and appointed Jiří RUSNOK (independent) prime minister as well as a 15-person "government of experts." Zeman insisted that the new appointments were qualified technocrats, but critics denounced them as political cronies of the president. They also accused the president of trying to circumvent the legislative branch. On July 16, Rusnok's government raised the minimum wage, the first increase since 2007. The Chamber of Deputies voted 96–92 on July 17 to dissolve the parliament, falling short of the 120 needed. On August 7, parliament rejected Rusnok and his cabinet, 100–93. Both submitted their resignations on August 13. Zeman could decline to appoint a replacement and let Rusnok's government stay on as a caretaker government until May 2014, when elections are due, or parliament could opt for a snap election. Members of TOP 09 announced plans to draft a constitutional amendment limiting the powers of the president.

Ironically, the downfall of Nečas appeared to indicate the success of his anti-corruption drive. After three years of investigations, the police are no longer afraid to enforce the rule of law within the highest echelons of power. However, on July 17, the Supreme Court ruled that the three MPs were entitled to immunity protection for any deal made while they were in office.

POLITICAL PARTIES AND GROUPS

From 1948 to 1989 Czechoslovakia was under effective one-party rule, although the National Front of the Czechoslovak Socialist Republic (*Národní Fronta*—ČSR), controlled by the Communist Party (*Komunistická Strana Československa*—KSČ), included four minor parties in addition to trade-union, farmer, and other groups. Termed by its most visible leader, Václav Havel, as a "temporary organization" to assist in the transition to democratic rule, the Civic Forum (*Občanské Fórum*—OF) was formally launched by a number of anti-Communist human rights groups on November 19, 1989; nine days later, in conjunction with its Slovak counterpart, it negotiated the settlement under which the KSČ agreed to give up its monopoly of power. Having won the June 1990 general election, the OF in February 1991 split into two wings, a majority of its leadership later voting to establish the Civic Democratic Party (ODS), while others participated in the launching of the Civic Movement (see under ČSNS, below).

During 1992, specifically Czech and Slovak parties became far more influential than those attempting to maintain federal constituencies, thus setting the stage for the breakup of the federal system at the end of 1992. On the establishment of the independent Czech Republic on January 1, 1993, the parties that had claimed a federal identity ceased to do so.

Parliamentary Parties:

Civic Democratic Party (*Občanská Demokratická Strana*—ODS). The ODS resulted from the inability of the Civic Forum leadership in early 1991 to transform the somewhat diffuse movement into a formal party. Intensely anticommunist, the ODS quickly built a strong organization and concluded an electoral alliance with the Christian Democratic Party (*Křesťansko-Demokratická Strana*—KDS), which had originated in the mid-1980s as an unofficial ecumenical Christian group calling for political pluralism and had been registered as a party in December 1989 under the leadership of Václav BENDA, a leading dissident in the Communist era. In the June 1992 election the ODS/KDS became the leading formation both at the federal level and in the Czech National Council, ODS leader Václav Klaus heading the Czech regional administration. Upon formal separation from Slovakia on January 1, 1993, the Czech coalition headed by the ODS became the government of the independent Czech Republic, with Klaus continuing as prime minister.

In November 1995 the ODS formally merged with the KDS under the ODS rubric, although five of the ten KDS deputies preferred to join the KDU-ČSL. The ODS lost ground in the spring 1996 balloting for the Chamber of Deputies, falling to 68 seats, but Klaus was able to form a minority coalition. However, allegations of irregularities regarding campaign finances intensified in 1997, contributing to the collapse of the Klaus government in late November. Klaus was reelected chair at the ODS Congress in December, and he finally decided that the party would not participate in the "transitional" government led by Josef Tošovský. Many party dissidents, reportedly upset with Klaus's autocratic style and the alleged financial improprieties, objected to the chair's directive, and four ODS members accepted positions in the January 1998 government. Anti-Klaus legislators subsequently resigned from the ODS to form the new Freedom Union (see US-DEU, below), and several cabinet members reportedly also left the party. Klaus was unable to forge a coalition government following the June 1998 legislative balloting (at which the ODS secured 63 seats, second to the ČSSD) and subsequently endorsed an "opposition contract" that permitted installation of a ČSSD minority government.

Following the November 2000 partial Senate election, the ODS held 22 seats in the upper house, second to the Quad Coalition (see KDU-ČSL, below). In regional assembly contests, the party won control of six and tied the Quad Coalition in a seventh. In the June 2002 Chamber of Deputies elections, the ODS won 58 seats and continued as the leading opposition party. Klaus resigned as party leader on November 2, 2002, to run for the presidency and was replaced at a party conference by Mirek Topolánek on December 15. After three contentious rounds of balloting in parliament, Klaus was elected president on February 28, 2003. The ODS dominated the balloting in 2004 for the country's 13 regional councils (established in 2000) with 36 percent of the vote.

In the run-up to the 2006 legislative elections, Topolánek's platform emphasized tax reform, with implementation of a 15 percent flat tax rate for the VAT, personal income, and corporate income taxes. He also promised increased anticorruption measures.

The ODS won a plurality in the June 2006 Chamber of Deputies election with 81 seats on a 35.4 percent vote share. Topolánek's subsequent struggle to form a majority government generated tension between him and President Klaus, and the latter questioned publicly whether the government appointed in January 2007 would survive long.

In March 2007 Topolánek announced that Czech conservative MEPs (the ODS had nine European Parliament seats in 2007) would form an alliance with British conservatives to create a new parliamentary group starting in 2009. News reports in the same month detailed that the ODS was cooperating with the KSČM in 65 municipal governments despite a ban against cooperation with the communists at the local level issued by the ODS leadership in November 2006.

President Klaus announced in February 2007 that he would seek a second presidential term. Despite initial concerns about Klaus's earlier public statements deriding the survival chances of the Topolánek premiership, by May the ODS parliamentary members had closed ranks and voted unanimously in their caucuses to support his candidacy. At a national party congress held in Prague in November, the ODS MPs reaffirmed their unanimous support for Klaus. Party leader Topolánek addressed the congress to defend the ODS-led government's performance and appeal for an end to infighting. He also emphasized that there should be no cooperation with communist parties, even in local government coalitions.

At an ODS national conference in April 2008 Topolánek again defended the party's record in government, claiming that the ODS ministers had defended the party's policy program but had to moderate some goals to accommodate coalition partners. Topolánek publicly criticized ODM Deputy Vlastimil TLUSTÝ in early June 2008, suggesting that Tlustý was no longer welcome in the party after obstructing the finance reforms in August 2007 and derailing legislation on restitution to the Catholic Church in 2008.

Tlustý was back in the news in September when he collaborated with investigative journalists to expose the activities of fellow ODS delegate Jan MORAVA, who allegedly sought sensitive information that could be used to compel MPs in the coalition parties (including Tlustý and SZ MP Olga ZUBOVÁ) to vote with the government. Morava resigned from his seat in parliament on September 8. Another ODS deputy closely allied with Tlustý, Juraj RANINEC, resigned from the party (he remained an MP) the following week in protest over the party's response to the scandal. A third deputy, Jan SCHWIPPEL, followed suit in quitting the ODS but remaining in parliament as an unreliable vote for the government. The internal dissention and resignations weakened the tenuous ODS position in the Chamber of Deputies, making it more difficult for the ODS-led government to survive future no-confidence motions.

The ODS won only three races in the October 2008 Senate elections and was soundly defeated by the opposition parties in many of the regional elections, a disastrous showing for Topolánek in his bid to maintain control of the government and lead the national party. Pavel BEM, mayor of Prague and a rival for the ODS leadership, called for an extraordinary party congress and signaled his willingness to unseat Topolánek as party leader. The embattled Topolánek responded to the mounting internal criticism by saying he would resign if new leadership emerged that could forge consensus in the party ranks, but Bem in his view was not that leader. At the party congress in December Topolánek was able to consolidate support from the regional party bosses and beat back Bem's challenge, securing reelection with 284 votes over 162 for Bem. Meanwhile, President Klaus announced that he was leaving the party due to its ideological move toward the center.

Despite his resilience in retaining leadership of the party, Topolánek's ability to maintain discipline within the ODS parliamentary group and the reeling coalition partners was fatally compromised in 2008. The opposition parties brought down the government with a no-confidence measure in late March 2009.

In the European Parliament elections in June 2009 the ODS rebounded somewhat as it won nine seats with a 31 percent vote share. Shortly thereafter, the ODS formed a new right-wing faction in the European Parliament with the British Conservative Party and the Polish Law and Justice Party.

In March 2010 Petr NEČAS was elected to succeed Topolánek as party leader. In the legislative balloting in May, the ODS placed second with 20.2 percent of the vote and 53 seats, compared with 81 seats following the 2006 balloting. Nonetheless, Nečas was appointed prime minister and negotiated an agreement with TOP 09 and the VV to form a center-right coalition government. Following local balloting in October, the ODS and ČSSD formed a controversial coalition city government that was criticized by members of both parties. Nečas formed a new government in May 2012 but resigned in disgrace in June 2013.

Leaders: Martin Kuba (Acting Chair), Miroslava NĚMCOVÁ (Deputy Leader), Pavel BLAŽEK, Tomáš CHALUPA, Jiří POSPÍŠIL (Vice Chairs).

TOP 09. This new party, whose initials stand for "tradition, responsibility, and prosperity" (*Tradice Odpovědnosti Prosperita*), was formed in mid-2009 after the fall of the coalition government and its replacement by an interim government. Most of the new party's leadership split from the KDU-ČSL to join TOP 09 after Cyril Svoboda regained leadership of the KDU-ČSL, most notably TOP 09 founder Miroslav Kalousek. The party soon attracted other disaffected KDU-ČSL leaders and former ministers, including former defense minister Vlasta Parkanová. Karel Schwarzenberg, the former foreign minister, joined TOP 09 and was immediately designated to head the new party's ticket for the autumn 2009 legislative elections, given his stature as the most popular former member of the Topolánek cabinet.

The party's ideological orientation is center-right, with a platform that emphasizes social conservatism, fiscal responsibility, and Christian values. Soon after forming, the party worked out an alliance with the **Movement for Mayors and Independents.**

An influence-peddling scandal ensnared MP Ladislav ŠUSTR in September 2009. Šustr, one of the KDU-ČSL deputies who joined TOP 09 in 2009, was alleged by an investigative news report to have agreed to alter lottery legislation in exchange for a large contribution to party coffers. He resigned immediately from parliament and claimed he acted without knowledge of the party.

TOP 09 received 16.7 percent of the vote in the May 2010 chamber elections. It secured 41 seats to become the third largest party in the legislature and joined the ODS-led coalition government with party leader Schwarzenberg becoming deputy prime minister and minister of foreign affairs. In Senate balloting in October, TOP 09 lost 4 seats, lowering its total to 5. In 2012 TOP 09 was the only member of the governing coalition to support Czech participation in the EU fiscal compact. In February Jan BŘEZINA, an influential member of the KDU-ČSL, defected to TOP 09.

Leaders: Karel SCHWARZENBERG (President), Miroslav KALOUSEK (First Vice President), Jaromír DRÁBEK (Vice President), Pavol LUKŠA, Helena LANGŠÁDLOVÁ, Marek ŽENÍŠEK (Vice Presidents).

LIDEM. Loosely translated as "for the people," *LIDEM* is also a play on the initials for liberal democrats. Formed in 2012 by dissidents from the VV, *LIDEM* was led by Deputy Prime Minister Karolina PEAKE and included seven other members of parliament who were formerly in the VV. The grouping joined the ODS-led coalition government in May 2012. It did not contest the 2012 Senate election.

Leaders: Karolina PEAKE (President); Dagmar NAVRATILOVA (Vice President).

Czech Social Democratic Party (*Česká Strana Sociálne Demokratická*—ČSSD). First organized in 1878, the ČSSD was the plurality party in Czechoslovakia's first parliamentary election in 1920 but went underground in 1939. In 1948 it was forced to merge with the KSČ, resurfacing as a separate party in late 1989. It won no seats at the 1990 federal election, after which its Czech and Slovak wings became, in effect, separate parties. In the June 1992 election the ČSSD won 16 seats in the Czech National Council. It mounted strong opposition to the proposed "velvet divorce" between Czechs and Slovaks, arguing in favor of a "confederal union," but eventually accepted the inevitability of the separation. At its first postindependence congress in February 1993, the party formally renamed itself the "Czech" SSD and said it would seek to provide a left-wing alternative to the neoconservatism of the ruling coalition.

Benefiting from public unease over the social consequences of economic transition, the ČSSD achieved a major advance in the 1996 Chamber election, to 61 seats and 26.4 percent of the vote. It opted to give qualified external support to a further center-right coalition, the immediate reward being the election of the ČSSD Chair Miloš Zeman as president of the new Chamber of Deputies. At its congress of March 1997 the party reelected Zeman as chair and endorsed his call for confrontation with the coalition government. The ČSSD supported the transitional government of Josef Tošovský in the January 1998 parliamentary confidence vote with the provision that early elections would be called. The party won a plurality of 74 seats in the June 1998 legislative balloting (on the strength of 32.3 percent of the vote), leading to the installation of a minority ČSSD government led by Zeman, with external ODS support. Objecting to the continuing pact with the ODS, Petra BUZKOVÁ resigned as deputy chair in January 2000.

The ČSSD fared poorly in 13 regional assembly elections in November 2000, winning control of none and capturing only 15 percent of the vote. At simultaneous balloting for 27 Senate seats, the party won just 1, for a loss of 8, leaving it far behind the Quad Coalition and the ODS.

In the 2002 Chamber of Deputies elections, the ČSSD won 70 seats, making it the largest party in the lower house. Vladimír Špidla replaced Zeman as prime minister and chair of the party. Špidla formed a coalition government with the KDU-ČSL and US-DEU. In the October 25–26, 2002, Senate elections, the ČSSD won just 7 seats, bringing its representation in the upper house down to 11 from 15 (compared with 26 for the ODS). In 2003 dissidents within the ČSSD refused to support Špidla's presidential candidate, Jan Sokol, which contributed to the victory by Václav Klaus of the ODS. In response, Špidla forced the leader of the dissidents, Trade and Industry Minister Jiří RUSNOK, to resign. In EU elections in June 2004, the ČSSD came in fifth and won only 2 seats. Špidla resigned on June 26, 2004, and was replaced by Stanislav Gross as prime minister and party leader. Gross stepped down from the premiership in April 2005 in the wake of a crisis over his financial affairs. He resigned as party chair on September 24, 2005. Deputy chair Jiří Paroubek was appointed prime minister on April 25, 2005, and elected chair at a party conference on May 13, 2006.

In the run-up to the 2006 legislative balloting, Prime Minister Paroubek steered the party toward themes of "Security and Prosperity," with promises to reduce unemployment, reform the health care system along the German model, increase public assistance, raise the average annual salary, increase monthly pensions, reduce (modestly) the corporate income tax rate, and increase investment in public infrastructure, research, and development. The ČSSD won 74 seats with a 32.3 percent vote share, an increase of 4 seats over the previous election, but, due to the ODS's gains, the ČSSD was the second largest party in the lower house. After losing the plurality in the chamber, Paroubek offered his resignation as prime minister. However, with no clear majority coalition government in waiting immediately after the election, President Klaus refused to accept Paroubek's resignation. Unable to form a rival coalition government after the failure of the ODS's first attempt in August 2006, Paroubek's standing in the party was further undermined by tepid results in the October 2006 Senate elections (ČSSD candidates won 6 seats) and the actions of two members of the party's parliamentary delegation, Miloš MELČÁK and Michal POHANKA, who broke ranks and deliberately were absent from the vote of confidence for the ODS-led coalition government in January 2007. Pohanka resigned from the party immediately thereafter. Paroubek moved in February to expel Melčák from the party, bringing the ČSSD lower house delegation down to 72 seats. Soon thereafter Paroubek appealed to both former members to continue to support the ČSSD party line in future votes in parliament.

Soon thereafter the party faced a major embarrassment over unpaid legal fees and penalties owed to Zdenek ALTNER, the lawyer who successfully defended the party from 1997 to 2000 in its battle to establish ownership of the Prague party headquarters. Altner claimed his contract, signed with then ČSSD Chair Miloš Zeman, entitled him to over 19 billion koruna for his services plus outstanding interest and penalties. Zeman subsequently announced his resignation from the ČSSD in the face of a legal proceeding initiated against him by the party over the matter. Paroubek repeatedly sought an out-of-court settlement with Altner, but the lawyer refused to make a deal and initiated proceedings to have the party declared bankrupt, which the trial court dismissed. The party countered with a libel lawsuit against Altner in July.

Paroubek emerged from the March 2007 party conference with his leadership position intact, but his support among the delegates was the lowest of all the ČSSD leaders selected, with only 60 percent of the votes. Political observers speculated that Deputy Chair Bohuslav Sobotka was the most likely replacement should Paroubek's support in the party collapse with future missteps.

In a 2007 by-election the party picked up 1 additional seat in the Senate for a total of 13.

The party expelled Deputy Evžen SNÍTILÝ in February 2008 after he broke ranks with the party and voted for the reelection of President Klaus instead of voting for Jan Švejnar, the candidate endorsed by the ČSSD. Snítilý, however, refused to resign his seat in parliament. Petr Wolf announced he was leaving the party deputies group in late June, charging that party leader Paroubek had pressured him to vote for the challenger Jan Švejnar in the presidential election and to pledge to vote against the radar base agreement by threatening to publicly release sensitive information about Wolf if he failed to comply.

Paroubek called a two-day party conference in late May to set the party's policy agenda for the October 2008 Senate elections. The ČSSD, with a sizable and consistent lead over the ODS in public opinion polls throughout 2008, emphasized discipline among its members behind its positions against the ratification of the radar base treaty with the United States, for elimination of the new medical fees, against university tuition fees, and for the reinstatement of child benefits. Meanwhile, former party chair, prime minister, and presidential candidate Miloš Zeman announced that he would consider a presidential bid if parliament changed the rules to permit direct election of the president. In July his supporters officially registered the Friends of Miloš Zeman Civic Association with the Interior Ministry. Zeman subsequently founded the **Party of Civic Rights—Zemanovci** (*Strana Práv Občanů—Zemanovci*—SPOZ) (see below).

In the October 2008 Senate election the ČSSD won an overwhelming majority of the races, securing 23 of the 27 seats. However, in the European Parliament elections in June 2009 the ČSSD won 7 seats, 2 fewer seats than rival ODS, a disappointing result after soundly defeating the ODS in the Senate and regional elections the previous year. Moreover, ČSSD leaders, especially Paroubek, were targeted by egg-throwing protestors at the election rallies. The protests over the party's role in bringing down the ODS-led government prompted the ČSSD to ask the interim government for extra police protection.

Internal leadership of the ČSSD remained relatively stable in 2009. Party Chair Paroubek won reelection at a party conference in 2009. The party did not choose a female vice party chair, however, despite rules requiring at least one woman in the post. After the party's disappointing showing in the May 2010 elections, in which gained 56 seats compared with 74 in the 2006 balloting, Paroubek resigned as party leader. He was replaced by Bohuslav SOBOTKA.

Sobotka was formally elected chair at a party congress in March 2011. Reports in August indicated that Paroubek had left the ČSSD to form a new political party. In May 2012 ČSSD parliamentarian David RATH was caught with $375,000 in alleged bribes in his possession. The corruption scandal undermined public confidence in the party, which had been leading in opinion polls. The ČSSD lost 75 seats in the October 2012 local elections but still was the leading party, with 23.6 of the vote. It also secured a majority in the Senate with 46 seats.

Leaders: Bohuslav SOBOTKA (Chair), Jiří PAROUBEK, Stanislav GROSS (Former Prime Ministers), Alena GAJDŮŠKOVÁ, Martin STAREC, Milan CHOVANEC, Lubomír ZAORÁLEK (Vice Chairs).

Public Affairs (*Věci Veřejné*—VV). Formed in 2001, the VV was initially a small, regional party, based in Prague. The center-right party emphasized fiscal conservatism and anticorruption. In June 2009 investigative journalist Radek JOHN was elected leader of the VV. His fame and reputation helped the party in the 2010 chamber elections in which the VV received 10.9 percent of the vote and 24 seats in the lower house. The VV subsequently joined the ODS-led coalition government and John became a deputy prime minister. In May 2011 John resigned as deputy prime minister, claiming the government did not support his anticorruption efforts. In July Karolina PEAKE was appointed deputy prime minister. Following the conviction of two VV members of parliament of corruption charges, Peake and other leading figures left the party to form a new grouping, **LIDEM,** in May 2012. The VV subsequently joined the opposition. Vit BÁRTA won 80 of 98 to become party chairman at the February 2013 party congress.

Leaders: Vit BÁRTA (Chair), Petra QUITTOVÁ (First Vice Chair), Michael BABAK, Jiří LEXA (Vice Chairs), Radek JOHN (Honorary Chair).

Communist Party of Bohemia and Moravia (*Komunistická Strana Čech a Moravy*—KSČM). Established under its present name in March 1990, the KSČM is descended from the Communist Party of Czechoslovakia (KSČ) founded in 1921 by the pro-Bolshevik wing of the ČSSD. The KSČ was the only East European Communist Party to retain legal status in the 1930s, until it was banned in the aftermath of the 1938 Munich agreement. Its leaders returned from Moscow at the end of World War II as the dominant element of a Soviet-sponsored National Front and effectively seized sole power in 1948. In March 1990, as non-Communists took over leading government posts, the Czech component of the KSČ relaunched itself as the KSČM, with a socialist rather than a Marxist-Leninist orientation. At the June 1990 multiparty election, the Communists took second place in the Czech National Council, winning 32 of the 200 seats. They then went into opposition for the first time since 1945, amid a continuing exodus of party members.

In mid-1991 the KSČ was officially dissolved, but both the KSČM and its Slovak counterpart remained "Czechoslovak" in orientation. In the June 1992 election the KSČM-led Left Bloc won 35 of the 200 Czech National Council seats and subsequently resisted dissolution of the federation. Following the creation of the independent Czech Republic in January 1993, the party experienced much internal strife, including the resignation of Jiří Svoboda as leader over the rejection of his proposal to drop "Communist" from the party's title. He was replaced in June 1993 by the conservative Miroslav GREBENÍČEK, whose election precipitated the formation of the two breakaway factions that later reorganized as the SDS (see below). The secessions meant that the KSČM had lost a majority of its ten deputies elected in 1992; however, it recovered strongly in the 1996 balloting, winning 22 seats, whereas the various breakaway groups failed to obtain representation. The KSČM fared even better in the 1998 balloting for the Chamber of Deputies, winning 24 seats on the strength of 11 percent of the vote. Following the November 2000 Senate election, it held 3 seats (a loss of 1) in the upper house.

In balloting for the Chamber of Deputies in June 2002, the KSČM won 41 seats. It joined the conservative ODS as the opposition to the coalition government. In the 2004 elections for the European Parliament, the party exceeded analysts' expectations, apparently because of growing popular discontent with the coalition government. The KSČM received the second-largest number of votes with 20.3 percent of the total vote and won 6 seats. Considered one of the "least reformed" communist parties among the countries recently admitted to the EU, the KSČM in 2005 campaigned against the proposed new EU Constitution. The party took an important modernizing step when on September 20, 2005, hard-line leader Miroslav Grebeníček stepped down as chair. Vojtech Filip was elected chair on October 1, defeating rival Vaclav EXNER for the post.

Filip led the party into the 2006 elections with public assurances that the KSČM would not seek to nationalize Czech industries or assets or engage in a "bloody" class war. However, he pledged that the party would seek withdrawal from NATO, increased security for workers, and expanded public housing with 50,000 new apartments every year. The KSČM won 26 seats with a 12.8 percent vote share, a step back from its 2002 showing, but it remained the third largest party in the lower house. It subsequently joined the ČSSD in opposition to the ODS-led coalition government. After the October 2006 Senate election the KSČM had 2 seats in the Senate. In a 2007 Senate by-election the party picked up 1 additional seat.

Filip made controversial remarks at a February 2007 KSČM central committee meeting during which he inquired whether the party's members were ready "to initiate and take the lead in possible revolutionary processes" and called for a return to a Leninist ideology. His remarks prompted a police investigation and condemnation from anticommunist political opponents.

Political observers contended that the party was facing a potential membership crisis: The party's declining percentage of the national vote and its average member age of over 70 years indicate that the KSČM is failing to attract younger Czech voters dissatisfied with aspects of capitalism and globalization. In this regard, the party has lost ground to the ČSSD and the Green Party.

KSČM Deputy Josef Vondruška was charged with abuse of office in 2008 for the mistreatment of political prisoners during the 1980s at the Minkovice jail. The Chamber of Deputies voted in late 2007 to remove his immunity to prosecution.

The KSČM leadership created controversy once again in late February by announcing that it embraced the ideals of the party circa 1948, the time of the Communist putsch, which the party defended as a constitutionally sound revolution. The Communist leaders acknowledged, however, that this era contained "inadequacies and tragic deformations."

The KSČM held a party congress on May 17, 2008, where Vojtěch Filip was reelected as party leader. Filip was challenged by three candidates for the leadership but won handily with 176 of 275 total votes.

The KSČM won one Senate race in the October 2008 election, maintaining a total of three seats in that chamber. In the elections for the European Parliament in June 2009 the KSČM won 14 percent of the vote and four seats. An investigative news report published in September alleged that two KSČM vice party chairs were implicated in an influence-peddling scheme. Party leader Filip called for the resignation of Jiří Dolejš and Čeněk Milota soon thereafter.

The party received 11.3 percent of the vote in the May 2010 legislative balloting and maintained its 26 seats in the Chamber of Deputies. In July the government asked the interior ministry to investigate whether the KSČM should be banned following a Senate report that was highly critical of the party's actions since the demise of the communist government.

Leaders: Vojtěch FILIP (Chair), Petr SIMUNEK, George DOLEJŠ, Miloslava VOSTRÁ (Vice Chairs), Pavel KOVARČÍK, Zdenék LEVÝ, Otakar ZMÍTKO.

Northern Bohemians (*Severočeši.cz*). The Northern Bohemians is a small regional party in Northern Bohemia. It surprised election pundits by winning two seats in the October 2010 Senate elections.

Leader: František RIBA (Chair).

Other Parties That Contested the 2010 Elections:

Christian and Democratic Union–Czech People's Party (*Křest'anská a Demokratická Unie–Česká Strana Lidová*—KDU-ČSL). The KDU-ČSL is descended from the Czechoslovak People's Party that had been founded in 1918, banned in 1938, and revived in 1945 as a component of the Communist-dominated National Front. From late 1989 the People's Party had sought to reestablish its independence, joining the broad-based coalition government appointed in December. The party contested the election of June 1990 in an alliance that won 19 seats in the Czech National Council. Included in the postelection Czech coalition government, the alliance suffered defections in late 1991, and in April 1992 it was officially redesignated as the KDU-ČSL, which in the June 1992 election won 15 seats in the Czech National Council. The party became a member of the ODS-led Czech coalition government that took the republic to independence in

January 1993, after which it no longer advocated autonomy for Moravia, from which it had long drawn the bulk of its support.

In late 1995 the KDU-ČSL was strengthened by the adhesion of five deputies of the KDS (see ODS, above), who rejected the latter's decision to merge with the dominant ODS; however, the party fell back to 18 seats in the 1996 Chamber balloting.

The KDU-ČSL increased its representation to 20 in the 1998 balloting for the Chamber of Deputies. Josef LUX, chair of the party, subsequently resigned his post and withdrew from political life in September due to illness.

The KDU-ČSL was a founding member of the center-right Quad Coalition that was formed prior to the November 1998 Senate and municipal elections. (Other members included the US, ODA, and the DEU. See the 2007 *Handbook* for additional information.) Jan Kasal was elected KDU-ČSL chair in May 1999, with Kasal then being succeeded by Cyril Svoboda at a May 2001 party conference. In the elections for the Chamber of Deputies in 2002, the KDU-ČSL won 21 seats.

At a party conference on November 8, 2003, Miroslav Kalousek defeated incumbent party leader Svoboda by a vote of 164 to 131 to become the chair of the KDU-ČSL. Kalousek positioned the party for the 2006 elections with assurances that the KDU-ČSL would work to hold the line on taxes and prevent any communist influence in the government.

In the June 2006 Chamber of Deputies election, the KDU-ČSL won only 13 seats on a 7.2 percent vote share. Following the election, the KDU-ČSL engaged in unsuccessful negotiations first with the ODS and SZ and then the ČSSD and the KSČM to form a government, before finally entering into the coalition agreement with the ODS and SZ in late December 2006. The poor election performance and failed negotiations with the ČSSD and the KSČM proved costly to Kalousek; he resigned as chair in late August after the KDU-ČSL senior leadership balked at joining any coalition involving the communist KSČM. Jan Kasal took over on an interim basis until Jiří Čunek, a senator, was selected chair at a party congress in December 2006. Čunek brought the party into coalition with the ODS and Green Party and was named deputy prime minister in the new cabinet, one of the five cabinets posts for the KDU-ČSL.

Corruption allegations surfaced against Čunek in early 2007, creating more tension within the party. Čunek was accused by a former aide of accepting a bribe from a real estate developer while mayor of Vsetin, the town where he rose to national prominence after evicting Roma rent squatters. As the investigation got under way, Čunek issued a public denial and received the full support of the party presidium in mid-February, but some party members expressed frustration that the case was hurting the party's public image and standing in the coalition government. The party's national committee issued a one-line statement of support for Čunek on March 6, but several KDU-ČSL senators issued a public statement asking Čunek to step down until the investigation was completed. Political observers noted that with only 7 percent of the vote in the 2006 election and declining public support in the wake of the allegations, the KDU-ČSL was in danger of slipping below the 5 percent threshold in future elections. Nevertheless, the party's official position was that Čunek would remain chair and that any move to remove him from the cabinet would threaten the KDU-ČSL's support for the government. The charges against Čunek were dropped in August, but a new corruption investigation prompted him to resign from the cabinet on November 1. He was reinstated to his previous cabinet positions by President Klaus on April 2, 2008, after he was cleared by the investigation and a subsequent audit of his finances.

At a party conference in Pardubice in April Čunek's leadership mandate was reaffirmed, as only 5 of 300 delegates voted for a proposal to elect a new party chair. Čunek's address to the conference blamed disunity within the party for its decline in popular support and apologized for the ordeal party members experienced because of his investigations on bribery charges. The party also chose its list of 15 candidates for the European parliamentary elections in 2009.

The KDU-ČSL generally has supported the ODS-led coalition in most areas. It did take a more cautious approach to the question of recognition of Kosovo's independence from Serbia and was against proposals for direct election of the president if the powers of the office were thereby expanded. The KDU-ČSL platform has included efforts to restrict abortion, a position at odds with the coalition partners and counter to the weight of public opinion.

The KDU-ČSL did not win any additional seats in the October 2008 Senate election. Party leader Čunek was dismissed from the cabinet in January. In the European Parliament elections in June 2009 the KDU-ČSL held on to its two seats with 7.6 percent of the vote. Meanwhile, at the May 30 party conference Cyril Svoboda returned to leadership of the party. Soon thereafter, many members left the KDU-ČSL to join a new party, **TOP 09**, formed by former KDU-ČSL leader Miroslav Kalousek along with four other deputies. Jiří STODŮLKA, the party's general secretary, resigned in September after public disclosure by the media that Stodůlka was implicated in an influence peddling investigation.

In the May 2010 legislative balloting, the KDU-ČSL received only 4.4 percent of the vote and failed to gain any seats in the chamber, the first instance since 1990 that the party was not represented in the lower house. Svoboda resigned as a result of the KDU-ČSL's performance. Deputy chair Michaela ŠOJDROVÁ took over as interim leader of the party. She was replaced by Pavel Bělobrádik.

Leaders: Pavel BĚLOBRÁDIK (Chair), Marian JUREČKA, Zuzana ROITHOVÁ, Jan BARTOŠEK, Roman LINEK, Klára LIPTÁKOVÁ (Vice Chairs), Pavel HORÁVA (Secretary General).

Green Party (*Strana Zelených*—SZ). Originally founded in 1989 and prominent in the "Velvet Revolution," the SZ failed to win representation in the 1990 election. For the 1992 poll it joined the broader Liberal Social Union but reverted to independent status in November 1993. The party was barred from the 1996 legislative elections for failing to put up the required deposit. The SZ received 2.4 percent of the vote in the 2002 legislative elections for the Chamber of Deputies, below the minimum threshold for securing representation.

Martin Bursík was elected party chair in autumn 2005. He led the party into the 2006 elections with a message that it was the party most concerned with the environment, human rights, and the rights of women and minorities and would help eliminate the perceived corruption and vote-trading of the last decade. The election proved to be a breakthrough for the SZ as it finally transcended the 5 percent threshold for securing seats in the lower house with a 6.3 percent vote share, good for 6 seats. In the postelection cabinet negotiations, the SZ, despite its small block of seats, was the most sought after partner for the two major parties because of the SZ's growing public profile. Bursík took the party into a coalition government with the ODS and the KDU-ČSL and secured four cabinet posts for the party. However, Karel SCHWARZENBERG, Bursík's designee for foreign minister, was not an SZ member. The Schwarzenberg nomination sparked a controversy within the party, with 50 members delivering a signed statement to Bursík complaining about the lack of communication between the chair and party members over the appointment. The dissidents also raised concerns about Schwarzenberg's support for the U.S.-Czech bilateral negotiation on a proposed radar base (see Foreign relations, above). Bursík downplayed the dispute, maintaining that the SZ supported the radar base only on the condition that it be under NATO's control. At the party's national congress in mid-February 2007, this position was moderated somewhat, with the party pledging not to seek a national referendum on the base and to advocate for debate over the base issue at the level of the European Parliament and NATO.

The Green Party went on record in opposition to the reelection of President Klaus in 2008 because of the president's persistent denials of the importance of global climate change. The Greens instead endorsed the candidacy of Jan Švejnar, in league with the ČSSD. After the messy election process and aftermath, Bursík announced in late May that the Greens had drafted a proposal for a referendum to authorize direct election of the president.

Dissension within the party grew in the wake of the forced resignation of Education Minister and SZ party Deputy Chair Dana Kuchtová from the cabinet in October 2007. Dissatisfaction began with an internal struggle over naming a successor to Kuchtová. After two months of wrangling, Bursík finally nominated Ondřej Liška instead of the candidate recommended by the party's national council, prompting the resignation of the council's chair. In the wake of Bursík's compromise positions within the government in the first half of 2008, especially on support for the U.S. radar treaty, the left-of-center elements within the party, including Kuchtová, charged that Bursík was ruling from the top down and was too concerned with preserving the coalition at the expense of faithfulness to the party's platform. An April 2008 national party conference in Prague reaffirmed that the Greens would remain in the government, even after KDU-ČSL leader and Deputy Prime Minister Jiří Čunek was reinstated, something the Greens had previously opposed. By July Bursík announced an extraordinary party congress to convene in September to reaffirm his mandate (and remove Kuchtová as deputy leader) or select new leadership. Moreover, he proposed new party rules to be promulgated at the meeting designed to strengthen the hand of party leaders and weaken the power of the party's national council. The meeting was also expected to clarify the party's position on ratifying the U.S. radar agreement and the Lisbon Treaty. Kuchtová announced on July 23 that she would run against Bursík for party leader in the SZ congress. In August the national council proposed that the congress be held after the October 2008 Senate and local elections, but Bursík prevailed and the congress was scheduled for September.

At the party congress, held in Teplice on September 6–7, Bursík defeated Kuchtová in the race for party leader 227 votes to 109; Kuchtová also lost the post of deputy party leader to Ondřej Liška. Bursík's new party rules were not considered but his opponents on the SZ national council were dismissed. Several unhappy SZ deputies demanded soon thereafter more open discussion within the party of issues and positions that were at odds with the coalition government's programs and proposals as the price for continued support of the government.

The turmoil within SZ ranks led to a disastrous result for the party in the October 2008 Senate elections, having won no new seats. Following the defeat, Olga Zubová, head of the SZ national council, resigned from that post. During a party congress in Pardubice in late November 2008, Zubová and Věra JAKUBKOVÁ both announced that they were leaving the SZ deputies group but for the time being would support the coalition government.

With the collapse of the coalition government in March 2009, the SZ's infighting boiled over. A faction of the party split off and formed a rival Green party, the **Democratic Green Party,** in anticipation of the new parliamentary elections, despite the dismal electoral support the party received in the 2008 Senate election and the June 2009 European Parliament election, in which the SZ only won 2 percent of the vote. After the miserable European parliamentary poll results, Bursík resigned as leader and was replaced by Deputy Chair Liška as acting leader. The party also performed poorly in the May 2010 elections, securing only 2.4 percent of the vote and no seats in the lower house. Liška was formally elected as leader of the SZ in November.

Leaders: Ondřej LIŠKA (Chair), Přemysl RABAS (First Deputy Chair), Martin ANDER, Kateřina JACQUES (Deputy Chairs).

Sovereignty—Jana Bobošíková Bloc (*Suverenita—Blok Jana Bobošíkové*). The bloc was an electoral alliance formed by the **Common Sense Party** (*Strana Zdravého Rozumu*—SZR), founded in 2002 and led by Petr HANNIG, and **Politika 21,** led by Jana BOBOŠÍKOVÁ. The conservative, anti-EU grouping received 3.7 percent of the vote in the 2010 elections for the lower house, but no seats. A May 2012 poll found Bobošíková the fifth most popular Czech politician.

Leader: Jana BOBOŠÍKOVÁ.

Czech National Social Party (*Česká Strana Národně Sociální*—ČSNS). The ČSNS adopted its current name in September 1997, having previously been called the Free Democrats–Liberal National Social Party (*Svobodní Demokraté–Liberálni Národně Sociální Strana*—SD-LNSS). The centrist SD-LNSS was formed as a merger of the SD and LNSS in late 1995, although most LNSS deputies rejected the union and later launched a separate, short-lived parliamentary group, the Civic National Movement (*Občanské Národní Hnutí*—ONH). The SD component, dating as such from 1993 and led by Jiří Dienstbier, grew out of the Civic Movement (OH) wing of the Civic Forum (OF) launched in 1991 but was unrepresented in the 1992–1996 parliament. The LNSS was descended from the National Socialist Party (founded in 1897), which played a dominant role in the interwar period and was a member of the postwar Communist-led National Front, becoming the Czechoslovak Socialist Party (*Československá Strana Socialistická*—ČSS) in 1948. Unsuccessful in the 1990 election, the ČSS in 1991 merged with the former Agrarian Party (*Zemědělská Strana*—KS) and the Green Party (SZ, see above) to form a Liberal Social Union (*Liberálně Sociální Unie*—LSU) that won 16 Czech National Council seats in 1992 but thereafter suffered dissension and broke up. Most of the old ČSS component opted in June 1993 to form the centrist-inclined LNSS.

Dienstbier, a prominent dissident during the Communist era and subsequently Czechoslovakia's foreign minister, later left the SD-LNSS. In November 2000 he competed unsuccessfully as a ČSSD senatorial candidate. A year earlier the ČSNS had indirectly achieved lower house representation when Marie MACHATÁ, who had been elected from the Freedom Union, joined the party. (She technically sat as an independent.) In the 2002 lower house elections, the ČSNS received only 0.81 percent of the vote; by 2006 its share had fallen to 0.02 percent. The party received a similar vote share in the 2010 chamber elections.

Leader: Michael KLUSÁČEK (Chair).

The Moravians (*Moravané*). The Moravians were formed by the December 17, 2005, merger of the Moravian Democratic Party (*Moravská Demokratická Strana*—MDS) and the Movement for an Independent Moravia and Silesia–Moravian National Union (*Hnutí Samosprávné Moravy a Slezska–Moravské Národní Sjednocení*—HSMS-MNS). The MDS was formed in April 1997 by merger of the Moravian National Party (*Moravská Národní Strana*—MNS) and the Bohemian-Moravian Center Union (*Českomoravská Unie Středu*—ČMUS). The ČMUS was derived from the Movement for Self-Governing Democracy–Association for Moravia and Silesia (*Hnutí za Samosprávnou Demokracii–Společnost pro Moravu a Slezsko*—HSD-SMS), founded in 1990 in support of a demand that the historic province of Moravia-Silesia should have status equivalent to Bohemia and Slovakia. In the 1990 election the HSD-SMS took third place in the Czech National Council, winning 22 seats, 8 of which were lost in 1992. Thereafter, strains developed between moderates and a radical faction favoring extraparliamentary action. The proparliamentary Bohemian-Moravian Center Party (*Českomoravská Strana Středu*—ČMSS) was announced in January 1994, the new title indicating the party's intention to extend its activities to Bohemia. Later in the year it joined other centrist groups, including the Liberal Social Union (*Liberálně Sociální Unie*—LSU), the Farmers' Party (*Zemědělské Strany*—ZS), and the Christian Social Union (*Křest'ansko Sociální Unie*—KSU), in a loose alliance, the ČMUS. Formal merger occurred in February 1996. For the 1998 election the party cooperated with the HSMS-MNS.

Ivan DŘÍMAL, the former MNS leader, was reelected MDS chair in April 2000. In elections for the Chamber of Deputies in 2002, the MDS received just 0.27 percent of the vote. With the long-term goal of self-rule for Moravia and Silesia, the Moravians hoped for a better showing in the June 2006 election for the Chamber of Deputies but received only 0.23 percent of the vote. In March 2009 Jiří NOVOTNÝ became leader of the party. The MDS received 0.2 percent of the vote in elections for the lower house in 2010.

Leaders: Milan TRNKA (Chair), Zdenek ZBOŽÍNEK (First Deputy Chair), Ondrej HÝSEK (Deputy Chair).

Independent Democrats (*Nezávislí Demokraté*—ND, or NEZ/DEM). The NEZ/DEM was founded on June 23, 2005, by former ČSSD member of parliament Jana VOLFOVÁ with the help of Vladimír Železný, at that time leader of the Independents (*Nezávislí*). The Independents (the NEZ) had been founded in 1995 by Železný, a former Nova TV general director, as a center-right, euroskeptic party. In the 2002 senatorial elections, the NEZ won two seats. In the 2004 EU parliamentary elections, the NEZ received 8.2 percent of the vote and gained two seats. Bowing to the fact that Železný's name was better known than that of the ND, the party was renamed Independent Democrats (Chair V. Železný), with the chair's name becoming a formal component of the party name. (The Independents [the NE] carried on as a separate entity under the leadership of Frankisek ZWYRTEK.) The NEZ/DEM then merged with the Party for a Secure Life (*Strana za Životní Jistoty*—SŽJ), which focused on senior citizens and other economically vulnerable groups, under the name Independent Democrats. (See the 2005–2006 *Handbook* for history of the SŽJ.)

Party leader Železný formed a Czech branch of the euroskeptic European parliamentary grouping Libertas.eu in January 2009 with two former ODS MPs, Vlastimil Tlustý and Jan Schwippel, to contest the EP elections in June. The new party, **Libertas.cz** failed to win any seats. Both groupings appear to be defunct.

Leader: Vladimír ŽELEZNÝ (Chair).

Party of Civic Rights—Zemanovci (*Strana Práv Občanů—Zemanovci*—SPOZ), a social democratic grouping founded in 2009 by former ČSSD leader and prime minister Miloš ZEMAN. The party received 4.33 percent of the vote in the 2010 Chamber of Deputies election. Zeman won the first popular presidential election in January 2013.

Leaders: Miloš ZEMAN (President of the Czech Republic, Honorary Chair), Martin Nejedly (Deputy Chair).

Czech Pirate Party (*Česká Pirátská Strana*—ČPS), an Internet-oriented party inspired by its Swedish counterpart and concerned with reform of copyright and patent law as well as privacy rights. The Pirates won one seat in the October 2012 Senate election.

Leader: Kamil HORKÝ.

New or minor parties that participated in the 2010 elections included (unless noted, the parties received less than 1 percent of the vote) the following: the **Party of Free Citizens** (*Strana Svobodných Občanů*—SSO), a euroskeptic party that was opposed to ratification of the Lisbon Treaty, led by Petr MACH; the **Humanist Party** (*Humanistická Strana*—HS), registered in 1996 and led by Jan TAMÁŠ; the **Czech Crown** (*Koruna Česká*—KČ), a monarchist party for Bohemia, Moravia, and Silesia led by Václav SRB; the **Liberals.cz** (*Liberállové.cz*), formerly the Liberal Reform Party—LiRA, which in 2007 had one affiliated candidate in the Senate and was led by Milan HAMERSKÝ; **Ob˘cané.cz,** led by Petr HAVLIK; the **Vote Pravý Bloc** (*Volte Pravý Blok*), led by Peter CIBULKA, and the **Conservative Party** (*Konzervativní Strana*), led by Jan MIKULECKÝ.

The far-right **Workers' Party** (*Delnická Strana*—DS), led by Tomáše VANDASE, was targeted in 2008 and 2009 in the government's crackdown on anti-Roma activities and acts of violence by far-right nationalists. It was ordered dissolved in 2010, but reformed as the **Workers Party of Social Justice** (*Delnická Strana Sociální Spravedlnosti*—DSSS), still led by Vandase. The DSSS received 1.1 percent of the vote in May 2010.

Other Parties or Groups:

Freedom Union–Democratic Union (*Unie Svobody–Demokratická Unie*—US-DEU). The US-DEU had its origins in the dissension in the ODS over the leadership of Václav Klaus and his handling of a campaign finance scandal as nearly half of the ODS's 69 deputies reportedly left the party to form the Freedom Union (*Unie Svobody*—US) on January 17, 1998. In late 2001 the US and the Democratic Union (*Demokratická Unie*—DEU) merged into a new party to be known as the US-DEU, which won ten seats in the 2002 balloting for the Chamber of Deputies. Defections in 2003 and 2004 yielded a new party name, the **New Freedom Union** (*Nová Unie Svobody*—NUS), in April 2006 before the June legislative elections. The name change was seen as an effort to recast the party as a libertarian party of freedom and protest, with a platform that advocated legalization of some drugs and euthanasia, drastic reduction of income taxes, and public provision of universal Internet access. Despite the image makeover, the NUS secured only 0.3 percent of the vote. The party returned to its US-DEU designation in 2007, but continued electoral losses led to its dissolution in January 2011. (For more on US-DEU, please see the 2013 *Handbook*.)

Association of Independent Candidates and European Democrats (*Sdružení Nezávislých a Evropští Demokraé*—SNK–ED). The merger of the SNK and the ED was formalized on December 12, 2005. Formed prior to the 2002 elections and led by former ODS leader Josef ZIELENIEC and Igor PETROV, the Association of Independents (SNK) was a center-right party that, unlike the ODS, was highly supportive of European integration. The party sought to appeal to young conservatives who were dissatisfied with the more nationalistic ODS. In the 2002 elections for the Chamber of Deputies, the SNK received 2.8 percent of the vote. However, it won two seats in the 2002 Senate elections. The SNK formed a coalition with the European Democrats (ED) in 2004, having substantial success in the June 2004 balloting for the European Parliament (three seats on an 11 percent vote share).

The SNK-ED received only 2.1 percent of the vote in the June 2006 legislative elections, below the 5 percent threshold for securing a seat. In 2007 three senators were affiliated with the SNK-ED.

New party leaders were selected at a party conference on May 12, 2007, with Helmut Dohnálek as the new chair.

Sen. Josef NOVOTNÝ made allegations following the 2008 presidential election that an ODS senator offered him a 2-million-koruna bribe to vote for the reelection of President Klaus. No charges were drawn up by investigators, however, since there was no tangible evidence to corroborate the allegation.

In February 2010 first deputy chair Markéta REEDOVÁ left the party and joined the newly formed VV. The SNK-ED did not participate in the May or October 2010 legislative elections and was reported to be defunct in 2012.

Leaders: Helmut DOHNÁLEK (Chair), Josef MARTINIC (Deputy Chair).

In 2007 several minor parties were organized, including the **Republican Party of Bohemia, Moravia, and Silesia** (*Republikánská Strana Čech, Moravy a Slezska*—RSČMS) and the **Party for Dignified Life** (*Strana Důstojného Života*—SDŽ), led by former ČSSD deputy and then Independent Democrats founder Jana VOLFOVÁ. Additional parties that formed in 2008 and early 2009 included the **European Democratic Party** (*Evropská Demokratická Strana*—EDS), a pro-European party founded in November 2008 to promote Czech development and European integration, led by Jana HYBÁŠKOVÁ.

Other minor parties (*strana*) and movements (*hnutí*) that contested legislative elections or elections for the European Parliament between 2002 and 2010 included (all of the parties in the list below received less than 1 percent of the vote in the various elections): **Balbín's Poetic Party** (*Balbínova Poetická Strana*—BPS), founded in 2002 and led by Jiří HRDINA; the **Czech Movement for National Unity** (*České Hnutí za Národní Jednotu*—ČHNJ), led by Pavel SVOBODA; the **Czech Right** (*Česká Pravice*—CP), a conservative party registered in January 1994 and led by Michal SIMKANIČ; **Helax-Ostrava Is Having Fun** (*Helax-Ostrava se baví*—HOB), formed in 2002 and led by Gabriela ZIMERMANOVÁ; the **Movement of Independents for a Harmonic Development of Community and Town** (*Hnutí Nezávislých Za Harmonický Rozvoj Obcí a Měst*—HNHRM), which in 2008 had one affiliated candidate in the Senate; the **National Party** (*Národní Strana*—NS), an ultranationalist party, currently led by Petra EDELMANNOVÁ, that was registered in 2002 and drew increasing media attention with a series of protests targeting foreigners and ethnic minorities, including Sudeten Germans, Jews, and Roma, and formed a paramilitary corps called the National Guard; the **Republicans** (*Republikáni*), a right-wing, euroskeptic party founded on March 4, 2002, by former members of the SPR-RSČ (see the 2008 *Handbook* for history of the SPR-RSČ) and led by Jan VIK; the **Republicans of Miroslav Sládek** (*Republikáni Miroslava Sládka*—RMS), a far-right party formed in 2002 by Miroslav SLÁDEK and former members of the SPR-RSČ which was suspended for one year by the Czech Supreme Court in February 2008 for failure to submit annual financial reports for several previous years; the **Right Bloc** (*Pravý Blok*—PB) led by Petr CIBULKA; the **Romany Civic Initiative** (*Romská Občanská Iniciativa*—ROI), a party promoting the interests of Roma led by Štefan LIČARTOVSKÝ; the **Party of Democratic Socialism** (*Strana Demokratického Socialismu*—SDS), made up of disaffected former members of the KSČM and now led by Jiří HUDEČEK; and the **Party for an Open Society** (*Strana pro Otevřenou Společnost*—SOS), led by Pavel RYTÍŘ.

For information on the **Coalition for the Czech Republic** (*Koalice pro Českou Republiku*—Koal ČR), the **Equality of Prospects Party** (*Strana Rovnost Šancí*—SRŠ), the **Folklore as Well as Society** (*Folklor i Společnost*—FiS), the **Law and Justice Party** (*Právo a Spravedlnost*—PaS), the **4 Visions** (*4 VIZE*), the **Romany Social Democratic Party** (*Romská Demokratická Sociální Strana*—RDSS), and the **Czech-Roma Civic Movement** (*Česko-romské občanské sdružení*), please see the 2012 *Handbook*.

For information on the **Path of Change** (*Cesta Změny*), the **Communist Party of Czechoslovakia** (*Komunistická Strana Československa*—KSČ), and the **Civic Democratic Alliance** (*Občanská Demokratická Aliance*—ODA), see the 2009 *Handbook*.

LEGISLATURE

The **Parliament of the Czech Republic** (*Parlament České Republiky*) consists, under the 1992 constitution, of a Senate and a Chamber of Deputies. To achieve the transition to separate statehood on January 1, 1993, the composition of the lower house was decreed to be identical to that of the previous Czech National Council (*Česká Národní Rada*) elected in June 1992. The parliament operated as a single-chamber legislature until an entirely new Senate was elected in 1996.

Senate (*Senát*). Under legislation enacted in September 1995, the 81 members of the upper house are elected on a majoritarian basis for a six-year term from single-member constituencies, with one-third of the seats normally being renewed every two years. All 81 seats were filled in the first election held November 15–16 and November 22–23, 1996.

Elections for 27 seats in the Senate were held on October 12–13, 2012. The Czech Social Democratic Party won 13, an increase of 7, giving it a majority with 46 seats. Other results were as follows: the Civic Democratic Party, 4 seats (15 total); the Christian Democratic Union–Czech People's Party, 1 seat (6 total); the TOP 09–Movement for Mayors and Independents, 1 seat (4 total); the Communist Party of Bohemia and Moravia, 1 seat (2 total); the Pirate Party, 1seat (1 total), Green Party 1 seat (1 total), Movement Ostravak 1 seat (1 total), North Bohemians, 0 seats (2 total), independents, 2 seats (2 total).

President: Milan ŠTĚCH.

Chamber of Deputies (*Poslanecká Snemovna*). The lower house consists of 200 deputies directly elected for a four-year term by universal suffrage of those ages 18 and older. Under the controversial electoral reform legislation passed in July 2000, with effect from 2002 the thresholds for representation were raised to 5 percent for single parties, 10 percent for two-party alliances, 15 percent for three-party alliances, and 20 percent for alliances of four or more parties. The reforms also increased the number of electoral districts from 8 to 35.

At the most recent election of May 28–29, 2010, the seats in the Chamber were distributed as follows: the Czech Social Democratic Party, 56; Civic Democratic Party, 53; TOP 09, 41; Communist Party of Bohemia and Moravia, 26; and Public Affairs, 24.

President: Miloslava NĚMCOVÁ.

CABINET

[as of July 19, 2013] (*See headnote.*)

Prime Minister	Jiří Rusnok (ind.)
Deputy Prime Ministers	Jan Fischer (ind.)
	Martin Pecina (ind.)
Ministers	
Agriculture	Miroslav Toman (ind.)
Culture	Jiří Balvín (ind.)
Defense	Vlastimil Picek (ind.)
Education, Youth, and Sport	Dalibor Štys (ind.)
Environment	Tomáš Podivínský (ind.)
Finance	Jan Fischer (ind.)
Foreign Affairs	Jan Kohout (CSSD)
Health	Martin Holcát (ind.)
Industry and Trade Information Technology	Jiří Cienciala (ind.)
Interior	Martin Pecina (ind.)
Justice	Marie Benešová (CSSD) [f]
Labor and Social Affairs	František Koníček (CSSD)
Local Development	František Lukl (ind.)
Transportation	Zdeněk Žák (ind.)

[f] = female

INTERGOVERNMENTAL REPRESENTATION

Ambassador to the U.S.: Petr GANDALOVIC.

U.S. Ambassador to the Czech Republic: Norman L. EISEN.

Permanent Representative to the UN: Edita HRDÁ.

IGO Memberships (Non-UN): CEUR, EIB, EU, ICC, IEA, IOM, NATO, OECD, OSCE, WTO.

DENMARK

Kingdom of Denmark
Kongeriget Danmark

Political Status: Constitutional monarchy since 1849; under unicameral parliamentary system established in 1953.

Area: 16,629 sq. mi. (43,069 sq. km).

Population: 5,566,856 (2013E—UN); 5,556,452 (2013E—U.S. Census).

Major Urban Center (2011E—UN): COPENHAGEN (541,989; metropolitan area, 2,050,000).

Official Language: Danish.

Monetary Unit: Krone (market rate November 1, 2013: 5.53 kroner = $1US).

Sovereign: Queen MARGRETHE II; proclaimed queen on January 15, 1972, following the death of her father, King FREDERIK IX, on January 14.

Heir to the Throne: Crown Prince FREDERIK, elder son of the queen.

Prime Minister: Helle THORNING-SCHMIDT (Social Democratic Party); appointed by the Queen on October 3, 2011, to succeed Lars Løkke RASMUSSEN (Liberal Party) following the general election of September 15; formed a coalition government on October 3.

THE COUNTRY

Encompassing a low-lying peninsula and adjacent islands strategically situated at the mouth of the Baltic, Denmark has a largely homogeneous population, although controversy has emerged over increasing numbers of asylum seekers and immigrant workers. A vast majority (95 percent) of the inhabitants belong to the state-supported Evangelical Lutheran Church. Approximately 48 percent of the wage labor force is female, with 40 percent of working women concentrated in "female-intensive" service and textile manufacturing jobs. In government the prime minister and 8 of 22 other ministers are women. Women occupy 70 of the 179 seats in the unicameral parliament, with significantly less representation at the local level.

About three-quarters of Denmark's terrain is devoted to agriculture, and most of the agricultural output is exported (chiefly meat, dairy products, and eggs). However, industrialization was substantial after World War II, especially machinery and electrical equipment, processed foods and beverages, chemicals and pharmaceuticals, textiles, clothing, and ships. It is a leader in renewable energy, clean technology, and biotechnology. Although a member of the European Community/European Union (EC/EU) since 1973, Denmark does not use the euro as currency.

The global recession triggered Denmark's worst economic slump since World War II, although not as severe as many other EU members. The economy began to slowly recover in 2010, growing by 1.3 percent, followed by 1.1 percent in 2011 but fell by -0.6 percent for 2012. Unemployment rose to 7.5 percent in 2010 and then dropped to 6.1 percent in 2011, but rose to 7.6 percent for 2012.

GOVERNMENT AND POLITICS

Political background. The oldest monarchy in Europe, Denmark has lived under constitutional rule since 1849. Its multiparty system, reflecting the use of proportional representation, has resulted since World War II in a succession of coalition governments, most of minority status. The Social Democratic Party (*Socialdemokratiet*—SD) maintained its prewar position as the strongest single party, heading coalition governments in 1947–1950, 1953–1968, and 1971–1973, the last under the premiership of Anker JØRGENSEN. After two years of a nonsocialist minority government under Poul HARTLING of the Liberal Party (*Venstre*), Jørgensen returned following the 1975 election, heading a series of minority coalitions until 1982, when he was succeeded by Poul SCHLÜTER of the Conservative People's Party (*Konservative Folkeparti*—KF) as head of another minority government that included the Liberals, Center Democrats (*Centrum-Demokraterne*—CD), and Christian People's Party (*Kristeligt Folkeparti*—KrF).

The first Conservative prime minister since 1901, Schlüter faced heavy opposition to his proposed austerity measures. For the first time since 1929, the budget failed, and he was forced to call an early election on January 10, 1984, which yielded a decrease in class-alliance voting, with Danes supporting the traditional Conservative outlook on economic issues, including lowered interest rates. As a result, Schlüter remained in office as head of the preexisting four-party government.

On April 14, 1988, the opposition SD secured legislative approval of a resolution requiring that vessels from the North Atlantic Treaty Organization (NATO) be formally "reminded" of Denmark's 31-year-old ban on nuclear weapons. Prime Minister Schlüter responded by calling a snap election for May 10, at which the socialist bloc suffered a marginal loss, while the stridently anti-immigrant Progressive Party (*Fremskridtspartiet*—FP), unacceptable as a government coalition partner, increased its parliamentary seats from 9 to 16. Since the anti-NATO forces retained a narrow majority, the prime minister submitted his resignation on May 11 but continued in government while negotiations over government composition took place. A fourth Schlüter cabinet, comprising the Conservatives, the Liberals, and the Radical Liberal Party (*Det Radikale Venstre*—RV), was announced on June 3.

In a referendum on June 2, 1992, Danish voters by a 50.7 to 49.3 percent majority rejected the Maastricht Treaty, which provided for a common European currency and pledged EC members to seek common foreign and security policies. While both EC and Danish leaders were surprised by the outcome, it reflected a widely held view that increased European integration would lead to a loss of Danish national identity. The rejection came despite a number of safeguards that had been built into the treaty, including optional adherence to the common currency.

Unwilling to accept the electorate's decision on the Maastricht Treaty, the government on October 27, 1992, secured a "national compromise" agreement among seven of the eight parliamentary parties (the exception being the FP) setting out terms of joint support for the treaty in a second referendum. Its main stipulations were that Denmark would be able to opt out of the proposed single European currency, defense policy coordination, cooperation on legal and police matters such as immigration control, and EU citizenship arrangements. These requirements were largely accepted by the EC heads of government meeting in Edinburgh (Scotland) on December 11–12.

Having headed five minority center-right governments since 1982, Schlüter resigned in January 1993 after a judicial report found that he had misled parliament in 1989 over government policy on the admission of the relatives of Tamil refugees from Sri Lanka already in Denmark (the so-called Tamilgate scandal). The SD leader, Poul Nyrup RASMUSSEN, thereupon formed Denmark's first majority government since 1971, securing the agreement of the RV, CD, and KrF for a center-left coalition that commanded a one-seat majority in parliament. The new administration promptly called a further referendum on the Maastricht Treaty on May 18, 1993. This time the Danish version of the instrument, including the opt-outs agreed upon in Edinburgh, received endorsement by 56.8 percent of those voting.

Despite government efforts to combat unemployment and to reform tax policies, economic progress was slow, and the coalition parties performed poorly in local elections in November 1993. Rasmussen encountered further difficulty in February 1994, when the newly appointed social affairs minister, Bente JUNCKER, was obliged to resign over a leak of controversial and unsubstantiated information about a political opponent. She subsequently sat as an independent in the *Folketing* (Parliament), and the government was thus reduced to technical minority status with 89 of the 179 seats.

The ruling coalition suffered an overall reversal in the June 1994 European Parliament balloting and to a lesser extent in national balloting on September 21. The SD remained the largest party with 34.6 percent of the vote. The opposition Liberals made significant gains, overtaking the Conservatives as the second leading party, but that advance was partially offset by entry of the Red-Green Unity List into the *Folketing.* The outcome was the appointment on September 26 of a minority center-left coalition, headed by Rasmussen and consisting of his SD, the RV, and the CD. Although the government as formed commanded only 76 seats (including one of the two Greenland deputies) in the 179-member *Folketing,* it could rely on the external support of the Socialist People's Party (*Socialistisk Folkeparti*—SF) and the Red-Green Unity List on most issues. Its position was nevertheless precarious, faced by a center-right opposition with a seat total of 83.

The Rasmussen administration in 1995 focused on reducing unemployment, which was still about 11 percent in a country that had enjoyed full employment for most of the postwar period. However, the government's scope for concrete policy action continued to be circumscribed by an equal commitment to preserving the parity of the krone within the unofficial narrow band of the EU's exchange rate mechanism. Meanwhile, the center-right opposition contended that the government was shirking necessary pruning of Denmark's generous welfare provision and of the extensive rights and benefits accorded to Danish labor. Two CD cabinet members resigned their posts in mid-December 1996 to protest the 1997 budget process.

The SD maintained its front-runner status in the November 1997 municipal elections and in the February 1998 parliamentary balloting, in which the "anti-immigration" Danish People's Party (*Dansk Folkeparti*—DFp) made a strong electoral debut with nearly 7 percent support and 13 seats. The 1998 election came six months early, in part to prepare for the upcoming national referendum on the EU's Amsterdam Treaty (see entry on EU for details). Together with coalition allies the SD once again managed to secure a narrow (90-seat) majority in the *Folketing* with the support of two deputies from the Faroes and Greenland. In a separate referendum on May 28, the Danish voters endorsed the Amsterdam Treaty by a 55–45 percent vote, although on September 28, 2000, in a major reversal for the government, they rejected participation in the EU's eurozone by 53–47 percent.

In what proved to be a disastrous political miscalculation, Prime Minister Nyrup Rasmussen called an early election on October 31, 2001, expecting to ride a recent surge in popularity to another term. Instead, voters on November 20 awarded a plurality of 56 seats to the center-right Liberal Party, and on November 27 Liberal leader Anders Fogh RASMUSSEN announced formation of a minority government in coalition with the KF, which had won 16 seats. Eighteen seats short of a majority in the 179-seat *Folketing,* Rasmussen was forced to rely on external support from the DFp, which held 22 legislative seats.

Danish attention in 2002 turned to immigration, an issue brought increasingly to the forefront due to concerns about international terrorism and the growing demands on the country's welfare system. In June the legislature approved a new law tightening restrictions on asylum seekers and reducing welfare benefits for immigrants. In 2004 immigration laws were amended (on the recommendation of the DFp) to restrict the entry of Muslim clerics, or *imams.* Despite criticism by the United Nations High Commissioner for Refugees (UNHCR) and by the Council of Europe's human rights commissioner, polls indicated public support for further limits on immigration. Danish voters sent a mixed message to the government in the elections held on February 8, 2005. Both the ruling Liberal Party and the largest opposition party (the SD) declined slightly in representation, while the right-wing DFp gained two seats for a total of 24. Following the election, Prime Minister Rasmussen became the first Liberal leader to win a second consecutive term of office and formed another minority government in coalition with the KF, again relying on the DFp for legislative support. He appointed a new cabinet on February 18. As the one-year anniversary of the publication of caricatures of the Prophet Mohammed approached in September 2006 (see Foreign relations, below), authorities arrested nine Muslims suspected of plotting to bomb *Jyllands-Posten*, the newspaper, which originally published the cartoons. (Four of them were convicted and sentenced to 12 years in prison in June 2012.) Tensions increased a month later after far-right groups invited more potentially offensive cartoons, provoking outrage in the Muslim community.

In mid-2006, with broad backing by conservative, liberal, and opposition parties, the government laid out wide-ranging plans for reforming the welfare system, effective in 2017, an agenda that prompted large public protests in Copenhagen. Under the agreement, the retirement age would be raised by two years, and the early retirement age would be pushed back by two years. Hailed by the IMF as a plan that would "safeguard pension and health-care costs" over the long term (through 2027), the proposal also included provisions to improve integration of immigrants in an effort to boost the country's labor supply.

Rasmussen formed another Liberal-KF government on November 23, 2007, following snap elections on November 13 in which the Liberals had secured a plurality of 46 seats. In February 2009 the Rasmussen government announced a stimulus package that included increased spending and plans to cut the top marginal income tax from 63 to 55 percent. Prime Minister Rasmussen resigned on April 5, 2009, after accepting appointment as the secretary general of NATO. He was succeeded the same day by the Liberal Party's Lars Løkke RASMUSSEN (no relation), who formed a government with the same coalition partner and supporters as the previous administration.

New prime minister Lars Løkke Rasmussen and the Liberal Party appeared to face an uncertain political future. Polls showed an approval rating for Rasmussen of only 16 percent, more than 20 points behind his leading rival, Helle THORNING-SCHMIDT of the Social Democrats. Polls conducted throughout the spring predicted that the Social Democrats would win a 25–28 percent vote in the June 2009 balloting for the EU Parliament, but on election the two parties virtually tied, with the Social Democrats taking 21 percent of the actual vote to the Liberals' 20 percent. Danish voters showed strong interest in the EU elections, with their highest-ever EU election turnout of 60 percent. Voters also gave two euroskeptic parties, the Danish People's Party and the Socialist People's Party, one extra seat each. The results left the 13-member Danish delegation with 5 euroskeptic members.

The Liberals and Social Democrats suffered large seat losses in the November 2009 regional and municipal elections, both parties losing more than 10 percent of the seats they held by virtue of the 2005 balloting. The biggest winner was the SF, which more than doubled its seat totals at both levels, to stand as the third-largest party across governments of the 5 regions and 98 municipalities. The DFp increased its seats at both levels by about one-third.

Disquiet over the 2005 cartoon controversy was renewed in 2010 after a January 1 assassination attempt on one of the cartoonists. The issue reemerged in February when one major newspaper broke ranks with other media and apologized for republishing the offending 2005 cartoon in 2008.

In February 2010 based on the local election results and the looming 2011 parliamentary elections, Prime Minister Rasmussen substantially reshuffled his cabinet. At the same time his coalition government reset the government's agenda with a ten-goal plan to be achieved within ten years. Both actions came on the heels of a budget agreement, including support from the DFp, which included an expansionary stimulus to counteract sluggish economic growth. The budget also provided for defense cuts that foretold a reduced commitment to NATO projects, a policy action that drew criticism from former prime minister and current NATO secretary general Fogh Rasmussen. The incumbent prime minister rejected the criticism, calling it wide of the mark on Denmark's solidarity with NATO efforts.

Another cabinet shuffle occurred in March 2011, after Immigration Minister Birthe Roenn HORNBECH admitted her knowledge of the illegal denial of passports to Palestinians born in Denmark. Roenn

Hornbech was dismissed from the cabinet, and the ministerial responsibilities of refugees, immigration, integration, and ecclesiastical affairs were split between the ministers of development, cooperation, and culture. Additionally, Taxation Minister Troels Lund POULSEN was appointed as the new education minister.

In an effort to cut spending, the government unveiled an unemployment reform package in early 2011. Under the plan, unemployed persons would only be allowed to collect benefits (*dagpenge*) for a maximum of two years, down from four years; and they would have to pay into the system for a year before becoming eligible, instead of paying in for just six months.

In May 2011 Prime Minister Rasmussen announced the resumption of 24-hour customs controls for persons entering Denmark. EU members denounced the move as a violation of the Schengen Agreement. Although prevention of drugs and weapons smuggling was the stated purpose behind the border checks, Rasmussen acquiesced to the measure in return for the Danish People Party's support for pension reform. The deal backfired, as DFp supporters accused the party of selling out, and Tax Minister Peter CHRISTENSEN (V) was ridiculed internationally for mistakenly insisting that six other EU members had already implemented similar checkpoints.

In August 2011 Rasmussen unveiled his 2012 budget, which included a $2 billion stimulus package and a deficit of 4.6 percent of GDP ($16.4 billion). When the DFp rejected the budget, Rasmussen admitted he could not pass the bill and scheduled parliamentary elections for September 15. The run-up to the elections focused on competition between the "blue" center-right alliance, led by Rasmussen and encompassing the Liberals, Christian Democrats, KF, DFp, and Liberal Alliance, and a "red" left-wing alliance, headed by Social Democrat leader Helle Thorning-Schmidt and supported by the Socialist People's Party, the Radical Liberal Party, and the Red-Green Unity List. In contrast to the previous election, which had focused heavily on immigration issues, the economy dominated the 2011 elections. Rasmussen's campaign focused on tightening Denmark's finances, including reigning in the debt and forgoing tax increases, while Thorning-Schmidt advocated increased taxes on Danish banks, cigarettes, and junk food; increased spending on health and education; and adding an extra 12 minutes to the workday.

With 87.71 percent turnout, voters rejected the past decade of center-right government in favor of Thorning-Schmidt's red alliance. Despite the loss of 1 seat by the Social Democrats, the red alliance was able to pick up enough seats to hold a 92–87 advantage over the blue alliance. The victory was largely due to the electoral gains made by the Red-Green Unity List and the Social Liberal Party. Despite the ascendance of the red alliance, Rasmussen's Liberal Party placed first in the election, winning 47 seats, 3 more than the Social Democratic Party. Rasmussen conceded defeat the day after the election and oversaw a caretaker government until October 3, when the queen appointed Thorning-Schmidt as Denmark's first female prime minister.

Constitution and government. The constitution adopted in 1953 abolished the upper house of parliament while leaving intact the main outlines of the Danish political system. Executive power is nominally vested in the monarch, which proceeds by equal primogeniture as decided in a 2009 referendum that overturned male preference. Actual executive power is exercised by a cabinet responsible to the *Folketing*, a legislative body that includes representatives from the Faroe Islands and Greenland. The judicial system is headed by a 15-member Supreme Court and encompasses two high courts, local courts, specialized courts for labor and maritime affairs, and an ombudsman who is appointed by the *Folketing*. Judges are appointed by the Crown on the advice of the minister of justice.

Under a major reform enacted in 1970, the former 25 regional districts were reduced to 14 counties (*amtskommuner*), each governed by an elected council (*amtsiåd*) and mayor (*amtsborgmester*). The counties in turn are divided into 277 local administrative units, each with an elected communal council (*kommunalbestyrelse*) and mayor (*borgmester*).

To streamline governance, on January 1, 2007, the preexisting 14 counties were reduced and reorganized into 5 regions and the 270 municipalities were reduced to 98. Councils of 41 members, elected every four years, govern the regions. Regional governments' principal responsibility is delivery of hospital and health services. The regions have no power to tax; their revenues come from municipal subsidies and the central government. The city of Copenhagen is governed by a city council (*borger repræsentation*) and an executive consisting of a head mayor (*overborgmester*), two deputy council chairs (*næstformand*), and six deputy mayors (*borgmestie*).

Reporters Without Borders ranked Denmark 6th, up from 10th in 2012. In 2012 Transparency International rated Denmark the least corrupt country in the world.

Foreign relations. Danish foreign policy, independent but thoroughly Western in outlook, emphasizes support for the United Nations, the economic integration of Europe, and regional cooperation through the Nordic Council and other Scandinavian programs. Formerly a member of the European Free Trade Association (EFTA), Denmark was admitted to the EC on January 1, 1973; dissatisfaction with fishing agreements led to the withdrawal of newly autonomous Greenland from the EC in 1982, followed by sporadic conflict with individual community members, particularly the United Kingdom, over North Sea fishing rights. Although committed to collective security, the Danish government long resisted pressure by NATO to increase its defense appropriations in real terms. Responding to widespread popular agitation, in May 1984 the Social Democrats and their allies forced legislation making Denmark the first NATO member to withdraw completely from missile deployment. Danish voters in February 1986 endorsed (by popular referendum) continued participation in the EC; however, leftist opposition parties in the *Folketing* succeeded in enacting measures to further reduce effective involvement in NATO, including, in April 1988, legislation reiterating a long-standing (but unenforced) ban on visits by nuclear-equipped vessels. While the EC issue dominated Danish policy in 1992–1993, the government continued to attach importance to regional cooperation. In 1992 it became a founding member of the ten-nation Council of the Baltic Sea States and an enthusiastic signatory of the European Economic Area treaty between the EC and most EFTA countries. In May 2011 Denmark and the seven other nations of the Arctic Council signed an historic agreement to coordinate the prevention and clean-up of offshore oil spills.

Denmark contributed a warship, a submarine, and 160 troops to the 2003 attack on Iraq. After the downfall of the Saddam Hussein regime, a 460-member Danish peacekeeping force was sent to Iraq. Despite deep divisions within parliament and the public over the decision to participate in the invasion, the issue of the subsequent occupation of Iraq was not particularly contentious in Denmark. The government withdrew its combat troops in 2007 because the Iraqi security capability had improved. A small contingent remained in Baghdad to guard Danish diplomats.

On August 6, 2004, Denmark and Greenland signed a pact with the United States allowing the latter to upgrade its early-warning radar facility in Thule. The science minister made a controversial announcement in October that Demark was going to map the seabed north of Greenland to explore a geological case for claiming the international territory of the North Pole—a vast source of oil and natural gas—for Denmark.

Denmark's relationship with many Muslim countries was seriously damaged when the *Jyllands-Posten*, the country's largest-circulation newspaper, published political cartoons of caricatures of the Prophet Mohammed on September 30, 2005. Many Muslims were offended because depictions of the Prophet are forbidden under Islamic religious law. The following month, Prime Minister Rasmussen declined to meet with ten ambassadors from Muslim countries where the cartoons prompted large-scale protests, saying that he neither possessed nor wanted the power to limit freedom of the press. The reappearance of the caricatures in publications in 2006 provoked violent protests by Muslims throughout the world. Subsequently, Iran, Libya, and Syria withdrew their ambassadors from Denmark, and radical Islamists declared a *fatwa* (religious edict) against the Danes serving in Iraq. Muslim countries boycotted Danish goods, severely affecting dairy sales in particular. Ultimately, Danish-Muslim relations began to stabilize, with Denmark reopening its embassies in Muslim countries by midyear and Muslim countries ending their boycott.

In August 2007 Russia planted a flag on the North Pole seabed while a Danish expedition was collecting evidence on whether the Pole is geologically linked to Greenland. Prime Minister Rasmussen responded to the Russian action by saying the North Pole is shared property for the world, but his science minister said he believed it belonged to Denmark. At stake are natural resources, including as much as a quarter of the world's energy reserves, and the power to regulate navigable sea routes if the polar ice continues to melt. Denmark sponsored an expedition of researchers in August 2012 to prove its territorial claim.

On January 1, 2012, Denmark assumed the rotating presidency of the EU. Prime Minister Thorning-Schmidt devoted a considerable part of her first year in office to the EU presidency and the eurozone crisis.

She steered discussions that led to the Fiscal Compact and signed on to the budget deficit limits even though Denmark does not use the euro.

As a member of the Global Counterterrorism Forum, Denmark has formed a partnership with Burkina Faso, providing $22 million over five years to address the root causes of terrorism. In 2013 Denmark provided non-combat support to French troops in Mali (see entry on Mali).

Current issues. With a slim, five-seat edge over the opposition, Prime Minister Thorning-Schmidt's left-wing coalition must find common ground on a range of problems or risk collapse. So far, this has proven difficult. Her Social Democrats have steadily fallen in opinion polls since election day. By April 2013 the SD was polling at just 14.4 percent, a huge drop from the 24.8 percent approval in the September 2011 election and the lowest level since 1898.

Domestic opposition led Prime Minister Thorning-Schmidt to drop the idea of a referendum on participating in the EU common security and defense policy and justice and home affairs policy, and she declined to endorse the creation of an EU banking union. The Red-Green Unity List, Liberal Alliance, and Danish People's Party all took exception with Thorning-Schmidt's decision to sign the Fiscal Compact, saying the decision needed to be put before the Danish people in a referendum.

At the May 2012 NATO summit, Denmark expanded its contributions to the ongoing mission in Afghanistan and reaffirmed its commitment to training missions in the country after other countries withdraw in 2014. The prime minister also announced that Denmark would purchase five drones as well as donate 100 million kroner ($16.6 million) to fund Afghanistan's new security forces. Her statement drew criticism over the use of state pension funds to buy weapons.

In October 2012 Thorning-Schmidt announced a 2012 budget with infrastructure projects that would create 135,000 jobs by 2020 and expand the labor force by raising the retirement age and extending the work day by 12 minutes. A "fat tax" on foods high in saturated fats was imposed (and withdrawn a year later), after Danes swarmed Swedish and German border towns buying meat, cheese, and junk food. The new government abolished the immigration ministry, broadened immigrant access to social benefits, and granted automatic citizenship to children born in Denmark. It also canceled plans for customs checkpoints. She also reversed a campaign promise and canceled the popular early retirement program.

Once Denmark's presidency of the EU ended in 2012, the SF held up the government with drawn-out party elections, eventually choosing Annette VILHELMSEN as chair in October. The prime minister then reshuffled her cabinet, including Vilhelmsen and former SF chair Holger Nielsen, to mark a new emphasis on domestic matters.

The 2013 budget process was extremely contentious. Prime Minister Thorning-Schmidt's "Denmark at Work" proposal raised the top tax bracket and earned income credit, increased property taxes, and slowed cost-of-living adjustments for benefit programs. The government ultimately struck a compromise with the opposition Liberals in June 2012, believing support from the largest party in parliament would be more durable, even though it meant alienating the progovernment Red-Green alliance. This scenario repeated in July, when the government left its erstwhile allies out of discussions to raise funds by scaling back job-sharing and early-age pension programs. Furious, the Red-Green faction announced it was "in opposition to the government" in late June.

Leaders of the Red-Green Unity List dug in their heels over the planned expiration of the *dapenge* unemployment benefit, calling on the government to put off scheduled cuts in benefits for another six months and to continue benefits at current levels. List members argued that 23,000 citizens were slated to lose their income. Ten public-service unions, representing teachers, nurses, and more, warned of "social disaster" if the government cut *dagpenge*. The three-party coalition was divided, with the Socialist People's Party arguing that the issue was too important to be put off again, while Radical Liberal economy minister Margrethe VESTAGE insisted that the government should focus on creating jobs so people would not need unemployment benefits. After months of negotiations, a budget was finally announced in November that cut the deficit by half while postponing the planned cuts in unemployment assistance until July 2013. Predictably, the unemployment benefits issue returned in June 2013, with the government agreeing to extend training programs and continue benefits at 60 percent of the full level through 2016. The extension will be funded by cuts in Danish-language courses for immigrants.

One year after ending a decade of center-right governance in Denmark, Prime Minister Thorning-Schmidt's slim leftist coalition appears deeply divided and fragile. The Red-Green Unity List has nearly doubled its popularity since the parliamentary elections.

Although the DFp finished third in the 2011 elections, its anti-immigrant, anti-Islam agenda is beginning to lose influence across Europe. In July 2013 the government blamed the DFp for a sharp decline in tourism, saying their anti-Muslim visa policies and talk of border controls had damaged Denmark's international reputation as a "pleasant, progressive, and diverse nation."

In 2013 Thorning-Schmidt launched "Growth Plan DK," a $15 billion economic package designed to create 150,000 jobs by improving the investment climate, increasing education, and curbing the generous welfare state. The government wants to raise the labor supply through work incentives and raising the early retirement threshold. The Red-Green Unity List denounced the plan, details of which included cutting the corporate tax from 25 percent to 22 percent and reducing a tax on beer and soft drinks. The lost revenue would be balanced by cuts in student aid and unemployment benefits.

Teachers rejected Thorning-Schmidt's plan to extend the school day and increase the authority of principals. Schools shut down for the entire month of April 2013, when the government locked out 70,000 teachers. The standoff ended June 7, when the governing coalition reached a reform agreement with the DFp and VS.

Thorning-Schmidt signed a long-term partnership agreement with Afghan President Hamid Karzai in May 2013 that included 2 billion kroner ($350 million) in financial aid and pledges to help develop the Afghan police. Danish troops, which have been active in Afghanistan since 2002, are scheduled to exit the country by August 2013, instead of December 2014. The prime minister linked the early departure to the British decision to withdraw ahead of schedule. In August, Thorning-Schmidt reshuffled some of her cabinet and merged the Ministry for European Affairs with the Ministry of Trade and Investment.

POLITICAL PARTIES

Government and Government-Supportive Parties:

Social Democratic Party (*Socialdemokratiet*—SD). Founded in 1871, the SD mainly represents industrial labor and advocates economic planning, full employment, extensive social security benefits, and environmental planning. The SD has been the ruling party of Denmark for most of the past 75 years. Most recently, the SD led the ruling government coalition from 1993 until 2001. In 2003 the SD, along with the RV (Radical Liberal Party; see below), refused to support the government's bid to send soldiers to Iraq following the U.S. invasion.

In the 2005 elections the SD won 47 seats in the *Folketing,* a loss of 5 seats from the previous elections. On April 12, 2005, Helle Thorning-Schmidt was elected leader of the SD, becoming the first woman to head the party. In the 2007 legislative balloting the party won 45 seats—2 fewer than in 2005 and 1 shy of the Liberals' plurality—and 25.5 percent of the vote. In the 2011 elections the Social Democrats lost 1 seat, winning a total of 44 seats with 24.8 percent of the vote. However, the red electoral alliance, led by the Social Democrats, won a majority of seats in the legislature, making Thorning-Schmidt Denmark's new prime minister. SD leaders feared heavy losses in the November 2013 local elections—it controls 48 of 98 mayorships—and there was sentiment to replace Thorning-Schmidt as party leader at the September party congress.

Leaders: Helle THORNING-SCHMIDT (Party Leader and Prime Minister), Frank JENSEN, Mogens JENSEN (Vice Chairs), Lars MIDTIBY (Secretary).

Socialist People's Party (*Socialistisk Folkeparti*—SF). The SF was formed in 1958 by former Communist Party chair Aksel LARSEN, who had disagreed with Moscow over the suppression of the 1956 Hungarian Revolution. It has often acted as an unofficial left wing of the SD, concentrating on influencing the platform and voting patterns of the larger party. Traditionally anti-EU, the party was split during its August 1997 congress when parliamentary leader Steen GADE resigned to campaign for ratification of the EU's Amsterdam Treaty. In the February 2005 elections the SF attracted 6 percent of the vote and 11 seats. The SF more than doubled its vote to 13.0 percent in the 2007 balloting and won 23 seats, becoming the fourth largest party in parliament, and its substantial gains in the November 2009 regional and municipal elections made it the third largest party at those levels. The Socialist People's Party won only 16 seats with 9.2 percent of the vote in 2011. On August 15, 2012, the Socialist People's Party disciplined Özelm Cekic, stripping the legislator of her role as party spokesperson due to her vocal criticism of the government tax deal. Party chair Villy SØVNDAL resigned in September and was replaced by Annette VILHELMSEN in October.

Leaders: Annette VILHELMSEN (Chair), Mattias TESFAYE, Mette TOUBORG (Deputy Chairs), Anne BAASTRUP (Parliamentary Leader), Turid LEIRVOLL (National Secretary).

Radical Liberal Party (*Det Radikale Venstre*—RV). Also characterized in English as a "Social Liberal" grouping, the RV was founded in 1905; it represents mainly small landowners and urban intellectual and professional elements. The party advocates strengthening private enterprise in a social-liberal context and has become more pro-European. With a record of often joining or endorsing SD-led governments, it nevertheless supported the Schlüter (KF)-led coalition in 1982. Following the September 1987 election, (then) parliamentary leader Niels Helveg PETERSEN rebuffed Anker Jørgensen's appeal to realign with the Social Democratic and Socialist People's parties, thereby precluding the establishment of a new socialist administration. The RV was awarded five cabinet posts in the 1988 Schlüter government but withdrew from formal participation in 1990.

The party has attracted liberal voter support in the wake of the victory of the center-right parties in the 2001 elections. The RV increased its seats in the February 2005 election, bringing its total to 17. In 2007 internal division over the party's close ties to the Social Democrats led Danish parliamentarian Naser KHADER and EU parliamentarian Anders Samuelsen to leave the RV and form the New Alliance (see below). The RV won only 5.1 percent of the vote and 9 seats in the 2007 legislative poll. In the 2011 balloting, however, the RV's performance improved, with 17 seats and 9.5 percent of the vote.

Leaders: Margrethe VESTAGER (Minister of Economics and Interior), Klaus FRANDSEN (President), Emil Dyred (Vice President).

Red-Green Unity List (*Enhedslisten-De Rød-Grønne*). The Red-Green formation was launched in 1989 as a coalition of three left-wing/environmentalist groups: the VS (Left Socialist Party) and DKP (Communist Party of Denmark) (see below) and the Trotskyist **Socialist Workers' Party** (*Socialistisk Arbejderparti*—SAP). The Maoist **Communist Workers' Party of Denmark** (*Danmarks Kommunistisk Arbejderparti*—DKA) joined the coalition in 1991. Strongly opposed to EU membership and the Maastricht process, the Unity List achieved a breakthrough in the September 1994 general election, winning 3.1 percent of the vote and 6 seats. Officially, the party has no chair but rather is directed by a 21-person collective leadership. The Unity List lost 1 of its 6 seats in the March 1998 elections with a vote share of 2.7 percent. It lost another in 2001, when its vote share totaled 2.4 percent. The party did significantly better in the February 2005 election, attracting 3.4 percent of the vote and increasing its seats in parliament to 6. In the November 2007 legislative elections party support dropped to 2.2 percent, good for 4 seats, but support for the party rebounded in 2011, when it won 12 seats with 6.7 percent of the vote. The List agreed to support the governing red coalition, but cooperation broke down in mid-2012. The List is governed by an Executive Committee.

Executive Committee: Bruno JERUP, Jakob SØLVHØJ, Katrine Toft MIKKELSEN, Line BARFOD, Lole MØLLER, Mikael HERTOFT, Per CLAUSEN.

Left Socialist Party (*Venstresocialisterne*—VS). The VS split from the SF in 1967 and achieved representation in the legislature for the first time from 1968 to 1971. In 1984 the party's "revolutionary" wing broke with the leadership over its unwillingness to organize cadres along traditional communist lines. Two members defected to the SF in July 1986. Subsequently, the party was weakened by growing factionalization, with the "Red Realists" favoring cooperation with the SF and the "Left Oppositionists" following a rigid Marxist-Leninist line. The VS has maintained a distinct identity within the Red-Green Unity List. The party has no titular chair, instead operating via collective leadership.

In 2006 Danish authorities arrested several VS members and charged them with supporting Palestinian and Colombian terrorist organizations, but they were cleared of it in December 2007 when a Copenhagen court ruled that the supported organizations were not terror groups.

The party sparked controversy in July 2013 when a spokesperson, Inger Støjberg, told Danish Muslims to assimilate or "find somewhere else to live."

Leaders: Karen NYGARD, Henrik FORCHAMMER, Albert JENSEN, and Michael SCHOELARDT.

Communist Party of Denmark (*Danmarks Kommunistiske Parti*—DKP). The DKP was formed in 1919, achieved parliamentary representation in 1932, and participated in the immediate postwar coalition government. The party was greatly weakened by the 1956 Hungarian revolt and the schism that subsequently led to the formation of the Socialist People's Party. Its representation in the *Folketing* following the 1973 election was its first since 1956. However, it lost all of its 7 legislative seats in the 1979 balloting. As a member of the Red-Green Unity List coalition, the DKP remains a loose network of militants rather than a full-fledged party. In 1990 a Marxist-Leninist faction of the group opposed to participation in the Unity List formed the **Communist Forum** (*Kommunistisk Forum*), which became the **Communist Party in Denmark** (*Kommunistisk Parti i Danmark*—KPiD) in November 1993 under the leadership of Betty Frydensbjerg CARLSSON. After a period of collective leadership, Henrik Stamer Hedin subsequently became chair.

Leader: Henrik Stamer HEDIN (Chair)

Opposition Parties:

Liberal Party (*Venstre*—V). Founded in 1870 as the Agrarian Party but currently representing some trade and industrial groups as well as farmers, the Liberal Party (commonly referenced in Danish as *Venstre* [Left] rather than *Liberale Parti*) stands for individualism as opposed to socialism in industry and business, reduction of taxation through governmental economy, relaxation of economic restrictions, and adequate defense. Its parliamentary representation rose from 22 in 1988 to 29 in 1990, and the party was the main victor in the September 1994 national election, winning 23.3 percent of the vote and 42 seats, although it chose to remain in the opposition.

In the 2001 election the Liberals won 31 percent of the national vote and a plurality of 56 seats, permitting the party chair, Anders Fogh Rasmussen, to forge a center-right minority government on November 27. In February 2005, the Liberal Party won 29 percent of the vote and 52 seats in parliament, 4 fewer than it had won in the previous election. Nevertheless, the party's showing was strong enough to allow party leader and Prime Minister Rasmussen to win a second term at the head of a minority coalition government with the KF (see below). The Liberals won a 26.2 percent vote share and 46 seats in the November 2007 elections. Following brief negotiations, a third Rasmussen government (again comprising the Liberals and the KF, with pledged support from the DFp and a Faroe Islands member) took office on November 23. When Rasmussen was named secretary general of NATO in April 2009, Lars Løkke Rasmussen, the former vice chair of the party, was named acting party leader.

In the 2011 balloting the Liberals became the largest party in the legislature with 26.7 percent of the vote and 47 seats. However, their blue alliance was defeated by the Social Democratic Party–led coalition in the election, placing the party in the opposition for the first time in 10 years.

Leaders: Lars Løkke RASMUSSEN (President and Former Prime Minister), Kristian JENSEN (Vice President), Claus Søgaard-Richter (Secretary General).

Conservative People's Party (*Konservative Folkeparti*—KF). Founded in 1916 as an outgrowth of an earlier Conservative grouping (*Højre*), the KF mainly represents financial, industrial, and business groups. It supports adequate defense, protection of private property, sound fiscal policy, and lower taxation. Under the leadership of Poul Schlüter, the party recovered from a low of 5.5 percent of the vote in 1975 to 14.5 percent in 1981, enabling Schlüter to form a center-right coalition in 1982, which remained in office for more than a decade. A further surge to 23.4 percent in 1984 was followed by a decline to 16 percent in 1990 and the resignation of Schlüter in January 1993.

The KF has not recovered from its decline in popularity in the early 1990s. In the 1998 general elections, the party lost 11 seats, winning a total of only 16, a loss attributed in part to the emergence of the right-wing Danish People's Party. Nevertheless, the party sustained a high profile as the junior partner in the coalition government led by the Liberal Party. In the 2005 general election, the KF marginally improved its representation, winning 10.3 percent of the vote and 18 seats. The KF maintained its seats in the 2007 elections on a vote share of 10.4 percent and returned as the junior partner in the coalition government. In the 2011 elections, the KF's vote share dropped to 5.9 percent, which gave the party only 8 seats.

Leader: Lars BARFOED (Party Leader).

Liberal Alliance (*Liberal Alliance*—LA). This party was known until August 2008 as the New Alliance (*Ny Alliance*—NA), which was founded in May 2007 by Naser Khader, a former RV member of the Danish parliament; Anders Samuelsen, a former RV member of the European Parliament; and Gitte SEEBERG, a former KF member of the Danish parliament. The NA announced its intention to offer a middle-ground party with an emphasis on liberal market policies (including calls for tax reductions beyond those proposed by the Liberal Party), reformed and relaxed immigration policies, greener energy, a pro-EU stand, and increased foreign aid. The Syrian-born Khader rose in prominence in Denmark as a well-received voice of moderation in the wake of the cartoon controversy (see Foreign relations, above), and early polls indicated the NA could capture as many as 15 seats in a parliamentary election. However, the party's mixed policy signals and refusal to announce whether it would support a new Rasmussen-led government cost it in the November 2007 balloting, when the party won only 5 seats on a 2.8 percent share of the vote. In February 2008 two members resigned from the party, including Seeberg, who left to sit in parliament as an independent. In July Seeberg stood down from parliament altogether and was replaced by an appointed NA member. In January 2009 Khader also left the party, leaving it with only two members in parliament. Despite these defections, the LA won 9 seats with 5 percent of the vote in the 2011 balloting.

Leader: Anders SAMUELSEN (Chair).

Danish People's Party (*Dansk Folkeparti*—DFp). The DFp was launched in October 1995 by dissident deputies of the right-wing Progress Party (FP; see below), including former FP leader Pia Kjærsgaard. While espousing similar policies, the DFp is regarded as being to the right of the parent party. The nationalistic DFp, openly anti-immigrant, did very well in the November 1997 municipal elections and was one of the biggest winners in the March 1998 national election, winning 13 seats compared with the FP's 4. Its vote share rose to 12 percent in the November 2001 general election, in which it won 22 seats, making it the third largest political party in Denmark. The party retained that position in the February 2005 general election, winning 24 seats and the 2007 elections, winning 13.9 percent of the vote and 25 seats. In the 2011 elections the DFp maintained its position as the third largest party, winning 12.3 percent of the vote and 22 seats. Kjærsgaard resigned as party leader in September 2012 and endorsed Kristian Thulesen Dahl to succeed her.

Leaders: Kristian Thulesen DAHL (Chair), Peter SKAARUP (Deputy Chair), Poul Lindholm NIELSEN (Party Secretary).

Other Parties That Contested the 2011 Elections:

Christian Democrats (*Kristelig Demokraterne*—KD). The KD was originally formed as the Christian People's Party (*Kristeligt Folkeparti*—KrF) in 1970 in opposition to abortion and liberalization of pornography regulations. The party achieved representation in the *Folketing* for the first time in 1973 and placed two representatives in the center-left coalition formed in January 1993. The KrF vote slipped to 1.1 percent in the June 1994 European elections (insufficient for representation) and took only 1.8 percent in the September national balloting, thereby exiting from both the *Folketing* and the government. The KrF returned to the *Folketing* following the March 1998 election, in which it won four seats on a vote share of 2.4 percent. It retained all four in 2001.

The KrF changed its name to Christian Democrats in October 2003 in an attempt to enhance its public image, prompting the resignation of party chair Jann SJURSEN. He was replaced by Marianne KARLSMORE. The KD won only 1.7 percent of the vote in the 2005 general election, which was not enough to win any seats in parliament, and Karlsmore resigned soon after. The CD vote share sank to 0.9 percent in 2007 and 0.8 percent in 2011, below the 2 percent threshold needed for parliamentary representation. Per Ørem Jørgensen replaced Bjarne Hartung Kirkegaard as president at the 2011 party congress. Jørgensen resigned in October 2013 and formed the **Democratic Party** in February 2013.

Leader: Stig GRENOV (President).

Other Parties:

Progress Party (*Fremskridspartiet*—FP). The right-wing FP was formed in 1972 by Mogens GLISTRUP, who was convicted in February 1978 of tax evasion. The party advocated gradual dissolution of the income tax and abolition of the diplomatic service and the military. The second largest parliamentary group after the 1973 balloting, it had slipped to eighth place by 1984, with one of its six representatives subsequently joining the Conservatives and another becoming an independent. In an unexpected recovery, it won 9 seats in 1987, but the FP was unable to join in what would have been a six-party Schlüter majority because of a Radical Liberal refusal to ally itself with a party viewed not only as extremist but also as racist because of a strong anti-immigrant posture. The FP registered the largest single-party gain in the 1988 balloting, winning 16 seats, only to lose 4 in 1990. The FP vote slumped to 2.9 percent in the June 1994 European Parliament balloting but recovered to 6.4 percent in the September national poll. Internal divisions in 1995 resulted in the ouster of Pia Kjærsgaard as FP leader, after which she and three supporters withdrew to form the DFp (above). The party lost 7 of its 11 seats in the 1998 elections and won no seats in 2001 with only 0.6 percent of the vote. The FP did not contest subsequent parliamentary elections.

Leaders: Niels HØJLAND (President), Holger THOMSEN (Vice President), Berit DISSING (Secretary).

See the 2013 *Handbook* for information on two defunct parties, the **Center Democrats** (*Centrum-Demokraterne*—CD) and **Civil Center** (*Borgerligt Centrum*—BC).

Danish political movements that contested the 1994, 1999, 2004, and 2009 European Parliament elections included the **June Movement** (*Juni Bevægelsen*), led by Keld ALBRECTHSEN and named after the month of the 1992 initial rejection of the Maastricht Treaty. In the June 2009 EU elections the party lost its one seat and decided to disband. The **People's Movement against the European Union** (*Folkesbevægelsen mod EU*) took 10.3 percent of the vote and two seats (against 18.9 percent and four seats in 1989) in the 1994 European Parliament balloting and one seat in 1999, 2004, and 2009.

LEGISLATURE

The ***Folketinget*** (also frequently rendered as *Folketing*) is a unicameral legislature whose members are elected every four years (subject to dissolution) by universal suffrage under a modified proportional representation system. Of its present membership of 179, 135 are elected in 17 metropolitan districts, with 40 additional seats being divided among those parties that have secured at least 2 percent of the vote but whose district representation does not accord with their overall strength. In addition, the Faroe Islands and Greenland are allotted two representatives each.

In the most recent election, held on September 15, 2011, the Liberal Party won 47 seats; the Social Democratic Party, 44; the Danish People's Party, 22; the Radical Liberal Party, 17; the Socialist People's Party, 16; the Red-Green Unity List, 12; the Liberal Alliance, 9; and the Conservative People's Party, 8. The Faroe Islands are represented by Union and Social Democratic party members; Greenland's members come from the Eskimo Brotherhood and Forward parties (see Related Territories, below).

President: Mogens LYKKETOFT.

CABINET

[as of November 7, 2013]

Prime Minister	Helle Thorning-Schmidt (SD) [f]
Deputy Prime Minister	Margrethe Vestager (RV) [f]
Ministers	
Business Affairs and Growth	Henrik Sass Larsen
Children	Christine Edda Antorini (SD) [f]
Climate, Energy, and Buildings	Martin Lidegaard (RV)
Culture	Marianne Jelved (RV) [f]
Defense	Nicolai Halby Wammen (SD)
Development and Cooperation	Christian Friis Bach (RV)
Economics and Interior	Margrethe Vestager (RV) [f]
Employment	Mette Frederiksen (SD) [f]
Environment	Ida Margrete Meier Auken (SF) [f]
Finance	Bjarne Fog Corydon (SD)

Food, Agriculture, and Fisheries	Karen Angelo Hækkerup (SD) [f]
Foreign Affairs	Villy Søvndal (SF)
Gender Equality, Ecclesiastical Affairs, and Nordic Cooperation	Manu Sareen (RV)
Health and Prevention	Astrid Krag Kristensen (SF) [f]
Justice	Morten Bødskov (SD)
Science, Innovation, and Higher Education	Morten Østergaard Kristensen (RV)
Social Affairs and Integration	Annette Vilhelmsen (SF) [f]
Taxation	Holger K. Nielsen (SF)
Trade and Investments	Nick Hækkerup (SD)
Transport	Pia Olsen Dyhr (SF) [f]
Urban, Housing, and Rural Affairs	Carsten Mogens Hansen (SD)

[f] = female

INTERGOVERNMENTAL REPRESENTATION

Ambassador to the U.S.: Peter TAKSØE-JENSEN.

U.S. Ambassador to Denmark: Rufus GIFFORD.

Permanent Representative to the UN: Carsten STAUR.

IGO Memberships (Non-UN): ADB, AfDB, CEUR, EBRD, EIB, EU, IADB, ICC, IEA, IOM, NATO, OECD, OSCE, WTO.

RELATED TERRITORIES

Faroe Islands (*Faerøerne,* or *Føroyar*). The Faroe Islands (numbering 18) in the North Atlantic have been under Danish administration since 1380. Their area is 540 square miles (1,399 sq. km), the population is approximately 50,000 (2010E), with residents of the capital Tórshavn accounting for some 17,200. The principal language is Faroese, with most inhabitants also Danish-speaking. Fishing and sheep raising are the most important ingredients of the islands' economy.

The islands, which send two representatives to the *Folketing,* constitute a self-governing territory within the Danish state. A local legislature (*Løgting*) with between 27 and 33 members (currently 33) elects an administrative body (*Landsstýri*) headed by a chair (*løgmadur*). The Crown is represented by a high commissioner (*ríkisumbodsmadur*). The islands have been represented on the Nordic Council since 1969.

The principal political groups are the **Union Party** (*Sambandsflokkurin*), which urges the retention of close links to metropolitan Denmark; the **Social Democratic Party** (*Javnarflokkurin*); the conservative-liberal **People's Party** (*Fólkaflokkurin*); the left-wing **Republic** (*Tjóđveldi*), which advocates secession from Denmark (the party changed its name in 2007 from the Republican Party [*Tjøđveldisflokkurin*]); the **Home Rule Party** (*Sjálvstýrisflokkurin*); the **Progressive and Fisheries Party** [and] **Christian People's Party** (*Framburs–Fiskivinnuflokkurin Kristeligt Folkeparti*) the **Labor Front** (*Verkmannafylkingin*), founded in 1994 by dissident Social Democrats and trade unionists; and the **Center Party** (*Miflokkurin*); and the Progressive Party (Framsókn), founded in 2011 by former members of the People's Party.

In elections on July 7, 1994, all of the above parties won representation in the islands' 32-member legislature. The leading formation was the Union Party (8 seats), whose leader was sworn in on September 15 as prime minister of a center-left coalition that also included the Social Democrats, the Home Rule Party, and the Labor Front. The previous coalition had consisted of the Social Democratic, Republican, and Home Rule parties.

In the national election of September 21, 1994, the two Faroe Islands' seats in the Danish *Folketing* were won by candidates of the Union and People's parties. In 1996 the Social Democratic Party was replaced in the government coalition by the People's Party, while the Social Democratic Party and the People's Party each secured one seat in the March 1998 Danish *Folketing* balloting.

In the legislative elections of April 30, 1998, the dominant issue was the islanders' growing demand for sovereignty, which was embraced in varying degrees by candidates across the political spectrum. Anti-Copenhagen sentiment was inflamed by continuing controversy over the Faroese government's 1993 purchase of a failing Danish-owned bank, one of only two on the islands, whose condition the Faroese alleged had been misrepresented by the Danes. The Republican Party led the 1998 balloting, winning 8 seats with a vote share of 23.8 percent, followed closely by the Social Democratic Party and the People's Party. The Labor Front lost its three seats. Anfinn KALLSBERG, leader of the People's Party, subsequently formed an 18-seat coalition government consisting of his own party, the Republicans, and the Home Rule Party. In August the new government said it would seek independence while remaining under the Danish monarchy and monetary system, hoping to submit independence to a referendum.

Meanwhile, after two decades of talks, the failure of island and British negotiators to settle a boundary dispute over a potentially large oil and gas field on the ocean floor, in the so-called White Zone in the North Atlantic, prevented the Faroese from going forward with exploration of the site. Finally, in May 1999 representatives from the Faroe Islands, Denmark, and the United Kingdom reached a settlement of the dispute over the maritime border. The islands were granted sovereignty over some 40 square miles of the area in question, further fueling the drive for independence in view of the potential new oil wealth. However, the Danish government in March 2000 hardened its stance on the independence question, announcing that Danish subsidies (estimated at $110 million per year) would cease 4 years after independence rather than being phased out over 15–20 years as proposed by Faroese leaders. In February 2001 the Faroese government announced May 26 as the date for a referendum on the issue of full sovereignty by 2012, but in March the vote was called off because of declining support in the face of Copenhagen's firm position on the subsidies.

In January 2003 government officials from the Faroe Islands and Denmark began talks aimed at transferring responsibility in several policy areas to the Faroese government. On June 26, 2003, the talks culminated in the signing of an agreement that transferred authority over the Faroese judicial system, police, and civil law. Responsibility for security for the Faroe Islands remains with Denmark. In December 2003 the governing coalition collapsed when the Republican Party withdrew its support as the result of charges of an accounting scandal involving the administration of Prime Minister Anfinn Kallsberg (People's Party). On January 20, 2004, parliamentary elections resulted in the anti-independence Union Party winning 23.7 percent of the vote. While this was the highest percentage won by any party, it was down 2.3 percent from the Union Party's showing in the 2002 elections. On February 3, 2004, the Union Party, the Social Democratic Party, and the People's Party formed a new coalition government with Social Democrat Jóannes EIDESGAARD as prime minister. In the January 2008 balloting the Republic party won vote and seat pluralities. On February 5 Prime Minister Eidesgaard formed a new three-party center-left government of the Social Democratic, Republic, and People's parties. That coalition subsequently broke up and was replaced on September 26 by a right-of-center coalition comprising the Union, People's, and Social Democratic parties, headed by Union Party leader Kaj Leo Johannesen.

Early elections on October 29, 2011, resulted in a center-right coalition government made up of the Union, People's, Center, and Independence parties, with Johannesen again as prime minister. The Social Democratic Party moved to the opposition, while the new pro-independence Progressive Party won two seats.

The EU moved to impose sanctions on the Faroes in May 2013 due to overfishing of herring in the North Atlantic.

High Commissioner: Dan KNUDSEN.

Prime Minister: Kaj Leo JOHANNESEN (Union Party).

Greenland (*Grønland,* or *Kalaallit Nunaat*). Encompassing 840,000 square miles (2,175,600 sq. km), including an extensive ice cover, Greenland is the second-largest island in the world, after Australia. The population, which is largely Eskimo, totals approximately 56,500 (2010E), with residents of the capital, Nuuk (Godthåb), accounting for some 15,300. The indigenous language is Greenlandic. Fishing, mining, and seal hunting are the major economic activities. A number of oil concessions were awarded to international consortia in 1975, but most were subsequently abandoned.

Although under Danish control since the 14th century, the island was originally colonized by Norsemen and only through an apparent oversight was not detached from Denmark along with Norway at the Congress of Vienna in 1815. It became an integral part of the Danish state in 1953 and was granted internal autonomy, effective May 1, 1979, on the basis of a referendum held January 17. The island continues to elect two representatives to the Danish *Folketing*. After achieving autonomy, the island government sought compensation from the United States for the 1953 relocation of indigenous villagers during the construction of U.S. airbases in the northwest. Also persistently controversial was the crash in 1968 of an American B-52 bomber near the Thule base and the eventual disclosure that it had been carrying nuclear weapons, in breach of the Danish ban on nuclear weapons on its territory.

In a preautonomy general election held April 4, 1979, the socialist **Forward** (*Siumut*) party obtained 13 of 21 seats in the new parliament (*Landsting*), and *Siumut* leader Jonathan MOTZFELDT subsequently formed a five-member executive (*Landsstyre*). Other participating groups included the **Solidarity** (*Atássut*) party, led by Lars CHEMNITZ, which obtained the remaining 8 seats, and the proindependence **Eskimo Brotherhood** (*Inuit Ataqatigiit*—IA).

In the balloting of April 1983 for an enlarged *Landsting,* the *Siumut* and *Atássut* parties won 12 seats each, Motzfeldt again forming a government with the support of two IA representatives. A further election on June 6, 1984, necessitated by a nonconfidence vote two months earlier, yielded a formal coalition of the *Siumut* and IA parties, which had obtained 11 and 3 seats, respectively. However, a disagreement ensued regarding the prime minister's alleged "passivity" over the projected installation of new radar equipment at the U.S. airbase in Thule, forcing another early election on May 26, 1987, the results of which were *Siumut* and *Atássut,* 11 seats each; *Inuit Ataqatigiit,* 4; and a new political party, *Issittup Partiia* (Polar Party), representing the business community and fishing industry, 1. On June 9 Motzfeldt succeeded in forming a new administration based on the previous coalition.

The "Thule affair" returned to prominence in January 1995, when the metropolitan government announced a parliamentary inquiry into the 1968 crash, amid continuing demands from Greenlanders for compensation for its alleged consequences, including a high local incidence of cancer. Controversy intensified in July when the Danish foreign minister disclosed that as early as 1957 the U.S. government had informed the then prime minister that nuclear weapons were present in Greenland and that he had raised no objection. (In May 2003 Greenland and Denmark signed an agreement stipulating that in exchange for Greenland's support for modernization of the U.S. radar station in Thule, Greenland would be consulted on all foreign affairs matters relating to the island.)

In September 1997 former prime minister Motzfeldt returned to the premiership when Lars Emil JOHANSEN, a strong proponent of the exploitation of Greenland's mineral and oil wealth, moved into the business sector. In the Danish *Folketing* balloting of March 11, 1998, *Siumut* and *Atássut* each won 1 seat, with the *Siumut* deputy becoming allied with the government coalition. In the *Landsting* election of February 16, 1999, *Siumut* won 11 seats, *Atássut,* 8; the IA, 7; and independents, 5. Among the major issues were calls for more autonomy from Denmark, proposed adoption of the euro should Denmark join the EU's Economic and Monetary Union, and oil exploration. Following the election, *Siumut* and the IA formed a new coalition government under the leadership of Motzfeldt, *Atássut* returning to opposition.

In September 1999 Danish Prime Minister Rasmussen formally apologized to Greenland's indigenous population for the forced relocation of villagers in 1953 in connection with the construction of U.S. bases.

While autonomy remained an ongoing issue in the country's politics, domestic issues were highlighted in the December 3, 2002, parliamentary elections. The new Democratic Party (*Demokratüt*), which stressed issues of improving Inuit education and relieving the housing shortage, received 15.6 percent of the vote and won five seats in the *Landsting.* The biggest winner of the election was the ruling Forward Party (*Siumut*), which secured ten seats and formed a new coalition government under Prime Minister Hans Enoksen. The left-wing Eskimo Brotherhood Party (*Inuit Ataqatigüt—IA*) won eight seats, and the pro-independence Solidarity Party (*Atussut*) won seven seats. A month later the coalition collapsed after a political disagreement, and on January 17, 2003, the Forward Party formed a new coalition with just the Solidarity Party.

In September 2003 the Forward Party again formed a new government in coalition with the pro-independence Eskimo Brotherhood Party after a rift with the Solidarity Party over a budgetary issue. In the most recent election of November 22, 2005—called a year early by the prime minister after the coalition parties failed to reach agreement on a budget—the Forward Party retained ten seats, the Eskimo Brotherhood and the Democratic parties won seven each, and the Solidarity Party secured six. A new left-right coalition government was formed under Prime Minister Enoksen, including all but the Democratic Party. Observers reported that social matters, not independence, were the overriding issues of the election.

In 2006 Greenland, Denmark, and the EU signed an agreement in which the EU would pay millions in subsidies to Greenland in exchange for control over policies regarding climate change and scientific research, prompted by reports of the significant retreat of Greenland's ice sheet, revealing huge mineral resources. The Eskimo Brotherhood Party withdrew from government in May 2007 in a dispute over prawn fishing regulations. Also in 2007 the EU and Greenland signed a new fisheries agreement meant to support the latter's policies in the wake of declining fish populations. Spurred by the prospects of oil revenue, Prime Minister Enoksen proposed a November 2008 referendum to expand the scope of Greenland's self-governance.

On November 25, 2008, 75 percent of those voting in a referendum endorsed the proposed expansion of the island's autonomy, which supporters hoped would lead to full independence from Denmark by 2020. Starting June 21, 2009, the home-rule government in Greenland assumed greater responsibility for police affairs, the justice system, immigration, the coast guard, and other policy areas, although Denmark retained control over most security and foreign policies. Collaterally, Greenland was also scheduled to begin to receive much of the income from oil, gas, and gemstone deposits, whose value was expected to increase dramatically in coming years. The annual subsidy from Copenhagen continued, but the amount was frozen at the 2009 rate. Prime Minister Enoksen called for early parliamentary elections to be held on June 2, 2009.

With financial scandals swirling around Enoksen's government, the Forward Party in June 2009 lost its place in government for the first time. The Eskimo Brotherhood received 44 percent of the vote, far ahead of Forward's 27 percent. Two seats short of an outright majority, the Eskimo Brotherhood formed a government with the centrist Democrats (*Demokraatit*) and the single center-right independent candidate elected under the party label of the Association of Candidates (*Kattusseqatigiit*). The three-party coalition assumed office June 12 under the leadership of Prime Minister Kuupik Kleist. On December 7, 2012, Kleist's government passed a controversial "large-scale" law allowing foreign mining companies to import cheap labor.

On March 12, 2013, Forward won 14 seats to the IA's 11. Voters were concerned over an influx of Chinese workers and potential environmental damage from mining. Forward's Aleqa HAMMOND formed a government with Solidarity and the new Inuit Party (*Partii Inuit*), recently established by Eskimo Brotherhood members unhappy with the large-scale law. Hammond became Greenland's first female prime minister.

High Commissioner: Mikaela ENGELL.
Prime Minister: Aleqa HAMMOND (*Siumut*)

DJIBOUTI

Republic of Djibouti
République de Djibouti (French)
Jumhuriyah Djibouti (Arabic)

Political Status: Former French dependency; proclaimed independent June 27, 1977; new constitution with provisions for limited multiparty elections in effect as of September 1992; limit on the number of parties lifted in September 2002; presidential term limits removed in 2010.

Area: 8,958 sq. mi. (23,200 sq. km).

Population: 925,817 (2012E—UN); 792,198 (2013E—U.S. Census).

Major Urban Center (2005E): DJIBOUTI (599,000).

Official Languages: French and Arabic.

Monetary Unit: Djiboutian Franc (official rate November 1, 2013: 179.00 francs = $1US).

President: Ismail Omar GUELLEH (Popular Rally for Progress); elected on April 9, 1999, and inaugurated for a six-year term on May 8 in succession to Hassan GOULED Aptidon (Popular Rally for Progress); reelected (as the sole candidate) to another six-year term on April 8, 2005; reelected under a new constitutional provision on April 8, 2011, for a five-year term.

Prime Minister: Abdoulkader KAMIL Mohamed (Popular Rally for Progress); appointed by the president on March 31, 2013, and sworn in on April 1, to succeed Dileïta Mohamed DILEÏTA (Popular Rally for Progress).

THE COUNTRY

Formerly known as French Somaliland and subsequently as the French Territory of the Afars and the Issas, the Republic of Djibouti is strategically located in East Africa just south of the Bab el Mandeb, a narrow strait that links the Gulf of Aden to the Red Sea. Djibouti, the capital, was declared a free port by the French in 1949 and has long been an important communications link between Africa, the Arabian peninsula, and the Far East. The largest single population group (40 percent) is the ethnically Somalian Issa tribe, which is concentrated in the vicinity of the capital, while the Afar tribe (35 percent) is essentially nomadic and ethnically linked to the Ethiopians. The remaining 25 percent consists largely of Yemeni Arabs and Somalis.

Serviced by a number of international airlines and heavily dependent on commerce, Djibouti also provides Ethiopia with its only railroad link to the sea. The country is largely barren, with less than 1 percent of its land under cultivation, few known natural resources, and little industry; consequently, the government relies extensively on aid from France and other Western donors, several Arab countries, and various multilateral organizations.

Pervasive poverty and high unemployment remained priorities in the 2000s. In a significant boost to the economy, Djibouti undertook a major expansion of the port of Doraleh with financial backing from the United Arab Emirates. One of the largest and most modern terminals in Africa, the port opened in early 2009 and moved the country closer to its goal of becoming a regional hub for transport, trade, and finance. Despite an unemployment rate of nearly 60 percent, widespread poverty, and a ballooning budget deficit as government spending increased to meet social and security pressures, annual GDP growth remained strong, averaging 4.5 percent in 2010–2011.

But in 2012 Djibouti was hard hit by the combined impact of high global commodity prices and drought in the Horn of Africa, widening the account deficit to 12 percent of GDP in 2011 (from 6 percent in 2010). Despite $47 million pledged by international donors for 2011–2013 to cope with the impact of the drought, the government requested an additional $15 million from the IMF to meet a shortfall. In 2011 GDP grew by 4.5 percent, and inflation reached 5 percent (up from 4 percent in 2010). Driven by port activity, a recovery of trade with Ethiopia, construction, and the ongoing surge in foreign direct investment, in 2012 GDP grew by 4.8 percent, while inflation was 3.7 percent. In May 2013 agreements were signed for China to provide $2.0 billion to construct a railway from Ethiopia to Djibouti's port at Negad.

GOVERNMENT AND POLITICS

Political background. The area known as French Somaliland was formally demarcated by agreement with Emperor Menelik II of Ethiopia in 1897 following a half-century of French penetration that included a series of treaties with indigenous chiefs between 1862 and 1885. Internal autonomy was granted in 1956, and in 1958 the voters of Somaliland elected to enter the French Community as an Overseas Territory. Proindependence demonstrations during a visit by President de Gaulle in August 1966 led to a referendum on March 19, 1967, in which a majority of the predominantly Afar voters opted for continued association with France. Somali protest riots were severely repressed, and the name of the dependency was changed to Territory of the Afars and the Issas to eliminate exclusive identification with the Somali ethnic group.

On December 31, 1975, a UN General Assembly resolution called on France to withdraw from the territory, and during 1976 extensive discussions were held in Paris between leading tribal representatives and the French government. In the course of the talks, France tacitly

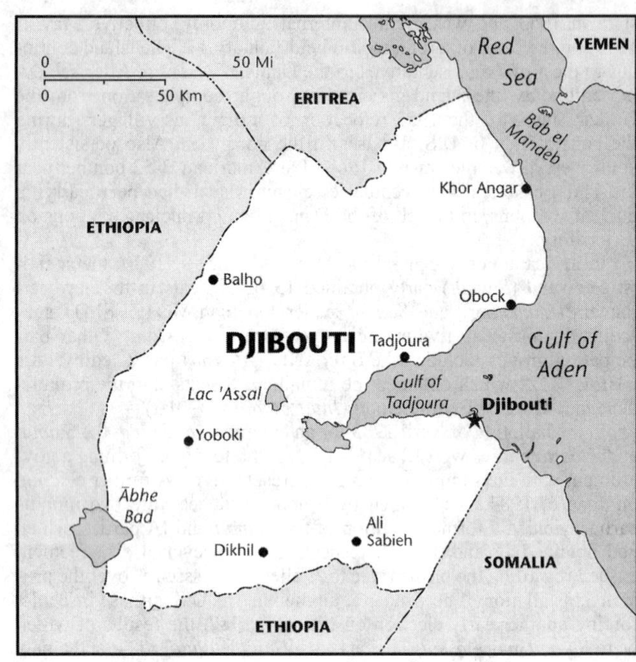

agreed that the Afar president of the local Government Council, Ali AREF Bourhan of the National Union for Independence, no longer represented a majority of the population; consequently, Paris approved a new nationality law governing eligibility for a second referendum on independence. Aref subsequently resigned, and on July 29 a new ten-member council, composed of six Issas and four Afars, was formed.

On May 8, 1977, 98.8 percent of the electorate voted for independence while simultaneously approving a single list of 65 candidates for a Chamber of Deputies. Negotiations with the French that culminated in the referendum were conducted by a United Patriotic Front representing five of the territory's major political groups. In the assembly election, the Front acted under the name of the Popular Independence Rally (*Rassemblement Populaire pour l'Indépendance*—RPI). Following the passage of relevant legislation by the French parliament, the territory became independent as the Republic of Djibouti on June 27. Three days earlier, Issa leader Hassan GOULED Aptidon of the African People's League for Independence had been unanimously elected president of the republic by the chamber. On July 12 President Gouled named Afar leader Ahmed DINI Ahmed to head a 15-member Council of Ministers.

On December 17, 1977, Dini and four other Afar cabinet members resigned amid charges of "tribal repression," the duties of prime minister being assumed by the president until the designation of a new government headed by Abdallah MOHAMED Kamil on February 5, 1978. Mohamed Kamil was in turn succeeded by Barkat GOURAD Hamadou on September 30, 1978. Gourad, an Afar advocate of "detribalization," formed subsequent governments on July 7, 1981 (following the reelection of President Gouled on June 12); on June 5, 1982 (after a legislative election on May 21); and on November 23, 1987 (after balloting on April 24).

Although the cabinets formed since independence had been designed to strike a careful balance in tribal representation and all three prime ministers named by President Gouled were Afars, charges of Issa domination persisted, and most members of the opposition Djibouti People's Party (*Parti Populaire Djiboutien*—PPD) formed in August 1981 were from the ethnic minority. The regime's immediate response was to arrest PPD leader Moussa Ahmed IDRISS and the party's entire 12-member executive committee. However, all were released by January 1982, after the enactment of legislation establishing Gouled's Popular Rally for Progress (*Rassemblement Populaire pour le Progrès*—RPP) as the sole authorized party.

Despite a constitutional limit of presidential tenure to two terms, Gouled was permitted to run again in 1987 on the ground that he had initially been appointed by the Chamber of Deputies rather than having been popularly elected. As sole candidate, the incumbent was reported to have secured 90 percent of the vote in the April 24 poll.

In 1990 the regime's reported backing of the rebels in Somalia sparked internal conflicts between the Issa majority and Afar/Gadabursi kinsmen of Somalian leader Siad Barre; as a consequence, the government on January 9, 1991, arrested 68 people for alleged involvement in a "vast plot" to incite "civil war" between the Afar and Issa communities. While most were soon released, the detention of seven "ringleaders," including former chief minister Ali Aref Bourhan, was confirmed by the interior ministry on January 17; three days later it was announced that "about 20" individuals had been formally charged with attempting to overthrow the government. At midyear, there were ethnic clashes between Issas and Oromos, and in October Afar rebel forces, having coalesced as the Front for the Restoration of Unity and Democracy (*Front pour la Restauration de l'Unité et de la Démocratie*—FRUD), launched attacks on government installations.

In response to the fighting, France urged Djibouti to institute "rapid" liberalization of its political system, and on November 27, 1990, the government revealed plans for a referendum "to consult" the population "on changes to be made in the political domain." On December 19 it announced that the referendum would be held in May 1992, but only if rebel activity had ceased. Eleven days later an RPP spokesperson reported that legislative elections to be held immediately after the referendum would be open to candidates from "several parties." Meanwhile, the slaying by government forces of 40 Afars and the wounding of 50 others in a Djibouti slum severely eroded what support remained for the regime. Thereafter, 14 parliamentarians led by Mohamed AHMED Issa ("Cheiko") formed a parliamentary opposition group, and in January 1992 the health and public service ministers resigned, with the former decrying the regime's "war logic." Concurrently, a French spokesperson insisted that the escalating civil war was an "internal matter" not covered by a defense agreement concluded between the two countries in 1977. Nonetheless, a French military contingent was deployed in February to implement a cease-fire between government and FRUD units. Subsequently, a committee formed by President Gouled presented a preliminary draft of a new constitution, which was not acceptable to the rebels, however, because it would retain a strong presidency.

On June 20–24, 1992, representatives of most of the leading opposition groups (under the banner of the United Opposition Front of Djibouti [*Front Uni de l'Opposition Djiboutienne*—FUOD] in Political Parties and Groups, see below) met in Paris to forge a common front against the Gouled regime. The session concluded with a demand for a "transitional government led by a prime minister from the ranks of the opposition," who would be charged with initiating a democratic transitional process that would include the drafting of a multiparty constitution.

In a national referendum on September 4, 1992, a reported 97 percent of the voters approved the draft constitution presented by the administration, providing for, among other things, multiparty activity, although a separate vote also endorsed a proposal to limit the number of legal parties to four. Subsequently, FRUD and other opposition members of FUOD boycotted the legislative balloting of December 18 (at which the RPP was awarded all of the seats) as well as the presidential election of May 7, 1993, at which President Gouled defeated four other candidates by a wide margin in securing reelection to a fourth term.

In mid-1994 a split developed within FRUD between supporters of its newly designated president Ali MOHAMED Daoud, who favored peace talks with the government, and his recently ousted predecessor, former prime minister Dini, who, along with most of the FUOD leadership, supported continued resistance. The peace talks, which reportedly had commenced as secret negotiations between Prime Minister Gourad and the "New FRUD" secretary general, Ougoureh KIFLE Ahmed, eventually yielded a reconciliation agreement on December 26 that in a cabinet reshuffle of June 8, 1995, provided the Kifle faction with two ministerial portfolios.

The December 1994 accord yielded greatly reduced hostilities in 1995, although by early 1996 dissension within the government had become intense, with the justice minister and RPP secretary general, Moumin BAHDON Farah, leading those who contended that the agreement had not brought real peace and stability to Djibouti. The dominance of the pro-accord camp was demonstrated on March 27 when Bahdon was dismissed from the government, together with Ahmed BOULALEH Barre, the defense minister. Bahdon and his allies subsequently launched a new opposition group, Group for the Democracy of the Republic. Collaterally, the episode showed that in the bitter contest between possible successors to an increasingly infirm Gouled, ascendancy had been gained by the president's nephew and *chef de cabinet*, Ismail Omar GUELLEH.

To contest the 1997 Assembly elections, the Group for the Democracy of the Republic (GDR) formed a coalition with the United Opposition Front of Djibouti (FUOD) and a faction of the Party of Democratic Renewal (PRD). However, a strong opposition failed to materialize as, in addition to the PRD, both FRUD and the National Democratic Party (PND) suffered from factionalization.

In assembly elections on December 19, 1997, the RPP–"New FRUD" electoral coalition captured all 65 seats (54 by the RPP and 11 by "New FRUD"), garnering a reported 78.55 percent of the vote tally compared to 19.19 percent for the Party of Democratic Renewal and 2.25 percent for the National Democratic Party. On December 28 President Gouled reappointed Gourad as head of a reshuffled government.

In February 1999 President Gouled announced that he would not seek reelection in balloting scheduled for the following April, and the RPP promptly chose Guelleh as its presidential candidate. A number of opposition leaders declared their intention to campaign for the chief executive's post, including Abbate Ebo ADOU of the Action for Revision of Order in Djibouti (AROD), the PRD's Abidillahi HAMAREITEH, and Aden Robleh AWALEH of the National Democratic Party's (*Parti National Démocratique*—PND). However, in February the aforementioned withdrew from the race as their parties, under the reported direction of the GDR, formed an electoral alliance, subsequently styled the Unified Djiboutian Opposition (*Opposition Djiboutienne Unifiée*—ODU), which then chose Moussa Ahmed IDRISS, a former independence fighter who had only recently resigned from the RPP, as its standard-bearer.

Guelleh captured 74.09 percent of the vote on April 9, easily outdistancing Idriss. Despite gaining the endorsement of the newly formed Unified Djiboutian Opposition (see Political Parties, below), Idriss garnered just 25.78 percent of the vote. Prime Minister Gourad was reappointed on May 10, and a reshuffled cabinet was formed two days later. Idriss was arrested in September for "attacking the morale of the armed forces" by publishing an article critical of the government in *Le Temps*. Idriss and 19 of his supporters were found guilty and sentenced to four months' imprisonment; however, Idriss was later released and granted amnesty. Subsequently, he was invited to resume his role as a member of the Chamber of Deputies.

After 22 years in office, Prime Minister Gourad announced his resignation in February 2001; he was succeeded on May 7 by Dileïta Mohamed DILEÏTA, a former chief of the presidential staff. In the wake of a comprehensive agreement between the administration and FRUD, several FRUD members were included in the new cabinet installed on July 4. In addition, in September 2002 President Guelleh announced the establishment of a full multiparty system. The ruling Union for a Presidential Majority (*Union pour la Majorité Présidentielle*—UMP) still won all 65 seats in balloting for the Chamber of Deputies on January 10, 2003. Also undercutting the administration's stated goal of broader governmental participation, Guelleh was the only candidate in the April 8, 2005, presidential balloting. He appointed a new government on May 22.

Former president Gouled died on November 21, 2006, at age 90.

The UMP again won all 65 seats in assembly elections on February 8, 2008; opposition parties boycotted the balloting on grounds that it was "undemocratic." Prime Minister Dileïta was reappointed on March 26, and the cabinet was reshuffled the following day.

Under constitutional provisions adopted in 2010, President Guelleh was allowed to run for a third term, reduced to five years, on April 8, 2011. The election was boycotted by the opposition, leaving only one challenger, the former head of the Constitutional Council, Mohamed Warsama RAGUEH, who secured just 19.4 percent of the vote. Guelleh was sworn in on May 8 and reappointed Prime Minister Dileïta and named a new government, retaining only nine ministers from the previous cabinet, on May 12.

Ahead of legislative elections on February 22, 2013, opposition parties formed a new coalition, the Union for National Salvation (*Union pour le Salut National*—USN), including the PDD, the PND, Republican Alliance for Democracy (*Alliance Republicaine pour la Démocratie*—ARD), the Movement for Democratic Renewal and Development (*Mouvement pour le Renouveau Démocratique et le Développement*—MRDD), the Union for Democracy and Justice (*Union pour la Démocratie et la Justice*—UDJ), the Movement for Development and Liberty (*Mouvement pour le Développement et la Liberté*—MoDel), and the Rally for Action on Democracy and Development (*Rassemblement pour l'action, la démocratie et le développement*—RADD). Another newly formed opposition grouping, the centrist Center for Unified Democrats (*Le Centre Des Démocrates Unifiés*—CDU), also contested the balloting. In the balloting, the UMP won 49 seats, and the USN, 16 (see Current issues, below). Following the balloting, Guellah replaced Prime Minister Dileïta with defense minister Abdoulkader KAMIL Mohamed on March 31. A new cabinet was named the next day.

Constitution and government. The Chamber of Deputies established under the 1977 independence referendum was empowered to act as a constituent assembly pending adoption of a formal constitution. In that capacity it approved a number of measures in 1981 dealing with the presidency and the legislature. On February 10 it decreed that candidates for the former could be nominated only by parties holding at least 25 chamber seats, with balloting by universal suffrage and election for a six-year term that could be renewed only once. Following the presidential election of June 12 (in which the incumbent was the only candidate), the opposition PPD was organized, but it was denied legal status on the basis of a "National Mobilization" law approved on October 19 that established a one-party system. As a result, all of the candidates in the parliamentary elections of 1982 and 1987 were presented by the government-supportive RPP. A new constitution providing for a qualified multiparty system (with a maximum, for at least ten years, of four parties being permitted) became effective in September 1992. The president, who appoints the prime minister and otherwise exercises broad authority, was limited to two six-year terms. In September 2002 the government eliminated all restrictions on party registration.

The colonial judicial structure, based on both French and local law, was technically abolished at independence, although a successor system based on Muslim precepts remains imperfectly formulated. For administrative purposes the republic is divided into five districts, one of which encompasses the capital. Local elections to regional assemblies, envisioned under recent decentralization plans negotiated by the government with groups such as FRUD, were held in March 2006.

Constitutional amendments approved by the Chamber of Deputies on April 19, 2010, and promulgated on April 21 removed presidential term limits and reduced the presidential term to five years, among other things (see Current Issues, below.)

The media is heavily regulated in Djibouti. In 2013 Reporters Without Borders described the country as a "media black hole" and ranked it 167th out of 179 countries in freedom of the press.

Foreign relations. Djibouti's small size and its mixed population of Ethiopian-oriented Afars and Somali-oriented Issas make it highly vulnerable in a context of historic friction between its two neighbors. Despite bilateral accords in 1986 and 1987, Somalia has long regarded Djibouti as a "land to be redeemed," while the nearly 500-mile railroad between the port of Djibouti and Addis Ababa was viewed by Ethiopia as vital to its export-import trade during the lengthy revolt in its Red Sea province of Eritrea. The country's security depends in part on a French garrison, which was of crucial importance during the prolonged Soviet military presence in Ethiopia and South Yemen.

In January 1986 President Gouled hosted a six-nation conference to set up an Intergovernmental Authority on Drought and Development in East Africa (IGADD, subsequently the Intergovernmental Authority on Development—IGAD), which marked the first meeting between the Ethiopian head of state, Lt. Col. Haile-Mariam, and President Siad Barre of Somalia since the two countries went to war in 1977. The other states participating in the conference as IGADD members were Kenya, Sudan, and Uganda. Subsequently, peace talks between the 1977 combatants, mediated by Djibouti, were held in Addis Ababa in May, with Gouled reaffirming his country's role in the peace negotiations during a state visit to Ethiopia in September. A second IGADD summit was held in March 1988, with the Djibouti president being elected to a second term as the authority's chair.

The repatriation of some 50,000 Ethiopians who had fled to Djibouti during the Ogadan conflict began in 1983 but was subsequently halted because of the drought; it was resumed in December 1986 amid charges that the "voluntary" program would in fact expose the refugees to potential mistreatment. By 1987 it was estimated that fewer than 20,000 expatriates remained, with Djibouti insisting that they too would have to leave since resources were lacking for their assimilation.

The early 1990 intensification of the Somalian civil war, coupled with Djibouti's continued tacit support of the Somalian National Movement (SNM), an Issa rebel group, resulted in a deterioration of relations between Djibouti and Mogadishu and mutual border militarization. In October Somalian claims of military intrusion yielded closure of the maritime border while igniting ethnic hostilities in Djibouti. Meanwhile, observers described Djibouti's dependence on French security forces and aid (renewed for ten years in July) as motivation for publicly siding with allied forces in the Gulf crisis, despite a number of Djibouti-Baghdad military and economic agreements.

The outbreak of ethnic violence in 1991 severely strained Djiboutian–French relations. Paris, which had deployed troops in March to disarm Ethiopian soldiers fleeing into Djibouti, dismissed the government's claims that Ethiopian Afars were seeking to establish a "greater Afaria" and in October ordered its troops to remain in their barracks. Concurrently, France pressed the Gouled regime to accelerate political liberalization and enter into cease-fire negotiations with the rebels. In November France rejected Djibouti's request for supplies and labeled the regime's international efforts to solicit weapons as "intolerable." Following the government's violent suppression of Afar slum dwellers in Djibouti in December, Paris warned Djibouti that it would suspend economic aid unless there was immediate "democratization," and in February 1992 France intervened to enforce a standoff between government and rebel forces that continued for the remainder of the year. Relations with Paris improved in the wake of the December 1994 peace accord that the government signed with a FRUD faction, with French defense minister Charles Dillon confirming, during a visit to Djibouti in January 1996, that France would maintain its military presence in the republic.

An unresolved territorial dispute flared up in mid-April 1996 when Djiboutian and Eritrean forces clashed in a northern border area claimed by Eritrea on the strength of a 1935 colonial-era map. In June the Organization of African Unity (OAU, subsequently the African Union—AU) authorized Djibouti, Burkina Faso, and Zimbabwe to mediate the border dispute; however, in November Eritrea severed relations with Djibouti, accusing the Gouled administration of supporting Ethiopia's military campaign. (In early 1999 the OAU named a new negotiating team after the delegates from Burkina Faso and Zimbabwe refused to enter Eritrea without their banned Djiboutian colleagues [see separate entries on Eritrea and Ethiopia for more details].) Normal relations were reestablished with Eritrea following the conclusion of the conflict, in part assisted by the two countries' similar stances regarding events in Somalia.

In late 2001 and early 2002 Djibouti's potentially strategic geographic location in regard to the West's war on terrorism was noted internationally. President Guelleh agreed to allow the United States to establish a military base in Djibouti, while also endorsing an ongoing French military presence. At the same time, the Guelleh regime, cognizant of the status of Islam as the nation's majority religion, evinced a strongly pro-Arab and pro-Palestinian posture in regard to the turmoil in the Middle East. In September 2003 Djibouti expelled some 80,000 illegal immigrants, mostly Ethiopians and Somalis. It was subsequently reported that U.S. concerns over possible attacks on Western interests had led the government of Djibouti to detain several hundred suspects. In 2006 Djibouti opposed an AU decision to send peacekeeping troops to Somalia and denied accusations by the UN that it was supplying weapons to Somali Islamists. At the AU summit in early 2007, following renewed fighting in Somalia, Djibouti agreed to the proposed AU peacekeeping mission, which was to be replaced by a UN peacekeeping force within six months.

With piracy becoming a growing threat to coastal countries in East Africa, in 2009 nine countries in the Indian Ocean and Red Sea regions, including Djibouti, announced plans to cooperate on combating the threat. The resulting Djibouti Code of Conduct allows for the countries that are party to the agreement to send troops into other signatory countries' territorial waters to pursue pirates.

Also in 2009, Iran and Djibouti agreed on bilateral cooperation following a visit to Djibouti by Iranian president Mahmoud Ahmadinejad.

In May 2010 the International Criminal Court (ICC) asked the UN Security Council to take action against Djibouti after the government failed to arrest Sudanese president Omar Hassan al-Bashir when he visited Djibouti. The Sudanese president had been indicted on war crimes charges in connection with genocide in Darfur.

In December 2011 Djibouti sent the first 100 (of a planned 850) soldiers to join the African Union Mission in Somalia (AMISOM) supporting Somalia's transitional government against Al Shabaab militants, despite the group's threats to retaliate against participating countries.

In January 2012 U.S. commandos launched a raid to free two kidnapped aid workers in Somalia from the U.S. military base in Djibouti at Camp Lemonnier. During a visit to the camp a month before, U.S. defense secretary Leon Panetta had called Djibouti "the central location for continuing the fight against terrorism." Meanwhile, in February, Djibouti signed a memorandum of understanding with landlocked South Sudan, which was in a dispute with Sudan over the cost of transporting and exporting oil through its territory, to build a pipeline to its port on the Red Sea.

In April 2013 Djibouti announced it would deploy additional troops with AMISOM. Djibouti and Yemen finalized an accord to enhance cooperation against maritime smuggling and human trafficking. The UN World Food Program began construction of a regional hub and distribution center in Djibouti in June. In July Djibouti and Ethiopia signed a series of agreements designed to further integrate the economies of the two countries.

Current issues. On April 19, 2010, the all-UMP Chamber of Deputies approved amendments removing term limits on the presidency, reducing the mandate to five years, and setting the upper age limit to 75. Other amendments provided for the creation of a senate, abolition of the death penalty, and prohibition of the overlapping of parliamentary mandates and ministerial posts. The following day, thousands of supporters demonstrated in front of the presidential palace, and shortly thereafter, Guelleh indicated he would seek a third term in 2011.

In June 2010 Djibouti and Eritrea agreed to an offer by Qatar to mediate the border dispute, with resolution to be determined by a panel that was to include two members each from Djibouti and Eritrea. Eritrean forces immediately withdrew from the disputed area.

Attention in 2011 turned to the upcoming presidential election, drawing the ire of the opposition in protest of the constitutional amendment allowing Guelleh to run again. Tensions escalated in February with unprecedented protests of antigovernment demonstrators—likely influenced by similar protests in North Africa and the Middle East—calling for Guelleh's resignation and for the election to be postponed to allow for a more credible process. (For more on the demonstrations and crackdowns in the run-up to the election, see the 2012 *Handbook.*) In April the opposition boycotted the presidential election, which Guelleh easily won with 80.6 percent of the vote, defeating a single challenger, the former president of the Constitutional Court. President Guelleh, who had previously announced that he would not seek a fourth term, called for national unity.

On October 8, 2011, Guelleh dismissed national education minister Adawa Hassan Ali, who had served in the position for only five months. Although no reason was given for his departure, local media reports claimed it was related to a meeting he had with a leader of the opposition Djibouti Democratic Coalition during an official trip to Canada. By November 2011 Guelleh's cabinet shuffle had done little to make the regime any less fragile, according to the *Indian Ocean Newsletter,* which reported that a new wave of arrests took place on November 21 targeting political opponents.

Opposition groups agreed to participate in legislative polling on February 22, 2013, after the Assembly voted to allow 20 percent of the seats to be allocated on a proportional basis. The USN rejected the official results following the balloting and filed suit with the Constitutional Council alleging voting fraud and intimidation. The opposition challenge was rejected by the court on March 13. Meanwhile, sporadic protests and riots took place in the capital throughout the remainder of February and into March, leading to an estimated 600 arrests and at least 6 deaths.

POLITICAL PARTIES AND GROUPS

On September 4, 2002, President Guelleh announced the introduction of a full multiparty system. Eight parties participated in the 2003 legislative elections, four each in progovernment and opposition electoral blocs. In the 2008 legislative elections, only the UMP fielded candidates. Opposition parties, united under the Union for a Democratic Alternative (*Union pour l'Alternance Démocratique*—UAD) boycotted the balloting, claiming it was undemocratic. Six opposition groups formed the USN ahead of the February 2013 elections.

Government-Supportive Parties:

Union for a Presidential Majority (*Union pour la Majorité Présidentielle*—UMP). Formed as an electoral bloc prior to the 2003 legislative elections by the RPP, FRUD, PND, and PPSD, the UMP secured all 65 seats in that balloting with a reported 62 percent of the vote. The four groups also backed Guelleh in the 2005 presidential election. In the 2008 legislative balloting, the UMP, this time including the four groups and the UPR, again won all 65 seats.

In March 2010 following President Guelleh's announcement that he intended to amend the constitution so that he could stand for a third term, the UMP, as expected, supported the measure to extend his mandate by removing term limits. According to official results, the UMP secured 61.5 percent of the vote in the February 2013 elections, winning 49 seats.

Leaders: Ismail Omar GUELLEH (RPP), Ali Mohamed DAOUD (FRUD), Aden ROBLEH Awaleh (PND), Moumin BAHDON Farah (PPSD).

Popular Rally for Progress (*Rassemblement Populaire pour le Progrès*—RPP). The RPP was launched on March 4, 1979, its leading component being the socialist African People's League for Independence (*Ligue Populaire Africaine pour l'Indépendance*—LPAI). Long the principal spokesperson for the Issa majority, the LPAI was not represented in the Afar-dominated preindependence Chamber of Deputies, although two of its members held ministerial posts.

The RPP was the first political group to be legalized under the "pluralist" constitution of 1992 and was credited with a clean sweep of chamber seats in December. In September 1996, Gouled announced his intention to serve out his presidential term (despite his failing health) and also to retain the party leadership until 1999.

In September 1996 the party announced the composition of its reshuffled Executive Committee, highlighted by the appointment as third deputy chair of Ismail Omar Guelleh, the apparent front-runner in the party's bitter contest to succeed the increasingly infirm Gouled. At a party congress in 1997, Gouled was reelected chair, while party delegates also elected a 125-member Central Committee and adopted a resolution confirming its alliance with the "New FRUD." Guelleh, who had succeeded Gouled as president of the republic in 1999, was also elected as the new RPP chair in March 2000, Gouled having retired from party activity.

The party won a majority in all five regional and three communal area elections in March 2006. Subsequently, tensions developed with FRUD, which had hoped to gain more power on the local level. In September 2012 the RPP elected a new 17-member executive committee and Abdoulkader KAMIL Mohamed replaced Dileïta Mohamed DILEÏTA as vice president of the party (he succeeded Dileïta as prime minister in April 2013), while Ilyas Moussa DAWALEH was elected secretary general of the party.

Leaders: Ismail Omar GUELLEH (President of the Republic and President of the Party), Abdoulkader KAMIL Mohamed (Prime Minister and Vice President of the Party), Ilyas Moussa DAWALEH (Secretary General).

Front for the Restoration of Unity and Democracy (*Front pour la Restauration de l'Unité et de la Démocratie*—FRUD). The Afar-dominated FRUD was organized in Balho in northern Djibouti in August 1991 by nominal merger of the three groups below on a platform calling for the overthrow of President Gouled's "tribal dictatorship" and the installation of a democratic multiparty system.

In September 1991 leaders of FRUD and the MNDID (see under PND, below) met in Ethiopia, and one month later their combined forces clashed with government troops in Djibouti's southern Yokobi region. Meanwhile, a second rebel summit, this time including the Democratic Union for Djiboutian Justice and Equality, was held in Somaliland.

The FRUD representative in the capital, Abbate Ebo Adou of the AROD (below), was arrested in December 1991 but was released following French intervention in February 1992. Two months later a small armed Gadabursi movement, the **Front of Democratic Forces** (*Front des Forces Démocratiques*—FFD), led by Mahmoud ABAR Derane and Omar CHARDIE Bouni, was reported to have linked up with FRUD. The following August, during a congress in an area "liberated" by FRUD, the incumbent president, Mohamed ADOYTA Yusuf, was named first vice president, while former Prime Minister Ahmed DINI Ahmed, theretofore resident in Yemen, was named FRUD president.

Meanwhile, FRUD had been instrumental in the June 1992 formation in Paris of the United Opposition Front of Djibouti (*Front Uni de l'Opposition Djiboutienne*—FUOD), an alliance of Afar and antiregime Issa groups. (See 2000–2002 *Handbook* for additional information on FUOD.)

On February 22, 1994, it was reported that Dini had been ousted and a new executive committee appointed with Ougoureh Kifle Ahmed as its secretary general. Subsequently, Kifle was said to have been engaged in a series of peace talks with the government that were opposed by supporters of Dini. At a "reconciliation" meeting of FRUD factions on June 21–25, Ali Mohamed Daoud (a.k.a. Jean Marie) was formally designated as the successor to

Dini, who, from residence in Ethiopia, continued to reject the posture of political conciliation displayed by the current leadership. By late July the latter itself appeared to back away from continued peace talks by issuing a series of demands calling for ethnic balance in the government and armed forces. Meanwhile, FUOD had refused to recognize the new FRUD leadership, continuing to support the FRUD-Dini group, which, during a September congress named a rival seven-member executive committee sworn "to pursue the armed struggle against the Gouled regime."

In December 1994 the "New FRUD" leadership concluded an agreement with the government (from which the group's deputy secretary general, Ibrahim Chehem Daoud, dissociated himself) that called for an end to armed resistance and integration of FRUD units into the regular military, an alliance with the RPP that would include cabinet portfolios for two FRUD faction members, and the reform of electoral lists prior to the next election. In accordance with the agreement, the legalization of FRUD as the fourth political party permitted under Djibouti's constitution was announced by the interior minister on March 9, 1996, although the split between the legalized "New FRUD" and the FRUD-Dini faction remained unresolved at that stage.

Ending over 19 years in exile, FRUD-Dini Vice President Adoyta Yusuf returned to Djibouti in November 1996, along with some 15 supporters. Their return was facilitated by high-level negotiations between the Djiboutian prime minister and his Ethiopian counterpart and sparked speculation that Adoyta would join the Gouled cabinet. In March 1997 the FRUD's longtime European representative, Ismael Ibrahim Houmed, also returned from exile.

The "New FRUD" held its first congress on April 15–16, 1997, officials revealing that they had signed a secret political platform with the ruling party in December 1994 that included provisions for both higher profile joint governmental activities and the preparation of a shared list of candidates for the legislative balloting scheduled for December 1997. Furthermore, party delegates elected a multiethnic, 21-member Executive Committee and a 153-member National Committee. The former's composition underlined the party's pledge to include non-Afars in leadership positions.

Meanwhile, the "New FRUD's" tightened alliance with the government widened the chasm between it and the FRUD-Dini faction. Underscoring the reportedly widespread antipathy felt toward the "New FRUD," demonstrators on May 1, 1997, disrupted the group's attempt to open an office in a predominantly Afar neighborhood in the capital. Following the FRUD-Dini's alleged attack on government forces in September, the Gouled administration authorized a military offensive against the rebel militants and urged its allies abroad to deny asylum to the FRUD-Dini's exiled leadership. Consequently, a number of FRUD-Dini faction leaders were extradited to Djibouti, while others were reported to have been forced to leave their safe havens. On November 10–12 the FRUD-Dini organized a congress within Djibouti's borders where delegates reelected Dini chair and elected a 13-member political bureau. Furthermore, the faction asserted that, while it was committed to further warfare, it remained open to establishing a dialogue with the government.

On November 26, 1997, FUOD president Ahmed Issa died. He was succeeded by Mahdi Ibrahim Ahmed, who in November 1998 called for an interim government, including the main opposition parties prior to the 1999 presidential balloting. However, there were few subsequent reports of FUOD activity, attention focusing on government negotiations with the remaining FRUD antigovernment forces.

In March 1998 FRUD-Dini and PRD delegates appealed to IGAD ministers meeting in Djibouti to intervene in the strife, claiming that foreign mercenaries were assisting government forces in the latest outbreak of fighting. The militants' entreaties were shelved by IGAD, and skirmishes were reported throughout the year and into 1999.

Following a series of secret meetings in France, an accord was signed on February 7, 2000, in Paris providing for an immediate cessation of hostilities, reciprocal prisoner releases, the eventual reintegration of the militants into their former jobs, and further discussions regarding the proposed devolution of political authority to the regions (primarily in the north of the country) involved in the rebel activity. Dini returned to Djibouti in late March from his long exile in France, and a FRUD-Dini congress on April 5–6 endorsed the Paris accord and reaffirmed its confidence in Dini's leadership, although the faction's fighters were to remain armed pending negotiation of a comprehensive peace settlement.

A final agreement was reached in May 2001 for, among other things, the demobilization of FRUD forces, which subsequently proceeded smoothly, facilitated by a September amnesty bill. FRUD also contributed several ministers to the July 2001 "postwar cabinet." However, friction continued within FRUD, particularly when Dini announced plans to launch a party called FRUD-National, which would seek countrywide membership that would include a significant non-Afar segment. Reports indicated that some FRUD continued to object to Dini's perceived efforts to place his personal imprint on the movement, while the so-called "Armed-FRUD" still remained skeptical of the peace process in general.

FRUD formalized its relationship with the RPP with the launching of the UMP prior to the 2003 legislative poll, while Dini established his own opposition party (see ARD, below). By that time there did not appear to be an armed FRUD of any consequence, though in late 2005 battles between Afar rebels and government troops were reported in the northern area of the country.

Following the RPP's overwhelming victory in local elections in 2006, disputes within FRUD over criticism of the election led to the ouster of at least one local FRUD party leader. In 2008 FRUD secretary general Ougoureh Kifleh Ahmed was reelected to the Chamber of Deputies on the UMP candidate list.

Tensions in the north turned into violent clashes in September 2009 and May 2010, when FRUD rebels, who claimed they were attacked by Djibouti military forces, killed seven soldiers and wounded scores. The military wing of FRUD, under the leadership of Mohamed KADAMY, blamed the government for failing to find a peaceful resolution. Some observers said the army was under pressure from the president, "who wanted immediate results."

Meanwhile, in early 2010 FRUD opposed the government's decision to send troops to Somalia, calling it "counterproductive" in light of the country's struggles with Eritrea and saying it would open the door to "importing terrorism" from Somalia.

Party secretary general Ougoureh Kifleh Ahmed was replaced as defense minister when a new government was named on May 12, 2011, following the presidential election on April 8. In November 2012 members of an armed faction of the grouping, the FRUD-*armé*, were reportedly responsible for a series of attacks on security forces.

Following the 2013 Assembly balloting, FRUD member Mohamed Ali HOUMED was elected deputy speaker of the legislature.

Leaders: Ali Mohamed DAOUD (President), Hassan MOKBEL (Spokesperson), Ougoureh KIFLEH Ahmed (Secretary General).

For information on **Action for Revision of Order in Djibouti** (*Action pour la Révision de l'Ordre à Djibouti*—AROD), the most prominent of the FRUD partners but one for which no recent activity has been reported, see earlier editions of the *Handbook.*

People's Social Democratic Party (*Parti Populaire Social Démocrate*—PPSD). The PPSD was launched in 2002 under the leadership of Moumin Bahdon Farah, who had been dismissed as justice minister in March 1996 and had subsequently helped to establish the Group for the Democracy of the Republic (*Groupement pour la Démocratie de la République*—GDR) to oppose President Gouled. (For additional information on the GDR, see the 2000–2002 *Handbook.*) Bahdon stayed on as the leader of the PPSD, and the party backed Guelleh in the 2005 presidential election.

In 2008 accusations were levied against Bahdon concerning his alleged involvement in the murder of a French judge. The judge was reported to have been investigating arms smuggling or money laundering, allegedly involving major figures in Djibouti, nearly a decade earlier. When the judge's death was determined to be a homicide, allegations followed against government officials in France and Djibouti, including Bahdon, who was said to have ordered the judge to conduct the investigation. Bahdon denied any role in the matter. He died in September 2009.

In April 2011 Bahdon's daughter Hasna Bahdon Mounim became the first woman elected to head the party.

Leader: Hasna BAHDON Mounim.

Union of Reformed Partisans (*Union des Partisans Reformés*—UPR). The launching of the UPR was announced in early 2005 under the leadership of Ibrahim Chehem Daoud, a former FRUD leader. The UPR endorsed President Guelleh in the 2005 presidential balloting. In 2008 the UPR joined the UMP electoral bloc for the assembly elections, and in 2009 party leader Chehem supported the constitutional amendment that permitted President Guelleh to seek a third term.

Leaders: Ibrahim CHEHEM Daoud, Adou Ali ADOU (Secretary General).

Opposition Parties:

Union for National Salvation (*Union pour le Salut National*—USN). Formed in January 2013, the USN sought to unite the opposition ahead of the 2013 Assembly balloting and included the PND, ARD, MRDD, UDJ, PDD, MoDel, and RADD. The coalition secured 35.6 percent of the vote in the election and 16 seats. However, the USN challenged the election results in court and on the streets through protests. On June 1–2, 17 leading members of the group were arrested, although most were subsequently released.

Leaders: Ahmad Youssouf HOUMED (Chair), Abdourahman Mohamed GUELLAH (Secretary Generral), Daher Ahmed FARAH (Spokesperson).

National Democratic Party (*Parti National Démocratique*—PND). The PND was reported to have been launched in Paris in late 1992 by Aden Robleh Awaleh, theretofore leader of the Djiboutian National Movement for the Installation of Democracy (*Mouvement National Djiboutien pour l'Instauration de la Démocratie*—MNDID). A former Gouled cabinet member and vice president of the RPP, Robleh had formed the MNDID in early 1986 (for more information on the MNDID, please see the 2013 *Handbook*).

In September 1993 Robleh met in Paris with the PRD's Djame, the two leaders subsequently reiterating the opposition's 1992 appeal for a transitional government of national unity. Nonetheless, Robleh joined his PRD counterpart in endorsing the December 1994 accord between "New FRUD" and the government.

In April 1996 a Paris judge issued an international arrest warrant against Robleh and his wife in connection with a French inquiry into a September 1990 grenade attack on a cafe in Djibouti, in which a six-year-old French child was killed and 15 people (mostly French nationals) were injured. Suspected by French investigators of having been the brains behind the attack, the PND leader reportedly fled Paris to seek refuge in Morocco.

In May 1997 Robleh's decision to suspend party spokesperson Farah ALI Wabert exacerbated a growing chasm between the chair and his opponents on both the Political Bureau and National Council. Subsequently, all of the Political Bureau members, with the exception of Mahdi AHMED Abdillahi, who was also wanted for the 1990 attack, endorsed a letter urging Robleh to resign by August 31, 1997. A Paris court sentenced five defendants in absentia to life imprisonment for the 1990 attack. However, the case against Robleh was deferred, and he was briefly considered as the potential PND candidate for president in 1999. A number of PND members were reportedly arrested in late 1999 for what the government termed an illegal street demonstration. In April 2001 Robleh was given a six-year suspended sentence after being convicted of complicity in the 1990 attack. By 2003 the PND agreed to participate in the electoral bloc under the UMP, and in 2005 Robleh announced the party's endorsement of President Guelleh's reelection bid. In 2007 Robleh was reelected president of the party, and in 2008 he was reelected to parliament on the UMP list, having been seated for the first time in 2003. In 2008 he was a representative in the Pan-African Parliament. In 2010 the PND broke with the UMP over the constitutional amendment that allowed Guelleh to seek a third term.

In January 2013 the PND joined the opposition USN.

Leaders: Aden ROBLEH Awaleh (President of the Party and 1993 presidential candidate), Saida FALCOU, Moussa HUSSEIN, Abdallah DABALEH.

Republican Alliance for Democracy (*Alliance Republicaine pour la Démocratie*—ARD). The ARD was registered in 2002 under the leadership of former FRUD leader Dini, who subsequently became the most prominent spokesperson for the UAD. Dini's death in September 2004 reportedly left both the ARD and the URD at sea in regard to leadership. In 2006 a new executive committee was formed to reactivate the party, and although some called for a return to militancy, a majority of party members favored less radical means of promoting democratic reforms. ARD leader Ahmad Youssouf HOUMED was selected as chair of the USN ahead of legislative elections in February 2013. Following opposition protests against the results of the Assembly balloting, Houmed was arrested on June 1, 2013, but released the following day.

Leader: Ahmad Youssouf HOUMED (Chair).

Movement for Democratic Renewal and Development (*Mouvement pour le Renouveau Démocratique et le Développement*—MRDD). Legalized in 1992, the MRDD is an offshoot of the Party of Democratic Renewal (PRD), which had been formed in 1992 and served as a leading opposition grouping. (See 2000–2002 *Handbook* for additional information on the PRD.) MRDD leader Daher Ahmed Farah is editor of the opposition weekly *Le Renouveau*, which has been the object of repeated closures by the government.

Farah was active in trying to organize the opposition ahead of the 2011 presidential election. In February the party participated in demonstrations calling for President Guelleh to step down. After going into exile, Farah returned to Djibouti in January 2013. Farah was named in a series of libel lawsuits in 2013, which critics argued were politically motivated.

Leaders: Daher Ahmed FARAH, Souleiman Farah LODON.

Union for Democracy and Justice (*Union pour la Démocratie et la Justice*—UDJ). The UDJ was established in 2002 under the leadership of Ismail Guedi Hared, a former cabinet director for President Gouled. UDJ Secretary General Farah Ali WABERI resigned from his post in March 2005 to protest the UAD's decision to boycott the upcoming presidential election.

The party opposed the constitutional amendment that allowed the president to run for a third term.

Leader: Ismael Guedi HARED (President).

Djibouti Development Party (*Parti Djiboutien pour le Développement*—PDD). The PDD served as a founding component of the UAD, but PDD leader Mohamed Daoud Chehem angered the other UAD parties in early 2005 by flirting with a possible presidential candidacy (subsequently abandoned).

Chehem was among the opposition leaders detained following antigovernment protests in early 2011. Chehem was instrumental in the formation of the USN.

Leader: Mohamed Daoud CHEHEM (President).

Movement for Development and Liberty (*Mouvement pour le Développement et la Liberté*—MoDel). The moderate Islamist grouping, MoDel, was formed in 2012 by Abdourahman BARKAT God (Falfalos) and Abdourahman Soueiman BACHIR. The party joined the USN ahead of the 2013 balloting. Barkat and Bachir, along with party leader Sheikh Guirreh MEIDAL, were arrested in February during a government crackdown on opposition figures.

Leader: Sheikh Guirreh MEIDAL.

Rally for Action on Democracy and Development (*Rassemblement pour l'action, la démocratie et le développement*—RADD). RADD was formed in 2012 by Abdourahman Mohamed GUELLAH. Guellah was elected mayor of Djibouti in 2012 and selected as the USN secretary general, the following year.

Leader: Abdourahman Mohamed GUELLAH.

Center for Unified Democrats (*Le Centre Des Démocrates Unifiés*—CDU). The centrist CDU was formed in 2012. The CDU received 2.96 percent of the vote in the 2013 Assembly balloting. Subsequent reports indicated that the party had joined the opposition USN. In February 2013, party leader Omar Elmi KHAIREH was arrested along with other opposition figures.

Leader: Omar Elmi KHAIREH.

LEGISLATURE

The **Chamber of Deputies** (*Chambre des Députés*) is a unicameral body of 65 members elected for five-year terms. Prior to 1992 there was no alternative to a single list presented by the Popular Rally for Progress (RPP). Under the system of limited pluralism approved in September 1992, a total of four parties was permitted to compete for chamber seats. However, the limit on the number of parties was eliminated in 2002.

In the most recent balloting on February 22, 2013, the Union for a Presidential Majority, 49; and the Union for National Salvation, 16.

President: Idriss ARNAOUD Ali.

CABINET

[as of November 5, 2013]

Prime Minister	Abdoulkadar Kamil Mohamed
Ministers	
Agriculture, Livestock, and Marine Affairs	Mohamed Ahmed Awaleh
Budget	Bodeh Ahmed Robleh
Communication, Posts and Telecommunications; Government Spokesperson	Ali Hassan Bahdon
Economy and Finance, in Charge of Industry and Planning	Ilyas Moussa Dawaleh
Energy and Water, in Charge of Natural Resources	Ali Yacoub Mahamoud
Equipment and Transportation	Moussa Ahmed Hassan
Foreign Affairs and International Cooperation	Mahamoud Ali Youssouf
Health	Kassim Issak Osman
Higher Education and Research	Nabil Mohamed Ahmed
Housing, Urban Planning, and Environment	Mohamed Moussa Ibrahim Balala
Interior	Hassan Omar Mohamed Bourhan
Justice, Penal Affairs, and Human Rights	Ali Farah Assoweh
Labor, in Charge of Administration Reform	Abdi Houssein Ahmed
Muslim Affairs and Endowment	Aden Hassan Aden
National Defense	Hassan Darar Houffaneh
National Education and Vocational Training	Djama Elmi Okieh
Promotion of Women and Family Planning, and Relations with Parliament	Hasna Barkat Daoud [f]
Delegate Ministers	
Attached to the Minister of Economy and Finance (Trade, Small and Medium Enterprises, Handicrafts, Tourism, and Formalization)	Hassan Ahmed Boulaleh
Attached to the Minister of Foreign Affairs (International Cooperation)	Ahmed Ali Silay
Secretaries of State	
Prime Minister's Office, in Charge of National Solidarity	Zarah Youssouf Kayad [f]
Minister of Housing, Urban Planning, and Environment's Office, in Charge of Housing	Amina Abdi Aden [f]
Youth and Sport	Badoul Hassan Badoul

[f] = female

INTERGOVERNMENTAL REPRESENTATION

Ambassador to the U.S. and Permanent Representative to the UN: Roble OLHAYE.

U.S. Ambassador to Djibouti: Geeta PASI.

IGO Memberships (Non-UN): AfDB, AU, Comesa, OIC, LAS, NAM, WTO.

DOMINICA

Commonwealth of Dominica

Political Status: Former British dependency; joined West Indies Associated States in 1967; independent member of the Commonwealth since November 3, 1978.

Area: 290.5 sq. mi. (752.4 sq. km).

Population: 71,293 (2012E—UN); 73,286 (2013E—U.S. Census).

Major Urban Center (2011E): ROSEAU (14,000).

Official Language: English (a French patois is widely spoken).

Monetary Unit: East Caribbean Dollar (official rate November 1, 2013: 2.70 dollars = $1US).

President: Charles SAVARIN (Dominica Labour Party); elected by the House of Assembly on September 30, 2013, and sworn in on October 2, succeeding Eliud Thaddeus WILLIAMS (Dominica Labour Party).

Prime Minister: Roosevelt SKERRIT (Dominica Labour Party); sworn in January 8, 2004, succeeding Pierre CHARLES (Dominica Labour Party), who died on January 6; remained in office following elections of May 5, 2005, and December 18, 2009.

THE COUNTRY

Dominica, located between Guadeloupe and Martinique in the Windward Islands of the eastern Caribbean, is the largest of the West Indies Associated States as constituted in 1967. Claimed by both France and Great Britain until coming under the latter's exclusive control in 1805, the island continues to reflect a pronounced French influence. Most of its inhabitants are descendants of West African slaves who were brought as plantation laborers in the 17th and 18th centuries, although a few thousand descendants of the Carib Indian tribe, which once controlled the entire Caribbean and gave the area its name, remain. Roman Catholicism is the dominant religion, but there are also long-established Anglican and Methodist communities. Women constitute 12.5 percent of the current legislature.

One of the world's poorest and least developed countries, Dominica's growth and development have been hindered by several hurricanes and a poor infrastructure. In August 2007 Hurricane Dean inflicted widespread damage on both agriculture and infrastructure and, coupled with the global financial crisis, yielded a contraction of 0.7 percent in 2009. That year, the IMF estimated unemployment at 10 percent. Recovery since the crisis has been slow, with growth below 2 percent. Following further natural disasters in 2011, the IMF disbursed $3.1 million and the Caribbean Development Bank gave $10.9 million in January 2012. Meanwhile, Dominica has invested in the tourism sector, becoming a major stakeholder of the regional airline LIAT in late 2012. In 2013 GDP expanded by 1.3 percent, with inflation of 2.3 percent.

GOVERNMENT AND POLITICS

Political background. An object of contention between Britain and France in the 18th century, Dominica was administered after 1833 as part of the British Leeward Islands. In 1940, it was incorporated into the Windward Islands, which also included Grenada, St. Lucia, and St. Vincent. It participated in the Federation of the West Indies from 1958 to 1962 and became one of the six internally self-governing West Indies Associated States in March 1967.

In July 1978 both houses of British Parliament approved an Order in Council terminating the West Indies Association as of November 3. Pending a new election, the existing premier, Patrick Roland JOHN, was designated prime minister, while the incumbent governor, Sir Louis COOLS-LARTIQUE, continued as interim president. Following government rejection of an opposition nominee for president, the Speaker of the House, Fred E. DEGAZON, was elected president on

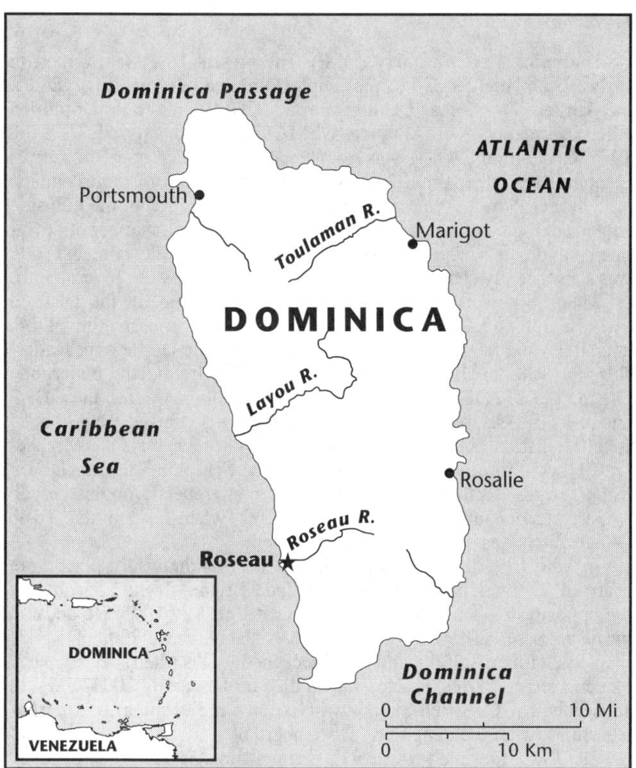

December 22, 1978. In the wake of an extended general strike, he retired to Britain in June 1979. His successor, Cools-Lartique, was also forced to resign only 24 hours after his return to office, and six days later, Prime Minister John, who headed up the Dominica Labor Party (DLP), stepped down.

The interim president, Jenner ARMOUR, designated former agriculture minister Oliver James SERAPHINE as his successor. In the legislative balloting on July 21, 1980, neither Seraphine nor John were reelected. President Aurelius MARIE, who had succeeded Armour in late February, asked Mary Eugenia CHARLES of the victorious Dominica Freedom Party (DFP) to form a new government. Charles was the region's first female prime minister.

There were two failed attempts by supporters of former prime minister John to overthrow the government in 1981, the second of which included an effort to free him from a jail term that had been imposed under a state of emergency. (For more on the history of John and his supporters, see the 2011 *Handbook.*)

Despite the challenges it faced in the early 1980s, the DLP contested the July 1985 parliamentary election, ultimately without success. Prime Minister Charles remained in office following the May 1990 election, in which the DFP retained a bare one-seat Assembly majority. While continuing as prime minister, Charles stepped down as party leader on August 14, 1993, to be succeeded by Brian ALLEYNE. The DFP lost power in the June 12, 1995, election when the United Workers' Party (UWP) won a one-seat majority. UWP party leader Edison JAMES led the formation of a new government.

Since the DFP and DLP had each won five seats, Alleyne accepted appointment as leader of the opposition with the agreement that he would withdraw after one year to be replaced by the DLP's Roosevelt (Rosie) DOUGLAS; however, the change was mandated only a month after the election when a DFP victor was declared ineligible for parliamentary service (although subsequently reinstated). In August 1996, Alleyne resigned his parliamentary seat to accept a judicial appointment in Grenada. The DFP was again reduced to third-party status by losing the ensuing by-election.

The DLP won 10 of 21 elective Assembly seats in the election of January 31, 2000, and Douglas was sworn in on February 7 as prime minister, heading up a coalition cabinet with the DFP. Following Douglas's death on October 1, the deputy DLP leader, Pierre CHARLES, was sworn in as his successor. No major government changes were made at that time, although a downsized and reshuffled cabinet was announced in June 2001. Charles died on January 6, 2004, and was succeeded two days later by Roosevelt SKERRIT, who, at age 31, became the world's youngest head of government and remained in office following the election of May 5, 2005. The DFP failed to win parliamentary representation.

Skerrit secured a third term in the December 18, 2009, election, in which the DLP won a landslide victory of 18 seats, the UWP securing just 3 seats. The election, monitored and declared free and fair by both the Organization of American States (OAS) and CARICOM, saw high turnout rates. The three victorious UWP members challenged the results and refused to take their seats in protest. Speaker of the house Alix BOYD-KNIGHTS mandated that after boycotting three sessions, the seats would be vacated. Two of the three members refused to assume their seats in parliament, and a special by-election was held in July 2009. The UWP retained both seats.

In August 2012 parliamentarians were informed that President Nicholas LIVERPOOL would resign because of health issues. Eliud Thaddeus WILLIAMS (DLP) was elected in a special sitting of parliament on September 17, 2012, which was boycotted by the UWP (see Current issues, below). Williams was succeeded by Charles SAVARIN (DLP) in October 2013 (see Current issues below).

Constitution and government. Under the constitution the Commonwealth of Dominica is a "sovereign democratic republic" based upon principles of social justice. The president, the head of state, is elected by the legislature after joint nomination by the prime minister and the leader of the opposition, or by secret ballot in the event of disagreement between the two. The president may not hold office for more than two five-year terms. Parliament consists of the president and a House of Assembly, which includes one representative from each electoral constituency, as defined by an Electoral Boundaries Commission, and nine senators who, according to the wishes of the legislature, may be either elected or appointed (five on the advice of the prime minister and four on the advice of the leader of the opposition). The term of the House is five years, subject to dissolution. The president appoints as prime minister the elected member who commands a majority in the House; in addition, he may remove the prime minister from office if, following a no-confidence vote, the latter does not resign or request a dissolution.

Provision is made for a Public Service Commission to make appointments to and exercise disciplinary control over the public service, as well as for a Police Service Commission and a Public Service Board of Appeal.

Partially elected local government bodies function in the principal towns and villages, with Roseau and Portsmouth controlled by town councils consisting of both elected and nominated members.

The court system embraces the Supreme Court of the West Indies Associated States (redesignated, in respect of Dominica, as the Eastern Caribbean Supreme Court), courts of summary jurisdiction, and district courts (the latter dealing with minor criminal offenses and civil cases involving sums of not more than $EC500). In late 2004 Parliament approved legislation for Dominica's participation in the Trinidad-based Caribbean Court of Justice (CCJ), replacing the London-based Privy Council as the country's final court of appeal. Since Dominica approved the legislation, Prime Minister Skerrit has encouraged the OECS to act on the matter. Although he reaffirmed his commitment to the issue as recently as April 2012, the matter has not yet been settled with the Privy Council in London.

Although not legally guaranteed, freedom of the press is generally respected. In May, Dominican leaders indicated their intention to repeal criminal defamation laws.

Foreign relations. Although Dominica was admitted to the Commonwealth at independence and to the United Nations shortly thereafter, its diplomatic ties are limited. It maintains only token representation in the United States, and most official contact with Washington is maintained through the U.S. ambassador to Barbados, who is also accredited to Roseau. Regional memberships include the Organization of American States (OAS) and various Caribbean groupings, including the Organization of Eastern Caribbean States (OECS).

Dominica has long been allied with the United States because of its reliance on American foreign aid and its support of U.S. military actions in Grenada and Libya in the 1980s. Dominica also signed several social and economic cooperation agreements with Cuba in 2001. In early 2004, Dominica switched relations with Taiwan to the People's Republic of China after China had offered a $12 million aid package. Despite criticism from opponents concerning the DLP's financial reliance on the PRC, the administration has worked with the PRC to secure funding for several public works projects, including a $30 million education facility at Dominica State College due to be completed in October 2013. In October 2012 the government announced the PRC will fund construction of a new hospital.

A long-standing dispute centered on the status of tiny Bird Island (Isla de Aves), 70 miles west of Dominica but controlled by Venezuela, located some 350 miles to the south. In 2001 Dominica asked its Caribbean neighbors for support in pursuing its claim to the island, which falls within competing maritime economic zones. The action was sharply rebuffed by Venezuela, which in 2005 established a naval base on the island. In June 2006 Prime Minister Skerrit conceded that the international community recognized Venezuelan sovereignty over the island and announced that a bipartisan commission would be established to delineate the maritime boundary.

The Bird Island issue notwithstanding, in 2008 Dominica entered the controversial Bolivarian Alternative for the Americas (ALBA), a Venezuelan-led trade organization launched in response to the U.S.-backed Free Trade Area of the Americas. The UWP opposition party condemned membership in ALBA after Venezuelan president Hugo Chávez had called on ALBA states, including Bolivia, Cuba, and Nicaragua, to form a military alliance to protect the region from potential attacks by the United States. Undeterred, Prime Minister Skerrit defended participation in the trade grouping as of benefit to Dominica and committed to joining the proposed military alliance.

Dominica and the five other OECS members agreed in June 2010 to form an Economic Union, which came into effect on January 21, 2011. The accord also provides a framework for an OECS Commission and an executive body with decision-making capability.

In January 2013 Prime Minister Skerrit announced plans to sever ties with the London-based Privy Council and to join the Trinidad-based Caribbean Court of Justice by the end of the year.

Current issues. Dominica is exploring geothermal energy resources, hoping to lower domestic energy costs and potentially export to Martinique and Guadeloupe. In December, Dominica signed an $18.1 million contract with Iceland Drilling Company (ICD) for two wells.

On August 24, 2012, parliamentary speaker Alix Boyd-Knight informed legislators that President Liverpool intended to resign due to health issues. Opposition leader Hector JOHN ended talks with Prime Minister Skerrit when he refused to produce Liverpool's resignation letter. On September 17, retired public servant Eliud Williams was elected president with 21 votes and inaugurated the same day. The UWP boycotted the election, claiming the process unconstitutional.

On September 30, 2013, Charles Savarin, the minister for national security, immigration, and labor, was elected by the Assembly to succeed Williams. Savarin received 19 votes. The UWP again boycotted the balloting.

POLITICAL PARTIES

The Dominican party system has been in a state of considerable flux since independence. In early 1979 a number of parliamentary members of the original Dominica Labour Party (DLP) withdrew under the leadership of Oliver Seraphine to form the Democratic Labour Party (subsequently the Dominica Democratic Labour Party—DDLP), while the cabinet named by Seraphine on June 21 drew on a recently organized Committee of National Salvation (CNS)—an alliance of former opposition groups that included the Dominica Freedom Party (DFP), headed by Mary Eugenia Charles. The CNS was, however, divided between a left-wing faction, representing trade-union interests, and the traditionally conservative DFP. Another component of the CNS, the National Alliance Party (NAP), had recently been formed by Michael A. DOUGLAS, who subsequently became finance minister in the Seraphine government.

The 1980 election was contested by a rump of the DLP, led by Patrick John; the DDLP; the DFP; and a recently organized Dominica Liberation Movement Alliance (DLMA). The principal contenders in 1985 were the DFP and the Labour Party of Dominica (LPD), with the recently formed United Workers' Party (UWP) becoming a serious contender in 1990 and securing a legislative majority in 1995. In 2000 the DLP won a plurality and formed a coalition government with the DFP as its junior partner.

Government Party:

Dominica Labour Party (DLP). The present DLP was formed in early 1985 by merger of the preexisting **Dominica Labour Party** (DLP), the **United Dominica Labour Party** (UDLP), and the **Dominica Liberation Movement Alliance** (DLMA). The dominant party after the 1975 election, the DLP was weakened by the defection of Oliver Seraphine and others in 1979 as well as by a variety of charges against party leader Patrick John, including an allegation that, as prime minister, he had attempted to secure South African backing for a number of developmental projects. The DLP won no seats in the 1980 election, and John was subsequently charged with attempting to overthrow the government.

The 1980s were a period of change and reunion for the DLP. In 1979 Seraphine and his supporters formed their own party, the DDLP, and additional factions arose from splits within the DDLP over leadership. In 1983 the DLP reunited with the DDL. After having undergone one merger, the DLP united with two other factional parties, the UDLP and the DLMA, in 1985. Now a reunited party, the DLP was faced with the difficult choice of choosing a party leader. In 1986, Michael DOUGLAS, former UDLP leader, defeated Seraphine, former DDLP leader, in an election during the merger conference. Douglas served as party leader until his retirement in 1992, when his brother, Rosie DOUGLAS, was chosen as his replacement.

In June 1995 the DLP won five House seats on a third-place vote share of 29.6 percent. Douglas succeeded Brian Alleyne as leader of the opposition when a DFP seat was vacated in July 1995. He became prime minister following the election of January 31, 2000. Douglas died on October 1, 2000, and was succeeded by his (then) deputy party leader, Pierre Charles. Pierre Charles died on January 6, 2004, and was succeeded by Roosevelt Skerrit, who secured reelection as prime minister in May 2005 and again in December 2009.

Leaders: Roosevelt SKERRIT (Prime Minister and Party Leader), Ambrose GEORGE (Deputy Leader), Peter ST. JEAN (Party President).

Opposition Party:

United Workers' Party (UWP). The former general manager of the Dominica Banana Marketing Corporation launched the UWP in July 1988 to "promote sound and orderly development" in the face of an "erosion of basic democratic rights" and a "state of fear in the nation." The party won 6 House seats in the 1990 election, supplanting the DLP as the principal opposition grouping. In 1995 it secured a narrow majority of 11 seats on a second-place vote share of 34.4 percent; its margin was strengthened by the acquisition of an additional seat in a by-election in August 1996. It returned to opposition after winning only 9 Assembly seats in January 2000, 1 of which was lost in 2005.

Earl WILLIAMS resigned as party leader and leader of the opposition on July 30, 2008, following allegations of financial irregularities in the purchase of Dominican land for a U.S.-based investor. Rob Green assumed leadership but failed reelection in December 2009. In the wake of the UWP's poor showing in 2009, its three elected members boycotted parliamentary sessions, albeit to little avail. The speaker of the House ruled that the seats would be declared vacant after a boycott of three sittings. By-elections were held on July 9, 2010, for two of the three seats (the third dissident having temporarily ended his boycott), both of which were easily regained by the UWP.

Former Prime Minister Edison James, who assumed party leadership in January 2012, announced in mid-2013 that he would not seek reelection in the polling due in March 2015.

Leaders: Hector JOHN (Deputy Leader and Parliamentary Leader of the Opposition), Edison JAMES (Party Leader), Ezekiel BAZIL (President).

Parties Contesting the 2009 Election:

Dominica Freedom Party (DFP). A right-of-center grouping long associated with propertied interests in Roseau, the DFP held the majority in the House of Assembly from 1980 to 1995. The DFP won a plurality of 35.8 percent of the votes in the balloting of June 12, 1995, but captured only 5 of 21 house seats, 1 of which was briefly vacated in July 1995 by the High Court, which ruled that the incumbent was a public service employee.

The DFP won two legislative seats in January 2000, thereafter joining the DLP in a government coalition. It secured no parliamentary representation in the May 2005 poll, although party leader, Charles SAVARIN, served briefly as foreign minister in the Skerrit administration. The appointment was criticized by most of his colleagues, who elected businessman Michael Astaphan to succeed him as party leader in August 2007. Subsequently, Astaphan was succeeded by hotelier Judith Pestaina.

In the July 2009 election, the party won no legislative seats on a paltry vote share of 2.39 percent.

Pestaina stepped down in October 2012 ahead of the 2015 election, and Astaphan became interim leader.

Leader: Michael ASTAPHAN (Acting Leader).

People's Democratic Movement (PDM). The PDM was formed by former DLP general secretary William Para Riviere in mid-2006 as a political party seeking to unite the citizens of Dominica around the central ideal of national development. The party's motto is "Dominica for Dominicans at Home and Abroad."

Leaders: William Para RIVIERE (Party Leader), Augustus COLAIRE (General Secretary).

Also active is the **Dominica Progressive Party**, led by Leonard (Pappy) BAPTISTE, which secured no legislative representation in 2009.

LEGISLATURE

Parliament consists of the president, ex officio, and a **House of Assembly** that sits for a five-year term and encompasses 21 elected representatives and 9 senators who, at the discretion of the House, may be either appointed or elected, in addition to the speaker and the attorney general. The members of the House of Assembly are responsible for electing its speaker. The speaker of the house may or may not be a member of the House of Assembly when chosen. If the speaker is not a representative when selected, he or she will become a member by virtue of the office. Following the election of December 18, 2009, the Dominica Labour Party held 18 representative seats; and the United Workers' Party, 3.

Speaker: Alix BOYD-KNIGHTS.

CABINET

[as of November 11, 2013]

Prime Minister	Roosevelt Skerrit
Ministers	
Agriculture and Forestry	Matthew Walter
Attorney General	Levi Peter
Caribbean Affairs	Ashton Graneau
Culture, Youth, and Sports	Justina Charles [f]
Education and Human Resource Development	Peter St Jean
Employment, Trade, Industry, and Diaspora Affairs	Colin McIntyre
Environment, Natural Resources, Physical Planning, and Fisheries	Kenneth Darroux
Finance, Foreign Affairs and Information Technology	Roosevelt Skerrit
Health	Julius Timothy
Information, Telecommunication, and Constituency Empowerment	Ambrose George
Lands, Housing, Settlements and Water Resource Management	Reginald Austrie
National Security, Immigration, and Labor	(vacant)
Public Works, Energy, and Ports	Rayburn Blackmoore
Social Services, Community Development, and Gender Affairs	Gloria Shillingford [f]
Tourism and Legal Affairs	Ian Douglas
Ministers of State	
Minister of State for Foreign Affairs	Alvin Bernard
Parliamentary Secretary in the Prime Minister's Office	Kelvar Darroux
Parliamentary Secretary in the Ministry of Public Works, Energy, and Ports	Johnson Drigo
Parliamentary Secretary in the Ministry of Lands, Housing, Settlements and Water Resource Management	Ivor Stephenson

[f] = female

Note: All ministers belong to the Dominica Labour Party (DLP).

INTERGOVERNMENTAL REPRESENTATION

Ambassador to the U.S.: Hubert John CHARLES.

U.S. Ambassador to Dominica: Larry L. PALMER.

Permanent Representative to the UN: Vince HENDERSON.

IGO Memberships (Non-UN): Caricom, CWTH, ICC, NAM, OAS, WTO.

DOMINICAN REPUBLIC

República Dominicana

Political Status: Independent republic established in 1844; under constitutional regime reestablished July 1, 1966.

Area: 18,816 sq. mi. (48,734 sq. km).

Population: 10,339,068 (2012E—UN); 10,219,630 (2013E—U.S. Census).

Major Urban Centers (2011E): SANTO DOMINGO (1,126,306), Santiago de los Caballeros (757,933).

Official Language: Spanish.

Monetary Unit: Dominican Peso (market rate November 1, 2013: 42.44 pesos = $1US).

President: Danilo MEDINA Sanchez (Dominican Liberation Party); elected on May 20, 2012, and inaugurated on August 16 for a four-year term, succeeding Leonel Antonio FERNÁNDEZ Reyna (Dominican Liberation Party).

Vice President: Margarita CEDENO DE FERNANDEZ (Dominican Liberation Party); elected on May 20, 2012, and inaugurated with the president on August 16 for a term concurrent with that of the president, succeeding Rafael ALBUQUERQUE De Castro (Dominican Liberation Party).

THE COUNTRY

The Dominican Republic occupies the eastern two-thirds of the Caribbean island of Hispaniola, which it shares with Haiti. The terrain is varied, including mountains, fertile plains, and some desert. About 70 percent of the population is biracial, claiming Spanish and Amerindian or African ancestors, with small minorities (about 15 percent each) of pure Spanish and African origin. The cultural tradition is distinctly Spanish, with 98 percent of the people professing allegiance to the Roman Catholic Church. According to 2004 World Bank data, women comprised 35 percent of the labor force. Though female representation in government has long been virtually nonexistent, President Leonel FERNÁNDEZ named two women to cabinet posts during his first term and three in his second and third. In the 2012 presidential election, Margarita Cedeño de FERNÁNDEZ, wife of Leonel Fernández, became the second woman to serve as vice president.

The Dominican Republic's economy is primarily agricultural, the leading cash crops being sugar, coffee, cocoa, and tobacco. The

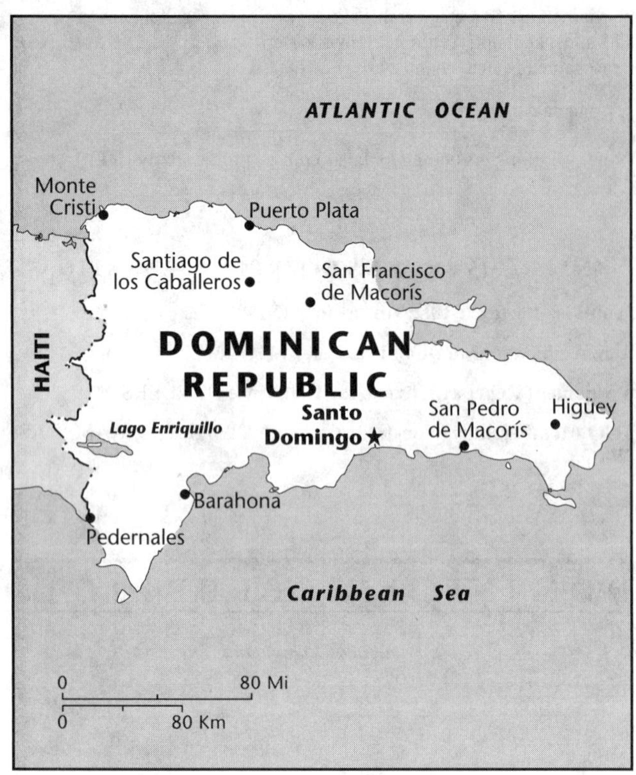

agricultural sector employs nearly 50 percent of the labor force and accounts for nearly half of the country's foreign exchange earnings. Manufacturing is largely oriented toward agricultural processing, but deposits of gold, silver, ferronickel, and bauxite contribute significantly to export earnings. In the 1980s spiraling foreign indebtedness and plummeting commodity prices severely crippled the economy, with austerity measures further inhibiting the capacity of most individuals to meet basic food and shelter needs. During the period unemployment was consistently in excess of 20 percent, with inflation soaring to more than 60 percent in 1989. Tourism gave rise to an increasingly active service sector. As a result, economic growth in 2000–2008 averaged 5.3 percent per year, and inflation averaged 14.4 percent per year. GDP growth slowed to 3.5 percent in 2009 due to the global economic downturn but rebounded in 2010 to 7.8 percent. Growth slowed since, with GDP expanding by 2.2 percent in 2013 and inflation at 4.5 percent. Meanwhile, unemployment in 2013 was 12.5 percent, down from a peak of 18.4 percent in 2004. The International Monetary Fund (IMF) commended the government's efforts to limit public expenditures, implement structural reforms, and enhance "targeting of assistance to the poorest," but a funding agreement disintegrated in February 2012 over electricity tariffs (see Current issues, below).

GOVERNMENT AND POLITICS

Political background. Since winning its independence from Spain in 1821 and from Haiti in 1844, the Dominican Republic has been plagued by recurrent domestic conflict and foreign intervention. Administered by a U.S. military governor from 1916 to 1924, the country entered into a 30-year period of control by Gen. Rafael Leonidas TRUJILLO Molina in 1930. Trujillo ruled from 1930 to 1947 and indirectly thereafter until his assassination in 1961, his death giving rise to renewed political turmoil. An election in December 1962 led to the inauguration of Juan BOSCH Gaviño, a left-of-center democrat, as president in February 1963. Bosch was overthrown in September 1963 by a military coup led by Col. Elías WESSIN y Wessin. Subsequently, the military installed a civilian triumvirate that ruled until April 1965, when civil war erupted. U.S. military forces—later incorporated into an Inter-American Peace Force sponsored by the Organization of American States (OAS)—intervened on April 28, 1965, and imposed a truce while arrangements were made to establish a provisional government and prepare for new elections. Dr. Joaquín BALAGUER Ricardo, a moderate who had been president at the time of Trujillo's assassination, defeated Bosch in an election held in June 1966. Emphasizing material development and political restraint, Balaguer was reelected in 1970 and successfully dealt with an attempted coup in 1971. In 1974 he was virtually unopposed for election to a fourth term, all of his principal opponents having withdrawn in anticipation of election irregularities. After the election Silvestre Antonio GUZMAN Fernández, speaking on behalf of the opposition coalition, demanded annulment of the results; however, he agreed not to press the demand after securing Balaguer's assurance that he would not seek further reelection in 1978. Despite his pledge, Balaguer contested the 1978 election but lost to Guzmán Fernández by a three-to-two majority. The inauguration of the new president on August 16 was the first occasion in Dominican history that an elected incumbent had yielded power to an elected successor.

In late 1981 four-time former chief executive Balaguer surprised many observers by announcing that he would seek to regain the presidency in 1982, despite his age at 74 and failing eyesight. Meanwhile, economic problems deepened and President Guzmán lost influence within the ruling Dominican Revolutionary Party (*Partido Revolucionaria Dominicana*—PRD). At midyear, Guzmán declared that he would not seek reelection and formally endorsed Vice President Jacobo MAJLUTA Azar as his successor. However, at a PRD convention in November Majluta was decisively rejected in favor of Guzmán's archrival, Salvador JORGE Blanco, who had been defeated for the 1978 nomination and whom Guzmán had succeeded in ousting from the party presidency in late 1979.

In the May 1982 election, Jorge Blanco defeated Balaguer by a 10 percent margin, while the PRD retained its majority in both houses of Congress. On July 4 President Guzmán died of an apparently self-inflicted gunshot wound. Majluta Azar served in the interim until Jorge Blanco's inauguration on August 16.

In the vote on May 16, 1986, Balaguer was elected to a fifth term, narrowly defeating Majluta after the PRD had succumbed to severe internal friction attributed primarily to a left-wing faction led by José Francisco PEÑA Gómez.

Announcement of the 1990 presidential outcome was delayed for nearly a month, with Balaguer credited in mid-June with a 14,000-vote victory over former president Juan Bosch. In the Senate, Balaguer's Social Christian Reformist Party (*Partido Reformista Social Cristiano*—PRSC) retained control by a margin of only one seat; in contrast, the opposition secured an overwhelming majority in the Chamber of Deputies.

Balaguer was initially declared the winner of the May 1994 presidential race by fewer than 30,000 votes. However, only three weeks before the August 16 constitutional deadline for swearing in a new president, the Santo Domingo electoral board responded to numerous complaints by voiding the results (40 percent of the total) at the capital. On August 2 the Junta Electoral Central (JCE) ignored a report by its electoral committee in overruling the Santo Domingo body. However, the action drew intense opposition, including a threat of military intervention, and on August 10 Balaguer concluded a "Pact for Democracy" ("*Pacto por la Democracia*") with José Peña Gómez, who had succeeded Majluta as PRD leader, to shorten the presidential term to 18 months, with new balloting on November 16, 1995. While Bosch's Dominican Liberation Party (*Partido de la Liberación Dominicana*—PLD) also supported the accord, it subsequently reversed itself and joined with the PRSC in endorsing a two-year term. On August 14 Congress hurriedly approved a constitutional amendment to such effect, along with amendments banning future presidents from serving consecutive terms, reforming the JCE, creating a National Judiciary Council to ensure the independence of the judiciary, and establishing dual citizenship for Dominicans living outside the country. The PRD responded to revision of the August 10 agreement by withdrawing from the congressional session and boycotting Balaguer's inauguration of his seventh term.

At first-round presidential balloting on May 16, 1996, the PRD's Peña Gómez was accorded a 45.9 percent plurality, substantially outdistancing the PLD's Leonel Fernández Reyna (38.9 percent) and Vice President Jacinto PEYNADO Garrigoza of the PRSC (15.0 percent). Before the second round on June 30, President Balaguer joined with the leaders of a number of small right-wing groups in endorsing Fernández, who won a narrow (51.3 to 48.8 percent) victory over Peña Gómez and was installed as Balaguer's successor on August 16.

Despite the death of Peña Gómez on May 10, 1998, the PRD won a sweeping legislative victory (83 seats in an enlarged 149-seat body) on May 16, while gaining control of about 90 percent of the island's 115 municipalities. By contrast, President Fernández's PLD won only 49 seats.

In the May 2000 presidential election, the PRD's Hipólito MEJÍA received a near majority of 49.86 percent and was declared the winner when his opponents withdrew from runoff contention. In congressional balloting on May 16, 2002, the PRD lost its lower house majority, although it retained a plurality and increased its Senate representation.

Seeking reelection in 2004, President Mejía faced opposition within his party. His administration was plagued by problems, including rampant inflation, a breakdown in electrical-generating capacity, and the collapse of the nation's second largest bank. The PLD's Leonel Fernández won a landslide victory, avoiding a runoff by securing 57.1 percent of the first-round vote.

After working with a PRD-dominated legislature for the first two years of his term, Fernández's public approval ratings soared and on May 16, 2006, the PLD secured 96 seats in the Chamber of Deputies and 22 of 32 Senate seats. The PRD was hampered by a lingering public perception of the group's mismanagement of the economy and corruption during the Mejía administration. In a move that many party members found unnecessary, the PRD formed an electoral alliance with the PRSC, another major opposition group, and several smaller parties.

On the back of strong voter support for the president's measures to improve and stabilize the economy, the PLD's winning record extended to the 2008 presidential elections, when incumbent president Fernández secured 54 percent of the vote and a third term in office. His center-left PRD rival, Miguel VARGAS, won 40.5 percent. The conservative PRSC placed a distant third with 4.59 percent. Seven smaller parties also participated in the election. The PLD and its allies also retained their legislative dominance, and Fernández named a new government after his inauguration on August 16.

The PLD won 41.7 percent of the votes during the May 2010 legislative election and took 54.6 percent with its allies. The PRD won 38.4 percent of the ballots and 41.9 percent combined with its allies. The PRSC was the third largest vote getter, with 6.2 percent. Though legislative members were normally voted in for four-year terms, the successful candidates of 2010 were to serve six years under a constitutional change predating the election that aligned legislative and presidential elections beginning in 2016. Voter turnout was low at 56 percent, and violence resulting in five deaths marred the election. Some complaints by opposition parties of electoral shenanigans by the PLD were leveled but not pursued.

The constitution prohibited Fernandez from seeking a fourth term in the election of May 20, 2012, but the PLD retained power as Danilo MEDINA secured the presidency with a narrow majority of 51.2 percent, avoiding a runoff. Former president Mejía ran for the PRD and lost with 47 percent of the vote (see Current Issues, below).

Constitution and government. The constitution of November 28, 1966, unchanged in its structural components by a 1991 successor, established a unitary republic consisting of 26 (later 32) provinces and a National District. Executive power is exercised by the president, who is elected (together with the vice president) by direct vote for a four-year term, save for the truncated two-year mandate imposed in 1994. Members of the bicameral Congress of the Republic, consisting of a Senate and a Chamber of Deputies, are likewise elected for four-year terms, except for those elected in the May 2010 elections, who were authorized to serve a six-year term to align congressional and presidential elections. The judicial system is headed by a Supreme Court of Justice, which consists of at least nine judges elected by the Senate. The Supreme Court appoints judges of lower courts operating at the provincial and local levels. All three branches of government participate in the legislative process. Bills for consideration by the legislature may be introduced by members of either house, by the president, and by judges of the Supreme Court. In July 2002 a Special Constituent Assembly reversed a requirement that the president be limited to a single term.

For administrative purposes the provinces are divided into 95 municipalities and 31 municipal districts. The president appoints provincial governors, while elected mayors and municipal councils govern the municipalities. Suffrage is universal and compulsory for those over 18 or married, if younger. Women have had the right to vote since 1942. Members of the armed forces and national police are not allowed to vote.

In January 2009 Congress began debating a major constitutional reform package being championed by President Fernández. Following endorsement of the reforms by a constitutional assembly, Fernández struck a deal with PRD opposition leader Miguel Vargas Maldonado that allowed Congress to approve the amendments, which went into effect on January 26, 2010. The amendments replaced the current two-term maximum for presidents with an allowance for former presidents to run again after a four-year hiatus from office; increased the number of seats in the Chamber of Deputies from 183 to 190; and synchronized presidential and legislative elections beginning in 2016. Provisions were also made for referendums; judiciary reform; investment in education, science, and technology; environmental protection; independent oversight of government; efforts to shut down human trafficking operations; and prohibitions against abortion and same-sex marriage in all circumstances.

Though freedom of expression is constitutionally guaranteed under the 2010 constitutional reforms, which guarantee journalists' right to protect confidential sources, defamation is a criminal offense. Violence and intimidation against journalists is common. In 2013 the Dominican Republic ranked 80th on Reporters Without Borders's Press Freedom Index.

Foreign relations. A member of the United Nations and most of its Specialized Agencies, the Dominican Republic also participates in the OAS. Traditionally it maintained diplomatic relations with most Western but not communist countries, although in response to a 1986 cut in the U.S. sugar import quota, President Balaguer announced in mid-1987 that his government intended to restore trade links with Cuba after a 26-year hiatus. Relations with the United States were long strained by the latter's history of intervention, but they substantially improved with the reestablishment of constitutional government in 1966. Recurring tensions and frontier disputes with Haiti have also influenced Dominican external affairs, periodically resulting in closure of the 193-mile common border. In June 1991 the Dominican government launched a systematic expulsion of illegal Haitian residents, most of whom had been working on sugarcane plantations (some for several decades), seen, in part, as a response to foreign allegations that child laborers were being inhumanely treated on state-owned plantations. Expulsions escalated in 1997, with some 15,000 Haitians deported in January and February. At a summit of the Caribbean Community and Common Market (Caricom) on February 20–21, President Fernández reached an agreement with Haitian President Préval to halt large-scale repatriations while securing acknowledgment of his country's right to expel illegal immigrants. However, a new wave of expulsions in November 1999 further exacerbated relations between the two countries. Tensions again eased in February 2002 during a visit by Haitian President Jean-Bertrand Aristide that yielded an agreement to provide jobs for Haitians at the countries' common border. The cyclical pattern resumed in mid-2005 with the recall of the Haitian ambassador after the lynching of three Haitians in Santo Domingo. The Fernández administration responded by deporting 2,000 of the Dominican Republic's estimated 1 million Haitians in August.

On September 7, 2005, the Dominican Republic joined Petrocaribe, a regional initiative by Venezuela to provide preferential financing of oil to Caribbean and Central American countries. Under the deal, the Dominican Republic is required to provide a fraction of the money for oil purchases up front and can pay for petroleum purchases with agricultural products.

In November 2006 the government reiterated a long-standing contention that it did not mistreat Haitians but indicated that it would continue to deport illegal immigrants and, drawing international criticism, refused to grant citizenship to Haitian offspring born within its borders. In September 2007 the government activated the Specialized Frontier Security Corps (Cesfront) to patrol the 193-mile border the Dominican Republic shares with Haiti. The group, which was expected to expand to 2,000 members in 2008, was given the mandate to control cross-border movement of immigrants, drugs, and other contraband.

Although not a member of Caricom, the Dominican Republic established a free trade agreement with the organization in 1998. A similar pact with the United States was proposed in mid-2002 by President Mejía. In early 2004 his administration conducted negotiations for accession to the trade pact between the United States and the recently launched Central American Free Trade Agreement (CAFTA), which provided for immediate elimination of 80 percent of intragroup tariffs, with the remaining tariffs to be phased out over a ten-year period. Though signed on August 5, 2006, technical reasons delayed its implementation until March 1, 2007. CAFTA was expected to partially offset the Dominican Republic's competitive losses to China in the garment industry.

President Fernández at the end of July 2007 signed an accord with Belize to increase cooperation between the two countries, indicative of the country's strengthening links with Central America. The Dominican Republic also entered into negotiations to sign bilateral free trade agreements with Mexico and Haiti, the latter offering the possibility of formalizing over $700 million in unregulated commerce between the two neighbors.

Tensions between the Dominican Republic and Haiti again frayed in November 2008, following an attack on a Dominican, which resulted in violent reprisals on Haitians in the country. The Fernández administration deported 500 Haitians in an attempt to quell the violence and ordered an additional 600 troops to patrol the border area. In September 2009, the government also began relocating soldiers and their families to the western border provinces to counter rising proportions of Haitians there.

The massive January 12, 2010, earthquake in Haiti highlighted the Dominican Republic's fragile relationship with its neighbor. Just before the country's legislature approved a constitutional amendment in January 2010 that prevented the descendants of illegal Haitian immigrants from claiming Dominican Republic citizenship, the country sent thousands of doctors, rescue teams, and mobile kitchens to Haiti, allowed Dominican airports to be used while international relief efforts were ongoing, and allowed the severely injured to cross the border for treatment.

During legislative elections on May 16, 2010, Dominican voters for the first time elected 20 parliamentarians to represent them in the Central American Parliament (Parlacen), the legislative arm of the Central American Integration System.

Dominican public hysteria over a cholera outbreak in Haiti slightly cooled relations between the two neighbors in January 2011, when President Fernández approved resuming deportations of undocumented Haitians from the country. More than 3,000 undocumented Haitians were forced out of the Dominican Republic, and security was tightened along the border in the first two weeks of the year. A new immigration law implemented on June 1, 2012, required non-Dominican workers to have a special permit.

The 2012 International Narcotics Control Strategy Report issued by the U.S. government listed "endemic" corruption and rising drug-related violence as two of the largest threats to stability in the Dominican Republic. In April 2013 the former director of the Dominican Republic's National Drug Control Agency was extradited to the United States on drug smuggling charges.

At a Caricom meeting in July 2013, President Medina made a direct appeal for the Dominican Republic to become a member of the organization, which was supported by current Caricom Chair Trinidad Prime Minister Kamla Persad-Bissessar.

Current issues. Though the country's economy showed strong growth of nearly 8 percent in 2010, and the government's 2011 budget was considered by observers to be well designed, the IMF was asked to provide emergency funds in 2011 to mitigate a growing deficit triggered by an energy crisis. The agency agreed to help in June on the stipulation that the government increase tax revenues by 1.5–2 percentage points in 2011–2013. The IMF said the imbalance had been caused by the failure of the Dominican authorities to predict the impact of surging crude prices on the country's economy, which is highly dependent on oil imports. In February 2012, the government refused to implement an IMF-recommended 18 percent increase on electricity tariffs, triggering the $1.7 billion loan agreement to end three months early. In October the IMF and Dominican Republic began drawing up plans for a new stand-by arrangement, but complications arose the following month when the government was unwilling to comply with IMF requests to allow market forces to determine electricity rates, which were reiterated in March 2013. The energy situation continued to worsen, with independent power producers reporting in April that they would be unable to guarantee energy supplies until the state settles $700 million worth of debt. That month, the government secured an agreement with Russia's state-owned Gazprom for an undisclosed amount of natural gas.

In June 2011 Danilo Medina assumed the leadership of the PLD from President Fernández, who was barred from seeking a third consecutive term. Fernández's wife, Margarita Cedeño, who had started and abandoned her own presidential run, was named PLD's vice presidential candidate in November 2011. Hipolito Mejía, who narrowly secured the PRD nomination over Miguel Vargas in March 2011, campaigned against PLD corruption and prioritized agriculture, education, and public health. Medina similarly pledged to implement a code of ethics in public administration, to improve education and health care, and to add 1.4 million citizens to the social security system. Although early polls in January showed Mejía with a nearly 20-point lead over Medina, months of campaigning saw a major reversal of public opinion.

Medina won 51.21 percent of the votes in the May 20 balloting. Mejía, who took 47 percent, initially protested the results, accusing his opponent of vote buying. He conceded two days later and assumed minority leadership. The remaining votes were split among four other presidential candidates: Guillermo MORENO, of the Peace Alliance (*Partido Alianza País*—ALPAIS), 1.37 percent; Eduardo ESTRELLA, of the Dominican Party for Change (*Partido Dominicanos por el Cambio*—DXC), 0.21 percent; Julián SERRULLE, of the Frente Amplio, 0.14 percent; and Max PUIG, of the Alliance for Democracy (*Alianza por la Democracia*—APD), 0.11 percent. An OAS election monitoring group confirmed some isolated cases of vote buying but reported that it was not significant enough to affect the normal functioning of the election and declared the results valid.

Medina was sworn in on August 16, 2012. His new cabinet retained several members from the Fernández administration. Following the PRD's loss, a rift emerged between the party's Vargas-led and Mejía-led factions (see the PRD entry in Political Parties, below).

POLITICAL PARTIES

The shifting political groupings that have appeared in the Dominican Republic since the fall of Trujillo reflect diverse ideological viewpoints as well as the influence of specific personalities. Party divisions and splinter groups are common. A total of 27 parties were registered for the May 16, 2010, legislative election.

Presidential Party:

Dominican Liberation Party (*Partido de la Liberación Dominicana*—PLD). A breakaway faction of the PRD (see below), the PLD was organized as a separate party under PRD founder Juan Bosch Gaviño during the 1974 campaign. Bosch ran unsuccessfully as PLD presidential candidate in both 1978 and 1982, securing 9.8 percent of the vote on the latter occasion. Subsequently, he was highly critical of the Blanco regime's economic policies as well as its often harsh anti-protest tactics. Although popular opinion polls showed Bosch running second to Balaguer in late 1985, the PLD nominee placed third, with 18.4 percent of the vote, in the 1986 presidential balloting; in an extremely close contest, he ran second to Balaguer in 1990.

In March 1991 Bosch stepped down as PLD leader and withdrew from party membership to protest deep-rooted animosity between right- and left-wing factions; he reversed himself two weeks later in response to appeals from his colleagues.

In April 1992 the PLD experienced a severe crisis when 47 of its left-wing members, including one senator and ten members of the Chamber of Deputies, resigned in protest at the expulsion of a popular trade unionist who had criticized the party's position on a proposed new labor code. The intraparty split had first emerged at a PLD congress in February 1991, when a right-wing group under Chamber president Jorge Botello had won control of the governing Political Committee. In May several additional persons were expelled from the party, including its former vice-presidential candidate, José Francisco Hernández Castillo, the mayor of San Pedro de Macorís, Manuel Rodríguez Roblés, and three deputies, all of whom, characterized by Juan Bosch as "rotten mangos," subsequently participated in organization of the APD (below).

Bosch, with the support of the right-wing **Progressive National Force** (*Fuerza Nacional Progresista*—FNP), headed by Marino Vinicio (Vincho) CASTILLO, ran a distant third in the presidential balloting of May 16, 1994, and on June 19 announced his resignation as PLD president. He died on November 1, 2001.

Although the PLD held only 12 of 120 lower house seats, its candidate, Leonel Fernández Reyna, secured a narrow victory in second-round presidential balloting on June 30, 1996, with the support of former president Balaguer. It ran second to the PRD in the 1998 legislative and 2000 presidential polls, and continued as runner-up to the PRD in the 2002 Chamber elections, losing 3 of its 4 Senate seats. Fernández was elected to a second presidential term in 2004, and the PLD won majorities in both legislative houses in 2006, illustrating growing support for the president during the midterm election. Fernández took 71.5 percent of the votes during the primary on May 6, 2007, besting former presidential secretary Danilo MEDINA before securing a third presidential term in 2008 with 53.83 percent of the vote.

Voters' desire for change and a strategy for addressing the economic downturn placed their confidence in the PLD platforms highlighting constitutional, judicial, and economic reforms along with a belt-tightening austerity program advocated by Fernández Reyna. Party advances continued in the 2010 legislative elections, when the PLD took 41.7 percent of ballots nationwide and gained nearly a two-thirds majority in the Chamber of Deputies. Political observers said the party's gains were the result of implementation of two popular social welfare programs and Fernández's perceived success in getting the country through the global economic downturn.

Small parties allied with the PLD in 2010 included the FNP, APD, BIS, PQD, UDC, PTD, PPC, PLRD, and PDP (see below for details on the last eight of these groups), as well as the **National Unity Party** (*Partido de Unidad Nacional*—PUN), the **Green Socialist Party** (*Partido Socialista Verde*—PSV), and the **Liberal Action Party** (*Partido Acción Liberal*—PAL).

Although speculation mounted in 2010 that Fernández would seek reelection (despite a constitutional ban on consecutive terms), he announced in April 2011 that he would not run. The next day, a PLD convention voted on a list of seven candidates, including Vice President Rafael Albuquerque, Danilo Medina, and First Lady Margarita Cedeño de FERNÁNDEZ, to stand during the coming primary. In June Medina, the leader of the internal opposition to Fernández, won the primary to become the PLD's candidate in the 2012 presidential election. Medina selected Fernández as his running mate in November 2011.

After the selection of Medina as the PLD's standard bearer, the smaller parties that united around the PLD in the previous election to form a progressive bloc again coalesced around the candidate, including the BIS, UDC, PTD, PLRD, FNP, PQD, PDP, and PRSC.

Leaders: Leonel FERNÁNDEZ Reyna (President of the Party), Danilo MEDINA (President of the Republic), Reinaldo PARED Pérez (Secretary General).

Other Legislative Parties:

Dominican Revolutionary Party (*Partido Revolucionario Dominicano*—PRD). Founded as a left-democratic grouping by former president Juan Bosch Gaviño in 1939, the PRD has rejected both communism and Castroism but has been critical of U.S. "imperialism" and "neo-colonialism." A member of the Socialist International since 1966, the party boycotted both the 1970 and 1974 elections but won the presidency and a majority in the Chamber of Deputies under the relatively conservative leadership of Antonio Guzmán Fernández in 1978, repeating the performance under Salvador Jorge Blanco in 1982. A three-way split within the PRD in the run-up to the 1986 election raised two distinct possibilities: that former vice president Majluta Azar might compete as the nominee of his right-wing *La Estructura* faction, or that Blanco supporters, unhappy with the president's endorsement of left-leaning José Peña Gómez, would rally for reelection of the incumbent. In July 1985 Majluta registered *La Estructura* as a separate party, but in January 1986 was named the PRD candidate with Peña Gómez succeeding him as party president. Majluta attributed his defeat in the May balloting to Peña Gómez, many of whose followers were reported to have supported Juan Bosch of the PLD. Lacking a congressional majority after the election, President Balaguer named a number of PRD/*La Estructura* members to the cabinet formed in late August. In 1990 Majluta and his associates ran separately (see PRI, below).

In July 1993 the PRD nominated Peña Gómez as its 1994 presidential candidate; supporters of President Balaguer then launched an intense personal attack against Peña Gómez, who was black and of Haitian extraction.

For the 1994 campaign, the PRD concluded pacts with a number of minor parties, including the **Democratic Assembly** (*Concertación Democrática*—CD), the **Democratic Unity** (*Unidad Democrática*—UD), and the PTD (under PRSC, see below). However, the UD, which was awarded three upper and seven lower house seats, refused to support the PRD's postelectoral boycott, thus substantially reducing the effectiveness of the action.

In August 1995 the PRD concluded a 1996 electoral pact with three parties that had formerly supported the PRSC: the PQD (see below), the **Institutional Democratic Party** (*Partido Democrático Institucional*—PDI), and the **National Party of Civil Veterans** (*Partido Nacional de Veteranos Civiles*—PNVC). PRD candidate Peña Gómez led the first-round presidential poll on May 16, 1996, with 45.8 percent of the vote, but was defeated in the June 30 runoff after the PRSC's Balaguer had endorsed the PLD's Fernández. Gravely ill, Peña Gómez announced his retirement from politics in April 1997 and died on May 10, 1998.

Having won control of both houses of Congress in May 1998, the PRD completed its sweep with the election of Hipólito Mejía as president two years later. However, in 2002 it lost its majority in the Chamber, securing 73 seats. In 2004 the party divided over whether President Mejía should run for reelection; he was, however, nominated and overwhelmingly defeated by former president Fernández in the balloting of May 16. In the 2006 legislative poll, the PRD ran a poor second to the resurgent PLD, falling from 29 seats to 6 in the Senate and from 73 to 60 in an enlarged Chamber of Deputies. PRD presidential candidate Miguel Vargas received 40.48 percent of the popular vote during the 2008 elections, 13 percent less than the winning PLD incumbent but far ahead of the other contesting parties.

Small parties that allied themselves with PRD for the 2010 elections included the PNVC; MIUCA and PDI (see below); the **Alternative Democratic Movement** (*Movimiento Democratico Alternativo*—MDA); the **Dominican Humanist Party** (*Partido Humanista Dominicano*—PHD); and the **Civic Renewal Party** (*Partido Civico Renovador*—PCR).

Significantly, the PRD lost its voice in the Senate during the 2010 legislative elections, when the PLD swept all PRD senators out, a reflection of the public's grudge against the corruption scandals and economic downturn of Mejía's presidency, and the failure of the PRD to block Fernández's 2009 constitutional reform package. With 36.4 percent of ballots won, the PRD gained 14 seats (for a total of 74) in the Chamber of Deputies.

After a strongly contested primary in March 2011, the PRD selected Mejía over Vargas to be its candidate for the 2012 presidential election. Mejía campaigned on a platform of cutting government spending and reform. Mejía lost the May 20 balloting with 47 percent of the vote.

Following Mejía's loss, a rift emerged in the party with Vargas leading an effort to expel the former presidential candidate and suspend the secretary general and other key party members. In January 2013 the PRD disciplinary committee voted to expel Mejía, a move the executive committee subsequently dismissed as invalid. A confrontation between the two factions at a January 27 meeting erupted into violence, leaving six people shot. In February attempts at mediated talks between the two factions stalled.

Leaders: Miguel VARGAS Maldonado (2008 presidential candidate and President of the Party), Hipólito MEJÍA Domingues (2012 presidential candidate and Former President of the Republic), Orlando Jorge MERA (Secretary General).

Social Christian Reformist Party (*Partido Reformista Social Cristiano*—PRSC). Created in 1963 by Joaquín Balaguer, the PRSC stresses a policy of economic austerity, national reconstruction, and political consensus. Drawing heavily on peasant and middle-class support, it won the elections of 1966, 1970, and 1974 but lost in 1978 after its leader had withdrawn a pledge not to become a candidate for another term. It lost again in 1982, Balaguer being defeated in the presidential election by a 37 to 47 percent margin; however, public recollection of a strong economy under Balaguer gave the ex-president a narrow victory over his PRD opponent in May 1986; his margin of victory was even narrower (0.7 percent) in winning a sixth term in May 1990, while the PRSC lost its former plurality in the Chamber of Deputies. Balaguer resigned as PRSC party president in February 1991, citing the time-consuming nature of government leadership; he won a seventh presidential term in 1994, which was shortened to two years. In 1996 he offered only lukewarm first-round support to his party's presidential nominee and backed the PLD's Leonel Fernández in the second round. He ran for an unprecedented eighth term in the balloting of January 2000, gaining third place on a 24.6 percent vote share. He died on July 14, 2002.

In the 2008 presidential election, the party's candidate, Amable Aristy Castro, placed a distant third with 4.59 percent of the vote. PRSC president Federico ANTÚN Batlle resigned because of the party's poor showing.

The PRSC came in third with 6.15 percent of votes cast during the May 16, 2010, legislative elections, in part due to a cleavage in the party, leading some members to align with the PLD. During a major party meeting in July 2011, however, PRSC activists voted to conduct a sweeping reorganization of the party from the municipality level up and to put forward their own candidate for the 2012 presidential election. The party also joined a progressive bloc of parties supporting the PLD's candidate, Danilo Medina.

Leaders: Carlos MORALES Troncoso (President of the Party), Ramón Rogelio GENAO (Secretary General), Amable ARISTY Castro (2008 presidential candidate).

Other Parties:

Independent Revolutionary Party (*Partido Revolucionario Independiente*—PRI). The PRI was launched before the 1990 election by Jacobo Majluta Azar, the leader of the PRD's *La Estructura* faction, after his defeat for control of the party by José Peña Gómez. Before his death on March 2, 1996, Majluta committed the PRI, which had no congressional representation but voting strength of about 100,000, to the support of the PRD's Peña Gómez in the 1996 presidential race. In December 2001 President Mejía accepted the honorary presidency of the PRI, and the party secured congressional representation in May 2002 by running candidates under the PRD banner. The party garnered 0.2 percent of the vote in the 2006 and 2010 legislative elections.

In the 2008 presidential election, PRI candidate Trajano Santana, who had campaigned for public investment in higher education, won 0.04 percent of the vote.

In March 2008 the party expelled several high-ranking members, including the vice president and secretary general, for supporting the candidacy of incumbent president Leonel Fernández. In July 2011 the party announced it would throw its support—which Santana said would total 100,000 votes—behind the PRD presidential candidate Hipólito Mejía.

Leaders: Trajano SANTANA (President of the Party and 2004 and 2008 presidential candidate), Leonidas RODRÍGUEZ (Secretary General).

Alliance for Democracy (*Alianza por la Democracia*—APD). Launched in mid-1992 by a group of left-wing PLD dissidents, the APD indicated interest in joining a broad front in 1994 to prevent the reelection of President Balaguer. However, in April 1993 it split into two factions led, on the one hand, by Sen. Max Puig and former PLD vice-presidential candidate José Francisco HERNÁNDEZ, and, on the other, by economist Vicente BENGOA and union leader Nelsida MARMOLEJOS. The latter group, which sought to forge an alliance with the PRD, was suspended for six months by an "emergency secretariat" organized by the Puig/Hernández faction. The party seeks broad alliances as a bridge to increasing public participation. The APD received 1.41percent of the vote in the 2010 legislative elections. In July 2011 Puig resigned from his position as labor minister in President Fernández's cabinet and announced that he would be the APD's candidate in the 2012 presidential election. The party distanced itself from the center-left alliance it had joined in previous elections; Puig said the APD would not look to be part of a progressive bloc with other parties. Puig secured just 0.11 percent of the vote in the May 2012 balloting.

Leaders: Max PUIG (President of the Party and 2012 presidential candidate), Carlos SANCHEZ (Secretary General).

Christian Democratic Union (*Unión Demócrata Cristiana*—UDC). The UDC was created on March 12, 1998. It received less than 1 percent of the vote in the 2010 legislative elections. The party organizes and conducts outreach programs in the poorest communities. The party joined the progressive bloc supporting the presidential candidacy of the PLD's Danilo Medina in the 2012 presidential election.

Leader: Luis Acosta MORETA (President).

Dominican Workers' Party (*Partido de los Trabajadores Dominicanos*—PTD). The PTD is a revolutionary socialist and democratic party that advocates for the universal adoption of democracy, social justice, freedom, and development. The party came into existence on Dec. 21, 1980, as two communist groups merged: the June 14 Red Line and the Proletarian Flag. The party won 0.5 percent of the vote in the 2006 and 2010 legislative elections. The PTD supported the candidacy of the PLD's Danilo Medina in the 2012 presidential elections, and its president, José González Espinosa, in joining the progressive bloc of parties, said that only a grand coalition of political and social forces could tackle the Dominican Republic's internal problems and external pressures.

Leaders: José González ESPINOSA (President), Esteban Díaz JAQUEZ (First Vice President), Antonio FLORIÁN (Secretary General).

Liberal Party (*Partido Liberal de República Dominicana*—PLRD). An autonomous component of the PRI, the PLRD joined the Liberal International in 1986. It endorsed former president Joaquín Balaguer as its candidate for the 2000 race. As part of the Progressive Bloc coalition, it received less than 0.5 percent of the vote in the 2006 and 2010 legislative elections. The PLRD joined the progressive bloc of parties supporting the candidacy of the PLD's Danilo Medina for the 2012 presidential election.

Leaders: Andrés VAN DER HORST (President), Vinicio Lorenzo ARIAS (Secretary General).

Institutional Social Democratic Bloc (*Bloque Institucional Social Démocrata*—BIS). The BIS splintered from the PRD in the May 2006 legislative elections to support the PLD and President Fernández and received 2.5 percent of the vote. It received 1.3 percent of ballots in the 2010 legislative elections. The BIS joined the center-left progressive bloc of parties supporting the PLD's Danilo Medina in the 2012 presidential election.

Leader: Franklin PERSIA (President).

Popular Alliance Party (*Partido Alianza Popular*—PAP). Recognized by the Central Election Board in October 2007, the PAP fielded its only candidate during the 2008 presidential election, founder Pedro de Jesus Candelier. The party's platform focused on advancing participatory democracy and the economy by fighting corruption, government abuse, and social inequality. Candelier, former police chief of the country, was dismissed by President Mejía in 2002 in response to high numbers of civilian killings at the hands of the police. He received 0.15 percent of the vote in the 2008 presidential election. The party's activities seemingly ceased in recent years, but Candelier, a polarizing figure in Dominican society, threw his support behind the PRD and Mejía's candidacy for the 2012 presidential election.

Leader: Pedro de Jesus CANDELIER Tejada (2008 presidential candidate).

Quisqueyan Democratic Party (*Partido Quisqueyano Demócrata*—PQD). A right-wing group, the PQD was formed by Gen. Elías Wessin y Wessin following his exile to the United States after the civil disturbances of 1965; two years earlier, the general had led the military coup that overthrew President Juan Bosch. The PQD supported Wessin y Wessin in the 1970 presidential campaign and participated in the coalition that boycotted the 1974 election. In September 1977 General Wessin announced his candidacy for the 1978 presidential election but subsequently withdrew in favor of MID candidate Francisco Augusto Lora. Wessin ran a distant fourth in the 1982 presidential balloting. In November 1986 he was named interior minister in the Balaguer administration, to which the armed services portfolio was added in June 1988; he continued as armed services minister after a cabinet reshuffle in August 1989, with the PQD being credited with Balaguer's margin of victory in May 1990.

The party received 0.8 percent of the vote in the 2006 legislative elections and 1.1 percent in the 2010 balloting. It rejoined the progressive bloc of parties supporting the presidential candidacy of the PLD's Danilo Medina in the 2012 election.

Leaders: Elias WESSIN Chavez (President), Lorenzo VALDEZ Carrasco (Secretary General).

Broad Front for National Dignity (*Frente Amplio por la Dignidad Nacional*-FADN). On March 20, 2011, representatives of a group of leftist parties signed a proclamation forming the FADN. The party sought to end political patronage and improve social equality by reorganizing the political system. The FADN primarily comprised the **Movement for Independence, Unity and Change** (*Movimiento Independencia, Unidad y Cambio*—MIUCA), a small leftist group associated with the international communist movement led by former attorney general Guillermo MORENO. MIUCA received 0.32 percent of the 2006 legislative election vote. Moreno stood as the party's nominee in the 2008 presidential elections, winning 0.44 percent of the vote on a platform supporting development, small business, and improved living conditions and jobs for the poor. MIUCA received greater support in the country's municipal elections. It won 0.95 percent of the vote during the 2010 legislative elections.

The FADN also absorbed the **Revolutionary Force** (*Fuerza de la Revolución*—FR) and the **Dominican Popular Movement** (*Movimiento Popular Dominicano*—MPD), among other smaller groups. The delegates selected lawyer Ángel Julián Serulle Ramia to lead the party and to be its 2012 presidential candidate. Serulle received 0.14 percent of the vote in the election.

Leaders: Ángel Julián SERULLE Ramia (President of the Party and 2012 presidential candidate), Juan Dionisio RODRIGUEZ Restituyo (Secretary General).

Peace Alliance (*Alianza País*). Former attorney general Guillermo Moreno broke away from MIUCA in 2009 to form Alianza País. He contested the 2012 presidential election and won 1.37 percent of the vote. In November 2012 Moreno filed a legal complaint charging that the fiscal deficit was caused by corruption during the Fernández administration.

Leader: Guillermo MORENO (Party Founder and 2012 presidential candidate).

Revolutionary Social Democratic Party (*Partido Revolucionario Social Demócrata*—PRSD). The PRSD, a splinter of the PRD led by former PRD president Hatuey De Camps, embraces the tenets of the social democratic movement, which seeks to incorporate elements of socialism and capitalism. The party garnered 1.56 percent of the vote in the 2006 legislative elections and 0.63 percent in the 2010 legislative balloting.

The party's nominee for the 2008 presidential elections, Eduardo ESTRELLA, running under the banner of The Fourth Way, received 0.47 percent of the vote. De Camps threw his support behind Mejía and the PRD in March 2011.

Leaders: Hatuey De CAMPS Jimenez (President), Rafael GAMUNDI Cordero (Secretary General).

Dominicans for Change Party (*Partido Dominicanos por el Cambio*—DXC). Eduardo Estrella left the PRSD in 2010 to found the DXC. Estrella took 0.21 percent of the vote in the May 2012 presidential election.

Leader: Eduardo ESTRELLA (Party Founder and 2012 presidential candidate).

Other parties presenting presidential candidates in recent elections have been the **Christian Popular Party** (*Partido Popular Cristiano*—PPC), backed by representatives of the Unification Church and led by Héctor Peguero MÉNDEZ; the right-wing **National Progressive Force** (*Fuerza Nacional Progresivo*—FNP), led by Dr. Marino Vinicio Castillo; the **New Power Movement** (*Movimiento Nuevo Poder*—MNP), led by Antonio REYNOSO; and the **Dominican Social Alliance** (*Alianza Social Dominicana*—ASD), whose presidential candidate, Carlos RAMON Bencosme, also ran in 2004. Other minor parties and their candidates in 2004 included the **National Solidarity Movement** (*Movimiento Solidaridad*—MSN), led by Ramon Emilio CONCEPCION; the **New Alternative Party** (*Partido Nueva Alternativa*—PNA), led by Ramon María ALMANZAR; and the **Popular Democratic Party** (*Partido Demócrata Popular*—PDP), led by Ramon Nelson DIDIEZ.

For more information on the **Revolutionary Social Christian Party** (*Partido Revolucionario Social Cristiano*—RSC), the **Democratic Integration Movement** (*Movimiento de Integración Democrática*—MID), and the **Movement of National Conciliation** (*Movimiento de Conciliación Nacional*—MCN), see the 2008 *Handbook.*

LEGISLATURE

The **Congress of the Republic** (*Congreso de la Republica*) consists of a Senate and a Chamber of Deputies, both directly elected for four-year terms, except for those elected during the May 16, 2010, legislative contest, who will serve a six-year term ending in 2016 because of a change in election law that will synchronize legislative and presidential elections.

Senate (*Senado*). The Senate currently consists of 32 members, 1 from each province and the National District. Following the election of May 16, 2010, the Dominican Liberation Party controlled 31 seats and the Social Christian Reformist Party held 1.

President: Reinaldo PARED Pérez.

Chamber of Deputies (*Cámara de Diputados*). The Chamber presently consists of 178 members elected on the basis of 1 deputy for every 50,000 inhabitants per province, with at least 2 from each province, and 5 elected by the accumulation of votes nationwide. After the election of May 16, 2010, the Dominican Liberation Party and its allies controlled 105 seats; the Dominican Revolutionary Party and its allies, 75; and the Social Christian Reformist Party and its allies, 3.

President: Abel Atahualpa MARTÍNEZ Durán.

CABINET

[as of August 1, 2013]

President	Danilo Medina Sánchez
Vice President	Margarita Cedeño de Fernández [f]
Secretaries of State	
Administrative Secretary of the Presidency	José Ramón Peralta
Agriculture	Luis Ramón Rodríguez
Armed Forces	Sigfrido Aramis Pared Pérez
Justice; Attorney General	Francisco Domínguez Brito
Controller General	Haivanjoe N. G. Cortinas
Culture	José Antonio Rodríguez
Economy, Planning and Development	Juan Temistocles Montas Dominguez
Education	Josefina Pimentel Valenzuela [f]
Environment and Natural Resources	Bautista Rojas Gómez
Finance	Simón Lizardo Mezquita
Foreign Relations	Carlos Morales Troncoso
Higher Education, Science and Technology	Ligia Amada Melo de Cardona [f]
Industry and Commerce	José del Castillo Saviñón
Interior and Police	José Ramon Fadul
Labor	Martiza Hernández [f]
Presidency	Gustavo Montalvo
Public Administration	Ramón Ventura Camejo
Public Health and Welfare	Freddy Hidalgo
Public Works and Communication	Gonzalo Castillo
Sports, Physical Education and Recreation	Jaime David Fernández Mirabal
Tourism	Francisco Javier García
Women's Affairs	Alejandrina German [f]
Youth	Jorge Minaya
Ministers without portfolios	
Citizen Safety Programs	Franklin Almeyda
Regional Integration Affairs	Miguel Mejía
(unassigned)	Antonio Isa Conde

[f] = female

INTERGOVERNMENTAL REPRESENTATION

Ambassador to the U.S.: Anibal de Jesus de Castro RODRIGUEZ.

U.S. Ambassador to the Dominican Republic: Raul H. YZAGUIRRE.

Permanent Representative to the UN: Héctor Virgilio ALCÁNTARA MEJÍA.

IGO Memberships (Non-UN): IADB, IBRD, ICC, IMF, IOM, NAM, OAS, WTO.

ECUADOR

Republic of Ecuador
República del Ecuador

Political Status: Gained independence from Spain (as part of Gran Colombia) in 1822; independent republic established in 1830; present constitution approved by a constituent assembly elected September 30, 2007, and in effect from September 28, 2008.

Area: 109,482 sq. mi. (283,561 sq. km), excluding the region previously in dispute with Peru, but including the Galápagos Islands.

Population: 15,495,016 (2013E—UN); 15,439,429 (2013E—U.S. Census).

Major Urban Centers (2012E): QUITO (1,608,000), Guayaquil (2,279,000), Cuenca (330,000), Ambato (165,000).

Official Language: Spanish.

Monetary Unit: U.S. Dollar. The dollar was phased in from January 2000 to March 2001 to replace the sucre as Ecuador's legal tender.

President: Rafael CORREA Delgado (Country Alliance); elected in second-round voting on November 26, 2006, and inaugurated on January 15, 2007, succeeding Alfredo PALACIO Gonzáles (independent); reelected in first-round balloting on April 26, 2009, and inaugurated on August 10 for a four-year term; reelected in first-round balloting on February 17, 2013, and inaugurated on May 24 for a four-year term.

Vice President: Lenin MORENO Garcés (Country Alliance); elected in second-round voting on November 26, 2006, and inaugurated on January 15, 2007, for a term concurrent with that of the president, succeeding Alejandro SERRANO Aguilar; reelected in first-round balloting on April 26, 2009, and inaugurated on August 10; reelected in first-round balloting on February 17, 2013, and inaugurated on May 24.

THE COUNTRY

South America's fourth-smallest republic has four main geographic regions: the Pacific coastal plain (*Costa*), the Andes highlands (*Sierra*), the sparsely populated eastern tropical rainforest (*Oriente*), and the Galápagos Islands (*Archipélago de Colón*) in the Pacific. The population is roughly 40 percent Indian, 40 percent mestizo, 10 percent white, and 10 percent black. Although Spanish is the official language, numerous Indian languages are spoken, the most important of which is Quechua. Approximately 95 percent of the population professes Roman Catholicism, but other religions are practiced, including tribal religions among the Indians. With an average life expectancy of 75 years and an adult literacy rate of just 84 percent, 36 percent of Ecuadorans live below the poverty line. According to the World Bank, 54 percent of the labor force is female, primarily in domestic service, market trade, and transient agricultural labor. Female participation in government is relatively high; the president and both vice presidents of the National Assembly elected in 2013 were women.

Adverse climate, rainforest terrain, volcanic activity, and earthquakes limit the country's habitable area and have slowed its economic development. The economy is primarily agricultural, with approximately one-half of the population engaged in farming, mainly on a subsistence level. The most important crops are bananas (of which Ecuador is the world's largest exporter), coffee, and cocoa. Following the lowering of tariff barriers for exports to the United States, cut flowers, broccoli, and mangoes emerged as important cash crops. Hardwoods and balsa are harvested from the forests, while Ecuadoran Pacific waters are a prime tuna-fishing area. Gold, silver, and copper continue to be mined, and production from Amazonian oil fields has placed Ecuador fifth among South American countries in output of petroleum, the country's leading export commodity (Ecuador has the third largest oil reserves in South America) and fourth among the continent's suppliers of crude oil to the United States. Other energy resources include natural gas deposits in the Gulf of Guayaquil and considerable hydroelectric potential.

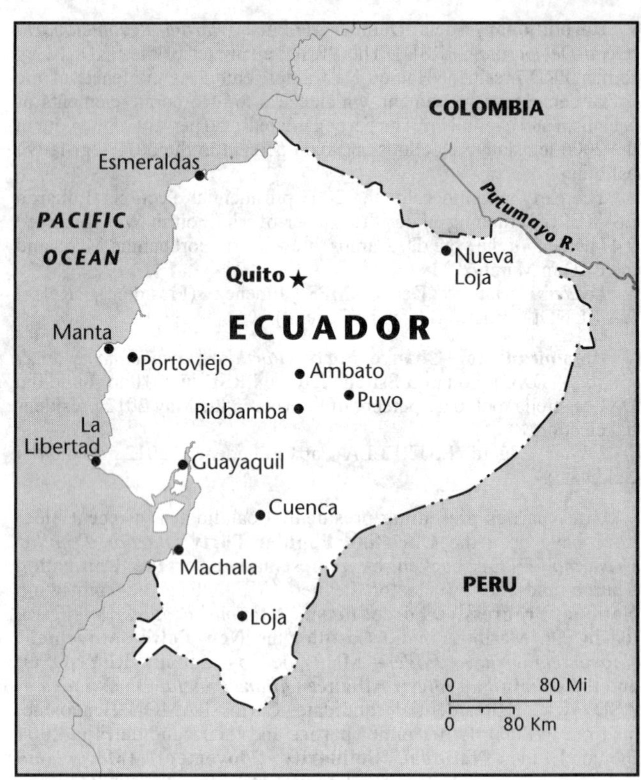

Following the adoption of the U.S. dollar as the medium of exchange in 2000, inflation declined to 5.2 percent by 2010, and stable growth resumed, due in large part to the strength of high worldwide oil prices. The global economic crisis caused growth to grind to a near-standstill at 0.4 percent in 2009, before resuming at 3.6 percent in 2010, 7.8 percent in 2011, and 5.0 percent in 2012. Unemployment hit 7.6 percent in 2010, but fell to 5.83 percent by 2012. Remittances to family members from some 2 million Ecuadorans who have emigrated to the United States and Europe (primarily Spain) have fallen in recent years from around $700 million in 2007 to $596 million in 2012.

GOVERNMENT AND POLITICS

Political background. Charismatic individuals rather than political platforms have dominated Ecuador's political life through most of the period since the country's liberation from Spanish rule in 1822 and its establishment as an independent republic in 1830. A historic division between Conservatives and Liberals (now of little practical significance) emerged in the 19th century, with the Conservatives based in the highlands and the Liberals on the coast. More recently, Ecuador has experienced tremendous political instability, with nine chief executives from 1988 to 2007, politicized high courts, and little popular support for the legislature.

A bright spot in Ecuadoran political life occurred in 1948 with the election of Galo PLAZA Lasso as president. The first chief executive since 1924 to complete his full term, Plaza created a climate of stability and economic progress, while his successor, José María VELASCO Ibarra, stood out in a lengthy catalog of interrupted presidencies and military juntas. Before his election in 1952 (his only full term), Velasco had served twice as president, in 1934–1935 and in 1944–1947. He was subsequently elected in 1960 and in 1968, but coups ended both terms prematurely. A military junta also ousted his 1961 successor, Carlos Julio AROSEMENA Monroy, in July 1963. During his last term in office, Velasco in mid-1970 dissolved the National Congress and assumed dictatorial powers to cope with a financial emergency. He was deposed for a fourth time in February 1972, the stimulus to military intervention being the approach of a presidential election in which Assad BUCARAM Elmhalim, a populist politician, appeared the likely winner. The military leadership, under Gen. Guillermo RODRÍGUEZ Lara, canceled the election, nominally restored the Liberal constitution of 1945, and advanced a "nationalist, military, and revolutionary" program emphasizing the objectives of social justice and popular welfare.

In December 1975 President Rodríguez announced his intention to make way for a return to civilian rule, but his actual departure in January 1976 was precipitated by a government crisis during which the entire cabinet resigned. A three-man junta headed by Vice Adm. Alfredo POVEDA Burbano succeeded Rodríguez, declaring that the 1972 program of the armed forces would be honored and that the nation would be returned to civilian leadership within two years; however, it was not until July 16, 1978, that a presidential election, in which no candidate obtained a majority of votes, was held. In a runoff on April 29, 1979, the center-left candidate, Jaime ROLDÓS Aguilera, defeated his conservative opponent, Sixto DURAN-BALLEN Córdovez, by a more than two-to-one majority and was inaugurated, without incident, on August 10.

Roldós, his minister of defense, and a number of others were killed in a plane crash on May 24, 1981, and the Christian Democratic vice president, Osvaldo HURTADO Larrea, was immediately sworn in to complete the remainder of Roldós's five-year term. On June 2 the late president's brother, León ROLDÓS Aguilera, by a legislative margin of one vote, was elected to the vice presidency.

A dispute between the president and vice president in early 1982, ostensibly over rapprochement with neighboring Peru (see Foreign relations, below), led to the resignation of two *Roldosista* ministers and, amid mounting economic problems, a period of uncertain legislative support for Hurtado, who was constitutionally precluded from seeking reelection in 1984. In the balloting on January 29, with 17 parties competing, the opposition Democratic Left (*Izquierda Democrática*—ID) won 24 of 71 legislative seats, while its presidential candidate, Rodrigo BORJA Cevallos, obtained a slim plurality. However, the nominee of the conservative National Reconstruction Front (*Frente de Reconstrucción Nacional*—FRN), León FEBRES Cordero, narrowly defeated Borja in a second-round poll on May 6. Subsequently, a major constitutional struggle erupted between the executive and legislative branches over control of the judiciary, with the president refusing to recognize a new Supreme Court appointed by the National Congress. The issue was eventually resolved in December, when the congress agreed to the resignation of both judicial panels and the appointment of a new court composed of progovernment and opposition members.

In June 1985 two ID deputies joined five members of the independent Radical Alfarista Front (*Frente Radical Alfarista*—FRA) in shifting their allegiance to the president, thereby, with the support of the Concentration of Popular Forces (*Concentración de Fuerzas Populares*—CFP), providing the government with its first legislative majority since the 1984 election. However, the government was shaken in mid-March 1986 by a brief revolt led by Lt. Gen. Frank VARGAS Pazzos, who had been dismissed as armed forces chief of staff after demanding the discharge and imprisonment of Defense Minister Luis PIÑEIROS Rivera and army commander Gen. Manuel ALBUJA for alleged misuse of public funds.

At midterm legislative balloting in June 1986 (postponed from January to allow for voter recertification), the pro-government parties again lost control of the congress by a decisive margin of 27–43, while the referendum on independent candidacies was defeated by an even more impressive 25.2 to 58.8 percent vote. The result was a renewal of friction between the two branches, with the president rejecting a congressional amnesty granted to General Vargas in September.

On January 16, 1987, Febres was kidnapped by dissident paratroopers at Taura air base and held for 11 hours, until agreeing to the release of Vargas. The legislature then approved a nonbinding resolution calling on the president to resign. The chief executive responded by declaring that he intended to remain in office until the expiration of his term in August 1988.

In the general election of January 31, 1988, Social Christian (*Partido Social Cristiano*—PSC) presidential candidate Sixto DURÁN-BALLÉN ran a poor third to the ID's Borja Cevallos and Abdalá BUCARAM Ortiz of the Ecuadoran Roldosist Party (*Partido Roldosista Ecuatoriano*—PRE). Buttressed by a comfortable legislative majority, Borja defeated Bucaram in runoff balloting on May 8 and formed a largely ID administration following his inauguration on August 10.

The president's legislative supporters were reduced to a minority in the biennial election of January 31, 1990, with Averroes BUCARAM Saxida (a cousin of Abdalá) being elected congress president. In late October, however, with the creation of a "Political Ethics Bloc" (*Bloque de Etica Política*), the body tilted briefly in favor of Borja, who was thereby able to secure Bucaram's ouster as presiding officer. Subsequently, legislative control again passed to the opposition, which displayed its hostility toward the president by impeaching no less than six of his ministers by mid-1991.

At second-round presidential balloting on July 5, 1992, Durán-Ballén, who had been denied renomination by the PSC, defeated his former party's candidate, Jaime NEBOT Saadi, by sweeping 19 of the country's 21 provinces. The PSC had, however, secured a legislative plurality, with Durán-Ballén's recently organized Republican Unity Party (*Partido Unidad Republicano*—PUR) in third place after the PRE. The most conspicuous loss in the presidential election was the formerly dominant ID, whose candidate attracted a vote share of only 8.2 percent.

In the midterm legislative election of May 1, 1994, the PSC won 22 of the 65 contested seats, while Durán-Ballén's PUR plummeted from 12 seats to 3. The result was an intensification of the long-standing legislative-executive rift, with the congress forcing changes in most leading ministries either by impeachment or the threat of impeachment.

In August 1995 Vice President Alberto DAHIK became the center of a corruption scandal concerning the illegal use of funds and bribery of legislative and judicial officials. In late September President Durán-Ballén urged Dahik to resign. He refused and in early October escaped dismissal by the failure of a legislative vote of impeachment. However, also facing charges by the Supreme Court, he resigned on October 11 and fled to Costa Rica. A week later the president secured approval for the naming of former education minister Eduardo PEÑA Triviño as Dahik's successor. The Durán-Ballén administration suffered a further embarrassment when all 11 of its constitutional reform proposals were rejected in a plebiscite on November 26 (see Constitution and government, below).

In the first-round presidential poll of May 19, 1996, the PSC's Jaime Nebot and the PRE's Abdalá Bucaram qualified for runoff balloting with vote shares of 27.4 and 25.5 percent, respectively. In the second round on July 7, the populist Bucaram confounded earlier opinion polls by easily defeating his opponent (54.3 to 45.7 percent) and was sworn in on August 10. However, the PRE held only 19 of 82 legislative seats, leaving Bucaram, like his predecessor, with the difficult task of seeking support from a deeply divided National Congress.

Following his inauguration, President Bucaram abandoned most of his populist campaign promises and advanced an economic reform program that included privatization of state-owned enterprises, elimination of guaranteed job security, and devaluation of the Ecuadoran sucre. The result was a wave of domestic unrest amid plummeting presidential popularity. On February 6, 1997, the National Congress ousted Bucaram because of "mental incapacity" and designated its presiding officer, Fabián ALARCÓN Rivera, as his successor. Two days later the congress yielded to the constitutional claim of Vice President Rosalía ARTEAGA Serrano, electing her interim president. On February 11 Arteaga submitted her resignation, and Alarcón was reinstated as chief executive for an 18-month term, with new elections scheduled for May 1998. Alarcón's incumbency was endorsed by 65 percent of those participating in a May 25 referendum, the voters also approving a call for a constituent assembly that was elected on November 30 with a party distribution not significantly different from that of the National Congress. The assembly's principal output was a new set of electoral rules that included an increase in the number of legislative seats from 82 to 121 and the abolition of midterm replenishment.

In nationwide election on May 31, 1998, the Popular Democracy (*Democracia Popular*—DP), a restyled Christian Democratic grouping, won a plurality of congressional seats, while its presidential nominee, Jamil MAHUAD Witt, bested five opponents with a 35 percent vote share. In a second-round contest on June 12, Mahuad secured 51.3 percent of the vote, defeating the *Roldosista* runner-up, Alvaro Fernando NOBOA Pontón.

President Mahuad assumed office in August 1998 amid severe economic problems. The new government proposed austerity measures in January 1999 designed to reduce the budget deficit, but it was forced to abandon planned increases in taxes and fuel prices at the insistence of the PSC, on which the DP was relying for a legislative majority.

By August 1999 President Mahuad's popularity had declined from 68 percent to 12 percent, and by January 1, 2000, had plummeted further to an unprecedented 2 percent in the wake of a debt-restructuring effort that generated a new wave of protests. The president responded by declaring a state of emergency and adopting the dollar as the Ecuadoran currency. On the streets, the native *Confederación de Nacionalidades Indígenas del Ecuador* (Conaie) launched a campaign to oust not only Mahuad but also members of Congress and the Supreme Court in favor of a "patriotic government of national unity." On January 21 Mahuad was overthrown in a coup led by a group of colonels who had joined forces with Conaie leaders. However, Gen. Carlos MENDOZA, who had been installed with Conaie president Antonio VARGAS and former Supreme Court president Carlos SOLORZANO as a ruling triumvirate, promptly mounted a countercoup that endorsed the "constitutional" elevation of Vice President Gustavo NOBOA Benjarano to the post that Mahuad had ostensibly abandoned. Conaie responded by charging the military with betrayal and called for a plebiscite to remove legislative and judicial incumbents, reverse the use of the dollar as the currency, end the U.S. military presence at an airbase in Manta, and secure amnesty for those participating in the January 21 uprising.

On November 24, 2002, Lucio GUTIÉRREZ Borbúa, a retired colonel who had participated in the ouster of Mahuad (an event commemorated in the full title of his small group, the Patriotic Society Party of January 21 [*Partido Sociedad Patriótica 21 de Enero*—PSP]), defeated Alvaro Noboa Pontón, now running as leader of the Institutional Renewal Party of National Action (*Partido Renovador Institucional de Acción Nacional*—PRIAN), in second-round presidential balloting. Nine months later, in the wake of an apparent shift to the right after Gutiérrez had attempted to introduce a number of IMF-mandated economic reforms, his administration was severely weakened by the withdrawal of the Conaie-based New Country—Pachakutik Movement (*Movimiento Nuevo País–Pachakutik*—MNPP). The president then entered briefly into an implausible alignment with the two leading legislative parties, the center-right PSC and the center-left ID. The effort soon failed, with both of the erstwhile allies joining an opposition drive for the president's impeachment. By mid-2004 poll results showed 68 percent of the public felt Gutiérrez should resign. However, he persevered by courting the *Roldosistas*. Although having earlier opposed the return of Abdalá Bucaram from exile in Panama, Gutiérrez met with the former president on September 1. Less than three months later, Gutiérrez deflected impeachment by negotiating a "new majority" that included the far-left Democratic Popular Movement (*Movimiento Popular Democrático*—MPD), the right-wing PRIAN, and the PSP, the PRE, and the CFP. Emboldened by an opposition suddenly in disarray, Gutiérrez recalled Congress in early December and pushed through a constitutionally questionable measure that removed all 31 Supreme Court justices. This allowed new appointees who would clear the way for former president Bucaram's return by dismissing the charges against him. On March 31, 2005, the charges were annulled, and Bucaram returned on April 2. These maneuvers aroused the public, and a wave of demonstrations in Quito, including an incursion of rioting students into the congressional building, yielded a 60–2 legislative vote on April 20 to remove Gutiérrez in the wake of a spurious finding that he had abandoned his post. Also purged were all 31 members of the Supreme Court.

Vice President Alfredo PALACIO Gonzáles, assuming the presidency after election by Congress on the same day in 2005 that Gutiérrez was removed, encountered an equally intractable legislature. In June 2005 he called for a referendum to establish "more democratic representation" by breaking with party-controlled electoral lists in favor of constituency-specific candidates (single-member districts) but was rebuffed by Congress.

On October 4, 2005, Gutiérrez returned from exile and was arrested on charges of attempting to destabilize the government by not recognizing the legitimacy of Palacio as his successor. Gutiérrez was released by judicial order in March 2006 after a high court ruling that his actions did not threaten national security.

During his brief tenure in office, Palacio faced a series of public protests over the status of a foreign oil company operating in Ecuador and the government's negotiations over a bilateral free trade agreement with the United States. Palacio's government was also plagued with a constant stream of cabinet reshuffling during his tenure in office; at least 55 ministers served from April 2005 until the swearing in of his successor in January 2007.

First-round balloting for president on October 15, 2006, resulted in a runoff from an original list of 13 candidates between Alvaro Noboa Pontón of the PRIAN, a right-of-center populist millionaire, and Rafael CORREA Delgado, an economist, former finance minister, and leader of a new left-wing bloc, the Country Alliance (*Alianza País*—AP). Noboa advocated a diplomatic distance from Chávez and Cuba, offering instead to embrace closer ties with the United States and a resurrection of the free trade agreement. Correa's election platform drew on themes from anti-U.S. Andean leftist populism. Correa called for an increase in social spending, the suspension or restructuring of repayment on foreign debt, a renegotiation of investment contracts with foreign oil companies, and nonrenewal of the agreement for the U.S. military base. He opposed the U.S. free trade agreement, suggesting that it would hurt small agricultural producers. Correa was elected in the second round on November 26, having prevailed in a particularly bitter campaign in which Noboa won the first round. Noboa challenged the final results, which gave Correa 57.1 percent of the vote to Noboa's 43.0 percent, and refused to concede. Correa was inaugurated on January 15, 2007, and formed a new government, drawn mostly from AP members, the same day. Legislative elections concurrent with the 2006 presidential election gave the PRIAN a plurality in Congress, with nine other parties also holding seats. Since the AP did not field any legislative candidates, the party had no dedicated support in Congress other than from the small number of seats won by the left-wing MPD and from the MNPP.

In October 2008 an interim legislative commission (known as the "*Congresillo,*" or "Little Congress") became the country's temporary legislative body after a new constitution was approved by referendum in September (see Constitution and government, below), pending the election and inauguration of a new National Assembly scheduled for mid-2009. Named by the outgoing constituent assembly, the interim congress was dominated by the AP, with 46 of 76 members. It was empowered to name a provisional 21-member Supreme Court, the directors of the temporary electoral authorities who would oversee the 2009 presidential and legislative elections, and the members of the Council of Citizen Participation and Social Control, a new and powerful fifth branch of government that would make permanent appointments to electoral and oversight institutions. The opposition claimed that AP domination of the interim congress would effectively weaken checks on executive power.

Presidential and legislative elections were held on April 26, 2009, as required by the new constitution. President Correa was reelected with 51.9 percent of the vote, enough to avoid a runoff and well ahead of former president Lucio Gutiérrez of the PSP, with 28.2 percent, and the PRIAN's Noboa, with 11.4 percent. Correa's victory was the first time an Ecuadoran candidate had won in the first round since the restoration of democracy in 1979. The AP secured a plurality in concurrent legislative elections, with 45.9 percent of the vote, followed by the PSP with 14.9 percent, the PSC with 13.5 percent, and the PRIAN with 5.8 percent. Thirteen smaller parties also won representation.

Facing public criticism of his education, mining, and water rights reforms, Correa's approval rating dropped precipitously from 73 percent in 2007 to 41 percent in early 2010, according to one poll. On April 8 Conaie mobilized 8,000 indigenous members who were concerned that the 2008 constitution allowed for the privatization of the public water system for a march on Quito. On another front, the constitutional court ruled against the indigenous groups on April 26, deciding that mining sector reforms were legal under the constitution. Conaie started nationwide protests on May 1, and by May 20 Correa had backtracked on his demand for the water law reform.

A truth commission convened to investigate human rights abuses by the Ecuadoran government released its report in June 2010. It found that 456 people had been victims of abuse—from illegal detention to murder—at the hands of the government over the past 25 years. Though Correa had set it up, the commission revealed that the current president's first administration had been guilty of 17 such abuses.

On September 30 Correa faced the deepest crisis of his tenure to date when a protest by about 800 police officers over a cut in public-employee benefits turned violent. As Correa left the police barracks, where he had gone to negotiate with the officers, a violent skirmish ensued in which he was exposed to tear gas and hurried to a nearby hospital, where he was detained for 10 hours. Appearing before the crowd at a hospital window, Correa ripped open his shirt and challenged protesters to kill him, vowing to leave the hospital "either as a president or a corpse." He declared a state of national emergency and, after he was rescued by an army unit, described the incident, in which eight people died and hundreds were wounded, as an attempted coup d'état. UNASUR, the United States, and other foreign governments expressed support for Correa. Six police officers involved in the incident were convicted in July. Correa also intensified his criticism of the media and the judicial branch. Four prominent newspapermen were sentenced to prison in July for libel against the president. In August an executive-controlled commission, created by the May 2011 constitutional referendum to assume power from the Judiciary Council to hire and fire judges, dismissed 48 judges, prompting concern over judicial branch independence.

Following years of litigation, on February 14, 2011, a provincial court in Sucumbios fined the Chevron Corporation almost $9 billion for dumping crude oil into the waterways of the Amazon rainforest in the early 1990s. Although Chevron rejected the ruling, saying the pollution was caused by Texaco before Chevron bought the company in 2001, the plaintiffs promised to go after Chevron in other Latin American countries where it had operations.

Correa was elected to an unprecedented third term on February 17, 2012, and the AP won a majority in the National Assembly in concurrent parliamentary elections.

Constitution and government. In a referendum held on January 15, 1978, Ecuadorans approved a new constitution that came into force with the retirement of the military junta and the inauguration of Jaime Roldós Aguilera in August 1979. The new basic law provided for a unicameral legislature and a single four-year presidential term, extension of the vote to illiterates (presumed to be about 30 percent of the population), and establishment of a framework of social rights for citizens. The Supreme Court, which is responsible for supervising superior courts, heads the judicial system. The superior courts in turn supervise lower (provincial and cantonal) courts.

On March 1, 1994, President Durán-Ballén launched a program of constitutional reform by announcing an eight-part plebiscite coincident with the May 1 congressional poll that included provisions for presidential reelection, compulsory voting, creation of an upper legislative chamber, and four-year terms for all representatives. However, the Supreme Electoral Tribunal (*Tribunal Supremo Electoral*—TSE) immediately struck down the proposal as "illegal and impractical." The TSE also rejected a call on June 10 for a July 31 plebiscite on formation of a constituent assembly to consider the changes, with the president insisting that the TSE's action was itself illegal since he had the right to "consult the people" on any matter that he wished. Subsequently, a scaled-down plebiscite was held on August 28, following the August 10 commencement of a new congressional session. An unusually low turnout of voters by a 2–1 majority approved most of the package, including a limitation on congressional power to determine public spending, authorization for nonparty candidates to stand for elective posts, and reelection of elected officials, including the president.

A second set of reform measures was rejected by approximately 56 percent of the participants in a plebiscite on November 26, 1995. Among the proposals were election of all legislators from single-member constituencies for four-year terms, presidential authority to dissolve the legislature, a ban on public service strikes, administrative decentralization to the provinces and municipalities, and partial privatization of the social security system. The constituent assembly elected in 1997 redrafted the constitution; the changes, which went into force on August 10, 1998, provided for a National Congress of a size (then 100) determined by a somewhat complex population-based formula, with members sitting for four-year terms; it also lowered the first-round cutoff for presidential balloting to 45 percent, with the victor serving a four-year term.

Rafael Correa campaigned for the presidency in 2006, promising a referendum on rewriting the constitution. Congress approved the referendum on February 13, 2007, and the electoral tribunal set the date for April. Eighty percent of voters approved the national referendum on April 15, 2007. A group of more than 50 legislators argued that the tribunal was giving too many powers to the presidency, leading to a lawsuit, gunfire, and the expulsion of 57 members of parliament (MPs). More than a dozen lawmakers briefly fled to Colombia, requesting asylum and seeking international intervention. Ultimately, the crisis abated as Congress continued to operate without the suspended legislators (for details on the contentious tribunal process, see the 2013 *Handbook*).

In subsequent elections for delegates to the constituent assembly tasked with drafting a new constitution, the PAÍS won a large majority, and the new assembly was seated on November 29, 2007. Delegates overwhelmingly voted to declare congress in recess without pay, effectively dissolving it, until approval of a new constitution in a referendum scheduled for 2008. The constituent assembly then assumed the powers of congress in addition to rewriting the country's constitution. Critics blasted the assembly's action, claiming that it was giving too much power to the executive branch, particularly after the attorney general, the banking chief, and other top officials were suspended. In a symbolic gesture, Correa declined to step down. After missing a May 2008 deadline, the assembly approved 257 articles in the final 30 days leading up to its July 24 deadline.

The new draft constitution was approved by 64 percent of voters in a national referendum on September 28. The new constitution permits two consecutive four-year presidential terms and enhances presidential authority by granting the president greater control over the central bank and the energy and telecommunications sectors. It also authorizes the president, once per term, to disband congress and call new elections for obstructing the president's "development plan." Additionally, the new charter sets forth provisions for immediate elections if a president is impeached or if the legislature is dissolved, and it allows for a presidential recall referendum. Further, the new constitution overhauls the judicial system and creates a fifth branch of government (executive, legislative, judicial, electoral, and now social) known as the Council of Citizen Participation and Social Control to appoint the committees that nominate the attorney general, ombudsman, comptroller, and National Electoral Council. The new basic law also grants the president greater fiscal control over provincial authorities and guarantees that all citizens have access to water, health care, pensions, and free university education. It is the world's first basic document to guarantee rights of nature, granting sensitive ecosystems legal protection from destruction. The establishment of foreign military bases and the concentration of large landholdings are prohibited. Supreme Court judges subsequently voiced their opposition, protesting a provision that would reduce their 31-member court to a 21-member national court of justice, subject to oversight by a constitutional court.

Voters approved all ten proposed amendments in a further constitutional referendum, held on May 7, 2011. Among the amendments were a ban on unjustified wealth, a lengthening of the time criminal suspects can be held without trial, and requiring banks to divest nonfinancial assets, such as newspapers or television stations.

Administratively, the country is divided into 24 provinces, including the Galápagos Islands. The provinces are subdivided into municipalities.

Ecuador's Constitution guarantees freedom of speech, but in recent years, the watchdog group Reporters Without Borders noted that press freedom had deteriorated under the administrations of President Lucio Gutiérrez Borbúa and President Rafael Correa. It ranked Ecuador 119th out of 179 countries in its 2013 Index of Press Freedom. Correa has called Ecuador's media "a corrupt instrument of the oligarchy" and introduced new media restrictions in July 2013 (see Current issues, below).

Foreign relations. The most enduring foreign-affairs issue for many years was a boundary dispute with Peru that dated to the 16th century and involved a 125,000-square-mile tract of land between the Putumayo and Marañón rivers, both tributaries of the upper Amazon. The dispute resulted in periodic conflict and a number of agreements, including the Rio Protocol of January 1942, which awarded the greater part of the area to Peru and was formally repudiated by Velasco Ibarra in 1960 on the ground that Ecuador had been pressured into acceptance of its terms by the guarantor states (Argentina, Brazil, Chile, and the United States). The frontier established by the Rio Protocol was itself never fully delineated, a 50-mile stretch in the vicinity of the Condor Mountains remaining to be charted along the presumed watershed of the Zamora and Santiago rivers, in an area where a new tributary of the Marañón was subsequently discovered.

In January 1981 Ecuador and Peru engaged in five days of fighting in the Condor region, while representatives of the guarantor states convened in Brasília, Brazil, for negotiations on a cease-fire that was accepted by the combatants on February 2. However, it was not until March 17 that the two sides began to withdraw their forces from the disputed area.

The dispute flared up again in August 1991, when Peruvian border units reportedly discovered Ecuadoran troops clearing woods for raising cattle inside Peruvian territory. Subsequently, Ecuador reiterated its rejection of the Rio Protocol, while the Peruvian popular press headlined the incident as a full-scale invasion by its neighbor.

In October 1993 a suggestion by Foreign Minister Paredes Delgado at the United Nations that Ecuador would seek an accord with Peru not to resort to force over the territorial issue promoted a "clarification" by Quito that it was not proposing a nonaggression pact with its neighbor. Two months earlier President Durán-Ballén had announced that he would repay the compliment of three visits to Ecuador by Peruvian president Alberto Fujimori in 1992 by embarking on the first state visit by an Ecuadoran president to Lima, Peru. However, in the wake of widespread criticism within Ecuador, the trip had not materialized by late January 1995, when troops, tanks, and fighter planes massed on both sides of the border. While Peruvians outside the contested area were reported to be largely indifferent to the latest confrontation, Ecuador charged its neighbor with "launching a massive offensive" and vowed a "fight for the fatherland."

Despite the announcement of a cease-fire on February 1, 1995, renewed fighting erupted the following day, with peace talks in Rio de Janeiro, Brazil, being broken off on February 5. Thereafter, in another about-face, the two sides signed a peace agreement in Brasília on February 17, though fighting did not cease until the end of the month. Under the so-called Itamaraty Declaration, the guarantor states would dispatch a team of observers on a renewable 90-day mission to oversee a gradual and mutual demobilization of the area and initiate talks aimed at resolving the long-standing dispute. In a remarkable display of warmth accompanying the July accord, Durán-Ballén congratulated his Peruvian counterpart on his reelection, while Fujimori indicated that he would attend a Rio Group summit in Quito in early September. Although the two did not formally meet on the latter occasion, Fujimori stated that their countries were undergoing a "recovery of mutual trust" and extended an invitation to Durán-Ballén to reinstate his earlier intention to visit Lima.

Tension again flared in late 1995, when Peru learned that Ecuador was about to take delivery of four military aircraft from Israel in a deal approved by the United States, despite its status as a guarantor of the Rio Protocol. A number of border incidents ensued, with Israel declaring on January 1 that it would not proceed with delivery of the planes until peace negotiations had been concluded. Finally, on January 19, 1998, agreement was reached in Rio de Janeiro on a timetable leading to a peace treaty. Under the accord, four commissions dealing with major aspects of the controversy would be established, including one dealing with the thorniest issue: border demarcation.

The lengthy dispute was formally settled with a "global and definitive" accord signed by presidents Mahuad and Fujimori in Brasília on October 26, 1998. While the disputed territory was awarded to Peru, control (but not sovereignty) of the principal town of Tiwintza, in addition to a corridor from the border, was assigned to Ecuador, which was also granted free navigation rights along the Amazon and the right to establish two port facilities within Peruvian territory. Provision was also made for linkup between the two countries' electrical grids and oil pipelines. Resolution of the lengthy controversy appeared to be confirmed by the presence of the two countries' chief executives at a frontier marker ceremony on May 13, 1999.

In September 2005 Ecuador and Colombia became involved in controversy over whether the Colombian guerrilla group, the Colombian Revolutionary Armed Forces (FARC), should be considered a "terrorist" organization, as claimed by Colombia, or an "irregular armed group," as defined by Ecuador. The Palacio administration agreed in January 2006 to let the border area serve as an "anvil" against which the Colombian military could "hammer" the guerrillas, but did not fundamentally alter Ecuador's long-standing policy of nonintervention in Colombia's domestic conflict. Less than two weeks later, however, relations again soured in the wake of an incursion by Colombia in pursuit of rebel forces. Nonetheless, Ecuadoran army units were deployed in February to disrupt FARC activities in the eastern Amazonian provinces, where they found and destroyed several FARC bases and captured several guerrillas. Similar activity by Ecuadoran troops in May demonstrated that despite the noninterference rhetoric, FARC activities were receiving greater attention.

Ecuador's relations with Europe have largely revolved around trade issues (particularly banana exports to the European Union [EU]) and of late on the growing number of Ecuadoran émigrés in the region. In November 2006 Ecuador renewed its complaints against the EU's import restrictions on its banana exports. Ecuador's suit before the World Trade Organization claimed that the EU banana import tariff introduced in January 2006 was discriminatory and had the effect of reducing its market share vis-à-vis the shares of African and Caribbean former colonies, contrary to a 2001 agreement guaranteeing Ecuador's share of the EU banana trade.

By 2006 Ecuador's relations with Peru had improved, with the two countries finalizing a deal for electricity from Peru to help Ecuador supplement its hydroelectric power generation deficit. Also, Ecuador's military redeployed troops that had been on the border with Peru to the Colombian border, closing down the bases left behind.

Like its Andean neighbors Colombia and Peru, Ecuador pursued negotiations with the United States over a bilateral free trade agreement in 2006. The agreement was meant to codify and extend trade preferences granted to Ecuador under the U.S. Andean Trade Promotion and Drug Eradication Act (ATPDEA), but negotiations subsequently broke down when, in March 2006, the Ecuadoran congress passed legislation that imposed a higher tax on foreign oil companies, increasing the windfall profit tax rate from 30 percent to 60 percent. The government also seized a U.S.-based energy firm's Ecuadoran assets. Palacio subsequently moderated his position, announcing that the free trade agreement would be adopted only if it was in the country's best interest. Palacio also proposed a 50 percent windfall profit tax rate, which congress ratified on April 19. The move prompted the United States to halt negotiations on the trade agreement. In May the indigenous group Conaie and others again put pressure on the government to cancel the Occidental Petroleum contract (though the company had offered to pay a $20 million penalty and windfall profit taxes), and on May 15 the contract was canceled. The United States then formally suspended negotiations over the free trade agreement, and Occidental filed a lawsuit against Ecuador with the World Bank Group.

Meanwhile, the government announced that it would seek to enhance commercial links with Chile and Mexico and to work out trade agreements with Central American neighbors who have bilateral free trade agreements with the United States. The United States, for its part, claimed that Ecuador acted in violation of the bilateral investment treaty between the two nations. Ecuador turned to Venezuela for energy cooperation and assistance after the 2006 cancellation of the Occidental Petroleum contract, signing an agreement to cooperate broadly for the initiation of joint enterprises between the state petroleum companies in May 2006. Ecuador also considered an arrangement to have Venezuela refine a portion of its oil output for domestic use, an arrangement with favorable terms that was expected to save Ecuador hundreds of millions of dollars. Given the tense relations between the United States and Venezuela, however, the Palacio government announced less extensive strategic alliances with Brazilian and Argentine state-owned oil companies, thus avoiding the appearance of being too friendly with Venezuela's president Hugo Chávez. In early 2008 Ecuador and Venezuela announced plans to build a huge oil refinery in the coastal province of Manabí, Ecuador.

Relations with Colombia deteriorated after a March 1, 2008, Colombian Army raid about a mile inside Ecuadoran territory that killed 1 FARC leader and 25 other people, including an Ecuadoran citizen and 4 Mexican university students. To protest the breach of Ecuador's sovereignty, President Correa suspended diplomatic relations with Colombia. Relations with Venezuela warmed in 2008, as President Hugo Chávez was the most vocal proponent of Ecuador's position in the regional crisis spurred by Colombia's March 1 raid inside Ecuador. In August presidents Correa and Chávez signed a series of economic cooperation agreements, including joint oil ventures.

Relations with Brazil grew tense in 2008, largely due to a dispute over Ecuador's expulsion of a Brazilian construction company because of a faulty dam it built in San Francisco, and a collateral request for international arbitration to determine whether Ecuador must repay its $258 million loan for the project.

Tensions over the border situation with Colombia heightened again in November 2008, when the Correa government accused the United States of covert involvement in the March 1 raid. President Correa subsequently denounced the FARC and rejected the Colombian government's claims that it had received no response from Quito after providing the coordinates of FARC encampments detected in Ecuador. In December the Correa government announced an "Enhanced Registration" program to provide refugee status to 50,000 Colombians fleeing the conflict.

Also in December 2008, Correa and Iranian president Mahmoud Ahmadinejad signed 12 agreements aimed at increased cooperation in the energy, oil, banking, and health sectors.

The FARC insurgency produced new tensions in February 2009, when a former Ecuadoran vice-minister was accused of having frequent contact with the FARC and possibly with Colombian drug traffickers (see Current issues). Subsequently, Ecuador announced that it would bolster its military and police presence along the border with Colombia. Later that month Ecuador expelled two diplomats from the U.S. embassy in Quito. Relations with the United States warmed somewhat in June 2009, when President Barack Obama commended Ecuadorans' "commitment to democracy" following Correa's election. In September, that warming seemed to continue when the two sides agreed to work together against the drug trade and contraband. The United States said it would provide guidance, technical support, and equipment to help Ecuador create two special police units to target the drug trade. Meanwhile, Correa enhanced Ecuador's relations with

Venezuela by agreeing to enter the Caracas-influenced Bolivarian Alliance of the Americas (ALBA) after years of reluctance.

In 2009 tensions were reignited when Colombian intelligence officials alleged that top FARC leaders were seeking refuge in Ecuador and may have been given Ecuadoran identity documents. In June Ecuador announced plans to seek an international investigation into the death of an Ecuadoran citizen during the March 1, 2008, raid inside Ecuador.

The two countries began to mend relations at the end of 2009. Ecuador began to crack down on FARC as the group used Ecuador as a conduit in its drug trade; authorities on October 1 seized eight tons of FARC's cocaine in Quito and along the border. The two countries' foreign ministers met several times and agreed to restart the Binational Border Commission (*Comisión Binacional de Frontera*—Combifron), an instrument to foster talks on difficult issues between the two. They also agreed to exchange diplomatic personnel up to the level of chargé d'affaires. On November 14 Colombia was quick to come to Ecuador's aid when Ecuador unexpectedly suffered a deficit in it supply of electricity. Peru also said it would divert electricity to Ecuador's grid to help make up for the shortfall. In January 2010 Ecuadoran authorities said they killed three Colombians who were part of FARC, and the Colombians said they killed nine members of the group, both confrontations happening along the border region between the two countries. On November 26 Correa and Colombian president Juan Manuel Santos announced the resumption of full diplomatic relations between their countries.

Ecuador signed the Quito-based, 12-member Union of South American Nations on July 15, 2009. Modeled on the EU, the *Union of South American Nations* (UNASUR) was designed to create a South American trade area and, eventually, a common currency. After a brief respite in 2010, when Correa's diplomacy brought U.S. Secretary of State Hillary Clinton to Quito to make a policy statement on Latin America, relations with the United States soured amid the WikiLeaks scandal. In a leaked diplomatic cable, U.S. ambassador Heather Hodges described widespread corruption in the Correa government. On April 7 Correa expelled Hodges; the United States responded by expelling Ecuadoran ambassador Luis Gallegos and suspending bilateral trade negotiations.

China stepped in to close a financing deal with Ecuador in June 2010 for a major hydroelectric power plant east of Quito. The Chinese agreed to provide a $1.7 billion loan to build the estimated $2 billion project and additional financing that would cover building 58 percent of seven other power plants. Correa has established warm ties with Iran, and Iranian President Mahmoud Ahmadinejad visited Quito in January 2012.

On August 17 Ecuador granted diplomatic asylum to Wikileaks founder Julian Assange, who had taken refuge at the Ecuadorian embassy in London. Assange faced deportation to Sweden where he is wanted for questioning on sexual assault accusations. The announcement triggered a major diplomatic row between the two countries, as the UK government announced it had the right to enter the embassy and, presumably, seize Assange. The Ecuadorean government responded that it would host Assange indefinitely, despite the strain placed on its relations with the United Kingdom and the United States. Critics accused Correa of hypocrisy and grandstanding ahead of his reelection bid.

In June 2013, Correa reportedly considered offering asylum to Edward Snowden, wanted by the United States for espionage, but was dissuaded by a June 28 telephone call from U.S. Vice President Joe Biden.

Correa renounced its trade benefits with the United States and pulled out of the ATPDEA program in June 2013, declaring that the pact made the country vulnerable to blackmail by Washington, D.C. However, the U.S. Congress was expected to cancel the program in July.

The China Development Bank provided a $2 billion loan in July 2013 as part of a two-year deal that provides PetroChina with 40,000 barrels of oil per day.

Current issues. President Correa's Yasuní ITT Initiative gained momentum and international support in late 2011. First proposed in 2010, the landmark environmental policy commits Ecuador to refrain from exploiting the estimated 1 billion barrels of crude oil in the Ishpingo-Tambococha-Tiputini oilfield beneath Yasuni National Park, a lush and exceptionally bio-diverse section of the Amazonian rainforest, if the government receives $3.6 billion, half the estimated value of the oil. The project, which would also protect two indigenous tribes from extermination, was supported by nearly 90 percent of the country.

Other government projects have been much less popular among indigenous peoples. Conaei organized a 435-mile cross-country trek to Quito in March to protest against plans to build an open-cast copper mine in El Pangui province. Conaei maintains that the project, funded by $1.4 billion from China's Ecuacorriente mining company, will force native peoples from their lands and contaminate the water. They also insist that the 2008 constitution's provision to protect nature requires the government to consult with affected populations before undertaking such a project. Several opposition parties, as well as the teachers union, supported the protest march. Correa dismissed the protestors as being "stupid and closed-minded."

With presidential and parliamentary elections approaching, Correa moved to repair his image as an enemy of the media, with mixed results. First, he ended his war with *El Universo* in February, pardoning the four individuals convicted of libeling him in coverage of the September 2010 police uprising and waiving their $42 million fine. But he also announced a new "Democracy Code" that prevents media from endorsing candidates or favoring one candidate over another in any fashion. Journalists complained that the new regulations were so strict that even an interview with a candidate could be interpreted as bias or favoritism. By July the government had closed down 17 radio and television stations and confiscated broadcasting equipment, ostensibly due to expired broadcast licenses. Correa also began to harangue journalists by name during his weekly radio and television addresses, targeting *El Universo* editor Gustavo Cortez in particular.

Educational reform has spread to the university sector, as the government began to evaluate universities on the quality of the education they provide. Of the country's 71 universities, 24 private and two public schools received failing grades and have been ordered to raise standards. Of those, 14 were given notice to shut down within 12 months. After eliminating tuition at public universities in the 2008 constitution, the government implemented entrance exams to screen applicants, many of whom previously relied on personal connections to gain admission.

In May a single-engine Cessna airplane crashed in northwestern Ecuador. Investigators discovered traces of cocaine, $1.3 million in cash, and two (dead) pilots with known ties to Mexican drugs and weapons dealers. While the incident raised concerns about cartels trying to establish a new "air bridge" linking Mexico and Colombia, the even more worrisome aspect was that Ecuador's new $60 million Chinese radar system did not detect the plane.

The Democratic Code promulgated in January 2012 instructed parties to select candidates internally by holding primaries and submit 157,946 signatures before they would qualify to be placed on the ballot for the 2013 presidential and parliamentary elections. In August the National Electoral Council extended the registration period for parties hoping to get on the February 17, 2013, ballot due to issues with questionable signatures on applications.

Correa announced his intention to run for a third term, explaining that the 2008 constitution's two-term limit did not apply, as this would only be his second term since the constitution was enacted.

Both presidential and parliamentary elections were held on February 17, 2013. Eleven parties participated, down from 43 in 2009. As expected, Correa was reelected in the first round with 57 percent of the vote—30 points ahead of the second-place Guillermo LASSO Mendoza of Creating Opportunities (CREO). Correa's Country Alliance swept the legislative races, taking 100 of 137 seats. CREO finished a distant second with 11. Some Correa supporters reportedly voted against him in hopes of forcing a runoff, thinking a narrower victory might curb his growing ego.

Correa was sworn in on May 24 and almost immediately sent the National Assembly the restrictive communications law he had tried to pass in the previous session. The AP majority quickly approved the law on June 14, which imposes penalties for reporting that harms an individual's reputation, restricts coverage of court trials, bans media lynching (publishing material meant to damage an individual's reputation or credibility), and prohibits publication of conversations and other personal communications. The law also establishes a Superintendency of Information and Communication and a five-member Council for the Regulation and Development of Information and Communication, appointed by the president.

Also in June the parliament passed a new mining law to regulate operations and clarify taxation guidelines. Ecuador's undeveloped mining sector could help diversify the national economy, which is heavily dependent on oil exports.

In August Correa abandoned the Yasuní ITT Initiative, which had only raised $13 million of the $3.6 billion needed. "The world has failed us," lamented Correa, who called it "one of the hardest decisions of my government."

POLITICAL PARTIES

Historically dominated by the Conservative and Liberal parties and long complicated by pronounced personalist tendencies, the Ecuadoran party system has recently been in a state of considerable flux. Many of the traditional parties have been built around particular candidates or families, consistent with the elite character of the country's political culture for many generations. Party organizations have therefore been weak. Party alliances and coalitions have tended to form to win particular election contests or deal with immediate crises, then dissolve after the elections or crises have receded. (For details on the principal electoral alliances formed before the 2009 electoral campaign, see the 2010 *Handbook.*)

Following the 2009 legislative elections, 13 legislators from the PRE and smaller parties formed an alliance called the National Agreement for Decentralization and Equity (*Acuerdo Democrático por la Descentralización y la Equidad*—ADE) in support of President Correa and the AP, thus giving the administration control of 72 of the 124 assembly seats.

Government Party:

Country Alliance (*Alianza País*—AP). The AP is a loose collection of socialist organizations, civil-society groups, indigenous leaders, and left-of-center personalities organized in 2006 largely by Rafael Correa, its presidential candidate. Correa chose not to participate in the presidential primaries sponsored by Conaie (below), instead forming alliances with the PS-FA, PSP, and the MNPP, among others, for support in the second round of balloting.

During his 2006 campaign, Correa had targeted for radical reform what he labeled the "*partidocracia*" of traditional parties that had long controlled the National Congress and brought down or crippled successive presidential administrations. Subsequently, the AP refused to field candidates in the 2006 legislative elections amid corruption allegations among various parties. After winning the election, President Correa successfully steered the AP toward securing a majority of seats in the constituent assembly election in September 2007. Correa rejected an attempt by some advisers to launch a party whose acronym would match his initials, deriding this as another example of the destructive pattern of personalization of politics in Ecuador.

The party was fined close to $1 million by the electoral tribunal in 2007 for concealing campaign spending from the November 2006 presidential runoff, but the tribunal backed away from that decision after Correa claimed that the investigation had not treated the AP and the opposition PRIAN equally with regard to overspending.

Correa's reelection in 2009 did little to bolster the AP, which won only a plurality of 59 seats (45.8 percent) in concurrent legislative elections. Fractures began to emerge between Correa and other members of the party in March 2010 when 19 of the 59 AP members of the assembly said they wanted to censure the president's attorney general. The row was triggered by the attorney general's interference in the investigation of a fatal traffic accident involving his wife and his subsequent refusal to step down.

In February 2011, Gustavo DARQUEA, an AP founder, left the party to protest its support of proposed constitutional amendments restricting freedom of the press and independence of the judiciary. After the amendments were approved in the May 2011 referendum, the AP continued to lose prominent members, who claimed Correa was strengthening his grip on power instead of seeking the promised reforms.

Leaders: Rafael CORREA Delgado (President of the Republic and Leader of the Alliance), Lenin MORENO Garcés (Vice President of the Republic), Galo MORA Witt (Secretary General), Fernando CORDERO (Assembly President).

Other Legislative Parties:

Creating Opportunities (*Movimiento Creo*—CREO) is a center-right party founded by César MONGE in 2010. Guillermo LASSO Mendoza resigned as president of the Banco de Guayaquil on July 10, 2012, to seek the presidency on the CREO ticket. He placed second in the February 2013 elections, on a 22.68 vote share, while CREO won 11 legislative seats and 11.42 percent of the vote.

Leaders: César MONGE (President); Guillermo LASSO Mendoza (2013 presidential candidate).

Social Christian Party (*Partido Social Cristiano*—PSC). A moderately right-of-center party, the PSC was founded in 1951 by former president Camilo PONCE Enríquez. Subsequently, it joined in a coalition with the PCE and the Ecuadoran Nationalist Revolutionary Action (*Acción Revolucionaria Nacionalista Ecuatoriana*—ARNE), a rightist group that was denied electoral registration in 1978 and was later dissolved. The PSC's sole member to become president to date was León FEBRES-CORDERO, who served from 1984 to 1988. Sixto Durán-Ballén, the PSC's 1988 presidential candidate who failed to secure sufficient votes in first-round balloting, eventually embarked on an ultimately successful race for the presidency as the PUR nominee.

The PSC's legislative representation increased from 9 seats in 1988 to a plurality of 16 in 1990; it retained its plurality in 1992 by capturing 21 seats. In 1996 the PSC held 27 seats.

In 2006 the PSC presidential candidate, Cynthia Viteri, won 9.6 percent of the vote in the first round. In concurrent legislative elections, the PSC list won 13.5 percent of the vote.

In the 2009 presidential election, the party backed PRIAN candidate Álvaro Noboa. In legislative voting, the PSC finished third with 13.6 percent, gaining 11 seats. The party has expanded its base of support from Quito to include the populous coastal provinces.

The PSC again finished third in the 2013 elections but dropped to 6 seats with an 8.99 percent share.

Leaders: Pascual DEL CIOPPO Aragundi (President), Pedro Carlos FALQUEZ Batallas (Vice President), Xavier Eduardo BUITRÓN Carrera (Secretary General).

January 21 Patriotic Society Party (*Partido Sociedad Patriótica 21 de Enero*—PSP). Launched in the run-up to the 2002 election, the center-right PSP was joined by the MNPP (below) in supporting the successful candidacy of Lucio Gutiérrez, the PSP's charismatic founder and leader, whose platform emphasized anticorruption measures and support for the poor. After Congress removed Gutiérrez in April 2005, he fled the country, and upon his return in October he was arrested on sedition charges. The case against him was dismissed in March 2006. Two months prior to his release, Gutiérrez was nominated by the PSP as their presidential candidate for the October election. Gutiérrez promised to call a constituent assembly to reform what he described as the dysfunctional political system. However, the supreme electoral tribunal barred Gutiérrez's candidacy for two years because of an alleged campaign finance violation. Nevertheless, Gutiérrez continued to campaign in defiance of the electoral board ruling. Subsequently, the PSP announced that it would form an alliance with the PRIAN for the presidential election, backing the PRIAN's Alvaro Noboa for president and Gilmar Gutiérrez (the brother of Lucio) for vice president. By September, however, the parties had gone their separate ways, with Gilmar Gutiérrez registering under the PSP banner. The PSP list won 17.5 percent of the vote in the legislative election, giving it the second largest bloc of seats in the congress. The PSP renewed its loose alliance with the PRIAN for the November 26 presidential runoff, supporting Noboa in exchange for promises that a Noboa government would prosecute perpetrators of the 2005 "coup" against Lucio Gutiérrez.

After its defeat in the presidential elections, the PSP eventually agreed to support a national referendum to create a constituent assembly. Soon thereafter some PSP legislators joined other opposition members in voting to dismiss the electoral tribunal chief in the wake of a dispute over the constituent assembly's authority, and the lawmakers were subsequently dismissed. In the 2007 constituent assembly elections, the PSP won 7.3 percent of the vote, with Gilmar Gutiérrez elected as a delegate.

Lucio Gutiérrez ran again in the April 2009 presidential elections, finishing second with 28.24 percent of the vote. PSP candidates won the second-largest legislative bloc, 19 seats, on a vote share of 14.9 percent. Gutiérrez ran again in 2013, receiving 6.73 percent of the vote, while the party won 5 seats on a 5.64 percent vote share.

Leaders: Col. (Ret.) Lucio Edwin GUTIÉRREZ Borbúa (Former President of the Republic and 2009 and 2013 presidential candidate), Gilmar GUTIÉRREZ Borbúa (Party President and 2006 presidential candidate), Leonardo ESCOBAR (Vice President).

Plurinational Unity of the Lefts (*Unidad Plurinacional de la Izquierdas*—UPI) is an alliance comprised of unions, teachers, and indigenous groups, as well as former Correa allies, and began as a parliamentary faction in 2011. Originally comprised of the **Pachakutik Multiethnic Unity Movement–New Country** (*Movimiento de Unidad Plurinacional Pachakutik—Nuevo País*—MNPP) and the **Democratic Popular Movement** (*Movimiento Popular Democrático*—MPD), the **Ethics and Democracy Network** (*Red Ética y Democracia*—RED), the **Socialist Party/Broad Front** (*Partido Socialista/Frente Amplio*—PS/FA), the **Marxist-Leninist Communist Party of Ecuador** (*Partido Comunista Marxista-Leninista del Ecuador–PCMLE*); **Montecristi Lives** (*Montecristi Vive*), founded by Alberto Acosta in 2011; **National Democratic Consensus-Building** (*Concertación Nacional Democrática*), headed by César Montúfar; **Radical Democracy Movement** (*Movimiento Participa Democracia Radical*); **Popular Power** (*Poder Popular*); **Party of Revolutionary Socialism** (*Partido Socialismo Revolucionario*); and the **Call for Provincial Unity Movement** (*Movimiento Convocatoria por la Unidad Provincial*).

Alberto ACOSTA Espinosa cofounded the ruling Country Alliance, chaired the constituent assembly that wrote the 2008 constitution, and won UPI's September 1, 2012, presidential primary election. The coalition secured five seats with 4.72 percent of the vote, while Alberto returned 3.26 percent.

Leaders: Fanny CAMPOS (Coordinator); Alberto ACOSTA Espinosa (2013 presidential candidate).

Pachakutik Multiethnic Unity Movement—New Country (*Movimiento de Unidad Plurinacional Pachakutik—Nuevo País*—MNPP). The New Country Movement (*Movimiento Nuevo País*—MNP) was formed as an antiestablishment grouping that backed the television journalist Freddy EHLERS Zurita, who had entered the 1996 presidential race in February as an independent candidate on an anticorruption, environmentalist platform. Ehlers finished in third place (21 percent vote share) in the first round of presidential balloting. Subsequently, he insisted that the *Nuevo País* was the real winner because it had led in the 11 highland provinces, and he predicted that the group would prevail over the old country parties in 2000.

In 1998 the MNP joined with Pachakutik, the political wing of the 2.5 million-strong Conaie, in a coalition styled like the MNPP, which supported Lucio Gutiérrez for president but went into opposition in August 2003. Most of the MNPP's electoral strength has been based in the Andean highlands and Amazonian provinces, where the 11 indigenous and ethnic groups it represents are concentrated.

In 2006 the party's presidential candidate, Luis MACAS, finished a distant sixth in the first-round balloting, with 2.2 percent of the vote. The party secured 3 percent of the vote in concurrent legislative balloting. Its alliance with the PS–FA to contest the constituent assembly elections netted less than 1 percent of the overall vote. The MNPP won 1.4 percent of the vote and four seats in the 2009 legislative elections.

In August 2013 Deputy Coordinator Fanny CAMPOS was elected the first woman to lead the party.

Leader: Fanny CAMPOS (National Coordinator).

Democratic Popular Movement (*Movimiento Popular Democrático*—MPD). Although initially banned from participation in the 1978 election, the MPD was subsequently registered as a legal party. Drawing much of its support from trade unions and teachers, the MPD, described as a far-left party, won just two seats in 1998 and three seats in 2002.

In 2004 the MPD was part of the new majority that helped President Lucio Gutiérrez avoid impeachment and push through a measure that removed all 31 Supreme Court justices. In 2006 the party's presidential candidate, Luis VILLACIS, won just 1.3 percent of the vote in first-round balloting. Subsequently, the MPD supported Correa.

In the 2009 legislative elections, the MPD won 4 percent of the vote and five seats. The party subsequently joined the ADE coalition in support of the AP but withdrew its support of Correa over his alleged power grabbing in the May 2011 constitutional referendum.

Leaders: Luis VILLACIS (National Party Director), Mery ZAMORA (First Assistant Director), Geovanii ATARIHUANA (Second Assistant Director), Marco CADENA (Secretary General).

Ethics and Democracy Network (*Red Ética y Democracia*—RED). Formed in January 2005 by its leader and former vice president of the republic León ROLDÓS Aguilera, the social democratic party focused on reform of the constitution to create a bicameral legislature with elements of party-list proportional representation and geographic constituencies, greater autonomy for local and regional authorities, eradication of political corruption, and reform of the education system.

RED formed an alliance for the 2006 presidential election with the ID, with Roldós standing as the coalition's presidential candidate. In the legislative elections, the RED won six of the ten seats won by the ID/RED alliance.

In the 2007, constituent assembly elections, the RED, no longer in alliance with the ID, won just over 2 percent of the vote.

In 2009 presidential candidate Martha Roldós finished fourth with 4.3 percent of the vote, and the RED won 1.9 percent in the parliamentary vote.

Leaders: León ROLDÓS Aguilera (President), Dolores PADILLA (Vice President), Ney BARRIONUEVO (Second Vice President), Carlos AGUINAGA (Secretary General).

Socialist Party/Broad Front (*Partido Socialista/Frente Amplio*—PS/FA) is a left-wing party that traces its origins to the 1932 Ecuadorian Socialist Party (*Partido Socialista Ecuatoriano*). In 1995 the Socialist Party merged with the Broad Left Front (*Frente Amplio de Izquierda*) to create the current party. The PS/FA secured one seat in the 2009 legislative elections. It polled 0.80 percent of the vote in 2013.

Leader: Rafeal Quintero, Fabián SOLANO (President).

Partido Avanza (Forward—PA) is a youth-oriented party founded in 2012 by Ramiro GONZÁLEZ, head of the national social security agency. He wants to build on the government's progressive educational policies, such as raising university standards, in order to build human capital. The party supported Correa's reelection bid. In the 2013 elections, Avanza polled 2.92 percent, for five seats in the National Assembly.

Leader: Ramiro GONZÁLEZ.

Society United for More Action (*Movimeinto Sociedad Unida Más Acción*—SUMA) was established in January 2012 by Mauricio RODAS, the 37-year-old founder of the Ethos Foundation, a center for research on public policy in Latin America. Rodas compiled a program of Model Responsible Government and the Ethnos Poverty Index and has challenged President Correa to debates on the benefits of his model of citizen engagement. Rodas ran for president in 2013 and placed fourth, with 3.90 percent of the vote. The SUMA party polled 3.22 percent and received one parliamentary seat on a platform that favored term limits.

Leader: Mauricio RODAS.

Ecuadoran Roldosist Party (*Partido Roldosista Ecuatoriano*—PRE). A center-left populist party founded in 1982, the PRE is closely associated with former president Abdalá Bucaram Ortiz, who remains exiled in Panama. The party was named for former president Jaime Roldós Aguilera, Bucaram's brother-in-law, who died under suspicious circumstances along with his wife in a plane crash in 1981. The party stronghold is in Bucaram's home city of Guayaquil. In 2009 the party won 4.1 percent of the votes and three legislative seats. The PRE subsequently backed the AP as part of the ADE coalition. In 2013 the party vote share rose slightly, to 4.51 percent, but secured only one seat.

Leaders: Abdalá BUCARAM Pulley (President); Nelson Martín ZAVALA Avellán (2014 presidential candidate).

In addition, three regional parties each won a single seat: **Regional Action for Equity/Latin American Popular Alliance** (*Movimiento Acción Regional por la Equidad*—ARE), **"Believing in Our People" Peninsular Movement** (*Movimiento Peninsular Creyendo en Nuetra Gente*—MPCNG), and **Movement for the Democratic Integration of Carchi** (*Movimiento Integración Democratica del Carchi*—MIDC).

Other Parties That Contested the 2013 Elections:

Institutional Renewal Party of National Action (*Partido Renovador Institucional de Acción Nacional*—PRIAN). The PRIAN, a right-of-center party, was founded by former *Roldosista* Álvaro NOBOA Pontón, a banana grower and reportedly Ecuador's wealthiest man, to support his presidential bid in 2002.

In July 2006 the PRIAN and the PSP formed an alliance to contest the presidential election, with Noboa as the presidential candidate, despite his earlier statements that he would not run. The PRIAN won 24.5 percent of the national vote in concurrent legislative elections of 2006, displacing the PSC as the largest bloc in the congress.

Despite its opposition to Correa's proposed constituent assembly, the PRIAN fielded candidates for the assembly election in 2007, winning 6.6 percent of the vote, with Noboa elected as a delegate. Jorge Cevallos Macías, president of Congress, was expelled from the party in June, reportedly because he opposed the dismissal of 57 lawmakers ordered by the Supreme Electoral Tribunal, a stance that broke with the party's position.

Noboa ran again in the 2009 presidential elections, finishing third with 11.4 percent of the vote. Meanwhile, PRIAN candidates won 5.8 percent of votes and seven seats in concurrent legislative elections. In 2013 Noboa finished fifth with 3.72 percent of the vote. PRIAN candidates won 3.00 percent of votes and lost all seven seats in the legislature.

Leaders: Wilson SÁNCHEZ (President and National Director), Álvaro NOBOA Pontón (2002, 2006, 2009, and 2013 presidential candidate).

Rupture (*Ruptura 25*) is a youth-oriented party led by María Paula ROMO, a legal scholar and member of the Constituent Assembly that wrote the 2008 constitution. Founded in 2004, the party grew out of the youth and women's movements in the 1980s and calls for observing the rule of law in a culturally diverse society. In the 2013 presidential election, environmental lawyer Norman WRAY won 1.31 percent of the vote, while Ruptura candidates polled 2.48 percent of the vote and no assembly seats.

Leader: María Paula ROMO.

Parties That Did Not Participate in 2013:

Municipalist Movement for National Integrity (*Movimiento Municipalista por la Integridad Nacional*—MMIN). The MMIN was founded in 2008 by mayors and councilmen from several parts of the country. Its most visible figure has been former Quito mayor Paco Moncayo, a former ID member. The party won 1.8 percent of votes and five seats in the 2009 legislative elections.

Leaders: Juan SALAZAR (President), Paco MONCAYO.

Democratic Left (*Izquierda Democrática*—ID). The ID, a moderate social democratic party, fielded Rodrigo Borja Cevallos as its presidential candidate in 1978, endorsing Jaime Roldós Aguilera in the subsequent runoff and offering partial support to the Hurtado Larrea government after Roldós's death. It narrowly lost the presidency in the May 1984 runoff after having captured a substantial legislative plurality in January.

In 1988 Borja Cevallos was the front-runner in the first round of presidential balloting and went on to defeat the PRE's Abdalá Bucaram in a runoff to become president of the republic, but in 1992 Raúl Baca Carbo ran a distant fourth in the first-round presidential vote. In 1996 the party's legislative representation plummeted from 8 seats to 4, but it won 17 seats in 1998. In 2002 the party held 16 seats.

The ID joined forces with Leon Roldós's RED party to contest the 2006 presidential elections, throwing its support behind Roldós. In 2009 the ID again joined with the RED in backing Martha ROLDÓS, who was placed fourth. In concurrent legislative balloting, the ID won 1.4 percent of the votes and three seats.

Leaders: Dalton BACIGALUPO Buenaventura (President), Andrés PAÉZ Benalcázar (Vice President).

National Democratic Consensus-Building Movement (*Movimiento Concertación Nacional Democrática*—MCND). Formed in 2008, the MNCD incorporates three right-of-center groups: **Citizen Vision** (*Visión Ciudadana,* headed by Mae Montaño); the **Future Now** (*Futuro Ya,* headed by Pablo Lucío Paredes); and the **National Democratic Consensus-Building** (*Concertación Nacional Democrática,* headed by César Montúfar). The grouping won 1.9 percent of legislative votes in 2009 and 1 seat.

Leaders: Mae MONTAÑO, Pablo Lucío PAREDES, César MONTÚFAR.

For other single-seat parties and the **Christian Democratic Union** (*Unión Demócrata Cristiana*—UDC), please see the 2013 *Handbook.*

Indigenous Organizations:

Confederation of Ecuadorian Indigenous Nationalities (*Confederación de Nacionalidades Indígenas del Ecuador*—Conaie). The confederation serves as an umbrella organization for nearly a dozen indigenous groups. It has advanced claims to most of the Andean province of Pastaza. To reinforce their demands, which included administrative autonomy and control of natural resources, including oil, the Indians mounted a brief insurrection in June 1990 and staged a protest march in Quito in April 1992. They were instrumental in forcing the ouster of President Mahuad in January 2000. With nearly 2.5 million members, the organization has proved a powerful political force.

Antonio VARGAS, the former president of Conaie, hoped to be the 2002 presidential candidate of Conaie and its political arm—the Pachakutik Movement (see under MNPP, above), but he resigned as president of the confederation because of a scandal involving signatures on a referendum petition.

In 2006 Conaie played a major role in organizing and staging the March protests against the free trade agreement negotiations with the United States and against any accommodation for Occidental Petroleum with regard to the alleged breach of its oil production contract with Ecuador. Conaie also appealed to the UN and human rights groups to monitor the situation in Ecuador to safeguard against excessive use of force to stop the protests.

Conaie proposed a single primary in late July for all of the left-of-center parties to select a candidate for the October 2006 elections. Its leader, Luis Macas, secured the nomination under the MNPP banner and won 2.19 percent of the vote.

Humberto CHOLANGO was elected president in 2011, and in 2013, Conaie backed the Plurinational Unity of the Lefts.

Leaders: Humberto CHOLANGO (President), Pepe ACACHO (Vice President).

Federation of Indigenous People, Peasants, and Negroes of Ecuador (*Federación de Pueblos Indígenas, Campesinas y Negros del Ecuador*—Fedepicne). Fedepicne was launched in 1996 by a group of Conaie dissidents. In 2005, former party president Marco MORILLO was identified as a member of the ID.

Leaders: Luis PACHALA (President), Ricardo GUAMBO, Pedro GUAMBO.

LEGISLATURE

The current legislature is a unicameral **National Assembly** (*Asamblea Nacional*) of 137 members, popularly elected, serving four-year terms. In August 2012, the National Election Council added 13 seats by divided the populous Pichincha, Guayas, and Manabi provinces. Following the most recent elections on May 9, 2013, the seat distribution was as follows:

Country Alliance, 100; Creating Opportunities Movement, 11; Social Christian Party, 6; January 21 Patriotic Society Party, 5; Pachakutik Multiethnic Unity Movement–New Country, 5; Avanza Party, 5; Society United for More Action, 1; "Believing in Our People" Peninsular Movement, 1; Movement for the Democratic Integration of Carchi, 1; Ecuadoran Roldosist Party, 1; Regional Action for Equity/Latin American Popular Alliance, 1.

(The number of seats held by parties frequently changes as a result of legislators' shifting alliances.)

President: Gabriela RIVADENEIRA.

CABINET

[as of October 5, 2013]

President	Rafael Correa Delgado
Vice President	Lenin Moreno Garcés
Ministers	
Agriculture, Livestock, and Fisheries	Javier Ponce Cevallos
Coordinating Minister for Cultural and Natural Heritage	
Coordinating Minister for Economic Policy	Patricio Rivera Yanez
Coordinating Minister for Internal and External Security	Homero Arellano
Coordinating Minister for Policy and Autonomous Governments	Betty Tola [f]

Coordinating Minister for Production, Employment, and Competitiveness	Santiago Leon
Coordinating Minister for Social Development	Richard Espinosa
Coordinating Minister for Strategic Sectors	Jorge Glas Espinel
Culture	Erika Sylva Charvet [f]
Defense	Carlos Larrea
Education	Gloria Vidal [f]
Electricity and Renewable Energy	Esteban Albornoz Vintimilla
Environment	Lorena Tapia [f]
Finance	Fausto Herrera
Foreign Relations, Commerce, and Integration	Ricardo Patiño
Government, Religious Affairs, Police, and Municipalities	José Serrano
Human Resources	Augusto Espinosa
Industry and Competitiveness	Verónica Síon [f]
Justice and Human Rights	Johana Pesántez [f]
Labor Relations	Juan Francisco Vacas
Mines and Oil	Pedro Merizalde
Planning and Development	Fander Falconi
Public Health	David Chiriboga
Social and Economic Inclusion	Doris Soliz [f]
Sport	José Francisco Cevallos
Telecommunications and the Information Society	Jaime Guerrero
Tourism	Freddy Ehlers
Transportation and Public Works	Maria de los Ángeles Duarte [f]
Urban Development and Housing	Pedro Jaramillo

[f] = female

INTERGOVERNMENTAL REPRESENTATION

Ambassador to the U.S.: Nathalie CELY.

U.S. Ambassador to Ecuador: Adam E. NAMM.

Permanent Representative to the UN: Xavier LASSO.

IGO Memberships (Non-UN): IADB, ICC, IOM, Mercosur, NAM, OAS, OPEC, WTO.

EGYPT

Arab Republic of Egypt
Jumhuriyat Misr al-Arabiyah

Note: Despite early indications that the Egyptian military sought a permanent governing role after president Morsi was deposed in July 2013, elements of the "roadmap" for return to civilian governance were being put into place by the interim government in late 2013. Following a proposed constitutional referendum in late December, interim prime minister Beblawi suggested parliamentary elections would take place in March 2014, with presidential voting in June 2014. However, the interim government's ban of the Muslim Brotherhood made reconciliation between Egypt's secularists and Islamists doubtful, and stoked fears of an increase in domestic terrorism extending outward from the Sinai region.

Political Status: Nominally independent in 1922; republic established in 1953; joined with Syria as the United Arab Republic in 1958 and retained the name after Syria withdrew in 1961; present name adopted September 2, 1971; under limited multiparty system formally adopted by constitutional amendment approved in referendum of May 22, 1980; provision for direct, multicandidate presidential election formally adopted by constitutional amendment approved in referendum of May 25, 2005.

Area: 386,659 sq. mi. (1,001,449 sq. km).

Population: 84,567,625 (2012E—UN); 85,294,388 (2013E—U.S. Census).

Major Urban Centers (2010E): AL-QAHIRA (Cairo, 7,248,671), al-Giza (3,122,041), al-Iskandariyah (Alexandria, 4,358,439), Es-Suweis (Suez, 556,655), Bur Said (Port Said, 610,468).

Official Language: Arabic.

Monetary Unit: Egyptian Pound (market rate November 1, 2013: 6.89 pounds = $1US).

Interim President: Adly MANSOUR, appointed July 3, 2013.

Interim Vice President: Mohamed ELBARADEI, appointed by President Mansour on July 9, 2013; resigned August 14, 2013.

Interim Prime Minister: Hazem EL-BEBLAWI, appointed by President Mansour on July 9, 2013.

THE COUNTRY

Situated in the northeast corner of Africa at its juncture with Asia, Egypt occupies a quadrangle of desert made habitable only by the waters of the Nile, which bisects the country from south to north. Although the greater part of the national territory has traditionally been regarded as wasteland, Egypt is the most populous country in the Arab world: 90 percent of the people are concentrated in 4 percent of the land area, with population densities in parts of the Nile Valley reaching 6,000 per square mile. (Ambitious projects inaugurated in the late 1990s created massive irrigation canals from Lake Nasser [formed by the Aswan High Dam] in the south and from four new lakes in the northwest [formed after flooding], permitting industrial and agricultural development in the desert. Another major irrigation canal was built eastward from the Nile along the northern coast into the Sinai Peninsula.) Arabic is universally spoken, and more than 80 percent of the ethnically homogeneous people adhere to the Sunni sect of Islam, much of the remainder being Coptic Christian. Women were listed as 29 percent of the paid labor force in 1996, with the majority of rural women engaged in unpaid agricultural labor; urban employed women tend to be concentrated in lower levels of health care and education.

Completion of the Aswan High Dam in 1971 permitted the expansion of tillable acreage and of multiple cropping, while the use of fertilizers and mechanization also increased production of such crops as cotton, wheat, rice, sugarcane, and corn, although Egypt still imports more than 50 percent of its food. Much of the population continues to live near the subsistence level, high rural-to-urban migration having increased the number of urban unemployed. A growing industrial sector, which employs 30 percent of the labor force, has been centered on textiles and agriprocessing, although the return by Israel of Sinai oil fields in 1975 permitted Egypt to become a net exporter of petroleum. Other natural resources include gas, iron ore, phosphates, manganese, zinc, gypsum, and talc.

The reopening of the Suez Canal (closed from the 1967 war until 1975) helped stimulate the gross domestic product, which displayed average annual real growth of 9 percent from mid-1979 to mid-1983. By 1985 economic conditions had sharply deteriorated as the decline in world oil prices not only depressed export income but severely curtailed remittances from Egyptians employed in other oil-producing states; in addition, tourism, another important source of revenue, declined because of regional terrorism and domestic insecurity. Compounding the difficulties were rapid population growth (an increase of approximately 1 million every nine months), an illiteracy rate estimated at nearly 50 percent, a high external debt, and an inefficient, bloated, and often corrupt bureaucracy of some 6 million civil servants.

Though annual GDP growth slowed to an average of about 5 percent in 2009–2010, the International Monetary Fund (IMF) said that the country's economic performance was better than expected, owing in large part to consumer spending and progress in the communication, construction, and trade sectors. The IMF urged Egypt to resume policies toward privatization and greater transparency.

The fall of the Mubarak government in February 2011 produced serious obstacles for the Egyptian economy. The manufacturing sector slumped 12 percent and tourism declined 40 percent. According to the IMF, Egypt's 2011 GDP growth was 1.8 percent. With a budget shortfall of 10 percent in 2011, Egypt at first sought—then rejected—a $3 billion loan from the IMF. To make up its approximately $10 billion deficit, Egypt accepted pledges for $4 billion in cash from Saudi Arabia and billions more in development projects from Qatar.

In 2012 and 2013 the tourism industry continued its slump, and anticipated outside investment did not materialize. These domestic factors, when combined with worldwide increases in energy costs and a global economic slowdown, kept 2012 GDP from rising to more than 2.2 percent, while inflation rose by 8.6 percent. GDP in 2013 rose 2.0 percent, while inflation decreased slightly to 8.2 percent. IMF forecasts for 2014 suggest GDP growth of 3.2 percent offset by an inflation rate of 13.6 percent.

After becoming president, Mohammed Morsi resurrected the IMF loan request, increasing it to $4.8 billion. However, the approval process languished. While Morsi was in office, Qatar became Egypt's preeminent benefactor, as Muslim Brotherhood–friendly Doha extended Cairo grants and loans in excess of $8 billion. As soon as the Egyptian military ousted Morsi and started sidelining the Brotherhood (see Current issues below), Saudi Arabia, Kuwait, and the United Arab Emirates (UAE) pledged more than $12 billion in cash, grants, and fuel shipments to Egypt. In August 2013 Egypt officially withdrew its IMF loan request.

GOVERNMENT AND POLITICS

Political background. The modern phase of Egypt's long history began in 1882 with the occupation of what was then an Ottoman province by a British military force, only token authority being retained by the local ruler (*khedive*). After establishing a protectorate in 1914, the United Kingdom granted formal independence to the government of King FUAD in 1922 but continued to exercise gradually dwindling control, which ended with its evacuation of the Suez Canal Zone in 1956. The rule of Fuad's successor, King FAROUK (FARUK), was abruptly terminated as the result of a military coup on July 23, 1952. A group of young officers (the "Free Officers"), nominally headed by Maj. Gen. Muhammad NAGIB, secured Farouk's abdication on June 18, 1953, and went on to establish a republic under Nagib's presidency. Col. Gamal Abdel NASSER, who had largely guided these events, replaced Nagib as prime minister and head of state in 1954, becoming president on June 23, 1956.

The institution of military rule signaled the commencement of an internal social and economic revolution, growing pressure for the termination of British and other external influences, and a drive toward greater Arab unity against Israel under Egyptian leadership. Failing to secure Western arms on satisfactory terms, Egypt accepted Soviet military assistance in 1955. In July 1956, following the withdrawal of a Western offer to help finance the High Dam at Aswan, Egypt nationalized the Suez Canal Company and took possession of its properties. Foreign retaliation resulted in the "Suez War" of October–November 1956, in which Israeli, British, and French forces invaded Egyptian territory but subsequently withdrew under pressure from the United States, the Soviet Union, and the United Nations.

On February 1, 1958, Egypt joined with Syria to form the United Arab Republic under Nasser's presidency. Although Syria reasserted its independence in September 1961, Egypt retained the UAR designation until 1971, when it adopted the name Arab Republic of Egypt.

Egypt incurred heavy losses in the six-day Arab-Israeli War of June 1967, which resulted in the closing of the Suez Canal, the occupation by Israel of the Sinai Peninsula, and an increase in Egypt's military and economic dependence on the USSR. Popular discontent resulting from the defeat was instrumental in bringing about a subsequent overhaul of the state machinery and a far-reaching reconstruction of the Arab Socialist Union (ASU), then the nation's only authorized political party.

A major turning point in Egypt's modern history occurred with the death of President Nasser on September 28, 1970, power subsequently being transferred to Vice President Anwar al-SADAT. The new president's authority was affirmed by voter approval of a new national constitution. At the same time, Moscow's increasing reluctance to comply with Egyptian demands for armaments generated tension in Soviet-Egyptian relations. This fact, coupled with Sadat's desire to acquire U.S. support in the return of Israeli-held territory, culminated in the expulsion of some 17,000 Soviet personnel in mid-1972.

The apparent unwillingness of U.S. President Nixon in 1972 to engage in diplomatic initiatives during an election year forced Sadat to return to the Soviet fold to prepare for another war with Israel, which broke out in October 1973. After 18 days of fighting, a cease-fire was concluded under UN auspices, with U.S. Secretary of State Henry Kissinger ultimately arranging for peace talks that resulted in the disengagement of Egyptian and Israeli forces east of the Suez Canal. Under an agreement signed on September 4, 1975, Israel withdrew to the Gidi and Mitla passes in the western Sinai and returned the Ras Sudar oil field to Egypt after securing political commitments from Egypt and a pledge of major economic and military support from the United States.

Although he had intimated earlier that he might step down from the presidency in 1976, Sadat accepted a second six-year term on September 16. On October 26, in the first relatively free balloting since the early 1950s, the nation elected a new People's Assembly from candidates presented by three groups within the ASU. Two weeks later, the president declared that the new groups could be termed political parties but indicated that they would remain under the overall supervision of the ASU. The role of the ASU was further reduced in June 1977 by a law that permitted the formation of additional parties under carefully circumscribed circumstances, while its vestigial status as an "umbrella" organization was terminated a year later.

On October 2, 1978, Sadat named Mustafa KHALIL to head a new "peace" cabinet that on March 15, 1979, unanimously approved a draft peace treaty with Israel. The People's Assembly ratified the document on April 10 by a 328–15 vote, while in a referendum held nine days later a reported 99.95 percent of those casting ballots voiced approval. At the same time, a series of political and constitutional reforms received overwhelming support from voters. As a result, President Sadat dissolved the assembly two years ahead of schedule and called for a two-stage legislative election in June. Sadat's National Democratic Party (NDP) easily won the multiparty contest—the first such election since the overthrow of the monarchy in 1953.

By 1981 Egypt was increasingly dependent on the United States for military and foreign policy support, while growing domestic unrest threatened the fragile political liberalization initiated in 1980. In an unprecedented move, the government imprisoned more than a thousand opposition leaders, ranging from Islamic fundamentalists to journalists and Nasserites. On October 6, 1981, President Sadat was assassinated by a group of Muslim militants affiliated with al-Jihad ("Holy War"). The assembly's nomination of Vice President Muhammad Hosni MUBARAK as his successor was confirmed by a national referendum on October 13.

During the first 24 years of Mubarak's tenure, he was approved by plebiscite for four presidential terms. The period was characterized by continued monopolization of authority by the NDP, though both the New

Wafd Party (NWP) and the Nationalist Progressive Unionist Party (NPUP) gained both recognition and legislative seats. Repression of dissent from parties less inclined to admit subservience to Mubarak's regime—most notably Islamists in the Muslim Brotherhood and certain liberal groups—became commonplace. Though garden-variety political dissent could be met by indiscriminate imprisonment, the Mubarak government was significantly harder on Islamist dissent, amounting to what some called an "all out war" against political Islam that included torture and targeted killing. However, even as Mubarak continued to appease Egyptians with promises of future political reforms, until 2005 his rule was focused upon perpetuation of the status quo. (For more information about the Mubarak presidency from 1981–2005, see the 2012 *Handbook.*)

Under increasing pressure from prodemocracy activists, as well as from the United States, President Mubarak called for a constitutional amendment to allow multicandidate elections in February 2005. Unprecedented public demonstrations and calls for Mubarak to step down preceded his historic announcement. The amendment was approved in a referendum in May 2005, but the government still faced vehement criticism for the restrictive conditions it placed on potential candidates. Opposition parties immediately announced a boycott of the presidential elections scheduled for September 2005. Egyptian authorities had attempted to ban referendum-day protests, but large demonstrations took place nonetheless.

The leftist Tomorrow Party (*al-Ghad*), the one new party granted a permit, saw its leader Ayman NOUR jailed for six weeks on charges of forging signatures on his political party application. His June 2005 trial was postponed until after the presidential elections, in which Mubarak was elected with 88 percent of the vote, defeating Nour, NWP leader Numan GOMAA, and seven other candidates. Nour was sentenced in December to five years in prison.

While the 2005 presidential election was trumpeted as a move toward democratization, most observers considered the election to be a very limited step toward reform. Some 19 candidates were disqualified, the government refused to allow international monitors, turnout was extremely low, and laws severely restricting political activity remained in place. Assembly elections a few months later were marked by violence, with at least nine people killed by government security forces, who blocked some polling stations in opposition strongholds. Hundreds of supporters of Muslim Brotherhood–backed candidates were arrested during the three-stage elections. While the NDP again dominated the results, independent candidates allied with the Muslim Brotherhood increased their representation more than fivefold, strengthening the group's position as the major opposition force. In what was regarded as a move to preserve the NDP's power, the government postponed local elections (scheduled for April 2006) for two years, saying the delay was necessary to give the assembly more time to adopt laws that would increase the role of local governments.

Tensions increased in 2006 following parliament's approval of a two-year extension to the 1981 emergency law. In a subsequent blow to political reform, the courts took disciplinary action against a judge who lost his judicial immunity after publicly charging electoral fraud in the 2005 parliamentary elections. Thousands of riot police attempted to disperse massive demonstrations in Cairo following the court ruling, and hundreds were arrested. The protests were backed by the country's 7,000 judges, who demanded they be granted independent oversight of all aspects of elections, as provided for in the constitutional amendments of 2000. The judges contended that they were restricted to monitoring polling places, not vote counting. Observers saw the demands of the judges as a challenge to the NDP's ability to retain control and, ultimately, to handpick Mubarak's successor. The latter was a topic of considerable speculation, particularly after Mubarak's son, Gamal MUBARAK, gained a more prominent leadership role in the NDP. The court cases against the judges, the imprisonment of prominent members of the political opposition, and the arrest and detainment of hundreds of protesters appeared to observers to have weakened the president's popularity, despite the country's substantial economic progress.

Attention in 2007 turned to controversial constitutional amendments, the most significant of which granted the government the authority to ban political parties based on religion (which observers said was aimed at the Muslim Brotherhood), froze most of the restrictions in effect under the emergency law (including broad police authority to circumvent legal processes while combating "terrorism"), gave the president the authority to dissolve parliament, and reduced judicial oversight over balloting. Egypt's judges rejected the results of the plebiscite and vowed not to supervise future balloting. Opposition and human rights groups were vociferous in their criticism, saying the changes were a major setback to Egyptians' basic freedoms and were designed to consolidate the ruling party's control.

Partial elections to the Shura Council in 2007 were dominated by the NDP. The Muslim Brotherhood participated by backing independent candidates for the council, though none secured a seat. Other independents won three seats, and the Nationalist Progressive Unionist Party was the only other party to win a seat. Despite their lack of electoral success in 2007, observers said the Muslim Brotherhood appeared to have gained strength, even as the government's increasing repression resulted in the arrest of hundreds of the group's members.

In early 2008 attention turned to the long-delayed local elections, seen by some as another benchmark for the administration's commitment to democracy. In the run-up to the elections, hundreds of Muslim Brotherhood members were arrested on the grounds of belonging to an illegal political group. Undaunted, the Brotherhood chose to back independent candidates for some of the 52,000 seats on the local councils, though the government reportedly blocked 90 percent of the Islamist candidates from registering. Opposition groups and labor activists staged a general strike the weekend before the elections, followed by demonstrations by thousands of supporters of the Muslim Brotherhood that turned violent when police intervened. Eventually, the Brotherhood announced that it was boycotting the elections, and in balloting marked by an extremely low turnout, the NDP won 92 percent of the seats—the overwhelming majority of which had been unopposed. The Muslim Brotherhood called the elections a fraud and contemplated legal action.

In May 2008 the Assembly approved the government's request to extend emergency law for two more years. Opposition groups and human rights organizations immediately criticized the action, claiming that emergency law was primarily used against the political opposition. Parliament extended the law for another two years on May 11, 2010, stating that the measure covered only terrorism and drug-related crimes.

In midterm elections for the Shura Council held in June 2010, the NDP won 80 of the 88 contested seats. In the two-stage elections for the assembly held later that year, the NDP again won a commanding majority. Independent candidates representing the Muslim Brotherhood were all unseated—a net loss of 88 seats. Brotherhood representatives repeated their claim that fraud, intimidation, and violence marred the election process. Since Egypt did not allow outside observers to monitor the elections—which Mubarak described as "largely lawful"—several human rights advocates called on the president to void the results and reschedule fairer elections.

In 2010 Egypt's political scene witnessed the return of Mohamed ElBaradei, former head of the International Atomic Energy Agency (IAEA) and 2005 Nobel Peace Prize winner. After an absence of 30 years, ElBaradei indicated that he would challenge President Mubarak in the 2011 presidential election. ElBaradei met with opposition leaders and announced the formation of a nonparty movement called the Coalition for Change, which would campaign for constitutional reform ahead of presidential balloting. Meanwhile, domestic unrest ramped up, as for days hundreds of workers from across the country staged massive demonstrations outside parliament, protesting low wages. Sustained protest by political activists also sought an end to emergency law.

Against the backdrop of rising food and fuel prices, public discontent over the 2010 parliamentary elections, a more visible and vocal opposition, continued repression of the Muslim Brotherhood, and the example set by a Tunisian uprising that toppled the autocratic regime of Zine Abidine BEN ALI, a trickle of popular protest aimed at the Mubarak government became a tsunami of antigovernment sentiment by the end of January 2011. Anti-Mubarak demonstrations grew in size and scope during the last week of January, driven by a variety of self-styled "youth movements" using social networking Websites to encourage the overthrow of Mubarak. Protestors overtook Tahrir Square in Cairo, as well as prominent sites in Alexandria and other cities, vowing not to leave until Mubarak stepped down. Protestors were forced into confrontations with both security forces and Mubarak loyalists and responded by burning down the headquarters of the NDP in Cairo.

Mubarak attempted to appease the public by appointing a new prime minister—Ahmed SHAFIK—and a vice president—Omar SULEIMAN, a man reviled by most of the demonstrators for his association with state-sponsored political repression. Predictably, popular discontent intensified. By February 10 consultation with leaders of the Egyptian military had convinced Mubarak to resign. On February 11 he publicly announced his departure, handing authority to the Supreme Council of the Armed Forces (SCAF), a group composed of the 20 most-tenured military men in Egypt and led by Field Marshall Mohammed Hussein TANTAWI, who was named head of state when the presidency was vacated. The SCAF immediately dissolved the Assembly and suspended the constitution. From the start of the uprising on January 24 through the resignation of Mubarak, 840 people had been killed and over 6,000 injured.

The SCAF declared that its limited mission was only to see the country through to parliamentary elections and the ratification of a new constitution. However, despite high approval of the military in the eyes of most Egyptians, some elements of the protest movement were concerned that the military government had too many holdovers from the Mubarak regime. Prime Minister Shafik, who the public closely identified with the former regime, became a liability for Tantawi, and was forced to resign in March. A few days later the SCAF installed Essam SHARAF as prime minister in deference to popular concerns. In another attempt to win popular support for the caretaker government, Interior Minister Mansour al-ESSAWY declared that the secret police organization—the loathsome State Security Investigations agency—had been abolished.

In June and early July 2011 growing frustration with the pace of reforms coupled with sectarian and philosophical divides in the body politic drew protestors back to Tahrir Square in Cairo. Violent clashes between demonstrators and the police were a new aspect of the Tahrir protest experience, and caused some protesters to criticize the SCAF for not doing enough to stop the violence. In late July the secular, prodemocracy demonstrators in Tahrir were overrun by Islamists, who crammed the square while calling for the imposition of sharia law. This show of force on the street highlighted the sectarian divisions occurring in Egypt's political realm, as new parties and coalitions formed around either secular or Islamic philosophies of governance.

In October 2011 sectarian violence intensified as Copts and liberal Muslims protesting in Cairo's Maspero district over the burning of a church were attacked by a larger group of conservative Muslims wielding homemade weapons. The initial attack and two days of subsequent skirmishes resulted in 25 deaths and scores of injuries.

In April 2011 former president Mubarak was arrested and charged with murder for the deaths of 840 protesters. In August Mubarak appeared in his own defense in a Cairo courtroom and before a television audience of millions. Later, a judge suspended proceedings for weeks due to Mubarak's deteriorating health. In September the trial resumed, but Field Marshall Tantawi's testimony—which was subjected to a media blackout—exonerated both the army and the regime of wrongdoing.

In late September the SCAF formally announced the dates for parliamentary elections that would begin in November 2011 and conclude in February 2012 (see Legislature, below). As the election neared, protests against the military regime intensified. For seven days security forces clashed with protestors, and 40 civilians were killed with more than 3,500 injured. In response to public discord, the caretaker government of Prime Minister Sharaf resigned, and Kamal Ahmed GANZOURI was named prime minister.

As the second round of parliamentary balloting concluded in December 2011, street violence aimed at the Tantawi regime flared again. For three days clashes broke out around the country, mostly centered on vote-counting centers where members of the military denied judges access to ballots. The election results favored the Islamist parties—especially the Freedom and Justice Party (FJP). The four expressly Islamic parties controlled more than 70 percent of Assembly seats and more than 80 percent of Shura Council seats. The remainder of seats in both houses was split between center and center-left parties.

In March 2012 the Assembly demanded that it be allowed to select a cabinet, and insisted that the Ganzouri government resign. In April the SCAF promised a cabinet realignment, but before such a shake-up could occur, street protests calling for the military to relinquish its authority returned in both frequency and fervor. Distrust of the SCAF led the Muslim Brotherhood's FJP to reverse its decision that it would not run a candidate in the 2012 presidential election.

The SCAF revealed in late April that presidential polling would take place in June. The election commissioners reported that ten aspiring candidates had been disqualified—chief among them the Muslim Brotherhood's Khairat al-SHATER. Also excluded was Mubarak's final prime minister, Ahmed SHAFIK, who later appealed and was reinstated as a candidate. The FJP candidate, Mohammed MORSI, received almost 25 percent of the vote, and Ahmed Shafik polled almost 24 percent. A runoff election between candidates Morsi and Shafik was scheduled for June.

On the eve of the election, several events conspired to unsettle Egyptian society and politics. First, Hosni Mubarak was found guilty of murder and sentenced to life in prison. Second, the SCAF reimposed the Mubarak-era emergency law. Third, a Mubarak-era panel of judges ruled that the duly elected parliament be dissolved. Both Islamists and secularists strenuously criticized what they characterized as a coup perpetrated by the SCAF. Observers noted that the new president would enter office with neither a constitution nor a legislature to check his power.

The runoff election turned out almost 52 percent of eligible voters. Egyptians learned on June 24 that Morsi had won 51.7 percent of the vote, compared to 48.3 percent for Shafik. Morsi was sworn in on June 30 and immediately tested the limits of his presidential authority vis-à-vis the military leadership. The president ordered the Parliament to reconvene: In response, the military elite and the Supreme Constitutional Court (SCC) dismissed Morsi's order. Egypt's Parliament met for a very brief session on July 10—just long enough to appeal the court decision authorizing its shutdown. The SCC maintained that its order dissolving Parliament was still valid and that the president could be found in contempt of court if he continued to violate its rulings.

In late July President Morsi selected Hesham QANDIL as his prime minister and tasked him with assembling a cabinet. The makeup of the cabinet selected by Qandil, which included longtime state employees and at least six former government ministers, dismayed many liberals and Islamists alike. The selection of five ministers from Mr. Morsi's FJP and the exclusion of cabinet members from other major political parties prompted complaints that the Muslim Brotherhood was attempting to dominate government.

A serious domestic security event in the Sinai near Egypt's border with both Israel and Gaza provided Morsi the opportunity to increase his authority as president. In early August an attack by gunmen disguised as Bedouins on an army checkpoint near the Rafah border left 16 Egyptian soldiers dead and 7 injured. President Morsi condemned the attacks as criminal and fired both his intelligence chief and the governor of Northern Sinai. The military undertook an antiterrorist campaign in the Sinai that resulted in the deaths of 20 so-called terrorists. The new president turned the crisis to his advantage when he forced the retirement of Defense Minister Tantawi, the army chief of staff, and other senior generals. In September 2012 Morsi's new defense minister, Abdel Fattah AL-SISI, forced the resignation of 70 army generals and removed six members of the SCAF.

Constitution and government. Under the 1971 constitution, executive power was vested in the president, who was nominated by the People's Assembly and elected for a six-year term by popular referendum. The president could appoint vice presidents in addition to government ministers and might rule by decree when granted emergency powers by the Assembly, which functioned primarily as a policy-approving rather than a policy-initiating body. In May 1990 the Supreme Constitutional Court invalidated the 1987 assembly elections, claiming the electoral system discriminated against opposition and independent contenders. Consequently, the government abolished electoral laws limiting the number of independent candidates, rejected the "party list" balloting system, and enlarged the number of constituencies.

In 2005 a constitutional amendment allowed for Egypt's first direct, multicandidate presidential elections—only after candidates gained backing from Assembly members and municipal councilors. The amendment was approved in a public referendum, albeit marked by huge public demonstrations over what was perceived as too much government control over potential candidates.

As provided by 2011 law, the Consultative Council (*Majlis al-Shura*), also referred to as the Shura Council, is composed of 180 elected and 90 appointed members who serve six-year terms. It serves in an advisory capacity as an "upper house" of the parliament. In addition to the Supreme Constitutional Court, the judicial system included the Court of Cassation, geographically organized Courts of Appeal, Tribunals of First Instance, and District Tribunals. A Supreme Judicial Council was designed to guarantee the independence of the judiciary. Emergency laws, in effect almost continuously from 1981 until May 2012, provided the government with broad arrest and detention powers. In addition, special military courts were established in late 1992 for the prosecution of those charged with "terrorist acts" in connection with the conflict between the government and militant Islamic fundamentalists.

For administrative purposes Egypt is divided into 26 governorates, each with a governor appointed by the president, while most functions are shared with regional, town, and village officials. In April 1994 the People's Assembly approved legislation whereby previously elected village mayors would thenceforth be appointed by the Interior Ministry.

Constitutional amendments passed by the assembly on April 30, 1980, and approved by referendum on May 22 included the following: designation of the country as "socialist democratic," rather than "democratic socialist," and designation of sharia as "the" rather than "a" principal source of law.

Though as it assumed authority in February 2011 the SCAF suspended the Egyptian constitution and called for a new one to be written once parliamentary elections could be held, the military regime broadly adhered to the former constitution. In order to facilitate parliamentary elections, the SCAF commissioned a panel of legal experts to draw up constitutional amendments delimiting the term of the president (two 4-year terms), instructing the president to appoint a vice president, requiring judicial supervision of the election process, and lowering the requirements for candidacy. Remnants of the old-guard National Democratic Party and the bulk of Muslim Brotherhood members supported the "yes" vote as they had the most to gain from hastily called elections. The "no" vote supporters—composed of the prodemocracy "revolutionary youth" along with members of the established center and center-left political parties—believed that more radical constitutional changes providing greater protections for democracy should be enacted *before* parliamentary elections. The national vote in March 2011 drew 41 percent of eligible voters, with 77.3 percent of the electorate voting "yes."

When the post-Mubarak parliament was seated in January 2012, one of its first tasks was to appoint a 100-member Constituent Assembly (CA) that would direct the writing of a new constitution, one that featured a presidential-parliamentary system of government, protected freedom of religion and expression, and embraced Islam no more or less than the 1971 constitution. As the first set of names selected for the CA drew criticism for excluding women and Christians, MPs struggled with selecting an acceptable mix of appointees.

However, these squabbles were mooted in April when a SCAF-supervised administrative court suspended the constituent assembly, all but guaranteeing that Egypt would elect a president before it ratified a new charter. In June, the SCAF ordered MPs to reconstitute the constituent assembly immediately or the military would do it for them. Within days, a new constituent assembly was appointed. The assembly considered a multitude of options, but settled upon a semi-presidential system, with a president as head of state and a prime minister as head of government. The assembly also decided to rename the two houses of the legislative branch: the former People's Assembly would be called the House of Representatives, and the former Shura Council would be called the Senate. However, primary legislative power would remain in the new House of Representatives. The assembly was divided on mention of Islamic law in the constitution: a Coptic member insisted that no mention of sharia be made, while many Islamists were insistent that sharia should be identified as the basis of law.

Liberals and secularists criticized the draft constitution for its weakness in protecting rights and liberties—especially in regard to religious liberty and gender rights. In addition, both Salafists and liberals criticized the special status preserved for the military in the draft. Observers noted that the draft gave the executive vast authority over the legislative branch and even granted the president the power to propose referenda without oversight. In addition, mechanisms for amendments were vague and unwieldy.

National polling for ratification of the constitution held in December 2012 drew slightly less than 33 percent of eligible voters. Of those 64 percent cast their approval, while 36 percent voted against. Once ratified, the new constitution invalidated all previous decrees by the SCAF and President Morsi, former NDP members were barred from political participation, and the 19-member High Constitutional Court was reduced to 11 members.

After President Morsi was removed by the military in July 2013, the 2012 Constitution was suspended. As part of a road map to return Egypt to civilian rule, the caretaker government headed by Interim President Mansour established a committee of legal scholars to amend the suspended constitution. Proposed amendments eliminated the Shura Council, changed the name of the lower house to the People's Assembly, and slightly increased the authority of the legislative branch. However, critics on the left found the changes fell short of protecting individual rights and liberties. The secular-Islamist divide carried into the writing of the draft constitution; the lack of a suitable compromise might delegitimize the document before it can even be adopted.

Egypt's press freedoms have never been robust. In its 2013 World Index, Reporters Without Borders characterized Egypt as hostile to the country's journalists and news organizations, ranking it 158th out of 179 countries. After the January 2011 revolution, the SCAF clamped down on Egypt's news organizations, warning them that criticism of the military would not be tolerated. After the election of President Morsi, members of Egypt's Journalist's Syndicate claimed that Shura Council appointments to state-run newspaper boards were calculated to stifle dissent and smother criticism of the Muslim Brotherhood, the FJP, and the Morsi government. The number of blasphemy cases soared after Morsi was elected, with more than 13 citizens receiving prison sentences for the offense. The government also attempted to silence media critics, such as Egyptian satirist Bassem YOUSSEF. After Morsi was removed from office, the interim military government shut down media outlets run by the Muslim Brotherhood, other sympathetic groups, and an affiliate of Al-Jazeera.

Foreign relations. As the most populous and most highly industrialized of the Arab states, Egypt has consistently aspired to a leading role in Arab, Islamic, Middle Eastern, African, and world affairs and has been an active participant in the UN, the Arab League, and the Organization of African Unity (subsequently the African Union). For years, its claim to a position of primacy in the Arab world made for somewhat unstable relations with other Arab governments, particularly the conservative regimes of Jordan and Saudi Arabia, although relations with those governments improved as a result of the 1967 and 1973 wars with Israel. Relations with the more radical regimes of Libya and Syria subsequently became strained, largely because of their displeasure with the terms of the U.S.-brokered disengagement. Thus a January 1972 agreement by the three states to establish a loose Federation of Arab Republics was never implemented.

Formally nonaligned, Egypt has gone through a number of distinct phases, including the Western orientation of the colonial period and the monarchy, the anti-Western and increasingly pro-Soviet period initiated in 1955, a period of flexibility dating from the expulsion of Soviet personnel in 1972, and a renewed reliance on the West—particularly the United States—following widespread condemnation of Egyptian-Israeli rapprochement by most Communist and Arab governments.

With supervision and prodding by the United States, in 1977 President Sadat began a diplomatic process with his counterpart in Israel, Prime Minister Menachem BEGIN, that led to the two unprecedented documents—a "Framework for Peace in the Middle East" and a "Framework for a Peace Treaty Between Israel and Egypt"—that were signed in September 1978. The finalized treaty was signed by Begin and Sadat at a White House ceremony hosted by U.S. president Jimmy Carter, and the 31-year state of war between Egypt and Israel officially came to an end. In May 1979 the first Israeli troops withdrew from the Sinai under the terms of the treaty, and negotiations on autonomy for the West Bank and Gaza opened in Israel.

The Arab League responded to the Egyptian-Israeli rapprochement by calling for the diplomatic and economic isolation of Egypt. The country succeeded in weathering the hardline Arab reaction largely because of increased economic aid from Western countries; the United States committed more aid on a per capita basis than had been extended to Europe under the post–World War II Marshall Plan.

Although Egypt and Israel formally exchanged ambassadors in February 1980, negotiations on the question of Palestinian autonomy were subsequently impeded by continued Jewish settlement on the West Bank, the Israeli annexation of East Jerusalem in July 1980, and the invasion of Lebanon in June 1982. Following the massacre of Palestinian refugees at Sabra and Chatila in September 1982, Cairo recalled its ambassador from Tel Aviv.

The Soviet intervention in Afghanistan in December 1979 generated concern in Egypt, with the government ordering Moscow in February 1980 to reduce its diplomatic staff in Cairo, while offering military assistance to the Afghan rebels. In 1981, accusing the remaining Soviet embassy staff of inciting Islamic fundamentalist unrest, Cairo broke diplomatic relations with Moscow. Relations were resumed in September 1984, as the Mubarak government departed from the aggressively pro-U.S. policy of the later Sadat years.

Relations with most of the Arab world also changed during President Mubarak's first term, Egypt's stature among moderate neighbors being enhanced by a virtual freeze in dealings with Israel after the 1982 Lebanon invasion. Although relations with radical Arab states, particularly Libya, remained strained, Egypt's reemergence from the status of Arab pariah allowed it to act as a "silent partner" in negotiations between Jordan and the PLO that generated a 1985 peace plan (see entries on Jordan and the Palestinian Authority).

During an Arab League summit in November 1987, the prohibition against diplomatic ties with Egypt was officially lifted. The threat of

Iranian hegemony in the Gulf was the principal factor in Cairo's rehabilitation. Egypt, which had severed relations with Iran in May 1987 upon discovery of a fundamentalist Muslim network allegedly financed by Tehran, possessed the largest and best-equipped armed force in the region. Following the League summit, Egypt instituted joint military maneuvers with Jordan, increased the number of military advisers sent to Iraq, and arranged for military cooperation with Kuwait, Saudi Arabia, and the United Arab Emirates.

Lebanon and Syria restored diplomatic relations with Cairo in 1989, and relations with Libya also improved as President Mubarak journeyed to Libya to meet with Col. Muammar al-QADHAFI, the first such visit by an Egyptian president since 1972. Meanwhile, Cairo increased pressure on Jerusalem to begin negotiations with the Palestinians in the West Bank and Gaza Strip.

In what was clearly his boldest foreign relations move, President Mubarak spearheaded the Arab response to Iraq's incursion into Kuwait in August 1990. The Egyptian leader successfully argued for an Arab League declaration condemning the invasion and approving Saudi Arabia's request for non-Arab troops to help it defend its borders. Overall, more than 45,000 Egyptian troops were deployed to Saudi Arabia, elements of which played a significant role in the liberation of Kuwait.

In the wake of Iraq's defeat in 1991, Western creditors quickly rewarded Cairo for its support during the Desert Shield and Desert Storm campaigns: Shortly after the defeat of Iraq, the United States and Gulf Arab states forgave about $14 billion of Egypt's $50 billion external debt, and other countries agreed to write off another $11 billion. Globally, Egypt's prestige was enhanced by the selection of its leading diplomat, former deputy prime minister Boutros BOUTROS-GHALI, as the secretary general of the United Nations in 1992.

Egyptian officials played an important advisory role in the secret talks that led up to the accord between Israel and the PLO in September 1993. Cairo's relations with Amman improved after the rift caused by Jordan's pro-Iraqi stance during the Gulf crisis. In 1995 President Mubarak hosted Jordan's King HUSSEIN, Israeli Prime Minister Yitzhak RABIN, and PLO Chair Yasir ARAFAT in a summit designed to revitalize the Israel/PLO peace accord. The summit also addressed growing tension between Egypt and Israel regarding nuclear weapons.

By mid-1995 tension with Egypt's southern neighbor, Sudan, had intensified because of President Mubarak's intimation that Sudanese officials had played a role in the June attempt on his life in Ethiopia. Sudan accused Egypt of provoking a clash in the disputed border region of Halaib, with Mubarak declaring his support for exiled opponents of the fundamentalist Khartoum regime. In 2004, Egypt reluctantly agreed to send military officers as observers to Sudan, but stopped short of getting involved in attempting to resolve the Sudanese civil war.

President Mubarak welcomed the election of Ehud BARAK as prime minister of Israel in May 1999 as a hopeful sign that a peace settlement between Israel and the Palestinians was possible. However, Egypt recalled its ambassador to Israel in November 2000 in response to Israeli bombing of the Gaza Strip. Egyptian-Israeli relations cooled even further following the election of hard-liner Ariel SHARON as prime minister in February 2001. By 2004, however, after Sharon had unveiled his unilateral disengagement plan for the Gaza Strip, relations between Egypt and Israel began to thaw. Egypt's role in security arrangements in Gaza were vital to the Israeli withdrawal process, and enhanced its status as a power broker in the region. In February 2005, Mubarak again helped mediate between Israel and the Palestinians, while his diplomatic efforts in the latter part of 2006 focused on negotiations toward a unity government in Palestine that would include both Hamas and Fatah. However, this strained Egypt's relations with Israel, which refused to accept Hamas as a legitimate partner in a Palestinian government.

In June 2007 Egypt called a summit with leaders of Israel, Jordan, and the Palestinian Authority to address ways to further isolate Hamas, including an international arrangement to secure the border with Gaza. Border issues involving Egypt's monitoring of the flow of weapons to and from the Gaza Strip flared in 2007 with accusations that Egypt's vigilance was lacking. In December the U.S. Congress voted to freeze $100 million in aid to Egypt pending a further assessment of progress against arms smuggling.

Events took a dramatic turn in January 2008 when Egypt allowed the border to be breached by tens of thousands of Palestinians seeking food and other emergency supplies in the wake of Israel's blockade of Gaza. Mubarak said he would allow the Palestinians to return to Gaza as long as they were not taking weapons with them.

In the wake of Israel's intensive ground and bombing attacks in Gaza in response to Hamas' continued attacks on southern Israel (see article on Israel for details), President Mubarak came under increasing criticism by Arab nations in January 2009 for his government's refusal to open its border with Gaza to allow the flow of humanitarian aid. Egyptian officials were also criticized for their lack of diplomatic pressure on Israel to halt the bombing, yet President Mubarak and other officials blamed Hamas for breaking the cease-fire. Meanwhile, Egypt refused to allow international troops to use the Egyptian side of the Gaza border to stage troops as part of any cease-fire agreement between Israel and Hamas.

In March 2009 Egyptian officials welcomed Sudan's President BASHIR to Cairo, by all accounts "undeterred" by the arrest warrant issued against Bashir by the International Criminal Court (ICC). (Egypt was not a signatory to the ICC agreement obliging its member states to arrest Bashir if he entered their territory.) In March President Mubarak boycotted the Arab League summit, reportedly because of its differences with Qatar over the countries' stances on the conflict between Israel and Gaza.

The spotlight was on Cairo in June 2009, when U.S. president Barack OBAMA delivered a speech aimed at the Muslim world, calling on American citizens and Muslims to do more to stem violent extremism. The speech came at a time of strained relations between the United States and Muslim countries, as well as tense relations with Israeli prime minister Binyamin NETANYAHU over the issue of Jewish settlements in the West Bank. A month later President Mubarak visited the White House, his first such trip in five years.

Tensions with Gaza erupted in January 2010, when an Egyptian border guard was killed and 15 Palestinians were injured in fighting after an aid convoy tried to enter the territory. Observers said the flare-up signaled heightened frustration among Gaza residents as Egypt attempted to seal the border, including building a steel wall underground to shut down hundreds of tunnels used for smuggling.

In May 2010 Egypt condemned Israel's attack on a flotilla trying to breach the blockade of Gaza. A month later, after three years of cooperating with Israel in the blockade, Egypt announced it would leave open its border with the Palestinian territory for humanitarian reasons.

The forced resignation of Mubarak in February 2011 required a reassessment of foreign relations in the greater Middle East. Outwardly, the United States and other Western countries declared their hope that the Egyptian revolution would allow democracy to flourish in a country sorely lacking it, while internally Western leaders were relieved that their close relationship with the Egyptian military ensured that their voices—at least to some extent—would still be heard in Cairo. Israel was concerned about the future status of the Egyptian-Israeli peace accord and the potential for the rise of Islamism in Egyptian society and government. Tel Aviv also worried about Egypt's underlying foreign policy calculus when in February Cairo allowed two Iranian Navy ships to pass through the Suez Canal—the first such occurrence since the 1979 Iranian Revolution. Meanwhile, the states in the Gulf Cooperation Council (GCC)—especially Saudi Arabia and Qatar—extended a financial hand to Egypt for pragmatic reasons, the most basic of which was to ensure Egyptian counterbalance against Iran's regional hegemonic ambitions.

Egypt did not succumb to introspection in 2011: instead it embarked upon a more aggressive foreign policy position in the region, exemplified by its role in brokering a unity agreement between Hamas and Fatah in May (see the Palestinian Authority/Palestine Liberation Organization entry in the 2012 *Handbook*). Displaying support for the Palestinian cause won Egypt respect in Lebanon, Syria, and Iran, while it showed the West and Israel that the era of Mubarak's support for their policy preferences was over.

Egypt's focus shifted to the border with Israel in August 2011, as the Egyptian military launched a campaign in the Sinai to thwart al-Qaida cells and lawless Bedouins, both of whom used the period after the revolution to expand their freedom of action. Just days after the campaign began, militants from Gaza entered southern Israel from Egyptian territory, attacking and killing eight Israeli citizens near the town of Eilat. The Israeli counterattack caused the deaths of three Egyptian security officers. In Cairo the public was outraged, as demonstrators converged on the Israeli embassy and burned Israeli flags. A month later unruly demonstrators entered the embassy and vandalized some offices before army forces arrived.

In March 2012 incoming FJP MPs began pressuring Hamas to reconcile completely with Fatah so a united Palestinian front allied with Egypt could force Israel into accepting an independent Palestinian state. Again in April, the Egyptian-Israeli relationship was tested when Egypt's national gas company canceled a long-term contract with the Israelis. In June Egypt learned the Israelis were deploying their Iron Dome missile shield on the border near Eliat. The following month terrorists crossed into Israel from Egypt, killing an Israeli construction worker. (For more information about terrorism in the Sinai, see Current issues, below.)

Egypt's relations with the United States were tumultuous in 2012. First, four U.S.-financed nongovernmental organizations (NGOs) that had been formally authorized to monitor Egypt's parliamentary elections had their offices raided and files confiscated by government agents. Then, the government prevented many of the employees of those organizations—including Sam LaHood, son of U.S. transportation secretary Ray LaHood—from leaving Egypt. When the government sought to arrest the Americans, the U.S. embassy in Cairo gave them shelter, and later all but one of the Americans was flown out of the country by the U.S. State Department. During the crisis, the United States informed the Egyptian government that its annual $1.5 billion aid package was in serious jeopardy of being terminated.

The second source of friction between Egypt and the United States involved statements made by FJP officials in February regarding their willingness to reopen the Camp David Accords for review, suggesting the treaty could be altered in the near future. This message was directed at Washington for its use of Egypt's annual aid as a bargaining chip in bilateral negotiations regarding the detained NGO workers. The third, and perhaps most egregious, point of conflict between the two countries involved the storming of the U.S. embassy in Cairo on September 11, 2012, by a large crowd of Islamists augmented by soccer hooligans known as Ultras. Though ostensibly the crowd attacked the embassy because of an obscure American film negatively portraying Islam's prophet Mohammed, reports indicated that Jamaa Islamiya (see Political Parties and Groups, below) had on August 30—days before the video started circulating on the Internet—called for a protest at the embassy on September 11. The protest was called to petition for release of the "Blind Sheik," Omar Abdel Rahman, who has been in a U.S. prison since 1996 for his role in the 1993 World Trade Center bombing. Morsi was slow to condemn the embassy assault, a fact that rankled U.S. officials. In a message aimed at Cairo, President Obama remarked in an interview that Egypt was neither an ally nor an enemy of the Unites States.

Egypt's relationships with its Arab neighbors in 2012 concerned both security and the economy. In late January protestors defaming Syrian president Bashar AL-ASSAD besieged the Syrian embassy in Cario—the second such assault in five months. Observers indicated that public opinion in Egypt was decidedly anti-Assad: Liberals decried his brutal authoritarianism, and Muslim Brotherhood members hoped to see Syrian Sunnis defeat the Alawite regime in Damascus. In July, 14 soldiers were injured and two security forces vehicles were destroyed in front of the Syrian embassy in Cairo after clashes erupted between security forces and protesters. Demonstrators had gathered in front of the embassy calling for the ouster of the Syrian ambassador. When President Morsi attended the Non Aligned Movement conference held in Tehran in late August, he shocked his hosts by declaring Egypt's support for Assad's opposition: Morsi even referred to Syria's regime as "oppressive." The president's remarks took the Iranians—key supporters of the Assad regime—by surprise.

Iran made diplomatic overtures to Egypt during 2012, first in February when it suggested that a revival of commercial relationships could hasten the revival of diplomatic relationships, and again in June after Morsi was elected. After the Egyptian presidential election results were released, the Iranian state news agency reported that President Morsi had declared his interest in restoring ties with Tehran. However, Morsi aides quickly denied the interview ever took place. Undaunted, a week later Iran's foreign minister Ali Akbar SALEHY said that his country was eager to exchange ambassadors with Egypt.

Egypt's relationship with Saudi Arabia was tested in 2012, as a protest staged in front of the Saudi embassy in April caused the Saudis to close the mission and recall its ambassador. The Kingdom reopened the embassy a week later, but only after Egyptian authorities spent significant time reassuring the Saudis that such an affront would not occur again. Despite past differences, Egypt sees the Saudis as significant allies, especially in terms of access to Gulf petrodollars. In 2012 the Saudis floated a billion dollar loan to Egypt for currency support, and signed off on another loan and investment package for $3.2 billion. Morsi's first foreign trip as president was to Riyadh, and his status as a statesman rose greatly when he helped broker a cease-fire between Israel and Hamas in November 2012.

Over the course of his shortened term in office, Morsi made more trips abroad than had former president Mubarak during his last decade in office. Among these foreign excursions were visits to Brazil, Russia, India, China, and South Africa (BRICs countries). President Morsi warmly welcomed Iran's president Mahmoud Ahmadinejad when he came to Cairo in February 2013 for the Organization of Islamic Cooperation gathering. However, Morsi made clear the differences between Egypt, which opposes Assad, and Iran, which supports Syria's president as a vital ally.

Relations between Egypt and Israel during Morsi's tenure were marked by cooperation—despite video evidence from 2010 that revealed Morsi describing Zionists as "descendants of apes and pigs." Israeli and Egyptian intelligence personnel worked closely to reduce security threats in northern Sinai, and Cairo refrained from aiding Hamas by keeping the Rafah border crossing closed for most of 2012 and 2013. In fact, Egypt stepped up efforts to close tunnels on its border with Gaza.

Ethiopia and its plans for the Renaissance Dam project on the Blue Nile continued to be a source of conflict in Egyptian foreign relations. Concern that the dam would divert a significant amount of water away from Egypt drove the country's leaders to scheme about plans to stop the project from proceeding—even to the extent of assembling a rebel force to blow up the dam.

Just weeks before being removed from office, Morsi clarified Egypt's stance on Syria by declaring an end to formal diplomatic relations with Damascus. Morsi's move may have been conditioned by decidedly anti-Syrian public opinion as the arrival of an estimated 120,000 Syrian refugees had strained Egypt's already fragile social fabric.

After Morsi was ousted, Egypt's foreign relations became more complicated. Though the United States would not characterize the military action as a coup, many other Western countries did. Denmark suspended all aid to Egypt, the UK tabled joint programs with Egyptian intelligence services, and Germany ended debt relief talks. Other European Union (EU) members discussed halting planned weapon sales. For its part, the United States canceled the sale to Egypt of four F-16 aircraft, declined to take part in a planned joint training exercise, and suspended some military aid, forcing Egypt to turn to Russia for a $2 billion dollar arms deal. Closer to home, Turkey condemned the coup as the work of Israel, Saudi Arabia, and the UAE. Syria's president Assad welcomed Morsi's downfall, pointing to it as evidence that political Islam was not workable. Israel's response to Morsi's exit was muted, though officials indicated a preference for an Egyptian government run by secularists rather than Islamists.

Current issues. Just prior to the November 2012 referendum on Egypt's draft constitution, President Morsi granted himself extra-constitutional power exempting his authority from judicial review. Morsi's decision was part of an ongoing dispute between high court judges—mostly Mubarak-era appointees—and a president who spent six months advocating proposed legislation that would have eliminated more than 3,000 judges by lowering the retirement age from 70 to 60. In addition, Morsi unsuccessfully attempted to remove from office Abdul Meguid MAHMOUD, Egypt's chief prosecutor, prompting the threat of a judges' strike and criticism from liberal leaders.

Both the content of the draft constitution and President Morsi's November edict elicited a strong public response, as protestors returned to Egypt's streets in opposition to the Muslim Brotherhood-dominated government. Secularists resented the lack of liberties offered by the draft constitution, and liberals despised what they believed was a power grab orchestrated by the president and his Muslim Brotherhood cohorts. As protests flared across the country, offices of the FJP in Suez and Alexandria were ransacked and burned. Anti-Morsi sentiment increased even after Morsi partially rescinded his November edict and continued to grow as the political opposition suggested that the victorious "yes" vote on the constitutional referendum came about as a result of widespread fraud.

December protests near the presidential palace in Cairo forced Morsi to leave temporarily, with the violence causing eight deaths and hundreds of injuries. In January 2013 the second anniversary of the fall of Hosni Mubarak became the spark for more anti-Morsi protests, as multiple Muslim Brotherhood offices were attacked and the government lost its control over an entire city—Port Said. Forty-five people were killed in the coastal city, and hundreds were injured. In Suez and Ismailia street violence caused at least eight deaths and more than 300 injuries, forcing Morsi to declare a state of emergency and issue curfews. In late February anti-Morsi protestors shut down a major access road to the Suez Canal, the closest that public demonstrations had ever come to disrupting canal operations.

In March the Supreme Constitutional Court upheld a lower court decision canceling parliamentary elections originally scheduled for April. In addition to this challenge posed to Morsi by the judiciary, the Egyptian military also displayed its willingness to defy presidential authority by refusing to enforce the curfew in Suez. Rumors credited to the Muslim Brotherhood suggested that the president was planning to dismiss popular Defense Minister Al-Sisi.

Increasing pressure brought upon Muslim Brotherhood members and their followers in the first half of 2013 ratcheted up sectarian tensions, resulting in an April attack upon Christians attending a funeral outside the most important Coptic church in Egypt. Coptic activists noted that sectarian violence had been rare during the age of Sadat and Mubarak but had increased exponentially under Morsi.

General anti-Morsi sentiment—driven primarily by public apprehension over the president's governing ability, the deplorable state of the economy, and endemic resource shortages—was given focus by members of the former *Kifaya* (Enough!) movement (see Political parties and groups, below). Their new movement, known as *Tamarod* (Rebellion), sought the recall of Morsi as well as early presidential elections. In 90 days of canvassing, Tamarod members and affiliated groups reported the collection of 15 million petition signatures calling upon Morsi to step down. The Muslim Brotherhood countered Tamarod with a movement of their own—*Tagarod* (Impartiality)—and tasked it with collecting signatures in support of the president. Undeterred, Tamarod called for nationwide anti-Morsi protests on June 30. Meanwhile, most Egyptians were shocked when the embattled president appointed a former member of the Islamic Group—the organization banned for domestic terrorism at major tourist sites in 1997—as governor of Luxor, the center of Upper Egypt's tourism industry.

Tamarod's efforts produced obvious results, as an estimated 14 million Egyptians—almost 20 percent of the population—took part in nationwide protests against the Morsi government from June 30 to July 3. Violent clashes between partisans left 34 dead and hundreds injured. Defense Minister Al-Sisi issued an ultimatum to both the president and the opposition, demanding cessation of violence and the start of negotiations, or else the military would assume control of the country. Morsi and his followers rejected the ultimatum as a breach of democratic legitimacy and suggested military action would trigger a civil war in Egypt. On July 3, with no apparent path to political reconciliation in place, Al-Sisi had Morsi and many of his aides detained, dissolved the Shura Council, suspended the constitution, and announced the formation of an interim government to be led by former Supreme Constitutional Court chief justice Adly Mansour as interim president. Al-Sisi also introduced a road map intended to return Egypt to civilian rule under an amended constitution. The plan called for ratification of a constitution first followed by parliamentary elections within six months and a presidential election shortly thereafter. The trial of Morsi and other Muslim Brotherhood leaders will not resume until January 2014. Either conviction or acquittal could provoke massive protest and military intervention.

Supporters of Morsi were encouraged by Muslim Brotherhood leaders to stay on the streets, demanding his full reinstatement. Though blame was difficult to establish, violent confrontations between the protestors and security forces on July 8 and 28 resulted in a reported 123 civilian deaths and four police deaths. However, the Brotherhood claimed more than 300 protestors had been killed. In response to continued provocation by the Brotherhood for Morsi followers to keep protesting, the interim government arrested the group's front-line leadership as well as a number of second-tier leaders. Pro-Morsi demonstrators set up camp at two Cairo locations, causing widespread transportation problems and disrupting normal commerce. Threatened with forced dispersal, the crowds did not budge. On August 14, the military government cleared both camps using fatal techniques. The result was what many observers referred to as a massacre: According to official sources, in Cairo alone, more than 800 protestors were killed, though the Brotherhood placed that figure at 1,500. Over the course of the following eight days, the government reported 900 deaths and more than 4,000 injuries across the country. In random violence in the south, as many as 60 churches were burned and a dozen Christians killed. Interim Vice-President Mohammed ElBaradei resigned his position in response to the force used to clear the Cairo protest sites, and the threat of continued violence led Interim Prime Minister Hazem EL-BEBLAWI to revive the dreaded emergency law.

Though the Sinai region had become the scene of instability and random violence since the fall of the Mubarak regime, in the aftermath of Morsi's ouster, the rate of violence and lawlessness escalated sharply. Several security outposts were attacked in July and August 2013, with more than 30 military personnel killed. Intelligence services reported that more than 12,000 fighters affiliated with Bedouins, al-Qaida, and the Muslim Brotherhood were distributed throughout the peninsula, working in small groups. In July one the affiliated groups bombed the Egytian-Jordanian gas pipeline for the tenth time in 26 months. In September Defense Minister Al-Sisi initiated a comprehensive military campaign to force terrorists and foreign fighters from the region. Though the interim government lifted the state of emergency in early November 2013, it could be reimposed at any time.

POLITICAL PARTIES AND GROUPS

(For background discussion of Egypt's political parties prior to January 2011, see the 2012 *Handbook.*)

In the aftermath of Hosni Mubarak's departure in February 2011, the political status quo came to an end. The National Democratic Party (NDP) was outlawed, and a new election law was passed establishing a Political Parties Affairs Committee to review applications for new parties. Each aspiring party had to produce 5,000 signatures from 10 of the country's 26 provinces, and could not be based solely on a religion or have militias. As new parties were approved in 2011 and 2012, several coalitions formed, broke apart, and re-formed, as members jockeyed for advantage within a very fluid political environment.

Former Government Party:

National Democratic Party—NDP (*al-Hizb al-Watani al-Dimuqrati*). The NDP was officially dissolved by the Supreme Administrative Court on April 16, 2011. In May former NDP members applied for the recognition of a new party, the Freedom Party, but were the first group to have its application rejected by the Political Affairs Committee. (For information about the NDP prior to April 2011 see the 2011 *Handbook.*) However, by late summer 2011 the SCAF had pushed the Committee to approve applications received from parties led by former NDP members (see Post-revolutionary Parties, below).

Other Parties:

Prior to the assembly elections of 2005, opposition leaders announced they had formed a coalition of ten parties and movements seeking greater representation in the legislative body. The resultant **National Front for Political and Constitutional Change,** led by former prime minister Atif SIDQI, was a successor to the **Consensus of National Forces for Reform** (*Tawafuq al-Qiwa al-Wataniyah lil-Islah*), a group of eight opposition parties formed in 2004. Notably excluded from the ten-member 2005 coalition was the **Tomorrow Party** (*al-Ghad*). Among those included were **Arab Dignity** (*Karama al-Araybia*), established by disenchanted Nasserists and led by Hamdeen SABAHI; **Enough** (*Kifaya*), also referenced as the **Egyptian Movement for Change,** which included leftists, liberals, and Islamists, cofounded in 2004 by George ISHAQ and Amin ESKANDAR; the **Labor Party,** which secured one seat in the 2011–2012 Assembly elections; the **Popular Campaign for Change;** and three parties represented in the assembly (the NWP, the NPUP, and the Nasserist Arab Democratic Party). However, after the fall of Mubarak, the status of parties and coalitions as they existed prior to January 2011 was drastically altered.

New Wafd Party—NWP (*Hizb al-Wafd al-Gadid*). (For information concerning the NWP prior to 2011, see the 2011 *Handbook.*)

After the ousting of Mubarak in 2011, the party's secretary general, Mounir Fakhry Abdel NOUR, accepted the post of minister of tourism in the caretaker government. Nour's position annoyed a subset of NWP members, who perceived the cabinet as composed of Mubarak apparatchiks. Internecine discord forced Nour to resign. When the party joined with the Muslim Brotherhood's Freedom and Justice Party (FJP) in the Democratic Alliance (DA) many members objected, and some left the party. Eventually NWP leaders decided to part ways with the DA and remain independent. In 2011–2012 parliamentary elections, NWP contested almost 80 percent of available seats, winning 41 in the Assembly and 14 in the Shura Council.

Leaders: Sayyid al-BADAWI (Chair), Fouad BADRAWI (Deputy Chair), Ahmed Ezz el-ARAB (Vice Chair), Mounir Fakhry Abdel NOUR (Secretary General).

National Progressive Unionist Party—NPUP (*Hizb al-Tagammu al-Watani al-Taqaddumi al-Wahdawi*). (For information concerning the NPUP prior to 2010, see the 2011 *Handbook.*) Also known as Tagammu, the NPUP was the party of the left beginning in 1976. In 2010 party leader Rifaat al-SAID criticized Mohamed ElBaradei for "courting" the Muslim Brotherhood in a possible bid for the presidency and for saying he was not opposed to the formation of a political party on a religious basis. In June 2011 the party joined the Democratic Alliance—anchored at the time by New Wafd and the Muslim Brotherhood's FJP—but left in August to join the secular Egypt Bloc (EB) alliance. The party won three seats in 2011 Assembly voting, and backed a candidate in the presidential election, Hisham BASTAWISY, who polled less than 30,000 votes. In 2013 Sayed Abdel AAL was elected NPUP chair, narrowly defeating Hussein Razeq.

Leaders: Sayed Abdel AAL (Chair), Hussein Abdul RAZEQ (Secretary General), Hisham BASTAWISY (2012 presidential candidate).

Tomorrow Party (*al-Ghad*). Officially recognized by the government in October 2004, this leftist party became only the third party allowed since 1977. Espousing a commitment to social justice, the party was founded by dissidents from the NWP. Former party leader Ayman NOUR came in a distant second to Mubarak in the September 2005 presidential election. A rift over leadership occurred after the election between Nour's supporters and those led by Musa Mustafa Musa, whose splinter group elected him the new party leader in October 2005. The party won one seat in the 2005 assembly elections.

Throughout 2007 rifts in the party intensified, with reports of two separate *Al-Ghad* parties—one loyal to Musa and the other led by Nour's wife, Gamila ISMAIL. In February 2010 the party nominated Nour as its 2011 presidential candidate (in an election that was never held). The party won 1 seat in June 2010 mid-term election for the Shura Council. In 2011 the return of internal dissent led to the emergence of two separate parties: *al-Ghad Al-Thawra* (the Revolution's Tomorrow) controlled by Nour, and the original *al-Ghad* still led by Musa.

After securing its official status, Nour led *al-Ghad Al-Thawra* into the Democratic Alliance, though many observed that the Egypt Bloc—dominated by liberal parties—would have been a more likely choice. The party fielded 15 candidates on DA lists in the 2011 parliamentary elections but won no seats. The Musa-led *al-Ghad* party fielded candidates in the 2011 parliamentary election on independent lists but were not competitive.

Al-Ghad Leader: Musa Mustafa MUSA (*Chair*).

Al-Ghad Al-Thawra Leader: Ayman NOUR (Chairman and President).

Other Parties That Contested Elections Prior to 2011:

Nasserist Arab Democratic Party—NADP. Also referenced simply as the Nasserist Party or Nasserite party, the NADP, formed in 1992, won one seat in the 1995 assembly balloting, three in the 2000 poll, and none in the 2005 elections. Its platform called for the government to retain a dominant role in directing the economy and to increase the provision of social services.

Rifts widened in the party in 2007 among the "old guard" who backed the 80-year-old Diaeddin Daoud's leadership, supporters of the party's secretary general, Ahmed HASSAN (blamed by many for the party's downfall), and a reformist wing headed by Sameh ASHOUR, who had left the party in 2002. Some of the dissidents joined the Arab Dignity party.

The party won one seat in the Consultative Council elections in June 2010. In April 2011 Daoud died, and Ashour was elected president of the party. Hassan was removed from his position as secretary general due to his close association with the Mubarak government. Ashour led the party into the Democratic Alliance, but withdrew in October 2011 in order to run candidates for the parliamentary elections independently. In 2011–2012 parliamentary voting the Nasserite party won one seat in the People's Assembly but none in the Shura Council. Ashour helped form a new coalition, the United Nasserist Party, with three other Nasserist groups—Al-Karama, Al-Wefaq, and the Nasserist Popular Conferenece—in January 2013.

Leaders: Sameh ASHOUR (President), Mohammed Abu al-ALA (Vice President).

Other parties that participated in parliamentary elections from 2005 until the resignation of Hosni Mubarak in 2011 were the Liberal Socialist Party (see the 2011 *Handbook*); the National Party (see the 2011 *Handbook*); the Green Party (see the 2011 *Handbook*); the **Democratic Unionist Party** (*Hizb al-Itahadi Democrati*), formerly led by Ibrahim TURK, the party's presidential candidate, until his death in 2006; the **Egyptian Arab Socialist Party,** led by Wahid al-UQSURI; the **Generation Party** (*al-Gayl*), founded in 2002 and led by Naji al-SHAHABI, it won one Assembly seat in 2010 and fielded a presidential candidate, Mohammed Fawzi ISSA, in 2012; the **National Conciliation Party,** led by Al-Sayyid Rifaat al-AGRUDI; **Solidarity** (*al-Takaful*), a socialist grouping led by Usama Mohammad SHALTOUT; the **Egypt 2000 Party** (*Misr*), led by Fawsi Khalil Mohammad GHAZAL; and the **Social Constitutional Party,** led by Mamduh Mohammad QINAWI.

Other Parties and Groups:

Muslim Brotherhood (*al-Ikhwan al-Muslimin*). Established in 1928 to promote creation of a pan-Arab Islamic state, the Brotherhood was declared an illegal organization in 1954 when the government accused its leaders, many of whom were executed or imprisoned, of plotting a coup attempt. However, for many years the Mubarak government tolerated some activity on the part of the Brotherhood since it claimed to eschew violence, as a means of undercutting the militant fundamentalist movement. With much of its support coming from the northern middle class, the Brotherhood retained the largest following and greatest financial resources among Egypt's Islamic organizations despite the emergence of more radical groups. It dominated many Egyptian professional associations, collaterally providing a wide range of charitable services in sharp contrast to inefficient government programs.

The Brotherhood won indirect Assembly representation in 1984 and 1987. Although they boycotted the 1990 assembly balloting, Brotherhood candidates contested a number of seats in November 1992 municipal elections. Many Brotherhood adherents were removed from local and national appointive positions in 1992–1993 as a side effect of the government's antifundamentalist campaign. Friction with the government intensified further in early 1995 when a group of Brotherhood members were charged with having links to the militant Islamic Group (see below). The government arrested more than 50 members of the group in July on charges of belonging to an illegal organization. The Brotherhood urged a boycott of the April 1997 local elections, claiming that many of its supporters and preferred candidates had been subjected to government "intimidation."

In January 1996 a number of former Brotherhood members, along with representatives of the Coptic community, launched the **New Center Party** (*Hizb al-Wasat al-Jadid*) in an avowed effort to heal divisions within Egyptian society. However, the government denied the party's request for recognition and arrested some 13 of its founders. The defendants were convicted of antigovernment activity by a military court and sentenced to three years in prison. *Al-Wasat* was again denied legal status in May 1998. However, after Mubarak's departure in 2011, the party again sought legal recognition, and on February 19, 2011, the New Center Party became the first party recognized by the SCAF (see below).

A number of independent candidates in the 2000 assembly balloting were clearly identifiable as belonging to the Brotherhood, and 17 of them were elected, permitting the return of the Brotherhood to the assembly after a ten-year absence. Though Brotherhood leaders subsequently denied any connection to militant groups, a number of Brotherhood members were arrested in the government crackdown on Islamists in late 2001 and early 2002.

The death of 83-year-old leader Mamoun al-HODAIBI in 2004 was seen as an opportunity to attract the younger generation, but the party selected an "old guard" successor: Muhammad Mahdi AKEF, 74, who maintained that the Brotherhood would not change its course. Akef had been convicted in 1954 of the attempted assassination of President Nasser and served 20 years in prison.

While Akef called for dialogue with the government, in May 2004 security forces arrested 54 members of the Brotherhood and for the first time targeted the organization's funding sources, closing various businesses and the group's Website. In March 2005, some 84 members were arrested in police raids in the midst of massive demonstrations. The Brotherhood ran 120 candidates as independents in the November–December 2005 assembly elections, securing 88 seats in balloting marked by violence. Arrests of Brotherhood members continued throughout 2006 and 2007, and intensified in 2008 prior to the

April municipal elections, with some 900 members arrested for belonging to an illegal political organization. More than 1,000 members were arrested in early 2009 during demonstrations in Cairo. At a large April rally more than 100 members of the People's Assembly, most of them Brotherhood members, were arrested.

The conservative wing of the party gained control in December 2009, when the Brotherhood named a new governing body dominated by old-guard members, to the exclusion of younger reformists. Mohammad BADIE, described as an ultra-conservative, was named the Brotherhood's new leader in January 2010 following a dispute between the group's ideological conservatives and reformists. Months later, as arrests of Brotherhood members continued, the group embraced Mohammed ElBaradei's push for political reform, indicating that it would work with the former Nobel Peace Prize winner.

In the wake of the January 2011 revolution, the Brotherhood sought and received legal status for a new party—the Freedom and Brotherhood Party (FJP)—to represent its interests in electoral politics. However, the Brotherhood experienced internal challenges, primarily a schism between older members and reform-minded younger members. Factions of younger members broke away to form splinter groups or parties of their own. A former deputy supreme guide for the Brotherhood, Mohammed HABIB, left the group to join another former Brotherhood member, Abdel Moneim Abou el-FOTOUH, who had been expelled for announcing his intention to run for president. Fatouh sought recognition for a new Islamist party, el-Nahda Party (see Postrevolutionary parties, below).

After President Morsi was deposed by the Egyptian military in July 2013, many of the Brotherhood's top leaders were arrested for inciting violence and other offenses. Mohammad Badie, Khairat al-Shater, Ahmed Aref, Saad al-Katatni, and many others were rounded up, while most of the secondary leaders were either in custody or in hiding. Observers speculated that the military was attempting to crush the Brotherhood, relegating the group to the place it occupied in the 1950s.

Leaders: Mohammad BADIE (Supreme Guide), Khairat al-SHATER (First Deputy Supreme Guide), Mahmoud EZZAT (Deputy Supreme Guide), Ahmed AREF (Spokesman), Saad al-KATATNI (Speaker of the People's Assembly), Ahmed FAHMY (Speaker of the Shura Council).

The **Democratic Peace Party,** led by Ahmed Mohammad Bayoumi al-FADALI, was approved in 2005. Democratic Peace ran candidates in the 2011–2012 parliamentary elections, winning two seats in the People's Assembly. In addition, the party supported the unsuccessful presidential candidacy of Houssam KHAIRALLAH in 2012. In 2008 the **April 6 Youth Movement** was formed through the online social networking site Facebook by Israa RASHID and Ahmad MAHER in support of industrial workers who were planning to strike on April 6. The founders, who said their group was not a political party, were arrested in May in an apparent attempt to shut down the movement, and Maher was arrested again in July for alleged "incitement against the regime." In 2008 and 2009 the group participated in pro-Gaza demonstrations. Reports in July 2011 indicated that the group had suffered internal discord, though the movement was still active through late 2013. After President Morsi was ousted in 2013, members of April 6 took part in the formation of a new organization, Third Square, predicated on rejection of both the Muslim Brotherhood and military rule.

Illegal Groups:

Holy War (*al-Jihad*). A secret organization of militant Muslims who split from the Muslim Brotherhood in the second half of the 1970s because of the latter's objection to the use of violence, *al-Jihad* was blamed for attacks against Copts in 1979 and the assassination of President Sadat in 1981. In the first half of the 1980s it appeared to be linked to the Islamic Group (see below), but the two organizations emerged with more distinct identities during the mid-1980s. Although some observers described *al-Jihad* as continuing to seek recruits, its influence appeared to have diminished in the late 1980s as the result of government infiltration of its ranks and growing support for the Islamic Group. However, security officials charged that a revival of the group was attempted in the first half of the 1990s in conjunction with the increasingly violent fundamentalist/government conflict. A number of reported *al-Jihad* supporters were imprisoned in the 1990s on charges of plotting the overthrow of the government. Meanwhile, members of an apparent splinter, the New *Jihad* or the Vanguards of Conquest (*Talai al-Fath*), were subsequently given death sentences for complicity in assassination plots against top government officials. Some reports linked that activity to Ayman al-ZAWAHIRI, a former Cairo surgeon who had been imprisoned and tortured for three years following the assassination of President Sadat. Al-Zawahiri was also linked to the bombing of the Egyptian embassy in Pakistan in 1995.

In 1998, in the wake of the Luxor attack of 1997, Ayman al-Zawahiri and his brother, Mohammad al-ZAWAHIRI, were described as attempting to "reorganize" *al-Jihad* from Afghanistan, where they had reportedly established ties with the al-Qaida network of Osama bin Laden. (Ayman al-Zawahiri had not been seen in Egypt since 1986.) By 1998 it appeared that a portion of *al-Jihad,* having been effectively suppressed in Egypt, had shifted away from a goal of overthrowing the Egyptian government to a global anti-Western campaign in concert with al-Qaida. However, some members of *al-Jihad* reportedly objected to that new focus and split from Ayman al-Zawahiri.

A number of alleged *al-Jihad* adherents received long prison terms in early 1999, while nine were sentenced to death in absentia, including Ayman al-Zawahiri and Yasser al-SIRRI, a London-based leader. Al-Zawahiri was also indicted in absentia in 1999 in the United States for his alleged role in the planning of the bombings of the U.S. embassies in Kenya and Pakistan in 1998. Following the attacks on the United States in September 2001 that were attributed to al-Qaida, al-Zawahiri was described as the number two leader, after bin Laden, in that network. Reports linked al-Zawahiri to the July 2005 bombings in Sharm El-Sheikh, Egypt, that killed at least 64 people, and in 2006 al-Zawahiri claimed that the Islamic Group had joined *al-Jihad,* which he said was linked to al-Qaida.

In May 2007 Egypt released 135 prisoners, all said to be members of *al-Jihad,* after they signed statements renouncing violence. A guerrilla leader of *al-Jihad,* Abdul-Aziz al-SHERIF, described as a longtime associate of al-Zawahiri, had also prepared a renunciation of extremism from his prison cell. Al-Sherif was also affiliated with the Islamic Group, and known as the man who "crafted al-Qaida's guide to jihad." Such prison dissensions were said to have caused rifts within al-Qaida.

Islamic Group (*Al-Gamaa al-Islamiya*). The Islamic Group surfaced in the late 1970s as the student wing of the Muslim Brotherhood, subsequently breaking from that organization and aligning (until the mid-1980s) with *al-Jihad* in seeking overthrow of the government. Popular among the poor in Cairo slums and villages in southern Egypt, it served as a loosely knit, but highly militant, umbrella organization for many smaller organizations. The government accused the group of spearheading attacks on security forces, government officials, and tourists beginning in 1992, and hanged a number of its members who had been convicted of terrorist activity.

Egyptian authorities in the mid-1990s asked the United States to extradite Sheikh Omar ABDEL RAHMAN, the blind theologian who is reputed to be the spiritual leader of the Islamic Group and had been in self-imposed exile in the New York City area since 1990. In April 1994 Sheikh Abdel Rahman was sentenced in absentia by an Egyptian security court to seven years in prison for inciting his followers to violence. In January 1996 Sheikh Abdel Rahman was sentenced to life in prison in the United States following his conviction on charges of conspiring to commit a series of bombings in the New York City area, including as mastermind of the 1993 World Trade Center bombing. Meanwhile, Safwat Abd al-GHANI, viewed as the political leader of the Group, was confined to prison in Egypt on a charge of illegal weapons possession.

Talaat Yassin HAMMAN, described by Egyptian authorities as the "military commander" of the Islamic Group, was killed by security forces in April 1994. His "intended successor," Ahmad Hassan Abd al-GALIL, also died in a shoot-out with police. After Galil died, Group military activities were led by Mustapha HAMZA and Rifai TAHA, apparently based in Afghanistan.

Two members of the Group were executed in February 1995 after being convicted of a bombing in which a German tourist was killed, while two others were executed in late March for the attempted killing of Nobel laureate Naguib MAHFOUZ in October 1994. The Egyptian government also accused the Group of being behind a June 1995 attempt on the life of President Mubarak in Ethiopia.

In mid-1996 a faction of the Islamic Group signaled an interest in negotiations with the government. However, that possibility was rejected by the Mubarak administration. Still, spokespersons for the Group emphasized that it had reached "political maturity" and had renounced violence in favor of joining the political process. Through mid-2005, Islamic Group members still committed to violence reportedly joined al-Qaida. In April 2006, it was reported that Egyptian authorities had released 950 members of the organization, though officials denied having released that number and said those who were released posed no risk to national security.

After the fall of Mubarak in 2011, Group members Tareq and Aboud al-ZUMR were released after 30 years of imprisonment for their roles in the assassination of Anwar Sadat. Tareq Zumr applied for recognition of the Group's political wing—the **Building and Development Party** (*al-Banna' wa al-Tanmiyya*)—but the party was found in violation of the March 2011 law forbidding parties formed solely around religious tenets. However, the government reversed its initial decision, granting the party official status in October. It joined the Islamist Alliance (see Coalitions, below), and won 13 seats in the People's Assembly during 2011–2012 parliamentary voting.

Building and Development Party Leaders: Tareq ZUMR (Secretary General), Safwat Abdel GHANY, Shathly Al-SAGHEER and Ashraf TAWFIK.

Also subject to government crackdowns have been the fundamentalist **Islamic Liberation Party** (*Hizb al-Tahrir al-Islami*), banned since 1974, and the obscure Islamic group **Islamic Pride Brigades of the Land of the Nile** that claimed responsibility for a 2005 bombing in Cairo.

Postrevolutionary Parties:

After the fall of Hosni Mubarak in 2011, a host of groups applied for and were granted legal status. These parties include the following:

Freedom and Justice Party—FJP (*Hizb al Horriya W'Alaadala*). The political arm of Egypt's Muslim Brotherhood, the FJP identified itself as civic-minded so as to allay public fears of an Islamist agenda. The largest and best organized of Egypt's parties, the FJP parlayed its organizational strength into unheralded success during parliamentary polling in 2011–2012. Running as the senior member of the Democratic Alliance, the FJP won more than 43 percent of the Assembly's elective seats, and over 58 percent of the available seats in the Shura Council. FJP member Mohammed Saad Tawfik al-KATATNI was elected speaker of the Assembly, and member Ahmed FAHMY was named Shura Council speaker. In February 2012, FJP put forward Muslim Brotherhood strategist Mohammad Khairat al-Shater as its candidate for the May presidential elections. However, the military government rejected al-Shater's candidacy, forcing the FJP to turn to its chair Mohammed Morsi to be its presidential candidate. In early 2013 Saad Al-KATATNI was elected party chair.

Leaders: Saad Al-KATATNI (Chair), Essam el-ERIAN (Vice Chair), Rafiq HABIB (Deputy), Mohammad Al-BELTAGI (Secretary General).

Reform and Development-Misruna Party (*al-Islah wal-Tanmiya*). Founded in 2009 by a nephew of former president Anwar Sadat, Esmat Sadat, this leftist-oriented party gained legal status in May 2011. The following month it merged with Ramy LAKKAH's party, **Our Egypt** (*Misruna*), but retained the name Reform and Development. The party ran independently in the 2011–2012 parliamentary elections, winning ten seats in the Assembly.

Leaders: Mohammed Anwar Esmat al-SADAT (President), Ramy LAKKAH.

Egyptian Socialist Democratic Party (*Hizb Al-Masri Al-Democrati*)—ESDP. Licensed March 2011, this leftist and secular party drew its inspiration from founding member Mohammed Abul GHAR, the physician who formerly spearheaded the Enough (*Kifaya*) movement. It also incorporated members from both the National Association for Change and the Justice and Freedom youth movement. The ESDP joined the Egyptian Bloc, and represented 40 percent of Bloc candidates. In 2011–2012 elections the party won 16 seats in the People's Assembly and 3 seats in the Shura Council.

Leaders: Mohammed Abul GHAR (Chair), Hazem EL-BEBLAWI, Farid ZAHRAN, Ziad al-ELEIMI, Samer SOLIMAN.

The Egyptians Citizen Party (*Hizb al-Mowaten al-Masri*). A refuge of former NDP members, this party is led by the former secretary general of the NDP, Mohamed RAGAB. Construction mogul Alaa HASABALLAH was a key figure in the founding of the party in July 2011. The party won four seats in the People's Assembly in 2012.

Renaissance Party (*Hizb el-Nahda*). Former Muslim Brotherhood member Abd El-Monem Abou El-FOTOUH formed el-Nahda after he was expelled from the Brotherhood in 2011 for announcing his candidacy for president. Fotouh was joined in the party by former Brotherhood deputy supreme guide Mohamed HABIB. Fotouh ran for president in 2012 as an independent.

Free Egyptians Party (*Hizb Al-Massreyeen al-Ahrrar*). This liberal party was founded by the Coptic businessman Naguib SAWIRIS and identified itself as a secular alternative to the FJP. Coptic Christians flocked to the party, with some estimating that Copts represented 70 percent of the membership. Free Egyptians allied with the Egyptian Bloc in 2011, and won 15 seats in the Assembly and 3 seats in the Shura Council.

Light Party (*Hizb al-Nour*). Al-Nour was the first post-revolutionary Salafist party given legal status by the government. Led by Emad Abdel GHOFOUR, the goals of al-Nour—such as the establishment of sharia and the end of bank usury—placed it squarely in the Islamist group of parties. In 2011 al-Nour established the Islamic Alliance with two other Salafist parties in order to compete in the 2011–2012 parliamentary elections. Al-Nour's success in polling surprised many observers, as they took the second-highest amount of seats in both the Assembly (109) and Shura Council (45). However, party members found that shared Islamic identities did not endear them to the FJP as political partners. In fact, al-Nour was only offered one post in the Morsi government, a post they rejected in protest.

Leaders: Younis MAKHYOUN (Chair), Emad Abdel GHOFOUR (Cofounder), Yasser BORHAMI, Hazem SHOUMAN.

Union Party (*Hizb al-Ithad*). The Union Party was founded on September 19, 2011, by Hossam BADRAWI, former secretary-general of the NDP in the waning days of the Mubarak regime. Despite his close ties to Mubarak, Badrawi was widely perceived as a reformist. The party fielded candidates independently in the 2011–2012 parliamentary elections, winning three seats in the Assembly.

Freedom Party (*Hizb al-Horreya*). Another party with roots in the NDP, Freedom Party was founded in July 2011 by the sons of business mogul Mohammad Mahmoud Ali Hassan, Mamdouh and Moatz HASSAN. The majority of party members are from Upper Egypt, with strong support coming from Luxor. Freedom ran candidates independently in the 2011–2012 parliamentary elections, winning three seats in the Assembly and two seats in the Shura Council.

Beginning Party (*Hizb al-Bedaya*). Beginning attracted many former NDP members with its centrist, business-oriented program. The party became official in August 2011, thanks to the efforts of founder Mahmoud Hossam Eddin GALAL—a former police officer and current businessman. Reportedly, many Egyptian expatriates have joined the party. In the 2012 presidential election, Galal ran as the Beginning Party candidate, receiving almost 24,000 votes.

Arab Egyptian Union Party. Secular and centrist in philosophy, the Arab Egyptian Union is committed to unifying Egypt with the Sudan in order to create an Arabist commercial and cultural bloc, thereby returning Egypt to a predominate political role in the Middle East. The party won one seat in the 2011–2012 Assembly elections.

Leader: Amr Al-Mukhtar SAMIDA (Chairman).

Justice Party (*Hizb al-Adl*). Most members of this party migrated to it from the National Association for Change, a decentralized group of young people whose efforts in the mobilization of popular protest helped bring down the Mubarak government. *Al-Adl* adopted a centrist agenda that differentiated it from the Islamists but at the same time accepted that Islam and Egyptian society are inextricably linked. Founder Mostafa NAGGAR had been a member of both the Muslim Brotherhood and the Revolution's Youth Coalition. In 2011 the party briefly allied with the DA, but later reversed course, running its candidates independently. The party won two seats in 2011–2012 People's Assembly balloting.

Leaders: Mostafa NAGGAR, Mohammed GABAR, Ahmed SHOUKRI, Abdel Muniem IMAM, Hisham AKRAM.

The **Center Party** (*Hizb al-Wasat*). As an offshoot of the Muslim Brotherhood founded by Abdul-Ela MADI, *al-Wasat* predates the January 25 revolution that toppled the Mubarak regime, yet it did not obtain official party status until February 2011. The party ran its candidates for parliament in 2011–2012 independently, winning nine seats in the Assembly. Both Madi and leading member Essam SULTAN were arrested in July 2013 for their criticism of the military coup that ousted President Morsi as well as for inciting violence.

Leaders: Abdul-Ela MADI (Founder and President), Essam SULTAN (Leading Party Member), Salah Abd al-KARIM.

Socialist Popular Alliance Party (*Hizb al-Tahaluf al-Shabi al-Ishtiraki*)—SPA. The party is secular and socialist in orientation and was officially recognized as a political party in September 2011. It has attracted former members of a variety of leftist organizations, including from parties such as Tagammu. It became affiliated with both the Coalition of Socialist Forces and The Revolution Continues Alliance. The latter alliance won eight seats in the 2011–2012 parliamentary elections, but since the SPA was the only licensed party in the grouping its candidates were awarded all eight seats. The party's candidate in the 2012 presidential election, Abul Ezz al-HARIRI, polled 40,000 votes.

Leaders: Amr Abdel RAHMAN (Cofounder), Khaled Al-SAYED, Emad ATEYYA, Wael GAMAL.

Egyptian Civilization Party (*Hizb al-Hadara*). Officially recognized in April 2011, the Egyptian Civilization Party is a secular party that advocates a centrist approach to governance, with a focus upon renewing Egypt's civilization through art and culture. It joined the Democratic Alliance and shared in the success of being teamed with the FJP. In won two seats in the 2011–2012 parliamentary polling.

Leaders: Mohamed al-SAWY (President and Founder, People's Assembly MP), Hatem KHATER (Leading Member), Hatem Abu Bakr Ahmed AZZAM (People's Assembly MP).

Dignity Party (*Hizb al-Karama*). Founded in 1996 by Hamdeen SABAHI, Dignity was not sanctioned by the government until August 2011. Sabahi had once represented the defunct Democratic Arab Nasserite Party in the Assembly, explaining this party's leftist, socialist, Nasserite orientation. During the 2011–2012 parliamentary elections, the party won eight seats in the Assembly. Sabahi ran as the party's candidate in the 2012 presidential elections, coming in third in the preliminary round of balloting with 21 percent of the vote.

Authenticity Party (*Hizb al-Asala*). The second Salafist party to become recognized by the government, *al-Asala* gained official status in August 2011. The party was founded by Salafi preacher Adel Abd al-Maqsoud AFIFY and garnered support from other Salafi clerics. As a junior member of the Islamic Alliance anchored by al-Nour, *al-Asala* benefitted from the former party's strong electoral success. The party won three seats in the 2011–2012 People's Assembly election and placed a candidate, Abdullah ALASHAAL, on the 2012 presidential election ballot.

Leaders: Adel Abd al-Maqsoud AFIFY (Founder and President), Mamdouh ISMAEL (Vice President), Ihab Mohammed Ali SHEEHA (Founder), Mohamed Ibrahim Abdel Fattah SULTAN (Founder).

National Party of Egypt (*Hizb Masr Al-Qawmi*). This party was founded by and attracted former NDP members. It received official status in August 2011, aided by its founding member Talaat al-SADAT—nephew of the late president Anwar Sadat. Key members include television and magazine producers, with a bulk its members situated in Lower Egypt. Running independently, the party won five Assembly seats in 2011–2012 voting.

Leader: Talaat AL-SADAT (Founder).

Constitution Party (*Hizb al-Dostour*). Led by Nobel Prize winner Mohammed ElBaradei, *al-Dostour* offers a centrist option between political Islam and military autocracy. Aimed at the disaffected youth who drove the 2011 revolution, the party sought to unite disparate groups that have a viable political message but no effective structure or leadership. In 2013 the party experienced significant infighting that resulted in the loss of many rank-and-file members as well as Deputy Chairman Hossam EISSA.

Leaders: Mohammed ELBARADEI (Founder), Ahmed El-HAWARY (Cofounder), Gameela ISMAIL (Secretary).

A number of parties licensed in 2011 and early 2012 were unable to produce electoral gains in parliamentary or presidential elections. The **Unity and Freedom Party,** primarily a Shia party, advocates secular goals and attracted some prominent Egyptian intellectuals such as Rasem al-NAFIS. **The Pioneers** (*Al-Riyada*) is a splinter group from the reformist camp of the Muslim Brotherhood. **Egypt Revival Party** (*Misr El-Nahda*), a refuge for former NDP members, presented a secular agenda mixed with free-market economics. The **Egypt Renaissance Party** (*Hizb Nahdet Masr*) was formed by Ahmed Abul-NAZAR, a prominent businessman from Lower Egypt and former NDP member of parliament (MP). The **Reform and Awakening Party**, based in Alexandria, is a centrist party that has called for social reform with an Islamic reference. The **Arab Justice and Equality Party** was founded by former development minister Hassaballah al-KAFRAWI and draws its support from Egypt's Bedouins. **Modern Egypt Party** (*Masr al-Hadytha*) is another party that attracted businesspeople with ties to the former NDP. Founder Nabil DEIBIS fashioned a liberal, secular agenda that featured a free-market political economy. **Freedom Egypt Party** was founded by Amr HAMZAWY, a young parliamentarian from Heliopolis. **Reform and Renaissance Party** (*Hizb al Eslah w Alnahdha*) is a centrist-oriented party founded by Ayman MORSI and Hisham Mostafa ABDEL AZIZ. **Al-Haq** was founded by Meriam MELAD and is the first Egyptian party concerned primarily with human rights. The **Flag Party** (*Hizb al-Raya*) is a Salafist party led by influential cleric and disqualified presidential candidate Hazem Salah ABU-ISMAIL. Ismail was arrested in August 2013 for murder and intimidation of citizens. The **Egyptian Popular Current** (*Al-Tayer al-Shabi al-Masr*) was founded late 2012 by Hamdeen Sabahi as a Nasserite party dedicated to counterbalancing the Islamist orientation of the Morsi government.

In January 2013 former al-Nour Party chair Emad Abdel Ghofour founded the **Homeland Party** (*Hizb Al-Watan*). *Al-Watan* sought to build a wide coalition of Salafist parties including *Al-Raya*, *Al-Asala*, the newly formed **People's Party** (*Hizb al-Shaab*), and three others. Former presidential candidate and ousted Brotherhood member Abdel-Moneim Abul-Fotouh founded the **Strong Egypt Party** (*Hizb Masr al-Qaweya*) as a reaction to the Morsi presidency. Another former presidential candidate, Ahmed Shafik, established the **Egyptian Patriotic Movement** along with former Free Egyptians Party vice-chairman Mohamed Abu HAMED.

Coalitions: Three main electoral coalitions formed after the 2011 revolution, and two more formed after the election of President Morsi in 2012. At one point the **Democratic Alliance** (DA) contained most of the Islamist parties in league with such liberal and secularist parties as the NWP and *al-Ghad.* The **Egypt Bloc** (EB) attracted liberal and secular parties—15 of them at one point. The third major alliance, formed exclusively by Islamist parties, solidified only two months before the 2011 Assembly elections. The **Islamic Alliance** included three parties: *al-Nour, al-Asala,* and Building and Development.

One minor coalition also played a role in the 2011–2012 parliamentary elections. **The Revolution Continues** Alliance, also referred to as **Completing the Revolution** (*Istikmal al-Thawra*), included the **Egypt Freedom Party, Egyptian Current Party** (*Al-Tayar al-Masry*), **Egyptian Liberation Party** (*Al-Tahrir al-Masry*), **Socialist Popular Alliance Party, *al-Nahda*,** and **Equality and Development Party**—as well as some unofficial groups. The alliance won eight seats in the 2011–2012 parliamentary elections.

Two broad coalitions formed after Morsi became president in July 2012: the **National Salvation Front** (NSF) and the **Egyptian Conference Party** (ECP). The ECP was composed of 25 left-leaning parties and secular groups and led by former Arab League general secretary Amr MOUSSA. In July 2013 Moussa stepped down and was replaced by Mohammad EL-ORABY, the former foreign affairs minister during SCAF rule in 2011. The NSF was formed a few months after the ECP and also represented many leftist parties—such as the Constitution Party, NPUP, and NWP. Before his departure, Moussa yoked the ECP to the National Salvation Front and, along with Mohammad ElBaradei and Hamdeen Sababi, became part of the NSF's leadership. After the military overthrew of Morsi, the NSF's raison d'etre was mooted, and observers conjectured that the coalition would not hold because it was not suited to electoral politics.

LEGISLATURE

As sanctioned by a popular referendum in April 1979, President Sadat dissolved the unicameral People's Assembly (*Majlis al-Shaab*) and announced expansion of the body from 350 to 392 members, in part to accommodate representatives from the Sinai. Prior to the election of May 27, 1984, the assembly was further expanded to 458 members, including 10 appointed by the president. In 1990 the assembly was reduced to 454 members, including the 10 presidential appointees.

In 2009 a new law expanded the assembly to 518 seats, with 64 seats being reserved for women. The measure created 32 new districts for women candidates only, as well as another 4 seats for women in densely populated districts, and 2 designated seats for rural areas. The Muslim Brotherhood and other opponents claimed the new law was unconstitutional and circumvented the right to equal opportunity.

In 2011 the military caretaker government instituted new rules for the People's Assembly, deciding that parliamentary elections would be held in September for a body consisting of 498 popularly elected seats and 10 seats appointed by the government. The provision of seats and districts carved out for female candidates was struck from the law. In July secular party leaders pushed for radical constitutional revisions prior to the election, a factor that delayed the elections until late November.

The election law approved by the SCAF in July 2011 created a hybrid in which one-third of the seats in the People's Assembly were decided by a majoritarian system in 83 two-member districts, where one winning member was required to be a worker or farmer. The remaining two-thirds of the seats were decided by a proportional representation system in large districts where from 4 to 12 seats were awarded to candidates heading closed party lists. Such an electoral system favored the Muslim Brotherhood because of its strong nationwide system of organization, as candidates used to relying on personal popularity in small districts found it necessary to ally with the Brotherhood's FJP—the party best suited to compete in the new, greatly expanded constituencies.

The first round of legislative elections took place November 28–29, 2011, with runoffs December 5–6. Polling stations were overwhelmed, and the turnout rate was more than 52 percent. The coalition of parties led by the FJP captured almost 50 percent of the seats, while the Salafist coalition led by al-Nour won 24 percent. The Egyptian Bloc parties won 13 percent of the seats, followed by New Wafd with 7 percent. The second round of the election was held December 14–15, with runoffs December 21–22. The 43 percent turnout rate for this round was significantly lower than round one, but the distribution of votes was very similar. The third and final round of People's Assembly voting spanned January 3–4, with runoffs taking place January 10–11. Again, the FJP and the Islamic Alliance took more than 70 percent of the vote.

When it met for the first time on January 23, 2012, the seats in the People's Assembly were dominated by Islamist MPs, with the following seat distribution: the FJP, 216; *al-Nour,* 109; New Wafd, 41; ESDP, 16; Free Egyptians, 15; Building and Development, 13; Reform and Development, 10; *al-Wasat,* 8; *al-Karama,* 6; Egypt National Party, 5; Egyptian Citizen Party, 4; *al-Asala,* 3; Union Party, 3; Freedom Party, 3; *al-Tagammu,* 3; *al-Hadara,* 2; *al-Adl,* 2; Democratic Peace Party, 2; Labor, 1; Arab Egyptian Union Party, 1; Naserite Party, 1; and various independents, 25. Together the Islamist parties—FJP, *al-Nour, al-Asala,* and Building and Development—occupied over 68 percent of all the seats. Of the 508 MPs, only 12 were women and 13 were Christians.

The Constitution of 2012 renamed the assembly the House of Representatives and expanded the number of seats to 546. However, other than one ad-hoc session immediately after Morsi was elected president, the assembly did not meet throughout his brief tenure.

Former Speaker: Mohammed Saad Tawfik Al KATATNI (FJP).

Elections for 180 seats in the 270-seat Shura Council (*Majlis al-Shura*), the consultative body sometimes referred to as the Upper House, were held in two stages spanning 21 days in January and February 2012. Turnout was 10 percent, with the Islamic parties taking over 83 percent of the seats. The party distribution for the elective seats was FJP, 105; *al-Nour,* 45; New Wafd, 14; Egyptian Bloc, 8; Freedom Party, 2; Democratic Peace Party, 2; and independents, 4. The remaining 90 seats were to be appointed by the president.

With the People's Assembly dissolved, the Shura Council assumed the role of chief legislative body from June 2012 until July 2013. However, the Supreme Constitutional Court undermined the council's legitimacy when it invalidated the election of its members with a June 2013 ruling. When the military removed President Morsi from power a month later, it also dissolved the Shura Council.

Former Speaker: Ahmed FAHMY (FJP).

CABINET

[as of September 1, 2013]

Prime Minister	Hazem El-Beblawi
Deputy Prime Minster and Minister of Defense	Abdel-Fattah Al-Sisi
Deputy Prime Minster and Minister of Higher Education	Hossam Eissa
Deputy Prime Minister and Minister for International Cooperation	Ziad Bahaa El-Din
Ministers	
Agriculture	Ayman Abu Hadid
Civil Aviation	Abdel-Aziz Fadel
Culture	Mohamed Saber Arab
Education	Mahmoud Abul-Nasr
Electricity and Energy	Ahmed Imam
Foreign Affairs	Nabil Fahmy
Industry and Foreign Trade	Mounir Fakhry Abdel-Nour
Health	Maha El-Rabat [f]
Housing, Utilities, and Urban Development	Ibrahim Mehleb
Information	Dorreya Sharaf El-Din [f]
Interior	Mohamed Ibrahim
Planning	Ashraf El-Arabi
Investment	Osama Saleh
Irrigation	Mohamed Abdel-Muttalib
Local Development	Adel Labib
Manpower	Kamal Abu-Eita
Petroleum and Mineral Resources	Sherif Ismail
Religious Endowments	Mohamed Mokhtar Gomaa
Social Solidarity and Social Justice	Ahmed El-Borai
Tourism	Hisham Zaazou
Antiquities	Mohamed Ibrahim
Youth	Khaled Abdel-Aziz
Environment	Laila Rashed Iskandar [f]
Sports	Taher Abu Zeid
Military Production	Reda Hafez
Scientific Research	Ramzy George
Telecommunications and Information Technology	Atef Helmy
Finance	Ahmed Galal
Manpower	Kamal Abu-Eita
Supply	Mohamed Abu Shadi
Transitional Justice and National Reconciliation	Mohamed Amin El-Mahdy
Justice	Abdul Abdul-Hamid
Administrative Development	Hany Mahmoud
Transport	Ibrahim Al-Demeri

[f] = female

INTERGOVERNMENTAL REPRESENTATION

Ambassador to the U.S.: Mohamed Mostafa Mohamed TAWFIK.

U.S. Ambassador to Egypt: Anne W. PATTERSON.

Permanent Representative to the UN: Mootaz Ahmadein KHALIL.

IGO Memberships (Non-UN): AfDB, AU, Comesa, IOM, LAS, NAM, OIC, WTO.

EL SALVADOR

Republic of El Salvador
República de El Salvador

Political Status: Part of the Captaincy General of Guatemala that declared independence from Spain in September 1821; member of the United Provinces of Central America that was launched in 1823; status as independent political entity formalized in constitution of 1841; the Republic of El Salvador formally established in constitution of 1859; constitution of 1962 suspended following the military coup of October 15, 1979; provisional government superseded following promulgation of new constitution on December 20, 1983; peace treaty with Farabundo

Martí National Liberation Front (FMLN) guerrillas (effective February 1) signed January 16, 1992.

Area: 8,124 sq. mi. (21,041 sq. km).

Population: 6,251,495 (2013E—UN); 6,108,590 (2013E—U.S. Census).

Major Urban Centers (2005E): SAN SALVADOR (508,000), Soyapango (295,000), Mejicanos (189,000), San Miguel (183,000), Santa Ana (179,000).

Official Language: Spanish.

Monetary Unit: Effective January 1, 2001, El Salvador adopted the U.S. dollar as its currency.

President: Carlos Mauricio FUNES Cartagena (supported by the Farabundo Martí National Liberation Front); elected on March 15, 2009, and inaugurated for a five-year term on June 1, succeeding Elías Antonio ("Tony") SACA González (Nationalist Republican Alliance).

Vice President: Salvador SÁNCHEZ CERÉN (Farabundo Martí National Liberation Front); elected on March 15, 2009, and inaugurated on June 1 for a term concurrent with that of the president, succeeding Ana Vilma ALBANEZ de Escobar (Nationalist Republican Alliance).

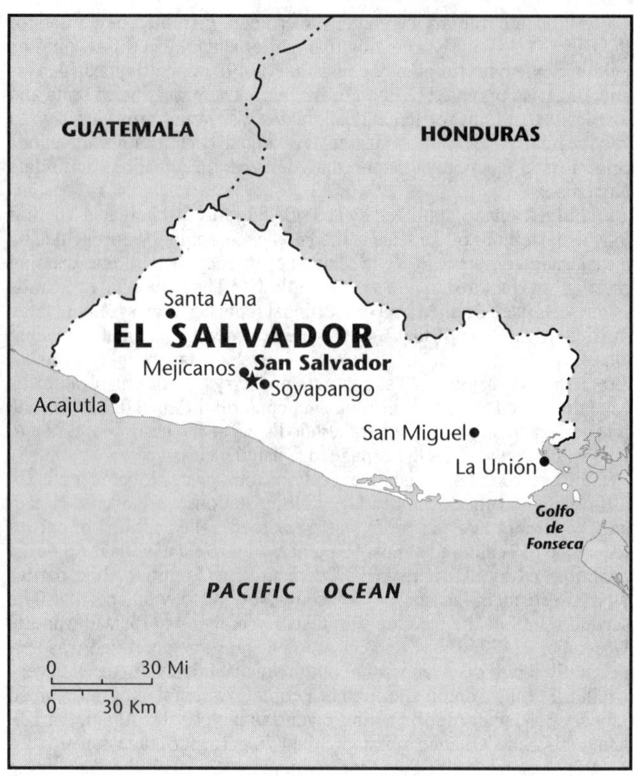

THE COUNTRY

The smallest of the Central American countries and the only one whose territory does not touch the Caribbean Sea, El Salvador is oriented geographically and, to some extent, psychologically toward the Pacific and the other isthmus countries. Its population density is the highest in the Americas, while its per capita income is among the lowest. Although there is a small Indian minority, the people are largely of mixed Spanish and Indian descent, with 86 percent classified as mestizo. The Catholic Church is predominant, but Protestant and Jewish faiths are represented. Women constitute approximately 47 percent of the paid labor force, concentrated largely in domestic and human service sectors and in manufacturing; female participation in government is minimal.

Traditionally dependent on agriculture, with coffee as the primary cash crop, El Salvador—before the domestic instability generated by the coup of October 1979—had become the region's leading exporter of manufactured goods. The industrial sector as a whole now accounts for about 30 percent of GDP, while agriculture contributes only 10 percent and services, 60 percent. Most of the country's trade occurs with the United States and neighboring Central American nations.

In 2001 El Salvador adopted the U.S. dollar as its currency in an effort to stabilize exchange rates and attract foreign investment. Growth averaged 2.0 percent annually in 2000–2010, registering 1.4 percent in 2011 and 1.3 percent in 2012. Unemployment stood at 5.8 percent for both 2010 and 2011 but rose to 6.9 percent in 2012. Remittances equaled $3.64 billion in 2011. In January 2009 the IMF approved $800 million in standby funds to bolster the economy in the wake of the global downturn, while noting that Salvadoran authorities did not intend to draw on the funds. An IMF Standby Agreement (SBA) valued at $790 million replaced the earlier 2009 arrangement in March 2010, and the World Bank and Inter-American Development Bank have provided loans of $600 million and $450 million, respectively.

In October 2011, Tropical Depression 12E unleashed one of the worst disasters in El Salvador's history. Total losses were estimated at $840 million—4 percent of GDP.

GOVERNMENT AND POLITICS

Political background. After the colonies comprising the Captaincy General of Guatemala declared their independence from Spain in 1821, a period of conflict ensued with Mexico over perceived Mexican domination efforts. El Salvador subsequently joined Costa Rica, Guatemala, Honduras, and Nicaragua in forming the United Provinces of Central America in 1823. In the wake of the collapse of that star-crossed federation into civil war in 1838, El Salvador formally declared its status as an independent entity in a constitution adopted in 1841. Many constitutional revisions were subsequently enacted during ongoing political turbulence throughout the rest of the 1800s, which also included several abortive attempts to recreate a Central American Federation. However, El Salvador enjoyed periods of relative calm during the first three decades of the 20th century and again from 1950 to 1960. Lt. Col. Oscar OSIRIO ruled from 1950 to 1956 and was succeeded by an elected president, Lt. Col. José María LEMUS, but a coup d'état in 1960 overthrew Lemus and inaugurated a period of renewed instability.

A new constitution was promulgated in January 1962 and an election was held the following April, although the opposition did not participate. Col. Julio Adalberto RIVERA, candidate of the recently organized National Conciliation Party (*Partido de Conciliación Nacional*—PCN), was certified as president and served a five-year term. Subsequent PCN victories brought Gen. Fidel SÁNCHEZ Hernández and Col. Arturo Armando MOLINA Barraza to power in 1967 and 1972, respectively, but announcement of the 1972 results provoked an unsuccessful coup by leftist forces, in the wake of which their candidate, José Napoleón DUARTE Fuentes, was exiled.

Following the election of February 20, 1977, the PCN candidate, Gen. Carlos Humberto ROMERO Mena, was declared president-elect with a majority of 67 percent of the votes cast, although the opposition, as in 1972, charged the government with massive electoral irregularities. The PCN won 50 of 54 seats in the legislative election of March 18, 1978, which was boycotted by most of the opposition because of inadequate assurances that the tabulation of results would be impartial.

In the wake of rapidly escalating conflict between right- and left-wing groups, General Romero was ousted on October 15, 1979, in a coup led by Col. Jaime Abdul GUTIÉRREZ and Col. Adolfo Arnoldo MAJANO Ramos, who were joined by three civilians on October 17 in a five-man ruling junta. While appealing to extremist forces to respect "the will of the majority" and aid in the installation of a "true democracy," the junta was actively opposed by leftist elements protesting military rule, and a state of siege, lifted on October 23, was reimposed three days later. On March 3 the Christian Democratic Party (*Partido Demócrata Cristiano*—PDC) presidential candidate, José Napoleón Duarte, who had returned from exile after the October coup, was added to the cabinet after a minister resigned.

In April 1980 the Revolutionary Democratic Front (*Frente Democrático Revolucionario*—FDR), a coalition of 18 leftist and far-leftist groups, including a dissident faction of the PDC, superseded the **Revolutionary Coordination of the Masses** (*Coordinadora Revolucionaria de las Masas*—CRM), an earlier group organized to oppose the PDC-military coalition. Subsequently, the major guerrilla organizations formed the Farabundo Martí National Liberation Front (*Frente

Farabundo Martí para la Liberación National—FMLN) to serve as the FDR's military affiliate. In the wake of these and other developments, the junta was reorganized on December 3, with Duarte and the increasingly hard-line Gutiérrez being sworn in as its president and vice president, respectively, on December 22.

In the election of March 28, 1982, the Christian Democrats secured the largest number of seats (24) in the 60-member assembly. However, four right-wing parties collectively constituted a majority and refused to permit Duarte to continue as president. The ensuing interparty negotiations resulted in a deadlock, with the Christian Democrats insisting on representation in the new government proportional to their share of the vote. On April 22 the assembly convened for its first session and elected Major d'Aubuisson as its president by a vote of 35–22. In a presidential election limited by the military's list of acceptable candidates, an independent, Dr. Alvaro MAGAÑA Borja, was accepted by the assembly on April 29 and sworn in on May 2. Two days later a tripartite administration was formed.

The move toward democracy generated no reprieve from insurgent activity. Nonetheless, the five parties represented in the Constituent Assembly agreed in August 1983 to establish a multiparty commission to prepare a timetable for new elections. Following promulgation of a revised constitution on December 20, the assembly approved presidential balloting for March 1984 and legislative and municipal elections for March 1985.

The 1984 election was contested by eight candidates, the acknowledged front-runners being d'Aubuisson and Duarte, neither of whom secured a majority. In a runoff on May 6, Duarte emerged the clear winner, with 53.6 percent of the vote, and was inaugurated on June 1.

The FDR-FMLN refused to participate in the election and increased military activity, but agreed to peace talks in late 1984. The talks, held in the guerrilla-held town of La Palma on October 15, were hailed as "historic," but FMLN insistence on "purification" of the armed forces through the integration of guerrilla elements proved a stumbling block for future talks, which were suspended altogether in January 1985.

The Christian Democrats unexpectedly swept the March 1985 election, winning 33 seats in the National Assembly and control of 200 of the country's 262 municipalities. The defeat of Arena, which had inhibited land reform measures and blocked Duarte's efforts in the areas of human rights and peace negotiation, was taken as evidence that traditional rightists in the business sector and the military had shifted to the PDC, the former heartened by negotiations with the IMF and the latter welcoming U.S. military aid funds and training that had measurably enhanced the armed forces' firepower and counterinsurgency capability.

Public discontent was fueled by the government's 1986 economic austerity plan, which included a 100 percent currency devaluation, tax increases, and a doubling of gasoline prices. Business leaders charged Duarte with "bowing to the dictates of the IMF," while labor unrest intensified. On February 21 thousands marched in San Salvador to protest sharp increases in the cost of living, which had risen by more than 125 percent since 1980.

Through the mediation of Peruvian President Alan García, the first meeting in more than a year between government and rebel representatives was held in Lima, Peru, in May 1986. However, Duarte's close advisor, Minister of Culture Julio REY Prendes, insisted that the administration had been "deceived" into believing that the opposition leaders would be speaking for their individual parties rather than on behalf of the FMLN, and the talks were quickly suspended.

On the basis of a peace plan advanced by the five Central American presidents in August 1987, discussions with FDR-FMLN representatives resumed in San Salvador in early October. However, the government insisted that the rebels lay down their arms as a precondition for inclusion in the "democratic" process and the talks again foundered. In legislative balloting in March 1988, Arena won a near majority of 30 seats, with the PDC and PCN winning 23 and 7, respectively. Two months later Arena secured an absolute majority as the result of a PCN crossover.

In November 1987, Dr. Guillermo UNGO and Rubén ZAMORA Rivas, leaders, respectively, of the National Revolutionary Movement and the Popular Social Christian Movement, had announced the formation of a leftist Democratic Convergence (*Convergencia Democrática*—CD), with the declared aim of seeking a resolution to the conflict through electoral participation. Since the two also served as president and vice president of the FDR, the action provided a linkage between the legal political process and the insurgency. Following the 1988 legislative elections (for which the CD did not present candidates), it was announced that the new grouping would participate in the 1989 presidential campaign. (For background on the now-defunct CD, see the 2008 *Handbook.*)

In early 1989 the FMLN leadership advanced a plan whereby the rebels would lay down their arms if the government would agree to a number of stipulations, including a six-month delay in the balloting scheduled for March 19. While rejecting the plan as unconstitutional, the government (responding in part to intense U.S. pressure) agreed to participate in formal talks with the insurgents that commenced February 22 in Qaxtepec, Mexico. Four days later President Duarte offered to postpone the first-round voting until April 30, leaving sufficient time for a second round, if necessary, before the June 1 expiration of his five-year term. However, both the rebels and Arena rejected this proposal, with Arena candidate Alfredo CRISTIANI Burkard securing the presidency on the basis of a 53.8 to 36.6 percent single-round victory over the PDC nominee, Fidel CHÁVEZ Mena.

Protracted negotiations, punctuated by a series of rebel offensives, culminated in a meeting in Mexico City (the first to be attended by FMLN field commanders) held April 4–27, 1991, which yielded a tentative package of constitutional amendments. During further talks in Caracas, Venezuela, in late May the two sides endorsed the formation of a human rights monitoring team, the United Nations Observer Mission in El Salvador, whose initial contingent was deployed on July 26. Two months later, during a New York meeting on September 25, Cristiani and FMLN representatives reached general agreement on a permanent cease-fire to end the bloody 12-year conflict. On January 16, 1992, a treaty (incorporating a formal cessation of hostilities on February 1) was signed in Mexico City. Despite setbacks that delayed completion of the peace process by two months, demobilization of both rebel units and the government's notorious Immediate Reaction Infantry Battalions was completed on December 15, 1992, at which time the war was declared over and the FMLN was legally certified as a political party.

Heading a leftist coalition, Rubén Zamora was defeated in second-round presidential balloting on April 24, 1994, by Arena's Armando CALDERÓN Sol. Subsequently, splits within both Arena and the FMLN led to withdrawals and the formation of new parties by the dissidents.

In the legislative balloting of March 16, 1997, Arena barely outpaced the FMLN, while in local contests leftists captured most of the country's major cities, including the capital, San Salvador. However, the leftist surge subsequently lost momentum, and Arena's Francisco FLORES easily outpolled six challengers to win the presidential poll of March 7, 1999, his nearly 52 percent of the vote precluding the need for runoff balloting. In the legislative election of March 2000, the FMLN captured a slim plurality of seats, but not enough to wrest control from the allied conservative forces of Arena, the Christian Democrats, and the PCN. The result was the same in March 2003, while Arena retained the presidency with the election of Antonio ("Tony") SACA on March 21, 2004.

The legislative distribution was not radically altered in the triennial balloting of March 12, 2006, although Arena replaced the FMLN as the plurality grouping by a gain of six seats.

Attention turned to the government's response to the economic crisis in the run-up to separate parliamentary and presidential elections in 2009. President Saca attempted to maintain support for the Arena party by appointing a committee of ministers to recommend solutions for dealing with rising food and fuel prices, and by cracking down on violent crime. Some 45 members of Mara Salvatrucha, a notorious gang, were subsequently detained in arrests across the country.

In parliamentary elections on January 18, 2009, the FMLN won 42 percent and 35 seats. Arena lost 2 seats but remained close behind the FMLN with a total of 32 seats in the new assembly. Three smaller parties won a total of 17 seats. While the FMLN won the most seats in the January 2009 legislative elections, it failed to gain a majority, paving the way for the Arena party to form minority coalitions to counter the new political heavyweight. The FMLN and Arena faced off again in the March presidential election following an acrimonious campaign season in which the Arena's Rodrigo AVILA, the former head of the national police, tried to maintain the party's hold on the government, implying that civil unrest would return if the FMLN's Mauricio FUNES, a popular television personality, was elected. Funes, the FMLN's first nonmilitant candidate, countered the attacks by alleging that Arena was prepared to carry out voter fraud to stay in power. Funes further distanced himself from party hard-liners and radical leftists by framing himself as a moderate similar to Brazilian president Lula da Silva, and he did not run as a member of the FMLN despite its support for his candidacy. Funes won a narrow victory in March, marking the end of Arena's power for the first time in 18 years.

Shortly after the new FMLN-led assembly was seated in June, political tensions heightened as Arena members in Congress blocked the confirmation of five Supreme Court judges and the attorney general, positions traditionally held by Arena members. The president's attempts to change these key officeholders posed an institutional crisis for the country as Arena initially refused to relinquish its authority over them. After weeks of deadlock in the legislature, the FMLN and Arena reached an agreement in which the presidency of the assembly went to Arena's ally Ciro Cruz ZEPEDA of the PCN and Arena's preferred candidate was named to head the Supreme Court.

President Funes launched a broad menu of new social programs, including free seeds for farmers and free shoes, milk, and books for students. Social spending rose from $35 million in 2008 to $201 million in 2012. He also promoted a moderate, business-friendly agenda and often turned to the new right-wing faction, **Grand Alliance for Change** (*Gran Alianza por la Unidad Nacional*—GANA), to back his efforts to win loans from international groups for infrastructure and social projects and to reform the voter registration system.

Funes strengthened ties with Washington, winning valuable endorsement and economic support from the Obama administration. He signed two agreements with the Millennium Challenge Corporation, one to develop the impoverished northern region of El Salvador, and a second in 2012 that would focus on airports, ports, and coastal zones. El Salvador also was one of four countries selected for the Partnership for Growth, an Obama administration program that identifies "constraints to economic growth in the country" (crime and uncompetitive produces) and devises strategies to overcome them.

In January 2010 Funes offered the first formal apology by the state for abuses committed during the 12-year conflict that ended in 1992. Congress decreed on March 24 that the day henceforth would be celebrated as Msgr. Oscar Arnulfo Romero day. Critics derided the public pronouncements as insufficient and demanded that Funes repeal an amnesty law that prevented the prosecution of war crimes.

In July 2010 the Supreme Court ruled that the electoral system of closed-list ballots that required candidates to be members of political parties was unconstitutional. Under the system as it stood, the electorate voted for parties, and no candidates were listed on ballots. Seats were filled based on the percentage of votes won by a party and a list of candidates provided to the electoral authorities by the party leadership. In December the legislature passed a decree allowing independents to run. The new electoral rule took effect in time for the 2012 elections.

Congress approved a new law that made gang membership illegal on September 1, 2010. The government estimated that about 20,000 people were involved in gangs in late 2010. In response the Mara Salvatrucha and Barrio-18 gangs called a 72-hour nationwide bus strike on September 7–9 that brought the economy to a grinding halt. The gangs threatened violence against bus network employees who did not participate in the strike. As crime continued to surge, Funes reiterated in February 2011 that he did not see an end to the domestic deployment of soldiers from the armed forces, 7,000 of whom had been working in concert with the national police since November 2009 on orders of the president to battle lawlessness.

In April 2011 the Supreme Court decreed that the PDC and the PCN be stripped of official recognition as political parties because each had failed to garner 3 percent of the national vote during the 2004 presidential election. An earlier ruling was stayed in 2005 by the supreme electoral tribunal on the grounds that eliminating the parties would violate the constitution's guarantee of a plural political system, and the 3 percent minimum was waived by a legislative decree. The April Supreme Court ruling reversed the waiver, and the PDC and the PCN, two of the oldest parties active in El Salvador, were given six months to each collect 50,000 signatures of support to contest the March 2012 legislative and municipal elections.

The court's ruling, along with fears of judicial overreach, set the branches of government against each other. In June the legislation passed, and Funes signed a bill requiring the consent of all five of the court's justices for a ruling to have the force of law. The legislation was one of several actions seeking to reel in the independent court, created in 2009 to stop the politicization of the judiciary from eroding the entrenched power of political parties. Opponents of the law called it a "tragedy for democracy," and citizens and civil society groups protested. The legislature repealed the unanimity law at the end of July because of the widespread public outrage. The repeal was seen to strengthen the concept of an independent judiciary and civil society groups in El Salvador.

Reporters Without Borders ranked El Salvador 38th out of 179 countries in its 2013 Index of Press Freedom.

Constitution and government. The constitution adopted by the Constituent Assembly on December 6, 1983, provides for a president and vice president, both elected by direct popular vote for five-year terms, and for a unicameral National Assembly elected for a three-year term. The judicial system is headed by a Supreme Court, whose 15 members are elected by the assembly. Justices serve for nine years, and five are replaced every three years. The Supreme Court is divided into four chambers: constitutional, civil, penal, and administrative conflict. Governors appointed by the chief executive head the country's 14 departments.

Foreign relations. In the early 1980s, following allegations of aid to the FMLN by the Sandinista National Liberation Front (*Frente Sandinista de Liberación Nacional*—FSLN), or *sandinista,* regime in Nicaragua, cooperation between El Salvador, Guatemala, and Honduras increased. In October 1983, at the urging of the United States, a revival of the Central American Defense Council (Condeca), originally a four-member group that included Nicaragua, was announced in support of a joint approach to "extra-continental aggression of a Marxist-Leninist character." Although the truncated council undertook no formal action, El Salvador and Honduras cooperated during U.S. military maneuvers in the region in 1983–1984, as well as in attempts to interdict Nicaraguan arms shipments to Salvadoran rebel forces. On November 26, 1989, Cristiani severed diplomatic relations with Managua after a Nicaraguan-registered plane, loaded with Soviet SAM-7 missiles allegedly consigned to the FMLN, crashed in El Salvador.

During 1987–1988 El Salvador came under increasing criticism for the alleged misuse of U.S. aid funds, the economic and military components of which totaled more than $400 million in 1987 alone. Relations were further complicated by a U.S. district court ruling in April 1988 that a long-standing exodus of Salvadorans to the United States consisted largely of economically motivated illegal entrants, rather than of political refugees.

In October 1990 the U.S. Senate voted to withhold half of an $85 million military aid appropriation for El Salvador until the Cristiani government "demonstrated good faith" in talks with the FMLN, curbed military assassinations and abductions, and mounted a meaningful inquiry into a number of murders, including those of six Jesuit priests a year earlier. U.S. president George H. W. Bush finally released the funds after the killing of two U.S. airmen by rebels in January 1991. In September, 2 of 11 military personnel (a colonel and a lieutenant) were convicted of the Jesuit massacre.

In September 1992 a long-standing territorial dispute that had provoked a brief war between El Salvador and Honduras in 1969 was resolved by a World Court judgment. In addition to ruling on control of a number of coastal land "pockets" (*bolsones*), two-thirds of which were awarded to Honduras, the court decided that the waters of the Gulf of Fonseca were not international but a closed condominium of El Salvador, Honduras, and Nicaragua, which benefited Honduras by providing it with access to the Pacific Ocean. In September 1995 a Bi-National Commission set up to implement the judgment agreed that residents of the territory could choose either Salvadoran or Honduran nationality. In February 1998 Honduran and Salvadoran representatives signed two treaties on demarcation of their borders, about 70 percent of which remained in dispute. However, approval of the treaties by Honduras was not immediately forthcoming because of opposition objections to their terms. Claiming that the Goascoran River, used to define the border, had changed its course over the past 200 years, El Salvador in late 2002 appealed the 1992 ruling, but the bid was unsuccessful.

In June 1997 President Calderón met with U.S. legislators in Washington to seek relief from tough new U.S. immigration laws under which more than 300,000 undocumented Salvadorans could be subject to deportation. In addition to hardship for the expatriates, El Salvador could have lost up to $1 billion a year in remittances (which then accounted for 60 percent of export earnings and 15 percent of the country's GDP).

In 1996 El Salvador and Guatemala, with a combined 60 percent of Central America's GDP, agreed to combine their customs agencies. In early 2000 the accord was amplified by the signing of an Investment and Service Trade Treaty, with a free flow in goods and services expected by 2002.

In March 2000 the Flores government came under attack for agreeing to let the United States set up a logistics base for its war on drugs at a military sector of the international airport in Comalapa, 20 miles from the capital. The Legislative Assembly approved the pact on July 7 by a 49–35 vote, despite objections by the FMLN, which insisted that a three-quarters majority was necessary because the issue impinged on the nation's sovereignty.

In December 2004 El Salvador became the first Central American country to ratify the Central American Free Trade Agreement (CAFTA) with the United States. In April 2006 the presidents of Honduras and El Salvador signed documents marking the end of 26 years of border demarcation dispute and announced they would reactivate the plan to build the joint El Tigre hydroelectric power plant on the Honduras side of the river.

In early September 2005 El Salvador joined the United States, Mexico, Guatemala, and Honduras in a joint operation against the Mara Salvarucha gangs. Nearly 200 individuals were arrested and, in late November of that year, a military deployment was ordered against 10,000 Mara gang members estimated to be active in El Salvador.

El Salvador enjoys normal diplomatic and trade relations with all its neighbors, including Honduras, with whom it has disputes over maritime borders in the Gulf of Fonseca. Both countries agreed to settle the dispute in the International Court of Justice. The case remained unresolved in 2011.

Prospects for better relations with the United States improved with the inauguration of President Funes in June 2009. Concern had grown that the United States would cut economic aid after the left-wing FMLN took control of the government. However, Funes presented a pragmatic agenda upon taking office, emphasizing economic growth and social progress over the anti-imperialist focus voiced by the FMLN in the past. At the same time, in his first month in office, Funes restored trade and diplomatic relations with Cuba and in October 2010 went on a state visit to Havana. It was the first such meeting between the Salvadoran and Cuban heads of state in more than 50 years. The two sides signed several accords, including agreements to bolster cooperation in health care, in increasing literacy, and in deepening cultural ties. Closer ties to Cuba did not disturb relations with the United States, as was made evident by the state visit of U.S. president Barack Obama to El Salvador in early 2011. The two sides agreed to a raft of new joint initiatives to bolster El Salvador's economy and infrastructure and fight poverty and crime.

In December 2010 El Salvador formed a united diplomatic front with its neighbors Honduras and Guatemala to press Mexico to protect the human rights of Central Americans traversing Mexico on their way to the United States.

The United States designated Mara Salvatrucha as a significant transnational criminal organization in October 2012, imposing sanctions on members.

El Salvador concluded a European Union (EU) association agreement in June 2012. Trade barriers were lifted as of October 1, 2013. The Millennium Challenge Corporation awarded El Salvador an unprecedented second compact in September 2013, worth $277 million, for infrastructure and transportation projects.

Current issues. El Salvador has the second-highest per capita murder rate in the world, with 69 homicides per 100,000 citizens in 2012, more than 4,000 per year. Police statistics indicate an average of seven murders and three carjackings every day. Crime continues to be a major policy challenge for officials, and it dominated the 2012 elections for parliament and provincial assemblies.

The murder rate fell from 13.6 per day to 5.7 per day ahead of the 2012 elections, causing speculation that the government had secretly negotiated a cease-fire among rival gangs. On March 23, however, leaders of MS-13 and Barrio-18 announced that they had tired of conflict and negotiated a truce themselves. Later, Monsignor Fabio Colindres revealed that he had led the negotiations.

Arena was declared the winner of the March 8 parliamentary elections with 33 seats, 14 more than in 2009. The FMLN won 31 seats, losing 2 seats and its plurality. Funes created an alliance with third-place GANA to pass legislation. Arena also dominated the municipal elections, winning 114 of 262 mayoral races, including San Salvador. Once the votes were tallied, the focus immediately shifted to the 2014 presidential ballot. Since Funes cannot run for a second term, on April 10, 2012, the FMLN selected Vice President and Minister of Education Salvador Sánchez Céren as its presidential candidate and Santa Tecla mayor Oscar ORTIZ for vice president. Arena nominated San Salvador mayor Norman QUIJANO as its candidate for president.

Before the new, Arena-led parliament convened, the FMLN appointed five new members of the Supreme Court and a new attorney general, triggering a constitutional crisis that paralyzed the government and judicial system for two months. At issue was how many Supreme Court slates one assembly could choose. On June 5 the constitutional chamber of the Supreme Court rejected the 2012 nominations because the 2009–2012 Assembly had already selected justices in 2009. The constitutional chamber also rejected the appointees from 2006 on similar grounds. Arguments between Arena and FMLN escalated into street demonstrations, with the newest appointees forcibly entering the court building to claim their place on the bench. After 17 negotiating sessions, President Funes announced a compromise solution on August 20, with the 2006 and 2012 appointees being reelected. The attorney general post remained vacant until a December vote in the legislature. In January 2013 the constitutional chamber invalidated the process for selecting judges to the Court of Auditors. The legislators voted for new members in March, and the chamber duly rejected those as well.

The gang truce continued to hold through the summer, but the public grew increasingly uncomfortable about the details, such as transfers of top gang leaders from maximum-security prisons to less restrictive facilities that allowed family visits and other benefits. Gang leaders proposed a second phase of the truce in November. Specifically, they wanted help reintegrating into society. The government agreed to create peace zones, known as violence-free municipalities, where gangs would turn in their weapons, renounce violence, and work at legitimate enterprises set up with government help, such as farms and bakeries. The first peace zone was established in January 2013 in Ilopango.

Arena expelled four of its legislators on November 7, 2012, after they voted for the government's budget. They formed a States for El Salvador (*Unidos por El Salvador*) faction. Arena's parliamentary group dropped from 33 seats to 29, behind the FMLN's 31. Altogether, the FMLN-GANA-CN-PDC bloc now had 55 seats, one less than the supermajority that would enable it to pass legislation without any Arena support.

The Legislative Assembly passed law in January 2013 allowing the Salvadoran diaspora to vote in Salvadoran elections. Vice President Sánchez Cerén visited California and Virginia in August to drum up support for his presidential bid; 92 percent of Salvadorans living abroad live in the United States.

Former president Tony Saca announced his candidacy for the presidency in February. He leads **Unity** (*Unidad*), an electoral alliance of GANA, the Party of Hope, and the National Coalition. Rivals questioned the constitutionality of Saca's candidacy, given term limits.

In September the Constitutional Court ruled that ballots for the 2014 presidential election would be marked with political party flags, not photos of the candidates. This decision was a blow for Saca, a familiar face leading a new political alliance.

POLITICAL PARTIES

In 1988 electoral laws were reformed, requiring political parties to obtain citizens' signatures in support of national party recognition, establishing a threshold minimum percentage of the national vote, which has varied over time from 0.5 to 3, to retain party status and to participate in at least every other election.

Prior to the 2009 elections, the FMLN formed coalitions with the Revolutionary Democratic Front (FDR) and the CD in 34 municipal races. Despite speculation about a potential coalition between Arena and the PCN, both parties fielded their own candidates. Following the election the FDR was deregistered because it failed to gain enough votes to meet the threshold requirement. The PDC and the PCN were also stripped of official recognition in 2011.

Government Parties:

Farabundo Martí National Liberation Front (*Frente Farabundo Martí para la Liberación Nacional*—FMLN). The FMLN was organized in October 1980 as the paramilitary affiliate of the Revolutionary Democratic Front (*Frente Democrático Revolucionario*—FDR, below), an umbrella formation of dissident political groups. Headed by a National Revolutionary Directorate (*Dirección Revolucionaria Nacional*—DRN) composed of representatives of participating armed units, the FMLN was in active rebellion until the late 1991 agreement that led to a formal cessation of hostilities on February 1, 1992. During ensuing months the FMLN engaged in a process of phased disarmament and on December 15 was recognized by the Supreme Electoral Tribunal as a legal political party.

At its first congress on September 6, 1993, the FMLN endorsed Rubén Zamora of the CD (below) as its 1994 presidential candidate. Following the election an internal split emerged between the People's

Renewal Expression (*Expresión Renovadora del Pueblo*—ERP) and the National Resistance (*Resistencia Nacional*—RN), on the one hand, and the Salvadoran Communist Party (*Partido Comunista Salvadoreño*—PCS), the Popular Liberation Forces (*Fuerzas Populares de Liberación*—FPL), and the Central American Workers Revolutionary Party (*Partido Revolucionario de los Trabajadores Centroamericanos*—PRTC), on the other. While surfacing as a dispute over the selection of legislative officers, a major factor of the split appeared to be resistance by the tripartite group to the ERP leader's advocacy of a departure from Marxism-Leninism, and in December 1994 both the ERP and RN left the Front, save for a rump RN faction headed by Eugenio CHICA and Marco JIMÉNEZ. In early 1995 the remaining FMLN components agreed to changes designed to yield a unitary organization and by midyear had begun to dissolve their respective party structures to become "currents" or "tendencies" within the revamped larger grouping. In 2004 and 2005, five members of the Legislature split from FMLN to from the Democratic Revolutionary Front (*Frente Democratico Revolucionario*—FDR). However, FDR maintained just one legislative seat in the 2006 elections and failed to win representation in the 2009 elections. (For information on the FDR, see the 2009 *Handbook.*)

The PCS was formerly a pro-Moscow group that was repudiated by most mass and guerrilla organizations for its "revisionist" outlook. In early 1980 it adopted a more militant posture, becoming under its secretary general, Schafik Jorge HANDAL, a de facto component of the FMLN. Following his party's break with the Democratic Nationalist Union (*Unión Demócrata Nacionalista*—UDN), Handal became official coordinator and subsequently coordinator general of the legitimized FMLN.

The FPL was previously the FMLN's largest military component. In May 1993 a scandal erupted as the result of an explosion at a clandestine FPL arsenal in Managua, Nicaragua, of arms that were supposed to have been turned over to the United Nations Observer Mission in El Salvador for destruction. A number of other such caches were subsequently discovered, tarnishing the credentials of the FMLN as a legal party.

The PRTC was a small FMLN component, which advocated a regional, as opposed to state, revolution. One of its leaders, Francisco VELIS, was assassinated in October 1993.

Having gained as much public support as the governing Arena party in the 1997 legislative poll, the FMLN held high hopes of achieving government control in the March 1999 presidential balloting. However, friction between orthodox Marxists and the modernist wing ("renovators") caused sustained difficulty in choosing a candidate. The ultimate selection, Facundo GUARDADO, a former guerrilla leader supported by the "renovators," generated little enthusiasm among the non-FMLN voters and won only 28.9 percent of the vote. Having failed even to force a runoff ballot, Guardado resigned as the FMLN's general coordinator on March 15, with his successor, Fabio Castillo, heading a new leadership in which traditional Marxists held a slim majority.

The FMLN rebounded to win a legislative plurality in March 2000 but was unable to gain control in the face of an Arena-led conservative coalition. Thereafter, the sharp division between the orthodox and reform wings persisted, and in October 2001 it was reported that Guardado had been "expelled," although he announced he would continue to participate in FMLN activity. Hard-liner Salvador Sánchez Cerén was elected as the new general coordinator in November. Subsequently, in early 2002, it was reported that a group of reformist FMLN legislators had left the party's parliamentary bloc, including Héctor SILVA, who stood for president in 2004 as the candidate of a PDC/CDU coalition (see under PDC, below).

Although retaining its legislative plurality of 31 in March 2003, the FMLN, led by Schafik Jorge Handal, was again rebuffed in its bid for the presidency in March 2004.

In March 2005 the party was weakened by the withdrawal of seven of its legislative deputies who joined with other FMLN dissidents to form a new party, the Revolutionary Democratic Front (which was deregistered following the 2009 elections for failure to meet the electoral threshold.) Subsequently, the death of Handal on January 24, 2006, appeared to provide an opening for reconciliation between his supporters and the FDR; however, his hard-line deputy, Sánchez Cerén, was named to head the FMLN legislative bloc, and in the March 12 election the party, while gaining one slot, lost its plurality to Arena.

In the January 2009 legislative elections, the FMLN gained three seats to overcome Arena as the party with the most seats, though the two parties were separated only by a three-seat margin, forcing both to form alliances. The FMLN's greatest victory came in the March presidential election when its preferred candidate, Mauricio Funes, among the most recognizable media personalities in the country, defeated Arena candidate Rodrigo Avila by a narrow margin. However, Funes was neither a party member nor an ex-guerrilla commander, in contrast to previous FMLN candidates. His election accordingly led to increased dissension between the Funes camp and party hard-liners regarding the president's policies and his moderate cabinet choices.

The government has faced ongoing disagreements between the moderates and radicals. The most public dispute occurred in November 2009 when Vice President Sánchez announced in Venezuela that he would re-create the Chávez model of socialism in El Salvador, undermining the president. For months, Funes had been trying to distance his administration from the Venezuelan leader. The party also split with the president in the legislature, where its members approved laws opposed by Funes. The president sought support from members of other parties, including Arena dissidents.

In February 2011 the FMLN assumed the leadership of the legislature with the presidency of Sigfrido REYES Morales—the first time the Left has presided over the assembly. The party gained control after the new GANA party split from Arena, which forced it to make a power-sharing deal with the FMLN. President Funes's relationship with the FMLN remained complicated throughout 2011, with the president's positions on issues relating to indefinite deployment of the armed forces to control criminality and approval of a law to rein in the Supreme Court, among others, exercising the party's left wing. The party captured 31 seats in the March 2012 elections, a loss of 4 seats since 2009 and 2 seats less than Arena.

Leaders: Carlos Mauricio FUNES Cartagena (President of the Republic), Salvador SÁNCHEZ Cerén (Vice President of the Republic, 2014 presidential candidate); Oscar ORTIZ (2014 vice presidential candidate); Medardo GONZÁLEZ (General Coordinator).

Party of Hope (*Partido de la Esperanza*). Party of Hope is the reorganized and re-registered name of the former **Christian Democratic Party** (*Partido Demócrata Cristiano*—PDC), which was dissolved by the Supreme Court in 2011 because it received less than 3 percent of the vote in the 2004 presidential election. An essentially centrist grouping, the PDC was the core component of the National Opposition Union (*Unión Nacional Opositora*—UNO), which won 8 legislative seats in 1972 and 14 in 1974 but boycotted the 1976 and 1978 balloting. Its best-known figure, José Napoleón Duarte, returned from exile following the October 1979 coup, joined the junta on March 3, 1980, and became junta president on December 22. He was succeeded by Provisional President Alvaro Magaña in May 1982 after the PDC had failed to secure a majority at the March Constituent Assembly election. Although Duarte continued as president under the new constitution in May 1984, the PDC did not win legislative control until March 1985; it returned to minority status as a result of the 1988 legislative balloting (an outcome attributed, in part, to intraparty bickering) and lost the presidency in 1989. Duarte died on February 23, 1990, For the 1991 election the party appealed to the left by forming an alliance with two labor-based groups, the **National Union of Peasant Labor** (*Unión Nacional Obrera Campesina*—UNDC) and the **Salvadoran Workers' Central** (*Central de Trabajadores Salvadoreños*—CTS).

Two leading factions, led by Fidel Chávez Mena and Abraham RODRÍGUEZ, competed for the party's presidential nomination in 1994, Chávez Mena (the 1989 nominee) receiving the designation and finishing third in the March first-round balloting. At a party convention in late November the party elected a *fidelista* directorate loyal to Chávez Mena, leading dissident *abrahamistas* (loyalists of Rodríguez) to withdrawal from the party on December 11 to form the Social Christian Reform Party (*Partido Reformista Social Cristiano*—PRSC).

The election of Ronald Umaña, representing a relatively young new guard or new political class as secretary general at the 1995 convention yielded a dispute with long-time old guard leader Julio SAMAYOA, who succeeded in forcing his opponent's expulsion from the party. In March 1996 the electoral tribunal confirmed the dismissal of Umaña and six associates, who promptly challenged the ruling's legality, and in December the tribunal reinstated Umaña.

For some constituencies in the March 1997 balloting, the PDC formed a "Great Center Coalition" with the Democratic Party (*Partido Democrático*—PD), which elected three deputies as compared with seven elected by the PDC outright.

Indicative of internal problems within the PDC was its replacement in January 1998 of Secretary General Ronald Umaña by Horacio TRUJILLO only to have Umaña reinstated in March by the electoral tribunal. Rodolfo Antonio Parker Soto, former legal adviser to the military during the civil war, was the PDC standard-bearer in the March 1999 presidential campaign, during which the PDC attacked what it perceived as widespread corruption in the Arena governments of the 1990s. Parker secured 5.8 percent of the vote, thereby dropping the PDC to fourth place behind the newly formed United Democratic Center (*Centro Democrático Unido*—CDU) in party rankings.

For the 2004 presidential race the PDC joined with the CDU in sponsoring former FMLN leader Héctor Silva Arguello; however, Silva's vote share of 3.9 percent was less than the joint minimum required to maintain the parties' registrations. In 2005 three PDC legislators left the party to help form the new **Popular Social Christian Party** (*Partido Popular Social Cristiano*—PPSC) under the leadership of former PDC secretary general René AUILEZ. Those legislators subsequently joined with members of the newly formed FDR and the CDU to create a bloc of 14 legislators known as the G-14. However, G-14 influence declined substantially following the 2006 assembly poll, when most of its members ran under the CD banner. Meanwhile, the PDC won six assembly seats in 2006, one more than in 2003. In 2009 the party won five seats. The party lost three of its assembly members to the newly formed LC party in June 2010, leaving it with a representative party larger than only the CD. The three legislators split off after the party expelled the popular mayor of San Miguel as part of an internal power struggle.

Competing under its new name in the March 8, 2012, parliamentary election, Party of Hope received 2.76 percent of the vote and one seat.

Leader: Rodolfo Antonio PARKER Soto (1999 presidential candidate and Secretary General).

Democratic Change (*Cambio Democrática*—CD). The center-left CD was founded in 1988 as a coalition of three political parties called the *Convergencia Democrática.* The CD won eight seats in 1989. The CD supported the unsuccessful bid of FMLN candidate Rubén Zamora for president in 1992, and in 1999 the party participated in elections as part of the United Democratic Center (*Centro Democrático Unido*—CDU). In 2005 the CDU became *Cambio Democrática.* The party won one legislative seat in both 2009 and 2012.

Leaders: Héctor Miguel Dada HIREZI (Minister of the Economy), Óscar Abraham KATTÁN Milla (Secretary General), Yanira CRUZ (Former Secretary General).

Other Legislative Parties:

Nationalist Republican Alliance (*Alianza Republicana Nacionalista*—Arena). The Arena party was launched in 1981 as an outgrowth of the Broad National Front (*Frente Amplio Nacional*—FAN), an extreme right-wing grouping organized a year earlier by ex-army major Roberto d'Aubuisson. D'Aubuisson was arrested briefly in May 1980 as the instigator of an attempted coup against the junta, which he had accused of "leading the country toward communism." Runner-up in the 1982 election with 19 assembly seats, the Alliance formed a conservative bloc with the PCN, which succeeded in scuttling most of the post-coup land-reform program and secured the appointment of a right-wing judiciary. Although remaining second-ranked in the March 1985 balloting, Arena's legislative representation dropped to 13 seats on the basis of a 29 percent vote share. Amid mounting evidence that his leadership and reputation had become a liability to the group, d'Aubuisson formally resigned as secretary general in September, holding thereafter the title of honorary president until his death in February 1991.

Arena secured a 53.8 percent popular vote victory in presidential balloting in March 1989 but slipped to a plurality of 44.3 percent in 1991 that gave it only 39 of 84 legislative seats. The party's legislative representation was unchanged in 1994, although Armando Calderón Sol defeated the FMLN's Rubén Zamora Rivas by a better than two-to-one margin in the second round of the presidential race. In 1997 a number of prominent Arena members defected to the PCN (below), with the party benefiting, in turn, by desertions from the PDC (above). The net result in the March balloting was a 1-seat Arena plurality over the FMLN.

As its 1999 presidential candidate, Arena chose Francisco Guillermo Flores Pérez, a 39-year-old economist who had held several ministerial posts and most recently had served as president of the Legislative Assembly, where he had earned a reputation as a skillful negotiator. Flores outflanked six other candidates to win the March 1999 presidential poll with nearly 52 percent of the vote. His successor, Elías Antonio ("Tony") Saca, also won easily in March 2004, with a 57.7 percent vote share.

Theretofore second-ranked, Arena gained plurality status in the 2006 legislative poll with 34 seats. It also won a plurality of municipalities in the 2006 local balloting.

Arena legislators revived civil war tensions in 2007 by proposing legislation to make party founder Roberto d'Aubuisson a "blessed son of the motherland," despite his alleged role in the 1980 slaying of Archbishop Óscar Romero. In February three Arena members (including a son of the late D'Aubuisson) were killed in Guatemala. The motive for the slayings was unclear.

In the January 2009 legislative elections, Arena lost two seats and its overall lead to the FMLN, but a last-minute deal with the PCN allowed it to hold on to the presidency of the assembly. Meanwhile, the nomination of Rodrigo Ávila, a congressman and former national police chief, as party standard-bearer in the March presidential election caused a rift as some members accused him of campaign fraud. Despite efforts to move the party to the center, the FMLN's Carlos Mauricio Funes narrowly defeated Avila, marking the first time in 18 years that Arena was not the governing party. In October 2009, as the party reeled from its first loss, 12 of its assembly members split off to form the new party GANA. The defection was said to be instigated by former President Tony Saca, who the party went on to expel from its ranks in December. The split caused Arena to lose representation in the assembly and forced Arena to forge a deal with the FMLN to rotate the assembly president's seat. Arena gained back 1 member after the short-lived LC party disintegrated in October 2010. The party placed first in the March 2012 parliamentary elections, with 39.76 percent of the vote and 33 seats.

The party rifts continued, with four more legislators expelled in November 2012 for voting in favor of the national budget, costing the party its plurality in the assembly. Cristiani resigned as party president in February 2013 and was replaced by Jorge VELADO, the vice president of ideology.

Leaders: Jorge VELADO (President), Hugo BARRERA (Vice President), Norman QUIJANO (Mayor of San Salvador, 2014 presidential candidate), René PORTILLO Cuadra (2014 vice presidential candidate).

Grand Alliance for Change (*Gran Alianza por la Unidad Nacional*—GANA). The GANA is a right-wing party formed in October 2009 when 12 deputies split from Arena (see above). GANA's leading member is former president Tony SACA, who was expelled from Arena in December 2009. Saca and Arena have a tense relationship, and Saca sued Arena for libel and defamation in 2013.

Though its roots were on the right, the group said that it would not rule out voting with FMLN for the good of the country. The Assembly initially had a bloc of 13 members in the legislature. It lost 1 assembly representative in June 2010 to the new LC party, but it then picked up 3 new representatives after the LC disintegrated in October. GANA polled third with 9.7 percent support in March 2012, giving it 11 seats, down from 16. GANA supported President Funes and the FMLN in the assembly.

Leaders: José Andrés ROVIRA Canales (President), Tony SACA (Former President of the Republic, 2014 presidential candidate).

National Coalition (*Concertación Nacional*—CN). National Coalition is the reorganized and re-registered name of the former **National Conciliation Party** (*Partido de Conciliación Nacional*—PCN). In April 2011 the Supreme Court stripped the PCN of its official standing because it received less than 4 percent of the vote in the 2004 presidential election. Members were given six months to collect 50,000 signatures to compete in the March 2012 legislative and municipal elections.

At the time of its founding in 1961, the PCN enjoyed a fairly broad range of political support and displayed some receptivity to social and economic reform. Over the years, however, it became increasingly conservative, serving the interests of the leading families and the military establishment. Following the declared willingness of its leadership to support peace talks with the rebels in mid-1982, 9 of its 14 assembly members withdrew to form the **Salvadoran Authentic Institutional Party** (*Partido Auténtico Institucional Salvadoreño*—Paisa). The PCN's Francisco GUERRERO, running as a candidate of moderation, placed third in the March 1984 presidential balloting, and his refusal to back d'Aubuisson in the runoff was considered crucial to Duarte's victory. The party won 12 legislative seats in March 1985, 5 of which were lost in the 1988 poll. Its 1989 presidential candidate, Rafael MORAN Casteñeda, ran third in the March 19 balloting, winning only 4.2 percent of the vote. Its legislative representation rose from 4 to 11 seats in 1997, when it also performed well in mayoralty races. However, PCN Co-Secretary General Rafael Hernán Contreras finished fifth in the March 1999 presidential poll, his 3.8 percent of the vote just barely surpassing the required 3 percent for continued party registration.

The party won 16 legislative seats in 2003 but placed fourth, with 2.7 percent of the vote, in the 2004 presidential race. The party won 11 seats in 2009. The party requalified in time to compete in the March 2012 legislative and municipal elections and received 7.18 percent of the vote, enough for 7 seats.

Leaders: Manuel Alfonso RODRIGUEZ Zaldaña (Secretary General), Rubén ORELLANA (Former President of the Assembly), José Rafael MACHUCA Zelaya (National Secretary and 2004 presidential candidate), Tomás CHÉVEZ.

Other Parties:

The following parties failed to win seats in 2009 and did not enter the 2012 parliamentary election: the **Christian Force** (*Fuerza Cristiana*—FC), the **National Liberal Party** (*Partido Nacional Liberal*—PNL), and the **United Democratic Center** (*Centro Democratico Unido*—UDC).

Leaders for Change (*Lideres por el Cambio*—LC). Five members of the 2009–2012 Assembly broke off from the PDC and the newly formed GANA to form the LC on June 30, 2010. The party said it was breaking off to be an independent voice in the legislature and did not reveal a guiding ideology, though its members did say they had ruled out any alignment with the FMLN. The party disintegrated in October after three of its members resigned and joined GANA. Another member joined Arena, and the last one became independent.

Leaders: Francisco ZABLAH, Juan Carlos MENDOZA.

LEGISLATURE

Formerly a 60-member body, the **Legislative Assembly** (*Asamblea Legislativa*) currently consists of 84 directly elected legislators, 64 elected from multimember constituencies and 20 by proportional representation, serving three-year terms.

Following the most recent election on March 11, 2012, the seat distribution was as follows: Nationalist Republican Alliance, 33; the Farabundo Martí National Liberation Front, 31; Grand Alliance for National Unity, 11; National Coalition, 7; Party of Hope, 1; and independent, 1.

President: Sigfrido REYES Morales.

CABINET

[as of October 4, 2013]

President	Carlos Mauricio Funes Cartagena (FMLN)
Vice President and Education Minister	Salvador Sánchez Cerén (FMLN)
Ministers	
Agriculture and Livestock	José Guillermo López Suárez (ind.)
Defense	José Atilio Benitz (ind.)
Economy	Héctor Miguel Antonio Dada Hirezi (CD)
Environment and Natural Resources	Herman Humberto Rosa Chávez (ind.)
Foreign Affairs	Jaime Miranda (ind.)
Interior	Gregorio Zelayandia (ind.)
Labor and Social Welfare	Humberto Centeno (FMLN)
Public Health and Social Assistance	María Isabel Rodríguez (ind.) [f]
Public Security and Justice	David Munguía Payés (ind.)
Public Works	Gerson Martínez (FMLN)
Tourism	José Napoleón Duarte Durán (PDC)
Treasury	Juan Carlos Cáceres Chávez (ind.)
Secretaries	
Private Secretary	Francisco José Cáceres Zaldaña (FMLN)
Secretary for Communications	David Rivas (ind.)
Secretary for Culture	Héctor Jesús Samour Canán (ind.)
Secretary of Legislative and Judicial Affairs	Ricardo Guillermo Marroquin Peñate (ind.)
Secretary for Social Inclusion	Vanda Guiomar Pignato (FMLN) [f]
Secretary for Strategic Affairs	Francis Hato Hasbún (FMLN)
Technical Secretary	Alexander Ernesto Segovia Cáceres (ind.)

[f] = female

INTERGOVERNMENTAL REPRESENTATION

Ambassador to the U.S.: Ruben Ignacio ZAMORA Rivas.

U.S. Ambassador to El Salvador: Mari Carmen APONTE.

Permanent Representative to the UN: Carlos Enrique GARCIA González.

IGO Memberships (Non-UN): IADB, IOM, OAS, WTO.

EQUATORIAL GUINEA

Republic of Equatorial Guinea
República de Guinea Ecuatorial

Area: 10,830 sq. mi. (28,051 sq. km).

Population: 743,600 (2012E—UN); 704,001 (2013E—U.S. Census).

Major Urban Centers (2011E—UN): MALABO (137,000).

Official Language: Spanish. (French was adopted as a "commercial" language in September 1997 during a period of friction between Malabo and Madrid. In addition various African dialects are spoken, and pidgin English serves as a commercial lingua franca.)

Monetary Unit: CFA franc (official rate November 1, 2013: 486.52 CFA francs = $1US). The CFA franc, previously pegged to the French franc, is now permanently pegged to the euro at 655.957 CFA francs = 1 euro.

President: Gen. Teodoro OBIANG Nguema Mbasogo (Democratic Party of Equatorial Guinea), assumed power as president of a Supreme Military Council following the ouster of MACIE (formerly Francisco Macías) Nguema Biyogo Ñegue Ndong on August 3, 1979; inaugurated October 12, 1982, following confirmation for a seven-year term by constitutional referendum on August 15; reelected for seven-year terms on June 25, 1989, February 25, 1996, and, in early elections, on December 15, 2002, and November 29, 2009.

Prime Minister: Vicente Ehate TOMI (Democratic Party of Equatorial Guinea), appointed by the president on May 21, 2012, succeeding Ignacio Milam TANG, who was appointed vice president; Tomi formed a new government on May 24.

THE COUNTRY

The least populous and the only Spanish-speaking African nation, Equatorial Guinea consists of two sharply differing regions: the mainland territory of Río Muni, including Corisco, Elobey Grande, and Elobey Chico islands as well as adjacent islets; and the island of Bioko (known prior to 1973 as Fernando Póo and from 1973 to 1979 as

Macías Nguema Biyogo), including Pagalu (known prior to 1973 as Annobón) and adjacent islets in the Gulf of Guinea. Río Muni, whose area is 10,045 square miles (26,017 sq. km), accounts for more than nine-tenths of the country's territory and about three-quarters of its total population; Bata is the principal urban center. Bioko's area covers 785 square miles (2,034 sq. km); Malabo is the chief town and the capital of the republic.

The two basic ethnic groups, both Bantu subgroupings, are the Fang, who reportedly account for the majority of the population, and the Bubi, primarily located in Bioko. (Bubi/Fang friction remains an important issue on Bioko, while resentment has also reportedly surfaced among the rest of Fang over the dominance within that group of President Obiang's Mongomo sub-clan.) Other elements include the Kombe and various coastal tribes in Río Muni, and Fernandinos (persons of mixed racial descent) in Bioko. Roman Catholicism is the religion of approximately 80 percent of the population. Women constitute 44.7 percent of the labor force and 22 percent of the current legislature.

Until the discovery of oil in the mid-1990s, the economy was dominated by agriculture, the principal exports being cocoa, coffee, and timber. Industry consisted primarily of small-scale agriprocessing operations, while a small fishing sector also operated. Following the August 1979 coup, substantial aid was tendered by Spain, France, and other international donors to help Equatorial Guinea recover from the economic devastation of the Macie era, during which most skilled workers were killed or fled the country, cocoa production and per capita GNP plummeted, and such essential urban services as power and water were disrupted. In contrast to the Eastern-bloc affiliation of its predecessor, the post-Macie government adopted generally pro-Western, free-market policies. Economic recovery was initially slow, the adverse effects of high budget and trade deficits, inflation, and a burdensome external debt only partially offset by improvements resulting from Equatorial Guinea's admission to the franc zone in 1985. Cocoa and timber prices declined in the late 1980s, further complicating the situation.

Economic growth averaged 37 percent annually from the mid-1990s to the mid-2000s, buoyed by additional discoveries of oil and potentially lucrative gas deposits. The increased revenue provided the government with regular budget surpluses in the early 2000s, although critics continued to cite perceived corruption and inefficiency, and widespread poverty persisted. Oil production peaked at close to 400,000 barrels per day in 2004 before flattening out in 2005 and declining slightly in 2006, in part due to a cap imposed by the government. Although GDP growth overall began to slow, the non-oil sector continued to expand at a significant pace, which the International Monetary Fund (IMF) cited as an indicator of progress in economic diversification. Annual GDP growth, though declining, averaged a robust 16.2 percent in 2007–2008. However, growth contracted, receding by an average of about 3.1 percent in 2009–2010, owing in large part to a decline in oil production, which fund managers cited, along with widespread poverty, as a "cause for concern." They also urged that public spending be directed toward improving living standards and productivity.

After the recent decline in oil production, the start-up of the Aseng oil and gas-condensate field in late 2011 boosted production and led to increased exports in the first half of 2012. The IMF estimated GDP growth of 4.5 percent in 2011, though it slowed to 2 percent in 2012. The African Economic Outlook 2012 listed Equatorial Guinea as one of Africa's ten richest countries, with a GDP per capita of $35,797.

Equatorial Guinea continues to court foreign investment, hosting a Forum for Attracting Investment in Houston, Texas, in June 2012 to present investment opportunities to U.S. businesses. President Obiang noted the role U.S. investment had played in his country's development, estimating the total at nearly $30 billion, mostly in its oil and gas sector. In 2013, GDP contracted by 2 percent. Inflation was 5 percent.

GOVERNMENT AND POLITICS

Political background. The former territory of Spanish Guinea, with Spanish sovereignty dating from 1778, was granted provincial status in 1959 and internal autonomy in 1964, achieving full independence under the name of Equatorial Guinea on October 12, 1968. The pre-independence negotiations with Spain had been complicated by differences between the mainland Fang, whose representatives sought the severance of all links with Spain, and the island Bubi, whose spokespeople advocated retention of some ties with Spain and semiautonomous status within a federal system. A compromise constitution and electoral law, submitted for popular approval in a UN-supervised referendum on August 11, 1968, was accepted by 63 percent of the people, the substantial adverse vote reflecting Bubi fears of mainland domination as well as Fang objections to the degree of self-rule accorded the islanders. In presidential balloting a month later, MACÍAS Nguema Biyogo, a mainland Fang associated with the Popular Idea of Equatorial Guinea (*Idea Popular de Guinea Ecuatorial*—IPGE), defeated the head of the pre-independence autonomous government, Bonifacio ONDO Edu of the Movement for the National Unity of Equatorial Guinea (*Movimiento de Union Nacional de Guinea Ecuatorial*—MUNGE).

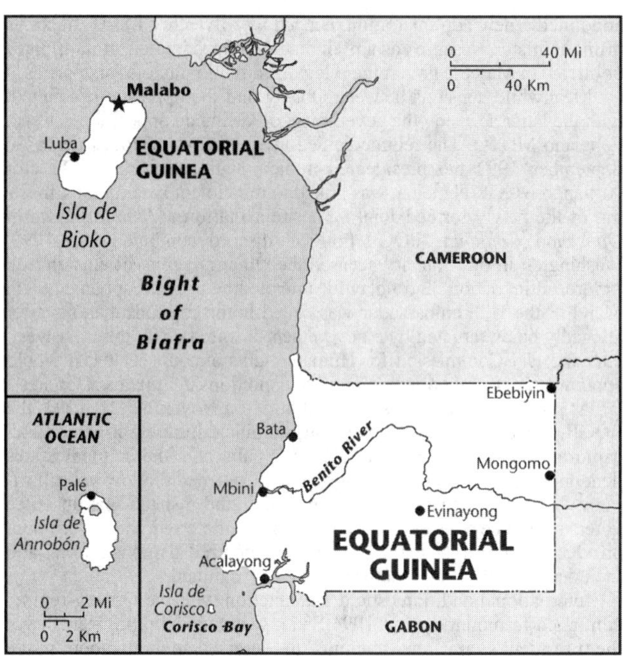

In 1969 President Macías seized emergency powers during a major international crisis involving tribal rivalries, allegations of continued Spanish colonialism, and conflicting foreign economic interests. Following an unsuccessful coup d'état led by Foreign Minister Atanosio NDONGO Miyone, 200 individuals were arrested and executed, and Macías subsequently instituted a highly centralized single-party state and assumed his presidency for life in 1972. (For more on Macías's assumption of the presidency, see the 2012 *Handbook.*) Along with other Equatorial Guineans, Macías dropped his Christian name (Francisco) on September 26, 1975; in 1976 he also changed his surname from Macías to Macie. The 11-year rule of Macías/Macie (during which the country became widely known as the "Auschwitz of Africa") was terminated on August 3, 1979, in a coup led by the president's nephew, Lt. Col. Teodoro OBIANG Nguema Mbasogo. Macie was executed on September 29, 1979, for crimes that included genocide, treason, and embezzlement.

Concurrent with the adoption, by referendum, of a new constitution on August 15, 1982, Colonel Obiang was confirmed as president for a seven-year term. Subsequently, Captain Seriche was named prime minister, the two vice-presidential roles being eliminated. The first National Assembly election mandated by the new constitution was held on August 28, 1983.

Between 1981 and 1986 there were several coup attempts; most notably one attempt in July 1986 that led to the execution of several members of the government and parliament. (For more on the coup attempts on President Obiang, see the 2012 *Handbook.*)

In late 1987 President Obiang launched a government formation, the Democratic Party of Equatorial Guinea (*Partido Democrático de Guinea Ecuatorial*—PDGE), as a precursor to political liberalization, but there was little immediate movement: Obiang was the only candidate in presidential balloting in June 1989. Although Obiang hailed his reelection as the launching of a democratization process and invited political exiles to return, he rejected the idea of a multiparty system, arguing that "political pluralism would send convulsions through the population." However, in 1990 failure to implement political reforms severely constricted foreign aid and investment. As a result, an extraordinary PDGE congress in August endorsed the adoption of a democratic constitution, which was overwhelmingly approved in a referendum of November 17, 1991. On January 23, 1992, the president appointed a new administration, headed by Silvestre SIALE Bileka as prime minister, to serve "as a prelude to the introduction of multiparty politics." In May the government legalized the first two of six parties.

Meanwhile, tensions between Obiang and the opposition mounted, with the latter accusing the government of killing an opposition activist, Feliciano MOTO. The regime denied involvement in Moto's death. In September 1992 the president's brother, National Security Director Armando NGOR Nguema, was linked to the violent breakup of a meeting of the newly formed Joint Opposition Platform (*Plataforma de la Oposición Conjunta*—POC). Political discord continued into 1993. Washington in mid-January accused the Obiang regime of engaging in torture, intimidation, and unlawful imprisonment of its opponents. On March 3 the U.S. ambassador was called home for consultations after allegedly being targeted by a government-inspired death threat. A week later the UN Commission for Human Rights announced that it would appoint a special rapporteur to monitor conditions in Equatorial Guinea.

At poorly attended legislative balloting on November 21, 1993, the PDGE, aided by the POC's boycott, dominated the eight-party field, capturing 68 of the 80 seats. Both Spain and the United States denounced the proceedings, while the POC termed the low voter turnout a "slap in the face to the dictatorship" and insisted that absentee voters should be considered its supporters. Undeterred, the government on December 6 imposed a ban on unauthorized demonstrations and included no opposition members in the new cabinet.

International and domestic dissatisfaction with the Obiang regime continued to mount, and in 1994 Spain suspended aid payments over the president's apparent attempts to derail democratization while Amnesty International condemned the government's human rights record.

Following the President's urging of opposition members to participate in a voter registration drive, in August negotiations with the Progress Party of Equatorial Guinea (*Partido del Progresso de Guinea Ecuatorial*—PPGE) were suspended after its leader, Severo MOTO Nsa, criticized the government, and on October 5 two people were killed in a clash between government troops and demonstrators in Malabo. The nation's first multiparty municipal elections were held on September 17, 1995, the PDGE being credited with victories in 18 of the 27 localities. However, domestic and international observers challenged the government's voting tally, the POC arguing that the opposition had really garnered about 80 percent of the votes. Subsequently, House speaker Felipe Ondo OBIANG Alogo and his deputy, Antonio Pascual Oko EBOBO, both prominent PDGE members, resigned on October 25.

On January 12, 1996, Obiang decreed that presidential elections would be held on February 25, three months before his term was set to expire. Opposition leaders denounced the president's actions as unconstitutional and designed to preclude effective organization on their part. By late January a number of opposition candidates had emerged, including the PPGE's Moto and three from the POC. However, the subsequent run-up was reportedly marked by gross malfeasance, including harassment of opposition activists and replacement of a UN-compiled electoral list with a government list that excluded voters in regions that had supported the opposition in previous polling. Consequently, most opposition candidates ultimately withdrew and called on their supporters to boycott the election.

At the February 25, 1996, polling, President Obiang was credited with 97.85 percent of the votes. However, citing irregularities both before and on election day, most observers dismissed the election as a sham. On March 29 Obiang appointed Angel Serafin Seriche DOUGAN to succeed Prime Minister Siale Bileka. On January 15, 1998, Dougan and his cabinet resigned in accordance with a requirement that the prime minister to submit his government for review after two years in office. But Dougan was reappointed head of a reshuffled government two days later.

In mid-January 1998 ethnic Bubi separatists reportedly attacked government offices on Bioko Island. (The Bubi were the dominant group on the island until independence but since then have been surpassed in numbers by the Fang.) Denying a role in the violence, leaders of the Movement for the Self-Determination of the Island of Bioko—MAIB (see Political Parties, below) nonetheless charged the government with a "veritable genocide" and reaffirmed their desire for self-rule. In March the Obiang administration denied charges by Amnesty International that it was torturing separatist prisoners. Thereafter, a military court sentenced 15 of the separatists to death in June for their alleged roles in the uprising, although the president commuted the death sentences in September following the prison death of a dissident who had reportedly been beaten by security forces. (The clemency came amid speculation that international economic sponsors were reconsidering their support.) Meanwhile, the government had reportedly arrested dozens of opposition activists in an apparent attempt to disrupt their preparations for legislative balloting (scheduled for late 1998, but postponed until early 1999).

In balloting on March 7, 1999, the PDGE increased its legislative dominance, capturing 75 of the 80 posts in polling that was reportedly again marked by widespread irregularities. The PDGE reportedly won 230 of 244 seats and control of all 30 municipal councils in the local elections of May 28, 2000. Observers described the balloting as generally free and fair, although its significance was greatly undercut by the fact that three leading independent parties boycotted what they described as an "electoral farce." Some analysts suggested that Western capitals were ignoring the lack of democratic progress (as well as continued human rights violations) due to the dramatic surge in oil production.

In February 2001 Dougan resigned, allegedly at the president's urging, over continued corruption allegations against government officials. Incoming prime minister Cándido Muatetema RIVAS, a former deputy secretary general of the PDGE, pledged the new government, which included members of several small parties in junior positions, would protect what he described as the economic and social rights of all citizens, but the opposition charged proceeds from oil sales were being used to consolidate power for the president's ethnic group. Amid continuing political turmoil, President Obiang moved the next presidential balloting up from February 2003 to December 15, 2002. Most opposition parties boycotted the election, and Obiang was reelected with 97.1 percent of the vote. Although Obiang had promised to appoint a government of national unity, he reappointed Rivas to head a reshuffled cabinet that was again dominated by the PDGE and included two of Obiang's sons.

The PDGE and its allies (the newly formed Democratic Opposition coalition) won 98 of 100 seats in the April 25, 2004, balloting for the House of People's Representatives. They also secured nearly all of the seats in concurrent municipal elections. Prime Minister Rivas resigned on June 11 and was succeeded three days later by Miguel Abia Biteo BORICO.

Borico and the entire cabinet resigned on August 10, 2006, and President Obiang appointed Ricardo Mangue Obama NFUBE as prime minister on August 14. On August 15 the president appointed two vice prime ministers, both from the PDGE. On August 16 Nfube named a new cabinet, which again was dominated by the PDGE but also included members of the Democratic Opposition coalition.

Following dissolution of the House of People's Representatives on February 29, 2008, President Obiang called for early elections on May 4 to coincide with municipal elections. The PDGE dominated the legislative balloting, winning 89 seats. The Democratic Opposition, a coalition of eight parties with whom the PDGE had formed an electoral alliance, won ten seats. The PDGE was victorious in the municipal elections as well. On June 8, the president appointed Ignacio Milam TANG, the country's ambassador to Spain, to replace Prime Minister Nfube, whom the president had dismissed on July 4. Following the resignation of the cabinet on the same day, the president referred to the outgoing government as "one of the worst ever," levying blanket accusations of corruption and mismanagement. On July 14 the president appointed a new cabinet, composed entirely of PDGE members.

In October 2009 President Obiang announced that presidential balloting would be held on November 29 (superseding a presidential decree in 2008 that set the election for 2010). Plácido MICÓ Abogo of the CPDS immediately criticized the date, arguing that 45 days was not sufficient time for the opposition to prepare, and he claimed that the PDGE was planning to manipulate the polls. The government, for its part, promised to hold a fair and democratic election, though observers noted the country's lack of an independent, impartial panel to oversee elections or to handle complaints. Despite the alleged irregularities, Micó did not abandon his candidacy and finished a distant second with 3.6 percent of the vote. President Obiang, having declared himself the victor after only a fraction of the votes were counted, garnered 95.4 percent on reported turnout of 93.4 percent. Three minor party candidates each secured less than 0.5 percent of the vote. The president reappointed Prime Minister Tang on January 12, 2010, and named a new, expanded government on January 14.

On January 27, 2011, the president announced a major cabinet reshuffle, declaring a government of national unity that included one member of the opposition party **Convergence for Social Democracy**

(*Convergencia para la Democracia Social*—CPDS). The party vehemently objected, calling the president's decree "fake," and immediately suspended its deputy secretary general for accepting the post. The new government also included the country's first female economy minister and representatives of three small parties supportive of the PDGE. Several days after naming his more inclusive government, President Obiang was elected chair of the African Union (AU).

In line with constitutional reforms proposed by the president, the government resigned on May 18, 2012, as a formality to allow President Obiang to form a new Cabinet. Vicente Ehate Tomi was appointed prime minister on May 21, announcing a new cabinet on May 24 (See Constitution and government, below).

On May 26, 2013, Equatorial Guinea held legislative elections, including balloting for the inaugural senate, which was established in the 2011 constitutional reforms. The PDGE-led electoral alliance won a landslide victory, securing 99 House seats and 54 Senate seats. The CPDS won a seat in each chamber (see Current issues, below).

Constitution and government. The 1982 constitution provided for an elected president serving a seven-year term and for a Council of State, one of whose functions was to screen candidates for presidential nomination. A National Council for Economic and Social Development was linked to the administration in a consultative capacity, while legislative functions were assigned to a unicameral National Assembly, whose members were elected for five-year terms.

In late 1980 the country was divided into six provinces (four mainland and two insular) as part of a process of administrative reform, while there are currently 30 elected municipal governments.

The basic law of November 1991 called for a separation of functions between the president and prime minister, while authorizing competing parties. Meanwhile, it severely limited opposition activity by banning from presidential or parliamentary eligibility all individuals who had not been continuously resident in the country for the preceding two years. In addition, it stipulated that the head of state could "not be impeached, or called as a witness before, during and after his term of office." Subsequent legislation on the formation of political parties specified that no such group could be organized on a tribal, regional, or provincial basis.

The president is the head of the judiciary, and the Supreme Court justices are his advisers. Press freedom is virtually nonexistent in Equatorial Guinea, with few independent outlets beyond government-controlled media. There were reports of intimidation of foreign reporters covering the Africa Cup of Nations in January 2012. In 2013, Reporters Without Borders ranked it 166th of 179 countries on its annual press freedom index.

From late 2011 the country began to implement constitutional reforms, including changing presidential term limitations, reshuffling the cabinet, and creating a senate, the balloting for which took place for the first time on May 26, 2013 (see Current issues, below).

Foreign relations. While officially nonaligned, the Macie regime tended to follow the lead of the more radical African states. Diplomatic relations were established with—and aid received from—several Communist regimes, including the Soviet Union, the People's Republic of China, Cuba, and North Korea. Relations with Gabon and Cameroon were strained as a result of territorial disputes, while by 1976 the mistreatment of Nigerian contract workers had led Lagos to repatriate some 25,000 people, most of them laborers on cocoa plantations. By contrast, the Obiang regime has striven for regional cooperation, with a Nigerian consulate opening in Bata in 1982 and a joint defense pact being concluded during a three-day official visit to Lagos by President Obiang in January 1987. Economic agreements were signed with Cameroon and the Central African Republic in 1983, and Obiang was active in the formation of the Central African Economic Community, announced in October 1983. Two months later, Equatorial Guinea became the first non-French-speaking member of the Central African Customs and Economic Union (UDEAC). As the only African country with Spanish as its official language, Equatorial Guinea was also anxious to develop links with Latin America and was accorded permanent observer status with the Organization of American States (OAS).

At the time of Macie's ouster, France was the only Western power maintaining an embassy in Malabo. Madrid made its first overture to the new regime in December 1979 with a state visit by King Juan Carlos; in 1983, Spain played a leading role in renegotiating Equatorial Guinea's $45 million foreign debt. Following Equatorial Guinea's admission to the franc zone in 1985, Malabo emphasized rapidly expanding ties with France and francophone West African countries.

Frayed by Spain's criticism of Equatorial Guinea's political and human rights practices, ties between the two countries weakened steadily in 1993. In August the government of Equatorial Guinea charged Madrid with inciting antigovernment violence on Annobon Island. In November Spain formally refused to underwrite the legislative balloting, saying it failed to meet "minimum requirements," and following the expulsion of its consul general in Bata, Madrid recalled its ambassador. Only France openly supported the electoral process, with the United States and the United Nations refusing to provide poll watchers.

In September 1997 Equatorial Guinea temporarily suspended diplomatic relations with Spain after Madrid refused to repeal the refugee status of PPGE leader Severo Moto Nsa. (For further details about the Moto case, see the PPGE below and the 1998 *Handbook.*)

In mid-1999 Equatorial Guinea filed a complaint against Cameroon with the International Court of Justice over territorial claims to a section of the Gulf of Guinea that included Bioko Island, which was resolved by the ICJ in 2002. Recent discoveries of offshore oil deposits fueled the dispute. In an effort to reduce tensions and increase cooperation in the Gulf region, a Gulf of Guinea Commission was established. In September 2000 Equatorial Guinea and Nigeria settled their ongoing border dispute, each country gaining sovereignty over one of the two major disputed oil fields.

Full economic ties with Spain were restored by 2001, and Madrid in 2003 forgave some $65 million of Equatorial Guinea's external debt. In addition, Spain offered diplomatic support to Equatorial Guinea when Gabonese troops occupied the disputed island of Mbagne. President Obiang rejected Gabon's offer to withdraw its troops in exchange for an oil-sharing agreement that would cover the island and its surrounding waters. Also in 2003, the United States reopened its embassy in Equatorial Guinea as U.S. companies continued to dominate oil exploration and production.

After Gabon and Equatorial Guinea agreed in 2004 to abide by the decision of a UN mediator appointed to investigate the island dispute, the case was submitted to the International Court of Justice in 2006. In June 2008, UN Secretary General Ban Ki-Moon began mediation to help facilitate a resolution. Meanwhile, China committed $2 billion to Equatorial Guinea for projects restricted to Chinese companies using Chinese products.

In November 2008 relations with Cameroon strained, when a nephew of President Obiang was kidnapped in Yaoundé, allegedly by two Cameroonian police officers who received $30,000 for their effort. Cameroon arrested the officers, denied any involvement, and accused the Equatorial Guinean embassy of being involved in the plot, which the embassy denied. Tensions with Cameroon were strained further in 2009 following the death of a Cameroonian fisherman in Equatorial Guinean waters, along a contentious maritime border. In January Cameroon released three sailors from Equatorial Guinea in exchange for three Cameroonian fishermen detained by Equatorial Guinean troops near the southern border.

In February 2009 an attack on the presidential palace was blamed on rebels from the Niger Delta region of Nigeria. Subsequently, 16 men were arrested, including 11 members of the Popular Unión (Union Popular—UP). The Nigerian government denied any involvement. In March the national security minister urged the army and security forces to stop violence against foreigners suspected of breaking the law, though reportedly that month, 12 Nigerians had been killed and 128 imprisoned in Equatorial Guinea for allegedly belonging to militant groups. In April 2010 seven Nigerian fishermen and traders were sentenced to 12 years in prison for attempting to assassinate the president in connection with the palace attack the previous year. Two UP members tried with the Nigerians were acquitted, but following a second arrest in August, they were convicted.

In June 2010, the United Nations Educational, Scientific, and Cultural Organization (UNESCO) refused President Obiang's offer of a $3 million scientific award due to Western nations' concerns about the regime's alleged corruption.

Equatorial Guinea sought to expand its ties with Egypt in 2010 as the two countries signed several bilateral agreements and Malabo sought support for its hosting of the AU summit in June 2011. Trade relations increased with Brazil.

In February 2011 the leaders of Equatorial Guinea and Gabon met for the first time to address their border dispute and agreed to participate in UN-facilitated mediation efforts. Following a "trilateral" meeting with UN Secretary General Ban-Ki Moon, they submitted their dispute to the International Court of Justice on February 26.

In March 2011 the president, as chair of the AU, worked to block AU support for the antigovernment protesters in North Africa and the region. When Libyan rebels began fighting in an attempt to overturn the regime, President Obiang expressed support for his longtime friend Col. Muammar Qadhafi. Subsequently, however, many African states voted in favor of the UN Security Council resolution for military action against the regime, leaving only Obiang and the AU's Peace and Security Council backing the Libyan leader.

President Obiang represented the AU at the G-20 Summit in Cannes, France, in November 2011 and urged the G-20 to work with African economies to insulate them from financial volatility.

In February 2012 Equatorial Guinea and Zimbabwe signed an oil deal worth $1.5 billion, in which Equatorial Guinea will provide a line of credit to Zimbabwe in exchange for mining rights.

In April 2012, Equatorial Guinea tightened its border with Cameroon to stop economic migrants from entering the country illegally, but stressed this action would not affect relations with Cameroon. Equatorial Guinea joined a Global Environment Facility (GEF) backed by international organizations and nongovernment organizations (NGOs) to combat illegal logging and promote sustainable forestry practices.

Close ties between China and Equatorial Guinea were reinforced as China increased its West African oil imports in 2012. The fourth China–Equatorial Guinea economic and trade joint commission meeting was held in China in April 2012.

In April 2013 a French appeals court threw out a defamation suit filed by Obiang against a French NGO that had alleged in a 2009 report that the administration had embezzled some $26.5 million from the nation's oil income.

The growing piracy problem in the Gulf of Guinea has fostered regional antipiracy cooperation efforts. In August 2013, Equatorial Guinea hosted regional leaders for a summit on maritime security.

Current issues. In July 2010 the president's son, Teodoro "Teodorin" Nguema OBIANG Mangue, was elected chair of the youth wing of the PDGE, a seat that automatically made him vice president of the party and, according to observers, one step closer to succeeding his father as leader of the country.

When President Obiang made his ministerial changes in January 2011, the CPDS was highly critical of his having appointed one of the party's officials to a junior post, blasting Obiang's "unilateral, Machiavellian act of poor intentions" and citing the lack of negotiations with or agreement from the party. The president's decree of a unity government came days before his election to head the AU. Following criticism for his human rights record from international observers, Obiang signed an agreement with the Red Cross of Central Africa to allow a permanent mission to monitor activities in the country. However, the administration continues to be dogged with questions about corruption. In February the president's son "Teodorin" was widely reported to have commissioned a $380 million super-yacht, the price noted by observers to be three times the nation's annual expenditure on health and education. News reports also cited the younger Obiang's $35 million mansion in Malibu, California, $33 million jet, and fleet of luxury cars—all managed on a monthly salary of $6,700 as agriculture minister. Watchdog groups claimed that the bulk of Teodorin's wealth was the result of extortion and urged Washington to impose sanctions or freeze whatever assets he held in the United States. Meanwhile, a U.S. Senate investigation reported in February that over the past several years the president's son had circumvented money-laundering controls and used suspect funds and hidden assets to pay for real estate and other expensive purchases in the United States.

As massive civil unrest spread through Tunisia, Egypt, and other countries in North Africa and the region in 2011, President Obiang blocked news reports of the tumultuous events, including radio broadcasts from Spain, and prohibited any reporting of it by media inside the country. The opposition called for a mass prodemocracy protest in Malabo on March 23. President Obiang accused the organizers of provoking a rebellion and banned the protests, unleashing a massive police force on the day of the planned demonstration, which did not materialize.

In March 2011, with widespread uprisings against rulers in Africa and the Middle East, President Obiang announced the "advisability of reforming the constitution," and in May stated that his goal was to foster broader participation of people across the political spectrum, promising more democratic institutions and creating audit and supervision bodies for the economy and government. A referendum on constitutional reform secured an overwhelming positive vote in November 2011. Human Rights Watch expressed concern that the changes would only strengthen the near-absolute powers of President Obiang and further curtail civil and political rights. Opposition parties UP and CPDS publicly distanced themselves from the reforms, under which the president is limited to two 7-year terms, and can appoint a Senate and a vice president. In May 2012, President Obiang appointed his son, Teodoro Obiang Nguame, as "Second Vice President" (a position that was not mentioned in the draft constitution) in charge of defense, a move interpreted by opposition groups as a sign that Obiang is grooming his son as a successor.

International efforts to address corruption intensified in 2012. In February France conducted an enquiry into the assets held by Equatorial Guinea after anticorruption group Transparency International claimed government officials had plundered state funds to build personal fortunes. In April French judges sought an arrest warrant for Teodorin on suspicion of acquiring property in France by fraudulent means. In response, the government warned this "provocation" might lead to negative consequences for French companies in Equatorial Guinea. In support of the earlier U.S. Senate investigation, in June an amended complaint was filed at a federal district court in Washington, D.C., laying out evidence that Teodorin had orchestrated a scheme to use U.S. financial institutions to funnel millions of dollars from Equatorial Guinea into the United States.

In January 2013 President Obiang called the legislative elections for May 26. On March 30, ten of the 12 opposition parties entered an electoral alliance with the PDGE, leaving just the CPDS and the APGE to campaign independently. The UP was reportedly among the PDGE-aligned parties, though party officials denied it and joined leaders of the nonrecognized Democratic Party for Social Justice in organizing a demonstration on May 15 to appeal to France and the United States for help ousting Obiang. The demonstration of some 200 people was greeted with heavy police presence, with at least four organizers arrested. Meanwhile, the government implemented a partial Internet ban, blocking access to Facebook and other Websites (including the CPDS site). Reporters Without Borders, which lists Obiang as a predator of freedom of information, condemned the action.

The PDGE reportedly won a landslide victory, securing 99 of 100 House seats, while the CPDS maintained its single seat. In the first senatorial contest, the PDGE won 54 seats and the CPDS, 1. (The remaining 15 seats are appointed by the president.) Opposition leader Plácido Micó of the CPDS denounced the results as fraudulent.

POLITICAL PARTIES

Political parties were banned in the wake of the 1979 coup. In late 1987 President Obiang announced the formation of a government party (the Democratic Party of Equatorial Guinea—PDGE), as part of what he called a democratization process that might eventually lead to the legalization of other groups. In late 1991 and early 1992 the Obiang regime approved legislation that (albeit with restrictive provisions, including a requirement that applicant groups pay a deposit of approximately $110,000) provided a legal framework for the formation of political parties. In May 1992 two parties, the Liberal Democratic Convention (CLD) and the Popular Union (UP), were registered, and by the end of the year four more had been legalized.

During February 10–March 18, 1993, the government sponsored an assembly of the PDGE and the (then) ten legal opposition parties to discuss ways to improve the "democratization process," including lessened restrictions on party activities and increased access to state funds and media. Nevertheless, charging a lack of government action, most opposition parties declared that they would boycott elections then scheduled for August. Ultimately, eight parties, including the PDGE, took part in the November balloting; however, the three leading members of the Joint Opposition Platform (POC) refused to participate. After suffering from what they perceived as government electoral abuses in the September 1995 municipal elections, many opposition parties boycotted the February 1996 presidential poll. (For more on the POC, see the 2013 *Handbook*.)

In October 1997 the two most prominent former POC members, the Progress Party of Equatorial Guinea (PPGE) and the UP, joined with the Union for Democracy and Social Development (UDDS) and the Republican Democratic Force (FDR) to form a new coalition, the **National Liberation Council.** The council's platform was highlighted by a pledge to "bring a change of government ... at all costs." In December the legislature passed a law forbidding the formation of coalitions prior to legislative balloting (then scheduled for mid-1998, but subsequently postponed until March 1999).

In early 2000 Victorino BOLEKIA Bonay, the leader of the opposition **Progressive Democratic Alliance** (*Alianza Demócratica y Progresiva*—ADP) and former mayor of Malabo, announced that the opposition, including the Convergence for Social Democracy (CPDS) and the UP, would boycott municipal balloting scheduled for May, protesting, among other things, restrictions on opposition freedom of expression and the lack of international observers.

Various, and at times overlapping, opposition alliances were formed in 2000 and 2001, the most prominent of which was the **Democratic Opposition Front** (*Frente de la Oposicion Demócratica*—FOD) that included the UP, ADP, the CPDS, the PPGE, and the Social Democratic Party (PSD). The FOD was launched in November 2000. In December the **Equatorial Guinea National Resistance** (*Resistencia Nacional Guinea Ecuatorial*—RENAGE) was launched in Barcelona, Spain; it included the UP, the UDDS, the FDR, the MAIB, and the Union of Independent Socialists (UDI). In March 2001 a new opposition alliance was reportedly formed by the UP, the CPDS, the PPGE, the FDR, the UDI, the MAIB, the National Alliance for the Restoration of Democracy (ANRD), the UDDS, the Party of the Democratic Coalition, and the Forum for Democracy in Equatorial Guinea (see below). Although instrumental in the formation of all of the above opposition alliances, the Popular Union (UP) accepted a junior cabinet post in March 2001. However, the UP campaigned against the dominant PDGE in the 2004 elections. In 2004 eight pro-presidential parties formed the **Democratic Opposition** electoral coalition and campaigned in both legislative and local elections. The coalition gained 30 seats in the legislature, and legislators from two of the parties—the Liberal Democratic Convention and the Social Democratic Union—were appointed to posts in the government. The Democratic Opposition also campaigned with the PDGE in the concurrent municipal elections, winning, with the PDGE, 237 of 244 posts.

In 2008 the coalition won 10 assembly seats in an electoral alliance with the PDGE, but no posts in the new government. In 2011 a CPDS member accepted a junior cabinet post against the wishes of the party. Ahead of the 2013 legislative election, the PDGE formed an alliance with ten of the 12 opposition parties.

Government and Government-Supportive Parties:

Democratic Party of Equatorial Guinea (*Partido Democrático de Guinea Ecuatorial*—PDGE). The PDGE was launched in October 1987 by President Obiang, who said it would be used to address the country's development problems while promoting national unity and "respect for the constitution and freedoms." Shortly thereafter, the House of Representatives approved a law requiring all public officials and salaried employees to contribute 3 percent of their salaries to the new formation.

During an extraordinary party congress in Bata on August 4–6, 1991, party delegates urged the government to establish short-, medium-, and long-term plans to lead to the legalization of other political groups and approved resolutions calling for the adoption of a multi-candidature presidential system and the drafting of a law on press rights.

At the PDGE's second national congress on March 20–26, 1995, President Obiang reaffirmed the party's preeminent role in the implementation of public policy and the PDGE has since remained the dominant government party. In legislative elections in 2004 the PDGE and its allies in the Democratic Opposition received 87.9 percent of the vote and 98 of the 100 seats in the legislature. In local elections, the PDGE and its allies won 237 of 244 posts. In 2008 the party won 89 seats in the assembly elections and also swept the concurrent local elections. Because of its electoral alliance with the Democratic Opposition, the PDGE effectively controlled 99 of the 100 legislative seats.

The party came under harsh criticism for allegedly planning fraud during the campaign for the early 2009 presidential election.

On March 30, 2013, the PDGE became the leader of an 11-party progovernment alliance. In May 26 balloting, the PDGE maintained its 99-seat majority in the House. In the first Senate elections, the party won 54 of 55 available seats.

Leaders: Brig. Gen. Teodoro OBIANG Nguema Mbasogo (President of the Republic), Vicente TOMI (Prime Minister), Teodoro "Teodorin" Nguema OBIANG Mangue (Vice President of the Party and Chair of the Party's National Youth Federation), Ricardo Mangue Obama NFUBE (Former Prime Minister), Miguel Abia Biteo BORICO (Former Prime Minister), Lucas NGUEMA ESONO MBANG (Secretary General).

Liberal Democratic Convention (*Convención Liberal Democrática*—CLD). Also identified as the Liberal Party (*Partido Liberal*—PL), the CLD was legally recognized in May 1992. In November Santos Pascual BIKOMO Nanguande, who had previously been linked to the **People's Alliance** (*Alianza del Pueblo*—AP), was named to serve as CLD chair until the party's first congress. An attempt to hold such a congress in January 1994 was blocked by the government after Bikomo had charged it with election irregularities.

The CLD was credited with winning one legislative seat in November 1993. Although an original member of the POC, the CLD supported President Obiang in the February 1996 presidential balloting, and Bikomo was named information minister in the new April government. Although Bikomo left his post in 1997, the CLD remained a government-supportive party and held junior ministries following the 1999 and 2004 elections. The party held no ministry posts following the July 14, 2008, cabinet reshuffle, when the president named an all-PDGE government, though in 2011 party president Alfonso Nsue Mokuy was appointed a junior cabinet post. The party joined the PDGE electoral alliance in March 2013.

Leader: Alfonso Nsue MOKUY (President).

Social Democratic Union (*Unión Demócrata Social*—UDS). Formerly a Gabon-based grouping affiliated with the ADP (Progressive Democratic Alliance) and the **Democratic Social Union** (*Unión Social Democrática*—USD), the UDS was officially recognized in October 1992 under the leadership of Carmelo MODÚ Acusé Bindang. In November the UDS leadership had expelled Modú for pursuing "ideals which ran counter to the principles" of the party and had named Angel Miko Alo Nchama as interim chair. However, Modú was subsequently again described as the leader of the UDS, which won five legislative seats in November 1993. After supporting President Obiang for reelection, Modú was named minister of state for labor and social security in the April 1996 cabinet and has subsequently held several government posts. The party's former secretary general, Aquilino Nguema Ona NCHAMA, who originally sought political refuge in Gabon, was reportedly living in exile in Spain and was secretary general of the UDDS (see Other Parties and Groups, below).

Leader: Miguel Mba NSANG (Secretary General).

Social Democratic and Popular Convention (*Convención Social Demócrata y Popular*—CSDP). The CSDP is reportedly split into two factions. The first, led by Rafael Obiang, apparently remained aligned with the POC, having boycotted the 1993 parliamentary elections and the 1996 presidential balloting. The second, led by Secundio Oyono Awong, participated in the 1993 legislative campaign, winning six seats. The latter also forwarded Oyono Awong as a presidential contender in 1996, several reports describing him as the only opposition candidate not to withdraw from the campaign prior to balloting.

Leaders: Santiago Ondo NTUGU, Secundio OYONO Awong (1996 presidential candidate).

Social Democratic Coalition Party (*Partido de Coalición Social Demócrata*—PCSD). The PCSD was officially registered in 1993. In early 1996 party leader Buenaventura Mezui Masumu announced his presidential candidacy; however, he withdrew from the campaign to protest the government's allegedly fraudulent pre-election activities. In the 2004 legislative and municipal elections, the PCSD garnered less than 1 percent of the vote.

In the 2009 presidential election Masumu finished fourth, with 0.17 percent of the vote.

Leader: Buenaventura Mezui MASUMU (2009 presidential candidate).

Social Democratic Party (*Partido Social Demócrata*—PSD). Formed by Marcellino Mangue MBA and recognized as a party in 1992, the PSD was formerly affiliated with the anti-Obiang group, the Party of the Democratic Coalition. However, it joined the pro-presidential coalition in 2004 and again allied with the PDGE in 2013.

Leaders: Benjamín BALINGA (President), Francisco Mabale NSENG.

Socialist Party of Equatorial Guinea (*Partido Socialista de Guinea Ecuatorial*—PSGE). Citing legislative constraints on party activity, the PSGE in January 1992 described President Obiang's multiparty advocacy as an attempt to deceive international observers. Subsequently, party leader Tomás Mecheba FERNÁNDEZ called for foreign intervention, military if necessary, to force the regime to cease human rights violations. The PSGE later supported cooperation with the PDGE, and Fernández accepted a junior post in the cabinet in 2001. However, the party did not win seats in the 2004 legislative election (gaining just 0.21 percent of the vote) and did not participate in the subsequent cabinet.

In January 2011, when President Obiang reshuffled the cabinet, a few members of smaller parties were appointed, including Fernández, who was named to a junior cabinet post. He was appointed minister for social health and welfare in May 2012.

Leader: Tomás Mecheba FERNÁNDEZ Galilea (President).

Popular Union (*Unión Popular*—UP). The UP was legally recognized in May 1992. However in October party members were detained and beaten by government security forces, and in March 1993, the group reportedly concluded a merger agreement with the PPGE (although there was no confirmation of the accord).

In August 1993 the government announced that UP activist Pedro MOTU Mamiaka had committed suicide while in detention. However, Amnesty International accused security forces of torturing him to death, and the UP called his death another demonstration of the government's persecution of dissenters.

The UP presented Andrés Moisés MBA Ada as a candidate in the 1996 presidential campaign, reportedly angering more senior politicians in the POC. In April 1998 the UP claimed that the government had detained 200 of its activists during a nationwide crackdown on opposition members.

The UP won four seats in the 1999 legislative balloting, but party leaders ordered the UP legislators to refuse to take their seats as a protest against perceived electoral fraud on the part of the government. A party split emerged when two legislators disobeyed UP orders over whether there should be cooperation with the PDGE. The election of Jeremia ONDO Ngomo as party president in October 2000 ushered in an era of cooperation, as the party reversed its boycott of the assembly, and Ondo accepted a junior post in the new government formed in March 2001. UP Secretary General Fabián NSUE Nguema, arrested for treason, was pardoned in November 2002. The UP reportedly remained active in various opposition alliances, and it joined the boycott of the 2004 legislative election.

Under pressure by the government in 2007 to elect a new leader, the UP held a party congress in October and chose Faustino Ond EBANG as its president, whom the government refused to recognize. In the aftermath of the attack on the presidential palace in February 2009, 11 members of the UP, including Ebang's brother and two others (former members of the outlawed PPGE) were arrested, detained without charge, and tortured, according to Amnesty International.

In the 2009 presidential election Archivaldo Montero BRIBÉ finished third, with 0.34 percent of the vote. Ebang, who the government claimed was the mastermind behind the 2009 attack, fled to Spain. In 2010 he was tried in absentia and ordered to pay $610,000. Two UP members were acquitted of the charges relating to the attack in April 2010 but were arrested and charged again in August.

In March 2011, in the wake of mass protests in North Africa and the Middle East, the UP tried to organize a prodemocracy demonstration in Malabo, but the effort was quickly quashed by the government. In August 2011 the UP issued a statement distancing the party officially from the constitutional reform process.

Party leaders have been arbitrarily arrested, including Nsue's mysterious disappearance in October 2012 and party president Daniel DARÍO Martínez Ayécaba's arrest in the airport two months later. Both were subsequently released. Ahead of the 2013 elections, the UP reportedly joined the PDGE-led electoral alliance. UP leaders subsequently denied the report. The party led an antigovernment rally on May 15 (see Current issues, above). Government forces swiftly broke up the 200-strong demonstration and arrested nine activists, including Secretary General Jerónimo NDONG.

Leaders: Daniel DARÍO Martínez Ayécaba (President), Archivaldo Montero BIRIBÉ (2009 presidential candidate), Jerónimo NDONG (Secretary General), Fabián NSUE Nguema, Andrés Moisés MBA Ada (Former President).

Other members of the 2013 electoral alliance include the **Progressive Democratic Alliance** (*Alianza Demócrata Progresista*—ADP), led by Victorino Bolekia BONAY, former mayor of Malabo, and Francisco Mba Oló BAHAMONDE, who was given a junior cabinet post in January 2011; the **Democratic National Union of Equatorial Guinea** (*Unión Demócráta Nacional*—UDENA), led by Pedro Cristino BUERIBERI; and the **Liberal Party** (*Partido Liberal*—PL), led by Salvador Nguema MANGUE.

Convergence for Social Democracy (*Convergencia para la Democracia Social*—CPDS). The CPDS was launched in Paris in May 1984 by the two groups below, which set as their goal talks with President Obiang designed "to democratically transform all the state institutions, to guarantee fundamental liberties, and to promote a policy of cooperation with neighboring countries and the Western world." The party was legally recognized in February 1993; however, on September 19, two days after he was convicted of murder in a summary military trial, CPDS activist Romualdo Rafael NSOGO was executed. Subsequently, CPDS leaders denounced the regime, accusing it of killing Nsogo in an attempt to intimidate the opposition.

In early 1996 the CPDS presented Anoncio NZE Angue as its presidential candidate, although he withdrew, along with the other POC candidates, to protest the government's tactics prior to the balloting. Nze was reportedly arrested in March for possessing CPDS documents referring to the Obiang administration as "an unreconstructed family dictatorship." At that time *Africa Confidential* referred to the CPDS as the "most radical" opposition group and the least likely to participate in national unity talks with the government.

In early 1998 a CPDS spokesperson reportedly accused the West of refusing to put pressure on the Obiang administration to enact political and social reforms because of Western "economic interests" in the country. In April the group claimed that nearly 50 of its members had been arrested by government security forces.

The CPDS won one seat in legislative polling in March 1999 but its representative subsequently refused to assume the post in protest over the government's alleged electoral malfeasance. On May 9, 2002, Secretary General Plácido Micó Abogo was arrested on charges of conspiracy to assassinate the president. He was pardoned in August 2003.

The CPDS won two seats in the 2004 legislative balloting but denounced the results because of alleged voting problems.

In January 2005 Santiago Obama Ndong was elected party president. In May the party's publication, *The Truth* (*La Verdad*), reportedly was shut down by the government, a month after several CPDS activists were arrested following clashes with security forces.

In the run-up to the 2008 legislative elections, the party's headquarters were reportedly raided by police. The CPDS won just one seat in the assembly. The secretary general alleged fraud.

Ahead of the 2010 presidential election, Plácido Micó Abogo, President Obiang's most vocal critic,, accused the president of spending millions in campaign funds and controlling state media coverage and criticized him for not holding any public debates.

The party was highly critical of President Obiang's appointment of CPDS deputy secretary general, Celestino Bonifacio Bacale, as minister delegate in the cabinet reorganization of January 2011. Party leaders reportedly ridiculed Obiang's references to a "unity" government and immediately suspended Bacale from his party post. In March the CPDS was denied permission to hold meetings in Malabo and Bata as opposition members sought to stage prodemocracy protests.

In March 2012 Doctor Wenceslao MANSOGO, a prominent member of the party, was sentenced to three years in prison after what Human Rights Watch described as a "politically motivated" trial. Mansogo, a doctor, was convicted of medical negligence after a patient died during an operation. After international outcry, President Obiang pardoned Mansogo in June.

The CPDS was one of two opposition parties to contest the May 2013 elections. The government cracked down on opposition parties ahead of the election, with security forces harassing CPDS members at a May 15 demonstration and access blocked to the party Website. The CPDS secured one seat in the House and one in the Senate. Micó denounced the results as fraudulent.

Leaders: Santiago Obama NDONG (President), Celestino Bonifacio BACALE (2002 presidential candidate), Pio OBAMA, Plácido MICÓ Abogo (Secretary General and 2009 presidential candidate).

Democratic Movement for the Liberation of Equatorial Guinea (*Reunión Democrática para la Liberación de Guinea Ecuatorial*—RDLGE). Formed in 1981, the Paris-based RDLGE announced a provisional government-in-exile in March 1983 following the failure of reconciliation talks between its leader and

Colonel Obiang in late 1982. The RDLGE was considered a relatively moderate opposition group, the formation of the CPDS apparently representing its response to the creation by more strident groups of the *Junta Coordinadora* (below, under ANRD).

Leader: Manuel Rubén NDONGO.

African Socialist Party of Equatorial Guinea (*Partido Socialista Africano de Guinea Ecuatorial*—PSAGE). Based in Oviedo, Spain, the PSAGE was little known prior to its CPDS alliance with the RDLGE.

Other Parties That Contested the 2013 Legislative Election:

Popular Action of Equatorial Guinea (*L'Action Populaire de Guinée Equatoriale*—APGE). Formed in 2003, the APGE was among six opposition groups that established themselves in exile in Spain, influenced by Severo Moto of the PPGE (above). The APGE, led by Miguel Esono Eman, fielded candidates in the 2004 parliamentary and municipal elections, but garnered just 0.25 percent of the vote.

In the 2009 presidential election APGE candidate Carmelo Mba Bacale withdrew a day ahead of the poll, accusing the PDGE of fraud, claiming that PDGE members were also heading polling stations. Bacale received 0.16 percent of the vote, finishing fifth. Bacale is the sole opposition member on the country's commission for constitutional reform. He said in May 2011 his party would not take part in the referendum on the reforms because they were "a sham."

As one of two independent parties, the APGE unsuccessfully contested the May 2013 election.

Leaders: Miguel Esono EMAN, Carmelo Mba BACALE (2009 presidential candidate).

Other Parties and Groups:

Progress Party of Equatorial Guinea (*Partido del Progreso de Guinea Ecuatorial*—PPGE). Also referenced as the People's Party of Equatorial Guinea, the PPGE was formed in Madrid in early 1983 by Severo Moto Nsa, a former secretary of state for information and tourism. Moto and other PPGE leaders returned to Malabo in mid-1988, apparently believing that the government had adopted a conciliatory attitude toward its opponents. However, a PPGE petition for recognition as a legal party was denied, and Moto returned to exile. In September several PPGE members, including Secretary General José Luis Jones, were jailed in connection with an alleged coup plot. Given a lengthy prison sentence shortly after his arrest, Jones received a presidential pardon in January 1989.

In August 1991 Moto planned a second termination of exile to campaign for a multiparty system and the holding of free elections, but the government refused to renew his passport until May 1992, when he returned to Malabo. In early September PPGE members were among those detained in another government crackdown on dissident activity. Nonetheless, the party was legalized in October.

In July 1994 the government severed relations with the PPGE after Moto allegedly defamed the Obiang regime, and in November the PPGE leader accused Obiang of involvement in the death of his brother, Vincente MOTO. Subsequently, in March 1995, Moto was sentenced to 18 months in prison for allegedly bribing a government official and defaming the head of state. A far more severe sentence of 28 years was imposed on Moto in April by a military tribunal investigating an alleged coup plot. The sentences were condemned by a number of Western governments, and, following the intercession of French President Jacques Chirac, President Obiang granted amnesty to Moto on August 3.

Moto announced his candidacy for president in early 1996; however, like most other opposition candidates, he withdrew prior to the balloting and urged PPGE supporters to boycott the election. Nevertheless, at midyear Moto was reported to have indicated the willingness of the PPGE and some of the other remaining POC component groups to reopen discussions with the Obiang government. In June 1997 the government banned the PPGE after it was revealed that Moto had allegedly been planning to overthrow the Obiang government. The following month the party ousted Moto after he restated his willingness to use violence to topple the government. On August 18 Moto was convicted in absentia of high treason and sentenced to at least 30 years in jail. Concurrently, the government ordered the PPGE to dissolve.

In October 1997 Moto, who was still being identified by observers as the PPGE's leader, surfaced in the Democratic Republic of the Congo as the organizer of a new antigovernment coalition. Subsequently, the PPGE suffered another blow when its first and second deputy leaders reportedly defected to the PDGE in early 1998.

In early 1999 Moto filed suit in Spain against the Obiang government, charging it with engaging in "state terrorism and genocide." Furthermore, Moto announced that his party would boycott legislative polling in March. The government called on Madrid to expel Moto, who had reportedly been residing there for two years. The PPGE also boycotted the 2004 elections, joining with other exile groups to form a government-in-exile in Spain with Moto as its leader.

In late 2005 Spain revoked political asylum for Moto but refused to return him to Equatorial Guinea or any other country that would not guarantee his safety.

In March 2008 eight party members were arrested in Equatorial Guinea, one of whom was reported to have died in custody. Subsequently, Moto was arrested in Spain in April on charges of arms trafficking to Equatorial Guinea. The PPGE was banned from participating in Equatorial Guinea's legislative elections in May. Meanwhile, Moto, who had been arrested in Spain on charges of arms trafficking, was sentenced in absentia to 62 years in prison for his alleged involvement in a 2004 coup attempt. In 2009 President Obiang said he would grant Moto amnesty if he would return to Equatorial Guinea and serve some of his sentence, but Moto remains in exile.

Leaders: Severo MOTO Nsá (President, in exile), Armengol ENGONGA (Vice President), José Luis JONES (Secretary General).

Republican Democratic Force (*Fuerza Demócrata Republicana*—FDR). In October 1997 this grouping was reported among the founders of the National Liberation Council. Subsequently, its cofounders, Felipe Ondo Obiang and Guillermo Nguema Ela, were described by party members as having been "abducted"; however, the government then admitted holding the two, and in mid-November they were released without explanation. In March 1998 the two were rearrested and charged with making defamatory comments about the president. They were released in March 2000, at which time they vowed to continue their campaign against the administration. In 2002 exiled resistance leader Daniel Oyono (see UDI, below) accused the government of tossing Nguema's body into the ocean from a plane and of torturing and killing Ondo. In 2003 Amnesty International reported that Ondo was being held by the government and tortured. The government denied reports that security forces had killed Ondo, saying that he had been transferred from one prison to another. Nguema was released from the country's notorious Black Beach prison in June 2009. His wife at one point was held in prison in Malabo without charge or trial for four months.

Leaders: Felipe ONDO Obiang, Guillermo NGUEMA Ela, Bonifacio NGUEMA, German Pedro Tomo MANGUE.

Union for Democracy and Social Development (*Unión para la Democracia y el Desarrollo Social*—UDDS). The UDDS was the core component of the Opposition Coordination of Equatorial Guinea (*Coordinación Oposición de Guinea Ecuatorial*—COGE), launched in March 1992 by several groups, including the PR, the Zaire-based **Movement for the National Unification of Equatorial Guinea** (*Movimiento para la Unificación Nacional de Guinea Ecuatorial*—MUNGE); the **Republican Party of Equatorial Guinea** (*Partido Republicano de Guinea Ecuatorial*—PRGE); the **National Movement for the Reliberation of Equatorial Guinea** (*Movimiento Nacional para la Reliberación de Guinea Ecuatorial*—Monarge); and the PSGE, which subsequently joined the POC.

Led by vociferous regime critic Antonio Sibacha Bueicheku, the UDDS in early 1993 called on the Guinean clergy to publicly denounce the Obiang administration's human rights record and urged the European Community (EC, subsequently the European Union—EU) and France to impose sanctions to stem the "perpetual violations." On May 31 five UDDS members were detained when security forces raided a party meeting. Consequently, in early June the party exhorted opposition members to fight the "last dictatorship." In early 1994 the party applauded Spain's decision to suspend aid to Equatorial Guinea and urged other donors to follow suit. In 2004 the UDDS renewed its request for intervention by the UN, the United States, France, and Spain to help bring about political change.

In June 2012 Buiecheku returned from self-imposed exile after 35 years in Spain, met with President Obiang, and praised developments in infrastructure and development, urging other leaders in self-imposed exile to return. Ahead of the 2013 election, the UDDS called for an electoral boycott.

Leaders: Antonio SIBACHA Bueicheku, Aquilino Nguema Ona NCHAMA (Secretary General).

National Alliance for the Restoration of Democracy (*Alianza Nacional de Restauración Democrática*—ANRD). Founded in 1974, the Swiss-based ANRD announced in August 1979 that it would regard the ouster of Macie as nothing more than a "palace revolution" unless a number of conditions were met, including the trial of all individuals for atrocities under the former dictator and the establishment of a firm date for termination of military rule.

In April 1983 the ANRD was instrumental in the launching of the Coordinating Board of Opposition Democratic Forces (*Junta Coordinadora de las Fuerzas de Oposición Democrática*), formed by a group of Spanish-based exile formations, then including the PPGE, to present a united front against President Obiang, whom it accused of failing to live up to the people's expectations and exhibiting a lack of respect for the law. The *Junta* denounced the August 1983 legislative balloting as a sham and called for an economic embargo of the Obiang regime by regional governments. Other participants in the *Junta* included the **Movement for the Liberation and Future of Equatorial Guinea** (*Movimiento de Liberación y Futuro de Guinea Ecuatorial*—Molifuge), the **Liberation Front of Equatorial Guinea** (*Frente de Liberación de Guinea Ecuatorial*—Frelige), and the **Democratic Reform** (*Reforma Democrática*). The ANRD boycotted the 2004 legislative elections.

Leader: Luis Ondo AYANG.

Union of Independent Democrats (*Unión Democrática Independiente*—UDI). Formation of the Revolutionary Command Council of Socialist Guinean Patriots was announced in September 1981 by Daniel Oyono, a former secretary of state for economy and finance, as a union of three internal groups: the Union of Independent Democrats (*Unión de Demócratas Independientes*—UDI), the Revolutionary Movement, and the Socialist Front. In addition to political liberalization, the new formation called for the withdrawal of foreign troops from Equatorial Guinea, a reference to the Moroccan and Spanish troops in the presidential guard. The extent of the council's subsequent activity has been unclear, although in mid-1999 it was reported that the council and Bubi nationalists had agreed to coordinate their activities. The UDI rubric was routinely referenced in news reports in the early 2000s.

Leader: Daniel OYONO.

Three other anti-Obiang groups are the Party of the Democratic Coalition, led by Francisco JONES; the Forum for Democracy in Equatorial Guinea; and the National Movement for the Liberation of Equatorial Guinea (*Movimiento Nacional de Liberación de la Guinea Ecuatorial*—Monalige), a continuation of a historic group (see Political background).

In April 2005 it was reported that former prime minister Christino Seriche Malabo BIOKO had joined exiled opposition activists in Spain and founded the **Vanguard for the Defense of Citizens' Rights** in December 2004 to "promote the establishment of a real democratic state" in Equatorial Guinea.

Two days before a scheduled antigovernment demonstration on May 15, 2013, two leaders of the officially unrecognized political group the **Democratic Party for Social Justice** were arrested.

Separatist Groups:

April 1 Bubi Nationalist Group. The Bubi Nationalist coalition was launched in Madrid in April 1983 by a number of groups advocating independence for the island of Bioko (formerly Fernando Póo) where the Bubi people then constituted a majority. The Bubi organizations had been excluded from the *Junta Coordinadora* because of their opposition to its goal of promoting a "national identity." The new Bubi formation subsequently issued a number of calls for an end to alleged human rights abuses against the islanders.

Leader: Bwalalele BOKOKO Itogi (Secretary General).

Movement for the Self-Determination of the Island of Bioko (*Movimiento par la Autodeterminación de la Isla de Bioko*—MAIB). The role of the Movement, established in 1993 in the Bubi nationalist movement, came under increased scrutiny following the arrest of a number of its members in July 1995. In late January 1998 the Movement denied government charges that it had organized deadly attacks on Bioko Island, countering that, following the incidents earlier in the month, the island's residents had been subjected to killing and torture by government forces and that 800 people had been arrested.

In June 1998, 15 Movement members were sentenced to death for their alleged roles in the January uprising. In addition, one of the group's leaders, Martin PUYE, was given a 20-year prison term; however, Puye, who, along with a number of the other Movement defendants, had showed signs of being tortured, died in jail in July. In August the president commuted the remaining death sentences to terms of life imprisonment.

Party activist Weja Chicampo returned from exile in Spain in 2003. In 2004, according to Amnesty International, he was arrested by hooded police officers, beaten, and imprisoned. He was freed by President Obiang in 2005. In February 2006 the group alleged that the government had killed one of its founders, Laesa Atanasio Bita ROPE, who had been sentenced to death in absentia by Equatorial Guinea in 1998. Rope was killed in the Côte d'Ivoire.

Leaders: Anacleto BOKESSA, Weja CHICAMPO, Paco AUDIJE.

LEGISLATURE

The constitutional reforms of 2011 converted the previously unicameral system to bicameral legislature.

House of People's Representatives (*Cámara de Representantes del Pueblo*). House representatives are elected to a five-year term. The PDGE-dominated, 41-member legislature elected in July 1988 was dissolved by the president in early July 1993. In balloting on March 7, 1999, for the 80-member House (enlarged to its current size in 1993), the Democratic Party of Equatorial Guinea (PDGE) won 75 seats; the Popular Union (UP), 4; and the Convergence for Social Democracy (CPDS), 1. The legislators from the UP and the CPDS refused to fill their seats as a protest against the government's conduct of the election. However, the UP later reversed its decision. In 2003, the legislature was enlarged to 100 seats in preparation for the 2004 elections.

In the most recent election on May 26, 2013, the PDGE won 99 seats, and the CPDS, 1.

President: Gaudencio Mohaba MESU.

Senate (*Senado*). Established in constitutional reforms ratified in November 2011, the Senate comprises 55 elected members and 15 presidential appointees serving five-year terms. In the first election, held on May 26, 2013, the PDGE won 54 seats and the CPDS, 1.

President: María Teresa Efua NSANG.

CABINET

[as of September 1, 2013]

Prime Minister	Vicente Ehate Tomi
First Deputy Prime Minister, in Charge of Political and Democracy Affairs	Clemente Engonga Nguema Onguene
Second Deputy Prime Minister, in Charge of Social and Human Rights Affairs	Alfonso Nsue Mokuy
Vice President, Head of Presidential Affairs	Ignacio Milam Tang
Second Vice President of the Republic, Head of Defense and State Security	Teodoro Nguema Obiang Mangue
Ministers	
Defense	Gen. Antonio Mba Nguema
Economy, Trade, and Promotion of Business	Celestino Bonifacio Bakale Obiang
Finance and Budget	Marcelino Owono Edu
Fisheries and Environment	Crescencio Tamarite Castaño
Foreign Affairs, International Cooperation, and Francophone Affairs	Agapito Mba Mokuy
Information, Culture, and Tourism, and Government Spokesperson	Jerónimo Osa Ekoro
Justice, Religious Affairs, and Penal Institutions	Francisco Javier Ngomo Mbengono
Labor and Social Security	Miguel Abia Biteo Borico
Mines, Industry, and Energy	Gabriel Mbega Obiang Lima
National Security	Nicholás Obama Nchama

Planning, Economic Development, and Public Investment	Conrado Okenve Ndoho
Presidency, in Charge of Administrative Coordination	Vicente Ehate Tomi
Presidency, in Charge of Civilian Cabinet	Braulio Ncogo Abegue
Presidency, Regional Integration	Baltasar Engonga Edjo
Secretary General of the Presidency of the Government	Tomás Esono Ava
Social Affairs and Promotion of Women	Maria Leonor Epam Biribe [f]
Transport, Technology, Posts, and Telecommunications	Francisco Mba Olo Bahamonde
Youth and Sports	Francisco Pascual Obama Asue
Ministers Delegate	
Economy, Commerce, and Business Development	Jose Angel Borico Moises
Foreign Affairs, International Cooperation, and Francophone Affairs	Pedro Ela Nguema Buna
General State Treasury	Monserrat Afang Ondo [f]
Health and Social Welfare	Tomas Mecheba Fernandez Galilea
Information, Culture, and Tourism	Guillermina Mokuy Mba Obono [f]
Energy	Fidel-Marcos Meñe Nkogo
Planning, Economic Development, and Investments	Fortunato Ofa Mbo Nchama
Posts and Transportation	Joaquín Elema Borengue
Ministers of State	
Agriculture and Forests	Miguel Oyono Ndong Mifumu
Education, Science, and Sport	Maria del Carmen Ekoro [f]
Interior and Local Corporations	Clemente Engonga Nguema Onguene
Presidency, in Charge of Parliamentary Relations and Judicial Affairs	Ángel Masie Mibuy
Presidency, in Charge of Missions	Alejandro Evuna Owono Asangono
Public Works and Infrastructure	Juan Nko Mbula

[f] = female

INTERGOVERNMENTAL REPRESENTATION

Ambassador to the U.S.: Purificación Angue ONDO.

U.S. Ambassador to Equatorial Guinea: Mark ASQUINO.

Permanent Representative to the UN: Anatolio NDONG MBA.

IGO Memberships (Non-UN): AfDB, AU, NAM.

ERITREA

State of Eritrea
Hagere Ertra (Arabic)
Dawlat Iritriyá (Tigrigna)

Political Status: Former Italian colony; became part of UN-sponsored Ethiopian-Eritrean Federation in September 1952; annexed as a province of Ethiopia in November 1962; declared independent on May 24, 1993, following secessionist referendum of April 23–25; new constitution approved by the Constitutional Assembly on May 23, 1997, but largely unimplemented as of mid-2013.

Area: 46,774 sq. mi. (121,144 sq. km).

Population: 5,596,059 (2012E—UN); 6,233,682 (2013E—U.S. Census). (A national census has not been conducted since 1984, when the population was reported to be 2,748,304. The World Bank in 2012 estimated the population at 5.4 million or less, citing a large exodus of Eritreans in recent years.)

Major Urban Centers (2005E): ASMARA (554,000), Keren (89,000).

Principal Languages: Tigrinya, Arabic, and English.

Monetary Unit: Nakfa (government rate of exchange as of November 1, 2013: 10.47 nakfa = $1US).

State President and Chair of the Executive Council of the People's Front for Democracy and Justice: ISAIAS Afwerki (People's Front for Democracy and Justice); named secretary general of the Eritrean People's Liberation Front in 1987; named head of Provisional Government of Eritrea following defeat of Ethiopia's Mengistu regime in May 1991; named state president on May 22, 1993; named chair of the Executive Council of the People's Front for Democracy and Justice on February 16, 1994.

THE COUNTRY

With a coastline stretching some 750 miles along the African border of the Red Sea, Eritrea is bordered on the northwest by Sudan, on the south by Ethiopia, and on the southeast by Djibouti. It is home to many ethnic groups (including the Afar, Bilen, Hadareb, Kunama, Nara, Rashida, Saho, Tigray, and Tigrigna); its people are almost equally divided between Christians and Muslims.

The leading agricultural products are cereals, citrus fruits, cotton, and livestock (including camels and goats). Approximately 80 percent of the population is involved in subsistence agriculture. Fish are plentiful in the vicinity of the islands off the Red Sea port of Massawa, while mineral resources include copper, gold, iron ore, potash, and nickel. The region's economic infrastructure was severely crippled by a long (1962–1991) war of independence from Ethiopia, the output of most industries being reduced during the conflict to a fraction of capacity. Conditions improved following the end of that war, and although annual GNP per capita ($115) remained one of the world's lowest, agricultural production had increased four-fold by May 1993. With the installation of a famine early warning system and infrastructural improvements, a return to agricultural self-sufficiency was reported by late 1994. However progress came to a halt with the outbreak of a border war with Ethiopia (Eritrea's main export market) in May 1998. By the time hostilities ended (at least temporarily) in 2000, it was estimated that GDP had fallen by 9 percent.

The government launched a five-year, $249 million economic recovery program in 2000, concentrating on agriculture, infrastructure, and support for the private sector. However, the economy subsequently continued to languish, particularly as a final resolution of the conflict with Ethiopia proved elusive and the expense of an army of 200,000 soldiers (one of Africa's largest) siphoned resources away from development programs. Meanwhile, remittances from the estimated 850,000 Eritreans living abroad declined substantially. In 2007 the government accepted a World Bank recommendation to emphasize improvements in food production through, among other things, the creation of an extensive irrigation system. Meanwhile, China cancelled much of Eritrea's debt and offered additional trade and cooperation accords.

Tension with Ethiopia continued to undermine the Eritrean economy as the port of Massawa, which formerly handled goods to and from Ethiopia, was described as a "ghost town" due to Ethiopia's use of the port in Djibouti. Eritrea's limited private industry also suffered from a lack of access to Ethiopian markets. On a more positive note, mining prospects improved significantly in the second half of 2008 when final guidelines were established in regard to the state's participation in joint ventures with foreign companies.

Growth of more than 8 percent was reported for 2011, in part due to expansion of gold mining, a significant revenue source for the government. However gold production reportedly declined in 2012, and global prices for metals in general weakened, resulting in moderately lower growth (6.3 percent) for the year.

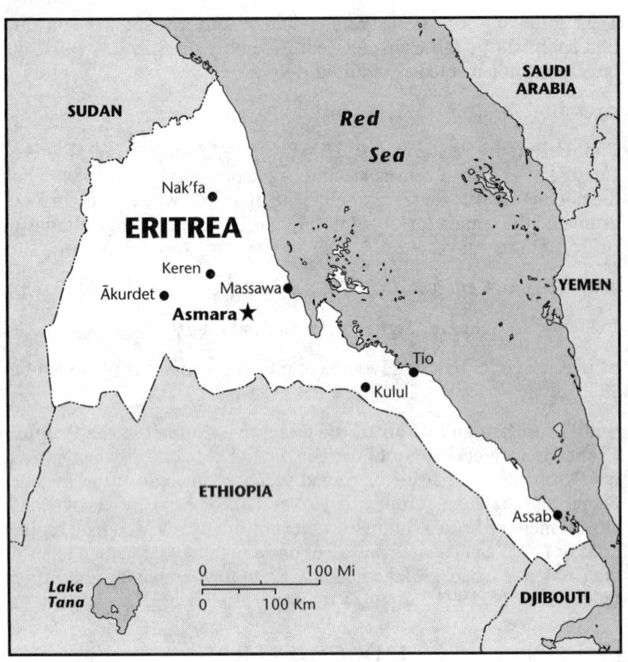

GOVERNMENT AND POLITICS

Political background. After several centuries of intermittent Ethiopian and Ottoman control, the coastal area of what became known as Eritrea was occupied in the 1880s by Italy, which in 1890 proclaimed it a colony and in 1935–1936 used it as a staging area for its conquest of Ethiopia. Administered by Britain in the immediate post–World War II era, the region was declared by the United Nations in 1952 to be an autonomous component of an Ethiopian federation. Ten years later it was annexed by Ethiopia, with Eritreans who opposed the action mounting a guerrilla campaign that lasted until the downfall of the Mengistu regime in May 1991 (see article on Ethiopia for additional information).

On June 15, 1992, the Eritrean People's Liberation Front (EPLF) announced the formation of a Provisional Government of Eritrea (PGE), headed by EPLF Secretary General ISAIAS Afwerki. In a referendum on April 23–25, 1993, 99.8 percent of those participating voted for independence, which was accepted by Ethiopia on May 3 and became effective on May 24, with Isaias assuming the title of president. The EPLF was succeeded by the People's Front for Democracy and Justice (PFDJ) in February 1994.

Following independence Eritrea's overriding concern was recovery from decades of economic neglect and military devastation. The damage to its infrastructure during the war of independence had been estimated at more than $2 billion. In addition, the port of Massawa had been all but destroyed by enemy bombardment. The divorce from Ethiopia was nonetheless described by *Africa Confidential* as "pragmatic," with no reparations being sought by Eritrea from Ethiopia and no indication that a return of Ethiopian assets was being considered. The new Eritrean state subsequently exhibited a decided assertiveness on territorial issues, as evidenced by strained relations with Yemen, Djibouti, Sudan, and ultimately Ethiopia (see Foreign relations, below).

The ferocity of the 1998–2000 border war with Ethiopia was very difficult for the international community to comprehend, since the narrow strip of land in question held few natural resources and was generally considered a poor candidate for development. The estimates of the number of Eritrean deaths in the conflict ranged from 20,000 to 50,000, while some 60,000 people were displaced. In addition, the Eritrean government reportedly spent $1 billion on armaments to conduct the campaign against its former Ethiopian allies, thereby dealing a severe blow to an economy already in desperate need of investment. Some analysts attributed Eritrea's intensity in the dispute to a "sense of indomitability" arising from the long war of independence and to a degree of hubris on the part of President Isaias. Although Isaias and his administration continued to maintain that Eritrea had been waging a defensive war and declared "victory" in the final settlement, most observers concluded that Ethiopia had, in fact, achieved military superiority prior to the cease-fire.

President Isaias appeared to retain broad popular support throughout the 1998–2000 war, although what one journalist called "quiet questions" were raised over the possibility that the president may have misjudged Eritrean capabilities. Following the war, criticism intensified noticeably, beginning with the issuance in late 2000 of the so-called "Berlin Manifesto" on the part of PFDJ supporters outside the country who argued that constitutional implementation was being unnecessarily delayed and that power remained inordinately concentrated in the president's hands. Subsequently, in May 2001, a number of influential government and party officials also broke ranks with Isaias (see PFDJ under Political Groups, below). Disconcerting many international donors, Isaias responded with a crackdown in September, arresting a number of government and party officials for "disloyalty." He also clamped down on the independent press. Isaias's critics subsequently accused him of focusing on the "false issue" of sovereignty (particularly in regard to ongoing conflict with Ethiopia [see Foreign relations, below]) at the expense of political reform.

Constitution and government. On May 22, 1992, the Provisional Government of Ethiopia issued a proclamation on Eritrea's transitional government structure. It stated that, prior to the adoption of a permanent constitution, the EPLF Central Committee would serve as the country's legislative body. Executive authority was invested in a 28-member Advisory Council (subsequently a 24-member State Council), chaired by the EPLF secretary general. In addition, a judiciary was authorized to function independently of the EPLF Central Committee, the Advisory/State Council, and the secretary general. The new basic law provided for the country's ten provinces to be headed by governors, each of whom was also authorized to serve on the Advisory/State Council.

On May 22, 1993, EPLF Secretary General Isaias was proclaimed president of Eritrea. Concurrently, a transitional National Assembly was established. (By a resolution of the PFDJ congress a year later, the assembly became a 150-member body encompassing the 75 members of the PFDJ's Central Committee, plus a number of indirectly elected members.) In March 1994 the National Assembly approved a resolution to establish a 50-member Constitutional Commission to prepare a draft basic law for the country. The commission issued its recommendations in 1996, and a special 527-member Constitutional Assembly was subsequently elected in direct balloting and charged with preparing a final document. As unanimously approved on May 23, 1997, by the Constitutional Assembly (which subsequently dissolved), the new constitution provided for a directly elected National Assembly, which was authorized to select a president, who was granted strong executive authority. The president's term was set at five years, renewable once. A multiparty system was envisioned, although a decision on its final structure was left to the National Assembly, as were details regarding other electoral matters. No precise timetable was established for the final implementation of the new constitution. Among other things, the 1998–2000 border war with Ethiopia served as an obstacle to implementation, while critics of President Isaias continued as of mid-2013 to accuse him of dragging his feet on the issue by not formally ratifying the constitution or scheduling new elections.

In May 1995 the National Assembly approved legislation dividing the country into six provinces, each of which would be further divided into regions, subregions, and villages. In early November the legislators decided that 30 percent of the provincial council seats would be reserved for women and gave the provinces nonethnic names (Southern Red Sea Region, Northern Red Sea Region, Anseba Region, Gash Barka Region, South Region, and Central Region).

In September 2001 the government closed down all 12 of the nation's privately owned newspapers and arrested a number of journalists in the wake of growing dissent over the authoritarian rule of the Isaias administration. The crackdown elicited an international outcry, but the government did not ease its hard-line position. Reporters Without Borders in 2007 strongly criticized the government and the PFDJ for an "ultra-nationalist" stance that characterized any criticism from journalists or reformists as a threat to national security and therefore an appropriate target for suppression. In 2013 the journalism watchdog continued to decry the "disastrous" conditions in Eritrea, which ranked among the world's worst countries in regard to freedom of information and was characterized as "Africa's biggest prison" for journalists, a number of whom have reportedly died while in detention.

Foreign relations. A number of countries, including the United States, recognized Eritrea on April 27, 1993, and the all-important recognition by Ethiopia on May 3 paved the way for the proclamation of independence three weeks later. On October 10 Eritrea and Ethiopia concluded an agreement on freedom of cross-border transit for citizens of the two countries. By the end of the year Eritrea had been admitted to the United Nations and most of its affiliated bodies.

In late 1993 Eritrea complained of an attack by an armed Islamic group that had infiltrated from Sudan. A similar outbreak in November 1994 yielded a rupture in diplomatic relations with Khartoum, which the Asmara leadership had privately charged with "Islamic and imperialistic ambitions." Subsequent peace talks in Yemen broke down in late December after Sudan refused to condemn infiltrators that Eritrea accused of destabilizing activities.

On November 11, 1995, a simmering dispute between Eritrea and Yemen over claims to three small islands in the Red Sea erupted into armed confrontation. The three islands, Greater Hanish (Hanish Al Kubra), Lesser Hanish (Hanish Al Suhrah), and Zukar (Jabel Zukar) had been retained by Britain when it withdrew from Aden in 1967 but were handed over to South Yemen three years later. Subsequently, the archipelago came under Yemeni development as a center for tourists, particularly French scuba enthusiasts. The November firefight, occasioned by the presence of Yemeni troops on Greater Hanish, was followed by a bloodier encounter on December 15–17. Thereafter Eritrea and Yemen agreed to a cease-fire monitored by a four-member committee composed of one representative each from Eritrea and Yemen, plus diplomats from the U.S. embassies in Eritrea and Yemen.

Mediated by the UN and France, subsequent talks yielded the signing of an accord in Paris on May 21, 1996, under which Eritrea and Yemen renounced the use of force and agreed to submit the dispute to binding arbitration by a panel of five judges, with Eritrea and Yemen appointing two each and these four naming the fifth. Nevertheless, the dispute flared up again in early August, when Eritrean troops occupied Lesser Hanish; they withdrew at the end of the month only on the express order of the UN Security Council. (In October 1998 the International Court of Justice [ICJ] ruled largely in Yemen's favor in the dispute, granting it sovereignty of the so-called Zukar-Hanish island groups, while ceding Eritrea control over a smaller island grouping. Moreover, the ICJ asserted that traditional fishing patterns—both Eritrean and Yemeni—should be protected. Both countries promptly agreed to comply with the decision.)

The relationship between Eritrea and Sudan continued to deteriorate as the former joined forces with Ethiopia and Uganda to form a regional front to contain militant Islamic fundamentalism. In late July 1996 Sudan claimed that its troops had repulsed an incursion by Eritrean forces as tensions mounted along their shared border. Sudanese-Eritrean relations plummeted further in June 1997 when Eritrean officials announced that they had uncovered an alleged Sudanese-backed plot to assassinate President Isaias.

Many international observers expressed surprise in May 1998 when a crisis erupted between Eritrea and Ethiopia over a disputed territory within their ill-defined border region. On May 13 Ethiopia accused Eritrea of having forcibly occupied the Badme Triangle region in "northwest Ethiopia." On the following day, Eritrea claimed that Ethiopian troops had in fact initiated the skirmish on "sovereign Eritrean territory." Subsequently, with both sides claiming to possess colonial Italian maps as evidence of their sovereignty claims, open warfare erupted in the region in late May. Meanwhile, in an attempt to explain the outbreak of fighting, analysts suggested that relations between the two countries had been deteriorating since Eritrea introduced its own currency, the nakfa, in 1997. That decision had been followed by Ethiopia's insistence that all trade between the two must be in hard currency—a move that adversely affected the Eritrean economy and set off a series of tit-for-tat exchanges.

Amid reports of continued fighting, the Organization of African Unity (OAU, subsequently the African Union—AU) and the United Nations spearheaded diplomatic attempts to settle the dispute in the second half of 1998. However, Eritrea rejected cease-fire proposals in both June and November, asserting that the proposals favored Ethiopia. In late January 1999 Eritrea also opposed a troop withdrawal plan backed by the UN and OAU, and within a week full-scale warfare had recommenced, with Ethiopia reported to have launched massive offensives on the Badme front and against the Eritrean port city of Assab. In late February Eritrea acknowledged having lost the Badme territory and agreed to abide by the earlier OAU proposal. Nevertheless, fierce fighting continued through March.

The July 1999 Algiers Summit of the OAU formally endorsed a peace plan that would have returned both sides to their prewar positions and would have established a border demarcation mechanism. However, the proposed deal collapsed in September, in part due to Ethiopian concerns over technical aspects of the plan, particularly regarding the proposed Eritrean withdrawal. The subsequent months saw relatively little fighting, but Ethiopia launched a major offensive in May 2000 that concluded in a June truce after Ethiopian forces had reclaimed all the land previously lost and had advanced deep into Eritrea. In addition to a cease-fire, the combatants also agreed to eventual deployment of international peacekeepers. A final peace accord was signed by Isaias and President Meles of Ethiopia in Algeria on December 12.

Following the tentative conclusion of the Eritrean/Ethiopian border war in late 2000, Eritrea concluded a border security agreement with Sudan in July 2001, though it was widely reported that Sudan subsequently continued to support antigovernment movements in Eritrea.

Meanwhile, in April 2001 an independent boundary commission (the Eritrea-Ethiopia Boundary Commission—EEBC) had established a 15-mile-wide buffer zone comprised exclusively of territory that belonged to Eritrea prior to the conflict. A UN Mission for Ethiopia and Eritrea (UNMEE)—comprised of some 4,200 peacekeepers from about 40 nations—was charged with monitoring the buffer zone.

In April 2002 the EEBC allocated sufficient territory to each side to permit each to claim it was satisfied with the outcome, although overall the decision appeared to favor Ethiopia. In March 2003 the border commission officially awarded the disputed town of Badme to Eritrea, but the Ethiopian government did not announce its acceptance of the ruling "in principle" until November 2004. Despite the EEBC's decision, border skirmishes continued to flare up, land mines were periodically detonated, and the UN expressed concerns over Eritrea's lack of cooperation with the peacekeeping force patrolling the border. Although his external reputation continued to decline, Isaias still clung to his hard line.

In October 2005 the Eritrean government banned UNMEE helicopter flights and other activity in the disputed border area to protest Ethiopia's unwillingness to accept the proposed final demarcation and return Badme to Eritrean control. Although the Security Council threatened to impose sanctions on Eritrea for its unilateral action, Isaias continued to maintain that sanctions would be more appropriate if leveled at Ethiopia. (Isaias claimed that Eritrea was the "law-abiding party" in the dispute and that Ethiopia was receiving preferential treatment from the West because of President Meles's assistance in the U.S.-led "war on terror.") The two countries were described as once again "on the brink" in November in view of continued troop and tank buildups and an Eritrean demand (reluctantly accepted by the Security Council) that all Western troops be withdrawn from UNMEE. Complicating matters for Eritrea was a report in mid-December by an independent claims commission at the Permanent Court of Arbitration that adjudged that Eritrea had initiated the 1998 war by invading Badme. (The commission collaterally held both sides liable for property damage and abuse of civilians during the conflict.)

Concerns grew in late 2006 that war might reignite with Ethiopia when Eritrean forces, stating a goal of helping to harvest crops, moved into the Temporary Security Zone (TSZ) that had been established at the border by the UN. Tensions subsequently intensified even further when Ethiopian troops (with U.S. backing) entered Somalia in December to assist the transitional Somali government, led by President Abdullahi Yusuf Ahmed, in its battle for control with Islamists led by the Islamic Courts Union (ICU). Although the Yusuf Ahmed administration regained the upper hand in Mogadishu with the Ethiopian support, an ICU guerrilla campaign subsequently continued, most analysts concluding that the insurgents were being armed in large part by Eritrea in what was seen as a Eritrean-Ethiopian "proxy war" in Somalia. In July 2007 Ethiopian President Meles Zenawi announced he was expanding the Ethiopian army to protect against a possible attack by Eritrea, and President Isaias described Ethiopia as a "U.S. mercenary" in the region.

Relations with the United States, EU, and UN had been tenuous since 2006 due to what was perceived in the West as President Isaias's "confrontational approach" to UNMEE (see Political background, above). Meanwhile, Eritrea reportedly by that time had significantly increased its ties with Pakistan in regard to oil exploration and other "entrepreneurial" activity. Eritrea also continued to provide aid to numerous Ethiopian opposition groups as an expression of its anger over the impasse in final border demarcation.

In April 2007 Eritrea announced it was suspending its membership in the Inter-Governmental Authority on Development (IGAD) in response to what Eritrea perceived as the regional body's support for the recent Ethiopian intervention in Somalia, which Eritrea opposed. In a related vein, the United States and the UN accused Eritrea of supplying arms to Islamist insurgents in Somalia, Washington going so far as to suggest it might place Eritrea on the U.S. list of countries that sponsor terrorism because of the issue. Meanwhile, President Isaias denied his country was providing arms to Somalia's antigovernment Islamists and accused Ethiopia and the United States of "destabilizing" the region with their efforts in Somalia and anti-Eritrean rhetoric.

In early 2008 Eritrea blocked fuel supplies to UNMEE forces in the TSZ, forcing the 1,700-strong UN force to relocate to the Ethiopian side of the border. The UN Security Council condemned Eritrea's "hostility" toward the peacekeeping force, as concern remained high that an "unintended" skirmish could reignite a full-scale border war. Ethiopia called for new negotiations, arguing that permanent border markers were required on the ground before the demarcation issue could be considered settled. However, the Isaias administration insisted on Ethiopian withdrawal from Badme before talks could begin, prompting renewed international criticism. In July the UN Security Council terminated the UNMEE's mandate, accusing Eritrea of "obstruction."

In 2008 Sudan suspended the activity of all Eritrean opposition groups on Sudanese soil, an apparent show of support for the Eritrean government in its multifaceted conflict with Ethiopia, which, among other things, had allegedly prompted Eritrean assistance for antigovernment Islamists in Somalia.

A long-standing border dispute with Djibouti erupted into small-scale military conflict in June 2008 after Eritrea reportedly sent troops into the disputed Ras Doumenia peninsula on the Red Sea. The United States (which relies on bases in Djibouti for military activity in the region), the AU, Arab League, and IGAD condemned the Eritrean actions, while Eritrea claimed sovereignty over the territory (experts agreed that the border had never been definitively demarcated). A UN team was dispatched to investigate the conflict, which had the potential to impact vital shipping lanes in and out of the Red Sea, and the UN Security Council subsequently expressed "deep concern" over the continuing border tension.

Following the withdrawal of Ethiopian forces from Somalia early in 2009 and the subsequent offensive by antigovernment Islamists there, the AU and IGAD asked the Security Council to impose sanctions on Eritrea for its alleged support for the Somali insurgents. The Security Council obliged in December by imposing an arms embargo on Eritrea and providing for penalties against military or political leaders who violated the embargo. In setting the sanctions, the Security Council also condemned Eritrea's refusal to withdraw its troops from disputed territory at the border with Djibouti. A cease-fire and tentative settlement was reached between Eritrea and Djibouti in 2010 under Qatari mediation. (Formal implementation of the accord between Eritrea and Djibouti had not been completed as of mid-2013, one sticking point appearing to be President Isaias's unwillingness to confirm that Eritrea was still holding prisoners of war from Djibouti.)

In September 2010 Ethiopian security forces reportedly captured 300 rebels who had been armed and equipped in Eritrea. An additional 30 fighters were detained in Djibouti. The Ethiopian government charged that both groups were part of an Eritrean effort to destabilize Djibouti.

Eritrea in July 2011 formally requested reinstatement in IGAD, but the organization put the application on hold until

Asmara halted "destabilization" activities in the region, particularly support for Islamist insurgents in Somalia.

Following the killing of several tourists in Ethiopia in March 2012, the Ethiopian army invaded Eritrea to attack three camps of the Ethiopian rebel group adjudged by Addis Ababa to have been responsible for the deaths. However, Eritrea did not retaliate for the incursion. It was not immediately clear what effect the death of Meles (announced in August 2012) would have on regional affairs, although observers noted that the deep personal animosity between the two presidents had fueled the border conflict as well as the proxy war in Somalia. Some observers perceived a possible softening of Ethiopia's stance toward Eritrea in the first half of 2013, although the new Ethiopian government subsequently alluded to ongoing Eritrean support for enemies of the Ethiopian administration.

Current issues. In March 2010 the United States again strongly criticized the Eritrean government for systematic human rights abuses and for "destabilizing" the region. Some analysts subsequently perceived an effort on behalf of the Isaias administration to improve its international reputation, although it continued to resist pleas for the release of political opponents and journalists in custody since 2001. In addition, a UN report ultimately accused the Eritrean government of having been behind a foiled terrorist plot in which commandos were sent to detonate bombs during an AU summit at Addis Ababa in January 2011. Although President Isaias vehemently denied the allegations, most neighboring countries and Western nations subsequently intensified their denunciation of what some observers concluded had become a rogue state. (Eritrea has regularly been referenced in recent years as Africa's North Korea.)

In January 2013 some 200 mutinous soldiers briefly seized the building housing the information ministry in Asmara in what some observers called a coup attempt and the government dismissed as a small incident. The soldiers were apparently permitted to return to their barracks, although a number of arrests (of both officers and civilians) were subsequently reported. At the very least, the incident reflected ongoing low morale in some segments of the army, which reportedly has suffered mass desertions. Subsequently, Amnesty International reported that more than 10,000 political prisoners (including deserters) had been jailed since President Isaias had taken power in 1993, with many of them still being detained under "unimaginably atrocious conditions."

POLITICAL GROUPS

In late 2000 the National Assembly approved statutes providing for eventual formation of political parties, although critics argued that accompanying restrictions represented an effective barrier to genuine multiparty activity. While describing party activity as "acceptable" in theory, the assembly in early 2002 upheld a ban on the legalization of parties, and the PFDJ remained the sole legal party as of mid-2013.

Opposition to the EPLF/PFDJ has primarily involved shifting, often overlapping, and mostly ineffective coalitions, usually led by the ELF (below). In November 1996 it was reported that the ELF had initiated formation of an Eritrean National Alliance (ENA), with the **Eritrean Liberation Front–National Council** (ELF-NC). Reportedly established with the assistance of Sudan, the ENA, whose components were described as having "fundamentalist tendencies," called for the ousting of the Isaias government and the installation of a multiparty system. ENA Chair Abdella Idriss of the ELF also called for investigation of alleged human rights violations on the part of the administration. Significantly, the **Eritrean Liberation Front–Revolutionary Council** (ELF-RC), a predominately Muslim but nonfundamentalist and nonmilitary group, declined to join the ENA because of the inclusion of the fundamentalist factions in the alliance.

In March 1999 the ENA appeared to be superseded by a broader coalition of opposition groups styled the Alliance of Eritrean National Forces (AENF) that included the ELF, ELF-NC, ELF-RC, and a number of small Marxist formations. Despite enjoying the support of Ethiopia, the AENF was described as maintaining a low profile during the Eritrean-Ethiopian war, supporting the 2000 truce while continuing to call for the ouster of the Isaias government.

In late 2002 reports once again began to reference the ENA, described at that time as comprising some 13 parties and groups under the leadership of the ELF's Idriss as president and HIRUY Tedla Bairu of the small, recently formed **Eritrean Cooperative Party** (ECP) as secretary general. Although the revitalized ENA reportedly initially indicated it would not use military force to try to overthrow the government, it was reported in May 2003 that an ENA military wing had been established. By that time, it appeared that the ENA was receiving financial aid from Ethiopia, Sudan, and Yemen. Once again undermining effective opposition cohesion, the ELF-RC refused to participate in the alliance, arguing that Hiruy was under "foreign influence."

In early 2004 four ENA members (the ELF-NC, RSADO, DMLEK, and the **People's Democratic Front for the Liberation of Eritrea** [PDFLE]) joined the EPM in forming an opposition alliance called the Four Plus One. In October additional small parties joined the grouping, which described itself as a means of strengthening the ENA rather than replacing it.

New ENA leaders were reportedly elected in January 2005, Hiruy replacing Idriss as president and Husayn KHALIFA succeeding Hiruy as secretary general. However, the ENA was again apparently superseded in February by the formation in Sudan of the **Eritrean Democratic Alliance** (EDA), which included the ELF, ELF-RC, EDP, EPM, the small **Eritrean Federal Democratic Movement** (EFDM), the "newly emerging" **Eritrean National Salvation Front** (ENSF, led by Jabir AHMAD), and, apparently, the **Eritrean Islamic Islah Movement** (EIIM). The role of the EIIM was controversial, since it supported the use of violence against government forces (EIIM fighters killed a number of Eritrean soldiers in early 2005) while other EDA components (notably the EDP and EPM) opposed the use of such force. Meanwhile, Hiruy and his ECP remained outside the EDA, with Khalifa being referenced as the EDA leader and Abdallah Aden of the EPM as his deputy. Hiruy subsequently criticized the EDA for "monopolizing" financial aid from Ethiopia, Sudan, and Yemen designed to support opposition activity in Eritrea. The EDA was described in early 2006 as "virtually paralyzed" by a lack of effective coordination. In March 2007 it was reported that Ethiopian President Meles Zenawi was supporting the EDA faction that comprised the ENSF, ELF-RC, and the EDP.

The EDA general congress in the spring of 2008 opened its doors to all organizations dedicated to the overthrow of the "despotic" Isaias regime. At that point the EDA membership reportedly included the DMLEK; EPM; EFDM, led by Bashir ISHAQ; the **Islamic Congress Party** (ICP); EDP; EIIM, led by Khelil AMER; ELF; ELF-RC; the **Eritrean *Nahda* Party**, led by Nur IDRIS; ENSF, led by Abdallah Aden; EPC, led by Taher SHENGEB; the **Eritrean Popular Democratic Front** (EPDF), led by Tewelde GEBRESELASSIE; and RSADO. (Gebreselassie was described in 2011 as the chair of the EDA, which reportedly was subsequently in competition with the recently formed EPDP [below] for the support of various opposition organizations.)

It was reported in late 2011 that regime opponents outside Eritrea had established the **Eritrean National Council for Democratic Change** (ENCDC), with the goal of forming a government-in-exile under the leadership of an executive committee chaired by Yusuf BERHANU. In addition, Eritrean refugees in Ethiopia announced the formation of the **Eritrean Movement for Democracy and Justice** (EMDJ), claiming to have an armed wing within Eritrea.

Government Party:

People's Front for Democracy and Justice (PFDJ). The PFDJ's predecessor—the Eritrean People's Liberation Front (EPLF)—was launched in 1970 as a breakaway faction of the Marxist-oriented ELF (below). The EPLF was an avowedly nonsectarian, left-wing formation supported by both Christians and Muslims in pursuit of Eritrean independence. With an estimated 100,000 men and women under arms, the EPLF for much of its preindependence existence controlled large areas of the Eritrean countryside, establishing schools, hospitals, a taxation system, and other government services.

After the EPLF revised its ideology to accommodate multipartyism and a "regulated" market economy, in May 1991 the United States for the first time supported the EPLF's call for a self-determination referendum. Immediately after the subsequent Ethiopian defeat, Isaias Afwerki, who had been named secretary general of the EPLF at its 1987 congress, announced that the group was establishing a provisional government in Eritrea until a UN-supervised independence vote could be conducted. At independence on May 24, 1993, Isaias was installed as Eritrean president. At its 1994 congress, the EPLF adopted its present name and elected a 75-member Central Council and a 19-member Executive Council chaired by Isaias.

In the wake of the 1998–2000 war with Ethiopia, which, among other things, directed attention away from proposed political reform, a group of 15 prominent PFDJ leaders (including members of the Executive Council) published a letter in May 2001 criticizing Isaias's "autocratic" rule and demanding a "legal and democratic transition to a truly constitutional government." Isaias reacted harshly to the challenge, and some of the so-called G-15 were among those arrested in a government crackdown in September 2001. Subsequently, PFDJ dissidents who had escaped arrest by fleeing the country announced the formation of an EPLF-Democratic Party in exile (see EPDP, below).

Leaders: ISAIAS Afwerki (President of Eritrea and Chair of PFDJ Executive Council); Yemane GHEBREAB, Hagos GEBHREHIWET, Abdeller JABER, Haile TEWOLDEBHRAN, and Zemeheret YOHANNES (PFDJ Department Heads); Ahmad al-Amin Mohammed SAÏD (Secretary General).

Opposition Groups:

Eritrean Liberation Front (ELF). The predominantly Muslim ELF initiated anti-Ethiopian guerrilla activity in 1961 in pursuit of Eritrean autonomy. Its influence plummeted following the formation of the EPLF, and numerous splinter groups subsequently surfaced. By 1992 the ELF was considered to have become virtually nonexistent within Eritrea. However, in November 1996 it helped to launch the first of several opposition alliances (see introductory text above for subsequent developments).

In May 2009 it was reported that the ELF had established the Eritrean Solidarity Front (ESF, "*Tadamun*") with the EIIM and EFDM in pursuit of the "restoration of the rights" of Muslims and other "marginalized" elements of the population. The ESF, reportedly led by Sheikh Abu SIHEL, indicated it would continue to operate under the EDA umbrella. Reports in 2010 indicated that the ELF had increasingly been receiving arms and financial support from Ethiopia.

Leaders: Abdella IDRISS, Hussein KHELIFA.

Eritrean People's Democratic Party (EPDP). The formation of the EPDP in 2010 was reported as a merger of a number of opposition organizations, including the Eritrean Democratic Party (EDP), the Eritrean People's Party (EPP), and the Eritrean Democratic Resistance Movement–Gash-Setit (EDRM-GS).

The EDP was a successor to the EPLF-Democratic Party that was formed in exile by PFDJ dissidents after the government crackdown of 2001. The founding EDP congress was held in Germany in early 2004, the party committing itself to nonviolent opposition to the Isaias government. The EDP subsequently announced a planned merger with the EPP (chaired by Woldeyesus AMAR) and the EDRM-GS (chaired by Ismail NADA).

At the founding of the EPDP, its leaders stated their hope that the new party would eventually serve as an umbrella for all "mainstream" opposition groups, with a particular emphasis on bridging the divide that had historically separated groups emanating from the EPLF (such as the EDP) and those from the ELF (such as the EPP and the EDRM-GS). The EPDP platform called for nonviolent opposition to the PFDJ regime, democratization (including a multiparty system), and "peaceful coexistence" with neighboring countries.

Leader: Menghesteab ASMERON (Chair).

Red Sea Afar Democratic Organization (RSADO). The RSADO joined the ENA in 2002 to advocate for the rights of the Afar ethnic group in the southern Red Sea region. In 2004 its chair, Ibrahim HAROUN, survived an assassination attempt, which some critics alleged may have been plotted by the ruling PFDJ.

RSADO attacks on Eritrean military posts were reported in late 2008 and early 2009, the attackers apparently operating out of Ethiopia with the support of the Ethiopian military. In mid-2009 the RSADO announced plans to establish a Democratic Movement of Eritrean Nationalists (DMEN) in conjunction with the DMLEK (below), while remaining under the EDA umbrella. In early 2010 the RSADO claimed responsibility (along with the ENSF) for several recent attacks on government troops. In September 2013 the RSADO announced that it had agreed to conduct military action against the Eritrean regime in conjunction with the **Sako People's Democratic Movement** (SPDM), another opposition grouping based in Ethiopia.

Leaders: Yasin Mohamed ABDELA, Nerredin ALI.

Democratic Movement for the Liberation of Eritrean Kunama (DMLEK). This group was a founding member of the ENA. It calls for more autonomy for the Kunama—an ethnic group indigenous to the Gash-Setit areas of western Eritrea.

Leader: Kerneleos UTHMAN.

Eritrean People's Movement (EPM). The EPM was founded in May 2004 to bypass the ELF/EPLF divide. It reportedly had the support of Sudan, Ethiopia, Australia, Europe, and the United States. In 2010 reports indicated that the EPM had merged with the EPDF (although subsequent reports announced that the EPM had been expelled from the grouping).

Leaders: Adhanom GEBREMARIAN (Former Ambassador to Nigeria), Mekonen HAILI, Abdallah ADEN (Former Ambassador to Sudan), Mohammed IBRAHIM.

For information on the **Eritrean Islamic Jihad Movement** (EIJM-*Jihad Islammiya*), and the **Afar Revolutionary Democratic United Front** (ARDUF), see the 2011 *Handbook.*

LEGISLATURE

The proclamation by the Provisional Government of Eritrea on May 22, 1992, called for legislative authority to be exercised by the Eritrean People's Liberation Front's Central Committee, which was subsequently augmented by representatives of provincial assemblies to form a transitional **National Assembly** (*Hagerawi Baito*). A resolution by the People's Front for Democracy and Justice (PFDJ) on May 1994 provided for the establishment of a successor body encompassing the 75 members of the PFDJ Central Council, 3 members from each provincial council (currently a total of 18 members following the establishment of six provinces in 1995), and 45 representatives of professional groups, women's organizations, and other social bodies. (The latter were selected by the State Council from lists recommended by the organizations involved.) The 1997 constitution provided for a unicameral legislature of directly elected members. However, elections were subsequently delayed for several reasons, notably the 1998–2000 war with Ethiopia and ongoing failure to finalize border arrangements. In early 2000 the assembly endorsed a new electoral law, declaring, among other things, that 30 percent of the seats in the next assembly election would be reserved for women. As of September 2013 new assembly elections had not been scheduled.

Chair: ISAIAS Afwerki.

STATE COUNCIL

[as of September 1, 2013]

President	Isaias Afwerki
Councilors	
Agriculture	Arefaine Berhe
Defense	Gen. Sebhat Ephrem
Education	Semere Russom
Energy and Mines	Ahmad Haji Ali
Finance and Development	Berhane Abrehe
Foreign Affairs	Osman Saleh
Health	Amna Nur-Hussein [f]
Information	(Vacant)
Justice	Fawzia Hashim [f]
Labor and Human Welfare	Selma Hassan [f]
Land, Water, and Environment	Tesfai Gebreselassie
Marine Resources	Tewelde Kelati
National Development	Giorgis Teklemikael
Public Works	Abraha Asfaha
Regional Administration	(Vacant)
Tourism	Askalu Menkerios [f]
Transportation and Communications	Woldemichael Abraha

[f] = female

INTERGOVERNMENTAL REPRESENTATION

Ambassador to the U.S.: (Vacant).

U.S. Ambassador to Eritrea: (Vacant).

Permanent Representative to the UN: Araya DESTA.

IGO Memberships (Non-UN): AfDB, AU, Comesa, NAM.

ESTONIA

Republic of Estonia
Eesti Vabariik

Political Status: Absorption of independent state by the Soviet Union on August 6, 1940, repudiated by Estonian Supreme Council on March 30, 1990; resumption of full sovereignty declared August 20, 1991, and accepted by USSR State Council on September 6; present constitution approved in referendum of June 28, 1992.

Area: 17,462 sq. mi. (45,227 sq. km).

Population: 1,400,417 (2012E—UN); 1,266,375 (2013E—U.S. Census).

Major Urban Centers (2005E—UN): TALLINN (399,816), Tartu (103,512).

Official Language: Estonian.

Monetary Unit: Euro (market rate November 1, 2013: 0.74 euro = $1US). Estonia adopted the euro on January 1, 2011.

President: Toomas Hendrik ILVES (Social Democratic Party); elected by parliament for a second five-year term on August 29, 2011; elected by electoral college on September 23, 2006, and sworn in for a five-year term on October 9, succeeding Arnold RÜÜTEL (People's Union of Estonia).

Prime Minister: Andrus ANSIP (Estonian Reform Party); nominated by the president on March 31, 2005, following the resignation of Juhan PARTS (Union for the Republic) and sworn in (along with a new government) on April 13; nominated by the president to form a new government following legislative elections of March 4, 2007, and inaugurated on April 5; nominated by the president to form a government following elections on March 6, 2011, and sworn in on April 6.

THE COUNTRY

The northernmost of the three former Soviet Baltic republics, Estonia is bordered on the north by the Gulf of Finland, on the east by Russia, and on the south by Latvia. In June 1990 the government established quotas for the admission of "foreign citizens," though these were eased by 2000. According to the 2012 Census, 68.7 percent of the population was Estonian, 24.8 percent Russian, and 4.9 percent are from other specified ethnicities.

The economy is based on services, which contributed 70 percent of GDP in 2010, followed by industry (29.1 percent) and agriculture (2.7 percent). Estonia is a net importer of gas from Russia, although Tallinn is supplied with gas extracted from extensive deposits of oil shale. The country is well-endowed with peat, some of which is used for the generation of electricity, and with phosphate, from which superphosphate is refined.

Estonia in June 1992 became the first former Soviet republic to abandon the ruble in favor of its own national currency, the kroon. The immediate impact of the action was to slow the rate of inflation from over 1,000 percent to 90 percent in 1993, although real GDP plunged by 26.3 percent that year. Under the influence of free-market reforms introduced in 1992 as well as the return of most of the "Baltic gold" held by the Bank of England and other Western depositaries since the Soviet takeover in 1940, signs of recovery began to emerge in mid-1993, and Estonia subsequently became one of the best-performing transition economies. Growth averaged more than 8 percent annually over the first half of the last decade, earning the government high marks for its fiscal policies from the EU and the International Monetary Fund (IMF). Unemployment also declined. Estonia's remarkable economic expansion, however, was abruptly curtailed in 2008 by the collapse of its real estate, retail, and export markets. The government then introduced a series of austerity measures in 2009, with growth resuming at 3.1 percent in 2010 and increasing in 2011 to 7.6 percent, making it the fastest growing economy in the EU.

Following years of consideration, the country adopted the euro as its currency from January 2011, having remarkably met all of the EU's monetary criteria through genuine monetary and budgetary reforms. Despite pessimism about prospects for the currency given the sovereign debt crises in peripheral EU economies, the Estonian economy continued to grow, with a rising demand for workers boosting domestic confidence and consumption. The eurozone crisis prompted growth to slow, but despite the economic difficulties, Estonia saw growth of 3.0 percent in 2013, according to the IMF. The unemployment rate was 7.8 percent, significantly reduced from the peak of 17.3 percent in 2010. Inflation was 3.2 percent.

GOVERNMENT AND POLITICS

Political background. Ruled by the Livonian Knights for the greater part of the 13th to 15th centuries and by Sweden until its defeat by Peter the Great in the Great Northern War of 1700–1721, Estonia was granted local autonomy by Russia in April 1917. A declaration of independence in February 1918 was followed by German occupation, but the country's sovereign status was recognized by the Versailles peace treaty of June 28, 1919, and by the Soviet-Estonian Tartu treaty of February 2, 1920. In September 1921 Estonia was admitted to the League of Nations.

In March 1934 Estonia succumbed to the virtual dictatorship of Konstantin PÄTS but was formally returned to a democratic system under a basic law of July 29, 1937, that provided for a presidency and a two-chambered parliament. On August 6, 1940, it was incorporated into the USSR under a secret protocol of the German-Soviet nonaggression pact of August 23, 1939. German occupation in 1941–1945 was followed by the restoration of Estonia's status as a Soviet republic.

On November 12, 1989, the Estonian Supreme Soviet unilaterally annulled the 1940 annexation, and in February 1990 it abolished provisions in its constitution that accorded a "leading role" to the Communist Party.

At legislative balloting on March 18, 1990, a majority of seats had been won by proindependence groups, notably the Estonian Popular Front (*Eesti Rahvarinne*), whose chair, Edgar SAVISAAR, was named prime minister on April 3. Savisaar's appointment had been preceded on March 29 by the reappointment of Arnold RÜÜTEL as legislative chair (de facto president of the republic).

A referendum on March 3, 1991, yielded a 77.8 percent vote in favor of independence; a declaration to this effect on August 20 was accepted by the USSR Supreme Soviet on September 6.

Prime Minister Savisaar resigned on January 23, 1992, after the government had failed to win enough legislative votes to support a state of emergency for coping with post-Soviet food and energy shortages. In general elections on September 20, Rüütel won a substantial plurality (42.2 percent) of the votes cast in presidential balloting, although in the legislative returns his Secure Home (*Kindel Kodu*) grouping ran second to the Fatherland ("Pro Patria") National Coalition (*Rahvuslik Koonderakond Ismaa*—RKEI), which supported Lennart MERI. Since neither presidential candidate had secured a majority, the choice was constitutionally assigned to the legislature, where a three-party nationalist alignment on October 5 endorsed Meri by a narrow margin. On October 21 a coalition government of the RKEI, the Moderates (*Rahvaerakond Mõõdukad*—M), and the Estonian National Independence Party was sworn in under the premiership of the RKEI's Mart LAAR.

On September 2, 1994, the president of the Bank of Estonia, Siim KALLAS, revealed that in 1992 Prime Minister Laar had secretly ordered the sale of 2 billion rubles to the breakaway Russian republic of Chechnya, in contravention of an agreement with the IMF that the rubles would be transferred to the Russian central bank. On September 26 a no-confidence motion was carried with the support of 60 deputies, and Laar was replaced on October 20 by Andres TARAND.

Following parliamentary elections on March 5, 1995, a conservative alliance, the Coalition Party and Rural Union (*Koonderakonna ja Maarahva Ühendus*—KMÜ) (see Estonian Coalition Party [*Eesti Koonderakond*—KE] in Political Parties, below), headed by the 1992 caretaker prime minister, Tiit Vähi, formed a new coalition government with Edgar Savisaar's Estonian Center Party (*Eesti Keskerabond*—EK) on April 12. Six months later, Savisaar was dismissed as interior minister over allegations that he had authorized secret tape recordings of the recent coalition negotiations. When the Center Party backed Savisaar, Vähi formed a new coalition with the Estonian Reform Party (*Eesti Reformierakond*—RE), led by Kallas.

Allegations that President Meri's sympathies inclined toward Moscow on bilateral issues underscored contentious presidential balloting in the *Riigikogu* in August 1996. Nominated for a second term by a cross-section of deputies, the incumbent was at first opposed, as in 1992, only by Arnold Rüütel of the Estonian Rural People's Party (*Eesti Maarahva Erakond*—EME). Meri defeated him in a second round of voting after the balloting had been referred to the electoral college. The reelected president pledged to use his further term to press for Estonia's full integration into European structures

In November 1996 Vähi renewed the alliance between his Estonian Coalition Party (*Eesti Koonderakond*—KE) and Savisaar's Center Party. Following EK dissidents' rejection of the government, Vähi formed an exclusively KMÜ minority government that President Meri approved on December 1.

On February 25, 1997, Vähi resigned, two weeks after narrowly surviving a no-confidence vote. The KE named Mart SIIMANN, its caucus head, as its candidate for prime minister. The KE secured only seven seats in the election on March 7, 1999. Although a resurgent Center Party won a plurality of seats, the Fatherland Union (*Erakond Isamaaliit*—IL), RE, and Moderates coalesced to form a center-right government, with Mart Laar returning to the prime minister's post.

With President Meri ineligible for a third term, the 2001 presidential election was again decided by electoral college vote. The second ballot on September 21 selected Arnold Rüütel, now of the opposition People's Union of Estonia (*Eestimaa Rakvaliit*—ERL), over the RE's Toomas SAVI by a vote of 186–155.

Due to increasing conflict among the government coalition partners (see Current issues in the entry on Estonia in the 2000–2002 *Handbook* for details), Prime Minister Laar on December 19, 2001, announced his intention to resign. He was succeeded by Siim Kallas, former finance minister and current chair of the RE, who formed a new Center Party/RE cabinet on January 28.

Municipal elections in October 2002 were most notable for the strong performance by the recently launched Union for the Republic (*Res Publica*—RP). Campaigning on an anticorruption and anticrime platform, the RP won nearly one-quarter of the votes in the March 2, 2003, legislative balloting. Declining a coalition offer from the Center Party, the RP subsequently agreed to an RP/RE/ERL government that was inaugurated on April 10 under the leadership of the RP's Juhan PARTS.

The RP-led center-right coalition government in 2003 endorsed the previous government's plans for Estonian accession to NATO and the EU. EU membership was formally achieved on May 1, 2004. Prime Minister Parts resigned on March 24, 2005, in response to the *Riigikogu*'s adoption of a nonconfidence motion against the administration's justice minister. With the EK replacing the RP in the government coalition, a new three-party government was installed on April 13 under the premiership of the RE's Andrus ANSIP.

Toomas Hendrik ILVES of the Social Democratic Party (*Sotsiaaldemokraatlik Erakond*—SDE) was elected president on September 23, 2006, after three rounds of balloting in the parliament. Ilves defeated incumbent president Rüütel by a vote of 174–162 in the electoral college.

The RE led all parties in the March 4, 2007, legislative balloting with 31 seats, followed by the EK with 29 and the newly formed Pro Patria and Res Publica Union (*Isamaa ja Res Publica Liit*—IRL), composed of the RP and Fatherland Union (see Political Parties, below). Eschewing further cooperation with the EK, which had previously blocked economic reforms, Andrus Ansip formed an RE/IRL/SDE coalition in April. Policy differences over how to manage the budget deficit resulted in the exit of the SDE from government in May 2009, rendering the government a minority coalition composed of the RE and the IRL.

A subsequent center-right coalition led by Prime Minister Ansip was formed following elections on March 6, 2011. This coalition resulted in the creation of an entirely RE-IRL-led cabinet, a marked change from the previous cabinet. The EK nominated independent Indrek TARAND for the August 2011 presidential elections, who advocated increased transparency and a presidential term limit. Although the EK did not promise to organize a campaign in the legislature on his behalf, it implicitly endorsed his support for a referendum on instituting direct presidential elections. Tarand was defeated by incumbent President Ilves, 73 votes to 25.

In May 2012 Minister of Defense Mart Laar resigned after suffering a stroke in February and was succeeded by IRL chairman and MP Urmas REINSALU. As a sign of the growing strength of the RE-IRL Coalition, Ansip announced that Reinsalu would serve as acting prime minister when Ansip had to be absent.

Constitution and government. In September 1991 the Supreme Council appointed a Constitutional Assembly (*Põhiseaduslik Assamblee*), composed of 60 members drawn equally from itself and the Congress of Estonia, a 495-member body elected in March 1990 by citizens of prewar Estonia and their descendants. The new basic law that emerged from the assembly's deliberations provided for a parliamentary system and a presidency with defined powers. Providing no national voting rights for Russians residing in Estonia unless they qualified for citizenship, the document was approved by a reported 93 percent majority on June 28, 1992. Following its first election in 1992, presidential elections were to be by parliamentary ballot, with the successful candidate needing a two-thirds majority of all the deputies. If after three ballots no candidate has succeeded, the decision passes to an electoral college in which the deputies are joined by a larger number of local representatives and in which a simple majority vote suffices. The president serves a five-year term and is limited to two terms. (For information on conditions specific to the 1992 presidential election, see the 2010 *Handbook.*)

The president nominates the prime minister and approves the latter's nominations for the cabinet, all subject to legislative approval. The *Riigikogu* is elected via direct party-list balloting in 11 districts. Most seats are distributed on a proportional basis within each district, although some are allocated as "national compensation mandates" to parties securing at least 5 percent of the national vote.

Administratively, the country is divided into 15 counties (*maakond*), which are subdivided into communes (*vald*), and 6 major towns (the other urban areas being subordinate to the counties).

The constitution protects rights to freedom of speech and the press, and libel is not a criminal offense. In 2013 Estonia ranked 11th in the world for press freedom on the annual index by Reporters Without Borders.

Foreign relations. Soviet recognition of the independence of the Baltic states on September 6, 1991, preceded the admission of the three to the CSCE on September 10 and admission to the UN on September 17. Prior to the Soviet action, diplomatic recognition had been extended by a number of governments, including, on September 2, the United States, which had never recognized the 1940 annexations. Estonia was admitted to the IMF in 1992 and to the Council of Europe in 1993.

Regionally, Estonia, Latvia, and Lithuania concluded a Baltic Economic Cooperation Agreement in April 1990, which led on September 24, 1991, to a customs union agreement intended to permit free trade and visa-free travel between their respective jurisdictions. Nevertheless, with each state adopting its own currency and establishing customs posts on its borders, the development of trade among them was slow. Estonia was a founding member of the Council of the Baltic Sea States in 1992, which served as a conduit for Swedish and other Scandinavian involvement in Estonia's quest for modernization.

Postindependence Estonia's key objective of securing the withdrawal of Russian troops from its territory was complicated in 1993 by Moscow's intense criticism of alleged discrimination against ethnic Russians under Estonia's new citizenship law. Western pressure persuaded Moscow to adhere to an August 1994 deadline for withdrawal, subject to Russian retention of the Paldiski communications base for an additional year. Prior to the Russian withdrawal, President Yeltsin on June 26 decreed that the Russian-Estonian border should be based on the Soviet-era line, thus effectively rejecting the Estonian contention that the 1920 border should be restored. In November 1995 Estonia bowed to reality by agreeing in principle to the maintenance of the existing border, but relations with its powerful neighbor remained tense. In December 1998 Estonia adopted legislation allowing children who had been born in Estonia to ethnic Russians to become Estonian citizens, a measure that was welcomed by the Council of Europe, the OSCE, and, to a certain extent, Moscow. The status of ethnic Russians in Estonia continued to be a contentious issue. It was estimated in 2004 that 120,000 had opted for Russian citizenship because of language and other restrictions, while more than 170,000 remained "stateless." (Noncitizens are ineligible to vote in national elections, although all permanent residents, regardless of citizenship status, can participate in local balloting.) On May 18, 2005, Russia and Estonia signed a treaty clarifying the common land border and the delimitation of the maritime zones in the Gulf of Finland and Gulf of Narva. However, Russia withdrew from the agreement a month later after the *Riigikogu* made references to the Russian occupation while ratifying the treaty in June.

Estonia became a signatory of NATO's Partnership for Peace in February 1994, subsequently reiterating its desire for full NATO membership and also for eventual accession to the EU. Estonia became a formal member of NATO in March 2004 and later joined the EU in May that year, confirming its place in Europe.

Estonian foreign policy has held coordination with Western interests as essential to its national security since independence. In June 2003, upon the request of the Iraqi Interim Government, Estonia deployed a light infantry platoon to support troops stationed in Iraq. In addition to contributing troops to such military operations, Estonia subsequently sought to strengthen diplomatic ties with the United States and the EU. (President Ilves, an American-raised career diplomat, indicated that he viewed the Western allies as a balance against perceived efforts by Russia to reassert its influence in the Baltics.) The last Estonian troops returned from Iraq in December 2008. The government planned to retain between 160 and 165 personnel in Afghanistan in 2012. In March 2013, the ministry of defense announced all remaining troops would withdraw by April 2014.

The RE/IRL/SDE government in Estonia faced a diplomatic dilemma almost immediately upon taking office in 2007 with regard to the Bronze Soldier, a statue then located in central Tallinn in commemoration of Soviet soldiers killed in Estonia during World War II, long a source of conflict between Russian nationalists and ethnic Estonians. In late April 2007 the government ordered the statue transferred from the city center to a cemetery in a less prominent location, prompting mass protests by ethnic Russians in May that occasionally turned violent. Many of the protestors reportedly belonged to the Kremlin-sponsored Nashi youth movement. Demonstrators also blockaded the Estonian embassy in Moscow, with no apparent intervention by Russian authorities to ensure the safety of embassy personnel. In addition, Estonian officials claimed that Russia had launched a "cyberspace war" by "attacking" Estonian government Websites during the disturbances. The Russian involvement was widely viewed as an unusually direct attempt to pressure Estonia, possibly as a precursor to a broader Russian effort to reestablish influence in the region.

Hopes for improved relations with Russia upon Dmitry Medvedev's May 2008 inauguration were undercut by Russia's subsequent military confrontation with Georgia in regard to South Ossetia and Abkhazia (see entry on Georgia for details). The Baltic states deemed the situation to be a threat to Georgia's integrity, prompting the Estonian *Riigikogu* to post an affirmation of Georgia's sovereignty on its official Website. Estonia continues to reject the de facto sovereignty of Georgia's separatist regions. The Russian government accused Estonia of paranoia and poor communication, while Estonia views the potential deployment of additional Russian warships to the Baltic Sea with concern.

In addition to its relations with Russia, the most significant recent development in Estonia's external affairs is the adoption of the euro currency, with effect from January 2011 (see The Country, above). President Ilves indicated in August 2011 that use of the euro currency could be limited to more disciplined economies in the aftermath of the sovereign debt crisis. This observation, while widely acknowledged by external observers, led some analysts to suggest that Estonia was preparing to play a pivotal role in an elite "New North" of EU members, definitively replacing its unwanted "eastern European" designation. However, both President Ilves and his challenger for the presidency, Indrek Tarand, opposed the Finnish condition that aid to Greece be granted with a guarantee that Greece would repay its debt to specific countries in proportion to their donations to the bailout fund.

Most of Estonia's foreign relations in 2012 were focused on matters pertaining to the eurozone crisis and a proposed EU bailout. The EU established the European Stability Mechanism (ESM), an international finance organization similar to the International Monetary Fund (IMF), to assist with easing the economic crisis. The ESM is designed to assist the 17 countries of the eurozone by offering loans and economic assistance packages to help the struggling economies recover. The Estonian cabinet approved the ratification treaty in July 2012 and sent it to parliament for ratification. Certain members of parliament viewed the ESM as a violation of Estonia's constitution, resulting in its appeal to the Supreme Court of Estonia. The court ruled that joining the ESM was constitutional, and the treaty was ratified by parliament in late August. Estonia also voted in September to ratify Croatia's accession to the EU, making them the 13 of the 27 states to approve the Croatian bid for membership.

The year 2012 also marked the expansion of Estonia's diplomatic core, as established diplomatic relations with Nauru, Trinidad and Tobago, and Cote d'Ivoire. On June 1, 2012, an agreement for visa-free travel took effect between Kazakhstan and Estonia.

A fresh effort to resolve the border dispute emerged in the spring of 2013 after Ansip and Russian Prime Minister Dmitry Medvedev held a successful meeting in April. On May 23, the cabinet approved the 2005 text of the treaty, updated to clarify that the treaty only applies to the border path and does not address other territorial claims, Following approval by Russian President Vladimir Putin on September 20, the treaty must be signed by both foreign ministers and ratified by each parliament.

Current issues. Controversy regarding the appropriate strategy for eliminating the budget deficit animated the ruling coalition in 2009. The SDE focused on higher taxes and extended social services, while the IRL emphasized structural reform. Policy differences were exacerbated by a dispute over redundancy payments and unemployment benefits (see Political Parties, SDE, below) resulting in the exit of the SDE from government in May 2009, rendering the government a minority coalition composed of the RE and the IRL.

Public approval of the RE government amidst tough economic conditions reflects widespread support for the adoption of the euro from January 2011, which Estonians see as further confirmation of their identity in Europe, as well as a consensus on an orthodox free market platform to secure future growth.

Estonians remain generally skeptical about their political institutions, including the parties. Many parties face financial constraints (see Political Parties, below), leaving them vulnerable to corruption. The party financing supervision committee reported that political parties saw revenue decline by an average of 15 percent in 2012. Smaller parliamentary parties, such as the SDE, have endorsed public funding for electoral campaigns, as well as coordinated dates for local and national elections to ensure integrity, transparency, and financial efficiency in the electoral process.

Leaders of the SDE and the Russian Party of Estonia (VEE) signed an agreement merging the two parties in January 2012. The assimilation was subsequently approved by the VEE and SDE congresses on January 29 and February 19, respectively. In the agreement, former VEE chair Stanislav TŠEREPANOV became SDE deputy chair.

In March 2012, the Estonian parliament passed an amendment to its penal code establishing human trafficking as a specific criminal offense, thus becoming the final EU country to pass such legislation in accordance with EU protocols on human trafficking. The law includes sexual exploitation and forced labor as forms of human trafficking.

Scandal erupted in May 2012 when Justice Minister Kristen MICHAL was accused of trying to transfer money of an unknown origin to the RE's account. Legally, the source of party funding must be transparent so as to ensure donations are not accepted from corporations. Amid a barrage of attacks, Michal resigned in December, maintaining his innocence but explaining that the attacks had hindered the work of the party and the government.

In June 2013, the RE expelled two members, including European Parliament member Kristiina Ojuland, for manipulating votes in internal party election of 2011 and 2013. Ansip resisted calls within the party for a new election in light of the 2013 fraud, noting that the 39 fraudulent votes did not affect the outcome of the election. Ojuland retained her seat in the European Parliament.

POLITICAL PARTIES

Following independence in 1991, the broad liberation and pro-Russian movements gradually broke up into a large array of smaller parties and groupings, which formed a variety of electoral alliances in 1992 and 1995. In November 1998 the Parliament banned electoral alliances in future balloting, reducing the number of small parties.

Government Parties:

Estonian Reform Party (*Eesti Reformierakond*—RE). The RE was founded in late 1994 by Siim Kallas, who as president of the Bank of Estonia had played a key role in the downfall of the Pro Patria prime minister, Mart Laar, in September, but had then failed to secure legislative endorsement as his successor. Described as "liberal rightist" in orientation, the RE incorporated the Estonian Liberal Democratic Party (*Eesti Liberaaldemokraatlik Partei*—ELDP). The RE won 16.2 percent of the vote in the March 1995 legislative poll.

Having at first remained in opposition, the RE replaced the Estonian Center Party in the coalition government in October 1995 but withdrew from the government in late 1996. As was the case with the Fatherland Union and the Moderates, the RE was given five cabinet posts in the new government formed after the March 1999 legislative balloting, in which the RE had secured 18 seats on a 15.9 percent vote share. After the collapse of that three-party coalition, the RE in January formed a new government with the Center Party, with Kallas assuming the post of prime minister.

The RE secured 19 seats on a 17.7 percent vote share in the March 2003 *Riigikogu* poll and accepted "junior" status in the subsequent RP/RE/ERL government. The replacement of the RP by the Center Party in the government coalition in April 2005 allowed the RE to name Andrus Ansip to the post of prime minister. The RE won the governing mandate in the 2007 elections with 27.8 percent of votes and 31 seats, allowing it to form a coalition with the IRL and the SDE. (Ansip became the first prime minister to be returned to office since independence.)

Proposed austerity measures led to more frequent disagreements with RE coalition partners in 2009. However, the 2011 elections showed broad political support for continued fiscal restraint and integration in Western institutions. Following the adoption of the euro currency in January, the RE won a subsequent term of government in the general balloting held in March 2011, in which it was awarded 33 seats and 28.6% of votes. The party is expected to govern with the IRL for the balance of its term, and the prime minister enjoys cooperative relations with President Ilves.

At a party congress held in June 2011, Prime Minister Ansip was appointed to another two-year stint as RE chair. The party platform continues to support private ownership, low taxes, targeted social spending, and "the primacy of personal freedom." He was re-appointed in May 2013. The following month, two members were expelled from the party for committing voter fraud (see Current Issues, above).

Leaders: Andrus ANSIP (Party Chair and Prime Minister), Siim Kallas (Honorary Chair of the Board), Jaanus TAMKIVI (Parliamentary Faction Chair).

Pro Patria and Res Publica Union (*Isamaa ja Res Publica Liit*—IRL). The IRL was formed in June 2006 by a merger of the RP and the IL in the hopes of improving the right's representation in the 2007 *Riigikogu* elections. However, the IRL secured only 17.9 percent of the vote and 19 seats (compared with 35 percent in 2003 for the RP and IL combined). Nevertheless, the IRL was subsequently invited to join the new RE-led coalition government. At a party council on February 7, 2009, the chair called for extensive structural reform in order to save the economy from the global economic crisis. The IRL leadership has suggested merging the Baltic stock markets and cutting welfare payments to counter the recession and widening government debt.

Internal divisions threatened to undermine the IRL and alter the form of the governing coalition following the 2011 elections, in which the party won 20.5 percent of the vote and 23 seats. The IRL announced that an emergency conference would be held on August 13 in response to complaints that the party's decision-making process was opaque and its staff support was insufficient. The conference also aimed to address concerns that the Pro Patria faction, which is generally more conservative, has been given a junior role in the party. Dissenters were led by Tõnis LUKAS, the erstwhile education minister. In January 2012 Parliamentary Chair Urmas REINSALU was elected as chairman after Mart LAAR stepped down due to failing health. In May Reinsalu was named minister of defense and was subsequently chosen by Prime Minister Ansip to serve as acting prime minister in the event of Ansip's absence.

Leaders: Urmas REINSALU (Chair), Ene ERGMA (Vice Chair and Speaker of the Riigikogu), Jaak AAVIKSOO (Vice Chair and Minister of Education and Research), Kaia IVA (Parliamentary Faction Chair).

Union for the Republic (*Res Publica*—RP). Formed originally by young anti-Soviet activists (including several prominent academics) as a political "club" in 1989, the rightist RP became a formal party in December 2001. The RP gained about one-quarter of the vote in the local and regional elections in 2001. Similar results (24.6 percent of the vote nationally) in the 2003 national legislative polls secured 28 seats for the RP, which then formed a coalition government with the RE and ERL under the leadership of the RP's Juhan Parts.

Fatherland Union (*Erakond Isamaaliit*—IL). Also referenced as the Pro Patria Union, the IL was launched in December 1995 by merger of the Fatherland ("Pro Patria") National Coalition (*Rahvuslik Koonderakond Isamaa*—RKEI) and the Estonian National Independence Party (*Eesti Rahvusliku Sõltumatuse Partei*—ERSP). Having dominated the previous government, the two parties had contested the March 1995 election in alliance as the Pro Patria/ERSP Bloc (*Isamaa ja ERSP Liit*) but had retained only eight seats on a 7.9 percent vote share and thus went into the opposition.

Following independence in 1991, the ERSP was the country's strongest party. In September 1992 the RKEI elected a plurality of

29 deputies, who joined the ERSP contingent and others to elect Lennart Meri president the following month. With the RKEI surpassing the ERSP in the election, RKEI leader Mart Laar turned the alliance into a unitary formation and was named to head a coalition government. After failing to sustain coalition unity, he was ousted as prime minister in September 1994.

Mart Laar returned to the prime minister's post in March 1999 as head of the new three-party coalition government installed following legislative balloting. However, his coalition collapsed in late 2001, and the IL moved into opposition following the installation of the new RE/Center Party government. Laar resigned as chair of the Fatherland Union following the party's poor performance in the October 2002 local elections. The Fatherland Union's electoral slide continued in the March 2003 legislative poll, in which it secured only seven seats on a vote share of 7.3 percent. (For more on the RKEI and ERSP, see the 2012 *Handbook.*)

Opposition Parties:

Estonian Center Party (*Eesti Keskerakond*—EK). Launched in October 1991 as the Estonian People's Center Party (*Eesti Rahva-Keskerakond*—ERKE), the party adopted its current name in April 1993. Founded by Edgar Savisaar, the Center Party is an offshoot of the Estonian Popular Front (*Eesti Rahvarinne*), a broad proindependence movement that coalesced in 1988 but split into various parties after independence. The Center Party used the Front's designation in the 1992 election, winning 15 seats (with 12.2 percent of the vote) and achieving a creditable third place for its presidential candidate, Rein TAAGEPERA. As Front party chair, Savisaar was prime minister from April 1990 to January 1992, having previously been chair of the Soviet-era Estonian Planning Committee.

The Center Party absorbed the Estonian Entrepreneurs' Party (*Eesti Ettevõtjate Erakond*—EEE) prior to the March 1995 balloting, at which it won 14.2 percent of the vote. In October 1995 Savisaar's dismissal over an alleged phone-tapping scandal precipitated his party's exit from the government, with Savisaar himself being replaced as party chair by Andra VEIDEMANN. Having initially declared his retirement from political life, Savisaar made a comeback at the head of anti-Veidemann elements in early 1996, securing reelection as chair in late March. Two months later, the Veidemann group launched the Progress Party (see New Estonia Party, below, under ERL), to which the Center Party lost 7 of its 16 deputies. In July the state prosecutor closed the Savisaar case, having found nothing criminal in the former minister's conduct.

In May 1998 the Center Party absorbed the Estonian Greens (*Eesti Rõhelised*), which had been launched in 1991 as a coalition of several organizations and had secured one legislative seat in 1992. The movement drew attention to the huge environmental damage resulting from the Soviet military presence in Estonia.

Described as a "canny populist," Savisaar led the EK to a first-place finish in the March 1999 balloting (28 seats and 23.4 percent of the vote) on a platform designed to appeal to segments of the populace wary of free-market economic reforms. The Center Party then remained in opposition to the three-party coalition government formed in March. After the demise of the government in January 2002, the Center Party was admitted to the new cabinet.

Savisaar was reelected mayor of Tallinn in 2002, and the party retained its popularity at the March 2003 legislative poll, leading all parties with 25.4 percent of the vote. However, it was unable to persuade the RE to pursue a coalition government and subsequently returned to opposition status. When the RP dropped out of the government in March 2006, the EK took its place a month later and formed a new government with the remaining governing parties. However, that government's tenure ended following the March 2007 legislative elections, despite a strong showing by the Center Party (29 seats on a 26.1 percent vote share).

Among other things, the exit of the EK from the government in 2007 permitted the RE to pursue economic policies previously blocked by the EK. Links with other parties have suffered due to the EK's hesitation to clearly condemn the Russian presence in Georgia and its opposition to the relocation of the Bronze Soldier memorial.

The EK is now largely viewed as a pro-Russia party, affording the opposition SDE space to make inroads with center-left Estonian voters. This was evidenced in the 2011 election results, in which the EK won 23.3 percent of votes and 26 seats, representing a loss of 3 seats. The EK was particularly damaged in the 2011 elections by revelations that Savisaar had solicited funds to construct an Orthodox church in Tallinn from Vladimir Yakunin, a Russian businessman and ally of Russia's prime minister, Vladimir Putin. The party subsequently nominated an independent, Indrek Tarand, as their candidate in the presidential elections in August that year. The incumbent president Ilves retained support across party lines, however, and secured reelection.

Leaders: Edgar SAVISAAR (Chair and Mayor of Tallinn), Enn EESMAA, Kadri Simson (Vice Chairs), Priit TOOBAL (Secretary General), Laine RANDJÄRV (Vice President of the Riigikogu), Jüri RATAS (Second Vice President of the Riigikogu).

Social Democratic Party (*Sotsiaaldemokraatlik Erakond*—SDE). The SDE is the successor (as of 2003) to the Moderates, launched in 1990 as an electoral coalition of the Estonian Social Democratic Party (*Eesti Sotsiaaldemokraatlik Partei*—ESDP) and the Estonian Rural Center Party (*Eesti Maa-Keskerakond*—EMKE).

The ESDP had descended from the historic party founded in 1905 and maintained in exile during the Soviet era. Relaunched in Estonia in 1990 as a merger of three social democratic and workers' parties, it became part of the independence movement. Founded in 1990 to represent the interests of Estonia's farming community, the EMKE differed from other agrarian formations in that it gave full backing to promarket policies.

Mõõdukad won 12 legislative seats in the 1992 election and subsequently joined the new Pro Patria–led government, although the ESDP sought to preserve a social welfare dimension to the promarket reforms favored by the other members of the coalition. *Mõõdukad* lost half of its representation in the 1995 balloting, despite the endorsement of Prime Minister Andres Tarand. The alliance established a more formal structure in April 1996, with Tarand being elected chair.

The Moderates ran on a joint list for the 1999 legislative poll with the newly formed Estonian People's Party (*Eesti Rahvaerakond*—R); the two groupings formally merged after that balloting, resulting in the party's new Estonian name (*Rahvaerakond Mõõdukad*). The People's Party had been launched in March 1998 by the Estonian Farmers' Party (*Eesti Talurahva Erakond*—ETRE) and the Republican and Conservative People's Party (*Vabariiklaste ja Konservatiivide Rahvaerakond "Parempoolsed"*—VKRE). The VKRE won five seats in the March 1995 election on a 5 percent vote share.

In the March 1999 election the *Mõõdukad*/People's Party joint list won 17 seats on a 15.2 percent vote share. Collaterally, *Mõõdukad* Chair Tarand was elected to head the nine-member council established by the governing parties to coordinate their activities and legislative initiatives.

At a party congress on May 18, 2001, Tarand stepped down as chair and was succeeded as chair by Ilves. Like the Fatherland Union, the Moderates performed poorly in the 2002 local elections, prompting the resignation of Ilves as party chair. The decline continued in the March 2003 legislative balloting (six seats on a 7 percent vote share), and in early 2004 party delegates approved the adoption of the SDE rubric to reflect the party's policies more accurately. Ilves, an American-raised career diplomat, heightened the SDE's relevance through his election to the presidency, which is typically imbued with only ceremonial power domestically but holds practical influence in affairs abroad. The SDE secured a 10.6 percent vote share in the 2007 legislative poll and joined the subsequent RE-led coalition government.

The SDE took issue with RE policies for employment contracts in January 2008, and friction with the RE increased as it became apparent that the government would cut social spending in 2009 to respond to the crisis. Policy disputes continued, with the SDE ultimately exiting government in May 2009 in response to the government's move to reduce redundancy payments in order to allow more firms to cut costs and avoid bankruptcy. The cuts were to be accompanied by increased unemployment benefits.

The SDE saw its support levels rise in advance of the 2011 balloting, in which it increased its representation from 10 to 19 seats, capturing 17.1 percent of the votes. The party is increasingly the preferred choice for center-left Estonian voters who view the EK as excessively pro-Russian. The last party congress was held in October 2010, in which Sven Mikser was appointed chair.

In January 2012, the SDE merged with the VEE when leaders of both parties signed an agreement. The SDE subsequently ratified the unification on February 20.

Leaders: Sven MIKSER (Chair and Parliamentary Chair); Indrek SAAR (Secretary General); Toomas Hendrik ILVES (President of the Republic and Former Chair); Ivari PADAR (Council Chair); Stanislav TŠEREPANOV (Deputy Chair and former VEE Chair).

Russian Party of Estonia (*Vene Erakond Eestis*—VEE). The VEE was formed in 1994 under Sergei KUZNETSOV and competed in the *Meie Kodu* coalition of ethnic Russian groupings in 1995. In 1996 the VEE absorbed much of the Russian People's Party of Estonia (EVRP), but VEE membership was undercut in 1997 by the formation of the breakaway Russian Unity Party (*Veni Üntsuspartei*—VÜP), which participated in the EÜRP joint list in the 1999 legislative balloting. Running independently in that poll, the VEE failed to gain representation on a 2.0 percent vote share.

In December 2002 the VÜP announced it was merging back into the VEE, along with two other parties—the Russian Baltic Party in Estonia (*Vene Balti Erakond Eestis*—VBEE) and the Unity of Estonia Party. (For more on the VBEE, see the 2007 *Handbook.*)

Although the enlarged VEE claimed a bigger constituency than the EÜVRP, it secured only 0.18 percent of the vote in the 2003 legislative elections, and only 0.3 percent of the June 2004 vote for the European Parliament. Subsequently, the VÜP, VBEE, and Unity were occasionally referenced as still maintaining separate identities. In 2007 the VEE secured just 0.2 percent of the vote share, underscoring the fact that the KK remains a more popular organized political medium for ethnic Russians in Estonia. The VEE ruled out a merger with the KK in 2009 but increased its vote share to 0.9 percent in the 2011 legislative election.

On January 29, 2012, the VEE congress voted to approve assimilation into the SDE.

Other Parties Contesting the 2011 Legislative Elections:

Estonian Greens (*Erakond Eestimaa Rohelise*—EER). The EER was launched in 2006 after a long respite on the part of the Greens from politics in Tallinn. The Greens began as the Estonian Green Movement in 1988, which then splintered when a political wing, the Estonian Green Party (*Eesti Rohelised*—ER), split off in 1989. The Greens nevertheless won 8 of 105 seats in the first democratic election to the Estonian Supreme Council in 1990. Their chair, Toomas FREY, subsequently became the first Green to be given the environment portfolio.

The ER fared poorly in the first elections following independence, securing one seat and a 2.62 percent vote share in the 1992 parliamentary elections. A merger with the Estonian Royalist Party (*Rojalistlik Partei*—PR) in 1995 afforded no seats in that year's election. In 1998, membership dipped below the 1,000-member threshold required by Estonian electoral law. Green parties did not participate in the 2003 national elections.

Party organization improved in 2006 with a membership drive sponsored by the Green Party Initiative Group (*Rohelise Erakonna Algatusgrupp*). The EER had received over 1,000 membership applications by November and was consequently registered as an official party for the 2007 legislative poll. Campaigning on the platform of "New Energy," which combined green politics with probusiness energy innovations, the EER won six seats on a 7.1 percent vote share.

Following the party's loss of legislative representation in the 2011 elections, in which the ER received 3.8 percent of the votes, it was announced that all leadership positions would be reviewed. At the party congress in November 2011, Aleksander LAANE assumed party leadership.

Leader: Aleksander LAANE (Chair).

People's Union of Estonia (*Eestimaa Rahvaliit*—ERL). The ERL was established in October 1999 as a successor to the EME. In June 2000 the ERL absorbed the Estonian Rural Union (*Eesti Maaliit*—EM) and the Estonian Pensioners' and Families' Party (*Eesti Pensionäride ja Perede Erakond*—EPPE).

The EME, also often referenced as the Country People's Party, had been founded in September 1994 and helped rally agrarians to the KMÜ. The EME leader, Arnold Rüütel, was chair of the Estonian Supreme Soviet in the Soviet era but had supported moves to throw off Moscow rule, becoming independent Estonia's first head of state.

Although the EME was a prominent member of the KMÜ-led government, it distanced itself from the KE (below) and the KMÜ in early 1999, when it announced plans to form a postelectoral coalition government with Edgar Savisaar's Center Party. A number of members of the Progress Party, including the prominent politician Andra Veidemann, subsequently agreed to run on the EME list, but the party nonetheless managed only seven seats (7.3 percent of the vote).

The EM was founded in March 1991 and took eight of the KMÜ seats in March 1995. The EM reached an agreement in January 1998 with the opposition Center Party to support each other in the Parliament in order to protect Estonian farmers and their markets. The EM then ran on the KE list in the March 1999 legislative balloting, as did the EPPE.

The EPPE descended from the Estonian Democratic Justice Union/ Pensioners' League (*Eesti Demokraatlik Õigusliit/Pensionäride Ühendus*—EDÕL/PÜ), which dated from 1991 but was not represented in the Parliament until it was elected in 1992. The EPPE's immediate predecessor, the Estonian Pensioners' and Families' League (*Eesti Pensionäride ja Perede Liit*—EPPL), won six legislative seats in 1995 as part of the KMÜ.

Following the formation of the ERL, the new grouping was reported to have the largest membership among Estonian parties. The ERL's Rüütel won the presidency on September 21, 2001, in a second-round electoral college ballot. The ERL went on to win 13 percent of the vote and 13 seats in the March 2003 legislative balloting, its membership having been bolstered by a proposed merger with the New Estonia Party (*Erakond Uus Eesti*—UE). (See the 2000–2002 *Handbook* for details on the UE.)

The ERL's representation fell to six seats (on a 7.1 percent share of the vote) in the 2007 legislative elections. The decline was partly attributed to the reconstituted Greens, whose appeal to traditional values and concern for environmental issues appealed to portions of the ERL's base. The EK and the ERL had agreed to govern together as coalition partners if sufficient seats were secured, but the pact was nullified in August 2007 following disappointing electoral returns.

The ERL's congress in December criticized the ruling coalition's economic policies as inequitable, citing the need to address the impact of inflation. A planned merger with the SDE failed to materialize in 2010, prompting the defection of four deputies, three of whom joined the SDE. The remaining deputy joined the Reform-led governing coalition. These defections combined with party finances to highlight the ERL's continued fragility, despite its occasional role as kingmaker. The party was further undermined by a court ruling in May 2010, which held that its former chair, Villu REILJAN, was guilty of soliciting bribes in connection with sales of state-owned real estate in 2006. The most recent party congress was in July 2010.

In the 2011 legislative elections, the ERL received 2.1 percent of the votes. Following the balloting the party held new leadership elections on May 28, naming Margo Miljandi, an entrepreneur and former council chair, as the new head of the party.

In August 2011 the party announced that it had begun negotiations to "cooperate" with the heretofore unknown Estonian National Movement (*Eesti Rahvuslik Liikumine*—ERL), led by Aivar KOITLA, a reserve officer and business owner.

Leaders: Margo MILJANDI (Chair), Mai TREIAL (Vice Chair), Arnold RÜÜTEL (Former President of the Republic).

Estonian Christian Democrats (*Eesti Kristlikud Demokraadid*—EKD). This party was formerly known as the Estonian Christian People's Party (*Eesti Kristlik Rahvapartei*—EKRP). Established in December 1998, the EKRP earned 2.4 percent of the vote in the 1999 legislative poll and 1.1 percent in 2003. Prominent EKD platform proposals included addiction management and limiting pornography and obscenity in public places. The party also supports philanthropy by churches and initiatives that provide social and economic incentives for Estonians to remain in Estonia. The EKD increased its vote share to 1.7 percent in the 2007 elections, the best performance by the parties that failed to win seats. The EKD received 0.5 percent of the vote at the time of the 2011 legislative elections.

Leaders: Peeter VÕSU (Chair), Paul RÄSTA (Vice Chair).

Estonian Independence Party (*Eesti Iseseivuspartei*—EIP). An opponent of Estonia's accession to the EU, the EIP was founded in November 1999 after its predecessor, the Future's Estonia Party (*Tuleviku Eesti Erakond*—TEE), was denied ballot access for failing to meet registration requirements. The EIP won 0.55 percent of the vote in the 2003 legislative balloting and 0.2 percent in 2007. In April 2008 the EIP was reportedly considering a merger with the EDP (subsequently the LEE) and the PK. The alliance remained a possibility in 2009 (see LEE, below), but diplomatic clippings listed the EIP as an independent party in 2010. The party garnered 0.4 percent of all votes in the 2011 legislative elections.

Leaders: Vello LEITO, Peeter PAEMURRU (Chairs); Sven SILDNIK, Kaido NÕMMIK (Vice Chairs).

Other Parties:

Libertas Eesti (*Libertas Eesti Erakond*—LEE). The LEE is the rubric adopted in March 2009 by the Democrats–Estonian Democratic Party (*Demokraadid–Eesti Demokraatlik Partei*—EDP). The EDP was formally established in February 2001 as the successor to the Estonian Blue Party (*Eesti Sinine Erakond*—ESE). The EDP won 1.2 percent of the vote and no seats in the 2004 European Parliament elections. No votes were recorded for the EDP in 2007, implying that party membership had tapered off below the 1,000-member minimum.

The LEE designation was adopted in 2009 to identify the party with the broader European "euroskeptic" movement, Libertas. No election returns were recorded for the LEE in 2011.

Leaders: Jaan LAAS, Jüri Heldur ESTAM (Chairs); Endel KALJUSMAA (Vice Chair); Märt MEESAK (Secretary).

United Left Party of Estonia (*Eestimaa Ühendatud Vasakpartei*—EUVP). The EUVP was formed through a merger of the EVP (below) and KK (below) in 2008. The party has extensive contacts with Russian and European counterparts and supports the promotion of leftist causes, albeit from a position of relatively limited influence.

Leaders: Sergei JÜRGENS (KK Chair), Heino RÜÜTEL (EVP Cochair).

Estonian Left Party (*Eesti Vasakpartei*—EVP). The EVP is a successor to the Estonian Social Democratic Labor Party (*Eesti Sotsiaal demokraatlik Tööpartei*—ESDTP). Undeterred by the ouster from power of the Estonian Communist Party (*Eestimaa Kommunistlik Partei*—EKP) during the transition to independence, elements of the old party adopted the name of Estonian Democratic Labor Party (*Eesti Demokraatlik Tööpartei*—EDTP) in 1992, asserting that the party now had a democratic-socialist orientation. It unsuccessfully contested the 1995 election within the Justice (*Õiglus*) alliance, which also included the Party for Legal Justice (*Õigusliku Tasakaalu Erakond*—ÕTE), led by Peeter TEDRE. The EDTP's subsequent efforts to establish ties with the ESDP were rebuffed. The party changed its name to the Estonian Social Democratic Labor Party in December 1997. The ESDTP contested the 1999 poll on the joint list of the EÜRP (below). Running independently in the 2003 balloting, the ESDTP won only 0.42 percent of the vote. In the 2007 legislative poll, the newly renamed EVP secured 0.1 percent of the vote. In May 2008 the EVP announced plans for a merger with the KK (below).

Leaders: Sirje KINGSEPP (Chair), Malle SALUPERE (Vice Chair).

Constitution Party (*Konstitutsioonierakond*—KK). A successor to the Estonian United People's Russian Party (*Eestimaa Ühendatud Vene Rahvapartei*—EÜVRP), also formerly known as Estonian United—People's Party (*Eestimaa Ühendatud Rahvapartei*—EÜRP), the KK was widely viewed as the most active political faction for minority ethnic Russian concerns. Then considered the strongest of the numerous ethnic Russian parties in Estonia, the EÜRP participated in the March 1995 election in the alliance known as Our Home Is Estonia (*Meie Kodu on Eestimaa*), along with the Russian Party of Estonia (see VEE, above) and the EVRP. *Meie Kodu* strongly opposed the 1993 Estonian citizenship law, which, by limiting the franchise to citizens, prevented the alliance from obtaining a higher vote among the estimated 20–30 percent ethnic Russian component of the populace. The grouping secured six seats, the legislators subsequently coalescing as a parliamentary Russian Faction.

The EÜRP contested the March 1999 balloting on a joint list with the ESDTP and the VÜP (see 2006 *Handbook*); the list secured six seats. EÜRP legislators voted to approve the new coalition government formed in January 2002 (for more information on EÜRP activities between 2000 and 2002, see the 2010 *Handbook*). The EÜRP adopted the EÜVRP rubric in December 2002. The EÜVRP secured only 2.24 percent of the vote in the 2003 legislative balloting, marking the first time since independence that no Russian party would be represented in the *Riigikogu*. The KK in May 2008 announced a merger with the EVP (see EVP, above).

Leader: Sergei JÜRGENS (Chair).

Unofficial political groupings in 2011 included the E-party, the Pirate Party of Estonia (reportedly defunct from late 2009), the Estonia's National Conservative Union, and the Free Association of Citizens.

For more information on the **Farmers' Assembly** (*Põllumeeste Kogu*—PK) and the **Estonian Coalition Party** (*Eesti Koonderakond*—KE), see the 2010 *Handbook*.

LEGISLATURE

The former Supreme Soviet/Council (Ülemnõukogu) ceased to exist on September 14, 1992, prior to balloting on September 20 for a new unicameral **Parliament** (*Riigikogu*) of 101 members elected by proportional representation for four-year terms. In the most recent election of March 6, 2011, the Estonian Reform Party won 33 seats; the Estonian Center Party, 26; the Pro Patria and Res Publica Union, 23; and the Social Democratic Party, 19.

Speaker: Ene ERGMA.

CABINET

[as of November 18, 2013]

Prime Minister	Andrus Ansip (RE)
Ministers	
Agriculture	Helir-Valdor Seeder (IRL)
Culture	Rein Lang (RE)
Defense	Urmas Reinsalu (IRL)
Economic Affairs and Communications	Juhan Parts (IRL)
Education and Research	Jaak Aaviksoo (IRL)
Environment	Keit Pentus-Rosimannus (RE) [f]
Finance	Jürgen Ligi (RE)
Foreign Affairs	Urmas Paet (RE)
Internal Affairs	Ken-Marti Vaher (IRL)
Justice	Hanno Pekvur (RE)
Regional Affairs	Siim Valmar Kiisler (IRL)
Social Affairs	Taavi Roivas (RE)

[f] = female

INTERGOVERNMENTAL REPRESENTATION

Ambassador to the U.S.: Marina KALJURAND.

U.S. Ambassador to Estonia: Jeffrey D. LEVINE.

Permanent Representative to the UN: Margus KOLGA.

IGO Memberships (Non-UN): CEUR, EBRD, EIB, EU, ICC, IOM, NATO, OECD, OSCE, WTO.

ETHIOPIA

Federal Democratic Republic of Ethiopia

Political Status: Former monarchy; provisional military government formally established September 12, 1974; Marxist-Leninist one-party system instituted September 6, 1984; communist constitution approved by referendum of February 1, 1987, resulting in redesignation of the country as the People's Democratic Republic of Ethiopia; "state responsibility" assumed by rebel coalition upon surrender of the former regime's military commander and acting president in Addis Ababa on May 27, 1991; national charter and transitional government approved by multiparty National Conference that met on July 1–5, 1991; present constitution promulgated December 8, 1994; Federal Democratic Republic of Ethiopia proclaimed August 22, 1995.

Area: 436,349 sq. mi. (1,130,138 sq. km).

Population: 86,886,572 (2012E—UN); 93,877,025 (2013E—U.S. Census).

Major Urban Centers (2005E): ADDIS ABABA (2,890,000), Dire Dawa (270,000), Nazret (218,000), Gondar (186,000), Dese (161,000), Jimma (151,000), Harer (117,000).

Working Language: Amharic (all Ethiopian languages enjoy equal state recognition).

Monetary Unit: Birr (official rate November 1, 2013: 18.99 birr = $1US).

President: MULATU Teshome (Oromo Peoples' Democratic Organization); elected by the Parliament on October 7, 2013, to a six-year term, succeeding GIRMA Wolde Giorgis (initially elected as an independent but joined the Ethiopian People's Revolutionary Democratic Front [EPRDF]).

Prime Minister: HAILEMARIAM Desalegn; designated by the Ethiopian Peoples' Revolutionary Democratic Front and sworn in on September 21, 2012, succeeding MELES Zenawi (Tigray People's Liberation Front), who died on August 20, 2012.

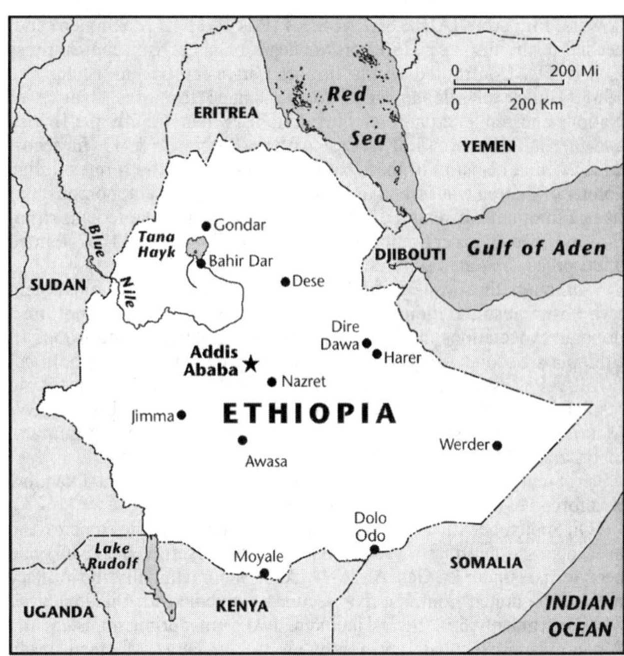

THE COUNTRY

One of the oldest countries in the world, Ethiopia exhibits an ethnic, linguistic, and cultural diversity that has impaired its political unity and stability in spite of the preponderant position long occupied by the Christian, Amharic- and Tigrinya-speaking inhabitants of the central highlands. Among the more than 70 different ethnic groups, the Amhara and the largely Muslim Oromo (Galla) account for approximately 40 percent of the population each. Amharic, the working language, is spoken by about 60 percent of the people; Galla, Tigrinya, Arabic, Somali, and Tigray are also prominent among the country's 70 languages and over 200 dialects, while English, Italian, and French have traditionally been employed within the educated elite. The Ethiopian Orthodox (Coptic) Church embraces about 40 percent of the population, as does Islam (most Ethiopian Muslims are Sunnis). Christians have long dominated governmental affairs. In 1994 women accounted for 37 percent of the labor force, the vast majority as unpaid agricultural workers. Although females have traditionally influenced decision making among the Amhara and Tigrayan peoples, their representation in the Mengistu government was minimal. There are 116 women in the current House of Peoples' Representatives, up from 42 in the previous membership, while several females have been appointed to recent cabinets.

One of the world's poorest countries, Ethiopia remains dependent on agriculture, with over 85 percent of its rapidly expanding population (the largest in Africa) engaged in farming and livestock-raising. (Despite free-market reforms initiated in the second half of the 1990s, most land remains owned by the government.) Coffee, the principal crop, accounts for more than 40 percent of export earnings (Ethiopia is the continent's largest coffee grower). Cotton and sugar are also widely harvested. Agricultural success waxes and wanes in response to variable rainfall, and drought and famine have routinely stalked the land, often generating massive, albeit not always sufficient, international aid shipments. Gold and marble are mined commercially, and deposits of copper, potash, and natural gas are awaiting exploitation. Oil exploration rights have been granted recently, although they reportedly remain highly speculative. The 1962–1991 civil war in Eritrea and guerrilla activity in other regions severely hampered industrial development, which is primarily concentrated in nondurable consumer goods. Industry currently accounts for about 13 percent of GDP, compared to 48 percent for agriculture.

The World Bank negotiated forgiveness of some of Ethiopia's commercial debt in the mid-1990s, although nearly $4 billion of additional external debt continued to constrain economic advancement. The International Monetary Fund (IMF) also supported the government's pursuit of structural reforms in the second half of the decade. Although in 1998 Ethiopia was considered to be positioned for sustained economic improvement, the 1998–2000 border war with Eritrea (see Political background and Current issues, below) severely eroded the confidence of investors and redirected national funds desperately needed for social services toward the military. The conflict also slowed down the government's privatization campaign and plans to strengthen the financial sector.

According to the IMF, the country averaged 6.5 percent annual GDP growth in 2000–2006, though drought contributed to economic contraction in 2003. The IMF announced additional debt relief for Ethiopia in late 2005 and called for increased donor assistance. Russia also cancelled more than $1 billion of Ethiopia's debt, while new lending from China was subsequently reported. However, the United Kingdom and other western donors temporarily suspended some direct aid in the wake of severe political discord that erupted in late 2005 and the subsequent government crackdown on the opposition. Aid distribution was described as returning to normal in late 2007 as the government pursued "reconciliation" with its opponents. Meanwhile, the IMF called upon the government to reinvigorate its privatization program, pursue additional reforms, and direct greater public resources toward infrastructure, health, and education. (Ethiopia's army of more than 180,000 troops, one of Africa's largest, currently consumes the lion's share of expenditures.) In a related vein, Ethiopia continued to seek membership in the World Trade Organization (WTO), while promoting increased exports of flowers, tea, and textiles. However, President Meles indicated that he did not by any means fully accept the "neoliberal," free-market "orthodoxy" of the major international financial institutions, saying that state intervention in the economy for the sake of development remained an important policy component.

Inflation spiked from 2005, when it was at 6.8 percent year on year, to 2009, when it hit a 13-year peak of 36.4 percent because of rapidly rising food prices. In 2010 the IMF forecast that inflation would plummet to a more reasonable 3.8 percent. Meanwhile, GDP continued to grow by 11.8 percent in 2007 and 11.2 percent annually in 2008, then declined to 9.9 percent in 2009. The IMF approved several special disbursements in 2009 to support government efforts to combat price increases and effects of the global recession.

In 2010 GDP grew by 8 percent, while inflation was 8.1 percent. In its annual Doing Business survey that year, the World Bank ranked Ethiopia 104th out of 183 countries. In November 2010 Ethiopia launched the five-year Growth and Transformation Plan that aims to double the size of the economy by 2015, mostly by supporting the development of small and medium-scale industries. Growth in 2011 continued the high-growth trajectory of recent years. In 2012 the spring rains arrived late, hampering food production and slowing growth. Expansionary policies had driven high inflation, but the IMF noted the success of tighter fiscal and monetary policy in reducing inflation to 24.1 percent. The IMF reported that GDP grew by 8.6 percent in 2012. The country ranked 173th out of 186 countries in the UN's 2013 Human Development Index, and annual per-capita GDP equaled $490. The UN's human poverty index revealed that almost 51 percent of citizens lived below the poverty threshold. Ethiopia remains one of the world's biggest per-capita recipients of emergency assistance.

GOVERNMENT AND POLITICS

Political background. After centuries of medieval isolation, Ethiopia began its history as a modern state with the reign of Emperor MENELIK II (1889–1913), who established a strong central authority and successfully resisted attempts at colonization by Italy and other powers. Emperor HAILE SELASSIE I (Ras TAFARI Makonnen) succeeded to the throne in 1930 on the death of his cousin, the Empress ZAUDITU. Confronted with a full-scale invasion by Fascist Italy in 1935, Haile Selassie appealed for assistance from the League of Nations and remained abroad until Ethiopia's liberation by the British and the liquidation of Italy's East African Empire in 1941. In accordance with a decision of the UN General Assembly, the former Italian colony of Eritrea was joined to Ethiopia in 1952 as an autonomous unit in an Ethiopian-Eritrean federation. Abandonment of the federal structure by formal incorporation of Eritrea into Ethiopia in 1962 fanned widespread separatist sentiment in Eritrea.

Although the post–World War II period witnessed a movement away from absolute monarchy, the pace of liberalization did not meet popular expectations, and in early 1974 an uprising among troops of Ethiopia's Second Army Division gradually escalated into a political revolt. As a result, Prime Minister Tshafe Tezaz AKLILU Habte-Wold resigned on February 28 and was replaced by ENDALKACHEW Makonnen, who also was unable to contain discontent among military, labor, and student groups. By late spring many aristocrats and former government officials had been imprisoned, and on July 22 Endalkachew was forced to resign in favor of Mikael IMRU.

On September 12, 1974, the military announced that the emperor had been deposed and that a Provisional Military Government (PMG) had been formed under Lt. Gen. AMAN Mikael Andom. Initially, the military presented a united front, but rival factions soon emerged. On November 24 approximately 60 officials, including two former prime ministers and Aman, were executed, apparently on the initiative of (then) Maj. MENGISTU Haile-Mariam, strongman of the little-publicized Armed Forces Coordinating Committee, or *Dergue,* as it was popularly known. After November 28 the *Dergue* acted through a Provisional Military Administrative Council (PMAC), whose chair, Brig. Gen. TEFERI Banti, served concurrently as acting head of state and government.

On March 21, 1975, the PMAC decreed formal abolition of the monarchy, while declaring its intention to organize a new national political movement "guided by the aims of Ethiopian socialism." Former emperor Haile Selassie, in detention since his deposition, died in August.

On February 3, 1977, following reports of a power struggle within the *Dergue,* General Teferi and six associates were killed in an armed encounter in the Grand Palace in Addis Ababa. Eight days later, Mengistu and Lt. Col. ATNAFU Abate were named chair and vice chair, respectively, of the PMAC in a proclamation that also modified the *Dergue* structure. However, Atnafu was executed on November 11 for alleged "counter-revolutionary crimes." Collaterally, antigovernment violence, dubbed the "white terror," flared in Addis Ababa amid indications of growing coordination between several opposition groups, including the Marxist Ethiopian People's Revolutionary Party (EPRP) and the more conservative Ethiopian Democratic Union (EDU). The Mengistu regime responded by mounting an indiscriminate "red terror" in December 1977–February 1978 based in part on the arming of civilians in urban dweller associations (*kebeles*).

The struggle for control in Addis Ababa was accompanied by military challenges on three major fronts. By March 1977 virtually all of northern Eritrea was under the administration of Eritrean rebels, while EDU guerrillas in the northwest were subjecting government forces to increased pressure. Moreover, in late July the government conceded that the greater part of the eastern region of Ogaden had fallen to insurgents of the Western Somalia Liberation Front (WSLF), who were supported by Somali regular forces. On September 7 Ethiopia severed relations with Somalia because of the "full-scale war" that existed between the two countries. By mid-December, however, a massive influx of Cuban personnel and Soviet equipment had shifted the military balance in Ethiopia's favor, and most of the region was recovered prior to formal Somali withdrawal in March 1978. Government forces in Eritrea then mounted a renewed offensive, and in late November recaptured the last two major cities held by the rebels—the strategically important Red Sea port of Massawa and Keren, some 70 miles northwest of Asmara.

Despite the success of the 1978 anti-insurgent campaigns, a major offensive in mid-1979 to wipe out remaining resistance in Eritrea proved ineffectual, with government control remaining limited to the principal towns and connecting corridors. Similar conditions prevailed in the Ogaden, where the WSLF and its ally, the Somali Abo Liberation Front (SALF), continued to launch guerrilla attacks. In response, Ethiopia was reported to have initiated a scorched-earth policy—poisoning water supplies, killing herds of livestock, strafing settled areas—that further aggravated what the UN Office of the High Commissioner for Refugees had earlier described as the world's worst refugee problem.

Following a number of unsuccessful attempts to unite existing Marxist parties, a Commission for Organizing the Party of the Working People of Ethiopia (COPWE) was formed in December 1979 to pave the way for a Soviet-style system of government. On September 10, 1984, authorities declared the COPWE's work complete, and Mengistu was designated secretary general of the new Workers' Party of Ethiopia (WPE); however, the PMAC remained in effective control, pending completion of a civilian governing structure.

A commission appointed and chaired by Mengistu presented the draft of a new constitution in early 1987. A reported 81 percent of voters approved the document during a referendum on February 1, the government announcing three weeks later that the country would thenceforth be styled the People's Democratic Republic of Ethiopia (PDRE).

A unicameral national legislature (*Shengo*), elected on June 14, 1987, convened on September 9, and on the following day selected Mengistu as the country's first president. The Shengo also named Lt. Col. FISSEHA Desta, theretofore deputy secretary general of the PMAC Standing Committee, as PDRE vice president and elected a 24-member State Council, headed by Mengistu and Fisseha as president and vice president, respectively. The former deputy chair of the PMAC Council of Ministers, Capt. FIKRE-SELASSIE Wogderes, was designated prime minister of an administration whose composition, announced on September 20, was largely unchanged from that of its predecessor.

The new government was greeted by vigorous rebel offensives—the Eritrean People's Liberation Front (EPLF) claimed a succession of victories over government troops beginning in September 1987 and, in March 1988, the Tigray People's Liberation Front (TPLF) took advantage of Addis Ababa's setbacks in Eritrea to launch a renewed offensive in its 13-year struggle for autonomy. In April, Mengistu, buffeted by military reversals and deteriorating troop morale, signed a cease-fire with Somali president Siad Barre, thus freeing Ethiopian troops for redeployment to Eritrea, most of which, despite the recapture of some rebel-held villages, remained under EPLF control.

Conditions worsened substantially for the central government in 1989. A failed military coup in mid-May, during which the defense and industry ministers were killed, provoked a purge of senior officers that yielded the loss of most seasoned commanders. Three months earlier the Ethiopian People's Revolutionary Democratic Front (EPRDF), a base-broadening coalition recently established by the TPLF, had launched another offensive that dealt the government a series of major setbacks. In August Mengistu felt obliged to augment his army (already one of Africa's largest at more than 300,000 personnel) by mass mobilization and conscription. A month later Mengistu accepted an overture by former U.S. president Jimmy Carter to open peace talks with the EPLF, subsequently accepting Carter and former Tanzanian president Julius Nyerere as cochairs of the discussions. Meanwhile, preliminary negotiations with the EPRDF were launched in Rome in October, although the Tigrayans linked them to "the irrevocable fall of the current regime." In November, with EPRDF forces moving toward the capital, Prime Minister Fikre-Selassie was dismissed for "health reasons" and replaced, on an acting basis, by Deputy Prime Minister HAILU Yimanu. Shortly thereafter, fighting also broke out in the east between government troops and rebel forces of the Oromo Liberation Front (OLF). Faced with continued military adversity, diminished Soviet support, and renewed projections of widespread famine, Mengistu in March 1990 formally terminated his commitment to Marxism. However, the regime remained on the brink of collapse as EPRDF troops advanced to within 150 miles of Addis Ababa and EPLF forces gained control of all of Eritrea except for several major cities.

In January 1991 the EPRDF and the EPLF, which had been coordinating military operations for two years, devised a "final" battle plan after the TPLF reportedly agreed to a self-determination referendum in Eritrea to be held following the anticipated rebel victory. With the OLF also a participant, the anti-Mengistu alliance launched a decisive offensive in February.

In what was seen as a last-ditch effort to salvage his regime, Mengistu on April 26, 1991, announced the appointment of former Foreign Minister TESFAYE Dinka, a moderate with ties to the United States and Western Europe, to the vacant position of prime minister and named Lt. Gen. TESFAYE Gebre-Kidan as vice president. However, on May 21, as EPRDF troops encircled Addis Ababa, Mengistu resigned as head of state and fled to Zimbabwe under pressure from U.S. officials who sought to prevent further bloodshed. Vice President Tesfaye became acting president. Three days later the EPLF sealed its control of Eritrea by capturing the towns of Asmara and Keren, and, with EPRDF fighters poised to attack the capital, General Tesfaye "effectively surrendered" on May 27. Under an agreement reached at a U.S.-brokered conference in London, the EPRDF took control of Addis Ababa on May 28 with only minimal resistance from holdout government troops. On the same day TPLF leader MELES Zenawi announced the impending formation of an interim government that would assume responsibility for "the whole country" until Ethiopia's political future could be further defined. Concurrently, however, EPLF leader Isaias Afwerki announced the establishment of a separate provisional government for Eritrea. Although some friction was subsequently reported between the two groups, a multiparty National Conference was launched on July 1 to chart the country's political future. On July 3 the EPRDF and the EPLF (technically attending as an observer) announced an agreement whereby the former would support a referendum in 1993 on Eritrean independence in return for access to the Red Sea port of Assab. At the conclusion of the conference two days later, a National Charter was adopted that offered guarantees of basic human rights, freedom of association, access to mass media, judicial independence, and substantial autonomy for the country's numerous ethnic groups. In addition, an 87-member Council of Representatives was named, which on July 21 formalized Meles' status as head of state. Subsequently, on July 29, the acting chief of government, TAMIRAT Layne, was confirmed as prime minister, with a 16-member cabinet being announced on August 10.

At the long-awaited referendum in Eritrea on April 23–25, 1993, 99.8 percent of those participating voted for independence, and on May 3 Addis Ababa endorsed the action, which was formalized on May 24. Subsequently, balloting for a 547-member Ethiopian Constituent Assembly was held on June 5, 1994, with the EPRDF winning an overwhelming majority in reporting districts (polling in Dire Dawa and elsewhere in the east and southeast being postponed until August 28 because of unsettled conditions in the largely Somali-dominated region).

While most of the major non-EPRDF groups participated in the 1993 Constituent Assembly poll, all but the largely progovernment Ethiopian National Democratic Party (ENDP) objected to the constitution adopted on December 8, 1994, and declared their intention to boycott the federal and state elections of May 7, 1995. Despite two negotiating sessions between government and opposition delegates, no resolution of the impasse was found. Representatives of the opposition Council of Alternative Forces for Peace and Democracy in Ethiopia (CAFPDE), led by BEYENE Petros, complained of a "stranglehold" by the EPRDF on the police and armed forces, the detention of numerous regime opponents, and a ban on many party activities. For its part, the government, through its chief negotiator, DAWIT Yohannes, called for acceptance of Ethiopia's existing state bodies and denied that it held political prisoners, insisting that those incarcerated encompassed only "warmongers." As a result of the stalemate, the EPRDF and its constituent groups swept the May balloting.

On August 21, 1995, the recently elected House of Peoples' Representatives convened to accept a transfer of power from its military-backed predecessor, and on August 22, after formal proclamation of the Federal Democratic Republic of Ethiopia, the legislature elected NEGASO Gidada to the essentially titular office of federal president. On August 23 the legislators elected former interim president Meles Zenawi to the far more powerful office of prime minister.

In late December 2006 the High Court found Mengistu, Fikre-Selassie, Fisseha, and many other Dergue officials guilty of genocide. Mengistu, living in Zimbabwe, was sentenced in absentia to life imprisonment [later changed by the Supreme Court to a sentence of death], though he was not expected to return to Ethiopia. (For more on the trial, see the 2012 *Handbook.*)

In March 1997 social discontent surfaced in segments of the Amhara population, resulting from the government's "land reform" projects, which were seen by opponents as a policy to serve the interests of the peasants close to the ruling EPRDF. Attention throughout the rest of the year focused on efforts by the EPRDF to negotiate agreements with Oromo, Somali, and Afar groups that would permit implementation of the delayed regional autonomy plan (see various sections below for further information).

With a swiftness that stunned observers, a border dispute between Ethiopia and Eritrea escalated from what was initially depicted as a minor skirmish in early May 1998 into full-scale fighting by June. Among the many casualties of the war was their joint effort, along with Uganda, to contain Sudan's regional influence, in particular Khartoum's effort to spread militant Islamic fundamentalism. Indeed, in its quest for regional allies, Addis Ababa reportedly toned down its anti-Sudanese rhetoric and opened a dialogue with Khartoum.

The war with Eritrea dominated Ethiopian affairs for the remainder of 1998 through 2000. (See Political background in entry on Eritrea for an extensive history of the conflict.) Nearly every segment of Ethiopian society, including the opposition parties, appeared to support the Ethiopian military campaign, and the EPRDF dominated the balloting that began in May 2000 for the House of Peoples' Representatives, while Meles was reelected to a second five-year term as prime minister on October 10, 2000, by acclamation in the House of Peoples' Representatives. On October 8, 2001, GIRMA Wolde Giorgis was selected to succeed President Negaso, who had become embroiled in a dispute with Meles and his supporters over the outcome of the war. Tension over the perceptions that Meles had given too much ground to Eritrean negotiators in creating a peace accord to end the 1998–2000 war culminated in an attempt by TPLF hard-liners to remove Meles from his party post in early 2001. Although Meles survived, the rebellion had spread to other components of the EPRDF, and Meles's position remained fragile. Student protests in April contributed to the sense of instability, and the government subsequently launched an extensive crackdown on its opponents, against many of whom it leveled corruption charges. Meanwhile, President Negaso sealed his political fate after siding with critics of Meles, who subsequently worked to have him expelled from the Oromo Peoples' Democratic Organization (OPDO) and the EPRDF. Girma Wolde Giorgis, Negaso's successor, was not widely known, even though he was a member of the House of Peoples' Representatives. Significantly, however, Girma was a member of the Oromo ethnic group (as was Negaso), his selection apparently reflecting the TPLF's intensifying concern over the growing unease in Oromia and other southern regions regarding TPLF dominance at the national level. Meanwhile, battles were reported in 2002 between Ethiopian forces and fighters from the OLF, Ogaden National Liberation Front (ONLF), and other, smaller secessionist and/or anti-EPRDF groups.

The political turmoil triggered by the peace accord concessions was expected to give the newly reorganized opposition parties an opportunity to present a genuine challenge to the EPRDF in the legislative balloting of May 15, 2005. For the first time, opposition candidates were allowed to "campaign openly" and were granted some access to state-run media. The election was also keenly observed by the West, which hoped the poll would represent an important step in the maturation of Ethiopia's fledgling democratic process and solidify Meles's credentials as one of the new breed of reformist African leaders.

Initial results indicated a strong challenge to the EPRDF from two new opposition alliances—the Coalition for Unity and Democracy (CUD) and the United Ethiopian Democratic Forces (UEDF). After allegations of widespread election fraud and vote-rigging, a new round of balloting was held in a number of constituencies. The EPRDF was credited with winning all of the seats subject to reballoting, and the final results accorded the EPRDF and its allies an even greater majority than originally projected, prompting severe domestic turmoil. EU observers concluded that the election had failed to meet international standards.

Meles was reelected by a show of hands in the legislature in a session on October 10 that was boycotted by more than 100 opposition members. The new cabinet was reshuffled the next day, although the portfolios remained primarily within the EPRDF.

Unrest culminated in another conflict between protesters and government forces in early November 2005 during an AU summit in Addis Ababa. The government blamed "stone-throwers" for initiating the battle, while the opposition blamed unnecessarily harsh reactions by security forces to a peaceful demonstration. Nearly 50 people died in the clashes, to which the government responded by detaining thousands of protesters and arresting nearly all of the CUD leadership, prominent members of other opposition parties, and a number of journalists and human rights activists. Those arrested were charged with treason, promoting violence, and attempting to overthrow the government.

Human rights groups expressed outrage over the 2005 crackdown, and the World Bank, EU, and United Kingdom suspended aid to Ethiopia to pressure Meles to adopt a more conciliatory stance. However, the trials of the detainees opened in May 2006, with Meles dismissing accusations about his "dictatorial rule." By that time, the prime minister was also facing growing international pressure regarding Ethiopia's continued refusal to accept the final decisions of the UN commission established to demarcate the border with Eritrea.

Reports surfaced in October 2006 that the Ethiopian commission created to investigate the events of 2005 initially intended to characterize the attacks on civilians as a "massacre." However, after several members of the commission had fled the country, the final report, accepted by the legislature in March 2007, concluded that security forces had taken "necessary measures" to quell the disturbances. In contrast, Amnesty International accused security forces of carrying out a systematic campaign of intimidation, detention, and even torture of its opponents.

In early April 2007 the federal High Court dismissed the controversial charges of attempted genocide and treason against the 2005 defendants and dropped all charges against some of the detainees. However, in June the court found more than 40 defendants guilty of various charges ranging from armed rebellion to "outrage against the constitution" and imposed harsh sentences (including life in prison in some cases). Most of the defendants subsequently signed a carefully crafted "letter of apology" in which they accepted responsibility for "mistakes" that had contributed to the unrest. Shortly thereafter, Prime Minister Meles announced that President Girma had pardoned the defendants and restored their civil rights in the name of "reconciliation." The United States reportedly helped mediate the resolution of the conflict, which had tarnished Meles's image despite his "pro-Western" role in Somalia and the "war on terror" in general (see Foreign relations, below). The international community also expressed concern that the proxy war in Somalia might combine with the unresolved border dispute to reignite fighting between Ethiopia and Eritrea (see entry on Eritrea for additional information). Although President Girma was initially not expected to run for a second term due to his advanced age and poor health, he was nominated again by the EPRDF and reelected to a second term by Parliament on October 9, 2007.

The Ethiopian government continued its military buildup in case of a renewed border war with Eritrea, which Ethiopia accused of arming and training Ethiopian rebels, most notably the ONLF, against whom the government had been waging an intense campaign since the spring of 2007 (see ONLF under Political Parties and Groups, below). For its part, the ONLF accused the government of having perpetrated a "reign of terror" against civilians in the Ogaden region. Human rights activists echoed at least some of the charges and warned of a potentially massive humanitarian crisis as the result of the government crackdown. The Meles administration also faced heavy domestic criticism for the alleged intimidation and harassment of opposition candidates in the April 2008 local elections, which were dominated by the EPRDF.

A total of 63 political parties put forward 2,188 candidates for the May 23, 2010, legislative elections, the fourth since the ousting of the Dergue. The National Electoral Board announced 93.4 percent of the country's nearly 32 million eligible voters turned out to cast ballots. The board's final tally gave the EPRDF and its allies near total control of both the federal and regional state governments. Out of 547 total seats available in the House of People's Representatives, the EPRDF took 499. Counting allied seats, the government held 545 seats, giving up only 1 to the new opposition coalition FORUM (see Political Parties, below) and to 1 independent. The government restricted movement of the foreign diplomatic corps, harassed independent journalists, and blocked international broadcasts in the lead-up to the election. Analysts said the EPRDF's actions were part of a strategy to narrow the political space before the elections. EU observers said the election was peaceful and organized but did not meet international standards, including a number of reports of harassment and intimidation. The nongovernmental organization Human Rights Watch released a report following the election highlighting the many ways the EPRDF had been systematically applying pressure to opposition party members since 2005. African Union observers said the balloting met that organization's standards for democratic elections, but international and domestic commentators questioned whether the country was slipping back into a one-party state. Meles was reelected prime minister by the House of People's representatives on October 5, and he appointed a reshuffled cabinet the next day.

In April 2009 the government reported it had uncovered an alleged coup plot, which eventually led to the convictions of 27 people, including death sentences for 5. But critics charged that the government was manufacturing threats to secure support in advance of the 2010 legislative elections.

The United States, United Kingdom, and EU all criticized the lopsided victory of Meles's EPRDF in the May 2010 elections, saying it did not meet international standards. Observers, though, commented that repercussions from the West would be mitigated by Meles's strong stance against the Islamic radicalization of East Africa by fundamentalist groups like Somalia's al-Shabaab.

The protests and revolts against regimes in North Africa and the Middle East in early 2011 (the "Arab Spring") led Meles to take steps to suppress dissent. In March more than 400 opposition leaders and figures were arrested on various charges. Meles also purged propresidential groupings, arresting more than 150 members of parties within the governing coalition.

Meles died in office on August 20, 2012 (see Current issues, below). Deputy Prime Minister HAILEMARIAM Desalegn was sworn in as Meles's successor on September 21. A minor cabinet reshuffle was undertaken on November 29.

Hailemariam again reshuffled the cabinet on July 4, 2013. On October 7, MULATU Teshome (Oromo Peoples' Democratic Organization) was unanimously elected president by the parliament.

Constitution and government. An imperial constitution, adopted in 1955, was abrogated when the military assumed power in 1974. The 1987 constitution provided for a communist system of government based on "democratic centralism." In July 1991, two months after the overthrow of the Mengistu regime, a National Conference was convened that approved a transitional government charter providing for an 87-member quasi-legislative body, the Council of Representatives, drawn from the various national "freedom units." The council, intended to serve for a 24-month period, was empowered to designate a chair to serve as head of a transitional government. Subject to council approval, the chair was authorized to appoint a prime minister and other cabinet members. Meanwhile, the council was directed to oversee the drafting of a constitution that would ensure the realization of "a completely democratic system" and to prepare the country for elections to a National Assembly under the new basic law.

The document promulgated in December 1994 provided for a new House of Peoples' Representatives, which serves as "the highest organ of State authority." In addition, representatives of Ethiopia's "nations, nationalities, and peoples" constitute a senate-like House of the Federation, whose functions include that of constitutional interpretation. The president of the republic is nominated by the House of Peoples' Representatives and elected for a once-renewable six-year term by a two-thirds vote of the two houses in joint session. A prime minister, who serves as chair of the Council of Ministers and commander in chief of the armed forces, is elected by the House of Peoples' Representatives from among those sitting as members of the majority party or coalition for a term normally coincident with the legislative mandate. The judiciary includes both Federal and State Supreme Courts, appointed by their respective legislative councils; there is also a federal High Court and a Court of Constitutional Inquiry, whose principal activity is to review disputes for submission to the House of the Federation.

Ethiopia was traditionally divided into 15 provinces, exclusive of the capital. However, in late 1987 legislation was enacted to redraw the internal boundaries in favor of 24 administrative regions, plus (in an apparent effort to placate separatists) five "autonomous regions," four of which (Assab, Dire Dawa, Tigray, and Ogaden) would be coterminous with administrative regions, while Eritrea would contain three administrative regions. The present republic encompasses the following nine states: Afar; Amhara; Beneshangul-Gumuz; Gambela Peoples; Harari People; Oromia; Somalia; Southern Nations, Nationalities, and Peoples; and Tigray. The federal capital, Addis Ababa, is a separate entity, although it also serves as the capital of Oromia. In addition, there is a separate Dire Dawa Administrative Council. (Both cities enjoy the same autonomy as the states; for example, each elects its own representatives to the national legislature.) New states may be created following majority approval by a nationality group and endorsement by a two-thirds vote of the relevant state council. A somewhat unusual guarantee of self-determination includes a right of secession if requested by a two-thirds majority of the group's legislative body, endorsed by a similar state council majority, and approved by a majority vote in a referendum called by the federal government.

The media have been strictly controlled since the Mengistu government. In late 2003 the government proposed a controversial new press law that would have limited the number of newspapers, but protests prevented its official adoption. However, in April 2005 it was reported that many of the measures perceived to be repressive had been "discreetly" introduced, forcing some journalists into exile. More than 20 journalists were among those arrested in the government crackdown of late 2005 and were held until 2007, when they signed a controversial letter of "apology" (see Political Background, above). International press watchdogs protested the "climate of fear" that existed for journalists. In 2013 Reporters Without Borders listed Ethiopia as 137th out of 179 in terms of press freedom, citing government harassment of critics.

Foreign relations. A founding member of both the United Nations and the Organization of African Unity (OAU, subsequently the African Union—AU), Ethiopia under Emperor Haile Selassie was long a leading advocate of regional cooperation and peaceful settlement in Africa. Addis Ababa was the site of the first African summit conference in 1963 and remains the seat of the AU Secretariat and the UN Economic Commission for Africa.

As a result of the emperor's overthrow in 1974, Ethiopia shifted dramatically from a generally pro-Western posture to one of near-exclusive dependence on the Soviet bloc. Moscow guided Addis Ababa in the formation of a Soviet-style ruling party and provided weapons and other assistance to military units (including some 11,000 Cuban troops) during the Ogaden war in 1977–1978. While Russia initially maintained a low profile in regard to the Eritrean secessionist movements (the two most important of which were Marxist-inspired), it gradually increased its support of counterinsurgency efforts. In 1988 the Soviets provided the government with 250,000 tons of grain for relief purposes, thus avoiding repetition of criticism it had received for failing to provide assistance during the 1984 famine. Meanwhile, despite the continued presence of 1,400 Soviet military advisors, Moscow's interest in supporting the Mengistu government's war against the rebels appeared to be waning, and, in September 1989, Cuba announced plans to withdraw all its troops.

Because of ethnic links to Somalia and the presence of virtually equal numbers of Muslims and Christians in Eritrea, most Arab governments (with the exception of Marxist South Yemen) remained neutral or provided material support to the guerrilla movements. Most black African governments, on the other hand, tended to support Addis Ababa, despite an OAU posture of formal neutrality.

During the 1980s, relations with neighboring countries were strained by refugees fleeing Ethiopia because of famine or opposition to the Mengistu regime's resettlement policies. Tensions with Somalia, including sporadic border skirmishes in 1987, centered on the Ogaden region, with Addis Ababa accusing Mogadishu of backing the secession efforts of the Somalian-speaking population. However, in April 1988 Mengistu and Somalia President Siad Barre signed a treaty calling for mutual troop withdrawal, an exchange of POWs, and an end to Somalian funding of the rebels.

Relations with Sudan also fluctuated after the Sudanese coup of April 1985. In mid-1986 Khartoum announced that it had ordered the cessation of Eritrean rebel activity in eastern Sudan, apparently expecting that Addis Ababa would reciprocate by reducing its aid to the Sudanese People's Liberation Army (SPLA). Subsequently, Khartoum denounced continued Ethiopian support of the SPLA as "aggression." In 1988 the continued SPLA insurgency forced more than 300,000 southern Sudanese refugees across Ethiopia's border, many starving to death en route.

Although Ethiopia remained strongly linked to the Soviet Union, anti-American rhetoric became manifestly subdued during an influx of U.S. food aid, valued at more than $430 million, from 1984 through 1986. Following the Ethiopian government's March 1988 expulsion of international aid donors from rebel-held areas, Washington reportedly began channeling food supplies to northern Ethiopian drought areas through Sudanese and rebel organizations. The U.S. policy of limiting its support to humanitarian aid continued into 1989, despite the decision of international creditors to fund Addis Ababa's agricultural reform program. In April 1989 the Mengistu regime indicated a desire to resume full diplomatic relations with Washington (reduced to the chargé level in 1980) but withdrew the overture in the face of a cool U.S. response. Washington reportedly exerted considerable pressure on Colonel Mengistu to resign in May 1991, named an ambassador to the new government in June, and was one of a dozen foreign governments to send a team of observers to the National Conference in July.

According to many observers, the Ethiopian, Eritrean, and Ugandan governments tried to coordinate efforts in 1996–1997 to control the spread of Islamic fundamentalism in the Horn of Africa, a policy that was also promoted by the United States. The campaign was primarily directed toward isolating Sudan's government, the Ethiopian government providing support to the Sudanese opposition, mainly the SPLA. It also endorsed the Sodere agreement signed in January 1997 by 26 Somalian factions, which was intended to sideline Somalia's self-declared "president" and United Somali Congress—SNA leader, Hussein Mohamed FARAH AIDID (see entry on Somalia). In addition, Ethiopia reportedly convinced those factions to assist in the fight with the Islamic Union guerrillas that were operating along the border of Ethiopia and Somalia.

In describing the 1998–2000 border war between Ethiopia and Eritrea, the *New York Times* said it was "hard to think of a more pointless and wasteful international conflict." As many as 60,000 Ethiopians lost their lives in the fighting, which, while sporadic, was described at its most intense moments as the "biggest war in the world." The Ethiopian military dominated the Eritreans and the populace embraced the cause with enthusiasm. However, critics said Meles gave away too much in the peace accord (see Current issues in entry on Eritrea for details), which subsequently proved highly controversial in Ethiopia. Among other things, critics decried the failure to gain guaranteed access to Eritrean seaports even though Eritrean secession had caused Ethiopia to become landlocked.

By November 2004 it was clear that final peace talks between Eritrea and Ethiopia had broken down. Among other things, Meles, under heavy domestic pressure, refused to accept the UN's proposed demarcation of the border, particularly the decision that the town of Badme would be Eritrean. Despite the presence of 4,200 UN peacekeepers, Ethiopia deployed its own troops to control Badme.

In a separate matter, Ethiopia immediately expressed concern over the takeover of the Somalian capital of Mogadishu in mid-2006 by followers of the Islamic Courts Union (ICU), and Ethiopia was subsequently perceived to be playing a covert role in supporting Somalia's Transitional Federal Government (TFG) against the Islamist militants. Finally, with apparent U.S. endorsement, Ethiopian forces invaded Somalia in late December, Meles declaring that an ICU victory in Somalia would endanger Ethiopia's "sovereignty." The Ethiopian campaign, which included the use of warplanes and heavy tanks, quickly turned the tide in favor of the TFG (see entry on Somalia for details). U.S. elite troops subsequently used bases in Ethiopia to launch attacks on suspected al-Qaida leaders in several nearby countries.

Ethiopian forces remained in Somalia (often under attack by anti-government Islamists) as efforts to achieve a negotiated settlement there produced little progress by mid-2008 (see entry on Somalia for details). Among other things, President Meles called for the deployment of a large international peacekeeping force in Somalia that would permit the withdrawal of Ethiopian troops. Tensions remained high with Eritrea throughout the rest of 2008 and first half of 2009 as the mandate of UN peacekeepers was terminated in the face of Eritrean "obstruction." Meanwhile, Ethiopian troops withdrew from Somalia in early 2009, prompting a surge by Islamic militants against Somalia's transitional government (see entry on Somalia for details). Ethiopia in 2010 continued to support the Somali transitional government and allied Sufi groups that had mobilized in the country to counter fundamental Wahabi insurgents. It provided training and equipment and did not rule out incursions into the country, such as one two-day operation across the border to drive out fundamentalist fighters in Belet Weyne. It also backed rebel groups within Eritrea that had attacked an Eritrean military base in the Denakil region early in the year in the continuing problems between the neighbors. Ethiopian troops made an incursion into the northern semiautonomous region of Somaliland on May 21, 2010, killing at least 12 civilians who had begun to fight the soldiers after having their trucks searched and being detained. Ethiopian troops also declared a curfew in southwestern Somalia after capturing the Bakol region from al Shabaab.

In April 2011 Ethiopia began construction on a $4.8 billion dam project on the Nile River, the Grand Ethiopian Renaissance Dam (GERD). The dam would be the largest hydroelectric facility in Africa. It was opposed by regional powers, including Egypt and Kenya, because the dam would change the Nile water quota, which had been agreed upon in a nine-country accord in 1959.

Following the independence of South Sudan in July 2011, Ethiopia hosted negotiations on border demarcation between the new nation and Sudan. One result of the talks was that Ethiopia agreed to deploy military observers to help monitor the border between the two countries. Meanwhile, fighting in Somalia created a wave of an estimated 80,000 additional refugees, who fled into Ethiopia in 2011.

Relations with Egypt improved considerably following the revolution, with the two countries agreeing to set up a technical committee to evaluate the impacts of Ethiopia's dam project.

During 2012 Ethiopian officials were said to be concerned about its role in Somalia fostering an image of the country as a regional bully and wanted its troops replaced by the AU Mission in Somalia. In November, Ethiopia and Kenya finalized a range of economic agreements to expand markets for both countries.

In April 2013 Ethiopia announced that it would withdraw its forces from Somalia. Also in April, Prime Minister Hailemariam traveled to

Brussels to confer with European Union (EU) officials in his first official foreign trip. Following the meeting, the EU pledged $30 million for maternal health in Ethiopia.

In May 2013 Ethiopia began to divert water from the Blue Nile in order to complete the GERD project. The action led to vigorous protests by Egypt and Sudan. Meanwhile, Ethiopia, Burundi, Kenya, Rwanda, Tanzania, and Uganda signed the Nile Cooperative Framework Agreement (CFA), which called for the creation of an international body to regulate water usage and rights. Egypt and the Sudan opposed the CFA. In July Ethiopia announced its intention to join the World Trade Organization (WTO) in 2015.

Current issues. In late November 2011 Dawit Kebede, managing editor of *The Awramba Times,* fled the country after the state newspaper called for his arrest. The paper's deputy editor was still in detention on terrorism charges since his arrest in June. Observers described it as a function of Meles' growing fears of unrest and sensitivity to criticism in the local press and around the region of the country's dam project.

The July 14–16, 2012, AU summit in Addis Ababa was surrounded by riot police and heavy security. The day before it began, more than 70 Muslims at a nearby mosque were arrested for staging a demonstration, defying an official warning. Meles, under medical treatment in Brussels, was unable to attend the summit. Deputy Premier and Foreign Minister Hailemariam Desalegn, his agreed-upon successor, took over the day-to-day management of the government. On August 20, following a campaign of misinformation about his whereabouts, Meles died in Brussels, reportedly from an infection while recovering from an operation.

Following Meles's death, the Justice Ministry withdrew charges against two weekly newspapers, and the Committee to Protect Journalists expressed guarded optimism about the country's future under the new leadership. One week after his unanimous election as chair of the EPRDF, Hailemariam was sworn in as prime minister on September 21, marking the first nonviolent transition in Ethiopia's modern history.

In November 2012, a government study found that the rate of human immunodeficiency virus and acquired immune deficiency syndrome (HIV/AIDS) in Ethiopia had declined by more than 90 percent since 2002, while the death rate from the disease fell by 53 percent as the government increased the number of counseling, testing, and treatment centers.

Abune MATHIAS (TEKLEMARIAM Asrat) was elected as the patriarch of the Ethiopian Orthodox Church on February 28, 2013, following the death of Abune PAULOS (GEBREMEDHIN Woldeyohannes), the fifth patriarch, on August 16, 2012.

Thirty-three opposition parties boycotted local elections on April 16, 2013, which were overwhelmingly won by the EPRDF. In May MELAKU Fenta, the director general of Ethiopia's revenues and customs authority, was arrested on corruption charges along with 30 others. On June 2 the opposition *Semayawi* Party (see Political parties and groups, below) sponsored the first major antigovernment protest since 2005. An estimated 10,000 people marched through Addis Ababa to demand the release of political prisoners.

POLITICAL PARTIES AND GROUPS

Political parties were not permitted under the monarchy, while legal party activity during the period of rule by the Provisional Military Administrative Council did not emerge until the formation of the regime-supportive Workers' Party of Ethiopia (WPE) in 1984. The 1987 constitution reaffirmed the WPE's position as the country's only authorized party, describing it as the "leading force of the state and society" and granting it wide authority, including the right to approve all candidates for the National Assembly. As the Mengistu regime faced accelerating rebel activity and declining Soviet support, the WPE in March 1990 abandoned its Marxist-Leninist ideology, changed its name to the Ethiopian Democratic Unity Party (EDUP), and opened its ranks to former members of opposition groups in an unsuccessful effort to broaden its base of public support. Following the overthrow of the Mengistu government in May 1991, leaders of the interim government announced that the EDUP had been dissolved. The Ethiopian National Election Board labeled 79 political parties as active in mid-2010, and 63 of those campaigned for seats in the May 2010 elections for either the House of People's Representatives or on state councils (22 parties were certified to run federal candidates and 57 were eligible to run in states). A total of 2,188 candidates, of whom 272 were women, vied for federal seats.

Government Parties:

Ethiopian People's Revolutionary Democratic Front (EPRDF). The EPRDF was launched in May 1988 by the TPLF in an effort to expand its influence beyond Tigray Province, over which it had recently achieved military dominance. Although the TPLF had long subscribed to Marxist-Leninist ideology, an EPRDF congress in early 1991 called for development of a "small-scale" economy in which farmers would lease land from the government and control the sale of their products. While the new platform called for tight government control of foreign trade, it also endorsed an expanded role for private investment in the economy. In another significant policy shift, the congress, while displaying a clear preference for a united Ethiopia, accepted Eritrea's right to self-determination.

Joined in a loose military alliance with the Eritrean People's Liberation Front (see entry on Eritrea) and the OLF (below), the EPRDF led the march on Addis Ababa that ousted the Mengistu regime in May 1991. Assuming power in the name of the EPRDF, Meles Zenawi was confirmed as head of state by the National Conference pending the outcome, under a new constitution, of multiparty elections originally scheduled for 1993 but not held until May 1995. The EPRDF won over 90 percent of the seats in that balloting, and Meles was elected prime minister by the House of Peoples' Representatives in August, the office of president (which he had previously held) having been reduced to figurehead status. The EPRDF dominated the 2000 legislative balloting and unanimously reelected Meles as EPRDF chair at a congress on September 1, 2001, the prime minister having survived serious dissension within the TPLF and other EPRDF component groups (see below). The congress also selected a new 140-member council, a 38-member Executive Committee, and an 8-member "Control Commission." Meles was reelected as chair at the September 2006 EPRDF congress, and, in light of the surprising success of the opposition in the 2005 elections, the EPRDF subsequently intensified its organizational efforts for the 2008 municipal balloting, which it dominated.

Meles was reelected as the EPRDF chair at the September 2008 congress. Prior to a September 2009 party meeting he surprisingly announced that he and other long-standing leaders might step down to make room for a "new generation." However, it was subsequently reported that Meles had been endorsed at the meeting for at least one more term as prime minister. In the May 2010 legislative elections the EPRDF increased its domination of national-level politics. It secured 499 of the 547 total seats up for grabs in the House of People's Representatives. International observers and opposition groups accused the EPRDF of widespread vote rigging, intimidation, and harassment after its landslide victory. Meles was reelected prime minister in October 2010.

Meles's plan was to step down in 2013, giving his agreed-upon successor Hailemariam Desalegn time to get ready for the 2015 election. That timetable was sped up by Meles's death on August 20, 2012. A Protestant from the Southern Region, Hailemariam is somewhat of an anomaly as a leader in a party dominated by northern highlanders and Orthodox Christians, a fact that reportedly met with disapproval among some factions. Reports in October 2012 indicated that renegade EPRDF members had formed a new grouping, the **Ethiopian People's Revolutionary Democratic Front-Democratic** (EPRDF-D).

Leaders: HAILEMARIAM Desalegn (Prime Minister of the Republic and Party Chair), GIRMA Wolde Giorgis (Former President of the Republic), SHIFERAW Jarso (Parliamentary Leader).

Tigray People's Liberation Front (TPLF). Formed in 1975 by former students who had been strongly influenced by Marxism-Leninism, the TPLF initially pursued independence or at least substantial autonomy for Tigray Province. However, the front's subsequent goal became the overthrow of the Mengistu regime and establishment of a new central government involving all ethnic groups. Established in 1985, a pro-Albanian Marxist-Leninist League of Tigray (MLLT) gained ideological ascendancy within the TPLF, and MLLT leader Meles Zenawi was elected TPLF chair at a 1989 congress. By that time the TPLF had become one of the country's most active antigovernment groups, its fighters having gained control of Tigray and having pushed south toward Addis Ababa. The TPLF subsequently began to shed its ideological rigidity, reflecting both the growing worldwide disillusionment with communism and a need to broaden the front's philosophical base in preparation for a possible government takeover. Consequently, by the time TPLF soldiers captured Addis Ababa in the name of the

EPRDF in May 1991, the front's leaders were describing themselves as supporters of Western-style multiparty democracy and limited private enterprise. However, disagreement was subsequently reported within the TPLF regarding the proposed privatization of state-run enterprises.

Following the tentative conclusion of the border war with Eritrea in 2000, hard-liners in the TPLF reportedly came close to ousting Meles in March 2001. Among other things, the dissidents, who included TEWOLDE Wolde-Mariam, then vice chair of the TPLF, strongly objected to the perceived lack of results in the peace accord as well as the imposition of economic austerity measures requested by the IMF and World Bank. Meles and his "reformist" supporters subsequently launched a purge of many of the critics. The TPLF won all 152 council seats in the state of Tigray. In September 2010 eight members resigned from the central committee amid rumors that there was a split in the ethnic-based party. Following the death of Meles in August 2012, ABAY Weldu, the governor of Tigray state, was elected party chair.

Leaders: ABAY Weldu (Chair), Seyoum MESFIN (Deputy Chair).

Amhara National Democratic Movement (ANDM). The ANDM was initially established in 1980 as the Ethiopian People's Democratic Movement (EPDM) by former members of the EPRP (below) under the guidance of the TPLF. In 1986 a number of pitched battles were reported in Wollo Province between EPDM forces and government troops. Subsequent ideological controversy generated the creation of an Ethiopian Marxist-Leninist Force (EMLF) to serve the same function in the EPDM as the MLLT was serving in the TPLF. The EPDM joined the TPLF in the 1988 formation of the EPRDF and adopted the ANDM rubric at its third congress in January 1994.

In October 1996 it was reported that former prime minister Tamirat Layne had been dismissed as ANDM secretary general during an emergency meeting of the Central Committee for "acting contrary to the principles for which the ANDM has stood during the last 16 years." Tamirat was also subsequently fired from his posts of deputy prime minister and minister of national defense as part of what was widely viewed as an anticorruption campaign. He was sentenced in 1999 to 18 years in prison on corruption charges.

Divisions were reported within the ANDM in 2005–2006, as some members objected to what they perceived as growing anti-Amhara rhetoric on the part of members of the TPLF and OPDO. Factionalization reportedly continued into mid-2009. During the 2010 regional state council elections, the ANDM won all 294 seats in Amhara state. In September 2010, at a party congress, Demeke Mekonnen was elected chair of the party. He was appointed deputy prime minister in March 2013.

Leaders: DEMEKE Mekkonen (Chair and Deputy Prime Minister of the Republic), GEDDU Andargachew (Deputy Chair), HILAWE Yosef, Ayalew GOBEZE, Yoseph RETA.

Oromo Peoples' Democratic Organization (OPDO). The OPDO was formed in April 1990 under the direction of the TPLF, its membership reportedly comprising Oromo prisoners of war captured by the TPLF in sporadic clashes with the OLF (below). The OLF immediately challenged the creation of the OPDO as an "unfriendly and hostile gesture," and the OPDO's existence remained a source of friction between the TPLF and the OLF. During 1992 the OPDO was reported to have been weakened by the desertion of a number of its followers to the OLF.

The OPDO, as expected, dominated the May 2000 elections in the state of Oromia, securing 173 of 178 seats in the House of Peoples' Representatives and 535 of 537 seats on the State Council. The OPDO declined to 110 seats in the 2005 balloting for the House of Peoples' Representatives. During the May 2010 regional state council elections, the OPDO won all 537 council seats in Oromia state and half of the council seats in Harari. In September 2010, at the sixth OPDO conference, Alemayehu Atomsa was chosen as the new party president. In October ABADULA Gemeda Dego was elected speaker of the lower house of the legislature.

Leaders: ALEMAYEHU Atomsa (Party President and President of the State of Oromia), ABADULA Gemeda Dego (Speaker of the House of People's Representatives), Girma BIRU.

Southern Ethiopia Peoples' Democratic Front (SEPDF). The SEPDF comprises many small, mostly ethnically based parties. It secured 112 of 123 seats from the state of Southern Nations, Nationalities, and Peoples in the 2000 balloting for the House of Peoples' Representatives. (For a list of component parties that gained representation, see Legislature in the entry on Ethiopia in the 2005–2006 *Handbook.*) A number of members of the SEPDF's Central Committee were dismissed in 2002 in the wake of friction attributed to ethnic disputes, as well as disagreement, reflective of similar problems in the OPDO and TPLF over the policies of Prime Minister Meles. At the 2008 EPRDF congress, SEPDF leaders reportedly sought greater funding and additional government posts for SEPDF members. During the May 2010 regional state council elections, the SEPDF won all 348 seats available in the Southern Nations, Nationalities, and People's state. In August 2011 the Southern Nations, Nationalities, and People's State Executive Council reelected SHIFERAW Shigute as council president. In July 2013 Shiferaw was appointed education minister.

Leaders: HAILEMARIAM Desalegn (Prime Minister and Chair), SHIFERAW Shigute (Minister of Education), KASSU Illala.

Somali Peoples' Democratic Party (SPDP). The SPDP was launched in Jijiga in Ethiopia's state of Somalia in June 1998 by the Ethiopian Somali Democratic League (ESDL) and a progovernment faction of the ONLF (below) that split from its parent grouping regarding the question of independence. (The ESDL, which had been formed in February 1994 by a number of progovernment eastern region groups [see the 2007 *Handbook* for details], and the ONLF faction had formed a victorious coalition in the 1995 elections in the region.)

ESDL leader Abdulmejid HUSSEIN, who had been the target in July 1996 of an assassination attempt that the government blamed on separatist rebels, was named leader of the SPDP at its formation. He was succeeded in 2000 by Mohammad Drir, who had already taken over Hussein's cabinet post.

A pro-EPRDF formation, the SPDP won 19 of the 23 seats from the state of Somalia in the House of Peoples' Representatives and 148 of the 168 Somali State Council seats in 2000. Severe fractionalization was reported within the party in 2002, although the SPDP won all 23 house seats from the state of Somalia in the 2005 poll. The party increased its holdings in the 2010 legislative elections to 24 House seats and all 168 regional state council seats and thousands of local seats in Somali state.

Leaders: Mohammad DRIR (Chair), Abdulrashid Dulene RAFLE (Vice Chair), Sultan Ibrahim (Secretary General).

Other Legislative Parties:

Beneshangul-Gumuz Peoples' Democratic Party (BGPDP). Described as a pro-EPRDF party, the BGPDP secured 6 of the 9 seats from the state of Beneshangul-Gumuz in the 2000 balloting for the House of Representatives and 71 of 80 State Council seats. In the 2010 legislative elections the party won 9 seats in the House and 98 of 99 seats in the Beneshangul-Gumuz regional state council.

Leader: Mulualem BESSE.

Afar National Democratic Party (ANDP). The ANDP was formed in August 1999 by the merger of five groups in the state of Afar: the Afar Peoples' Democratic Organization (APDO), the Afar Revolutionary Democratic Union Front (ARDUF), the Afar National Democratic Movement (ANDM), the Afar National Liberation Front (ANLF), and the Afar Liberation Front Party (ALFP).

The APDO, established originally as the Afar Democratic Union, had adopted the APDO rubric in 1992. Having benefited from dissension within the ALF (see below), the APDO was subsequently described as exercising dominant political authority, in alignment with the EPRDF, in the Afar region under the leadership of Ismail ALISERIO.

The ARDUF was formed in 1991 to "liberate Afar territories" of the former autonomous region of Assab from Eritrean domination. The ARDUF subsequently became an anti-EPRDF secessionist movement under the leadership of former WPE first secretary and Assab governor Mohamoda Ahmed GAAS. Sporadic fighting was reported in 1996 between the ARDUF's armed wing, *Ugugumo* (Revolution), and TPLF forces. During 1997, however, the government initiated a policy of dialogue with the ARDUF to reach a reconciliation over the future of the Afar National Regional State. The discussions brought about a division within the ranks of the ARDUF between pro- and anti-agreement factions. The former reportedly formally discontinued its armed struggle in 2002. Meanwhile, hard-liners led by Gaas apparently reached an agreement with the ONLF to coordinate the opposition to the current regime. (The rump ARDUF was described in 2007 as an active rebel group in the northeast of the country.)

The ANDM, a pro-EPRDF formation, was launched in February 1995 by Ahmed Mohamed AHAW, a son of the influential Sultan of Biru in the northwestern Danakil region.

The ANDP secured all of the 8 seats from the state of Afar in the 2000 balloting for the House of Peoples' Representatives and all but 3 of the Afar State Council seats, the grouping being widely perceived as a pro-EPRDF, pro-Meles party. During the 2010 legislative and state council elections, the group again took 8 seats in the House and all but 3 of the 96 seats available in the Afar state council.

Leader: Ismail ALISERO (Chair).

Ethiopia Federal Democratic Unity Forum (FORUM). FORUM is a registered opposition coalition that began in early 2009 with talks between UEDF leader Beyene Petros and former Ethiopian president Negaso Gidada with the goal of presenting a unified list of opposition candidates in 2010 legislative balloting. Participants eventually included the UEDF, UDJ, OFDM, ARENA, and others. Known also as *Medrek,* meaning forum in Amharic, the group advocates land ownership for farmers and economic improvement by bolstering manufacturing and services in the country. For the May 2010 elections, FORUM fielded 421 federal legislative candidates and 861 regional council candidates, making it the most formidable opposition to the EPRDF. However, the wide spectrum of ideologies represented by the coalition's constituent parties made problems from the start, including finding points of agreement for a unified platform. The group won only one House of People's Representatives seat in the May 2010 legislative elections. Members SEPDU, ARENA, OPC, and SDAF were certified to contest only regional elections. During its fourth general assembly in January 2011, Gebru Asrat was elected FORUM chair. The assembly also voted to extend the term of the rotating presidency from six months to one year. In June 2013 FORUM rejected calls from Egypt to oppose the construction of the GERD.

Leaders: MERARA Gudina (Chair), NEGASO Gidada (Former President of the Republic), TILAHUN Endeshaw (Secretary General), BEYENE Petros, Siye ABRACHA (Former Minister of Defense).

United Ethiopian Democratic Forces (UEDF). Launched in mid-2003 by the following groups and other parties (both within Ethiopia and in the diaspora) opposed to the EPRDF government, the UEDF (comprising mostly southern parties and dominated by Oromos) called for peaceful regime change, land reform, privatization of state-run enterprises, greater press freedom, and greater free-market influence in the economy. With the primary goal of defeating the EPRDF, the UEDF cooperated informally with the CUD in the May 2005 elections, the two groups pledging to forge a coalition government if successful in the balloting. However, opposition to the EPRDF regime appeared to be the only genuine shared position between the UEDF and the CUD, as UEDF officials made it clear they strongly opposed the CUD's plan to redraw regional boundaries and establish a more highly centralized government. Many UEDF supporters also criticized the CUD's proposed land privatization proposal as a pretext for "Amhara land grabs" in the south.

The UEDF was credited with winning 52 seats in the House of Peoples' Representatives in 2005, all but one of the successful candidates reportedly taking their seats despite a CUD call for a boycott of the legislature. UEDF President Beyene Petros and (then) Vice President Merera Gudina supported the decision to participate in the legislature and called for a national dialogue with the EPRDF and other parties toward installation of a national unity government. As a result, hard-line UEDF dissidents meeting in October announced that Beyene and Merera had been relieved of their UEDF leadership posts in favor of the EPRP's Fasika BELETE and Ayalsew DERSIE and that an "underground" antigovernment movement was being considered. However, Beyene rejected the validity of the dissident action and continued to serve as UEDF spokesperson, initialing a memorandum of understanding with the EPRDF and the OFDM providing for ongoing negotiations to resolve the nation's political problems in a peaceful manner and with respect for constitutional structures. However, the UEDF accused the government of illegally blocking the candidacies of many UEDF members in the April 2008 local elections. Merera was elected chair and Beyene vice chair at the April 2009 UEDF congress. Leaders of the group, including Merera and Beyene, subsequently formed the FORUM coalition of parties.

Leaders: MERERA Gudina (Chair), BEYENE Petros (Vice Chair).

Ethiopian Social Democratic Party (ESDP). In 2006 the group formerly known as the Council of Alternative Forces for Peace and Democracy in Ethiopia (CAFPDE) changed its name to the ESDP in an effort to merge several factional components into a single party. An umbrella organization for a number of opposition groupings, the CAFPDE was formed under the leadership of Beyene Petros, also the leader of the SEPDU, the core component of the CAFPDE. In 1994 Beyene described the constitutional revision then underway as "undemocratic" and inappropriately dominated by the TPLF. The CAFPDE declined to participate fully in the 1995 elections on the grounds that insufficient arrangements had been made for foreign observation of the polls.

The CAFPDE participated with other leading groups in forming the Coalition of Ethiopian Opposition Political Organizations (CEOPO) in Paris in September 1998. However, Beyene subsequently withdrew the CAFPDE from the CEOPO and declared the CAFPDE's intention to contest the 2000 legislative elections on its own. As a result, hard-liners within the CAFPDE announced that Beyene had been replaced as chair by KIFLE Tigneh Abate. However, the National Electoral Board ordered Beyene reinstated in January 2000.

The CAFPDE was credited with winning four seats in the House of Peoples' Representatives in the 2000 balloting, while the SEPDU secured two and the **Hadiya National Democratic Organization** (HNDO), a small grouping also led by Beyene, won three. Following the balloting, Beyene strongly criticized the EPRDF for the perceived "intimidation" of members of the CAFPDE and other opposition parties.

Leader: BEYENE Petros (Chair).

Southern Ethiopia Peoples' Democratic Union (SEPDU). The SEPDU was launched in 1992 by a number of small parties representing some 34 different tribal groups and holding 16 seats in the 87-member Council of Representatives. In March 1993 the SEPDU organizations participated in a "Peace for Ethiopia" conference in Paris. In a statement issued at the conclusion of the conference, participants strongly condemned the regime in Addis Ababa for its alleged repressive tendencies, while calling on it to permit nonviolent opposition activity. The Council of Representatives reacted by calling on SEPDU members to repudiate the conference resolutions. Beyene Petros, at the time the leader of the SEPDU and HNDO, left his post as a vice minister in the transitional government as a result of the events of 1993. He subsequently became chair of the CAFPDE.

After having agreed to participate in the 2000 legislative elections, the CAFPDE and the SEPDU boycotted local elections in December 2001 in the state of Southern Nations, Nationalities, and Peoples.

Leaders: TILAHUN Eadeshaw (Chair), KASSU Illala.

Unity for Democracy and Justice (UDJ). UDJ leader Birtukan Mideksa, a former judge and former vice chair of the CUD, was arrested with other opposition leaders in 2005 and released in 2007. However, after publicly questioning the terms of her release she was rearrested in early 2009, the reinstatement of her life sentence prompting heavy domestic and international criticism of the government. She was freed on October 6, 2010. The party pushed for a range of constitutional and government reforms but was plagued by infighting in the lead-up to the May 2010 elections. The UDJ, with more than 40,000 members and almost 60 offices nationwide, was seen as the strongest component of FORUM. In January 2011 the UDJ announced it would merge with the smaller Berhan for Unity and Democracy Party. UDJ member GIRMA Seifu Maru was the lone FORUM deputy elected to the House of People's Representatives.

Leaders: Birtukan MIDEKSA (President of the Party), NEGASO Gidada (Vice President and Former President of the Republic), Siye ABRACHA (Vice President and Former Minister of Defense).

Oromo Federal Congress (OFC). The OFC was formed in August 2012 by the merger of the **Oromo Federalist**

Democratic Movement (OFDM) and the **Oromo People's Congress** (OPC). After winning 11 seats in the May 2005 balloting for the House of Peoples' Representatives, the recently organized OFDM, which had resisted preelection overtures from the CUD and UEDF, called for a "national dialogue" between the opposition parties and the EPRDF. Among other things, the OFDM urged that no changes be made in the powers or boundaries of the nation's states.

The OPC was originally named the **Oromo National Congress** (ONC) when it was formed by political science professor MERARA Gudina in 1998. The ONC pledged to support the rights of the Oromo people, including preservation of the right to self-determination. Although the ONC won only 1 seat in the 2000 elections in the House of Peoples' Representatives, it reportedly secured some 39 of the UEDF's 52 seats in the 2005 poll, dominating balloting in several southern areas. Most of the successful ONC candidates, including Merera, subsequently took their legislative seats, although debate was reported within the ONC on the question. The party was subsequently severely split as dissidents announced in September that they had expelled Merera from the ONC and had withdrawn the ONC from the UEDF. However, Merera dismissed those measures as invalid actions on the part of only a few disgruntled ONC members. The national election board subsequently indicated that it believed the dissident faction had the strongest legal claim to the ONC rubric, and Merera in October announced the formation of the OPC, which was authorized by the government to compete only in elections in Oromia Regional State.

Leader: MERARA Gudina (Chair).

Union of Tigrians for Democracy and Sovereignty (ARENA). Led by Meles critic Gebru Asrat, the former president of Tigray Regional State, this grouping was launched in October 2007 by TPLF dissidents to challenge the TPLF in local balloting in Tigray. In 2008 former president Negaso Gidada agreed to join Arena in establishing FORUM. An ARENA candidate was murdered in the Tigray region in advance of the 2010 legislative elections. Opposition groups said the killing was part of deepening intimidation by the government to control the elections.

Leader: GEBRU Asrat (Chair).

FORUM members were also joined by the **Ethiopian Democratic Unity Movement** (EDUM), which was led by GUESH Gebre Selassie, and the **Somali Democratic Alliance Forces** (SDAF), the political opponent to EPRDF ally SPDP in Somali state that was being led by Buh HUSSIEN.

Gambela Peoples' Unity Democratic Movement (GPDM). The GPDM was formed in 2003 following the dissolution of the Gambela Peoples' Democratic Front (GPDF), which had secured all three of the seats from the state of Gambela in the House of Peoples' Representatives in the 2000 balloting and most of the Gambela State Council seats. Although the GDPF had presented its candidates in 2000 without declaring a cooperative stance with any other parties, it was later described as supportive of the pro-Meles faction of the TPLF and the EPRDF.

The GPDF resulted from a merger of the Gambela People's Liberation Party (GPLP)—a party representing the Anyuak ethnic group that, allied with the EPRDF, had won the 1995 elections in Gambela—and the Gambela People's Democratic Unity Party (GPDUP), a Nuer party. However, the GPDF was reportedly later dissolved following the collapse of power-sharing arrangements and the outbreak of sporadic deadly fighting between the Anyuak and the Nuer.

The GPDM secured 3 seats in the 2005 voting for the House of Peoples' Representatives and nearly all of the Gambela State Council seats. It subsequently concluded a cooperation agreement with the EPRDF. It won all 156 seats of the Gambela State Council during the May 2010 elections. In April 2013 the GPDM voted to remove Gambela state governor, Umod UBONG, and GPDM chair, Gatluak Tut KHOT was appointed acting governor and Olero OPIEW interim chair of the party.

Leader: Olero OPIEW (Acting Chair).

Other parties securing 1 seat each in the 2010 balloting for the House of Peoples' Representatives included the **Argoba People's Democratic Organization** (APDO), a new party that also won 3 state council seats in Afar in 2010 and resulted from the merger of the **Argoba National Democratic Organization** (ANDO), the **Argoba People's Democratic Movement** (APDM), and the **Harari National League** (HNL), a pro-EPRDF formation that also won 18 seats in the Harari State Council in 2010. The HNL was led by Murad ABDULHADI.

Other Parties and Groups:

All Ethiopian Unity Party (AEUP). This party is an outgrowth of factionalization within the All-Amhara People's Organization (AAPO), which initially supported the EPRDF but went into opposition over the issues of ethnic regionalization. The AAPO's president, Dr. ASRAT Woldeyes, was one of several AAPO leaders sentenced to prison in June 1994 for inciting armed opposition to the government. Asrat remained incarcerated until late 1998. Upon his release, the ailing former physician for Emperor Selassie left the country for medical treatment.

After winning only 1 seat in the 2000 balloting for the House of Peoples' Representatives, the AAPO suffered internal division. Hailu Shawel, the vice president of AAPO, lost a bid for the AAPO presidency, and he formed his own grouping under the AEUP rubric in consonance with its stated goal of downplaying its Amharic orientation in favor of outreach to "all Ethiopians." By that time a number of former AAPO members reportedly had joined the new EDP (see UEDP-Medhin, below). Hailu subsequently became prominent in the formation of the CUD in 2005, although CUD factionalization prompted him to return to the AEUP as his primary political affiliation following his release from prison in 2007.

Following the apparent demise of CUD, to which it joined in coalition, AEUP emerged on its own in advance of the May 2010 legislative elections. The party won 1 regional state council seat out of 99 in Benishangul-Gumuz state and was unable to secure any seats at the federal level.

On June 2013 AEUP Deputy Chair MELES Ashire was arrested along with an AEUP official, TADLO Tefera.

Leaders: HAILU Shawel (President), Makonnen BISHAW (Secretary General).

Ethiopian Democratic Party (EDP). The EDP, a moderate grouping espousing "unity and peace," was launched in December 1999 and secured two seats from Addis Ababa in 2000 in the House of Peoples' Representatives. The EDP was subsequently reported to be opposed to the conditions of the peace accord accepted by the Meles government with Eritrea. Founding members of the EDP included Lidetu Ayelaw, a former head of the AAPO youth wing. The EDP joined with several groups, including the Ethiopian Democratic Action Group, to found the United Ethiopian Democratic Party–Medhin (UEDP-Medhin) in 2003. The relationship of the UEDP with another group with a similar name—the Ethiopian Democratic Union Party (EDUP)—was unclear, although it was reported that the UEDP-Medhin rubric had been adopted prior to the 2005 national balloting as a result of several formal mergers of former single parties. It formerly was joined to the CUD coalition of parties.

Lidetu (who had been serving as the group's acting leader) was reportedly elected chair of the UEDP-Medhin in late 2005 after he broke with CUD components on the issue of participation in the legislature. (Lidetu supported the decision by most of the successful UEDP-Medhin candidates to take their seats.) Among other things, Lidetu accused CUD leader Hailu of trying to form a single party of the CUD components that would be dominated by the AEUP. In early 2009 a party congress readopted the EDP rubric in advance of the 2010 elections, pledging to campaign as a center-right party focused on "individual rights" rather than the rights of ethnic groups. Lidetu championed the Third Way platform that looked to walk the line between EPRDF policies and those of FORUM. The group did not win representation during the 2010 legislative balloting. At its fifth party congress in 2011, the party elected Mushe Semu as its leader. In 2013 CHANNIE Kebede was elected EDP president.

Leader: CHANNIE Kebede (President).

Coalition for Unity and Democracy (CUD). Launched in 2004 as an electoral coalition in advance of the 2005 legislative balloting by RE:MDSJ and the EDL, the CUD called for constitutional changes to reduce the authority of the executive branch and to promote democratization and human rights. Other campaign promises included intensified land privatization and a switch to proportional legislative balloting. Supported primarily by urban Amharas, the CUD also called for a more highly centralized government in which the ethnically based states would be replaced by a return to the former provincial structure. Under the CUD proposals, the constitution would also no longer include provisions for legal regional secession.

The CUD was the leading opposition force in the May 2005 national and state elections, dominating the balloting in Addis Ababa and other cities. The government ultimately credited the CUD with winning 109 seats in the House of Peoples' Representatives, although the coalition strongly challenged the accuracy of the final results and a number of its successful candidates refused to take their seats in the house. CUD members also declined to accept their council seats in Addis Ababa, and a "caretaker" administration was subsequently appointed for the capital by the federal government.

The question of whether or not to boycott the legislature in 2005 apparently caused significant dissension within the coalition, and undercut efforts by CUD Chair Hailu Shawel to merge the CUD components into a single party. In September the AEUP, RE:MDSJ, and EDL reportedly announced support for the proposed merger and creation of a Coalition for Unity and Democracy Party (CUDP). However, the UEDP-Medhin resisted that initiative, prompting the national election board to refuse recognition of the CUDP on the grounds that the CUDP required full participation of all of its electoral components.

Many of the CUD leaders (including Hailu and CUD legislators who had refused to take their seats in the House of Peoples' Representatives) were arrested in the government crackdown of November 2005, which reportedly scuttled the single-party proposal for good. Following their conviction on various charges in April 2007, Hailu and the other CUD detainees were pardoned in July, although the 14 CUD seats won in Addis Ababa in the 2005 election to the House of Peoples' Representatives were declared vacant by the government. Hailu reportedly dismissed the letter of apology he and others had signed as having been coerced by the government, but he subsequently reportedly denied making such comments. In any event, the CUD was later described as riven with internal disputes, particularly after the government recognized a faction under the name of **CUD/*Kinjit*** (under the leadership of Ayele Chamiso) as the "official" party. Chamiso, described by critics as having been co-opted by the government, was elected to the local council in Addis Ababa in April 2008, although the EPRDF was credited with winning the remaining 137 of the council's 138 seats. In addition, the EPRDF won the 14 former CUD seats from Addis Ababa in concurrent by-elections to the House of Peoples' Representatives. Meanwhile, Hailu continued to urge the United States to withhold aid from the Meles regime, although the Bush administration in Washington displayed a strong preference to dealing with other, less "radical," opposition groups. The CUD consequently appeared unlikely to serve as a significant force in subsequent elections, some former leaders having opted to help form new parties recently. By the 2010 legislative election season, observers considered the CUD moribund and began referring to it in the past tense. In July 2011 Ayele Chamiso went into voluntary exile in the United States. CUD was critical of the conduct of local balloting in 2013.

Leader: Ayele CHAMISO (Exiled Leader of the CUD/*Kinjit*).

Rainbow Ethiopia: Movement for Democracy and Social Justice (RE:MDSJ). Launched by prominent human rights activists in November 2004, the RE:MDSJ called upon the country's myriad opposition parties to coalesce in advance of the May 2005 legislative elections.

Leader: BERHANU Nega (Chair).

Ethiopian Democratic League (EDL). The EDL was launched in 2002 by opponents of the Meles administration. The new party described itself as open to all Ethiopians, regardless of ethnicity or regionality. Founding members reportedly included Berhanu Nega (a prominent economist) and Mesfin Wolde Mariam (a human rights activist). Both men were arrested in 2002 on charges of having incited disturbances at the University of Addis Ababa the previous year, but they were subsequently released, in part due to heavy international pressure. They were also arrested in the November 2005 government crackdown, Berhanu and Mariam then being referenced as the leaders of the newly formed RE:MDSJ. The two later migrated to separate parties—Berhanu went to Ginbot 7 and Mariam moved to UDJ. The UDJ led a protest against Ethiopia's antiterrorism law in September 2013.

Leaders: Chekol GETAHUN, MULENEH Eyuel.

Ginbot 7: The Movement for Justice, Freedom, and Democracy (Ginbot 7). The party's leader, Berhanu Nega, was one of the founders of RE:MDSJ, which was part of the CUD. Berhanu reportedly declined a government post following the election, and he was among the prominent opposition politicians who were arrested in November 2005. He was pardoned along with other CUD officials following their conviction in 2007 and moved to the United States, where he helped to launch the opposition grouping Ginbot 7, which means May 15, a reference to the May 15, 2005, balloting. In April 2009 the Ethiopian government arrested some 45 people for involvement in what the government described as a plot to assassinate Ethiopian officials. Berhanu, who was charged in absentia, described the allegations as "scurrilous" and said Ginbot 7, although dedicated to the ouster of the Meles regime, was committed to the rule of law. On December 22, 2009, Berhanu and four other opposition figures were sentenced to death on the charge of conspiring to assassinate high-ranking government officials, while 33 other members of Ginbot 7 received life sentences. Berhanu, who was a U.S. university professor and a U.S. national at the time of his sentencing, strongly condemned the verdict, saying witnesses for the prosecution were tortured for their confessions. After he was freed from prison, Nega moved to the United States and returned to academia. Reports in June 2013 revealed that Ginbot 7 had received $500,000 in financing from Eritrea.

Leader: BERHANU Nega (Chair).

Ogaden National Liberation Front (ONLF). The secessionist, ethnically Somali ONLF was organized in January 1986, reportedly by militant members of the Western Somalia Liberation Front (WSLF) opposed to Ethiopian-Somalian talks on the future of the Ogaden that did not involve participation by regional representatives. (For additional information on the WSLF, now disbanded, see the 2007 *Handbook.*) The ONLF reportedly began fighting for independence of the Ogaden/Somali region in the early 1990s, many supporters calling for creation of a "Greater Somalia" that would include Somalia and the Somali-populated areas of Ethiopia, Djibouti, and Kenya. The Ethiopian government responded to that campaign with a crackdown that included the arrest of a number of ONLF leaders and, reportedly, the killing of others. In September 1996 the Ethiopian army conducted cross-border operations inside Somaliland against ONLF guerrillas.

In June 1998 an ONLF faction that had reportedly been cooperating with the progovernment ESDL since 1995 formed a separate grouping— the SPDP (see above). For their part, ONLF secessionists continued to clash with government troops.

In April 2006 the ONLF claimed responsibility for several attacks on government troops. Approximately 1,000 ONLF fighters were reportedly training in Eritrea at that point. In April 2007 the ONLF claimed responsibility for an attack on a Chinese-owned oil site in the state of Somalia, having previously warned foreign companies to leave the region. The Ethiopian government subsequently launched heavy countermeasures that, among other things, attracted international criticism for the effects on civilians, many of them impoverished nomads. Sporadic but severe fighting between the ONLF and government forces continued for the next year, the Meles regime accusing Eritrea of supporting the ONLF as a way of destabilizing Ethiopia. In May 2008 the ONLF announced it had merged with the Western Somali Democratic Party (WSDP) and called upon all "ethnic Somalis" to join the antiregime "struggle." In September the ONLF called upon the international community to address the "humanitarian crisis" arising from the government offensive. Significant fighting between government troops and ONLF adherents continued throughout 2009.

In 2012 negotiations between the Ethiopian government and the ONLF failed after the rebel group refused to accept the legitimacy of the Ethiopian constitution as a precondition for a settlement.

Leaders: Mohamed Omar OSMAN (Chair), Abdirahman MAHDI, Mohamed Ismaïl OMAR, Shimber Abdel KADIR, Mohamed HUSSEIN.

Oromo Liberation Front (OLF). Initially centered in the eastern and mid-country regions, the OLF in the late 1980s expanded its activities to the west and south. Although it represented the largest ethnic group in Ethiopia, the OLF was the least powerful militarily of the rebel units that toppled the Mengistu government. Previously committed to the creation of a new country of "Oromia" in what is currently southern Ethiopia, OLF leaders said in June 1991 that they would consider remaining part of an Ethiopian federation that provided for substantial regional autonomy. In mid-July the OLF concluded a "unity" pact with four other Oromo groups: the **Islamic Front for the Liberation of Oromia** (IFLO), the **Oromo Aba Liberation Front** (OALF), and the **United Oromo People's Liberation Front** (UOPLF), and the OPDO (above). Earlier the OLF had occasionally allied itself with the EPLF (see under Eritrea entry) in skirmishes with the EPRDF, and it withdrew from the EPRDF-led coalition in June 1992 because of alleged electoral fraud, harassment of its members, and perceived inadequate tribal representation in the government. In the spring of 1994 the

OLF and IFLO were reported to have agreed to offer coordinated opposition to the forthcoming draft constitution. In early 1995 a number of skirmishes took place between government troops and OLF militants, and it was subsequently reported that several hundred OLF supporters had been imprisoned as a result of the front's low-level guerrilla campaign.

In mid-1996 the OLF announced that it had signed a cooperation pact with the hard-line faction of the ONLF. The two groups pledged, according to the *Indian Ocean Newsletter,* to coordinate their diplomatic, political, and military activity to secure self-determination referendums for their respective regions. Minor skirmishes between security forces and OLF militants continued throughout 1997 as the front reportedly remained divided between pro- and antidialogue factions. The party engaged in reportedly fruitless discussions with the government in 1997, and at an extraordinary OLF congress in early 1998 the antidialogue faction appeared to have won control of the group's policy-making Executive Committee. The OLF was subsequently described as "reinvigorated," partly as the result of aid from Eritrea. OLF antigovernment military activity in pursuit of independence was reported in mid-2002, although severe factionalization was reported between OLF militants, led by Daoud Ibsa, and moderates inclined to negotiate with the government. The OLF remained "at war with the regime" in early 2005, although Gelasa Dilbo, the OLF chair who had been under house arrest, had been permitted to leave for Kenya in late 2004.

Prime Minister Meles reportedly offered in late 2005 to negotiate with the OLF toward a possible peace settlement, but the OLF continued to support "mobilization" against the EPRDF regime. Meanwhile, the front reportedly remained split between supporters of Gelasa and supporters of Ibsa. The government accused the OLF of having taken part in recent attacks on security forces in the state of Somalia in 2007 and also alleged OLF cooperation with the ONLF in subsequent antigovernment activity. OLF members were reportedly among those arrested in November 2008 for alleged involvement in bomb attacks in Addis Ababa.

In February 2013 KEMAL Gelchu, an OLF militia leader, was detained and placed under house arrest in Asmara, Eritrea.

Leaders: GELASA Dilbo (Former Chair, in exile), Daoud IBSA (Chair), Hassan HUSSEIN (Spokesperson), Shigat GELETA (resident in Berlin, Germany), Beyan AROBA.

Afar Liberation Front (ALF). Long considered the most important of the Afar groups, the ALF was organized in 1975. Although its leadership was then based in Jeddah, Saudi Arabia, the ALF also operated in Ethiopia's Hararge and Wollo Provinces, where it was supported by followers of Ahmed ALI Mirah, the sultan of Awsa. In July 1991 the sultan returned from 17 years in exile and nominally endorsed Eritrea's right to self-determination, although his nomadic subjects occupied a lengthy portion of the Red Sea coast and had long had as their principal objective an Afar state within an Ethiopian federation. In April 1995 the sultan suspended his son, Hanfareh ALI Mirah, as ALF chair in response to preelectoral dissension within the Front; however, the ALF Executive Committee refused to endorse the action. The leadership of the ALF subsequently remained unclear as some reports suggested that the sultan and at least one of his sons had expressed support for the new Afar party (see ANDP, above), while other sons (including Umar ALI Mirah, Habib ALI Mirah, and Ousman ALI Mirah) continued to oppose the EPRDF. Renewed fighting between ALF hard-liners and Ethiopian forces was reported in mid-2002.

In 2006 it was reported that antigovernment "remnants" from the ALF, ARDUF (including *Uguguma* militants), and the ANLF had launched (with Eritrean support) the **Afar National Democratic Front** (ANDF) under the leadership of Mohamed IBRAHIM.

Ethiopian People's Revolutionary Party (EPRP). The EPRP initiated an unsuccessful antigovernment guerrilla campaign in north-central Ethiopia in 1977. Its forces also battled with the TPLF in Tigray Province, its defeat there in 1978 precipitating a sharp split within the party. One faction served as the formative core of the EPDM in alliance with the TPLF while a rump group was relatively quiescent until a series of kidnappings and other guerrilla acts in Gojam Province in early 1987. Although the EPRP was committed to the overthrow of the Mengistu regime, its relations with the EPRDF and the EPLF were strained. Following the rebel victory in May 1991, the EPRP, with an estimated 5,000 fighters controlling parts of Gojam and Gondar Provinces, was described as the "only really organized opposition" to the TPLF-dominated interim government. Like the country's other previously Marxist formations, the EPRP now supports multiparty democracy.

In 2001 the EPRP called for renewed action against the "racist" TPLF-led regime, and there were several reports in 2002 of fighting between the EPRP and government forces. Some reports described the EPRP as a participant in the UEDF in 2005, although the government continued to describe the EPRP as an illegal organization. Reports in 2013 indicated that the government had launched an initiative to convince leaders and former officials of the EPRP to return to Ethiopia.

Leaders: Col. TADERSE Muleneh, Iyassu ALEMAYEHU (in exile).

Islamic Union (*al-Itahad al-Islami*). Operating along the southern part of the border between Ethiopia and Somalia, the Islamic Union conducted guerrilla activity in the early 1990s in support of the establishment of an "Ethiopian Ogaden State." The grouping was accused by the government of several bomb attacks, prompting military countermeasures in the second half of 1996. On July 8, 1996, minister of transport and communication and the chair of the ESDL, Abdulmejid Hussein, was shot and wounded by *Al-Itahad* members. Government forces subsequently conducted territorial and extraterritorial military operations against *Al-Itahad,* the organization losing its last major bases to an Ethiopian assault in July 1997. (See entry on Somalia for information on *al-Itahad* activity in that country.)

Blue Party (*Semayawi*). *Semayawi* was an opposition group formed in August 2012. The party led the first antigovernment protests in eight years in June 2013. However, subsequent efforts to conduct demonstrations were blocked by the government, and 100 party members were arrested in September 2013.

Leader: YILEKAL Getachew.

Other parties winning single seats in the 2000 balloting for the House of Peoples' Representatives were the **Gambela Peoples' Democratic Congress** (GPDC), an anti-EPRDF formation with support within the Nuer ethnic group; the **Sidama Hadicko Peoples' Democratic Organization;** and the **Siltie Peoples' Democratic Party**.

Small formations include the **Tigray Democratic Union** (TDU), an anti-TPLF grouping that launched an armed struggle in 2000 under the leadership of AREGAWE Bereh, one of the founders of the TPLF; the **Sidama Liberation Movement** (SLM), led by Yilma CHAMOLA; the **Oromo National Liberation Party** (ONLP), launched in October 2000 under the leadership of ESAYAS Shegaw to "liberate Oromia from poverty and suffering."

Groups formed in advance of the 2005 legislative poll included the **Afar Liberation Party;** the **All Ethiopian Democratic Party,** launched by former members of the EDUP; the **Dal-Webi Democratic Movement,** which operates in the state of Somalia; and the **Ethiopian Pan-Africanist Party,** led by Abd al-Fatah HULDAR.

In 2006 the government announced several "victories" over fighters from an allegedly Eritrean-backed Amhara group called the **Ethiopian People's Patriotic Front** (EPPF), although some analysts expressed skepticism that the EPPF represented a significant threat. In November 2007 the EPPF participated in the launching of the antiregime **Unity of Ethiopians for Democratic Change** (UEDC), which included other armed groups such as the TPDM, the **Southern Ethiopia People's Front for Justice and Equality,** and the **Beneshangul People's Movement.**

For more information on the **Oromo People's Liberation Front** (OPLF), the **Ethiopian Democratic Union Party** (EDUP), the **Coalition of Ethiopian Democratic Forces** (COEDF), the **Ethiopian People's Democratic Alliance** (EPDA), the **All-Ethiopian Socialist Movement** (*Meison*), the **Tigray People's Democratic Movement** (TPDM), and the **Tigrayan Alliance for National Democracy** (TAND), please see the 2013 *Handbook.*

LEGISLATURE

The constitution of December 1994 provides for an Ethiopian **Parliament** encompassing a House of the Federation selected by the states and a popularly elected House of Peoples' Representatives. Both bodies have five-year mandates.

House of the Federation (*Yefedershein Mekir Bete*). The upper House currently consists of 108 members (serving five-year terms) who represent Ethiopia's "nations and nationalities," each of which is entitled to at least one member, with an additional representative for each one million of its population (The regional distribution of seats is as follows: Southern Nations, Nationalities, and Peoples, 54; Amhara,

17; Oromia, 16; Tigray, 6; Somalia, 4; Beneshangul-Gumuz, 4; Gambela Peoples, 4; Afar, 2; Harari People, 1). Members are designated by state councils, which may elect them directly or provide for their popular election. The House of the Federation was most recently replenished in 2010 following State Council elections on May 23. The new president of the House was elected on October 4.

Speaker: KASSA Tekeleberihan Gebrehiwot.

House of Peoples' Representatives (*Yehizb Tewokayoch Mekir Bete*). The House of Peoples' Representatives consists of no more than 550 members (minority nationalities being accorded at least 20 seats) directly elected for a five-year term from single-member districts by a plurality of votes cast. The most recent balloting was held on May 23, 2010. The national electoral board released final results on June 21. Results for 547 contested seats were as follows: Ethiopian People's Revolutionary Democratic Front, 499; Somali Peoples' Democratic Party, 24; Benshangul-Gumuz Peoples' Democratic Unity Front, 9; Afar National Democratic Party, 8; Gambela Peoples' Unity Democratic Movement, 3; Argoba Peoples' Democratic Organization, 1; Harari National League, 1; Ethiopia Federal Democratic Unity Forum, 1; independent, 1.

Speaker: ABADULA Gemeda Dego.

CABINET

[as of October 15, 2013]

Prime Minister	Hailemariam Desalegn
Deputy Prime Minister	Demeke Mekonnen
Deputy Prime Minister for Finance and Economy	Debretsion Gebremikael
Deputy Prime Minister for Good Governance and Reforms	Muktar Kedir
Ministers	
Agriculture	Tefera Deribew
Civil Service	Muktar Kedir
Communication Affairs Office	Redwan Hussein
Communications and Information Technology	Debretsion Gebremikael
Culture and Tourism	Ahmin Abdulkedir
Defense	Siraj Fergesa
Economic Development and Finance	Sufian Ahmed
Education	Shiferaw Shigute
Employment Protection and Forestry	Belete Tafese
Federal Affairs	Shiferaw Teklemariam
Foreign Affairs	Tewodros Adhanom
Government Whip	Roman Gebreselassie
Health	Keseteberhan Admassu
Industry	Ahmed Abtew
Justice	Getachew Ambaye
Labor and Social Affairs	Abdulfeta Abdulrahman
Mines	Sinkenesh Ejgu [f]
Revenue and Customs Authority	Beker Shale
Science and Technology	Demitu Hambisa
Trade	Kebebe Chane
Transport	Workneh Gebeyehu
Urban Development and Construction	Mekuria Haile
Water and Energy	Alemayehu Tegenu
Women, Children and Youth Affairs	Zenebu Taddesse [f]

[f] = female

INTERGOVERNMENTAL REPRESENTATION

Ambassador to the U.S.: Girma B. BIRRU.

U.S. Ambassador to Ethiopia: Donald BOOTH.

Permanent Representative to the UN: Tekeda ALEMU.

IGO Memberships (Non-UN): AfDB, AU, Comesa, NAM.

FIJI

Republic of the Fiji Islands
Matanitu Tu-Vaka-i-koya ko Viti (Fijian)
Fiji Ripablik (Hindustani)

Political Status: Voluntarily assumed the status of a British dependency in 1874; became an independent member of the Commonwealth on October 10, 1970; republic declared on October 15, 1987; current constitution promulgated on July 25, 1997, with effect from July 27, 1998; constitution abrogated by presidential decree on April 10, 2009; country led by military-backed interim government.

Area: 7,055 sq. mi. (18,272 sq. km).

Population: 880,391 (2012E—UN); 890,057 (2012E—U.S. Census).

Major Urban Center (2007C): SUVA, 74,481 (center), 173,137 (urban area).

Official Languages: English, Fijian (*Na Vosa Vakaviti*), and Hindustani (Fijian Hindi).

Monetary Unit: Fiji Dollar (official rate November 1, 2013: 1.83 dollars = $1US).

President (Interim): Ratu Epeli NAILATIKAU; appointed vice president on April 17, 2009, by President Josefa ILOILO; became acting president upon Iloilo's retirement, effective July 30, 2009; appointed interim president by the interim cabinet and sworn in on November 5, 2009.

Vice President (Interim): (Vacant).

Prime Minister (Interim): Commodore Frank Vorege BAINIMARAMA (Josaia Voreqe BAINIMARAMA); sworn in January 5, 2007, succeeding Jona Baravilalala SENILAGAKALI, who had been designated by Bainimarama on December 5, 2006, to replace ousted Prime Minister Laisenia QARASE (United Fiji Party); reappointed by President Iloilo on April 10, 2009, for a further five years.

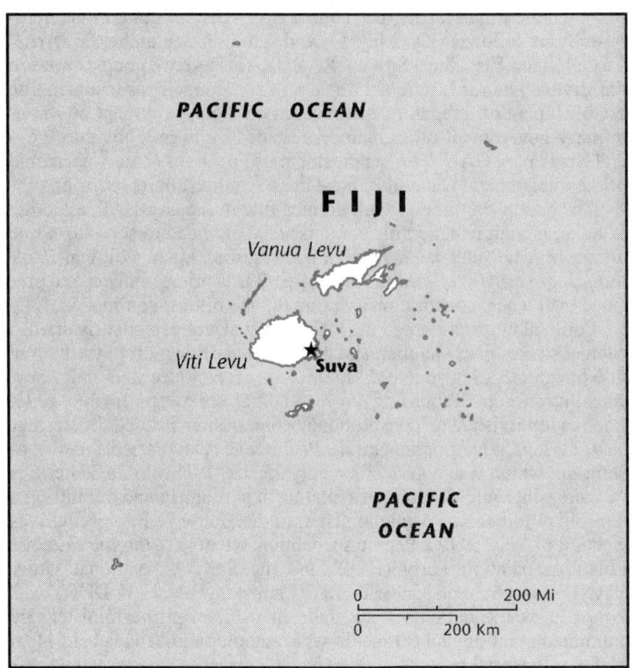

THE COUNTRY

Situated in the South Pacific east of Australia and north of New Zealand, Fiji consists of a group of some 330 islands, many of them mountainous and only about one-third inhabited, together with 500 islets spread over an area of 250,000 square miles of ocean. Viti Levu, the largest island, accommodates close to 80 percent of the population and is the site of Suva, the capital, and of the airport in Nadi, an important hub for air routes throughout the South Pacific islands. Native Fijians (mainly Melanesians, save for Polynesians in the far northern island of Rotuma) became a minority of Fiji's mixed population in consequence of the introduction of numerous Indian indentured laborers following the establishment of British rule in 1874. In the 1976 census Fijians constituted about 44 percent of the population; Indo-Fijians, 50 percent; other Pacific Islanders, 2 percent; Europeans and part-Europeans, 3 percent; and Chinese, 1 percent. By contrast, the percentages of ethnic Fijians and Indo-Fijians in the 2007 census were 57 and 37, respectively, largely as the result of Indian emigration following military coups in 1987, 2000, and 2006. Virtually all ethnic Fijians are Christian, approximately 85 percent being Methodist and 12 percent Roman Catholic. The Indo-Fijian population is predominantly Hindu, with a Muslim minority. In 2005 women constituted 34 percent of the employed labor force, with a higher proportion self-employed and engaged in nonmonetary subsistence activities such as agricultural cultivation and processing.

Traditionally, Fiji's economy was based on agriculture. Although that sector now accounts for approximately 12 percent of GDP, it employs over 70 percent of the workforce. Sugar remains the country's most important export, valued at 20 percent of exports in 2009, despite declining production because of lack of capital investment in new technology and disputes between Fijian landowners and Indo-Fijian leaseholders over tenure and rentals. Fish, garments, gold, timber, and small manufactured goods also are significant exports. Industry, led by food processing and garment production, contributes about one-fifth of GDP and employs one-third of the labor force. Gold mining remains the most important extractive industry and a significant export earner. Within the services sector, tourism is the major source of income, accounting for one-fifth of GDP. In 2012 Fiji's main export markets were the United States (13.3 percent), Australia (12 percent), Japan (6.3 percent), Samoa (5.8 percent), and Tonga (5.1 percent); its main sources of imports were Singapore (32.6 percent), Australia (15.4 percent), New Zealand (14.4 percent), and China (10.7 percent).

The December 2006 coup precipitated a flight of capital and skilled people and a 25 percent contraction of tourism earnings over the next four years. The government reduced expenditures by 14.2 percent during 2007, which slowed public works and raised unemployment. The economy, further depressed by floods and lagging international demand, shrank by over 10 percent the following three years. Population subsisting below the poverty line, mainly in rural areas and proliferating urban squatter settlements, was estimated at 31 percent in 2009.

In April 2009 the interim prime minister dismissed the governor of the Reserve Bank of Fiji, ordered the devaluation of the Fiji dollar by 20 percent to attract tourists, and decreed the retirement of civil servants aged 55 and over to reduce government expenditure. In 2012 the inflation rate eased to 4.4 percent, the trade deficit 6.1 percent of GDP, and the external debt 52 percent of GDP. The International Monetary Fund forecasts a GDP growth rate of 2.2 percent in 2013 and 2.0 percent in 2014.

GOVERNMENT AND POLITICS

Political background. Discovered by the Dutch explorer Abel Tasman in 1643 and visited by Captain James Cook in 1774, Fiji became a British possession in 1874 when the Fijian paramount chief ceded sovereignty to the United Kingdom to end internecine wars. Modern administration originated with the Fijian Affairs Ordinance in 1945, which laid the foundations for local government. A ministerial system was introduced in 1966 providing for a Legislative Council elected in such a way as to ensure robust Fijian representation. Following compromises negotiated at a constitutional conference in London in May 1979, Fiji became independent on October 1.

The Alliance Party (AP), with Ratu Sir Kamisese K. T. MARA at its head, dominated pre- and postindependence governments, winning elections in 1977 and 1982. At the next election in 1987 a National Federation Party (NFP)–Fiji Labour Party (FLP), comprising mainly Indo-Fijians, defeated the AP and formed a government headed by the

FLP's ethnic Fijian leader, Dr. Timoci BAVADRA. Ethnic Fijian demonstrations followed. On May 14, and again on September 25, Army Lt. Col. (later Brigadier) Sitiveni RABUKA staged two coups, replaced the civilian administration with a military council, proclaimed the establishment of a republic, and announced the appointment of a nonmilitary government of 23 members headed by former governor general Sir Penaia GANILAU as president of Fiji. Ratu Mara was named prime minister and General Rabuka became home affairs minister.

The country returned to full civilian rule in January 1990, although Rabuka, having resigned his commission, continued to serve as home affairs minister and later, leading a revitalized Fijian Political Party (*Soqosoqot ni Vakavulewa ni Taukei*—SVT), as prime minister and presided over a new constitution assuring Fijian political dominance.

Political unrest mounted in 1993 in the wake of personal rivalries, a cabinet shake-up in October, and parliamentary rejection of the budget in November. A legislative dissolution, a general election, and a new constitution kept Rabuka in power another six years. In mid-1994, Rabuka established a constitutional commission headed by former New Zealand governor general Sir Paul Reeves that drafted a new constitution, which was approved on July 25, 1997. This mollified critics by increasing Indo-Fijian representation in parliament and permitting a non-Fijian to become prime minister. In the House of Representatives election of May 1999 a People's Coalition, encompassing the FLP, the Fijian Association Party (FAP), and the Party of National Unity (PANU), won 51 seats, and the FLP's Mahendra Pal CHAUDHRY was sworn in as the nation's first ethnic Indo-Fijian prime minister. He appointed a multiracial cabinet in which ethnic Indo-Fijians held 11 of 17 full ministerial posts.

A year later, on May 19, 2000, feeding on ethnic Fijian resentment at growing Indo-Fijian influence, a group of gunmen led by George SPEIGHT, a failed Suva businessman, stormed the Parliament building, took hostage Prime Minister Chaudhry, many cabinet members, and a number of MPs, and declared himself prime minister. On May 29 Commodore Frank Vorege BAINIMARAMA, commander in chief of the armed forces, declared martial law, negotiated the release of hostages, and named Vice President Josefa ILOILO as interim president. Speight was convicted in February 2002 of treason and sentenced to life imprisonment; in March 2011 another alleged conspirator, Ratu Inoke TAKIVEIKATA, was given the same sentence for inciting mutiny and attempting to murder Bainimarama.

A complex series of events ensued in which the High Court declared the new government invalid, two inconclusive elections were held, the elected leaders challenged each other's legitimacy, and Bainimarama lost confidence in the civilian leadership. (See the 2010 *Handbook* for details.)

The general election of May 2006 produced an outright majority in the House of Representatives for Laisenia Qarase's United Fiji Party (*Soqosoqo Duavata ni Lewenivanua*—SDL), and Qarase was designated prime minister by President Josefa Iloilo.But five months later Bainimarama called the Qarase government "corrupt and unjust," insisted that it withdraw a legislative initiative giving the 2000 plotters amnesty, objected to a police investigation of Bainimarama's involvement in that coup, and called for Qarase's resignation. The confrontation climaxed when Bainimarama spearheaded Fiji's fourth coup on December 5, 2006, deposed the civilian government, and assumed the role of acting president. President Iloilo, despite misgivings, was persuaded by the military leaders to dissolve Parliament, name Bainimarama as interim prime minister, and legitimize the installation of an interim government of military officers and cooperative civilians. Bainimarama in turn reinstated Iloilo as president on January 5, 2007.

In March 2007, under pressure from EU representatives and at the urging of Pacific Islands Forum (PIF) leaders, Bainimarama lifted the state of emergency that had been imposed at the time of the coup and pledged to conduct an election leading to return to constitutional civilian government by the end of March 2009. But the government was slow to undertake necessary preparatory measures, such as the appointment and staffing of an electoral boundaries commission and appropriation of funds for the administration of the election. Policies restricting the registration of political parties such as the SDL and hampering public activities by candidates such as Qarase remained in place.

In February 2008 Bainimarama appointed himself as chair of the Great Council of Chiefs (which chose the president) and in June withdrew from the Forum-Fiji Joint Working Group consultations regarding election preparations. On June 22, 2009, the interim government renewed the Public Emergency Regulations that legalized censorship of the media and the banning of public meetings, and in July it banned the annual conference of the Methodist Church and temporarily detained six Methodist leaders. Bainimarama also announced that no election would take place until electoral reforms were completed, and on July 1, 2009, he extended the target date for a new constitution to 2013 and elections to 2014. Meanwhile, Bainimarama initiated and appointed a National Council for Building a Better Fiji and directed the drafting of a People's Charter for a Better Fiji. After a series of managed public consultations, the People's Charter, described as a "supplement to the Constitution," was completed on December 5, 2008, and approved and promulgated by President Iloilo on December 19.

Doubt regarding Bainimarama's commitment to restoring constitutional government was raised by actions to suppress dissent, such as the imposition of a temporary state of emergency in September 2007, the arrest and beating of 16 alleged antigovernment conspirators in November 2007, the sacking of the chief justice and the chief of police, the summary expulsion of four New Zealand and Australian diplomats and the blacklisting and deporting of two New Zealand journalists and two Australian editors of the *Fiji Times* in the following two years, an intimidating search of the premises of the Fiji Law Society in 2009, and the threat in early 2010 to terminate the pension of any retired official who criticized the interim government. Fiji's Council of Trade Unions general secretary Attar SINGH voiced concern about draft decrees restricting union membership and activity in industries declared "critical" by the regime, and in July the Public Service Act was amended by decree to prohibit civil servants from paying union dues.

Media suppression intensified in 2009 as the interim government dispatched Ministry of Information officials to the newsrooms of the main broadcast stations and newspapers, warning journalists not to disseminate "negative" reports about the government on pain of closure. In September Bainimarama ordered government bodies to terminate all connections to the Australian-owned and edited *Fiji Times.* One Australian and two New Zealand journalists were deported, and three local journalists were temporarily detained. The Fiji Media Council (Suva), the Pacific Island News Association–PACNEWS (Suva), the International Federation of Journalists (Brussels), Reporters Without Borders (Paris), and the Committee to Protect Journalists (New York) decried these actions as censorship and stifling of legitimate political reporting. The Media Industry Development Decree, issued on June 28, 2010, required 90 percent Fijian ownership of news media and institutionalised other restraints. Internet blogs Fiji Democracy Now and Fiji Today sprang up to fill the vacuum of political news from Fiji.

In the wake of a Court of Appeal ruling denying the legitimacy of the government, President Iloilo, backed by the military, on April 10, 2009, dismissed all of Fiji's judges, declared the constitution abrogated and a state of emergency in force, and appointed Bainimarama interim prime minister for a further five years. Bainimarama reshuffled his cabinet on April 11, 2009. Six days later, Iloilo named Epeli NAILATIKAU as vice president, filling a post that had been vacant since the 2006 coup. When Iloilo, 88, retired on July 30, Nailatikau became acting president.

Constitution and government. Fiji's 1970 constitution established Fiji as a fully sovereign and independent state with a titular head, the British monarch, represented locally by a governor general. Executive authority was vested in a prime minister and cabinet appointed by the governor general and responsible to a bicameral Parliament consisting of an appointed Senate and an elected House of Representatives. A complex electoral system was devised to ensure strong representation for the Fijian community, encompassing both communal and national electoral rolls. The judicial system included a Fiji Court of Appeal, a Supreme Court (the superior court of record), magistrates' courts, and provincial and district courts. A High Court above the courts of first instance and below the Court of Appeal was added in 1990. Judicial appointments were assigned to the governor general, with provision for an ombudsman to investigate complaints against government officials.

Below the center, Fiji was partitioned into four administrative divisions (Northern, Southern, Eastern, and Western), each headed by a divisional commissioner assisted by district officers. Divisions and lower-level districts are headed by appointed commissioners and officers, respectively. Urban areas include cities and towns, each of which elects a governing council. There also are local rural authorities responsible primarily for matters of public health. Native Fijian affairs are governed through a separate overlapping system based on the village (*koro*) and extending up to the provincial level. Each of 14 communal provinces has a partially elected provincial council and an executive head (*roko tui*). Executives are named by the Fijian Affairs Board, which oversees administration of ethnic Fijian matters. At the apex of the provincial councils, a Great Council of Chiefs (*Bose Levu Vakaturaga*) was empowered to advise the government on Fijian affairs. A National Land Trust Board was given administrative responsibility over four-fifths of the nation's land, which could not be alienated, on behalf of village groups. Indians were restricted to leasing holdings for up to 10 years (later expanded to 30 years), a situation that, along with the system of representation, remained the object of persistent Indian dissatisfaction.

The 1970 constitution was abrogated after the second coup of September 1987. Its successor, similar to the 1970 constitution, was promulgated on July 25, 1990, and assured that Fijians would retain the presidency and a majority in the legislature and local government bodies including the Fiji Affairs Board and Native Land Commission. The manifestly discriminatory constitution of 1990 was superseded in 1997 by a constitution that provided for continued Fijian predominance in the Senate but opened the door to possible Indo-Fijian control of the House through the election of 25 members on a nonracial basis (see Legislature, below). The ensuing victory of Mahendra Chaudhry, an Indo-Fijian, as prime minister in 1999 triggered the coup led by George Speight in 2000, but no constitutional changes.

After the December 5, 2006, coup the 1997 constitution remained nominally in force, but its civil liberties provisions were violated when the interim government dismissed the legislature, postponed the holding of an election to return Fiji to civilian rule, curbed political party activity, intimidated the media, and packed the human rights commission with political appointees.

On May 5, 2009, the Court of Appeal ruled that the December 2006 seizure of power was illegal and the interim government was illegitimate. President Iloilo responded by dismissing first the judges of the Court of Appeal, then the entire judiciary, abrogating the 1997 constitution, declaring a state of emergency, and reappointing Commodore Bainimarama as interim prime minister for five years. On March 14, 2012, Bainimarama decreed the abolition of the Great Council of Chiefs, terminating an institution established in 1876.

A commission to draft a new constitution was appointed in April 2012. Its chair, Professor Yash GHAI, submitted a draft in December. In January 2013 the interim government took charge of the process, altered the Ghai Draft, and in the Fiji Constitutional Process (Adoption of Constitution) Decree #12 of March 21, 2013, promulgated a new draft and invited submissions from the public during the month of April. The revised draft constitution prescribed a 45-member Parliament elected by proportional representation from four multimember constituencies. By majority vote the Parliament was to elect the president of Fiji and the prime minister who in turn was empowered to appoint a cabinet. A Bill of Rights specified a list of socioeconomic rights as well as civil liberties. A new Human Rights and Anti-discrimination Commission and an Accountability and Transparency Commission were prescribed. The new constitution was to be approved by the president and ratified by a constitutent assembly whose members were to be appointed by the interim government.

Foreign relations. Fiji is a member of the United Nations (UN) and of many of its associated agencies as well as of several regional organizations, including the Pacific Community. It was a founding member of the 16-member Pacific Islands Forum (PIF, formerly the South Pacific Forum), and Suva is the site of its Secretariat. Since 1978 Fiji has been a major contributor of soldiers to UN peacekeeping forces, from which it earned a substantial but undisclosed amount of foreign exchange for the government. In June 2011, in response to a United Nations request to cope with the anticipated withdrawal of U.S. troops at year-end, Fiji agreed to dispatch 55 more soldiers to Iraq, bringing the total in that country to 221. A further 380 troops for Golan Heights peacekeeping were pledged in July 2013 to join 183 already deployed in the region. In addition, retired Fijian soldiers and policemen engaged by international agencies for security work in the Middle East remitted home an estimated F$20 million a year, making official peacekeeping and private security work the third most important source of Fiji's foreign earnings, behind only tourism and sugar exports.

Upon independence Fiji joined the Commonwealth. But in October 1987, in response to criticism from London, the leaders of the military coup declared Fiji a republic, whereupon the Commonwealth Heads of Government Meeting in Vancouver, Canada, declared that Fiji's membership in the Commonwealth had "lapsed." The adoption of a new constitution in 1997 led to Fiji's readmission on October 1. The May 2000 coup precipitated suspension from meetings of the Commonwealth. Full participation in the Commonwealth was restored following the August–September 2001 democratic election.

Fiji was again excluded from Commonwealth meetings in the wake of the 2006 coup, and on September 1, 2009, the Commonwealth suspended Fiji's membership, citing the interim government's failure to schedule a legislative election for 2010 as promised. Fiji's latest coup was strongly condemned also by the UN Security Council and the European Commission. Numerous foreign governments, including Australia, New Zealand, the United States, and member states of the EU, ceased diplomatic and military contacts, suspended aid, curtailed migrant work permits, and imposed travel bans on the Bainimarama regime. In May 2009 the European Commissioner for Development Louis Michel canceled an allocation for Fiji sugar industry reform worth $33.4 million. As of mid-2013 an estimated $86 million in EU funds have been withheld.

The unconstitutional actions by President Iloilo in April 2009 stimulated international condemnations by Australia, New Zealand, Great Britain, the United States, the Commonwealth Secretariat, the Commission of the EU, and the UN Security Council, and also by international lawyers' groups, such as the International Bar Association and the Commonwealth Lawyers Association. Reporters Without Borders in 2013 ranked Fiji 107th out of 179 countries in press freedoms, citing the Media Industry Development Decree and a conviction of the editor of *Fiji Times*.

Interim Prime Minister Bainimarama responded by diversifying Fiji's contacts. In July 2010 he invited island leaders to an "Engagement With The Pacific" meeting that attracted high-ranking representatives from ten Pacific states. In April 2011 he hosted the Melanesian Spearhead Group's 18th summit in Suva, whose communiqué included a call for Fiji to be reinstated in regional trade and economic negotiations, and was elected chair of the group. He subsequently secured Fiji's chairmanship of the Groups of 77 and the International Sugar Council.

Relations with China deepened when the China Development Bank in 2009 loaned Fiji $60 million for the Somosomo hydroelectric development scheme. This and other grants for the new Navua Hospital and infrastructure and agricultural projects brought the total of China's loan and aid commitments since the December 2006 coup to over $253 million, equivalent to 9 percent of GDP. In 2011 Fiji leased land to a Chinese bauxite mining company and in June 2012 a Chinese ship departed with bauxite worth $1 million, with further shipments scheduled monthly for the following two years. The defense ministries of the two governments signed a Memorandum of Understanding in April 2011 to facilitate cooperation in counterterrorism, controlling cybercrime, and curbing smuggling, trafficking, and money laundering. In May 2013 Bainimarama was invited to meet the new Chinese president Xi Jinping in Beijing, who pledged further support to Fiji. In June Bainimarama signed a series of agreements with Russia covering military and technical cooperation, money laundering, air services, and educational exchange.

During the period 2010–2013, Interim Prime Minister Bainimarama visited Beijing, Tokyo, Kuala Lumpur, Abu Dhabi, and Moscow; hosted delegations from China, Russia, North Korea, Cuba, India, and the Middle East; and opened Fiji embassies in Jakarta, Pretoria, Seoul, Brazilia, and Abu Dhabi in search of diplomatic acceptance, loans, and aid to offset the deterioration of relations with Fiji's traditional partners Australia and New Zealand.

Allegedly for making comments critical of the interim government, the Australian acting high commissioner was expelled in July 2010. New Zealand reaffirmed its travel ban on Fiji's military rulers and their families during the Rugby World Cup competition starting in October 2011 in Auckland. The United States, despite concern about the growing influence of China in the region, shifted a planned regional aid office from Suva to Port Moresby and omitted Fiji from a State Department–led mission to eight Pacific islands in June 2011. Starting in 2012 the United States, followed by Australia and New Zealand, indicated that sanctions were to be eased in step with Fiji's preparations for an election in 2014. As of mid-2013 Fiji's diplomatic relations with Australia and New Zealand were conducted by acting heads of missions, although ministers continued to meet informally at international fora.

Current issues. After several postponements, in September 2011 Bainimarama promised the drafting of a new nonracial constitution and the establishment of an electronic voter register in anticipation of elections in 2014. He lifted the Emergency Regulations on January 7, 2012, but issued a Public Order Decree the same day offsetting the reform by enlarging the powers of the military and police. In August 2012 ousted prime minister Qarase was convicted of corruption and fraud and sentenced to one year in jail, thus being disqualified from running in the anticipated election. Permission for his SDL party to contest the anticipated election also remained in doubt. The interim government in April named a constitutional commission to be chaired by academic Yash Ghai and in May new voter registration institutions commenced work. The Ministerial Contact Group of the PIF noted approvingly that Fiji was "in transition" to a return to democracy, and in July the foreign ministers of Australia and New Zealand lifted travel bans as had the United States shortly before, and the three governments pledged funds to assist in voter registration and administration. Military contracts remained suspended.

The Ghai Draft of the constitution, submitted in December 2012, did not find favor with the interim government, which criticised it as overly bureaucratic and not sufficiently democratic. The interim government promulgated a new draft on March 21, 2013, and forshadowed its ratification by a Constituent Assembly. (See Constitution and Government, above.) Meanwhile, the government issued the Political Parties (Registration, Conduct, Funding, and Disclosures) Decree #4 on January 15 and invited political parties to apply for registration. Because of the short deadline, requirement of a paid-up membership minimum of 5000 Fiji dollars, and prohibition of foreign, union, or civil servant funding or membership, only four parties qualified by the deadline of April 14, 2013. (See Political Parties, below.) The government in July hosted a team of election experts from New Zealand, the European Commission, and the Commonwealth Secretariat to advise the Elections Office and claimed that by June 17, 518,148 voters had been registered.

The Commonwealth Heads of Government meeting in November declined to re-admit Fiji until a democratically elected government is installed, whereupon Fiji's foreign minister declared the Commonwealth "irrelevant."

POLITICAL PARTIES

Political party activity was first suspended in October 1987, although most parties remained active in preparation for parliamentary elections, which were ultimately held in May 1992. Formal party activity was again temporarily suspended in the wake of the May 2000 coup, with considerable realignment then occurring in preparation for the August–September 2001 general election. In early 2005, looking toward the general election scheduled for 2006, Prime Minister Qarase stepped up efforts to unite the major ethnic Fijian parties, resulting in formation of the Grand Coalition Initiative Group (GCIG). In the election of May 2006, only 3 of 13 contesting parties won seats.

The coup of December 5, 2006, and imposition by the military of a state of emergency again halted political party activity. Despite the lifting of the state of emergency in March 2007 the SDL and its leader Qarase remained banned. Other parties remained nominally free, but their leaders remained wary of attracting threats and reprisals from the military authorities. An exception was the Fiji Labor Party (FLP), which supported the interim government and whose leaders were rewarded by appointment to government bodies. The Political Parties (Registration, Conduct, Funding, and Disclosures) Decree of January 15, 2013, set down stringent rules for registration for the 2014 election, which were met by only four parties by the April deadline (see below). The interim government in February declared all unregistered parties defunct.

Parties Achieving Registration in 2013 for the 2014 Election:

Fiji Labour Party (FLP). Launched in July 1985 by leaders of the Fiji Trades Union Congress, the FLP presented itself as a "multi-racial political vehicle for all working people," although drawing most of its support from the Indo-Fijian community. It won eight Suva city council seats in November 1985 and subsequently gained three parliamentary seats held by NFP defectors.

Partly to neutralize criticism that an Indo-Fijian might become prime minister, an ethnic Fijian, Dr. Timoci Bavadra, was named to head a FLP-NFP coalition slate, with the NFP's Harish SHARMA as his deputy. Both were forced from office by the Rabuka coup. Bavadra, in ill health, died on November 3, 1989, and the FLP leadership was assumed by his widow, Adi Kuini SPEED. In August 1991 Adi Kuini Speed stepped down and eventually left the party to join the All National Congress (ANC, under FAP, below).

The FLP backed Rabuka for prime minister in June 1992 but withdrew its support of the Rabuka administration in June 1993.

In August 1998 the FLP formed an electoral alliance called the People's Coalition with the FAP and the PANU (see under PANU, below) to promote a multiracial approach to government and to halt the privatization of many public sector posts. In the balloting of May 1999 the FLP obtained a majority of 37 lower house seats, with its leader, Mahendra Chaudhry, serving as prime minister until his ouster after the coup of May 19, 2000.

The FLP went on to finish second in the August–September 2001 election and Chaudhry served as leader of the parliamentary opposition.

In the 2006 legislative poll, the FLP, even though supported in a People's Coalition by the UPP, FAP, and PANU, still finished second to the SDL but some of its members were invited into the cabinet, which precipitated a rift among party leaders. In January 2007, Chaudhry, despite attacks on his leadership from within his party, accepted appointment as finance minister in Bainimarama's interim administration, where he played an active role as civilian spokesperson for the government and defender of current policies while weathering media criticism. He resigned from the government in August 2008 and Commodore Bainimarama assumed his portfolio, whereupon he became a critic of interim government policies, particularly the mishandling of the sugar industry reforms. In July 2010 he was formally charged with tax evasion and on October 1 he was arrested for allegedly breaching the emergency regulations but was subsequently cleared and returned to lead the FPL again. Other leaders including Felix ANTHONY, Boseci BUNE, Krishna DATT, and Atu BAIN left the party and in 2013 gave their support to the Social Democratic Liberal Party (see below).

The FLP regrouped and, claiming 8,172 members, was granted registration on May 3. In April it joined with the NFP and the SODELPA (below) in the United Front for a Democratic Fiji, led by Mick BEDDOES, former leader of the UPP (below).

Leaders: Mahendra Pal CHAUDHRY (Former Prime Minister); Jokapeci KOROI (President); Monica RHAGWAN, Lavenia PADARATH (Executive Members).

National Federation Party (NFP). The NFP was formed in 1963 by A. D. PATEL, Siddiq KOYA, and Jai Ram REDDY as a union of two parties: the Federation, a predominantly ethnic Indian party, and the National Democratic Party, a Fijian party. Most of its support came from the Indo-Fijian community because of its advocacy of the "one man, one vote" principle.

In the elections of 1977 and 1982, the NFP remained in opposition but in 1987, in tandem with the FLP, it won cabinet portfolios. However, its ministers were ousted by the coup of May 14. In May 1989 it entered into a coalition with the FLP (above) under the leadership of the FLP's Adi Kuini Speed, but split in late 1991.

The party's only successful candidate in the 2001 general election was Prem SINGH, who was named leader of the opposition in the House of Representatives; the Supreme Court in August 2002 voided Singh's victory because of electoral irregularities.

At its annual convention in August 2004, the NFP elected a new leadership as part of a restructuring effort. In February 2005 the party's new general secretary noted that in view of the country's shrinking Indo-Fijian population, the NFP should seek to participate in the government rather than remain in opposition.

In 2006 the NFP emerged as the third most popular party, attracting 6.2 percent of the popular vote, but it won no seats. It was excluded from an all-party forum called by Commodore Bainimarama on April 6, 2009.

Nevertheless it successfully claimed 7,385 paid members and qualified for official registration on May 3, 2013. In April its leaders agreed to work with the FLP and the PDP (below) in the United Front for a Democratic Fiji.

Leaders: Raman Pratap SINGH (President), Mohammad RAFIQ (Vice President), Vishwa NADAN (General Secretary), Sanjeev PATEL (Treasurer).

Social Democratic Liberal Party (SODELPA). This is a reincarnation of the **United Fiji Party** (better known as the SDL—*Soqosoqo Duavata ni Lewenivanua*) led by deposed prime minister Laisenia Qarase. The SDL was established in 2001 by Qarase, at that time the caretaker prime minister. The new party attracted members from the principal indigenous formations, including the Fijian Political Party (SVT, below), the Fijian Association Party (FAP, below), and the Christian Democratic Alliance (*Veitokani ni Lewenivanua Vakarisito*—VLV). The latter faded and was deregistered in February 2004.

The SDL emerged from the August–September 2001 balloting with a plurality of 32 seats in the House of Representatives. Having negotiated a coalition arrangement with George Speight's Conservative Alliance Party (MV, below), Qarase formed a new government that also included a representative of the New Labour Unity Party (NLUP).

In 2005 the SDL and three other Fiji nationalist parties formed the so-called Grand Coalition Initiative Group (GCIG), which was committed to the maintenance of a Fiji-dominated government. Only the SDL won seats and its coalition partners remained politically without substantial influence. The SDL party won a majority of 36 seats in May 2006 and formed a government. The interim government from December 2006 banned public assemblies by the SDL and intimidated its leaders, particularly Qarase. The SDL remained hostile toward the interim government, and although its leaders participated in some of the public meetings on the People's Charter, they were excluded by the interim prime minister from an all-party forum on April 6, 2009.

Excluded from political activity for seven years, its leaders in late 2012 changed the SDL party's name to SODELPA, enlisted 8,689 paid-up members, and achieved official registration in April 2013. It attracted several defectors from the FLP (above) who objected to Chaudhry's collaboration with the interim government. In May it agreed to work with the FLP and NFP in the United Front for a Democratic Fiji and with the breakaway Fiji Islands Council of Trade Unions. Its first General Assembly convened on June 19 and elected an interim president and officers, appointed a Management Board and a National Executive Committee, and made plans to contest the 2014 election. Former prime minister Qarase was acknowledged as the party's figurehead leader although he was ineligible for formal office.

Leaders: Ro Teimumu KEPA (Interim President), Silivanusi WAQAUSA (Interim Vice President), Lote YAVUCA (Interim Vice President), Pio TABAIWALU (Interim General Secretary).

People's Democratic Party (PDP). Promoted by Felix Anthony, leader of the Fiji Trades Union Congress, the PDP was established on January 13, 2013, and achieved official registration on May 29. Spokesperson Nirmal SINGH asserted that the party is not sponsored by the union movement but is sympathetic to workers, employees, youth, and the poor. Its leaders refused to join the United Front for a Democratic Fiji but to remain an independent voice critical of the interim government.

Leaders: Adi Sivia QORO (Interim President); Jone BARAVILALA, Vijay SINGH, Sat NARAYAN, Jakob ETIKA (Executive Members).

Parties Contesting the 2006 Election, Now Declared Defunct by the Interim Government

United People's Party (UPP). In an effort to broaden its appeal, the former United General Party (UGP) changed its name in 2003 to the UPP. The UGP, representing "General Electors" (those not belonging to either the ethnic Fijian or Indo-Fijian communities), was formed in September 1998 by merger of the General Voters' Party (GVP) and the smaller General Electors' Party (GEP). In the May 1999 election the UGP won two parliamentary seats. In May 2001 President David PICKERING was succeeded by Mick Beddoes, and in June Pickering joined the NFP (below). Beddoes won the party's only seat at the 2001 general election. In 2002–2004, while the FLP's right to join the government remained in the courts, Beddoes served as leader of the opposition in the House.

Running in tandem with the FLP in 2006, the UPP won two legislative seats in its own right, with Beddoes being redesignated opposition leader in the wake of the Chaudhry tax evasion controversy. Beddoes was consistently critical of the interim government in 2007 and 2008, and he and his party were not invited to the all-party forum convened by Commodore Bainimarama on April 6, 2009.

Leader: Millis (Mick) BEDDOES (Party Leader).

National Alliance Party of Fiji (NAPF). Based on the multiracial model of the defunct AP, the NAPF was launched in early 2005 by veteran political leader Ratu Epeli Ganilau, former chair of the Great Council of Chiefs. Bolstered by a merger with the **Justice and Freedom Party** in April 2006, the NAPF emerged as the fourth most popular party in the 2006 election, with 22,504 votes, but it won no seats. In 2008 it participated in the six-party **People's Movement for Political Reform** and supported the interim prime minister's political initiatives.

Leader: Ratu Epeli GANILAU.

Party of National Unity (PANU). The PANU emerged originally in April 1998 to provide greater legislative representation for Viti Levu's northern province of Ba. For the May 1999 balloting the PANU joined the FLP and the Fijian Association Party (FAP, below) to present coalition candidates, winning four House seats. In April 2001 PANU leader Ponipate Lesavua joined Sitiveni Rabuka of the Fijian Political Party (SVT, below), the FAP's Adi Kuini Speed (the widow of former prime minister Timoci Bavadra, who had been ousted in the coup of May 1987), FLP leader Tupeni Baba, and Mick Beddoes of the UGP in calling for adherence to the rule of law and a commitment to political multiethnicity. Regarded as one of Fiji's "moderate" parties, the PANU failed to retain any House seats in the subsequent national election.

In 2004 the PANU and another Ba party, the Protector of Fiji (*Bai Rei Viti*—BKV), led by Ratu Tevita MOMOEDONU, merged as the People's National Party (PNP), but the merger quickly disintegrated. In early 2006 the BKV and the remnants of the PNP decided to merge into the restored PANU. Among those drawn to the new formation were key members of the Taukei Movement (below), including Minister of Agriculture Apisai TORA, of the former PANU.

The PANU contested the 2006 legislative poll as an ally of the FLP but won no seats. It was a founder of the People's Movement for Political Reform in 2008 and gave its approval to the interim prime minister's proposed reforms.

Leader: Ponipate LESAVUA.

Nationalist *Vanua Tako Lavo* Party (NVTLP). A strongly anti-Indian communal organization, the NVTLP is a descendant of the Fijian Nationalist Party (FNP) launched in 1974. The FNP drew many votes from the AP and contributed to the latter's reversal in the election of 1977. The FNP won no seats in 1982 or 1987.

The FNP was reorganized as the Fijian Nationalist United Front (FNUF) prior to the 1992 balloting. Subsequently, FNUF leader Sakeasi BUTADROKA broke with Brigadier Rabuka and moved the party into opposition, urging the deportation of all Indo-Fijians. The FNUF won five lower house seats in 1992 but lost them in 1994 under the banner of the Fijian-Rotuman Nationalist United Front Party. The NVTLP entered the 1999 election campaign opposing the existing constitution and demanding that Fijian customary law be restored to primacy. It won two seats at the balloting of May 8–15. Butadroka died in December 1999.

A number of Nationalists were directly involved or implicated in the May 2000 coup, including the party's president, Iliesa DUVULOCO and a vice president, Viliame SAVU, both of whom were subsequently sentenced to prison. Duvuloco, having served his sentence, resumed party leadership in 2005.

In the 2001 national election the NVTLP failed to win any House seats. In late 2001 Josaia WAQABACA, the party's general secretary, was charged with conspiring to kidnap Prime Minister Qarase, Commodore Bainimarama, and the attorney general, but was acquitted the following year. In 2006 the party attracted fewer than 3,700 votes. The NVTLP was critical of the December 2006 coup and the interim prime minister, who reciprocated by excluding the NVTLP leaders from an all-party meeting he convened on April 6, 2009. On April 27 Duvuloco and five party members were arrested for distributing leaflets urging President Iloilo to resign and the public to resist Bainimarama's decrees.

Leaders: Iliesa DUVULOCO, Saula TELAWA, Samisoni BOLATAGICI.

Fijian Political Party (*Soqosoqo ni Vakavulewa ni Taukei*—SVT). The SVT was launched by the Great Council of Chiefs in mid-1991 to fill the vacuum created by the demise of the Fijian Association and to appeal to ethnic Fijians. In October Deputy Prime Minister Sitiveni Rabuka won the party presidency, despite not having chiefly status. The party secured pluralities in the election of May 1992 and February 1994, with Rabuka forming governments that included representatives of the General Voters' Party (GVP) on both occasions. In May 1999, running on a multiracial platform with UGP and the NFP, the SVT placed third in the election, winning eight House seats.

In January 2001 the SVT, the former Christian Democratic Alliance (*Veitokani ni Lewenivanua Vakarisito*—VLV), and the Tu'uakitau Cokanauto faction of the FAP announced an alliance, the Combined Fijian Political Parties (CFPP), subsequently called the Fijian Political Parties Forum (FPPF), to represent indigenous Fijians. But having lost the endorsement of the Great Council of Chiefs, the SVT failed to win any seats in the August–September 2001 House election.

In April 2004 Rabuka again floated the concept of an alliance, this time for a "Fijian Multiracial Alliance." Six months later the SVT called for the release of all those convicted in connection with the May 2000 incidents, which earned them the enmity of Commodore Bainimarama. In the 2006 election the SVT garnered only 238 votes. Nevertheless, it was among six parties that formed the People's Movement for Political Reform to support Bainimarama's Forum and Charter initiatives in 2008.

Leaders: Ratu Sitiveni RABUKA (Former Prime Minister), Ema DRUAVESI (Secretary General).

Conservative Alliance Party (*Matanitu Vanua*—MV, or CAMV). Formation of the CAMV was announced in April 2001, and the party was formally launched in mid-June by supporters of coup leader George Speight. It won six seats in the August–September 2001 election (including one by the incarcerated Speight) and then entered into a coalition government with the plurality SDL.

Two other leaders, Rakuita VAKALALABURE and Naiqama LALABALAVU, followed Speight to jail in the mid-1980s, further weakening the party. In February 2006 it was reported that the SDL and CAMV had merged, but elements of the CAMV opposed the merger and vowed to keep the CAMV alive. With its nominal leader George Speight serving a life sentence for treason, the party is barely viable; nevertheless, in 2008 it lent its support to the interim government as part of the People's Movement for Political Reform.

Leaders: George SPEIGHT (Ilikimi NAITINI), Ropate SIVO (Secretary General).

Other Minor Parties:

The **Coalition of Independent Nationals** (COIN), formed originally by six independents to contest the 1999 election and led by Prince Vyas Muni LAKSHMAN; the **Party of the Truth** (POTT), led by Nimilote FIFITA; the **Social Liberal Multi-Cultural Party** (SLMCP), led by Jokentani DELAI; the Fiji Democratic Party (FDP), formed in late 2002 by a group of SVP and FAP dissidents, including former foreign minister Felipe BOLE; the Girmit Heritage Party (GHP), led by Beni SAMI; the Voice of the Rotuman (*Lio 'On Famor Rotuma*—LFR), led by Sakumanu PENE; the General Voters Party (GVP), led by Fred CAINE; the New Nationalist Party, led by Saula Telawa, a splinter of the NVTLP; and the New Labour Unity Party (NLUP).

LEGISLATURE

Under the 1970 Constitution, **Parliament** consisted of an appointed Senate of 22 members and an elected House of Representatives of 22 Fijian, 22 Indian, and 8 "general" members. Both bodies were suspended in the wake of the May 1987 coup. The 1990 constitution provided for a bicameral legislature that was overtly discriminatory in favour of ethnic Fijians, while its 1997 successor, without restoring ethnic parity, made substantial concessions to Indo-Fijian demands. Under pressure from the leader of the December 2006 coup, President Iloilo dissolved Parliament, and it has not reconvened since.

Senate (*Seniti*). The 1990 basic law called for a nonelective upper house of 34 seats, 24 for Fijians nominated by the Great Council of Chiefs, 9 for Indo-Fijians and others, and 1 for inhabitants of Rotuma. Under the 1997 document the chamber's size was reduced to 32, with the president appointing 14 members nominated on a provincial basis, 9 named by the prime minister, 8 designated by the leader of the opposition, and 1 chosen by the Rotuma Council.

The Senate term is concurrent with that of the lower house.

President (at dissolution): Taito WAQAVAKATOGA.

House of Representatives (*Vale*). The 1990 Constitution called for an elective lower house of 70 seats (37 reserved for Melanesians, 27 for Indians, 5 for others, and 1 for the island of Rotuma). In 1997 the size of the House was increased to 71, of which 25 were to be open to all races, with 23 reserved for Melanesians, 19 for Indo-Fijians, 3 for general voters, and 1 for Rotuman Islanders. The House term is five years, subject to early dissolution. At the election of May 6–13, 2006, the Fiji United Party won 36 seats; the Fiji Labour Party, 31; the United People's Party, 2; and independents, 2. Ten other parties contested the election but none won a seat.

Speaker (at dissolution): Ratu Epeli NAILATIKAU.

INTERIM CABINET

[as of November 1, 2013]

Prime Minister (Interim)	Commodore Frank Vorege Bainimarama
Ministers	
Defence, National Security, and Immigration	Joketani Cokanasiga
Education, National Heritage, Culture, and Arts	Filipe Bole
Finance, Strategic Planning, National Development, and Statistics	Commodore Josaia Voreqe Bainimarama
Foreign Affairs and International Co-operation	Ratu Inoke Kubuabola
Health	Dr. Neil Sharma
Industry and Trade	Aiyaz-Sayed-Khaiyum
Information, National Archives, and Library Services of Fiji	Commodore Josaia Voreqe Bainimarama
Lands and Mineral Resources	Commodore Josaia Voreqe Bainimarama
Local Government, Urban Development, Housing, and Environment	Aiyaz Sayed-Khaiyum
Primary Industries	Inia Seruiratu

INTERGOVERNMENTAL REPRESENTATION

Ambassador to the U.S.: Winston THOMPSON.

U.S. Ambassador to Fiji: Frankie Annette REED.

Permanent Representative to the UN: Peter THOMSON.

IGO Memberships (Non-UN): ADB, CWTH (suspended), ICC, NAM, PIF (suspended), WTO.

FINLAND

Republic of Finland
Suomen Tasavalta (Finnish)
Republiken Finland (Swedish)

Political Status: Independent since December 6, 1917; republic established July 17, 1919, under presidential-parliamentary system.

Area: 130,119 sq. mi. (337,009 sq. km).

Population: 5,411,080 (2013E—UN); 5,266,114 (2013E—U.S. Census).

Major Urban Centers (2013E): HELSINKI (604,000), Espoo (257,000), Tampere (217,000), Oulu (191,000).

Official Languages: Finnish, Swedish.

Monetary Unit: Euro (market rate November 1, 2013: 0.74 euro = $1 US).

President: Sauli NIINISTÖ (Kok); elected in second-round balloting on February 5, 2012, and inaugurated for a six-year term on March 1, 2012, succeeding Tarja HALONEN (Finnish Social Democratic Party).

Prime Minister: Jyrki KATAINEN (Kok); approved by the legislature and sworn in on June 22, 2011, as the leader of a six-party coalition government to replace Mari KIVINIEMI (Finish Center), following legislative elections on April 17, 2011.

THE COUNTRY

A land of rivers, lakes, and extensive forests, Finland is, except for Norway, the northernmost country of Europe. More than 93 percent of the population is Finnish-speaking and belongs to the Evangelical Lutheran Church. The once-dominant Swedish minority, now numbering about 7 percent of the total, has shown occasional discontent but enjoys linguistic equality; there also is a small Lapp minority in the north. Women constitute approximately 48 percent of the labor force, concentrated in textile manufacture, clerical work, human services, and the public sector (with women holding 70 percent of all public sector jobs). Female participation in elective bodies is currently around 40 percent. Notably, the new cabinet installed in 2007 included 12 women, or 60 percent total, the highest percentage in the world at the time (there were 9 women in the 2011 cabinet). In addition, there were 86 women elected to the Finnish Parliament in 2011, the largest number ever.

Finland was a founding member of the European Union's (EU) Economic and Monetary Union on January 1, 1999 (for information on the Finnish economy prior to 2008, please see the 2012 *Handbook*). The global financial crisis caused an economic contraction in Finland in 2008–2009. In 2009 Finland officially entered a recession, with GDP declining by 8.2 percent that year. Meanwhile unemployment rose from 6.4 percent in 2008 to 8.2 percent in 2009. In 2010 GDP grew by 3.4 percent, and 2.7 percent the next year. In 2011 inflation increased to 3.3 percent, and unemployment fell slightly to 7.8 percent. The country entered a recession in 2012, as GDP dropped slightly (–0.8 percent), while inflation and unemployment held steady at 3.2 percent and 7.7 percent, respectively. Government debt equaled 3.4 percent of GDP in 2012, slightly above the EU's 3 percent threshold.

GOVERNMENT AND POLITICS

Political background. Finnish independence followed some eight centuries of foreign domination, first by Sweden (until 1809) and subsequently within the prerevolutionary Russian Empire. The nation's formal declaration of independence dates from December 6, 1917, and its republican constitution from July 17, 1919, although peace with Soviet Russia was not formally established until October 14, 1920. Soviet territorial claims led to renewed conflict during World War II, when Finnish troops distinguished themselves both in the so-called Winter War of 1939–1940 and again in the "Continuation War" of 1941–1944. Under the peace treaty signed in Paris in 1947, Finland ceded some 12 percent of its territory to the Soviet Union (the Petsamo and Salla areas in the northeast and the Karelian Isthmus in the southeast) and paid an estimated $570 million in reparations through 1952. A Treaty of Friendship, Cooperation, and Mutual Assistance with the Soviet Union, concluded under Soviet pressure in 1948 and repeatedly renewed, precluded the adoption of an anti-Soviet foreign policy.

Finnish politics from World War II to the late 1980s was marked by the juxtaposition of a remarkably stable presidency under J. K. PAASIKIVI (1946–1956), Urho K. KEKKONEN (1956–1981), and Mauno KOIVISTO (1981–1994) and a volatile parliamentary system that yielded a sequence of short-lived coalition governments based on shifting alliances. Most were center-left administrations in which the Finnish Social Democratic Party (*Suomen Sosiaalidemokraattinen Puolue*—SSDP) played a pivotal role, especially under the premierships of Kalevi SORSA between 1972 and 1987. But in the election of March 15–16, 1987, the conservative National Coalition (*Kansallinen Kokoomus*—Kok) gained nine seats, drawing to within three of the plurality Social Democrats. On April 30, for the first time in 20 years, a Kok leader, Harri HOLKERI, became prime minister, heading a four-party coalition that included the SSDP, the Swedish People's Party (*Ruotsalainen Kansanpuolue/Svenska Folkpartiet*—RKP/SFP), and the Finnish Rural Party (*Suomen Maaseudun Puolue*—SMP), the last eventually withdrawing in August 1990. In second-round electoral college balloting on February 15, 1988, President Koivisto (SSDP) easily won election to a second six-year term.

In the face of surging unemployment, high interest rates, and a drastically weakened GDP, both the Kok and the SSDP fared poorly at the parliamentary poll of March 17, 1991. The opposition Finnish Center (*Suomen Keskusta–Finlands Centern*—Kesk), led by Esko AHO, emerged as the core of a new center-right coalition that included the Kok, the RKP/SFP, and the Finnish Christian Union (*Suomen Kristillinen Liitto*—SKL). The balloting produced a record number of legislative turnovers, approximately two-thirds of the incumbents being denied reelection.

Following the 1991 election, Prime Minister Aho announced a drastic stabilization program to alleviate the country's worst recession since World War II. In November, with the economy continuing to worsen, the markka was devalued by 12.3 percent, while labor agreed to a wage freeze until 1993. In an effort to avoid further devaluation, the government in April 1992 announced public sector cuts equivalent to approximately 2 percent of GDP. Another devaluation, in the form of a decision to let the markka float vis-à-vis other European currencies, was nonetheless ordered in September.

Unexpectedly selected as the SSDP candidate over former premier Sorsa, career diplomat Martti AHTISAARI comfortably won presidential elections held in two rounds on January 16 and February 6, 1994. In the runoff balloting, he took 53.9 percent of the vote, against 46.1 percent for Defense Minister Elisabeth REHN of the RKP/SFP.

Having agreed with Brussels in March 1994 on terms for entry into the European Union (EU, formerly the European Community—EC), Finland became the first of the three Scandinavian aspirants to conduct a referendum on the issue. Most of the political establishment favored entry, and Prime Minister Aho had deflected opposition from the farming constituency of his own Kesk party by appointing a vocal EU critic, Heikki HAAVISTO, as foreign minister in charge of the entry negotiations. The decision of the small anti-EU SKL in June to leave the coalition proved to be only a minor setback. Held on October 16, the referendum yielded a 53 to 47 percent margin in favor of entry, the majority "yes" vote of urban southern areas outweighing the mainly "no" verdict of the rural north.

Finland joined the EU on January 1, 1995. Meanwhile, the Aho government faced a general election amid continuing economic adversity, a modest upturn in 1994 not having reduced unemployment appreciably (unemployment peaked at 22 percent). The result of the balloting on March 19 was a swing to the left, the Social Democrats achieving their highest postwar vote share and the Left-Wing Alliance (*Vasemmistoliitto*—Vas) also gaining ground. A month later SSDP leader Paavo LIPPONEN formed an ideologically diverse ("rainbow") coalition government that included the RKP/SFP, Kok, the Vas, and the Green League.

The electoral swing to the left in 1995 was attributed to public disenchantment with the harsh economic consequences of the previous government's free-market, deregulatory policies, which were seen as having accentuated the damaging effects of international economic recession. There was nevertheless consensus within the new coalition that the austerity program instituted by the previous government should be continued, albeit with greater emphasis on job creation.

The SSDP retained its plurality in the legislative balloting of March 21, 1999, although its seat total declined from 63 to 51. The Kok finished second with 48 seats, followed by the Kesk, whose total jumped from 39 in 1995 to 46. After several weeks of negotiations, the five parties of the previous coalition agreed to form a new government, which was installed on April 15 under Lipponen's continued leadership.

Foreign Minister Tarja HALONEN of the SSDP led seven candidates in first-round presidential balloting on January 16, 2000, with 40 percent of the vote. She defeated Aho, 51.6 to 48.4 percent, in the runoff poll on February 6 and was inaugurated as Finland's first female president on March 1.

The 2003 Iraq War influenced Finnish domestic and foreign policy. In early 2003 President Halonen and Prime Minister Lipponen called for Iraqi compliance with the UN Security Council resolutions, although UN weapons inspectors had not found any clear evidence justifying an attack against Iraq. During the March 2003 elections Kesk leader Anneli JÄÄTTEENMÄKI allegedly leaked foreign ministry documents to the news media that seemed to indicate that Prime Minister Lipponen would ultimately support the U.S. coalition against Iraq. In the March 16, 2003, parliamentary elections, the Kesk captured 55 seats and formed a three-party coalition government on April 15 with the former ruling SSDP (53 seats) and the RKP/SFP (8 seats) headed by the Kesk's Jäätteenmäki. With the appointment of Jäätteenmäki, Finland became the only country in Europe with both a female president and prime minister. However, Jäätteenmäki resigned on June 18 following a major dispute over the aforementioned leak of secret documents. She was succeeded on June 24 by Matti VANHANEN of the Kesk. Jäätteenmäki apologized for the release of the papers but denied they were secret. In March 2004 she was acquitted on all charges related to the matter.

President Halonen won reelection in January 2006, narrowly defeating Sauli NIINISTÖ, 51.8 to 48.2 percent, in the second round of balloting. The election largely focused on the future direction of Finland's relationship with Europe, the North Atlantic Treaty Organization (NATO), and the effects of globalization.

The Kesk narrowly retained a plurality in the March 18, 2007, legislative election, securing 51 seats, compared to 50 for Kok and 45 for the SSDP. In view of the better than expected showing by the conservative parties, the SSDP was dropped from the four-party (Kesk, Kok, RKP/SFP, and Green League) coalition installed under Vanhanen's continued premiership on April 19.

In 2008 the new center-right coalition government quickly announced an ambitious job creation program that called for tax cuts of $3.5 billion, centered on a reduction of the value-added tax from 17 percent to 12 percent. At the same time, increases in taxes on alcohol, tobacco, and fuel were announced, and a nationwide smoking ban in public places was enacted. The ruling coalition also began a multiyear program to increase the pay of health and social workers, along with increased spending on social services. The government also continued its privatization program, selling its shares in the Kemira fertilizer company for $890 million. By 2008, the government still had investments of more than $38 billion in 19 Finnish firms that employed approximately 200,000 people.

In municipal elections in September 2008, the Kok secured the highest number of votes, followed by the SDP and the Kesk, which both saw their vote totals decline from 2004. The True Finn Party (*Perussuomalaiset*—PS), which placed fifth in the polling, gained the largest percentage of votes with an increase of 4.5 percent. The elections were marred by an e-voting pilot program that had numerous problems, resulting in the loss of approximately 2 percent of the votes. The Finnish Supreme Court later annulled the results of the districts that used e-voting machines and ordered a new round of balloting.

In February 2009 the government announced a €2 billion stimulus program, equal to 1.7 percent of GDP, in an effort to counter the nation's recession. Additional spending was directed to construction projects and worker retraining. In late 2009 allegations of illicit fundraising eroded public support for the Kesk. In December Vanhanen announced his intention to resign as prime minister and Kesk leader in light of the fundraising investigation and subsequent revelations about his personal life that emerged in a book by a former girlfriend. Kiviniemi, who was not implicated in the Kesk allegations, was elected to succeed Vanhanen in June 2010. She became Finland's second female prime minister and made only minor changes to the previous cabinet. Meanwhile, in May the government approved the construction of two new nuclear power plants, in a compromise with the Green Party, which opposed any new construction.

In legislative elections on April 17, 2011, Kok placed first, securing 44 seats, followed by the SSDP with 42. The PS was placed third with 39, its greatest electoral showing to date. On June 22 Jyrki KATAINEN of the Kok was elected prime minister of a six-party coalition government (see Current issues, below).

Sauli NIINISTRÖ (Kok) was elected president in the second round of balloting on February 5, 2012 (see Current issues, below). Niiniströ's victory marked the first time in 30 years that Kok won the presidency.

Constitution and government. The constitution of 1919 provided for a parliamentary system in combination with a strong presidency, which in practice has tended to grow even stronger because of the characteristic division of the legislature (*Eduskunta/Riksdagen*) among a large number of competing parties. The president is directly elected (since 1994) for a six-year term in two rounds of voting if no candidate obtains an absolute majority in the first. The head of state is directly responsible for foreign affairs and, until recently, shared domestic responsibilities with the prime minister and the cabinet. The *Eduskunta,* a unicameral body of 200 members, is elected by proportional representation for a four-year term, subject to dissolution by the president. The judicial system includes a Supreme Court, a Supreme Administrative Court, courts of appeal, and district and municipal courts.

Administratively, Finland is divided into 12 provinces (*läänit*), which are subdivided into 415 municipalities and rural communes. The 11 mainland provinces are headed by presidentially appointed governors, while the Swedish-speaking island province of Åland enjoys domestic autonomy (see Related Territory, below).

After decades of piecemeal reform, the March 1, 2000, constitution strengthened the powers of Parliament at the expense of the presidency by, among other things, limiting the president's authority in domestic matters (e.g., subsequent prime minister-designates were named by the Parliament, not the president).

Finland enjoys complete freedom of the press; broadcasting is largely over government-controlled facilities. In 2013 Finland topped the Reporters Without Borders Index of Press Freedom for the third year in a row.

Foreign relations. Proximity to the Soviet Union was the decisive factor in the shaping of post–World War II Finnish foreign policy, although Helsinki followed a course of strict neutrality. Finland actively and independently participated in such multilateral organizations as the United Nations (UN), the Nordic Council, and the Organization for Economic Cooperation and Development. Finland also was a leading proponent of the Conference on (later Organization for) Security and Cooperation in Europe (CSCE/OSCE), in recognition of which the landmark CSCE Final Act of 1975 was concluded in Helsinki.

Joining the European Free Trade Association (EFTA) at its inception in 1960 as an associate member, Finland, on a similar basis, became in 1973 the first free-market economy to be linked to the Soviet bloc's Council for Mutual Economic Assistance. In 1985 it became a full member of EFTA. Trade with the Soviet Union declined sharply after 1988, with the country moving to adopt EC industrial standards to protect its access to the EC's impending unified market. On January 20, 1992, the 1948 treaty was formally superseded by a new Russo-Finnish mutual cooperation pact, and on March 18 Finland applied for EC membership. As a prelude to EC entry, Finland became a signatory on May 2 of the European Economic Area treaty between the EC and EFTA countries. Earlier in March it had become a founding member of the Council of the Baltic Sea States.

Negotiations on EC/EU membership were successfully completed in March 1994, entry being duly accomplished January 1, 1995. In April 1994 Finland became linked to NATO by joining the alliance's Partnership for Peace program.

Finland joined the International Reconstruction Fund Facility for Iraq and pledged $6.2 million for reconstruction in 2004. While the government rejected U.S. requests for Finnish peacekeeping forces in Iraq, Helsinki donated €2 million to help organize Iraq's 2005 parliamentary election.

A key factor in the Finnish vote to enter the EU was a belief that membership would afford protection against a revival of Russian imperialism. Much discussion had been generated by the strong showing of Vladimir Zhirinovsky's ultra-nationalist Liberal Democrats in the 1993 Russian election and of Zhirinovsky's declared aim of restoring Finland to the Russian empire. The subsequent course of Moscow's external policy provided little reassurance for the Finns. Thus Finland sought to maintain friendly relations with Moscow by signing six economic and military cooperation accords with Russia during a visit to Helsinki by Prime Minister Viktor Chernomyrdin in May 1996. Relations with Russia subsequently continued to improve as President Halonen and Russian president Vladimir Putin forged a strong working relationship; this yielded agreements in 2006 on immigration along their common border and a Russian pledge to pay off its outstanding debt, originating back in the Soviet era.

In September 2007 Finland and Vietnam signed an accord in which the Finnish government agreed to provide $26.7 million in technical and logistical support for integration of minority groups in Vietnam. Finland hosted peace talks between rival Iraqi groups in an attempt to end sectarian violence in the same month.

Finland agreed to contribute troops to the EU-led peacekeeping operation in the Central African Republic in January 2008. On March

7, Finland recognized Kosovo's independence, attracting opposition from Serbia's ally Russia. The Parliament also approved the participation of Finnish troops in NATO's rapid reaction force in March.

The Parliament approved the EU's Lisbon Treaty on a vote of 151 in favor and 27 opposed in June 2008. Finland also announced support for Turkish membership in the EU. In October former president Ahtisaari received a Nobel Peace Prize for his role in mediating conflicts around the globe.

Finland agreed in 2009 to allow the construction of the Nord Stream gas pipeline through its territorial waters. The pipeline was to run from Russia to Germany.

In April 2010 Finland announced that it would send additional military forces to Afghanistan to help train local security forces. There were 100 Finnish troops in Afghanistan by 2011. Also in April, Finland pledged more than €18 million in aid for reconstruction projects in Haiti after that country's devastating earthquake (see entry on Haiti). In May Finland established diplomatic relations with the Federated States of Micronesia. That month the government announced that it would lend Greece €1.6 billion as part of an EU-sponsored aid package (see entry on Greece).

In April 2011 Finland, Norway, and Russia launched a trilateral program to study and mitigate the dangers of a potential nuclear accident or radioactive leak on the Arctic Circle. In May Finland joined the seven other members of the Arctic Council in an agreement to establish a secretariat and an annual budget for the group. Also in May the Finnish legislature approved an EU bailout package for Portugal, ending the stalemate among EU members over aid to the troubled country (see entry on Portugal). Meanwhile, in November, Finland announced it would reduce its peacekeeping force in Afghanistan. However, it pledged to increase its aid to the country to €20 million per year beginning in 2014.

Finland provided ten troops for the European Union Training Mission to Mali in April 2013.

Current issues. In legislative elections in April 2011, the Kok won a plurality of seats in the assembly, while Kesk dropped from first place to fourth. Kok leader Jyrki Katainen was appointed prime minister, but negotiations over a coalition government stalled over differences in economic policy. On June 17 an agreement was reached on a six-party "rainbow" coalition government that included the Kok, SSDP, Vas, Green League, and the RKP/SFP. The government was approved on June 22. In one of its first acts, the new government announced tax increases on capital gains and some products, including fuel, alcohol, and tobacco. It sought to stem the rising the debt ratio by 2015, through spending cuts and tax hikes worth €5 billion.

With a rapidly aging population, the government has moved to trim health care costs by consolidating 320 municipal units into fewer than 200 and by creating 34 social services and health care regions. The Social Services and Healthcare Act was conceived to create economies of scale and uniform health services. But Kesk and PS oppose the Act, believing it will reduce rural medical access.

The government tightened gun control laws with new regulations introduced in June 2011. The minimum age of gun ownership was raised from 15 years with adult supervision to 20, and potential owners must prove their involvement in hunting or shooting as a sport. The change came after two high-profile school shootings in 2007 and 2008 (for details, see the 2013 *Handbook*). Finland had the highest rate of gun ownership in Western Europe and fourth highest in the world.

In the first round of presidential balloting on January 22, 2012, Niiniströ of the Kok secured 36.9 percent of the vote and Pekka HAAVISTO of the Green League received 18.8 percent to advance to run-off polling, beating six other candidates. In the second round of voting, Niiniströ won with 62.6 percent of the vote to Haavisto's 37.4 percent in a campaign that revolved around economic issues. For the first time in Finland's history, both the prime minister and president were from the same party.

However, the growing support for the Euroskeptic True Finns confirmed that voters are tiring of tightening their own belts while bailing out other EU members. Consequently, in February 2012 Finland made the unprecedented request for collateral before agreeing to a second economic bailout package for Greece. Athens ultimately agreed to fund a €880 million escrow account to back the loan. A similar deal was made for Finland's €2 billion contribution to the Spanish bank rescue in July.

Kok prevailed in the October 28 municipal elections, taking the largest share of votes at 21.9 percent. Combined, the parties of the governing coalition secured 63.2 percent, while the populist True Finns received 12.3 percent—higher than its 5.3 percent in the 2008 local elections, but less than its 19.1 percent tally in the 2011 parliamentary race.

The parliament ratified the EU fiscal compact on December 21, 2012, with a vote of 139–38.

Finland's lackluster economy led the government in March 2013 to abandon its efforts to reduce the government deficit to 1 percent of GDP (well below the EU's 3 percent ceiling) and find ways to stimulate growth. Following Kok's lead, the government slashed the corporate tax rate from 24.5 percent to 20 percent, despite objections by the SSDP, and introduced other budgetary adjustments (such as higher consumption taxes on alcohol, tobacco, candy, soda, and electricity) meant to generate €600 million. Meanwhile, unemployment hit 9 percent in March.

As promised in the 2011 coalition agreement, Deputy Prime Minister Jutta JUPILAINEN reshuffled the SSDP cabinet seats in May 2013, bringing in two new female ministers, in a bid to attract female voters. Mid-way through this parliament's mandate, polls indicated that Kesk and its new leader, Juha SIPILA, had overtaken Kok in popularity. Kok's reputation suffered when a loophole favoring the wealthy was discovered in the tax reform package and also because of the lack of progress on health care reform. The European Commission has recommended that Finland raise its retirement age to cut spending, but such a move would have significant consequences for the governing coalition's fate in the 2015 parliamentary elections.

POLITICAL PARTIES

Finland's multiparty system, based on proportional representation, typically prevents any single party from gaining a parliamentary majority. The traditional classification of parties as "socialist" and "nonsocialist" became less relevant in the 1980s, as policy differences eroded and coalitions were formed across what remained of the right-left ideological divide.

Government Parties:

National Coalition Party (*Kansallinen Kokoomus*—KK or Kok). A conservative party formed in 1918, the Kok is the prime representative for private enterprise and the business community as well as for landowners. In the March 1979 general election, it displaced the SKDL (see Vas, below) as the second-largest parliamentary party. Retaining this position in 1983 and 1987, the Kok's success in the latter election enabled it to return to government (after 21 years in the opposition) as head of a coalition government. The party dropped to third place in 1991, when its representation plummeted from 53 to 40 seats and it became a junior coalition partner. It had a marginal decline to 17.9 percent in the 1995 balloting. However, in 1999 the Kok made the biggest gain of any of the 13 parties by picking up 7 additional seats. Riitta UOSUKAINEN, speaker of the Parliament, gained 12.8 percent of the vote in the first round of the 2000 presidential balloting.

In the March 2003 parliamentary elections the Kok won 40 seats. The Kok favored enlargement of the EU while simultaneously calling for clarifying and strengthening the rules that govern that institution. Sauli Niinistö continued these themes in his unsuccessful 2006 presidential bid. Embracing globalization and free trade, Niinistö called for a greater role for Finland in both European and transatlantic affairs.

In the 2007 legislative elections the Kok secured 50 seats and became the second largest party in Parliament. Niinistö was subsequently elected speaker of Parliament. The Kok placed first in the 2008 municipal balloting and won 23.5 percent of the vote and elected 2,021 councilors. The Kok also came in first in the June 2009 balloting for the EU parliament with 23.2 percent and 3 seats. The Kok became the largest party in the legislature following the 2011 elections, where it won 44 seats. Party leader Jyrki Katainen was subsequently appointed prime minister of a coalition government. Niinistö was elected president in February 2012.

Leaders: Sauli NIINISTRÖ (President of the Republic); Jyrki KATAINEN (Prime Minister and Chair); Janne SANKO, Anne-Mari VIROLAINEN, Henna VIRKKUNEN (Vice Chairs); Petteri ORPO (Chair of Parliamentary Group); Taru TUJUNEN (Secretary General).

Finnish Social Democratic Party (*Suomen Sosiaalidemokraattinen Puolue*—SSDP). The SSDP was formed in 1899 as the Finnish Labor Party. It is supported mainly by skilled laborers and lower-class, white-collar workers, with additional support from small farmers and professionals. It was the largest party in almost every legislature since 1907, one of the most conspicuous exceptions being in 1991, when, running second to the Center Party (*Keskustapuolue*), its parliamentary representation dropped from 56 to 48 seats. Having been in office continuously since 1966, the party went into opposition in 1991. Paavo Lipponen led the party to a major victory (in Finnish terms) in the 1995 elections, the SSDP vote share increasing by over 6 points to 28.3 percent. However, the SSDP declined to 51 seats on a vote share of 22.9 percent in 1999.

After Martti Ahtisaari decided not to run in the May 1999 primary for the party's 2000 presidential nomination, the SSDP elected Foreign Minister Tarja Halonen as its candidate. As is the custom for Finnish presidents, Halonen resigned from the party following her election in order to serve in a nonpartisan capacity. In the March 2003 parliamentary elections, the SSDP held onto its 53 seats but was unable to maintain its majority position in the coalition government. Lipponen stepped down as prime minister and assumed the role of the speaker of Parliament.

President Halonen stood for reelection in January 2006 and won after the second round of voting. Support from the labor unions played a critical role in her victory. Party chair Paavo LIPPON announced in March 2006 that he would resign his position after holding the post for more than 12 years. In June 2006 former party secretary Eero HEINALUOMA was elected chair.

The SSDP suffered its worst electoral defeat since 1962 in the 2007 legislative balloting, falling to the third largest parliamentary group, and became part of the opposition. In June 2008 a party conference elected Jutta Urpilainen chair of the SSDP. Support for the SSDP also declined in the October municipal elections, where its vote share declined by 2.9 percent. In voting for the EU parliament in June 2009, the SSDP received 17.5 percent of the vote and two seats.

In the 2011 parliamentary balloting, the SSDP placed second and secured 42 seats. It joined the Kok government, and Urpilainen was appointed deputy prime minister. Paavo LIPPONEN, the 2012 SSDP presidential candidate, polled fifth with 6.7 percent of the vote. The SSDP youth wing won a victory when 25-year-old Eero Vainio was elected vice chair at the May 2012 party congress.

Leaders: Jutta URPILAINEN (Deputy Prime Minister and Chair); Reijo PAANANEN (General Secretary); Krista KIURU, Antti LINDTMAN, Eero VAINIO (Vice Chairs).

Left-Wing Alliance (*Vasemmistoliitto*—VL or Vas). Vas was launched in April 1990 during a congress in Helsinki. Following the congress, the Communist Party of Finland (*Suomen Kommunistinen Puolue*—SKP) and its electoral affiliate, the Finnish People's Democratic League (*Suomen Kansan Demokraattinen Liitto*—SKDL), voted to disband. (The SKP reorganized in 1994; see SKP, below.)

The SKDL front had been created in 1944 by the pro-Soviet SKP (founded in 1918) and had established a sizable electoral constituency, winning a narrow plurality in 1958 and participating in various center-left coalitions until 1982. Meanwhile, in 1969 the SKP had split into majority revisionist and minority Stalinist wings, the latter being formally ousted in 1984. In 1986 the SKP launched its own Democratic Alternative front, which did little more than weaken the SKDL. The alliance and adoption of a left-socialist and anti-EC/EU platform at the 1990 congress healed most of these old rifts, with Vas advancing to 11.2 percent of the vote in 1995 and joining a coalition government headed by the Social Democrats. Vas won 20 seats in the 1999 poll, down 2 from 1995.

Vas gained an additional seat in the 2003 parliamentary elections to reach a total of 19 seats. Reacting against the economic pressures associated with globalization and the free movement of capital, Vas defined its role as a defender of Finnish labor and agriculture.

In May 2006 Vas elected Martti KORHONEN as party chair. The alliance secured 17 seats in the 2007 election. In the local elections the following year, Vas secured 833 council seats. In the EU parliamentary elections in 2009, Vas received 5.9 percent of the vote but failed to gain any seats. Also, in June Paavo Arhinmäki was elected party leader. In the 2011 balloting Vas secured 14 seats and subsequently joined the Kok-led governing coalition. Arhinmäki was the Vas 2012 presidential candidate. He was sixth in the election with 5.5 percent of the vote.

Leaders: Paavo ARHINMÄKI (Minister of Culture and Sport, Chair, and 2012 presidential candidate); Aino-Kaisa PEKONEN, Sari MOISANEN, Kalle HYÖTYNEN (Vice Chairs); Marko VARAJÄRVI (Party Secretary).

Green League (*Vihreä Liitto*—VL or Vihr). The Vihr was launched in 1988 as an unstructured alliance of several mainstream environmental organizations, including the **Green Parliamentary Group** (*Vihreä Eduskuntaryhmä*), which had won 2 seats in 1983, 4 in 1987, and 10 in 1991. The Vihr fell back to 9 seats in 1995 (but nevertheless entered government for the first time) before rebounding to 11 seats in 1999. Heidi HAUTALA, a member of Parliament, served as the Vihr presidential candidate in 2000, collecting 3.3 percent of the first-round votes. Vihr earned its best ever result in the March 2003 parliamentary elections, increasing its number of seats from 11 to 14.

In the 2007 legislative balloting the Vihr gained 15 seats and subsequently joined the Kesk-led coalition government. Vihr gained 370 seats on municipal councils in the 2008 local elections. In June 2009 the Vihr received 12.4 percent of the vote in elections for the EU parliament and secured 2 seats.

Ville Niinistö was elected party chair in 2011. In that year's national elections, the Vihr secured 10 seats and joined the subsequent Kok-led government. The party's 2012 presidential contender Pekka HAAVISTO was the country's first openly gay candidate. Haavisto placed second in runoff balloting on February 5.

Leaders: Ville NIINISTÖ (Minister of the Environment and Chair); Timo JUURIKKALA, Krista MIKKONEN (Deputy Chairs); Lasse MIETTINEN (Secretary); Pekka HAAVISTO (2012 presidential candidate).

Swedish People's Party (*Ruotsalainen Kansanpuolue/Svenska Folkpartiet*—RKP/SFP). Liberal in outlook, the SFP has represented the political and social interests of the Swedish-speaking population since 1906. Consistently taking 5–6 percent of the overall vote and with strong indirect support in the predominantly Swedish Åland Islands (see Related Territory, below), it has participated in a variety of postwar coalitions. In the 1994 presidential balloting its candidate, Elisabeth Rehn, was the surprise runner-up in the first round but lost in the runoff to Ahtisaari. The RKP/SFP won 12 seats in the 1995 and 1999 legislative polls, while Rehn declined to 7.9 percent of the vote in the first-round presidential balloting in 2000. The RKP/SFP suffered a serious setback in the March 2003 parliamentary elections by retaining only 7 of its 10 seats. In June 2006 Stefan Wallin was elected party chair. In the 2007 elections the party secured 9 seats and reentered the governing coalition after securing the support of the lone representative of the Åland Islands, a member of the independent voters' bloc, the **Bourgeois Alliance** (*Borgerlig Allians*).

In the 2008 municipal balloting, the RKP/SFP secured 510 seats, maintaining majorities in ethnically Swedish areas. In the June 2009 EU parliamentary balloting, it gained 6.1 percent of the vote and 1 seat. The party maintained its 9 seats in the 2011 legislative balloting and joined the Kok coalition government. The party's 2012 presidential candidate, Eva BIAUDET, placed seventh in the balloting with 2.7 percent of the vote. In June Carl HAGLUND was elected chair of the party, succeeding Stefan WALLIN. In July Haglund also replaced Wallin as minister of defense.

Leaders: Carl HAGLUND (Chair); Anna-Maja HENRIKSSON, Päivi STORGÅRD, Ulla ACHRÉN (Deputy Chairs); Johan JOHANNSON (Secretary General); Eva BIAUDET (2012 presidential candidate).

Christian Democrats in Finland (*Suomen Kristillisdemokraatit*—KD). The KD adopted its present name at a May 2001 party conference, having previously been called the Finnish Christian Union (*Suomen Kristillinen Liitto*—SKL). The SKL was formed in 1958 to advance Christian ideals in public life. It won 8 legislative seats in 1991 and joined a center-headed coalition before withdrawing in 1994 because of its opposition to EU accession. It lost 1 of its seats on a 3 percent vote share in 1995 and won 10 seats in 1999. Emphasizing the need to reform the Finnish economy to be more socially and ecologically responsible, the KD suffered a setback in the March 2003 parliamentary elections, losing 3 of its 7 seats. For the 2007 poll the KD emphasized increased employment, enhancement of family life, and guaranteed access to basic public services for all of the population, and it won 7 seats. In the 2008 balloting the KD gained 351 seats on the municipal councils. It secured 14 percent of the vote and 2 seats in the 2009 EU parliamentary voting in an alliance with the True Finn Party (see below). In the 2011 national elections, the KD won 6 seats. It joined the Kok-led government in June, and party leader Paivi Räsänen was appointed interior minister. Party secretary Sari ESSAYAH placed eighth in presidential balloting in 2012 with 2.5 percent of the vote.

Leaders: Paivi RÄSÄNEN (Minister of the Interior and Chair); Tuevo RIIKONEN, Sauli AHVENJÄRVI, Sari MÄKIMATTILA (Vice Chairs); Asmo MAANSELKÄ (Secretary General).

Other Parliamentary Parties:

True Finn Party (*Perussuomalaiset*—PS). Formerly known as the Finnish Rural Party (*Suomen Maaseudun Puolue*—SMP), the PS has roots that extend back to a small Poujadist faction—a conservative reactionary movement seeking to protect small business—that broke from the Agrarian Union in 1956. The SMP made substantial gains in the 1983 election, winning 17 seats and subsequently joining the government coalition; its representation fell to 9 seats in 1987, and it was awarded only one cabinet post as a member of the Holkeri coalition. It withdrew from the coalition in August 1990, slipped to 7 seats in 1991, and, having opposed EU membership, retained only 1 seat in 1995. The renamed grouping won 1 seat in 1999. During the March 2003 election, the PS adopted a platform that mixed socialism with a hard-line, right-wing populist stance that emphasized low taxes, encouraged small businesses, and advocated relief for personal debt. Its resurgence as an alternative party has been in part credited to the charismatic personality of its leader, Timo Soini.

The party gained 2 additional seats in the 2007 legislative elections to bring its representation to 5. It also increased its representation in the 2008 local elections, securing 443 council seats, up from 106 in 2004. The PS ran with the KD in an electoral alliance in the 2009 EU elections, securing 2 seats.

The PS was placed third with 19 percent of the vote in the 2011 parliamentary balloting and secured 39 seats. The election marked the emergence of the party as a major force in Finnish politics. The PS refused to participate in the Kok-led government because of opposition to EU economic bailout packages. Soini placed fourth in the 2012 presidential balloting with 9.4 percent of the vote. The party received 12.3 percent of the vote in the October 2012 municipal elections. Looking ahead to the 2015 legislative race, members elected a new, female party secretary, Riikka Slunga-Poutsalo, and scaled back its anti-EU, anti-immigration rhetoric.

Leaders: Timo SOINI (Chair and 2003 and 2012 presidential candidate); Hanna MÄNTYLA, Juho EEROLA, Reijo OJENNUS (Vice Chairs); Riikka SLUNGA-POUTSALO (Secretary).

Finnish Center (*Suomen Keskusta–Finlands Centern*—Kesk). The group that was formed in 1906 as the Agrarian Union (*Maalaisliitto*) and renamed the Center Party (*Keskustapuolue*) in 1965 has traditionally represented rural interests, particularly those of the small farmers. Because of major population shifts within the country, it now draws additional support from urban areas. The party surged from 40 parliamentary seats in 1987 to a plurality of 55 in 1991, with the 37-year-old Esko AHO becoming the youngest prime minister in Finnish history and also, amid economic recession, the most unpopular by 1994. The party slumped to 44 seats in the 1995 balloting, after which it went into the opposition. It secured 48 seats in 1999.

Aho also served as the Kesk standard bearer in the 2000 presidential campaign, finishing second with 34.4 percent in the first-round voting and nearly defeating the SSDP's Tarja Halonen in the second round on the strength of a last-minute popularity surge based in part on his opposition to EU sanctions against Austria. The Kesk continued to gain strength and earned 55 seats in the 2003 elections.

Prime Minister Vanhanen opted to run for the January 2006 presidential elections and finished third in the first round of voting with 18.6 percent of the vote. He aggressively integrated Finland into the European and global economy while adopting a more moderate position on social issues.

In the March 2007 elections, the Kesk lost 4 seats but remained the largest single party in the legislature with 51. In the 2008 municipal balloting, Kesk won 20.1 percent of the vote. In the June 2009 EU parliamentary elections, the Kesk secured 19 percent of the vote and 3 seats. In December Vanhanen announced that he would resign as party leader and prime minister at the Kesk conference in June 2010. Mari Kiviniemi was elected to replace him, defeating Mauri PEKKARINEN at a party congress. The Kesk lost 16 seats in the 2011 parliamentary elections and placed fourth in the balloting. Kesk presidential candidate Paavo VÄYRYNEN was third in the 2012 balloting with 17.5 percent of the vote. Following their poor showing, the party selected a new leadership team in June 2012.

Leaders: Juha SIPILÄ (Chair); Annika SAARIKKO, Riikka PAKARINEN, Juha REHULA (Vice Chairs); Timo LAANINEN (Secretary); Mari KIVINIEMI (Former Prime Minister).

Other Parties Contesting the 2011 Legislative Election:

Communist Party of Finland (*Suomen Kommunistinen Puolue*—SKP). A descendant of the original SKP (see Vas, above), the current SKP emerged at a congress in 1994 held by communists wishing to maintain a separate identity outside Vas. The reforged grouping opposed many policies of the subsequent rainbow government coalition and formally registered as a party in February 1997. The SKP secured only 0.8 percent of the vote in the 1999 legislative poll and also failed to capture any seats in the 2003, 2007, or 2011 parliamentary elections. The SKP did gain nine council seats in the 2008 local elections.

Leaders: Juha-Pekka VÄISÄNEN (Chair); Emmi TUOMI, Pauli SCHADRIN (Vice Chairs); Heikki HETOHARJU (General Secretary).

Communist Workers' Party (*Kommunistinen Tyoväenpuolue*—KTP). The KTP was launched in May 1988 by a group of former Democratic Alternative Stalinists. The party contested the 1991, 1995, 1999, and 2003 elections under the rubric "For Peace and Socialism," winning less than 0.1 percent of the vote in 2003, 2007, and 2011. It did not secure any seats in the 2008 municipal elections.

Leaders: Hannu HARJU (Chair), Hannu TUOMINEN (General Secretary).

Pirate Party (*Piraattipuolue*). The Pirate Party was formed by Pasi Palmulehto in August 2009 to advocate for the removal of restrictions on Internet downloading and copyright reforms. It received 0.5 percent of the vote in the 2011 parliamentary elections.

Leaders: Harri KIVISTÖ (Chair), Pasi PALMULEHTO, Ahto APAJALAHTI, Lasse KÄRKKÄINEN (Vice Chairs).

Other parties contesting the 2011 election included (all received less than 1 percent of the vote) the following: the **Finnish Worker's Party** (*Suomen Työväenpuolue*—STP), led by Juhani TANSKI; **For the Poor** (*Köyhien Asialla*—Köyh), led by Terttu SAVOLA; **Change 2011** (*Muutos 2011*—M11), led by Jiri KERONEN; and the **Freedom Party** (*Vapauspuolue Suomen Tulevaisuus*—VP). The **Senior Citizen Party** (*Suomen Senioripuolue*—SSP) merged with the **Independence Party** (*Itsenäisyyspuolue*—IP), led by Antti PESONEN, in 2012.

For information on the **Liberals** (*Liberaalit*), see the 2009 *Handbook.* For information on the **Finnish Islamic Party** (*Soumen Islamilainen Poulue*—SIP), the **Finnish Patriotic Movement,** and the **Finnish People's Blue-Whites,** see the 2011 *Handbook.*

LEGISLATURE

The **Parliament** (*Eduskunta/Riksdagen*) is a unicameral body of 200 members elected by universal suffrage on the basis of proportional representation in 15 districts. Its term is four years, although the president may dissolve the legislature and order a new election at any time. Following the election of April 17, 2011, the seat distribution was as follows: National Coalition Party, 44; Finnish Social Democratic Party, 42; True Finn Party, 39; Finnish Center, 35; Left-Wing Alliance, 14; Green League, 10; Swedish Peoples Party, 10 (Swedish Peoples Party, 9, and the Bourgeois Alliance, 1); and Christian Democrats in Finland, 6.

Speaker: Eero HEINÄLOUMA.

CABINET

[as of August 3, 2013]

Prime Minister	Jyrki Katainen (Kok)
Deputy Prime Minister	Jutta Urpilainen (SSDP) [f]
Ministers	
Agriculture and Forestry	Jari Koskinen (Kok)
Culture and Sport	Paavo Arhinmäki (Vas)
Defense	Carl Haglund (RKP/SFP)
Economic Affairs	Jan Vapaavuori (Kok)
Education and Science	Krista Kiuru (SSDP) [f]
Environment	Ville Niinstö (Vihr)
European Affairs and Foreign Trade	Alexander Stubb (Kok)
Finance	Jutta Urpilainen (SSDP) [f]
Foreign Affairs	Erkki Toumioja (SSDP)
Health and Social Services	Susanna Huovinen (SSDP) [f]
Housing and Communications	Pia Viitanen (SSDP) [f]
Interior	Päivi Räsänen (KD) [f]
International Development	Heidi Hautala (Vihr) [f]

Justice	Anna-Maja Henriksson (RKP/SFP) [f]
Labor	Lauri Ihalainen (SSDP)
Public Administration and Local Government	Henna Virkkunen (Kok) [f]
Social Affairs and Health	Paula Risikko (Kok) [f]
Transport	Merja Kyllönen (Vas) [f]

[f] = female

INTERGOVERNMENTAL REPRESENTATION

Ambassador to the U.S.: Ritva KOUKKU-RONDE.

U.S. Ambassador to Finland: Bruce J. ORECK.

Permanent Representative to the UN: Jarmo VIINANEN.

IGO Memberships (Non-UN): ADB, AfDB, CEUR, EBRD, EIB, EU, IADB, ICC, IEA, IOM, OECD, OSCE, WTO.

RELATED TERRITORY

Åland Islands (*Ahvenanmaa*). Lying in the Gulf of Bothnia between Finland and Sweden, the Ålands encompass more than 6,500 islands, fewer than 10 percent of which are populated. The total land area is 599 square miles (1,552 sq. km), inclusive of inland water. The capital is Mariehamn (*Maarianhamina*) on Åland Island. The inhabitants, an overwhelming majority of whom are Swedish-speaking, were estimated to total 28,500 in 2012.

The islands were under Swedish rule until 1809, when Finland was ceded to Russia and they became part of the Finnish Grand Duchy. When Finland declared its independence in 1917, the islanders expressed a desire for reversion to Sweden but were obliged to settle for internal autonomy, a status that was confirmed by a League of Nations decision in 1921.

While constitutionally one of Finland's 12 provinces, the islands were granted expanded autonomy in 1951 and again in 1991 (effective January 1, 1993). Provisions included enhanced legislative and fiscal authority, in addition to a recognition of regional citizenship, the right to tax alcohol sales, and full control of postal services. In 1988 the principle of majoritarian parliamentary government was introduced, supplanting a system whereby any party electing at least 5 deputies to the 30-member legislature (*Lagting*) could secure representation in the Executive Council (*Landskapsstyrelse*). The leading political groups are the **Center Party** (*Åländsk Center*), the **Moderate Party** (*Frisinnad Samverkan*), the **Åland Social Democratic Party** (*Ålands Socialdemokrater*), the **Liberal Party of Åland** (*Liberalerna på Åland*), the independent **Nonaligned Rally** (*Obunden Samling*), the **Free-Thinking Cooperation Party** (*Frisinnad Samverkan*), the **List for Åland's Future** (*Ålands Framtid*), and the **Greens of Åland** (*Gröna på Åland*), the first three of which formed a coalition government after the election of October 20, 1991. (For information on elections between 1995 and 2007, please see the 2012 *Handbook.*)

The islands' single representative in the Finnish Parliament had consistently been returned by the **Åland Coalition** (*ÅlAÅländsk Samling*), grouping all the main local parties. Elisabeth NAUCLÉR was elected in 2007 and 2011 as the islands' representative. She was a member of the independent coalition **Bourgeois Alliance** (*Borgerlig Allians*) who followed tradition and supported the Swedish Peoples Party grouping in the Finnish Parliament.

In the October 21, 2007, elections, the Liberal Party of Åland won 10 seats; the Center Party, 8; the Nonaligned Rally, 4; the Social Democrats, 3; the Free-Thinking Cooperation Party, 3; and the List for Åland's Future, 2. Following the elections, Viveka Eriksson, the leader of the Liberal Party, became the first female head of government for the islands. Her predecessor, Roger Nordlund, was elected speaker of the *Lagting*.

In a separate referendum on EU accession, held on November 20, 1994, the Åland islanders followed the rest of Finland (and Sweden) by voting in favor, but by a much larger margin of 73.7 to 26.3 percent. During negotiations over ratification of the EU's Lisbon Treaty in 2008, the islands received concessions from the Finnish government and the EU on several issues, including recognition of Åland's language autonomy and separate participation of the islands in several EU bodies. The concessions required changes to the formal 1991 act on autonomy. In July the government rejected a plan to build a tunnel between two of the larger islands.

In elections on October 16, 2011, the Center Party won 7 seats; the Liberal Party, 6; the Social Democrats, 6; the Moderate Party, 4; the independent Nonaligned Rally, 4; and the List for Åland's Future, 3. After the election, Camilla GUNELL of the Social Democrats formed a coalition government. Gunnell's government focused on economic diversification, sustainable development, and tourism. Shipping now contributes 28 percent of GNP, down from 40 percent, and the islands are becoming self-sufficient in energy production by shifting to wind-generated electricity.

Chair of the Executive Council and Prime Minister: Camilla GUNELL (Social Democrats).

Speaker of the Legislature: Britt LUNDBERG (Center Party).

FRANCE

French Republic
République Française

Political Status: Republic under mixed parliamentary-presidential system established by constitution adopted by referendum of September 28, 1958, and instituted on October 4.

Area: 211,207 sq. mi. (547,026 sq. km).

Population: 64,280,060 (2013E—UN); 65,952,000 (2013E—U.S. Census). Area and population figures are for metropolitan France (including Corsica); for overseas departments and other dependent jurisdictions, see Related Territories, below.

Major Urban Centers (2008E): PARIS (2,211,297), Marseille (851,420), Lyon (474,946), Toulouse (439,553), Nice (344,875), Nantes (283,288), Strasbourg (272,116), Montpellier (252,998), Bordeaux (235,891), Rennes (206,655), Le Havre (178,769), Saint-Étienne (172,696).

Official Language: French.

Monetary Unit: Euro (market rate November 1, 2013: 0.74 euro = $1US).

President: François HOLLANDE (Socialist Party); elected for a five-year term in runoff balloting on May 6, 2012, and inaugurated May 15, succeeding Nicolas SARKOZY (Union for a Popular Movement).

Premier: Jean-Marc AYRAULT appointed by the president on May 16, 2012, succeeding François FILLON (Union for a Popular Movement).

THE COUNTRY

The largest country of Western Europe in area and once the seat of a world empire extending onto five continents, France today is largely concentrated within its historical boundaries, maintaining its traditional role as the cultural center of the French-speaking world but retaining only a few vestigial political footholds in the Pacific and Indian Oceans and the Americas. While 94.4 percent of the population of metropolitan France, which includes the island of Corsica, are citizens, immigration has become a major political issue, the principal foreign ethnic groups being of North African (Arab), Portuguese, Turkish, Italian, Spanish, and German origins. French is the near-universal language, although German has co-official status in Alsace schools, and Alemannic, Basque, Breton, Corsican, and other languages and dialects are spoken to some extent in outlying regions. The Roman Catholic Church, officially separated from the state in 1905, is predominant, but there are substantial Protestant and Jewish minorities as well as a growing Muslim population, and freedom of worship is strictly maintained. Female representation in the national legislature has risen in recent

years, reaching 27 percent in the National Assembly as of July 31, 2012.

In addition to large domestic reserves of iron ore, bauxite, natural gas, and hydroelectric power, France was the world's sixth largest exporter and fifth largest importer of merchandise in 2010; it is notably an important exporter of chemicals, iron and steel products, automobiles, machinery, precision tools, aircraft, ships, textiles, wines, perfumes, and *haute couture.* The industrial sector contributes 21 percent of GDP and 21 percent of employment, with the service sector accounting for most of the balance. Agriculture accounts for only 2 percent of GDP and under 3 percent of employment.

The French economy has been struggling ever since global financial crisis of 2008, initially showing a modest recovery in 2010 and 2011 only to be plunged back into zero growth stagnation in 2012 and 2013 as the eurozone debt crisis took hold.

GOVERNMENT AND POLITICS

Political background. For most of the century after its Revolution of 1789, France alternated between monarchical and republican forms of government, the last monarch being NAPOLEON III (Louis Napoleon), who was deposed in 1870. The republican tradition has given rise to five distinct regimes: the First Republic during the French Revolution; the Second Republic after the Revolution of 1848; the Third Republic from 1870 to 1940; the Fourth Republic, proclaimed in October 1946 but destined to founder in the 1950s on dissension occasioned by the revolt in Algeria; and the Fifth Republic, established in 1958 by Gen. Charles DE GAULLE, who had headed the first postwar government.

Reentering public life at a moment when civil war threatened, de Gaulle agreed in May 1958 to become premier on the condition that he be granted decree powers for six months and a mandate to draft a new constitution. Following adoption of the constitution by referendum and his designation by an electoral college, de Gaulle took office on January 8, 1959, as president of the Fifth Republic. De Gaulle's initially ambiguous policy for Algeria eventually crystallized into a declaration of support for Algerian self-determination, leading in 1962 to the recognition of Algerian independence. In November 1962 Georges POMPIDOU was confirmed as the new prime minister, following an election that gave the Gaullists a majority in the National Assembly. A 1962 constitutional amendment introduced a system of direct election of the president. This consists in a run-off system whereby if one candidate does not receive a majority of votes cast in the first round, the two highest-scoring candidates proceed to compete against one another in a second round. Under this system, de Gaulle won a second term in 1965 in a runoff against François MITTERRAND, leader of the newly formed Federation of the Democratic and Socialist Left (*Fédération de la Gauche Démocrate et Socialiste*—FGDS). In the 1967 National Assembly election, reflecting a further decline in the president's popularity, the Gaullists lost their majority and required the support of the Independent Republicans (*Républicans Indépendants*—RI), led by Valéry GISCARD D'ESTAING.

The Fifth Republic was shaken in May–June 1968 by a period of national crisis that began with student demonstrations and led to a nationwide general strike and an overt bid for power by leftist political leaders. After a period of indecision, de Gaulle dissolved the National Assembly and called for a new election, which yielded an unexpectedly strong Gaullist victory. Following popular rejection of regional devolution and other constitutional proposals in a referendum held in April 1969, de Gaulle resigned, and the president of the Senate, Alain POHER, succeeded him on an interim basis. (De Gaulle died in November 1970.)

Former premier Pompidou, the Gaullist candidate for president, defeated Poher—a centrist accorded reluctant support by the left—in a June 1969 runoff. President Pompidou's death in April 1974 led to what was essentially a three-way presidential race among François Mitterrand, joint candidate of the Socialist Party (*Parti Socialiste*—PS), the French Communist Party (*Parti Communiste Français*—PCF), and other left-wing parties; Giscard d'Estaing for the center-right Independent Republicans; and Chaban-Delmas for the Gaullists. In the end, Giscard d'Estaing narrowly defeated Mitterrand in the May runoff. Although he was the first non-Gaullist president of the Fifth Republic, Giscard d'Estaing appointed a Gaullist, Jacques CHIRAC, as premier.

In August 1976 Premier Chirac resigned, charging that the president would not grant him sufficient authority to deal with the nation's problems; he was immediately replaced by the politically independent Raymond BARRE, an economist. Chirac then proceeded to reorganize the Gaullist party into the new Rally for the Republic (*Rassemblement pour la République*—RPR). Seeking reelection in 1981, President Giscard d'Estaing narrowly led a field of ten candidates (including Chirac for the RPR) in the first round, but he was defeated by Mitterrand in the May runoff. During 1985 the prospect of "cohabitation" between a Socialist president and a rightist government loomed as former premier Chirac forged a conservative alliance between the RPR and the UDF. While the Socialists remained the largest single party in the National Assembly after the election of March 1986, the RPR/UDF grouping drew within a few seats of a majority, and with Chirac's redesignation as premier, a "grand coalition" became a reality. Chirac's move to change the election system to proportional representation benefited the far-right National Front party led by Jean-Marie LE PEN, which won 35 seats. A delicate balance persisted until the 1988 presidential election, in which Mitterrand was the principal candidate of the left, while the rightist vote was split between Chirac, former premier Barre of the UDF, and Le Pen's National Front. Mitterrand obtained a plurality of 34.1 percent in first-round balloting and a 54.3 percent majority in the May runoff against Chirac.

In May 1991 the country's first female premier, Edith CRESSON, was appointed. Cresson's approval rating soon fell, however, and after an unprecedented Socialist drubbing in regional elections in March 1992, she was replaced by her finance minister, Pierre BÉRÉGOVOY.

In 1992 the Bérégovoy government convinced a narrow majority of voters to support the European Community's (EC) Maastricht Treaty (see Foreign relations, below) but was beset by a series of scandals and pervasive public fears over third world immigration—fears that both the FN and the "respectable" conservative parties encouraged. The first round of the 1995 presidential election gave the Socialist Lionel JOSPIN a surprise lead with 23.3 percent, but the crucial outcome was Chirac's second-place showing (20.8 percent) over Balladur (18.6 percent). In the May runoff Chirac took 52.6 percent of the vote against Jospin. After a speedy transfer of power from the terminally ill Mitterrand, Chirac named Alain JUPPÉ, his campaign manager and the incumbent foreign minister, to head a new RPR/UDF government.

The Juppé government quickly ran into problems, beginning with the disclosure in June 1995 that luxury Paris apartments owned by the city had been allocated to senior Gaullists (including Chirac and Juppé) at strikingly low rents. By-election and Senate election reversals for the center-right parties in September, combined with plummeting opinion poll ratings, impelled Juppé to resign in November so that he could form a slimmer, reshaped government.

In a surprising decision, President Chirac in April 1997 announced that parliamentary elections would be held ten months earlier than required. The first round was a disaster for the government, as the RPR/UDF secured only 30 percent of the vote. With support from the

Communists, who had won 38 seats, Jospin was sworn in as prime minister and named a multiparty cabinet.

In the first round of presidential voting on April 21, 2002, President Chirac emerged as the front runner, with a lackluster 19.8 percent of the vote in a field of 16 candidates, but the second-place finish of the FN's Le Pen (16.9 percent) sent shockwaves through the political system. Undercut by a splintering among left and green parties, which had eight candidates on the ballot, and humiliated by his 16.2 percent showing, Premier Jospin immediately announced that he would retire from politics. The mainstream left, facing no viable alternative, joined with the center-right in rallying around Chirac, and in the runoff balloting on May 5 the incumbent received 82.2 percent of the vote. Buoyed by his success, Chirac then authorized formation of a new electoral coalition, the Union for the Presidential Majority (*Union pour la Majorité Présidentielle*—UMP), at the opening of the legislative campaign later in May.

With the RPR, much of the UDF, and most of the Liberal Democracy (*Démocratie Libérale*—DL) as its principal components, the UMP swept the National Assembly election of June 2002, claiming 355 seats, to 140 for the PS, 21 for the PCF, and none for the FN. On June 17 President Chirac appointed as premier Liberal Democrat Jean-Pierre RAFFARIN, who had been serving as interim premier since May 6. In November 2002 the UMP was reorganized as a unitary party, the Union for a Popular Movement (*Union pour un Mouvement Populaire*—UMP).

On February 28, 2005, paving the way for a national referendum on a European Union (EU) constitution, a joint session of the Senate and National Assembly amended the French constitution to make it compatible with the proposed EU document. Despite Parliament's 730–66 vote (with 96 abstentions) in favor of the changes, nearly 55 percent of the voters rejected the May 29 referendum, dealing another blow to Chirac. Two days later Premier Raffarin tendered his resignation, with Chirac thereupon naming the minister of the interior, Dominique de VILLEPIN, as Raffarin's successor. A streamlined cabinet, announced on June 2, was most notable for the appointment of the UMP's president, Nicolas SARKOZY, as minister of state, a position second to premier.

On October 28, 2005, in the Paris suburb of Clichy-sous-Bois, young Muslims, mainly of North African and sub-Saharan descent, initiated a wave of violent rioting triggered by the deaths of two youths during a police chase. The disturbances soon expanded into other Parisian suburbs, long notorious for high unemployment, decrepit public housing, crime, and conflicts with police. Moreover, the growing Muslim community in France, numbering 5–10 million according to various estimates, continued to face major social barriers to integration, including widespread discrimination in housing and employment. By November 8 the riots had spread to some 300 communities, prompting Prime Minister de Villepin to declare a state of emergency, which was not lifted until January 4, 2006. More than 250 schools and 200 other public buildings had been burned or attacked and 10,000 vehicles destroyed. Arrests totaled 4,800.

Firmly supported by the UMP, Sarkozy entered the 2007 presidential campaign in the lead against the Socialist Ségolène ROYAL. The first round of voting on April 8 concluded with Sarkozy (31.2 percent of the vote) and Royal (25.9 percent) finishing ahead of the UMP's François BAYROU (18.6 percent), the FN's Le Pen (10.4 percent), and eight other candidates. Bayrou refused to endorse either Sarkozy or Royal in the second round, while Le Pen called upon his supporters to boycott the April 22 contest. In the end, Sarkozy won 53.1 percent to Royal's 46.9 percent. The day after his May 16 inauguration Sarkozy named the UMP's François FILLON as prime minister, after which he focused his energies on winning the National Assembly election scheduled for June 3 and 17. After the first round some analysts predicted that the UMP might collect as many as 400–500 seats, but in the end Sarkozy had to settle for a reduced majority of 313 seats—36 fewer than the UMP had held before the election.

President Sarkozy's tenure as president was marked, on the foreign policy front, by his strong interest in renewing the transatlantic alliance. He increased France's contribution of troops to the NATO mission in Afghanistan and played a leading role in the NATO offensive in Libya in 2011, which led to the overthrow of Libyan leader Muammar Gaddafi. Within Europe, Sarkozy developed a close working relationship with German Chancellor Angela Merkel, although he was at times accused of being the weaker partner in the relationship, especially as Germany's economy continued to outperform France's. As the EU's sovereign debt crisis, triggered by the global recession of 2009, intensified in 2010 and 2011, Sarkozy and Merkel emerged as the key political figures directing Europe's response. They were architects, for example, of EU and IMF-sponsored bailout loans given to Ireland, Greece, and Portugal that aimed at preventing them from defaulting on their debts. Indeed, his focus on EU affairs left him vulnerable to accusations of having neglected French affairs during his reelection campaign in 2011 and early 2012.

France's often tense relations with its Muslim immigrant population continued to simmer. In January 2010 a majority—although not all—of members serving on a parliamentary commission recommended introducing a ban on burqas and face-covering niqabs in all public places where being able to identify the wearer had potential consequence, such as in government offices, banks, hospitals, and public transport. (It was estimated that only some 1,900 women out of the total Muslim population of 5–6 million actually wore burqas.) The ban was approved by the National Assembly and took effect in April 2011. In addition, Sarkozy sparked a row with the EU in late 2009 by moving to deport en masse Roma immigrants, mostly citizens of Romania and Bulgaria. French authorities justified the deportations, which began in August, as necessary to counter such illegal activities as prostitution, drug trafficking, and exploitation of children as well as to end the "deplorable" living conditions in many of the camps. EU Commissioner for Justice Viviane Reding condemned the deportations were "disgraceful" and probably contrary to EU law, which led to a reversal of policy, with Roma no longer singled out for group deportations, but rather being assessed on a case-by-case basis.

In June 2010 the government announced plans to reduce public pension costs and government borrowing by raising the retirement age for most workers from 60 to 62 by 2018. Unions, public sector workers, and the PS-led opposition strongly opposed the move. In October, as the Senate worked its way through the plan, which the lower house had already approved, a series of massive strikes brought hundreds of thousands of opponents—among them, transit workers, teachers, postal workers, and truckers—into the streets. The proposal nevertheless won final approval in November 2010.

In June 2011 Christine LAGARDE resigned as finance minister to become managing director of the International Monetary Fund (IMF) after the resignation of the disgraced Dominique STRAUSS-KAHN who became embroiled in a sex scandal involving a chambermaid in a New York hotel. Before the scandal, Strauss-Kahn had been considered the most likely Socialist to be nominated against Sarkozy in the 2012 presidential election, so his departure from the race was expected to increase Sarkozy's chances of reelection.

In December 2011 the former President Jacques Chirac received a two-year suspended sentence for embezzling public funds to fund his political party. On account of his advanced age (79 years) and poor health, the courts chose not to send Chirac to jail. (On October 30, 2009, Chirac had already made history by becoming the first former head of state to be arraigned for criminal acts.)

In the first round of voting in the presidential elections on April 22, 2012, incumbent President Sarkozy won only 26 percent of the vote, falling slightly behind the Socialist Party's nominee, François HOLLANDE. The other big surprise in the ballot was the strong performance of the far-right National Front, whose candidate, Marine LE PEN, daughter of Jean-Marie Le Pen, won nearly 20 percent of the vote, coming in third place. In the runoff vote on May 6, Hollande defeated Sarkozy by 51.6 percent to 48.4 percent.

Upon taking office, Hollande followed up on his presidential campaign promises by seeking to differentiate himself from Sarkozy especially on economic policy. Hollande had criticized Sarkozy for emphasizing deficit-slashing austerity policies too much, and has pledged to re-balance fiscal and economic policies to favor growth more than austerity. However, within months of him taking office, disillusionment with this government had grown as France continued to languish economically, with little sign of an end in sight to the low growth and high unemployment. On foreign policy, Hollande was more successful, in particular receiving widespread praise internationally for successfully deploying troops to the North African state of Mali in early 2013 to help the government there reclaim large territories that had fallen into the hands of Islamist militants following a March 2012 coup.

Constitution and government. The constitution of the Fifth Republic has retained many traditional features of France's governmental structure while significantly enhancing the powers of the presidency in a mixed presidential-parliamentary system. The president, originally chosen by an electoral college but now directly elected in accordance with a 1962 constitutional amendment, holds powers expanded not only by the terms of the constitution itself but also by

President de Gaulle's broad interpretation of executive prerogative. In addition to having the power to dissolve the National Assembly with the advice (but not necessarily the concurrence) of the premier, the president may hold national referenda on some issues and is granted full legislative and executive powers in times of emergency. A partial check on the president's authority is the existence of a Constitutional Council, which supervises elections, passes on the constitutionality of organic laws, and must be consulted on the use of emergency powers.

The broad scope of presidential authority has curtailed the powers of the premier and the Council of Ministers, whose members are named by the president (upon the recommendation of the premier) and over whose meetings the president is entitled to preside. In July 2008 Parliament passed a major constitutional reform package by the narrowest of margins, 539–357, only one vote more than the required three-fifths majority. Described as encompassing the most significant changes ever made to the 1958 document, the package amended 47 of the 89 articles and added 9 new ones. Among other changes, presidents were limited to two terms in office, the assembly was given veto power over some presidential appointments, and troop deployments of more than four months now require legislative assent. In addition, a new article provided for an office of defender of rights (ombudsman). The assembly must still give priority to bills presented by the government "during two weeks of sittings out of four" (with additional priority for finance and social security bills as well as bills concerning states of emergency), and the government may still open debate on a bill and propose amendments.

The legislative capacity of the once all-powerful National Assembly remains circumscribed. It can pass legislation in such fixed areas as civil rights and liberties, liability to taxation, the penal code, amnesty, declarations of war, electoral procedure, and the nationalization of industries; however, it can only determine "general principles" in the areas of national defense, local government, education, property and commercial rights, labor, trade unions, and social security. Unspecified areas remain within the jurisdiction of the executive, and no provision is made for the National Assembly to object to a government decree on the ground that it is within a parliamentary mandate. The assembly has, however, played a more assertive role recently, making greater use of its powers of parliamentary oversight to investigate the conduct of foreign policy and to judge the conduct of government ministers.

The Senate, most of whose members are indirectly elected by an electoral college, was reduced under the Fifth Republic to a distinctly subordinate status, with little power other than to delay the passing of legislation by the National Assembly. The 1958 constitution further provides that if the presidency of the republic becomes vacant, the president of the Senate will become president ad interim, pending a new election. A separate consultative body, the Economic and Social Council, represents the country's major professional interests and advises on proposed economic and social legislation.

The higher judiciary consists of courts of assize (*cours d'assises*), which handle major criminal cases; courts of appeal (*cours d'appel*), for appeals from lower courts; and the Court of Cassation (*Cour de Cassation*), which judges the interpretation of law and the procedural rules of the other courts. Courts of instance (*tribunaux d'instance*) function locally.

In 1999 both houses of the legislature approved an amendment "favoring equal access to women and men to elected positions," the most direct consequence being a requirement that political parties nominate men and women in equal proportion for public office, effective with the 2001 local elections (in towns of 3,500 or more). In September 2000 French voters approved a referendum reducing the presidential term from seven to five years, effective with the 2002 election. A February 2006 joint session of Parliament passed a constitutional amendment permitting either chamber, by a two-thirds vote, to begin presidential impeachment proceedings for dereliction of duty. France's traditional freedom of the press has been maintained under the Fifth Republic. A long-standing restriction that offensive criticism may not be directed against the head of state is now largely ignored. The territory of metropolitan France (outside Paris) is divided into 22 regions and 96 departments (*départements*), the latter subdivided into more than 340 arrondissements, 4,000 cantons, and some 37,000 communes. In addition, there are 4 overseas regions and 4 coterminous departments—French Guiana, Guadeloupe, Martinique, and Réunion—as well as a number of other overseas jurisdictions (see Related Territories, below). The administrative structure is identical in all metropolitan regions and departments. Each metropolitan department is headed by a commissioner of the republic (*commissaire de la république*), the traditional title of prefect (*préfet*) technically having been abandoned with the enactment of decentralization legislation in 1982, although continuing in general use. While the commissioner continues to be appointed by and responsible to the central government, some of the commissioner's traditional administrative and financial functions have been transferred to locally elected departmental assemblies (*conseils généraux*) and regional assemblies (*conseils régionaux*). The smallest political unit, the commune, has a popularly elected municipal council (*conseil municipal*) headed by a mayor.

In December 1999 negotiations opened between the central government and Corsican representatives on autonomy for Corsica, which culminated in an agreement between the negotiating parties. However, on July 6, 2003, Corsican voters narrowly rejected, 51 percent to 49 percent, a referendum on administrative devolution for the island. A number of overseas dependencies have, however, accepted devolution.

Foreign relations. French foreign policy as developed under President de Gaulle was dominated by the objective of restoring France's former leading role in international affairs and its independence of action. This was particularly evident in de Gaulle's strenuous effort to establish an independent nuclear force and his refusal to sign treaties banning nuclear testing and proliferation. Within the Europe of "the Six" (the founding members of the EC: Belgium, France, the Federal Republic of Germany, Italy, Luxembourg, and the Netherlands), de Gaulle accepted the economic provisions of the Treaty of Rome but resisted all attempts at political integration on a supranational basis and twice vetoed British membership in the EC. Within the Atlantic community, he accepted the provisions of the North Atlantic Treaty but withdrew French military forces from North Atlantic Treaty Organization (NATO) control in 1966—France would not be fully represented again at a meeting of NATO defense ministers until 1994 and did not rejoin the military command structure until 2009—and refused the use of its territory for Allied military activities. De Gaulle caused a major strain in Franco-Canadian relations when, during a visit to Montreal on July 24, 1967, he uttered the phrase *Vive Le Québec Libre*, meaning "long live free Québec," a popularly used phrase by French-speaking Québec separatists who were campaigning for their province to secede from Canada and form its own country.

The most pronounced foreign policy change under President Pompidou was the adoption of a more flexible attitude toward British admission to the EC, which led to the community's enlargement in 1973 to also include the United Kingdom, Ireland, and Denmark. President Giscard d'Estaing introduced a more positive posture of cooperation with the United States and other Western powers. The international standing of President Mitterrand was undercut by the sinking, at the hands of French agents, of the antinuclear Greenpeace vessel *Rainbow Warrior* in Auckland harbor, New Zealand, in 1985. The Socialist-led government was not without its successes, however, including its strong support for the EC's Maastricht Treaty on political and economic union, which the French electorate endorsed in 1992 by a narrow majority (51 percent).

French forces participated in the U.S.-led multinational expedition that liberated Kuwait from Iraqi occupation in 1991 and also contributed significantly to the unsuccessful U.S.-led UN effort in 1992–1993 to prevent Somalia's descent into anarchy. Non-UN French forces were rapidly deployed in June 1994 to contain the carnage in Rwanda but were withdrawn in late August. France shared responsibility for the failure of the EC and other European structures to make an effective response to the escalating conflict in former Yugoslavia in 1992, later becoming a member of the Contact Group (with Britain, Germany, Russia, and the United States) charged with expediting a Bosnian settlement. French troops continue to be deployed as peacekeepers both to Bosnia and Kosovo.

Newly installed President Chirac generated intense controversy in June 1995 by announcing the resumption of French nuclear testing at Mururoa Atoll in the South Pacific, where a moratorium on testing had been declared in 1992 and had been followed by France's signing of the UN Treaty on Non-Proliferation of Nuclear Weapons. Following the sixth test in the series in January 1996, President Chirac announced that he had decided to end French nuclear tests "permanently," and in September France signed the UN-sponsored Comprehensive Nuclear Test Ban Treaty, which it ratified in 1998.

Although relations between Paris and London were strengthened in the early years of Chirac's presidency, the cornerstone of French external policy remained the alliance with Germany and the determination of the two governments to be the joint driving force of a new phase of EU integration, starting with the move to a single currency by the end of the century. France actively supported NATO's policy toward Serbia, both by committing ground troops to a peacekeeping force based in Macedonia and by participating in the NATO air strikes against Yugoslavia—which by then was a greatly reduced state in size comprising Serbia and Montenegro—during the Kosovo crisis in March–June 1999. At the same time, France supported establishment of a separate European military capability and subsequently committed significant personnel to the new EU-backed rapid reaction force.

From 1970 the principal vehicle for cooperation with other French-speaking nations was the Agency for Cultural and Technical Cooperation (*Agence de Coopération Culturelle et Technique*—ACCT). The ACCT was succeeded in 1998 by the International Organization of the Francophonie (*Organisation Internationale de la Francophonie*—OIF), which in 2013 had 57 full and 20 observer members.

After the September 11, 2001, attacks on the United States, France spearheaded European efforts to halt terrorism and break up underground terrorist cells. Dozens of suspected terrorists, the majority of them North African, were arrested and put on trial; many radical Muslim clerics were deported; and new antiterrorism measures were enacted. However, France's sharp opposition to the U.S.-led invasion of Iraq in March 2003 provoked a period of anti-French sentiment in the United States. The Sarkozy presidency from 2007–2012 witnessed a warming of relations between the United States and France. This was a result both of Sarkozy's stronger personal affinity with American culture than Chirac and due to the election of Barack Obama as U.S. president in 2008. After an initially slow response to the 2011 political upheavals in Egypt and Tunisia, the Sarkozy government moved decisively to help the Libyan rebels. France successfully pushed for a UN no-fly resolution in March 2011, after which it immediately attacked Gaddafi's forces from the air. At the end of April, France and Italy sent military advisors to assist the rebels. Also in June 2011 Sarkozy, following the U.S. lead, announced plans to reduce the French contingent in Afghanistan by 4,000 soldiers. All these actions seemed to improve Sarkozy's standing at home, although the worsening state of the French economy ultimately dashed his reelection chances in 2012.

Current issues. From 2010 to 2012, the overarching economic concern for France, as for the rest of Europe, was the eurozone sovereign debt crisis. Greece, with a debt of approximately €350 billion, more than 150 percent of the GDP, was in grave danger of national default, perhaps of abandoning the euro as a currency. However, through a series of tense summits, EU leaders took actions aimed both at keeping Greece inside the eurozone and preventing the euro's overall collapse, as more and more eurozone members fell deeper in debt. Thus, France and Germany helped to craft bailout packages from Greece, Ireland, and Portugal and set up a $650 billion so-called firewall—the European Stability Mechanism—essentially a giant bailout fund for eurozone countries at risk of defaulting. In December 2011 EU leaders managed to agree on a new Fiscal Treaty that imposed stricter limits on deficit and debt. The United Kingdom refused to sign on to the new treaty, as well as the Czech Republic, with both claiming it went too far in eroding the sovereignty of national governments.

Following his election, France's new president, François Hollande, in June 2012 pushed through a controversial change to France's pension system, rolling back Sarkozy's plan to raise the minimum retirement age to 62 years, keeping it instead at its existing level of 60 years. However, he failed to secure adoption of another proposal—a new income tax rate of 75% on individuals earning more than $1.3 million (€1 million) after France's constitutional court in December 2012 annulled the plan. The prospect of such a severe tax being levied had caused some wealthy French nationals, such as renowned actor Gerard Depardieu, to leave the country. Hollande also mostly failed in his pledge to get Germany to agree to a substantive reform of the EU's new Fiscal Pact to make it more growth oriented and less focused on slashing public spending. France's economic situation continued to worsen, with unemployment topping 11 percent by mid-2013 and GDP growth flat-lining. The president's approval rating consequently tumbled from 65 percent to just 25 percent in less than a year.

A very bitter debate erupted in early 2013 when the Hollande-led socialist government made good on an election campaign pledge by introducing legislation to legalize same-sex marriage. Despite massive and often violent street protests from right-wing and Catholic groups, and a constitutional challenge from the main opposition party, the UMP, France in May 2013 became the 14th country to allow gay couples to marry. It left open the question of their ability to adopt children, about which French public opinion was more evenly divided.

France made a crucial intervention in its former African colony, Mali, in January 2013, deploying troops and authorizing air strikes, in a successful bid to drive out Islamist militants who had seized swathes of territory in the north. Building on this military victory, the United Nations authorized deployment of a peacekeeping force in July 2013, with France's troop levels there scheduled to be gradually reduced from 4,500 to 1,000 by the end of the year. In the trade policy arena, France made headlines in summer 2013 by emerging as the country most resistant to launching talks between the 28-country European Union and the United States for a free trade agreement. While those talks—strongly backed by the United Kingdom, Germany, and the United States—managed to get started on time in July, it was not before France got the others to exclude audio-visual services from the agreement's scope. Meanwhile, the nation began to have a debate on its future energy and environmental policies, with major legislation scheduled for 2014. France currently gets 75 percent of its energy from nuclear power, and while President Hollande would like to reduce that dependency to 50 percent, the French nuclear industry is resisting this. Others are worried that such a shift could cause France to embark on environmentally harmful extractions of shale gas using hydraulic fracturing or "fracking" technology. For the time being, fracking is banned in France.

POLITICAL PARTIES

Although the particulars have changed almost beyond recognition since World War II, the current French party system nevertheless displays, in its broad structure, many similarities with that prevailing more than half a century ago. The left continues to be dominated by the Socialists and Communists, save that the former, since a relaunch in the early 1970s, has far outstripped the latter as an electoral force. An array of small formations still compete in the political center. De Gaulle's political heirs, campaigning from 1976 until 2002 as the Rally for the Republic (RPR) and now as the Union for a Popular Movement (UMP), are the main force on the conservative right; however, there remains a substantial populist far-right constituency, most prominently represented by the National Front (FN). One significant new phenomenon of the last half-century has been the "green" movement.

Party of Government:

Socialist Party (*Parti Socialiste*—PS). Originally established in 1905 and known for many years as the French Section of the Workers' International (*Section Française de l'Internationale Ouvrière*—SFIO), the French Socialist Party headed the 1936–1938 Popular Front government of Léon BLUM as well as several postwar coalitions, party leader Guy MOLLET being prime minister of the Fourth Republic's longest-lasting administration in 1956–1957. The advent of the Fifth Republic in 1958 accelerated the party's electoral decline, and in 1965 it joined the broader Federation of the Democratic and Socialist Left (*Fédération de la Gauche Démocrate et Socialiste*—FGDS) chaired by François Mitterrand, leader of the small Convention of Republican Institutions (*Convention des Institutions Républicains*—CIR).

After further false starts and bickering between the factions, in 1971 a "congress of socialist unity" elected Mitterrand as leader of the new Socialist Party, which embarked upon a strategy of left-wing union. Major gains in the 1973 legislative election were followed by a narrow second-round defeat for Mitterrand, as presidential candidate of the combined left, in 1974. In a 1981 rematch against Giscard d'Estaing, Mitterrand was victorious, and the PS then swept the National Assembly election in June. Despite a Socialist defeat in the 1986 assembly election, Mitterrand won a second term by defeating Jacques Chirac in May 1988, and a month later the PS secured a sufficient plurality to regain control of the National Assembly.

Following a massive defeat in the 1993 legislative elections, the PS chose former prime minister Michel ROCARD as first secretary, but he was forced to step down when the Socialists fared poorly in the June election for the European Parliament.

Straitened financial circumstances and the implication of various PS officials in corruption cases added to the Socialists' problems in the run-up to the 1995 presidential election. Their candidate, a former PS leader and education minister, Lionel Jospin, defied most expectations, taking the lead in the first round and winning 47.4 percent in the second. In June Jospin replaced Henri EMMANUELLI as PS first secretary, promising to carry out a thorough reform of party structures and policies. In the 1997 legislative elections, Jospin led the PS to a plurality of 241 seats in the National Assembly.

In the 2002 presidential race a divided left contributed to Jospin's third-place finish, with 16.2 percent of the vote. Humiliated, Jospin announced his retirement from active politics. In the June parliamentary election the PS won only 140 seats, and several months later former first secretary Emmanuelli launched a "New World" caucus within the PS in an effort to redirect the party toward its socialist roots and away from the social liberalism of the party's new first secretary, François Hollande. In May 2003, however, the party reelected Hollande as leader.

At a party congress in November 2005, Hollande's "modernizers" and the "traditionalists" attempted to heal the rift that had split the party into half a dozen factions. Among other things, the party agreed to unite behind a platform that called for an increase in the minimum wage, opposition to the controversial new youth labor legislation, and reversal of the government's decision to sell a minority stake in the principal state-owned electrical utility company. In other decisions, Laurent Fabius was restored to the party's executive, and the selection of a 2007 presidential candidate was deferred until November 2006.

In September 2006 Lionel Jospin withdrew from the contest for the presidential nomination. In November Ségolène Royal, a former minister of family affairs, won 61 percent of the vote in a party primary, easily defeating former finance minister Dominique Strauss-Kahn (21 percent) and Fabius (19 percent). Initially regarded as the front-runner in the race, Royal fell behind early in 2007 and never regained the lead. She won 25.9 percent of the first-round vote and then lost to Nicolas Sarkozy in the runoff, with 46.9 percent. In the June National Assembly election the PS somewhat unexpectedly improved on its 2002 performance, winning 186 seats.

In late May 2007 Bernard KOUCHNER, long a prominent figure on the left and cofounder of the international aid organization Doctors Without Borders (*Medecins sans Frontieres*), was expelled from the party for agreeing to serve as minister of foreign affairs in the Fillon cabinet. The more streamlined 15-member cabinet unveiled by President Sarkozy was notable for including a broad mix of ages, races, political backgrounds as well as near gender parity, with seven women appointed to it. Four months later, Strauss-Kahn was named to head the International Monetary Fund.

In March 2008 François Hollande announced that he would not seek reelection as first secretary at the party congress on November 14–16. Leading contenders for the post were Ségolène Royal, who had considerable grassroots support; the more moderate mayor of Paris, Bertrand DELANOË; the mayor of Lille, Martine Aubry, who was backed by Fabius and other "elephants" in the party's old guard; and Benoît HAMON, a member of the European Parliament. After the first round of voting Royal held the lead, but in the second round Aubry defeated her by the narrowest of margins—0.08 percent—after Hamon threw his support to Aubry.

One of the leading lights in the party, Dominique Strauss-Kahn, saw his fortunes rise and fall in rapid succession in 2010–2011. Having been appointed as managing director of the IMF in 2007, Strauss-Kahn had enhanced his standing both at home and abroad as the IMF played an increasingly important role in helping to get Europe through its sovereign debt crisis. However, just as he was being tipped as the hot favorite to be the party's nominee in the 2012 elections, the rape allegation in the New York hotel came to light, effectively dashing his hopes, even though the charges were later dropped. Instead, François Hollande became the party's nominee and went on to narrowly defeat Nicolas Sarkozy in the 2012 presidential elections. The socialists also won a convincing victory in the June 2012 parliamentary elections, taking 48.5 percent of the vote and 280 seats.

Leaders: Martine AUBRY (First Secretary), Ségolène ROYAL (2007 presidential candidate), Harlem DÉSIR (National Secretary for Coordination), Jean-Marc AYRAULT (Prime Minister), David ASSOULINE (Spokesperson).

Main Opposition Party:

Union for a Popular Movement (*Union pour un Mouvement Populaire*—UMP). The present UMP was established as a unitary party at a congress on November 17, 2002. It had been launched in May 2002 as the Union for the Presidential Majority (*Union pour la Majorité Présidentielle*—UMP), a center-right electoral alliance that included, principally, the Rally for the Republic and elements of both the Liberal Democracy (*Démocratie Libérale*—DL), led by former presidential candidate Alain MADELIN, and the Union for French Democracy (but not the Democratic Force faction of UDF leader François Bayrou—see MoDem, below). In the June 2012 elections, its support slipped significantly, losing 112 seats and consequently going from being the majority party to the main opposition party.

The Rally for the Republic (*Rassemblement pour la République*—RPR) had been established in 1976 as successor to the Union of Democrats for the Republic (*Union des Démocrates pour la République*—UDR), itself heir to various formations descended from the Union for the New Republic (*Union pour la Nouvelle République*—UNR), launched by de Gaulle in 1947. The RPR was organized as the personal vehicle of Jacques Chirac in his political rivalry with President Giscard d'Estaing. In 1998 the RPR aligned with the UDF and the DL in The Alliance, an unsuccessful effort to provide cohesion for the center-right parties. Subsequently, a segment of the RPR led by Charles PASQUA broke from the party's leadership to join with Philippe de Villiers's Movement for France (MPF, below) and contest the upcoming election for the European Parliament (EP) on a platform opposing further European integration.

Following his massive reelection victory against the FN's Jean-Marie Le Pen in May 2002, Chirac used his revived standing to organize the Union for a Presidential Majority and then to lead it to a sweeping victory at the June National Assembly elections. In preparation for conversion of the alliance to a unitary party, the RPR voted to dissolve in September 2002. The new formation also incorporated the DL, which had been organized in 1977 as the Republican Party (*Parti Républican*) by Giscard d'Estaing supporters, and attracted much of the UDF and many members of the RPF-IE. In October 2002 the Radical Party (PR, below) voted to associate with the UMP while retaining its separate identity.

During its November 2002 founding congress, at which it presented its guiding values as liberty, responsibility, solidarity, the nation, and Europe, the UMP elected Alain Juppé as chair and Philippe DOUSTE-BLAZY as secretary general. Juppé, who was convicted in January 2004 of misusing public funds in 1988–1995 while an aide to Chirac and secretary general of the RPR, received an 18-month suspended sentence and was banned from public office for ten years (reduced to one year, on appeal). In July he resigned as UMP chair, with Nicolas Sarkozy then being elected as his replacement in November. Although President Chirac did not announce that he would not seek a third term until March 11, 2007, Nicolas Sarkozy had received the party's endorsement in January. In the April 2007 election Sarkozy finished first in the initial round, with 31.2 percent of the vote, and won the presidency with 53.1 percent in the runoff. In mid-May, when Sarkozy resigned the party presidency, Jean-Claude Gaudin assumed the post on an acting basis. In June the UMP, in pursuit of a "presidential majority," won 313 National Assembly seats, considerably less than in 2002. Following Sarkozy's defeat in the 2012 presidential election, the UMP held an election for a new leader. The party's General Secretary from 2010 to 2012, Jean-François Copé, was elected in the November 2012 ballot, although his narrow margin of victory—with 50.03 percent—caused his opponent, François Fillon, to contest the victory.

Leaders: Jean-François COPÉ (President); Laurent WAUQUIEZ (Vice President), Luc CHATEL (Deputy Vice President), Michèle TABAROT (Secretary General), Valérie PÉCRESSE (Deputy Secretary General) Jean-Pierre RAFFARIN (President of the National Council), Catherine VAUTRIN (National Treasurer).

Other National Parties:

Left Radical Party (*Parti Radical de Gauche*—PRG). A splinter from the Radical Party, the PRG was organized as the Left Radical Movement (*Mouvement des Radicaux de Gauche*—MRG) prior to participating in the 1973 election as part of the Left Union (*Union de la Gauche*—UG).

The MRG was relaunched under new leadership in 1996, when it absorbed the small Reunite (*Réunir*) group led by Bernard Kouchner (a former Socialist minister who subsequently rejoined the PS). With the aim of sharpening its image, the party also adopted the new single-word name "Radical"—much to the chagrin of the main Radical Party, which in March secured a court ruling that the MRG title should be restored. Reorganized as the Radical Socialist Party (*Parti Radicale Socialiste*—PRS), the party took part in the 1997 elections under a withholding agreement with the PS. The PRS was given one ministerial position and two subministerial positions in the subsequent Socialist government. The courts again forced the party to choose another name, resulting in adoption of the present designation at a congress in 1998.

In the 2002 presidential balloting the PRG's Christiane TAUBIRA, from French Guiana, finished 13th, with 2.3 percent of the vote.

In the 2012 parliamentary elections, the party almost doubled its representation, winning 12 seats, an increase of 5, and attracting 2 percent of the vote nationwide.

Leader: Jean-Michel BAYLET (President).

Europe Ecology–The Greens (*Europe Écologie–Les Verts*). The Greens, which organized as a unified environmental party in 1984, began as an outgrowth of an Ecology Today (*Aujourd'hui l'Écologie*) movement that had offered candidates in the 1981 National Assembly election. The Greens declined to present candidates for the 1988 election on the grounds that only a return to proportional representation would assure them an equitable number of seats.

Les Verts secured no assembly seats on a minuscule vote share in 1993. Partly because of its poor showing, the party, in a decisive move to the left, then elected Dominique VOYNET. As the *Les Verts* candidate, Voynet ran eighth of nine contenders in the first round of the 1995 presidential balloting, taking 3.3 percent of the vote. For the 1997 legislative election the Greens cooperated in some districts with the Socialists or the PRS (now the PRG). Having won seven seats, they entered the Socialist Jospin government.

In October 2001 the Greens abandoned their initial 2002 presidential candidate, Alain LIPIETZ, a former Maoist who had previously supported Corsican and Basque separatists. In his place the party nominated Noël MAMÈRE, who ran seventh, with 5.3 percent of the vote, in the first round. In January 2003 Voynet was replaced by Gilles LEMAIRE, who was then succeeded by Yann WEHRLING two years later. Voynet received the party's endorsement for president in 2007 but won only 1.6 percent of the first-round vote. Two years later, in the June 2009 election for the European Parliament, the Greens led formation of the **Europe Écologie** alliance, which tied the PS for second place, with 14 of France's 72 seats. Those elected on the list included antiglobalization campaigner José Bové (see Small Farmers' Confederation, below) and Daniel COHN-BENDIT, a Franco-German environmental activist who was a leader of the 1968 student demonstrations and who had previously been elected to the European Parliament from Germany. On November 13, 2010, the alliance became a fully formed political party. The party took 3 percent of the vote in the June 2012 parliamentary elections and formed part of the presidential majority led by the socialist party. It nominated Eva JOLY as its candidate in the 2012 presidential elections, but she was eliminated in the first round after securing just 2.3 percent of the vote.

Leaders: Pascal DURAND (National Secretary), Françoise ALMARTINE, Marie BOVÉ, Jean-Philippe MAGNEN, Elise LOWY, Eva SAS.

Republican and Citizen Movement (*Mouvement Républicain et Citoyen*—MRC). The MRC traces its origins to the Citizen's Movement (*Mouvement des Citoyens*—MdC), which was founded in 1993, primarily by former PS adherents who favored a "weaker" EU and who opposed the proposed single EU currency.

In August 2000 the MdC president, Jean-Pierre Chevènement, resigned as interior minister because of his objections to the proposed Corsican autonomy plan. Running for president in 2002 on a platform that combined leftist economics, law and order, and French independence, he finished sixth, with 5.3 percent of the first-round vote. In the June National Assembly election, running on a Republican Pole list (*Pôle Républicain*—PR), the party failed to win any seats. It subsequently reorganized as the MRC. A party congress in June 2010 elected Jean-Luc Laurent as the MRC's new president. In the 2012 parliamentary elections the MRC won two seats in the national assembly.

Leaders: Jean-Luc LAURENT (President), Jean-Pierre CHEVÈNEMENT (Honorary President), Georges SARRE (President of the National Council).

New Center (*Nouveau Centre*—NC). The NC was formed in late May 2007 by members of the UDF, including 18 members of the National Assembly, who objected to François Bayrou's decision to establish the Democratic Movement (MoDem, below) as successor to the UDF. Whereas Bayrou sought independence from the UMP, the NC supported the newly elected president, Nicolas Sarkozy, and participated in the government of the new prime minister, François Fillon.

The party's founding congress was held May 16–17, 2008, at which time Hervé Morin won the presidency with 87 percent support, versus 13 percent for Mireille BENEDETTI. The party won 12 seats and 2 percent of the vote in the June 2012 parliamentary elections.

Leaders: Hervé MORIN (Minister of Defense and President of the Party); Philippe VIGIER (Secretary General); Jean-Marie CAVADA, Catherine MORIN-DESAILLY, Jean-Léonce DUPONT, Yvan LACHAUD, Rudy Salles (Vice Presidents).

Democratic Movement (*Mouvement Démocrate*—MoDem or MD). The MoDem held its founding conference on December 2, 2007, at which time it absorbed what remained of the Union for French Democracy (*Union pour la Démocratie Française*—UDF). Founder François Bayrou stated that a key purpose of the new party would be to overcome the left-right divide in French politics.

The UDF had been established in 1978 by a number of right-centrist parties, including the Radical Party (PR, above), plus several smaller groups in the governing coalition. For two decades its most prominent figure was Valéry Giscard d'Estaing (for details, see the 2007 or earlier editions of the *Handbook*). He stood down as UDF leader in 1996 and attempted to confer the succession on Alain Madelin. However, delegates at a UDF conference preferred former defense minister and Republican President François LÉOTARD.

After dropping from 213 seats in the 1993 legislative poll to 198 in 1997, the UDF also was shaken (as was the RPR) by a poor performance in the 1998 regional elections. Prompting an immediate crisis within the UDF, five UDF incumbent presidents of regional councils accepted the support of the extreme-right FN to retain their posts. Two resigned shortly thereafter, and the UDF eventually expelled the other three.

Among those who attacked Léotard for failing to make a "clean break" with the FN was François Bayrou of the Democratic Force (*Force Démocrate*—FD), which had been launched in 1995 within the UDF as a merger of the Center of Social Democrats (*Centre des Démocrates Sociaux*—CDS) and the Social Democratic Party (*Parti Social-Démocrate*—PSD). Bayrou suggested that the UDF be abolished in favor of a new, single center-right party. In September 1998 Bayrou assumed the UDF presidency and continued to lobby for the remaining UDF components to merge. The resultant "New" (*Nouvelle*) UDF was established in 1999, although the leading constituent parties retained de facto identities. (Léotard subsequently left politics.)

Bayrou finished fourth (with 6.8 percent of the first-round vote) in the 2002 presidential election. Although some of the UDF joined Chirac's new UMP prior to the June 2002 National Assembly election, Bayrou's supporters, clustered in the FD faction, ran independently under the UDF label, winning 29 seats, for third place.

Attacking what he termed the "perpetual war" between the UMP and the Socialists, Bayrou again sought the presidency in 2007, winning 18.6 percent of the vote, for third place, in the first round. He then declined to endorse either the UMP's Sarkozy or the Socialist Royal in the runoff, which contributed to a rupture in the party. Bayrou's announcement on May 10 that he was forming a new Democratic Movement prior to the June National Assembly election then led to the defection of 22 out of 29 UMP legislators, 18 of whom formed the UMP-aligned New Center (NC, above). In the subsequent legislative election MoDem won only three seats.

At the same time, three members of the European Parliament (EP) who had been elected under the UDF banner but who objected to formation of MoDem reorganized within the EP as the Civic Alliance for Democracy in Europe (*Alliance Citoyenne pour la Démocratie en Europe*—ACDE). The three, Jean-Marie CAVADA, Claire GIBAULT, and Janelly FOURTOU, subsequently adopted the name Democratic Future (*Avenir Démocrate*—AD). In June 2009 Cavada, running on the UMP list as a member of the New Center, retained his seat.

In the April 2012 presidential elections, Bayrou ran once more for the presidency, but on this occasion he scored a disappointing 9 percent, half of what he had won in the 2007 ballot. His party also competed in the June 2012 parliamentary elections, winning two seats in the national assembly.

Leader: François BAYROU (President).

National Front (*Front National*—FN). The FN, an extreme right-wing formation organized in 1972 on an anti-immigration program, startled observers in 1984 by winning 10 of the 81 French seats in the European Parliament. Leader Jean-Marie Le Pen secured 14.4 percent of the vote in the first round of the 1988 presidential election. In the 1995 presidential poll, Le Pen took a first-round share of 15 percent.

In December 1997, for a second time, Le Pen was convicted under anti-racism laws for dismissing Nazi gas chambers as a "detail in history" and was fined some $50,000. In April 1998 Le Pen was found guilty of assaulting a female Socialist candidate during the 1997 legislative election campaign. The sentence included the suspension of civil rights for two years, which was reduced to one year on appeal.

Internal conflicts came to a head in December 1998 when deputy leader Bruno Mégret and several of his supporters were expelled from the FN for advocating alliances with parties of the moderate right. The schism led to the coexistence of two parties, each claiming to be "the" FN, but in May the courts ruled that Mégret's group had usurped the FN designation, which led to the new party's selecting National Republican Movement (MNR, below) instead.

Although the FN/MNR bifurcation initially appeared to split the far-right vote, Le Pen subsequently took advantage of rising anti-immigrant, anticrime, and "French first" sentiment (as well as a divided left) to pull off an unexpected second-place finish—16.9 percent of the vote—in the April 2002 first-round vote for the presidency. However, Le Pen's success had the adverse consequence of drawing all his opponents together in support of President Chirac's reelection, and in the second-round voting in June Le Pen could manage only 17.8 percent of the vote.

Le Pen again sought the presidency in 2007, but this time he finished fourth in the first round, with 10.4 percent of the vote. Subsequently, Le Pen continued to run afoul of the authorities. In February 2008 he was fined and given a suspended sentence for describing the German occupation during World War II as relatively benign, and in March he was fined for incitement because of anti-Muslim comments.

The January 2011 party conference chose his daughter Marine to succeed him. She ran a strong campaign and surprised many by finishing with 18 percent of the vote in the first round of the presidential ballot in April 2012. However, her strong personal performance was not quite equaled by her party in the June 2012 parliamentary elections, with the party picking up 13.6 percent in the first round but winning only two seats in the national assembly.

Leaders: Marine LE PEN (President); Jean-Marie LE PEN (Honorary President); Alain JAMET, Louis ALIOT (Vice Presidents); Steeve BRIOIS (Secretary General).

The Alternatives (*Les Alternatifs*). The Alternatives was launched as the Red and Green Alternatives (*L'Alternatives Rouge et Verte*—ARV) in 1989 by merger of the Unified Socialist Party (*Parti Socialist Unifié*—PSU), which dated from 1960, and the New Left (*Nouvelle Gauche*—NG), which had been organized by Pierre JUQUIN following his expulsion from the PCF in 1987. Initially a self-proclaimed anarcho-syndicalist group, the ARV also described itself as "feminist, ecologist, and internationalist."

The ARV adopted its current name in 1998, when new statutes described the organization as a political movement dedicated to creating a post-capitalist society based on human liberation, social justice, and harmony with nature. In 2002 it supported President Chirac's reelection in the second round ("for the first and last time") and in June ran candidates unsuccessfully for various National Assembly seats. In 2007 it supported the presidential candidacy of José BOVÉ, France's most prominent antiglobalization advocate and founder of the Small Farmers' Confederation (*Confédération Paysanne*), and ran, unsuccessfully, as part of the alternative left movement in the subsequent National Assembly election.

Leaders: Jean-Jacques BOISLAROUSSIE, Rachel LAFONTAINE (Spokespersons).

Ecology Generation (*Génération Écologie*—GE). The GE was formed in 1990 by Brice LALONDE, a former presidential candidate and subsequently environment minister. "*Les Bleus*" has had no success in national elections, and in 2002 Lalonde failed to obtain the necessary number of signatures to appear on the presidential ballot. Another party president, France GAMERRE, tried to run in 2007 but also failed to obtain sufficient signatures. For the 2007 National Assembly election the GE concluded an accord with three like-minded organizations: the **Independent Ecological Movement** (*Mouvement Écologiste Indépendant*—MEI), led by former Green presidential candidate Antoine WAECHTER; Albert LEPEYRE's **Clover–New Ecologists** (*Le Trèfle—Les Nouveaux Écologistes*); and Jacques LE BOUCHER's **Man-Animal-Nature Movement** (*Mouvement Homme-Animaux-Nature*—MHAN).

In 2008 France Gamerre chose not to seek a third term as party president and was succeeded by former vice president Jean-Noël Debroise.

Leader: Jean-Nöel DEBROISE (President).

Radical Party (*Parti Radical*—PR). Founded in 1901, the Radical Party was the leading party of the prewar Third Republic and a participant in many Fourth Republic governments. Technically called the Radical and Radical Socialist Republican Party (*Parti Républicain Radical et Radical-Socialiste*—RRRS) but also known as the *Parti Valoisien* from a Rue de Valois address in Paris, the Radicals maintained their traditional anticlerical posture but were more conservative than the Socialists in economic and social matters.

The Radical majority's refusal to join the Union of the Left with the Socialists and Communists caused the exit of a left-wing faction in 1972 to form the Left Radical Movement (see Left Radical Party, below).

In 1978 the Radicals became founding members of the UDF. Almost eliminated from the National Assembly in the 1981 Socialist landslide, the PR recovered somewhat in the 1986 elections and held office in the subsequent "cohabitation" government. However, the party fell back to three seats in 1988 and again went into opposition. It returned to office following the center-right assembly landslide of March 1993. In 2002 it aligned with the UMP while maintaining its separate identity, but in May 2011 it voted overwhelmingly to separate. In the June 2012 parliamentary elections, the party won 6 seats, having secured 1 percent of the vote, a decline of 12 seats compared to its previous total number of assembly members.

Leaders: Jean-Louis BORLOO (President of the Party); André ROSSINOT (Honorary President); Laurent HÉNART (Secretary General); Arlette FRUCTUS, Jean-Paul ALDUY (Deputy Secretaries General).

Before the end of 2007, two new movements took shape, both representing the Sarkozy-supportive left. **The Progressives** (*Les Progressistes*), describing itself as social democratic, was established by a defector from the Socialist Party, Éric BESSON, who served as secretary of state for forward planning, assessment of public policies, and development of the digital economy; was subsequently named an assistant secretary general of the UMP; and is now minister for immigration, integration, national identity, and mutually supportive development. Defining itself as social-liberal, the **Modern Left** (*La Gauche Moderne*—GM) was formed by Jean-Marie BOCKEL, mayor of Mulhouse and secretary of state for justice in the Fillon government.

Workers' Struggle (*Lutte Ouvrière*—LO). The LO is a small Trotskyite party whose leader, Arlette Laguiller, has entered six presidential races since 1974, "not at all to be elected" but to "make heard the workers' voice amid the . . . hypocritical declarations" of the leading candidates, including those of the Socialist and Communist parties. In the 2002 presidential contest Laguiller attracted 5.7 percent of the vote in the first round, her best performance to date. In 2007 Laguiller won 1.3 percent of the vote in the first round of the presidential election. In the 2012 election LO nominated Nathalie Arthaud as its candidate, and she won 0.56 percent of the vote.

Leaders: Arlette LAGUILLER, Nathalie ARTHAUD.

Regional Parties and Groups:

Parties and groups seeking Corsican autonomy or separation have long been active, but they drew increased international attention as proposals for greater Corsican autonomy made their way through Parliament. Closest to the political mainstream, the Corsican Nation (*Corsica Nazione*—CN) alliance, led by Jean-Guy TALAMONI, competed with some success against branches of national parties in regional elections. The largest and most prominent of the militant organizations was the **Corsican National Liberation Front** (*Front de Libération Nationale de la Corse/Fronte di Liberazione Naziunale di a Corsica*—FLNC), which was established in 1976 but which in 1990 split into two organizations: the FLNC–Historic Wing (FLNC–*Canal Historique*—FLNC-CH), which was later called the Corsican National Liberation Front–Union of Combatants (FLNC–*Union des Combatants*—FLNC-UC), and the FLNC–*Canal Habituel,* which dissolved in 1997.

The history of the FLNC has been marked by bombings, other terrorist activities, and interfactional feuding, interspersed with periodic cease-fires. An FLNC-CH splinter, the *Armata Corsa,* was established in 1999 by François SANTONI, a former secretary general of *A Cuncolta Indipendentista* (ACI), the legal wing of the banned FLNC-CH; Santoni was murdered in August 2001. In May 2001 the ACI had announced that three additional groups—*Corsica Viva, Associu per a Suvranita,* and *U Cullettivu Naziounale*—were joining it in formation of Independence (*Indipendenza*). In February 2004 the CN and *Indipendenza* were among the groups organizing a

National Union (*Unione Naziunale*—UN) list headed by Jean-Guy Talamoni and another moderate nationalist, Edmond SIMÉONI. With the support of the FLNC-UC, the list won 17 percent of the second-round vote in the March elections. In November the CN and *Indipendenza* merged as the Independent Corsican Nation (*Corsica Nazione Indipendente*—CNI).

Six months later, the FLNC-UC ended its cease-fire to protest the trial of 22 nationalists, one of whom, Charles PIERI, was reputedly the FLNC-UC commander. In May 2005 Pieri was convicted and sentenced to ten years in prison for involvement in illegal fund-raising. Nineteen codefendants also were convicted, but 2 were acquitted, including Talamoni. In the following three years, the FLNC and the FLNC–October 22 claimed responsibility for hundreds of bombings. In May 2008 a new Corsican National Liberation Front 1976 (FLNC 1976) claimed responsibility for some two dozen recent attacks.

In February 2008 the CNI announced that it would contest upcoming local elections independent of the other UN participants, the National Call (*A Chjama Naziunale*—CAN) and the **Party of the Corsican Nation** (*Partitu di a Nazione Corsa*—PNC), which was established in December 2002 by merger of several groups that rejected the use of violence. In February 2009 the CNI, still led by Talamoni, joined three other smaller separatist groups, most prominently Renovation (*Rinnovu*), under one banner, the **Corsica Libera** (CL), which won 4 of 51 Corsican Assembly seats in the March 2010 regional elections. The PNC-led proautonomy **Femu a Corsica** list, headed by Gilles SIMÉONI, won a surprising 11, only 1 less than the UMP. Earlier, in August 2009, the FLNC-UC, the FLNC 1976, and the FLNC–October 22 announced that they were reuniting under the FLNC banner. There are a number of additional regional organizations of varying degrees of militancy. The **Union of the Alsatian People** (*Union du Peuple Alsacien/Elsass Volksunion*—UPA/EVU) has campaigned for regional autonomy and restoration of links to German-speaking Lorraine. The **Breton Democratic Union** (*Union Démocratique Breton*—UDB), a socialist-oriented group, seeks autonomy for Brittany by nonviolent means. Other regional groups include the federalist **Party for the Organization of a Free Brittany** (*Parti pour l'Organisation d'une Bretagne Libre*—POBL); the separatist **Liberation Front of Brittany–Breton Republican Army** (*Front Libération de la Bretagne–Armée Républicain Breton*—FLB-ARB); and the French Basque **Those of the North** (*Iparretarrak*), which was outlawed in July 1987 following the conviction of its leader, Philippe BIDART, for murder. Bidart was freed in 2007.

The various regionalist and separatist parties of France won only 0.59 percent of the vote nationwide in the June 2012 parliamentary elections, which secured them two seats.

LEGISLATURE

The bicameral **Parliament** (*Parlement*) consists of an indirectly chosen Senate and a directly elected National Assembly.

Senate (*Sénat*). The French Senate, which under the Fifth Republic has been reduced to a limiting and delaying role, currently consists of 348 members. The 312 senators from metropolitan France (including Corsica) are designated by an electoral college that is dominated by municipal council members but also includes National Assembly deputies and regional and departmental council members. Nineteen senators are indirectly elected by the overseas jurisdictions, and 12 are named by the Higher Council of French Abroad (*Conseil Supérieur des Français à l'Étranger*) to represent French nationals overseas.

Under a 2003 reform, the number of senators was increased from 321 to 331 in 2004 and to the present number of 343 in September 2008; 5 more were added in 2011, thus bringing the total membership to 348. (Metropolitan and overseas departments were to be represented by 326, other overseas territories by 10, and French citizens abroad by 12.) In addition, the senatorial term was shortened from nine years (selected by thirds every three years) to six years (to be selected by halves every three years).

As of August 2012 the distribution of seats by senatorial grouping was as follows: Socialists and allies, 128; Union for a Popular Movement, 132; Centrist Union (mainly former members of the Union for French Democracy), 31; Communist, Republican, Citizen, and Left Party (mainly members of the French Communist Party), 21; Democratic and European Social Rally, 17; Ecologists, 12; and unattached, 7.

President: Jean-Pierre BEL.

National Assembly (*Assemblée Nationale*). The French Assembly presently consists of 577 deputies, elected by two-round, majoritarian voting in single-member districts for five-year terms (subject to dissolution). Candidates receiving a majority of the vote in the first round are declared elected; in all other districts, those who receive 12.5 percent of the vote in the first round may proceed to the second, in which a plurality is sufficient for election.

At the most recent elections on June 10 and 17, 2012, the final results from both rounds produced the following distribution: Socialist Group, 295 seats; Union for a Popular Movement (UMP), 196; Union of Democrats and independents, 29; Ecologist Group, 18; Democratic and republican left, 15; Radical, republican, democrat and progressist, 15; and nonaligned, 9 (includes miscellaneous right, 2; National Front, 2; miscellaneous left, 1; MoDem, 1; Arise the Republic, 1; Movement for France, 1, and Far Right, 1).

President: Claude BARTOLONE.

CABINET

[as of August 1, 2013]

Ministers	
Agriculture and Food	Stéphane Le Foll
European Affairs	Thierry Repentin
Culture and Communication	Aurélie Filipetti [f]
Decentralization	Anne-Marie Escoffier [f]
Defense	Jean-Yves Le Drian
Ecology, Sustainable Development, and Energy	Philippe Martin
Economic and Industrial Recovery	Arnaud Montebourg
Economy and Finance	Pierre Moscovici
Equality of the Regions and Housing	Cécile Duflot [f]
Food Processing	William Garo
Foreign Affairs	Laurent Fabius
Foreign Trade	Nicole Bricq [f]
French Nationals Abroad	Hélène Conway-Mouret [f]
Higher Education and Research	Genevieve Fioraso [f]
Interior	Manuel Valls
Justice; Keeper of the Seals	Christiane Taubira [f]
Labour, Employment, and Social Dialogue	Michel Sapin
National Education	Vincent Peillon
Overseas France	Victorin Lurel
Social Affairs and Health	Marisol Tourane [f]
Sport, Youth, Popular Education, and Community Life	Valérie Foureyron [f]
State Reform, Decentralization, and Civil Service	Marylise Lebranchu [f]
Women's Rights; Government Spokesperson	Najat Vallaud-Belkacem [f]

[f] = female

Note: All ministers are members of the PS.

INTERGOVERNMENTAL REPRESENTATION

Ambassador to the U.S.: François M. DELATTRE.

U.S. Ambassador to France: Charles H. RIVKIN.

Permanent Representative to the UN: Gérard ARAUD.

IGO Memberships (Non-UN): ADB, AfDB, CEUR, EBRD, EIB, EU, G-8, G-20, IADB, ICC, IEA, IOM, NATO, OECD, OSCE, WTO.

RELATED TERRITORIES

The former French overseas empire entered a state of constitutional and political transformation after World War II, as a majority of its component territories achieved independence and most of the others modified their links to the home country. The initial step in the process was the establishment in 1946 of the French Union (*Union Française*) as a single political entity designed to encompass all French-ruled territories. As defined by the constitution of the Fourth Republic, the French Union consisted of two elements: (1) the "French Republic," comprising metropolitan France and the overseas departments and territories, and (2) all those "associated territories and states" that chose to join. Vietnam, Laos, and Cambodia became associated states under this provision; Tunisia and Morocco declined to do so. The arrangement proved ineffective, however, in stemming the tide of nationalism, which led within a decade to the independence of the Indochinese states, Tunisia, and Morocco; the onset of the war of independence in Algeria; and growing pressure for independence in other French African territories.

In a further attempt to accommodate these pressures, the constitution of the Fifth Republic as adopted in 1958 established the more flexible framework of the French Community (*Communauté Française*), the primary purpose of which was to satisfy the demand for self-government in the African colonies while stopping short of full independence. Still composed of the "French Republic" on the one hand and a group of "Member States" on the other, the community was headed by the president of the French Republic and endowed with its own Executive Council, Senate, and Court of Arbitration. Initially, 12 French African territories accepted the status of self-governing member states, with only Guinea opting for complete independence. In response to the political evolution of other member states, the French constitution was amended in 1960 to permit continued membership in the community even after independence, but no previously dependent territory elected to participate. The community's Senate was abolished in 1961, at which time the organization became essentially moribund.

As a consequence of constitutional changes instituted in March 2003 and legislation passed in July 2003 and February 2007, the present French Republic encompasses, in addition to mainland France and Corsica, five overseas departments, six overseas collectivities, and two overseas collectivities *sui generis*, each of whose history and present status are discussed below.

Overseas Departments:

The overseas departments (*départements d'outre-mer*—DOM) all have similar political institutions. Like the metropolitan departments, their chief administrative officers are commissioners of the republic or prefects, appointed by the French Ministry of the Interior. Unlike the metropolitan departments, which are grouped into regions, each overseas department is geographically coterminous with an overseas region (*région d'outre-mer*). Each overseas department elects a General Council (*Conseil Général*) to which many of the earlier day-to-day prefectural powers, particularly in financial affairs, were transferred in 1982. General councillors are elected to represent individual districts (cantons). Voters also elect, from party lists, a Regional Council (*Conseil Régional*) to which enhanced policy and planning powers in economic, social, and cultural affairs were accorded in 1983. In addition, there are directly elected mayors and municipal councils for the various townships (communes).

In January 2010 voters in French Guiana and Martinique, despite a low turnout, approved separate reform referenda authorizing replacement of their General and Regional councils with new assemblies. Subsequently, on June 17, the presidents of French Guiana, Guadeloupe, and Martinique established a Regional Union of the Antilles and French Guiana. Although in recent years all three overseas departments had rejected autonomy proposals, creation of the union was interpreted as an effort to coordinate their positions on regional issues and, as stated in a final declaration by the presidents, to ensure that their citizens are not burdened by "choices [presumably imposed from Paris] that are not welcomed by them."

French Guiana (*Guyane*). Situated on the east coast of South America between northern Brazil and Suriname, French Guiana became a French possession in 1816, after two centuries of strife involving, at various times, most of the Western European sea powers. It was ruled as a colony until 1946, when it became a department. From 1852 to 1947 it was utilized as a penal colony, including, most notoriously, Devil's Island (*Île du Diable,* one of the Salut group), where political prisoners were incarcerated. In 1968 a major rocket-launch facility was established in Kourou, from which the European Space Agency has launched satellites and space probes since 1983. The economy is heavily dependent on French subsidies and on the European Space Center, which contributes about one-quarter of the department's GDP. Fishing, agricultural production (principally legumes, sugarcane, fruit, and rice), and tourism also contribute to the economy. Among the largely undeveloped natural resources are significant gold deposits.

The department covers an area of 35,135 square miles (91,000 sq. km). Of its population (2006C) of 205,954, some 90 percent inhabit the coastal region and are mainly Creoles, interspersed with Chinese, Lebanese, Brazilians, Haitians, Surinamese, and others, while the 10 percent living in the interior are largely Indian and *Noir Marrons* (descendants of fugitive slaves). The capital, Cayenne, had a population of 59,977 in 2006. The department elects two deputies to the French National Assembly and, since September 2008, two senators to the Senate. Local government is based on 2 districts, comprising 19 cantons and 22 communes.

The two main parties are the local branch of the Union for a Popular Movement (UMP) and the **Guianese Socialist Party** (*Parti Socialiste Guyanais*—PSG), an affiliate of the French Socialist Party whose longtime advocacy of internal self-rule was recently augmented by a demand for autonomy as a "necessary and preparatory stage" for full independence. There is also a pro-independence **Movement for Decolonization and Social Emancipation** (*Mouvement pour la Décolonisation et l'Émancipation Sociale*—MDES).

Pressure from government and political leaders within the department for increased autonomy led to a meeting in Paris in December 2000 between recently installed Secretary of State for Overseas Departments and Territories Christian Paul and leaders of the PSG, the RPR (the predecessor of the UMP), the **Guiana Democratic Forces** (*Forces Démocratiques Guyanaises*—FDG) of Sen. Georges OTHILY, and the leftist **Walwari** movement (but not the MDES, which had refused an invitation). In November 2001 the French government endorsed a series of locally drafted autonomy proposals, which included greater legislative and administrative control.

In an unprecedented development, Guianese politician Christiane TAUBIRA, founder of *Walwari,* ran for the French presidency in 2002 as the nominee of the Left Radical Party (PRG). She won 2.3 percent of the national vote in the first round. In October 2006 the French government suspended authorization for development of an open-cast gold mine near Cayenne. Opponents of the facility had convinced Paris that pollution from the mine would cause significant harm to an adjacent nature preserve. Exploitation of the department's gold reserves remains a contentious issue, however, especially in the south, where "informal gold mining" is largely conducted by miners who have illegally crossed the border. Moreover, their activities have created significant pollution problems along thousands of miles of rivers. Illegal immigration from Suriname and Guyana also remains a significant issue, as does smuggling.

On January 10, 2010, some 70 percent of those voting rejected greater autonomy for the department, a principal reason being fear of reduced economic support from Paris. In a second referendum on January 24, however, 57 percent approved creation of a new legislature that would combine the powers and duties of the Regional and General councils. In May 2012, Christiane Taubira was appointed Minister of Justice in the newly formed French government, serving under Prime Minister Jean-Mark Ayrault and President François Hollande.

Prefect: Eric SPITZ.

President of the General Council: Alain TIEN-LIONG (Diverse Left).

President of the Regional Council: Rodolphe ALEXANDRE (UMP).

Guadeloupe. Situated in the Lesser Antilles southeast of Puerto Rico, the Caribbean territory of Guadeloupe was first occupied by the French in 1635, was annexed as a colonial possession in 1815, and became a French department in 1946. It encompasses the main islands of Basse-Terre and adjacent Grande-Terre as well as a number of smaller islands, including Marie-Galante, La Désirade, Les Saintes (Terre-de-Haut and Terre-de-Bas), and the uninhabited Îles de la Petite Terre. (The island of Saint Barthelemy and the northern half of Saint Martin were separated from Guadeloupe in 2007—see separate write-ups, below.) Guadeloupe has an area of 630 square miles (1,632 sq. km) and a population (2010C) of 407,205, of whom approximately 12,000 are residents of the capital, Basse-Terre. The largest town is Les Abymes (60,147). Guadeloupians are predominantly black and mulatto, with a few native-born whites and many metropolitan French. The department's economy is based principally on tourism and the export of bananas, sugar, and rum. High unemployment remains a perpetual problem. The department elects four deputies to the French National Assembly and three senators to the Senate. Local administration is based on 2 districts, divided into 40 cantons and 32 communes.

Long-present aspirations on the part of leftist organizations erupted in a series of bombings in the 1980s but gave way, by the 1990s, to calls for greater autonomy. At present, the leading parties are branches of the PS and the UMP, plus the **Guadeloupian Democratic Progressive Party** (*Parti Progressiste Démocratique Guadeloupéen*—PPDG), which was formed in the early 1990s by dissidents from the **Communist Party of Guadeloupe** (*Parti Communiste Guadeloupéen*—PCG).

In the June 2007 election for the National Assembly two seats were won by *Divers Gauche* candidates (Éric JALTON and Jeanny MARC), one by the UMP's Gabrielle LOUIS-CARABIN, and one by the PS's Victorin Lurel. (Lurel was elected from the fourth district, which at the time still included St. Barth and St. Martin. Accordingly, he will continue to represent both new overseas collectivities until the next National Assembly election.) The department's senators are Lucette Michaux-Chevry (UMP), Jacques Gillot (GUSR), and Daniel MARSIN of the **Socialist Renewal** (*Renouveau Socialiste/Divers Gauche*). In May 2012 Victorin Lurel of the PS was appointed to the French government as the Minister for Overseas France. In the May 2012 presidential elections, the voters in Guadalupe sided heavily with the Socialist candidate François Hollande, who secured 72 percent of the vote in the runoff vote compared to 28 percent for Nicolas Sarkozy.

Prefect: Marcelle PIERROT.

President of the General Council: Jacques GILLOT (GUSR).

President of the Regional Council: Josette BOREL-LINCERTIN (PS).

Martinique. Occupied by the French in 1635, the Lesser Antilles Caribbean island of Martinique was annexed as a colonial possession in 1790 and became a department in 1946. It has an area of 425 square miles (1,100 sq. km). Its population of 402,000 (2010E) is predominantly black, with a small number of native-born whites and many metropolitan French. The capital, Fort-de-France, had a population of 90,347 in 2006. The economy, based largely on sugarcane, bananas, and rum, is, like that of the other overseas departments, heavily dependent on direct and indirect subsidies from the French government. Martinique is represented in the French Parliament by four deputies and two senators. Local administration encompasses 4 districts, divided into 45 cantons and 34 communes.

The leading parties include the PS-affiliated **Socialist Federation of Martinique** (*Fédération Socialiste de la Martinique*—FSM) and the UMP. There also is a **Martinique Communist Party** (*Parti Communiste Martiniquais*—PCM). In local politics, however, the most successful parties have recently been the separatist **Martinique Independence Movement** (*Mouvement Indépendantiste Martiniquais*—MIM) and the proautonomy **Martinique Progressive Party** (*Parti Progressiste Martiniquais*—PPM). Alfred MARIE-JEANNE, a leader of the MIM and mayor of Rivière-Pilote, was described as the first pro-independence leader of a French regional body following his election as president of the Regional Council in 1998.

The June 2007 National Assembly election saw three incumbents returned, but Edmond-Mariette lost in the second round to the PPM's Serge Letchimy. At the March 2008 communal elections the left easily retained control of the General Council despite a split in the PPM that saw the departure of Claude Lise to form the **Martinique Democratic Rally** (*Rassemblement Démocratique Martiniquais*—RDM). The department is currently represented in the Senate by Lise and Serge LARCHER (*Divers Gauche*).

To ease economic discontent, in March 2009 the Sarkozy government agreed to an aid package for small and medium-sized businesses and to assist the tourism industry, which was suffering the effects of the ongoing international recession.

On January 10, 2010, some 80 percent of those voting in a referendum rejected greater autonomy for Martinique, but a second referendum on January 24 saw 68 percent approval of creating a new assembly that will replace the General and Regional councils. Meanwhile, in the Regional Council election of March 14 and 21, the PPM list, which won 26 seats, ousted the MIM, which won only 12. The UMP took 3 seats. As a consequence, Serge Letchimy assumed the presidency. In the March 2011 General Council elections Josette Manin (BPM) became the first woman to win the presidency. The voters in Martinique came out strongly for François Hollande in the May 2012 presidential elections, giving him 68.4 percent, compared to 31.6 percent for Nicolas Sarkozy in the second round. In the legislative elections of June 2012, socialist or other left-wing candidates won two seats in the national assembly and regionalist candidates took the other two.

Prefect: Laurent PRÉVOST.

President of the General Council: Josette MANIN (BPM).

President of the Regional Council: Serge LETCHIMY (PPM).

Mayotte (*Mahoré*). Encompassing Grande-Terre, one of the four principal islands of the Comoros archipelago northwest of Madagascar, as well as the much smaller Petite-Terre and some 30 islets, Mayotte (known locally as Mahoré) was initially settled by Africans and later colonized by Arabs. From the 15th century it was visited by European ships traveling to and from the East Indies. In the aftermath of a devastating period of internal strife that began in the late 1700s, Mayotte was ceded to France in 1841 by a Malagasy sultan.

Mayotte has an area of 145 square miles (375 sq. km) and a population of 212,600 (2012C). The chief towns are Dzaoudzi (the administrative center, on Petite-Terre), Mamoudzou, and Koungou, with populations (2005E) of 12,800, 55,500, and 19,700, respectively. Although French is the official language, most citizens speak Shimaoré, a Comoran dialect. Economic activity, centered in Mamoudzou on Grande-Terre, was traditionally based on agriculture, the principal export products being vanilla and ylang-ylang (a fragrant tree and its products), but since 2000 fishing and aquaculture have moved to the fore. The territory is administered by a prefect and an elected General Council of 19 members; it is represented in the French Parliament by one deputy and two senators.

In two referenda held in 1976, voters rejected inclusion in the new Muslim-dominated Republic of the Comoros in favor of French department status. The following December Mayotte was made a territorial collectivity (*collectivité territoriale*) of France, a category construed as being midway between an overseas department and an overseas territory. In 1979 this status was extended by the French National Assembly for another five years, at the conclusion of which a third referendum was to have been held; however, in 1984 the assembly adopted a bill that indefinitely postponed a final decision. The UN General Assembly on several occasions voted in support of Comoran sovereignty over the island, while the Organization of African Unity (OAU, predecessor of the African Union—AU) demanded that France end its "illegal occupation."

Visiting Mayotte in 1994, Prime Minister Balladur announced that a referendum on the island's status would be held by 2000. Shortly thereafter, the introduction of visa requirements for incoming Comoran nationals, intended to curb illegal immigration, provoked protest demonstrations in the Comoros, where the government's hostility to French rule over Mayotte was undiminished by the desire of many Comorans to emigrate to French-ruled territory. Mayotte's economy continued to perform well, particularly relative to the Comoros, where a sense of "deprivation" vis-à-vis the more prosperous Mayotte was considered a contributing factor to the secessionist movement on Anjouan (see article on Comoro Islands).

Negotiations between officials from Mayotte and the French government in 1998 led to a tentative agreement that Mayotte would initially become a "departmental collectivity" (*collectivité départemental*). It was reportedly understood that an "evolutionary process" would subsequently lead to full-fledged departmental status for the island. French officials remained cautious, however, about the implications of any formal settlement that lacked UN and AU endorsement of French sovereignty over Mayotte.

Over the objections of Mayotte's Senate and National Assembly representatives, Marcel HENRY and Henry JEAN-BAPTISTE, who renewed their call for full overseas departmental status for the island, the General Council and 16 out of 17 communes ultimately approved the *collectivité départemental* proposal, which was formally signed in Paris on January 27, 2000. In a referendum on July 2 nearly three-fourths of the voters supported the plan, although the precise procedures and dates remained to be worked out for the gradual transfer, over a ten-year period, of selected powers from the prefect to the General Council. Mayotte's status was formally changed from departmental collectivity to overseas collectivity under the 2003 constitutional amendments.

In the June 2007 National Assembly election Abdoulatifou ALY of the MDM defeated Kamardine's reelection bid. He then chose to sit with the New Center group but later moved to François Bayrou's MoDem. Following the March 2008 local elections, the UMP's Ahmed Attoumani DOUCHINA was elected president of the General Council. The UMP had won eight council seats, followed by *Divers Droit* with four.

Also during March 2008, Mayotte drew international attention following the flight of Col. Mohammed Bacar from the Comoran island of Anjouan, where his rebellious administration had been deposed by Comoran and AU troops. On Mayotte, Bacar and some two dozen supporters were charged with weapons possession and with illegally entering French waters. Anti-Bacar riots led the authorities to transfer the fugitives to Reunion, and on July 18, having been given suspended sentences for importing arms, Bacar and three others were expelled to Benin.

On March 29, 2009, voters in Mayotte overwhelmingly endorsed changing the collectivity to a department. The vote in favor of departmental status was 95 percent, which did not dissuade the AU and the government of the Comoros from denouncing the referendum. The change in status was completed on March 31, 2011. The change left a number of structural reforms to be implemented, including adoption of a secular code of laws and formation of a judicial system that, under the French constitution, cannot retain the present Muslim and customary influences. During a visit to the island in January 2010, President Sarkozy, in addition to promising increased funding for schools and housing, focused on the problem of illegal immigration from the Comoros. As many of one-third of Mayotte's current residents may have arrived illegally, and during 2009 Mayotte accounted for half of the 29,000 expulsions from French territory. Daniel Zaïdani was elected president on April 3, 2011. He beat Douchina by one vote. Left-wing and socialist candidates won both national assembly seats in the June 2012 legislative elections in Mayotte, although Nicolas Sarkozy edged out François Hollande in the May 2012 presidential ballot by 51 percent to 49 percent.

Prefect: Jacques WITKOWSKI.

President of the General Council: Daniel ZAÏDANI (*Divers Gauche*).

Reunion (*La Réunion*). The island of Reunion, located in the Indian Ocean about 600 miles east of Madagascar, has been a French possession since 1642, although it did not assume its present name on a permanent basis until 1848. It has been an overseas department since 1946. The island has an area of 970 square miles (2,510 sq. km). Its population of 817,000 (2009E), located mainly on the coast, is composed of Creoles, whites, Malabar Indians, blacks, Malays, Vietnamese, and Chinese. The capital, Saint-Denis, had a population of 140,733 in 2007. The economy is based primarily on sugarcane cultivation, tourism, and public sector employment. Reunion elects five members of the French National Assembly and four senators. Local administration is based on 24 communes and 49 cantons.

Currently active parties include the local branches of the PS, the UMP, and MoDem. Other organizations include the **Reunion Communist Party** (*Parti Communiste Réunionnais*—PCR) and the **Reunion Greens** (*Les Verts Réunion*). In the late 1990s a proposal to divide Reunion into two departments generated controversy, with President Chirac being the most prominent French official to voice support for the idea. In 2000, however, both the Senate and the National Assembly voted down any such division. In the June 2007 National Assembly election only one incumbent, the UMP's Bertho AUDIFAX, lost his seat, which was won by the PS's Jean-Claude FRUTEAU. René-Paul VICTORIA (UMP) and Huguette BELLO (PCR) won reelection, while the two open seats were won by Patrick LEBRETON (PS) and Didier Robert (UMP), the latter having easily defeated President Vergès in a runoff. The department's senators are Anne-Marie PAYET, who was elected as a member of the UDF; Gélita HOREAU, who joined the Communist, Republican, and Citizen group in the Senate; and Jean-Paul VIRAPOULLE (UMP).

Speaking in Brussels at a May 2010 Forum for Outermost Europe 2010, hosted by the EU's European Commission, President Robert commented on the EU's free trade agreements with Asian and Pacific countries and on the organization's common fisheries policy. He cautioned that Reunion had no desire to "fall a victim to the external policies of the EU." In the second round of the presidential elections of May 2012, François Hollande easily defeated Nicolas Sarkozy, winning 71.5 percent of the vote.

Prefect: Jean-Luc MARX.

President of the General Council: Nassimah DINDAR (UMP).

President of the Regional Council: Didier ROBERT (UMP).

Overseas Collectivities:

Through the years, various amendments and statutes have defined and redefined the six jurisdictions discussed below. These changes have often been accompanied by revisions in legislative structures. The status overseas collectivity (*collectivité d'outre-mer*) was established by the constitutional reform of March 2003. Legislation passed in February 2007 raised Saint Barthelemy and Saint Martin from communes, within the overseas department of Guadeloupe, to separate overseas collectivities.

French Polynesia (*Polynésie Française*). Scattered over a wide expanse of the South Pacific, the 35 islands and 83 atolls of French Polynesia—comprising the Austral (Tubuai) Islands, the Gambier Islands, the Marquesas Archipelago, the Society Archipelago, and the Tuamotu Archipelago—have a combined area of 1,622 square miles (4,200 sq. km) and a population of 267,000 (2010E), of whom approximately 26,050 are settled in the territorial capital, Papeete, on the island of Tahiti. A French protectorate from 1843, in 1880 Tahiti was annexed under a treaty signed by King POMARE V. The colony gradually expanded and was renamed French Oceania in 1903. Designated as an overseas territory in 1946, French Polynesia assumed its present name in 1957.

Renewed French nuclear testing in the territory, conducted from September 1995 to January 1996, was met with international protests and serious violence in Papeete. France began dismantling the Mururoa nuclear test site in 1997, and the project was completed in mid-1998.

The economy relies heavily on tourism, with additional earnings coming from the harvesting of black pearls, the sale of commercial fishing licenses, and the export of coconut products. The territory is represented in the French Parliament by two National Assembly deputies and two senators.

In November 1995 the Territorial Assembly adopted an accord providing for greater autonomy in such areas as transportation, communications, the offshore economic zone, and fishing rights. France retained responsibility for defense and security as well as judicial oversight in the accord, which was approved by the French National Assembly in December and entered into effect in April 1996.

In March 2003, as specified by French constitutional revisions, French Polynesia was reclassified from overseas territory to overseas collectivity, with the provision that additional autonomy could be granted by legislative action. A statute to that effect was passed by the Senate in December 2003 and the National Assembly in January 2004, with the Constitutional Council approving the Autonomy Act for French Polynesia on February 27. Under the act local executive responsibilities are vested in a Council of Ministers headed by a president responsible to the Assembly of French Polynesia, which is directly elected for a five-year term.

An election for the new, 57-member Assembly of French Polynesia was held on May 23, 2004, but a near-stalemate resulted. The UMP-allied TH won 28 seats and a newly organized coalition, the **Union for Democracy** (*Union pour la Démocratie*—UPD), led by Oscar Temaru of the *Tavini Huira'atira,* won 27, including 24 seats in the Windward Islands of Tahiti and Moorea. The balance of power was thus held by Nicole BOUTEAU of the **This Country Is Yours** (*No Oe E Te Nunaa*) party and *Fe'tia Api*'s Philip SCHYLE, who had become party president as a consequence of Boris Léontieff's death in a 2002 plane crash. Elected president by the legislature on June 15, Temaru indicated his intention to move French Polynesia toward a goal of independence within 20 years.

In January 2006 President Temaru disbanded the Polynesia Intervention Group (*Groupement d'Intervention de la Polynesie*—GIP), a 1,300-person quasi-security force that had been established in the mid-1990s by Flosse to assist in national and regional disaster relief but had since taken on additional land and maritime responsibilities. Several times during 2005 some 300 GIP militants had blockaded the port of Papeete and its industrial zone over a disputed employment contract.

On December 13, 2006, having failed to hold the support of several cabinet members and legislators whom he had recruited in April, Temaru lost a censure motion, by a vote of 29–0, that was boycotted by the UPD. On December 26 the TH's Tong Sang, backed by Vernaudon's

Ai'a Api and Bouissou's *Rautahi,* was elected president. Although President Tong Sang pledged to restore cordial relations with France and to refocus the government's attention to economic development, tensions with Paris continued to exist not only over the autonomy/independence divide, but also over endemic corruption and cultural matters. In 2006 France refused to permit use of indigenous languages in assembly debates, and French courts refused to acknowledge any legal role for a restored Indigenous Land Tribunal. Efforts by traditionalists to create a formal customary institution, comparable to one in New Caledonia, have also been rebuffed.

In the June 2007 National Assembly election Michel BUILLARD (UMP) won reelection, defeating Oscar Temaru, and the TH's Bruno SANDRAS won the other seat. The collectivity is represented in the Senate by Gaston FLOSSE from People's Rally for the Republic Party (*Tahoera'a Huiraatira*) and the UPD's Richard TUHEIAVA. On September 14, Temaru reassumed the presidency, two weeks after he and Flosse had engineered the ouster of Tong Sang, who subsequently established his own party, the **Polynesia, Our Home** (*O Porinetia, To Tatou Ai'a*—OPTTA).

The French secretary of state for overseas territories, Christian ESTROSI, responding to Polynesia's seeming inability to establish a stable government, then convinced the French Parliament to reform the collectivity's electoral system. Among other changes, to be elected in a first round of voting, assembly candidates would have to achieve 50 percent of the vote. In all other constituencies, only those candidates winning at least 12.5 percent could advance to a second round. Despite the objections of many Polynesians, including Temaru, who accused Paris of interfering in internal Polynesian affairs, the Council of State approved the reform package in December, thereby permitting an early assembly election.

On February 9, 2009, facing a no-confidence vote engineered by Assembly Speaker Temaru, his UPD, the TH, and *Rautahi,* Tong Sang resigned as president. Two days later, Tong Sang faced former president Temaru, Edouard Fritch, and an independent, Sandra LEVY-AGAMI, in yet another presidential election. Temaru, with 24 votes, and Tong Sang, with 20, proceeded to a runoff, from which Temaru emerged with a 37–20 victory. Only two months later, however, Gaston Flosse announced that the TH was ready to join the opposition, in part because of a government proposal to adopt an income tax. President Temaru thereupon formed a surprising alliance with Tong Sang's TTA, cementing his hold on the presidency. A new cabinet announced on April 17 included, in addition to the UPD and the TTA, two members of an assembly group led by Jean-Christophe Bouissou, and two TH defectors.

On November 24, 2009, President Temaru lost a no-confidence vote 29–24, and Tong Sang was elected as his successor the following day by a vote of 29–28. The resultant government was led by the newly allied TTA and TH, which, however, parted ways once again in April 2010 over the government's lack of support for Flosse's becoming assembly speaker. That post went instead to Oscar Temaru. A month later, Flosse was convicted and fined for obstructing an investigation into a disbanded intelligence unit.

The continuing governmental instability had led President Sarkozy to announce in January 2010 that additional electoral reforms would be introduced before the end of the year. A council of traditional chiefs was among those who had requested Paris's intervention. In September French Polynesian government leaders met with French government representatives in Paris. The French side reportedly threatened to cut off aid to French Polynesia, unless the government there managed to become more stable, and to focus more on economic development. In October the French government unveiled, and in July 2011 passed, some changes to the territory's electoral system in the hope of improving its stability. Representation from Tahiti was increased and that of the outer islands reduced.

In the presidential elections of May 2012, French Polynesia voted for Nicolas Sarkozy, who won 53 percent of the vote in the second ballot, compared to 47 percent for François Hollande. Similarly, right-wing candidates picked up all three of French Polynesia's seats in the national assemble in the June 2012 legislative elections, defeating regionalist candidates in the second-round runoff. In territorial elections held in May 2013, Gaston Flosse's proautonomy, anti-independence party won a majority of seats, 38 out of 57, and he consequently was returned to the presidency at the age of 82. The economic situation in Reunion is bleak, with unemployment at 30 percent, its tourist industry having been hit hard by the recession in France. Since taking office, Flosse has been searching for outside investment from mainland France and China to lift the collectivity out of its slump.

High Commissioner: Jean-pierre LAFLAQUIERE.

President of the Government: Gaston FLOSSE (*Tahoera'a Huiraatira*).

Speaker of the Assembly: Édouard FRITCH (*Tahoera'a Huiraatira*).

Saint Barthelemy (*Saint-Barthélemy*). Lying east of the Virgin Islands in the Leeward Islands of the Lesser Antilles in the Caribbean, with St. Martin to the northwest and St. Kitts and Nevis to the South, St. Barth (also St. Bart, St. Barts, St. Barths) came under French control in 1648, was sold to Sweden in 1784, and was sold back to France in 1878, at which time it was administratively linked to Guadeloupe. On February 21, 2007, President Chirac signed into law legislation converting the island from a commune of the Department of Guadeloupe to a separate overseas collectivity. The process of amicable separation from Guadeloupe had been put in motion by passage of a referendum on December 7, 2003, in which 96 percent of those voting approved becoming a collectivity.

St. Barth is France's smallest overseas collectivity, with an area of 9 square miles (24 sq. km) and a population of approximately 8,902(2009E). The seat of government and largest town is Gustavia (named after a Swedish king). The vast majority of the population is white, and although French is the official language, English is also widely spoken. With no natural resources to exploit and virtually no arable land, the economy depends heavily on high-end tourism.

The government of St. Barth combines aspects of a commune, a department, and a region. The representative of the French government is a deputy prefect (*préfet délégué*). The Territorial Council comprises 19 members serving five-year terms. The council elects from its membership a president and a six-member Executive Council. In the new collectivity's first election, held July 1, 2007, the **St. Barth First** (*St.-Barth d'Abord*) list, headed by Bruno MAGRAS (UMP), the communal mayor, won an easy victory, taking 72 percent of the vote and 16 council seats. The other 3 seats were split among the other three competing lists: **Together for Saint Barthelemy** (*Ensemble pour Saint-Barthélemy*), headed by Benoît CHAUVIN (MoDem and Cap 21); **All United for Saint Barthelemy** (*Tous Unis pour Saint-Barthélemy*), led by Karine MIOT; and **Action-Balance-Transparency** (*Action-Equilibre-Transparence*), led by Maxime DESOUCHES. Magras was elected president by the council when it convened on July 15.

The island's first senator, Michel MAGRAS (UMP), was elected in September 2008. The island held its second territorial elections in March 2012, in which the UMP, led by Bruno Magras, secured an absolute majority in the first round of balloting. The island received its first member of the National Assembly following the June 2012 legislative elections, with Hélène VAINQUEUR-CHRISTOPHE (PS) winning the seat.

Deputy Prefect: Philippe CHOPIN.

President of the Territorial Council: Bruno MAGRAS (UMP).

Saint Martin (*Saint-Martin*). Lying east of the Virgin Islands in the Leeward Islands of the Lesser Antilles, with Anguilla to the north and Saint Barthelemy to the southeast, the island of St. Martin is divided roughly in half, with the French overseas collectivity of *Saint-Martin* in the north and the Dutch dependency *Sint Maarten* in the south. First claimed by Spain following the early voyages of Christopher Columbus (who, despite legend, neither named nor made explicit reference to the island), Saint Martin was partitioned by the Dutch and French in 1648, although up until 1815, as a consequence of various European wars, the French sector repeatedly fell under Dutch or English control. During this period the island's economy was based on the extraction of salt from salt ponds and the cultivation of cotton, tobacco, and, from the late 1700s, sugarcane, which led to the importation of African slaves far in excess of the white population. Emancipation came in 1848, after which sugar declined in importance.

From 1946 the French half of the island comprised two communes in the Department of Guadeloupe. Seventy-six percent of St. Martin's voters approved establishment of a separate overseas collectivity in a referendum held on December 7, 2003. On February 21, 2007, President Chirac signed the necessary legislation, which accorded the same collectivity status to nearby Saint Barthelemy. St. Martin became fully established as a collectivity when its first Territorial Council convened on July 15, 2007.

The overseas collectivity of St. Martin encompasses about 20 square miles (53 sq. km) and has a population of 37,461 (2009E). The administrative center and largest community is Marigot. The population is primarily of African, British, Dutch, French, and Creole ancestry.

French is the official language, but English is spoken universally. Today, the economy largely depends on tourism, followed by trade and offshore financial services.

Representing the French government is a deputy prefect. Local legislative responsibility is held by the Territorial Council, which comprises 23 members serving five-year terms. The council elects from its membership a president and an Executive Council. Five lists competed in the collectivity's first election, held July 1 and 8, 2007: the **Union for Progress** (*Union pour le Progrès*—UPP), led by Louis CONSTANT-FLEMING (UMP), which won 40 percent of the first-round vote; **Togetherness, Responsibility, Success** (*Rassemblement, Responsabilité, Réussite*—RRR), led by Alain RICHARDSON (32 percent); **Succeed Saint-Martin** (*Réussir Saint-Martin*—RSM), led by Jean-Luc HAMLET (11 percent); **Alliance for the Overseas Collectivity of Saint Martin** (*Alliance pour le COM de Saint-Martin*), headed by Dominique RIBOUD (9 percent); and the **Democratic Alliance for Saint Martin** (*Alliance Démocratique pour le Saint-Martin*), led by Wendel COCKS (8 percent). The first three proceeded to the second round, in which the UPP won 16 seats, the RRR won 6, and the RSM won 1.

In the March 2012 territorial elections, Alain Richardson from the Triple R party (*Rassemblement Responsabilite Reussite*) was elected President of the Territorial Council, defeating Daniel Gibbs. In April 2013 the Territorial Council elected its first female president, Aline Hanson, from the RRR party.

Deputy Prefect: Philippe CHOPIN.

President of the Territorial Council: Aline HANSON.

Saint Pierre and Miquelon (*Saint-Pierre et Miquelon*). Located off Newfoundland in the North Atlantic, St. Pierre and Miquelon consists of eight small islands covering 93 square miles (242 sq. km). Until recently rich in fish, the surrounding waters were regularly visited by Basque fishermen well before the advent of British and French territorial claims, which were not definitely resolved, in France's favor, until 1814. The population in 2009 was 6,345 of whom almost 90 percent lived in the capital, St. Pierre. Formerly an overseas territory, the islands were raised to the status of an overseas department in 1976 following a referendum; by 1982, however, popular sentiment clearly favored the status of a territorial collectivity, which came into effect in 1985.

The most serious subsequent issue was a dispute between France and Canada involving a French claim to a 200-mile maritime economic zone—Canada acknowledged only the traditional 12-mile limit—and a related controversy centered on fishing quotas. In 1992 an international arbitration tribunal awarded the islands an exclusive economic zone of 3,600 square miles (8,700 sq. km), or about one-fifth of what France had sought. More recently, severe overfishing of cod and the consequent closure of fishing grounds have had a dramatic effect on the economy. In May 2009 France lodged claims at the UN Commission on the Limits of the Continental Shelf to tracts of the seabed extending as far as 350 nautical miles. Tourism and fish farming are among the industries now being promoted.

An overseas collectivity since 2003, St. Pierre and Miquelon has an elected Territorial Council (previously called the General Council), in addition to elected municipal councils, and is represented in the French Parliament by one deputy and one senator. Members of the Territorial Council serve six-year terms.

The 2012 French presidential elections were easily won by François Hollande, who defeated Nicolas Sarkozy in the second round by 65 percent to 35 percent. In the June 2012 legislative elections, Annick GIRARDIN (Radical Left) won the collectivity's seat in the national assembly. The collectivity's representative in the French Senate since 2011 has been Karine CLAIREAUX (PS).

Prefect: Patrice LATRON.

President of the Territorial Council: Stéphane ARTANO (AD).

Wallis and Futuna Islands (*Wallis et Futuna*). The inhabitants of Wallis and Futuna, French protectorates from 1888, voted in 1959 to exchange their status for that of a French overseas territory. An overseas collectivity since 2003, Wallis and Futuna covers 106 square miles (274 sq. km) in the South Pacific just west of Samoa, with a population of 12,835 (2010E), excluding some 20,000 Wallisians residing in New Caledonia and Vanuatu. The capital, Mata'utu, has a population of approximately 1,200. The economy relies heavily on French aid, public sector jobs, and remittances sent home from New Caledonia.

The islands are governed by a chief administrator and an elected Territorial Assembly and are represented in the French Parliament by one deputy and one senator. There is also a six-member Territorial Council encompassing the kings of the islands' three traditional kingdoms plus three members appointed by the chief administrator. Monarchical powers are limited to traditional matters and customary law, but the kings remain influential.

A political crisis was precipitated in 2005 when a grandson of Tomasi KULIMOETOKE, the traditional king of Wallis, sought refuge in the royal palace to avoid serving an 18-month prison sentence for vehicular homicide. Although he surrendered in June and was taken to New Caledonia to serve his sentence, what began as a conflict between customary law and the French penal code had become an impasse between traditionalists, who continued to support the administration of Wallis's prime minister, Kapeliele FAUPALA, and a reformist group led by the UPWF and the **Alliance of Wallis and Futuna** (*Alliance de Wallis et Futuna*—AWF), with tacit backing from Futuna's two royal clans. On May 22 the reformists announced a rival administration, headed by Kolovisi (Clovis) LOGOLOGOFOLAU, that was subsequently recognized by the chief administrator, Xavier de Furst. In September, when the reformists moved forward in an effort to depose the 86-year-old Kulimoetoke, who had ruled on Wallis since 1959, the king's supporters blockaded roads and shut down the airport to prevent the coronation of a new king. A special envoy from New Caledonia, Louis Lefranc, was called in to mediate the conflict, and on September 26 he reaffirmed French recognition of King Kulimoetoke. As a consequence, Logologofolau and a number of his supporters fled to New Caledonia. Early in the year, the AFW's Apeleto (Albert) LIKUVALU had been elected president of the Territorial Assembly, but on November 23 he was replaced by Ermenigilde SIMETE, who had center-right backing.

In March 2006 the two kings of Futuna, Soane Patita MAITUKU and Visesio MOELIKU, met in Paris with President Chirac, who gave his support to their request for Futuna to be made a subprefecture, which would accord the island a greater degree of administrative independence from Wallis. (The island's first subprefect took office in November 2006.) In February 2007 the French government and island representatives reached agreement on a $50 million developmental aid package for 2007–2011 that focused on needed infrastructure, health, and education.

On Futuna, disagreements within the traditional hierarchies have recently led to some changes. In February 2008 the chiefly clans of Alo removed King Maituku from office over opposition to his style of management. The coronation of his successor, Petelo VIKENA, took place on November 6, but King Vikena stepped down on January 22, 2010, reportedly because of vandalism and criticism from clan leaders. No successor had been chosen by midyear by late 2011. Meanwhile, King Moeliku of Sigave, the other traditional kingdom of Futuna, left office in August 2009, and his successor, Polikalepo KOLIVAI, was not crowned until July 3, 2010.

In mid-March 2010 Wallis and Futuna suffered significant damage from Cyclone Tomas. On hard-hit Futuna, the majority of crops were destroyed and at least 70 percent of the buildings reportedly suffered severe damage or were destroyed. The French military rushed aid from New Caledonia, but the response was widely criticized as inadequate. In June the French secretary of state for overseas territories, Marie-Luce Penchard, promised that additional rebuilding aid would be forthcoming.

In July 2010, following several months of labor discord and disruptions to electricity and water supplies on Wallis, strikers claimed to have taken over the principal utility operator, Electricity of Wallis and Futuna (EWF), which was owned by a French company. A week earlier, King Faupala had terminated the contract with EWF, which disputed the legality of the action. Pending resolution in the courts, the strikers on Wallis began restoring services to the island. In the second round of the legislative elections of June 2012, the right-wing candidate David Vergé narrowly defeated the left-wing candidate Mikaele Kulimoetoke by 41.61 percent to 41.04 percent. In the presidential ballot runoff in May 2012, François Hollande defeated Nicolas Sarkozy by 56 percent to 44 percent. In April 2013 the islands elected their first female president of the Territorial Assembly since that institution was first established in 1962, Nivaleta Iloai.

Prefect: Michel AUBOUIN.

Chief Administrator: Michel JEANJEAN.

President of the Territorial Assembly: Nivaleta ILOAI.

Overseas Collectivities Sui Generis:

As recently as 2002 there were three overseas territories (*territoires d'outre-mer*): French Polynesia, Wallis and Futuna, and the French Southern and Antarctic Lands (TAAF). The constitutional amendments of March 2003 eliminated the category from the French constitution, although the TAAF remained an overseas territory by dint of legislation passed in 1955.

The classification "overseas country" (*pays d'outre-mer*) was established to recognize New Caledonia's unique constitutional status under 1998's Nouméa Accord between Paris and what was then the overseas territory of New Caledonia. The February 2007 legislation categorized both the TAAF and New Caledonia as collectivities sui generis (*collectivités sui generis*)—that is, as unique collectivities. Both nevertheless continue to be referenced, for descriptive rather than legal purposes, as a territory and an overseas country, respectively.

French Southern and Antarctic Lands (*Terres Australes et Antarctiques Françaises*—TAAF). The Southern and Antarctic Lands comprise the Antarctic continent between 136 and 142 degrees east longitude and south of 60 degrees south latitude (Adélie Land) plus four additional districts: the islands of Saint Paul and Amsterdam; the Kerguélen Archipelago; the Crozet Archipelago; and, since February 2007, the Scattered Islands (*Îles Éparses*) in the Indian Ocean. The Scattered Islands are Tromelin Island, situated off the northeast coast of Madagascar, and several islands located in the Mozambique Channel between Madagascar and the west coast of Africa: Bassas da India, Europa Island, Juan da Nova Island, and the Glorioso Islands.

The TAAF embraces some 170,000 square miles (440,000 sq. km), with a fluctuating population of scientific personnel numbering about 150 in the winter and 300 in the summer. Most are based in the Kerguélen Archipelago, located in the southern Indian Ocean, and Adélie Land. In January 2001 the seat of administration was moved from Paris to St. Pierre, Reunion. A Consultative Council that assists the territory's administrator meets at least twice yearly. The legal status of the Antarctic portion of the territory remains in suspense under the Antarctic Treaty of 1959 (see Antarctica in main alphabetical listing).

Chief Administrator: Pascal BOLOT.

New Caledonia (*Nouvelle-Calédonie*). Covering 7,375 square miles (19,000 sq. km) in the Pacific Ocean east of Queensland, Australia, New Caledonia includes, in addition to the main island of Grande Terre, the Loyalty Islands (*Îles Loyauté*) to the east, the Belep Islands (*Îles Bélep*) to the north, and a number of smaller islands. European contact dates from 1774, with the arrival of English explorer James Cook. France took possession in 1853, but a number of revolts by the indigenous Kanak population followed. After serving as a major base for U.S. Pacific forces in World War II, in 1946 New Caledonia was made an overseas territory.

New Caledonia has a population of 248,000 (2007E), of whom about 95,000 reside in Nouméa, the capital. The largest ethnic group is Melanesian (45 percent), followed by those of European origin (34 percent). Local government is based on 33 communes. New Caledonia is represented in the French Parliament by two deputies and two senators. An important mining center, the territory possesses some of the world's largest nickel reserves; the metal accounts for 90 percent of export earnings.

A long-term economic development plan, which included a proviso that the territory could not become independent for at least 19 years, was approved by the Territorial Assembly in 1979. In an assembly election the following July that was widely interpreted as a referendum on the issue, the Independence Front (*Front Indépendantiste*—FI), encompassing a group of parties demanding the severance of all links to France, obtained a little over one-third of the vote. Subsequently, the FI succeeded in concluding a legislative coalition with the autonomist Federation for a New Caledonian Society (*Fédération pour une Nouvelle Société Calédonienne*—FNSC), which had theretofore been allied with the anti-independence Rally for Caledonia in the Republic (*Rassemblement pour la Calédonie dans la République*—RPCR). In June 1982 the new de facto majority ousted the RPCR-led government and installed an FI-led "government of reform and development" headed by Jean-Marie TJIBAOU. The change in government without an intervening election precipitated widespread demonstrations by right-wing elements, who invaded the Territorial Assembly chamber in July, injuring three FI deputies. Following a restoration of order, the high commissioner announced that a new constitution for New Caledonia, to be promulgated by mid-1983, would give the territory increased internal autonomy.

Under the proposed statute of autonomy, as presented by the French government in March 1983, substantial powers would be transferred from the French high commissioner to a new territorial government headed by a president, who would be elected by the Territorial Assembly and empowered to name his own ministers. At the conclusion of an all-party conference near Paris in mid-July, the FI and the FNSC accepted the French offer on the basis of an anticipated vote on self-determination that would be confined to Melanesians and other New Caledonians with at least one parent born in the territory. The RPCR, dominated by white planters, declared its opposition to any reform that excluded from the franchise persons other than French military and civil service personnel.

In 1984 the French National Assembly approved the autonomy statute, without, however, calling for electoral reform. As a result, the FI position hardened into a demand that the vote be confined exclusively to Melanesians. Subsequently, the FI joined with a number of other pro-independence groups in forming the **Kanak Socialist National Liberation Front** (*Front de Libération Nationale Kanak Socialiste*—FLNKS). The FLNKS boycotted the November legislative election, at which the RPCR won 34 of 42 seats. One week later, amid mounting acts of terrorism and the deaths of a number of separatists, the FLNKS announced the formation of a provisional Kanaki government under Tjibaou's presidency.

In the face of an FLNKS boycott, an independence referendum conducted in September 1987 yielded a 98 percent vote in favor of remaining within the republic. A month later, Pons introduced a new autonomy statute that by means of boundary redefinition left the FLNKS dominant in two, rather than three, of the four regions. In April 1988 the RPCR won 35 of 48 seats in the new Territorial Congress.

Following the Socialists' return to power in 1988, the Rocard government concluded an agreement with pro- and anti-independence forces on a plan whereby the French government, through its high commissioner, would administer the territory for a year, in the course of which New Caledonia would be divided into three new autonomous regions, one (in the south) dominated by settlers and two (in the north and in the Loyalty Islands) by Kanaks. The arrangement, to commence in 1989, would remain in effect for a ten-year period, near the end of which a territory-wide referendum on independence would be held. The "Matignon Accord" ultimately received the FLNKS's backing and was approved by both territorial and mainland voters in November.

Hard-line separatists subsequently branded the 1988 pact as a sellout to the colonists, and in May 1989 FLNKS leader Tjibaou and his deputy, Yeiwene YEIWENE, were assassinated during a tribal ceremony on the island of Ouvéa. Despite the bloodshed, elections to provincial assemblies for the three regions were conducted, as scheduled, in June 1989, with the RPCR winning in the south and the FLNKS ahead elsewhere. A week later, the restructured Territorial Congress, with limited powers and an RPCR majority, elected its president.

Although he headed one of the FLNKS's relatively hard-line components, Tjibaou's successor, Paul NÉAOUTYINE, called in early 1990 for the coalition to redirect its immediate energies to economic development. He also indicated that as part of its effort to bring all pro-independence groups into a single organization, the FLNKS would not rule out talks with the extremist **United Kanak Liberation Front** (*Front Uni de Libération Kanak*—FULK), which had rejected the 1988 accord and whose leader, Yann Céléné UREGEI, had left New Caledonia in the wake of the Tjibaou assassination. Earlier, Nidoïsh NAISSELINE, leader of the equally radical **Kanak Socialist Liberation** (*Libération Kanak Socialiste*—LKS), had announced that the LKS would join the FULK in a front with a structure paralleling that of the FLNKS.

In the 1995 provincial election the RPCR retained a majority in the Territorial Congress and the FLNKS again took second place. Under the new leadership of Rock WAMYTAN of the **Caledonian Union** (*Union Calédonienne*—UC), in February 1996 the FLNKS agreed that a consensus proposal on the territory's future, rather than the stark options of independence or continued French territorial status, should be put to a referendum in 1998. The FLNKS withdrew from discussions with the French government several months later, however, partly because Paris had removed full independence from the list of possible outcomes. Negotiations resumed sporadically later in the year, but no progress was achieved as attention focused on a major dispute over the proposed opening of a new nickel smelter in the north. Some FLNKS elements viewed as "blackmail" French insistence that the facility could be opened only after resolution of the autonomy issue. As a result of the conflict, the FLNKS boycotted the 1997 French National Assembly election, at which the two RPCR incumbents were reelected, and blockaded nickel operations in the south for much of the year. Some FLNKS members questioned its tactics, however, which resulted in formation of the **Federation of Independence Coordination Committees** (*Fédération des Comités de Coordination des Indépendantistes*—FCCI).

On April 21, 1998, representatives of the FLNKS and RPCR concluded an agreement with French officials providing for a period of "shared sovereignty" during which power would gradually devolve to the island. A final referendum on the question of independence would be held in 15–20 years. The "Nouméa Accord" was formally signed on May 5 during a ceremony in the capital attended by French Prime Minister Jospin, and the French Parliament endorsed the pact on July 6. A referendum in New Caledonia on November 8 produced a 72 percent "yes" vote, despite opposition from the local branch of the National Front (FN) and other right-wing parties. The French National Assembly approved the required implementing legislation in December, followed by the Senate in February 1999.

In elections for three new provincial assemblies in May 1999, the RPCR secured a majority in South Province, while pro-independence alliances won majorities in North Province and the Loyalty Islands. Disagreements over the power-sharing arrangement persisted, however, which contributed to President Lèques's decision to step down following the March 2001 provincial elections. On April 3 the Congress elected the RPCR's Pierre FROGIER to head a new government in which the FLNKS's Déwé GORODEY assumed the vice presidency. With the UC and Palika in conflict over leadership of the FLNKS, Wamytan subsequently lost the front's presidency.

In the National Assembly election in June 2002 the two incumbents were returned under the banner of President Chirac's new UMP. In runoff balloting Pierre Frogier defeated the FLNKS's Paul Néaoutyine, and Jacques LAFLEUR of the RPCR defeated the APLC's Didier Leroux.

Meanwhile, the government was increasingly beset by internal policy disputes, which ultimately led to its dissolution and reorganization in November 2002, again under the leadership of Frogier. In the new Council of Ministers the RPCR-FCCI coalition remained dominant, holding seven of the ten ministerial posts, to two for the FLNKS and one for the UC.

The May 9, 2004, assembly elections saw a new pro-autonomy party, the **Future Together** (*Avenir Ensemble*—AE), unseat the RPCR in the south, winning 19 seats to 16 for the RPCR and then forming a provincial government with the support of the FN, which had won the remaining 4 seats. (None of the pro-independence parties had met the 5 percent threshold needed for representation under the proportional distribution system.) In Northern Province the pro-independence parties continued to dominate, led by the UNI and the UC, while in the Loyalty Islands the assembly's 14 seats were split among six parties. In the resultant Congress the AE and RPCR each held 16 seats, followed by the UNI-FLNKS, 8; the UC, 7; the FN, 4; the LKS, 1; the **Renewed Caledonian Union** (*Union Calédonienne Renouvea*—UCR), 1; and the **Union of Cooperating Committees for Independence** (*Union des Comités de Coopération pour l'Indépendance*—UCCI), 1.

On February 17, 2007, in keeping with a commitment in the Nouméa Accord to prevent an influx of Europeans from diluting the indigenous vote, the French Parliament temporarily froze the New Caledonian electoral roll. As a consequence, only those resident in 1998 were to be permitted to vote in the local elections in 2009 through 2014. The measure, which affected some 7,000 French nationals, was strongly opposed by the RPCR and other anti-independence parties. It is expected that after 2014 a minimum residency requirement will be instituted.

In the June 2007 National Assembly election the RPCR/UMP claimed both seats. In runoff balloting, incumbent Pierre Frogier defeated Charles PIDJOT (FLNKS), and Gaël YANNO won against Charles WASHETINE (FLNKS). Losing candidates included incumbent Jacques Lafleur, who, after 29 years in office, failed to make it to the second round. He had been ousted as RPCR leader in August 2006 and consequently set up a new party, the **Rally for Caledonia** (*Rassemblement pour la Calédonie*—RPC). In both districts the AE candidates finished third in the first round, which left analysts questioning the durability of the AE government.

The elections for the three provincial assemblies on May 10, 2009, concluded with anti-independence parties holding a decided overall advantage among the 76 seats. As a consequence, the pro-French contingents in the 54-seat Congress controlled 31 seats, led by **The Rally–UMP** (*Le Rassemblement–UMP,* the renamed RPCR/UMP); the **Caledonia Together** (*Calédonie Ensemble*—CE), a new party formed by Philippe GOMÈS upon his departure from the AE; a coalition of the AE and Sen. Simon LOUECKHOTE's **The Movement for Diversity** (*La Mouvement de la Diversité*—LMD); and the RPC. Successful pro-independence parties and coalitions (24 seats), led by the UNI (Palika and the UCR) and the UC, also included the FLNKS, Louis Kotra UREGEI's new **Labor Party** (*Parti Travailliste*—PI), and the LKS.

Despite the recent divisions in their camp, the principal anti-independence parties, with encouragement from Paris, hammered out a "stability pact" that saw Gomès, the outgoing president of the Southern Province assembly, elected president of the collectivity on June 5, 2009. His predecessor, Harold Martin, was named president of the Congress, while Pierre Frogier took over as Southern Province assembly president. Election of a vice president took until June 15, when the Congress chose Pierre NGAIOHNI of the FLNKS.

On February 17, 2011, the government collapsed on the withdrawal of the UC from the coalition. The UC accused President Gomès of not honoring a promise to fly the Kanak flag alongside the French tricolor. The assembly met again on March 4, its only business being to elect a new government. Harold Martin (AE) was elected president, but, as he had previously promised, Gomès immediately took his party out of the coalition, thus forcing the government's collapse. Gomès intended to make France intervene and call new general elections. Instead, while the President Martin government was operating as a caretaker, the Sarkozy administration in July changed New Caledonia's basic law, ensuring any government at least 18 months' stability before it could be removed by a vote of no-confidence.

In late August 2011 Sarkozy visited New Caledonia. He urged all parties to cooperate more and declared that, while he preferred the territory to remain French, he would not interfere if a referendum voted for total independence. In the presidential elections of 2012, Sarkozy easily defeated François Hollande, winning 63 percent of the vote compared to Hollande's 37 percent. Of New Caledonia's two seats in the national assembly, the right-wing candidate Sonia Lagarde won one, while the other was won by Philippe Gomès, another right-wing candidate, who defeated Jean Pierre Djaiwe. Anti-independence candidates in the June 2012 legislative elections scored 70 percent of the vote, while pro-independence candidates won 30 percent.

High Commissioner: Jean-Jacques BROT.

President of the Government: Harold MARTIN (AE).

President of the Congress: Gérard POADJA.

Insular Possession:

Clipperton Island (*Île Clipperton*). Uninhabited Clipperton Island is located in the North Pacific, roughly 800 miles southwest of Mexico. A coral atoll with an area of about 3.5 square miles (9 sq. km), Clipperton was named after the sea captain who claimed it for Great Britain in 1705. The French claim dates from 1708, when the island was given the competing name Passion Island (*Île de Passion*). Occupied by Mexico in 1897, Clipperton was ultimately awarded to France in 1931 and was then administered, from 1936 until early 2007, by the high commissioner of French Polynesia. Legislation passed in February 2007 assigned the minister for overseas France direct responsibility.

GABON

Gabonese Republic
République Gabonaise

Political Status: Independent since August 17, 1960; present constitution, providing for "semi-presidential" regime, adopted March 14, 1991.

Area: 103,346 sq. mi. (267,667 sq. km).

Population: 1,576,207 (2012E—UN); 1,640,286 (2013E—U.S. Census).

Major Urban Center (2005E): LIBREVILLE (metropolitan area, 659,000).

Official Language: French.

Monetary Unit: CFA Franc (official rate November 1, 2013: 486.52 francs = $1US). The CFA franc, previously pegged to the French franc, is now permanently pegged to the euro at 655.957 CFA francs = 1 euro.

President: Ali Ben BONGO Ondimba (Gabonese Democratic Party), elected in controversial balloting on August 30, 2009, resolved by Constitutional Court rulings on September 4 and October 12, succeeding Interim President Rose Francine ROGOMBÉ (Gabonese Democratic Party), who, on June 9, had constitutionally succeeded Ali Ben Bongo Ondimba's father, El Hadj Omar (formerly Albert-Bernard) BONGO Ondimba (Gabonese Democratic Party), who died on June 8; sworn in for a seven-year term on October 16, 2009.

Prime Minister: Raymond Ndong SIMA (Gabonese Democratic Party), appointed by President Bongo on February 27, 2012, to succeed Paul Biyoghe MBA (Gabonese Democratic Party), who resigned on February 13.

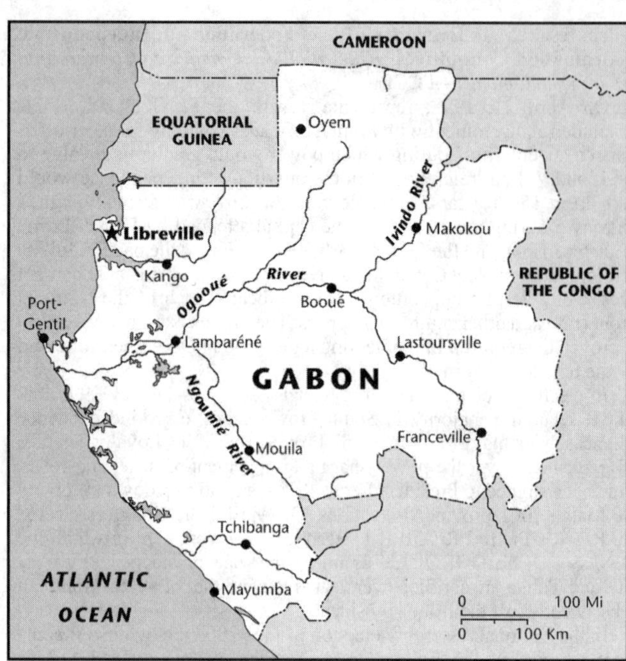

THE COUNTRY

A tropical, heavily forested country on the west coast of Central Africa, Gabon is inhabited by a sparse population whose largest components, among more than 40 distinct ethnic groups, are the Fang and Eshira tribes. A sizable European (predominantly French) community also is resident. Indigenous Gabonese speak a variety of Bantu languages, with Fang predominating in the north. About 60 percent of the population is Christian (largely Roman Catholic), with most of the rest adhering to traditional beliefs; there also is a small Muslim minority. Women constitute over half of salaried workers in the health and trading sectors, although female representation in party and government bodies is minimal. Women comprised 15.8 percent of the seats in the lower house (18 of 114) and 17.6 percent of the seats in the upper house (18 of 102).

Abundant natural resources that include oil, high-grade iron ore, manganese, uranium, and timber provided Gabon with a per capita GNP of over $4,200 in the early 1980s. Oil output accounted for about three-fourths of Gabon's export earnings until 1986. By 1988 the economic impact of recession in the oil industry significantly affected Gabon, though a subsequent recovery was noted by 1993. (For more on the history of Gabon's economy, please see the 2013 *Handbook.*)

Since 2003 the economy has rebounded, aided by higher oil prices, external-debt rescheduling, and an increase in non-oil revenues. Annual GDP growth averaged 3.7 percent in 2004–2008, fluctuating due to the non-oil sector, particularly timber and minerals. As a result of its economic recovery and significant progress in structural reforms and transparency, Gabon was able to negotiate early repayment of its $2.3 million debt to the Paris Club of creditors in January 2008. Meanwhile, the International Monetary Fund (IMF) commended Gabon for its progress in oil-revenue administration, including a reduction in oil subsidies in 2009, and for structural reforms "essential to improving the business climate." GDP growth contracted to less than 1 percent in 2009, in part due to a decline in oil prices. Noting the "painful social developments" domestically and the international economic crisis, the IMF said it would still help Gabon even though authorities had failed to meet the terms of a stand-by loan arrangement. Fund managers commended the administration, however, for improved governance but urged greater progress in structural reforms and transparency. As oil prices climbed higher, annual growth rebounded to an average of 5.6 percent in 2010–2011. The IMF also cited greater public investment and a recovery in the mining sector, as well as Gabon's having abolished "burdensome regulations," thus enhancing the business environment.

Economic activity was boosted by public investment in building and improving roads and stadiums ahead of the January 2012 Africa Cup of Nations. GDP growth remained moderately high in 2012, at 6.2 percent. Inflation that year grew by 3 percent, while GDP per capita was $11,929, one of the highest in the region. Nonetheless, there are widespread inequities in the distribution of wealth, with 20 percent of the population living on less than $2 per day. In April 2012 Gabon signed a deal with a South Korean firm to build a new oil refinery in Port Gentil that is expected to more than double the old refinery's output, to 50,000 barrels a day by 2016. Planning is also underway on several power plants to triple electrical output by 2020, and the Russian company Gunvor launched a $500 million joint Russo-Gabonese project to distribute oil throughout the region.

GOVERNMENT AND POLITICS

Political background. Colonized by France in the latter half of the 19th century and subsequently administered as a part of French Equatorial Africa, Gabon achieved full independence within the French Community on August 17, 1960. Its longtime political leader, President Léon MBA, ruled in a conservative yet pragmatic style and supported close political and economic relations with France. However, Mba's attempts to establish a one-party state based on his Gabon Democratic Bloc (*Bloc Démocratique Gabonais*—BDG) were resisted for several years by the Gabonese Democratic and Social Union (*Union Démocratique et Sociale Gabonais*—UDSG), led by Jean-Hilaire AUBAME. Only after an attempted coup by Aubame's army supporters had been thwarted by French military intervention in February 1964 and Mba's party had gained a majority in legislative elections two months later was the UDSG formally outlawed.

Mba was reelected to a seven-year presidential term in March 1967, but he died the following November and was succeeded by Vice President Albert-Bernard (subsequently El Hadj Omar) BONGO Ondimba. Officially declaring Gabon a one-party state in March 1968, Bongo announced a "renovation" policy that included conversion of the former ruling party into a new, nationwide political grouping, the

Gabonese Democratic Party (*Parti Démocratique Gabonais*—PDG). The incumbent was the sole candidate for reelection to a fourth term on November 9, 1986, having survived a coup attempt by military officers in 1985.

Pressured by a deteriorating economy and mounting protests against his regime, President Bongo announced in early March 1990 that a national conference would be called to discuss the launching of an inclusive political organization that would pave the way for eventual adoption of a multiparty system. However, the conference ended its month-long deliberations on April 21 with a call for the immediate introduction of democratic pluralism. The president responded by granting legal status to all of the participating organizations. Moreover, on April 29 he announced that longtime Prime Minister Léon MEBIAME would be succeeded by Casimir OYÉ MBA as head of a government that would include a number of opposition leaders.

First-round legislative balloting was held on September 23, 1990, the results of which were annulled in 32 of 120 constituencies because of alleged improprieties. At the conclusion of second-round balloting on October 21 and 28, 62 seats were declared to have been won by the PDG (including 3 seats by pro-PDG independents). Subsequently, the PDG tally was augmented by 4 seats, with 7 opposition parties being credited with a total of 54.

In May 1991 six of the seven opposition parties with legislative representation announced a boycott of parliamentary proceedings, called for a dissolution of the government, and demanded that the Bongo regime comply with the dictates of the 1990 national conference and the constitution adopted on March 14 (see Constitution and government, below). On June 7, two days after an opposition-led general strike, President Bongo announced the resignation of Oyé Mba's government and called on the opposition, now united in the Coordination of Democratic Opposition (*Coordination de l'Opposition Démocratique*—COD), to join a "government of national consensus." On June 15 the opposition rejected his offer; three days later Oye Mba was reappointed, and a new government was named that included a limited number of opposition figures.

In July 1992 the PDG-dominated National Assembly rejected an unprecedented no-confidence motion by a vote of 72 to 45. The motion, filed by the opposition to protest the government's rescheduling of local elections, closely followed assembly approval of a new electoral code, which opposition leaders described as "antidemocratic." Despite their drawing together in mid-1993 to form the Committee for Free and Democratic Elections, opposition groups failed to unite behind a single slate, and at balloting on December 5 President Bongo was credited with winning reelection over 13 competitors by a narrow 51.18 percent majority. The result was immediately challenged by runner-up Paul MBA-ABESSOLE of the National Rally of Woodcutters (*Rassemblement National des Bûcherons*—RNB), who accused Bongo of "high treason against the nation by an electoral coup d'état," declared himself president, and announced the formation of a parallel "government of combat" headed by his party's secretary general, Pierre-André KOMBILA Koumba. On December 12 Mba-Abessole announced the formation of the High Council of the Republic (*Haut Conseil de la République*—HCR), which included a majority of the opposition presidential candidates, to serve as an advisory body for his parallel government. On December 14 Bongo, promising a multiparty government of "broad consensus," termed the formation of the alternative body an "anticonstitutional act," and postelectoral unrest quickly subsided as the regime deployed heavily armed regular and paramilitary forces. Meanwhile, legislative balloting originally scheduled for December 26 was postponed until March 1994.

In January 1994 consumer prices skyrocketed, and widespread disturbances were reported after France halved the value of the CFA franc. On February 15 Mba-Abessole urged his supporters to "disobey all government directives" and threatened to expel party members who took part in Bongo's proposed unity government. One week later, nine people were killed when government troops supported by tanks destroyed the RNB's radio station and attacked Mba-Abessole's residence as a "punitive measure" for his having incited "hatred, violence, and intolerance." In addition, elections were rescheduled for August 1994.

On March 11, 1994, Prime Minister Oyé Mba resigned, stating that the country had entered a "new political phase"; however, Bongo reappointed him two days later, and on March 25 Oyé Mba named a new government, which included no opposition members. On April 8 Libreville lifted the state of alert and curfew that had been imposed almost without interruption since December 9, 1993.

On September 27, 1994, following three weeks of internationally supervised negotiations in Paris, government and opposition representatives signed an agreement calling for the establishment of a transitional coalition government and an independent electoral commission empowered to oversee an electoral timetable providing for local and legislative elections in 12 and 18 months, respectively. Consequently, on October 11 Oyé Mba again resigned, and two days later the president named a PDG confidant, Paulin OBAME-NGUEMA, as interim prime minister. Although Obame-Nguema's appointment was generally well received, the RNB continued to urge its members to refuse to participate in a Bongo-affiliated government and denounced the 27-member cabinet named by Obame-Nguema, which included 6 opposition members, for failing to reflect the opposition's legislative strength.

On February 3, 1995, the Constitutional Court, acting at the opposition's urging, ruled that the mandate of the current assembly could continue for the duration of the transition period defined by the 1994 accord. Three days later, opposition deputies ended their legislative boycott, and on April 21 President Bongo agreed to submit a package of constitutional reforms to voters, who provided an overwhelmingly positive response at balloting on June 25. The Bongo administration, however, proved reluctant to implement the Paris Accord, and in February 1996 the opposition called on France to pressure the government to adhere to the transitional schedule. Thereafter, in May, Bongo agreed to organize an electoral commission to schedule and oversee local and, subsequently, national legislative elections.

Local polling, originally scheduled for July 1996, was delayed until October 20 by organizational problems that remained largely unresolved as of election day. Consequently, there were widespread reports of incomplete electoral lists and ballot-box shortages, as well as a voter turnout rate as low as 10–15 percent in some areas. Such problems were so severe in Libreville that balloting there was suspended and completed in late November. Opposition leaders claimed that the disorganization was part of a "deliberate" government attempt to undermine the electoral system. Meanwhile, opposition candidates, led by the RNB, captured a clear majority of the contests.

The opposition fared far less well at National Assembly elections conducted on December 15 and 29, 1996, and January 12, 1997, as the governing PDG scored a decisive victory, securing 82 of the 120 assembly seats. At subsequent balloting on January 26 and February 9, 1997, to fill the Senate for the first time, the governing party again secured a substantial majority. Meanwhile, on January 27 President Bongo reappointed Obame-Nguema, who announced a cabinet the following day.

On March 20, 1997, the National Assembly approved draft constitutional amendments that included provisions for the creation of a vice-presidential post and lengthening of the presidential term to seven years (following the next election). Following Senate approval of the amendments in April, the president named Didjob DIVUNGUI DI NDINGE, leader of the Democratic and Republican Alliance (*Alliance Démocratique et Républicaine*—ADERE), as his vice president on May 28.

In mid-April 1998 the government announced the formation of the National Democracy Council (*Conseil pour la Démocratie Nationale*—CND), a consultative body comprising the former and current leaders of a broad spectrum of governmental and opposition groups, and charged it with assisting in the organization of presidential elections then tentatively scheduled for late 1998. In October the government announced that the first round of balloting would be held on December 6, with a second round, if necessary, on December 20. The Bongo administration rebuffed subsequent opposition requests for additional preparation time, and in early November the HCR and other leading opposition groups withdrew from the national electoral commission to protest what they described as a perfunctory revision of an already suspect voter-registration list. Meanwhile, intraparty factionalization undermined the ability of prominent opposition groups to coalesce behind a competitive challenger to the incumbent.

On December 6, 1998, President Bongo won a seven-year term at polling that his opponents charged was tainted by "massive fraud." Bongo's 66.6 percent vote share dwarfed the returns of six other presidential aspirants, with his nearest competitors, the HCR's Pierre MAMBOUNDOU and the RNB's Paul Mba-Abessole, capturing 16.6 and 13.4 percent, respectively. On January 24, 1999, Bongo named Jean-François NTOUTOUME EMANE to succeed Obame-Nguema, who had resigned two days earlier, and on January 25 a new government was named.

The PDG retained its legislative stranglehold in assembly balloting in December 2001, securing 88 seats. On January 27, 2002, President Bongo reappointed Prime Minister Ntoutoume Emane; notably, however, the new cabinet announced the same day included three members of the RNB (including Mba-Abessole) and the leader of another opposition grouping, the Social Democratic Party (*Parti Social-Démocratique*—PSD).

In local elections in 2002, the PDG achieved an overwhelming victory, albeit with voter participation estimated at less than 20 percent in some areas. In Senate elections held in 2003, the PDG won 60 of the chamber's 91 seats, followed by the Rally for Gabon (*Rassemblement pour le Gabon*—RPG), which took 8 seats.

On November 27, 2005, President Bongo won another seven-year term at balloting that was again challenged as fraudulent by his opponents. Bongo garnered 79 percent of the vote, easily defeating four challengers, most notably Pierre Mamboundou, whose affiliation was listed as the Union of Gabonese People (*Union du Peuple Gabonais*—UPG), 13.6 percent; and Zacharie MYBOTO, an independent affiliated with the newly formed Gabonese Union for Democracy and Development (*Union Gabonaise de la Démocratie et du Développement*—UGDD), 6.6 percent. Two other candidates each received less than 1 percent of the vote: Augustin Moussavou KING of the Gabonese Socialist Party (*Parti Socialiste Gabonaise*—PSG) and Christian-Serge MAROGA of the Rally of the Democrats (RDD). Turnout was recorded at 63.6 percent, with security forces voting on November 25 in a move decreed by Bongo to maintain order at civilian polling on November 27. Bongo was sworn in on January 19, 2006, retaining Vice President Divungui Di Ndinge and appointing a new prime minister, Jean Eyéghe NDONG, on January 20. A new government was installed on January 21.

Bongo announced in 2006 that he would seek another term in the 2012 election, effectively halting discussion about his successor. Some opposition parties, meanwhile, reportedly suggested that the ruling PDG be replaced by a coalition styled as the *Union pour la Majorité Présidentielle Gabonaise* (UMPG), intended to more evenly distribute power among the smaller parties and the PDG. The latter, not surprisingly, opposed the idea. However, midyear talks between the opposition and majority parties resulted in their members being seated on the newly created electoral commission. While the opposition balked at the provision allowing the president veto power over any of the commission's decisions, they were appeased by other provisions allowing access to state-run media, a review of voter registration lists, public financing of legally registered parties, and limits on campaign spending.

Following another overwhelming victory by the PDG in National Assembly elections of December 17 and 24, 2006, Ndong was reappointed on January 24, 2007, and a new government, dominated by the PDG but including members of at least four other parties, was named on January 25.

Corruption charges against President Bongo were in the spotlight in 2007, when he was found guilty in a French court of accepting a bribe to free a French citizen from jail in 1996 and ordered to pay a fine of nearly $720,000. Subsequently, allegations surfaced that Bongo and his father-in-law, Denis SASSOU-NGUESSO, president of the Republic of the Congo, had embezzled money to buy property in France, straining relations between the countries.

Following polling on June 10, 2007, in 20 constituencies where the courts had annulled the 2006 results because of irregularities, the PDG won in 11 constituencies, retaining its 82 seats, while independents reportedly added 1 seat. Allies of the PDG were reported to have won 6 seats and others, 2 seats. A major reshuffle of the cabinet took place on December 27, 2007; additional cabinet changes were made on February 4, 2008, after the minister of foreign affairs was named chair of the African Union Commission. The PDG retained its stronghold in local elections on April 27, 2008, winning 1,100 of 1,990 municipal and departmental seats. On October 7 the cabinet was reshuffled.

The PDG dominated a reshuffled cabinet appointed on January 14, 2009, though the government did include two members of the opposition UGDD and two other parties. The UGDD officially rejected participation in the government and dismissed the two party members who had accepted posts. In Senate elections on January 18, the PDG won 75 of the enlarged chamber's 102 seats, followed by independents with 9 seats, and the RPG with 6.

Following the death of President Bongo at age 73 on June 8, 2009—a report that the government initially denied—Senate president Rose Francine ROGOMBÉ became interim president on June 9, in accordance with the order of succession under the constitution. Vice President Didjob Divungui Di Ndinge resigned on June 10, but was reappointed by Rogombé on June 27. Though the constitution stipulates that elections were to be held within 45 days, they were delayed due to the government's stated need to update voter lists and due to opposition complaints about problems with the electoral process. Further, protests mounted over presidential candidates not resigning from government, including President Bongo's son, Ali Ben BONGO Ondimba. On July 15 Prime Minister Ndong resigned in order to run for the presidency (he later withdrew), and on July 17, Rogombé named agriculture minister Paul Biyoghe MBA to replace him. She then announced a minor reshuffle of the cabinet on July 22, and two ministers resigned on August 7 and August 15, respectively, to run for president, prompting another minor reshuffle.

In presidential balloting on August 30, 2009, Ali Ben Bongo received a plurality of the votes—41.8 percent—to defeat 16 other candidates (after six others withdrew), only two of whom received a significant number of votes: the UPG's Pierre Mamboundou and former minister André Mba OBAME, each with a fraction over 25 percent of the vote. None of the other candidates received more than 3.9 per cent of the vote. The initial results prompted violent protests, some opposition members calling Bongo's victory "an electoral coup d'etat." In subsequent recounts, the Constitutional Court confirmed the results on September 4 and again on October 12, paving the way for Bongo to assume office on October 16. President Bongo reappointed Mba as prime minister the same day, and on October 17 Mba named a new, smaller government, comprised largely of technocrats and few ministers from the previous regime. The positions of vice president, deputy prime minister and minister of state were abolished, and the cabinet numbered 14 fewer members than in the previous government.

Despite speculation that Prime Minister Mba would not be retained, he was reappointed by the president and named an extensively reorganized government on January 14, 2011. On January 25, challenger Obame declared himself president and named a new "government" while taking refuge in a UN office in Libreville. The following day the government charged him with treason, dissolved his newly formed political party, and put down pro-Obame demonstrations in the days that followed (see Current issues, below). In legislative balloting on December 17, 2011, the PDG won an absolute majority, although opposition groups heavily criticized the polling (see Current issues, below).

On February 12, 2012, the Constitutional Court confirmed the December election results. The next day the cabinet and prime minister resigned as required by the Constitution. A new cabinet was announced on February 28. The outgoing agricultural minister, Raymond Ndong SIMA, was appointed prime minister—the first time the post was held by someone from outside the ethnic Fang region of the capital.

Constitution and government. Until 1991, when a qualified multiparty system was introduced, popular election was pro forma because of a requirement that all candidates be approved by the PDG. Constitutional amendments approved by the legislature on April 18, 1997, provided for a lengthening of the presidential term from five to seven years; in addition, the amended basic charter empowered the president to name both a vice president (appointees to the newly created post are not eligible to succeed the chief executive) and a prime minister, who must enjoy the confidence of the legislature. The head of the government is the prime minister, who is appointed by the president. The prime minister, in consultation with the president, appoints the Council of Ministers. In 2003 the National Assembly voted to revoke the constitutional limit on the number of terms to which the president may be reelected. This effectively guaranteed Bongo the presidency for life. In December 2010 the National Assembly adopted a constitutional amendment allowing the president to extend his mandate in the event of an emergency requiring a delay of regularly scheduled elections.

Members of the bicameral legislature, which comprises a Senate (created in March 1994 and filled in April 1997) and a National Assembly, are directly elected for six-year and five-year terms, respectively. There is an appointed Economic and Social Council, whose advice on relevant policy issues must be given legislative consideration. The judiciary includes a Supreme Court (divided into judicial, administrative, and accounting chambers) and Courts of Appeal, as well as a Constitutional Court and an extraordinary High Court of Justice to hear impeachment cases.

For administrative purposes Gabon is divided into 9 provinces and subdivided into 37 departments, all headed by presidentially appointed executives. Libreville and Port-Gentil are governed by elected mayors and Municipal Councils, while four smaller municipalities have partly elected and partly appointed administrations.

Freedom of speech and the press are guaranteed in the 1991 Constitution, although censorship is common. For instance, on August 3, 2012, Gabon's state-run media regulator, the National Communications Council, suspended the weekly newspapers *Ezombolo* and *La Une* for disrespecting public institutions "and the personalities that embody them." Reporters Without Borders ranked Gabon 89th out of 179 countries in media freedom.

Foreign relations. Following his accession to power in 1967, President Bongo sought to lessen the country's traditional dependence on France by cultivating more diversified international support. Regionally, Gabon withdrew in 1976 from membership in the Common African and Mauritian Organization, while diplomatic relations with Benin, broken in 1978 after Gabon's alleged involvement in a mercenary attack in Cotonou in 1977 and the expulsion in 1978 of 6,000 Beninese workers, were restored in February 1989. Relations with neighboring Equatorial Guinea suffered until the overthrow of the Macie regime in August 1979, by which time as many as 80,000 Equatorial Guinean refugees had fled to Gabon. Relations with Cameroon deteriorated in May 1981 with the expulsion of nearly 10,000 Cameroonians in the wake of violent demonstrations in Libreville and Port-Gentil. Subsequently, an overt campaign against immigrant workers further strained ties between Gabon and its neighbors. Libreville nonetheless continued to participate in the Economic Community of Central African States, hosting its third summit meeting in August 1987. During the same month, a presidential visit to the United States served to strengthen relations between the two countries, with Bongo pledging to protect American investments of more than $200 million and Washington agreeing to debt restructuring of some $8 million owed by Gabon for military purchases. Earlier, following a meeting with the Palestine Liberation Organization's Yasir Arafat in Tunisia, the regime reiterated its opposition to "apartheid, Zionism, and neocolonialism."

In 1988, despite President Bongo's stated intent, Gabon continued to be heavily dependent on French support, with annual aid hovering at $360 million. In February the government granted the European Economic Community fishing rights to Gabonese territorial waters; thereafter, cooperation agreements were negotiated with the Congo in June and Morocco in October. Meanwhile, the regime's battle with Libreville's large illegal population continued: 3,500 foreigners were arrested in July following Bongo's warning that tougher measures would be used to stop "clandestine immigration."

In late 1992, following two years of negotiations, Gabon and South Africa, which had long been trading partners, established full diplomatic relations. Meanwhile, Libreville's crackdown on illegal immigrants was underscored by the deportation of 7,000 Nigerians.

Angered at Paris's "silence" over French press reports critical of President Bongo, Libreville recalled its ambassador on April 21, 1995. However, relations were quickly restored as Paris reasserted its support for Bongo who, in turn, called for an end to anti-French demonstrations in Libreville.

In the late 1990s President Bongo returned to the role of regional mediator, assuming a prominent position in efforts to reduce tensions in the Republic of the Congo and Côte d'Ivoire. In November 1999 Libreville hosted a summit of the heads of state and foreign ministers of seven Gulf of Guinea nations (Angola, Cameroon, Democratic Republic of the Congo, Republic of the Congo, Equatorial Guinea, Nigeria, and São Tomé and Príncipe) that yielded agreement to form a cooperative commission.

In 2003 relations with Equatorial Guinea became tense following Gabon's occupation of the uninhabited islands of Mbagne, Cocotiers, and Congas in the potentially oil-rich Corisco Bay, north of Libreville. In 2004 both countries agreed to negotiations under the auspices of the UN, but a summit scheduled for October was canceled after it was reported that Gabon intended to "sell" the islands, thus trying to stake its claim to legitimate ownership. (The case was submitted to the International Court of Justice in 2006; progress toward a resolution was reported in 2010.)

French support declined in 2005 along with Gabon's oil supply, leaving Bongo to look increasingly to China, which previously had agreed to import large quantities of Gabonese oil and had funded and built Gabon's parliamentary complex. China subsequently loaned Gabon $3 billion to tap iron ore reserves in Belinga. A controversial iron-ore project backed by Chinese financing in 2009 reportedly was suspended because of an outcry over the ultimate destruction of the storied Kongou Falls. Meanwhile, relations with France continued to deteriorate in 2009, as in March the PDG accused France of having conducted "a vast campaign to destabilize Gabon," largely based on legal actions in France regarding corruption allegations against President Bongo and other Gabonese officials (see Current issues, below). Further, the government, through the PDG, made what was described as an appeal for a "thorough" reexamination of cooperative agreements with France.

Following the election of President Ali Ben Bongo Ondimba in 2009, relations with France warmed, marked by a February 2010 visit by French president Nicolas Sarkozy. France had earlier decided to maintain its permanent military base in Libreville.

In June 2010, in a meeting with President Obama in Washington, D.C., President Bongo was urged to take major steps to curb corruption and reform the judiciary. *Africa News* noted that the fact that Bongo was at the White House and that there continued to be cordial relations with the United States was a signal that "reform was hardly at the top of the list in U.S. relations with . . . the oil-rich state."

On July 15, 2012, Gabon's Jean Ping—President Bongo's brother-in-law—lost his post as chairman of the African Union to Nkosazana Dlamini-Zuma, South Africa's home affairs minister and the ex-wife of President Jacob Zuma. The vote ended months of gridlock after neither secured the required two-thirds majority at an AU summit in January. Ping had the support of mostly French-speaking members—plus Kenya, Nigeria, and Ethiopia—and Dlamini-Zuma was mostly supported by English-speaking countries.

In July 2013 Gabon and the EU signed a new fisheries agreement which increased the number of EU vessels authorized to fish in Gabonese waters. In exchange, the EU would pay Gabon an annual subsidy of $1.8 million.

Current issues. In March 2009, in the midst of a months-long strike by public health workers demanding better wages and working conditions, the president's 45-year-old wife, Dr. Edith Lucie BONGO, died after a long illness. She was the daughter of Denis Sassou-Nguesso, president of the Republic of the Congo, and instrumental in the close relationship between the two countries' leaders. Some observers said that his wife's death delayed President Bongo's response to the health workers' strike and a concurrent strike by teachers and that the aging president had been handing over more responsibility to his son, defense minister Ali Ben Bongo Ondimba. Meanwhile, corruption charges against Bongo and his wife continued to be the focus of sustained attention in 2009.

Bongo, who was Africa's longest-serving head of state, died in June 2009; rumors of his ill health had spread since May, when he traveled to Spain for treatment. Defense Minister Ali Ben Bongo Ondimba—the president's son, who had recently named a new army chief of staff and a new chair of the National Security Council—immediately closed the borders and ordered soldiers to the streets, orders he relaxed the following day. Meanwhile, the government, which had denied that Bongo was ill, suspended two newspapers and a satellite television service for reporting on his medical condition. His death set off "frantic electioneering," according to *Africa Research Bulletin*, and calls for delaying the election beyond the 45-day period called for under the constitution. After a series of reshuffles in the government, including the immediate succession of Senate President Rose Francine Rogombé as interim president, the resignation and then reappointment of the vice president, and the resignation of the prime minister, candidates began shifting for position. For the first time, a group of five opposition parties, styled as the alliance for Change and Restoration, backed a single candidate—the UPG's Pierre Mamboundou. The PDG, for its part, sidestepped former prime minister Ndong and other party stalwarts in favor of the president's son, Ali Ben Bongo Ondimba, who headed the reform wing of the party, as flag-bearer. In the rush to elections, set for August 30, some 23 candidates announced their intentions. Ultimately, 17 contested the election, the majority of them as independents. Prior to the start of the campaign on August 15, the opposition, which accused the government of preparing to rig the poll, sought a postponement, demanding, among other things, that candidates who held government posts resign. Some 10,000 protesters took part in a violent demonstration in Libreville, demanding Bongo's resignation as defense minister. Interim president Rogombé called for calm, and, following a meeting with numerous candidates, Bongo resigned his government post at the start of the official campaign period. Among the candidates lining up to challenge Bongo were former PDG member André Mba Obame, who ran as an independent, and the UGDD's Zacharie Myboto. PDG member and former prime minister Casimir Oyé Mba, who had declared as an independent, withdrew the day before the election, but his name remained on the ballot.

Bongo's plurality of 41.7 percent of the vote was not officially announced until September 3, 2009, following peaceful voting on August 30. However, immediately after the vote Bongo declared himself the victor, as did Obame and Mamboundou, each of whom subsequently was reported to have received 25 percent of the vote. The announcement of the results sparked protests in which at least two people were killed and fires were set at a police station and a French consulate. More than 50 people were arrested, and 16 candidates immediately called for a recount, claiming "grave manipulations" of the vote. On September 4 the Constitutional Court confirmed the results, resulting in Bongo's receiving the mandate with far less than a majority. Violent protests resumed, and a week later the opposition called for a three-day general strike, which was largely ignored. The Constitutional Court, meanwhile, responded to additional requests for a recount, and it again confirmed the results on October 12, with Bongo said to have received a slight increase (41.8 percent), as did Mamboundou, who moved into second place (25.6 percent), followed by Obame (25.3 percent). Following his swearing in on October 16, Bongo pledged to uphold justice and fight corruption.

In February 2010, in preparation for legislative elections scheduled for 2011, a number of defectors from the governing PDG, under the leadership of the UGDD's Myboto, formed a new opposition party, the National Union (*Union Nationale*—UN; see Political Parties and groups, below). Meanwhile, troubles began to mount for the new president, as a government audit in March found one-tenth of the public payroll to be "ghost workers," i.e., fictitious. The money saved was ultimately used to pay for civil service bonuses. In May President Bongo was reported to have bought a luxury home in Paris worth $120 million, demonstrating taste "which appears to be inherited from his father," according to Deutsche Presse-Agentur. The president's power was further secured in parliamentary elections in June, when the PDG lost only two seats to the newly formed UN, and again in December, when the assembly approved a constitutional amendment allowing the president to extend his mandate in case of an emergency. The opposition claimed that the new authority could pave the way to a dictatorship.

President Bongo further bolstered his authority by undertaking, through the reappointment of Prime Minister Mba, an extensive cabinet reshuffle in January 2011. Blaming key officials for the slow pace of reforms, he also reorganized the management of the presidency. These moves, together with the constitutional amendment that the PDG- dominated assembly had pushed through, were undertaken with an eye on legislative elections slated for December, according to *Africa Confidential*. The president was said by observers to be uncertain of the outcome of assembly elections given Bongo's weak mandate, increasing tensions among the country's ethnic groups, and a noticeable lack of funds moving into his personal account since the death of his father. Reports noted that Bongo "maintained a dignified silence..." over a claim, revealed in documents released by WikiLeaks, that he and his father had allegedly benefited from some $36 million that Gabonese officials had embezzled from the central bank under orders from government officials. To add to his difficulties, on January 25, challenger André Mba Obame declared himself president of the republic and named a cabinet while taking refuge in the office of the United Nations Development Program with some of his supporters. Obame set himself forth as the rightful winner, following the example of Alassane Dramane Ouattara in Côte d'Ivoire, who refused to concede after the disputed 2010 presidential election and was ultimately successful in ascending to the presidency. However, in Obame's case the government charged him with treason and abolished his political party. Two violent protests followed as Obame's backers rallied in Libreville. Tear gas was used to break up the rallies, where demonstrators clashed with riot police. Subsequently, the opposition called for a political dialogue, but there was no immediate response from the government. Meanwhile, several members of Obame's UN party were arrested after they allegedly set cars on fire and looted stores in Libreville.

In March 2011 observers said Bongo was trying to co-opt former challenger Pierre Mamboundou into a broad presidential alliance in advance of the legislative elections. The Constitutional Court refused to allow the government to postpone the elections until 2012 to put in place biometric voter registration measures, and elections were scheduled for December 17. On November 2 a declaration signed by 13 opposition parties was made public that called on the public to "oppose and prevent" the election, claiming it would be rigged in favor of the ruling party. The same day the Union for the New Republic, headed by Louis-Gaston MAYILA, announced it would take part in the election. On November 3 the Union of the Gabonese People, whose leader Pierre Mamboundou died of a heart attack on October 15, announced the party would participate even though spokesman Thomas Ibinga had signed the statement opposing elections. On November 4 the PDG threatened to use the full force of the law to respond to any group that tried to obstruct the election. On November 19 former prime minister Jean Eyeghe Ndong, now an opposition leader, called on the public to boycott the vote, denouncing the lack of transparency and antifraud measures. The elections went forward on December 17, albeit with a turnout of just over 34 percent. The results were announced December 21. The ruling PDG won a landslide victory, claiming 114 of the 120 seats in the National Assembly, after a number of opposition parties boycotted the balloting. Despite some irregularities, the African Union observer mission said the vote was credible and peaceful.

In January 2012 Gabon cohosted (with Equatorial Guinea) the Africa Cup of Nations, which succeeded in spurring investment in the country but was described as a political headache: visiting teams arrived to find inadequate lodging; after tourists failed to materialize, officials resorted to handing out free tickets to the opening match. In June Gabon delayed payment on a $1 billion bond, triggering fears of a default. However, payments were resumed over the following months. The country's main opposition leader, Andre Mba Obame, returned on August 11 after 14 months in France. His return was met by opposition demonstrations that were suppressed by security forces, leaving one dead and dozens injured or arrested on August 15.

A 2013 joint Gabonese government–World Wildlife Fund study found that poachers had killed more than 11,000 elephants in Gabon's national parks between 2004 and 2012. The report prompted new calls for increased security, but no new steps were taken through 2013. Noted environmental activist Marc Ona ESSANUI was arrested on May 15, 2013, and charged with libel for alleging corruption between the government and an agro-industrial developer from Singapore. Independent observers charged that the arrest was the result of a campaign by Essanui to stop a massive timber, palm oil, and rubber plantation development. Reports during the summer of 2013 revealed that Bongo had replaced a number of officials in Gabon's nine regions with loyalists, apparently to bolster support ahead of the 2016 presidential election.

POLITICAL PARTIES

Officially declared a one-party state in March 1968, Gabon, in practice, had been under one-party government since the banning of the former opposition group, the Gabonese Democratic and Social Union (*Union Démocratique et Sociale Gabonais*—UDSG), in 1964. Twenty-six years later, in February 1990, President Bongo announced that the ruling Gabonese Democratic Party (PDG) would be dissolved in favor of a Gabonese Social Democratic Rally (*Rassemblement Social-Démocrate Gabonais*—RSDG), which would pave the way for a multiparty system. In early March he retreated somewhat by announcing that the PDG would continue as a unit within the RSDG. However, delegates to a national political conference in late April rejected the RSDG as a vehicle for phasing in pluralism over a three- to five-year period; Bongo responded by granting legal status (initially for one year) to all of the 13 opposition groups participating in the conference, 7 of which obtained parliamentary representation late in the year. In May 1991, 6 of the 7 parties announced a boycott of parliamentary proceedings and called for dissolution of the coalition government. Meanwhile, a short-lived Coordination of Democratic Opposition (*Coordination de l'Opposition Démocratique*—COD) had been launched by 9 opposition groups, 3 of which merged in early 1992 to form the African Forum for Reconstruction (FAR).

On June 30, 1993, members of Gabon's major opposition parties, meeting in the United States, agreed to form the Committee for Free and Democratic Elections, dedicated to establishing a "democratic state." Following presidential balloting on December 5, the committee was supplanted by the High Council of the Republic (*Haut Conseil de la Republique*—HCR), which had been organized by Paul Mba-Abessole, leader of the National Rally of Woodcutters (RNB) and runner-up in the controversial elections, to function as an advisory body for his "administration." The HCR, which reportedly included a majority of the opposition presidential candidates and parties, named Mba-Abessole and PGP leader Pierre-Louis AGONDJO-OKAWE president and vice president, respectively. On January 27, 1994, the HCR was restyled the High Council of Resistance (*Haut Conseil de Résistance*—HCR) and announced that it would no longer refer to Mba-Abessole as the president of the republic, although it vowed to continue to resist the Bongo regime.

At an HCR meeting in December 1997, party delegates elected a new executive bureau headed by Pierre Mamboundou of the Union of Gabonese People (UPG). Furthermore, four HCR members (the FAR, the Movement for People's Social Emancipation [MESP], the RNB, and the UPG) signed a new cooperation accord on which they reportedly expected to base their 1998 presidential campaign. In May 1998 the HCR chose Mamboundou as its standard-bearer for the presidential elections due in December; however, in subsequent months the viability of the movement was cast in doubt by reports that it had been reduced to only four or five parties, including the RNB, which had decided to field its own presidential candidate. In November the HCR withdrew from the national electoral commission, declaring that the commission's "hasty" revision of the electoral list had set the stage for "massive fraud" at the presidential balloting.

Of Gabon's 35 registered political parties, most belong to the presidential majority in what Bongo euphemistically called "convivial democracy." Ahead of the 2009 presidential election, a coalition styled the Alliance for Change and Restoration backed the UPG's Pierre Mamboundou. In addition to the UPG, the alliance included the Gabonese Socialist Party (*Parti Socialiste Gabonais*—PSG), the RNB, and a group called the Union for the New Republic, as well as the National Alliance of Builders.

A new party, the National Union (*Union Nationale*—UN), was formed in 2010 in preparation for legislative elections scheduled for 2011.

Government and Government-Supportive Parties:

Gabonese Democratic Party (*Parti Démocratique Gabonais*—PDG). Officially established by President Bongo in 1968, the PDG succeeded the earlier Gabon Democratic Bloc (*Bloc Démocratique Gabonais*—BDG) of President Mba. The PDG's most powerful body is its Political Bureau, although the party congress is technically the highest organ. There also is an advisory Central Committee, which oversees a variety of lesser bodies. In September 1986 the Third PDG Congress expanded the Central Committee from 253 to 297 members and the Political Bureau from 27 to 44 members to give "young militants" more access to leadership roles. In 1988 party membership was approximately 300,000. On May 17, 1990, amid increasing political turmoil and criticism of the regime's reform efforts, Bongo resigned as party chair, citing a desire to serve above "partisan preoccupations."

In early 1993 (then) National Assembly President Jules BOURDÈS-OGOULIGUENDE joined Alexandre Sambat in resigning from the PDG to run as an independent presidential candidate. On October 19 President Bongo officially declared his candidacy for reelection, and on November 4 the PDG organized a "New Alliance for Democracy and Change" electoral pact that included the **Association for Socialism in Gabon** (*Association pour le Socialisme au Gabon*—APSG) and the **People's Unity Party** (*Parti de l'Unité du Peuple*—PUP), led by Louis-Gaston Mayila, both of which had gained legislative representation in 1990, as well as the previously FAR-affiliated **Gabonese Socialist Union** (*Union Socialiste Gabonais*—USG). The PUP won 1 seat in the assembly balloting of 2001.

In 2006 reports surfaced of a rift in the PDG between a faction led by state minister Paul Toungui and his wife (President Bongo's daughter), Pascaline BONGO, and those supporting Ali Ben Bongo Ondimba, the president's son and likely successor. The party retained an overwhelming majority of seats (82) in the 2006 National Assembly elections. In June 2007 the PDG secured its legislative standing by retaining its total of 82 seats following partial elections in 20 constituencies where the 2006 results had been annulled by the courts due to irregularities. The PDG reportedly won in 11 of the 20 constituencies. The party further underscored its authority with overwhelming victories in the 2008 local elections and the 2009 Senate elections.

Party secretary general Simplice Guedet MANZELA lost his post of 10 years when Faustin Boukoubi was elected at a party congress in September 2008.

Following the death of President Bongo in June 2009, Prime Minister Ndong sought to secure the PDG nomination for the presidency. Failing that, as the nomination went to the president's son Ali Ben Bongo Ondimba over Casimir Oyé Mba and nine others, Ndong said he would contest the election as an independent, but ultimately he withdrew and threw his support behind independent candidate André Mba Obame. Meanwhile, Ali Ben Bongo retained his post as defense minister but ultimately stepped down at the start of the official campaign on August 15 as a result of protests registered by eight other candidates who claimed that any candidates still serving in government could use their position to unfair advantage.

In March 2010 Ali Ben Bongo Ondimba was elected president of the party, and Boukoubi was reelected secretary general. In April 2013 Bongo was reelected party president.

Leaders: Ali Ben BONGO Ondimba (President of the Republic and President of the Party), Jean Eyéghe NDONG (Former Prime Minister of the Republic and Vice President of the Party), Georgette KOKO (Vice President of the Party), Faustin BOUKOUBI (Secretary General).

Circle of Liberal Reformers (*Cercle des Libéraux Réformateurs*—CLR). The CLR was formed in late 1992 by former minister of security Jean-Boniface Assélé, the brother of President Bongo's former wife, who was expelled from the PDG along with two other founders of the new group. The party won representation in the assembly in 2001. In 2006 the party won two seats in the assembly, and Assélé retained his cabinet position. After his dismissal from the cabinet in January 2009, Assélé was elected as a senator and in February 2009 was elected fourth vice president of the Senate; he subsequently declined as he was seeking a higher post. Assélé was a strong supporter of Ali Ben Bongo's presidential bid in August. In September Assélé was again elected fourth vice president of the Senate, and this time he accepted the post. The party won one seat in the 2011 Assembly balloting.

Leader: Gen. Jean-Boniface ASSÉLÉ.

Democratic and Republican Alliance (*Alliance Démocratique et Républicaine*—ADERE). At balloting in 1996 and early 1997 the ADERE won a number of town council and Senate seats after reportedly forming alliances with local PDG chapters. Furthermore, in May 1997 President Bongo named a senior ADERE leader, Didjob Divungui Di Ndinge, vice president of the republic.

Following the death of President Bongo, the party left the presidential majority, and Ndinge resigned as vice president of the republic. He was subsequently reappointed to the position by Interim President Rogombé and later announced that he would not seek the presidency. By early August 2009 the party had not endorsed any candidate, Ndinge instructing members to vote their conscience. Ndinge's vice presidency was abolished after Ali Ben Bongo Ondimba took office in October.

In January 2010 the party rejoined the presidential majority.

Leader: Didjob DIVUNGUI DI NDINGE (Former Vice President of the Republic).

Social Democratic Party (*Parti Social-Démocrate*—PSD). The PSD became a member of the COD following its formation in 1991. During its first congress in Libreville, on April 21, 1992, party president Pierre Claver Maganga-Moussavou was chosen as its 1993 standard-bearer, but he secured a vote share of under 4 percent.

In October 1996 Maganga-Moussavou was ousted from the Obame-Nguema cabinet after he led a vociferous protest against the government's rescheduling of elections. Subsequently, the party reportedly dismissed another PSD leader, Senturel Ngoma MANDOUNGOU, when he assumed Maganga-Moussavou's vacant post.

In November 1998 the PSD withdrew from the national electoral commission to protest its administration of the voter registration lists. Subsequently, at polling in December, Maganga-Moussavou once again secured less than 4 percent of the vote. The PSD leader joined the PDG-led cabinet of January 2002 as the minister of state for agriculture, livestock, and rural development. In June 2004 the group joined the parties making up the ruling coalition, and Maganga-Moussavou was named to the cabinet in September.

In July 2009 party leader Maganga-Moussavou was nominated as its candidate in the upcoming presidential election. He retained his ministerial post, despite lengthy and vocal protests of eight other candidates. Maganga-Moussavou subsequently resigned on August 6, days before the start of the official campaign period on August 15. He finished the election in sixth place, with 0.76 percent of the vote. Maganga-Moussavou returned to his assembly seat, and in February 2010, he said the PSD remained part of the presidential majority. The party won one seat in the 2011 Assembly elections.

Leader: Pierre-Claver MAGANGA-MOUSSAVOU (President of the Party and 1993, 1998, and 2009 presidential candidate).

Gabonese Party of Independent Centrists (PGCI). The PGCI is led by Jean-Pierre Lemboumba, one of President Bongo's closest advisers. In 2002 the party signed on to be included in the presidential majority. The party reiterated its commitment to the presidential majority in July 2010.

Leaders: Jerôme OKINDA, Luccherie GAHILA (Secretary General).

In August 2009 PDG member Jean Rémy Pendy BOUYIKI announced that he was forming a new party, the **Democratic Party for Action and Freedom**, as part of the presidential majority and to support Bongo's candidacy.

Other Parties That Contested Recent Elections:

National Rally of Woodcutters/Rally for Gabon (*Rassemblement National des Bûcherons/Rassemblement pour le Gabon*—RNB/RPG). Formerly the National Rectification Movement–Woodcutters (*Mouvement de Redressement National—Bûcherons*/Morena–*Bûcherons*), the party adopted the RNB rubric in February 1991 in an effort to distinguish itself from its parent.

A southern grouping, whose claimed membership of over 3,000 (mostly from the Fang ethnic group) supported nonviolent change, the Woodcutters on June 22–24, 1990, mounted the first opposition congress since the multiparty system was legalized. In the 1990–1991 legislative balloting, the group became the leading opposition party, securing more than twice as many seats as Morena–*Originels*. Despite its success, the formation accused the government of electoral fraud and intimated that it would refuse to participate in assembly proceedings. In 1991 the Woodcutters joined an opposition call for dissolution of the National Assembly and the mounting of internationally supervised elections.

In mid-1992 West Africa reported that strained relations between the RNB and the Gabonese Progress Party (PGP, below) threatened the COD coalition. The enmity reportedly stemmed from the PGP's charge that the RNB's boycott of the later rounds of the 1990 election caused the opposition's defeat, as well as PGP bitterness at the RNB's failure to consult other parties prior to calling a general strike in February 1992. Meanwhile, Fr. Paul Mba-Abessole, the RNB's leader, labeled PGP president Pierre-Louis Agondjo-Okawe a "dangerous Marxist." (Mba-Abessole, who was dismissed by Morena in 1990, returned to Libreville that year at Bongo's invitation, after 13 years in exile.)

In June 1993 the party's secretary general Pierre-André Kombila Koumba was named chair of the opposition Committee for Free and Democratic Elections. Five months later, during the run-up to presidential balloting, the Woodcutters and the **National Convention for Change** (*Convention Nationale pour le Change*—CNC) issued a joint statement accusing the Bongo regime of electoral fraud.

In February 1994 RNB members and the party's radio station, Radio Liberté, were attacked by government forces deployed to quell antigovernment unrest in Libreville, with RNB leaders subsequently claiming that a number of its members had been detained. The attack on the RNB facilities coincided with the launching of a union-led general strike, which the RNB had publicly supported. Thereafter, the RNB was the most prominent of the opposition parties opposed to any cooperation with the Bongo regime.

At local balloting in October and November 1996, the RNB reportedly secured 62 of 98 contested posts; however, the party fared poorly in subsequent assembly balloting, falling eight seats short of its 1990 total. On January 19, 1997, the RNB-dominated Libreville municipal council elected Mba-Abessole as mayor.

In January 1998 the RNB newspaper, *Le Bûcheron*, was suspended by the government for two separate three-month periods for publishing articles "insulting" to the president. In addition, Kombila Koumba, the paper's editor, was fined and given a suspended sentence. In June Mba-Abessole announced that Kombila Koumba had been removed from his party post because of alleged "indiscipline"; however, Kombila Koumba rejected Mba-Abessole's authority to oust him, and at a mid-July congress of his supporters, Kombila Koumba was pronounced RNB president. Subsequently, both Mba-Abessole and Kombila Koumba announced their intention to campaign for the presidency under the splintered RNB banner. Furthermore, in October the Constitutional Court approved the campaign application of another RNB stalwart, Alain ENGOUNG-NZE, thus leaving the party with three presidential contenders. At balloting in December Mba-Abessole finished a distant third with 13 percent of the vote, while Kombila Koumba and Engoung-Nze finished near the bottom of the seven-candidate field.

In October 2000 the party reportedly adopted a new name (the Rally for Gabon [RPG]), but subsequent news stories referenced the grouping as the RNB/RPG. Several months earlier, the RNB also had reportedly announced the formation of a **Front of Parties for Change** (*Front des Parties pour le Changement*—FPC) with three smaller parties—the Congress for Democracy and Justice, the Rally of Republican Democrats, and the Republican Union for Democracy and Progress.

Following the December 2001 legislative balloting, Mba-Abessole, who had recently adopted a stance favoring "convivial democracy," accepted an invitation from President Bongo for the RNB/RPG to participate in an opening up of the government, although some party members remained hostile to the initiative. Mba-Abessole and two other RNB/RPG members were included in the new cabinet installed in January 2002. Mba-Abessole, a deputy prime minister, supported Bongo in the 2005 presidential election, although a year earlier he had accused the government of being the leading violator of human rights in the country. By the 2006 legislative elections, references were made strictly to the RPG as the main faction, which won eight seats, and the RNB/Kombila, which in 2006 retained the single seat it had won in 2001. Although Mba-Abessole lost his seat, he was retained in the cabinet as deputy prime minister. Kombila Koumba also was appointed to the cabinet in 2006 and has since retained his post. In the 2008 Senate elections the RPG won six seats.

In 2009 Mba-Abessole received the party's nod as its standard bearer in the August presidential election. Though he received the backing of Morena (see below) and an opposition grouping known as the Party of Equal Opportunity, he subsequently withdrew and supported former PDG member André Mba Obame, who ran as an independent and subsequently claimed he was the legitimate winner of the disputed election. In the days following the election, Mba-Abessole was refused entry into Côte d'Ivoire, where authorities said they had been ordered not to allow in members of the Gabon opposition. The party won three seats in the 2011 Assembly balloting.

Leaders: Paul MBA-ABESSOLE (1993 and 1998 presidential candidate), Pierre-André KOMBILA Koumba (leader of dissident faction and 1998 presidential candidate), Vincent Moulengui BOUKOSSO.

African Forum for Reconstruction (*Forum Africain pour la Réconstruction*—FAR). Also referenced as the Action Forum for Renewal (*Forum d'Action pour le Renouveau*), FAR was launched in early 1992 by merger of the National Rectification Movement–Originals (*Mouvement de Redressement National*—Morena–*Originels*), which had secured seven legislative seats in 1990–1991, and two smaller formations, the Gabonese Socialist Union (*Union Socialiste Gabonais*—USG), which had secured three seats, and the extralegislative Gabonese Socialist Party (*Parti Socialiste Gabonais*—PSG). The party's platform advocates the establishment of a "state of law and social justice" and a market economy, tempered by the "interests of the State."

Organized in 1981, Morena operated clandestinely within Gabon for the ensuing nine years, during which time, with support from the French Socialist Party, it formed a self-proclaimed government-in-exile in Paris. In 1981–1982 its domestic leaders were repeatedly arrested for distributing leaflets calling for a multiparty system. Many were sentenced to long prison terms, but by 1986 all had been released under a general amnesty that had been urged by French President François Mitterrand. By early 1990 the party had given rise to a number of dissident factions, the most important of which was Morena–*Bûcherons* (above) as distinguished from the essentially northern, ethnic Fang parent group led by Noël Ngwa-Nguema. At a Morena party congress on August 30, 1991, Executive Secretary Jean-Pierre Zongue-Nguema called for a revival of the COD and denounced the "duplicity" of opposition colleagues who had joined the Bongo government.

At presidential balloting in December 1993, party leader León Mbou-Yembit captured a bare 1.83 percent of the vote while Adrien NGUEMA Ondo, running under the National Rectification Movement–Unionist (*Mouvement de Redressement National*—Morena–*Unioniste*) banner, secured less than 1 percent.

In August 1998 the Forum's Morena wing reportedly split into two camps, which subsequently held separate congresses in Libreville and Lambarene under the leadership of Jean Clement BOUTAMBA and Felix Martin Ze MEMINI, respectively.

In the 2005 presidential election, Augustin Moussavou King ran as a candidate affiliated with the PSG, coming in a distant fourth.

Ahead of the 2009 presidential election, Morena resurfaced and supported the RNB/RPG's Mba-Abessole, though Morena member Luc Bengono NSI announced his candidacy, and Morena–*Unioniste* fielded Bienvenu Maro NGUEMA as its candidate for the poll. Nguema finished 14th, with 0.09 percent of the vote, while Nsi finished 15th with 0.07 percent.

Leaders: León MBOU-YEMBIT, Pierre ZONGUE-NGUEMA (COD Chair and Former Morena–*Originel* Leader), Noël NGWA-NGUEMA (Former Morena–*Originel* Executive Secretary), Vincent ESSOLOMONGEU (Secretary General).

Gabonese Progress Party (*Parti Gabonais du Progrès*—PGP). The president of the PGP, Pierre-Louis Agondjo-Okawe, called in April 1990 for dissolution of the transitional government on the grounds that it was inadequately representative of the Gabonese people. In May the death of party secretary general Joseph Rendjambe was a catalyst for renewed unrest throughout the country. Second runner-up in the 1990 legislative poll, the PGP is composed primarily of members of the Myéné ethnic group.

In July 1998 the party announced that Benoit Mouity-Nzamba would be its standard-bearer at presidential balloting in December; however, there were no further reports regarding his candidacy.

In February 2000 the PGP reportedly accused the government of "organizing electoral fraud" and called on the president to convene talks on electoral and "institutional" reforms. The party won three seats in the 2001 assembly elections. Party leader Agondjo-Okawe died on August 27, 2005. Following Seraphim Ndaot Rembogo's succession to party leadership, some sources referenced the PGP/Ndaot as winning two seats in the 2006 assembly elections. The government reported the results as the PGP winning two seats. Reports indicated that the PGP boycotted the 2011 Assembly balloting.

Leaders: Seraphim NDAOT Rembogo, Benoit MOUITY-NZAMBA, Anselme NZOGHE (Secretary General).

Union of the Gabonese People (*Union du Peuple Gabonais*—UPG). In July 1989 the UPG, which is supported largely by the southern Bapounou ethnic group, was reported to have circulated leaflets critical of President Bongo in Paris; the following October, three of its members were arrested in Gabon for alleged involvement in a coup plot. In February 1990 party founder Pierre Mamboundou was expelled from France to Senegal, despite his denial of complicity in the attempted coup. (Mamboundou died of a heart attack on October 15, 2011.)

On July 14, 1992, UPG activists demonstrated in Libreville, calling for Mamboundou's amnesty. On November 2, 1993, the UPG leader was allowed to return from Senegal; however, his bid to stand as a presidential candidate in the December elections was rejected. Subsequently, on November 8–9 UPG demonstrators rioted in Libreville in a futile attempt to force the government to overturn the ban.

Mamboundou's preeminent role within the UPG was diminished on September 25, 1995, when party members elected his former co-leader and recent nemesis, Sebastien Mamboundou MOUYAMA, chair. In August 1996 it was reported that Mouyama had launched a new political party called the **Alternative Movement** (*Mouvement Alternatif*—MA). However, Mamboundou ran as the UPG and HCR's presidential candidate in 1998, and he was routinely referenced as the UPG leader in the 2001 legislative campaign, calling for a boycott of the second round of balloting in view of what he termed the "indescribable disorder" of the first round. The legal status of the new group and its relationship with the UPG was not immediately clear.

Defying a ban on demonstrations, members of the UPG participated in a mass protest near Libreville in November 2005 over alleged irregularities in organizing the upcoming elections, and seven party members were arrested.

In March 2006 government authorities raided the UPG offices to "recover arms" following a demonstration by party members, some allegedly armed, in which a protester was killed by government security forces. The party denied there were weapons at its headquarters. Mamboundou, for his part, sought refuge in the South African embassy in Libreville. A month later tensions apparently eased after Mamboundou left the embassy and met with President Bongo.

The party won eight seats in the 2006 legislative elections and 90 members were elected in local balloting in 2008, third after the PDG and the UGDD. Mamboundou returned to Gabon in January 2009, and the party won two seats in the Senate elections on January 18.

Ahead of the 2009 election, a coalition called the Alliance for Change and Restoration backed UPG leader Pierre Mamboundou for the presidency. Four minor candidates later joined the grouping. Mamboundou, who had called for Ali Ben Bongo to resign his ministry once he became a candidate, initially claimed to have won the election with some 39 percent of the vote, but the electoral commission held to Bongo's victory. Mamboundou was slightly injured during a protest against the results, which were not officially announced until September. In the Constitutional Court's final ruling on the results in October, Mamboundou's result increased slightly, moving him into second place with 25.6 percent of the vote. Mamboundou died on October 15, 2011. Unlike other opposition groups, the UPG participated in the 2011 Assembly balloting, but failed to win any seats.

Leader: Richard MOULOMBA (Secretary General).

Minor parties include the *Cercle Omega*, which fielded Marcel Robert TCHORERET as its 2009 presidential candidate; **Circle for Renovation and Progress** (*Cercle pour le Renouveau et le Progrès*—CRP); the **Congress for Democracy and Justice** (*Congrès pour la Démocratie et la Justice*—CDJ); and the **Union for Democracy and Social Integration**.

For more information on the **Bongo Must Go** (*Bongo Doit Partir*—BDP), the **Rally of the Democrats** (RDD), please see the 2013 *Handbook.*

Outlawed Group:

National Union (*Union Nationale*—UN). The opposition UN was established in February 2010 by former PDG members, including 2009 independent presidential candidate André Mba Obame, who most recently had been a member of the Gabonese Union for Democracy and Development (*Union Gabonaise de la Démocratie et du Développement*—UGDD). The UGDD, which started in France on April 30, 2005, under the leadership of Zacharie Myboto, a PDG defector, was officially recognized in Gabon in April 2006. It merged with the UN in 2010, ahead of legislative elections scheduled for December 2011. (For more information on the history of the UGDD, see earlier editions of the *Handbook.*)

The UN also included two minor groups—the African Development Movement (MAD), led by Pierre-Claver ZENG EBOME, and the Rally of Republican Democrats (*Rassemblement des Démocrates Républicains*—RDR), which won one seat in the 2006 assembly elections.

Obame, who had claimed that he was the rightful winner of the controversial 2009 presidential election, in January 2011 declared himself president. Obame took refuge in UN offices in Libreville and named a new "government" of 18 ministers. In response, President Bongo shut down the party and nullified Obame's parliamentary mandate. A serious health condition forced Obame to travel to Paris for treatment in October 2012, but he pledged to undertake a new political campaign against the regime in January 2013.

Leaders: Zacharie MYBOTO (President of the Party and 2005 and 2009 presidential candidate), Casimir Oye MBA (Former Prime Minister), André Mba OBAME (Secretary General and 2009 presidential candidate).

LEGISLATURE

In March 1994 the (then) unicameral National Assembly adopted a draft constitutional reform bill that provided for a Senate, or upper legislative house. Elections to fill the body were held for the first time in January–February 1997.

Senate (*Sénat*). Created by a constitutional amendment in 1994, the Senate originally was a 91-member body. Senators are indirectly elected for a six-year term by members of municipal councils and departmental assemblies. First-ever balloting to fill the body was held on January 26 and February 9, 1997. The chamber was enlarged to 102 seats in the most recent balloting on January 18, 2009, in which the seat distribution was as follows: the Gabonese Democratic Party, 75; independents, 9; Rally for Gabon, 6; Gabonese Union for Democracy and Development, 3; Circle of Liberal Reformers, 2; Union of the Gabonese People, 2; Gabonese Party of Independent Centrists, 2; Social Democratic Party, 2; and Democratic and Republican Alliance, 1.

President: Léonard ANDJEMBÉ.

National Assembly (*Assemblée Nationale*). The sole legislative organ prior to 1997, the National Assembly is a 120-seat body whose members are elected for five-year terms. Following the most recent balloting on December 17, 2011, the allocation of seats was as follows: the Gabonese Democratic Party, 114; the Rally for Gabon, 3; the Circle of Liberal Reformers, 1; the Social Democratic Party, 1; the Union for the New Republic, 1.

President: Guy NDZOUBA-NDAMA.

CABINET

[as of August 1, 2013]

Prime Minister	Raymond Ndong Sima
Ministers	
Agriculture, Livestock, and Rural Development	Julien Nkogue Bekale
Budget, Public Accounts and Civil Service, in Charge of State Reform	Christiane Rose Ossoucah Raponda [f]
Communications, Posts, and Digital Economy	Blaise Louembé
Defense	Rufin Pacome Ondzouga
Economy, Employment, and Sustainable Development	Luc Oyoubi
Foreign Affairs, Cooperation, and Francophone Affairs	Emmanuel Issozet Ngondet
Forests and Water Affairs	Gabriel Ntchango
Health	Léon Nzouba
Health, Social Affairs, Solidarity, and the Family	Honorine Nzet Biteghe [f]
Industry and Mines	Régis Immongault
Interior, Civil Security, and Immigration, and Decentralization	Jean François Ndongou
Investment Promotion, Public Works, Transport, Habitat, and Tourism	Magloire Ngambia
Justice and Keeper of the Seals	Ida Reteno Assonouet [f]
National Education, Higher Education, Scientific Research and Innovation, in Charge of Culture, Youth and Sports	Séraphin Moundounga
Oil, Energy and Hydrocarbons	Etienne Ngoubou
Small and Medium-Sized Enterprises, and Handicrafts	Fidèle Mengue Mengouang

[f] = female

INTERGOVERNMENTAL REPRESENTATION

Ambassador to the U.S.: Michael MOUSSA-ADAMO.

U.S. Ambassador to Gabon: Eric D. BENJAMINSON.

Permanent Representative to the UN: Noel Nelson MESSONE.

IGO Memberships (Non-UN): AfDB, AU, IOM, NAM, OIC, WTO.

GAMBIA

Republic of The Gambia

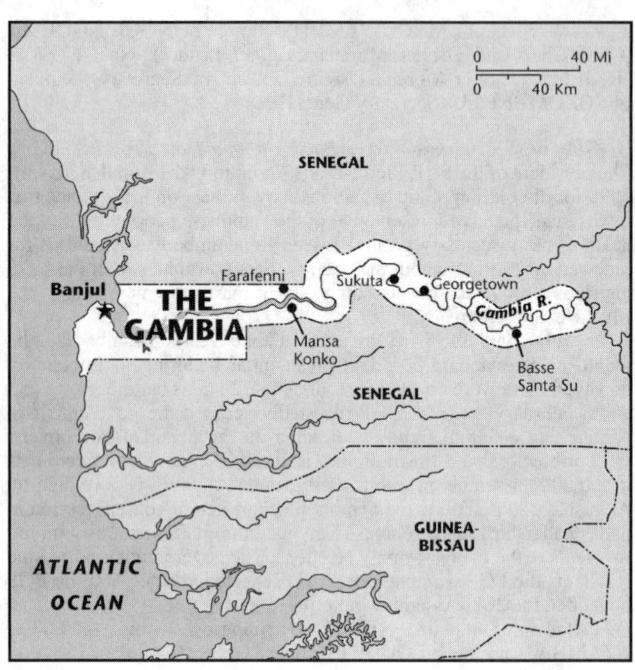

Political Status: Became an independent member of the Commonwealth on February 18, 1965; republican regime instituted April 24, 1970; Gambian-Senegalese Confederation of Senegambia, formed with effect from February 1, 1982, and dissolved as of September 30, 1989; most recent constitution approved by national referendum on August 8, 1996.

Area: 4,361 sq. mi. (11,295 sq. km).

Population: 1,847,753 (2013E—UN); 1,883,051 (2013E—U.S. Census).

Major Urban Center (2005E): BANJUL (metropolitan area, 568,000).

Official Language: English.

Monetary Unit: Dalasi (market rate November 1, 2013: 35.32 dalasis = $1US).

President: Yahya JAMMEH (Alliance for Patriotic Reorientation and Construction); installed as chair of the Armed Forces Provisional Ruling Council following military coup that overthrew the government of Alhaji Sir Dawda Kairaba JAWARA Sanyang (People's Progressive Party) on July 22, 1994; popularly elected to five-year presidential terms on September 26, 1996, October 18, 2001, September 22, 2006, and November 24, 2011.

Vice President: Isatou NJIE-SAIDY (Alliance for Patriotic Reorientation and Construction); appointed by the president on March 21, 1997, to fill previously vacant post; reappointed by the president on December 21, 2001, October 19, 2006, and February 3, 2012.

THE COUNTRY

Situated on the bulge of West Africa and surrounded on three sides by Senegal, Gambia is a narrow strip of territory (varying from 6 to 10 miles wide) that borders the Gambia River to a point about 200 miles inland from the Atlantic. The population is overwhelmingly African, the main ethnic groups being Mandingo (40 percent), Fula (13 percent), Wolof (12 percent), and Jola and Serahuli (7 percent each); in addition, there are small groups of Europeans, Lebanese, Syrians, and Mauritanians. Tribal languages are widely spoken, although English is the official and commercial language. Islam is the religion of 80 percent of the people. Poverty is widespread (an estimated 67 percent of the population lives on less than $1.25 per day), while approximately one-half of the people are illiterate.

The economy has traditionally been based on peanuts, which are cultivated on almost all suitable land and which, including derivatives, typically account for upward of 80 percent of export earnings. Industry is largely limited to peanut-oil refining and handicrafts; unofficially, smuggling into Senegal has long been important. Tourism has grown steadily in recent decades and now contributes an estimated 20 percent of GDP.

In the early 1990s the government implemented an economic recovery program sponsored by the International Monetary Fund (IMF) that emphasized agricultural development, reductions in external borrowing, promotion of the private sector, and government austerity; those measures were credited with stimulating an improvement in GDP and a decline in inflation.

Western aid was severely curtailed following the military coup of 1994, the Jammeh regime consequently turning to new donors such as Libya and Taiwan to finance an ambitious infrastructure program.

Thereafter, the government adopted another IMF-prescribed structural adjustment program with an emphasis on economic and financial reform. Meanwhile, the Fund urged the government to continue to increase its support for the private sector. In early 2000 Gambia called on the international investment community to assist African countries in their privatization efforts, asserting that state assets were being treated as "scrap" and sold off at extremely low prices.

Gambia experienced a severe economic downturn in 2002, partly due to a collapse in the peanut harvest. The currency lost 60 percent of its value against the euro and 45 percent of its value against the dollar, and unemployment approached 50 percent. However, the economy subsequently rebounded, although, with unemployment and poverty "at record highs," the IMF urged additional widespread reforms. Meanwhile, potentially significant oil deposits were discovered offshore, raising the possibility of dramatic revenue enhancement in the future.

Severe regional drought dramatically reduced agriculture production in 2011, contributing to economic contraction of 4.3 percent for the year. The IMF subsequently approved new lending to assist with Gambia's "acute" balance-of-payments problem, and a much-improved harvest underpinned GDP growth of 5.3 percent for 2012. At the same time, international concern over the repressive nature of the Jammah administration intensified (see Current issues, below).

GOVERNMENT AND POLITICS

Political background. Under British influence since 1588, Gambia was not definitively established as a separate colony until 1888. It subsequently acquired the typical features of British colonial rule, achieved internal self-government in 1963, and became fully independent within the Commonwealth on February 18, 1965. Initially a parliamentary regime (with the British monarch serving as head of state), Gambia changed to a republican form of government following a referendum in 1970.

For nearly three decades after independence, leadership was exercised by the People's Progressive Party (PPP), headed by President Dawda K. JAWARA, although opposition candidates secured approximately 30 percent of the popular vote in the elections of 1972, 1977, and 1982. At the May 1979 PPP congress—the first in 16 years—President Jawara rebuffed demands by some delegates that a one-party system be instituted, commenting that such a change could occur only through the ballot box. However, in 1980, amid allegations of a widespread antigovernment conspiracy, two opposition movements described by the president as "terrorist organizations" were banned, despite protests from the legal opposition parties.

A more serious threat to the Jawara regime developed in July 1981 when the capital was taken over by elements of Gambia's paramilitary Field Force and the Socialist and Revolutionary Labor Party, a Marxist-Leninist group led by Kukoi Samba SANYANG. The uprising was quelled with the aid of Senegalese troops dispatched under the terms of a 1965 mutual defense and security treaty. Subsequently, President Jawara and Senegalese President Diouf announced plans for a partial merger of their respective states in the form of a Senegambian Confederation, which came into effect on February 1, 1982.

The confederation, which critics branded as the equivalent of annexation by Senegal, was a major issue in the May 1982 presidential election in Gambia, the first to be conducted by direct vote. However, with the government branding several members of the demonstrably divided opposition as participants in the 1981 coup attempt, Jawara secured a 73 percent majority. The president subsequently appeared to defuse the confederation issue by resisting immediate monetary union with Senegal, a proposal viewed with skepticism by many Gambians.

While President Jawara was returned to office at the general election of March 11, 1987, with a reduced majority of 59 percent, the PPP increased its representation in the 36-member House of Representatives from 28 to 31, most observers attributing the latter success to the recent economic upturn. Subsequently, amid widespread concern about Gambia becoming "Senegal's eleventh region," the administration evinced little interest in pursuing genuine Senegambian integration, and the confederation was dissolved with the consent of both countries as of September 30, 1989.

After declaring his intention to retire at a PPP congress in December 1991, Jawara reversed himself and stood for a fifth consecutive five-year term in April 1992, reportedly to avoid further electoral slippage that might result in defeat for the ruling party. The outcome was Jawara's reelection and a marginal decline of five elected House seats for the PPP on a vote share virtually identical to that of 1985.

The Jawara government was overthrown on July 22, 1994, in a bloodless coup by junior army officers, who installed Lt. Yahya JAMMEH as chair of a five-member Armed Forces Provisional Ruling Council (AFPRC). Three days later the council named a 15-member government composed almost equally of military and civilian members. Antagonism toward the Jammeh government subsequently emerged from several quarters. In mid-August tension between the AFPRC and older military officials, who complained of being shunted aside, was underscored by the arrest of two high-ranking officers. Collaterally, friction continued between the AFPRC and members of Jawara's former government. Finally, on October 10 the European Union (EU) and the United Kingdom suspended economic and military assistance following Jammeh's dismissal of Finance Minister Bakary Bunja DARBO, the sole holdover from the previous administration.

In an attempt to mollify his critics, Jammeh in late 1994 announced a four-year transitional timetable that included plans for the drafting of a new constitution, an investigation into government corruption, a crackdown on crime, and a presidential election in November 1998. However, the four-year time frame drew widespread criticism, and in early February 1995 the AFPRC reduced it to two.

On April 10, 1995, the regime named a constitutional commission and charged it with drafting a document that would provide a legal framework for the holding of multiparty elections. However, in October the defection of AFPRC spokesperson Capt. Ebou JALLOW, amid charges that he had attempted to overthrow the regime, underscored the internal turmoil that had plagued the AFPRC and Jammeh's cabinet throughout 1995.

The draft constitution was released by the AFPRC in March 1996 and approved (according to government figures) by 70.4 percent of the voters in a national referendum on August 8, 1996, despite opposition charges that the new basic law had been carefully written to ensure that the Jammeh regime would continue in power. Jammeh subsequently announced that presidential elections would be held in September (months earlier than anticipated), with national legislative balloting to follow before the end of the year.

In voting on September 26, 1996, Jammeh was elected to a five-year presidential term as the candidate of the newly formed Alliance for Patriotic Reorientation and Construction (APRC). Official results credited him with 55.8 percent of the votes, his closest pursuer among the three other candidates being Ousainu DARBOE of the United Democratic Party (UDP) with 35.3 percent.

On November 8, 1996, the government announced that legislative elections, due on December 11, would be postponed until January 1997. The decision came after weeks of UDP-orchestrated antigovernment demonstrations. Subsequently, at balloting on January 2, 1997, President Jammeh's APRC captured 33 of the 45 contested seats (the president is empowered to name 4 additional legislators), giving the party the two-thirds majority necessary to pass legislation and make constitutional changes unimpeded. With 7 seats, Darboe's UDP finished a distant second.

Rebuffed in his attempt to name Edward SINGHATEY (a former member of the AFPRC) as vice president (the 27-year-old Singhatey failed a constitutional requirement that the deputy chief executive be at least 30 years old), Jammeh appointed a new 13-member cabinet on March 7, 1997, which did not include a vice president but placed Singhatey in the powerful post of minister to the president. However, following opposition criticism that the constitution mandated the appointment of a vice president, the president named Isatou NJIE-SAIDY (his minister of health, social welfare, and women's affairs) to the post on March 21. Njie-Saidy thereby became the first female vice president in western Africa. The transformation from military to civilian rule was completed on April 17 when Jammeh replaced the last four military governors with civilians.

President Jammeh was reelected to a second term with 53 percent of the vote on October 18, 2001, the UDP's Darboe again proving to be his nearest competitor among four opposition candidates. The APRC dominated the assembly balloting in January 2002 as well as the April local and regional elections as the result of a boycott by the major opposition grouping.

In assembly by-elections on September 29, 2005, to replace four ousted members, three seats went to a newly formed opposition coalition, the National Alliance for Democracy and Development (NADD), and one seat was secured by the APRC. Assembly speaker Sherif Mustapha DIBBA, who was arrested in connection with an alleged March 21, 2006, coup attempt, was replaced in April. Although Dibba was released without charge after spending several days in jail, he was subsequently dismissed from the assembly by the president.

On September 22, 2006, President Jammeh was reelected for another five-year term with 67.3 percent of the vote, again defeating the UDP's Darboe, with 26.7 percent, and another opposition candidate, Halifah SALLAH of the NADD, with just under 6 percent of the vote. Strengthened by Jammeh's victory and a divided opposition, the APRC won an overwhelming majority in the National Assembly elections of January 25, 2007, with few seats going to the UPD and the NADD. The APRC also retained its dominance in municipal elections held on January 24, 2008.

President Jammeh was reelected to a fourth term in balloting on November 24, 2011, being credited with 72 percent of the vote. Darboe finished second among the three candidates with 17 percent. Opposition parties strongly criticized the conduct and results of the election, and most of them boycotted the March 29, 2012, assembly poll, at which the APRC won 43 of the 48 elected seats.

Constitution and government. During the 12 years following adoption of a republican constitution in 1970, Gambia was led by a president who was indirectly elected by the legislature for a five-year term and was assisted by a vice president of his choice. The procedure was changed in 1982 to one involving direct election of the chief executive, who retained the authority to designate his deputy. The 1996 constitution provided for a directly elected president with broad powers (including the authority to appoint the cabinet) and a National Assembly of elected legislators and presidential appointees. The assembly may order the resignation of the head of state or cabinet ministers by a two-thirds vote. The judicial system is headed by a Supreme Court and includes a Court of Appeal, magistrates' courts, customary tribunals, and Muslim courts.

At the local level the country is divided into districts administered by chiefs in association with village headmen and advisers. The districts are grouped into seven regions, which are governed by centrally appointed commissioners and area councils thus far containing a majority of elected members, with district chiefs serving ex officio. Banjul is governed by an elected city council.

Conditions for journalists in Gambia have been considered among the worst in the world since draconian curbs were instituted in 2004. Reporters and commentators are routinely jailed, and several have not emerged from prison. Reporters Without Borders accuses the Jammeh administration of fostering an "extremely threatening environment," and the few independent, privately owned newspapers and radio stations are "stifled" at any hint of dissent. The government's intimidation of the media has attracted widespread international condemnation, most recently in regard to a new law passed in July 2013 authorizing the arrest of Internet bloggers accused of spreading "fake news" or "caricaturing" government officials.

Foreign relations. While adhering to a formal policy of nonalignment, Gambia has long maintained close relations with the United Kingdom, its principal aid donor, and the African Commonwealth states. By far the most important foreign policy question, however, has turned on relations with Senegal. In 1967 the two countries signed a treaty of association providing for a joint ministerial committee and secretariat, while other agreements provided for cooperation in such areas as defense, foreign affairs, and development of the Gambia River basin. In early 1976 a number of new accords were concluded that, coupled with the need for Senegalese military assistance to Gambia in 1980 and 1981, paved the way for establishment of the Confederation of Senegambia in February 1982. However, few of its goals had been seriously addressed at the time of the confederation's dissolution in 1989.

Relations deteriorated in the wake of the breakup with Senegal in 1989, with Banjul accusing Dakar of economic harassment (largely in connection with Senegalese attempts to limit the clandestine flow of reexport goods). However, a meeting between Presidents Jawara and Diouf in December 1989 proved beneficial, the Jawara administration reportedly attempting to stabilize relations so as not to jeopardize Gambia's recent economic improvement. Ties were further strengthened by the conclusion of a treaty of friendship and cooperation on January 8, 1991, that provided for annual political summits and the establishment of joint commissions to help implement summit agreements. However, in September 1993 Senegal closed its borders with Gambia, voicing renewed frustration with illegal commerce. In November the two countries agreed to the establishment of a technical committee charged with creating a mechanism to alleviate the problem.

In April 2000 Gambia and four other West African nations (Ghana, Guinea, Nigeria, and Sierra Leone) agreed to share a common currency by the end of 2002. (The deadline has been extended several times, most recently to at least 2015.)

In November 2000 the Commonwealth Ministerial Action Group visited Gambia, signaling a relative easing of relations that had reportedly been lukewarm since 1995, although Gambia continued to be criticized for its human rights record.

Relations between Gambia and Senegal remained tense in the early 2000s amid repeated claims that the Jammeh government provided aid to antigovernment forces in Senegal. Subsequently, a 100 percent increase in duties on vehicles traveling through Gambia and a doubling of the cost of ferries between northern and southern Senegal temporarily led to the closing of the border between the two countries, to the detriment of both countries' economies. Negotiations brokered by Nigeria in late 2005 resulted in Senegal's agreeing to remove its border blockade following Gambia's partial removal of the ferry charges and an apology by Jammeh.

Renewed fighting along the border between Senegalese government forces and antigovernment rebels in late 2006 led to an influx of 10,000 refugees into Gambia, with reports that some rebel fighters had also entered the republic. President Jammeh, for his part, refused to respond to inquiries from Senegal as to the whereabouts of the rebels. Despite the death of a key rebel leader in Paris in January 2007, heavy fighting between Senegalese rebels and Senegalese forces reignited in March. Some nine Senegalese rebels were charged by the end of the year with conspiracy to commit acts of terrorism against Senegal from Gambian soil. In early 2008 the two countries reaffirmed their commitment to military cooperation aimed at peacekeeping in the region.

Relations with Britain continued to be strained (President Jammeh not having visited since 1997) due to what was described as a "damning" report by London-based Amnesty International detailing abuses by government forces, including the alleged killing of thousands of people suspected to be witches.

Nigeria reportedly discovered a cache of weapons being shipped from Iran through Nigeria to Gambia in October 2010. Although some observers speculated that the arms had in fact been intended for President Jammeh or the Gambian military, Gambia in November severed diplomatic ties with Iran, a former ally, over the mysterious shipment.

In response to prolonged antigovernment protests in Libya and Libyan government attacks on civilians in early 2011, Gambia withdrew its support for the embattled Qadhafi regime in April and recognized the Transitional National Council, established by rebels and protesters. In May Gambia's High Court ordered the government to take control of all Libyan assets in the country until a government recognized by the UN was established in Libya.

In December 2012 President Jammeh facilitated the release of hostages held by rebels in the Casamance region of Senegal, and he subsequently continued to present himself as a potential mediator in that separatist conflict. However, Gambia's relations with Senegal had turned sour again by September 2013 as Jammeh alleged that Gambian dissidents were still being harbored in Senegal.

Current issues. The Economic Community of West African States refused to send observers for the November 2011 presidential balloting after determining that the electorate had been "cowed by repression," making free and fair elections impossible. Although President Jammeh's reelection was universally considered preordained, the opposition weakened its prospects by failing to coalesce behind a single candidate. The UDP's Darboe (the second-place finisher) called the official results "bogus" and accused the administration of having abused its incumbency by, among other things, encouraging overt pressure from the military on the electorate. At the same time, at least some of Jammeh's support was attributed to public appreciation of the schools, hospitals, and roads that had been built under his administration.

All but one of the opposition parties boycotted the March 2012 assembly elections, claiming they had been given insufficient time to campaign and that voting in any event would be unduly influenced through the inappropriate use of state resources. Meanwhile, many voices in the international community continued to question Jammeh's "intolerant and unpredictable" behavior, such as his August order for the mass execution of 47 prisoners, including some held for political offenses. Intense international condemnation (most notably from the EU and African Union) greeted the first nine executions, and Jammah subsequently suspended his order regarding the other prisoners to see if "criminal activity" would decline as he had intended with his original decision.

In January 2013 the EU formally called upon the administration to discontinue human rights abuses and otherwise improve the country's governance. However, Jammah responded that he would not "change a thing," contributing to the decision by most opposition parties to boycott the April local elections. (At least half of the seats held by the APRC went uncontested.)

POLITICAL PARTIES

Prior to the 1994 coup, Gambia was one of the few African states to have consistently sanctioned a multiparty system, despite the predominant position held since independence by the ruling People's Progressive Party (PPP). Following the coup, all party activity was proscribed until August 14, 1996, when, in the wake of the recent approval of a new constitution, the government announced that the ban had been lifted. However, the regime's opponents described the new "preconditions" for party registration as "onerous" and accused President Jammeh of lacking commitment to genuine democratization. Such fears appeared justified when Jammeh announced shortly thereafter that the three main parties from the pre-coup era (the PPP, NCP, and GPP) had been banned. Under intense regional and other international pressure, Jammeh lifted the ban in July 2001 to permit full-party participation in the upcoming presidential election.

In early 2011 a number of civic organizations launched the Coalition for Change–Gambia to confront the current "dictatorship" through nonviolent action. Four members of the coalition, including former minister of communications and information Amadou JANNEH, were subsequently sentenced to life in prison for producing and printing anti-Jammeh T-shirts. Janneh was released in 2012 after U.S. activist Rev. Jesse Jackson had intervened on his behalf.

Government Party:

Alliance for Patriotic Reorientation and Construction (APRC). Founded on August 26, 1996, as a vehicle for Col. Yahya Jammeh's presidential campaign, the APRC was a successor to the July 22 Movement (named in reference to the date of Jammeh's takeover in 1994), which had been launched in mid-1995. (Among other things, the leaders of the July 22 Movement had committed it to "national unity," apparently in the hope of bridging the nation's ethnic divisions. However, the bulk of the support for the Jammeh regime at that point was described as emanating from the Jola ethnic group, which constitutes less than 10 percent of the population.) APRC founders announced they would pursue economic development based on free-market principles and cooperation with neighboring countries. Jammeh resigned his military position (as required by the constitution) shortly before the September 1996 presidential balloting. The party underscored its ruling power with definitive victories in the 2006 assembly by-elections and presidential election and in the 2007 assembly balloting, at which it won 42 of the 48 elected seats.

Following his reelection in November 2011, President Jammeh handpicked the APRC candidates for the March 2012 assembly poll, some 26 members reportedly being expelled from the party after they apparently attempted to be designated as candidates without his imprimateur. The APRC won 43 seats on a vote share of 51.8 percent, 25 of its candidates having run unopposed.

Leaders: Yahya JAMMEH (President of the Republic and Chair of the Party), Isatou NJIE-SAIDY (Vice President of the Republic), Musa BITTAYE.

Other Party That Contested the 2012 Assembly Elections:

National Reconciliation Party (NRP). Formed quickly in August 1996, the NRP presented Hamat Bah as its candidate in the September 1996 presidential election, the well-known hotel owner garnering 5.5 percent of the votes. Bah ran again in 2001, securing 7.7 percent of the vote, and the NRP won one seat in the 2002 assembly elections.

In 2005 the party joined the newly formed opposition coalition (the National Alliance for Democracy and Development—NADD), but in March 2006 some 2,500 NRP members reportedly defected to the APRC at a massive rally in Sankuba. The NRP subsequently split from the NADD and teamed up with the UDP and the GPDP under the name Alliance for Regime Change prior to presidential balloting in September, backing UDP candidate Darboe. The NRP and the UDP formed an electoral alliance in the 2007 assembly elections, although the alliance's four successful candidates were from the UDP.

Although Bah officially ran as an independent in the 2011 presidential poll (in which he finished third with 11.1 percent of the vote), he was supported by a United Front of the NRP, NADD, GPDP, and PDOIS. The NRP was the only opposition party to contest the March 2012 assembly elections, winning one seat on a vote share of 9.4 percent. The party also participated in the April 2013 local elections, again rejecting the boycott supported by most other opposition parties.

Leader: Hamat BAH.

Other Parties:

People's Democratic Organization for Independence and Socialism (PDOIS). The leftist PDOIS was formed at a 1986 congress to approve a lengthy manifesto that accused the PPP of compromising the country's sovereignty by agreeing to the establishment of Senegambia on the basis of an "unequal relationship." Party leader Sidia Jatta, who also had contested the 1992 election, secured a reported 2.87 percent of the vote in the 1996 presidential balloting and 3.2 percent in the 2001 presidential elections. The PDOIS was one of two opposition parties to participate in the 2002 legislative elections, winning two seats.

In January 2005 the PDOIS was one of the founding members (along with the NDAM, NRP, PPP, and UDP) of the NADD (the new opposition coalition), with Halifa Sallah (the secretary general of the PDOIS) being referenced as the chair of the NADD. Sallah served as the NADD's 2006 presidential candidate, finishing a distant third. (Earlier the UDP and NRP had dropped out of the NADD, although a lengthy court battle ensued in that regard [see section on the NADD in the article on Gambia in the 2012 *Handbook*].)

In the 2007 assembly elections the NADD, then comprising the PDOIS, the PPP, and the NDAM, was credited with winning one seat. In April the NDAM withdrew from the coalition, and it was reported that the NADD was "on the verge of disintegration."

Halifah Sallah was arrested in March 2009 and charged with sedition for writing about the government's crackdown on witches. The government withdrew the charges several days later "in the interest of peace and justice."

The PDOIS launched a movement called Agenda 2011 in advance of the 2011 presidential election, urging the opposition to form an alliance and support a single candidate. It also proposed holding primaries as a way of resolving the issue of who should be the opposition standard-bearer. However, the party itself was subsequently criticized for not supporting the perceived strongest potential opposition candidate (the UDP's Ousainu Darboe). The PDOIS instead backed the NRP's Hamat Bah. At that point the government continued to reference the NADD as a separate entity, and some news reports referenced its support (separately from the PDOIS) for Bah. However, the de facto status of the NADD subsequently remained unclear.

Leaders: Sidia JATTA (1992, 1996, and 2001 presidential candidate), Halifa SALLAH (Secretary General).

People's Progressive Party (PPP). The moderately socialist PPP, which merged with the Congress Party (CP) in 1967, governed the country from independence until the 1994 coup. It sponsored adoption of the republican constitution in 1970 and long favored increased economic and cultural links with Senegal as well as maintenance of the Commonwealth association.

PPP Secretary General Dawda Jawara was reelected president of the republic in 1992, defeating four principal rivals with a 58.4 percent vote share. Following the July 1994 coup Jawara was granted political asylum by Senegal.

In November 1994 a number of PPP members were arrested for their alleged involvement in a failed coup plot. In June 1995 President Jammeh granted amnesty to the alleged conspirators; however, six months later at least 35 PPP activists were jailed and similarly charged. In 1996 the AFPRC formally charged Jawara with embezzlement, and his assets were seized.

In mid-1996 Jawara, in an announcement issued in London, strongly criticized the new constitution drafted by the Jammeh regime, describing the document as "tailor-made" to elect Jammeh and designed to "confuse" matters in regard to basic individual rights. As with the NCP and the GPP, the PPP was banned from participating in the 1996 elections by the Jammeh government. After the ban was lifted in July 2001 the PPP teamed with the GPP and the UDP in launching an opposition coalition, which supported the UDP's Ousainu Darboe in the October 2001 presidential election. Jawara returned to Gambia in mid-2002 in response to the government's offer of amnesty. He resigned as leader of the PPP in December 2002 and was replaced by Omar Jallow. The PPP joined the NADD in 2005, and months later Jallow was one of three opposition leaders arrested on security charges, which were later dropped.

Following disagreement with some of its former NADD partners on the matter, the PPP supported the UDP's Darboe in the 2011 presidential poll.

Leaders: Yaya CEESAY (President), Omar JALLOW (Secretary General).

United Democratic Party (UDP). Launched in August 1996 after the snap presidential election was announced, the UDP was described as having the support of the three parties (the PPP, NCP, and GPP) that had been banned by the Jammeh regime. UDP presidential candidate Ousainu Darboe, a prominent lawyer, ran second to Jammeh in the September 26 balloting, securing a reported 35.34 percent of the votes.

In May 1998 nine UDP members, including party leader Lamin Waa Jawara, were detained by government security forces. Darboe and a group of UDP members were arrested in June 2000 in connection with an alleged confrontation with APRC militiamen. Darboe was released on bail and served as the presidential candidate of a UDP/PPP/GPP coalition, securing 32.7 percent of the vote in the October 2001 election. (The criminal case against Darboe and the other UDP members was ultimately dismissed.)

The UDP/PPP/GPP coalition boycotted the January 2002 assembly elections. In November 2002 Jawara accused Darboe of misappropriating funds, and Jawara was subsequently expelled from the UDP. He then formed a new political party, the NDAM (below). In 2005 the UDP joined the NADD in an effort to unseat President Jammeh. In the run-up to the 2006 presidential election, however, the UDP dropped out of the NADD and backed its own leader, Darboe, for the presidency. Darboe also gained backing from the NRP and the GPDP in a coalition referenced as the **Alliance for Regime Change**, but the additional support did little to bolster his showing in the polls. The UDP and the NRP participated in an electoral alliance in the 2007 assembly balloting, with the alliance's four successful candidates coming from the UDP.

After failing to convince all of the opposition parties to coalesce behind him for the 2011 presidential poll, Darboe ran with the support of the UDP, PPP, and the **Gambia Moral Congress** (GMC), led by Mai FATTY, who had recently returned to Gambia after four years in exile. Darboe finished second again with 17.4 percent of the vote, and he strongly challenged the validity of the balloting, alleging that many non-Gambians had been permitted (even encouraged) to vote by the administration. Darboe strongly criticized the execution of nine prisoners in August 2012 (see Current issues, above), while the GMC subsequently called for demonstrations to protest perceived arbitrary arrests and other human rights abuses on the part of the government.

Leaders: Yaya JALLOW (Deputy Secretary General), Momodou Shyngle NYASSI, Ousainu DARBOE (Secretary General and 1996, 2001, 2006, and 2011 presidential candidate).

Gambia Party for Democracy and Progress (GPDP). The GPDP was formed as an opposition party in 2004 by Henry Gomez, who was based in Germany. The party's platform focused on contributing to the development of Gambia, and in that respect supported the efforts of President Jammeh. (Gomez was quoted as saying that being in the opposition did not mean being hostile to the government.) Prior to the 2006 presidential election, Gomez's candidacy was rejected by the electoral commission because of his failure to meet residency requirements. The GPDP then threw its support behind the UDP's Darboe.

The GPDP did not present any of its own candidates in the 2007 assembly elections, Gomez saying the party wanted to concentrate on the next presidential elections. However, the GPDP appeared to support the UDP/NRP assembly candidates as a continuation of the earlier three-party alliance. Two years in advance of the next presidential election, Gomez in 2009 wrote a letter to President Jammeh seeking a political alliance, commending Jammeh for his "visionary and purposeful moves."

In February 2011 the GPDP declined to take part in local elections. Although Gomez initially expressed an interest in running for president in 2011, the GPDP ultimately joined the United Front in support of the NRP's Hamat Bah. Like most of the other opposition parties, the GPDP boycotted the 2012 assembly elections, Gomez criticizing the shortness (11 days) of the government-decreed campaign period.

Leader: Henry GOMEZ (Secretary General).

National Democratic Action Movement (NDAM). Formed by Lamin Waa JAWARA after he was expelled from the UDP in 2002, the NDAM emerged as one of the leading opposition parties in spite of its short existence. Jawara was arrested in 2004 on charges of sedition and served six months in prison, the sentence reportedly increasing his popularity in the opposition. In 2005 the NDAM joined the NADD, but it withdrew in April 2007, saying it was time to "go it alone."

In November 2007 Jawara was named by the president to head a local council, a move observers saw as a test of the new legislation granting the president authority over local affairs. For his part, Jawara said he did not consult with the party before accepting the president's offer. Subsequently, in May 2008 Jawara was reported to have defected to the APRC during a political rally, declaring that he shared President Jammeh's ideology and wanted to promote unity. Jawara was later appointed as a regional governor, and he supported Jammeh in his 2011 reelection bid. Jawara was named to the cabinet following the May 2012 legislative elections, and the status of the NDAM subsequently remained unclear.

Gambia People's Party (GPP). The GPP was launched in early 1985 by former vice president Aassan Musa CAMARA and a number of other defectors from the PPP to oppose President Jawara at the 1987 general election. As the balloting approached, it was felt by many that the GPP had overtaken the NCP as the principal opposition grouping; however, Camara obtained only 13 percent of the presidential vote, with the GPP securing no legislative representation. Camara again finished third in the 1992 presidential poll, while the GPP returned to the House of Representatives with two seats. Banned from participating in the 1996 elections (together with the PPP and the NCP), the GPP supported the UDP's candidate in the December 2001 presidential balloting. Camara died in September 2013. (The reference in previous *Handbooks* to Camara having died in 2007 was incorrect.)

National Convention Party (NCP). The NCP was organized in late 1975 by Sherif Mustapha Dibba, former vice president of the Republic and cofounder of the PPP. Although jailed in August 1981 on charges of involvement in the July coup attempt, Dibba challenged Jawara for the presidency in 1982, securing 28 percent of the vote. The five legislative seats won by the NCP in 1977 were reduced to three in 1982. A month after the election, Dibba was released from confinement, the charges against him having been vacated by a Banjul court. The NCP won five House seats in 1987 and six in 1992, Dibba running second to Jawara in the presidential balloting on both occasions. The NCP was banned from participating in the 1996 elections but regained legal status in July 2001, with Dibba winning 3.7 percent of the vote in the October presidential poll. Despite his previous criticism of President Jammeh and the APRC, Dibba announced an "alliance" between the NCP and the APRC prior to the legislative balloting of January 2002. Dibba was subsequently nominated by the president to the assembly, of which he was then elected speaker, thereby eliciting criticism from a number of other NCP stalwarts who wished to remain in strict opposition to the APRC. Dibba was dismissed as speaker by the president in 2006, following allegations that Dibba had been involved in a plot to overthrow the government. After Dibba's removal, the status of the party was unclear, although in September an announcement from the party urged NCP members to support Jammeh in the upcoming presidential election. The party did not present candidates in the 2007 or 2012 assembly elections. (Dibba died of a heart attack in June 2008.)

Leader: Ebrima Janko SANYANG.

LEGISLATURE

Prior to its dissolution following the 1994 coup, the unicameral House of Representatives contained 50 members—36 directly elected by universal adult suffrage, 5 indirectly elected chiefs, 8 nominated members, and the attorney general (ex officio). The 1996 constitution provided for a 49-member **National Assembly,** 45 elected by popular vote in single-member constituencies and 4 appointed by the president. (The size of the assembly was increased to 53 [48 elected, 5 appointed] for the January 17, 2002, election in view of the recent population increase.) The term of the assembly is five years, unless it is dissolved earlier by the president.

In the most recent elections (boycotted by most opposition parties) on March 29, 2012, the Alliance for Patriotic Reorientation and Construction won 43 of the 48 elected seats; the National Reconciliation Party, 1; and independents, 4.

Speaker: Abdoulie BOJANG.

CABINET

[as of September 15, 2013]

President	Yahya Jammeh
Vice President	Isatou Njie-Saidy [f]
Ministers	
Agriculture	Solomon Owens
Basic and Secondary Education	Fatou Lamin Faye [f]
Energy	Teneng Mba Jaiteh [f]
Environment, Parks, and Wildlife	Fatou Ndeye Gaye [f]
Finance and Economic Affairs	Kebba S. Touray
Fisheries and Water Resources	Mass Axi Gai
Foreign Affairs	Susan Waffa-Ogoo [f]
Health and Social Welfare	Omar Sey
Higher Education, Research, Science, and Technology	Yahya Jammeh
Information and Communication Infrastructure	Nana Grey-Johnson
Interior	Ousman Sonko
Justice and Attorney General	Mama Fatima Singhateh [f]
Presidential Affairs	Momodou Sabally
Regional Administration and Land	Momodou F. K. Kolley
Secretary General and Head of Civil Service	Momodou Sabally
Tourism and Culture	Fatou Mas Jobe-Njie [f]
Trade, Industry, Regional Integration, and Employment	Abdou Kolley
Transport, Works, Infrastructure, and National Assembly Matters	Bala Garba-Jahumpa
Women's Affairs	Isatou Njie-Saidy [f]
Youth and Sports	Alieu K. Jammeh

[f] = female

INTERGOVERNMENTAL REPRESENTATION

Ambassador to the U.S.: Alieu Momodou NGUM.

U.S. Ambassador to The Gambia: Edward ALFORD.

Permanent Representative to the UN: Mamadou TANGARA.

IGO Memberships (Non-UN): AfDB, AU, CWTH, ECOWAS, IOM, NAM, OIC, WTO.

GEORGIA

Georgia
Sakartvelo

Note: In first-round balloting on October 27, 2013, Giorgi Margvelashvili, the Georgian Dream candidate, was elected president with 62 percent of the vote; Davit Bakradze of the United National Movement finished second with 22 percent of the vote. Following his inauguration on November 17, Margvelashvili appointed (upon the recommendation of Georgian Dream) Irakli Garibashvili, theretofore the minister for internal affairs, as prime minister, incumbent Prime Minister Bidzina Ivanishvili having announced prior to the election that he would vacate the post. The Georgian Parliament on November 20 approved a vote of confidence in Garibashvili and his new cabinet, which was identical to the outgoing cabinet for the inclusion of Aleksandr Chikaidze as minister of internal affairs. Margvelashvili and Garibashvili, close allies of Ivanishvili, pledged to pursue Georgia's proposed accession to the European Union and NATO while also working to mend the relationship with Russia.

Political Status: Formerly the Georgian Soviet Socialist Republic, a constituent republic of the Union of Soviet Socialist Republics (USSR); renamed Republic of Georgia on November 14, 1990; declared independence on April 9, 1991; renamed Georgia under new constitution promulgated on October 17, 1995. (The autonomous republics of Abkhazia and South Ossetia have unilaterally declared their independence and have defied Georgia's political and military efforts to integrate them into the national structure. However, their independent status had not been recognized by any other country until they were recognized by Russia on August 26, 2008, following the Russian-Georgian military conflict earlier in the month. As of September 2013 Nauru, Nicaragua, Tuvalu, and Venezuela were the only other countries to have joined Russia in recognizing the independence of Abkhazia and South Ossetia.)

Area: 26,900 sq. mi. (69,700 sq. km).

Population: 4,355,673 (2002C); 4,448,820 (2012E—UN).

Major Urban Center (2010E): TBILISI (1,157,500). (Under the Saakashvili administration, the Georgian Parliament was relocated from Tbilisi to a new building in Kutaisi, the country's second-largest city.)

Official Language: Georgian (Abkhazian is recognized in Abkhazia).

Monetary Unit: Lari (official rate November 5, 2013: 1.67 lari = $1US).

President: (*See headnote.*) Mikhail SAAKASHVILI (United National Movement); popularly elected on January 4, 2004, and sworn in for a five-year term on January 25 succeeding Nino BURJANADZE, who had been declared interim president on November 23, 2003, by opposition leaders participating in the ouster of Eduard Amvrosiyevich (Georgi) SHEVARDNADZE (Citizens' Union of Georgia); reelected in the first round of early elections on January 5, 2008, and inaugurated for a five-year term on January 20. (Burjanadze, then the chair of the parliament, served as acting president of Georgia from November 25, 2007 [when President Saakashvili resigned his post in order to campaign for the upcoming election], until January 20, 2008.)

Prime Minister: (*See headnote.*) Bidzina IVANISHVILI (Georgian Dream–Democratic Georgia); nominated by the president (upon the recommendation of the Georgian Dream coalition) on October 17, 2012 (following the legislative elections of October 1), and inaugurated with his new government on October 25 (following confirmation by the Georgian Parliament on the same day) to succeed Vano MERABISHVILI (United National Movement).

THE COUNTRY

Located in western Caucasia, Georgia is bordered on the north and northeast by Russia, on the southeast by Azerbaijan, on the south by Armenia and Turkey, and on the west by the Black Sea. It includes three Muslim-dominated areas: Abkhazia (estimated population of 200,000) on the northwestern border with Russia, the autonomous republic of Ajaria on the southwestern border with Turkey, and South Ossetia (estimated population of 30,000–50,000) on the north-central border with Russia. Ajaria has long enjoyed formal autonomous status, while Abkhazia and South Ossetia, the source of conflict with the central government throughout most of the 1990s and 2000s, declared their independence (recognized only by Russia and a few other nations) following the military conflict between Georgia and Russia in August 2008. (See Political background, below.)

According to the government, approximately 84 percent of the population (including the disputed territories) is Georgian, 7 percent Azerbaijani, 6 percent Armenian, and 1.5 percent ethnic Russian. An estimated 80 percent of the population adheres to Orthodox Christianity, which has also played an increasingly important political role as a voice of nationalist sentiment and, in the opinion of some critics, as a source of intolerance toward religious minorities. Approximately 10 percent of the population is Muslim.

The country's terrain is largely mountainous, with a subtropical region adjacent to the Black Sea that supports the production of tea, tobacco, grapes (Georgian wines are highly prized in Russia), and citrus fruits. Approximately 50 percent of the workforce is employed in small-scale agriculture. Mineral resources include manganese, coal, and peat, and there also is abundant hydroelectric capacity. Industrial

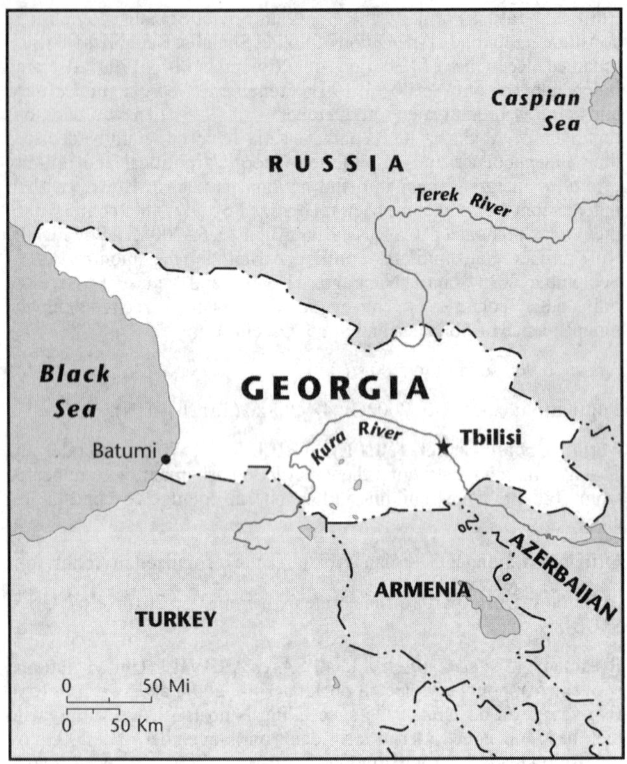

output includes iron and steel, chemicals, machine tools, plastics, and paper.

At independence, Georgia's combination of fertile land, scenic coastline, and broad cultural background provided what one journalist described as "all the ingredients for a rich and prosperous nation." However, domestic turmoil and political transition yielded an economic decline of more than 60 percent in 1990–1994 (including large drops in industrial production and agricultural output), accompanied by hyperinflation of around 10,000 percent in 1993 and 7,400 percent in 1994. Remedial action recommended by the International Monetary Fund (IMF) began to produce results in 1995, notably a fall in the inflation rate to 65 percent and output contraction of only 5 percent. Robust annual GDP growth (11 percent) was recorded in 1996 and 1997.

Double-digit growth also was anticipated for 1998, but conditions were severely compromised by the Russian financial crisis of that year. Consequently, GDP growth of less than 3 percent annually was achieved in 1998–2000.

The economy was described in 2001 as having "hit rock bottom," with more than half of the population living below the poverty line in a country that had been one of the most prosperous republics in the USSR. Problems included widespread corruption, an "old-style" (i.e., Soviet) mentality among government leaders, faltering legal reform, and the plight of an estimated 260,000 refugees of Georgian ethnicity who had fled the civil war in Abkhazia in 1992–1993. However, significant assistance continued from Western capitals, particularly Washington, which had provided more than $1 billion since independence in an effort to shift Georgia away from Russian influence. On the other hand, private foreign investors remained generally wary, although great attention was given to the construction of an oil pipeline (opened in mid-2006) from Azerbaijan through Georgia to a port in Turkey (see article on Azerbaijan for details).

The new government installed in 2004 implemented broad structural reforms designed to revive the economy through, among other things, the extensive privatization of state-run enterprises and the introduction of a simplified tax system. The administration also launched an anticorruption drive with the goal of reducing the role of the "gray" economy, estimated at that point to be responsible for 80 percent of economic activity. By 2006 the government was broadly praised for having increased tax collections fourfold, reduced bureaucratic inefficiencies, and returned basic services to the population. In fact, the World Bank described Georgia as one of the top economic reformers among transition nations. However, despite such progress, foreign investors remained wary of the "frozen conflicts" in Abkhazia and South Ossetia, which also were seen as hindering Georgia's hopes for accession to the European Union (EU) and the North Atlantic Treaty Organization (NATO). The IMF also continued to call for judicial reform, particularly in regard to the protection of property rights, while domestic critics charged the government with antidemocratic tendencies.

Tensions with Russia contributed to gas shortages in 2006, which forced Georgia (with little gas or oil of its own) to seek alternative sources such as Azerbaijan and, at least temporarily, Iran. Growth declined to only 2 percent for 2008, primarily as the result of the war with Russia in early August in South Ossetia (see Political background, below). The global economic crisis subsequently generated a second major shock, and GDP contracted by 3.8 percent in 2009. Consequently, the IMF authorized several special disbursements to support government efforts to reform the tax system, reorient spending from the military to the social sphere, and improve the nation's antiquated roads. Attention also focused on another proposed line to pipe natural gas from eastern Turkey across Georgia to EU countries.

GDP grew by 6.5 percent in 2012, and inflation was negligible for the year, although unemployment remained high at more than 15 percent (significantly higher for young people) as of early 2012. The IMF approved new support in April 2012 for the government's economic policies, while the World Bank continued to rank Georgia as one of its easiest countries in which to do business.

GOVERNMENT AND POLITICS

Political background. Having been absorbed by Russia in the early 19th century, Georgia proclaimed its independence in May 1918, with Soviet recognition being extended two years later. However, in February 1921, after having been overrun by the Red Army, Georgia was proclaimed a Soviet republic. In 1922 it entered the USSR as a component of the Transcaucasian Federated Soviet Republic, and in 1936 it became a separate union republic.

In balloting in October–November 1990 for the Georgian Supreme Soviet, a pro-independence Round Table–Free Georgia coalition secured a parliamentary majority, and on December 8 the Georgian Communist Party withdrew from the Communist Party of the Soviet Union, announcing that it would seek Georgia's secession from the USSR. In January 1991 the Georgian Supreme Soviet voted to establish a 20,000-member National Guard, and on April 9 it declared the country's independence. Five days later, the Supreme Soviet named its chair, Zviad GAMSAKHURDIA, to the new post of executive president of the republic. On May 26 Gamsakhurdia retained the post by winning 87 percent of the vote in Georgia's first direct presidential poll, although opponents criticized his "dictatorial" tendencies. On August 18, immediately prior to the attempted coup in Moscow, Prime Minister Tengiz SIGUA resigned, with Gamsakhurdia assuming personal control of the foreign, interior, and justice ministries, as well as of the republican security force. On September 16 the leader of the opposition National Democratic Party (NDP), Georgi CHANTURIA, was arrested as he tried to leave the country. Other arrests followed, and on September 24 Gamsakhurdia declared a state of emergency. Violence nonetheless intensified, culminating in full-scale armed conflict in late December.

On January 2, 1992, after meeting with opposition party leaders, rebel commanders Dzhaba IOSELIANI and Tengiz KITOVANI announced the deposition of the president (who subsequently fled to Armenia) and the establishment of a ruling Military Council. On March 6 Eduard SHEVARDNADZE, who had served for 13 years as first secretary of the Georgian Communist Party before being named Soviet foreign minister, returned to Georgia. On March 10 he was named chair of a State Council, whose 50 members included virtually all of the anti-Gamsakhurdia leadership, including Tengiz Sigua, who was reappointed to his former position as nominal head of government. In national elections on October 11, Shevardnadze received a 95 percent popular mandate as head of state, while simultaneous legislative balloting yielded seats for over 30 parties and alliances, none gaining a decisive advantage.

In addition to the struggle for control of Georgia's central administration, the republic was racked by ethnic strife in the early 1990s. In September 1990 the Supreme Soviet of the autonomous *oblast* (region) of South Ossetia, in a move branded as invalid by the Georgian Supreme Soviet, proclaimed itself a full republic (within the USSR) independent of Tbilisi. In January 1991 USSR president Mikhail Gorbachev issued a decree annulling South Ossetia's act of secession, and in March Georgian president Gamsakhurdia and new Russian president Boris Yeltsin agreed to establish a joint Georgian-Russian militia to disarm Georgian and Ossetian paramilitary groups, which had become engaged in what was termed a "mini–civil war." The conflict nonetheless continued, with Yeltsin rejecting appeals for South Ossetia's inclusion within the Russian Federation on the basis of union with North Ossetia. A referendum on January 19, 1992, in which an overwhelming majority of South Ossetians voted for integration with its Russian counterpart, was rejected by Georgia's new Military Council as "a blatant attempt to violate the territorial integrity of a sovereign state."

During the first half of 1992, intermittent fighting continued between government and pro-Gamsakhurdia forces, particularly in western Georgia, where the former president's supporters were entrenched. Tbilisi's problems were compounded on July 23 when Abkhazia's Supreme Soviet proclaimed Abkhazia's "state sovereignty," an action that the Georgian State Council immediately branded as null and void. Although the area's inhabitants were only 18 percent Abkhazian (as contrasted with 46 percent Georgian), the conflict continued, with rebel forces being repulsed during a three-day effort in March 1993 to capture Sukhumi, the government-occupied capital of Abkhazia. During the offensive, Shevardnadze denounced the participation of "thousands of Russian troops" on the Abkhazian side. The charge drew an admission from Moscow that some Russians might be involved; however, Moscow argued that the Russians were being used by President Yeltsin's hard-line opponents to destabilize the Caucasian region.

On August 5, 1993, Georgian prime minister Sigua resigned, and on August 10 he was replaced by Otar PATSATSIA. Three days later Shevardnadze met with Yeltsin to arrange for "final settlement" of the Abkhazian conflict, while the UN Security Council agreed on August 25 to dispatch a team of military observers to monitor a cease-fire that had been concluded on July 27. However, the Abkhazians responded with renewed hostilities that on September 27 yielded the capture of Sukhumi. Subsequently, forces loyal to former president Gamsakhurdia overran a number of strategic towns in western Georgia, including the Black Sea port of Poti. Russian units were then deployed to secure road and rail links cut off by the "Zviadists," and most of the area was recaptured. On December 31 Gamsakhurdia was reported to have committed suicide after a rebel band he was leading was surrounded by government troops.

On December 1, 1993, the Georgian government and its Abkhazian opponents signed an agreement in Geneva that seemed to pave the way for peace in the war-torn former Soviet republic. The accord provided for a cease-fire, the deployment of a team of international observers, the drafting of proposals on the future of Abkhazia by a team of representatives of the UN and the Conference on (later Organization for) Security and Cooperation in Europe (CSCE/OSCE), the return of refugees, and an exchange of prisoners. During second-round talks in Geneva in January 1994, it was decided that Russian troops, acting on behalf of the Commonwealth of Independent States (CIS), would be deployed as a buffer between Georgian and Abkhazian forces. Two weeks later, during a Russian-Georgian summit in Tbilisi (hailed by Shevardnadze as "one of the major events in 200 years of history between our two peoples"), a memorandum was signed authorizing the establishment of three Russian military bases within Georgia.

Georgian and Abkhazian officials concluded a further agreement in Moscow on April 4, 1994, that reaffirmed the December 1993 accord, while asserting, in principle, that Abkhazia should be granted the status of an autonomous republic within Georgia. However, the basic conflict of aspirations was again evident in November when the Abkhazian legislature adopted a new constitution enshrining the republic's self-declared sovereignty and elected its chair, Vladislav ARDZINBA, as president, drawing protests from the United States, the UN, and Russia, all of which continued to recognize Georgian sovereignty over the region.

Earlier, in November 1993, President Shevardnadze had sought to broaden his political base by launching the Citizens' Union of Georgia (CUG), while in May 1994 a declaration of "national unity and accord" was signed by 34 parties and groups, including the opposition NDP. Nevertheless, the president continued to face fierce nationalist opposition to his policy of rapprochement with Moscow and acceptance of Abkhazian autonomy. One casualty of the deadly hostilities was NDP leader Chanturia, who was assassinated in Tbilisi on December 3.

In January 1995 government forces successfully resisted an advance by members of the National Liberation Front (NLF) intended to "liberate" Abkhazia, with Tengiz Kitovani being arrested for leading the attempt. In May the government made another effort to confront the NLF-associated *Mkhedrioni* paramilitaries, now led by Dzhaba Ioseliani.

The unremitting violence of Georgian politics was highlighted by a bomb attack on Shevardnadze on August 29, 1995, while he was en route to sign a new presidential constitution approved by the legislature five days earlier. He escaped with minor injuries, and the constitution was duly promulgated on October 17 amid a security crackdown and the dismissal of the security minister, Igor GIORGADZE, who was named as one of bombing's three instigators, all of whom were believed to have fled to Russia. The complete disbandment of the *Mkhedrioni* was announced on October 1, with Ioseliani being arrested on November 15 and charged with complicity in the assassination attempt. (Ioseliani was sentenced in November 1998 to 11 years in prison following his conviction on charges related to the attack as well as a count of armed robbery.)

The breakaway Abkhazian parliament categorically rejected the definition of Abkhazia as part of Georgia in the new Georgian constitution, but, despite the continuing instability, presidential and parliamentary elections (boycotted by the separatists) went ahead peacefully, and to all appearances fairly, on November 5, 1995, followed by a second legislative round on November 19 and further balloting for unfilled seats on December 3. Standing as candidate of both his own CUG and the Socialist Party of Georgia (SPG), Shevardnadze easily won the presidential contest against five other candidates, obtaining 76.8 percent of the popular vote. The legislative elections yielded a substantial plurality for the CUG, with the seats won by allied parties ensuring a commanding pro-Shevardnadze majority. A new government appointed on December 11 included Nikoloz LEKISHVILI (former mayor of Tbilisi) as minister of state, the next highest political post after the president. Meanwhile, having denounced the inclusion in the new Georgian Parliament of the 12 Abkhazian deputies elected in 1992, Abkhazia conducted elections to its own 35-member People's Assembly in November 1996, the Georgian government and legislature condemning the balloting as illegal. (The Georgian administration announced that it had polled the ethnic Georgian refugees from Abkhazia and that over 99 percent of them were opposed to the separatist initiative.)

Brokered by Moscow and the OSCE, a security and confidence-building accord was initialed by Georgian and South Ossetian representatives on April 17, 1996, yielding direct talks in September between Shevardnadze and the chair of the South Ossetian legislature, Ludvig CHIBIROV. However, tension rose again when the South Ossetians held a direct presidential election on November 10 (returning Chibirov on a separatist platform), despite the Georgian government's dismissal of the exercise as illegal.

Negotiations with Abkhazia stalled in 1997, despite mediation efforts by Russia, the UN, and Western powers. Shevardnadze and Abkhazian president Ardzinba signed a nonaggression pact on August 15 but could agree on little else. Among other things, Tbilisi favored replacing the CIS force with an international one organized by the UN, but Abkhazia would not consent.

On the other hand, Georgia appeared to reach an agreement with South Ossetia in March 1997, preserving Georgia's territorial integrity while giving "special powers of self-determination" to the separatist region. A joint commission for economic reconstruction of South Ossetia also was established. However, in December, South Ossetia canceled further negotiations, and a final settlement remained in doubt.

President Shevardnadze was the target of a second assassination attempt on February 9, 1998, when a band of attackers opened fire on his motorcade. They were subsequently reportedly identified as former members of the private army of the late President Gamsakhurdia. Shevardnadze subsequently renewed his demand that Moscow extradite former security minister Igor Giorgadze, who was suspected of being a ringleader in the 1995 assassination attempt. The president also speculated that "powerful interests" opposed to the transit of Caspian Basin oil across Georgia may have been involved in the 1998 attack.

Tension intensified in Abkhazia in mid-May 1998, as heavy fighting broke out when Abkhazian forces entered the "security zone" along the border with Georgia proper and met resistance from Georgian troops. (Some observers suggested the Abkhazian initiative had been fueled by the region's negative response to a recent CIS proposal that autonomy within a confederal Georgia was Abkhazia's appropriate ultimate political status, not independence.) Some 35,000 ethnic Georgians reportedly fled from Abkhazia and the security zone to escape the fighting. Although a cease-fire was announced at the end of May, sporadic clashes were reported throughout the rest of the year.

The Georgian government faced another serious threat in October 1998 when several hundred soldiers (reportedly Gamsakhurdia loyalists) revolted at an army base in the town of Senaki. The soldiers seized tanks and advanced on Kutaisi, the country's second-largest city, before being crushed by government troops. Shevardnadze again attributed the unrest to opponents of the trans-Georgia oil pipeline from Azerbaijan.

Discussions toward economic cooperation were reportedly launched with officials from South Ossetia in January 1999, although relations were strained by that region's plan to conduct new legislative balloting in May. Meanwhile, little progress was apparent regarding the Abkhazian stalemate, although a plan was announced in March for repatriating the refugees from the 1998 unrest. Collaterally, the mandates of the CIS and UN missions were extended to at least the middle of the year. On the domestic front, the Shevardnadze administration, perhaps with an eye on the legislative elections scheduled for the fall, announced several anticorruption measures during the first half of 1999, including plans to forcibly dismiss judges (many of whom had been appointed during Communist rule) and replace them with jurists selected through competitive examination.

Legislative balloting was conducted in South Ossetia in May 1999, although the Georgian government denounced the balloting as contrary to the national constitution; the OSCE also refused to recognize the poll's legitimacy. Subsequently, on October 3, Abkhazian president Ardzinba was reelected without opposition in Abkhazia's first-ever popular vote, securing a reported 99 percent of the votes. On the same day, a reported 97 percent of those participating in a referendum in Abkhazia endorsed the 1994 Abkhazian constitution and its declaration of the region's status as an independent republic. The Georgian government challenged the legality of the voting in Abkhazia, noting that, among other things, ethnic Georgians who had fled Abkhazia during the civil war had been excluded from the balloting. Underlining the apparent stalemate in negotiations toward a compromise settlement, the Abkhazian legislature subsequently approved another declaration of sovereignty.

In balloting for the Georgian Parliament in October–November 1999, the CUG retained a solid majority, although a strong challenge was posed by the Revival for Georgia bloc, led by Aslan ABASHIDZE, the chair of the Ajarian Supreme Council and longtime "strongman" of Ajaria. (Opposition parties claimed there had been significant irregularities in the poll, and international observers, while not as harsh, did not fully endorse the balloting.) Abashidze also was expected to be the main challenger to Shevardnadze in the Georgian presidential balloting of April 9, 2000, but the Ajarian leader withdrew shortly before polling day. Abashidze's sudden withdrawal led some analysts to suggest a deal had been struck. Lending support to that assessment, shortly after Shevardnadze was reelected with 79 percent of the vote, the parliament revised the constitution to recognize the "Republic of Ajaria" as an official autonomous region. Moreover, in June, when the Supreme Council of Ajaria adopted a new constitution, flag, and anthem, Shevardnadze announced that those initiatives did not violate the Georgian constitution, in contrast to the administration's consistent rejection of constitutional moves on the part of separatists in Abkhazia and South Ossetia. Meanwhile, Shevardnadze appointed a new cabinet that included Gia ARSENISHVILI in the post of minister of state, whose responsibilities had been expanded in late 1999 to approach those of a prime minister.

Following a series of protest demonstrations, President Shevardnadze reshuffled the cabinet in late 2001, naming Avtandil JORBENADZE as the new minister of state. However, many CUG legislators subsequently left the party to form new opposition groupings.

In balloting that was sanctioned by the Georgian government, on November 4, 2001, Abashidze was elected unopposed as president ("Head of the Republic") in Ajaria, voters there also electing a new bicameral legislature (comprising a 35-member Council of the Republic and a 10-member Senate). Subsequently, in unsanctioned first-round presidential balloting in South Ossetia on November 18, President Chibirov finished third among six candidates in controversial balloting. The runoff, held on December 6, was won by businessman Eduard KOKOITY over Stanislav KOCHIYEV, speaker of the South Ossetian legislature and leader of the local Communist Party. The Georgian government and most international organizations deemed the South Ossetian balloting illegal, adopting a similar stance toward the legislative elections held in Abkhazia on March 2, 2002.

Independents and parties led by CUG defectors dominated the June 2002 local elections in Georgia. Preliminary results of the national legislative balloting on November 2 indicated a victory for progovernment candidates, but international observers cited widespread irregularities, including apparent falsification of results. Thousands of protesters demonstrated in Tbilisi and other cities, while several Western capitals argued that the Georgian opposition had been denied its rightful victory. Subsequently, some 30,000 demonstrators under the leadership of Mikhail SAAKASHVILI, a former cabinet minister who had quit the CUG in 2001 to protest perceived rampant corruption in government, marched on the parliament building on November 22 to prevent the legislature from convening. When troops declined to intervene, Shevardnadze was evacuated from the building, and he declared a nationwide state of emergency. However, reportedly heeding Russian advice, Shevardnadze resigned the next day (apparently in return for immunity from prosecution), and Nino BURJANADZE, the chair of the parliament, assumed presidential authority pending new national elections. The peaceful overthrow of Shevardnadze became known as the "Rose Revolution," a reference to the fact that oppositionists had carried roses during their demonstrations as a symbol of their commitment to nonviolence.

In presidential balloting on January 4, 2004, Saakashvili won 97 percent of the vote, and he was inaugurated on January 25. Upon Saakashvili's recommendation, the parliament on February 17 approved a new cabinet (whose members averaged 35 years of age and were mostly Western educated) headed by Zurab ZHVANIA in the reintroduced post of prime minister. Subsequently, new elections were held on March 28, 2004, to fill the 150 proportional seats in the parliament, with Saakashvili's National Movement–Democrats (NMD) reportedly winning 68 percent of the vote and more than 130 seats.

In March 2004 Ajarian leader Abashidze agreed to hold new legislative elections, but he was forced to step down in April and leave for Moscow after Tbilisi emboldened the local population and police to rise against him. (Saakashvili immediately announced the imposition of his own presidential authority in the region.) Saakashvili's Victorious Ajaria Party won an overwhelming majority in June balloting for the Ajarian legislature, and Levan VARSHALOMIDZE, an ally of the president, was named to head the council of ministers in Ajaria. Meanwhile, the Georgian Parliament adopted several constitutional amendments reducing the level of autonomy for Ajaria.

Saakashvili having also pledged to restore the central government's control over Abkhazia and South Ossetia, Georgia mounted a massive show of military forces along the border with South Ossetia in September 2004, but the deployment backfired when the assault was repulsed by South Ossetian fighters.

New, unsanctioned presidential balloting was held on October 3, 2004, in Abkhazia, with Abkhazian prime minister Raul KHAJIMBA (supported by Russia) and former prime minister Seregey BAGAPSH as the main contenders to succeed ailing president Ardzinba. Bagapsh was initially announced as the winner, but disorder broke out over the results, prompting a series of takeovers of government buildings by supporters of the two camps. Following the threat of a Russian intervention, Bagapsh and Khajimba agreed to run in new elections on a joint ticket, with Bagapsh as the presidential candidate and Khajimba as the vice-presidential candidate. The "unity" ticket secured more than 90 percent of the vote in reballoting on January 20, 2005, and the two were inaugurated on February 12. Aleksandr ANKUAB was subsequently named prime minister of the region.

Georgian Prime Minister Zhvania died on February 3, 2005, in what was ultimately ruled an accident involving a faulty gas heater. He was succeeded on February 17 by Zurab NOGHAIDELI.

In December 2005 President Saakashvili appeared to signal a shift to a less confrontational approach in regard to South Orsetia by proposing a settlement plan calling for "demilitarization" of the conflict and the eventual granting of broad autonomy to South Ossetia, albeit still under Georgian sovereignty. Saakashvili also reportedly reached out to the separatist leaders in Abkhazia, suggesting that peace negotiations could lead to a mutually acceptable refinement of a 2000 UN plan that would accord significant autonomy to Abkhazia.

Russia initially appeared to support the broad plans for Abkhazia and Ossetia but backed away from that stance in early 2006, apparently in part in response to a row with Georgia in January over gas supplies. Tensions in the "cold war" between Georgia and Russia subsequently continued to escalate, the Saakashvili administration accusing Russia of engaging in a "creeping annexation" of South Ossetia and Abkhazia. Exacerbating the hostility was Saakashvili's reassertion of Georgia's goal of joining NATO (anathema to Russia). Meanwhile, on the domestic front, opposition parties charged Saakashvili with having violated the spirit of the Rose Revolution by overconsolidating his authority and "packing" governmental bodies with his supporters.

In July 2006 the central government reasserted its control over portions of the Kodori Gorge (which straddles Abkhazia) that had previously been held by militias loyal to a local strongman. Consequently, Georgians who previously had been expelled from Abkhazia established an Abkhazian "government-in-exile" in the region.

In September 2006 the government arrested some 29 people in connection with an alleged coup plot. The detainees were described as supporters of former security minister Igor Giorgadze, who had been residing in Russia since being charged with complicity in the 1995 assassination attempt against President Shevardnadze. Amid the growing conflict with Russia, Saakashvili's United National Movement (UNM) dominated the October 2006 municipal elections, which international observers described as generally free and fair. However, opposition parties strongly criticized constitutional changes approved by the parliament in December that extended the legislative term and shortened the president's term so that simultaneous balloting could be held in October 2008. The opposition claimed that the measures were meant to help the UNM extend its control.

On November 12, 2006, Eduard Kokoity was reelected president of South Ossetia with 96 percent of the vote against three rivals. In addition, a concurrent referendum yielded a reported 99 percent "yes" vote regarding independence. However, as expected, the Saakashvili administration described the votes as "illegal" and symptomatic of Russian "provocation." Subsequently, in April 2007, Saakashvili established a "provisional administration" under the presidential leadership of former South Ossetian prime minister Dmitry SANAKOYEV to govern the areas of South Ossetia inhabited by ethnic Georgians. (Sanakoyev, who had previously fought for the region's independence from Georgia, said he had been persuaded by the Rose Revolution to pursue accommodation with the central government.)

In the March 4 and 18, 2007, elections to the People's Assembly in Abkhazia, most of the successful candidates were reportedly supporters of President Bagapsh. The federal government again denounced the poll.

By the fall of 2007 reports were circulating that President Saakashvili's popularity had declined in the wake of rising inflation, ongoing widespread poverty despite overall economic growth, and the strange developments surrounding former defense minister Irakli OKRUASHVILI (see For a United Georgia under Political Parties, below).

Energized by the arrest of Okruashvili, opposition forces began mobilizing large-scale demonstrations in Tbilisi that reached critical mass in early November 2007 when police cracked down on the protesters and Saakashvili, arguing that Russia was fomenting a coup plot, imposed a ten-day state of emergency that reportedly caused concern among his Western allies. The state of emergency was lifted on November 16 after Saakashvili accepted the demand from opposition parties that snap presidential elections be held. On the same day, Saakashvili appointed Vladimir GURGENIDZE, a prominent banker, to succeed Prime Minister Noghaideli, who had resigned, ostensibly for health reasons. Saakashvili resigned as president on November 25 to campaign for the presidential poll. Nino Burjanadze (the chair of parliament) served as acting president until Saakashvili was reinaugurated on January 20, 2008, following his first-round victory in balloting on January 5, in which he was credited with 53.5 percent of the vote. Runner-up Levan GACHECHILADZE (credited with 25.7 percent of the vote) described the balloting as "rigged," and new demonstrations were held in support of a recount. International observers cited irregularities in the conduct of the poll but suggested that the flaws probably did not affect the outcome. A new cabinet, again headed by Gurgenidze, was approved by parliament on January 31. The opposition also derided the accuracy of the official results from the May 21 early legislative balloting, in which Saakashvili's United National Movement (UNM) won 119 of the 150 seats. Observers described electoral conditions for balloting as improved over the January election, but the opposition again accused the government of gross violations, and most opposition legislators boycotted subsequent sessions of the parliament. The poll was conducted with a background of growing tension between Georgia and Russia, particularly in regard to Abkhazia, where a series of incidents had prompted Russia to lift trade restrictions on the separatist enclave. At the same time, the Abkhazian legislature appealed to the international community for recognition as an independent nation, citing as a precedent the recent recognition of Kosovo's independence by the United States and other Western nations. The South Ossetian legislature issued a similar request, and sporadic firefights were reported in early August between South Ossetian fighters and Georgian forces in Georgian villages in the enclave. (Each side accused the other of provoking the turmoil.)

Upon the orders of President Saakashvili, who had campaigned on a platform calling for the return of Georgia's "territorial integrity," Georgian forces shelled the South Ossetian capital of Tskhinvali during the night of August 7–8, 2008. Georgian troops entered the city the next day and overpowered the South Ossetian fighters. However, Russia responded dramatically by sending its own forces into South Ossetia and quickly routing the Georgian army. Significantly, the Russian army subsequently moved deep into Georgia proper before a tentative ceasefire was negotiated under EU mediation. Concurrently, Russian forces easily took control of Abkhazia. Late in the month Russia formally recognized the independence of both enclaves and pledged to keep its forces deployed in them for protective purposes. Hundreds of civilians died in the conflict (some as the result of suspected ethnic cleansing on the part of both South Ossetians and Georgians in South Ossetia), while many cities and villages in South Ossetia were reduced to rubble. Although most of its troops withdrew from Georgia proper in the fall, Russia kept an estimated 10,000 soldiers in South Ossetia and Abkhazia and in what it called "zones of responsibility" outside the borders of those regions. Meanwhile, domestic discontent with President Saakashvili's handling of the conflict grew, although the president denied that it had contributed to Prime Minister Gurgenidze's October resignation, which was attributed to a "joint consensual decision" made prior to the war. In addition to remaining vigilant regarding "external aggression," new prime minister Grigol MGALOBLISHVILI, an investment banker and theretofore ambassador to Turkey, pledged to pursue financial stability in the wake of sharp economic contraction resulting from war expenses, a collateral decline in tourism, and the effects of the global recession. Mgaloblishvili's cabinet was approved by the parliament on November 1. However, Mgaloblishvili resigned on January 30, 2009; he was succeeded by Nika GILAURI, theretofore a deputy prime minister and finance minister.

The regional parliaments of South Ossetia and Abkhazia again endorsed independence for their regions following the Georgian-Russian military conflict of mid-2008. Aslanbek BULATSOV, a former official from North Ossetia, was named prime minister of South Ossetia in October, while parties supportive of President Kokoity dominated the elections (again denounced as illegal by the Georgian government and most of the international community) to the South Ossetian legislature on May 31, 2009. Kokoity dismissed the government in early August amid criticism of economic conditions and the perceived ineffective (if not corrupt) disbursement of financial assistance from Russia. On August 5 Kokoity announced the appointment of Vadim BROVTSEV, the director of a construction company, as the new prime minister.

President Bagapsh was elected to a second term in Abkhazia on December 13, 2009, by securing 59.4 percent of the vote in first-round balloting that was again deemed illegitimate by the Georgian government. Former Abkhazian prime minister Khajimba, credited with 15 percent of the vote and a second-place finish, alleged that the balloting was marred by widespread fraud and other irregularities. Bagapsh appointed longtime Abkhazian foreign minister Sergey SHAMBA as prime minister in February 2010.

Abkhasian president Bagapsh died in office on May 29, 2011. He was succeeded on an acting basis by vice president Aleksandr ANKVAB, who was subsequently elected president on August 27 with 55 percent of the vote against two other candidates, including prime minister Shamba. Ankvab subsequently named Leonid LAKERBAIA to replace Shamba as premier.

Former education minister Alla DZHIOYEVA won the runoff presidential balloting in South Ossetia on November 27, 2011, but the results were voided by the South Ossetian Supreme Court due to alleged irregularities in Dzhioyeva's campaign. The court ordered new elections for March 25, 2012, and declared that Dzhioyeva would not be allowed as a candidate. However, an accord (reportedly brokered by Russia) was reached in early December, with Dzhioyeva apparently being reclassified as a legal candidate. As part of the agreement, President Kokoity resigned on December 10 and was succeeded on an interim basis by Prime Minister Brovtsev. Subsequently, Dzhioyeva announced in January 2012 that she was rejecting the earlier agreement and planned to hold her inauguration (based on the 2011 results) on February 10. However, on February 9 she was hospitalized under mysterious circumstances and did not participate in the new balloting, which was won in the second round on April 8 by Leonid TIBILOV, a pro-Russian former security chief. Tibilov in April named Rostik KHUGAYEV as prime minister, and in May Dzhioyeva was named deputy prime minister, apparently resolving the dispute.

On June 30, 2012, President Saakashvili appointed Vano MERABISHVILI to succeed Prime Minister Gilauri, reportedly with directions to focus on unemployment and to shepherd the UNM's campaign for the upcoming legislative poll. However, Merabishvili was succeeded in October by Bidzina IVANISHVILI, the billionaire whose recently organized Georgian Dream coalition had swept to a remarkable victory over the UNM in the October 1 legislative balloting.

Constitution and government. The constitution given legislative approval on August 24, 1995, and promulgated on October 17 defines Georgia as a democratic state with freedom of speech, thought, conscience, and faith being guaranteed. The president, who serves as head of state, commander in chief, and chief executive, is elected for a once-renewable five-year term by universal adult suffrage. The position of prime minister was reintroduced on February 11, 2004, with the president being designated to nominate a candidate for the post, subject to ratification by the legislature. The prime minister presides over a Council of Ministers, members of which he nominates subject to approval by the president and confirmation by the legislature. (Constitutional amendments were passed in 2010 that were to transfer some authority from the president to the prime minister following the 2013 presidential election.) Legislative authority is vested in a parliament, which is to have two chambers when conditions permit but is currently unicameral (see Legislature, below). In 1997 parliament approved a law giving the president the right to appoint the mayors of the six largest cities as well as regional governors. A National Security Council (inaugurated in January 1996) has a consultative role in defense and security matters.

The country's territory is defined as being established by the Act on the Restoration of the State Independence of Georgia of April 9, 1991. Thus the Soviet-era autonomous republics of Abkhazia and Ajaria and the autonomous region of South Ossetia (each containing a substantial Muslim population) are officially regarded as being under Georgian sovereignty, despite the fact that separatist governments assumed control in all three regions in the early 1990s. Ajaria's autonomous status was codified in June 2002 (see Political background, above), while South Ossetia and Abkhazia declared their independence in 2008 following the military conflict between Georgia and Russia.

Judicial power is exercised by independent courts, normally sitting in public. Final authority resides in the Supreme Court, whose members are elected by parliament on the president's recommendation. A Constitutional Court of nine members serving ten-year terms oversees the constitutionality of legislative and executive acts.

Although the Saakashvili administration was elected on a reformist platform, it was subsequently described by critics as exerting "subtle pressure" on media owners in an alleged effort to curtail press freedom. Despite the fact that criticism of the government is sometimes reported in newspapers and national broadcasts, journalistic watchdogs have recently voiced their disappointment over the lack of balance in coverage, particularly in regard to a perceived progovernment bias on the part of the two major independent television stations (at least prior to the October 2012 legislative elections).

Foreign relations. In part because of the civil strife that was then raging, Georgia did not become a member of the CIS at the latter's launching on December 21, 1991. In April 1992 State Council Chair Shevardnadze asserted that Georgian public opinion strongly opposed entry into the CIS. However, Georgia sent observers to CIS meetings and, reversing itself, agreed in October 1993 to join the group, with ratification by the Georgian legislature on March 1, 1994.

Georgia joined the IMF on May 5, 1992. It did not, however, become a member of the UN until July 31, when it became the last former Soviet republic to gain admission to the world body.

The United States recognized Georgia's independence on December 25, 1991, but, because of the conditions in Georgia, did not establish full diplomatic relations until March 24, 1992, one day after recognition by the European Community (EC, later the EU). Coincident with the U.S. action, Georgia was admitted to the CSCE. On April 15 it became a member of the North Atlantic Cooperation Council (NACC), linking NATO to its former adversaries in Eastern Europe. In March 1994 Georgia became a signatory of NATO's Partnership for Peace initiative, having the previous month signed a friendship and cooperation treaty with Russia.

With Georgia's concurrence, the UN Security Council gave its approval in July 1994 to the deployment of Russian peacekeeping forces in Abkhazia (having in May ruled out sending any more than a handful of UN observers to the region). In March 1995 President Shevardnadze initialed a further agreement with Moscow providing for Russia's retention of four military bases in Georgia in exchange for economic assistance. The accord was confirmed when the Russian prime minister visited Tbilisi in September, and in January 1996 the Georgian Parliament ratified the 1994 friendship treaty with Russia.

The government's strategy of alignment with Russia to secure Moscow's backing for the resolution of Georgia's internal conflicts remained controversial in Tbilisi. Shevardnadze justified the granting of military base rights to Russia by pointing out that Moscow had reciprocated by upholding the territorial integrity of Georgia within its Soviet-era borders, meaning that Russia had formally agreed that Abkhazia and South Ossetia were sovereign Georgian territory. Nevertheless, the nationalist parties opposed ratification of the 1994 friendship treaty with Russia and repeatedly called for the withdrawal of all Russian forces from Abkhazia, claiming that the Russian troops were protecting the separatist regime in Sukhumi and preventing the return of ethnic Georgian refugees.

In April 1996 Georgia joined with Armenia and Azerbaijan in signing partnership and cooperation accords with the EU. Collaterally, Georgia sought to improve its relations with neighboring states, although strains with Turkey remained.

The presence of Russian troops on the four military bases leased from Georgia continued to be an irritant for nationalists, who lobbied for a complete withdrawal. Meanwhile, the parliament threatened to annul the leasing agreement unless Russia supported Georgia's efforts to reassert control over Abkhazia. Georgia also sought backing among CIS states to tighten economic sanctions on the separatist region, Shevardnadze declaring in January 1997 that Georgia would not remain in Russia's "sphere of influence" unless Russia helped Georgia restore its sovereignty over Abkhazia and South Ossetia. The president also indicated that Georgia saw more advantage in joining the EU rather than NATO but did not rule out the possible political involvement of NATO in resolving the Abkhazian conflict. He called on the CIS either to broaden the mandate of its Russian peacekeeping force to more effectively protect Georgians displaced by the conflict in Abkhaz or to comply with the parliament's resolution calling for withdrawal of the force. At its summit in March 1997, the CIS agreed to a broader mandate that would extend the peacekeepers across a wider area to facilitate the return of 200,000 refugees displaced by fighting in 1993, but the CIS failed to implement the redeployment, apparently due to Russian opposition.

Despite the discomfort of Russia, an informal but growing Azerbaijan-Georgia-Ukraine alliance, the "Union of Three," continued to take form in 1997. The alignment, created in late 1996 as an alternative to reliance on the CIS, was Western-oriented and interested in military cooperation independent of Russia. One of its goals was to export Azerbaijan's Caspian oil to Europe via Georgia and the Black Sea, completely bypassing Russia. Moldova declared that it shared strategic interests with the Union of Three in a quadrilateral communiqué issued in November 1997, necessitating the coining of a new abbreviation, GUAM (for Georgia, Ukraine, Azerbaijan, Moldova). (The abbreviation was updated to GUUAM in April 1999 with the addition of Uzbekistan to the grouping; however, Uzbekistan announced in mid-2002 that it was suspending its participation because of the grouping's lack of effectiveness.)

Georgia joined the Council of Europe in February 1999, the Shevardnadze administration describing the accession as indicative of the country's movement toward "European political and economic standards." Concurrently, the government continued to question its ties with the CIS, which it called ineffective as far as economic and security issues were concerned.

In the early years of the 21st century, Georgia drew closer to the West and away from the Russian orbit. Meanwhile, Georgia continued to accuse Russia of fueling separatist sentiment in South Ossetia and Abkhazia, while Russia alleged that Georgia was preventing effective action against Chechen rebels operating out of the Pankisi Gorge in the mountainous border region between Georgia and the secessionist-minded Russian region of Chechnya. Adding another layer of nuance to the matter was the presence of U.S. special forces, who had arrived earlier in the year to help train Georgian forces in antiterrorism tactics. (Washington believed that members of al-Qaida or other terrorist networks may have also found a safe haven among Muslim refugees from Chechnya in the border area.)

U.S. influence was perceived in the ouster of President Shevardnadze in 2003 and the installation of the U.S.-educated Mikhail Saakashvili as president after the "Rose Revolution." The United States also continued to maintain troops on Georgian soil and to provide substantial economic aid to Georgia.

For Russia, influence in Georgia remained a vital national security interest, in part because Georgia has two ports that offer access to the Black Sea. Among other things, Russia granted Russian passports to the residents of Abkhazia and South Ossetia, in effect conferring Russian citizenship upon them. Other ongoing points of contention between Russia and Georgia were the Russian military bases maintained in Georgia by treaty rights and Russia's control over Georgia's supplies of oil and gas.

In 2005 the Georgian Parliament issued a national security report that listed the country's foreign policy priorities as strategic cooperation with the United States, Ukraine, Azerbaijan, and Turkey and partnership with Russia. During a visit to Tbilisi in May 2005, U.S. President George W. Bush called upon "all nations" to respect Georgia's "sovereignty," a remark widely construed as critical of Russian support for the breakaway republics. In a possibly related matter, Russia later in the month announced that it would close its two remaining military bases in Georgia by the end of 2008.

Georgia arrested four Russians on espionage charges in September 2006, provoking a sharp Russian response. Although Western pressure influenced the release of the detainees to Russia in only a week, Russia severed transportation and rail links with Georgia, imposed a partial trade embargo, and deported a small number of the estimated 500,000 Georgians living and working in Russia. Subsequently, Russia imposed a massive increase in the price of its gas exports to Georgia, forcing the Saakashvili administration to make emergency arrangements with non-Russian suppliers. Saakashvili also asked the EU to denounce Russia for attempting "to extend its sphere of influence" through manipulation of its oil and gas reserves. With relations with Russia still at a low point, Georgia in February 2007 launched "intensified dialogue" about NATO membership and in April committed additional troops to the U.S.-led forces in Iraq as evidence of its "worthiness" as a Western ally.

In a nonbinding referendum held concurrently with the January 2008 presidential balloting, 72.5 percent of those voting endorsed Georgia's proposed membership in NATO, and at the April NATO summit President Bush called for a Membership Action Plan to be signed for Georgia immediately. Although the summit rejected that request, the alliance was sufficiently positive about Georgia's prospects for eventual membership to anger Russia, which called NATO expansion "provocative." NATO condemned the Russian military initiative in Georgia (and Russia's subsequent recognition of South Ossetia and Abkhazia as independent nations) in August. However, it was widely conceded that Georgia had little hope for NATO membership soon, although the EU included Georgia in the Eastern Partnership launched in May 2009 to promote closer relations with former Soviet states without the promise of eventual EU membership. Meanwhile, Georgia announced its withdrawal from the CIS in August.

An EU report issued in October 2009 blamed Georgia for starting the 2008 conflict in South Ossetia, although it also criticized Russia for having fomented violence previously in the breakaway territories as well as for its inordinately strong military response, which the EU said "went far beyond the reasonable limits of defense." Russia in early 2010 announced that full ties would not be restored with Georgia while President Saakashvili remained in office. Meanwhile, U.S. officials continued to criticize Russia's "invasion and ongoing occupation" of Georgia and urged negotiations to peacefully resolve the status of Abkhazia and South Ossetia.

As of mid-2013 Georgia was still contributing some 1,500 troops to the U.S.-led mission in Afghanistan, although the deployment had generated increased criticism in Georgia.

Current issues. After leading mass demonstrations in 2008 calling for President Saakashivili's resignation, most opposition party leaders in May 2009 agreed to talks with the administration, and in July President Saakashvili announced plans for a number of judicial and electoral reforms, including the direct election of mayors and expanded access for the opposition to state television. Meanwhile, although Saakashvili continued to pursue the return of South Ossetia and Abkhazia to Georgian sovereignty, there appeared to be no likelihood of success in that regard as Russia completed army and naval bases in the enclaves and signed border protection agreements with the de facto governments of both regions. Sentiment in South Ossetia clearly favored eventual absorption into Russia (possibly in union with North Ossetia), although Moscow remained formally opposed to that option. Meanwhile, Abkhazian leaders firmly ruled out unification with Russia or reintegration with Georgia.

Antigovernment riots in Tbilisi on May 21–22, 2011, left 2 dead and 40 injured and resulted in more than 90 arrests. Sporadic protests continued through the rest of the year and the first half of 2012, many of them led by the Georgian Dream (GD) movement founded by Bidzina Ivanishvili, who had been quietly funding many philanthropic initiatives for a decade but had previously eschewed political ambitions. Most observers initially were convinced that the UNM would be able to resist the GD challenge without great difficulty. However, the tide began to turn in favor of the opposition in September when videos were broadcast of guards abusing prisoners in Tbilisi, lending heft to the arguments of critics who had already perceived deterioration in the administration's commitment to human rights. For his part, Saakashvili characterized the upcoming poll as a referendum on the nation's progress since the Rose Revolution, citing dramatic economic improvement and the curtailment of corruption and crime. Meanwhile, some analysts described the election as pitting the advantages of the incumbency against the seemingly unlimited resources of Ivanishvili, who essentially financed the entire GD effort by himself.

Following the surprisingly strong GD victory in the October 2012 elections, Saakashvili earned broad international praise for his unhesitating acceptance of Ivanishvili's ascendancy to the prime ministership. For his part, Ivanishvili (a political neophyte facing what one analyst called a "steep learning curve") indicated he would maintain Georgia's recent pro-Western policies (including support for eventual NATO and EU membership) but would also try to improve relations with Russia by, first, reestablishing economic ties.

As expected the subsequent "cohabitation" between President Saakashvili (ineligible to run for reelection in the 2013 balloting due to term limits) and Prime Minister Ivanishvili proved contentious, particularly in view of the arrest in late 2012 and the first half of 2013 of a number of former UNM-affiliated officials, including former prime minister Vano Merabashvili and others who had served in Saakashvili's cabinet. (Western organizations cautioned the Ivanishvili administration against "selective justice.") Attention subsequently focused on the first round of presidential balloting, which was scheduled for October 27, 2013, and local elections due in May 2014.

POLITICAL PARTIES

The formerly dominant Georgian Communist Party (GCP) was dissolved following the abortive Moscow coup of August 1991, with its deputies being expelled from the Georgian Supreme Soviet in mid-September. The secessionist Round Table–Free Georgia coalition that had supported President Gamsakhurdia became largely moribund following his ouster in January 1992.

Legislative elections in October 1992 gave representation to more than 30 parties or alliances, none gaining a meaningful number of seats. Most were as much military as political groupings, being commonly based on clan or regional loyalties. In November 1993 President Shevardnadze launched a new progovernment grouping called the Citizens' Union of Georgia (CUG); however, the revival in June 1994 of the GCP (as the United Communist Party of Georgia) showed that old allegiances remained powerful.

In April 2003 supporters of President Shevardnadze launched the **For a New Georgia** bloc, which included, among others, the CUG, the SSP, the Christian Democratic Union, the NDP, and the Party for the Liberation of Abkhazia. The bloc was reportedly the top performer in the November 2003 legislative balloting. However, following the ouster of Shevardnadze shortly after the poll, the bloc factionalized, and it did not present candidates in the 2004 presidential or legislative polls. Many of the other older parties also lost their relevance after Shevardnadze's fall. (For a complete history of the CUG as well as information on other defunct or diminished parties and groups, see the 2007 *Handbook*.)

Nearly 50 parties reportedly participated in the 2003 and 2004 legislative elections, many of them in newly organized (and often unstable) blocs or coalitions that sometimes lacked clearly formulated ideologies or agendas.

Several blocs were credited with securing legislative seats in the 2003–2004 elections. One of the most important was the **Right Opposition, Industrialists, and News** bloc, an alliance that included the New Rights Party, the Georgian Liberal Party, Industry Will Save Georgia, and other groupings. The well-financed bloc supported private enterprise and included some of the country's most successful

business leaders. However, it also suffered at the polls because of its image as a "party of oligarchs." Industry Will Save Georgia reportedly subsequently left the bloc, whose parliamentary faction later was referenced as the Political Union–New Rights, News.

Three blocs and nine individual parties were permitted to present candidates in the May 2008 legislative poll, the Central Election Commission having rejected the application of nearly 40 other groups for insufficient signatures (30,000 signatures are required for registration). Meanwhile, analysts continued to describe the Georgian party system as "immature," with many groupings focused on leaders rather than ideology.

The **United Opposition (National Council/New Rights)** bloc finished second to the UNM in the 2008 legislative elections, at which time the bloc comprised For a United Georgia, the New Rights Party, the Conservative Party of Georgia, Georgia's Way, the People's Party, the Georgian Group, the National Forum, Freedom, and **We Ourselves** (also referenced as "On Our Own"), a party devoted to the issues of displaced Georgians from Abkhazia and led by Paata DAVITAIA, (then deputy chair of the Georgian Parliament). The grouping was an outgrowth of the United National Council that was formed in September 2007 to oppose the Saakashvili administration. The council called for the president's resignation, establishment of a purely parliamentary system, greater judicial independence, Georgia's integration into NATO and the EU, and early elections in the spring of 2008. At that time the council included the RPG and the GLP but did not include the New Rights Party. The National Council, whose coordinator was Konstantine Gunrsadze of For a United Georgia, was described as the governing body of the United Opposition (or the United Public Movement), which presented independent Levan Gachechiladze as the primary challenger to Saakashvili in the January 2008 presidential poll. (The grouping had been reduced to nine members by that time, following the exit of the GLP.) Gachechiladze, a prominent businessman who had once served as Saakashvili's campaign manager, accused the president of "authoritarianism" and denounced the official poll results (which credited Gachechiladze with 26.7 percent of the vote) as fraudulent. The RPG ran on its own in the May 2008 legislative elections, analysts suggesting that some RPG members considered the United Opposition's approach to be too radical. It also appeared that the members of the United Opposition lacked significant mutual interests other than the ouster of Saakashvili. Using the rubric United Opposition (National Council/National Rights) after the New Rights Party became affiliated, the coalition was credited with winning 17 seats in the legislative poll on a vote share of 17.7 percent. However, some of the bloc's deputies subsequently declined to take their seats to protest the actions of the administration.

The National Council (at that time comprising the Conservative Party of Georgia, People's Party, former prime minister Zurab Noghaideli's Movement For a Just Georgia, and three smaller parties) secured 6.9 percent of the vote in the 2010 municipal elections. Two electoral blocs (comprising eight parties) and 14 individual parties contested the October 2012 legislative elections. Nearly 50 candidates, including many independents, were registered for the presidential poll scheduled for late October 2013.

Government Coalition:

Georgian Dream (GD). Launched as a "political movement" in late 2011 by Bidzina Ivanishvili (described as the richest man in Georgia), the GD invited Georgian opposition parties to coalesce behind joint candidates for the 2012 legislative elections. The GD quickly faced several barriers, including issues surrounding the citizenship of Ivanishvili, who had left Georgia in 1982 to work in the metals and banking industries in Russia before returning 20 years later to live as a reclusive philanthropist (with an estimated net worth of $6.4 billion) in his homeland. (Ivanishvili subsequently gave up both his Russian and French citizenships.) New laws, apparently directed at Ivanishvili, were also adopted in December to limit the amount of campaign donations individuals could make to parties. (Ivanishvili was eventually heavily fined for such violations of the new restrictions.)

After a number of parties had aligned in the GD (including Ivanishvili's GD-DG), the GD led several antigovernment protest demonstrations in Tibilsi in mid-2012, and a number of GD activists were arrested in the run-up to the October parliamentary poll. Completing a remarkable surge, the "Bidzina Ivanishvili–The Georgian Dream" list (including the parties below and supported by other small parties) secured a solid legislative majority (85 seats, including 44 based on 55 percent of the vote in the nationwide proportional balloting). Ivanishvili, who had not been a legislative candidate due to the citizenship question, was subsequently named prime minister, his Georgian citizenship having been formally restored by President Saakashvili.

As anticipated, friction was reported in 2013 within the GD, whose components espoused widely divergent policies and had appeared united prior to the election primarily by their antipathy toward Saakashvili. Giorgi Margvelashvili, who had been named education and science minister in Prime Minister Ivanishvili's cabinet, was nominated as the GD candidate for the October 2013 presidential poll, thereby assuming the mantle of early frontrunner for the post.

Leaders: Bidzina IVANISHVILI (Prime Minister), David SAGANELIDZE (Chair of the Parliamentary Majority), Zakaria KUTSNASHVILI (Chair of the Georgian Dream faction in Parliament), Giorgi MARGVELASHVILI (2013 presidential candidate).

Georgian Dream–Democratic Georgia (GD-DG). Organized as a formal political party in April 2012 by Bidzina Ivanishvili and his supporters, the GD-DG pledged to pursue better relations with Russia while still pursuing NATO and EU membership for Georgia. The party's platform also promised basic health insurance for Georgians and support for the agricultural sector. Manana Kobakhidze, a prominent human rights lawyer, served as GD-DG chair until Ivanishvili's citizenship status was resolved later in 2012.

Leaders: Bidzina IVANISHVILI (Prime Minister and Chair), Manana KOBAKHIDZE, Sozar SUBARI (Political Secretary), Nodar KHADURI (Executive Secretary), Kakha KALADZE.

Republican Party of Georgia (RPG). Launched in 1990, the RPG participated in the October 1992 legislative elections as a member of the "October 11 Bloc" and later was a founding member of the United Republican Party (URP). (For information on the URP, which the RPG left in 1995, see the Popular Front of Georgia section in the 2011 *Handbook*.) The RPG participated in the 1999 legislative elections in an electoral alliance called the National Democratic Alliance–The Third Way, which also included the NDP and the Party of National Industry and Economic Revival (recently formed under the leadership of Besik JUGELI, a former NDP legislator).

The RPG was allied with the Saakashvili–National Movement bloc for the 2003 legislative elections and joined the "parliamentary majority" in support of President Saakashvili in 2004. However, a number of RPG legislators subsequently split with the government following conflict between the RPG and the UNM over elections in Ajaria, and the RPG became one of the leading opposition parties calling for Saakashvili's resignation. The RPG aligned with the Conservative Party of Georgia for the 2006 municipal elections, the coalition securing more than 12 percent of the votes. Although the RPG participated in the formation of the opposition coalition in late 2007 and supported Levan Gachechiladze in the January 2008 presidential poll, it quit the United Opposition prior to the May 2008 legislative balloting, reportedly in an effort to serve as a more moderate anti-Saakashvili force than some of its former coalition partners. The RPG secured two seats in the 2008 legislative elections on a vote share of 3.8 percent, but the RPG deputies reportedly subsequently relinquished their seats. The RPG aligned in the Alliance for Georgia with the New Rights Party and Our Georgia–Free Democrats for the 2010 municipal elections.

As of mid-2013 it was reported that nine of the GD legislators had formed a Georgian Dream–Republicans faction in the legislature.

Leaders: Davit USUPASHVILI (Chair of the Party and Chair of the Georgian Parliament), Davit BERDZENISHVILI (Political Secretary and Chair of the Georgian Dream–Republicans faction in Parliament), Gigla AGULASHVILI (Executive Secretary).

Our Georgia–Free Democrats. Launched in July 2009, this moderate opposition party is led by Irakli Alasania, who stepped down as Georgia's ambassador to the UN in late 2008 and became a critic of the Saakashvili administration, particularly in regard to the midsummer war with Russia. In February 2009 Alasania was named one of the leaders of the informal Alliance for Georgia, which also included the New Rights Party and the RPG.

Alasania, a strong supporter of greater Georgian integration with the EU, secured 19 percent of the vote in the election for mayor of Tbilisi in May 2010 as the candidate of the Alliance for Georgia, which was credited with 9.2 percent of the nationwide vote in the municipal elections. Alasania's performance was considered disappointing, and in June he announced the de facto dissolution of the alliance. (When this party served as an important component of the GD for the 2012 legislative elections, it was often referenced simply as the Free Democrats.) Alasania was named deputy prime minister and defense minister in the October 2012 cabinet. Four other Free Democrats were also appointed to the cabinet. It was subsequently reported that there were 10 members of the Georgian Dream–Free Democrats faction in the legislature.

Leaders: Irakli ALASANIA, (Chair and Defense Minister), Tea TSULUKIANA (Deputy Chair), Irakli CHIKOVANI (Secretary General and Chair of the Georgian Dream–Free Democrats faction in Parliament).

Conservative Party of Georgia. This grouping was formed in 1995 as a successor to the Liberal-Conservative Party, which had been founded by former members of the Georgian Conservative Monarchists' Party (GCMP). (The GCMP had been launched in late 1989 in support of the Georgian monarchy, for which there was no obvious claimant.) Previously aligned with the UNM, the center-right Conservative Party secured representation in the 2004 legislative poll as part of the New Right bloc. In early 2006 the party was among the opposition groups that organized public demonstrations calling for the resignation of President Saakashvili. At that point, several of the party's legislators were participating in an opposition parliamentary faction called the Democratic Front that also included the RPG and Industry Will Save Georgia. In April 2006 the front, led by Davit ZURABISHVILI, announced a boycott of parliament pending action on the front's demands for representation on the national election commission, the direct election of the mayor of Tbilisi (currently appointed by the president), and other reforms. The Conservatives participated in the 2006 local elections in alliance with the RPG and as part of the United Opposition (National Council/New Rights) coalition that won 17 seats in the May 2008 parliamentary poll. In 2008 and 2009 the Conservatives called for a campaign of civil disobedience to prompt the resignation of President Saakashvili.

Following the October 2012 legislative poll, it was reported that the Georgian Dream–Conservatives legislative faction comprised six members.

Leaders: Zviad DZIDZIGURI, Giga BUKIA (Chair of the Georgian Dream–Conservatives faction in Parliament).

National Forum. Formed in late 2006 by Kakha Shartava, the National Forum was a member of the United Opposition (National Council/New Rights) bloc for the 2008 legislative poll. The party, which opposes the proposed accession of Georgia to NATO and the EU (preferring a neutral stance), nevertheless aligned with the GD in February 2012. Six of the GD candidates elected in the October 2012 legislative poll subsequently formed a Georgia Dream–National Forum faction.

Leaders: Kakha SHARTAVA, Malkhaz VAKHTANGASHVILI (Chair of the Georgian Dream–National Forum faction in Parliament).

Industry Will Save Georgia. Launched in 1999, this nationalist, protectionist grouping was described as comprising "well-heeled business leaders" (including Gogi Topadze, a "beer magnate") opposed to the sale of government assets to foreign investors. It also objected to many of the economic strictures recommended by the IMF.

For the 1999 legislative balloting the party formed an electoral alliance with the URA (see below) and a number of smaller parties, including the center-right Political Union "Sporting Georgia," formed in 1998 under the leadership of economist Roman RURUA; the **Movement for the Georgian State,** a center-right grouping formed in 1998 under the leadership of Irakli BATIASHVILI; and the **National Movement "Georgia First of All,"** a right-wing grouping led by Guram SHARADZE. The bloc won 7.8 percent of the proportional vote in the 1999 legislative balloting. It was described in mid-2006 as controlling seven seats in the parliament.

In the May 2008 legislative poll the Industrialists participated in the Rightist Alliance (also referenced as the Rightist-Alliance–Topadze Industrialists) that also included the NDP and Unity (see UCPG, below). The alliance won 0.9 percent of the vote.

Six of the successful GD candidates in the October 2012 legislative elections subsequently formed a Georgian Dream–Entrepreneurs faction in parliament with Topadze as chair.

Leaders: Gogi TOPADZE (Chair), Zurab TKEMALADZE.

People's Party. Formed by former members of the NDP, the People's Party contested the 1999 legislative elections in a coalition with two other small groupings—the **Popular Union** and the **Party of Independence and Unity of Georgia.** The People's Party formed an alliance with the KTK (below) for the June 2002 local elections.

Koba Davitashvili, the current chair of the party and a former member of the Conservative Party, initially supported the UNM as part of the Conservative Party, but he subsequently clashed severely with Mikhail Saakashvili. Although the party participated in the GD for the October 2012 legislative poll, observers suggested its right-wing, nationalistic ideology might eventually lead to friction with the centrist and left-leaning members of the coalition. Supporting such analysis, Davitashvili was nominated as a candidate for the October 2013 presidential poll, despite most of the other GD components having agreed on a consensus candidate.

Leaders: Koba DAVITASHVILI (Chair and 2013 presidential candidate), Mamuka GIORGADZE.

Opposition Party:

United National Movement (UNM). Also referenced as the National Movement Party or simply as the National Movement, the center-right, nationalist UNM was founded in 2001 in support of governmental and economic reform, closer ties with the EU and the United States, and restoration of Georgian control over Abkhazia and South Ossetia. The UNM platform also called for raising pensions, enhancing social services for the poor, fighting corruption, and increasing state revenues by curtailing the power of the oligarchs.

The UNM was led at its formation by Mikhail Saakashvili, a former cabinet minister who quit the CUG in late 2001 to protest what he considered to be acceptance on the part of the government of widespread corruption. Campaigning with the motto of "Georgia Without Shevardnadze," Saakashvili led a National Movement–Democratic Front to notable success in the June 2002 local elections.

In 2003 the UNM joined with the United Democrats, the Union of National Security, and the youth movement *Kmara* ("Enough") to form the United People's Alliance, which played a central role in the forced resignation of President Shevardnadze. (Candidates for the November 2003 legislative balloting were presented through a Saakashvili–National Movement bloc that reportedly also included the RPG and others.) The alliance subsequently presented Saakashvili as the dominant presidential candidate in the January 2004 balloting, and the UNM served as the core component of the National Movement–Democrats (NMD) that was credited with winning 133 of 150 seats in the March balloting for the legislature. Other components of the NMD included the United Democrats, a centrist grouping formed in June 2002 by former CUG leader and former speaker of the parliament Zurab Zhvania. (The United Democrats in 2002 claimed the allegiance of some 25 legislators. Subsequently, Zhvania formed an electoral alliance with Nino

Burjanadze [chair of the parliament] called the Burjanadze–Democrats Bloc, which won a number of seats in the November 2003 legislative poll. Several other groups reportedly participated in the 2003 bloc, including the Union of Georgian Traditionalists and the Christian-Conservative Party of Georgia.) Zhvania, an ally of Saakashvili in the Rose Revolution, was named prime minister in February 2004.

The formation of the NMD in early 2004 was described variously as a "merger" or "amalgamation" of the UNM and the United Democrats. However, a degree of tension was subsequently reported between the UNM and the United Democrats, particularly following the death in 2005 of Zhvania. Consequently, references to the NMD subsequently declined, with the UNM being regularly described as the nation's ruling party and many members of the United Democrats (including Burjanadze) having apparently been absorbed into the UNM.

The UNM reportedly secured approximately two-thirds of the vote in the October 2006 municipal elections, while Saakashvili was elected to a second presidential term in January 2008 on a platform that called for restoration of Georgia's "territorial integrity," NATO membership for Georgia, closer ties with the EU, and the expansion of social welfare programs. Similar themes were stressed by the UNM for the May legislative balloting, at which its candidates (minus Burjanadze, who withdrew from the UNM proportional list to protest the perceived low placement of her supporters on the list) were presented under the rubric of the UNM–For a Victorious Georgia, which secured 119 of 150 seats (71 in single-member constituencies and 48 on a vote share of 59 percent in the proportional component). Burjanadze subsequently launched a new anti-Saakashvili party (see Democratic Movement–United Georgia, below).

The UNM dominated the June 2010 municipal elections, securing a reported 66 percent of the vote nationwide and retaining the important mayoralty of Tbilisi.

The UNM "More Benefit to the People" list fell to 65 seats (including 33 on a vote share of 40 percent in the proportional balloting) in the October 2012 legislative poll, after which President Saakashvili announced the UNM would serve as the "constructive opposition."

A number of UNM members who had served in previous cabinets were arrested by the new Ivanishvili administration in late 2012 and the first half of 2013. Included was former prime minister Vano Merabishvili, who was charged with misuse of public funds and abuse of power. His trial was subsequently postponed until the fall of 2013. By that time public opinion polls indicated that support had dropped significantly for the UNM, which nominated former parliamentary speaker Davit Bakradze (considered open to compromise with the GD) as its candidate for the October presidential poll.

Leaders: Mikhail SAAKASHVILI (Chair and President of the Republic [term scheduled to expire in November 2013]), Davit BAKRADZE (Chair of the Parliamentary Minority, 2013 presidential candidate, and Former Speaker of Parliament), Giorgi GABASHVILI (Chair of the United National Movement faction [40 members] in Parliament), Akaki BOBOKNIDZE (Chair of the National Movement–Majoritarians faction [six members] in Parliament), Tariel LONDARIDZE (Chair of the National Movement–Regions faction [six members] in Parliament), Gigi UGULAVA (Mayor of Tbilisi), Vano MERABISHVILI (Secretary General and Former Prime Minister [under arrest as of mid-2013]).

Other Parties That Contested the 2012 Legislative Elections:

Georgian Labor Party (GLP). The GLP is a successor to the Union for a Law-Governed State (ULGS), founded in August 1995 and rendered in English as the State Justice Union. The ULGS, an ideologically centrist grouping, won one legislative seat in 1995, while the GLP (founded in 1997) secured two seats in 1999 in single-member constituencies despite just barely missing the 7 percent threshold for proportional representation with 6.85 percent of the vote. The GLP also performed well in the June 2002 local elections and won seats in the 2003 and 2004 national legislative polls.

One of the few Georgian parties with a clear ideology, the left-wing GLP enjoys its greatest support in Tbilisi. At its founding, the GLP was considered "pro-Russian," but its stance subsequently shifted to one that favors eventual membership for Georgia in NATO. The GLP was among the parties calling for the resignation of President Saakashvili in the first half of 2006. It was credited with approximately 10 percent of the vote in the 2006 municipal elections.

The GLP was initially described as one of the founders of the opposition coalition formed in late 2007, but GLP leader Shalva Natelashvili was presented as a single-party candidate in the January 2008 presidential poll, securing 6.5 percent of the vote. Having strongly criticized the administration for recent economic reforms perceived by the party as having failed to assist the poor, the GLP won six seats in the May legislative balloting on a vote share of 7.4 percent. However, the GLP subsequently announced a boycott of the legislature to protest what it described as flawed electoral results. In 2011 the GLP called for the impeachment of President Saakashvili for his conduct in the 2008 war with Russia. The party list failed to secure any seats in the 2012 legislative poll (1.2 percent of the vote in the proportional component), some of its supporters having apparently voted for the new GD opposition bloc.

Leaders: Shalva NATELASHVILI (Chair and 2013 presidential candidate), Giorgi GUGAVA (Secretary).

Christian Democratic Movement. Founded in early 2008 by Giorgi Targanadze, a popular ex-television anchor from *Imedi TV* (the focus of a recent government crackdown), this grouping described itself as a member of the "moderate opposition." Among other things, its campaign platform called for the Georgian Orthodox Church to be established as the state religion. The party won six seats in the May legislative poll on a vote share of 8.7 percent and gained another seat following subsequent by-elections. Among the parties reportedly participating in the movement were **Forward Georgia,** which had been launched under the leadership of Irakli BATIASHVILI in the wake of the Rose Revolution to provide opposition to the Saakashvili administration; the **Green Party,** a left-leaning grouping led by Giorgi GACHECHILADZE; and the **Party of the Future,** led by Gia MAISASHVILI, who had won 0.8 percent of the vote in the January 2008 presidential poll.

Although Targanadze had emerged as one of President Saakashvili's most strident critics, the Christian-Democratics were reportedly not recruited to participate in the opposition GD bloc for the 2012 legislative poll, at which the Christian Democratic Union list (which also included the **European Democrats**) fell to 2 percent of the vote in the proportional component and won no seats. (The Green Party reportedly supported the GD.) In August 2013 it was reported that the European Democrats had nominated Zurab KHARATISHVILI as a candidate for the October presidential poll, with the support of the NDP (below). Kharatishvili had recently generated criticism from the major parties by resigning as chair of the Central Election Commission to run for the presidency.

Leaders: Giorgi TARGANADZE (Leader and 2013 presidential candidate), Levan VEPHKHVADZE.

National Democratic Party (NDP). Claiming to be the heir of a pre-Soviet party of the same name, the NDP was organized in 1988 as a secessionist grouping with a "Christian outlook." It favored restoration of the monarchy as a means of national unification. Allied with the smaller and more secularist Democratic Party (DP), it won 32.6 percent of the vote in the 1990 republican election, while in the October 1992 legislative balloting the NDP took 12 seats and the DP 10.

Having initially supported Shevardnadze's assumption of power in 1992, the NDP subsequently became critical of his policy of rapprochement with Moscow and opposed Georgia's CIS membership. In December 1994, NDP leader Georgi Chanturia was assassinated in Tbilisi in an attack that also seriously injured his wife, Irina SARISHVILI-CHANTURIA, who took over the party leadership despite having one of three bullets that struck her lodged close to her heart.

The former DP chair, Kartlos GHARIBASHVILI, took only 0.5 percent of the vote in the November 1995 presidential election; however, in the legislative balloting the NDP came in second place, with 8 percent of the proportional vote and 34 seats in total. In January 1996, NDP deputies unsuccessfully opposed ratification of the 1994 friendship treaty with Russia, claiming that it contained unacceptable "military union" provisions.

Following the NDP's participation in the For a New Georgia bloc in the November 2003 legislative poll, Irina Sarishvili-Chanturia resigned as NDP leader to form a new grouping, referenced as the **Hope Party** for the January 2008 presidential balloting in which Sarishvili-Chanturia was credited with 0.2 percent of the vote. Meanwhile, the NDP participated in the Rightist Alliance for the May legislative poll. (Some reports indicated that an NDP member secured a legislative seat following subsequent by-elections.) Running on its own, the NDP received only 0.1 percent of the vote in the proportional component of the 2012 legislative poll.

Leader: Bachuki KARDAVA.

New Rights Party. Formed in October 2000 as the "New Faction" by dissident CUG legislators, this grouping adopted its current name in June 2001 and scored significant victories in the June 2002 local elections. For the 2003 legislative balloting, the New Rights Party formed the **New Right** bloc with the GLP, the Conservative Party of Georgia, and others. It participated in the 2004 legislative poll as part of the Right Opposition, Industrialists, and News bloc, which won 17 proportional seats. Although the bloc's electoral success was built in part on its cooperation with the NMD, a number of legislators from the bloc supported the drive in early 2006 by opposition parties to force the resignation of President Saakashvili. Davit Gamkrelidze, chair of the New Rights Party, won 4.0 percent of the vote in the January 2008 presidential poll, the party's support in the business sector having earned Gamkrelidze the endorsement of Industry Will Save Georgia and the NDP. However, the New Rights Party joined the United Opposition for the May legislative balloting, reportedly securing 5 of the bloc's 17 legislative seats. (The party's legislators subsequently declined to take their seats.)

In September 2008 Gamkrelidze called for President Saakashvili's resignation in view of the "catastrophic consequences" of the 2008 war with Russia. The New Rights Party subsequently aligned with the new Our Georgia–Free Democrats (above) in the Alliance for Georgia for the 2010 municipal elections. The Political Union "New Rights" list secured 0.4 percent of the vote in the proportional component of the 2012 legislative elections.

Leaders: Davit GAMKRELIDZE (Chair), Kakha KATSITADZE.

Other parties that participated in the 2012 parliamentary elections included **Free Georgia** (0.3 percent of the proportional vote), led by former legislator Kakha KUKAVA (previously a leader of the Conservative Party), who called for the reestablishment of economic ties with Russia and Abkhazia; **Freedom** (0.05 percent), led by Konstantine GAMSAKHURDIA, a son of Georgia's first president; the **Georgian Group** (*Kartule Dasi*) movement (0.1 percent), a left-wing, nationalist formation led by former GLP member Jondi BAGHATURIA; the ***Merab Kostava* Society** (0.05 percent), a rightist grouping led by Vaja ADAMIA; **For the Future of Georgia** (0.03 percent), an Ajaria-based grouping led by Nino KVIRIKADZE; the **Sportsmen's Union of Georgia** (SUG—0.07 percent), launched in 1994 in support of "consolidation of the nation" and close ties with other CIS countries and currently led by Valery GIORGOBIANI; the **Labor Council of Georgia** (0.03 percent); the **Public Movement** (0.03 percent); and **Justice for Georgia** (0.19 percent), which nominated Sergo JAVAKHIDZE for the October 2013 presidential elections.

Other Parties and Groups:

For a United Georgia. This party was formed in September 2007 by supporters of Irakli Okruashvili, a former ally of Mikhail Saakashvili in the Rose Revolution who had been dismissed from the cabinet in November 2006. Okruashvili in September 2007 accused Saakashvili of plotting to kill opponents and charged the administration in general with widespread corruption, prompting large-scale antigovernment demonstrations. In a bizarre series of events, Okruashvili himself was arrested on corruption charges and subsequently reportedly acknowledged that he could not produce evidence for his accusations against Saakashvili. Okruashvili was released on bail and announced his retirement from politics, but he later said that his retraction had been coerced. Meanwhile, his initial arrest had prompted widespread protest demonstrations, and For a United Georgia (also referenced as the Movement for a United Georgia) served as a core component of the new anti-Saakashvili opposition coalition.

Okruashvili was arrested on an Interpol warrant in December 2007 in Germany but was later granted asylum in France. In March 2008 a Georgian court sentenced him in absentia to a prison term of 11 years following his conviction on extortion charges.

Okruashvili resigned from For a United Georgia in October 2010 and helped to found the new Georgian Party, whose leaders also included 2008 presidential candidate Levan Gachechiladze, Erosi Kitsmarishvili (a former ambassador to Russia), and human rights activist Sozar Subari, who was named chair. The new party endorsed further Georgian integration into the EU but called for normalization of relations with Russia as well.

In June 2011 the Georgian government charged Okruashvili in absentia of leadership of an illegal armed formation, and in September 15 of his supporters were convicted of plotting to aid his return to Georgia. Later in the year Okruashvili announced that the Georgian Party had merged back into For a United Georgia, Subari having left the party for the GD. Okruashvili returned to Georgia in November 2012, and, despite his initial arrest, the 2008 verdict was overturned in early 2013 and other charges against him were subsequently dismissed.

Leaders: Irakli OKRUASHVILI (Cochair), Erosi KITSMARISHVILI (Cochair), Konstantine GUNRSADZE, Giorgi TORTLADZE, Eka BESELIA (Secretary General).

Georgia's Way. This party (also known as Georgia's Way) was formed by Salome ZOURABISHVILI, a French citizen who received Georgian citizenship in 2004. A former French diplomat, Zourabishvili served as Georgian minister of foreign affairs until being dismissed in the fall of 2005. With Georgia's Way by then firmly in the opposition camp, Zourabishvili in 2007 announced plans to run for president in 2008. However, the party subsequently joined the United Opposition and supported Levan Gachechiladze in the presidential poll. Zourabishvili resigned as president of the party in November 2010 and was replaced by Kakha Seturidze. Although apparently not a formal member of the GD, Georgia's Way opted not to present 2012 legislative candidates in deference to the GD, Zourabishvili having endorsed the political aspirations of Bidzina Ivanishvili. Zourabishvili planned a run for president of the republic in 2013, but her candidacy was rejected because she holds dual citizenship, which has been ruled an automatic disqualification.

Leader: Kakha SETURIDZE.

Georgian Politics. Formed in early 2008 by, among others, several former members of the Georgian Supreme Council, Georgian Politics called for economic cooperation with Abkhazia and opposed Georgia's proposed NATO membership. The party secured 0.5 percent of the May legislative vote.

Leader: Gocha PIPIA.

Union of Reformers and Agrarians (URA). The URA is a successor to the Reformers' Union of Georgia (RUG), a "liberal-centrist" grouping founded in 1993 in support of closer relations with Russia as well as market reforms designed to facilitate the emergence of a middle class. The RUG had competed in the 1995 legislative balloting as a member of the bloc Reformers' Union of Georgia–National Concord (*Sakartvelos Reformaforta Kavshiri–Erovnuli Tankhmoba*), which won two parliamentary seats. Other members of that 1995 bloc were the **Georgian Citizens' Political Association** (GCPA), launched in August 1995 as a centrist-traditionalist grouping in favor of "unification of national mentality," and the Sportsmen's Union of Georgia. The URA participated in the Rightist Alliance in the 2008 legislative poll.

Leader: Bakur GULUA (Chair).

Union of Georgian Traditionalists (*Kartvel Traditsionalista Kavshiri*—KTK). Also known as the Traditionalist Party, the conservative KTK won seven seats in the Supreme Council in 1992. Its 4.2 percent share of the vote in 1995 was insufficient for proportional seats in the Georgian Parliament, but it elected two deputies in the constituency contests.

Eleven of the successful candidates from the Revival of Georgia bloc in the 1999 legislative balloting subsequently joined the KTK parliamentary faction. (For detailed information on the Revival of Georgia bloc [led by Aslan Abashidze, the dominant figure in Ajarian affairs at the time], see the 2008 *Handbook*.) The KTK competed in the June 2002 local elections in an electoral alliance with the People's Party (see above). For the 2008 legislative poll the KTK participated in the Traditionalists, Our Georgia, and Women's Party bloc, which won 0.4 percent of the proportional vote.

Leader: Akaki ASATIANI (2013 presidential candidate).

Our Georgia. This party was established in early 2008, mainly by supporters of the late Badri PATARKATSISHVILI, who had finished third in the January 2008 presidential poll with 7.1 percent of the vote.

Leader: Gocha JOJUA.

Women's Party. This party was established in early 2008 by legislator Guguli Magradze, a recent defector from the UNM. It reportedly informally supported the GD in the 2012 legislative poll.

Leader: Guguli MAGRADZE.

Democratic Movement–United Georgia. Formed by Nino Burjanadze, the former chair of the Georgian Parliament who split with President Saakashvili in 2008 (see UNM, above), this new party was one of the most influential opposition groups calling for Saakashvili's resignation in 2009. Ten members of the party were arrested on weapons charges in 2009, which Burjanadze characterized as a "campaign of terror" against her supporters in advance of antigovernment rallies. Burjanadze and her party decided not to contest the 2012 legislative poll so as not to compromise the prospects of the opposition GD coalition. However, Burjanadze was the party's candidate for the October 2013 presidential poll, announcing that Saakaskvili would be arrested if she won the election.

Leader: Nino BURJANADZE (2013 presidential candidate).

United Communist Party of Georgia—UCPG (*Sakartvelos Komunisturi Partia*). The UCPG was launched in June 1994 in an attempt to unite the various factions that claimed descent from the Soviet-era Georgian Communist Party (GCP). The old GCP had been somewhat less tainted by corruption and abuse of power than its counterparts elsewhere; it was nevertheless dissolved in August 1991 as Georgia moved to independence and its leaders shifted their support to other parties. (For information on the UCPG in 1995–2000, see the 2013 *Handbook.*)

The UCPG leader is the father of Igor Giorgadze, former chief of the Georgian Security Service, who officials have claimed was a key figure in the attempt to assassinate Shevardnadze in 1995. The government demanded in July 1997 that Moscow extradite the alleged conspirator, but Maj. Gen. Panteleimon Giorgadze said his son was not in Moscow.

Igor Giorgadze, who claimed the charges against him were "utterly groundless," helped launch the Party of Justice (registered in 2004 in Georgia) from exile. After having reportedly spent time in some eight countries over the past 11 years, he announced from Moscow in 2006 that he was not seeking Russian citizenship or permanent asylum in Russia but rather intended to attempt to regain political influence in Georgia through the Party of Justice. Subsequently, UCPG leaders claimed that the Georgian government was withholding pension payments from party adherents. Reports in 2011 indicated that many UCPG members had left the party for other groupings.

Leader: Maj. Gen. Panteleimon GIORGADZE.

Parties supporting South Ossetian president Eduard Kokoity in the 2009 elections for the South Ossetian legislature included the **Republican Party "Unity"**; the **Communist Party**, led by Stanislav KOCHIV (speaker of the legislature); and the formally recognized branch of the People's Party. The primary opposition party was the **Republican Socialist Party "Fatherland,"** which, under the leadership of Vyacheslav GOBOZOV, accused Kokoity of using governmental authority to repress dissent. (An unrecognized grouping led by Roland KELEKHSAYEV also claimed the People's Party rubric in announcing cooperation with Fatherland in an anti-Kokoity Civic Forum.) Following the election of President Tibilov in April 2012, a number of new parties were established, including **New Ossetia**, led by David SANAKOYEV, who had finished second in the presidential poll, and ***Alans*** (named after an ancient tribal group), led by Roin KAZAYEV. Meanwhile, Kokoity reportedly left Unity in mid-2013, although he pledged to remain active politically.

In Abkhazia, President Sergei Bagapsh was reelected in the December 2009 poll as the candidate of **Unified Abkhazia**, a previously informal vehicle for his supporters that was officially recognized as a political party in early 2009. Among the four other candidates was Beslan BUTBA, a wealthy businessman and former parliamentarian who recently launched the centrist **Economic Development Party of Abkhazia** (EDPA). Yakub LAKOBA, the leader of the **People's Party of Abkhazia**, announced a cooperation agreement with Butba for the presidential balloting. Butpa finished fourth in the balloting according to official results, with 8 percent of the vote. Unified Abkhazia, which had supported Alexandr Ankvab in his successful bid in the special presidential election held following Bagapsh's death in 2011, won three seats in the March 2012 elections to the Abkhazian legislature, while the opposition **Forum for National Unity of Abkhazia** (FNUA), led by former Abkhazian prime minister Raul Khajimba, secured four seats. The remaining seats were won by independents. It was reported in 2013 that United Abkhazia had withdrawn its supported for President Ankvab, although some loyalists apparently left the party because of that decision. Subsequently, leaders of the FNUA, EDPA, People's Party, and other groups announced the formation of a Coordinating Council to press for reform in South Ossetia.

For more information on the **Popular Front of Georgia** (PFG) and the **Christian-Conservative Party of Georgia**, see the 2011 *Handbook.* For information on the **All-Georgian Union of Revival**, the **Socialist Party of Georgia**, and small parties that competed in the 1999 and/or 2003–2004 legislative balloting, see the 2012 *Handbook.*

LEGISLATURE

The 1995 constitution specifies that when territorial and political conditions permit, the **Georgian Parliament** (*Sakartvelos Parlamenti*) will consist of two chambers, namely a Council of the Republic elected by proportional representation and a Senate composed of deputies elected in the country's territorial units. In the interim, the legislature consists of a single chamber, currently comprising, under revisions approved in March 2008, 150 members (77 elected in single-number constituencies and 73 elected via proportional balloting from party lists in one nationwide constituency). The term of office is four years. First-round candidates in the single-member constituencies must receive more than 30 percent of the vote to be elected; if no candidate reaches that level, a runoff is held between the top two vote getters. The threshold for gaining representation in the proportional poll is 5 percent (reduced prior to the 2008 balloting from 7 percent).

At the most recent balloting of October 1, 2012, the Georgian Dream coalition won 85 seats (41 in single-member constituencies and 44 in the proportional balloting), and the United National Movement (UNM) won 65 seats (32 in single-member constituencies and 33 in the proportional balloting). It was reported in mid-2013 that some 13 legislators had left the UNM legislative faction to sit as independents.

Chair: David USUPASHVILI.

CABINET

[as of September 1, 2013] (*See headnote.*)

Prime Minister	Bidzina Ivanishvili
Deputy Prime Ministers	Kakhi Kaladze
	Giorgi Kvirikashvili
State Ministers	
Diaspora Issues	Konstantin Surguladze
European and Euro-Atlantic Integration	Aleksi Petriashvili
Reintegration	Paata Zakareishvili
Ministers	
Agriculture	Shalva Pipia
Corrections and Legal Assistance	Sozar Subari
Culture and Monument Protection	Guram Odisharia
Defense	Irakli Alasania
Economy and Sustainable Development	Giorgi Kvirikashvili
Education and Science	Tamar Sanikidze [f]
Energy	Kakhi Kaladze
Environmental and Natural Resources Protection	Khatuna Gogoladze [f]
Finance	Nodar Khaduri
Foreign Affairs	Maia Panjikidze [f]
Health, Labor, and Social Affairs	David Sergienko
Internal Affairs	Irakli Garibashvili
Internally Displaced Persons from the Occupied Territories, Accommodation, and Refugees	David Darakhvelidze
Justice	Tea Tsulukiani [f]
Regional Development and Infrastructure	David Narmania
Sports and Youth Affairs	Levan Kipiani

[f] = female

INTERGOVERNMENTAL REPRESENTATION

Ambassador to the U.S.: Archil GEGESHIDZE.

U.S. Ambassador to Georgia: Richard B. NORLAND.

Permanent Representative to the UN: (Vacant).

IGO Memberships (Non-UN): CEUR, EBRD, ICC, IOM, OSCE, WTO.

GERMANY

Federal Republic of Germany
Bundesrepublik Deutschland

Note: Angela Merkel (Christian Democratic Union [CDU]) was sworn in for a third term as chancellor on December 17. Her CDU won the September 22 federal elections but were five seats short of a majority. After mooting an alliance with the Green party, Merkel spent nearly three months convincing the Social Democrats to form a coalition, which the SPD was initially reluctant to do, after suffering heavy electoral losses following its previous coalition with the CDU. .

Political Status: Divided into British, French, Soviet, and U.S. occupation zones in July 1945; Federal Republic of Germany under democratic parliamentary regime established in Western zones on May 23, 1949; German Democratic Republic established under Communist auspices in Soviet zone on October 7, 1949; unified as the Federal Republic of Germany on October 3, 1990.

Area: 137,854 sq. mi. (357,041 sq. km).

Population: 81,932,216 (2013E—UN); 81,147,265 (2013E—U.S. Census).

Major Urban Centers (2011E): BERLIN (3,375,222), Hamburg (1,734,272), Munich (1,388,308), Cologne (1,024,373), Frankfurt am Main (687,775), Stuttgart (597,176), Düsseldorf (581,122), Bremen (547,769), Hannover (514,137), Leipzig (510,512), Dresden (507,939), Nürnberg (495,121), Bonn (309,869). Parliament voted in June 1991 to relocate the capital from Bonn to Berlin; the actual transfer occurred during 1999–2000. A 1994 Berlin-Bonn law defined the former capital as a "federal city," and many government and international offices continue to operate there.

Official Language: German.

Monetary Unit: Euro (market rate November 1, 2013: 0.74 euro = $1US).

Federal President: Joachim GAUCK (Independent); elected by the Federal Convention on March 18, 2012, and sworn in on March 23 for a five-year term, succeeding Christian WULFF (Christian Democratic Union), who resigned on February 17, 2012.

Federal Chancellor: (*See headnote.*) Angela MERKEL (Christian Democratic Union); elected by the Federal Assembly and sworn in on November 22, 2005, to succeed Gerhard SCHRÖDER (Social Democratic Party) following legislative elections of September 18; reelected by the Federal Assembly following Federal Assembly elections on September 27, 2009, and again on September 22, 2013.

THE COUNTRY

Germany's commanding position in Central Europe and large population have made it a significant factor in modern European and world affairs, despite the political fragmentation that has characterized much of its history. Flat and low-lying in the north and increasingly mountainous to the south, the country combines abundant agricultural land with rich deposits of coal and other minerals and a strategic position astride the main European river systems. A small group of Danish speakers is located in the northwest, and a group who speak Sorbian, a language related to Polish, inhabits the southeast of the former German Democratic Republic (GDR, or East Germany); otherwise, the indigenous population is remarkably homogeneous. On the other hand, large numbers of Turkish and other foreign workers who entered the Federal Republic of Germany (FRG, or West Germany) after World War II have more recently been joined by a flood of asylum seekers and other immigrants. (Germany's once substantial Jewish population was virtually destroyed during the Nazi period in 1933–1945 and presently numbers only about 100,000, mostly immigrants from the former Soviet Union.) Protestantism, chiefly Evangelical Lutheranism, is the declared religion of about 38 percent of the population, with Roman Catholics numbering about 34 percent. Women made up 47 percent of the labor force in 2009 but remained greatly underrepresented in federal and state governmental and legislative bodies.

Although highly industrialized prior to World War II, the German economy exhibited major regional variations that, coupled with quite dissimilar postwar military occupation policies in the east and the west, yielded divergent patterns of reconstruction and development. West Germany, with a greater resource base than East Germany, substantial financial assistance from the Western allies, and a strong commitment to a market economy, recovered rapidly. Its industry expanded greatly, and by the 1960s the country had become the strongest economic power in Western Europe. Communist East Germany recovered more slowly, but by 1990 it placed among the top dozen nations in industrial output and second only to the Union of Soviet Socialist Republics (USSR) in Eastern Europe.

Political reunification on October 3, 1990, was preceded by the entry into force on July 1 of a State Treaty establishing an economic, monetary, and social union of the two Germanies. The principal objectives of the treaty were transition from a socialist to a market economy in the east, replacement of the East German currency by the West German deutsche mark, and economic integration. Particular attention was given to largely obsolete capital stock, severe environmental pollution, and uncertainties about property rights in the former Communist territory.

The economic problems surrounding reunification proved to be much greater than anticipated. GDP fell by 2 percent in 1993, the most severe decline since 1945. Growth of more than 2 percent in the following years did not halt the rise in unemployment, which was particularly severe in the east, where even in 2005 more than 20 percent of workers were jobless. Germany's economy expanded modestly through the early and middle of the century's first decade. (For details, see the 2010 *Handbook*.) However in mid-2008 the economy began to contract as a result of the global economic recession. The economy felt the effects of the global downturn in 2009, as demand for exports slowed and unemployment neared 9 percent. Annual GDP declined by 5.1 percent in 2009 but rebounded in 2010 (3.6 percent) and 2011 (3.1 percent) and 0.9 percent in 2012. The government reported a budget surplus of €8.3 billion for the first half of 2012. Unemployment stood at 7.7 percent in 2009 and dropped steadily thereafter, reaching 5.5 percent in 2012, a 20-year low.

GOVERNMENT AND POLITICS

Political background. Germany's history as a modern nation dates from the Franco-Prussian War of 1870–1871 and the proclamation in 1871 of the German Empire, the result of efforts by Otto von BISMARCK and others to convert a loose confederation of German-speaking territories into a single political entity led by the Prussian House of Hohenzollern. Defeated by a coalition of powers in World War I, the German Empire disintegrated and was replaced in 1919 by a democracy known to history as the Weimar Republic, whose chronic economic and political instability paved the way for the rise of the National Socialist (Nazi) Party and the installation of Adolf HITLER as chancellor in 1933. Under a totalitarian ideology that stressed nationalism, anti-Communism, anti-Semitism, and elimination of the disabled, Hitler converted the Weimar Republic into an authoritarian one-party state—the so-called Third Reich (empire). His policy of aggressive expansionism led to the outbreak of World War II in 1939 and, ultimately, to the defeat of the Nazi regime by the Allies in 1945.

Following Germany's unconditional surrender on May 8, 1945, the country was divided into zones of military occupation assigned to forces of the United States, Britain, France, and the Soviet Union, whose governments assumed all powers of administration pending the reestablishment of a German governmental authority. Berlin, likewise divided into sectors, was made a separate area under quadripartite control with a view to its becoming the seat of the eventual central German government. Elsewhere, the territories east of the Oder and Neisse rivers were placed under Polish administration; East Prussia was divided into Soviet and Polish spheres; and the Saar was attached economically to France.

At the Potsdam Conference in July–August 1945, the American, British, and Soviet leaders agreed to treat Germany as a single economic unit and to ensure parallel political development in the four occupation zones, but the emergence of sharp differences between the Soviet Union and its wartime allies soon interfered. Among other things, Soviet occupation policies prevented implementation of the plan for a single economic unit, forcing the Western powers to adopt joint measures for their zones only. Protesting a proposed currency reform by its Western counterparts, the Soviet Union in June 1948 instituted a blockade of the land and water routes to Berlin that was maintained until May 1949, prompting Britain and the United States, with French ground support, to resort to a large-scale airlift to supply the city's western sectors.

Having failed to agree with the Soviet Union on measures for the whole of Germany, the three Western powers resolved to merge their zones of occupation as a step toward establishing a democratic state in western Germany. A draft constitution for the West German federal state was approved by a specially elected parliamentary assembly on May 8, 1949, and the Federal Republic of Germany (FRG), with its capital in Bonn, was proclaimed on May 23. The Soviet Union protested these actions and on October 7 announced the establishment in its occupation zone of the German Democratic Republic (GDR), with East Berlin as its capital. An anti-Communist workers' uprising in East Germany in 1953 was ruthlessly suppressed by GDR and Soviet forces.

In West Germany the occupation structure was gradually converted into a contractual relationship based on the equality of the parties involved. Under the London and Paris agreements of 1954, the FRG gained sovereignty on May 5, 1955, when it was admitted to the North Atlantic Treaty Organization (NATO) and the Western European Union (WEU), while on January 1, 1957, the Saar was returned as the result of a plebiscite held in 1955. The Soviet-backed GDR had meanwhile also been declared fully sovereign and was accorded formal recognition by Communist, but not Western, governments. Although Berlin remained technically under four-power control, East Berlin was incorporated into the GDR as its capital, while West Berlin, without being granted parliamentary voting rights, was accorded a status similar to that of a *Länd* (state) of the FRG. The FRG-GDR border served as the focal point for much of the Cold War confrontation in the 1950s and 1960s, with intermittent crises triggered by Soviet or East German interruptions or threats of interruption of land access to West Berlin. This tension, accompanied by accelerating immigration from the East to the West via the open borders inside Berlin, induced the eastern authorities in August 1961 to build the Berlin Wall, closing off East from West Berlin.

During the eight years following proclamation of the FRG in 1949, the Christian Democratic Union—CDU (*Christlich Demokratische Union Deutschlands*) under Chancellor Konrad ADENAUER maintained coalition governments with the Free Democratic Party (*Freie Demokratische Partei*—FDP) and other minor groups, thereby excluding the Social Democratic Party (*Sozialdemokratische Partei Deutschlands*—SPD) from power. In 1957 the CDU and its Bavarian affiliate, the Christian Social Union (*Christlich-Soziale Union*—CSU), won a clear majority of legislative seats, but in 1961 and again in 1965 they were forced to renew their pact with the FDP. In 1966 disagreements over financial policy led the FDP to withdraw from the coalition, and Ludwig ERHARD, who had succeeded Adenauer as chancellor three years earlier, was obliged to resign. On December 1 a CDU-CSU/SPD "grand coalition" government was inaugurated, with Kurt-Georg KIESINGER of the CDU as chancellor.

As a result of the election of September 1969, Willy BRANDT, SPD leader as well as vice chancellor and foreign minister of the CDU-CSU/SPD government, became chancellor at the head of an SPD/FDP coalition. Although the coalition was renewed after the November 1972 balloting, widespread labor unrest early in 1974 attested to the increasing inability of the Brandt administration to cope with domestic economic difficulties, including a record postwar inflation rate of more than 7.5 percent; however, it was the revelation that one of the chancellor's personal political aides was an East German espionage agent that prompted Brandt's resignation on May 6 and his replacement shortly thereafter by former finance minister Helmut SCHMIDT. Former FDP foreign minister Walter SCHEEL, who had served briefly as interim chancellor following Brandt's resignation, was elected federal president on May 15 and was sworn in on July 1, succeeding the SPD's Gustav HEINEMANN.

In a close election on October 3, 1976, the SPD/FDP coalition emerged with a substantially reduced majority of 253 out of 496 seats in the *Bundestag* (Federal Assembly), and on December 15 Schmidt was reconfirmed as chancellor. However, growing Christian Democratic strength at the state level gave the CDU-CSU an overall majority in the Federal Convention, which is responsible for electing the president; as a result, *Bundestag* president Karl CARSTENS, the CDU candidate, was elected on May 23, 1979, to succeed President Scheel, who had decided not to seek a second term after being denied all-party support.

Chancellor Schmidt remained in office following the *Bundestag* election of October 5, 1980, in which the SPD gained 4 seats and the FDP gained 14. The CDU-CSU, led in the campaign by Franz-Josef STRAUSS, minister-president of Bavaria and CSU chair, lost 17 seats.

An extensive reorganization of the Schmidt cabinet in April 1982 pointed up increasing disagreement within the SPD/FDP coalition on matters of defense and economic policy. On September 17 all four FDP ministers resigned, precipitating a "constructive vote of no confidence." This procedure, a vote on a specific replacement for the chancellor, resulted on October 1 in the appointment of Dr. Helmut KOHL as head of a CDU-CSU/FDP government. Subsequently, in mid-December, Kohl called for a regular confidence vote that was deliberately lost by CDU abstentions, thus permitting the chancellor to call an early election. In the balloting on March 6, 1983, the three-party coalition won 278 of 498 lower house seats, allowing Kohl to form a new government on March 29.

The governing coalition's mandate was renewed in balloting on January 25, 1987, although the CDU-CSU share of the vote (44.3 percent) was the lowest since the founding of the West German state in 1949. The SPD did marginally better than opinion polls had predicted, drawing 37 percent, compared with 38.2 percent in 1983. Gaining strength at the expense of the major parties were the FDP, which was awarded an additional ministry (for a total of four) in the government formed on March 11, and the Greens, whose parliamentary representation increased from 27 to 42.

In October 1989, in response to political upheavals elsewhere in Eastern Europe, anti-regime demonstrations took place in East Berlin and other major cities. In an attempt to quell the growing unrest, East German authorities abolished the restrictions on foreign travel for GDR citizens on November 9 and immediately began dismantling sections of the infamous Berlin Wall that had long divided the city. Subsequently, as the Communist regime faced imminent collapse (for details, see the 1990 *Handbook*), appeals for reunification resurfaced. On February 6, 1990, Kohl announced his readiness "to open immediate negotiations on economic and monetary union." A positive GDR response resulted in agreement on a common monetary system by the German finance ministers in mid-May, effective July 1. On the same day, all border restrictions between East Germany and West Germany were eliminated.

The crucial succeeding stages toward reunification were (1) Chancellor Kohl's agreement with Soviet leader Mikhail Gorbachev on July 15–16, 1990, that a unified Germany could be a member of NATO; (2) agreement at the "two-plus-four" (the two Germanies plus the four wartime Allies) forum in Paris on July 17 that international legality should be bestowed on a unified Germany by a "treaty of settlement" rather than a peace treaty; (3) the East German parliament's resolution on August 23 that the five newly restored eastern *Bundesländer* (or *Länder,* federal states)—Brandenburg, Mecklenburg–West Pomerania, Saxony, Saxony-Anhalt, and Thuringia—should accede to the Federal Republic; (4) the signing in Berlin on August 31 of a formal unification treaty between East Germany and West Germany; and (5) the signing in Moscow on September 12 by the two-plus-four states of the Treaty on the Final Settlement with Respect to Germany, formally terminating the wartime victors' responsibilities for Germany and Berlin.

On October 1, 1990, the four World War II Allies formally suspended their occupation rights, and in a jubilant midnight ceremony in Berlin on October 2–3 the two Germanies were united. On October 4, 144 members of East Germany's disbanded legislature (*Volkskammer*) joined West German legislators in the inaugural session of an expanded *Bundestag* at Berlin's *Reichstag* building, while 4 ministers from the former GDR, including its only non-Communist minister-president, Lothar DE MAIZIÈRE, entered the Kohl government as ministers without portfolio. At elections held October 14 in the re-created eastern *Länder,* the CDU won control in all but one parliament (Brandenburg, where it ran second to the SPD).

On December 2, 1990, at the first free all-German election in 58 years, Kohl's CDU-CSU/FDP coalition captured 398 of 662 *Bundestag* seats with 54.8 percent share of the vote, while the opposition SPD secured 239 seats on a vote share of 33.5 percent. On January 17, 1991, Kohl was formally reinvested as chancellor to head a new government containing 11 CDU, 4 CSU, and 5 FDP ministers.

The unexpected pace of German unification strongly influenced the policy agenda of the now-enlarged Federal Republic, particularly in regard to its ongoing commitments to the West and the European Community (EC, subsequently the European Union [EU]). Among other acute problems, the government faced a need for near-total economic renewal in the east, a wave of immigration coupled with mounting anti-foreigner feeling, and a variety of political and legal entanglements involving secret police activities in the former GDR and human rights violations committed by the East German government.

Because of the involvement of West German expertise and capital, the process of converting the centrally planned East Germany to a "social market economy" moved forward more quickly and with less short-term difficulty than in neighboring ex-Communist countries. Most leaders conceded, however, that the challenges far exceeded pre-unification expectations. The conversion process was spearheaded by the Trust Agency (*Treuhandanstalt*), responsible for privatizing nearly 8,000 state-owned firms and large agricultural enterprises. After a slow start, the number of sales reached 500 per month by early 1992, although returns were substantially less than anticipated, in part because of the obsolescence of most East German industry, chronic environmental pollution, and the legal uncertainty of deeds subject to claim from pre-Communist owners.

Economic problems resulting from unification heightened popular disquiet over immigration, as reflected in substantial electoral gains for the extreme right in successive state and local elections in 1991–1992 and in widening antiforeigner violence. The government responded by banning a number of extremist groups, while also securing an amendment to the law on asylum (in May 1993) that allowed authorities to refuse entry to so-called economic migrants. However, the government in mid-June indicated that it would ease restrictions on the attainment of citizenship by aliens, while maintaining the "blood principle" of 1913 that conferred the right to nationality on those of ethnic German ancestry irrespective of place of birth or current location. In January 1999 reform of the citizen law granted automatic citizenship to German-born children of long-term residents and allowed immigrants to seek naturalization following eight years of residence.

Alarmed by the spiraling costs of unification, the Kohl government on January 19, 1993, led a drive for a "solidarity pact" designed to finance the estimated $60 billion annual cost of the subsidies required by the eastern region through increased taxation and expenditure cuts. While initially rejected by the SPD for being socially unjust, federal/state negotiations resulted in formal signature of the pact on March 13.

The coalition's standing, already damaged by economic recession, was further impaired in 1993 by a series of ministerial resignations for alleged misconduct. In addition, Kohl's credibility suffered when his controversial nominee for the federal presidency was forced to withdraw because of media reaction to his intensely right-wing views. Subsequently, another CDU nominee, Constitutional Court president Roman HERZOG, was elected to the presidency on May 23, 1994, by a slim 53 percent majority of Federal Convention votes.

State and local balloting in the early months of 1994 yielded no clear pattern of voter sympathies, much attention thereby being focused on the all-Germany European Parliament poll on June 12. The results showed that the CDU-CSU had overcome a Europe-wide swing against incumbent parties by increasing its seat total from 32 to 47 in a German contingent that increased from 81 to 99. The European results proved to be a portent, in that the Kohl coalition retained a narrow majority in the federal elections held on October 16. The crucial outcome was the FDP's unexpected surmounting of the 5 percent barrier, its 6.9 percent giving it 47 seats, enough to provide a 10-seat majority for another CDU-CSU/FDP coalition.

The new *Bundestag* duly reelected Kohl as chancellor on November 15, 1994, by 338 votes to 333. Two days later the fifth Kohl government, again a coalition of the CDU-CSU and the FDP, was sworn in, with much the same personnel as its predecessor but with the FDP contingent reduced from five to three ministers.

The Kohl forces suffered a string of defeats in the 1998 state elections, which included a surprising 13 percent showing in Saxony-Anhalt by the German People's Union (*Deutsche Volksunion*—DVU), which became the first extreme-right party to win seats in an eastern state legislature. The state elections foreshadowed the results of the September 27 *Bundestag* contest in which the SPD, running its reelected minister-president of Lower Saxony, Gerhard SCHRÖDER, defeated Kohl's CDU-CSU, 40.9 percent to 35.1 percent. Kohl thus became the first incumbent chancellor to be turned out in postwar Germany, and Schröder became the first Social Democratic chancellor in 18 years. Schröder took office on October 27 as the leader of a center-left ("red-green") coalition government with the environmentally oriented Greens (*Die Grünen*), who had won 47 seats with a 6.7 percent vote share.

On May 23, 1999, the SPD's Johannes RAU, former minister- president of North Rhine–Westphalia, was elected federal president in a second round of balloting by the Federal Convention. Sworn in on July 1, Rau became the first president from the SPD since 1974.

Facing polls that showed severe erosion in support for the administration in advance of the September 23, 2002, balloting for the *Bundestag,* Chancellor Schröder launched a highly vocal campaign against U.S. policy toward Iraq that appeared to resonate with the electorate. Consequently, the SPD and Alliance "90/The Greens combined for 206 seats, enough for the two parties to maintain their governing coalition. Later in the year, Schröder announced that priorities for his second term would include a number of potentially unpopular fiscal reforms, including cuts in social spending. These cuts appeared to contribute to a series of disappointing SPD performances in state elections. By early 2004 public opinion had again turned against the SPD, and Horst KÖHLER of the CDU was elected president of the republic in the first round of balloting in the Federal Convention.

With the SPD's popularity continuing to decline, Chancellor Schröder deliberately lost a no-confidence vote on July 1, 2005, and asked for early elections. President Köhler dissolved the *Bundestag* on July 21. In new balloting on September 18, the SPD led all parties with 222 seats, although the governing SPD/Greens coalition failed to secure a majority. Meanwhile, the CDU-CSU combined for 225 seats, although the conservatives too were unable to put together a working legislative majority with their longtime ally, the FDP. (Both the CDU and the SPD rejected forming a coalition with the Left, a new alliance that had won 54 seats [see Political Parties, below].) Consequently, after six weeks of intense negotiation it became clear that a CDU-CSU/SPD "grand coalition" represented the only hope for even short-term stability. Angela MERKEL of the CDU was sworn in on November 22 as chancellor and head of a government that included eight ministers from the SPD, six (including Merkel) from the CDU, and two from the CSU. Merkel was the first woman and the first former citizen of East Germany to become chancellor, and, at 51, the youngest person to hold that position since the end of World War II. The *Bundestag* elected Merkel on the first ballot with 397 votes, well above the simple majority required but below the combined 448 seats of the new coalition. Observers said many SPD deputies did not support Merkel because they regarded the coalition's program as too politically conservative.

In late October 2008, the government approved a series of measures to bolster the financial system. Some German banks had been heavily invested in the U.S. housing market and were suffering from its collapse. All personal bank deposits were guaranteed by the government, and $862 billion was approved to shore up banks, resulting in several of them becoming partially owned by the state. The SPD successfully lobbied for a measure aimed at banks that had received a government bailout, requiring them to impose a salary cap of $650,000. In November another two-year fiscal stimulus package of $22 billion was approved in an effort to further mitigate the effects of the recession. All of the measures prompted intense debate between the moderate and conservative wings of the CDU-CSU.

After heavy lobbying by France and the United Kingdom, which believed that the stimulus package fell short of what was needed, Merkel agreed to an additional $86 billion in January 2009. Another $175 billion was approved for the creation of a "Germany fund" to provide companies an alternative to banks for loans and credit guarantees. For more information on Merkel's first chancellorship, see the 2010 *Handbook*.

While domestic concerns were focused primarily on the economic downturn, the popular president, Horst Köhler, was reelected in May 2009 by a single vote, or 614 total, in first-round Federal Assembly balloting, thereby sparing the CDU a serious political blow ahead of September parliamentary elections. In a setback for the SPD, the party's vote share plunged to a record low 20.8 percent in the June European parliamentary election behind the CDU, with 30.7 percent. Trailing the SPD, the Alliance '90/The Greens took 12 percent, while the FDP, the Left, and the CSU also won seats.

Federal Assembly elections were held on September 27, 2009, giving the following seat distribution: Christian Democratic Union/ Christian Social Union (CDU/CSU), 239; Social Democratic Party, 146; Free Democratic Party (FDP), 93; the Left, 76; and Alliance '90/ The Greens, 68. Merkel, now with a clear plurality in alliance with the center-right Free Democrats (FDP) instead of the SPD, was reelected as chancellor by the Federal Assembly on October 28, 2009.

On May 31, 2010, President Köhler resigned—an unprecedented event for a German president—after being heavily criticized for commenting in a radio interview that German troops were in Afghanistan to defend Germany's economic interests, a view contrasting with the official position (that the role of German troops was completely humanitarian). German presidents are not supposed to express controversial opinions in public. On June 30 the Federal Convention replaced Köhler with Christian WULFF (CDU), the minister-president of Lower Saxony.

Constitution and government. Germany, under the Basic Law (*Grundgesetz*) of May 23, 1949, is a federal republic in which areas of authority are both shared and divided between the component states (*Länder*) and the federal government (*Bundesregierung*). Responsibility in such areas as economic, social, and health policy is held jointly, with the federal government establishing general guidelines, the states assuming administration, and both typically providing funds. Each state (*Land*) has its own parliament elected by universal suffrage, with authority to legislate in all matters—including education, police, and broadcasting—not expressly reserved to the federal government. The latter is responsible for foreign affairs, defense, and such matters as citizenship, migration, customs, posts, and telecommunications.

The major federal components are the head of state, or federal president (*Bundespräsident*); a cabinet headed by a chancellor (*Bundeskanzler*); and a bicameral parliament consisting of the Federal Council (*Bundesrat*) and the Federal Assembly (*Bundestag*). *Bundesrat* members are appointed and recalled by the state governments. Thus a change in government at the state level will likely cause a change in the political composition of the *Bundesrat*. The role of the *Bundesrat* is limited to those areas of policy that fall under joint federal-state responsibility, although it has veto powers where specified *Land* interests are involved. The *Bundestag*, elected by universal suffrage under a mixed direct and proportional-representation system, is the major legislative organ. It elects the chancellor by an absolute majority but cannot remove the chancellor except by electing a successor. A political party must achieve at least 5 percent of the popular vote in order to win any seats in the *Bundestag*. The president, whose functions are mainly ceremonial, is elected by a special Federal Convention (*Bundesversammlung*) consisting of the members of the *Bundestag* and an equal number of members chosen by the state legislatures. Ministers are appointed by the president on the advice of the chancellor.

The judiciary is headed by the Constitutional Court (*Bundesverfassungsgericht*), with the two houses of parliament each electing half its judges. It also includes a Supreme Federal Court (*Bundesgerichtshof*) as well as federal administrative, financial, labor, and social courts. While the constitution guarantees the maintenance of human rights and civil liberties, certain limitations in time of emergency were detailed in a controversial set of amendments adopted in 1968. In addition, the Constitutional Court is authorized to outlaw political parties whose aims or activities are found to endanger "the basic libertarian democratic order" or its institutional structure. The court gains its information from the Federal Office for the Protection of the Constitution (*Bundesamt für Verfassungsschutz/BfV*), a part of the Ministry of the Interior. This office performs surveillance, both covert and open, on groups, including political parties, that it suspects of being a danger to German democracy.

The Federal Republic of Germany currently encompasses 16 *Länder*, 10 from the former West Germany and 6 (†; identified in the following table) from the former East Germany. (The government proposed reducing the number of states to 8 in the mid-1990s, but that plan ran into difficulty at its first electoral test in May 1996 when Brandenburg voted against merger with Berlin.)

State and Capital	*Area (sq. mi.)*	*Population (2012E)*
Baden-Württemberg (Stuttgart)	13803	10,569,111
Bavaria (Munich)	27238	12,519,571
Berlin (Berlin)†	341	3,375,222
Brandenburg (Potsdam)†	15044	2,449,511
Bremen (Bremen)	156	654,774
Hamburg (Hamburg)	291	1,734,272
Hesse (Wiesbaden)	8151	6,016,481
Lower Saxony (Hannover)	18311	7,778,995
Mecklenburg–West Pomerania (Schwerin)†	6080	1,600,327
North Rhine–Westphalia (Düsseldorf)	13149	17,554,329
Rhineland-Palatinate (Mainz)	7658	3,990,278
Saarland (Saarbrücken)	992	994,287
Saxony (Dresden)†	6839	4,050,204
Saxony-Anhalt (Magdeburg)†	7837	2,259,393
Schleswig-Holstein (Kiel)	6053	2,800,119
Thuringia (Erfurt)†	5872	2,170,460

† = formerly part of East Germany.

A 32-member commission was appointed in 2003 to propose revision of the constitution to redistribute certain authority from the states to the federal level in order to provide greater efficiency in, among other areas, implementing economic policy and providing social services. Part of the proposal was that the *Bundesrat* (controlled by the states) would accept reduced veto authority over federal legislation. Negotiations in the commission collapsed in December 2004 over the question of reducing regional control of education. However, general agreement was reached in early 2006 on legislation regarding "federalism reform," prompted in part by the recent installation of a "grand coalition" government. Under the accord, the number of laws subject to veto by the *Bundesrat* would be reduced from 60 percent of the total to approximately 35 percent. In return for the dilution of power at the national level, the states were to be given greater authority over education, the penal system, and the civil service. The constitutional amendments were approved by the parliament during June–July, and a schedule for their gradual implementation was established. Significantly, however, the amendments did not address the contentious issues of revising the formula for distribution of tax revenues between the states and the national government or the proposed merger of small states to make them more "competitive" with the larger states.

The drive to reform federalism was successful in modifying Germany's antiterrorism laws, giving federal law enforcement "preventative power" in averting terrorism, and in handing the federal government sole authority to enact environmental law. Freedom of speech and press is constitutionally guaranteed except to anyone who misuses it in order to destroy the democratic system, such as advocating Nazi views, fomenting racial hatred, and denying the Holocaust. Political parties likewise can be (and sometimes are) banned as anti-democratic. In Reporters Without Borders ranked Germany 17th out of 179 countries in freedom of the press in its 2013 Index of Press Freedom.

Foreign relations. The post–World War II division of Germany and the anti-Soviet and anti-Communist outlook of most West Germans resulted in very close relations between the Federal Republic and the Western Allies, whose support was long deemed essential both to the survival of the FRG and to the eventual reunification of Germany on a democratic basis. The FRG became a key member of NATO, the EC, and the WEU as well as of the Organization for Economic Cooperation and Development (OECD), the Council of Europe, and other multilateral bodies aimed at closer political and economic cooperation. Participation by the GDR in multilateral organizations was for more than two decades limited primarily to the Soviet-backed Council for Mutual Economic Assistance and the Warsaw Treaty Organization.

In August 1970 FRG chancellor Willy Brandt signed a nonaggression treaty with the Soviet Union. The following December he concluded a treaty with Poland by which the Federal Republic gave de facto recognition to Polish acquisition of nearly one-quarter of Germany's pre–World War II territory.

The "two Germanies" concept acquired legal standing with the negotiation in November 1972 of the Basic Treaty (*Grundvertrag*) normalizing relations between the FRG and the GDR. While the agreement stopped short of a mutual extension of full diplomatic recognition, it affirmed the "inviolability" of the existing border and provided for the exchange of "permanent representative missions" by the two governments, thus seeming to rule out the possibility of German reunification. On September 5, 1974, following ratification of the Basic Treaty, both Germanies were admitted to the United Nations.

A treaty voiding the 1938 Munich Agreement on dismembering Czechoslovakia was negotiated with that country in June 1973 and ratified a year later. The initiation of this program of postwar "reconciliation" earned a Nobel Peace Prize for Brandt in 1971. (The territorial implications of the treaty were reaffirmed by the Final Act of the 1975 Helsinki Conference on Security and Cooperation in Europe [CSCE] and by a treaty between Poland and newly unified Germany on November 14, 1990.)

The Treaty on the Final Settlement with Respect to Germany (see Political background, above) was, in actuality, a long-delayed World War II peace treaty, under which the wartime Allies terminated "their rights and responsibilities relating to Berlin and to Germany as a whole," with corresponding "quadripartite agreements, decisions, and practices" and "all related Four Power institutions" being dissolved. For their part, the German signatories agreed to assert no territorial claims against other states; to forswear aggressive war; to renounce the manufacture or possession of nuclear, biological, and chemical weapons; to station only non-NATO forces in the east until completion of Soviet troop withdrawals by the end of 1994; and to reduce their overall armed forces from 577,000 (including East German units) to 370,000 by 1995. West Germany for its part on September 13 signed a Treaty on Good-Neighborliness, Partnership, and Cooperation with the USSR, a treaty later accepted by Russia and the other Soviet successor states.

Because of the constitutional ban on deployment of German forces outside the NATO area, Germany did not participate in the 1991 Gulf war, although it sent air force units to Turkey (a NATO member) and made a substantial financial contribution to the U.S.-led effort. In November 1991 Bonn issued a ban on arms shipments to Turkey in the wake of charges that German weapons had been used against minority Kurds.

Predictions before unification that the newly enlarged Germany would play a larger role in world affairs materialized in the early 1990s. Thus, Germany led the world in direct monetary assistance to the Russian Federation. More controversially, Germany used its new diplomatic leverage to insist on speedy EC recognition of the secessionist Yugoslav republics of Slovenia and Croatia (and later Bosnia and Herzegovina), overriding the more cautious approach of Britain and France. When the former Yugoslavia descended into bloody ethnic conflict in 1992, the government authorized a German warship and three reconnaissance aircraft to join a sanctions-monitoring UN/WEU force in the Adriatic, although the German opposition claimed that the deployment was illegal.

Seeking to ground German unification in an EC framework, the Kohl government was firmly committed to the EC's Maastricht Treaty on political and economic union. Ratification of the treaty was completed by the *Bundestag* in December 1992, subject to a Constitutional Court ruling that any future steps toward European Union required specific German parliamentary approval. Germany also signed an agreement with France on May 22, 1992, providing for the creation by 1995 of a joint Franco-German army corps, envisaged as the nucleus of a future European military force.

Responding to international criticism of Germany's nonparticipation in the 1991 Gulf war, the government in January 1993 introduced draft constitutional amendments that would enable German troops to be deployed in UN-approved peacekeeping and humanitarian operations. The immediate urgency of the issue lay in whether German air force personnel could participate in implementing the Security Council's decision of March 31, 1993, to enforce a "no-fly" zone over Bosnia and Herzegovina. On April 21 cabinet approval was given to the dispatch of 1,600 German troops to participate in the UN operation in Somalia. In a definitive ruling on July 12, 1994, the Constitutional Court decreed that German forces could participate in collective defense or security operations outside the NATO area, provided *Bundestag* approval was given in each case.

Russian troops completed their withdrawal from Berlin on August 31, with the last Allied troops leaving the city on September 8. Finally cleared of Russian troops, Germany stepped up its diplomatic initiatives in Eastern Europe, supporting the quest of its immediate eastern neighbors to join the EU.

The Franco-German axis remains strong in the EU; the two countries were the driving force behind economic and monetary union. Chancellor Angela Merkel and French president Nicolas Sarkozy worked closely together on the eurozone crisis until Sarkozy lost his bid for reelection in May 2012. Although his successor, Socialist François Hollande, had campaigned on a very anti-EU platform, he backed Merkel's tough line regarding Greece's request to relax the terms of the country's bailout package. (For more on German-French relations, see entry on France and also earlier *Handbooks*.)

Meanwhile, Germany's relations with the United States were severely compromised by Schröder's strong opposition to Washington's Iraq policies. The United States responded, in part, by announcing that 35,000 of the 75,000 U.S. troops in Germany would be deployed to other countries.

In January 2006 Chancellor Merkel visited Washington and promised a "new chapter" in U.S.-German relations. She also initially endorsed Schröder's concept of a "strategic relationship" with Russia, reportedly concluding that business interests trumped German concerns over the perceived "autocratic drift" in Russia. Following her appointment to the rotating presidency of the EU in January 2007, Merkel earned praise for facilitating the apparent revival of the EU's constitutional reform process and for promoting improved EU-U.S. economic relations.

Germany contributed naval and air forces to the UN peacekeeping force in Lebanon in 2006 after the Israeli-Hezbollah war and increased its troops in the NATO-led mission in Afghanistan by 500 (bringing its total commitment to approximately 3,500 troops) in March 2007. In October the *Bundestag* extended the Afghanistan mission for another 12 months, capped German personnel there at 3,500, and limited the operation to the safer northern areas of the country and to the capital of Kabul, provoking a diplomatic spat with U.S.-led allies over which country would be responsible for the more dangerous operations in Afghanistan. In March 2012 Merkel confirmed that German troops would leave Afghanistan by 2014.

In March 2008 Merkel became the first German chancellor to address the Israeli Knesset, declaring that Germany would be "a loyal partner and friend" to Israel and characterizing Iran's threats against Israel as tantamount to threats against Germany.

Beginning in late 2008, Merkel's relationships with other European leaders were marked by tension, as some viewed her as taking an isolationist approach to the global financial crisis. Dubbed "Madam No" for her refusal to embrace a massive EU stimulus package, Merkel later accepted a spending package and other measures, although many leaders grew frustrated by her slow, deliberate pace (see Current Issues, below).

U.S.-German relations under President Barack Obama have been cordial but not warm. When candidate Obama wanted to deliver a high-profile speech at the Brandenburg Gate in July 2008, Merkel's disapproving reaction to the "odd" request prompted Obama's campaign staff to move to Tiergarten Park instead. After Obama's election, friction between the two administrations arose over his support for a bailout of the U.S. auto industry, which Merkel saw as giving American automakers a competitive advantage. Additionally, a rift occurred in June 2009 over Germany's refusal to accept nine prisoners of the Chinese ethnic Uigher minority from the U.S. detention center at Guantánamo Bay, Cuba, citing a lack of information on whether they were a security risk. Obama awarded Merkel the Presidential Medal of Freedom at a state dinner in June 2011 and has frequently encouraged her to find a solution to the EU's economic woes. However, relations cooled again in 2013, with November revelations that the United States had been spying on Germany, even monitoring Merkel's cellphone conversations.

In August 2011 Germany increased support for Georgia to join NATO eventually, and called for a halt to all military action following Russian attacks against it in what was widely regarded as a violation of Georgia's sovereignty. Russian-German relations cooled when Vladimir Putin was reelected president in 2012. While Merkel had served as a link to outgoing president Dmitry Medvedev, whom she regarded as progressive, she is reportedly put off by Putin's antidemocratic policies.

Germany refused to become involved in the popular uprising against Libyan strongman Muammar Qadhafi in 2011, angering allies by refusing to support the NATO air campaign and abstaining from UN Security Council votes backing the rebels. However, Foreign Minister Westerwelle endorsed the rebels during a visit to Benghazi in June 2011 and Defense Minister Thomas de Maziere raised the possibility of sending German troops to help reconstruction efforts.

Merkel continued to press austerity as the solution to the struggling economies of many EU member states throughout 2012 and 2013. She hosted UK Prime Minister David Cameron and his family at her country residence in January 2013, trying to dissuade London from exiting the union. Meanwhile the once strong German-French partnership frayed under new French President Francois Hollande, whose party referred to Merkel as the "chancellor of austerity."

Current issues. The government began to monitor radical Islamic groups following the revelation that the terrorists who attacked the United States in September 2001 had spent time in Hamburg. The government quickly passed new domestic antiterrorism legislation and began investigations that led to the arrest of a number of Muslims charged with ties to radical Islamic groups abroad. In September 2007 officials claimed to have averted massive bomb attacks on the Frankfurt international airport and the U.S. air base at Ramstein.

Officials have focused in particular on Salafist groups, an ultraconservative form of Islam. The Federal Office for the Protection of the Constitution (*Bundesamt für Verfassungsschutz*—BfV) issued a report in April 2012 estimating that some 38,000 of the 4 million Muslims living in Germany could be "potential extremists." One month later, a group of Salafist youths attacked police during a demonstration in Bonn, and on June 14 Federal Interior Minister Hans-Peter FRIEDRICH banned the Salafist Millatu Ibrahim group.

An April 2011 BfV report called attention to the rising number of crimes committed by left-wing groups. Such attacks rose by an alarming 39 percent in the first three months of 2011, compared to the same period in 2010. The "Hekla Reception Committee—Initiative for More Societal Eruptions" [Hekla is a volcano in Iceland] claimed responsibility for bombing Berlin's Ostkreuz railway station in May 2011, while 18 more bombs were discovered along Berlin's railroad tracks in October 2011. In May 2012 the "Friends of Loukanikos" claimed responsibility for bombing a car belonging to Horst Reichenbach. "As leader of the EU task force on Greece," the group explained in a letter to *Berliner Morgenpost,* Reichenbach "is responsible for holding the Greek authorities to austerity measures, which have extremely worsened the lives of Greek people."

Right-wing neo-Nazi groups are active in the former GDR lands, which still have high regional unemployment rates. The National Democratic Party (NPD) has 5 seats in the parliament of Mecklenburg-Western Pomerania and 8 seats in Saxony, giving it access to public funding. According to Interior Minister Friedrich, the ranks of neo-Nazi and "nationalist anarchists" may be thinning in Germany, but the remaining members are becoming increasingly radicalized and dangerous.

Germans were stunned by the discovery of a domestic right-wing terrorist group on November 4, 2011. Over a period of seven years, members of the neo-Nazi Nationalist Socialist Underground (*Nationalsozialistischer Untergrund*—NSU) carried out two bombings, 14 bank robberies, and the murders of nine immigrant businessmen and one policewoman. Heinz Fromm resigned as head of the BfV in July 2012 following widespread accusations of incompetence.

As Germany dealt with the issue of potential terrorism, the government struggled to balance a person's right to privacy with the information needs of national security, as well as with how to define the rights of minorities, especially the 2.7 million Muslim residents, primarily of Turkish descent. In November 2010 Merkel asserted that a national action plan, with specific targets, was needed to make integration a reality. The "National Action Plan on Integration" debuted in January 2012 and sets targets in 11 different sectors, including education, health care, and sports.

Merkel introduced an austerity package in June 2010 that sought to cut €85 billion from the budget by 2014 in order to keep the national debt below the 0.35 percent of GDP ceiling mandated by parliament and a 3 percent of GDP cap from the EU. Billed as the biggest austerity drive since World War II, Merkel's savings were to come primarily from spending cuts, not tax increases and government spending to stimulate growth. She ignored criticism from EU neighbors accusing Germany of not doing its part to boost consumption. She would later advocate the same approach for EU members deeply in debt.

Merkel and Foreign Minister Karl-Theodorzu GUTTENBERG sought savings from streamlining and modernizing the armed forces. Conscription was scrapped, and the last recruits were drafted in January 2011. After discussing a variety of options, a blueprint was adopted in April 2012. Total forces would be reduced from 240,000 to 185,000, and further savings would come from closing and combining military facilities.

Merkel's domestic austerity policies, taken in combination with her eventual decision to help Greece, cost her much popularity. This was reflected in the May 9, 2010, election in North-Rhine-Westphalia, Germany's largest *Land*, where the CDU suffered a humiliating defeat by the SPD. This defeat caused Merkel to lose her majority in the *Bundesrat*.

Mayors in Western Germany appealed to the *Bundestag* on March 20 to end the "solidarity pact" implemented in 1990 to help the six states that once made up the GDR. While the average income in the eastern states still hovers around 70 percent of the rest of the country, the mayors argued that they could not justify the assistance while cutting services for their own constituents.

The high price tag—and limited results—from 20 years of these transfer payments has left many Germans wary of the EU bailout program, seeing it as a similar transfer from thrifty countries to undisciplined, spendthrift countries.

While Merkel's domestic economic measures have been criticized by opposition political parties, Germans generally regard her tough stance toward EU bailouts favorably. She has consistently preached austerity and fiscal responsibility for EU debt-strapped members. As the combined total of the bailout packages for Greece, Ireland, and Portugal grew, German public opinion has been strongly against any further action to prop up the zone's weaker economies. In late 2011 Merkel rejected a proposal to issue "euro-bonds" backed by all 17 eurozone members. With many of the 17 economies already struggling, she feared Germany would be left to foot the bill alone. Instead, she convinced the other member states to negotiate a new treaty that would enforce budget discipline in order to prevent future debt crises.

Merkel's personal approval rating stood at 76 percent in early August 2012, but the CDU/CSU lost critical seats to the SPD in regional elections in 2011 and 2012. The CDU racked up its worst performance ever in her native Mecklenburg-Western Pomerania in May 2011. Junior coalition party FDP was completely shut out of the local parliament and has encountered similar results in other states.

The CDU lost another key post when President Wulff resigned on February 17, 2012, following accusations that he had improperly received a €500,000 loan from the wife of a business associate in 2008. (He was indicted on 21 counts in April 2013.) On March 18, Joachim Gauck, a pastor who had narrowly lost to Wulff in 2010, won on the first ballot.

The FDP lost all of its seats in the Saarland's parliament in March 2012, but the CDU remained the dominant party by forming a grand coalition with the second-place SPD. The Left won 9 seats, followed by the Pirate Party with 4 and the Greens with 2. A Social Democrat/Green coalition took majority control of the North Rhine-Westphalia parliament in May 2012, where the CDU dropped from 35 percent support in 2010 to 26 percent. The SPD picked up 32 new seats in Germany's largest state in a race framed as a referendum on Merkel's austerity program. The Pirate Party (see below) polled 8 percent—as did the more mainstream FDP—and won 20 seats.

The CDU and FDP lost control of the parliament in Lower Saxony in January 2013, taking 68 seats to the combined 69 of the SPD and Greens. The results also cost the shifted the balance of power in the *Bundesrat* to the opposition parties.

Federal Education and Research Minister Annette Schavan (CDU) resigned in February after it was discovered that she had plagiarized portions of her doctoral dissertation. Bavaria and Hesse filed suit in the Federation Constitution Court on February 5, questioning the legality of the solidarity pact.

Merkel's government announced in March 2013 that it would not try to ban the far-right NDU, fearing a ban too much resembled a Nazi or Communist policy. Jewish, Turkish, and Roma groups denounced the decision, accusing Merkel of failing to protect the rights of minorities. In April police broke up the Aryan Defense Prison Crew, a network of far-right prisoners hoping to contact the NSU.

The number of refugees seeking asylum in Germany nearly doubled in 2013, due to the crisis in Syria and Germany's economy making it an attractive destination. The increase in arrivals soon outpaced available facilities, especially in Berlin. The NDU took advantage of the situation in an election season and began staging protests outside shelters. Anti-NDU protestors soon joined them, and the Alliance '90/Greens highlighted the plight of the asylum-seekers. In August, a *Bundesdag* panel released the findings of an investigation into the NSU. The report noted "major failures" on the part of the security services that simply were not attuned to neo-Nazi groups. Meanwhile the trial of Beate Zschäpe and four other NSU members began in Munich.

The economy remained strong, with a record GDP, high employment levels, and a budget surplus. But like much of Europe, Germany faces a rapidly aging population promised high pensions. A new census released in June showed 1 million fewer residents than expected. The society must decide whether they will welcome immigrants to maintain population levels.

Germans opted for continuity in the federal elections of September 22, 2013. The CDU/CSU won 41.5 percent of the vote, followed by the SPD, with 25.7 percent, and The Left with 10.2 percent. The Greens slipped to fourth place, with 8.4 percent, while the FDP failed to pass the 5 percent threshold and lost parliamentary representation. Merkel secured a third term as chancellor but had difficulty forming a government without the FDP. After discussions with Alliance '90/The Greens, she revisited the idea of a grand coalition with the SPD and indicated a willingness to consider implementing a national minimum wage—a key SPD demand. For the first time, Germany will have MPs of African descent, and 5.7 percent of MPs have family roots outside of Germany.

POLITICAL PARTIES

Following unification in 1990, the established West German parties extended their operations into the former GDR, with considerable success, although the Party of Democratic Socialism (PDS)—successor to the former ruling (Communist) Socialist Unity Party of Germany (SED)—retained significant support. In federal and state elections, meeting the threshold of 5 percent of the vote made it difficult for minor parties to achieve legislative representation. Of the 22 parties that contested the October 1994 *Bundestag* election, only 6 were awarded seats, and 1 of those, the PDS, on an ancillary provision.

Under Germany's federal system, power at the state level provides opposition parties with an important counterbalance to the central government. As of October 1, 2013, state governments are configured as follows.

In Brandenburg the SPD governed with the Left instead of the CDU. In Thuringia sole control by the CDU was replaced by an SPD-CDU coalition. In Saxony the CDU governed with the FDP instead of the SPD, while in Schleswig-Holstein the ruling coalition is made up of the SPD, Alliance '90/The Greens, and the local South Schleswig Voter's Union. In Saarland the CDU, previously governing alone, were forced into alliance with the FDP and the Greens.

The CDU governed in coalition with the FDP in Hesse, Lower Saxony, and Saxony but lost control of Baden-Württemberg to Alliance '90/The Greens and the SPD. In Saarland the CDU/FDP/Green coalition was replaced with a CDU/SPD government. In Hamburg an all-SPD government replaced a CDU/Green coalition, while the CDU and SPD governed in Saxony-Anhalt. The CSU had a majority government in Bavaria. The SPD governed with Alliance '90/The Greens in Rhineland-Palatinate, and it led a coalition with the CDU in Mecklenburg-West Pomerania. The SPD governed with the Greens in Bremen and North-Rhine-Westphalia, with the Left in Brandenburg, and with the CDU in Berlin.

Germany has dozens of other parties in addition to those discussed below, but none has a national following of electoral significance. (See earlier editions of the *Handbook* for information on additional parties.)

Governing Parties:

Christian Democratic Union (*Christlich Demokratische Union Deutschlands*—CDU). Founded in 1945 as a middle-of-the-road grouping with a generally conservative policy and broad political appeal, the CDU espoused united action by Catholics and Protestants to sustain German life on a Christian basis, while guaranteeing private property and freedom of the individual. Dominated from 1949 to 1963 by Chancellor Konrad Adenauer, the CDU and its Bavarian affiliate, the CSU (below), continued as the strongest party alignment within the Federal Republic until 1969, when it was forced into opposition. Following a transfer of support by the FDP from the SPD to the CDU on October 1, 1982, chancellor Helmut Schmidt (SPD) was obliged to step down as in favor of the CDU's Helmut Kohl. After a poor showing in the European Parliament election in June 1989, Kohl regained much of his popularity by waging a vigorous campaign for German unification, which was formally consummated on October 3, 1990.

In late 1997 the CDU nominated Kohl for the September 1998 election, but the aging chancellor could not overcome an early lead by his younger and more telegenic opponent, Gerhard Schröder, who capitalized on high unemployment and a desire for change. The CDU-CSU vote share dropped from 41.4 to 35.1 percent (28.4 percent for the CDU), a loss of 49 seats that toppled the ruling coalition. Kohl even failed to win his home seat, returning to the *Bundestag* only because of his position at the top of the party list. The first postwar chancellor to lose as an incumbent, Kohl subsequently resigned as party chair, and in early November Kohl's handpicked successor, Wolfgang Schäuble, secured the position of CDU chair.

In late 1999 both Kohl and Schäuble subsequently fell victim to a major party financing scandal. Schäuble announced his resignation as party chair and parliamentary leader on February 16, 2000, having acknowledged receiving undeclared contributions from an arms dealer in 1994. On April 10, 2000, a party congress elected Angela Merkel as chair, making her the first woman and the first Easterner to head the CDU.

In February 2001 Kohl agreed to pay a fine of more than $140,000 in connection with the financing scandal, thereby avoiding probable criminal charges but not a parliamentary inquiry. By that time the party had already been fined approximately $23 million, pending appeal. Financial scandals in the party continued that year.

Merkel vied for the party's endorsement as candidate for chancellor in the 2002 national election, but she eventually withdrew from the race when it became clear that support had grown for Edmund Stoiber of the CSU to serve as the joint CDU-CSU candidate. The CDU's Horst Köhler was elected president of the republic on the first ballot in May 2004 as the joint candidate of the CDU, CSU, and FDP. In June 2004 the CDU-CSU alliance continued its electoral recovery by winning the European Parliament elections with 44.5 percent of the vote and 49 of Germany's 99 seats.

In May 2005 Merkel was nominated without opposition as the CDU-CSU candidate in the upcoming early elections. Although the CDU fell from 190 seats in the 2002 *Bundestag* balloting to 179 in the 2005 poll, it managed to secure a small plurality (in conjunction with the CSU) that subsequently propelled Merkel to the chancellorship.

The CDU struggled to maintain its stronghold in a number of *Länder* as voting trended toward the left. Seeking to secure the position as the political mainstream, the party adopted a new program at its December 2007 conference, defining itself as "the people's party of the center," and agreed to relax some of its economic reforms in favor of extending social benefits. Nevertheless, in early 2008 state elections, the CDU lost its plurality in Hesse and Hamburg and lost substantial ground in Lower Saxony. The losses were seen as major setbacks for the conservatives and for Merkel's authority ahead of national elections in 2009.

CDU membership has fallen to 484,397, down from 530,755 in July 2008, making it virtually tied with the SPD. While significant rifts appeared within the CDU concerning the bailout of failing German firms, the party has largely supported Merkel's austerity prescription for EU members.

Merkel was reelected party chair in December 2012 with nearly 98 percent of the votes. She also led the CDU/CSU to victory in the September 2013 federal election, receiving 40.5 percent of the vote and 255 seats.

Leaders: Angela MERKEL (Chancellor and Party Chair), Volker KAUDER (Parliamentary Leader), Norbert LAMMERT (President of the *Bundestag*), Hermann Gröhe (General Secretary).

Christian Social Union (*Christlich-Soziale Union*—CSU). The Bavarian affiliate of the CDU, which by mutual agreement is unopposed by the CDU in Bavaria and does not present candidates elsewhere, espouses policies similar to its federal partner but tends to be more conservative. Party chair Franz-Josef Strauss became minister-president of Bavaria following the state election of October 15, 1978, and was the unsuccessful CDU-CSU candidate for chancellor in the 1980 national election.

The CSU's vote share dropped to 6.7 percent in the September 1998 election, costing the party 3 seats and helping turn out of power the CDU-CSU coalition. Following that electoral setback, in January 1999 Edmund Stoiber, the minister-president of Bavaria, succeeded Theodor WAIGEL as party head. In January 2002 Stoiber, who had won praise for his handling of economic affairs in Bavaria, was selected as the CDU-CSU candidate for chancellor in the 2002 balloting as public leader of the coalition. Stoiber led the CSU to victory in Bavarian state elections in September 21, 2003, with 124 of 180 seats. However, two years later in the 2005 national elections its seat total in the *Bundestag* fell from 58 to 46.

Following several disagreements with the CDU and reported friction with some CSU members, Stoiber resigned as chair of the CSU and minister-president of Bavaria at a CSU congress in September 2007. He was succeeded as minister-president of Bavaria by Günther BECKSTEIN, the hard-line Bavarian interior minister noted for his support for stricter security laws and regulations on noncitizens. Meanwhile, Erwin HUBER, previously Bavaria's economy minister and a Stoiber supporter, was elected CSU chair by a 58 percent vote in the congress against several other rivals. The separation of the two posts formerly held by Stoiber was credited with facilitating a "fairly bloodless leadership succession" within the party. A new party platform adopted in late September emphasized the need for climate protection and the duty of immigrants to integrate into German culture as well as the demand that the *Bundeswehr* be deployed on missions only with "clear guidelines" and limited scope.

By early 2008 the dual leadership structure faced difficulties maintaining the party's historic lead in Bavaria. The CSU suffered heavy losses in the March 2008 election in the two major Bavarian cities of Munich and Nuremberg, a portent of the September state elections, in which the party lost its overall majority, which it had held since 1962, with only 43 percent of the vote. In the Bavarian legislature, the CSU's loss amounted to one-quarter of its seats, while advances were made by Alliance '90/The Greens and the FDP, the latter regaining representation for the first time since 1990 with 8 percent of the vote. The CSU's defeat resulted in a major shake-up in leadership as Huber and Beckstein ceded their posts to deputy chair and agriculture minister Horst Seehofer.

One of Seehofer's most significant early decisions was securing the appointment in early February 2009 of zu Guttenberg to Merkel's cabinet as economics minister. The 37-year-old "Baron from Bavaria" proceeded to strike a hard stance against propping up flailing German firms, a move that resonated with a public deeply angered by corporate abuses that became apparent during the economic recession. Guttenberg's term as defense minister in Merkel's second cabinet came to an end in March 2011, when it emerged that he had plagiarized much of his PhD thesis. He resigned in disgrace, having acquired, among others, the nickname of "Baron Googleberg."

In May 2013 Seehofer confirmed that many state ministers had improperly hired family ministers as "assistants" and ordered them to repay their salaries. Georg SCHMID, chair of the Bavarian parliament, had used his wife as his secretary for 23 years. The CSU won 8.9 percent of the vote and 56 seats in the September 2013 *Bundestag* election.

Leaders: Horst SEEHOFER (Chair and Minister-President of Bavaria, President of the Bundesrat), Hermann GROHE (General Secretary).

Opposition Parties:

Social Democratic Party of Germany (*Sozialdemokratische Partei Deutschlands*—SPD). Founded in the 19th century and reestablished in 1945, the SPD discarded its original Marxist outlook in 1959 and embraced the concept of the "social market." With a powerful base in the larger cities and the more industrialized states, the SPD subsequently stressed a strong central government and social welfare programs and was an early advocate of normalized relations with Eastern Europe. It was the principal opposition party before participating in a coalition with the CDU-CSU from 1966 to 1969. After the election of October 1969 the SPD's Willy Brandt formed a governing coalition with the FDP. Brandt was replaced as chancellor in May 1974 by Helmut Schmidt, following an espionage scandal. The coalition continued until October 1982, when the FDP transferred its support to the CDU, thus forcing the SPD into opposition.

Brandt resigned as SPD chair in March 1987. Parliamentary leader Hans-Jochen VOGEL was designated as his successor, but the party's relatively poor showing at the 1990 election led Vogel to resign on December 4. He was succeeded by the minister-president of Schleswig-Holstein, Björn ENGHOLM.

Damaged by the revival of an old political scandal, Engholm resigned as chair on May 3, 1993, and was succeeded on June 13 by Rudolf SCHARPING (then minister-president of Rhineland-Palatinate), who led the SPD to its fourth successive federal election defeat in October 1994. However, concurrent SPD advances at the state level gave it a majority in the *Bundesrat,* although the party lost ground in North Rhine–Westphalia and Bremen in May 1995 and in October suffered a major defeat in Berlin (once an SPD stronghold).

Scharping was ousted as SPD chair in November 1995 and was replaced by the more left-leaning Oskar LAFONTAINE, the Saarland minister-president (and 1990 SPD candidate for chancellor). Lafontaine advocated cooperation with the Greens and the ex-Communist PDS but expressed doubts about the plan for a single European currency and questioned the automatic granting of citizenship to ethnic Germans from Eastern Europe. The first electoral test of such policies, in three state elections in March 1996, yielded a lower SPD vote in each case.

In March 1998 the party selected Gerhard Schröder, the minister-president of Lower Saxony, to be its 1998 candidate for chancellor on the strength of his reelection victory in the state elections. Claiming to represent the "new center," Schröder led the SPD to a 40.9 percent vote share at the September *Bundestag* election, moving the party from 252 to 298 seats.

Belying reports that he controlled the party, Lafontaine quit his SPD leadership post in March 1999 after Schröder appeared to wrest control of the party's agenda during a struggle over economic policymaking. In April, Schröder formalized his victory, winning the party chair at a special SPD congress.

Although there was growing discontent with the party leadership because of Schröder's reform efforts, the SPD won the 2002 legislative elections, and Schröder formed another coalition government with the Greens. In September 2003 SPD member Johannes Rau announced that he would not seek reelection as president of Germany. The SPD and the Greens choose Gesine SCHWAN, the first female candidate to run for the office. Schwan was defeated by the CDU-CSU/FDP candidate, Horst Köhler, in the May presidential poll. In February 2004 Schröder announced his resignation as party leader, and Franz Müntefering was elected chair at a party congress in March. Schröder's subsequent efforts to move the party to the center, epitomized by Agenda 2010, led a group of dissidents to leave the party and form a new left-wing group (see WASG below). In May 2005 Lafontaine resigned from the SPD to become the PDS/WASG standard-bearer, claiming the SPD was pursuing "antisocialist policies."

The SPD fell from 251 seats in the 2002 *Bundestag* balloting to 222 seats in the 2005 poll (at which it secured 34.3 percent of the party-list votes). An SPD congress in mid-November elected Matthias PLATZECK, the minister-president of Brandenburg, as the new SPD chair to succeed Müntefering. However, Platzeck resigned for health reasons in April 2006 and was succeeded by Kurt BECK, the minister-president of Rhineland-Palatinate. By that time, concern was reportedly being voiced within the SPD over its declining membership, its perceived secondary status in the government coalition, and the increasing popularity of the farther Left. In the fall of 2007 Beck, apparently securing dominance over the centrist Müntefering camp, won the party's endorsement for a leftward shift that would promote the expansion of social programs and government-funded benefits and was dubbed as a return to the party's traditional social democratic roots. However, by moving further left, the SPD signaled a lack of unity with its CDU coalition partner, assuring further difficulty in co-governance, and opened the way for the CDU to take the stage as the political center going into the 2009 national election.

In April 2009 the SPD launched a platform calling for higher taxes for top wage earners, the introduction of a minimum wage, free day care for children, the reintroduction of a stock exchange turnover tax, and a ban on the far-right NPD. However, the platform seemingly had little resonance with the public. In June the SPD garnered 20.8 percent of the vote in the European parliamentary elections, its worst-ever return in a national election. Müntefering resigned as party chair following the SPD's disastrous showing in the September 2009 federal elections, being replaced by Sigmar GABRIEL, previously environment minister in the CDU/SPD coalition.

The SPD recovered in 2013, taking 25.7 percent of the vote and 192 seats in the September 22 parliamentary election.

Leaders: Sigmar GABRIEL (Chair), Frank-Walter STEINMEIER (Parliamentary Floor Leader), Andrea NAHLES (General Secretary), Peer STEINBRUCK (2013 Candidate for Chancellor), Martin SCHULZ (President of the European Parliament).

The Left (*Die Linke*). This electoral alliance was quickly formed by the two left-wing parties PDS and WASG (see below) after Chancellor Gerhard Schröder in May 2005 called for early elections. Showing strength mainly in the ex-Communist eastern states, the alliance secured 54 seats in the September *Bundestag* balloting on a "hard-left" platform with populist undertones. The alliance led to a formal merger, and the new party was formally launched on June 16, 2007, under the leadership of PDS chair Lothar Bisky and Oskar Lafontaine, the former finance minister under Schröder who resigned from the SPD in 1999 in protest of the government's move toward neoliberal policies, subsequently joining the WASG. The Left, its membership bolstered by disaffected SPD members, subsequently rose to 11 percent support in public opinion polls as it called for a lower retirement age, increased unemployment benefits, and expansion of other social programs. State elections in early 2008 demonstrated the further popularity of the party in western states, as it entered state legislatures in Hamburg, Hesse, and Lower Saxony for the first time. In 2008 it claimed the third-largest political party membership in Germany and was particularly strong among the working class.

Once dismissed by the major political parties, the Left has been courted by the SPD as a coalition partner in several states. However, SPD leaders have rejected overtures by the Left to align at the federal level.

In advance of the 2009 federal elections, the Left reported having 76,000 members. The party nominated actor and director Peter Sodann as its 2009 presidential candidate; he received 91 delegate votes, the least of three candidates. Also in May, the party adopted a platform to sharply define itself as the leftmost leaning party, advocating the nationalization of banks, a ban on layoffs at profitable firms, and an end to stock options and hedge funds.

Lafontaine's long-standing critique of inadequate government control over financial markets began to look prescient as German firms buckled under the 2008–2009 economic recession. Lafontaine and Bisky did not stand in the May 2010 party elections, being replaced by Gesine Lötzch and Klaus Ernst. The Left has suffered greatly from internal divisions, with some western members, who have never experienced communism, expressing a nostalgia for the GDR not shared by their eastern comrades. In early 2012 *Der Spiegel* revealed that the federal intelligence agency had 27 of the party's 76 members of the *Bundesrat* under surveillance due to the party's alleged "unconstitutional tendencies."

The party replaced Lötzch and Ernst at its June 2012 congress with two obscure individuals. Bernd Riexiger is a hardliner from western Germany, while Katja Kipping is an easterner. The Left retained its place as the third-largest party in the *Bundestag*, winning 64 seats on a 10.2 percent share in the September 2013 federal elections.

Leaders: Bernd RIEXIGER, Katja KIPPING (Cochairs), Gregor GYSI (Parliamentary Leader).

Alliance '90/The Greens (*Bündnis '90/Die Grünen*). Constituted as a national "antiparty party" during a congress held January 12–14, 1980, in Karlsrühe, *Die Grünen* was an amalgamation of several ecology-oriented groups formed in the late 1970s. Internal divisiveness contributed to a poor showing in the October 1980 federal election, when the party won only 1.5 percent of the vote. At the 1983 balloting, however, it won 27 *Bundestag* seats on the basis of a 5.6 percent vote share, and by late 1987 it had secured representation in 8 of the 11 western state parliaments.

In late 1989 a Green Party (*Grüne Partei*) was launched in East Germany, and joined with the Independent Women's League (*Unabhängige Frauenbund*) in offering a Greens list at the March 1990 *Volkskammer* poll. Not having endorsed unification, the group was unwilling to join forces with its western counterpart for the all-German balloting in December, entering instead into the anti-unification Alliance '90 coalition, which was able to win eight *Bundestag* seats by meeting the minimum 5 percent vote-share requirement in the former GDR, even though its percentage in the whole of Germany was only 1.2. By contrast, the original Greens, with a 3.9 percent share, were unable to secure the necessary 5 percent in the West.

At parallel congresses in Hannover on January 16–17, 1993, the western Greens and Alliance '90 decided to unite under the official name Alliance '90, while styling themselves informally as the "Greens." The merger was formalized during a congress in Leipzig on May 14. At their Mannheim congress in February 1994, the Greens opted in principle for a "red-green" coalition with the SPD after the October federal elections.

The Greens made a further advance in the October 1994 federal balloting, to 7.3 percent and 49 seats. The new parliamentary arithmetic precluded a coalition with the SPD, but the Greens' presence was acknowledged by the election of a party deputy as one of the *Bundestag*'s four vice presidents. A party congress in December 1995 endorsed the Greens' opposition to any external German military role, although 38 percent of the delegates favored participation in UN peacekeeping missions. The Greens subsequently registered gains in state elections, as a result of which "red-green" coalitions governed five states by the end of 1997. At their convention in February 1998, party leaders said their task was to make clear that the Greens' agenda was not limited to environmental policy and that the party was the best hope for comprehensive change.

On the heels of a setback in Hesse state elections, the Greens convened a conference in March 1999 that reportedly focused on "philosophical" issues and ended with a pledge to move the group's platform back toward its "roots."

In early 2001 Vice Chancellor Joschka FISCHER of the Greens came under attack for his role as a far-left activist in the 1970s, which was said to have included participation in violent street demonstrations and association with various members of such militant organizations as the Baader-Meinhof gang, which later became the Red Army Faction. Despite calls from the CDU and other conservative elements for his resignation, Fischer retained the support of Chancellor Schröder, and in January 2002 he was formally designated as leader of the Greens, a new post in the party, which had previously preferred a collective leadership.

The Greens declined slightly from 55 seats in the 2002 *Bundestag* balloting to 51 in the 2005 poll, at which it received 8.1 percent of the party-list vote. Fischer subsequently stepped down as the party leader after the Greens went into opposition. Following two years without representation in any state administration, the Greens joined the SPD in a coalition government in Bremen in June 2007. The party had mixed results in the early 2008 state elections and formed a coalition government with the CDU for the first time in Hamburg, long an SPD stronghold. The unusual alliance signaled the Greens' willingness to compromise for political ends as it backed away from its long-standing opposition to a deepening of the Elbe River in exchange for the cancellation of a new coal-fired power plant in the city.

In November 2008 ethnic Turk Cem Özdemir was elected co-chair of the party, becoming the first member of an ethnic minority to lead a major German political party. He succeeded Reinhard BÜTIKOFER, who had announced in March that he would not seek reelection. Özdemir was previously the first ethnic Turk to be elected to the *Bundestag*, but was forced to resign in 2002 for using "air miles" accumulated from official trips for personal travel. Subsequently, he was elected to the European Parliament in 2004.

In response to the economic recession, the Greens' 2009 federal election platform included the so-called Green New Deal to create 1 million jobs in Germany over the next four years through investment in combating climate change, education, and health care. The Greens had their best performance ever in the European Parliament elections in June, garnering 12 percent of the vote.

By 2012 the Greens held seats in all 16 state legislatures and controlled Baden-Wurttemberg. The party has shifted its ideology to tap into a strain of German conservatism that values protecting nature and communities through slower growth and industrialization. They stumbled in the 2013 *Bundestag* election, finishing fourth with 8.4 percent of the vote and 63 seats. Voters were put off by a proposed 49 percent tax on persons making over €80,000 per year and resurrected allegations that party members promoted pedophilia in the 1980s. The party leadership subsequently resigned en masse. Co-chair Claudia Roth declined to seek another term, while Cem ÖZDEMIR was re-elected at the October party conference.

Leaders: Simone PETER, Cem ÖZDEMIR (Cochairs), Winfried KRETSCHMANN (Minister-President of Baden-Wurttemberg).

Other Parties That Contested Recent Elections:

Free Democratic Party (*Freie Demokratische Partei*—FDP). A moderately rightist party that inherited the tradition of economic liberalism, the FDP stands for free enterprise without state interference but advocates a program of social reform. In the 1980 parliamentary election it won 53 seats (14 more than in 1976), in part because of the defection of Christian Democratic voters dissatisfied with their candidate, Franz-Josef Strauss. The FDP's representation fell to 34 in 1983 but rose to 46 in 1987 and went up to 79 members in 1990, before falling back to 47 in October 1994.

The FDP had formed a governing coalition with the SPD following the elections of 1972, 1976, and 1980 but shifted its support to the CDU in October 1982 after a dispute over the size of the 1983 budget deficit, thereby causing the fall of Helmut Schmidt's government. FDP leader Hans-Dietrich GENSCHER retained his positions as vice chancellor and foreign minister under the successor government of Helmut Kohl, but he resigned on May 18, 1992.

The failure of the party to win representation in a series of state elections from 1992 to 1994 generated much criticism of new leader Klaus KINKEL. He obtained a reprieve when the FDP unexpectedly retained a 47-seat *Bundestag* presence in October 1994 (with a 6.9 percent share of the vote); however, further electoral failures in Bremen and North Rhine–Westphalia in May 1995 obliged Kinkel to vacate the leadership while remaining foreign minister. Named at a special party congress in June, his successor, longtime Hesse leader Wolfgang GERHARDT, distanced himself somewhat from Chancellor Kohl by calling for relaxed citizenship laws, termination of the arms embargo against Bosnian Muslims, and an end to the "solidarity" tax that was financing economic recovery in the former East Germany; with an eye toward the challenge posed by the rise of the Greens, he also called for a greater focus on environmental issues. In January 1996 the FDP staged a relaunch on a more right-wing economic platform, quickly winning representation in three state elections in March and confirming its new orientation at a party congress in Karlsrühe in June.

In the *Bundestag* elections of September 1998 the FDP lost 4 seats, with a vote share of 6.2 percent. In early January 2001 Gerhardt resigned the party chair, with the FDP secretary general, Guido WESTERWELLE, being formally elected as his successor on May 4 at a party congress. In May 2002 Westerwelle was named as the FDP's first solo candidate for chancellor, having announced in January that the FDP would compete independently in the upcoming federal elections, thereby severing the party's alliance with the CDU. In the 2002 election the FDP won 7.4 percent of the vote and 47 seats. The FDP improved to 61 seats (its best performance since 1990) in the 2005 *Bundestag* poll, at which it secured 9.8 percent of the proportional votes.

The party made minor improvements in seats in the early 2008 state elections, and in January 2009 it entered its fifth state government alliance in Hesse. In May Westerwelle was reelected party chair by an overwhelming 96 percent. The party emerged stronger from the European Parliament elections in June 2009 with 11 percent of the vote, up from 6.1 percent in 2004.

In the run-up to the 2009 federal election the FDP campaigned for more tax cuts to jump start the economy and an end to state bailouts of German firms. The party has nearly imploded since 2009, losing all of its seats in Berlin, Bremen, Mecklenburg–West Pomerania, Rhineland-Palatinate, the Saarland, and Saxony-Anhalt. Polling at less than 3 percent nationally in December 2011, down from 14.6 percent in 2009, the current junior coalition partner may not secure the 5 percent minimum to enter parliament in the 2013 election.

The FDP has suffered a leadership crisis that has voters wondering if it would be capable of governing. Longtime leader Guido WESTERWELLE resigned in April 2011 in favor of vice chancellor Philipp Rösler. At 32 years old, the new general secretary, Christian Lindner, was heralded as the next generation of FDP. Instead, he suddenly resigned after just two years, when he botched a party referendum on Merkel's EU rescue program. Voting was to have continued for several days, but Lindner announced the motion had failed due to insufficient turnout—with two days of voting still to go. Following the FPD's loss in Lower Saxony in January 2013, Rösler turned responsibility for the party's campaign for the *Bundestag* in September to Rainier BRUEDERLE, the party's floor leader in the *Bundestag*. The change did not help the party's fortunes. The FPD secured only 4.8 percent of the vote and lost all of its seats.

Leaders: Philipp RÖSLER (Chair), Patrick DÖRING (Secretary General).

Alternative for Germany (*Alternative für Deutschland*—AfD) was a surprisingly strong contender in the September 2013 federal election, taking 4.7 percent of the vote. The Euroskeptic party, registered only in April 2013, calls for German's exit from the Eurozone and the re-establishment of the deutschmark. It does not advocate leaving the EU altogether, but does want to see some responsibilities returned to state control. AfD was established by economics professor Bernd LUCKE and several former members of the CDU. It won a seat in the Hesse regional parliament in elections also held in September 2013.

Leader: Bernd LUCKE.

Pirate Party (*Piratenpartei Deutschland*—PiratenP). The Pirate Party advocates Internet freedom and direct participation in policymaking. The party surged in 2012, winning seats in the parliaments of Berlin, Mecklenburg–West Pomerania, North Rhine–Westphalia, and Saarland. It has branches in all 16 states and claims to have 35,000 members. The Pirates' call for transparency and participatory democracy appears to have resonated with the many Germans who feel their concerns regarding the EU bailouts have been ignored. Some analysts believe the Pirates' emphasis on data privacy and human rights may attract former FDP voters turned off by the latter party's increasing emphasis on tax cuts and other probusiness policies.

By 2013 the Pirate Party appeared to have lost its appeal as a protest party. It secured only 2.2 percent of the vote in the Bundestag elections.

Leader: Bernd Schlöemer (Chair).

Party of Democratic Socialism (*Partei der Demokratischen Sozialismus*—PDS). Pressure exerted by Soviet occupation authorities led in April 1946 to the formation of the Socialist Unity Party of Germany (*Sozialistische Einheitspartei Deutschlands*—SED) by merger of the preexisting Communist and Social Democratic parties. The SED controlled all East German organizations, except the churches, for the more than four decades of Communist rule.

Longtime party leader Erich HONEKER resigned on October 18, 1989, and was replaced as general secretary by Egon KRENZ. On November 11, in the face of rapidly escalating opposition to the dominance of the SED, all of the party's 22 Politburo incumbents, save Krenz, quit and were replaced by a substantially smaller body of 11 members. On December 3 Krenz also resigned. Six days later, during an emergency congress, the party abandoned Marxism and renamed itself the Socialist Unity Party of Germany–Party of Democratic Socialism (SED-PDS) under a new chair, Gregor GYSI. It formally dropped the SED component of the name at an election congress in late February 1990.

In the all-German balloting of December 1990, the PDS, campaigning jointly with a Left List (*Linke List*), won 17 *Bundestag* seats, with almost all of its combined 2.4 percent vote share coming from the former GDR. The party gained further ground in the October federal elections when it won 30 *Bundestag* seats. A PDS congress in January 1995 endorsed a more moderate "left-wing democratic" program. In the September 1998 federal elections, the PDS won more than 5 percent of the vote nationwide for the first time, with most of its support from the east, thereby increasing its representation to 36 seats.

In November the PDS formed its first formal governing coalition since reunification when it joined the SPD in a state government in Mecklenburg–West Pomerania, with the PDS getting three posts in the eight-member cabinet On October 14, 2000, Gabrielle ZIMMER succeeded Lothar Bisky as chair, reflecting an effort by the party's reform wing to move toward the political center. The party subsequently indicated that it would be prepared to enter the federal government in partnership with the SPD after the 2002 election, a possibility that the SPD immediately rejected. Following the election, party disputes continued over Zimmer's leadership. On June 28, 2003, a special party congress again elected Bisky as chair, to succeed Zimmer. In state elections in Brandenburg in September 2004, the PDS had its best electoral success since reunification with 28.3 percent of the vote. The PDS gained seven seats in the 2004 European Parliament elections.

The PDS, which had secured only 2 seats in the 2002 *Bundestag* balloting, was "rejuvenated" by its electoral alliance with the smaller WASG in 2005, gaining a combined 54 seats. The spring 2007 merger between the PDS and WASG into the Left ended the tenure of the PDS as an autonomous party; members of parliament elected as PDS are listed with the Left faction, and the PDS has adopted the newer party's platform.

Electoral Alternative for Labor and Social Justice (*Wahlalternative Arbeit und Soziale Gerechtigkeit*—WASG). Comprising mostly disaffected members of the SPD and trade unionists led by former foreign minister Oskar Lafontaine, the WASG was launched as a formal party in early 2005. The leaders of the new group accused the SPD leadership, particularly Gerhard Schröder, of having moved to the right in the interest of the business sector. The WASG merger with the larger PDS in the spring of 2007 into the Left effectively ended the WASG as an independent political party.

The Republicans (*Die Republikaner*). The Republicans party was launched in November 1983 by two former Bavarian CSU deputies who objected to Franz-Josef Strauss's "one-man" leadership, particularly in regard to East-West relations. The manifestly ultra-rightist group was self-described as a "conservative-liberal people's party" that favored a reunited Germany, environmental protection, and lower business taxes. Although the party claimed a nationwide membership of only 8,500, its West Berlin section obtained 11 legislative seats on the basis of a 7.5 percent vote share in January 1989.

As reunification became a leading German concern, the party's appeal ebbed. It obtained only 2 percent of the vote at state elections in North Rhine–Westphalia and Lower Saxony in early 1990, and in late May its increasingly controversial chair, former Waffen SS officer Franz SCHÖNHUBER, was obliged to resign, although he recovered the post at a party congress in July. The party made a comeback in the Baden-Württemberg state election in April 1992, winning 11 percent of the vote and 15 seats; in May 1993, moreover, it secured *Bundestag* representation by the defection from the CDU of Rudolf KRAUSE. Prior to the October 1994 *Bundestag* election Schönhuber was again deposed as leader, officially because of an unauthorized meeting with the leader of the DVU (below) but also because of his negative media image. In 2006 state protection authorities delisted the Republicans as a right-wing extremist group, although its positions on issues such as immigration, where it stated there is "no place for Islam in Germany," were still considered far right. The Republicans also called for an end to Germany's participation in the EU.

The party received only 1.9 percent of the *Bundestag* proportional vote in 1994, 1.8 percent in 1998, 0.6 percent in 2002, and 0.6 percent in 2005 as it struggled for votes against the more popular NPD and DVU. In the 2009 European Parliament elections, the Republicans fielded Uschi WINKELSETT as a candidate and won 1.3 percent of the vote. In the 2009 its proportional vote in the *Bundestag* was further reduced to 0.4 percent.

Leader: Rolf SCHLIERER (Federal Chair).

National Democratic Party—The People's Union (*Nationaldemokratische Partei Die Volksunion*—NPD). The original NPD was formed in 1964 by a number of right-wing groups and was subsequently accused of neo-Nazi tendencies but avoided providing clear-cut grounds for legal prohibition. Unrepresented in the state parliaments or in the *Bundestag,* its appeal at the federal level slipped to a record low 0.2 percent of the popular vote in 1980 and recovered only marginally thereafter. In April 1995 NPD leader Günter DECKERT received a prison sentence for incitement to racial hatred and other offenses.

On December 8, 2000, the *Bundestag* approved a government effort to ban the NPD as "anti-Semitic, racist, xenophobic, and violence-supporting." The proposal had already been backed by 14 of 16 state interior ministers and by the *Bundesrat,* although some elements of the CDU as well as the FDP opposed a ban as counterproductive. On March 18, 2003, the Constitutional Court, which had banned only two parties in the previous 50 years, rejected a ban on the party because some members of the party who had given evidence were police informers.

The NPD has consistently been part of governing coalitions in two eastern provinces for a decade. In 2004 state elections, the NPD gained 9.4 percent of the vote and 8 seats in Saxony in its greatest electoral showing to date. The party contested the 2005 *Bundestag* elections in alliance with the DVU (below), securing 1.6 percent of the proportional vote. In the 2006 state elections in Mecklenburg–West Pomerania, the NPD secured 7.3 percent of the vote and six seats in the legislature. It also retained its one seat in the May 2007 balloting in Bremen.

In recent years, the NPD has been beset by a series of criminal indictments, funding problems, and renewed political efforts to ban the party. In the wake of a spate of attacks by right-wing youth on individuals of foreign descent in 2007, SPD regional leaders began pushing again for a ban, while several German banks closed accounts belonging to the NPD because they wanted no part in the party's financial dealings.

The party's financial situation worsened when government prosecutors in December 2007 began investigating the group for fraud for allegedly cheating the government out of political matching funds. Police later arrested the NPD treasurer on embezzlement charges.

Another high-profile right-wing attack in December 2008, this time against a police officer in Bavaria, fueled more support for a ban on the NPD. Chancellor Merkel announced that the government was looking for ways to outlaw the party, but would be careful in doing so to avoid a second failure in the courts.

Short of a ban, German officials explored ways to curb the NPD's strength by blocking more than $1 million in public financing. One proposal that gained attention in late 2008 was a constitutional amendment to prevent political parties from receiving state aid if they were deemed to be "agitating against the principles of the constitution." In May 2009 the party was fined $1.7 million for accounting irregularities and ordered to return more than $1 million in public money. Former NPD chair Udo Voigt said the party was suffering an "existential crisis" due to lack of funds.

Voigt and two senior party members were also convicted of inciting racial hatred because of pamphlets they had distributed before the 2006 World Cup that impugned a German football player of Nigerian descent.

Despite these problems, the NPD has become the largest and most prominent far-right political party in Germany, with some 7,000 members. It sought to broaden its appeal among women through ties to new right-wing women's organizations. As of the results of municipal elections in June 2009, the NPD claimed more than 100 seats on regional and city councils. The party's success at the local level has been part of a strategy to make itself appear "mainstream." Nonetheless, Germany's Office for the Protection of the Constitution has described the NPD as racist, revisionist, and inspired by Nazi ideology. In the 2009 federal election the NPD received 1.5 percent of the proportional vote, a slight decline of 0.1 percent from 2005. Interior ministers from all 16 stated tried to ban the party, but the CPU/CSU declined to pursue a ban. Party member Sebastian SCHMIDTKE staged protests outside asylum shelters in Berlin and encouraged other xenophobic responses in the run-up to the 2013 parliamentary elections. The NPD secured only 1.5 percent of the vote, however.

Leaders: Holger APFEL (Chair), Udo PASTORS, Karl RICHTER (Deputy Chairs), Peter MARX (Secretary General).

Other minor parties that participated in the 2013 elections include the **Animal Protection Party** (*Tierschutzpartei*—TP); the **Ecological Democratic Party** (*Ökologisch-Demokratische Partei*—ÖDP); the **Family Party of Germany** (*Famlienpartei Deutschlands*—FPD); **Free Voters** (*Freie Wähler*—FW); and the **Citizens in Rage** (*Bürger in Wut*).

Other Parties:

German Communist Party (*Deutsche Kommunistische Partei*—DKP). West Germany's former Communist Party, led by Max REIMANN, was banned as unconstitutional in 1956; Reimann returned from exile in East Germany in 1969. Meanwhile, plans to establish a new Communist party consistent with the principles of the Basic Law had been announced in September 1968 by a 31-member "federal committee" headed by Kurt BACHMANN. At its inaugural congress in April 1969, the new party claimed 22,000 members, elected Bachmann as chair, and announced its intention to seek a common front with the SPD in the 1969 *Bundestag* election (an offer that was promptly rejected by the SPD). Subsequently, it received financial support from the East German SED, with which it cooperated in a series of "alternative" postwar anniversary celebrations in 1985. This support ended with the changes in East Germany in late 1989, forcing the DKP to curtail its activities. The party's longtime chair, Herbert MIES, resigned in October 1989 and was replaced by a four-member council at the tenth congress in March 1990. In the 2009 national legislative election, the DKP received only 929 votes.

Leader: Patrik KÖBELE.

South Schleswig Voters' Union (*Südschleswigscher Wählerverband*—SSW/*Sydslesvigk Vaelgerforening*—SSV). Founded in 1948 with the approval of the British occupation authorities, the SSV represented the interests of ethnic Danes in northern Schleswig-Holstein. Exempted from the 5 percent threshold rule, it consistently obtained representation in the state legislature, increasing from one to two seats in March 1996 on a 2.5 percent vote share and then to three in 2000 with 4.1 percent of the vote. It fell back to two seats in 2005 with 3.6 percent of the vote. The party also has representation in a number of local and regional councils, and in June 2012 it joined the governing coalition in Schleswig-Holstein after receiving 3 seats for its 4.6 percent of the vote.

Leaders: Flemming MEYER, Rüdiger SCHULZE, Anke SPOORENDONK, Lars HARMS.

Democratic Party of Germany (*Demokratische Partei Deutschlands*—DPD). The DPD was founded in October 1995 to represent the interests of foreigners in Germany and to oppose racism, being based in the 2-million-strong Turkish community. The DPD's prospects for electoral progress are limited by the fact that most non-German immigrants do not have citizenship and are therefore not entitled to vote.

Leader: Markus GIERSCH (Chair).

For information on the **German People's Union** (*Deutsche Volksunion*—DVU) and the **Law-and-Order Offensive Party** (*Partei Rechtsstaatlicher Offensive*—PRO), see the 2013 *Handbook.*

Extremist Groups:

Although terrorist activity receded in the 1980s, armed groups on the right and the left remained active in postunification Germany. Neo-Nazi groups, whose overall membership was estimated in early 1985 at 22,000, were particularly active in the early 1990s, mounting attacks on foreign residents and Jews. (By the late 1990s the extremists' numbers were reported to have climbed to more than 50,000.) They included the **Free Workers' Party** (*Frei Arbeiterspartei*—FAP), reputedly the largest neo-Nazi group at the time of its banning in February 1995; the much smaller, Hamburg-based **National List** (*Nationale Liste*—NL), which also was banned in February 1995; the **German League for People and Homeland** (*Deutsche Liga für Volk und Heimat*—DLVH); the **National Socialist Action Front/National Action** (*Aktionsfront Nationaler Sozialisten/Nationale Aktion*—ANS/NA); various "military sport groups" (*Wehrsportgruppen*), including the *Wehrsportgruppe Hoffman* led by Odfried HEPP and allegedly supported by the Palestine Liberation Organization; and the **Viking Youth** (*Wiking Jugend*—WJ), banned in October 1994. In January 2004 Bavaria banned the far-right **Franconian Action Front** (*Aktionsfront Fränkische*—FAF). The federal government banned another neo-Nazi organization, the **Blood and Honor Group**, in 2000, and in 2008 banned two groups for Holocaust denial, the Collegium Humanum, based in Vlotho, and the Association for the Rehabilitation of People Persecuted for Denying the Holocaust.

A surge in violent, right-wing activity in late 2008 and 2009, including the wounding of a Bavarian police officer in a stabbing incident, prompted renewed efforts to find and prosecute members. Of particular concern was an Interior Ministry report in March 2009 that found that among 15-year-old boys, 1 in 20 were members of a right-wing group; the rate was significantly higher, 1 in 8 boys, in the former East Germany. In response, authorities banned the **Patriotic German Youth** (*Heimattreue Deutsche Jugend*—HDJ).

On the left in the 1970s, the **Red Army Faction** (*Rote Armee Fraktion*—RAF), an outgrowth of the Baader-Meinhof group, emerged with an estimated strength of about 500. Following the emplacement of Pershing missiles in 1984, the RAF declared an "anti-imperialist war" and claimed responsibility for more than 20 bombings in 1985, mainly at U.S. military and diplomatic installations, which left four dead; the group also claimed credit for the assassination of the arms manufacturer Ernst ZIMMERMAN in February 1985. In April 1992 the RAF announced that it would cease its attacks on public officials if the government released several of its long-incarcerated members. In an apparent response, former RAF activist Günter SONNENBERG was released in mid-May after serving 15 years of a life sentence. In September 1995, however, an RAF member was sentenced to life imprisonment for involvement in terrorist actions in 1977 and 1982. In April 1998 the RAF announced that it had formally disbanded. In May the government pardoned Helmut POHL, an RAF member who had urged the group to disband in 1996; he had been convicted for the 1981 bombing of a U.S. Air Force base. In February 2007 former RAF member Brigitte MOHNHAUPT was pardoned after being imprisoned for 24 years. In March 2009 RAF co-founder Horst MAHLER was sentenced to five years on top of a six-year sentence for denying the Holocaust.

In August 1998 the government outlawed the **Revolutionary People's Liberation Party/Front** as well as the **Turkish People's Liberation Party/Front**, splinters of **Dev-Sol** (*Devrimce Sol*), a leftist Turkish group founded in Turkey in 1978 on a platform advocating the creation of a "communist society." (Dev-Sol had been originally banned in Germany in 1983.) The government claimed the outlawed groups were extremists who financed their activities through blackmail and violence. The Marxist Turkish group DHKP-C, also banned that year, became active again in late 2002, recruiting new members from poor areas of Germany's big cities. Five suspected members were charged with belonging to a terrorist organization in late 2007. Renewed violence by members of the Kurdish Workers Party (PKK) in 2007 was attributed to Turkish military operations along the border of northern Iraq. In 2008 the head of the German intelligence agency said up to 700 members of radical Islamic groups were under surveillance. In June 2009 Turkish and German authorities discussed restricting the flow of capital to the PKK and extraditing two PKK members from Germany to Turkey. In December 2010 three members of the banned group were imprisoned for raising funds for the PKK and for recruiting new members in Germany.

LEGISLATURE

The bicameral parliament consists of an indirectly chosen upper chamber, the *Bundesrat,* or Federal Council, and an elective lower chamber, the *Bundestag,* or Federal Assembly.

Federal Council (*Bundesrat*). The upper chamber currently consists of 69 members appointed by the state governments, each of whose three to six votes (depending on population) are cast *en bloc.* Lengths of term vary according to state election dates. The presidency rotates annually among heads of the state delegations, usually state minister-presidents. As of October 2013, the seat distribution was as follows: Christian Democratic Union (CDU), 14; Social Democratic Party (SPD), 34; Christian Social Union (CSU), 5; Free Democratic Party (FDP), 4; the Left, 2; and Alliance '90/The Greens, 10.

President: Winfried KRETSCHMANN.

Federal Assembly (*Bundestag*). The lower chamber, which currently has 630 members, is the world's largest democratically elected legislative body. The president can dissolve the assembly, prompting a federal election, upon a chamber vote of no confidence in the chancellor. Deputies are chosen for four-year terms by popular vote under a complicated electoral system combining direct and proportional representation. Following the Federal Assembly elections on September 22, 2013, for 630 seats, the seat distribution was as follows: CDU/CSU, 306 seats (236 constituency and 75 party list); SPD, 192 seats (58, 135); the Left, 64 (4, 60); Alliance '90/The Greens, 63 (1, 62).

President: Norbert LAMMERT.

CABINET

[as of October 20, 2013]

Chancellor	Angela Merkel (CDU) [f]
Vice Chancellor	Philipp Rösler (FDP)
Head, Federal Chancellery	Ronald Pofalla (CDU)
Ministers	
Consumer Protection, Food, and Agriculture	Hans-Peter Friedrich (CSU)
Defense	Thomas de Mazière (CDU)
Economic Cooperation and Development	Dirk Niebel (FDP)
Economics and Technology	Philipp Rösler (FDP)
Education and Research	Johanna Wanka (CDU) [f]
Environment, Nature Conservation, and Nuclear Safety	Peter Altmaier (CDU)
Family Affairs, Senior Citizens, Women, and Youth	Kristina Schröder (CDU) [f]
Finance	Wolfgang Schäuble (CDU)
Foreign Affairs	Guido Westerwelle (FDP)
Health	Daniel Bahr (FDP)
Interior	Hans-Peter Friedrich (CSU)
Justice	Sabine Leutheusser-Schnarrenberger (FDP) [f]
Labor and Social Affairs	Ursula von der Leyen (CDU) [f]
Transport, Building, and Urban Development	Peter Ramsauer (CSU)

[f] = female

INTERGOVERNMENTAL REPRESENTATION

Ambassador to the U.S.: Niels Peter Georg AMMON.

U.S. Ambassador to Germany: John EMERSON.

Permanent Representative to the UN: Peter WITTIG.

IGO Memberships (Non-UN): CEUR, EU, G-8, G-20, ICC, IEA, IOM, NATO, OECD, OSCE.

GHANA

Republic of Ghana

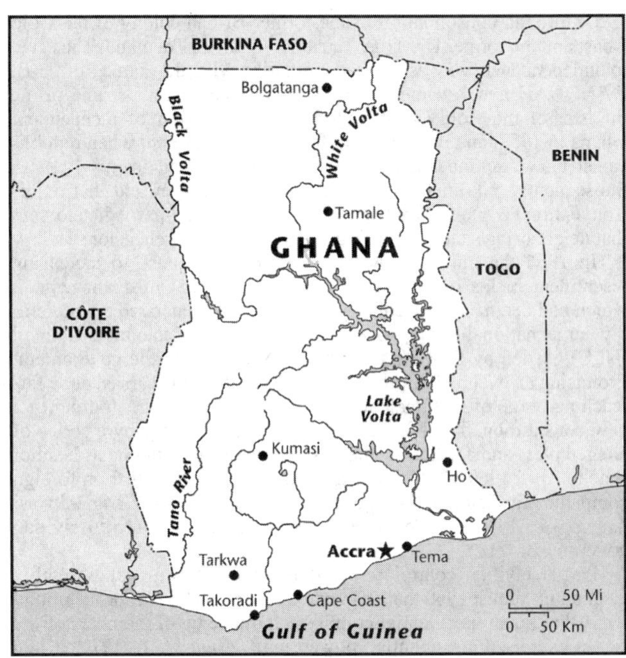

Political Status: Independent member of the Commonwealth since March 6, 1957; under military control 1966–1969 and 1972–1979; Third Republic overthrown by military coup of December 31, 1981; constitution of Fourth Republic, approved in referendum of April 28, 1992, formally launched on January 7, 1993.

Area: 92,099 sq. mi. (238,537 sq. km).

Population: 25,677,793 (2012E—UN); 25,199,609 (2013E—U.S. Census).

Major Urban Center (2011E—UN): ACCRA (2,263,785).

Official Language: English.

Monetary Unit: New Cedi (market rate November 1, 2013: 2.21 cedi = $1US).

President: John Dramani MAHAMA (National Democratic Congress); sworn in on July 24, 2012, to succeed John Evans Atta MILLS (National Democratic Congress), who died in office after being elected for a four-year term in runoff balloting on December 28, 2008, and January 2, 2009, and sworn in on January 7; reelected on December 7, 2012, and sworn in on January 7.

Vice President: Kwesis AMISSAH-ARTHUR (National Democratic Congress); sworn in on August 6, 2012, to succeed John Dramani MAHAMA (National Democratic Congress) after the latter was sworn in as president; reelected on December 7, 2012, and sworn in on January 7 for a term concurrent with that of the president.

THE COUNTRY

Located on the west coast of Africa just north of the equator, Ghana's terrain includes a tropical rain forest running north about 170 miles from the Gulf of Guinea and a grassy savanna belt that is drained by the Volta River. While the official language of the country is English, the inhabitants are divided among more than 50 linguistic and ethnic groups, the most important being the Akans (including Fanti), Ashanti, Ga, Ewe, and Mossi-Dagomba. About 40 percent of the population is Christian, and 12 percent Muslim, with most of the rest following traditional religions. Over 40 percent of households are headed by women, who dominate the trading sector and comprise nearly 50 percent of agricultural labor; a smaller proportion of salaried women is concentrated in the service sector. Following the 2012 legislative balloting, women held 30 of 275 seats in the parliament (10.9 percent).

Agriculture employs nearly 60 percent of the population and accounts for about 39 percent of GDP, in large part owing to cocoa production. Other important export commodities include timber, jewelry, and coffee (and in recent years, oil). Manufacturing centers on food processing and the production of vehicles and textiles. Mining accounts for more than one-half of foreign exchange; in addition to gold, there are important deposits of diamonds, bauxite, and manganese.

Battered by tumbling cocoa and gold prices, the economy grew by only 1 percent in 2000, with inflation running at more than 30 percent annually. (For more on the economy prior to the 2000s, please see the 2012 *Handbook.*)

By 2005 GDP growth was more than 5 percent, although inflation was close to 15 percent. The International Monetary Fund (IMF) noted progress in structural reforms and private-sector investment. However, poverty was unabated, particularly in the north. Annual GDP growth averaged just over 6 percent in 2006–2007, with inflation declining to about 10 percent. The IMF, the World Bank, and the African Development Bank canceled $3.2 billion of Ghana's debt to allow resources to be used for poverty-reduction efforts. Meanwhile, the World Bank approved a $75 million loan for what was described as a model gold-producing project, predicted to generate between $300 million and $700 million for the country over the next 20 years. In 2007 it was reported that gold, for the first time, had surpassed cocoa as the largest source of foreign revenue, each commodity bringing in more than $1 billion, as a result of rising international gold prices and a bumper cocoa harvest. Annual growth averaged 5.3 percent in 2008–2009, the IMF noting that Ghana had made "remarkable success" in developing its financial sector (which, only a year earlier, fund managers had said required urgent agent). As inflation rose to a five-year high of 20.3 percent in February 2009 due chiefly to rising food prices and the global economic downturn, the cedi lost one-third of its value against the U.S. dollar, and Ghana was reported to be facing a financial crisis. Meanwhile, the IMF and the World Bank pledged about $1 billion through 2011 to help bolster the country's economy.

Ghana's financial outlook improved greatly as oil production came online in late 2010, the country said to be capable of producing 120,000 barrels per day (bpd), increasing to 250,000 bpd in 2014. Meanwhile, offshore reserves of 3 billion barrels were reported.

Bolstered by investments from the offshore oil sector, the economy grew 7.7 percent in 2010, while inflation slowed to 10.7 percent, due in large part to a marked decrease in imports. Exports increased by $2 billion in 2011, owing in large part to high global prices for cocoa and gold. In addition, direct investment in oil helped boost revenue, and the European Union (EU), which contributed more than 60 percent of total foreign investment, pledged its continued support. The IMF urged stronger fiscal management and more progress on structural reforms, while commending Ghana for adopting regulations to manage oil revenues. GDP grew by 7 percent in 2012, while inflation rose by 9.2 percent. The World Bank ranked Ghana 64th out of 185 countries in its 2013 Doing Business survey, the highest rating among West African nations. However, the government's deficit rose to 12.1 percent of GDP, prompting new measures, including improvements in tax collections, aimed to reduce the deficit to 9 percent of GDP in 2013.

GOVERNMENT AND POLITICS

Political background. The first West African territory to achieve independence in the postwar era, Ghana was established on March 6,

1957, through consolidation of the former British colony of the Gold Coast and the former UN Trust Territory of British Togoland. The drive to independence was associated primarily with the names of J. B. DANQUAH and Kwame N. NKRUMAH. The latter became prime minister of the Gold Coast in 1952, prime minister of independent Ghana in 1957, and the country's first elected president when republican status within the Commonwealth was proclaimed on July 1, 1960. Subsequently, Nkrumah consolidated his own power and that of his Convention People's Party (CPP), establishing a one-party dictatorship that neighboring states increasingly viewed with apprehension.

In 1966 the military ousted Nkrumah in response to increasing resentment of his repressive policies and financial mismanagement, which had decimated the country's reserves and generated an intolerably large national debt. An eight-man National Liberation Council (NLC) headed by Lt. Gen. Joseph A. ANKRAH ran the government. Promising an eventual return to civilian rule, the NLC carried out a far-reaching purge of Nkrumah adherents and sponsored the drafting of a new constitution. The NLC era was marked, however, by a series of alleged plots and corruption charges, with Ankrah resigning as head of state in April 1969 after admitting to solicitation of funds from foreign companies for campaign purposes. He was replaced by Brig. Akwasi Amankwa AFRIFA, who implemented plans for a return to civilian government.

Partial civilian control returned following a National Assembly election in August 1969 that designated Kofi A. BUSIA as prime minister. A three-man presidential commission, made up of members of the NLC, exercised presidential power until August 31, 1970, when Edward AKUFO-ADDO was inaugurated as head of state. The Busia administration was unable to deal with economic problems generated by a large external debt and a drastic currency devaluation, and in January 1972 the military, under (then) Col. Ignatius Kutu ACHEAMPONG, again seized control. The National Redemption Council (NRC), which was formed to head the government, immediately suspended the constitution, banned political parties, abolished the Supreme Court, and dissolved the National Assembly. In 1975 the NRC was superseded by the Supreme Military Council (SMC).

In the wake of accusations that "governmental activity had become a one-man show," General Acheampong was forced to resign as head of state on July 5, 1978, and he was immediately succeeded by his deputy, (then) Lt. Gen. Frederick W. K. AKUFFO. Promising a return to civilian rule by mid-1979, Akuffo quickly reconstituted a Constitution Drafting Commission, which subsequently presented its recommendations to an appointed, but broadly representative, Constituent Assembly that convened in mid-December.

In the wake of badly received efforts to secure constitutional immunity from future prosecution for existing government officials, Akuffo was ousted on June 4, 1979, by a group of junior military officers. The next day, an Armed Forces Revolutionary Council (AFRC) was established under Flt. Lt. Jerry John RAWLINGS, who had been undergoing court-martial for leading an unsuccessful coup on May 15. Having dissolved the SMC and the Constituent Assembly, the AFRC launched a "house cleaning" campaign, during which former presidents Acheampong, Afrifa, and Akuffo, in addition to a number of other high-ranking military and civilian officials, were accused of corruption and executed. Although the AFRC postponed promulgation of a new constitution until autumn, it did not interfere with scheduled presidential and legislative balloting on June 18. In a runoff presidential poll on July 9, Dr. Hilla LIMANN of the People's National Party, which had won a bare majority in the new National Assembly, defeated Victor OWUSU of the Popular Front Party; Limann was inaugurated on September 24.

The Limann government proved unable to halt further deterioration of the nation's economy and, in the wake of renewed allegations of widespread corruption, was overthrown on December 31, 1981, by army and air force supporters of Lieutenant Rawlings, who was returned to power as head of a Provisional National Defense Council (PNDC). Three weeks later a 17-member cabinet was appointed that included a number of prominent individuals known for their "spotless integrity." Despite a number of subsequent coup attempts (two in 1985 alone), the flight lieutenant became Ghana's longest postindependence ruler, while district elections in late 1988 and early 1989 were viewed as heralding a return to civilian government.

In January 1991 Rawlings instructed the National Commission for Democracy (NCD), which had recently sponsored a series of debates on the creation of regional and national assemblies, to draw on its findings, together with the content of past constitutions, in assembling a new national charter. Four months later the regime officially endorsed the NCD's plans for installation of a multiparty system and authorized a nine-member, ad hoc Committee of Experts to draft a constitution. On August 26 the document was submitted to a 258-member consultative assembly, Rawlings announcing that a referendum on the new basic law would be followed by presidential and legislative elections on November 3 and December 8, respectively.

On April 28, 1992, the new constitution, which included provisions for a National Assembly, was approved by 90 percent of the voters, and on May 17 the ban on political parties was lifted. Nevertheless, nine days later the High Court upheld the decision by the Interim National Electoral Commission (INEC) to continue a political-parties law proscribing 21 parties outlawed in 1981 (see Political Parties, below). On September 14 Rawlings resigned from the air force to campaign for the presidency as a candidate for the National Democratic Congress (NDC), the political-party successor to the PNDC.

At presidential balloting on November 3, 1992, Rawlings led the five-candidate field with 58.3 percent of the vote. Although international observers described the polling as "fair," attributing irregularities to deficient "organization and training," the four opposition contenders alleged widespread fraud, including NDC ballot stuffing. On November 13 the opposition announced it would boycott parliamentary balloting until a new electoral register was created (a demand rejected by the administration). Consequently, only 29 percent of eligible voters took part in the legislative poll of December 29 for the 200 assembly seats, with pro-Rawlings candidates securing all but 2.

In 1995 Dr. Kwesi BOTCHWEY, who had championed Ghana's adoption of an IMF-prescribed economic reform program as well as a rescinded value-added tax, resigned as finance minister. Meanwhile, the withdrawal of Vice President Kow Nkensen ARKAAH's National Convention Party (NCP) from the presidential coalition in May reflected ruptured relations between Arkaah and Rawlings.

At presidential balloting on December 7, 1996, Rawlings and his vice-presidential running mate, John Evans ATTA MILLS, defeated by a vote of 57.2–39.8 percent their main rivals, a Great Alliance ticket headed by the New Patriotic Party's (NPP) John KUFUOR, with Arkaah in the vice-presidential slot. At concurrent legislative balloting the NDC retained a nearly 2 to 1 legislative majority, capturing 133 seats to the Great Alliance's 65. Subsequently, in January 1997 the Great Alliance disbanded acrimoniously.

President Rawlings's efforts to name a new government in early 1997 were complicated by difficulties in satisfying the various factions within the NDC as well as by the opposition's insistence that all prospective cabinet members, even incumbents, were subject to assembly approval. As a result, the full cabinet was not completed until midyear.

Rawlings being constitutionally prevented from seeking a third term, the NPP's Kufuor led seven candidates in the first round of presidential balloting on December 7, 2000, with 48 percent of the vote and defeated the NDC's Atta Mills by 6 percent in the second round 3 weeks later. Meanwhile, the NPP had also secured a legislative majority in assembly balloting on December 7, setting the stage for installation of an NPP-led cabinet early in 2001.

Kufuor's majority of 52.5 percent of the vote in the presidential balloting of December 7, 2004, secured his second-term victory in the first round of balloting over the NDC's Atta Mills, who received 44.6 percent. The NPP also fared well in the concurrent assembly elections, winning 128 seats in the newly enlarged body of 230 seats. A new government was sworn in on February 1. The cabinet was reshuffled on April 28, 2006, with additional changes made on May 13. The cabinet was reshuffled on July 11, after eight ministers resigned on July 6 to begin campaigning for the presidential election in December 2008 (ministers are required to resign when they apply to be nominated). The cabinet was again reshuffled on January 12, 2008, and a minor reshuffle took place in May.

A field of eight candidates, including one independent, contested the 2008 presidential elections. After the first-round on December 7, the NPP's Nana Dankwa AKUFO-ADDO garnered 49.1 percent of the vote, while the NDC's John Evans Atta Mills secured 47.9 percent, neither candidate receiving the required 50 percent to clinch the nomination. The results of a subsequent runoff on December 28 were too close to call, leading the electoral commission to schedule one more round of balloting in a single constituency where voting had been postponed due to alleged irregularities. After Atta Mills received 50.2 percent in the runoff in the Tain constituency on January 2, 2009, the electoral commission certified the victory on January 3. Atta Mills and his running mate, John Dramani MAHAMA, a former communications minister, were sworn in on January 7. The president named a new cabinet, dominated by the NDC and technocrats, which was vetted and approved by parliament in stages from January to mid-February, with most of the 23 ministers seated by February 13. Three ministers of state took office on March 11. The minister of youth and sport announced his resignation on June 26, despite having been cleared of allegations of malfeasance. A minor reshuffle occurred on October 13 following the resignation of two ministers linked to bribery allegations.

The NDC was also victorious in concurrent legislative elections on December 7, 2008, becoming the largest party with 114 seats, followed by the previously dominant NPP with 107. On January 7, 2009, Joyce BAMFORD-ADDO became the first woman to be elected speaker of Ghana's National Assembly.

The cabinet was reshuffled on January 25, 2010, with all members being seated by March 10 following approval by parliament. Extensive cabinet changes were announced on January 4, 2011, taking effect on January 21.

Following allegations of corruption, the attorney general and the minister of education resigned, and the cabinet was reshuffled on January 23, 2012 (see Current Issues, below). Another reshuffle occurred on March 6.

On July 24, 2012, Atta Mills, who had been reportedly battling throat cancer, died following a stroke. Vice president Mahama was sworn in to succeed him on the same day. Kwesis AMISSAH-ARTHUR, the chief of Ghana's central bank, was named vice president on August 1 and sworn in on August 6.

Mahama was reelected on December 7, 2012, winning 50.7 percent of the vote and avoiding a run-off. In concurrent balloting for an expanded 275-seat assembly, the National Democratic Congress won 148 seats, following by the New Patriotic Party, 123, and the People's National Convention, 1. Three independents were also elected. A new cabinet was named on January 10, 2013, and approved between February 15 and March 7.

Constitution and government. On August 26, 1991, a consultative assembly of 258 members (117 drawn from district assemblies, 119 representing "identifiable" groups, and 22 governmentally appointed) began deliberations on a new constitution, a draft of which had been published by the government two weeks earlier. The document, which drew from Ghana's previous four constitutions as well as French basic law, was a multiparty instrument featuring a directly elected president; a presidentially appointed vice president; a military–civilian Security Council chaired by the president; a nonpartisan Council of State; a unicameral, directly elected legislative body; and a special committee on human rights and administrative justice.

The new constitution was approved by referendum on April 28, 1992, and on June 10 the PNDC was disbanded, though its ministerial personnel remained in office until March 22, 1993, despite the formal proclamation of Ghana's Fourth Republic on January 7.

Freedom of the press is guaranteed by the constitution. In 2013 Reporters Without Borders ranked Ghana 30th out of 179 countries in media freedom, behind only Namibia and Cape Verde among African nations.

Foreign relations. External relations since independence have been pragmatic rather than ideological, the government unilaterally renouncing certain portions of the foreign debt and further disturbing creditor nations by taking partial control of selected foreign enterprises.

Relations with neighboring Togo had been strained since the incorporation of British Togoland into Ghana at the time of independence. In 1977 Ghana accused Togo of smuggling operations aimed at "sabotaging" the Ghanaian economy, while Togo vehemently denied accusations that it was training Ghanaian nationals to carry out acts of subversion in the former British territory. The border between the two countries was periodically closed, Accra repeatedly charging Togolese officials with spreading "vicious lies" about the Rawlings regime and "providing a sanctuary" for its opponents. In a February 1988 effort to interdict commodity smuggling (Togo, without mining, was being credited with multimillion-dollar gold export earnings), Rawlings declared a state of emergency in a number of Ghanaian towns along the Togolese border. The estrangement was substantially alleviated by an October 1991 treaty that resulted in the reopening of border crossings. However, in March 1993 Togolese President Eyadéma accused Ghana of involvement in an attack on his compound, and in early January 1994 the two countries were reportedly "close to war" after Lomé charged Accra with supporting, at least tacitly, a second attack in Togo. On January 7 the Rawlings administration claimed it had no interest in "getting involved in Togo's internal affairs" and urged the Eyadéma government to stop blaming Ghana "whenever there is an armed attack or political crisis." The tension heightened on January 12 when Togolese troops killed 12 Ghanaians at a border post and Togolese naval officers imprisoned 7 Ghanaian fishermen.

In April 1994 Lomé blamed Accra for the "presence of bombs in Togo," thus igniting yet another round of acrimonious exchanges. On a more positive note, Accra appointed an ambassador to Togo in November, and on December 26 the border between the two countries was reopened. In July 1995 Rawlings and Eyadéma signed a cooperation agreement after which Togo appointed an ambassador to Ghana for the first time in over a decade.

Relations with other regional states have been mixed since the 1981 Ghanaian coup. The PNDC moved quickly to reestablish links with Libya (severed by President Limann in November 1980 because of the Qadhafi regime's presumed support of Rawlings), thereby clearing the way for shipments of badly needed Libyan oil. In April 1987 an agreement was signed with Iran for the delivery of 10,000 barrels of crude per day. Concurrently, a number of joint ventures were proposed in agriculture and shipping.

The 1987 overthrow of Burkina Faso's Thomas Sankara by Blaise Compaoré dealt a political and personal blow to Rawlings, who had hoped to form a political union with his northern neighbor by the end of the decade; instead, he encountered in the new Burkinabé president an ally of the Côte d'Ivoire's Houphouët-Boigny, with whom relations were strained. In April 1988, on the other hand, Rawlings and Nigeria's (then) president Gen. Ibrahim Babangida sought to ease tensions stemming from Nigeria's expulsion of Ghanaian workers in 1983 and 1985. In January 1989 the rapprochement yielded a trade agreement that removed all trade and travel barriers between the two countries.

Relations with Côte d'Ivoire worsened further in November 1993, when Ivorians seeking revenge for a murderous attack on supporters of their soccer team in Ghana killed 23 Ghanaian nationals and injured more than 100 others in Abidjan. Although Ivorian authorities established security areas for the Ghanaians, over 9,000 had reportedly fled the country by mid-month. In early 1997, on the other hand, Ivorian president Henri Konan Bédié made the first official visit to Ghana by an Ivorian head of state in nearly four decades. During his stay Bédié proposed broader economic and social ties between the two nations. Tensions heightened somewhat in 2005 after Ghanaian arms smugglers were arrested in the Ivorian town of Tantama. Meanwhile, Ghana opened a new embassy in Dakar, Senegal. In 2006 Ghana deployed 120 peacekeeping troops to Côte d'Ivoire under the mandate of the United Nations. UN concern was further focused on reports of illegal diamond smuggling into Ghana from Côte d'Ivoire, in violation of UN sanctions and of the Kimberley Process. The UN criticized Ghana for allegedly failing to respond to its own evaluators' reports of suspicious activity.

In 2007 Kufuor was elected president of the African Union (AU). Shortly thereafter, Ghana sent a battalion to help support the AU mission in Somalia. Meanwhile, Ghana signed a 10-year development agreement with Britain.

Hundreds of Liberian refugees were expelled from Ghana and returned to Monrovia in March 2008, despite the refugees' pleas and protests, amid a dispute between the two countries over how to handle the more than 40,000 refugees still in Ghana following the Liberian civil war that began in 1989.

President Barack Obama visited Ghana in July 2009—his first visit to sub-Saharan Africa since the need for partnership with African countries. In discussions in November 2011, the Ghanaian and Chinese defense ministers pledged to increase military ties between the two countries.

In January 2012 Ghana and China reached agreement on a $3 billion economic development loan. The country also secured a $500 million loan from the IMF. Meanwhile, Ghana and Côte d'Ivoire launched new negotiations to resolve disputes over the maritime boundaries of the two countries. On September 21 sections of the land and seas borders and joint airspace were closed between Ghana and Côte d'Ivoire after an incursion by anti-government rebels attacked a village in Côte d'Ivoire. Authorities reported that the rebels were based in Ghana. The border was reopened three days later.

In January 2013 Ivorian militia leader Charles Blé GOUDÉ was arrested by Ghanaian security forces and extradited to Côte d'Ivoire. The arrest reportedly significantly improved relations between the two countries. In July Ghana and Japan signed an educational agreement to increase the number of Ghanaian students able to study in Japan.

Current issues. Long-simmering tensions between NDC and NPP supporters in northern Ghana erupted in violence prior to the 2008 general elections, leaving 3 people dead and 12 wounded, with each side accusing the other of looting and stockpiling weapons. However, aside from that episode, there was a marked absence of turmoil surrounding the elections, observers attributing the 69.5 percent turnout to improved security at polling places and a surge in interest by younger voters. Though the NDC edged out both parliamentary and presidential victories in the general elections, the results proved far less than a solid mandate for President Atta Mills, whose margin of victory was less than 50,000 votes, and whose party secured just seven more legislative seats than the NPP. Observers saw little hope for cooperation between the two leading parties, let alone a unity government, citing a "sour political climate" in which many NPP loyalists felt "cheated" after the close elections. Meanwhile, the new president came under attack from his former mentor, former president Jerry Rawlings, who publicly criticized him for "mediocre" cabinet appointments and for being "too slow" to prosecute NPP leaders for corruption. (Observers noted that Atta Mills's choice of John Mahama as his running mate, rather than a candidate favored by Rawlings, had been intended, in part, to distance himself from Rawlings in order to counter a commonly held view that Rawlings was likely to direct the new president.)

In addition to the political divisions, the economy was described in dire terms by the World Bank in 2009, and even the newly appointed trade minister declared that Ghana was "broke," which some analysts said was the NDC's way of pointing blame at the NPP's previous failures and explaining why the new administration was unable to follow through on some of its campaign promises, such as cutting gas prices. Nevertheless, Atta Mills began to move forward with plans to stabilize the declining currency, reduce the spiraling budget deficits, and reign in inflation. But in April, the administration raised the minimum wage by 18 percent, despite a provision in the budget of a month earlier that provided for only a 12 percent increase. Atta Mills also ordered a review of former president Kufuor's severance package, and security officers seized some of the former president's property thought to have been state-owned (though some of it was not). He also began tackling corruption, firing some under suspicion from various ministries and the Central Bank (most notably, Mahamudu BAWUMIA, the NPP vice presidential candidate), as well as overhauling public-sector management boards. As Ghana began to deal with an anticipated oil boom as a result of its starting up oil production in 2010, international agencies applauded Atta Mills's announcement that all current and future contracts with oil companies would be made public, described as a "significant move in a sector known more for its secrecy than its openness."

In September 2009 a new political party was formed in honor of former leader Kwame Nkrumah, reflected in the name Nkrumah Never Dies (NNDP) (see Political Parties, below).

In what was described as a "bizarre" series of events in early 2010, fires were set at several government offices, including the Ministry of Information and the Ministry of Foreign Affairs, and at the home of former president Rawlings, who was away at the time. He and his wife subsequently asked to be housed at government expense, and Rawlings firmly denied a suggestion on the radio by NPP member *Nana Darkwah BAAFI* that the former president had somehow set fire to his own house (known as Boom Junction). Baafi was arrested but later released after the president issued a "statement of concern" and criticism voiced by other NPP members. As attention began turning to presidential elections scheduled for December 2012, members of the four parties represented in the assembly proposed holding concurrent presidential and parliamentary polls on November 7, a measure that would require a constitutional amendment. Also, women organizers from the same four parties called for a constitutional amendment to guarantee that at least 30 percent of parliamentary seats be designated for women. In July the arrest of radio commentators who aired views critical of a huge oil deal with Ireland negotiated under Kufuor's NPP government drew widespread criticism aimed at the country's "antiquated" libel laws. The Atta Mills administration at one point tried to block the oil deal, claiming contravention of anticorruption laws on the part of one of the partners (whose directors had close ties to Kufuor).

The politically charged atmosphere in August 2010 gave rise to allegations against the NDC of "going on a rampage" against public employees suspected of being NPP members, while police supposedly stood by as workers were driven out of their offices and regional ministers were "terrorized." Shortly thereafter, the NDC called on the chief justice to purge the judiciary of "corrupt and politically biased members," escalating a months-long battle between the party and judges angry over what they claimed were the murders of colleagues as a consequence of their judicial decisions. That same month, Atta Mills confirmed that he would seek reelection in 2012, and Nana Dankwa Akufo-Addo again won the NPP bid to be its standard-bearer.

In January 2012 revelations surfaced that Alfred Agbesi WOYOME had illicitly financed NDC and NPP candidates and party officials. Woyome had earlier received $30 million from the government following questionable claims about past "consulting" work done on building projects. The scandal led to the resignations of the attorney general and the minister of education, who had served as attorney general. Woyome was arrested for fraud on February 6.

Ahead of the presidential election in 2012, Atta Mills overcame rifts within his party to secure the nomination over former president Rawlings's wife, Nana Konadu Agyeman RAWLINGS. The subsequent death of Atta Mills was reported to have created sympathy for the NDC and new president Mahama prior to presidential polling scheduled for December 7 and 28. Mahama won the first round of voting on December 7, against seven other candidates, and the NDC secured a majority in parliament. International observers cited the balloting as generally free and fair. However, the NPP's Akufo-Addo, and opposition parties, protested the results. After the new parliament convened in January 2013, the NPP members initiated a boycott of the legislature while the party filed suit with the Supreme Court, alleging vote rigging and other electoral fraud. The subsequent televised hearing transfixed the nation as they continued through the summer of 2013.

POLITICAL PARTIES

Political parties, traditionally based more on tribal affiliation than on ideology, were banned in 1972. The proscription was lifted in early 1979. (For more on political parties prior to 1992, please see the 2012 *Handbook.*) Four new opposition parties (the New Patriotic Party [NPP], National Independence Party [NIP], People's Heritage Party [PHP], and People's National Convention [PNC]) presented candidates in the November 1992 presidential election. However, the opposition parties boycotted the December legislative elections, charging electoral fraud in presidential balloting on behalf of the National Democratic Congress (NDC), which had been formed to support the presidential campaign of PNDC Chair Jerry Rawlings.

In January 1993 the Coordinating Committee of Democratic Forces of Ghana (CCDFG), an 11-party "Nkrumahist" coalition formed in 1991, was effectively superseded as the major opposition grouping by the new Inter-Party Coordinating Committee (ICC), which agreed to accept the "present institutional arrangements" but rejected the recent election results, calling for a new round of voting. However, the ICC was weakened somewhat the following August when the NPP (one of the strongest of the new groupings) decided to recognize the disputed election tallies.

Coordinated opposition activity next surfaced in early 1995, under the banner of the Alliance for Change. The NPP-dominated alliance subsequently organized antigovernment demonstrations that forced the Rawlings administration to rescind the recently imposed value-added tax, the coalition's success encouraging it to announce its intention to present an electoral front in 1996. After drawn-out negotiations, which prompted the withdrawal of some components of the Alliance for Change, a new Great Alliance was announced in August 1996 by the NPP and the PCP. Despite being roiled by debate over the choice of legislative candidates until just prior to election day, alliance-affiliated candidates captured over 60 legislative seats in December balloting. Nevertheless, the coalition subsequently collapsed as the NPP and PCP blamed each other for the opposition's failure to secure greater gains.

In the run-up to the 2008 presidential elections, the four legislative parties (the NPP, PNC, CPP, and NDC) signed an agreement that was proposed to be the basis for a law outlining procedures for the orderly transition of power. However, no formal coalitions were formed, and only a few minor parties (including the newly formed Reformed Patriotic Democrats [RPD], below) endorsed the NDC's candidate in the presidential runoff balloting.

Government and Government-Supportive Parties:

National Democratic Congress (NDC). The NDC was formed on June 10, 1992, as a coalition of pro-Rawlings and pro-PNDC political and social clubs, including the New Nation Club and the Development Union. A number of factions emerged within the NDC from 1995 to 1996, including the December 31 Women's Movement (led by the president's wife, Nana Konadu RAWLINGS), which advocated sponsoring female candidates in 30 percent of the constituencies in the upcoming legislative elections. Despite concern over how the party would be able to accommodate its various strains, Jerry Rawlings was selected by acclamation as the NDC presidential nominee at the party's third annual national conference on September 6, 1996. Rawlings, who had been involved in a widely publicized conflict with Vice President Kow Nkensen Arkaah, subsequently selected little-known law professor John Evans Atta Mills as his 1996 running mate.

At the NDC's congress in December 1998, party delegates named Rawlings the NDC "Leader for Life" and, consequently, the president of the party's newly designated decision-making body. Rawlings's ascension to the supreme party post was denounced by members of the NDC Reform Group, who had become increasingly combative following Rawlings's selection of Atta Mills as his would-be successor. In March 1999 the Reform Group announced it intended to form a separate party to compete in the 2000 elections (see National Reform Party, below).

A rift between those loyal to Rawlings and those who supported Chair Obed Yao ASAMOAH surfaced in late 2005, Rawlings blaming Asamoah for the NDC losing in the 2004 elections. Following the party's election of pro-Rawlings candidate Kwabena Adjei to the chairship at its December 2005 congress, Asamoah resigned in 2006 and formed a new party (see Democratic Freedom Party, below). Meanwhile, Adjei left the party to become a member of the NPP, and later formed the RPD (below).

In 2007 the NDC staged a two-week parliamentary boycott in protest of the jailing of one of its assembly members on charges of financial irregularities. Subsequently, the party tapped Atta Mills over three other contenders as its 2008 presidential candidate, a move some observers said was meant to demonstrate the party's independence from Rawlings's control. Rawlings had declined to openly support any of the potential NDC candidates. In the run-up to the 2008 elections, several smaller parties were reported to have rejected an electoral alliance with the NDC.

In April 2008 Atta Mills chose as his running mate John Mahama, a 50-year-old former communications minister, in the midst of the ongoing feud between Mills's backers and those loyal to Rawlings and his wife, Nana Konadu Rawlings. Mrs. Rawlings favored another candidate who she thought would challenge the NPP's base in the Ashanti Region. Following a campaign that emphasized the NPP's lack of success in fighting corruption and restoring a battered economy, Atta Mills eked out a narrow victory over the NPP's Akufo-Addo in December 2008, the contest ultimately determined by the results in a single constituency in January 2009. Atta Mills's victory was due, in part, to the RPD's support in the runoff balloting, which split off votes from the NPP. Meanwhile, in the legislative elections the NDC overcame the NPP, albeit by just seven seats, restoring the party to power for the first time since the 1990s, though requiring it to form coalitions in order to achieve a strong majority.

In 2009, Foreign Affairs Minister Alhaji Muhammed Mumuni, under pressure to resign in the wake of a monetary fraud case against him, refused to step down until a court ruled in the matter. President Atta Mills, who had considered replacing the minister, postponed action pending a court decision. Meanwhile, barely 100 days into the new administration, Rawlings was publicly critical of Atta Mills' performance, raising what observers said were fears that someone other than the new president might end up directing the government.

In August 2010, Atta Mills announced his intention to seek reelection in the 2012 poll. In a surprising and unprecedented development, the wife of the former president and head of the party's women's wing, Nana Konadu Agyeman Rawlings, challenged Atta Mills for the party's 2012 presidential nomination. She accused Atta Mills of not acting quickly enough to curb corruption. Though her faction claimed one million members, observers saw Atta Mills as the clear favorite. At the party congress in July 2011, Atta Mills won the nomination by a landslide, claiming 96.9 percent of the vote.

In December 2011, the **Democratic Freedom Party** (DFP) reintegrated with the NDC. The DFP was founded in 2006 by former NDC chair Obed Yao Asamoah and was launched as an alternative opposition group after Asamoah lost his fight for control of the NDC to a pro-Rawlings faction.

After Atta Mills died in office on July 24, 2012, Mahama succeeded him. On August 31, at a special party congress, Mahama secured the party's nomination for the 2012 presidential election. He won the general election with 50.7 percent of the vote, while in legislative balloting, the NDC secured 46.4 percent of the vote and 148 seats.

Leaders: John Dramani MAHAMA (President of the Republic), Kwesis AMISSAH-ARTHUR (Vice President of the Republic), Flt. Lt. (Ret.) Jerry John RAWLINGS (Former President of the Republic), Nana Konadu Agyeman RAWLINGS (Women's Organizer), Johnson Asiedu NKETIA (General Secretary).

Other Legislative Parties:

New Patriotic Party (NPP). The center-right NPP was launched in June 1992, its founders including former members of the old Progress Party, which had governed Ghana from 1969 to 1972 under Prime Minister Kofi Busia. The NPP's platform advocated the protection of human rights, the strengthening of democratic principles, and the holding of "free and fair elections." At the same time, the new grouping was widely viewed as devoted to the interests of the business class.

In 1994 the NPP sought to forge ties with other opposition groups, agreeing in November to back a single candidate in the next presidential election. Collaterally, it broke off negotiations with the NDC (below), stating that the government was uninterested in maintaining a dialogue. Meanwhile, the party experienced internal debate over its own presidential candidates. At midyear the decision was postponed until 1995 as leaders sought to placate the party's influential Young Executives Forum wing, which had funded Albert Abu BOAHEN's candidacy in 1992 but reportedly sought a new standard-bearer.

At the NPP congress in 1996, delegates chose John Kufuor as the party's presidential candidate. Kufuor declared his intent to forge a coalition with the PCP (see CPP, below), which was achieved in August with the establishment of the Great Alliance. The new alliance selected Kufuor as its common presidential candidate and thereby the main threat to the Rawlings campaign.

After a number of postponements that NPP officials attributed to poor regional organization, the party convened its fourth congress in 1998. At balloting for leadership posts, Secretary General Agyenim BOATENG was ousted in favor of 39-year-old Dan BOTWE, whose victory highlighted what observers described as a youth movement within the party. At further intraparty balloting in October, Kufuor outpolled five other NPP would-be presidential candidates and secured the party's backing for another national campaign in 2000. In part, the NPP's success in the 2000 legislative balloting (100 seats versus 60 in 1996) was attributed to its "clean sweep" in areas dominated by the Ashanti ethnic group. Meanwhile, Kufuor secured 48.2 percent of the vote in the first round of the presidential election before winning the post with 56.9 percent in the second round.

In 2005 a rift developed over allegations attributed to party chair Haruna ESSEKU concerning contributors' kickbacks to the president. Esseku denied he had made such allegations, which some observers claimed were made up to keep him from retaining chairship of the party. The president also denied the allegations. Subsequently, Peter Mac Manu was elected party chair at the December congress.

Dr. Charles WEREKO-BROBBY, former chair of the defunct United Ghana Movement (UGM) and its 2000 presidential candidate, rejoined the NPP sometime after the UGM dissolved in 2007. He had left the NPP in 1996 to form the UGM.

As President Kufuor's second term drew to a close, the party's attention turned to naming a possible successor. However, infighting marked the run-up to the NPP congress in December 2007, when it selected Akufo-Addo as its presidential candidate over Alan Kyerematen, who was favored by Kufuor. In light of large sums of money having been spent on the campaigns of many of the 17 candidates vying for the party's nod, Kyerematen became widely known by the nickname "Alan Cash." Kyerematen ultimately conceded to avoid a runoff "for the sake of unity." Another rift occurred in late 2007 when Kwabena Adjei, a key political figure in the Ashanti Region, and a number of youthful followers formed the Reformed Patriotic Democrats (RPD, above). Adjei had shifted alliances a few times, having been a member of the NDC prior to 2007.

Further tension, albeit short-lived, ensued in April 2008 when Kyerematen abruptly left the party, citing harassment of his supporters following the party's selection of Akufo-Addo as its standard-bearer. Two weeks later, however, President Kufuor persuaded him to return to the fold.

In the run-up to the 2008 general elections, the NDC alleged vote-rigging by the NPP via "bloated" voter-registration rolls, and following an investigation by the electoral commission, some discrepancies were found. Although violent clashes occurred between NPP and NDC supporters in northern Ghana in August, the subsequent elections were reported to be peaceful. However, the NPP lost its dominant status as Akufo-Addo was defeated in presidential balloting by a slim margin, along with running mate Mahamudu Bawumia, and ultimately in a January 2009 single-constituency runoff, which the NPP sought unsuccessfully to delay. The NPP also finished second in the legislative elections, albeit by just seven seats, but suffered a net loss of 20 seats from the 2004 balloting.

Akufo-Addo was chosen as the party's presidential candidate for the 2012 balloting. He again picked Bawumia as his running mate in December 2011. Akufo-Addo placed second in the balloting with 47.7 percent of the vote, while the NPP secured 47.5 percent of the vote in concurrent legislative balloting and 123 seats.

Leaders: Nana Dankwa AKUFO-ADDO (2008 and 2012 presidential candidate), John Agyekum KUFUOR (Former President of the Republic), Alhaji Aliu MAHAMA (Former Vice President of the Republic), Jake Okanta Obetsebi LAMPTEY (Chair), Mahamudu BAWUMIA (2008 vice presidential candidate), Jacob Otanka OBETSEBI-LAMPLEY (Chair), Kwadwo Owusu AFIRIYIE (Secretary General).

People's National Convention (PNC). The PNC was launched on May 30, 1992, by former president Dr. Hilla Limann, who finished third in the November presidential balloting. In late 1993 the party was divided by Limann's initial antipathy toward opposition party unity talks and subsequently by his reported insistence that he be named the leader of any group that emerged therefrom. In October *West Africa* reported that among the PNC members opposing Limann was his close aide, Dr. Ivan ADDAE-MENSAH, who accused the former president of unconstitutional party activities, and by November a number of the PNC's constituent parties had reportedly broken off to join the PCP. In December Limann announced that despite the party schism he would continue to fend off merger efforts and "serve as a watchdog of the constitution."

Criticizing Rawlings's performance as leaving "much to be desired," Limann asserted in April 1994 that he "could prove equal to the task of leading Ghana again." However, at a party congress in 1996 Limann agreed to step aside to allow delegates "to inject fresh blood into the party." Subsequently, Edward Mahama was named the PNC's 1996 presidential candidate by acclamation, the PNC deciding to "go it alone" rather than participate in the Great Alliance formed by the NPP and the PCP. At balloting on December 7, Mahama secured just 3 percent of the presidential tally and the party won 1 legislative seat.

On January 23, 1998, former president Limann died. At the PNC's congress in September, Mahama was elected chair and chosen to represent the party at 2000 presidential polling, at which he secured 2.92 percent of the vote in the first round. (The PNC supported the NPP's John Kufuor in the second round.) During the 2000 presidential and legislative campaigns, the PNC claimed to be the legitimate successor to Kwame Nkrumah's original CPP, although it had lost a legal battle to use the CPP's rubric. The PNC's platform was described as "populist," albeit with a noticeable capitalistic bent. In 2004 Mahama again ran for the presidency as the PNC's candidate, with the backing of the EGLE (below) in what was called the Grand Coalition, but received only 1.9 percent of the vote. In concurrent assembly balloting, the PNC contested the election with the EGLE and the GCPP (below) under the mantle of the Grand Coalition, the PNC being credited with winning four seats.

In 2006 First Vice Chair John NDEBUGRE was suspended because of his support for ROPA (see Current issues, above), in opposition to the party's position on the new law. Ndebugre subsequently resigned and was replaced by Alhaji Ahmed Ramadan.

The party again chose Edward Mahama to be its presidential candidate in the 2008 elections. A tentative electoral alliance with the CPP collapsed due to "mistrust," the PNC subsequently contesting the elections on its own. Mahama, who had chosen Petra Amegashie as his running mate, secured 0.87 percent of the vote, fourth among the eight candidates. The party, which won two seats in concurrent legislative balloting, remained neutral during the presidential runoff election.

In 2011 the PNC was said to be considering electoral alliances with the CPP in some regions for the 2012 elections. Hassan AYARIGA was the PNC candidate for the 2012 presidential election. He won 0.2 percent of the vote, while the party maintained its sole seat in the parliament.

Leaders: Hassan AYARIGA (2012 presidential candidate), Dr. Edward MAHAMA (Chair and 1996, 2000, 2004, and 2008 presidential candidate), Petra AMEGASHIE (2008 vice presidential candidate), Ahmed RAMADAN (National Chair), Bernard MONARH (General Secretary).

Other Parties That Contested the 2012 Legislative Elections:

Convention People's Party (CPP). The CPP considers itself the legitimate successor to the party of the same name formed by former president Nkrumah during the independence campaign. The revived grouping was launched in 1999 under the name Convention Party (due to a legal dispute over the use of the original rubric) as a result of a merger agreement between the People's Convention Party (PCP) and the National Convention Party (NCP).

The PCP had been formed in December 1993 as an apparent successor to the Nkrumahist ICC by the National Independence Party (NIP), the People's Heritage Party (PHP), and the People's Party for Democracy and Development (PPDD). (For further information on the NIP, PHP, and PPDD, see the 1999 *Handbook.*) A faction of the PNC also participated in the launching. (Organizers had reportedly rejected a demand from PNC leader Dr. Hilla Limann that he be named the new party's leader; consequently, only dissident PNC members joined the PCP.)

In early 1996 somewhat confusing reports indicated that the CPP rubric had been revived following a "merger" of the PCP and the NCP, the latter having split from the ruling Progressive Alliance the previous year. However, subsequent news stories routinely still referenced the PCP, and at least a portion of the NCP appeared to remain independent.

In the wake of its disappointing performance (five seats) at December 1996 balloting, the PCP blamed the NPP for the opposition's failure to secure greater representation.

In January 1996 Vice President Kow Nkensen Arkaah participated in the announcement of the "merger" of the NCP and the PCP in a revived CPP. However, other NCP leaders subsequently denounced that coalition, arguing that Arkaah was no longer the leader of their party or its presidential candidate. Some influential party members later also criticized the Great Alliance formed in August by the NPP and the PCP.

Ending an eight-year legal battle on the issue, the CP was officially permitted to resume use of the CPP rubric in mid-2000. It campaigned for the December elections on a center-left platform that called for increased social spending and deceleration of the pace of economic reform. CPP candidate George HAGAN secured 1.78 percent of the vote in the first round of presidential balloting, the party throwing its support behind the NPP's John Kufuor in the second. The CPP accepted a cabinet post in January 2001, although the party subsequently emphasized that it disagreed with the NPP on many important issues. In the 2004 presidential election, party chair George Aggudey secured just 1 percent of the vote.

In mid-2005 the party reportedly was engaged in unity discussions with the PNC in a move toward gaining political dominance, particularly as more youthful members defected to the CPP from the NPP and the NCP. Three CPP assembly members were dismissed by the party late in the year because they supported the ROPA (see Current issues, above), contrary to the party's position. In 2007 party member Kwaku Emmanuel OSAFO declared his candidacy for the 2008 presidential election. He was endorsed by a group within the party referenced as the Patriots, who vowed to restore Nkrumah's seven-year development plan. Detractors said the so-called Patriots were causing a split in the party with their plans to restructure it.

At the party's congress on December 16–17, 2007, the CPP overwhelmingly elected former minister of public sector reform Paa Kwesi Nduom as its standard-bearer for the 2008 elections. Though Nduom had created a rift in the party when he campaigned for the NPP in 2001, he enjoyed great popular support and political stature. He was reported to have the backing of two key Nkrumahists, both wealthy businessmen who observers note could bring private sector support to the socialist-leaning party. At the same congress, Ladi Nylander, a supporter of Nduom, was elected party chair. Nduom, who subsequently chose Michael Abu SAKARA Foster as his running mate, secured 1.34 percent of the vote in the 2008 presidential balloting, a far distant third in the field of eight candidates. The party, which remained neutral during the presidential runoff, won one seat in the concurrent legislative elections.

CPP member Kwabena DUFFUOR, a former central bank governor, stirred controversy when he was named finance minister in 2009, in the wake of 40 percent inflation during his tenure that led to the NPP government firing him in 2000.

In August 2010 party secretary general Ivor Kobbina GREENSTREET and the party's youth leader were suspended for allegedly having "brought the image of the party into disrepute" by making disparaging remarks. Subsequently, it was reported that they were expelled. That same month the CPP reportedly was prepared to accept a merger with the PNC (below), but subsequently it was reported that the parties would try to form electoral alliances in some regions for the 2012 poll. Meanwhile, Nduom left the party in December 2011 and formed the Progressive People's Party.

Sakara was the party's 2012 presidential candidate. He received 0.2 percent of the vote, while the CPP failed to secure any seats in the legislature with less than 1 percent of the vote.

Leaders: Samia NKRUMAH (Chair), Michael Abu SAKARA Foster (2012 presidential candidate and and 2008 vice presidential candidate), George AGGUDEY (2004 presidential candidate), Hajia Hamdatu IBRAHIM-HARUNA, William DOWOKPOR (Communications Director), Ivor Kobbina GREENSTREET (Secretary General).

Reformed Patriotic Democrats (RPD). Considered a breakaway group from the NPP, the RPD was subsequently reported to have close ties with the NDC. The party was formed in October 2007 by Kwabena Adjei, a former NDC chair who more recently had been a member of the NPP. The party has its stronghold in the Ashanti Region (which likely helped bolster the NDC in the 2008 presidential runoff election) and among its members were dissident youthful supporters of Ekwow Spio-Garbrah, who lost his bid to be NDC flagbearer in 2008. Adjei said the party would focus on the youth of Ghana, with emphasis on "human capacity" and creating jobs, among other things. Following the party's certification in March 2008, its strategy was described by observers as an effort to split the votes between the two main contenders, force a runoff, and then enter into a "serious pact" with the winning party. (The RPD rejected a request in July by the NPP to refrain from contesting the presidential elections.)

Adjei, the party's 2008 presidential candidate, with Rosemond Abraham as his running mate, secured only 0.08 percent of the vote, coming in last among the eight candidates. Subsequently, the RPD strengthened its ties to the NDC by supporting John Evans Atta Mills in the presidential runoff. In September 2012 the RPD announced it would support the NDC's Mahama in the upcoming presidential election. In the 2012 balloting, the RPD endorsed Mahama for the presidency, and failed to gain any seats in the parliament.

Leaders: Kwabena ADJEI (2008 presidential candidate), Rosemond ABRAHAM (2008 vice presidential candidate), Hagan BROWN Jr. (National Chair), John BEDIAKO (Vice Chair), Sarpong MANU (Secretary General).

Democratic People's Party (DPP). Founded in 1992 after the ban on political parties was rescinded, the DPP is a small party with a Nkruhmaist orientation. Party founder and leader Thomas Ward-Brew, often described as a maverick, missed the filing deadline for the 2004 presidential election. In 2007 the DPP brought a suit against a Dutch-based organization for allegedly illegally funding four political parties in Ghana. Ward-Brew was again nominated to be the party's flagbearer in the 2008 presidential election, choosing Peter Dwamena, a retired banker, as his running mate. Ward-Brew secured just 0.10 percent of the vote, finishing seventh among the eight candidates. While the DPP officially remained neutral during the presidential runoff, a group of DPP members from the northern region allegedly accepted money from the NPP and led the public to believe the party was supporting the NPP. Four of the accused DPP members were subsequently expelled from the party in 2009. The DPP supported incumbent president Mahama in the December presidential balloting but received 0.03 percent of the vote in legislative balloting and no seats in parliament.

Leaders: Thomas WARD-BREW (Chair and 2008 presidential candidate), Peter DWAMENA (2008 vice presidential candidate), Mohammed Salisu SULEMANA (Secretary General).

New Vision Party (NVP). Founded in June 2008 by the Rev. Daniel Yaw Nkansah, the party endorsed democratic socialist principles, though some observers viewed it as more of a religious-based group. "Prophet Nkansah," as he was known, pledged to help the poor by providing free access to health care and free education up to the senior high school level, and he invited members of all religions to join the party and help unseat "wicked politicians." Though five candidates from the party contested the 2008 legislative elections, none was elected, while the party only received 0.01 percent of the vote in 2012 legislative balloting.

Leaders: Rev. Daniel Yaw NKANSAH, Aaron KING, Prince GAMBRAH (Regional Chair), Zurkanain ADAMS (Vice Chair), Samuel DUODU (Regional Secretary).

Great Consolidated Popular Party (GCPP). Formed in 1996, the GCPP, having lost its bid to be designated as the legitimate successor to the original CPP, presented its chair, Daniel Lartey, as a presidential candidate in 2000. He won only 1.04 percent of the vote in the first round and endorsed the NPP's John Kufuor in the second round. The GCPP did not put forth a candidate for president in 2004, but it supported the PNC's Mahama as part of the Grand Coalition with the PNC and the EGLE. In concurrent assembly elections, the GCPP also was represented in the Grand Coalition.

Though the party nominated Lartey to contest the 2008 presidential elections, his candidacy was rejected by the electoral commission, which said the GCPP had not complied with rules regarding regional party congresses. Though the GCPP threw its support behind the NDC in the presidential runoff, Lartey subsequently vowed to unseat Atta Mills in 2012, when Lartey would be 86 years old. Lartey died in December 2009 after a short illness. In mid-2010 observers said there was growing support for the party leader's son Henry Lartey to succeed him.

In June 2011 party chair John THOMPSON and secretary general Adams ALI were expelled for alleged "misbehavior" that resulted in bringing "public ridicule" to the party and for allegedly not paying their dues. Subsequently, Henry Lartey was named interim, and then permanent, chair. He was the party's candidate for the 2012 presidential election, receiving 0.4 percent of the vote. The GCPP secured 0.01 percent of the vote in the concurrent parliamentary elections.

Leader: Henry LARTEY (Chair and 2012 presidential candidate).

Other parties that contested the 2012 balloting include the **National Democratic Party**, formed in 2012; the **United Front Party**, whose 2012 presidential candidate, Akwasi Addai ODIKE, won 0.1 percent of the vote; **United Renaissance Party** (for more information, see the 2012 *Handbook*); the **Independent People's Party**, led by Kofi Percival APALOO; the **Yes, People's Party**; and the **Ghana Freedom Party**. None received more than 0.4 percent of the vote.

Other Parties and Groups:

National Reform Party (NRP). Originally organized to function as a reform-minded faction within the NDC, the NRP formally registered as an independent party in June 1999 with the intent of forwarding a candidate at the 2000 presidential elections. The reform faction's decision to break with the NDC was reportedly precipitated by alleged attempts by the Rawlings camp to "undemocratically" control the party, in particular the president's pledge to back the presidential candidacy of Vice President Atta Mills.

Augustus Tanoh, a lawyer and businessman and former Rawlings ally, secured 1.21 percent of the vote in the first round of presidential balloting in December 2000. The NRP subsequently supported the NPP's John Kufuor in the second round, although party leaders resisted overtures to join the new cabinet, denying that Cecilia BANNERMAN, the new minister for manpower development and employment, was an official member of the NRP as claimed by the administration.

The party did not field a candidate in the 2008 presidential election. In May 2011 party chair "Goosie" Tanoh said the NRP would back Atta Mills in the 2012 presidential election, citing the president's economic policies. Following the president's death, the NRP reportedly supported his successor, Mahama.

Leaders: Augustus Obuadum "Goosie" TANOH (Chair and 2000 presidential candidate), Peter KPORDUGBE, Kyeretwie OPOKU (General Secretary).

United Love Party (ULP). Publicity on this group appeared in February 2008, when its leader, Ramon Osei Akoto, announced its formation to support his bid for the presidency. Akoto was unsuccessful in getting nominated as an independent prior to the 2004 presidential election and subsequently joined the NDC. However, he later became an outspoken critic of the NPP and the NDC, and as ULP leader made wide-ranging pledges, including free utilities and uninterrupted electricity under his government, the creation of 5 million high-paying jobs within four years, and greater emphasis on the fight against malaria.

In 2010 the party was reported to have started a free United Love Party University online, billed as "the first political party global university in the world."

In 2011 presidential flag bearer Akoto promoted free electricity for all Ghanians and breaking ties with the IMF, the World Bank, and the United Nations. Akoto was named the party's candidate for the 2012 presidential election but failed to register his candidacy for the balloting.

Leaders: Ramon Osei AKOTO (Chair), Robert ARMANU, Ken AMOAH (Secretary General).

Every Ghanaian Living Everywhere Party (EGLE). The (then) Eagle Club was formed in 1991, allegedly as a political affiliate of the PNDC. However, in mid-1992 the renamed EGLE party declined to offer a blanket endorsement for all PNDC–NDC legislative candidates, positioning itself only as a pro-Rawlings grouping. EGLE did not put forth its own presidential candidate for the 2004 election, and instead joined in a Grand Coalition with the PNC and the GCPP (below) to support the PNC's Edward Mahama. The coalition also contested the concurrent assembly elections, with only the PNC credited as having won seats.

Party leader Nana Yaa OFORI-ATTA died in May 2007.

The party supported the NDC's Atta Mills in the 2008 presidential election, and reports indicated it would support the NDC's Mahama in 2012.

Leaders: Alhasan Alhaji BENE (National Chair), Alhaji Rahman JAMATUTU (Vice Chair), Henry GIDI, Sam Pee YALLEY (General Secretary).

For more information on the **Real Democratic Patriotic Party** (RDPP), the **Nkrumah Never Dies** (NNDP), and the **Ghana National Party** (GNP), please see the 2013 *Handbook*.

LEGISLATURE

The unicameral **National Assembly** elected in June 1979 was dissolved following the coup of December 31, 1981. The new constitution, approved in April 1992, provided for the establishment of a directly elected body of 200 members, each to serve a four-year term.

In 2012, based on census figures, the assembly was expanded to 275 seats.

In the most recent election, on December 7, 2012, the seat distribution was as follows: the National Democratic Congress, 148; the New Patriotic Party, 123; the People's National Convention, 1; and independents, 3.

Speaker: Joyce BAMFORD-ADDO.

CABINET

[as of August 1, 2013]

President	John Dramani Mahama
Vice President	Kwesis Amissah-Arthur
Ministers	
Chieftancy and Traditional Affairs	Henry Seidu Danaa
Communications	Omane Boamah
Defense	Mark Owen Woyongo
Education	Jane Nana Opoku Agyemang [f]
Employment and Social Welfare	Nil Armaah Ashitey
Energy and Petroleum	Emmanuel Kofi Buah
Environment, Science, and Technology	Oteng Agyei
Finance	Seth Tekper
Fisheries and Aquaculture	Nayon Bilijo
Food and Agriculture	Clement Kofi Humado
Foreign Affairs and Regional Integration	Hannah Tetteh [f]
Gender, Children, and Social Protection	Nana Oye Lithur [f]
Health	Hanny Sherry Ayitey [f]
Information	Mahama Ayariga
Interior	Kwesi Ahwoi
Justice and Attorney General	Marietta Brew Appiah Oppong [f]
Lands, and Natural Resources	Inusah Fusani
Local Government and Rural Development	Akwasi Oppong-Fosu
Presidential Affairs in Parliament	Benjamin Kunbuor
Roads and Highways	Amin Amidu Sulemani
Security	John Dramani Mahama
Tourism, Culture, and Creative Arts	Elizabth Ofosu Agyare [f]
Trade and Industry	Haruna Iddrisu
Transport	Dzifa Ativor
Works and Housing, Water Resources	Collins Dauda
Youth and Sports	Elvis Afriyie Ankrah
Ministers of State	
Office of the President	Fifi Kwetey
	Abdul Rashid Hassan Pelpuo
	Alhassan Azong
	Mustapha Ahmed
	Comfort Doyoe Cudjoe Ghansah [f]
Regional Ministers	
Ashanti	Eric Opoku
Brong Ahafo	Paul Evans Aidoo
Central	Samuel Sarpong
Eastern	Helen Adjoa Ntoso [f]
Greater Accra	Julius Debrah
Northern	Bede Anwataazumo Ziedeng
Upper East	Limuna Muhammed Muniru
Upper West	Ephraim Avea Nsoh
Volta	Joseph Nil Laryea Afotey Agbo
Western	Ebenezer Kwodwo Teye Addo

[f] = female

INTERGOVERNMENTAL REPRESENTATION

Ambassador to the U.S.: Daniel Ohene AGYEKUM.

U.S. Ambassador to Ghana: Gene CRETZ.

Permanent Representative to the UN: Ken KANDA.

IGO Memberships (Non-UN): AfDB, AU, CWTH, ECOWAS, IOM, NAM, WTO.

GREECE

Hellenic Republic
Elliniki Dimokratia

Political Status: Gained independence from the Ottoman Empire in 1830; military rule imposed following coup of April 21, 1967; civilian control reinstituted July 23, 1974; present republican constitution promulgated June 11, 1975.

Area: 50,944 sq. mi. (131,944 sq. km).

Population: 12,017,476 (2012E—UN); 10,772,967 (2013E—U.S. Census).

Major Urban Centers (2011E—UN): ATHENS (789,166, urban area, 3,074,160), Thessaloniki (Salonika, 385,406, urban area, 1,104,460), Patras (168,530), Iraklion (135,761), Larissa (131,095).

Official Language: Greek.

Monetary Unit: Euro (market rate November 1, 2013: 0.74 euro = $1US).

President: Karolos PAPOULIAS (Panhellenic Socialist Movement); elected by Parliament on February 8, 2005, and sworn in on March 12 for a five-year term, succeeding Konstantinos (Kostis) STEPHANOPOULOS (Democratic Renewal), who was constitutionally precluded from a third term; reelected by Parliament on February 3, 2010, and sworn in on March 13 for a second, and final, five-year term.

Prime Minister: Antonis SAMARAS (Democratic Renewal) appointed as prime minister by the president on June 20, 2012, following legislative

elections on June 17, and sworn in on June 21, to succeed Panagiotis PIKRAMMENOS (Independent), who had served as interim prime minister of a caretaker government since May 16.

THE COUNTRY

Occupying the southern tip of the Balkan Peninsula and including some 3,700 islands in the Ionian and Aegean seas, the Hellenic Republic is peopled overwhelmingly by Greeks but also includes small minority groups of Turks, Pomaks, Roma, and others. Since the early 1990s immigrants from Albania, other Balkan and East European countries, the Middle East, and South Asia have settled in Greece and significantly changed the country's social fabric. More than 95 percent of the people speak modern (*dimotiki*) Greek, a more classical form (*katharevoussa*) no longer being employed in either government or university circles. The majority of the population belongs to the Eastern Orthodox Church, whose status is regulated by Article 3 of the Constitution. (Ecclesiastical decisions are subject to appeal at the Supreme Administrative Court and clergy salaries are paid by the state.) In 2010 women constituted 40 percent of the paid workforce, with three-fifths of those classed as "economically active" in rural areas performing unpaid agricultural family labor; urban women are concentrated in the clerical and service sectors. Female representation in government at all levels is low in comparison to other European Union (EU) states. Women secured 63 seats in the legislature in the June 2012 elections, or 21 percent of the seats.

Greece's budget deficit and public debt in 1997 remained well above the criteria set by the Maastricht Treaty for admission to the EU's proposed Economic and Monetary Union (EMU); the Greek inflation rate of 5.4 percent was also too high to qualify. (For more information on the Greek economy prior to the 1990s, please see the 2012 *Handbook.*) Consequently, when the European Commission announced its recommendations in early 1998 on the matter, Greece was the only 1 of the 12 EU members interested in the EMU not to be invited to participate in its launching in January 1999. The Greek drachma became part of the EU's Exchange Rate Mechanism in March 1998 (for more information on the Greek economy prior to 2000, see the 2010 *Handbook*).

Inflation fell to about 3 percent in 2000, and the budget deficit declined to 1.5 percent of GDP, sufficient to permit Greece's formal entry into the EMU and adoption of the euro effective January 1, 2001. The nation's economic growth subsequently slowed as public spending increased, causing the deficit to rise to 6 percent of GDP. This prompted disciplinary action by the European Commission. In March 2005 the administration announced broad tax increases in order to enhance revenue. On May 16, 2007, the European Commission recommended ending disciplinary action as the deficit fell to 3 percent of GDP. Economic growth contracted by 3.3 percent in 2009 and 3.5 percent in 2010 due to the global financial crisis. Unlike other European states, Greece was not able to implement a comprehensive stimulus program due to its heavy indebtedness, which exceeded 140 percent of GDP by 2010 (see Government and Politics, below). A continuing debt crisis and political instability led to further reductions in GDP (please see Current Issues, below), which declined by 7.1 percent in 2011 and 6.4 percent in 2012. Inflation fell from 3.1 percent in 2011 to 1 percent the next year. Meanwhile, GDP per capita fell from $31,700 in 2008 to $22,055 by 2012, and the unemployment rate rose from 12.5 percent in 2010 to 17.3 percent in 2011 and a record high 24.2 percent in 2012. In 2013 the watchdog group Transparency International ranked Greece 94th out of 176 nations, the lowest rating among the EU members.

GOVERNMENT AND POLITICS

Political background. Conquered by the Ottomans in the later Middle Ages, Greece emerged as an independent kingdom in 1830 after a protracted war of liberation conducted with help from Great Britain, France, and Russia. Its subsequent history has been marked by championship of Greek nationalist aspirations throughout the Eastern Mediterranean and recurrent internal upheavals, reflecting, in part, a continuing struggle between royalists and republicans. The monarchy, abolished in 1924, was restored in 1935 and sponsored the dictatorship of Gen. Ioannis (John) METAXAS (1936–1941) before the royal family took refuge abroad upon Greece's occupation by the Axis powers in April 1941. The resumption of the monarchy in 1946 took place in the midst of conflict between Communist and anti-Communist forces that had erupted in 1944 and was finally terminated when the Communists were defeated with British and subsequent U.S. military assistance in August 1949. A succession of conservative governments held office until 1964, when the Center Union, a center-left coalition led by Georgios (George) PAPANDREOU, achieved a parliamentary majority. Disagreements with the young King Konstantinos (CONSTANTINE) on military and other issues led to the resignation of Papandreou in 1965, initiating a series of crises that culminated in a coup d'état and the establishment of a military junta on April 21, 1967. An unsuccessful attempt by the king to mobilize support against the junta the following December yielded the appointment of a regent, the flight of the king to Rome, and a reorganization of the government whereby Col. Georgios (George) PAPADOPOULOS, a junta member, became prime minister.

In May 1973 elements of the Greek navy attempted a countercoup in order to restore the king, but the plot failed, resulting in formal deposition of the monarch and the proclamation of a republic on June 1. Papadopoulos's formation of a civilian cabinet and the scheduling of an election for early 1974 resulted in his ouster on November 25 by a conservative military group under the leadership of Brig. Gen. Dimitrios IOANNIDIS. However, following the abortive junta-supported Cyprus coup of July 15, 1974, and the Turkish invasion of the island on July 20, the new regime was forced on July 24 to call on Konstantinos Karamanlis to form a caretaker government in advance of a return to civilian rule. Karamanlis was confirmed as prime minister following a parliamentary election on November 17, and Michael STASSINOPOULOS was designated provisional president a month later. Stassinopoulos was succeeded as president by Konstantinos TSATSOS on June 19, 1975. On November 28, 1977, eight days after an early election in which his New Democracy (ND) party retained control of the legislature by a reduced majority, Karamanlis formed a new government. He resigned as prime minister on May 6, 1980, following his parliamentary designation as president the day before, and he was succeeded on May 9 by Georgios RALLIS.

At the general election of October 18, 1981, the Panhellenic Socialist Movement (PASOK) swept to victory with a margin of 22 seats on a vote share of 48.1 percent, and Dr. Andreas PAPANDREOU (son of the pre-coup premier) formed Greece's first socialist administration three days later. Despite ongoing complaints that the PASOK leadership had failed to make good on its election promises, the government was given a vote of confidence at the European Parliament election in June 1984, winning 41.6 percent of the vote and capturing 10 of the 24 available seats.

President Karamanlis resigned on March 10, 1985, after Papandreou had withdrawn an earlier pledge to support his reelection. In a legislative poll on March 29, the PASOK nominee, Christos SARTZETAKIS, was elected to a regular five-year term as head of state. Subsequently, PASOK remained in power, with a reduced legislative margin of 11 seats on a vote share of 45.8 percent, as the result of an early general election on June 2.

Damaged by a series of scandals, PASOK was defeated at legislative balloting on June 18, 1989, by the ND, which itself fell six seats short of a majority. Two weeks of intense negotiations followed, with the ND and the Communist-led Progressive Left Coalition agreeing on July 1 to form an anti-PASOK administration on condition that its mandate be for only three months and limited to "restoring democratic institutions and cleansing Greek political life." On September 20 Papandreou, his parliamentary immunity having been lifted, was ordered to stand trial on charges of having authorized illegal wiretaps while in office; eight days later the former prime minister and four associates were also indicted for a variety of offenses, which included bribery and the receipt of stolen funds.

On October 11, 1989, the president of the Supreme Court, Ioannis GRIVAS, was asked to form an essentially nonpartisan caretaker administration, which was sworn in the following day. At the year's second parliamentary poll on November 5, the ND registered a net gain of only three seats (three short of a majority), with PASOK gaining an equal number. In consequence, the three main parties agreed on November 21 to form a coalition government under a former governor of the Bank of Greece, Xenophon ZOLOTAS.

The all-party Zolotas government collapsed on February 12, 1990, because of continuing disagreement among the coalition partners over economic policy, and it was succeeded by a caretaker administration. At the ensuing poll the ND fell one seat short of a majority, but, with the support of the sole Democratic Renewal (DIANA) member, it was able to secure the installation of a government headed by Konstantinos (Constantine) MITSOTAKIS on April 11. Meanwhile, with the ND abstaining, Parliament had been unable to elect a new state president in three rounds of balloting on February 19, February 25, and March 3. The impasse was broken on May 4 by the new Parliament, which returned former president Karamanlis to office.

On January 17, 1992, PASOK leader Papandreou was acquitted of the corruption charges. He led his party on October 10, 1993, to decisive victory at an early election necessitated by a series of ND parliamentary defections. The defectors led by former foreign minister Antonios SAMARAS formed a new political party, the now-defunct Political Spring (*Politiki Anixi*—POLAN), which won ten seats in the 1993 elections. Samaras won an MP seat on the ND ballot in the 2007 parliamentary elections.

In September 1994 the Greek Parliament voted, without the participation of ND deputies, to indict three former ND ministers, including former prime minister Mitsotakis, on financial corruption charges. However, arguing that a trial would be politically divisive, Papandreou in mid-January 1995 induced Parliament to drop the charges against Mitsotakis.

In parliamentary balloting for a new president, center-right politician Konstantinos (Kostis) STEPHANOPOULOS was elected on the third ballot on March 8, 1995, with 181 votes to 109 for an ND nominee. The votes for the successful candidate, amounting to one more than the required three-fifths majority, came from PASOK and the small POLAN grouping.

Growing divisions within PASOK were highlighted by the resignation in September 1995 of the commerce, industry, energy, and technology minister, Konstantinos (Kostas) Simitis, because of opposition to his modernization policies in the PASOK executive. When the elderly prime minister fell seriously ill in November, a full-scale succession struggle ensued, with the influence of Papandreou's wife, Dimitra (Mimi) LIANI, proving to be a controversial factor. The recently appointed interior minister, Apostolos-Athanassios (Akis) TSOCHATZOPOULOS, became acting prime minister and appeared to be well placed in the leadership battle. However, following Papandreou's resignation on January 15, 1996, balloting of PASOK deputies on January 18 resulted in a narrow second-round victory for Simitis, who was sworn in as prime minister four days later.

Simitis called an early general election on September 22, 1996. The outcome was a reduced but still comfortable majority of 162 seats (out of 300) for PASOK, with the added bonus that the main opposition ND slipped to 108 seats, while three small left-wing parties polled strongly to win the remaining 30 seats among them. A further PASOK administration sworn in on September 25 contained a number of personnel changes designed to strengthen Simitis's position, although Tsochatzopoulos, a former general secretary of PASOK and leader of its populist wing, remained in the government, moving to the influential defense portfolio.

The elevation of Konstantinos Simitis to the premiership in January 1996 was seen as bringing to an end the Papandreou era and marking Greece's effective Europeanization. A commercial lawyer by profession, Simitis declared a commitment to the modernization of party and government structures, pursuit of a social democratic program, and closer integration within the EU.

On the domestic front, the government continued in 1997 and early 1998 to face serious protests over its economic austerity measures. Although the 1997 budget (announced in late 1996) had prompted a large-scale demonstration by farmers and a series of strikes by public- and private-sector workers, Prime Minister Simitis subsequently unveiled yet another tight budget for 1998. Civil servants again went on strike in February 1998 to protest cuts in benefits as well as measures designed to facilitate the privatization of state-run enterprises. Despite continued opposition from workers and other segments of the population supportive of increased spending (such as pensioners and students), the government held fast to its austerity approach in the 1999 budget, Simitis declaring EMU accession on January 1, 2001, to be his top priority.

Simitis called for early elections on April 9, 2000, which produced a surprisingly slim victory of only 1 percent (43.79 percent to 42.73 percent) by PASOK over the ND, which was led by political newcomer Konstantinos (Kostas) KARAMANLIS, the nephew of former prime minister and president Karamanlis. However, due to Greece's complicated proportional-representation system (designed to preclude the need for coalition governments), PASOK secured 158 legislative seats, a sufficient majority to permit Simitis to form a new government on April 13.

Among other things, Simitis and PASOK appeared to have suffered some loss of support because of declining social services (necessitated by budget austerity). Following elections, Simitis quickly promised "a new cycle of change" that would return social welfare to the forefront of his government's agenda. At the same time, however, the realities of EMU accession (implemented on January 1, 2001) demanded continued conservative structural reforms, including revision of liberal labor and pension regulations. Vehement opposition to austerity measures continued to plague the administration in 2002. Three months of public-sector strike action disrupted tourism and hampered government services in the spring in response to the proposed refinancing of the state pension fund.

While the Simitis government enjoyed some successes in 2003, particularly in regard to the apprehension of terrorists, social reform initiatives and construction projects required for hosting the Olympics progressed slowly in 2003–2004. The 2004 legislative elections were held early (in March) in part to avoid conflict with the summer games. In the wake of growing discontent over several issues, primarily related to public-sector wages and halting preparations for the Olympic Games, Prime Minister Simitis resigned on February 10, 2004, although he returned to the premiership three days later in a caretaker capacity pending early elections on March 7. Ten years of socialist government under PASOK ended with the legislative balloting, in which PASOK won only 40.5 percent of the votes and 117 seats and quickly conceded defeat to the ND, whose leader, Konstantinos Karamanlis, was named prime minister. He was sworn in on March 10 and formed a new government the same day. Prime Minister Karamanlis also assumed the culture portfolio in order to direct Olympic Games affairs, gaining widespread praise when the August games were held without major problems. However, Greece exceeded recommended EU budget deficit limits while hosting the games, requiring increased fiscal discipline in order to avoid EU sanctions. Karamanlis addressed the issue, winning a vote of confidence (165–135) in parliament on June 13, 2005, for his plan to change labor laws and pension benefits in an attempt to rein in deficit spending. The measures, however, did not prevent a series of strikes that plagued the country's economy in 2005–2006.

In an unprecedented vote by 279 of its 300 members, parliament on February 8, 2005, elected Karolos PAPOULIAS, a former foreign minister, as the country's next president, the first to come from the center-left. Papoulias not only received the endorsement of PASOK, of which he is a founding member, but also that of the ND, which nominated him. He was inaugurated for a five-year term on March 12. The cabinet was reshuffled on February 15, 2006.

The ND and Karamanlis narrowly retained control in the snap legislative poll of September 16, 2007, failing to receive the larger mandate desired by the prime minister. Meanwhile, PASOK's seats decreased to 102, while the Communist Party of Greece (*Kommounistiko Komma Elladas*—KKE) and the Coalition of the Radical Left (*Synaspismos Rizospastikis Aristeras*—SYRIZA) both nearly doubled their number of seats. Further, for the first time, parliament was represented by five parties, as the far-right Popular Orthodox Rally (*Laikos Orthodoxos Synagermos*—LAOS) won 10 seats. Karamanlis formed a new government on September 19, 2007. The cabinet was reshuffled on January 8, 2009. In the EU elections of June 7, 2009, PASOK scored a clear victory for the first time in nine years. The elections were marked by record abstention rates and the increased popularity of the far-right party LAOS.

On September 3, 2009, Karamanlis announced snap elections due to the "need to make painful decisions in the field of economy." PASOK won the balloting on October 4, 2009, with 160 seats to 91 for the ND. George PAPANDREOU of PASOK was appointed prime minister. The new government announced a dramatic revision of the country's financial statistics. The budget deficit was revised to 13.6 percent of the GDP. The public-debt-to-GDP ratio was also projected to be 113.4 percent (it would rise to 126 percent by the year's end). This shocked the financial markets and eventually eliminated Greece's fiscal ability to borrow.

On March 25, 2010, Papandreou announced the country would accept EU-IMF aid to avoid bankruptcy. The details of the bailout were finalized on May 2. The European Union and the International Monetary Fund (IMF) agreed to commit up to €110 billion in loans to Greece. On May 9 the European Union and the IMF agreed on a more comprehensive and ambitious €750 billion Euro bailout plan, of which €440 billion would come from Eurozone governments, €60 billion from an EU emergency fund, and €250 billion from the IMF. The Greek government agreed to implement an unprecedented extensive fiscal austerity and structural reform program. The program was highly unpopular and met with widespread public resistance (see Current issues, below). Disagreements over the austerity program led to an extensive cabinet reshuffle in September.

By 2011 it became evident that the country would need a second major bailout, but the EU required additional austerity measures (see Current issues, below). Papandreou conducted another major cabinet reorganization on June 16 in an effort to ensure support for more savings and revenue enhancements. Five days later the government survived a no-confidence measure in the parliament, on a vote of 155–143. However, the popularity of the government continued to decline. On November 6 Papandreou announced his resignation (see Current issues, below). Four days later the president named Lucas PAPADEMOS, a political independent, as interim prime minister of a coalition government that included PASAK, the ND, and LAOS, and was sworn in on November 11.

In legislative balloting on May 6, 2012, opposition to the austerity measures imposed by the EU bailout led a record number of voters to back extremist parties of the left and right. Although the ND placed first in the balloting, it secured only 108 seats, followed by SYRIZA with 52, and PASOK with 41. Both the ND and PASOK were unable to form coalition governments, and efforts to create a broad unity government also failed (see Current Issues, below). A caretaker cabinet was sworn in on May 17 with independent Panagiotis PIKRAMMENOS as prime minister and new elections scheduled for the following month. In balloting on June 17, the ND increased its seats and was able to form a coalition with PASOK and the **Democratic Left** (*Dimokratiki Aristera*—DIMAR). ND leader Samaras became prime minister on June 20 (see Current issues, below).

On June 21, 2013, DIMAR withdrew from the coalition (see Current issues, below). Samaras reshuffled the cabinet on June 25 and the number of PASOK ministers was increased.

Constitution and government. The possibility of a return to monarchy was decisively rejected at a plebiscite on December 8, 1974, the Greek people, by a two-to-one margin. The republican constitution adopted in June 1975 provided for a parliamentary system with a strong presidency. Under the new basic law (branded as "Gaullist" by political opponents of Prime Minister Karamanlis), the president had the power to name and dismiss cabinet members (including the prime minister), to dissolve Parliament, to veto legislation, to call for referenda, and to proclaim a state of emergency. These powers were lost by a constitutional amendment that secured final parliamentary approval on March 6, 1986. The action restored full executive power to the prime minister, assuming retention of a legislative majority. The unicameral Parliament, whose normal term is four years, elects the president by a complex procedure that requires a two-thirds majority on a first or second ballot, three-fifths on a third or fourth ballot (a legislative dissolution and election being required prior to the fourth), an absolute majority on a fifth ballot, or a relative majority between the two leading contenders on a sixth. A requirement that the head of state be elected by secret ballot was rescinded by a second amendment, also effective in March 1986. The judicial system is headed by the Supreme Court and includes magistrates' courts, courts of the first instance, and justices of the peace.

Traditionally administered on the basis of its historic provinces, Greece is currently divided into 51 prefectures (plus the self-governing monastic community of Mount Athos), with Athens further divided into four subprefectures. In January 1987 the government approved a plan to divide the country into 13 new administrative regions to facilitate planning and coordinate regional development. In 1997 a major local government reform, the Kapodistrias Plan (*Schedio Kapodistria*), mandated the merger of most of the existing 5,757 communities into 1,034 municipalities, inspiring widespread local resistance. Shortly after its election on October 4, 2010, the Papandreou government announced a sequel to the Kapodistrias Plan, the Kallikratis Plan (*Schedio Kallikratis*). This mandated the merger of the 1,034 municipalities into 370, the abolition of the 54 Greek prefectures, and their replacement by 13 regions. The Kallikratis Plan was approved by the Parliament on May 27, 2010.

The news media operated under severe constraints while the military was in power. Upon the return to civilian rule, censorship was lifted and a number of theretofore banned papers reemerged, although some have since experienced major shifts in circulation. The Karamanlis government enacted legislation in January 2005 banning individuals with large shareholdings in media from owning shares in companies that bid for public contracts. The European Commission has called on Greece to change the law, indicating that it violated EU directives. In 2013 Reporters Without Borders ranked Greece 84th out of 179 countries in freedom of the press.

Foreign relations. Greece has historically been Western oriented, and throughout most of the post–World War II era has been heavily dependent on Western economic and military support. The repressiveness of the 1967–1974 military regime was, however, a matter of concern to many European nations, and their economic and political sanctions were instrumental in Greece's withdrawal from the Council of Europe in 1969. Relations with the United States remained close, primarily because Greece, a member of the North Atlantic Treaty Organization (NATO) since 1952, continued to provide a base for the U.S. Sixth Fleet, but the return to democratic rule was accompanied by increased evidence of anti-American feeling.

The most important issue in Greek foreign affairs is its relationship with Turkey, particularly in regard to the Cyprus question, which has been a source of friction since the mid-1950s. The Greek-inspired coup and subsequent Turkish invasion of Cyprus in July 1974 not only exacerbated tension between the two countries, but also served to bring down the military regime of General Ioannidis and precipitated Greek withdrawal from the military flank of NATO. The return of civilian government, on the other hand, brought a renewal of cooperation with Western Europe. Greece announced in September 1974 that it was rejoining the Council of Europe and subsequently applied for full, as distinguished from associate, membership in the European Economic Community (EEC), with preliminary agreement being reached in Brussels in December 1978 and entry achieved on January 1, 1981.

Greece returned to the NATO military command structure after a six-year lapse, in October 1980. The action was accepted by Turkey's recently installed military regime, although a lengthy dispute between the two countries over the delineation of territorial waters, continental shelf, and air space in the Aegean Sea remained unresolved.

Prior to the 1981 electoral campaign, PASOK had urged withdrawal from NATO and the EEC, in addition to cancellation of the agreement with the United States regarding military bases. During the campaign these positions were modified, Papandreou calling only for "renegotiation" of the terms of membership in the two international organizations.

Although continuing his criticism of the U.S. military presence, the prime minister signed an agreement on September 9, 1983, permitting U.S. military bases to continue operation until the end of 1988. In early 1986 Papandreou again reiterated his intention to "rid the country of foreign bases," and in September he declared, without indicating a timetable, "our decision to remove... nuclear weapons from our country is final and irrevocable." Nonetheless, on May 30, 1990, a new eight-year cooperation agreement was announced that ensured continued operation of two of four U.S. facilities in return for about $350 million a year in military aid. Symptomatically, Parliament approved the agreement in late July by a straight party, one-vote margin.

Meanwhile, controversy with Turkey continued, with tension again escalating as the result of a confrontation between Greek and Turkish fighter planes over the Greek Aegean islands during Turkish military maneuvers in early 1989. The Aegean controversy turns on Turkish refusal to recognize territorial waters and airspace wider than six miles, on the grounds that to do otherwise would convert the area into a "Greek lake," denying Greece's demarcation of the Athens Flight Information Region (FIR).

In early 1992 there was widespread Greek opposition to former Yugoslavia's southernmost republic proclaiming its independence as "Macedonia," a name that historically had embraced parts of modern Greece, Bulgaria, and Albania, as well as Yugoslavia. As a result of Greek pressure, most Western nations, including the United States, refused for 15 months to recognize the new state, pending resolution of the highly charged dispute. It was not until April 7, 1993, that the two neighbors agreed to open discussion on the issue, with United Nations membership being granted the following day to "The Former Yugoslav Republic of Macedonia" (referenced as FYROM).

In a substantial hardening of Athens's position following the October 1993 election, the incoming Papandreou government closed Macedonia's principal trade route through the port of Thessaloniki on February 17, 1994. The action was taken after six of Greece's EU partners (followed by the United States) had extended diplomatic recognition to FYROM, thus complicating Greece's assumption of the EU presidency on January 1. In a highly unusual action against one of its members, the EU challenged the Greek embargo in a suit filed with the European Court of Justice (ECJ) on April 13. The Greek government was unabashed, reasserting that it would "never recognize a state bearing the name of Macedonia or one of its derivatives." It accordingly welcomed a decision by the ECJ on June 29 denying the commission's application for an interim injunction ordering the lifting of the blockade. Subsequent UN and U.S. mediation yielded the signature of an "interim accord" in New York on September 13, under which Macedonia agreed to modify its national flag to meet Greek concerns and to affirm that it had no territorial claim on Greece. The thorniest issue, that of the name "Macedonia," was referred to further talks; nevertheless, Greece lifted the trade embargo on October 14.

In September 1994 Greece declared that it would formally extend its jurisdiction to 12 nautical miles upon entry into force of the UN Convention on the Law of the Sea (UNCLOS) on November 16. Turkey immediately warned that the move would be considered an "act of aggression," and on October 30 Athens announced that it would defer the introduction of what it continued to view as a "sovereign right." It further angered Ankara by reiterating its right to the extension when ratifying the convention in June 1995, although it made no move to apply it.

The Turkish government also disputed Greek sovereignty over an unidentified number of islets in the Aegean in 1996, with both countries deploying warships in the area. U.S. diplomatic intervention defused the immediate crisis, with the result that both the Greek and the Turkish governments were assailed by right-wing opposition leaders for giving in to U.S. pressure. In a previous escalation in February, Turkey had recalled its ambassador from Athens after Greece had blocked an EU aid grant to Turkey, thereby again demonstrating its opposition to the EU-Turkey customs union effective since the beginning of 1996.

Simitis continued to foster improved ties with Turkey in the second half of 1998, as evidenced by his role in convincing the Cyprus government to deploy Russian-made missiles on the Greek island of Crete rather than in Cyprus (see entry on Cyprus). However, a full-scale diplomatic crisis erupted between Athens and Ankara in February 1999 following the arrest of PKK leader Abdullah Öcalan in Nairobi, Kenya, minutes after he had left the home of the Greek ambassador. It was subsequently revealed that Öcalan had been smuggled into Greece by pro-Kurdish factions, apparently without the knowledge of the government, which nevertheless then had assumed responsibility for Öcalan's protection and transfer to a safe haven; South Africa was reportedly Öcalan's final destination. Öcalan's arrest was a disaster for the Greek government on several fronts. Ankara strongly denounced Athens's actions, suggesting that Greece should be declared an "outlaw state" for "supporting terrorists." At the same time, Greek embassies and foreign missions became targets for militant Kurdish protesters, who accused Greece of having conspired in the arrest. Some domestic critics accused the government of incompetence for being unaware of Öcalan's entry into Greece. Meanwhile, the government's failure to protect Öcalan once it had accepted that responsibility was perceived as a significant blow to national pride.

Relations between Greece and Turkey improved unexpectedly in the aftermath of an earthquake that hit western Turkey in August 1999. Greece contributed to rescue efforts and extended other aid, gestures that were reciprocated by Turkey when an earthquake struck Athens in September. Underscoring the rapprochement, Greece finally lifted its veto on EU financial aid earmarked for Turkey and, in December, withdrew its opposition to Turkey's eventual EU accession, contingent on resolution of the Cyprus and Aegean questions.

In the early 1990s, Greece refused to recognize the name adopted by Macedonia, citing the lack of distinction between that name and the territory of ancient Greek Macedonia. Instead, Greece used the provisional name—Former Yugoslavian Republic of Macedonia (FYROM). Former U.S. undersecretary of state Matthew Nimetz was appointed to mediate the dispute, which escalated after Greece blocked FYROM's accession to NATO in 2008, and Macedonia subsequently referred Greece to the International Court of Justice (ICJ), accusing the country of violating a 1995 pact between the two countries.

Greece's relations with its NATO and EU partners were seriously tested over the former's bombardment of Yugoslavia, which started in late March 1999. With an overwhelming majority of its citizens against the bombing, the Greek government decided not to let its troops join the campaign but to provide logistical support for the NATO force stationed in neighboring Macedonia—a decision highly criticized by the domestic opposition. U.S. president Bill Clinton visited Greece in November 1999 amid fierce protests largely due to widespread anti-Western feelings, further fueled by the NATO action in Yugoslavia. During the visit Greece initially withdrew from a proposed antiterrorism pact with the United States; however, the accord eventually went into effect in September 2000.

Greece's progress toward normalization of relations with Turkey continued through 2000 when a number of cooperation agreements were signed. In November agreement was reached on a procedure for the readmission by Turkey of approximately 700,000 illegal immigrants who had entered Greece from Turkish territory. In March 2002 Greece and Turkey signed an agreement for a 285-kilometer natural gas pipe-line through which Turkey would supply Greece with 500,000 cubic meters of gas each day. Finally, improved Greek-Turkish relations contributed to the decision in December by Greek and Turkish Cypriots to resume talks after a four-year hiatus. In November 2007 Karamanlis became the first Greek prime minister in almost 50 years to make an official visit to Ankara. Bilateral talks focused on economic relations.

Greece opposed the U.S.-led invasion of Iraq in March 2003. Opposition to the war led to widespread antiwar protests during that year. Nonetheless, the PASOK government granted the United States overflight and basing privileges during the conflict and did not join fellow NATO members France, Germany, Belgium, and Luxembourg in attempting to block the U.S. alliance's military assistance to Turkey on the eve of the invasion.

Greece's relations with the other members of the EU were strained in 2004 when an EU investigation determined that the country had provided misleading data upon joining the euro currency system in 2001, when deficit spending had been above the 3 percent limit stipulated by the EU. The Karamanlis government blamed the previous PASOK-led government for the false reporting.

In April 2005 Greece became the sixth country to ratify the EU constitutional treaty, with legislators from both the governing ND party and the leading opposition, PASOK, supporting the treaty. On June 11, 2008, Greece became the 18th country to ratify the now-defunct EU Lisbon Treaty (see 2009 Ireland entry). The ratification was supported by the ND and PASOK, although PASOK stated that a referendum should be held. Smaller parties voted against ratification.

Increased cooperation with Russia became a priority under the Karamanlis government, and two major pipeline projects were announced. In March 2007 Russia, Greece, and Bulgaria signed an agreement for the construction of an oil pipeline from the Bulgarian port of Burgas to the Greek port of Alexandroúpolis. A second agreement signed in April 2008 provided for a Russian natural gas pipeline, connecting the Greek portion of the pipeline to another section in Italy. The increased Greek-Russian cooperation was met with concern by American and European partners, who worried that the ventures strengthened Russian leverage in a market already dominated by the energy giant.

In May 2010 Turkish prime minister Erdoğan paid an official visit to Athens. Twenty-one bilateral agreements were signed, which highlighted significant improvement in relations. On October 25 the EU agreed to deploy border patrol forces to help Greece monitor its border with Turkey. The action followed increased illegal immigration from Turkey, with an estimated 45,000 crossing the border in the first part of 2010. On November 1 and 2 there were attempts to mail 14 explosive devices from Greece to selected targets, including the leaders of France, Italy, and Germany. Although no one was seriously harmed by the devices, Greece suspended the shipment of international parcels for two days, beginning November 3. Two members of a small extremist group, the Conspiracy of Fire Nuclei (see Political Parties, below), were arrested on November 1. In December Human Rights Watch criticized the Greek government over conditions at its immigrant camps, citing widespread overcrowding and poor sanitation.

On December 5, 2010, the ICJ ruled that Greece had violated the terms of the 1995 agreement by blocking Macedonia's bid to join NATO. Talks between the leaders of Greece and Macedonia in January 2011 failed to resolve Greece's continuing refusal to recognize its northern neighbor. In April a Greek firm announced the construction of an undersea electricity cable to Cyprus and Israel (see entry on Cyprus).

In August 2012 the number of border guards was tripled from 600 to 1,800 along the Greek frontier with Turkey, following a dramatic rise in illegal immigration (see Current issues, below). In September the Greek and Macedonian foreign ministers met in New York and agreed to further dialogue on the Macedonian name issue. However, in meetings through September 2013, no resolution had been achieved.

In May 2013 Greece and China signed a range of agreements designed to increase trade and develop Greece as a hub for Chinese products being transported into Europe.

Current issues. The deteriorating Greek economy led Karamanlis to call early elections on October 4, 2009. Following the parliamentary elections of October 4, 2009, the new government announced that the deficit and debt figures had to be substantially revised upwards. This in effect froze Greek bonds markets. On March 25, 2010, despite initial objections Greece announced it would agree to a rescue plan organized by the Eurozone and the International Monetary Fund (IMF). In return the country committed to a politically unpopular long-term fiscal austerity and structural reform program. Following his resounding victory, new Prime Minister Papandreou pledged that all corruption cases would be brought to justice and culprits would be punished. Yet legal privileges enjoyed by ministers and delegates meant that many of the alleged corruption cases had already lapsed. The admittance of PASOK's former minister Anastassios (Tassos) MANDELIS on 2009 that he had been bribed by Siemens sent shockwaves as corruption appeared to be prevalent in both leading political parties and punishment of corruption appeared impossible. Meanwhile, the unprecedented public-sector salary reductions and other benefit cuts harshly hit the Greek low- and middle-class, while the long-due reform of the social security system also meant large losses for Greece's active working population and pensioners. It was estimated that the total decline of civil servant and pensioner income would be up to 20 percent. The implementation of the targets and the reforms outlined in the EU-IMF memorandum met with the fierce reaction of the opposition parties, as well as trade unions that staged repeated strikes and protests. Internal disputes within the government and parliament slowed planned economic reforms. In balloting on November 7 and 14, 2010, PASOK candidates were elected to head 8 of the country's 13 regions. The ND won the remaining 5. PASOK also secured the majority of mayoral posts and seats on local councils. Papandreou argued that the electoral success represented a mandate to continue economic reforms.

In April 2011 the EU reported that Greece's deficit was 10.5 percent of GDP, well above the 9.6 percent target required by the EU/IMF rescue package. Fears that Greece would default led to further reductions in the country's bond ratings. Under pressure from the EU and creditors, the Papandreou government introduced an initiative to save €26 billion through tax hikes and government cuts, as well as raise €50 billion from the privatization of state-owned enterprises. The austerity program would eliminate 150,000 government jobs. The new measures were approved in June and prompted the EU, on July 21, to agree to provide €109 billion in additional financing.

Support for the government eroded through the fall of 2011. Meanwhile, on October 31, 2011, Papandreou announced that the government would hold a referendum on the EU bail-out program. The planned vote created additional uncertainty in international financial markets and prompted harsh domestic and international criticism. On November 3 Papandreou withdrew plans for the referendum. On November 6 he announced his resignation, and the president appointed political independent Lucas Papademos as prime minister of a coalition government on November 10.

Following intense negotiations in February 2012, the EU/IMF agreed to a second bailout package. Greece would receive €130 billion in additional financing and investors would accept a voluntary 46.5 percent reduction of the value of their bonds, worth a further €100 billion. In exchange, Greece had to enact €3.3 billion in budget cuts, equal to 1.5 percent of GDP. Parliament approved the deal on February 12 that included the loss of 150,000 government jobs, a 22 percent reduction in the minimum wage, and cuts in social welfare programs. The measures were met with widespread protests and strikes, prompting the interim government to call for new elections in May.

The May 6, 2012, balloting was won by the ND, but the party did not gain a majority and antibailout parties, including SYRIZA and the far-right Golden Dawn (*Chryssi Avgi*), won the most seats. Efforts to form a coalition government failed, and a caretaker cabinet was installed with new elections scheduled for June. The strength of the antibailout parties led to speculation that Greece would leave the eurozone rather than comply with the terms of the EU-IMF rescue proposal. The June elections were cast as a referendum on eurozone membership. The ND and PASOK increased their seats and were able to form a coalition government with DIMAR on June 21. Both PASOK and DIMAR took the unusual step of nominating independents for the cabinet, instead of appointing party members. The outcome reassured financial markets, although Finance Minister Vassilis RAPANOS resigned on June 25, citing ill health. He was replaced by Yannis STOURNARAS. The government survived a no-confidence vote, 179–121, on July 9.

In October an IMF report revealed that Greece would not be able to meet its target of reducing its debt-to-GDP ratio to 120 percent by 2020. In December, the EU/IMF agreed to provide €49.1 in bailout payments that had been stalled because of delays in implementing austerity measures and a broad privatization initiative. Meanwhile, the government's austerity measures had reduced the deficit from 10.9 percent of GDP in 2011 to 8.2 percent of GDP in 2012.

As required by the EU/IMF, the parliament on January 12, 2013, approved austerity measures, including an increase on taxes for everyone earning more than €20,000 and a rise on the corporate tax rate from 20 percent to 26 percent. In addition, a range of tax breaks were eliminated. The reforms were expected to raise €2.5 billion annually but sparked continuing protests and demonstrations. Through January a succession of strikes paralyzed Athens and other municipalities as government workers protested pay cuts and reductions in benefits. Meanwhile, the government launched what was described as a "fire sale" of assets, including islands and other properties,

In March the EU/IMF delayed payment of €2.8 billion in aid after the government failed to follow-through on a pledge to fire 7,000 civil service workers who were guilty of various minor crimes and to transfer 25,000 others to a reserve pool of workers whose positions would eventually be eliminated. The EU/IMF agreed in July to disperse €6.8 billion and granted Greece additional time to trim its public sector. By 2015 Greece was supposed to eliminate 180,000 public sector jobs.

On June 11, 2013, Samaras announced the closure of the state broadcasting company, along with the loss of 2,656 jobs. DIMAR opposed the decision and withdrew from the governing coalition in protest on June 21. The loss of DIMAR left the ND-PASOK coalition with a slim three-seat majority in the legislature (see Political parties, below). Through the summer of 2013, there was a marked increase in attacks on immigrants and a concurrent rise in far-right activities as anti-immigrant sentiment rose across the country.

POLITICAL PARTIES

Government Parties:

New Democracy (*Nea Dimokratia*—ND). Formed in 1974 as a vehicle for Konstantinos Karamanlis, New Democracy was, under Karamanlis, a broadly based pragmatic party committed to parliamentary democracy, social justice, an independent foreign policy, and free enterprise. Georgios (George) Rallis, generally viewed as a moderate rightist, was elected party leader on May 8, 1980, and was designated prime minister the next day, following Karamanlis's election as president of the republic. In the wake of the ND's defeat at the 1981 election, Rallis lost an intraparty vote of confidence, and, in a move interpreted as reflecting the ascendancy of right-wing influence within the parliamentary group, he was succeeded in December by the leader of the party's conservative bloc, Evangelos AVEROFF-TOSSITSAS. The latter resigned as leader of the opposition in August 1984, following the ND's poor showing at the European Parliament balloting in June, the moderates rallying to elect Konstantinos Mitsotakis as his successor over Konstantinos Stephanopoulos.

Stephanopoulos, in turn, withdrew with a number of his center-right supporters to form the Democratic Renewal (*Dimokratiki Ananeosi*—DIANA) in September 1985 after Mitsotakis's August redesignation as ND leader, despite the party's legislative loss to PASOK two months earlier. (DIANA was dissolved in June 1994, following its inability to win European Parliament representation.)

The party secured a plurality of 145 seats at the legislative balloting of June 18, 1989, following which it agreed to an unlikely (albeit interim) governing alliance with the Progressive Left Coalition (below, under Coalition of the Left, Movements and Ecology) to ensure parliamentary action that would permit the lodging of indictments against former prime minister Papandreou. After the ensuing election of November 5, at which it again fell short of a majority, it joined in a three-way coalition that included PASOK to govern until new balloting on April 8, 1990, at which it won exactly half of the seats. With DIANA's external support, Mitsotakis on April 11 was able to form a new single-party administration, which survived until the early election of October 10, 1993. As a result of the ND defeat, Mitsotakis on October 26 announced his resignation as party leader, and Miltiadis EVERT defeated Ioannis VARVITSIOTIS in a race for the succession.

The party was second to PASOK in the June 1994 European Parliament balloting, winning 9 of 25 seats, and won the Athens mayoralty in October. In the September 1996 balloting the ND slipped to 38.1 percent of the vote and 108 seats, remaining in opposition. Evert resigned as ND leader in the wake of the poll but decided to contest the resultant leadership election, thereby aggravating a long-running internal feud that was not resolved by his reelection as leader in October. Ranged against Evert was former prime minister Mitsotakis, who backed the candidacy of his daughter, former ND culture minister Dora Bakoyannis, as well as the candidacies of Stephanos MANOS (former finance minister) and Georgios SOUFLIAS (former education minister). Souflias received the backing of the other two contenders in the unsuccessful bid to prevent Evert from regaining the leadership, following which the party stepped back from the brink of an open split by referring the leadership issue to a full party congress in 1997.

Konstantinos (Kostas) Karamanlis, a nephew of former president Karamanlis (who died in April 1998), was elected as the new president of the party during the fourth congress on March 21, 1997, Evert losing in the first round. Intraparty friction continued in 1998 and 1999, contributing, among other things, to the defection of Manos. However, Manos and the Liberals agreed to support Karamanlis in the April 2000 legislative balloting in which the ND came within one percentage point of assuming governmental control.

In local elections on October 20, 2002, Dora Bakoyannis, the wife of Pavlos BAKOYANNIS, a prominent party member assassinated in 1989 by the terrorist November 17 Revolutionary Organization, was elected the first female mayor of Athens with 61 percent of the vote. The ND won other local races as well, demonstrating the growing decline of voter support for PASOK. In the March 7, 2004, elections, the ND wrested control of government from the long-governing PASOK, winning 165 seats and the prime ministership for Karamanlis.

Eleftherios Zagoritis replaced Evangelos MEIMARAKIS as party secretary in 2006 when Meimarakis accepted the post as defense minister. The party is informally split into two major factions: the Karamanlis supporters, who claim to be the continuation of the pre-1967 right, and the Mitsotakis supporters, who represent the pre-1967 center, which joined ND after 1974. The Mitsotakis faction has opted for full support of Karamanlis but could reassert itself if Karamanlis declared his intention to withdraw from politics or suffered a serious electoral defeat.

Following the line of Prime Minister Karamanlis, the party has carefully avoided raising thorny political issues, such as acceleration of the privatization program, despite rhetoric in favor of reform. This has secured high levels of public opinion support, which only wavered after the August 2007 fires. Despite clumsy attempts to fault previous PASOK governments for "foreign sabotage," the party was able to survive the crisis with minor losses in the 2007 elections.

Beginning in 2009 public opinion of New Democracy deteriorated, due to recurrent incidents of corruption, which have led Greeks to question the sustainability of the two-party system that has characterized Greek politics since the 1970s.

In the EU elections of June 7, 2009, the ND won 32.3 percent of the vote and 8 seats, second to PASOK. The party suffered the bitterest defeat in its history as it collected only 33.5 percent of the vote and 91 seats in the 2009 parliamentary elections. This was 8.4 percent less than in the 2007 elections and the lowest percentage that the party had ever garnered. On the very night of the elections, Karamanlis announced his resignation from the party presidency. Dora BAKOYANNIS, former foreign minister and daughter of Konstantinos Mitsotakis, promptly announced her intention to run for the post. She was followed by former ministers Dimitrios AVRAMOPOULOS and Antonios SAMARAS. The contenders agreed to significantly increase the number of electors voting for the new party leader. Following Avramopoulos's endorsement of Samaras, the election took place on November 29, 2009, and Samaras won a clear victory. Yet the party continued to suffer in opinion polls, as public opinion considered it to be the primary culprit for the plight of Greek economy. Investigations into ND-era corruption cases and Karamanlis's repeated refusal to defend the policies of his government deteriorated the situation even further. In addition, party unity was threatened by apprehension over Samaras's nationalistic and populist record. Samaras led opposition to the EU-IMF–backed plan at the parliament. Former party presidential contender Dora Bakoyannis was the only party MP to disobey Samaras's line and vote for the plan. This cost her position in the party. She subsequently formed the **Democratic Alliance** (*Dimokratiki Symmachia*) a centrist, pro-EU grouping, which aimed to fill the gap between PASOK and ND. Following a party conference in July 2010, Alexandros Lykourentzos became the new party secretary. The ND placed second in local balloting in November 2010 with 32.8 percent of the vote. In June 2011 Samaras rejected an offer to participate in a government of national unity.

The ND won the May 2012 parliamentary balloting with 108 seats, but Samaras was unable to form a government. The ND secured 129 seats in the June voting, and Samaras was appointed prime minister of a coalition government. In June 2013 an unknown grouping, the Group of Popular Rebels, claimed responsibility for an attack on the ND party's Athens headquarters. The following month, two former ND legislators who left the party to become independents, returned to the party, increasing the ND-led coalition's parliamentary majority from three to five seats.

Leaders: Antonios Samaras (Prime Minister and President of the Party), Konstantinos (Kostas) KARAMANLIS (Former Prime Minister), Konstantinos MITSOTAKIS (Former Prime Minister and Honorary President of the Party), Dimitris AVRAMOPOULOS (Vice President of the Party), Alexandros LYKOURENTZOS (Party Secretary).

Panhellenic Socialist Movement (*Panellinio Sosialistiko Kinima*—PASOK). Founded in 1974 by Andreas Papandreou, PASOK endorsed republicanism and economic socialism. In foreign affairs it committed to the dissolution of European military alliances, abolition of U.S. military installations in Greece, and renegotiation of Greek membership in the EEC. In 1975, in the first of a series of internal crises, the party was weakened by the withdrawal of members who disagreed with Papandreou over a lack of intraparty democratic procedure. However, most of the dissidents rejoined PASOK prior to the 1977 election, at which it won 93 parliamentary seats. The 1981 balloting yielded a PASOK majority, permitting Papandreou to form the country's first socialist government.

On March 9, 1985, PASOK announced that it would not support the reelection of President Karamanlis, offering as its candidate Christos Sartzetakis, who was elected to a five-year term by the legislature in procedurally controversial balloting on March 29. In early parliamentary balloting on June 2, the party secured a somewhat diminished majority that permitted Papandreou to continue as prime minister.

PASOK suffered major reverses at local balloting in October 1986 and was runner-up to the ND at the parliamentary elections of June and November 1989. The party experienced a further, albeit marginal, decline in April 1990 but rebounded at the municipal balloting in October, both alone and in coalition with the Communists. The depth of continuing fissures within PASOK was illustrated at its second congress held September 20–23, when Akis Tsochatzopoulos, Papandreou's choice for election to the newly created post of general secretary of the Central Committee, was approved by a bare majority of one vote. By contrast, Papandreou himself was unanimously reelected party leader and eventually returned as prime minister in October 1993. Subsequently, Papandreou was reelected leader by voice vote at the 1994 congress, with Tsochatzopoulos being reconfirmed by the Central Committee.

Growing divisions within PASOK intensified when Papandreou fell seriously ill in November 1995, the succession struggle being complicated by the political ambitions of his wife, Dimitra Liani. Following Papandreou's resignation in January 1996, four candidates stood for the PASOK parliamentary leadership (and thus the premiership), the victor in balloting of PASOK deputies being the reformist Konstantinos Simitis, who defeated establishment candidate Tsochatzopoulos 86 votes to 75 in the second round. Papandreou died on June 23 and was succeeded as PASOK president by Simitis, who on June 30 again defeated Tsochatzopoulos in balloting at a special party congress, winning 53.5 percent of delegates' votes. He went on to lead PASOK to a further election victory in September, a reduced vote share of 41.2 percent yielding an overall majority of 162 seats.

Simitis was reelected as PASOK leader at a March 1999 congress, although populist influence reportedly grew in the new 180-member Central Committee. Of particular concern to the populist wing were the government's tight economic policies, seen as constituting a threat to organized labor and other traditional PASOK constituencies. After PASOK narrowly won the April 2000 legislative balloting, Simitis was reelected as party leader during an October 2001 congress at which he rebuffed a challenge from the leader of the populist wing, Akis Tsochatzopoulos, who was subsequently replaced as Greece's minister of national defense.

By 2003 polls showed growing support for PASOK's main political rival, the ND. In response, Simitis resigned as leader of the party and was replaced by Foreign Minister Georgios (Giorgos) Papandreou. Papandreou faced voter discontent with corruption, the government's management of the economy and the stock exchange crisis, and the preparations for the 2004 Olympics. In legislative elections in March 2004, PASOK received 40.55 percent of the vote, thereby losing governmental control to the ND for the first time in a decade.

Papandreou's election as party leader shortly before the 2004 elections brought a popular, liberal politician to the PASOK leadership. However, Papandreou soon came under pressure from the conservative leftist faction within his party, which firmly opposed his reform agenda. He then moderated his positions, disappointing the reformist segment of Greek society without maintaining PASOK's appeal to more leftist voters. This ambivalence contributed to PASOK's decreased representation in parliament in the 2007 elections, in which the party lost 15 seats compared to its 2004 showing.

Papandreou was elected president of Socialist International, the worldwide organization of socialist parties, on January 31, 2006.

In direct balloting for party leadership on November 11, 2007, Papandreou secured reelection, winning significantly with 56 percent of the vote, while Venizelos collected 38 percent and the third candidate, Konstantinos (Kostas) SKANDALIDIS, secured 6 percent. Despite Papandreou's easy victory, opinion polls showed that the party was persistently failing to capitalize on rising discontent with the government, while the party continued to lose voters to more-leftist parties.

A major party crisis occurred on June 12, 2008, when, following Ireland's rejection of the Lisbon Treaty (see 2009 Ireland entry), former prime minister Simitis opposed Papandreou's proposal that a similar referendum be held in Greece. Papandreou refrained from expelling Simitis from the party but did expel him from PASOK's parliamentary group. This unprecedented move against a former prime minister and party president manifested the deep internal divide that plagued PASOK. In the EU elections of June 7, 2009, PASOK won 36.64 percent of the vote and eight seats. This was PASOK's first victory under George Papandreou, the victory solidifying his position in the party's leadership and demonstrating the party's potential to win back a majority in the next parliamentary elections.

PASOK returned to power with a resounding victory in the 2009 parliamentary elections. It garnered 43.9 percent of the vote and 160 seats, thus improving its electoral performance by 5.8 percent compared to the 2007 parliamentary elections. However, Papandreou faced discontent within the party over the government's austerity program. Papandreou's leadership was tested when he nominated Sokratis XYNIDIS for the post of the party's general secretary. While Xynidis was finally elected on October 23 with about 58 percent of the vote, Georgios PANAGIOTAKOPOULOS, a candidate representing statist and nationalist party members, garnered more than 41 percent of the vote. Party opposition also emerged in May 2010, when party MPs Ioannis DIMARAS, Sophia SAKORAFA, and Vassileios OIKONOMOU refused to vote for the EU-IMF-backed reform package brought to the Parliament by the PASOK government. They were immediately removed from the party's parliamentary ranks by Papandreou. Following Xynidis's appointment to an alternate minister's position, Michael KARCHIMAKIS was elected as new party secretary on September 14. In local elections PASOK was placed first with 34.7 percent of the vote. Papandreou resigned as prime minister on November 11. He was subsequently replaced as party leader by Evangelos VENIZELOS.

PASOK suffered one of its worst electoral defeats in the May 2012 legislative balloting when it fell to third place and secured only 41 seats. Its decline continued the next month when it lost an additional 8 seats in new elections. On December 28 PASOK expelled former finance minister Georgios PAPACONSTANTINOU after reports revealed that he had allegedly erased the names of family members from a computer disk that listed more than 2,000 wealthy Greeks who had banks accounts in Switzerland and who may have been attempting to evade Greek taxes.

During a cabinet reshuffle in June 2013, Venizelos was appointed deputy prime minister.

Leaders: Evangelos VENIZELOS (Deputy Prime Minister and Party Leader), Konstantinos SIMITIS (Former Party Leader), Michael KARCHIMAKIS (General Secretary).

Opposition Parties:

Democratic Left (*Dimokratiki Aristera*—DIMAR). The Democratic Left was formed in 2010 by dissident members of the moderate wing of SYRIZA. Four SYRIZA members of parliament joined the new grouping. At the party's first congress in April 2011, Fotis Kouvelis was elected chair of the grouping. In local polling in November 2010 the Democratic Left secured 2.2 percent of the vote and seven seats on municipal councils. DIMAR won 19 seats in the May 2012 balloting and 17 in the June polling. It subsequently joined the ND-led government but withdrew in June 2013 over a dispute about the closure of the state-run broadcasting corporation.

Leader: Fotis KOUVELIS.

Independent Greeks (*Anexartitoi Ellines*—ANEL). A conservative, antibailout party formed in February 2012 by former ND deputy Panos KAMMENOS and other party members who had been expelled for opposing the EU-IMF rescue package. In the May parliamentary elections, ANEL surprised observers by winning 33 seats. However, in the June balloting, its seat total declined to 20. Kammenos suffered minor injuries during an attack by anti-fascist demonstrators in September 2013.

Leaders: Panos KAMMERNOS (Party Leader), Mihalis GIANNAKIS (General Secretary).

Golden Dawn (*Chryssi Avgi*). A far-right party, formed in 1993, the Golden Dawn remained an extremist fringe party through most of its history. However, its opposition to the austerity measures mandated by the EU-IMF bailout package and its anti-immigration stance dramatically increased the party's popularity ahead of the May 2012 elections. Golden Dawn placed fifth in the balloting with 21 seats. In the June parliamentary polling, the party secured 18 seats. Through 2013 members of Golden Dawn were blamed for a series of attacks on immigrants and leftist groups. For instance, in September, a member of the Golden Dawn stabbed and killed Pavlos Fyssas, a popular rapper, known for his anti-racism lyrics. The attack led to ongoing efforts to ban the Golden Dawn.

Leader: Nikolaos MICHALOLIAKOS.

Communist Party of Greece (*Kommounistiko Komma Elladas*—KKE). The KKE is Greece's historic communist grouping, from which the more moderate wing, KKEs (see under Coalition of the Radical Left, above), split in 1968. KKE became the fourth-largest party in Parliament at the 1977 election but experienced numerous membership defections during 1980 in reaction to leadership support of the Soviet intervention in Afghanistan. It recovered to become the only group other than PASOK and New Democracy to secure parliamentary representation in 1981.

Following the 1984 election for the European Parliament, the KKE distanced itself from PASOK, seeking to attract voters from the latter's left wing and hoping to increase its leverage in the next Parliament should PASOK fail to secure a majority. The KKE's continued unwillingness to support PASOK in second-round balloting contributed to the governing party's poor showing in the 1986 municipal elections.

During the latter half of 1989 the KKE experienced renewed internal dissonance. A dispute with the party's youth organization resulted in the dismissal of the latter's entire Central Committee in late September, while a number of trade union affiliate members withdrew to form an anti–Coalition "Militant Initiative" in mid-October. Additional defections followed, including the resignation of eight Central Committee members in late November in protest of the formation of an ecumenical administration.

During the party's 1991 congress "conservatives" won control of the Central Committee over reformists, 60–51, and proceeded to confound earlier expectations by electing Aleka Papariga, a hard-liner, as general secretary. Although the chances of realignment within *Synaspismos* appeared to have been improved by the selection of a KKE reformist to succeed Florakis as Coalition president on March 18, Papariga announced in mid-June that she was taking the KKE out of the alliance. Subsequently, seven reformers, including Coalition leader Damanaki, were suspended from the party's Central Committee.

The KKE won 9 parliamentary seats in a vote share of 4.5 percent in October 1993 and 2 European Parliament seats in June 1994. It improved further to 5.6 percent (and 11 seats) in the September 1996 general election. After organizing many of the antigovernment protests and orchestrating anti-West sentiments during and after the NATO bombing of Yugoslavia (see Foreign relations, above), the KKE won 5.5 percent of the vote at the general election in April 2000, thereby retaining its 11 seats. In the 2004 elections the KKE received 5.9 percent of the vote and 12 seats in the Parliament. Harilaos Florakis, the party's general secretary from 1972 to 1989 and honorary president, died in March 2005.

To widen its electoral appeal, the party has increasingly imbued its antiglobalization, anti-U.S. rhetoric with nationalism. As chair, Papariga has forged an alliance with nationalist media personalities, such as Liana KANELLI, who was elected to parliament on the KKE ticket in 2004 and 2007. This move paradoxically increased the appeal of KKE within the ranks of rightist, hard-line religious voters, who shared similar views. The party also firmly opposed all reform programs and eschewed any offers of cooperation from more moderate leftist parties.

In the September 2007 elections, however, the party increased its number of seats to 22, subsequently furthering its anti-EU, anti-U.S. stance by criticizing PASOK and SYRIZA for their alleged half-hearted opposition to government policies and support of EU and U.S. positions. In the 2009 EU elections the KKE garnered 8.4 percent of the vote and 2 seats. This performance appeared to confirm the electoral strength of the party as well as its leading position on the Greek left, which was briefly challenged by SYRIZA. In the 2009 parliamentary elections KKE garnered 7.5 percent of the vote and 21 seats, 0.6 percent less than in the 2007 elections. This was a rather poor performance for the party, which had expected to benefit from the social unrest that had characterized Greece since 2007. Following the announcement of the EU-IMF-backed fiscal austerity and structural reform program, KKE attempted to spearhead popular opposition and supported civil disobedience. The KKE was third in local elections in November 2010 with 10.9 percent of the vote.

In May 2012 the KKE secured 36 seats in parliamentary elections, but its total declined to 12 seats in the subsequent June balloting. Longtime party leader Papariga resigned in April 2013 and was replaced by Dimitris KOUTSOUMBAS.

Leader: Dimitris KOUTSOUMBAS (General Secretary).

Coalition of the Radical Left (*Synaspismos Rizospastikis Aristeras*—SYRIZA). SYRIZA was formed in January 2004 by *Synaspismos*/SYN, independent activists, and several small leftist groups, including the **Renewing Communist Ecological Left** (*Ananeotiki Kommounistiki Oikologiki Aristera*—AKOA), the **Internationalist Workers Left** (*Diethnis Ergatiki Aristera*—DEA), the **Movement for the Unity of Action of the Left** (*Kinima gia tin Enotita Drasis tis Aristeras*—KEDA), and **Active Citizens** (*Energoi Polites*). The coalition secured 3.3 percent of the vote and 6 seats (all held by members of *Synaspismos*/SYN) in the March 2004 elections. Alexandros (Alekos) Alavanos was subsequently elected president of *Synaspismos*/SYN, thereby becoming the leader of SYRIZA.

Despite persistent efforts to establish communication and cooperation with the KKE (below), SYRIZA met with KKE's rejection, while SYRIZA rebuffed attempts by PASOK to establish political cooperation. However, a number of other parties joined SYRIZA prior to the September 2007 elections, at which SYRIZA, benefiting from public discontent with PASOK, significantly increased its electoral support by winning 5 percent of votes and 14 seats. This trend continued through late 2007 and early 2008, as SYRIZA capitalized on PASOK's recurrent crisis as well as the popularity of new *Synaspismos*/SYN president Alexis Tsipras. At one point, opinion polls suggested that SYRIZA might be able to challenge PASOK's supremacy on the left of the Greek political spectrum. However, while SYRIZA succeeded in collecting much of the protest vote against the two big political parties, it failed to produce a comprehensive political program. The December 2008 riots proved to be the turning point for SYRIZA's high ambitions. Its tolerant stance against the rioters alienated a large share of SYRIZA's potential voters.

In the 2009 EU elections SYRIZA won 4.7 percent of the vote and 1 seat, disappointing party leaders who had fostered hopes at one time of challenging PASOK's leading political position in the left-of-center. The poor result sparked a feud among radicals and moderates within the party, which was further complicated by deteriorating relations between party leader Tsipras and parliamentary leader Alavanos. While many feared that internal strife would make SYRIZA miss the 3 percent electoral threshold and its parliamentary presence, it collected 4.6 percent and 13 seats in the 2009 parliamentary elections. This was 0.4 percent less than in the 2007 parliamentary elections, but given the ominous pollster predictions it appeared as a relative success. Like KKE, SYRIZA appeared unable to benefit from social upheaval and the rise of severe economic and social problems, as it failed to provide a convincing alternative. Following the June 2010 SYN conference, Parliament members Fotios KOUVELIS, Nikolaos TSOUKALIS, Grigorios PSARIANOS, and Athanassios LEVENTIS withdrew from the SYRIZA parliamentary group. They later joined the newly formed Democratic Left (*Dimokratiki Aristera*) party (see below). In local balloting in November 2010 SYRZIA secured 5 percent of the vote.

SYRZIA's opposition to the austerity measures of the EU bailout propelled it to second place in the May 2012 parliamentary polling. It secured 52 seats and emerged as the leading antibailout party. In the June polling, the party again placed second and increased its seats to 71. Through the fall of 2013, SYRIZA played a leading role in organizing anti-austerity demonstrations and strikes, both to protest government actions and to undermine the ND-led coalition.

Leaders: Alexios (Alexis) TSIPRAS (Leader), Alexandros (Alekos) ALAVANOS (Former Leader).

Coalition of the Left, Movements and Ecology (*Synaspismos tis Aristeras ton Kinimaton Kai tis Oikologias*—SYN). Also referenced as SYN, *Synaspismos* is a successor to the Progressive Left Coalition (*Synaspismos tis Aristeras kai tis Proodou*), which was formed prior to the June 1989 balloting as an alliance of the KKE (below) and the Greek Left (*Elliniki Aristera*—EAR), plus a number of minor leftist formations. The action served to mitigate a deep rupture that had existed in Greek Communist ranks since 1968. While the drive to promote a broad alliance (*symparataxis*) of the "forces of the Left" had been initiated in early 1988 by the KKE's Harilaos FLORAKIS, the Coalition's eventual leaning was closer to that of the EAR.

The Greek Left had been formally launched in 1987 during an April 21–26 constituent congress of the majority faction of the Communist Party of Greece–Interior (*Kommounistiko Komma Elladas–Esoterikou*—KKEs). (For more on the early history of the SYN, please see the 2013 *Handbook.*) The action implemented a decision of the KKEs's fourth national conference in May 1986 to reorganize as a more broadly based party of the left, thereby rejecting an appeal by its (then) secretary, Ioannis (Yannis) BANIAS, that a long-standing specific identification with Marxism-Leninism be retained. The KKEs had been founded in 1968 as the result of a split in the KKE, although the two formations joined with the United Democratic Left (*Eniaea Dimokratiki Aristera*—EDA) to contest the 1974 election as members of a United Left coalition. Ultimately emerging as Greece's principal "Eurocommunist" group, the KKEs participated in the 1977 election as a member of the Alliance of Progressive and Left-Wing Forces (*Symmachia Proodeftikon kai Aristeron Dynameon*), winning one of the Alliance's two seats. Unsuccessful in 1981, it regained a single seat in 1985 and subsequently increased its representation under its new name as a member of *Synaspismos*. The EAR dissolved itself in June 1992, being merged into *Synaspismos,* which became a single party.

Following the 1993 election, at which the Coalition fell marginally short of the 3 percent threshold needed for parliamentary representation, Maria DAMANAKI resigned as president, with a party congress electing Nikolaos (Nikos) KONSTANTOPOULOS as her successor. Subsequently, the group recovered to win two seats at the June 1994 European Parliament poll and ten seats in the September 1996 general election (on a vote share of 5.1 percent). The Coalition secured only 3.2 percent of the vote (6 seats) in the 2000 legislative balloting.

At a party conference in June 2003 *Synaspismos* formally changed its name from the Progressive Left Coalition to the

Coalition of the Left, Movements and Ecology in order to appeal to "Green" voters. However, the party continued to use *Synaspismos/* SYN as its official designation.

Synaspismos became the senior partner to smaller, hitherto unknown leftist groups at the formation of SYRIZA in January 2004. After the March elections, in which SYRIZA had barely managed to surpass the electoral threshold, economist Nikolaos Konstantopoulos resigned as party leader after a decade in the post and was succeeded by Alexandros Alavanos. Alavanos aimed to give the party a more radical image and furthered cooperation with small leftist groups, which vehemently opposed globalization, privatization, and the reform agenda, which the ND and PASOK claimed to support. Special attention was given to educational reform, and SYRIZA spearheaded the opposition against a proposed constitutional amendment banning non-state universities. An unexpectedly high electoral performance in the Athens municipal elections of October 2006 promoted the reputation of Alexios (Alexis) Tsipras, a strong secondary candidate for the mayorship, as a potential party leader. Meanwhile, the center-left faction of the party was informally led by Michael PAPAGIANNAKIS who died after a long illness on May 26, 2009.

The strengthening of Tsipras's position following the 2009 elections led to his clear victory in a party conference held in June 2010. In the aftermath of this conference, the moderate wing of the party withdrew, citing its opposition to the unconstructive and polemical politics of Tsipras, as well as his identifications with marginal leftist groups.

Leaders: Alexios (Alexis) TSIPRAS (President), Alexandros (Alekos) ALAVANOS (Former President), Nikolaos (Nikos) HOUNTIS (Secretary), Andreas KARITZIS.

Other Parties:

Popular Orthodox Rally (*Laikos Orthodoxos Synagermos*—LAOS). The LAOS party was formed in 2000 by ND dissident Georgios Karatzaferis as a far-right, anti-immigrant party that emphasized populism and the cultural "superiority" of the Greek Orthodox religion. During the snap election of 2007, when the party received 3.8 percent of the vote and 10 seats (for more on the early history of LAOS, please see the 2013 *Handbook*).

In 2009 LAOS focused on the issue of illegal immigration. In the EU elections in June, LAOS received 7.2 percent of the vote and 2 seats, a significant increase over previous EU elections. In the 2009 parliamentary elections LAOS garnered 5.6 percent of the vote and 15 seats, 1.8 percent more than in the 2007 parliamentary elections. This was a significant success for a party that had struggled to avoid the fate of other far-right parties and to establish itself in the Greek political scene. While the election of Antonis Samaras to the leadership of ND was expected to put additional pressure on LAOS, given Samaras's nationalistic and populist credentials, Karatzaferis changed course by taking a more constructive stance, and LAOS was the single parliamentary party that offered partial support to the government on the EU/IMF reform and austerity package. This implied Karatzaferis's interest in rebranding LAOS as a "moderate" right-wing party. During local balloting in November 2010, LAOS secured 4 percent of the vote and was placed fifth among the parties that contested the elections.

In the May 2012 polling, LAOS secured less than 3 percent of the vote and therefore no seats in the legislature. In the June balloting, LAOS received less than 2 percent of the vote. In 2013 former LAOS member Adonis GEORGIADIS, who left the party to join the ND, was appointed minister of health.

Leaders: Georgios KARATZAFERIS (President), Othon FLORATOS (Director General).

Ecologists-Greens (*Oikologoi-Prasinoi*). Following a brief rise of Ecologists-Alternatives (*Oikologoi-Enallaktikoi*) in the late 1980s-early 1990s, this party, founded in December 2002, represents the most serious attempt at the establishment of a green party in the Greek political spectrum. Led by a group of prominent environmentalists, among them Michael (Michalis) TREMOPOULOS, who frequently made headlines with his campaigns, the party benefited from growing popular discontent with established political parties.

In the 2007 parliamentary elections the Greens won just 1 percent of the vote. In the 2009 EU elections the party won 3.5 percent of the vote and one seat. This was a clear success, although opinion polls had suggested even higher numbers as the party entered the European Parliament for the first time. In the 2009 parliamentary elections, the Greens secured 2.5 percent of the vote, thus failing to cross the 3 percent threshold for parliamentary representation. Following the parliamentary election they rejected the offer of Prime Minister Papandreou to participate in the cabinet. In the November 2010 local elections the Greens garnered 2.8 percent of the vote.

In the May 2012 elections, the Greens received 2.9 percent of the vote. Its share declined to just 0.9 percent in the June balloting.

Leaders: Philippos DRAGOUMIS, Eleonora ZOTOU, Orestis KOLOKOURIS, Aekaterini (Katia) LEMBESSI, Eleni (Lenio) MYRIVILI, Nikolaos (Nikos) CHRYSSOGELOS (Members of the Executive Secretariat).

Other formations and parties that participated unsuccessfully in the 2012 legislative elections include (all received less than 1 percent of the vote), the **Centrists' Union** (*Enosi Kentroon*—EK); the **Marxist-Leninist Communist Party of Greece** (*Marxistiko-Leninistiko Kommounistiko Komma Ellados*—M-L KKE); the **Recreate Greece** (*Dimiourgia Xana*) electoral alliance; the **Anticapitalist Leftist Cooperation** (*Antikapitalistiki Aristeri Synergasia-ANT.AR.SY.A*); the **Greek Ecologists** (*Ellines Oikologoi*); the **Society Political Party of Kapodistrias Followers** (*Koinonia Politiki Parataxi Synechiston tou Kapodistria*); the **Labor Revolutionary Party** (*Ergatiko Epanastatiko Komma*); **OAKKE—Organization for the Restructuring of KKE** (*Organosi gia tin Anasyngrotisi tou KKE*—OAKKE); the **Peasant Labor Movement of Greece** (*Panagrotiko Ergatiko Kinima Ellados*—PAEKE); **National Hope** (*Ethniki Elpida*); the **Pirate Party**; the **I Don't Pay Party**; the **Panathinaikos Movement** (PANKI); the **Liberal Party** (LIBERTAS); and the **Democratic Alliance** (*Dimokratiki Symmachia*—DISY).

For more information on the **Democratic Social Movement** (*Dimokratiko Kinoniko Kinima*—DIKKI), and the **Democratic Renaissance** (*Dimokratiki Anagennisi*—DA), please see the 2012 *Handbook.*

Extremist Groups:

November 17 Revolutionary Organization (*Epanastatiki Organosi 17 Noemvri*—EO17N). The EO17N is a leftist urban guerrilla organization named after the date of the famous Athens Technical University (*Polytechneio*) insurrection, which had been violently crushed by the military junta on November 17, 1973. The grouping surfaced in 1975 and subsequently claimed responsibility for numerous assassinations and violent attacks. Among its victims were CIA Station Chief Richard Welch, former police officer Evangelos MALLIOS, ND MP Pavlos Bakoyannis, and steel magnate Dimitrios (Dimitris) ANGELOPOULOS. In October 1991 the group claimed responsibility for the attempted murder of a press attaché at the Turkish Embassy in Athens. In July 1992 the EO17N unsuccessfully attempted to assassinate the minister of finance, while in July 1994 it claimed responsibility for the assassination of a Turkish diplomat. In February 1996 an unsuccessful attack on the U.S. Embassy in Athens was believed to have been planned by the EO17N. Subsequently, the EO17N claimed responsibility for the assassination in Athens in June 2000 of a British defense attaché, saying the killing was a response to the NATO air attacks in Yugoslavia in 1999. Greek authorities subsequently came under intensified pressure for the lack of arrests in regard to EO17N activities.

In 2003 Greek authorities made a series of arrests and gained convictions of the top leadership of EO17N. Leader Alexandros GIOTOPOULOS and the group's alleged main assassin, Dimitris KOUFONTINAS, both received multiple life sentences during trials in December 2003. In addition, 12 others were convicted of terrorism charges. The sentences of 13 of the defendants were upheld by the Court of Appeals on May 14, 2007. The convictions effectively ended the operational capabilities of EO17N.

Other terrorist groups include the **May 1st Revolutionary Organization,** the **People's Revolutionary Struggle** (*Epanastatikos Laikos Agonas*—ELA), and the **Revolutionary Nucleus** (*Epanastatikos Pyrinas*—EP), all of which allegedly carried out attacks against "capitalist" and "imperialist" targets throughout the 1980s and 1990s. The People's Revolutionary Struggle split into several factions in 1995. One of these groups, the **Revolutionary Struggle** (*Epanastatikos Agonas*—EA), exploded three bombs in Athens on May 5, 2004, to protest the Olympics. On May 13 another bomb exploded outside of a bank, while a second device was found and detonated by police. The police also found and destroyed a bomb near an Olympic site on May 19. Terrorism made an alarming reappearance on January 15, 2007, when an antitank missile was fired against the U.S. Embassy in Athens, causing material damages only. The Revolutionary Struggle group took responsibility for the attack. Following a series of bomb attacks causing only minor damages, on March 10, 2010, two men were spotted by police breaking into a car. Following an exchange of fire one person, later identified as Lampros FOUNTAS, was shot dead, while the other escaped. On March 27, 2010, a 15-year-old Afghan immigrant was killed when a bomb planted on Patission Street exploded in his hands. Following intensive police investigation, on April 10, 2010, six persons were arrested and charged with membership of the Revolutionary Struggle, while the police discovered ammunition in a home of one of the defendants. In April 2013 three members of the EA were convicted for a 2009 attack and each was sentenced to 25 years in prison.

Following the arrests of members of the Revolutionary Struggle, a group identified as the **Revolutionaries Sect** (*Sechta Epanastaton*) resumed terrorist activity, raising concerns about a renewal of terrorist violence in Greece. On June 25, 2010, a parcel bomb addressed to the minister of citizens' protection, Michael CHRYSSOCHOIDIS, exploded within the ministry building. Chryssochoidis's aide Georgios VASSILAKIS, who opened the parcel, was killed in the attack. On July 19, 2010, journalist Sokratis GIOLIAS was murdered in front of his apartment. The Revolutionaries Sect later claimed responsibility for the attack.

The **Conspiracy of Fire Nuclei** (*Synomosia Pyrinon tis Fotias*—SPF), an extreme anarchist group, emerged in 2008 during a series of arson attacks in Athens against banks and car dealerships. Six members of the SPF were arrested in September 2009 in connection with additional bombings and convicted in 2011. In November 2010 the SPF attempted to mail small bombs to a range of targets, including the German, Swiss, and Russian embassies. Two members of the group were arrested for their role in the abortive attacks, which caused only minor injuries. The group claimed responsibility for a letter-bomb attack on a prosecutor in September 2013 (no one was injured in the attack).

LEGISLATURE

The unicameral **Parliament** (*Vouli*) consists of 300 members elected by direct universal suffrage for four-year terms, subject to dissolution. Since 1926 the procedure for allocating seats, usually a form of proportional representation, has tended to vary from one election to another. At the October 1993 balloting, simple proportional representation based on the Hagenbach-Bischoff quota was used in the first distribution, with the Hare quota employed in the second for all parties securing a minimum national vote share of 3 percent. The introduction of the 3 percent electoral threshold in 1990 prompted minority candidates to run on mainstream-party ballots.

Following early elections on June 17, 2012, the seat distribution was as follows: New Democracy, 129; Coalition of the Radical Left, 71; Panhellenic Socialist Movement, 33; the Independent Greeks, 20; Golden Dawn, 18; Democratic Left, 17; and the Communist Party of Greece, 12.

Speaker: Evangelos-Vasileios MEIMARAKIS.

CABINET

[as of September 15, 2013]

Prime Minister	Antonis Samaras (ND)
Deputy Prime Minister	Evangelos Venizelos (PASOK)
State Minister	Dimitris Stamatis (ND)
Ministers	
Administrative Reform and E-Government	Kyriakos Mitsotakis (ND)
Culture and Sports	Panos Panagiotopoulos (ND)
Development and Competitiveness	Kostis Hatzidakis (ND)
Education, Religious Affairs, Culture, and Sport	Konstantinos Arvanitopoulos (ND)
Environment, Energy, and Climate Change	Yannis Maniatis (PASOK)
Finance	Yannis Stournaras (ind.)
Foreign Affairs	Evangelos Venizelos (PASOK)
Government Spokesperson	Simos Kedikoglou (ND)
Health	Adonis Georgiadis (ND)
Infrastructure, Transport, and Networks	Michalis Chryssohoidis (PASOK)
Interior	Yannis Michelakis (ND)
Justice, Transparency, and Human Rights	Charalambos Athanassiou (ND)
Labor and Social Security	Giannis Vroutsis (ND)
Macedonia, Thrace	Theodoris Karaoglou (ND)
Merchant Marine and Aegean	Miltiadis Varvitsiotis (ND)
National Defense	Dimitris Avramopoulos (ND)
Public Order and Citizen Protection	Nikos Dendias (ND)
Rural Development and Food	Athanasios Tsaftaris (ind.)
Tourism	Olga Kefalogianni (ND) [f]

[f] = female

INTERGOVERNMENTAL REPRESENTATION

Ambassador to the U.S.: Christos PANAGOPOULOS.

U.S. Ambassador to Greece: Daniel B. SMITH.

Permanent Representative to the UN: Michel SPINELLIS.

IGO Memberships (Non-UN): CEUR, EBRD, EIB, EU, ICC, IEA, IOM, NATO, OECD, OSCE, WTO.

GRENADA

State of Grenada

Political Status: Independent member of the Commonwealth since February 7, 1974.

Area: 133 sq. mi. (344 sq. km).

Population: 107,247 (2012E—UN); 109,590 (2013E—U.S. Census).

Major Urban Center (2005E): ST. GEORGE'S (3,600).

Official Language: English.

Monetary Unit: East Caribbean Dollar (official rate November 1, 2013: 2.70 EC dollars = $1US).

Sovereign: Queen ELIZABETH II.

Governor General: Cecile LA GRENADE; sworn in on May 7, 2013, succeeding Carlyle GLEAN Sr.

Prime Minister: Keith MITCHELL (New National Party); sworn in on February 20, 2013, succeeding Tillman THOMAS (National Democratic Congress), following legislative election of February 19.

THE COUNTRY

Located close to St. Kitts and Nevis, Grenada encompasses the southernmost of the Caribbean's Windward Islands, about 90 miles north of Trinidad. The country includes the main island of Grenada, the smaller islands of Carriacou and Petit Martinique, and a number of small islets. The population is approximately 75 percent black, the balance being largely mulatto, with a small white minority. English is the official language, while a French patois is in limited use. Roman Catholics predominate, with Anglicans constituting a substantial minority. Women comprise one third of the house of representatives.

Grenada's economy is based on agriculture; bananas, cocoa, nutmeg, and mace are its most important products. Tourism, an important source of foreign exchange, declined substantially in the mid-1970s but subsequently revived. Unemployment has long been a major problem, encompassing upward of 40 percent of the adult population in 1994

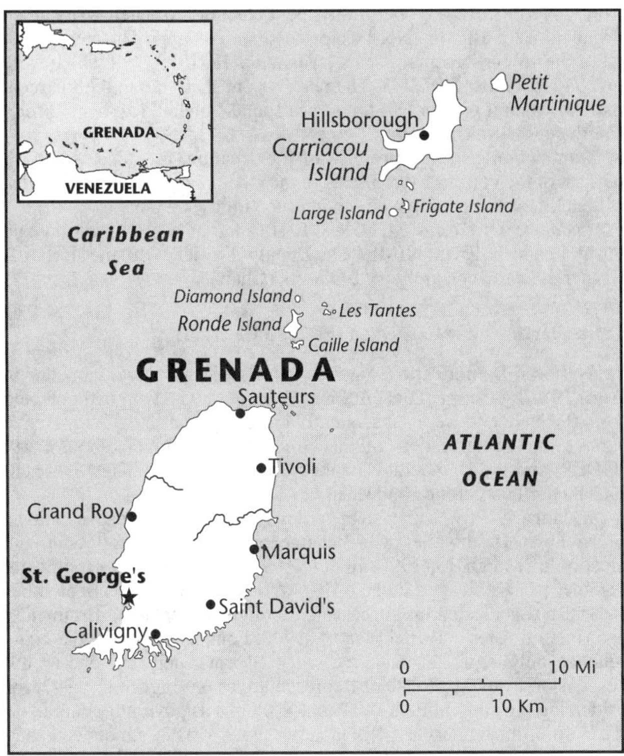

before declining to a reported 13 percent in 2000, only temporarily, before rising to 30 percent by 2010. The country's economy has suffered as a result of several strong hurricanes; Hurricane Ivan, on September 7, 2004, destroyed 90 percent of the country's buildings, with damages estimated in excess of $2 billion and economic contraction of at least 3.5 percent, and a less severe hurricane in July 2005 yielded additional destruction estimated at $200 million. GDP plummeted to -5.7 percent in 2009 with the global recession and declined further in 2010. Due to the lingering impact of the global financial crisis, the economic situation continued to worsen through 2012, leading the government to restructure its debt for the second time in eight years. In 2013 GDP stagnated with 0.5 percent growth, according to the IMF, and inflation was 2.6 percent.

GOVERNMENT AND POLITICS

Political background. Discovered by Columbus on his third voyage in 1498, Grenada was alternately ruled by the French and British until 1783, when British control was recognized by the Treaty of Versailles. It remained a British colony until 1958, when it joined the abortive Federation of the West Indies. In 1967 Grenada became a member of the West Indies Associated States, Britain retaining responsibility for external relations. Eric M. GAIRY, who had been removed from office by the British in 1962 for malfeasance, was redesignated prime minister upon the assumption of internal autonomy.

On February 7, 1974, Grenada became an autonomous member of the Commonwealth, two years after an election that the British interpreted as a mandate for independence. Many Grenadans, however, were opposed to self-rule under Gairy, whom they compared to Haiti's "Papa Doc" Duvalier. United primarily by their dislike of Gairy, the nation's three opposition parties—the Grenada National Party (GNP), the New Jewel Movement (NJM), and the United People's Party (UPP)—contested the election of December 7, 1976, as a People's Alliance. Although failing to defeat the incumbent prime minister, the Alliance succeeded in reducing the lower house strength of Gairy's Grenada United Labour Party (GULP) to 9 of 15 members.

In the early morning of March 13, 1979, while the prime minister was out of the country, insurgents destroyed the headquarters of the Grenada Defense Force, and a People's Revolutionary Government (PRG) was proclaimed. Led by Maurice BISHOP, the PRG ruled Grenada until 1984, when the revolution was finally ended by U.S. military forces with OECS endorsement (for more on the revolutionary government, see the 2011 edition of the *Handbook*). Subsequently, a provisional administration under Nicholas A. BRATHWAITE was established, which held office until the installation of Herbert A. BLAIZE as prime minister of a new parliamentary regime on December 4, 1984.

In an unusual development, the allegedly "authoritarian" Blaize lost the leadership of the New National Party (NNP) to Dr. Keith MITCHELL at a party convention held January 21–22, 1989. Six months later Blaize dismissed Mitchell from the cabinet and announced the formation of a new grouping, the National Party (NP). Faced with the certainty of an adverse confidence vote, the prime minister prorogued the legislature on August 23. After a long illness, Blaize died on December 19 and was immediately succeeded by his deputy, Ben JONES, who dissolved Parliament in anticipation of an election that was constitutionally mandated by March 1990.

The election of March 13, 1990, yielded a plurality of seven legislative seats for the National Democratic Congress (NDC), whose leader, Brathwaite, formed an administration that moved from minority to majority status with the May 7 defection to the NDC of a GULP representative. Brathwaite resigned as NDC leader in July 1994 and stepped down as prime minister on February 1, 1995. George BRIZAN succeeded him in both capacities. Brizan was unable to lead the NDC to a legislative victory five months later on June 20 and was replaced by Mitchell, whose NNP had captured 8 of 15 lower house seats. The NNP won all 15 seats in the election of January 1999 but was reduced to a narrow 1-seat margin in November 2003. In early elections on July 8, 2008, the NDC won 11 house seats, and NDC leader Tillman THOMAS succeeded Mitchell as prime minister.

After internal divisions resulting in the expulsion of 10 party members in September 2012, the NDC suffered a major blow in the legislative elections of February 19, 2013, when the NNP, led by Mitchell, won a landslide victory of all 15 seats (see Current issues, below).

Constitution and government. Grenada's constitution, originally adopted in February 1967 and modified only slightly on independence, was suspended following the March 1979 coup but restored in November 1984, the legitimacy of laws enacted in the interim being confirmed by Parliament in February 1985. The British monarch is the nominal sovereign and is represented by a governor general. Executive authority is exercised on the monarch's behalf by the prime minister, who represents the majority party in the House of Representatives, the lower house of the bicameral legislature. The House is popularly elected for a five-year term, while the upper chamber, the Senate, consists of 13 members appointed by the governor general: 10 on the advice of the prime minister, 3 of whom represent interest groups, and 3 on the advice of the leader of the opposition. The judicial system includes a Supreme Court composed of a High Court of Justice and a two-tiered Court of Appeal, the upper panel of which hears final appeals from the High Court. There are also eight magistrates' courts of summary jurisdiction.

Grenada is administratively divided into 6 parishes encompassing 52 village councils on the main island, with the minor islands organized as separate administrative entities.

Freedom of the press, legally protected in Grenada, improved in July 2012 when the legislature decriminalized defamation. However, the government is often accused of taking measures to oppress the media.

Foreign relations. The United Kingdom and the United States recognized the Bishop government in March 1979, but relations subsequently deteriorated. By mid-1982 all of the other six members of the OECS (Antigua, Dominica, Montserrat, St. Kitts-Nevis, St. Lucia, and St. Vincent) were generally hostile. The intervention by U.S. and Caribbean forces following Bishop's murder, coupled with Reagan's assertion that Grenada had become "a Soviet-Cuban colony being readied for use as a major military bastion to export terror," left little opportunity for an improvement in relations between St. George's and Havana under either the interim administration of Nicholas Brathwaite or the restored parliamentary government of Herbert Blaize. Thus, the last Cuban diplomat remaining in Grenada (a chargé d'affaires) departed in March 1984. Subsequently, Grenada participated in the U.S.-backed regional security plan designed to avert future leftist takeovers. On a May 1997 visit to Cuba, Prime Minister Mitchell signed an economic cooperation agreement between the two countries. Grenada has maintained support for Cuba since. (For more on foreign policy under the Bishop regime and Grenada's relationship with Cuba, see the 2012 *Handbook.*)

In 2005 Grenada abruptly severed diplomatic relations with Taiwan, thereby paving the way for ties with the People's Republic of China (PRC), which had offered funding to help with recovery from Hurricane

Ivan. Taiwan responded to the move by demanding full repayment of a $28.1 million debt from the 1990s. In U.S. court, Taiwan secured an order allowing the country to seize payments from airlines and cruise lines due to Grenada's airport and port authority. The U.S. district court overturned the court order in June, releasing Grenada from the mandate. Meanwhile, Grenada has continued to benefit from foreign direct investment by the PRC. In 2011 the PRC pledged $200 million for public works projects, and in March 2012 made plans to renovate a track and field and football stadium that was damaged by Hurricane Ivan in 2004.

In June 2010 Grenada joined with the five other OECS members in an agreement to create an Economic Union, which provided a framework for an OECS Commission, an executive body with decision-making capability. The OECS Economic Union was officially created on January 21, 2011. In addition to the creation of the Economic Union, Grenada became one of the main countries pushing for the integration of the OECS states by allowing free movement of people and goods through the country from other OECS member states. This multilateral decision was finalized at an OECS summit chaired by Prime Minister Thomas in January 2011 and became effective on August 1. Though plans for an integrated economy stalled with the lingering impact of the global financial crisis on the region, Thomas and others expressed hope that the single economy will be achieved by 2015, but some OECS representatives, including Barbados prime minister Freundel Stewart, say that the 2015 deadline is unrealistic. In January 2012, Grenada joined the other states of the OECS in committing to acceding to the appellate jurisdiction of the Caribbean Court of Justice, which would replace the London-based Privy Court as the highest court. In March 2013 Governor General Carlyle GLEAN announced in parliament that a referendum, necessary to adopt the CCJ, will be held within the next two years.

Current issues. In the first half of 2012, three cabinet officials left their posts amid scandal, leading Prime Minister Thomas to reshuffle the cabinet in June—the fourth reorganization in as many years. Facing a motion of no confidence in August, Thomas temporarily suspended and eventually, on September 17, prorogued parliament, ending the legislative session six months early. Tensions within the NDC culminated at the September 30 annual convention, when 10 party members, including five former cabinet ministers, were expelled. After leaving the NDC, former environment minister Glynis BROWN launched a new party, the National United Front (NUF) on November 27 (see Political Parties, below).

In January 2013 Thomas scheduled the next legislative election for February 19. With the NDC weakened by internal divisions, the NNP took a clear lead. The country's soaring unemployment rate and the worsening economy were the election's dominant issues. The NNP won all 15 seats with 58.8 percent of the vote, shutting out the NDC, with 40.7 percent. Six other parties contested unsuccessfully, taking only a small fragment of the vote. More than 80 percent of registered voters participated, and the observers from the OAS declared the election "civil and peaceful." Keith Mitchell was sworn in for his fourth term as prime minister on February 20, 2013.

On May 7, 2013, Cecile LA GRENADE was sworn in as Governor General, succeeding Carlyle Glean, who had announced his retirement in April.

POLITICAL PARTIES

Government Party:

New National Party (NNP). The NNP was launched in August 1984 as an amalgamation of the **Grenada National Party** (GNP), led by Herbert Blaize; the **National Democratic Party** (NDP), led by George Brizan and Robert Grant; the **Grenada Democratic Movement** (GDM), led by Dr. Francis Alexis; and the **Christian Democratic Labour Party** (CDLP), led by Winston WHYTE. In its 1984 campaign manifesto, the NNP formally endorsed the 1983 military intervention and urged that foreign military and police units not be withdrawn. It dominated the elections of December 3, winning 14 of 15 lower house seats. Disagreements and struggles for leadership, causing disarray in the coalition in mid-1985, continued until the former GNP members controlled most of the party, most notably Herbert Blaize as NNP party leader. Consequently, several key leaders defected in 1987.

A far more critical cleavage was revealed in January 1989 when (theretofore) General Secretary Keith Mitchell, who had previously criticized Blaize for contributing to a "lack of camaraderie" among senior members, defeated the prime minister for the party leadership. However, Mitchell asserted that he would not seek the Blaize's removal from government office before the next election. Mitchell was named prime minister after the NNP victory of June 20, 1995. The NNP swept all of the 15 parliamentary seats on January 18, 1999, 7 of which were lost on November 27, 2003. The party's vote share fell to 47.8 percent in 2008 when it won only 4 house seats, and Mitchell lost his bid for a fourth consecutive term.

Campaigning on the promise of job creation, the NNP won 58.8 percent of the vote and all 15 seats in the election of February 19, 2013. Mitchell took office as prime minister the following day.

Leaders: Dr. Keith MITCHELL (Leader of the Opposition and Party Leader), Elvin NIMROD (Deputy Leader), Roland BHOLA (General Secretary), Gregory BOWEN (Chair).

Other Parties That Contested the 2013 Election:

National Democratic Congress (NDC). The NDC was launched in April 1987 by George BRIZAN and Francis Alexis, who had defected from the NNP and were subsequently joined by a variety of anti-Blaize figures, including leaders of the Grenada Democratic Labour Party (GDLP) and the Democratic Labour Congress (DLC). The NDC held its inaugural conference on December 18, 1987.

In January 1989 Brizan stepped down as opposition leader in favor of Nicholas Brathwaite, who became prime minister following the election of March 13, 1990. In July 1994 Prime Minister Brathwaite resigned as party leader; at the NDC's annual convention on September 4, Brizan was elected his successor, although not replacing Brathwaite as prime minister until February 1, 1995. Four months later the NDC retained only 4 of 15 legislative seats. Brizan received a one-month suspension from the House of Representatives on August 27, 1997, for criticizing the appointment of Daniel Williams as governor general.

Before the January 1999 legislative vote, Brizan announced that, because of his declining health, Deputy Chair Joan Purcell would serve as the NDC standard-bearer and attempted, without success, to negotiate an alliance with several smaller parties. The NDC consequently presented its candidates (including Brizan and Purcell) but lost all of its seats in parliament. Brizan subsequently retired, and in October 2000 former tourism minister Tillman Thomas was elected party leader. The NDC won 7 of 15 house seats (on a vote share of 45 percent) in 2003 and became the governing party in 2008, securing 11 seats with 51.2 percent of the vote. Thomas became prime minister on July 9, 2008.

At the September 2012 NDC congress, 10 party members were expelled, accused by Thomas of working against party interest. After running on a platform of increased investment in agriculture and renewable energy, the NDP lost all parliamentary seats in the February 19, 2013, election, winning 40.7 percent of the vote.

Leaders: Tillman THOMAS (Prime Minister and Party Leader), Nazim BURKE (Deputy Leader), Peter DAVID (General Secretary), Simon STANFORD (Chair).

National United Front (NUF). The NUF was launched in November 2012 by former members of the NDC as an alternative to the then-majority party. In the February 2013 election, three candidates unsuccessfully contested.

Leaders: Glynis ROBERTS (Party Leader), Siddiqui SYLVESTER (Chair).

Movement of Independent Candidates (MIC). Founded by Abdurraheem JONES in March 2012, the MIC aims to oppose the partisan system by offering independent candidates. Three candidates unsuccessfully contested the February 2013 balloting.

Leader: Abdurraheem JONES (Party Leader).

Good Ole Democracy (GOD). The GOD offered three candidates in the 1999 election, capturing a minuscule 0.2 percent of the total vote that was, nevertheless, an improvement over its 1995 vote share. It contested only two constituencies, without success, in 2003 and was also unsuccessful in 2008. Two candidates ran and lost in the 2013 election.

Leader: Justin McBURNIE.

Grenada Renaissance Party (GRP). The GRP is a small formation that failed to elect its sole candidate in 2003. Three candidates unsuccessfully contested the 2013 election.

Leader: Martin W. EDWARDS.

Grenada United Patriotic Movement (GUPM). Launched in August 2012, two GUPM candidates ran without success in the February 2013 election.

Leader: Oswald McBURNIE.

People's United Labor Party (PULP). Party founder Winston FREDERICK, the party's sole candidate, unsuccessfully contested the February 2013 election.

Leader: Winston E. FREDERICK (Party Leader).

Other Parties:

Grenada United Labour Party (GULP). The GULP was founded in 1950 as the personal vehicle of Eric M. Gairy, who headed governments from 1951 to 1957, 1961 to 1962, and 1967 to 1979. Having acquired a reputation for both corruption and repression while in office, Gairy did not present himself for election in 1984, when the GULP secured 36 percent of the popular vote. Marcel Peters, the party's only successful candidate, was expelled from the GULP in early 1985, thus leaving the party with no parliamentary representation.

Although Gairy had announced in December 1987 that he was retiring from politics, he faced no opposition in reelection as GULP president at the party's annual convention in December 1988. The party was runner-up to the NDC in the March 1990 balloting, winning four legislative seats, Gairy being among those defeated. Within a year of the 1990 election, three of the four GULP representatives defected from the party, and the fourth was expelled in March 1992 by the party's Executive Council. The GULP won two legislative seats in June 1995.

The GULP contested the January 1999 legislative poll jointly with the DLP (see under PLM, below). The coalition, GULP/United Labour, secured only 12 percent of the vote (and no seats), despite the support of Marcelle GAIRY (the daughter of Eric Gairy), who resigned as Grenada's high commissioner to London to participate in the campaign. For the 2008 legislative poll, the GULP formed a United Labor Platform (ULP) with the PLM, but the electoral alliance was able to secure only 0.8 percent of the vote. Collin FRANCIS resigned as party leader in 2009 and has yet to elect a replacement.

In January 2013 the GULP announced that it would not contest the February 19 general election because of a lack of suitable candidates.

Leaders: Wilfred HAYNES (President), Wayne FRANCIS (Acting Party Leader).

People's Labour Movement (PLM). The PLM was initially launched as the **Democratic Labour Party** (DLP) in December 1995 by four NDC dissidents, led by former attorney general Francis Alexis, who had resigned in July from the parent party claiming it was "finished and done with." It competed in the January 1999 legislative poll in alliance with the GULP (above); a similar alliance was formed for the 2008 balloting. However, the party was weakened by a dispute between Alexis and Dr. Terrence MARRYSHOW that led to the latter's resignation as party president. The party did not contest the 2013 elections.

LEGISLATURE

The bicameral **Parliament** consists of an appointed Senate of 13 members and a popularly elected 15-member House of Representatives.

Senate. Of the 13 members of the upper house, 10 are nominated by the government and 3 by the leader of the opposition. Of the 10 government-nominated senators, 3 are appointed by the prime minister upon the recommendation of the organizations or interests that he or she believes those senators should be selected to represent.

President: Lawrence JOSEPH.

House of Representatives. The lower house comprises 15 members elected for a five-year term subject to dissolution. In the most recent election, of February 19, 2013, the New National Party won all 15 seats.

Speaker: Michael PIERRE.

CABINET

[as of November 1, 2013]

Prime Minister	Keith Mitchell
Deputy Prime Minister	Elvin Nimrod
Ministers	
Agriculture, Lands, Forestry, Fisheries, and the Environment	Roland Bhola
Communications and Works, Physical Development, Public Utilities, and Information Communication Technology	Gregory Bowen
Economic Development, Trade, Planning, and Cooperative	Oliver Joseph
Education and Human Resource Development	Anthony Boatswain
Finance, Energy, National Security, Public Administration, Disaster Preparedness, Homeaffairs, Implementation, and Information	Keith Mitchell
Foreign Affairs and International Business	Nickolas Steele
Health and Social Security	Clarice Modeste-Curwen [f]
Legal Affairs, Attorney General, Labor, Local Government, and Carriacou and Petite Martinique Affairs	Elvin Nimrod
Social Development, Housing, and Community Development	Delma Thomas [f]
Tourism, Civil Aviation, and Culture	Alexandra Otway-Noel [f]
Youth Empowerment, Sports, and Ecclesiastical Relations	Emmalin Pierre [f]
Ministers of State	
Housing, Lands, and Community Development	Glen Noel
Information, Information Communication Technology, and Culture	Arley Gill

[f] = female

INTERGOVERNMENTAL REPRESENTATION

Ambassador to the U.S.: Angus FRIDAY.

U.S. Ambassador to Grenada: Larry Leon PALMER.

Permanent Representative to the UN: Denis G. ANOTINE.

IGO Memberships (Non-UN): Caricom, CWTH, ICC, NAM, OAS, WTO.

GUATEMALA

Republic of Guatemala
República de Guatemala

Political Status: Independent Captaincy General of Guatemala proclaimed 1821; member of United Provinces of Central America, 1824–1838; separate state established 1839; most recent constitution (adopted May 31, 1985, with effect from January 14, 1986) amended by referendum of January 30, 1994.

Area: 42,042 sq. mi. (108,889 sq. km).

Population: 15,263,427 (2012E—UN); 14,373,472 (2013E—U.S. Census).

Major Urban Centers (2005E): GUATEMALA CITY (991,000), Mixco (307,000), Villa Nueva (237,901), Quetzaltenango (114,000), Escuintla (72,000).

Official Language: Spanish.

Monetary Unit: Quetzal (market rate November 1, 2013: 7.94 quetzales = $1US). Since May 1, 2001, foreign currencies have been permitted to circulate and may be used in business transactions.

President: Otto Pérez Molina (Patriotic Party); elected in runoff election on November 6, 2011, and sworn in for a four-year term on January 13, 2012, succeeding Álvaro COLOM Caballeros (National Unity of Hope).

Vice President: Roxana Baldetti (Patriotic Party); elected on November 6, 2011, and sworn in for a term concurrent with that of the president on January 13, 2012, succeeding José Rafael ESPADA (National Unity of Hope).

THE COUNTRY

The northernmost of the Spanish-speaking Central American countries, Guatemala is also the most populous, with an annual population growth rate close to 3 percent. Noted for its high proportion (65 percent) of Indians, the population is concentrated in the southern half of the country. The other major population group, the *ladinos*, is composed of mestizos and assimilated Indians. Although Spanish is the official language, about two dozen Indian languages are spoken, of which the most important are Cakchiquel, Caribe, Chol, Kekchi, Mam, Maya, Pocoman, and Quiché. The dominant religion is Roman Catholicism, although recent inroads by Pentecostal Protestantism have prompted Guatemalan bishops to take a new look at "the discovery of America" and issue calls for a "new evangelism" capable of incorporating indigenous rites and rituals. Women constitute approximately 27 percent of the official labor force, not including subsistence farming and unreported domestic service; employed women are concentrated in sales, clerical jobs, and the service sector and make up 40 percent of professionals. Female participation in government has traditionally been virtually nonexistent but is on the rise. In the 2003 election, women won 15 of 158 seats (9.4 percent); in 2007, the number rose to 17 (10.8 percent). In the 2011 election, women won 21 seats (13.29 percent), and Roxana Baldetti became the country's first female vice president.

The Guatemalan economy is still largely agricultural. Coffee remains by far the single most important source of foreign revenue; cotton, bananas, and sugar are also exported. Significant progress is currently being registered in manufacturing, which, like commercial farming, is predominantly in the hands of *ladinos* and foreign interests. The latter, including investors from the United States, Europe, and Asia, are deeply involved in the *maquiladoras*, virtual sweatshop industries that turn imported materials into finished products (such as textiles) for export.

Severe budgetary difficulties have persisted since the early 1980s, and both poverty and income inequality remain fundamental problems. As of 2011, the World Bank estimated 54 percent of the population lived below the national poverty line. By 2011 about half the children under five years of age were chronically malnourished, the highest child malnutrition rate in Latin America and the fourth highest in the world.

The economy grew at a yearly average of 3.6 percent from 1990 to 2000 and continued that trend with growth averaging 3.9 percent per year from 2001 to 2007, but it fell to 0.5 percent in 2009 with the global recession before rebounding slightly to 2.9 percent in 2010. The economy has shown steady improvement since, with the IMF projecting 3.4 percent growth in 2013. Inflation reached 11.4 percent in 2008, the highest level since the 1990s, due to high fuel and commodity prices but then plummeted in 2009 to 1.9 percent. After reaching a second peak of 6.2 percent 2011, it was 4.3 percent in 2013.

GOVERNMENT AND POLITICS

Political background. Guatemala, which obtained its liberation from Spanish rule in 1821 and its independence as a nation from the breakup of the United Provinces of Central America in 1839, has existed through much of its national history under a series of prolonged dictatorships, including that of Gen. Jorge UBICO from 1931 to 1944. The deposition of Ubico in 1944 by an alliance of students, liberals, and dissident members of the military known as the October Revolutionaries inaugurated a period of reform. Led initially by President Juan José ARÉVALO and then by Jacobo ARBENZ Guzmán, the progressive movement was aborted in 1954 by rightist elements under Col. Carlos CASTILLO Armas. The stated reason for the coup was the elimination of communist influence, Castillo Armas formally dedicating his government to this end until his assassination in 1957. Still another coup, in 1963, overthrew the government of Gen. Miguel YDÍGORAS Fuentes. A new constitution drawn up under Ydígoras's successor, Col. Enrique PERALTA Azurdia, paved the way for the election in 1966 of a civilian president, Julio César MÉNDEZ Montenegro, and the restoration of full constitutional rule with his inauguration on July 1. Col. Carlos ARANA Osorio succeeded Méndez as president in an election held March 1, 1970, amid widespread terrorist activity that included the kidnapping of the nation's foreign minister.

The 1974 presidential and legislative balloting presented a confusing spectacle of charges and countercharges. Initially, it appeared that Gen. Efraín RÍOS Montt, the candidate of the National Opposition Front (a coalition of the Christian Democrats and two minor parties) had placed first in the presidential race by a wide margin. Subsequently, however, the government declared that Gen. Kjell Eugenio LAUGERUD García, the candidate of the ruling right-wing coalition, had obtained a plurality of the votes cast. Since neither candidate was officially credited with a majority, the Congress, controlled by the conservatives, was called on to designate the winner, and named General Laugerud.

Similar confusion prevailed in the election of March 5, 1978, evoking numerous allegations of fraud and threats of violence during five days of indecision by the National Electoral Council, which eventually ruled that the center-right candidate, Maj. Gen. Fernando Romeo LUCAS García, had narrowly outpolled his far right-wing opponent, Colonel Peralta Azurdia.

In the election of March 7, 1982, Gen. Angel Aníbal GUEVARA, the candidate of a new center-right grouping styled the Popular Democratic Front, was declared the victor over three opponents representing far-right, centrist, and center-left interests, with no far-left organizations participating. Two days later the defeated candidates joined in a public demonstration protesting the conduct of the election and calling for annulment of the results. Outgoing president Lucas rejected the public appeal, and on March 23 a group of military dissidents seized power in a bloodless coup aimed at the restoration of "authentic democracy." On March 24 a three-member junta consisting of Ríos Montt, Brig. Gen. Horacio Egberto MALDONADO Schaad, and Col. Francisco Luis GORDILLO Martínez assumed formal authority. Subsequently, on June 9, Ríos Montt dissolved the junta and assumed sole authority as president and military commander.

Although taking office with strong military and business support, Ríos Montt became increasingly estranged from both by a series of anticorruption and economic reform proposals, while incurring mounting opposition from the Catholic Church because of overt proselytizing by a U.S. Protestant sect to which he belonged. Following a number of apparent coup attempts, he was ousted on August 8, 1983, by a group of senior army officers under Brig. Gen. Oscar MEJÍA Víctores, who promised that an election would be held in 1984 to pave the way for "a return to civilian life."

The balloting of August 1, 1984, in which 17 parties participated, was for a National Constituent Assembly, which drafted a new basic law (adopted on May 31, 1985) modeled largely on its 1965 predecessor. In the subsequent general election of November 3, 1985, the Guatemalan Christian Democratic Party (*Partido Democracia Cristiana Guatemalteca*—PDCG) obtained a slim majority of legislative seats, and in a runoff presidential poll on December 8, its candidate, Marco Vinicio CEREZO Arévalo, defeated the National Center Union (*Union del Cambio Nacionalista*—UCN) candidate, Jorge CARPIO Nicolle, with a margin of 68 to 32 percent of the vote. Assuming office on January 14, 1986, Cerezo Arévalo became the first civilian president of Guatemala since Méndez Montenegro in 1966.

From the early 1960s Guatemala was beset by guerrilla insurgency. Initially two groups, the Rebel Armed Forces (*Fuerzas Armadas Rebeldes*—FAR) and the 13th of November Movement (M-13), operated in the country's rural northeast. After 1966 counterinsurgency actions drove the guerrillas into the cities, generating urban violence that claimed the lives of many Guatemalans as well as some members of the foreign diplomatic community. In 1976 a new left-wing group, the Guerrilla Army of the Poor (*Ejército Guerrillero de los Pobres*—EGP), claimed credit for a wave of increased terrorism following a devastating earthquake in February. Both left- and right-wing extremism intensified after the 1978 balloting, with the principal left-wing groups forming in January 1981 a unified military command called Guatemalan National Revolutionary Unity (*Unidad Revolucionaria Nacional Guatemalteca*—URNG). In August 1982 Ríos Montt, describing his counterinsurgency strategy as "scorched earth," established the most extensive Civil Self-Defense Patrol (*Patrullas de Autodefensa Civil*—PAC) network in the world, encompassing virtually every adult male in the countryside and eventually constituting a counter-guerrilla force of nearly 1 million men. Thousands of civilians in the countryside were massacred, mostly by the army and civil patrols, with reports of an estimated 18,000 people killed in 1982. The rebels attempted to establish a "liberated corridor" from Guatemala City to the Mexican border, populated by Indians fleeing army resettlement into "protected" villages; however, vigorous offensive action by the government was reported by late 1983 to have substantially weakened guerrilla operations.

In October 1986 President Cerezo signaled his willingness to enter into peace talks with the country's rebel organizations, including URNG. However, no formal contacts were made with the insurgents until after the August 1987 Esquipulas II Central American peace accord brokered by Costa Rican president Óscar Arias, whose efforts won him the Nobel Peace Prize. A series of exploratory talks began in Madrid under Spanish government auspices in October 1987.

Although the ruling Christian Democrats had won a majority of municipal elections in April 1988, military unrest was evidenced by a failed coup in mid-May, and the administration was forced to cancel a meeting in Costa Rica between the National Reconciliation Commission (*Comisión de Reconciliación Nacional*—CRN) and representatives of the URNG guerrillas. By fall, the president faced mounting opposition from both right-wing extremists buoyed by the recent electoral success of anti-Duarte forces in El Salvador and the human rights Mutual Support Group (*Grupo de Apoyo Mutuo*—GAM), which had long campaigned for the appointment of an independent body to inquire into the fate of the country's missing persons. Civil-military relations were a frequent challenge for Cerezo, the country's first elected civilian leader since Arbenz was deposed in 1954. The president was the target of two serious, but failed, coup attempts from far-right officers in May 1988 and May 1989.

The leading presidential contenders in the run-up to nationwide balloting in November 1990 appeared to be former president Ríos Montt, heading a No Sell-Out (*No-Venta*) coalition of right-wing parties, and Carpio Nicolle of the UCN. In late October, however, the Court of Constitutionality vacated Ríos Montt's final appeal against disqualification because of his involvement in the 1982 coup. Thereafter, Carpio's failure to secure a majority on November 11 forced a runoff on January 6, 1991, which Jorge SERRANO Elías of the recently organized Solidarity Action Movement (*Movimiento de Acción Solidaria*—MAS), with substantial backing from *No-Venta* supporters, won by a better than two-to-one margin.

President Serrano faced four major problems: the fragile state of the nation's economy, an array of human rights abuses by the military, a surge in drug trafficking, and the inconclusive status of negotiations with the URNG. In early February the three leading union federations indicated that they would not join in a new "social pact" before the reversal of a number of government economic policies that included the recent abandonment of price controls and large-scale layoffs of public-sector employees. Concurrently, an official commission reported that there had been 304 killings by "death squads" and 233 "disappearances" in 1990, with Guatemala ranked third, worldwide, in the latter regard. For its part, the United States announced a suspension of military aid in December because of the government's failure to "criticize or exhaustively investigate" those chargeable with human rights abuses, including those responsible for the 1990 death of a U.S. citizen. Earlier, Guatemalan Treasury police revealed that a total of 4,770 kilos of cocaine had been seized in 1990, most of it originating in Colombia, with Guatemala serving not only as a bridge for shipments to the United States but also as a major money-laundering center.

In March and October 1990 the third and fourth rounds of negotiation with URNG representatives were held in Oslo, Norway, and Metepec, Mexico, respectively. The talks proved unproductive because of the Guatemalan military's insistence that it would join in a "dialogue with the subversive delinquents" only after they had laid down their arms. However, the army reversed itself in early 1991, agreeing, for the first time, to participate in a new round of talks launched in Mexico City in late April. The 1991 talks continued in Mexico in June and July, where agreement was reached on the need for "a negotiation process [having] as its final objective the search for peace through political means." A further meeting in Mexico City in September yielded a series of rebel demands, including abolition of the PAC units and an end to military conscription; however, no substantive results were reported.

A round of talks that concluded in late February 1992 also failed to yield a breakthrough, despite pressure on both sides stemming from formal settlement in mid-February of the conflict in neighboring El Salvador. In August a compromise was reached on the Civil Self-Defense Patrols, URNG dropping its demand for their immediate dissolution and the government agreeing not to expand them. In October an agreement (subsequently formalized in a tripartite accord involving the United Nations High Commissioner for Refugees—UNHCR) was concluded on the return of approximately 43,000 Guatemalan refugees, many of whom had spent more than a decade in camps on the Mexican side of the border. By early 1993, however, the parties had become deadlocked over a timetable for implementation of human rights guarantees and the establishment of a truth commission to investigate human rights violations during the lengthy armed conflict.

On May 25, 1993, scarcely more than two weeks after the ruling MAS registered a sweeping victory in municipal balloting, President Serrano attempted to assume near-dictatorial powers that included dissolution of the Congress and dismissal of the Supreme Court. Initially, the action appeared to be supported by the military, but on June 1 the defense minister, Gen. José Domingo GARCÍA Samayoa, responded to widespread popular protests by announcing that both Serrano and Vice President Gustavo ESPINA Salguero had resigned and that Congress would reconvene to select a successor to the ousted head of state. However, the president of the Supreme Court concurred with Espina's contention that he had remained in office, and the military indicated that on constitutional grounds they would accept him as the new chief executive. An unlikely grouping of business, labor, and other leaders then advanced a National Consensus Petition (*Instancia Nacional de Consenso*) that contended that Espina was barred from office because he had supported Serrano's *autogolpe*. The Constitutional Court agreed, and on June 5 the Congress, in a surprising move, selected the country's human rights ombudsman, Ramiro DE LEÓN Carpio, to serve the balance of Serrano's presidential term.

The new chief executive offered the URNG rebels a two-track peace plan that called for the establishment of a representative forum within Guatemala to discuss resolution of the issues that had provoked the conflict, in addition to revival of the talks with rebel leaders in Mexico City. However, the insurgents rejected the overture, as well as a substantially modified plan tendered in early October.

In November 1993, in an effort to purge institutions of unsavory elements, De León proposed a Contract for the Restructuring of the State with Congress, with a referendum encompassing a series of constitutional reforms, including the shortening of congressional and judicial mandates; an increase in the size of the court to 13 members; the review of parliamentary immunity cases by the court, rather than by Congress; increased autonomy for the attorney general and comptroller general; and limitations on the discretionary appointive powers of both president and Congress. A 67.9 percent popular majority approved the proposals on January 30, 1994. However, the turnout was only 16.1 percent, meaning that passage involved only 10.9 percent of the electorate. Despite such dubious authorization, the reforms became law on April 8, paving the way for the election of a new Congress on August 14.

An agreement with URNG representatives on January 10, 1994, to reopen peace talks led two months later to a Global Human Rights Accord and a timetable for continued negotiations. Subsequently, during a UN-mediated meeting in Oslo the two sides agreed to set up a three-member commission to look into Guatemala's unhappy record of human rights violations and acts of violence.

In August 1994 balloting for a truncated congressional term (to January 1996), a turnout of scarcely more than 20 percent of the registered voters gave an unexpected plurality to former president Ríos Montt's Guatemalan Republican Front (*Frente Republicano Guatemalteco*—FRG). Initially excluded from the new congressional directorate by a coalition of other rightist groups, among them the second-ranked National Advancement Party (*Partido de Avanzada Nacional*—PAN), the FRG eventually succeeded in forging an alliance with the PDCG and UCN that yielded the designation of Ríos Montt as legislative president on December 2.

During the first half of 1995 the FRG waged a strenuous campaign to overcome Ríos Montt's disqualification as a candidate in the November 12 presidential elections. In mid-February the Constitutional Court, on technical grounds, rejected a series of *ríosmontista* electoral reforms, with the FRG, despite retention of a slim legislative majority, subsequently losing ground on the issue. On August 9, in the wake of a final ruling by electoral authorities, the general's wife, Teresa Sosa DE RÍOS, requested inscription as the FRG candidate for the November poll, but she was also rejected on constitutional grounds a week later. On August 22 URNG announced a temporary cease-fire to facilitate electoral participation, while declining to endorse any of the contestants.

After failing to win a majority in presidential balloting on November 12, 1995, the PAN's Alvaro Enrique ARZÚ Irigoyen narrowly defeated the FRG's Alfonso PORTILLO Cabrera in a second-round vote on January 7, 1996. Earlier, the PAN had secured outright control of the National Congress by winning 43 of its 80 seats.

Skirmishes with URNG resumed only two days after Arzú's inauguration on January 14, 1996. Talks with rebel leaders did, however, resume in Oslo on February 6 and in Rome on February 12. Two weeks later the president traveled to Mexico for a secret meeting with URNG representatives. The action led to a cease-fire on March 20 and formal negotiations that yielded an agreement on socioeconomic and agrarian affairs on May 6. Earlier, the Guatemalan defense minister, Gen. Julio BALCONI Turcios, had declared that the conflict was over, while the president of the government's peace commission, Presidency Secretary Gustavo PORRAS, expressed his confidence that a definitive peace agreement would be signed by mid-September. However, such a target became increasingly problematic because of heightened hard-line activity within the military by a group styling itself Reclaiming the Guatemalan Army (*Recuperando el Ejército Guatemalteco*—PREGULA), which on August 12 issued a document charging 16 civilians and 57 military officers with treason for their support of the peace negotiations. On the other hand, tangible progress in negotiations with the rebels culminated in the signing in Mexico City on September 19 of a UN-mediated agreement, under which the Guatemalan military undertook to reduce its 46,000-strong complement by one-third in 1997 and to concentrate on defending the country's borders rather than on internal security. Another cease-fire on December 4 was followed by a formal peace accord on December 29 that laid out procedures for reincorporating the guerrillas into civilian life and legalizing URNG, while providing amnesty for a wide range of civil rights violations on both sides of the conflict.

In a May 16, 1999, referendum, an extremely low turnout of voters (18 percent) rejected about 50 constitutional reforms mandated, in large part, by the 1996 accord. As a result, completion of the peace process was substantially imperiled. Earlier, on February 26, an independent Historical Clarification Commission that had been established with UN backing submitted an unexpectedly severe assessment of the 36-year civil war. The commission's report declared that the military had committed "acts of genocide" against the Mayans, including responsibility (together with the PACs) for 85 percent of civilian deaths. It also confirmed earlier reports that the U.S. Central Intelligence Agency had provided both money and training in support of the government effort.

In first-round presidential balloting on November 7, 1999, Alfonso Portillo Cabrera secured 47.8 percent of the vote and went on to defeat the PAN's Oscar BERGER Perdomo by a two-to-one majority in a December 26 runoff. The FRG also won a majority of legislative seats. Portillo oversaw modest reforms to the security forces, most notably the 2003 dissolution of the Presidential General Staff, a notoriously abusive army intelligence unit whose abolishment was stipulated in the 1996 peace agreement.

At the subsequent balloting of November 9, 2003, Oscar Berger's recently organized Grand National Alliance (*Gran Alianza Nacional*—GANA) won a plurality of 49 legislative seats, while Berger himself led in the presidential race and went on to defeat Álvaro COLOM Caballeros of the center-left National Unity of Hope (*Unidad Nacional de Esperanza*—UNE) in a runoff on December 28.

In mid-2003 the Constitutional Court ruled that Ríos Montt could contest the November poll, observing that a ban on persons who had participated in a coup could not be applied retroactively. However, Ríos Montt's third-place finish precluded his involvement in the December runoff. In March 2004 the former president was charged with criminal behavior during disturbances leading up to the court's decision. He was placed under house arrest to prevent his leaving the country but remained politically influential. Meanwhile, former president Portillo fled the country in the face of embezzlement and money laundering charges.

President Berger's post-election 89 percent approval rating plummeted to 25 percent, reflecting soaring crime rates brought on by the *mara* street gangs challenging the drug cartels for control of the drug trade. The police force, which was often subject to corruption, was overwhelmed and failed to prosecute a large proportion of criminals. Violence increased ahead of the September 2007 elections. In February three Salvadoran members of the Central American Parliament (based in Guatemala) and their driver were killed. Four police officers who were arrested in connection with the killings were shot in their cells a few days later, prompting the resignation of the interior minister. Subsequently, two party coordinators for the center-left UNE were killed after leaving a political gathering near the border with El Salvador in April. By the end of May, two other political officials had been killed: a mayoral candidate backed by the Encounter for Guatemala (*Encuentro por Guatemala*—EG) and an activist with the FRG. As public outrage mounted, support grew for the reinstatement of the death penalty, promoted by the UNE presidential candidate Álvaro Colom as well as the *Partido Patriota* (PP) the presidential candidate Otto PÉREZ Molina. Pérez's slogan, "A strong hand now!" highlighted crime control as the centerpiece of his platform. Colom, for his part, pledged to strengthen the attorney general's office and the National Civil Police to curtail the violence that fueled public disenchantment with the traditional parties.

UNE won the largest percentage of the vote (27.1) in the September 9, 2007, legislative election, followed by the PP with 25 percent. The GANA fell to third place with 18.3 percent. In concurrent presidential balloting, the UNE's Colom defeated 13 other candidates in the first round, including Alejandro GIAMMATTEI of the GANA (which declined to support either runoff candidate). Colom secured 52 percent of the vote in runoff balloting on November 4 to defeat the PP's Gen. Otto PÉREZ Molina.

Colom, the first social-democratic president elected in over 50 years, formed a new government on January 14, 2008. Spiraling crime was the main domestic concern for Colom's administration. Several top army officers were fired in 2008, likely for ties to the drug trade. Colom announced a plan to increase the size of the armed forces by 2010 for public security.

In March 2008 Colom formed a panel to declassify military documents connected with the torture, killings, and human rights violations perpetrated during the 36 years of civil war, in the wake of confidential documents that had been leaked to the press a year earlier alleging abuses carried out by Ríos Montt (who won a seat in Congress in 2007). Despite army resistance, Colom succeeded in declassifying the files in June 2011. The International Commission Against Impunity in Guatemala (CICIG), a U.S.-backed UN initiative established to investigate organized crime, helped combat domestic crime. The commission issued its first report in September 2008, stating that 98 percent of crimes committed in Guatemala, and 93 percent of murders, went unpunished. The CICIG subsequently recommended that the Supreme Court create special tribunals for high-profile cases. President Colom created a National Security Council to coordinate internal security strategy the following month. Later that year, after two more drug-related killings claimed 33 lives, Colom abruptly fired the entire military high command. In October 2009, the UN released a crime report that revealed Guatemala had Central America's third highest homicide rate. Separately, the Guatemalan government announced it had confiscated 11 tons of cocaine in 2009—five times as much as it did the year before. A U.S. State Department drug report released in 2010 called Guatemala the "epicenter of the drug threat."

Facing constant opposition from the PP in Congress and lacking enough seats to move its agenda through the legislature, the Colom administration became reliant on negotiating with a new dissident legislative bloc, Renewed Democratic Freedom (*Libertad Democrática Renovada*—LIDER). In order to ease friction with the legislature, in May 2010 Colom's UNE forged an electoral alliance with GANA.

In the legislative election of September 11, 2011, the PP won 56 seats, a slim margin over the UNE-GANA coalition, with 48. As no presidential candidate secured the minimum number of votes in the first round of voting, the presidential contest was decided in the runoff elections of November 6, in which the PP's Otto Pérez Molina defeated LIDER's Manuel Antonio BALDIZÓN (see Current issues, below).

In January 2013 Pérez conducted a minor cabinet reshuffle. That month, the FRG disbanded and reorganized under the banner the **Republican Institutional Party** (*Partido Republicano Institucional*—PRI). Former president Ríos Montt was charged with crimes against humanity in March (see Current issues, below).

Constitution and government. The 1985 constitution, as amended in 1993, mandates the direct election for four-year, nonrenewable terms of a president and a vice president, with provision for a runoff between the two leading slates in the absence of a majority. The president is responsible for national defense, security, and naming a cabinet. Legislative power is vested in a unicameral Congress of 158 members serving four-year terms. The Congress selects the 13 members of the Supreme Court, with the president of the court supervising the judiciary throughout the country; the Supreme Court head also presides over a separate Constitutional Court. Local administration includes 21 departments and the municipality of Guatemala City, each headed by a governor appointed by the president. In December 1986 Congress approved legislation organizing the departments into eight regions.

From 1978 to 1985, 47 Guatemalan journalists were killed, and more than 100 were forced into exile. A 1991 report said "freedom of expression is severely restricted by direct violence targeted at journalists and by an ever-present climate of fear and repression" in Guatemala. A 2008 UN report labeled Guatemala a "country of risk" for journalists, and five journalists were killed in the next three years. Intimidation reportedly came principally from organized crime and clandestine groups. Watchdog groups reported that Guatemalan journalists declined to report on organized crime, human rights violations during the civil war, or corruption. As of September 2013, four journalists had been killed that year. Reporters Without Borders ranked Guatemala 95th out of 179 countries on its 2013 press freedom index.

A new law went into effect in May 2009 that strengthened the rules related to judicial appointments. The new measures, recommended by the CICIG, introduced an evaluation system for determining the qualifications for candidates and regulated the nominations process by which the Congress selected new judges. The new law was not initially put effectively into practice during appointments in September, CICIG and the UN said, when 13 supreme justice court magistrates and 90 appeals court judges were selected for the 2009–2014 term. Several candidates were dropped from the appointment list after their connections to UNE came to light.

Foreign relations. The principal focus of Guatemalan foreign affairs has long been its claim to Belize (formerly British Honduras), which became independent in 1981. Guatemalan intransigence in the matter not only delayed Belizean independence but also adversely affected relations with the United Kingdom, which dispatched military reinforcements to the area in 1975 after receiving reports that Guatemala was massing troops at the border. Despite talks in 1975 and 1976 and a joint commitment in 1977 to a "quick, just, and honorable solution" to the controversy, no agreement was reached. Thus, when the United Kingdom granted independence to Belize in September 1981, the Lucas government severed all diplomatic ties with London and appealed unsuccessfully to the UN Security Council to intervene. In August 1984, representatives of the three leading groups offering presidential candidates for the forthcoming election met in Washington, D.C., with U.S. officials to formulate a policy that would permit formal recognition of Belize and withdrawal of British forces. While no immediate results were forthcoming, the conciliatory posture was continued by the Cerezo administration, and direct discussions were held with Belizean representatives in Miami, Florida, in 1987. Meanwhile, consular relations with the United Kingdom were resumed in August 1986, with full diplomatic ties restored the following January.

After tensions flared with Belize in May 1990 when Guatemalan agricultural workers unknowingly planted crops over the border, Cerezo and Belizean prime minister George Cadle Price met on the Honduran island of Roatán on July 9. The impasse settled after the installation of President Serrano in January 1991. In mid-February Serrano asserted that "Belize has the recognition of the international community" and seven months later overruled his foreign minister (who resigned over the issue) by extending diplomatic recognition to the country. Amid continued domestic controversy the Guatemalan Constitutional Court ruled by a narrow margin in November 1992 that the recognition of Belize was valid, subject to approval by a popular referendum.

A series of cross-border killings and arrests in 1999 and 2000 prompted a meeting between Foreign Minister Gabriel ORELLANA Rojas and Belizean prime minister Said Musa (for more, see the 2013 *Handbook*). Though they reached an agreement on a mechanism for resolving further border and territorial disputes, incidents involving Guatemalan peasant squatters continued into mid-2001. Agreement was reached in September 2002 on the deployment of Organization of American States (OAS) observers to the disputed area pending the holding of referenda on the issue in the two countries. However, the accord was repudiated by Guatemala in August 2003, and in May 2004 new discussions were launched at OAS headquarters in Washington, D.C., on finding an "equitable and permanent solution" to the long-standing controversy. In December 2008 Guatemala and Belize signed an agreement allowing the International Court of Justice (ICJ) to arbitrate Guatemala's territorial claim and calling for simultaneous referenda on the matter to be held in both countries on October 6, 2013. In April 2013, however, Guatemala indefinitely suspended the referendum, reportedly after Belize refused Guatemala's request to move up the date and revise its referendum procedure.

Generally cordial relations with the United States yielded crucial military and other aid that supported relatively successful counterinsurgency efforts during the late 1960s. Subsequently, however, the United States evidenced concern over the diminishing effectiveness of such assistance in a context of increased polarization between right and left. In March 1977 Guatemala repudiated U.S. military support after the Carter administration had announced that human rights considerations would be used in setting allocation levels. Although the Reagan administration resumed military and economic assistance, all aid (except for cash sales) was suspended by the U.S. Congress in November 1983 following publication of the Kissinger Commission report on Central America, which attributed thousands of recent civilian deaths to "the brutal behavior of the security forces." The program was again reinstituted in mid-1984, but in December 1990 the U.S. Congress imposed a new ban on military assistance and in June 1991 extended it to most categories of economic aid, pending evidence of "progress [in] eliminating human rights violations and in investigating and bringing to trial those responsible for major human rights cases." In May 1993 the United States joined other foreign governments in condemning Serrano's bid for full power and helped set in motion OAS procedures that may have influenced the military's about-face in the matter.

In August 1994, a week before leaving office, Panamanian president Guillermo Endara rejected a request for the extradition of Serrano Elías, on the grounds that the accusations against the former Guatemalan chief executive were political in nature. Endara's decision was upheld by his successor, Ernesto Pérez Balladares, whose September 1 inauguration was boycotted by his Guatemalan counterpart. A third extradition request was rejected by Panama in February 1998.

On September 19, 1994, the UN General Assembly announced the establishment of a Human Rights Verification Mission in Guatemala (MINUGUA). The mission began its work on November 21 with a staff of 200 foreign human rights observers, 60 police officers, and 10 military officers to monitor compliance with the human rights agreement signed by the government and URNG on March 29. However, high levels of violence continued, prompting MINUGUA to warn in late 2002 of a breakdown of law and order in several regions of the country. Meanwhile, the U.S. government curtailed assistance to an anti-drug police unit that it had helped to establish in 1998, after high-ranking members of the unit were accused of drug trafficking, murder, and kidnapping. The unit was dissolved shortly afterward. As drug trafficking continued, in 2003 the United States "decertified" Guatemala for having "failed demonstrably" to meet its obligations under international counternarcotics agreements. However, the Berger administration in 2005 pledged refreshed cooperation with the U.S. Drug Enforcement Agency in overhauling the corrupt Anti-Narcotics Analysis and Investigation Service (SAIA).

Despite widespread opposition, Congress approved the Central American Free Trade Agreement (CAFTA) with the United States on March 10, 2005, by a vote of 126–12. CAFTA (implemented on July 1, 2006), eliminated customs tariffs on a number of goods and created clear, enforceable regulations for all aspects of cross-border trade.

Calls to regulate the movement of drugs in the Americas increased in 2007, as did demands for improved regulation of Guatemala's private adoption agents, due to the high number of Guatemalan babies adopted by Americans. While the government attempted to increase the transparency of the process, critics claimed that children were being unlawfully taken from their parents to meet U.S. demand. After two years of negotiations, Guatemala signed a bilateral free trade agreement with Panama on February 28, 2008, securing concessions for all Panamanian exports to Guatemala. Exports from other countries were granted access through quotas. Also in 2008, the CICIG was established, with 11 countries contributing a $20 million budget. During a visit to the United States in April, President Colom and U.S. president George W. Bush agreed to a collective effort involving more than $4 million in new anti-drug and public security assistance, increased judicial assistance, and additional funding for the CICIG. Subsequently, Guatemala inaugurated a U.S.-supported elite anti-drug unit.

In December 2008 President Colom and El Salvador's president, Elías Antonio Saca, agreed to establish a binational customs union to allow the free transit of goods and services.

In an effort to shore up relations with Cuba, President Colom visited Havana in February 2009, 12 years after the Arzú government had restored relations. Colom presented former leader Fidel Castro with the Order of the Quetzal, the highest honor conferred by the Guatemalan government. The awarding of the honor, a controversial issue in Guatemala, was meant to thank Havana for carrying out medical and literacy programs in Guatemala. Meanwhile, Colom also apologized publicly in Cuba for Guatemala's role as a staging area for the 1961 Bay of Pigs invasion by U.S.-trained Cuban exiles. In June Guatemala and Cuba signed economic cooperation agreements. Meanwhile, Brazil agreed to loan Guatemala $99 million over 12 years to buy Brazilian aircraft and radar equipment.

The Guatemalan judicial selection process attracted international criticism in October 2009 after a number of judges were installed in the Supreme Court based on political connections (see Constitution and government, above), culminating in UN Secretary General Ban Ki-moon's declaration that the legislature must pick independent and competent judges to combat near total impunity from prosecution in the country. The same month the country celebrated the completion of an electricity connection with Mexico. The presidents hailed the link, which began sending 200 megawatts of electricity to Guatemala and cost $55 million to complete, as the first to connect power grids throughout the region under the Central American Electrical Interconnection System project. Guatemala strengthened economic ties to the south in November, when free trade agreements entered into force between the country and Chile and Colombia.

In October 2010 U.S. President Barack Obama apologized to Guatemala following revelations that thousands of Guatemalans had been infected with syphilis in a U.S. Public Health Service experimental program in 1946–1948.

In October 2011, Guatemala became one of the nonpermanent members of the United Nations Security Council for the 2012–2013 session, winning an unchallenged contest to take the Latin America seat vacated by Brazil.

At a March 2012 summit of Central American leaders, President Pérez tried to encourage serious debate among the region's countries on the possibility of decriminalizing drugs as a strategy of combating rising transborder, narcotics-related violence, a measure opposed by regional governments and the United States.

In February 2013 a partial free trade agreement between Guatemala and Ecuador took force, kicking off increased opportunities for bilateral trade between the two countries.

On May 24, 2013, after a two-year-long legal battle, former president Alfonso Portillo was extradited to the United States where he faced charges for using U.S. banks to launder some $70 million during his presidency (see Current issues, below).

Following talks in August, Guatemala and Mexico announced an initiative to increase military cooperation along the border zone, including interchange of military personnel and combined patrols, in an effort to crack down on human and drug trafficking across the notoriously porous border.

Current issues. Thanks to the CICIG's efforts, Guatemala's first genocide case went to trial in July 2011, when former Gen. Héctor Mario LÓPEZ Fuentes was charged with the massacre of some 300 Mayans in the state of Quiche during the civil war. Among other cases brought against civil war figures, former GANA presidential candidate Alejandro Giammattei was acquitted in August of carrying out extrajudicial executions while he was prison chief. In another setback for the CICIG, after a drawn-out extradition and trial process, former president Portillo was acquitted in May of embezzlement. The UN General Assembly extended the mandate for the CICIG in December 2010 for two years until 2013.

Ahead of September 2011 balloting, UNE's hopes for continuing President Colom's center-left agenda were dashed in July, when the Constitutional Court disqualified Sandra Torres Colom, presidential candidate for a UNE-GANA coalition, on grounds that her recent divorce from the president had been obtained solely as a means of sidestepping the constitutional provision barring close relatives of sitting presidents from seeking that office. Ten candidates contested the presidential race. The PP fielded former civil war military general Otto Pérez Molina, vowing to crack down on crime and Mexican drug cartels operating in the country. LIDER nominee Manuel Antonio Baldizón, a lawyer and businessman, also adopted an anticrime platform, pledging to enforce the death penalty at a rate of 10 executions per month. Eduardo SUGER ran for the Commitment, Renewal, and Order Party (CREO) on a platform of fighting poverty, and Mario ESTRADA was the National Change Union (UCN) candidate.

In the first round of the presidential election on September 11, Pérez finished first, with 36 percent of the vote, far ahead of his closest rival, LIDER candidate Baldizón, with 23.2 percent, and CREO's Suger, in third with 16.4 percent. Though Pérez won by a definitive margin, he failed to secure the necessary 50 percent, so the two candidates proceeded to a second round of balloting in November. Meanwhile, the PP came in first in legislative voting on September 11, winning 26.6 percent of the vote and 56 seats. The UNE-GANA won 48 seats but dissolved their alliance by the end of the month. Nine other groupings secured legislative representation. Independent observers deemed the elections free and fair.

The presidential runoff election in November was a contest between Pérez and Baldizón, who had recently won the UNE-GANA coalition's endorsement. Pérez defeated Baldizón with nearly 54 percent of the vote. Pérez took office on January 14, 2012.

In March 2012 a court handed down prison sentences totaling 7,710 years to five men for the 1982 Plan de Sanchez massacre, resolving a 2004 ruling from the Inter-American Court of Human Rights holding Guatemala responsible and calling for legal action on the slaughter of 256 people. Pedro PIMENTAL Ríos was sentenced earlier in the month to 6,060 years in prison for the Dos Erres massacre.

During the summer of 2012, the Pérez administration drafted a constitutional reform package that included a controversial amendment allowing the state to acquire as much as a 40 percent stake in new mining companies. A barrage of criticism led the administration to drop the controversial amendment, and a significantly reduced package was presented in September. In November the administration asked that debate on the reform package be postponed as funds reserved for a referendum were redirected to the recovery effort from the earthquake of November 7.

The mandate for the CICIG was in January 2013 officially extended for another two years past the September 2013 expiration date. In November 2012 the CICIG had made an unusual move, providing the government with a list of 18 of the country's judges with links to organized crime.

Also in January, the Pérez administration launched its latest security reform effort: a new violence observatory to track violent deaths across the country over the next five years.

In March 2013 former president Ríos Montt went on trial for crimes against humanity for the killing of 1,771 people during his 17-month rule. The United Nations High Commissioner for Human Rights lauded the proceedings, noting it was "the first time, anywhere in the world, that a former head of state is being put on trial for genocide by a national tribunal." On May 11 the three-judge tribunal found Ríos Montt guilty of genocide. However, on May 21, the constitutional court overturned the landmark verdict, annulling everything that occurred in the trial after April 19, when Ríos Montt was briefly left without his lawyer. Later that week, on May 24, former president Alfonso Portillo, who had previously been cleared of domestic embezzlement charges, was extradited to the United States where he faced charges of laundering more than $70 million through U.S. banks during his presidency.

POLITICAL PARTIES AND GROUPS

Political power in Guatemala, described by Brookings Institution analyst Kevin Casas-Zamora as a "party-less democracy," has traditionally been personal rather than institutional, with parties developing in response to the needs or ambitions of particular leaders.

Under current law, parties must maintain a minimum vote share to retain legal status; however, unrecognized groups may, upon petition by a sufficient number of signatories, secure recognition before any given election. In 1995, 14 of 23 participating groups failed to qualify for continued registration. Of the 9 that survived, only incoming President Arzú's PAN, Ríos Montt's FRG, and the left-of-center FDNG were viewed as fully viable formations. The leading parties in 1999 were the FRG and the PAN, with the recently formed New Nation Alliance (ANN) a distant third. In 2003 Oscar Berger's Grand National Alliance (GANA) led a field that included Álvaro Colom's National Unity of Hope (UNE), the FRG, the PAN, and the ANN.

In January 2009 dissident UNE members of Congress formed a legislative bloc under the rubric **Renewed Democratic Freedom** (*Libertad Democrática Renovada*—LIDER).

Government Party:

Patriotic Party (*Partido Patriota*—PP). Founded in 2001 and initially part of GANA (see below), the PP withdrew from the presidential alliance in May 2004. Its principal founder, former general Otto Pérez Molina, known for supporting the 1996 peace process, formed the party shortly after being forced into retirement by the Portillo government in 2000. He moved immediately to the opposition, throwing his new center-right party's support behind Oscar Berger's successful 2003 candidacy. One of the PP's most prominent members, Rodolfo VIELMAN Castellanos, was killed in March 2006.

As the party's presidential candidate in 2007, Pérez responded to public discontent over the violence by promising to expand the police force, reinstate the death penalty, and crack down with an "iron hand, head, and heart." Aura Marina SALAZAR Cutzal, an assistant to Pérez, and her bodyguard were shot dead in early October 2007. Pérez blamed organized crime for the killings.

Pérez's anticrime message made him popular with urban voters but attracted less rural support in the 2007 elections. He finished second in the first round of voting and lost to UNE's Álvaro Colom in runoff balloting, securing 47.2 percent of the vote. The PP won 30 seats in the concurrent legislative election, finishing third with 15.9 percent of the vote.

In the first balloting of 2011, Pérez placed first in the presidential election with 36 percent of the vote, while party secured a legislative majority with 56 seats. Pérez won the presidency in the November runoff election with 54 percent of the vote.

At a May 2013 party congress, Roxana Baldetti was reelected secretary general.

Leaders: Otto PÉREZ Molina (President and Party Leader), Ingrid Roxana BALDETTI Elías (Vice President and Secretary General).

Other Legislative Parties:

National Unity of Hope (*Unidad Nacional de la Esperanza*—UNE). Center-left UNE was founded in 2001 by ANN (below) secessionist Álvaro Colom Caballeros, nephew of a leftist Guatemala City mayor killed in 1979. A former vice minister and director of the National Peace Fund, an IMF-supported government entity that made investments in rural areas, Colom first ran for president in 1999 as the candidate of the ANN, a broad leftist coalition that included former guerrilla leaders, among others. He finished third.

UNE, a more centrist grouping than the ANN, fared well in the 2003 elections, as Colom's message of fighting poverty resonated with rural voters. The party won 30 congressional seats in 2003, with Colom the runner-up in first-round presidential balloting. He lost to the GANA's Oscar Berger in the second round on December 28.

In the run-up to the 2007 presidential election, Colom pledged an improved justice system and increased social expenditures. In the first round of voting Colom finished first, but fell short of a majority with 28.2 percent of the vote. UNE also led all parties in the concurrent legislative poll by winning 48 seats and 22.8 percent of the vote. Colom defeated the PP's Pérez in the second round, with 52.8 percent of the vote. Outside of Guatemala City, which he lost in the second round by 19 points, Colom won 57.3 percent of the vote, indicating that the rural poor were an important base of support.

Reportedly conflicts emerged within the party over Colom's cabinet appointments. The party's representation in Congress fell significantly between 2008 and late 2011, from 48 to 31 seats, as a result of multiple defections to the new dissident LIDER party. In response, UNE leaders forged an electoral alliance with the opposition party GANA in May 2010. Former first lady Sandra Torres Colom, the UNE-GANA alliance presidential candidate, was disqualified from running by an August 2011 court ruling (see Current issues, above). In balloting the following month, the alliance won 48 seats. In late September, the parties announced the dissolution of the alliance, noting that it had been formed primarily to support Torres's presidential bid.

Leaders: Jairo Joaquin FLORES (Party Leader), Sandra TORRES (Secretary General).

Grand National Alliance (*Gran Alianza Nacional*—GANA). Launched in early 2003, the GANA is a center-right grouping that presidential aspirant Oscar Berger joined following his defection from the PAN (below). Its founding parties included the **Guatemalan Reform Party** (*Partido Reformador Guatemalteco*—PRG), also known as the **Reform Movement** (*Movimiento Reformador*—MR), and the **Party of National Solidarity** (*Partido Solidaridad Nacional*—PSN), as well as the PP (above). The GANA secured a plurality of 49 seats in the November 2003 legislative elections, and Berger won the December presidential runoff. However, the GANA lost 7 of its legislative seats when the PP withdrew in May 2004 to protest an apparent rapprochement between President Berger and former president Ríos Montt.

The GANA lost its legislative plurality in the September 2007 balloting, finishing second with 37 seats and 16.5 percent of the vote. Giammattei finished third in the concurrent first round of presidential elections with 17.2 percent of the vote. The GANA lost a significant number of seats in Congress over the 2008–2012 legislative term to defections to new dissident groups LIDER and BG. The party dropped from 37 representatives after the election to 17 by late 2011. The party forged an electoral alliance with opponent UNE to counter the losses. Though the UNE-GANA presidential candidate, Sandra Torres, was disqualified from running (see Current issues, above), the parties together secured 48 seats in September balloting. The alliance subsequently dissolved.

Leaders: Jaime Antonio MARTÍNEZ Lohayza (Secretary General), Carlos Alberto MARTÍNEZ Castellanos (Deputy Secretary), Oscar José BERGER Perdomo (Former President of the Republic).

Renewed Democratic Freedom (*Libertad Democrática Renovada*—LIDER). LIDER formed concurrently with the decline in popularity of President Colom. In December 2008, 11 UNE deputies defected from the governing party to form the new legislative bloc. In July 2009 three PP dissidents also joined the party, which continued to increase its numbers until it was the third most powerful voting bloc, with 27 seats by late September 2011. Members of LIDER said they would not consistently oppose UNE, but they would also not promise to support the government party.

After coming in second in the first round of voting in September 2011, LIDER presidential candidate Manuel Baldizón proceeded, unsuccessfully, to the second round. In concurrent legislative balloting, the party secured 14 seats.

Leader: Manuel BALDIZÓN (Secretary General and 2011 presidential candidate).

Commitment, Renovation and Order (*Compromiso, Renovación y Orden*—CREO). CREO is a right-wing party launched in October 2010. The new party's presidential candidate Eduardo SUGER, formerly of the **Center of Social Action** (*Centro de Acción Social*—CASA, below), won 16.4 percent of the vote, placing third. CREO secured 12 legislative seats.

Leaders: Roberto GONZALEZ (Secretary General), Eduardo SUGER (2011 presidential candidate).

Republican Institutional Party (*Partido Republicano Institucional*—PRI). The PRI was launched in 1988 as the **Guatemalan Republican Front** (*Frente Republicano Guatemalteco*—FRG). The right-wing FRG participated in Ríos Montt's *No-Venta* coalition for the

1990 campaign. Deregistered thereafter, its legislative members joined the government grouping as an independent bloc that was awarded the leadership of four congressional commissions. In late 1993 the party failed to secure legislative approval for revocation of the constitutional provision banning heads of state who had participated in coups from running for the presidency. It registered a dramatic victory in the 1994 legislative contest, winning 32 seats, with Ríos Montt subsequently being named congressional president.

In 1999 the party won the presidency and a majority of congressional seats. However, by mid-2001 factional differences erupted, with supporters of President Portillo aligned against those loyal to Ríos Montt and Vice President Reyes López. During 2003, allegations of corruption were made against Portillo, and in early 2004 he left the country.

The party won 15 seats in the September 2007 legislative election, finishing fourth with 9.8 percent of the vote. Presidential candidate Luis Rabbé finished fifth in the concurrent first round of presidential balloting with 7.3 percent of the vote. In September 2011 balloting, the FRG's legislative presence was reduced to one seat.

Party leaders voted in January 2013 to dissolve the FRG and reorganize under the PRI banner. (Though bearing the same name and a similar logo to Mexico's *Partido Republicano Institucional*, they are not officially affiliated.) The move, which came days before the announcement of the crimes against humanity trial of Ríos Montt (see Current issues, above), was likely in part to distance the party from its history. Meanwhile, the PRI adopted the ideologies and leadership of the now-dissolved FRG.

Leaders: Luis Fernando PÉREZ (Secretary General), Alberto Salazar GUILLERMO Ortiz (Deputy Secretary), Gen. (Ret.) José Efraín RÍOS Montt (Former President of the Republic, Former President of Congress, and FRG 2003 presidential candidate), Luis RABBÉ (FRG 2007 presidential candidate).

Union of National Change (*Union del Cambio Nacionala*—UCN). The UCN advocates a constitutional, democratic, and republican regime focused on uniting the country. The party, whose slogan was "better times" (*tiempos mejores*), campaigned for the September 2007 elections on a platform that pledged to advance women's and workers' rights, to fight corruption, and to limit social and economic polarization. Presidential candidate Mario Estrada finished sixth in the first round of the 2007 presidential balloting with 3.2 percent of the vote. The UCN won four legislative seats and held six by late 2011. Estrada again stood for president in 2011, coming in fourth with 8.6 percent of the vote. At that time, the party secured 14 legislative seats.

In April 2013 internal elections, Marío ESTRADA was not only reelected secretary general but selected as the 2015 presidential candidate.

Leader: Mario Amilcar ESTRADA Orellana (Secretary General, 2007, 2011 and 2015 presidential candidate).

Unionist Party (*Partido Unionista*—PU). The PU was organized by former president Alvaro Arzú in the wake of inconsistent support for his policies within the PAN (below). Subsequently eclipsed within the new party by Gustavo PORRAS, a center-left former guerrilla member and government peace negotiator, Arzú eventually regained control. He succeeded in having Guatemala City's center-right mayor, Fritz García-Gallont, named the PU secretary general and standard-bearer for the 2003 presidential campaign. García-Gallont placed fifth in the November poll, with a 3 percent vote share.

In 2007 García-Gallont finished eighth in the first round of presidential balloting with 2.9 percent of the vote. The PU won eight legislative seats with 6.1 percent of the vote but held just five seats in late 2011. Patricia de Arzú, Alvaro Arzú's wife, finished eighth in the 2011 presidential election for the PU, with 2.2 percent of the vote. The PU won one seat.

In February 2013 the PU formalized an alliance with **Victory** (*Victoria*—below) and **TODOS**, founded in August 2012. The alliance backs Todos-founder Roberto ALEJOS for the 2015 presidential election.

Leaders: Alvaro Enrique ARZÚ Irigoyen (Former President of the Republic and Secretary General), Patricia de ARZÚ (2011 presidential candidate), Fritz GARCÍA-Gallont (Former Mayor of Guatemala City, 2003 and 2007 presidential candidate).

National Advancement Party (*Partido de Avanzada Nacional*—PAN). The PAN was organized before the 1990 election by the former mayor of Guatemala City, Alvaro Arzú Irigoyen, who was placed fourth in the presidential poll and entered the Serrano Elías cabinet as foreign minister. A disagreement with the president over the recognition of Belize prompted Arzú's resignation in September 1991, thereby shattering the existing governmental coalition. The party was runner-up to the FRG in 1994, winning 24 congressional seats; it secured a legislative majority in 1995, with Arzú winning the presidency in second-round balloting on January 7, 1996. By late 1997 three factions were reported to have emerged within the party: one led by congressional president Arabello Castro and backing Interior Minister Rodolfo MENDOZA for president in 1999, one united behind Guatemala City mayor Oscar Berger, and one loyal to President Arzú. Berger won the party's presidential nomination in early 1999 but lost decisively to Portillo Cabrera in the November runoff.

The division of the party between followers of Arzú and Berger, largely over support for an FRG bill permitting Ríos Montt's reelection as legislative president, prompted 15 PAN deputies to announce in June 2000 that they intended to sit as independents.

Berger defeated Secretary General Leonel López for the PAN's 2003 presidential nomination; subsequently, Berger and nine other legislators defected to join the GANA. López thereupon became the PAN standard bearer, finishing fourth in November's first-round balloting.

The party's original 2007 presidential candidate was Francisco ARREDONDO. However, he refused to accept the PAN nominee for vice president, Oscar Rodolfo Castañeda, as his running mate. The party executive ultimately removed Arredondo from the ballot, nominating Castañeda for president. Castañeda finished ninth in the first round of the presidential poll with 2.6 percent of the vote. The PAN won four legislative seats with 4.6 percent of the vote and held three in late 2011. Party secretary Juan Gutiérrez finished seventh in the first round of the 2011 presidential election, with 2.8 percent of the vote. The PAN won two seats.

Leaders: Juan GUTIÉRREZ (Secretary General and 2011 presidential candidate), Leonel Eliseo LÓPEZ Rodas (2003 presidential candidate), Oscar Rodolfo CASTAÑEDA (2007 presidential candidate).

Guatemalan National Revolutionary Unity (*Unidad Revolucionaria Nacional Guatemalteca*—URNG). URNG was formed in January 1981 as a largely exile-based umbrella organization designed to provide various guerrilla groups with a unified military command, which was never fully implemented. Its political wing, led by Raúl MOLINA Mejía, was styled United Representation of the Guatemalan Opposition (*Representación Unitaria de la Oposición Guatemalteca*— RUOG).

In October 1987 inconclusive "low-level" talks aimed at seeking "peace and democracy" were held with government representatives in Madrid, Spain. Another inconclusive round of talks with government representatives was held in Oslo, Norway, during March and April 1990, but at discussions in Madrid in June, party representatives agreed on the need for elections to a constituent assembly in 1991 in which the guerrillas could participate.

Reversing its original call for Guatemalans to boycott elections, URNG appealed in May 1995 for a voter turnout in favor of "alternative candidates," though failing to indicate specific candidates.

Government and URNG representatives in Oslo, Norway, signed a definitive cease-fire on December 4, 1996, paving the way for the conclusion of a formal peace accord on December 29 (see Political background, above).

URNG's longtime leader and former secretary general Ricardo Arnoldo RAMÍREZ de León (a.k.a. Rolando MORÁN) died on September 4, 1998. On October 19 URNG formally filed for registration as a legal party. URNG participated in the 1999 and 2003 balloting as a member of the ANN (below), but that alliance had splintered by 2007, when URNG won two seats in the September legislative poll with 3.3 percent of the vote, while Miguel Angel Sandoval finished tenth with 2.1 percent of the vote in the concurrent first round of presidential balloting.

For the 2011 election, the URNG formed a coalition with Winaq (below) and ANN, wining 3 seats.

Leaders: Hector Alfredo NUILA Ericastilla (Secretary General), Carlos Enrique MEJÍA Paz (Deputy), Miguel Angel SANDOVAL (2007 presidential candidate).

Winaq. An indigenous grouping founded in 2005 by Nobel Peace Prize winner Rigoberta Menchú, *Winaq* gets its name from a Mayan word that means "the wholeness of the human being." Since *Winaq* is not recognized as a party, Menchú represents EG. A member of the Quiché Maya indigenous nation, Menchú first came to prominence with a 1983 autobiography detailing the violence and discrimination she and her family suffered in Guatemala's conflict, and her own experience as a labor and indigenous-rights organizer. She was awarded the Nobel Prize in 1992. Menchú made only marginal gains in 2011, when she came in sixth, with 3.3 percent of the vote, as the presidential candidate for a coalition representing *Winaq,* the URNG, and the ANN.

At a party congress in June 2013, *Winaq* signaled intentions to form a leftist alliance ahead of 2015 balloting.

Leaders: Amílcar de Jesús POP Ac (Secretary General), Rigoberta MENCHÚ (Deputy Secretary General).

New Nation Alliance (*Alianza Nueva Nación*—ANN). ANN was formed in February 1999 as a left-of-center electoral alliance of the URNG (above), DIA (below), and a number of smaller groups. Its 2003 presidential candidate, Rigoberto QUEME, withdrew in September after an internal dispute over candidacies, prompting its principal components, the URNG and DIA, to compete separately from the party in the presidential race. ANN won 7 legislative seats in 2003, two less than in 1999.

Presidential candidate Jorge Ismael SOTO García (a.k.a. Pablo Monsanto, a former guerrilla leader), received 0.6 percent of votes in the initial round of the 2007 presidential contest, because the URNG and DIA each presented its own candidate. After ANN failed to win a legislative seat with 1.4 percent of the vote, the party lost its registration. ANN joined a coalition with *Winaq* and URNG in 2011, which won three seats.

Leaders: Jorge Ismael SOTO García (2007 presidential candidate), Alfonso BAUER Paiz (Secretary General).

Encounter for Guatemala (*Encuentro por Guatemala*—EG). Left-wing EG was organized in 2006 by Nineth Varenca Montenegro Cottom (a member of Congress) and César Montes, who had recently resigned from the ANN (above) along with several other legislators. In February 2007 EG reached an agreement with the indigenous grouping *Winaq* (above) that guaranteed *Winaq* a 50 percent share of EG's legislative and mayoral candidates for the September election. *Winaq* leader Rigoberta Menchú finished seventh as the EG's candidate in the first round of the 2007 presidential balloting with 3.1 percent of the vote. EG won four seats in the concurrent legislative elections with 6.2 percent of the vote but held just one seat by late 2011.

Ahead of the 2011 elections, EG formed an alliance with center-right party **Vision With Values** (*Visión con Valorés*—VIVA) behind VIVA secretary general Harold CABALLEROS for president. Caballeros secured 6.16 percent of the vote, and the alliance won six seats.

Leaders: César MONTES, Rigoberta MENCHÚ (2007 presidential candidate), Nineth Varenca MONTENEGRO Cottom (Secretary General).

Victory (*Victoria*). Victory was founded in 2008. In September 2011 balloting, the party won one legislative seat. Ahead of the 2015 election, Victory formed an alliance with the PU and TODOS (see PU, above).

Leader: Abraham RIVERA.

Parties Contesting the 2011 Elections:

Center of Social Action (*Centro de Acción Social*—CASA). CASA was launched in 2003 to represent the interests of indigenous peoples. In 2007 CASA won 5 legislative seats with 4.9 percent of the vote, and its presidential candidate, Eduardo Suger, finished fourth in the concurrent first round of presidential balloting with 7.5 percent of the vote. By late 2011 CASA held 2 seats. Alejandro Giammattei, formerly of GANA, finished ninth as CASA's presidential candidate, with 1 percent of the vote, in 2011.

Leaders: Alejandro GIAMMATTEI (2011 presidential candidate), Rigoberto QUEMÉ Chay, Feliz Adolfo RUANO de Leon.

Winning less than one percent of the vote were **National Development Action** (*Acción de Desarrollo Nacional*—ADN), a center-right Christian party launched in 2010, and the **National Convergence Front** (*Frente de Convergencia Nacional*—FCN).

Other Parties:

Authentic Integral Development (*Desarollo Integral Auténtico*—DIA). DIA was formerly known as Authentic Comprehensive Development (*Desarollo Inclusivo Auténtico*). The party's 2007 presidential candidate, Héctor Rosales, was shot at while campaigning in August in a rural area close to the town of Cunen. He escaped unhurt and blamed the FRG for the attempt. Rosales won 0.6 percent of the vote in the first round of the presidential poll. In 2007 the party failed to win a legislative seat, with 1.4 percent of the vote, and was stripped of its registration.

Leaders: Héctor ROSALES (2007 presidential candidate), Jorge Luis ORTEGA Torres (Secretary General).

Democratic Union (*Unión Democrática*—UD). Launched before the 1994 election, UD campaigned vigorously as a party "without a past." However, despite a nationwide campaign that relied heavily on television ads, it secured only 1 congressional seat in both 1995 and 1999, in coalition, on the latter occasion, with the Greens (*La Organización Verde*—LOV, below). The party won 2 seats in 2003, while supporting GANA's Berger for the presidency.

UD secured 1 legislative seat in the September 2007 elections with 1.4 percent of the vote, while its presidential candidate, Manuel Conde Orellana, received just 0.8 percent in the concurrent first round of presidential balloting, finishing 11th.

Leaders: Manuel CONDE Orellana (2007 presidential candidate), Gen. Rodolfo Ernesto (Fito) PAIZ Andrade (Secretary General), Edwin Armando MARTINEZ Herrera.

Front for Democracy (*Frente por la Democracia*—EL FRENTE). Founded in January 2006 by dissidents from the FRG and the PDCG, the center-right party did not field a presidential candidate in 2007, and failed to keep its registration after winning 0.9 percent of votes in the concurrent legislative elections.

Leader: Alfonso CABRERA Hidalgo (Secretary General).

Guatemalan Christian Democratic Party (*Partido Democracia Cristiana Guatemalteca*—PDCG). Founded in 1955 as a centrist party of liberal and reformist views, the PDCG secured a majority of 51 congressional seats in 1985, with its longtime leader, Vinicio Cerezo Arévalo, defeating the UCN's Carpio Nicolle in a runoff for the presidency. Its 1990 standard-bearer, Alfonso CABRERA Hidalgo, withdrew from candidacy in late October, ostensibly because of failing health, but was nonetheless credited with a third-place finish. Its congressional representation fell from 28 to 13 seats in 1994.

In April 1995 the PDCG formed an electoral coalition styled the National Alliance (*Alianza Nacional*—AN) with the UCN and Social Democrat Party (*Partido Social Demócrata*—PSD). With the formation of the AN, nine PDCG members of Congress resigned their party memberships and set themselves up as an independent bloc to protest AN's decision to support the presidential candidacy of Andrade DÍAZ Durán. The PDCG's representation dwindled to three congressional seats in 1995 and in 1999 fell to two, both of which were retained in 2003.

After the September 2007 legislative election, in which it failed to win a seat with 0.8 percent of the vote, PDCG lost its registration due to its failure to meet the vote threshold. Meanwhile, its presidential candidate, Vinicio CEREZO Blandón, son of former president Marco Vinicio Cerezo Arévalo, won 0.5 percent of votes in the first round of balloting.

Leaders: Marco Vinicio CEREZO Arévalo (Former President of the Republic), Ana Catalina Reyes SOBERANIS (Former President of the National Congress), Dr. Francisco VILLAGRAN Kramer (Former Vice President of the Republic and Leader of the Right-Wing Faction), René DE LEÓN Schlotter (Leader of the Left-Wing Faction), Vinicio CEREZO Blandón (2007 presidential candidate), Jacobo ARBENZ (2003 presidential candidate).

Guatemalan Independent Bloc (*Bloque Independiente Bancada Guatemala*—BG). In the run-up to the 2007 balloting, the BG was formed by a group of GANA dissidents, including 13 of GANA's 37 legislative deputies, and led by Luis Alberto CONTRERAS Colindres. The splinter group consisted of two factions, one led by Alfredo VILA and the other by Jaime MARTINEZ, which also had the backing of 2007 presidential candidate Alejandro Giammattei. Despite the rift, BG members often voted with GANA. The party held 13 seats in Congress late in the 2008–2012 term.

Leader: Rubén Eduardo MEJÍA Linares.

(For information on the **National Liberation Movement** [*Movimiento de Liberación Nacional*—MLN], **Nationalist Authentic Central, Social Democrat Party, New Guatemala Democratic Front, The Green Organization** [*La Organización Verde*—LOV], **We Can** [*Podemos*], and a number of other parties and groups that were active in the 1990s, see the 2008 and 2009 *Handbooks.*)

Clandestine Groups:

Anti-Communist Secret Army (*Ejército Secreto Anticomunista*—ESA). A right-wing group presumed to be an outgrowth of the former White Hand (*La Mano Blanca*), the ESA is reportedly linked to the more extreme faction of the MLN. It is known to maintain a "death list" of numerous left-wing activists and has been prominently involved in the escalation of political assassinations that began in late 1978. In early 1980 it threatened to kill 20 leftists for each assassination of a rightist and in mid-1988 issued a communiqué stating it would ensure that communist journalists "either leave the country or die inside of it."

Other extreme right-wing formations include the **Squadron of Death** (*Escuadrón de la Muerte*—EM) and the **Officers of the Mountain** (*Oficiales de la Montaña*—OdeM).

LEGISLATURE

Guatemala's legislative body is the unicameral **Congress of the Republic** (*Congreso de la República*), which currently consists of 158 members elected for four-year terms. In the September 11, 2011, election for the 2012–2016 term, the seat distribution was as follows: Patriotic Party, 56 seats; National Unity of Hope and Grand National Alliance, 48; Renewed Democratic Freedom, 14; Union of National Change, 14; Commitment, Renewal, and Order, 12; Vision with Values and Encounter for Guatemala, 6; Winaq, Guatemalan National Revolutionary Unity–Broad Left Movement, and Alternative New Nation, 3; National Advancement Party, 2; Guatemalan Republican Front, 1; Unionist Party, 1; and Victory, 1. In January 2013 the FRG reorganized under the banner Republican Institutional Party (PRI), retaining their singly congressional seat.

President: Pedro MUADI.

CABINET

[as of September 15, 2013]

President	Otto Fernando Perez Molina
Vice President	Ingrid Roxana Baldetti Elias [f]
Ministers	
Agriculture and Food Policy	Elmer Lopez Rodriguez
Communications, Infrastructure, and Housing	Alejandro Sinibaldi
Culture and Sports	Carlos Batzin
Economy	Sergio de la Torre
Education	Cythia del Aguila [f]
Energy and Mines	Erick Archila
Environment and Natural Resources	Roxana Sobenes [f]
Foreign Affairs	Luis Fernando Carrera Castro
Interior	Mauricio Lopez Bonilla
Labor and Social Welfare	Carlos Contreras
National Defense	Ulises Anzueto Giron
Public Finances	Pavel Centeno
Public Health and Social Services	Jorge Villavicencio Alvarez
Social Assistance	Luz Lainfiesta [f]
Head, Peace Secretariat	Antonio Arenales

[f] = female

INTERGOVERNMENTAL REPRESENTATION

Ambassador to the U.S.: Jose Francisco VILLAGRAN DE LEON.

U.S. Ambassador to Guatemala: (Vacant).

Permanent Representative to the UN: Gert ROSENTHAL.

IGO Memberships (Non-UN): IADB, IOM, NAM, OAS, WTO.

GUINEA

Republic of Guinea
République de Guinée

Political Status: Independent republic since October 2, 1958; under one-party presidential regime until military coup of April 3, 1984; multiparty constitution approved by referendum of December 23, 1990, providing for five-year transition to civilian government; constitution suspended following military coup of December 23, 2008; constitutional order restored following Supreme Court ratification of presidential election results in December 2010.

Area: 94,925 sq. mi. (245,857 sq. km).

Population: 10,522,509 (2012E—UN); 11,176,026 (2013E—U.S. Census).

Major Urban Center (2005E): CONAKRY (1,478,000).

Official Language: French, pending adoption of Soussou or Malinké. (Six other tribal languages are also spoken.)

Monetary Unit: Guinean Franc (market rate November 1, 2013: 7042.25 francs = $1US).

President: Alpha CONDÉ (Rally of the Guinean People), elected after multiparty balloting on June 27 and November 7, 2010, and sworn in on December 21 to succeed Acting President Gen. Sékouba KONATÉ (nonparty), who had ascended to head of state on December 4, 2009, following an assassination attempt on December 3 against Capt. Moussa Dadis CAMARA, who had been appointed by the National Council for Democracy and Development on December 24, 2008, after military coup following the death of Gen. Lansana CONTÉ (Party of Unity and Progress) on December 22.

Prime Minister: Mohamed Said FOFANA (independent), appointed by the president on December 24, 2010, to succeed Interim Prime Minister Jean-Marie DORÉ (Union for the Progress of Guinea).

THE COUNTRY

Facing the Atlantic on the western bulge of Africa, Guinea presents a highly diversified terrain that ranges from coastal flatlands to the mountainous Foutah Djallon region where the Niger, Gambia, and Senegal rivers originate. The predominantly Muslim population includes over 2 million Fulani (Fulah); over 1.25 million Malinké (Mandingo, who have long been the dominant tribe); over 500,000 Soussou; 350,000 Kissi; and 250,000 Kpelle. While women are responsible for an estimated 48 percent of food production, female participation in government is minimal.

The majority of the population is dependent upon subsistence agriculture. Bananas, coffee, peanuts, palm kernels, and citrus fruits are important cash crops, although much foreign exchange is derived from mining. Guinea is one of the world's largest producers of bauxite, its reserves being exploited largely with the assistance of foreign companies. There are also valuable deposits of iron ore, gold, diamonds, uranium, and oil, in addition to substantial hydroelectric capability.

In May 2001 the IMF approved a three-year arrangement for Guinea to "foster macroeconomic stability, promote growth, improve social services and reduce poverty." (Please see the 2013 *Handbook* for an overview of the economy prior to 2001). The country underwent a dramatic economic slowdown in 2003, with GDP growth declining to 1.2 percent. In addition, inflation rose to 14.8 percent. The economic contraction was the result of a range of factors, including poor harvests and a slump in manufacturing caused by significant problems with public utilities. The most significant negative consequence was a major rise in unemployment, with some estimating it as high as 70 percent. Meanwhile, food and fuel prices doubled. Government reform of its tariff and auditing systems, along with other reforms, led to promises of $800 million in debt relief and up to $82 million in economic aid as part of its arrangement with the IMF. However, delays in addressing structural problems, such as privatizing key industries, led some sources to withhold aid.

In the wake of continuing poor economic performance, the IMF approved a staff-monitored program for Guinea for 2005–2006 in an effort to improve structural reforms, reduce poverty, and bolster economic stability, noting that initial benchmarks had been met. Still, fund advisers cited the need for better monetary control, reform of public utilities, and a flexible exchange rate. Meanwhile, annual GDP growth for 2006 was recorded at 2 percent, partially due to a series of union strikes over rising food and fuel prices that disrupted the lucrative bauxite industry. In early 2007 a general strike virtually shut down the country's economy for several weeks. Inflation rose to about 30 percent annually, and food and fuel prices reportedly tripled. Observers described the economy as "teetering on the verge of collapse," and Transparency International ranked Guinea as the most corrupt country

in Africa. After the strikes ended, the government received multimillion-dollar pledges from European donors for infrastructure improvements, the fishing industry, and various reform programs. Also, the IMF approved a three-year poverty-reduction program, and in early 2008 the Paris Club of creditors agreed to cancel $180 million of Guinea's debt and reschedule another $120 million. GDP growth of 2.4 percent in 2009 was overshadowed by the September massacre (see Current issues, below), which resulted in the Africa Development Bank (AfDB) suspending aid, including funding for a $300 million mining project, and sanctions being imposed by the United States and the African Union (AU). Political instability also led to China's postponing plans to invest $5 billion in various projects around the country. However, in May 2010 a Hong Kong firm that reportedly had ties to the Chinese government agreed to invest $2.7 billion in Guinea in exchange for access to vast mining and oil rights. Meanwhile, annual average growth in 2010–2011 was reported to be about 3.1 percent. With political stability returning to the country and the installation of a civilian government in 2011, annual GDP growth was 3.6 percent, and the mining sector became the key focus of foreign investors. GDP grew by 3.9 percent in 2012, while inflation was 15.3 percent, a decline from 21.5 percent the previous year. GDP per capita in 2012 was $518. In 2013 the World Bank ranked Guinea as 178th out of 185 countries in its annual Doing Business survey, reflecting the nation's continuing domestic difficulties in attracting foreign investment.

GOVERNMENT AND POLITICS

Political background. Historically part of the regional kingdom of Ghana, Songhai, and Mali, Guinea was incorporated into the French colonial empire in the late nineteenth century. Post-World War II colonial policy led to increasing political activity by indigenous groups, and in 1947 the Democratic Party of Guinea (PDG) was founded. Under the leadership of Ahmed Sékou TOURÉ, the PDG pushed for independence, and, following rejection of membership in the French Community in a referendum held September 28, 1958, Guinea became the first of France's African colonies to achieve complete independence. Since the PDG already held 58 of the 60 seats in the Territorial Assembly, Sékou Touré automatically became president upon establishment of the republic on October 2, 1958. Although the Soviet Union came to Guinea's aid following the abrupt withdrawal of French technical personnel and a collateral crippling of the new nation's fragile economy, Soviet nationals were expelled in 1961 after being charged with involvement in a teachers' strike.

Foreign intervention has dominated Guinea's history. The most dramatic incident occurred in November 1970 when Guinea was invaded by a force composed of Guinean dissidents and elements of the Portuguese army. The action was strongly condemned by the United Nations and resulted in a wave of arrests and executions. In July 1976 Diallo TELLI, the minister of justice and former secretary general of the Organization of African Unity (OAU, subsequently the African Union—AU), was arrested on charges of organizing an "anti-Guinean front" supported financially by France, the Côte d'Ivoire, Senegal, and the United States. Observers viewed Telli's possible complicity in a conspiracy, coupled with evidence of discontent within the people's militia, as indicative of a potentially serious threat to the Touré regime (the severity of which reportedly prompted the flight of nearly one-quarter of Guinea's population to neighboring countries). Subsequently, French sources reported that Telli had been assassinated in prison while awaiting trial.

President Touré was sworn in for the fifth time on May 14, 1982, after an election five days earlier in which he was credited with close to 100 percent of the votes. However, on March 26, 1984, Africa's longest-serving chief executive died while undergoing heart surgery in the United States. Prime Minister Lansana BEAVOGUI immediately assumed office as acting president, but on April 5 a group of junior military officers seized power in a bloodless coup and announced the appointments of Col. Lansana CONTÉ as president of the Republic and Col. Diarra TRAORÉ as prime minister. Despite Touré's legendary status, the military found themselves in control of what had been described as a police state, with widespread corruption permeating both governmental and party bureaucracies and an economy in shambles. While immediate action was taken by the postcoup administration to reduce political repression, the malfunctioning state-controlled economy presented a more intractable challenge.

Following the April 1984 takeover, power struggles were reported between President Conté and the internationally visible Traoré, the former consolidating his power by abolishing the prime minister's post and demoting Traoré to education minister in a December cabinet reshuffle. Subsequently, on July 4, 1985, while President Conté was out of the country, army elements led by Traoré declared the dissolution of the "corrupt" Conté administration and occupied sections of Conakry. The coup attempt was quelled by loyalist forces prior to the president's return on July 5, most of those involved being arrested, pending trial by military courts. Traoré and his co-conspirators were executed shortly after their imprisonment, although there was no official confirmation of their deaths until 1987.

In late 1988, in an effort to counter domestic opposition to his stringent economic programs and inspire the return of Guinean expatriates, Conté called on men and women "without regard to their abode" to join in the drafting of a bipartisan constitution, which was approved by referendum on December 23, 1990.

On January 9, 1992, in keeping with the spirit of the new basic law, which called for a separation of powers between executive and legislative organs of government, General Conté relinquished the presidency of the quasi-legislative Transitional Committee for National Recovery (CTRN, under Constitution and government, below), while remaining president of the republic. Despite widespread popular protests during the remainder of 1992, the regime rejected appeals for a national conference and countered objections to the pace and breadth of reform by adopting draft laws increasing penalties for the organization of violent demonstrations and banning unauthorized public meetings.

In April 1993 the administration announced plans to hold presidential and legislative elections in the last quarter of the year; however, unrest continued as General Conté rebuffed the opposition's call for an independent electoral commission and all-party talks. In September the government, ignoring the opposition's demand for simultaneous polling, scheduled presidential elections for December 5, with legislative balloting to follow 60 days later. Furthermore, in the wake of violent clashes September 28 and 29 in Conakry, Conté banned all opposition demonstrations until after the elections.

On December 19, 1993, Lansana Conté retained the presidency, leading an 8-candidate field with 51 percent of the vote in polling marred by at least 12 deaths and charges of widespread irregularities. On December 23 the Supreme Court annulled voting results in two opposition districts where second-place finisher Alpha CONDÉ of the Rally of the Guinean People (RPG) had reportedly secured 90 percent of the vote, and on January 4, 1994, the court confirmed the incumbent's victory, ignoring opposition calls for a second round of balloting.

After three postponements, a National Assembly poll was held on June 11, 1995, with 21 of 46 legalized parties participating. Conté's Party of Unity and Progress (PUP) was credited with an absolute majority of 71 of 114 seats and the runner-up RPG with 19, the remainder being distributed across eight other contestants. Most opposition groups challenged the results, although foreign observers indicated that irregularities had been relatively isolated.

On July 5, 1995, the RPG, the Party for Renewal and Progress (*Parti pour le Renouveau et le Progrès*—PRP), and the Union for the New Republic (UNR), who among them controlled 37 seats, announced their intention to boycott the assembly and joined with nine other opposition parties to form the Coordination of Democratic Opposition (Codem). The new formation was denounced by the government, and Conté refused its entreaties to engage in extraparliamentary negotiations. Subsequently, Codem abandoned the boycott, and the inaugural session of the first democratically elected Guinean Assembly opened on October 5, 1995.

On February 2 and 3, 1996, 50 people were killed and more than 100 others wounded when approximately 2,000 soldiers demonstrating for higher wages and better working conditions rampaged through Conakry, ultimately attacking the presidential palace and taking the president hostage. During his brief captivity Conté reached agreement with the soldiers on amnesty for the mutineers, salary increases, and reform of the armed services; however, following the retreat of the rebellious troops, Conté dismissed reports that their attack on his government had occurred spontaneously and accused opposition activists of helping organize the failed "coup" attempt. Thereafter, despite warnings from the insurgents that the "entire army" would retaliate if any of their comrades were arrested, by June at least 52 people had been detained for their roles in the incident, including Lt. Lamine DIARRA, one of the two alleged masterminds of the rebellion, his alleged co-conspirator, Cmdr. Gbago ZOUMANIGUI, having reportedly fled to Libya. (In August some 40 of the detainees were released after the state prosecutor ruled there was insufficient evidence against them.)

On July 9, 1996, Conté named an economist, Sidya TOURÉ, as Guinea's first prime minister since 1984. Touré's appointment was followed on July 17 by a major cabinet reshuffling that included the departure of interior minister Alseny René GOMEZ, theretofore considered the president's second-in-command. On November 3 Conté, in an apparent attempt to reestablish control of military and security forces, appointed himself to head a newly created national defense ministry. The decision came just one day after government forces allegedly orchestrated an attack against Alpha Condé and his RPG supporters that left over 50 people injured. In early 1997 the president proclaimed executive authority over the national bank.

In February 1998 the newly created State Security Council convened the trial of the military personnel allegedly responsible for the February 1996 uprising. However, in March the court proceedings were overshadowed by deadly clashes between opposition activists and government security forces in Conakry that left at least nine dead and a number of opposition figures imprisoned. In response to the government's subsequent refusal to release the jailed militants, opposition legislators affiliated with Codem boycotted the National Assembly. In September relations between the opposition and government deteriorated further when the government dismissed the opposition's call for the establishment of an independent electoral commission and created an electoral affairs committee, which it charged with preparing for presidential elections in December. In October tensions between the Conté administration and National Assembly President El Hadj Boubacar Biro DIALLO reached a nadir as the latter was suspended from the ruling party for criticizing the government's treatment of the alleged February 1996 insurgents (most of whom had been convicted and sentenced to prison in late September).

At presidential elections on December 14, 1998, President Conté won reelection, capturing 56.12 percent of the vote and easily outdistancing his four competitors. As anticipated, the polling results were immediately challenged by the opposition, whose top two contenders, Mamadou Boye BA of the Union for Progress and Renewal (UPR) and Alpha Condé, had officially secured 24.63 and 16.58 percent, respectively. On March 8, 1999, the president appointed Lamine SIDIMÉ (theretofore head of the Supreme Court) as prime minister, with no official explanation given for the change; on March 12 Conté named a moderately reshuffled government, which was sworn in on April 10.

Twice-postponed municipal elections were held on June 25, 2000, with the PUP winning more than three-quarters of the seats. Subsequently, on November 11, 2001, 98 percent of those voting in a national referendum endorsed a controversial constitutional amendment permitting President Conté to run for a third term in 2003, with the term of office extended from five to seven years.

The PUP dominated the June 30, 2002, legislative balloting, securing 85 seats; the UPR finished second with 20 seats. Amid severe controversy over electoral procedures and government control of the media, the major opposition parties boycotted the presidential election of December 21, 2003, at which Conté was reelected with an official 95.6 percent of the vote.

In late February 2004 President Conté dismissed Prime Minister Sidimé without explanation, and François Lonseny FALL was appointed on March 1 to head a reshuffled cabinet with a broad mandate to improve economic conditions. However, following a breakdown in relations with Conté, Fall resigned on April 29 and went into exile in the United States. A new prime minister was not appointed until December 9, when Cellou Dalein DIALLO was named to the post.

The PUP swept the postponed municipal elections on December 18, 2005, securing more than three-quarters of the seats. On April 5, 2006, the president ordered a cabinet reshuffle that granted more control to Diallo, but hours later, after a surprise rescinding of the cabinet changes, the prime minister was dismissed for alleged gross misconduct. On May 29 the president reportedly removed all of Diallo's supporters from the cabinet in a major reshuffle that did not include a prime minister.

Following massive strikes in early 2007, the president appointed one of his confidants, Eugène CAMARA, as prime minister on February 9, resulting in further public protests. Camara, who weeks earlier had been appointed by the president as minister of state for presidential affairs, served as prime minister for only three weeks. On February 26 President Conté named Lansana KOUYATÉ as prime minister with enhanced authority, and Camara returned to his ministerial post. On March 28 Kouyaté named a new cabinet, which included only one member of the previous administration. Following three days of rioting by members of the military over salary and other issues, President Conté replaced the minister of defense on May 12 (see Current issues, below). Subsequently, legislative elections scheduled for June 2007 were postponed until December and subsequently delayed again (with the approval of opposition parties) until December 2008. Those elections never took place.

On May 20, 2008, President Conté dismissed Kouyaté, replacing him the same day with Ahmed Tidiane SOUARÉ, an economist and former minister. A new, expanded cabinet, which included four women, several members of Conté's PUP, and one post each for the UPR, Union of Democratic Forces of Guinea (*Union des Forces Démocratiques de Guinée*—UFDG), and UPG, was appointed on June 19.

President Conté, who had been in ill health for years, died at the age of 74, on December 22, 2008. Hours after his death a group of junior military officers, calling themselves the National Council for Democracy and Development (*Comité National pour le Developpement et la Démocratie*—CNDD), seized power by proclaiming over the airwaves that a coup had taken place. The seated government challenged the claim, but on December 24 the CNDD named its leader, Capt. Moussa Dadis CAMARA, as president, and he immediately dissolved the government, suspended the constitution, and imposed a moratorium on the activities of all political parties and unions. On December 30 the CNDD named a civilian, Kabiné KOMARA, as prime minister, despite calls by supporters of former prime minister Souaré for him to head an interim government and insisting that the speaker of the assembly, Aboubacar SOMPARÉ, be installed as president in accordance with constitutional provisions. Meanwhile, Souaré, Somparé, and other government officials were sent to a military camp for an "informational meeting" and subsequently endorsed the junta. A new, enlarged government composed of technocrats and soldiers (and no members of political parties) was announced on January 14, 2009. Though Camara had pledged that presidential and parliamentary elections would be held in 2010, civilian and political groups urged a December 2009 date, following proposed legislative elections in October. In late March 2009 the government agreed to set presidential balloting on December 13 (with a second round scheduled for December 27, if necessary), owing to intense pressure from international donors, the AU, and the Economic Community of West African States (ECOWAS), with Camara ultimately declaring that neither he nor members of the junta would participate. However, following what came to be known as the "September massacre" (see Current issues, below), electoral plans began to unravel. One minister resigned in protest on October 12, and three others followed suit the following week. Minor cabinet reshuffles occurred on October 29 and November 5. In the wake of the December 3 assassination attempt on Camara by one of his military aides, he left the country for medical treatment, and the minister of defense, Gen. Sékouba KONATÉ, assumed presidential duties on December 4.

On January 12, 2010, Camara attended talks with Konaté and opposition leaders in Burkina Faso, mediated by President Blaise Compaoré, and agreed to return Guinea to civilian rule, conditioned on the military not contesting the elections and Camara's continuing his recovery outside the country. Subsequent meetings between Konaté and opposition leaders resulted in accord on the January 20 appointment of the UPG's Jean-Marie DORÉ as prime minister for a period of six months. He was sworn in on January 26 and named an interim government on February 15. On March 7 Konaté announced that multiparty presidential balloting would be held on June 27. Former prime minister Cellou Dalein Diallo of the UFDG finished at the top of the list of 24 candidates, with 44 percent of the vote, followed by Alpha Condé with 18 percent, forcing a runoff, scheduled for July 18. Following accusations of fraud by some candidates, including Sidya Touré of the small Union of Republican Forces (*Union des Forces Republicains*—UFR), who finished third, the Supreme Court began a review of the claims, Konaté threatened to resign, and the runoff was postponed until August 1. Meanwhile, Prime Minister Doré banned demonstrations ahead of the election, and the Supreme Court rejected efforts by Doré and others in the government to be involved in organizing the second round, subsequently rescheduled for August 14. However, on August 9 the poll was further postponed to September 19. On September 10 two elections officials were charged with vote tampering and sentenced to a year in prison, and four days later the head of the electoral commission, who had been convicted of falsifying the results of first-round voting, died in a Paris hospital. After several more delays, the runoff was held on November 7. Condé was declared the winner with 52.5 percent of the vote in what was internationally hailed as the country's first free and fair election since independence. Diallo, who secured 47.4 percent, challenged the results and refused to concede until the official tally was confirmed by the Supreme Court on December 2. Condé was sworn in on December 21, and Doré and his government resigned the same day. On December 24 the president named Mohamed Said FOFANA, an economist, as prime minister and began forming a new government, giving himself the defense portfolio and including members of several other parties that had supported him in the second round. He appointed a former adviser to the critical mines portfolio on January 5, 2011, as well as 10 more ministers, with one additional appointment on January 7.

Following suppression of opposition protests in August 2012 (see Current Issues, below), the minister of planning and the minister of economic control and audits resigned in protest. Both were members of Kouyaté's newly formed grouping, the Party of Hope and National Development (*Parti de l'Espir pour le Développement National*—PEDN). The resignations were part of an opposition boycott of the government and legislature.

On October 5, 2012, Condé conducted a major cabinet reshuffle, creating a government that, for the first time since 2008, did not included serving members of the military. In addition, the last three senior generals involved in the 2008 coup resigned.

Legislative elections were held on September 28, 2013, after having been postponed multiple times since their orginally planned date in June of 2007 (see Current Issues, below). RPG won 53 of 114 seats followed by UDFG with 37 seats and UFR with 10 seats. The remaining 14 seats were divided between 12 minor parties. While a number of irregularities have been cited by observers, the Guinea Supreme Court has upheld the election.

Constitution and government. The 1982 constitution was suspended and the Democratic Party of Guinea dissolved by the Military Committee for National Recovery (*Comité Militaire de Redressement National*—CMRN) in the wake of the April 1984 coup. Subsequently, Guinea was ruled by a president and Council of Ministers named by the CMRN, although the committee itself was dissolved on January 16, 1991, in favor of a Transitional Committee for National Recovery (*Comité Transitoire de Redressement National*—CTRN). The new body, which was to govern the country until the election of an all-civilian administration, included equal numbers of military and civilian personnel.

In a decree issued in May 1984, President Conté ordered that the name "People's Revolutionary Republic of Guinea," adopted in 1978, be dropped in favor of the country's original name, the Republic of Guinea. Subsequently, he announced the formation of a "truly independent judiciary" and revival of the theretofore outlawed legal profession. In August 1985 a Court of State Security was established, with a supreme court judge, two military officers, and two attorneys, to try "crimes against the state."

A 50-member committee, led by Foreign Affairs Minister Maj. Jean TRAORÉ, was appointed in October 1988 to draft a new constitution, which was reportedly approved by 99 percent of the participants in a referendum on December 23, 1990. The new *loi fondamentale* validated replacement of the CMRN by the CTRN, which in turn yielded authority in 1995 to a civilian regime consisting of a president and unicameral legislature, both popularly elected under two-party (subsequently multiparty) auspices, and an independent judiciary. A presidential decree on June 19, 1997, established a consultative Economic and Social Council whose 45 members are appointed by the president upon the recommendation of various civic institutions.

The 1990 constitution was suspended by the president of the transitional CNDD, composed of 26 military officers and 6 civilians, following the coup of December 2008. Constitutional order was restored following the presidential election in late 2010. In 2013 Reporters Without Borders ranked Guinea 86th out of 179 countries in freedom of the press.

The country is administratively organized into four main geographic divisions—Maritime, Middle, Upper, and Forest Guinea—which are subdivided into eight regions—Boké, Faranah, Kankan, Kindia, Labé, Mamou, N—Zérékoré, and Conakry. The Conakry region is subdivided into five "urban communes," while the remaining seven regions are subdivided into a total of 33 prefectures.

Foreign relations. President Touré's brand of militant nationalism and his frequent allegations of externally provoked conspiracy led to strained international relations, including diplomatic ruptures with France (1965–1975), Britain (1967–1968), and Ghana (1966–1973). By January 1978, however, Conakry had moved to ease long-standing tensions with its immediate neighbors. Shortly thereafter, diplomatic relations with Senegal and the Côte d'Ivoire were restored. In October 1980 Guinea acceded to the Mano River Union (MRU), formed seven years earlier to promote economic cooperation between Liberia and Sierra Leone, while in March 1982 Touré called for the unification of Guinea and Mali, arguing that economically the two countries were "two lungs in a single body." In subsequent years Conakry also increased its visibility in the ECOWAS.

In December 1978 French President Giscard d'Estaing visited Guinea, the first Western leader to do so in over two decades. The extremely warm reception he received was viewed as part of a broad effort to scale down assistance from Soviet and other Eastern bloc countries in favor of Western aid and investment. In keeping with the policy shift, President Touré made a number of trips to the United States, Canada, and Western Europe from 1979 to 1983. However, distrust of the "father of African socialism" and an overvalued local currency discouraged large-scale Western involvement. By contrast, in the wake of the 1984 coup, Prime Minister Traoré negotiated a broad aid package with France, while French and other foreign investment increased significantly upon the adoption of monetary and fiscal reforms recommended by the IMF.

Despite Guinean fears of a new "colonialism," raised by the influx of foreign merchants and military advisers into the capital, Conakry continued to pursue external assistance in developing its infrastructure and mineral resources, while concluding resource-development agreements with Morocco, Guinea-Bissau, and Liberia in 1989.

In early 1990 an influx of refugees fleeing the Liberian civil war quickly exhausted the reserves of Guinea's southern border region, and in May, President Conté called for international aid to support refugees claimed to number 200,000. In August, Conakry deployed troops to seal its southern border after a rebel incursion in alleged reprisal for Guinea's participation in ECOWAS activity in Liberia.

In September 1992, after a three-month cease-fire aimed at inducing Liberian and Sierra Leonean rebels to disarm and accept a full amnesty, Guinean and Sierra Leonean troops resumed their joint efforts to repel rebels in eastern and southern Sierra Leone. Meanwhile, the publication of a report claiming that Guinea had trained a Liberian paramilitary force assigned to interim Liberian president Amos Sawyer led to the detainment of its author. In August 1994, 35,000 Liberians were reported to have fled into Guinea, raising the five-year total to approximately 500,000.

In April 1996 Mali recalled its ambassador and criticized the Conté administration after Guinean troops stormed into the Malian embassy in Conakry in search of a leader of the February military uprising. Clashes between Malian and Guinean residents were subsequently reported in April and October near the border.

In April 1997 Belgium closed its consular offices after Conakry refused to release three Belgian nationals it had arrested in March for allegedly plotting to overthrow the government. Meanwhile, observers reported that Guinean security forces had arrested and then released 75 Liberian refugees on similar charges.

Amid reports that rebels from Sierra Leone had attacked a town in southern Guinea, in early December 1998 Conakry announced that it was closing its borders until after the presidential polling scheduled for December 14. Further Sierra Leonean cross-border activity was reported in early 1999, and in April Liberian troops threatened to enter Guinean territory in pursuit of Liberian antigovernment rebels, whom Monrovia accused Conakry of at least tacitly supporting. In August at least two dozen people died when militants, allegedly operating from a base in Liberia, attacked a town in southern Guinea, and in mid-September Charles Taylor claimed that Guinean forces had killed several hundred Liberians during raids in April and August. Conté subsequently called his Liberian counterpart a "warmonger," although at the same time insisting that no problems existed between the two countries' peoples.

In March 2000 Guinea, Liberia, and Sierra Leone reportedly agreed to the immediate reactivation of the MRU secretariat. (Due to civil wars the body had been dormant since 1990.) However, Guinea and Liberia were subsequently described as still "trading destabilization accusations." (See article on Liberia for additional information.)

Economic relations between France and Guinea continued to remain strong through the early 2000s, but Conakry also began to develop stronger security ties with the United States, which had provided military training and equipment to improve Guinea's military capabilities for regional peacekeeping missions. The appointment of Prime Minister Fall, an English speaker and widely seen as pro-American, as opposed to pro-French, was perceived as a sign of Conté's desire to improve relations with the United States. One manifestation of the increased ties between the two countries was a decrease in Guinean support for Liberian rebel groups, and broad support from Conakry for the United Nations peacekeeping mission in Liberia after the departure of President Charles Taylor from that country. By mid-2006, a marked decrease in violence at the border with Liberia was reported. In August, Guinea and South Korea agreed to establish bilateral relations.

Relations with regional neighbors and the United States deteriorated quickly in the wake of the 2008 coup by a military junta. Both the AU and ECOWAS suspended Guinea pending democratic elections, and the United States and the European Union (EU) condemned the coup and immediately suspended all aid except for emergency and humanitarian assistance. Nigeria refused to acknowledge the coup leaders, while Senegal urged the international community to recognize the junta.

The support of Libya was reaffirmed in 2010 after acting president Konaté and what was reported as "a large delegation of his government" attended the 41st anniversary celebration of the Libyan Revolution on September 1.

In June 2012 France canceled €53.7 million of Guinea's debt and rescheduled an additional €97.1 million. In September the World Bank and the IMF announced that Guinea had qualified for $2.1 billion in debt relief under the Heavily Indebted Poor Countries (HIPC) initiative. This would eliminate two-thirds of Guinea's external debt.

In June 2013 Guinea was one of 16 African countries cited by France as the future beneficiaries of a new focus on international economic assistance. During a March visit by Russian Foreign Minister Sergei Lavrov, a long-running dispute that had idled a Russian-own aluminum facility was settled. Russia agreed to pay $832 million, to settle back taxes and royalty payments.

Current issues. In December 2008, following the death of President Conté, a bloodless coup was staged by junior military officers in a grouping called the CNDD. Moussa Dadis Camara, a 44-year-old junior officer appointed president by the CNDD, broadcast news of the takeover early on December 23, announcing that a transitional "consultative council" of military and civilian personnel would run the country with the dual aims of reviving the economy and fighting corruption. Camara's immediate dissolution of the government and suspension of the constitution and all political parties were challenged by Prime Minister Souaré and by the assembly speaker, Aboubacar Sompаré, the latter asking the Supreme Court to name him president as stipulated by the constitution. Camara quickly moved to quash support for such requests, stating that the National Assembly's mandate had ended in 2007. Camara subsequently promised to renegotiate and monitor mining contracts and to fight corruption. Souaré and others subsequently made positive pronouncements about the junta. Meanwhile, Conté's funeral in Conakry on December 26 was attended by 20,000 people, including leaders from neighboring countries, but not by Camara. With tensions still simmering, soldiers were sent to search the home of former prime minister and current UFDG leader Cellou Diallo in an effort to quell suspicions of what the junta reportedly said might be another coup plot. Meanwhile, former prime minister Kouyaté returned to Conakry from Côte d'Ivoire for the first time since his dismissal by President Conté, to attend the funeral and to meet with Camara.

Despite initial confusion and a short-lived curfew after the announcement of Conté's death, the military takeover was reported to be well-received by the public. Opposition groups were said to have greeted news of the coup "with delight," extending to the naming of the new prime minister, a banker, on December 30, 2008, and a new cabinet appointed two weeks later. The transitional government included numerous economists and technocrats who were seen as the appropriate choices to lead the country out of economic and civil crises. Meanwhile, the coup was also popular with more junior members of the military who had been alienated by the Conté government's perceived favoritism to senior officers. Camara, for his part, promised to reform the military by upgrading salaries and promotion structures, among other things.

Among Camara's first announcements was that elections would be held in 2010 (in order to provide enough time to prepare for free and fair balloting), but he later bowed to internal and external pressures and revised the date to sometime in 2009. In the days following the coup, 11 political parties and groups had proposed a transition scheme to the junta, including provisions for a national transition council, a transitional period not to exceed 12 months, prohibitions against Camara and other CNDD officials participating in national elections, and the establishment of a special court to resolve constitutional and electoral disputes. In February 2009 Camara presented his own transition plan, proposing a process to restore constitutional order, register voters, and lift the suspension of political parties and union activities. He also called for the establishment of a truth and reconciliation committee to review charges against the previous government. Meanwhile, the most vocal public criticism of the junta was directed toward a few appointees in the cabinet who allegedly had been involved in fraud or linked to drug trafficking. Camara, in a follow-up to his anti-corruption promises, quickly ordered the arrests of numerous former government officials, among them Conté's son, Ousmane, and three former ministers in charge of mines, including former prime minister Ahmed Tidiane Souaré. All three ministers were accused of stealing millions of dollars from the mining ministry. Ousmane Conté made a public confession on television to having smuggled cocaine. The junta also investigated numerous business executives in connection with alleged corruption. A fourth former mines minister was arrested in March; the three who had been arrested earlier were released on bail in April after they agreed to repay the stolen money.

While the anti-corruption efforts gained Camara popular support, as did his call for "free, credible, and transparent elections," it was unclear whether Camara would adhere to his original declaration that junta members should not contest the elections, as he later insisted he had the right to run. He also said that those who had been in power under President Conté should not contest the elections, referring to leaders of the PUP, UFR, and UFDG, observers said. In April 2009 Camara agreed to proposals by various groups calling for parliamentary elections on October 11 and presidential balloting on December 13, with a second round, if necessary, on December 27. Further, Camara excluded himself and other junta members from contesting the elections. However, in August the electoral commission postponed presidential elections to January 31, 2010, to be followed by legislative elections in March. Political tensions heightened in the midst of the electoral confusion, culminating in what was subsequently called a "massacre" on September 28 when at least 150 people were killed and 1,200 wounded when security forces opened fire in a football stadium in Conarky filled with 50,000 people protesting against the regime. International condemnation was swift, with France calling an emergency EU meeting to address punishment for those responsible. Four ministers resigned within weeks, and opposition parties rejected a proposal to form a unity government. Camara, for his part, said he was sorry about the events, blaming "uncontrollable elements" in the military, but the remarks did not sway the international community, which imposed extensive sanctions against the regime. Political turmoil was unabated, as on December 3 Camara was shot and wounded by one of his closest aides, Aboubacar DIAKITÉ. Camara was flown to Morocco for treatment after the assassination attempt, and on December 4 the minister of defense, Gen. Sékouba Konaté, took over as acting president. In early January 2010 Camara, who had remained out of the country, was flown to Burkina Faso for mediated talks with Konaté and opposition leaders.

It was agreed that Guinea would be returned to civilian rule within six months, the military would not contest the elections, and Camara would continue his recovery outside of the country. Also, accord was reached on the appointment on January 20 of interim prime minister Jean-Marie Doré of the UPG, who was among those wounded during the September 2009 "massacre" that Diakité had allegedly ordered, an event observers said led to deep divisions in the military and, consequently, the attempt on Camara's life. Diakité admitted to the assassination attempt, saying he had been threatened with arrest. Further, he blamed the September killings on Camara.

With the installation of Doré on January 26, 2010, and the regime's pledge toward steps to establish a civilian government, France agreed to cooperate in the process. In March 2010 acting president Konaté announced that presidential elections would be held on June 27, and he appointed a 155-member council to oversee the transition. Subsequently, the EU lifted some sanctions, and attention focused on the upcoming poll, which was contested by 24 candidates and conducted in "a festive atmosphere," according to the *International Herald Tribune*. Since none of the candidates garnered a majority, however, a runoff was scheduled for July 18 for the top vote-getters, former prime minister Cellou Dalien Diallo of the UFDG (who received 44 percent of the vote) and Alpha Condé of the RPG (18 percent). Sidya Touré of the UFR, who finished third with 15.6 percent, threw his support behind Diallo for the second round. In fourth place, with just 7.7 percent of the vote, was former prime minister Lansana Kouyaté of the Party of Hope for National Development (*Parti de l'Espir pour le Développement National*—PEDN), which he founded in 2009. Despite observers" declarations that the elections were free and fair, almost all of the candidates complained of irregularities, and subsequently, the second round, originally set for July 18, was again postponed from August 14 to September 19 after the Supreme Court found evidence of fraud. The head of the electoral commission, Ben Sekou Sylla, and another top elections official were convicted of fraud and sentenced to a year in prison. On September 12 fighting erupted between supporters of the two leading candidates, resulting in the death of 1 person and injuries to 50. A few days later, Sylla died in a Paris hospital of an undisclosed illness. In the wake of the violence, second-round balloting was again postponed. On October 10 Konaté announced that official campaigning would begin on October 11 in preparation for second-round balloting on October 24. However, violent clashes in the capital on October 19 prompted another delay. Konaté appointed a Mali national of the International Organization of the Francophonie to head the electoral commission, which subsequently announced that the run-off would be held on October 31. The RPG agreed, but the UFDG alternatively proposed November 7 to allow more time to resolve problems. Two broad electoral alliances formed ahead of the runoff: the Alliance Cellou in Diallo's camp and the *Alliance Arc-en-Ciel* (Rainbow Alliance), which included former prime ministers Kouyaté and Fall, backing Condé. Following Condé's victory in the election, which ended years of military rule and was attributed in large part to his having made alliances "across the board," Diallo immediately challenged the results, claiming voter intimidation and electoral fraud, and refused to concede. On November 15 the election commission declared Condé the winner, and the president called for national unity. However, Diallo vowed to take his challenge to the Supreme Court. Tensions heightened across the country, and though Diallo and Condé urged calm, violence broke out between the two main ethnic groups, the Malinké, who largely supported Condé, and the Fulani, who backed Diallo. At least 10 people were reported killed and 200 injured in Conarky and two other cities. On November 17 General Konaté decreed a state of emergency in the country. Following the Supreme Court's ratifying the election results on December 2, restrictions imposed during the state of emergency were eased, and the country's sea and air borders were reopened, but the land borders remained closed. The new head of the armed forces announced the end of the state of emergency on December 10. Constitutional order was officially restored, and the AU acknowledged the event by lifting tsanctions it had imposed after the junta took control. On December 24 the president began making appointments to his new government, including prime minister Fofana and members of several parties who had challenged him in the first round of the presidential poll but rallied to support him in the long-delayed runoff.

Foremost among President Condé's concerns in 2011 was a review of major mining contracts and establishing new regulations for future investment in an effort to rid the process of corruption. He invited U.S. philanthropist George Soros to help formulate a new mining code, a move that drew protests from several international entities, including China. In March the EU lifted sanctions (imposed after the junta took over) against 84 of 89 people allegedly involved in a crackdown on political protesters in 2009. Among those still under sanction was junta leader Camara. On March 17 the president established a national human rights commission headed by Mamady KABA, former president of the Guinea chapter of the African Assembly for the Defense of Human Rights. The country's calm was soon broken following the president's ban on demonstrations to welcome arrival the Conarky arrival of Diallo on April 3. Nevertheless, supporters greeted Condé's main political rival in defiance of the ban, which, *Africa Confidential* noted, "does not augur well for democracy." Demonstrators clashed with police, and some reports listed three UFDG activists killed and 60 wounded. A total of 27 people in Conarky and another city were arrested and sentenced to a year in jail, while 17 others were freed after being fined.

Attention turned to elections for the National Assembly, which had been dissolved following the coup in 2008, when the political affairs minister recommended in July 2011 that a census for a new voter register be held in advance of any polling. The UFDG and the UFR opposed the proposal, claiming that a census would be weighted in favor of the governing RPG. Meanwhile, the EU promised to release its grant money for Guinea once the country holds legislative elections, which were scheduled to take place before the end of the year. However, repeated postponements led to a series of protests and demonstrations. On September 27, 2011, two protestors were killed and 322 arrested during a demonstration in Conkary. Meanwhile, in December, Condé demobilized 4,000 troops as part of a broader effort to reduce government spending and lessen the power of the military.

In February 2012 Col. Mouse Camara, an official in the president's office in charge of combatting organized crime, was charged for his involvement in the 2009 Conkary stadium massacre. In March elections were set for July 8 but were subsequently postponed to March 2013. On August 27 police blocked an opposition demonstration. Scores of demonstrators and police were injured, and 38 were arrested. In response, opposition parties announced a boycott of the government and legislature.

A 2012 report by Doctors Without Borders found that 1.5 percent of Guinea's population were infected with HIV/AIDS and only 40 percent of those had access to anti-retroviral drugs. In October 2012 the Global Fund for AIDS, Tuberculosis, and Malaria gave Guinea $120 million to combat the chronic diseases.

Following further delays in scheduling legislative balloting in March 2013, anti-government protests spread from Conakry to other cities. During the increasingly violent demonstrations, five were killed and more than 200 injured. A new wave of protests in May left 12 dead and 90 wounded. In response, President Condi announced an investigation into the protests and replaced his Minister of the Interior. Elections were scheduled for September 24 in an effort to avoid the suspension of international aid by the EU. But tensions continued to rise in July, August, and September when the government refused to allow the opposition to hold a march in Conakry. Parliamentary elections were finally held on 28 September with an election run up marred by widespread protest and suspected election fraud. President Alpha Condi's RPG party won 53 of 114 seats, failing to obtain the absolute majority needed to govern. Opposition has continued to demand the election be voided despite a court ruling supporting the election results. Protests have continued into November with one killed and nine wounded in a clash over the alleged attempted kidnapping of a popular radio host who had been critical of President Condi.

POLITICAL PARTIES AND GROUPS

Prior to the 1984 coup, Guinea was a typical one-party state, according a monopoly position to the now defunct Democratic Party of Guinea (*Parti Démocratique de Guinée*—PDG) in all aspects of public life. The Military Committee for National Recovery's initial promise of an introduction of "democracy" was reaffirmed in 1989 by President Conté, and the constitution approved in December 1990 included provisions for two parties, with numerous others being recognized in 1991 and 1992.

During 1993 a number of somewhat transitory opposition coalitions emerged, including Democratic Change (*Changement Démocratique*—CD), a 30-party grouping under whose banner activists clashed with police in Conakry in September. The principal opposition alliances in the run-up to the December presidential balloting were AGUNA (below) and the BPG, while nine of the nearly four dozen recognized parties were reportedly members of a "Presidential Tendency" headed by the PUP (below).

In August 1995 the "Presidential Tendency" splintered because of the failure of the PUP and a number of its erstwhile allies to reach agreement on a new assembly president; subsequently, the defecting parties formed the **Alliance of Democratic Forces** (*Alliance pour les Forces Démocratiques*—AFD), under the leadership of Oumar CAMARA.

Two somewhat overlapping opposition alliances were formed in 2001 to attempt to stop Conté from running for a third term. In July the UFR, the UFDG, and others formed the **Democratic Change in 2003** (*Alternance Démocratique en 2003*) to oppose the upcoming referendum on amending the constitution. Subsequently, opposition activity focused on the **Movement against the Referendum and for Democratic Change** (*Mouvement Contre le Référendum et pour l'Alternance Démocratique*—Morad), formed by the Codem, UFR, PGP, and four other parties.

In advance of the next legislative elections, postponed until late 2008 (but never held), it was reported that 13 small parties had left the governing coalition of the PUP in May 2007 to form a new coalition referenced as the **National Alliance for Democracy**, organized by the UFR's Sidya Touré. Among the minor parties participating were the **National Union for Progress of Guinea**, the **Liberal Party of Guinea**, and the **National Alliance for Progress**.

A coalition styled as the **Republican Front for Democratic Change** (*Front de L'Alternance Démocratique*—FRAD) was originally formed by a coalition of four parties in 2002 and then grew to include seven of the main opposition parties. FRAD emerged from previous anti-Conté groupings, principally the Coordination of the Democratic Opposition (*Coordination de l'Opposition Démocratique*—Codem). The Codem was formed by the RPG, PRP, UNR, and a number of other smaller parties to mount a legislative boycott in response to alleged ballot fraud in the June 1995 poll. In early February 1996 the group supported President Conté's handling of the military unrest in Conakry; however, after the president alleged that opposition activists had been involved in the uprising, Codem parliamentarians boycotted the assembly. Thereafter, intracoalition conflict was reported between the PRP's Siradiou DIALLO, who advocated establishing a dialogue with the administration, and the RPG's Alpha Condé, who accused the regime of harassment and the illegal detention of opposition activists.

In late 1996 the Codem announced that it was forming a "resistance militia" in response to violent attacks against its members and to fend off security forces attempting to arrest its supporters. Thereafter, the coalition criticized the Conté administration for reducing the prime minister's powers. Underscoring its increasing hostility toward Conté's policies, the Codem in early 1998 established an Executive Secretariat to coordinate "acts of resistance" against the government. In March a number of opposition leaders, including the UNR's Mamadou Ba, were arrested after violent clashes erupted in Conakry between opposition protesters and government forces. Subsequently, the Codem boycotted legislative proceedings in an effort to persuade the government to release its imprisoned members. (In June, Ba was given a "lenient verdict" and released.) Codem boycotted the 2001 presidential referendum and announced that it would also boycott the upcoming legislative elections. In 2002 a split emerged in Codem over participation in the presidential elections, leading to the breakup of Codem and the creation of the FRAD by parties that planned to boycott the elections. The main difference between Codem and the FRAD was the absence of the UPR. Nonetheless, many of the most prestigious and well-respected opposition figures, including Condé, Ba, Touré, and Boubacar Biro Diallo (the then president of the assembly), joined the coalition. The FRAD led the opposition to the presidential election in 2003 and organized a succession of protests and demonstrations against the regime. In response, most of the FRAD's leadership figures, including Condé, Ba, and Touré, were arrested for brief periods. In 2005 FRAD leaders called on the president to resign to allow for transition to a government of national unity. At that time, the FRAD included the RPG, UFR, UPG, UFDG, and two minor parties: the **African Democratic Party** (*Parti Démocratique Africain*—PDA), led by Marcel CROS, and the **Djama Party** (*Parti Djama*), a moderate Islamist party led by Mohamed Mansour KABA. (The status of FRAD at the time of the 2010 presidential election was unclear.)

Political parties were suspended by the military junta in December 2008. Soon after the coup, a group of 11 political parties and groups presented the junta with a plan for transitional governance and called for elections in 2009. Among the political parties were the PDA, UFD, RPG, UFDG, Djama, and UPG.

Eighteen new parties were formed ahead of the June 2010 presidential election.

Government and Government-Supportive Parties:

Rally of the Guinean People (*Rassemblement Populaire Guinéen*—RPG). In early 1991 Alpha Condé received an enthusiastic welcome from RPG members upon his return from exile. Subsequently, on May 19 government troops violently disrupted the party's attempt to hold an inaugural meeting.

In February 1993 the RPG and the UNR were accused of inciting antigovernment violence in rural communities, and Condé subsequently appealed unsuccessfully for a joint opposition candidate in the December presidential poll, in which he was runner-up with a 19.55 vote share.

In 1994 the RPG adopted a new platform urging "peace, justice, and solidarity," and in April Condé reiterated the party's desire "to prepare for parliamentary elections in a transparent manner." Nonetheless, RPG activists subsequently accused the government of attempting to assassinate their leader, and in September 1995 at least one person was killed when RPG militants clashed with government security forces in Nzérekoré.

On November 2, 1996, already confrontational relations between the RPG and the government reached their nadir when government security forces allegedly organized an attack on a motorcade carrying Condé and an RPG building was attacked by arsonists. Furthermore, on November 19 two prominent RPG leaders, Saliou CISSÉ and Keita BENTOUBA, were arrested. RPG leaders derided the arrests, reportedly describing them as a "dangerous, resounding slip-up," and in late December Codem officials cited the November incidents as catalysts for their decision to launch a militia.

The Codem's legislative boycott in early 1998 was prompted in part by the ransacking of the RPG's headquarters and the arrest of two RPG parliamentarians. Thereafter, in early December Alpha Condé returned from self-imposed exile to campaign for the presidency. Despite the large turnouts that greeted his public appearances, the RPG candidate finished a distant third in the polling. Furthermore, on December 15 Condé was arrested as he prepared to enter Côte d'Ivoire, and a number of RPG activists were jailed for their alleged participation in the violent unrest that followed the release of the polling results. Having garnered substantial regional and global interest, the trial of Condé and more than 40 codefendants concluded in September 2000 with Condé being found guilty of sedition. His prison sentence was cut short by a presidential pardon in May 2001. Condé returned to Conakry in 2005 after two years of self-imposed exile in Paris, to help organize the party ahead of the December municipal elections (in which the RPG won only a handful of seats). The RPG backed the unions' demands in their 2006–2007 strikes and urged party members to participate in civil disobedience. Numerous party members reportedly were arrested during the protests. In May 2007 the RPG refused to participate in negotiations with the government and other political parties on preparations for the next legislative elections, but the party was planning to participate in the elections.

Following the 2008 coup, Condé called the members of the junta "patriots" but said he would never participate in a government that was not democratically elected.

Following talks in Burkina Faso in January 2010, in which Camara agreed to allow Konaté to pursue the necessary steps toward civilian rule, Condé applauded the appointment of Doré as a "big step" in resolving the political crisis.

Following Condé's second-place finish (by nearly 20 percentage points) in the first round of multiparty presidential balloting in June 2010, many observers believed former prime minister Diallo would win the runoff. However, the lengthy delays gave Condé time to put together alliances "across the board," observers said, pushing him ahead of Diallo in what was Condé's third run at the presidency.

In January 2012, the RPG formed a new version of its 2010 electoral coalition, the RPG Rainbow Alliance, along with the small **Rally for the Defense of the Republic** and the **Democratic Rally for Development** (see below). Ahead of the planned September 2013 legislative balloting, reports indicated that the RPG Rainbow Alliance had grown to more than 40 parties. RPG won 53 seats of 114 in the much delayed and opposition protested September elections.

Leaders: Alpha CONDÉ (President of the Republic), Ahmed CISSÉ, Ibrahima Kalil KEITA.

Union for Progress and Renewal (*Union pour le Progrès et le Renouvellement*—UPR). The UPR was launched in September 1998 as a merger of the PRP and the UNR. While leadership of the new grouping was assumed by Siradiou Diallo, the PRP's secretary general and

1993 presidential candidate, the UNR's Mamadou Boye Ba, was named the UPR's presidential candidate. Ba, who had been detained from March to June for his alleged role in the violent clashes in Conakry, finished second in the December balloting with 22 percent of the vote.

The UPR factionalized in 2002, with members who advocated dialogue with Conté and participation in elections remaining in the UPR under Diallo. Those UPR members who supported boycotting the upcoming legislative elections joined the Union of Democratic Forces of Guinea, of which Ba became president. Diallo died on March 14, 2004, of a heart attack, and the UPR elected Ousmane Bah as leader of the party. The UPR reportedly withdrew from the assembly in protest following the municipal elections of December 2005, which the party claimed were "nothing short of electoral robbery." The UPR legislators ultimately returned to parliament, and in 2007 party members participated in talks with Prime Minister Kouyaté regarding postponement of the 2007 legislative elections.

The UPR was represented in the new government formed by Prime Minister Souaré in June 2008.

Ahead of the 2010 presidential poll, the UDR was seen as attracting many Fulani votes in central Guinea, and thus posing something of a challenge to the UFDG's Diallo, but the party was not seen as an electoral threat nationwide. Bah, the party's flagbearer, finished 11th with 0.6 percent of the vote. He pledged his party's support to Alpha Condé in the second round of presidential balloting and was appointed minister of state for public works and transport, a post he retained in the October 2012 cabinet reshuffle.

UPR secured one seat in the September 28, 2013, parliamentary elections.

Leader: Ousmane BAH (President of the Party and 2010 presidential candidate).

Party of Hope for National Development (*Parti de l'Espir pour le Développement National*—PEDN). Former prime minister Lansana Kouyaté started the PEDN in March 2009 following his return to the country after he was dismissed from the government by President Conté. According to its Web site, the liberal democratic party was founded on several principles, including duty, giving youth a chance, fighting poverty and demagoguery, and promoting cultural and traditional values. It also stated that the party adheres to the charters of the UN and the AU.

In the June 2010 presidential balloting, Kouyaté finished fourth with 7.8 percent of the vote. Ahead of the second-round balloting in September, the PEDN formed the Rainbow electoral alliance with the RPG, among others, to back Alpha Condé. Two members of PEDN were appointed to cabinet positions but resigned in August 2012 as part of an opposition boycott of the government. In May 2013 the PEDN announced it would boycott legislative elections scheduled for September but ended up securing 2 seats during the September 28 elections.

Leader: Lansana KOUYATÉ (Former Prime Minister and 2010 presidential candidate).

United Front for Democracy and Change (*Front Uni pour la Démocratie et le Changement*—FUDEC) Former prime minister and diplomat François Lonseny Fall formed the FUDEC "for a democratic and prosperous Guinea" ahead of the 2010 presidential election, in which he finished 14th with 0.4 percent of the vote. As head of the Rainbow Alliance that backed Condé, Fall was subsequently appointed secretary general of the presidency in the new government. In October 2012 Fall became the minister of state for foreign affairs.

Leader: François Lonseny FALL.

Minor parties that supported Condé in the second round of presidential balloting in 2010 were the **Rally for the Defense of the Republic,** led by Papa Koly KOUROUMAH, a first-round candidate who finished fifth with 4.8 percent of the vote, and the **Rally for the Integral Development of Guinea** (RDIG), led by Jean Marc TELLIANO, who finished seventh in the first round with 1.9 percent. Both Kouroumah and Telliano were named to cabinet posts in the new administration. RDIG secured one seat in the September 2013 parliamentary elections.

Other Parties That Contested the 2010 Presidential Election:

Union of Democratic Forces of Guinea (*Union des Forces Démocratiques de Guinée*—UFDG). The UFDG was one of the first parties applying for legal status in 1991. Its leader, Amadou Bâ OURY, was arrested on October 27, 1992, for alleged involvement in an attempted assassination of President Conté 11 days earlier, but he was released shortly thereafter in apparent acknowledgment by authorities that false testimony had been given against him.

In May 1996 the UFDG resurfaced as the leading opponent to the National Assembly's adoption of a law that rehabilitated former president Sékou Touré, calling it a "trivialization" of Touré's crimes. After he left the UPR, Mamadou Ba joined the UFDG and was elected president in October 2002. In 2005, Ba distanced himself from some FRAD members and expressed support for Prime Minister Diallo.

In 2007 Ba backed the choice of Kouyaté for prime minister, along with the unions.

Following former prime minister Diallo's return to Guinea in April 2007, it was reported that Ba had taken over leadership of the party.

In 2008 the party received one post in the government formed by Prime Minister Souaré. Following the military coup in December, Diallo's home was raided by soldiers, who accused him of providing arms for a plot against the junta. Prime Minister Kabiné Komara met with Diallo the next day to smooth over the incident.

Diallo, who was credited with bringing key supporters to the UFDG, was tapped by observers and analysts as the front-runner in the 2010 presidential election, which proved to be the case in the first round. Following his defeat in the long-delayed runoff, the UFDG became the main opposition, and Diallo, claiming fraud and irregularities, initially refused to concede. In April 2011 Diallo called for nationwide civil disobedience after scores of UFDG members were detained after they had gathered at the airport in Conarky to greet Diallo upon his arrival. The demonstrations had been prohibited by the president. In May security forces reportedly raided Diallo's home, searching for weapons. President Condé was said to be out of the country at the time.

In October 2011 reports indicated that the UFDG had formed a new opposition coalition, the Front for Democracy and Progress (FDP). Ahead of elections scheduled for September 2013, Diallo urged opposition parties to participate in the balloting and not boycott the polling. UDFG won 37 seats in September 28, 2013 elections.

Leaders: Cellou Dalien DIALLO (Former Prime Minister and 2010 presidential candidate), Mamadou BA.

Party of Unity and Progress (*Parti de l'Unité et du Progrès*—PUP). The PUP nominated Gen. Lansana Conté as its presidential candidate in August 1993, subsequently becoming the core component of an informal regime-supportive coalition that included the **Democratic Rally for Development** (*Rassemblement Démocratique pour le Développement*—RDD), led by Georges Koly GUILAVOGUI.

At the PUP's first national congress, held April 4–7, 1997, Conté was named as the party's candidate for upcoming presidential elections, and Aboubacar Somparé's theretofore interim appointment as PUP secretary general was made permanent.

In January 1998, members of the PUP's youth wing launched the **Movement for Lansana Conté's Reelection** (*Mouvement pour la Réélection de Lansana Conté*—MORELAC). In June the presidential supporters formed the **Association of Movements Affiliated to the Party of Unity and Progress**, a coalition of some 200 parties and groups chaired by Karim KANE. The groups were successful in the 2001 referendum to allow Conté to stand for a third term. In early 2005 feuding between Conté loyalists and those supporting the president's unofficial heir apparent, Youth Minister Fode Soumah, was reported. Late in the year, the party made a strong showing in both rural and urban areas in municipal elections. During the strikes in 2006 and 2007, the PUP criticized the unions for moving beyond their social realm with their political goals.

On May 25, 2007, the party unanimously approved Mamadou Sylla, who had once faced corruption charges, as honorary chair of the party, granting him shared leadership with President Conté, who was long reported to be in ill health. Controversy surrounded Sylla (see Current issues, above), provoking trade unions and civil societies in particular, even though Sylla reportedly had helped bring about the appointment of a prime minister by consensus in response to unions' demands earlier in the year. It was subsequently reported that the situation within the PUP was becoming "increasingly volatile" as the president fought off efforts to diminish his authority. Tensions within the party heightened following Conté's death in December 2008, when six members of the party's national political bureau subsequently were dismissed for trying to install Sylla as interim chair until the next party congress. Sylla started a new party, the Democratic Union of Guinea (below), in advance of the 2010 presidential election.

(Party secretary general Sékou Konaté is not the same as acting president Konaté.)

Ahead of the 2010 presidential elections, many of the key members of the PUP, including Somparé and Konaté, reconciled, and Somparé was named the party's standard-bearer. He finished eighth with a little over 1 percent of the vote. PUP led a series of protests in 2012 against the repeated postponement of legislative elections.

Leaders: Aboubacar SOMPARÉ (2010 presidential candidate), Sékou KONATÉ (Secretary General).

Union of Republican Forces (*Union des Forces Republicains*—UFR). A small grouping formed in 1992, the UFR elected former prime minister Sidya Touré as its president in May 2000. The UFR subsequently was reported to have filed a suit against the government for having prevented its candidates from contesting the June municipal balloting. In 2004 Touré was cleared of charges accusing him of plotting to overthrow the government.

The UFR supported the unions' strikes in 2006–2007.

In 2009 the junta named Touré to a committee formed to review mining agreements as part of the junta's crackdown on corruption. Ahead of the 2010 presidential elections, it was reported that the UFR was financed largely by wealthy allies of acting head of state Gen. Konaté and former prime minister Kouyaté, among others. The UFR was seen as gaining strength under Touré's leadership, though he finished third, with 15.6 percent of the vote. He threw his support behind Diallo in the second round. Touré charged that security forces fired on him and other opposition figures during the August 27 protest in Conkary. He subsequently led calls for an opposition boycott of the government and legislature. UFR secured 10 seats in the September 2013 parliamentary poll despite initially announcing a planned boycott of the legislative elections.

Leaders: Sidya TOURÉ (President of the Party and 2010 presidential candidate), Bakary ZOUMANIGUI (Secretary General).

Liberal Party for Unity and Solidarity (*Parti Libéral pour l'Unité et la Solidarité*—PLUS). Founded by Ousmane KABA, an economist, former finance minister, and UFR dissident, ahead of the 2010 presidential election. Kaba finished 12th with 0.5 percent of the vote.

Other minor parties formed in advance of the 2010 presidential elections and their candidates were: **Guinea for All** (Ibrahima Kassory FOFANA, who finished ninth, with 0.7 percent of the vote; secured one seat in September 2013 parliamentary elections; **Rally for the Defense of the Republic** (Papa Koly Kouroumah, fifth with 4.8 percent, backed Condé in the second round); **New Generation for the Republic** (Ibrahima Abe SYLLA, sixth, with 3.4 percent, backed Diallo in the second round; secured one seat in September 2013 parliamentary elections): **National Renewal Party** (Boubacar BARRY, 10th, with 0.6 percent; secured one seat in September 2013 parliamentary elections); **Democratic Union of Guinea** (Mamadou Sylla, former honorary chair of the PUP, finished 13th, with 0.4 percent); **Workers and Solidarity Party** (Mamady DIAWARA, 15th with 0.3 percent); **Democratic Prosperous Future for Guinea** (Boubacar BAH, 16th, 0.3 percent); **Development and Unity Party** (Mbemba TRAORE, 17th, 0.2 percent); **Union for the Integrated Development of Guinea** (Joseph BANGOURA, 18th, 0.2 percent); **Republican Party** (Alpha Ibrahima KEIRA, 19th, 0.2 percent); **Union of Democratic Forces** (Mamadou Baadiko BAH, 20th, 0.2 percent): **Generation of Citizens** (Fode Mohamed SOUMAH, 21st, 0.1 percent): **Pan-African Democratic Convention** (Saran Daraba KABA, 22nd, 0.1 percent; the only female candidate, Kaba supported Condé in the second round); **Guinean Rally for Unity and Development** (Abraham BOURE, 23rd, 0.1 percent); and **Rally for a Prosperous Guinea** (Bouna KEITA, 24th, with 0.1 percent).

Other Parties:

National Alliance for Progress (*Alliance Nationale pour le Progrès*—ANP). The ANP was formed prior to the 1995 legislative elections but remained a minor party for most of its history. However, it was one of the few opposition parties not to boycott the 2002 legislative elections, and it won two seats in the assembly.

Leader: Sagno MOUSSA.

Union for the Progress of Guinea (*Union pour le Progrès de Guinée*—UPG). In the December 1993 balloting UPG secretary general Jean-Marie Doré secured less than 1 percent of the vote; nevertheless, Doré emerged as a prominent Codem spokesperson after the UPG secured 2 seats at the 1995 assembly balloting.

In presidential balloting in December 1998 Doré secured just 1.73 percent of the vote. The UPG left Codem in May 1996. Although the UPG took part in the 2002 legislative elections and won three seats, it boycotted the 2003 presidential elections. Doré is one of the main spokespersons for the FRAD. In 2006 the UPG called for President Conté's resignation due to his medical problems.

In 2008 the UPG participated in unity talks with the new prime minister, Ahmed Tidiane Souaré, and accepted a post in the cabinet. Following the 2008 coup, Doré called for a peaceful transition.

Following Doré's appointment in January 2010 as interim prime minister, he was prevented as a member of the ruling regime from seeking the presidency in the June election.

Doré was the opposition spokesperson during negotiations in November 2011 with the government over legislative elections. Doré opposed the scheduled September 2013 balloting, contending that the opposition groups needed more time to prepare for the elections. UPG won 2 seats during the September 28, 2013, parliamentary elections.

Leader: Jean-Marie DORÉ (Former Interim Prime Minister and 1998 presidential candidate).

For more on the **People's Party of Guinea** (*Parti Guinéen du Peuple*—PGP), the **Democratic Party of Guinea–African Democratic Rally** (*Parti Démocratique de Guinée—Rassemblement Démocratique Africain*—PDG-RDA), and the **Union for National Progress–Party of Unity and Development** (*Union pour le Progrès National—Parti pour l'Unité et le Développement*—UPN-PUD), please see the 2012 *Handbook.* For information on rebel groups that were active within Guinea in the past decade, see earlier editions of the *Handbook.*

LEGISLATURE

The 210-member People's National Assembly (*Assemblée Nationale Populaire*), elected from a single PDG list for a seven-year term on January 27, 1980, was dissolved in April 1984. Balloting for a successor body, originally scheduled for November 1992, was rescheduled in April 1993 for the last quarter of the year but did not in fact occur until June 11, 1995.

The assembly was dissolved following the military coup of December 24, 2008.

National Assembly (*Assemblée Nationale*). The current assembly is a 114-member body with a five-year mandate. One-third of its deputies are elected by majority vote in single-member districts, two-thirds on a national list vote with proportional representation.

National Assembly elections were originally scheduled for June 2007 but have been continuously and repeatedly postponed until September 28, 2013. In legislative balloting widely regarded as corrupt President Conde's Rally of the Guinean People won 53 seats; Union of Democratic Forces of Guinea won 37 seats; Union of Republican Forces won 10 seats; Party of Hope for National Development won two seats; Union for the Progress of Guinea won two seats; Rally for the Integral Development of Guinea won one seat; Guinea for All won one seat; Union for Progress and Renewal won one seat; Guinean Union for Democracy and Development won one seat; Work and Solidarity Party won one seat; New Generation for the Republic won one seat; Guinean Party for Renaissance and Progress won one seat; Guinea United for Development won one seat; Generation for Reconciliation, Union and Prosperity won one seat; and National Party for Renewal won one seat.

President: Unfilled since 2008 coup as of November 18, 2013.

CABINET

[as of September 1, 2013]

Prime Minister	Mohamed Said Fofana
Ministers	
Agriculture	Emile Yombouno
Communications	Togba Césaire Kpoghomou
Culture and Heritage	Ahmed Tidiane Cissé
Employment and Technical and Professional Education	Damantang Albert Camara
Environment, Water, and Forests	Saran Mady Touré
Fisheries and Aquaculture	Moussa Condé
Health and Public Hygiene	Edouard Gnankoye Lama
Higher Education and Scientific Research	Tèliwel Bailo Diallo

Human Rights and Civil Liberties	Kalifa Gassama Diaby
Industry and Small and Medium Enterprises	Ramatoulaye Bah [f]
International Cooperation	Mustafa Koutoubou Sanoh
Mines and Geology	Mohamed Lamine Fofana
National Defense	Alpha Condé
Planning	Sékou Traoré
Pre-University Education	Ibrahima Kouroumah
Secretary General, Presidency	Mohamed Diané
Security, Civil Protection, and Reform of the Security Services	Madifing Diane
Social Affairs and Promotion of Women and Children	Diaka Diakité [f]
Telecommunications and Information Technologies	Oyé Guilavogui
Territorial Administration and Political Affairs	Alhassane Condé
Tourism, Hotels, and Handicrafts	Mariam Baldé [f]
Trade	Mohamed Dorval Doumbouya
Urban Affairs, Construction, and Housing	Ibrahima Bangoura
Youth, Youth Employment, and Sports	Sanoussy Bantama Sow

Ministers of State

Economy and Finance	Kerfalla Yansané
Energy and Environment	Papa Koly Kouroumah
Foreign Affairs and Guineans Overseas	François Lonseny Fall
Justice	Christian Sow
Public Works and Transport	Ousmane Bah
Security and Civil Defense	Mamadouba Toto Camara

Ministers Delegate

Budget	Mohamed Diarré
Guineans Overseas	Rougui Barry [f]
Health	Naman Keita
National Defense	Abdul Kabélé Camara
Social Affairs and Promotion of Women and Children	Mimi Koumbassa [f]
Transport	Tidiane Traoré

[f] = female

INTERGOVERNMENTAL REPRESENTATION

Ambassador to the U.S.: Blaise CHÉRIF.

U.S. Ambassador to Guinea: Alexander Mark LASKARIS.

Permanent Representative to the UN: Mamadi TOURÉ.

IGO Memberships (Non-UN): AfDB, AU, ECOWAS, IOM, NAM, OIC, WTO.

GUINEA-BISSAU

Republic of Guinea-Bissau
República da Guiné-Bissau

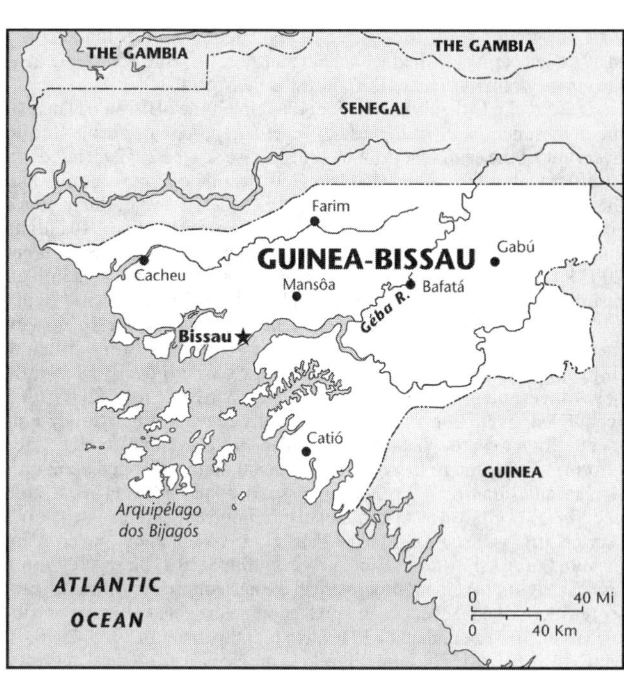

Political Status: Achieved independence from Portugal on September 10, 1974; under rule of Revolutionary Council following coup of November 14, 1980; new constitution of May 16, 1984, amended on May 4, 1991; military control imposed following coup of May 8, 1999; present constitution promulgated July 7, 1999, under direction of military junta; interim national transition council appointed on April 15, 2012, following military coup.

Area: 13,948 sq. mi. (36,125 sq. km).

Population: 1,585,440 (2012E—UN); 1,660,870 (2013E—U.S. Census).

Major Urban Center (2007E): BISSAU (407,424).

Official Language: Portuguese (several local languages are also spoken).

Monetary Unit: CFA Franc (official rate November 1, 2013: 486.52 francs = $1US). The CFA franc, previously pegged to the French franc, is now permanently pegged to the euro at 655.957 CFA francs = 1 euro.

Interim President: Manuel Serifo NHAMADJO (Ind.), appointed by the Military Command on May 11, 2012; succeeding interim president Raimundo PEREIRA (African Party for the Independence of Guinea and Cape Verde), who was forced from power in a coup on April 13.

Interim Prime Minister: Rui DUARTE DE BARROS (PRS), appointed by the interim president on May 16, 2012; succeeding acting prime minister Adiato Djaló NANDIGNA (African Party for the Independence of Guinea and Cape Verde), who was forced from power on April 13.

THE COUNTRY

Situated on the west coast of Africa between Senegal on the north and Guinea on the south, the Republic of Guinea-Bissau also includes the Bijagóz Archipelago and the island of Bolama. The population is primarily of African descent (principal tribes include the Balante, Fulani, Mandyako, and Malinké), but there are smaller groups of mulattoes, Portuguese, and Lebanese. The majority continues to follow traditional religious beliefs; however, there is a significant Muslim population and a small Christian minority. Women remain underrepresented in most social, economic, and political structures. Following the 2008 elections, women held 14 percent of the seats in the Assembly (14 out of 100).

Agriculture employs the vast majority of the population, with peanuts and cashews typically producing two-thirds of export earnings. Other important exports are palm products, fish, and cattle, while such crops as cotton, sugar, and tobacco have been introduced in an effort to diversify the country's output; industry is dominated by state enterprises and mixed ventures. The chief mineral resource may be petroleum (the extent of on- and offshore reserves is uncertain, although a number of Western oil companies have signed exploration contracts with the government). Economic development has been hindered by insufficient capital, skilled labor, and transport facilities. Consequently, the country remains one of the poorest in the world.

In 2001 the IMF suspended debt relief to Guinea-Bissau because of the government's unwillingness to enact agreed-upon reforms (for an overview of the economy prior to 2001, please see the 2012 *Handbook*). Conflict within the country led to a GDP decline of 7 percent in 2002; there was no measurable GDP growth in 2003. That year, donor states suspended aid after the government failed to demobilize ex-soldiers and continue economic restructuring. Following the coup of September 2003 and subsequent legislative elections, donors announced a limited resumption of aid in 2004, including $13 million from the World Bank.

Real GDP growth of about 2 percent was recorded for 2004, with the IMF describing the country's economic situation as "very difficult" following years of political instability, increasing poverty, and little new investment. However, economic activity for 2005–2006 rebounded, averaging 3.8 percent annually, owing in part to government efforts toward what the IMF termed "long-overdue" civil service reforms. At the end of the year, international donors pledged $262 million in aid, about half of Guinea-Bissau's goal, based on its sizable debt. In 2007 GDP growth contracted to 2.7 percent, largely due to civil service arrears, according to the IMF. However, the new government installed in April instituted an emergency financial plan, resulting in a significant improvement. Recovery in the agriculture sector, significant increases in donor revenue, and greater domestic consumption contributed to an average annual GDP growth of 3.8 percent in 2008–2010. In May 2010 the IMF, citing authorities' progress in structural reforms, approved a three-year, $33.3 million loan to support the country's economic program. Meanwhile, the Paris Club of creditors canceled $256 million of Guinea-Bissau's debt. In March 2012, the IMF commended the government for its progress in stabilizing the economy, noting that economic growth reached 5.3 percent in 2011 on the back of exceptional cashew prices and a strong harvest. GDP declined by 1.5 percent in 2012, partially as a result of the economic disruptions caused by a military coup in April (see Political background, below). That year inflation expanded by 2.2 percent, while GDP per capita was $551.

GOVERNMENT AND POLITICS

Political background. First discovered by the Portuguese mariner Nuno Tristão in 1446, the territory long known as Portuguese Guinea did not receive a final delimitation of its borders until 1905. Initially, the country was plundered by slave traders, and consequent hostility among the indigenous peoples resulted in uprisings in the early twentieth century. The area was eventually pacified by military means, and in 1952 it was formally designated as an Overseas Province of Portugal.

In 1956 a group of dissatisfied Cape Verdeans under the joint leadership of Amílcar CABRAL, Luís de Almeida CABRAL, Aristides PEREIRA, and Rafael BARBOSA formed the African Party for the Independence of Guinea and Cape Verde (*Partido Africano da Independência da Guiné e Cabo Verde*—PAIGC). Failing to win concessions from the Portuguese, the PAIGC, with assistance from Warsaw Pact nations, initiated an armed struggle in 1963, and by the early 1970s the PAIGC claimed to control two-thirds of the mainland territory. On January 20, 1973, Amílcar Cabral was assassinated in Conakry, Guinea, allegedly by PAIGC dissidents but with the apparent complicity of the Portuguese military. Six months later, Aristides Pereira and Cabral's brother, Luís, were confirmed as party leaders by a PAIGC congress.

A government was formally organized and independence declared on September 23 and 24, 1973. The Portuguese authorities claimed the move was a "propaganda stunt," but the coup in Portugal in April 1974 led to an informal cease-fire and negotiations with the rebel leaders. Although the talks failed to resolve the status of the Cape Verde Islands, an agreement signed August 26, 1974, provided for the independence of Guinea-Bissau as of September 10, 1974, and the removal of all Portuguese troops by October 31.

In the first balloting since independence, 15 regional councils were elected during December 1976 and January 1977, the councils in turn selecting delegates to a second National People's Assembly, which convened in March 1977; Cabral was reelected president of the republic and of the 15-member Council of State, while (then) Maj. João Bernardo VIEIRA was designated vice president of the republic and reconfirmed as president of the assembly. Vieira became principal commissioner (prime minister) on September 28, 1978, succeeding Maj. Francisco MENDES, who died on July 7.

The principal political issue of the late 1970s was a projected unification of Cape Verde with Guinea-Bissau, many mainland leaders—including President Cabral and other high officials of the binational PAIGC—being Cape Verdean *mestiços.* On November 10, 1980, an extraordinary session of the National People's Assembly adopted a new constitution that many black Guineans construed as institutionalizing domination by islanders; four days later a coup led by Vieira, a native Guinean, deposed the president. On November 19 the Council of State and the assembly were formally dissolved by a Revolutionary Council that designated Vieira as head of state, and, on the following day, the council announced a provisional cabinet, all but one of whose members had served in the previous administration. Shortly thereafter, President Vieira identified the basic reasons for Cabral's ouster as the country's social and economic difficulties, including severe food shortages; "progressive abandonment of the principle of democratic centralism"; and "corruption of the meaning of unity between Guinea-Bissau and Cape Verde."

At a PAIGC conference in November 1981 it was announced that presidential and legislative elections under a new constitution would be held in early 1982 and that the party would retain its existing name, despite the fact that in the wake of the coup its Cape Verdean wing had formally repudiated the goal of unification with the mainland. In May 1982 President Vieira instituted a purge of reputed left-wingers within the government and the PAIGC. Furthermore, he named Vítor SAÚDE Maria as prime minister, a post that had been vacant since the 1980 takeover. Continued instability persisted for the next two years, culminating in the ouster of Saúde Maria on March 8, 1984, for alleged antistate activity. The return to constitutional rule followed on March 31 with the election of eight regional councils, which, in turn, chose 150 deputies to a new National People's Assembly. The assembly convened on May 14 and two days later approved a new basic law that combined the offices of head of state and chief of government into the presidency of a revived Council of State, to which Vieira was unanimously elected.

A further attempt to overthrow the Vieira regime was reported on November 7, 1985, when security forces arrested some 50 individuals, including the first vice president, Col. Paulo CORREIA, and a number of other prominent military and civilian officials, who were, apparently, opposed to economic austerity moves and upset by a military anticorruption drive. Despite international appeals for clemency, Correia and five of his associates were executed in July 1986.

A new National Assembly was designated on June 15, 1989, by and from the regional councils, for which direct single-party balloting had been conducted on June 1. On June 19 General Vieira was reelected to a second term as president of the Council of State, which two days later named its former vice president, Col. Iafai CAMARA, as first vice president, and its former secretary, Dr. Vasco CABRAL, as second vice president. Both of the vice presidencies were abandoned in a government restructuring of December 27, 1991, that marked another restoration of the post of prime minister, to which former agriculture minister Carlos CORREIA was appointed.

In July 1992 the PAIGC agreed to the formation of a national commission with responsibility for facilitating the country's first multiparty balloting. However, the elections, originally scheduled for November and December, were rescheduled in October for March 1993, at which time they were again postponed. In July the Council of State set March 27, 1994, as the new date for simultaneous presidential and legislative balloting, with a further postponement in February 1994 to late May. At the poll that was finally held on July 3, Vieira, who had resigned his commission to qualify as a candidate under a 1991 constitutional revision, was credited with winning 46 percent of valid presidential votes, as contrasted with 21.9 percent for runner-up Kumba YALA of the opposition Social Renewal Party (*Partido para a Renovação Social*—PRS); concurrently, the ruling PAIGC was awarded 64 of 100 parliamentary seats. Vieira went on to secure reelection by defeating Yala, who had been accorded unanimous opposition endorsement, in a runoff on August 7.

On October 25, 1994, Vieira named a senior PAIGC official, Manuel Saturnino da COSTA, to succeed Correia as prime minister. Observers attributed the delay between the election and Costa's appointment to a deep division in the ruling party between its founding members, including Costa, and their younger colleagues, who desired more "pragmatic" economic policy-making. On November 11 Costa named a new government, which included members of both PAIGC tendencies.

On May 27, 1997, President Vieira dismissed Costa in the midst of what the president described as a "serious political crisis." Costa's ouster came as government troops were deployed to quell riots sparked by state workers who were angered at poor working conditions and the government's failure to pay salary arrears. On June 5 Vieira reappointed Carlos Correia as prime minister, and Correia formed a new government the following day. However, Correia's appointment was immediately contested by opposition legislators, who asserted that the president was constitutionally required to consult with the assembly prior to naming a prime minister. Subsequently, a virtual legislative deadlock ensued as opposition legislators refused to consider the government's initiatives while their legal challenge was being considered by the courts. On October 7 the Supreme Court ruled that the administration had erred, and on October 11 the president dismissed Correia; however, following negotiations with legislative leaders, on October 13 Vieira reappointed Correia.

In January 1998 President Vieira dismissed his military chief of staff, Gen. Ansumane MANE, charging him with "dereliction of duty" for allegedly failing to stem the illegal transfer of arms from Guinea-Bissau to Senegalese rebels. Subsequently, in early June, troops directed by General Mane overran the national airport and an army base in Bra as part of a declared effort to remove Vieira from power. Facing minimal resistance from a small contingent of pro-presidential forces, the rebels quickly secured control of a majority of the country. However, bolstered by Senegalese and Guinean troops, Vieira's loyalists fought the rebels to a standstill in Bissau. On August 26 regional mediators in Cape Verde brokered a cease-fire agreement that held until October, when fierce fighting was once again reported. In November the two sides signed a second cease-fire accord in Abuja, Nigeria. The accord included provisions for presidential and legislative balloting in March 1999, as well as the formation of a unity government comprising representatives selected by the president as well as the rebels. In addition, the agreement called for the replacement of the Senegalese and Guinean troops with a regional peacekeeping force supplied by the Economic Community of West African States (ECOWAS). On December 3 Vieira, under strong pressure from the military rebels, named Francisco FADUL, General Mane's aide-de-camp, to replace Correia as prime minister.

In early January 1999 the national balloting envisioned for March was indefinitely postponed as contentious debate continued in Bissau over implementation of the Abuja accord. Fierce fighting was reported in the capital in early February; however, a new cease-fire agreement (based on the Abuja document) was reached on February 4, and ECOWAS troops began arriving en masse soon thereafter. On February 20 Fadul and his nine-member cabinet were sworn in.

Amid reports that troops loyal to the president were seeking to rearm, fresh fighting erupted on May 6, 1999, and the following day General Mane claimed that his forces had overthrown Vieira, who agreed to the unconditional surrender of the government on May 10. (Vieira left the country in June.) On May 14 Mane named the president of the assembly, Malan Bacai SANHÁ, interim president; furthermore, Mane announced that election preparations could continue as scheduled and that he would not be a presidential candidate. In early July the military junta promulgated a new constitution (see Constitution and government, below).

In the first round of presidential balloting on November 28–29, 1999, the PRS's Kumba Yala led a field of 11 presidential aspirants with 34.81 percent of the vote, while interim president Sanhá finished second with 23.34 percent. Meanwhile, at concurrent legislative polling the PRS led a crowded field with 38 seats while the PAIGC's representation fell to 24, which was 4 less than the second-place Guinea-Bissau Resistance—Bah Fatah Movement (*Resistência da Guiné-Bissau—Movimento Bah-Fatah*—RGB-MB).

Having failed to garner the vote share necessary to stave off a second round of balloting, Yala faced off against Sanhá on January 16, 2000. Yala won easily, capturing 72 percent of the vote, and on January 24 he named a PRS leader, Caetano NTCHAMA, prime minister. On February 19 Ntchama was sworn in as the head of a government that included representatives from four political parties and a number of independents, but no members of the PAIGC. However, Ntchama was buffeted by tensions between the PRS and the RGB-MB; in September the RGB-MB ministers were dismissed, but they were reinstated shortly thereafter. In the meantime, conflict between President Yala and the former head of the junta, Ansumane Mane, resurfaced. In November, uneasy with some recent military appointments, Mane announced that he had "reinstated" himself as the chief of staff, and clashes were reported between a few troops following Mane and the majority of the army, which remained loyal to Yala. Some opposition figures, most prominently from the PAIGC, the Union for Change (*União para a Mudança*—UM), and the Democratic Alliance (*Aliança Democrática*—AD), were arrested for allegedly supporting Mane. On November 30, Mane was killed by government troops surrounding his enclave in Quinhamel, north of Bissau.

In January 2001 the RGB-MB left the governing coalition in reaction to an earlier reshuffle the party claimed unfairly favored the PRS. In March, Yala dismissed Ntchama, who was reportedly having medical problems, and named an independent, Faustino Fadut IMBALI, as the new prime minister. Imbali had run in the 1999 presidential elections and had supported Yala in the second round in January 2000. He had also served in Ntchama's government as the deputy prime minister. Imbali formed a government including the PRS, the RGB-MB, the PAIGC, the Guinean Civic Forum (*Foro Civico da Guiné*—FCG), the Social Democratic Party (*Partido Social Democrata*—PSD), the Democratic Convergence Party (*Partido da Convergência Democrática*—PCD), and independents. The PAIGC and the RGB-MB, however, reportedly continued their critical stance toward Yala's presidency and some of Imbali's policies. Yala dismissed Imbali on December 7, 2001, and appointed Alamara NHASSE of the PRS as the new prime minister the following day. Nhasse's new government, formed on December 12, included members from the PRS and the PCD as well as independents.

In the wake of increasing tension between President Yala and Prime Minister Nhasse concerning ministerial and judicial appointments, Yala dismissed Nhasse on November 15, 2002. On November 16 Yala appointed Mario PIRES of the PRS to head a temporary caretaker government. Yala also dissolved the assembly and announced that new legislative elections would be held in early 2003. However, that balloting was postponed several times as the government was perceived as becoming increasingly authoritarian.

The military deposed President Yala on September 14, 2003, in a takeover that appeared to have broad domestic support. The army's chief of staff, Gen. Verissimo Correia SEABRA, proclaimed himself interim president and named a military council to conduct governmental affairs pending the appointment of a new civilian government. (Yala was permitted to "resign" as of September 17.) On September 28, Henrique ROSA, a prominent businessman with no formal political ties, was appointed interim president, while Antonio Artur SANHÁ of the PRS was designated head of a caretaker cabinet.

Negotiations between the major political groups and the military subsequently yielded an agreement providing for legislative elections within 6 months and presidential balloting within 18 months. Concurrently, a 56-member civilian Transitional National Council was appointed to advise the government, pending the new elections. The PAIGC secured a plurality of 45 seats in the March 28 and 30, 2004, assembly poll, followed by the PRS with 35 seats. Carlos GOMES Júnior, the president of the PAIGC, was appointed prime minister on May 12 to head a cabinet comprising the PAIGC and independents.

In the first round of presidential balloting on June 19, 2005, the PAIGC's Malam Bacai Sanhá received 35.45 percent of the vote, followed by Vieira (running as an independent) with 28.87 percent, and Yala of the PRS with 25 percent. Ten other candidates, representing 6 other parties and independents, each won less than 3 percent of the vote. Since Sanhá failed to gain a clear majority, he faced Vieira in a runoff on July 24. Several weeks later, Vieira was declared the winner with 52.35 percent of the vote. In August the Supreme Court rejected Sanhá's request to annul the election, and the PAIGC government finally conceded defeat on September 27. Amid continuing friction with Prime Minister Carlos Gomes, Vieira was sworn in on October 1, and on October 30 he dismissed the prime minister in favor of PAIGC dissident Aristides GOMES (see PAIGC under Political Parties, below). On November 9 Vieira appointed a five-party coalition government comprising the PAIGC (split into pro-Vieira and pro–Carlos Gomes factions), the PRS, the PCD, the United Social Democratic Party (*Partido Unido Social Democrata*—PUSD), and the Electoral Union (*União Eleitoral*—UE). In early 2006, court rulings upheld the appointment of Aristides Gomes, striking down the PAIGC's argument that it was unconstitutional since Gomes had been suspended from the party (for his support of Vieira) and that the president was obligated to appoint a majority-party member to head the government.

Following a parliamentary no-confidence vote on March 19, 2007, Prime Minister Aristides Gomes announced his resignation on March 29. On April 10 the president appointed a new prime minister, Martinho Ndafa CABI. On April 17 Cabi named a new government comprising members of the PAIGC, the PRS, and the PUSD (and only one minister from the previous government). In what was described as a cost-saving measure, President Vieira announced in July that legislative elections would be postponed from March 2008 to coincide with presidential polling in 2009. (However, in December he revised the date for legislative elections to November 2008.) Following the withdrawal of the PAIGC, again in an opposition stance, from the unity government on July 25, President Vieira dismissed Prime Minister Cabi on August 5, replacing him with former Prime Minister Carlos Correia. A new government was formed on August 9, dominated by PAIGC supporters of the president but also including members of the PRS, the United Popular Alliance (*Aliança Popular Unida*—APU), and the Republican Party for Independence and Development (*Partido Republicano para a Independência e o Desenvolvimento*—PRID), a PAIGC breakaway party led by Aristides Gomes. Days later, the president suspended the navy commander, Rear Adm. José Americo Bubo NA TCHUTO, accusing him of plotting a coup. Na Tchuto escaped house arrest and fled by boat but was soon rearrested in Gambia.

In the parliamentary elections on November 16, 2008, the PAIGC won an overwhelming majority of 67 seats, followed by the PRS with 28, and the PRID with 3. The PRS challenged the results, claiming electoral fraud, but the Supreme Court ultimately upheld the outcome, with the official results announced on November 21. President Vieira survived a coup attempt two days later, leading to the arrest of a nephew of former president Yala. On December 25, President Vieira appointed PAIGC leader Carlos Gomes as prime minister. He was installed along with a new, all-PAIGC government on January 7, 2009. Meanwhile, the armed forces chief of staff, Gen. Baptista TAGMÉ Na Wai, was shot at by members of the president's militia, who later claimed the attack was accidental. The militia was subsequently disarmed. However, on March 1, Tagamé, a longtime critic of Vieira, was killed in a bomb explosion at armed forces headquarters in Bissau. Political turmoil culminated in the early hours of March 2, when Vieira was killed by army troops while he was asleep in his palace. Analysts said the assassination was to avenge Tagamé's death and was likely also a tribal battle. Assembly speaker Raimundo PEREIRA became interim president in accordance with constitutional order. In presidential balloting on June 28, none of the 11 candidates (including one woman) won a majority, forcing a runoff between top vote-getters Kumba Yala of the PRS (27.9 percent) and the PAIGC's Sanhá (37.5 percent), who ran unsuccessfully in 2005. A second round was held on July 26, pushed back from August 2 after the electoral commission declared that the earlier date was more compatible with harvest time. Sanhá won with 63.3 percent of the vote, with Yala a distant second with 36.7 percent on turnout of 61 percent. Sanhá was sworn in on September 8 and retained Gomes as prime minister.

The cabinet was restructured on October 29, 2009, the number of ministerial posts being reduced from 21 to 16. A minor reshuffle occurred on February 14, 2010. The minister of interior, who was suspended in October 2010 for allegedly disrupting the reform process in the security sector, resigned on December 21.

President Sanhá died on January 9, 2012 (see Current issues, below). Speaker Pereira again became interim president. Meanwhile, Gomes resigned as prime minister to run for the presidency on February 10, and was replaced, on an interim basis, by Adiato Djaló NANDIGNA (PAIGC). No candidate secured the required majority in presidential polling on March 18, but before a run-off could be conducted, a military coup forced Pereira from power and arrested Gomes. The Assembly was dissolved and a 32-member National Transitional Council (NTC) was appointed. Manuel Serifo NHAMADJO (ind.) was named acting president on April 19 by the military, and he named Rui Duarte DE BARROS prime minister of a unity cabinet on May 16 (see Current issues, below). The cabinet was reshuffled on June 6, and the NTC was revised and expanded to 34 members.

Constitution and government. The constitution of May 1984 gave the PAIGC the right to define "the bases of state policy in all fields"; for legislative purposes it reestablished the National People's Assembly, members of which were to be designated by eight regional councils. The assembly was, in turn, empowered to elect a 15-member Council of State, whose president was to serve as head of state and commander in chief of the armed forces.

In early 1989 a six-member National Commission, headed by Fidélis Cabral DALMADA, was established by the PAIGC Central Committee to revise the constitution in accordance with recent economic reform and structural adjustment policies. Thereafter, in April 1990, President Vieira promised "freer and more democratic elections," and in August he characterized the democracy movement as "irreversible." On January 9, 1991, he formally committed himself to political pluralism in a speech that was promptly endorsed by the PAIGC. On May 4 the assembly approved a constitutional amendment voiding the republic's "revolutionary" character and stripping the PAIGC of its status as the "leading force in society." Both president and legislators were henceforth to be popularly elected for five-year terms. Four days later a framework law on political parties won legislative approval, with numerous opposition groups subsequently being recognized in preparation for the country's first contested elections (originally scheduled for late 1992, but not held until mid-1994).

In July 1999 the military junta led by Gen. Ansumane Mane discarded the 1991 basic law in favor of a new constitution that included provisions for presidential term limits (two five-year terms), the abolition of the death penalty, and the establishment of strict residency requirements for government officeholders. In November the junta drafted a new document, a so-called *Magna Carta*, reportedly styled after the basic law imposed in Portugal following its 1974 military coup; however, General Mane withdrew the controversial draft law (which provided for ten years of military rule) following an outcry from Bissau's political leaders. Furthermore, the junta amended the article of the July document that excluded would-be presidential candidates whose parents were foreign-born. In October 2000 President Yala named a State Council to "advise him on decisions such as declaration of war and state of emergency." Some observers suggested that the establishment of the council substantively finalized the transition to civilian rule. (For details of governmental arrangements following the September 2003 coup, see Political background, above.)

Under the constitution, freedom of the press is guaranteed, but following the 2012 military coup, a temporary news blackout was imposed and journalists reported intimidation and harassment. In 2013 Reporters Without Borders ranked Guinea-Bisseau 92nd out of 170 countries, a decline from 75th the previous year.

Foreign relations. During the struggle for independence, Guinea-Bissau received economic and military assistance from many Communist countries, including the Soviet Union, Cuba, and China. A subsequent deterioration in relations with the USSR because of alleged encroachment upon the country's fishing grounds appeared to have been reversed in early 1978 with a promise of Soviet assistance in modernizing the country's fishing industry. In May 1982, on the other hand, President Vieira replaced two strongly pro-Soviet cabinet ministers with Western-trained "technocrats" and appealed for development aid from non-Communist sources.

In November 1980 Guinea was the first country to recognize Guinea-Bissau's Revolutionary Council; earlier disputes over offshore oil exploration rights had been defused by former Guinean President Sékou Touré's announcement that Guinea would cooperate with other African states in developing on- and offshore resources. Similar controversy with Senegal erupted in early 1984, involving questions about the legality of offshore borders drawn by the French and Portuguese governments before independence. In February 1985 the International Court of Justice (ICJ) offered a settlement of the Bissau-Conakry border question that was accepted by both governments, while in March a meeting between Vieira and Senegalese President Diouf resulted in assignment of the latter dispute to an ad hoc international tribunal. A decision by the tribunal on July 31, 1989, in favor of Senegal, was immediately rejected by Bissau in an appeal to the ICJ.

A meeting with President Pereira of Cape Verde in Mozambique in 1982 yielded an announcement that diplomatic relations would be restored. Despite "reconciliation," the unification sought by Cabral became more and more distant as island influence was purged from the mainland party, with no reference to eventual merger being mentioned in the 1984 Guinea-Bissau constitution. The last vestige of the PAIGC alliances, a joint shipping line, was liquidated on February 29, 1988; both countries cited the nonviolent action as a sign of their "political maturation."

A further border clash with Senegal occurred in April and May 1990, leaving 17 dead and drawing charges by Dakar that Bissau was harboring Casamance separatist guerrillas (see the entry on Senegal). Tensions eased, however, in the wake of a meeting in the border town of São Domingos on May 29 at which the two countries agreed to a mutual troop withdrawal and termination of aid to each other's insurgent movements. In April 1991 Vieira called for the Casamance rebels to lay down their arms and take advantage of Senegal's multiparty system. Subsequently, in May, Guinea-Bissau was the site of cease-fire talks between Dakar and Casamance representatives. However, in early February 1995 relations between Bissau and Dakar were again strained when Senegal bombed a Guinea-Bissau border village in retaliation for Bissau's alleged support of two recent Casamance rebel attacks against Senegalese military sites. Relations again eased on June 12, when a visit by Senegalese President Abdou Diouf produced a declaration to abandon border hostility and an agreement to share equally in offshore mineral and energy resources.

In early 1996 the Vieira administration agreed to ratify a 1993 maritime joint-exploration pact with Senegal, ignoring its domestic critics' charges that the agreement unfairly favored the neighboring state, and in June, Bissau and Dakar signed a security collaboration accord. (On the basis of such accords Senegal and Guinea dispatched troops to Guinea-Bissau in 1998 in an effort to quell the military uprising.)

In February 1999 the leaders of rebel forces in Guinea-Bissau claimed that French battleships had fired on their positions. Paris denied the charges. Following the military coup in May, ECOWAS peacekeeping forces departed, with both the junta and its regional sponsors agreeing that they were "redundant." On the other hand, a United Nations contingent arrived in Bissau in June in accordance with provisions in the February cease-fire. The UN officials were charged with organizing elections, and in March 2000 their mandate was extended. Among the myriad problems confronting international mediators was the need to smooth relations between Bissau and the Senegalese and Guinean governments, both of whom had sent troops in an ultimately futile attempt to reinforce the Vieira administration. Guinea-Bissau's relations with Senegal were further strained in April, following an attack by Casamance rebels, who had (according to Senegal) infiltrated from Guinea-Bissau's territory. In March 2002 the leader of one of the main rebel factions was arrested and deported to Senegal. The situation subsequently improved, and in September the border was reopened and a joint security commission was formed.

Although the international community initially condemned the overthrow of Yala, Guinea-Bissau's external relations were quickly repaired. Once Rosa assumed office, he made diplomatic visits to a number of neighboring states, and Portugal as well. International aid was resumed soon after the March 2004 elections and included pledges to provide the funds needed to pay the military and civil service until after the June 2005 presidential elections. In addition, the small UN mission charged with monitoring the border between Senegal and Guinea-Bissau had its mandate extended for one year. Conflict at the border reignited in early 2006 (see Current issues, below), with the Casamance rebel leader reportedly refusing to participate in peace talks. In early 2007 Senegalese refugees again fled to Guinea-Bissau following renewed violence in the Casamance region.

In 2008 Guinea-Bissau extradited five suspected al-Qaida members to Mauritania in connection with the killing of French tourists in Mauritania in December 2007. The killings raised concerns that Islamic extremists were broadening their scope of operations to include sub-Saharan West Africa. That same year the United States reopened a diplomatic office in Guinea-Bissau after an absence of 10 years, and the U.S. ambassador in Senegal, who oversees affairs in Guinea-Bissau, said a full embassy would soon be reinstated in the country. Following an attack on President Vieira's residence after the November elections, Senegal deployed troops to its shared border and made a plane available for the Guinea Bissau leader "to evacuate him and his family in case of absolute necessity."

China pledged $48.5 million to help modernize Guinea Bissau's telecommunications network in 2009.

In 2011 Angola pledged $32 million toward reform of Guinea-Bissau's military, a step analysts said was part of a West African effort to pare down what was widely regarded as an unwieldy and corrupt armed forces.

The April 12, 2012, coup, prompted widespread international condemnation, including suspension of most of the EU's aid and strong rebukes from the UN, the AU, the United States, and Portugal. Guinea-Bissau's membership in the African Union was suspended on April 17. On April 30, 2012, ECOWAS imposed sanctions against the junta leaders. The day before, talks between the organization and junta representatives collapsed over ECOWAS's demands for new elections to be held within the year and the restoration of the interim president. Nonetheless, ECOWAS recognized the new regime and urged the international community to follow suit in a communiqué on July 2.

A planned speech by Raimundo Pereira at the General Assembly created a diplomatic stir. Ultimately, he failed to appear as planned on September 28, 2012, reportedly because ECOWAS officials stopped him. Officials from the EU and the UN were said to be upset with ECOWAS for legitimizing the coup by recognizing the transitional government.

In February 2013 ECOWAS pledged to increase economic assistance to Guinea-Bissau and, again, urged international recognition of the transitional government.

Current issues. On June 5, 2009, Territorial Minister Baciro DABÓ, a PAIGC ally of assassinated president Vieira, running as an independent in the upcoming presidential election, was killed by military forces. The assassination was reportedly part of a failed coup attempt aimed at Prime Minister Gomes, who was in Portugal at the time, as well as his chief of staff, José Zamora INDUTA. Vieira ally and former defense minister Helder PROENÇA, reported to have been behind the coup attempt, was killed in a separate attack the same day, as was former Prime Minister Faustino IMBALI, the presidential candidate of the Party for Development, Democracy, and Citizenship (PADEC), who had publicly accused the military of corruption. Authorities said Dabó and Proença had been plotting a coup. The killings were immediately condemned by the international community; the African Union (AU) urged that elections not be postponed. Meanwhile, one of the remaining presidential candidates, Pedro INFANDA of the Guinea-Bissau League for the Protection of Ecology (*Liga da Guiné-Bissau para Protecção Ecologia*—LIPE), withdrew, saying he feared for his life. (Infanda, a lawyer who had represented navy commander Na Tchuto, was arrested by military officials in March and severely beaten.) Interim president Pereira decided to keep the June 28 polling date after consulting with government and political party officials. Former interim president of the republic and PAIGC stalwart Malam Bacai Sanhá won handily in second-round balloting on July 26 over former president Yala, both having defeated nine other candidates—five of them independents—in the first round.

Sanhá's efforts toward political and economic reforms, cited by the international community, were shattered on April 1, 2010, when a mutiny attempt was spearheaded by renegade troops under the command of the army's deputy chief of staff, Gen. Antonio INDJAI, and former navy commander and accused 2008 coup plotter José Americo Bubo Na Tchuto, who had taken refuge in a UN building in Bissau. The coup attempt prompted immediate condemnation from the United States, the UN, and others in the international community, as well as mass public protests in Bissau, leading to Gomes's release the same day. Induta remained in detention, where he was allegedly tortured. Later in the day, Indjai declared that the "incident," as it was publicly referred to, was a "purely military problem." The following day Gomes met with President Sanhá and then stated at a press conference that all had returned to normal and that he would be retaining his post as prime minister. (He also had the support of the Council of Ministers.) During the same press conference, Na Tchuto warned against public demonstrations in support of Gomes, as did Indjai. Meanwhile, President Sanhá attributed the April 1 episode to "confusion" among soldiers that ultimately reached high levels of government. Days later, the U.S. government named Na Tchuto and air force chief Ibraima Papa CAMARA "international drug kingpins" and narco-traffickers, opening the way to freeze any U.S. assets they held and banning them from doing business with U.S. citizens. In a stunning announcement on June 28, Sanhá appointed General Indjai as army chief of staff, replacing Induta, who was still in detention. The appointment resulted in the suspension of U.S. military assistance, the early termination of the European Union's (EU) mission to reform Guinea Bissau's security forces, and cancellation of a meeting of ECOWAS chiefs of defense staff scheduled for late June. U.S. officials, for their part, said they would not back the country's military reforms because there was no "clear proof that the armed forces will respect democracy."

In January 2011 Induta, who had been in charge of reforming the army, was released from prison, along with several other officers, after the EU threatened sanctions. Induta reportedly remained under house arrest. An economic setback occurred in 2011, when in May cashew traders went on strike to protest a new export tax. Meanwhile, the government continued to draw down the military in its effort to bolster civilian rule and bring the size of the military more in proportion with the civilian population. The relative quiet during the first half of 2011 was shattered when protesters, said to have been organized by seven opposition parties, took to the streets twice in mid-July, demanding the resignation of Prime Minister Gomes. The protesters cited his failure to rein in rising prices and claimed he was holding up the investigation into the assassination of former president Vieira. Government officials said the case had stalled because of lack of evidence. Around the same time, health workers went on strike to protest working conditions and pay issues.

On December 26 a coup d'état was launched while Sanhá was under treatment in a Paris hospital. The coup was put down, and troops arrested at least 31 people, including its leader Na Tchuto. On January 9 Sanhá died in Paris from an undisclosed condition. The speaker of the

Assembly, Raimundo Pereira, took over as interim president. Meanwhile, an alliance of the PRS and some minor parties, called the Democratic Opposition Collective, claimed that Gomes's decision to run for president, after handing over the premiership to Adiato Djalo Nandigna, was unconstitutional. The alliance launched protest rallies demanding his resignation and the end of the Angolan military's involvement in Guinea-Bissau.

In the March 18, 2012, presidential election, Gomes won 49 percent of the vote, while Yala secured 23 percent, and Manuel Serifo Nhamadjo (Independent) won 16 percent. Since none had more than 50 percent, a runoff was slated for April 22. Although foreign electoral observers declared the vote largely free and fair, Yala disputed this, saying he would not participate in a rerun without a new voter registration. On March 19 uniformed men assassinated former military intelligence chief Sambo Djalo. The next day Yala and four other candidates accused Gomes of electoral fraud. But the national electoral commission overruled the objections on March 28.

On the night of April 12–13 mutinous soldiers toppled the government, launching heavy gunfire and mortar attacks on government offices, the state-owned radio station, and the PAIGC headquarters. A military junta announced an interim government headed by the PRS's Ibrahima Sori Djaló in a statement also signed by the Democratic Opposition. The coup was defended as an effort to prevent an alleged plot between the government and Angolan military officials to destroy the country's armed forces. Gomes and Pereira were briefly detained; released on April 27, following talks with senior military officials from ECOWAS; and flown to Côte d'Ivoire.

According to *Africa Confidential*, the coup reflected an alliance among Yala, some extra parliamentary parties, and officers opposed to security reform. Surprised by the force of international condemnation that followed, however, some of those politicians who initially lent support to the coup soon began to retreat. Gomes, who had been the front-runner in the runoff election suspended by the new junta, had won widespread international support for his economic and security sector reforms, which were intended to end the army's involvement in drug trafficking.

On May 11, 2012, the junta appointed Manuel Serifo Nhamadjo, the speaker of the National Assembly, as interim president. On May 16, from Portugal, Gomes refused to recognize the new interim government. The same day Nhamadjo named Rui Duarte de Barros as interim prime minister. Meanwhile, a 600-troop ECOWAS force began to arrive in the country. On May 18 the UN Security Council unanimously adopted a resolution imposing targeted sanctions against five members of the junta and requested UN secretary-general Ban Ki Moon's engagement to help restore constitutional order. On May 22 the junta announced a new cabinet, drawn mostly from opposition parties, and stated that a transitional civilian government would assume power for the year while the cabinet organized elections. On May 31 EU officials added 15 more junta members to the list of targeted sanctions, freezing their assets within the EU and refusing to recognize the interim government. In June Angolan troops begin to withdraw from Guinea-Bissau, a move observers expected would ease tensions. On June 21 military officials announced that Na Tchuto, detained since the failed December coup, had been released. On October 21 fighting broke out at an air force base near Bissau in what reports indicated was a counter-coup. Six people were killed, and five military officers were subsequently arrested.

On January 17, 2013, the PAIGC, and other opposition groups, signed the Pact of Transition and agreed to participate in the political process with elections planned for November 2013. On April 2, 2013, Na Tchuto and three others were arrested by U.S. and Cape Verde law enforcements in international waters on drug trafficking charges and extradited to the United States. In response, the government dismissed Col. Serifo MANÉ, the chief of the country's domestic intelligence. Meanwhile, on April 18, Army chief of staff Indjai was indicted by the United States for drug smuggling. Meanwhile, international reports indicated that the drug trade had increased dramatically since the coup.

In July 2013 the UN reported that a steep decline of 63 percent in cashew prices had devastated the economy. Exports declined from 100,000 tons in 2011 to 60,000 in 2012. Aid organizations warned that almost half of the population faced malnutrition or starvation.

POLITICAL PARTIES

On May 8, 1991, the National People's Assembly approved the formation of opposition parties, thereby formalizing events set in motion in April 1990. The principal requirements for registration are that each group present to the Supreme Tribunal of Justice a petition signed by 1,000 eligible voters, at least 50 of whom must reside in each of the country's regions and the district of Bissau. By early 1993 more than two dozen parties had been formed, most of which had been legalized. Following the 2012 April coup, 22 parties agreed to participate in the interim National Transitional Council (NTC) after the dissolution of the Assembly.

Former Government Party:

African Party for the Independence of Guinea and Cape Verde (*Partido Africano da Independência da Guiné e Cabo Verde*—PAIGC). Formed in 1956 by Amílcar Cabral and others, the PAIGC established external offices in Conakry, Guinea, in 1960 and began armed struggle against the Portuguese authorities in 1963. During its 28 years as the country's only lawful party, the PAIGC was formally committed to the principle of "democratic centralism." Its policymaking and administrative organs include a Central Committee (the Supreme Council of the Struggle), a National Council, a Permanent Committee, and a Secretariat.

Until the coup of November 1980 the party leadership was binational, with Aristides Pereira, president of Cape Verde, serving as secretary general and President Luis Cabral of Guinea-Bissau as deputy secretary. On January 19, 1981, the Cape Verdean branch decided to break with the mainland organization, proclaiming, on the following day, an autonomous African Party for the Independence of Cape Verde (PAICV).

In May 1990 General Vieira instructed the party to begin preparations for the introduction of political pluralism. Accordingly, the Central Committee in July proposed the adoption of "integral multipartyism." At its congress in November 1991 the PAIGC voted to widen intraparty democracy and restructure its executive apparatus by dropping the post of secretary general in favor of a party president and national secretary.

At the party's congress in May 1998, delegates reelected Vieira to the PAIGC presidency and approved the appointment of Paulo Medina to the newly created post of permanent secretary. Despite Vieira's positive account of the meeting, observers asserted that the PAIGC emerged from the congress further factionalized. Thereafter, it was unclear what effect the military uprising of June 1998 would have on the PAIGC, although the vehemently anti-Vieira stance of Francisco Fadul, a long-time party member who was sworn in as prime minister in February 1999, appeared to portend further cleavage.

In the wake of Vieira's removal from office, Manuel Saturnino da Costa was chosen on May 12, 1999, to assume the PAIGC party presidency, and Flavio Provenca was named interim secretary. The party held an extraordinary congress in Bissau September 3–9, with the stated goal of preparing for presidential and legislative polling. Delegates voted to expel Vieira, Carlos CORREIA, and a number of former ministers affiliated with Vieira, and the (then) defense minister and ally of the Mane junta, Francis Benante, was elected as the new PAIGC president.

The PAIGC won 24 seats in the 1999 legislative elections, and its candidate, interim president of the republic Malam Bacai Sanhá, won 23.34 percent of the votes in the first round in November 1999 presidential elections. He lost in the second round in January 2000, with 28 percent of the vote.

The PAIGC assumed an opposition stance to the PRS-led government formed in February 2000. The party reportedly came under intense scrutiny after allegedly supporting Ansumane Mane's failed bid to reinstate himself as the chief of staff in November. Benante was subsequently arrested and then released for alleged possession of arms, as were other opposition figures. The PAIGC accepted a post in the cabinet announced in March 2001 but remained highly critical of some of the administration's policies. In May the PAIGC voted in the legislature to approve the government's program, but only after amnesty was granted to prisoners from the events of the previous November. The new government appointed in December reportedly did not include any PAIGC members. In 2004 the PAIGC became the largest party in the assembly, receiving 33.88 percent of the vote and 45 seats. Party leader Carlos Gomes became prime minister on May 12, 2004, and subsequently formed a government of PAIGC members and independents. Gomes declared that he would not seek the presidency in 2005 and would instead concentrate on his role as prime minister. Following the election of Vieira in July, friction intensified within the party between those who supported Vieira, including party vice president Aristides Gomes, and those who remained loyal to Carlos Gomes. In September, Aristides Gomes and several other dissident members were suspended, and a month later 14 of the party's 45 legislators resigned, declaring themselves independents. Aristides Gomes joined with some of those dissidents and others from various opposition groups to form the **Forum for the Convergence of Development** (FCD), reportedly in an attempt to create a new majority in the assembly. The continued dissension between Vieira and the Carlos Gomes supporters in the PAIGC resulted in a delay in Vieira's inauguration until October because the pro-Gomes faction refused to recognize his authority. The rift culminated in Vieira's dismissal of the prime minister on October 30, and his appointment on November 2 of Aristides Gomes as the new prime minister. For its part, the PAIGC postponed indefinitely its extraordinary congress scheduled for October, and in November named a new chair, Martinho Ndafa Cabi. Meanwhile, Carlos Gomes's faction of the party continued to contest the appointment of Aristides Gomes, claiming it was unconstitutional, but court rulings in 2006 upheld Vieira's action. The status of Aristides Gomes and his supporters in the PAIGC remained unclear throughout 2007.

The PAIGC, in a "stability pact" with the PRS and the PUSD, was instrumental in the change in government in 2007 through a no-confidence vote in parliament that culminated in the consensus choice of Prime Minister Cabi to replace Aristides Gomes, following negotiations with President Vieira.

In March 2008 Aristides Gomes started a new political party, (see PRID, below), with plans to participate in the legislative elections scheduled for later in the year. In July, Carlos Gomes was elected to head the PAIGC, defeating Malam Bacai Sanhá, who had been unsuccessful in his bid to become president of the republic in 2000 and 2005.

Meanwhile, party veteran Saturnino da Costa, who was given a cabinet post in the government named by Gomes in January 2009, had sought the PAIGC presidential nod for the June 2009 election, along with four other party members. However, in April the party named Sanhá, a member of the Balanta ethnic group, as its presidential candidate over former prime minister Cabi. Carols Gomes, for his part, had backed Raimundo Pereira, who had ascended to interim president following the assassination of Vieira in March 2009.

The PAIGC initially rejected participation in the interim national transitional council in the aftermath of the April 2012 coup but agreed to the planned transition period in January 2013.

Leaders: Carlos GOMES Júnior (Former Prime Minister and Chair of the Party), Maria Djaló NANDINGNA (Vice Chair), Martinho Ndafa CABI (Former Prime Minister), Manuel Saturnino da COSTA, Paulo MEDINA.

Other Legislative Parties:

Social Renewal Party (*Partido para a Renovação Social*—PRS). The PRS was formed in January 1992 by seven defectors from the FDS (below) led by Kumba Yala, who accused the parent group of secretly collaborating with the PAIGC. Yala was runner-up to Vieira in the 1994 presidential balloting, with the party winning 12 of 100 assembly seats. In November, Yala rejected an offer to join the Costa government. Meanwhile, the PRS reportedly teamed with the Union for Change (UM, below) and the Front of Struggle for the Liberation of Guinea (FLING, below) to form a voting bloc in the assembly.

On November 10, 1995, Yala told a Portuguese daily, *Jornal de Notícias*, that the PAIGC was bereft of both "international credibility" and the "confidence of the people." Calling for early elections, Yala warned that while the PRS was opposed to a civil war, its wide support within the military would allow it to take power in "five or ten minutes."

In January 1998 Yala announced that he would form a parallel government if elections (then scheduled for midyear) were postponed. Thereafter, the PRS joined with other opposition groups demanding Vieira's resignation in early 1999. The PRS won 38 seats in the 1999 legislative elections, and Yala won the presidency in January 2000 with 72 percent of the vote in the second round. In 2003 the party was rife with conflict between those who supported Yala and those who did not. This divide led party president Alamara Nhasse to resign his post and lead a group of defectors to form a new group, the National Reconciliation Party (see below).

In the March 2004 elections, the PRS came in second with 24.76 percent of the vote and 35 seats. After Yala's defeat in the June 2005 presidential election, at least three people were killed during a protest by his supporters.

Rifts in the party resulted in a legal challenge to Yala's presidency in 2007, but a court ruling allowed him to retain his post. In November 2008 President Vieira accused Yala of being behind an attack on the palace, claiming the renegade soldiers involved were linked to the former president. The attack came shortly after the release of official results of the parliamentary elections, in which the PRS won 28 seats, a distant second to the PAIGC.

In 2009, while some in the party backed Baltazar Lopes FERNANDEZ as the party's candidate for president, Yala ultimately won the bid.

The party advocated the dismissal of Prime Minister Gomes after the April 2010 coup attempt and was among the organizers of mass demonstrations in July 2011 demanding Gomes's resignation.

Following the 2012 coup, party member Rui DUARTE DE BARROS was appointed prime minister in May.

Leaders: Rui DUARTE DE BARROS (Interim Prime Minister), Kumba YALA (Former President of the Republic and 2005 and 2009 presidential candidate), Ibrahima Sori DJALÓ (Acting Chair), Austino DACOSTA, Alberto NAMBEIA, Caetano NTCHAMA (Former Prime Minister), Antonio Artur SANHÁ (Former Prime Minister and Secretary General).

Republican Party for Independence and Development (*Partido Republicano para a Independência e o Desenvolvimento*—PRID). PAIGC dissident Aristides Gomes, a Vieira supporter, formed the PRID in March 2008, in advance of the November parliamentary elections, and won one of the three legislative seats his new party captured. Following the assassination of Vieira in 2009, Gomes left the country but subsequently applied to be a presidential candidate in the June election. His bid was rejected by the Supreme Court, which ruled that he was out of the country during the mandated time for candidates to be in residence. PRID was given one ministry in the post-coup government in 2012.

Leaders: Aristides GOMES (President and former Prime Minister), José Braima DAFE (Spokesperson).

New Democracy Party (*Partido da Nova Democracia*—PND). Little is known about the PND, which emerged in 2008 and won one seat in the November parliamentary elections. It is led by Mamadu Djaló, formerly of the **Party of Renovation and Progress** (*Partido da Renovação e Progresso*—PRP), who ran as an independent candidate in the 2005 presidential election placing sixth. Djaló had promised that if his party won, he would build a mosque and two schools and help create jobs for youth. The PND joined the PAIGC in initially opposing the transitional government.

In the 2009 presidential election, Djaló finished fourth with 2.95 percent of the vote.

Leader: Mamadu DJALÓ (2009 presidential candidate).

Democratic Alliance (*Aliança Democrática*—AD). The AD coalition, of which the PDC (below) was a core component, was credited with winning four seats (including one by the PCD's Victor Mandinga) in the 1999 legislative balloting. In the 2008 legislative elections, the AD was referenced as a party and credited with winning one seat.

Other Parties That Contested Recent Elections:

United Social Democratic Party (*Partido Unido Social Democrata*—PUSD). The PUSD was led by former prime minister Vítor Saúde Maria, who left the PAIGC in 1984 and was a member of the FDS before launching the present formation in June 1991.

In March 1993 Saúde Maria denounced PRD leader da Costa's detainment for alleged involvement in a coup attempt, accusing the government of launching an unprovoked opposition crackdown. Saúde Maria died in October 1999. His replacement as party president, Francisco José Fadul, was chosen at a party congress in late 2000. In the 2004 elections the PUSD became the third-largest parliamentary party with 16.1 percent of the vote and 17 seats. On April 5, 2006, it was reported that the PUSD had withdrawn from the government in a dispute regarding the justice minister, although it subsequently rejoined the government.

Following a dispute with the government for its refusal to dismiss a PUSD cabinet member whom Fadul accused of corruption, Fadul quit the party and started a new party, the PADEC (see below), in 2007. Collaterally, he claimed in a legal challenge that he was the PUSD president. PUSD opposed the post-coup interim government but joined the transitional process in January 2013.

Leader: Francisco José FUDAL.

Social Democratic Party (*Partido Social Democrata*—PSD). Founded by dissident RGB-MB members, the PSD was legalized on August 21, 1995. It won three seats in the legislative elections in 1999 and backed the PRS's Kumba Yala in the second round of the presidential elections in January 2000. Although some PSD members had previously taken part in PRS-led coalition governments, the cabinet installed in

December 2001 reportedly did not include any PSD members. In 2002 the party was part of the **Electoral Union** (*União Eleitoral*—UE), along with a few other small leftist and center-left parties. Party leader Joaquim Balde was the spokesman for the National Transition Council, following the coup in 2003.

Leaders: João Seco MANE (President), Joaquim BALDE (1999 presidential candidate), Gaspar FERNANDES (Secretary General).

Guinea-Bissau League for the Protection of Ecology (*Liga da Guiné-Bissau para Protecção Ecologia*—LIPE). The LIPE, also formerly referenced as the LGBPE, applied for legalization in July 1993. The league's president, Bubacar Rachid Djaló, ran in the first round of the presidential elections in November 1999 and backed the PRS's Kumba Yala in the second round in January 2000. Djaló was given a junior cabinet post in the PRS-led government in February but was not reappointed in the new government formed in March 2001.

In 2009 party member Pedro Infanda, who had planned to run as an independent, withdrew as a presidential candidate, stating that he feared for his life. Infanda, a lawyer who had represented José Americo Bubo Na Tchuto (see Current issues, above), had been arrested in March and allegedly beaten and tortured by military officials. He said his decision was made in the wake of the killing of another candidate, Territorial Minister Baciro Dabó, in June.

Leader: Bubacar Rachid DJALÓ (President and 1999 presidential candidate).

National Union for Democracy and Progress (*União Nacional para a Democracia e o Progresso*—UNDP). The UNDP was formed in December 1997 by Aboubacar Baldé, a former PAIGC official, who was reportedly angered at the ruling party's failure to organize a congress in mid-1997. The party was officially recognized in April 1998 and won one legislative seat in 1999. The UNDP reportedly came under scrutiny after Ansumane Mane's failed bid to reinstall himself as the chief of staff in November 2000. In the 2004 elections, the UNDP received 1.1 percent of the vote. Baldé dropped out as a 2005 presidential candidate for financial reasons. In the post-coup government, Baldé was appointed minister of commerce and industry.

Leader: Aboubacar BALDÉ (Minister of Commerce and Industry and 1999 presidential candidate).

National Reconciliation Party (*Partido Nacional do Reconciliation*—PRN). Formed in October 2004 by former PRS leader Alamara Nhasse, the PRN drew a large number of senior PRS figures away from the PRS, including a former defense minister and the former mayor of Bissau.

In 2009 the PRN called on the government of Prime Minister Gomes to step down, blaming it for Guinea Bissau's political turmoil.

Leader: Alamara NHASSE (Former Prime Minister).

Party for Development, Democracy, and Citizenship (*Partido para Democracia, Desenvolvimento e Cidodania*—PADEC). Former prime minister, PAIGC member, and PUSD leader Francisco Fadul formed the PADEC in 2007 after a dispute with the PUSD leadership.

In April 2009, in what human rights organizations described as a government crackdown on critics, party leader Fadul was allegedly beaten at his home by "men in uniform." In May the Supreme Court rejected Fadul's application to be a presidential candidate in the June election, saying he could not run because he had not resigned as head of the court of auditors. The party nominated former prime minister Faustino Imbali, who was assassinated in June 2009.

Leader: Francisco FADUL.

Other minor parties that contested the 2008 legislative elections were: the **Guinean Democratic Party** (*Partido Democrático Guinéense*—PDG), led by Manuel CA; **Movement for Democracy in Guinea-Bissau** (*Movimento Democrático Guiné-Bissau*—MDG), led by Silvestre ALVES; the **Socialist Party of Guinea-Bissau** (PS-GB); **Labor Party** (*Partido dos Trabalhadores*—PT); **Democratic Social Party** (*Partido Democrático Social*—PDS); **Alliance of Patriotic Forces** (*Aliança de Forças Patrióticas*—AFP); **Democratic Center** (*Centro Democrático*—CD); **Popular Democratic Party** (*Partido Popular Democrático*—PPD); **Progress Party** (*Partido de Progresso*—PP); and **Guinean Patriotic Union** (*União Patriótica Guinéens*—UPG), whose 2009 presidential candidate, Francisca Vaz TURPIN, was the only woman to contest the election. She finished ninth with 0.3 percent of the vote.

In the 2009 presidential election, Serifo BALDE of the **Young Party** finished sixth with 0.5 percent of the vote, and Aregado Mantenque TÉ of the **Workers Party** (*Partido dos Trabalhadores*), formed in Portugal in 2002, finished seventh with 0.5 percent.

Other Parties and Groups:

Electoral Union (*União Eleitoral*—UE). The UE was formed in 2002 to contest legislative elections by a group of four small leftist and center-left parties. In the 2004 elections the UE gained two seats in the assembly. Other minor parties in the UE include the **Guinean Socialist Party** (*Partido Socialista Guineense*—PSG), led by Cirilo VIEIRA.

Leader: Joaquim BALDE.

United Popular Alliance (*Aliança Popular Unida*—APU). The APU was formed prior to the 2004 legislative elections as an electoral coalition between the ASG (below) and the small **Guinean Popular Party** (*Partido Popular Guineense*—PPG), led by Joao Tatis SA. It won one seat in the 2004 assembly election. In May 2004 the APU signed an agreement with the PAIGC and the UE to "ensure stability." Sa ran last in the field of 13 first-round presidential candidates in 2005.

Socialist Alliance of Guinea-Bissau (*Aliança Socialista da Guiné-Bissau*—ASG). The ASG was launched in May 2000 under the leadership of Fernando Gomes, a human rights advocate. Gomes had run as an independent candidate in the first round of presidential elections in November 1999, receiving 7 percent of the vote. He backed Kumba Yala in the second round. Gomes and the ASG, however, were subsequently among the fiercest critics of the government, especially on the issues of human rights and freedom of the press. Gomes was briefly detained in late May 1999 for having released a communiqué strongly critical of the government. Party president Gomes, who was also the founder of the Guinea-Bissau Human Rights League, was arrested in 2002, an event Amnesty International said was "politically motivated."

Leader: Fernando GOMES.

United Platform (*Plataforma Unida*—PLATAF). This electoral coalition, led by Helder VAZ and Victor Mandinga, was formed to contest the 2004 legislative elections. Two members of the coalition, the Democratic Front and the Democratic Convergence Party, were also linked in a separate coalition as the Democratic Alliance (see Democratic Convergence Party, below). In 2004, the former leader of the PLATAF, Francisca VAZ Turpin, filed papers to form a new party, the UPG (above).

Democratic Convergence Party (*Partido da Convergência Democrática*—PCD). The PCD first surfaced in the early 1990s under the leadership of a former PAIGC member, Victor Mandinga. The PCD apparently served as the core component of the Democratic Alliance coalition that was credited with winning four seats (including one by Mandinga) in the 1999 legislative balloting. Mandinga supported Ansumane Mane in the events of late 2000, and he was briefly detained by security forces. Mandinga, routinely referenced as leader of the AD, subsequently remained a highly vocal and visible critic of President Yala. Meanwhile, several cabinet ministers installed in March 2001 and December 2001 were referenced as PCD members. In 2005 Mandinga was named minister of finance.

Leader: Victor MANDINGA.

Democratic and Social Front (*Frente Democrática e Social*—FDS). The FDS was launched in early 1990 by former PAIGC president Rafael Barbosa to fight against the "dictatorship" of the existing system. A cofounder of the PAIGC, Barbosa had been accused of collaboration with the Portuguese during the liberation struggle, convicted of treason in 1974, and imprisoned. He was released briefly upon Vieira's seizure of power in 1980 but was again imprisoned after calling for the expulsion of Cape Verdeans from Guinea-Bissau. He was formally amnestied in 1987.

Following a contentious FDS leadership meeting on January 15, 1992, the two-year-old group suffered its third split as seven members left to form the PRS. The FDS won a single seat in the legislature in 1999. In advance of the 2004 assembly election, the FDS formed a coalition with the PUSD, the PRD, and the LGBPE. Longtime party leader Rafael BARBOSA died in January 2007 at age 81.

Other minor parties in the PLATAF include the **Group of Independent Democrats** (*Grupo de Democratas Independentes*—GDI), which was formed by Helder Vaz and dissidents from the RGB-MB; and the **Democratic Front** (*Frente Democrática*—FD), led by Canjura INJAI.

Guinea-Bissau Resistance–Bah Fatah Movement (*Resistência da Guiné-Bissau—Movimento Bah-Fatah*—RGB-MB). Launched in Lisbon, Portugal, in 1986, the RGB-MB was technically precluded from using "Bafata" in its official title because of a legal prohibition of the use of an ethnic, regional, or (in this case) town name for political parties. As a result it substituted "Bah-Fatah" for "Bafata" prior to registration in December 1991. RGB-MB founder Domingos Fernandes Gomes returned after six years in exile on May 18, 1992. The party was runner-up to the PAIGC in the 1994 legislative poll, winning 19 seats. In November, Fernandes refused an invitation to join the Costa government.

In late 1998 the RGB-MB announced that it would not participate in reconciliation talks with President Vieira and called for his resignation. The party had been a vocal critic of Vieira throughout the military uprising, which it had allegedly described as an internecine struggle within the PAIGC.

In the 2004 legislative elections, the RGB-MB received only 1.85 percent of the vote and consequently no seats in the assembly. Party leader Domingos Fernandes Gomes announced he would run in the 2005 presidential election, but his name did not appear on the list of candidates. Party leader Salvador Tchongo dropped out the 2005 presidential race, citing financial difficulties and a lack of confidence in the process.

Leaders: Domingos FERNANDES Gomes (1994 presidential candidate), Salvador TCHONGO (President), Mario Ujssumane BALDE (Secretary General).

Union for Change (*União para a Mudança*—UM). The UM was originally organized prior to the 1994 election as a six-party electoral coalition that included the left-of-center Democratic Front (*Frente Democrática*—FD), led by Marcelino BAPTISTA; the United Democratic Movement (*Movimento para a Unidade e a Democracia*—Mude), led by Felintro Vaz MARTINS; the Democratic Party of Progress (*Partido Democrático do Progresso*—PDP); and the Party of Renovation and Development (*Partido da Renovação e Desenvolvimento*—PRD), a grouping of PAIGC dissidents led by João da Costa; as well as the FDS and LGBPE, which did not join their partners in a formal merger in November 1995. The Union secured six seats in 1994 and three in 1999. The party reportedly came under scrutiny after Ansumane Mane's failed bid to reinstate himself as the chief of staff in November 2000 and party president Manuel Rambout Barcelos was arrested. The group's secretary general, Agnello Regala, also was arrested for allegedly supporting Mane. He was released in December. In the 2004 election the UM received only 2 percent of the vote and therefore no seats in the assembly. The UM rejected participation in the interim national transitional council formed after the April 2012 coup.

Leaders: Manuel Rambout BARCELOS, Amine Michel SAAD (PDP), Agnello REGALA (Secretary General).

Guinean Civic Forum (*Foro Civico da Guiné*—FCG). The FCG's Antonieta Rosa Gomes competed in the 1999 presidential election, and in 2000 she was appointed to the Ntchama government. However, she was dismissed in November 2001. The new government appointed in December 2001 reportedly did not include any FCG members. The FCG received less than 1 percent of the vote in the 2004 elections. Gomes ran for president in 2005 on the FCG ticket in affiliation with the **Social Democracy** (SD) group. She was the only woman to contest the elections.

Leader: Antonieta Rosa GOMES (1999 and 2005 presidential candidate).

Other minor parties include the **Manifest Party of the People** (PMP) and the **Party of National Unity** (*Partido da Unidade Nacional*—PUN), led by Idrissa DJALÓ.

LEGISLATURE

The current **National People's Assembly** (*Assembleia Nacional Popular*) is a directly elected body of 102 members elected for five-year terms. At the most recent balloting of November 16, 2008, for 100 seats, the distribution was as follows: African Party for the Independence of Guinea and Cape Verde, 67; Social Renewal Party, 28; Republican Party for Independence and Development, 3; New Democracy Party 1; and Democratic Alliance, 1. The Assembly was dissolved on April 16, 2012, following a military coup.

CABINET

[as of August 1, 2013]

Prime Minister	Rui Duarte De Barros (PRS)
Ministers of State	
	Fernando Vaz (FOD)
	Orlando Mendes Viegas
	Aristedes da Silva
Ministers	
Agriculture and Rural Development	Nicholau Santos
Civil Service, State Reform, Labor, and Social Security	Aristedes da Silva
Commerce and Industry	Abubacar Baldé (UNDP)
Defense	Celestino de Carvalho
Economy and Regional Integration	Soares Sambu
Energy and Natural Resources	Daniel Gomes
Finance	Gino Mendes
Fisheries	Mário Lopes da Rosa
Foreign Affairs and International Cooperation	Fernando Delfim da Silva
Health	Agostinho Cá
Infrastructure, Transport, and Communication	Rui Araujo Gomes
Interior	António Suka Ntchama (PRS)
Justice	Mamadú Saido Baldé
National Education, Youth, Culture, and Sport	Alfredo Gomes
Natural Resources	Certório Biote
Presidency and the Council of Ministers	Fernando Vaz
Territorial Administration and Local Government	Baptista Té (PRID)
Transport and Telecommunications	Orlando Mendes Viegas
Women, Family, and Social Solidarity	Gabriela Fernandes [f]

[f] = female

INTERGOVERNMENTAL REPRESENTATION

Ambassador to the U.S.: (Vacant).

U.S. Ambassador to Guinea-Bissau (and Senegal, based in Senegal): Lewis A. LUKENS.

Permanent Representative to the UN: João Soares DA GAMA.

IGO Memberships (Non-UN): AfDB, AU, ECOWAS, IOM, NAM, OIC, WTO.

GUYANA

Cooperative Republic of Guyana

Political Status: Formerly the colony of British Guiana; independent member of the Commonwealth since May 26, 1966; under republican regime instituted February 23, 1970; present constitution approved February 11, 1980, with effect from October 6.

Area: 83,000 sq. mi. (214,969 sq. km).

Population: 763,099 (2012E—UN); 739,903 (2013E—U.S. Census).

Major Urban Center (metropolitan area, 2003E): GEORGETOWN (231,000).

Official Language: English.

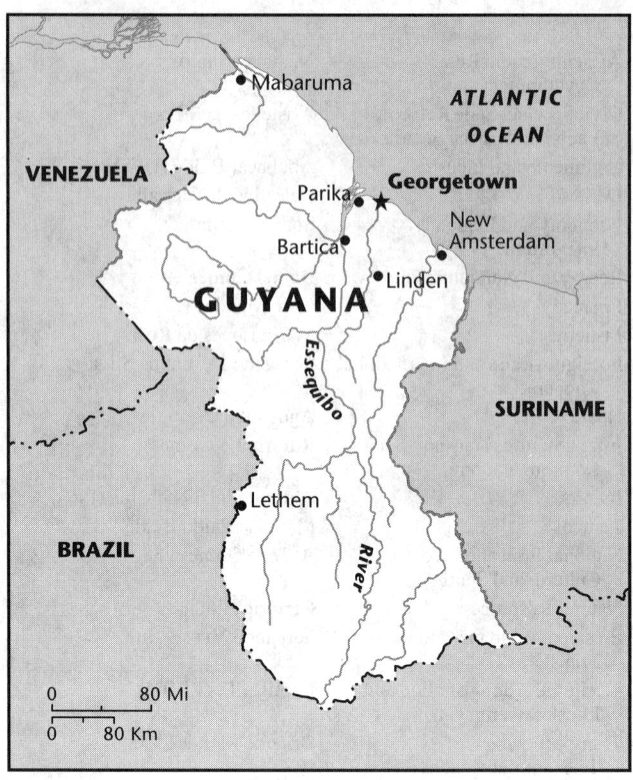

Monetary Unit: Guyanese Dollar (market rate November 1, 2013: 202.95 dollars = $1US).

President: Donald Ramotar (People's Progressive Party/Civic); sworn in December 3, 2011, to succeed Bharrat Jagdeo (People's Progressive Party/ Civic), who had been in office since August 11, 1999.

Prime Minister: Samuel A. (Sam) HINDS (Civic); sworn in December 19, 1997, succeeding Janet JAGAN (People's Progressive Party); reappointed by the president on August 11, 1999; April 4, 2001; September 4, 2006; and December 5, 2011.

THE COUNTRY

Noted for its dense forests and many rivers, Guyana, whose name is an Amerindian word meaning "land of many waters," is situated on the northern Atlantic coast of South America, with Venezuela and Suriname on the west and east, respectively, and Brazil on the south and southwest. Its inhabitants are concentrated along a narrow coastal belt, the only area suitable for intensive agriculture. Most of their ancestors arrived during the centuries of British colonial rule: African slaves before 1800 and East Indian plantation workers during the nineteenth century. According to the 2002 census, 43.5 percent of the population are of East Indian origin, mainly engaged in agriculture; 30.2 percent are African, including mostly civil servants; 16.7 percent claim multiple heritages; 9.1 percent are Amerindian; and the remainder are European or Chinese. The principal religions are Christianity (58 percent), Hinduism (28 percent), and Islam (7 percent), according to a 2002 census. In 2009, 34 percent of adult women were in the paid labor force, concentrated chiefly in agriculture and cottage industries, and 21 women were elected to the National Assembly in 2011.

The Guyanese economy is based primarily on agriculture, with sugar and rice being the principal crops, although exploitation of mineral resources, including bauxite, alumina, gold, diamonds, and manganese, has become increasingly important. Since 1975 Guyana has experienced severe economic difficulties, with falling export prices generating large balance-of-payments deficits and shortages of basic commodities creating a vast underground economy supported by widespread smuggling. In 1986 Prime Minister Hoyte attempted to alleviate the situation by launching a "reconstructive" liberalization program that departed significantly from his predecessor's socialist policies. Despite a 70 percent currency devaluation in April 1989 and the removal of most trade restrictions and price controls, lengthy talks with the International Monetary Fund (IMF) failed to yield agreement on standby and structural adjustment facilities until mid-1990, in the wake of another devaluation of 26.7 percent. From 1990 to 2000 GDP growth averaged 4.25 percent per year, according to the IMF, though that number obscures an economy that swung considerably throughout the decade from booms to contractions. From 1998 to 2007 the economy contracted four times before reaching a decade peak of 7 percent growth at the end. Unemployment, however, remained in the double digits.

In an effort to counter the effects of the global economic recession, the government in 2009 unveiled its largest budget ever, reflecting an 8 percent year-on-year increase. New initiatives in education, health, housing, and water increased spending in those areas by 15.9 percent. The spending inoculated Guyana against the global economic downturn, bringing growth of 3.3 percent in 2009. The IMF commended the Guyanese authorities for reducing inflation from a 2007 peak of 12.2 percent to 3 percent in 2009 and for successfully implementing a value-added tax. Inflation averaged 5.9 percent from then through 2013. GDP has continued to rise since the recession, with growth of 5.5 percent in 2013.

GOVERNMENT AND POLITICS

Political background. Guyana's political history during its first decade of independence was largely determined by an unusual ethnic structure resulting from the importation of African slaves and, subsequently, of East Indian laborers to work on the sugar plantations during the centuries of British colonial rule. The resultant cleavage between urbanized Africans and the more numerous rural East Indians was reflected politically in an intense rivalry between the communist-led, East Indian-supported People's Progressive Party (PPP) of Dr. Cheddi B. JAGAN and the African-backed People's National Congress (PNC), led by Linden Forbes BURNHAM, a former PPP leader who broke with Jagan in 1955. Jagan's party, with a numerically larger constituency, came to power in British Guiana under a colonial constitution introduced in 1953 but was removed from office later that year because of British concern over a veer toward communism. Jagan's party again emerged victorious in general elections held in 1957 and 1961 but was defeated in 1964, when the introduction of a new system of proportional representation made possible the formation of a coalition government embracing Burnham's PNC and the small United Force (TUF). In spite of earlier internal disorders, Burnham's administration successfully negotiated with the British for independence and remained in office following the achievement of full Commonwealth status in 1966 and the adoption of a republican form of government in 1970. However, the PNC's continued dominance in 1968 and 1973 generated widespread controversy. Contributing to opposition charges of fraud and withdrawal of the TUF from the governing coalition was a revision of the electoral law to allow Guyanese residing overseas to vote.

The 1970 redesignation of Guyana as a "cooperative republic" attested to the ruling party's increased commitment to socialism. In his "Declaration of Sophia," published on the tenth anniversary of his premiership, Burnham referred to the PNC as a socialist party committed to government land control, the nationalization of foreign business interests, and a domestic economy of three sectors, "public, cooperative, and private," with the cooperative sector predominant. He also called for revision of the nation's constitution to expunge the "beliefs and ideology of our former imperialist masters." Subsequently, in a referendum held July 10, 1978, more than 97 percent of those voting were said to have approved extension of the legislature's term beyond its July 23 expiration date so that the PNC-dominated National Assembly could serve, additionally, as a constituent body to consider a series of drastic changes in the nation's basic law.

Guyana's new constitution came into effect on October 6, 1980. Burnham assumed the office of executive president and designated Ptolemy A. REID as prime minister. On December 15, in an election branded by an international team of observers as "fraudulent in every possible respect," the PNC was credited with an overwhelming popular mandate, and on January 1, 1981, the government was substantially expanded to include five vice presidents and additional ministers.

In the wake of worsening fiscal conditions, the regime faced mounting internal and external political challenges, culminating in the arrest by Canadian authorities in December 1983 of six persons, including a member of the Toronto-based right-wing Conservative Party of Guyana, who were charged with plotting to assassinate Burnham and other key officials. A number of subsequent leadership changes included the appointment in August 1984 of Vice President Hugh

Desmond HOYTE to succeed the reportedly ailing Reid as first vice president and prime minister.

President Burnham died on August 6, 1985, while undergoing surgery in Georgetown, and was succeeded by Hoyte, who was accorded a regular five-year mandate on December 9 in balloting that, as in 1980, yielded allegations of widespread fraud.

Elections that should have been held in late 1990 were postponed to permit the compilation of new electoral rolls, with the National Assembly (due to expire on February 2, 1991) being accorded a series of two-month extensions before formal dissolution on September 28. On November 10 President Hoyte announced that the long-delayed balloting would take place on December 16; on November 22, however, he responded to continued domestic and international criticism of the voter-registration procedure by again postponing the poll. The assembly validated President Hoyte's action in December when it reconvened under a state of emergency decree; the parliamentary session was prolonged to September 30, 1992.

In contrast to the two previous elections, a team of 100 foreign observers characterized the balloting on October 5, 1992, as largely fair and impartial. The ongoing 1991 alliance of the PPP and a small social and political party of business owners and professionals—Civic (PPP/C)—won a majority of the popular vote. Dr. Jagan was installed as president four days later, and his party, after lengthy negotiations with TUF and the Working People's Alliance (WPA), secured control of the National Assembly and approval for a government headed by Civic leader Samuel A. (Sam) HINDS.

The PPP/C won 48 of 65 Neighborhood Democratic Councils (NDCs) and three of six municipalities in local government elections on August 8, 1994. The principal loss was in the capital, where 12 of 30 seats were captured by Good and Green for Georgetown (GGG), a new formation led by former prime minister Hamilton Green, who served a one-year term as the city's mayor before defeat in August 1995 and reelection in 1996.

President Jagan suffered a fatal heart attack on March 6, 1997, and was immediately succeeded, for the balance of his term, by Prime Minister Hinds, who also held the post of vice president. On March 17 Hinds appointed his predecessor's wife, Janet JAGAN, as first vice president and prime minister, additionally naming Agriculture Minister Reepu Daman PERSAUD as second vice president.

Mrs. Jagan became president in the general election of December 15, 1997 (which yielded a largely unchanged distribution of legislative seats), thereafter naming Hinds as first vice president and prime minister, and Bharrat JAGDEO as second vice president. The election generated intense controversy, however, and the PNC did not agree to take up its assembly seats until mid-1998.

Mrs. Jagan resigned for medical reasons on August 1, 1999, and a somewhat complicated scenario ensued: as constitutionally prescribed, Prime Minister Hinds again assumed the presidency on a provisional basis. He then named Jagdeo as first vice president and prime minister and resigned in the latter's favor. Following his installation as president, Jagdeo reappointed Hinds as prime minister, and Hinds proceeded to name a cabinet virtually identical to its predecessor.

In January 2001 a Guyanese Supreme Court judge declared the 1997 election null and void because of the introduction of voter-identification cards. However, in a March 1 clarification the judge ruled that the Jagdeo government was not illegitimate, despite having been installed under unconstitutional legislation. Shortly thereafter, the issue became moot with the March 19 victory of the PPP/C (characterized by international observers as "basically fair") and the incumbent's reinstallation.

A new election had been anticipated in August 2006. However, in March 2006 the Guyana Election Commission announced that the balloting would be delayed beyond the constitutional deadline of August 4 due to difficulties in assembling a valid electoral list. Regional and general elections were held on August 28. Following the assassination of Agriculture Minister Satyadeow SAWH, the new National Assembly was delayed in convening until September 28, over three weeks after the constitutionally required date of September 2 and four months after the May 2 dissolution. The opposition immediately argued that the deferral would require a constitutional amendment, but the chief justice dismissed their claims; the PNC and allied Reform party (PNC/R) thereupon indicated that it would appeal the decision to the Caribbean Court of Justice. Jagdeo continued in office following the election, in which the PPP/C increased its parliamentary majority by two seats.

In an effort to conduct the country's first local elections since 1994, President Jagdeo proposed legislation in May 2011 that would reestablish the polls, which had been suspended due to an impasse between the government and the Corbin-led opposition over election reforms. In January 2013 ambassadors from the United States, U.K., Canada, and E.U. issued a joint statement urging the elections to be held within the year. The following month, the legislature approved a bill approving an extension of the date for local elections, which PPP/C leaders said would pave way from progress, but that opposition members criticized as a further mechanism to postpone them. As of late 2013, no date had been set for local elections.

In the November 28, 2011, general election, the PPP/C retained the presidency for the fifth consecutive election. Donald RAMOTAR replaced President Jagdeo, who was constitutionally prohibited from seeking a third consecutive term, as the PPP/C won 49 percent of the vote. The APNU, an opposition coalition led by the PNCR, took 41 percent. Despite Ramotar's victory, the PPP/C lost the parliamentary majority for the first time in 19 years by 1 seat, taking 32 seats. The APNU won 26 seats and the AFU 7 (see Current Issues, below).

Constitution and government. The 1966 constitution established Guyana as a parliamentary member of the Commonwealth under the sovereignty of the British queen. The monarchical structure was abandoned in 1970 in favor of a titular president elected by the National Assembly.

The 1980 constitution provided for a president who is selected each time voting occurs (normally every five years) for a new National Assembly. (The successful presidential candidate is the nominee of the party that receives the most votes in the legislative balloting.) The president's extensive powers include the authority to appoint and dismiss an unspecified number of vice presidents and a prime minister, to dissolve the legislature, and to veto all legislative enactments. The National Assembly includes 65 popularly elected members; its normal term is five years. In an unusual procedure, voters cast their ballots for party slates, with selection of new assembly members a postelectoral internal party matter. Universal adult suffrage has existed in the country since 1953. The judicial branch consists of ten magistrates' courts, one for each judicial district, and a Supreme Court, encompassing a High Court and a Court of Appeal; however, the National Assembly in November 2004 approved a bill transferring jurisdiction of the Court of Appeal to the Caribbean Court of Justice (CCJ) as of the launching of the Trinidad-based regional body in March 2005. There are elected councils in the country's ten regions, in addition to municipal administrations in Georgetown and four towns, although the balloting of August 1994 was their first replenishment since 1970. Local councilors elect from their membership a National Congress of Local Democratic Organs, which, together with the National Assembly, constitutes a deliberative body known as the Supreme Congress of the People of Guyana.

Constitutional amendments must be approved by the assembly and, if not endorsed by a two-thirds majority, submitted to a popular vote (the legislative extensions of 1991 being technically in the form of constitutional amendments carried by the PNC's [then] overwhelming assembly majority).

Freedom of the press is generally respected, but the state and media have an uneasy relationship. For instance, in October 2011, President Jagdeo ordered the suspension of a privately owned opposition TV station over a comment that an opposition MP made on a program earlier in the year. Meanwhile, the opposition claims they do not have free access to state-owned media. In May 2013 Legal Affairs Minister Anil NANDLALL announced that the government was reviewing the law criminalizing defamation. International media watchdog Reporters Without Borders ranked Guyana 69th of 179 countries for press freedom in 2013.

Foreign relations. Guyana's major foreign policy problems stem from boundary disputes with both its eastern and western neighbors. The disagreement with Suriname centers on the delineation of a riparian boundary between the two countries: Guyana claims that the boundary follows the Corentyne, while Suriname claims it follows the New River. To the west, meanwhile, Venezuela has long claimed all territory west of the Essequibo River, which amounts to more than half of Guyana's total area (see map). In 1966 the two countries agreed to settle the issue by diplomatic means, and in 1970, after talks had failed, Venezuela agreed to a 12-year moratorium on its claim. The 1970 protocol provided that if the dispute was not resolved by September 18, 1982, it would be referred to an "appropriate international organ" or, failing agreement on such an organ, to the secretary general of the United Nations. In the wake of a series of border incidents that accompanied expiration of the moratorium, Venezuela rejected a Guyanese request to seek a ruling from the International Court of Justice and formally requested the mediation of United Nations Secretary General Javier Pérez de Cuéllar. In March 1983 Venezuela announced that Guyana had acquiesced in the action, but no further progress was reported until February 1985, when the Venezuelan foreign minister indicated that his government was prepared to adopt a conciliatory attitude in furtherance of a "new spirit of friendship and cooperation" between the two countries. Following a November 1989 meeting in Caracas with Venezuelan president Carlos Andrés Pérez, President Hoyte announced that the two governments had agreed to seek the "good offices" of the vice chancellor of the University of the West Indies, Alister McIntyre, in formulating a resolution of the long-standing dispute. Evidence of the changed climate was provided by Guyana's admission to the Organization of American States (OAS) in January 1991, after Venezuela had withdrawn an objection stemming from the boundary issue.

The Essequibo dispute rekindled in October 1999 after Guyana awarded offshore oil concessions in waters claimed by Venezuela to three foreign firms. Guyana claimed that the contested territory had been awarded to Guyana under an 1899 arbitration award and was "internationally accepted" thereafter. A constituent assembly, then considering changes in the Venezuelan constitution, responded by insisting that it would reject any modifications to the original Captaincy-General of Venezuela that had been "vitiated by nullity." A subsequent agreement to accept a Barbadian diplomat as mediator proved unproductive.

The dispute with Suriname was resolved in September 2007 when a UN tribunal ruling gave Guyana rights to 12,800 square miles, almost twice the area awarded to Suriname. The offshore area is thought to hold 15 billion barrels of oil and 42 trillion cubic feet of natural gas. On May 19, 2008, an anticrime agreement with Suriname dealt with piracy, money laundering, and trafficking in people, drugs, and firearms. On May 23 Guyana joined 11 other South American countries in founding the Union of South American Nations (Unasur) to continue the process of regional integration.

Tensions with Suriname heightened briefly in 2008 when Surinamese authorities seized a Guyanese vessel on the Corentyne River in October. The boat, on a mission to load sugar upriver, was released after a fine was paid for not being captained by a Surinamese citizen.

In February 2009 Norway agreed to pay Guyana $250 million over a five-year period to slow deforestation. The compensation was meant to encourage Guyana to limit greenhouse gas emissions from deforestation. (In 2010 Denmark and Germany also signed agreements with Guyana to help counter climate change; Denmark agreed to pay $250 million between 2010 and 2015 and Germany pledged to pay $11 million to counter deforestation in Guyana.)

April 2009 marked the completion of the Takutu Bridge linking Guyana and Brazil, strengthening ties between the two countries. Subsequently, leaders finalized plans for a $2 billion hydroelectric power plant to serve Brazil.

Two U.S. government reports in 2010 criticizing Guyana's effort in drug- and human-trafficking prompted Guyanese officials to claim the reports were filled with misrepresentations and falsities. In April the UN appointed Jamaican diplomat Norman GIRVAN to mediate the border dispute between Venezuela and Guyana after the two sides agreed to restart talks that had been suspended since 2007. The two countries had already begun to improve relations, including two July 2009 agreements on a new highway linkage between the two and a deal for Venezuela to ship 10,000 barrels of oil a day to Guyana.

In bilateral talks with Suriname in September 2010, the two sides agreed to cooperate on the exploitation of natural resources, on climate change policy, and on a possible bridge linking the two countries over the Courantyne River. In July 2011 the Surinamese foreign minister ruled out any military option in pursuit of the country's claims in the New River Triangle.

Tensions between Guyana and Venezuela resurfaced in September 2011 when Venezuela learned that in 2009, Guyana applied to the United Nations to extend its continental shelf by 150 miles, in accordance with a changing regulation that previously stipulated a 200–nautical mile outer limit of exclusive economic zones. Guyana filed for the extension through the UN Laws of the Sea, of which Venezuela is not a signatory. Border tensions between Guyana and Venezuela were reignited in September 2011 when Venezuela was notified of Guyana's 2009 bid to extend its maritime border by 150 miles. The expansion, under the UN Commission on the Limits of the Continental Shelf, of which Venezuela is not a member, would impact Venezuela's eastern maritime boundary. In May 2012 Caricom foreign ministers voted to throw their support behind Guyana's bid, over Venezuela's objections. The following month, territorial tensions heightened between the uneasy neighbors when Guyana approved a contract for the offshore exploration of crude oil in the Essequibo region, Guyanese maritime territory that Venezuela claims.

In August 2012 the Guyanese government went on the offense after the U.S. State Department published a report contending that the country does not comply with minimum standards for eliminating human trafficking.

In March, Guyana and the United States signed an open skies agreement, which replaced a 1946 U.K.-U.S. agreement grandfathered in from before independence. The treaty will ease travel and trade between the two countries.

Guyana satisfied Millennium Development Goal of halving "proportion of hungry people" ahead of the 2015 deadline.

Current issues. In October 2011 President Jagdeo called for parliamentary elections on November 28. Ahead of the election, the PNCR allied with other opposition parties in June to create **A Partnership for National Unity** (APNU) against the PPP/C (see Political Parties, below). Leading up to the 2011 election, the APNU campaigned that the incumbent PPP/C had cut social programs and ignored the poor, while the ruling party, seeking a fifth consecutive five-year term, boasted vibrant average annual economic growth, a significantly lower debt-to-GDP ratio, a positive forecast by the IMF, and the lowering of tax rates. President Jagdeo, constitutionally barred from seeking a third time, endorsed Donald Ramotar as the PPP/C candidate. The APNU put forward David GRANGER of the PNCR.

Four parties contested in the November 28, 2011, election. The PPP/C won 32 parliamentary seats with 48.6 percent of the vote, remaining the party with the most representation in the assembly, but losing its majority. The APNU won 26 seats (40.8 percent), and the AFC, seven (10.3 percent), and the parties subsequently formed a parliamentary coalition. Observers from the Organization of American States (OAS) lauded Guyana's "inclusive and clean electoral process," but noted instances of voter confusion because of change of polling station venues. Voter turnout was 72.9 percent. Election officials delayed announcement of the results by two days in order to verify them.

Guyana is widely recognized as a conduit for South American drugs into the North American and European markets and is also plagued by gunrunning and gang violence. The U.S. government reported that almost 20 percent of Guyana's GDP comes from trafficking drugs and that the illicit trade is so deeply embedded in the country's operations that drugs systematically enter the U.S. through airports and shipping containers ostensibly filled with agricultural and mining exports. Highlighting the country's security problems spurred directly by the drug trade, PNCR opposition leader Robert CORBIN in May 2008 claimed drug gangs had infiltrated Guyanese law enforcement and security services. In response to several cases of corruption, the government began polygraph testing for enforcement officials. Several drug enforcement officers, including the agency's chief, were fired because of the results of the tests. Also in May protests against the government's failure to improve security turned violent when demonstrators attacked the culture ministry and surrounding buildings with Molotov cocktails and gunfire. The government claimed Corbin, who had called for the protests, was inciting acts of political extremism in an attempt to pressure the administration over security concerns. In 2012, the U.S. State Department said Guyana is a transit country for narcotics, primarily cocaine, destined for North America. The 2012 International Narcotics Control Strategy Report states that heavy drug traffic has warped the country's political and judicial infrastructures. Although legislation recently passed to aid prosecutors in the investigation and conviction of drug crimes, there were no convictions under the law in 2011. A request in July 2013 from the U.S. government for Guyanese officials to be more active in combating human trafficking prompted Guyana to respond that the country will no longer cooperate with American requests for information on trafficking.

Partisan divisions between the PPP/C president and the PNCR and AFC legislature slowed the legislative process throughout 2012 and 2013. In June 2012 Ramotar said he would not approve bills drafted by the opposition without "the full agreement of the executive and the full involvement of the executive." A proposed hike in electricity rates provoked demonstrations in the mining town of Linden in July 2012. The government drew sharp criticism from the AFC and the PNCR for the handling of the protests, which resulted in the deaths of at least three protesters. That month, the legislature approved a motion of no confidence against Home Affairs Minister Clement Rodhee, but it was not enforced. In an address on January 1, 2013, the president called for an end to the partisan stalemates, but the year brought further disagreement; members of the administration, frustrated with the lack of PPP/C leadership in parliament, hinted in March at the possibility of snap elections. The opposition halted majority-supported firearms trafficking and money laundering initiatives, in March and April, respectively. Meanwhile, fissures within the coalition emerged in April 2013 when the AFC proposed a $40 billion budget cut that the APNU wanted to avoid.

POLITICAL PARTIES

Government Parties:

People's Progressive Party/Civic (PPP/C). Launched on January 1, 1950, by Dr. Cheddi B. Jagan and his wife, Janet Jagan, the PPP began as an anticolonial party speaking for the lower social classes but subsequently came to represent almost exclusively the large East Indian racial group. It long adhered to a pro-Soviet line, and at a June 1969 Moscow meeting Dr. Jagan formally declared the PPP to be a communist party. While the PPP and other opposition groups charged that the PNC fraudulently manipulated the overseas vote in the 1973 election, Dr. Jagan offered his critical support to the PNC in August 1975. The PPP Central Committee narrowly approved participation in the December 1980 legislative balloting, in which the party was officially credited with winning ten seats. It was awarded eight seats in 1985.

In June 1991 Jagan retreated from his earlier insistence on state ownership by saying that the PPP would "critically examine" enterprises in the public sector and consult with both business and labor "as to the best means of insuring their viability." Dr. Jagan died on March 6, 1997. Under the leadership of his wife, the PPP won a majority of directly elected legislative seats in the balloting of December 15, 1997. Janet Jagan resigned the presidency for medical reasons on August 1, 1999.

Since 1991 the PPP has been allied with the **Civic Party** (PPP/C), a group of local business owners and professionals headed by former interim president and current prime minister Samuel HINDS. Relations between the PPP/C and main opposition party PNC deteriorated over time and culminated in several charges against the opposition, including voter irregularities and inciting extremism. As the cost of living continued to climb, several protests were staged against the ruling party, including one in April 2008 by sugar workers in the town of New Amsterdam. The PNC staged street protests in the capital.

In 2008 the party and the administration of president Bharrat Jagdeo were implicated in the case of drug trafficker Roger Khan. Khan told a U.S. court he had helped Jagdeo's administration fight crime and conduct surveillance. In 2009, Khan's lawyer said PPP party member and government health minister Leslie Ramsammy helped his client buy advanced surveillance equipment. The party and the government denied the claim.

Following the death of the former president of the republic and party stalwart Janet Jagan on March 28, 2009, the country observed two days of mourning.

Meanwhile, since President Jagdeo was ineligible for reelection in 2011, observers began speculating about a likely successor and the potential for party infighting in the process. At the end of 2009 the party distanced itself from a campaign to hold a referendum that would allow Jagdeo to run for a third term in office. The election marked an important turning point for the PPP/C, representing the first time a candidate was neither a member of the Jagan family nor handpicked by a Jagan. The primary process itself became a fractious issue when Jagdeo came out in opposition to holding a secret ballot for it.

In April 2011 the party selected Donald Ramotar uncontested as its presidential candidate for that year's election. Of the four other primary candidates, three withdrew before election day, and the fourth failed to show up for the vote.

In June 2012 long-time party member Ralph RAMKARRAN resigned from the party after he had made public his concerns about corruption within the party leadership. He remained a harsh critic of the party after his exit.

Leaders: Donald RAMOTAR (President of the Republic and General Secretary), Zulfikar MUSTAPHA (Executive Secretary).

The United Force (TUF). The TUF, a small party founded by Peter D'AGUILAR in the early 1960s, represents conservative business and other interests. It favors racial integration, closer ties to the West, and it draws support from white, Amerindian, and other minority groups.

In 1968 the TUF withdrew from the governing coalition to protest the enfranchisement of overseas voters. The party won two seats in the 1980 legislative elections, which it held until 1992, when it lost one. It held on to one seat in balloting in 1997 and 2001. Party leader Manzoor Nadir became an "opposition" participant in the Hinds government in 2001 and continued in that capacity after the 2006 election.

On February 19, 2008, the TUF signed an agreement with the PPP/C and opposition parties to support the administration in garnering international support to help fight the country's burgeoning crime problem.

In May 2009, in the wake of a five-day strike by air traffic controllers, parliament approved a controversial bill introduced by Nadir, the minister of labor, that limited the ability of workers to strike by requiring that all parties involved in a potential walkout first meet with an arbitration panel appointed by the labor minister. The *Stabroek News* in 2010 said the party had been suffering from dwindling support over the years and that it was in danger of extinction. In an attempt to shake up the party and distance itself from its association with the PPP/C in the lead-up to the 2011 general elections, TUF's new leader and presidential candidate, Valerie Garido-Lowe, publicly asked Nadir to step down from his ministerial seat in August. Nadir said he would relinquish his seat if a majority of TUF representatives on the party's 2006 roll asked for his resignation.

In the 2011 general election, Nadir, initially the party's presidential candidate, stepped down and handed the post to Garido-Lowe, who left the party to join the AFC in October and was replaced by Peter PERSAUD. In November, TUF lost its single parliamentary seat, winning just 0.26 percent of the vote.

Leader: Peter PERSAUD (Party Chair and 2011 presidential candidate).

Principal Opposition Party:

A Partnership for National Unity (APNU). Formed in July 2011 before the November general elections, APNU is an alliance of the Guyana Action Party (GAP), the Justice for All Party (JAP), the National Front Alliance (NFA), the People's National Congress Reform (PNCR), and the Working People's Alliance (WPA). The alliance was headed by presidential candidate David GRANGER, who has served as parliamentary leader of the opposition since January 2012.

People's National Congress Reform (PNCR). Linden Forbes Burnham created the PNC in 1957 after he broke with PPP leader Cheddi Jagan. Primarily an urban-based party, it represented the African racial bloc, or about one-third of the population, including most of the nation's intellectuals. Initially, it advocated a policy of moderate socialism, anticommunism, and hospitality to private investment, but a swing to the left, culminating in Prime Minister Burnham's 1974 "Declaration of Sophia" (see Political background, above), brought the PNC close to the opposition People's Progressive Party on most domestic issues. In 1987 President Hoyte denied that the party was shifting to the right and insisted that the PNC remain committed to, given local conditions, an innovative form of socialism. The PNC drew heavily on the overseas vote in securing a two-thirds legislative majority in 1973 and was accused of massive fraud in obtaining better than three-quarter majorities in 1980 and 1985. It was runner-up to the PPP/C in 1992, winning 27 assembly seats with 43.6 percent of the vote.

Severe intraparty differences, which had broken out before the 1992 election, continued. Former prime minister Green, Viola BURNHAM (widow of the former president), and 13 other ex-ministers were dropped from the PNC's new parliamentary delegation. In February 1993 Green was expelled from the party following a disciplinary inquiry into misconduct charges. He then filed a High Court writ against Hoyte and other PNC leaders, claiming violation of his constitutional rights and in May announced that he would stand for election as mayor of Georgetown later in the year. Although subsequently identified with a group styled the Forum on Democracy, Green stated that his objective was not to form a new party but "to capture the PNC and bring it back to the people." As leader of the Good and Green for Georgetown (see GGG, below), he became mayor of Georgetown in September 1994.

Despite Hoyte's 1987 position, the PNC at its biennial congress in May 1994 adopted a new constitution that omitted reference to it as a "socialist" party, the former prime minister describing the word as a "chameleon term" endorsed by a variety of groups that had "only a ritual jargon in common." Former president Hoyte died on December 22, 2002; Viola Burnham died on October 10, 2003. During the 2001 legislative balloting, the PNC absorbed **Reform** (R), a group comprising a number of prominent business owners and professionals, one of whom, Stanley MING, was slated to be prime minister if the PNC/R had prevailed in the election. When it failed to oust the PPP/C, the party renamed itself the People's National Congress Reform–One Guyana (PNCR-1G) to broaden its appeal to the electorate for the 2006 elections. The One Guyana grouping came together before the country's

2006 elections and involved several smaller parties, including the **National Front Alliance** (NFA), led by member of parliament Keith SCOTT, a former founding member of the WPA who broke off to form the **National Democratic Movement**, which was later incorporated into the NFA. At the same time the **National Republican Party** (NRP), led by Fiesal Ferose ALI, joined the NFA. The NFA last fielded its own candidates in 2001.

In May 2008 PNCR-1G organized street protests in the capital against the rising cost of living. President Jagdeo subsequently met with Corbin, who had fiercely criticized the ruling party's response to crime, to discuss security concerns.

In February 2009, members of the party criticized the PPP/C for not responding to the global economic crisis, concerned the unemployment rate would rise. After Corbin left the country to seek medical treatment in May, Richard Van West Charles, a former minister of health, took over the party's helm, causing friction with party members who had backed Aubrey ARMSTRONG. The rift over Charles's accession was another sign of weakening in the party following the ouster of Corbin critic James MCALLISTER, who had attempted to challenge the party leadership. The squabbling led to internal calls for Corbin to step down.

In March 2010 Corbin said he would not run as the party's presidential candidate in the 2011 general election and pledged to reconcile with McAllister and others. The party dropped the 1G suffix from its name and once again referred to itself as PNCR, though the component remained a part of the party. After a contentious primary fight, the party picked by a narrow margin Guyana defense force brigadier (Ret.) David Arthur Granger in February 2011 to be its presidential candidate for that year's election. Many observers were surprised when the PNCR announced in July that it would officially unite in a coalition, including the **Guyana Action Party** (GAP), the NFA, and the WPA, to form the APNU, a unified opposition against the PPP/C. The coalition, which released a 16-point plan to defeat the PPP/C, put forward a unified list of candidates led by Granger.

At a party congress in July 2012, Granger was elected PNCR leader, replacing Corbin, who did seek reelection.

Leaders: David Arthur GRANGER (Leader and 2011 presidential candidate), Basil WILLIAMS (Chairman).

Guyana Action Party (GAP). GAP was launched in January 1989 as the Guyanese Action for Reform and Democracy (Guard). A self-described civic movement that did not seek power as a political party, Guard organized a series of public rallies on behalf of political (particularly electoral) reform in mid-1990. A charge by President Hoyte that the formation was "a political party masquerading as a nonpolitical, apolitical faction" appeared to be substantiated by the issuance of a statement in November that it might take part in a "third slate" involving the now-defunct URP (see 2008 *Handbook*). The situation was further clouded in December, when businessman Sam Hinds resigned as Guard chair to accept designation as PPP shadow prime minister.

While continuing to emphasize the need for reform, Guard announced in August 1991 that it would contest the forthcoming election with Nanda K. GOPAUL, a former trade union official, as its presidential candidate. However, in early 1992 Gopaul emerged as the founder of the **Guyana Labor Party** (GLP).

Under the GAP rubric, the formation won 2 legislative seats in 2001 as a partner of the WPA (below).

An indigenous rights party called Rise, Organise, and Rebuild (ROAR; founded in 1999) joined in coalition with GAP in the August 2006 elections, winning a legislative seat for GAP leader Everall Franklin. ROAR ceased operations after the 2006 election and has been subsumed into the GAP coalition.

In July 2011 GAP joined the APNU, a broader grouping of parties led by presidential candidate David Granger. Besides GAP, the coalition included the WPA, PNCR, and NFA.

Leader: Paul HARDY.

Justice for All Party (JFAP). Led by Chandra Narine Sharma, a local television station owner, the JFAP claimed that electoral irregularities cost it a seat in the 2001 legislative balloting; it was also unsuccessful in 2006. Sharma, an outspoken critic of President Jagdeo, was ordered to shut his station down for four months beginning April 12, 2008, after the repeated airing of a threat from a caller who wanted to kill the president. Several opposition parties complained about the closure. The JFAP joined the APNU in October 2011. In May 2013 Charma stood trial for allegations that he raped a minor in 2010.

Leader: Chandra Narine SHARMA.

Working People's Alliance (WPA). The WPA was organized in late 1976, following the tender of PPP support to the (then) ruling PNC, as a coalition of left-wing groups that included the African Society for Cultural Relations with Independent Africa (ASCRIA), founded by Eusi Kwayana during his affiliation with the PNC. Three of its principal leaders, Dr. Omawale, Dr. Rupert Roopnaraine, and Dr. Walter RODNEY, were indicted on arson charges in July 1979, the last being killed by a bomb explosion in June 1980. The party has been described as having "the appearance of a genuine bridge across the racial barrier in Guyana" in that its membership is drawn from both the African and Indian ethnic communities. It refused to participate in the December 1980 election on the ground of anticipated irregularities. It won 1 seat in 1985 and 2 in 1992.

In January 1994, following a weeklong public fast by Walter Rodney's son Shaka, the government announced that a special committee would be appointed to review the files on the 1980 bombing, for which, despite a 1988 ruling of death by "accident or misadventure," the PNC was widely believed to have been responsible. The inquiry led in June 1996 to the issuance of a warrant for the arrest of a former Guyana Defense Force sergeant, Gregory SMITH, who had been living in French Guiana since the 1980 assassination.

A consultative member of the Socialist International, the party contested the 1997 election as the Alliance for Guyana (AG), reverting to its original name for the 2001 campaign, in which it won only 2 legislative seats in conjunction with the Guyana Action Party (GAP, above).

The social democratic party has recently declined (in part because of the defection of one of its legislators to the AFC in 2005), and it secured no assembly representation in 2006. In 2008 the party condemned the "assault on press freedom and freedom of expression being launched by the PPP/C government" on JFAP leader Chandra Narine Sharma's television station. A statement released by the party in April said the government was limiting the opportunity of the poor to air their grievances through the media. In June 2010 the party strongly protested what was reported to be government intimidation when a party executive, Dr. David Hinds, was searched for drugs as he was boarding a flight to leave the country. The party said the PPP/C became irritated with Hinds because of a critical speech he gave and his taking part in two protests against the government. In July 2011 the WPA joined the APNU.

In June 2013 the government announced the launch of an inquiry into Rodney's death. Though WPA is now in an alliance with the PNCR, long implicated in the bombing, WPA leaders welcomed the inquiry as "overdue" and important for reconciliation.

Leaders: Dr. Rupert ROOPNARAINE (Chair), Nigel WESTMAAS, Bonita HARRIS, Eusi KWAYANA.

Other Legislative Parties:

Alliance for Change (AFC). In October 2005 Khemraj Ramjattan (a lawyer and legislator who had been expelled from the PPP/C in 2004 because he accused the PPP/C leadership of corruption) and Raphael Trotman (a PNC legislator) launched the AFC. Former members of the WPA and GAP (below) also reportedly joined the new formation, which argued that the Guyanese were eager to support a racially integrated party after so many years of conflict between the nation's racially divided major parties. The AFC pledged to pursue higher living standards in Guyana based on free-market policies, which led some observers to suggest that it enjoyed support from the United States.

In 2008 the AFC supported opposition groups backing the administration's attempts to garner international help to combat crime. In May Ramjattan joined PNCR-1G leader Robert Corbin and GAP in implicating the PPP/C in the case of drug trafficker Roger Khan. The groups called for a probe into the matter.

A court challenge initiated by the AFC in 2008 over a disputed Region 10 parliamentary seat awarded to the PPP/C remained unresolved in 2009. The AFC claimed it should have been awarded the seat.

In early 2009 Ramjattan criticized the expanded government budget, saying the statistics used to create it were not real and that it failed to acknowledge the country's high unemployment rate. He also accused the Jagdeo administration of not having consulted other groups before releasing the spending plan. He recommended shutting down nonessential government ministries to save money. Another party official, Raphael Trotman, joined in the criticism, saying that the budget did not address three key issues that most concerned Guyana's population: poverty, the high cost of living, and unemployment. In mid-2010 the AFC entered into talks with PNCR to run a unified campaign against the PPP/C in the upcoming 2011 general election. Nothing came of those talks, and the AFC chose Ramjattan as its presidential candidate for the 2011 elections during a special convention in October 2010.

In January 2012 Trotman was elected speaker of the national assembly.

Leaders: Khemraj RAMJATTAN (Party Leader), Nigel HUGHES (Chair), Moses NAGAMOOTOO (Vice Chair).

Other Parties:

Unity Party (UP). Cheddi Jagan Jr. launched the UP on February 13, 2005, after a dispute with the leadership of his parents' PPP. The party's stated goal was to pare down government and help increase private sector growth. In April 2011 Jagan said the UP would be contesting the 2011 elections.

Leader: Cheddi JAGAN Jr.

Good and Green for Guyana (GGG). Former prime minister Hamilton Green, who had been expelled from the PNC in February 1993, formed the GGG as the Good and Green for Georgetown before the 1994 Georgetown municipal campaign. The new party won a plurality of 12 of 30 seats in the September 1994 election with its leader, now Georgetown mayor, signaling a return to national politics under the more inclusive rubric in mid-December. In August 1995 a coalition of PNC and PPP/C councilors succeeded in denying Green election to an additional one year as mayor; however, he was reelected to the post in August 1996.

Starting in 2009 Hamilton Green fought efforts to have local elections, which could unseat him, and contended with claims of executive mismanagement. He took to the campaign trail prior to the 2011 general elections but was said by observers to have set aside the GGG party.

Leaders: Hamilton GREEN (Mayor of Georgetown), Ramesh KISSOON (Former Deputy Mayor of Georgetown).

LEGISLATURE

National Assembly. The unicameral legislature, which sits for five years, barring dissolution by the president, currently consists of 65 elected members, plus not more than 4 non-elected, non-voting members and 2 parliamentary secretaries appointed by the president. Before 2001, 53 members were directly elected on a proportional basis, regional councils selected 10 (1 by each of the ten councils), and the National Congress of Local Democratic Organs, to which each regional council had elected 2 members, designated 2. Constitutional amendments in early 2001 provided for direct election of all 65 members, 40 on a proportional basis from national lists and 25 on a "geographic" basis that assigned from 1 to 7 seats to each of the 10 regions.

Following the most recent election on August 28, 2006, the seat distribution was as follows: the People's Progressive Party/Civic, 36 seats; the People's National Congress Reform, 22; the Alliance for Change, 5; The United Force, 1; and a coalition of the Guyana Action Party and Rise, Organise, and Rebuild, 1.

Speaker: Raphael TROTMAN.

CABINET

[as of November 12, 2013]

Prime Minister	Samuel A. Hinds
Ministers	
Agriculture, Forestry, Fisheries, Crops, and Livestock	Leslie Ramsammy
	Ally Baksh (second minister)
Amerindian Affairs	Pauline Campbell-Sukhai [f]
Culture, Youth, and Sports	Frank Anthony
Education	Priya Manickchand [f]
	Desrey Fox (second minister) [f]
Finance	Ashni Kumar Singh
	Juan Edghill (second minister)
Foreign Affairs	Carolyn Rodrigues-Birkett [f]
Health	Bheri Ramsaran
Home Affairs	Clement Rohee
Housing and Water	Mohamed Irfan Ali
Human Services and Social Security	Jennifer Webster [f]
Labor	Nanda Kissore Gopaul
Legal Affairs and Attorney General	Anil Nandlall
Local Government and Regional Development	Ganga Persaud
	Norman Whittaker (second minister)
Natural Resources and the Environment	Robert Montgomery Persaud
Presidential Secretariat, Head	Roger Luncheon
Public Service	Jennifer Westford [f]
Public Works	Robeson Benn
Tourism, Industry, and Commerce	(Vacant)

[f] = female

Note: All cabinet members from People's Progressive Party/Civic.

INTERGOVERNMENTAL REPRESENTATION

Ambassador to the U.S.: Bayney KARRAN.

U.S. Ambassador to Guyana: D. Brent HARDT.

Permanent Representative to the UN: George W. TALBOT.

IGO Memberships (Non-UN): Caricom, IADB, ICC, NAM, OAS, OIC, WTO.

HAITI

Republic of Haiti
République d'Haïti

Political Status: Independent state proclaimed in 1804; republic established in 1859; military-backed regime installed following coup of September 30, 1991; constitutional government reinstated on November 8, 1994.

Area: 10,714 sq. mi. (27,750 sq. km).

Population: 10,308,644 (2012E—UN); 9,894,000 (2013E—U.S. Census).

Major Urban Centers (2005E): PORT-AU-PRINCE (1,249,000), Carrefour (446,000), Cap-Haïtien (112,000).

Official Languages: French, Creole.

Monetary Unit: Gourde (market rate November 1, 2013: 43.40 gourdes = $1US).

President: Michel MARTELLY (*Repons Peyizan*); elected in second-round balloting on March 20, 2011, and sworn in on May 14 for a five-year term in succession to René PRÉVAL (Front for Hope).

Prime Minister: Laurent S. LAMOTHE; nominated by the president on March 1, 2012, approved by the Senate on April 10, approved by the Chamber of Deputies on May 3, and inaugurated on May 14 (along with his cabinet) in succession to Garry CONILLE, who had announced his resignation on February 24; formed new government on August 6, 2012.

THE COUNTRY

The poorest country, on a per capita basis, in the Western Hemisphere, Haiti occupies the western third of the mountainous Caribbean island of Hispaniola, which it shares with the Dominican Republic. Approximately 95 percent of the population is of predominantly African descent, with the remainder mostly comprising whites and people of mixed black-white background. Roman Catholicism, which coexists with a folk cult based on various voodoo practices, is the official religion, but other faiths are permitted. Women constitute close to 50 percent of the agricultural labor force and 60 percent of the urban workforce, concentrated in domestic service and manufacturing.

The economy has long been handicapped by political instability, underdeveloped infrastructure, and a paucity of mineral resources, the extraction of limited amounts of bauxite having ceased in 1983. (Promising exploration continued as of mid-2013 of potential offshore oil deposits and of potential gold, copper, and silver reserves in the mountainous northeastern region.) While the manufacturing sector has grown, with an emphasis on the assembly and reexport of imported components, agriculture remains the country's economic mainstay, drawing two-thirds of the workforce. Important crops include sugarcane, cacao, sisal, and coffee, the principal commodity, which accounts for about 30 percent of export earnings.

Observers currently estimate that between 60 and 80 percent of the potential workforce remains outside formal employment, while more than half the school-age children are not attending school. Nearly 50 percent the population is illiterate, and the maternal mortality rate is the highest in the Western Hemisphere. In addition, inequality is extreme: 1 percent of the population controls almost half of the country's wealth. Remittances are the principal source of foreign exchange, equaling almost a quarter of GDP and double the earnings from exports. Two-thirds of the population subsists on less than $1 per day.

The economy was wracked in early 2008 by a dramatic increase in prices for fuel and imported food (particularly rice), which set off massive protest demonstrations. Later in the year a series of savage hurricanes damaged much of the country's infrastructure and agricultural production. The government, backed by substantial new aid and debt relief from international lenders and donors, pledged in 2009 to pursue long-term structural reform to create jobs, reduce poverty, and increase food production. In support of those efforts, the International Monetary Fund (IMF) and World Bank approved $1.2 billion in debt relief. The small flicker of hope for improved conditions was extinguished, however, by a massive earthquake on January 12, 2010, that by government estimates killed more than 200,000 people and demolished most of the nation's productive capacity. The IMF forgave additional Haitian debt and approved special lending to assist in recovery and reconstruction efforts. Meanwhile, international donors promised $4.6 billion in assistance at a March 2010 conference, although disbursement and utilization subsequently proved difficult in view of the nation's greatly diminished "economic capacity." GDP declined by more than 5.5 percent in 2010, while unemployment exceeded 30 percent. Despite a poor harvest, growth rebounded to 5 percent in 2011, assisted by increased remittances from the estimated 3 million Haitians living abroad (many with dual citizenship).

Government officials in 2012 continued to encourage international donors (whose pledges by then had exceeded $10 billion) to carry through on disbursements (approximately 50 percent to date). Drought and hurricanes (Isaac in August and Sandy in October) contributed to a decline in the growth rate to 2.8 percent for the year, and the IMF called for better mobilization of aid resources, citing the negative impact of bureaucratic bottlenecks and a lack of transparency in public finances. It was estimated by mid-2013 that 325,000 survivors of the earthquake still lived in "increasingly wretched" temporary tent cities, while more than 7,500 people had died from a nearly three-year cholera epidemic across the nation.

GOVERNMENT AND POLITICS

Political background. Since a slaves' revolt that established Haiti in 1804 as the first independent republic in Latin America, the nation's history has been marked by violence, instability, and mutual hostility between blacks and biracial persons. After a period of U.S. military occupation (1915–1934), biracial presidents held office until 1946, when power passed to a black president, Dumarsais ESTIMÉ. His moderate administration was terminated in 1950 by an army coup that paved the way for the regime of another black, Gen. Paul MAGLOIRE, who was himself overthrown in December 1956. Five interim regimes followed before the 1957 election in which François DUVALIER, a country doctor, won the presidency with the support of poor blacks, beating Louis DÉJOIE, the candidate of biracial persons and the urban middle class. Contrary to expectations, the Duvalier administration degenerated into a dictatorship, as recurring threats to the regime fed a prolonged period of repression. In 1961 Duvalier forced an unconstitutional reelection that secured him a second term, and in May 1964 he staged another election that made him president for life (official results recorded a 100 percent ballot share for Duvalier).

Throughout his incumbency President Duvalier maintained a tight grip on the country. With many of its opponents in exile, the regime maintained a balance of terror using a blend of persuasion, voodoo symbolism, and a personal army of thugs and enforcers, the so-called *Tontons Macoutes* (Creole for "bogeymen"). In early 1971 Duvalier had the constitution amended to allow him to designate a successor; his son, Jean-Claude DUVALIER, was promptly named to the position, and he assumed the presidency following his father's death on April 21.

The younger Duvalier proved popular internationally, and by 1975 U.S. aid to Haiti had risen to over $35 million, up from an annual average of $3.8 million under his father's rule. However, following the election in 1976 of Jimmy Carter (a U.S. president with a dedicated interest in human rights), Duvalier appeared to yield somewhat under continuing U.S. pressure to ameliorate the more corrupt and repressive aspects of his family's two decades of rule.

In the legislative election of February 11, 1979, an independent candidate running on a human rights platform won a clear victory against a government-endorsed opponent, thus becoming the legislature's first member who was not a Duvalier loyalist. In June, in an unprecedented act of public defiance, some 200 intellectuals issued a manifesto protesting the censorship of plays and films. Most startling of all was the appearance at midyear of three new political parties after publication of a book by Grégoire EUGÈNE, a law professor, which pointed out that such organizations were technically permissible under the Haitian constitution. By the end of the year, however, any stirrings of liberalization appeared to have been beaten back, with the passing of a repressive press law and further *Macoutes* attacks on dissidents.

The first municipal elections in 26 years were held in mid-1983. No opposition candidates presented themselves, several potential candidates having disappeared before the balloting. In August the national legislature dissolved itself after accepting a new, presidentially drafted constitution. While balloting for a new chamber on February 12, 1984, resulted in the defeat of numerous Duvalierists, foreign observers became convinced that the government, wishing to create the appearance of change, had asked incumbents not to campaign vigorously. Six months later, a regime-supportive Progressive National Party (PNP) was launched under legislation permitting partisan activity by groups agreeing to the life presidency. In November the government announced the discovery of a "communist" plot against the regime, in what was widely perceived as another bid for support from anticommunist donor nations, particularly the United States.

In early 1985, under pressure from the United States and France (another major donor), the government released a number of political prisoners, and in April President Duvalier announced a series of "democratic" reforms. These included the legalization of political parties, increased power for the National Assembly, and provision for a new post of prime minister, to be filled by presidential appointment from the parliamentary majority. However, restrictions on party registration ensured the exclusion of known regime opponents, while the life presidency remained intact.

Riots and demonstrations began to multiply in late 1985, sparked by the killing of several teenagers during an antigovernment protest in Gonaïves. Not yet willing to relax its hold on the country, the Duvalier government in December moved to concentrate power among an inner circle of loyalists. The disturbances intensified, however. On January 8, 1986, schools and universities were closed in the wake of widespread student boycotts, and ten days later police dispersed the first major protest in the capital. With pressure for democratization building internationally as well as domestically, Duvalier on February 7 departed on a U.S. plane to France with an entourage of family and close associates.

Between 1986 and 1991, the army once again moved to the center of Haitian politics, throwing its weight behind a series of six short-lived, nondemocratic governments. The first of these was inaugurated when, immediately upon Duvalier's departure, army chief of staff Gen. Henri NAMPHY assumed power as head of a 5-member National Council of Government (*Conseil National du Gouvernement*—CNG) that included two other officers and two civilians. A 19-member provisional government, which initially contained a number of Duvalier loyalists, was announced on February 10, 1986. On March 20 the one prominent anti-Duvalierist in the new administration, human rights leader Gérard GOURGUE, resigned from both the CNG and the justice ministry, alleging "resistance" to liberalization. General Namphy responded by excluding Duvalierists from a reconstituted council that included himself, (then) Col. Williams REGALA (the interior and defense minister), and Jacques FRANÇOIS (succeeded as foreign minister in a cabinet reshuffle on March 24 by retired general Jean-Baptiste HILAIRE).

In June 1986, in the face of continued unrest, municipal elections were scheduled for July 1987, to be followed by presidential and legislative balloting in November and the installation of a new government in February 1988. In September 1986 an election was held for 41 of 61 members of a Constituent Assembly charged with drafting Haiti's 23rd constitution since independence. The new basic law, incorporating a number of safeguards to prevent the return of a Duvalier-type dictatorship, was overwhelmingly approved by a referendum on March 29, 1987.

By mid-1987 the Namphy regime had proven to be unwilling or unable to curb a mounting campaign of terror by disbanded *Macoutes,* and the promised local elections were postponed. Presidential and legislative balloting commenced on the morning of November 29, but within hours that voting was also called off because of widespread violence and voter intimidation. The four principal opposition leaders thereupon withdrew as presidential candidates, and Leslie MANIGAT, a self-proclaimed "democratic centralist" believed to have CNG backing, emerged from the rescheduled poll of January 17, 1988, with a declared majority of 50.3 percent.

On June 17, 1988, President Manigat attempted to remove General Namphy as army commander, but Manigat was himself overthrown by a military coup two days later. On June 20 Namphy announced the formal deposition of the Manigat administration, declaring that he would thenceforth rule by decree as the country's chief executive. Less than three months thereafter, a revolt by noncommissioned officers of the Presidential Guard, led by Sgt. Joseph HEBREUX, resulted in Namphy's ouster, with power passing to Lt. Gen. Prosper AVRIL on September 18. Subsequently, Avril successfully resisted countercoup efforts by army units on April 2 and 5, 1989, and on September 24 he announced a series of local, national legislative, and presidential elections for 1990.

Following the assassination of a Presidential Guard colonel on January 19, 1990, General Avril declared a nationwide state of siege and instituted a roundup of opposition leaders, some of whom were deported after reportedly being brutalized by police. While the emergency decree was rescinded on January 30, popular unrest continued, forcing the general's resignation on March 10. His acting successor, Army Chief of Staff Herard ABRAHAM, promised to remain in office for no more than 72 hours, and on March 13 Supreme Court justice Ertha PASCAL-TROUILLOT was sworn in (also on an acting basis) as the country's first female president and its fifth chief executive since the Duvalier ouster.

Presidential and legislative elections, initially scheduled for September 1990, were deferred due to voter-registration problems until December 16. Fr. Jean-Bertrand ARISTIDE, a radical Catholic priest who had been expelled from his order two years earlier, won a landslide victory in the presidential poll with 67 percent of the vote, in what was, given the country's electoral record, an atypically democratic and peaceful process. However, Aristide's somewhat hastily organized coalition, the National Front for Change and Democracy (*Front National pour le Changement et la Démocratie*—FNCD), was able to nominate only 50 candidates for the 110 seats in the two legislative houses. Following his inauguration on February 7, 1991, the new head of state was obliged to settle for his second-choice candidate for prime minister, the politically inexperienced René PRÉVAL, who took office on February 13.

On September 30, 1991, scarcely more than seven months after his installation as Haiti's first democratically elected chief executive, Aristide was ousted and sent into exile in a bloody coup headed (although reportedly not instigated) by the armed forces commander, Brig. Gen. Raoul CÉDRAS. On October 8 a rump group of senators was induced to declare the presidency vacant and approve the installation of Supreme Court president Joseph NERETTE as interim head of state. Nerette, in turn, named Jean-Jacques HONORAT, a former diplomat and government official who had been exiled by the younger Duvalier in 1981, to head a government formed on October 16.

On October 29, 1991, the United States imposed strict economic sanctions, which induced the military-backed regime to enter into negotiations with a mission from the Organization of American States

(OAS) aimed at restoring Aristide to office. By late November the talks were at an impasse, with the Haitians demanding an end to the embargo but refusing to reinstate the ousted president. Honorat then challenged the OAS by announcing that new elections would be held in early January, although most of December was spent in an effort to find a prime ministerial candidate who would be acceptable to Aristide, Cédras, and Haitian political and business leaders.

In January 1992 a compromise was reached in Caracas, Venezuela, that called for the appointment of René THEODORE, secretary general of the Unified Party of Haitian Communists (*Parti Unifié des Communistes Haïtiens*—PUCH), as prime minister. However, the accord was repudiated by the military leadership. In an understanding reached in Washington, D.C., on February 23 among Aristide, Theodore, and a Haitian parliamentary delegation, Aristide dropped a demand for Cédras's removal and offered immunity from prosecution for all those involved in the coup. Subsequently, however, Aristide withdrew the pledge, while the military-dominated National Assembly refused to endorse the plan after Nerette had characterized it as "unconstitutional."

On May 9, 1992, military, government, and legislative leaders in Port-au-Prince proposed the appointment of a new government and Nerette's resignation "at a suitable moment," with no mention of a successor. Pro-Aristide deputies succeeded in blocking passage of the unilateral scheme, but a more specific version was approved on May 20 that provided for Nerette's departure upon the installation of a new administration, with no presidential replacement envisioned until an overall political solution had been reached. Accordingly, Nerette on June 2 named conservative businessperson and former World Bank official Marc Louis BAZIN to head a government that was installed on June 19.

In early July 1992 Aristide demanded a United Nations (UN) presence in Haiti and declared that he would meet with Bazin only after the latter had relinquished office. On the other hand, the head of Aristide's "presidential commission," Rev. Antoine ADRIEN, agreed on September 12 to the deployment of 18 human rights observers (3 per department, as contrasted with 18 per department sought by Aristide). However, in mid-December, after being permitted only one brief probe beyond Port-au-Prince, the UN team was declared by the Bazin government to have "no legal basis" to continue its activities. Subsequently, under strong pressure from both the United States and the UN, the government reversed track, and in mid-March the first of several hundred observers arrived under the leadership of UN mediator Dante Caputo.

In mid-April 1993 Caputo left Port-au-Prince after failing to obtain General Cédras's assent to a UN/U.S. plan by which the general would step down in return for an amnesty for his involvement in Aristide's ouster. The regime's intransigence was further reflected by its refusal on May 24 to accept a multilateral military force to supervise Aristide's return to office. On June 15 the Haitian legislature agreed to Aristide's reinstatement as president but set no date for his return and attached conditions (including a general amnesty for his military opponents) that he had long declared unacceptable. Shortly thereafter, the army agreed to "proximity talks" between General Cédras and Aristide, which began on June 27 in New York. Meanwhile, Prime Minister Bazin was obliged to submit his resignation after four of his ministers refused to step down in what appeared to be a failed *autogolpe* (self-coup).

The New York meeting in June 1993 yielded an agreement that provided for Aristide's return to Haiti on October 30, assuming the following sequence of events: (1) a "dialogue" under UN and OAS auspices among Haiti's parties, leading to the annulment of a partial senatorial election that had been conducted, despite an opposition boycott, in January; (2) the naming by Aristide of a prime minister; (3) acceptance of Aristide's nominee for prime minister by the "normalized" Haitian parliament; (4) the lifting of UN and OAS sanctions against Haiti; (5) the modernizing of Haiti's armed forces, with the assistance of a 2,000-member international force (half from the United States); (6) an amnesty for those involved in the 1991 coup; (7) the creation of a new police force under an Aristide-appointed commander; and (8) General Cédras's "early retirement."

On August 3, 1993, it was announced that Robert MALVAL, a wealthy Port-au-Prince businessman, had been asked by President Aristide to become the next prime minister. Malval, characterized as a "profoundly reluctant public figure," was reported to have accepted the job on condition that he play a purely transitional role and be replaced by a permanent successor no later than December 15. On August 25 the Haitian parliament, after extensive wrangling between pro- and anti-Aristide blocs, approved the appointment of Malval, who was sworn in by the exiled president five days later at the Haitian embassy in Washington. However, the military, headed by General Cédras but apparently under the effective control of police chief Michel FRANÇOIS, mounted a concerted effort to block Aristide's return. Perhaps most importantly, it refused to counter a wave of domestic violence by thousands of armed military "attachés" modeled after the *Macoutes*.

On October 15, 1993, U.S. president Bill Clinton dispatched a flotilla of six warships to Haitian waters to enforce an oil and arms embargo ordered by the UN Security Council after a contingent of American and Canadian advisers for a UN peacekeeping force had been prevented from disembarking in Port-au-Prince. The Haitian military responded by pressing for completion of the first major highway linking Haiti to the neighboring Dominican Republic.

Prime Minister Malval's formal resignation on December 15, 1993, coincided with the conclusion of a two-week foreign trip, during which he failed in an attempt to mount a national conference to break the country's political stalemate. Malval characterized the impasse between Cédras and Aristide as involving "a man who refuses to resign and a man who has made a choice to remain abroad as a sort of flag bearer, a mystic symbol."

On February 15, 1994, Aristide rejected a U.S.-backed peace plan that called for the appointment of a broad-based government without setting dates for the exiled president's return or a military step-down. Another U.S. plan in late March that called for Cédras's removal, but not that of François, was also rejected by Aristide. Washington then called for a global trade embargo of Haiti, which, along with a freeze on the foreign assets of about 600 army officers, was approved by the UN Security Council, effective May 22. Meanwhile, anti-Aristide legislators had on May 11 declared the presidency vacant, thus permitting the 80-year-old president of the Supreme Court, Émile JONASSAINT, to assume the office on a "provisional" basis. On June 24 direct flights to and from the United States were terminated, with all international commercial flights ending on July 30. Finally, on July 30 the Security Council authorized a U.S.-led invasion if Haiti's military attempted to continue in office.

On September 17, 1994, former U.S. president Jimmy Carter, U.S. armed forces chief of staff Gen. Colin Powell, and Senator Sam Nunn flew to Port-au-Prince for a "last best effort" meeting with Cédras and Jonassaint. The talks yielded an agreement signed by Carter and Jonassaint the following day that provided for the "honorable retirement" of "certain military officers of the Haitian armed forces," the approval of a general amnesty by the Haitian parliament, the lifting of economic sanctions "in accordance with United Nations resolutions" (which required President Aristide's return), coordination by U.S. and Haitian military units, and formal approval of the accord by the U.S. and Haitian governments.

On September 19, 1994, an initial contingent of 2,000 U.S. troops landed without incident on Haitian soil. On October 10 General Cédras resigned his command, and he flew to exile in Panama three days later. On October 15 President Aristide received an exuberant welcome on his return to Haiti, and on October 18 he appointed wealthy U.S.-educated businessman Smark MICHEL as prime minister. A new government was named by Michel on November 6 and sworn in November 8 amid pledges to revitalize the economy, in part by privatizing most large industries. Other objectives included "relaunching" the agricultural sector, improving tax collection, creating an autonomous university, and establishing a "truth commission" to investigate human rights abuses during the period of military-backed rule. For his part, President Aristide, bowing to pressure from the Catholic hierarchy, agreed on November 16 to leave the priesthood.

In two-stage balloting for partial Senate replenishment and a new Chamber of Deputies (originally scheduled for June 4 and 25, 1995, but not completed until September 17), President Aristide's Lavalas Political Organization (*Organisation Politique Lavalas*—OPL) gained control of both houses by wide margins.

By mid-1995 Prime Minister Michel was warning of "drastic consequences" if an economic program backed by the IMF should fail. He also reportedly complained of President Aristide's lack of support for one of the plan's crucial components: the privatization of nine state enterprises. Michel resigned on October 16, 1995, and was succeeded by Foreign Minister Claudette WERLEIGH, who was believed to share the president's doubts about divestiture, particularly in view of the anticipated loss of 6,000 jobs.

Despite considerable uncertainty as to his intentions, President Aristide on November 30, 1995, reiterated an earlier pledge that he would not attempt to extend his term to discount his years in exile, and on December 17 the Lavalas candidate, former prime minister René Préval, secured an overwhelming mandate, albeit on a turnout of substantially less than half of the electorate, as Haiti's next head of state. Although Préval reportedly favored the installation of former Lavalas leader Gérard PIERRE-CHARLES as prime minister, the selection was vetoed by the outgoing president, who preferred retention of the incumbent. It was not until March 6, 1996, that Rosny SMARTH, having secured legislative approval, was sworn in as the new head of government.

Subsequently, a rift emerged between the essentially populist Aristide and Prime Minister Smarth, who sought to implement the IMF-approved structural-adjustment program that included substantial privatization. In November 1996 the former president broke with the existing Lavalas organization by forming a competing Lavalas Family (*La Fanni Lavalas*—FL) movement that applied for registration as a party in early 1997. While Smarth survived a no-confidence vote on March 27, he felt obliged to submit his resignation on June 9 amid a mounting wave of strikes and demonstrations against his policies. On June 25 President Préval named an economist, Ericq PIERRE, as Smarth's successor. However, Pierre failed to secure legislative approval, and on August 20 Smarth announced that he would no longer continue in a "caretaker" capacity. On November 3 Préval nominated another economist, Hervé DENIS, as the next prime minister, but Denis was also rejected by the legislature, on December 23. A third nominee, Jacques-Édouard ALEXIS, fell two votes short of approval by the Chamber of Deputies in early January 1999.

On January 12, 1999, President Préval ruled that the term of office of nearly all members of the National Assembly (as well as those of mayors and many other municipal officers) had expired the previous day under the law governing the 1995 election. He therefore declared the assembly dissolved and announced he would rule by decree, with Alexis serving as prime minister, pending negotiations with various political groups regarding new elections. Discussions with opposition parties yielded an agreement in early March on a transition government, which was sworn in on March 26 under the leadership of Alexis, and establishment of a nine-member Provisional Electoral Council (*Conseil Electoral Provisoire*—CEP) to oversee balloting that the government hoped to conduct before the end of the year.

In June 1999 the CEP called for a new poll the following November. The date was subsequently postponed to March 21, 2000, then to April 9, and finally to May 21, at which time first-round balloting was conducted for municipal councils, the full Chamber of Deputies, and 19 Senate seats. Opposition parties, many having coalesced under the banner of the Democratic Convergence (*Convergence Démocratique*—CD), charged the government with fraud in counting the votes from the balloting and called for a boycott of the second round on July 9, arguing that only complete new elections would expunge the irregularities. Meanwhile, on June 17 the CEP president, Léon MANUS, fled the country because of alleged threats over his refusal to certify the May 21 results.

On August 16, 2000, the CEP announced that the Lavalas Family had won 72 of the lower house seats, 18 of the contested Senate seats, and about 80 percent of the municipal seats. The CD-led opposition also boycotted the presidential balloting on November 26, at which Aristide was credited with 92 percent of the vote over six other candidates. Following his inauguration on February 7, 2001, Aristide appointed Jean-Marie CHÉRESTAL, a former finance minister and trade negotiator, to form a new government, which was installed on March 2. However, in light of the continued debilitating impasse with the opposition and rapid economic decline, Chérestal in January 2002 announced his intention to resign as prime minister. He was succeeded on March 14 by Yvon NEPTUNE, theretofore president of the Senate.

During the ensuing two years, the Aristide regime encountered a mounting wave of strikes and mass protests, culminating in an armed uprising that yielded the fall of Haiti's fourth largest city, Gonaïves, to insurgents on February 5, 2004. On February 22, Haiti's second largest city, Cap-Haïtien, also fell. With rebel forces led by Guy PHILIPPE and Louis-Jodel CHAMBLAIN approaching the capital, President Aristide resigned on February 29 and was flown into exile (under duress, he subsequently maintained) on a U.S. aircraft. Concurrently, U.S. president George W. Bush ordered the dispatch of 500 marines to Port-au-Prince, with France announcing that 200 of its troops would be similarly deployed and the UN Security Council authorizing the formation of a multinational interim peacekeeping force.

In the wake of Aristide's departure, his constitutionally designated successor, Supreme Court president Boniface ALEXANDRE, was sworn in as acting head of state on March 8, 2004. On March 9 a U.S.-backed Council of Elders announced that it had appointed as interim prime minister Gérard LATORTUE, who proceeded to name a largely nonpartisan cabinet. On December 9 Latortue stated that he would not contest the presidential balloting originally scheduled for November 2005.

After four postponements, presidential and legislative elections were held on February 7, 2006. Former president Préval won the presidential balloting, narrowly avoiding a runoff with 51.2 percent of the vote in the first round. However the result was considered questionable because the CEP, on somewhat dubious legal grounds, had eliminated some 85,000 blank ballots from the tabulation, thereby drawing intense opposition criticism (despite the fact that the official second-place finisher [former president Manigat] had been credited with only 12.4 percent of the vote). Préval's installation was delayed until May 14 because of inconclusive legislative results that necessitated a runoff poll on April 21 in which a mere 15–20 percent of eligible voters were reported to have participated. Préval took office on May 14, and three days later he nominated Alexis to serve again as prime minister, a nomination that was ratified almost unanimously by Parliament. Alexis's new cabinet comprised members of five parties.

In a speech at the National Palace in October 2007, President Préval proposed constitutional changes to allow the government greater flexibility to target corruption, promote development, and prepare for the eventual departure of UN peacekeepers. Préval also called for parliament to initiate amendments to allow a president to serve for two consecutive terms, as opposed to the nonconsecutive terms currently permitted. In addition, he proposed that future elections be held at five-year intervals and recommended the creation of a constitutional court and the expansion of presidential powers to include the right to dismiss the prime minister, a prerogative currently reserved for parliament. Recognizing that his call for an expansion of presidential authority could raise suspicions about his intentions, Préval reiterated that his tenure would end in 2011 no matter what action was taken. However, Préval's proposals failed to gain sufficient support in the legislature and never reached the floor for a vote.

In the wake of massive protest demonstrations ignited by dramatic price increases on food, fuel, and other basic goods, Prime Minister Alexis lost a censure motion (the equivalent of a nonconfidence vote) by a 16–1 vote in the Senate on April 12, 2008, and was thereby constitutionally required to resign. Late in the month Préval nominated Ericq Pierre, the nation's representative to the Inter-American Development Bank, for prime minister, but the Chamber of Deputies rejected Pierre (as had happened in 1997) because he could not produce a birth certificate for one of his grandmothers (prime ministers must be descended from native-born Haitians). Préval's second choice, Robert MANUEL (a former minister of public security and the manager of Préval's 2006 campaign), was also blocked in the Chamber in June, ostensibly on technical grounds, including the facts that Manuel had not lived in Haiti for five consecutive years (as constitutionally required), had only recently registered to vote, and did not own property in Haiti. (Manuel's supporters argued that drug traffickers and other criminals had "paid off" deputies to reject Manuel.) As had been the case with Pierre, much of the opposition to Manuel in the Chamber came from the recently formed Conference of Progressive Parliamentarians (*Concertation des Parlementaires Progressistes*—CPP), which reflecting deep divisions within Préval's Front for Hope (*Fwon Lespwa/Front de l'Espoir—Lespwa)*, included many *Lespwa* deputies.

On June 23, 2008, President Préval nominated a third prime ministerial candidate, Michèle PIERRE-LOUIS, a respected economist and grassroots advocate for Haiti's poor and youth. Her nomination was ratified by the Chamber of Deputies on July 17, with 61 deputies voting in favor, 1 against, and 20 abstaining. On July 31, Pierre-Louis was approved by the Senate by a 12–5 vote, and on September 6 she became the nation's second female prime minister. Her new cabinet contained members of *Lespwa*, Aristide's FL, and several smaller parties.

Hurricane Gustav and two other storms killed upwards of a thousand people in the second half of 2008, inflicted an estimated $1.5 billion in damage, and left more than 1 million people food deprived and homeless. President Préval called for massive international assistance, arguing that Haiti had reached the "tipping point" and could become a "base for terrorism" or a regional "hub for drug trafficking" if total collapse occurred.

Despite recent debt relief and significant aid pledges from international donors, the Senate cited a lack of economic improvement when it voted on October 30, 2009, to oust Prime Minister Pierre-Louis. (Some analysts attributed the dismissal to Pierre-Louis's recently launched anticorruption campaign.) Pierre-Louis was succeeded by Jean-Max BELLERIVE, theretofore the minister for planning and external cooperation, whose new government, which included a number of incumbents, was inaugurated on November 11. The administration (described as enjoying better support among the political elite than its predecessor) quickly faced nearly unfathomable challenges when an earthquake on January 12, 2010, devastated much of Port-au-Prince and surrounding areas. As many as 250,000 people died as a result of the earthquake and some 50 aftershocks, and an estimated 1.5 million were left homeless. In addition, most of the hospitals, schools, government buildings, highways, and industries in the region were destroyed or heavily damaged. The international community rallied strongly to Haiti's aid, pledging billions in reconstruction assistance, forgiving most of the country's foreign debt, and increasing the size of the UN force to help oversee the tent cities housing refugees.

According to the results released by the government for the first round of presidential balloting on November 28, 2010, Mirlande MANIGAT of the Rally of Progressive National Democrats won 31.37 percent of the vote, followed by Jude CÉLESTIN of Unity (*Inite*—a grouping formed recently by supporters of President Préval, who was constitutionally precluded from seeking reelection), with 22.48 percent, and the singer Michel MARTELLY, with 21.84 percent. However, charges immediately spread of widespread irregularities in the balloting, and protest demonstrations erupted among Martelly's supporters, who claimed he had been defrauded of second place and the right to participate in the runoff with Manigat. In February 2011 the CEP accepted the view of observers from the OAS and elsewhere that Martelly had indeed finished second. Despite the fact that Manigat enjoyed the support of much of the political elite, Martelly, whose bawdy stage persona was Sweet Micky, capitalized on the youth vote and popular interest in dramatic change in the second round of presidential balloting on March 20, 2011, at which he secured victory over Manigat with 67.6 percent of the vote. Meanwhile, *Inite* and its allies dominated the balloting for the Senate and Chamber of Deputies, although revisions were required in the final official tallies for those bodies as well.

President Martelly quickly faced difficulties with the *Inite*-dominated legislature, which in June rejected the nomination of businessman Daniel ROUZIER for prime minister. Bernard GOUSSE, a lawyer and former justice minister, met a similar fate in August. As had been the case with other nominees in the past, citizenship issues dogged Rouzier, and both men were criticized in some circles for their connection to earlier discredited regimes. The international community, concerned that the political deadlock was compromising reconstruction efforts, welcomed the relatively smooth confirmation in October of new prime minister Garry CONILLE, who among other things, had served on the board of directors of the reconstruction commission. However, Conille resigned on February 24, 2012; he was succeeded by Laurent S. LAMOTHE, theretofore minister of foreign affairs and a member of the "Team of Martelly."

Constitution and government. The 1987 constitution, repudiated by General Namphy in July 1988, was restored by President Pascal-Trouillot in 1990 and remained nominally intact after the 1991 coup. (Haiti returned to constitutional rule in October 2004, but the constitution was not properly enforced until May 2006.) The document provides for a directly elected president, who may serve no more than two five-year terms (which must be nonsequential), and a prime minister, who is responsible to a legislature composed of a Senate and Chamber of Deputies. The president negotiates and signs all treaties and presides over the Council of Ministers; the prime minister must come from the legislative majority or, if there is none, must be appointed after consultation with the chamber presidents, subject to parliamentary endorsement. Constitutional amendments, which must be supported by a two-thirds majority in each house and approved by a majority of two-thirds of the votes cast in a joint legislative sitting, can come into effect only after the installation of the next elected president. The judiciary encompasses a Supreme Court (*Cour de Cassation*), whose president serves as acting head of state in the event of a vacancy; courts of appeal; courts of first instance; justices of the peace; and special courts as prescribed by law.

The 1987 basic law divided the traditionally monolithic armed forces into distinct military and police components; accorded the universally spoken Creole language official status in addition to French; banned Duvalierists from public office for ten years; authorized an independent commission to supervise elections; asserted the previously nonexistent rights of free education, decent housing, and a fair wage; and eliminated sanctions (theretofore largely ignored) against the practice of voodoo.

Haiti is presently divided into ten departments, each headed by a presidentially appointed prefect and subdivided into *arrondisements* and communes. In May 2011 the National Assembly approved a constitutional revision authorizing Haitians with dual citizenships to vote in Haitian elections, to hold local government positions, and to own land in Haiti. The changes were designed to promote the return to Haiti of well-educated members of the diaspora, many of whom had become citizens of the United States and other regional countries. The revisions went into effect in June 2012, along with amendments providing for, among other things, a new Constitutional Court, a new Permanent Electoral Council, and a special Supreme Court panel to administer the judicial system. The basic law revision also stated that 30 percent of public sector employees must be female.

Reporters Without Borders reported a dramatic increase in press freedom following the ouster of President Aristide in 2004. However, journalists were described by the media watchdog as "focusing on survival rather than freedom" in the wake of the January 2010 earthquake that destroyed many radio stations and forced the two main daily newspapers to publish only on the Internet. One of the dailies resumed publication in April, and the other subsequently launched a weekly print edition. Nearly all radio and television stations were back on the air by 2012.

Foreign relations. Despite its membership in a number of international bodies, Haiti has avoided close ties with neighboring countries and before joining the Association of Caribbean States (ACS), founded in 1994, had distanced itself from most moves toward Caribbean economic and political integration. Its historically most sensitive foreign affairs issue, the border relationship with the Dominican Republic, has been periodically aggravated by activities of political exiles from both countries. Relations with the United States, which were briefly suspended in 1963, have fluctuated, the Duvalier government frequently using its votes in international bodies to bargain for increased foreign assistance from Washington.

In early 1983 long-standing litigation regarding the rights of Haitian refugee "boat people" being detained in Florida was resolved by a U.S. landmark decision, which allowed about 1,700 detainees to apply for political asylum while establishing constitutional protection for those remaining incarcerated. In September 1985 Haiti concluded an agreement with the Bahamas that would require all illegal Haitian immigrants in the Bahamas to register with Bahamian authorities, with only those resident in the Bahamas before December 30, 1980, married to Bahamians, or owning real estate being permitted to remain.

In the wake of President Aristide's ouster in 1991, a new wave of Haitians attempted to flee by boat to the United States. By early 1992 several thousand had been picked up at sea by the U.S. Coast Guard and accorded temporary refuge in Guantánamo Bay, Cuba. By midyear the exodus had largely ended, in the wake of an order by President George H. W. Bush on May 24 that all Haitians intercepted at sea be returned immediately to their homeland without determination of whether they qualified for political asylum. The order was overturned on July 26 by a New York appeals court but was upheld by the U.S. Supreme Court on August 1. In early 1993 it was estimated that of more than 40,000 Haitians attempting to reach the United States since the 1991 coup, nearly three-quarters had been returned to Haiti by the U.S. Coast Guard. By mid-1994 the Clinton administration had demonstrated considerable ambivalence on the matter, initially adhering to the Bush policy of repatriation, then supporting ship-based processing of refugees for possible transfer to third countries. However, a less-than-enthusiastic response to the latter policy, particularly from Panama, led, in early July, to an announcement that the processing facilities in Guantánamo would be reactivated. Thus, despite the ease with which Cubans had thenceforth been able to claim eligibility for asylum in the United States, the number of Haitians that could look forward to such status was severely limited.

The United States, which had favored the conservative Marc Louis Bazin in the 1991 presidential poll, subsequently joined the OAS embargo against the military-backed government and was a prime mover in the June 1993 talks that established the original timetable for Aristide's return to office. By the end of September 1994, the U.S. military intervention involved 20,000 troops, with their eventual replacement, a 6,900-member UN Mission in Haiti (UNMIH), being assembled in Puerto Rico. By late December the U.S. contingent had been reduced to approximately 9,000 personnel, of whom only 5,000 remained upon transfer of responsibility for Haitian security to the UNMIH on March 31, 1995. The balance of the U.S. force, apart from about 200 noncombatant personnel, withdrew on January 18, 2000.

The UNMIH mandate was extended for six months from March 1, 1996, albeit only after China (which objected to Haitian relations with

Taiwan) had insisted on a reduction to 1,200 troops; however, Canada announced that it would provide an additional 700 personnel at its own expense to bring the total up to the Security Council's target of 1,900. The peacekeeping mission was renewed for an additional five months on July 1 (and renamed the UN Support Mission in Haiti—UNSMIH), after China had dictated a new cut to 600 (exclusive of a 700-member force from Canada, Pakistan, and Bangladesh, funded jointly by Canada and the United States). In early December the Security Council voted to extend the UNSMIH until May 31, 1997, subject to renewal at that time for two additional months. Although it had been agreed that the mission would not continue past July 31, the mandate was further extended to November 30, with the last UN troops departing from Haiti during the ensuing month, save for a 300-member police monitoring unit (the United Nations Civilian Police Mission in Haiti [*Mission de Police Civile des Nations Unies en Haïti*—MIPONUH]) that was to remain for another year.

In March 1996 President Préval met with his presidential counterpart from the Dominican Republic in the first visit by a Haitian president to the neighboring state in more than six decades. Despite the rapprochement, more than 15,000 Haitians were expelled from the Dominican Republic in late January and early February 1997. In an effort to avert a crisis, the two presidents agreed during a summit of the Caribbean Community and Common Market (Caricom) on February 20–21 to an immediate halt to large-scale repatriation, while acknowledging the right of the Dominican Republic to deport illegal immigrants. Despite the accord, Haitian officials claimed in November that as many as 40,000 Haitians (of an estimated 500,000 without legal status) had been forced to leave the Dominican Republic during the year.

Reciprocating Préval's 1996 visit to the Dominican Republic, Leonel Fernández on June 18–20, 1998, became the first head of state from the Dominican Republic to visit Haiti since Rafael Trujillo in 1936. A meeting of the two presidents was preceded by a session of a joint Dominican-Haitian commission, which reached agreement in a number of areas without resolving such major issues as migration and trade.

The U.S. military presence in the wake of Aristide's second departure from office in 2004 quickly grew to a 3,600-member force, which on June 1 formally transferred its peacekeeping mandate to a UN Stabilization Mission in Haiti (*Mission des Nations Unies pour la Stabilisation en Haïti*—MINUSTAH), which had 7,413 troops and civilian police deployed as of April 2005. (The mandate for MINUSTAH, focused to a large degree on quelling urban gang warfare and, more recently, on providing security in the wake of the January 2010 earthquake, has been extended routinely since 2006.)

In March 2007 Venezuela and Cuba announced the creation of a $1 billion fund to aid Haiti, while Venezuelan president Hugo Chávez, during a visit to Port-au-Prince, promised additional assistance, including an increase in oil shipments from 3,000 to 14,000 barrels per day. Venezuela also provided aid to help Haiti cope with the economic shocks of price increases and hurricanes in 2008 and the earthquake in 2010, as did the United States and other donors.

Current issues. As part of his administration's "reconciliation" campaign, President Martelly conferred with former presidents Aristide and "Baby Doc" Duvalier, both of whom had unexpectedly returned to Haiti amid great fanfare in early 2011. Martelly, whose staff reportedly included several former Duvalierists, said it would be the job of the judiciary to determine whether or not to proceed with criminal charges against Duvalier. (A Haitian judge ruled in early 2012 that Duvalier could face corruption charges but not charges regarding human rights abuses, declaring, to the consternation of international watchdog organizations, that the statute of limitations had expired for prosecution of such crimes. However in March 2013 the Court of Appeal, considering the possibility of reinstating the human rights charges, began hearing testimony from people who claimed they or their relatives had been victims of the Duvalier regime.)

Prime Minister Conille's resignation in February 2012 was attributed to tensions between him and legislators and between him and Martelly, the latter reportedly involving Conille's insistence on investigating allegations of corruption in connection with reconstruction contracts. Although the confirmation of Laurent Lamothe as Conille's successor proceeded relatively quickly by Haitian standards ("only" two months), international donors said that Haiti's drawn-out political process over the past two years had compromised reconstruction efforts. Lamothe, the former president of an international telecommunications company and a close ally of the president, promised stability, although several key political parties reportedly participated in the fall in anti-Martelly demonstrations prompted by concerns over rising prices and perceived corruption among government officials.

In late October 2012 Hurricane Sandy killed more than 50 people in Haiti, damaged or destroyed nearly 20,000 homes and other buildings, and ruined an estimated 70 percent of the crops in the south. In addition to contributing to worries about food security (already a concern in the wake of a severe drought earlier in the year), the storm appeared to exacerbate the cholera epidemic, which by mid-2013 had affected more than 600,000 people. Most investigators concluded that the epidemic had started when cholera-infected soldiers from Nepal had joined MINUSTAH after the 2010 earthquake. However the UN declined to accept or deny responsibility and argued that, in any event, it was held harmless by international law from damage claims.

The international community in the first half of 2013 intensified its pressure on the Haitian government to set a date for the local elections and partial Senate elections that were more than a year overdue. (Many local governing bodies were being led by that time by temporary presidential appointees rather than elected officials pending new balloting.) Observers warned that the electoral delay was causing hesitation among foreign investors, as were perceived undue governmental influence on the judiciary, human rights abuses (particularly in prisons), rising crime, and a lack of accountability and efficiency regarding reconstruction aid.

POLITICAL PARTIES

All parties were outlawed during the first six years of the François Duvalier dictatorship. In 1963 a regime-supportive National Unity Party (*Parti de l'Unité Nationale*—PUN) was organized with an exclusive mandate to engage in electoral activity. Its Jean-Claudiste successor, the National Progressive Party (*Parti Nationale Progressiste*—PNP), was launched in September 1985. Six years earlier, three unofficial groups had surfaced—the PSCH and PDCH (below), plus a Haitian National Christian Party (*Parti Chrétien National d'Haïti*—PCNH) organized by Rev. René des RAMEAUX. All three were subjected to intermittent repression for the remainder of the Duvalier era.

In March 1987 it was reported that more than 60 new parties had been formed. Two months earlier, a National Congress of Democratic Movements (*Congrès National des Mouvements Démocratiques*—CNMD/Konakom) had been organized in opposition to the Namphy regime by delegates from nearly 300 political groups, trade unions, peasant and student organizations, and human rights associations. Subsequently, the CNMD became the core of a loosely organized "Group of 57" that conducted a variety of antigovernment protests (including a general strike in Port-au-Prince on June 29) before being amalgamated into a National Front for Concerted Action (*Front National de Concertation*—FNC) in September. The FNC joined the PDCH in boycotting the election of January 1988.

Although a large number of groups participated in the December 1990 balloting, the FNCD (under *Alternativ*, below), Panpra (under PFSDH, below), and the MIDH (below) emerged as the principal formations. By 1995 the PPL (under OPL, below) had become the dominant group, most opposition groups boycotting the legislative balloting of June–August and the December presidential poll; in late 1997, however, the PPL's dominance was challenged by the Lavalas Family, a new formation launched by former president Aristide.

Following the disputed first-round elections of May 21, 2000, about 15 opposition parties formed the Democratic Convergence (*Convergence Démocratique*—CD), which became the primary anti-Aristide coalition. United primarily (if not solely) by their "common hatred" of Aristide, the CD parties boycotted the second round of balloting on July 3 as well as the presidential and Senate polls on November 26. Calling the Aristide government "illegitimate," the CD in February 2001 announced that it had named Gérard Gourgue of the FNC as "alternative president." The CD declined an offer to join the government of Prime Minister Neptune in March 2002, demanding instead the installation of a "consensus" administration to oversee new presidential and legislative elections.

About 70 political groups existed before the 2006 elections, of which 10–50 were active in the run-up to the first-round poll on February 7. Numerous changes among the parties were reported before the second-round legislative balloting on April 21.

In 2008 a new cross-party voting bloc, the Conference of Progressive Parliamentarians (*Concertation des Parlementaires Progressistes*—CPP), was formed in the Chamber of Deputies by legislators concerned over the government's economic approach. Bringing together 53 of the 99 deputies, including around 20 dissident *Lespwa* members, the new bloc was also initially seen as a challenge to the authority of President Préval, who lost his lower house coalition. In the

Chamber poll held on May 12, 2008, some 20 CPP members of Préval's party voted against their leader's first prime ministerial candidate, Ericq Pierre, who subsequently alleged that CPP members had wanted him to buy their support. The CPP also opposed Robert Manuel (Préval's second nominee) but endorsed Michèle Pierre-Louis for the premiership. It was reported in late 2009 that some 35 members of the CPP had realigned with Préval in the new *Inite* party (see below).

Legislative Parties:

Unity (*Inite*). Formed in late 2009, *Inite* is a successor (at least partially) to the Front for Hope (*Fwon Lespwa/Front de l'Espoir—Lespwa*), which was launched by René Préval (theretofore a member of Lavalas) in his successful bid for a second presidential term in 2006. Upon completion of the legislative balloting in December 2006, *Lespwa* held a plurality of 22 Chamber seats, although the party was fractured (at least temporarily) by the participation of *Lespwa* deputies in the CPP (see introductory text, above). *Lespwa* won 6 of the 11 contested seats in the 2009 Senate elections, bringing its total to 12.

Lespwa was disbanded in November 2009 in favor of the new pro-Préval *Inite*, which, in addition to former *Lespwa* supporters, reportedly included at least factions of the UNCRH (below), MRN (below), PLB (below), MOP (see OPL, below), and defectors from other small parties. *Inite* nominated Jude Célestin, the head of the state construction company, as its candidate for the November 2010 presidential election. Célestin was initially credited with a second-place finish in the first round of the presidential poll, but the CEP subsequently placed him third, and he was therefore ineligible for the runoff. Under intense international pressure, *Inite* officials ultimately accepted that decision, although Célestin personally objected. *Inite* subsequently secured a plurality in the elections for the Chamber of Deputies.

Leaders: René PRÉVAL (Former President of the Republic), Jude CÉLESTIN (2010 presidential candidate), Sen. Joseph LAMBERT, Sorel JACINTHE (Former President of the Chamber of Deputies), Rodolphe JOAZIDE (Former President of the Senate).

Peasant Response (*Respons Peyizan*). This grouping served as the vehicle for the successful 2010–2011 presidential campaign of Michel Martelly, who ran on a populist, right-of-center platform. It was also credited with winning three seats in the 2010–2011 balloting for the Chamber of Deputies. In mid-2011 it was reported that the members of *Respons Payizan* had launched a Peasants Political Party.

Leaders: Michel MARTELLY (President of the Republic), Varnel DURAND (National Director), Fednel MONCHERY, Evelyne THANI.

Alternative for Progress and Democracy (*Alternativ*). This coalition was formed prior to the 2010 elections by the OPI, Fusion, and the **Convention for Democratic Unity** (*Komite Inite Democratik*—KID), led by Evans PAUL, the former mayor of Port-au-Prince. In 2006 the KID had participated in an electoral coalition called the Democratic Alliance (*Alliance Démocratique*—AD/*Alyans*) with the **People's Party for Haiti's Rebirth** (*Parti Populaire Du Renouveau Haïtien*—PPRH), led by Claude ROUMAIN. The PPRH had been forged in January 2005 as a merger of Roumain's party Generation 2004 and the Haitian Liberal and Social Party.

Paul, who was campaign manager for Jean-Bertrand Aristide in 1990, had formerly been the head of the National Front for Change and Democracy (*Front National pour le Changement et la Démocratie*—FNCD), formed in late 1990 as an alliance of more than a dozen left-of-center groups supporting Aristide. In 1999 he had launched the Harmonious Space for Preservation of Democracy (*Espace de Concertation pour la Sauvegarde de la Démocratie*—EC/*Espace*) as an alliance of the FNCD and other groups to contest the legislative balloting conducted on May 21, 2000.

The AD placed third in the 2006 lower house poll. Evans and the leaders of the other *Alternativ* components ultimately called for a boycott of the 2010 elections, but many *Alternativ* legislative candidates participated in the balloting anyway. Eleven of them were successful in the Chamber of Deputies and five in the Senate.

Leader: Evans PAUL (Former Mayor of Port-au-Prince).

Organization of the Struggling People (*Organisation du Peuple en Lutte*—OPL). The current OPL is an offshoot of the center-left Lavalas Political Organization (*Organisation Politique Lavalas*—also OPL), which emerged after its founding in 1991 as the principal pro-Aristide formation. In 1995 the latter group launched the Lavalas Political Platform (*Plateforme Politique Lavalas*—PPL) as an alliance that also included the PLB (below) and the Movement for the Organization of the Country (*Mouvement d'Organisation du Pays*—MOP), a center-right formation whose leader, Jean MOLIERE, had been the third-ranked presidential candidate in 1988.

In 1996 the original OPL split into two groups—the pro-Aristide Lavalas Family (FL, below) and the Organization of the Struggling People, which retained the OPL abbreviation and became a "bitter opponent" of Aristide and a leading rival of the FL. The new OPL initially joined the Democratic Consultation Group in negotiations with President Préval in February 1999. However, it withdrew from the group following the assassination of OPL senator Jean-Yvon TOUSSAINT in early March, demanding that the crime be solved as a prerequisite to the party's return to discussions with the government. Consequently, the OPL was not represented in the new cabinet installed in late March. The OPL was one of the leading parties in the 2000 election.

OPL leader Paul Denis headed an inquiry that in 2005 accused Aristide of misusing $50 million in public money. Denis ran for president unsuccessfully in 2006, and in 2008, after the exit of Prime Minister Alexis, he was considered a potential prime ministerial nominee. However, despite Denis's experience as a former senator and as an adviser to President Préval, analysts suggested that his anti-Lavalas credentials rendered him too controversial to secure the position.

When Ericq Pierre received the prime ministerial nomination from Préval in April 2008, the OPL worked unsuccessfully to form a majority in favor of his ratification. Subsequently, the OPL strongly objected to decisions made by the CEP in regard to the 2009 Senate elections.

Although Denis joined the Bellerive cabinet in November 2009, the OPL subsequently organized demonstrations to protest the perceived inappropriate and ineffective use of reconstruction aid by the administration following the January 2010 earthquake.

Leaders: Paul DENIS (2006 presidential candidate), Edgard LEBLANC (Coordinator).

Haitian Social-Democratic Fusion Party (*Parti Fusion des Sociaux-Démocrates Haïtiens*—PFSDH or Fusion). Fusion was launched before the 2006 elections by Serge Gilles, who had previously led the Nationalist Revolutionary Progressive Party (*Parti National Progressiste Révolucionnaire*—Panpra), which in 1989 had become the first Haitian party to be admitted to the Socialist International. In 2004 Gilles had also organized the Haitian Socialist Grand Party (*Grand Parti Socialiste Haïtien*—GPSH), which became a component of Fusion.

Fusion was runner-up to *Lespwa* in the 2006 Chamber of Deputies balloting. In 2007–2008 Micha Gaillard, a professor and the former spokesperson for the anti-Aristide coalition (the CD), emerged as a key voice within Fusion. Gaillard was a critic of the perceived slow pace of social change in Haiti under President Préval and of the government's response to spiking food costs. In mid-2010 Serge Gilles called upon Préval to resign.

Leaders: Victor BENOIT (Chair), Serge GILLES (2006 presidential candidate), Micha GAILLARD (Spokesperson).

Together We Are Strong (*Ansanm Nou Fò*). Upon the formation of this coalition under the leadership of Pierre Eric JEAN-JACQUES (the outgoing president of the Chamber of Deputies) and other legislators in 2010, it initially appeared that it would nominate the musician Wyclef JEAN as its candidate for the November presidential balloting. However, Jean ultimately attempted to run as the candidate of **Live Together** (*Viv Ansanm*), but his candidacy was rejected on residency grounds. Meanwhile, the *Ansanm Nou Fò* candidate, Leslie Voltaire (an architect with an extensive government background), received 1.51 percent of the vote in the first round of presidential balloting.

Jean Tholbert ALEXIS, elected to the Chamber of Deputies in 2010 as an *Ansanm Nou Fò* candidate, was named in September 2012 to head a new progovernment legislative bloc called Parliamentarians for Stability and Progress, which claimed the support of some 60 legislators, including members of *Ansanm Nou Fó*, the AAA, MAS, PLAPH, Liberation Platform, Mochrena, and apparently *Inite.* (Alexis was widely referenced as a member of *Inite* when he was elected president of the Chamber of Deputies in January 2013.)

Leaders: Eric JEAN-JACQUES (Former President of the Chamber of Deputies), Leslie VOLTAIRE (2010 presidential candidate).

The Lavalas Family (*La Fanmi Lavalas*—FL). The FL was launched by former president Aristide in November 1996. While Aristide denied that the new group was intended as an "instrument of division," it reflected his growing disenchantment with President Préval's economic policies and served as a vehicle for Aristide's return to the presidency in November 2000.

Activist and a former priest Gérard JEAN-JUSTE, the FL's initial 2006 presidential candidate, was disqualified by the CEP for not personally submitting his registration by the deadline (which would have been impossible, as he was imprisoned at the time). The party formally boycotted the election, although a portion of its membership endorsed Préval.

On April 30, 2008, four years after the latest ouster of Aristide, some 5,000 of his supporters marched in the streets of Port-au-Prince to demand his return from exile. Reflecting longstanding internal divisions within the FL, two separate FL candidate lists were initially presented for the 2009 Senate elections, prompting the CEP to reject both lists and seek endorsement of a candidate list from Aristide, who called the election a sham and declined to be involved in the process. The competing FL factions subsequently agreed on a single list, which was again rejected by the CEP because of the lack of Aristide's signature on accompanying documents. FL officials noted that such formalities had not surfaced for the 2006 balloting and argued that Aristide had "not been actively making decisions about the party's activities for several years now." The FL, which had been expected to perform well in the Senate balloting, called for a boycott of the elections, while many international observers described the party's exclusion as a setback for democratization. The FL was also subsequently barred from participating in the November 2010 elections because the CEP said it could not verify the authenticity of Aristide's signature on application papers. Several FL members subsequently registered as presidential candidates of other parties, and many FL leaders endorsed the candidacy of Jean Henry CÉANT, a prominent lawyer, who finished fourth in the first round of presidential balloting (with 8.18 percent of the vote) as the candidate of the small ***Renmen Ayiti*** party.

Aristide attracted widespread international and domestic attention when he returned to Haiti from exile in South Africa on March 18, 2011, after having received the required authorization to do so from the Préval administration. Although Aristide strongly criticized the decision that banned the FL from the recent legislative poll, he subsequently indicated that he would concentrate on social issues rather than political affairs in the future.

Although the FL was subsequently described as being "in tatters," Aristide reportedly retained a significant following, and he was greeted by thousands of supporters when in early 2013 he was seen in public for the first time in nearly two years. He predicted the FL would perform well if permitted to contest the next local and Senate elections.

Leaders: Jean-Bertrand ARISTIDE (Former President of the Republic), Luis GÉRARD-GILLES (2006 presidential candidate), Maryse NARCISSE (Head of Executive Council).

Haiti in Action (*Ayiti an Aksyon*—AAA). The AAA is the rubric recently adopted by the party formerly called Standard-Bearer in Action (*Latibonit an Aksyon/l'Arbonite en Action*—LAAA). The LAAA was formed prior to the 2006 poll, at which it won two Senate and four Chamber seats. Party leader Youri Latortue was the leading voice among the 16 senators who removed Prime Minister Alexis from office in April 2008. Latortue said that legislators ousted Alexis because he failed to boost food production, protect people against crime, establish a national security force, or set a timetable for the departure of UN peacekeepers. The AAA reportedly received the portfolio for the ministry of youth, sports, and civic action in the October 2011 cabinet.

Leader: Sen. Youri LATORTUE.

Organization for the Future (*Organizasyon Lavni—Lavni)*. Yves CHRISTALIN, theretofore the minister for social affairs and labor, finished ninth with 1.51 percent of the vote in the first round of presidential balloting in November 2010. *Lavni*'s Simon Dieuseul DESRAS, elected to the Senate in 2010, was chosen as president of that body in 2012.

Leaders: Simon Dieuseul DESRAS (President of the Senate), Yves CHRISTALIN (2010 presidential candidate).

Christian Movement for a New Haiti (*Mouvement Chrétien pour une Nouvelle Haïti*—Mochrena). A center-right party formed in 1991 by evangelical Protestant churches (reportedly with financial support from their U.S. counterparts), Mochrena won three seats in the 2000 balloting for the Chamber of Deputies, all of which were retained in 2006. Its 2006 presidential candidate, Luc Mésadieu, placed fifth with a 3.4 percent vote share.

Leaders: Luc MÉSADIEU (2006 presidential candidate), Gilbert N. LEGER.

Cooperative Action to Build Haiti (*Konbit pou Bati Ayiti*—Konba). Konba, which means "fight" or "combat" in Creole, won three lower house seats in 2006.

Leader: Chavannes JEAN-BAPTISTE.

Respect (*Respè/Respect*). Respect is a small group launched before the 2006 presidential poll, at which its leader, Charles Henri Baker, finished third with 8.2 percent of the vote. Baker, the leader of a prominent business umbrella organization, finished sixth in the first round of presidential balloting in November 2010 with 2.38 percent of the vote.

Leader: Charles Henri BAKER (2006 and 2010 presidential candidate).

Other parties securing legislative seats in 2010–2011 included **For Us All** (*Pou Nou Tout*—PONT), led by former prime minister and 2006 presidential candidate Jean Marie CHÉRESTAL; the **Platform of Haitian Patriots** (*Plateforme des Patriotes Haïtiens*—PLAPH), an anti-Préval grouping formed in 2009 under the leadership of Himmler REBU; **Assembly** (*Rasamble*), whose leaders called for a boycott of the November 2010 elections but some of whose legislative candidates continued to campaign; ***Konbit pou Refe Ayiti***, a new party whose leader, Claire Lydie PARENT, was rejected by the CEP as a 2010 presidential candidate; the **Socialist Action Movement** (*Mouvman Aksyon Sosyalis*—MAS); ***Veye Yo*** (We Are Watching), a pro-Aristide grouping (with roots in the diaspora in Miami, Florida), whose leader, Lavarice GAUDIN, was rejected by the CEP as a 2010 presidential candidate; the **Democratic Movement for the Liberation of Haiti–Democratic Revolutionary Party of Haiti,** led by François LATORTUE; and **Liberation Platform** (*Platforme Libération*), led by Serge Jean LOUIS, who called for a boycott of the 2010 balloting in concert with the UCADDE, *Rasamble,* and *Alternativ.*

Other Parties:

Rally of Progressive National Democrats (*Rassemblement des Démocrates Nationaux Progressistes*—RDNP). The RDNP was organized by Leslie Manigat while in exile in Venezuela during the 1970s. Strongly anticommunist, Manigat called in mid-1986 for a "solidarity pact" between the centrist parties. The lack of an effective response was attributed, in part, to Manigat's reputation as a *noiriste* and hence a threat to the country's powerful biracial elite. He was credited with securing a bare majority of the presidential vote in the highly controversial balloting of January 17, 1988, but was ousted in a coup on June 19. He returned from exile in 1990 but was barred from another presidential bid. In 2002 Manigat was reported to have organized a four-party opposition coalition styled the Patriotic Union (*Union Patriotique*—UP), which was followed in 2004 by the National Democratic Progressive Coalition (*Coalition des Démocrates Nationaux Progressistes*—CDNP). Manigat placed second in the 2006 presidential race, with 12.4 percent of the vote, while the RDNP secured four seats in the 2006 balloting for the Chamber of Deputies.

In April 2008 RDNP secretary general and former first lady Mirlande Hyppolite Manigat joined the voices of those involved in food and fuel price demonstrations, expressing disappointment that the government, and in particular President Préval, had not done enough to answer people's concerns. As one of the leading contenders in the November 2010 presidential election, Mirlande Manigat, a constitutional law professor, campaigned on a center-right platform focusing on the restoration of basic services and other "small steps" toward recovery from the devastation of January's earthquake. Having been endorsed by a number of current and former legislators, she was credited with a first-place finish in the first round of balloting with 31.4 percent of the vote, but she was soundly defeated in the runoff in March 2011.

Leaders: Leslie François MANIGAT (Former President of the Republic and 2006 presidential candidate), Mirlande Hyppolite MANIGAT (Secretary General and 2010 presidential candidate).

Mobilization for Haiti's Progress (*Mobilisation pour le Progrès d'Haïti*—MPH). The MPH won four lower house seats in 2006. As its 2010 presidential candidate, the MPH nominated former prime minister Jacque-Edouard Alexis, who had earlier failed in his attempt to secure the nomination of the new pro-Préval Unity coalition. Alexis finished fifth with 3.07 percent of the vote in the first round of balloting.

Leaders: Samir Georges MOURRA, Jacque-Edouard ALEXIS (Former Prime Minister and 2010 presidential candidate).

National Christian Union for the Reconstruction of Haiti (*Union Nationale Chrétienne pour la Reconstruction d'Haïti*—UNCRH). The UNCRH candidate, Jean Chevannes Jeune, a pastor and civil engineer, placed fourth in the 2006 presidential balloting with a vote share of 5.6 percent. Perhaps reflecting previously noted internal party turmoil, at least one UNCRH faction reportedly joined the pro-Préval *Inite* for the November 2010 elections, although Jeune was presented as a presidential candidate of the **Christian Citizen's Alliance for the Reconstruction of Haiti** (*Alliance Chretiénne Citoyenne pour la Reconstruction d'Haïti*—ACCRHA). Jeune finished seventh in the first round of balloting with 1.80 percent of the vote.

Leader: Jean Chavannes JEUNE (2006 presidential candidate).

National Reconstruction Front (*Front de la Reconstruction Nationale*—FRN). The FRN was launched in late February 2004 by a group of former rebels led by Guy Philippe, who played a significant role in the ouster of President Aristide. Despite being wanted on drug charges by both U.S. and Haitian authorities, Philippe openly presented himself as a candidate for the 2009 Senate elections; his application was rejected by the CEP.

Leaders: Buteur METAYER (President), Guy PHILIPPE (Secretary General).

Bridge (*Pont*). The Bridge party won two northwest Senate seats in 2006.

Leader: Evallière BEAUPLAN.

Movement for National Reconstruction (*Mouvement pour la Reconstruction Nationale*—MRN). Launched in 1991 by René Théodore, the leader theretofore of the Unified Party of Haitian Communists (*Parti Unifié des Communistes Haïtiens*—PUCH), the MRN was prohibited from participating in the 1995 elections, ostensibly because of a dispute as to whether Théodore or Jacques Rony MODESTIN (also of the MRN) controlled the party name. Subsequently, Théodore, once an Aristide ally, called for annulment of the election results.

The party secured one lower house seat in 2006. Although the MRN reportedly supported *Inite* candidate Jules Célestin in the November 2010 presidential poll, it appeared to present its own candidates in the concurrent legislative elections.

Leaders: René THÉODORE, Jean-Enol BUTEAU.

Heads Together (*Tèt Ansanm*). Tèt Ansanm won a lower house seat in 2006, although the Electoral Council rejected the candidacy of its leader on the grounds that he was a U.S. citizen.

Leader: Dumarsais SIMÉUS.

Open the Gate Party (*Parti Louvri Barye*—PLB). Originally launched as a pro-Aristide party in mid-1992, the PLB won two seats in the 2000 balloting for the Chamber of Deputies. It was subsequently perceived as adopting a middle ground in the nation's political impasse, calling for negotiations between the FL and CD. The PLB reportedly joined the pro-Préval *Inite* for the November 2010 elections.

Leaders: Renaud BERNARDIN, François PIERRE-LOUIS (Secretary General).

Movement for the Installation of Democracy in Haiti (*Mouvement pour l'Instauration de la Démocratie en Haïti*—MIDH). The MIDH was founded in 1986 by Marc Louis Bazin, a former World Bank official, who participated in the 1988 electoral boycott. As the 1990 presidential candidate of the National Alliance for Democracy and Progress (*Alliance Nationale pour la Démocratie et la Progrès*—ANDP) that also included Panpra, Bazin was runner-up to Aristide with a 15 percent vote share, while the ANDP ran second to the FNCD in the legislative poll.

Bazin subsequently endorsed the September 1991 coup that resulted in Aristide's ouster and was named prime minister by Interim President Nerette on June 2, 1992. Bazin resigned from the position on June 8, 1993. The MIDH boycotted the 1995 legislative poll but participated (unsuccessfully) in the 2000 balloting. Bazin died in mid-2010.

Patriotic Movement for National Salvage (*Mouvement Patriotique pour le Sauvetage National*—MPSN). The MPSN was formed in 1999 as a coalition of right-wing groups led by the Duvalierist head of the MDN. The MPSN participated unsuccessfully in the 2000 legislative balloting, decrying the government's "inappropriate control" of the electoral process.

Leader: Hubert de RONCERAY.

Mobilization for National Development (*Mobilisation pour le Développement National*—MDN). The runner-up to Leslie Manigat in the 1988 presidential balloting and subsequently one of the most outspoken critics of General Avril, MDN leader Hubert de Ronceray was among those expelled from the country in January 1990. He supported Aristide's ouster in 1991, and the MDN became prominent in the opposition following his return in 1994. In August 1996 two leading MDN members were shot dead in Port-au-Prince by unknown assailants. De Ronceray again went into temporary exile in October 1997 following the late August assassination of MDN deputy leader Pastor Antoine LEROY.

Leaders: Hubert de RONCERAY (President), Max CARRÉ (Secretary General).

Haitian Social Christian Party (*Parti Social Chrétien d'Haïti*—PSCH). The PSCH was launched on July 5, 1979, as one of two parties styling themselves the Haitian Christian Democratic Party (see PDCH, below). The party subsequently added the issue date of its manifesto to its name (PDCH—27 Juin), before becoming commonly identified by the Social Christian label. Its leader, Grégoire EUGÈNE, was deported to the United States in December 1980 and was prohibited from returning until after the February 1984 election, when he resumed his position as professor of constitutional and international law at Haiti University. For the remainder of the Duvalier era, he and his daughter, Marie, were sporadically subjected to either detention or house arrest. Eugène was credited with running fourth in the 1988 presidential poll. The party is now led by Eugène's son.

Leader: Grégoire EUGÈNE Jr.

Haitian Civic and Political Front (*Front Civico-Politique d'Haïtien*—Fronciph). Fronciph was launched on September 15, 1999, as a right-wing electoral alliance of the PDCH and PAIN and about 30 other parties and civic organizations, including the **National Cooperative Movement** (*Mouvement Koumbite National*—MKN), led by Volvick Rémy JOSEPH, and the **National Party of Labor** (*Parti National du Travail*—PNT), led by Thomas DESULMÉ.

Haitian Christian Democratic Party (*Parti Démocratique Chrétien d'Haïti*—PDCH). The PDCH was formed on July 5, 1979, by Silvio CLAUDE, who had been arrested and deported to Colombia after standing unsuccessfully for election to the legislature in February. Rearrested on his return to Haiti, he was sentenced in August 1981 to a 15-year prison term for attempting to create "a climate of disorder." Although the sentence was annulled in February 1982, periods of arrest and/or detention continued for the remainder of the Duvalier era. The PDCH refused to participate in the election of January 1988, while its leader placed fourth in the 1990 presidential balloting. A forceful critic of Aristide, Claude was killed in an act of apparent retribution by followers of the ousted president during the 1991 coup. His daughter, Marie Denise Claude, later became a leading member of the party, although she ran for a Senate seat in 2006 under the Fusion banner.

Leaders: Marie Denise CLAUDE (Leader), Osner FEVRY (Branch Leader).

National Agricultural and Industrial Party (*Parti Agricole et Industriel National*—PAIN). The PAIN was formed by Louis Déjoie (the son of a prominent Duvalier opponent), who participated in the 1988 boycott. Déjoie ran third in the 1990 presidential race with a 5 percent vote share. Although the PAIN endorsed the overthrow of the Aristide government in 1991, its leader, Louis DÉJOIE II (Déjoie's son) was named Malval's minister of commerce and industry in September 1993. The elder Déjoie died in early 1998.

Leader: Toussaint DESROSIERS (Spokesperson).

National Front for Concerted Action (*Front National de Concertation*—FNC). The FNC was organized in September 1987 through a merger of the "Group of 57" (see introductory text, above) with a number of other moderate left-wing formations. Led by Gérard Gourgue, a prominent lawyer and human rights activist who had resigned as minister of justice in the Namphy administration in March 1986, the party joined the PDCH in boycotting the January 1988 balloting.

On February 6, 2001, the opposition party group, Democratic Convergence (*Convergence Démocratique*—CD), named Gourge the provisional president of their "alternative government," a symbolic gesture to protest what the CD regarded as the flawed process that led to the election of Aristide.

Leader: Gérard GOURGUE.

Other small parties and groups that presented presidential candidates in November 2010 included the following: **Force 2010** (*Fòs 2010*), whose candidate, Wilson JEUDY (the mayor of the Port-au-Prince suburb of Delmas), received 0.57 percent of the vote in the first round of balloting; **Haiti for Haitians** (*Ayisyen pou Ayiti*), an FL offshoot whose candidate, former prime minister Yvon Neptune, received 0.39 percent of the vote; the **Democratic Movement of Haitian Youth** (*Mouvement Démocratique de la Jeunesse Haïtienne*—MODEJHA), whose candidate, Jean ANACACIS, received 0.39 percent of the vote; **Konbit Economic Liberation** (*Konbit Liberasyon Ekonomik*—KLE), whose candidate, Léon JEUNE (a former secretary of state for public security), received 0.35 percent of the vote; the **National Konbit for Haitian Development** (*Konbit Nasyonal pou Devlopman Ayiti*—KNDA), whose candidate, Axan Delson ABELLARD, received 0.29 percent of the vote despite officially withdrawing from the race shortly before the election; the **Wozo Political Organization** (*Organisation Politique Wozo*—WOZO), whose candidate, Garaudy LAGUERRE, received 0.26 percent of the vote; the **December 16 Platform** (*Platfòm 16 Désanm*), whose candidate, Gérard Marie Necker BLOT, received 0.24 percent of the vote; and the **Party for Haitian National Evolution** (*Parti de l'Evolution Nationale Haïtienne*—PENH), whose candidate, Eric Smarcki CHARLES, received 0.24 percent of the vote. The **Democratic Institutional Party** (*Parti Démocrate Institutionnaliste*—PDI) failed in its attempt to present Raymond Alcide JOSEPH, then the Haitian ambassador to the United States, as a presidential candidate.

Other groups winning one Chamber seat each in 2006 were the **Haitian Democratic and Reform Movement** (*Mouvement Démocratique et Renovateur d'Haïti*—Modereh), led by Dany TOUSSANT and Prince Pierre SONSON; the **Independent Movement for National Reconciliation** (*Mouvement Indépendent pour la Réconciliation Nationale*—MIRN), led by Luc FLEURINORD; **Justice for Peace and National Development** (*Justice pour la Paix et le Développement National*—JPDN), led by Rigaud DUPLAN; the **Liberal Party of Haiti** (*Parti Liberal Haïtien*—PLH), led by Gehy MICHEL; and the **Union of National and Progressive Haitians,** led by Edouard FRANCIQUE.

Other parties and groups have included the **Alliance for the Liberation and Advancement of Haiti** (*Alliance pour la Libération et l'Avancement d'Haïti*—ALAH), led by Reynold GEORGES; the **Alternative for the Development of Haiti** (*L'Alternative pour le Développement d'Haïti*—ADH), led by attorney Gerard DALVIUS; the **Citizens Union of Haitians for Development, Democracy, and Education** (*Union des Citoyens Ayisyen pour le Développement, la Démocratie, et L'Éducation*—UCADDE) whose executive secretary, Jeantel JOSEPH, charged the CEP with inappropriate conduct in declaring the UCADDE candidate the loser in a closely contested Senate race in 2009; **Credo,** a right-wing party led by Prosper AVRIL; **Democratic Action to Build Haiti** (*L'Action Démocratique de Bâtir Haïti*—Adebha), led by René JULIEN; the **Effort of Solidarity to Build a National and Popular Alternative** (*Effort de Solidarité pour la Construction d'une Alternative Nationale et Populaire*—ESCANP), a party based in the western region of Grand-Anse that cooperates with the influential grassroots group called the **Resistance Committee of Grand-Anse** (*Komite Reziztans Grand-Anse*—KOREGA); the anti-FL **Haitian Democrats' Party** (*Parti des Démocrates Haïtiens*—PADEMH), led by Jean-Jacques Clark PARENT; the far-left **Haitian National Popular Party** (*Parti Populaire National Haïtien*—PPNH), a pro-Aristide group formerly led by Bernard SANSARICQ (who narrowly escaped death in a shooting incident with government troops in August 1987) and now led by Ben DUPUY, the editor of the weekly *Haiti Progress;* the **Konbit National Movement** (*Mouvman Konbit Nasyonal*—MKN), led by Volvick Remy JOSEPH; the **Movement for the Advancement, Development, and Innovation of Democracy in Haiti** (*Mouvement pour l'Avancement, le Développement, et l'Innovation de la Démocratie en Haïti*—MADIDH), led by Marc Antoine DESTIN; the **National and Patriotic Movement of November 28** (*Mouvement Nationale et Patriotique du 28 Novembre*—MNP-28), led by former Senate president Déjean BÉLIZAIRE; the anti-FL **National Progressive Democratic Party of Haiti** (*Parti National Démocratique Progressiste d'Haïti*—PNDPH), led by Turneb DELPE; the **National Unity Party** (*Parti de l'Unité Nationale*—PUN), a remnant of the Duvalierist party of the 1960s that has reportedly been gaining new followers recently following Jean-Claude Duvalier's apology (from exile) in 2007 for "wrongs" committed by his administration; the **National Unity Movement** (*Mouvement d'Unité National*—MUN), led by Georges SAATI; the **Organization for the Advancement of Haiti and of Haitians** (*Organisation pour l'Avancement d'Haïti et des Haïtiens*—OLAHH), led by Joel BORGELLA; the extreme-right **Organization for Democracy in Haiti** (*Organisation pour la Démocratie en Haïti*—OPDH), whose leader, Carl DENIS, was arrested in August 1995 for allegedly plotting against the government; the **Papaye Peasants Movement** (*Mouvement Paysan de Papaye*—MPP), described as the nation's largest peasant organization and a member of the CD; the **Party for a Development Alternative** (*Parti pour un Développement Alternatif*—PADA), led by Gerard DALVIUS; the **Party of Haitian Manufacturers, Workers, Merchants, and Development Agents** (*Parti des Industriels, Travailleurs, Commercants, et Agents du Développement d'Haïti*—PITACH), led by Jean Jacques SYLVAIN; the **Party of the Patriotic Camp and of the Haitian Alliance** (*Parti du Camp Patriotique et de l'Alliance Haïtienne*—PACA-PALAH), led by Franck François ROMAIN; **Popular Star,** a "people's organization" led by Alexis CLAIRIUS, a supporter of the CD; the **Rally of Christian Democrats** (*Rassemblement des Démocrates Chrétiens*—RDC), led by Eddy VOLEI; the Social **Renovation Party** (*Parti Social Rénovation*—PSR), led by François PIERRE-LOUIS; the **Union for National Reconstruction** (*Union pour la Reconstruction Nationale*—URN), led by neo-Duvalierist Evans NICOLAS, a presidential candidate in 2000; and the **Union of Democratic Patriots** (*Union des Patriotes Démocratiques*—UPD), led by Rockefeller GUERRE. (Some of the above parties are no longer functioning.)

LEGISLATURE

The present **Parliament** (*Parlement*) is a bicameral body which, when meeting as a whole for purposes such as constitutional amendment, is styled the **National Assembly** (*Assemblée Nationale*). On January 11, 1999, President Préval declared that the terms of most legislators had expired and that the assembly was therefore dissolved. Under arrangements negotiated by Préval with several political parties in March, new legislative elections were expected by the end of the year; however, the first round was not held until May 21, 2000, with a disputed second round held on July 9. The terms of all of the members of the Chamber of Deputies and two-thirds of the members of the Senate elected in 2000 expired on January 11, 2004, and the assembly consequently ceased functioning. New elections were initially scheduled for September 2005, but it was not until February 7, 2006, that presidential and first-round legislative balloting (for all seats in the Senate and Chamber of Deputies) took place. The second legislative round was held April 21.

Senate (*Sénat*). The upper house comprises 30 members (3 senators per department), elected via majoritarian voting for six-year terms, with rotation of one-third of the members every two years. Balloting was erratic in the 1990s due to the nation's political turmoil, and the 1997 election results were set aside by the Provisional Electoral Council (CEP). Consequently, new elections for 19 seats were conducted on May 21 and July 9, 2000. However, most opposition parties boycotted the second-round voting to protest perceived improper calculation of first-round results by the government. The Lavalas Family (FL) was credited with winning 18 of the seats, with 1 going to an independent. The FL was also declared the winner of 8 additional seats contested on November 26, 2000, in a contest boycotted by the major opposition parties. The Senate stopped functioning in January 2004 when the mandates of two-thirds of its members expired, and new balloting was postponed amid the turmoil surrounding the ouster of President Aristide.

First round balloting for all 30 seats (increased from 27) was held on February 7, 2006. Following a second round of balloting on April 21, 2006, coupled with deferred voting for 3 seats on December 3, the Front for Hope (*Lespwa*) held 11 seats; the Haitian Social-Democratic Fusion Party (Fusion), 5; the Organization of the Struggling People (OPL), 4; the Lavalas Family (FL), 3; the Bridge Party, 2; the National Christian Union for the Reconstruction of Haiti, 2; the Standard-Bearer in Action (LAAA), 2; and the Democratic Action Party, 1.

The mandates for ten senators expired on May 11, 2008, elections to fill those seats having been postponed in late 2007 due to turmoil within the CEP and subsequent consideration of proposed electoral law revisions. The balloting for those seats and one other unfilled seat was held on April 19 (first round) and June 21, 2009. (Voting for one other unfilled seat was postponed due to disturbances at polling places.) Of the 11 contested seats, *Lespwa* secured 6; Fusion, 1; OPL, 1; Cooperative Action to Build Haiti (Konba), 1; Haiti in Action (AAA, as the LAAA had been renamed), 1; and independent, 1. New elections for 11 seats, whose mandates expired in May 2010, were held on November 28, 2010 (first round) and March 20, 2011. Five of the seats were won by Unity (*Inite*), 5 by the Alternative for Progress and Democracy (*Alternativ*), and 1 by the Organization for the Future (*Lavni*). Following the balloting, the total distribution of seats was as follows: *Lespwa*, 10; *Inite*, 5; *Alternativ*, 5; Fusion, 3; AAA, 2; For Us All, 1; the FL, 1; *Lavni*, 1; the OPL, 1; and Konba, 1. (Some reports simply credited the *Lespwa* seats to its successor [*Inite*], while others noted that Fusion and the OPL had participated in *Alternativ*.)

New balloting for 10 seats was due by January 2012, but no election date had been scheduled as of mid-2013, leaving the Senate at that time with only 20 seated members. Further complicating the electoral landscape, the mandates of 10 other senators were scheduled to expire in early 2014.

President: Simon Dieuseul DESRAS.

Chamber of Deputies (*Chambre des Députés*). The lower house is currently composed of 99 members, directly elected for four-year terms via majoritarian voting in 99 single-member districts. (For results of the 2006 balloting, see the 2012 *Handbook*.) All mandates in the chamber expired in May 2010.

The first round of balloting for all 99 seats was most recently held on November 28, 2010, followed by a second round on March 20, 2011. Following is the distribution of seats from that balloting (reports on the results varied somewhat): Unity, 32; the Alternative for Progress and Democracy, 11; the Together We Are Strong party, 10; Haiti in Action, 8; the Organization for the Future, 7; Assembly, 4; Peasant Response, 3; *Konbit pou Refe Ayiti*, 3; the Christian Movement for a New Haiti, 3; For Us All, 3; Liberation Platform, 3; the Socialist Action Movement, 2; *Veye Yo*, 1; the Democratic Movement for the Liberation of Haiti–Revolutionary Party of Haiti, 1; the Platform of Haitian Patriots, 1; Respect, 1; independents, 2; and vacant, 4.

President: Jean Tholbert ALEXIS.

CABINET

[as of August 1, 2013]

Prime Minister	Laurent S. Lamothe
Ministers	
Agriculture, Natural Resources, and Rural Development	Thomas Jacques
Commerce and Industry	Wilson Laleau
Communication (Acting)	Josette Darguste [f]
Culture	Josette Darguste [f]
Defense	Jean Rodolphe Joazile
Economy and Finance	Wilson Laleau
Environment	Jean François Thomas
Foreign Affairs and Religious Affairs	Pierre Richard Casimir
Haitians Living Abroad (Acting)	Pierre Richard Casimir
Interior and Territorial Collectives	David Bazile
Justice and Public Security	Jean Renal Sanon
National Education and Professional Training	Vanneur Pierre
Planning and External Cooperation	Laurent S. Lamothe
Public Health and Population	Florence Duperval Guillame [f]
Public Works, Transport, and Energy	Jacques Rousseau
Relations with Parliament	Ralph Ricardo Théano
Social Affairs and Labor	Charles Jean-Jacques
Tourism	Stéphanie Balmir Villedrouin [f]
Women's Affairs and Women's Rights	Marie Yanick Mézil [f]
Youth and Sports	Magalie Racine [f]
Ministers Delegate to the Prime Minister	
Energy Security	René Jean-Jumeau
Human Rights and the Fight Against Extreme Poverty	Marie Carmelle Rose Ann Auguste [f]
Promotion of the Peasantry	Marie Mimose Felix [f]
Secretary General of the Council of Ministers	Enex Jean-Charles
Secretary General of the Prime Minister's Office	Lucien Francoeur

[f] = female

INTERGOVERNMENTAL REPRESENTATION

Ambassador to the U.S.: Paul Getty ALTIDOR.

U.S. Ambassador to Haiti: Pamela A. WHITE.

Permanent Representative to the UN: Denis REGIS.

IGO Memberships (Non-UN): Caricom, IADB, IOM, NAM, OAS, WTO.

HONDURAS

Republic of Honduras
República de Honduras

Note: In the presidential election of November 24, 2013, Juan Orlando Hernandez of the National Party secured 36.9 percent of the vote, followed by Xiomara Castro (Libre) with 28.8 percent. Castro challenged the results the following day, but on December 12, the High Electoral Court confirmed Hernandez's victory.

Political Status: Part of the independent Captaincy General of Guatemala, 1821; member of United Provinces of Central America, 1824–1838; separate republic established 1839; present constitution promulgated January 20, 1982, following a decade of military rule.

Area: 43,277 sq. mi. (112,088 sq. km).

Population: 7,984,288 (2012E—UN); 8,448,465 (2013E—U.S. Census).

Major Urban Centers (2011E—UN): TEGUCIGALPA (1,088,000).

Official Language: Spanish.

Monetary Unit: Lempira (market rate November 1, 2013: 20.42 lempiras = $1US).

President: (*See headnote.*) Porfirio LOBO Sosa (National Party); elected on November 29, 2009, and inaugurated on January 27, 2010, for a four-year term, succeeding Roberto MICHELETTI Baín (Liberal Party), who was appointed by the congress on June 28, 2009, for a six-month term following a bloodless coup the same day that ousted José Manuel (Mel) ZELAYA Rosales (Liberal Party).

First Vice President: María Antonieta Guillen de BOGRÁN (National Party); elected on November 29, 2009, and inaugurated on January 27, 2010, for a term concurrent with that of the president, filling a vacancy after the June 28, 2009, removal of Vice President Commissioner Aristides MEJIA Carranza (Liberal Party).

THE COUNTRY

Honduras, the second largest of the Central American republics, is mountainous, sparsely inhabited, and predominantly rural. Approximately 90 percent of the population is racially mixed; Indians constitute about 7 percent, blacks and whites the remainder. Roman Catholicism is the religion of more than 95 percent of the people, three-quarters of whom are functionally illiterate. Women constitute about 7 percent of the rural labor force, exclusive of unpaid family workers, and 32 percent of the urban workforce, primarily in domestic service; departing from tradition, each of the last six governments has contained at least one female cabinet member.

The nation's economy traditionally depended on agriculture, and coffee, bananas, and shrimp remain important exports. However, industry, with an emphasis on nondurable consumer goods, now accounts for a higher share of GDP (27 percent versus 12 percent for agriculture), largely because of the growth during the 1990s of foreign-owned *maquila* companies, which produce garments and other goods for export using materials imported on a virtually duty-free basis. GDP growth during the 1990s averaged 2.8 percent and expanded at a robust annual average of 5.1 percent in 2000–2008, according to the International Monetary Fund (IMF). The expansion was helped along in part by the 2006 implementation of the Central American Free Trade Agreement with the United States, the destination for 60 percent of Honduras's exports and family remittances (chiefly from some 900,000 Hondurans living in the United States), which accounted for more than 25 percent of the country's gross domestic product.

Honduras's largely rural and young population, coupled with the prevalence of droughts, hurricanes, and mudslides, has contributed to its cycle of poverty and high underemployment, according to the World Bank. It has remained one of the least developed countries in the region, with 59 percent of the population living below the poverty line and 36.2 percent in extreme poverty.

The combined effects of the global economic downturn and the six-month political crisis resulted in an economic contraction of 2.1 percent in 2009. On a positive note, inflation dropped to 5.5 percent in 2009 from a decade-high 11.4 percent in 2008, mainly due to declining consumer and investment spending, remittances, and tourism. In August 2010 the IMF reported that Honduras had begun to rebound from the global economic downturn, noting authorities' efforts to improve tax administration and collection, control spending, and improve targeting of subsidies to the poor. GDP grew by 3.7 percent in 2010, and unemployment stood at 4.6 percent. Remittances accounted for a lower but significant 16 percent of GDP, nearly four times higher than foreign direct investment the same year. The drop in remittances from the 2006 level was the result of continuing hard economic times globally. Remittances rebounded year on year in 2010 and moved closer to the pre-downturn level. GDP growth stayed at 3.7 percent in 2011 before decreasing slightly to 3.3 percent in 2012. The IMF projected growth of 3.3 percent in 2013 and noted a decline in coffee production was expected to have an adverse effect. Inflation was 5.7 percent and unemployment, 4.4 percent.

GOVERNMENT AND POLITICS

Political background. Honduras declared its independence from Spain in 1821 as part of the Captaincy General of Guatemala. After a brief period of absorption by Mexico, the states of the Captaincy General in 1824 organized as the Central American Federation, which broke up in 1838. Decades of instability, revolution, and governmental change followed, with Honduras experiencing 67 different heads of state between 1855 and 1932, and U.S. military forces intervening on three occasions between 1912 and 1924. A measure of internal stability, accompanied by a minimum of reform and progress, was achieved between 1932 and 1954 under the presidencies of Tiburcio CARIAS Andino and Juan Manuel GALVEZ. Three years after a military coup in 1954, Ramón VILLEDA Morales was installed as constitutional president and served until his 1963 overthrow in another military action mounted by (then) Col. Oswaldo LÓPEZ Arellano. Subsequently, a Constituent Assembly, with a National Party (*Partido Nacional*—PN) majority, approved a new constitution and designated López Arellano as president.

Immediately before the 1971 election, López Arellano organized the framework for a new government under a Pact of National Unity, which called for equal representation in the congress, the cabinet, the Supreme Court, and other government organs for the PN and the Liberal Party (*Partido Liberal*—PL) and for the two parties to put up separate candidates for the presidency. After 18 months in office, the administration of President Ramón Ernesto CRUZ was overthrown by the military under former president López Arellano, who served the remainder of Cruz's presidential term. On March 31, 1975, Arellano was replaced as military commander in chief by (then) Col. Juan Alberto MELGAR Castro after a group of dissident junior officers had seized control of the Supreme Council of the Armed Forces, and on April 22 Melgar Castro replaced him as head of state. The new president was in turn ousted on August 7, 1978, by a three-man junta headed by Brig. Gen. Policarpo PAZ García.

On July 25, 1980, the Constituent Assembly that had been elected on April 20 named Paz García to serve as sole executive pending adoption of a new basic law and the popular election of a successor. Dr. Roberto SUAZO Córdova led the PL to a surprisingly conclusive victory in nationwide balloting on November 29, 1981, and assumed office on January 27, 1982, promising "a revolution of work and honesty."

On March 31, 1984, General Gustavo ALVAREZ Martinez was dismissed and sent into exile, following charges of plotting a coup and misappropriating government funds. The latter allegations turned largely on the activities of the Association for the Progress of Honduras (APROH), a right-wing grouping of military and business leaders that, a year earlier, had accepted a $5 million contribution from the intensely anticommunist Unification Church of Sun Myung Moon for the purpose of countering Honduran "subversives." APROH, which was formally outlawed in November 1984, had also advocated direct U.S. military intervention against the Nicaraguan *sandinistas* as a necessary precondition of regional economic development.

In late 1984, amid deepening fissures within the ruling PL, President Suazo Córdova endorsed the former interior minister, Oscar MEJÍA Arellano, as the party's 1985 presidential candidate. However, a majority of the party's congressional delegation backed chamber president Efraín BU Girón, leaving the chief executive with the minority support of only 29 deputies. The split yielded a constitutional crisis in early 1985, with Congress removing five of the nine Supreme Court justices on grounds of corruption and the president responding by ordering the arrest of the new chief justice. In April the old court was reinstalled after the leading parties agreed to an open contest in the forthcoming presidential balloting that would permit any faction of a recognized party to present a presidential candidate; an electoral change approved later in the year declared that the winner would be the leading candidate within the party that secured the most votes. Under the new arrangement, José Simón AZCONA del Hoyo, an anti-*suazocordovista* PL member, was declared president-elect after the election of November 24, despite placing second to the leading PN nominee, Rafael Leonardo CALLEJAS Romero.

Azcona's victory yielded the first transition involving elected civilians in more than half a century. However, because of party fissures, he could look forward to controlling only 46 of 132 legislative seats. As a result, before his inauguration on January 27, 1986, the incoming chief executive concluded a "National Accord" (an echo of the 1971 pact) with the Nationalists that gave the opposition effective control of the judiciary and representation in the cabinet and other influential bodies, thus dimming prospects for major policy changes, including meaningful land reform. Although the accord subsequently deteriorated (see PN under Political Parties, below), PL-PN cooperation at midyear yielded the indefinite suspension of municipal elections scheduled for November, neither party apparently favoring a public test before the presidential and legislative balloting scheduled for 1989.

In the November 1989 election, PN candidate Callejas secured 50.2 percent of the presidential vote, and his party returned to power after 18 years. The new president named two PL members to cabinet posts.

Oswaldo RAMOS Soto secured the PN presidential nomination in 1993 but went on to lose by a wide margin to the PL nominee, Carlos Roberto REINA Idiáquez. The Liberals also won decisively in the legislative balloting, defeating the *nacionalistas* by 71 seats to 55.

In a move reminiscent of the Pact of National Unity, the PL and PN joined with the Innovation and Unity Social Democratic Party (*Partido Innovación y Unidad Social Demócrata*—PINU-SD) and the Christian Democratic Party of Honduras (*Partido Demócrata Cristiano de Honduras*—PDCH) in organizing the National Council of Convergence (*Consejo Nacional de Convergencia*—Conacon) in September 1995 to promote consensus on social, economic, and political issues. Excluded from the grouping, the Democratic Unification Party (*Partido Unificación Democrática*—PUD) charged that it was launched in an effort to preserve the dominance of the traditional parties.

In the balloting of November 30, 1997, the Liberal presidential nominee Carlos Roberto FLORES Facussé won with nearly 53 percent of the vote. The PL also retained control of the National Congress by a reduced majority of 67 seats. Flores was inaugurated on January 27, 1998, at which time he appointed a cabinet that included only one incumbent minister.

At the president's request, the congress on September 18, 1998, passed a number of constitutional amendments designed to bring the military under civilian control. The administration's efforts to implement the changes, including the abolition of autonomous military spending and designation of the nation's first civilian defense minister, triggered an apparent coup attempt on July 30, 1999.

The PN's Ricardo MADURO Joest defeated the PL's Rafael PINEDA Ponce in the election of November 25, 2001, although the incoming president's party was limited to a plurality (61 of 128 seats) in the National Congress.

The 2005 election was reminiscent of 1993. The Liberals, led by Manuel (Mel) ZELAYA, turned back a *nacionalista* effort to retain the presidency, while winning a legislative plurality that was close to being a reversal of the 2001 result (see Political Parties, below).

President Zelaya reshuffled the cabinet on February 1, 2009, after Vice President Elvin Ernesto SANTOS resigned on December 18, 2008, to seek election in the 2009 presidential poll. Former defense minister Aristides MEJIA Carranza was appointed to succeed Santos on January 6, 2009. On June 28 about 100 soldiers stormed the presidential palace in the wake of a secret Supreme Court order two days earlier and removed Zelaya in the first bloodless coup in the country in decades. Zelaya was immediately flown to Costa Rica. Later that day, in accordance with the constitutional order of succession, congress named the PL leader, Roberto MICHELETTI Bain, as provisional president until elections scheduled for November. Congress also voted to accept a letter of resignation purportedly written by Zelaya (though he denied producing it), and Micheletti reshuffled the cabinet.

Zelaya returned to Honduras clandestinely on September 21, 2009, and was granted sanctuary in the Brazilian embassy. The two competing political camps, with pressure from the United States, in late October reached an agreement designed to resolve the crisis by, among other things, authorizing congress to determine whether Zelaya should be reinstated in the presidency for the remainder of his term. In November, days ahead of the general election, the main presidential candidates signed an agreement to respect the choice of voters. An independent candidate, Carlos REYES, dropped out close to the election in protest of failed efforts to bring back Zelaya.

In controversial presidential balloting on November 29, in which Zelaya and his supporters called for a boycott, Porfirio LOBO Sosa of the PN was elected with 56.6 percent of the vote. His closest challenger was Elvin Santos of the PL, with 38.1 percent. During concurrent parliamentary balloting, the PN won control of the legislature with 71 seats, while the PL secured 45. Turnout was reported to be less than 50 percent. On December 2 the outgoing congress voted 111–14 not to restore Zelaya to the presidency.

On January 26, 2010, the legislature passed an amnesty law that shielded all those involved in the ouster of the former president, including any actions taken by Zelaya, from recrimination. The same day, the Supreme Court absolved top military commanders of charges that they abused their power in the ouster. Zelaya was also given free passage to leave the country. Lobo was inaugurated and installed a new cabinet that included members of several parties on January 27. Hours later, Zelaya was escorted to the airport by Lobo and boarded a flight to the Dominican Republic, where he went into exile.

In February 2011 the congress finalized a constitutional reform package that would allow the president a minimum of 10 representatives or 2 percent of voters to petition for a plebiscite or referendum. A referendum would require a simple majority in the congress to move forward, and a plebiscite would need approval by a two-thirds majority.

A series of cabinet reshuffles took place from September 2011 to August 2012. In September Lobo replaced three ministers in an attempt to bring new life to his cabinet and make it more "dynamic." In January Lobo replaced another minister, followed by another minor reshuffle of four ministers in February. Another minister was replaced in March, while the finance minster resigned in August and was subsequently replaced. In all, ten ministries changed leaders during the series of cabinet reshuffles.

In April 2012, the National Congress took a step forward in ensuring greater political participation for women in the government. Under the existing law, only 30 percent of the government had to be composed of women. In passing a new law, the National Congress raised that percentage to 40 percent from 2012 to 2015, and set it at 50 percent beginning in 2016.

Following up on a UN report that Honduras was the most murderous country in the world in 2012, President Lobo announced a reshuffle of the national security team on April 15, 2013, the same day that congress removed Attorney General Luis RUBI and the head of police purification from office. Former minister of the exterior Arturo CORRALES was inaugurated on May 1 as minister of security, with added responsibility for the newly created National Defense and Security Council.

Constitution and government. The current constitution provides for a directly elected president, who may serve for only one term, and a unicameral legislature whose members serve four-year terms concurrent with that of the chief executive. The judiciary includes a Supreme Court and five courts of appeal, each of which designates local justices within its territorial jurisdiction.

Internal administration is based on 18 departments headed by centrally appointed governors. The departments are subdivided into a total of 283 municipalities, each with an elected mayor and municipal assembly (including the capital, which for most of the half century prior to 1985 had been denied local government status).

The constitution promulgated in 1982 guarantees freedom of the press. However, in September 1993 the legislature gave the government the right to censor all media material, including films and novels, found to "offend [Honduran] culture, morality, family unity, and traditions." Journalists were frequently attacked and killed in the period following the 2009 coup. The international media watchdog Reporters Without Borders ranked Honduras 127th on its 2013 press freedom index.

Foreign relations. A member of the Organization of American States (OAS) and the United Nations, Honduras has long inclined toward a conservative position in inter-American and world affairs (though the country moved to the left under the Zelaya administration, beginning in 2005). It joined in founding the now-inactive Organization of Central American States in 1951 and the Central American Common Market (CACM) in 1960. In 1982 Honduras participated in the U.S.-sponsored formation of a Central American Democratic Community (Condeca), which included Costa Rica, El Salvador, and Guatemala, while excluding Nicaragua; however, the alliance quickly became moribund. In May 1986 Honduras joined with the other four CACM countries in endorsing the creation of the Central American Parliament (*Parlamento Centroamericano*—Parlacen), although neither Costa Rica nor Nicaragua was represented at Parlacen's October 1991 inauguration. In May 1992 the three Parlacen countries announced the formation of a Northern Triangle (*Triángulo Norte*) for trade, which became the Central American Group of Four (*Grupo América Central 4*—AC-4) with the addition of Nicaragua in

April 1993. Meanwhile, at a *Triángulo Norte* summit in October 1992 its presidents called for a new effort to establish a regional political grouping in the form of a Central American Federation, with Parlacen as its legislative forum. The projected Federation was advanced as an outgrowth of a Central American Integration System that had been supported by all five regional executives during a December 1991 meeting in Honduras, although subsequently ratified only by Honduras, El Salvador, and Nicaragua.

A series of disagreements with neighboring El Salvador in 1969 led the two countries to an undeclared "soccer war," during which invading Salvadoran forces inflicted hundreds of casualties. The OAS arranged a cease-fire on July 18. Renewed hostilities broke out in July 1976, and it was not until October 30, 1980, that a formal peace treaty was signed in Lima, Peru. Relations remained tense because of a border controversy and continuing clashes between Salvadoran government forces and guerrilla groups operating from sanctuaries in the ostensibly demilitarized territorial pockets (*bolsones territoriales*).

The boundary dispute centered on claims by Honduras that El Salvador (and, to a lesser extent, Nicaragua) had attempted to block its access to the Pacific Ocean by controlling egress through the Gulf of Fonseca. Honduras and El Salvador agreed in 1986 to submit the issue to the International Court of Justice (ICJ), with Nicaragua participating as a limited observer. In a decision handed down in September 1992 the ICJ awarded most of the disputed territory to Honduras, while ruling that the Gulf waters were not international but a closed condominium of the three countries that, in effect, guaranteed Honduras its long-sought access to the Pacific. On the other hand, the Honduran territorial gains stimulated widespread protests by Salvadoran settlers, who insisted that the transferred areas be declared "peace zones," free of Honduran government or military control. In response, the Honduran foreign ministry affirmed that the territories were Honduran. In September 1995 a Bi-Zonal Commission set up to implement the 1992 judgment agreed that residents of the territory could choose either Honduran or Salvadoran nationality. Further moves to alleviate border tensions were undertaken by the two countries' foreign ministers in late 1996, and in January 1998 the countries' presidents met in Tegucigalpa to sign an accord finalizing the border demarcation. Nonetheless, El Salvador reopened the issue in early 2002 by requesting a review of the boundaries established by the 1992 decision. At issue was delineation of the last 4 miles of the 145-mile border, which was settled during a meeting of Honduran president Manuel Zelaya and Salvadoran president Tony Saca on April 18, 2006, thus terminating the 37-year controversy.

Conflict between Honduras and Nicaragua arose in early 1995. Nicaragua contended that Honduran vessels in the Gulf of Fonseca had repeatedly destroyed boundary markers and then crossed over into the more fertile shrimp beds in their territory. In late January 1996 the controversy appeared to have been defused by agreement on an area of tolerance within which vessels from both countries could operate pending a World Court decision on maritime demarcation.

A new crisis with Nicaragua erupted in November 1999 following ratification by the Honduran Congress of a 1986 maritime border treaty with Colombia that involved some 50,000 square miles of coastal waters, portions of which were alleged to have been forcibly ceded to Colombia during the U.S. occupation of Nicaragua in the 1920s. In reprisal, Nicaragua imposed a 35 percent duty on all goods imported from Honduras. In January 2000 the two countries agreed to submit the dispute to another World Court ruling; however, less than a month later peace in the Gulf of Fonseca was again threatened by an exchange between Honduran and Nicaraguan patrol boats, each claiming that it had been attacked by the other. Friction continued into 2002, with periodic seizures of Honduran boats accused of illegally fishing in Nicaraguan waters and Nicaragua authorizing oil prospecting in the region. On November 28, 2006, the Nicaraguan president-elect, Daniel Ortega, offered President Zelaya a partnership agreement including proposals to end the border dispute, reduce poverty, and minimize military presence. Both countries agreed to a final border demarcation set by the ICJ in October 2007. The ruling gave Honduras 80 percent of the disputed 34,500 square kilometers in the Caribbean Ocean, including sovereign control over the islands of Bobel, Sabana, Port Royal, and Sur.

In January 2002 outgoing president Flores reestablished relations with Cuba, which had been suspended since 1961. Seemingly prompted by Cuban aid after the 1974 and 1998 hurricanes, the new Maduro administration faced mixed reactions to its rapprochement with the Marxist regime but made no attempt to rescind the action. In October 2007 Zelaya became the first Honduran president to visit Cuba, meeting with its interim leader Raúl Castro.

Honduras participated in the conclusion of negotiations on establishment of a Central America Free Trade Agreement (CAFTA) in December 2003. Under the U.S.-sponsored initiative, most intraregional trade would, over time, become tariff free. The treaty was formally launched on April 1, 2006.

Honduras continued to cooperate with the United States against the drugs trade. In June 2006, following the creation of a special military unit to support police work, Zelaya asked U.S. president George W. Bush for special forces personnel to counter trafficking in drugs bound for the United States in the country's eastern Mosquitia coast region.

In May 2007 the U.S. government granted an 18-month extension of the Temporary Protected Status (to March 2009), affecting 78,000 Hondurans, 230,000 Salvadorans, and 4,000 Nicaraguans. The status allowed foreign nationals whose homeland conditions are recognized by the U.S. government as being temporarily unsafe to continue residing in the United States but precludes their acquisition of permanent resident status.

On January 15, 2008, Honduras signed an agreement with Venezuela to purchase oil from the state oil company (Petrocaribe) at preferential rates. In October Honduras joined Alianza Bolivariana para los Pueblos de Nuestra America (ALBA), a trade organization begun by Venezuela president Hugo Chávez as an alternative to the Free Trade Area of the Americas being proposed by the United States. The increasing ties with Venezuela were in direct contrast to Honduras's declining relationship with the United States.

Following the military coup that ousted President Zelaya in June 2008, the OAS on July 4 suspended Honduras. After President Porfirio Lobo's controversial election in November 2009, he urged other Latin American leaders to recognize him as the head of state. The United States, Panama, Costa Rica, Peru, and Colombia immediately accredited the election's results. While the U.S. government called the election a "significant step" in Honduras's return to the community of nations after the ouster of former president Zelaya, Brazil's president Luiz Inácio Lula da Silva said the election was illegitimate and that cooperating with Lobo would pose a serious threat to democracy in Latin America. Argentina and other countries across Latin America also refused to accept the election results. After an OAS report in July that said Honduras had made significant advances to rectify problems as a consequence of Zelaya's removal, Chile and Mexico restored full diplomatic relations.

In March 2010 the U.S. government announced that it would restore $31 million in military and social aid to Honduras that it had frozen after Zelaya's ouster. In April the two countries signed a security cooperation agreement under the U.S. government's Mérida Initiative, a regional program designed to combat organized crime, gangs, and the trafficking of drugs and firearms. Under the multi-year deal, the U.S. agreed to provide $4.4 million in funding to the Honduran police.

Former Colombian president Álvaro Uribe was honored by Honduras's congress in November 2010 for his efforts toward promoting democracy in the country. Uribe, who was among the first to recognize the Lobo presidency, was greeted by protesters upon his arrival at the airport. In December Honduras formed a rare united diplomatic front with neighbors El Salvador and Guatemala to press Mexico to protect the human rights of Central Americans traversing Mexico on their way to the United States, triggered by that month's mass kidnapping of 50 Central Americans from a freight train in Oaxaca, Mexico, which the Mexican government attempted to ignore. The event and the diplomatic push forced a promise from the main left-wing Mexican Democratic Revolution Party to do more to uphold the human rights of Central American immigrants transiting through Mexico.

In a move to put pressure on South American countries that had not yet renewed ties with Honduras because of Zelaya's removal, the country's government announced in March 2011 that it would shutter its embassies in Argentina, Bolivia, Brazil, Ecuador, and Venezuela. These countries had said that they would not recognize the Lobo government until Zelaya was allowed to return without threat of prosecution. After the two sides agreed to an accord signed in Colombia and Zelaya was allowed to return to Honduras (see Current issues, below), the OAS in June approved the country for readmission into the organization. Member states agreed to allow Honduras back in after a vote of 32–1, with Ecuador being the only country to register disapproval on the grounds that those responsible for the ouster had not been punished and citing Honduras's human rights record.

Tensions over the Gulf of Fonseca arose again in March 2013 when Honduras claimed an armed Nicaraguan naval vessel had attacked a Honduran fishing boat in disputed waters. The incident triggered renewed efforts to settle the dispute, resulting in a trilateral agreement among President Lobo, Nicaraguan President Daniel Otega, and El Salvadoran President Mauricio Funes on May 8 to establish an economic zone in the gulf. Lobo noted that the agreement was not a solution but a signal of cooperation toward resolution of the conflict.

Drug trafficking continued to be a major problem, as the U.S. State Department in June 2013 blacklisted the Honduran trafficking group Cachiros.

Current issues. Violence marred the political process in November 2008 when two members of the PL, including the vice president of congress, who was a supporter of aspiring presidential candidate Roberto Micheletti, and two members of the PN were killed by unidentified attackers. In nationwide primaries held by the PL and the PN in November, the PL's Mauricio VILLEDA, a lawyer and political novice, defeated four other PL aspirants, including Micheletti, who had widely been regarded as the front-runner. Villeda was standing in for former vice president Elvin Santos, who had resigned to participate but whose bid was blocked by the Supreme Electoral Tribunal. Subsequently, congress validated Santos's candidacy, and Villeda stepped down and backed Santos. Meanwhile, the PN's Porfirio Lobo easily defeated three other candidates to win his party's nomination.

In the early months of 2009 controversy heightened over Zelaya's plan for a nationwide referendum to determine public support for establishing a Constituent Assembly to draft a new constitution. Both the PL and the PN opposed the referendum, scheduled for June 28, arguing against the lifting of term limits. In the days leading up to the poll, the Supreme Court, following a similar vote by congress, ruled the referendum unconstitutional. Further, the military confiscated ballots to prevent the vote from taking place. On June 25 Zelaya led hundreds on a peaceful protest to an air force base where the crowd attempted to retake the ballots, and he subsequently fired the commander of the armed forces for refusing to order the military to implement the poll. The leaders of the army, navy, and air force resigned in a show of support for the commander. Meanwhile, the Supreme Court ruled that the removal of the commander was illegal and reinstated him. Ultimately, the electoral tribunal also ruled that the referendum was illegal. Nevertheless, Zelaya vowed to hold the poll as scheduled on June 28. That morning, however, soldiers stormed the palace and arrested Zelaya in a bloodless coup and immediately put him on a plane to Costa Rica. Micheletti, president of congress, ascended to the presidency, and congress voted to accept a letter of resignation purportedly written by Zelaya. (The former president denied having written such a letter.) The coup set off opposing demonstrations on June 29 and prompted widespread condemnation from Zelaya's supporters in Venezuela, Cuba, and Bolivia, as well as from the OAS, the United States, and the United Nations, all of whom refused to recognize the new government. The European Union (EU) and Latin American countries withdrew their ambassadors, and the military was dispatched to patrol the streets and guard government buildings. Numerous assassinations, including those of journalists and supporters and opponents of the government occurred following the coup.

U.S. and EU financial assistance was put on hold, as was aid from the Inter-American Development Bank, the World Bank, and the Central American Bank for Economic Integration.

On July 10, 2009, Costa Rican president Oscar Arias began mediating talks between Zelaya and the de facto government. Proposals put forth by Arias would allow Zelaya to return to the country and finish his term as president, move up new elections to October, grant amnesty for political crimes before and after the coup, and include all major political parties in a government of national unity. However, the interim government rejected the proposals, prompting Zelaya to threaten to walk away as well. On July 16 Zelaya stationed himself in Nicaragua with hundreds of supporters as the standoff over negotiations continued. Honduran soldiers on the border subsequently blocked a demonstration by about 1,000 Zelaya supporters, and ultimately the protesters returned to Honduras.

On September 21, 2009, Zelaya secretly reentered Honduras and took refuge in the Brazilian embassy. Micheletti demanded that the Brazilians hand over the president, but they refused to comply. In late October, amid mounting pressure from the international community, including the United States, the two sides agreed to let the National Congress decide whether to restore the government to its status before Zelaya's ouster. However, on November 5 the Micheletti administration formed a so-called unity government without the participation of Zelaya and his supporters, prompting Zelaya to threaten to pull out of the reconciliation agreement and boycott the upcoming presidential election. On November 25 the Supreme Court ruled that Zelaya could not legally return to office, a ruling that was to be passed on to congress for its consideration during a planned December 2 floor debate over the issue. On the same day, the presidential candidates signed an agreement that they would respect the voters' decision.

Parliamentary and presidential polling took place on November 26, 2009, amid greatly heightened security, as some 30,000 police and military personnel were ordered to patrol the streets and oversee the electoral process. The police reportedly asked mayors to turn over the names of "enemies" of the process, a move that drew condemnation from international watchdog groups. There were also reports that military forces suppressed a rally in one town, and that at least one person was killed and others were beaten and arrested. In the presidential election, the PN's Lobo won 56.6 percent of the vote, easily defeating the PL's Elvin Santos, who had served as vice president under Zelaya. Santos garnered 38 percent on turnout of slightly less than 50 percent of the electorate. In concurrent parliamentary elections, the PN won 71 seats of the total 128 contested seats in congress. The PL secured the second-highest number of seats with 45. On December 2 the outgoing congress voted against reinstating Zelaya as president.

The election did little to quell the crime boiling over in Honduras, as in December 2009 there were more reports of abductions and murders of activists and Zelaya supporters, as well as the assassinations of the country's former anti-drug-trafficking agency chief and a retired colonel who was related to Micheletti. During that period, president-elect Lobos unsuccessfully called for Micheletti to step aside in favor of a consensus transition team. Lobo also asked congress to grant Zelaya political amnesty in order for the country to begin to move past the ouster and to pass an amnesty law for all those involved in the former president's removal. The legislature passed the initiative in time for him to sign on inauguration day, January 27, 2010, allowing Lobo to grant Zelaya safe passage from his five-month refuge at the Brazilian embassy to the airport. Dominican Republic president Leonel Fernández escorted Zelaya to his country as an honored guest.

In February 2010, in an effort to signal the government was beginning to move past the ouster, President Lobo appointed a government that included members of all the country's political groups. Meanwhile, a delegation from the OAS arrived in Honduras to help set up a truth commission to review the events leading to the coup and its aftermath. Lobo also removed the country's armed forces chief, who had played a key role in Zelaya's ouster, in an effort to mollify at least ten heads of state who refused to return to normal relations with Honduras. Meanwhile, Honduras restored diplomatic relations with 29 other countries.

Administration critics began a movement on April 20, 2010, to press for a national Constituent Assembly to draw up a new constitution, and for the unconditional return of Zelaya. The campaign was spearheaded by the National Popular Resistance Front (*Frente Nacional de Resistencia Popular*—FNRP), a broad coalition that had emerged in mid-2009 to protest the removal of the former president, and subsequently became the primary opposition to the Lobo government, organizing numerous massive street protests and acts of civil disobedience. In the months that followed, nearly a dozen resistance members were reported to have been killed, threatened, or intimidated.

On May 4, 2010, President Lobo formally inaugurated a truth commission established to investigate events surrounding the 2009 coup. The commission members pledged to interview both supporters and opponents of the coup, but backers of ousted president Zelaya immediately rejected the commission as "a farce" and vowed not to cooperate. In June President Lobo fired three judges and one magistrate in the wake of disciplinary proceedings against them for being critical of the 2009 coup, prompting severe criticism from Amnesty International.

Momentum began building for a national constituent assembly as the FNRP reported in September that it had collected more than 1.3 million signatures in its petition drive.

In October 2010 President Lobo, in what analysts said was an attempt to engage leftist opposition and encourage more international recognition of his presidency, asked congress to create a special parliamentary commission to investigate reforming the constitution's requirements to hold plebiscites. Observers said the move signaled that Lobo was open to the convening of a constituent assembly. Meanwhile, the FNRP declined an invitation for a dialogue offered by the president, rejecting it as "a political maneuver . . . guided by the U.S. State Department." The group, which did not recognize Lobo's government, said no dialogue could take place until former president Zelaya was allowed to return to the country. Adding to Lobo's woes, the teachers resumed their strike on November 3, protesting Lobo's retraction of a minimum wage increase that was to have taken effect in January 2010 and his introduction of a new wage scale that reduced the pay for many teachers. An overwhelming number of teachers had opposed the coup, and 13 were killed in its aftermath, including a prominent teachers union member. In late November the International Criminal Court announced that it had opened preliminary investigations into Honduras, focusing on the 2009 coup. On a positive note, the government in November pledged to investigate the deaths of nine journalists in 2010, due in part to pressure from several groups in the region committed to freedom of expression. The same month Lobo announced that the national police and the army had begun an operation to sweep the coastal province of Colón of heavily armed groups, possibly with ties to Mexican drug cartels. The year's violent crime figures showed a worsening situation in the country, though government officials said the worst was focused in the north, where drug gangs were fighting for territory. The government said the homicide rate had swollen to 77 per 100,000 in 2010, totaling 6,236 violent deaths that year.

Spurred into action by Lobo's more energetic attempts to reconcile the nation to the ouster of Zelaya, the congress in January 2011 approved a measure by a vote of 103–25 to reform the 1983 constitution to make it easier for referendums and plebiscites to be held over issues concerning presidential reelection and term limits. The legislature approved the constitutional change a second time in February, a step required by law. The FNRP rejected the constitutional reform on the grounds that major changes could only be accomplished by convening a constituent constitutional assembly.

In March 2011 the criminal charges brought against former President Zelaya, who was ousted from office for attempting to hold such a referendum, were annulled by the Supreme Court, except those related to financial corruption and embezzlement. The right-wing judges who constituted the court had for months refused to remove any of the charges they had previously instituted. Zelaya remained in exile in the Dominican Republic, saying he would not return to Honduras until all charges were dropped. In early May the Honduran court of appeals annulled the final set of charges, and the prosecutors said they would not appeal the decision; this last action cleared the way for Zelaya's return. A nine-point agreement between President Lobo and Zelaya, brokered by the presidents of Venezuela and Colombia, was reached in Cartagena, Colombia; that spelled out the former president's right to return and paved the way for his arrival in Tegucigalpa and repatriation on May 28. The agreement also contained guarantees given by the Lobo administration to make progress on human rights issues and to hold a constituent assembly.

The Honduran Truth and Reconciliation Commission, set up by Lobo to investigate the 2009 ouster of Zelaya, released its 500-page report in July 2011. The commissioners concluded that Zelaya's removal amounted to an illegal coup d'état but that the former president was at least partially to blame for it, as his insistence on holding a public survey on a possible constituent assembly pressed more conservative state institutions into action. They also faulted the Honduran constitution for neither having a mechanism for removing a sitting president nor giving the congress the power to impeach him. The commissioners recommended that the constitution be amended to provide proper channels for the removal of a president who is acting extraconstitutionally.

In August 2011 the congress approved the flagship initiative under the Lobo presidency, a "model cities" project that would create sophisticated free trade zone–like administrative regions in the likeness of places like Hong Kong to facilitate economic development. The cities were envisioned to have their own local laws and fiscal autonomy but to be subject to the Honduran constitution on issues concerning defense, foreign relations, and electoral rules. Critics said there was a lack of transparency in the creation of the Special Development Regions (*Regiones Especiales de Desarrollo*) and worried that large pieces of Honduran land could be sold off to foreign actors.

In a move toward reclaiming control of the government, the FNRP formed an official political party, the Freedom and Refoundation Party (Libre) in November 2011. Under the banner of resistance to the Lobo government, Libre began its political mobilization in an effort to contest the upcoming presidential election.

In January 2012, the National Congress passed a law establishing the Commission of the Reform of Public Security. This commission is responsible for designing and implementing a series of comprehensive reforms of all institutions within public security. The primary focus of the commission is to implement the systematic debugging of the national police, but it is also authorized to begin the process of purging officials from the judiciary and public prosecutor's office to ensure justice for all the citizens of Honduras.

On September 4, 2012, president of the National Congress, Juan Orlando Hernandez, announced that an agreement had been reached to begin the first of three model cities. The Commission for the Promotion of Public-Private Alliances (COALIANZA), the government organization overseeing the model cities project, claimed that the project will create 95,000 jobs by 2015. On September 7, 14 opposition groups filed a legal challenge to the project, claiming it was unconstitutional and a violation of sovereignty.

As the country's struggle with crime increased, congress approved legislation easing the use of phone tapping by authorities in February 2013. President Lobo conducted a reshuffle of the national security team in April (see Political background, above).

After years of negotiations, congress agreed upon provisions of a measure to strengthen and clarify the presidential impeachment process in January 2013. The legislation was overwhelmingly approved on March 20 with 110 of 128 votes, as the main opposition PL strongly supported it. Zelaya's Libre party opposed the measure on the grounds that it should be decided by constitutional tribunal, rather than by the PN-dominated congress.

POLITICAL PARTIES

Government Parties:

National Party (*Partido Nacional*—PN). Created in 1923 as an expression of national unity after a particularly chaotic period, the PN is a right-wing party with close ties to the military. While traditionally dominated by rural landowning interests, it has, in recent years, supported programs of internal reform and favors Central American integration. Factionalism within the PN was evidenced in the wake of November 1982 balloting for the party executive, former president Gen. Juan Melgar Castro accusing the *oficialista* faction, led by former president Ricardo Zúñiga, of perpetrating a "worthless farce." In July 1983 two separate PN conventions were held, and three presidential candidates were nominated in 1985. Rafael Leonardo Callejas, supported by most of the party, led all contenders in the 1985 balloting with 43 percent of the total votes. However, the other two PN candidates garnered less than 2 percent each. As a result, under existing electoral procedure, the presidency was awarded to PL, whose nominees had collectively obtained a 51 percent vote share. The PN quickly reached a power-sharing agreement with the PL, but Callejas, after declaring the accord's commitments no longer binding, announced in January 1987 that the PN would move into "more critical" opposition. The PN won the 1989 presidential race with a slight majority of the popular vote but lost in 1993 under the candidacy of former Supreme Court President Oswaldo Ramos Soto. As in the case of the PL, the party contains a number of internal factions.

In the 1997 election the PN legislative delegation declined by 1, to 54, although César CASTELLANOS narrowly defeated his PL opponent to win the Tegucigalpa mayoralty. Castellanos, considered a potential presidential candidate, was killed in a helicopter crash in late 1998.

In November 2001 PN candidate Ricardo Maduro won the presidency with a 53 percent vote share, although the party failed to secure a legislative majority. During the 2005 presidential elections, Porfirio ("Pepe") Lobo Sosa received 46.2 percent of the vote, finishing second to the PL's Manuel Zelaya. The PN also dropped to second in 2005's legislative balloting and has since cooperated intermittently in the passage of PL-sponsored legislation. Capitalizing on public frustration with the ruling party, the PN led thousands in a Tegucigalpa march aimed at pressuring the government to control rising crime rates in April 2007.

PN members of congress twice abstained from voting on Honduras's accession to two Venezuelan organizations, including the ALBA trade group. The party did not want to appear to be blocking the country from receiving benefits for the poor from the two organizations, but since the PN represents Honduras's conservative and business interests, it sought to ensure that that it was viewed as not having a role in the agreements.

In 2008 then party president Lobo was named the PN's presidential candidate for the 2009 election. To attract more liberal voters, Lobo softened his platform by naming education, social issues, and job creation his top issues, abandoning the tough anti-crime stance he had campaigned on in his failed bid for the presidency in 2005.

In the November 2009 legislative elections the PN won 55.5 percent of the vote and wrested control from the PL. It increased its representation in the legislature by 16 with its win of 71 seats. Across the country, the PN also won 17 of 18 departments and more than half of Honduras's 298 municipalities.

Seeking to strengthen its position further ahead of the 2013 general elections, the PN entered into talks with the PDCH in March 2011 on forming an electoral alliance. The two groups already shared a long and productive working relationship that saw PDCH members in high-level positions during the Lobo administration. Juan Orlando HERNÁNDEZ Alvarado, the president of the National Congress, secured the nomination in November 18, 2012, elections, narrowly defeating Ricardo ALVAREZ, who also claimed victory.

Leaders: Porfirio ("Pepe") LOBO Sosa (President of the Republic); Ricardo Antonio ALVAREZ Arias (President of the Party), Carlos Áfrico MADRID Hart (Vice President of the Party); Ricardo MADURO Joest, Ricardo ZÚÑIGA Augustinus, Gen. Juan Alberto MELGAR Castro, Rafael Leonardo CALLEJAS Romero (Former Presidents of the Republic); Juan Orlando HERNÁNDEZ Alvarado (Secretary General, President of the National Congress, and 2013 presidential candidate).

Democratic Unification Party (*Partido Unificación Democrática*—PUD). The PUD was launched in September 1993 by the merger of four left-wing groups drawn, at least in part, from demobilized elements of the Honduran Revolutionary Movement (*Movimiento Revolucionario Hondureño*—MRH), the Honduran Revolutionary Party (*Partido Revolucionario Hondureño*—PRH), the Morazanista Liberation Party (*Partido Morazanista de Liberación*—PML), the Party for the Transformation of Honduras (*Partido para la Transformación de Honduras*—PTH), and the Patriotic Renovation Party (*Partido Renovación Patriótica*—PRP), which now included the Communist Party of Honduras (*Partido Comunista de Honduras*—PCH), led by Mario SOSA Navarro. In its 1994 legalization of the new formation, the National Congress ruled that the PUD could not engage in electoral activity until 1997. In late 1994 the party called for "the overthrow of [President] Reina and his family" as a means of averting "total disaster." Its founder secured an assembly seat in 1997, while PL defector Filiberto ISAULA captured the mayoralty of La Paz, the stronghold of former PL president Suazo Córdova. It won five assembly seats in 2001, all of which were retained in 2005. Party leader Juan Ángel Almendares Bonilla won 1.5 percent of the vote in the concurrent presidential election.

César Ham, who supported President Zelaya's controversial proposal for a constitutional referendum, received the party's bid as its 2009 presidential candidate. The PUD opposed the 2009 coup that ousted President Zelaya.

In the November 2009 general election, Ham received 1.7 percent of the popular vote, placing last out of the field of five candidates. PUD legislative candidates won 3.1 percent of votes, securing 4 seats, 1 less than the party had previously held. After the election, Ham was appointed by President Lobo as director of the National Institute of Agriculture. The party's sympathies fell with the FNRP, the group led by Zelaya that sought official recognition as a political party and pressed for a constituent assembly to be held. The FNRP reciprocated the PUD's support, and in March 2011 FNRP members attended the party's annual general meeting. In May 2013 the PUD formalized an alliance with the FAPER (*Frente Amplio Político Electoral en Resistencia*), which was formed in 2012, and backed Andrés PAVÓN in the November elections.

Leaders: César David Adolfo HAM Peña (President of the Party and 2009 presidential candidate), Suyapa ALEMAN (Vice President), Andrés PAVÓN (2013 presidential candidate).

Christian Democratic Party of Honduras (*Partido Demócrata Cristiano de Honduras*—PDCH). The PDCH, a small centrist party with some trade union support, was accorded legal recognition by the Melgar Castro government in December 1977. The action was reversed in November 1978 after complaints by the PN that the PDCH had broken the electoral law by receiving funds from abroad. The party was permitted to contest the 1981 election, at which it ran fourth, with 1.6 percent of the vote. In 1985 it barely secured the 1.5 percent vote share needed to maintain registration; in 1997 it drew only 1.25 percent. Its legislative representation rose from two seats to three in 2001 and to four in 2005. The PDCH 2005 presidential candidate, Juan Ramón Martínez, won 1.4 percent of the vote.

Labor leader Felicito Ávila was nominated as the party's presidential candidate for the 2009 elections. The party opposed the constitutional referendum proposed by President Zelaya in 2009 on the grounds that it was illegal.

Ávila finished fourth with 1.8 percent of the vote in the November 29, 2009, presidential election. The PDCH secured five seats in congress in concurrent legislative elections. Based on agreement on a number of governance issues, the party announced in March 2011 that it had begun discussing an alliance with the ruling PN for the general elections in 2013. Despite reports that the party sought an alliance with the PN in early 2013, the PDCH nominated its own presidential candidate Orle Aníbal SOLÍS Meraz in May.

Leaders: Orle Aníbal SOLÍS Meraz (2013 presidential candidate), Felicito ÁVILA Ordoñez (President of the Party and 2009 presidential candidate), Lucas Evangelisto AGUILERA (Vice President of the Party), Carlos Andino BENÍTEZ, Elsa MARINA, Marco Antonio REYES (Secretary General).

Innovation and Unity Social Democratic Party (*Partido Innovación y Unidad Social Demócrata*—PINU-SD). Another centrist group, PINU was granted legal status in 1977. It ran third in the 1981 balloting, although securing only 2.5 percent of the vote, and was fourth in 1985 with 1.9 percent. In mid-1986 the party announced that it had become a social democratic formation, although several other groups indicated that they intended to seek formal recognition under the rubric, including one launched the following October as the PSDH. The party increased its legislative representation from two seats to three in 1997 and to four in 2001, only two of which were retained in 2005. PINU-SD's 2005 presidential candidate, Carlos Sosa Coello, received 1 percent of the vote.

The party had adopted the PINU-SD designation as of 2008. As a minority party, it most often has supported the PL in congress.

In February 2009, 46-year-old union leader Bernard Martinez was nominated as the first black presidential candidate in the country's history. He received 1.9 percent of ballots in the November presidential election, finishing a distant third. The party won three seats in concurrent legislative elections.

On March 17, 2013, the party unanimously nominated party president Jorge AGUILAR Paredes to be the PINU-SD candidate in the November 2013 presidential elections.

Leaders: Jorge AGUILAR Paredes (President and 2013 presidential candidate), Rosa Esther LOVO (Vice President), Bernard MARTINEZ Valerio (2009 presidential candidate), Carlos SOSA Coello (2005 presidential candidate), Olban VALLADARES Ordoñéz (1993, 1997, and 2001 presidential candidate).

Liberal Party (*Partido Liberal*—PL). Tracing its political ancestry to 1890, the PL is an urban-based, center-right grouping that has historically favored social reform, democratic political standards, and Central American integration. With the active support of a social-democratic faction, Alipo (below), it secured an impressive victory over the Nationalists in the 1981 balloting, winning the presidency and a clear majority in the National Congress. Following the inauguration of President Suazo Córdova in January 1982, Alipo's influence waned, while the non-*alipista* group split into an "old guard" *rodista* faction (named after former Liberal leader Modesto Rodas Alvarado), composed primarily of traditionally antimilitarist conservatives, and a presidential faction (*suazocordovistas*), encompassing right-wing technocrats with close links to the business community and the armed forces. The latter cleavage resulted in the president's loss of legislative support in early 1985 and the generation of a major constitutional crisis (see Political background, above).

One of four PL candidates, José Azcona del Hoyo, with partial *rodista* and Alipo support, won the presidency in 1985 without the backing of Suazo Córdova, who, with the remaining *rodistas,* supported Oscar Mejía Arellano. In 1987 rightist Carlos Flores Facussé, a strong supporter of U.S. policy, was elected PL president and in 1989 was runner-up to the PN's Rafael Leonardo Callejas for the national presidency, a position that he won in 1997. After losing to the *nacionalistas* in 2001, the PL regained power in the legislature in 2005, but did not gain an overall majority. In concurrent presidential balloting, former minister of the Honduran Social Investment Fund, Manuel Zelaya, a wealthy rancher and logging magnate, was elected by only a 3.7 percent margin. He had campaigned on a platform of government openness and a slogan of "citizen power," which stressed a more responsive government and wider participation in civil society. Under Zelaya, a former three-term congressman, the PL shifted from center-right to center-left as a result of a more socialist agenda. His decision in 2008 to align with President Chávez's ALBA trade organization pulled the country closer to Venezuela, Cuba, Bolivia, and Nicaragua and caused major rifts in the PL, which traditionally had favored closer U.S. ties. The party subsequently was divided between those who supported or opposed the president's move to join ALBA.

In the run-up to the 2009 presidential election, Zelaya and party stalwart Roberto Micheletti, president of the National Congress, reportedly joined forces to prevent Vice President Elvin Santos from running in the party's primary. The electoral commission ruled late in the process that Santos was ineligible since he had temporarily served as commander-in-chief during his vice presidency, thus making him subject to the constitutional ban on presidential reelection. The PL subsequently nominated Mauricio VILLEDA of the "Elvincista movement" (Movimiento Elvincista, which backed former vice president Elvin Santos) as its candidate for the primary election, and Santos resigned as vice president to pursue his presidential candidacy. Villeda was widely accepted as a stand-in for Santos. Villeda subsequently backed out, clearing the way for Santos, who defeated Micheletti in the primary to become the party's flag bearer.

Zelaya's push in 2009 to rewrite the country's constitution provoked much opposition from within his own party, as well as from other branches of government, and was among the factors that ultimately led to his ouster. Following a bloodless coup on June 28, 2009, and Zelaya's exile to Costa Rica, it was Micheletti, one of Zelaya's fiercest critics, who, as president of congress, ascended to the presidency of the republic, in accordance with the constitutional order of succession.

During the controversial general election in November 2009, Santos placed a distant second with 38 percent of the vote and left the party shortly thereafter. The PL also lost control of the legislature, securing a total of 45 seats. It gave up 17 seats, mainly to its chief rival, the PN. Former President Zelaya was officially expelled from the PL in June 2011, the party saying the decision was made because he was organizing another party under the FNRP banner and attempting to spread socialism in Honduras. The party experienced serious internal strife in the years after the 2009 coup, and several factions formed that either embraced the actions that led to Zelaya's removal or tried to distance themselves from it. Among those attempting to take the PL's flag for primaries before the 2013 elections were Mauricio Villeda, son of the former president and former running mate of Elvin Santos, who campaigned on a platform of being less stained by the 2009 coup than Micheletti. Villeda secured the party's presidential nomination in November 2012 voting. In September 2013 ten party deputies faced disciplinary action for voting to support Oscar CHINCHILLA's nomination against the party line. Santos returned to the party in support of Villeda later that month.

Leaders: Mauricio VILLEDA (2013 presidential candidate), Roberto MICHELETTI Bain (President of the Party and former Provisional President of the Republic), Elvin Ernesto SANTOS (2009 presidential candidate), Bill O'Neill Santos BRITO (Secretary General).

Other Parties and Groups:

Freedom and Refoundation (*Libertad y Refundacion*—Libre). The Libre party was established in November 2011 supporting former president Zelaya. The party was established by the National Popular Resistance Front (FNRP) and is largely a manifestation of the existing FNRP structure. In November 2012 balloting Xiomara CASTRO de Zelaya, the wife of the former president, secured the Libre nomination for the 2013 presidential election.

Leader: Xiomara CASTRO de Zelaya (2013 presidential candidate).

National Popular Resistance Front (*Frente Nacional de Resistencia Popular*—FNRP). The FNRP coalesced from a number of protest groups in the wake of the 2009 ouster of President Zelaya. It consisted of workers' organizations and other grassroots groups, all with the aim of promoting a national constituent assembly to rewrite the constitution and securing the return of former president Zelaya.

The group organized a number of mass protests against Zelaya's removal, and, after the election of Porfirio Lobo, in protest of alleged human rights abuses. The FNRP also reported violence against its members, with more than 30 members killed after Zelaya's ouster.

The group, which did not recognize the current government as legitimate, called on the Lobo administration to create the conditions necessary for Zelaya to return to Honduras and participate in the political process, but in October 2010 it refused to participate in a dialogue at the invitation of the government. It was reported that the group was taking steps to be recognized as a political party.

One of its leaders, Carlos Reyes, was an independent candidate in the 2009 presidential elections but dropped out in protest over failed efforts to reinstate Zelaya. As part of the agreement that returned Zelaya to the country in May 2011, the government agreed to recognize the FNRP as a legitimate political movement and to guarantee the holding of a constituent assembly. The group intended to register as a party before the 2013 general elections. Zelaya, meanwhile, said he hoped to build an alliance between the officially recognized FNRP and his former PL. The group began calling itself **The Broad Front of Popular Resistance** (*el Frente Amplio de Resistencia Popular*—FARP) in June, though its leaders had not yet filed their nominations with the election authorities, and continues to be known as the FNRP. The group formally organized as a party in November 2011 (see Libre, above).

Leaders: José Manuel (Mel) ZELAYA Rosales (Coordinator General and Former President of the Republic), Juan BARAHONA (Deputy National Coordinator), Edgardo CASAÑA (Secretary General).

Wide Movement for Dignity and Justice (*Movimiento Amplio por la Dignidad y la Justicia*—MADJ). Founded in late May 2008 with the support of prosecutors, social groups, workers' organizations, and religious figures, the MADJ represents a range of civil society constituencies intent on curbing the widespread corruption plaguing Honduras, particularly at official levels, and safeguarding natural resources as well as worker and human rights. Led by the president of the Association of Prosecutors, Víctor Fernández, leading party members held a hunger strike against corruption from April 7 to May 14, 2008, based in a "dignity tent" located near the Congress.

In 2010 the MADJ joined a number of Honduran organizations to create the **Strategic Group EPU-Honduras** (*Grupo Estratégico EPU-Honduras*) to advocate in front of the UN Human Rights Council against recent human rights violations in the country. The MADJ joined the FNRP in calling for a constituent assembly in 2010 and early 2011 to reform the Honduran constitution but issued a statement imploring the other group not to lose focus by putting its energy behind eventually becoming a political party.

Leader: Víctor FERNÁNDEZ.

Patriotic Action (*Acción Patriótica*—AP). The AP was launched in March 2006 by a group of left-leaning politicians and trade union leaders who felt that the PUD had failed to live up to its promise to end the "political duopoly" of the PL and PN.

Following the 2009 coup, labor leader Israel Salinas became one of the main supporters of ousted president Manuel Zelaya. Along with other labor leaders, he threatened general strikes and resistance at border crossings in late July. Salinas, the president of the United Confederation of Honduran Workers, died in an airplane crash on February 14, 2011.

Leader: Agapito ROBLEDA (PUD Dissident).

Socialist Party Morazánico of Honduras (*Partido Socialista Hondureño Morazánico*—PSHM) José Leonidas Martínez and Santos Eliodoro Briones founded the PSHM, a new leftist grouping, in March 2008. The group was active in the demonstrations against the 2009 coup and strongly supported the reinstatement of President Manuel Zelaya. The group called the 2009 general election a "farce" and posted videos on its website of what it called government repression and police brutality in San Pedro Sula on voting day.

Leaders: José Leonidas MARTÍNEZ (Secretary General), Santos Eliodoro BRIONES.

For more information on the **Popular Liberal Alliance** (*Alianza Liberal del Pueblo*—Alipo) see the 2010 *Handbook.*

Extremist Groups:

For details on these groups, which have been inactive since the 1990s, see previous editions of the *Handbook*: **the Honduran**

Revolutionary Movement (*Movimiento Revolucionario Hondureño*—MRH); the **Cinchonero Popular Liberation Movement** (*Movimiento Popular de Liberación Cinchonero*—MPLC), led by Raúl LÓPEZ; the **Lorenzo Zelaya People's Revolutionary Front** (*Frente Popular Revolucionario–Lorenzo Zelaya*—FPR-LZ), led by Efraín DUARTE; and the **Morazanista Front of Honduran Liberation** (*Frente Morazanista de Liberación Hondureña*—FMLH), led by Gustavo GARCÍA España, Fernando LOPEZ, and Octavio PEREZ (both of the latter names are reportedly aliases).

LEGISLATURE

Under the 1982 constitution the former Congress of Deputies has been replaced by a **National Congress** (*Congreso Nacional*) that consists of 128 members elected on a proportional basis for four-year terms.

In the most recent election of November 29, 2009, the seat distribution was as follows: the National Party, 71; Liberal Party, 45 seats; Christian Democratic Party of Honduras, 5; Democratic Unification Party, 4; and Innovation and Unity Social Democratic Party, 3.

President: Juan Orlando HERNÁNDEZ Alvarado.

CABINET

[as of November 19, 2013] (*See headnote.*)

President	Porfirio Lobo Sosa (PN)
First Vice President	Maria Antonieta Guillen de Bogran (PN) [f]
Second Vice President	Samuel Armando Reyes (PN)
Third Vice President	Victor Hugo Barnica (PN)
Ministers	
Agriculture and Livestock	Jacobo Regalado Weizemblut (PL)
Culture, Arts, and Sports	Tulio Mariano Gonzales (PN)
Defense	Marlon Pascua Cerrato (PN)
Education	Marlon Escoto
Family Support	Maria Elena Zepeda (PN) [f]
Finance	Wilfredo Ceratto (PN)
Foreign Affairs	Mireya Aguero [f]
Human Rights	Miguel Ángel Bonilla González (PN)
Industry and Commerce	Adonys Lavaide
Interior and Justice	Carlos Áfrico Madrid Hart (PN)
Labor and Social Security	Felicito Avila Ordoñez (PDCH)
National Institute for Women's Affairs (INAM)	María Antonieta Botto (PN) [f]
Natural Resources and Environment	Rigoberto Cuellar Cruz (PL)
Planning and International Cooperation	Julio Raudales (PL)
Presidency	Maria Antonieta Guillen de Bogrlan (PN) [f]
Public Health	Arturo Bendaña Pinel (PN)
Public Works, Transportation and Housing	Miguel Angel Gamez (PN)
Security	Arturo Corrales (PDCH)
Social Development	Hilda Rosario Hernández Alvarado (PN) [f]
Tourism	Nelly Karina Jerez Caballero (PN) [f]
Directors	
Honduran Fund for Social Investment	Miguel Edgardo Martinez Pineda (PN)
National Institute of Agriculture	Cesar David Ham Peña (PUD)

[f] = female

INTERGOVERNMENTAL REPRESENTATION

Ambassador to the U.S.: Jorge Ramon HERNANDEZ-ALCERRO.

U.S. Ambassador to Honduras: Lisa KUBISKE.

Permanent Representative to the UN: Mary E. FLORES.

IGO Memberships (Non-UN): IADB, ICC, IOM, NAM, OAS, WTO.

HUNGARY

Hungary
Magyarország

Political Status: Independent kingdom created in 1000; republic proclaimed in 1946; Communist People's Republic established August 20, 1949; pre-Communist name revived as one of a number of constitutional changes approved on October 18, 1989.

Area: 35,919 sq. mi. (93,030 sq. km).

Population: 10,355,110 (2012E—UN); 9,939,470 (2013E—U.S. Census).

Major Urban Centers (2011): BUDAPEST (1,740,000), Debrecen (208,000), Szeged (168,000), Miskolc (168,000), Pécs (156,000), Györ (131,000).

Official Language: Hungarian.

Monetary Unit: Forint (official rate November 1, 2013: 220.58 forints = $1US).

President: János ÁDER; elected (as the candidate of the Federation of Young Democrats–Hungarian Civic Alliance and the Christian Democratic People's Party [FiDeSz-MPP]) in first-round balloting by the National Assembly on May 2, 2010, sworn in for a five-year term on May 2 and assumed office on May 10, succeeding Pál SCHMITT (FiDeSz-MPP).

Prime Minister: Viktor ORBÁN (Federation of Young Democrats–Hungarian Civic Alliance); nominated by the president to form a government following the legislative elections of April 11 and 25, 2010, and elected by the National Assembly on May 29 and sworn in as head of a two-party coalition on the same day in succession to Gordon BAJNAI (nonparty).

THE COUNTRY

Masters for over 1,000 years of the fertile plain extending on either side of the middle Danube, the Hungarians have long regarded their country as the eastern outpost of Western Europe in cultural pattern, religious affiliation, and political structure. More than 90 percent of the present Hungarian population is of Magyar origin; Roma (Gypsies), Germans, Southern Slavs (Croats, Serbs, and Slovenes), Slovaks, and Romanians are the main ethnic minorities. Despite more than four decades of Communist-mandated antireligious policies from the mid-1940s until the late 1980s, about 37 percent of the population identified as Roman Catholic in the 2011 census; there are also Protestant (13 percent), Eastern Orthodox, and Jewish adherents. In 2007 the employment rate for women was 51 percent, although their pay was 11 percent lower, on average, than men's, at a rate below the European Union (EU) average.

Although the Hungarian economy was traditionally dependent on the agricultural sector, agriculture now accounts for less than 3 percent of GDP. However, the country remains a net food exporter, with one of the largest agricultural trade surpluses in Eastern Europe. Industry contributed 37 percent of GDP in 2010. In addition to processed foods, leading industrial products, almost all of which require imported raw materials (iron ore, petroleum, copper, and crude fibers), are machinery, transportation equipment, electrical and electronic equipment

(including computers), chemicals, and textiles. Bauxite, coal, and natural gas are the chief mineral resources.

Largely because of the collapse of trade with other ex-Communist states, Hungary's GDP fell by 20 percent from 1989 through 1993, and both inflation and unemployment registered in double digits. Growth resumed in 1994 and averaged 4.8 percent annually in 1997–2000, while unemployment and consumer price inflation declined by half over the decade. For the 1990s as a whole, Hungary led the region in direct foreign investment, and trade burgeoned, especially with the EU. Led by Germany, EU countries now purchase three-fourths of Hungary's exports and provide two-thirds of its imports.

Hungary was described in a 2000 report from the International Monetary Fund (IMF) as "in the vanguard of the transition economies" seeking EU accession. However, budget deficits began to increase in the early 2000s, prompting the government (under EU pressure) to implement austerity measures. Overall, the EU considered the economic progress of 2002–2003 sufficient to include Hungary among the ten new countries admitted to the EU on May 1, 2004.

Solid growth (4 percent) was achieved in both 2004 and 2005 on the strength of increased exports and rising investment. However, the IMF and the EU warned that the budget deficit and public debt remained unacceptably high. In early 2006, the government announced comprehensive tax increases and budget cuts to reduce the budget deficit (then running at about 10.7 percent of GDP annually). The EU subsequently extended the deadline from 2008 to 2009 for Hungary to meet the EU standard (an annual budget deficit no more than 3 percent of GDP) that is necessary for Hungary's planned adoption of the euro as its official currency. Although the budget initiatives prompted major protest demonstrations, they were endorsed by the IMF.

Growing political resistance to further spending cuts threatened to derail achievement of the economic goals necessary for euro adoption. In March 2008 the European Central Bank issued a report urging Hungary to press ahead with economic reforms, however unpopular, if it expected to join the eurozone and have a competitive market economy.

As the global economic recession descended in the second half of 2008, Hungary quickly appeared among the hardest hit in Europe, its unprecedented growth collapsing to a GDP uptick of just 0.5 percent in 2008 and a decline of 6.3 percent in 2009. Of particular impact to the economy was the dramatic drop in the value of the forint, which hit an historic low relative to the euro in October. A boom in foreign currency borrowing, especially of low-interest loans in Swiss francs, exposed the country to a high risk of default as the forint tumbled in value. Some 80 percent of the assets in Hungary's banks were foreign owned. Hungary responded by imposing a series of extreme fiscal constraints in order to qualify for loan packages offered by the European Central Bank, IMF, World Bank, and the EU. However, the unpopular measures, which curbed social benefits, led to the resignation of Prime Minister Ferenc GYURCSÁNY in March (see Current issues, below) and prevented Hungary from offering the kind of stimulus packages available in other EU countries. GDP growth was renewed at 1.2 percent in 2010 and 1.7 percent in 2011. Recent government austerity measures have contributed to an unemployment rate at 11.5 percent in February 2012. Predicted GDP growth for 2012 is 0 percent. In March 2013 Prime Minister Viktor ORBÁN stated that the government did not anticipate joining the eurozone until 2020 at the earliest.

GOVERNMENT AND POLITICS

Political background. Part of the Austro-Hungarian Empire, the former Kingdom of Hungary lost two-thirds of its territory (including Transylvania) and the bulk of its non-Magyar population at the end of World War I under the 1920 Treaty of Trianon. A brief Communist dictatorship under Béla KUN in 1919 was followed by 25 years of right-wing authoritarian government under Adm. Miklós HORTHY, who bore the title of regent. Having regained Northern Transylvania from Romania under the 1940 Vienna Award, Hungary joined Germany in the war against the Soviet Union in June 1941 and was occupied by Soviet forces in late 1944. Under a definitive peace treaty with the Allied Powers signed in February 1947, Hungary reverted to its 1920 borders.

Communists obtained only 17 percent of the vote in a free election held in November 1945, but with Soviet backing they assumed key posts in the coalition government that proclaimed the Hungarian Republic on February 1, 1946. Seizing de facto control in May–June 1947, the Communists proceeded to liquidate most opposition parties and to establish a dictatorship led by Mátyás RÁKOSI, formally establishing the Hungarian People's Republic in August 1949.

The initial years of the People's Republic were marked by purges and the systematic elimination of domestic opposition. In the post-Stalin era, however, gradual liberalization led to the outbreak in October 1956 of a popular revolutionary movement, the formation of a coalition government under Imre NAGY, and the announcement on November 1 of Hungary's withdrawal from the Warsaw Pact. Massive Soviet military force was employed to crush the revolt, and a pro-Soviet regime headed by János KÁDÁR was installed on November 4.

Concerned primarily with consolidating its position, the Kádár government was initially rigid and authoritarian. However, the 1962 congress of the Hungarian Socialist Workers' Party (*Magyar Szocialista Munkáspárt*—MSzMP) marked the beginning of a trend toward pragmatism in domestic policy that was exemplified by the implementation of a program known as the New Economic Mechanism, which allowed for decentralization, more flexible management strategies, incentives for efficiency, and expanded production of consumer goods. At the same time, Hungary strictly adhered to Soviet pronouncements in foreign affairs, as most dramatically demonstrated by the participation of Hungarian troops in the Warsaw Pact invasion of Czechoslovakia in August 1968.

The retreat from Communist domination commenced somewhat earlier in Hungary than elsewhere in Eastern Europe. In May 1988 Kádár was replaced as party general secretary by Károly GRÓSZ, who had been premier since June 1987. Grósz was succeeded as premier in November by Miklós NÉMETH. In early 1989 the National Assembly legalized freedom of assembly and association, and in mid-March 75,000 demonstrators were permitted to assemble in Budapest to demand free elections and the removal of Soviet troops. On May 2, acting on behalf of the Németh government, security forces began dismantling the barbed-wire fence along the border with Austria, and on May 13, five days after Kádár had been forced into retirement from his ceremonial post as party president, talks began with opposition leaders on transition to a multiparty system. On June 16 the martyred Imre Nagy was formally "rehabilitated" by means of a public reburial attended by some 300,000 persons. On October 7 the MSzMP renounced Marxism and renamed itself the Hungarian Socialist Party (*Magyar Szocialista Párt*—MSzP). On October 23 the non-Communist speaker of the National Assembly, Mátyás SZÜRÖS, became acting president of the republic in the wake of legislative action that abolished the Presidential Council, purged the constitution of its Stalinist elements, and paved the way for the first free elections in more than four decades.

At second-stage legislative balloting on April 8, 1990, the recently formed Hungarian Democratic Forum (*Magyar Demokrata Fórum*—MDF) won a substantial plurality of seats, and on May 3 its chair, József ANTALL, was asked to form a center-right government, consisting of the MDF, the Christian Democratic People's Party (*Kereszténydemokrata*

Néppárt—KDNP), and the Independent Smallholders' Party (*Független Kisgazda Párt*—FKgP), that was installed on May 23. Earlier, on May 2, the new parliament had named a noted former dissident, Arpád GÖNCZ, to the post of acting state president. A referendum on direct election of the president (favored by 86 percent of those participating) failed on July 29 because of insufficient turnout, and on August 3 the assembly elected Göncz to a regular five-year term.

In 1991–1992 the Antall government secured the passage of legislation providing compensation for property expropriated during the Fascist and Communist eras, as well as for individuals killed, imprisoned, or deported for political reasons between 1939 and 1989. In addition, an amendment was approved in October 1993 allowing the prosecution of certain crimes committed by state authorities during the 1956 Hungarian uprising.

In February 1992 the FKgP withdrew from the ruling coalition because its blueprints for the restoration of land to pre-Communist owners had not become government policy. However, three-quarters of the 44 FKgP parliamentary deputies continued to support the government, initially as the FKgP "Historical Section" (*Történelmi Tagozat*). Antall carried out a controversial ministerial reshuffle in February 1993, but the government was further weakened at midyear when a right-wing MDF faction led by István CSURKA was expelled from the party and formed the Hungarian Justice and Life Party (*Magyar Igazság és Élat Párt*—MIÉP).

The MDF sought to ensure political continuity despite Antall's early death in December 1993 at the age of 61, with succession passed to longtime heir-apparent Péter BOROSS, theretofore the interior minister. However, the change of prime minister did nothing to restore the political fortunes of the MDF, which was overwhelmingly defeated in the May 1994 general election by a resurgent MSzP led by Dr. Gyula HORN. Despite his party's commanding majority, Horn sought to dispel overseas concern about the return to power of Hungary's ex-Communists by forming a coalition with the centrist Alliance of Free Democrats (*Szabad Demokraták Szövetsége*—SzDSz).

The Horn government declared its commitment to completing its predecessor's successful privatization program, while giving priority to the investigation of alleged corruption in the disposal of state-owned assets. However, in January 1995 the highly respected László BÉKESI resigned as finance minister, claiming that promarket reform was being resisted by other ministers. In February a new finance minister, Lajos BOKROS, and a special privatization minister were appointed amid government admissions that Hungary's economic difficulties were chronic, largely because of spiraling public debt. The announcement of draconian economic austerity measures in March precipitated the resignation of two more MSzP ministers.

The Horn government also faced deep conflict over its effort to draft a new constitution to replace the much-amended Communist-era text. One area of contention was an FkgP-led effort for direct, popular election of the president, although the party's proposed referendum on the change was struck by the Constitutional Court shortly before the scheduled presidential vote in the National Assembly. On June 19, 1995, the National Assembly handed Arpád Göncz an easy victory to a second five-year term against an independent conservative nominee, Ferenc MÁDL.

In February 1996 Finance Minister Bokros resigned after his colleagues had declined to endorse the next stage of his deficit-reducing plans. However, by early 1998 the MSzP/SzDSz government was being credited with having achieved significant economic progress. In the first round of voting on May 10, the MSzP secured 32.3 percent of the vote, followed by the center-right Federation of Young Democrats–Hungarian Civic Party (*Fiatal Demokraták Szövetsége–Magyar Polgari Párt*—FiDeSz-MPP) with 28.2 percent. Following the second round on May 24, the FiDeSz-MPP emerged with a plurality of 148 seats, with the MSzP winning 134 and the SzDSz claiming only 24. Consequently, the president asked the 35-year-old FiDeSz-MPP leader, Viktor Orbán, to form a new government. After rejecting cooperation with the MSzP and the ultranationalist MIÉP, Orbán reached agreement with the MDF (with which the FiDeSz-MPP had presented joint candidates) and the FKgP. Orbán was sworn in on July 6, and the new cabinet took office on July 8.

On June 6, 2000, the National Assembly elected Ferenc Mádl as President Göncz's successor.

Somewhat earlier than expected, and with preparations for accession to the EU in mind, on December 13, 2001, President Mádl announced a National Assembly election for April 2002. Although opinion polls had forecast a repeat victory for Prime Minister Orbán, the opposition Socialists won 42.1 percent of the party-list vote in first-round balloting on April 7, compared to 41.1 percent for the FiDeSz-MPP-MDF. A leftist government composed of the MSzP and the SzDSz took office under former Socialist finance minister Péter Medgyessy on May 27.

In a national referendum on April 12, 2003, voters approved proposed accession to the EU with an 84 percent "yes" vote. (The National Assembly ratified the measure on December 15, and Hungary joined the EU with nine other new members on May 1, 2004.) However, concurrent austerity measures on the part of the government eroded support for Prime Minister Medgyessy, and the government parties fared poorly in the June 2004 European Parliament balloting. Following a dispute between Medgyessy and junior coalition partner SzDSz, Medgyessy announced his resignation on August 25 after apparently having also lost the support of his own party. He was succeeded on September 26 by the MSzP's Ferenc GYURCSÁNY, a wealthy young businessman who had been serving as minister of youth and sports.

On June 7, 2005, László SÓLYOM, who was nominated by the FiDeSz-MPSz (as the FiDeSz-MPP had been renamed [see Political Parties, below]), was elected president in the third round of balloting in the assembly. Solyom was best known for his former post as president of the Constitutional Court.

The governing coalition of the MSzP and SzDSz extended its legislative majority at the assembly balloting of April 9 and 23, 2006. Gyurcsány's government program was approved by a vote of 206–159 in the assembly on June 9, and Gyurcsány on the same day was again sworn in as prime minister to head a reshuffled MSzP/SzDSz cabinet.

Following the public's rejection of major reforms in a March 2008 referendum, Gyurcsány restructured the cabinet. He immediately dismissed health minister Agnes HORVATH and following the SzDSZ's pullout from the coalition he appointed seven new ministers in April and created a new Ministry of National Development and Economy (to replace the former Ministry of Economy and Transport); transportation became a separate ministry. The coalition remained a minority government into 2009, leading the opposition to call for a snap election (see Current issues, below). Facing open hostility from the opposition and from within his own party. Gyurcsány announced his resignation on March 21, 2009, to a party congress by saying that some regarded him as an obstacle to reform. FiDeSz's calls for early elections were backed by the president, who said that a popular vote would be the best way for Hungary to establish a stable government. After rejecting Gyurcsány's nominations for successors, senior figures in the MSzP and SzDSz settled on Gordon BAJNAI, an independent, as a consensus candidate. Bajnai demanded written guarantees from MSzP and SzDSz leaders to approve his fiscal austerity plans as a condition of his nomination. On April 14 the National Assembly passed a "constructive" vote of no confidence in Gyurcsány and formally approved Bajnai as the new prime minister, with 204 in favor and 8 abstentions. FiDeSz-MPSz boycotted the vote. Bajnai, a former economy minister, announced a new cabinet, of which six ministers were politically unaligned. Solyom formally appointed the cabinet on April 20.

In September 2006 a recording was leaked to the media of a supposedly private speech Prime Minister Gyurcsány had made to senior members of the MSzP. Among other things, Gyurcsány admitted in the speech that he had falsely claimed during the legislative campaign that Hungary's budget deficit was only 4.7 percent of GDP, contrary to estimates twice that high from the central bank and international financial institutions. Gyurcsány's acknowledgment that "we lied in the morning, we lied in the evening, and we lied at night" about economic data prompted massive street protests, most notably outside the assembly building. More than 300 people were injured during the demonstrations, and violence also broke out in October during celebrations to commemorate the 50th anniversary of the failed 1956 uprising.

The MSzP suffered major losses in the October 2006 municipal elections, with the opposition FiDeSz-MPSz and KDNP winning majorities on 18 of 19 county councils and 19 of 23 city councils. However, the government survived a no-confidence motion in October by a 207–165 vote in the assembly, and the assembly also endorsed the prime minister's budget plans in December, despite intense opposition from major sectors of the population. Another massive protest demonstration in March 2007 also appeared to threaten a government collapse, but the MSzP and SzDSz announced a new coalition agreement in July that they hoped would keep the government intact.

In an effort to improve accountability, public trust, and the economy, the governing coalition and several opposition parties agreed in August 2007 to establish an independent budget-monitoring office to ensure a predictable budget, tracking changes through political administrations, and to inform the general public about progress in meeting budget targets. Hungary had built up huge budget deficits in 2002 and 2006, resulting in the package of austerity measures that are part of the current euro convergence program.

The National Assembly also approved a major overhaul to the health care system in December 2007, replacing the ailing state-run National Healthcare Insurance Fund Administration with a quasi-private National Health Insurance Center that would provide health care through potentially dozens of health funds. The new system, part of a privatization drive that included the postal, railway, and telecommunications sectors, mandated the government's sale of 49 percent of its shares in its health care system to private industry in an attempt to reduce its public deficit. As part of the provisions, citizens would pay fees for doctor and hospital visits for the first time. However, as part of the agreement that led to the legislation's passage, the FiDeSz-MPSz arranged for these fee provisions, as well as university tuition fees, to be put to a public referendum. On March 9, 2008, in a highly symbolic referendum organized by the FiDeSz-MPSz, voters overwhelmingly censured core health care reform initiatives considered essential for Hungary's beleaguered economy. The rejection by 80 percent of voters was considered a vote of no confidence in the coalition leadership.

Soon after the vote, Gyurcsány dismissed health minister Agnes HORVATH, prompting further coalition turmoil. The Horvath dismissal was the final blow to a steadily deteriorating relationship between the governing parties over the pace and content of economic reforms. SzDSz announced at the end of March it would pull out of the coalition and remove its three cabinet ministers.

The MSzP's minority government was tasked with unilaterally discerning how to realize increasingly unpopular economic reform goals while fending off calls by leading opposition party FiDeSz-MPSz to hold early elections. Opposition parties stood against any plan that did not sizably reduce spending, while members of Gyurcsány's own party objected to reducing social benefits. Gyurcsány sought outside financial support from the IMF, World Bank, and EU in October 2009, but the $33.7 billion in loans were conditioned on Hungary reducing its 2009 budget deficit to below the EU mandatory cap of 3 percent of GDP. Gyurcsány reduced the capital gains tax and cut a host of popular social programs, winning praise from the European Commission but obtaining no further support from Western European leaders now concerned about domestic economic problems. Additionally, Hungary's call for fast-track membership into the Eurozone as a means to rid itself of the unstable forint was rebuffed. (See this entry in the 2013 *Handbook* for details on Gyurcsány's economic policies in this period.)

Gyurcsány's resignation brought little immediate change in economic policy. Bajnai entered office in March promising to continue advancing economic austerity measures, including $2.7 billion in spending cuts. In late June the parliament passed a tax reform bill to enter into force in 2010 that shifted the overall tax burden from businesses to individuals as a means to improve investor sentiment and bring down debt. Additionally, the National Assembly passed a revised plan to meet a deficit target of 3.9 percent in 2009 and 3.8 percent in 2010.

The alliance of the FiDeSz-MPSz and the KDNP won a landslide victory in balloting for the National Assembly in April 2010. Former president Viktor Orbán of the FiDeSz-MPSz formed a coalition government with the KDNP on May 29.

On June 29, 2010, the National Assembly elected Pál SCHMITT as President Sólyom's successor. Nominated by the FiDeSz-MPSz, Schmitt won with 263 votes to 59 votes for András BALOGH, who was nominated by the MSzP. Schmitt resigned on April 2, 2012, following allegations that he committed plagiarism in his doctoral thesis and the decision by Semmelweis University to withdraw his degree. Speaker of the National Assembly László KÖVÉR became acting president. On May 2, 2012, the National Assembly elected János ÁDER as president. Nominated by the FiDeSz-MPSz, Áder won with 262 votes to 40 votes for Krisztina MORVAI, who was nominated by *Jobbik*. The MSzP and the LMP both boycotted the election.

Constitution and government. The constitution of 1949 (as amended in 1972) declared Hungary to be a state in which all power belonged to the working people, the bulk of the means of production was publicly owned, and the (Communist) Hungarian Socialist Workers' Party was the "leading force" in state and society. Under the October 1989 revision, Hungary is described as an "independent democratic state" adhering to "the values of both bourgeois democracy and democratic socialism." In addition, civil and human rights are protected; a multiparty parliamentary system is to be maintained; and executive, legislative, and judicial functions are separated. The former 21-member Presidential Council was replaced by an indirectly elected state president who serves as commander in chief of the armed forces and has the capacity to negotiate international agreements. Subsequently, the unicameral National Assembly approved a law on the activity and financing of political parties, prohibited parties from operating in the workplace (thus invalidating the traditional role of Communist party cells), and approved an electoral law based on a mixed system of proportional and direct representation. The judicial system is jointly administered by the Supreme Court, whose president is named by the legislature, and the ministry of justice. Below the Supreme Court are county, district, and municipal courts. A Constitutional Court was also added in 1989 as successor to a Constitutional Law Council established by the assembly five years before.

The constitution was revised again in 2011 and took effect on January 1, 2012, raising some controversy (see Current issues, below). The name of the country was changed to Hungary from the Republic of Hungary (*Magyar Köztársaság*). The preamble stressed traditional values and a Christian basis for Hungary, as well as proclaiming responsibility for "Hungarians living outside her borders." It altered executive and legislative functions to restrict the ability of the state to increase public debt, including the weakening of the Constitutional Court's oversight on budgetary matters when state debt is above 50 percent of GDP. Finally, it stipulated that issues such as family law, changes to the tax system, and state budgets could henceforth only be changed by "cardinal laws" (e.g., those passed by a two-thirds supermajority of the parliament).

On March 11, 2013, a series of amendments were passed by a 265–11 vote of parliament. The amendments limited the power of the constitutional court to review laws (including invalidating the court's decisions before 2012, eliminating them for legal precedence), required state-funded students to work in Hungary after graduation or repay tuition fees, banned electoral advertising in private media, and defined the family as a married heterosexual couple with children.

The country is administratively divided into 19 counties and 23 cities and towns of county status (including Budapest), about 200 other towns, and nearly 3,000 villages. Council members at the local levels are directly elected, while those at the county level are elected by the members of the lower-level councils. Each council elects an executive committee and a president.

Formerly pervasive censorship was relaxed in 1988, and in June 1992 a 1974 decree authorizing government supervision of radio and television was declared unconstitutional. However, the Orbán government of 1998–2002 was widely criticized for apparent efforts to control broadcasting and print media, a criticism that has been renewed since 2010. In particular, a new media law passed on December 21, 2010, created the National Media and Infocommunications Authority to regulate media content and allows for fines for violations of coverage that is "unbalanced" or has "violated human dignity." The Hungarian Constitutional Court repealed elements of the media law in November 2011 as unconstitutional. In 2012 Freedom House ranked Hungary as only "partly free" with regard to press freedom, citing a decline in the media environment created by the government's new laws.

Foreign relations. Following the failure of the 1956 revolution, Hungary faithfully followed the Soviet lead in international issues. However, relations with its closest Eastern-bloc neighbors were not always smooth (see the 2012 *Handbook*). On June 26, 1990, the National Assembly voted unanimously to suspend Hungary's participation in the Warsaw Pact and to withdraw from the alliance by late 1991.

Hungarian foreign policy throughout the 1990s pursued membership in a variety of Western European international governmental organizations, along with other members of the "Visegrád" cooperation bloc formed on February 15, 1991, including Poland and Czechoslovakia (subsequently the Czech Republic and Slovakia) Membership in Council of Europe in 1990, Organization for Economic Cooperation and Development (OECD) in 1993, and NATO's Partnership for Peace program in 1994, which reflected a larger goal of close relations with the EU. (See the entry in the 2010 *Handbook* for details on Hungary's admission to these organizations.)

Although Hungary repeatedly stated its acceptance of existing borders, its keen interest in the status of the 2.5 million ethnic Hungarians in neighboring countries caused regional strains in the post-Communist era. Despite Hungarian attempts to curb the inflow, ethnic Hungarians continued to cross the border from Transylvania in substantial numbers. The civil war in former Yugoslavia also resulted in an exodus of ethnic Hungarians from the Serbian-ruled province of Vojvodina, once part of the Austro-Hungarian Empire. Moreover, Slovakia's move to independence on January 1, 1993, increased concern in Hungary over Slovakia's ethnic Hungarian minority.

The Horn government elected in May 1994 sought to improve relations with Romania and Slovakia. In February 1995 Hungary signed the Council of Europe's new Convention on the Protection of National Minorities, and the following month it concluded a friendship and cooperation treaty with Slovakia, which guaranteed the existing border and provided formal protection for minority groups (principally ethnic Hungarians in Slovakia).

A long-negotiated treaty dealing with minority rights and other bilateral issues was signed by the Hungarian and Romanian prime ministers on September 16, 1996, in Timişoara in Romanian Transylvania, where 1.6 million ethnic Hungarians form Europe's largest nonimmigrant ethnic minority. The text represented a compromise, but, inevitably, the treaty was fiercely condemned by the nationalist parties of both countries as a capitulation. Both governments considered finalization of the treaty as an important step toward membership in the EU and the North Atlantic Treaty Organization (NATO).

On April 1, 1994, Hungary submitted an application to the EU for full membership following the coming into force of an association agreement two months earlier. In December 1997 the EU issued a formal invitation to Hungary and five other "first-wave" nations to begin discussions in March 1998 regarding membership protocols.

In January 1996 the government committed 400 Hungarian troops to the NATO-commanded International Force (IFOR) charged with implementing the Dayton Accords for Bosnia. Further important integration into Western structures was achieved in March when Hungary enrolled as a full member of the OECD.

In July 1997 NATO invited Hungary, Poland, and the Czech Republic to join the alliance in 1999, but the extreme extraparliamentary parties in Hungary continued to oppose membership. Voters approved NATO accession overwhelmingly (85 percent) in a popular referendum on November 16, and Hungary quickly submitted its formal membership application. Accession was achieved on March 12, 1999, at a ceremony in the United States, although the timing was poor for the new NATO members in view of the conflict between the alliance and Yugoslavia. The NATO military action was particularly sensitive for Hungary, since the 340,000 ethnic Hungarians resident in Vojvodina were considered possible targets of Serbian reprisals. Budapest permitted NATO planes access to Hungarian airspace for attacks on Serbia but otherwise was not involved in the campaign.

Hungary supported U.S. policy toward Iraq in 2003 and deployed 350 troops to the U.S./UK-led coalition following the fall of Saddam Hussein. However, Hungary's stance strained relations with France and Germany, and, with more than half of the Hungarian population indicating opposition to the war, the Hungarian troops were withdrawn from Iraq by the end of 2004. Hungary has also contributed to the NATO-led peacekeeping mission in Afghanistan, including 364 troops in June 2013.

Upon his installation as prime minister in 2002, Péter Medgyessy announced that EU membership would be his administration's top priority. His successor, Ferenc Gyurcsány, in 2004 moved to complete agricultural reform demanded by the EU and to pursue the fiscal policies necessary to permit Hungary to adopt the euro by 2010. (The assembly in December 2004 had ratified the proposed new EU constitution by a vote of 322–12.)

On December 17, 2007, Hungary became the first EU country to ratify the Lisbon Treaty, the successor to the failed 2005 EU constitution, tallying 325 votes and 14 abstentions in the National Assembly. (The Lisbon treaty was rejected by Ireland, tabling its adoption throughout the rest of Europe. See the Ireland entry in the 2008 *Handbook*.) On December 21 Hungary became one of nine countries in Eastern Europe to join the EU's border-free Schengen zone.

In recent years Hungary has sought to secure a more reliable stream of oil and supplies, given concerns that it was overly dependent upon Russia, which has used its energy reserves as formidable leverage in its foreign policy. Hungary, which receives 80 percent of its gas from Russia, was one of the countries most affected by gas outages in 2006 when Russia cut gas deliveries through a pipeline passing through Ukraine. In February 2008, seemingly contradicting its goal for energy diversification, Hungary signed an agreement with Russia to jointly partner the building of the "South Stream" gas pipeline through Hungary, bypassing Ukraine. Following a second dispute between Ukraine and Russia in January 2009 that resulted in gas shutoffs to Europe and the Balkans, the Hungarian gas company MOL secured a $277 million loan from the European Bank for Reconstruction and Development to build a new natural gas storage facility in Hungary. This advanced the prospects of the EU-backed Nabucco pipeline (to bring gas to Europe from Azerbaijan) by forming a consortium with Austria's OMV gas company to pump from Iraq's Kurdistan region.

In June 2009 a diplomatic spat erupted with Slovakia over that country's adoption of a language law making it a punishable offense to use minority languages, such as Hungarian, in official communication. Relations between the two countries worsened in May 2010, when the National Assembly in Hungary approved a new law that would allow ethnic Hungarians in other countries to apply for Hungarian citizenship if they spoke Hungarian and could prove Hungarian ancestry. Slovakia subsequently threatened to strip citizenship from any Slovak citizen who sought dual citizenship with Hungary. Tension increased in 2011 following the passage of the new Hungarian constitution and its provision for "responsibility" over Hungarians abroad.

Criticism by EU institutions of Hungarian government policy (see Current issues, below) led to tensions between Budapest and Brussels in 2012. Citing Hungary's failure to keep its budget deficits below 3 percent of GDP, the EU suspended 495 million euros of funding in March 2012. Orbán rejected EU criticism in a speech that month, accusing the EU of colonialism and attempting to turn Hungarians into "second-class European citizens." EU criticism continued through 2012 and was reinvigorated by the 2013 amendments to the constitution. On July 3, 2013, the European Parliament approved a resolution criticizing the rapid modification of the "constitutional and legal framework" of Hungary, arguing that FiDeSz-MPSz was failing to comply with EU common values. Orbán rejected the criticism as unjust to efforts by his regime to address economic and social problems in the country.

Current issues. The state of the economy, the austerity measures enacted by the MSzP government, and an unemployment rate of 11.4 percent (the highest since 1994) became the talking points in the run-up to the April 2010 legislative elections. The FiDeSz-MPSz campaigned on a platform that rejected further cuts to social programs and promised to cut taxes and generate economic growth. Meanwhile, the far-right Movement for a Better Hungary (*Jobbik Magyarországért Mozzalom—Jobbik*) pledged to end "preferences" for foreign investors and to seek state protection for Hungarian industries. The election notably saw not only the weakening of the MSzP, which fell to a distant second place in the assembly, but also the eclipse of the established liberal MDF and SzDSz to the point that domestic commentators speculated whether either party could recover as a force in Hungarian politics.

In July 2010 the IMF and EU suspended ongoing talks with Hungary over its existing loan packages, stating that Hungary must further reduce its state deficit. Despite this, the government passed a series of tax reforms in November 2010 that reduced what had been one of the heaviest tax burdens in the region, instituting a flat rate on personal income and a decreased corporate tax rate.

The FiDeSz-MPSz further reinforced its political position in the municipal elections on October 3, 2010. Of the 649 positions elected, the FiDeSz-MPSz won 596, with the MSzP winning only 49. The FiDeSz-MPSz also secured 22 of 23 mayoralties (including Budapest) and control of all 19 county assemblies.

The FiDeSz-MPSz holds sufficient seats in parliament to pass the two-thirds threshold needed to approve constitutional amendments, and it has controversially used that power to limit the purview of the Constitutional Court. For example, after the court found a proposed retroactive tax to be constitutional, FiDeSz deputies voted to limit the court's power to review budgetary matters.

Such efforts were solidified in the 2011 constitution, which provoked controversy domestically and abroad. Opposition parties and NGOs had limited input into the new constitution, which was passed by a 262–44 vote on April 18, 2011. The MSzP and LMP both boycotted the vote in protest, with *Jobbik* voting in opposition. The new constitution was criticized on the one hand for significantly changing the checks and balances between the executive, legislative, and judicial branches. Tax and budgetary issues would now require a two-thirds majority to be changed, the Constitutional Court's power over budgetary issues was curtailed, and the budget dramatically curtailed parliament's ability to increase public debt. Social provisions were also criticized, including specific references in the preamble that Hungary is a Christian state, that the life of a fetus is protected from conception, that marriage is between a man and a woman, and that Hungary asserts a "sense of responsibility" for ethnic Hungarians outside its borders.

In July 2011 a new law on religion restricted state recognition of churches and religious associations. Only 14 of the existing 358 registered religious groups were given legal recognition (expanded to 32 by amendment in February 2012). To obtain recognition, other groups must possess 1,000 members, a 20-year presence in Hungary, and obtain a two-thirds vote of approval in parliament.

The domestic media raised concerns that the electoral law of November 2011 "gerrymandered" electoral district borders of the National Assembly in favor of the FiDeSz-MPSz.

After the new constitution took force on January 1, 2012, the European Commission of the European Union began legal proceedings against the government concerning the independence of the central bank, judiciary, and data protection authority (the last institution being concerned with the privacy and use of personal information). The Venice Commission (the European Commission for Democracy through Law), an advisory body to the Council of Europe, issued critical opinions in March 2012 regarding the laws on the judiciary and on churches. On April 25, 2012, the European Commission referred Hungary to the Court of Justice of the European Union over continued concerns regarding the judiciary and data protection authority.

There were multiple commemorations of interwar leader Miklós Horthy in 2012, including the renaming of a small town square in his honor in May, the erection of statues in two towns in May and June, and the planned unveiling of a large equestrian statue in Budapest in October. These events, and others, led to accusations by the left opposition that the FiDeSz-MPP was encouraging a "Horthy cult."

Planned parliamentary elections in the spring of 2014 have led to ongoing negotiations for electoral alliances between leading opposition parties, with particular domestic media attention to the possibility of an alliance between MSzP and *Együtt 2014*.

POLITICAL PARTIES

As of late 1988 the sole authorized political party was the Hungarian Socialist Workers' Party (*Magyar Szocialista Munkáspárt*—MSzMP), supported by a Communist-controlled umbrella organization, the Patriotic People's Front (*Hazafias Népfront*), which, prior to the emergence of a number of unofficial formations, embraced virtually all organized groups and associations in the country. In January 1989 the National Assembly legalized freedom of assembly and association, and a month later the MSzMP approved the formation of independent parties, some of which had begun organizing on an informal basis as early as the previous September. In May 1989 talks began on transition to a multiparty system, yielding a historic accord on September 19 that sanctioned broad-ranged participation in national elections.

In 1994 some 40 parties (out of well over 100 officially registered) competed for National Assembly seats, with 8 winning representation. In 1998, 26 offered candidates, 6 successfully; in 2002, 4 of 39 won representation; in 2006, 5 of 48; in 2010, 5 of 21.

Government Parties:

Federation of Young Democrats–Hungarian Civic Alliance (*Fiatal Demokraták Szövetsége–Magyar Polgari Szövetség—FiDeSz-MPSz*). Founded in 1988, the right-wing group then styled simply as the Federation of Young Democrats (FiDeSz) ran fifth in the 1990 parliamentary balloting, winning only 22 of 378 elective seats. Six months later, however, it captured mayoralties in nine of the country's largest cities. Weakened by defections thereafter, the party's national representation declined further to 20 seats in May 1994. A 35-year age limit on membership was abandoned in April 1993, paving the way for merger with the Hungarian Civic Party (*Magyar Polgari Párt*—MPP) and creation of the FiDeSz-MPP. In September 1997 the parliamentary caucus of the party voted to admit 11 members of the KDNP parliamentary group, which had dissolved, making the FiDeSz-MPP the largest opposition group in the parliament.

The FiDeSz-MPP competed for a number of seats in the May 1998 legislative balloting on a joint list with the MDF. In addition, several FiDeSz-MPP candidates came from the MKDSz, an association recently formed by the former KDNP members. The FiDeSz-MPP emerged from the balloting as the leading party (148 seats) and became the senior member of the coalition cabinet subsequently formed with the MDF and the FKgP under the leadership of the FiDeSz-MPP's young chair, Viktor Orbán. At a party congress in January 2000 the posts of prime minister and party chair were separated.

On September 1, 2001, the FiDeSz-MPP concluded an agreement with the MDF establishing an electoral alliance for the 2002 National Assembly balloting. In January 2002, 14 Roma parties and groups also agreed to participate in the pact. Although opinion polls had anticipated an Orbán victory, the FiDeSz-MPP/MDF coalition's 188 seats (164 won by the FiDeSz-MPP) were insufficient to organize a new government after the April election.

In May 2003 the FiDeSz-MPP adopted the FiDeSz-MPSz rubric. In July centrists from the FiDeSz left the party to form a new political entity, the **New Hungary Party,** which pledged to pursue more moderate policies than the FiDeSz. In May 2004 the FiDeSz-MPSz reached an agreement with the KDNP to run joint candidates in the 2004 EU parliamentary elections and the 2006 legislative elections.

The alliance won 164 seats (141 for the FiDeSz-MPSz) in the 2006 assembly balloting, the poll having been widely perceived as a battle for national supremacy between Prime Minister Gyurcsány and Orbán, who campaigned on a populist platform calling for tax cuts and increased government spending. Orbán offered to resign as leader of the FiDeSz-MPSz after the legislative defeat, but a party congress in May reelected him. Orbán's popularity reportedly increased significantly due to his role in leading antigovernment protests in 2006–2007. Under Orbán, the FiDeSz-MPSz has become the leading opposition party in government. A much publicized poll in late 2007 reported that FiDeSz-MPSz was twice as popular as the governing MSzP. However, analysts attributed public support largely as a reaction to disenchantment with the ruling coalition and its economic policies.

In late 2007 the FiDeSz-MPSz battled accusations that it was linked to a newly formed right-wing group called the Hungarian Guard (associated with the Movement for a Better Hungary), whose members wear nationalist insignia and are considered anti-Semitic. Orbán insisted that the FiDeSz-MPSz is not anti-Semitic, but he did not condemn the Guard, whose membership is in the hundreds. Political analysts attributed Orbán's ambiguous response to the party's need to court right-wing voters.

In September 2008, a major spy scandal erupted involving accusations that two FiDeSz-MPSz parliamentary delegates had used a security company to infiltrate state agencies and illegally surveyed Socialist politicians. The suspicions were brought by the minister of intelligence and were allegedly based on taped phone conversations.

In the run-up to the EU parliamentary election in June 2009, Orbán prompted outrage in neighboring Slovakia when he said that the election would determine how many deputies would represent ethnic Hungarians in the "Carpathian Basin," a nationalist reference to an historical Hungarian homeland. Nevertheless, alliance of the FiDeSZ-MPSz and the KDNP won a landslide 56 percent of the vote, amounting to 14 of Hungary's 22 seats and a result that confirmed the FiDeSZ as the probable leading party going into Hungary's 2010 parliamentary election. Orbán was reelected unopposed at a party congress on June 13.

The FiDeSZ-MPSz and the KDNP continued their alliance for the April 2010 assembly elections, adding such additional partners as the **Party of Entrepreneurs** (*Vállalkozók Pártja*—VP) in the contests for some regional seats. Overall, the alliance won 263 seats, which represented not only the majority needed to form a government but also the two-thirds supermajority sufficient to amend the constitution.

The FiDeSZ-MPSz drafted and ratified a new constitution in 2011, stressing both traditional values and financial austerity in the new law. Domestic critics, however, argued that the structure of the constitution would make it difficult for future governments to overturn FiDeSZ-MPSz's current policies and that it subverted the democratic process.

Leaders: Viktor ORBÁN (President and Prime Minister), László KÖVÉR (Chair, Speaker of the National Assembly), Tibor NAVRACSICS (Parliamentary Leader).

Christian Democratic People's Party (*Kereszténydemokrata Néppárt*—KDNP). A right-of-center grouping, the KDNP claims to be a revival of the Popular Democratic Party, the leading opposition formation in the immediate post–World War II period. The party won 21 assembly seats in 1990 and 22 in May 1994. In 1997 the Christian Democrats signed a cooperation pact with the FKgP in preparation for the 1998 elections. However, the leadership's subsequent alliance-building efforts went too far for the European Union of Christian Democrats, which expelled the KDNP in July for "unacceptable links" to the extremist MIÉP; dissidents within the KDNP also criticized the party leadership for cooperating with extreme nationalists. The divisiveness culminated in the dissolution of the KDNP's parliamentary caucus in mid-1997, with 11 members deciding to work with the FiDeSz-MPP and forming the MKDSz. The fractured KDNP won no seats in the May 1998 legislative poll, having secured only 2.6 percent of the party-list votes in the first round of balloting.

After failing to secure representation in 2002 in the *Centrum* alliance (see below), the KDNP won 23 seats in the 2006 assembly poll in an alliance with the FiDeSz-MPSz. In September 2007 KDNP chair and parliamentary leader Zsolt Semjén caused an uproar by using the opening session of Parliament to issue inflammatory remarks about Jews and SzDSz policies. The KDNP opposed a government bailout of financial institutions and cuts to pensioner incomes in the wake of the 2008–2009 economic crisis.

Leader: Zsolt SEMJÉN (Chair and Parliamentary Leader).

Opposition Parties:

Hungarian Socialist Party (*Magyar Szocialista Párt*—MSzP). The origin of the MSzP lies in the June 1948 merger of Hungary's Communist and Social Democratic parties. Known initially as the **Hungarian Workers' Party** (*Magyar Munkáspárt*—MMP), the merged grouping was reorganized as the **Hungarian Socialist Workers' Party** (*Magyar Szocialista Munkáspárt*—MSzMP) when János Kádár took over the leadership in the wake of the 1956 revolution. At an extraordinary party congress on October 6–10, 1989, the party renounced Marxism, adopted its current name, and appointed Rezsó NYERS to the newly created post of presidium president. Gyula Horn was, in turn, chosen to succeed Nyers in May 1990. He led the party to a decisive victory in the May 1994 general election.

In the wake of a financial scandal and unpopular austerity measures, a dissident faction within the MSzP, called the Socialist Democratic Group, demanded the replacement of Prime Minister Horn as chair of the party in early 1997. Following the MSzP's decline in the May 1998 legislative poll (which eventually forced the party into opposition), Horn resigned as party leader at the September 1998 MSzP congress. He was succeeded by Lászlo KOVÁCS, former foreign minister and leader of the MSzP's parliamentary group. In October 2000, although refusing to accept a new leadership role, Horn asserted that the party under Kovács had become "too defensive."

A party congress in June 2001 chose a former nonparty finance minister, Péter Medgyessy, as the MSzP candidate for prime minister in the next national election. The decision paid off at the polls in April 2002, when the MSzP secured 178 seats, sufficient for it to form a governing coalition with the SzDSz.

Voter discontent with economic reforms, electoral losses in the June 2004 EU parliamentary polls, and the dissatisfaction of the Free Democrats all subsequently combined to undermine support for Medgyessy. At an MSzP conference in August 2004, party members voted to replace him with Ferenc Gyurcsány, a millionaire businessman who pledged to pursue a "third way," under which socialism would be "tempered" by free-market policies. Gyurcsány was widely credited with "rescuing" the MSzP from internal strife, and the success of the MSzP/SzDSz coalition in the 2006 assembly poll was attributed to his popularity. Gyurcsány's public standing plummeted following the election (see Current issues), but he was reelected as MSzP chair in February 2007 after threatening to resign as prime minister if he lost his party post.

In October 2007, during anniversary celebrations commemorating the 1956 uprising, a 30,000-strong demonstration turned against Gyurcsány, demanding his resignation. The FiDeSz-led rally accused the prime minister of betraying democracy and of failing to defend Hungary against a resurgent Russia.

Gyurcsány's growing unpopularity had much to do with latent distrust emanating from his 2006 leaked speech. Following the March 2008 referendum the MSzP officials discussed bringing "fresh faces" into the party, while FiDeSz used the moment to demand a "vote of confidence" in Gyurcsány and called for early parliamentary elections, which would likely have led to further MSzP and SzDSz losses. In June the MSzP maintained minority status in the National Assembly and faced difficulties in advancing any new policies. The opposition, led by FiDeSz-MPSz, threatened to block the MSzP legislation as a means to force an early election.

By the time he resigned in March 2009, Gyurcsány's public approval ratings had sunk to 18 percent, though the MSzP as a whole faired only slightly better at 23 percent. Gyurcsány's resignation prompted an ambiguous response within the party. Though increasingly isolated, Gyurcsány offered a degree of stability leading into the 2010 federal elections. He relinquished party leadership on March 28; on April 5 Ildikó LENDVAI won party chair with 91 percent of the delegates' votes. After the party posted dismal returns of 17 percent at the EU parliamentary election in June, MSzP leaders reviewed ways to revamp the party and concluded that the past seven years in power had "made the party's voter base unsure, and have exhausted its organizational force" and that the party's goal to modernize the economy while guaranteeing a social net had broken down. Lendvai called on her party to search within its ranks for a new, young candidate it could run for prime minister who would be capable of restoring voter trust.

The MSzP's defeat in the April 2010 assembly election (leading to Lendvai's resignation later that month) drew significant attention from domestic and international analysts. Of particular concern was the fact that the Hungarian political system had moved from a relative balance between the center-left and center-right to a position in which the MSzP was nearly equaled by the far-right *Jobbik* party.

In October 2011, Gyurcsány and his faction split from the MSzP and founded a new party, the **Democratic Coalition** (*Demokratikus Koalíció*—DK).

Leaders: Attila MESTERHÁZY (Chair), Imre SAZEKERES (Deputy Chair).

Movement for a Better Hungary (*Jobbik Magyarországért Mozgalom*). Popularly known as *Jobbik,* the party was launched by Dávid Kovács in 2003 as an outgrowth of the university student organization Right-Wing Youth Community (*Jobboldali Ifjúsági Közösség—Jobbik*). Calling itself a "radical patriotic Christian" party, *Jobbik* is considered an extreme right-wing party with nationalistic roots. It advocates withdrawal from the EU, greater rights for ethnic Hungarians living in other countries (including dual citizenship), and a crackdown on "Gypsy crime." The party has frequently been accused of anti-Semitism, although *Jobbik*'s leaders have disputed the charges.

The Movement for a Better Hungary was said to be partially responsible for attacks against demonstrators in a gay pride march in Budapest on July 7, 2007. A month later the group formed a uniformed paramilitary arm called the **Hungarian Guard** (*Magyar Gárda*), led by Gábor Vona and former defense minister Lajos FUR. The Guard's charter includes "training to help maintain public order, preserve Hungarian culture, and defend the nation in extraordinary situations." Major political parties condemned the civil defense group, labeling it as "fascist," while the World Jewish Council called for the group to be banned because the Guard's coat of arms is associated with Hungary's World War II–era fascist Arrow Cross party. The National Roma Council demanded it be banned along with other paramilitary groups after the Guard marched several times outside Roma villages to protest "Gypsy criminality." The association between the Guard and *Jobbik* led to the resignation of Kovács and several other leaders of the movement. Following the killings of a Roma man and his young son, a July 2009 appellate court upheld a lower court ruling that banned the group for rejecting equal rights to Romas and inciting resentment against them. The Guard defied the court decision with a mass rally in Budapest, subsequently relabeling itself as the Hungarian Guard Foundation (*Magyar Nemzeti Gárda*).

Jobbik polled third highest in the European Parliament election in June 2009, taking 15 percent of the vote and winning 3 seats. The results confirmed that *Jobbik* had emerged as the dominant far-right party in Hungary. Significantly, it entered the National Assembly for the first time after the 2010 elections, in which the party secured 47 seats.

In 2011 *Jobbik* supported actions by the Civil Guard Association for a Better Future (*Szebb Jövőért Polgárőr Egyesület*), which began patrols of the town of Gyöngyöspata in March 2011 to combat alleged acts of "Gypsy terror." Domestic and international rights groups claimed that the Civil Guard had ties with both *Jobbik* and the Guard.

On November 27, 2012, Márton GYÖNGYÖSI, *Jobbik*'s deputy group leader in parliament, called on the government to create a register of members of parliament and civil servants who were of "Jewish origin," triggering widespread international and domestic condemnation.

Leaders: Gábor VONA (President), Jozsef INANCSI (Hungarian Guard Chair), Lajos PÕSZE, Krisztina MORVAI.

Politics Can Be Different (*Lehet Más Politika!*—LMP). Founded in February 2009, the LMP is a liberal and green party with a platform that calls for sustainable development, transparency in governance, and social justice. In the campaign for the 2010 assembly elections the LMP notably criticized the SzDSz, MDF, and other liberal parties as inauthentic and led by "used-up politicians." In November 2012 the party was divided at its congress over whether to participate in an alliance with *Együtt 2014*. The split led one faction of the party, the Dialogue for Hungary, to break away under former parliamentary group leader Benedek JÁVOR in February 2013.

Leaders: András SCHIFFER, Bernadette SZÉL (Cochairs).

Other Parties Registered for the 2010 Elections:

Alliance of Free Democrats (*Szabad Demokraták Szövetsége*—SzDSz). Founded in May 1988 as the Network of Free Initiatives (*Szabad Kezdeményezések Hálózata*—SzKH), the SzDSz was reorganized as a political party the following November and held its first general assembly in March 1989. It won 93 legislative seats in 1990, becoming the leading opposition party of the post-Communist era. Factional strife between "pragmatists" and "ideologues" appeared to be healed in November 1992 by the election of Iván PETÓ as party chair.

The party slipped to 69 seats in the May 1994 general election, its first-round voting share being 19.4 percent. Pető subsequently could not contain disagreements over whether the SzDSz should stay in the government coalition, a division that was aggravated by a privatization scandal in October 1996 that implicated both coalition partners. The scandal seriously damaged the party in public opinion polls. Pető resigned in April 1997, although he denied any role in the scandal. He was replaced by Interior Minister Gábor KUNCZE, who in November was named the party's candidate for prime minister in 1998. Kuncze resigned as party leader following the May 1998 legislative balloting, at which the SzDSz declined sharply to 24 seats.

A party congress in December 2000 elected the mayor of Budapest, Gábor Demszky, as chair over Gábor FODOR. Demszky stated that his goals included defeating the government in 2002, denying the Socialists a National Assembly majority, and preventing an alliance between the FiDeSz-MPP and the MIÉP. Immediately after the election, the party's parliamentary leader, Gábor Kuncze, resigned his post in view of Demszky's strong criticism of the deputy group. Demszky in turn resigned in June 2001 and was succeeded as chair by Kuncze.

At the 2002 National Assembly election the SzDSz won 20 seats (1 in alliance with the MSzP), all but 3 of them on a proportional basis. A formal coalition agreement with the Socialists was negotiated over the next month, and the government that took office on May 27 included four SzDSz ministers, although cabinet reorganizations later reduced that number to three. The SzDSz was instrumental in forcing the resignation of Prime Minister Medgyessy in 2004 because of fears of potential future electoral losses.

In March 2005 the SzDSz announced that it would henceforth be known as the SzDSz–Hungarian Liberal Party. However, news reports subsequently continued to refer regularly to the original rubric. The SzDSz suffered heavy losses in 2006 municipal elections, apparently in part due to voter discontent with its coalition partner, the MSzP. Kuncze subsequently announced his resignation as party chair, and he was replaced in March 2007 by János Kóka.

However, Kóka barely lasted a year as chair following an internal investigation that confirmed suspicions of fraud during previous party elections that secured his seat. In June 2008 the state party convened, and in a closely contested race replaced Kóka with the more popular and charismatic Gábor Fodor, then the current minister of environment and water management.

Fodor's election was interpreted as increasing the chances of the SzDSz to reform the coalition government with the MSzP, though he preconditioned such a move on Gyurcsány's departure. Fodor promised to widen voter support for the SzDSz, which has suffered heavy losses in recent years because of its role in drafting the painful austerity measures. However, the June 2009 European Parliament election resulted in the SzDSz losing all seats with a mere 2.2 percent of the vote. Taking this as a sign of failed leadership, Fodor and four members of the party leadership offered to resign. On July 12 the SzDSz elected Attila RETKES as the new party chair. However, conflict between Retkes and Kóka subsequently created dissatisfaction within the party, and Retkes resigned his office in May 2010 after the party's poor showing (despite an electoral alliance with the MDF) in the April assembly balloting.

Leaders: Viktor SZABADAI (Chair), Gábor DEMSZKY.

Democratic Community of Welfare and Freedom (*Jólét és Szabadság Demokrata Közösség*—JESz). Originally founded as the **Hungarian Democratic Forum** (*Magyar Demokrata Fórum*—MDF). The MDF is a right-of-center nationalist group founded in September 1988 with the avowed purpose of "building a bridge between the state and society." The group claimed 15,000 members at the opening of its first national conference at Budapest in March 1989, when it demanded that Hungary again become "an independent democratic country of European culture." It won 165 of 378 elective seats at the April 1990 election. In January 1993 Prime Minister József Antall survived a challenge to his leadership of the MDF from the party's ultranationalist right, led by István Csurka. In early June, Csurka and three parliamentary colleagues were expelled from the party, and they formed the MIÉP. Antall died on December 12, 1993, and was succeeded, on a temporary basis, by Sándor LEZSÁK, who was named chair of the MDF Executive Committee on February 23, 1994, after yielding the party presidency to Defense Minister Lajos FÜR on February 18. Lezsák withdrew completely from the leadership on June 1, 1994, in view of the MDF's severe decline to 37 legislative seats at the May balloting. On being confirmed as MDF chair in September, Für ruled out a merger with the KDNP "for the time being."

Following Für's decision to stand down, an MDF congress in March 1996 returned Lezsák to the MDF chair, a decision provoking a centrist faction to form the breakaway **Hungarian Democratic People's Party** (*Magyar Demokrata Néppárt*—MDNP), leaving the rump MDF with approximately 20 parliamentary deputies. The MDF contested many seats in the May 1998 legislative balloting jointly with the FiDeSz-MPP, emerging with 17 seats and joining its electoral partner in the coalition government named in July.

At a party congress on January 30, 1999, Justice Minister Ibolya Dávid defeated Lezsák for the MDF chair. She was overwhelmingly reelected in January 2001 despite criticism from some members and from coalition partners for her efforts to strengthen cooperation with the MDNP and other groups accepting "moderate, center-right, Christian-Democratic or Christian values."

In April 2002 the MDF won 24 of the National Assembly seats captured by the FiDeSz-MPP/MDF electoral coalition. However, it slipped to 11 seats running on its own in 2006.

In April 2008 the MDF led cross-party discussions on tax cut proposals, securing agreements from the participating parties that tax cuts should be a priority in upcoming years. The MDF advocated an 18 percent flat tax and elimination of the inheritance tax. In late 2008 the MDF was critical of the ruling MSzP for not taking action quickly enough in the unfolding economic crisis, although the two parties reached agreement on several measures that became part of fiscal reform packages.

The party lost faction status in May 2009, after three parliamentary delegates opted out of the party caucus in protest of their leadership's supposed ties to the SzDSz; the three were later formally expelled from the party. The MDF narrowly won one seat in European parliamentary elections in June, taking 5 percent of the vote. The party entered into an electoral alliance with the SzDSz in the 2010 elections, but the alliance failed to pass the threshold.

On March 5, 2011, a party congress of the MDF formally voted to change the party's name but reelected the existing leadership and confirmed the existing party program.

Leaders: Zsolt MAKAY (Chair), István HORVATH (Vice Chair), Károly HERÉNYI.

Center Party (*Centrum Párt*). The Center Party was formed in November 2001 as an alliance of the KDNP (above), the MDNP and ZD (see Other Parties, below), and the Third Side for Hungary (*Harmadik Oldal Magyarországért Egyesület*—HOM), a nonpartisan civic forum that had been organized the preceding February by Mihály KUPA, at that time an independent in the National Assembly, and István GYENESEI, a county official. In founding the *Centrum*—more formally, the Center of Solidarity for Hungary (*Összefogás Magyarországért Centrum*)—the four organizations agreed to contest the 2002 general election jointly, but the alliance won only 3.9 percent of the party-list vote and no seats. The KDNP left the Center Party to participate in an electoral coalition with the FiDeSz-MPP in 2006, and the rump Center Party also presented (unsuccessfully) its own candidates.

Leader: Lajos SZABÓ (President).

Independent Smallholders' Party (*Független Kisgazda Párt*—FKgP). Advocating the return of collectivized land to former owners, the FKgP was launched in November 1989 as a revival of the party that dominated Hungary's first postwar election in 1945. The party—formally, the Independent Smallholders,' Agrarian Workers' and Civic Party (*Független Kisgazda, Földmunkás és Polgári Párt*)—was subsequently deeply divided over the nature of reparations for property lost during the Communist era. Thus, in December 1989 a number of dissidents led by Imre BOROS withdrew to form the National Smallholders and Bourgeois Party (*Nemzeti Kisgazda és Polgári Párt*—NKgP), most members of which, however, rejoined the parent party in 1991. On February 21, 1992, FKgP leader József Torgyán announced that the party was withdrawing from the government coalition because the MDF had denied it an opportunity to influence policy; the action was accompanied by the expulsion of most of the FKgP's 44 parliamentary deputies, who proceeded to reaffirm their support for the Antall administration. They subsequently announced formation of an FKgP "Historical Section" (*Történelmi Tagozat,* which evolved into the now-defunct United Smallholders' Party [*Egyesült Kisgazda Párt*—EKgP]). In the May 1994 general election the FKgP recovered to win 26 seats.

Following the MDF split in March 1996, the FKgP became the largest opposition party and stepped up its criticism of the Socialist-led government while rebuffing overtures by the nonparliamentary MIÉP for a three-party merger with the KDNP, whose members were described by Torgyán as "disgusting pseudo-liberal worms and vultures." In August Torgyán rejected a proposal by the leader of the nonparliamentary MIÉP for a three-party merger that would have also embraced the KDNP. However, in February 1998 the FKgP reached an agreement with the KDNP for an electoral alliance in the second round of the general elections scheduled for May; the FKgP won 48 seats in that balloting, thereby becoming the third leading party in the assembly. Its subsequent participation in the coalition government led by the free market–oriented FiDeSz-MPP surprised some observers.

On February 8, 2001, Torgyán resigned as minister of agriculture as a result of a financial scandal that also involved his son, and on February 22 his acting replacement, Imre BOROS, ordered an investigation into Torgyán's financial management of the ministry. Party powers responded, unsuccessfully, in March by demanding Boros's dismissal from the government. With the party clearly divided between Torgyán loyalists and reformers, Torgyán was reelected party leader on May 5, but on the same day the FKgP parliamentary faction, meeting separately, elected Zsolt Lányi as party chair. The latter group attempted to expel Torgyán four days later. A May 17 court decision ordered his reinstatement, but, in a further twist, the National Assembly Procedural Committee on May 28 determined that he should sit as an independent.

In the second half of 2001 the FKgP rupture became a collapse, and at the April 2002 election the party won only 0.8 percent of the party-list vote and no seats.

In July 2001 members of the Lányi group had formed a **Reform Smallholders' Party** (*Reform Kisgazdapárt*—RKgP), which elected Katalin LIEBMANN as chair in September. Lányi himself established the **Hungarian Smallholders' and Civic Party** (*Magyar Kisgazda és Polgári Párt*—MKgPP) in September. Sándor CSEH and a former FKgP parliamentary leader, Attila BÁNK, led another agrarian grouping, the **Smallholders' Party–Party of the Smallholders' Federation** (*Kisgazdapárt a Kisgazda Svövetség Pártja*), into the 2002 national election. None of the smallholder formations elected any parliamentary candidates.

In December 2007 former Smallholder party officials met to discuss forming a new political party in the wake of the upcoming referendum on economic reforms. The Smallholder dissidents were severely critical of the ruling coalition's reform policies.

Leader: Péter HEGEDÜS (Chair).

Hungarian Justice and Life Party (*Magyar Igazság és Élet Párt*—MIÉP). The extreme right-wing MIÉP was launched in June 1993 by dissidents of the then-ruling MDF after István Csurka unsuccessfully challenged József Antall for the MDF leadership in January. Conspicuously anti-Semitic, the party stated that Hungary's national revival was being thwarted by a "Jewish-Bolshevik-liberal conspiracy." By late November 1993 the MIÉP boasted 11 assembly deputies, but in the May 1994 balloting it won only 1.6 percent of the first-round vote and no seats. In October 1996 the party attracted tens of thousands of demonstrators to an antigovernment rally in Budapest, while a March 1997 rally against European integration was attended by an estimated 50,000 protesters. The MIÉP's growing influence was also apparent in the May 1998 legislative elections, in which it secured 14 seats—its first ever via the ballot box. The MIÉP was the only parliamentary party in early 1999 to oppose Hungary's accession to NATO.

The party reelected Csurka as chair at a December 2000 conference at which it also encouraged former Hungarian territories toward "a sense of nationhood" and called for formation of a national guard to "expel foreign mafias." Earlier in the year, Csurka had compared Romania's pollution of the Tisza River to genocide.

At the 2002 general election the MIÉP won only 4.4 percent of the list vote, below the threshold for proportional National Assembly seats.

In March 2004 Ernoe ROZGONYI tried to oust Csurka from his leadership position. When this effort failed, Rozgonyi launched a new political party, the **Hungarian National Front** (MNF). The new right-wing party opposed EU membership and Hungarian support for the U.S. intervention in Iraq. The MIÉP contested the 2006 assembly balloting in a Third Way coalition with *Jobbik.*

After the 2010 elections, Csurka and the MIÉP broadly supported the policies of the FiDeSz-MPSz–led government. Csurka died on February 4, 2012, leaving the future of the MIÉP uncertain.

Leader: László KOVÁCS (Vice Chair).

Hungarian Social Democratic Party (*Magyarországi Szociáldemokrata Párt*—MSzDP). Founded in January 1989, the MSzDP was a revival of the party that was forced to merge with Hungary's Communist Party in 1948. During a congress in October 1989, the party split into "historic" and "renewal" wings, but they reunited in October 1993. The MSzDP secured less than 1 percent of the first-round party-list vote in the May 1994 general election. For the 1998 poll it cooperated with the MSzP and, in a few cases, the MP, but it again secured no seats. In 2002 it ran four unsuccessful candidates in conjunction with the MSzP.

However by late 2007 and early 2008 the MSzDP was seeing an uptick in membership, powered primarily by disaffected MSzP members, including a number of lower ranking Budapest officials, critical of the ruling party's move toward neo-liberal economic policies. MSzDP Chair László KAPOLYI, whose representation in parliament is under the MSzP party, sought to stem the tide by tightening the rules required for MSzDP membership. He offered "temporary membership" for the first year, pending the approval of local party units.

The decision may have to do with an MSzDP-MSzP cooperation agreement as well as concern about splitting the liberal vote in the next parliamentary election. The MSzDP promotes an "eco-socialist market economy." Kapolyi has said the party was seeking links with the Center Party in advance of EU parliamentary elections. The MszDP grew in 2008 by siphoning members from the MSzP.

Leader: László KAPOLYI (Chair).

Hungarian Workers' Party (*Magyar Munkáspárt*—MM). Following the October 1989 party congress of the then-ruling MSzMP, a group of hard-line Communists who were opposed to formation of the MSzP announced the launching of the **János Kádár Society** (*Kádár János Baráti Társaság*) as the "only legal heir" to the parent party. Prior to the 1990 balloting the group reappropriated the MSzMP name, but it succeeded in winning only 3.7 percent of the vote. It adopted the name Workers' Party in 1992.

Improving on its 1994 performance, in the May 1998 poll the MP received 4.1 percent of the first-round party-list votes, but it again failed to win any seats. Gyula Thürmer was reelected chair at the party's 18th congress in February 1999. In April 2002 the party won 2.8 percent of the party-list vote and then threw its support behind the MSzP in the second round. It was renamed the Hungarian Communist Workers' Party in November 2005. In 2006 a breakaway faction called the **Worker's Party of Hungary 2006** (*Magyarországi Munkáspárt 2006*—MMP 2006) was created under the leadership of János FRATANOB. The breakaway faction advocated closer cooperation with the ruling MSzP on certain policies and taxing wealthy citizens at an income rate of 50 percent.

One-time vice chair Attila VAJNAI was convicted of wearing a red star symbolizing Communism on his jacket during a demonstration in 2003; he was acquitted by Hungary's Supreme Court in 2009.

On May 11, 2013, it adopted its current name, as any reference to communism in political names was banned by the 2011 constitution.

Leaders: Gyula THÜRMER (Chair); Lajosné KARACS, Zsuzsanna FOGARASI (Vice Chairs).

Other small parties that registered for the 2010 elections included the **Civil Movement** (*Civil Mozgalom*—CM), led by Mária SERES; the **Unity Party** (*Összefogás Párt*—OP), led by Zsolt SZEPESSY; the **Green Left** (*Zöld Baloldal*); and the **Party of the Greens** (*Zöldek Partja*).

Dialogue for Hungary (*Párbeszéd Magyarországért*—PM). The PM emerged as a faction at the party congress of the LMP in November 2012, advocating cooperation with *Együtt 2014.* The group, including eight sitting members of parliament, subsequently left the LMP and founded the PM on February 3, 2013. On March 8, 2013, the PM joined *Együtt 2014* in an electoral alliance for the 2014 parliamentary elections.

Leaders: Benedek JÁVOR, Timea SZABÓ (Cochairs).

Other Parties:

Modern Hungary Movement (*Modern Magyarország Mozgalom*—MoMa) was founded on April 21, 2013, by Lajaos BOKROS, the MDF's member of the European Parliament who left the MDF in 2011 during its transformation into the JESz. MoMa is a self-described liberal party advocating the free market, individual freedoms, and entrepreneurship.
Leader: Lajos BOKROS (Chair).

Together 2014 (*Együtt 2014*). Founded on October 26, 2012, as an alliance of three civic organizations, the *Haza és Haladás Egyesület* (Patriotism and Progress Association), *Egymillióan a Magyar Sajtószabadságért Egyesület* (One Million for the Freedom of Press in Hungary), and *Maygar Szolidaritás Mozgalom* (Hungarian Solidarity Movement), brought together by opposition to FiDeSz-MPSz. The movement's expressed goal was to seek an alliance of parties to gain a two-thirds majority in parliament in the 2014 parliamentary elections and dismantle FiDeSz-MPSz's changes to the constitution. The movement was registered as a party on March 8, 2013, and announced an electoral alliance with the LMP on the same day. The party received widespread media attention as it represented former prime minister Gordon Bajnai's return to politics.
Leader: Gordon BAJNAI (Chair).

4K!–Fourth Republic (*4K!–Negyedik Köztársaságot!*) was founded in 2007 as a civic organization focusing on youth empowerment and the use of public spaces in Budapest. It participated in the 2010 municipal elections but rose to national attention during the 2011 protests against the new constitution. It was refounded as a national political party on April 28, 2012, critical of both FiDeSz-MPSz and MSzDP.
Leader: András ISTVÁNFFY.

Roma Organizations:

Roma, who are estimated to represent up to 10 percent of the Hungarian population, are the largest ethnic minority and endure abysmal socioeconomic conditions. Recent reports estimate that the Roma suffer 70 percent unemployment, with fewer than 5 percent of children completing high school. In 2007–2008, Hungary hosted the EU's Roma Inclusion Program, a 15-year integration measure spanning nine Eastern European states that seeks to improve social and economic conditions for Roma. Roma organizations, including the Roma Civil Rights Foundation and the National Roma Council, have become increasingly active in 2007 and 2008 because of threats posed by the newly founded paramilitary organization, the Hungarian Guard (see Movement for a Better Hungary). In 2009 tensions heightened between Roma and far-right extremists following the sentencing of a Roma family in the 2006 murder of a school teacher. The crime triggered a wave of hostility and killings of Roma. Police doubled the size of a task force investigating anti-Roma attacks. In an EU survey released in April 2009, 90 percent of Roma in Hungary said discrimination due to ethnic origin was widespread. In response, one Roma group announced plans in early 2009 to establish its own "Gypsy Guard" to counter the Hungarian Guard. However, the plan was widely denounced as incendiary by Roma and other party politicians.

A large number of Roma (Gypsy) parties and civic organizations were established in the post-Communist era. Few, however, have more than a local or regional following. The larger groups include the **Lungo Drom Alliance,** led by Flórián FARKAS; the **Hungarian Gypsies' Peace Party,** led by Aladar HORVÁTH, who also chairs the Roma Civil Rights Foundation; the **Hungarian Roma Parliament;** the **Brotherhood Independent Gypsy Organization** (*Phralipe Független Cigány Szervezet*); and the MCF **Roma Unity Party** (*MCF Összefogás Párt*—MCFÖP), led by Orbán KOLOMPÁR.

On April 9, 1995, the Roma elected a 53-member National Autonomous Authority of the Romany Minority (*Országos Cigány Kisebbségi Önkormányzat*—OCKÖ; also translated as the National Gypsy Minority Self-Government), the first such officially sanctioned advisory body in Eastern Europe. All of the seats were won by the *Lungo Drom,* as they also were at the election held January 23, 1999. In February 2011, the OCKÖ changed its name to the National Roma Self-Government (*Országos Roma Önkormányzat*—ORÖ).

LEGISLATURE

The **Hungarian National Assembly** (*Országgyülés*) is a unicameral body consisting of 386 elective deputies (including 8 seats reserved for ethnic minority representation), of whom 210 are returned from regional and national lists on a proportional basis and 176 from single-member constituencies on a majoritarian basis. (The electoral law of December 2011 reduces the number of deputies in the next national elections to 199, of whom 93 are returned from national lists on a proportional basis and 106 by a majority vote in single-member constituencies.) The legislative term is four years. Following two-stage balloting on April 4 and 25, 2010, the party distribution was as follows: the electoral alliance of the Federation of Young Democrats–Hungarian Civic Party (FiDeSz-MPSz) and the Christian Democratic People's Party (KDNP), 263 (FiDeSz-MPSz, 226; KDNP, 36; and 1 seat won in alliance with the Association of Entrepreneur's Party); the Hungarian Socialist Party, 59; the Movement for a Better Hungary, 47; Politics Can Be Different, 16; and independents, 1.
Speaker: László KÖVÉR.

CABINET

[as of November 1, 2013]

Prime Minister	Viktor Orbán (FiDeSz-MPSz)
Deputy Prime Minister	Zsolt Semjén (KDNP)
Deputy Prime Minister	Tibor Navracsics (FiDeSz-MPSz)
Ministers	
Defense	Csaba Hende (FiDeSz-MPSz)
Foreign Affairs	János Martonyi (FiDeSz-MPSz)
Human Resources	Zoltán Balog (FiDeSz-MPSz)
Interior	Sándor Pintér (ind.)
National Development	Zsuzsanna Németh (ind.) [f]
National Economy	Mihály Varga (FiDeSz-MPSz)
Public Administration and Justice	Tibor Navracsics (FiDeSz-MPSz)
Rural Development	Sándor Fazekas (FiDeSz-MPSz)

[f] = female

INTERGOVERNMENTAL REPRESENTATION

Ambassador to the U.S.: György SZAPÁRY.

U.S. Ambassador to Hungary: Colleen Bradley BELL (nominee).

Permanent Representative to the UN: Csaba KŐRÖSI.

IGO Memberships (Non-UN): EBRD, EIB, EU, ICC, IEA, IOM, NATO, OECD, OSCE, WTO.

ICELAND

Republic of Iceland
Lýðveldið Ísland

Political Status: Independent republic established June 17, 1944, when present constitution was adopted, under democratic parliamentary system. Constitution last amended on June 24, 1999.

Area: 39,768 sq. mi. (103,000 sq. km).

Population: 318,006 (2013E—UN); 315,281 (2013E—U.S. Census).

Major Urban Center (2010E): REYKJAVÍK (118,488).

Official Language: Icelandic.

Monetary Unit: Króna (market rate November 1, 2013: 120.35 krónur = $1US).

President: Dr. Ólafur Ragnar GRÍMSSON (previously People's Alliance); elected on June 29, 1996, and inaugurated on August 1 for a four-year term, succeeding Vigdís FINNBOGADÓTTIR (nonparty); ran unopposed in June 2000; reelected on June 26, 2004; ran unopposed in June 2008; reelected with 52.78 percent of the vote, defeating five other candidates, on June 30, 2012; inaugurated for an unprecedented fifth four-year term on August 1.

Prime Minister: Sigmunder Davið GUNNLAUGSSON (Progressive Party), sworn in on May 23, 2013, to succeed Jóhanna SIGURÐARDÓTTIR (The Alliance), who did not seek reelection.

THE COUNTRY

The westernmost nation of Europe, Iceland lies in the North Atlantic Ocean just below the Arctic Circle. Although one-eighth of the land surface is glacier, the warm Gulf Stream assures a relatively moderate climate and provides the country's rich reserve of fish, which accounts for one-quarter of GDP. The population is quite homogeneous, the preponderant majority being of Icelandic descent. More than 80 percent of the population adheres to the Evangelical Lutheran Church, although other faiths are permitted. Approximately 80 percent of adult women work outside the home, mainly in clerical and service sectors. The four-term presidency of Vigdís FINNBOGADÓTTIR (1982–1996) yielded a significant increase in female political representation.

Although fishing and fish processing employ only about 9 percent of the labor force, marine products typically account for nearly three-fourths of Iceland's export trade; other leading activities include dairy farming and sheep raising. Recent development efforts have focused on exploiting the country's considerable hydroelectric and geothermal energy supply. Energy production and smelting are currently estimated to account for about 35 percent of the GDP. Iceland has invested heavily in hydrogen fuel technology, which has resulted in a 75 percent decline in domestic energy costs. High-tech industry, information technology, and gaming are also growing sectors.

Iceland was one of the first countries to experience the 2008 global economic crisis. The króna declined by 44 percent in 2008 in relation to the euro, and all four major credit firms lowered Iceland's bond rating. In order to stem inflation and protect the currency, the Central Bank increased interest rates several times (see Political background, below). The government nationalized the banking industry after the collapse of a number of major financial institutions and a period of dramatic monetary destabilization that affected Iceland's financial partners. The International Monetary Fund (IMF) and leading European states provided a $10 billion loan to stabilize the economy. In 2008, GDP rose by 0.3 percent, inflation soared from 4 to 12.4 percent, and the unemployment rate climbed from 1.9 to 7 percent. The next year, GDP declined by 6.9 percent, while inflation remained high at 12 percent and unemployment exceeded 8 percent. In 2010, GDP again declined by 4 percent, before rising to 3.1 percent the next year as the economy stabilized. Unemployment in 2012 fell to 5.8 percent, and GDP grew 1.6 percent. On February 17, 2012, Iceland's credit rating was upgraded in response to continued economic improvements. By June 2012, Iceland had repaid, early, about two-fifths of the $910 million it borrowed from the IMF during the height of its financial crisis.

GOVERNMENT AND POLITICS

Political background. Settled by disaffected Norsemen in the last quarter of the ninth century, Iceland flourished as an independent republic and convened its first parliament (Althing) in 930. However, it came under Norwegian rule in 1262 and in 1381 became a Danish dominion, stagnating for 500 years under neglect, natural calamities, and rigid colonial controls. The island achieved limited home rule in 1874 under the leadership of Jón SIGURDSSON and in 1918 became an internally self-governing state united with Denmark under a common king. Iceland's strategic position in World War II resulted in British occupation after the fall of Denmark in 1940, with military control being transferred to American forces when the United States entered the war in 1941. Full independence was achieved on June 17, 1944.

Coalition government has dominated politics throughout Iceland's history. A significant change in the postwar era was the defeat of a 12-year centrist coalition of the Independence Party (IP) and the Social Democratic Party (SDP) in 1971. The election of June 1974 resulted in a coalition involving the IP and the Progressive Party (PP), while that of June 1978 yielded a center-left government of the PP, SDP, and the People's Alliance (PA). The latter government fell in October 1979 and, in the wake of an inconclusive legislative election in December, was replaced by a minority SDP administration that was in turn succeeded in February 1980 by a group of IP deputies led by Gunnar THORODDSEN in coalition with the PA and the PP. On June 29 Vigdís FINNBOGADÓTTIR, director of the Reykjavík Theatre since 1972, became the world's first popularly elected female head of state when she defeated three other candidates seeking to succeed Kristján ELDJÁRN, who had declined to seek a fourth term.

In March 1983, Prime Minister Thoroddsen requested dissolution of the Althing and announced that he would not be a candidate for reelection. After another inconclusive poll in April, each of the three major party leaders failed in efforts to form a viable coalition. With the president having threatened to name a nonparty administration, Steingrímur HERMANNSSON of the PP finally succeeded, in May, in organizing a cabinet of his own and IP members.

At the election of April 1987, which was marked by an IP loss of five seats and a doubling (to six) of representation by the feminist Women's Alliance (WA), the coalition fell one seat short of a majority. The prime minister remained a caretaker until the installation in July of the IP's Thorsteinn PÁLSSON as head of an administration that included PP and SDP representatives. Pálsson resigned in September 1988. Hermannsson returned as head of a new government that included the SDP and the PA; the coalition's marginal legislative strength was significantly enhanced by addition of the recently organized Citizens' Party in September 1989.

Backed by all of the major parties, President Finnbogadóttir was elected to a third four-year term in June 1988. In the first Icelandic challenge to a sitting head of state, Sigrún THORSTEINSDÓTTIR of the small Humanist Party obtained only 5.3 percent of the popular vote.

At the election of April 20, 1991, Independence parliamentary representation rose from 18 to 26, while the Citizens' Party lost all of its seats. On April 30 Davíð ODDSSON, who had succeeded Pálsson as IP leader on March 10, was sworn in as head of a bipartisan administration that included the SDP.

The Social Democrats split in September 1994 (see Political Parties, below). A modest economic upturn in 1994 yielded a narrow 32–31 majority for the coalition parties in legislative balloting on April 8, 1995, although the SDP lost many votes to the new Awakening of the Nation list headed by its former deputy chair. Moves to reconstitute the existing coalition proved abortive, and Oddsson managed an IP–PP partnership that commanded a comfortable majority of 40 seats.

On October 1, 1995, President Finnbogadóttir announced that she would not seek reelection when her fourth four-year term expired. In popular balloting on June 29, 1996, the former finance minister and former leader of the leftist PA, Ólafur Ragnar GRÍMSSON, defeated four other candidates, winning 40.9 percent of the vote.

In mid-1998, the PA, SDP, and WA agreed to establish an electoral coalition in an effort to unseat Prime Minister Oddsson's government. The resultant Unified Left (The Alliance) failed to make any inroads, however, and Oddsson was returned for a third term in the election of May 8, 1999. A year later, President Grímsson's term was extended for an additional four years when no potential challenger met the nomination deadline. The IP/PP coalition remained in power following the legislative balloting of May 10, 2003, with Oddsson retaining the prime ministership after agreeing to turn the post over to Halldór ÁSGRÍMSSON of the PP part way through his anticipated four-year term. (Ásgrímsson was inaugurated as prime minister on September 15, 2004.) Other factors contributing to the September 2004 "transition" reportedly included Oddsson's compromised health and his indecorous dispute with President Grímsson over a proposed new media law. Among other things, Grímsson's veto of the bill, reportedly the first use of the office's veto power since independence, suggested to some observers that further exercise of presidential authority, strongly encoded in the constitution but rarely exercised, might be in the offing. No formal policy changes accompanied the transfer of the prime ministership. However, analysts noted that Ásgrímsson and the PP were noticeably "more EU-friendly" than Oddsson and the IP. Meanwhile, Grímsson won a third presidential term with 86 percent of the vote on June 26, 2004.

When his party received only 12 percent of the vote in the local elections held on May 27, 2006, Ásgrímsson resigned as prime minister. He was succeeded, on June 15, 2006, by Geir HAARDE, leader of the IP, who immediately announced a cabinet reshuffle. Haarde, most recently the foreign minister but also a widely respected former finance minister, quickly addressed the economic concerns, halting government spending on a number of infrastructure projects and negotiating wage concessions with the labor unions.

In the May 2007 legislative elections, the IP again won the majority of seats, and Haarde was reappointed as prime minister to head a new coalition government that included The Alliance instead of the PP. The Left-Green Alliance, which focused on the environment and denounced the Iraq war, won five new seats. Following the elections, a poll found that the new government had an approval rating of 83 percent—the highest ever recorded for an Icelandic government (for more on the 2007 election see the 2010 *Handbook*). Grímsson's tenure was extended for a fourth term in August 2008, when no presidential challengers met the registration deadline.

In March 2008 the Central Bank raised interest rates to 15.5 percent, a record high, in response to a spike in inflation, which rose 11.8 percent, its highest level in six years. In an effort to contain inflation and a growing consumer credit crisis, the central banks of Denmark, Norway, and Sweden agreed to provide up to $775 million to commercial banks in Iceland. In October, Iceland's leading banks collapsed causing a massive devaluation of the króna and the loss of billions in savings and pension funds. Inflation rose to record levels and the Central Bank raised interest rates to 18 percent. The government responded by nationalizing the banks and adopting a budget that included a $150 billion krónur deficit in order to stabilize the financial sector. It also secured more than $10 billion in loans after agreeing to first compensate foreign investors for losses related to the successive bank failures. Massive protests and demonstrations began in October in response to the government's management of the crisis, culminating on January 20, 2009, when thousands of citizens took to the streets of Reykjavik, banging pots and pans and throwing fruit and yogurt at the parliament building.

The growing economic recession led to tensions within the governing coalition, with The Alliance demanding it be given the post of prime minister in exchange for remaining in the government. When Haarde refused, the coalition collapsed and the government resigned on January 26, 2009. He subsequently announced that he had cancer and would not seek reelection. Social Affairs Minister and member of The Alliance Jóhanna SIGURÐARDÓTTIR was appointed to lead an interim minority government that included The Alliance and the Left-Green Alliance (VGF).

New Althing elections were held on April 25 and resulted in a coalition government of The Alliance, which placed first, and the VGF, which placed third, along with two independents. Sigurðardóttir became the first female and first openly gay prime minister of Iceland. The new government faced severe economic challenges. The IMF estimated that Iceland's foreign debts could exceed 300 percent of GDP by the end of 2010. Therefore, in November 2009 the government implemented a new income tax system (with a top rate of 46.1 percent), raised the VAT, and increased taxes on commodities such as fuel. It also sharply raised fees for commercial fishing and slashed healthcare spending by 20 percent. International credit-rating services downgraded Iceland to the lowest level possible.

In August 2009 the parliament approved a controversial bill, dubbed Icesave, which would provide $5.44 billion to the United Kingdom and the Netherlands to repay the countries for a loan they provided Iceland to compensate British and Dutch citizens who lost deposits when Icelandic banks collapsed. The measure was immensely unpopular and was amended in December. Grímsson vetoed Icesave on January 5, 2010, and the measure was defeated in a March 6 national referendum by 93.2 percent of the votes. In reply, London and Amsterdam blocked further negotiations on Iceland's entry into the European Union (EU).

In municipal elections in May 2010, voters fled the traditional parties. Former comedian, Jón GNARR, leader of the newly formed Best Party (*Besti Flokkurinn*—BF) was elected mayor of Reykjavik.

A cabinet reshuffle on September 2, 2010, reduced the number of posts from 12 to 10. On December 9 the Icelandic negotiators finalized a new Icesave agreement that would enable the country to repay the British and Dutch governments at lower interest rates. On February 20, 2011, Grímsson vetoed the new Icesave agreement, forcing another referendum. On April 9 the second agreement was defeated by 58.9 percent of the voters. After the referendum, the coalition government survived a no-confidence measure by a vote of 32–30.

A minor cabinet reshuffled occurred on December 31, 2011, after two ministers resigned over the government's pro-EU membership policies. Parliamentary elections on April 27, 2013, saw victory for the PP–IP coalition, which promised to end austerity, lower taxes, forgive household debt, and halt further steps toward EU membership.

Constitution and government. Iceland's constitution, adopted by referendum in 1944, vests power in a president (whose functions are mainly titular), a prime minister, a legislature, and a judiciary. The president is directly elected for a four-year term. The unicameral legislature (Althing) is currently a 63-member body also elected for four years (subject to dissolution by the president) under a proportional system. The prime minister, who performs most executive functions, is appointed by the president but is responsible to the legislature. Eight district courts occupy the lower level of the judicial system, while the Supreme Court sits at the apex. There are also special labor and impeachment courts.

The number of general electoral districts (*Kjöroemi*) was reduced from eight to six, beginning with the 2003 elections. The number of independent towns (*Kaupstaðir*) and other municipalities (*sveitarfelög*) was progressively reduced from 204 in 1990 to 104 in 2003 through voluntary consolidation.

In 2013 Reporters Without Borders ranked Iceland 9th out of 179 countries, in freedom of the press. This was a decline from 6th place the previous year.

Foreign relations. Nordic links, North Atlantic Treaty Organization (NATO) membership, and the fish-based economy are the principal determinants of Icelandic foreign relations. Attempts to extend its territorial waters from 1952 to 1975 embroiled the country in disputes with a number of maritime competitors. The first "cod war" resulted from the proclamation of a 12-mile limit in 1958 and was terminated by agreements with Britain, Ireland, and West Germany in 1961; a second period of hostilities followed the proclamation of a 50-mile limit in 1973 and was ended by a temporary agreement with Britain the same year. In 1975, a third "cod war" erupted following Iceland's extension of the limit to 200 miles despite an adverse ruling in 1974 by the International Court of Justice on the 50-mile limit. The dispute led Iceland to break relations with the United Kingdom for a period of months in 1976, before reaching a compromise. Less volatile confrontations over economic zones, fishing rights, species depletion, and quotas continued to occur with various countries (Norway, Denmark, Russia) over the ensuing two decades. Iceland subsequently intensified its efforts to settle remaining fishing disputes, and in May 1999, it signed an agreement with Norway and Russia regulating catches in the Barents Sea.

Traditionally opposed to maintenance of an indigenous military force, the government in 1973 announced its intention to close the U.S.-maintained NATO base at Keflavík in order "to ensure Iceland's security." The decision was reversed in August 1974 by the conservative administration, although the government requested that Icelanders be employed for nonmilitary work previously done by Americans at the base. Relations with Washington were momentarily strained in March 1985 by press reports that Pentagon contingency plans included the movement of nuclear depth charges to the Keflavík base. Shortly thereafter, U.S. officials assured Reykjavík that no such weapons would be deployed without Icelandic approval, while in May the Althing, by unanimous vote, declared the country to be a nuclear-free zone. In January 1994 a new Icelandic-U.S. accord provided for continued U.S. use of the Keflavík base.

In a move indicative of Scandinavia's historic links to the Baltic states, Iceland on August 26, 1991, became the first country to reestablish diplomatic relations with Estonia, Latvia, and Lithuania. In May 1992 it became a signatory of the European Economic Area (EEA) treaty between the European Free Trade Association (EFTA) and the European Community (EC, later the EU) states, although unlike most other EFTA members it made no effort to join the EC. In November 1992 Iceland became an associate member of the Western European Union (WEU).

An agreement signed in October 1995 provided for Iceland, together with Norway, to accede (as nonvoting members) to the Schengen Accord envisaging the abolition of internal border controls between most EU states. The arrangement went into effect on March 25, 2001, enabling Denmark, Finland, and Sweden, as EU members, to preserve the 40-year-old Nordic Passport Union with their two non-EU Nordic partners.

Iceland has not consistently complied with the global moratorium on whaling passed by the International Whaling Commission (IWC) in 1986. Instead, Iceland withdrew from the IWC in 1992, and it has not signed the UN Convention on International Trade in Endangered Species. In March 1999 the Althing voted to rescind a ten-year-old ban, arguing that limited harvests will cause no harm and may even increase fish populations. By a very close vote, the IWC readmitted Iceland in October 2002. The country observed the commercial ban from 1989 to 2006 but allowed hunting for research purposes. In August 2003 Iceland permitted the killing of some 38 minke whales for "scientific purposes," prompting international protest and boycotts of the country's increasingly lucrative ecotourism industry. In March 2006 Greenpeace, which claimed the total had reached 100, announced it would be sending its ship MV *Arctic Sunrise* to Iceland as a part of its ongoing efforts to convince Iceland to give up whaling. Nevertheless, in October 2006 Iceland announced that it would resume limited commercial whaling, a decision that prompted a written protest from 25 countries, including the United States and the majority of the EU states. Both minke whales and fin whales have been harvested.

The United States withdrew its last warplanes from the Keflavík NATO base on September 8, 2006. The Icelandic government and population responded with alarm about being left "without air defenses" and about the possibility the country might eventually need to create its own military forces. In September 2006, Iceland and the United States signed a new defense agreement in which Washington pledged that it would continue to defend Iceland even though it would not station forces in the country. The former U.S. military facilities were turned over to Iceland. In 2011 Verne Global, a UK-based IT company, opened a $700 million zero-carbon data center in part of the former base.

The Icelandic Crisis Response Unit (ICRU), established in 1997 as a volunteer peacekeeping unit, successfully managed an airport during NATO operations in Kosovo in 2003 and performed a similar function in Kabul, Afghanistan, in 2004–2005.

Iceland recognized Kosovo's independence in March 2007. In April 2007, Iceland signed separate defense agreements with Denmark and Norway. The accords allowed both countries to undertake military training exercises in Iceland. Later in the month, NATO agreed to take over supervision of Iceland's airspace if the host country covered the cost of facilities. In November 2012, Finland and Sweden agreed to form a pan-Nordic Air Police unit to help Denmark and Norway patrol Iceland's air space.

The economic downturn of 2008 reignited debate over entry into the EU, and the Alliance-led government initiated negotiations over membership. Meanwhile, a decision by the UK government to use antiterrorism measures to freeze some Icelandic assets in the Icesave dispute led the government to respond by opposing the deployment of a British air force unit as part of the NATO mission at Keflavik air base.

In February 2010, the European Commission officially recommended that the EU begin negotiations with Iceland for membership. On June 17, EU leaders accepted the recommendation but tied Iceland's entry into the organization to the country's settlement of debt issues with the United Kingdom and the Netherlands (see Current issues, below). In December, the European Commission determined that Iceland had met the requirements to begin EU negotiations. Mackerel quotas are a point of contention, with Iceland objecting to the EU and Norway controlling 90 percent of the recommended level.

By 2012, Iceland had completed 8 of the 35 policy areas required for EU membership. But in May 2013, newly elected Prime Minister Sigmunder Davið GUNNLAUGSSON halted talks pending a referendum on membership.

China has reached out to Iceland as a possible entrée to membership in the Arctic Council. A large delegation led by Prime Minister Wen Jiabao visited Iceland in 2012, and a bilateral free-trade agreement is under discussion.

Current issues. The ruling Alliance–VGF government sought to draft and enact a new constitution to improve economic oversight. On November 27, 2010, voters elected 25 members to a constitutional committee charged to review Iceland's basic law. (For more on the committee see the 2013 *Handbook*.) The committee reviewed proposals submitted by the public through Facebook and other social media. A referendum was to coincide with the June 2012 presidential election, but the PP–IP blocked the bill with a filibuster. Voters approved all six proposals in a national referendum on October 20, 2012, including common ownership of natural resources and having a national established church. But the government took no further action, and the PP–IP threatened another filibuster. Þór SAARI (Movement) introduced a vote of no confidence in the government in parliament on March 11, 2013, citing the government's failure to pass a new constitution. The motion failed, 32 votes to 29. Prime Minister Sigurðardóttir called the constitutional failure the "saddest day" of her 35 years in parliament.

President Ólafur Ragnar Grímsson won an unprecedented fifth term on June 30, 2012, defeating five other candidates. In August, the number of government ministries was reduced from ten to eight. The Economic Affairs, Agriculture, and Fisheries Ministry was divided, with agriculture and fisheries combined with the Industry, Energy, and Tourism Ministry to form a new industry and innovation portfolio. The economic affairs sector was added to the finance portfolio to create the Ministry of Finance and Economic Affairs.

Following the defeat of the second Icesave agreement by referendum in May 2011, Icelandic officials reported that the funds recovered from the bankruptcy of the major banks would be used to compensate the British and Dutch creditors. The announcement came after the two countries threatened to take Iceland to court to recover the funds. Icelandic banks and financial companies sued to stop the repayment plan. In a surprise verdict, the European Free Trade Association Court dismissed all claims against Iceland in January 2013, ruling that it had not violated deposit guarantees due to the magnitude of the country's financial crisis. In March 2013, a special prosecutor indicted the former chiefs of several failed banks for manipulating share prices.

The traditional PP–IP coalition returned to power after parliamentary elections on April 27, 2013. They pledged to write off as much as 75 percent of foreign-held debt and use the cash to help citizens struggling to pay their mortgages. Each party secured 19 seats, with the IP taking slightly more of the popular vote (50,454 votes to 46,173 for the PP). But the PP had a relative victory, jumping from 9 seats to 19, while the IP gained only 3 seats above the 16 it secured in 2009. President Grímsson thus opted to invite IP leader Sigmunder Davið Gunnlaugsson to form the government. While the PP–IP had presided over the financial collapse, Gunnlaugsson only entered parliament in 2009 and was not tainted by the mess. The Alliance dropped to third place, down from 20 seats to 9, while the VG lost half its seats, going from 14 to 7. Ten new parties competed, and two passed the 5 percent threshold to gain seats: Bright Future, with 6 seats, and the Pirate Party, with 3. Twenty-five (40 percent) of the new members of parliament are women. Turnout was a record low, 83.3 percent, suggesting voter fatigue.

POLITICAL PARTIES

Government Parties:

Progressive Party—PP (*Framsóknarflokkurinn*). Founded in 1916 as a representative of agrarian interests, the Progressive Party has been responsible for many social and economic reforms benefiting agriculture and the fisheries. In the past it expressed qualified support for NATO while advocating the withdrawal of military forces as soon as possible. Although the party placed second in the 1983 balloting, its chair, Steingrímur Hermannsson, succeeded in forming a coalition government. The PP did better than anticipated in the 1987 balloting, retaining 13 of its 14 seats, although Hermannsson was unable to form a new government. The party was awarded four ministries in the Pálsson government of July 8, with Hermannsson returning as head of a three-party coalition in September 1988. The PP went into opposition following the election of April 1991, in which its parliamentary representation was unchanged. It returned to government after the 1995 balloting, in which it secured 23.3 percent of the vote.

The PP saw its vote share drop to 18.4 percent in the May 1999 election, giving it 12 seats (a loss of 3), but it remained the junior partner in the governing coalition. The PP retained its 12 seats (on a 17.7 percent vote share) in the 2003 balloting. Under an agreement reached following that election, PP leader Halldór Ásgrímsson was sworn in as head of the ongoing PP/IP coalition government in September 2004. However, he resigned in 2006.

Jón SIGURDSSON resigned as party chair in 2007 after the PP suffered its worst electoral showing in decades, losing 5 seats to become the fourth-largest party in the Althing.

In January 2009 at a party congress, the PP reversed its previous opposition to EU membership. At the same meeting, Sigmunder Davið Gunnlaugsson was elected as the new chair of the PP. In the April Althing elections, the PP secured 14.8 percent of the vote and 9 seats. Gunnlaugsson rebranded the PP as the party of the Icelandic nation, opposed to the EU in general and the Icesave deal.

The PP returned to power following the April 27, 2013, parliamentary elections, winning 19 seats, the same number as the IP but far better than the 9 seats it gained in the 2009 vote. Based on this factor, President Grímsson invited Gunnlaugsson to form the government.

Leaders: Sigmunder Davið GUNNLAUGSSON (Chair, Prime Minister), Sigurður Ingi JÓHANNSSON (Vice Chair), Sigurdor EYTHORSSON (Secretary General).

Independence Party—IP (*Sjálfstæðisflokkurinn*). Formed in 1929 by a union of conservative and liberal groups, the IP has traditionally been the strongest party and has participated in most governments since 1944. Although primarily representing commercial and fishing interests, it draws support from all strata of society and is especially strong in the urban areas. It stands for a liberal economic policy, economic stabilization, and the continued presence of NATO forces. A major split occurred in February 1980 when Vice Chair Gunnar THORODDSEN, backed by several Independence MPs, broke with the regular party leadership and formed a coalition government with the Progressive and People's Alliance parties.

The party lost 5 of its 23 seats in the election of April 1987, largely because of the defection of Albert GUMUNDSSON, who had been forced to resign as industry minister in March because of a tax scandal. Party Chair Thorsteinn Pálsson stepped down as prime minister in September 1988 because of a dispute over economic policy. In March 1991 Reykjavík mayor Davíð Oddsson succeeded Pálsson as party chair and formed a government on April 30, following an election in which the party's plurality rose from 18 to 26. The IP lost only 1 seat in the 1995 balloting, winning 37.1 percent of the vote. However, because of losses by its Social Democratic coalition partner, it felt obliged to form a new center-right coalition with the PP.

Oddsson was returned to office in the election of May 1999, after the IP won 26 Althing seats on an improved vote share of 40.7 percent, and again in the May 2003 balloting, after the IP secured 22 seats on a vote share of 33.7 percent. On September 27, 2005, Oddsson stepped down from the government and relinquished his post in the party's leadership to become chair of the Board of Governors of the Icelandic Central Bank. He was replaced the next month by Geir Haarde, who in June 2006 became the new prime minister. Haarde was reappointed prime minister following the May 2007 legislative elections in which the IP increased its representation by 3 seats, to 25. Former communications minister and party member Sturla BÖÒVARSSON was elected president of the parliament following the legislative balloting.

Haarde resigned as prime minister and party chair in 2009. He was replaced by Bjarni BENEDIKTSSON at a party congress in March 2009. In the 2009 legislative balloting, the IP won 16 seats with 23.7 percent of the vote. The IP offered to join a coalition government with The Alliance, but the initiative was rejected, and the IP instead became the main opposition party in the Althing, marking the first time in 18 years that the party had not been part of the government. On April 23, 2012, Haarde was convicted on one count of official negligence for his role in the Icelandic financial crisis. The conviction was symbolic, and Haarde received no punishment.

Party members called for Benediktsson's resignation two weeks ahead of the 2013 election, accusing him of being out of touch with regular voters. He responded by granting a rare television interview and his popularity rebounded. The IP increased its parliamentary representation from 16 to 19, with 26.7 percent of the valid votes.

Leaders: Bjarni BENEDIKTSSON (Chair), Hanna Birna KRISTJÁNDÓTTIR (Vice Chair), Kjartan GUNNARSSON (Secretary General).

Opposition Parties:

The Alliance (*Samfylkingarinnar*). The Alliance was established as a unified party on May 5, 2000, having originated prior to the May 1999 Althing election as an electoral coalition of three parties: the People's Alliance—PA (*Althýðubandalagið*), the Social Democratic Party—SDP (*Althýðuflokkurinn*), and the Women's Alliance—WA (*Kvennalistinn*). The three were frequently referred to as the Unified Left.

The PA was launched in 1956 as an electoral front of Communists and a smaller group of disaffected Social Democrats. It traditionally advocated a radical socialist domestic program and a neutralist policy in foreign affairs, including Icelandic withdrawal from NATO. Its parliamentary representation rose from eight to nine in 1991 and remained at that level following the 1995 election. Having been the party chair since 1987, Ólafur Ragnar Grímsson stood down in the fall of 1995 in order to contest the June 1996 presidential election, in which he secured a comfortable victory. By then, the PA had moved to an explicitly democratic socialist orientation. Formation of the Unified Left caused a number of PA Althing members to resign from the party, arguing that it had moved too far to the center in accommodating Social Democrats.

The SDP, which dated from 1916, long advocated state ownership of large enterprises; increased social welfare benefits; and continued support for NATO. In the 1987 election, the party's legislative strength rose from six seats to ten, all of which were retained in 1991, when it joined in coalition with the IP. Unrest over government austerity measures yielded an unsuccessful challenge to the leadership and the formation of the breakaway Awakening of the Nation-People's Movement (*Thjóðvaki-Hreyfing Fólksins*), which was launched for the 1995 election by former SDP deputy chair and social affairs minister Jóhanna SIGURÐARDÓTTIR. In the 1995 balloting the SDP won only 11.4 percent of the vote and seven seats, while the *Thjóðvaki* won 7.2 percent and four seats. The two groups subsequently reconciled, and Sigurðardóttir became a prominent leader in the Unified Left before the 1999 election.

The WA, which has also been known as the Alliance of the Women's List (*Samtök um Kvennalista*), was organized prior to the 1983 balloting, when it won three seats. Said to be the first feminist group in the world to secure such representation, it doubled its seats to six in 1987, one of which was lost in 1991. In 1995, it slipped further to three seats. Its 1996 presidential candidate, Guðrún AGNARSDÓTTIR, finished third, with 26 percent of the vote. Like the PA, the WA lost a number of members who objected to formation of the Unified Left.

In the run-up to the 1999 Althing election, The Alliance called for an expansion of social services and family-oriented government policies (such as longer parental leave) while arguing that Iceland should not consider applying for EU membership for at least four years. It also proposed that the U.S. military presence in Iceland should be reduced but did not challenge continued membership in NATO. Unity proved elusive for the coalition, particularly between the centrist SDP and its more strongly leftist partners, and it won only 26.8 percent of the vote and 17 seats.

In May 2000, The Alliance announced that a former SDP leader, Össur SKARPHÉÐINSSON, had been elected chair, and a former PA leader, Margrét FRÍMANNSDÓTTIR, was named deputy chair. The Alliance increased its vote share to 31 percent and its seat total to 20 in the 2003 legislative election. In 2005 Skarphéðinsson was replaced as party leader by Ingibjörg Gísladóttir.

In the May 2007 balloting, The Alliance lost two seats, but it subsequently joined the IP-led coalition government. In 2008 the Alliance launched an initiative to end a special provision within the Kyoto Protocol that allowed the country to increase its greenhouse emissions by up to 10 percent per year.

Sigurðardóttir was appointed prime minister and asked to form an interim government following the resignation of the IP-led government in January 2009. In March 2009 **Iceland's Movement–Living Land** (*Íslandshreyfingin–Lifandi Land*) merged with The Alliance. Founded in March 2007 in Reykjavík by environmental activist Omar Ragnarsson, Iceland's Movement campaigned on a green platform stressing stricter environmental regulation.

Sigurðardóttir was elected party chair of The Alliance at a congress in March 2009, after Gísladóttir declined to seek another term due to health reasons. Sigurðardóttir subsequently led The Alliance to victory in the April Althing elections. The party won 29.8 percent of the vote and secured 20 seats. The Alliance formed a coalition government with the VGF with Sigurðardóttir again as prime minister. After the balloting, party member Ásta R. JÓHANNESDÓTTIR was elected speaker of the Althing. In municipal balloting in May 2010, The Alliance secured a disappointing three of 15 seats on the Reykjavik council. Polls indicated a deep decline in support for The Alliance because of the country's economic woes. Sigurðardóttir resigned as party chief before the 2013 election.

Leaders: Árni Páll ÁRNASON (Chair), Jóhanna SIGURÐARDÓTTIR (Former Prime Minister), Katrín JÚLÍUSDÓTTIR (Vice Chair).

Left-Green Alliance (*Vinstrihreyfing-Grœnt Frambod*—VGF). Also referenced as the Red-Green Party and the Left-Green Party, the VGF was formed in 1998 by left-leaning Althing members of the People's Alliance and the Women's Alliance who opposed joining the Unified Left. It won 9.1 percent of the vote and six Althing seats in 1999 and 8.8 percent of the vote and five seats in 2003. The VGF became the third-largest party in the Althing following the May 2007 elections when it won nine seats.

The VGF participated in The Alliance-led interim government in January 2009. In the 2009 elections, the VGF won 21.7 percent of the vote and secured 14 seats in the Althing. It again joined in a governing coalition with The Alliance and secured three cabinet posts. In April 2011, two VGF members of the Althing left the party and declared themselves independents to protest the coalition's management of the Icesave crisis. The party opposes EU membership and supports the draft constitution.

Leaders: Katrín JAKOBSDÓTTIR (President and former Minister of Education, Science, and Culture), Björn GÍSLASON (Vice President), Tómasdóttir SOLELY (Secretary General).

Bright Future (*Björt framtíð*) is a liberal political party established on February 4, 2012; it favors EU membership and the eurozone and promotes environmental protection. Prior to the 2013 parliamentary election Bright Future had two MPs who had switched parties: Guðmundur Steingrímsson (PP) and Róbert MARSHALL (Alliance). It secured six seats in the 2013 election.

Leaders: Heiða Kristín HELGADOTTIR (Chair), Guðmundur STEINGRÍMSSON (Chair of parliamentary faction).

Pirate Party of Iceland (*Píratar*). Iceland's Pirate Party was founded on November 24, 2012, and observes the standard Pirate platform of direct democracy and Internet freedom. Founding member Birgitta Jónsdóttir was already a member of parliament, giving the international movement its first seat in a national parliament. The Pirates won three seats in the 2013 election and introduced a bill to offer citizenship to Edward Snowden, who leaked U.S. intelligence secrets to the media.

Leader: Birgitta JÓNSDÓTTIR.

Other Parties in the 2013 Election:

Dawn (*Dögun*) was created in March 2012 through the merger of **Movement** (*Hreyfingin*), the **Liberal Party** (*Frjálslyndi Flokkurinn*), and the **Democratic Movement** (*Lýðræðishreyfingin*). It advocates household debt relief and staunchly backs the draft constitution. Movement was originally formed as the **Citizens' Movement** (*Borgarahreyfingin*), which grew out of antigovernment protests in January 2009. The populist, center-right party advocated economic reforms in response to the 2009 recession and won four seats in the April 2009 Althing balloting. One of the party's members of parliament became an independent in August 2009. The remaining three members of parliament formed the Movement in 2010.

The Liberal Party was formed in 1998 by Sverrir HERMANNSSON, former cabinet minister and former director of the national bank of Iceland. It supported decentralization, a free-market system, a social safety net, lower taxes, and continued participation in NATO; it opposed EU membership. The Liberals won two seats in the May 1999 Althing election, four seats in 2003 and four again in 2007. The small **New Force** (*Nýtt Afl*) political party merged with the Liberals at the beginning of 2007, but the enlarged party won only 2.2 percent of the vote in 2009 elections and failed to gain any seats. The Democratic Movement was founded in January 2009 and received 0.6 percent of the vote in the April 2009 Althing elections, (For more on these parties see the 2010 *Handbook.*)

Other minor or newly formed parties include the following: **Rainbow** (*Regnboginn*), founded in March 2013 by VGF deputy Bjarni HAROARSON; **Solidarity**, founded in 2012 by Lilja Mósesdóttir of the VGF, did not field a candidate for parliament; the **Iceland Democratic Party** (Lýðræðisvaktin), founded February 16, 2013, to promote the draft constitution; the anti-EU **Right-Greens** (*Haegri-Graenir*), formed in 2010 and led by Guðmundur Franklin Jónsson; and the **Household Party** (*Heimilanna*), formed in March 2013 as a union of the **Sovereign Union** (*Samtök Fullveldissinna*) and seven other small groups, led by Pétur Gunnlaugsson; and **Best Party** (*Besti Flokkurinn*—BF) formed in November 2009 and led by comedian Jón Gnarr. Originally a joke party, Gnarr was elected mayor of Reykjavik on November 16, 2009, and 6 out of 15 seats on the city council in 2010.

LEGISLATURE

Iceland's parliament, the **Althing** (*Alingi*), consists of 63 members elected for four-year terms by a proportional system. In the election of April 27, 2013, the Independence Party won 19 seats; the Progressive Party, 19; the Alliance, 9; the Left-Green Alliance, 7; Bright Future, 6, and the Pirate Party, 3.

President: Einar K. GUÐFINNSSON.

CABINET

[as of November 8, 2013]

Prime Minister	Sigmunder Davið Gunnlaugsson (PP)
Ministers	
Agriculture and Fisheries	Sigurður Ingi Jóhannsson (PP)
Education, Science, and Culture	Illugi Gunnarsson (IP)
Environment and Natural Resources	Sigurður Ingi Jóhannsson (PP)
Finance and Economic Affairs	Bjarni Benediktsson (IP)
Foreign Affairs	Gunnar Bragi Sveinsson (PP)
Health	Kristján Þór Júlíusson (IP)
Industry and Commerce	Ragnheiður Elín Árnadóttir (IP) [f]
Interior	Hanna Birna Kristjándóttir (IP) [f]
Social Affairs and Housing	Eygló Harðardóttir (PP) [f]

[f] = female

INTERGOVERNMENTAL REPRESENTATION

Ambassador to the U.S.: Gunmundur Arni STEFANSSON.

U.S. Ambassador to Iceland: Robert C. BARBER (nominated).

Permanent Representative to the UN: Gréta GUNNARSDÓTTIR.

IGO Memberships (Non-UN): CEUR, EBRD, EFTA, ICC, NATO, OECD, OSCE, WTO.

INDIA

Republic of India
Bharat

Political Status: Independent since August 15, 1947; republican system instituted by constitution of January 26, 1950.

Area: 1,222,559 sq. mi. (3,166,414 sq. km), excluding approximately 30,160 sq. mi. (78,114 sq. km) of Jammu and Kashmir presently held by Pakistan and 16,480 sq. mi. (42,685 sq. km) held by China.

Population: 1,267,286,430 (2012E—UN); 1,220,800,359 (2013E—U.S. Census).

Major Urban Centers (urban areas, 2011C): NEW DELHI (16,753,235); Mumbai, formerly Bombay (18,414,288); Kolkata, formerly Calcutta (14,112,536); Chennai, formerly Madras (8,696,010); Bengalooru (Bangalore, 8,499,399); Hyderabad (7,749,334); Ahmadabad (6,240,201).

Official Languages: Hindi, English (in addition to other languages that are official at state levels).

Monetary Unit: Rupee (market rate November 1, 2013: 62.33 rupees = $1US).

President: Pranab MUKHERJEE (United Progressive Alliance); elected July 19, 2012, by an electoral college and inaugurated July 25 for a five-year term, succeeding Pratibha Devisingh PATIL (United Progressive Alliance).

Vice President: Mohammad Hamid ANSARI (United Progressive Alliance); elected by Parliament on August 10, 2007, and inaugurated August 11 for a five-year term, succeeding Bhairon Singh SHEKHAWAT; reelected on August 7, 2012.

Prime Minister: Manmohan SINGH (Indian National Congress); appointed by the president on May 19, 2004, and sworn in on May 22, in succession to Atal Bihari VAJPAYEE (*Bharatiya Janata Party*), who had submitted his resignation on May 13, following the election of April–May; invited to form a new government by the president on May 20, 2009, following the legislative election of April–May 2009, and sworn in as the head of a new Council of Ministers on May 22.

THE COUNTRY

Forming a natural subcontinent between the Arabian Sea and the Bay of Bengal and stretching from the Himalayas in the north to the Indian Ocean in the south, the Republic of India encompasses a mélange of ethnic, linguistic, and socioreligious groups that together constitute a national population second in size only to that of mainland China. India embraces over 1,600 different languages and dialects, most of Indo-European derivation, followed in importance by Dravidian, Austro-Asiatic, and Sino-Tibiti. Although India has the largest Hindu population in the world (about 83 percent of the people), the Muslim component (over 11 percent) makes India the country with the world's fourth-largest Muslim population, after Indonesia, Pakistan, and Bangladesh. Smaller religious groups include Christians, Sikhs, Buddhists, and Jains. All religions enjoy equal status under the constitution, and caste discrimination, although still practiced in rural areas, is outlawed. Despite a rising participation rate, women make up only 28 percent of the active labor force. Under a 1993 constitutional amendment, one-third of local council seats and executive positions are reserved for women. A proposal currently under discussion would extend the one-third reservation to Parliament and the state legislatures. Female representation in the most recently elected lower house of Parliament is 11 percent (60 of 545 seats), and 10.6 percent in the upper house (26 of 245 seats).

Agriculture employs about 54 percent of Indian workers and contributes 18 percent of GDP; the principal crops are rice, cotton, and jute (fall harvest); wheat (summer harvest); and oilseeds, sugarcane, coffee, tea, spices, and nuts. Despite employing only 18 percent of the labor force, industry is considerably diversified, producing manufactures ranging from transport equipment (principally two-wheeled vehicles) and diesel engines to aluminum, petroleum products, and televisions as well as such long-established mainstays as cotton textiles and processed foods. Industry as a whole accounts for 29 percent of GDP, compared with 53 percent for services. Leading merchandise exports include mineral products; textiles and garments; gems and jewelry; base metals and related products; chemicals and related products; machinery, appliances, and electrical equipment; and such traditional agricultural commodities as oil cakes, rice, coffee, tea, spices, and cashews.

Annual GDP growth averaged 6.1 percent between 2001–2009 (for an overview of the economy prior to 2000, please see the 2013 *Handbook*). In 2010, India's GDP grew at 10.6 percent, and it continued to expand at an annual rate of 8.5 percent in 2010–2011. The rapid economic growth, however, precipitated a high rate of inflation, which stood at 11.9 percent at year-end in 2010, far above the 5 percent that Indian economists believe to be the maximum acceptable level. In 2011, GDP grew by 7.2 percent, and it grew by 4 percent in 2012. That year inflation grew by 9.3 percent, while GDP per capita was $1,491. In January 2013, the Reserve Bank cut interest rates to 7.75 percent, after 11 consecutive increases, and eased credit in a bid to spur economic growth. The World Bank ranked India 132nd out of 185 countries in its 2013 annual Doing Business survey, citing corruption and the country's regulatory framework.

GOVERNMENT AND POLITICS

Political background. After a prolonged struggle against British colonial rule, which had been entrenched in 1858, India attained independence within the Commonwealth on August 15, 1947, when Britain put into effect the Indian Independence Act, thereby partitioning the subcontinent into the sovereign states of predominantly Hindu India and Muslim Pakistan. However, the act applied only to former British India, thus setting the stage for confrontation between the two new nations over accession of various princely states and feudatories that had retained nominal independence under the Raj, including Jammu and Kashmir, where a militarized Line of Control (LoC) still separates Indian and Pakistani sectors.

Jawahar Lal NEHRU, leader of the politically dominant Indian National Congress (INC), served as India's first prime minister. A follower of the charismatic advocate of nonviolence Mohandas Karamchand GANDHI, who was assassinated in 1948, Nehru enunciated India's basic principles of democracy, secularism, socialism, and nonalignment. Upon his death in 1964 Nehru was succeeded by Lal Bahadur SHASTRI, who died in 1966 and was in turn succeeded by Indira GANDHI, Nehru's daughter.

In 1969, the INC split into Gandhi and conservative factions, the latter subsequently entitled the INC-Organization, or Congress (O). With Gandhi's "New Congress" group having swept the parliamentary election of March 1971, she controlled enough seats in the lower house (*Lok Sabha*) to amend the constitution. Between 1971 and 1974 new constitutional amendments were adopted permitting parliamentary restriction of fundamental rights, and legislation was enacted authorizing the use of preventive detention as an antiterrorism measure. In June 1975, however, the High Court of Allahabad ruled in favor of a petition filed by Raj NARAIN, who charged that Gandhi had committed election irregularities in 1971. The ruling disqualified Gandhi from membership in the *Lok Sabha,* but she was granted a 20-day stay to appeal to the Supreme Court.

Opposition party leaders immediately launched a civil disobedience campaign to force Gandhi's resignation, and on June 26, 1975, President Fakhruddin Ali AHMED declared a state of emergency at her request. Nearly 700 opposition leaders were promptly arrested, and press censorship was introduced for the first time since independence. In July Parliament approved the state of emergency, after which a majority of the opposition members withdrew from the lower house in protest. In November the Indian Supreme Court unanimously upheld the prime minister's appeal, and in February 1976 Parliament voted to extend the term of the sitting *Lok Sabha* beyond its five-year mandate.

In January 1977, Gandhi called an election for March. In spite of the short, six-week campaign, a multiparty *Janata* (People's) Front was able to organize behind anticorruption campaigner Jaya Prakash NARAYANAN and Congress (O) leader Moraji R. DESAI. Pledging to end the state of emergency and restore democracy, *Janata* swept the election, Gandhi being among the defeated candidates. Desai was designated prime minister, and the state of emergency was revoked on March 27.

In December 1977, Gandhi resigned from the INC Working Committee and, in January 1978, organized the Indian National Congress–Indira (universally rendered as Congress [I]), which by mid-year had become the nation's major opposition party. Gandhi returned to the *Lok Sabha* after winning a November by-election, but in late December, she was stripped of her seat and imprisoned for the duration of the parliamentary term by action of the *Janata* majority.

The fragility of the *Janata* coalition was highlighted in mid-1978 by a major leadership dispute between Prime Minister Desai and his home affairs minister, Charan SINGH. Moreover, a series of communal riots in a number of states effectively split the party into Hindu and secular factions and provoked demands by Raj Narain and others that *Janata* adopt the posture of a secular "third force" opposed to both Hindu extremism and Gandhi's "authoritarianism." In mid-July Singh and a number of others resigned to join Narain's recently formed *Janata* Party–Secular (JP-S), thus depriving the government of its majority in the *Lok Sabha* and forcing Desai's resignation as prime minister. Invited by President Neelam Sanjiva REDDY to form a new government, Singh was sworn in on July 28, but he submitted his own resignation three weeks later following the defection of a number of Congress (O) members and an announcement that Congress (I) would not support him in a confidence vote. President Reddy therefore dissolved the *Lok Sabha* on August 22.

Gandhi swept back into power in the *Lok Sabha* election of January 1980. However, her administration failed to curb mounting domestic violence. A continuing influx of illegal Bengali immigrants generated reprisals in Assam, while riots broke out in Karnataka over a recommendation that Kannada be adopted as the language of instruction. Muslims and Hindus battled sporadically in Uttar Pradesh and Gujarat, and *Harijans* ("Untouchables") were targets for numerous atrocities. Maoists, Naxalites (named after a peasant revolt in the 1960s in Naxalbari, West Bengal), and other extremists continued their frequently violent activities in Manipur, Mizoram, Nagaland, and West Bengal, while demands for autonomy by Sikhs in Punjab led to the storming of Parliament in October 1982 by several thousand individuals as part of a continuing *morcha* (mass agitation).

The Sikh agitation of the early 1980s was directed by the relatively moderate leader of the *Shiromani Akali Dal* (SAD), Harchand Singh LONGOWAL. During early 1984 Hindu-Sikh violence intensified, fueled in part by supporters loyal to Sikh fundamentalist Jarnail Singh BHINDRANWALE, who operated from sanctuary within the Golden Temple in Amritsar. A series of assassinations, reportedly ordered by Bhindranwale, led to an assault on the Golden Temple by Indian security forces during the night of June 5–6, in the course of which over 1,000 persons, including Bhindranwale, were killed. The action provoked an even deeper Sikh resentment, which reached a climax on October 31 with Gandhi's assassination by two Sikh members of her personal bodyguard.

Mrs. Gandhi's son, Rajiv GANDHI, was immediately sworn in as prime minister, and an election was called at which Congress (I) won an unprecedented 401 of 508 contested seats. In July 1985, the government concluded a peace accord with *Akali Dal.* Sikh extremists responded by assassinating Longowal on August 20, and violence in Punjab and elsewhere persisted through 1986.

In mid-1988, the Gandhi administration lost a critical series of state elections as evidence emerged of extensive corruption, particularly in arms contracts with Western companies. The government also came under serious challenge from Vishwanath Pratap SINGH, whose anticorruption campaign as defense minister had led to his expulsion from Congress (I) in mid-1987. Singh then played a key role in organizing a seven-party opposition National Front (*Rashtriya Morcha*) within which a three-party *Janata Dal* (People's Party) grouping was formed in October.

Prime Minister Gandhi called an early lower house election for November 1989, at which the National Front and its allies gained a clear-cut majority of seats. On December 2 Singh, although not favored by supporters of *Janata Dal* leader Chandra SHEKHAR, was sworn in as head of a new administration with external support from the right-wing Hindu *Bharatiya Janata* Party (BJP) as well as the two leading leftist formations, the Communist Party of India (CPI) and the Communist Party of India–Marxist (CPI-M).

In September 1990, BJP leader Lal Krishna ADVANI began a religious pilgrimage (*rath yatra*) to the site of an abandoned Muslim mosque in Ayodhya, Uttar Pradesh, where Hindu efforts to construct a temple had led to serious ethnic unrest. On October 23 Prime Minister Singh ordered Advani's arrest, whereupon the BJP withdrew its support. With the National Front government thus weakened, *Janata Dal* split on November 5, 1990, Chandra Shekhar and Deputy Prime Minister Devi LAL forming *Janata Dal*–Socialist (JD-S). Two days later Singh became the first Indian prime minister to be defeated on the floor of the *Lok Sabha,* losing a confidence vote 346–142, and on November 10 Shekhar, with Congress (I) backing, was named as his successor.

Prime Minister Shekhar, whose parliamentary group counted only 54 members, felt obliged to resign on March 6, 1991, in the wake of a rift with Gandhi. On March 13, President Ramaswamy VENKATARAMAN, acceding to a request by the Congress (I) leader, dissolved Parliament. At first-stage legislative balloting on May 20, Congress (I) was the victor in a substantial proportion of completed contests, but on May 21, the election was thrown into chaos by Gandhi's assassination at the hands of Sri Lankan Tamil separatists angered over India's 1987–1990 intervention in support of the Sri Lankan government (see Foreign relations, below). Second- and third-stage polling were immediately postponed, with longtime party stalwart P. V. Narasimha RAO being named Congress (I) president on May 29. Completion of the election on June 15 yielded, as anticipated, less than a legislative majority for the Congress (I) and its allies. Rao nonetheless succeeded in forming a coalition administration and then, through a series of by-election victories and opposition defections, was able to convert his plurality to a majority over the ensuing two years.

During 1994, Prime Minister Rao became increasingly beleaguered by critics of his market-oriented economic policies. In March 1995, Congress (I) suffered the latest in a series of state electoral defeats. The losses generated an open revolt within the party, and a dissident rally on May 19 named a longtime rival of the prime minister, Narain Dutt TIWARI, to succeed Rao as party leader. Tiwari and his ally Arjun SINGH subsequently formed the All India Indira Congress (AIIC).

Balloting for the 11th *Lok Sabha,* held in several rounds beginning on April 27, 1996, delivered a heavy defeat for Congress (I), which had been sullied earlier in the year by a major corruption scandal and the consequent resignations of ten government ministers. Whereas Congress (I) retained only 140 *Lok Sabha* seats, the fundamentalist BJP won 161. A 14-party center-left alliance, which included *Janata Dal* and which was subsequently redesignated the United Front (UF), secured 177 seats.

President Shankar Dayal SHARMA invited the BJP parliamentary leader, Atal Bihari VAJPAYEE, to form a government. A BJP administration was announced on May 15, 1996, but resigned on May 28 rather than face a confidence vote. The president then turned to the UF, which had selected the Karnataka chief minister, H. D. DEVE GOWDA (*Janata Dal*), as its overall leader. Crucially, Deve Gowda obtained a prompt pledge of support from the Congress (I) leadership. A UF minority government, containing representatives of nine component parties, was sworn in on June 1.

Facing corruption and bribery charges, former prime minister Rao resigned as Congress party president on September 21, 1996. (Although he was convicted in October 2000, the verdict was overturned in March 2002.) He was succeeded two days later, initially in an acting capacity, by the party treasurer, Sitaram KESRI, the first member of a lower caste to head Congress. (By then, having outlasted or reabsorbed most rival Congress formations, the party had largely dropping the appended "I.")

On March 30, 1997, Congress announced that it was withdrawing support from the government. The UF administration consequently lost a confidence motion on April 11, prompting Deve Gowda to resign. With neither the Congress nor the UF strong enough to form a government on its own, Deve Gowda announced that he would step down as head of the UF, thereby permitting a "face-saving" change of leadership that would facilitate further UF-Congress cooperation. As a result, the highly respected foreign minister, Inder Kumar GUJRAL of the *Janata Dal,* was sworn in as prime minister on April 22. He reappointed most of the incumbent ministers to his new cabinet.

In electoral college voting on July 14, 1997, Vice President Kicheril Raman NARAYANAN, who had the support of all major parties, was elected president, thereby becoming the first head of state with a *Dalit* (formerly "Untouchable" or *Harijan*) heritage.

In August 1997, the public learned that the government-appointed Jain Commission, in the course of its investigation into the 1991 assassination of Rajiv Gandhi, had considered evidence of a possible indirect connection between the Dravidian Progressive Federation (*Dravida Munnetra Kazhagam*—DMK), a member of the UF government, and the suspect Sri Lankan rebels. Consequently, Congress and the UF's *Tamil Maanila* Congress (TMC), which was in competition with the DMK for control of Tamil Nadu, demanded that Gujral oust the DMK. When Gujral refused, Congress withdrew its support from the government, triggering its collapse on November 28. Congress and the BJP both failed in separate efforts to form a new government, prompting President Narayanan to announce an election for February–March 1998.

Although the 1998 election failed to produce a majority for any of the major national parties, the BJP and its allies emerged with a parliamentary plurality of some 252 seats, while the UF lost nearly half of its former representation. Having secured the support of a patchwork coalition of some 20 other national and regional parties, the BJP's Vajpayee was sworn in as prime minister on March 19.

Meanwhile, the Congress Party, had turned increasingly toward Sonia GANDHI, Rajiv's widow, who, although not a candidate herself, had campaigned heavily in the final weeks before the election. On March 9, 1998, Sitaram Kesri announced his decision to retire as party leader, clearing the way for Gandhi's assumption of the presidency. On March 16 Gandhi was additionally named the party's parliamentary chair and thus the de facto leader of the opposition even though she had never held elective office. Earlier, on January 28, a New Delhi court had sentenced 10 Indians and 16 Sri Lankans to death for conspiring in her late husband's 1991 assassination.

On May 11 and 13, 1998, India conducted nuclear weapons tests for the first time since 1974, exploding five devices underground in the Rajasthan desert near Pokaran. (Pakistan responded on May 28 and 30 with six explosions of its own.) Domestically, the news prompted widespread expressions of national pride, although international condemnation and imposition of sanctions by the United States and other countries quickly followed.

Meanwhile, Prime Minister Vajpayee found himself facing ultimatums from his own coalition partners, particularly Jayalalitha JAYARAM, the flamboyant leader of the All India Dravidian Progressive Federation (All India *Anna Dravida Munnetra Kazhagam*—AIADMK) and a former chief minister of Tamil Nadu. Vajpayee's rejection of her demands for policy and personnel changes led Jayalalitha (as she is universally known) to withdraw her support, and on April 17, 1999, the government lost a confidence motion 270–269 in the *Lok Sabha.* The prime minister resigned the following day, and after Sonia Gandhi proved unable to forge a Congress-led coalition, President Narayanan dissolved the lower house on April 26.

The ensuing election campaign was marked by considerable political reshuffling, with the BJP announcing in May 1999 the formation of a National Democratic Alliance (NDA) that, by late August, included 24 parties. Significantly, the NDA election manifesto emphasized economic reforms and infrastructural development while omitting Hindu nationalist goals. The most important development of the preelection period, however, was renewed hostilities in the mountainous Kargil area of Kashmir, where Islamic militants and Pakistani troops had crossed the long-established LoC. A negotiated withdrawal was completed late in July, although sporadic artillery exchanges persisted.

The NDA won a clear victory in the 1999 *Lok Sabha* balloting. On October 13, with the support of some 18 parties and just over 300 MPs, Prime Minister Vajpayee was sworn in at the head of a massive 70-member cabinet (including ministers of state). Numerous cabinet reshuffles occurred in the following three years. In July 2002, Vajpayee elevated the hard-line minister of home affairs, Lal Krishna Advani, to the post of deputy prime minister.

On February 27, 2002, Muslims burned train cars carrying Hindu activists from the disputed sacred site in Ayodhya. Nearly 60 died in the attack, which generated reprisals by Hindu vigilantes that cost an additional 1,100 Muslim and Hindu lives and forced over 100,000 Muslims to flee their homes. Reports prepared by the United Kingdom and the European Union (EU) subsequently alleged that the anti-Muslim riots were not spontaneous, as some officials had claimed, but were instead an organized campaign conducted with the acquiescence—in some cases, the assistance—of government personnel.

On July 15, 2002, A. P. J. Abdul KALAM, a scientist and the architect of India's ballistic missile program, was elected president of India. Although a political novice, the widely popular Kalam, a Muslim, drew support from most of the opposition as well as the NDA. On August 12 Bhairon Singh SHEKHAWAT, a former chief minister of Rajasthan, was elected vice president, his predecessor, Krishan KANT, having died in office on July 27.

In late January 2004 Prime Minister Vajpayee advised President Kalam to dissolve the *Lok Sabha* and call an early election. Although public opinion polls indicated that Vajpayee would easily lead the NDA to victory, there were perceptions that the plight of the rural poor was slighted. In addition, what was widely viewed as an inadequate government response to the communal violence that followed the 2002 train-burning incident had raised questions about the government's commitment to a secular union. As a result, voters confounded expectations, and in balloting in April–May Sonia Gandhi's Congress and its allies registered an upset victory, winning 219 seats, versus 185 for the NDA.

On May 13, 2004, Vajpayee submitted his resignation, and on May 19 the president named the INC's Manmohan SINGH prime minister. Singh, a Sikh senator and former finance minister, had been credited with instituting reforms that saved India's faltering economy. A day earlier, Gandhi had withdrawn her name from consideration, in part to defuse the divisive issue of her Italian birth. Having obtained the external support of the CPI-M, and an assortment of other parties, Singh and a multiparty United Progressive Alliance (UPA) government were sworn in on May 22.

On July 21, 2007, Pratibha PATIL, the UPA candidate and most recently governor of Rajasthan, was elected as president of India with 65.8 percent of the vote, defeating Vice President Shekhawat, who had been endorsed by the BJP and most of the other NDA parties. Earlier, a newly formed "third force" United National Progressive Alliance (UNPA) of regional parties failed to convince President Kalam to seek a second term. On August 10, the UPA's Mohammad Hamid ANSARI was elected vice president, defeating the NDA's candidate, Najma HEPTULLAH, by a 2–1 margin.

On July 8, 2008, the Left Front withdrew its support from Prime Minister Singh over objections to a U.S.-India nuclear power deal (see Foreign relations, below). Staking the survival of his minority government on gaining parliamentary approval of the program, Singh managed to attract sufficient backing from the SP, some smaller parties, and independents, which produced on July 22 a 275–256–10 vote in favor of the pact.

The election of April–May 2009 was preceded by several changes in the makeup of the governing UPA and the opposition NDA as well as by the formation of alternative Third Front and Fourth Front alliances, led, in the first case, by the Left Front and the pro-*Dalit Bahujan Samata* Party (BSP) and, in the second, by the Uttar Pradesh–based *Samajwadi* Party (SP). The multistage balloting saw the Congress-led

UPA expand its plurality to 262 seats, which, with the external support of the BSP and the SP, enabled Prime Minister Singh to claim another term in office.

On January 19, 2011, Singh conducted a major cabinet reshuffle (see Current issues, below), followed by another extensive reorganization on July 12 in response to ministerial resignations over the preceding seven months.

Former finance minister Pranab MUKHERJEE of the UPA was elected president on July19, 2012, defeating Purno SANGMA, the candidate of the NDA. Tensions between the All India Trinamul Congress (AITC) and the INC over economic reforms led the former to withdraw from the UPA in September 2012, causing the ruling coalition to lose its majority. However, the SP agreed to support though not join the government. In October, Singh reshuffled the cabinet. In March 2013, the DMK withdrew from the government in protest over the failure of the cabinet to strongly condemn the Sri Lankan government for atrocities against ethnic Tamils during that country's civil war. Singh reshuffled the cabinet in June to fill the vacancies created by the resignation of the DMK ministers, but the government remained dependent on external support and was vulnerable to a no-confidence vote.

Constitution and government. India's frequently amended constitution of January 26, 1950, provides for a republican form of parliamentary government in a secular union (despite Hindu numerical predominance) that currently embraces 28 states and 7 centrally administered territories. Under the Indian constitution, all legislative subjects are divided into three jurisdictions: the union list, comprising subjects on which the union Parliament has exclusive authority; the state list, comprising subjects on which the state assemblies have authority; and the concurrent list, comprising subjects on which both may legislate, with a union ruling predominating in the event of conflict and where state questions assume national importance.

The head of state, a president who serves a five-year term, is chosen, under a weighted voting system, by an electoral college comprising the elected members of both the bicameral Parliament and the state legislatures. The vice president is elected by the members of the full Parliament and serves as ex officio chair of the upper house of the legislature, the Council of States (*Rajya Sabha*). The lower House of the People (*Lok Sabha*), elected for a five-year term (subject to dissolution), is presided over by a speaker elected by its members. The speaker must be a member of Parliament but by convention abandons party affiliation while serving as presiding officer. The prime minister is elected by the parliamentary members of the majority party or coalition of parties and heads a government that is collectively responsible to the legislature.

Each state has a governor, who is appointed by the president for a term of five years, and a popularly elected legislature. The legislatures may be bicameral or unicameral, but all are subject to maximum terms of five years. Administration is carried out by a chief minister heading a cabinet subject to parliamentary responsibility. In the event that constitutional processes in a state are rendered inoperative, the union constitution provides for the institution of direct presidential rule, with the concurrence of both houses of Parliament. The president can also appoint an agent to act as presidential surrogate, while the prime minister can call for new state elections.

The union territories, some of which are former foreign territories or are located in outlying regions, are administered by appointed officials (called lieutenant governors or administrators) responsible to the president. Puducherry and the National Capital Territory of Delhi also have elected assemblies and chief ministers.

In December 2009 the central government approved the reestablishment of the state of Telangana, which had been merged with Andhra in 1956 to form Andhra Pradesh. The government's 2009 decision provoked heated opposition, including the mass resignation of over 100 legislators from the Andhra Pradesh state assembly. Final approval was granted by the government in July 2013 (see Current issues, below).

State and Capital	*Area (sq. mi.)*	*Population (2011C)*
Andhra Pradesh (Hyderabad)	106,204	84,665,533
Arunachal Pradesh (Itanagar)	32,333	1,382,611
Assam (Dispur)	30,285	31,169,272
Bihar (Patna)	36,356	103,804,637
Chhattisgarh (Raipur)	52,197	25,540,196
Goa (Panaji)	1,429	1,457,723
Gujarat (Gandhinagar)	75,684	60,383,628
Haryana (Chandigarh)	17,070	25,353,081
Himachal Pradesh (Shimla)	21,495	6,856,509
Jammu and Kashmir (Srinagar)*	39,146	12,548,926
Jharkhand (Ranchi)	30,778	32,966,238
Karnataka (Bengalooru)	74,051	61,130,704
Kerala (Thiruvananthapuram)	15,005	33,387,677
Madhya Pradesh (Bhopal)	119,013	72,597,565
Maharashtra (Mumbai)	118,808	112,372,972
Manipur (Imphal)	8,620	2,721,756
Meghalaya (Shillong)	8,660	2,964,007
Mizoram (Aizawl)	8,139	1,091,014
Nagaland (Kohima)	6,401	1,980,602
Orissa (Bhubaneswar)	60,118	41,947,358
Punjab (Chandigarh)	19,445	27,704,236
Rajasthan (Jaipur)	132,138	68,621,012
Sikkim (Gangtok)	2,740	607,688
Tamil Nadu (Chennai)	50,215	72,138,958
Tripura (Agartala)	4,045	3,671,032
Uttarakhand (Dehradun)	20,650	10,116,752
Uttar Pradesh (Lucknow)	93,022	199,581,4770
West Bengal (Kolkata)	34,267	91,347,736
Union Territory and Capital		
Andaman and Nicobar Is. (Port Blair)	3,185	379,944
Chandigarh (Chandigarh)	44	1,054,686
Dadra and Nagar Haveli (Silvassa)	190	342,853
Daman and Diu (Daman)	43	242,911
Lakshadweep (Kavaratti)	12	64,429
Puducherry (Puducherry)	185	1,244,464
National Capital Territory		
New Delhi (Delhi)	573	16,753,235

**Indian-held portion*

Indian news media are protected by the constitution. Nevertheless, state and local officials have sometimes attempted to intimidate publishers and journalists, some of whom have been detained for such alleged violations as "offending religious feelings." Journalists have also come under attack in areas subject to Maoist and separatist insurgencies, especially in the northeast. In 2013 the media watchdog group Reporters Without Borders ranked India 140th among 179 countries in terms of freedom of the press, a significant decline from three years before, when it was ranked 105th out of 175 countries.

Foreign relations. India's policies as a member of the Commonwealth, the United Nations, and other multilateral organizations have been based on nonalignment, peaceful settlement of international disputes, self-determination for colonial peoples, and comprehensive efforts to ameliorate conditions in the developing nations. Following independence, it avoided participation in regional defense pacts and exclusive alignment with either Western or Communist powers, although it accepted economic and military aid from both groups.

India's foreign policy has often focused on Pakistan. The centuries-old rivalry between Hindus and Muslims in the subcontinent was directly responsible for the partition in 1947 and continued to embitter Indo-Pakistani relations thereafter, particularly in the long-standing dispute over Jammu and Kashmir. Fighting over that territory in 1947–1948 resulted in a de facto division into Pakistani- and Indian-held sectors. The Indian portion was subsequently absorbed as a separate state of the Indian Union. That action was strongly protested by Pakistan, and renewed armed conflict between the two countries erupted in 1965. In December 1971, following a political crisis in East Pakistan and the flight of some 10 million Bengali refugees to India, the two nations again went to war. The brief conflict ended with Pakistani acceptance of a cease-fire on the western front and the emergence in the east of the independent state of Bangladesh.

In March 1972, India and Bangladesh concluded a 25-year Treaty of Friendship and Cooperation, and relations remain close despite recent disagreements over boundaries; conflicting claims to newly formed islands in the Bay of Bengal; and the continued presence in

Bangladesh of Indian insurgents from Assam, Tripura, and Manipur. (See the Bangladesh entry for details.) In December 1996, the two countries concluded a pact on sharing the Ganges River, while an agreement signed on October 1, 2003, covers seven other rivers.

India and Pakistan agreed to resume normal relations in mid-1972, but ambassadors were not exchanged until 1976. In the following decade bilateral sessions focused on economic, educational, cultural, and technical cooperation as well as on illegal border crossings, drug trafficking, smuggling, and terrorism. The Jammu and Kashmir issue continued to poison relations, however, particularly after separatists and Islamic fundamentalists began increasing their attacks in 1989 and Kashmir's most senior Islamic leader, Moulvi Mohammed FAROOQ, was assassinated in 1990.

To diffuse external criticism of nuclear weapons tests conducted in May 1998, Indian Prime Minister Vajpayee and Pakistani Prime Minister Nawaz Sharif conferred briefly during the July 1998 South Asian Association for Regional Cooperation (SAARC) session in Colombo, Sri Lanka. They met again in September in New York and agreed, among other things, to renew bilateral talks on Kashmir in October.

Of even greater import, on February 20–21, 1999, Vajpayee and Sharif met in Lahore, Pakistan, the first such visit across the border by an Indian leader in a decade and only the third bilateral summit since the 1947 partition. Among the provisos in the resulting "Lahore Declaration" was a commitment by both governments to reduce the possibility of accidental nuclear war. The heightened hostilities in Kashmir in May–July 1999 temporarily halted the peace process, while the coup by the Pakistani military in October 1999 further undermined regional relations. In July 2001 Prime Minister Vajpayee conferred with Pakistan's chief executive, Gen. Pervez Musharraf, in Agra, but the meeting concluded without significant progress.

Meanwhile, attacks by Islamic separatists led India to charge not only that Pakistan was not taking adequate measures to stop infiltration by terrorists but that its Inter Services Intelligence agency was abetting the attacks. On October 1, 2001, militants carried out an assault on the state assembly building in Srinagar, the summer capital of Jammu and Kashmir, causing nearly 40 deaths. India dispatched additional armed forces to Kashmir, with Pakistan responding in kind. On December 13, terrorists attacked India's Parliament, leaving 14 dead, including the terrorists, and by May 2002, when three gunmen stormed a Kashmiri army base and left nearly three dozen dead, India and Pakistan had a combined million troops or more stationed along the LoC. Diplomatic intervention, led by the United States, ultimately helped defuse the situation, but in Kashmir the familiar pattern of hostilities continued: clashes between Indian forces and separatist guerrillas, shelling by Indian and Pakistani forces across the LoC, bombings, and assassinations.

On April 18, 2003, Prime Minister Vajpayee called for "open dialogue" with Pakistan, and the gesture quickly led to a mutual upgrading of diplomatic relations. On November 26 the two governments instituted a cease-fire, the first in 14 years, between Pakistani and Indian forces in the disputed border region. Meeting in New Delhi on April 17, 2005, Manmohan Singh, the new Indian prime minister, and Pakistan's President Musharraf jointly declared that the peace process was "irreversible." In December 2006 Singh described the destinies of the two countries as linked and reiterated the need for peace, security, and friendship, but India temporarily brought a halt to the dialogue following a November 2008 assault on Mumbai by Pakistani-based terrorists (see Current issues, below).

India initially attempted to maintain friendly relations with the People's Republic of China; however, border tensions between the two nations escalated into military conflict in October 1962. At issue were 14,500 square miles of territory in the Aksai Chin area of eastern Kashmir and some 36,000 square miles of Arunachal Pradesh in the northeast (below the so-called McMahon line, established in 1913–1914), from which China withdrew after the 1962 war. Following a thaw in relations during 1976, ambassadors were exchanged for the first time in nearly 14 years. During a state visit by Prime Minister Rajiv Gandhi to China in December 1988 (the first by an Indian head of government since 1954), "in-depth discussions" on the boundary question were reported. An agreement to reduce troop levels and respect the existing Line of Actual Control (LAC) without prejudice to the rival claims was signed by Chinese Premier Li Peng and Prime Minister Rao in Beijing on September 7, 1993. In April 2005 the two countries agreed to a framework for settling the border issue (see the entry on the People's Republic of China for additional information about the border dispute).

The United States was a strong supporter of Indian independence, and U.S. aid to India for some years thereafter far exceeded that received by any other nation. Politically, relations have fluctuated, the most severe strain occurring in the course of the 1971 conflict between India and Pakistan. Differences also arose over India's explosion of an underground nuclear device in May 1974 and its subsequent refusal to permit international inspection of nuclear facilities. Following the collapse of the Soviet Union in 1991, Washington increased its pressure on New Delhi to sign the Nuclear Non-Proliferation Treaty (NPT) and join with Pakistan and China in limiting nuclear development in East and South Asia. India refused to do so on the grounds that "the treaty in its present form is discriminatory" in that it legitimizes possession of nuclear weapons by a handful of countries. Without referencing the nuclear issue, a U.S.-Indian military accord was concluded in mid-January 1995 that called for joint military exercises, training, defense research, and weapons production.

In February 2000, Prime Minister Vajpayee stated that India would not sign the Comprehensive Nuclear Test Ban Treaty (CTBT) until a national consensus was achieved. Meanwhile, the last of the U.S. sanctions that had been imposed after the May 1998 nuclear tests were lifted on September 23, 2001, as the administration of George W. Bush marshaled support for an impending assault on the al-Qaida terrorist network and the Taliban regime in Afghanistan.

Despite India's opposition to the U.S.-led invasion of Iraq in 2003 and the American public's concerns about India's role in the outsourcing of U.S. service jobs, relations with the United States continued to strengthen, at least in part because the Bush administration viewed India as a counterweight to China. During a visit by Prime Minister Singh to Washington in July 2005, plans were announced for a new nuclear partnership. The plan for sharing civilian nuclear technology and fuel requires India to separate its civil and military nuclear programs, permit international monitoring of its civil operations, and refrain from further nuclear tests and the transfer of nuclear technology to third countries. With the Singh government having won a confidence vote in the *Lok Sabha* in July 2008, on August 1 the International Atomic Energy Agency (IAEA), whose approval was required because India remains outside the NPT regime, endorsed the deal, as did the 45-country Nuclear Suppliers Group on September 6. President Bush signed the legislation on October 8.

During 1987, India became directly involved in the ethnic strife engulfing Sri Lanka. Sri Lanka's Tamil dissidents had long enjoyed support in the south Indian state of Tamil Nadu, which is predominantly ethnic Tamil. It was not until 1985 that Rajiv Gandhi retreated from the overtly pro-Tamil posture of his recently assassinated mother by declaring that he opposed any attempt by the Tamil minority to establish an autonomous state in Sri Lanka. In late 1986 he proposed the merger of Sri Lanka's largely Tamil Northern and Eastern provinces as a basis of settling the dispute, and in July 1987, during his first official visit to Sri Lanka, he offered military assistance to the Jayawardene government in support of the regionalization plan. Within days, 3,000 Indian troops had been dispatched to the island's Jaffna peninsula to assist in the disarming of the guerrillas. Although some 70,000 Indian troops were deployed by early 1988, the mission proved to be a political liability for both governments, and by March 1990 the Indian troops had been withdrawn. New Delhi made no effort to send them back when the Tamil insurgency in Sri Lanka resumed with even greater ferocity, after which Gandhi himself became a victim.

The Sri Lankan military's impending defeat of the Liberation Tigers of Tamil Eelam (LTTE) insurgency in the second quarter of 2009 generated expressions of concern in New Delhi for the civilians caught in the crossfire, but the Singh government also noted that the LTTE was a "terrorist" organization. Politicians from ethnically Tamil areas were often less circumspect, with former Tamil Nadu chief minister Jayalalitha of the AIADMK calling for Indian intervention to establish a separate Tamil country.

In 1996, India and Nepal signed the Mahakali Integrated Development Treaty and a subsequent agreement providing Nepal with transit rights across Indian territory to Bangladeshi ports. A continuing bilateral dispute involves the Kalapani border area, which Indian troops have occupied since the 1962 Sino-Indian war.

In August 2009, India and the ten-member Association of Southeast Asian Nations (ASEAN) concluded negotiations on a free trade area.

From 1994, India has lobbied extensively for a permanent seat on the UN Security Council, insisting that such action would permit the council to reflect more accurately the distribution of the world's population. The United States, which has actively supported bids by Germany and Japan, threw its support behind the Indian request during President Obama's visit in November 2010. Both Pakistan and China declared their strong opposition pending resolution of the Kashmir dispute.

Export controls were relaxed for Indian companies involved in defense industries and nuclear energy by the United States in January 2011.

Although India and Russia signed the biggest military procurement deal in Indian history, worth $36 billion, in December 2010, relations between the two countries became rocky in 2011. In April that year, Russia abruptly pulled out of naval exercises with India, reportedly because of India's purchase of military equipment from other countries.

On September 6, 2011, Prime Minister Singh signed agreements with Bangladesh to settle border disputes, which had been the chief obstacle to peace between the two countries. However, the contentious issue of water rights remained unresolved. Fifty-four rivers run through both India and Bangladesh.

In October 2011, India deployed additional troops to the state of Arunachal Praddesh, which borders China-controlled Tibet, and over much of which China has claimed sovereignty in response to a buildup of Chinese troops on the border. India planned to increase its troop strength in the region by 90,000 and to deploy advanced weaponry, including fighter aircraft and cruise missiles. Since it was planning to build dams to generate hydroelectric power in the area, India feared that China might divert water from rivers that flow into India for its own hydroelectric use.

In September 2011, Pakistan granted India most-favored nation trade status after the two countries finalized an agreement to "normalize" economic relations. Also in September, Singh became the first Indian prime minister to visit Bangladesh since 1999. During the trip, Singh signed ten accords, including agreements to end bans on 46 Bangladeshi products and to better demarcate the mutual border.

On October 4, 2011, Afghan President Hamid Karzai and Singh singed a far-reaching series of economic and security accords, including an agreement for India to train Afghan security forces. The accords were promoted as a new "strategic partnership" between the two countries.

On February 16, 2012, two Italian marines on the merchant vessel *Enrica Lexie* fired on an Indian fisher vessel, killing two. Indian authorities arrested the two marines and seized the *Enrica Lexia* when it entered port in Kerala. On May 2, the Indian Supreme Court ordered the release of the vessel but not the marines. Italy recalled its ambassador on May 18, arguing that the incident took place in international waters and the marines should be tried in Italy.

In March 2012, the United States filed a complaint with the World Trade Organization (WTO) over an Indian ban on the import of poultry and eggs. In April, following a "private" visit by Pakistani Prime Minister Ali ZARDARI, it was announced negotiations were under way to allow direct investment from Pakistan in financial Indian markets.

Beginning on January 6, 2013, a series of military exchanges along the LoC left two Indian and three Pakistani soldiers dead and prompted boarder closures. Talks between senior Indian and Pakistani military officers on January 16 reduced tensions and led to the border being reopened on January 28. Also in January, India and Bangladesh signed an extradition treaty. India and Thailand followed the treaty with a similar accord in May.

In March 2013, India and Australia were able to soften a UN Human Rights Council resolution that was critical of Sri Lanka's human rights record during that country's civil war. The resolution passed 25–13 (with 8 abstentions) on March 21. Both India and Australia supported the final draft. On April 15, more than 30 Chinese soldiers crossed some 6.2 miles into the Ladakh region and set up a camp, prompting denunciations from the Indian government and the deployment of troops to the region.

Meanwhile, in March 2013, Italy announced that it would not return the two marines in the *Enrica Lexie* incident to India for trial. In response, India imposed a travel ban on Italy's ambassador. On April 2, the ban was lifted, although the Indian Supreme Court ordered a new investigation into the incident. Meanwhile, in April, India opposed the UN Arms Trade Treaty, contending that unfairly disadvantaged countries with significant weapons imports. It lobbied against the measure and abstained, along with 22 other countries, from the final vote.

Current issues. Despite major defections from the first-term UPA—chiefly, that of the Left Front parties because of their opposition to the Indian-U.S. nuclear technology agreement—Congress pulled together a reconfigured UPA that easily won the April–May 2009 *Lok Sabha* election. Singh thereby became the first prime minister since Nehru to continue in office after completing a full five-year term. Indian voters had expressed concerns about rising commodity prices and inflation, but the government's relative economic success may have been the major factor in their decision to endorse a second term for Singh, an economist who offered stability in the context of the ongoing international recession.

Currently ranked fifth among all countries in terms of carbon dioxide emissions, India has rejected efforts to set legally binding targets for emission reductions, but it has introduced plans for massive increases in solar and nuclear energy generation. Shortly before the December 2009 UN Summit on Climate Change in Copenhagen, Denmark, the Singh government also pledged to cut the ratio of pollution to GDP to 20–25 percent of 2005 levels by 2020. Other efforts to lower emissions are to include introducing mandatory fuel efficiency standards, adopting building codes that mandate greater energy efficiency, and requiring coal-fuel power plants to use cleaner technology.

Another factor in the UPA's 2009 win may have been rejection of the ardent Hindu nationalism represented by some factions of the BJP. In April 2006 Prime Minister Singh had labeled the Maoist insurgency, affecting more than a dozen states, as the biggest threat to national security, but in the year before the election there had been a marked increase in Hindu violence directed against Christians and Muslims, particularly after the murder of Swami Laxmanananda SARASWATI, a leader of the fundamentalist World Council of Hindus (*Vishwa Hindu Parishad*—VHP), in Orissa in August 2008. Although Maoists claimed responsibility, Hindi anger was directed against Christians, prompting violence that Prime Minister Singh labeled a "national disgrace" and that subsequently spread elsewhere, leaving an estimated 16,000 Christians temporarily in refugee centers in just one district of Orissa. At the same time violence in the volatile northeast and elsewhere also escalated, most dramatically in Assam, where, for example, nearly 80 people were killed and some 450 injured on October 30 in a dozen coordinated bombings. The police implicated the extremist *Harkat-ul-Jihad-i-Islami* (HJI) in the bombings, the suggested motive being retaliation for attacks earlier in the month by Bodo tribes people against Muslims, over 80,000 of whom fled to refugee camps. In June 2008, a proposal to transfer 40 hectares of state land in Jammu and Kashmir to a board managing the Hindu shrine of Amarnath led to demands by Muslims that the transfer be halted. During the next two months dozens of people were killed and hundreds injured in the resultant unrest throughout Muslim-dominated Kashmir and Hindu-majority Jammu.

Commuter trains and stations in Mumbai were bombed in a coordinated attack on July 11, 2006, leaving 180 dead and nearly 800 injured. India accused Pakistan's Musharraf government of failing to prevent infiltration by terrorists from such Islamist organizations as *Lashkar-i-Taiba* (LiT), which New Delhi has linked to many other bombings, assaults, and assassinations (see the discussion of Kashmiri separatist and Islamic militant groups in the Political Parties and Groups section).

An audacious attack by 10 Islamic militants on Mumbai on November 26–29, 2008, left 166 people dead and another 300 hurt and jeopardized the India–Pakistan rapprochement. Having landed by inflatable boat at night, the assailants made their way to predetermined targets in a well-planned mission that Prime Minister Singh later described as demonstrating "sophistication and military precision," raising the prospect that "official agencies" of the Pakistani government had been involved in the planning. A previously unknown group calling itself the Deccan Mujaheddin claimed responsibility, but the possibility remained that it was merely a front name for another organization. The attack resulted in the immediate resignation of Home Affairs Minister Shivraj PATIL, the tightening of the Unlawful Activities Prevention Act, and the creation of a National Investigation Agency to pursue terrorists.

All of the assailants, including the lone survivor, Ajmal Amir AMIN (a.k.a. Ajmal KASAB), whose trial began in April 2009, were ultimately shown to have Pakistani addresses, and in February 2009 Islamabad acknowledged that the assault had been at least partially planned there. In July Amin surprised onlookers by changing his plea to guilty, after which he described in detail not only his participation but also the training he had received from the LiT. In the same month,

Prime Minister Singh and Pakistan's prime minister, Yusuf Gilani, conferred on the sidelines of a Nonaligned Movement meeting in Egypt, at which time they reiterated a common commitment to fighting terrorism. Subsequently, Pakistan put seven suspects on trial for planning the attack, but the slow-moving proceedings have caused friction between the two countries. In March 2011 the home secretaries for both countries met and agreed to a joint investigation of the bombing. In July, on a visit to India, U.S. secretary of state, Hillary Clinton, urged Pakistan to prosecute "fully and urgently" the culprits in the 2008 attack. To make matters more complex, Mumbai was hit by three bombs in a coordinated attack on July 13, 2011. The blasts killed 26 and injured 130. On September 14, another three bombs were exploded in Mumbai, killing 20 and injuring 100. On June 21, 2012, Indian security officials arrested Syed Zabiuddin ANSARI, one of the alleged planners of the 2008 attack.

The Maoist rebellion in northern and eastern parts of the country intensified in 2010. By July, approximately 800 people had been killed, and the rebels, estimated to number 10,000–20,000, had reportedly spread to some 200 of India's 626 districts. Operation Green Hunt, a multistate offensive involving more than 60,000 troops and policemen, was considered largely ineffective against the rebels, who presented themselves as the champions of the oppressed in extremely poor areas. Between January and September 2011, 46 civilians and 109 security personnel were killed as a result of Maoist violence. Prime Minister Singh announced on September 13 that government planned to launch rural development programs to reduce the appeal of the Maoist revolutionaries among the poor.

Kashmir also remained restive in 2010. During the summer, there were almost 900 confrontations between Indian security forces and various elements opposed to Indian rule. More than 50 Kashmiris, mostly teenagers, were killed, and. schools were closed for three months. September was a particularly bloody month. A Kashmiri mob, numbering in the tens of thousands, reacted to a report of a Koran burning in the United States by vandalizing government vehicles and offices and by burning a Christian school to the ground. The violence was so severe that the government closed the airport and imposed a curfew. In 2011, the violence subsided somewhat, and Kashmir once again became a tourist destination. Commentators attributed the relative peace to the improving relations between India and Pakistan and the conciliatory measures taken by the Indian government, such as the release of separatist protestors.

Corruption problems plagued the UPA in late 2010 and 2011. In November 2010, Andimuthu RAJA, the minister of communications and information technology, resigned his post because of a sale of mobile phone licenses to select companies that cost the government $39 billion in revenue. This scandal helped force a cabinet reshuffle in January 2011. Continued revelations prompted various forms of protest, including hunger strikes and marches. The demonstrations were met by violent suppression. In August, bowing to public pressure, the Indian parliament passed a resolution supporting a strong anticorruption bill that was advocated by the social activist Anna HAZARE, who undertook a hunger strike to protest against corruption. On February 2, 2012, the high court ruled that the government had to cancel the mobile telephone licenses of 122 telecommunications companies and undertake a new round of bids in response to the earlier scandal. The companies served an estimated 69 million Indians.

In state assembly balloting in February and March 2012, the INC won a majority in only one of five states, Manipur, and a plurality in Uttrakhand, where it formed a coalition with the BSP. The SP won Uttar Pradesh, while the BJP won Goa and the SAD won Punjab. The worst flooding in a decade in June 2012 killed at least 27 and affected more than 900,000 people in Assam state.

In December 2012, following contentious and often bitter debate, Parliament voted to allow direct foreign investment in India's retail sector. Opponents of the measure claimed that it would undermine domestic companies.

On December 16, 2012, 23-year-old Jyoti Singh PANDEY was brutally attacked and gang raped. She later died of her injuries. The attack sparked a public outcry against violence toward women and problems within the criminal justice system in prosecuting perpetrators of sexual crimes. A 2011 report found that out of 256,329 reported violent crimes, 228,650 were against women. Six men were arrested on January 3, 2013. One hanged himself in prison on March 11, while the trials of the others, including one juvenile, were still ongoing in August 2013. Five special courts were subsequently appointed to fast-track the prosecution of sexual crimes and enacted new legislation on violence toward women. Rights groups asserted that the government's measures did not go far enough to address gender violence.

On April 5, 2013, a building collapsed in Mumbai, killing 74 and injuring 36. The structure, which had been built illegally, highlighted continuing problems with substandard construction. Nine people were arrested for bribery and homicide in connection with the collapse. Thirty-six police officers were suspended after they were found accepting bribes related to illegal buildings.

In July 2013, the government announced the creation of a new state, Telangana. The new state, India's 29th, would have a population of 40 million and include 10 districts from the existing state of Andhra Pradesh.

POLITICAL PARTIES AND GROUPS

Although there were more than 100 parties and groupings in the first general election in 1952, the undivided Indian National Congress dominated the political scene until 1969, when it split into ruling (Gandhi) and opposition factions. The latter, although repudiating the designation, was subsequently styled the Indian National Congress–Organization, or Congress (O), by the Election Commission. The Gandhi Congress easily won the election of 1972. Following the declaration of emergency in June 1975, however, a national *Janata* (People's) Front, comprising Congress (O), the Indian People's Party (*Bharatiya Lok Dal*), the Socialist Party, the Indian People's Union (*Bharatiya Jana Sangh*), and the Congress for Democracy, formed to oppose the Gandhi Congress. In May 1976 the widely respected Jaya Prakash Narayanan announced that the front would be converted into a unified political party in order to present a "democratic national alternative" to Congress rule. In March 1977, the resultant *Janata* Party swept to victory. The Gandhi Congress became increasingly divided after its defeat, and in January 1978 those remaining loyal to Mrs. Gandhi organized separately as the Indian National Congress–Indira (INC-I), or the Congress (I).

Janata split in July 1979, and in 1980, the Congress (I) secured a near two-thirds majority in the lower house. In the wake of Indira Gandhi's assassination, Congress (I) swept nearly 80 percent of contested seats in the *Lok Sabha* election of December 1984. Since 1989, however, broad coalitions have been required to form governments.

The *Janata Dal* (People's Party) formed the core of a seven-party centrist National Front—NF (*Rashtriya Morcha*) alliance that failed to outpoll Congress (I) in November 1989 but was able to form a government with the external support of the two main Communist parties—the Communist Party of India (CPI) and the CPI-Marxist (CPI-M)—and the fundamentalist *Bharatiya Janata* Party (BJP). The BJP's withdrawal of support a year later and a split in *Janata Dal* precipitated the government's fall. Although the NF was broadened to include the Communist and other left-wing parties for the June 1991 election, becoming the NF/Leftist Front (NF/LF), Congress (I) and its allies returned to power.

The April–May 1996 election was a success for the BJP, but its inability to attract other support enabled an even larger, 14-party NF/LF, subsequently renamed the United Front (UF), to form a minority government under H. D. Deve Gowda of the *Janata Dal*. The ministerial lineup included representatives of nine parties, including *Janata Dal*, Dravidian Progressive Federation (DMK), *Samajwadi* Party (SP), CPI, Assam People's Council (AGP), and the *Telugu Desam* Party (TDP). (For more on the UF, please see the 2013 *Handbook.*)

On May 16 the BJP and a dozen of its allies announced formation of a National Democratic Alliance (NDA) that by the time of the September–October *Lok Sabha* election victory numbered some 24 mostly regional organizations. Although many of the smaller NDA parties had left the fold since the 1999 balloting, the NDA entered the 2004 election campaign as the odds-on favorite. Most of the BJP's major allies in 1999, including *Shiv Sena* (SS), the *Biju Janata Dal* (BJD), the SAD, and the *Janata Dal* (United), remained in place, and two state governing parties, the TDP of Andhra Pradesh and the AIADMK of Tamil Nadu, had joined. Despite dire predictions of record losses, the Congress had cemented alliances with the main Tamil Nadu opposition parties, including former NDA member DMK; had repaired relations with the leaders of the Nationalist Congress Party (NCP); and had gained the support of a new Andhra Pradesh formation, the *Telangana Rashtra Samithi* (TRS). Congress and its allies prevailed, and with external support from the four-party Left Front alliance and others, they succeeded in forming a minority government.

For the 2009 *Lok Sabha* election, the country's 7 "national" parties—the *Bahujan Samaj* Party (BSP), BJP, CPI, CPI-M, INC, NCP, and *Rashtriya Janata Dal* (RJD)—38 "state" parties, and a number of India's 1,000 additional registered parties offered candidates. The main contestants were, once again, the UPA and NDA (both somewhat reconfigured), this time joined by two additional alliances. The Third Front, which was launched in March 2009 and included several of the erstwhile UNPA parties, was led by the four parties of the Left Front and the BSP, while the three-party Fourth Front included the SP and the RJD. Only the UPA parties fared better than they had in 2004, gaining 79 seats, while the NDA parties collectively lost 17; the Third Front parties, 30; and the Fourth Front parties, 37.

In addition to India's myriad political parties, many unregistered or proscribed separatist or militant groups exist. The principal ones are based in Kashmir or the northeast states. The 2004 Unlawful Activities (Prevention) Amendment Ordinance banned 32 groups, including the Maoist Communist Center (MCC), the Jammu and Kashmir Liberation Front (JKLF), the *Hizb-ul-Mujaheddin,* the *Lashkar-i-Taiba,* and many of those discussed under the subhead Principal North and Northeast Militant Organizations.

United Progressive Alliance (UPA):

Indian National Congress (INC). Founded in 1885 and led from 1966 to 1977 by Indira Gandhi, the INC experienced the withdrawal in 1969 of an anti-Gandhi conservative faction that became India's first recognized opposition party, the Indian National Congress–Organization (Congress-O), prior to joining *Janata.* The INC was further weakened by the defection or expulsion of numerous leaders both before and after the 1977 election, at which the party suffered its first defeat. In January 1978 Gandhi's supporters designated the former prime minister as the president of a new national opposition party, the Indian National Congress–Indira (INC-I), or Congress (I). Building from a political base in the traditionally pro-Gandhi south, Congress (I) quickly displaced the rump INC as the principal opposition force. In July 1981 the Election Commission ruled that the Congress (I) was the "real" Congress in that the majority of INC leaders and legislative officeholders at the time of the 1978 division had since become members of Indira Gandhi's party. By late 1982 the anti-Gandhi Congress had, for all practical purposes, disintegrated.

Under the leadership of Indira Gandhi's son Rajiv, Congress (I) easily won the December 1984 *Lok Sabha* election, but in November 1989 its representation plummeted, forcing it into opposition. Following the 1991 poll, however, Congress (I) and its allies formed a minority government under the premiership of P. V. Narasimha Rao, successor to the assassinated Rajiv.

The Rao government's pursuit of rapid economic liberalization and deregulation, coupled with corruption disclosures and other scandals, contributed to a defeat in the 1996 election. After helping bring about the speedy collapse of the BJP government, the Congress opted to give external support to a minority United Front administration. Rao resigned as party chief in September 1996 and was replaced by the Congress treasurer, Sitaram Kesri—the party's first non-Brahmin leader.

The late Rajiv Gandhi's Italian-born widow, Sonia Gandhi, brought support back to the ailing party during the legislative campaign in January 1998. Despite winning only 141 seats, the party emerged as the largest opposition formation. Party President Kesri announced his resignation on March 9, after which Sonia Gandhi was chosen as his replacement and as the party's parliamentary leader, despite holding no elective office.

Meanwhile, Congress welcomed the return of former dissidents who had formed splinter parties because of opposition to the policies of Mrs. Gandhi or Rao. Among these leaders were Sharad Pawar of the Indian National Congress (Socialist), Madhavrao SCINDIA of the Madhya Pradesh Vikas Party (MPVP), Arjun Singh of the All India Indira Congress (AIIC), and Sis Ram OLA of the All India Indira Congress (Secular). With most of the splinter parties no longer functioning, Congress was increasingly being referenced without the appended "I."

In May 1999, Gandhi resigned as INC president when several prominent party leaders, principally Sharad Pawar, proposed a constitutional amendment that would restrict the national presidency, vice presidency, and prime ministry to native-born Indians. Three days later Pawar and two others were expelled by the party, and on May 24 Gandhi withdrew her resignation. Pawar went on to cofound the Nationalist Congress Party (see NCP, below).

At the September–October 1999, *Lok Sabha* election the Congress turned in its worst performance in nearly half a century, winning only 114 seats. On October 17 Gandhi, who had been elected to the lower house in her first contest, was chosen leader of the opposition.

Prior to the 2004 election, the Congress picked up additional support through mergers with a number of parties, most prominently the Tamil Maanila Congress (TMC) of the late G. K. MOOPANAR, who had left the Congress in April 1996 in opposition to reactivation of an alliance with the Tamil AIADMK (below). Another 1996 splinter, the Haryana Vikas Party (HVP), led by former Haryana chief minister Bansi LAL and a son, Surender SINGH, also reunited with the Congress shortly before the election. The Himachal Vikas Congress (HVC) of Sukh RAM did likewise. In August 2003, the main body of the Sikkim Sangram Parishad (SSP, below), led by former Sikkim chief minister Nar Bahadur BHANDARI, also merged with Congress.

Following its unexpected *Lok Sabha* victory in the election of April–May 2004, when it won 145 seats, Congress elected Sonia Gandhi as its parliamentary leader, paving the way for her designation as prime minister. The BJP and other Hindu parties had already announced, however, their strong objection because of her foreign birth. Despite wide support from most non-NDA parties, on May 18 she withdrew from consideration, asserting that she had never sought to be prime minister. It was also widely believed that her children, having seen their grandmother and father assassinated while in office, had urged her to step aside. In her stead Gandhi put forward Manmohan Singh, a Sikh and respected economist, who thus became the first member of a minority to serve as prime minister.

In March 2006, Gandhi resigned her seat in the *Lok Sabha* to deflect criticism that she had violated a technical provision of a law prohibiting elected politicians from holding salaried positions. Prior to reclaiming her seat in a May by-election, she resigned from her positions in several foundations and other organizations, including as unsalaried chair of the extraconstitutional National Advisory Council, which she had established in May 2004 to direct government policy.

The April–May 2009 general election saw the INC increase its *Lok Sabha* plurality to 206 seats. Prime Minister Singh, who had undergone heart bypass surgery earlier in the year, began a second term on May 22, although there was speculation that he might not serve a full five-year term. Many observers predicted that Rahul Gandhi, the son of Sonia Gandhi, would eventually ascend to leadership of the INC and then the government. Nevertheless, the INC's success in three state elections (including the election in Maharashtra, where Mumbai is located) in October was attributed to the continued effective leadership of Sonia Gandhi, who was rewarded with her fourth term as party president in 2010. In addition, she was given the power to choose the presidents and other leaders for the state organizations of the INC in about a dozen states. Her added control of the apparatus of state parties certainly solidified her hold on power, but it was called "undemocratic" by critics in the party. On September 7, 2011, Sonia Gandhi underwent treatment for an unspecified illness. In June 2011 Pranab MUKHERJEE was elected president of India.

In December 2012, the INC won a majority of seats in the Himachal Pradesh assembly, defeating the incumbent BJP government. The INC's Virbhadra SINGH became chief minister of the state.

At a party congress on January 2013, Rahul GANDHI was elected vice president of the party.

Leaders: Sonia GANDHI (President of the Party), Pranab MUKHERJEE (President of the Republic), Dr. Manmohan SINGH (Prime Minister), Motilal VORA (Treasurer), Ahmed PATEL (Political Secretary), Rahul GANDHI (Vice President of the Party).

Nationalist Congress Party (NCP). Formation of the NCP was announced in May 1999 by three Congress members who had been expelled from the parent party for proposing, in a direct affront to Sonia Gandhi, a constitutional amendment requiring that only "natural-born" Indian citizens be permitted to serve as national president, vice president, or prime minister. At its formal launch in June the NCP absorbed what remained of the Indian National Congress (Socialist)—the INC-S or Congress (S)—which traced its origin to the anti-Gandhi Congress of 1977–1978. (The NCP president had served as leader of the INC-S from 1981 until his return to the Congress in 1986.)

The new party won eight seats in the 1999 *Lok Sabha* election. Despite its differences with the parent party, in Maharashtra State the NCP joined the INC and a number of independents in forming a state government under a Democratic Front. In May 2002 the Kerala branch of the NCP reestablished the Congress (S) under Ramachandran KADANNAPPALLY.

The NCP campaigned in 2004 with Congress and won nine seats. In March, a faction led by Purno Sangma had broken away, largely because of opposition to the foreign-born Sonia Gandhi as a prospective prime minister, and joined the AITC (above). Sangma himself returned to the NCP in December 2005. Another faction, based in Chhattisgarh and led by V. C. SHUKLA, also broke away in 2004 and formed the short-lived Rashtriya Janatantrik Dal, which then merged with the BJP. In 2006 the NCP absorbed the Kerala-based Democratic Indira Congress–Karunakaran (DIC-K), which had been established in May 2005 by former Congress leader and Kerala chief minister K. KARUNAKARAN and his son, K. MURALEEDHARAN.

In March 2008, Sangma was a prime mover in the Meghalaya Progressive Alliance, a coalition that won sufficient support in the Meghalaya State election to unseat a Congress-led government. In May 2009, however, a Congress-led Meghalaya United Alliance won control of the government after two months of presidential rule. At the union level, the NCP remained within the UPA. In November, however, the NCP suffered a blow in the state of Assam when 85 percent of its leadership there left the NCP to join the INC. The defectors cited dissatisfaction with the national leadership as a reason for the move. In the same month, however, the NCP formed an alliance with the INC to govern the populous state of Maharashtra. However, dissension emerged in May 2011 between the NCP and the INC. NCP leader Sharad Pawar blamed Congress for the poor financial health of Maharashtra State Cooperative Bank, due to bad loans made to industries controlled by Congress members. He threatened to pull out of the coalition that governed Maharashtra.

Sangma resigned from the NCP in June 2012 to campaign for the presidency after the NCP agreed to back INC candidate Pranab Mukherjee. Mukherjee defeated Sangma with 69.3 percent of the vote. Ajit PAWAR, the deputy chief minister of Maharashtra and party leader Pawar's nephew, was forced to resign in September 2012 after being implicated in a corruption scandal over irrigation.

Leaders: Sharad PAWAR (President of the Party and Minister of Agriculture), Tariq ANWAR, T. P. Peethambaran MASTER, V. RAJESHWARAN, Devi Prasad TRIPATHI (General Secretaries), Y. P. TRIVEDI (Treasurer), Praful Manoharbhai PATEL (Minister of Heavy Industries and Public Enterprises).

Jammu and Kashmir National Conference (JKNC). The dominant party in Jammu and Kashmir following independence, the JKNC continued to be led by Sheikh Mohammed ABDULLAH, who was primarily responsible for the 1947 decision to join India, until his death in 1982. From then until the late 1990s, the JKNC, led by the sheikh's son, Farooq Abdullah, was typically allied with Congress, which backed the JKNC in a state election in 1996 (the first since 1987), assisting the party to a decisive overall majority and enabling Farooq Abdullah to resume the post of chief minister. The JKNC then won three seats in the 1998 *Lok Sabha* balloting as a United Front party. In the 1999 election the party picked up an additional seat, after which it joined the NDA government.

In June 2002, Farooq Abdullah turned over the presidency of the party to his son, Omar. In the following September–October state election the JKNC finished with a plurality of seats but lost control of the government to a coalition of the Congress and the Jammu and Kashmir People's Democratic Party (PDP). In July 2003, the JKNC left the NDA, and in the *Lok Sabha* election of 2004 it won two seats while remaining outside both the UPA and the NDA.

In the state election of November–December 2008, the JKNC won a leading 28 seats. At the end of December, it reestablished ties to the Congress and ousted the PDP from the government. In the 2009 general election, it ran within the UPA, winning three seats and joining the Singh government. In 2009, Farooq was again elected president of the party and appointed minister of New and Renewable Energy.

Leaders: Farooq ABDULLAH (Minister of New and Renewable Energy and President of the Party), Omar ABDULLAH (Chief Minister of Jammu and Kashmir), Sheikh Nazir AHMAD (General Secretary).

Jharkhand Mukti Morcha (JMM). The JMM (Jharkhand Liberation Front) was organized in 1980 to represent the tribal people of Bihar and Orissa. It was allied with the National Front/Leftist Front in the 1991 national election, winning six *Lok Sabha* seats, but its main faction remained outside the alliance for the 1996 poll, at which its representation was reduced to two members. As an ally of Congress in 1998, the party lost its remaining lower house seats.

In 1999, a factional dispute between Shibu Soren and Suraj MANDAL threatened to split the party, which failed again in its bid for lower house seats. The Soren wing of the party supported Prime Minister Vajpayee's government but broke with the NDA when the alliance backed a BJP candidate for chief minister of the new state of Jharkhand in November 2000. (Mandal, having been expelled from the JMM, went on to form the Jharkhand Vikas Dal, which merged with the JD[U] after the 2004 general election.)

In March 2004, the JMM concluded a pact with the Congress, and it then won five *Lok Sabha* seats, after which Soren joined the Singh cabinet. He was forced to resign as minister of coal and mines in late July, however, following issuance of an arrest warrant related to his alleged involvement in a 1975 riot that cost ten lives. He returned to the cabinet in November, resigned in March 2005 in an unsuccessful effort to become chief minister of Jharkhand, again rejoined the Singh cabinet in January 2006, and then resigned once more in November 2006, following his conviction for murdering his secretary. He received a life sentence and was temporarily replaced as party president by his wife, but his conviction was overturned in August 2007.

In August 2008, following the JMM's decision to withdraw its support for the state government, Soren became chief minister of Jharkhand. In January 2009, however, Soren was forced to resign as chief minister of Jharkhand after losing a state by-election. With no party or coalition able to command a majority in the state legislature, president's rule was imposed and then extended for an additional six months in July. In May 2009 Soren was one of two JMM members elected to the *Lok Sabha*. The other, Kameshwar BAITHA, a former Maoist commander, has been under detention since 2005 in Bihar State. Soren held his post as president of Jharkhand until May 2010, when he was forced to resign because the BJP, his coalition partner in the state government, withdrew its support because Soren had voted against a BJP motion in parliament. The BJP and the JMM, however, formed a coalition government in September 2010 in Jharkhand. In September 2012, the JMM reportedly threatened to leave the UPA over the relaxation of restrictions on foreign direct investment in the retail sector, which the party claimed would undermine local business. In January 2013, the JMM withdrew its support for the BJP-led coalition government in Jharkhand, prompting the formation of a new state government.

Leaders: Shibu SOREN (President), Vinod PANDEY (Vice President), Sudhir MAHATO (General Secretary).

Indian Union Muslim League (IUML). The IUML (regularly also referenced simply as the Muslim League—ML) is a remnant of the prepartition Muslim League led by Mohammad Ali JINNAH. It opposes both secularism and Hindu nationalism. It won two lower house seats in 1996, 1998, and 1999, when its successful candidates entered the *Lok Sabha* under the banner of the **Muslim League Kerala State Committee** (MLKSC). In 2004 its general secretary, E. Ahamed, the only winning candidate on the MLKSC list, was named a minister of state in the Ministry of External Affairs. At the time, the IUML was allied with Congress in Kerala's United Democratic Front government, but the coalition lost the 2006 state election. In November 2005 K. T. JALEEL and other dissidents within the IUML organized the CH Secular Forum, which called for closer ties to Left Front parties.

The death of the longtime national president, G. M. BANATWALA, was followed in September 2008 by the election of E. Ahamed as his successor. In the 2009 general election, the IUML won two seats. In August 2013, the IUML announced it would hold district, state, and national conventions in September to prepare for the 2014 elections.

Leaders: E. AHAMED (Minister of State for Railways and President of the Party), K. M. Kader MOHIDEEN (General Secretary), Dastgheer Ibrahim AGA (Treasurer), Panakkad Mohammed Ali Shihab THANGAL (Kerala State President), P. K. KUNHALIKUTTY (Kerala General Secretary).

All India Majlis-e-Ittehadul Muslimeen (AIMIM). Based in Hyderabad and aiming to represent India's Muslims, the AIMIM (All India Muslim Federal Assembly) won a *Lok Sabha* seat in a 1994 by-election and expanded to two seats in the 1996 general election. It retained one seat in 1998, 1999, 2004, and 2009.

Longtime leader Sultan Salahuddin OWAISI died in September 2008 and was succeeded as president by a son. The AIMIM supported Mukherjee of the INC for the presidency in 2012. The AIMIM demanded the establishment of a minimum quota system for Muslim candidates ahead of the 2014 elections.

Leaders: Asaduddin OWAISI (President), Akbaruddin OWAISI (Floor Leader in the Hyderbad Assembly).

Kerala Congress (KC). Long subject to internal rifts, the KC remains divided into several factions. In the 1999 election the **Kerala Congress (Mani)** and the **Kerala Congress (Joseph),** the latter led by P. J. Joseph, each won one *Lok Sabha* seat. The KC (Joseph) won the party's sole seat in 2004. It later picked up a second seat by absorbing the Indian Federal Democratic Party (IFDP), led by P. C. Thomas, which had originated in 2001 as a loose alliance of *Lok Sabha* independents. In November 2006 a Kerala court threw out Thomas's victory because of a campaign violation, but the Supreme Court stayed the disqualification. Another faction, the **Kerala Congress (Jacob),** merged into the Democratic Indira Congress–Karunakaran (see the NCP, above) in 2005 but was revived following the 2006 Kerala State election. In June 2007 the KC faction under P. C. Thomas joined in forming that year's short-lived UNPA.

In 2009, the only faction to win a *Lok Sabha* seat was the KC (Mani). In state elections in Kerala in May 2011, the KC was part of the winning United Democratic Front coalition, gaining 11 of 72 seats. In 2011, the KC (Joseph) merged with the KC (Mani), but a faction under P. C. Thomas broke away to form a new grouping, the **Kerali Congress (Thomas).**

Kerala Congress (Mani) Leaders: K. M. MANI (Chair), Jose K. MANI (Member of the *Lok Sabha*).

Kerala Congress (Joseph) Leader: P. J. JOSEPH.

Kerala Congress (Balakrishna Pillai) Leader: R. Balakrishna PILLAI.

Kerala Congress (Jacob) Leader: T. M. JACOB.

Kerala Congress (Secular) Leader: P. C. GEORGE.

Keral Congress (Thomas) Leader: P. C. THOMAS.

Viduthalai Chiruthaigal Katchi (VCK). The VCK (Liberation Panthers Party, *Dalit* Panthers Party) is a small party based in Tamil Nadu. It won two state assembly seats in 2006 and currently participates with the DMK and Congress in the Tamil Nadu government. The VCK won one *Lok Sabha* seat in 2009. Party leader Thol THIRUMAVALAVAN and 225 supporters were arrested in September 2012 during protests against a visit by Sri Lanka's president. In 2013 Thirumavalavan led demonstrations in Bangalore following the alleged honor killing of a young man who married a woman from a higher caste.

Leader: Thol THIRUMAVALAVAN (General Secretary).

Republican Party of India (RPI). Founded in 1956 by Bhimrao Ramji AMBEDKAR, the Maharashtra-based RPI is dedicated to carrying out the equality clauses of the Indian constitution for its largest constituency, the *Dalits* (from the Hindu for "Oppressed"), formerly called "Untouchables" or *Harijans.* The party's intense factionalism has not helped its cause, although in the 1998 elections three factional leaders were among the four RPI candidates to win *Lok Sabha* seats. With part of the party linked to the Congress and another part favoring the new NCP, all four seats were lost in 1999. The party subsequently split, with one faction led by Prakesh AMBEDKAR, rebranding itself as the ***Bharatia* Republican Party** (*Bharatia Republican Paksha—Bharipa Bahujan Mahasangh*—BRP).

In 2004, running as an ally of Congress, the Ramdas Athawale faction, RPI(A), won one seat in the lower house but was not offered a ministerial portfolio in the Singh cabinet, an "injustice" that led Athawale to question his faction's future loyalty to Congress at the state level. In June 2006 faction leader R. S. GAVAI was named governor of Bihar, where he served for two years before becoming governor of Kerala.

In 2009, the RPI(A) failed to retain its *Lok Sabha* seat. The RPI(A) joined a coalition government in Mumbai with the SS and the BJP following municipal elections in 2012, while the BRP remained in the NCP-led coalition.

Leaders: Prakash AMBEDKAR (BRP), Ramdas ATHAWALE (RPI[A]), Rajendra GAVAI, Jogentra KAWADE, T. M. KAMBLE.

Rashtriya Lok Dal (RLD). The current RLD was established by the September 1998 merger of the preexisting RLD and the *Bharatiya Kisan Kamgar Party* (BKKP). The BKKP had been launched in opposition to the BJP in September 1996 by *Lok Sabha* member Ajit Singh, a former Congress (I) agriculture minister and son of Charan Singh, with the support of Mahendra Singh TIKAIT, a peasant leader in Uttar Pradesh. In the 1999 national election, the RLD was allied with the Congress and won two seats. In July 2001, it joined the NDA, although Ajit Singh resigned from the cabinet in May 2003. In the 2004 general election, the RLD won three seats. Allied with the *Samajwadi* Party, it added a *Rajya Sabha* seat in 2006.

In the 2009 general election, the RLD picked up two *Lok Sabha* seats, for a total of five. In December, the *Rashtriya Lok Dal* (RLD) joined the UPA, and Singh was appointed minister of civil aviation. Divisions within the state party organization in Utter Pradesh prompted the resignation of RLD spokesperson KK TRIPATHI in August 2013.

Leader: Ajit SINGH (President and Minister of Civil Aviation).

National Democratic Alliance (NDA):

Bharatiya Janata Party (BJP). The BJP (Indian People's Party) was formed in April 1980 by the bulk of *Janata*'s *Jana Sangh* group, which opposed efforts by the *Janata* leadership to ban party officeholders from participation in the activities of the National Volunteer Corps (*Rashtriya Swayamsevak Sangh*—RSS), a secretive paramilitary Hindu communal group that is generally regarded as the BJP's parent organization. By 1982 the BJP was widely viewed as the best-organized non-Communist opposition party.

In 1988, the BJP won 88 *Lok Sabha* seats. It supported the National Front government of V. P. Singh until October 1990, when BJP leader L. K. Advani was detained in connection with the Ayodhya temple dispute. The party's legislative representation rose to 119 in 1991 as the leading component of an electoral alliance that included Shiv Sena (below). Its anti-Muslim populism then helped it emerge from the April–May 1996 *Lok Sabha* election as the plurality party, with 161 seats, after which it formed a minority government under Atal Bihari Vajpayee. The administration resigned after 13 days, however, rather than face defeat in a confidence vote.

In 1997, the party tried to expand its support through moderating its Hindu nationalist (Hindutva) image and forging ties to state and regional parties. In the 1998 election, it again emerged as the plurality party, winning 181 seats, with Vajpayee then cobbling together a governing coalition. In 1999 it won 182 seats, and Vajpayee succeeded in forming his third government.

Between then and 2004, the BJP absorbed several smaller parties, including the Manipur State Congress Party (MSCP), the Tamil Nadu–based M. G. R. Dravidian Progressive Federation (M. G. R. Anna Dravida Munnetra Kazhagam—MGR ADMK, named after AIADMK founder M. G. Ramachandran), a 1997 offshoot of the AIADMK; and the Chhattisgarh-based Rashtriya Janatantrik Dal of former NCP leader V. C. Shukla.

Confounding expectations, the BJP-led NDA fell to Congress and its allies in the 2004 *Lok Sabha* elections, with the BJP winning only 22 percent of the vote and 137 seats. Shortly after the election, L. K. Advani was named leader of the opposition, while former prime minister Vajpayee was awarded the new position of parliamentary party chair. The following October, Advani also took over as BJP president, after the resignation of Venkaiah NAIDU. In May–June 2005 Advani traveled to Pakistan, where he made conciliatory remarks that raised the ire of the party's militant elements. He was further weakened in July when charges of incitement were reinstated against him and seven others in connection with the 1990 Ayodhya mosque incident. (In March 2007 the Supreme Court rejected a petition that could have further delayed the case or led to its dismissal.) Apparently pressured by the RSS and the fundamentalist World Council of Hindus (Vishwa Hindu Parishad—VHP), Advani stepped down as party president but remained leader of the opposition.

Late in 2005, several other significant developments occurred, beginning with the expulsion of former secretary general Uma BHARATI, a former chief minister of Madhya Pradesh and a leader of hard-line fundamentalists within the party, for "indiscipline and anti-party activities." Shortly thereafter, she formed a new party, the Bharatiya Janshakti Party. Near the end of December RSS figure Sanjay JOSHI resigned as party secretary general for organization after allegations of sexual misconduct surfaced. After being exonerated, Joshi returned to his post in April 2006, but he was again replaced as part of a January 2007 reorganization.

The BJP fell back to 116 seats in the April–May 2009 *Lok Sabha* election, which the Bharatiya Janshakti Party did not contest. As of November 2009, BJP chief ministers headed the state governments in Chhattisgarh, Gujarat, Himachal Pradesh, Karnataka, Madhya Pradesh, and Uttarakhand.

Moderate party leader Jaswant SINGH, a key cabinet minister from 1998 to 2004, was expelled by the BJP in August 2009 because of its objections to a recently published book in which he deviated from the party's interpretation of events surrounding the 1947 partition. Nitin Gadkari was elected to a three-year term as national party president in

December 2009. He was reelected in 2012. In April of that year, former BJP president Bangaru LAXMAN was convicted of bribery and sentenced to four years in prison. The BJP supported opposition candidate Sangma in the 2012 presidential election.

Following the revelation of corruption charges in January 2013, Gadkari resigned. He was replaced by Rajnath SINGH at a party congress on January 23. Reports in 2013 indicated that Narenda MODI, chief minister of Gujarat, would be the BJP's candidate for prime minister in the 2014 elections.

Leaders: Rajnath SINGH (President), Lal Krishna ADVANI (Chair, BJP Parliamentary Party), Sushma SWARAJ (Leader of the Opposition in *Lok Sabha*), Atal Bihari VAJPAYEE (Former Prime Minister), Arun JAITLEY (Leader in the Rajya Sabha), Shivraj PATIL, Narendra MODI (Chief Minister of Gujarat).

Janata Dal (United)—JD(U). *Janata Dal* was created by the merger in 1988 of the *Janata* (People's) grouping, led by Subramanian Swamy; *Lok Dal* (confusingly also meaning "People's Party"); and *Jan Morcha* (People's Front), led by Vishwanath Pratap Singh. *Janata* had been established as a formal merger of several diverse parties following their collective victory in the 1977 elections; *Lok Dal* had been founded in 1979 by a number of dissident *Janata* factions; and *Jan Morcha* had been launched in 1987 by Congress (I) dissidents.

Janata Dal obtained 141 of the 144 seats won by NF candidates in 1989 but only 55 of the 128 NF/LF seats obtained in 1991. The latter election was precipitated by a split in *Janata Dal* that led to the creation of what became the *Samajwadi* Party (below). A further split in 1994 eventually led to formation of the BJP-allied *Samata* Party. The rump *Janata Dal* led the United Front (UF) to a plurality in the 1996 general elections, although its seat tally fell to 45. The party was further reduced by corruption charges against its president, Lalu Prasad Yadav, chief minister of Bihar, whose rebel Rashtriya Janata Dal (RJD) substantially eroded the Janata Dal's role in Parliament and in the UF government. In the election of 1998 the party captured only 6 seats.

The party further splintered because of differences between Sharad Yadav and former prime minister H. D. Deve Gowda. With both factions claiming to be the "real Janata," on August 8, 1999, the Election Commission recognized the competing factions as separate entities, with the Deve Gowda branch being called the Janata Dal (Secular) and the Yadav branch, Janata Dal (United). At the same time, it approved joint use of the arrow symbol by the JD(U), the Samata Party, and Ramakrishna HEGDE's Lok Shakti (LS), the three having been negotiating a common list for the upcoming election. A week later the JD(U), as expected, joined the NDA, and in the subsequent election the JD(U) list won 21 seats in the *Lok Sabha*.

The Samata (Equality) Party had resulted from the Janata Dal split in early 1994 that yielded a Janata Dal (G); led by George FERNANDES, the new party adopted the Samata designation late in the year. Remaining outside the center-left alliance that became the United Front, it won 6 *Lok Sabha* seats in the 1996 balloting, all in the state of Bihar. In 1998 its 12 seats were important to the formation of the BJP-led coalition government.

An anticipated formal merger of the JD(U), the LS, and the Samata Party failed to materialize in January 2000 when the Samata Party, which had wanted Yadav to step down in favor of Fernandes, rejected unification. The status of the LS and the Samata Party was compromised, however, by a decision of the Election Commission that derecognized officeholders of both who had been elected on the JD(U) list. In September 2000 the LS itself was derecognized, and in November former LS leader Ram Vilas Paswan formed the Lok Janshakti Party (LJP, below). In March 2001, Samata President Jaya JAITLEY, who had replaced Fernandes following the earlier Election Commission ruling, resigned after being videotaped accepting a bribe in a sting operation. Fernandes, although not implicated, resigned as defense minister, but he returned to the post in October.

In December 2003, the long-anticipated merger of the Samata Party and the JD(U) was achieved, with Fernandes then becoming JD(U) president. The merger met with objections from a minority of both parties, including former JD(U) parliamentary leader Devendra Prasad YADAV, who instigated formation of a JD(U-Democratic) faction in the *Lok Sabha*. He as well as a number of other dissenters ultimately joined the RJD before the 2004 lower house election, at which the JD(U) won only eight seats.

In the Bihar State elections in October–November 2005 the JD(U) finished first and formed an NDA government with the second-place BJP. In April 2006 Sharad Yadav was elected president of the party over the ailing George Fernandes, who had refused to step aside. In January 2007, Jaya Jaitley and Bhahmanand MANDAL, who had opposed the merger, revived the Samata Party. In August, however, a faction led by N. K. SINGH and Shiv KUMAR tried to oust Mandal. The Election Commission declined to recognize either faction.

In 2009, the JD(U) was the only NDA party to show a significant improvement over its 2004 results, gaining 12 *Lok Sabha* seats, for total of 20. George Fernandes, 79, having been denied a party nomination, ran independently but failed to win a seat. In July 2012, several BJP regional leaders defected to the JD(U). Reports in 2013 indicated that the JD(U) had ended its alliance with the NDA and would seek another coalition for the 2014 balloting.

Leaders: Sharad YADAV (President), Nitish KUMAR (Chief Minister of Bihar).

Shiv Sena (SS). Since its formation in 1966 the Maharashtra-based *Shiv Sena* (Army of Shivaji, referencing a 17th-century Hindu king who repulsed the armies of the Muslim Moghul empire) has articulated Hindu nationalism even more forcefully than has the BJP. Led by Bal Thackeray, a former newspaper cartoonist turned populist orator, the movement was prominent in the anti-Muslim violence that led to the destruction of the Ayodhya mosque in December 1992. It won 15 *Lok Sabha* seats in the April–May 1996 election and was represented in the resultant very short-lived government led by the BJP. Closely linked to the BJP, the SS brought its remaining 6 seats into the BJP-led government following the 1998 election. In the 1999 *Lok Sabha* balloting the party returned to its earlier strength, winning 15 seats even though Thackeray had been disenfranchised for six years in July 1999 because of a conviction for inciting communal hatred in a 1987 speech. In the 2004 general election it retained 12 seats.

In early 2003, a dispute between Bal Thackeray's youngest son, Uddhav, and a nephew, Raj THACKERAY, over who would accede to the party leadership concluded with Uddhav's elevation. In December 2005 Raj resigned from the party, and in March 2006 he formed the Maharashtra Navnirman Sena—MNS (Maharashtra Reconstruction Army), to which he hoped to attract SS dissidents. In October 2008, he was charged with inciting violence against migrant workers. Earlier in 2008, a former northern party leader, Jai Bhagwan GOYAL, announced that he was forming the Rashtrawadi Sena in response to negative comments by Uddhav about northerners living in Maharashtra.

The SS attracted considerable criticism in June 2008 when an editorial in the party newspaper, Saamana, called for Hindus to adopt the tactics of Islamist suicide bombers. In the 2009 general election the SS won 11 seats. (The MNS ran 12 candidates without success.) In 2010, Raj Thackery accused the SS of bribery, after Bal Thackeray had complained that the MNS had supported the INC and NCP candidates in local elections. In the 2012 Mumbai municipal elections, 44 of the 75 SS assembly candidates elected were women (60 percent). Bal Thackeray died following a heart attack on November 17, 2012, at age 86.

Leaders: Uddhav THACKERAY (Executive President), Anant GHEETE (Leader in the *Lok Sabha*).

Shiromani Akali Dal (SAD). Although the Sikh *Shiromani Akali Dal* (Akali Religious Party) contests elections nationally, its influence is confined primarily to Punjab, where it campaigns against excessive federal influence in Sikh affairs. Prior to the June 1984 storming of Amritsar's Golden Temple, leadership of the Sikh agitation had effectively passed from the *Akali Dal* to the more extremist followers of Jarnail Singh Bhindranwale. In July 1985, a year after Bhindranwale's death, the moderate *Akali Dal* leader, Harchand Singh Longowal, concluded a peace agreement with Prime Minister Rajiv Gandhi, but Longowal was assassinated in August.

In 1986, a number of *Akali Dal* leaders, including Parkash Singh Badal, a former chief minister, withdrew to form a separate party, but in 1987 the party reunited under Simranjit Singh Mann, a former police official. Factionalism nevertheless persisted. In 1994–1995 the Sikh religious leadership, led by Manjit SINGH, attempted to unify the party, with half a dozen of the more distinctly nonsecular factions—the most notable exception being the Badal group—adopting an "Amritsar declaration" and briefly appending "Amritsar" to their collective identity. However, Mann, asserting that other party leaders were not abiding by the declaration, subsequently formed a separate party (see SAD [Mann], below).

In 1998–1999, a serious internal feud saw a faction led by Gurcharan Singh TOHRA defect to form the All India Shiromani Akali Dal (AISAD), which may have contributed to the SAD's losing six of its eight *Lok Sabha* seats in the 1999 election. Three years later, it lost the state poll. Tohra and Badal reconciled in 2003, but Tohra died in March 2004. Less than a month later Jaswant Singh MANN organized a new anti-Badal All India Shiromani Akali Dal, one of several minor SAD formations.

At the 2004 general election, the SAD won eight seats as a component of the NDA. Shortly afterward a dissident SAD leader, Prem Singh CHANDUMAJRA, announced formation of another anti-Badal offshoot, the Shiromani Akali Dal (Longowal), but he rejoined the parent party in January 2007. A month later, in alliance with the BJP, the SAD won the Punjab State election, permitting Badal to again become chief minister. In 2009 Badal's SAD won only four *Lok Sabha* seats. The BJP–SAD coalition again won state balloting in Punjab in March 2012. In March 2013, the anti-Badal grouping Shiromani Akali Dal (Amritsar) reintegrated with the party.

Leaders: Parkash Singh BADAL (Chief Minister of Punjab), Sukhbir Singh BADAL (President), Sukhdev Singh DHINDSA (Secretary General).

Telangana Rashtra Samithi (TRS). The TRS was founded in April 2001 by former members of the *Telugu Desam* Party (TDP). They advocated restoration of a separate Telangana State, which had been absorbed by Andhra Pradesh in 1956. In the 2004 general election the party won five seats in the *Lok Sabha.* It joined the UPA government but withdrew in August 2006 over the statehood issue.

In March 2008, the party's 4 remaining *Lok Sabha* members resigned, as did 16 members of the Andhra Pradesh legislature, forcing by-elections at both levels over the statehood issue. The TRS suffered significant defeats, however, returning only 2 of the 4 to the *Lok Sabha* and only 7 to the state legislature. In 2009, having obtained a pledge of support for reestablishing Telangana, the party's president, K. Chandrasekhar Rao, backed the NDA in the national election despite maintaining an alliance with the Third Front's Telugu Desam Party (TDP, below) at the state level. The TRS won only 2 seats in the *Lok Sabha* and 10 in the Andhra Pradesh legislature, prompting Rao, not for the first time, to submit his resignation in June. Two days later, however, responding to a unanimous resolution by the party's General Body, he withdrew it. Despite lengthy discussions in 2012, the TRS officially announced it would not merge with the INC.

Leader: K. Chandrasekhar RAO (President).

Assam People's Council (*Asom Gana Parishad*—AGP). The AGP was launched in October 1985 as a coalition (but not a merger) of the All-Assam Students' Union (AASU) and the All-Assam *Gana Sangram Parishad* (AAGSP), which were united by their call for the deportation of (largely Bangladeshi) "aliens" from Assam. It won two *Lok Sabha* seats in 1991 and five in 1996 (and regained a substantial plurality in concurrent state balloting in Assam) but claimed none in 1998 or 1999. In May 2001 it lost the state election to the Congress.

The AGP returned to the *Lok Sabha* in the 2004 election, winning two seats. It remained the leading opposition party in Assam following the 2006 state election, despite a September 2005 split that saw the party's founder, Prafulla Kumar MAHANTA, a former chief minister of Assam, expelled. Mahanta then formed a new Assam People's Council (Progressive), but the party reunited in October 2008. In 2009 the AGP won one *Lok Sabha* seat. Jayanta DAS, a senior BJP leader, defected to the AGP in August 2013, along with other party members.

Leader: Prafulla Kumar MAHANTA (President).

Indian National Lok Dal (INLD). The INLD was announced by octogenarian politician Devi Lal in October 1996 under the name *Haryana Lok Dal* (HLD). Lal was a leader of the early *Samajwadi* Party but switched to the *Samata* Party before breaking from it to form the HLD, which campaigned as the HLD (*Rashtriya*), or HLD-R, after another political group appropriated the HLD designation. The HLD-R contested the 1998 elections in alliance with the BSP (below) and won four *Lok Sabha* seats, but it subsequently backed the Vajpayee government. In mid-February 1999, however, it withdrew its support to protest subsidy cuts for food grains and fertilizer. By the time the NDA was formed in May 1999, the party was almost uniformly referred to as the INLD, and went on to win five seats in the September–October general election.

In July 1999, Lal's son, Om Prakash Chautala, had returned as chief minister of Haryana following the resignation of Bansi Lal of the now-defunct *Haryana Vikas* Party (HVP; see under INC, above). At a premature state election in February 2000, the INLD won a clear mandate, with the BJP joining the Chautala administration as a junior partner. At the national level, Chautala broke with the BJP shortly before the 2004 general election, at which the INLD won no seats. The INLD lost control of the 90-seat Haryana legislature in the March 2005 state elections, dropping from 47 to 9 seats. In 2009 it failed to win any of the state's 10 *Lok Sabha* seats.

In September 2012, investigators recommended forgery and conspiracy charges against Chautala and other INLD leaders in a scandal involving recommendations for government positions. In August 2013, the INLD announced it would support Narenda Modi of the BJP to be prime minister in 2014.

Leaders: Om Prakash CHAUTALA (Former Chief Minister of Haryana and President of the Party), Ajay Singh CHAUTALA (Secretary General).

Left Front (LF):

Communist Party of India–Marxist (CPI-M). Organized in 1964 by "leftist" deserters from the CPI (below) favoring a more radical line, the CPI-M called for small-scale, rural-oriented, labor-intensive development as well as political decentralization. In 1969 some of its more extreme and overtly pro-Chinese members withdrew to form the CPI-ML (below). At its annual conference in January 1992, the CPI-M responded to events in the former Soviet Union by proclaiming itself "the strongest Communist party in the world."

At the party's 16th congress in 1998, it attacked the "multiple threat of communalism and retrograde economic policies" offered by the BJP-led government. In 1998 it retained its 32 seats in the *Lok Sabha* and then added 1 more in 1999. Prior to the latter election the CPI-M and the CPI jointly identified the defeat of the BJP as their primary goal. However, the Revolutionary Socialist Party (RSP) and the Forward Bloc (both below) contended that the left should also disavow any association with the Congress. As a result, the left entered the contest without a unified "Left Front" platform.

In the 2004 general election, the CPI-M led a unified Left Front once again, winning 43 *Lok Sabha* seats and subsequently extending external support to the Congress-led government.

At the state level, the CPI-M continued to hold an overall majority in Tripura and West Bengal, and in April–May 2006 it led a Left Democratic Front alliance to an upset victory over Congress in Kerala. Party leader Jyoti Basu served as chief minister of West Bengal from 1977 until ill health forced him to step down in November 2000.

In 2009, the CPI-M lost the majority of its *Lok Sabha* seats, dropping to 16. The bad news continued in 2010 when the party suffered a crushing defeat in the municipal elections in West Bengal, a state where it had been in control for over 30 years. In the elections of May 2011 the CPI–M lost control of the state of Kerala to the INC.

The CPI-M supported Mukherjee of the INC for the presidency in 2012. The part won 49 of 60 seats in the Tripura legislative elections in February 2013.

Leaders: Basudeb ACHARIA (*Lok Sabha* Leader), V. S. ACHUTHANANDAN, Buddhadev BHATTACHARJEE, Manik SARKAR (Chief Minister of Tripura), S. Ramachandran PILLAI (All India Kisan Sabha President and Politburo Member), Prakash KARAT (General Secretary).

Communist Party of India (CPI). Established in 1925, the CPI was India's largest opposition party, following the new country's first general election in 1952. Although the CPI-M took with it the majority of CPI members when it broke away in 1964, most of the party bureaucracy, legislative representatives, and trade unionists remained in the CPI. In 1980 supporters of former chair S. A. DANGE established the All India Communist Party—from 1989, called the United Communist Party of India—following rejection of Dange's proposal to support the Congress (I).

Throughout the 1990s, the party's *Lok Sabha* representation gradually diminished, falling to four in 1999, but in the 2004 general election, it won ten seats. It dropped to four again in 2009. At a party congress in March 2012, Suravaram Sudhakar REDDY was elected general secretary of the CPI. The CPI won one seat in the 2013 Tripura legislative balloting.

Leaders: Suravaram Sudhakar REDDY (General Secretary), Gurudas DASGUPTA (AITUC General Secretary and *Lok Sabha* Leader).

All India Forward Bloc (AIFB). Frequently referenced simply as the **Forward Bloc,** the AIFB is a leftist party confined primarily to

West Bengal. Its program calls for land reform and nationalization of key sectors of the economy. It won two *Lok Sabha* seats in 1991, three in 1996, and two in 1998 and 1999. The party suffered the loss of one of its most important modern leaders with the death of General Secretary Chita BASU in 1997. In 2009 it won two *Lok Sabha* seats, down from three in 2004.

In 2010, a fissure began to emerge between the AIFB and the Left Democratic Front. In the state of Kerala the CPI-(M) blocked the move of the AIFB to join the front in the civic elections of October. The Forward Block in Kerala then made an alliance with the BJP, although the BJP cautioned against overemphasizing the importance of what it characterized as only a "local arrangement." In September 2012, the AIFB led a series of protests against government price hikes on fuel.

Leaders: Debabrata BISWAS (General Secretary), N. Vellapan NAIR (Chair), Amar Singh KUSHWAHA (Deputy Chair).

Revolutionary Socialist Party (RSP). The RSP is a Marxist–Leninist grouping based in West Bengal, Kerala, and Tripura. It won five *Lok Sabha* seats in 1996, when it was a UF party, but it chose not to join the new UF government.

In May 1999, a rebel faction under the leadership of party veteran Shibhu Baby JOHN held its own convention, where it argued for leftist unity in the effort to prevent the BJP's return to power. The "official" RSP, however, joined the Forward Bloc in advocating a policy of equidistance from both the BJP and the Congress in the forthcoming national election, at which it won three seats, down from five in 1998. It again won three in 2004 but only two in 2009.

Leaders: Abani ROY, Debabrata BISWAS (General Secretary).

Other Third Front Parties:

Bahujan Samaj Party (BSP). Representing India's disadvantaged and *Dalits,* the BSP (Party of the Majority) advances no ideological program, save nonsecularism and "power to the majority." It is based in Punjab and in Uttar Pradesh, where it is a principal rival of the SP. The party's founder, Kanshi RAM, died in October 2006.

The party's tally of 11 *Lok Sabha* seats in the 1996 national election dropped to 5 in 1998 before recovering to 14 in 1999. In partnership with the BJP, it regained leadership of the Uttar Pradesh government in May 2002, but the coalition dissolved in August 2003, and Chief Minister Mayawati Kumari stepped down. Five months earlier a scandal had erupted over a videotape that recorded Mayawati asking BSP loyalists to donate to the party money that they had obtained from public projects.

In 2004, the BSP won 18 *Lok Sabha* seats in alliance with Congress. In December 2005 its parliamentary leader, Raja Ram PAL, was one of 11 legislators expelled by the lower house after being caught accepting bribes in a sting operation.

In the April–May 2007 Uttar Pradesh election, the BSP won an outright victory, taking a majority in the Legislative Assembly and ousting the SP-led government. Mayawati thereupon returned as chief minister. In June 2008 the BSP withdrew from the UPA, in part over economic policy but also because Congress was allegedly trying to win greater support from the BSP's voter base. Another factor may have been Mayawati's acknowledged ambition to be prime minister. In the 2009 general election, the party won 21 *Lok Sabha* seats and then gave external support to the Singh government.

In September 2009, the Supreme Court ordered Mayawati's government to discontinue using public funds for erecting statues and other monuments honoring BSP figures, including Mayawati herself. The cost of the program was reported to be $425 million.

In May 2010, Mayawati expelled 500 party workers who had what she characterized as dubious or criminal backgrounds. The move came in response to the continued criticism of her and the party for alleged corrupt practices. In 2011 Mayawati came under renewed criticism for her extravagant lifestyle. A U.S. embassy cable from 2008 that was released by Wikileaks reported that she sent a private jet to Mumbai to buy a pair of sandals. It also called her a "corrupt and virtual paranoid dictator."

Mayawati was turned out of office following state elections in Uttar Pradesh in March 2012, where the BSP placed second behind the SP. In April 2013, the BSP announced it would jointly contest elections in Mysore with the small **Social Democratic Party of India** (SDPI).

Leaders: Mayawati KUMARI (Former Chief Minister of Uttar Pradesh and BSP President), Satish Chandra MISHRA (General Secretary).

Biju Janata Dal (BJD). An Orissa party established in 1997, the BJD is led by Naveen Patnaik, the son of a former important state leader, Biju PATNAIK. Naveen, who had taken over his late father's national legislative seat in 1996 while a member of the *Janata Dal,* subsequently left the parent grouping in protest over that party's failure to ally with the BJP. The BJD won nine seats in the March 1998 national balloting, and Patnaik was named minister of mines. In the 1999 election the BJD won ten seats.

Patnaik stepped down as minister of mines to become chief minister of Orissa following a BJD-BJP victory in state balloting in February 2000. Patnaik won a second term as chief minister in the April 2004 state election, while the BJD took 11 *Lok Sabha* seats in simultaneous union balloting. In 2009 the BJD retained its overwhelming majority in the state assembly and, as part of the Third Front, increased its *Lok Sabha* representation to 14 seats.

Leaders: Naveen PATNAIK (Chief Minister of Orissa and President of the Party), Braja Kishore TRIPATHY (Leader in the *Lok Sabha*).

All India Dravidian Progressive Federation (All India *Anna Dravida Munnetra Kazhagam*—AIADMK). The AIADMK is a Tamil party that split from the DMK (above) in 1972. Its founder, former matinee idol Maruthur Gopala RAMACHANDRAN, died in 1987, provoking a succession struggle. In 1991, as an ally of Congress (I), the AIADMK retained the 11 *Lok Sabha* seats won in 1989 and also assumed power in Tamil Nadu under Jayalalitha Jayaram, a former actress. Accused by the opposition of massive financial corruption, Jayalalitha resumed the AIADMK's alliance with the Congress for the 1996 *Lok Sabha* and state elections, but her party was wiped out by the DMK in the former and retained only 4 seats in the latter.

The party won 18 *Lok Sabha* seats in March 1998 and joined the BJP coalition government, from which Jayalalitha repeatedly threatened to withdraw because of her objections to ministerial and military appointments and dismissals. Making good on her threat, she precipitated the confidence vote of April 17, 1999, that brought down the government and led to the September–October election, at which the party, once again allied with Congress, won 10 seats. In February and October 2000, Jayalalitha was sentenced to prison following corruption convictions, but she ultimately prevailed on appeal. Numerous other cases against her have been similarly unsuccessful.

Although she was barred from competing, in the May 2001, state election Jayalalitha once again led her party and its Secular Front alliance to a lopsided victory over the DMK. She then won a by-election in February 2002, permitting her to again become chief minister.

Prior to the April–May 2004 general election the AIADMK joined the NDA, but it was rejected by the electorate, losing all 33 seats it contested. In early 2006, in preparation for the Tamil Nadu assembly election, the AIADMK forged a Democratic People's Alliance that included the MDMK, the JD(S) (above), splinter groups of the IUML (above) and AIFB (above), and several other small parties. The coalition was routed, however, by a DMK-led alliance. In 2007, Jayalalitha, having parted ways with the NDA, joined in forming the new UNPA, but she soon departed. Having backed the BJP candidate for president, she was expected to seek a renewed alliance with that party before the next general election, but instead the AIADMK aligned itself with the Third Front, returning to the *Lok Sabha* with nine seats. AIADMK supported Sangma in the 2012 presidential contest. A number of prominent members of the **Pattali Makkal Katchi** (PMK) and the **Dravidian Progressive Federation** (*Dravida Munnetra Kazhagam*—DMK) (see below) were reported to have defected to the AIADMK in 2013.

Leader: Jayalalitha JAYARAM (Former Chief Minister of Tamil Nadu and General Secretary of the Party).

Telugu Desam Party (TDP). An Andhra Pradesh–based party, *Telugu Desam* (*Telugu* Nation) was reported to have disbanded in March 1992, but a revitalized party, led by former film star Nandmuri Tarak (N. T.) Rama RAO, swept into power in the 1994 state election. Subsequent intraparty divisions ultimately saw the reform-minded Chandrababu Naidu replace Rao as chief minister in September 1995. The leadership of the Rao faction passed, after Rao's death in January 1996, to his widow, Lakshmi PARVATHI.

In the 1996 national election, the TDP-Naidu (or TDP-Babu) won 16 lower house seats as a member of the United Front. In 1998 the Parvathi faction, having organized separately as the **NTR Telugu Desam Party,** won no seats, while the Naidu faction slipped from 16 to 12. In March 1999 the TDP leadership voted to leave the United Front, in part because the alliance's central committee had decided to support a Congress Party candidate for speaker of the *Lok Sabha*.

Under Naidu the TDP achieved major gains in 1999, winning 29 *Lok Sabha* seats and extending its support to the NDA government without, however, joining the Council of Ministers. In 2004, as part of the NDA, the TDP saw its *Lok Sabha* representation plummet to 5 seats as the Congress Party successfully exploited a widening gap between the rising fortunes of the state's urban elite and the plight of its rural farmers. In the simultaneous state election the TDP lost all but 45 of its 180 assembly seats.

In 2009, the TDP won 6 seats in the *Lok Sabha* and made a significant recovery in the state assembly election, claiming 105 seats but failing to topple Congress. As in 1999 and 2004, Parvathi's group won no *Lok Sabha* seats. The TDP opposed the creation of a separate state of Telangana, and a number of TDP elected and appointed officials resigned to protest the decision.

Leader: N. Chandrababu NAIDU (Former Chief Minister of Andhra Pradesh and President of the Party).

Janata Dal (Secular)—JD(S). The JD(S) name was applied by the Election Commission to the Deve Gowda faction of *Janata Dal* (see JD[U], above) in August 1999. Although the party contested nearly 100 seats in the subsequent national election, it captured only 1, with Deve Gowda himself going down to defeat.

In April 2004, the JD(S) won three *Lok Sabha* seats, including one contested by Deve Gowda, and placed third in the Karnataka State Assembly. In May, Deve Gowda announced that the JD(S) would form a coalition government with the second-ranked Congress, rather than the plurality BJP, in Karnataka. In January 2006, however, H. D. Kumaraswamy, son of Deve Gowda, led 39 JD(S) members of the Legislative Assembly in a revolt that brought down the Congress-JD(S) government. Realigned with the BJP, Kumaraswamy formed a new administration. Deve Gowda suspended the defectors in February but then, late in the year, welcomed them back into the fold. That outcome precipitated a further split, with Deve Gowda's continuing leadership being opposed by Surendra MOHAN, who formed a breakaway "real" JD(S), the Janata Dal (Left).

Following a lengthy political impasse, in November 2007 Kumaraswamy agreed to step down as chief minister and permit the BJP to head the government, as had previously been agreed by the coalition partners. The JD(S) unsuccessfully sought to realign with Congress before the May 2008 state election, at which it suffered significant losses. As part of the Third Front in 2009, it won three *Lok Sabha* seats, including one by Deve Gowda and another by Kumaraswamy. The JD(S) subsequently agreed to support the UPA government. The JD(S) tied with the BJP for second in the legislative balloting in Karnataka in May 2013, with each party winning 40 of 223 seats.

Leaders: H. D. DEVE GOWDA (Former Prime Minister and Chair of the Party), H. D. KUMARASWAMY (Former Chief Minister of Karnataka), H. D. REVANNA.

Haryana Janhit Congress (HJC). The HJC is a breakaway from the INC. It was formed in 2007 by former Haryana chief minister Bhajan Lal and a son, Kuldeep Bishnoi, after the latter's suspension from the INC for antiparty activity. Another factor in the party's formation was the INC's decision not to name Lal as chief minister following the 2005 state election.

In the 2009 general election, Lal won the party's only *Lok Sabha* seat. Two months later, party leader Subhash BATRA announced that he was forming the Samasat Haryana Janhit Congress (SHJC) because he objected to the Lal family's domination of the HJC and recent efforts by Lal to draw closer to the BJP. The HJC agreed to an alliance with the BJP in Haryana for the 2014 elections.

Leaders: Kuldeep BISHNOI (President), Bhajan LAL.

Marumalarchi Dravida Munnetra Kazhagam (MDMK). The MDMK is a strongly Tamil nationalist grouping, occasionally accused of being too close to Sri Lanka's separatist Liberation Tigers of Tamil Eelam (LTTE) for easy cooperation with national parties. The Jain Commission report on the assassination of Rajiv Gandhi caused the party some difficulties, although its long-standing antipathy to the DMK contributed to its participation in the AIADMK alliance in 1998 and in the subsequent BJP-led government coalition. The party had run five candidates in Tamil Nadu, winning three seats.

In April 1999, the MDMK broke ranks with the AIADMK over the latter's withdrawal of support for the Vajpayee government, which led to a rapprochement with the DMK and the MDMK's participation in the NDA.

As a consequence of urging support for the LTTE, the MDMK's general secretary, Vaiko, was detained by the AIADMK-led Tamil Nadu government from July 2002 until he was released on bail in February 2004. Responding to an imminent NDA-AIADMK pact, the MDMK had left the Vajpayee government in December 2003. It contested the 2004 election with Congress (and the DMK), winning four *Lok Sabha* seats, as it had in 1999.

Somewhat surprisingly, in March 2006, the MDMK aligned with the AIADMK for the May Tamil Nadu assembly election, prompting the DMK to demand the MDMK's removal from the UPA. Subsequently, a dissident faction formed under *Lok Sabha* members L. GANESAN and Ginje RAMACHANDRAN, who objected to the AIADMK alliance and Vaiko's continuing leadership. Both were expelled from the party after backing the government in a July 2008 confidence vote related to the proposed nuclear technology agreement with the United States. In March 2007 Vaiko had broken from the UPA, charging that it had failed to implement most provisions of its program and to address the needs of the common people.

After having initially participated in the UNPA, it joined in forming the Third Front in March 2009 but won only one *Lok Sabha* seat in the April–May national election. Vaiko and a number of supporters were arrested during protests against a visit by the president of Sri Lanka. In 2013, the MDMK attempted unsuccessfully to prevent the distribution of the John Abraham Bollywood film, *Madras Café*, because the movie portrayed Tamils in a negative light.

Leaders: VAIKO (V. GOPALASWAMI, Secretary General), A. GANESHAMURTHI (Member of the *Lok Sabha*).

Pattali Makkal Katchi (PMK). Based in the disadvantaged Vanniyar community of northern Tamil Nadu, the PMK (Pattali People's Party) emerged in 1997 as a bitter opponent of the AIADMK, although in the interests of political power it subsequently joined a coalition with its enemy. It won all four seats it contested in the 1998 national election, and five of eight in 1999. In February 2001 it left the NDA, but after a lack of success in the subsequent state elections, it rejoined the alliance in late July. It departed again in January 2004 and joined the DMK and MDMK (below) as allies of Congress for the April–May general election, at which it won six seats.

For the 2006 Tamil Nadu assembly election, the PMK participated in the victorious DMK-led Democratic Progressive Alliance, but in June 2008 it was dismissed from the government. In March 2009, with the national election approaching, it left the UPA and allied with the AIADMK in the Third Front, but it lost all of its *Lok Sabha* seats at the polls. Reports in 2011 indicated that the party had rejoined the UPA. Senior PMK official Kaudvetti GURU was arrested for the third time in August 2013 for his role in an April demonstration that turned violent.

Leaders: G. K. MANI (President), Dr. S. RAMDOSS (Founder), Anbumani RAMDOSS.

Fourth Front:

Samajwadi Party (SP). The *Samajwadi* (Socialist) Party, based in Uttar Pradesh, held its inaugural convention in October 1992. The new formation was an outgrowth of the *Janata Dal*–Socialist (JD-S), which had been organized by former *Janata Dal* leaders Chandra Shekhar and Devi Lal following their withdrawal from the National Front in November 1990. Shekhar, with Congress (I) support, subsequently served as prime minister until March 1991.

The party won 17 *Lok Sabha* seats in the 1996 election; 20 seats in 1998, second to the CPI-M among UF members; and 26 in 1999, although an attempt by President Mulayam Singh Yadav and the NCP's Sharad Pawar to forge a "Third Force" front in opposition to the NDA and the Congress failed to materialize. After winning 36 seats in the 2004 *Lok Sabha* election, the party backed formation of the Congress-led government in May but remained independent of the Congress in Uttar Pradesh, where it led the state government until ousted by the BSP (below) in the April–May 2007 state election. In August 2007 the SP's Rashid Masood ran as the UNPA's candidate for vice president but finished a distant third in the three-way race.

The largest party in the Fourth Front, the SP finished third overall in the 2009 *Lok Sabha* election, winning 23 seats, but that total was far behind the INC and the BJP and represented a net loss of 13 from 2004. The SP then extended external support to the Singh government. The SP won balloting in Uttar Pradesh in March 2012, and Yadav was named chief minister of the state. In March 2013, reports indicated that the SP would withdraw support from the UPA-led government.

Leaders: Mulayam Singh YADAV (President of the Party and Chief Minister of Uttar Pradesh), Janeshwar MISRA (Vice President), Ram Gopal YADAV (*Rajya Sabha* Leader), Amar SINGH (General Secretary).

Rashtriya Janata Dal (RJD). Formed in 1997 in the state of Bihar, the RJD (National People's Party) emerged from the conflict between the charismatic leader of Bihar state, L. P. Yadav, and his successor as president of the *Janata Dal,* Sharad Yadav. After his indictment on charges stemming from alleged misallocation of $250 million in agricultural support funds, L. P. Yadav was ousted from the *Janata Dal* and formed the RJD. In the March 1998 national balloting the party held its 17 seats in Bihar but failed to move significantly into other states.

In mid-February 1999, L. P. Yadav and his wife, Rabri Devi, the controversial chief minister of Bihar State, were arrested while protesting New Delhi's decision to assume governance of the state in the wake of two massacres of peasants, allegedly at the instigation of private landlords. The central takeover was rescinded in March when the Vajpayee administration could not muster support for the move from a majority of the Rajya Sabha.

In the September–October 1999 election, the RJD lost all but 7 *Lok Sabha* seats despite an alliance with Congress. In the Bihar State election in February 2000, however, it showed unexpected strength, capturing a plurality of legislative seats. In 2004, the RJD took 21 *Lok Sabha* seats as a Congress ally, but in the February 2005 state election it won only 75 assembly seats and was forced to surrender power. The failure of the BJP and its allies to form a government ultimately led to another state election in October–November 2005, in which the RJD lost another 21 seats and finished third. In the meantime, Yadav had been charged with embezzling agricultural subsidies in 1996, when he was chief minister. As of May 2006 dozens of former government officials and businessmen had been convicted of involvement in "fodder scam." In December 2006 Yadav and his wife were acquitted of having "disproportionate assets" above his known income.

Shortly before the April–May 2009 general election, Yadav stated that the SP, RJD, and LJP had united not in opposition to the UPA but to stop communalism. In the election the RJD lost 20 of its 24 seats but gave external support to the new UPA government. In the 2012 Bihar elections, the RJD placed third and secured just 22 seats. The death of MP Umashankar SINGH in January 2013 reportedly created divisions within the party over the candidate to replace him.

Leaders: Lalu Prasad YADAV (President of the Party), Rabri DEVI (Former Chief Minister of Bihar).

Lok Janshakti Party (LJP). The LJP was formed as the *Janshakti* Party in November 2000 by government minister Ram Vilas Paswan and three other members of the lower house, all formerly of the derecognized *Lok Shakti* (LS; see JD[U], below). The new party was recognized by the Elections Commission under its present name in December 2000.

In April 2002, Paswan resigned as minister of coal and mines and pulled his party out of the governing NDA, citing the government's inability to resolve the ongoing sectarian violence in Gujarat. Allied with Congress in 2004, the LJP won four seats, all from Bihar, and Paswan was again appointed to the cabinet.

In 2005, the LJP did not support the RJD-Congress coalition in the Bihar State elections, prompting the RJD leadership to demand Paswan's ouster from the UPA government. Paswan, a leading advocate for the minority rights of Dalits, Muslims, and others, led the LJP into the newly organized Fourth Front for the April–May 2009 general election, but the party failed to retain any *Lok Sabha* seats and only won three seats in state elections in Bihar in 2010. In August 2013, Paswan's son, Chirag PASWAN, was named as his father's successor for the 2014 balloting.

Leader: Ram Vilas PASWAN (President of the Party).

Other Parliamentary Parties:

Dravidian Progressive Federation (*Dravida Munnetra Kazhagam*—DMK). The DMK, which dates back to the early years of Indian independence, is an anti-Brahmin regional party dedicated to the promotion of Tamil interests and more autonomy for the states. A major split in 1972 led to formation of the AIADMK (below), which outpaced the DMK in most subsequent Tamil Nadu elections. However, in an unprecedented swing occasioned in part by the alleged corruption of the AIADMK state administration, the DMK in 1996 not only won 17 *Lok Sabha* seats but also returned to power with a landslide majority in the concurrent state election. Allegations related to the DMK's possible indirect involvement in the assassination of Rajiv Gandhi split the informal coalition holding the United Front in power and brought about the elections of 1998, at which the party won only 6 seats.

In preparation for the 1999 *Lok Sabha* election, in mid-May the DMK joined several other Tamil Nadu parties, including the PMK and MDMK (see below), as participants in the NDA. Having carried 12 seats, the DMK agreed to join the Vajpayee cabinet.

In the May 2001 state election, the DMK was handily defeated by its nemesis, the AIADMK, and at the end of June, party leader M. Karunanidhi was arrested on corruption charges. Mass demonstrations and a governmental crisis followed, and intervention by federal authorities soon led to his release.

The DMK pulled out of the NDA government in December 2003 and then allied itself with Congress. It won 16 *Lok Sabha* seats in the 2004 union election and was awarded several portfolios in the resultant Singh cabinet. As in past elections, for the May 2006 Tamil Nadu assembly balloting the DMK led a multiparty Democratic Progressive Alliance that included Congress as well as the PMK, IUML, CPI-M, and CPI (see below). Reversing its 2001 defeat, the alliance captured 163 of 234 seats in ousting the AIADMK.

In May 2007, the DMK forced party member Dayanidhi MARAN to resign from the union cabinet following a disagreement within the party leadership that persisted into 2008. Observers saw the matter as largely a family dispute, since Maran, Karunanidhi, and most of the other leaders are closely related. In the 2009 general election the DMK gained 2 *Lok Sabha* seats, for a total of 18, but initially rejected joining the new Singh government because of dissatisfaction with potential cabinet posts. In late May, however, the dispute was resolved, and the DMK joined the government. In April 2011 the former minister of communications and information technology Andimuthu Raja was indicted on corruption charges relating to the improper awarding of mobile telephone licenses. The scandals undermined the DMK's popularity and contributed to the party's losses in the Tamil Nadu legislative elections in April, where the DMK placed third. Reports indicated a potential power struggle between the two sons of 87-year-old Karunanidhi, M. K. Stalin and M. K. Azhagiri, to succeed their father upon his retirement. In March 2013, the DMK withdrew from the UPA and the cabinet over the government's refusal to endorse a resolution that was highly critical of Sri Lanka's human rights record.

Leaders: Dr. Kalaignar Muthuvel KARUNANIDHI (President of the Party), M. K. AZHAGIRI (Union Minister of Chemicals and Fertilizers), M. K. STALIN, K. ANBAZHAGAN (Secretary General).

All India Trinamul Congress (AITC). The AITC, which is often referenced simply as the **Trinamul Congress,** emerged in September 1997 out of the bitter struggle to wrest control of West Bengal from the CPI-M and its state leader, Jyoti Basu. Formed by Mamata Banerjee, the party won seven seats in the 1998 national election and eight in 1999 as part of the NDA.

In March 2001, Banerjee resigned as minister of railways (for the second time in six months) and pulled her party from the NDA. She allied with Congress and sought the office of chief minister of West Bengal. However, the Left Front, led by the CPI-M, easily won the June election, after which Banerjee briefly resigned as AITC leader. In August, having severed its ties to Congress, the party again joined the NDA.

In March 2004, a faction of the Nationalist Congress Party (see NCP, below) under Purno Sangma merged with the AITC to form the Nationalist Trinamul Congress (NTC), although the AITC designation was to be retained until after the April–May general election. The party suffered a major setback, however, winning only 2 seats—2 short of the 4 required for registration under its new name as a national party. Prior to a February 2006 by-election, Sangma returned to the NCP. Meanwhile, in August 2005, Banerjee distanced her party from the NDA in anticipation of running independently in the April–May 2006 West Bengal assembly election, at which the AITC managed to hold only 30 of the 60 seats it had previously claimed. Despite reaching an agreement with Congress for the September 2006 *Lok Sabha* by-elections, the AITC remained aligned with the NDA at the national level.

On December 30, 2006, at the urging of her followers, Banerjee ended a 25-day hunger strike she began as a protest against the forced acquisition of farmland for an automobile factory. Shortly before the 2009 *Lok Sabha* election, Banerjee and INC leaders reached a seat-sharing arrangement that brought the AITC into the UPA and resulted in its winning 19 seats (all in West Bengal), second only to the INC itself among the UPA parties. Banerjee, once again, was offered the post of railway minister in the new cabinet, from which she resigned again in May 2011, when she was elected chief minister of West Bengal, the first woman to hold that office. Her victory was stunning because the communists had held power for 34 years in the state. AITC member Dinesh TRIVEDI was made minister of railways but forced to resign on March 14, 2012, after proposing a highly unpopular increase in railway fees. Mukul ROY was named to replace him; however, lingering strife with the INC led the AITC to withdraw from the government in September. The AITC rebuffed efforts to form a third-front electoral coalition in West Bengal.

Leaders: Kumari Mamata BANERJEE (Party Chair and Chief Minister of West Bengal), Mukul ROY (General Secretary).

Assam United Democratic Front (AUDF). The AUDF is a nonsectarian party committed to ending the regional insurgency and promoting the rights and economic betterment of minorities, women, and the disadvantaged. It currently holds ten seats in the Assam legislature, and in 2009 won one *Lok Sabha* seat. In September 2012, an investigation was launched into party leader Baruddin Ajmal al-Qasimi's role in violent protests in Assam that left more than 100 dead.

Leaders: Baruddin AJMAL al-Qasimi (President), Hafiz Rashid Ahmad CHOUDHURY (Working President).

Bodoland People's Front (BPF). In February 2003 the Bodo Liberation Tiger Force (BLTF) agreed to end an insurgency in Assam that dated from 1968. The agreement followed a March 2000 cease-fire. On December 6, 2003, a Bodoland Territorial Council (BTC) was established and an amnesty extended to some 2,600 BLTF members who laid down their arms. Former BLTF commander in chief Hagrama Mohilary, now heading the newly formed BPF, was inaugurated as chief executive of the BTC. In 2009, the BPF won its first *Lok Sabha* seat and extended support to the UPA government. The party won 12 seats in the 2011 state balloting in Assam. Reports in 2013 indicated that the party had temporarily suspended operations.

Leaders: Hagrama MOHILARY (a.k.a. Hagrama BASUMATARY), Sansuma Khunggur BWISWMUTHIARY (Member of the *Lok Sabha*).

Jharkhand Vikas Morcha (JVM). The JVM was formed in 2006 by Babulal Marandi, a former Jharkhand chief minister and BJP vice president who had resigned his previous affiliation because of differences over the state government. It participated in the abortive UNPA in 2007 but ran independently for the *Lok Sabha* in 2009, with Marandi winning the party's sole seat.

Leader: Babulal MARANDI.

Mizo National Front (MNF). A leading force in Mizoram State, the MNF won the state's one *Lok Sabha* seat in the election of April–May 2004. In December 2008, however, it lost control of the state government to the INC, which also took away the MNF's *Lok Sabha* seat in 2009. It continues to hold one seat in the upper house.

Leaders: Pu ZORAMTHANGA (Former Chief Minister of Mizoram), Lalhming LIANA (Secretary).

Nagaland People's Front (NPF). In addition to belonging to the governing Democratic Alliance of Nagaland, the NPF claimed the state's only *Lok Sabha* seat in the 2004 election as part of the NDA. In 2009, running independently, it retained the seat, after which it agreed to support the new UPA government and endorsed the UPA presidential candidate Mukherjee in the 2012 balloting. The NPF won a majority in the Nagaland legislative elections in February 2013 with 37 of 59 seats.

Leaders: Neiphiu RIO (Chief Minister of Nagaland), C. M. CHANG (Member of the *Lok Sabha*).

Sikkim Democratic Front (SDF). Formed in opposition to the then-ruling *Sikkim Sangram Parishad* (SSP), which had dominated Sikkim politics since 1985, the SDF obtained a commanding majority in the Sikkim State election of December 1994 and went on to win the state's single *Lok Sabha* seat in 1996. It retained the seat in 1998, swept the simultaneous state and national elections in 1999, and held both the *Lok Sabha* seat and the state in 2004. In November 2005, decrying the state government's failure to meet the needs of the people, dissidents led by Chiten Dorjee LEPCHA announced their intention to form a "third force."

In February 2006, the SDF joined the UPA, although it ran independently in May 2009. At that time the SDF won all 32 seats in the state assembly, after which P. K. Chamling was sworn in for a fourth time as chief minister. The SDF retained its one *Lok Sabha* seat at the central level and then extended its external support to the UPA government.

Leader: Pawan Kumar CHAMLING (Chief Minister of Sikkim and President of the Party).

Two other parties, both based in Maharashtra State, won single seats in the 2009 *Lok Sabha* elections: the **Bahujan Vikas Aaghadi,** drawn from the Kunbi community and led by Jadhav Baliram SUKUR, and the **Swabhimani Paksha,** the political arm of the farmer-oriented Swabhimani *Shetkari Sanghatana,* led by Raju SHETTI. Both gave their support to the new UPA government. In addition, the **Swatantra Bharat Paksh,** also based in Maharashtra, was awarded one *Raja Sabha* seat in the June 2009 election; its leader is Sharad JOSHI. The **Bodoland People's Progressive Front** (BPPF), led by Rabiram NARZARY, was formed in opposition to the BPF.

The **United Liberation Front of Assam** (ULFA), established in 1979, is led by military commander Paresh BARUA and political chair Arabinda RAJKHOWA. The largest and best organized of the northeastern separatist organizations, it is responsible for a significant number of terrorist acts against Indian authorities. In the 1990s the ULFA and several other militant organizations began operating from camps set up in nearby Bhutan. Bangladesh began concerted efforts to suppress the ULFA in 2010. In September 2011, the ULFA signed a cease-fire. In 2012, the estimated strength of the ULFA was 2,000.

Other Parties:

Autonomous State Demand Committee (ASDC). The ASDC emerged in 1986 seeking greater autonomy for the predominantly tribal Karbi Anglong district of Assam. It won a *Lok Sabha* seat in a 1994 by-election in Assam and retained it in the 1996 and 1998 general elections. In 1999 the party's then-president, Jayanta Rongpi, ran successfully under the banner of the Communist Party of India–Marxist-Leninist (Liberation)—see under CPI-ML, below. Since then, the party has split, more than once, into competing factions. In May 2008 the Assam state government declared that it had evidence of links between ASDC leaders and militant organizations, such as the National Socialist Council of Nagaland (Isaac Muivah) and the *Dima Halam Daogah* (see under the subhead Principal North and Northeast Militant Organizations, below).

Leaders: Holiram TERANG (President), Jotson BEY, Babu RONGPI, Chomang KRO (Secretary General), Daniel TERON (General Secretary, ASDC-Progressive).

Communist Party of India–Marxist-Leninist (CPI-ML). As the result of disagreement over operational strategy for the spread of communism in rural India, an extreme faction within the CPI-M organized the CPI-ML in 1969. Committed to Maoist principles of people's liberation warfare, the party was actively involved in the Naxalite terrorist movement in West Bengal and was banned during the state of emergency. Some members subsequently rejected revolutionary Marxism in favor of parliamentary democracy, but none of the party's many splinters ever secured *Lok Sabha* representation until 1999, when the ASDC's Jayanta Rongpi agreed to run under the banner of the legal **Communist Party of India–Marxist-Leninist (Liberation)** (CPI-ML-L). The party failed to retain the seat in 2004.

In early 2007, the CPI-ML strongly opposed seizures of farmland in West Bengal, where the Left Front government was seeking to establish a special economic zone.

Leaders: Dipankar BHATTACHARYA (General Secretary), Jayanta RONGPI, Abhijit MAJUMDER (CPI-ML–Liberation), Indramil BHATTACHARYA (CPI-ML–Provisional Central Committee), Sridhar MUKHERJEE (CPI-ML–New Democracy).

Desiya Murpokku Dravida Kazhagam (DMDK). The DMDK (National Progressive Dravidian Party) was launched in September 2005 in Tamil Nadu by film star Vijayakant and former AIADMK minister Panruti S. Ramachandran. Advocating "progressive programs and policies," Vijayakant has directly linked himself to the founder of the AIADMK, M. G. Ramachandran, and is widely called "*Karuppu* MGR" (dark-skinned MGR). The DMDK failed to win any seats in the 2009 general election. It won 29 seats in the 2011 assembly election in Tamil Nadu. Reports in 2013 indicated that the DMDK was in negotiation with the NCP for an electoral alliance ahead of the 2014 balloting.

Leaders: VIJAYAKANT (President), Panruti S. RAMACHANDRAN (Presidium Chair).

Jammu and Kashmir People's Democratic Party (PDP). Established in 1999, the PDP has called for demilitarization of Jammu and Kashmir. It finished third in the 2002 Jammu and Kashmir State election and went on to join the second-ranked Congress in unseating the Jammu and Kashmir National Conference (JKNC, above) government. In the 2004 national election the PDP won one *Lok Sabha* seat.

In November 2005, the PDP's founder, Mohammed Sayeed, who had served as chief minister of Jammu and Kashmir for three years, was replaced by senior Congress leader Ghulam Nabi AZAD, in accordance with the 2002 coalition pact. The arrangement subsequently collapsed, and in the wake of the 2008 state election, despite gaining 5 assembly seats, for a total of 21, the PDP saw the JKNC and Congress form a new government. In January 2009, the PDP withdrew from the UPA, and it failed to hold its *Lok Sabha* seat in the subsequent general election.

Leaders: Mehbooba MUFTI (President), Mufti Mohammed SAYEED (Former Chief Minister of Jammu and Kashmir).

Shiromani Akali Dal (Mann)—SAD(M). The SAD(M), also frequently referenced as the **Shiromani Akali Dal (Amritsar),** was formed by radical *Akali Dal* faction leader S. S. Mann in the mid-1990s because, he claimed, other leaders had failed to adhere to the 1994 Amritsar declaration (see SAD, above). Mann successfully competed for a *Lok Sabha* seat in 1999. In 2004 and 2009, the party ran a small number of candidates, all unsuccessful.

In a case dating back to 1991, in November 2006, Mann was acquitted of sedition for allegedly advocating establishment of Khalistan, a Sikh homeland. In March 2013, SAD(M)'s leadership in Malwa defected to the SAD.

Leader: Simranjit Singh MANN (President).

The following additional state parties, all unrepresented at the national level, were registered at the time of the 2009 general election: the **Arunachal Congress** (AC), based in Arunachal Pradesh; the **Jammu and Kashmir National Panthers Party** (JKNPP); the **Maharashtrawadi Gomantak** (MAG), of Goa; the **Manipur People's Party** (MPP); the **Mizoram People's Conference** (MZPC); the **National People's Party** (NPP) of Manipur; the **Puducherry Munnetra Congress** (PMC); the **Save Goa Front** (SGF); the **United Democratic Party** (UDP) of Meghalaya; the **Uttarakhand Kranti Dal**—UKD (Uttarakhand Revolution Party) of Uttarakhand; and the **Zoram Nationalist Party** (ZNP) of Mizoram; the **Janata Party** (JP), led by Subramanian SWAMY. The **Communist Party of India–Maoist** (CPI-Maoist) was banned in 2009 (for more information, see the 2012 *Handbook*).

Kashmiri Separatist and Radical Islamic Groups:

All Parties Hurriyat Conference (APHC). Founded in March 1993 as a coalition of 26 political parties and other groups, the APHC seeks to end the division of the "occupied territories" through peaceful means, including civil disobedience and protests. With offices both in Jammu and Kashmir and in Pakistan, the APHC maintains that it constitutes the sole political representative of the Kashmiri people. It does not participate in state or general elections.

Among the current APHC participants are Mirwaiz Umar Farooq's **Awami Action Committee;** the **Azad Kashmir People's Party,** a Pakistan People's Party splinter founded and led by Sardar Khalid IBRAHIM; the **Democratic Freedom Party,** founded in 1998 by Shabir Ahmed SHAH; the **Islamic Political Party (Jammu and Kashmir),** led by Muhammad Yousuf NAQASH; the **Ittihad-ul-Muslimeen,** led by Maulana Muhammad Abbas ANSARI; the Muhammad Yasin MALIK faction of the **Jammu and Kashmir Liberation Front** (JKLF); the **Jammu and Kashmir Liberation Forum,** led by Javaid Ahmad MIR; the **Jammu and Kashmir National Front** (JKNF), led by Nayeem Ahmad KHAN; Abdul Ghani BHAT's Muslim Conference, which also includes as prominent leaders Jahangir Gani BHAT and Shabir Ahmad DAR; and the People's Political Front, led by Fazal-ul-Haq QURESHI. A major figure in the APHC, Abdul Ghani LONE of the People's Conference, was assassinated in May 2002. The conference is currently headed by a son, Bilan Ghani LONE, whose brother, Sajjad LONE, stirred up considerable controversy in 2009 when he became the first separatist in two decades to seek a *Lok Sabha* seat. (The seat was won by a member of the JKNC.) Another APHC participant, the People's League, lost its leader on August 11, 2008, when Sheikh Abdul AZIZ was killed by police during a protest march generated by a land dispute near the Hindu shrine of Amarnath. Mukhtar Ahmad WAZA was named as his acting successor.

APHC leaders have been detained on numerous occasions. In September 1999 New Delhi arrested 15 APHC leaders under the Jammu and Kashmir Public Safety Act and proceeded to hold them without trial. In April–May 2000 the Indian government released a number of the detainees, including the APHC chair, Syed Ali GILANI (GEELANI) of the Jamaat-e-Islami. Shortly afterward, speaking in New Delhi, Gilani repeated that the Kashmir question could be resolved only through tripartite talks involving India, Pakistan, and the Kashmiri people. In July 2000 Abdul Ghani Bhat succeeded Gilani as APHC chair.

In July 2003, the election of Muhammad Abbas Ansari as chair of the Executive Council precipitated a split in the organization, and two months later the more hard-line members, led by Gilani, attempted to replace him with Masrat ALAM. Since then, the organization has remained divided, with the more radical Gilani branch, encompassing about 16 groups, closely identified with the party Gilani formed in 2004, the Tehrik-e-Hurriyat Jammu and Kashmir (Jammu and Kashmir Movement for Freedom), as successor to the Jamaat-e-Islami.

On January 22, 2004, responding to overtures from New Delhi, a number of moderate APHC leaders, including former chairs Abdul Ghani Bhat and Mirwaiz Umar Farooq, met with representatives of the Indian government and agreed to seek an "honorable and durable solution" through dialogue and step-by-step measures. The delegation met Prime Minister Vajpayee the next day. In July, Ansari resigned as APHC chair in order to facilitate reconciliation, a task undertaken by APHC founder Farooq.

On June 2, 2005, a dozen moderate APHC representatives crossed the LoC into Pakistan's Azad Kashmir for the first time since 1947. Led by Farooq, who addressed the Azad Kashmir Legislative Assembly, the delegation then traveled to Islamabad for meetings with Pakistani officials, including President Musharraf.

In February 2006, Farooq became the first separatist leader to hold a public rally in Hindu-dominated Jammu in over a decade and urged those in attendance to "build bridges" between their various communities. A round table proposed by Indian Prime Minister Singh drew a rejection from the APHC moderates, who argued that the talks would not advance the negotiations. Hard-liner Gilani termed the proposed talks a "futile exercise." In contrast, a March 10–12 conference in Islamabad, organized by the Washington-based Pugwash Conferences, was attended not only by various APHC leaders—among them, Yasin Malik, Sajjad Lone, and Abdul Ghani Bhat—but also by civil society leaders, officials from both Azad Kashmir and Indian Kashmir, and "back-channel" diplomats. Moderates and hard-liners alike boycotted a second round table, held May 24–25, in Srinagar.

In December 2006, elaborating a strategy he had previously proposed, Pakistani President Musharraf set forth a four-point plan for Kashmir: greater self-government, demilitarization, opening of the LoC to permit greater freedom of movement within existing borders, and joint supervision by India and Pakistan. The APHC moderates labeled the plan "realistic and bold," and over the next several months even some hard-liners appeared more willing to consider aspects of the plan, particularly demilitarization of Kashmir. Following a January 26, 2007, meeting with Musharraf, Farooq called for an end to violence. On March 16–17 Bhat and Malik were among the Kashmiri leaders who attended an International Kashmir Conference held in Islamabad.

By June 2008, the focus of attention had become the Amarnath dispute, which involved a proposal to transfer 40 hectares of state land to a board managing the Hindu shrine. During the next two months dozens of people were killed and hundreds injured in the resultant unrest throughout Muslim-dominated Kashmir and Hindu-majority Jammu. Most prominent APHC leaders, including Umar Farooq and Syed Gilani, were detained or placed under house arrest at various times during this period. Relations with the Singh government failed to improve thereafter, with Farooq stating in July 2009 that a dialogue with New Delhi would resume only after the central government revoked "draconian" laws, began to withdraw Indian troops from Kashmir, and released political prisoners. Separatist sentiments had been further inflamed by the alleged rape and murder of two Muslim women by Indian soldiers in late May. In February 2013, Farooq was placed under house arrest following protests over the execution of Afzal GURU who had been convicted in the 2001 Indian Parliament attack.

Leader: Mirwaiz Umar FAROOQ (Chair).

United Jihad Council (UJC). A grouping of a dozen or more organizations committed to the separation of Jammu and Kashmir from

India, the UJC was established in 1994, allegedly under the auspices of Pakistan's Inter Services Intelligence agency. Participants include the *Hizb-ul-Mujaheddin,* whose chair, Syed Salahuddin, also heads the UJC, and the *Lashkar-i-Taiba* (both discussed separately below). Other member organizations include the **Jamiat-ul-Mujaheddin,** the **al-Umar Mujaheddin** of Mushtaq ZARGAR, and the Pakistan-based **Jaish-e-Muhammad** and **Harkat-ul-Mujaheddin.** Some support Kashmiri independence, but others advocate Kashmir's inclusion in Pakistan. The UJC called for a boycott of the 2008 Jammu and Kashmir legislative election and the 2009 national election.

Chair: Syed SALAHUDDIN (a.k.a. Mohammad Yusuf SHAH).

Hizb-ul-Mujaheddin (HuM). Founded in 1990, the HuM is the largest of the Islamic militant organizations seeking separation of Jammu and Kashmir from India and establishment of a fundamentalist regime. Unlike many other separatist groups, which typically have bases in the Pakistani territory of Azad Kashmir, the HuM has asserted that it is an exclusively Kashmiri organization, although it has close links to Pakistan's *Jamaat-e-Islami* party. The HuM has claimed responsibility for or been implicated in many of the most widely reported violent incidents in Kashmir in recent years.

On July 24, 2000, the organization's operational chief, Abdul Majid DAR, announced a three-month cease-fire that was rescinded in early August when talks with Indian officials broke down. In May 2002 Dar was expelled for "violating discipline." He was murdered in March 2003, after which his followers announced their separation from the organization's leadership, headed by Syed Salahuddin, whom some opponents accused of ordering the elimination of influential opponents. Dar's successor as operational chief, Saiful ISLAM, died in a gun battle in April 2003, and Islam's successor, Ghulam Rasool DAR, met a similar fate in January 2004. Since then, in an apparent effort to confound authorities, the HuM has tended to identify key field commanders only by aliases.

In January 2009, Mohammad Ahsan DAR, an HuM cofounder and current leader of Muslim Mujaheddin, was arrested by Jammu and Kashmir police. Officials indicated that he had recently returned from Pakistan's Azad Kashmir and was engaged in coordinating the activities of militant organizations. A major offensive by Indian security forces in October 2011 resulted in the arrest of Mohammad SHAFI, the operational chief of the group. In 2013, Salahuddin claimed the UJC militants were responsible for the deaths of five Indian soldiers in Poonch.

Leader: Syed SALAHUDDIN.

Indian Mujahideen (IM). A militant Islamic group identifying itself as the IM surfaced with a series of bombings in Uttar Pradesh in November 2007. The group also claimed responsibility for bombings in Rajasthan in May 2008, Gujarat in July 2008, and New Delhi in September 2008, resulting in dozens of deaths and hundreds of injuries. Although the IM's origins remain shadowy, speculation has centered on connections to the LiT and the proscribed **Students' Islamic Movement of India** (SIMI) and **Harkat-ul-Jihad-i-Islami** (HJI).

Lashkar-i-Taiba (LiT). The LiT (Army of the Pure) was established between 1990 and 1993 as the military wing of the religious group, the *Markaz ud-Dawa Wal Irshad,* which was formed in 1986 to organize Pakistani Sunni militants participating in the Afghan revolution. The *Markaz* was officially dissolved in December 2001 and all its assets transferred to the "new" charity **Jamaat-ud-Dawa** (JuD, Party of the Calling) in an effort to avoid proscription.

The LiT, which the United States has labeled a terrorist group, was banned by India in October 2001 and by Pakistan in January 2002. The JuD was placed on a "watch list" but not banned by the Pakistani government in November 2003. It has denied any connection to the LiT, although Hafiz Mohammed Sayeed continues to be identified in most sources as head of both. Following the terrorist assault on Mumbai in November 2009, the UN Security Council added the JuD to its list of terrorist organizations and Pakistan banned it.

Further complicating matters, the LiT is suspected of using other front names, including al-Mansurian and the Islami Inqilabi Mahaz (Islamic Revolutionary Group). The LiT has claimed responsibility for and been implicated in innumerable bombings, suicide missions, and other attacks within Kashmir and elsewhere. Many of its members have been jailed in India and Pakistan. An LiT commander, Bashir Ahmad KHAN, was killed by Indian forces in April 2004. Indian authorities have linked it to the August 2003 Mumbai bombings, which killed over 50 people; the New Delhi bombings of October 2005 (some 60 fatalities); the March 2006 bombing of Hindu shrines in Varanasi (about 15 dead); and the July 11, 2006, coordinated bombings in Mumbai (180 dead). In November 2006 Indian authorities labeled LiT leader Azam CHEEMA as the mastermind behind the July Mumbai attacks. The group's alleged "all-India" coordinator, Abu UMAR, was killed by security personnel in July 2007. India has presented evidence of the LiT's involvement in planning the November 26–28, 2008, Mumbai attack. In 2012, the United States offered a $10 million reward for information leading to the capture of Sayeed.

Leaders: Hafiz Mohammed SAYEED, Zaki ur-Rehman LAKHVI, Haji Muhammad ASHRAF, Mahmoud Muhammad Ahmed BAHAZIQ.

For information on other Kashmiri separatist groups, many of which are based in Pakistan's Azad Kashmir, see the entry on Pakistan.

Principal North and Northeast Militant Organizations:

In Assam, the **National Democratic Front of Bodoland** (NDFB) denounced a 2003 accord between New Delhi and the Bodo Liberation Tiger Force (BLTF), which led to establishment of a Bodoland Territorial Council. The NDFB remained in militant opposition until announcing a cease-fire that entered into effect in March 2005. More recently, rivalry between the NDFB and the Bodoland People's Front (BPF, above), which descended from the BLTF, has contributed to the emergence of a **Bodo Royal Tiger Force** (BRTF), which reportedly was organized by former members of the BLTF. Another group, the **Bodo People's Progressive** years of efforts by the Bhutanese government to negotiate their departure, the Royal Bhutanese Army took to the field against some 30 insurgent bases (for more, please see the 2013 *Handbook*). In September 2005 the ULFA's Barua indicated a willingness to begin peace talks, but on September 25, 2006, the Indian army responded to a recent upsurge in violence by ending a cease-fire and resuming military action against the ULFA. In June 2008, some ULFA leaders declared a unilateral cease-fire, which led to their expulsion from the organization. In September 2011, the ULFA signed a cease-fire with the government, and more than 600 fighters turned their weapons over to the government. Other groups forced from Bhutan in 2003–2004 were the NDFB and the **Kamatapur Liberation Organization** (KLO), which has sought creation of a Kamatapur state from districts in Assam and West Bengal. In August 2013, NDFB military commander Ranjan DAIMARY was captured in Bangladesh.

The **Dima Halam Daogah** (DHD), led by Dilip NUNISA, has sought to create, primarily from part of Assam, a separate state for the Dimasa people. A cease-fire entered into effect at the start of 2003, but it has not been observed by a "Black Widow" faction led by a former DHD president, Jewel GARLOSSA, who was arrested in Bangalore in June 2009. Shortly thereafter, his faction declared a three-month unilateral cease-fire. The **Achik National Volunteers Council** (ANVC), led by Dilash MARAK, has sought to carve an Achik Land from parts of Assam and Meghalaya; it accepted a cease-fire agreement in July 2004, but a competing **Achik National Liberation Front Army** (ANLFA) has since emerged. Another group, the **Adivasi National Liberation Army** (ANLA), led by Mangra ORAN, has been linked to some bombings. Oran was arrested in Jharkhand in December 2008. The Karbi-Anglong district of Assam has also been the focus of a tribal dispute between the **Kuki Revolutionary Army** and the Karbi **United People's Democratic Solidarity.** Many Kukis had fled to Assam from Manipur, where they had been under attack by elements of the **National Socialist Council of Nagaland** (NSCN).

The separatist conflict in Nagaland, dating from 1954, has cost an estimated 200,000 lives and the creation of Nagaland State in 1963 failed to halt the insurgency. The principal separatist group, the NSCN, subsequently split into S. S. KHAPLANG (NSCN-K) and Isaac Muivah (NSCN-IM) factions. In October 2005, peace talks opened in Bangkok, Thailand, with the NSCN-IM (for more information on the conflict prior to 2005, please see the 2013 *Handbook*). In June 2009 a recently formed civil society organization, the Forum for Naga Reconciliation, announced that the NSCN-IM, the NSCN-K, and the **Federal Government of Nagaland** (FGN), led by S. SINGYA, had signed a "Covenant of Reconciliation" in an effort to overcome their differences and present a unified front.

In Manipur, the umbrella organization for the separatist insurgency is the **Manipur People's Liberation Front** (MPLF), which was formed by the **United National Liberation Front** (UNLF), the **People's Revolutionary Party of Kangleipak** (Prepak), and the **People's Liberation Army** (PLA). The UNLF, which was established in 1964 by Areambam Samrendra SINGH, formed a **Manipur People's Army** (MPA) in 1990 in an effort to achieve independence for Manipur. Singh was killed in 2001, and succeeded by Rajkumar MEGHEN (a.k.a. Sana YAIMA). The PLA's political wing is the **Revolutionary People's Front of Manipur** (RPFM. The **Kangli Tawoi Kanna Lup** (KYKL) and the **Kangleipak Communist Party** (KCP) have also been involved in recent bombings. Other Manipur groups include the **Kuki National Organization** (KNO) and the **United People's Front** (UPF), both of which are umbrella organizations for various Kuki and Zomi rebel groups. In Meghalaya, the **Hynniewtrep National Liberation Council** (HNLC), led by Cheristerfield THANGKHIEW and Bobby MARWEIN, has claimed to represent the interests of the Khasi tribe.

In December 2004, the faction of the insurgent **National Liberation Front of Tripura** (NLFT) led by Nayanbasi JAMATIA (NLFT-NB), following up on an April 2004 cease-fire, reached a tripartite peace agreement with the central and state governments, although Jamatia himself had withdrawn from peace negotiations. At issue in Tripura has not only been independence or autonomy but also the expulsion of Bengali settlers. Another separatist group, the **All Tripura Tiger Force** (ATTF), led by Ranjit DEBBARMA. The ATTF, which is based in Bangladesh, reportedly has a political wing, the **Tripura People's Democratic Front** (TPDF). Other separatist groups include the **Babbar Khalsa International** (BKI), which is led by Wadhwa SINGH. The BKI is one of several banned groups that have demanded creation of a Sikh state of Khalistan, primarily from Punjab but also encompassing parts of adjoining states. A more moderate Sikh group, **Dal Khalsa,** established in 1978, is led by Haracharanjit Singh DHAMI.

For more information on the **United Gurkha Revolutionary Front** (UGRF), please see the 2013 *Handbook.*

LEGISLATURE

The union-level **Parliament** (*Sansad*) is a bicameral body consisting of an indirectly elected upper chamber (*Rajya Sabha*) and a directly elected lower chamber (*Lok Sabha*).

Council of States (*Rajya Sabha*). The upper chamber is a permanent body of not more than 250 members, up to 12 of whom may be appointed for six-year terms by the president on the basis of intellectual preeminence; the remainder are chosen for staggered six-year terms (approximately one-third retiring every two years) by the elected members of the state and territorial assemblies, according to quotas allotted to each. As of July 2009 the 231 occupied seats were distributed as follows: Indian National Congress, 67; *Bharatiya Janata* Party, 47; Communist Party of India (Marxist), 15; *Samajwadi* Party, 13; *Bahujan Samaj* Party, 11; All India Dravidian Progressive Federation, 7; *Janata Dal* (United), 6; Communist Party of India, 5; Dravidian Progressive Federation, 4; Nationalist Congress Party, 4; *Rashtriya Janata Dal,* 4; *Shiv Sena,* 4; *Biju Janata Dal,* 3; *Shiromani Akali Dal,* 3; *Telugu Desam* Party, 2; All India *Trinamul* Congress, 2; Assam People's Council, 2; *Janata Dal* (Secular), 2; All India Forward Bloc, Bodoland People's Front, Indian National *Lok Dal,* Indian Union Muslim League, Jammu and Kashmir National Conference, Jharkhand *Mukti Morcha,* Mizo National Front, Nagaland People's Front, *Lok Janshakti, Pattali Makkal Katchi, Rashtriya Lok Dal,* Revolutionary Socialist Party, Sikkim Democratic Front, *Swatantra Bharat Paksh,* 1 each; independents and other, 7; nonparty nominees, 9. Fourteen seats were vacant.

Chair: Mohammad Hamid ANSARI.

House of the People (*Lok Sabha*). Serving a five-year term (subject to earlier dissolution), the lower chamber currently has 545 seats, of which 543 are allocated to directly elected members from the states and union territories, with 2 filled by presidential nomination to represent the Anglo-Indian community. Seventy-nine seats are reserved for members of scheduled castes, and 41 are reserved for members of specified tribes. General elections held in five stages on April 16, 22–23, and 30 and May 7 and 13, 2009, resulted in the following distribution: United Progressive Alliance, 262 (Indian National Congress, 206; All India Trinamul Congress, 19; Dravidian Progressive Federation, 18; Nationalist Congress Party, 9; Jammu and Kashmir National Conference, 3; Jharkhand *Mukti Morcha,* 2; Indian Union Muslim League, 2; Kerala Congress [M], 1; All India *Majlis-e-Ittehadul Muslimeen,* 1; *Viduthalai Chiruthaigal Katchi, 1*); National Democratic Alliance, 159 (*Bharatiya Janata* Party, 116; *Janata Dal* [United], 20; *Shiv Sena,* 11; *Rashtriya Lok Dal,* 5; *Shiromani Akali Dal,* 4; *Telangana Rashtra Samithi,* 2; Assam People's Council, 1); Third Front, 79 (Left Front, 24 [Communist Party of India (Marxist), 16; Communist Party of India, 4; All India Forward Bloc, 2; Revolutionary Socialist Party, 2]; *Bahujan Samaj* Party, 21; *Biju Janata Dal,* 14; All India Dravidian Progressive Federation, 9; *Telugu Desam* Party, 6; Janata *Dal* [Secular], 3; Haryana *Janhit* Congress, 1; *Marumalarchi Dravida Munnetra Kazhagam,* 1); Fourth Front, 27 (*Samajwadi* Party, 23; *Rashtriya Janata Dal,* 4); Assam United Democratic Front, *Bahujan Vikas Aaghadi,* Bodoland Peoples Front, Jharkhand *Vikas Morcha* (*Prajantantrik*), Nagaland People's Front, *Swabhimani Paksha,* Sikkim Democratic Front, 1 each; independents, 8; nominated members, 2; vacancy, 1.

Speaker: Meira KUMAR.

CABINET

[as of November 5, 2013]

Prime Minister	Manmohan Singh (INC)
Ministers	
Agriculture	Sharad Pawar (NCP)
Atomic Energy	Manmohan Singh (INC)
Civil Aviation	Ajit Singh (RLD)
Commerce and Industry	Anand Sharma (INC)
Communications and Information Technology	Kapil Sibal (INC)
Coal	Sriprakash Jaiswal (INC)
Culture	Chandresh Kumari Katoch (INC) [f]
Defense	A. K. Antony (INC)
Earth Sciences	Jaipal Sudini Reddy (INC)
External Affairs	Salman Khurshid (INC)
Finance	Palaniappan Chidambaram (INC)
Health and Family Welfare	Ghulam Nabi Azad (INC)
Heavy Industries and Public Enterprises	Praful Manoharbhai Patel (NCP)
Home Affairs	Sushil Kumar Shinde (INC)
Housing and Urban Poverty Alleviation	Girija Vyas (INC) [f]
Human Resource Development	M. Mangapati Pallam Raju (INC)
Labor and Employment	Sis Ram Ola (INC)
Law and Justice	Kapil Sibal (INC)
Micro, Small, and Medium Enterprises	Vayalar Ravi (INC)
Mines	Dinsha J. Patel (INC)
Minority Affairs	K. Rahman Khan (INC)
New and Renewable Energy	Farooq Abdullah (JKNC)
Overseas Indian Affairs	Vayalar Ravi (INC)
Panchayati Raj	V. Kishore Chandra Deo (INC)
Parliamentary Affairs	Kamal Nath (INC)
Personnel, Public Grievances, and Pensions	Manmohan Singh (INC)
Petroleum and Natural Gas	M. Veerappa Moily (INC)
Planning	Manmohan Singh (INC)
Railways	Mallikarjun Kharge (INC)
Road Transport and Highways	Oscar Fernandes (INC)
Rural Development	Jairam Ramesh (INC)
Science and Technology	Jaipal Sudini Reddy (INC)
Shipping	G. K. Vasan (INC)
Social Justice and Empowerment	Kumari Selja (INC)
Space	Manmohan Singh (INC)
Steel	Beni Prasad Verma (INC)
Textiles	Kavuri Samba Silva Rao (INC)
Tribal Affairs	V. Kishore Chandra Deo (INC)
Urban Development	Kamal Nath (INC)
Water Resources	Harish Rawat (INC)
Ministers of State (Independent Charge)	
Chemicals and Fertilizers	Srikant Kumar Jena (INC)
Consumer Affairs	Kuruppassery Varkey Thomas (INC)

Corporate Affairs	Sachin Pilot (INC)
Development of North Eastern Region	Paban Singh Ghatowar (INC)
Drinking Water and Sanitation	Bharatsinh Madhaysunh Solanki (INC)
Environment and Forests	Jayanthi Natarajan (INC) [f]
Information and Broadcasting	Manesh Tewari (INC)
Micro, Small, and Medium Enterprises	K. H. Muniyappa (INC)
Parliamentary Affairs	Paban Singh Ghatowar (INC)
Power	Jyotiraditya Madhavrao Scindia (INC)
Statistics and Program Implementation	Srikant Kumar Jena (INC)
Tourism	K. Chiranjeevi (INC)
Women and Child Development	Krishna Tirath (INC) [f]
Youth Affairs and Sport	Jitendra Singh (INC)

[f] = female

INTERGOVERNMENTAL REPRESENTATION

Ambassador to the U.S.: Nirupama RAO.

U.S. Ambassador to India: Nancy Jo POWELL.

Permanent Representative to the UN: Hardeep Singh PURI.

IGO Memberships (Non-UN): ADB, AfDB, CWTH, G-20, IOM, NAM, SAARC, WTO.

INDONESIA

Republic of Indonesia
Republik Indonesia

Political Status: Independent republic established August 17, 1945; original constitution reinstated by presidential decree in 1959; under modified military regime from March 12, 1966, until democratic multiparty system reestablished following change of government on May 21, 1998.

Area: 735,354 sq. mi. (1,904,569 sq. km).

Population: 249,851,054 (2013E—UN); 251,160,124 (2013E—U.S. Census).

Major Urban Centers (2010E): JAKARTA (9,607,787), Surabaya (2,765,487), Bandung (2,394,873), Medan (2,097,610), Tangerang (1,798,601), Semarang (1,555,984), Palembang (1,455,284), Ujung Pandang (formerly Makassar, 1,338,633), Padang (833,562), Malang (820,243), Yogyakarta (388,627).

Official Language: Bahasa Indonesia (a form of Malay).

Monetary Unit: Rupiah (market rate November 1, 2013: 11,129.90 rupiahs = $1US).

President: Susilo Bambang YUDHOYONO (Democrat Party); elected on September 20, 2004, and inaugurated on October 20 for a five-year term, succeeding Megawati SUKARNOPUTRI (Indonesian Democratic Party of Struggle); reelected on July 8, 2009, and sworn in on October 20.

Vice President: BOEDIONO (BUDIYONO, nonparty); elected July 8, 2009, and sworn in October 20 for a term concurrent with that of the president, succeeding Muhammad Jusuf KALLA (Golkar Party).

THE COUNTRY

The most populous country of Southeast Asia and fourth in the world, Indonesia is an archipelago of over 13,500 islands straddling the equator for a distance of 3,000 miles from the Asian mainland to Australia. Java, Sumatra, and Borneo (whose territory Indonesia shares with Malaysia and Brunei) are the principal islands and contain most of the population, which is predominantly of Malay descent but includes a significant Melanesian component in the east and some 3.5–4 million ethnic Chinese. The country embraces the world's largest Muslim population in addition to small minorities of Christians (9 percent), Hindus (2 percent), and Buddhists (1 percent). Overall, a total of more than 500 languages and dialects are in use. Women make up 37 percent of the active labor force, with the majority engaged in agriculture, retail occupations, manufacturing, and hospitality industries. Islamic strictures and, until 1999, the predominance of the military in government have restrained female participation in politics; women held about 17 percent of the 550 seats in the People's Representation Council elected in 2009.

Agriculture contributed 14.4 percent of GDP but employed 38 percent of the workforce in 2012, industry accounted for 47 percent of GDP and 22 percent of employment, and sevices comprised 39 percent of GDP and 48 percent of the workforce. As the leading petroleum producer in the Far East, the country benefited from high oil prices for several decades. But in 2008, Indonesia announced that it was withdrawing from the Organization of Petroleum Exporting Countries (OPEC) because it had become a net importer of oil. Since then, the government has promoted diversification into agribusiness and manufacturing, including food products, garments and other textiles, transportation equipment, and electrical appliances. Indonesia has long been one of the world's principal exporters of rubber, palm oil, coffee, tea, spices, and tin, and more recently, liquefied natural gas has become a major source of export earnings. Principal export destinations in 2012 were Japan (16 percent), China (11 percent), Singapore (9 percent), South Korea (8 percent), and the United States (8 percent); principal sources of imports were China (15 percent), Singapore (14 percent), Japan (12 percent), Malaysia (6 percent), and South Korea (6 percent).

After more than a decade of rapid economic expansion, the Asian financial crisis of 1997 triggered a precipitous decline in the value of the rupiah, a negative GDP growth, and high inflation. Reforms in the banking and energy industries, privatization and invitation of foreign participation in state enterprises, restructuring of corporate debt, and greater provincial fiscal autonomy restored GDP growth to more than 5 percent throughout the 2000s and reduced unemployment to 6.1 percent in 2012 and the percent of the population remaining below the poverty line to 12.5. The International Monetary Fund (IMF) forecasts GDP growth of 6.3 percent in 2013 and 6.4 percent in 2014.

GOVERNMENT AND POLITICS

Political background. Colonized by the Portuguese in the 16th century and conquered by the Dutch in the 17th century, the territory formerly known as the Netherlands East Indies was occupied by the Japanese in World War II. Upon the Japanese withdrawal, Indonesian nationalists took control, proclaiming the independent Republic of Indonesia on August 17, 1945. After four additional years of war and negotiation, the Netherlands government recognized the new state on December 27, 1949, and relinquished claim to all its possessions in the East Indies except West New Guinea (Irian Jaya). In 1963 the United Nations brokered the transfer of Irian Jaya (subsequently renamed Papua, currently encompassing the provinces of Papua and West Papua) to Indonesian control. In December 1975 Indonesian troops invaded the Portuguese Overseas Territory of East Timor, and on July 17, 1976, the government proclaimed it a province of Indonesia, an action that neither Portugal nor the United Nations recognized.

SUKARNO, one of the leaders of the nationalist struggle, served as constitutional president from 1949 until the late 1950s, when he responded to a series of antigovernment rebellions by proclaiming martial law and, in 1959, imposing a so-called "guided democracy" under which he exercised quasi-dictatorial powers. The Indonesian Communist Party (*Partai Komunis Indonesia*—PKI) assumed an increasingly prominent role and by 1965 had embarked, with Sukarno's acquiescence, on a campaign to arm its supporters. When the PKI attempted to purge the army leadership by assassination on October 1, 1965, the military struck back. Army assaults and vigilante actions by

Javanese villagers led to mass killings of PKI supporters (and innocent Chinese) in rural areas and the eradication of what had been the world's third-largest communist party. In succeeding months President Sukarno attempted to restore order, but public confidence in his leadership had seriously eroded. In March 1966 he was forced to transfer key political and military powers to Gen. SUHARTO, who had achieved prominence by turning back the attempted Communist takeover.

In March 1967, the People's Consultative Assembly (*Majelis Permusyawaratan Rakyat*—MPR) removed Sukarno from office, and he retired to private life until his death in June 1970. Suharto, who had proclaimed a "New Order" as acting president, was elected by the MPR in 1968 for a five-year term as president.

In 1984, Suharto sponsored legislation that required all political, social, and religious organizations to adopt the five-point *Pancasila* state philosophy of belief in a supreme being, humanitarianism, national unity, consensus democracy, and social justice. Despite discontent among Muslim leaders, a decade of relative stability ensued. At the nationwide election in June 1992 the government-supported coalition of functional groups called Golkar retained overwhelming control of the largely elective People's Representation Council (*Dewan Perwakilan Rakyat*—DPR), and on March 10, 1993, the MPR unanimously elected President Suharto to a sixth five-year term.

Opposition to Suharto's New Order regime arose in the 1990s, led by the Indonesian Democratic Party (*Partai Demokrasi Indonesia*—PDI), which was headed from December 1993 by Sukarno's eldest daughter, Megawati Sukarnoputri (familiarly identified as Megawati). Government suppression of the PDI in July 1996 triggered Indonesia's worst civil disorder since 1984. The May 1997 election returned Golkar with an increased majority; a weakened PDI and the United Development Party (*Partai Persatuan Pembangunan*—PPP) remained in opposition.

In March 1998, the MPR elected President Suharto for a seventh term. It also confirmed Suharto's choice of Bacharuddin Jusuf HABIBIE, a longtime associate, as vice president. By then, however, the financial crisis, which had spread in the second half of 1997 from Thailand to East Asia, had given new impetus to antigovernment protesters. Student demonstrators began demanding far-reaching *reformasi* (political reform). In May 1998 the government's deep cuts in subsidies for fuel, electricity, and transportation precipitated widespread outrage that degenerated into looting and rioting as civic, religious, ex-military, and political leaders began taking up the call for reform and urging the president to resign. Among the most outspoken critics was Amien RAIS of *Muhammadiyah,* the country's second-largest Muslim organization, with some 28 million members. In May violence claimed nearly 1,200 victims, and thousands of businesses and buildings in Jakarta were destroyed. On May 21, having lost support within Golkar and the military leadership, Suharto resigned. Vice President Habibie immediately took the oath of office as president.

Despite a series of political reforms, Habibie's reign was ineffective and contributed to Golkar's poor showing in the June 1999 DPR election. Of the 48 contesting parties, the other principal contenders were Megawati's newly registered PDI-Struggle (PDI-*Perjuangan,* or PDI-P); the National Awakening Party (*Partai Kebangkitan Bangsa*—PKB), led by Abdurrahman WAHID, who was also head of the country's largest Muslim organization, the 30-million-member Council of Scholars (*Nahdlatul Ulama*—NU); and Rais's National Mandate Party (*Partai Amanat Nasional*—PAN). The PDI-P was eventually credited with 153 seats, well ahead of Golkar's 120 seats. Habibie's popularity waned, and on October 20–21, 1999, the MPR elected the PKB's Wahid as president and the PDI-P's Megawati as vice president.

During the same period !ndonesia was confronted by unprecedented violence in the annexed province of East Timor. An August 1999 pro-independence vote in the territory had precipitated a wave of aggression by pro-Jakarta militias, which ceased only when a UN peacekeeping force intervened in September. In October the MPR rescinded East Timor's 1976 annexation. Following a quarter-century of strife, including allegations of genocide and other human rights abuses by Indonesia, and after two years of administration by the UN, the annexed territory became independent as the Democratic Republic of Timor-Leste on May 20, 2002. (For additional details, see the Timor-Leste entry.)

The "Cabinet of National Unity" announced by President Wahid on October 26, 1999, constituted an ethnic, religious, and regional cross section, with all of the leading parties represented. Within months of taking office, however, the patched-together coalition government was disparaged for inexperience and inefficiency. Moreover, although widely respected, Wahid displayed erratic decision making and failed to take effective initiatives to resolve separatist and sectarian conflicts, and so he lost political legitimacy. On July 23, 2000, the MPR voted 591–0 to remove Wahid and elected Megawati as his successor (see the 2010 *Handbook* for details).

On April 5, 2004, Indonesia elected members of the DPR, the new Regional Representatives Council (*Dewan Perwakilan Daerah*—DPD), which had been established as an upper house of the MPR by a 2002 constitutional amendment, and local legislators—a total of more than 15,200 offices contested by nearly 450,000 candidates. Golkar won a plurality, 127 seats, in the DPR, followed by Megawati's PDI-P with 109. Somewhat unexpectedly, 58 seats were won by the recently organized Democrat Party (*Partai Demokrat*—PD), headed by Megawati's former coordinating minister for political and security affairs, Lt. Gen. (Ret.) Susilo Bambang YUDHOYONO.

Encumbered by a perceived lack of progress in eliminating corruption and resolving regional conflicts, President Megawati was defeated in the presidential election on September 24, 2004, by Lt. Gen. (Ret.) Susilo Bambang Yudhoyono, leader of the new Democrat Party (*Partai Demokrat*—PD). Inaugurated on October 20, President Yudhoyono formed a new "United Indonesia Cabinet" (*Kabinet Indonesia Bersatu*) that included representatives of his own PD, Golkar, the PKB, the PPP, the recently organized Prosperous Justice Party (*Partai Keadilan Sejahtera*—PKS), the PAN, and the Crescent Star Party (*Partai Bulan Bintang*—PBB).

A political consequence of the earthquake and tsunami that struck on December 26 was a new initiative to resolve the decades-old secessionist conflict in Aceh. In the 1990s, secessionist sentiment in northwest Sumatra, led by the Free Aceh Movement (*Gerakan Aceh Merdeka*—GAM), had surged, and clashes with security forces multiplied. The 2004 tsunami spurred the government and the GAM leaders to return to the negotiating table to deal with the crisis. Talks in early 2005, mediated by former Finnish president Martti Ahtisaari's Crisis Management Initiative team, devised an agreement on "special autonomy" for Aceh, and a peace agreement was signed on August 15. By late December the GAM had disarmed, and Jakarta had removed a significant proportion of nonlocal troops and security personnel from Aceh. On July 11, 2006, the DPR unanimously passed legislation granting the province political autonomy, 70 percent of revenues from its oil and natural gas resources, extra reconstruction allocations from the national budget, special permission to form local political parties (only national parties are permitted elsewhere), and Muslims permission to practice Islamic law (sharia).

Despite a peace agreement in February 2002 and the disbanding of the *Laskar Jihad* (Holy Warriors), communal strife between Muslims and Christians, many of them ethnic Chinese, peristed in Maluku (the Moluccan Islands). Secessionism also persisted, with members of the Christian Maluku Sovereignty Front (*Front Kedaulatan Maluku*—FKM) intermittently raising the banned flag of the South Maluku Republic, which had been proclaimed in 1950, resulting in clashes with security forces, arrests, and additional prosecutions of FKM members for subversion. Nearby Sulawesi had also experienced sectarian strife before conclusion of a peace agreement in December 2001, and Kalimantan suffered from a long-running dispute between native Dayaks and immigrant Madurese. In predominantly Melanesian West Papua (now officially Papua) separatists continued to seek independence. (See Annexed Territory, below.)

The DPR election of April 9, 2009, concluded with President Yudhoyono's PD winning a plurality of 148 seats, followed by Golkar with 106 and the PDI-P with 95. In the July 9 presidential election, Yudhoyono won with 60.2 percent of the vote, beating Megawati and the Golkar candidate, incumbent vice president Jusuf KALLA. In October the president named a new cabinet that included the PD, Golkar, the PAN, the Prosperous Justice Party (*Partai Keadilan Sejahtera*—PKS), the PKB, the PPP, and 5 independents.

Constitution and government. In the wake of unsuccessful efforts to draft a permanent constitution in 1950 and 1956, the government in 1959 readopted by decree the provisional constitution of 1945, which allocated most powers to the president under a strong executive system. The five guiding principles (*Pancasila*) identified in the preamble are monotheism, humanitarianism, national unity, democracy by consensus, and social justice.

The president, who is now directly elected and limited to two five-year terms, serves as commander in chief of the military; "may declare war, make peace and conclude treaties," with legislative concurrence; and may declare a state of emergency under conditions set by the legislature.

Prior to constitutional reforms passed in 2001 and 2002, the People's Consultative Assembly (MPR) was considered the highest state organ, interpreting the constitution and electing the president and vice president. Effective from the 2004 general election, the MPR became a bicameral legislature, the new upper house—the Regional Representatives Council (*Dewan Perwakilan Daerah*—DPD)—being indirectly elected. The DPD, whose membership may total no more than one-third that of the DPR, can propose legislation on regional autonomy, regional boundaries, the allocation of resources between the central government and the regions, and management of natural resources. It may also advise the lower house, the DPR, on such matters as taxation, the budget, religion, and education. The DPR exercises legislative functions and may impeach the president by a two-thirds vote, precipitating investigation, trial, and concurrence by the Constitutional Court. If two-thirds of the MPR assented, the president could then be dismissed. The MPR also oversees the inauguration of the president and vice president and is empowered to consider constitutional amendments.

At the apex of the judicial system is the Supreme Court, whose members are proposed by the Judicial Commission of the DPR and appointed by the president. There are also lower public courts, religious courts, military tribunals, and state administrative courts. In addition, a 2002 constitutional change authorized creation of a nine-member Constitutional Court (the president, the DPR, and the Supreme Court each nominate three judges), which, in addition to its role in the presidential dismissal process, has authority to review the constitutionality of legislative acts, to resolve disputes between state organs, to review contested election results, and to consider the dissolution of political parties.

Indonesia is at present divided into 33 provinces, including 3 special regions (Papua, West Papua, and Yogyakarta), 1 special capital district (Jakarta), and since 2006 Nanggroe Aceh Darussalam (the special region of Aceh).

Each province has an elected legislature (*Dewan Perwakilan Rakyat Daerah*) and, under the post-Suharto reforms, an elected governor; government at the regency (*kabupaten*) and municipal (*kotamadya*) levels includes elected legislatures and elected executives (*bupati* and *walikota,* respectively).

Foreign relations. Following independence, Indonesia initially sought to play a prominent role in Asian affairs while avoiding involvement in conflicts between the major powers. In the early 1960s, however, President Sukarno attempted to project Indonesia as the spearhead of the "new emerging forces." While officially nonaligned in foreign policy, his regime formed close ties with the Soviet Union and the People's Republic of China; induced the Netherlands to transfer West New Guinea (Irian Jaya) to Indonesia; and instituted a policy of *konfrontasi* (confrontation), supported by guerrilla incursions, against the new state of Malaysia.

Most of these policies were reversed under his successor, President Suharto, who moved Indonesia, although still formally nonaligned, closer to the West. Membership in the United Nations (UN) and many of its related agencies resumed in 1966, Indonesia having withdrawn in 1965 because of international opposition to its annexation of West New Guinea. The three-year confrontation with Malaysia ended in 1966, after which diplomatic relations were established with Malaysia and Singapore, and Indonesia took the lead in forming the Association of Southeast Asian Nations (ASEAN) in 1967 as an instrument of regional cooperation.

Formal diplomatic ties to China, having been suspended in October 1967, were restored in August 1990. Relations suffered as a consequence of attacks against Chinese in the upheaval leading to Suharto's resignation, but in May 1999 President Habibie issued a decree outlawing ethnic discrimination and ended a ban against using or teaching Mandarin Chinese. Ties warmed further as China emerged in the top five among Indonesia's trade and investment partners, and on January 1, 2010, Indonesia joined other members of ASEAN in instituting a free trade agreement with China. President Yudhyono visited Beijing in March 2012 to promote further trade and investment ties despite complaints by Indonesian producers about competition from cheap imports from China.

In December 1995 Indonesia and Australia signed a security cooperation agreement, and in 1997 the two neighbors completed a treaty defining their maritime boundaries.

However, Indonesia's invasion of and harsh security policies in East Timor attracted continued Australian public criticism. In January 1999 the Australian government switched from recognition of Indonesian sovereignty to advocacy of an act of self-determination in East Timor, and President Habibie, similarly advised by officials in Jakarta, allowed the UN to conduct a referendum. The post referendum paramilitary violence of September 1999, followed by Australia's leading role in the resultant UN peacekeeping force, led to a chilling of relations. Under President Wahid relations initially improved, but Jakarta's failure to discourage a flow of boats carrying asylum seekers from Afghanistan and the Middle East to Australia's outer territories in 2001–2002 drew sharp criticism from the government of Prime Minister John Howard. Relations were further complicated by the threat of terrorism and Jakarta's unwillingness to acknowledge the presence of the *Jemaah Islamiah* (JI) terrorist organization until an October 12, 2002, bombing of a Bali tourist resort claimed 202 lives, 88 of them Australian.

Australian skepticism was reinforced by Indonesian appeals court reversals in 2004 of convictions of four high-ranking officers for abuses in East Timor (now Timor-Leste) and of the former civilian governor of East Timor, Abílio Soares. In April 2008 the Supreme Court also overturned the conviction of militia leader Eurico GUTERRES. Jakarta had previously refused to allow extradition of 311 Indonesians, including Gen. WIRANTO, indicted by the Timor-Leste Special Crimes Unit. In January 2005 Timor-Leste and Indonesian leaders agreed to establish a Commission of Truth and Friendship to examine remaining human rights cases but without prosecutorial authority. The commission's report detailed the violence perpetrated by Indonesian forces but did not recommend further action, and President Yudhoyono and Prime Minister José Alexandre Gusmão in August 2009 pledged to forego further recriminations in order to pursue good relations. Yudhoyono in May 2012 attended the inauguration of Timor-Leste's new president, Taur Matan Ruak.

In January 2005, President Yudhoyono warmly acknowledged Australia's pledge of A$1 billion in aid following the previous December's earthquake and tsunami disaster, and in April the two countries signed a framework partnership agreement that included among its provisions closer military cooperation. In March 2006, however, Indonesia protested Australia's decision to grant temporary protection visas to a group of proindependence Papuans who sought asylum. Relations were largely repaired in November, when the two countries' foreign ministers signed a ten-point security agreement that included pledges to respect each other's sovereignty and unity and not to support separatist movements. Yudhoyono in 2009 agreed to enforce laws against people-smuggling and illegal transit, in return for which Australia offered to contribute funds and technical expertise for the processing in Indonesia of refugees and would be permitted to send search-and-rescue aircraft into Indonesian airspace in response to asylum-seeker boat distress calls. In 2013 Yudhoyono conferred with successive Australian prime ministers Gillard, Rudd, and Abbott to coordinate policies to curb people smuggling, but cooperation ended in November upon revelations of Australian electronic eavesdropping on Yudhoyono, his wife, and top officials.

Relations with the United States strengthened during the 1980s, with the Ronald Reagan administration identifying Indonesia as a staunch anticommunist state. However, Indonesian military heavy-handedness in East Timor in 1991 and again in 1999 induced the U.S. Congress to cut off direct military funding. Following Suharto's resignation, the Clinton administration voiced its support for the Habibie government and, later, the Wahid presidency.

President George W. Bush described Indonesia as a key ally in the war on terrorism despite massive Indonesian demonstrations in October–November 2001 to protest the U.S. intervention against the Taliban government of Afghanistan. Widespread Indonesian opposition also greeted the 2003 U.S.-led invasion of Iraq. Nevertheless, the Bush administration announced in May 2005 that it was relaxing restrictions on the sale of nonlethal military equipment to Indonesia and restored military links, including weapons sales, in November. In February 2009, U.S. Secretary of State Hillary Clinton included Indonesia in her first official visit to the Far East, and President Obama visited in November 2010, both visits reinforcing efforts by the new U.S. administration to strengthen ties to moderate Islamic governments. U.S. military training of Indonesian Special Forces troops resumed in July 2010, although U.S. human rights groups and some U.S. senators objected; an offer by Secretary Gates to sell F-16 fighters was likewise deflected by human rights concerns. Secretary Clinton visited again in September 2012, and Secretary of Defense Chuck Hagel visited in August 2013, reflecting the U.S. "rebalancing" of policy toward Asia. In February 2013 the purchase of U.S. Apache helicopters was announced, and in June the commander of the U.S. 7th Fleet visited Indonesia aboard the command ship USS *Blue Ridge* to discuss closer naval cooperation; also in June an interoperability exercise labelled Garuda Shield brought U.S. and Indonesian army units together.

In September 2007, during a visit to Indonesia by Vladimir Putin, the Russian president and President Yudhoyono signed nine agreements, including, most significantly, a deal for the purchase of Russian weaponry. Other agreements covered a range of topics, from combating terrorism to protecting the environment. Indonesia in November 2012 agreed to buy 150 tanks from the German firm Reinmetall and in January 2013 signed a Memorandum of Understanding on military cooperation and sales with the United Kingdom.

Indonesia, already a dialogue partner of the Pacific Islands Forum, was invited by the Melanesian Spearhead Group in March 2011 to participate as an observer. In April Fiji's interim prime minister opened an embassy in Jakarta and solicited Indonesia's support for Fiji's bid for observer status in ASEAN. In 2012 Indonesia negotiated diplomatic links with Tuvalu, Nauru, Haiti, and Botswana, bringing its worldwide bilateral ties to a total of 182.

Indonesia hosted the 19th summit of ASEAN in November 2011 and, as part of the Bali Concord III on security, economic, and sociocultural cooperation, in 2012 set up the ASEAN Coordinating Center for Humanitarian Assistance on Disaster Management in Jakarta and invited the 12-nation Transpacific Partnership negotiators to a summit meeting in Bali in October 2013.

Current issues. The first Yudhoyono administration was credited with effective management of the simmering separatist conflicts in Aceh, Maluku, and Papua. In response to the bombings at the Marriott and Ritz-Carlton hotels in Jakarta in July 2009, Jakarta vigorously hunted members of the terrorist cells. Security personnel killed JI mastermind Noordin Mohammed TOP in September 2009 and arrested a JI founder, cleric Abu Bakar BASHIR, who in June 2011 was convicted and sentenced to 15 years in prison. In March 2012, police shot dead five terrorists affiliated with Jamaah Ansharut Tauhid, and in June, Umar PATEK, affiliated with JI, was convicted for his part in the 2002 Bali bombing.

The government took initiatives to curb graft and corruption. Despite allegations of partiality and overzealousness in wiretapping, Indonesia's Corruption Eradication Commission (*Komisi Pemberantasan Korupsi*—KPK) in 2009 successfully prosecuted several high-profile cases.In January 2010 Yudhoyono set up a task force chaired by Kuntoro MANGKUSUBROTO to eliminate corruption in the courts, and two weeks later the Constitutional Court announced establishment of anticorruption courts in seven provinces, one of which in May convicted four legislators for taking bribes. In April 2012, the Corruption Eradication Commission succeeded in prosecution for bribery of former Democratic Party Treasurer Muhammad NAZRUDDIN, and in September, the Democratic Party's former deputy secretary general Angelina SONDAKH went on trial for allegedly receiving $3.6 million in kickbacks. Further arrests in mid-2013 include Bandung mayor Dada ROSADA and the chief of the oil and gas regulatory agency SKK Migas, Rudi RUBIANDIRI; also under investigation were North Sumatra police and commerce officials and the treasurer of the governing coalition party Golkar, Setya NOVANTO. Nevertheless Indonesia fell from 100th to 118th on the Transparency International index for 2012.

President Yudhoyono's initiatives in response to the international financial crisis that began in 2008 included infusing funds into the economy to stimulate consumer spending, enabling labor-intensive infrastructure projects, and stabilizing the stock market and banks. As a consequence, Indonesia avoided a recession and achieved a positive trade balance and a 6.3 percent GDP growth rate in 2013, among the best in Asia, with 6.4 percent growth in 2014 forecast by the International Monetary Fund (IMF).

Frontrunners for the 2014 presidential election were Jakarta's governor Joko "Jokowi" WIDODO (PDI-P), retired general Probowo SUBIANTO (Gerindra), former vice president Jusuf KALLA (Golkar), and former economics minister Aburizal BAKRIE (Golkar), with Megawati a possible candidate but undeclared as of mid-December 2013. In 2013 Freedom House rated Indonesia "free" with above-average scores for political rights and civil liberties, and Reporters Without Borders noted that Indonesia had risen on its press freedom index from 146 to 130.

POLITICAL PARTIES

Prior to May 1998, the government was supported by a government-managed coalition of functional groups called by its acronym, Golkar, with only two other parties—the United Development Party (PPP) and the Indonesian Democratic Party (PDI), both dating from 1973—allowed to contest elections. Muslim associations, including the two largest—the long-established NU, and *Muhammadiyah,* chaired by Amien Rais—increasingly assumed a quasi-political character, as did the Association of Indonesian Muslim Intellectuals (*Ikatan Cendikiawan Muslim Indonesia*—ICMI), which was formed in December 1990.

In 1998, the political landscape, was transformed by the end of Suharto's guided democracy. The Habibie government eased restrictions, and 48 political parties subsequently qualified for the 1999 DPR election.

By 2004, roughly 300 parties had formed, but only 24 qualified for the April DPR elections. A new electoral law passed by the DPR in 2007 allowed more than 100 parties to be registered, but the Ministry of Justice and Human Rights reduced the number eligible for the 2009 DPR election to 38, 9 of which subsequently won seats.

The electoral law passed in October 2008 specified that only parties winning 20 percent of the seats or 25 percent of the overall vote in the April 2009 DPR election could nominate candidates, 30 percent of which must be women, for the July 2009 presidential race. The viability of small parties was uncertain in light of the 2011 Political Parties Law, which required parties to have branch offices in all 33 provinces, and the Legislative Election Law, raising the threshold to gain a DPR seat to 3 percent of the national vote.

As of April 2013 the General Elections Commission had declared 15 parties (out of 46 applicants) eligible to participate in the 2014 election: National Democratic Party (Nasdem), National Awakening Party (PKB), Prosperous Justice Party (PKS), Indonesian Democratic Party of Struggle (PDIP), Golkar Party, Gerindra, Democratic Party (PD), National Mandate Party (PAN), United Development Party (PPP), Hanura, Aceh's Peace Party (PDA), Aceh's National Party (PNA), Aceh Party (PA), Crescent and Star Party (PBB), and Indonesian Justice and Unity Party (PKPI).

Presidential Party:

Democrat Party (*Partai Demokrat*—PD). The centrist PD (also translated as the Democratic Party, Democrats Party, or Democracy Party) was established in 2002 to promote its principal founder, Lt. Gen. (Ret.) Susilo Bambang Yudhoyono, then a coordinating minister for political and security affairs in the Megawati cabinet. On the strength of Yudhoyono's popularity, the PD won 7.5 percent of the vote and 56 seats in the DPR election in April 2004 and then won

party that was dissolved during the Sukarno era, the PBB won 13 seats and a 2 percent vote share at the June 1999 legislative election.

In April 2004, the PBB won about 2.6 percent of the vote and 11 seats in the DPR election and supported Yudhoyono for president. Party chair Yusril MAHENDRA, formerly justice and human rights minister in the Megawati cabinet, was named to the powerful post of state secretary in the Yudhoyono cabinet and served until the May 2007 reshuffling. In the DPR the PBB joined four smaller parties—the PPDK, the PP, the PPDI, and the PNIM (all below)—in forming the Democratic Star Pioneer faction.

In May 2005, Malam S. Kaban replaced Mahendra as chair. Defeated rival Hamdan Zoelva attempted to organize a new formation, the Star Crescent Party (*Partai Bintang Bulan*—PBB) and planned to merge the two parties to qualify. But the 2008 election law change eliminated the need for the maneuver, and Zoelva rejoined the mainstream PBB. The party won only 1.8 percent of the vote, however, and thus no DPR seats.

Mahendra was the party's prospective nominee for the 2009 presidential election, but PBB's lackluster performance in the DPR election excluded it from putting forth a candidate.

Leaders: Malam S. KABAN (Chair), Hamdan ZOELVA (Deputy Chair), Yusril Ihza MAHENDRA (Chair of Advisory Board), Abdul Sahar HASSAN (Secretary General).

Democratic Nationhood Party (*Partai Demokrasi Kebangsaan*—PDK). The PDK was established in July 2002 as the National Democratic Unity Party (*Partai Persatuan Demokrasi Kebangsaan*—PPDK, also known in English as the United Democratic Nationhood Party). The PPDK drew support from reform-minded, nationalist members of the middle class. Its chair, Ryaas Rasyid, was until 2001 minister of state for administrative reforms in the Wahid cabinet. In the 2004 DPR election, the PPDK won 1.2 percent of the vote and four seats. The party's support of Golkar's Wiranto for president precipitated the resignation of cofounder Andi Alfian MALLARANGENG in July. The PPDK was relaunched as the PDK in October 2007.

In the April 2009 DPR election, the PDK won only 0.6 percent of the vote and thus no seats.

Leaders: Muhammad Ryaas RASYID (Chair), ALIUDDIN HAMMERING (Secretary General).

Pioneer Party (*Partai Pelopor*—PP). The PP was established in August 2002 by Rachmawati Sukarnoputri, a younger sister of President Megawati, to advance her father's Marhaenist philosophy of "self-reliance and support for ordinary people." Her ambition to seek the presidency was thwarted when the PP won only 1 percent of the vote and three DPR seats in the 2004 DPR election; she then supported Amien Rais of the PAN. In January 2006 Rachmawati was named an adviser to President Yudhoyono.

In 2009 the PP won only 0.3 percent of the DPR vote and thus no seats. It supported President Yudhoyono's reelection in July 2009.

Leaders: Rachmawati SUKARNOPUTRI, Eke Surya SANTOSO (Chair), KRISTIYANO (Secretary General).

Concern for the Nation Functional Party (*Partai Karya Peduli Bangsa*—PKPB). The PKPB, which is also rendered in English as the National Concern Workers' Party, was founded in September 2002 with the support of former President Suharto and his eldest daughter, Siti Hardiyanti Rukmana. When the PKPB won only 2 percent of the vote and two DPR seats at the April 2004 legislative election, thereby precluding Rukmana's nomination for the presidency, the party decided to support Golkar's Wiranto. The PKPB's representatives chose to sit with the Golkar faction in the DPR.

The PKPB won only 1.4 percent of the vote in the April 2009 DPR election.

Leaders: R. HARTONO (Chair), Ari MARDJONO, Siti Hardiyanti RUKMANA, Hartarto SASTROSOENARTO (Secretary General).

Indonesian Justice and Unity Party (*Partai Keadilan dan Persatuan Indonesia*—PKPI). The PKPI began as the PKP, which was formed in mid-December 1998 by former Golkar members. One of its leaders, former general and defense minister Edi SUDRAJAT, had resigned from Golkar in November after having lost an election for Golkar chair the previous July. Another founder, Gen. Try Sutrisno, had served as Suharto's vice president from 1993 to 1998. The PKP won 1 percent of the vote and four seats in the DPR at the June 1999 election. Having reconstituted itself as the PKPI, in April 2004 it won only one seat. In the 2004 presidential contest the PKPI backed Susilo Bambang Yudhoyono.

Sudrajat died in December 2006 and was succeeded as chair by Meutia Swasono, minister of women's empowerment in the Yudhoyono cabinet. In 2009 the PKPI failed to retain its four DPR seats, having won only 0.9 percent of the vote. It backed President Yudhoyono's reelection in July.

Leaders: Meutia Farida SWASONO (Chair), Samuel SAMSON (Secretary General).

Indonesian Democratic Vanguard Party (*Partai Penegak Demokrasi Indonesia*—PPDI). Also identified in English as the Upholders of Indonesian Democracy Party, the PPDI was established in 2003. It won under 0.8 percent of the vote and one DPR seat at the April 2004 election and subsequently supported the PAN's Amien Rais for president.

Although the party was officially registered for the 2009 DPR election, an internal split threatened its prospects. It ended up winning only 0.1 percent of the vote.

Leaders: Mentik BUDIWIYONO (Chair), Joseph Lea WEA (Secretary General).

Indonesian National Party (Marhaenism) (*Partai Nasional Indonesia [Marhaenisme]*—PNIM). Formed in May 2002 by another of Sukarno's daughters, Sukmawati Sukarnoputri, the PNIM is a leading Marhaenist party, claiming descent from Sukarno's PNI, which he had established in 1927 and which was consolidated into the PDI in 1973. Sukmawati planned to compete for the presidency in 2004 against her sisters, the incumbent Megawati and the PP's Rachmawati Sukarnoputri, but her PNIM won only one DPR seat and 0.8 percent of the vote at the April DPR election. In the end, the PNIM backed the PAN's Amien Rais.

In December 2008, a former general and governor of Jakarta, SUTIYOSO, stated that the PNIM was prepared to support his run for the presidency in 2009, but the party performed poorly in the April 2009 DPR election, winning only 0.3 percent of the vote.

Leaders: Sukmawati SUKARNOPUTRI (Chair), Ardi MUHAMMAD (Secretary General).

New National Parties:

National Democrat Party (*Nasional Demokrat*—NasDem). The NasDem Party originated as the mass organization National Democrat founded February 1, 2010, by Surya Paloh upon his failure to achieve leadership of Golkar and with the support of Sultan Hamengku Buwono X and other notables disillusioned by the established parties. The NasDem Party was registered by the Law and Human Rights Ministry on July 27, 2011, and in November 2012 approved by the General Elections Commission for 2014 electoral participation. Populist, nationalist, and reformist, it attracted new members from Golkar and PPP. But Sultan Hamengku Buwono X rejected the transition from mass organization to political party and retired from party politics. In January 2013 Paloh summarily replaced Patrice Rio Capella as party chief, who shifted to become secretary general. Paloh's takeover precipitated the departure of wealthy patron Hary Tonoesoedibjo, who joined the People's Conscience Party (Hanura), and numerous party members in Jakarta, Maluku, and West Java. In February DPR member Akbar FAIZAL left Hanura to join the NasDem Party. The Indonesian Survey Circle (LSI) in March 2012 found NasDem to be the fourth most popular party, but the Political Weather Station in November 2012 found only 6 percent of voters favored the party, putting it in fifth place.

Leaders: Surya PALOH (Chair), Sugang SUPARWOTO (Deputy Chair), Patrice Rio CAPELLA (Secretary General).

Other new political parties emerging in 2011–2013 included the **National Republic Party** (Nasrep), cofounded by Golkar defector Hutomo "Tommy" MANDLA PUTRA, son of the late president Suharto; the **Indonesian National Sovereignty Party** (PKBI), set up by Zanuba Arifah CHAFSOH (Yenny WAHID); the **National Union Party** (PPN); and the **Indonesia Nation Sovereignty Party** (PKBI). The newest party to be registered, the **Union of Independent People** (SRI), put forward former finance minister Mulyani INDRAWATI as its candidate for the presidency in the 2014 election despite her implication in the controversial Bank Century bailout two years earlier.

Other National Parties Failing to Win DPR Seats in 2004 or 2009:

Democratic Renewal Party (*Partai Demokrasi Pembaruan*—PDP). Also translated as the Renewal of Democracy Party, the PDP began as a reform group within the PDI-P, but its leaders were expelled in May 2005 after challenging Megawati's reelection as party chair. Charging that Megawati had turned away from Sukarno's teachings, the dissidents announced formation of the PDP the following December under the leadership of Roy B. B. Janis, who had previously served as an associate chair of the PDI-P. The PDP was officially registered in 2006. It won 0.9 percent of the vote in the 2009 DPR election.

Leaders: Roy B. B. JANIS (Executive Chair), Abdul MADJID (Chair of Advisory Council), Laksamana SUKARDI (Coordinator), Didi SUPRIYANTO (Secretary).

Indonesian Populist Fortress Party (*Partai Nasional Banteng Kemerdekaan Indonesia*—PNBKI). The PNBKI was established in 2002 as the *Partai Nasional Bung Karno* (incorporating in its title a nickname for former President Sukarno) by former PDI-P members who no longer supported President Megawati. Later renamed because of a new law prohibiting the naming of parties after individuals, it won 1.1 percent of the vote but no DPR seats in 2004. In 2009 it won 0.5 percent of the vote.

Leaders: Erros DJAROT (Chair), Zulfan LINDAN (Secretary General).

Indonesia Unity Party (*Partai Sarikat Indonesia*—PSI). The PSI was formed in December 2002 by eight ideologically diverse parties, each of which had won only one seat at the 1999 DPR election and which therefore did not meet the threshold for contesting the 2004 election. Regarded as a coalition of convenience, the PSI attracted only 0.6 percent of the vote in 2004. Its 2004 presidential candidate, Siswono YUDOHUSODO, eventually became the running mate of the PAN's Amien Rais. In 2009 it won only 0.1 percent of the vote.

Leaders: H. MARDINSYAH (Chair), Nazir MUCHAMAD (Secretary General).

Seventeen other national parties, many of them newly registered since 2004, unsuccessfully contested the 2009 DPR election. Of them, only 2 won more than 1.0 percent of the vote: the **Ulema National Awakening Party** (*Partai Kebangkitan Nasional Ulama*—PKNU), established by former members of the PKB and chaired by Choirul ALAM, which won 1.5 percent, and the **National People's Concern Party** (*Partai Peduli Rakyat Nasional*—PPRN), led by Amelia Achmad YANI, which won 1.2 percent.

The other 15 unsuccessful parties were the following: the **Archipelagic Republic Party** (*Partai Republik Nusantara*—PRN), led by Letjen SYAHRIR; the **Freedom Party** (*Partai Merdeka*—PM), formed in 2002 by former government minister Adi SASONO; the **Indonesian Democratic Devotion Party** (*Partai Kasih Demokrasi Indonesia*—PKDI), led by Stefanus Roy RENING; the **Indonesian Nahdlatul Community Party** (*Partai Persatuan Nahdlatul Ummah Indonesia*—PPNUI), which emerged from the NU as the *Nahdlatul Ummat* Party and won five seats in 1999 under the leadership of Syukron MAKMUN; the **Indonesian Workers and Businessmen's Party** (*Partai Pengusaa dan Pekerja Indonesia*—PPPI), led by Daniel HUTAPEA; the **Indonesian Youth Party** (*Partai Pemuda Indonesia*—PPI), chaired by Hasanuddin YUSUF; the **Labor Party** (*Partai Buruh*—PB), led by labor union leader Mochtar PAKPAHAN, who had organized the National Labor Party (*Partai Buruh Nasional*—PBN) after being released from prison in 1998; the **National Front Party** (*Partai Barisan Nasional*—Barnas), chaired by Vence RUMANGKANG; the **National Sun Party** (*Partai Matahari Bangsa*—PMB), led by Imam ADDARUQUTNI, a former PAN member; the **New Indonesia Struggle Party** (*Partai Perjuangan Indonesia Baru*—PPIB), led by Nurmala Kartini SJAHRIR; the **Patriot Party** (*Partai Patriot*—PP), formed in 2001 and led by Yapto Sulistio SOERJOSOEMARNO; the **Prosperous Indonesia Party** (*Partai Indonesia Sejahtera*—PIS), led by Budiyanto DARMASTONO; the **Regional Unity Party** (*Partai Persatuan Daerah*—PPD), founded in 2002 and chaired by Oesman SAPTA; the **Sovereignty Party** (*Partai Kedaulatan*) led by H. Ibrahim BASRAH; and the **Workers' Struggle Party** (*Partai Karya Perjuangan*—PKP), led by Jackson KUMAAT.

Aceh Parties:

Aceh Party (*Partai Aceh*—PA). The PA was established in May 2008 through the conversion of the Free Aceh Movement (*Gerakan Aceh Merdeka*—GAM) into a legal party.

The GAM, which had fought for Aceh's independence from 1976 until 2005, was closely associated with the Aceh Sumatra National Liberation Front (ASNLF), which dated from 1989.

Peace talks, which were indecisive in the early 2000s, were made urgent by the December 2004 tsunami. The GAM declared a ceasefire and dropped its demand for independence, opening the way for resumption of peace negotiations with the government. The peace agreement signed on August 15, 2005, effectively ended the secessionist conflict (despite the continuing presence of small proindependence militant groups), and by the end of the year the GAM had decommissioned its weapons and disbanded its armed wing, the *Tentara Nasional Aceh* (TNA).

Following approval by the DPR of Aceh autonomy legislation, a GAM candidate, Irwandi YUSUF, won the 2006 provincial gubernatorial election.

GAM's transformation into a legal political party made it eligible for legislative elections held in April 2009, when the PA was the clear leader among regional parties in contests for the provincial and district assemblies. In April 2012, Aceh completed a peaceful election for governor and district mayors in which a former GAM leader Zaini ABDULLAH, now a PA leader, was elected by a 55.8 percent majority.

Leaders: Muzzakir MANAF (Chair, Former GAM Commander), Malik MAHMUD (Patron), Adnan BEURANSAH (Spokesperson), Muhammad YAHYA (Secretary General).

In addition to the PA, the following 5 Aceh-based parties were registered for the 2009 elections: **Acehnese People Party** (*Partai Rakyat Aceh*—PRA); **Peaceful, Prosperous Aceh Party** (*Partai Aceh Aman Sejahtera*—PAAS), **Independent Voice of the Acehnese Party** (*Partai Suara Independen Rakyat Aceh*—SIRA); **Sovereign Aceh Party** (*Partai Daulat Aceh*—PDA); **United Aceh Party** (*Partai Bersatu Aceh*—PBA).

In April 2013 the General Elections Commission declared the Aceh Party (PA), the Aceh Peace Party (PDA), and the Aceh National Party (PNA) eligible to participate in the 2014 poll.

Illegal and Insurgent Groups:

Communist Party of Indonesia (*Partai Komunis Indonesia*—PKI). Founded in the 1920s, the PKI was banned in 1966 in the wake of the failed 1965 coup attempt. It subsequently split into pro-Peking and pro-Moscow factions. A number of imprisoned party leaders were executed in 1985 and 1986. In April 1996 the government restored the suffrage rights of over 1 million people alleged to have been involved in the 1965 PKI insurgency. Voicing support for the *reformasi* movement, in 1998 the party called for formation of a Patriotic and Democratic Alliance.

Three PKI members, all of whom had been in prison for over 30 years, were among 28 political prisoners freed by the Habibie government in August 1998. In February 2004 the Constitutional Court restored the political rights of former PKI members, and in 2009 former party members were permitted to run for DPR seats, but discrimination against members and their families remained common.

Jemaah Islamiah (JI). In the days after the September 11, 2001, al-Qaida attacks on the United States, the shadowy *Jemaah Islamiah* (Islamic Congregation) emerged as the principal Southeast Asian terrorist organization. Operating in cells located throughout the region, the JI was believed to have direct ties to al-Qaida. JI-attributed bombings and other plots have taken place or been uncovered in a number of countries, including the Philippines, Singapore, and Malaysia as well as Indonesia, which is generally regarded as the organization's home base. The JI has as an overarching goal the creation of a single, regional Islamic state.

The militant cleric Abu Bakar Bashir (Baasyir) has been labeled as the organization's spiritual leader—an accusation that he has denied. After serving four years in jail for subversion during the Suharto era, Bashir moved to Malaysia but subsequently returned to Indonesia, purportedly to promote the establishment of a regional Islamic state through his participation in an umbrella organization known as the **Indonesian Mujahidin Council** (*Majelis Mujaheddin Indonesia*—MMI). In the wake of the 2002 Bali bombing Bashir was detained and in 2003 and was convicted of crimes that included subversion for authorizing a series of bombings and for plotting to assassinate then vice president Megawati. Bashir was released in April 2004 but was immediately rearrested for his alleged leadership of the JI and involvement not only in the Bali case but also in the August 2003 bombing of a Marriott Hotel in Jakarta that killed 12. In 2005 he was found guilty of conspiracy in the Bali bombing, but in 2006 the Supreme Court quashed his conviction and he was freed.

In August 2003, another allegedly key figure in JI operations, Riduan ISAMUDDIN (also known as HAMBALI), was apprehended by Thai officials, with assistance from the U.S. Central Intelligence Agency. Hambali, flown to the United States for interrogation, has since been held incommunicado, originally at an undisclosed location but more recently at the U.S. Guantánamo Bay detention center. Among the three dozen suspects arrested for the Bali bombing, the JI-linked AMROZI bin Nurhasyim, his brother Ali GUFRON (MUKHLAS), and Imam SAMUDRA were convicted and executed in November 2008.

In September 2004, a suicide bombing outside the Australian embassy in Jakarta killed 11. Azahari HUSIN and Noordin Mohammed Top, both suspected JI members, were believed to have planned the attack. In October 2005 suicide bombers again struck Bali, killing 44. A month later, Husin was killed by security personnel in East Java.

By then, some analysts were reporting a split in the JI between hard-line militants and those who rejected the tactic of inflicting civilian casualties. In mid-2006 Top and his associates formed an al-Qaida organization identified as **Tanzim Qaedat al-Jihad** (Organization for the Basis of Jihad) and a small group of militants split off in 2009 to set up a small al-Qaida branch in Aceh.

In March 2006, Indonesian officials indicated that they had arrested some 270 alleged JI members since 2000, including Bashir's apparent successor, Abu RUSDAN. In June 2007 military leader Abu Dujana and political leader ZARKASIH (alias Zainuddin FAHMI) were captured. In April 2008 both were convicted of terrorism and given 15-year prison sentences.

Despite government efforts, a major domestic terror attack took place on July 17, 2009, when coordinated explosions inside Jakarta's Marriott and Ritz-Carlton hotels killed six foreigners and one Indonesian in addition to the two bombers. Noordin Top was again reported to be the mastermind of the bombings. He was killed in a police raid in Solo two months later. One of the JI-affiliated Bali bombers, Umar PATEK, was convicted and jailed in April 2012.

Bashir, who after his release in 2006 had set up an above-ground organization **Jemaah Ansharut Tauhid** (JAT) linked to al-Qaida Aceh, was arrested again on August, 9, 2010, along with five other activists, for plotting attacks on foreigners and assassinations of public officials, including President Yudhoyono. In June 2011, Bashir was convicted of financing an armed camp set up by al-Qaida in Aceh and sentenced to 15 years in prison, and in March 2012, five JAT militants allegedly planning bank robberies were killed by police. The United States in February 2012 formally declared JAT a foreign terror network.

Leaders: Ainal BAHRI (Abu DUJANA), ZULKARNAEN (Arif SUNARSO).

Islamic Defenders Group (Front Pembela Islam—FPI) This militant Islamic movement was founded in 1998 by cleric Muhammad Rizieq SYIHAB. Among its demands is the closing of Christian churches in Sumatra, Java, and Lombok, cessation of performances of Lady Gaga and sales of *Playboy* magazine, and institution of sharia law. It provoked confrontations in Kalimantan and Aceh in February 2012.

For a discussion of the **Free Papua Movement** (OPM) see the Annexed Territory section, below.

LEGISLATURE

People's Consultative Assembly (*Majelis Permusyawaratan Rakyat*—MPR) was originally the Provisional People's Consultative Assembly (*Majelis Permusyawaratan Rakyat Sementara*—MPRS) set up by President Sukarno in 1960. Reforms passed by the DPR in January 1999 reduced the MPR's membership from the 1,000 decreed by the Suharto government to 700, including 135 regional representatives and 65 civic and social delegates in addition to the 500 DPR members. As a result of constitutional changes passed in August 2002, Indonesia's legislative functions are now performed by two bodies: the People's Representation Council (DPR), which deliberates on and passes laws, and the Regional Representatives Council (DPD), which functions as an upper house with limited powers related primarily to regional concerns. Also in 2002 the MPR ceased electing Indonesia's president, who is now popularly elected.

Speaker: Sidarto Danusubroto.

Regional Representatives Council (*Dewan Perwakilan Daerah*—DPD). The DPD was created by constitutional amendment in August 2002. Members (familiarly styled "senators") are indirectly elected for five-year terms on a nonpartisan basis by provincial assemblies and must convene at least once a year. The most recent election for 132 members (4 from each of Indonesia's 33 provinces) was held April 9, 2009.

Speaker: Irman GUSMAN.

People's Representation Council (*Dewan Perwakilan Rakyat*—DPR). An outgrowth of the Mutual Cooperation House of Representatives (*Dewan Perwakilan Rakyat–Gotong Rojong*—DPRGR) set up by President Sukarno in 1960, the DPR encompassed 425 elected members and 75 military appointees until the June 1999 election, when military representation was cut to 38 seats. Additional reforms passed in August 2002 eliminated all reserved seats and increased the number of members to 550. Representatives are directly elected through a province-based proportional system that permits voters to cast ballots for individual candidates or parties, which must achieve a minimum threshold of 2.5 percent of the popular vote to claim seats.

In 2009, the size of the house was increased to 560 seats. The April election produced the following party distribution: Democrat Party, 148; Golkar Party, 106; Indonesian Democratic Party of Struggle, 94; Prosperous Justice Party, 57; National Mandate Party, 46; United Development Party, 38; National Awakening Party, 28; Great Indonesia Movement Party, 26; People's Conscience Party, 17.

Speaker: Marzuki ALIE.

CABINET

[as of September 1, 2013]

President	Susilo Bambang Yudhoyono (DP)
Vice President	Boediono (PD)
Coordinating Ministers	
Economy	Hatta Radjasa (PAN)
People's Welfare	Agung Laksono (Golkar)
Political Affairs, Security, and Social Welfare	Air Chief Mar. (Ret.) Djoko Suyanto (ind.)
Ministers	
Agriculture	H. Suswono (PKS)
Defense	Purnomo Yusgiantoro (ind.)
Energy and Mineral Resources	Jero Wacik (PD)
Education and Culture	Mohammad Nuh (ind.)
Finance	Muhammad Chatib Basri (ind.)
Foreign Affairs	Marty Muliana Natalegawa (ind.)
Forestry	Zulkifli Hasan (PAN)
Health	Nafsiah Mboi [f]
Home Affairs	Gamawan Fauzi (ind.)
Industry	M. S. Hidayat (Golkar)
Information and Communication	Tifatul Sembiring (PKS)
Justice and Human Rights	Amir Syamsuddin
Manpower and Transmigration	Muhaimin Iskandar (PKB)
Maritime Affairs and Fisheries	Syarif Cicip Sutardjo
Public Works	Djoko Kirmanto (ind.)
Religious Affairs	Suryadharma Ali (PPP)
Social Affairs	Salim Segaf Al Jufri (PKS)
Trade	Gita Wirjawan
Transportation	Evert Ernest Mangindaan (PD)
Tourism and Creative Economy	Mari Elka Pangestu (ind.) [f]
Ministers of State	
Administrative Reform	Aswar Abubakar (DP)
Cooperatives and Small and Medium-sized Enterprises	Syarifuddin Hasan (PD)
Disadvantaged Regions	Ahmad Helmi Faisal Zaini (PKB)
Environment	Baltazar Kambuaya
Public Housing	Djan Faridz
Research and Technology	H. Gusti Muhammad Hatta (ind.)
State-owned Enterprises	Dahlan Iskan

Women's Empowerment	Linda A. Gumelar (ind.) [f]
Youth and Sports	Roy Suryo (PD)
Attorney General	Jaksa Agung
Chair, National Development Planning Board	Armida Alisjahbana (ind.) [f]
State Secretary	Sudi Silalahi (ind.)

[f] = female

INTERGOVERNMENTAL REPRESENTATION

Ambassador to the U.S.: Dino Patti DJALAL.

U.S. Ambassador to Indonesia: Robert BLAKE.

Permanent Representative to the UN: Desra PERCAYA.

IGO Memberships (Non-UN): ADB, APEC, ASEAN, G-20, NAM, OIC, WTO.

ANNEXED TERRITORY

Papua (Papua and West Papua provinces). The western half of the island of New Guinea, Papua has an area of 159,375 square miles (412,781 sq. km) and a population of 2.8 million (2010E). As a consequence of recent transmigration, mainly from Java, native Papuans now number barely half of the total. Jayapura is the principal city and the capital of Papua Province. Manokwari is the capital of West Papua Province (previously called West Irian Jaya). As a result of special autonomy legislation passed in 2001 and 2008, respectively, each has an elected governor as chief administrator and an elected legislatures, the Papua People's Representative Council (*Dewan Perwakilan Rakyat Papua*) for Papua and the Regional People's Representative Council (*Dewan Perwakilan Rakyat Daerah*—DPRD) for West Papua. The territory's extensive resources include natural gas, gold, copper, nickel, and tropical woods, and the provincial governments are guaranteed a portion of royalties resulting from resource exploitation.

Long known as Netherlands New Guinea and more recently as Irian Jaya, Papua was formerly a Dutch colony that was turned over to Indonesian administration on May 1, 1963, under a UN-sponsored agreement pending a decision on self-determination. Indonesia conducted an "act of free choice" in mid-1969 by convening eight hand-picked regional consultative assemblies, all of which voted for annexation by Indonesia. Papuans opposed to Indonesian rule founded a resistance body, the **Free Papua Movement** (*Organisasai Papua Merdeka*—OPM), in 1964.

In 1971, the Papuan nationalists proclaimed a "Provisional Revolutionary Government of West Papua New Guinea" that controlled a shifting territory west of the border with Papua New Guinea. An offensive by the Indonesian Army in 1984 precipitated the flight of hundreds of Papuans into Papua New Guinea. A border cooperation agreement in October 1985 and the Status of Forces Agreement in 1992 eased tensions between Jakarta and Port Moresby but did not end refugee flows or cross-border raids by Indonesian forces. In September 1998, the newly installed Habibie government and the OPM, led by Moses WERROR, announced a cease-fire, bringing a formal end to three decades of conflict that had caused an estimated 40,000 fatalities.

In June 2000 some 3,000 delegates to a Papua People's Congress, chaired by Theys ELUAY, declared their desire to secede from Indonesia. The Wahid administration rejected Papuan sovereignty claims but ordered security forces to avoid violence, organized a human rights fact-finding team, and temporarily allowed Papuans to fly their flag, although beneath that of Indonesia. Eluay and other leaders of the Papuan Presidium Council (*Presidium Dewam Papua*—PDP) were subsequently charged with subversion, and in November 2001 Eluay was murdered. Seven Indonesian soldiers were convicted for the murder but given short sentences by the Indonesian court.

In October 1999, the Habibie administration announced reforms that led to the division of Irian Jaya into two provinces, Papua and West Papua.

On October 23, 2001, the Indonesian legislature approved Law No. 21/2001 creating special autonomy for the Papua territory under which some 70–80 percent of revenues from the exploitation of natural resources would be retained for local use. In October 2005 the central government, citing the Aceh autonomy agreement as a model, created the Papua People's Council (*Majelis Rakyat Papua*—MRP), composed of Papuan religious, traditional, and women's leaders, to which local officials appointed 42 members. But the Papuan lower house in June 2010, amid popular demonstrations in Jayapura, Manokwari, and Sorong, resolved to reject special autonomy status and instead begin exploratory talks with Jakarta regarding a referendum on future independence. West Papua's special autonomy was established in 2008 by Law 35/2008.

In March 2006, 43 Papuan men associated with the independence movement fled to Australia and were granted temporary protection visas, a move deeply resented in Jakarta. They and other Papuan leaders met in Port Vila, Vanuatu, in March–April 2008 to establish the **West Papua National Coalition for Liberation** (WPNCL), chaired by Gen. Richard YOWENI of the OPM's National Liberation Army (*Tentara Pembebasan Nasional*—TPN), with Otto ONDAWAME serving as vice chair and Rex RUMAKIEK as secretary-general. Working from a secretariat based in Port Vila, the WPNCL hoped to generate international support for Papuan self-determination. But in August 2010, it was rebuffed by the Pacific Islands Forum (PIF) when it sought observer status, and in 2011 and again in 2013 its bids for observer status in the Melanesian Spearhead Group failed. Prime Minister Somare of neighboring PNG has consistently distanced his government from the Papuan independence leaders, and Prime Minister O'Neill in June 2013 reaffirmed PNG's recognition of Indonesia's sovereignty in Papua and West Papua.

Reports by the nongovernmental organization (NGO) Human Rights Watch (HRW) and the U.S. State Department in 2012 accused Indonesian security personnel of committing human rights abuses, including prisoner abuse, torture, and murder, during efforts to track down OPM guerrillas in Papua and West Papua. Low-level, violent altercations including shoot-outs between independence advocates and the authorities and OPM counterdemonstrations persisted in 2012, exemplified by the alleged targeted killing of Mako TABUNI in June. Arrests and prosecutions for flying the banned OPM Morning Star flag (adopted in 2007 by the Papuan Tribal Council) continued with the jailing in March 2012 of five activists for three years. A TNI/Police attack of a village in Sorong flying the OPM flag killed three OPM fighters and the arrest commander Isak KAWAIBIN. An OPM ambush in February 2013 left eight TNI soldiers and four civilians dead, and another attack in June killed a policeman and a civilian. In August two boats carrying West Papua independence advocates left Cairns bound for Merauke despite Indonesian threats to deny them entry and Canberra's disapprobation of Papuan activist groups operating in Australia.

Meanwhile, Papua's new governor Lukas ENEMBE, supported by the Papua Peace Network and a Netherlands NGO, in April offered to negotiate with OPM leaders to give them a role in provincial governance and revealed that he had been in informal contact with Papua Liberation Army Front (TPN) commander Goliat TABUNI. Also in April, New Zealand announced a Papua Community Policing Project valued at US$2 million. Both initiatives followed a January declaration of loyalty to Indonesia by an OPM breakaway group of over 200 led by Daniel KOGOYA.

IRAN

Islamic Republic of Iran
Jomhori-e Islami-e Irân

Political Status: Former monarchy; Islamic Republic proclaimed April 1–2, 1979, on basis of referendum of March 30–31; present constitution adopted in a referendum of December 2–3, 1979.

Area: 636,293 sq. mi. (1,648,000 sq. km).

Population: 76,415,323 (2012E—UN); 79,853,900 (2013E—U.S. Census).

Major Urban Center (2011E—UN): TEHRAN (7,803,883), Mashhad (2,427,316), Esfahan (1,602,110), Tabriz (1,398,060).

Official Language: Persian (Farsi).

Monetary Unit: Rial (official rate November 1, 2013: 24,981.26 rials = $1US).

Supreme Religious Leader: Ayatollah Seyed Ali KHAMENEI; elected President October 2, 1981, and sworn in October 13, following the assassination of Mohammad Ali RAJAI on August 30; reelected August 16, 1985, and sworn in for a second four-year term on October 10; named Supreme Religious Leader by the Assembly of Experts on June 4, 1989, following the death of Ayatollah Ruhollah Musavi KHOMEINI on June 3.

President: Hassan ROUHANI (Society of Combatant Clergy); popularly elected on June 14, 2013, confirmed on August 3 by the Supreme Religious Leader, and sworn in before the legislature for a four-year term on August 4, succeeding Mahmoud AHMADINEJAD.

First Vice President: Eshaq JAHANGIRI (Servants of Construction); appointed by the president on August 4, 2013, to succeed Mohammad Reza RAHIMI, following elections on June 14, 2013.

THE COUNTRY

A land of elevated plains, mountains, and deserts that is semiarid except for a fertile area on the Caspian coast, Iran is celebrated both for the richness of its cultural heritage and for the oil resources that have made it a center of world attention. Persians make up about one-half of the population, while the principal minority groups are Turks and Kurds, who speak their own languages and dialects. English and French are widely spoken in the cities. More than 90 percent of the people belong to the Shiite sect of Islam, the official religion. Prior to the 1979 Islamic revolution, women constituted approximately 10 percent of the paid labor force, with substantial representation in government and the professions. Since 1979 female participation in most areas of government has been limited, and many working women still serve as unpaid agricultural laborers on family landholdings. On the other hand, the government of President Ali Akbar Hashemi RAFSANJANI was less willing than its predecessor to enforce Islamic social codes, and women successfully ran for parliamentary seats.

In 2002, GDP growth of 4.8 percent was recorded (for information on the economy prior to 2002, please see the 2013 *Handbook*). Also contributing to economic advances were increased privatization, tax incentives for corporations, and loosening of trade regulations. A dual exchange rate—one for state imports of many basic goods and another, much higher, for all other transactions—was eliminated with the adoption of a unified exchange rate in 2002.

High oil prices continued to buoy the economy, with annual average GDP growth of 6.2 percent in 2005–2008. However, the unemployment rate was reported to be 18 percent, and the annual inflation rate was 20 percent. The International Monetary Fund (IMF) commended Iran for accelerating privatization efforts, particularly with its largest banks, and noted progress in structural and tax reforms. Inflation declined to single digits, while annual GDP growth contracted to 4 percent in 2009 and 5.9 percent in 2010. Iran moved to reduce energy subsidies with the aim of exporting more oil to generate revenue, which the government planned to redistribute among its citizens. Iran's plan was to phase out all subsidies by early 2014. In 2011, GDP growth slowed to 3 percent. The following year, GDP declined by 1.9 percent, while inflation continued to rise, from 21.3 percent in 2011 to 30.1 percent in 2012, and unemployment was 12.5 percent. GDP per capita was $7,211.

GOVERNMENT AND POLITICS

Political background. Modern Iranian history began with nationalist uprisings against foreign economic intrusions in the late 19th century. In 1906, a coalition of clergy, merchants, and intellectuals forced the shah to grant a limited constitution. A second revolutionary movement, also directed largely against foreign influence, was initiated in 1921 by REZA Khan, an army officer who, four years after seizing power, ousted the Qajar family and established the Pahlavi dynasty. Although Reza Shah initiated forced modernization of the country with Kemalist Turkey as his model, his flirtation with the Nazis led to the occupation of Iran by Soviet and British forces in 1941 and his subsequent abdication in favor of his son, Mohammad Reza PAHLAVI. The end of World War II witnessed the formation of separatist Azerbaijani and Kurdish regimes under Soviet patronage; however, these crumbled in 1946 because of pressure exerted by the United States and the United Nations (UN). A subsequent upsurge of Iranian nationalism resulted in expropriation of the British-owned oil industry in 1951, during the two-year premiership of Mohammad MOSSADEQ.

In the wake of an abortive coup in August 1953, Mossadeq was arrested by loyalist army forces with assistance from the U.S. Central Intelligence Agency (CIA) and British intelligence operatives. The period following his downfall was marked by the shah's assumption of a more active role, culminating in systematic efforts at political, economic, and social development that were hailed by the monarchy as a "White Revolution." However, the priorities established by the monarch, which included major outlays for sophisticated military weapon systems and a number of "showcase" projects (such as a subway system for the city of Tehran), coupled with a vast influx of foreign workers and evidence of official corruption, led to criticism by traditional religious leaders, university students, labor unions, and elements within the business community.

In March 1975, the shah announced dissolution of the existing two-party system (both government and opposition parties having been controlled by the throne) and decreed the formation of a new National Resurgence Party to serve as the country's sole political group. In the face of mounting unrest and a number of public-services breakdowns in overcrowded Tehran, Emir Abbas HOVEYDA, who had served as prime minister since 1965, was dismissed in August 1977 and replaced by the National Resurgence secretary general, Jamshid AMOUZEGAR.

By late 1977, both political and religious opposition to the shah had further intensified. On December 11 a Union of National Front Forces was formed under Karim SANJABI, a former Mossadeq minister, to promote a return to the constitution, the nationalization of major industries, and the adoption of policies that would be "neither communist nor capitalist, but strictly nationalist." Conservative Muslim sentiment, on the other hand, centered on the senior mullah, Ayatollah Ruhollah KHOMEINI, who had lived in exile since mounting a series of street demonstrations against the "White Revolution" in 1963, and the more moderate Ayatollah Seyed Kazem SHARIATMADARI, based in the religious center of Qom. Both leaders were supported politically by the long-established Liberation Movement of Iran, led by Mehdi BAZARGAN.

By mid-1978, demonstrations against the regime had become increasingly violent, and Prime Minister Amouzegar was replaced on August 27 by the Senate president, Jaafar SHARIF-EMAMI, whose parliamentary background and known regard for the country's religious leadership made him somewhat unique within the monarch's inner circle of advisers. Unable to arrest appeals for the shah's abdication, Sharif-Emami was forced to yield office on November 6 to a military government headed by the chief of staff of the armed forces, Gen. Gholam Reza AZHARI. The level of violence nonetheless continued to mount; numerous Kurds in northwest Iran joined the chorus of opposition, as did the well-financed Tudeh Party, a communist group. The oil fields and major banks were shut down by strikes, bringing the economy to the verge of collapse. Thus, after an effort by Golam-Hossein SADIQI to form a new civilian government had failed, the shah on December 29 named a prominent National Front leader, Shahpur BAKHTIAR, as prime minister designate.

Ten days after Bakhtiar's formal investiture on January 6, 1979, the shah left the country on what was called an extended "vacation." On February 1, amid widespread popular acclaim, Ayatollah Khomeini returned from exile, and a week later he announced the formation of a provisional government under a Revolutionary Council, which was subsequently reported to be chaired by Ayatollah Morteza MOTAHARI. On February 11 Prime Minister Bakhtiar resigned, and Bazargan was invested as his successor by the National Consultative Assembly immediately prior to the issuance of requests for dissolution by both the assembly and the Senate.

Despite a series of clashes with ethnic minority groups, a referendum on March 30–31, 1979, approved the proclamation of an Islamic Republic by a reported 97 percent majority. A rising tide of political assassinations and other disruptions failed to delay the election on August 3 of a constituent assembly (formally called the Assembly of Experts) delegated to review a draft constitution that had been published in mid-June. The result of the council's work was subsequently approved in a national referendum on December 2–3 (see Constitution and government, below).

The most dramatic event of 1979 was the November 4 occupation of the U.S. embassy in Tehran and the seizure of 66 hostages (13 of whom were released on November 17, while another was freed for health reasons in early July 1980), apparently in an effort to secure the return of the shah for trial; he had been admitted to a New York hospital for medical treatment. The action, undertaken by militant students, was not disavowed by the Revolutionary Council, although the government appeared not to have been consulted. Prime Minister Bazargan felt obliged to tender his resignation the following day, without a successor being named. On December 4 the UN Security Council unanimously condemned the action and called for release of the hostages, while the International Court of Justice (ICJ) handed down a unanimous decision to the same effect on December 15. Both judgments were repudiated by Iranian leaders.

Notwithstanding the death of the shah in Egypt on July 27, 1980, and the outbreak of war with Iraq in late September (see Foreign relations, below), no resolution of the hostage issue occurred in 1980. American frustration at the lengthy impasse was partially evidenced by an abortive helicopter rescue effort undertaken by the U.S. Air Force on April 24, and it was not until November 2 that Tehran agreed to formal negotiations with Washington, proposing the Algerian government as mediator. The remaining 52 hostages were ultimately freed after 444 days of captivity on January 20, 1981, coincident with the inauguration of Ronald Reagan as U.S. president. In return for their freedom, Washington agreed (1) to abstain from interference in internal Iranian affairs; (2) to freeze the property and assets of the late shah's family pending resolution of lawsuits brought by the Islamic Republic; (3) to "bar and preclude" pending and future suits against Iran as a result of the 1979 revolution or the hostage seizure, with an Iran-U.S. Claims Tribunal to be established at The Hague, Netherlands; (4) to end trade sanctions against Tehran; and (5) to unfreeze $7.97 billion in Iranian assets.

Internal developments in 1980 were highlighted by the election of the relatively moderate Abol Hasan BANI-SADR, a former adviser to Ayatollah Khomeini, as president on January 25, and the convening of a unicameral assembly, the *Majlis-e Shoura-e Islami*, on May 28, following two-stage balloting on March 14 and May 9. On August 9 Bani-Sadr reluctantly agreed to nominate Mohammad Ali RAJAI, an Islamic fundamentalist, as prime minister after three months of negotiations had failed to yield parliamentary support for a more centrist candidate.

Despite the support of secular nationalists, political moderates, much of the armed forces, and many Islamic leftists, Bani-Sadr was increasingly beleaguered by the powerful fundamentalist clergy centered on the Islamic Republican Party (IRP) and its (then) secretary general, Chief Justice of the Supreme Court Ayatollah Mohammad Hossein BEHESHTI. The IRP had emerged from the 1980 legislative balloting in firm control of the *Majlis,* enabling the clergy, ultimately with the support of Ayatollah Khomeini, to undermine presidential prerogatives during the first half of 1981. Moreover, on June 1 an arbitration committee, which had been established in the wake of violent clashes on March 5 between fundamentalists and Bani-Sadr supporters, declared that the president had not only incited unrest but had also violated the constitution by failing to sign into law bills passed by the *Majlis.* Nine days later, Khomeini removed Bani-Sadr as commander in chief, and on June 22, following a two-day impeachment debate in the assembly that culminated in a 177–1 vote declaring him incompetent, the chief executive was dismissed.

On June 28, 1981, a bomb ripped apart IRP headquarters in Tehran, killing Ayatollah Beheshti, 4 government ministers, 6 deputy ministers, 27 *Majlis* deputies, and 34 others. Prosecutor General Ayatollah Abdolkarim Musavi ARDEBILI was immediately appointed chief justice, while on July 24 Prime Minister Rajai, with more than 90 percent of the vote, was elected president. Having been confirmed by Ayatollah Khomeini on August 2, Rajai named Hojatolislam Mohammad Javad BAHONAR (Beheshti's successor as leader of the IRP) as prime minister, the *Majlis* endorsing the appointment three days later. Meanwhile, in late July deposed president Bani-Sadr, accompanied by Massoud RAJAVI of the *Mujaheddin-e Khalq* (see Political Parties and Groups, below), had fled to Paris, where he announced the formation of an exile National Resistance Council.

On August 30, 1981, President Rajai and Prime Minister Bahonar were assassinated by an explosion at the latter's offices, and on September 1 the minister of the interior, Hojatolislam Muhammad Reza MAHDAVI-KANI, was named interim prime minister. On October 2 Hojatolislam Seyed Ali KHAMENEI, Bahonar's replacement as secretary general of the IRP and a close associate of Khomeini, was elected president with 95 percent of the vote. Sworn in on October 13, he accepted the resignation of Mahdavi-Kani on October 15, with Mir Hosein MUSAVI, the foreign minister, being named the Islamic Republic's fifth prime minister on October 31, following confirmation by the *Majlis.* President Khamenei was elected to a second four-year term on August 16, 1985, defeating two IRP challengers. On October 13, following nomination by the president, Musavi was reconfirmed as prime minister.

At *Majlis* elections on April 8 and May 13, 1988, reformists won a clear majority. The elections, which were boycotted by the sole recognized opposition party, the Liberation Movement of Iran, also highlighted the increasing power of *Majlis* speaker Hojatolislam Ali Akbar Hashemi Rafsanjani, who on June 2 was named acting commander in chief of the armed forces. On June 6 Rafsanjani was renamed to his parliamentary post, despite the reported efforts of Ayatollah Hussein Ali MONTAZERI, Khomeini's officially designated successor, to force him to concentrate exclusively on his military responsibilities.

On March 27, 1989, following a meeting of the Presidium of the Assembly of Experts at which the "future leadership of the Islamic Republic" was discussed, Montazeri, declaring his "lack of readiness" for the position, submitted his resignation as deputy religious leader. On June 3 the 89-year-old Khomeini died, the Assembly of Experts designating President Khamenei as his successor the following day. On July 28 Iranians overwhelmingly voted their approval of constitutional changes that abolished the office of prime minister and significantly strengthened the powers of the theretofore largely ceremonial presidency. On August 17 Speaker Rafsanjani, who had been elected to succeed Khamenei as chief executive, was sworn in before the *Majlis,* and two days later he submitted a 22-member cabinet list that secured final approval on August 29.

In nationwide elections on October 8, 1990, to the Assembly of Experts, supporters of President Rafsanjani won a majority of seats, thus dealing a major setback to hard-line leaders. Rafsanjani further depleted the hard-liners' influence by, ironically, making assembly membership contingent on successful completion of an Islamic law examination. Furthermore, in parliamentary balloting in April and May 1992 Rafsanjani supporters captured an unexpectedly large majority of the seats, aided in part by the pro-Rafsanjani Council of Guardians' elimination of a number of hard-line *Majlis* candidates in March.

On June 11, 1993, President Rafsanjani was reelected to a second four-year term. However, despite lackluster opposition from three challengers selected by the Council of Guardians from a list of 128 presidential candidates, he won only 63.3 percent of the vote, a severe decline from the 94.5 percent registered in 1989. The president's slippage was also evident when the *Majlis,* while approving the remainder of the reshuffled cabinet on August 16, voted against the reappointment of Mohsen NURBAKHSH as minister of economic affairs and finance. Notwithstanding the obvious legislative dissatisfaction with current policies, Rafsanjani subsequently named Nurbakhsh to the newly created post of vice president for economic affairs, which did not require approval by the *Majlis*.

Cuts in state subsidies and consequent price increases triggered a series of riots in several cities in 1994, the assembly authorizing police to "shoot to kill" in any subsequent outbreaks. An estimated 30 people died when police opened fire during a disturbance near Tehran in April 1995. Nevertheless, President Rafsanjani vowed to persevere with his free-market reform policies, although it was widely conceded that little progress had been achieved in making the economy more efficient or the government bureaucracy less corrupt.

Elections to a new *Majlis* were held on March 8 and April 19, 1996, the balloting failing to produce a clear-cut victor in the battle between conservatives and moderates for political dominance. The results reflected the continued "quiet power struggle" between President Rafsanjani and Ayatollah Khamenei, whose supporters had accused the administration of having "wandered" from the path set by the 1979 revolution. With political primacy still apparently hanging in the balance, attention subsequently focused on the presidential election scheduled for May 1997, ruling clerics having emphasized that no constitutional amendments would be considered to permit a third term for Rafsanjani.

In what was considered an extraordinarily high voter turnout of 88 percent, Hojatolislam Seyed Mohammad KHATAMI, a moderate cleric, won the May 23, 1997, presidential poll with 20 million votes (69.5 percent) to 9 million combined votes for the three other candidates, including second-place (25 percent) Ali Akbar NATEQ-NURI, the conservative speaker of the *Majlis*, who was supported by Ayatollah Khamenei and the Society of Combatant Clergy, the majority conservative faction of the *Majlis*. Khatami, backed by various leftist groups as well as the moderate Servants of Construction, reportedly did well among women, students, the urban middle class, and other voters who apparently desired an end to Iran's international isolation, an easing of Islamic "vigilantism," and economic reform. The *Majlis* approved Khatami's cabinet recommendations on August 20; meanwhile, outgoing President Rafsanjani was named as president of the newly expanded Council for the Expediency of State Decrees (see Constitution and government, below), which included former cabinet members rejected by Khatami.

The election of President Khatami in May 1997 precipitated an extended tug-of-war for political and economic control between his reformist camp, which enjoyed widespread popular support, and the conservative clerics, who retained broad institutional power, often in alliance with intelligence services and businessmen. For his part, Khatami steadfastly pursued the "rule of law" and a civil society marked by greater nonclerical participation in governing bodies, expanded freedoms for individuals and the media, and tolerance for divergent religious and political views (including the legalization of parties). He also steadfastly called for warmer ties with the West based on a "dialogue of civilizations" and attempted to convince neighboring states that Iran had no interest in establishing regional dominance. Conservatives tried to block democratization at many levels, including the *Majlis* (which forced the dismissal of several cabinet members) and the judiciary (which banned newspapers and took legal action against a number of reformists). The conservative cause appeared to receive a boost in the October 23, 1998, balloting for the Assembly of Experts, although their success was tainted by a relatively low turnout and the fact that many reform candidates had been barred from running by the conservative Council of Guardians. However, pro-Khatami candidates did very well in the municipal balloting of late February 1999, winning all of the seats on the Tehran Council and some 70 percent of the seats they contested overall. Significantly, Ayatollah Khamenei, often associated with the conservative cause, did not support hard-liners in their efforts to ban reform candidates in the local elections.

Reformist candidates reportedly won about 70 percent of the seats in *Majlis* elections of February–May 2000, but the new membership's legislative efforts faced constant resistance from the Council of Guardians and the judiciary. The reformists maintained their electoral momentum in June 2001, when President Khatami was reelected with a reported 78 percent of the vote against nine challengers. The reformists suffered a major defeat in local elections held on February 28, 2003, with conservative candidates winning majorities in most major cities, as former supporters of the reformists chose to stay away from the polls. The conservative Builders of an Islamic Iran Council won 14 of 15 city council seats in Tehran. Turnout in the capital was reported at about 10 percent, with turnout nationwide reported at 39 percent.

In parliamentary elections on February 20, 2004, conservatives won a sweeping victory after the Council of Guardians disqualified more than a third of the candidates. Some 80 incumbent reformist MPs were among those barred from standing for election. The Interior Ministry reported turnout at 28 percent in Tehran and 50.57 percent nationwide, the lowest since the 1979 revolution. After a second round, held on May 7 to determine remaining seats, the conservatives had secured at least 200 of 290 seats. Within the conservative majority, the Builders of an Islamic Iran Council controlled about 195 of those. Lesser-known reformists without formal ties to established political parties and associations were left with a small bloc of about 40 seats.

In the 2005 presidential elections, conservative candidate Mahmoud AHMADINEJAD, the mayor of Tehran, won a runoff vote against former president Rafsanjani on June 24, with 61.64 percent of the vote vs 35.93 percent, respectively, a difference of more than 7 million votes. Turnout for the runoff was reported at 59.72 percent compared to 62.66 percent in the first round (in which seven candidates competed). Reformist and former *Majlis* speaker Mehdi KARUBI, who stood as a candidate in the first round on June 17, alleged rampant voter fraud and irregularities in an open letter to the supreme leader.

In the elections for the Assembly of Experts on December 15, 2006, conservatives retained control, the Council of Guardians having again disqualified a third of the candidates. Rafsanjani retained his seat, receiving the most votes of any Tehran candidate. In concurrent elections for local councils, moderate conservatives won the majority of seats, followed by reformists. Following the death in July 2007 of the speaker of the Assembly of Experts, Ali MESHKINI, Rafsanjani was elected on September 4 to fill the post.

Following the resignation of five ministers within four days, including the oil minister, the cabinet was reshuffled on August 12, 2007.

In parliamentary elections on March 14, 2008, conservatives repeated their strong performance of four years earlier, securing about 60 percent of the seats in the first round of balloting after the Council of Guardians disqualified nearly 40 percent of the reformist candidates, including many former *Majlis* members. Supporters of President Ahmadinejad won fewer seats than anticipated, owing in large part to gains by independent candidates, who won more than 30 percent of the seats. So-called pragmatic conservatives, who were said to be dissatisfied with Ahmadinejad's economic policies, also made a strong showing. Turnout nationwide was reported to be 60 percent, nearly 10 percent higher than in 2004. Following second-round balloting on April 25 to decide 82 seats, the pragmatic conservatives, or principlists, added nearly a dozen seats to the 42 they had secured in the first round. Ahmadinejad's supporters secured a total of 170 of the 290 seats, including at least 38 seats in the runoff. Overall, reformists gained 6 seats over the 40 they held following the 2004 elections, and independents secured 71 seats. Results for 3 seats were annulled by the Interior Ministry, though no reason was given. Reformists called for a recount after the first round; a subsequent investigation by the Council of Guardians validated the initial results.

President Ahmadinejad dismissed the ministers of economic affairs and the interior, replacing both on April 22, 2008. The new minister of interior, Ali KORDAN, was impeached by parliament for false claims he made about his education. Meanwhile, an aide to Ahmadinejad was fired for allegedly trying to bribe legislators to keep them from voting for impeachment. The subsequent vote was seen as underscoring parliament's increasing rift with Ahmadinejad (see Current issues, below).

On June 12, 2009, Ahmadinejad was reelected for a four-year term in controversial balloting in which he secured 62.63 percent of the vote, compared to 33.75 percent for his main rival, former prime minister Mir Hosein Musavi, a political moderate. Two other candidates received only a small percentage of the vote. Immediately after the results were announced and Ahmadinejad's victory subsequently confirmed by the supreme leader, violent protests broke out across the country in the wake of allegations of irregularities (see Current issues, below). After a partial recount of the votes, the Guardian Council confirmed the election results on June 29.

On July 16, 2009, the head of the Atomic Energy Organization, Gholamreza AGHAZADEH, resigned, and President Ahmadinejad replaced him in a reshuffled cabinet, naming one of his vice presidents, Esfandyar Rahim MASHAEE, as first vice president. The move prompted outrage from hard-line conservatives, who denounced the choice because of remarks Mashaee made in 2008 to the effect that Iranians were friends with Israelis. More significantly, Ahmadinejad insisted on retaining Mashaee over the objections of Supreme Leader Ayatollah Khamenei, who had been the president's foremost defender following the controversial election. (The first vice president is first in line to succeed the president if he dies or becomes incapacitated and also leads cabinet meetings in the president's absence.) However, on July 24 Ahmadinejad submitted to the pressure—after the public broadcast of Khamenei's order on state television—and accepted Mashaee's resignation on July 24. Following his inauguration on August 5, Ahmadinejad nominated a new government on August 20, and parliament approved all but three ministers, two of whom were women. One of the vice presidents was transferred to a new portfolio on August 25, and two ministers named on September 6 were rejected by parliament. On September 13, the president promoted the vice president for legal and parliamentary affairs, Mohammad Reza RAHIMI, to fill the vacant post of first vice president. Two ministers were approved on October 20 to replace those who had been rejected in September. The last three ministers to fill the cabinet were approved on November 15, and a further reshuffling of vice presidents occurred the same month. The dismissal of the foreign minister on December 13 prompted criticism by conservatives. His portfolio was assumed by the vice president in charge of the atomic energy organization, described as a protégé of the president.

One minister was replaced on February 7, 2011, and on February 13, a replacement was named for the atomic energy portfolio. The minister of intelligence resigned on April 18, but while the president accepted his resignation, the spiritual leader did not. Following the dismissal of three ministers on May 12, President Ahmadinejad took over the oil portfolio, a move that was challenged on legal grounds by the Council of Guardians. The president named a caretaker to the post on June 2.

In parliamentary elections on March 2 and May 4, 2012, conservatives allied to Khamenei won 182 seats (see Current issues, below). In May, Ahmadinejad carried out a minor cabinet reshuffle, reassigning three vice presidents to different portfolios.

In presidential balloting on June 14, 2013, moderate Hassan ROUHANI won in the first round of polling, defeating conservative candidate and mayor of Tehran, Mohammad Baqer QALIBAF (United Front of Conservatives) and four other candidates (see Current issues, below). His cabinet was approved between August 15–17, including the appointment of Elham AMINZADEH, the country's first woman vice president for legal affairs.

Constitution and government. The constitution of December 1979 established Shiite Islam as the official state religion, placed supreme power in the hands of the Muslim clergy, and named Ayatollah Ruhollah Khomeini as the nation's religious leader (*velayat-e faqih*) for life. The *velayat-e faqih* is also supreme commander of the armed forces and the Revolutionary Guard, can declare war, and can dismiss the president following a legislative request or a ruling of the Supreme Court. He is formally responsible for the "delineation" of national policies in all areas, although some de facto authority was assumed by other officials following Ayatollah Khomeini's death in 1989.

An elected 86-member Assembly of Experts appoints the country's spiritual leader and has broad powers of constitutional interpretation. (Members of the assembly are popularly elected for eight-year terms. Previously, only mullahs were permitted to run; however, revisions approved prior to the 1998 balloting permitted nonclerics to stand for the assembly, although their candidacies were still subject to approval by the Council of Guardians.) The president, the country's chief executive officer, is popularly elected for a maximum of two four-year terms. Members of the unicameral *Majlis,* to which legislative authority is assigned, also serve four-year terms. The post of prime minister was eliminated as part of basic law revisions approved by referendum in July 1989, the president being authorized to appoint members of the Council of Ministers, subject to legislative approval. The *Majlis* was also empowered to impeach the president by a one-third vote of its members and to request his dismissal by a two-thirds vote. In the event of a presidential vacancy, an election to refill the office must be held within 50 days.

A Council of Guardians, encompassing six clerics specializing in Islamic law appointed by the *velayat-e faqih* and six nonclerical jurists elected by the legislature from nominees selected by the High Council of the Judiciary, is empowered to veto candidates for the presidency, *Majlis,* and Assembly of Experts and to nullify laws considered contrary to the constitution or the Islamic faith. (No constitutional provision having been made for the vetting by the Council of Guardians of candidates in municipal elections, the *Majlis* established a special committee for that purpose prior to the February 1999 local balloting.) In addition, a Council for the Expediency of State Decrees, composed of six clerics and seven senior governmental officials, was created in February 1988 to mediate differences between the *Majlis* and the more conservative Council of Guardians. (The authority and size of the Expediency Council were expanded in March 1997 by Ayatollah Khamenei, transforming the Council from an arbitrative panel to an "august consultative body," comprising a wider range of members, such as technocrats and faction leaders.) There is also a Supreme Council for National Security, established under the 1989 constitutional amendments to replace the National Defense Council. The new council, which coordinates defense and security policies and oversees all intelligence services, comprises the president, who serves as chair, two members appointed by the *faqih,* the chief justice of the Supreme Court, the speaker of the *Majlis,* and several military and ministerial representatives. Political parties are technically authorized to the extent that they "do not violate the independence, sovereignty, national unity, and principles of the Islamic Republic."

The civil courts instituted under the monarchy were replaced by Islamic Revolutionary Courts, judges being mandated to reach verdicts on the basis of precedent or Islamic law. The legal code subsequently underwent numerous changes, and on several occasions Ayatollah Khomeini called for the purging of judges who were deemed unsuitable or exceeded their authority. In August 1982, it was announced that all laws passed under the former regime would be annulled if contrary to Islam, while on September 23 homosexuality and consumption of alcohol were added to an extensive list of capital offenses. Although individuals are guaranteed a constitutional right to counsel, summary trials and executions were common following the 1979 revolution, many victims being suspected leftists or guerrillas.

Iran is administratively divided into 30 provinces (*ostans*); in addition, there are about 400 counties (*shahrestan*) and nearly 900 municipalities (*bakhsh*). The first municipal elections ever were conducted in February 1999. Reformers hoped that substantial authority would eventually be shifted from the national government to the local councils.

The press is highly censored and controlled. In 2013, the media group Reporters Without Borders ranked Iran 174th out of 179 countries in freedom of the press.

Foreign relations. Although a charter member of the UN, Iran momentarily curtailed its participation in the world body upon the advent of the Islamic Revolution. It boycotted the 1979 Security Council debate on seizure of the U.S. embassy in Tehran but joined in UN condemnation of the Soviet presence in Afghanistan late in the year.

An active member of OPEC, Iran was long in the forefront of those urging aggressive pricing policies, as opposed to the more moderate posture of Saudi Arabia and other conservative members. After 1980, however, a combination of the world oil glut and the need to finance its war effort forced Iran to sell petroleum on the spot at market at prices well below those set by OPEC; concurrently, it joined Algeria and Libya in urging a "fair share" strategy aimed at stabilizing prices through drastic production cutbacks.

A major international drama erupted in late 1986 with the revelation that members of the U.S. Reagan administration had participated in a scheme involving the clandestine sale of military equipment to Iran, the proceeds of which were to be used to support anti-Sandinista *contra* forces in Nicaragua. In early 1989 relations with the West, which had recently improved, again plummeted when British authorities refused to enjoin publication of Salman Rushdie's *Satanic Verses,* a work considered deeply offensive to Muslims worldwide, with Khomeini issuing a death decree against the author in February.

Iran and its western neighbor, Iraq, have long been at odds over their borders, principally over control of the Shatt al-Arab waterway linking the Persian Gulf to the major oil ports of both countries. Although the dispute was ostensibly resolved by a 1975 accord dividing the waterway along the *thalweg* (median) line, Iraq abrogated the treaty on September 17, 1980, and invaded Iran's Khuzistan Province on September 22. Despite early reversals, Iran succeeded in retaining control of most of the larger towns, including the besieged oil center of Abadan, and by the end of the year the conflict had resulted in a military stalemate. The war had the immediate effect of accentuating disunity within the Islamic world, the more radical regimes of Libya, Syria, and South Yemen supporting Tehran, and the more conservative governments of Jordan, Egypt, and the Gulf states favoring Baghdad. (In March 2009, Iran and Iraq agreed on joint technical teams to demarcate the border.)

Despite mediation efforts by the UN, the Organization of the Islamic Conference, the Nonaligned Movement, and various individual countries, fighting continued, with Iran advancing into Iraqi territory for the first time in July 1982. Rejecting a cease-fire overture, Tehran demanded $150 billion in reparations, the ouster of the Saddam Hussein government, and Iraqi repatriation of expelled Shiites. By early 1984 Iranian forces had made marginal gains on the southern front, including capture of the bulk of the Majnoon oil fields north of Basra, with what was essentially a stalemate prevailing for the ensuing three years.

A renewal of Iranian military offensives in late 1987 proved futile, as Iraqi troops drove Iranian troops from Basra and half of the Iranian Navy was reported lost during fighting with U.S. battleships protecting oil tankers in the Gulf. In February 1988 the "war of the cities" recommenced, with Iran and Iraq bombarding each other's capitals and other densely populated centers. Thereafter, the combination of Iraq's increasing use of chemical weapons and major military supply shortages led Iran to agree to a cease-fire on July 18. Ensuing peace talks, mediated by the UN, were slowed by friction over the return of prisoners, the Iraqi demand for free passage through the Shatt al-Arab waterway, and Iranian insistence that Iraq be condemned for initiating the fighting. However, despite allegations by both sides that the other was rearming, the cease-fire continued into 1990, being succeeded by a peace agreement on what were essentially Iranian terms (i.e., a return to the 1975 accord) in the wake of the crisis generated by Iraq's seizure of Kuwait in August 1990. (Still, Iran contends that its "cessation of hostilities" agreement with Iraq has never been replaced by a formal peace accord.)

Iran played a somewhat ambivalent role during the Gulf drama of 1990–1991, declaring its "full agreement" with those condemning the Kuwaiti invasion but opposing the deployment of U.S. troops to the region. In September 1990, it denied that it had secretly agreed to help break the UN embargo by importing some 200,000 barrels a day of Iraqi crude oil. Subsequently, it provided "haven" for upward of 100 Iraqi warplanes upon commencement of Operation Desert Storm in January 1991. Iran retained the planes upon the conclusion of hostilities and a year later confiscated them in what it termed partial satisfaction of reparations stemming from the Iran–Iraq conflict.

As the Gulf crisis subsided, Iran's top two leaders, Ayatollah Khamenei and President Rafsanjani, appeared to have reached an unspoken understanding to cooperate in countering the influence of their more radical colleagues by seeking a reduction in friction with the United States and other Western powers, as well as with regional Arab governments, including Iraq. In the wake of Saddam Hussein's humiliating military defeat, Tehran voiced sympathy for Iraq's Shiites while insisting that it was providing no military support for the southern rebels. Iran appeared to try to position itself midway between two former antagonists: Iraq, which it wished to see weakened but not destroyed, and the United States, whose power it acknowledged but which it did not welcome as a permanent arbiter of Middle Eastern affairs.

In April 1991, Iran generated concern among its Persian Gulf neighbors by expelling Arab residents from Abu Musa, a small island in the middle of the waterway that, along with two adjacent islands, Large Tunb and Small Tunb, had long been viewed as belonging to the United Arab Emirates but had been jointly administered since Iranian occupation of Abu Musa in 1971. Iran subsequently rejected the Arab League's call for ICJ arbitration. (Iran has continued to maintain that it owns the islands. The Gulf Cooperation Council [GCC] has backed the Emirates' claim to the islands and has "demanded" that Iran enter into negotiations and end its "occupation" of Abu Musa.)

In May 1991, the administration of U.S. President George H. W. Bush announced that it would not welcome improved relations until Tehran used its influence to secure the release of hostages held by pro-Iranian groups in Lebanon. The Iranian foreign ministry indicated in return that the hostage issue might soon become a "non-problem," particularly if some $10 billion of impounded Iranian assets were released by Washington. Shortly thereafter, the United States agreed to resume purchasing Iranian oil, with the stipulation that all payments would go into an escrow account established by the ICJ.

For the remainder of 1991, Tehran continued its efforts to emerge from political and economic isolation, hosting an international human rights conference in September and taking an active role in the release of the remaining American and British hostages in Lebanon. However, despite a U.S. agreement in December to compensate Iran $278 million for undelivered military equipment, further rapprochement was stymied by Tehran's opposition to U.S.-brokered Middle East talks and President Rafsanjani's condemnation of American efforts to persuade China and India to stop transferring nuclear equipment to Iran.

Further complicating relations with the United States was a decision in March 1995 by Conoco Inc., under heavy pressure from Washington, to abandon a proposed $1 billion contract with Iran for the development of offshore oil and natural gas fields, and the subsequent imposition by U.S. President Bill Clinton of a full embargo on U.S. trade and investment with Iran. Describing Iran as an "outlaw state" because of its alleged complicity in international terrorism and its pursuit, according to U.S. officials, of nuclear weapons capability, Washington also called upon Moscow and Beijing to forgo their respective plans to sell nuclear reactors to Iran for the production of electricity.

In January 1996, it was revealed that some $18 million had been approved for the American CIA to support efforts to "change the nature" of the Iranian government. Washington subsequently attempted to intensify pressure on Tehran by authorizing sanctions against foreign companies that invest significantly in Iran's oil and gas industries.

A German court appeared to support American charges that Iran had engaged in "state-sponsored terrorism" when it ruled in April 1997 that senior Iranian officials were involved in the 1992 assassinations of Iranian Kurdish separatists in a German restaurant. Bonn withdrew its ambassador to Tehran following the ruling, with other European Union (EU) members (except Greece) following suit. The EU's action, however, was temporary (the ambassadors returned in November) and did little to dissuade critics of the United States' unilateral policy of sanctions against Iran. Former U.S. national security advisers Zbigniew Brzezinski and Brent Scowcroft, for example, said the costly sanctions were not isolating Iran but were instead alienating American allies while driving Tehran and Moscow closer. Iran had reportedly been receiving Russian help with a ballistic missile program. According to the *New York Times*, Moscow agreed to withdraw support of the program under American and Israeli pressure in 1997. Meanwhile, in November, the United States bought 21 Soviet-era MIG-29s from Moldova to keep them from being sold to Iran.

Washington seemed more receptive to rapprochement with Tehran following the election of moderate President Khatami in May 1997. At the end of July, Secretary of State Madeleine Albright confirmed that the United States would not oppose the construction of a transnational Central Asian gas pipeline that would cross northern Iran, the first major economic concession to Iran since the 1979 revolution. Tehran's relations with Iraq, Syria, and the Gulf states, especially Saudi Arabia, also improved following Khatami's victory.

In a televised interview in January 1998, President Khatami proposed cultural exchanges with the United States. He also expressed a willingness to reconsider Iran's severed relationship with the United States and, in reply, the U.S. State Department suggested direct negotiations. However, Iran's powerful conservative spiritual leader, Ayatollah Ali Khamenei, subsequently lashed out at the United States, reconfirming deep internal divisions in the Iranian leadership.

The most significant regional tension in 1998 involved neighboring Afghanistan, where Taliban forces launched a midyear campaign to gain control of those parts of the country previously held by opposition forces. Tehran, angered at the unexplained killing of a number of its diplomats in Afghanistan and concerned over the fate of the anti-Taliban Shiite community in the central area of that country, massed more than 200,000 troops along the border in September, and war seemed imminent. Both sides subsequently showed a degree of restraint; however, moderates in Tehran reportedly expressed the fear that a military venture would compromise Iran's hope to become the "gateway" for the economic markets opening up in Central Asia. Similar motivation also partially explained Tehran's announcement in September that it had disassociated itself from the *fatwa* against Salman Rushdie, a decision that prompted the reestablishment of full relations with the United Kingdom. President Khatami's "charm offensive" toward Europe subsequently included a visit to the Vatican in March 1999.

Toward the end of the Clinton administration in 1999–2000, trade restrictions against Iran were reduced, and Secretary of State Albright announced official "regret" over the U.S. role in the 1953 coup and for supporting Iraq in the 1980–1988 Iran-Iraq war. However, the new George W. Bush administration adopted a much less conciliatory stance in the first half of 2001, based on what it claimed was Iranian support for militant Palestinian groups, such as Islamic Holy War and Hamas, as well as Hezbollah guerrillas in Lebanon. (The Iranian government contended that it provides only "moral support" and humanitarian aid for such groups and does not belong on the U.S. list of state sponsors of terrorism.) Moderate Iranians had hoped that a new era in relations with Washington would develop following the U.S.-led campaign against al-Qaida and Taliban forces in Afghanistan in late 2001, Iran having reportedly supplied useful intelligence and other assistance to support that effort in light of its different view of Islam than that expressed by al-Qaida and the Taliban. However, expectations of rapprochement with Washington were dashed in January 2002, when President Bush accused Iran of forming, along with Iraq and North Korea, an "axis of evil" threatening global security. That characterization prompted widespread anti-American demonstrations in February, and President Khatami accused Washington of "bullying" many other countries in the world through its "war on terrorism." Nevertheless, the United States continued its pressure, with Bush in August accusing Iran of seeking to develop weapons of mass destruction and demanding that Russia cease assistance to Iranian nuclear activities. The EU, on the other hand, considered Iran's posture in a much less provocative light and launched new talks with Tehran on possible trade-liberalization measures.

Iran officially opposed the U.S.-led invasion of Iraq in 2003 but nevertheless welcomed the ouster of President Saddam Hussein and allowed Iraqi opposition figures to travel freely from Iran to northern Iraq on the eve of the war. Meanwhile, the U.S.-led campaign in Afghanistan against the Taliban removed another hostile regime on Iran's western border.

Iran has had close ties in Iraq to prominent Shiite political figures, especially those from the Supreme Council of Islamic Revolution in Iraq (SCIRI). Iran had provided refuge and assistance to SCIRI during the 1980–1988 Iran-Iraq war, arming the group's military wing, the Badr Brigade. Iran reportedly has operated an extensive intelligence network in Iraq and has provided support to Shiite mosques and influential religious charities. U.S. officials have accused Iran of "meddling" in Iraq and failing to police its border with Iraq.

Iran's nuclear program became the focus of international scrutiny following revelations—revealed in satellite photographs provided by the exiled *Mujaheddin-e Khalq* in August 2002 (see reference to MKO, under Political Parties, below)—that it had failed to disclose an elaborate underground uranium-enrichment facility in Natanz and a heavy-water plant in Arak. Iranian officials obstructed inspectors from the International Atomic Energy Agency (IAEA) and provided contradictory explanations to them when they inquired about the nature of Iran's nuclear program. Facing possible referral to the UN Security Council, Iran negotiated a tentative agreement in October 2003 with Britain, France, and Germany—acting as representatives of the EU—to allow more intrusive inspections and to divulge the full history of its program in return for access to civilian nuclear technology. Iran also volunteered to temporarily suspend uranium-enrichment activities while negotiations continued with the Europeans. In the meantime, additional questions were raised about the nature of Iran's nuclear program and the government's intentions when the IAEA found traces of highly enriched uranium. Iran insisted that its activities were solely for the purpose of producing electricity, but the United States accused Tehran of secretly working to build nuclear weapons.

Tensions over the nuclear issue heightened following the election of President Ahmadinejad in June 2005. Talks between Iran and European governments had made little progress, and Iran, dismissing European proposals as "insulting," announced that it would end its voluntary suspension of uranium-enrichment activities and would refuse further IAEA inspections. The Iranians reopened a uranium conversion plant in Isfahan in August 2005, declaring that it was fully within its rights under the Nuclear Non-Proliferation Treaty to pursue uranium enrichment and activities associated with it. On February 4, 2006, member states on the IAEA's board of governors voted to refer Iran to the UN Security Council for its failure to dispel concerns over its nuclear program. The Security Council urged Iran on March 29 to suspend uranium enrichment but did not threaten punitive sanctions amid reluctance voiced by Russia and China. Striking a defiant tone, President Ahmadinejad announced on April 11 that Iran had successfully enriched uranium at low levels, saying the country had taken a major step toward mastering nuclear technology. He reiterated the regime's view that Iran regarded uranium enrichment as an inalienable right under the Nuclear Non-Proliferation Treaty.

In 2006, the United States reversed its long-standing policy and said on May 31that it was ready to hold direct talks with Iran on the nuclear issue and that it would join European governments in negotiations aimed at resolving the crisis. In a fresh diplomatic initiative, the United States, other permanent members of the UN Security Council, and Germany agreed to offer Iran a package of incentives if it suspended uranium enrichment and cooperated with IAEA inspectors. The proposal, which included offers of access to civilian nuclear technology, trade concessions, and some security assurances, was presented to Iran by an EU envoy in June. However, Iran insisted it would not respond to the offer until late August, despite Western demands for an answer within weeks. In August, Ahmadinejad said that Iran would not yield to international pressure to dismantle its nuclear program. Consequently, the Security Council unanimously voted on December 23 to impose sanctions on Iran. For its part, Iran condemned the resolution as illegal.

While the United States said it would continue to seek a diplomatic solution to the nuclear dispute, it refused to rule out possible military action. Iranian officials warned that any U.S. or Israeli military action against its nuclear sites would result in retaliation against U.S. and Israeli targets. In March 2007, the UN Security Council unanimously agreed to tighten sanctions as Iran continued to insist that it was developing its nuclear program solely for peaceful purposes. The UN resolution included a ban on arms sales to Iran and an expanded freeze on its assets. Iran again countered that the sanctions were illegal. Iranian and U.S. officials met in Baghdad in May 2007, in the most high-profile contact between them, but the talks focused on Iraq. Iran continued to maintain that it would not halt its nuclear research program, even as the Bush administration asserted that there would be "serious consequences" if Tehran did not end its enrichment process. In September the IAEA reported that it had reached agreement with Tehran on a "work plan" to resolve outstanding questions about nuclear activity, but Western diplomats continued to step up pressure on Iran. The EU decided to impose its own sanctions outside of those adopted by the UN because some countries wanted to distance themselves from the broader U.S. actions. Subsequently, in October, the Bush administration announced sweeping new sanctions against Iran's Revolutionary Guard, accusing the guard of proliferating weapons of mass destruction and supporting terrorism through the guard's elite Quds division. The United States also called for other countries to stop doing business with four of Iran's largest banks. Iran's chief nuclear negotiator, Ali LARIJANI, resigned in October, reportedly over differences with Ahmadinejad on how to conduct the talks. By early November, the UN had agreed to consider yet another set of sanctions if Iran did not answer key questions by December about its nuclear program, though a month earlier the IAEA had said that it had no evidence Tehran was seeking nuclear arms. Meanwhile, it was reported that Iran and Russia had resolved all disagreements over payments for the Bushehr nuclear power plant and that Russia subsequently delivered fuel for the plant. The Bush administration backed Russia's supplying fuel rods to Iran because it meant Iran no longer needed enriched uranium.

In 2007, Iran and Nicaragua restored diplomatic relations and signed extensive trade agreements. Iran also entered into several economic agreements with Venezuela in 2007. A diplomatic dispute with Canada ended in December, when Iran expelled the Canadian ambassador for allegedly "breaching diplomatic protocols." Denmark closed its embassy in Tehran in 2008 following a student protest related to the reprinting in Danish newspapers of a controversial cartoon originally published in 2006 that depicted the prophet Mohammad. Iran had demanded an apology.

Tensions between Iran and the United States heightened in January 2008 amid claims that Iranian speedboats had threatened U.S. Navy ships in international waters in the Strait of Hormuz. The speedboats pulled away just as the navy vessels were about to fire on them, an incident that coincided with President Bush's trip to the Middle East. Meanwhile, in what was described as an "unexpectedly critical" report, the IAEA said that Iran had failed to give clear answers to Western intelligence agencies regarding a military link to its nuclear program. Iran called the allegations "baseless." In May the London-based Institute for Strategic Studies said that Iran's controversial nuclear program had spurred "a wave of interest" in atomic energy across the Middle East, with at least 13 countries already having announced plans to explore nuclear energy or revive existing programs.

Morocco suspended its diplomatic ties with Iran in March 2008 over public comments by an Iranian official that allegedly questioned the sovereignty of Sunni-majority Bahrain. Outrage by Sunni Muslims prompted Moroccan leaders to recall their envoy to Iran.

Meanwhile, Iran's relations with Iraq warmed in March 2008 during President Ahmadinejad's landmark visit to Baghdad, the first time an Iranian leader had traveled there since 1979. (It was also recorded as the first "full-fledged" state visit to Iraq by any foreign head of state since the U.S. invasion in 2003.) Ahmadinejad, in a direct denial of U.S. allegations, said that Iran was not arming Shiite militias in Iraq. Subsequently, the two countries signed several agreements, including some encompassing the development of mining and other industries.

However, Iraq refused a $1 billion Iranian loan for projects to be headed by Iranian firms. In June Iraq's prime minister, Nouri al-Maliki, made a reciprocal visit to Iran.

In May 2008, the United States and Britain were considering what was described as "an overture for wide-ranging political talks" from Iran. The Western allies had renewed their offer of "incentives" if Tehran would suspend uranium enrichment and engage in negotiations on its nuclear program. However, Iran's continued development of its nuclear program, discerned by Israeli intelligence overflights, prompted one Israeli minister to warn that an attack on Iran's nuclear sites was becoming "unavoidable."

The nuclear issue continued to be the focal point of contention between Iran and the West. Following the election of U.S. president Barack Obama, who had sent a conciliatory message to Iran during his campaign, the new administration offered to hold direct talks with Iran, without preconditions. However, U.S. Defense Secretary Robert Gates remained skeptical about the possibility of relations between the two countries, particularly in the aftermath of Iran's successful test launch of a missile capable of striking U.S. and Israeli bases in the Persian Gulf. The test launch resulted in the Italian foreign minister canceling his trip (that same day) to Iran, after Ahmadinejad insisted the two meet at the launch site.

The UN Security Council unanimously adopted a new resolution of concern over the threat of nuclear proliferation and reaffirmed previous resolutions related to the development of Iran's nuclear program in September 2009. In October, Iran agreed to international demands that it allow inspectors at its nuclear site near Qom and begin substantive negotiations regarding its nuclear program. However, observers noted, the supposed agreement came at the same time Iran was allegedly attempting to develop a nuclear warhead.

Tensions heightened with Yemen in November 2009 when the latter accused Iran of supporting antigovernment Huthi rebels as part of its effort to spread Shiite influence throughout the Middle East. The nuclear issue again came to the forefront the same month, when Brazil's president Lula da Silva publicly expressed support for Iran's right to enrich uranium while encouraging authorities to participate in nonproliferation talks. President Hugo Chavez of Venezuela expressed similar support for Iran.

In January 2010, Iran blamed the United States and Israel for the death of an Iranian nuclear scientist after a remote-controlled bomb exploded outside his home. Later that month, President Obama, in his State of the Union address, warned of "growing consequences" if Iran continued to pursue its nuclear program. The United States subsequently announced plans to step up arms sales to friendly regimes in the Gulf region and enhance its military presence there. In February President Ahmadinejad said he supported the October 2009 Geneva agreement that called for Iran to ship some three-quarters of its nuclear fuel to Russia and France for conversion into fuel rods for medical isotopes. However, the deal unraveled, and shortly thereafter, Ahmadinejad ordered Iran's atomic energy agency to begin enriching its uranium to a higher level. Over the next several months, further warnings were issued by the United States; the IAEA reported on what it believed to be Iran's plans to design nuclear warheads and accused Iran of failing to cooperate with inspectors; and President Obama urged China to increase pressure on Iran over its nuclear program. In April, President Ahmadinejad declared that Iran's nuclear path was "irreversible," and in May, delegates from the United States, the United Kingdom, and France walked out on Ahmadinejad's address to the parties to the Nuclear Non-Proliferation Treaty. Iran then formed a new alliance, announcing that it would ship some of its nuclear fuel to Turkey. Subsequently, in June the UN Security Council passed a resolution imposing a fourth round of sanctions on Iran, including an expansion of the arms embargo and greater restrictions on financial and shipping enterprises. Meanwhile, the IAEA reported that Iran had enough stockpiles to make two nuclear weapons if the uranium was further enriched. Further U.S. and EU sanctions were imposed later in June. In September, the Obama administration blacklisted eight Iranian officials for their alleged role in the postelection violence, citing, for the first time, human rights violations. The same month, Ahmadinejad, speaking at the UN, claimed that most people believed the 9/11 terrorist attacks were orchestrated by the U.S. government, prompting the U.S. delegation to walk out and drawing a swift rebuke from President Obama. Ahmadinejad also said he hoped negotiations on swapping enriched uranium could resume in October. Ten days earlier, Iran had released one of three Americans jailed in July 2009 on charges of spying after they allegedly crossed the Iranian border while hiking in northern Iraq.

In late October 2010, Iran yielded to international pressure after suffering the economic consequences of extensive sanctions and agreed to nuclear talks with the EU's foreign policy chief in November. Meanwhile, proposed nuclear talks moved forward as the EU agreed to December 5, one of two dates suggested by Iran. Following failed discussions in January 2011, the United States imposed new sanctions, including against Iran's shipping line and against its Revolutionary Guard.

On December 1, 2011, the EU applied further diplomatic and economic sanctions against Iran because of the country's nuclear program. Meanwhile, on December 4, Iran downed an unmanned U.S. aerial surveillance drone.

One of Iran's leading nuclear scientists was assassinated on January 11, 2012. Iran claimed that Israel was behind the attack. On January 23, EU leaders agreed to phased sanctions on Iranian oil imports, beginning on July 1 (see Current issues, below).

On February 13, 2012, Israeli embassy staff in New Delhi were attacked with an explosive device, wounding one, while a second bomb was detected and defused near the Israeli embassy in Tbilisi. The following day, three Iranians were arrested in a failed bombing of the Israeli embassy in Bangkok. Israel blamed the incidents on Iranian intelligence forces. Also in February, the IAEA reported positive discussions with Iran over its nuclear program and offered to restart negotiations. However, an IAEA team left Iran on February 20, citing an impasse over Iran's refusal to allow inspection of some facilities. Subsequent talks between Iran and world powers in April and June failed to resolve any major issues over Tehran's nuclear program. In August, Iran hosted the Non-Aligned Movement (NAM) summit in Tehran. The location of the meeting was criticized by some human rights groups and international organizations. President Mohammed Morsi became the first Egyptian president to visit Iran since 1979 when he attended the NAM meeting.

On September 3, Bahrain restored diplomatic relations, which had been suspended since 2011, with Iran. However, on September 7, Canada cut diplomatic relations with Iran, describing Tehran as a "threat" to international security. Also in September, the IAEA reported that Iran had doubled the number of centrifuges at one of its enrichment facilities and cited a variety of forms of interference with its efforts to investigate Iran's nuclear program. Meanwhile, Israeli leaders openly speculated about the possibility of a preemptive strike on Iranian nuclear sites. Reports indicated that the United States actively discouraged an Israeli strike and, instead, redoubled diplomatic efforts, while pledging the deployment of an advanced radar system in the region to better protect Israel. The EU announced new sanctions on Iran in October. In December, Iran claimed that it had captured a U.S. aerial drone and was able to reverse engineer the device and construct its own drones.

In January 2013, Iran and Argentina agreed to establish a "truth commission" to investigate the 1994 bombing of a Jewish center in Buenos Aires, an attack widely believed to have been supported by Tehran (see Current issues, below). Negotiations in April between Iran and the permanent members of the UN Security Council, plus Germany (known collectively as the P5+1 Group), failed to achieve any progress on Tehran's nuclear program. Reports in March 2013 alleged that Iran was actively training and arming Syrian rebels. The election of Rouhani in 2013 seemed to offer the potential for a breakthrough on Iran's nuclear program as the new leader adopted a less aggressive stance than his predecessor. On November 24, Iran and the P5+1 reached a temporary agreement whereby Tehran agreed to restrictions on the production of nuclear materials, along with more international inspections and the surrender of some existing equipment and supplies, in exchange for the relaxation of economic sanctions. The accord was hailed by Iran and the West, but criticized by Israel and Gulf states, including Saudi Arabia.

Current issues. Despite increasing oil revenues, Iran's spiraling inflation and widespread unemployment made the economy the most important issue in the 2008 parliamentary elections. President Ahmadinejad's economic policies alienated many conservatives, who split into two main factions: the hard-line supporters of Ahmadinejad (and the Revolutionary Guard), who sought to maintain their hold on parliament; and a broad coalition of principlists, who were aligned with the clerics, Ali Larijani, the former chief nuclear negotiator, and Tehran's mayor, Mohammad Baqer QALIBAF. Reformists, too, were divided, the main coalition including 18 groups allied with former president Khatami and the National Trust Party of former *Majlis* speaker Mehdi Karubi. More than 2,000 candidates from the Reformist Coalition were disqualified by the Council of Guardians, provoking widespread criticism. Similarly, the candidate list of the pro-reform

National Trust Party was reduced by half. Thus conservatives, as expected, won an overwhelming majority of seats following two rounds of voting, though reformists were able to increase their representation somewhat over the number they had held in the outgoing parliament. Independents won a significant number of seats, but since none was reported to have appeared on the lists of any political groups, it was unclear as to which factions they ultimately aligned themselves with in the *Majlis*. According to observers, the parliament, though overwhelmingly conservative, would not be fully supportive of President Ahmadinejad, as the broad principlists were expected to form alliances with pro-reform factions to challenge the administration on economic policies that fueled public discontent. Just prior to the second round of elections, Ahmadinejad dismissed the economic affairs and interior ministers in the wake of severe criticism of their alleged mismanagement and lack of accountability. The reshuffle reportedly marked a further consolidation of the power of the Revolutionary Guard, 12 former members of which were said to hold cabinet posts, while only one cleric retained a ministry title. The *International Herald Tribune* reported the elections as another "triumph for the supreme leader's consolidation of conservative authority," reinforcing Ayatollah Khamenei's claims of "political hegemony."

Tensions between parliament and Ahmadinejad heightened in late 2008, as the replacement interior minister was impeached in an episode reported by the *Washington Post* as a "tumultuous parliamentary session broadcast live on Iranian state radio. He caused a storm by linking the lawmakers opposing him to foreign groups and anti-Iranian governments, often referred to here as 'the enemy.'" Ahmadinejad, for his part, said the impeachment (over false education credentials) was illegal and "unfair." The ousted interior minister was the tenth to resign or be impeached since Ahmadinejad was elected in 2005.

Attention soon turned to the 2009 presidential election, amid growing public dissatisfaction with the economic policies of the Ahmadinejad administration, as unemployment and inflation continued to soar, along with prices, especially gas and housing. Meanwhile, major increases in state spending—particularly on the nation's nuclear program, with little domestic benefit, and increasing civil service wages and pensions ahead of the election—and Ahmadinejad's unpopular remarks about Israel and his denial of the Holocaust turned a significant portion of the population against him, according to observers. In March, a political moderate who had not been active in politics for 20 years, former prime minister Mir Hosein Musavi, announced his candidacy for the June election. He gained the support of many reformists after their candidate, Mohammad Reza Khatami, former deputy speaker of parliament and a leader of the Islamic Iran Participation Front (*Jebhe-ye Mosharekat-e Iran-e Eslami*—IIPF), withdrew. (Khatami, who had only reluctantly become a candidate when pressured by reformists, stepped down to support Musavi.) While a few conservatives announced their endorsement of Musavi, most of his backers were avid reformists, though Musavi reportedly did not characterize himself as such. However, he campaigned on a platform of greater personal freedom and women's rights and was said to be trying to gain ground with conservatives who had become disillusioned with Ahmadinejad. Two other challengers also entered the race: Mohsen REZAI, former commander of the Revolutionary Guard, described as an independent conservative, and former *Majlis* speaker and reformist Mehdi Karubi of the National Trust Party. As the challengers began increasingly to use the online social networking site Facebook, the government on May 23 blocked the site, though it subsequently lifted the ban in response to public outcry. That same month Ayatollah Khamenei urged the populace not to vote for pro-Western candidates (i.e., the reformists). Meanwhile, in the midst of the presidential campaign, Iran successfully test-fired a medium-range missile capable of striking as far as Israel and U.S. bases in the Persian Gulf, according to news reports.

Immediately following the 2009 election, which Ahmadinejad won with nearly 63 percent of the vote on an inordinately high turnout of 85 percent, according to official government results, Musavi denounced the outcome, claiming widespread fraud. The other two challengers also questioned the official outcome, alleging widespread abuses and vote rigging. As soon as the official results were announced (and subsequently confirmed by Ayatollah Khamenei), mass demonstrations erupted in Tehran and across the country, overwhelmingly by supporters of Musavi. The protests resulted in violent clashes with police and plainclothes paramilitary Basiji and the arrest of more than 100 members of reformist groups who were charged with having organized the protests. Meanwhile, shortly before a victory rally for the president, Ahmadinejad praised the outcome of the election as "very accurate." Despite the president's remarks, reports surfaced of a crackdown on independent media in the country, as well as restrictions on mobile phone use for calls and text messaging, measures designed to prevent the organization of further demonstrations. As the protests were unfolding, Musavi and Mohammad Reza Khatami, brother of the former president, were said to have been taken into custody at their homes by security forces. Subsequently, challenger Mohsen Rezai, who won just 1.73 percent of the vote, and former speaker of parliament Ali Larijani, expressed their support for Ahmadinejad.

Within days of the initial protests in June 2009, the administration banned international media from covering demonstrations in Tehran after video was aired that showed police battling with supporters of Musavi. Meanwhile, news reports said Iranian television aired rallies in favor of Ahmadinejad. As protests continued for several weeks, there were reports of journalists being beaten, and amateur video captured the shooting death of one female protester, prompting further international condemnation. In Tehran, stores closed, universities suspended classes, and security forces hurled tear gas inside Musavi's campaign headquarters. An estimated 250 demonstrators were reported killed, and some 500 journalists, protesters, and government officials were arrested. On June 29 the Guardian Council of 12 clerics appointed to oversee elections dismissed all complaints and confirmed the official results.

While international officials and human rights organizations denounced the violence, the initial response to the 2009 election results was generally muted. Secretary of State Hillary Clinton said that the United States hoped the election reflected "the genuine will and desire" of the Iranian people (though weeks later, President Obama said he was appalled and outraged by the violence in Iran). The Iranian government, for its part, accused Great Britain, the United States, and other Western nations of fueling the protests and otherwise interfering in Iran's affairs. The EU "categorically rejected" all such allegations. Subsequently, Iran arrested several British embassy employees but later began releasing some of them.

In the weeks after the election, demonstrations continued to be met with resistance by security police, and the elite Revolutionary Guard was said by the *New York Times* to have emerged "as a driving force behind efforts to crush a still-defiant opposition movement." On July 16, 2009, President Ahmadinejad named minister Esfandyar Rahim Mashaee, his son-in-law, as first vice president, angering conservatives because of remarks Mashaee made in 2008 indicating that Iran was friends with Israel. Further, Ahmadinejad showed "rare defiance" to Supreme Leader Ayatollah Khamenei, the president's foremost defender following the controversial election, by refusing to dismiss Mashaee as Khamenei ordered. The president's refusal to obey marked a major rift among the hard-line conservatives, according to analysts, who said Ahmadinejad feared the hard-liners would try to exert power over the government. Meanwhile, leaders in parliament said the legislature planned to force Ahmadinejad to replace Mashaee. Ultimately, however, Ahmadinejad relented and accepted Mashaee's resignation on July 24. A further rift developed between Khamenei, backed by the Revolutionary Guard and the hard-line clerics, and cleric and former president Ali Akbar Hashemi Rafsanjani, who delivered a sermon criticizing officials' handling of the postelection crisis. Rafsanjani thus "reignited the opposition, emerging as its leading patron," according to the Associated Press. During the president's inauguration on August 5, hundreds protested outside the *Majlis,* while inside the ceremony was boycotted by numerous senior leaders, including former president Rafsanjani and presidential challengers Khatami and Musavi, the latter having declared Ahamdinejad's government illegitimate. Four days later, a Revolutionary Guard commander called for the arrest of Musavi and Khatami, claiming they were behind the "soft revolution." Musavi, who subsequently formed a new political movement, the Green Path of Hope (see Political Parties and Groups, below) and Khatami fueled further tensions when they denounced what they claimed were the "show trials" of political dissidents charged with stirring up antigovernment sentiment following the elections. They accused the government of torture (which the police chief confirmed) and using forced confessions. In televised trials on August 25, a prosecutor called for "full punishment" to be handed down against reformist Saeed HAJARIAN of the IIPF. Meanwhile, following more protests against the government for shutting down a reformist newspaper, the new head of the judiciary vowed to prosecute those who had tortured detainees arrested in the postelection crackdown. Ahmadinejad subsequently promoted legal and parliamentary affairs vice president Mohammad Reza Rahimi as first vice president. Meanwhile, many of the president's ministerial nominations were rejected by parliament, which observers attributed to the president reportedly having filled the list with "inexperienced cronies" while removing all critics. Ultimately, a cabinet of hard-liners was approved, according to observers. One of the president's most controversial appointments, Defense Minister Ahmad VAHIDI, had been accused of planning the 1994 bombing of a Jewish center in Buenos Aires that killed 85 people. Iran denied any involvement.

Violence erupted again in December 2009 during antigovernment protests across the country on the Ashura holiday when 13 people were killed and some 1,500 reportedly arrested, including several opposition leaders and a nephew of Musavi. The arrests prompted an angry rebuke by Karubi, who had also been attacked by security forces.

Addressing the postelection violence of the previous year, a parliamentary committee issued a report in January 2010 acknowledging that official abuses had occurred and stating that the deaths of three detainees was a result of overcrowding and other poor conditions inside the prison. Further, the report blamed the former chief prosecutor, an ally of President Ahmadinejad, for the deaths. Also in January, in the wake of an announcement that several foreign nationals were among those arrested in the previous month's protests, intelligence officials banned Iranians from having any contact with some 60 international organizations, including the Voice of America. On January 28, two people who had been sentenced to death following the postelection protests were executed by hanging. The two men had been found guilty of belonging to an outlawed monarchist group, the Kingdom Assembly of Iran. Shortly thereafter, death sentences were announced for another five protesters who were arrested in December 2009.

While Iran's nuclear program dominated the international airwaves throughout the first part of 2010, other concerns received domestic attention when, in March, the regime revoked the license of a reformist newspaper that supported the views of Musavi, who aired a video message online calling for a "year of resistance" against the government. Musavi accused the regime of violating the constitution and destroying the economy. Meanwhile, the government announced death sentences for six more people arrested in December 2009. In May, a former minister, who had served in government in the early 2000s and was recently reported to have been aligned with Musavi's new Green political movement, was seriously wounded in an attack at his university office. Subsequently, in a move observers said was meant to mollify the Green movement on the anniversary of the June 2009 postelection violence, Supreme Leader Ayatollah Khamenei commuted the sentences of 85 protesters who had been convicted on charges related to those demonstrations. Days later, a rally of a few thousand Green supporters in Tehran was reported to have been outnumbered by security forces and disbanded without violence. Another execution took place on June 20, this time of the leader of a Sunni insurgent group who had been found guilty of plotting terrorist attacks with the alleged involvement of the United States, Britain, and Pakistan. The group, known as the Soldiers of God, claimed responsibility for killing Revolutionary Guard commanders and other Iranians in fighting at Iran's border with Pakistan and Afghanistan.

The regime stepped up pressure on the opposition in September 2010 when officials raided Musavi's office and seized his computers and other property. It was also reported that the Basiji militia attacked the home of Musavi's Green movement colleague, Karubi. The two reformists, who claimed the 2009 presidential election was fraudulent, were accused of inciting postelection protests, and their case was set for trial. Shortly thereafter, and one day after President Ahmadinejad had defended Iran's record of allowing dissent, two journalists were sentenced to six years in jail on charges of "propaganda against the state" and "inciting public opinion." An online blogger was sentenced to death for allegedly insulting the supreme leader.

Tensions heightened in 2011 as Musavi and Karubi sought permission in February to hold a rally in support of civil uprisings in Tunisia and Egypt. Thousands of backers used social networking sites to promote a demonstration on February 14, but on February 9, the state prosecutor refused to allow any such rally and warned of repercussions if demonstrators went ahead with their plans, even though the Ayatollah and other government officials had pronounced their support for the uprisings elsewhere (unless they were pro–United States). In the interim, hundreds of thousands of people demonstrated in Tehran on February 11 to mark the 23rd anniversary of the Islamic Revolution. Some 20,000 demonstrators turned out on February 14, despite threats from the Revolutionary Guard, and many protesters were beaten. Musavi and Karubi were arrested ahead of the event and prevented from attending. A day later, 222 members of parliament issued a statement condemning the leaders of the Green movement, calling for their trial and execution. In March, security forces clashed with demonstrators who were protesting the arrests of the Green movement's leaders. Several days later it was reported that regime loyalists cracked down further by removing former president Rafsanjani as chair of the Assembly of Experts, a post he had held for nearly four years. Observers said he was replaced by "a moderate conservative." The struggle for power among conservative factions in the government emerged in May when Ahmadinejad's attempt to dismiss the intelligence minister was blocked by the Ayatollah. Later that same month, the president was forced out of his plan to assume the post of oil minister on a caretaker basis—in time to preside over an OPEC meeting.

Iran's ability to enrich uranium, leading to the development of nuclear weapons, continued to be of great concern as in June 2011 government officials said they would speed up uranium production. This came despite new sanctions imposed by the United States and repeated calls by the UN to cease all enrichment. Iranian authorities continued to maintain that the entire effort was for peaceful purposes.

A $2.8 billion financial scandal led to resignations and arrests of 32 leading economic and political figures in October 2011, many of whom were allies of Ahmadinejad. Following the imposition of new sanctions by the UK (and other Western powers) on Iran because of the country's nuclear program, the Iranian parliament voted to downgrade diplomatic relations with the UK on November 27, 2011. Two days later, protestors stormed the British embassy in Tehran. The next day, the UK evacuated all diplomatic personnel from Iran, ordered the Iranian embassy in London closed, and expelled all Iranian diplomats.

After the EU announced restrictions on Iranian oil imports in January 2012, desperate Iranians endeavored to convert rials into dollars and euros. The value of the Iranian currency dropped by 50 percent, forcing the government to officially devalue the rial. A further devaluation occurred in August. Meanwhile, on January 3, Faezah Hashemi RAFSANJANI, daughter of the former president, was sentenced to six months in prison for spreading "propaganda" critical of the regime. Mahdi Hashemi Rafsanjani, the son of the former president, was also reportedly detained after he returned to Iran following three years in exile in the United Kingdom.

Prior to parliamentary elections on March 2, reports indicated that more than 1,500 reformist candidates were denied registration by the Council of Guardians. Consequently, many reformists groups boycotted the balloting. Allies of Khamenei swept the balloting. Also in March, Amnesty International reported that Iran had increased its use of capital punishment, executing at least 360 in 2011 for various offences.

Reports in October 2012 indicated the growing impact of international sanctions on Iran. The value of the rial dropped to a record low, while inflation continued to accelerate, officially rising past 25 percent, with speculation that the real rate was above 50 percent. Demonstrators protesting the deteriorating economy clashed with police in Tehran on October 3, leaving scores wounded and 16 arrested.

Tensions between Ahmadinejad and the legislature increased significantly throughout the final months of 2012 and into 2013. In October, Ahmadinejad publically denounced Sadeq LARIJANI for refusing to allow the president to visit Evin Prison where his press advisor, Ali Akbar JAVANFEKR was incarcerated. The president also suggested that Larijani was protecting his brother, Ali LARIJANI, the speaker of the Majlis, from prosecution on corruption charges. In January 2013, the Majlis voted to investigate the Central Bank. Concurrently, Ahmadinejad ally and Central Bank Governor Mahmoud BAHMANI was asked to resign. Ahmadinejad was called before the legislature to answer questions on the economy in January 2013.

A major earthquake on April 9, 2013, struck near Bushehr, the site of a nuclear plant, killing 32 and injuring hundreds. The government rejected reports that the nuclear facility had been damaged.

Prior to presidential balloting on June 14, 2013, the Guardian Council reviewed 680 candidates who had filed to run. The Council approved eight, but two later withdrew. Moderate Hassan Rouhani won the balloting with 50.9 percent of the vote. The surprise election of Rouhani reflected public dissatisfaction with Ahmadinejad's stance on the nuclear issue and his management of the economy.

POLITICAL PARTIES AND GROUPS

Although political parties are permitted under the constitution, none was recognized following the formal dissolution of the government-sponsored Islamic Republican Party in June 1987, despite Tehran's announcement in October 1988 that such groupings would thenceforth be welcomed if they "demonstrated commitment to the Islamic system."

A number of new political formations were identifiable during the *Majlis* elections of 1996, although it was carefully noted by the government that they were not official parties. Meanwhile, some former parties appeared to remain informally tolerated. Supporters of President Mohammad Khatami were reported in 1998 to have achieved recognition as the first full-fledged political party since the 1979 revolution (see Islamic Iran Solidarity Party, below), and several others also subsequently achieved legal status. However, the main political formations have continued to be organizations acting in a "pseudo-party" capacity by, among other things, presenting candidate lists for legislative elections without having sought formal party registration. Political parties in Iran tend to operate as small clubs, personal platforms, or loosely defined ideological associations rather than as large organizations with grassroots networks or formal, disciplined structures. Membership in one does not preclude membership in another, and the associations tend to lack detailed policy manifestos. Some appear before an election and quickly fade afterward.

Though many of the candidates contesting the 2008 *Majlis* elections ran as independents, four main lists of candidates were presented by two conservative and two reformist groupings. The conservative United Fundamentalist Front (also known as the United Principalist Front or the United Front of Conservatives) was led by deputy *Majlis* speaker Reza BAHONAR and speaker Gholam-Ali Haddad-Adel, both leaders of the Builders of an Islamic Iran Council. The group was comprised largely of staunch supporters of President Ahmadinejad. The other conservative grouping, the Inclusive Fundamentalist Coalition (or Broad Principalist Coalition), included those opposed to the president's economic and foreign policies, aligned with Ali Larijani, the former chief nuclear negotiator and former speaker of parliament; clerics; and the mayor of Tehran, Mohammad Baqer Qalibaf. The Reformists Coalition, led by Mohammad SALAMATI of the Islamic Revolution Mujaheddin Organization, included 18 groups allied with former president Khatami. The reformist National Trust Party, led by former *Majlis* speaker Mehdi Karubi, included a number of candidates who were also allied with the Reformists Coalition. A Nationwide Coalition of Independent Candidates was also established in February 2008.

In 2009, the Guardian Council approved only four of the 476 potential candidates, men and women, for the June presidential election. Reformists were inclined to back former prime minister Mir Hosein Musavi, along with some conservatives who became increasingly angry with Ahmadinejad over his domestic policies and inflammatory rhetoric.

In the 2012 *Majlis* election, conservatives formed five broad coalitions. Two pro-Khamenei coalitions emerged: the United Front of Conservatives (UFC) and the Insight and Islamic Awakening Front. The Front of Stability of the Islamic Revolution, formed in 2011, and the Monotheism and Justice Party were made up primarily of Ahmadinejad's supporters. The other conservative group was the moderate People's Voice, led by Ali MOTAHARI. Reformists were divided among the Democratic Coalition of Reformists, the Labor Coalition, and the Moderate Reformists.

Builders of an Islamic Iran Council (*Etelaf-e Abadgaran-e Iran-e Eslami*). This group, whose name is also translated as Developers of an Islamic Iran Council, first emerged in the local elections of February 2003, presenting largely unknown, younger candidates on the Tehran ballot with strong backing from senior conservatives in the political establishment. The party won control of the Tehran city council, which had been paralyzed by feuds among reformist council members. The council elected Mahmoud Ahmadinejad as mayor. The group in some cases operated under alternative names outside of Tehran. Employing vague slogans calling for economic progress and adherence to "Islamic values," the party launched a well-financed campaign for the 2004 parliamentary elections. With more than 2,300 reformist candidates barred from appearing on the ballot, the group secured a large majority of at least 195 seats in the *Majlis*. Divisions and defections have emerged within the party's bloc in parliament, sharply reducing the number of seats held by the party, although not affecting the overall conservative majority. A significant number of the newly elected MPs included former officers in the Revolutionary Guards. The most powerful figure in the party has been Gholam-Ali Haddad-Adel, son-in-law of the supreme leader, who was selected speaker of the *Majlis*. The group originally endorsed Mohammad Baqer Qalibaf, the former chief of police forces, before the first round of the 2005 presidential elections, but later backed Ahmadinejad in his successful bid. Although encompassing a range of views on economic policy but without a clear ideological vision, the group has become the most prominent conservative party, at least in the public arena.

The party has drawn membership from the Society of Islamic Engineers, which has roots in traditional conservative circles and helped publicize the Builders of an Islamic Iran Council (Ahmadinejad comes from the society). Following their election, the party's MPs adopted strident, populist language; impeached Khatami's transport minister; urged an uncompromising stance on the nuclear issue; and adopted measures hostile to foreign investment. The party has been widely perceived as a vehicle for the supreme leader, with the supreme leader's son, Mojtaba Khamenei, allegedly playing an influential role in the party.

In the run-up to the 2008 parliamentary elections, the conservatives were divided between the party's hardline supporters of President Ahmadinejad and others who opposed his economic policies and brash approach to international issues. The party subsequently participated in the United Fundamentalist Front, which won 69 percent of the *Majlis* seats. Though Ahmadinejad has been recognized as a member of this group, he ran for president in 2009 as an independent. In the 2012 elections, the party was divided between supporters of the president and those of the Ayatollah. In 2013, the party supported conservative candidate, Saeed JALILI, who placed third in the balloting.

Leaders: Mahmoud AHMADINEJAD (Former President of the Republic), Mehdi CHAMRAN (Party President), Gholam-Ali HADDAD-ADEL (Former Speaker of the *Majlis*), Nasrin SOLTANKHAH (Deputy Chair).

Society of Combatant Clergy (*Jame'e Rohaniat Mobarez*—JRM). This hard-line, conservative group has continued to exert influence within the political establishment, although, like other older conservative groups, it has been overshadowed on the public stage by the Builders of an Islamic Iran Council. Along with the Islamic Coalition Society (see below), the group vehemently opposed the reformist agenda and has remained committed to perpetuating the country's rigid political and cultural restrictions. With strong ties to the clergy, the party sees Iran as representing the interests of the Islamic world.

The JRM was formed in late the 1970s in support of the then-exiled Ayatollah Khomeini. (The JRM has often been referenced, as it was in recent *Handbooks,* as the Association of Combatant Clergy. The JRM abbreviation and translation of "Jame'e" as "society" has been adopted for this edition of the *Handbook* in order to assist the reader in differentiating between the conservative JRM and its influential moderate offshoot, the Assembly of Combatant Clergy [see MRM, below]. Readers are cautioned to assess news reports carefully, as the two groupings are routinely confused because of the similarity of their names.) The JRM served as the primary vehicle for clerical political representation following the installation of Khomeini as the nation's leader in 1979, with the JRM and Servants of Construction (SC) considered breakaway groups. Although the JRM essentially concurred with the SC in the mid-1990s regarding proposed economic reform, it argued that ultimate political authority should remain with the nation's religious leaders, adopting a conservative stance on such issues as proposed expanded press freedoms and reinstitution of a formal party system.

As of late 1995, the society was believed to control about 150 seats in the *Majlis*, giving it significant policy influence under the leadership of Speaker Ali Akbar Nateq-Nuri. Having apparently done poorly in the first round of voting for the new *Majlis* in March 1996, the JRM adopted a hard-line approach for the second round, denouncing "liberals" as a threat to the ideals of the 1979 revolution. According to a number of observers, that campaign was assisted by *Hezbollah* militants, who, among other things, reportedly disrupted meetings of "un-Islamic" groupings.

It was subsequently estimated that society supporters had secured about 110 seats in the new *Majlis* in 1996. Although this represented the loss of its former "overall majority," the JRM was nevertheless able to secure the reelection of Nateq-Nuri as speaker by a reported vote of 146–105. JRM adherents later served as the core of the new *Hezbollah* faction in the *Majlis,* with Nateq-Nuri unsuccessfully carrying the standard of the conservative clerics in the May 1997 presidential election. He received 7.2 million votes to 20 million for the victorious Mohammad Khatami. However, Nateq-Nuri was reelected as *Majlis* speaker in both 1997 and 1998. The JRM was not widely referenced in regard to the 1999 municipal balloting. Many of its 2000 *Majlis* candidates were presented in conjunction with the Islamic Coalition Society. The JRM did not endorse a candidate in the 2001 presidential balloting, thereby diluting the conservatives' chances of mounting an effective challenge to President Khatami. In the 2005 presidential elections, the group initially backed Ali Larijani, former director of the state television and radio monopoly and former chief nuclear negotiator, prompting criticism from Ahmadinejad's supporters that the group was causing divisions within the conservative camp.

By 2007, rifts reportedly had developed among some progovernment factions, with Nateq-Nuri criticized for not being conservative enough. In March, Nateq-Nuri said that he would not be a candidate in any election. In June 2008 Nateq-Nuri was detained by Iranian authorities for allegedly accusing some clerics of corruption.

In the run-up to the 2009 presidential election, a rift reportedly developed between Nateq-Nuri and group leader Mohammad Reza Mahdavi-Kani, with the former remaining silent on the candidacy of Ahmadinejad, while the latter spoke out in support of the president. Mahdavi-Kani's declaration angered members in the wake of an official vote that failed to reach the threshold for its public pronouncement of support for Ahmadinejad. Other members turned against the Ahmadinejad administration in the wake of soaring housing and gas prices and double-digit inflation. In October 2009, a cleric agreed to mediate the dispute between the factions. In 2011, Mahdavi-Kani was elected chair of the Assembly of Experts. In the 2012 parliamentary elections, the JRM was part of the UFC. JRM moderate Hassan Rouhani has won the 2013 presidential elections, although some hardliners in the party supported more conservative candidates.

Leaders: Hassan ROUHANI (President of the Republic), Ali Akbar NATEQ-NURI (Former Speaker of the *Majlis*), Assadollah BADAMCHIAN, Mohammad Reza MAHDAVI-KANI (Founder), Hojatoleslam Jafar SHOJOUNI (General Secretary).

Islamic Coalition Society (*Jameyat-e Motalefe-ye Eslami*). An umbrella organization of hard-line conservative clerics and merchants with links to the late Ayatollah Khomeini, the Islamic Coalition Society is influential in the judiciary as well as the quasi-charitable foundations that, having originally been formed to aid war victims and the poor, now control much of the non-oil economic sector. Although consensus within the society opposes political liberalization, there reportedly has been factionalization concerning economic reform, which is endorsed by some of the business community. In the 2005 presidential elections, the party initially backed Ali Larijani but later withdrew its support in favor of Ahmadinejad, reportedly on the orders of the office of the supreme leader.

In the 2006 Assembly of Experts elections, the party supported candidates of the Society of Combatant Clergy. In advance of the 2008 parliamentary elections, the party backed the candidate list of the United Fundamentalist Front.

In the 2009 presidential election, the party supported Ahmadinejad.

In 2010 party secretary general Mohammad Nabi Habibi backed the idea of political parties in the country, saying that political groups should become parties only when they have laid down a platform of specific plans and ideas. The party was one of the pro-Ahmadinejad groupings in the 2012 parliamentary balloting. The party's 2013 presidential candidate was Ali Akbar VELAYATI, who received 6.2 percent of the vote.

Leaders: Hamid Reza TARAQQI, Habibollah ASGAROWLADI (Former Commerce Minister), Assadollah BADAMCHIAN (Deputy Secretary General), Mohammad Nabi HABIBI (Secretary General).

Islamic Iran Development and Justice Party (IIDJP). The principlist grouping held its first congress on December 13, 2007, with a stated goal of increasing public participation in politics. Concerns about unemployment, inflation, and social ills led to the formation of the party in the run-up to the 2008 parliamentary election, with party leaders expressing their support for Ali Larijani, who subsequently won a seat. In the 2009 presidential election, the party supported independent conservative Mohsen Rezai.

Leaders: Kamal DANESHYAR, Amir Ali AMIRI, Reza TALAINIK (Secretary General).

May 23 Movement. Prior to the reformist victory in the parliamentary elections of 2000, some 20 parties and organizations (including important student organizations) committed to political reform and broadly supportive of President Khatami formed the May 23 Movement. (The coalition was named in honor of Khatami's election victory, which occurred on May 23, 1997; it is also known as the Second Khordad Movement [or Front], the second day of the month of Khordad in the Iranian calendar corresponding to May 23.) Once in power, serious divisions within the coalition emerged, as reformists argued over how to respond to the successive vetoes of parliamentary bills and measures stifling dissent and press freedom. The coalition failed to agree on a unified candidate list in Tehran for the 2003 local elections. During the disputed 2004 parliamentary elections, members of the coalition were deeply divided over whether to boycott the vote or to participate in hopes of limiting the size of a conservative victory. Although the coalition leaders continued to hold meetings, they could not reach agreement on a single, reformist candidate for the 2005 presidential elections, splitting reformist votes during the first round. One of the group's early leaders, Abbas Abdi, was said to be among the most influential reformists in Iran. Abdi was also reported to be the first person to storm the U.S. embassy in Tehran, leading other students in the 1979 takeover and hostage crisis. Abdi subsequently joined the IIPF (below).

Islamic Iran Participation Front (*Jebhe-ye Mosharekat-e Iran-e Eslami*—IIPF). Established in December 1998 by pro-Khatami forces, the IIPF presented candidates in the 1999 municipal elections, some in coalition with the SC (below). For the 2000 *Majlis* balloting, it served as a core component of the May 23 Movement, subsequently reporting that approximately 80 of its members had been elected. The IIPF is led by Mohammad Reza Khatami, the brother of former president Khatami. Several senior members of the party had been involved as student activists in the seizure of the U.S. embassy in 1979 but have since evolved into proponents of liberal democratic change. After the 2000 elections, members of the IIPF were the most outspoken advocates for sweeping reforms, arguing as cabinet ministers and MPs for greater media freedom, cultural openness, women's rights, environmental safeguards, and engagement with Western governments. Regarding economic policy, some elements of the IIPF and other reformists remain reluctant to embrace market reform measures.

Some prominent members of the party were targeted and harassed by the conservative judiciary, paramilitaries, and parallel security services. Abbas Abdi, who formerly was reported to have been a leader in the May 23 Movement (above) and among those who stormed the U.S. embassy in Tehran in 1979, was sentenced to four years in prison after publishing a poll in October 2002 showing a majority of Iranians supporting dialogue with the United States. Judges closed newspapers sponsored by the party, including *Sobh-e Emrooz*. Its editor, Saeed Hajarian, was a senior adviser to President Khatami when Khatami was shot and nearly killed in an assassination attempt in 2000. Hard-line paramilitaries sometimes broke up IIPF rallies and events. Frustrated with the obstruction of the Council of Guardians and judicial repression, IIPF members lobbied to confront the conservatives, advocating that Khatami resign or hold a referendum, but the president refused. By the end of Khatami's second term, the IIPF had concluded that reform within the parameters of the current system was unattainable and that the constitutional framework had to be amended to deliver genuine parliamentary democracy. During the crisis preceding the 2004 elections, in which most IIPF candidates were banned from appearing on the ballot, IIPF leaders wrote an unprecedented open letter to the supreme leader questioning the legitimacy of his rule and warning of a betrayal of the revolution. Out of power, some members turned to promoting new civil society groups and civic education efforts. The party also sought to reach out to liberal activists in the banned but tolerated Liberation Movement of Iran led by Ibrahim YAZDI (see below). The party supported Mostafa Moin, former minister of scientific research in Khatami's cabinet, in the first round of the 2005 presidential elections. In the second round, the party endorsed Rafsanjani, largely as a vote against the conservative Ahmadinejad.

In 2007, divisions were reported over attempts to form a reformist coalition in advance of the 2008 *Majlis* election. However, following the government's barring most of the party's members from contesting the election, the IIPF participated in the Reformists Coalition, backing its list of candidates.

In 2009, the IIPF backed Mir Hosein Musavi for president, though Abbas Abdi was said to have been an adviser to presidential challenger Mehdi Karubi of the National Trust Party (below). Following the disputed election, during a period of mass protests, reports surfaced that police had stormed IIPF party headquarters and had arrested several people, including Saeed Hajarian, Mohsen Mirdamadi, and Mohammad Reza Khatami, who was later released. Claiming the confessions had been coerced, the group condemned the arrests and called on the government to release all political prisoners.

The party's license was revoked in April 2010, and Mirdamadi was returned to prison in May. In September the IIPF and the IRMO were officially banned by the judiciary. Several members of the IIPF joined the opposition call for a boycott of the 2012 legislative election. Mohammad-Reza AREF of the IIPF was a presidential candidate for the 2013 elections but withdrew from the campaign. The IIPF and Aref subsequently endorsed Rouhani in the balloting.

Leaders: Mohammad Reza KHATAMI (Former Deputy Speaker of the *Majlis*), Saeed HAJARIAN, Seyyed Safdar HOSEYNI, Azar MANSURI, Abbas ABDI, Mohsen MIRDAMADI (Secretary General), Abdollah RAMEZANZADEH (Deputy Secretary General).

Islamic Revolution Mujaheddin Organization (IRMO). Described by some observers as the "third major grouping" (after the JRM and the SC) during the 1996 *Majlis* campaign, IRMO was supported by a number of leftist organizations and former parties. It was reportedly aligned to a certain degree with the SC in 1996, although its support was considered "feeble" in contrast to *Hezbollah*'s efforts on behalf of the SC's main rival, the JRM. IRMO supported Mohammad Khatami in the 1997 presidential election and served as one of the most liberal components of the May 23 Movement in the 2000 *Majlis* balloting. Although it supported Khatami in his reelection effort in 2001, IRMO subsequently distanced itself from the government by insisting upon more active resistance to the antireform influence of conservative clerics.

A prominent member of the party, university academic Hashem Aghajari, was convicted of apostasy and sentenced to death in November 2002 for a speech in which he questioned absolute clerical authority and called on Iranians to interpret the Koran for themselves. Following student demonstrations, the supreme leader intervened, ordering the courts to lift the death penalty. Aghajari was later sentenced to a five-year prison term. In the 2005 presidential elections, IRMO supported Mostafa Moin.

Most, if not all, of the party's candidates were reportedly among the thousands of reformists disqualified by the government prior to the 2008 parliamentary elections. Following the 2009 presidential election, IRMO leaders urged unsuccessful independent challenger Mir Hosein Musavi, whom the party supported, to form a new political party (see Green Path of Hope, below).

The party vowed to appeal the government's April 2010 revocation of its license, in which the minister of interior accused the IRMO and the IIPP of spreading rumors, plotting to create differences in the country, and violating Islamic standards, among other things. In September the court officially ordered the group to be dissolved.

Leaders: Behzad NABAVI (Former Deputy Speaker of the *Majlis*), Mohsen ARMIN (Spokesperson), Mohammad SALAMATI (Secretary General).

Islamic Labor Party (ILP). An outgrowth of a workers' movement launched in the 1980s in opposition to Marxist groups, the ILP reported that 15 of its members had been elected to the *Majlis* in 2000 as part of the May 23 Movement. ILP leader Ali Reza Mahjoub is also head of the House of Workers, the nation's primary federation of unions. One of the few well-known reformists to return to the *Majlis* in 2005 balloting, Mahjoub managed to win a seat in the new parliament, representing a Tehran district (determined in a third round of voting that coincided with the first round of presidential polling on June 17).

In 2007, the party participated in protests demanding job security and rights for workers, including the right to form unions; it subsequently joined the Reformists Coalition in advance of the 2008 parliamentary elections. In the run-up to the 2009 presidential election, the ILP was among several reformist parties that pressed for a single candidate to represent their interests. The ILP formed the Labor Coalition ahead of the 2012 balloting. The Coalition elected Hossein Kamali as its presidential candidate in November 2012, but he withdrew in May 2013. The grouping subsequently supported Rouhani in the presidential balloting.

Leaders: Ali Reza MAHJOUB, Abolqasem SARHADIZADEH, Hossein KAMALI (Secretary General).

Assembly of Combatant Clergy (*Majma' Ruhaniun Mobarez*—MRM). The MRM was launched in 1988 by members of the Society of Combatant Clergy (JRM) who split from the parent group because of their objections over the JRM's unwillingness to support political liberalization. (The MRM was referenced as the Assembly of Militant Clerics in the 1999 *Handbook,* and its name has been routinely translated in news reports as the Association of Militant Clerics [or Clergy], the League of Militant Clerics, and other variations. See the section on the JRM, above, for an explanation of the naming conventions adopted for this edition of the *Handbook* to assist in identifying the two groups.)

Members of the MRM were prominent in the reformists' victory in 1988 *Majlis* balloting, although their influence declined following the 1992 balloting. The MRM returned to center stage on the political front with the surprise presidential victory in 1997 by MRM member Mohammad Khatami, who had been eased out of his position as minister of Islamic culture in 1992 after critics accused him of maintaining too liberal a stance regarding Western influences. A member of the May 23 Movement in the 2000 *Majlis* balloting, the MRM currently serves as one of the primary moderate groupings within the reform movement.

Within the May 23 Movement, the MRM favored a more gradualist approach to reform, seeking to work solely within the confines of the theocratic system and avoid antagonizing conservative institutions. The MRM opposed boycotting the 2004 elections and supported a rival presidential candidate in the 2005 presidential elections, backing party leader Mehdi Karubi instead of the IIPF's Mostafa Moin. After losing in the first round of the election and alleging fraud, Karubi resigned as the organization's secretary general to form his own party (see the National Trust, below). The MRM elected Mohammad Khatami to head its Central Council on August 8, 2005, days after he completed his second and final four-year term as president. Khatami has been associated with the party since the 1980s.

In 2008, MRM leader Seyyed Abdolvahed Musavi-Lari had a key role in the Reformists Coalition prior to the parliamentary elections. Khatami, for his part, announced that he would not be a candidate. In April Khatami announced that he was retiring from political activity, but he later decided to contest the 2009 presidential election. However, he withdrew in March 2009 to support Mir Hosein Musavi. In April, the MRM voted against backing Ahmadinejad, due to a "variety of criticisms" against the president, according to the group's spokesperson.

In 2010, Khatami urged reformists to abandon the Green movement (below), claiming leaders Karubi and Musavi had "stained the Reformists Front's integrity in a huge way." Khatami called for a boycott of the 2012 parliamentary elections.

Leaders: Seyyed Abdolvahed MUSAVI-LARI, Gholamreza MESBAHI (Spokesperson), Mohammad KHATAMI (Secretary General).

National Trust Party (*Etemaad-e Melli*). Shortly after the 2005 presidential election, Mehdi Karubi, former parliamentary speaker and former leader of the MRM, registered the National Trust as a new party. Party founders included Rassoul MONTAJABNIYA, a former prominent member of the Assembly of Combatant Clergy, and Reza HAJATI, a former student activist. Karubi also owns a newspaper that carries the party's name.

The reformist National Trust Party, which reportedly was allowed to field candidates for 55 percent of the seats in the 2008 parliamentary election, initially rejected overtures to join the Reformists Coalition formed in advance of the balloting. However, following its unsuccessful bid in the first round in March, the National Trust Party joined the Reformists Coalition for the second round in April. The loose coalition also included the **Democracy Party** (*Mardom Salari*), led by Mostafa KAVAKEBIAN.

In the run-up to the 2009 presidential election, a rift developed between the National Trust Party and backers of former president Khatami. Party leader Mehdi Karubi subsequently announced his candidacy in May; he received 0.85 percent of the vote and later joined the Green movement.

In 2011, Karubi was imprisoned along with fellow Green movement leader Mir Hosein Musavi and their wives, following their call for the February 14 antigovernment demonstrations. The party was part of the Moderate Reformist bloc in the 2012 balloting. The party initially endorsed former president Rafsanjani in the 2013 balloting, but after he was disqualified, backed Rouhani.

Leader: Mehdi KARUBI (2005 and 2009 presidential candidate and Former Speaker of the *Majlis*).

Green Path of Hope. The Green movement, as it is often referenced, was formed by presidential candidates Mir Hosein Musavi and Mehdi Karubi in August 2009 in response to the election of President Ahmadinejad. According to some observers, the movement was an attempt to prevent Musavi's arrest following postelection demonstrations and to build resistance to the regime. According to news reports, the grouping became increasingly radical, as some supporters called for the creation of a secular state, and Musavi declared himself ready to become a martyr.

Mehdi Karubi, who finished fourth in the 2009 presidential election with 0.85 percent of the vote and subsequently joined the Greens, was reportedly shot at, but unharmed, by unidentified gunmen in January 2010. Meanwhile, some reformists criticized the Green movement for being anti-Islam. Musavi was placed under house arrest in February 2011. The grouping endorsed Rouhani in the 2013 presidential elections.

Leaders: Mir Hosein MUSAVI (Former Prime Minister and 2009 presidential candidate), Mehdi KARUBI (Former Speaker of the *Majlis* and 2009 presidential candidate).

Servants of Construction—SC (*Kargozaran-e Sazandegi*). The SC (also sometimes referenced as the Executives of Construction) was launched in January 1996 by 16 top members of the Iranian executive branch, leading to its being informally referenced as the "G-16." Widely viewed as allied with (then) President Rafsanjani, the SC founders called for continued economic reform and moderate political liberalization.

About 90–100 SC supporters were believed to have been elected to the *Majlis* in 1996, a strong "antiliberal" campaign on behalf of the JRM/*Hezbollah* having apparently prevented what some observers had expected to be a clear-cut SC victory. The SC supported Interior Minister Abdullah NOURI in his unsuccessful bid to be elected speaker of the new *Majlis*.

The SC supported Mohammad Khatami in the May 1997 presidential election. Although the *Majlis* subsequently approved all of Khatami's cabinet recommendations, some of the harshest debate was over two SC candidates, Nouri and Seyed Ataollah Mohajerani. Early in 1998 the conservative judiciary arrested some Khatami supporters, including the SC's Gholan Hussein Karbaschi, mayor of Tehran, for alleged corruption in an election backlash that was seen by pro-Khatami elements as an escalation of political warfare. The popular mayor, who had been a leading figure in Khatami's surprise presidential victory, was subsequently sentenced to 18 months in prison. By that time, however, the SC had reportedly elected him as its secretary general after the grouping had apparently been officially recognized as a party. After 7 months in jail, Karbaschi was pardoned in December 1999 by Ayatollah Ali Khamenei. The SC was subsequently reported to have been fractionalized on the issue of how close to remain aligned with the Khatami administration, some members criticizing the president for failing to take stronger action to challenge the prosecution of SC members by the conservative judiciary.

The SC presented candidates in the 1999 municipal elections, some in alliance with the IIPF. Nouri was the top vote-getter in the local balloting in Tehran, but later in the year he was sentenced to five years in prison for having questioned the powerful role of the religious hierarchy, his case becoming one of the most prominent of the reformist versus conservative battles.

The "centrist, economics-oriented" SC presented joint candidates with other members of the May 23 Movement for many of the seats in the 2000 *Majlis,* although SC candidates competed on an independent SC list for some seats in Tehran. Included in that group was Rafsanjani, who had stated his goal of returning to the speakership of the *Majlis.* Indicative of the ongoing lack of harmony between Rafsanjani and Khatami (as well as their respective supporters), Rafsanjani was also included on the candidate list of the conservative JRM. Although he was elected to the *Majlis,* Rafsanjani ultimately declined his seat in the wake of controversy surrounding electoral decisions in his favor on the part of the Council of Guardians. He, however, remained head of the influential Expediency Council. Meanwhile, the SC claimed representation in the *Majlis* of some 55 members. Following the SC's defeats in the municipal elections of 2003, the parliamentary elections of 2004, and Rafsanjani's crushing loss in the 2005 presidential vote, the group announced plans for a major reorganization and "restructuring" that would result in new leadership.

Despite opposition calls to boycott the 2012 parliamentary balloting, the SC participated in the elections. The SC backed Rouhani in the 2013 presidential balloting, and SC member Eshaq Jahangiri was appointed first vice president in August.

Leaders: Eshaq JAHANGIRI (First Vice President of the Republic), Mohammad-Ali NAJAFI (Chair), Hossein MARASHI (Deputy Chair).

Liberation Movement of Iran (*Nehzat-e Azadi-e Irân*). A liberal Islamic grouping established in 1961 by Mehdi Bazargan, the Liberation Movement, also referenced as the Freedom Movement of Iran, supported the opposition religious leaders during the anti-shah demonstrations of 1978. Named prime minister in February 1979, Bazargan resigned in the wake of the U.S. embassy seizure the following November. Subsequently, he remained one of the most outspoken critics tolerated by the government. In a letter authored in November 1982, he accused the regime of responsibility for an "atmosphere of terror, fear, revenge, and national disintegration." *Nehzat-e Azadi,* which was linked to the Paris-based National Resistance Council, boycotted the legislative balloting in 1984 and in 1988 because of government-imposed electoral restrictions. In May 1988, the publication of a second letter from Bazargan to Ayatollah Khomeini highly critical of the government's war efforts and other "erroneous plans" led to the arrest of leading members of his party and of the Association for the Defense and Sovereignty of the Iranian Nation, which had been formed in opposition to continuation of the war with Iraq in March 1986 by Bazargan and others who had participated in the 1979 provisional government. Bazargan charged that the movement was not permitted to participate freely in the 1992 legislative campaign, and supporters were urged to boycott the 1993 presidential balloting.

Bazargan died of heart failure in January 1995, and his longtime assistant, Ibrahim Yazdi, was subsequently named as the movement's new secretary general. Yazdi later called on the government to permit the movement to present candidates in the March 1996 legislative elections. However, the Council of Guardians ruled that movement candidates per se would not be permitted to do so, although four members could run as independents. Those potential candidates subsequently declined to participate in the campaign to protest the council's decision. For his part, Yazdi argued that, while Iranians remained "loyal" to the "ideals" of the revolution, there was growing discontent over the government's "violation" of "rights and liberties." Yazdi was arrested in December 1997 (and later released) after signing a letter with 50 other government critics appealing for protection for Ayatollah Hussein Ali Montazeri, a cleric whose home was attacked by demonstrators after he questioned the authority of Ayatollah Khamenei. Montazeri had once been in line to succeed Ayatollah Khomeini (see Political background, above, for details). He has been under house arrest for several years for his remarks, prompting mass protests by his supporters in the city of Isfahan.

The Liberation Movement, a strong supporter of the reform tendency since 1997, was not permitted to present candidates in 2000 *Majlis* balloting, and the crackdown on the party by the conservative judiciary resulted in the arrest of some 60 party members in late 2000 and early 2001 on charges of seeking to overthrow the government in relation to, among other things, student unrest. The party was formally outlawed in July 2002. It condemned the Council of Guardians' ban on hundreds of reformist candidates in the 2004 parliamentary elections and speaks out frequently on human rights abuses. The most significant case has been that of Akbar Ganji, a journalist jailed in 2001 for reporting on an alleged conspiracy of assassinations orchestrated against dissidents. He was released after having served his full sentence in 2006, despite pressure for years by world leaders for his early release.

Since 2005, when Yazdi tried to run for president but was disqualified, the party has been tolerated, but by most accounts it has no influence in the affairs of the country.

In 2009, an activist member of the group was arrested for allegedly disseminating propaganda against the government. Yazdi was arrested for participating in postelection protests in June and again following violent protests in December. He was released in March 2011 and the next day resigned as party leader. Mehdi Bazargan's son Abdolali took over the leadership position. The grouping backed Rouhani in the 2013 presidential polling.

Leader: Abdolali BAZARGAN.

Office for Consolidation of Unity (*Daftar-e Takhim-e Vahdat*). This student organization has served as a platform for outspoken critics of the regime and in 1999 led street demonstrations protesting a crackdown on press freedom. The organization played an important role in the 1979 revolution, supporting the seizure of the U.S. embassy, and many of its leaders participated in the taking of American hostages. The group allied itself with the May 23 Movement (Second of Khordad) but later broke ranks with President Khatami and the reformists, criticizing their refusal to confront the conservatives and arguing that the Islamic Republic is inherently undemocratic. Several leaders have been imprisoned since 1997. Ahmad BATEBI, a student demonstrator with no links to the organization's leadership, was imprisoned in 1999 after his photograph appeared in newspapers and on the cover of the *Economist* holding the bloodied T-shirt of a fellow student. He remains in prison, after having been allowed several furloughs for medical care; he was rearrested in 2006. In February 2007, Batebi's wife, a dentist, reportedly was "snatched from the street," arrested by men thought to be security and intelligence agents, according to Human Rights Watch. A government crackdown on student activists in midyear included the arrest of six members of the organization during a sit-in at a university in July and the subsequent use of tear gas against students protesting an appearance by President Ahmadinejad at the University of Tehran in October. Following the disputed 2009 presidential election, student members of the group in Great Britain protested, demanding the expulsion of the British ambassador from Tehran after Iranian leaders accused Western nations of being behind the postelection violence. The group later condemned the British decision to expel Iranian diplomats following the storming of the British embassy in Tehran in November 2011.

Devotees of the Party of God (*Ansar-e Hezbollah*). This is a hardline paramilitary organization known for breaking up antiregime street demonstrations and attacking those considered to be flaunting social restrictions imposed by the authorities. Its roots date back to the 1979 revolution, when gangs of urban poor organized as *Hezbollah* to support Ayatollah Khomeini. Most members are veterans of the Iran-Iraq war or former members of the Basij militia, which was formed by the revolutionary leadership. The group has been accused of carrying out political assassinations and was highly critical of Ahmadinejad.

National Front (*Jebhe-e Melli*). The National Front was established in December 1977 as an essentially secular antiregime coalition of nationalist factions, including followers of former prime minister Mohammad Mossadeq. One of its founders, Shahpur Bakhtiar, was formally expelled upon designation as prime minister by the shah in late 1978; another founder, Karim SANJABI, resigned as foreign minister of the Islamic Republic in April 1979 to protest a lack of authority accorded to Prime Minister Bazargan. Prominent in the front is the long-standing **Iranian Nation Party** (INP), formed by Dariush FORUHAR, a former minister in the post-revolution Bazargan government. The INP (also sometimes referenced as the Iran People's Party) was tolerated by the government, despite remaining technically illegal. The party's newsletter regularly published harsh criticism of the regime, particularly in regard to human rights violations. Foruhar and his wife, Parvaneh ESKANDARI-FORUHAR, were murdered in November 1998, the killings ultimately being attributed to "rogue elements" within government security forces. Several INP members were arrested in July 1999 in connection with student unrest. For the 2000 *Majlis* balloting the INP, now led by Bahran NAMAZI, attempted to present joint candidates with the Liberation Movement of Iran and other groups in a Coalition of National Religious Forces in support of the reformist movement.

Among some of the other parties and groups are the **Islamic Labor Welfare Party**, the **Youth Party**, the **Modernist Muslim Women's Association**, and the **Association of the Women of the Islamic Revolution**. For more information on the **Islamic Iran Solidarity Party,** the **Party of the Masses** (*Hezb-e-Tudeh*), the **Moderation and Development Party** (*Hezb-e E'tedāl va Towse'eh*), led by Mohammad Bagher; and the **Front for Freedom and Equality** (please see the 2012 *Handbook*).

The largest guerrilla group—which at one time claimed some 100,000 members but is now considered to have much less support—is the **Mujaheddin-e Khalq** ("People's Warriors," also referenced as the *Mujaheddin Khalq* Organization—MKO or MEK), founded in 1965 in opposition to the shah. Leftist but also Islamic, the *Mujaheddin* confined most of their activities after the revolution to urban areas, frequently engaging in street battles with the Revolutionary Guards and the regular army; many of the political assassinations of 1979–1982 were apparently carried out by its members. The political leader of the *Mujaheddin,* Massoud RAJAVI, accompanied former president Abol Hasan Bani-Sadr into exile in Paris in July 1981 but subsequently came under pressure from French authorities and left, with 1,000 of his followers, for Iraq in June 1986; within Iran, guerrilla leader Mussa KHIABANI was killed in February 1982, his successor being Ali ZARKESH. In mid-1988 the *Mujaheddin* captured three Iranian towns before the Iranian army drove them back into Iraq in early August. The 15,000-member guerrilla force reportedly met with stiff resistance from "locals" who considered its attacks on the weakened army treasonous. Subsequently, the *Mujaheddin* claimed that thousands of its adherents had been executed by government forces. In December 1991, many *Mujaheddin* members were arrested during a government crackdown on opposition street protests, while President Rafsanjani ordered air strikes against its bases in Iraq during the run-up to the 1992 balloting.

In late 1993, Tehran strongly criticized Paris's decision to permit Maryam RAJAVI (wife of Massoud Rajavi and recently elected, according to *Middle East International,* as "president of Iran" by the *Mujaheddin* executive committee) to remain, with 200 supporters, in France. In January 1994 some 17 *Mujaheddin* members were arrested for participating in a bombing in the Iranian capital, with leaders of the group denying complicity and accusing the government of routinely linking them to all such disturbances for political purposes. Later in the year the U.S. State Department accused the *Mujaheddin* of engaging in terrorism, Washington's animosity apparently stemming in part from *Mujaheddin* links to the Iraqi regime of Saddam Hussein. The group was reportedly used to assist Hussein's forces in crushing Kurdish and Shiite rebellions. In the summer of 1997, apparently as a gesture of goodwill toward the new moderate Khatami government, Israel ordered an end to *Mujaheddin* broadcasts via an Israeli-owned satellite. The *Mujaheddin,* now operating out of Iraq, claimed responsibility for sporadic attacks in Tehran in 2000 and 2001. Subsequently, the group was designated a foreign terrorist organization by the United States, Canada, Iraq, Iran, and the EU. (In 2009, the Council of the European Union removed the group from the EU's terror list.)

In August 2002, the group's political wing, the National Council of Resistance of Iran (NCRI), presented satellite photographs and details of an underground uranium-enrichment center in Natanz and a heavy-water nuclear production facility in Arak. The satellite imagery prompted speculation that the group was supplied with intelligence from the United States or Israel, as it would lack sufficient resources to monitor Iran's nuclear activities. The revelations, subsequently confirmed by UN inspectors, indicated that Iran had made substantial progress in its nuclear research and renewed suspicions that the regime was pursuing a clandestine weapons project (possibly involving the purchase of materials and know-how from Pakistani scientists). The group lost its primary sponsor after the fall of Saddam Hussein and was briefly bombarded by U.S. forces. The MKO agreed to a cease-fire and was later disarmed and confined to designated camps under U.S. guard. Some 4,000 MKO members have remained under U.S. military supervision or "detention" at Camp Ashraf in Iraq, and, after a lengthy review by the U.S. State Department and the Federal Bureau of Investigation (FBI), none has been charged as suspected terrorists. The political wing, the NCRI, continues to enjoy support from a small number of parliamentary representatives in Europe and in the U.S. Congress.

Meanwhile, the U.S. State Department listed the NCRI as an "alias" for the exiles fighting in Iraq. Rajavi, described as the leader of the NCRI, met on separate occasions with leaders of Belgium and Norway, drawing criticism from Iran after Rajavi was quoted as saying the Iranian mullahs were a threat to the people of Iran and "to all humanity."

In 2007 as many as 3,800 members were said to be living in Iraq under some degree of supervision by the United States. Though Iraq was trying to evict the group for security reasons, the United States reportedly was reluctant to change course because the *Mujaheddin* were said to be providing important information about Iran's nuclear program. In April 2011, Iraqi security forces attacked Camp Ashraf, home to NCRI refugees, killing 36 and wounding more than 300. Another attack on Ashraf in September 2013 killed 52 and prompted calls from U.S. security officials to evacuate the remaining 3,000 members.

Of the separatist groups, the largest is the primarily Sunni Muslim **Kurdish Democratic Party of Iran** (KDPI), also referenced as the Democratic Party of Iranian Kurdistan (DPIK), which was outlawed in August 1979. Campaigning under the slogan "Democracy for Iran, Autonomy for the Kurds," the KDPI, like the *Mujaheddin,* has been a principal target of government forces; its guerrilla wing is often referred to as the *Pesh Mergas* (as is a similar Kurdish group in Iraq). Its former secretary general, Abdur Rahman QASSEMLOU, was assassinated in Vienna in July 1989, while his successor, Sadeq SHARAFKANDI, and four KDPI colleagues were murdered in Berlin in September 1992. In 1993 German prosecutors charged that the Iranian government had been involved in the latter attack. (Former Iranian prime minister Bani-Sadr testified at a trial in Germany in 1996 that Ayatollah Khamenei had personally signed a death warrant for Sharafkandi.) Late in 1993 it was also reported that KDPI guerrillas had engaged government troops near the Iraqi border. Another KDPI leader, Ghafur HAMZEKI, was reported to have been assassinated in Baghdad in August 1994, while, in what was described as an effort to "crush" the guerrillas, Iranian bombers and missiles attacked KDPI bases in Iraq the following November. In May 1995, it was reported that Abdallah HASSANZADEH had replaced Mustafa HEJRI as KDPI leader and secretary general. The KDPI claimed that its fighters had been attacked by Iranian troops in late 1996 in the wake of the incursion by the Iraqi military into the Kurdish "safe haven" in northern Iraq. In April 1997, a German court ruled that unnamed senior Iranian officials were responsible for the 1992 assassinations in Berlin, a finding that strained Iran's relations with the EU as well as with Germany. Perhaps indicating a reduction in tensions between the KDPI and the government, the KDPI was described as openly supporting candidates in Kurdish-populated areas in the 1999 municipal elections. As of 2005 the secretary general of the Iraq-based KDPI was Mustafa HEJRI. In December 2006 the KDPI reportedly split into two factions: one led by Hejri, and a breakaway group led by Abdullah Hassan ZADEH, the **Democratic Party of Kurdistan** (DPK), also in Iraq. In August 2012, the KDPI and the Revolutionary Society of Iranian Kurdistan Workers (*Komala*) signed a strategic partnership agreement. Reports in 2013 indicated ongoing negotiations between the KDPI and the DPK to reunite under a single banner.

Another separatist group, identified as the **Party for a Free Life in Kurdistan**, also known as Pejak, was operating in 2007 just miles from Iran in the northern region of Iraq. It claimed responsibility for numerous cross-border attacks in Iran, including the killing of 24 Iranian soldiers in 2006 in retaliation for the deaths of 10 Iranian Kurds. The group, which some reports said was an offshoot of the Kurdistan Workers' Party in Iraq, claimed to have several thousand members living in its base camp in northern Iraq and identified two of its leaders as Akif ZAGROS and Gulistan DUGAN. In February 2007 three members of Pejak were killed by Iranian forces near the border with Turkey; earlier Pejak claimed it had shot down an Iranian helicopter. Despite ongoing clashes within Iran and Iraq, the U.S. State Department said in August that Pejak was not included on its list of foreign terrorist organizations but noted that its activities were being monitored. Subsequently, in April 2008 Pejak leaders, reported to be hiding in the mountains in Iraq, threatened bomb attacks inside Iran unless Tehran changed its anti-Kurdish policies. The *New York Times* reported that Pejak and the Kurdistan Workers' Party (PKK), recognized as a terrorist organization that has engaged in violent conflict with Turkey, "appear to a large extent to be one and the same, and share the same goal: fighting campaigns to win new autonomy and rights for Kurds in Iran and Turkey." The PKK's leader was Abdullah OCALAN (imprisoned in Turkey). In April 2009 the group was blamed for an attack on a police station in a western province bordering Iraq. A week later, Iranian forces attacked Kurdish villages near the border and inside Iraq that were thought to be Pejak strongholds, according to *Agence France-Presse*.

In 2010, a high-ranking Iranian commander called for Iraq to crack down on Pejak, which he claimed had reorganized and mobilized forces in Iraq's Kurdish region. The same official stated that there was no longer any Pejak activity on Iran's border with Turkey. In May 2010, five Kurdish activists, said to have been members of Pejak, were executed. They had been found guilty in the bombing deaths of Revolutionary Guard members and of being "enemies of God." In 2011 Pejak rebel leader Abdul Rahman AHMADI, who was living in exile in Germany, said he believed the civil unrest and protests in Syria and other countries in the Middle East would reach Iran as well. By 2012, estimates were that Pejak had 3,000 members. Reports in 2013 asserted that Iranian forces had suppressed most of the Pejak militias.

LEGISLATURE

The unicameral **Islamic Consultative Assembly** (*Majlis-e Shoura-e Islami*) has 290 members serving four-year terms. Members are popularly elected in multiple-member constituencies in which each voter votes for as many candidates as there are seats. (Successful candidates must receive a minimum percentage of the total votes. If some seats remain unfilled after the first round of balloting, a runoff round is held.) Political groups are permitted to present candidate lists, many of the leading groups serving in a quasi-party capacity. All candidates must be approved by the Council of Guardians, which regularly rejects many prospects. Five of the 290 seats are reserved for religious minorities, including 2 for Armenian Christians, 1 for Assyrian Christians, and 1 each for Jewish Iranians and Iranian Zoroastrians.

In the most recent election of March 2 and May 4, 2012, conservatives secured 182 seats; reformists, 75; and independents, 33.

Speaker: Ali Ardeshir LARIJANI.

CABINET

[as of November 5, 2013]

President	Hassan Rouhani
First Vice President	Eshaq Jahangiri
Vice President, Chief of Atomic Energy Organization	Ali Akbar Salehi
Vice President, Chief of Executive Affairs	Mohammad Shariatmadari
Vice President, Director of Martyrs and Veterans Foundation	Mohammad-Ali Shahidi
Vice President, Chief of Cultural Heritage and Tourism	Mohammad Ali Najafi
Vice President, Chief of the Environmental Protection Organization	Masoumeth Ebtekar [f]
Vice President, Chief of Legal Affairs	Elham Aminzadeh [f]
Vice President, Chief of Parliamentary Affairs	Majid Ansari
Vice President, Chief of the Political and Security Affairs	Ali Younesi
Vice President, Science and Technology Affairs	Sorena Sattari
Vice President, Supervision and Strategic Affairs	Mohammad Bager Nobakht
Vice President, Women and Family Affairs	Shahindokht Molaverdi [f]
Ministers	
Agriculture	Mahmoud Hojjati
Communications and Information Technology	Mahmoud Vaezi
Cooperatives, Labor and Social Welfare	Ali Rabiei
Culture and Islamic Guidance	Ali Jannati
Defense	Brig. Gen. Hossein Dehqan
Economic Affairs and Finance	Ali Tayebnia
Education (Acting)	Ali Asghar Fani
Energy	Hamid Chitchian
Foreign Affairs	Mohammad Javad Zarif
Health	Hassan Qazizadeh Hashemi
Industry, Mines and Trade	Mohammad Reza Ne'Matzadeh
Intelligence	Mahmoud Alavi
Interior	Abdolreza Rahmani Fazli
Justice	Mostafa Pour-Mohammadi
Labor, Cooperatives, and Social Welfare	Ali Rabiei
Petroleum	Bijan Namadar Zanganeh
Roads, Housing, and Urban Development	Abbas Akhoundi
Scientific Research and Technology	Reza Faraji Dana
Youth and Sports (Acting)	Mohammad-Ali Shahidi

[f] = female

INTERGOVERNMENTAL REPRESENTATION

The United States severed diplomatic relations with Iran on April 4, 1980. Iranian diplomatic interests in Washington were handled by an interests section at the Algerian embassy until March 1992, when a successor section was established at the Pakistani embassy. The embassy of Switzerland handles U.S. interests in Iran.

Permanent Representative to the UN: Mohammad KHAZAEE.

IGO Memberships (Non-UN): IOM, NAM, OIC, OPEC.

IRAQ

Republic of Iraq
al-Jumhuriyah al-Iraqiyah

Political Status: Independent state since 1932; declared a republic following military coup that overthrew the monarchy in 1958; provisional constitution issued September 22, 1968, and substantially amended thereafter; de facto one-party regime ousted following invasion by U.S./UK-led forces in March 2003; interim constitution (Transitional Administrative Law) adopted by the U.S.-appointed Iraqi Governing Council on May 8, 2004, providing for popular election of a Transitional National Assembly; new constitution adopted by referendum on October 15, 2005, providing for popular election of a permanent National Assembly and a mixed presidential/parliamentary system.

Area: 167,924 sq. mi. (434,923 sq. km).

Population: 33,844,529 (2012E—UN); 31,858,481 (2013E—U.S. Census).

Major Urban Centers (2005E): BAGHDAD (5,925,000), Irbil (Arbil, 3,216,000), al-Mawsil (Mosul, 1,325,000), Basra (1,250,000).

Official Languages: Arabic, Kurdish.

Monetary Unit: New dinar (market rate November 1, 2013: 1,165.00 new dinars = $1US).

President of the Presidency Council: Jalal TALABANI (Patriotic Union of Kurdistan); elected by the Transitional National Assembly on April 5, 2005, and inaugurated on April 7; reelected by the National Assembly on April 22, 2006, and sworn in on May 3 for a four-year term; reelected by the National Assembly on November 11, 2010.

Vice Presidents of the Presidency Council: Tariq al-HASHIMI (Renewal List) (see Current issues, below) and Khodeir al-KHAOZAI (State of Law Coalition); elected by the National Assembly on May 12, 2011, and sworn in on May 30 for a term concurrent with the remaining term of the president. One vice-presidential position is vacant following the resignation of Adil Abdul-MAHDI (Supreme Council for the Islamic Revolution in Iraq) on May 31.

Prime Minister of the National Government: Nuri Jawad al-MALIKI (Islamic Call); nominated by the president (upon the recommendation of the United Iraqi Alliance) on April 21, 2006, and approved by the National Assembly and sworn in (along with his new national unity government) on May 20 in succession to Ibrahim al-JAAFARI (Islamic Call/United Iraqi Alliance); reelected by the National Assembly on November 11 and sworn in along with the new government on December 21.

President of the Kurdish Region: Massud BARZANI (Democratic Party of Kurdistan); approved by the Iraqi Kurdistan National Assembly on June 12, 2005, and inaugurated for a four-year term on June 14; popularly elected on July 25, 2009, and inaugurated for another four-year term on August 20.

Prime Minister of the Kurdish Regional Government: Barham SALIH (Patriotic Union of Kurdistan); appointed by the president to form a new government (upon the nomination of the Kurdistan List) on September 30, 2009, and inaugurated on October 28 (following ratification by the Kurdistan Iraqi Parliament) in succession to Nechirvan BARZANI.

THE COUNTRY

Historically known as Mesopotamia ("land between the rivers") from its geographic position centered in the Tigris-Euphrates Valley, Iraq is an almost landlocked, partly desert country whose population is overwhelmingly Muslim and largely Arabic speaking but also includes a Kurdish minority of over 4 million in the northeastern region bordering on Syria, Turkey, and Iran. A majority (60 percent) of the Muslims are Shiite, although the government was dominated by Sunnis prior to the 2003 U.S./UK-led invasion. Women were given the right to vote and run for office in the interim constitution adopted in 2004 (for information on the status of women under the Saddam regime, please see the 2012 *Handbook*).

The most important agricultural crops are dates, barley, wheat, rice, and tobacco. Oil is the leading natural resource and, under normal conditions, accounts for over half of GNP. Iraq has known reserves of 115 billion barrels of oil, although many fields have yet to be explored. Iraq's reserves (estimated as high as 350 billion barrels) are believed to be among the four largest in the world. The predominantly Kurdish north is rich in oil, as is the mainly Shiite south. However, the central region (where most Sunnis live) has fewer proven reserves, an issue that has contributed significantly to recent difficulties in negotiating final political stability at the national level. Other important natural resources include phosphates, sulfur, iron, copper, chromite, lead, limestone, and gypsum (for more information on Iraq's economy and society prior to 2002, see the 2010 *Handbook*).

The March 2003 invasion of Iraq by U.S./UK-led forces further damaged Iraq's infrastructure, although significant international aid flowed into the country. Oil production and exports resumed in the second half of 2003 but remained below prewar levels. Particularly damaging to production were numerous attacks on Iraq's oil pipelines, installations, and oil security personnel on the part of disaffected supporters of the former Hussein regime and other Sunni insurgents as well as militant Islamists from other countries. The conflict also compromised rebuilding efforts. In 2003 Iraq's GDP declined by 41.4 percent, but it recovered in 2004 to grow by 46.5 percent before slowing to 3.7 percent growth in 2005.

In 2008 the national government announced that foreign companies would be invited to submit bids for oil and gas contracts for the first time in more than 30 years. Meanwhile, the International Monetary Fund credited the government's "fiscal discipline" with having helped reduce annual inflation to 14 percent (down from 70 percent in 2006).

Economic prospects also appeared to advance as security conditions improved in 2008, although public services remained "dilapidated" and the private sector "anemic."

Corruption in government and the business sector continued to dampen the enthusiasm of foreign investors in the 2000s. The IMF approved $2.38 billion in February 2010 to assist in the repayment of the country's foreign debt and a $3.6 billion loan in March to help implement economic reforms. GDP grew by 5.6 percent in 2010, 8.6 percent the next year, and 10.2 percent in 2012. Inflation in 2012 was 6.1 percent, and the official unemployment rate was 16 percent. GDP per capita was $6,305. In 2012, Iraq was the world's sixth fastest growing economy. In August 2012, the IMF approved the extension of a $3.95 billion to support the Iraqi currency. In October, the International Energy Agency announced that Iraq could increase its oil production to 8.3 million barrels per day by 2035, making it the world's second largest oil producer.

GOVERNMENT AND POLITICS

Political background. Having previously been conquered successively by Arabs, Mongols, and Turks, the region now known as Iraq became a British mandate under the League of Nations following World War I. British influence, exerted through the ruling Hashemite dynasty, persisted even after Iraq gained formal independence in 1932. The country continued to follow a generally pro-British and pro-Western policy until the overthrow of the monarchy in July 1958 by a military coup that cost the lives of King FAISAL II and his leading statesman, Nuri al-SAID. Brig. Gen. Abd al-Karim QASIM, leader of the revolt, ruled as head of a left-wing nationalist regime until he was killed in a coup on February 8, 1963, that brought to power a new military regime led by Lt. Gen. Abd al-Salam ARIF and, after Arif's accidental death in 1966, by his brother, Gen. Abd al-Rahman ARIF. The Arif regime terminated in a bloodless coup on July 17, 1968, which established Maj. Gen. Ahmad Hasan al-BAKR, a former premier and leader of the right wing of the Arab Socialist Renaissance Party (*Hizb al-Baath al-Arabi al-Ishtiraki*), as president, prime minister, and chair of the Revolutionary Command Council (RCC), which was designated the country's highest authority by the provisional constitution issued on September 22.

Under President Bakr, a number of alleged plots were used as excuses to move against internal opposition. The most prominent took place in June 1973 when a coup attempt by Col. Nazim KAZZAR, head of national security, led to numerous arrests and executions. Domestic instability was further augmented by struggles within the Baath and by relations with the Kurdish minority.

The Kurds, under the leadership of Mullah Mustafa al-BARZANI, resisted most Baghdad governments in the two decades after World War II and, with Iranian military support, were intermittently in open rebellion from 1961 to 1975. A 1970 settlement with the Kurds ultimately broke down over distribution of petroleum revenues and exclusion of the oil-producing Kirkuk area from the proposed "Kurdistan."

In May 1974, Iraq and Iran agreed to a mutual withdrawal of troops along their common frontier, pending a settlement of outstanding issues. However, the Iraqi army subsequently launched a major offensive against the Kurdish rebels, and over 130,000 Kurds fled to Iran to escape the hostilities. Concessions were ultimately made on both sides in an agreement concluded in March 1975 during a meeting of the Organization of Petroleum Exporting Countries (OPEC) in Algiers; a "reconciliation" treaty was signed in Baghdad the following June. Iraq agreed to abandon a long-standing claim to the Shatt al-Arab waterway at its southern boundary with Iran and accepted a delimitation of the remaining frontier on the basis of agreements concluded prior to the British presence in Iraq. Iran, in return, agreed to cease all aid to the Kurds, whose resistance momentarily subsided. In mid-1976, however, fighting again erupted between Iraqi forces and the Kurdish *Pesh Merga* guerrillas, ostensibly because of the government's new policy of massive deportation of Kurds to southern Iraq and their replacement in the north by Arabs.

On July 16, 1979, President Bakr announced his resignation from both party and government offices. His successor, Saddam HUSSEIN, had widely been considered the strongman of the regime, and his accession to leadership of the Baath and the RCC came as no surprise. Earlier in the year, the Iraqi Communist Party (ICP) had withdrawn from the six-year-old governing National Progressive Front, following what Hussein himself had termed a purging of Communists from the government. Reports in late July of a "failed conspiracy" against the new president provided further evidence that he had effectively eliminated opponents from the RCC.

Although former president Bakr was known to be experiencing health problems, his resignation was apparently linked to differences within the RCC in regard to three policies: (1) containment not only of the Kurds but, in the aftermath of the Iranian Revolution, the increasingly restive Shiite community, led by Ayatollah Muhammad Bakr al-SADR until his execution in April 1980; (2) an Iraqi-Syrian unification plan (see Foreign relations, below), aspects of which Hussein found objectionable; and (3) suppression of the ICP, including the removal from the cabinet of its two ministers. Although a broad amnesty was proclaimed on August 16, 1979, Kurdish, Shiite, and Communist opposition to the Hussein government persisted and appeared to expand following Baghdad's September 17, 1980, abrogation of the 1975 Algiers agreement and the invasion five days later of Iran's Khuzistan Province, which yielded a debilitating conflict that was to preoccupy the regime for the next eight years (see Foreign relations, below).

Iraq also suffered extensive physical destruction from the Western-led Operation Desert Storm in early 1991, which had been precipitated by the Iraqi invasion of Kuwait the previous August. (For a chronology of relevant events, see the 1991 *Handbook,* Appendix A-II.) Upon formal termination of the conflict on March 3, Baghdad faced major rebellions by Kurds in the north and Shiites in the south, both of which were largely contained by early April. Many Shiite refugees fled into southeastern Iran, and the Kurds retreated into the mountainous northern region bordering Iran and Turkey. Late in the month autonomy talks were launched in Baghdad between Kurdish leaders and the Iraqi government. Meanwhile, on March 23, President Hussein announced the formation of a new government, including the appointment of Saadoun HAMMADI to assume the prime ministerial duties theretofore performed by Hussein himself. On May 18 the Kurdish leadership reported that the regime had accepted its demands for a democratic government, separation of the Baath from the government, a free press, and elections. Moreover, on July 4, the National Assembly endorsed a bill providing for a limited democracy, wherein political party formations would be legalized but membership in the armed forces and security apparatus would continue to be limited to Baath members.

Although President Hussein formally approved the National Assembly bill on September 3, 1991, he subsequently retreated from liberalization measures and moved to consolidate power within a cabinet increasingly dominated by family members. On September 13, the president named Muhammad Hamzah al-ZUBAYDI to replace Hammadi as prime minister after Hammadi, whom analysts had described as the only independent in the regime, had called for a more conciliatory posture in negotiations with UN coalition members and the Kurds.

In January 1992, 80 military officers charged with participating in a coup attempt were executed along with 76 antiregime demonstrators. Four months later elections were held in the north to an Iraqi Kurdistan National Assembly. However, Baghdad immediately branded the poll as violating a constitutional prohibition of elections by armed groups; the Kurdish leaders defended the action as being in conformity with the 1970 autonomy agreement. On June 4 the new Kurdish Assembly named Fuad MASUM, a member of the political bureau of the Patriotic Union of Kurdistan (PUK), as the first Kurdish prime minister, and a Kurdish cabinet was appointed shortly thereafter. Masum resigned on March 18, 1993, amid reported discontent over fuel and food shortages in the north; he was succeeded on April 11 by Kosrat Abdulla RASUL, a popular veteran guerrilla fighter, who announced a new Kurdish cabinet on April 26. (The Kurdish coalition government collapsed in 1994 as renewed fighting broke out between the PUK and its long-standing rival, the Democratic Party of Kurdistan [DPK]. Kurdish territory was subsequently partitioned informally into PUK and DPK spheres of influence until the DPK invited Iraqi troops into the area to participate in an anti-PUK campaign in August 1996. See DPK under Political Parties and Groups, below, for details.) Meanwhile, President Hussein remained firmly in control of the Iraqi government, although growing popular discontent was reported, particularly in regard to the economic and social effects of UN sanctions in place since the Gulf crisis. A number of civilians and army officers (apparently including former supporters of the regime) were executed following the discovery of an alleged coup plot in August 1993, which may also have contributed to a surprise cabinet reshuffle on September 5 in which Prime Minister Zubaydi was replaced by Ahmad Hussein KHUDAYYIR, a longtime Baath member and close associate of the president who had served as finance minister since 1991.

Citing the damage inflicted on Iraq by the UN sanctions, President Hussein took formal control of the Iraqi administration on May 29, 1994, by assuming the additional post of prime minister in succession to Khudayyir, who retained the finance portfolio. Numerous ministerial changes were reported over the next 15 months as the regime faced continuing economic and political pressures.

In mid-August 1995, two of President Hussein's sons-in-law and their wives fled the country and accepted political asylum in Jordan. The most important of the defectors appeared to be Lt. Gen. Hussein Kamil al-MAJID, who, as head of the Iraqi weapons program, had been one of the most powerful figures in President Hussein's inner circle. Majid, reported to have been locked in an intense power struggle with Saddam Hussein's eldest son, Udai HUSSEIN, immediately called for the overthrow of the Hussein regime in order to have the UN sanctions lifted.

Apparently in part to counter perceptions that the defections represented a serious threat to the government's future, the RCC on September 7 amended the constitution to provide for popular confirmation of its chair as president of the republic. Three days later the National Assembly endorsed the RCC's "nomination" of Saddam Hussein for a seven-year presidential term, and a national referendum on October 13 produced a reported 99.96 percent "yes" vote on the question. Voter turnout was also announced at over 99 percent, a tribute, in the eyes of some observers, to the organizational capabilities of a "revitalized" Baath, which also supplied nearly all the candidates for new assembly elections in March 1996. Meanwhile, any genuine concern the regime may have felt as the result of the much-publicized defections of 1995 evaporated in February 1996 when Lt. Gen. Majid accepted a "forgiveness" offer from President Hussein, only to be killed in a gunfight shortly after his return to Iraq.

Following the recommendation of the RCC, the National Assembly on August 19, 2002, unanimously nominated President Hussein for another seven-year term. The government reported that 100 percent of those voting in a national referendum on October 15 approved the measure.

After declaring the Iraqi regime to be in violation of UN resolutions relating to inspections designed to determine Iraq's status in regard to weapons of mass destruction, the United States and the United Kingdom launched an invasion in March 2003 that resulted in the ouster of Hussein. (See Foreign relations, below, for additional information.) On April 21 U.S. Gen. (Ret.) Jay GARNER arrived to head a U.S. Office for Reconstruction and Humanitarian Assistance (ORHA), which, among other things, was to set up an Iraqi Interim Authority (IIA) as an advisory body to the ORHA. However, the Iraqis slated to participate in the authority (many of whom had just returned from exile) balked at the lack of day-to-day government responsibilities assigned to the proposed IIA. On May 6, U.S. President George W. Bush named L. Paul BREMER, a former U.S. ambassador, as head of the civil administration and the Coalition Provisional Authority (CPA). The UN Security Council endorsed the CPA's legal status as an occupying power in a resolution on May 22 and called upon the CPA (formally launched June 1) to facilitate a quick transition to Iraqi rule. Bremer attempted to "de-Baathify" the government and military by dissolving the security forces, a decision that was later perceived to have had negative consequences.

With membership determined by the CPA, a new Iraqi Governing Council (IGC) was established on July 13, 2003. The 25 members were carefully divided across religious and ethnic lines (13 Shiites, 5 Sunnis, 5 Kurds, 1 Assyrian Christian, and 1 Turkman). A rotating presidency was instituted for the IGC, which on September 1, announced the formation of a 25-member interim cabinet authorized to assist in drafting an interim constitution and preparing for elections for a transitional government. (The Arab League did not recognize the IGC as Iraq's legitimate government, although OPEC allowed the IGC oil minister to attend OPEC meetings.)

Security continued to deteriorate as foreign fighters, former regime elements, and Iraqi Sunnis engaged in a bloody insurgency. A truck bomb destroyed the UN compound in Baghdad, leading to a UN withdrawal from Iraq, and car bombs and improvised explosives subsequently took a toll on coalition forces and Iraqi leaders. In a major development, Hussein's two sons were killed in a battle in Mosul in late July 2003. Meanwhile, efforts to identify or discover banned weapons produced no results, even after the deployment of the 1,000-member Iraq Survey Group, which was composed of U.S. and international weapons experts. (In January 2005, the Bush administration confirmed that no banned weapons or chemical agents had been found.)

Insurgents also began to kidnap foreign workers and Iraqi government and political figures. Over time, the insurgency appeared to become more organized, and many analysts concluded that one of the ringleaders was Jordanian-born Abu Musab al-ZARQAWI, who was known to have links to al-Qaida.

On December 13, 2003, Saddam Hussein was captured near Tikrit, and by January 2004, the coalition had captured or killed 42 of its 55 "most-wanted" former Iraqi leaders. Meanwhile, security improved in the Kurdish north and the Shiite south; the ongoing insurgency was concentrated in the central region in an area that became known as the Sunni Triangle.

During negotiations on the interim constitution in early 2004, the Shiites on the IGC demanded that the document be based on sharia (Islamic law); they also opposed a clause that permitted any three provinces to block a permanent constitution with a two-thirds vote in each of the three provinces. Because there were three Kurdish provinces, that provision gave the Kurds a de facto veto over the future constitution. However, the country's highest Shiite leaders eventually agreed to the "Kurdish veto." In return, a plan to use regional bodies to elect representatives to the Transitional National Assembly (TNA) was revised in favor of direct elections.

The draft interim constitution was presented on March 1, 2004, and was approved by the United States and the IGC on March 8. On June 28, the IGC was dissolved in favor of the new Iraqi Interim Government (IIG), which accepted the transfer of sovereignty from the CPA (as endorsed by the UN Security Council on June 8). Ayad ALLAWI, a Shiite from the Iraqi National Accord, was named prime minister of the interim administration, and Ghazi Ajil al-YAWAR, a Sunni, was named to the largely ceremonial post of interim president.

In March 2004, Bremer announced the reconstruction of the Iraqi security forces in response to growing unrest in Fallujah among followers of Shiite cleric Muqtada al-SADR, the son of a popular cleric killed by the Hussein regime. After two sieges in April and May and a second assault, which included members of the new Iraqi security forces, Fallujah was returned to relative calm. Al-Sadr subsequently announced his intention to participate politically and to form a party.

Internal problems continued to plague the IGC and the CPA through 2004. (On May 17, 2004, the chair of the IGC, Izzedin SALIM, was assassinated.) Meanwhile, the credibility of the United States was undermined by revelations of a prisoner-abuse scandal at the U.S. military prison at Abu Ghraib in which U.S. troops mistreated and degraded Iraqi prisoners.

After contentious negotiations within the Sunni community, Muhsin Abd al-HAMID, leader of the Iraqi Islamic Party (the largest mainstream Sunni party), urged Sunnis to boycott the balloting for the TNA on January 30, 2005. After contentious negotiations within the Sunni community, Muhsin Abd al-HAMID, leader of the Iraqi Islamic Party (the largest mainstream Sunni party), urged Sunnis to boycott the balloting for the 275-member TNA on January 30, 2005. The turnout was thereby only approximately 60 percent, although international observers described the balloting, dominated by the Shiite United Iraqi Alliance, as generally free and fair. The poll also marked the first time women voted in an Iraqi election. In the balloting, the main Shiite coalition (the United Iraqi Alliance [UIA]) secured 140 seats, followed by the Democratic Patriotic Alliance of Kurdistan (DPAK) with 75 and the multiethnic, multireligious Iraqi List (led by Allawi) with 40. Concurrent balloting was held for a new Iraqi Kurdistan National Assembly, as well as for various regional councils.

After intense and often contentious negotiations, the TNA, on April 5, 2005, elected Jalal TALABANI, a Kurd from the PUK, as president of a new Presidency Council that also included Shiite and Sunni vice presidents. On April 7 the Presidency Council appointed Ibrahim al-JAAFARI, a Shiite from Islamic Call (*al-Dawah,* a party that was part of the winning UIA list), to head a new cabinet, which was inaugurated on May 3. On October 15 a proposed permanent constitution, drafted by a committee appointed by the TNA, was adopted by referendum with a "yes" vote of 79 percent (see Constitution and government, below). On December 15 elections for a permanent National Assembly (with 275 seats) were held, the UIA repeating its January victory by winning a plurality of 128 seats. The DPAK finished second with 53 seats, followed by the Iraqi Accord Front (IAF) with 44 and the Iraqi National List (INL, as the Iraqi List had been renamed) with 25. (Iraq's Sunni community participated more heavily in the December poll than it had in January; many of its votes were directed to the IAF or the Iraqi National Dialogue Front.)

Throughout 2005, violence in Iraq developed an increasingly sectarian character, prompting speculation that the country was about to plunge into all-out civil war. Foreign troops and Shiites were targeted by insurgents (see section on al-Qaida in article on Afghanistan for additional information). Hopes that Iraq would stabilize in the near-term were dealt a severe blow on February 22, 2006, by the bombing in Samarra of the al-Askariya shrine, a Shiite holy site. The bombing confirmed for some observers that Iraq was in a civil war, and the civilian death toll rose dramatically in February and March.

Because the formation of a government depended on a two-thirds majority ratification in the National Assembly, several months passed before a cabinet could be submitted to the body for approval. The major problem involved divisions within the UIA over its choice for prime minister. Al-Jaafari won an internal poll within the alliance against Adil Abd al-MAHDI in February 2006 by just one vote. However, groups representing Kurds and Sunnis refused to participate in any national unity government with al-Jaafari as prime minister. Consequently, al-Jaafari was eventually forced to relinquish the premiership to a fellow *al-Dawah* candidate, Nuri Jawad al-MALIKI, under a deal brokered by Grand Ayatollah Ali al-SISTANI. On May 20, al-Maliki formed a coalition cabinet.

Saddam Hussein was hanged in December 2006 following his conviction of crimes against humanity, including his ordering the execution of Shiites in the village of Dujail following an attempt on his life in 1982.

Six Shiite ministers who were supporters of hard-liner Muqtada al-SADR (see Al-Sadr Movement under Political Parties and Groups) resigned from the cabinet on April 16, 2007. Further damaging governmental stability, IAF ministers suspended their participation in the cabinet in August, while several INL ministers resigned their posts as directed by former prime minister Allawi. The IAF returned to the cabinet in July 2008, the al-Maliki administration having been strengthened by improving security conditions.

In August 2009, ahead of legislative elections the following year, a new coalition, the Iraqi National Alliance (INA) was formed from the parties of the UIA. However, al-Maliki declined to join the new grouping and instead emerged as the leader of a rival body, the State of Law Coalition (see Political parties, below). Meanwhile, Allawi's grouping, the INL, was relaunched ahead of the balloting as the Iraqi National Movement (INM).

In voting on March 7, 2010, no party received a majority. The INM secured the most seats with 91, followed closely by the State of Law Coalition with 89. Wrangling over the creation of a new coalition government continued into the fall, with al-Maliki leading a caretaker government. The inability to establish a new government also delayed the election of a new president. On November 11, an agreement was reached whereby Talabani was reelected president by the parliament and al-Maliki was reappointed prime minister. Meanwhile, Allawi was promised a prominent role as the head of a newly created national political and security council (see Current issues, below). Al-Maliki named a coalition government that was approved by the legislature on December 21 and included the INM, the State of Law Coalition, and the PUK.

In December, 2011, after the government issued an arrest warrant for First Vice President Tariq al-HASHIMI of the Renewal List (see Current issues, below), the INM initiated a boycott of the cabinet and the Council of Representatives. The INM ended its boycott of the legislature on January 29, 2012, but refused to participate in the government for another month.

On March 7, 2012, Nechirvan BARZANI (DPK) was appointed prime minister of a reshuffled cabinet for the Kurdish regional government under a power-sharing agreement in which the DPK and the PUK rotate government control every two years.

Constitution and government. Constitutional processes were largely nonexistent during the two decades after the 1958 coup, despite the issuance of a provisional basic law in 1968 and a 1971 National Action Charter that envisaged the establishment of local governing councils and the reconvening of a legislature. It was not until 1980 that elections were held for a unicameral National Assembly and a Kurdish Legislative Council, respectively. However, the Revolutionary Command Council (RCC), the nation's supreme authority since 1968, was not dissolved, effective power remaining concentrated in its chair, who continued to serve concurrently as president of the republic and commander in chief of the Armed Forces. (Amendments approved by the RCC in September 1995 directed that its chair's assumption of the presidency would henceforth be subject to the approval of the National Assembly and a national referendum.) RCC decrees had the force of law and were not automatically subject to any legislative or judicial review, although some bills were passed on to the assembly for approval. The RCC was also solely responsible for electing and dismissing its own members, who had to come from the leadership of the Baath. The judicial system was headed by a Court of Cassation and included five courts of appeal, courts of the first instance, religious courts, and revolutionary courts that dealt with crimes involving state security.

As a concession to northern minority sentiment, the Kurds in 1970 were granted autonomy as "defined by law," and in 1976 Iraq's 16 provincial governorates were expanded to 18, 3 of which were designated as Kurdish Autonomous Regions. However, it was not until after the 1991 Gulf war that Baghdad agreed to enter into a dialogue with Kurdish leaders to achieve meaningful implementation of what had been promised more than two decades earlier. After the new talks broke down, Kurdish groups in 1992 established an elected Iraqi Kurdistan National Assembly, which in turn selected a prime minister to oversee a Kurdish government broadly responsible for most services in the region until the collapse of Kurdish cooperation in 1994.

In January 1989, it was announced that the Iraqi constitution would be replaced prior to the National Assembly balloting of April 1; however, a draft of the new basic law did not appear until July 30, 1990, after having secured legislative approval 12 days before. The published version of the document provided for direct election of the president for an eight-year renewable term; replacement of the RCC by a 50-member Consultative Council, composed of an equal number of appointed and directly elected members; and the registration of new political parties, with a proviso that only the Baath would be permitted to have branches in the army and security forces. In a speech on March 16, 1991, Saddam Hussein declared that the time had come to begin building the "pillars" of the "new constitutional order" despite the many problems facing the country. On September 3, 1991, Hussein approved a law technically ending 23 years of one-party rule; however, the other changes were never submitted to a referendum.

The interim constitution adopted in March 2004 following the overthrow of Saddam Hussein in 2003 provided for an appointed Interim Iraqi Government (IIG) to assume sovereignty from the U.S.-led Coalition Provisional Authority (CPA) for a short time pending the election of transitional government bodies. The 275-member Transitional National Assembly (TNA—elected by popular vote on January 20, 2005) was authorized to elect the Presidency Council, dissolve the cabinet, and oversee the drafting of a new permanent constitution. The Presidency Council (elected in April 2005) was empowered to appoint the prime minister, cabinet, and members of the judicial council and to veto legislation passed by the assembly. Day-to-day governmental responsibility was given to the prime minister and the cabinet (installed in May 2005).

The TNA was supposed to produce a draft permanent constitution by August 15, 2005, but deep divisions regarding issues such as the role of Islam, the powers of regions under a federalist system, and the distribution of oil wealth pushed negotiations well past that deadline. Most Sunni representatives boycotted the discussion, in part due to their concern over proposed "regionalization" articles that Sunnis feared might lead to the eventual breakup of the country. However, some Sunni leaders accepted a last-minute agreement regarding future constitutional revision and encouraged Sunnis to participate in the referendum on October 15. The proposed constitution was approved by 79 percent of the voters, receiving overwhelming support in Shiite- and Kurdish-dominated areas. However, the new basic law almost failed as the result of a provision that it could not be passed if two-thirds of the voters in three provinces rejected it. The "no" vote easily exceeded the two-thirds threshold in two Sunni-dominated provinces but reached only about 55 percent in the third province where passage had seemed questionable.

The new 2005 permanent constitution codified Iraq as a federal republic with a mixed presidential/parliamentary system. Although regions (of which Kurdistan was recognized as one) were granted broad autonomy, the "unity of Iraq" was "guaranteed." A region was defined as comprising one or more provinces, leaving open the possibility of provinces joining together to form more powerful regions. (A Kurdish Regional Government [KRG] was subsequently formed in the provinces of Arbil, Sulaimaniya, and Dohuk.) However, many of the provisions in that regard and other controversial areas were considered temporary at best because the constitution authorized the National Assembly to appoint a new panel following the upcoming legislative elections to propose additional changes and refinements to the constitution. Meanwhile, Islam was enshrined as the state religion (and a basic source of legislation), although freedom of religion was guaranteed. The directly elected National Assembly (1 seat for every 100,000 inhabitants, or 325 seats in 2010) was authorized to elect the president by a two-third's majority for a four-year term. Significant responsibilities (including the role of commander in chief of the armed forces) were reserved for the prime minister, nominated by the president upon the recommendation of the bloc with a majority of seats in the assembly.

In October 2006, the assembly passed legislation permitting provinces throughout the country to form regional administrations similar to the KRG.

Following the overthrow of the Hussein regime in 2003, the CPA and the interim and transitional Iraqi governments promoted establishment of a free press. Several hundred small, often fleeting, newspapers were subsequently launched, many of them serving as outlets for Iraqi political parties. More than 150 journalists were killed in 2003–2007, and others were kidnapped, primarily by insurgents who particularly targeted Iraqis working for foreign news outlets. Intensified sectarian conflict in 2006–2007 also contributed to imposition of press restrictions by the al-Maliki administration, especially on what the government perceived as "inflammatory" reporting. Some foreign correspondents and Iraqi journalists who had fled the violence returned to the country in 2008 as security conditions improved. Under heavy domestic and international pressure, the government established a special police force to investigate violence against journalists. In 2013 Reporters Without Borders ranked Iraq 150th out of 179 countries in freedom of the press.

Foreign relations. After adhering to a broadly pro-Western posture that included participation in the Baghdad Pact and its successor, the Central Treaty Organization (CENTO), Iraq switched abruptly in 1958 to an Arab nationalist line that was subsequently largely maintained. Relations with the Soviet Union and other Communist-bloc countries became increasingly cordial after 1958, whereas diplomatic links with the United States (and temporarily with Britain) were severed in 1967. In 1979, however, Baghdad moved against Iraqi Communists, veering somewhat toward the West, particularly France, for military and development aid. The change in direction was reinforced following a June 7, 1981, Israeli air raid against the Osirak nuclear reactor being built outside Baghdad, France indicating that it would consider assisting in reconstructing the facility.

Relations with Arab states have fluctuated, although Iraq has remained committed to an anti-Israel policy. A leading backer of the "rejection front," it bitterly denounced the 1977 peace initiative of Egyptian President Sadat and the Camp David accords of September 1978, after which, on October 26, Syria and Iraq joined in a "National Charter for Joint Action" against Israel. This marked an abrupt reversal in relations between the two neighbors, long led by competing Baath factions. The "National Charter" called for "full military union," and talks directed toward its implementation were conducted in January and June 1979. At the latter session, held in Baghdad, presidents Assad of Syria and Bakr of Iraq declared that their two nations constituted "a unified state with one President, one Government and one Party, the Baath." However, the subsequent replacement of Bakr by Saddam Hussein, whom the Syrians had long considered an instigator of subversion in their country, coupled with Hussein's accusations of Syrian involvement in an attempted coup, abruptly terminated the rapprochement.

Relations with Tehran have long been embittered by conflicting interests in the Gulf region, including claims to the Shatt al-Arab and to three islands (Greater and Lesser Tunb and Abu Musa) occupied by Iran in 1971, as well as by Iranian support for Iraq's Kurdish and Shiite communities. Following the advent of the Khomeini regime in Iran in 1979, Iraq bombed a number of Kurdish villages inside Iran, and on September 22, 1980, having repudiated a 1975 reconciliation treaty, Iraq invaded its eastern neighbor. Despite overwhelming Iraqi air superiority and early ground successes, the Iranian military, reinforced by a substantially larger population with religious commitment to martyrdom, waged a bitter campaign against the Western-supplied Iraqi forces, the brief campaign projected by Hussein soon being reduced to a stalemate. In the course of the protracted conflict, numerous Iraqi cease-fire proposals were rebuffed by Tehran, which called for the payment of $150 billion in reparations and Hussein's ouster. It was not until a failed siege of the Iraqi city of Basra, coupled with an increasingly intense political struggle within Tehran, that Ayatollah Khomeini on July 20, 1988, called for a suspension of hostilities. A cease-fire was subsequently concluded with effect from August 20, although it was not until August 15, 1990, in the midst of the crisis generated by its seizure of Kuwait, that Iraq agreed to a comprehensive settlement based on the 1975 Algiers accord, a rejection of which by Baghdad had precipitated the lengthy conflict. A number of issues, including Iranian demands for reparations, subsequently remained unresolved, however, and a final peace accord was not signed, the status between the two countries being described as "no war, no peace."

The "annexation" of Kuwait in August 1990 was preceded by Saddam Hussein's delivery of a July 17 Revolution Day speech, during which the Iraqi president insisted that Kuwait had not only exceeded OPEC production quotas but had also stolen oil from Iraqi wells by "slant drilling." Other areas of contention were historic uncertainties regarding the precise demarcation of the Iraq-Kuwait border, plus the status of certain offshore territories (including Bubiyan Island) that had been operationally "loaned" to Iraq as a gesture of Arab solidarity during the Iran-Iraq war (see article on Kuwait). However, there was little international support for Baghdad's position, and the UN Security Council reacted strongly, demanding an unconditional withdrawal within hours of the Iraqi action on August 2, imposing a trade embargo on August 6, and approving on November 29 the use of any methods needed to force Iraqi compliance as of January 15, 1991. On January 16, following a five-month buildup of U.S. and allied military units, the UN coalition commenced offensive action, which yielded the liberation of Kuwait City on February 26–27 and a suspension of military operations on February 28, followed by Iraqi acceptance of terms for ending the conflict on March 3.

Although most coalition military units withdrew from the Gulf by mid-1991, the UN economic embargo remained in effect, in part because of U.S. displeasure at Saddam Hussein's continuance in office. Nevertheless, although Washington had long demanded that the Iraqi president step down, the George H. W. Bush administration did not wish to trigger dismemberment of the country. Thus, it stood aside as Iraqi forces crushed a Shiite insurrection in the south, and U.S. aid to the northern Kurds was confined largely to humanitarian supplies.

Seemingly encouraged by the coalition's unwillingness to intervene on behalf of either the Kurds or Shiites, the Hussein regime subsequently refused to comply with cease-fire provisions requiring its assistance in the location and destruction of Iraq's nonconventional weapons. Nevertheless, by October 1991, the International Atomic Energy Agency (IAEA) had accumulated enough information to charge that an Iraqi atomic weapon had been within 18 months of completion at the outset of the Gulf war and that enough material had survived allied bombing to allow the completion of other such weapons within five years. Consequently, on October 11 the Security Council approved additional restrictions, branded by Baghdad as "colonial," to prevent Iraq from ever again acquiring the means to build weapons of mass destruction.

During 1992 and early 1993, tension continued unabated between Baghdad and UN authorities. On August 27, 1992, U.S. and British warplanes began patrolling a southern "no-fly" zone below the 32nd parallel to protect Shiite Muslims from Iraqi air attacks. In January 1993 Iraq was obliged to remove surface-to-air missiles that had been moved into the zone, and a series of cross-border raids to retrieve abandoned military equipment from Kuwait were countered by retaliatory allied air strikes. Meanwhile, a northern "no fly" zone, similar to the one in the south, remained in effect to protect the Kurds, although Kurdish secession was effectively blocked by opposition from virtually all interested parties save for the Kurds themselves.

U.S. Tomahawk missiles struck the Iraqi intelligence headquarters in Baghdad on June 26, 1993; Washington claimed it had "compelling evidence" that Iraq had been involved in a plot to kill former president Bush in Kuwait several months earlier. Moreover, Western powers threatened further military action if the Hussein regime continued to resist measures designed to prevent the development of chemical and nuclear weapons and long-range missiles by the Iraqi military.

An estimated 70,000 Iraqi soldiers massed near the Kuwaiti border in early October 1994, prompting the United States to order "overwhelming" air power and send 40,000 of its troops back to the region in fear of a repetition of the 1990 invasion. In addition, the UN Security Council warned Baghdad against any further "provocative" behavior, and other Arab states (including some, such as Jordan, that had been relatively pro-Iraqi in the previous conflict) strongly condemned the Iraqi buildup. Consequently, the Iraqi forces quickly withdrew, and on November 10, in a major policy shift, the RCC issued a decree, signed by President Hussein and approved by the National Assembly, that accepted Kuwait's sovereignty, political independence, and territorial integrity, based on a recent UN border demarcation.

Despite Iraq's conciliatory measures, the Security Council kept its economic sanctions in place, the United States insisting it would not support their lifting until Baghdad had returned Kuwaiti property seized in 1990–1991, had accounted for numerous missing Kuwaitis (some presumed to still be held in Iraqi prisons), and had established permanent safeguards to protect the rights of the Kurds in the north and the Shiites in the south. Western powers also insisted on full compliance with the demands of the UN weapons monitors; concern focused on a perceived lack of candor from Baghdad regarding its biological weapons program.

In view of the enormous hardships being endured by the populace as the result of continued UN sanctions, the regime finally agreed in December 1995 to a UN Security Council plan permitting the sale of a limited amount of Iraqi oil to pay for food and medicine. (Baghdad had previously resisted the proposal, saying it represented a compromise of its sovereignty.) The Security Council gave its final approval to the project in May 1996, but implementation was delayed over U.S. concerns that appropriate monitoring mechanisms had not been established. Washington reluctantly accepted the arrangements for the oil sale in early August, but action was again suspended later that month when Iraqi troops entered Kurdish territory in the north at the invitation of the DPK. (See the DPK under Political Parties and Group for details.)

In early September 1996, the United States launched more than 20 cruise missiles at Iraqi air defense installations in the south as an "indirect punishment" for Iraq's recent military actions in the north. Tension escalated over the next several weeks as Washington dispatched aircraft carriers and additional troops to the Gulf and President Hussein threatened to fire upon Western planes patrolling the "no-fly" zones. Both sides subsequently retreated from the brink of open warfare, however, as Iraqi forces withdrew from the north and the United States discovered a paucity of support from its former coalition allies for renewed hostilities. Consequently, with Iraq facing a potentially catastrophic winter, attention again focused on the oil-for-food plan, which was finally implemented in mid-December. The plan authorized Iraq to sell $2 billion in oil over the next six months. Some of the revenue was earmarked for victims (primarily Kuwaitis) of Iraq's 1990 aggression; the Kurds were also scheduled to receive assistance. However, the bulk of the new income was slated for distribution (under UN supervision) throughout Iraq, where it was estimated that nearly 5,000 children had been dying each month from malnutrition or normally treatable diseases.

The UN Special Commission on Iraq (UNSCOM) reported in April 1997 that, although progress was being made in the dismantling of weapons, Iraq was still not cooperating as fully as desired. The issue erupted into a major crisis in October when Baghdad threatened to block all further UN inspections unless the economic sanctions were lifted and U.S. personnel (described as a threat to Iraqi "national sovereignty") were removed from the UN teams. At the same time, new UNSCOM head Richard Butler (former Australian ambassador to the UN) reported that "no remotely credible account" had emanated from the Iraqi government regarding its former biological weapons program. In November the RCC ordered the expulsion of all U.S. inspectors, prompting Washington to send additional forces to the region and to solicit support for a possible military response. However, the United States found little enthusiasm for its plan among Arab states, many of whom accused the Clinton administration of applying a double standard by taking such a hard line toward Iraq but failing to pressure Israel to proceed with implementation of the peace accord with the Palestinians. Nevertheless, U.S. planes, ships, and soldiers continued to pour into the region in early 1998 in preparation for an attack, despite opposition from fellow Security Council members China, France, and Russia. With time apparently running out, UN Secretary General Kofi Annan met with Hussein in Baghdad in late February, finally securing the Iraqi president's signature on a memorandum of understanding permitting the resumption of inspections at all proposed sites, including the "presidential palaces" previously declared off-limits. Tensions having been reduced, at least temporarily, regional leaders subsequently launched a quiet campaign to pursue the reintegration of Iraq into the international community, while a number of countries, including France and Russia, continued to promote the lifting of the UN sanctions. Among other things, many countries were eager to join Iraq in oil and natural gas projects as soon as the sanctions were removed. Meanwhile, the new phase of the oil-for-food program permitted $5.2 billion in oil sales over the next six months.

Encouraged by the apparent moderation in the Iraqi stance on inspections, the United States in the spring of 1998 reduced its forces in the Gulf, and UNSCOM head Butler spoke of a possible breakthrough in negotiations with the Iraqi regime. However, a fresh crisis erupted in August when Baghdad, declaring its disarmament "complete," demanded a reduction in U.S. representation in UNSCOM and suspended cooperation with UNSCOM in some areas. The Security Council adopted a hard line toward the demands, and the Iraqi government subsequently announced it was ending all cooperation with UNSCOM until the UN sanctions were lifted and Butler was replaced as chief of the inspectors. A new U.S./UK assault on Iraqi sites appeared imminent in mid-November before Hussein, reportedly under heavy pressure from other Arab leaders, agreed to permit UNSCOM to return to work. Significantly, in addition to ordering a continued buildup of U.S. military capabilities in the region, President Clinton and other U.S. officials indicated that U.S. policy now sought a regime change in Iraq, not just "containment." To that end, the U.S. Congress authorized Clinton to allocate $97 million in military and financial assistance to Iraqi opposition groups.

In early December 1998, UNSCOM's Butler reported that the Iraqi government was not living up to its mid-November pledge of cooperation but was in fact refusing inspectors access to some sites and withholding requested documents. Consequently, on December 16, U.S. and UK forces launched Operation Desert Fox, an intensive bombing and missile campaign on military sites throughout Iraq. U.S. and UK officials said the attacks were designed to degrade the weapons capabilities of the Hussein regime and reduce its collateral threat to nearby countries, although China, France, and Russia (the other permanent members of the Security Council) criticized the action. Extensive damage was inflicted by the campaign (which ended on December 20), but Baghdad remained defiant, declaring a permanent cessation in its interactions with UNSCOM and announcing it would no longer respect the no-fly zones. Subsequently, Iraqi pilots routinely challenged the zones, prompting retaliatory strikes by U.S. forces, now operating under expanded rules of engagement and having been authorized to attack a wider array of targets, such as government buildings and communication facilities. U.S. and UK planes continued to pound Iraqi sites into May. However, the Security Council remained divided on how to proceed, support for military action having been further eroded by revelations that some UNSCOM inspectors had conducted intelligence-gathering activities for Washington while engaged in their inspection duties.

In December 1999, the UN Security Council authorized the establishment of the UN Monitoring, Verification, and Inspection Committee (UNMOVIC) to succeed UNSCOM and offered to suspend the UN sanctions against Iraq if Baghdad were to cooperate with the new disarmament body and the IAEA for 120 days. Iraq quickly rejected the proposal. Hans Blix of Sweden, a former IAEA director, was chosen in January 2000 as a compromise candidate to head UNMOVIC, and technical appointments to UNMOVIC in March were designed to produce a broad base of inspectors. Nevertheless, Iraq displayed no inclination to let the new inspectors into the country, in part, according to some analyses, because international commitment to the sanctions appeared to be waning. President Hussein subsequently launched a "charm offensive" to reestablish regional ties, particularly through trade accommodations. In addition, he was seen as attempting to deflect attention from the Iraqi disarmament issue by adopting a vocal pro-Palestinian stance.

As part of Baghdad's efforts to rejoin the Arab mainstream, it negotiated a free-trade pact with Egypt in January 2001 and promoted economic ties with Syria, one destination for inexpensive Iraqi oil. In addition, Iraq was formally reintegrated into the Arab League at the March 2002 summit, during which Baghdad pledged its support for Kuwaiti "sovereignty." Moreover, President Hussein continued to emphasize his regime's support for the Palestinian cause by, among other things, halting oil exports for one month in the spring of 2002 to protest Israeli actions.

The tone of the Iraqi/UN impasse changed significantly with the installation of the George W. Bush administration in Washington in early 2001, the new U.S. president announcing he would give heightened attention to enforcement of the no-fly zones and intensify pressure on Baghdad. Lending support to the call for renewed vigilance, UNMOVIC in March 2001 indicated that the Iraqi regime probably still retained the ability to deploy biological or chemical weapons.

Following the terrorist attacks on the United States in September 2001, President Bush quickly expanded the global U.S.-led "war on terrorism," arguing that Iraqi weapons of mass destruction could someday end up in the hands of terrorists. Branding Iraq as a member (along with Iran and North Korea) of an "axis of evil," Bush directed the Central Intelligence Agency to use "all available tools" to overthrow Hussein. In mid-2002 the Bush administration started planning a U.S.-led invasion of Iraq that would begin if complete disarmament were not quickly forthcoming. Although Washington initially indicated it believed previous Security Council resolutions were sufficient to support military action against Iraq, the U.S. administration ultimately responded to domestic and international pressure and decided to seek another "last chance" resolution. Iraq having agreed in September to "unconditional" inspections (while continuing to maintain that it possessed no prohibited weapons or weapon-delivery systems), the Security Council on November 8, 2002, adopted Resolution 1441, which threatened Iraq with "serious consequences" if it failed to comply with the new inspection regime. UNMOVIC inspectors arrived in Iraq later in the month.

The growing possibility of the overthrow of the regime of Saddam Hussein presented a paradox for leaders in the Kurdish north, which in recent years had enjoyed de facto self-rule, the region having been divided into separate areas administered by the PUK and the DPK. Some Kurds believed that a war to remove Hussein would jeopardize the authority they exercised, although most of the Kurdish political organizations remained committed to a federal Iraq. In addition, the Kurds were leery of Turkey's intentions should hostilities erupt. (Turkey, home to some 20 million Kurds, had battled its own Kurdish separatist movement since the early 1980s [see article on Turkey for details] and was naturally perceived as concerned that a breakup of Iraq could lead to renewed demands for creation of an independent Kurdistan.) Further complicating political and military assessment was the presence of major oil fields near the northern city of Kirkuk, which was controlled by the Hussein regime but claimed by the Kurds.

UN weapons inspectors arrived in Iraq in late November 2002 to resume the search for banned weapons. Meanwhile, Iraq gave the UN a list of its weapons and information on past weapons programs. However, the 12,000-page report was heavily criticized as misleading and incomplete. The UN demanded greater cooperation from Iraq, citing numerous incidents of interference.

In January 2003, the inspectors discovered 12 unreported chemical warheads and Iraqi missiles that violated range limitations. Iraq subsequently pledged to be more forthcoming and cooperative, and opposition to a potential U.S.-led military strike grew in France, Germany, and a host of other nations. In February UN inspectors reported that Iraq had agreed to the UN's use of aerial reconnaissance, and the inspectors asked for more time to complete their mission. However, the United States and the United Kingdom presented a draft UN Security Council resolution on February 24 that would authorize military action against Iraq if the regime did not meet a deadline of March 17. By this point, the Security Council and NATO seemed locked into pro- and anti-invasion blocs. In response, the Bush administration announced that it would develop a "coalition of the willing" to pursue military action. The pro-war camp withdrew its draft UN resolution on March 17 in light of a threatened French veto. Meanwhile, as the United States and the UK deployed more troops to the region and conducted a diplomatic campaign to convince more countries that Iraq was in violation of its UN commitments, Arab leaders tried unsuccessfully to convince Hussein to resign and go into exile.

As the threat of invasion grew, the Iraqi regime undertook a number of steps designed to forestall military engagement. On February 4, 2003, Iraqi officials offered to renegotiate terms with the UN to address any remaining major concerns of the weapons inspectors. The regime also began destroying its stocks of prohibited missiles in March. At the same time the country was divided into four military districts, each led by a relative or close ally of Hussein, and Iraq began defensive deployments of troops around Baghdad.

On March 20, 2003, the United States launched a series of missile attacks (the "shock and awe" initiative); American, British, Australian, and Polish troops began a ground offensive shortly thereafter. The coalition forces drove quickly into Iraq and engaged in both conventional and psychological warfare to convince the Iraqi military to surrender. Both efforts were successful: the rapid advance to Baghdad was eased by the surrender of major Iraqi commands. Meanwhile, some of the most intense fighting of the war took place between coalition forces and Iraqi special militias known as the *Fedayeen* (martyrs) *Saddam*. (Some of the *Fedayeen* were reportedly non-Iraqis recruited on the eve of the campaign.) The U.S./UK coalition attempted, with limited success, to prompt a Shiite uprising in the South. However, Kurdish forces in the north operated effectively with U.S. special operations forces, and airborne troops and were able to capture the key towns of Mosul and Kirkuk. By April 7 U.S. forces were in Baghdad; the last battle of the campaign took place in Hussein's hometown of Tikrit on April 14.

The overthrow of Saddam Hussein's regime in April 2003 significantly altered the dynamics of Iraq's role in the region. The fall of Baghdad in just three weeks raised U.S. hopes that a post-Hussein Iraq would serve as an impetus for regional transformation in the Middle East, but the more immediate goal became stability in Iraq. The first step in building a new Iraqi government was the appointment of the IGC by the U.S.-led CPA. The creation of this body was met with skepticism by Iraq's Arab neighbors but was endorsed by Iran, which was willing to cooperate with the council because it included Iraqi Shiite parties that had been in exile in Iran. Following the dissolution of the CPA in 2004, Iraq's interim government, led by Ayad Allawi, cooperated with U.S.-led forces in an effort to defeat insurgents. Iraq's transitional and permanent governments, led, respectively by Ibrahim al-Jaafari and Nuri al-Maliki, continued Allawi's policy of cooperation with the United States.

In 2006, Prime Minister al-Maliki backed the full withdrawal of foreign troops by 2008. The United States, however, tied its withdrawal to security conditions in Iraq, not to a specific timetable. In November 2006, President Talabani met with Iranian President Ahmadinejad in an attempt to solicit Iran's assistance in quelling the sectarian violence that had wracked Iraq since early in the year. Ahmadinejad pledged to assist "brother Iraq" but insisted that stability was dependent on the withdrawal of U.S.-led "occupation forces" from Iraq. Talabani also visited Syria in January 2007, diplomatic relations between Iraq and Syria having been resumed the previous November. Syria's President Assad declared that a "safe and secure Iraq" would be a "benefit" for Syria. Iran and Syria also were among some 16 countries from the region and the West that held a regional security conference in Baghdad in March, Iraqi Prime Minister al-Maliki imploring Iraq's neighbors to discontinue financial and military aid to militant groups in Iraq. Subsequently, some 60 countries meeting in Egypt in May adopted a five-year plan for Iraqi reconstruction and security. Concurrently, several creditor nations announced that they were forgiving additional Iraqi debt.

President Bush in late January 2007 announced that some 30,000 additional troops would be sent to Iraq as part of a military "surge" intended to restore security. At the same time, the United States reportedly began to enlist previously anti-U.S. Sunni tribal leaders in a campaign against al-Qaida forces.

Tensions with Turkey intensified significantly in October 2007, when Turkish forces began cross-border shelling of suspected bases of the Kurdistan Workers' Party (PKK), which had been conducting a campaign against the government in Ankara since the late 1970s. Turkey in 2008 launched several more offensives against the PKK in Iraq, prompting criticism from the Iraqi government and messages of concern from Washington. However, state visits between Turkish and Iraqi officials continued, while a number of Sunni Arab countries (including Syria) also extended their diplomatic relations with the

Shiite/Kurd–dominated Iraqi government. Among other things, the United Arab Emirates forgave some $7 billion of Iraqi debt. Meanwhile, Iran's president Mahmoud Ahmadinejad visited Iraq in March 2008, pledging additional economic assistance.

Friction developed with Syria in the second half of 2009 as the Iraqi government strongly objected to the border with Syria being used as a transit route for insurgents heading into Iraq. In September Iraq deployed troops along the border after several major bomb attacks in Baghdad and other locations. In October Iraq and Turkey signed an accord that led to increased cooperation on, among other things, a proposed oil pipeline from Kirkuk to Turkey and rail and canal transportation between the two countries.

In December 2010, the UN Security Council ended the last remaining sanctions on Iraq dating from the 1990–1991 Gulf War. It also terminated the "oil-for-food" program.

Turkey's prime minister travelled to Iraq on a state visit in March 2011 to discuss trade and security issues with al-Maliki and to attempt to improve bilateral relations. However, tensions between the countries increased following a series of cross-border incursions by Turkey against Kurdish rebels, including a campaign in August of widespread aerial and artillery attacks. The strikes were in response to attacks from PKK bases in northern Iraq. The UK's military mission in Iraq officially ended in May with the withdrawal of the last British combat troops, although some training personnel remained. In July, Iraq called for Kuwait to cease construction of a port on the disputed island of Bubiyan.

After Kurdish rebels launched attacks into Turkey from Iraq in October 2011, the Turkish government approved cross-border operations by security forces. Despite protests by Iraq, Turkish forces continued to operate inside Kurdistan for several weeks. In December, Turkey undertook air attacks on suspected Kurdish bases in Northern Iraq.

The Iraqi government warned in November 2011 that an agreement between the Kurdistan regional government and international energy firm Exxon-Mobil was illegal because it had not been negotiated through the national oil ministry. Royal-Dutch Shell had earlier withdrawn from a similar agreement under pressure from the central government. Exxon-Mobil suspended the contract in March 2012.

In February 2012, Saudi Arabia appointed its first ambassador to Iraq in more than 20 years. Iraq and NATO signed a security agreement in September whereby the alliance would continue training and technical assistance for Iraqi defense forces. In October, Turkey extended, by one-year, a measure that authorized military incursions into Iraq. The Iraqi government protested the extension. Also in October, Iraq announced it would purchase 18 F-16 fighters from the United States, bringing its total to 36. In December, the United Kingdom reported that it had paid $22.4 million to more than 400 Iraqis as compensation for illegal detainment or torture during the Iraq War.

In March 2013, 48 Syrian soldiers who fled into Iraq were killed in an ambush by militants while being escorted back to Syria. The attack also killed 9 Iraqi soldiers and was cited as evidence of the growing spillover of the Syrian conflict into Iraq. In April, the PKK announced it would withdraw its fighters from Turkey to bases in Iraq. Iraq and India signed an agreement to expand energy cooperation in August (in 2013 Iraq became India's largest supplier of oil).

Current issues. Prime Minister al-Maliki faced a serious political threat in August 2007 when the IAF and the INL suspended participation in his cabinet. As a result, al-Maliki in September reportedly intensified his efforts to placate Sunnis by releasing Sunnis who had been arrested in the recent crackdown and by endorsing proposed legislation that would permit former Baath members to return to government service. However, the hydrocarbons law (considered a crucial element in a lasting political settlement) remained unresolved in the assembly. Meanwhile, President Bush cited what he described as the success of the nine-month surge and urged continued support for the al-Maliki administration despite its failure to achieve many of the benchmarks established earlier to measure progress.

In mid-2007, the UN terminated UNMOVIC's mandate and also announced that the scope of the UN Assistance Mission for Iraq would be expanded to assist the Iraqi government in fostering political reconciliation as security conditions continued to improve. One so-called benchmark was reached in early 2008 with passage of legislation permitting many former Baath members to return to their jobs and resume political activity. A general amnesty was also issued for many of those detained in security sweeps of recent years. On the other hand, major fighting erupted in the spring between Iraqi security forces and Shiite militias (some possibly linked to al-Sadr) that had previously controlled many neighborhoods in Baghdad and other cities. The government's apparent success in those encounters strengthened al-Maliki's position and facilitated the IAF's return to the cabinet in July. Al-Maliki subsequently suggested that conditions had improved sufficiently to consider the potential withdrawal of most foreign troops from Iraq by 2011. Although still loathe to produce a formal timetable for withdrawal, U.S. officials also expressed the hope that the "endgame" had been reached, although they were careful to acknowledge that recent gains remained "fragile" and "reversible," as evidenced by continued deadly bomb attacks throughout the country. Among the remaining outstanding political issues was the status of oil-rich Kirkuk, which the Kurds claimed should become part of the Kurdish autonomous region, even though some 40 percent of its population was Arab or Turkmen.

In September 2008, Iraqi forces assumed responsibility for security in Anbar Province, the "heartland" of the former Sunni insurgency, and in November the Status of Forces Agreement (SOFA) was concluded with the United States, providing for final U.S. withdrawal from Iraq within three years. Provincial elections on January 31, 2009, also provided evidence of potential stability after the national legislature finally agreed upon the extent of provincial authority. (The ongoing dispute over Kirkuk precluded balloting in its province, while the three Kurdish provinces voted in July for their autonomous regional legislature.) Candidates vied for 444 seats on 14 provincial councils. Parties and groups that had coalesced behind Prime Minister al-Maliki dominated the provincial elections because his Shiite supporters were joined by Sunnis who appreciated his reaching across sectarian lines with recent policies. In the balloting, the State of Law coalition placed first with 126 seats, followed by the al-Mihrab Martyr List, an SIIC-led electoral coalition, with 52 seats, and the al-Sadr Movement with 43.

In February 2009, new U.S. president Barack Obama announced an exit plan under which U.S. forces would be reduced in Iraq from 142,000 to 50,000 by August 2010. In early June, Obama reassured Iraqis that the United States was not pursuing permanent military bases in Iraq and held "no claim" on Iraqi territory or resources. Later that month most U.S. combat troops withdrew from Baghdad and other major population centers. Although deadly insurgent attacks subsequently increased in number significantly as the U.S. presence declined, the Iraqi government in the fall described the security situation to be sufficiently controlled to permit national legislative elections in early 2010. During September civilian casualties dropped to their lowest level since the U.S. invasion, although a twin car-bomb attack killed 125 and injured more than 700 in October. Most noteworthy among the preelection political developments was al-Maliki's formal separation from the UIA (see below).

Prior to and during national parliamentary elections on March 7, 2010, violence escalated sharply. Attackers killed more than 220 during the campaign and balloting as insurgents attempted to disrupt the elections. Following the balloting, both al-Maliki and Allawi called for recounts, prompting a lengthy review of the balloting, but results announced by the electoral commission confirmed the earlier tallies. Neither the INM nor the State of Law grouping was able to create a majority coalition through the summer. Negotiations between the parties continued until an agreement was reached in November on the formation of a coalition government with al-Maliki as prime minister. Reports indicated that the agreement was reached after the INA agreed to back the coalition government in exchange for the release of several thousand Mahdi Army militia fighters imprisoned by the government.

U.S. President Obama announced in August 2010 an end to U.S. combat operations, withdrew the last combat brigades, and tasked the 50,000 remaining U.S. troops with support and training operations. In September the United States formally ended combat operations in Iraq, although U.S. personnel continued to undertake security missions.

Al-Sadr returned to Iraq in January 2011 following three years in Iran. Al-Sadr assumed an increasingly visible political role and emerged as one of the foremost proponents of the withdrawal of all foreign troops from Iraq. In March Allawi announced that he would not head the proposed new security and political council because of al-Maliki's failure to devolve powers from the prime minister's office.

In May 2011, the National Assembly approved the creation of a third vice-presidential post. However, Vice President Adil Abdul-MAHDI resigned on May 31, leaving one position vacant. Two months later, al-Maliki reached an agreement with the parties in his coalition government to streamline the cabinet by eliminating 12 ministries. Violence increased through 2011 as insurgents continued a campaign of assassinations of government and security officials and bombings, including a suicide bombing on January 18 in Tikrit, which killed 60 and injured more than 150, and another attack in Tikrit in May that left

58 dead and 100 wounded. In a coordinated series of attacks on March 20, there were 40 bombings in 20 cities. In 2011, the UN estimated that 21,499 civilians were killed or injured in Iraq that year as a result of the continuing violence.

On December 19, 2011, an arrest warrant was issued for First Vice President Tariq al-Hashimi (Renewal List), charging the Sunni leader with orchestrating terrorist attacks. Al-Hashimi subsequently fled into the Kurdish region of Iraq. The incident created a crisis within the Iraqi government, as Sunni groups boycotted the Council of Representatives. Meanwhile, on December 31, the last remaining U.S. troops withdrew from Iraq.

In April 2012, the Kurdish regional government announced it would not turn over al-Hashimi for trial on murder and terrorism charges. Al-Hashimi went into exile in Turkey. The government initiated a trial in absentia on May 15, and al-Hashimi and his son-in-law Ahmed QAHTAN were found guilty of murder and sentenced to death in September.

On December 17, 2012, President Talabani suffered a stroke and travelled to Germany two days later for medical treatment. Reports indicated that Kosrat Rasool ALI had been appointed as interim leader of the Patriotic Union of Kurdistan.

Through 2013, instability continued to affect the cabinet. Between March and September of that year, four ministers, all Sunnis, resigned for various reasons, including increasing violence between Sunnis and Shiites. The strife prompted the government to postpone regional elections in two provinces. Also in March, the DPAK ministers began a boycott of the government over a dispute about the 2013–2014 budget. The Kurds asserted that the budget did not provide adequate resources for oil exploration in Kurdish areas. The boycott ended on May 2.

A Sunni militant group, the Army of the Naqshbandia Order (*Jaysh Rijal al-Tariq al-Naqshabandi*—JRTN) led by former military officers of the Saddam regime, launched an increasing number of attacks. On April 25, the JRTN captured the city of Sulaiman Bek, in fighting that killed 128 and injured 269 before Iraqi security forces retook the town.

Insurgent attacks increased substantially through the fall of 2013. The UN reported that July 2013 was the deadliest month for insurgent attacks since June 2008, as 1,057 were killed, including 928 civilians, and 2,326 were wounded. Approximately one-third of all attacks occurred in Baghdad.

In August 2013, the Federal Supreme Court ruled that Maliki was eligible for a third term, overturning legislation enacted in July. In September, the prime minister, vice president, speaker of the parliament, president of the Kurdish region, and other political leaders signed an "honor pledge" to support Talabani and the current government as the president continued to recover from his stroke.

POLITICAL PARTIES AND GROUPS

Following the 1968 coup the dominant force within Iraq was the Arab Socialist Renaissance Party (*Hizb al-Baath al-Arabi al-Ishtiraki*), which under the National Action Charter of 1973 became the core of the regime-supportive National Progressive Front (NPF), subsequently the National Progressive and Patriotic Front (NPPF). (For details on the Baath, which was disbanded by the CPA following the ouster of Saddam Hussein in 2003, and other components of the NPPF, see the 2007 *Handbook.*) An inclusive opposition grouping, the 17-member Iraqi National Joint Action Committee (INJAC) was launched in Damascus in December 1990. Coordination of opposition activity passed in June 1992 to the Iraqi National Congress (INC, below). For an overview of opposition groups, including the Supreme Council of the Islamic Revolution of Iraq (SCIRI), prior to 2002, please see the 2012 *Handbook.*

Parliamentary Parties and Groups:

Iraqi National Movement (*al-Harakah al-Wataniyah al-Iraqiyah*—INM). Formed to contest the 2010 legislative elections, the INM was created from the **Iraqi National List** (INL) and the **Renewal List** (*Tajdid*). Formerly known as the Iraqi List, the INL was formed by Interim Prime Minister Ayad Allawi in December 2004 in advance of the 2005 legislative balloting. The INL includes members of several parties and groups, including Allawi's INA, as well as some tribal leaders. Although mostly Shiite, the group formally presents itself as secular and nonsectarian. It campaigned on a platform of promoting national unity by bridging ethnic and religious differences, but it polled only 13.8 percent of the vote in the January 2005 poll, winning 40 seats in the 275-seat TNA. The INL was therefore unable to form a government, and Allawi was succeeded as prime minister by Ibrahim al-Jaafari of the United Iraqi Alliance.

In preparation for the December 2005 poll for a permanent National Assembly, the INL expanded to include the Iraqi Communist Party and former president Ghazi al-Yawar's *Iraqiyun* List. Nevertheless, it once again polled poorly; its representation fell to 25 seats with just 8 percent of the vote. The group may have suffered from the formation of Sunni-based lists that were running for the first time. Despite the poor showing, the INL retained representation in the subsequent national unity government.

In August 2007, the INL leaders directed its ministers to resign from the cabinet to protest the perceived lack of reform efforts on the part of Prime Minister al-Maliki, with Allawi presenting himself as a candidate to return to the premiership. However, not all of the INL cabinet members followed the withdrawal directive.

The INL performed well in the January 2009 provincial elections, finishing second overall (behind the State of Law coalition and, significantly, ahead of the SIIC). Some INL members reportedly joined State of Law in advance of the 2010 national legislative poll, while the remainder joined the newly formed INM, The INM placed first in the 2010 election with 91 seats. In November Osama al-Nujaifi of the INM was elected speaker of the National Assembly after the party agreed to participate in a coalition government, in which it received 11 ministries.

In December 2012, INM offices were raided by security forces in Baghdad and approximately 15 party activists and officials were arrested. In January 2013, a breakaway faction of the INM formed a new grouping, the White Bloc.

Leaders: Ayad ALLAWI (Former Interim Prime Minister), Osama al-NUJAIFI (Speaker of the National Assembly).

Iraqi National Accord—INA (*al-Itilaf al-Watani al-Iraqi*). A predominantly Sunni grouping formed with support from Saudi Arabia following the Iraqi invasion of Kuwait, the INA was the focus of increasing attention in the mid-1990s in light of the disarray within the INC. The U.S. intelligence community in particular reportedly concluded that the INA represented one of the "most promising" of the Iraqi opposition formations, in part because its members included a number of defectors from the Iraqi military. The INA opened an office in Amman, Jordan, in February 1996 after King Hussein offered to support anti–Saddam Hussein efforts. An INA office also operated in Kurdish-controlled territory in northern Iraq until operations there were quashed by Iraqi troops in August–September 1996.

The INA was also one of the seven organizations deemed eligible by Washington in early 1999 to share in $97 million of U.S. aid designed to support antiregime activity. Subsequent reports regularly referenced the INA, which claimed clandestine support within the Iraqi military, as a member of the revamped INC. Although continuing to cooperate (from offices in London and Jordan) with the INC in attempting to establish a unified opposition front in 2002, the INA appeared to be making certain that it was identified as a separate grouping. Meanwhile, former INA members under the leadership of Tawfiq al-YASIRI and other former Iraqi military officers formed an Iraqi National Coalition to participate in opposition coordination efforts. In January 2012, the INA claimed that more than 40 of its members had been detained by the government for political reasons. Through 2013, reports indicated that INA officials were targeted by militants, including candidates for provincial offices.

Leaders: Dirgham KADHIM, Ayad ALLAWI (Secretary General and Former Interim Prime Minister).

Renewal List (*Tajdid*). Formed in 2009 by Vice President of the Republic Tariq al-HASHIMI, the Renewal List was a Sunni grouping but sought to become a party that "rose above" sectarian and ethnic divisions. The Renewal List formed the INM with the INA. In May 2010 al-Hashimi was reelected vice president of Iraq. He was subsequently convicted of murder in absentia and went into exile in Turkey.

Leader: Tariq al-HASHIMI (Vice President of the Republic).

Iraqiyun List. Established in December 2004 by Interim President Ghazi Ajil al-Yawar, the *Iraqiyun* List comprised independents and members of small parties from across the political, ethnic, and religious spectrum. It supported a federal system for Iraq.

After the *Iraqiyun* List secured five seats in the TNA in January 2005, al-Yawar was named one of Iraq's two vice presidents. The *Iraqiyun* List joined the Iraqi National List for the December 2005 election for the permanent National Assembly and the INM for the 2010 balloting. Osama al-NUJAIFI of the List was elected speaker of the Council of Representatives in November 2010. Divisions within the party emerged in 2013, with one faction advocating protests against growing violence and another, led by al-Nujaifi, rejecting calls for demonstrations.

Leaders: Osama al-NUJAIFI (Speaker of the Council of Representatives), Ghazi Ajil al-YAWAR (Former Vice President of the Republic).

Iraqi National Dialogue Front. This front, which contested the December 2005 legislative elections, is predominantly a Sunni political grouping, although its candidates included representatives from other ethnic and sectarian groups. It was formed to protest the IIP's acceptance of the draft constitution, which included provisions for regional authorities. The front's founder, Saleh al-Mutlaq, was the primary Sunni Arab negotiator on the constitutional drafting committee. The front secured just over 4 percent of the vote in the December 2005 poll, winning 11 seats. The front joined the INM in the 2010 legislative balloting. Its leader Saleh al-MUTLAQ was disqualified from campaigning because of ties to the former regime, so his brother Ibrahim al-MUTLAQ officially led the front during the balloting. Saleh al-Mutlaq was appointed deputy prime minister in 2011.

Leader: Saleh al-MUTLAQ (Deputy Prime Minister).

Iraqi Turkmen Front—ITF (*Irak Türkmen Cephesi*). A coalition of 26 small Turkmen parties and groups formed in 1995, the ITF advocated greater autonomy for the Turkmen ethnic group and official recognition as a minority. The ITF secured three seats in the January 2005 TNA elections, but its representation dropped to one seat after the December 2005 poll. The coalition joined with the INM in the 2010 assembly balloting. The ITF called for Kirkuk to become a "special province" and granted self-governance.

Leader: Sadettin ERGEÇ.

Iraqi Communist Party—ICP (*al-Hizb al-Shuyui al-Iraqi*). Founded in 1934, the ICP was legalized upon its entrance into the National Front in 1973. However, in May 1978 the government executed 21 Communists for engaging in political activities within the armed forces (a right reserved exclusively to Baath members), and by March 1979 several hundred ICP members had either fled the country or relocated in Kurdish areas. With the party having withdrawn from the National Front, (then) RCC Vice Chair Saddam Hussein confirmed in April that Communists were in fact being purged.

In 1993, an ICP congress rejected a proposal that it transform itself into a more centrist grouping and instead reaffirmed its Marxist identity. The congress also elected Hamid Majid Musa as the new ICP secretary general.

The ICP was not included on the list of opposition groups approved by Washington to receive U.S. assistance in early 1999, and it did not participate in the 2002 meetings led by the INC, SCIRI, and other groups in the hope of creating a unified opposition front. However, Musa was appointed a member of the Governing Council following the fall of Saddam Hussein, and the ICP campaigned for the January 2005 legislative election under a People's Union list that also included non-ICP candidates. In the December 2005 poll, the ICP joined the Iraqi National List. It joined the INM for the 2010 balloting. In November 2012, the ICP called for early elections.

Leader: Hamid Majid MUSA.

Other minor parties in the INM include the **National Movement for Development and Reform (*al-Hal*),** led by Jamal al-KARBULI, **al-Hadba**, led by Usama al-NUJAYFI and which won 19 seats in provincial balloting in 2009, and the **Assembly of Independent Democrats.**

State of Law Coalition—SL (*I'tilāf Dawlat al-Qānūn*). Formed in 2009 to compete in provincial balloting, the State of Law Coalition was a vehicle for prime minister al-Maliki after he led the **Islamic Call** (*al-Dawah al-Islamiyah*) out of the UIA. The coalition initially comprised some 40 parties and groups representing Shiites, Sunnis, Kurds, and Christians, with tribal leaders reportedly outnumbering clerics in its leadership. Among other things, al-Maliki pledged to support the "social diversity" of the country. In the 2009 elections the Coalition placed first with 19.1 percent of the vote and the majority of seats in provincial councils.

In the 2010 national elections, the State of Law Coalition placed second with 89 seats. Al-Maliki was subsequently reelected prime minister by the assembly to lead a coalition government that included the SL. Reports in 2013 indicated that Maliki would seek a third term as prime minister.

Leaders: Nuri Jawad al-MALIKI (Prime Minister), Khodeir al-KHAOZAI (Vice President of the Republic).

Islamic Call (*al-Dawah al-Islamiyah*). *Al-Dawah* was established in the 1950s with the support of Shiite leader Muhammad Bakr al-Sadr, who was executed by the Hussein regime in April 1980. Closely affiliated with the Iranian *Mujaheddin,* the Damascus-based *al-Dawah* claimed responsibility for seven assassination attempts on Saddam Hussein and for numerous bombings during the 1980s. Although it was a founding member of the INC, *al-Dawah* subsequently distanced itself from the congress because it was dissatisfied with its representation on the group's executive council. The United States refused to aid *al-Dawah*'s antiregime activities and some reports in April 1999 indicated that a deep political rivalry had developed between *al-Dawah* and the SCIRI leadership. By 2002 it was generally accepted that *al-Dawah* had broken away from SCIRI, and *al-Dawah* was not officially represented at the various Iraqi opposition meetings during 2002.

As a party in exile, *al-Dawah* had split into various branches in Tehran, Damascus, and London, but after the fall of Saddam Hussein its prominent leaders returned to Iraq and resumed political activity. Like SCIRI, whose leaders also returned from exile, al-Dawah cooperated with the U.S.-led occupation authority and gained representation on the IGC. Following the UIA's success in the January 2005 TNA balloting, Ibrahim al-Jaafari of al-Dawah was appointed prime minister. However, dissatisfaction with al-Jaafari's performance within the UIA eventually forced him to relinquish the post after elections for the permanent assembly in December 2005. In April 2006, al-Jaafari was replaced as the UIA candidate for prime minister by another al-Dawah member, Nuri al-Maliki. Al-Dawah formally withdrew from the UIA in August 2009, and al-Maliki subsequently focused on the State of Law coalition as the vehicle for his reelection effort. A no-confidence motion in al-Maliki failed to secure the requisite number of signatures of Iraqi members of parliament in June 2012.

Leaders: Nuri Jawad al-MALIKI (Prime Minister), Ali al-ADEEB.

Other minor parties in the coalition included, among others: the **Islamic Union of Iraqi Turkoman**, led by Abbas al-BAYATI, and the **Independent Bloc**, led by deputy prime minister Hussein al-SHAHRISTANI.

Iraqi National Alliance—INA (*Al-Itilaf al-Watani al-Iraqi*). Formed in August 2009, the two leading components of the INA were the Supreme Islamic Iraqi Council (SIIC, as SCIRI had been renamed) and the al-Sadr Movement. Although the INA clearly remained primarily a Shiite grouping, it also included several Turkmen parties, the INC, and several small Sunni groups, as well as a number of independents.

The INA was created to replace the **United Iraqi Alliance** (UIA), which had been formed in December 2004 as the brainchild of Grand Ayatollah Ali al-Sistani, the Shiite leader who wanted an umbrella organization for the major Shiite parties. Minor parties in the UIA included Hezbollah, a "Marsh Arab" Shiite grouping; the **Islamic Action Organization**, formed in the early 1960s and often referred to as the Islamic Task Organization (ITO); and the **Islamic Union of Iraqi Turkmen,** a grouping of Shiite Turkmen formed in 1991 and led by Abbas al-BAYATI. By the time of the January 30, 2005, balloting for the TNA, some 22 parties had reportedly joined the alliance. In the December 2005 assembly elections, the UIA won a plurality of 128 seats. The alliance subsequently served as a core component of the national unity government.

Prime Minster al-Maliki's *al-Dawah* ultimately declined to join the INA, reportedly because the INA would not agree in advance that al-Maliki would be the INA's candidate for prime minister. Instead, al-Maliki announced that the State of Law coalition (see below), which had been formed for the provincial elections, would be expanded for the national legislative poll.

Human Hamoudi of the SIIC was named the initial INA leader, but that role later went to former prime minister Jaafari prior to the 2010 balloting in which the grouping placed third with 71 seats. The INA was part of the coalition government formed in November 2010 and received 17 ministries. Jaafari called for the government to block the movement of PKK fighters into Iraq from Turkey.

Leader: Ibrahim al-JAAFARI (Chair).

Supreme Islamic Iraqi Council (SIIC). The SIIC is the new name adopted in May 2007 by the Supreme Council for the Islamic Revolution in Iraq (SCIRI), which had also been referenced as the Supreme Assembly of the Islamic Revolution in Iraq (SAIRI). SCIRI was formed in 1982 as an umbrella for a number of Shiite groups, including the **Holy Warriors** (*al-Mujahidin*), which was founded in 1979 in Iran. (The Holy Warriors had claimed responsibility for a variety of attacks on Baghdad, and in March 1980 the RCC had decreed the death penalty for members of the organization.) Other founding members of SCIRI were Islamic Call (*al-Dawah,* see above); the **Islamic Action Organization,** an *al-Dawah* splinter group formed in 1980 under the leadership of Sheikh Taqi MODARESSI; the **Islamic Movement in Iraq,** led by Sheikh Muhammad Mahdi al-KALISI; and the **Islamic Scholars Organization,** led by Sheikh al-NASERI.

Each of the SCIRI components was awarded representation in the INJAC in 1990. In late December 1991 the INJAC debated and ultimately rejected a plan formulated by SCIRI leader Hojatolislam Said Muhammad Bakr al-HAKIM (a founder of the Holy Warriors), which called for Syrian, Iranian, and Turkish assistance in overthrowing the Hussein regime.

In early 1994, spokespersons for SCIRI called for UN intervention to protect the Shiite population in southern Iraq from a government military offensive. In early 1999 the United States indicated an interest in providing assistance to SCIRI as part of the new U.S. initiative to topple Saddam Hussein. However, SCIRI leaders based in Iran declined the offer because they did not want to collaborate with the INC.

SCIRI declined to attend the INC rejuvenation meetings in 1999. It subsequently claimed responsibility for attacks on Iraqi government targets in May 2000 and June 2001. Although SCIRI participated in the 2002 sessions designed to promote a unified anti-Hussein front in advance of a potential U.S.-led military campaign, it was not operating in tandem with the INC and argued that Iraqis themselves should overthrow the Hussein regime. SCIRI reportedly had up to 12,000 fighters at its command, most in Iran but some already in Iraq. When Saddam Hussein fell, SCIRI leaders began returning to Iraq and pledged cooperation with the U.S.-sponsored political process. SCIRI was one of the early participants in the IGC established by the CPA.

Following the overthrow of the regime of Saddam Hussein in 2003, the SCIRI militia (the Badr Brigade) regrouped as a political entity, the Badr Organization, which maintained close ties to SCIRI. SCIRI leader al-Hakim was assassinated in August 2003; he was succeeded by his nephew, Abd al-Aziz al-HAKIM.

Abd al-Aziz al-Hakim met in December 2006 in Washington with U.S. President Bush, whose administration appeared to be emphasizing ties with SCIRI (despite SCIRI's Iranian association) in an attempt to "marginalize" the supporters of Muqtada al-Sadr. The adoption of the SIIC rubric in May 2007 was also seen, in part at least, as another effort to underscore the moderate stance of the group in relation to the Sadrists, with whom the SIIC and the Badr Organization (a dominant element in Iraqi security forces) subsequently battled for control of southern Iraq.

The SIIC formed a coalition, the al-Mihrab Martyr List, ahead of the January 2009 provincial elections. In the balloting, the SIIC grouping lost dominance in several Shiite provinces and only received 6.8 percent of the overall vote. Abd al-Aziz al-Hakim, who had functioned as one of Iraq's most influential leaders by maintaining good relations with the United States and Iran, died of illness in early 2009 just as the SIIC was forming the INA. He was succeeded as the SIIC leader shortly thereafter by his son, Ammar al-Hakim. In the 2010 balloting the SIIC secured 18 seats as part of the INA. In May 2012, the SIIC organized demonstrations to protest the Bahraini crackdown on opposition protestors (see entry on Bahrain). In 2013, the SIIC called for a national dialogue to reduce sectarian violence across the country.

Leaders: Ammar al-HAKIM (Leader), Adil Abd al-MAHDI (Former Vice President of the Republic), Haithem al-HUSSAIN, Human HAMOUDI.

Al-Sadr Movement. This group, an amorphous political, social, and military movement, coalesced around the personality of Shiite leader Muqtada al-Sadr, the son of Grand Ayatollah Mohammed Sadeq al-Sadr and a relative of Grand Ayatollah Mohammed Bakr al-Sadr, two prominent Iraqi Shiite clerics killed by Saddam Hussein's regime. After being underground since 1999, Muqtada al-Sadr rose to prominence almost immediately after the fall of Saddam Hussein in 2003. Al-Sadr did not have the religious credentials of his father, but he was able to claim his family's legacy. Although the majority of Iraqi Shiites backed the approach of the Shiite establishment toward the U.S. occupation of Iraq, Muqtada al-Sadr galvanized a minority of urban Shiite poor from East Baghdad's "Sadr City" (formerly known as Saddam City). After forming his own militia (the Mahdi Army), he also began to organize social services for Shiite communities.

Al-Sadr spurned the IGC, whose membership consisted of other Shiite parties such as SCIRI and *al-Dawah.* Throughout 2003, his followers opposed the presence of U.S.-led forces in Iraq, and tensions rose between occupying authorities and his movement. In early April 2004 full-blown hostilities erupted between al-Sadr's militia and U.S. forces in Sadr City, Najaf, and other Shiite population centers. U.S. forces prevailed then and also when another uprising broke out in August, the Mahdi Army suffering heavy losses. However, al-Sadr survived the fighting, which enhanced his reputation among Shiites who opposed the continued U.S. presence. His political and military actions also challenged other Shiite groups and the establishment in Najaf. However, al-Sadr was never able to command the allegiance of the majority of Iraq's Shiites, who still followed Grand Ayatollah Ali al-Sistani.

The Al-Sadr Movement did not confront coalition forces in Iraq militarily after the August 2004 failed uprising. However, al-Sadr refused to participate in the January 2005 elections for the TNA, although the closely allied "National Independent Cadres and Elites" list won three seats. Throughout 2005 al-Sadr sought a political role and was persuaded to join the UIA list before the December 2005 poll.

With the formation of a national unity government in May 2006, al-Sadr's followers were awarded five ministries (agriculture, education, health, trade, and transportation). However, the Mahdi Army was subsequently implicated in widespread attacks on Sunnis during sectarian violence that dominated the rest of the year. Under reported heavy U.S. pressure, the al-Maliki administration directed security forces to target Madhi Army elements as part of the security operation launched in early 2007, and in April the Sadrist ministers resigned from the cabinet, denouncing Maliki's support for the U.S. "occupation forces." In May al-Sadr called upon his supporters to operate "peacefully" in pursuit of the withdrawal of U.S. forces, and in August he declared a "suspension" of Mahdi Army activities for six months, although some breakaway factions reportedly continued to operate militarily.

In September 2007, the Sadrist bloc announced its formal withdrawal from the UIA's legislative faction due to what it perceived as the government's failure to provide adequate services or security. The rupture was partly attributable, in the opinion of many analysts, to the ongoing friction between the Sadrists and the SIIC for influence in southern Iraq.

Al-Sadr extended the "cease-fire" in regard to the Mahdi Army in February 2008 for six months. However, fighting subsequently broke out between al-Sadr's supporters and government forces attempting to quash Shiite militias in Baghdad and elsewhere. (Some analysts suggested that breakaway factions of the Mahdi Army were operating outside al-Sadr's control at that point.) Al-Sadr again urged his forces not to target government institutions or forces, while decrying the government's "haphazard raids." As many as 1,000 may have died in the seven-week conflict before al-Sadr authorized Iraqi forces (but no U.S. troops) to deploy in Sadr City. Al-Sadr subsequently announced the formation of a new "social wing" for his movement and extended the cease-fire against U.S. troops indefinitely, while continuing to call for an immediate withdrawal of the U.S. presence from Iraq.

The Sadrist bloc campaigned as the **Independent Free Movement** in the 2009 provincial balloting, securing just 6.1 percent of the vote. Emphasizing the movement's shift toward political and social activity, al-Sadr's supporters helped launch the INA with the SIIC in preparation for the 2010 national legislative elections. The Sadrists won 39 seats as part of the INA in the balloting. Meanwhile, al-Sadr remained in self-imposed exile in Iran until 2011. In September 2013, al-Sadr announced his intention to return to politics.

Leaders: Muqtada al-SADR, Sheikh Salah al-UBAYDI, Nassar al-RUBAYI (Parliamentary Leader).

Islamic Virtue Party (*Hizb al-Fadilah*). *Al-Fadilah* is led by Muhammad al-Yacoubi, a former student of Mohammad Sadeq al-Sadr. The party is particularly strong in the Basra region of Iraq and advocates the establishment of a regional government in the Shiite south, as well as installation of Islamic religious law throughout Iraq. *Al-Fadilah* was part of the UIA during the January and December 2005 legislative elections and joined the national unity government in 2006. However, *al-Fadilah* withdrew from the UIA and the cabinet in March 2007 in a dispute over cabinet posts. The party contested several provincial elections in 2009 on its own and won six seats. However, it joined the INA for the 2010 legislative balloting and gained six seats.

Leaders: Sheikh Muhammad al-YA'QUBI, Sheikh Arsad al-NASIRI, Bassam SHARIF.

Iraqi National Congress (INC). The INC was launched by a number of largely Kurdish exile groups in Vienna, Austria, in June 1992. More than 70 delegates from 33 opposition groups attended the congress's first conference within Iraq in the northern city of Shaqlawah in September. During a second such conference in Salahuddin in October, 170 representatives from virtually all the antiregime formations elected a 3-member presidential council and a 26-member executive council. The participants also committed themselves to the nonviolent overthrow of Saddam Hussein and the establishment of a federal system that would permit a substantial degree of ethnic autonomy without partition of the country. Delegates to a third conference in 1993 established a constitutional council and approved diplomatic initiatives intended to secure broader international support for their efforts. At that time, many groups (including the DPK, PUK, SCIRI, IMIK, and INA) were presenting themselves as components of the INC. However, infighting subsequently disrupted INC cohesion, and by 1996 the group was described as in complete disarray (see the 2005–2006 *Handbook* for details).

In early 1999, Washington designated the INC as one of the groups eligible to receive U.S. aid in the effort to topple the Iraqi regime. Consequently, in an apparent effort to regroup, the INC held its first general meeting in nearly three years in London in April 1999. The session appointed an "interim collective leadership" to oversee the revitalization effort.

The United States briefly halted aid to the INC in early 2002 to protest perceived insufficient accounting of the estimated $18 million previously allocated to the INC. However, later in the year the INC's international profile again increased as speculation grew over the role of long-standing Iraqi opposition groups following the potential overthrow of Saddam Hussein. A few observers suggested that INC leader Ahmad Chalabi might serve an important role in a new government. At the same time, however, it appeared that many of the INC's major founding components no longer considered themselves members of the INC. SCIRI, for example, clearly was maintaining its distance from the INC, and the PUK, DPK, and INA were also regularly being referenced as operating outside of the INC umbrella.

Chalabi and other INC members entered Iraq during the U.S./UK-led invasion in early 2003. Despite losing the support of the United States for alleged improper financial dealings, Chalabi became deputy prime minister in the Transitional National Government. Chalabi's INC was briefly part of the UIA but campaigned outside the UIA in the December 2005 elections, failing to win any assembly seats. In the 2010 balloting, the UIA secured one seat in the assembly. Chalabi called for al-Maliki to resign in August 2013.

Leaders: Ahmad CHALABI (Former Deputy Prime Minister), Gen. Najib al-SALHI.

Movement for Constitutional Monarchy. Led by a claimant to the Hashemite throne, which was abolished in 1958, this London-based movement was one of the groups declared eligible for special U.S. aid in early 1999. In 2002 it was described as a component of the INC. In the December 2005 poll the movement ran with Ahmad Chalabi's INC, but the list failed to win any seats, nor did it secure representation in the 2010 balloting.

Leaders: Sharif Ali ibn HUSSEIN, Salah al-SHAYKHLY.

Other parties in the coalition included, among others, the **National Reform Trend,** formed in 2008 by former minister Ibrahim al-JAAFARI, who became chair of the INA and which won 23 seats in the 2009 provincial elections, and the **Tribes of Iraq Coalition** (Anbar Salvation Council), a Sunni grouping formed in 2008 from the Awakening movement and led by Hamid al-HAIS.

Democratic Patriotic Alliance of Kurdistan (DPAK). The DPAK (or Kurdistan Alliance) was formed by the DPK, PUK, and other smaller groups in December 2004 to contest the January 2005 elections for the TNA. Other minor parties in the DPAK included the **Kurdistan Communist Party** (KCP), formed in 1993 and led by Kamal SHAKIR; the **Kurdistan Socialist Democratic Party** (KSDP), led by Muhammad Jahi MAHMUD; the **Kurdistan Toilers' Party,** formed in 1985 by dissidents from the Kurdistan Socialist Party under the leadership of Qadir AZIZ; the **Chaldean Democratic Union; the Iraqi Turkmen Brotherhood Party;** and the **Islamic Group of Kurdistan.**

The DPAK finished second in the January 2005 balloting with 75 seats and just over 25 percent of the vote, partly because of the widespread boycott of the election by Iraq's Sunni community. The PUK, DPK, and most of the other smaller DPAK parties presented a joint Kurdish National Democratic List for the January 2005 elections for the Iraqi Kurdistan National Assembly; the list won 104 of 111 seats.

PUK secretary general Jalal Talabani became president of Iraq after the January 2005 poll. In the December 2005 election for a permanent assembly, the DPAK again presented a joint ticket dominated by the DPK and PUK. Six other smaller parties joined the list, although the Kurdistan Islamic Union left to campaign on its own. Since more Sunni Arabs participated in the December elections than in January, the DPAK's seat total fell to 53 on a vote share of 21.7 percent. In addition to being an important component of the national government, the DPAK continued to dominate the Kurdish Regional Government.

The DPK and PUK presented a Kurdistani List for the July 2009 elections to the Kurdistan Iraqi Parliament, securing 59 seats on a 58 percent vote share. Meanwhile, the KCP and Toilers' Party participated in a Freedom and Social Justice List that also included the **Kurdistan Independent Work Party,** the **Kurdistan Pro-Democratic Party,** and the **Democratic Movement of Kurdistan Party.** The parties maintained their coalition for the 2010 legislative balloting. The List secured 42 seats in the balloting and was given six ministries in the subsequent government. Talabani was reelected president of Iraq in November 2010. Following a stroke in December 2012, Talabani remained hospitalized through the summer of 2013.

Leader: Jalal TALABANI (President of the Republic).

Democratic Party of Kurdistan—DPK (*Partîya Demokrata Kurdistan*). The DPK evolved from a KDP offshoot, the Kurdish Democratic Party (Provisional Leadership), which was formed in late 1975 following the Algiers agreement between Iraq and Iran and the collateral termination of aid to the Kurds by Iran and the United States. When Mullah Mustafa al-Barzani withdrew from the Kurdish insurgency (see Political background, above), the KDP splintered, and the Provisional Leadership declared itself the legitimate successor. It refused to cooperate with the National Front and undertook guerrilla activity through the military wing of the old party, the *Pesh Merga*s ("Those Who Face Death"). The Provisional Leadership consistently opposed government efforts to resettle Kurds in southern Iraq and engaged in clashes with its rival (the PUK, see below), and the Iraqi army. The group began to call itself the DPK following the death of Mullah Barzani in March 1979, although differences between "traditionalist" and "intellectual" factions continued.

In mid-July 1979, several hundred party members returned to Iraq from Iran, where they had resided since 1975. In the spring of 1980, however, there were reports that Iraqi Kurds (*Faili*), who had emigrated from Iran in the first half of the century, were being expelled at the rate of 2,000 a day. Collaterally, Massud Barzani, the son of Mullah Barzani and a leader of the DPK Iranian wing, voiced support for the Tehran regime because of collusion between "U.S. imperialism and its [Baath] lackeys... [in] relentlessly fighting against . . . our Shi'a brethren." A subsequent party congress in August 1981 concluded with a denunciation of the "fascist regime" in Baghdad and its "imperialist war."

In 1988, the DPK and the PUK served as the leading components of a new rebel coalition called the Kurdistan Front (KF) that also included the Kurdistan Socialist Party (KSP), the Kurdistan People's Party (a small Marxist grouping), and the IMIK (below). The DPK controlled the largest rebel force during the 1991 Kurdish uprising following the Gulf war and was represented at the Baghdad peace talks by Nechirvan BARZANI, a nephew of Massud Barzani and grandson of the KDP's founder. During the second half of 1991, the distance between Massud Barzani, who urged immediate negotiations with the Hussein regime, and the PUK's Jalal Talabani, who argued for continued military actions prior to talks, widened, thus hampering action by a coalition that had granted veto power to each of its members. (The revived KF by then included the Assyrian Democratic Party [a Kurdish-speaking Assyrian grouping], the Christian Union [another Assyrian formation], and the Kurdish Communist Party [KCP, an offshoot of the ICP, below].)

On May 19, 1992, the KF conducted an inconclusive election for executive leader, neither of the leading contenders (Massud Barzani and Jalal Talabani), with vote shares of 44.6 and 44.3 percent, respectively, being able to secure a majority; concurrently, a 105-seat Iraqi Kurdistan National Assembly was selected (see Legislatures, below). The DPK and the PUK decided to share power equally in the assembly as well as in a Kurdish "national government" located in Arbil. Moreover, immediately prior to an INC meeting in September 1992, the two groups agreed to place their guerrilla units under a single command. However, the accord was never implemented, and the DPK and PUK retained control of western and eastern "enclaves," respectively. Ongoing tension, fueled by the reported deep animosity between Barzani and Talabani, eventually erupted into open fighting in early 1994, and as many as 2,000 guerrillas were reported killed over the ensuing months. Although an agreement was announced in late November for a cease-fire leading up to new elections in May 1995, PUK forces shortly thereafter seized control of Arbil and expelled DPK representatives from the assembly and cabinet. Yet another cease-fire in the spring of 1995 also proved ineffective, and heavy fighting was reported to have broken out again in July, one correspondent describing the factions as "risking national suicide" at the time when unity was most crucial to Kurdish ambitions. Despite intense U.S. mediation efforts, the DPK/PUK infighting continued throughout the rest of the year and the first half of 1996 as each side retained control of its own territory and no region-wide governance was attempted.

Prompting intense international criticism, the DPK invited the Iraqi military to join it in a "final" offensive against the PUK in late August 1996. (DPK leaders subsequently argued that they had taken that action out of fear that the PUK was planning its own offensive in concert with Iranian forces, which had recently crossed the border to challenge guerrillas from the Kurdish Democratic Party of Iran.) Some 30,000 Iraqi soldiers moved into the north and quickly forced the PUK out of its stronghold in Salahuddin and toward the Iranian border.

On September 26, 1996, DPK leader Barzani announced the formation of a new coalition Kurdish government, led by Roz Nuri SHAWEZ of the DPK and including representatives from the IMIK and the KCP. Barzani also declared that the "temporary" military alliance with Baghdad had ended (Iraqi troops having already been withdrawn in the face of U.S. retaliatory measures in southern Iraq) and reiterated that he was not pursuing a separate political accord with the Iraqi regime. Subsequently, the PUK launched a counter-offensive and recaptured most of the territory it had recently lost. By late October, the DPK and PUK were again reported to be discussing a cease-fire and the possible reactivation of regional authority.

The DPK withdrew from negotiations in March 1997, and KF cohesion was further corroded when new hostilities broke out the following month between the PUK and the IMIK. Kurdish affairs were additionally complicated in May when some 10,000 Turkish troops crossed into northern Iraq to attack camps of the Kurdish Workers' Party (PKK, see article on Turkey). Although Baghdad formally objected to the encroachment on its sovereignty, its protest was apparently not heartfelt enough to stimulate any other action. Despite UN and other international condemnation of its cross-border offensive, Turkey sent even more forces into Iraq in September, claiming, among other things, that it had been invited to do so by the DPK. Subsequently, the PUK launched what it called a "pre-emptive strike" against DPK strongholds in October; however, the cease-fire was subsequently reinstated (reportedly under heavy U.S. pressure), and the uneasy DPK/PUK territorial and military standoff continued into 1998. At that time, it was estimated that there were approximately 10,000 DPK guerrillas loyal to Barzani, described as a publicity-shy "tribal leader" wary of Western influence in the region. Despite having been branded a "traitor" by other opposition groups for his brief collaboration with the Iraqi regime in 1996, Barzani was invited to Washington to meet with Talabani in the fall of 1998, their subsequent peace agreement reflecting U.S. recognition that the former remained a significant influence in the Kurdish region and thereby a necessary component of any effective anti-Hussein opposition. Among other things, the two Kurdish leaders agreed to share power in the region and to conduct new assembly elections in the second half of 1999. However, although "relative peace" transpired in the Kurdish-controlled regions, continued friction prevented new assembly balloting. Finally, in October 2002, the assembly reconvened amid a "display of friendship" between Barzani and Talabani, seemingly prompted by the prospect of the overthrow of Saddam Hussein and the concurrent need for Kurdish unity in discussions regarding a "post-Saddam" Iraq. (It has long been widely accepted that Kurdish sentiment overwhelmingly favors the creation of an independent Kurdish state. However, bowing to opposition to that concept from regional and Western capitals, the Kurdish groups in Iraq remain formally supportive of a federated Iraq with substantial regional autonomy.) As of late 2002, it was estimated that as many as 25,000 guerrillas were under the command of the DPK, which had governed northwestern Iraq on a de facto basis with an administration based in Arbil. (Most news reports currently reference this group as the Kurdish Democratic Party [KDP] in apparent recognition of its status as the genuine successor to the original KDP.) Roj Nouri Shawis of the party was appointed deputy prime minister in 2010. Nechirvan BARZANI was appointed prime minister of the Kurdish region in March 2012.

Leaders: Massud BARZANI (President of the Kurdish Region), Nechirvan BARZANI (Prime Minister and Vice President of the Party), Roj Nouri SHAWIS (Former Deputy Prime Minister).

Patriotic Union of Kurdistan—PUK (*Yeketî Niştîmanî Kurdistan*). The PUK, which has received support from the Syrian Baath, resulted from the 1977 merger of Jalal Talabani's Kurdish National Union (KNU) with the Socialist Movement of Kurdistan and the Association of Marxist-Leninists of Kurdistan. The KNU had been formed in mid-1975 when Talabani, a left-wing member of the original KDP, refused to accept Mullah Barzani's claim that the Kurdish rebellion had come to an end. Supported by *Pesh Merga* units, Talabani subsequently attempted to unify guerrilla activity under his leadership, but the PUK suffered significant losses in June 1978 during skirmishes in northern Iraq with the DPK, which Talabani accused of having links to both the shah of Iran and the U.S. Central Intelligence Agency.

In January 1984, it was reported that an agreement had been concluded between the PUK and government forces that called for a cease-fire, assurances of greater Kurdish autonomy, and the formation of a 40,000-member Kurdish army to counter Iranian incursions into Iraqi Kurdistan. The agreement was never implemented, however, and Iran's Islamic Republic News Agency asserted in November 1986 that the PUK had entered into an alliance with the DPK to pursue a joint struggle against Baghdad.

PUK forces battled with supporters of the IMIK (below) in late 1993, PUK leaders calling the pro-Iranian fundamentalists "dangerous" and uncommitted to basic Kurdish aspirations. Two years later the PUK was locked in open conflict with the DPK, Talabani accusing arch rival Massud Barzani, among other things, of "hoarding" revenue generated by trade across the Turkish border. Like the DPK, the PUK was estimated to control about 15,000–25,000 fighters, leading observers to the conclusion that a military resolution of their dispute seemed unlikely. Meanwhile, Talabani, described, in contrast to Barzani, as a "garrulous jet-setter," was considered to have the stronger support among Western powers. The PUK, in which a core of urban intellectuals and leftists could still be identified, also exhibited policy differences with the DPK. The PUK's antitribal stance, for example, attracted support from peasant farmers embroiled in land disputes with long-standing tribal leaders. Following attacks by DPK/Iraqi forces in August and September 1996, the PUK was reported to have received military support from Iran, facilitating its subsequent counteroffensive. In September 1998 Talabani reconciled with Barzani during a meeting in Washington in the interest of presenting a united front against the Iraqi regime (see DPK, above, for additional information). Subsequently, the PUK exercised de facto authority in the eastern half of northern Iraq, designating the city of Sulaimaniya as its regional "capital," until the formation of the Kurdish Regional Government following the overthrow of the Hussein national government. In June 2012, the PUK reaffirmed its strategic partnership with the DPK at a joint meeting in Erbil following reports of differences between the groups over support for al-Maliki.

Leaders: Jalal TALABANI (President of the Republic and Leader of the Party), Barham SALIH (Former Prime Minister of the Kurdish Regional Government), Ahmad BAMARMI, Kosrat Rasool ALI.

Iraqi Accord Front—IAF (*Jabahat al-Tawafuq*). The IAF (also referenced as the Iraqi Consensus Front or *Tawafiq*) is a Sunni coalition that won 44 seats in the December 2005 assembly poll. The biggest party in the IAF is the IIP, but the front also includes the hard-line **General Council for the People of Iraq**, led by Adnan al-Dulaimi; and the **National Dialogue Council**, led by Sheikh Khalaf al-ILYAN. The IAF helped formulate the early 2006 national reconciliation and joined the subsequent unity government. However, in early August 2007 the IAF announced that its ministers were suspending their cabinet participation to protest the al-Maliki administration's failure to disband Shiite militias or to release Sunnis who had been "arbitrarily arrested" in the 2006–2007 crackdown on sectarian violence. The IAF also demanded a greater role for Sunnis in security policies overall.

Apparently responding to the recent government crackdown on Shiite militias, which, among other things, had targeted Sunnis, the IAF in April 2008 announced its plan to rejoin the government. Six IAF members (four from the IIP and two from the National Dialogue Council) were installed in the cabinet in July. In May 2009 IAF leader Harith al-OBEIDI was assassinated.

The IAF secured 32 seats in provincial elections in 2009 and 6 seats in the 2010 national legislative balloting. In May 2013, Turkey hosted a conference for Iraqi opposition figures, including a number of exiled members of the IAF.

Leaders: Muhsin Abd al-HAMID, Salim al-JUBOURI, Adnan al-DULAIMI.

Iraqi Islamic Party (IIP). The IIP, formed in the 1950s, was suppressed during the reign of Saddam Hussein, and members of the party conducted an armed struggle against the regime. The IIP resurfaced after the fall of Saddam Hussein in 2003, and the party's secretary general, Muhsin Abd al-Hamid, was given a seat on the IGC. Leaders of the IIP called on followers to boycott the January 2005 legislative elections, but the party participated in the December 2005 poll as the main component of the IAF. (The IIP had caused some controversy among Sunni Arabs because of its support for the new constitution.)

Tariq al-HASHIMI, vice president of the republic, left the IIP to join the INM in the second half of 2009.

Leader: Iyad al-SAMMARRAI (Secretary General of the Party and former Speaker of the National Assembly).

Change (*Gorran*). This grouping was formed in opposition to the DPK-PUK alliance in the Kurdish region in early 2009. It surprised analysts by securing 25 seats in the July balloting for the Kurdistan Iraqi Parliament. *Gorran* received 8 seats in the 2010 national legislative balloting. Prior to balloting for the Kurdish regional assembly, clashes between *Gorran* supporters and PUK members on September 6, 2013, left 12 injured.

Leader: Nawshirwan MUSTAFA.

Unity Alliance of Iraq (*I'tilaf Wehdat al-Iraq*—IU). Usually referred to as "Iraq's Unity," this mainly Sunni coalition was created by groups that participated in the Awakening movement in Anbar province where Sunni militias fought insurgents (see Anbar Salvation Council, below). Initially formed by Sheikh Abu RISHA of the **Iraq Awakening and Independents National Alliance**, Jawal al-BOLANI of the **Iraqi Constitutional Party** led the coalition during the 2010 national legislative elections in which Iraq's Unity won four seats.

Leader: Jawal al-BOLANI.

Kurdistan Islamic Union (KIU). Led by Salah al-Din Baha al-DIN, the KIU was part of the Kurdish Alliance in the January 2005 elections. The KIU dropped out of the Kurdish Alliance and ran on its own in the December 2005 poll, winning 5 seats and 1.3 percent of the vote. In the 2009 balloting for the Kurdistan Iraqi Parliament, the KIU led a Reform and Services List that won 13 seats. Other members of the coalition included the Islamic Group in Kurdistan, the KSDP (see DPAK, above), and the **Future Party.** In the 2010 national balloting, the KIU won 4 seats. Reports in 2013 indicated that the KIU had joined *Gorran* in an electoral bloc for the regional balloting.

Kurdistan Islamic Group (KIG). Formed in 2001 by Muhammad Ali Bapir, the KIG, a conservative Sunni grouping, is comprised mainly of former members of the IMIK. The group was reportedly linked to *Ansar al-Islam* (an allegation denied by Bapir), and leaders were arrested by U.S. forces in 2003. In the January 2005 elections, the KIG secured two seats in the TNA. In the March 2010 balloting, the KIG also secured two seats in the national parliament.

Leaders: Muhammad Ali BAPIR, Marwan GALALY.

Other Parties and Groups:

For more on the **List for the Iraqi Nation** (*Mithal al-Alusi*), the **Assyrian Democratic Movement**—ADM (*al-Rafidain*), the **Reconciliation and Liberation Bloc** (*al-Risaliyun*), and the **Yazidi Movement for Reform and Progress**, please see the 2012 *Handbook.*

Ansar al-Islam (Supporters of Islam). A Kurdish extremist grouping launched initially as the *Jund al-Islam* (Army of Islam) by defectors from the **Islamic Movement of Iraqi Kurdistan**—IMIK (see the 2010 *Handbook* for more details) and other fundamentalist militants in mid-2001, *Ansar al-Islam* was subsequently blamed for a number of violent episodes in northern Iraq. One of the group's adversaries—the PUK—alleged that *Ansar al-Islam,* which controlled several villages with a guerrilla force estimated at 400–1,000 fighters, was connected with the al-Qaida terrorist network. In 2003 *Ansar al-Islam* leader Mullah Najm al-Din Faraj (a.k.a. Mullah Krekar) fled to Norway. In May 2010 one of the leaders of the organization, Abdullah al-Shafii, was captured by U.S. forces in Baghdad. In April 2012, Iraqi security forces captured 25 *Ansar al-Islam* fighters who were part of the group's main cell in Baghdad. Reports in 2013 indicated that many *Ansar al-Islam* fighters had joined other groups, including *Ansar al-Sunnah.*

Leaders: Mullah Najm al-Din FARAJ (a.k.a. Mullah KREKAR), Ahson Ali Abd al-AZIZ, Abdullah al-SHAFII.

Al-Qaida in Iraq. This group is an outgrowth of the *Tawhid* insurgent/terrorist organization formed, under the leadership of Jordanian militant Abu Musab al-Zarqawi, to combat U.S.-led forces following the overthrow of the Hussein regime in 2003. *Tawhid*'s initial relationship to Osama bin Laden's al-Qaida was unclear, but in late October 2004 al-Zarqawi pledged his allegiance to bin Laden, who in turn endorsed al-Zarqawi as leader of al-Qaida in Iraq. Al-Zarqawi claimed responsibility for the antigovernment attacks in Jordan in late 2005 in what was perceived as an attempt to expand his group's influence beyond Iraq. Concurrently, references to the group as "al-Qaida in Mesopotamia" increased.

The U.S. government consistently referred to al-Qaida in Iraq as comprising "non-Iraqi terrorists," although most independent analysts concluded that Sunni Iraqi insurgents also participated in the activities of the group, which was reportedly involved in many attacks on U.S. and Iraqi forces. In addition, al-Zarqawi's followers targeted Shiite Iraqi civilians perceived to be cooperating with the United States or the Iraqi government, which apparently cost al-Qaida in Iraq much support among those sectors in the population that might otherwise have sympathized with its goals.

Al-Zarqawi was killed during a U.S. airstrike in June 2006, and he was reportedly later succeeded as leader of al-Qaida by Sheikh Abu Hamza al-MUHAJIR, an Egyptian referred to by U.S. officials under a different pseudonym—Abu Ayyub al-Masri. Al-Muhajir subsequently reportedly claimed the allegiance of 12,000 fighters, although many observers considered that figure to be inflated.

In 2007, the United States reportedly convinced a number of Sunni tribal leaders (who may have previously supported the Sunni insurgency) to join with U.S. and Iraqi forces in a sustained campaign against al-Qaida in Iraq. In the fall, bin Laden reportedly urged al-Qaida supporters in Iraq to avoid fueling sectarian violence, although the extent of his authority in that matter appeared questionable. Meanwhile, al-Qaida in Iraq continued to operate as part of an umbrella organization of Sunni insurgent groups known as the Islamic State of Iraq.

Major offensives were launched against al-Qaida in Iraq by U.S. forces in January 2008 and by Iraqi forces in May. Al-Qaida in Iraq was subsequently described as severely weakened. In April 2010 the Iraqi government announced that the two senior leaders of al-Qaida in Iraq, al-Muhajir and Abu Omar al-BAGHDADI had been killed in a joint U.S.-Iraqi operation in Tikrit. In May Abu Bakr al-BAGHDADI was named the new head of al-Qaida in Iraq, but reports indicated that the most powerful figure in the organization was "war minister" Al-Nasser Ii-Deen Allah abu SULAYMAN. The organization increased the attacks after the death of Osama bin Laden in May 2011, including a series of 17 attacks across Iraq on August 16, which killed more than 90 and injured more than 200. In 2012, the group launched a series of attacks across Iraq in an effort to reignite sectarian violence.

By 2012, most of the al-Qaida-affiliated organizations had been brought together under the umbrella of the **Islamic State of Iraq and the Levant** (*Dawlat al-'Islāmiyya fi al-'Iraq wa-l-Sham*—ISIS or ISIL), led by Abu Bakr al-Baghdadi. In April, Abu Bakr al-Baghdadi released a tape claiming that the ISIS had merged with the Al-Nusra Front, the main al-Qaida affiliate in Syria (see entry on Syria). Both Al-Nusra and al-Qaida denied the merger. In July, the ISIS attacked Abu Ghraib prison, releasing more than 500 prisoners, including a number of al-Qaida fighters. By 2013, there were an estimated 2,500 ISIS fighters in Iraq.

Anbar Salvation Council. Also known as "Anbar Awakening," this group was formed in 2006 (apparently with the support of the al-Maliki administration) to represent progovernment Sunnis in Anbar Province. Components of the council in 2007 reportedly cooperated with U.S. and Iraqi forces in the campaign against al-Qaida fighters. One leader of the council, Sheikh Abd al-SATTAR Abu Reesha, was killed by a roadside bomb in September 2007.

The Awakening movement subsequently spread to other areas of Iraq as former Sunni insurgents joined the U.S.-led campaign against al-Qaida in Iraq. Members of numerous Awakening Councils (reportedly earning $300 per month from the United States) subsequently served as guards at checkpoints and buildings, their presence being credited as a major reason for the decline of violence in the country in 2008. In October 2008 the Shiite-dominated military assumed responsibility for the heavily armed councils in Baghdad. The following year a number of Sunni tribal leaders joined Prime Minister al-Maliki's State of Law coalition in anticipation of the 2010 legislative elections, and the movement won six seats on provincial councils. Others joined the **Iraq Awakening and Independents National Alliance**, part of the **Unity Alliance of Iraq.**

LEGISLATURES

The new constitution, approved by national referendum on October 15, 2005, provided for a unicameral **National Assembly** (also referenced as the Council of Representatives [*Majlis al-Nuwwab*]; for information on the legislature prior to 2005, please see the 2012 *Handbook*). The assembly comprises 325 members elected by proportional representation within the 18 provinces, whose seat distribution (based on population) ranges from 5 to 59. Twenty-five percent of the seats are reserved for women. Five seats are reserved for Christians, and three for other minority groups. The seat distribution following the March 7, 2010, election, was as follows: the Iraqi National Movement, 91; the State of Law Coalition, 89; the Iraqi National Alliance, 71; the Democratic Patriotic Alliance of Kurdistan, 42; Change, 8; the Iraqi Accord Front, 6; the Unity Alliance of Iraq, 4; the Kurdistan Islamic Union, 4; Kurdistan Islamic Group, 2; Christians (non-party), 5; minorities (non-party), 3.

Speaker: Osama al-NUJAIFI.

Kurdistan Iraqi Parliament. Created after the collapse of a new autonomy agreement with the Iraqi government in late 1991, a unicameral Iraqi Kurdistan National Assembly, as then constituted, contained 105 seats, 5 of which were reserved for Christian Assyrians. A minimum vote share of 7 percent was necessary for non-Assyrian representation. Following the balloting of May 19, 1992, the Democratic Party of Kurdistan (DPK) and the Patriotic Union of Kurdistan (PUK) agreed to fill 50 seats each; 4 were awarded to the Assyrian Democratic Party and 1 to the (Assyrian) Christian Union. However, renewed Kurdish infighting subsequently precluded legislative activity. On October 4, 2002, the assembly reconvened for the first time in eight years as part of a reconciliation initiative launched in anticipation of possible U.S. military action against the Iraqi regime of Saddam Hussein.

Following the ouster of Hussein in 2003, the interim national constitution adopted in 2004 provided for new elections for a 111-member Iraqi Kurdistan National Assembly. The first balloting was held on January 30, 2005.

The regional legislature (which covers the Iraqi provinces of Dohuk, Irbil, and Sulaimaniya) was renamed the Kurdistan Iraqi Parliament in 2009. One hundred of the 11 members (elected for a four-year term) are elected by party-list proportional balloting in a single nationwide constituency. The remaining 11 seats are reserved for minorities (5 for Turkmen, 5 for Christians, and 1 for Armenians), also elected by proportional balloting, except for the Armenian seat, which is majoritarian. At least 30 percent of the seats must be allocated to women.

In the balloting for the 100 general seats on July 25, 2009, the Kurdistani List (the DPK and PUK) won 59 seats; Change, 25; the Reform and Services List, 13; the Islamic Movement, 2; and the Freedom and Social Justice List, 1.

Speaker: Arsalan BAYIZ.

CABINET

[as of November 5, 2013]

Prime Minister	Nuri al-Maliki (SL)
Deputy Prime Ministers	Roj Nouri Shawis (DPAK) Saleh al-Mutlaq (INM)
Deputy Prime Minister for Energy Affairs	Hussein al-Shahristani (SL)
Ministers	
Agriculture	(Vacant)
Civil Society Affairs	Dakheel Kassem (DPAK)
Communications (Acting)	Torurhan Mudhir Hassan al-Mufti (INM)
Culture	(Vacant)
Defense (Acting)	Saadun al-Dulaimi (ind.)
Education	(Vacant)
Electricity	Raad Shallal al-Ani (INM)
Emigration and Immigration	Din Dar Najman Shafiq (KIU)
Environment	Sarkoun Lazar Salaywa (ADM)
Finance (Acting)	Ali Youssef Abdel Nabi (INA)
Foreign Affairs	Hoshyar al-Zebari (DPAK)
Health	Majid Mohamad Amin (DPAK)
Higher Education	Ali al-Adib (SL)
Human Rights	Mohamad al-Soudani (SL)
Industry and Minerals	Ahmad Nasser al-Dali Karbuli (INM)
Interior (Acting)	Nuri al-Maliki (SL)
Justice	Hassan al-Shummar (INA)
Labor and Social Affairs	Nassar al-Rubae (INA)
Municipalities and Public Works	Adel Mhoder (INA)
National Security (Acting)	Nuri al-Maliki (SL)
Oil	Abdul Kareem al-Luaibi (SL)
Planning	Ali Youssef Abdel Nabi (INA)
Reconstruction and Housing	Mohamad Sahib al-Darraj (INA)
Science and Technology	(Vacant)
Tourism and Antiquities	Liwaa Smaissem (INA)
Trade	Khairalla Hassan Babker (DPAK)
Transportation	Hadi al-Ameri (INA)
Water Resources and Irrigation	Muhannad Salman Saadi (INA)
Youth and Sport	Jassim Mohammed Jafar (SL)
Ministers of State	
Foreign Affairs	Ali al-Sajri (IU)
Government Spokesperson	Ali al-Dabbagh (SL)
National Assembly Affairs	Safa al-Safi (SL)
National Reconciliation	Amer al-Khuzai (ind.)
Provincial Affairs (Acting)	Safa al-Safi (SL)
Tribal Affairs	Jamal al-Bateekh (INM)

Women's Affairs	Ibtihal al-Zaidy (INA) [f]
Without Portfolio	Salah Muzahem Darwish (INM)
Without Portfolio	Abdel Saheb Kahraman (DPAK)
Without Portfolio	Yassin Mohammad Ahmad (INA)
Without Portfolio	Abdel Mahdi Hassan al-Matayri (INA)
Without Portfolio	Diaa Nejm al-Assadi
Without Portfolio	Hassan al-Sari (INA)
Without Portfolio	Bushra Hussein Saleh (INA) [f]

[f] = female

Kurdistan Regional Government:

[as of September 15, 2013]

Prime Minister	Nechirvan Barzani (DPK)
Deputy Prime Minister	Imad Sayfour (PUK)
Ministers	
Agriculture	Serwan Baban
Culture and Youth	Kawa Mahmoud Shakir
Education	Asmat Muhamad Khalid
Electricity	Yasin Sheikh Abu Bakir Muhammad Mawati
Endowment and Religious Affairs	Kamil Ali Aziz
Finance and Economy	Bayiz Saeed Mohammad Talabani
Health	Rekawt Hama Rasheed
Higher Education and Scientific Research	Ali Saeed
Housing and Reconstruction	Kamaran Ahmed Abdullah
Interior	Abdul Karim Sultan Sinjari
Justice	Sherwan Haidary
Labor and Social Affairs	Asos Najib Abdullah [f]
Martyrs	Sabah Ahmed Mohamed
Municipalities and Tourism	Dilshad Shahab
Natural Resources	Abdullah Abdulrahman Abdullah
Pesh Merga Affairs	Jafar Mustafa Ali
Planning	Ali Sindi
Trade and Industry	Sinan Abdulkhalq Ahmed Chalabi
Transportation and Communications	Jonson Siyaoosh
Secretary of the Cabinet	Mohammad Qaradaghi

[f] = female

INTERGOVERNMENTAL REPRESENTATION

Ambassador to the U.S.: Lukman FAILY.

U.S. Ambassador to Iraq: Robert Stephen BEECROFT.

Permanent Representative to the UN: Mohamed Ali ALHAKIM.

IGO Memberships (Non-UN): IBRD, LAS, NAM, OIC, OPEC.

IRELAND

Republic of Ireland
Éire

Political Status: Independent state since 1921; under republican constitution effective December 29, 1937.

Area: 27,136 sq. mi. (70,283 sq. km).

Population: 4,582,769 (2013E—UN); 4,775,982 (2013E—U.S. Census).

Major Urban Centers (2013C): DUBLIN (527,612), Cork (119,230), Galway (75,529), Limerick (57,106).

Official Languages: Irish (Gaelic), English.

Monetary Unit: Euro (market rate November 1, 2013: 0.74 euro = $1US).

President (*Uachtarán na hÉireann*): Michael D. HIGGINS (Labour); elected on October 27, 2011, and inaugurated for a seven-year term on November 11, succeeding Mary Patricia McALEESE (*Fianna Fáil*).

Prime Minister (*Taoiseach*): Enda KENNY (*Fine Gail*); nominated by the *Dáil* on March 9, 2011, and appointed by the president and sworn in the same day in succession to Brian COWEN (*Fianna Fáil*), who had resigned on March 8.

THE COUNTRY

The present-day Irish Republic, encompassing 26 of Ireland's 32 historic counties, occupies all but the northeastern quarter of the Atlantic island lying 50 to 100 miles west of Great Britain. Animated by a powerful sense of national identity, the population is approximately 88 percent Roman Catholic and retains a strong sense of identification with the Catholic minority in Northern Ireland. However, a constitutional provision according a privileged position to the Church was repealed by public referendum in 1972. In 2011 women constituted 53 percent of the paid labor force, concentrated in the clerical and service sectors; female participation in government, traditionally small, currently includes 2 cabinet ministers, 18 of 60 senators, and about 16 percent of *Dáil* representatives.

Historically dependent on farming and animal husbandry, Ireland's economy is now dominated by services and knowledge-based industries. Agriculture accounts for 2 percent of GNP and 5 percent of employment. Most farm activity centers on cattle raising and dairying; wheat, barley, sugar beets, and potatoes rank among the leading crops. The industrial sector now contributes about 27 of GNP and employs 19 percent of the workforce. Exported manufactures include chemicals, computers and electrical machinery, clothing, and textiles as well as beverages and processed foods. Low corporate taxes and other incentives have encouraged global high-tech firms such as Apple, Microsoft, and Amazon to establish operations in Ireland, and the service sector grew to comprise 72 percent of GDP and 76 percent of employment in 2012. Ireland has become the world's second-largest exporter of information technology and services. Tourism is another significant source of foreign exchange.

Ireland has been a substantial net financial beneficiary of the European Community (EC, subsequently the European Union—EU) since it became a member in 1973. At the same time, an Industrial Development Authority has had considerable success in attracting foreign investment that helped to generate economic growth averaging 3 percent a year through the 1980s and also in improving the trade balance. During the 1990s, Ireland's combination of low taxes and highly skilled, English-speaking workers attracted foreign investment, particularly U.S. computer firms and international financial companies. With the highest rate of GDP growth per annum in the EU, Ireland's economy became known as the Celtic Tiger.

Ireland was well positioned to meet the criteria for its entry into the European Economic and Monetary Union (EMU) in 1999, when economic expansion reached 8 percent. By July 2000, however, some analysts were expressing concern about an annualized inflation rate of 6.2 percent—more than double the average for the 11-country eurozone—fueled by labor shortages, low interest rates, a real estate bubble, and an expanding private-sector credit boom. With the highest GDP growth rates in the EU, the government enacted substantial spending increases and tax cuts. While the EU warned Dublin about the potential inflationary tendencies of recent budgets, Ireland's GDP growth remained strong through 2007, averaging nearly 6 percent annually.

The global financial crisis punished the Irish economy severely in 2008, when plummeting property values threatened bank solvency. By year's end, GDP had contracted by 11 percent, and unemployment tripled to more than 13 percent. As bank losses from bad loans approached 32 percent of GDP, the government was forced to underwrite the banking sector to stave off total collapse. The 2010 budget slashed public spending by $5.4 billion. Dramatic decline continued as GDP contracted by an additional 7.1 percent in 2009 and 0.4 percent in 2010.

The international financial community stepped in with a €85 billion bailout in November 2010, conditioned on stiff austerity measures. The economy began to stabilize in 2012, with GDP growing 0.9 percent, although unemployment remained at 14.7 percent.

GOVERNMENT AND POLITICS

Political background. Ireland's struggle to maintain national identity and independence dates from the beginning of its conquest by England in the early Middle Ages. Ruled as a separate kingdom under the British Crown and, after 1800, as an integral part of the United Kingdom, Ireland gave birth to a powerful revolutionary movement whose adherents first proclaimed the Republic of Ireland during the Easter Week insurrection of 1916 and, despite initial failure, reaffirmed it in 1919. A measure of national independence was accorded by Great Britain through a treaty in December 1921. Under its terms, the 26 counties of Southern Ireland were granted dominion status, the 6 Protestant-majority counties of Northern Ireland electing to remain within the United Kingdom. The partition was regarded as provisional by the Irish Republic, which until 1998 remained formally committed to incorporation of the northern counties into a unified Irish nation. Under the historic multiparty Good Friday Agreement of April 10, 1998, however, the Irish government acknowledged, as stated in the accompanying British-Irish Agreement, "the legitimacy of whatever choice is freely exercised by a majority of the people of Northern Ireland with regard to its status, whether they prefer to continue to support the Union with Great Britain or a sovereign united Ireland."

Officially known as the Irish Free State from 1922 to 1937, Southern Ireland became the Irish Republic, or simply Ireland (*Éire*), with the entry into force of its present constitution on December 29, 1937. The era's dominant leader was Éamon DE VALÉRA of the Republican (*Fianna Fáil*) party, who served as prime minister for most of the period between 1932 and 1959 and was then president until 1973. Ireland's association with the British Commonwealth was gradually attenuated and finally terminated on April 18, 1949. For most of the next decade governmental responsibility tended to alternate between the *Fianna Fáil* and United Ireland (*Fine Gael*) parties, while from 1957 to 1973 the former ruled under the successive prime ministries of De Valéra (1957–1959), Sean F. LEMASS (1959–1966), and John M. LYNCH (1966–1973).

After calling a surprise election in February 1973, *Fianna Fáil* failed to retain its majority, and a coalition government of the *Fine Gael* and Labour parties was installed under the leadership of Liam COSGRAVE. Lynch returned as prime minister following a *Fianna Fáil* victory in an election held June 16, 1977, but on December 5, 1979, announced his intention to resign and six days later was succeeded by Charles J. HAUGHEY. Haughey's investiture was widely regarded as the most remarkable comeback in Irish political history: Although ultimately acquitted, he had been dismissed as Lynch's finance minister in 1970 and tried on charges of conspiring to use government funds to smuggle arms to the outlawed Irish Republican Army (IRA).

At the election of June 11, 1981, *Fine Gael* gained 21 lower house seats over its 1977 total, and on June 30 Dr. Garret FITZGERALD, by a three-vote margin, succeeded in forming a government in coalition with Labour. The new administration quickly increased taxes, announced spending cuts, and permitted higher interest rates, but on January 27, 1982, its first full budget was defeated by a single vote. Following a new election on February 8, the Haughey-led *Fianna Fáil,* backed by three Workers' Party deputies and two independents, returned to office on March 9. Eight months later, unable to reverse economic decline and buffeted by a series of minor scandals within his official family, Haughey lost a no-confidence motion by two votes. The balance of power again shifted at an election on November 24, yielding the installation of another *Fine Gael*–Labour government under FitzGerald on December 14, 1982.

On October 22, 1986, FitzGerald survived a no-confidence motion by one vote, but he lost his parliamentary majority on December 10 with the resignation of a *Fine Gael* conservative. On January 21, 1987, the four-year-old coalition government fell over the issue of budget cuts, which Labour felt would impinge inequitably on welfare programs. At the ensuing general election of February 17 *Fianna Fáil* fell only three seats short of a majority, with a third Haughey administration being approved on March 10 by the barest possible margin on a vote of 83–82, with one abstention. On the basis of public opinion polls that suggested increased support for his administration, Haughey called an early election on June 15, 1989, but *Fianna Fáil*'s net loss of four parliamentary seats obliged him to join with the Progressive Democrats (PD), which had been formed by *Fianna Fáil* dissidents in 1985. On July 12 the *Fianna Fáil*–PD coalition won *Dáil* approval in an 84–79 vote, with Haughey returning as prime minister.

On December 3, 1990, Mary ROBINSON, a left-leaning lawyer who had long campaigned for birth control and legalized divorce, was inaugurated as president, after having defeated *Fianna Fáil* candidate Brian LENIHAN in runoff balloting on November 9. In November 1991, Prime Minister Haughey, besieged by the alleged improprieties of associates, overcame an intraparty vote of no confidence led by his finance minister, Albert REYNOLDS, who was promptly sacked. However, on January 30, 1992, after being further buffeted by the revival of a 1982 wiretapping scandal, Haughey submitted his resignation, with Reynolds, on February 11, assuming the office that had eluded him three months before. Although *Fianna Fáil* was obliged to retain the PD as its coalition partner, eight former ministers were swept away in an abrupt conclusion to the Haughey era.

On June 18, 1992, a referendum was held on the Maastricht Treaty on more inclusive EU, which voters approved by a 69 percent majority. In a referendum on November 25, Irish voters registered nearly 60 percent majorities in favor of guaranteeing the right to travel to other EC states for abortion and the right to obtain information on abortion availability (enacted into law in March 1995). On a third question decided in November, however, voters opted by a similar majority against a proposed relaxation of Ireland's strict abortion proscription.

The *Fianna Fáil*–PD coalition collapsed in early November 1992 after Reynolds had accused PD leader Desmond O'MALLEY of giving "dishonest" evidence in an inquiry into fraud in the beef-exporting industry. Defeated by a Labour-proposed no-confidence motion on November 5, Reynolds was forced to call an early election on November 25 and saw his party slump to its worst postwar electoral showing. *Fine Gael* also lost ground sharply, while the Labour Party, under the charismatic leadership of Richard (Dick) SPRING, registered its best-ever result, albeit remaining third-ranked. Having spent the election campaign attacking Reynolds, Labour subsequently found that the new parliamentary arithmetic and the attractions of office dictated the party's first-ever coalition with *Fianna Fáil.* The new government, enjoying an unprecedented 36-seat overall majority, took office on January 12, 1993, with Reynolds continuing as prime minister, Spring becoming deputy prime minister and foreign minister, and Labour nominees being awarded five other posts.

Apparently secure in office, Reynolds was unexpectedly brought down in November 1994, after his nomination of the incumbent attorney general as High Court president drew Labour opposition because the nominee had been reluctant to authorize the extradition to the North of a Catholic priest accused of pedophile offenses. Amid great political drama, featuring accusations that Parliament had been misled, Reynolds resigned on November 17 and was replaced as *Fianna Fáil* leader by his finance minister, Bertie AHERN. However, attempts to reconstitute the previous coalition proved abortive, and on December 15 a three-party minority government was formed under the leadership of John BRUTON (*Fine Gael*) that included Labour and the small Democratic Left. The coalition commanded 82 of the *Dáil*'s 166 seats but could rely on the support of the Green Party deputy, whereas *Fianna Fáil* and the PD had a combined strength of only 78 seats and so would require the support of all five independents to challenge the government.

In light of the IRA's cease-fire announcement at the end of August 1994 (see Foreign relations, below), the *Dáil* voted on February 1, 1995, to revoke the 1976 Emergency Powers Act, which had enhanced special police powers in force since 1939. The retention of the original 1939 powers, on the grounds that they were needed to combat organized crime, drew strong criticism from civil liberties groups. (The 1976 powers were not reinstated when the IRA called off its cease-fire in February 1996.)

The Bruton government narrowly prevailed when it called on voters to sanction the legalization of divorce in a constitutional referendum on November 24, 1995. With *Fianna Fáil* giving only half-hearted backing to the proposed change, and with the Catholic Church exerting all its influence against, the outcome was a 50.3 percent victory for the affirmative. New statutes facilitating the division of properties in divorce took effect in February 1997.

With a scandal involving alleged payments to political figures reaching longtime *Fianna Fáil* leader Haughey, the government coalition headed by *Fine Gael* decided to call for early *Dáil* elections in 1997. However, the coalition of *Fine Gael,* Labour, and the Democratic Left failed to close a slight gap in opinion polls and lost to *Fianna Fáil* and the allied Progressive Democrats in balloting on June 6. While no party commanded an outright majority, *Fianna Fáil* won 77 seats and the Progressive Democrats 4 seats, enough to secure, with the support of a few independents, a confidence motion and to form a minority coalition government on June 26. Bertie Ahern thus became, at 45, Ireland's youngest prime minister.

On October 30, 1997, the *Fianna Fáil* candidate, Mary McALEESE, won the presidential election to succeed Robinson, who had declined to run for a second term and had stepped down in September to become the United Nations (UN) High Commissioner for Human Rights. Inaugurated on November 11, McAleese, a Catholic from Northern Ireland and professor of law at Queens University in Belfast, had trounced her four opponents with 45 percent of the vote on the first count and then received 59 percent in the runoff against the *Fine Gael* candidate, Mary BANOTTI.

On April 10, 1998, after 22 months of negotiations, the British and Irish governments won agreement on a historic multiparty peace accord for Northern Ireland (see Foreign relations, below, and the United Kingdom: Northern Ireland entry). Prime Minister Ahern actively campaigned on behalf of the Belfast (Good Friday) Agreement, which received Parliament's overwhelming assent on April 22 and won the backing of 94.4 percent of republic voters (on a turnout of 56 percent) at a referendum on May 22. The approval constituted acceptance of constitutional changes voiding Ireland's claim to sovereignty in the North, although formal enactment of the amendments was delayed until the United Kingdom handed over devolved powers to the Northern Ireland Assembly and executive body on December 2, 1999.

Following years of revelations about political favors and donations, tax evasion schemes, and various gifts to politicians, the climate of "sleaze" was cited by the Labour Party at the end of June 2000 when it introduced a no-confidence motion against the government. However, the government won a confidence motion by a vote of 84–80 on the strength of independent support.

In *Dáil* balloting on May 17, 2002, *Fianna Fáil* won 41.5 percent of the vote and 81 seats, while *Fine Gael* declined to 22.5 percent and 31 seats. Prime Minister Ahern was reappointed on June 6 to head another *Fianna Fáil*–PD government. Subsequently, on October 19, voters approved the Nice treaty in a second referendum, 62.9 percent in favor and 37.1 percent opposed.

In January 2003, the Supreme Court ruled that non-Irish parents and relatives of children born in the country did not have an automatic legal right to remain in Ireland. This ruling was followed by a referendum in June in which voters overwhelmingly endorsed a constitutional amendment that prohibited the automatic extension of citizenship to non-EU babies born in Ireland. The court ruling and subsequent constitutional amendment were supported by the government as a means to end the practice of non-EU persons using residence in Ireland as a means to gain legal status within the union.

In June 2003, a commission found that Ahern and many other members of Parliament had violated limits on campaign spending in the 2002 elections. However, the commission ruled that the violations were not intentional and not criminal.

The June 11, 2004, elections for the European Parliament handed *Fianna Fáil* its worst electoral defeat to date, as *Fine Gael* defeated the ruling party for the first time. The election also marked the first time that *Sinn Féin* won a seat in the EU body. Apparently in response to its poor showing, the administration in December announced a significant increase in public spending for retired workers, people with disabilities, and other sectors of the population.

Prior to the 2004 presidential election, a range of parties, including *Fianna Fáil, Fine Gael,* and *Sinn Féin,* supported the incumbent President McAleese. The Green Party tried to present Éamon RYAN for the presidency, but it was unable to garner support for his candidacy. As a result, no other candidate filed to run for the presidency by the October 1 deadline, and McAleese was thus officially declared reelected on October 1.

Accusations of corruption began to plague Prime Minister Ahern in the summer of 2006. In an August television interview, he admitted to writing blank checks for *Fianna Fáil* party leaders while minister of finance (1991–1994) in the Haughey and Reynolds governments. In September a newspaper reported that in 1993 Ahern had allegedly also received payments from a wealthy businessman. A few days later Ahern admitted receiving these and other funds describing them as loans. He also said that, while some people making the payments had received government appointments, the decisions were made because the contributors were friends, not because money had changed hands. Ahern subsequently began to repay the contributors with 5 percent interest. Additional questions later arose over large deposits into his bank account in 1994 and whether he had paid market value for his Dublin house.

In December 2006 the Moriarty Tribunal, investigating the alleged financial improprieties of former *Fianna Fáil* prime minister Haughey, issued a scathing 600-page report on the corrupt practices of Haughey, the person who first named Ahern as minister of finance. Despite the timing of these and the preceding revelations, Ahern was required by the constitution to hold an election at least once every five years and thus had to call a general election before June 2007. Polls in April 2007 made continuation in government of *Fianna Fáil* and the Progressive Democrats look doubtful. However, the Mahon Tribunal (investigating allegations of Ahern's financial misdeeds) announced it was postponing its hearings until after the election, while on May 14 Ahern enhanced his image by being the first Irish leader to address a joint session of the British Parliament. Capitalizing on those developments (as well as on the nation's continued excellent economic conditions and the recent significant progress regarding Northern Ireland [see Foreign relations, below, for details]), *Fianna Fáil* secured only 3 fewer seats (77) in the May 24 *Dáil* elections than it had in 2002. Meanwhile, *Fine Gael* increased its vote share from 22.5 percent to 27.2 percent and picked up 20 more seats than in 2002. However, its seat gains came mostly at the expense of the Progressive Democrats and independents. *Fianna Fáil* was therefore able to form a majority coalition government, appointed on June 14, 2007, under the continued leadership of Ahern, by joining forces with the Green Party (6 seats), Progressive Democrats (2 seats), and 4 independents.

On September 13, 2007, corruption issues returned to the forefront of attention as Ahern began several days of sworn testimony before the Mahon Tribunal. His testimony raised substantial doubt about the accuracy of his varied accounts in the early and mid-1990s. On September 26 Enda KENNY, *Fine Gael* leader, entered a motion of no confidence in the government on the basis of Ahern's dubious testimony. However, the motion was defeated 81–76, with the Green Party, Progressive Democrats, and 4 independents remaining in support of the government.

In March 2008, testimony before the tribunal, Ahern's former constituency secretary contradicted significant aspects of Ahern's earlier testimony, prompting Ahern's coalition partners to call for a clear explanation. On April 2 Ahern announced his intention to resign on May 6, a date that permitted him to address a joint session of the U.S. Congress on April 30 as previously scheduled. On his final day in office Ahern met with Northern Ireland's soon-to-retire First Minister Ian Paisley for a commemorative ceremony in which Ahern praised Paisley and, implicitly, himself for their roles in the return of self-rule to Northern Ireland.

On the day after Ahern's resignation on May 6, 2008, Brian COWEN, who had been elected leader of *Fianna Fáil* in April, was nominated to the post by the *Dáil* and appointed by the president. Cowen quickly announced a reshuffled cabinet comprising the same parties as those in the Ahern administration.

Cowen's tenure was marked by economic mismanagement and tensions with the EU. Despite rising unemployment, declining revenues, and turbulent international markets, Cowen focused his efforts on the upcoming June 12, 2008, national referendum regarding the EU's proposed Lisbon Treaty, which would provide a political framework to ease implementation of economic coordination. Among the parties in Parliament, only *Sinn Féin* opposed ratification of the treaty, which was also endorsed by many business and labor leaders. However, 53.4 percent of the voters said "no" to the treaty, with exit polls revealing popular confusion over the treaty's meaning and implications. At a December meeting of the European Council—heads of the 27-member EU states—Cowen relayed the Irish people's concerns about the implications regarding taxes, military neutrality, and social policies of Ireland signing on to the Lisbon Treaty. In response, the council agreed that legal guarantees would be given to protect Irish sovereignty, and the Irish government set October 2, 2009, as the date for a second referendum.

By this time, the global financial crisis had hit Ireland particularly hard, and Irish voters pondered the potentially negative economic consequences of a "no" vote. On a turnout of 59 percent, voters supported ratification 67 to 33 percent, thereby salvaging the EU's prospects. However, the vote appeared to do little to buoy sagging public support for the prime minister or even to give assurances of the survival of his government until the next scheduled election in 2012. Within a week of the referendum, corruption charges associated with *Fianna Fáil* reemerged as John O'DONOGHUE resigned as speaker of the *Dáil* over a report of less than forthright disclosure of extravagant charges to his expense account. By mid-October, the Green Party was threatening to leave the government to avoid being tainted by the corruption charges; it also voiced objections to the government's bank rescue plan. However, the Green Party, fearing it would lose seats in a snap election, ultimately supported the government's decision to create a so-called bad bank that would acquire poorly performing property loans from Irish banks in exchange for government bonds. The program—the National Asset Management Agency (NAMA)—remained controversial, however, as critics described it as redistributing money from taxpayers to banks and risk from the banks to the public.

Meanwhile, the government's problems continued to mount. Prime Minister Cowen had to ask Defense Minister Willie O'DEA to resign, which he did in March 2010, or face losing the Green Party as a governing partner after it was revealed that O'Dea had filed a false affidavit against a political opponent. Cowen reshuffled the cabinet in March, which did little to boost public confidence in Cowen's leadership.

In a bid to slash government spending, Cowen and public sector unions signed the Croke Park Agreement on June 6, 2010. At a time when the private sector was laying off workers, the unions agreed to a 5–10 percent cut in public sector salaries in return for minimal layoffs.

In late November 2010, the finance ministers from the EU approved a $114 billion rescue package (underpinned by loans from the EU and the IMF) for Ireland's beleaguered financial sector, assuming adoption by the government of stringent austerity measures, such as reduced public-sector employment and tax increases. The bailout arrangements further eroded support for Cowen, who on January 22, 2011, resigned as leader of *Fianna Fáil* but maintained his post of prime minister and called for early elections. Public confidence in Cowen's government had now sunk to 4 percent. The following day, the Green Party withdrew from the government, although the party agreed to support the EU-mandated budget legislation. The *Dáil* was dissolved on February 1, and a new election scheduled for February 25. Foreign Minister Micháel Martin assumed leadership of *Fianna Fáil* going into the election.

When the votes had been counted, *Fianna Fáil* lost 58 of its previously held 78 seats, reducing it to the third-largest party in the legislature. Voters also punished the Green Party, which lost all six of its seats. The winners of the election were *Fine Gael*, with 76 of the 165 seats, and the Labour Party, which came in second with an impressive total of 37 seats. *Sinn Féin* also performed well in the election and received 14 seats, just 5 seats fewer than *Fianna Fáil*. Among the newly elected representatives was Gerry Adams, president of *Sinn Féin*, who had resigned his positions in the British House of Commons and the Northern Ireland National Assembly to contest and win a seat in the *Dáil*.

Enda Kenny, leader of *Fine Gael*, negotiated a coalition agreement with the Labour Party and was sworn in as prime minister on March 9, 2011. On the same day, Kenny formed a new cabinet that split the finance ministry into multiple departments. In recognition of the country's dire financial circumstances, the new departments would comprise an economic council and include ministers from both coalition parties. The two parties, which together controlled 113 of the 165 seats in the *Dáil,* agreed to follow Cowen's austerity measures for two years in an attempt to gain time to renegotiate the terms of the EU bailout. The two-year plan would be followed by revised austerity programs that would reduce the budget deficit to the EU-required level of 3 percent of GDP by 2015.

Constitution and government. Under Articles 2 and 3 of the Irish constitution as adopted by plebiscite on July 1, 1937, the document applied to "the whole island of Ireland," with Parliament and the government accorded jurisdiction, at least in theory, over the entire "national territory." (As a consequence, residents of Northern Ireland have long been considered citizens of the republic and, accordingly, eligible to hold office in the South.) In the referendum of May 22, 1998, however, Irish voters approved substitute texts for Articles 2 and 3, as specified by the Good Friday Agreement concluded the previous month. The new Article 2 acknowledges "the entitlement and birthright of every person born in the island of Ireland... to be part of the Irish nation," but the new Article 3 also recognizes "that a united Ireland shall be brought about only by peaceful means with the consent of a majority of the people, democratically expressed, in both jurisdictions in the island." In addition, Article 3 authorizes creation of shared North-South executive institutions that "may exercise powers and functions in respect of all or any part of the island."

The constitution provides for a president (*Uachtarán na hÉireann*) directly elected for a seven-year term and for a bicameral legislature (*Oireachtas*) consisting of a directly elected lower house (*Dáil*) and an indirectly chosen upper house (*Seanad*) with power to delay, but not to veto, legislation. The *Seanad* may also initiate or amend legislation, but the lower house must approve all such proposals. Presidential and *Dáil* elections are conducted under the single transferable vote system, in which voters indicate their first choices on their ballots and are invited to indicate a preference order for the other candidates. Multiple "counts," in which candidates getting lower "first-choice" vote totals are eliminated and some votes are transferred to second choices, are often required to determine final electoral outcomes. The cabinet, which is responsible to the *Dáil,* is headed by a prime minister (*Taoiseach*), who is the leader of the majority party or coalition and is appointed by the president for a five-year term on recommendation of the *Dáil.* The president has the power to dissolve the *Dáil* on the prime minister's advice. The judicial system is headed by the Supreme Court and includes a Court of Criminal Appeal, a High Court (called the Central Criminal Court for criminal cases), and circuit and district courts. Judges are appointed by the president with the advice of the government and may be removed only by approval of both houses of the legislature.

Local government is based on 4 provinces (Connacht, Leinster, Munster, and part of Ulster), 27 counties (Tipperary counting as two for administrative purposes), and 5 county boroughs (Dublin, Cork, Galway, Limerick, and Waterford), each with elected governing bodies. Eight regional authorities have as part of their mandate coordinating EU matters.

On August 19, 1998, responding to a car bombing in Omagh, in the North, that claimed 29 lives and injured more than 200 people, Parliament passed a controversial series of "extremely draconian" anti-terrorism measures that included negating the right to silence and adding penalties for withholding information about terrorist crimes.

A constitutional convention, comprised of 100 persons representing a cross section of the population, convened in December 2012 to consider a range of issues. It ultimately proposed keeping the single-transferable vote system, with minor modification, and declined to consider the issue of abolishing the upper house of Parliament (see Current issues).

Although free expression is constitutionally guaranteed, a Censorship of Publications Board under the jurisdiction of the Ministry of Justice is empowered to halt publication of books. Moreover, under the Broadcasting Act 1960, as amended in 1976 and interpreted by the Supreme Court in a July 1982 decision involving a ban against the Provisional *Sinn Féin,* individuals and political parties committed to undermining the state may be denied access to the public broadcasting media. Reporters Without Borders ranked Ireland 15th out of 179 countries in its 2013 Press Freedom Index.

Foreign relations. Independent Ireland has traditionally adhered to an international policy of nonalignment, remaining neutral throughout World War II and subsequently avoiding membership in any regional security structure, in part because of a reluctance to be a military partner of Britain. It has, however, been an active participant in the UN (since

1955), the EC/EU (since 1973), and other multinational organizations. In November 1992 it became an observer member of the Western European Union (WEU), following its endorsement of a defense/security dimension to European integration under the EU's Maastricht Treaty.

Beginning in 1969, Dublin's relations with the United Kingdom were complicated by persistent violence in Ulster and terrorism committed by both the IRA and ultra-unionists. Since the late 1970s the two governments have cooperated in security matters, but aspects of the Northern Ireland problem caused frequent strains. In an effort to improve relations, in 1981 Prime Ministers FitzGerald and Thatcher agreed to establish an Anglo-Irish Inter-Governmental Conference (AIIC) to discuss a range of mutual concerns. The conference convened in January 1982 but subsequently encountered a number of obstacles, including the Haughey government's opposition to UK proposals for devolution of power to the North, its unwillingness to endorse the British position during the UK–Argentinean Falklands conflict, and renewed IRA bombings in London. Further progress was, however, registered in discussions between the two prime ministers in November 1983, leading two years later to an Anglo-Irish Agreement that was subsequently ratified by the Irish and UK parliaments. The pact established a "framework" within which Dublin would have an advisory role in the devolution of power to Northern Ireland but also acknowledged British sovereignty for as long as such status should be desired by a majority of the territory's inhabitants.

In April 1991, what had become a lengthy, but inconclusive, series of AIIC talks on the future of Northern Ireland were suspended in favor of a new initiative that called for negotiations between political leaders in the North and the Dublin government, followed by a renewal of talks between the British and Irish representatives. After a series of procedural delays, punctuated by a revival of sectarian violence, Irish ministers in June 1992 met with both Catholic and Protestant leaders from Northern Ireland for the first time since 1973. However, the republic's constitutional claim to the North again proved to be a crucial obstacle to progress, the talks being formally terminated in November in favor of a continuation of the AIIC process.

The advent of the *Fianna Fáil*–Labour coalition in January 1993 brought a change of tone in Dublin, which held out the prospect of Irish constitutional changes to accommodate the Northern majority. In May, President Robinson became the first Irish head of state to confer with a British monarch by meeting privately with Queen Elizabeth II at Buckingham Palace. Familiar strains resurfaced during President Robinson's unofficial visit to Belfast the following month, when she met and shook hands with the *Sinn Féin* leader, Gerry ADAMS. Nevertheless, renewed impetus in UK-Irish consultations culminated in the Downing Street Declaration on Northern Ireland jointly issued by Prime Ministers Major and Reynolds on December 15, 1993.

Representing a new departure in Anglo-Irish relations, the declaration aimed at a cessation of hostilities in Northern Ireland. While assuming that "the people of the island of Ireland" might wish to opt for unification, it reiterated that "it would be wrong to attempt to impose a united Ireland in the absence of the freely given consent of a majority of the people of Northern Ireland." The Irish government then exerted its influence to bring *Sinn Féin* into the negotiating framework, as envisaged in the declaration, provided that *Sinn Féin* renounce violence. The government's efforts were rewarded by an IRA cease-fire announcement on August 31, 1994, after which *Sinn Féin* leader Adams was invited to Dublin, where in October the government launched an all-Ireland Forum for Peace and Reconciliation (FPR). The publication in February 1995 of a UK-Irish "framework document" setting out the parameters for all-party talks on Northern Ireland provided further impetus to the peace process.

A semiofficial visit by Britain's Prince Charles on May 31–June 1, 1995, which included meetings with both President Robinson and Prime Minister Bruton, was the first by a member of the royal family since Irish independence in 1922. Nevertheless, Dublin's efforts to expedite formal all-party talks on Northern Ireland became stalled by the UK government's insistence on prior "decommissioning" of terrorist groups' arms. U.S. President Clinton, during a visit in November to London, Northern Ireland, and Dublin, helped the parties work around this impasse with the two governments agreeing to a "twin-track" approach under which decommissioning would be dealt with separately by an international commission chaired by former U.S. senator George J. Mitchell.

Mitchell's report in January 1996 concluded that decommissioning of arms prior to talks was unachievable but called on all groups to renounce violence in favor of democratic means. While both Dublin and London accepted the Mitchell "principles," London's collateral decision to hold elections in the North for a consultative Northern Ireland Forum on Political Dialogue prior to renewed talks was seen in Dublin as responsible for the IRA's decision in February to call off the cease-fire. Nevertheless, the Bruton government supported the British position that *Sinn Féin* could not participate in formal talks without a reinstatement of the cease-fire. The resumption of IRA violence in mainland Britain enabled Dublin to extract from London a firm date of June 10 for the start of talks, in return for accepting that a preceding forum election would be held in Northern Ireland. Following the polling on May 30, Bruton and Prime Minister Major of Britain jointly opened the talks at Belfast's Stormont Castle and by June 12 had persuaded the Unionist representatives to accept former senator Mitchell as plenary chair. Thereafter, the process became bogged down in familiar procedural wrangling.

On June 25, 1997, Prime Minister Bruton and British Prime Minister Tony Blair agreed on a detailed mechanism for arms decommissioning and the need for an IRA cease-fire, which was restored on July 20, 1997, clearing the way for *Sinn Féin* to enter the broad-based peace talks held in Belfast the following September. With progress made on several issues and the cease-fire continuing to hold, newly installed Prime Minister Ahern reaffirmed that the Irish Republic would consider dropping its claim to sovereignty over Northern Ireland, if approved by Irish voters in a constitutional referendum.

In January 1998, Ireland and Britain jointly issued a document entitled "Propositions on Heads of Agreement" that provided the framework for the Good Friday Agreement of April 10. The propositions put forward "balanced constitutional change" by both governments; establishment of a directly elected Northern Ireland Assembly and a North-South ministerial council; formation of British-Irish "intergovernmental machinery"; and "adoption of practical and effective measures" concerning such issues as prisoners, security, and decommissioning of arms. Conclusion of the Good Friday Agreement (for details, see the Northern Ireland entry) was accompanied by a new British-Irish Agreement, which replaced the 1985 Anglo-Irish Agreement and committed both governments to carry through on the multiparty peace accord. On November 26 Tony Blair became the first UK prime minister to address the Irish Parliament, using the occasion to lobby for continuation of the peace process and for disarmament to begin.

The arms-decommissioning issue remained a sticking point, however, and the Good Friday Agreement was not fully implemented until December 2, 1999. The North-South Ministerial Council held its inaugural meeting on December 13, and four days later representatives of Ireland, the United Kingdom, the Channel Islands, the Isle of Man, and the devolved governments of Northern Ireland, Scotland, and Wales convened in London for the first session of the Council of the Isles. On the same day Prime Minister Blair hosted the first intergovernmental meeting under the British-Irish Agreement. Throughout 2000 and into 2001 Prime Minister Ahern remained actively involved in holding together the peace process in the face of IRA reluctance to begin active decommissioning. In March 2003 Ahern supported Blair's decision to postpone elections for the Northern Ireland Assembly in response to increasing violence in the North (the elections were held in November 2003). Ahern also participated in talks between the main Northern Irish political parties and the British and Irish governments in December 2003 and January 2004.

Relations between the Irish government and *Sinn Féin* and the IRA deteriorated sharply in late 2004 and early 2005 in the wake of allegations that the IRA was involved in massive money-laundering operations. The government launched raids on a number of alleged IRA locations and confiscated large sums of money, while criticizing *Sinn Féin* leaders for their perceived role (denied by *Sinn Féin*) in directing IRA activity. For his part, Prime Minister Ahern, long a champion of efforts to bring die-hard nationalists "in from the cold," was also reportedly upset by the *Sinn Féin* approach in the talks in December 2004 that failed to resolve the power-sharing dispute in Northern Ireland. However, in July 2005 the IRA announced that it would agree to permanently dismantle all of its weapons and allow two observers—a Catholic priest and a former president of the Methodist Church in Ireland—to witness the process. In September the disarmament was reported to have been carried out. However, the IRA's refusal to release details concerning the operation or to allow any visual documentation of the event fed the ongoing skepticism among members of Ian Paisley's Democratic Unionist Party (PUD). With the Democratic Unionists refusing to communicate with *Sinn Féin*, no resumption of negotiations regarding the sharing of power occurred. In April, UK Prime Minister Blair and Ahern gave the two sides until

November 24, 2006, to form a government, declaring that if this deadline was not met they would dissolve the Northern Ireland legislature, terminate the salaries of those involved, and select other means for governance of the province.

On October 13, 2006, Ahern and Blair announced that their three-day meeting, held in St. Andrews, Scotland, with leaders of the major Northern Ireland political parties had led to the St. Andrews Agreement (see entry on UK: Northern Ireland). It proposed a way forward for restoring devolved power through eventual restoration of the Northern Ireland Assembly. It also called for an executive power-sharing relationship between Unionist and Republican parties to be forged by November 24 and, if successful, for elections the following March. The parties reached sufficient understanding in November about power sharing as well as about the steps required by the agreement regarding policing and justice policy that elections were held on March 7, 2007. On March 26 the leading parties agreed to a shared executive arrangement, and on May 8 the first minister and deputy first minister were elected by the assembly, with other ministers being approved on May 12.

The UK contributed £7 billion toward the EU/IMF bailout package for Ireland in late 2010, a move Chancellor of the Exchequer George OSBORNE explained as being "absolutely in Britain's national interest." At the invitation of the Irish president, Queen Elizabeth II of England visited Ireland in May 2011. This marked the first time a monarch from the United Kingdom visited the country since Ireland was established as a state. The visit was meant to emphasize reconciliation and goodwill between the two countries, although *Sinn Fein* declined to participate. Perhaps due to public criticism of *Sinn Fein*'s 2011 snub, Martin McGUINNESS was on hand to greet the queen during her June 27 Diamond Jubilee celebration in Belfast. McGuinness acknowledged that their widely photographed handshake must have been very difficult for the queen, who lost family members in a 1979 IRA attack, but that their meeting was an essential step in the reconciliation process.

Alongside the Northern Ireland negotiations, Ireland revisited its long-standing military neutrality following publication in March 1996 of the first-ever government white paper on the subject. *Fianna Fáil* long opposed participation in any military organization of which Britain was a member, due to the attendant possibility that British troops would return to Irish Republic soil. Despite a concern by opponents that ratification of the June 1997 Amsterdam Treaty on greater EU integration would ultimately commit Ireland to participation in a unified military force, Irish voters approved the treaty by referendum on May 22, 1998, with 62 percent voting in favor. In 1999 the Ahern government confirmed its interest in joining NATO's Partnership for Peace, which the *Dáil* authorized by a 112–24 vote on November 9, thereby permitting Irish forces to participate in training for multilateral "peace support, search-and-rescue and humanitarian missions." In 2000 Ireland agreed to commit 1,000 troops to a new EU Rapid Reaction Force, although the government secured an agreement that its troops would be deployed only in UN-sanctioned operations.

During the prelude to the 2003 U.S.-led invasion of Iraq, the Irish government permitted U.S. planes to use Shannon airport for stopovers and refueling, despite several large protests.

Prime Minister Kenny paid a visit to China in March 2012 to encourage "substantial" Chinese investment in Ireland, saying that Beijing's interest was proof that Ireland's economy was on the road to recovery. Also in March, Chinese vice president Xi Jinping visited Ireland; one month later Minister for Agriculture, Food, and the Marine Simon COVENEY led an agri-services trade delegation to China; the 90 Irish businesses represented returned home with contracts valued at €35 million. The two countries formally established a strategic partnership that year, during which China invested $150 million in the Irish economy.

While eight Irish troops participated in a NATO cold-weather exercise in the Arctic Circle in March 2012, and NATO secretary general Anders Fogh Rasmussen encouraged Ireland to pursue full membership in NATO, in March 2013 Minister for Justice Alan SHATTER confirmed that the government would remain outside the alliance. Irish troops participated in the EU's 2013 Training Mission to Mali, and Dublin provided €700,000 in humanitarian aid to the war-torn country.

Current issues. Ireland's financial woes continued under the new *Fine Gael*-Labour government after a March stress test revealed that its four major banks were in need of an additional €46.3 billion in order to remain solvent. In response to this news, credit ratings agencies downgraded Ireland. Negotiations between Kenny's government and the EU resulted in even more EU funds being given to Ireland in order to prop up the country's failing banks. Compounding the crisis, the rising strength of the euro in 2011 raised the price of Irish labor, fueling unemployment and pushing Irish citizens to seek work abroad.

In July 2011, the EU agreed to lower the interest rate on Ireland's bailout loan and to extend the terms of the agreement. Meanwhile, the *Dáil* passed a resolution condemning the Vatican for "undermining child protection frameworks" by downplaying regulations for reporting abuse. The Vatican denied the charge and recalled its ambassador from Dublin in protest.

Irish voters went back to the polls on October 27, 2011, this time to choose a successor to term-limited president Mary McAleese. Just as Gerry Adams resigned from the UK House of Commons and the Northern Ireland National Assembly to contest the *Dáil* election, his *Sinn Féin* colleague, former IRA commander Martin McGuinness resigned his Northern Ireland mandate to run for president of the Irish Republic. Michael D. Higgins, leader of the Labour Party, won the presidential balloting, with 56.8 percent of the transferrable votes to the independent Séan GALLAGHER's 35.5 percent. McGuinness placed third with 13.7 percent of the vote. *Fine Gael*'s candidate, Gay MITCHELL, came in a distant fourth, possibly due to voters' frustration with the leading party's economic policies. In concurrent constitutional referendums, voters approved reductions in judicial salaries but rejected a measure to grant parliament greater investigatory powers. Higgins was sworn in November 11.

Following the presidential election, the government unveiled additional spending cuts and tax increases for 2012 worth €3.8 billion. The cuts targeted social benefits, including health care and child services.

In November, Dublin closed Ireland's embassy in Vatican City. Although explained as a "cost-saving measure," the move was a stinging rebuke of the Vatican's seemingly indifferent stance toward a majority-Catholic country. A series of investigations, including the Murphy commission in 2009, had accused several successive Dublin archbishops of covering up reports of physical and sexual abuse of children and charged the police with complicity inasmuch as they treated accusations against the church as being outside police purview. In March 2010, Pope Benedict issued a pastoral letter in which he apologized to the victims and expressed "shame and remorse" over the clergy's failings. The apology did not satisfy the Irish government.

Despite its precarious position, the Irish economy showed signs of modest growth by early 2012. The Kenny government announced a major job creation plan in February 2012 to address the unemployment rate, which rose to 14.5 percent in early 2012. The prime minister reported that the country had a balance of trade surplus for the first time in a decade.

The Mahon tribunal wrapped up its 15-year inquiry on March 22, 2012. Its final report concluded that "corruption in Irish political life was both endemic and systemic" until the late 1990s and singled out *Fianna Fáil* leaders, including former prime ministers Ahern and Reynolds, for corrupt practices. The tribunal's €250 million price tag is yet another *Fianna Fáil* expense borne by Irish taxpayers.

In a national referendum on May 31, 2012, Ireland voted in favor of the European Stability Mechanism. The EU did not need Ireland's approval for the agreement to pass, so the vote's importance came in its opportunity to measure popular sentiments regarding the EU-imposed austerity package.

The 2013 budget, released in December 2012, expected the budget deficit to fall from 8.2 percent of GDP for 2012 to 7.5 percent in 2013. Growth was projected to improve at 1.5 percent. Unemployment remained high, however, despite record levels of labor emigration. Dublin had the opportunity to highlight its economic recovery when it assumed the rotating presidency of the EU on January 1, 2013. Prime Minister Kenney announced plans to focus on stability, growth, and jobs. On April 12 EU financial leaders granted Ireland a seven-year extension to pay off its bailout loans. The country is on track to exit the bailout at the end of 2013, prompting Labour to question the need for a €3.1 billion adjustment scheduled for October.

The Croke Park Agreement expired in June 2013 and was credited with saving taxpayers €1.8 billion in wages. It was replaced with a similar pact, the Haddington Road Agreement, expected to save another €1 billion by 2013.

President Higgins in July 2013 signed a bill legalizing abortion up to 17 weeks if the mother's life is at risk, including from suicide. The bill passed the Daíl 127–31 but prompted the largest revolt inside *Fine Gael* since forming the government. The party had promised not to introduce an abortion bill during its 2011 campaign. The "Protection of Life During Pregnancy Bill" was proposed following the October 2012 death of Savita HALAPPANAVAR, who was denied an abortion while at a hospital suffering a miscarriage. Five *Fine Gael* MPs and two senators were expelled from the party for voting against the bill, including European Affairs Minister Lucinda CREIGHTON.

After making no public statements since his resignation, in September 2013, Emeritus Pope Benedict XVI issued a letter denying allegations of covering up instances of sexual abuse by priests.

On October 4, Irish voters went to the polls about a referendum on abolishing the Seanad, the upper house of Parliament. Leaders of *Fine Gael* described the Seanad as "elitist and irrelevant" and touted the €20 million in salaries that would be saved. Labour and *Fianna Fáil* denounced the initiative, while *Sinn Féin* supported it. In the end, the Seanad barely survived the vote, with 51.73 percent voting against abolishing the body. Also on October 4, voters gave their support to a constitutional amendment to establish a Court of Appeals, to assume some of the workload of the Supreme Court; 65.16 percent voted in favor of the measure.

POLITICAL PARTIES

Government Parties:

The results of the 2011 parliamentary and presidential elections may signal the beginning of a significant realignment among Ireland's political parties. Not only has *Fianna Fáil*, Ireland's longest-ruling party, slipped behind *Fine Gael* and Labour, some polls put it in fourth place behind Sinn Fein.

Fine Gael. *Fine Gael* ("Family of the Irish") was formed in September 1933 through the amalgamation of parties that had accepted the 1921 partition, led by *Cumann na nGaedheal* (the ruling party in 1923–1932). It advocates ultimate union with Northern Ireland, financial encouragement of industry, promotion of foreign investment, and full development of agriculture. Its inability to win a majority in the *Dáil* led to the formation of coalition governments with the Labour Party in 1948–1951, 1954–1957, 1973–1977, 1981–1982, and, under the premiership of Garret FitzGerald, 1982–1987. *Fine Gael*'s slump from 70 to 51 seats in the February 1987 election yielded the surprise resignation of FitzGerald, with former justice minister Alan DUKES being named opposition leader.

At the June 1989 election, the party increased its parliamentary representation to 55, remaining in the opposition. In November 1990 Dukes resigned and was replaced by his more rightist deputy, John Bruton. At the November 1992 balloting, *Fine Gael*'s legislative representation fell to 45 seats, its poorest showing since 1948. Nevertheless, the political crisis of late 1994 enabled Bruton to form a three-party coalition government with Labour and the Democratic Left (see Labour Party, below). In the June 1997 elections, *Fine Gael* increased its strength to 54 seats, but the poor showing of Labour forced *Fine Gael* to return to the opposition.

In mid-July 2000, Bruton proposed that *Fine Gael* and Labour consider a preelection pact before the next general election, but a Labour spokesperson responded that his party preferred to campaign on its own platform. On January 31, 2001, Bruton lost a confidence vote among the party's MPs, and on February 9, Michael NOONAN, a former minister of justice, succeeded him as leader of the opposition. Noonan in turn resigned after *Fine Gael*'s poor performance in the 2002 balloting for the House of Representatives (31 seats on a 22.5 percent vote share); he was succeeded by Enda Kenny, a former minister of tourism and trade. Kenny led *Fine Gael* to an increase of 20 seats in the 2007 elections. As the party's standing in polls began to slip in mid-2010, the then deputy leader Richard BRUTON explored a leadership challenge, but the initiative was strongly and effectively rebuffed by Kenny. In the February 2011 election, the party was propelled into first place with 46 percent of first-preference votes and 76 seats. The party entered a coalition with the Labour Party, with Kenny as prime minister. A July 2013 revolt over legalizing abortion resulted in the expulsion of five MPs and two Senators, who in September established the Reform Alliance with an eye toward the 2014 elections.

Leaders: Enda KENNY (Party Leader and Prime Minister), James REILLY (Deputy Leader).

Labour Party (*Páirtí Lucht Oibre*). Originating in 1912 as an adjunct of the Trades Union Congress (TUC), the Labour Party became a separate entity in 1930. It has traditionally advocated far-reaching social security and medical services, public ownership of many industries and services, better working conditions and increased participation of workers in management, expanded agricultural production, protection of the home market, and cooperation and ultimate union with Northern Ireland.

In October 1982, its leader in parliament, Michael O'LEARY, resigned from the party following its rejection of his proposal that Labour commit itself to the formation of a coalition government with *Fine Gael* should the Haughey government fall. His successor, Richard (Dick) Spring, promptly negotiated an interparty agreement that permitted a *Fine Gael*–Labour coalition to assume office on December 14. The coalition collapsed because of Labour's objection to budget cuts advanced by Prime Minister FitzGerald in January 1987. In opposition, Labour increased its parliamentary representation from 12 seats to 15 in the June 1989 balloting.

In 1990, Labour joined with the Workers' Party (below) in backing the successful presidential candidacy of Mary Robinson, who had twice been a Labour parliamentary candidate but had left the party in 1985. In November 1992 Labour achieved its best-ever election result, winning 33 seats. In January 1993 the party entered into a majority coalition with *Fianna Fáil,* which collapsed in November 1994, largely at Labour's instigation. The party then renewed its alliance with *Fine Gael,* joining a three-party coalition that also included the Democratic Left (DL). However, in the June 1997 elections, Labour's strength was cut to 17 seats, forcing its return to the opposition. The electoral decline precipitated the resignation of Dick Spring as party leader and the announcement by the Labour leadership that henceforth the party was prepared to discuss joining a governing coalition with any party.

For the 1997 election, the Labour Party joined forces with the DL, but the coalition's total of 21 seats was significantly below the 37 seats won in the 1992 poll by the two parties combined. Following months of discussions, Labour and the DL formally merged in January 1999, with Labour leader Ruairí QUINN becoming leader of the unified party and the former DL president, Proinsias DE ROSSA, becoming party president. (For additional information on the DL, see the 2007 *Handbook.*)

Despite heightened expectations, Labour won only 20 seats in the May 2002 elections, and Quinn did not contest the party leadership post again when his term expired in October. He was succeeded by Pat RABBITTE, who resigned in August 2007 after the party had failed to improve in the balloting held the previous May. In the elections of February, 2011, the Labour Party's seat share increased to 37, a gain of 17, with 19.5 percent of first-preference votes. In May it joined a coalition headed by *Fine Gael*, controlling 6 of 17 ministerial positions, but its popularity plummeted as it backed the unpopular austerity budgets that cut wages. In April 2013, Social Protection Minister Joan Burton warned that popular tolerance for austerity had reached its limit. By May 2013, seven high-profile members had tendered their resignations and the party received 5 percent of the vote in a by-election.

Leaders: Eamon GILMORE (Leader), Michael D. HIGGINS (President of the Republic), Joan BURTON (Deputy Leader).

Opposition Parties:

Fianna Fáil. Founded in 1926 by Éamon de Valéra, *Fianna Fáil* ("Soldiers of Destiny") advocates the peaceful ending of partition, the promotion of social justice, and the pursuit of national self-sufficiency. It held governmental responsibility in 1932–1948, 1951–1954, 1957–1973, 1977–1981, and March–November 1982, and was then in opposition for over four years. During this period Charles Haughey survived a number of challenges to his leadership, most notably from Desmond O'Malley (see PD, below), who withdrew from the party in 1985. O'Malley, sitting as an independent, was joined by one *Fianna Fáil* representative in voting to approve the Anglo-Irish Agreement in November 1985, the remainder of the party voting in opposition. Haughey returned as prime minister after the 1987 election, but the *Fianna Fáil* legislative plurality was reduced from 81 to 77 seats in the June 1989 balloting, creating, for the first time in Irish history, a governmental impasse. Consequently, Haughey turned to the PD and on July 12 formed *Fianna Fáil*'s first coalition government.

Haughey resigned in January 1992 and was succeeded by longtime party rival Albert Reynolds. In November the party suffered its worst electoral showing since World War II, winning only 68 seats, forcing Reynolds to seek support from the Labour Party (above). The coalition collapsed with Reynolds's resignation in November 1994, with *Fianna Fáil* going into opposition while remaining the largest parliamentary party. In the subsequent election of June 1997, however, *Fianna Fáil* increased its strength to 77 seats, enough for party chief Bertie Ahern to form a minority government in coalition with the PD and a few independents. Reynolds campaigned for but lost the party's nomination for the presidency in September 1997 to Mary McAleese, who won the nationwide election the following October.

In the 2002 legislative elections, *Fianna Fáil* won 81 seats in the *Dáil* and 30 seats in the Senate. Ahern formed a new coalition government with the PD on June 6, 2002. McAleese was reelected president, without opposition, in October 2004. Following the 2007 elections *Fianna Fáil* held 77 seats in the *Dáil* (plus the officially nonpartisan chair), having overcome predictions of a poor showing that had been based on the ongoing financial scandals involving Ahern and former party leader Haughey.

In September 2007, Ahern announced that the party planned to reorganize on an all-Ireland basis that would include the six counties in Northern Ireland.

After Ahern announced his impending resignation in early April 2008, Deputy Prime Minister Brian Cowen was elected unopposed as the new party leader. Micháel Martin assumed the position of party leader after Cowen resigned his post in early 2011 and led the party into a disastrous showing in the February election. The party's seat share fell dramatically to 20 seats with 17.5 percent of first-preference votes.

The Mahon tribunal's final report, issued on March 22, 2012, cited instances of corruption by former prime ministers Ahern and Reynolds, among others. Ahern immediately resigned from the party. A grassroots movement gained strength in 2013 as party members called for an end to the longstanding practice of collecting donations outside Catholic Churches for three months each year, saying the process was "outdated," in "bad taste," and aligned the party too closely with the Roman Catholic Church.

Leaders: Micheál MARTIN (Party Leader), Séan DORGAN (General Secretary).

Sinn Féin. The islandwide *Sinn Féin* (Ourselves Alone) was formed in 1905 to promote Irish independence and won a majority of the Irish seats in the 1918 UK elections. In conjunction with the IRA, which had been created in 1919 to conduct a guerrilla campaign against British forces, *Sinn Féin* helped lead the revolutionary movement that produced the Irish Free State. Many members left both *Sinn Féin* and the IRA at the formation in 1922 of the *Cumann na nGaedheal* (see *Fine Gael,* above) and in 1926 of *Fianna Fáil.* Its influence substantially reduced, *Sinn Féin* continued its strident opposition to partition while serving as the political wing of the outlawed IRA. A long-standing policy dispute within the IRA eventually led traditional nationalists, committed to continued violence, to form the Provisional IRA in 1969, while the Marxist-oriented rump, primarily devoted to nonviolent political action, continued to represent the "Official" IRA. The rump changed its party name to *Sinn Féin*–The Workers' Party in 1977 to differentiate itself from the Provisional *Sinn Féin* created by the Provisional IRA. In 1982 the Marxists relinquished the *Sinn Féin* identification entirely to the "Provos" and became the Workers' Party (below). (The "Provisional" label is sometimes still used, particularly in reference to the IRA.)

In supporting the IRA's goal of establishing a unified "democratic socialist republic," *Sinn Féin* contested several elections with the proviso that no successful candidate would sit in the *Dáil,* which it did not consider legitimate. In the February 1982 balloting, none of *Sinn Féin*'s seven candidates was successful, and it did not contest the national election in November. In November 1986, however, a party conference in Dublin voted 429 to 161 in favor of ending the policy against taking up *Dáil* seats. Party President Gerry Adams received support in the action by other leaders, including the Army Council of the IRA, while a splinter group left the conference in protest (see Republican *Sinn Féin,* below). The change in policy won no *Dáil* seats until June 1997, when *Sinn Féin* won one. *Sinn Féin* also scored significant electoral success in Northern Ireland in 1997 (see United Kingdom: Northern Ireland entry).

At a special party conference held in Dublin on May 10, 1998, *Sinn Féin* overwhelmingly endorsed the April 10 Good Friday Agreement and agreed to take up seats in the proposed Northern Ireland Assembly. Amid speculation that *Sinn Féin* might win sufficient seats at the next general election to warrant its inclusion in a coalition government, in July 2000 the party won the Sligo mayoralty, its first such victory in over three decades. In the 2002 elections *Sinn Féin* won five seats in the *Dáil.* The party also won its first seats in the EU Parliament in the 2004 elections, one from the republic and one from Northern Ireland. It secured four seats in the *Dáil* in 2007.

Sinn Féin performed well in the 2011 elections, receiving 14 seats with 8.5 percent of first-preference votes. One of these was won by Adams, who resigned from the UK House of Commons and the Northern Ireland National Assembly to contest the *Dáil* election. Former IRA commander Martin McGuinness similarly switched constituencies to run for president of the Irish republic in 2011, finishing in third place. The party has continued to gain support, thanks to its populist, anti-austerity stance.

Leaders: Gerard (Gerry) ADAMS (President), Mary Lou McDONALD (Vice President), Declan KEARNEY (National Chair), Dawn DOYLE (General Secretary).

Socialist Party (SP). The SP was founded in September 1996 by trade unionists, Dublin community activists, and members of Militant Labour. Advocating public ownership and democratic-socialist planning in key sectors of the economy, the islandwide, nonsectarian party won one *Dáil* seat in June 1997. In the parliamentary debate on the Good Friday Agreement of April 10, 1998, SP leader Joe Higgins called for "a democratic and socialist alternative" to the proposed constitutional changes and objected to seeking voter approval of the pact on May 22, arguing against holding simultaneous referenda on the Northern Ireland accord and the EU's Amsterdam Treaty. The SP won one seat in the 1997 and 2002 elections.

The SP supports the abolition of the office of president, and President McAleese's unopposed election in 2004 provided additional emphasis for the party's efforts. The SP lost its sole seat in the *Dáil* in 2007 when Higgins finished fourth (with 15 percent of the vote) in a three-seat constituency. However, Higgins was elected to the European Parliament in 2009. Prior to the 2011 elections, the SP cooperated in an informal alliance under the label of United Left Alliance, joining with People Before Profit Alliance (see below) and an independent candidate associated with a Tipperary group styled as the Workers and Unemployed Action Group in stated opposition to the incumbent government and the coalition anticipated to form after the election. Under its official party label in 2011, the Socialist Party won two seats with 1.2 percent of first-preference votes.

Leader: Joe HIGGINS.

People Before Profit Alliance. The People Before Profit Alliance is a left-wing alliance launched in October 2005 that received approximately 9,000 first-preference votes in the 2007 elections. In the 2011 elections, the Alliance received two seats in the *Dáil* with approximately 1 percent of first-preference votes.

Other Parties:

Green Party (*Comhaontás Glas*). Founded in December 1981 as the Ecology Party of Ireland by Christopher FETTES, *Comhaontás Glas* is an Irish expression of the European Green movement. The group adopted the name Green Alliance in 1983 but took its present name in 1987 to clarify its political status. It captured its first legislative seat at the June 1989 balloting, won a different seat in 1992, and has held 2 of Ireland's 15 European Parliament seats since 1994. The party backed the proposal legalizing divorce that was narrowly approved by referendum in November 1995.

In the June 1997 election, the Green Party increased its strength to two seats. With its poll standing on the rise, the party's May 2000 convention featured a contentious debate over possible participation in a coalition government after the next election. The Green Party won six seats in the 2002 elections but did not join the government. It again won six seats in 2007 and, in view of the depletion of the Progressive Democrats, joined the new cabinet. That decision prompted the resignation as party leader of Trevor SARGENT, who had pledged not to enter the government with *Fianna Fáil.* In the 2011 elections, the Green Party lost all six of its legislative seats, receiving less than 2 percent of the first-preference votes.

Leaders: Eamon RYAN (Party Leader), Roderick O'GORMAN (Chair), Catherine MARTIN (Deputy Leader).

Progressive Democrats—PD (*Dan Páirtí Daonlathach*). The PD was organized in December 1985 by former *Fianna Fáil* legislator Desmond O'MALLEY as an alternative to a "party system... based on the civil war divisions of 65 years ago." Accused by critics of being a "Thatcherite," O'Malley called for fundamental tax reform, government tax cuts, and support for private enterprise. The party won 14 *Dáil* seats in 1987, 8 of which were lost in the 1989 election, after which it joined with *Fianna Fáil* in a coalition government. It withdrew in 1992, and at the resultant November legislative poll its representation rose from 6 seats to 10. O'Malley resigned as leader in October 1993 and was succeeded by Mary HANEY, the first female head of a significant Irish party. In the June 1997 elections the PD won 4 seats and joined *Fianna Fáil* in the new government. In the 2002 elections for the *Dáil,* the PD won 8 seats, and it subsequently formed another coalition government with *Fianna Fáil.*

Haney resigned as party leader in September 2006 in favor of Michael McDOWELL. Following the party's poor showing in the 2007 elections (only two seats won), a series of leadership shifts culminated in the election of Ciarán CANNON as new party leader in April 2008. Members voted to disband the party at a special party conference in November 2008. Haney continued as minister of health, sitting as an independent.

Workers' Party (*Páirtí na nOibri*). Tracing its origin to the original *Sinn Féin* and known from 1977 until 1982 as *Sinn Féin*–The Workers' Party, the Workers' Party is a product of the independence and unification movements that have spanned most of the 20th century. Marxist in outlook and dedicated to the establishment of a united, socialist Ireland, the party captured its first *Dáil* seat in 20 years at the June 1981 election and expanded its representation to three at the February 1982 balloting. After slipping to two seats in November 1982, the party won four seats in 1987 and seven in 1989. In February 1992, however, six of the party's seven MPs, including its leader, Proinsias De Rossa, broke away to form the Democratic Left after their proposal to replace "Leninist revolutionary tactics" with "democratic socialism" was narrowly voted down at a party conference. The rump group failed to secure parliamentary representation in the elections from 1992 through 2011. Its Northern Ireland wing, formerly known as the Workers' Party Ireland Clubs, holds no seats in either the UK House of Commons or the Northern Ireland Assembly.

Leaders: Mick FINNEGAN (President), John LOWRY (General Secretary).

Republican Sinn Féin. The Republican *Sinn Féin* was formed at the parent party's 1986 conference by some 30 dissidents who were vehemently opposed to participation in a *Dáil* that did not include representatives from Northern Ireland. It is allegedly linked to Northern Ireland's violent Continuity IRA, although party leaders have denied any connection. The party president branded the IRA's May 2000 decision to put its arms dumps under international supervision as "an overt act of treachery."

Leaders: Des DALTON (President), Caít TRAINOR (Vice President).

Irish Republican Socialist Party (IRSP). Founded in 1974, the IRSP serves as the political wing of a fringe republican paramilitary group, the Irish National Liberation Army (INLA). The IRSP advocates a democratic socialist republic throughout all of Ireland's 32 counties. It opposed the April 1998 Good Friday Agreement as "a betrayal" that "institutionalizes sectarianism, fails to properly address the imperialist role that Britain has played . . . and locks the Irish people into a capitalist alliance." The INLA announced a cease-fire in August 1998 and in February 2010 confirming that it had disposed of its weapons. The party now presents itself as the first party to advocate on behalf of the gay and lesbian community in Ireland.

Leader: Martin McMONAGLE (Chair).

Communist Party of Ireland—CPI (*Páirtí Cummanach na hÉireann*). An islandwide grouping first formed in 1921 and reestablished in 1933, the CPI split into northern and southern factions during World War II and remained separate until 1970. The party continues to advocate a united, socialist Ireland.

Leaders: Lynda WALKER (Chair), Eugene McCARTAN (General Secretary).

Other parties include several small religious and profamily parties, many of which were formed in opposition to the legalization of divorce in the constitutional referendum held in November 1995. Perhaps the most widely known is the **National Party,** founded in 1995 under the leadership of Nora BENNIS. Others include the **Christian Solidarity Party,** founded by Gerard CASEY in July 1994 as the Christian Centrist Party and now led by party president Richard GREENE and the **People of Ireland Party** (*Muintir na nÉireann Páirtí Teoranta*), founded in 1995 and led by Richard GREENE.

An **Independent *Fianna Fáil*** was established in 1970 by the late Neil BLANEY, a former *Fianna Fáil* minister, and, following his death, was led by his son Harry BLANEY from 1997 to 2002, when he retired and was replaced by his son Niall BLANEY. In 2006 Blaney announced he was joining *Fianna Fáil;* he was reelected to the *Dáil* on the *Fianna Fáil* ballot in the 2007 elections, drawing sharp criticism from the rest of the Blaney family and leading to the dissolution of the Independent *Fianna Fáil.* Other parties with small followings include the **South Kerry Independent Alliance,** the **Natural Law Party,** the far-left **Socialist Workers' Party,** and the anarchist **Workers' Solidarity Movement.**

LEGISLATURE

The Irish **Parliament** (*Oireachtas*) is a bicameral body composed of an upper chamber (Senate) and a lower chamber (House of Representatives).

Senate (*Seanad Éireann*). The upper chamber consists of 60 members serving five-year terms. Eleven are nominated by the prime minister and 49 are elected—6 by graduates of the universities and 43 from candidates put forward by five vocational panels: cultural and educational interests, 5 seats; labor, 11; industry and commerce, 9; agriculture, 11; and public administration, 7. The electing body, a college of some 900 members, includes members of the *Oireachtas* as well as county and county borough councillors. The power of the Senate extends primarily to delaying for a period of 90 days a bill passed by the *Dáil.* Technically, the house does not function on the basis of party divisions; however, following the most recent balloting on February 25, 2011, its composition was as follows: *Fine Gael,* 19 seats; *Fianna Fáil,* 14; the Labour Party, 12; *Sinn Féin,* 3; and independents, 12.

Chair (*Cathaoirleach*)*:* Paddy BURKE.

House of Representatives (*Dáil Éireann*). The *Dáil* currently has 166 members (*teachtaí dála,* familiarly called TDs or deputies) elected by direct suffrage through a single-transferable-vote form of proportional representation for five-year terms, assuming no dissolution. At the most recent balloting, held on February 25, 2011, *Fine Gael* won 76 seats; the Labour Party, 37; *Fianna Fáil*, 20; *Sinn Féin*, 14; People Before Profit Alliance, 2; Socialist Party, 2; and independents, 15.

Chair (*Ceann Comhairle*)*:* Sean BARRETT.

CABINET

[as of September 24, 2013]

Prime Minister (*Taoiseach*)	Enda Kenny (FG)
Deputy Prime Minister (*Tánaiste*)	Eamon Gilmore (Lab)
Ministers	
Agriculture, Fisheries, and Food	Simon Coveney (FG)
Arts, Heritage and Gaeltacht	Jimmy Deenihan (FG)
Children and Youth Affairs	Frances Fitzgerald (FG) [f]
Communications, Energy and Natural Resources	Pat Rabbitte (Lab)
Defense	Alan Shatter (FG)
Education and Skills	Ruairí Quinn (Lab)
Environment, Community and Local Government	Phil Hogan (FG)
Finance	Michael Noonan (FG)
Foreign Affairs and Trade	Eamon Gilmore (Lab)
Health	James Reilly (FG)
Jobs, Enterprise and Innovation	Richard Bruton (FG)
Justice and Equality	Alan Shatter (FG)
Public Expenditure and Reform	Brendan Howlin (Lab)
Social Protection	Joan Burton (Lab) [f]
Transport, Tourism and Sport	Leo Varadkar (FG)

[f] = female

INTERGOVERNMENTAL REPRESENTATION

Ambassador to the U.S.: Anne ANDERSON.

U.S. Ambassador to Ireland: (Vacant).

Permanent Representative to the UN: David DONOGHUE.

IGO Memberships (Non-UN): CEUR, EBRD, EIB, EU, ICC, IEA, IOM, OECD, OSCE, WTO.

ISRAEL

State of Israel
Medinat Yisrael (Hebrew)
Dawlat Israil (Arabic)

Political Status: Independent republic established May 14, 1948; under multiparty parliamentary regime.

Area: 8,463 sq. mi. (21,920 sq. km), including inland water (172 sq. mi., 445 sq. km).

Population: 7,924,052 (2012E—UN); 7,707,042 (2013E—U.S. Census). Area and population figures include East Jerusalem (27 sq. mi. [70 sq. km] prior to subsequent unilateral expansion), which Israel occupied in 1967 and formally annexed in 1980 in an action not recognized by the UN or the United States (which maintains its embassy in Tel Aviv). Also included is a 444-square-mile (1,150 sq. km) sector of the Golan Heights to which Israeli forces withdrew under a 1974 disengagement agreement with Syria and which was placed under Israeli law in December 1981. The area figures do not include Gaza (most of which was turned over to Palestinian control in May 1994 prior to a total turnover in 2005) or the West Bank (from portions of which Israel began withdrawing in May 1994), which encompassed an area of about 2,320 square miles (6,020 sq. km). The combined population of Gaza and the West Bank in 2002 was approximately 3,449,000. The 2008 census figures and 2012 UN population estimate do not include the populations in Gaza and the West Bank, except for Jewish settlers in the West Bank (estimated at more than 350,000 in 2012).

Major Urban Centers (2005E): JERUSALEM (709,000, including East Jerusalem), Tel Aviv/Jaffa (375,000), Haifa (269,000), Rishon LeZiyyon (220,000), Ashdod (200,000).

Official Languages: Hebrew, Arabic. English, which was an official language under the British Mandate from the League of Nations, is taught in the secondary schools and is widely spoken.

Monetary Unit: New Shekel (market rate November 1, 2013: 3.54 shekels = $1US).

President: Shimon PERES (*Kadima*); elected by the *Knesset* in second-round balloting on June 13, 2007, and inaugurated for a seven-year term on July 15, succeeding Moshe KATSAV (*Likud*). (*Knesset* Speaker Dalia ITZIK [*Kadima*] had been serving in an acting presidential capacity since January 25, 2007. See Political background, below, for details.) The next election was scheduled for June 2014.

Prime Minister: Benjamin NETANYAHU (*Likud*); nominated by the president on February 20, 2009, to form a new government following the legislative elections of February 10 and sworn in as head of a new coalition government on March 31 in succession to Ehud OLMERT (*Kadima*), who had remained in a caretaker capacity after announcing his resignation on September 21, 2008; formed a new coalition government on March 18, 2013, following early legislative elections on January 22.

THE COUNTRY

The irregularly shaped area constituting the State of Israel is not completely defined by agreed boundaries, its territorial jurisdiction being determined in part by military armistice agreements entered into at the conclusion of Israel's war of independence in 1948–1949. The territory under de facto Israeli control increased substantially as a result of Israel's military occupation of Arab territories in the Sinai Peninsula (since returned to Egypt), Gaza, the West Bank of the Jordan River (including the Old City of Jerusalem), and the Golan Heights following the Arab-Israeli War of 1967. (The Gaza Strip is now under Palestinian control, as are sections of the West Bank.) More than 75 percent of those holding Israeli citizenship are Jewish, while approximately 20 percent are Arab. As of 2007 women constituted 47 percent of the paid workforce, concentrated in agriculture, teaching, administration, and health care. (According to recent estimates, 56 percent of Jewish women participate in the workforce, compared to less than 20 percent of Arab women.)

Following independence, Israel emerged as a technologically progressive, highly literate, and largely urbanized nation that achieved rapid development based on scientific exploitation of its agricultural and industrial potentialities. Agriculture has since diminished in importance but remains a significant economic sector, the most important products being citrus fruits, field crops, vegetables, and export-oriented nursery items. The industrial sector includes among its major components high-tech manufactures (which account for approximately 40 percent of exports), cut diamonds, textiles, processed foods, chemicals, and military equipment. U.S. financial assistance, tourism, and direct aid from Jews in the United States and elsewhere are also of major economic importance.

Defense requirements generated a highly adverse balance of trade and contributed to a rate of inflation that escalated to more than 400 percent prior to the imposition of austerity measures in mid-1985. However, inflation declined dramatically to less than 16 percent in 1988, and Israel experienced one of the highest GDP growth rates in the world in the first half of the 1990s, while unemployment, which had peaked at more than 11 percent in 1992, dropped to 6 percent by the end of 1996. The conservative government installed in 1996 pursued pro-business policies (most notably extensive privatization of state-run enterprises) and a commitment to budget restraint.

Economic conditions deteriorated sharply in the wake of renewed government/Palestinian violence in 2000, the subsequent "burst of the technology bubble," and the collateral decline in the global economy. Growth subsequently resumed, although unemployment remained unacceptably high at 9.1 percent in 2005.

Despite the war with Hezbollah in Lebanon in mid-2006, GDP grew by an average of 5.3 percent annually in 2006–2007, while unemployment declined to 7.5 percent in the latter year. Increased exports, the "innovative" technology sector, and heavy foreign investment were credited with underpinning that strong economic performance.

Although GDP grew by 4.3 percent in 2008, the effects of the global economic crisis were apparent by the last quarter of the year as exports fell and the credit crunch depressed investment and strained the financial sector. The government consequently implemented a stimulus plan, established a new regulatory structure for capital markets, provided guarantees for exporters, and negotiated new wage and benefit packages with business and workers. Although growth fell to only 0.1 percent in 2009, Israel weathered the financial storm better than many other developed countries, and expansion of 4.6 percent was achieved in 2011, with unemployment falling below 6 percent. Meanwhile, attention focused on the recent discovery offshore of major deposits of natural gas, which some analysts estimated might fulfill energy needs for a generation of Israelis, currently dependent on imported oil and gas. (The first offshore gas began flowing in 2013.) Despite the encouraging financial statistics, the government in 2011–2012 was confronted with major demonstrations protesting an inadequate supply of affordable housing and other social problems, including a widening wealth gap. Growth declined to 3.1 percent in 2012.

GOVERNMENT AND POLITICS

Political background. Israel's modern history dates from the end of the 19th century with the rise of the world Zionist movement and establishment of Jewish agricultural settlements in territory that was then part of the Ottoman Empire. In the Balfour Declaration of 1917 the British government expressed support for the establishment in Palestine of a national home for the Jewish people, provided that the rights of "existing non-Jewish communities" were not prejudiced. With the abrogation of Turkish rule at the end of World War I, the area was assigned to Great Britain under a League of Nations Mandate that incorporated provisions of the Balfour Declaration. British rule continued until May 1948, despite increasing unrest on the part of local Arabs during the 1920s and 1930s and Jewish elements during and after World War II. In 1947 the UN General Assembly adopted a resolution calling for the division of Palestine into Arab and Jewish states and the internationalization of Jerusalem and its environs, but the controversial measure could not be implemented because of Arab opposition. Nonetheless, Israel declared its independence coincident with British withdrawal on May 14, 1948. Although the new state was immediately attacked by Egypt, Syria, Lebanon, Jordan, and Iraq, it was able to maintain itself in the field, and the armistice agreements concluded under UN auspices in 1949 gave Israel control over nearly one-third more territory than had been assigned to it under the original UN resolution. (A second major military encounter between Israel and Egypt in 1956 resulted in Israeli conquest of Gaza and the Sinai Peninsula. In two further Arab-Israeli conflicts, Israel seized territories from Jordan [1967] and from Egypt and Syria [1967 and 1973]. Cease-fire disengagements resulted, however, in partial Israeli withdrawal from territory in the Syrian Golan Heights and the Egyptian Sinai. Withdrawal from the remaining Sinai territory, except for Taba [see Occupied and Previously Occupied Territories, below], was completed in April 1982 under a peace treaty with Egypt concluded on March 26, 1979. The Israeli sector of the Golan Heights, on the other hand, was placed under Israeli law on December 14, 1981.)

The internal governmental structure of modern Israel emerged from institutions established by the British administration and the Jewish community during the Mandate. For three decades after independence, a series of multiparty coalitions built around the moderate socialist Israel Workers' Party—enlarged in 1968 to become the Israel Labor Party—governed with relatively little change in policy and turnover in personnel. Save for a brief period in 1953–1955, David BEN-GURION was the dominant political figure until his retirement in 1963. He was succeeded by Levi ESHKOL (until his death in 1969), Golda MEIR (until her retirement in 1974), and Yitzhak RABIN, the first native-born Israeli to become prime minister.

Prime Minister Rabin tendered his resignation in December 1976, following his government's defeat on a parliamentary nonconfidence motion, but he remained in office in a caretaker capacity pending a general election. On April 8, 1977, prior to balloting scheduled for May 17, Rabin was forced to resign his party leadership post in the wake of revelations that he and his wife had violated Israeli law concerning overseas bank deposits. His successor as party leader and acting prime minister, Shimon PERES, proved unable to reverse mounting popular dissatisfaction with a deteriorating economy and evidence of official malfeasance. Consequently, a new reform party, the Democratic Movement for Change, captured a significant proportion of Labor's support in the May poll, and the opposition *Likud* political grouping, having obtained a sizable legislative plurality, subsequently formed a new governing coalition under Menachem BEGIN. The *Likud* front emerged with a one-seat advantage in the June 30, 1981, *Knesset* elections, and Begin formed a new coalition government on August 4.

Prime Minister Begin's startling announcement on August 28, 1983, of his intention to resign both his governmental and party positions for "personal reasons" (primarily the death of his wife) was believed by many observers also to have been influenced by severe Israeli losses in the 1982 war in Lebanon (see Foreign relations, below). The Central Committee of *Likud*'s core party, *Herut,* thereupon elected Yitzhak SHAMIR as its new leader on September 1, and the constituent parties of the ruling coalition agreed to support Shamir, who, after failing in an effort to form a national unity government, was sworn in as prime minister on October 10.

Amid increasing criticism of the Shamir administration, particularly in its handling of economic affairs, five *Likud* coalition deputies voted with the opposition in March 1984 in calling for legislative dissolution and the holding of a general election. In balloting in July, Labor (44 seats) marginally outpolled *Likud* (41 seats). Extensive interparty discussion followed, yielding agreement on August 31 on the formation of a national unity coalition on the basis of a rotating premiership. Thus, Labor's Peres was approved as the new prime minister on September 13 with the understanding that he would exchange positions with Vice Prime Minister and Foreign Affairs Minister Shamir midway through a full parliamentary term of four years. Therefore, on October 20, 1986, Shamir became prime minister, with Peres assuming Shamir's former posts.

The election of November 1, 1988, conducted in the midst of a major Palestinian uprising (intifada) that had erupted in the occupied territories 11 months earlier, yielded an even closer balance between the leading parties, with *Likud* winning 40 *Knesset* seats and Labor 39. Conceivably, *Likud* could have assembled a working majority in alliance with a number of right-wing religious parties. However, most of the latter refused to participate in an administration that did not commit itself to legislation excluding from provisions of the law of return (hence from automatic citizenship) those converted to Judaism under Reform or Conservative (as opposed to Orthodox) auspices. As a result, Shamir concluded a new agreement with the Labor leadership, whereby he continued as prime minister and Peres assumed the finance portfolio in a government installed on December 22.

By early 1990 the coalition was under extreme stress because of divergent views on the terms of peace talks with the Palestinians. The principal differences turned on *Likud*'s insistence that no Arabs from East Jerusalem participate in the talks or in future elections and that Israel should be accorded a right of withdrawal from the negotiations should the Palestine Liberation Organization (PLO) become even remotely involved. There were also deep fissures within *Likud* itself, caused primarily by a group of hard-liners, including Industry and Commerce Minister Ariel SHARON, who were opposed to a Palestinian franchise. Following an angry exchange with Shamir in the *Knesset* on February 12, Sharon resigned from the cabinet. Ten days later Labor issued an ultimatum to the prime minister to accept its peace formula (which called for at least one delegate each from Palestinian deportees and those maintaining partial residence in East Jerusalem) or face dissolution of the government. Rejecting that demand, Shamir on March 12 dismissed Peres from the cabinet, prompting Labor's other ministers to resign. Three days later, in the wake of a successful nonconfidence motion (the first in Israeli parliamentary history), Shamir assumed the leadership of a caretaker administration. A lengthy period of intense negotiation followed, with Shamir on June 11 forming a *Likud*-dominated right-wing government whose two-seat majority turned on the support of dissidents from Labor and *Agudat Yisrael,* a periodic Labor ally. In November *Agudat Yisrael* formally joined the ruling coalition, increasing the government's *Knesset* majority to six.

In February 1992 former prime minister Rabin gained control of the Labor Party from longtime rival Peres, who had been unable since 1977 to lead Labor to the formation of a government in its own right. Four months later, in what was termed more of a *Likud* debacle than a Labor triumph, Labor won a plurality of 44 *Knesset* seats. It subsequently formed a new administration (headed by Rabin) on July 12 in coalition with the recently organized *Meretz* (a coalition of three left-of-center parties) and the ultraorthodox Sephardi Torah Guardians (Shas).

On March 24, 1993, Ezer WEIZMAN, a former fighter pilot and former *Likud* hard-liner who had subsequently become a Labor leader and an outspoken advocate of peace with the Arabs, was elected by the *Knesset* as Israel's seventh president. The following day former deputy foreign minister Benjamin NETANYAHU, who called for "a much tougher line" in addressing the Palestinian issue, was elected in a party contest to succeed Shamir as *Likud* leader. The Labor/*Likud* split on the Palestinian question came into even sharper focus in September when Prime Minister Rabin signed the historic agreement with the PLO that launched the Palestinian self-rule process. (See the entry on the Palestinian Authority/Palestine Liberation Organization for details.)

In mid-July 1994 two MPs from *Yiud,* a breakaway faction of the ultranationalist *Tzomet,* agreed to enter the Labor government; however, they were prevented from doing so until late December because of a High Court ruling that their action would contravene antidefection legislation. Their support gave the Labor coalition 58 of 120 *Knesset* seats. However, on February 3, 1995, the six *Knesset* representatives of Shas, which had withdrawn from the ruling coalition in March 1994, announced that they were formally returning to opposition because of worsening security and the status of Jewish settlers in the West Bank.

Attention subsequently focused on negotiations over the second agreement in the Palestinian autonomy process, which was signed on September 28, 1995, and endorsed (in a non-mandatory vote) by the *Knesset* by 61–59 on October 6. However, domestic and regional political affairs were thrown into turmoil when Rabin was assassinated on November 4 by a right-wing Israeli opposed to the peace process. (Rabin's assailant, Yigul AMIR, was sentenced to life imprisonment in March 1996.) Foreign Minister Peres assumed the position of acting prime minister upon Rabin's death and was formally nominated by Labor on November 13 to proceed with forming his own cabinet. The leaders of Labor, *Meretz,* and *Yiud* signed a government agreement on November 21, and the new cabinet was approved by the *Knesset* the following day, at which time Peres became prime minister.

Likud's Netanyahu defeated Peres by a vote of 50.5 percent to 49.5 percent in the first-ever direct balloting for prime minister on May 29, 1996 (see Constitution and government, below, for details). The election turned primarily on security issues, as Netanyahu adopted a hard-line stance toward any further "concessions" to the Palestinians, categorically ruled out the eventual creation of an independent Palestinian state, and pledged additional support for the Jewish settlers in the West Bank. Although Labor led all parties by winning 34 seats in the concurrent *Knesset* elections, Netanyahu was subsequently able to form a coalition government comprising representatives from *Tzomet* and the newly formed *Gesher* (the two parties with whom *Likud* had presented joint *Knesset* candidates), Shas, The Third Way (a new centrist grouping), *Yisrael B'Aliya,* and two ultraorthodox groups (the National Religious Party [NRP] and United Torah Judaism [UTJ]). Netanyahu formally succeeded Peres as prime minister on June 18 after the *Knesset* approved the new government by a vote of 62–50.

In addition to growing pressure regarding the Palestinian question, Prime Minister Netanyahu confronted several other significant domestic problems in 1997 and early 1998. Most notable was the controversial demand by the Orthodox Jewish movement that it be formally confirmed as the ultimate authority concerning conversions to Judaism. (The Reform and Conservative movements, strongly represented in the United States, were seeking to have conversions completed under their auspices legally recognized in Israel.) With his coalition government so dependent on backing from Orthodox parties, Netanyahu initially announced support for legislation confirming the Orthodox monopoly; however, a special committee was subsequently established to attempt to produce a compromise position. The prime minister also faced dissension within *Likud* and growing restiveness over budget austerity, the latter contributing to the decision by *Gesher* to leave the coalition in January 1998. (The government's legislative majority was reduced to a razor-thin 61–59 by *Gesher*'s withdrawal.) In addition, the administration was buffeted in early 1998 by changes in the leadership of Mossad (Israel's external security apparatus, which had recently bungled an assassination attempt in Jordan) and the chaotic and incomplete distribution of gas masks during the most recent U.S./Iraqi crisis. Regarding that confrontation, the Israeli government had emphasized that, unlike in 1991, it had been prepared to respond militarily if it had been targeted by Iraqi missiles. On March 4, 1998, the *Knesset* by a vote of 63–49 reelected President Weizman, who had added a degree of political impact to the previously essentially ceremonial post by criticizing the Netanyahu government's handling of the peace process.

Under heavy international pressure, Prime Minister Netanyahu signed an accord with PLO Chair Yasir Arafat in late October 1998 calling for further Israeli withdrawals from West Bank territory (the so-called Wye agreement). However, implementation of the plan stalled in December as Netanyahu futilely attempted to address the growing popular demand for progress toward a resolution on the Palestinian front while maintaining the allegiance of the religious parties in his coalition, who steadfastly opposed any land-for-peace compromise and, in fact, urged additional construction of Jewish settlements in the occupied territories. The government also exhibited a lack of unity regarding policies to address the deteriorating economic climate. Consequently, in mid-December, Netanyahu, facing the threat of a no-confidence motion in the *Knesset,* agreed to early elections.

On May 17, 1999, Ehud BARAK of the Labor-led One Israel coalition was elected prime minister, defeating Netanyahu by 56–44 percent. (Three minor candidates had withdrawn shortly before the election.) Barak had staked out a more liberal peace posture than Netanyahu, announcing he would, if elected, revitalize the Wye agreement, initiate final status discussions with the Palestinians, withdraw Israeli forces from Lebanon within one year, and relaunch discussions with Syria regarding the Golan Heights. Barak had also emphasized his economic platform because domestic problems such as burgeoning unemployment, rising inflation, and declining growth appeared to be playing a greater role in voting considerations that year than in previous elections. In concurrent balloting for the *Knesset,* One Israel secured a plurality of 26 seats, followed by *Likud* (19 seats), Shas (17), *Meretz* (10), and 11 parties with 6 or fewer seats. Subsequently, in view of his poor showing (as well as *Likud*'s collective electoral decline), Netanyahu resigned as chair of *Likud* and was succeeded by his long-time rival, Ariel Sharon.

After difficult and extended negotiations (during which he ultimately abandoned efforts to form a national unity government with *Likud*), Barak on July 6, 1999, received *Knesset* confirmation of a new cabinet, including One Israel (Labor, *Gesher,* and *Meimad*), Shas, *Yisrael B'Aliya, Meretz,* the NRP, and the Center Party, which had been formed in mid-1998 by a group of prominent *Likud* members opposed to Netanyahu's policies. Barak immediately called for a comprehensive peace settlement with the Palestinians, Syria, and Lebanon within 15 months. In April Barak appeared to accept the eventual creation of an independent Palestinian "entity" (he avoided using the word "state") comprising Gaza and 60–70 percent of the West Bank. However, he indicated a "majority" of the Jewish settlers in the disputed areas would remain under Israeli sovereignty. At the same time, popular sentiment in Israel appeared to be turning away from the proposed return of the Golan Heights to Syria, and the construction of additional Golan settlements (suspended since the previous December) resumed in April.

Barak's coalition proved fractious in regard to his peace initiatives, and Shas, *Yisrael B'Aliya,* and the NRP left the cabinet on July 9, 2000, to protest potential "concessions" to the Palestinians. On July 31 the government suffered another setback when Moshe KATSAV of *Likud* defeated Shimon Peres for the Israeli presidency by a vote of 63–37 percent. (President Weizman had resigned his post, ostensibly because of poor health, although he had recently been subjected to an investigation concerning gifts he had received as a cabinet member a decade earlier.) In addition, *Gesher*'s minister resigned from the cabinet on August 2.

Prime Minister Barak attended a "make-or-break" summit with the PLO's Yasir Arafat and U.S. president Bill Clinton at Camp David in July 2000. Although agreement appeared close on several issues, the summit ended unsuccessfully when common ground could not be found regarding the status of Jerusalem and sovereignty over the city's holy sites. Although Barak subsequently indicated a willingness to endorse the establishment of two "separate entities" in Jerusalem, negotiations collapsed in October in the face of a second Palestinian intifada and heavy reprisals by the Israeli military that included the use of assault helicopter and rocket attacks.

Although he had previously survived several nonconfidence votes, Barak, faced with an apparent lack of support in the *Knesset* for his peace efforts, announced his resignation on December 9, 2000, and called for a special prime ministerial election as a national referendum of sorts on the matter. (Barak remained in his post in an acting capacity pending the new balloting.) The Israeli electorate illustrated a rightward shift on February 6, 2001, by electing the hawkish Sharon as prime minister by a 62.4–37.6 percent margin over Barak, who quickly resigned as Labor's leader.

Somewhat surprisingly, Labor agreed to join the national unity government formed by Sharon on March 7, 2001. *Likud*'s other coalition partners included Shas, *Yisrael B'Aliya,* the new One Nation, the UTJ (represented at the deputy ministerial level), and the new National

Union-*Yisrael Beiteinu* (NU-YB) *Knesset* faction (see National Union under Political Parties, below, for details). On October 15 the NU-YB ministers announced their intention to leave the cabinet, having adopted an even harsher stance toward the Palestinian question than Sharon. However, their resignation was temporarily rescinded following the assassination by Palestinian militants of Tourism Minister Rechavam ZE'EVI, leader of the NU-YB, on October 17. After the NU-YB faction finally departed the cabinet on March 15, 2002, Sharon bolstered his government by appointing new ministers from the NRP and *Gesher.* However, Sharon dismissed the Shas and UTJ ministers on May 20, when they failed to support his austerity budget proposals, although the Shas ministers were reinstated on June 3 after the package passed on a second vote in the *Knesset. Gesher* leader David Levy resigned his post as minister without portfolio on July 29.

The Labor ministers resigned from the cabinet on October 30, 2002, because of their opposition to the allocation of funding for Jewish settlements in the West Bank and Gaza. Faced with the potential collapse of his national unity government and the loss of a government majority in the *Knesset,* Prime Minister Sharon called for new *Knesset* elections to be held in early 2003.

On November 19, 2002, Maj. Gen. (Ret.) Avraham MITZNA, the mayor of Haifa, was elected as the new Labor leader. He subsequently proposed a "markedly dovish" approach to the Palestinian question, calling for the closure of Jewish settlements in Gaza, the immediate evacuation of Israeli forces from that region, and the eventual unilateral Israeli withdrawal from portions of the West Bank should a comprehensive peace agreement fail to materialize. For his part, Prime Minister Sharon pledged to maintain his hard line regarding negotiations with the Palestinians, announcing that negotiations would not proceed until all violence ceased.

Likud scored a major victory in the January 28, 2003, *Knesset* election, securing 38 seats compared to 19 seats for the Labor/*Meimad* coalition. Labor subsequently pulled out of negotiations regarding a new coalition government, and on February 28 Sharon formed a new cabinet comprising *Likud, Shinui,* the NRP, and the NU-YB. Subsequently, Sharon shifted political discourse significantly by warning that "painful concessions" regarding Palestinian statehood would eventually be required. In that regard, in June 2004 the cabinet endorsed Sharon's plan for unilateral disengagement from Gaza, while Labor agreed to provide a safety net in the *Knesset* for Sharon in order to allow him to proceed toward disengagement. (Sharon dismissed two NRP ministers who opposed his plan, placing the government in minority status in the *Knesset.*) In October the *Knesset* endorsed the proposal by a vote of 67–47. However, the government coalition finally collapsed on December 1 when the *Knesset* rejected Sharon's proposed 2005 budget. (Sharon dismissed the *Shinui* ministers who voted against the budget.) On January 10, 2005, Sharon secured *Knesset* approval (by a vote of 58–56) for a new cabinet comprising *Likud,* Labor, and the UTJ, with Labor leader Peres being named vice prime minister in the new government.

In February 2005 the *Knesset* approved $900 million in compensation for Israeli settlers displaced by the unilateral disengagement from Gaza, which began in August, prompting Netanyahu to resign as finance minister and opening up deep fissures within *Likud.* Subsequently, in November, the *Knesset* rejected Sharon's appointment of two *Likud* loyalists to his cabinet. Meanwhile, Amir PERETZ defeated Shimon Peres in an internal party ballot for the leadership of Labor, and Peretz subsequently promised to end the party's participation in Sharon's government. Sharon consequently called an election for early 2006 and then announced his resignation from *Likud* and the formation of a new party, *Kadima,* or "Forward."

In January 2006 Prime Minister Sharon suffered a debilitating stroke, and his deputy, former Jerusalem mayor Ehud OLMERT, became acting prime minister. Olmert steered *Kadima* to a plurality of 29 seats in the March 28 *Knesset* balloting, while the coalition of Labor and *Meimad* won 19 seats, and *Likud* fell to 12 seats. On April 11 the cabinet declared Sharon permanently incapacitated and named Olmert interim prime minister (effective April 14). Olmert was inaugurated as prime minister on May 4 as head of a coalition government (*Kadima,* Labor/*Meimad,* Shas, and the small Pensioners Party) that controlled 67 *Knesset* seats. Olmert expanded the coalition with the addition of *Yisrael Beiteinu* (which had separated from the National Union to campaign on its own in the recent legislative poll) to the cabinet in late October. The administration subsequently faced growing criticism for its handling of the July–August conflict with Hezbollah in Lebanon (see Foreign relations, below). Among other things, a leaked interim report from a special commission reportedly challenged Olmert's "judgment" and "prudence" in the matter. In addition, a number of scandals subsequently buffeted the cabinet, and corruption allegations apparently contributed to a demonstration in Tel Aviv in May 2007 by some 100,000 protesters demanding Olmert's resignation.

Former prime minister Shimon Peres (who had helped launch *Kadima*) was elected president of Israel with 86 votes in second-round balloting in the *Knesset* on June 13, 2007, after his two challengers from the first round dropped out of the race. Peres was inaugurated on July 15 after President Katsav had formally resigned effective July 2 as part of an apparent plea-bargaining arrangement involving charges of sexual harassment. (Katsav, at his own request, had been declared "temporarily incapacitated" by a *Knesset* committee in January in order to combat the charges, his presidential duties having been assumed at that time by *Knesset* Speaker Dalia ITZIK. In 2009 Katsav was indicted on rape and sexual harassment charges, and in December 2010 he was sentenced to seven years in prison after being found guilty on two counts.)

The government's legislative majority in the *Knesset* diminished in January 2008 (when *Yisrael Beiteinu* left the cabinet) and in July (when three legislators defected from the Pensioner's Party). Prime Minister Olmert on September 21 announced he would resign because of the impact of an ongoing corruption investigation on his ability to govern. However, he remained in his post in a caretaker capacity as Tzipi LIVNI, recently elected as the new *Kadima* leader, attempted to form a new coalition government and avoid early elections in order to pursue Olmert's recent diplomatic efforts with Hamas (which had recently endorsed a cease-fire) and Syria. When Livni on October 26 declared that those negotiations had collapsed, President Peres announced that new *Knesset* elections would be held in early 2009. Olmert subsequently dedicated the rest of his tenure to intensifying negotiations regarding Palestinian affairs as well as broader regional tensions. However, talks with the Palestinians collapsed in December when the resumption of Hamas rocket attacks prompted a massive (and controversial) Israeli offensive against Gaza (see the entry on the Palestinian Authority/Palestine Liberation Organization for details). "Operation Cast Lead" (as the offensive was called) also muted the campaign for the February 2009 *Knesset* balloting and once again propelled security issues to the forefront of Israeli concerns. Although Livni and *Kadima* (along with Labor) strongly supported the Gaza initiative, Livni continued to call for a two-state solution to the Palestinian impasse. Meanwhile, *Likud*'s Benjamin Netanyahu, rising in popularity polls, pledged to end Hamas rule in Gaza and to concentrate more on improving the economic conditions of Palestinians than on political negotiations.

Both *Kadima* (28 seats) and a resurgent *Likud* (27 seats) claimed victory in the February 2009 poll, but it quickly became clear that Netanyahu enjoyed better prospects of forging a new government than Livni, particularly in light of reportedly severe friction between Livni and Labor's Barak.

Netanyahu was inaugurated on March 31 as head of a center-right government that comprised *Likud,* Shas, *Yisrael Beiteinu* (which had jumped to third place [ahead of Labor] in the recent election), Jewish Home (*Habayit Hayehudi,* a successor to the NRP), and surprisingly, Labor. The new government was endorsed by 69 legislators on March 31, but its majority grew to 74 the following day when agreement was reached with the UTJ, which was assigned two deputy ministerial positions.

Netanyahu subsequently pledged to pursue a "full peace" with the Palestinians. However, skeptics noted the appointment of the very hawkish Avigdor LIEBERMAN, the leader of *Yisrael Beiteinu,* as minister of foreign affairs. The strength of the right-wing parties in his government also appeared to influence Netanyahu's subsequent resistance to heavy pressure from new U.S. president Barack Obama for a cessation of Jewish settlement construction in the West Bank and East Jerusalem. Meanwhile, a UN report accused the Israeli military of war crimes and human rights abuses during the Gaza campaign.

In late November 2009 the *Knesset* approved Netanyahu's proposed 10-month "restriction" of additional West Bank settlement construction. However, new construction was approved in March 2010 for East Jerusalem, which the United States called an "affront" to U.S. vice president Joe Biden, who was visiting the Middle East at the time.

Defense Minister and Deputy Prime Minister Ehud Barak and four other members of the *Knesset* resigned from Labor on January 17, 2011, and formed a new government-supportive parliamentary faction called Independence, which accepted cabinet positions in a cabinet reshuffle on January 19. Meanwhile, the eight remaining Labor legislators, reflecting growing party dissatisfaction with Prime Minister

Netanyahu's handling of peace negotiations with the Palestinians, moved into the opposition, and Labor relinquished its cabinet posts.

On May 9, 2012, new *Kadima* leader Lt. Gen. (Ret.) Shaul MOFAZ was named a vice prime minister, *Kadima*'s 28 *Knesset* seats providing the coalition with a solid legislative majority. However, Mofaz quit the government in July, and *Kadima* returned to opposition. The remaining coalition members were subsequently unable to agree on the 2013 budget, and early elections were held on January 22, 2013, with the recently announced electoral alliance of *Likud* and *Yisrael Beiteinu* securing a plurality of 31 of the 120 seats, a lackluster performance considering that the two parties had won 42 seats combined in 2009. Nevertheless, after extensive negotiations, Netanyahu on March 18 was able to form a government comprising *Likud*, *Yisrael Beiteinu*, Jewish Home, and two new parties (the centrist *Yesh Atid* [There is a Future], which had surprisingly finished second in the *Knesset* election with 19 seats, and *Habenua* [The Movement], a center-left grouping formed under Livni's leadership by former *Kadima* legislators).

Constitution and government. In the absence of a written constitution, the structure of Israeli government is defined by fundamental laws that provide for a president with largely ceremonial functions, a prime minister serving as effective chief executive, and a unicameral legislature (*Knesset*) to which the government is responsible and whose powers include the election of the president. Under legislation passed in March 1992, in what some observers initially construed as an historic change in the country's electoral system, the *Knesset* approved a law providing for the direct election of the prime minister. However, that legislation was reversed in March 2001, and the prime minister is now once again appointed by the president upon the recommendation of the *Knesset*. The prime minister's term of office corresponds to that of the *Knesset*.

The role of Judaism in the state has not been formally defined, but the Law of Return of 1950 established a right of immigration for all Jews (with a few exceptions, such as criminals). The judicial system is headed by a Supreme Court, and there are five district courts in addition to magistrates' and municipal courts. Specialized courts include labor courts and religious courts with separate benches for the Jewish, Muslim, Druze, and Christian communities, while military courts are important in the occupied areas.

In October 2010 the cabinet approved legislation requiring non-Jews applying for citizenship to swear allegiance to Israel as a Jewish state. Representatives of minority communities and civil rights groups strongly objected to the measure.

Israel is divided into six administrative districts (*mehozot*), each of which is headed by a district commissioner appointed by the central government. Regions, municipalities, and rural municipalities are the principal administrative entities within the districts.

Israeli newspapers are numerous and diverse, although many of the leading dailies reflect partisan or religious interests. Reporters Without Borders has recently described the media as enjoying "genuine freedom" but said that Israel's record has been "badly tarnished" by military abuses against journalists in the Palestinian territories.

Foreign relations. Israeli foreign relations have been dominated by the requirements of survival in an environment marked by persistent hostility on the part of neighboring Arab states, whose overt measures have ranged from denying Israel use of the Suez Canal (wholly mitigated upon ratification of the 1979 peace treaty between Israel and Egypt [see below]) to encouraging terrorist and guerrilla operations on Israeli soil. Although initially committed at independence to "nonidentification" between East and West, Israel subsequently encountered hostility from the Soviet Union and most other communist governments (Romania and Yugoslavia being the most conspicuous exceptions) and began to rely primarily on Western countries, principally the United States, for political, economic, and military support.

Having joined the United Nations in 1949, Israel frequently incurred subsequent condemnation by UN bodies because of Israeli reprisals against Arab guerrilla attacks and Israel's refusal to reabsorb or pay compensation to Arab refugees from the 1948–1949 war. Israel also rejected the internationalization of Jerusalem as envisaged in the 1947 UN resolution. (Enactment on July 30, 1980, of an Israeli law reaffirming a unified Jerusalem as the nation's capital evoked additional international condemnation.)

In May 1974 a Golan disengagement agreement was concluded with Syria, while Sinai disengagement accords were concluded with Egypt in January 1974 and September 1975. Under the latter, Israel withdrew its forces from the Suez Canal and evacuated the Abu Rudeis and Ras Sudar oil fields.

In what was hailed as a major step toward peace in the region, Egyptian President Anwar Sadat startled the world in November 1977 by accepting an Israeli invitation to visit Jerusalem. While Sadat yielded little during an unprecedented address to the *Knesset* on November 20, his very presence on Israeli soil kindled widespread hope that the lengthy impasse in Arab-Israeli relations might somehow be broken. Subsequent discussions produced potential basis for settlement in regard to the Sinai but no public indication of substantial rethinking of established positions, on either side, in regard to the West Bank and Gaza. Israel, in responding to Egyptian demands for a meaningful "concession," announced a willingness to grant Palestinians in Gaza and the West Bank "self-rule," coupled with an Israeli right to maintain military installations in the occupied territories. Egypt, on the other hand, rejected the idea of an Israeli military presence and continued to press for Palestinian self-determination.

The prospects for a meaningful accord fluctuated widely during the first eight months of 1978, culminating in a historic summit convened by U.S. President Jimmy Carter at Camp David, Maryland, on September 5. The unusually lengthy discussions yielded two major agreements—a "Framework for a Peace Treaty between Egypt and Israel" and a "Framework for Peace in the Middle East"—which were signed by President Sadat and Prime Minister Begin at the White House on September 17. In the course of subsequent negotiations in Washington, representatives of the two governments agreed on the details of a treaty and related documents, but the signing was deferred beyond the target date of December 17 because of disagreement about linkage to the second of the Camp David accords, which dealt with autonomy for the inhabitants of the West Bank and Gaza and provided for Israeli withdrawal into specified security locations. In addition, Egypt wished to modify an important treaty provision by an "interpretive annex," stating that prior commitments to other Arab states should have precedence over any obligations assumed in regard to Israel. Progress toward resolving the impasse was registered in early March 1979, and the treaty was formally signed in Washington on March 26, followed by an exchange of ratifications on April 25. In a set of minutes accompanying the treaty, the parties agreed that "there is no assertion that this treaty prevails over other treaties or agreements" and that, within a month after the exchange of instruments of ratification, negotiations would be instituted to define "the modalities for establishing the elected self-governing authority" for Gaza and West Bank. While no significant progress on autonomy for those two regions was immediately forthcoming, the sixth and final phase of withdrawal from the Sinai, save for Taba, was completed on schedule in April 1982.

On June 6, 1982, Israeli forces invaded Lebanon. While the immediate precipitant of the incursion appeared to have been the shooting on June 3 of Israel's ambassador to the United Kingdom, the attack was far from unanticipated in view of a recent substantial buildup of Israeli military strength along the border. Code-named "Peace for Galilee," the attack was initially justified by Israel as necessary to establish a PLO-free zone extending 40–50 kilometers inside Lebanon. However, Israeli forces had completely surrounded Beirut by June 14, and U.S. President Ronald Reagan had announced that he would approve the dispatch of 800–1,000 U.S. marines to participate in an international force that would oversee the evacuation of Palestinian and Syrian forces from the Lebanese capital. On August 6 U.S. envoy Philip Habib reached agreement, through Lebanese intermediaries, on the PLO withdrawal, which commenced on August 21.

In what was officially described as a "police action" necessitated by the assassination of Lebanese President-elect Bashir Gemayel on September 14, 1982, Israeli contingents entered West Beirut and took up positions around the Shatila and Sabra Palestinian refugee camps, where a substantial number of "terrorists" were alleged to have been left behind by the PLO. On September 18 it was revealed that a large-scale massacre of civilians had occurred at the hands of right-wing Phalangist Lebanese militiamen, who had been given access to the camps by Israeli authorities. While the Israeli cabinet subsequently expressed its "deep grief and regret" over the atrocities, the affair generated widespread controversy within Israel, with Prime Minister Begin resisting demands for the ouster of Defense Minister Sharon as well as for the establishment of a commission of inquiry into the circumstances of the massacre. Following the largest protest rally in Israeli history in Tel Aviv on September 25, the prime minister reversed himself and asked the chief justice of the Supreme Court to undertake a full investigation. The results of the inquiry (published in February 1983) placed direct responsibility for the slaughter on the Phalangists but also faulted Sharon and several senior officers for permitting the militiamen to enter the camps in disregard for the safety of the inhabitants. In addition, while absolving the prime minister of foreknowledge of the entry, the commission expressed surprise, in view of "the Lebanese situation as it was known to those concerned," that a decision on entry should have been taken without his participation.

An agreement was concluded in May 1983 among Israeli, Lebanese, and U.S. negotiators that provided for Israeli withdrawal, an end to the state of war between Israel and Lebanon, and the establishment of a jointly supervised "security region" in southern Lebanon. Although unable to secure a commitment from Syria to withdraw its forces from northern and eastern Lebanon, Israel redeployed its forces in early September to a highly fortified line south of the Awali River. However, a number of attacks by guerrilla groups had concurrently been mounted against Israeli troops and contingents of the international peacekeeping force, and they culminated in simultaneous bomb attacks on U.S. and French detachments in Beirut on October 23 that left over 300 dead.

In March 1984, following departure of the multinational force from Beirut, the Lebanese government, under pressure from Syria, abrogated the 1983 troop-withdrawal accord. However, the Israeli cabinet in January 1985 approved a unilateral three-stage withdrawal that was implemented in several stages over the ensuing six months. Despite the withdrawal announcement, Shiite Muslim militants in Lebanon mounted a terror campaign against the departing Israelis, who retaliated with an "iron-fist" policy that included the arrest and transfer to a prison camp in Israel of hundreds of Shiites. In June 1985 militants hijacked an American TWA jetliner, demanding release of those prisoners in exchange for hostages on the plane. After two weeks of negotiations, the passengers were freed, and Israel began a gradual release of the Lebanese prisoners, both Israel and the United States insisting that the two events were unrelated. Meanwhile, negotiations had been renewed with Egypt to resolve the Taba dispute—an initiative that was condemned by *Likud* and was further jeopardized by the assassination of an Israeli diplomat in Cairo in August, by an Israeli air attack on the PLO's Tunis headquarters (in retaliation for the murder of three Israelis in Cyprus) in September, and by the killing of seven Israeli tourists in Sinai during October.

Throughout 1986 Peres (as prime minister until October 30 and as foreign minister thereafter) continued his efforts on behalf of a comprehensive peace settlement. An unprecedented public meeting in July with King Hassan of Morocco was described as "purely exploratory" but was viewed as enhancing the position of moderate Arab leaders, including Jordan's King Hussein, whose peace discussion with the PLO's Yasir Arafat had broken down in January. Late in the year, the Israeli government was hard-pressed to defend its role in the U.S.-Iranian arms affair, Peres insisting that Israel had transferred arms to Iran at Washington's request and was unaware that some of the money paid by Tehran had been diverted to Nicaraguan *contras*. The government was also embarrassed by the March 1987 conviction in a Washington court of Jonathan Jay POLLARD on charges of having spied for Israel. Defense Minister Rabin insisted that Pollard was part of a "rogue" spy operation set up without official sanction and that no one else had engaged in such activity since Pollard's arrest in 1985. However, the case aroused deep pro-Pollard feeling within Israel, and it was later reported that "state elements" had paid approximately two-thirds of Pollard's legal expenses. (Pollard, serving a life sentence in the United States, was granted Israeli citizenship in January 1996.)

During 1989 the Israeli government drew increasing criticism from international civil rights groups for actions triggered by the continuing intifada in the occupied territories. It also experienced a cooling of relations with Washington because of Prime Minister Shamir's failure to respond positively to the so-called "Baker plan" for Palestinian peace talks, the essentials of which corresponded to proposals advanced by former prime minister Rabin. By the end of the year, the future of the occupied Arab lands had become increasingly important because of an escalation of Soviet immigrants, some of whom were settling in the disputed West Bank areas.

With the launching of military action against Iraq by UN-backed forces in mid-January 1991, Israel came under attack by Soviet-made Scud missiles. U.S. President George H. W. Bush's administration thereupon dispatched two batteries of Patriot surface-to-air missiles to Israel, while urging Israeli authorities not to retaliate against Baghdad, lest Israeli involvement weaken the Arab-supported coalition. Having obliged with a posture of restraint, the Shamir government requested that it be provided with $3 billion in compensation for damages, plus $10 billion in loan guarantees to resettle immigrants from the Soviet Union. Washington responded in late February by approving a $400 million housing loan guarantee, followed, in early March, by a $650 million aid package to help cover increased military and civil defense expenditures. Moreover, in October 1992 the U.S. Congress approved the $10 billion loan guarantee program after the new Labor government in Israel had announced that it would halt large-scale investment in the Jewish settlements in the occupied territories. Concurrently, a U.S. foreign aid appropriation bill was approved that included renewal of the annual $3 billion in economic and military aid earmarked for Israel in the wake of the 1978 Camp David accords.

Middle East peace talks began in October 1991 in Madrid, Spain, among Israeli, Lebanese, Syrian, and joint Jordanian-Palestinian delegations, with a number of other governmental and intergovernmental representatives present as observers. It was agreed at the meeting that further "two-track" negotiations would be held on Israeli-Palestinian and Israeli-Jordanian matters directed at an interim period of Palestinian self-rule and, eventually, a final settlement with Israel. However, no substantial progress was reported in three rounds of bilateral talks that concluded in mid-January 1992. Subsequently, the 19 participants in a revival of multilateral talks in Moscow on January 28–29 established working groups dealing with environment, water, disarmament and security, economic development, and refugee issues, although the Palestinians boycotted the meeting because of a dispute over the composition of its delegation. In addition, Syria and Lebanon refused to participate on the grounds that Israel had shown no territorial flexibility in the bilateral discussions.

In what was quickly branded a "public relations disaster," Israeli authorities on December 18, 1992, ordered the deportation from the occupied territories of more than 400 Palestinians charged with being leaders of the fundamentalist Islamic Resistance Movement (Hamas, see the article on the Palestinian Authority/Palestine Liberation Organization), which had recently been responsible for a series of attacks on Israeli military personnel and civilians. Because Lebanon refused to accept the deportees, they were confined to a portion of the buffer strip inside the Lebanese border. The action drew almost universal condemnation from abroad, including demands by both the U.S. government and the UN Security Council that the group be returned to the occupied territories. Subsequently, Israel agreed to permit 10 (later 16) of those "wrongly deported" to return. In early February 1993 Israel also authorized the return of 100 of the others, with the remainder to be repatriated by the end of the year. The latter offer was resisted by the deportees, who demanded that all those remaining be released immediately, but was nonetheless implemented by the Israelis.

On August 19, 1993, some 14 months of secret talks in Norway between Israeli and PLO representatives culminated in a Declaration of Principles on interim self-rule for Palestinians in the Israeli-occupied territories. The declaration provided for a five-year transitional period beginning with Israeli withdrawal from Gaza and the West Bank town of Jericho and culminating in a transfer (to "authorized Palestinians") of responsibility in most of the rest of the West Bank for all matters, save foreign relations, defense, and other "mutually agreed" areas. Formalized in an historic signing by Israeli prime minister Rabin and PLO chair Arafat in Washington on September 13, the process was targeted for completion by April 13, 1999.

A number of meetings to implement the Israeli/PLO accord were subsequently held in Egypt, but they failed to clear the way for commencement of the Israeli withdrawal from Gaza and Jericho on the agreed date of December 13, 1993. An initial dispute turned on Jericho's size, the Israelis proposing 21 square miles, with the PLO insisting on 39 square miles extending south to the Dead Sea. Subsequent disagreement centered on security provisions for Israeli settlers in Gaza, in addition to control over the passage of Palestinians from Egypt into Gaza and from Jordan into Jericho. These problems appeared to have been overcome in an agreement initialed by Israeli Prime Minister Rabin and PLO Chair Arafat in Cairo on February 9, 1994; however, the massacre of 29 worshippers at a Muslim mosque in Hebron by a follower of the late extremist Rabbi Meir KAHANE (see Kahane Lives, under Political Parties, below) brought the peace process to a sudden halt.

It was not until May 4, 1994, that a definitive accord implementing the 1993 declaration was signed in Cairo by Rabin and Arafat. Under the settlement, Israel was to withdraw from Gaza and Jericho within three weeks, legislative and executive powers for the two areas were to be assigned to a "Palestinian authority," and a 9,000-person Palestinian police force was to be established. On the other hand, Israel was to retain authority over Jewish settlements in Gaza, a military base on the Egyptian border, and external security. The actual degree of Palestinian autonomy was further constrained by annexes to the agreement that provided for an Israeli role at all levels of decision making for the territories. Nonetheless,

Palestinian policemen entered Gaza on May 10, and on May 13 Israeli troops withdrew from Jericho, ending a 27-year occupation.

Meanwhile, in a January 1994 meeting with President Clinton in Geneva, Syrian President Assad had declared that he was ready for "normal, peaceful relations" with Israel. However, it was noted that peace would require significant concessions by Israel, including withdrawal from the Golan Heights. Israel appeared to respond on May 17 by offering to withdraw from the Golan in three phases over a five- to eight-year period in return for peace and normalized relations with its longtime adversary. However, observers were quick to note the sticking point: disagreement as to whether normalization or withdrawal should come first.

Israel was more successful in its quest for normalization with Jordan, U.S.-brokered contacts yielding another important White House ceremony on July 25, 1994, when King Hussein and Prime Minister Rabin signed a declaration ending the 46-year-old state of war between their two countries. On October 26 a peace treaty was signed, and it was ratified shortly thereafter by their respective legislatures.

Relations with most other Arab states (Iraq, Libya, and Sudan being conspicuous exceptions) improved measurably as the peace process gained momentum. In mid-1994 first-ever joint naval exercises, involving Israel, Egypt, Tunisia, Qatar, Canada, Italy, and the United States, were held off the Italian coast. In August a senior Israeli foreign ministry official visited Bahrain and Kuwait; in early September agreement was reached with Morocco and Tunisia on the establishment of liaison offices; and on September 30 the Gulf Cooperation Council (GCC) lifted the "secondary" and tertiary" aspects of its economic boycott of Israel, although the ban on direct trade was retained. In early November, Tansu Çiller became the first Turkish prime minister to visit Israel, and on December 26 Rabin became the first Israeli prime minister to visit Oman. In addition, in an historic ceremony in Jerusalem on December 30, Israel and the Vatican agreed to establish diplomatic relations. Representatives from both sides expressed the hope that a 2,000-year rupture between Christians and Jews could thus be overcome.

The funeral of Yitzhak Rabin in November 1995 attracted Israel's largest-ever gathering of foreign leaders, including several from prominent Arab states, underscoring, among other things, international concern that the assassinated prime minister would be difficult to replace in the ongoing Middle East peace process. However, despite the shock of his death, the withdrawal of Israeli troops from six more West Bank towns (as authorized in the second Israeli/PLO accord) proceeded smoothly throughout the rest of the year. Meanwhile, Turkey and Israel signed an agreement in August 1996 for the exchange of "technical expertise" on defense matters, a development that was criticized in many Arab capitals. (The two countries also conducted a small yet highly symbolic joint military exercise in the Mediterranean in January 1998.)

As was widely expected, Benjamin Netanyahu's election as Israeli prime minister in 1996 slowed progress on the Palestinian front. (See the entry on the Palestinian Authority/Palestine Liberation Organization for details from 1996 through 1999.) Meanwhile, further heavy fighting occurred in Lebanon in 1996, and public support in Israel for additional involvement there subsequently declined, particularly after 73 Israeli soldiers were killed in a helicopter crash in February 1997.

The relationship between Israel and Jordan was severely tested in September 1997 when Israeli intelligence officers attempted to assassinate Khaled MESHAL, a Hamas official in Amman. The attack on a Jordanian citizen enraged King Hussein, who threatened to break diplomatic relations and put two captured Mossad agents on trial. Prime Minister Netanyahu and other Israeli leaders reportedly made a secret visit to Amman in an effort to reduce tension, and the agents were returned to Israel in early October following the release of Hamas leader Sheikh Ahmed YASSIN and a large group of Jordanian and Palestinian prisoners from Israeli jails.

Although previous negotiations between Israel and Lebanon had always been based on the premise of a comprehensive regional settlement, the Netanyahu government in early 1998 proposed a "Lebanon first" strategy through which Israel would withdraw from Lebanon in return for stringent security guarantees. During the prime ministerial campaign in Israel in early 1999, Labor's Ehud Barak pledged to withdraw Israeli forces from Lebanon if elected, although he hoped it would be as part of a peace agreement with Syria and the Palestinians. The broader initiatives having stalled in early 2000, the Israeli *Knesset* in March voted to initiate a unilateral withdrawal, which was completed on May 24 (see the entry on Lebanon for additional information).

A number of Arab states closed their offices in Israel following the outbreak of the "second intifada" in late 2000, and a March 2001 Arab League summit endorsed the Palestinian "right to resist" Israeli "aggression." Meanwhile, Ehud Barak's defeat by Ariel Sharon in the February 2001 special prime ministerial balloting appeared to doom prospects for any quick settlement of the Palestinian issue, particularly in view of the fact that the new Bush administration in Washington had announced it did not consider itself in any way bound by the "parameters" endorsed previously by the Clinton administration. For his part, Sharon pledged that Jerusalem would remain "whole and unified" under Israeli sovereignty and that no Jewish settlements would be dismantled. Suicide bombings continued unabated in early 2002, and Israel in April launched an offensive of unprecedented scale that left it in control of most West Bank towns. The Sharon government also announced at midyear that it would begin to construct a "security fence" around the West Bank.

In early 2002 Saudi Arabia proposed the full normalization of relations between Israel and Arab countries in return for complete Israeli withdrawal from the occupied territories. Arab leaders subsequently urged Washington to propose a specific timetable for creation of a Palestinian state, arguing that the lack of progress in resolving the Palestinian/Israeli conflict was generating widespread anti-U.S. sentiment in the Arab world. In April 2003 the Middle East Quartet (the European Union [EU], Russia, the UN, and the United States) formally unveiled a much-discussed "road map" toward a final comprehensive settlement of the dispute, calling for establishment of an "independent, democratic, and viable" Palestinian state. Final negotiations were slated for completion by the end of 2005, assuming Palestinian institutions had been "stabilized" and Palestinian security forces had proven adequate in combating attacks against Israel. Israeli Prime Minister Sharon offered "qualified" support for the road map, as did the *Knesset,* although the latter insisted that it be made clear that Palestinian refugees would not be guaranteed the right to return to their former homes in Israel.

In the face of a perceived lack of progress in subsequent "road map" negotiations, the Sharon government in February 2004 announced its intention to disengage unilaterally from Gaza, sending the message that it would not deal with Arafat's Palestinian Authority (PA) but instead would withdraw from Palestinian territories on its own terms. The decision was met with tacit approval from U.S. president George W. Bush, who, while still preferring that major decisions be made within the context of a negotiated solution, viewed Arafat's leadership of the PA as the major obstacle to such a solution.

Following Arafat's death in November 2004, the Israeli government called upon the new Palestinian leadership—headed by the new president, Mahmoud Abbas—to finally come to terms with "terrorism" on the part of Palestinian militants. At the same time, however, momentum regarding Sharon's unilateral disengagement plan continued to grow, and forced evacuation of Israeli settlements from Gaza (and a few in the northern West Bank) were conducted in August–September 2005, marking the end of 38 years of Israeli occupation of Gaza.

Upon assuming the acting prime ministership in January 2006, Ehud Olmert was immediately faced with the implications of Hamas's sweeping win in the January 2006 Palestinian legislative elections. Among other things, the United States and Israel declared they would refuse to deal with an authority governed by Hamas. Meanwhile, Olmert's government faced the challenge of implementing its policy of "convergence" (including further unilateral disengagement from parts of the West Bank), which it presented successfully to Israeli electors in March. Olmert promised that Israel's final borders would be drawn by 2010, unilaterally by Israel if he was unable to find a "Palestinian partner" other than Hamas with whom to negotiate a final treaty. He also praised the Israeli settlers in the West Bank and insisted that the larger settlements there would be expanded.

In mid-July 2006 attention shifted to the Israeli-Lebanese border when Hezbollah conducted a cross-border raid and abducted two Israeli soldiers. Israel subsequently launched a series of air raids on Lebanon, targeting not just Hezbollah-controlled areas in the south of Lebanon but also Beirut and other cities. Civilian deaths in Lebanon reached 340 in the first week of attacks, and the Israeli air force also bombed civilian infrastructure, including the Beirut airport, bridges, power plants, and fuel depots. Hezbollah, meanwhile, continued to fire rockets into northern Israel. On August 14 Israeli troops began to withdraw from southern Lebanon in support of a resolution adopted on August 11 by the UN Security Council calling for an end to the hostilities. The resolution proposed that the UN Interim Force in Lebanon be expanded from 2,000 to 15,000 troops to assist in preserving order along the Israeli-Lebanese border while negotiations continued toward the disarmament of Hezbollah. It was reported that 117 Israeli soldiers had been killed in the conflict, while 41 Israeli civilians had died, primarily from the 4,000 rocket attacks launched by Hezbollah. Following the Israeli withdrawal, the Olmert government faced increasing domestic criticism in Israel for its perceived failure to have accomplished its main goal in the war—the removal of Hezbollah as a security threat. The anti-Hezbollah campaign also drew heavy criticism from most Arab states, particularly in regard to the killing of Lebanese civilians and widespread damage to infrastructure throughout Lebanon. However, the United States firmly supported the initiative as a component of the "war on terrorism," and in mid-2007 Washington announced a new $30 billion, ten-year military-aid package for Israel.

In October 2007 Israeli jets reportedly bombed a desert site in Syria that some analysts had concluded might have been a nascent nuclear reactor. The charge was denied by Syria.

Prime Minister Olmert in 2007 appeared to base his future prospects on plans for renewed talks toward a comprehensive Middle East peace settlement, which were formally launched in the United States in November. By that time Olmert had signaled his readiness to discuss the eventual division of Jerusalem and the Israeli withdrawal from much of the West Bank as part of a final two-state settlement.

The Israeli offensive in Gaza in December 2008–January 2009 was strongly criticized by most Arab governments, and relations with Turkey were also strained by the matter. Following his installation as prime minister in March, Benjamin Netanyahu tried to shift the focus of international attention away from Palestinian affairs and toward Iran, whose perceived nuclear ambitions he characterized as Israel's top security concern. Among other things, Netanyahu reportedly traveled to Moscow in September to ask the Russian government not to deliver surface-to-air missiles to Iran.

On May 31, 2010, Israeli commandos attacked a flotilla of ships heading to Gaza with what those on the ships described as humanitarian supplies. Nine Turkish activists were killed by the Israelis, who argued that some of the supplies could have been used by Hamas for military purposes. In the face of intense international criticism (one subsequent report by UN human rights officials alleged that Israel had violated international law by confronting the flotilla in international waters and accused Israel, in any event, of a "brutal and a disproportionate" response), the Israeli government in late June agreed to lift most of the economic blockade against Gaza.

Meanwhile, Turkish officials accused Israel of "inhuman state terror" and demanded an apology before they would consider restoring ambassadorial ties. Israel also experienced heightened tension in August with Lebanon when a border firefight killed two Lebanese and one Israeli.

With Israeli-U.S. relations having improved significantly, direct talks between Netanyahu and Abbas opened with fanfare in mid-September 2010. However, they quickly foundered when Netanyahu declined to extend the moratorium on new West Bank settlement construction beyond its expiry on September 26, despite a reported offer of $3 billion in additional U.S. military aid in return for an extension. Other apparent concessions to right-wing elements of Netanyahu's cabinet also compromised prospects for progress, as did the ongoing absence of Hamas from the negotiations. Another clash at that border in May 2011 left seven pro-Palestinian demonstrators dead, prompting a UN report that accused Israeli forces of having used excessive force. Israeli-Lebanese relations deteriorated further in midyear when the two countries presented competing claims regarding their maritime border, suddenly a much more significant matter in view of the recently discovered gas fields under the Mediterranean.

Alleged Palestinian militants entered Israel in August 2011 and killed a number of Israelis in several attacks. Israeli forces chased the attackers to the Egyptian border, and several Egyptian officers were killed when the firefight extended across the border. Israel called the Egyptian deaths "inadvertent," but the incident prompted massive protests in Egypt, culminating in the storming of the Israeli embassy in Cairo. Analysts attributed the vehemence of the demonstrations to pressure from the Egyptian populace on its new government to display a tougher line regarding Israel than President Mubarak had adopted. Meanwhile, Israel's relations with Turkey remained strained, with Turkey having suspended its military ties with Israel while continuing to demand that Israel "pay a price" for the 2010 flotilla conflict. (A UN report on that matter upheld the legality of Israel's blockade but described the actions of the Israeli commandos as "excessive" and "unreasonable.")

In September 2011 Netanyahu denounced the Palestinian initiative to gain statehood recognition at the UN as premature, stating that such statehood was "not possible without peace" and that Israel needed to remain vigilant against "militant Islam."

Ramifications of the Arab Spring continued to be of major concern to Israel through 2012. Among other things, Israel expressed skepticism over the competence of Egyptian security in the Sinai, although the Netanyahu administration was described as working to avoid tension with the government of new Egyptian president Mohamed Morsi. Meanwhile, Israel adopted a generally neutral stance regarding the civil war in Syria despite an obvious interest in how the potential fall of Syrian President Assad might affect the status of the Golan Heights.

Under the mediation of U.S president Barack Obama, a rapprochement was reached between Israel in Turkey in March 2013 after Prime Minister Netanyahu expressed regret over the deaths in the 2010 flotilla incident. Turkey subsequently announced plans to move toward normalization of relations.

Israel took no formal stance in regard to the ouster of President Morsi by the Egyptian military in mid-2013, although it indicated that stability in Egypt was its primary concern. In that regard, Israel expressed dismay over developments in the northern Sinai, where a growing number of jihadists were reportedly operating with little interference from Egyptian authorities. Prime Minister Netanyahu also expressed skepticism in regard to the Russian plan for the elimination of chemical weapons in Syria (Israel had earlier endorsed a possible U.S. military strike in Syria) and in regard to the offer from new Iranian president Hassan Rouhani for talks with the West about Iran's nuclear program.

Current issues. Restiveness within Labor over the lack of progress in the peace process prompted the government reshuffle of January 2011 and the launching of Ehud Barak's new Independence movement (see Political background, above, and Political Parties, below, for details). The administration also faced a major domestic challenge in midyear when demonstrators in Tel Aviv and other cities protested the nation's inadequate supply of affordable housing as well as rising prices for food and other basic commodities. Netanayahu's governing coalition was buffeted again in early 2012 with the expiration of long-standing legislation that had exempted Orthodox religious students from military service. Other disputes focused on proposed cutbacks in the 2013 budget and the recent forced evacuation of Jewish settlers from several West Bank locations. Netanyahu initially considered early elections to try to resolve the policy disputes, but that plan was shelved when new *Kadima* leader Shaul Mofaz joined the government in May. However, Mofaz left the cabinet only two months later, having demanded a faster and fuller integration of the religious students into the military than was acceptable to Netanyahu and the religious parties in the coalition. In October Netanyahu called for early elections when the coalition partners could not agree on proposed austerity measures for 2013.

On November 13, 2012, Israel launched a series of air strikes against a number of targets in Gaza in what Israeli officials described as a response to an increase in rocket attacks into Israel in recent months. The Israeli air strikes prompted retaliatory rocket and missile attacks from Gaza, and more than 160 Palestinians and some 8 Israelis died in the eight-day conflict, which ended with an Egyptian-brokered cease-fire that precluded a possible Israeli ground offensive. The Israeli government reported after the conflict that it had significantly undermined the military capability of Hamas, but some of Netanyahu's critics characterized the action as an "election war." In the run-up to the new legislative poll, Netanyahu also stressed the possibility that Israel might feel compelled to attack Iran's nuclear installation.

Despite the prime minister's continued focus on security, many voters in the January 2013 *Knesset* election appeared more concerned about domestic economic issues, contributing to the success of the centrist and center-left parties, particularly the recently formed *Yesh Atid.* In March Netanyahu turned to *Yesh Atid* and Tzipi Livni's *Hatenua* to help form the next government, which excluded the ultraorthodox parties for the first time in many years. Surprising some observers, the new parties in May agreed to an austerity budget that cut spending (including for social programs) and raised taxes. On the other hand, their insistence on reopening talks with the Palestinians paid dividends when, after six months of lobbying on the part of U.S. Secretary of State John Kerry, direct Israeli-Palestinian negotiations resumed after a hiatus of nearly three years.

POLITICAL PARTIES

Government Parties:

Unity–National Liberal Party (*Likud–Liberalim Leumi*). With the "Unity" rubric reflecting the contention that Israel was entitled to all land between the Jordan River and the Mediterranean, *Likud* was formed under the leadership of Menachem Begin in September 1973 in an effort to break the legislative monopoly of the Labor Alignment (see ILP, below). Joining in *Likud* initially were the *Herut*-Liberal Bloc (*Gush Herut-Liberalim*—Gahal), composed of the *Herut* (Freedom) and Liberal parties, and the Integral Land of Israel movement. Peace to Zion (*Schlomzion*), Ariel Sharon's small right-wing party, entered *Likud* after the 1977 election. Although often maintaining a common outlook in regard to captured territory, the constituent parties subsequently differed somewhat on domestic policy, though generally tending to favor the denationalization of certain industries in the context of a free-enterprise philosophy.

In September 1985 *La'am* (For the Nation), a *Likud* faction that had been launched in 1969 from Rafi (a 1965 offshoot of Mapai, see ILP, below) by former prime minister David Ben-Gurion as the State List, merged with *Herut*. Prior to the 1988 election, two additional groups merged with *Likud*: the Movement for Economic Recovery/Courage (Ometz), founded in early 1984 by former Mapai member Yigael HURWITZ, and the Movement for Israel's Tradition (*Tenuat Masoret Yisrael*—Tami), an Oriental Orthodox party founded in 1981 as an offshoot of the NRP by Aharon ABU-HAZEIRA.

Relations between *Likud* leader Benjamin Netanyahu and former foreign minister David Levy became tense following the latter's loss to Netanyahu in the March 1993 party election. In early 1995 the situation worsened further, with Levy insisting that the adoption of a primary system to choose party candidates for the next election would marginalize the numerically dominant Sephardi community, of which he was a member. As a result, Levy formed the Bridge Party (*Gesher*) in February 1996 in an attempt to build a "social bridge" between the classes and a "political bridge" between the left and the right. (See the 2005–2006 *Handbook* for additional information on the defunct *Gesher*.) Despite the launching of *Gesher*, Levy supported Netanyahu in the May 1996 prime ministerial balloting. *Likud* also agreed to present joint candidates with *Gesher* and *Tzomet* (see below) for the concurrent *Knesset* balloting on a platform that emphasized security as the "first condition" in any peace agreement and opposed the establishment of an independent Palestinian state as well as "land-for-peace" negotiations with Syria regarding the Golan Heights.

Surprising many observers, Netanyahu won the 1996 prime ministerial election with 50.5 percent of the vote. At the same time, the *Likud/Gesher/Tzomet* alliance garnered 25.1 percent of the *Knesset* votes, thereby securing 32 seats, 22 of which went to *Likud* under the formula previously established with its electoral partners. Meanwhile, within *Likud* the most contentious issue involved a cabinet post for Sharon, who had reportedly agreed not to challenge Netanyahu for party supremacy in return for a major ministry in the event of a *Likud* victory. Last-minute negotiations finally produced agreement on the creation of a new ministry of national infrastructure for Sharon, who became one of eight *Likud* members to join Netanyahu in the new cabinet. However, friction between Netanyahu and Sharon continued, as evidenced by Sharon's vote against the new Israeli/Palestinian accord when it was presented to the cabinet for approval by Netanyahu in January 1997. Benjamin Begin, Menachem Begin's son and a longtime opponent of territorial negotiations with the Palestinians, also voted against the agreement and resigned as minister of science to protest Netanyahu's decisions in the matter. Factionalization was also apparent at the November party convention when Netanyahu's supporters pushed through a change whereby the former primary system for choosing legislative candidates was replaced by selection by the Central Committee, which was dominated by Netanyahu loyalists.

In January 1999 Netanyahu was named *Likud*'s candidate for prime minister, securing 82 percent of the primary vote against Moshe ARENS. (Arens, one of Netanyahu's mentors and a former defense minister, had challenged Netanyahu in order to "stop the hemorrhaging" within the party.) By that time, several prominent *Likud* dissenters had defected to the new Center Party (see the 2012 *Handbook* for information on the Center Party, which ceased operating in the early 2000s), while Benjamin Begin had founded his own party (see New *Herut*, below, under New Freedom) and decided to run for prime minister against Netanyahu.

Following his loss to Labor's Ehud Barak in the May 1999 balloting for prime minister, Netanyahu resigned as *Likud*'s leader. He was succeeded on an interim basis by Sharon, who was elected in a permanent capacity on September 3 with 53 percent support of the party membership over two other candidates. Although Netanyahu declined to challenge Sharon for the party's nomination for prime minister in the February 2001 election, in mid-2002 he positioned himself for another run at *Likud* leadership, his supporters sponsoring a resolution that was approved by the Central Committee stating that the party would never support the creation of an independent Palestinian state. However, Sharon easily defeated Netanyahu in the November 28 party balloting. Despite the often bitter previous history between the two men, Netanyahu was named finance minister in the Sharon cabinet appointed in February 2003.

Although Sharon had survived several confrontations with dissident *Likud* members opposed to his plan for unilateral Israeli withdrawal from Gaza (which took place in August 2005), he left *Likud* in November and launched *Kadima* (see below). Netanyahu assumed leadership of *Likud* after Sharon's departure, winning an internal party ballot held in December 2005. *Likud*'s electoral fortunes were severely compromised by the launching of *Kadima*, and *Likud* won only 12 seats in the March 2006 *Knesset* balloting (down from 39 seats in 2003) on a vote share of 9 percent. However, Netanyahu easily won reelection as party leader in an August 2007 vote against far-right candidate Moshe FEIGLIN, a West Bank settler.

In December 2008 *Likud* associated itself with the right-wing, religious Zionist Ahi Party, which, as the Renewed Religious National Zionist Party, had participated, under the leadership of Ephraim EITAM, in the National Union (see below) in 2006, winning two of the nine seats secured by the NRP–National Union electoral coalition. (Eitam and Yitzhak LEVY had formed the Religious National Zionist Party prior to the 2006 balloting after they had split from the NRP in a dispute over policy regarding Gaza.) Netanyahu reportedly at first rebuffed Eitam's overtures on the ground that Eitam, a vehement supporter of the controversial Jewish settlements in the West Bank and East Jerusalem, was too hawkish. However, the affiliation (variously described as a merger or an electoral coalition agreement) with Ahi was ultimately accepted due to campaign budgetary advantages.

Likud rebounded dramatically in the 2009 *Knesset* balloting, securing 27 seats on a vote share of 21.6 percent and propelling Netanyahu to the prime ministership as head of a center-right coalition. Netanyahu again handily defeated Feiglin in *Likud*'s January 2012 leadership election. *Likud* formed an electoral alliance with *Yisrael Beiteinu* for the 2013 *Knesset* poll, securing 20 of the 31 seats won by the alliance (which gained 23.3 percent of the popular vote).

Leaders: Benjamin NETANYAHU (Prime Minister and Chair), Yariv LEVIN (Parliamentary Leader), Israel KATZ (Chair of the Secretariat), Moshe KAHLON (Chair of the Central Committee).

Yisrael Beiteinu (Israel Is Our Home). Founded in 1999 as a party representing the interests of immigrants to Israel from the former Soviet Union, *Yisrael Beiteinu* adopted a hard-line stance on the Israeli–Palestinian conflict. The party won 4 seats in the May 1999 *Knesset* balloting with 2.6 percent of the vote, subsequently forming a *Knesset* faction with the National Union (see below). However, in the 2006 *Knesset* poll, *Yisrael Beiteinu* left the National Union coalition and campaigned on its own. It performed well, winning 11 seats with 9 percent of the vote. The party joined the *Kadima*-led coalition government in October 2006, with Lieberman serving as deputy prime minister and heading the new strategic affairs ministry. However, *Yisrael Beiteinu* left the cabinet in January 2008 to protest the government's decision to resume negotiations with the Palestinians.

Yisrael Beiteinu rose to third place in the February 2009 *Knesset* balloting by securing 15 seats on a vote share of 11.7 percent. Lieberman was subsequently named a deputy prime minister and minister of foreign affairs in the new *Likud*-led government, but he resigned from the cabinet in December 2012 after he was formally charged with breach of trust and fraud. Lieberman dismissed the charges as politically motivated, and his trial continued as of October 2013. Meanwhile, some observers attributed the less than stellar performance in the January 2013 *Knesset* poll by the alliance of *Likud* and *Yisrael Beiteinu* to Lieberman's legal troubles. *Yisrael Beiteinu* secured 11 of the alliance's 31 seats.

Leader: Avigdor LIEBERMAN (Chair).

Yesh Atid (There Is a Future). Founded in January 2012 by Yair Lapid, a popular television anchorman and the son of Tommy Lapid (see Change [Shinui], below), the centrist and secular *Yesh Atid* quickly attracted significant media attention and stunned the political establishment by finishing second (with 19 seats on a vote share of 14.3 percent) in the January 2013 *Knesset* poll. Lapid reportedly agreed to *Yesh Atid*'s participation in the March cabinet only with the understanding that the new government would restart peace negotiations with the Palestinians.

Leaders: Yair LAPID (Chair), Ofer SHELAH (Parliamentary Leader).

Jewish Home (*Habayit Hayehudi*). *Habayit Hayehudi* is the rubric adopted by a group of parties in November 2008 who were attempting to unite various religious camps under the leadership, in part, of the National Religious Party—NRP (*Mifleget Datit Leumit*—Mafdal).

Dedicated to the principles of religious Zionism, the NRP was formed in 1956 through the union of two older organizations, *Mizrahi* and the *Mizrahi* Workers (*Hapoel Hamizrahi*). The NRP subsequently evolved into a militantly nationalist group calling for outright annexation of the West Bank.

Formerly allied with Labor, the NRP went into opposition following the 1973 election because of a dispute over religious policy, but it subsequently reentered the government. In December 1976 Prime Minister Rabin expelled the three NRP members from his cabinet after nine of the party's ten legislative deputies had abstained on a no-confidence vote, thus precipitating a government crisis that led to a call for the May 1977 election. On the eve of the 1977 balloting, the NRP concluded a coalition with *Likud*, subsequently participating in the Begin government formed on June 20. The arrangement continued after the 1981 election, in which the NRP's representation fell from 12 to 6 seats. The electoral decline continued through 1984, when the NRP won only 4 seats.

Prior to the 1988 balloting (at which it won five seats) the NRP absorbed Heritage (*Morasha*), a religious grouping formed prior to the 1984 election by merger of the Rally of Religious Zionism (*Mifleget Tzionut Dati*—Matzad) with the *Agudat* Israel Workers (*Poalei Agudat Yisrael*). The party's legislative strength grew to six in 1992 and nine in 1996, and it secured two seats in the June 1996 government.

Underscoring the tenuous nature of the alliance between *Likud* and the ultra-religious parties, the NRP ministers voted against Prime Minister Netanyahu in January 1997 when the recent Israeli/Palestinian agreement was presented to the cabinet.

Zevulun HAMMER, longtime chair of the NRP and deputy prime minister in the Netanyahu cabinet, died in January 1998. He was succeeded as minister of education and culture and party chair by Yitzhak Levy, the NRP secretary general. The NRP, by then considered the primary political voice of the Jewish settlers in the occupied territories, strongly opposed the Wye agreement of October 1998, contributing significantly to the subsequent collapse of the Netanyahu government.

The NRP secured five seats in the May 1999 *Knesset* balloting on a vote share of 4.2 percent. It left the new Barak government in mid-2000 in protest over discussion of the possible return of the Golan Heights to Syria. Effi EITAM, a brigadier general in the national reserves, succeeded Levy as NRP chair in April 2002 as the NRP prepared to join the Sharon government. In the 2003 *Knesset* poll, the NRP won six seats, and the party again joined Prime Minister Sharon's government. However, Sharon's plan to disengage unilaterally from Gaza subsequently split the NRP, some of whose *Knesset* members joined the National Union (below) in February 2005. In the 2006 poll the NRP campaigned on a joint list with the National Union, with the combined slate winning nine seats on 7 percent of the vote. (Three of the seats went to members of the NRP.)

The formation of *Habayit Hayehudi* in November 2008 was intended to involve the formal merger of the NRP and the National Union. However, the leaders of *Moledet* and *Tequma* (two major components of the National Union) objected to the slots proposed for their members on the *Habayit Hayehudi* candidate list and subsequently broke away to reform the National Union. Consequently, the *Habayit Hayehudi* ticket, which won 3 seats on a vote share of 2.9 percent in the 2009 poll, was essentially an NRP grouping, with the addition of *Tequma* members who opted to remain in the new party. For the 2013 *Knesset* election, other National Union members (including *Moledet*) joined *Habayit Hayehudi*, which under the leadership of its new chair, software entrepreneur Naftali Bennett, improved to 12 seats on a vote share of 9.1 percent. The ultranationalist *Habayit Hayehudi* remained opposed to the notion of an independent Palestinian state but nevertheless joined the March 2013 government, which subsequently reopened negotiations with the Palestinians.

Leaders: Naftali BENNETT (Chair and Parliamentary Leader), Uri ARIEL, Uri OHRBACH.

Hatenua (The Movement). A "new party with veteran politicians," *Hatenua* was formed prior to the January 2013 *Knesset* election by former Kadima leader Tzipi Livni, who had resigned from the *Knesset* in May 2012, and a group of *Kadima* legislators who had recently abandoned *Kadima* to form their own *Knesset* faction. *Hatenua*, described as liberal and secular, secured 5 percent of the vote and six seats.

Leaders: Tzipi LIVNI (Leader), Meir SHEETRIT (Chair), Amir PERETZ, Amnon MITZMA.

Other Legislative Parties:

Israel Labor Party—ILP (*Mifleget Ha'avoda Ha'yisra'elit*). The ILP was formed in January 1968 through merger of the Israel Workers' Party (*Mifleget Poalei Eretz Yisrael*–Mapai), a Western-oriented socialist party established in 1929 and represented in the government by prime ministers David Ben-Gurion, Moshe SHARETT, Levi Eshkol, Golda Meir, Shimon Peres, and Yitzhak Rabin; the Israel Workers' List (*Reshimat Poalei Yisrael*–Rafi), founded by Ben-Gurion as a vehicle of opposition to Prime Minister Eshkol; and the Unity of Labor–Workers of Zion (*Achdut Ha'avoda–Poalei Zion*), which advocated a planned economy, agricultural settlement, and an active defense policy.

In January 1969 the ILP joined with Mapam (see *Meretz,* below) in a coalition known initially as the Alignment (*Ma'arakh*) and subsequently as the Labor Alignment (*Ma'arakh Ha'avoda*). The latter was technically dissolved upon Mapam's withdrawal to protest the formation of the national unity government, although the Labor Alignment rubric was subsequently used to reference a linkage between Labor and *Yahad* (Together), a party led by former air force commander and former *Likud* leader Ezer Weizman, who had urged direct talks with Arab leaders until his retirement from partisan politics before the 1992 election.

Following the assassination of Prime Minister Rabin in November 1995, Labor's Central Committee endorsed Shimon Peres, who had been serving as foreign minister and the lead Israeli negotiator regarding emerging Palestinian autonomy, to succeed Rabin as party leader and prime minister. Subsequently, in a significant policy change, the committee in April 1996 eliminated the long-standing section in the party platform that formally opposed the eventual creation of an independent Palestinian state.

Labor retained a slight majority in the May 1996 *Knesset* balloting (securing 34 seats on the strength of 26.8 percent of the vote); however, Peres was narrowly defeated in the concurrent election for prime minister. Later in the year, amid reports of intraparty friction, Peres announced he would not run for prime minister in 2000 or for reelection as party chair.

In May 1997 the party rejected the proposed creation of a new post of party president for Peres, setting the stage for a subsequent generational change of leadership. In early June, Ehud Barak, a hawkish former army chief of staff and foreign minister under Peres, was elected as Labor's new leader with 57 percent of the vote, easily defeating runner-up Yossi BEILIN, a Peres supporter who garnered 29 percent of the vote. Barak subsequently attempted to move the ILP closer to the center of the political spectrum, and after securing unanimous nomination in January 1999 as the party's candidate for prime minister, he announced in March that Labor would contest the upcoming legislative balloting in a One Israel coalition with *Gesher* and *Meimad.*

The ILP secured 23 of the 26 seats won by One Israel (20.2 percent of the vote) in the May 17, 1999, legislative elections, while Barak was elected prime minister with 56 percent of the vote. However, the ILP suffered major setbacks when Peres was defeated by *Likud*'s Moshe Katsav for state president in July 2000 and Barak was soundly beaten in the special prime ministerial balloting in February 2001. Barak subsequently resigned as ILP leader, and new elections for that post were held in September 2001. Initial results showed Avraham BURG, the speaker of the *Knesset,* with a small majority over Benjamin BEN-ELIEZER, then the defense minister. However, Ben-Eliezer's supporters challenged the results, and after a partial rerun in December, Ben-Eliezer, a hard-liner regarding the Palestinian question, was declared the winner.

Gen. (Ret.) Avraham Mitzna, the mayor of Haifa, was elected leader of the ILP in November 2002, and he subsequently proposed a "radical peace agenda" for the January 2003 *Knesset* balloting (which the ILP contested in a coalition with *Meimad*). Following his poor performance in the elections, Mitzna resigned the ILP leadership in May, and he was succeeded in an acting capacity by Peres. In December 2004 Labor cooperated with Ariel Sharon's *Likud* to form a unity government in order to implement Israel's disengagement plan from Gaza.

In November 2005 Shimon Peres was replaced (in an internal party ballot) as the leader of Labor by left-wing union leader Amir Peretz. Peretz had previously served as the leader of One Nation (*Am Ehad*), which had been formed in early 1999 by several dissident members of *Likud* with strong ties to organized labor, and Peretz stated his intention to reassert Labor's traditional domestic socialist orientation.

Labor concurrently left Prime Minister Sharon's government, prompting a call for an early election for March 2006, in which Labor/*Meimad* won the second highest number of seats (19). Peretz was subsequently appointed deputy prime minister and defense minister in the new government.

Peretz finished third in the first round of balloting for party leader in May 2007 after having faced severe criticism for his role in Israel's 2006 war with the Hezbollah in Lebanon. In the subsequent runoff, Barak (returning to politics after a six-year absence) secured the leadership post with 51.2 percent of the vote against Ami AYALON, the former head of Israel's internal security, who had promised to withdraw Labor from the government unless Prime Minister Olmert resigned. Upon being named deputy prime minister and defense minister, Barak pledged "level-headed" leadership, which included continued participation in the Olmert government, pending developments in the proposed rejuvenation of negotiations with Palestinian leaders.

Following Prime Minister Olmert's resignation in September 2008, Barak indicated that Labor would participate in a coalition government led by the new *Kadima* leader Tzipi Livni. However, friction was reported between Barak and Tivni following the February 2009 *Knesset* balloting (in which Labor, running without *Meimad*, fell to 13 seats on a vote share of 9.9 percent), and Labor joined the *Likud*-led coalition government formed in March. Although Labor's central committee approved the measure by a vote of 680–507, some members were reportedly "tormented" by the decision to cooperate with *Likud*, and the party was subsequently described as suffering from factionalization.

Labor's *Knesset* representation fell to eight in January 2011, when Barak and four other legislators left the party as it announced plans to move into opposition in light of frustration over Prime Minister Netanyahu's approach to peace negotiations with the Palestinians. Labor's cabinet posts were subsequently filled by members of Barak's new Independence faction (see above). In September 2011 Shelly Yachimovich, a former broadcast commentator described as a "staunch social democrat," was elected as the new Labor chair, defeating Amir Peretz for the post. In late 2012 Yachimovich called for the center-left parties to present a united front in the *Knesset* poll scheduled for January 2013, especially in view of what she described as the "extremist" union of *Likud* and *Yisrael Beiteinu*. Such cooperation proved elusive, however, but Labor, running on its own, improved to 15 seats on a vote share of 11.4 percent in the 2013 poll.

Leaders: Shelly YACHIMOVICH (Chair), Isaac HERZOG (Parliamentary Leader), Binyamin BEN-ELIEZER, Eitan CABEL (General Secretary).

Sephardi Torah Guardians (*Shomrei Torah Sephardim*—Shas). An offshoot of *Agudat Yisrael* (below), Shas was formed prior to the 1984 *Knesset* balloting, in which it won four seats. It is an orthodox religious party that draws support from Jews of Oriental (Sephardi) descent from North Africa and the Middle East.

In December 1984 Shas withdrew from the national unity coalition in a dispute with the NRP over the allocation of portfolios, with then Shas leader Yitzhak PERETZ subsequently returning to the interior ministry with a budget enhanced by a transfer of funds from religious affairs. Shas withdrew again in February 1987 over the issue of registering a U.S. convert as Jewish but rejoined the coalition after the 1988 election, in which it won six *Knesset* seats. Its *Knesset* representation was unchanged in the 1992 poll, after which it joined the Labor coalition. In September 1993 Shas leader Aryeh Deri was obliged to resign as interior minister after a lengthy inquiry into alleged corruption had yielded formal charges against him. The result was a six-month withdrawal of Shas from the government coalition, followed by the group's return to opposition status in February 1995.

Shas won 8.5 percent of the vote and 10 seats in the May 1996 *Knesset* balloting, thereby becoming the third-largest legislative party. Its success was in part attributed to the large Shas network of schools and social services, which had won growing grassroots support, even among relatively nonobservant Sephardic Jews. In June, Shas accepted an invitation to join the new Netanyahu government, in which its two portfolios included, not surprisingly, the ministries of labor and social affairs. In the national campaign of early 1999, Shas was described as "thoroughly domestic" in its political concerns and appeared to be surging in popularity, despite Deri's conviction in February on bribery and other charges. Shas won 17 seats on a 13 percent vote share in the May legislative balloting and joined Ehud Barak's subsequent Labor-led government.

Deri resigned as chair of Shas in June 1999. He was imprisoned in September 2000 after his four-year sentence was upheld by the appellate courts.

Shas won 11 seats in the 2003 *Knesset* elections and 12 in 2006, joining the *Kadima*-led coalition government formed by Prime Minister Olmert in May 2006. In mid-2008 Shas threatened to support a nonconfidence motion against the Olmert government unless additional funds were allocated for religious schools and welfare payments. The party also strongly opposed any negotiations with Palestinian officials regarding the status of East Jerusalem.

Following Prime Minister Olmert's resignation in September 2008, Shas declined to join a proposed coalition government under the leadership of *Kadima*'s Tzipi Livni, who charged Shas with making "economically and diplomatically illegitimate demands" in return for participation. Shas won 11 seats in the February 2009 *Knesset* elections on a vote share of 8.5 percent and readily joined the subsequent *Likud*-led coalition government.

Former Shas chair Deri returned to politics in 2012, prompting a reported leadership struggle within the party that was apparently resolved, at least temporarily, by a compromise reached in October under which leadership responsibilities were to be shared by Deri, Eliyahu YISHRAI (who had assumed the chairmanship in 1999), and (then) Housing and Construction Minister Ariel Atias. After retaining its 11 seats (on a vote share of 8.8 percent) in the January 2013 *Knesset* election, Shas did not participate in the formation of the new cabinet in March. Rabbi Ovadia YOSEF, the longstanding Shas spiritual leader, died in early October 2013.

Leaders: Aryeh DERI (Former Chair), Ariel ATIAS (Parliamentary Leader).

United Torah Judaism (UTJ). Also known as the Orthodox Torah bloc, the UTJ was formed prior to the 1992 balloting as a coalition of the two parties below. It won four *Knesset* seats in 1992 and 1996, and one of its members was appointed deputy minister for housing and construction in the June 1996 Netanyahu government. The UTJ won five seats in the May 1999 legislative balloting on a vote share of 3.7 percent and subsequently agreed to support the Barak government in the *Knesset,* albeit without cabinet representation. The UTJ was given several deputy ministerial posts in the Sharon government in March 2001 but lost those positions in May 2002 when the UTJ opposed Sharon's emergency budget cuts. (Rabbi Eliezer SHACH, the longtime spiritual leader of the UTJ and its two component groupings, died in November 2001.)

The UTJ won five seats (on a vote share of 4.3 percent) in the 2003 *Knesset* balloting but resisted repeated invitations to join Sharon's subsequent coalition governments because of the presence of Change (*Shinui,* below) in the cabinet. However, after *Shinui* fell out with *Likud* in late 2004, the UTJ agreed to join the cabinet formed in January 2005. The two factions of UTJ briefly split in 2005 but reunited in time for the 2006 poll, in which the UTJ won six seats on 4.7 percent of the vote.

The UTJ won five seats in the February 2009 *Knesset* balloting on a vote share of 4.4 percent. Although the party initially rebuffed an invitation to join the *Likud*-led coalition government installed on March 31 because of friction between the UTJ and *Yisrael Beiteinu*, the UTJ on April 1 signed an agreement with *Likud* under which the UTJ was given deputy ministerial posts in the ministries of health and education and leadership of the *Knesset*'s finance committee. The UTJ improved to 7 seats in the January 2013 *Knesset* election on a vote share of 5.2 percent but, significantly, was not included in the new government formed in March.

Leaders: Yaakov LITZMAN (Chair), Israel EICHLER.

Union of Israel (*Agudat Yisrael*). A formerly anti-Zionist Orthodox religious party, *Agudat Yisrael* was allied prior to the May 1977 election with *Poalei Agudat Yisrael* in the United Torah Front, which called for strict observance of religious law and introduced the no-confidence motion that led to Prime Minister Rabin's resignation in December 1976. The party's *Knesset* representation fell from four in 1981 to two in 1984 as a result of the loss of Oriental Jewish votes to the recently organized Shas. After winning five seats in 1988, *Agudat Yisrael* declined government representation at full ministerial level but agreed to the appointment of one of its representatives as deputy minister of labor and social affairs. It accepted a Jerusalem Affairs portfolio in November 1990 after Prime Minister Shamir agreed to endorse a number of the party's legislative objectives. *Agudat Yisrael* members secured four of the six seats that UTJ won in the 2006 *Knesset* polling.

Leader: Meir PORUSH.

Torah Flag (*Degel Hatorah*). Following its formation in 1988 by a group of *Agudat Yisrael* dissidents, the *Degel Hatorah*, a non-Zionist, ultraorthodox religious party, captured two *Knesset* seats in the 1988 poll. Its members secured two of the six *Knesset* seats won by the UTJ in the 2006 *Knesset* polling.

Rabbi Auraham RAVITZ, leader of Degal Hatorah and a longtime member of the *Knesset*, died in early 2009.

Leader: Moshi GAFNI.

Power–Democratic Israel (*Meretz–Yisrael Democrati*). *Meretz* was formed prior to the 1992 election as an electoral coalition of the Civil Rights and Peace Movement—CRM (*ha-Tenua le-Zechouot ha-Ezrakh*—Ratz), the United Workers' Party (*Mifleget Hapoalim Hamenchedet*—Mapam), and *Shinui* (see below). The *Meretz* platform called for a phased peace settlement with the Palestinians, Jordan, Lebanon, and Syria, based on withdrawal from the occupied territories and guarantees for the security of Israel through interim agreements, security arrangements, and demilitarization. It also advocated religious pluralism, liberalization of the "law of return," the adoption of a bill of rights, equal status for women, and strict enforcement of antipollution legislation. *Meretz* won 12 *Knesset* seats in 1992 and 9 (Ratz, 4; Mapam, 3; and *Shinui,* 2) in 1996, having prior to the latter endorsed the creation of an independent Palestinian state and "land-for-peace" negotiations with Syria.

In early 1999 Ratz and Mapam agreed to a formal merger of their groupings, with *Meretz* becoming a political party rather than a coalition. Some *Shinui* members also participated in that initiative, although *Shinui* ultimately retained its own identity and campaigned on its own for the May 1999 *Knesset* elections, in which *Meretz* won ten seats on a vote share of 7.6 percent.

Meretz won six seats in the 2003 *Knesset* balloting on a vote share of 5.2 percent. Subsequently, it was announced that *Meretz* would merge with several other left-wing groups to form a new party, known as *Meretz-Yahad* ("Together"), which opposed Prime Minister Sharon's disengagement plan, calling instead for negotiations with the Palestinians toward a comprehensive settlement. Party leaders hoped to draw support from disaffected ILP members. However, in the 2006 *Knesset* election, *Meretz-Yahad* won only five seats (on a 3.8 percent vote share), one less than *Meretz* had won in 2003 and just half of the representation it had after the 1999 election. In the 2009 *Knesset* elections *Meretz* ran on a joint list with the New Movement (*Tnu'a HaHadasha*), a recently formed grouping of left-wing activists led by Tzali REGHEF. The New Movement–*Meretz* list won three seats (two for *Meretz*) on a vote share of 2.95 percent. Longtime *Meretz* leader Chaim ORON retired from the *Knesset* in early 2011. *Meretz* improved to six seats on a vote share of 4.6 percent in the January 2013 *Knesset* election.

Leaders: Zahava GAL-ON (Chair), Ilon GILON (Parliamentary Chair), Dror MORAG (Secretary General).

United Arab List (UAL). The UAL was formed prior to the 1996 *Knesset* elections by Arab groups hoping to increase the electoral clout of the estimated 1 million Israeli Arabs by presenting a joint list of candidates. Although reports agreed that one core component of the new grouping was the Arab Democratic Party, there was confusion regarding other participants. Israeli government publications said that the other two components of the UAL were the Islamic Movement in Israel and an Arab Islamic List.

The UAL won four seats in the 1996 balloting, as several other Arab groupings decided to present their own candidates. The UAL increased its representation in the May 1999 Knesset election to five seats on the strength of 3.4 percent of the vote but fell to two seats in 2003. In the 2006 *Knesset* election, the UAL ran on a single list with the Arab Movement for Change, led by Ahmad Tibi (see National Democratic Alliance [*Balad*], below, for earlier information). The combined grouping won four seats with just over 3 percent of the vote.

In early 2009 the Central Elections Committee banned the UAL and *Balad* from participating in the upcoming *Knesset* balloting on the grounds that the parties supported terrorism and refused to recognize Israel as a democratic Jewish state. Tibi called the proponents of the ban (primarily the far-right National Union and *Yisrael Beiteinu*) "fascists and racists" determined to have "a country without Arabs." The Supreme Court subsequently revoked the electoral ban, and the UAL–Arab Movement for Change List (named *Ra'am-Ta'al*) won four seats in the February *Knesset* balloting, having campaigned on a platform calling for Israeli withdrawal (including settlers) from the West Bank and establishment of a Palestinian state. *Ra'am-Ta'al* retained its four seats in the January 2013 *Knesset* poll on a vote share of 3.7 percent.

Leaders: Ibrahim SARSUR, Ahmad TIBI (Parliamentary Leader).

Democratic Front for Peace and Equality—DFPE (*Hazit Democratit le-Shalom ve-Shivayon—Hadash*). The Democratic Front was organized prior to the 1977 election to present candidates drawn from the former New Communist List (*Rashima Kommunistit Hadasha*—Rakah), a section of the "Black Panther" movement of Oriental Jews, and a number of unaffiliated local Arab leaders. The DFPE retained its existing four *Knesset* seats in 1988, lost one in 1992, rebounded to five in 1996 (campaigning on behalf of an independent Palestinian state and "equality" for Israeli Arabs), and fell back to three in 1999. Described as supported primarily by secular Israeli Arabs, the party retained its three seats in the 2003 and 2006 *Knesset* elections and improved to four seats in the 2009 and 2013 balloting (the latter on a vote share of 3.0 percent).

Leaders: Muhammad BAREKA (Chair), Hanna SWAID (Parliamentary Leader), Awdah BISHARAT (Secretary General).

National Democratic Alliance (*Balad*). This pro-Arab grouping is led by Azmi Bishara, a former member of Rakah (see DFPE, above), who had been elected to the *Knesset* in 1996 on the *Hadash* list. In March 1999 Bishara, a Christian, announced his candidacy for prime minister, thereby potentially becoming the first non-Jew to run for that post. *Balad* campaigned primarily in opposition to perceived government discrimination against Israeli Arabs. It was subsequently reported that Ahmed Tibi, a Palestinian leader, had associated his Arab Movement for Change with *Balad.* Formed in early 1996 by Tibi (described as an adviser to Palestinian leader Yasir Arafat), the movement was one of the groupings expected to participate in the UAL. However, according to government publications, it presented its own candidates (unsuccessfully) in the 1996 *Knesset* elections before aligning with *Balad* for the 1999 balloting. (See UAL, above, for subsequent information on Tibi's party.)

Bishara withdrew from the prime minister's race shortly before the May 17, 1999, balloting; he did not specifically endorse Labor's Ehud Barak, but most Bishara supporters were expected to vote for Barak. *Balad* won two seats (filled by Bishara and Tibi) in the concurrent *Knesset* election. The *Knesset* stripped Bishara of his parliamentary immunity in November 2001, and the *Balad* leader went on trial in February 2002 on charges of "incitement to violence" by, among other things, a speech he had given in Syria supporting "popular resistance" on the part of Palestinians. (The charges were subsequently dropped after the courts ruled that Bishara's immunity had been in place when the statements were made.)

The Israeli government was unsuccessful in its efforts to have *Balad* disqualified from the 2003 *Knesset* balloting, in which *Balad* secured three seats on a 2.3 percent vote share. In 2006 *Balad* again won three seats, although Tibi had aligned with the UAL.

In April 2007 Bishara (by then resident abroad) reportedly resigned his *Knesset* seat after Israeli police confirmed that they were investigating him on suspicion of having "aided an enemy" during the 2006 war between Israel and Hezbollah in Lebanon. (Bishara had denounced Israel's actions in that conflict.)

Balad, described as supported mainly by secular Arab Israelis, faced another attempt to ban it from elections in 2009 (see UAL, above, for details). Following a Supreme Court ruling in its favor, *Balad* retained its three *Knesset* seats in 2009 and, on a vote share of 2.6 percent, in 2013.

Leaders: Azmi BISHARA (in exile), Jamal ZAHALKA (Chair and Parliamentary Leader).

Kadima (Forward). *Kadima* was formed by Prime Minister Sharon after he left *Likud,* then the leading party in the coalition government, in November 2005. Sharon's goal was a new centrist party that would grant him the freedom to carry out his policy of unilateral disengagement from Palestinian territories, a move that was staunchly opposed by some members of *Likud.* Senior figures from *Likud* and Labor joined the new party, including (from *Likud*) Finance Minister Ehud Olmert (the former mayor of Jerusalem), Justice Minister Tzipi Livni, and (from Labor) former prime minister Shimon Peres. Following Sharon's debilitating stroke in January 2006, Olmert became acting prime minister.

Kadima won the largest number of seats (29 out of 120) in the March 2006 *Knesset* balloting. Its platform included a pledge to make further disengagements from Palestinian territory, although Jerusalem and the larger settlement blocs in the West Bank would remain under Israeli control.

Facing a growing corruption investigation, Olmert in July 2008 announced his intention to resign as prime minister. He also subsequently decided not to run as a candidate in the new election for *Kadima*'s leader, the post being narrowly won in balloting on September 17 by Livni, theretofore deputy prime minister and a longtime rival of Olmert within the party. Livni, a centrist considered untainted by the corruption scandal, defeated runner-up Lt. Gen. (Ret.) Shaul Mofaz, a hawkish former army chief and then minister of transportation and road safety, by 43.1 percent of the vote to 42 percent.

Following Prime Minister Olmert's resignation in September 2008, Livni was unable to forge a new coalition government, necessitating early elections in February 2009. Although *Kadima* secured a plurality (28 seats) on a vote share of 22.5 percent, Livni proved unable to form a center-left government, and *Kadima* moved into opposition.

Shaul Mofaz defeated Livni for the *Kadima* leadership with 62 percent of the vote in the March 2012 balloting. He subsequently surprised observers by joining the new national unity government in May, although *Kadima* withdrew from that coalition in July amid acrimony between Mofaz and Prime Minister Netanyahu. (In addition to clashing with Netanyahu on the issue of draft reform [see Current issues, above], Mofaz also strongly criticized the prime minister for "heading to war" with Iran.) Fractionalization was subsequently reported within *Kadima* as both Livni and Olmert apparently considered a return to active politics. (Olmert was given a one-year suspended jail sentence following his conviction in July of "breach of trust" in regard to one of the corruption cases against him, although he was exonerated on two more serious charges.) Livni subsequently founded a new party, *Hatenua* (above), with a number of *Kadima* defectors, and *Kadima* collapsed to only two seats (on a vote share of 2.1 percent) in the January 2013 *Knesset* poll.

Leaders: Lt. Gen. (Ret.) Shaul MOFAZ (Party Leader), Shimon PERES (President of Israel), Yisrael HASSON (Member of the *Knesset*).

Other Parties That Contested the 2013 Knesset Elections:

Otzma Leyisrael (Strong Israel). Having been founded prior to the January 2013 *Knesset* election by former members of the National Union who declined to merge with Jewish Home, the right-wing *Otzma Leyisrael* narrowly missed gaining legislative representation with 1.8 percent of the vote.

Leaders: Arieh ELDAD, Michael BEN-ALI.

Am Shalem (Whole Nation). Formed by Rabbi Chaim Amsallem, who had recently left Shas, Am Shalem, campaigning on a pledge to bring the religious and secular parties together, won 1.2 percent of the vote in the January 2013 *Knesset* election.

Leader: Rabbi Chaim AMSALLEM.

Dor Bonei Haaretz (Generation of Nation Builders). This party is an outgrowth of the Pensioners Party (*Gimla'ey Yisrael LaKneset*—Gil). Gil's primary concerns were domestic, and it pledged to protect pensioner rights, including the right to housing. It also advocated the enlargement of national health insurance and other services for pensioners. Gil stunned electoral observers in the 2006 *Knesset* poll by winning seven seats with nearly 6 percent of the vote. The party's ascent was underscored by its invitation to join the coalition government formed in May.

Three Gil legislators, led by Moshe SHARONI, quit the party in mid-2008 and formed a "Justice for Pensioners" faction in the *Knesset.* The defectors criticized Gil leader Rafi Eitan for failing to push the Olmert administration sufficiently in regard to proposed pension increases. Although two of the earlier defectors reportedly later rejoined Gil, the party fell dramatically to 0.5 percent of the vote (and no seats) in the February 2009 *Knesset* balloting. *Dor* was credited with 0.2 percent of the vote in the 2013 poll.

Leaders: Efraim LAPID, Rafi EITAN.

The Greens. One of several environmentally oriented parties established recently, The Greens won 1.52 percent of the vote in the 2006 *Knesset* poll, which would have been sufficient to secure representation in previous elections for which the threshold was 1.5 percent (raised to 2 percent for 2006). The party won some 50 seats in 22 municipalities in the November 2008 local elections but declined to 0.37 percent of the vote in the 2009 *Knesset* balloting. The Green and Young for a Green Future in Israel slate won 0.21 percent of the vote in the 2013 *Knesset* poll.

Leaders: Pe'er VISNER (Deputy Mayor of Tel Aviv), Amir MELTZER.

Other small parties that participated in both the 2009 and 2013 Knesset elections included ***Brit Olam*** (0.02 percent of the vote in 2013), a grouping led by Ofer LIFSCHITZ and Kinneret Golan HOZ that promotes improved relations between the Jewish and Arab communities; the ***Da'am* Workers Party** (0.09 percent), a largely Israeli Arab organization founded in 1995 by Jewish and Arab activists as an offshoot of the Communist Party of Israel and currently led by Asma AGBARIEH-ZAHALKA; the left-wing **Green-Leaf** (*Ale-Yarok*) party (1.2 percent), a grouping currently led by comedian Gil KOPATCH that promotes, among other things, the liberalization of marijuana laws; ***Koah LaHashpi'a*** (Strength to Influence, 0.7 percent), a grouping dedicated to the rights of the disabled and led by Yochai DOK; ***Or*** (Light, 0.03 percent), a secular grouping formed in 2008 under the leadership of author Yaron YADAN to pursue uniform education; and **The Israelis** (*HaYisraelim,* 0.05 percent), led by Gideon DORON in pursuit of a revamping of the *Knesset* structure to include constituency seats in addition to national proportional seats.

Other Parties:

Independence Party (*Haatzma'ut*). Having been formed as a *Knesset* faction in January 2011 by Deputy Prime Minister Ehud Barak and four other Labor legislators in the wake of a split within Labor, Independence held its founding party congress in May and elected Barak as its chair. The new party described itself as "centrist, Zionist, and democratic." Barak and three other Independence members continued to serve in the *Likud*-led coalition government. However, Barak surprised observers by announcing his retirement from politics in late 2012, and the party did not present candidates in the January 2013 *Knesset* poll.

National Union (*Halchud HaLeumi*). Formed as an electoral alliance in early 1999 by *Moledet, Tequma*, and New *Herut,* the right-wing National Union won four seats (two for *Moledet* and one each for *Tequma* and New *Herut*) in the May *Knesset* elections on the strength of 3 percent of the vote. Shortly thereafter, the National Union formed a *Knesset* faction with *Yisrael Beiteinu,* although the New *Herut* legislator objected to that initiative, and New *Herut* left the National Union. The National Union–*Yisrael Beiteinu* (NU–YB) faction joined the Sharon government in March 2001 but subsequently found itself to the right even of Sharon regarding the Palestinian question. On October 15 the NU–YB ministers, including Tourism Minister Rechavam Ze'evi of *Moledet,* announced their intention to resign from the cabinet. However, that decision was temporarily rescinded after Ze'evi was assassinated on October 17 by Palestinian militants. In March 2002 the NU–YB finally left the coalition, subsequent efforts by Sharon failing to persuade the ultrarightists to return.

In 2003 the NU–YB won seven seats in the *Knesset* election. The NU–YB *Knesset* faction expanded in 2005 when legislators Ephraim Eitam and Yitzhak Levy defected from the NRP and formed the Renewed Religious National Zionist Party, which joined the National Union.

Yisrael Beiteinu left the electoral coalition prior to the 2006 *Knesset* balloting, in which the National Union ran with the NRP, their slate winning nine seats (six for the National Union parties). An attempt was made to merge the NU and NRP into a single party in late 2008, but the initiative collapsed in a dispute over the proposed candidate list (see Jewish Home, above, for additional information). Meanwhile, Eitam's group aligned with *Likud* (see section on *Likud*). Consequently, the National Union ticket that won four seats in the February 2009 poll comprised *Moledet*, most of *Tequma*, and several smaller parties, including *Hatikva*, led by Aryeh ELDAD, and Our Land of Israel (*Eretz Yisrael Shelanu*), led by Rabbi Sholom Dov WOLPO and Baruch MARZEL. The National Union collapsed prior to the January 2013 *Knesset* election, with *Moledet* and the rump Tequma joining Jewish Home and *Hatikva* and Our Land of Israel in launching *Otzma Leyisrael* (above).

Homeland (*Moledet*). *Moledet* is an ultra-Zionist secular party founded in 1988 by a reserve major general, Rechavam Ze'evi, who called for annexation of the occupied territories and the ouster of their Arab inhabitants. In a controversial move that was opposed by several senior ministers, Ze'evi was appointed to the Shamir cabinet in February 1991, but the party went into opposition after the 1992 election, in which it increased its representation from two to three seats. In early July 1994 plans were announced for a merger of *Moledet* with the equally right-wing Renaissance (*Tehiya*) party. (For additional information on *Tehiya,* see the 2007 *Handbook.*) *Moledet* won two seats in the 1996 *Knesset* balloting.

Revival (*Tequma*). Launched in late 1998 by spiritual leaders and activists among Jewish settlers in the occupied territories, *Tequma* subsequently joined the National Union electoral coalition with *Moledet* and New *Herut,* the right-wing parties having concluded they all would face difficulty passing the 1.5 percent vote threshold for *Knesset* representation running individually.

Dimension (*Meimad*). Founded in the late 1980s by former NRP members who believed the parent grouping had become too right-wing, *Meimad* competed unsuccessfully in the 1992 *Knesset* elections. In February 1998 *Meimad* announced its intention to participate in the next legislative balloting as an "Orthodox but open-minded and open-hearted" grouping that could provide a voice for Zionists who supported the peace process. In early 1999 *Meimad* agreed to join the One Israel electoral coalition with the Labor Party and *Gesher. Meimad* secured 1 of the 26 seats won by One Israel in the May *Knesset* balloting, and leader Rabbi Michael Melchior was named to the subsequent Barak cabinet. *Meimad* ran in coalition with Labor in the 2003 and 2006 *Knesset* elections but opted out of that electoral alliance for 2009 in a dispute over where *Meimad* members would be placed on the candidate list. (*Meimad* had previously been assured of gaining seats via its placement in the lists.) *Meimad* contested the 2009 poll in alliance with the new **Green Movement,** a social-environmental party recently established under the leadership of Eran BEN-YEMINI and Al TAL. The new alliance won only 0.8 percent of the vote.

Leaders: Rabbi Michael MELCHIOR, Rabbi Yehuda AMITAL.

Crossroads (*Tzomet*). Also known as the Zionist Revival Movement, *Tzomet* was formed by the defection of former army chief of staff Rafael EITAN from *Tehiya* prior to the 1988 balloting, in which *Tzomet* won two *Knesset* seats; *Tzomet* won eight seats in 1992, but in 1994, two of its legislators defected to form a separate faction, which in June took the name *Yiud* and subsequently joined the Labor coalition. *Tzomet* joined *Likud* and *Gesher* in an electoral coalition in early 1996, supporting Benjamin Netanyahu for prime minister and presenting joint Knesset candidates. *Tzomet* was allocated five of the *Knesset* seats won by the alliance in May, and Eitan was named deputy prime minister and minister of agriculture and rural development in the new cabinet formed in June. As was the case with several other ministers from hard-line groupings, Eitan voted against the accord providing for additional Israeli troop withdrawals from the West Bank when it was presented to the cabinet in January 1997. *Tzomet* contested the 1999 *Knesset* balloting on its own, securing only 0.1 percent of the vote.

Tzomet leader Eitan drowned in November 2004. *Tzomet* won only 1,509 votes in the 2006 *Knesset* poll and 0.05 percent of the vote in 2009.

Leader: Moshe GREEN.

Change (*Shinui*). The original *Shinui* movement under Amnon RUBINSTEIN joined in November 1976 with the Democratic Movement of former army chief of staff Yigael Yadin to form the Democratic Movement for Change (DMC), which, with 15 seats, emerged as the third-largest party in the 1977 election, after which it supported the Begin government. Following a split in the DMC in September 1978, the *Shinui* group and supporters of Transport and Communications Minister Meir AMIT withdrew to form the opposition Change and Initiative (*Shinui ve Yozma*—Shai). The DMC was formally dissolved in February 1981, its remnants regrouping with supporters of Shai to contest the June election under the *Shinui* label. A member of the national unity government after the 1984 balloting, *Shinui* withdrew from the coalition in May 1987. It presented a joint list with the New Liberal Party in 1988.

Two *Shinui* members were elected to the *Knesset* in 1996 as part of *Meretz.* However, *Shinui* in early 1999 opted to contest the upcoming *Knesset* balloting on its own under the leadership of Tommy LAPID, a political commentator and television personality who accepted the *Shinui* chairmanship in March. *Shinui*'s subsequent campaign was primarily devoted to opposing the increasing influence of ultraorthodox parties. It secured six seats in the May 1999 *Knesset* balloting on a vote share of 5 percent. *Shinui* subsequently maintained a position of refusing to join any government that included any ultraorthodox parties. Lapid resigned from the party in early 2006, and a number of *Shinui* members reportedly joined *Kadima.* The rump *Shinui* received only 4,675 votes in the March *Knesset* balloting. Lapid died in mid-2008.

New Freedom (*Herut Hahadasha*). New *Herut* was launched in 1998 by former *Likud* member Benjamin (Benny) BEGIN as a revival of the original *Herut,* which had been formed in the 1970s by his father, Menachem Begin. Benjamin Begin, a steadfast opponent of any "land-for-peace" agreement with the Palestinians, subsequently announced his candidacy for the prime ministerial election of May 1999. He also was a leading figure in the formation of the right-wing National Union electoral coalition with *Moledet* and *Tequma* for the concurrent *Knesset* balloting. However, Begin, who had withdrawn his prime ministerial candidacy shortly before the balloting, resigned his National Union leadership post following the election and retired from politics. New *Herut* left the National Union when the Union agreed to form a single *Knesset* faction with *Yisrael Beiteinu,* the New *Herut* legislator thereby becoming a single-member faction. The party won less than 0.1 percent of the vote in the 2006 *Knesset* balloting.

Leader: Michael KLEINER.

Movement for Israel and Immigration (*Yisrael B'Aliya*). *Yisrael B'Aliya* was originally launched in 1992 as the National Movement for Democracy and Aliya ("ingathering") as a means of promoting the economic well-being of the ex-Soviet immigrant community. *Yisrael B'Aliya* won six seats in the May 1999 legislative balloting on a vote share of 5.1 percent. After joining the subsequent Barak government, it left the cabinet in early August 2000 in opposition to consideration being given to a possible return of the Golan Heights to Syria. The party was awarded cabinet seats in the new Sharon government in early 2001, with Natan SHARANSKY serving as deputy prime minister. Following the poor showing of *Yisrael B'Aliya* in the January 2003 *Knesset* balloting (two seats on a 2.2 percent vote share), Sharansky resigned his cabinet post, with the stated goal of "rebuilding" the party. However, it was quickly announced that the deputies from *Yisrael B'Aliya* would "merge" with the *Likud* faction in the *Knesset.* Sharansky was subsequently named minister for diaspora affairs, but he resigned that post in May 2005 to protest Sharon's disengagement plan. *Yisrael B'Aliya* finally merged with *Likud* before the 2006 *Knesset* poll, and its former leader Sharansky subsequently served as a *Likud* representative in the *Knesset* before announcing his retirement from politics in October 2006.

Banned Party:

Kahane Lives (*Kahane Chai*). *Kahane Chai* is a derivative of Thus (*Kach*), which served as the political vehicle of Rabbi Meir KAHANE, founder of the U.S.-based Jewish Defense League. *Kach* elected its leader to the *Knesset* in 1984, after having competed unsuccessfully in 1977 and 1981. Linked to the activities of the anti-Arab "Jewish underground," the group advocated the forcible expulsion of Palestinians from both Israel and the occupied territories. It was precluded from submitting a *Knesset* list in October 1988 when the High Court of Justice ruled in favor of an Election Commission finding that the group was "racist" and "undemocratic." Kahane was assassinated in New York in November 1990, with a number of his followers, including his son, Rabbi Binyamin Zeev KAHANE, subsequently forming *Kahane Chai.*

Baruch GOLDSTEIN, the Jewish settler who killed 29 Muslim worshippers at a Hebron mosque on February 25, 1994, was a Kahane disciple. In March the Israeli cabinet voted to ban both *Kach* and *Kahane Chai,* although a subsequent official report on the incident found that Goldstein had acted alone.

Binyamin Kahane and his wife were killed in late December 2000 in a drive-by shooting allegedly conducted by Palestinian militants. In late 2001 the United States added *Kahane Chai* to its list of terrorist organizations, despite objections from the Israeli government. *Kahane Chai* was subsequently described as "highly visible" among Jewish settlers in the West Bank.

LEGISLATURE

The ***Knesset*** (Assembly or Congregation) is a unicameral legislature of 120 members elected by universal suffrage for four-year terms (subject to dissolution either by the *Knesset* itself or the prime minister [with the consent of the president]). The members are elected on a nationwide proportional basis, each voter casting one vote for the party or coalition of his or her choice. (The minimum vote percentage for a list to gain representation was raised from 1 percent to 1.5 percent in 1992 and to 2 percent in 2006.)

In the most recent balloting of January 23, 2013, the coalition of *Likud* and *Yisrael Beiteinu* won 31 seats (*Likud*, 20; *Yisrael Beiteinu*, 11); *Yesh Atid*, 19; the Israel Labor Party, 15; Jewish Home (*Habayit Hayehudi*), 12; the Sephardic Torah Guardians (Shas), 11; United Torah

Judaism, 7; *Hatenua*, 6; *Meretz*, 6; the United Arab List, 4; the Democratic Front for Peace and Equality (*Hadash*), 4; the National Democratic Alliance (*Balad*), 3; and *Kadima*, 2.

Speaker: Yuli-Yoel EDELSTEIN.

CABINET

[as of October 1, 2013]

Prime Minister	Benjamin Netanyahu (*Likud*)
Ministers	
Agriculture and Rural Development	Yair Shamir (*Yisrael Beiteinu*)
Communications	Gilad Erdan (*Likud*)
Culture and Sport	Limor Livnat (*Likud*) [f]
Defense	Lt. Gen. Moshe Ya'alon (*Likud*)
Development of the Negev and Galilee	Silvan Shalom (*Likud*)
Education	Shai Piron (*Yesh Atid)*
Energy and Water Resources	Silvan Shalom (*Likud*)
Environmental Protection	Amir Peretz (*Hatenua*)
Finance	Yair Lapid (*Yesh Atid*)
Foreign Affairs	Benjamin Netanyahu (*Likud*)
Health	Yael German (*Yesh Atid*)
Home Front Defense	Gilad Erdan (*Likud*)
Housing and Construction	Uri Yehuda Ariel (Jewish Home)
Immigrant Absorption	Sofa Landver (*Yisrael Beiteinu*) [f]
Industry, Trade, and Labor	Naftali Bennett (Jewish Home)
Intelligence	Yuval Steinitz (*Likud*)
Internal Affairs	Gideon Sa'ar (*Likud*)
Jerusalem Affairs	Naftali Bennett (Jewish Home)
Justice	Tzipi Livni (*Hatenua*)
Public Diplomacy and Diaspora Affairs	Benjamin Natanyahu (*Likud*)
Public Security	Yitzhak Aharonovitch (*Yisrael Beiteinu*)
Regional Cooperation	Silvan Shalom (*Likud*)
Religious Services	Naftali Bennett (Jewish Home)
Science and Technology	Yaakov Perry (*Yesh Atid*)
Senior Citizens	Uri Orbach (Jewish Home)
Social Affairs and Social Services	Meir Cohen (*Yesh Atid*)
Strategic Affairs	Yuval Steinitz (*Likud*)
Tourism	Uzi Landau (*Yisrael Beiteinu*)
Transport, National Infrastructure, and Road Safety	Yisrael Katz (*Yisrael Beiteinu*)
Without Portfolio (Responsible for International Relations)	Yuval Steinitz (*Likud*)

[f] = female

INTERGOVERNMENTAL REPRESENTATION

Ambassador to the U.S.: Michael Scott OREN.

U.S. Ambassador to Israel: Daniel Benjamin SHAPIRO.

Permanent Representative to the UN: Ron PROSOR.

IGO Memberships (Non-UN): EBRD, IADB, IOM, OECD, WTO.

OCCUPIED AND PREVIOUSLY OCCUPIED TERRITORIES

The largely desert Sinai Peninsula, encompassing some 23,000 square miles (59,600 sq. km), was occupied by Israel during the 1956 war with Egypt but was subsequently evacuated under U.S. and UN pressure. It was reoccupied during the Six-Day War of 1967 and, except for a narrow western band bordering on Suez, was retained after the Yom Kippur War of 1973. The Egyptian-Israeli peace treaty, signed in Washington, D.C., on March 26, 1979, provided for a phased withdrawal, two-thirds of which—to beyond a buffer zone running roughly from El Arish in the north to Ras Muhammad in the south—was completed by January 1980. Withdrawal from the remainder of the Sinai, to "the recognized international boundary between Egypt and the former mandated territory of Palestine," was completed on April 25, 1982 (three years from the exchange of treaty-ratification instruments), "without prejudice to the issue of the status of Gaza."

Title to Taba, a small Israeli-occupied area adjoining the southern port of Eilat, was long disputed. A 1906 Anglo-Egyptian/Turkish agreement fixed the border as running through Taba itself. However, a 1915 British military survey (admitted to be imperfect) placed the border some three-quarters of a mile to the northeast. A decision to submit the matter to arbitration was made during talks between Egyptian President Hosni Mubarak and Israeli Prime Minister Shimon Peres in Alexandria in September 1986. Two years later a five-member tribunal supported the Egyptian claim in regard to a boundary marker 150 yards inland from the shore, and in early 1989 Egypt acquired ownership of a luxury hotel on the beach itself, after agreeing to pay compensation to its owner.

Golan Heights. The mountainous Golan Heights, embracing a natural barrier of some 600 square miles (1,550 sq. km) at the juncture of Israel and Syria southeast of Lebanon, was occupied by Israel during the 1967 war. Its interim status (including demarcation of an eastern strip under UN administration) was set forth in a disengagement agreement concluded with Syria in May 1974. In an action condemned by many foreign governments, including that of the United States, the area under Israeli military control was formally made subject to Israeli "law, jurisdiction, and administration" on December 14, 1981. The Israeli-controlled area is largely Druze-populated, with a minority of Jewish settlers; the number of inhabitants in mid-2006 was approximately 40,000.

Note: For information on Gaza (formerly occupied by Israel) and the West Bank (which currently contains Israeli [Jewish] settlements as well as Palestinian-controlled areas), see the entry on the Palestinian Authority/Palestine Liberation Organization at the end of the Governments section of this book.

ITALY

Italian Republic
Repubblica Italiana

Political Status: Unified state proclaimed in 1861; republic established by national referendum in 1946; under parliamentary constitution effective January 1, 1948.

Area: 116,303 sq. mi. (301,225 sq. km).

Population: 60,850,782 (2013E—UN); 61,482,297 (2013E—U.S. Census).

Major Urban Centers (2012E): ROME (2,639,000), Milan (1,262,000), Naples (959,000), Turin (872,000), Palermo (655,000), Genoa (582,000).

Official Language: Italian (German is also official in Trentino-Alto Adige).

Monetary Unit: Euro (market rate November 1, 2013: 0.74 euro = $1US).

President of the Republic: Giorgio NAPOLITANO (Democrats of the Left) elected by the electoral college on May 8–10, 2006, and inaugurated on May 15 for a seven-year term, succeeding Carlo Azeglio CIAMPI (independent). Reelected on April 20, 2013, and inaugurated on April 22.

President of the Council of Ministers: (Prime Minister): Enrico LETTA (Democratic Party), nominated by the president on April 24, 2013, and sworn in along with a new government on November 16, to succeed Mario MONTI (Independent), who resigned on December 21, 2012.

THE COUNTRY

A peninsula rooted in the Alps and jutting into the Mediterranean for a distance of some 725 miles, the Italian Republic includes the large islands of Sicily and Sardinia and other smaller islands in the Tyrrhenian, Adriatic, Ionian, Ligurian, and Sardinian seas. Rugged terrain limits large-scale agriculture to the Po Valley, the Campagna region around Naples, and the plain of Foggia in the southeast. Among numerous socioeconomic cleavages, there is a vast difference between the industrialized north and the much less developed south. Ethnically, however, the Italians form a relatively homogeneous society, the only substantial minority being the approximately 250,000 German-speaking persons in the province of Bolzano (Alto Adige, or South Tirol), which is part of the region known as Venezia Tridentina from 1919 to 1947 and thereafter as Trentino-Alto Adige, whose more activist leaders have long sought a referendum on return of the province to Austrian sovereignty. Although Italian is the official language, regional variations of the standard Tuscan dialect exist, and in various parts of the country small minorities speak French, German, Ladin (similar to Romansch), Slovene, and Sard (Sardinian). Roman Catholicism is nominally professed by over 90 percent of the population; however, religious freedom is constitutionally guaranteed, and in March 1985 the Chamber of Deputies ratified a revised concordat with the Holy See that terminated Roman Catholicism's status as the state religion. In 2011 women constituted 38 percent of the paid labor force, concentrated mainly in education and the service sector. Women hold 30 percent of the seats in both chambers of Parliament.

Italy, a founding member of the Economic and Monetary Union (EMU) of the European Union (EU), is the world's eighth-largest economy (for information on the Italian economy prior to the 2000s, please see the 2012 *Handbook*). GDP declined by 1 percent in 2008 and 5.2 percent in 2009 amid rising inflation and the global economic recession. By 2010, sluggish GDP growth resumed at 1.3 percent, with 0.4 percent in 2011, but the trend reversed in 2012 with a 2.4 percent drop. At present, the agricultural sector accounts for 2 percent of GDP, while industry contributes about 25 percent and services, the balance.

Unemployment, a persistent problem, declined from 11.4 percent in 1998 to 6.8 percent in 2008 before rising to 8.4 percent in 2011 and 10.6 percent in 2012. Inflation fell to a 30-year low of just under 1 percent in 2009 in the wake of falling prices of goods and services as a result of the global recession. Inflation rose by 2.9 percent in 2011 and 3.3 percent in 2012. In recent years, the government has targeted tax evasion in an effort to bring the economy in line with EU standards for member states and to help reduce the spiraling deficit. A slowing economy and increasing welfare costs contributed to the deficit as well, reaching 4.6 percent of annual GDP in 2010, 3.9 percent in 2011, and 3 percent for 2012.

The real danger to Italy's economy was the country's debt burden, which remains stuck at about 120 percent of GDP, the second highest in Europe after Greece. Amid international concern about the EU's ability to resolve its debt crisis, interest rates on Italian government bonds rose sharply, fueling deeper concerns over the country's ability to service its obligations.

GOVERNMENT AND POLITICS

Political background. First unified in the 19th century as a parliamentary monarchy under the House of Savoy, Italy fought with the Allies in World War I. Having succumbed in 1922 to the Fascist dictatorship of Benito MUSSOLINI, while retaining the monarchy, it entered World War II on the side of Nazi Germany in June 1940 and switched to the Allies only after the king removed Mussolini from office in 1943. After this change of sides, Italy became the scene of several months' bitter fighting, not only between Allied and German forces, but also between supporters and opponents of Mussolini. The war ended with a period of provisional government, after which the monarchy was abolished by popular referendum in 1946, and a new, republican constitution went into effect on January 1, 1948. A Communist Party (*Partito Comunista Italiano*—PCI) bid for national power under the leadership of Palmiro TOGLIATTI was defeated in the parliamentary election of April 1948, which established the Christian Democrats (*Partito della Democrazia Cristiana*—DC), then headed by Alcide DE GASPERI, as Italy's strongest political force. Luigi EINAUDI (DC) was elected as the country's first president in May 1948, being succeeded by Giovanni GRONCHI (DC) in 1955 and Antonio SEGNI (DC) in 1962, with the DC leading a succession of center-right coalition governments. The first important modification in this pattern occurred in 1962 with the formation by the DC's Amintore FANFANI of a center-left coalition that, under a policy of an "opening to the left" (*apertura a sinistra*), sought parliamentary support from the Socialist Party (*Partito Socialista Italiano*—PSI) and from 1964 usually included PSI ministers in the government. As part of the realignment, Giuseppe SARAGAT of the Democratic Socialist Party (*Partito Socialista Democratico Italiano*—PSDI) was elected to replace the ailing Segni as president in December 1964. Saragat was succeeded by Giovanni LEONE (DC) in 1971.

In a bitterly contested election in June 1976, the PCI registered unprecedented gains at the expense of the smaller parties, running a close second to the DC. While another DC-PSI government could technically have been formed, the Socialists had indicated during the campaign that they would no longer participate in a coalition that excluded the PCI. For their part, the Communists agreed to abstain on confirmation of a new cabinet in return for a "government role" at less than the cabinet level. As a result, former prime minister Giulio ANDREOTTI succeeded in organizing an all-DC minority government that survived Chamber and Senate confidence votes in August. In practice, Communists governed many Italian regions and municipalities.

In January 1978, the Communists, Socialists, and members of the Italian Republican Party (*Partito Repubblicano Italiano*—PRI) withdrew their support of the Andreotti government following rejection by the DC of a renewed PCI demand for cabinet-level participation. Negotiations conducted by DC president Aldo MORO resulted, however, in a compromise whereby the Communists settled for official inclusion in the ruling parliamentary majority and a guarantee that they would be consulted in advance on government policy. Andreotti, directed by President Leone to form a new government, organized a cabinet that, with only two changes from the preceding one, took office on March 13. Three days later, on March 16, 1978, five-time prime minister Moro was abducted by the extremist Red Brigades; on May 9 his body was found in Rome after the government, with substantial opposition support, refused to negotiate with the terrorists. Moro had been considered a likely successor to President Leone, who resigned on June 15 in the wake of persistent accusations of tax evasion and other irregularities. Following the interim presidency of Amintore Fanfani, Alessandro PERTINI of the PSI was sworn in as head of state on July 8.

The withdrawal of Communist support led to the collapse of the Andreotti government in January 1979 and, ultimately, to early but inconclusive elections in June, after which Francesco COSSIGA (DC) formed a three-party centrist government that survived a confidence vote in the Chamber only because of abstentions by the Republicans and the PSI. The Cossiga government survived until September, when it was forced to resign after defeat of an economic reform package.

In October 1980, the PSI and PSDI concluded a "third force" agreement that did not, however, preclude a dialogue to "reconcile Christian and socialist values." Accordingly, the two parties and the Republicans joined a DC-led government under Arnaldo FORLANI that took office in October. Subsequently, it was revealed that a large number of leading officials, including several cabinet members, belonged to a secret Masonic lodge known as P-2, which had been implicated in a variety of criminal and antidemocratic activities. As a result of the scandal, Forlani was forced to submit his government's resignation in May 1981, and in June, Giovanni SPADOLINI of the Italian Republican Party (*Partito Reppublicano Italiano,* PRI) became the first non-Christian Democrat since 1945 to be invested as prime minister. The first Spadolini coalition, encompassing the four participants in the previous government plus the Liberals (*Partito Liberale Italiano*—PLI), lasted until August 1982. The prime minister was able to form a new government, but differences over economic policy persisted, forcing a second collapse in November.

In December 1982, former prime minister Fanfani returned as head of a four-party coalition that included the DC, PSI, PSDI, and PLI. Although Fanfani succeeded in enacting a number of tax reforms, friction arose during the 1983 regional election campaign, and in April, PSI leader Bettino CRAXI withdrew his party from the coalition, forcing parliamentary dissolution. In the election of June 1983, the Christian Democrats suffered their most severe setback since the party's formation, while the PCI also lost seats. The beneficiaries were the smaller parties, most notably the PRI. The PSI also gained, and on July 21 Craxi was asked to form Italy's first socialist-led administration. Craxi again resigned in June 1986, after an unexpected defeat on a local finance bill in which numerous coalition deputies played the role of secret-ballot defectors (*franchi tiratori,* or snipers), but he was eventually able to form a new government on the basis of the previous five-party alignment.

In February 1987, Craxi announced the "liquidation" of a 1986 pact with the DC that would have permitted them to lead the government for the last year of the parliamentary term; in March, with obvious reluctance, he submitted his resignation. After a series of abortive cabinet-building efforts, former prime minister Fanfani succeeded in organizing a minority administration that lasted only until late April; in a highly unusual move, the Christian Democrats voted to bring down their own government, leading President Cossiga (who had succeeded President Pertini) to call an early general election.

The June 1987 balloting yielded a significant shift of support from the PCI to the PSI, with a marginal gain for the DC and the parliamentary debut of Italy's Greens (*Federazione dei Verdi*—FdV). The Socialists strongly objected to the proposed choice of DC Secretary General Ciriaco DE MITA as prime minister, and President Cossiga somewhat unexpectedly called on the outgoing DC treasury minister, Giovanni GORIA, to head a revived five-party government that took office in July. Goria managed to retain coalition support only until March 1988, when the PSI and PSDI abstained on a controversial nuclear-power vote. Subsequently, after negotiating a record 200-page government program, De Mita, with PSI and PLI support, returned as head of a new administration. In October, De Mita succeeded in ending a 140-year tradition that permitted legislators to vote in secrecy on virtually all important measures. Thenceforth, budgetary matters, particularly, would no longer be subject to "sniper" attack, although secrecy was retained for selected issues, such as civil rights, abortion, and divorce, and for the electoral college selection of a president.

In May 1989, De Mita resigned as prime minister, and Andreotti replaced him in July. The government remained in power until March 1991, when Craxi's PSI withdrew its support, after which Andreotti fashioned a four-party coalition of the DC, PSI, PSDI, and PLI. It was Andreotti's seventh government.

The run-up to the general election of April 1992 was preceded by a number of significant changes in the Italian party system. Formation of the Democratic Party of the Left (*Partito Democratico della Sinistra*—PDS) as revisionist heir to the PCI prompted the collateral organization of a hard-line Communist Refoundation Party (*Partito della Rifondazione Comunista*—PRC). In addition, the long-dominant DC was severely challenged in the country's two major regions by the launching of the Northern League (*Lega Nord*—LN), with the Lombard League (*Lega Lombarda*—LL) at its core, and, in the south, by the emergence of an anti-Mafia grouping, The Network (*La Rete*). The new formations were the principal beneficiaries of the April balloting, in which the DC registered its poorest showing since World War II. On April 24 Prime Minister Andreotti announced his resignation, as did President Cossiga the following day, leaving the country without the constitutional capacity to form a new government. A prolonged deadlock over the selection of a new head of state ensued before being effectively broken by the assassination of the country's leading anti-Mafia judge, Giovanni FALCONE, on May 23. On May 25 a shocked electoral college, in its 16th round of voting, named the recently designated Chamber speaker, Oscar Luigi SCALFARO (DC), as Cossiga's successor. Four weeks later, after nearly three months of political paralysis, the PSI's Giuliano AMATO succeeded, on the basis of the same four parties as his predecessor, in forming Italy's 51st postwar administration.

The traditional parties were severely damaged from early 1992 onward by the country's biggest postwar corruption scandal, which started in Milan and centered at first on disclosures that PSI officials had enriched party coffers by systematic abuse of public service contracts. Arrests began in February and continued throughout the year, amid evidence of wrongdoing at all levels of the center-left political establishment. Some 200 Italian parliamentarians were under criminal investigation by early 1993. Although gravely weakened by the widening scandal, the Amato government clung to office through public approval of eight referendums on April 18–19 that called for major political and economic reforms.

On April 22, 1993, Amato announced his resignation, and he was replaced on April 29 by the politically unaffiliated governor of the Bank of Italy, Carlo Azeglio CIAMPI, whose seven-party coalition government included 3 former Communists (now members of the PDS) and 1 Green. However, less than 24 hours later the last 4 resigned because of the Chamber's unexpected refusal to lift Craxi's parliamentary immunity to corruption charges. On May 5 a new government was formed, 10 of whose 25 members were unaffiliated.

The meltdown of the postwar party structure accelerated in the run-up to a general election on March 26–27, 1994, and included the transformation of the once-dominant DC into the now-defunct Italian Popular Party (*Partito Popolare Italiano*—PPI). The result was a radically transformed Parliament dominated by the right-wing Freedom Alliance (*Polo della Libertà*—PL), headed by the new *Forza Italia*—FI formation of media tycoon Silvio BERLUSCONI. On May 11 Berlusconi was sworn in as prime minister of a five-party, right-wing government that included representatives of the LN and the postfascist National Alliance (*Alleanza Nazionale*—AN).

Policy and personal strains quickly paralyzed the new government, however, culminating in the withdrawal of the LN and the resignation of Berlusconi on December 22, 1994. Shortly before his exit, the prime minister had been called before Milan magistrates to answer charges of corrupt payments by parts of his business empire. Rebuffing Berlusconi's demand that he should be reappointed or new elections called, President Scalfaro appointed a nonparty banker, Lamberto DINI, as prime minister to head a cabinet of technocrats that took office on January 17, 1995, in the midst of an economic crisis. The discrediting of the old political elite reached new heights in September with the launching of judicial proceedings against Andreotti on charges of association with the Mafia. (He was ultimately acquitted in 1999.)

Having survived a right-wing nonconfidence motion in October 1995 by striking a deal with the PRC, Dini submitted his resignation on December 30 after parliamentary passage of the 1996 budget. An attempt to form a reformist government by former merchant banker Antonio MACCANICO (then nonparty) foundered, whereupon new elections were called three years ahead of schedule. The contest saw the emergence of a broad "Olive Tree" (*Ulivo*) alliance of center-left parties that was headed by Romano PRODI (a former left-wing DC minister) and included the PPI, the ex-Communist PDS, and new parties founded by Dini and Maccanico.

The results of the balloting on April 20–21, 1996, gave the Olive Tree parties decisive pluralities in both houses; as a result Prodi on May 17 became prime minister of Italy's 55th postwar government—technically a minority administration, but with promised external support by the PRC. Although the cabinet was predominantly leftist, the government was firmly pro-EU and soon adopted austerity measures to meet the criteria for entry into the proposed EU common currency in 1999, including reducing a budget deficit of 6.8 percent of GDP to less than the 3 percent required for participation. In late November the Prodi government claimed an important initial success when the Italian lira was readmitted to the EU exchange rate mechanism after four years of nonparticipation.

The Prodi government survived its first crisis in April 1997 when the PRC refused to endorse military action to restore order in Albania, forcing Prodi to solicit the support of the center-right parties. A more serious challenge arose when Prodi in late September announced his proposed 1998 budget, which called for pension reductions and further welfare cuts. The PRC denounced the budget, and Prodi resigned on October 9. However, public opinion turned on the PRC, which modified its stance sufficiently to permit reinstatement of the government. Subsequently, the Olive Tree alliance scored heavy victories in local elections in November.

Rejecting the proposed 1999 budget, the PRC again withdrew its support, and the government fell on October 9, 1998. Massimo D'ALEMA, leader of the Democrats of the Left (*Democratici di Sinistra*—DS, as the PDS had been renamed), the largest party in the Parliament, was called upon to form a government after Prodi's attempts to regroup proved futile. D'Alema put together a multiparty government that included not only the first formerly Communist cabinet ministers since a unity government in 1947 but also former president Cossiga's recently organized Democratic Union for the Republic (*Unione Democratica per la Repubblica*—UDR), a center-right grouping of moderate democrats and Christian reformers. Sworn in on October 21, D'Alema retained several key ministers, including those who had been the architects of austerity, and pledged to pass the budget that had been Prodi's downfall.

D'Alema submitted his resignation on December 12, 1999, after losing the support of the small, three-party *Trifoglio* (Clover) parliamentary alliance, which included Cossiga's new Union for the Republic (*Unione per la Repubblica*—UR). Asked to form a new administration by President Carlo Ciampi, who had handily won election as chief of state in May, D'Alema proposed a seven-party government that was largely unchanged except for the addition of the Prodi-sponsored Democrats (*Democratici*). However, D'Alema's second administration proved short-lived: Responding to major gains won by the resurgent center-right in regional elections, the prime minister resigned on April 17, 2000. President Ciampi then turned to former prime minister Amato, D'Alema's minister of treasury and budget, who succeeded in forming an eight-party Olive Tree government that was sworn in on April 26 and confirmed by the Chamber of Deputies two days later.

After Amato removed himself from consideration, the Olive Tree endorsed Rome's mayor, Francesco RUTELLI, a Democrat, to lead the alliance into the 2001 general election. On the center-right, Silvio Berlusconi asserted that the string of corruption charges against him was attributable more to overzealous prosecutors than to actual illegalities. Having reconfigured his Freedom Alliance as the House of Freedoms (*Casa delle Libertà*), on May 13 the former prime minister swept back into office with comfortable majorities in both houses of Parliament. The victory had been widely predicted as Italy's complex political dynamics increasingly came to resemble, in effect, a two-party system: the center-right House of Freedoms alliance won 368 seats in the Chamber of Deputies (58.4 percent) and 177 in the Senate (56.2 percent of the elective seats), while the center-left Olive Tree took 247 (39.2 percent) in the lower house and 128 in the upper (40.1 percent). Berlusconi's cabinet, which was sworn in on June 11, included members of his *Forza Italia,* the AN, the LN, and two Christian Democratic parties, plus a handful of independents. Subsequently, the Christian Democrats merged as the Union of Christian and Center Democrats (*Unione dei Democratici Cristiani e dei Democratici di Centro*—UDC), and the small Italian Republican Party (PRI) decided to join the governing coalition.

Despite his electoral successes, Berlusconi faced charges that he had bribed judges in the mid-1980s to gain control of a food company, an attack that he said was politically motivated. In an undisguised attempt to undercut the prosecution, Berlusconi's parliamentary majority passed legislation allowing a defendant to request a change of venue if there were "legitimate suspicions" of judicial bias. However, the Supreme Court rejected Berlusconi's bid to move his corruption trial from Milan. Parliament then passed a bill giving immunity from prosecution to the top five officeholders—the president, the prime minister, the presidents of the Senate and Chamber, and the head of the Constitutional Court—during their tenure, which meant that the charges against Berlusconi would fall under the statute of limitations by the end of his current term. In January 2004 the Constitutional Court ruled the immunity law unconstitutional, and in April the trial resumed. In the end, Berlusconi was acquitted, although several of his closest colleagues were convicted of corruption and linked to organized crime.

On April 15, 2005, the UDC leader and deputy prime minister, Marco FOLLINI, withdrew his party from the cabinet, demanding policy and ministerial changes in the wake of major setbacks for the House of Freedoms parties in the local elections of April 3–4. Berlusconi tendered his resignation on April 20 but quickly fashioned a new government. He was sworn in once again on April 23 at the head of a reshuffled Council of Ministers (dubbed Berlusconi II) that comprised all the House of Freedoms parties, including the UDC.

By the time the 2006 election campaign got under way, support for Berlusconi had been undermined by growing public discontent over Italy's anemic economy, Berlusconi's grip on the media, persistent charges of corruption against him and other government figures, and the continued presence of some 3,000 Italian troops in Iraq in support of the 2003 U.S. invasion. Nevertheless, the new coalition, the Union (*l'Unione*), headed by Prodi's center-left Olive Tree, narrowly won the April election in the Chamber (49.8 percent over Berlusconi's 49.6 percent). Ironically, a new electoral law that Berlusconi had shepherded through Parliament in December 2005 ended up giving Prodi's coalition a larger majority of Chamber seats, 348–281, than would otherwise have been the case. The House of Freedoms actually won more votes in the Senate (49.9 percent versus 49.8 percent), but the same electoral change handed the Union a two-seat advantage.

Berlusconi initially refused to accede to Prodi, attributing the result to fraud, and opposed Prodi's choice of Giorgio NAPOLITANO, an 80-year-old former Communist and speaker of Parliament, to succeed outgoing President Carlo Azeglio Ciampi. On May 10, 2006, Napolitano won approval by Parliament and regional representatives for a seven-year term and appointed Prodi as prime minister. Prodi was sworn in with a new government on May 17.

By early 2007, public discontent with crime and a sluggish economy strained support for the Prodi government, especially in the Senate, and prompted Union leaders to formulate a 12-point agenda that excluded more radical coalition priorities, including a proposal to grant legal rights to unwed and same-sex couples. This compromise initiative failed to prevent a major crisis in early March concerning Prodi's support for continuing the deployment of Italian peacekeepers in Afghanistan and for the expansion of a U.S. military base near Vicenza. After the Senate rejected both proposals, Prodi tendered his resignation but accepted Napolitano's request to submit to a parliamentary vote of confidence. The crisis subsided on March 27 when the Senate, having confirmed Prodi's tenure, narrowly approved both military measures.

Prodi's majority dissolved on January 16, 2008, when Clemente Mastella of coalition partner Democratic Union for Europe (UDEUR—see the 2010 *Handbook*) resigned following an investigation into allegations of corruption against him and his wife. Unable to muster a vote of confidence in the Senate, Prodi resigned on January 24. On February 6 President Napolitano dissolved both houses of Parliament and set early elections for April 13 and 14. Berlusconi's unnamed center-right grouping, consisting of his newly created People of Freedom (*Il Popolo della Libertà*—PdL), and two regional parties, the Northern League (*Lega Nord*—LN) and the Movement for Autonomy Allied for the South (*Movimento per l'Autonomia Alleati per il Sud*—MPA), won 43.7 percent of the vote, compared with 38 percent for the center-left coalition led by Walter VELTRONI. Berlusconi was sworn in as prime minister, along with a new government, on May 8. (For details on the center-right alliance before the 2008 election, see the 2011 *Handbook.*)

On April 6, 2009, an earthquake killed almost 300, injured 1,500, and destroyed much of the city of l'Aquila and surrounding villages in the central region of Abruzzo. Berlusconi's prompt outreach to the victims helped consolidate his hold on power. The PdL handily won the June elections for the European Parliament, securing 35 percent of the vote, for 29 of 72 seats for Italy, well ahead of the PD's 26 percent result, for 21 seats. The biggest winner in the polling was the right-wing LN, which doubled its percentage of the vote, to 10 percent, for 9 seats in the EU Parliament.

Amid falling popularity, on November 8, 2011, Berlusconi lost his Parliament majority. He resigned on November 12 (see Current issues, below) in exchange for the passage of an austerity plan. The economist and political independent Mario MONTI was nominated by the president as prime minister of a nonparty, technocratic government that was sworn into office on November 16. The government survived confidence votes in the Senate on November 17 and the Chamber the next day.

Monti's caretaker government collapsed when Berlusconi withdrew support in December 2012. Parliamentary elections were held February 24–24, 2013, with the PD, PdL, and upstart Five-Star Movement topping the polls. After protected negotiations, Enrico Letta (PD) formed a coalition with the PdL and was sworn in on April 24.

Constitution and government. The 1948 constitution, which describes Italy as "a democratic republic founded on work," established a parliamentary system with a president, a bicameral legislature, and an independent judiciary. The president, selected for a seven-year term by an electoral college consisting of both houses of Parliament plus delegates named by regional assemblies, appoints the prime minister and, on the latter's recommendation, other members of the Council of Ministers; he may dissolve Parliament at any time prior to the last six months of a full term. The Parliament consists of a Senate and a Chamber of Deputies; the two houses have equal legislative power, and both are subject to dissolution and the holding of new elections. The Council of Ministers is responsible to Parliament and must resign upon passage of a vote of nonconfidence.

Under a modification to electoral arrangements approved by referendum in April 1993, proportional representation was replaced by predominantly first-past-the-post, constituency-based elections. Subsequent parliamentary implementation of the mandate provided for single-member districts for both the Senate and Chamber, with 75 percent of the contests to be decided by plurality voting (hence no runoffs) and 25 percent by a system of proportional representation that would favor minor parties (subject, in the case of the Chamber of Deputies, to a vote threshold of 4 percent). A referendum held on April 18, 1999, called for abolishing the proportional component of Chamber elections. Although 91 percent of those voting backed the measure, the turnout was 0.4 percent below the 50 percent threshold needed to make the result binding. A repeat referendum on May 21, 2000, attracted only 32 percent of registered voters.

The judiciary is headed by the Constitutional Court (*Corte Costituzionale*) and includes (in descending order of superiority) the Supreme Court of Cassation (*Corte Suprema di Cassazione*), assize courts of appeal (*corti d'assise d'appello*), courts of appeal (*corti d'appello*), tribunals (*tribunali*), district courts (*preture*), and justices of the peace (*giudici conciliatori*).

Italy's historically centralized system was substantially modified under the 1948 basic law, which called for the designation of 19 (later 20) administrative regions (*regioni*), 5 of which (Friuli-Venezia Giulia, Sicily, Sardinia, Trentino-Alto Adige, and Val d'Aosta) enjoy special status. Each region has its own administration, including an elected Regional Council (*Consiglio Regionale*). Since April 2000, voters have directly elected presidents in the 15 ordinary regions. (Each special region has its own constitutional provisions.) Subdivisions include 103 provinces and some 8,100 municipalities, all administered by locally elected bodies. In October 2001 a national referendum endorsed a devolution proposal under which the regions would assume greater authority in agriculture, education, health, and other areas.

Although freedom of speech and the press is constitutionally guaranteed, the collection and release of official news is centered in the Information Service of the Presidency of the Council of Ministers. Reporters Without Borders ranked Italy 57th out of 179 countries in 2013 in freedom of the press.

Foreign relations. Italian rule outside the country's geographical frontiers was terminated by World War II and the Paris Peace Treaty of 1947, by which Italy renounced all claims to its former African possessions and ceded the Dodecanese Islands to Greece, a substantial northeastern region to Yugoslavia, and minor frontier districts to France. A dispute with Yugoslavia over the Free Territory of Trieste was largely resolved in 1954 by a partition agreement whereby Italy took possession of Trieste city and Yugoslavia acquired the surrounding rural area.

The province of Alto Adige (South Tirol), acquired from Austria after World War I, was a periodic source of tension between the two countries. In June 1992 they were at last able to notify the United Nations (UN) that outstanding issues related to the South Tirol question had been resolved. Under the settlement, South Tirol (Bolzano) was to be given substantial provincial autonomy, including guarantees for use of the German language, within the broader autonomous region of Trentino-Alto Adige.

Internationally, Italy has been a firm supporter of the Atlantic alliance, the UN and its related agencies, and European integration. Rome has also attempted to forge a special relationship with the Arab world. Although affirming a need for action against terrorism, Italian authorities, in the wake of widespread anti-American street demonstrations, reacted coolly to the April 1986 U.S. bombing raid on Libya. By contrast, Italy endorsed a hard-line response to Iraq's seizure of Kuwait in 1990, and Italian forces joined the U.S.-led expedition that liberated Kuwait in early 1991. In early 2003, despite wide public protests, the Berlusconi government backed the U.S.-led ouster of Iraq's Saddam Hussein and later committed some 3,000 troops to that country. Denouncing the war in Iraq as a "grave" mistake, Prime Minister Romano Prodi withdrew the remaining Italian forces from the country in December 2006. The next year Italy assumed command of ground troops for UNIFIL, the UN peacekeeping mission in Lebanon. In 2009 Italy became the first NATO member to respond to U.S. president Barack Obama's request for additional troops to fight the Taliban in Afghanistan, offering to deploy an additional 1,000 soldiers.

The post-1989 collapse of communism in Eastern Europe created some regional difficulties for Italy, notably an influx of refugees from Albania and later from former Yugoslavia. Responding to the new political realities, and in part to counter the economic power of reunited Germany, Italy sponsored the *Pentagonale* regional accord with Austria, Hungary, Czechoslovakia, and Yugoslavia; this became the *Esagonale* in 1991 with the accession of Poland, and in 1992, following the breakup of Yugoslavia, was relaunched as the Central European Initiative (CEI). In October 1994 Italy concluded a friendship and cooperation treaty with Russia.

As the former colonial ruler of Somalia, Italy displayed its concern at the descent of the country into anarchy in 1991 and provided 2,600 troops for the U.S.-led peacekeeping force in late 1992. In May 1993 it was one of the first to accord formal recognition to another former territory, the Ethiopian breakaway state of Eritrea. On a state visit to Addis Ababa in November 1997, then-President Scalfaro formally apologized for Italy's occupation of Ethiopia in 1936–1941.

In November 1995, Italy agreed to assign 2,300 troops to the International Force (IFOR) to be deployed in Bosnia under the Dayton peace agreement. In the wake of an influx of Albanian refugees in early 1997, Italy led a 6,000-strong multinational force which, with UN backing, was credited with helping restore order in Albania. In 1998, having joined the Contact Group for the former Yugoslavia as its sixth member, Italy backed the sanctions imposed on Belgrade over the Kosovo crisis and in March 1999 joined the air campaign launched by the North Atlantic Treaty Organization (NATO) (see entry on Serbia).

Long criticized for putting relations with the United States above those with the EU, Berlusconi also had to address the strong euro-skepticism espoused by the Northern League, a key member of his governing coalition after the 2008 elections. A growing stream of refugees fleeing unrest in North Africa swamped Italian immigration facilities on the island of Lampedusa in 2011, amid uprisings in Tunisia and Libya. Illegal immigrants streamed over Italy's borders, souring relations with France and other countries and prompting them to reestablish border controls that had been largely dismantled under the intra-EU Schengen agreement, allowing passport-free travel in most of the EU.

In December 2011, Italy and Libya agreed to reactivate a friendship treaty that was suspended in March during the Libyan civil war. Rome also released $3.4 billion in Libyan assets frozen during the conflict.

Italy protested that it was not consulted before a joint UK–Nigerian rescue mission on March 8, 2012, in which two Italian hostages were killed (see entry on Nigeria). On May 18, Italy recalled its ambassador to India after two Italian marines were arrested following the shooting of two Indian fishermen who were misidentified as pirates (see entry on India). The two were allowed to return to Italy to vote in the February 2013 elections, after which the Italian Foreign Ministry announced they would not return to India. Following diplomatic protests, the Italian government reversed course, prompting the resignation of Foreign Minister Giulio TERZI.

Prime Minister Letta pledged to continue support to Afghanistan following the NATO withdrawal in 2014.

Current issues. After years of fragmentation, the 2008 election suggested that Italy was moving toward a two-party system. Berlusconi's campaign promises to cut taxes, privatize state-owned industries, and crack down on illegal immigration prompted a number of parties to join his center-right People of Freedom (*Il Popolo della Libertà*—PdL) coalition. Already the center-left had consolidated and in 207 formed the Democratic Party (*Partito Democratico*—PD). However, by excluding several parties of the far left from, center-left leaders lost an opportunity to present a broad front to counter the center-right's ability to exploit voters' frustrations with the sagging economy and the perceived threat posed by illegal immigrants. Despite its clear majority in both houses of Parliament, the center-right's stability was jeopardized by its dependence on support from the anti-immigrant and protectionist Northern League, even after Berlusconi's PdL was established as a political party in March 2009, absorbing some 13 parties, including the National Alliance.

The ultra-right's influence on the new PdL and on Berlusconi's governing coalition was seen in police actions aimed mainly against illegal immigrants. Further, Berlusconi's refusal to condemn an initiative to reserve seats on Milan's public transportation for native Italians and his statement that his party did not envision "a multi-ethnic Italy" prompted outrage in Italy and abroad. In May, the Chamber passed a law imposing a $13,500 fine and deportation on illegal immigrants. Over the previous several years Italy had become less and less welcoming to illegal migrants from North Africa, many of whom crossed from Libya in dangerously overcrowded, small boats. In the spring of 2009 Italy began a policy of escorting boats intercepted in international waters back to Libya, with which it had very warm relations, without considering any claims for asylum. The policy, though widely criticized by domestic and international civil-rights groups, and by the Pope, was popular at home, particularly with supporters of the *Lega Nord.*

Berlusconi's problems mounted in May when his wife filed for divorce, citing his philandering and plans to include several TV starlets in the PdL lists for European Parliament elections in June. Just days before the elections, opposition leaders called on the prime minister to resign after a court accused him of having paid his British lawyer to lie about Berlusconi's business investments in the 1990s.

Despite the PdL's strong showing in the local elections that were held the same month, Berlusconi's political standing continued to erode amid an ongoing series of sex and corruption scandals. In 2008 the ruling coalition had passed an immunity law for senior-serving politicians, which was designed to negate previous rulings of the Constitutional Court. In October 2009 the court ruled the law unconstitutional, thus allowing two prosecutions of Berlusconi, for corruption and tax fraud, to resume. In November 2009 Berlusconi was struck in the face while signing autographs at a rally in Milan. He suffered a broken nose and spent several nights in the hospital. His attacker was later declared incompetent to stand trial.

A second round of local elections, held March 28–29, 2010, saw Berlusconi's coalition do unexpectedly well. However, most of the gains were made by the *Lega Nord.* The vote was interpreted as a protest against economic conditions, as well as an expression of anti-immigrant feeling.

Responding to European Commission warnings to cut the deficit to below 3 percent of GDP, in May 2010 the government announced an austerity program worth about $33 billion for the years 2011–2012, heavily targeted toward the public sector and expected to curb some 1.6 percent of GDP.

A cabinet shake-up occurred on November 15, 2010, when four ministers allied with former government supporter and Chamber president Gianfranco Fini quit after Berlusconi rejected Fini's call to resign. The government barely survived no-confidence votes in the Chamber and the Senate on December 14. Berlusconi's fall in public opinion was reflected in PdL losses in the local elections held on May 15–16, 2011, followed by a referendum on June 12–13 that defeated PdL-sponsored laws granting Berlusconi immunity from prosecution while in office, authorizing new nuclear power plant construction, and allowing for the privatization of water supplies. Meanwhile, on July 18, the prime minister appeared before the court on bribery charges; a separate trial also began that day in which Berlusconi was charged with paying for sex with a minor and abusing his office by obtaining her release after her arrest for theft.

In mid-July 2011, as the rating agency Standard & Poor's downgraded Italy's outlook from stable to negative, Parliament passed a new austerity measure of spending cuts and tax increases. Amid charges of corruption aimed at finance minister Giulio Tremonti and the arrest of a PdL deputy for corruption (after the Chamber lifted his immunity), Berlusconi initially rebuffed opposition calls for him to resign and call early elections. However, he lost his majority in Parliament on November 8 amid debate over additional austerity measures. Berlusconi offered his resignation four days later, after passage of his economic package. He left office on November 16 and was replaced by the political independent Mario MONTI, who formed a cabinet of technocrats. The cabinet cut the deficit by $30 billion during its first month in office through tax increases and cuts in local government spending. The government also raised the retirement age from 60 to 61 for women and 65 to 66 for men.

In January 2012, the Italian passenger liner, the *Costa Concordia,* wrecked and capsized near the island of Giglio, killing 32. The captain, who left the vessel before passengers were fully evacuated, was later charged with manslaughter.

In February 2012, international credit agencies downgraded Italy's debt, leading to higher borrowing costs. Also in February, the government ended a tax exemption on the Vatican commercial properties. In June, the cabinet approved an €80 billion series of economic measures designed to both reduce the debt and stimulate the economy. The package included the sale of state property and cuts to various public programs. Meanwhile, the legislature approved labor reforms that made it easier to hire and fire workers.

September brought mixed economic news. While a bond sale brought the treasury €6.5 billion at the lowest yield in years, Monti announced that GDP would likely contract by 2.4 percent for 2012, twice the level forecast in April. Reduced tax revenue, brought on by sagging consumer demand, meant less money to cut the budget deficit.

Berlusconi was convicted of tax fraud on October 26, in a case related to the purchase of television rights by his media conglomerate. He was ordered to pay €10 million in back taxes, sentenced to four years in jail (reduced to one year due to overcrowding), and barred from holding public office for five years. Only two days earlier, he had indicated that his party would revert to its former name, Forza Italia, for upcoming parliamentary elections and that he would not be that party's candidate for prime minister.

On December 6, the PdL abstained from confidence votes in both houses of Parliament. Two days later, Berlusconi reversed his earlier decision and stated that he would seek another term as prime minister. Prime Minister Monti declared that his government could not function without the support of the PdL and announced that he would resign once the 2013 budget had passed. That budget, which included €3.7 billion in spending cuts and predicted a 1.8 percent of GDP deficit, was approved 373–67 on December 21. Monti immediately submitted his resignation, and President Napolitano dissolved Parliament on December 23. New elections were scheduled for February 24–25, 2013, with Monti remaining as caretaker in the interim.

The political landscape going into the elections was divided between Italy Common Good, a center-left bloc led by Pier Luigi BERSANI's PD, and a center-right group under Berlusconi's PdL. After first declaring he would not run in the February election, Monti formed his own centrist party, Civic Choice, in the last days of 2012, giving him little time to mount a full-scale campaign. He received support from the Catholic Church and by big business. On election day Monti headed the With Monti for Italy alliance, comprised of Civic Choice, the Union of the Democratic Center, and Future and Freedom. The upstart, antiestablishment Five-Star Movement of comedian and blogger Beppe GRILLO surged in the polls, threatening to unseat more established parties.

As feared, election results were inconclusive, with the PD having a majority in the Chamber but not in the Senate. In the Chamber, the PD-led coalition took 345 seats, followed by PdL–NL with 125, Five-Star Movement with 109, and With Monti at 47 seats. In the Senate, the PdL–NL led with 125; followed by Italy Common Good with 119; Five-Star Movement, 54; and With Monti, 19.

On March 22, President Napolitano asked Bersani to form a government, but Grillo rebuffed Bersani's overtures, sticking to his campaign pledge to not join any coalition. Bersani next approached Berlusconi, who turned him down on March 26. Bersani made one last, unsuccessful effort with Grillo on March 27.

Amid the ongoing government confusion, President Napolitano's term expired. After Parliament rejected both of his nominees—former Senate speaker Franco MARINI and former prime minister Prodi—Bersani announced his resignation as PD leader on April 19. On April 20 Parliament opted for continuity and elected the 87-year-old Napolitano for an unprecedented second term.

On April 24, Napolitano tapped 46-year-old Enrico Letta of the PD to form a new government. Letta, nephew of one of Berlusconi's closest advisors, forged a PD—PdL grand coalition that was sworn in on April 28. PdL leader Angelino ALFANO was named deputy prime minister, Berlusconi demanded the reversal of Monti's tax on first-time homebuyers and cancellation of a scheduled value-added tax (VAT) increase in return for the PdL's participation. Letta's diverse cabinet included Italy's first black minister, Cécile KYENGE, an ophthalmologist originally from the Democratic Republic of Congo. Letta's premiership started on an ominous note when, during the inauguration ceremony, Luigi PREITI, a 46-year-old unemployed, desperate Italian man, shot two police officers outside the prime minister's office.

The economy received a boost in early April, when Monti's government announced it would begin paying €40 billion in arrears owed to the private sector. However, the government's ability to follow through was unclear as the ongoing political crisis had sapped consumer spending and thus tax revenue. Monti raised the projected budget deficit for 2013 from 2.4 percent of GDP to 2.9 percent.

The Five-Star Movement suffered heavy losses in local elections in May, as voters expressed disgust with the party's intransigence over forming a coalition government. The PD increased its authority, winning city hall in all 16 cities at stake, including Rome.

Minister of International Cooperation and Integration Kyenge quickly became the target of ugly racist and anti-immigrant sentiments. Northern League senator Roberto CALDEROLI described her as an "orangutan," and she was pelted with bananas during a rally in July. A naturalized citizen, Kyenge became a lightning rod for opponents of a law to grant citizenship to Italian-born children of immigrants. In May, the Court of Cassation overturned the Berlusconi-era state of emergency that had targeted the country's growing Roma population for intrusive registration procedures.

Letta's fragile government issued a package of 80 economic initiatives in June, including canceling the VAT hike and deferring the first home tax. Finance Minister Fabrizio SACCOMANNI warned that ending the home tax would leave a €8 billion hole in the budget. Letta also began work on constitutional reforms that would eliminate the bonus seats given to the top-finishing party and reduce the power of the Senate.

After years of escaping numerous legal charges, Berlusconi's luck ran out on July 30, when the Supreme Court upheld his tax fraud conviction. The ruling was controversial, as the Court had moved the case up by several months because the statue of limitations on the charges expired on August 1. (He has two other appeals pending; for his March 7 conviction for publicizing wiretapped phone call and his June conviction for prostitution.) The PdL immediately blocked all parliamentary activity in protest, while the Senate began impeachment proceedings. Berlusconi filed an appeal with the European Court of Human Rights, noting that the impeachment law was enacted only in 2012, long after his crime. On September 28, all PdL ministers threatened to resign if Berlusconi is impeached. But on October 2, 25 PdL senators rebelled against Berlusconi, allowing Letta's government to survive a confidence vote.

POLITICAL PARTIES

For more than four decades after World War II, the Italian political scene was dominated by the Christian Democrats (DC) on the center-right and the Italian Communist Party (PCI) on the left. The DC formed the major component of all postwar governments until 1994, while the PCI, although without government representation after 1947, remained the largest communist formation in Western Europe and by far the largest Italian opposition party (for more information on political parties prior to the 1980s, please see the 2012 *Handbook*). The reorganization of the prewar Fascist Party is constitutionally forbidden.

The established postwar party structure came under increasing challenge in the 1980s, before effectively disintegrating in the early 1990s. On the left, the PCI reacted to the collapse of communism in Eastern Europe by becoming a democratic socialist party. On the right, increasing popular disgust with political corruption in Rome gave rise to various regional movements, especially in the north, seeking the breakup of Italy as a unitary state. On the center-left, the miring of many political leaders in financial and other scandals led to the conversion of the DC into the Italian Popular Party (PPI). This did not prevent a hemorrhage of Christian Democratic support in the 1994 election, which featured a three-way alliance structure of the right, center, and left, covering most significant parties. Since the 1996 elections this has become a two-way center-left versus center-right contest.

Parliamentary Parties:

Democratic Party (*Partito Democratico*—PD). Founded on October 14, 2007, during the presidency of Romano Prodi, the center-left PD resulted from the merger of the **Democrats of the Left** (*Democratici di Sinistra*—DS) and **Daisy–Democracy Is Freedom** (*Margherita–Democrazia è Libertà*—M-DL) in an effort to unify the center-left into a single entity. Six smaller parties also joined the PD and were subsequently fully absorbed. (For more information on the now defunct subsets of the Democratic Party, including the DS, M-DL, and the **Italian Popular Party** [*Partito Popolare Italiano*—PPI], see the 2008 *Handbook.*)

The 2008 election handed the PD 33.2 percent of the vote for the Chamber and 33.7 percent for the Senate. On April 16, 2008, following the collapse of his Union government and electoral defeat, Romano Prodi resigned his leadership position in favor of Walter Veltroni, mayor of Rome and former DS leader. Although the PD remains the strongest center-left party, several factions have emerged that reflect the priorities of its two principal constituents. Former DS members and their supporters emphasize the party's social democratic roots and support affiliation with the European Socialist Party, while former Daisy advocates oppose that affiliation and continue to carry their Catholic and reformist standard.

Veltroni's quest to build a strong, unified party of the center-left collapsed in February 2009, when the party suffered heavy losses in regional elections in Sardinia. Veltroni resigned on February 21, leaving the center-left opposition in shambles and further strengthening Berlusconi's center-right coalition. Dario FRANCESCHINI, Veltroni's deputy, succeeded him as interim party leader.

The June 2009, EU elections caused the PD to lose 1 seat, retaining 21. In the March 2010 regional elections the PD lost control of Calabria, Campania, Piedmont, and Lazio to the PdL and kept Liguria, Emilia-Romagna, Tuscany, Marche, Umbria, and Basilicata.

At a party congress held on November 7, 2009, Pier Luigi Bersani, a former communist and cabinet member, defeated Franceschini to become leader of the PD. Bersani's election prompted past PD leader Francesco Rutelli to leave and form a new centrist party, **Alliance for Italy** (*Alleanza per l'Italia*—ApI; see below). Twelve deputies and 13 senators also abandoned the PD for more centrist parties. The PD won an additional 38 town councils in local balloting in May 2012.

Matteo RENZI, the 37-year old mayor of Florence, challenged Bersani in the 2013 parliamentary election primary. Bersani resigned as party leader on April 17, 2013, following unsuccessful efforts to form a government and two rejected candidacies for president. Party president Maria Rosaria BINDI also resigned.

Leaders: Guglielmo EPIFANI (Acting Secretary), Maria Rosaria (Rosy) BINDI (Acting President), Luigi ZANDA (Senate Leader), Roberto SPERANZA (Chamber Leader), Maurizio MIGLIAVACCA (Coordinator), Piero GRASSO (President of Senate).

People of Freedom (*Il Popolo della Libertà*—PdL). In an effort to coalesce Italy's myriad parties and movements of the right and center and as a response to the center-left's creation of the similarly inclusive, center-left Democratic Party (*Partito Democratico*—DP), Berlusconi launched the PdL coalition on November 18, 2007. Following the January 2008 collapse of the center-left coalition government of Romano Prodi, Berlusconi agreed to form a joint list with Gianfranco Fini, leader of the National Alliance (*Alleanza Nazionale*—AN) ahead of the April election.

On February 8, 2008, Berlusconi formed the new alliance, which also included *Forza Italia* (FI), the AN, and several smaller parties that continued to exist as separate entities. The PdL subsequently garnered 37.4 percent of the vote, winning 276 seats in the Chamber and 146 in the Senate, making it Italy's largest political organization and the first to win more than 35 percent of the vote since Christian Democracy in 1979. (The AN was the second-largest ally in the PdL's legislative victory, winning 90 seats in the Chamber of Deputies and 48 in the Senate.)

Further bolstering the PdL's authority was the decision by the AN to merge with the PdL (alongside FI) in early March 2009. To further secure the PdL's stronghold, Berlusconi presided with much fanfare over the PdL's inaugural congress at the end of March, announcing the consolidation of the various parties, including some 13 minor groups and parties, into the PdL fold. (For details about the parties that merged into the PdL, see the 2011 *Handbook.*)

PdL cohesion soon began to unravel. After repeated clashes with Berlusconi over the leader's conduct and policies, former AN leader Gianfranco Fini was expelled from the party in July 2010. He retained his position as president of the Chamber of Deputies and took 33 members with him to form a new party, **Future and Freedom** (*Futuro e Libertà*—FLI; see below), thus depriving Berlusconi of a majority. As Berlusconi's political clout waned amid mounting legal scandals, embarrassing defeats in the May 2011 local elections, and the country's stagnant economy, the prime minister announced in June that he would not seek another term when his mandate was up in 2013. In an apparent move to anoint a successor to the 74-year-old leader, the party's national council on July 1 appointed the 40-year-old justice minister, Angelino Alfano, to the new post of political secretary. Alfano resigned his cabinet post to prepare the party for the upcoming campaign. Berlusconi resigned as prime minister in November 2011.

In local elections in May 2012, the PdL won in only 6 of the 15 major cities it had previously controlled, and it lost the governorship of Sicily in October. Amid spreading corruption charges against PdL officials across the country, Berlusconi announced in October that he would reestablish the party under the Forza Italia banner but not seek the premiership in 2013. Two months later, he declared that he would seek the top office, because he had could not find any other worthy candidate. The PdL withdrew its support for Prime Minister Monti on December 6, 2012, paving the way for early elections in February 2013.

Berlusconi formed a grand coalition government with the PD in April 2013 but threatened to pull out in September when the Supreme Court upheld his conviction on tax fraud and the Senate began impeachment proceedings. A rebellion by PdL senators saved the Letta government in October, prompting speculation that the PdL might split into separate Berlusconi and Alfano parties.

Leaders: Silvio BERLUSCONI (Party President), Angelino ALFANO (Political Secretary), Renato SCHIFANI (Senate Leader), Renato BRUNETTO (Chamber Leader), Sandro BONDI, Denis VERDINI (Coordinators).

Five Star Movement (*Movimento 5 Stelle*—M5S). Comedian and blogger Beppe GRILLO and Internet mogul Gianroberto CASALEGGIO formed M5S in 2009. The party's platform is built around developing direct democracy through the Internet as well as promoting clean water, public transportation, and the environment. It is fiercely anti-EU, anti-austerity, and antiestablishment. Five Star candidates made impressive showings in local elections in 2012 and dominated the 2013 parliamentary elections, taking one-fourth of the vote.

Throughout the 2013 campaign, Grillo insisted he would not join any government coalition, a position he stuck to despite overtures from the Democratic Party. He has developed a reputation for authoritarianism, especially after expelling party members who disagreed with him. Grillo did not seek election himself and has been known to text his MPs with instructions during parliamentary debates.

Voters have become disillusioned with Grillo's lack of flexibility and disappointed with the performance of M5S officials, who are largely political novices. Several quit Parliament after serving a few months.

Leaders: Beppe GRILLO (Founder), Gianroberto CASALEGGIO (Cofounder), Riccardo NUTI (Chamber Leader), Nicola MORRA (Senate Leader).

Civic Choice (*Scelta Civica*—SC). Mario MONTI established SC following the collapse of his technocratic government in December 2012. The centrist, nominally Christian Democratic party sought to build on his economic program by promoting European integration and fiscal rigor. The **Toward the Third Republic** (*Verso la Terza Repubblica*) party founded in November 2012 by Ferrari chairman Luca Cordero di MONTEZEMOLO was folded into the new party. SC headed the With Monti for Italy coalition for the February 2013 parliamentary elections. SC finished fourth, with 37 seats in the Chamber and 20 in the Senate.

Leaders: Mario MONTI (Founder, former prime minister), Lorenzo DELLAI (Chamber Leader), Gianluca SUSTA (Senate Leader).

Left Ecology Freedom (*Sinistra Ecologia Libertà*—SEL) is a leftist party formed in 2010 by Nichi Vendola the openly gay governor of Puglia. SEL began as am umbrella group assembled to pass the 4 percent threshold in the 2009 European Parliament election. Originally known as **Left and Freedom**, the founding members were Vendola's **Movement for the Left** (*Movimento per la Sinistra*—MpS), the **Socialist Party** (*Partito Socialista*—PS), the **Democratic Left** (*Sinistra Democratica*—SD), **Federation of the Greens** (*Federazione dei Verdi*—FdV), and **Unite the Left** (*Unire la Sinistra*). The group did not win any seats in 2009 but organized as a formal party in 2010 with "ecology" added to its name. The FdV opted to remain a separate but allied party. The party supports a national minimum wage, relaxed immigration policies, and same-sex marriages.

Vendola, a harsh critic of austerity, refused to consider an alliance with Monti and instead joined the PD electoral alliance in February 2013. SEL polled at 3.2 percent, enough for 37 Deputies and 7 Senators. SEL member Laura Boldrini was elected president of the Chamber in March.

Leaders: Nichi VENDOLA (President), Laura BOLDRINI (President of Chamber)

Northern League (*Lega Nord*—LN). The LN formed in February 1991 as a federation of the Lombard League (*Lega Lombarda*—LL) and sister parties in Emilia-Romagna, Liguria, Piedmont, Tuscany, and Veneto. The party's name for the northern regions is "Padania" (the lands of the Po River), a term that the LN's parliamentary groups have included in their names.

Launched in 1979 and named after a 12th-century federation of northern Italian cities, the LL achieved prominence in the 1980s as the most conspicuous of several regional groups to challenge the authority of Rome, particularly its use of public revenues to aid the largely impoverished south. It advocated the adoption of a federal system with substantial regional autonomy in most areas, save defense and foreign policy. Its xenophobic and barely disguised racist outlook included a pronounced anti-immigrant posture.

The LN won 8.7 percent of the national vote in the 1992 general election and 8.4 percent as part of the PL in March 1994. Having joined the Berlusconi government in May, the LN pulled out in December amid much acrimony. The LN contested the April 1996 legislative elections independently, increasing its support to 10.1 percent of the national proportional vote and winning 59 seats in the lower house and 27 in the Senate, while becoming the strongest party in northern Italy. In opposition to the resultant center-left government, the LN convened a "parliament" in Mantua in late May, at which Bossi, flanked by green-shirted activists, reasserted the league's secessionist aims. In September Bossi led a three-day LN march and rally, the climax of which was a declaration of independence for the "Republic of Padania" and the formation of a provisional government. However, strong local opposition to the LN's aims, combined with warnings and appeals from senior politicians in Rome, apparently contributed to Bossi's subsequent announcement that he was prepared to negotiate new constitutional arrangements for northern Italy.

In January 1998, Bossi received a one-year suspended sentence for criminal incitement, and in July both he and his deputy, Roberto Maroni, received seven-month suspended sentences for resisting authorities and offensive behavior. Having reconciled with FI, the LN won a surprisingly small 3.9 percent of the proportional vote in 2001 as FI made significant inroads in the north.

Responding in part to anti-immigrant statements by the party leadership, in 2002 the Council of Europe issued a report describing the LN as "racist and xenophobic." In January 2004 Umberto Bossi resigned from the Council of Ministers because of inadequate progress on regional devolution. The LN nevertheless remained in the coalition, and in April 2005 the party's 28 deputies and 17 senators helped approve the "Berlusconi II" government. The LN saw minor losses in the April 2006 poll, winning 23 Chamber and 13 Senate seats.

The party subsequently softened its secessionist rhetoric and began to advocate federalism as the preferred means to securing greater regional autonomy. Riding a wave of anti-immigrant sentiment and disaffection with the center-left government, the LN emerged stronger than ever in the 2008 election, winning 8.3 percent of the vote—double its performance in 2006—and capturing 26 Senate and 60 Chamber seats. Reflecting its rising political status, the LN was awarded four cabinet posts. In the March 2010 regional elections the LN greatly enhanced its importance in Berlusconi's coalition by gaining control of Veneto and Piedmont. The previous June it had picked up 5 seats in the EU Parliament, for a total of 9.

At the June 2011 annual party convention in Pontida, Lombardy, Roberto Maroni, the interior minister and a leading critic of the LN's adhesion to the center-right, emerged as the strongest candidate to eventually succeed Bossi as party leader. When Bossi resigned in April 2012 following revelations of the misappropriation of party funds, Maroni was elected to replace him in June.

LN leaders only agreed to continue their alliance with the PdL for the February 2013 parliamentary elections if Berlusconi declined to run for prime minister. They were rewarded with 18 seats in the Chamber and 17 in the Senate.

Leaders: Roberto MARONI (Federal Secretary), Bitonci MASSIMO (Senate Leader), Giancarlo GIORGETTI (Chamber Leader), Roberto CALDEROLI (Coordinator).

Brothers of Italy—National Center-Right (*Fratelli d'Italia—Centrodestra Nazionale*—FdI-CN) is a center-right union of two factions spun off of the PdL in a December 2012 reorganization. It ran under the PdL umbrella in February 2013 and was rewarded with 9 Chamber seats. Former PdL national coordinator Ignazio LA RUSSA founded National Center-Right, while Guido CROSETTO and Giorgia MELONI headed Brothers of Italy. The party opposes austerity and tighter European integration

Leaders: Ignazio LA RUSSA (President), Guido CROSETTO (Coordinator).

Union of the Center (*Unione di Centro*—UdC). The UdC was founded on December 8, 2007, by Pier Ferdinando CASINI through the merger of his **Union of Christian and Center Democrats** (*Unione dei Democratici Cristiani e di Centro*—UDC) and the **Rose for Italy** (*Rosa per l'Italia*). (For more on UDC and Rose for Italy, please see the 2012 *Handbook.*) The party was formed to unite like-minded centrist parties and attracted many minor parties and movements. On February 28, 2008, it nominated Casini as its candidate for prime minister. The Christian Democratic Party and several other minor parties joined the UdC, which campaigned as an alternative to the expanding center-left and center-right coalitions. It was the only party in the 2008 election not aligned with either coalition to win seats in both chambers: 35 deputies and 3 senators. In the June 2009 EU elections the UdC retained its five seats. The UdC joined the Monti for Italy alliance for the February 2013 parliamentary elections, winning 8 Chamber and 2 Senate seats.

Leaders: Pier Ferdinando CASINI (Leader and Chamber Leader), Rocco BUTTIGLIONE (President), Lorenzo CESA (Secretary), Gianpiero D'ALIA (Senate Leader).

Democratic Center (*Centro Democratico*—CD) was founded on December 28, 2012, by former members of the Alliance for Italy and continues the center-left values of that party. Some Italy of Values members also switched to CD. Running in February 2013 as part of the Italy Common Good coalition, Democratic Center secured 0.49 percent of the vote and five Chamber deputies. Most CD politicians have switched parties many times over the years. Party leader Bruno Tabacci is a past member of the Union of Christian and Center Democrats and the founder of the defunct White Rose party.

Leader: Bruno TABACCI (President).

South Tirolean People's Party (*Südtiroler Volkspartei*—SVP). The SVP is a moderate, autonomist grouping representing the German- and Ladin-speaking inhabitants of South Tirol (Bolzano/Bozen or Alto Adige), where it is the largest party. In 1996 the SVP joined the Olive Tree alliance, with which it remained affiliated until May 2001, although it offered two candidate lists, the SVP list and the SVP–Olive Tree list. Together they won eight Chamber and five Senate seats. In 2004 the SVP ran with the Olive Tree alliance in the balloting for the European Parliament, winning one seat. The SVP won five seats in the Senate and four in the Chamber in 2006, but those numbers were cut to four in the Senate and two in the Chamber in 2008. The SVP joined the Italy Common Good alliance for the February 2013 parliamentary election, securing two Senate and four Chamber seats.

Leaders: Luis DURNWALDER (Leader), Richard THEINER (President), Martin ALBER (Secretary).

Movement for Autonomies (*Movimento per le Autonomie*—MPA). The MPA was founded in 2005 by Raffaele LOMBARDO, formerly president of the UDC in Catania and in the European Parliament. He left the party and joined forces with the Northern League after Prodi's Union abandoned a plan to build a bridge over the Straits of Messina to join the mainland with Sicily. Lombardo and his supporters had long sought the bridge as a way to end Sicily's economic isolation. In 2008 the MPA formed a political pact with the **Italy of the Center** (IdC), its leader, Vincenzo Scotti, becoming the president of the MPA.

With Berlusconi's promised support for the bridge project, the MPA joined his coalition in 2008, winning two Senate seats and eight Chamber seats. In 2009 the party shortened its name to Movement for Autonomies. The MPA was a founding member of the NPI parliamentary alliance. In July 2012, Lombardo resigned as secretary of the party and was replaced by Giovanni Pistorio. In 2012 the Sicilian branch retitled itself the **Party of the Sicilians** (*Partito dei Siciliani*—PdS). MPA-PdS joined Berlusconi's coalition in 2013 and was awarded one Chamber and two Senate seats, despite receiving less than 1 percent of the vote.

Leaders: Vincenzo SCOTTI (President), Giovanni PISTORIO (Federal Secretary).

Associative Movement Italians Abroad (*Movimento Associativo Italiani all'Estero*—MAIE). This party, which represents Italians residing in South America, succeeds Italian Associations in South America (*Associazioni Italiane in Sud America*). In 2008 the party won one seat in the Senate and one in the Chamber. The MAIE allied with the LD in a fruitless bid for seats in the 2009 EU elections. It secured two Chamber seats in 2013.

Leader: Riccardo MERLO.

Future and Freedom for Italy (*Futuro e Libertà per l'Italia*—FLI). In July 2010, after his ouster from the PdL, Gianfranco FINI, the controversial president of the Chamber and former neofascist leader, formed FLI as a new center-right parliamentary group. With 33 deputies and 8 senators, the group's continued support was crucial to Berlusconi's hold on power and enabled him to survive a confidence vote on December 14. The following day, FLI joined the UdC and several minor parties to form yet another centrist parliamentary group, the **New Pole for Italy** (*Nuovo Polo per l'Italia*—NPI).

At a congress in Milan held on February 11–13, 2011, FLI was inaugurated as an official party, with Fini as president, a title he subsequently relinquished to avoid the appearance of a conflict of interest with his ongoing role of president of the Chamber. Almost from the onset, FLI suffered repeated internal divisions, reflecting its heterogeneous makeup, including former neofascists, disgruntled progressives, and civil libertarians. Its parliamentary presence subsequently fell to 26 deputies and 5 senators. FLI joined the Monti for Italy alliance for the February 2013 parliamentary elections and received a single Senate seat. Fini subsequently resigned and the party is effectively defunct.

Leader: Roberto MENIA (Coordinator).

Other Parties That Contested the 2013 Elections:

Forty-seven parties competed in the February 24–24, 2013, Chamber elections. Thirty-one competed individually, while 16 parties participated in one of three coalitions. Seven parties secured seats. Fifty-nine parties vied for Senate seats, and eight succeeded. Many of these parties were regional and local entities, such as **The Freedomites** (*Die Freiheitlichen*), **Veneto State** (*Veneto Stato*), and the radical **Sardinian Action Party** (*Partito Sardo d'Azione*). **The Megaphone—List Crocetta** (*Il Megafono—Lista Crocetta*) captured one Senate seat for the governor of Sicily, Rosario CROCETTA. Others represented special interests, such as **No to the Closing of Hospitals** (*No Chiusura Ospedali*), the pro-music **All Together for Italy** (*Tutti Insieme per L'Italia*), **Enough Taxes** (*Basta Tasse*), **Women for Italy** (*Donne per L'Italia*), and **Gabrielle Nappi's Italian Naturalist Movement** (*Movimento Naturalista Italiana Gabriele Nappi*).

Italian Radicals (*Radicali Italiani*—PR). The Italian Radicals party is a predominantly libertarian, middle-class grouping advocating civil and human rights. The PR more formally identifies itself as a movement associated with the **Transnational Radical Party** (*Partito Radicale Trasnazionale*), which distances itself from national politics.

The PR's membership in the Chamber of Deputies increased from 4 seats in 1976 to 18 following the June 1979 election—by far the largest gain of any party. Gravitating to the right in the 1990s, the PR presented an unsuccessful Pannella List (*Lista Pannella*—LP) in the March 1994 poll as an ally of Berlusconi's Freedom Alliance. For the 1996 election, Pannella joined with television personality and critic Vittorio SGARBI to present a *Lista Pannella-Sgarbi.* In the May 2001 balloting, the PR offered a *Lista Pannella-Bonino,* which attracted considerable attention in late April and early May when party leader Emma Bonino staged a hunger strike to protest the media's failure to cover her party's platform. The list failed to win seats in either house, although the *Lista Bonino* won two seats in the European Parliament in 2004. Ahead of the 2008 election, the PR formed an electoral alliance with the PD, winning three seats on the Democratic Party list in the Senate and six in the Chamber. In the June 2009 EU parliamentary elections the PR lost its two seats.

Although the PR failed to win any seats in the February 2013 parliamentary election, Bonino was appointed Minister of Foreign Affairs in the Letta government.

Leaders: Silvio VIALE (President), Emma BONINO, Minister of Foreign Affairs.

Civil Revolution (*Rivoluzione Civile*—RC). Founded by Antonio INGROIA on December 29, 2012, as a leftist coalition for the 2013 parliamentary elections, RC was comprised of **Italy of Values,** the **Communist Refoundation Party**, the **Party of Italian Communists**, and the **Federation of the Greens**. Ingroia, a former prosecutor, espoused an anticorruption platform that failed to resonate with voters. RC received 2.2 percent of the vote and dissolved on April 2.

Italy of Values (*Italia dei Valori*—IdV). Italy of Values was established in 1998 as a liberal democratic, law-and-order, reformist organization by Antonio Di Pietro, a former magistrate who had attracted national attention early in the decade for winning convictions against a number of national politicians in the "clean hands" (*Mani Pulite*) anticorruption campaign. Refusing to reestablish ties to the center-left Olive Tree (despite having initially lent support to Romano Prodi's Democrats) and rejecting participation in the center-right Berlusconi alliance, Di Pietro put forward his organization's own list, the *Lista Di Pietro–Italia dei Valori,* for the May 2001 elections. It failed to win any Chamber seats, narrowly missing the 4 percent threshold for proportional seats, but retained 1 Senate seat. For the 2004 European Parliament elections IdV's two successful candidates were Di Pietro and former Communist leader Achille Occhetto. The party won 17 Chamber and 4 Senate seats in the 2006 election. The September 2006 defection from the party of Sen. Sergio DE GREGORIO reduced the Union's majority in the Senate to a single seat.

IdV's electoral fortunes improved greatly in the 2008 election when it won 28 seats in the Chamber and 14 in the Senate. In the wake of the Democratic Party's poor showing in regional elections and its leadership shift, the IdV emerged as the opposition's most vocal critic of government policies. IdV improved its standing in the June 2009 EU parliamentary elections, gaining 8 percent of the national vote and increasing its representation from 2 to 7 seats.

In 2011, IdV activists collected 2 million signatures in support of three referenda that resulted in the repeal of laws enabling the prime minister to postpone prosecution while in office, allowing for construction of nuclear power plants, and permitting privatization of water supplies. In July, the IdV boycotted a Senate vote to amend the Constitution to allow the direct election of the president. The party joined **Civil Revolution** for the 2013 parliamentary election. It regrouped at its June conference, electing a new leadership team. In September it removed Di Pietro's name from the party logo.

Leaders: Antonio DI PIETRO (Honorary President), Ignazio MESSINA (Secretary).

Communist Refoundation Party (*Partito della Rifondazione Comunista*—PRC). In February 1991 a dissident Communist Refoundation Movement (*Movimento di Rifondazione Comunista*) assembled in Rome to revive the old Communist Party, following the latter's conversion a week earlier to the PDS (see the DS, above). The new group was formally launched during a conference in Rome in May 1991; a month later Proletarian Democracy (*Democrazia Proletaria*—DP), a small party with roots in a 1976 leftist electoral alliance, voted to dissolve and join the new group.

Having won 5.6 percent of the vote in the 1992 Chamber of Deputies election, the PRC advanced to 6 percent in 1994 as a member of the Progressive Alliance (AP), from which it later distanced itself. In June 1995 the PRC was weakened by the defection of 14 of its 35 lower house deputies in protest at the alleged "isolationism" of the leadership. By mutual agreement, the rump PRC remained outside the center-left Olive Tree alliance in the April 1996 legislative elections, at which it increased its proportional vote to 8.6 percent. It then gave external backing to the minority Olive Tree government formed in May.

For more than two years, the PRC was the key player in keeping the Prodi government in power, taking disagreements to the brink on several occasions over economic priorities (a 35-hour work week and a plan to stem unemployment in the south) and foreign policy issues (intervention in Albania and expansion of NATO). But the PRC was itself divided in these confrontations, notably when it nearly forced Prodi to resign in October 1997 but backed down when rank-and-file members protested the party's action. A year later, as the PRC withdrew its support of the 1999 budget and Prodi's coalition collapsed, the strains within the PRC split the party. A progovernment faction defected and formed the Party of Italian Communists (PdCI, below). In the May 2001 election the PRC won 3 Senate and 11 Chamber seats, all of the latter because of its 5 percent vote share in the proportional balloting. In the 2006 election the party rebounded, winning 41 Chamber and 27 Senate seats.

The party failed to win any seats in Parliament in 2008 and remained divided along regional and factional lines. In 2009 the conservative wing formed a faction within the grouping titled **To the Left with Refoundation** (*A Sinistra con Rifondazione*). The party joined the Civil Revolution faction for the 2013 election but won no seats.

Leader: Paolo FERRERO (Secretary).

Party of Italian Communists (*Partito dei Comunisti Italiani*—PdCI). Formed shortly after the PRC withdrew support of the Prodi government in October 1998, the PdCI was largely composed of PRC defectors led by Armando COSSUTTA, formerly the PRC president. However, the 21 deputies who followed Cossutta out of the PRC were insufficient to salvage the Prodi government. Subsequently, the Communists reconciled themselves to being part of a coalition that included former Christian Democrats and received two cabinet posts in the D'Alema government, the first regime in half a century to include communists. The PdCI continued in the subsequent Amato administration and campaigned as part of the Olive Tree in 2001. After the 2006 election, during which the party won 16 Chamber seats, Cossutta resigned as president and later left the party.

The PdCI left the SA coalition after the coalition's 2008 electoral debacle, wherein the PcCI and other coalition members lost all their seats in Parliament and called for a new alliance of Italian communist parties. The party joined the Civil Revolution faction for the 2013 election but won no seats.

Leaders: Cesare PROCACCINI (Secretary), Antonino CUFFARO (President).

Federation of the Greens (*Federazione dei Verdi*—FdV). The FdV was officially launched in November 1986 as a union of regional green lists. In its first national election (June 1987) it took 1 Senate and 13 Chamber seats. After merging with the competing Rainbow Greens (*Verdi Arcobaleno*) in December 1990, the FdV in April 1992 improved its standing to 4 Senate and 16 Chamber seats on a national vote share of 2.8 percent. As a member of the Progressive Alliance in March 1994 its share slipped to 2.7 percent. The Greens won a 2.5 percent proportional vote share in the April 1996 legislative elections, following which Edo RONCHI of the FdV was appointed environment minister, a position he retained in the two D'Alema governments. Alfonso Pecoraro Scanio then served as minister of agriculture under Prime Minister Amato. The party won 9 Senate and 8 Chamber seats in May 2001 as part of the "Sunflower" alliance (with the Italian Democratic Socialists) within the Olive Tree. Although the FdV did not join in formation of the Olive Tree Federation in early 2005, it remained closely allied with the Olive Tree parties. The Greens won 15 Chamber seats at the April 2006 election. For the Senate contest, it joined with the PdCI (above) and the small **United Consumers** (*Consumatori Uniti*—CU), led by Bruno DE VITA, in a **Together with the Union** (*Insieme con L'Unione*) list that won 11 seats. In November 2006 a small number of Greens left the party and formed **Environmentalists for the Olive Tree** (*Ecologisti per l'Ulivo*), with the aim of merging into the Democratic Party the following year. The exodus left the party dominated by left-leaning members, led by president Alfonso Pecoraro Scanio, who was appointed minister of the environment in Prodi's cabinet.

In July 2008, after the FdV failed to win any seats as part of the SA coalition, Grazia Francescato replaced Pecoraro Scanio as party leader. In January 2009 the FdV formed a joint list for the European Parliament elections with the MpS, Democratic Left, and the Socialist Party but failed to win any seats. Angelo BONELLI became party president in 2009. The party joined the Civil Revolution faction for the 2013 election.

Leader: Angelo BONELLI (President).

Valdotanian Union (*Union Valdôtaine*—UV). This centrist party represents the Valle d'Aosta, where it is the largest party. It has been represented in Parliament almost constantly since 1976 and has dominated the regional government for most of that time as well. The UV was founded in September 1946 as a close ally of the Christian Democratic Party until the mid-1950s, when it began strengthening its ties to the center-left. In 2006, after leaving the center-left coalition, the party lost its presence in Parliament.

The UV won one Senate seat in 2008 and again in 2013. A faction broke away in January 2013 to found the **Progressive Valdotanian Union**.

Leader: Ego PERRON (President).

Italian Republican Party (*Partito Repubblicano Italiano*—PRI). The oldest Italian political party still in existence under its original name, the PRI was founded in 1897, espousing Giuseppe MAZZINI's moderate leftist principles of social justice in a modern free society. It has dwindled in popularity and no longer has any representation at the federal level and scant seats at the local level. (See the 2013 *Handbook* for a detailed party history.)

Autonomy Liberty Democracy (*Autonomie Liberté Démocratie*). This center-left coalition was created for the 2006 election in the Valle d'Aosta, which is guaranteed one deputy and one senator under the constitution. The coalition included ten parties: **Alé Vallée**, **Alternative Greens** (*Verdi Alternativi*), **Alternative Left** (*Sinistra Alternativa*), **Committee of Valdaostans** (*Comité de Valdôtains*), the **DS** (*Gauche Valdôtaine*), the **IdV**, the **Daisy** (*La Margherita*), the **Communist Refoundation Party** (*Partito della Rifondazione Comunista*), **Rose in the Fist** (*Rosa nel Pugno*), and **Valle d'Aosta Alive** (*Vallée d'Aoste Vive*). The coalition won a single Chamber seat in the 2008 poll but none in 2013.

For information on the **Democratic Union for Consumers** (*Unione Democratica per i Consumatori*—UD), **The Right** (*La Destra*), **Pensioners' Party** (*Partito Pensionati*—PP), **Social Movement–Tricolor Flame** (*Movimento Sociale–Fiamma Tricolore*—MS-FT), **The Left—The Rainbow** (*La Sinistra—L'Arcobaleno*—SA) coalition and the **For the Left** (*Per la Sinistra*) alliance for the 2009 European Parliament elections, see the 2013 *Handbook*.

Italy has numerous regional groupings, many of which allied with the **Northern League** and the **Autonomy Movement** for national elections. Exceptions include the **Venetian Republic League** (*Liga Veneta Repubblica*), **Independent Venice** (*Indipendenza Veneta*), the **Sardinian Action Party** (*Partito Sardo d'Azione*), and the **Padania Union** (*Unione Padana*).

Other Parties:

Alliance for Italy (*Alleanza per l'Italia*—ApI). On November 11, 2009, after leaving the PD, Francesco Rutelli, a senator and founding member of the party, formed the ApI as a centrist alternative to the governing and opposition coalitions. The new party drew a number of former leaders of the center-left, including former Socialist Party leader, Enrico BOSELLI. In December 2010 ApI joined the UdC, FLI, and several smaller parties to form the NPI parliamentary alliance. ApI had six members in the Senate and five in the Chamber. By 2012, defections from other parties raised the ApI's representation to seven in the Senate and seven in the Chamber, but many of those MPs joined the new **Democratic Center** and ran on its ticket in February 2013. The ApI sat out the 2013 election to regroup in time for the 2014 European Parliament elections.

Liberal Democrats (*Liberaldemocratici*—LD). A right-wing faction of M-DL established this party on September 18, 2007, upon the M-DL's decision to merge with the Democratic Party. Although the LD initially voiced support for Prodi's center-left government, it voted against it in the January 2008 confidence vote that led to the government's fall. After allying with Berlusconi's PdL on February 8, 2008, the LD won one seat in the Senate and three in the Chamber. Two elected LD members, including Lamberto Dini, later left the party to join the PdL. The two remaining LD deputies joined the "mixed" parliamentary group.

In November 2008, the party's deputies voted against Berlusconi's economic plan and withdrew its support for the government, returning to the center-left opposition. A faction of the LD joined the PdL in 2009. The LD gained no representation in the 2009 EU elections. In late 2012 party records revealed donations of nearly $1 million from the PdL, sparking accusations of vote buying. The party did not compete in the 2013 parliamentary election and began an internal reorganization. Italo Tanoni was elected party president in July 2013.

Leaders: Italo TANONI (President), Enzo MARRAZZO (Coordinator).

Terrorist Groups:

In the second half of the 20th century Italy was often buffeted by political terrorism, with over 200 names having been used by groups committed to such activity. The most notorious of the left-wing formations, the **Red Brigades** (*Brigate Rosse*), was founded in 1969, reportedly in linkage with the West German Red Army Faction terrorists. The *Brigate Rosse* engaged in numerous killings during the late 1970s, including that of former prime minister Aldo Moro; subsequently, one of its offshoots, the **Union of Fighting Communists** (*Unione dei Comunisti Combattenti*—UCC), claimed responsibility for the 1987 murder of an air force general and the 1988 assassination of Sen. Roberto RUFFILLI, a leading ally of Prime Minister De Mita. In 1998 Renato CURCIO, a cofounder of the Red Brigades and its last leading figure behind bars, was freed from prison after serving 24 years of a 30-year sentence. In May 1999 the Red Brigades apparently resurfaced, claiming responsibility for assassinating Massimo D'ANTONA, an adviser to the minister of labor.

More recently, the Red Brigades have claimed responsibility for several murders, including the assassination in March 2002 of government economic adviser Marco BIAGI. Members continue to be apprehended, including Leonardo BERTULAZZI, who was arrested in Argentina in November 2002. The reputed head of logistics for the organization, he had been convicted in absentia in 1977 for kidnapping. In May 2004 the EU added the Red Brigades to its list of terrorist organizations.

Members of the **Politico-Military Communist Party** (*Partito Comunista Politico-Militare*), an offshoot of the Red Brigades, were arrested in February 2007 on charges of plotting to attack several domestic targets and assassinate current prime minister Berlusconi.

The **Informal Anarchist Federation** (*Federazione Anarchica Informale*—FAI) claimed responsibility for the explosion of parcel bombs at the Swiss and Chilean embassies in Rome on December 23, 2010, injuring two people. On December 9, 2011, a tax collector in Rome was injured by a mail bomb sent by the FAI. Ten people with ties to the FAI were arrested on June 13, 2012, in coordinated operations in Italy, Germany, and Switzerland.

LEGISLATURE

The bicameral **Parliament** (*Parlamento*) consists of an upper house, the Senate, and a lower house, the Chamber of Deputies, of roughly equal power. A new electoral law passed in December 2005 restored the pre-1993 full proportional representation system for 617 out of 630 seats in 26 constituencies (autonomous Valle d'Aosta retains the first-past-the-post system for its single seat, while overseas Italian citizens elect the remaining 12 deputies). This legislation set minimum thresholds for parliamentary representation for a coalition (10 and 20 percent for the Chamber and Senate, respectively) and for a political party (4 percent for the Chamber and 3 percent for the Senate). When a coalition or a party with the largest number of votes fails to win 340 Chamber seats, the law stipulates that it will receive enough "bonus" seats to reach the 340-seat level.

Senate (*Senato della Repubblica*). The upper house consists of 322 members elected to a five-year term (except for senators for life, currently numbering 7, including Giorgio Napolitano, who is inactive during his tenure as president) by universal suffrage under a proportional representation system that was proposed by the Berlusconi government and adopted on December 21, 2005 (recognizing coalitions winning at least 20 percent of the vote and including at least one party winning at least 3 percent of the vote, and parties winning at least 8 percent running independently or in a coalition winning less than 20 percent of the vote). Under a new "majority prize" provision, a coalition winning a majority of votes in a region will automatically be allocated no less than 55 percent of the region's seats, with the rest distributed among other qualifying coalitions and parties. The majority prize applies to all regions but Molise (which elects only 2 senators), Valle d'Aosta (1 senator), and Trentino-Alto Adige (which falls under a separate election law dividing its 6 seats evenly between Italian- and German-speaking senators). Under a law passed in December 2001, Italian citizens residing abroad elect 6 senators representing four districts: Europe; North and Central America; South America; and Africa, Asia, Oceania, and Antarctica.

The February 24–25, 2013, election produced the following results: Center-left coalition Italy Common Good, 122 (Democratic Party, 105; Left Ecology and Freedom, 7; Megaphone, List of R. Crocetta, 1); Center-right coalition, 116 (People of Liberty, 98; Northern League, 17; Great South, 1); Five-Star Movement, 54;

With Monti for Italy Coalition, 18 (Civic Choice, 37; Union of the Center, 8); Associative Movement Italians Abroad (present only overseas), 1; and Valdotanian Union (present only in Valle d'Aosta), 1.

As of September 2013, senators were organized into the following parliamentary groups (senators may change their affiliation at any time): Democratic Party, 108 members; People of Freedom, 91; Five-Star Movement, 50; Northern League–Padania, 16; Civic Choice, 20; Large Autonomy and Freedom, and mixed, 16.

President: Pietro GRASSO.

Chamber of Deputies (*Camera dei Deputati*). The lower house consists of 630 members directly elected to a five-year term by universal suffrage, with 617 seats distributed under the new proportional representation system (recognizing coalition lists with a 10 percent threshold that include at least one party receiving at least 2 percent of the vote, separate party lists with a 4 percent threshold, and parties representing linguistic minorities that win at least 20 percent of the vote in their corresponding regions). Valle d'Aosta elects 1 member, and overseas Italian citizens elect the remaining 12 deputies representing the same four districts as in the Senate. Under the new majority prize provision, a coalition that receives a majority of the vote but less than 55 percent of the seats in Italy proper (340 out of 618) automatically is awarded the full 340 seats.

The February 24–25, 2013, election produced the following results: Center-left coalition Italy Common Good, 340 (Democratic Party, 292; Left Ecology and Freedom, 37; Democratic Center, 6; South Tirolean People's Party, 5); Center-right coalition, 125 (People of Liberty, 97; Northern League, 18; Brothers of Italy, 9); Movement for Autonomy Allied for the South, 8; Five-Star Movement, 108; With Monti for Italy Coalition, 47 (Civic Choice, 37; Union of the Center, 8).

As of September 2013, deputies (who may change their affiliation at any time) were organized into the following parliamentary groups, which do not necessarily correspond to party names: Democratic Party, 293 members; Five-Star Movement, 106; People of Freedom, 97; Civic Choice for Italy, 47; Left Ecology Freedom, 37; mixed, 21; Northern League–Padania, 20; and Brothers of Italy, 9.

President: Laura BOLDRINI.

CABINET

[as of September 28, 2013]

Prime Minister	Enrico Letta (PD)
Deputy Prime Minister	Angelino Alfano (PdL)
Ministers	
Agriculture, Food, and Forestry	Nunzi De Girolamo (PdL) [f]
Cultural Heritage and Activities	Massimo Bray (PD)
Defense	Mario Mauro (SC)
Economy and Finance	Fabrizio Saccomani (ind.)
Economic Development	Flavio Zanonato (PD)
Education	Maria Chiara Carrozza (PD) [f]
Environment	Andrea Orlando (PD)
Foreign Affairs	Emma Bonino (PR) [f]
Health	Beatrice Lorenzin (PdL) [f]
Infrastructure and Transport	Maurizio Lupi (PdL)
Interior	Angelino Alfano (PdL)
Justice	Annamaria Cancellieri (ind.) [f]
Labor and Social Policy	Enrico Giovannini (ind.)
Ministers without Portfolio	
Constitutional Reforms	Gaetano Quagliariello (PdL)
Equal Opportunities, Sport, and Youth Policy	(Vacant)
European Policy	Enzo Moavero Milanesi (SC)
Integration	Cecile Kyenge Kashetu (PD) [f]
Parliamentary Relations	Dario Franceschini (PD)
Public Administration and Simplification	Giampiero D'Alia (UDC)
Regional Affairs and Autonomy	Graziano Delrio (PD)
Territorial Cohesion	Carlo Trigila (PD)

[f] = female

INTERGOVERNMENTAL REPRESENTATION

Ambassador to the U.S.: Claudio BISOGNIERO.

U.S. Ambassador to Italy: John PHILLIPS.

Permanent Representative to the UN: Sebastiano CARDI.

IGO Memberships (Non-UN): ADB, AfDB, CEUR, EBRD, EU, G-8, G-20, ICC, IEA, IOM, NATO, OECD, OSCE, WTO.

JAMAICA

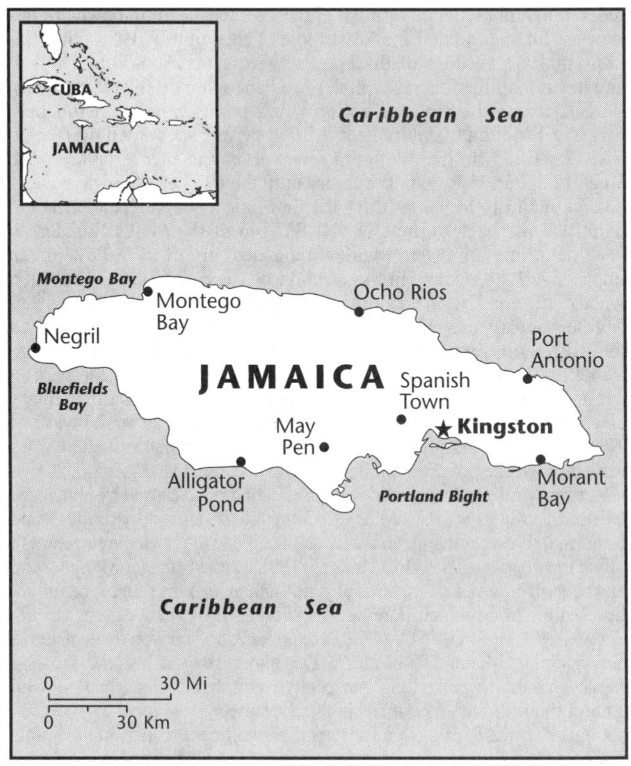

Political Status: Independent member of the Commonwealth since August 6, 1962; under democratic parliamentary regime.

Area: 4,411 sq. mi. (11,424 sq. km).

Population: 2,831,212 (2013E—UN); 2,909,714 (2013E—U.S. Census).

Major Urban Center (2011E): KINGSTON (579,137).

Official Language: English.

Monetary Unit: Jamaican Dollar (market rate November 1, 2013: 104.50 dollars = $1US).

Sovereign: Queen ELIZABETH II.

Governor General: Patrick ALLEN; sworn in on February 26, 2009, succeeding Kenneth Octavius HALL.

Prime Minister: Portia SIMPSON MILLER (People's National Party); inaugurated on January 5, 2012, to succeed Andrew HOLNESS (Jamaica Labour Party—JLP) following early legislative elections on December 29, 2011; formed new cabinet on January 6, 2012. (Holness had served as prime minister since October 23, 2011, following the resignation of the JLP's Bruce GOLDING.)

THE COUNTRY

Jamaica, whose name is derived from the Arawak Indian word *Xaymaca,* is a mountainous island located 90 miles south of Cuba. The third-largest island in the Caribbean, it is the largest and most populous of the independent Commonwealth nations in the area. About 77 percent of the population is of African descent; another 15 percent is of mixed Afro-European heritage. Population density is high, particularly in metropolitan Kingston, which contains more than 30 percent of the national total. The Anglican and Baptist creeds claim the most adherents, but numerous other denominations and sects are active. Women constitute approximately 46 percent of the official labor force, concentrated in agriculture and civil service, with a large proportion of the remainder serving as unpaid agricultural workers. There are eight women in the current House of Representatives and two women (in addition to the prime minister) in the cabinet. As a consequence of male urban migration, more than one-third of all households are headed by women, with 70 percent of all children reportedly being born to single mothers.

The Jamaican economy is based on sugar, bauxite mining, and tourism, the last being the second leading earner of foreign exchange after remittances from Jamaican expatriates (who constitute an estimated one-quarter to one-third of the total Jamaican population). Agricultural products including rum, molasses, bananas, coffee, and citrus fruits also underpin the economy, as does a thriving informal sector based primarily on the illegal production and export of marijuana and, in recent years (according to some analysts), the transshipment of cocaine from South America to North America and Europe.

In the mid-1970s the country began to experience severe economic difficulty, marked by high inflation, pervasive unemployment, a stifling foreign debt, and depression of the bauxite and sugar industries. Even before widespread devastation caused by Hurricane Gilbert in September 1988, the Seaga administration's acceptance of austerity measures mandated by the International Monetary Fund (IMF) had fueled growing public dissatisfaction with loss of services and decreased buying power. By late 1990 the only promising sector was the bauxite industry, which had launched a major expansion in both mining and refining because of increasing demand for aluminum.

Unemployment reached 16 percent at the turn of the century, while development prospects remained dim in view of extraordinarily high public debt, which appeared to preclude significant government investment in resolving widespread social problems such as income inequities, high illiteracy (30 percent), vast urban slums, and rising crime and violence (linked to the drug trade as well as political turbulence).

Tourism, the bauxite/aluminum sector, and remittances were all severely distressed by the global economic crisis of 2008–2009, and GDP contracted by 1.6 percent in the 2008/2009 fiscal year. The World Bank, Inter-American Development Bank, and other donors (including China) provided additional aid, but the government in mid-2009 was forced to pursue IMF lending for the first time since 1996 in order to offset declining public revenues and ongoing heavy debt repayment obligations on the nation's $19 billion debt. In February 2010 the IMF approved $1.27 billion in lending (over three years), which was expected to trigger an additional $1.1 billion in support from other international financial sources, including regional banks. In order to qualify for the assistance, the Jamaican government in January had convinced nearly all of its domestic creditors to trade in some $8.4 billion in government bonds for bonds with lower interest rates and longer maturities. The government also pledged to pursue "fiscal discipline" in the public sector, reform in the financial sector, and additional privatization of state-owned enterprises. GDP contracted by more than 3 percent in fiscal year 2009/2010, and recovery was compromised by Tropical Storm Nicole, which left $125 million in damage in its wake in September 2010.

Disbursements from the IMF were suspended in early 2011 because of the Fund's objections to recent salary increases for public employees and to the slow pace of tax and pension reforms. Other international financial institutions followed the IMF's lead in suspending loans.

Three years of recession ended in 2011, with GDP expanding by 1.2 percent. However, unemployment remained high (more than 14 percent), and the IMF warned that the outlook was poor unless significant fiscal and structural reforms were implemented.

In part due to the effects of Hurricane Sandy in October 2012, the economy contracted by 0.3 percent for the year, putting even greater pressure of the new government's efforts to secure reactivation of IMF support. The May 2013 accord (see Current issues, below, for details) was described as a "last chance" for Jamaica to avoid economic collapse. The government also pinned hopes for recovery on an ambitious plan for port, airport, and telecommunications expansion designed to position Jamaica as a "logistics hub" in advance of expansion of the Panama Canal.

GOVERNMENT AND POLITICS

Political background. A British colony from 1655 to 1962, Jamaica developed a two-party system before World War II under the leadership of Sir Alexander BUSTAMANTE and Norman W. MANLEY, founders, respectively, of the Jamaica Labour Party (JLP) and the People's National Party (PNP). A considerable measure of self-government was introduced in 1944, but full independence was delayed by attempts to set up a wider federation embracing all or most of the Caribbean Commonwealth territories. Jamaica joined the West Indies Federation in 1958 but withdrew in 1961 because of disagreements over taxation, voting rights, and location of the federal capital. (The Federation dissolved in 1962.)

Bustamante became the nation's first prime minister at independence in 1962; on his retirement in 1967 he was succeeded by Donald SANGSTER, who died within a few weeks. Sangster's replacement, Hugh L. SHEARER, led the country until the 1972 election gave a legislative majority to the PNP for the first time since independence and permitted Michael Norman MANLEY, son of the PNP's founder, to become prime minister. Manley remained in office following an impressive PNP victory in the election of December 1976. However, when confronted by an economic crisis and mounting domestic insecurity, he was forced to call an early election in October 1980 that returned the JLP to power under the conservative leadership of Edward SEAGA. Benefiting from a surge of popularity occasioned by Jamaican participation in the invasion of Grenada, Seaga called an early parliamentary election for December 15, 1983. The JLP swept all seats in the wake of a PNP boycott prompted by the PNP's assessment that outdated voter rolls favored the government party.

Prime Minister Seaga cited emergency conditions caused by Hurricane Gilbert in 1988 as the reason for extending the parliamentary term beyond its normal five-year mandate, but he was unable to avert Manley's return to office in February 1989. On March 15, 1992, Prime Minister Manley, who had been in poor health for several years, announced his retirement, effective March 23, at which time he was succeeded by his longtime deputy Percival (P. J.) PATTERSON. The PNP under Patterson won the legislative poll again in March 1993, and in December 1997 it became the first Jamaican party to gain a third consecutive term. In addition, the PNP won control in all 13 parish councils in the September 1998 local elections by taking 170 of 227 seats overall. Despite a significant reduction in its vote share and seats, the PNP maintained a majority in the national legislative election in October 2002.

Prime Minister Patterson retired on March 30, 2006, and was succeeded by Portia SIMPSON MILLER, who had been elected PNP leader on February 25. Known affectionately as "Mama Portia" or "Sister P," Simpson Miller, Jamaica's first female premier, commanded widespread popular support at her inauguration in March 2006. However, a major financial scandal in the cabinet late in the year cost the PNP support (see the 2008 *Handbook* for details), although the government survived a no-confidence vote in the legislature.

The JLP returned to power after 18 years in opposition by winning 31 of 60 seats in the September 3, 2007, legislative elections. Some analysts concluded that perceived foot-dragging on the part of the government in responding to a hurricane that had struck in late August contributed to the JLP's narrow victory (only 3,000 votes separated it from the PNP in the nationwide total). Other issues of popular concern included ongoing economic stagnation, government corruption, and chronic crime and violence, much of it crime- and/or drug-related. (Jamaica has one of the highest murder rates in the world.)

New prime minister Bruce GOLDING, who had been installed as the JLP leader in 2005, named an expanded 18-member cabinet on September 14, 2007. Golding, considered a technocrat, quickly launched a series of anticrime measures and pledged to address corruption within the police force and the judiciary. Subsequently, both houses of the legislature endorsed retention of the death penalty as a means of combating the crime wave. However, by mid-2009, it had become clear that the failing economy had become the new administration's top priority. Among other things, Golding announced large-scale spending cuts and collateral tax increases, while pursuing emergency lending from the IMF, which was approved in early 2010 (see The Country, above, for details).

In September 2011 Golding announced he would resign as prime minister and JLP leader in the face of sharply declining support for his administration. He was succeeded in both positions on October 23 by Andrew HOLNESS, who surprised observers by calling for early legislative elections on December 29. The PNP overwhelmed the JLP in that poll, and Simpson Miller returned to the prime ministership on January 5, 2012.

Constitution and government. Under the 1962 constitution, the queen is the titular head of state. Her representative, a governor general with limited powers, is advised, in areas bearing on the royal prerogative, by a 6-member Privy Council. Executive authority is centered in a cabinet of no fewer than 12 members (including the prime minister), who are collectively responsible to the House of Representatives, the elected lower house of the bicameral Parliament; the upper house (Senate) is entirely appointive. The judicial system is headed by a Supreme Court with both primary and appellate jurisdiction. Judges on the Supreme Court and a Court of Appeal are appointed by the governor general on the advice of the prime minister. There are also several magistrates' courts. For administrative purposes, Jamaica is divided into 13 parishes and the Kingston and St. Andrew Corporation, a special administrative entity encompassing the principal urban areas.

In May 1991 Prime Minister Manley revealed that the government had mounted a constitutional review, including the call for implementation of a change to republican status. The two leading parties had long agreed in the matter, the principal issue being whether the governor general should be replaced by a president with executive or ceremonial powers.

In September 1994 the search for an all-party consensus on constitutional reform foundered over a new issue—the PNP's move to dispense with the UK-based Privy Council as Jamaica's final court of appeal in favor of participation in the projected Caribbean Court of Appeal. The PNP government argued that the existing method of appeal was "culturally inappropriate and inconsistent" with Jamaica's sovereign status. Pressure for the change, which had been under discussion for some years, had intensified after the Privy Council had recommended that two individuals who had been under sentence of death for 14 years should, because of the lengthy delay, have their sentences commuted to life imprisonment. Prime Minister Patterson had responded that his administration was "unwavering" in its determination to execute convicted murderers. For its part, the opposition appeared to differ largely on procedural grounds, arguing that the government wished to alter the appellate process by simple legislative action without reference to the larger package of proposed amendments that included the JLP's call for an independent police services commissioner. In March 1997 opposition leader Seaga declared that a future JLP government might withdraw from the Caribbean appellate body on the ground that its members' appointments had been politically biased.

In September 2004 Prime Minister Patterson announced that a referendum on republican status would be held by March 2005. The (then) opposition JLP responded that it would not support the move unless the abandonment of judicial appeals to the Privy Council was also submitted to the voters, and the referendum remained in abeyance. Although both major parties continued to support the transfer of authority from the Privy Council to the Caribbean Court of Appeal, no action had been taken in the matter as of mid-2013 due to disagreement on the need for a national referendum (versus legislative approval). Meanwhile, Prime Minister Portia Simpson Miller reaffirmed her support for replacement of the queen as Jamaica's head of state with an elected president.

In 2008 the new JLP administration proposed a constitutional revision that would set fixed dates for elections, replacing the current system, which allows the governor general to dissolve Parliament at any time and call for new elections within three months of the dissolution. The JLP also subsequently pledged to pursue a constitutional amendment that would limit prime ministers to two terms. However, no action was taken by December 2011 (when the JLP lost its legislative majority) in regard to those proposed amendments, which require approval by two-thirds of each legislative chamber and endorsement in a national referendum. In a more definitive vein, the Parliament in 2011, after 16 years of assessment, approved a New Charter of Fundamental Rights and Freedoms to replace elements of the constitution previously considered too vague in such matters.

The press has traditionally been free of censorship and government control and is considered highly influential in the region. However, media owners have argued recently that outdated libel laws stifle investigative journalism by placing the burden of proof on defendants rather than plaintiffs and by permitting massive judgments that threaten to put newspapers and broadcasters out of business.

Foreign relations. Jamaica is a member of the United Nations and the Commonwealth as well as a number of regional organizations. Previously cordial relations with the United States were marred in the mid-1970s by Jamaican support for Cuban intervention in Angola and by subsequent allegations of U.S. involvement in destabilization activities similar to those that had led to the ouster of the Salvador Allende regime in Chile.

The designation of Edward Seaga as prime minister in November 1980 signified a return to a pro-U.S. posture. Seaga was widely regarded as a prime mover behind the Reagan administration's 1981 Caribbean Basin Initiative, and ties to Washington were further strengthened by Jamaica's participation in the U.S.-led action in Grenada in October 1983. In contrast, Prime Minister Manley moved in late 1989 to reestablish relations with Havana (severed in 1980).

In June 1994 Jamaica agreed to the anchoring of U.S. ships in its waters to determine if Haitian expatriates could qualify as refugees. In May 1997 an agreement was announced that would permit U.S. drug enforcement agents to pursue suspected traffickers into Jamaican airspace and territorial waters.

The Patterson and first Simpson Miller administrations signed a number of agreements with Venezuela, including an August 2005 contract in which Venezuela offered Jamaica preferential prices for oil imports. Simpson Miller and Venezuelan president Hugo Chávez signed a memorandum of understanding in March 2007 to supply Jamaica with liquefied natural gas for electricity generation and bauxite/alumina production.

In February 2010 China pledged $500 million for infrastructure improvements in Jamaica. Partial ownership by Chinese companies in Jamaican sugar and aluminum operations was subsequently approved by the Jamaican government. Additional Chinese support for harbor and road improvements was announced in 2012–2013.

Current issues. In August 2009 the United States requested the extradition from Jamaica to the United States of purported Jamaican crime boss Christopher "Dudus" COKE to face drug- and gun-trafficking charges. Among other things, the issue brought scrutiny to the pervasive influence in Jamaica of so-called garrison politics, under which political parties have for many years cooperated with criminal gangs in poor neighborhoods by providing government contracts and important social programs in return for voter support. The Golding administration delayed action against Coke, who was aligned with the JLP in West Kingston, until May 22, 2010, when, in the face of growing U.S. pressure, an arrest warrant was issued. Intense gun battles erupted soon thereafter in Coke's stronghold of Tivoli Gardens between his supporters and security forces attempting to enforce the warrant, leaving some 70 civilians and 3 officers dead and more than 3,400 under temporary arrest. Coke was finally arrested in late June and quickly extradited to the United States.

Although a Commission of Inquiry ruled in mid-2011 that no official misconduct had occurred, it nevertheless described Golding's role in the Coke affair as inappropriate. (In June 2012 Coke was sentenced by a U.S. court to a jail term of 23 years and fined $1.5 million after he pled guilty to racketeering and drug trafficking charges.) Ongoing economic difficulties (including the suspension of IMF assistance) also apparently contributed to Golding's decision to resign in October 2011. New prime minister Andrew Holness (at 39, the youngest Jamaican premier ever) pledged to follow most of Golding's policies, which did little to assist the JLP in the December elections. (Observers concluded that Holness had erred politically in calling the snap elections rather than giving his administration time to establish its own identity.) Meanwhile, PNP leader Simpson Miller charged the JLP with broad mishandling of the economy, and the center-left PNP romped to the largest-ever seat total (42) for a single party. The PNP also won control of 12 of the 13 parish councils in the March 2012 local elections.

Prime Minister Simpson Miller in 2012 described the restoration of positive relations with the IMF as the centerpiece of her government's economic recovery program. Although negotiations took longer than expected, the IMF in May 2013 approved a four-year, $932 million lending agreement, which also triggered more than $1 billion in support from the World Bank and the Inter-American Development Bank. For its part, the government agreed to cut 7,000 public sector jobs, privatize a number of state-run enterprises, reduce social spending, raise taxes, and reform pension programs. Meanwhile, unions representing public employees accepted wage restraints, and most private creditors agreed to another debt swap (the second in three years).

POLITICAL PARTIES

Jamaica's two leading parties, the Jamaica Labour Party and the People's National Party, have similar trade union origins. Both are well organized and institutionalized, but personal leadership within them remains very important.

Government Party:

People's National Party (PNP). Organized in 1938 by Norman W. Manley, the PNP became affiliated in 1943 with the Trade Union Council. After losing elections in 1945 and 1949 but winning those of 1955 and 1959, the PNP came to power for the first time since independence in March 1972, following ten years in opposition. Headed until 1992 by Michael Manley (son of its late founder), the PNP was based on the National Workers' Union and drew its principal support from middle-class, intellectual, and urban elements. Committed to a program of democratic socialism, the party was decisively defeated in the October 1980 election. Following its boycott of the 1983 balloting, the party functioned as an extraparliamentary opposition. It subsequently moved to the center and, in the 1986 municipal elections, removed the word "socialism" from its manifesto, rejecting a proposed electoral alliance with the Workers' Party of Jamaica (WPJ), a communist grouping formed in 1978 (see the 2008 *Handbook* for information on the defunct WPJ).

The PNP won control of 11 of 13 parish councils in July 1986 (securing 126 of 187 seats overall) and decisively defeated the JLP in the parliamentary balloting of February 1989 with a 56.7 percent vote share. It performed even better in the early national election of March 1993, winning 52 of 60 House seats on a 60 percent vote share.

Former prime minister and PNP leader Michael Manley died on March 6, 1997. On December 18 his successor, P. J. Patterson, led the party to its third consecutive legislative victory with a marginal loss of two seats. Patterson managed to win a fourth victory for his party in legislative balloting in October 2002, although the PNP majority declined even further. Reportedly because of the decreasing vote share of his party, Patterson subsequently declared that his current term would be his last, and he stepped down in favor of Portia Simpson Miller in March 2006.

Following the PNP's loss in the September 2007 legislative election (27 of 60 seats) and its lackluster performance in the December local balloting, Simpson Miller faced a strong challenge for the party's leadership at the September 2008 party conference from Peter PHILLIPS, a former minister of national security, who pledged to return the PNP to its "socialist roots." However, Simpson Miller (the first woman to head one of the country's two main parties) was reelected by a small margin, and her supporters captured three of the PNP's vice-presidential positions as well. Simpson Miller returned to the premiership in January 2012, following the PNP's dramatic rebound in the December 2011 legislative poll (42 of 63 seats).

Leaders: Portia SIMPSON MILLER (Prime Minister and President of the Party); Peter BUNTING (Chair); Angella BROWN-BURKE, Derrick KELLIER, Noel ARSCOTT, Fenton FERGUSON (Vice Presidents); Anthony HYLTON (Deputy Chair); Peter BUNTING (General Secretary).

Opposition Party:

Jamaica Labour Party (JLP). Founded in 1943 by Alexander Bustamante, the JLP originated as the political arm of his Bustamante Industrial Trade Union. The more conservative of Jamaica's two leading parties, the JLP supports private enterprise, economic expansion, and a generally pro-Western international stance. However, the party also identifies with black African states and other developing countries. Opposition to Prime Minister Seaga's leadership, particularly in regard to economic policy, contributed to the JLP's defeat in local elections in 1986, in the parliamentary poll of February 1989, and in municipal balloting in March 1990, with dissidents advancing the slogan "Three in a row, time to go." Seaga's principal opponents, a so-called gang of five led by Pearnel CHARLES, were unable to dislodge the JLP leader at the party's annual conference in June 1990 and were removed from the shadow cabinet during September and October. (For subsequent development on this front through 1995, see the 2012 *Handbook.*)

Although still under attack by party opponents, Seaga was reelected JLP leader on March 26, 1995. A month earlier, Bruce Golding, the shadow finance minister who had long been considered Seaga's successor, had resigned as JLP chair, reportedly after his supporters had asked Seaga to step down. Subsequently, Golding formed the rival National Democratic Movement (below). Seaga was again confirmed as JLP leader at the party's annual conventions in 1999 and 2000.

The JLP was runner-up to the PNP in the election of December 18, 1997, winning only 10 House seats. Although the JLP increased its vote share and won a total of 26 seats in legislative balloting in October 2002, the party's failure to displace the PNP as the ruling party reportedly prompted increasing internal criticism of Seaga. In mid-2004 Seaga announced that he would step down as JLP leader in November. Golding, who had returned to the party, was elected as Seaga's successor at a convention on February 20, 2005, and he was sworn in as Leader of the Opposition on April 21.

After nearly 20 years in opposition, the JLP returned to power (with Golding as prime minister) following the 2007 elections, by winning 33 of 60 seats. The JLP also won local elections in December, gaining majorities in 9 of the 13 parish councils. However, the party's fortunes declined significantly in the December 2011 legislative balloting (21 of 63 seats). Andrew Holness, the education minister who had been elected leader of the JLP and thereby prime minister following Golding's resignation in October, consequently became Leader of the Opposition.

Leaders: Andrew HOLNESS (Leader, Leader of the Opposition, and Former Prime Minister), Audrey SHAW, Desmond McKENZIE, Christopher TUFTON (NDM).

Other Parties Contesting the 2011 Elections:

National Democratic Movement (NDM). The NDM was launched on October 29, 1995, by former JLP chair Bruce Golding, who had resigned in early September as opposition finance spokesperson, and other JLP legislators. Golding, who had indicated earlier that he might challenge Edward Seaga for leadership of the JLP at its annual conference in November, declared that the new formation was needed to generate the "long-range stability" without which there could be "no significant investment and growth." However, the NDM lost all of its existing five seats in the legislative balloting of December 18, 1997. Golding stepped down from his leadership post in March 2000, and a May NDM conference selected Hyacinth BENNETT as his successor. She thereby became the first woman to head a Jamaican party. Before the legislative balloting in October 2002, the NDM initiated the formation of an electoral coalition called the **New Jamaica Alliance** (NJA) that also included the **Republican Party of Jamaica** (RPS), led by Denzil TAYLOR, and the Jamaica Alliance for **National Unity** (JANU), which had been launched the previous March by a church and civic group led by Rev. Al MILLER. The NJA failed to win any seats in the legislative balloting. Golding subsequently returned to the JLP.

The NDM contested only 10 seats in the September 3, 2007, elections, receiving fewer than 600 votes at the national level. (The NDM had threatened to boycott the poll after its principal candidate, Earle De Lisser, was not allowed to participate in televised debates between the JLP and PNP candidates.)

Leaders: Earle DE LISSER (President), Apollone REID (Vice President).

Two other parties presented candidates in 2011, securing only a handful of votes each. They were the **Jamaica Alliance Movement** (JAM), led by community advocate Ras Astor BLACK (the sole JAM candidate and the founder of the country's first Rastafarian party in 2001); and the **Marcus Garvey People's Progressive Party** (MGPPP), whose president, Moses Emanuel HENRIQUES, died in February 2012. He was succeeded by Leon BURRELL. (The MGPPP, which lacks formal political party status due to its small size, aligned with the NDM for the 2011 elections, the two parties agreeing not to present candidates in the same constituencies.)

LEGISLATURE

The bicameral **Parliament** consists of an appointed Senate and an elected House of Representatives. All spending bills must originate in the lower chamber.

Senate. The upper house presently consists of 21 members appointed by the governor general; 13 are normally appointed on advice of the prime minister and 8 on the advice of the leader of the opposition. Following the installation of the new Senate on January 17, 2012, the People's National Party controlled 13 seats and the Jamaica Labour Party controlled 8.

President: Stanley REDWOOD.

House of Representatives. The lower house includes 63 members (raised in 2011 from 60 to 63) elected from single-member districts by universal adult suffrage for five-year terms, subject to dissolution. In the early election of December 29, 2011, the People's National Party won 42 seats and the Jamaica Labour Party won 21.

Speaker: Michael PEART.

CABINET

[as of July 1, 2013]

Prime Minister	Portia Simpson Miller [f]
Ministers	
Agriculture and Fisheries	Roger Clarke
Defense, Development, Information, and Sports	Portia Simpson Miller [f]
Education	Ronald Thwaites
Finance and Planning	Peter Phillips
Foreign Affairs and Foreign Trade	Arnold Nicholson
Health	Dr. Fenton Ferguson
Industry, Commerce, and Investment	Anthony Hylton
Justice	Sen. Mark Golding
Labor and Social Security	Derrick Kellier
Local Government and Community Development	Noel Arscott
National Security	Peter Bunting
Science, Technology, Energy, and Mining	Phillip Paulwell
Transport, Works, and Housing	Omar Davies
Tourism and Entertainment	Dr. Kenneth Wykeham McNeill
Water, Land, Environment, and Climate Change	Robert Pickersgill
Without Portfolio (Finance and Planning)	Horace Dalley
Without Portfolio (Office of the Prime Minister [Information])	Sandrea Falconer [f]
Without Portfolio (Office of the Prime Minister [Sport])	Natalie Neita-Headley [f]
Without Portfolio (Transport, Works, and Housing)	Morais Guy
Youth and Culture	Lisa Hanna [f]
Attorney General	Patrick Atkinson

[f] = female

Note: All cabinet members belong to the People's National Party.

INTERGOVERNMENTAL REPRESENTATION

Ambassador to the U.S.: Stephen Charles VASCIANNIE.

U.S. Ambassador to Jamaica: Pamela E. BRIDGEWATER.

Permanent Representative to the UN: Courtney RATTRAY.

IGO Memberships (Non-UN): Caricom, CWTH, IADB, IOM, NAM, OAS, WTO.

JAPAN

Japan
Nippon

Political Status: Constitutional monarchy established May 3, 1947; under multiparty parliamentary system.

Area: 145,850 sq. mi. (377,750 sq. km).

Population: 135,210,095 (2012E—UN); 127,253,075 (2013E—U.S. Census).

Major Urban Centers (2010C): TOKYO (8,945,695), Yokohama (3,688,773), Osaka (2,665,314), Nagoya (2,263,894), Sapporo (1,913,545), Kobe (1,544,200), Kyoto (1,474,015), Fukuoka (1,463,743), Kawasaki (1,425,512), Saitama (1,222,434), Hiroshima (1,173,843), Sendai (1,045,986).

Official Language: Japanese.

Monetary Unit: Yen (market rate November 1, 2013: 98.77 yen = $1US).

Sovereign: Emperor TSUGUNOMIYA AKIHITO; ascended the throne on January 7, 1989, on the death of his father, Showa Emperor MICHINOMIYA HIROHITO.

Heir Apparent: Crown Prince NARUHITO.

Prime Minister: Shinzo ABE (Liberal Democratic Party), elected by the Diet on December 26, 2012, and formally appointed by the emperor on the same day to succeed Yoshihiko NODA (Democratic Party of Japan).

THE COUNTRY

Situated off the coast of Northeast Asia and stretching some 2,000 miles, the Japanese archipelago consists of over 3,000 islands, although the 4 main islands of Honshu, Hokkaido, Kyushu, and Shikoku account for 98 percent of the land area. While mountainous terrain has limited the farming acreage, the country's location has provided a stimulus to fishing, other maritime pursuits, and trading. The thickly settled, basically Mongoloid population is remarkably homogeneous; the only significant ethnic minority consists of 700,000 Koreans, most of whom are descended from some 2.5 million laborers brought to Japan in the period 1910–1945. The Ainu, an indigenous people concentrated on the northern island of Hokkaido, today number only about 50,000. Buddhism and Shintoism are the two major religions. Women constitute about 42 percent of the labor force but remain underrepresented in elective office. Following the 2012 balloting, women held 38 seats in the House (7.9 percent). In the 2013 upper house elections, women secured 39 seats (16.1 percent).

Japan was the economic superpower in Asia before World War II. Growth between 1954, when prewar economic levels were first regained, and 1970 proceeded at an average rate, in real terms, of at least 10 percent annually, vaulting Japan past West Germany and into second place, behind the United States, among the world's largest economies. It retained that position until overtaken by China in 2010. The role of agriculture (2 percent of GDP) in the Japanese economy has shrunk as industry and services have grown. Industry accounts for about 30 percent of GDP and 27 percent of employment, while services contribute 69 percent of GDP and 68 percent of employment.

GDP grew by 2.8 percent in 2000 but contracted to 0.4 percent in 2001 and 0.3 percent in 2002 (for more information on the economy prior to 2000, please see the 2012 *Handbook*). Growth was restored in 2003, when GDP rose by 1.4, and the unemployment rate dipped after peaking at a record 5.5 percent early in the year. Annual GDP growth averaged 1.4 percent in 2005–2007. However, in 2008 the onset of the international financial crisis reversed the positive trend, resulting in Japan recording its first recession in seven years. Nevertheless, Japan committed to a $100 billion loan to the International Monetary Fund (IMF) to temporarily support the Fund's assistance to its members during the crisis. Far from being immune to the financial turmoil, Japan's economy contracted by 5 percent in 2009. By 2010, however, robust annual growth of 4 percent was recorded, though the IMF urged the authorities to draw up fiscal policies to rein in Japan's high public debt. Following the devastating earthquake and tsunami in March 2011, the IMF cited the "tremendous resilience of the Japanese people in tackling the formidable challenges of reconstruction" and pledged supplemental assistance to help restore the affected regions. GDP declined by 0.6 percent in 2011 as the country fell back into recession, while inflation was –0.3 percent and unemployment 4.6 percent. The following year, GDP grew by 2 percent, inflation was –0.4 percent, and unemployment, 4.4 percent.

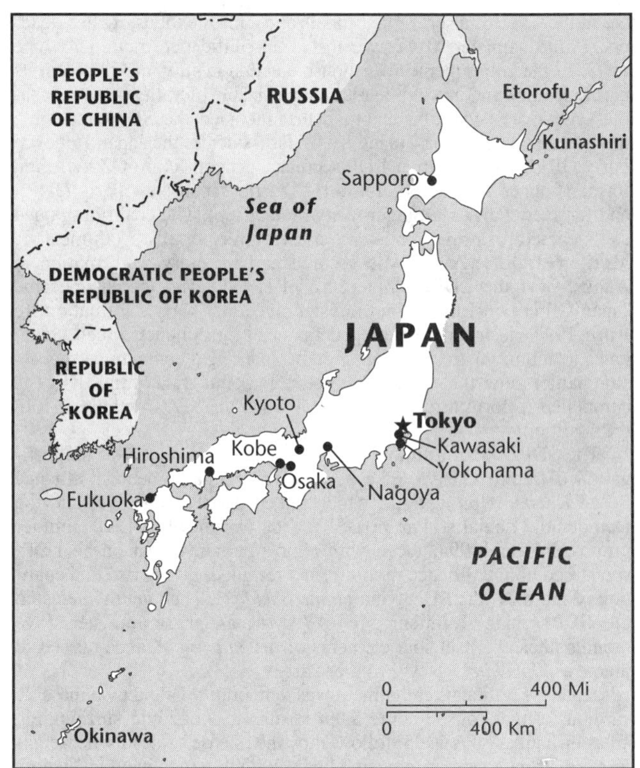

GOVERNMENT AND POLITICS

Political background. The armistice signed by Japan on September 2, 1945, concluded World War II and ended the era of imperial expansion that had begun with the Meiji Restoration in 1867. Stripped of its overseas territorial acquisitions, including Manchuria, Korea, Formosa (Taiwan), southern Sakhalin, and the Kuril Islands (in addition to the de facto loss of its "Northern Territories" to the Soviet Union—see Foreign relations, below), Japan was occupied by Allied military forces under Gen. Douglas MacArthur. A period of far-reaching social, political, and economic reforms ensued, overseen by U.S. occupation authorities. A constitution promulgated November 3, 1946, effective May 3, 1947, deprived Emperor HIROHITO of his claim to divine right and transformed Japan into a constitutional monarchy that expressly renounced war and the maintenance of military forces.

The Allied occupation was formally ended by a peace treaty signed in San Francisco on September 8, 1951, effective April 28, 1952; by its terms (still unrecognized by Moscow when the Soviet Union dissolved), the United States retained control of the Bonin and Ryukyu islands while informally recognizing Japan's "residual sovereignty" in those territories. Concurrently, a security treaty between Japan and the United States (modified in 1960 by a Treaty of Mutual Cooperation and Security) gave the latter the right to continue maintaining armed forces in and around Japan. The Bonin Islands were returned to the Japanese administration in 1968, while reversion of the Ryukyus (including Okinawa) occurred in 1972.

For six decades Japan's political fortunes rested mainly with a small group of conservative politicians, civil servants, and businesspeople identified with the Liberal Democratic Party (LDP), established in 1955 by merger of the Liberal and Democratic parties. Dedicated both to free enterprise and to continued close association with the United States, the LDP was periodically challenged until the 1980s by leftist forces associated primarily with the Social Democratic Party of Japan (SDPJ, formerly the Japanese Socialist Party), the small Japanese Communist Party (JCP), and a wide but volatile extraparliamentary opposition, including trade union, student, and intellectual groups. Until 1993 LDP rule continued without interruption under prime ministers Zenko SUZUKI (1980–1982), Yasuhiro NAKASONE (1982–1987), Noburu TAKESHITA (1987–1989), Sosuke UNO (1989), Toshiko KAIFU (1989–1991), and Kiichi MIYAZAWA (1991–1993).

In the wake of a series of scandals and a mass exodus of party leaders, Prime Minister Miyazawa lost a no-confidence motion in June 1993. In the consequent lower house election in July, the LDP lost its parliamentary majority while retaining a sizable plurality. An improbable seven-party coalition emerged that included the SDPJ and three new groups recently organized by LDP dissidents: the Japan Renewal Party (JRP), led by former LDP secretary general Ichiro OZAWA and former finance minister Tsutomu HATA; the Japan New Party (JNP); and the New Party Harbinger (*Shinto Sakigake*). The coalition named as its choice for prime minister a conservative populist from the JNP, Morihiro HOSOKAWA, who secured parliamentary confirmation in August over the LDP nominee, Yohei KONO, and thereby became Japan's first non-LDP prime minister since that party's formation. In April 1994 disclosures of alleged financial misconduct forced Hosokawa to submit his resignation, thereby sparking a contentious succession battle. Later that month the victor, Tsutomu Hata of the JRP, was compelled to form a minority cabinet when the SDPJ withdrew from the coalition.

The SDPJ's action followed the formation, principally at the instigation of Ichiro Ozawa, of a new center-left parliamentary alliance called *Kaishin* (Innovation), which linked the JRP, the JNP, and the Democratic Socialist Party (DSP) with two new ex-LDP splinter groups. In June 1994, faced with almost certain defeat on an LDP-sponsored nonconfidence motion, Hata resigned, giving rise to a coalition of the LDP, the SDPJ, and *Shinto Sakigake.* The Diet then elected the SDPJ chair, Tomiichi MURAYAMA, as prime minister. Five months later, the principal elements of the *Kaishin* alliance agreed to merge as *Shinshinto* (New Frontier Party).

Japanese political realignment was temporarily halted by a massive earthquake that caused some 5,000 deaths in Kobe and surrounding areas on January 17, 1995, followed by the release of deadly nerve gas in a Tokyo subway system on March 20. The latter incident, which resulted in ten deaths and injury to thousands of commuters, was the work of a millennial religious cult, *Aum Shinrikyo,* whose leader, Shoko ASAHARA, was arrested in May after an intensive manhunt. (A death sentenced imposed in 2004 has not yet been carried out.)

In a House of Councilors election in July 1995, the LDP and *Shinshinto* registered gains while the SDPJ regained only 16 of the party's 41 vacated seats. The LDP-SDPJ-*Sakigake* coalition continued in office until January 1996, when Prime Minister Murayama resigned, having been battered by a variety of economic and political problems. Murayama was succeeded by the country's outspoken LDP trade minister, Ryutaro HASHIMOTO, at the head of a new administration of the same three parties.

Encouraged by the failure of *Shinshinto* to sustain its early promise as a "government in waiting," the prime minister called an early lower house election for October 1995 and was rewarded by a significant increase in LDP representation to 239 seats in the 500-seat House of Representatives. The two smaller government parties both suffered heavy losses, in part because the new Democratic Party of Japan (DPJ) took 52 seats in its first election. Both the Social Democratic Party (SDP, formerly the SDPJ) and *Shinto Sakigake* declined to join a new LDP-dominated government, as did the DPJ, with the result that Hashimoto had to settle for a pledge of qualified external support from the SDP and *Shinto Sakigake* in return for formal policy consultation. On that basis, Hashimoto was reelected prime minister in November and announced an exclusively LDP cabinet.

At the end of 1997 *Shinshinto* collapsed, with the DPJ quickly emerging as the largest opposition party. In May 1998 both the SDP and *Shinto Sakigake* decided to withdraw their support from the LDP at the end of the legislative session in June, but the announcement posed no threat to the LDP, which, owing to defections from other parties since the last election, once again controlled a majority of lower house seats.

The Hashimoto administration approached the July 1998 election for half the House of Councilors with dim prospects amid economic turmoil triggered by what was then Japan's worst postwar recession (and the first since the international oil shock of 1974). Furthermore, charges of bribery and other corruption had generated a series of resignations and dismissals within the Ministry of Finance and the central bank. When the LDP captured only 44 of the 60 contested seats it had previously claimed in the upper house, Prime Minister Hashimoto resigned. Foreign Minister Keizo OBUCHI succeeded him as party leader and prime minister.

In January 1999 Prime Minister Obuchi announced the formation of a coalition with Ichiro Ozawa's new Liberal Party (LP), a successor to *Shinshinto.* The following October, the recently organized New *Komeito* formally joined the government, guaranteeing a majority in both houses to Obuchi. In December, however, with a general election due in less than a year, the LP's Ozawa threatened to pull his party from the tripartite coalition unless Obuchi put forward legislation reducing the size of the House of Representatives. Obuchi relented and in January–February 2000 forced through the Diet a bill that cut 20 proportional seats from the 500-member lower house.

The LDP-LP relationship remained tenuous, in part because the LDP would not support as many LP candidates for the upcoming lower house election as Ozawa demanded. Thus, on April 1, 2000, Obuchi announced that the two parties were severing connections. Later that day the prime minister suffered what would prove to be a mortal stroke. With Obuchi in a coma, the cabinet resigned, paving the way for the election of the LDP's Yoshiro MORI as prime minister on April 5. Two days earlier over two dozen Diet members had left Ozawa's LP and formed the New Conservative Party (NCP), which replaced the LP in the three-party government.

Following Obuchi's death, Mori announced a general election for June 25, 2000. In the context of continuing economic doldrums, and with Mori having committed several verbal gaffes since taking office, the LDP lost its lower house majority, winning only 233 seats. Despite having suffered significant losses themselves, New *Komeito* and the NCP provided enough additional seats to ensure Prime Minister Mori's reelection by the Diet.

With the economy verging on recession and with his administration plagued by corruption allegations as well as his personal unpopularity, Mori resigned in April 2001. His successor, former health minister Junichiro KOIZUMI, came into office on the strength of a reformist agenda that included limiting the influence of the LDP's factions, enabling faster deregulation, reducing the government deficit, and instituting additional banking and other structural reforms. In the House of Councilors election of July 29, both the LDP and the opposition DPJ gained seats at the expense of smaller parties.

In October 2001, responding to the previous month's al-Qaida attacks on the United States, the Diet passed legislation that permitted the government to deploy warships to the Indian Ocean in support of U.S.-led operations in Afghanistan. Such noncombat deployment of Japan's Self-Defense Forces (SDF) remained controversial, however, and the issue became even more inflammatory in 2003 when Koizumi won approval to commit additional SDF personnel in support of the U.S.-led invasion of Iraq.

Koizumi handily defeated three challengers for the presidency of the LDP in September 2003 and then announced a general election for November. Aided by the LDP's absorption of the NCP shortly before the balloting, the LDP and New *Komeito* maintained a slightly reduced majority, but the DPJ, bolstered by a September merger with the LP, gained 40 seats, apparently confirming speculation that Japan was moving toward a two-party system. That possibility was further supported by the results of the July 2004, election for half the House of Councilors: the DPJ won 50 seats and the LDP won 49, although together the latter and New *Komeito* retained an overall majority.

In August 2005 the prime minister called an early election following the defeat in the House of Councilors of reform legislation intended to privatize Japan Post—in effect, the largest savings bank in the world, with total assets of $2.9 trillion. In the September 11 election, the LDP registered the largest victory in Japan's post–World War II history, winning 296 seats and permitting Koizumi to pass his postal reform plan, which included dividing the agency into separate units responsible for mail delivery, banking, insurance, and management services. In September 2006, with Koizumi having announced that he was voluntarily stepping down after serving five years as prime minister, Cabinet Secretary Shinzo ABE was elected president of the LDP. The victory ensured Abe's election as prime minister.

At the July 29, 2007, election for half the House of Councilors, the LDP lost its plurality in the upper house for the first time in the party's history. The opposition DPJ claimed 60 seats, for a total of 109, while the LDP won only 37, which dropped its representation to 83. The defeat for the Abe government came in the midst of corruption scandals, a series of ministerial gaffes, and the disclosure of massive errors in the public pension system: underpayments to retirees, improper exemptions, and uncredited premium payments. Pressure mounted for Abe's resignation, and on September 12 he announced that he would step down. His successor as LDP president, Yasuo FUKUDA, a former cabinet secretary, easily won confirmation as prime minister on September 25.

On September 1, 2008, Fukuda also resigned, beset by falling poll numbers, economic difficulties, and an inability to advance his legislative agenda because of opposition from the DPJ-controlled Senate. On September 22 the LDP elevated Taro ASO from LDP secretary general to party president by a two-to-one margin over four rivals, and he was confirmed as prime minister two days later.

Aso fared no better than Fukuda. In early 2009, with Japan's economy succumbing to recession, his standing in public opinion polls dipped below 20 percent approval. In July, with the end of the lower house term approaching, Aso dissolved the House of Representatives and called an election for August 30. Dissatisfaction with LDP rule culminated in an unprecedented victory for the DPJ, which won 308 seats, compared to 119 for the LDP. On September 16 the DPJ's Yukio HATOYAMA, the finance minister, won confirmation as prime minister at the head of a government that included the SDP and the People's New Party (PNP) as junior partners.

On June 2, 2010, Hatoyama became the fourth prime minister in a row to serve less than a year. A major factor in his decision to resign was his inability to follow through on a campaign pledge to relocate a planned U.S. military heliport on Okinawa (see Foreign relations, below), a failure that had already precipitated the SDP's departure from the government on May 30. Hatoyama, who also urged party secretary general Ichiro Ozawa to resign, was succeeded by Naoto KAN, the deputy prime minister and one of the DPJ's founders, who received the assent of the Diet on June 4. He was formally appointed by the emperor on June 8. Kan's popularity plummeted quickly, however, as a result of his proposal in June to double the sales tax rate to 10 percent. Subsequently, in the July 11.House of Councilors midterm elections, the DPJ lost its majority. Kan reshuffled the cabinet on September 17, three days after his reelection as DPJ leader.

Kan reshuffled the cabinet again on January 14, 2011, appointing an economics minister who was described as being a fiscal hawk. The reshuffle was reportedly prompted by efforts to appease the opposition, which had threatened to block the budget and was critical of the administration's handling of a maritime dispute with China. Prime Minister Kan came under heavy criticism for his handling of affairs in the aftermath of the catastrophic earthquake and tsunami in March, but he rejected calls to step down. Ultimately, on August 10 he announced his intention to resign after 15 months in office, and on August 29 Finance Minister Yoshihiko NODA was elected in DPJ runoff balloting as party leader, thus virtually securing the post of prime minister. He was confirmed as prime minister by the Diet on August 30, and on September 2 he named a new cabinet, retaining the sole PNP representative.

Noda reorganized the cabinet and created the post of deputy prime minister on January 13, 2012. This was followed by another reshuffle on June 4, which included the resignations of two ministers who had been censured by the opposition-controlled upper house. As part of a broad effort to ease tensions with China (see Foreign relations, below) and improve the government's popularity ahead of elections, the cabinet was again reshuffled on October 1.

In elections for the House of Representatives on December 16, 2012, the LDP won an overwhelming majority, returning the party to power after three years as the opposition (see Current issues, below). Former prime minister Abe was returned to his old job on December 26, and he named a new cabinet the same day. The LDP further strengthened its power by winning balloting for the upper house on July 21.

Constitution and government. The constitution of May 3, 1947, converted Japan from an absolute to a constitutional monarchy by transferring sovereign power from the emperor to the people and limiting the former to a "symbolic" and ceremonial role. In addition, the peerage was abolished and a range of civil rights enumerated, including freedom of thought and conscience, free and equal education, an absence of censorship, and impartial and public judicial procedures.

Legislative and fiscal authority are vested in a bicameral parliament (Diet) consisting of a dominant House of Representatives and an upper chamber, the House of Councilors, which has the power to delay legislation. A bill's proponents in the lower house may overcome a defeat in the upper chamber by achieving a two-thirds majority upon reconsideration of the returned bill, but representatives have rarely exercised that option. (On January 11, 2008, the House of Representatives overrode the House of Councilors for the first time since 1951 on a measure authorizing a one-year extension of a two-ship mission in the Indian Ocean that was resupplying NATO forces in Afghanistan.)

The cabinet, headed by a prime minister, is collectively responsible to the Diet and must resign on passage of a no-confidence vote in the House of Representatives unless the house is dissolved and a new election held. Judicial power is vested in an appointive Supreme Court and in lower courts as established by law.

Administratively, Japan is divided into 47 prefectures, each with an elected mayor or governor and a local assembly. Smaller municipal units have their own elected mayors and assemblies.

Constitutional amendments require a two-thirds majority of both houses and subsequent ratification by a majority vote in a popular referendum. In 1999 the Diet passed a bill authorizing the formation in each house of a Research Commission on the Constitution to consider "widely and comprehensively" the provisions of the basic law. The two committees convened for the first time in January 2000 and submitted their final reports in April 2005. The process culminated in the passage in 2007 of the National Referendum Act, which set forth basic procedures for conducting a constitutional referendum. The act entered into effect in May 2010.

Article Nine of the constitution, which prohibits "the threat or use of force" internationally and renounces the maintenance of armed forces and "other war potential" for such purposes, has been central to consideration of whether the 1947 constitution should be amended or even replaced. Article Nine has been interpreted by the government as permitting the maintenance of Self-Defense Forces (SDF), currently totaling about 240,000 personnel. Presently, dispatch of SDF contingents abroad is limited to peacekeeping operations under the United Nations or, as in the case of the recent deployments to the Indian Ocean and Iraq, to the terms of specific legislation. In December 2006 the Diet voted to raise the status of the Defense Agency to that of a full ministry, but debate remains open as to whether the government should be granted a freer hand in deploying SDF forces overseas, including participation in mutual defense efforts.

Freedom of the press is constitutionally guaranteed. In 2013 Reporters Without Borders ranked Japan 53rd out of 179 countries in media freedom, a sharp decline from the previous when the country ranked 22nd. The media watchdog group attributed the fall to a "lack of transparency" and "almost zero respect for access to information" on the Fukushima nuclear disaster (see Current issues, below).

Foreign relations. Japan was admitted to the UN in 1956 and belongs to all of its specialized and related agencies. Japan is also a member of such bodies as the Organization for Economic Cooperation and Development (OECD) and the Group of Seven/Group of Eight.

Japan's failure to offer a clear apology for its 1941 surprise attack on Pearl Harbor, Hawaii, caused some lingering ill-feeling in the United States, as in Japan has Washington's refusal to apologize for the decision to drop atomic bombs on Hiroshima and Nagasaki in August 1945. Neither resentment has significantly affected Japan's continuing postwar reliance on the United States for its defense, and the 1960 mutual security treaty remains in effect.

Normal relations with South Korea were established in 1965–1966 after many years of hostility, which, in muted form, lingered because of Korean resentment over the Japanese occupation of 1910–1945 and over the alleged discrimination against Koreans born and living in Japan. It was not until a visit by South Korean president Roh Tae Woo in May 1990 that the residual bitterness was substantially eased by Emperor Hirohito tendering "deepest regret" for "the suffering . . . which was brought about by my country."

In 1992 Tokyo admitted that the Japanese army had forced tens of thousands of Korean women to serve as "comfort women" (unpaid prostitutes) during World War II. In all, up to 200,000 women had been so enslaved in the territories occupied by Japan. To atone for this, in 1994 the Murayama government announced a ten-year commitment of $1 billion, which, in part, would fund vocational training centers for women in neighboring countries. Controversial legislation passed in 1992 permitted, for the first time since World War II, the use of Japanese military personnel for international peacekeeping missions.

Issues related to Japan's imperialist past continue to affect relations with its neighbors, including Russia. The postwar normalization of relations with the Soviet Union proceeded slowly. Bilateral talks on a Japanese-Soviet peace treaty were instituted in 1972, but Soviet refusal to return the northern islands of Etorofu, Kunashiri, Shikotan, and Habomai, which were annexed after World War II, prevented any significant progress toward a treaty until the post-Soviet era. In 1996 Moscow and Tokyo agreed to resume negotiations on a peace treaty that would include resolution of the "northern territories" issue, which included the islands of Etorofu, Kunashiri, Shikotan, and Habomai.

Perhaps the most troublesome aspect of the U.S.-Japan defensive alignment has been the American military presence in Okinawa. In

December 1996 an agreement was reached on a 20 percent reduction in the land used by the U.S. military, without a collateral reduction in the number of U.S. forces stationed on the island. In 1997 the United States and Japan negotiated revised guidelines for military cooperation. For the first time, Japan agreed to commit military personnel to overseas support during Far East crises. Without specifying locales, legislation passed in 1999 permits Japan in an emergency to provide U.S. forces with fuel, food, and other logistic support, plus access to Japanese civilian airports and ports. In addition, Japanese ships may assist in such activities as minesweeping in international waters, while members of the Japan SDF deployed abroad may carry weapons to defend themselves and Japanese civilians.

In November 1996 the Japanese foreign ministry lodged a formal protest with South Korea because of a port facility being constructed in a group of small islands (called Takeshima by Japan and Tokto by South Korea) located midway between the two countries. Partly because of the territorial dispute, in January 1998 Tokyo scrapped a 1965 fishing treaty with its neighbor, but in September the two compromised on a treaty revision governing fishing zones and quotas.

In January 1998 a joint commission was formed to draft the text of a definitive accord to resolve the northern territories issue, and in November, during the first state visit to Moscow by a Japanese head of government in 25 years, Prime Minister Obuchi and Russian president Boris Yeltsin reaffirmed a 2000 target date for completing the peace accord and ending the insular impasse.

Relations with North Korea have been dominated by security concerns, especially after Pyongyang fired a three-stage missile over the Pacific in August 1998. The launch produced a strong rebuke from Tokyo, which temporarily froze food aid and development assistance to Pyongyang. North Korea's growing launch capability also contributed to Japan's announcement in September that it would participate with the United States in research on a theater missile defense system (MDS).

During a state visit by South Korean president Kim Dae Jung to Japan in 1998, Emperor TSUGUNOMIYA AKIHITO publicly communicated his "deep sorrow" for Japan's 35 years of colonial rule, while a concluding statement from the two governments included the first written "heartfelt apology" from Tokyo to Seoul.

A November 1998 visit to Japan by Chinese president Jiang Zemin, the first by a Chinese head of state since World War II, failed to produce the expected formal, written Japanese apology for its 1937–1945 occupation. Instead, Prime Minister Obuchi repeated an expression of "deep remorse" that Prime Minister Murayama had voiced in 1995.

Relations with North Korea were strained again in March 1999, when, in the first action of its kind since 1953, Japanese naval vessels chased and fired on two suspected North Korean spy ships in territorial waters. In December 2001 the Japanese coast guard intercepted a suspected North Korean spy ship within Japan's exclusive economic zone. An exchange of fire ended with the sinking of the North Korean vessel, which led Pyongyang to accuse Tokyo of "brutal piracy."

In October 2002, following a visit by Prime Minister Koizumi to North Korea and the latter's belated admission that it had kidnapped 13 Japanese citizens in the late 1970s and early 1980s, Japan and North Korea restarted normalization talks in Malaysia. No progress was made in two days of discussions, however, and further efforts were hindered by other developments, including Pyongyang's renewal of its nuclear weapons development program. In March 2003 North Korea objected to Japan's launch of two reconnaissance satellites and in December to Tokyo's confirmation that it would move ahead with deployment of the MDS. A one-day visit to Pyongyang by Koizumi in May 2004 concluded without progress on any bilateral issues.

A persistent insular dispute has centered on the uninhabited Senkaku Islands between Taiwan and Okinawa. Both China and Taiwan claim ownership of the islands, which are controlled and administered by Japan. In recent years there have been numerous incidents, including blockades, arrests, and efforts to intercept military aircraft, as the complex dispute remains unresolved.

In May 2006, following years of discussions, the United States and Japan completed a plan for relocation of a U.S. Marine heliport to Nago, in the north of Okinawa, and the transfer by 2015 of 8,000 Marines to Guam, at a cost of $10.3 billion (60 percent to be paid by Japan). Also, all or part of five military facilities were to revert to Japanese control. Nevertheless, many Okinawans have objected to the continued U.S. presence, while at the same time recognizing its positive economic impact.

In October 2006, responding to North Korea's October 9 underground nuclear weapons test, Japan imposed new unilateral sanctions, including banning all imports from North Korea and preventing its ships from entering Japanese ports. Japan nevertheless remained a key participant in the six-party talks (with China, Russia, South Korea, and the United States) on dismantling North Korea's nuclear weapons program. After Pyongyang agreed to terminate development of its nuclear capabilities, discussions between Japan and North Korea resumed in June 2008 in Beijing. North Korea agreed, among other things, to reexamine the case of the abducted Japanese. Tokyo, in turn, vowed to ease sanctions.

In February 2009 Prime Minister Aso became the first Japanese prime minister since the end of World War II to visit Russia's Sakhalin Island, which had belonged to Japan for many years prior to the Yalta Conference agreements in 1945. Aso and Russian president Dmitri Medvedev pledged to accelerate efforts to resolve the status of four neighboring islands.

On April 5, 2009, North Korea launched another rocket that it insisted was intended to carry a communications satellite into orbit, but Western observers declared that the launch was a failed military test. In response to broad international criticism, the North announced that it was once again quitting the six-party talks and would nullify all related agreements. On May 23 North Korea conducted its second nuclear weapons test, followed by a series of short-range missile launches. Another series, labeled as a further provocation by Tokyo, followed in early July.

The United States and Japan agreed in February 2012 to revise the 2006 agreement on U.S. force in Okinawa. Under the revised accord, the United States would immediately begin to relocate 8,000 of the 18,000 troops stationed on the island and Japan would pay for $3.1 billion of the estimated $8.6 billion costs of the redeployment.

In April 2012 Thein Sein became the first leader of Myanmar to visit Japan since 1984. During his visit, Japan announced it would cancel $3.7 billion in debt owed by Myanmar. In June Nado and Russian president Vladimir Putin agreed to restart negotiations on the Kuril Islands. Meanwhile, tensions over the Senkaku Islands resurfaced after the Japanese government bought three of the islands from a private owner. There were widespread protests and demonstrations in China and a boycott of Japanese goods and businesses. Noda responded by reshuffling the cabinet and appointing Makkio TANAKA, whose father helped open relations with China, as education minister.

In January 2013 Chinese surveillance vessels entered the waters of the Senkaku Islands, prompting an official complaint by Japan. Three days later, Japan sent fighter aircraft to the islands after a Chinese surveillance aircraft flew over the area. At the end of January, in a sign of increasing tensions, Japan announced it would increase military spending for the first time in 11 years.

Prime Minister Abe announced in March 2013 that Japan would join negotiations for a free trade area in the Pacific and launch talks with the EU for a bilateral free trade agreement. In April, Japan and Taiwan signed an agreement to allow Taiwanese fishing vessels in waters around the Senkaku Islands (see entry on Taiwan). Also in April, Japan and the United States signed an agreement to turnover or consolidate five U.S. military facilities on Okinawa by 2022. Both China and South Korea denounced the "Restoration of National Sovereignty Day" celebrations that commemorated the end of the U.S. occupation of Japan on April 28, 1952. Also in April, Abe further increased tensions with neighboring states when he announced support for revising Article 9 of Japan's constitution that renounced the use of offensive military force.

Current issues. Despite the steps taken in 2011 to strengthen the economy, including the introduction of a $62 billion stimulus package, Prime Minister Kan's accomplishments were quickly overshadowed by the catastrophic March earthquake and tsunami that struck in the eastern part of the country. The disasters resulted in the deaths of more than 15,000 people and unprecedented destruction, including severe damage to three nuclear reactors at the Fukushima nuclear power station in the northeast. Kan took steps to shut down aging nuclear power stations and halting plans to build new reactors. Meanwhile, the public was angered by what it perceived to be a slow government response to the calamity and its delayed release of information about the extent of the nuclear disaster. Kan initially rejected calls to step down, but he ultimately announced his intention to resign in August. Following the adoption of the bills he promoted on addressing the debt and on renewable energy, Kan resigned on August 26. Finance Minister Yoshihiko Noda was elected the new DPJ leader the same day and was confirmed as prime minister by parliament on August 30, becoming the country's sixth prime minister in five years. He sought political cooperation with the LDP, especially on economic, defense, and strategic issues, but was rebuffed in a number of votes in the House of Councilors.

A fiscal conservative, Noda ruled out any tax increase to pay for the $169 billion dollars reconstruction cost and stated that he did not favor raising taxes to pay for the national debt, which is now estimated as twice the size of the gross domestic production. The economy rebounded in late 2010, owing in large part to increased exports and consumer spending. In November the first nuclear reactor to have been shut down since the disaster started functioning again in the western part of the country, making it one of only 10 of the country's 54 reactors to be generating electricity.

In January 2012 the government reported that Japan ran a trade deficit for the first time since 1980. The imbalance was blamed on the lingering impact of the earthquake. In June the final two members of *Aum Shinrikyo* wanted for the 1995 subway attack were apprehended and arrested. Also in June, the legislature approved a controversial increase in the consumption tax, from 5 percent to 10 percent, after Noda agreed to drop other plans to reform the pension system. The increase was designed to help reduce Japan's ballooning debt. On August 29 the upper house approved a nonbinding censure of Noda, authored by seven small opposition parties, over the increase in the consumption tax. The opposition groups then boycotted the few remaining days of the legislative session.

In balloting for the House of Representatives on December 16, 2012, the LDP, along with their allies, the New *Komeito*, won 325 seats, a supermajority that allowed the coalition to override the upper chamber. The DPJ placed a distant second, with 57, while the newly formed right-wing grouping, the Japan Restoration Party—JRP (*Nippon Ishin no Kai*), was third with 54. Abe was again appointed prime minister. The LDP–New *Komeito* also won polling for the upper house on July 23, with 135 seats to 59 for the DPJ.

Once in office, Abe launched a series of economic reforms that came to be known as "Abenomics." Central to the new economic plan was a massive $104.3 billion stimulus program designed to create 600,000 jobs and add 2 percent to GDP, along with a break-up of the nation's utility monopolies and efforts to increase inflation to 2 percent per year by increasing the amount of money in circulation.

POLITICAL PARTIES

Throughout most of the postwar era, Japan's multiparty political structure featured the predominance of a single government party, the conservative Liberal Democratic Party (LDP), over a diversified opposition on the center and left of the political spectrum. Since 1996, however, the growth of the newly established Democratic Party of Japan (DPJ) may mean that Japan may be moving toward a two-party system.

Government Coalition:

Liberal Democratic Party—LDP (*Jiyu-Minshuto*). Born of a 1955 merger between the former Liberal and Democratic parties, the conservative LDP attaches more importance to organization and financial power than to ideology. It has favored private enterprise, alliance with the United States, and expansion of Japanese interests in Asia.

In December 1992 the influence of the party's long-dominant Takeshita faction was reduced as the result of a major cabinet reshuffle and by the creation from its ranks of a new faction effectively headed by former secretary general Ichiro Ozawa. Ozawa was one of a number of leaders to withdraw from the party prior to the July 1993 balloting, in which the LDP for the first time lost control of the lower house. On July 30 the battered party elected Yohei Kono as its new president. Although further weakened by postelection defections, the LDP rump seized the opportunity of a split in the new ruling coalition in April 1994 to establish an alliance with the Social Democrats and New Party Harbinger (*Shinto Sakigake*). This resulted in the party's return to government in June as the dominant member of a three-party coalition.

In January 1996, in the wake of SDP leader Tomiichi Murayama's withdrawal as prime minister, the LDP's Ryutaro Hashimoto was elected to the post. The party's lower house representation advanced to 239 out of 500 in the October general election, permitting formation of a minority government with the external support of the SDP and *Shinto Sakigake*. By fall 1997 the LDP had reestablished its majority through defections from other parties.

In the June 25, 2000, lower house election, the party lost its majority, winning only 233 seats in the 480-member chamber (it had held 271 of 500 seats before the balloting), but Prime Minister Yoshiro Mori continued in office with the support of coalition partners New *Komeito* and the New Conservative Party—NCP (*Hoshuto*). The latter had been formed in April 2000 by Transport Minister Toshihiro NIKAI and 25 other members of Parliament who had abandoned the Liberal Party (LP; see DPJ, below) upon the LP's departure from the governing coalition.

Despite having survived parliamentary no-confidence votes in November 2000 and March 2001, Mori resigned in April 2001. In the four-person contest to succeed him as LDP leader, Ryutaro Hashimoto, who was now head of the largest party faction, unexpectedly lost to Junichiro Koizumi, a reformer and former health minister who vowed to end the faction system. He was reelected, unopposed, to a two-year term in August 2001, but over the next year his policies met frequent resistance from the heads of other powerful LDP factions. In March 2002 he lost a key ally, Koichi KATO, who fell victim to a tax-evasion scandal involving an aide.

In the September 2003 election for the LDP presidency, Prime Minister Koizumi received over 60 percent support, defeating three other candidates: faction leader Shizuka, former transport minister Takao FUJII, and former foreign minister Masahiko. In the subsequent November election for the House of Representatives, the LDP won 237 seats. It then renewed its coalition with New *Komeito* and absorbed the NCP, which, having never won widespread support, had captured only 4 seats (down from 7 in 2000).

At the July 2004 House of Councilors election the LDP won 49 of 121 seats, slightly less than its target and 1 less than the DPJ. Its 114 total upper house seats (8 short of a majority) were supplemented by New *Komeito*'s 24. Following the replenishment, Chikage OGI, former NCP leader and transport minister, was elected the upper house's first female president.

In July 2004 former prime minister Hashimoto announced that he would surrender the leadership of his faction, still the LDP's largest, as a consequence of a political contributions scandal. The move was seen as strengthening Prime Minister Koizumi's position within the party. In late September, shortly before announcing a cabinet reshuffle, Koizumi reorganized the party leadership.

The defeat of postal reform legislation in August 2005 had been proceeded by a major split within LDP ranks, with the result that 37 LDP legislators voted against the package in the lower house. Reform opponents Mitsuo HORIUCHI and Shizuka KAMEI resigned as faction leaders, and Kamei then helped form the PNP. In the run-up to the September 2005 snap election, Prime Minister Koizumi refused to extend party backing to any of the rebels and instead ran other candidates, dubbed "assassins," against them. Most of the rebels were defeated. A number of those who had not formally resigned from the party prior to the election were expelled in October.

Koizumi had announced in 2005 that he would step down as president of the party when his term ended in September 2006. By early 2006 three leading presidential candidates had emerged: Chief Cabinet Secretary Shinzo Abe, Foreign Minister Taro Aso, and Finance Minister Tanigaki. In the September 20 election, Abe, who was generally considered Koizumi's choice, won with 464 votes to 136 for Aso and 102 for Tanigaki. Six days later both houses of the Diet made Abe, 52, Japan's youngest postwar prime minister. His prospects for completing the term in office were dimmed in July 2007, however, when the LDP, for the first time in its history, lost its plurality in the House of Councilors. In the election for half the upper house, the LDP won only 37 seats, for a total of 83. Under pressure, Abe resigned on September 12, and on September 23 the LDP elected Yasuo Fukuda, a former cabinet secretary, over Aso by a vote of 330–197. Fukuda quickly named three faction leaders, Bunmei OBUKI, Sadakazu TANIGAKI, and Toshiro Nikai, to key party posts. (In May 2008 the Tanigaki faction merged into the Koga faction.) He was then confirmed as prime minister on September 25.

Less than a year later, Fukuda resigned. On September 22, 2008, on his fourth attempt at the party presidency, Taro Aso was elected to the post with 351 of 527 votes. His opponents were Kaoru YOSANO, finance minister (66 votes), who in 2010 left the LDP to form the Sunrise Party of Japan (SPJ, below); Yuriko Koike, a former environment minister (46); Nobuteru Ishihara, former LDP policy chief (37); and Shigeru Ishiba, former defense minister (25 votes). Aso took office as prime minister on September 24, heading a substantially reconfigured cabinet. In January 2009 senior party member and former minister

Yoshima WATANABE, citing the LDP's lack of commitment to political reform, resigned from the party. He subsequently formed the Your Party (below).

The LDP entered the 2009 election campaign with all opinion polls showing it far behind the DPJ. It ended up winning only 119 seats (a loss of 177) and taking only 26.7 percent of the proportional votes. On September 16 Taro Aso resigned both as prime minister and as party president. A party election on September 28 concluded with Sadakazu Tanigaki, 64, easily winning the party presidency over two 46-year-old candidates, former deputy minister of justice Taro KONO and legislator Yasutoshi NISHIMURA. Both of the younger candidates argued for a generational change in leadership and attacked the party's faction-based politics.

In April 2010 former members of the LDP organized two new parties, the SPJ and the New Renaissance Party (below). In the July election for the House of Councilors, the LDP staged a minor comeback, winning 51 of the 121 open seats, compared to 44 for the DPJ, even though it obtained fewer prefectural and proportional votes.

In September 2012 Abe was again elected party president. The LDP won a majority in legislative balloting in December 2013, and Abe formed a coalition government with the New *Komeito*. The LDP subsequently won the July 2013 House of Councilors elections.

Leaders: Shinzo ABE (Prime Minister and Party President), Masahiko KOMURA (Vice President), Taro ASO (Deputy Prime Minister and Former Prime Minister, Aso Faction), Shigeru ISHIBA (Tsushima Faction), Yuriko KOIKE, Bunmei IBUKI (Ibuki Faction), Makoto KOGA (Koga Faction), Masahiko KOMURA (Komura Faction), Nobutaka MACHIMURA (Machimura Faction), Fukushiro NUKAGA (Nukaga Faction), Yuji TSUSHIMA (Tsushima Faction), Taku YAMASAKI (Yamasaki Faction), Nobuteru ISHIHARA (Secretary General).

New Komeito (New Clean Government Party). The New *Komeito* was formed by merger on November 7, 1998, of *Komei* with members of *Shinto Heiwa* (New Peace Party). The New *Komeito* is the latest incarnation of *Komeito* (Clean Government Party), which started as the *Komei* Political League, a political society, in 1961 and became a party in 1964 (for more on the history of *Komeito*, see the 2013 *Handbook*).

Sometimes also referred to as the New Clean Government Party, *Komei* was the smaller of two groups to emerge from *Komeito,* which disbanded in December 1994. The larger group, the *Komei* New Party, followed the *Komeito* chair, Koshiro Ishida, into *Shinshinto* five days later, while the smaller *Komei* held the loyalty of some 3,200 local assembly members and much of the *Komeito* delegation in the House of Councilors. Organized under the slogan "Reform Initiated Locally," it saw itself as the inheritor of *Komeito*'s "clean government" program, emphasizing grassroots democracy, humanism, protection of the global environment, and disarmament.

Following the breakup of *Shinshinto* in December 1997, some 18 members of the House of Councilors initially organized as the Dawn Club (*Reimei Kurabu*), which in January 1998 merged with *Komei,* while many *Shinshinto* lower house members formed *Shinto Heiwa* on January 4, 1998. *Shinto Heiwa* and another post-*Shinshinto* formation, the Reformers' Network Party—RNP (*Kaikaku Kurabu,* also known as the Reform Club), joined in a lower house alliance called the Peace and Reform Network, which soon constituted the second-largest opposition group in the House of Representatives.

Formation of the New *Komeito* by *Komei* and members of the defunct *Shinto Heiwa* in November 1998 served to broaden the alliance with the RNP in the lower house, where the two parties' 52 members formed a parliamentary group under the name *Komeito Kaikaku* (roughly, Clean Government Reform). At a convention in July 1999 the party voted to join the LDP–LP alliance, but expansion of the governing coalition was delayed until October. (The RNP accompanied the New *Komeito* into the Obuchi government as a junior partner, but by then it had already been weakened by defections to other parties, and it lost its remaining five lower house seats in the next election.)

In the June 2000 lower house election New *Komeito* fared poorly, winning 31 seats, 11 fewer than it had held upon dissolution but enough to help ensure continuation of the governing alliance. By early 2001, however, the party was publicly dissatisfied with Prime Minister Mori's leadership, and in February the New *Komeito* secretary general, Tetsuzo FUYUSHIBA, stated that it would leave the coalition if Mori did not resign soon, which he did less than two months later.

In the November 2003 election, the party won 34 lower house seats. Following the July 2004 House of Councilors election, New *Komeito* held 24 seats in the upper house, where it ranked third. In September 2005 it lost 3 of its lower house seats, and following the July 2007 election, its upper house delegation stood at 20.

Takenori KANZAKI was succeeded by Akihiro OTA in September. Wholesale leadership changes followed the defeat of the LDP–New *Komeito* government in the August 2009 election, in which Ota and the party's secretary general, Kazuo KITIGAWA, both lost their lower house seats. Having lost all 8 of its constituency seats, the party was left with only 21 block seats on the basis of 11.5 percent of the proportional vote. Natsuo Yamaguchi was elected party leader in September 2009 and reelected in September 2012. The party won 31 seats in the 2012 lower house balloting and had 20 seats following the 2013 upper chamber elections. Ota was appointed minister of land, infrastructure, transport, and tourism in the LDP-led government.

Leaders: Natsuo YAMAGUCHI (Chief Representative), Tetsuo SAITO, Yoshihisa INOUE (Secretary General).

Principal Opposition Parties:

Democratic Party of Japan—DPJ (*Nihon Minshuto*). The liberal DPJ was launched in September 1996 by a faction of the New Party Harbinger (*Shinto Sakigake*) led by Yukio Hatoyama and including the popular health and welfare minister, Naoto Kan. Grandson of a leader of the pre-1955 Democratic Party component of the LDP, Hatoyama had fallen out with the leadership of the *Shinto Sakigake* (established in 1993 by former LDP legislators) over electoral strategy. The DPJ quickly attracted parliamentary and popular support, winning 52 lower house seats in the October election.

In March 1998 the New Party Fraternity—NPF (*Shinto Yuai,* or Amity Party), the Democratic Reform League—DRL (*Minshu Kaikaku Regno*), and the Good Governance Party—GGP (*Minseito*) voted to dissolve and join the DPJ. All had previously agreed to work with the DPJ in a parliamentary bloc called *Minyuren.* The GGP had been established in January by the merger of three other parties: the Sun Party—SP (*Taiyo*), formed in December 1996 by former prime minister Tsutomu Hata and a dozen lower house members; the Voice of the People—VP (*Kokumin no Koe*); and the From Five Party (FFP) of former prime minister Morihiro Hosokawa. Like the NPF, the VP and FFP had emerged in January 1998, from the ruins of *Shinshinto* (New Frontier Party), which had been established in 1994 by nine opposition groups but had never coalesced into a viable alternative to the LDP. (For a detailed history of *Shinshinto,* see previous editions of the *Handbook.*)

Following the July 1998 election, the DPJ, supported in the House of Councilors by the affiliated *Shin-Ryokufukai* group, remained the largest opposition force in the Diet. At a DPJ convention in January 1999, Naoto Kan easily won reelection as party chief, despite earlier allegations of sexual misconduct. In September, however, he lost his leadership to Secretary General Yukio Hatoyama by a runoff vote of 182–130.

In the June 2000 election the DPJ made major gains, advancing to 127 seats, 32 more than it had held before the balloting. In March 2001 the DPJ absorbed much of *Sakigake,* as the reconfigured rump of *Shinto Sakigake* had been named in 1998. (In 2002 the remaining elements of *Sakigake* formed the Environmental Political Party Green Assembly [*Kankyosenta Midori no Kaigi*], which dissolved in 2004.)

In September 2002 Hatoyama won a narrow reelection victory over Kan, but a significant faction remained dissatisfied with his leadership. In December he resigned as president after other party leaders reacted strongly against his having unilaterally approached Ichiro Ozawa, then of the Liberal Party—LP (Jiyuto), about a merger aimed at uniting the opposition. Ozawa had formed the LP in January 1998 following the breakup of *Shinshinto.* While the LP was reported at its founding to have attracted the greatest number of *Shinshinto* members (including 54 lower house representatives), many analysts considered it unable to mount an effective campaign against the LDP because of its leader's autocratic style. Its membership in the lower house later fell to under 40, leaving it third among the opposition parties. In January 1999 the LP joined the LDP in a coalition government, reuniting conservative forces that had separated upon Ozawa's departure from the LDP in 1993. Ozawa's insistence on LDP support for additional LP candidates in the upcoming general election contributed to a parting of ways in April 2000. Rejecting Ozawa's leadership, more than half the LP Diet members abandoned the party and quickly formed the New Conservative Party (NCP), which reestablished the LDP linkage. In the June 2000 election the LP fared considerably better than the NCP, winning 22 seats, 4 more than it had held in the House of Representatives prior to dissolution.

The forced resignation of Hatoyama from the DPJ presidency in December 2002 over his unauthorized contact with Ozawa probably delayed, but did not prevent, unification of the DPJ and the LP. The merger ultimately occurred in September 2003, six weeks before a lower house election, in which the DPJ, now led by Naoto Kan, made significant gains, to 177 seats.

On May 10, 2004, Kan resigned as DPJ president, beset not only by an admission that he, like many other politicians, had not made all his required payments into the state pension plan but also by opposition from within the DPJ to his support for the LDP's pension reform bill. He was replaced on May 18 by the party's former secretary general, Katsuya OKADA, after the likely successor, Ichiro Ozawa, admitted six years of nonpayments into the pension plan.

In the House of Councilors election of July 2004, the DPJ won 50 seats, 1 more than the LDP, for a total of 83 seats, a gain of 24 over its total after the 2001 election. In late August Okada was elected to a two-year term as DPJ president, but the party's loss of more than one-third of its seats in the September 2005 general election led Okada to resign. His successor, the youthful Seiji MAEHARA, defeated Naoto Kan for the post, but on March 31, 2006, Maehara also resigned, accepting responsibility for the party's involvement in false accusations of financial impropriety directed against an LDP official. On April 7 the party's Diet members chose Ichiro Ozawa over Kan to fill the five-month balance of Maehara's term. In September, without challenge, Ozawa won a full term.

Capitalizing on public anger at the Abe government over financial and pension scandals, in July 2007 the DPJ won 60 of the 121 upper house seats up for election and thereby became the plurality party in the House of Councilors for the first time, with 109 of 242 seats. A crisis erupted in early November, however, when Ozawa resigned his leadership post after the DPJ refused to consider a grand coalition with the LDP. Two days later, at the urging of some party members, he withdrew his resignation. By mid-2008, with the People's New Party (PNP), the New Party Nippon (NPN), and some independents having agreed to sit as a bloc with the DPJ in the House of Councilors, the DPJ effectively controlled 120 upper house seats, enough to delay, if not thwart, government legislation.

In September 2008 Ichiro Ozawa was elected unopposed to a two-year term as party president. On May 11, 2009, however, he resigned in response to a scandal involving illegal political donations. Although Ozawa himself was not implicated, a senior aide had been indicted in the case, which, Ozawa feared, would undercut the party's chances to defeat the LDP in the upcoming legislative election. Five days later the party's secretary general, Yukio Hatoyama, was elected party president, easily defeating party vice president Katsuya Okada.

In the August 2009 elections to the House of Representatives, the DPJ and its allies, the SDP and the PNP, secured enough seats to permit Hatoyama's election as prime minister. Following Hatoyama's resignation in June 2010, Deputy Prime Minister Naoto Kan assumed leadership and subsequently was confirmed as prime minister. In September Kan defeated a challenge to his party presidency by Ozawa, by 721–491.

On August 29, 2011, in the fallout from criticism of Prime Minister Kan's handling of the aftermath of the earthquake and tsunami, the party elected Finance Minister Yoshihiko Noda as its leader, and Noda became the next prime minister.

In April 2012 Ozawa was found not guilty of violating campaign fundraising laws, he left the party to form the **People's Life First** (*Kokumin no Seikatsu ga Daiichi*). (See **Tomorrow Party**, below.) In September 2012 Noda was reelected as president of the DPJ. Also in September, Osaka mayor Toru HASIMOTO announced the creation of a new party, the **Japan Restoration Party**—JRP (*Nippon Ishin No Kai*), made up mostly of DPJ defectors (see below). Another group of defectors formed the **Kizuna Party** (*Shintō Kizuna*), led by Akira UCHIYAMA.

Following its defeat in the 2012 elections for the House of Representatives, in which the party dropped to 57 seats, Noda resigned. He was replaced by Banri Kaidea following a party election on December 25.

Leaders: Banri KAIEDA (President), Yoshihiko NODA (Former Prime Minister), Akira GUNJI, Akihiro OHATA (Secretary General).

Japan Restoration Party—JRP (*Nippon Ishin No Kai*). Formed in September 2012 by the Mayor of Osaka, Toru Hashimoto, the JRP was a right-wing, populist grouping that advocated deregulation, educational reform, and the abolition of the House of Councilors. The party was the first major party to be based in Osaka, and not Tokyo. In November 2012, the **Sunrise Party** (*Taiyō no Tō*) merged with the JRP. The SPJ was founded on April 10, 2010, and is also known as Rise Up, Japan! It was a conservative, nationalist (some critics have said xenophobic) formation that has called for reforming the taxation and social security systems and for revising the constitution. Sunrise Party leader, Shintaro ISHIHARA, became president of the combined grouping and led the party in the 2012 lower house balloting where the JRP won 54 seats. In January 2013 Hashimoto was again elected leader of the party.

Leaders: Toru HASHIMOTO (President), Ichiro MATUSI (Secretary General).

People's New Party—PNP (*Kokumin Shinto*). The PNP was formed in August 2005 under the leadership of former LDP legislator and Hashimoto faction leader Tamisuke WATANUKI and others who objected to Prime Minister Koizumi's plan for postal privatization. Many of the members of the new party had previously belonged to the LDP's Kamei faction, whose leader, Shizuka Kamei, had argued that postal reform would come at the expense of rural and needy constituents. In the September lower house election the PNP retained four seats (two of them proportional), including Kamei's. In July 2007 it won two seats in the House of Councilors, thereby maintaining its upper house representation at four, all of whom chose to sit in the DPJ opposition bloc.

In the August 2009 House of Representatives election, the PNP won three seats. Following the election, Shizuki Kamei was named party leader, after which the PNP joined the new DPJ-led government. Kamei stepped down as state minister of financial services and postal reform on June 11, 2010, because of the DPJ's decision not to make reversing some postal reforms a priority.

The PNP secretary general Mikio Shimoji was appointed minister of postal reform in October 2012. The PNP secured one seat in the 2012 House elections, and two seats in the upper chamber in 2013. However, in March 2013, party leader Shozaburo Jimi announced the dissolution of the PNP after the LDP rejected a merger bid.

Leaders: Shozaburo JIMI, Mikio SHIMOJI (Secretary General).

Social Democratic Party—SDP (*Shakai Minshuto*). Dating from 1945, the SDP was known until 1991 as the Japan Socialist Party (JSP) and then, until 1996, as the Social Democratic Party of Japan (SDPJ). The party long appeared to be more radical than its principal rival, the Japanese Communist Party, but a platform adopted in 1966 favored nonalignment, a nonaggression pact among the great powers, and a democratic transition from capitalism to socialism. In 1986 the party formally abandoned Marxist-Leninist doctrine.

Subsequently, the party's membership base was eroded by the decision of the pro-JSP *Sohyo* trade union federation to merge with the recently organized Private Sector Trade Union Confederation (*Rengo*). The SDPJ's lower house representation plummeted to 70 members in the June 1993 election (down from 136 in 1990), but the party remained second ranked and the LDP's overall defeat enabled the SDPJ to participate in the first non-LDP government in four decades. After leaving the new ruling coalition in April 1994, the SDPJ entered a coalition government with the LDP and *Shinto Sakigake* in June, providing Japan's first socialist prime minister, Tomiichi Murayama, since 1948.

In late 1994, 60 dissident members of the party's right wing, led by former chair Sadao YAMAHANA, formed a policy group within the SDPJ called the New Democratic Union—NDU (*Shin Minshu Rengo*). Early in 1995 Yamahana met with key members of three non-Socialist groups to create a new third party, and 24 SDPJ and other MPs subsequently agreed to form the Democratic League–Democratic New Party Club (*Minshu Rengo–Minshu Shinto Kurabu*). However, in the wake of the January 17, 1995, Kobe earthquake and, two months later, the Tokyo subway attack, the participants suspended their efforts, with most of them ultimately finding their way to the new DPJ.

Of 41 SDPJ seats up for election in the upper house poll of July 23, 1995, only 16 were retained. Weakened in 1996 primarily by the formation of the DPJ, the SDP suffered further electoral disaster in October, slumping to only 15 lower house seats. Fearing total domination by the LDP in a further coalition, the SDP opted instead to give qualified external support to a minority LDP government.

On May 30, 1998, the SDP announced it would end its loose alliance with the LDP at the end of the June legislative session. In the July upper house election, it recaptured only 5 of 12 contested seats it had previously held, but in June 2000 it increased its lower house membership to 19. Two months earlier, former prime minister Murayama had announced his retirement.

In the November 2003 lower house election the SDP won only six seats, which led longtime leader Takako Doi to resign as chair. Her deputy, Mizuho Fukushima, was named to succeed her. The SDP gained one seat in the September 2005 general election. At a party convention held in February 2006, it vowed to continue its opposition to Prime Minister Koizumi's policies and any constitutional change that would weaken the renunciation of war. In August 2009, allied with the DPJ, it retained seven lower house seats, but its share of the proportional vote fell to only 4.3 percent. The SDP then joined the DPJ-led government as a junior partner, with one cabinet post, but it withdrew on May 30, 2010, two days after State Minister of Consumer Affairs and Food Safety Fukushima was dismissed, because of the government's failure to negotiate a change in the planned U.S. military heliport on Okinawa. In August 2012 the SDP announced it would boycott the legislature after the passage of an increase in the consumption tax.

After securing only three seats in the December 2012 lower house balloting and two seats in the upper house in July 2013, Fukushima resigned.

Leaders: Tomiichi MURAYAMA, Takako DOI (Honorary Leaders); Seiji MATAICHI (Secretary General).

Japanese Communist Party—JCP (*Nihon Kyosanto*). Founded in the 1920s, the JCP traditionally relied on tight discipline to maximize its role in united front operations. Although it was "Eurocommunist" in outlook prior to the demise of the Soviet Union, the party focused primarily on domestic affairs, with an emphasis on the antinuclear issue. JCP strength in the House of Representatives crested at 39 in 1979 and fell to 15 after the 1993 poll.

No longer calling for abolition of the monarchy and immediate nationalization of core industries, the JCP attempted to recast itself as a democratic socialist party without abandoning its name. It had some success in the 1996 lower house election, rising to 26 seats by attracting disaffected left-oriented former supporters of the SDP, but it won only 20 in June 2000 and then fell to 9 in 2003. The party made no gains in the 2005 lower house election.

At the party's 24th Congress, held in January 2006, longtime leader Tetsuzo FUWA, citing age and health concerns as well as the need to "strengthen young energy" within party ranks, stepped down as chair of the Central Committee, a post that was temporarily left vacant. In July 2007 the JCP won only two seats in the House of Councilors, reducing its upper house representation to seven. Its platform for the August 2009 general election called for a "democratic revolution," foreign policy independence from the United States, and adoption of a rule-governed economy without "excessive probusiness policies." The JCP retained its nine block seats, based on 7 percent of the proportional vote, but after the July 2010 election it held only six in the upper house. In the 2012 balloting, it fell to 8 seats, but increased its number in the House of Councilors to 11 in 2013.

Leaders: Kazuo SHII (Chair), Tadayoshi ICHIDA (Secretary General).

Your Party (*Minna no To*). Formation of Your Party was announced on August 8, 2009, by Yoshimi Watanabe, a former state minister of administrative reform who had abandoned the LDP the preceding January because of opposition to the Aso government's policies, especially the slow pace of government reform. Watanabe called for reducing the control of the central government's bureaucracy, giving local governments more control, and reducing the size of both houses of the Diet. He also indicated that Your Party might cooperate with the DPJ if the DPJ won the September lower house election. At the polls Your Party won five seats, including three block seats based on a 4.3 percent share of the proportional vote.

Your Party entered the 2010 upper house election holding only one seat, but it picked up an additional ten, seven of them based on a third-best 13.6 percent of the proportional vote. Watanabe was reelected party leader in September 2012. In the 2012 balloting, the party won 18 seats, and then went on to secure 18 seats in the upper house.

Leaders: Yoshimi WATANABE (President and Leader in the House of Representatives), Keiichiro ASAO (Secretary General).

Other Parliamentary Parties:

New Party Daichi—True Democrats (*Shinto Daichi—Shinminshu*). New Party *Daichi* (Mother Earth) was established in August 2005 by former LDP member Muneo Suzuki, who had been convicted of bribery in 2003 but was free on bail. In the September 2005 lower house election Suzuki won a proportional seat and chose to sit as an independent.

In February 2008 a high court rejected Suzuki's appeal in the bribery case. He then appealed to the Supreme Court, which upheld his conviction and two-year prison sentence in September 2010. He was released on parole in December 2011. Three DPJ members of the House joined the grouping, which adopted its current name on January 5, 2012. The party won one seat in the House balloting in 2013.

Leader: Muneo SUZUKI.

New Renaissance Party—NRP (*Shinto Kaikaku*). The NRP, also known as the New Reform Party, was established in April 2010 under the leadership of Yoichi Masuzoe, a former LDP minister of health who, among other things, called for decentralization, an end to "money politics," and new economic policies. The NRP also attracted the members of the Japan Renaissance Party (JRP), which had been formed in 2008 by DPJ defector Hideo WATANABE, a member of the House of Councilors.

The NRP won one proportional seat in the July 2010 House of Councilors election, for a total of two. The NRP joined the boycott of the legislature following the passage of the consumption tax increase. After the 2013 House of Councilors elections, the NRP had three seats, including two independents who sat with the party.

Leaders: Yoichi MASUZOE (Chair), Testsuro YANO (Deputy Chair), Masakatsu KOIKE, Hiroyuki ARAI (Secretary General).

Okinawa Social Mass Party (*Okinawa Shakai Taishuto—Shadaito*). *Shadaito* was founded in 1950 on the island of Okinawa. It has long advocated the removal of U.S. military bases. Keiko Itokazu ran unsuccessfully as the opposition candidate in the November 2006 Okinawa gubernatorial election, but in 2007 she retained her seat in the national House of Councilors, where she sits as an independent. She maintained her seat in the July 2013 balloting.

Leader: Keiko ITOKAZU.

Tomorrow Party (*Mirai no To*). The Tomorrow Party was formed in November 2012 as an antinuclear party. Ichiro OZAWA and the small **People's Life First** (*Kokumin no Seikatsu ga Daiichi*) merged with the grouping in November 2012. The party won nine seats in the 2012 House elections. However, after the balloting, the Ozawa defected to form the **People's Life Party** (*Seikatsu no To*), and the Tomorrow Party subsequently dissolved in May 2013.

The small Green Wind (*Midori no Kaze*), formed in 2012 and led by Kuniko TANIOKA, gained representation in the House through defections from other parties.

Other Parties:

Happiness Realization Party—HRP (*Kofuku Jitsugento*). The conservative HRP, founded in May 2009, is associated with the Happy Science movement. It ran over 300 candidates in the August 2009 election, none successfully. In May 2010, however, a DPJ member of the House of Councilors, Yasuhiro OE, changed allegiance, giving the party its sole Diet member. The HRP failed to secure representation in the 2012 balloting.

Leader: Ryuho OKAWA (President).

New Party Nippon—NPN (*Shinto Nippon*). Formed on August 21, 2005, by Nagano's governor, Yasuo Tanaka, the NPN attracted four LDP lower house members who opposed postal privatization. The party won one proportional seat in the lower house election of September 2005 and also held one seat in the House of Councilors, but in early July 2007 both representatives resigned from the party over policy differences with Tanaka. On July 29 Tanaka won his own seat in the House of Councilors. He subsequently chose to join the DPJ-led opposition bloc.

In August 2009 Tanaka won a seat in the lower house, where he sat with the DPJ group. The party won no seats in 2012.

Leader: Yasuo TANAKA.

Other recently active minor parties include the Greens Japan (*Midori no Mirai;* literally, Green Future), which was formed in 2008 by merger of two parties: the Japan Greens, and the Rainbow and Greens. The **New Socialist Party** (*Shin Shakaito*) was founded in 1996 by left-wing elements of the SDP. Other groupings include the small **Tax Cuts Japan** (*Genzei Nippon*) led by Takashi KAWAMURA.

A variety of small right-extremist (*uyoku*) groups continue to function. Most are intensely nationalist "new wave" formations that espouse a revisionist view of Japan's imperialist history. There are also many small groups on the extreme left.

LEGISLATURE

The bicameral **Diet** (*Kokkai*) comprises an upper chamber (House of Councilors) and a lower chamber (House of Representatives). Real power resides in the lower chamber, although amendments to the constitution require two-thirds majorities in both houses. Both houses vote for prime minister, but the lower house results prevail in the absence of a consensus.

House of Councilors (*Sangiin*). The upper chamber, which replaced the prewar House of Peers, is renewed by halves every three years, each member serving a six-year term. The chamber cannot be dissolved. An October 2000 electoral law reduced the membership from 252 to 247 effective from the July 2001 election, and another 5 seats were eliminated in 2004. At each election, 73 members are chosen from 47 prefectural districts, returning from 1 to 4 members, and 48 members are elected on a proportional basis from national party lists.

As a result of the July 21, 2013, elections for 121 seats, the Liberal Democratic Party held 115 seats (65 newly won); Democratic Party of Japan and *Shin-Ryokufukai*, 59 (17); New *Komeito,* 20 (11); Your Party, 18 (8); Japanese Communist Party, 11 (8); Japan Restoration Party, 9 (9); Social Democratic Party, 3 (1); New Renaissance Party, 3 (1); People's New Party, 2 (1); Okinawa Social Mass Party, 1 (0); independent, 1 (0).

President: Masaki YAMAZAKI.

House of Representatives (*Shugiin*). An electoral reform bill adopted in 2000 specified that at the next election the existing 500-seat lower chamber would be reduced to 480 seats, of which 300 would be filled from single-member electoral districts by simple majority voting and 180 by proportional representation applied in 11 electoral blocks returning from 6 to 30 members. The term of office is four years. The election of December 16, 2013, produced the following results (block seats in parentheses): Liberal Democratic Party, 294 (57); Democratic Party of Japan, 57 (30); Japan Restoration Party, 54 (40); New *Komeito,* 31 (22); Your Party, 18 (14); Tomorrow Party, 9 (7); Japanese Communist Party, 8 (8); Social Democratic Party, 2 (1); People's New Party, 1 (0); New Party *Daichi,* 1 (1); independents, 5.

Speaker: Bunmei IIBUKI.

CABINET

[as of September 15, 2013]

Prime Minister	Shinzo Abe
Deputy Prime Minister	Taro Aso
Ministers	
Abduction Issue	Keiji Furuya
Administrative Reform	Tomoni Inada [f]
Agriculture, Forests, and Fisheries	Yoshimasa Hayashi
Chief Cabinet Secretary	Yoshihide Suga
Defense	Itsunori Onodera
Economic Revitalization	Akira Amari
Economy, Trade, and Industry	Toshimitsu Motegi
Education, Culture, Sports, Science, and Technology	Hakubun Shimomura
Environment	Nobuteru Ishihara
Finance	Taro Aso
Foreign Affairs	Fumio Kishida
Health, Labor, and Welfare	Norisha Tamura
Industrial Competitiveness	Toshimitsu Motegi
Information Technology	Ichita Yamamoto
Infrastructure Resilience	Keiji FuruyaKeiji Furuya
Internal Affairs and Communication	Yoshitaka Shindo
Justice	Sadakazu Tanigaki
Land, Infrastructure, Transport, and Tourism	Akihiro Ota (New *Komeito*)
Nuclear Incident Economic Countermeasures	Toshimitsu Motegi
Ocean Policy	Ichita Yamamoto
Reconstruction	Takumi Nemoto
Reform of Administration, Social Security, and Tax	Akira Amari
Regional Revitalization and Regional Government	Yoshitaka Shindo
Restoration From and Prevention of Nuclear Accident	Takumi Nemoto
Women's Empowerment and Childrearing	Masako Mori [f]
Ministers of State	
Consumer Affairs and Food Safety	Masako Mori [f]
Corporation in Support of Compensation for Nuclear Damage	Toshimitsu Motegi
Decentralization Reform	Yoshitaka Shindo
Disaster Management	Keiji Furuya
Economic and Fiscal Policy	Akira Amari
Financial Services	Taro Aso
Gender Equality	Masako Mori [f]
Measures for Declining Birthrate	Masako Mori [f]
Nuclear Emergency Preparedness	Nobuteru Ishihara
Okinawa and Northern Territories Affairs	Ichita Yamamoto
Regulatory Reform	Tomoni Inada [f]
Science and Technology Policy	Ichita Yamamoto
Space Policy	Ichita Yamamoto

[f] = female

Note: Except where noted, all members of the cabinet belong to the LDP.

INTERGOVERNMENTAL REPRESENTATION

Ambassador to the U.S.: Kenichiro SASAE.

U.S. Ambassador to Japan: Caroline KENNEDY.

Permanent Representative to the UN: Motohide YOSHIKAWA.

IGO Memberships (Non-UN): ADB, AfDB, APEC, EBRD, G-8, G-20, IADB, ICC, IEA, IOM, OECD, WTO.

JORDAN

Hashemite Kingdom of Jordan
al-Mamlakah al-Urduniyah al-Hashimiyah

Political Status: Independent constitutional monarchy established May 25, 1946; present constitution adopted January 8, 1952.

Area: 34,495 sq. mi. (89,206 sq. km), excluding West Bank territory of 2,270 sq. mi. (5,879 sq. km).

Population: Both figures exclude Palestinians in the West Bank, over which Jordan abandoned de jure jurisdiction in 1988. 6,491,738 (2012E—UN); 6,482,081 (2013E—U.S. Census).

Major Urban Center (2011E—UN): AMMAN (2,155,056).

Official Language: Arabic.

Monetary Unit: Dinar (official rate November 1, 2013: 0.71 dinar = $1US).

Sovereign: King ABDULLAH ibn Hussein (King Abdullah II); assumed the throne on February 7, 1999, following the death of King HUSSEIN ibn Talal; coronation ceremony held on June 9, 1999.

Heir to the Throne: Undesignated. Prince HAMZEH ibn Hussein, half-brother of the king, had been designated crown prince on February 7, 1999, but on November 28, 2004, Abdullah stripped him of the crown, making the king's eldest son, 11-year-old Hussein, heir apparent.

Prime Minister: Abdullah ENSOUR, appointed by the king on October 4, 2012, following the resignation of Fayez TARAWNEH, and sworn in with the new government on October 11, 2012; reappointed on March 9.

THE COUNTRY

Jordan, a nearly landlocked kingdom in the heart of the Middle East, is located on a largely elevated, rocky plateau that slopes downward to the Jordan Valley, the Dead Sea, and the Gulf of Aqaba. Most of the land is desert, providing the barest grazing for the sheep and goats of Bedouin tribesmen, whose traditional nomadic lifestyle has largely been replaced by village settlement. With Israeli occupation in June 1967 of the territory on the West Bank of the Jordan River, the greater part of the country's arable area was lost. The population is mainly Arab, but numerous ethnic groups have intermixed with the indigenous inhabitants. Islam is the state religion, the majority being members of the Sunni sect. Less than 10 percent of Jordanian women are in the workforce, mainly in subsistence activities and trading; more than half are illiterate (as compared with 16 percent of men), with the percentage of women enrolled in school dropping dramatically at marriage age. Although enfranchised in 1974, female participation in government has been minimal. Some cabinets have included several female appointees; in addition, a woman was elected to the House of Representatives for the first time in 1993. Although no women won seats in elections held June 17, 2003, six women were appointed to the house under a February 2003 amendment that reserved six seats for them. Reforms to the electoral law in 2012 increased the number of seats for women to 15, and 18 were elected in 2013.

Jordan's economy and its political life have been dominated in recent times by dislocations and uncertainties stemming from the Arab conflict with Israel. The original East Bank population of some 400,000 was swollen in 1948–1950 by the addition of large numbers of West Bank Palestinian Arabs and refugees from Israel, most of them either settled agriculturalists or townspeople of radically different background and outlook from those of the seminomadic East Bankers. Additional displacements followed the Arab-Israeli war of June 1967. The society has also been strained by a 3.5 percent annual natural increase in population, rapid urbanization, scarce water resources, and the frustrations of the unemployed refugees, many of whom have declined assimilation in the hope of returning to "Palestine." (It has been estimated that over 50 percent of the people currently residing in Jordan are of Palestinian origin, about two-thirds of them still formally considered refugees.)

Agricultural production is insufficient to feed the population and large quantities of foodstuffs (especially grain) have to be imported, while many of the refugees are dependent on rations distributed by the UN Relief and Works Agency for Palestine Refugees in the Near East (UNRWA). Major exports include phosphates, potash, and fertilizers. Manufacturing is dominated by production of import substitutes, mainly cement, some consumer goods, and processed foods.

Annual GDP growth averaged 6.7 percent from 2000 to 2008, though official unemployment was more than 12 percent, and unofficial estimates were as high as 30 percent (for information on the Jordanian economy prior to 2000, please see the 2010 *Handbook*). Inflation throughout the same period averaged 4.3 percent per year, although it spiked to 14.9 percent in 2008. The robust growth was attributed, in large part, to Jordan's far-reaching structural reforms, which included controlling public debt and increasing privatization. Also, strong performance in the construction and tourism sectors offset weaker demand for exports. Exports to the United States have grown since a bilateral free trade agreement took effect in 2001. In the wake of the global economic downturn, annual GDP growth slowed to 2.7 percent in 2009 but rose to 3.1 percent in 2010 and 2.6 in 2011. Inflation in 2011 was 4.4 percent, and official unemployment was 12.9 percent. That year, the government's deficit rose to 6.1 percent of GDP. In 2012, GDP grew by 2.8 percent, while inflation was 4.8 percent, and unemployment, 12.2 percent. GDP per capita was $4,878. That year, the IMF approved a special $2.3 billion program to promote economic growth in Jordan, while Kuwait, Saudi Arabia, Qatar, and the United Arab Emirates pledged $5 billion over a five-year period.

GOVERNMENT AND POLITICS

Political background. The territory then known as Transjordan, which only included land east of the Jordan River, was carved out of the Ottoman Empire in the aftermath of World War I, during which Arabs, with the assistance of British forces, had rebelled against Turkish rule. British administration of the region was formalized under a League of Nations Mandate, which also covered the territory between the Jordan River and the Mediterranean (Palestine). Over the next two decades, gradual autonomy was granted to Transjordan under the leadership of ABDULLAH ibn Hussein, a member of the region's Hashemite dynasty who had been named emir by the British in 1921. Full independence came when Abdullah was proclaimed king and a new constitution was promulgated on May 25, 1946, although special treaty relationships with Britain were continued until 1957. The country adopted its current name in 1949, its boundary having expanded into the West Bank under an armistice concluded with Israel, with which Arab states had been in conflict since Britain relinquished its Palestinian mandate in 1948.

Following the assassination of Abdullah in 1951 and the deposition of his son TALAL in 1952, Talal's son HUSSEIN ascended the throne at the age of 16 and was crowned king on May 2, 1953. Hussein's turbulent reign was subsequently marked by the loss of all territory west of the Jordan River in the 1967 Arab-Israeli War (see Israel map, p. 642), assassination and coup attempts by intransigent Arab nationalist elements in Jordan and abroad, and intermittent efforts to achieve a limited modus vivendi with Israel. The most serious period of internal tension after the 1967 war involved relations with the Palestinian commando (fedayeen) organizations, which began to use Jordanian territory as a base for operations against Israel. In 1970 in what became known as Black September, a virtual civil war ensued between commando and royalist armed forces, with the fedayeen ultimately being expelled, primarily to Lebanon, in mid-1971. The expulsion led to the suspension of aid to Jordan by Kuwait and other Arab governments; it was restored following Jordan's nominal participation in the 1973 war against Israel.

In accordance with a decision reached during the October 1974 Arab summit conference in Rabat, Morocco, to recognize the Palestine Liberation Organization (PLO) as the sole legitimate representative of the Palestinians, King Hussein announced that the PLO would thenceforth have responsibility for the West Bank but stopped short of formally relinquishing his kingdom's claim to the territory. The Jordanian government was subsequently reorganized to exclude most Palestinian representatives, and the National Assembly, whose lower house contained 30 West Bank members, entered what was to become a ten-year period of inactivity (see Legislature, below).

In a move toward reconciliation with Palestinian elements, King Hussein met in Cairo in March 1977 with PLO leader Yasir ARAFAT, a subsequent meeting occurring in Jordan immediately after the September 1978 Camp David accords. In March 1979 the two met again near Amman and agreed to form a joint committee to coordinate opposition to the Egyptian-Israeli peace treaty, while in December the king named Sharif Abd al-Hamid SHARAF to replace Mudar BADRAN as head of a new government that also included six West Bank Palestinians. Sharaf's death on July 3, 1980, resulted in the elevation of Deputy Prime Minister Dr. Qasim al-RIMAWI, whose incumbency ended on August 28 by the reappointment of Badran. Following a breakdown of negotiations with Arafat in April 1983 over possible peace talks with Israel and a continued deceleration in economic growth, the king reconvened the National Assembly on January 9, 1984, and secured its assent to the replacement of deceased West Bank deputies in the lower house. The next day the king appointed Interior Minister and former intelligence chief Ahmed OBEIDAT to succeed Badran as prime minister in a cabinet reshuffle that increased Palestinian representation to 9 members out of 20. Obeidat resigned on April 4, 1985, the king naming Zaid al-RIFAI as his successor.

In mid-1988, after the outbreak of the intifada and following an Arab League call for PLO governance of the West Bank, Hussein abruptly severed all "legal and administrative" links to it, discontinued the five-year (1986–1990) aid package for its Palestinian population, and dissolved the House of Representatives. Subsequently, a declared intention to elect a house composed exclusively of East Bank members was suspended pending amendments to the electoral law.

On April 24, 1989, Prime Minister Rifai resigned because of widespread rioting in response to price increases imposed as part of the IMF-mandated austerity program. Three days later a new government, headed by Field Marshal Sharif Zaid ibn SHAKER (theretofore Chief of the Royal Court), was announced, with a mandate to prepare for a parliamentary balloting.

On November 8, 1989, following a campaign revealing continued support for the monarchy but intolerance of martial law and government corruption, Jordan held its first national election in 22 years. Urban fundamentalist and leftist candidates won impressive victories, generating concern on the part of a regime whose principal supporters had long been the country's rural conservatives. Nevertheless, following the election, the king lifted a number of martial law restrictions, appointed a new Senate, and reappointed Badran as prime minister. The cabinet that was announced on December 6 included six Palestinians but no members of the Muslim Brotherhood, despite the latter's strong electoral showing.

During the first half of 1990 the regime signaled continued interest in a more inclusive political process, meeting with Palestinian and Communist Party leaders and in April appointing a broadly representative group of individuals to a newly formed National Charter Commission. Subsequently, in a move indicative of popular support for Iraq's position in the Gulf crisis and the enhanced status of the Muslim fundamentalists, the king on January 1, 1991, named a prominent Palestinian, Tahir al-MASRI, and five Muslim Brotherhood members to the cabinet.

At a national conference on June 9, 1991, the king and the leaders of all the country's major political groups signed an annex to the constitution that granted parties the right to organize in return for their acceptance of the legitimacy of the Hashemite monarchy. Additional political reform was also expected with the appointment on June 18 of the liberal and (despite his Gulf war stance) generally pro-Western Masri to replace the conservative Badran as prime minister. However, Masri's attempt to form a broad-based coalition government foundered as the Muslim Brotherhood, excluded from his cabinet because of its strident opposition to Middle East peace negotiations, and conservatives, apparently concerned over accelerated democratization as well as their dwindling cabinet influence, joined in October to demand the government's resignation. Their petition, signed by a majority of the members of the (then recessed) House of Representatives being tantamount to a nonconfidence vote, Masri felt obliged to step down on November 16. Signaling a reassertion of monarchical control and an apparent slowdown in the pace of democratization, the king reappointed Shaker to head a new government, which, accommodating the conservatives but not the Brotherhood, survived a nonconfidence motion on December 16 by a vote of 46–27.

On April 1, 1992, King Hussein abolished all that remained of martial law regulations introduced in the wake of the 1967 Arab-Israeli war. Several months later the political party ban was formally lifted, and party registration began in December.

On May 29, 1993, Prime Minister Shaker was replaced by Abd al-Salam al-MAJALI, whose initial mission was to oversee the election of a new house. Although the balloting on November 8 was the first to be conducted on a multiparty basis, the effect was minimal, some of the new groups charging that electoral law changes and campaign restrictions had hindered their effectiveness. Only the Muslim Brotherhood's Islamic Action Front—IAF (*Jabhat al-Amal al-Islami*), with 16 seats, secured significant representation, while 47 independents, many of them expected to be broadly supportive of the king, were elected.

Majali was reappointed to lead the new government announced on December 1, 1993, his caretaker status being extended pending the outcome of the talks launched between Amman and Tel Aviv in the wake of the recent Israeli-PLO accord. On January 5, 1995, following the signing of the Jordanian-Israeli peace treaty (see Foreign relations, below), Majali stepped down as prime minister in favor of Shaker, whose new government was appointed three days later. Included in the 31-member cabinet were 17 house members, although the IAF, leader of the anti-treaty opposition, was again unrepresented.

As on three earlier occasions, Shaker, the king's cousin and long-time confidant, assumed the prime ministership in 1995 at a time of some difficulty for the regime. Although the government preferred to emphasize its economic plans, public attention focused primarily on the peace treaty, opposition to normalizing relations with Tel Aviv having been wider, or at least more vocal, than expected. However, the king adopted a relatively hard line toward the accord's opponents, stifling dissent somewhat, even at the expense, in the opinion of some observers, of a slowdown in the democratization process. Consequently, a conference planned by antitreaty Islamic, leftist, and nationalist parties for late May was banned by the government. Perhaps partly as a consequence, the impact of many of the parties was minimal when the first multiparty municipal elections were conducted on July 11–12, entrenched tribal influence dominating the balloting.

On February 4, 1996, King Hussein appointed Abd al-Karim KABARITI, another close friend of his and the former foreign affairs minister, to succeed Shaker. Once again the IAF was excluded from the new cabinet, although members of several other fledgling parties were given portfolios. Charged with revitalizing the economy, Kabariti imposed IMF-mandated reforms that led to increases in the price of bread, precipitating Jordan's worst unrest of the decade when riots broke out in August in the northern city of Karak and the poorer sections of Amman. While many of the demonstrators were arrested, the king later in the year quietly ordered a rollback in the price of bread and granted amnesty to those involved in the riots.

On March 19, 1997, Hussein dismissed Prime Minister Kabariti and reappointed Majali, whose primary task once again was to oversee the election of a new lower house. Most opposition parties and groups (including the Muslim Brotherhood) boycotted the November 4 balloting, citing new press restrictions and perceived progovernment bias in the electoral law. A number of prominent personalities, including former prime ministers Obeidat and Masri, also urged voters to stay away from the polls. Consequently, the balloting was dominated by progovernment, independent tribal candidates. On November 22 Hussein appointed a new 40-member House of Notables, none of whom was a member of the Islamist opposition. Meanwhile Majali remained as prime minister, although the cabinet was extensively reshuffled on

February 17, 1998, in the wake of an outbreak of pro-Iraqi demonstrations, which had been quashed by security forces.

In mid-1998 it was confirmed that King Hussein was being treated for cancer, and on August 12 he delegated some authority to his brother, HASSAN ibn Talal, who had been crown prince and heir to the throne since 1965. Hassan quickly orchestrated the removal of the Majali government, which resigned on August 19, having become the focus of popular discontent over a number of issues, including the mishandling of a water crisis in Amman and the embarrassing overstatement of economic growth. On August 20 Crown Prince Hassan appointed a new cabinet headed by Fayez TARAWNEH, a U.S.-educated economist and former chief of the royal court. The crown prince also launched a dialogue with the nation's political parties and groups (including the Muslim Brotherhood), which had remained marginalized as Jordan's proposed democratization program stalled under the influence of ongoing regional tensions, and pledged that the administration of Prime Minister Tarawneh would provide a "safety net" to protect the poor from the effects of IMF-mandated fiscal reforms. Subsequently, Hassan attempted to effect changes at the top levels of the military, an initiative that angered Hussein, who returned in the fall to resume full monarchical authority. The perceived "meddling" in army matters was one of the reasons King Hussein cited for the dismissal of his brother as heir apparent on January 24, 1999. Other factors reportedly included the king's long-standing interest in reestablishing a direct father-to-son line of succession and his belief that his eldest son ABDULLAH (married to a Palestinian woman) would ultimately prove a more popular leader than Hassan.

King Hussein died on February 7, and Abdullah assumed the throne the same day, becoming Abdullah II and taking an oath to protect "the constitution and the nation" before the National Assembly. (Formal coronation ceremonies were held on June 9.) Representatives from some 75 countries (including nearly 50 heads of state) attended the funeral of King Hussein on February 8, 1999, underscoring the widespread respect he had earned for his peacemaking efforts and his skillful management of Jordanian affairs during his 46-year reign. World leaders also wanted to signal their support for King Abdullah II, a newcomer to the international stage suddenly forced into the role of a prominent participant in the Middle East peace process. The new king, who had been educated in the West and whose mother was from the United Kingdom, promised a more open government with fewer press restrictions and possible revision of the electoral code to facilitate greater party influence. However, he declared the economy to be his top priority, announcing his support for budget reduction and other reforms recommended by the IMF.

Immediately upon assuming the throne, King Abdullah announced that he was "absolutely committed" to peace with Israel, despite the fact that many Jordanians appeared to have become disenchanted with that particular aspect of his father's legacy. Underscoring its antimilitancy posture, the regime in the fall of 1999 ordered the closing of the Jordanian offices of Hamas and expelled several leaders of the Islamic fundamentalist movement, which spearheads hard-line anti-Israeli sentiment in the West Bank (and Gaza). In addition, security forces arrested a group of militants with reported ties to the alleged international terrorism organization of Osama bin Laden, charging the detainees with plotting to attack U.S. and Israeli targets. At the same time, Abdullah concentrated on improving ties with Syria, Lebanon, Kuwait, and other neighbors, and, in an apparent further attempt to promote Arab solidarity, called for the end of UN sanctions against Iraq.

On March 4 King Abdullah appointed a new 23-member cabinet headed by Abd al-Rauf al-RAWABDEH, a prominent proponent of economic reform. However, Rawabdeh, reportedly under pressure from the king and his government, resigned on June 18, 2000. Ali ABU al-RAGHEB, a businessman and former trade minister, was appointed to form a new government, which was sworn in on June 19. The change in prime ministers was attributed to the perceived failure of the Rawabdeh government to achieve effective economic change as well as to Rawabdeh's reported "autocratic" style, which had apparently contributed to friction between his administration and the National Assembly. The appointment of Abu al-Ragheb as prime minister was generally well received, the business community in particular endorsing his stated goals of attracting foreign investment and promoting tourism. Investors also welcomed the country's accession to the World Trade Organization in April 2000 and the signing of a rare free trade agreement with the United States later in the year. Meanwhile, political reform remained subordinate to the economic focus, King Abdullah reportedly relying even more heavily on secret security and intelligence services than his father had in the later years of his reign.

On April 23, 2001, Abdullah announced the postponement of legislative elections scheduled for November. On July 22, he approved a new electoral law calling for the redrawing of voting districts, increasing the number of seats in the House of Representatives from 80 to 104 (later raised to 110 to accommodate a six-seat quota for women), and lowering the voting age from 19 to 18.

On June 16, 2001, the king dissolved the National Assembly in anticipation of new balloting for the House of Representatives, expected in November. However, in view of the roiling Israeli-Palestinian conflict, polling was postponed until September 2002. The king in August 2002 further delayed new elections until March 2003, citing "difficult regional circumstances" that included a potential U.S. attack on neighboring Iraq. Analysts suggested that the government feared "radical elements" might take advantage of surging anti-Israel and anti-U.S. sentiment within the Jordanian population to present a significant electoral challenge to the establishment unless regional tensions were reduced. Elections were finally held on June 17, 2003, two months after the fall of Baghdad to U.S.-led invading forces and the removal of Saddam Hussein from power. Progovernment legislators held a clear majority in the new legislature, but Islamist and tribal members opposed the king's promotion of women's rights. Reforms allowing women to initiate divorce, raising the legal age for marriage to 18, and stiffening penalties for "honor killings" of women were weakened or blocked by legislators arguing that such measures threatened family stability. In the balloting the IAF made a significant showing with 17 seats. Meanwhile, a new 28-member cabinet, headed by al-Ragheb, was announced. Criticized for failing to bring about promised reform, al-Ragheb resigned in October and was replaced on October 25 by Faisal al-FAYIZ, formerly chief of the royal court.

Popular opinion presented the government with a difficult act in maintaining strong ties with the United States, and King Abdullah II called on Washington to establish a timetable for creation of a Palestinian state as a means of tempering Arab frustration over the lack of progress in the Middle East peace process. At the same time, Jordan was a solid supporter of the U.S.-led "war on terrorism" following the al-Qaida attacks on the United States in September 2001. In addition to contributing troops to peacekeeping forces in Afghanistan, following the attempted ouster of the Taliban and al-Qaida, the government announced in 2002 that it had thwarted planned attacks against U.S. and Israeli targets through several roundups of Islamic militants. However, critics of the government charged that the crackdown had undercut political liberalization by barring most public demonstrations, dampening legitimate dissent, and tightening restrictions on the media.

On October 28, 2002, Laurence Foley, senior U.S. diplomat, became the first Western official to be assassinated in Jordan. Of the 11 suspects tried for the crime, 8 were sentenced to death. Among them was Abu Musab al-ZARQAWI, who was tried in absentia and subsequently linked to the armed resistance to U.S. forces in Iraq. He was sentenced to death (in absentia) two more times for plotting failed attacks inside Jordan and at the border with Iraq. (Al-Zarqawi was killed in a U.S. airstrike near Baquba, Iraq, in June 2006.)

King Abdullah's effort to maintain Jordan's role as mediator in the Middle East resulted in his holding in June 2003 a summit in the Red Sea port of Aqaba with U.S. president George W. Bush, Israeli prime minister Ariel Sharon, and Palestinian National Authority (PNA) prime minister Mahmud Abbas to launch the U.S.-backed "road map" for peace.

U.S.-Jordanian relations were strained by the 2003 Iraq invasion, which Jordanians strongly opposed. In the run-up to war, Abdullah warned the United States and the United Kingdom that an attack on Iraq could lead to "regional destabilization." He ultimately adopted an ambivalent stance, allowing the stationing of U.S. forces near the Iraqi border while opposing the invasion. When Iraq's Sunnis boycotted legislative elections held January 30, 2005, the king warned of an impending "Shiite crescent" stretching from Iran to Lebanon that might destabilize the Sunni-led status quo in the Arab world. Relations with Iraq warmed in 2005 after King Abdullah agreed to pardon Iraqi deputy prime minister Ahmed Chalabi, who had been sentenced in absentia by a Jordanian court in 1992 for bank fraud. In October 2005 the interim Iraqi prime minister visited Amman, and the two countries signed a security cooperation agreement.

On April 4, 2005, Fayiz resigned amid criticism of his slow pace of reform. The king appointed Adnan BADRAN, a 70-year-old academic, to replace him and reduced the number of cabinet positions as part of his effort to streamline government. Widely reported to be unpopular, the finance minister, Bassam AWADALLAH, resigned on June 15, forcing Badran to shuffle eight ministers in the cabinet on July 3. Fifty-three legislators had threatened a no-confidence vote unless Badran overhauled his economic team and included more ministers from the south. The reshuffled cabinet included four women, and Adel QUDAH replaced Awadallah.

On November 9, 2005, near-simultaneous bombings in Amman at three hotels frequented by Westerners killed 60 people and injured more than 100, prompting King Abdullah to call for a "global strategy" against terrorism. Demonstrators filled the streets, denouncing the attacks and those who claimed responsibility: al-Zarqawi and al-Qaida (see al-Qaida under the article on Afghanistan). Eleven top officials, including the national security adviser, resigned on November 15, and days later Abdullah appointed Marouf BAKHET to the national security post. On November 24, Badran resigned amid reports that opinion polls rated the government the lowest of any administration after 200 days in office. Vowing that he would not allow the attacks to derail the government's National Agenda for reform, the king subsequently named Bakhet—widely regarded as a proponent of change—as prime minister.

Amid increased tensions in the region, Jordan, at the request of the Iraqi government, closed its border with Iraq to all Arab citizens (including Jordanians) in early 2006, and it subsequently temporarily closed its border to Palestinian refugees. Meanwhile, tensions heightened inside Jordan as the government increased fuel prices in anticipation of the expiration of oil grants from Saudi Arabia, Kuwait, and the United Arab Emirates. Islamist groups' requests to hold demonstrations against the increases, set to end by 2007, were repeatedly denied by the government.

In the wake of the Palestinian election victory by Hamas in 2006, King Abdullah adopted a moderate approach, stating that Jordan would not "disregard the new Palestinian government before reviewing its agenda," and he continued to endorse Israeli-Palestinian negotiations. However, Jordan subsequently took a harder line, accusing Hamas of smuggling arms and plotting attacks inside the country. According to reports, Jordan was fearful that the "rising tide of radical Islam it sees originating from Iran" threatened its stability.

A woman convicted in the 2005 hotel bombings was sentenced to death in September 2006, shortly after a gunman was arrested in an unrelated incident in which he was charged with killing one tourist and wounding six other people, including a Jordanian police officer. In several other cases throughout the year, numerous people identified as belonging to various terrorist organizations, including al-Qaida, were sentenced to death or lengthy prison terms. Among those convicted were nine men involved in a 2005 rocket attack on a U.S. warship in the port of Aqaba and two al-Qaida members who were planning to carry out attacks on Jewish and U.S. targets during the millennium celebration.

The cabinet was reshuffled on November 22, 2006, and the new government was sworn in on November 27. In March 2007 the parliament approved a new law that requires political parties to have a founding membership of 500 rather than 50 in order to be legally recognized (see Current issues, below). A minor cabinet reshuffle occurred on September 2, 2007, following the July resignations of the health and water and irrigation ministers in the wake of a crisis involving contaminated drinking water.

Municipal elections on July 31, 2007, marking the first time Jordanians could elect city mayors, were boycotted by the IAF, which accused the government of vote rigging. Following elections to the lower house of parliament on November 20, 2007, supporters of the king, described as mainly Bedouins and centrists—all independents—secured an overwhelming majority of the 110 seats, with representation of the IAF reduced to 6 seats. On November 22 the king appointed Nader DAHABI to succeed Bakhet as prime minister. Dahabi, 61, a former transport minister and the head of an economic development zone, was sworn in with a new government (including eight members of the previous cabinet and four women) on November 25.

The cabinet was extensively reshuffled on February 23, 2009. On November 23, after a protracted legislative paralysis in which a major income tax–reform measure languished without legislative action, King Abdullah II ordered the dissolution of the House of Representatives and called for early elections. Prime Minister Dahabi, whose government had been criticized for its handling of the recent economic downturn, resigned on December 9 and was succeeded by Samir al-RIFAI, a businessman and former minister to the royal court. Rifai announced a new cabinet on December 14. The Senate was renewed on December 20, and former prime minister Masri was appointed president of the chamber. Twenty-seven new senators were appointed, and 28 others had their mandates renewed. Meanwhile, new elections were postponed until November 9, 2010, to permit the new government to enact electoral reforms (see Current issues, below). Rifai reshuffled the cabinet on July 28, 2010. Following legislative elections to the House of Representatives on November 9, 2010, Prime Minister Samir al-Rifai resigned on November 21 but was reappointed prime minister of a reshuffled cabinet on November 24. The king appointed a new Senate the following day.

Following widespread protests over unemployment, King Abdullah II dismissed Rifai and the cabinet on February 1, 2011, and designated former prime minister Marouf al-BAKHIT to form a new government. Demonstrations continued through the spring, prompting the king to appoint a royal committee to revise the constitution (see Current issues, below). In July the cabinet was reshuffled following the resignation of two ministers who were accused of corruption. Bakhit resigned on October 17, and Awm al-KHASAWNEH was named to replace him (see Current issues, below). A new cabinet was appointed on October 24. The following day, the king appointed a new Senate.

Khasawneh subsequently resigned on April 26, 2012 (see Current issues, below). The king appointed Fayez Tarawneh to replace him. A reshuffled cabinet was sworn in on May 3, consisting mainly of new appointees, in an effort to accelerate political reforms. Tarawneh was dismissed on October 4, when the king appointed Abdullah Ensour as prime minister. A new government was sworn in on October 11.

Following legislative elections on January 23, 2013 (see Current issues, below), Ensour and his cabinet resigned, but remained in place as a caretaker government. The king reappointed Ensour on March 9, and a new cabinet was approved on March 30.

Constitution and government. Jordan's present constitution, promulgated in 1952, provides for authority jointly exercised by the king and a bicameral National Assembly. Executive power is vested in the monarch, who is also supreme commander of the armed forces. He appoints the prime minister and cabinet; orders general elections; convenes, adjourns, and dissolves the assembly; and approves and promulgates laws. The assembly, in joint session, can override his veto of legislation and must also approve all treaties. The House of Representatives is comprised of 110 members (increased from 80 in 2003) elected via universal suffrage, while members of the senate-like House of Notables are appointed by the king. The present multiparty system was authorized in a National Charter signed by the king and leaders of the country's major political movements in 1991. The judicial system is headed by the High Court of Justice. Lower courts include courts of appeal, courts of first instance, and magistrates' courts. There are also special courts for religious (both Christian and Muslim) and tribal affairs. Martial law, imposed at the time of the 1967 Arab-Israeli war, provided for military tribunals to adjudicate crimes against "state security." Although many other martial law elements—such as the ban on large public meetings and restrictions on the press and freedom of speech—were suspended by King Hussein in 1989 and 1991 decrees, the special courts were not abolished until martial law was totally repealed on April 1, 1992.

Local government administration is based on the five East Bank provinces (*alwiyah*) of Amman, Irbid, Balqa, Karak, and Man, each headed by a commissioner. The *alwiyah* are further subdivided into districts (*aqdiyah*) and subdistricts (*nawahin*). The towns and larger villages are governed by partially elected municipal councils, while the smaller villages are often governed by traditional village headmen (*mukhtar*s). Under an election reform law adopted in 2007, all mayors and local councils are directly elected, except in Amman, where half the council members continue to be appointed by the king. The law also includes a 20 percent quota for women in local councils.

The press has long been subject to censorship. Most newspapers have been suspended more than once for publishing stories considered objectionable by the government. In March 2007 the parliament adopted amendments to the press and publications law that allowed for heavy fines for journalists who committed perceived violations. However, following widespread criticism from media groups and human rights organizations, legislators struck down imprisonment for journalists. In 2012 the watchdog group Reporters Without Borders ranked Jordan 134th out of 179 countries in freedom of the press.

Foreign relations. Historically reliant on aid from Britain and the United States, Jordan has maintained a generally pro-Western orientation in foreign policy. Its pro-Iraqi tilt during the Gulf crisis and war of

1990–1991 (see below) was a notable exception, prompting the suspension of Western aid and imposition of a partial blockade of the Jordanian port of Aqaba to interdict shipments headed for Iraq in violation of UN sanctions. However, relations with the West improved rather quickly thereafter, several meetings between King Hussein and U.S. President Bill Clinton yielding preliminary agreement on external debt rescheduling and the resumption of aid.

Regional affairs have long been dominated by the Arab-Israeli conflict, Jordan's particular concerns being the occupation of the West Bank by Israel since 1967 and the related Palestinian refugee problem, both of which gave rise to policy disputes between King Hussein and PLO Chair Yasir Arafat. Jordan tended to be somewhat less intransigent toward Israel than many of its Arab neighbors. After initially criticizing the PLO for conducting secret talks with Israel, Hussein (who over the years had also had secret contacts with Israel) eventually endorsed the Israeli-PLO accord signed in September 1993. Subsequently, Jordanian and Israeli officials began meeting openly for the first time in decades to discuss such matters as water resources, the refugee problem, border delineation, and economic cooperation. Then, on July 25, 1994, King Hussein and Israeli Prime Minister Yitzhak Rabin signed a declaration ending the 46-year-old state of war between their two countries. The agreement was followed by the signing at the Jordanian-Israeli border on October 26 of a formal peace accord in which each nation pledged to respect the other's sovereignty and territorial integrity, based on a recently negotiated demarcation of their mutual border. Cooperation was also pledged on trade, tourism, banking, finance, and in numerous other areas. Significantly, President Clinton attended the treaty ceremony, promising substantial debt relief and increased aid to Jordan in return for its participation in the peace process. Arafat was conspicuously absent among the 5,000 invited guests, many Palestinians having been angered by the agreement's reference to Jordan's "special role" as "guardian" of Islamic holy sites in Jerusalem. However, the concern appeared to lessen somewhat in January 1995 when Jordan and the PLO signed an accord endorsing the Palestinian claim to sovereignty over East Jerusalem while also committing the signatories to wide-ranging cooperation in the financial, trade, and service sectors. In October 1996 King Hussein visited the West Bank for the first time since 1967, the trip apparently having been designed to underscore the king's support for the development of Palestinian autonomy under Arafat's direction. The king also played a significant intermediary role in the January 1997 agreement reached by Arafat and Israeli Prime Minister Benjamin Netanyahu regarding additional Israeli troop withdrawals from the West Bank.

Diplomatic relations with Egypt, suspended in 1979 upon conclusion of the latter's accord with Israel, were reestablished in September 1984. Prior to the Gulf crisis of the 1990s, relations with Saudi Arabia and other Middle Eastern monarchies were for the most part more cordial than those with such left-wing republics as Libya.

Relations with Syria have been particularly volatile, a period of reconciliation immediately after the 1967 war deteriorating because of differences over guerrilla activity. In September 1970 a Syrian force that came to the aid of the fedayeen against the Jordanian army was repulsed, with diplomatic relations being severed the following July but restored in the wake of the 1973 war. Despite numerous efforts to improve ties, relations again deteriorated in the late 1970s and early 1980s, exacerbated by Jordanian support for Iraq in the Gulf war with Iran. A cooperation agreement signed in September 1984 was immediately threatened by Syria's denunciation of the resumption of relations with Egypt; earlier, on February 22, relations with Libya had been broken because of the destruction of the Jordanian embassy in Tripoli, an action termed by Amman as a "premeditated act" by the Qadhafi regime. Thereafter, renewed rapprochement with Syria, followed by a resumption of diplomatic relations with Libya in September 1987, paved the way for a minimum of controversy during a November Arab League summit in Amman. A Syrian-Jordanian economic summit in February 1989 was preceded in January by a meeting between Hussein and Saudi Arabia's King Fahd to renegotiate an expiring agreement that in 1988 was reported to have provided approximately 90 percent of Jordan's foreign aid receipts.

Jordan's professed goal of maintaining neutrality in the wake of Iraq's occupation of Kuwait in 1990 was challenged by the anti-Iraqi allies who accused the regime of being sympathetic to Baghdad, citing the king's description of Saddam Hussein as an "Arab patriot" and Amman's resistance to implementing UN sanctions against Iraq. On September 19 Saudi Arabia, angered by King Hussein's criticism of the buildup of Western forces in the region, suspended oil deliveries to Jordan and three days later expelled approximately 20 Jordanian diplomats. Meanwhile, fearful that Jordan's location between Israel and Iraq made it a likely combat theater, King Hussein intensified his calls for a diplomatic solution, declared an intention to defend his country's airspace, and reinforced Jordanian troops along the Israeli frontier. In January 1991 Jordan temporarily closed its borders, complaining that it had received insufficient international aid for processing over 700,000 refugees from Iraq and Kuwait. Thereafter, in a speech on February 6, 1991, King Hussein made his most explicit expression of support for Iraq to date, assailing the allies' "hegemonic" aims and accusing the United States of attempting to destroy its neighbor. Following the war, the king quickly returned to a more moderate position, calling for "regional reconciliation" based on "forgiveness" among Arabs and a permanent resolution of the Palestinian problem.

In what was perceived as a further effort to rebuild relations with Arab neighbors, who before the war had provided annual aid estimated at $500 million, King Hussein called in late 1992 for the installation of a democratic government in Iraq. In May 1993 the king openly broke with Iraq, charging it with activities inimical to Jordanian interests and declaring his opposition to Saddam Hussein's continued rule. King Hussein also condemned the Iraqi buildup along the Kuwaiti border in October 1994 and, in August 1995, granted asylum to the members of President Hussein's family and governmental inner circle who had recently fled Iraq. In addition, he invited Iraqi opposition groups to open offices in Jordan. The king's unequivocal anti-Iraq stance assisted in the reestablishment of normal relations with all the Gulf states except Kuwait by August 1996, when he was greeted in Saudi Arabia by King Fahd for the first time since the 1990 invasion.

In December 1996 the United Nations implemented its "oil-for-food" deal with Iraq (see article on Iraq), which broke Jordan's informal "monopoly" on trade with its neighbor, and precipitated a decline in annual bilateral trade from $400 million in 1996 to just $250 million in 1997. As conflict loomed between the United States and Iraq in the early part of 1998, Amman managed to stay in the good graces of both countries by opposing any U.S. military attack while banning demonstrations in support of Iraq and calling on that country to abide by UN resolutions.

Efforts to normalize relations with Israel faced setbacks in early 1997 when Israel announced plans to build another settlement in East Jerusalem. Relations were in part assuaged when, following the shooting death of seven Israeli schoolgirls in Jordan on March 13 by a corporal in the Jordanian army, Hussein immediately responded by visiting the families of the Israeli schoolchildren and expressing sympathy for their losses. Nevertheless, relations again took a turn for the worse on September 25 when agents from the Israeli intelligence agency Mossad were caught in Amman attempting to poison Hamas leader Khaled Meshal. Furious at this attack on Jordanian soil, King Hussein demanded the antidote to the poison and threatened to break off relations with Israel. The Israeli government furnished the antidote and subsequently exchanged a large group of Jordanian and Palestinian prisoners held in Israel for the captured Mossad agents. (See Current issues, below, for subsequent developments.)

In February 2008 King Abdullah II met in Moscow with Russian president Vladimir Putin to enhance bilateral ties and begin talks on cooperation on a civilian nuclear energy program. The king also sought to incorporate Russia into the Middle East peace process initiated by the United States at its November 2007 summit in Annapolis, Maryland (see Current issues, below). In March the king visited the United States to urge a long-term U.S. commitment to development in the region, and in August, as the first Arab leader to visit Iraq since the fall of Saddam Hussein, he announced plans to reopen Jordan's embassy in Iraq. In December 2009 Jordan and Iraq announced an arrangement that would allow Iraqis in Jordan to vote in Iraqi elections at polling stations in Jordan.

On April 22, 2010, two missiles fired at Israel landed in Jordanian territory. Reports indicated that the rockets had been launched from Egypt but overshot their targets. Jordan and Egypt subsequently launched a joint investigation to discover the perpetrators.

On April 26 the United States and Jordan announced a four-year program of economic and technical assistance designed to grow the kingdom's economy. However, in July reports surfaced that the United States had threatened to withhold aid from Jordan if the country pursued a civilian nuclear energy program. Meanwhile, Jordan continued negotiations with MERCOSUR over a free trade agreement.

Unrest in Syria prompted the closure of border crossings with Jordan beginning in March 2011. Damascus accused its neighbor of allowing antigovernment groups to cross into Syria. The closures cut trade between the two nations by an estimated $700,000 per day. The Jordanian government in April announced new measures to control the border in an effort to convince Syria to reopen the crossings. In August Jordan called for the Syrian government to undertake reforms and curb violence against opposition groups. In December Jordan requested to be exempted from Arab League economic sanctions on Syria. Meanwhile, on November 21, the king traveled to the Israeli-occupied West Bank for the first time since 2000. During the visit, Abdullah met with Palestinian president Mahmoud Abbas.

In January 2012 Jordan hosted a new round of negotiations between Israelis and Palestinians in Amman, the first such discussions in more than one year. At an international Friends of Syria summit in Tunis in February, representatives from 70 countries agreed to provide humanitarian supplies and aid to Syrian refugees in Jordan, Lebanon, and Turkey. In June Jordan closed its border with Syria. In October a Jordanian soldier was killed during a battle with Islamic militants trying to enter Jordan from Syria. Five foreign fighters were captured in the incident. Also in October, Egypt announced the suspension of natural gas shipments to Jordan because of rising domestic demand (the shipments were later resumed, but cut by one-third).

In January 2013 the UN reported that 30,000 Syrians had fled into Jordan, bringing the total number of displaced Syrians in the country to 300,000. Reports in March indicated that Syrian rebels were being trained in Jordan by Western intelligence officers. In June 2013 Jordan approved a treaty with the United Kingdom that guaranteed alleged criminals a fair trial and forbade the introduction of evidence based on torture. The treaty was negotiated to allow the extradition of radical cleric Abu QATADA to Jordan.

Current issues. In the November 20, 2007, parliamentary elections, the IAF fielded 22 candidates but secured only two-thirds of the seats it had won in 2003. Observers attributed the decline to rifts in the party and the IAF's inability to follow through on its long-held pledges to reduce poverty and unemployment. Independents loyal to the king won handily, though turnout was reported to be low (with reports of only 32 percent turnout in Amman). A large percentage of the population was said to oppose the current electoral laws, which they claimed allow for greater representation in progovernment districts. Opposition groups, including the IAF, had been pressuring the government for reforms to move toward proportional representation to ensure greater pluralism, including greater representation in districts heavily populated by Palestinians, but no government proposals were forthcoming. Hamas's rise to power in the Palestinian government was cited as key to the Jordanian government's lack of movement on electoral reforms in its effort to contain the republic's "restive Palestinian majority and an activist Islamic opposition," according to the *New York Times*. Following the parliamentary balloting, in which the government had rejected the IAF's request for international observers, the IAF again registered allegations of fraud; subsequently, 17 people were arrested on charges of vote tampering.

With his renewed support in the legislature, King Abdullah urged lawmakers to focus on education, health, housing, and public sector salaries. Additionally, the king continued to press for a two-state solution to resolve Palestinian-Israeli violence and the resumption of peace talks, as well as dialogue between Fatah and Hamas. Meanwhile, the king reiterated his "full support" for the Palestinian National Authority (also referenced as the Palestinian Authority) and sought international aid for the Palestinians in Gaza. Israeli Prime Minister Ehud Olmert was reported to have made a secret visit to Jordan earlier in 2007 to discuss bilateral relations. In November Jordan was represented at the U.S.-sponsored Middle East peace talks in Annapolis, Maryland.

Tensions in the region increased in January 2008 in the wake of Israel's blockade of Gaza, forcing many Palestinians to flee the dire situation there, lacking food, water, and electricity. Olmert's visit to Jordan in early January was harshly criticized by the IAF, despite the king's condemnation of Israeli "aggression" in Gaza. The government, for its part, accused the IAF of having a "special relationship" with Hamas. In March dozens of pro-Hamas marches, reportedly organized by the IAF, attracted thousands of Jordanians calling for Hamas to stage suicide attacks against Israel. In April five Islamists, four of whom were said to be members of the Hamas Islamic Resistance Movement (see Political Parties and Groups, below), were on trial for allegedly supplying secret military information to Hamas. In a major turnaround in August, Jordan made overtures to Hamas in an effort to rebuild a relationship, reportedly amid fears of a major influx of refugees, potentially leading to civil unrest, should U.S.-backed Middle East peace efforts collapse. The move by Jordan was said by analysts to have been an effort at maintaining a delicate balance between reaching out to Hamas and avoiding angering the United States and Israel. Further protests against Israel's blockade were organized by the IAF in Amman in November. Following Israel's attacks inside Gaza in late December, in response to Hamas's firing of rockets into southern Israel, tensions ignited within Jordan over the Gaza issue. When the speaker of parliament postponed a proposal by the IAF to dispatch an aid ship to Gaza, 21 members, including two from the IAF, walked out in protest. The IAF claimed the postponement was meant to block the aid effort, which would circumvent Israel's blockade of Gaza. The ship was ultimately dispatched in mid-January 2009.

Pressure for greater democratic reforms was brought to the forefront in January 2009 when 100 people, described as national and political leaders, said they had formed a "national front" to promote that agenda. Subsequently, the minister for political development, Musa al-MAAYTAH, promised further reforms and said the administration would embark on an "era of openness" with the Islamic opposition. Maaytah, who was part of an extensively reshuffled cabinet installed on February 23, was reported to have been appointed to underscore the government's commitment to political reforms. Another key appointment, which analysts saw as a signal of Jordan's "reluctance" to engage with Hamas, was Nayif al-QADI as interior minister, a post he had held in the late 1990s when he deported several Hamas members. The cabinet overhaul came at a time when inflation was approaching 13 percent and food and fuel prices were soaring. The prime minister retained his post in the reshuffle, which was aimed at stabilizing the economy in the wake of the global financial crisis.

In April 2009 three members of Hamas were convicted in a military court for participating in military training in Jordan, thus jeopardizing the kingdom's safety, according to authorities. Some news reports said that Jordan had accused the men of being spies. The men were sentenced to five years in prison, and two other defendants were acquitted. Hamas responded by requesting amnesty for the prisoners.

A new electoral law was enacted in June 2010. The new measure increased the number of seats in the house by ten and reshuffled electoral boundaries mainly to benefit rural areas. It also increased the minimum number of women deputies to 12. The IAF announced in July that it would boycott the November elections because of the redistribution of seats away from its traditional strongholds in urban areas. In August opposition groups and parties protested after the electoral commission announced that various parties had objected to more than 400,000 voters (there were 3.4 million registered voters). Opposition leaders feared that a large number of voters would be disqualified. In the November 9 balloting, independent candidates who supported the monarch won a commanding majority in the house.

In response to massive antiregime protests, the king held direct discussions with the IAF for the first time in more than ten years. On March 13, 2011, in an effort to end the protests, the government created the National Dialogue Committee (NDC). Led by the speaker of the Senate, Taher al-MASRI, the committee opened talks with the opposition groups, but the negotiations were boycotted by the IAF. In April the king named a royal committee to consider recommendations from the NDC to revise the constitution. Meanwhile, the protests continued, including an incident in Zarqa that left 83 police officers injured and hundreds of Islamists wounded. In August constitutional amendments, including a provision that would allow the assembly to select the prime minister, instead of the monarch, were endorsed by the king. The opposition groups asserted that the reforms did not go far enough and continued the protests.

Bakhet was forced to resign on October 17 following allegations of corruption related to a casino project. His government had also been criticized for not enacting promised reforms more quickly. Bakhet was replaced by Khasawneh, who served as a justice at the International Criminal Court and had a reputation for honesty. Khasawneh resigned when the king extended the assembly's term, arguing instead for new elections. He was then replaced on April 26 by Tarawneh who pledged to speed reforms in the kingdom. In May the assembly passed legislation that would ban religious parties. The measure prompted protests and condemnation from Islamist groups. Following growing protests, the king replaced Tarawneh with Abdullah Ensour in October. Also in October, 11 Jordanians were arrested in what security authorities described as an "al-Qaeda terrorist plot" to kill Westerners.

Amid continuing anti-government protests, parliamentary elections were held on January 23, 2013. The IAF boycotted the polling that was dominated by promonarchist independents. Ensour was reappointed prime minister in March and named a new cabinet. In May, Ensour announced an end to electricity subsidies that cost $1.8 billion annually and were cited as a major reason for a growing budget deficit. Ensour conducted a cabinet reshuffle in August in an effort to boost the popularity of the government. The civil war in Syria caused a dramatic decline in Jordanian agricultural exports, creating a negative ripple effect through the economy. From January to September, direct losses were estimated to be $113 million.

POLITICAL PARTIES AND GROUPS

Parties were outlawed prior to the 1963 election. Subsequently, an "official" political organization, the Arab National Union (initially known as the Jordanian National Union), held sway from 1971 to February 1976, when it was disbanded. On October 17, 1989, King Hussein announced that some party activity could resume but left standing a prohibition against party-affiliated candidacies for the November legislative election. The National Charter signed in June 1991 recognized the right of parties to organize, on condition that they acknowledge the legitimacy of the monarchy. Legislation formally lifting the ban on parties was approved by the National Assembly in July 1992 and by King Hussein on August 31. The first groups were recognized the following December.

Legal Parties:

National Constitutional Party (NCP). The NCP was officially formed on May 1, 1997, reportedly by nine pro-government parties and the **Jordanian Arab Masses Party** (*Hizb al-Jamahir al-Arabi al-Urduni*), the **Popular Unity Party** (*Hizb al-Wahdah al-Shabiyah*), and the **Jordanian Popular Movement**. (Some reports indicated that the component groupings had dissolved themselves in favor of the NCP, although their institutional status, as well as that of the NCP, subsequently remained unclear.) Under the slogan "rejuvenation, democracy, and unity," the NCP ran in the November elections on an agenda of peace with Israel, support for the IMF economic program, and the "Jordanization" of political life. It won only two seats. Many observers believe that the NCP was meant by its leaders to serve as a counterweight to the historical dominance of the Islamic, leftist and pan-Arabist movements. The formation of the NCP was one of the reasons that the Islamic and most of the leftist and pan-Arabist parties decided to boycott the elections.

In 2002 the NCP was one of five centrist parties that urged the government to carry out political reforms. The NCP joined a host of other parties in 2007 in a campaign opposing the government's political parties law. The NCP was also generally critical of the 2010 electoral law, although it praised the increase in the minimum number of woman deputies. Throughout recent protests, the NCP remained generally supportive of the monarchy, although the grouping was very critical of the 2013 decision to rescind fuel subsidies.

Leaders: Abdul Hadi MAJALI (President of the Party), Amed ALSHUNNAK (General Secretary).

Islamic Action Front—IAF (*Jabhat al-Amal al-Islami*). The IAF was formed in late 1992 by the influential Muslim Brotherhood (below) as well as other Islamists, some of the latter subsequently withdrawing because of Brotherhood domination. Like the Muslim Brotherhood, the IAF promotes the establishment of a sharia–based Islamic state with retention of the monarchy. Although the IAF is generally perceived as opposing Israeli-PLO and Jordanian-Israeli peace talks, a significant "dovish" minority exists within the Front.

IAF leaders objected to electoral law changes introduced in mid-1993 and accused the government of interfering in the Front's campaign activities prior to the November house elections. However, after initially threatening to boycott the balloting, the Front presented 36 candidates, 16 of whom were elected. IAF candidates did not perform as well as anticipated in the July 1995 municipal elections, potential support having apparently gone instead to tribally-based parties. Subsequently, Front/Brotherhood leaders suggested that King Hussein was "trying to restore authoritarian rule." No IAF members were included in the new government announced in February 1996.

In view of the recently enacted press restrictions and continued complaints over electoral laws, the IAF boycotted the 1997 legislative balloting. A member of the IAF, Abd al-Rahim AKOUR, accepted a post in the new cabinet of June 2000 but was suspended from the party for that decision.

After winning 17 seats in the 2003 parliamentary elections, the IAF became the principal opposition party in the legislature. Following the suicide bombing attacks on hotels in Amman in 2005, which the IAF denounced, the Front urged the government to consider individual freedoms as it began drafting antiterror laws.

The victory of Hamas in the Palestinian elections in 2006 was seen by observers as likely to further widen the gap between hawks and doves in the IAF. The hawks, who contended that the government continued to marginalize Islamists, appeared to be strengthened by the Hamas victory, observers said. Subsequently, the IAF elected Zaki Said Bani-Irshayd, who was supportive of Hamas, as its new secretary general. (The dovish leader of the associated Muslim Brotherhood decided not to run for reelection in 2006.) A government crackdown on Islamists, including the dismissal of two deputies from the lower house of parliament, furthered the tensions between the government and the IAF, and resulted in a walkout by IAF deputies for several weeks in early 2007. The IAF continued lobbying for the elimination of the one-person, one-vote system (cited as an unfair system in multiple-candidate districts) and protested vehemently against a new law approved by the parliament in 2007, which required political parties to have a minimum of 500 members (instead of 50) in order to be officially recognized. Numerous other groups joined the IAF in a demonstration, in defiance of a government ban, against the political parties law, which they regarded as a "major setback to the country's democratic process." The IAF was highly critical of what it said was the king's lack of movement on promised political reforms, including a change to the press law involving imprisonment for journalists (later removed by legislators).

Also in 2007 the IAF elected the first Christian to its administrative board, but he resigned within a month. The IAF said the Christian member, who had been active in the group for years, probably resigned due to political and other pressures. Following its boycott of municipal elections in July (see Current issues, above), the IAF decided to participate in parliamentary elections in November. It secured only six seats, a significant erosion of power for what had been the leading opposition group in the lower chamber. The lack of support for the IAF was attributed to its inability to effect socio-economic changes and to rifts in the party between hawks and doves, the hawks opposing the doves decision to participate in polling, which the hawks believed would not be fair and transparent. Also, the hawks were said to be angered by the way the IAF candidates were chosen (without consultation with the full membership). Some observers said the party was facing "the biggest internal crisis in its history," furthered by Hamas's decision to form a Palestinian Muslim Brotherhood, prompting divisions in the IAF (see Muslim Brotherhood, below) between pro-Jordanian and pro-Hamas factions. In June the two factions resolved the contentious issue of whether Zaki Said Bani-Irshayd should retain his post as secretary general. He had been blamed by some for allegedly undermining the position of the group's parliamentary candidates in the 2007 elections, leading to a loss of IAF seats. Ultimately, Bani-Irshayd was allowed to retain his post, and four members who had resigned in protest returned, reportedly putting an end to the long-running conflict.

In March 2009 the IAF criticized Egypt for denying entry at the Rafa border crossing to 17 parliamentarians, including IAF members, who were on a mission to express solidarity with the people of Gaza. The IAF was also highly critical of Arab leaders who failed to accept an invitation to an emergency summit in Qatar to consider measures against Israel following the Gaza attacks.

In June 2010 Hamza MANSUR, leader of the moderate faction of the IAF, was elected secretary general in a close election by the Shura Council. He defeated the "hawk" candidate, Mohammad ZYOD, who favored closer ties with Hamas, on a vote of 62 to 55. The IAF announced in August that it would boycott the 2010 legislative balloting. Also in August the IAF called for an end to direct negotiations between Israel and the Palestinians. The IAF expelled five members who violated the boycott and ran in the assembly elections. One dissident, Ahmed QUDAH, won election to the assembly.

In May 2011 the IAF joined other opposition parties to form the opposition grouping the National Front for Reform. The party boycotted the 2013 elections. In 2013 the IAF condemned government plans to close the border with Syria in order to stem the flow of refugees into Jordan.

Leaders: Hamzah MANSUR (Secretary General), Abd al-Latif ARABIYAT, Ziad Abu GHANIMA, Jamil ABU-BAKR (Spokesperson), Rahil al-GHARAYIBAH (Deputy Secretary General).

Communist Party of Jordan—CPJ (*al-Hizb al-Shuyui al-Urduni*). Although outlawed in 1957, the small pro-Moscow CPJ subsequently maintained an active organization in support of the establishment of a

Palestinian state on the West Bank, where other communist groups also continued to operate. About 20 of its leaders, including (then) Secretary General Faik (Faiq) Warrad, were arrested in May 1986 for "security violations" but were released the following September. More than 100 members were detained for five months in 1989 for allegedly leading antigovernment rioting. One CPJ member, Isa Madanat, was elected to the House of Representatives in 1989 and the following spring he and several party associates participated in negotiations on the proposed National Charter, the January repeal of the nation's anti-Communist act having ostensibly put the CPJ on the same footing as other parties preparing for official recognition. After initially being rejected for legal party status in late 1992 on the ground that communism was "incompatible" with the Jordanian constitution, the CPJ was recognized in January 1993. By that time Madanat and his supporters had left the CPJ to form the JSDP (below, under JUDP). Despite the opposition of its youth wing, the CPJ participated in November 1997 national elections.

In 2010 the CPJ held discussions with several smaller parties including the **Jordan People's Democratic Party** (*Hizb al-Shaab al-Dimuqrati al-Urduni*—Hashd) and the **Jordanian Baath Arab Socialist Party**—JASBP (*Hizb al-Baath al-Arabi al-Ishtiraki al-Urduni*) to form an electoral coalition ahead of the 2010 house elections. In May 2010 the CPJ joined the IAF-led opposition coalition the National Front for Reform. The CPJ boycotted the 2013 balloting.

Leader: Munir HAMARENEH (General Secretary).

Jordanian Arab Democratic Party—JADP (*al-Hizb al-Arabi al-Dimuqrati al-Urduni*). The JADP is a leftist group recognized in mid-1993, its supporters including former Baathists and pan-Arabists. The two JADP members who were elected in the 1993 house balloting subsequently joined a parliamentary bloc called the Progressive Democratic Coalition, which also included representatives from the JSDP and *al-Mustaqbal* as well as 18 (mainly liberal) independents. The JADP subsequently announced its opposition to any "normalization" with Israel without full "restoration of Palestinian rights," a stance that aligned the JADP with Palestinian groups opposed to the Israeli-PLO peace accord. The issue appeared to divide the party, some 17 members reportedly resigning in early 1995 in support of the PLO and in protest over a perceived "absence of democracy" within the JADP. One of the party's leaders, Muhammad Daudia, is a former cabinet minister.

Leaders: Akram al-HOMSI (Secretary General), Muhammad DAUDIA, Abla Mahmoud abu TRAY.

Jordanian Baath Arab Socialist Party—JASBP (*Hizb al-Baath al-Arabi al-Ishtiraki al-Urduni*). The Baathists, who had supported a number of independent candidates in the 1989 house election, were initially denied legal status in December 1992 as the Baath Arab Socialist Party in Jordan because of apparent ties to its Iraqi counterpart. However, the Interior Ministry reversed its decision in early 1993 after the grouping revised its name and offered "assurances of independence" from Baghdad. An Arab nationalist party that opposes peace talks with Israel as "futile," the JASBP presented three candidates in the 1993 house balloting, one of whom was elected. In late 1996 the government accused the JASBP of having helped to incite "bread riots," and a group of Baathists were arrested in connection with those events. However, some observers questioned the government's assertions, a correspondent for *Middle East International* describing the party as too "splintered and shrunken" to be capable of generating effective action. The newspaper *al-Dustur* reported on May 15, 1997, that the JASBP had formed an alliance with two other pan-Arabist parties—the **National Action Front** (*Haqq*), led by Muhammad al-ZUBI, and the **Arab Land Party**, led by Mohammad Al OURAN. The new grouping was reportedly called the **Nationalist Democratic Front** (NDF), led by Hamad al-FARHAN. The NDF parties did not boycott the November 1997 elections, and the JASBP won one seat in the lower house. In 2011 the JASBP joined the opposition coalition the National Front for Reform. The JASBP joined the IAF-led National Front for Reform, but it withdrew from the grouping in 2012 in order to compete in the 2013 elections. The JASBP subsequently formed an electoral coalition with the **Jordanian People's Democratic Party** (*Hizb al-Shaab al-Dimuqrati al-Urduni*—HASHD) and the small **Progressive Arab Baath Party** (*Hizb al-Baath al-Arabi al-Taqaddumi*) (see below).

Leaders: Akram HOMSI (Secretary General), Abdullah al-AHMAR (Deputy Secretary General).

Jordanian People's Democratic Party (*Hizb al-Shaab al-Dimuqrati al-Urduni*—Hashd). The leftist Hashd was formed in July 1989 by the Jordanian wing of the Democratic Front for the Liberation of Palestine (DFLP), a component of the PLO (see separate article). Its initial application for recognition was rejected because of its DFLP ties, but, as an independent "on a friendly basis" with the DFLP, the party was legalized in early 1993. Like the DFLP, the Hashd opposed the Israeli/PLO accord of September 1993 although it supports the peace process in general as a means of resolving the Palestinian problem. In 2002 the party rallied in support of Iraq prior to the U.S. invasion. In 2004 the party joined other groups in calling on Muslims worldwide to support Iran in the wake of U.S. involvement in the region. The Hashd joined the CPJ and the JASBP in an electoral coalition for the 2010 house elections. HASHD joined the National Front for Reform but withdrew from the coalition in 2013 in a dispute over whether to participate in the 2013 balloting.

Leaders: Ahmad YUSUF (Secretary General), Ablah ABU-ULBAH.

Jordanian Unionist Democratic Party (JUDP). Formed in 1995 as a merger of the Jordanian Socialist Democratic Party—JSDP (*al-Hizb al-Dimuqrati al-Ishtiraki al-Urduni*) and the Jordanian Progressive Democratic Party—JPDP (*al-Hizb al-Taqaddumi al-Dimuqrati al-Urduni),* the JUDP supports "Arab unity, democracy, and social progress" and opposes the normalization of relations with Israel. The JSDP, whose secretary general (Isa Madanat) had been a former leader of the CPJ, had been recognized in early 1993 even though it had refused a government request to delete "socialist" from its name and references to "socialism" from its party platform. Meanwhile, the JPDP had been formed in late 1992 by the merger of three leftist groups—the Jordanian Democratic Party, the Palestinian Communist Labor Party Organization, and the Jordanian Party for Progress. (The latter subsequently withdrew from the JPDP, its leader later founding the Freedom Party, subsequently the Progressive Party, below.) The JPDP was recognized in January 1993 after its leaders bowed to government pressure and deleted references to socialist objectives from the party platform. Several leaders of the JPDP were former members of the Palestinian National Council.

The creation of the JUDP was widely attributed to the desire of its leftist components to develop a stronger electoral presence, their impact having been negligible in the 1995 municipal elections. However, in 1997 political differences precipitated the resignation of over 150 members, including former secretary general Mazen al-SAKET. The JUDP fielded four candidates in the November 1997 elections and won one seat.

In 2009 Musa al-Maaytah was named as minister of political development. It was unclear whether he was still affiliated with the JUDP.

Leaders: Isa MADANAT, Ali Abd al-Aziz AMER.

Progressive Party. Formed in 1993 as the Freedom Party (*Hizb al-Hurriyah*) by a former official of the CPJ, this grouping is described as "trying to combine Marxist ideology with Islamic tradition and nationalist thinking." The Progressive Party participated in the 1997 lower house election boycott but was represented in parliament in 2003. The Progressive Party held talks with the IAF, CPJ, and other parties on the establishment of a new opposition coalition in 2012. The party boycotted legislative elections in 2013.

Leader: Fuad DABBOUR (Secretary General).

Jordanian Democratic Popular Unity Party—JDPUP (*Hizb al-Wahdah al-Shabiyah al-Dimuqrati al-Urduni*). The leftist JDPUP was formed in 1990 by Jordanian supporters of the Popular Front for the Liberation of Palestine (PFLP, see article on the PLO). True to its PFLP heritage, the JDPUP opposes peace negotiations with Israel. The JDPUP joined the boycott of the 1997 lower house elections. In 2002 the JDPUP and five other opposition parties failed in their attempt to form a coalition, citing ideological differences. In 2007 the party was among several that protested the country's new political parties law. The party participated in the 2007 and 2010 parliamentary elections but did not secure any seats. The JDPUP called for joint action by opposition parties on electoral reform in 2012. The party boycotted the 2013 legislative elections.

Leaders: Saeed THIYAB (Secretary General), Esam AL-KHAWAJA.

Pan-Arab Action Front Party—PAAFP (*Hizb al-Jabhat al-Amal al-Qawmi*). Described as having close ties with Syria, the PAAFP was legalized in January 1994, its members reportedly including several prominent Palestinian hard-liners. Ideological differences subsequently led a faction of the PAAFP to form a new grouping, the **Nationalist Action Party**.

Leader: Muhammad al-ZUBI.

The first political party to be led by a woman was licensed in March 2007. The centrist **Jordanian National Party** was formed by Muna HUSSEIN ABU-BAKR, a U.S.-educated biologist, to promote equal rights, among other things. She was arrested in 2008 on charges of selling counterfeit medicine. Also licensed in 2007 was the **United Jordanian Front Party**, founded in September by the interior minister, Eid al-FAYEZ, and Amjad MAJALI as a party for reform and modernization.

Other legal parties include the **al-Ansar Party,** a moderate grouping recognized in December 1995 and headed by Muhammad MAJALI; the **Jordanian Arab Constitutional Front Party,** led by Milhem al-TALL, who in 1989 election campaign called for Jordanian-Syrian union and participated in the 1997 boycott; the **Jordanian Peace Party,** a strong supporter of the peace process with Israel and headed by Shaher KHREIS; the **Green Party**, founded in 2000 by Mohammad BATAYNEH, who later served as energy minister; the **Jordanian People's Committees Movement,** launched in 2001 under the leadership of Khalid SHUBAKI; the **Jordanian Welfare Party,** launched in 2001 and led by Mohammad Rijjal SHUMALI; the **Progressive Arab Baath Party** (*Hizb al-Baath al-Arabi al-Taqaddumi*), led by Fouad DABOUR and said to have a political philosophy similar to that of the Syrian Baath Party; the **Jordanian National Movement**, led by Samir AWAMLEH, was formed in 2004 and included 11 small parties in what was described as a pro-government centrist front; the **Prosperity** (*al-Rafah*) party, led by Mohammed AJRAMI after party infighting in 2002; the **Renaissance** (*al-Nahdah*) party, led by Mijhim al-KHURAYSHAH; the **New Dawn** (*al-Fajr al-Jadid*), a centrist party legalized in 1999; the **Muslim Center Party** (*Hizb Al-Wasat Al-Islamiy*); the **Islamic Centrist Party** (*Hizb Alwasat Al-Isalami*); **Stronger Jordan**; the **Homeland;** and the **Islamic al-Wasat** party, led by Marwan al-FAURI.

For information on the **Jordanian National Alliance Party** (*Hizb al-Tajammu al-Watani al-Urduni*—JNAP), the **Liberal Party** (*Hizb al-Ahrar*), the **Homeland Party** (*Hizb al-Watan*), the **Christian Democratic Party**, and the **Democratic Unionist Arab Party—The Promise** (*al-Hizb al-Wahdawi al-Arabi al-Dimuqrati—al-Wad*), see the 2009 *Handbook.* For information on the **Awakening Party** (*Hizb al-Yaqazah*), **Future Party** (*Hizb al-Mustaqbal*), and **Progress and Justice Party**—PJP (*Hizb al-Taqaddumi wa-al-Adl*), see the 2011 *Handbook.* For information on the **Democratic Arab Islamic Movement Party–Propagate** (*Hizb al-Harakah al-Arabiyah al-Islamiyah al-Dimuqrati—Dua*), the **Arab Land Party,** and the **Ummah Party** (Community), see the 2012 *Handbook.* For more on the **Pledge Party** (*Hizb al-Ahd*), see the 2013 *Handbook.*

Other Groups:

Muslim Brotherhood (*al-Ikhwan al-Muslimun*). An outgrowth of the pan-Arab Islamic fundamentalist group of the same name established in Egypt in 1928, the Brotherhood has played a prominent role in Jordanian political affairs. It promotes the creation of an Islamic state based on strict adherence to Islamic law (sharia) but does not advocate abolition of the monarchy, having generally maintained a cooperative relationship with King Hussein.

Following an impressive showing in the 1989 elections, the Brotherhood was given ten seats on the National Charter Commission formed in April 1990. In November one of its leaders, Abd al-Latif Arabiyat, was elected speaker of the House of Representatives while five of its members entered the government on January 1, 1991. However, it was unrepresented in the subsequent Masri or Shaker cabinets, underscoring the rift between the Brotherhood and the government regarding Jordan's participation in the U.S.-led Middle East peace negotiations. In December 1992 members of the Brotherhood and other fundamentalists established the IAF (above) as their official political party. Primarily because of the Brotherhood's strong opposition to the 1994 peace treaty with Israel, it was not represented in the January 1995 cabinet, reports surfacing that King Hussein and Prime Minister Shaker pointedly had failed even to consult new Brotherhood leader Abd al-Majid THUNIBAT concerning the formation of the government. Indicative of the credibility of the Muslim Brotherhood as an opposition force, it was its decision to boycott the November 1997 elections that led other Islamic as well as non-Islamic opposition parties to also suspend their participation. The dovish Thunibat decided not to run for a fourth term as leader in 2006.

In 2007 the Muslim Brotherhood was caught up in the divisive issue of support for Hamas. The Brotherhood, as part of a 14-party Coordination Committee, wanted the group of diverse parties to meet and discuss the Palestinian crisis, but political differences among the parties eventually scuttled the Brotherhood's efforts. The Brotherhood was also described by observers as facing a crossroads in its relationship with Iran as a result of increasing sectarian tensions between Sunni and Shiite Muslims in the region.

Hamas's decision to establish a Palestinian Muslim Brotherhood in 2008 was seen as a turning point in its alignment with the Jordanian Brotherhood and as contributing to pro-Hamas and pro-Jordanian factions within the group. Meanwhile, rifts between hawks and doves (see IAF, above) led to the dissolution in February of the Brotherhood's Shura (consultative) Council (its highest decision-making committee); subsequently the hawks were elected to a narrow majority of a new council in March, though in a compromise move, Abd al-Latif Arabiyat, a dove, was chosen head of the council. At the same time, Haman Said, described as a hawk of Palestinian origin, was elected as the Brotherhood's new overall leader with the support of those in the group who backed Hamas. (His opponent, Salim Falahat, held the post of the director general.) Meanwhile, the government stated its increasing concerns about links between the Brotherhood and Hamas, fearing a security threat highlighted by the trial of five Islamists (see Current issues, above).

In advance of Pope Benedict XVI's visit to Jordan in May 2009, the Muslim Brotherhood demanded that the pope apologize for remarks he had made in 2006 about the Prophet Muhammad, which many Muslims found "insulting." Though the pope said he was "deeply sorry" about the reaction to his speech, he said the passage he quoted did not reflect his opinion. Pope Benedict was scheduled to meet with Muslim religious leaders at Amman's largest mosque. It was unclear whether Brotherhood members would be invited.

The Muslim Brotherhood endorsed the IAF-led boycott of legislative elections in 2010. In December 2010 a leader of the movement, Abdul Majeed THNEIBAT, was ordered to face a party trial after he accepted an appointment as a senator. Through 2012 the Muslim Brotherhood organized a series of protests and demonstrations against the government. The Muslim Brotherhood condemned the 2012 draft electoral law that would ban religious parties. The Brotherhood called for a boycott of the 2013 balloting and led a series of increasing large demonstrations against the government through 2013.

Leaders: Haman SAID, Abd al-Latif ARABIYAT (Head of the Shura Council), Muhammad Abd al-Rahman al-KHALIFA, Abd al-Munim ABU ZANT, Salim FALAHAT.

For more information on the **Islamic Liberal Party,** the **Prophet Mohammad Army,** the **Vanguard of Islamic Youth** (*Shabab al-Nafir al-Islami*), the **Islamic Resistance Movement** (Hamas), and the **Renewal Party** (*Hizb al-Tajdid*), please see the 2012 *Handbook.*

LEGISLATURE

The bicameral **National Assembly** (*Majlis al-Ummah*) consists of an appointed House of Notables and an elected House of Representatives. The assembly did not convene between February 1976 and January 1984, a quasi-legislative National Consultative Council, appointed by King Hussein, serving from April 1978 to January 1984.

House of Notables (*Majlis al-Ayan*). The upper chamber consists of 60 members appointed by the king from designated categories of public figures, including present and past prime ministers, twice-elected former representatives, former senior judges and diplomats, and retired officers of the rank of general and above. The stated term is four years although actual terms, until recently, have been irregular because of various royal decrees directed primarily at the elected House of Representatives, whose suspension requires a cessation of upper house activity.

The House of Notables appointed in January 1984 consisted of 30 members, while the body designated in November 1989 was expanded to 40 in keeping with a requirement that the upper house be half the size of its elected counterpart. The king formed a new 55-member upper chamber, including 7 women, on November 17, 2003, although activity remained suspended pending new elections to the House of Representatives. In the wake of bombings at three hotels in Amman on November 9, 2005, and the subsequent resignations of several government officials, the king dissolved the upper chamber on November 16 and appointed a new House of Notables on November 17.

The upper chamber was expanded from 55 to 60 members in 2010. It was last renewed on October 25, 2011.

President: Abdul Karim DUGHMI.

House of Representatives (*Majlis al-Nuwwab*). The lower chamber consists of 150 members elected from 45 districts containing 1 to 7 seats each and 27 seats filled by a proportional representation system. Twelve seats are reserved for members of the Christian and Circassian minorities and 15 for women. The constitutionally prescribed term of office is four years, although no full elections were held from 1967 to 1989 as the result of turmoil arising from Israel's occupation of the West Bank.

The house seated in 1967 contained 60 members (30 from West Jordan and 30 from East Jordan) elected in nonparty balloting. After being dissolved by the king in November 1974, its members were called back into session by royal decree in February 1976, at which time the king was authorized to postpone new elections indefinitely and call future special sessions as needed. However, the house did not meet again until January 1984. By-elections were held two months later to fill 8 vacant East Bank seats; it being deemed impossible to conduct elections in the West Bank, the 6 vacant seats from the occupied territory were filled by voting within the house itself. The house continued to meet in special session until its dissolution on July 30, 1988, following which King Hussein announced the severance of all legal and administrative ties with the West Bank. Consequently, the November 8, 1989, election of a new house (expanded to 80 members) excluded the West Bank. Political party activity remained proscribed, although the Muslim Brotherhood (defined as a charitable organization rather than a party) was permitted to present candidates, 20 of whom were elected.

The number of seats was increased from 80 to 110 by a 2003 decree. The house was further expanded in 2013 to 150 seats. In the most recent elections on January 23, 2013, promonarchy independent candidates again won an overwhelming majority in the chamber.

Speaker: Saad Hayel SROUR.

CABINET

[as of September 15, 2013]

Prime Minister	Abdullah Ensour
Ministers	
Agriculture	Akef al-Zoubi
Communications and Information Technology	Azzam Talal Salit
Culture	Lana Mamkagh [f]
Defense	Abdullah Ensour
Education	Muhammad Dhneibat
Energy and Mineral Resources	Muhammad Hamed
Environment	Taher al-Shakhshir
Finance	Umayyah Touqan
Foreign Affairs	Nasir Judeh
Health	Ali al-Nahleh Hiaset
Higher Education and Scientific Research	Amin Mahmoud
Industry and Trade	Hatem Hafez al-Halwani
Interior	Hussein Hazza Majali
Justice	Bassam al-Talhouni
Labor	Nidal Mardi Qatamin
Municipal and Rural Affairs	Walid al-Masri
Planning and International Cooperation	Ibrahim Saif
Political and Parliamentary Affairs	Khaled Kaladeh
Public Sector Development	Khleif al-Khawaldeh
Public Works and Housing	Sami Halaseh
Religious Endowments and Islamic Affairs	Hayel Abdel Hafiz Dawood
Social Development	Reem Mamdouh Abu Hassan [f]
Tourism and Antiquities	Nidal Mardi Qatamin
Transportation	Lina Shabib [f]
Water and Irrigation	Hazam al-Nasser
Ministers of State	
Cabinet Affairs	Ahmad Nouri Zyadaat
Media Affairs and Communications	Mohammad Hussein Moumani
Without Portfolio	Salameh al-Nu'iamt

[f] = female

INTERGOVERNMENTAL REPRESENTATION

Ambassador to the U.S.: Alia Hatough BOURAN.

U.S. Ambassador to Jordan: Stuart JONES.

Permanent Representative to the UN: Prince Zeid Ra'ad Zeid AL-HUSSEIN.

IGO Memberships (Non-UN): ICC, IOM, LAS, NAM, OIC, WTO.

KAZAKHSTAN

Republic of Kazakhstan
Qazaqstan Respublikasy

Political Status: Entered the Russian Soviet Federative Socialist Republic as autonomous republic on August 26, 1920; became constituent republic of the Union of Soviet Socialist Republics on December 5, 1936; declared independence on December 16, 1991; current constitution approved by referendum of August 30, 1995, effective from September 6.

Area: 1,049,155 sq. mi. (2,717,300 sq. km).

Population: 16,566,675 (2012E—UN); 17,736,896 (2013E—U.S. Census). Emigration of ethnic Russians, Germans, and Ukrainians after independence, coupled with a declining birth rate (the lowest in Central Asia), caused a net decrease from the 1989 total of 16,536,511 to 14,953,100 in 1999.

Major Urban Centers (2009C): ASTANA (formerly Tselinograd and then Akmola, 678,000), Almaty (formerly Alma-Ata, 1,421,000). Formal transfer of the government from the former capital, Almaty, to Astana occurred in June 1998. Since 1999 Astana's population has more than doubled.

Official Language: Kazakh (replaced Russian in 1989); confirmed as official language in 1995 constitution, which also accords Russian special status as "the social language between peoples" while specifying that government officials are required to be proficient in Kazakh by the year 2010.

Monetary Unit: Tenge (official rate November 1, 2013: 154.38 tenge = $1US).

President: Nursultan Abishevich NAZARBAYEV (*Nur Otan*); elected by the Supreme Soviet as its chair on February 22, 1990, succeeding K. U. MEDEUBEKOV (Communist Party of Kazakhstan); reelected on April 24; sworn in to newly created post of president on December 10, 1991, following popular election on December 1; confirmed in office until 2000 by referendum on April 29, 1995; elected for a seven-year term on January 10, 1999; reelected on December 4, 2005, and sworn in on January 11, 2006; reelected on April 3, 2011, and sworn in on April 8.

Prime Minister: Serik AKHMETOV (*Nur Otan*); promoted from deputy prime minister by the president on September 24, 2012, succeeding Karim MASSIMOV (*Nur Otan*), who had resigned that day.

THE COUNTRY

The second largest of the former Soviet republics in area and the fourth largest (after Russia, Ukraine, and Uzbekistan) in population, Kazakhstan consists largely of a vast flatland, much of it desert, extending nearly 2,000 miles from the Altai Mountains in the east to the Caspian Sea in the west. It is bordered by Russian Siberia on the north, China on the east, and the republics of Kyrgyzstan, Uzbekistan, and Turkmenistan on the south. Its people are about 64 percent Turkic-speaking Kazakhs and 23 percent Russians, down from over 42 percent in 1960. Smaller groups include Uzbeks, Ukrainians, Uighurs, and Tatars. Relations between the dominant Kazakhs and the country's ethnic Russian population deteriorated after independence, and as a result over 1.7 million ethnic Russians had emigrated by 1999. Three-fifths of Kazakhstan's preindependence German population of 946,000 likewise left the country, as did a large number of ethnic Ukrainians. About 62 percent of the current population are Sunni Muslim, and most of the rest are Russian Orthodox. Women constitute about 49 percent of the active labor force and 24.3 percent (26 of 107 seats) of the current lower house of Parliament, and 4.3 percent (2 of 47 seats) of the upper house.

Prior to the breakup of the Soviet Union, Kazakhstan's northern tier of "virgin lands" produced most of the USSR's cattle and wool and a substantial amount of its wheat. Wheat, wool, and meat continue to be exported, with the agricultural sector currently contributing about 5 percent of GDP and employing 30 percent of the labor force. Kazakhstan ranked as one of the world's top wheat producers in 2012. Industry, which accounts for about 41 percent of GDP but employs only 12 percent of the active labor force, is concentrated in hydrocarbon and mineral extraction, the most important sectoral exports being oil and gas, copper and other metals, chemicals, and machinery. The country's deposits of barite, chromite, lead, manganese, silver, tungsten, uranium, and zinc rank among the world's largest; other extractable resources include coal, copper, iron ore, gold, and titanium.

Since 2000, growth has been explosive, owing primarily to the petroleum sector (please see the 2013 *Handbook* for information on the economy prior to 2000). Additional oil and gas discoveries and significant foreign investment in Kazakhstan's energy sector have made the nation one of the world's leading energy suppliers. In late 2001 a new oil pipeline opened, linking Kazakhstan's largest onshore field, Tengiz, to the Russian Black Sea port of Novorossiysk, while construction began in 2004 on a $700 million pipeline to China. In late 2008 Kazakh oil began flowing for the first time through the Baku-Tbilisi-Ceyhan pipeline route to the Turkish port of Ceyhan. Meanwhile, development began in the massive Kashagan field in the Caspian—reportedly the world's largest petroleum discovery in the last 30 years.

GDP grew by an average of 10.3 percent in 2000–2006, but growth slowed to 8.9 percent in 2007 and then to 3.2 percent in 2008 as the global financial crisis penetrated the economy. Kazakhstan managed to avoid the resultant widespread recession, but growth in 2009 was only 1.2 percent. GDP growth rebounded in 2010 to 7.3 percent, 7.5 percent in 2011, and 5 percent in 2012. However, inflation increased by 8.3 percent in 2011, before moderating to 5.1 percent in 2012. GDP per capita rose to $11,772, up from $7,308 in 2009. Unemployment rates have gradually decreased from a high in 2000 of 12.8 percent to 5.4 percent in 2012. General government gross debt has held steady at about 11 percent of total GDP, and the IMF predicts a steady decline into 2014. In 2013 the World Bank ranked Kazakhstan 49th out of 185 countries in its annual Doing Business index, one of the highest rankings in the region.

GOVERNMENT AND POLITICS

Political background. Subject to Russian incursion and influence since the 17th century, the Kazakh lands were gradually annexed by imperial Russia during the 19th century. After a brief attempt at independence in 1917–1920, Kazakhstan became an autonomous Soviet republic and then, in 1936, a full union republic within the USSR. Kazakh leaders long acted in close concert with Moscow, and Kazakhstan's current president, Nursultan Abishevich NAZARBAYEV, was viewed as a possible contender for the presidency of the Soviet Union. Thus, the Kazakh Republic approached secession from the USSR cautiously, issuing a declaration of state sovereignty only in October 1991 and withholding a declaration of independence until December 16.

In June 1989 Nazarbayev, who had been serving as chair of the Kazakhstan Council of Ministers, was named first secretary of the Kazakh Communist Party. On February 22, 1990, Nazarbayev was elected to succeed K. U. MEDEUBEKOV as chair of the Supreme Soviet (head of state), a post to which he was reelected In April, following a legislative replenishment. Nazarbayev stepped down as leader of the Socialist Party of Kazakhstan (the renamed Communist Party), prior to being popularly elected president of the republic on December 1, 1991, after which he appointed a government headed by Sergei TERESHCHENKO. In early 1993 Nazarbayev became the acknowledged but unofficial leader of the new People's Union of Kazakhstan Unity (*Soyuz Narodnoye Edinstvo Kazakhstana*—SNEK), which on March 7, 1994, won a plurality of 33 directly elective seats in the 177-seat Supreme Council (*Kenges*). Some 220 prospective candidates, many assumed to be opponents of the president, had been denied participation in the election. The alignment of the *Kenges* thereafter depended on the "state list" and independent deputies (together, about 100), who were broadly pro-Nazarbayev. Tereshchenko was replaced as prime minister by Akezhan KAZHEGELDIN in October, amid presidential reproaches about the slow pace of economic reform.

A major political crisis erupted in March 1995 when the Constitutional Court invalidated the 1994 poll because of numerous irregularities. The *Kenges* responded on March 11 by adopting a constitutional amendment enabling the legislature to overrule the court, but the latter refused to accept the action as lawful. The president appeared to back down by accepting the resignation of the Kazhegeldin government, dissolving the *Kenges,* and announcing a new election, which a substantial majority of deputies opposed. He then recaptured the initiative by calling an April 29 referendum at which he obtained a 95 percent mandate for the extension of his presidential term to December 2000. In a further referendum on August 30, Nazarbayev secured 89 percent support for a new constitution strengthening presidential powers.

Ruling by decree, President Nazarbayev dismissed the Constitutional Court in October 1995 and introduced a new government structure that pared down the number of ministries and state committees. Elections to the two legislative chambers created under the new constitution were held in early December. The January 1996 opening of the legislature, in which SNEK and its allies remained dominant, marked the end of rule by presidential decree. In October 1997 President Nazarbayev announced the resignation of Prime Minister Kazhegeldin and appointed Nurlan BALGIMBAYEV, head of the state oil company, as the new prime minister.

Adoption of constitutional amendments by a joint session of Parliament in October 1998 (see Constitution and government, below) was followed in January 1999 by a premature presidential election in which the incumbent received 79.8 percent of the votes cast. His closest competitor, Serikbolsyn ABDILDIN of the reorganized Communist Party of Kazakhstan (*Kommunisticheskaya Partiya Kazakhstana*—KPK), won 11.7 percent. Several potential candidates, including former prime minister Kazhegeldin, had been ruled ineligible for violating a law against participation in meetings of unregistered organizations. (In September 2001 Kazhegeldin was sentenced, in absentia, to ten years in prison for abuse of power and bribery.)

The recently formed presidential party, Fatherland (*Otan*), which in March had absorbed the Party of People's Unity (successor to the SNEK), emerged from the Assembly elections of October 1999 holding a plurality of 23 seats, with the progovernment Civic Party of Kazakhstan claiming 13 and independents (many of them progovernment), 22. The opposition was led by the KPK, which held only 3 seats in the expanded 77-seat body. As with the January presidential election, the Organization for Security and Cooperation in Europe (OSCE) refused to validate the results, citing campaign irregularities.

In October 1999 Kasymzhomart TOKAYEV, theretofore the foreign minister, became prime minister, replacing Balgimbayev, who had resigned to return to his previous post as head of the state oil monopoly. Prime Minister Tokayev, in turn, resigned in January 2002, citing the need for "new ideas" in government. He was succeeded by Imangali TASMAGAMBETOV, previously a deputy prime minister.

Expressing concerns about a lack of democratic progress, a number of government officials participated in the launching of the moderate Democratic Choice of Kazakhstan (*Demokraticheskii Vybor Kazakhstana*—DVK) movement in November 2001, provoking their dismissal. In the following year two prominent DVK founders—Galymzhan ZHAKIYANOV, who had been fired as governor of the northern Pavlodar region, and Mukhtar ABLYAZOV, a former minister of economy and trade—were sentenced to jail terms for having abused their former offices. (Ablyazov received a presidential pardon in April 2003 and retired from politics; Zhakiyanov was not paroled until January 2006.)

Prime Minister Tasmagambetov resigned on June 11, 2003, accusing the lower house of "crude violations of voting procedure" during a May 19 confidence vote that his government had won. Tasmagambetov was succeeded on June 13 by Daniyal AKHMETOV, former governor of the Pavlodar region.

Meanwhile, under the terms of a restrictive political party law that had come into force in July 2002, several opposition parties had been officially "liquidated." Others had decided not to seek reregistration, while the Ministry of Justice had used the law's technical provisions to block the registration of new opposition groups. Only 12 parties were eligible to contest the September 19–October 3, 2004, Assembly election, in which the propresidential *Otan* won a commanding 42 of 77 seats. The only opposition seat was won by the Democratic Party of Kazakhstan "White Road" (*Ak Zhol*), a DVK splinter. *Otan* also dominated the Senate replenishment of August 19, 2005.

Of some two dozen prospective presidential candidates, five made it onto the ballot of December 4, 2005. President Nazarbayev won 91.1 percent of the vote, while the principal opposition candidate, former Assembly speaker Zharmakhan TUYAKBAI, collected only 6.6 percent. Having been sworn in for another term on January 11, 2006, Nazarbayev reappointed Prime Minister Akhmetov. Later that year, *Otan*—subsequently renamed *Nur Otan* (roughly, Light of the Fatherland)—increased its total of Assembly seats to 57 out of 77 by absorbing three allied parties.

On January 10, 2007, Deputy Prime Minister Karim MASSIMOV was named prime minister and Akhmetov was appointed minister of defense. Under a proportional representation system that was instituted by constitutional amendment in May, *Nur Otan* won all 98 directly elected seats (with 88.4 percent of the vote) in a snap lower house election called by Nazarbayev for August 18. No other party achieved the 7 percent threshold for representation. In the Senate replenishment of October 4, 2008, *Nur Otan* won all 16 indirectly elected seats.

In early presidential elections on April 3, 2011, Nazarbayev was reelected with 95.5 percent of the vote. The opposition boycotted the balloting, which was criticized by domestic and international observers. Nazarbayev was confirmed on April 8 by Parliament and sworn in the same day. The ruling *Nur Otan* won all 16 seats in the elections for half of the Senate on August 19.

On November 16, 2011, Nazarbayev dissolved the Majlis in response to requests made by members of the body. The stated intent was for multiparty inclusion and to allow a newly elected body to focus on economic issues. Early elections were held on January 15, 2012 for 98 members, as well as indirect elections of an additional 9 members representing different ethnic groups. *Nur Otan* retained the vast majority of seats winning 83; however, changes in election law allowed for greater distribution regardless of the 7 percent threshold rule, with Ak-Zhol winning 8 seats and KPPK winning 7 seats. Nazarbayev reshuffled the cabinet on January 20 and 21.

On September 24, 2012, Massimov resigned as prime minister and was replaced by Serik AKHMETOV (*Nur Otan*) (see Current issues, below). A reshuffled cabinet was named over the next four days. Another reshuffle occurred on January 16, 2013, including the creation of the ministry of regional development. Concurrently five new regional governors were appointed. Further changes to the cabinet occurred in June.

Constitution and government. The constitution approved by referendum on August 30, 1995, was independent Kazakhstan's third in less than four years. It provided for a strong, popularly elected president with powers to appoint the prime minister (subject to parliamentary confirmation) and to dissolve the bicameral legislature. Parliament may remove the president, for treason or medical incapacity, by a three-fourths vote of a joint session.

Amendments adopted by Parliament in May 2007 limit future presidents—but not the current incumbent—to two terms in office. In addition, beginning in 2012 the presidential term will be five years instead of seven. Other amendments increased the size of both houses of Parliament—to 47 seats in the Senate and to 107 in the Assembly, with 98 of those elected by proportional representation and the remainder appointed by the Assembly of the Peoples of Kazakhstan, an advisory body on ethnic matters that had been established by presidential decree in 1995.

A Constitutional Council, the highest legal body, is appointed jointly by the chairs of the legislative houses and the president. The president may veto council decisions. A Supreme Court is the highest judicial body for criminal, civil, and other cases originating in the courts of general jurisdiction.

Kazakhstan encompasses a total of 16 "administrative-territorial units": 14 regions (*oblystar*), the capital, and Almaty, each governed by an elected council (*maslikhat*) and an executive body, the latter headed by a governor (*akim*) appointed by the president on the recommendation of the prime minister. Councils and executive bodies also function at lower administrative levels. The city of Baykonur (formerly Leninsk), which borders the Russian-run Baykonur space center, is under Russian administration.

Among other enumerated rights, the constitution guarantees private property and permits private ownership of land while retaining state control of water and other natural resources. Although the constitution prohibits censorship, most media outlets are directly or indirectly controlled by presidential family members or loyalists, including the powerful Khabar Agency, the country's leading media company. Opposition journalists can be targeted under libel and other criminal statutes for such offenses as insulting the honor of the president, undermining national security, encouraging violence, or inciting ethnic or religious hatred. In its campaign for the OSCE chairship, Kazakhstan pledged to reform its laws governing media, but in 2009 an OSCE official noted that Kazakhstan's media regulation "still fails to meet several international standards." In 2013 Reporters Without Borders ranked Kazakhstan 160th out of 179 countries.

Foreign relations. Kazakhstan became a sovereign member of the Commonwealth of Independent States (CIS) on December 21, 1991. By early 1992 it had established diplomatic relations with a number of foreign countries, including the United States. In March it was admitted to the United Nations, and it joined the IMF and World Bank in July. It also joined the Conference on (later Organization for) Security and Cooperation in Europe (CSCE/OSCE) and in May 1994 became a signatory of the NATO Partnership for Peace program. In January 1995 Kazakhstan signed a partnership and cooperation accord with the European Union, and the following December it joined the Organization of the Islamic Conference. In 1996 Kazakhstan applied for membership in the World Trade Organization (WTO) and began to negotiate preparatory bilateral market access agreements with WTO members. President Nazarbayev indicated in mid-2012 that he expected Kazakhstan would be ready for acceptance into the WTO by late 2012 or 2013.

During the Cold War, Soviet nuclear weapons were stationed inside Kazakhstan, and as a result disarmament became a leading foreign policy issue for the new republic. During a 1992 Washington visit, President Nazarbayev indicated that Kazakhstan was prepared to accede to the 1968 Nuclear Non-Proliferation Treaty (NPT) and agreed to sign a revised version of the Strategic Arms Reduction Treaty (START) initially concluded by U.S. president George H.W. Bush and Soviet president Mikhail Gorbachev in July 1991. Both actions were formalized during a visit by U.S. vice president Al Gore in December 1993. Thereafter, the United States provided technical and financial aid, including funds for dismantling nuclear weapons. On May 24, 1995, the Kazakh foreign ministry announced that all the country's nuclear weapons had been transferred to Russia or destroyed.

Regionally, the Caspian Sea has been a major focus of attention for Kazakhstan and the other littoral states, Russia, Azerbaijan, Turkmenistan, and Iran. Meeting in Moscow in 1998, Nazarbayev and Russian president Boris Yeltsin signed the first of several bilateral agreements concerning Caspian Sea boundaries and development, thereby clearing the way for exploitation of underlying oil reserves. In 2001 Kazakhstan and Azerbaijan concluded a related agreement, which, like the Kazakh-Russian accords, was harshly attacked by another littoral state, Iran. In April 2002 and October 2007, the leaders of the littoral countries held inconclusive meetings in an effort to resolve their differences over Caspian rights. In March 2010, on the sideline of talks held by the littoral states to complete a security cooperation pact, the Iranian envoy noted that 70 percent of the Caspian issues had been resolved. Caspian region states continue to develop naval assets in the region, with Kazakhstan setting up a naval aviation base in Aktau in 2011 and launching its first of three missile boats in 2012 to augment its nascent fleet of coastal craft.

Economic integration has also been a major regional consideration. In January 1994 an economic union with Uzbekistan and, six days later, Kyrgyzstan was announced. In July the scope of the new Central Asian Economic Union was extended to include cooperation in defense, foreign policy, and social affairs. In March 1998 Tajikistan agreed to join the union, which four months later adopted the name Central Asian Economic Community. Subsequently renamed the Central Asian Cooperation Organization (CACO), it welcomed Russia as the fifth member in October 2004. A year later, the CACO agreed to merge into the Eurasian Economic Community (EAEC), which began in 1996 as a CIS Customs Union of Belarus, Kazakhstan, Kyrgyzstan, and Russia. In 2009 Russia, Belarus, and Kazakhstan announced that a full customs union of the three would enter into effect at the beginning of 2010, although it took until midyear to complete the necessary customs code. Russia, Belarus, and Kazakhstan meet in November 2011 and signed the Treaty on the Eurasian Economic Commission, agreeing on a road map toward Eurasian Economic Union. The treaty came into force on February 1, 2012, and the Eurasian Economic Commission (EEC) was formed. It replaced the Commission of the Customs Union. This coincided with the launch of the Common Economic Space on January 1. Since 2005 President Nazarbayev had made an annual bid for Kazakhstan to become the first Central Asian state to chair the OSCE. Many member states opposed the bid citing Kazakhstan's poor record on human rights and its lack of democratic reforms. Nevertheless, at the 2007 OSCE meeting in Spain, all 56 member states voted to grant Kazakhstan the OSCE chair for 2010, the decision coming just three months after Kazakhstan's governing party won all 98 available seats in the Assembly. Kazakhstan assumed the presidency of the OSCE on January 1, 2010.

In April 1996 Kazakhstan, Kyrgyzstan, Russia, and Tajikistan undertook jointly with China to oppose separatist, terrorist, and Islamic fundamentalist activities in Central Asia, thus forming the Shanghai Five. With the continuing conflict in Afghanistan as a backdrop, the Shanghai Five defense ministers, meeting in Astana in March 2000, pledged their cooperation against terrorism. A month later, Nazarbayev joined the presidents of Kyrgyzstan, Tajikistan, and Uzbekistan in signing a mutual security agreement to combat terrorism, extremism, and other threats. In May 2001 Kazakhstan and the other members of the CIS Collective Security Treaty (Armenia, Belarus, Kyrgyzstan, Russia, and Tajikistan) authorized formation of a joint rapid reaction force, and in June 2001 the Shanghai Five plus Uzbekistan established the Shanghai Cooperation Organization. In April 2003 the six signatories of the CIS security treaty formed the Collective Security Treaty Organization.

The country's global profile was heightened by its support for the U.S.-led "war on terrorism" and the October 2001 invasion of Afghanistan, which elevated several Central Asian republics to the status of Washington's "newest strategic partners." Among other things, Kazakhstan granted overflight permission to U.S. planes, which were also permitted to use Kazakh airfields for refueling and emergency landings. In January 2009 Kazakhstan agreed to allow U.S. nonmilitary cargo to traverse the country en route to Afghanistan to supply American troops there.

In 1993 Kazakhstan and the other Central Asian republics joined in formation of the International Fund for Saving the Aral Sea (IFAS). Straddling the border between Kazakhstan and Uzbekistan, and at one time the world's fourth largest inland body of water, the Aral Sea has diminished to three discontinuous lakes that together hold only about 10 percent of the sea's volume in 1960, primarily because the USSR diverted the Amu Darya and Syr Darya rivers for irrigation. The IFAS is currently developing a 2011–2015 action plan focused on integrated use of water resources in the surrounding region.

In March 2009 another diplomatic effort among the Central Asian nations resulted in the implementation of a regional Nuclear Weapons Free Zone. In contrast, Kazakhstan viewed the 2010 overthrow of the Kyrgyzstan government as a threat to regional security and, in its role as chair of the OSCE, helped broker the departure of the ousted Kyrgyz president, Kurmanbek Bakiyev, from the country.

Relations between Kazakhstan and Kyrgyzstan continued to improve in January 2011 as President Nazarbayev announced plans to increase economic cooperation between the two countries. In late June an agreement to create a joint $100 million economic development fund was signed. Meanwhile in February, during a visit by Nazarbayev to China, seven bilateral economic agreements were signed, including a deal wherein Kazakhstan agreed to supply China with uranium in exchange for a $5 billion loan. The accords reflected the steady growth in trade. By 2010 bilateral trade between Kazakhstan and China was $20 billion per year, the same as trade between Kazakhstan and Russia. In September 2011 Prime Minister Massimov urged Kyrgyzstan to join the Commonwealth of Independent States' Customs Union, asserting that the membership would ease border tensions brought about by labor migrants.

On January 30, 2013, Kazakhstan and Russia agreed to create a joint air-defense system. Meanwhile, the two nations also initiated negotiations on a new bilateral friendship treaty. In February, Kazakhstan and Japan finalized an investment treaty and agreed to increase cooperation on nuclear technology. Russian exports of gasoline at below-market prices in the winter of 2013 prompted Kazakhstan to limit the import of Russian petroleum products to protect domestic producers. The United States announced in July that it supported a Kazak initiative to establish a nuclear fuel bank in Kazakhstan to better control the flow of nuclear materials.

Current issues. On January 31, 2011, Nazarbayev ordered early presidential elections on April 3. The incumbent won the balloting with more than 95 percent of the vote in polling that was boycotted by the opposition parties. The president ran against three contenders that all openly supported Nazarbayev. International monitors cited irregularities and lack of transparency in the process, noting a turnout rate of nearly 90 percent, artificially boosted by government-supported incentive programs and threats against those that failed to vote.

In May 2011 a major strike by oil workers over wages significantly slowed energy production in the Mangistau region. The protests continued and widened to broader political issues throughout the year, flaring up again on December 16 with police firing on demonstrators and killing at least 15. President Nazebayev declared a state of emergency on December 22, approving a heavy police and military presence in the affected regions and earning international condemnation. The state of emergency was lifted in February, although a number of increasingly diminishing protests continued through midyear. Mangistau deputy governor Amangeldy AYTKULOV was subsequently charged with bribery and abuse of power as officials blamed unrest in the region on corruption.

On October 13, 2011, President Nazarbayev signed into law two bills replacing 1992 legislation and guaranteeing religious freedom. The new laws, designed to curtail religious extremism, have been condemned by human rights defenders. The laws require religious groups to reregister with the government and define limits to where literature and other religious activities can be displayed. The laws also expand the list of criminalized religious activities.

On January 15, 2012, parliamentary elections were held with seven parties competing for 98 seats. The election was the first held after the election law changed, guaranteeing at least one seat in the lower house for the nonmajority party. International monitors noted that the election was technically well ran but was not pluralistic despite two competing parties crossing the 7 percent threshold for seats in parliament. Prior to the election, several opposition candidates and parties were declared ineligible on technical grounds.

On September 24, 2012, Nazarbayev appointed Prime Minister Massimov as presidential chief of staff. Massimov was a close ally of the president and the move was reportedly designed to strengthen the presidency. Serik Akhmetov was selected to replace Massimov in a change that helped balance clan representation within the government. A subsequent cabinet reshuffle in January 2013 further consolidated power among the president's close allies. In December, a plane crash near Shymkent, in south Kazakhstan, killed 27, including the acting head of the nation's border guards and 15 senior officers.

Beginning in 2013, polling was scheduled to allow the direct election of regional governors in Kazakhstan for the first time in the country's history. In March, minor protests were held in several cities against the rising utility costs, which increased as much as 30 percent in some areas. In April 2013, reports surfaced that Nazarbayev had undergone treatment for prostate cancer, renewing speculation about who would succeed the 72-year-old president. Former prime minister Massimov and current prime minister Akhmetov were seen as the most likely frontrunners, although the president's daughter Dariga NAZARBAYEV was also cited as a possibility (see Political parties, below).

POLITICAL PARTIES

In September 1991 the ruling Communist Party of Kazakhstan (KPK) renamed itself the Socialist Party of Kazakhstan (SPK) and adopted a platform of political pluralism and cautious economic reform. President Nazarbayev, the former KPK leader, withdrew from the SPK before his reelection in December 1991, and the party subsequently declined in importance. Nazarbayev was later associated with the Party of People's Unity of Kazakhstan (PPU), which was generally regarded as a "presidential" party prior to its 1999 merger with the newly established *Otan.*

The Kazakhstan Democratic Party "Citizen" (*Azamat*) was launched in April 1996 as an opposition movement aspiring to a government "of honest and competent people." *Azamat,* which did not register as a party until June 1999, was the first opposition grouping to feature eminent public figures in its leadership, including former government official and SPK chair Petr SVOIK. In February 1998 the current KPK, the SPK, *Azamat,* the nationalist *Azat* movement, and a number of other opposition groups formed a People's Front of Kazakhstan that suspended its activities ten months later, in the midst of the presidential campaign. By then, another movement, For Fair Elections, had been formed by *Azamat,* the KPK, and the Green Party (see *Tabiyghat,* below), among others. In mid-October a number of For Fair Elections leaders were arrested for participating in meetings of the unregistered movement, which ultimately led to their disqualification from presidential candidacy.

In July 1999 the KPK, the recently formed Republican People's Party of Kazakhstan (*Respublikanskaya Narodnaya Partiya Kazakhstana*—RNPK) of former prime minister Akezhan Kazhegeldin, and three public movements formed an opposition bloc, *Respublika,* to contest the October 1999 Assembly election on a platform that included abolition of the strong presidency and its replacement with a parliamentary system. Following the election, the KPK, RNPK, *Azamat,* Green Party, and various public associations formed an oppositionist Forum of Democratic Forces of Kazakhstan (*Forum Demokraticheskikh Sil Kazakhstana*—FDSK), which demanded that authorities invalidate the results for both parliamentary houses.

Launched in November 2001 as a movement, the Democratic Choice of Kazakhstan (DVK; see *Alga!,* below) brought together members of the opposition from a number of parties and movements—among them, the KPK, RNPK, and FDSK—and a number of government officials concerned over the slow pace of democratization. As a consequence of their involvement, the government officials were quickly dismissed. In another attempt to consolidate opposition forces, in December 2001 leaders of the RNPK, *Azamat,* and the newly established Kazakhstan People's Congress (*Narodnyi Kongress Kazakhstana*—NKK) announced that they were forming a United Democratic Party (UDP), but the UDP failed to cohere and was never registered.

Generating further criticism for its autocratic approach in dealing with political opponents, the government adopted a new Law of Political Parties in June 2002 that required a party to have 50,000 members, representing all regions, to obtain legal standing (the previous threshold had been 3,000 members). The new legislation also prohibited parties based on religion, ethnicity, or gender, and authorized the government to abolish any that did not register within two months of formation, failed to contest two consecutive elections, or failed to obtain 3 percent of the vote in an election. In response to the legislation, a number of opposition formations, including *Azamat,* the NKK, and the RNPK, refused to reregister and were therefore "compulsorily liquidated." Several others were denied registration, ostensibly for failing to meet technical provisions of the new law. They included the National Democratic Party "People's Wisdom" (*Yel Dana*), despite changing its name from the Democratic Party of Women of Kyrgyzstan and opening its membership to men.

A total of 12 parties were registered in time to contest the September–October 2004 legislative election, but only 4 parties met the 7 percent threshold needed to qualify for any of ten proportional seats. Following the election, the KPK, DVK, and the Democratic Party of Kazakhstan "White Road" (*Ak Zhol*) announced formation of an opposition Coordinating Council of Democratic Forces. Subsequently, in March 2005, most of the opposition parties established a Bloc of Democratic Forces "For Fair Kazakhstan" under former Assembly speaker and *Otan* member Zharmakhan Tuyakbai, who was designated as the bloc's 2006 presidential contender.

In September 2005 *Otan, Asar,* the Agrarian Party (APK), the Civic Party (GPK), the Democratic Party of Kazakhstan (see NSDP, below), and *Rukhaniyat* formed the propresidential People's Coalition of Kazakhstan in support of President Nazarbayev's reelection. In the following year *Asar,* the APK, and the GPK merged into *Otan,* which in

December 2006 adopted the new name *Nur Otan.* Further consolidations took place before the August 2007 Assembly election, in which *Nur Otan* took every seat in the lower house. At the time, there were eight registered parties. Since then, *Nur Otan* has dominated Kazakhstan's government at all levels.

Presidential Party:

People's Democratic Party "Light of the Fatherland" (*Narodno Demokraticheskaya Partiya "Nur Otan"*). In January 1999 former prime minister Sergei Tereshchenko, head of the reelection campaign for President Nazarbayev, announced that he planned to form the Republican Political Party "Fatherland" (*Otan*), which would adhere to "democratic and parliamentarian principles." *Otan* was officially launched at a founding congress on March 1, with Tereshchenko being named acting chair when Nazarbayev declined the leadership on constitutional grounds. Merging into *Otan* were the Party of People's Unity of Kazakhstan (PPU), the Kazakhstan Liberal Movement, the Democratic Party of Kazakhstan, and the For Kazakhstan–2030 Movement.

Beginning in February 1993 as a sociopolitical movement called the Union of People's Unity or the People's Union of Kazakhstan Unity (*Soyuz Narodnoye Edinstvo Kazakhstana*—SNEK), the PPU later emerged as a progovernment political party. With its leadership composed primarily of officials who had been associated with the Communist Party of Kazakhstan, it inherited much of the organization of the former ruling party. It advocated gradual economic reform and political pluralism. It also sought to serve as a bridge between the country's ethnic groups while opposing dual citizenship and language rights for ethnic Russians. Registered for the March 1994 legislative balloting, the PPU won a small plurality, amid claims of fraud. It remained the dominant party as the result of legislative elections in 1995 and 1996.

Otan emerged from the 1999 lower house election as the plurality party, with 23 seats. In September 2002 the People's Cooperative Party of Kazakhstan, which had been formed in 1994 as a pro-Nazarbayev formation with a predominantly rural base, merged with *Otan;* it had won 1 Assembly seat in 1999. The Republican Political Labor Party, which had been established in 1995, merged with *Otan* in 2002.

At the 2004 Assembly election *Otan* won a majority, achieving 61 percent of the party list vote and taking 42 of the 77 seats. Shortly thereafter, however, the speaker of the Assembly, Zharmakhan Tuyakbai, described the election as a "disgraceful farce" in which voters' rights were violated. He then resigned from *Otan* and joined the opposition.

In July 2006 *Otan* and the Republican Party "All Together" (*Asar*) agreed to merge. The *Asar* party had been established in September 2003 by the president's eldest daughter, Dariga Nazarbayeva, a prominent figure in the country's mass media industry. *Asar* had reportedly grown to be Kazakhstan's second-largest party (after *Otan*) by the time of the September–October 2004 Assembly election, in which it won four seats.

Meeting in November 2006, congresses of both the Agrarian Party of Kazakhstan—APK (*Qazaqstan Agrarlyk Partiyasi*) and the Civic Party of Kazakhstan (*Grazhdanskaya Partiya Kazakhstana*—GPK/ *Qazaqstan Azamattlyk Partiyasi*) also agreed to merge into *Otan.* The APK, founded in 1999 and pledging support for farmers and private land ownership, had won 3 seats in the 1999 Assembly election. In 2004 it and the GPK formed the Bloc of the Agrarian and Civic Parties "Agrarian Industrial Workers Union" (AIWU) to contest the Assembly election, in which the AIWU won 11 seats, second to *Otan.* The progovernment GPK had been formed in 1998 at the initiative of entrepreneurs in mining and heavy industry. In 1999 it had won 13 Assembly seats.

At an extraordinary congress held in late December 2006, *Otan,* which had raised its Assembly representation to 57 seats by absorbing *Asar,* the APK, and the GPK, changed its name to *Nur Otan.* On July 4, 2007, at a party congress in Astana, President Nazarbayev assumed the chairship, citing the constitutional amendments passed two months earlier. In the August 2007 snap Assembly election, the party claimed all 98 seats.

Dariga Nazarbayeva, who had been appointed deputy chair of *Nur Otan* after its merger with *Asar,* was removed from her position in 2007. Meanwhile, her husband, Rakhat ALIYEV, was charged with corruption and dismissed as deputy prime minister. Observers then speculated that Nazarbayev's second daughter, Dinara, and her husband, Timur KULIBAEV, would rise to power. In late 2007, however, the president dismissed Kulibaev without explanation as deputy head of a state company, signaling what appeared to be a fall from favor. In early 2008, Aliyev, in exile in Austria, was tried in absentia for kidnapping, conspiring to overthrow the government, and a host of other charges. He was sentenced to two 20-year terms in prison, but Austria refused to extradite him.

Nazarbeyev was reelected president of Kazakhstan in early elections on April 3, 2011. In an indirect balloting for the Senate on August 19, *Nur Otan* won all 16 seats. Nur Otan received 81 percent of the vote in the January 2012 Assembly elections for 83 seats.

In February 2013, Bauirzhan Baibek was appointed first deputy chair of the party, reportedly as part of an effort to usher in a younger generation of leaders within *Nur Otan.*

Leaders: Nursultan Abishevich NAZARBAYEV (Chair of the Party and President of the Republic), Bauirzhan BAIBEK (First Deputy Chair), Kazrat SATYBALDY (Secretary), Vladimir BOBROV (Secretary), Erlan Tynymbayuly KARIN (Secretary).

Other Registered Parties:

National Social Democratic Party–Azat (*Zhalpyulttyk Sotsial-Demokratiyalyk Partiya*—NSDP-*Azat*). The decision to unite the NSDP and *Azat* (Freedom) occurred in October 2009, although the possibility of such a merger had been broached as early as 2007, when *Azat* was still known by its original name, *Naghyz Ak Zhol.* In July 2010 the Ministry of Justice refused for technical reasons to register the merged opposition party but did not indicate that the separate registrations of the founding parties would be canceled.

Founded in September 2006 by former speaker of the Assembly and 2005 presidential candidate Zharmakhan Tuyakbai, and registered in January 2007, the NSDP was described by its leader as "a party of principled opposition to the current political course of the country's leadership." As an extension of the For Fair Kazakhstan movement, the party had as its primary goal the "country's fundamental political modernization and democratic state building." In the August 2007 Assembly election the NSDP finished second, but its 4.5 percent vote share was below the 7 percent threshold for seats.

The founding congress of the Democratic Party of Kazakhstan "True White Road" (*Qazaqstan Demokratiyalyk Partiyasi "Naghyz Ak Zhol"*) was held in April 2005, following its split with the leadership of the *Ak Zhol* (below). It was headed by three former *Ak Zhol* cochairs—Bulat Abilov, Altynbek Sarsenbayev, and Oraz Zhandosov. Unlike the *Ak Zhol,* the *Naghyz Ak Zhol* gave its support to For Fair Kazakhstan's Tuyakbai in the 2005 presidential race.

On February 13, 2006, Sarsenbayev, his driver, and a bodyguard were found murdered. At the end of August a former national security agent received a death sentence (commuted to life in prison) for planning the attack, while nine other defendants, all but one a security agent, were sentenced to between three years and life in prison.

In December 2006 founder Bulat Abilov went on trial for fraud involving an investment fund. In July he had been convicted of assaulting a police officer and given a three-year suspended sentence. The political opposition claimed that the charges were politically motivated.

On February 29, 2008, *Naghyz Ak Zhol* voted to adopt the name *Azat* in order to better distinguish itself from *Ak Zhol* (though its new name duplicated that of an earlier nationalist group). *Azat* claimed to be the true opposition party and sought to exert political pressures on the government from its position outside Parliament. The party called for nationwide demonstrations in February 2009, demanding the government's resignation over its handling of the financial crisis. However, officials refused to permit any public rally, except for one gathering in a small square in Almaty.

In April 2009 leaders of Azat, NSDP, *Alga!,* and the KPK met to explore the formation of what Abilov termed "an efficient political alliance." While nothing official developed from the meetings, opposition leaders, including Abilov, organized a number of unauthorized protests in the aftermath of the December 2011 social unrest. Abilov and other opposition leaders were detained on February 27, 2012. Abilov was released on March 11, which suggested to pundits that a split in the opposition was imminent.

AZAT was the only major opposition political party with valid registration during the January 2012 parliamentary elections and receiving 1.68 percent of the vote. Parliamentary rules require 7 percent for earning seats.

In July 2013, Abilov was arrested and briefly detained prior to an opposition meeting. Meanwhile, Abilov joined a group of opposition leaders in calling for the closure of Russian military bases in Kazakhstan.

Leaders: Bulat ABILOV, Zharmakhan TUYAKBAI, Amirzhan KOSANOV (Secretary General).

Democratic Party of Kazakhstan "White Road" (*Qazaqstan Demokratiyalyk Partiyasi "Ak Zhol"*). *Ak Zhol,* whose English-language variants include "Bright Path" and "Light Way," was formed in March 2002 by several defectors from the recently organized opposition movement Democratic Choice (see *Alga!,* below). Although *Ak Zhol* also took a position in moderate opposition to the government, its critics asserted that it was the product of a government effort to establish an officially approved opposition party. One of the founders, Oraz ZHANDOSOV, had previously served as deputy prime minister, and in January 2003 he was appointed as a presidential aide. Another founder, former Security Council secretary and ambassador to Russia Altynbek SARSENBAYEV, was named minister of communications in July 2004; he stepped aside as the September election approached and then resigned in September, in the course of a ministerial reorganization that, in effect, eliminated his position. A third founder, Assembly member Bulat ABILOV, was convicted of slandering a fellow MP in July 2004 and given a suspended sentence, which precluded his running for reelection.

At the September–October 2004 balloting *Ak Zhol* finished second to *Otan* in terms of the party list vote, but its 12 percent share was only good enough for a single Assembly seat—the only seat won by the opposition. Alikhan Baimenov, who had headed the *Ak Zhol* party list, immediately stated that he would not take up the seat as a protest against the conduct of the "illegitimate" election.

In early 2005 *Ak Zhol* split over policy differences and direction. As a consequence, a faction called the "True *Ak Zhol"* (see NSDP-*Azat,* above) formed in late April. In the December 2005 presidential election Baimenov finished third, with only 1.6 percent of the vote. In October 2006, however, following a meeting with President Nazarbayev, Baimenov announced that he would assume his Assembly seat in the interest of building a political consensus.

In December 2006 *Ak Zhol* and the Justice Party (*Adilet,* below) announced a cooperation agreement, and in July 2007 the two temporarily united under the *Ak Zhol* banner. When *Ak Zhol* managed to win only 3 percent of the vote in the subsequent election, *Adilet* reestablished its separate identity. The party claimed about 150,000 members prior to the election but in 2008 acknowledged a decrease in its membership. The party advocates maintaining good relations with *Nur Otan* in order to achieve change; toward that end, it signaled its intention to sign *Nur Otan*'s March 2009 memorandum of cooperation between the parties.

In 2011 *Ak Zhol* joined other opposition parties in supporting an initiative to end the special status of the Russian language

In November 2011 Azat Peruashev was elected party chair. Peruashev was previously chair of the Atameken Union National Economic Forum of Kazakhstan and a former member of *Nur Otan*, only joining *Ak Zhol* in July of that same year. The party won 7.48 percent of the vote in the January parliamentary elections, thus gaining eight seats in the lower house. *Ak Zhol* is considered a propresidential party.

In October 2012, noted Kazak poet Kazybek Isa was elected deputy chair of the party by *Ak Zhol*'s central committee.

Leaders: Azat PERUASHEV (Chair), Kazybek ISA (Deputy Chair).

Unity (*Birlik*). *Birlik* was formed in April 2013 by the merger of two small parties, **Justice** (*Adilet*) and **Spirituality** (*Rukhaniyat*). *Adilet* began as the Democratic Party of Kazakhstan (DPK), which was registered in June 2004. *Adilet* received 0.66 percent of the vote in the January 2012 parliamentary elections, not crossing the 7 percent threshold for seats. *Rukhaniyat* was registered in October 2003 under the leadership of writer Altynshash DZHAGANOVA, head of Kazakhstan's Migration and Demographics Agency. In December 2011, the Central Election Commission of Kazakhstan cancelled the registration of the party. The party was subsequently removed from ballots for the January 2012 parliamentary elections (for more information on the history of the two parties, please see the 2013 *Handbook*). Serik Sultangali was elected as *Birlik*'s first chair

Leader: Serik SULTANGALI (Chair).

Communist Party of Kazakhstan (*Kommunisticheskaya Partiya Kazakhstana*—KPK/*Qazaqstan Kommunistik Partiyasi*). A faction of the old ruling KPK opposed its conversion into the Socialist Party of Kazakhstan (*Sotsialisticheskaya Partiya Kazakhstana*—SPK) in September 1991 and eventually achieved legal registration as the new KPK in February 1994. The party favored close economic ties with other ex-Soviet republics, restoration of state ownership, and equality of ethnic groups. In 1996 the KPK eliminated references in its manifesto to "the struggle for proletarian dictatorship and the reinstatement of the USSR."

Party leader Serikbolsyn Abdildin finished second, with 11.7 percent of the vote, in the 1999 presidential election. The KPK won only three Assembly seats the following October, when it accused the progovernment Civic Party and the Agrarian Party, in particular, of vote manipulation.

In early 2004 differences over funding sources led supporters of Vladislav Kosarev to leave the KPK and establish the Communist People's Party (KNPK, below). In July the KPK and the newly registered DVK party (see *Alga!,* below) agreed to form an electoral bloc, Democratic Choice of Kazakhstan, which won only 3.4 percent of the party list vote and no seats in the September Assembly election. The KPK boycotted the August 2007 Assembly election, protesting the institution of party-list balloting; Abdildin called the election "a farce."

The KPK and *Alga!* partnered again in 2009 to form a radical bloc called Democracy. The two parties also held talks on creating a broader opposition coalition with the NSDP and Azat. The KPK, NSDP, and Azat refused to sign the memorandum on interparty consolidation initiated by *Nur Otan* in March.

On April 19, 2010, Abdildin resigned as first secretary. In October 2011 a court suspended the KPK as a political party for six months, after party leader Gaziz Aldamzharov was accused of trying to organize an unregistered political coalition with *Alga!*. On April 26, 2011, the ban was extended for another six months because party leader Aldamzharov was quoted in a local newspaper. In February 2013, the KPK's newspaper was suspended and the party fined after a court found that it had continued to operate during the KPK's 2011 ban.

Leaders: Gaziz ALDAMZHAROV (First Secretary), Serikbolsyn ABDILDIN.

Communist People's Party of Kazakhstan (*Kommunisticheskaya Narodnaya Partiya Kazakhstana*—KNPK/*Qazaqstan Kommunistyk Khalyk Partiyasi*). The KNPK, which is sometimes rendered in English as the National Communist Party of Kazakhstan, was registered in June 2004 by dissident KPK members who accused Serikbolsyn Abdildin of accepting suspect funds. The KNPK won 2 percent of the party list and no seats in the 2004 Assembly election. Its 2005 presidential candidate, maverick parliamentary deputy Yerasyl ABYLKASYMOV, won only 0.3 percent of the vote.

In March 2007 KNPK and KPK announced a merger that was quickly abandoned by June, and political and logistical differences were cited. In August 2007 the KNPK won only 1.3 percent of the Assembly vote. The KNPK's Marxist-Leninist platform has been modified to accommodate Kazakhstan's current economic realities. In presidential elections in April 2011, party candidate Zhambyl Akhmetbekov received 1.4 percent of the vote.

KNPK received 7.2 percent of the vote in January parliamentary elections gaining seven seats largely in response to KPKs ban from participating in the election.

In March 2013, the KNPK organized a rally in Astana to protest the increase in utility prices.

Leader: Vladislav KOSAREV (First Secretary).

Party of Kazakhstan's Patriots (PKP). Established in August 2000 by Gani Kasymov, an Assembly deputy and 1999 independent candidate for president, the PKP reregistered in 2003. In April 2004 the Officers' Union of Kazakhstan, an association of war veterans, joined the party, which was unsuccessful in the 2004 Assembly election, winning under 1 percent of the party list vote. In August 2007 the PKP won 0.8 percent of the vote.

Although the PKP supported President Nazarbayev's reelection in December 2005, it has differed with the government on some issues. Kasymov, now a senator, has been outspoken on environmental and human rights issues. In January 2009, in comments critical of proposed amendments on mass media regulation, he was quoted as saying, "We have reached a point where we have no opposition parties in the country, do we want to destroy newspapers, too?"

Kasimov ran as a presidential candidate in the April 2011 elections receiving 1.9 percent of the vote for a second place finish to incumbent Nazarbayev. PKP received 0.8 percent of the vote in January 2012 parliamentary elections not crossing the 7 percent threshold.

Leader: Gani KASYMOV (Chair).

Social Democratic Party "Village" (*Aul Sotsial-Demokratiyalyk Partiya—Aul*). *Aul* was first registered in March 2000 by parliamentary deputy Gani Kaliyev in support of rural dwellers and agro-industry. The party was reregistered in April 2003 but won under 2 percent of the party list vote and no Assembly seats in the 2004 election. It did, however, win a Senate seat in 2005. In August 2007 it captured 1.5 percent of the national vote. The party did not nominate a candidate for the April 2011 presidential race but did receive 1.2 percent of votes in January 2012 parliamentary elections, not crossing the 7 percent threshold. In February 2013, negotiations on a merger between *Aul* and *Azat* broke down.

Leader: Gani KALIYEV (Chair).

Unregistered Parties:

Forward! (*Alga!*). *Alga!* is the successor to the People's Party "Democratic Choice of Kazakhstan" (*Demokraticheskii Vybor Kazakhstana*—DVK/*Qazaqstannyn Demokratiyalyk Tandau*), which was deregistered in January 2005.

The DVK was considered more moderate than the Forum of Democratic Forces (FDSK) when it was launched as a movement in November 2001 by a number of government officials, including Minister of Labor Alikhan Baimenov, who were promptly dismissed. In March 2002 Baimenov and other DVK founders, including former deputy prime minister Oraz Zhandosov, departed to form *Ak Zhol.*

Two prominent DVK founders—Galymzhan Zhakiyanov, who had been dismissed as governor of the northern Pavlodar region, and Mukhtar Ablyazov, another former minister—were convicted in 2002 on charges of abuse of power. Critics of the government charged that the trials were politically motivated. Ablyazov was granted a presidential pardon in April 2003 and retired from politics, but Zhakiyanov, who had been sentenced to serve a seven-year prison term, remained incarcerated until January 2006.

After repeated attempts to register as a nonprofit organization, the DVK was ultimately registered as a political party in May 2004. In July it joined the KPK in forming the KPK-DVK electoral bloc, the Opposition People's Union, which was unsuccessful in the subsequent Assembly election.

In January 2005 an Almaty court ordered the DVK dissolved for promoting civil disobedience. Party leaders planned to appeal to a higher court but ultimately sought to form a successor party, Forward, DVK! (*Alga, DVK!*), although "DVK" was dropped from the name by the July 2005 founding congress. Since then, *Alga!* has repeatedly had its registration application denied by the Ministry of Justice, but its chapters and coordinating committee remain active. In 2009 the group was again in coalition with the KPK and participated in discussions to join an opposition bloc with *Azat* and the NSDP.

In 2011 KPK and *Alga!* were accused of attempting to coordinate political activities, which resulted in KPK losing its party status for the January 2012 parliamentary elections. On January 23, 2012, *Alga!* party leader Kozlov was arrested "for inciting social strife and organizing mass civil unrest." He was convicted on October 8 but filed an appeal to the Supreme Court.

Leaders: Asylbek KOZHAKHMETOV (Founder), Vladimir KOZLOV (Chair, Coordinating Committee).

Tabiyghat Party. The "green" *Tabiyghat* Party held its constituent congress in March 2006 under the leadership of environmental advocate Mels Yeleusizov. *Tabiyghat* (Nature) had been established as a nongovernmental organization in the early 1990s but has frequently been associated with opposition causes, particularly through the Party of Social Justice and Ecological Revival *"Tabiyghat"* and then the Green Party. Yeleusizov, who was disqualified as a 1999 presidential candidate because he had been convicted of participating in an unauthorized For Fair Elections meeting, ran in 2005 as an independent but won only 0.3 percent of the vote. Yeleusizov ran as an independent presidential candidate in the April 2011 elections receiving 1.2 percent of the vote.

Leader: Mels YELEUSIZOV.

Banned Organizations:

In October 2004 the Supreme Court labeled the following as terrorist organizations and banned them: **al-Qaida;** the **Kurdistan Worker's Party;** the **Islamic Movement of Uzbekistan;** and the **Islamic Party of East Turkestan,** based in China's Xinjiang Uygur Autonomous Region. The latter two organizations are no longer in operation as of 2008. Another group, the **Hizb ut-Tahrir,** which has sought to establish an Islamic state in the region but has not been directly linked to terrorist activities, was banned in March 2005; a number of its alleged members have been prosecuted by Kazakhstan in recent years. The **Jamaat of Mujahedins** was added to the list of organizations banned for terrorist activities by the Kazakh Prosecutor-General's Office in October 2006, after extremist religious literature and ammunition connected to the group were reportedly found in the nation's capital.

LEGISLATURE

The 1995 constitution provides for a bicameral **Parliament** (*Parlamenti*), which replaced the unicameral Supreme Council (*Kenges*).

Senate (*Senat*). The Senate has 47 members, increased from 39 following constitutional amendments of 2007. Of these, 15 are appointed by the president and 32 indirectly elected by officials representing the country's regions, Astana, and Almaty. Constitutional amendments passed in 1998 increased senatorial terms from four years to six, with half the elected seats renewable every three years. Members of the progovernment *Nur Otan* constitute the largest party bloc. *Nur Otan* won all 16 seats in the October 4, 2008, replenishment, as it did in the August 19, 2011, balloting.

Chair: Kairat MAMI.

Assembly (*Majilis*). The Assembly has 107 members, increased from 77 according to constitutional amendments promulgated in May 2007, which also eliminated district seats. In the snap election of January 15, 2012, *Nur Otan* won 83 directly elective seats. Two other progovernment parties crossed the 7 percent threshold for seats. *Ak Zhol* received 7.47 percent of the vote for 8 seats and KNPK received 7.19 percent of the vote for 7 seats. The other 9 members were indirectly elected in August by the 350-member advisory Assembly of the Peoples of Kazakhstan.

Chair: Nurlan NIGMATULIN.

CABINET

[as of August 1, 2013]

Prime Minister	Serik Akhmetov
First Deputy Prime Minister	Bakhytzhan Sagintayev
Deputy Prime Ministers	Asset Issekeshev
	Yerbol Orynbayev
	Kairat Kelimbetov
Ministers	
Agriculture	Asylzhan Mamytbekov
Culture and Information	Mukhtar Kul-Muhammed
Defense	Adelbek Dzhaksybekov
Economy and Budget	Yerbolat Dossayev
Economic Integration	Zhanar Aytzhanova [f]
Education and Science	Bakytzhan Zhumagulov
Emergency Situations	Vladimir Bozhko
Environmental Protection	Nurlan Kapparov
Finance	Bolat Zhamishev
Foreign Affairs	Yerlan Idrisov
Health	Salidat Qayirbekova [f]
Industry and New Technologies	Asset Issekeshev
Internal Affairs	Kalmukhanbet Kasymov
Justice	Berik Imashev
Labor and Social Welfare	Tamara Duisenova [f]
Macro-Economic Issues	Kairat Kelimbetov
Oil and Gas	Uzakbai Karabalin
Regional Development	Bakhytzhan Sagintayev
Transport and Communications	Askar Zhumagaliyev

[f] = female

INTERGOVERNMENTAL REPRESENTATION

Ambassador to the U.S.: Kairat UMAROV.

U.S. Ambassador to Kazakhstan: Kenneth J. FAIRFAX.

Permanent Representative to the UN: Byrganym AITIMOVA.

IGO Memberships (Non-UN): ADB, CIS, EBRD, IOM, OIC, OSCE.

KENYA

Republic of Kenya
Jamhuri ya Kenya

Political Status: Independent member of the Commonwealth since December 12, 1963; republic established in 1964; de facto one-party system, established in 1969, recognized as de jure by constitutional amendment on June 9, 1982; multiparty system approved by constitutional amendment on December 20, 1991; new constitution approved by referendum on August 4, 2011, providing for a mixed presidential-parliamentary system with a bicameral legislature.

Area: 224,960 sq. mi. (582,646 sq. km).

Population: 44,068,491 (2013E—UN); 44,037,656 (2013E—U.S. Census).

Major Urban Centers (2011E—UN): NAIROBI (urban area, 3,138,369); Mombasa (523,183).

Official Language: English (Kiswahili is the national language).

Monetary Unit: Kenyan Shilling (principal rate November 1, 2013: 85.50 shillings = $1US).

President: Uhuru KENYATTA (The National Alliance) elected by popular vote on March 4, 2013, and inaugurated for a five-year term on April 9, succeeding Emilio Mwai KIBAKI (Party of National Unity).

Deputy President: William Samoei arap RUTO (United Republican Party), elected on March 4, 2013, and sworn in for a term concurrent with the president on April 9, succeeding Vice President Stephen Kalonzo MUSYOKA (Orange Democratic Movement–Kenya).

THE COUNTRY

An equatorial country on the African east coast, Kenya has long been celebrated for its wildlife and such scenic attractions as the Rift Valley. The northern part of the country is virtually waterless, and 85 percent of the population and most economic enterprises are concentrated in the southern highlands bordering on Tanzania and Lake Victoria. The African population, mainly engaged in agriculture and stock-raising, embraces four main ethnic groups: Bantu (Kikuyu, Kamba, Luhya), Nilotic (Luo), Nilo-Hamitic (Masai), and Hamitic (Somali). Non-African minorities include Europeans, Asians (mainly Indians and Pakistanis), and Arabs. In addition to Kiswahili and English, the most important languages are Kikuyu, Luo, and Luhya. A majority of the population is nominally Christian (approximately 40 percent is Protestant, and 30 percent is Catholic), while approximately 10 percent adheres to traditional religious beliefs; there is also a growing Muslim minority currently comprising 10 percent of the population. Women remain underrepresented in politics. Following balloting in 2013, women held 65 of 350 seats in the assembly (18.6 percent) and 18 of 68 Senate seats (26.5 percent). Women also held six cabinet posts.

Although Kenya's economy was long considered one of the continent's healthiest, it has been subject since the mid-1980s to numerous pressures, including fluctuating fuel and commodity prices, an external debt of about $5 billion, high rates of natural population increase (currently estimated at 2.46 percent annually), escalating inflation, and large foreign exchange losses attributed to irregular banking activity. Kenya is still considered the banking, communications, and business center of East Africa, but the banking sector and the country's transportation infrastructure suffered greatly from the corruption and neglect under the Moi regime. Health and educational services also deteriorated significantly, while unemployment rose steadily. Kenya has one of the highest infant mortality rates in the world, and more than half the population lives on less than $1 a day (for more information on the Kenyan economy, please see the 2013 *Handbook*).

Kenya's relations with foreign financial donors were strained in the 1990s and early 2000s (please see the 2009 *Handbook*). By 2009 the World Bank had over $1 billion invested in national and regional development projects (for more details, see the 2012 *Handbook*). GDP growth averaged 4.1 percent between 2000 and 2010. During that same period inflation averaged 9.8 percent, while official unemployment averaged 15 percent (with some estimates as high as 40 percent). GDP growth in 2011 was 4.4 percent, and 4.7 percent in 2012. Inflation accelerated to 13.9 percent in 2011 but slowed to 9.4 percent the next year. Unemployment remained high in 2012, with unofficial estimates at 40 percent. In its 2013 Doing Business survey, the World Bank ranked Kenya 121st out of 185 countries.

GOVERNMENT AND POLITICS

Political background. Kenya came under British control in the late 19th century and was organized in 1920 as a colony (inland) and a protectorate (along the coast). Political development after World War II was impeded by the Mau Mau uprising of 1952–1956, which was inspired primarily by Kikuyu resentment over European control of the country's best land. Further difficulties arose in the early 1960s because of tribal and political rivalries, which delayed agreement on a constitution and postponed the date of formal independence within the Commonwealth until December 12, 1963. An election held in May 1963 had already established the predominant position of the Kenya African National Union (KANU), led by Jomo KENYATTA of the Kikuyu tribe, who had previously been imprisoned and exiled on suspicion of leading the Mau Mau insurgency. Kenyatta accordingly became the country's first prime minister and subsequently, upon the adoption of a republican form of government on December 12, 1964, its first president. The principal opposition party, the Kenya African Democratic Union (KADU), dissolved itself and merged with KANU in 1964. However, a new opposition party, the Kenya People's Union (KPU), emerged in 1966 under the leadership of the leftist Jaramogi Oginga Ajuma ODINGA, whose forced resignation as vice president in April 1966 caused a minor split in the ruling party and led to a special election in which the new group won limited parliamentary representation.

Both President Kenyatta and Vice President Daniel Teroitich arap MOI, a member of the small Kalenjin ethnic group, were unopposed for reelection in September 1974. Kenyatta died on August 22, 1978, and was immediately succeeded, on an interim basis, by Moi, who, as the sole KANU candidate, was declared president on October 10 to fill the remainder of Kenyatta's five-year term.

A veneer of apparent stability was shattered by an attempted coup by members of the Kenyan Air Force on August 1, 1982. Loyal military and paramilitary units quickly crushed the rebellion, and the government announced the disbanding of the existing air force. President Moi dissolved the National Assembly on July 22, 1983, and called for a premature general election. The balloting was conducted on September 26, although Moi on August 29 was guaranteed a return to the National Assembly as an unopposed candidate and reelected to another presidential term as KANU's sole candidate for the office. Thereafter, he dealt harshly with rebel leaders, 12 of whom were executed in 1985.

In early 1986 the government launched a crackdown on dissidents and dealt forcefully with unrest within the university community in late 1987. Internal and external critics continued to charge the government with human rights abuses. Notwithstanding such controversies, the government experienced little real electoral challenge in early 1988. As the only candidate presented by KANU on February 27, Moi was declared reelected, again without the formality of a public vote, while party preselection eliminated most dissenters from assembly balloting on March 21. Several days later, Moi replaced his longtime vice president, Mwai KIBAKI, with the relatively unknown Dr. Josephat KARANJA. However, in April 1989 the assembly, apparently with the tacit support of the president, declared its nonconfidence in Karanja, who resigned on May 1. Moi immediately appointed George SAITOTI to the position, noting that his new deputy, who had earned praise for his handling of economic affairs, would retain the finance portfolio.

In February 1990 the highly popular Foreign Minister Robert OUKO, was assassinated before he could complete an investigation of government and KANU corruption. Although domestic unrest intensified following the incident, in May Moi once again rejected calls for introduction of a multiparty system, insisting that such a change would exacerbate tribal cleavage. A KANU conference in December 1990 reendorsed the one-party system, while in February 1991 the government refused to recognize a National Democratic Party (NDP) organized by former vice president Odinga. However, multiparty advocates regrouped in midyear as the Forum for the Restoration of Democracy (FORD).

The administration's image was further tarnished on November 19, 1991, when Nicholas Kiprono BIWOTT, one of the president's closest political allies, was dismissed from the cabinet after an outside investigator had described him as a prime suspect in the Ouko murder. Shortly thereafter, international lenders and Western capitals informed Nairobi that economic assistance would be frozen until political and economic reforms were implemented. In response, Moi reluctantly reversed his position on multiparty pluralism, and following constitutional revision effective December 20, several new parties were legalized, prompting a number of cabinet and KANU officials to resign and join the opposition.

On October 28, 1992, Moi dissolved the National Assembly in preparation for the as yet unscheduled elections. Describing the action as his "secret weapon," Moi apparently sought to capitalize on the recent splintering of FORD into two factions, FORD–Kenya (FORD–K) and FORD–Asili (FORD–A), over the choice of a presidential candidate. In presidential balloting on December 29 Moi was challenged by two former vice presidents, Kibaki, founder of the Democratic Party (DP), and Odinga, leader of FORD–K, as well as FORD–A leader Kenneth MATIBA and four other candidates. Although winning only 36 percent of the vote, Moi easily outpolled his three top challengers. Meanwhile, in simultaneous legislative balloting KANU secured 100 assembly seats, well ahead of FORD–K and FORD–A, which won 31 seats each. Domestic and international observers criticized the polling as tainted by KANU intimidation tactics, electoral fraud, and vote rigging. Subsequently, on January 4, 1993, the two FORD groups and the DP, the latter controlling 23 assembly seats, announced the formation of an opposition coalition to "nonviolently" force the holding of new elections. However, only the DP honored a pledge not to sponsor candidates against other opposition parties. As a result, the coalition was in disarray in a by-election on June 27, 1994, that gave KANU 3 of 7 seats. More importantly, an increasing number of disillusioned opposition MPs were crossing over to KANU, with the latter edging toward the two-thirds majority needed for constitutional revision.

The government's violent crackdown on dissidents in late 1996 signaled both an intensification of Moi's desire to suppress the proreform movement and the apparent ascendancy of hard-liners within KANU. In early February 1997 the administration, citing "emergency" drought conditions, imposed the Preservation of National Security Act, which granted the government broad emergency powers, including the right to curtail political party activity. Thereafter, widespread antigovernment demonstrations were reported in late February 1997, and in April the ambassadors of 14 countries issued a joint statement condemning the government for using excessive force to suppress the continuing unrest and calling on the administration to remove restrictions on the opposition's freedoms of speech and assembly.

In mid-April 1997 the constitutional reform movement appeared to gain new focus when a number of prominent opposition leaders took part in a meeting of the National Convention Assembly (NCA), a proreform movement theretofore led by activist religious groups. For their part, KANU leaders dismissed the NCA as a "grouping of tribalists," and the NCA's attempt to convene a meeting of its executive wing was banned.

Under pressure from both domestic and international observers, President Moi on June 1, 1997, pledged to review the colonial-era laws that allowed security personnel to use force against illegal demonstrations; nevertheless, reports of government-initiated violence continued. Consequently, on July 17 the opposition announced its intention to launch a campaign of protest demonstrations culminating in a general strike in August. In response, the administration announced that it would establish a bipartisan parliamentary commission to review the constitution and expunge those laws designed to suppress the opposition. Real progress remained elusive, however, as the government rejected demands that NCA representatives be included on the commission.

On August 28, 1997, President Moi organized a meeting of over 120 KANU and opposition parliamentarians at which the two sides launched the Inter-Party Parliamentary Group (IPPG) to serve as a vehicle for drafting electoral reform measures. Subsequently, IPPG negotiators forged a series of draft constitutional amendments, which were approved by the legislature in late October and early November and signed into law by Moi on November 7. Meanwhile, the government approved the registration of 12 new parties, including, after some delay, Safina, a grouping launched in early 1995 by Paul MUITE (an opposition MP) and the noted paleontologist Dr. Richard LEAKEY (see Political Parties, below). On November 10 Moi dissolved the assembly, and the following day the government announced that presidential and legislative elections would be held in late December.

At the presidential balloting held December 29–30, 1997, President Moi won another five-year term by outdistancing a field of 14 candidates. The incumbent secured approximately 40 percent of the vote, while his nearest competitor, the DP's Kibaki, captured 31.1 percent. Meanwhile, in simultaneous legislative elections, KANU narrowly retained its majority, securing 113 seats. The DP finished second, with 41 seats overall, while a total of ten parties gained representation. Deriding the polling as fraudulent, a number of opposition officials immediately called for new elections, and Kibaki filed suit to have the results overturned. Dismissing criticism of the electoral process, on January 8, 1998, Moi named a new government, which did not, however, include a vice president.

The terrorist bombing of the U.S. embassy in Nairobi on August 7, 1998, and the resulting death of 247 Kenyans and 11 U.S. citizens caught the Moi government off guard. Security concerns surfaced again in early 1999 when it was revealed that a Kurdish militant, Abdullah Öcalan, had entered Kenya without going through proper immigration procedures, only to be captured and transported out of the country by Turkish security agents acting without Nairobi's consent. On February 18 Moi dismissed three top security officials and reshuffled his government in an apparent response to the incident.

Among those affected by the cabinet changes was finance minister Simeon NYACHAE, the government's most prominent anticorruption campaigner, who resigned from the government rather than accept a lesser post. Nyachae's demotion reportedly surprised observers, as it appeared to undermine the government's claims of greater economic accountability on the eve of fresh negotiations with the IMF. On April 3 Moi reappointed George Saitoti as vice president. (Saitoti had held the post until December 1997, after which Moi had left the post vacant, prompting speculation that his next deputy would be his hand-chosen successor.)

President Moi pulled a political rabbit out of his hat in June 1999 when he enticed Dr. Richard Leakey (a prominent member of the Safina opposition party) to join the administration as cabinet secretary and head of the civil service. Leakey and his economic reform team were subsequently given high marks for probity and enthusiasm, although it remained unclear whether progress would be sufficient for the IMF and World Bank (who were demanding improved fiscal discipline, privatization, and anticorruption measures) to resume aid. That question became moot in April 2001 when Leakey resigned after powerful groups within the government had blocked his anticorruption efforts.

On June 12, 2001, Moi appointed Raila ODINGA (the former vice president's son) and other members of the NDP to his cabinet, thereby forming a "coalition" government. (In March 2002 KANU and the NDP formally merged.)

A number of opposition alliances were formed in 2002 in preparation for the December presidential and legislative balloting. In February several groups (including the DP, FORD–K, NCA, the **United Democratic Movement** (UDM), and a faction of FORD–A launched a **National Alliance for Change** (NAC), which was later restyled as the **National Alliance of Kenya** (NAK) under the party registration for the **National Party of Kenya** (NPK). Concurrently, FORD–People, Safina, the **Kenya National Democratic Alliance** (KENDA), and others established the **People's Coalition of Kenya** (PCK), also sometimes referenced as the "Third Force for Change." In mid-October the NAK and PCK joined the newly formed **Liberal Democratic Party** (LDP) and its so-called Rainbow Alliance of former KANU and NDP faction leaders in an even larger opposition alliance called the **National Rainbow Coalition** (NARC), also referred to as the "Super Alliance." However, the selection of Kibaki as the NARC's presidential candidate caused problems with FORD–People leader Simeon Nyachae, who withdrew his party from the alliance and launched his own presidential campaign. These 15 opposition parties in the "Super Alliance" were held together by a Memorandum of Understanding (MoU) signed before the December 2002 elections by the leadership of the constituent parties of the NAK and the LDP, who agreed, if victorious, to divide cabinet positions equally in consultation among the party leaders and to name the LDP's Raila Odinga as prime minister once a new constitution was adopted.

Moi in July 2002 selected Uhuru KENYATTA, the son of independence leader Jomo Kenyatta, as his preferred successor. However, public sentiment subsequently appeared to be turning solidly against KANU, which was expected to face a serious electoral challenge in December from a united opposition. On August 30, 2002, Moi dismissed Saitoti, who had earlier opposed Moi's selection of Kenyatta as his presidential successor. (The post remained vacant until November 4, when Moi appointed Wycliffe Musalia MUDAVADI from KANU as the new vice president.) In the meantime four cabinet ministers, including Odinga, resigned from the cabinet over Moi's selection of Kenyatta, and, with Saitoti, joined the opposition (see Political Parties, below). Moi dissolved the assembly on October 26, 2002, prior to the elections and before it had an opportunity to review proposed changes to the constitution drafted by the constitutional review commission. Moi dissolved the constitutional commission the following day, and on October 28 he barred delegates from convening.

The results of the presidential and legislative balloting on December 27, 2002, swept KANU out of power in a decisive victory for the "Super Alliance." The NARC presidential candidate, Mwai Kibaki, secured 62.3 percent of the vote, while Moi's handpicked successor, Uhuru Kenyatta, captured only 31.2 percent. The remaining three presidential candidates won less than 6.4 percent of the vote. In the legislative elections, the constituent parties of NARC captured a majority of 125 of the 210 elected seats. KANU finished second with 64 seats and became the official opposition party for the first time. Five other parties secured seats in the National Assembly.

President Kibaki was inaugurated on December 30, 2002, and had a cabinet in place by January 6, 2003. Vice President Michael Kijana WAMALWA died of a serious illness on August 23, 2003. Kibaki named Arthur Moody AWORI the new vice president on September 25, 2003.

The NARC government, in its first major policy initiative in 2003, eliminated the fees for public primary schools and made school compulsory. NARC's campaign pledges for economic revival proved more difficult to realize because the graft and oppression of the Moi regime had left the Kenyan economy in bad shape. The economy, transportation infrastructure, and the once-strong banking and financial services sector were in serious disrepair. International pressure to eliminate corruption in the public and private sectors and to privatize state enterprises, resisted by Moi for years, forced action when the new government needed foreign aid and loans to deliver on its promises to revive the economy. President Kibaki promised to create 500,000 new jobs every year, a pledge that proved impossible because acts of terrorism and severe drought weakened the tourism and agriculture sectors early in his term. Moreover, the government made slow progress in the privatization of government-controlled enterprises, which had long been sources of political patronage and graft.

The NARC coalition pledged to crack down on public sector corruption with a zero-tolerance campaign platform. In 2003 President Kibaki was under popular and international pressure to end corruption and prosecute some of the worst abusers under the Moi regime. In early February 2003 Kibaki dismantled entrenched political patronage networks by purging senior civil service and security forces members and reassigning others. Soon thereafter, he dismissed the chief executives of three state enterprises. Kibaki opened the new session of the National Assembly on February 18, 2003, with the remarkably frank admission that "[c]orruption has undermined our economy, our politics, and our national psyche" and pledged to address the issue by introducing legislation. (A new law and code of ethics were later adopted requiring senior government officials to declare their assets upon entering and exiting office.) Within days of the speech Kibaki suspended the chief justice of the High Court pending an investigation into allegations of corruption and torture of prisoners. Kibaki also named a high-profile anti-graft crusader, John GITHONGO (former head of Transparency International in Kenya), as his anticorruption chief.

In March 2003 the government opened a public inquiry, closely followed by the news media and the Kenyan people, into the infamous Goldenberg International corruption scandal that first surfaced in the 1990s. The inquiry addressed a scheme whereby nearly $600 million was siphoned from the public coffers of the central bank to the Goldenberg firm (and, by implication, to a string of government officials) in the form of export credits and state subsidies for gold and jewelry exports that never existed. (As of 2008, however, few public officials under investigation had been formally indicted or put on trial.)

In October 2003 Kibaki, in the wake of a report issued by a special commission investigating the conduct of the Kenyan judiciary, suspended 6 of the 9 judges in the court of appeals, 17 out of the 36 high court judges, and 82 of the 254 magistrates on grounds of "corruption, unethical conduct, and other forms of misbehavior."

By December 2003, however, problems with the government's own anticorruption record emerged in press accounts of new irregularities in government procurement. By May 2004 additional allegations surfaced over irregularities in procurement contracts for police telecommunications equipment, forensic laboratories, and a new passport system (dubbed the Anglo-Leasing scandal). In July British High Commissioner Sir Edward Clay publicly criticized the Kibaki government for its renewed tolerance for the corrupt practices of the past and an appetite among senior government officials within the NARC coalition for the trappings of office. The British, United States, and European Union (EU) governments immediately stepped up diplomatic pressure on Nairobi to investigate and prosecute any wrongdoing. The IMF and World Bank joined the chorus of donors calling for zero tolerance for corruption and an end to lavish perks for senior government officials.

In a bid to shore up support for his government in the face of bitter factional infighting among the major parties within NARC, President Kibaki reshuffled the cabinet on June 30, 2004, and formed a "government of national unity" by including key opposition party leaders, including members of KANU and FORD–People.

On February 7, 2005, John Githongo resigned from his post as anticorruption chief, citing pressure from within the cabinet to close his investigations of the procurement irregularities. The United States immediately suspended $2.5 million in anticorruption aid to Kenya. President Kibaki reshuffled the cabinet again on February 14, 2005, transferring some cabinet ministers and announcing a number of changes in the civil service in response to the mounting pressure from foreign governments, and on February 16, 2005, government prosecutors filed charges against six former government officials implicated in the procurement scandals.

By mid-2005 the parliamentary groups of NARC were in disarray as members of the government and opposition camps crossed party lines to forge temporary and unstable alliances, and groups of MPs openly contemplated the formation of new political parties and party alliances in anticipation of the 2007 elections. The run-up to the constitutional referendum in November 2005 intensified this instability and maneuvering for political advantage.

Opposition to the November 2005 constitutional referendum united under the banner of the "Orange Team"; the "no" vote was symbolized by an orange. Building on the defeat of the proposed constitution, the LDP and KANU leadership, the power brokers behind the Orange Team, took steps to form a coalition, the **Orange Democratic Movement** (ODM). As a coalition of political notables and their parties and ethnic networks, ODM was subject to factional infighting even as its supporters were positioning the ODM to win control of the government in the 2007 elections.

In the wake of the no-vote for the referendum on constitutional reform in November 2005, Kibaki dismissed his entire cabinet on November 23; 7 of the 28 cabinet ministers campaigned against the proposed constitution (see Constitution and government, below). Political turmoil ensued as Kibaki announced the names of his new cabinet on national television on December 8 only to have many of the newly appointed officials refuse to serve. Final cabinet appointments were made on December 13.

In 2006 more details of the Goldenberg and Anglo-Leasing corruption scandals surfaced and threatened to bring down Kibaki's government. John Githongo, living in exile in the United Kingdom, alleged in a public letter to President Kibaki that the Kenyan government had issued phony contracts to a nonexistent British firm to upgrade its passport system and forensic science laboratories (the Anglo-Leasing scandal). The "Githongo Report" alleged that up to 30 members of the government had participated in the scheme, including Vice President Moody Awori, who denied any wrongdoing. In the fallout George Saitoti (education minister), Kiraitu MURUNGI (energy minister), and David MWIRARIA (finance minister) resigned their cabinet positions in February 2006. Githongo also claimed that the money raised by graft was intended to fund the forthcoming election campaign.

In response to members of his own cabinet defecting to ODM, President Kibaki announced in March 2006 that he no longer considered NARC a viable party and that he identified with (but never formally joined) the newly formed **National Rainbow Coalition of Kenya** (NARC–K) party. ODM, KANU, and other opposition parties responded to the president's statement and his subsequent support for NARC–K candidates in the July 2006 by-elections by challenging the legitimacy of his government and calling for a vote of no confidence in parliament.

Given the close margins on votes of no confidence in parliament, the July 24, 2006 by-elections for five assembly seats (to replace the five MPs who died in an April 2006 airplane crash) were hotly contested by the new NARC–K party and the opposition KANU and LDP elements of ODM. NARC–K candidates prevailed in three of the five constituencies; KANU candidates won the other two. The balloting was marred by charges of vote buying, violence, and allegations that government aircraft were used to transport campaigning NARC–K politicians and that government vehicles were used to ferry voters to the polls. LDP and KANU party leaders called on the Electoral Commission of Kenya (ECK) to nullify the results, and ECK officials complained of "the wanton violation of electoral rules by the Government."

By November the charges against Saitoti and Murungi were dropped or dismissed, and Kibaki reappointed them to their previous cabinet posts. David Mwiraria also returned to the cabinet in July 2007 but with a new portfolio (environment and natural resources). (Critics alleged that Kibaki was reluctant to jettison political allies who could deliver critical support in the 2007 elections.) Additionally, Kibaki refused to recall the National Assembly until March 22, 2006, out of fear that the parliament would pass a vote of no confidence.

Despite his pledge in 2002 to serve only for one term, Kibaki indicated in 2006 that he would seek reelection in 2007 under the banner of a new, but unnamed party. The formation by Kibaki's remaining supporters in government of a new splinter party, National Rainbow Coalition of Kenya (NARC–K), which drew Kibaki loyalists in the cabinet and National Assembly into its fold from the fractured NARC coalition's constituent parties, called into question the viability of the NARC government's election mandate. After five members of parliament died in an airplane crash in April 2006 (including two assistant cabinet ministers), the by-election held to replace them in July 2006 was the first electoral contest featuring NARC–K candidates. With Kibaki's endorsement and campaign support, the NARC–K candidates took three of the five seats. Kibaki did not formally join NARC–K, however, despite the party's public endorsement of him for another term in January 2007, choosing instead to keep his choice of reelection vehicle open until the formation of the Party of National Unity (PNU) in September 2007.

Kibaki dismissed two cabinet ministers in early October 2007 after NARC party leaders shifted their support to other presidential candidates before the presidential and legislative campaigns. Kibaki dissolved parliament on October 22 in preparation for the December general elections.

Legislative balloting was held on December 27, 2007, and 23 parties won seats in the National Assembly. The ODM secured a plurality of 99 seats; the PNU, 43 seats; Orange Democratic Movement–Kenya (ODM–K), 16; KANU, 14; Safina, 5; NARC–K, 4; FORD–People, 3; and NARC, 3. Fifteen other parties won 2 seats or fewer. The parliamentary elections were overshadowed, however, by the post-election chaos surrounding the presidential balloting held on the same day. The Electoral Commission of Kenya (ECK) hastily declared incumbent president Mwai Kibaki the winner over challenger Raila Odinga, despite allegations by opposition leaders and international observers of widespread irregularities and a flawed result. Kibaki was declared the winner by the ECK with 46 percent of the vote; Raila Odinga, the ODM candidate, placed second with 44 percent. Kalonzo MUSYOKA of ODM–K polled 9 percent. Six other candidates failed to poll more than 1 percent combined. Ethnic violence over the disputed results led to thousands of casualities and widespread unrest and provoked a police crackdown on demonstrations (see Current issues, below).

President Kibaki was hurriedly sworn in for a second term on December 30. He installed a partial cabinet on January 8 and named Kalonzo Musyoka as vice president. Following protracted negotiations between Kibaki and the ODM's Raila Odinga over a power-sharing arrangement (see Current issues, below), Kibaki acquiesced in broad changes in the structure of executive power and agreed that Odinga would serve as the Kenya's first prime minister in an agreement signed on February 28. On April 13 they jointly appointed a new, expanded cabinet, with 42 seats divided according to the strength of the two camps. The cabinet, the largest in Kenya's history, was sworn in on April 17.

Lands minister Kipkalya KONES died in an airplane crash on June 10. Finance Minister Amos KIMUNYA resigned on July 8 after a vote of nonconfidence passed several days before in the National Assembly. Kimunya had presided over the ministry during the sale to the Libyan government of a hotel property owned by the Kenyan government. The appearance of irregularities surrounding the sale and Kimunya's initial denials of rumors that the property had been sold prompted the action by parliament.

Kibaki reshuffled the cabinet on January 23, 2009, giving Deputy Prime Minister Uhuru Kenyatta the finance portfolio, bringing Amos Kimunya back into the cabinet as trade minister, and appointing a new minister for roads. Justice minister Martha KARUA resigned from the cabinet on April 6.

On August 4, 2010, a new constitution, which limited the powers of the presidency, created a bicameral legislative, and contained a new bill of rights, was approved in a referendum by a vote of 67 percent in favor and 30 percent opposed (see Constitution and government, below). The constitution was opposed by Kenyan churches because it permitted abortion under certain conditions, including medical emergencies. However, both the president and the prime minister supported the new basic law and campaigned for its approval. Difficulties in implementing the new constitution led to a postponement of elections scheduled for 2012 (see Current issues, below). On August 16 there was a minor cabinet reshuffle.

Throughout 2010 and into 2011, the government continued to be plagued by allegations of scandal, leading to the resignation of the minister of foreign affairs and the minister of industrialization (see Current issues, below). In response, a new attorney general was appointed in August 2011.

Following his indictment by the ICC, Kenyatta resigned his portfolio on January 26, 2012, but remained as deputy prime minister (see Current issues, below). The cabinet was reshuffled on March 25. The second deputy prime minister, Wycliffe Musalia MUDAVADI, left the ODM to join the UDF (see Political parties, below). He resigned his position as minister for local affairs on May 9 but retained his post as deputy prime minister.

Ahead of national elections in March 2013, Kenyatta's new grouping, The National Alliance (TNA), formed the broad-based Jubilee coalition, which included, among other parties, the newly formed United Republican Party (URP) and NARC (see Political parties, below). The main opposition to the Jubilee alliance was the Coalition for Reforms and Democracy (CORD), led by the ODM. Kenyatta won the presidential balloting as the Jubilee's candidate with 50.5 percent of the vote. Jubilee secured majorities in both the newly formed Senate and the National Assembly (see Current issues, below). Kenyatta was inaugurated on April 9. His cabinet was approved between May 15 and June 5.

Constitution and government. The 1963 constitution was amended several times (for more information, please see the 2013 *Handbook*). The National Assembly, initially bicameral in form, was reduced to a single chamber in 1967 by merger of the earlier Senate and House of Representatives. All candidates for election to the assembly were required to be members of KANU prior to the December 1991 amendment, which authorized multiparty balloting. Under controversial amendments approved in 1988 the president, who had been accorded the right in 1986 to replace the auditor and attorney generals, was further empowered to dismiss court of appeal and high court judges; concurrently, police were authorized to hold uncharged detainees for up to 14 days. An amendment passed in August 1992 required that successful presidential candidates secure 25 percent of the vote in at least five of the eight provinces. Defended by the government as a means to avoid election of a solely regional candidate, the law was criticized by the opposition for unduly favoring the incumbent, whose support was drawn from a number of small, geographically widespread tribes. Amendments in 1997 permitted the formation of a coalition government, mandated a broad review of the constitution, and expanded the number of directly elected seats in the assembly from 188 to 210.

A popular plank of the NARC government electoral platform promised to deliver a new constitution that would reduce the powers of the president within six months, with a deadline of June 2003. The mistrust between the National Alliance of Kenya (NAK) and Liberal Democratic Party (LDP) party factions of NARC (see Political Parties, below), however, led to a stalemate over the formula for the diminution of executive power. Raila Odinga of the LDP rallied support for the creation of a robust prime minister in a constitutional arrangement similar to that of France. President Kibaki and his closest advisors in the NAK wing of NARC lost their enthusiasm for specific arrangements that would force the executive to substantively share power with another single figure, and for other reforms that might weaken NARC's ability to maintain its electoral advantage. A constitutional review conference opened on April 30, 2003, in the Bomas of Kenya, comprised of all the members of the National Assembly plus 406 delegates, but the divisions over a new power-sharing formula only sharpened during the proceedings. The promised deadline passed without approval of a new constitution, and popular agitation over the stalemate presented the NARC with a serious crisis, as a majority of Kenyans expected concrete reforms to prevent future abuses of executive power associated with the graft, corruption, and oppression of the previous regime. The situation became more polarized with the suspicious murder in September 2003 of Crispin MBAI, a key figure in the negotiations over executive power sharing at the Bomas conference and a close associate of Odinga.

The stalemate continued into 2004 as the "Mt. Kenya" faction of the NAK wing of NARC sought assembly review and amendment of the Bomas draft, which supported the Odinga/LDP view of executive power sharing and was approved in March by most of the 629 delegates to the review conference. The LDP wing countered that the draft could only be passed or defeated in toto, a position also favored by a majority of the delegates who attended the review conference. The government withdrew from the conference and sought passage of legislation that would permit the assembly to amend the Bomas draft. On June 28, 2004, President Kibaki announced that the 2004 revised date for a new constitution would also be missed. Riots broke out at pro-Bomas constitutional rallies in Nairobi and Kisumu as riot police moved to enforce a ban on antigovernment protests.

In 2005, a Parliamentary Select Committee on Constitutional Review (PSC) was formed to consider the status of changes to the Bomas draft. The LDP pulled out of the PSC after six of its party members were removed from the committee. Eventually, the NAK wing of NARC prevailed as the assembly amended the Bomas draft to weaken the prime minister, retain a powerful presidency, and maintain a unicameral legislature. The changes also altered the basis for the administration of Kenya's provinces; previous arrangements would be changed to create elective district administration with accountability to the central government. On July 22, 2005, the National Assembly approved the key terms of the revised constitution bill. A national referendum on the new constitution, required by a ruling of the High Court before a new constitution could have effect, was held on November 21, 2005.

The constitution's key elements included provisions for land reform, women's rights, and the further establishment of regional religious courts. (Christian and other religious courts would be created to work in tandem with the Kadhi, or Muslim, courts, which apply religious law to issues such as personal status, marriage, and divorce.) Absent from the proposed constitution, generally referred to as the Wako draft, were provisions to establish a prime minister and to return to a bicameral legislature.

The referendum, which became known as the Banana and Orange Referendum (because the many illiterate voters were asked to choose from a symbol of a banana if they approved of the new constitution and an orange if they opposed it), was hotly contested. Both sides held a series of political rallies that were marred by violence; at least eight people were killed. The referendum ballot on November 21, 2005, drew a 53 percent voter turnout. The Wako draft constitution was soundly defeated, with approximately 58 percent voting against and only 42 percent favoring its passage. The failure dealt a blow to Kibaki's leadership and threatened the viability of his government.

The political settlement that emerged on February 28, 2008, following the political turmoil and ethnic violence over the disputed December 2007 presidential elections led to a constitutional reform bill—the National Accord and Reconciliation Act—which passed on March 18, 2008. The act codified the new post of executive prime minister and created two deputy prime ministers. On December 16, 2008 parliament passed a bill eliminating the Electoral Commission (ECK) and providing for the establishment of an interim commission as recommended by the Kriegler Report. A bill to create a special tribunal to try perpetrators of election violence, as recommended by the Waki Report, however, failed to pass in February 2009 (see Current issues).

A special court ruled in May 2010 that the country's Islamic Kahdi courts were unconstitutional since they allowed one religion to be treated differently than others. A new constitution was ratified by referendum and went into force on August 21. The new basic law created an upper house, the 67-member Senate (a minimum of 16 seats are reserved for women). In addition, the lower house, the National Assembly, was expanded to up to 349 members. At least 47 seats in the assembly must go to women (one from each county) under the new framework (see Legislature, below). The constitution limited the powers of the presidency and created a judiciary that included, at the appellate level, the supreme court, the court of appeals, and the constitutional court. It also contained a bill of rights that guaranteed a range of basic liberties for Kenyans. Finally, it abolished the office of the prime minister. Administratively, Kenya is divided into 47 counties, each headed by an elected governor and county assembly.

Following the 2002 election, Kenya made significant strides in advancing free speech and developing a free press. The press grew noticeably bolder, publishing news articles and analysis critical of the government as a matter of routine and without the fear of intimidation or reprisals that were ever present under the Moi regime. In 2012 the media watchdog group Reporters Without Borders ranked Kenya 71st out of 179 countries in freedom of the press, a rise from 84th the previous year and a ranking comparable with regional states, such as Tanzania (70th) and Zambia (72nd).

Foreign relations. Kenya devoted its primary attention following independence to regional and continental affairs, supporting African unity and liberation movements in southern Africa. Regionally, it signed the Treaty for East African Cooperation in Kampala, Uganda, on June 6, 1967, providing for the formal launching of the East African Community (EAC) on December 1. The grouping (initially perceived as a model for multinational economic integration) was designed to preserve and expand arrangements established under British colonial rule in areas such as transportation and communications. Supporters also envisioned eventual creation of a common market, and the East African Development Bank (EADB) was established as a related institution (see article on EADB under Regional and Subregional Development Banks). However, the EAC achieved little success, in part due to ideological differences between Kenya and socialist Tanzania and a variety of disputes between Kenya and Uganda. The EAC was terminated in mid-1977 amid significant acrimony over distribution of its assets and collateral developments, including Tanzania's decision to close its border with Kenya. In November 1983 final agreement was reached regarding the EAC assets, and the Kenyan-Tanzanian border was reopened; relations with Dar es Salaam were further stabilized by the reestablishment of diplomatic relations in December. Relations with Uganda also improved in the immediate wake of the November agreement, although new tensions subsequently arose, with each country accusing the other of harboring insurgents and Nairobi exhibiting what some observers described as an "obsession" with perceived Ugandan hostility.

In 1994 the three former EAC members established a Tripartite Commission for East African Cooperation with the hope of reviving integrationist sentiment, and in 1996 Francis MUTHAURA, Kenya's former ambassador to the United Nations, was named executive secretary of the commission's new secretariat, headquartered in Arusha, Tanzania. Kenya was subsequently viewed as the leading proponent of cooperation, and a treaty for the formal reactivation of the EAC had been drafted by the spring of 1999. The proposed accord called for the gradual reduction of tariffs between members and establishment of a common external tariff as initial steps toward a possible monetary union and even, in the minds of the most ardent integrationists, eventual political federation. The presidents of the three countries involved were scheduled to meet to approve the new treaty by the end of 1999. However, considerable negotiation reportedly was necessary on details of the plan; Tanzania expressed concern that it would be overwhelmed by Kenya's much larger economy, and continental leaders wondered how a revived EAC would interact with other groupings, such as the Common Market for Eastern and Southern Africa (Comesa) and the Southern African Development Community (SADC), which were promoting larger free-trade blocs. Meanwhile, Rwanda and Burundi were eager for membership once the EAC was relaunched successfully. (For details on the subsequent formal reestablishment of the EAC and the expansion to include Rwanda and Burundi, see separate article on the EAC in the Intergovernmental Organization section.) In 2004 the three EAC principals signed a customs union agreement that established a common external tariff, but left room for exceptions, which in 2007 materialized as Tanzanian requests to exempt pharmaceuticals, transport buses, millstones, and wheat. Comesa also moved to adopt a customs union in May 2007 with the common tariffs set to be in place by December 2008.

Kenyan-Somali relations frequently have been strained by the activities of nomadic Somali tribesmen (*shiftas*) in Kenya's northeastern provinces and by long-standing Somalian irredentist claims. They reached a nadir in mid-1977 with the outbreak of hostilities between Somalia and Ethiopia in the latter's Ogaden region, when a Kenyan spokesperson declared that an Ethiopian victory would be "a victory for Kenya." It was not until July 1984 that President Moi paid his first state visit to Mogadishu, in the course of which an agreement was concluded on border claims and trade cooperation, with Moi offering to help Somalian President Siad Barre "find a peaceful solution" to the dispute with Addis Ababa. The following September, several hundred ethnic Somali members of an exile group, the Northern Frontier District Liberation Front (NFDLF), responded to a government amnesty and returned to Kenya, declaring that the organization's headquarters in Mogadishu, Somalia, had been closed. Subsequently, in early December, Kenyan and Somalian representatives concluded a border security agreement, while other top *shifta* leaders responded to a second general amnesty in July 1985, declaring an end to the years of "banditry." With the subsequent collapse of the central state in Somalia, border incidents nonetheless continued throughout the 1990s and into the next century.

In early 1992 Nairobi, seeking to repair strained regional relations, signed cooperation agreements with Ethiopia and Sudan. Furthermore, on May 8 Nairobi established formal relations with Pretoria, and in June Moi became the first African head of state to visit South Africa in 21 years. Meanwhile, the encampment of approximately 300,000 Somalian, 70,000 Ethiopian, and 30,000 Sudanese refugees along Kenya's borders was described by the regime as an economic burden and source of insecurity. In August the United Nations High Commission for Refugees (UNHCR) criticized Kenya for detaining thousands of refugees in squalid conditions in Nairobi and Mombasa. Thereafter, in January 1993, amid rumors that it was considering an involuntary repatriation and describing the refugee situation as increasingly untenable, Kenya urged the UNHCR to hasten their departure.

On November 28, 2002, terrorists bombed an Israeli-owned hotel in Mombasa, killing 11 Kenyans and three Israeli tourists. On the same day a shoulder-launched missile was fired at an Israeli airliner but missed its target. In December al-Qaida claimed responsibility for the attacks as it had for the 1998 bombing of the U.S. Embassy in Nairobi.

President Kibaki's new government faced renewed pressure from the United States and the United Kingdom in 2003 to crack down on terrorist activity in Kenya with new internal security measures and reforms in the Kenyan security services. The United States threatened cuts in foreign aid to Kenya to encourage the new government, which reorganized the key security units responsible for antiterrorist intelligence. Both the United States and the United Kingdom announced in late May 2003 heightened security alerts for travel to Kenya, and British Airways and the Israeli airline El Al temporarily suspended flights. The travel alerts, warning of increased risk of a terrorist attack, were a blow to the Kenyan tourist industry already reeling from the November 2002 bombing and missile attacks. The alerts and threats of aid reduction prompted the government to submit a controversial Suppression of Terrorism Act in July 2003, which when introduced in the assembly was greeted with alarm by many government and opposition members, Muslim community leaders from the Coast and Mombasa, and leaders in human rights organizations; it prompted hundreds of protesters in Nairobi. The bill, which proposed to strengthen the government's powers of detention of persons and permit searches without court authorization, was blocked by an assembly committee. Since 2003, Kenya's cooperation with the United States antiterrorism policies for East Africa, while not complete (Kenya has refused to support immunity for U.S. personnel from war crimes prosecution), has nonetheless been substantial. Accordingly, direct aid to Kenya from the United States has increased since 2005, despite U.S. concerns over the persistence of public sector corruption.

Nairobi advanced its regional security objectives in East Africa in 2003 by signing in March a Strategy and Plan of Action for implementing a security agreement reached with Tanzania and Uganda in 2001. In May 2003 two Kenyan army battalions were deployed on the border with Somalia to guard against infiltration by potential terrorists, and in June the government responded to the heightened terror alerts by suspending flights to Somalia. As the violence escalated in Mogadishu and southern Somalia in early 2006 and as the drought conditions in the region worsened, these forces increasingly faced large numbers of refugees attempting to enter Kenya. By September 2006, with over 34,000 new refugees encamped in Kenya along the Somali border, the military was put on high alert and intensified patrols of territorial waters to fend off illegal shipments of arms and disrupt the transit of other illicit materials tied to terrorist cells among the Somali Islamic militias. The Kenyan military quietly cooperated with both Ethiopian and U.S. military forces in December strikes against the Somali militias by Ethiopian forces, offering intelligence assistance and air reconnaissance (this support of U.S. and Ethiopian forces was controversial and angered elements of Kenya's Muslim community). In January the Kenya-Somali border was closed. In the aftermath Human Rights Watch issued a report that accused Kenya of assisting the United States in rounding up Somali refugees suspected of ties to the Islamic militias and turning them over to Ethiopian authorities for detention.

In 2006, Chinese President Hu Jintao visited Kenya during his tour of Africa in 2006, and PRC diplomats offered expanded foreign aid and improved trade relations and sought in return Kenya's recognition of the PRC's One-China policy in regard to Taiwan. In April 2007 a delegation of nearly 100 Chinese business executives accompanied by PRC trade diplomats visited Nairobi; in August the Kenyan foreign ministry announced the opening of a new trade section in the Kenyan embassy in Beijing and assigned a trade attaché to the post.

Kenya experienced tremendous international pressure following the disputed 2007 presidential election. An EU election observation team immediately alerted the international community that there were irregularities and serious flaws in the tabulation of results at some polling locations and in the final counts certified by the ECK. As the unrest over the disputed presidential results spread across the country, fears of escalating ethnic violence between Luo and Kikuyu tribe members in major urban centers and between Kalenjin and Kikuyu in the Rift Valley, and the potential for continuing political and economic chaos, spurred a rapid, but uncoordinated diplomatic intervention. The strongest concerns were voiced by East African leaders and Western democracies, such as the United States, the EU (especially the United Kingdom), Canada, Australia, and international financial and security organizations, including the World Bank and the United Nations. Pressure from neighboring heads of state in East Africa and threats by Western governments to suspend aid, deny visas, freeze assets, and prosecute human rights cases finally convinced Kenyan elites that a domestic settlement was necessary to avert collapse of the constitutional order and to restore the regime's international legitimacy.

Ironically, once he became prime minister, Raila Odinga engineered pressure from Nairobi on Zimbabwe's president Robert Mugabe to reach a power-sharing agreement with his rival in that country's disputed presidential election. However, in September 2010 Kenya hosted the Sudanese president, Umar Hassan Ahmad al-BASHIR, violating an international arrest warrant issued by the ICC.

In February 2010 the United States again warned the government of the need to resolve differences and reach a political settlement during a visit by U.S. secretary of state Hillary Clinton. In March the Kenyan government rejected a plan by the Somali government to deploy 2,500 Somali troops that had been trained in Kenya as part of an offensive against Islamic militants. The Kenyan rejection was based on concerns that the deployment would destabilize the border area by alienating Somali clans in the region. Relations between Kenya and China continued to improve through 2010. The Chinese government provided $11.7 million in grants and loans to the government, bringing Chinese investment and aid in the country to more than $350 million since 2005.

Refugees continued to flood into Kenya from Somalia, with an estimated 44,000 arriving in the early months of 2011 alone and raising the number at the UN camp in Dadaab to more than 350,000. On May 4 more than 50 people were killed by Ethiopians of the Merille tribe during a border raid in a disputed area of northeast Kenya. The raid was reported to be in retaliation for an earlier incursion of members of the Kenyan Turkana tribe that killed five Merilles. Also in May tensions between Kenya and Uganda increased after Ugandan security forces occupied the disputed island of Ugingo in Lake Victoria. In July the United States issued arrest warrants for John Harun MWAU, a member of parliament from the ODM, and Naima Mohamed NYAKINIYWA, on charges of drug trafficking. The United States also froze the assets of the two. Reports indicated that U.S. law enforcement officials did not receive meaningful cooperation from their Kenyan counterparts in the investigation.

On October 16, 2011, more than 1,600 Kenyan troops entered Somalia as part of an operation to suppress the *al-Shabab* insurgency group (see entry on Somalia). The incursion was in response in to a series of kidnappings of Western tourists and aid workers in northern Kenya by *al-Shabab*. On November 17 Kenya, Ethiopia, and Somalia announced a coordinated military campaign against *al-Shabab*. Meanwhile, *al-Shabab* conducted escalating attacks in Kenya (see Current issues, below) and, in January 2012, declared a holy war against the Kenyan government. Meanwhile, on October 20, a Kenyan naval patrol boat captured six Somali pirates near Kiunga.

Sudan severed diplomatic relations with Kenya in November 2011 after a Kenyan court indicted Sudanese president Omar Hassan Ahmed al-BASHIR on war crimes for his role in the genocide in Darfur. By February 2012 Kenyan forces in Somalia numbered 4,600. They were placed under the command of the UN peacekeeping operation in Somalia. In September, Kenya and Ethiopia finalized a series of economic agreements.

In May 2013, Kenya and Somalia signed an agreement to begin the repatriation of an estimated 600,000 Somali refugees. In June, the United Kingdom announced it would spend more than $31 million to compensate an estimated 5,200 Kenyans who had been tortured or mistreated during the Mau Mau uprising of the 1950s. Also in June, Kenyan officials began trade negotiations with the United States in an effort to transform the U.S. African Growth and Opportunity Act, scheduled to expire in 2015, into a permanent agreement.

Current issues. Kibaki announced in September 2007, the formation of a new party coalition backing his reelection campaign, the Party of National Unity (PNU). The PNU was formed to replace the defunct NARC coalition with many of the same constituent parties that were still allied with Kibaki (who is Kikuyu). It also included the support of KANU after behind-the-scenes deal making by former president Moi.

The ODM, an opposition coalition that formed to defeat the Wako constitution referendum in late 2005, transformed into a political party in 2006. By August 2007, factional disputes cost ODM the support of its KANU wing and split the remaining wings of the party in two, with the strongest faction rallying behind the presidential candidacy of Raila Odinga (who is Luo) and another faction backing the candidacy of Kalonzo Musyoka (who is Kamba). With three major candidates in the race, each from a different ethnic group, the scramble by party operatives to knit together the necessary cross-ethnic political alliances began in "the season of defections," when the party affiliations of political figures changed at a dizzying pace as they sought to pick a party that would get them a nomination and a seat in parliament.

Prior to the election, Kibaki appointed all new members to the ECK (including his family lawyer), except for the chair whom he reappointed. Odinga's ODM camp warned that Kibaki, who had close ties to former president Moi and other politicians threatened by regime change and ongoing anticorruption investigations, was preparing to rig the presidential election. Kibaki's preelection maneuvers and allegations of conspiracy by the opposition led to a highly charged atmosphere when the polls opened on December 27, 2007.

The ODM won a plurality in the parliamentary elections, but the presidential balloting was marred by sporadic violence. Chaos ensued when irregularities occurred at several polling sites in Central Province (Kibaki and Kikuyu strongholds), which did not report results at the same time as other areas of the country. In other cases, results announced at the constituency level did not match the results later reported by the ECK. The ECK declared Kibaki the winner in the presidential election without an official explanation of the balloting irregularities. Odinga declared that he had won and that the election had been rigged. On December 30 Kibaki was hurriedly sworn in for a second term, despite warnings from the EU election monitoring team that the results were highly irregular and deeply flawed. Soon thereafter, Odinga and other ODM leaders threatened to take their protest over the disputed elections into the streets of Kenya's major cities. More disturbing were violent attacks by Luo and Kalenjin on Kikuyus who had settled in the western parts of the country. The worst violence occurred in and around Eldoret in the Rift Valley, where ethnic Kalenjin militias targeted and killed Kikuyus, including people who had sought shelter in a church, which the attackers burned down, killing many inside. The ethnic violence sparked reprisals by Kikuyu on Luo communities in several large cities including the capital Nairobi. Luos counterattacked, and the entire country was threatened by escalating ethnic violence and the internal displacement of Kenyans evicted by the hostilities or displaced by fears of more violence. Before the unrest subsided, estimates put the number of dead at more than 1,200 and the displaced at more than 300,000.

Efforts to mediate between the Kibaki and Odinga camps began almost immediately with the World Bank's country director Colin Bruce attempting to broker a memorandum of understanding on an election inquiry and a power-sharing arrangement; these negotiations were soon taken over by the African Union chair and president of Ghana John Kufuor. The negotiations broke down, however, when Kibaki announced cabinet appointments on January 8 and refused to sign any brokered agreements for power sharing.

In the midst of calls for massive protests organized by the ODM in Nairobi, Mombasa, Kisumu, and other large cities around the country, the assembly convened on January 15. The longtime speaker of parliament was displaced by an ODM candidate in the first session. Meanwhile, the government warned that the opposition's planned "mass action" rallies were a violation of the preelection ban on public rallies and would be suppressed by force. Security forces fired tear gas and live rounds to break up several rallies. ODM leaders condemned these actions, but they switched tactics and announced a boycott on business interests allied with Kibaki and the PNU.

Former UN secretary general Kofi Annan stepped in to take over the mediation efforts later in January and scored a breakthrough when he convinced Kibaki and Odinga to meet together January 24 for the first time since before the election. The two leaders and their negotiating teams met throughout February but made little progress. As international pressure to come to an agreement mounted, the goals and demands of the two sides remained far apart. With intervention from U.S. secretary of state Condoleezza Rice and the Ugandan and Tanzanian presidents, Annan was finally able on February 28 to get the two sides to sign a two-page memorandum of understanding that put in place a power-sharing arrangement between Kibaki and Odinga. The arrangement created an executive prime ministership (and two deputy prime ministerships) to be occupied by Odinga and included a pledge to share cabinet positions. Final agreement on the size of the cabinet (eventually 42 ministers, the largest cabinet in Kenya's history) and the actual appointments was delayed until April 13 because the two sides squabbled over details for six weeks and almost dissolved the agreement. The threat of renewed violence eventually convinced both leaders to overcome the final obstacles and implement a grand coalition government.

As part of the power sharing agreement a series of independent commissions was established to study and report on the irregularities in the election and to investigate the post-election violence. The reports and recommendations of these commissions dominated political calculations for the coalition partners well into 2009.

The first of these reports was produced by an Independent Electoral Review Commission (IREC), which was chaired by South African jurist Johann Kriegler. Released in September 2008, the Kriegler Report found a dizzying array of ballot irregularities attributable to both ODM and PNU operatives as well as ECK regional poll staff rendering any chance of recovering a definitive winner of the presidential election impossible. Moreover the polls excluded a third of eligible voters while counting votes from more than 1 million deceased persons. The IREC's final recommendation was a complete overhaul of the ECK or its abolishment and replacement by an interim election board independent from government interference. A bill amending the constitution to abolish the ECK and replace it with an Interim Independent Election Commission (IIEC) passed in December.

The second and even more contentious group released its report on October 15. The Commission of Inquiry into Post–Election Violence (CIPEV), chaired by Justice Philip Waki, investigated the horrifying attacks, reprisals, and general mayhem wrought by ethnic militias following the presidential polls, in some cases perpetrated at the behest of political and business leaders. The Waki Report concluded that some attacks were spontaneous in origin but soon morphed into organized violence, while others were planned in advance and executed by ethnic militias organized and funded by political and business elites at the highest national and regional levels. Moreover, state security forces ignored internal staff reports that warned of possible violence and deliberately took advantage of the chaos to perpetrate additional human rights violations. As part of the documentation of the crimes, Waki produced a large body of evidence and handed over a sealed envelope to Kofi Annan that reportedly contained the names of prominent politicians and business leaders, most notably some members of the cabinet, who should face further investigation by a special tribunal. Waki's recommendation gave the government 90 days to act on its own to create a special tribunal independent of the judiciary and attorney general and with international representation. If the government failed to act on this timeline he requested than Annan turn the envelope over to the International Criminal Court in The Hague for further investigation.

While both men initially pledged to implement the Waki report, the political ramifications of the sealed envelope soon put strains on both President Kibaki and Prime Minister Odinga's political alliances and therefore on their ability to work together to get past the crisis. Part of Odinga's ODM leadership and electoral support came from areas where some of the most shocking violence occurred in the Rift Valley—and these political allies, threatened by the potential for being named in the sealed envelope, began to maneuver for leverage in order to avoid the possibility of prosecution. For Kibaki's part, his closest political and business elite allies were also threatened, as rumors after the election placed members of the Mungiki criminal syndicate in the presidential State House to plan reprisals for the attacks on Kikuyu communities. Kibaki signaled that the tribunal might be empowered to grant amnesty for all crimes, which galvanized opposition against a special tribunal constitutional bill in parliament by reform MPs who feared yet another government investigation that served to quash prosecutions and give impunity to corrupt politicians. Together with those MPs who feared prosecution or political cronies whose careers were tied to such persons, these reform MPs defeated the special tribunal bill put forward by the government in February 2009 (following the first of several extensions on the deadline granted by Annan).

As the government stalled or sought further schemes for undermining the independence of a tribunal, several other international reports were released that further deepened the sense that corrupt Kenyan public officials were systematically escaping justice. The most important of these was a statement from the UN official rapporteur on extrajudicial executions in Kenya, which alleged that Kenyan police and military personnel had engaged in systematic torture and execution over a number of years, and had escaped punishment by complicity from officials charged with oversight and investigation. In the same month, two human rights activists were murdered in broad daylight by gunmen in Nairobi not long after calling attention to the same pattern of abuse and impunity for police "death squads."

In July Annan, out of patience that the government would create a tribunal with appropriate power and independence, turned the sealed envelope over to an ICC prosecutor, despite the announcement by Kibaki and Odinga that they would form a Truth and Reconciliation Commission to explore ethnic violence.

In January 2010, 5 people were killed and more than 20 injured in protests that followed the arrest of a radical Islamic cleric, Abdullah al-Faisal. Meanwhile, in March the ICC initiated an investigation into postelection violence in Kenya in 2008. A proposed pay raise for the prime minister and members of parliament prompted protests and strikes throughout the country in July. Most major parties supported the ratification of the new constitution in August 2010. The effort to secure passage of the new law eased existing tensions between the president and prime minister.

Six prominent Kenyans, known as the Ocampo Six (after ICC prosecutor Luis Ocampo), were charged by the ICC for their roles in election violence in 2007–2008. The accused included former cabinet ministers Henry KOSGEY and William Samoei Arap RUTO and current finance minister and deputy prime minister Uhuru Kenyatta.

Widespread protests against the rising costs of food and fuel led the government to cut taxes on corn, wheat, gasoline, and kerosene in April 2011. In an effort to counter charges of corruption, Kibaki replaced Attorney Gen. Amos WAKO with noted law professor and political outsider Githu MUIGAI in August. Also in August the cabinet appointed a task force to create a constitutional amendment that would overturn the requirement that one-third of the members of parliament be women. The government asserted that the quota would be too difficult to implement. Women's rights groups criticized the action.

Following the 2011 Kenyan deployment of troops in Somalia, three separate grenades attacks in November left 3 dead and 18 injured. The attacks were said to be the work of *al-Shabab.* Reports indicated that *al-Shabab* was active in recruiting terrorists from among Somali refugees in the country.

The ICC formally indicted four members of the Ocampa Six on January 23, 2012, including Kenyatta and Ruto. Both subsequently claimed that the indictments were politically orchestrated by Odinga to sabotage their respective presidential bids. There were 6 people killed and more than 60 injured on March 11 in a grenade attack in Nairobi. The government blamed the Somali *al-Shabab* group. Meanwhile, a British energy company announced on March 26 that it had discovered oil in northern Kenya and that it would expand exploration and start production activities. On June 10 the minister of state for provincial administration and internal security, George SAITOTI, was killed in a helicopter crash (see Political parties, below) along with four other officials.

Police in Nairobi foiled two *al-Shabab* attacks in September, including a plan to blow up the parliament building. On September 28, a new, broad, antiterrorism bill was enacted that strengthened penalties for terrorism convictions and increased the powers of security agencies. Meanwhile, ethnic clashes in the Tana Delta between the Pokomo and Orma tribes left 78 dead.

In January 2013, a series of *al-Shabab* attacks in and around Garissa left 11 dead and 13 injured. In February, the Supreme Court rejected a petition by human rights groups and civil organizations requesting that Kenyatta be barred from running for the presidency because of his ICC indictment.

Despite their indictments, Kenyatta and Ruto were elected president and deputy president in balloting on March 4, 2013. The indictees argued that the charges were a form of neocolonialism and foreign interference. Running as the candidate of the Jubilee Coalition, Kenyatta defeated Prime Minister Odinga, the candidate of CORD, 50.5 percent to 43.7 percent. There were six other candidates, none of whom received more than 4 percent of the vote. Meanwhile, Jubilee secured 21 Senate seats, compared with 20 for CORD, and 6 for the small Amani Alliance. In the assembly voting, Jubilee secured 167 seats, followed by CORD with 141 (see Legislature, below).

Through the summer of 2013, a succession of witnesses withdrew from the ICC case against Kenyatta prompting reports that prosecutors would not have enough evidence to try the president. Supporters of the president and deputy president continued to deny the charges, while opponents charged that the government was using various forms of intimidation to pressure witnesses. The ICC prosecutor asserted that the government continued to fail to cooperate fully and actively interfered with the investigation. In June, in response to negotiations with the AU, the ICC offered to hold Ruto's trial in Africa.

POLITICAL PARTIES

On September 16, 2007, Kibaki unveiled his reelection coalition under the banner of the **Party of National Unity** (PNU), an umbrella coalition of parties and the successor to the NARC coalition formed in 2002 (for information on parties and coalitions prior to 2007, please see the 2012 *Handbook*). As the PNU nominations process for parliamentary constituencies was subsequently bogged down by so many parties vying for a share of the nominations slate in November, affiliate parties and candidates began to make contingency plans so they could be on the ballot even if they failed to secure the PNU label. Other PNU-affiliated politicians succumbed to the appeals and promises of opposition leaders and bolted from the PNU and its affiliate parties. The ODM also lost to rival camps some politicians who had failed to win nomination by the party.

By December 27 there were nearly 2,550 registered candidates from 108 political parties (with a record 269 female candidates) eligible to run for the 210 elected seats in parliament. One parliamentary constituency had 33 separate candidates vying for a single seat. Unlike the presidential balloting held simultaneously, the parliamentary polling was conducted in relative calm and with few allegations of irregularities.

Once the PNU and ODM camps reconciled their bitter dispute over the presidential elections and the ethnic violence subsided, a grand coalition government emerged, with power sharing between rival presidential candidates and division of seats in an expanded cabinet. The practical result left only one opposition party among 23 in the legislature. All other parties were either part of the government or allied with government parties. An opposition caucus began to emerge in May 2008, however, which drew together nearly 65 politicians from some of the smaller parties and disgruntled MPs from the coalition parties.

The passage of a political parties bill in July 2008 requiring a stronger organizational basis for parties and more mass membership from each constituency across the nation created a scramble by parties to comply or face deregistration. If strictly enforced the law could reduce the number of parties certified to contest the next national election.

Government Parties:

Jubilee Alliance. Jubilee was founded in as a vehicle to support the presidential campaign of Uhuru Kenyatta in January 2013. The alliance initially included **The National Alliance** (TNA), the **National Rainbow Coalition** (NARC), the **United Republican Party** (URP), and the **Republican Congress Party** (RCP).

Leader: Uhuru KENYATTA (President of the Republic).

The National Alliance (TNA). The TNA was originally founded as the **National Alliance Party of Kenya** (NAK)/**National Party of Kenya** (NPK) but relaunched in 2012 to serve as the political base for Uhuru Kenyatta. The NPK was launched in June 2001 under Charity NGILU, who had been the **Social Democratic Party** (SDP) presidential candidate in 1997. By 2002 Ngilu had moved the NPK into the NAC grouping to help launch the restyled NAK, turning over to the opposition alliance the party registration for the NPK to avoid delays or obstruction in party certification from the Moi government.

The NAK brought together 14 parties under one tent (with the NAK as one of the two pillars of NARC, the other being the LDP). Before the LDP joined forces with the NAK to form NARC, Ngilu was in line to receive the prime minister's post under the anticipated new constitution. Once LDP's Rainbow Alliance entered the scene, the premiership was promised to Raila Odinga of the LDP. Ngilu was named a cabinet minister by President Kibaki, was made chair of NARC, and was selected to sit on the NARC Summit.

In the party dissolution crisis that followed in 2004, Ngilu initially supported Kibaki on the question of individual or corporate membership in NARC, but by early 2005 she and other NPK party leaders had reversed course and registered the NPK independently again. The NPK joined the LDP and FORD–K in asking the courts to block the March 2005 NARC effort to dissolve the constituent parties and hold direct NARC party elections. The high court, however, ruled against the injunction and cleared the way for NARC to hold grassroots elections. NPK was not consulted during the creation of the NARC–Kenya party, and Ngilu challenged the legitimacy of the new party by suggesting that NARC–K was little more than the DP in a different form. After running for parliament under the NARC banner in the 2007 election, the NPK party became dormant, while Ngilu emerged as a leader of NARC.

Kenyatta revived the party in 2012 and changed its name to the TNA. By September, the party had won six by-elections, including two seats in the assembly and four on local councils. The TNA continued to gather momentum as Kenyatta emerged as a strong presidential contender and led the effort to create the Jubilee Alliance. Kenyatta was elected president in the March 4, 2013, elections, while the TNA secured 17 Senate seats, 89 assembly seats, and 8 governorships. Despite the party's success, financial woes led to the layoff of staff as reports indicated an internal struggle between TNA chair Johnson Sakaja and vice chair Lydia Mokaya.

Leaders: Kenyatta UHURU (President of the Republic), Johnson SAKAJA (Chair), Lydia MOKAYA (Vice Chair), Onyango OLOO (Secretary General).

National Rainbow Coalition (NARC). The NARC was fashioned out of the October 2002 Super Alliance between the 14-party National Alliance for Kenya (NAK)—a restyled version of the National Alliance for Change—and the newly formed **Liberal Democratic Party** (LDP) and its Rainbow Alliance of KANU/NDP dissidents. From the beginning, this grouping of politicians, ethnic interests, and wide-ranging political ideologies was one of political expedience more than enduring ties or shared policy goals. *Africa Confidential* framed NARC's inherent challenge: "[I]t isn't a party, it's a loose alliance of individuals and 15 parties. Its members range from leftists and trade unionists to 'tribal rights' ethnic chauvinists who have found common political cause."

Uniting the opposition to defeat the ruling KANU necessitated constructing a "big tent." NAK and LDP achieved this with the 2002 preelection of MoU that equally divided job responsibilities and cabinet positions should NARC prevail. The NARC platform promised to revive the economy and create hundreds of thousands of jobs, crack down on official corruption (and get foreign aid flowing again), ratify a new constitution that limited presidential power within six months, and institute free universal primary education.

After the NARC electoral victory the underlying tensions within the coalition began to appear almost immediately. President Kibaki never convened the NARC Summit, the top party organ made up of the constituent major party leaders after the election, and the LDP neglected to designate one of its leaders as its Summit representative, perhaps due to the difficulty of choosing faction leaders. From the very beginning the ethnic rivalries, dissension over broken MoU promises, and the division of power undermined the cohesion of NARC in government.

President Kibaki's efforts throughout 2004 and 2005 to fashion a more cohesive NARC by dissolving the constituent parties and opening NARC to an individual rather than a corporate basis for membership had the opposite effect. His move to invite opposition members into the government and demote several LDP cabinet members exacerbated the tensions and drove some LDP assembly members to sit with the opposition parties. The February 5, 2004, NARC party meeting in Nanyuki, which convened to plan the dissolution of the constituent parties and broker a new consensus on power sharing, failed when only a fraction of the invited delegates attended. At a second Nanyuki meeting in April, members of the NARC committee for corporate membership voted down the plan to dissolve the member parties in favor of individual membership. The LDP, FORD–K, UDM, and IPK representatives voted in favor of retaining corporate membership, the FORD–A and SPARK delegates took a middle position, the DP representative remained neutral, and only the SDP and PPF leaders supported dissolution of parties and individual membership.

Calls for NARC party elections slated to begin February 26–27, 2005, at local levels, March 1 at the constituency level, and ending on March 11 were eventually scuttled. Opposition from three NARC factional leaders—Charity Ngilu (NPK), Raila Odinga (LDP), and Musikari Kombo (FORD–K)—led to a court battle over the NARC constitution.

In January 2005, 73 members of the assembly from the NAK wing of NARC formed a new lobby called National Reform Initiative (NARI) in response to their dissatisfaction with the pace and tenor of the government's economic, land, constitutional, and social service reforms. With the LDP wing of the coalition already in open rebellion, this left the future parliamentary cohesion of NARC in jeopardy. By mid-2005 National Assembly members from the Coast Province were openly meeting to discuss the formation of a regional party, further undermining NARC's cohesion.

The major party organs of NARC were the Summit, created by the MoU, the Party Council, and the Parliamentary Group. In theory the NARC Summit achieved some measure of party and ethnic balance among the coalition partners. The Summit consisted of the DP's Kibaki (Kikuyu), LDP's Odinga (Luo), Moody Awori (Luhya), Najib Balala (Coast and Muslims), UDM's Kipruto KIRWA (Kalenjin), and the NPK's Charity Ngilu (Kamba). All of these organs fell away because of factional tensions. In practice NARC had two de facto secretariats, one unofficial group loyal to Kibaki and another official group under the leadership of Ngilu.

The movement of the LDP into opposition and the formation of NARC–K in 2006 further divided NARC and undermined its viability. President Kibaki declared NARC "dead," and Ngilu retorted that the newly formed NARC–K was little more than the DP with a different name and should not be confused with the NARC, which was still the ruling government party. At least 80 MPs left the coalition, including Mutua Katuku and Alex KIBAKI (President Kibaki's son) as well as many cabinet ministers.

Leaders of the NPK, DP, and FORD–K met in June 2006, after the formal launch of NARC–K, to discuss reinvigorating the NARC party organs after Kibaki distanced himself politically from the coalition.

The NARC revival effort was renewed a year later in the maneuvering to strengthen the party in preparation for the 2007 presidential and legislative elections. Party representatives met three times in meetings chaired by Noah Wekesa to rewrite the coalition's constitution; the last meeting included representatives of constituent members DP, FORD–K, FORD–A, UDM, SPARK, the PPF, plus representatives of the independent parties Mazingira Green Party of Kenya and Saba Saba Asili and a representative from the LPK (part of ODM–K, see above). Most of these parties supported Kibaki's reelection.

Notably, the NARC party chair, Charity Ngilu, and other official party leaders declined to attend or review the new constitution and would not surrender NARC's registration certificate to others, thus keeping Kibaki from using NARC as his umbrella for contesting the 2007 elections. Ngilu, the health minister until her dismissal from the cabinet in October 2007, broke with Kibaki and moved closer to the ODM leadership in August 2007, finally joining the ODM senior leadership group, Pentagon, in October, but with agreement that she had the option to stand for election to the new parliament under the NARC banner.

NARC put forward 73 candidates, including Ngilu, for constituencies but won three seats in the National Assembly in the December 2007 election. After the election NARC was formally allied with the ODM and President Kibaki, and Prime Minister Odinga appointed Ngilu to the cabinet with the water and irrigation portfolio.

Ngilu initially pledged to support Odinga in the 2013 presidential balloting but then shifted the party's support to Kenyatta as NARC joined Jubilee. In the balloting, NARC won one Senate seat and three assembly seats. Ngilu was appointed Minister of Lands, Housing, and Urban Development in the subsequent cabinet.

Leaders: Charity NGILU (Chair and Minister of Lands, Housing, and Urban Development), Fidelis NGULI (Secretary-General), Bartha Mbata MBUVI (Vice Chair), Wanjala WELIME.

United Republican Party (URP). The URP was formed in January 2013 by William Samoei Arap Ruto and defectors from the ODM. The URP was one of the founding members of the Jubilee Alliance and Ruto was the coalition's vice presidential candidate in the 2013 general elections. In that balloting, the URP secured 12 Senate seats, 75 assembly seats, and 10 governorships.

Leaders: William Samoei arap RUTO (Deputy President of the Republic), Francis Ole KAPPARO (Chair).

Amani Coalition. The Amani Coalition was formed in 2013 to support the presidential candidacy of Deputy Prime Minister Musalia MUDAVADI. The alliance included the **United Democratic Forum** (UDF), the **Kenyan African National Union** (KANU), and **New Ford Kenya** (New Ford–K). After the elections, the coalition joined the Jubilee Alliance.

United Democratic Forum (UDF). Founded in 2012 by Deputy Prime Minister Musalia MUDAVADI and other defectors from the ODM, the UDF was a reformist party which promoted economic liberalism. Mudavadi was the UDF's 2013 presidential candidate. Mudavadi placed third in the balloting with 4 percent of the vote. The UDF won 3 Senate seats, 11 assembly seats, and 1 governorship, in the general elections.

Leaders: Musalia MUDAVADI (2013 Presidential Candidate), Hassan OSMAN (Chair), Abraham LIMO (Secretary General).

Kenya African National Union (KANU). Originally drawing most of its support from Kenya's large Kikuyu and Luo tribes, KANU was formed in 1960, established its leading position in the election of May 1963, and subsequently broadened its constituency through absorption of the Kenya African Democratic Union (KADU) and the African People's Party (APP), both supported by smaller tribes. KANU principles include "African socialism," centralized government, racial harmony, and "positive nonalignment."

Following President Moi's lead, KANU in December 1990 voted to retain the one-party system; however, on December 3, 1991, a special congress endorsed the president's about-face on the issue. A number of KANU adherents, including 11 National Assembly members, subsequently switched allegiance to new opposition parties, primarily FORD (below).

During the run-up to presidential and legislative balloting in late 1992, the party attempted to portray itself as a "stable alternative" to what it described as an internally divided, tribal opposition. On the other hand, it continued to suffer from a steady flow of defections as well as accusations that it was supporting Kalenjin tribesmen who were considered responsible for initiating ethnic clashes in the Rift Valley. Faring poorly in Nairobi, Nyanza, and Central Province, the party lost over half of its seats in assembly elections on December 29. Nevertheless, KANU retained an assembly majority, securing 100 seats, not including the 12 seats designated for presidential appointment.

In 1996 KANU was bolstered by the addition of a number of former opposition members as well as three legislative by-election victories. However, several factions subsequently emerged, notably KANU-A, ostensibly more open to political reform and internal party democracy, and KANU-B, which tended to reflect more centralized and traditionalist perspectives. With Moi's renomination for another (and possibly final) presidential term a foregone conclusion, the main issue within KANU in late 1996 was the selection of his vice presidential running mate for the 1997 campaign. Although George Saitoti retained a degree of support for continuing in office, it was reported that he and his supporters in the KANU-B faction (including Nicholas Biwott and party secretary general Joseph KAMOTHO) were being challenged by Simeon Nyachae, a cabinet minister, and his KANU-A colleagues.

At an October 1996 meeting the internecine competition reached a head as the two camps clashed over internal election policies, with the KANU-A wing seeking the introduction of a nationwide internal balloting system (apparently with the anticipation of snaring the secretary generalship), while KANU-B demanded continuation of the local branch elections (from which victors are chosen for top posts). For his part, President Moi came down firmly behind the KANU-B faction, either demoting or ousting KANU-A ministers in a sweeping government reshuffling in January 1997.

In early 1998 Moi called on the party to rally behind constitutional reform efforts and pledged to expand KANU's dialogue with FORD–K and the National Development Party (NDP), a previously minor grouping that had been pushed into the limelight when former FORD–K leader Raila Odinga had joined it in December 1996. Meanwhile, a third faction (KANU–C) emerged within the party under the leadership of Kipruto arap KIRWA and other "youth-oriented" activists. Angered at the organizational efforts of the Kirwa faction, Moi called on KANU dissidents to quit the party in June; subsequently, Kirwa and his associates withdrew from the constitutional review process. (In January 1999 they formally broke with the party and formed the UDM [see below].)

The supremacy of the KANU-B faction within the party and government was reinforced by the February 1999 cabinet reshuffling, which included the demotion of Nyachae (who then left the government and, ultimately, the party [see FORD–People, below]). However, a number of prominent KANU–B leaders were subsequently accused of corruption in a report published by the assembly in May 2000.

Growing cooperation between KANU and the NDP led to the inclusion of several NDP members (including Odinga) in the cabinet in June 2001. Subsequently, in March 2002, the NDP decided to merge into KANU, with Odinga becoming KANU's secretary general. However, severe internal problems arose in July when President Moi selected Uhuru Kenyatta as his preferred successor. Odinga subsequently helped form the so-called Rainbow Alliance within KANU in conjunction with several other disaffected former leaders, including Saitoti, who had been ousted as vice president of the republic in August.

President Moi's selection of Kenyatta (who was formally nominated at a party congress in October) was designed to put a Kikuyu candidate on the party ballot and maintain Moi's control over the party after he exited the presidency. The ploy split KANU and drove out the Rainbow dissidents. The Alliance formally left KANU in October to form the LDP (see above). NARC's nomination of Mwai Kibaki in October pitted two Kikuyu candidates as the presidential frontrunners, a fact that magnified the importance of the votes brokered by the other ethnic leaders in the LDP.

More KANU old guard resigned after the party's defeat in the December 2002 elections, throwing the party into turmoil. By April 2003, Moi announced that he would step down as party chair later in the year. Stepping into the role of official opposition party leader in the assembly, Kenyatta named a shadow KANU cabinet in June. At the September KANU executive meeting, Moi kept his pledge and resigned as chair without naming a successor. Kenyatta was subsequently named acting chair in April 2004.

KANU's party elections were held at a party congress in early 2005. Kenyatta took the chair in a landslide victory over rival faction leader Nicholas BIWOTT; Biwott disputed the outcome and moved to set up a rival KANU faction dubbed the New KANU Alliance Party. (This faction was given control over KANU's government registration by the Registrar of Societies and the ECK during a battle over the party's relationship to ODM in late 2006 through June 2007.)

As the principal opposition party uniting the Orange Team against the November 2005 constitutional referendum, KANU played a dominant role in shaping the ODM (see above). KANU signaled its willingness to work with their ODM partners to nominate a single opposition candidate for president and worked with ODM partners in the July 2006 by-elections, with KANU representatives picking up two of the five contested seats in parliament.

In parliament KANU MPs aggressively challenged President Kibaki's paper-thin, disorganized majority. For instance, in March 2006 six KANU members resigned their seats in the powerful House Business Committee after complaining that the government was underrepresenting KANU in committee assignments.

Kenyatta grew increasingly disenchanted with KANU's place within ODM in 2007, however, as it became clear that he was not likely to secure the ODM nomination for president and that other ODM leaders were inclined to move ODM away from a coalition of parties model toward a unified party structure. In June 2007 he delayed filing presidential candidacy papers with the ODM party organs pending a clarification on whether ODM was a coalition or a party and whether the parties had status as corporate members. (After a meeting of his KANU faction in Kasaranu, Kenyatta secured an understanding within ODM's leadership that seats in a new government would be divided according to a set formula, with 40 percent given to KANU.)

In the meantime, Biwott's faction actively maneuvered to support Kibaki in the elections (with the aid of Daniel arap Moi's rehabilitation by Kibaki and Moi's active deal brokering) and met at a Mombasa delegates meeting in June to continue the quest to take KANU outside ODM. Ultimately, the fight with Biwott for control over the KANU's registration forced Kenyatta's hand by July; moreover, Moi worked tirelessly behind the scenes to reconcile the factions, restore the party registration to Kenyatta's faction, and split KANU permanently from ODM (as Raila Odinga was getting the upper hand in the ODM nomination fight). By August Kenyatta announced that KANU was out of ODM and would run its own candidates in the legislative elections. Kenyatta also announced that he would not run for president but would instead support the reelection of Kibaki (the last a vindication for the king-making activities of Moi and a huge boost to Kibaki's reelection bid).

In September Kenyatta took part in the discussions forming the PNU coalition to reelect Kibaki, but KANU was given a special dispensation as a partner party and allowed to run candidates against PNU candidates in parliamentary races under the KANU banner.

Running candidates in 91 constituencies under its own banner, KANU won 14 seats in the parliamentary election in December 2007. Four KANU MPs were named to the cabinet in April 2008, including Kenyatta as deputy prime minister.

After yet another failed attempt to wrest back control of KANU leadership, Nicholas Biwott was elected party leader of a new party, the **National Vision Party** (NVP), on December 22, 2008. (The NVP joined the Amani Coalition in 2102.)

In June 2010 KANU was criticized by the election commission for failing to have party elections in more than five years. KANU led the opposition to the new constitution, ratified in August. In December 2010 KANU leader Uhuru Kenyatta was charged by the ICC with inciting election violence in 2007–2008 and formally indicted in 2012. He left the party in 2012 to form the TNA. In 2011 the party's executive committee approved a name change to the **Kenya Alliance for National Unity** (KANU); however, leading party figures resisted the alteration.

KANU joined the Amani Coalition for the 2013 balloting, and won 3 Senate seats, 6 assembly seats, and 1 governorship.

Leaders: Gideon MOI (Chair), Nick SALAT (Secretary General).

New Forum for the Restoration of Democracy in Kenya (New FORD–K). Formed as a splinter group from FORD–K in 2007, New FORD–K forged an alliance with the PNU in September 2007 to contest the December 2007 elections but later choose to run candidates under the party's own banner. Two New FORD–K candidates won seats in the December 2007 parliamentary election, and Peter Shitanda was appointed to the cabinet and remained through several cabinet reshuffles. After joining the Amani Coalition, New Ford–K won 6 seats in the assembly and 1 governorship in the 2013 general elections.

Leaders: Eugene WAMALWA (Chair and Justice Minister), Peter Soita SHITANDA (Housing Minister), Boni KHALWALE.

Forum for the Restoration of Democracy for the People (FORD–People). FORD–People was launched by Kenneth Matiba in October 1997, thus ending his battle with Martin SHIKUKU for control of FORD–A. Reportedly the most distinguishing salient feature of the FORD–People's charter (in comparison to the FORD–A's) is an intraparty electoral system wherein its candidates' nominations "will be under direct primary elections."

Upon Matiba's retirement in December 1998, his son Raymond MATIBA allegedly assumed control over the party; however, it was not immediately clear in what capacity the younger Matiba would function.

In December 2001 FORD–People invited former KANU minister Simeon Nyachae to join the party and serve as its presidential candidate. FORD–People subsequently participated in the formation of the PICK and NARC groupings. Nyachae pulled out of NARC almost immediately, however, after NARC refused to institute a primary to nominate a single candidate for the presidency. Nyachae ultimately ended up pursuing his own candidacy in the December 2002 election, a decision that reportedly caused serious rifts within FORD–People.

Nyachae and the other elected FORD–People ministers sat in opposition within the National Assembly, pledging to vote with NARC when it made good decisions. Nyachae was eventually brought into the cabinet by President Kibaki when he formed the government of national unification in June 2004. At a December 2004 party conference Kipkalya Kones, Reuben Oyondi, and Farah Maalim were elected chair, vice chair, and secretary general, respectively.

In preparation for the 2007 presidential elections, FORD–People met with FORD–Kenya with the aim of reviving the original FORD party. The talks were aimed at reaching an agreement on the process of determining a joint presidential nominee. Farah Maalim proclaimed that the "differences between party members have been ironed out and all were now united." The parties intended to play down the importance of reaching an agreement on a new constitution and instead made economic development, energy resources, and drought recovery the primary issues for FORD–People. Ultimately, the parties remained separate. Simeon Nyachae, roads and public works minister, announced in June 2006 that he planned to leave politics and not stand for election in 2007.

The FORD–People leadership found the NARC–K leadership team unacceptable as electoral partners, a factor which may have been decisive in Kibaki choosing not to embrace NARC–K as the banner behind his reelection campaign. FORD–People joined under the PNU banner for the 2007 elections.

Like other PNU allied parties however, FORD–People chose to run under its own banner in some 41 constituencies and ultimately won three seats in the National Assembly in the December 2007 election. One FORD–People MP, Henry Obwocha, was appointed to the coalition cabinet but lost his position in a cabinet reshuffle. Obwocha subsequently became party chair.

In the 2013 general elections, FORD–People won four seats in the assembly. After parliament convened, FORD–People joined Jubilee.

Leaders: Henry OBWOCHA (Party Chair), Simeon NYACHAE (2002 presidential candidate), Reuben OYONDI (Vice Chair), Farah MAALIM (Secretary General), Francis Munyialo OPAR (Party Organizing Secretary), Dominic MUTHUURI (Treasurer), Kimani WANYOIKE (Former Secretary General and 1997 presidential candidate).

National Rainbow Coalition of Kenya (NARC–Kenya or NARC–K). NARC–K claimed to be a "political vehicle" that would enable the current Kenyan leadership a "fresh start" to achieve "true Kenyan independence." Launched in June 2006 and composed primarily of former members of NARC and the DP who remain loyal to President Kibaki, NARC–K seeks to free itself from the political corruption that plagued the country under President Moi and the scandals and factional infighting that have marred the Kibaki presidency. Although billed as a multiethnic party, the leadership derives most of its support from the Kikuyu ethnic group, and skeptics have charged that the formation of NARC–K is little more than a political maneuver designed to bring the DP into power under a different name. (Kibaki is the founder of DP, see below.) At the very least, the formation of NARC–K appeared to be an attempt to reconstitute the DP with the objective of attracting wider support within the

Mt. Kenya region. Complicating matters further was Kibaki's ambiguous relationship with NARC–K. Kibaki stated that he identified with NARC–K, and Vice President Moody Awori (a Kibaki ally) declared that President Kibaki was "behind the inspiration of leaders knitting together the values, policies and vision of the party." However, Kibaki was noticeably absent from NARC–K's first public meeting, and he never registered as a member of the party. Kibaki's reluctance may be explained by the risk to his government of his joining NARC–K and thereby endangering the constitutional status of his fragile government elected under the NARC banner. Moreover, Kibaki may have lost the support of FORD–People and other ministers if he formally joined NARC–K.

Despite this ambiguity, the NARC–K leadership endorsed Kibaki as its presidential choice on January 7, 2007. When Kibaki subsequently spurned the invitation to run under the NARC–K banner and organized the PNU party coalition in September 2007, NARC–K joined as a corporate member of the new party. Soon thereafter many NARC–K notables, including Moody Awori, left the party to affiliate directly with PNU.

In the turmoil over the PNU nominations process, however, Martha Karua and Matua Katuku maneuvered to assume control over the NARC–K party registration. This effort created a safe haven for politicians allied with Kibaki: If they failed to secure the direct PNU nomination, aspirants could fall back to a NARC–K nomination and stand for election against the PNU choice.

NARC–K ran candidates in 59 constituencies and secured four seats under its own banner in the 2007 parliamentary election. Karua won a seat under the PNU label, was named to the cabinet by Kibaki after the election, and was part of Kibaki's negotiation team for brokering the power-sharing agreement between Kibaki and Odinga. She is jockeying with KANU's party leader, Uhuru Kenyatta, for the upper hand within the PNU alliance in the bid to be Kibaki's successor and the PNU's presidential candidate in 2012. In June 2012 Brian WEKE led a group of defectors from NARC–K to join the New FORD–K.

In 2013, NARC–K won one seat in assembly balloting. It subsequently joined Jubilee.

Leaders: Martha KARUA (Chair), Danson MUNGATANA (Secretary General), Asman KAMAMA (Deputy Chair).

People's Democratic Party (PDP). The PDP won one seat in the National Assembly in the December 2007 election. The party's MP affiliated with the ODM rather than the ODM–K/PNU alliance. It also won one seat in 2012 and one governorship. Reports indicated that the PDP joined the Jubilee coalition after the balloting.

Leader: Richard ONYONKA.

Chama Cha Uzalendo (CCU). A socialist party, the CCU secured two seats in the 2007 parliamentary election and two assembly seats in 2013. The party joined Jubilee after the parliament was sworn in.

Leaders: Koigi WAMWERE (Chair), Gitobu IMANYARA, Wavinya NDETI.

Other current members of the Jubilee Alliance include the **Republican Congress Party** (RCP), founded by Najib BALALA, which did not win any seats in the election, although Balala was appointed secretary of mining in the subsequent cabinet; the **Alliance Party of Kenya** (APK), formed in 2012 and led by Kiraitu Murungi, which won three Senate seats, five assembly seats, and one governorship in 2013.

Opposition Parties:

Coalition for Reforms and Democracy (CORD). CORD was a liberal, reformist, political alliance formed in December 2012 by the **Orange Democratic Movement** (ODM), the **Wiper Democratic Movement–K**, and the **Forum for the Restoration of Democracy–Kenya** (FORD–Kenya), among other parties. Prime Minister Raila Odinga (ODM) was the coalition's presidential candidate, and Vice President Stephen Kalonzo Musyoka (WDM–K), the deputy president candidate. The ticket placed second in the balloting with 43.7 percent of the vote. In the legislative balloting, CORD became the largest opposition party in both the Senate and National Assembly. The coalition won 23 governorships, more than any other grouping.

Leaders: Raila ODINGA (Former Prime Minister), Stephen Kalonzo MUSYOKA (Former Vice President of the Republic), Moses Masika WETANGULA (Senate Minority Leader and Former Foreign Minister).

Orange Democratic Movement (ODM). Originally known as the Orange Team, ODM began as a coalition of disparate political actors who came together in their opposition to the November 2005 constitutional referendum. ODM took shape after the referendum as an unsteady partnership between the LDP and KANU and the smaller LPK, allied by their common desire to defeat President Kibaki in the 2007 election. As a consequence, ODM lacked a common ideology or political philosophy and was best understood throughout 2006 as a pure opposition coalition. In the beginning ODM had no institutional structure and suffered from infighting among the leaders, many of whom were actively plotting paths for securing the ODM endorsement for the presidential nomination. Among the notable political figures who sought the ODM nomination for president were Raila Odinga (LDP), William Ruto (KANU), Najib Balala (LDP), Uhuru Kenyatta (KANU), Stephen Kalonzo Musyoka (LDP), Wycliffe Musalia Mudavadi (LDP), Julia Ojiambo (LPK), and Joseph Nyaga.

In September 2006 ODM registered as a political party under the initials ODM–K and began to create party organs to contest the 2007 elections, but as it did so the tensions between the party notables seeking the ODM presidential nomination and between the constituent parties increased. The formal structures included a plenary, a National Executive Council, a National Election Board, and a Council of Elders (later renamed the Consensus Committee). Disagreements about how the presidential nominee should be selected, whether by a direct vote of party delegates or by consensus, lingered well into July 2007, with the various candidates shifting their position on the method they preferred as their fortunes rose and fell. They also fought bitterly within the party over attempts to fill party offices with their loyalists. In June KANU leader Uhuru Kenyatta began pressing for clarification on the nature of the party itself, whether it was a coalition of parties or whether ODM would replace its constituent parties. Unhappy with the answers about KANU's membership, outmaneuvered for the ODM presidential nomination, and in a fight over control of KANU's legal status, Kenyatta pulled KANU out in late July. In September KANU joined the PNU and endorsed Kibaki. Meanwhile, the party subsumed the **Liberal Democratic Party** (LDP). (Please see the 2009 *Handbook* for more information on the LDP.)

Eventually the party settled on a direct vote by delegates to select the presidential candidate. Soon thereafter the rivalry for the ODM nomination between Musyoka and Odinga boiled over, with Musyoka bolting from LDP to the LPK in early August 2007 and refusing to permit the Registrar of Societies to install a new slate of leaders for ODM. The schism resulted in Musyoka forming a separate party and running as a presidential candidate under the original, registered party designation, ODM–K (see below). Odinga, Ruto, Mudavadi, and other leaders immediately acquired the rights to the ODM designation, registered their slate of leaders, and condemned Musyoka and Ojiambo for dividing the movement and thereby strengthening Kibaki's hand. In the meantime they actively courted stronger ties with NARC and NAK leader Charity Ngilu, in part as a hedge against losing support from Kamba voters following the departure of Musyoka. (Musyoka and Ngilu are both Kamba.) Odinga secured the party nomination on September 1 at a party nominating convention. He established the ODM Pentagon as the party's top strategic organ. Other members of the Pentagon included Ruto, Mudavadi, Najib Balala, and Joseph Nyaga.

Charity Ngilu joined the ODM Pentagon in late October after publicly endorsing Odinga in early October and subsequently being dismissed from the cabinet by Kibaki. Ngilu secured Odinga's agreement that she would contest her parliamentary constituency under the NARC banner, however. Another cabinet member, John KOECH, left KANU to join ODM in October and was also subsequently dismissed from the cabinet by Kibaki. (Koech later defected to ODM–K in November after failing to win an ODM nomination in his constituency.) After backing Odinga's candidacy in September, KADDU party chair Cyrus Jirongo withdrew his support in early November citing ODM's hostility to KADDU's attempt to run candidates in constituencies contested by ODM candidates.

ODM selected its candidates for parliament in primaries held in mid-November. The party then offered candidates in 190 constituencies in the December parliamentary elections and secured 99 seats in the National Assembly. Raila Odinga was credited with 44 percent of the national vote for president in the ECK official tally of results, which Odinga publicly disputed. Odinga and the ODM alleged that the election was rigged and immediately took steps to instigate massive public protests in Nairobi and other major urban centers in Western Province (the Luo tribe and ODM party stronghold), as ethnic violence erupted against Kikuyu peoples in Luo and Kalenjin majority regions in the west and the Rift Valley.

With a plurality in the National Assembly, the ODM elected one of their own MPs, Kenneth Marende, as the speaker after the National Assembly convened in January in the midst of unrest over the disputed presidential election. Two ODM MPs were murdered in late January, reducing the party's overall seat count to 96. (The speaker is ex officio and, thus, vacated his constituency seat.) In June by-elections, the ODM retained its three seats. ODM cabinet minister Kipkalya Kones and an ODM assistant minister died in a plane crash in June. These seats were retained by the ODM in a September by-election.

After the tenth parliament convened in January, ODM and MPs from PICK, PDP, and UDM forged alliances, which, with Charity Ngilu's NARC, gave the parties a solid plurality of the National Assembly votes. None of the ODM's selections for cabinet posts, however, except for the UDM representative, came from the Rift Valley or the Kalenjin tribe, which created a split during the election between Odinga and the Kalenjin politicians who backed ODM candidates, including William Ruto. Although Ruto was appointed minister of Higher Education, Science, and Technology, the rift expanded in 2010 as Ruto confirmed his intention to challenge Odinga as the party's candidate for the presidency in 2012. In December 2010 the ICC issued arrest warrants for Ruto and party chair Henry Kosgey on charges of orchestrating election violence in 2007–2008. Both Ruto and Kosgey were forced to resign from the government in 2011 because of allegations of corruption, unrelated to the ICC charges. Ruto subsequently left the ODM to form the URP.

In May 2012 former vice president and current deputy prime minister Mudavadi resigned from the party and joined the UDF after he was prevented from seeking the ODM nomination for the presidency. The ODM led the effort to form the ODM. The ODM won 17 Senate seats, 96 seats in the assembly, and 16 governorships in the 2013 general elections. In August 2013, a faction of "young Turks" in the ODM unsuccessfully attempted to challenge the party's leadership by calling for new leadership elections.

Leaders: Raila ODINGA (Party Leader, Prime Minister of the Republic, and 2007 and 2013 presidential candidate), Henry KOSGEY (Chair), Peter Anyang' NYONG'O (Secretary General), Omingo MAGARA (Treasurer), Franklin BETT (Elections Board Chair).

Wiper Democratic Movement–Kenya (WDM–K). The WDM K was originally founded as the **Orange Democratic Movement–Kenya** (ODM–K) in August 2007 from factional battles within the Orange Democratic Movement over the nomination of one of the party's many notables to be the candidate for president in the 2007 elections (see above). Outmaneuvered by Raila Odinga and his factional supporters for the ODM nomination, Stephen Kalonzo Musyoka, who controlled the party's official registration papers, established ODM–K, forcing Odinga and the remaining ODM leadership to register ODM separately.

Musyoka was nominated as the ODM–K presidential candidate on August 31, with LPK party chair Julia Ojiambo as his designated vice presidential candidate. ODM–K's new leadership summit consisted of Musyoka, Ojiambo, and Kennedy Kiliku, head of the NLP (see below).

The ODM–K won 14 assembly seats in the December 2007 parliamentary election. Musyoka ran in the presidential election and received 9 percent of the national vote. Soon after the election, Musyoka allied the party with Kibaki and the PNU. Kibaki then chose Musyoka as his vice president and minister for home affairs. After Kibaki and Odinga announced the power-sharing agreement, ODM–K retained 3 seats in the cabinet. Musyoka was expected to be the ODM–K presidential candidate in 2012. In 2012 the party had adopted a new name, the Wiper Democratic Movement–Kenya.

The party joined CORD for the 2013 general elections, with Musyoka as the coalition's deputy presidential candidate. The WDM–Kenya secured 5 Senate seats in the polling, 26 assembly seats, and 4 governorships.

Leaders: Kalonzo MUSYOKA (Party Leader, Vice President of the Republic, 2007 presidential candidate, and 2013 deputy presidential candidate), Samuel POGHISIO (Chair), Mutula KILONZO (Secretary General), David RIMITA (Election Board Chair), Joseph KHAMISI.

Forum for Restoration of Democracy–Kenya (FORD–K). The Luo-dominated FORD–K is the most direct outgrowth of the Forum for Restoration of Democracy (FORD), which was characterized by its multiparty founders in August 1991 as a "discussion group" in deference to the ban on political parties other than KANU. Despite seeming widespread support, FORD experienced problems in formulating a comprehensive platform and establishing a permanent party structure following its legalization in December 1992. Leadership disputes contributed to the difficulties; one faction supported the presidential ambitions of Martin Shikuku while another aligned itself with Jaramogi Oginga Ajuma Odinga, the aging former vice president of the republic, who succeeded in being named interim chair, with Shikuku as interim secretary general. However, the picture clouded further in May 1992 when Kenneth Matiba, a Kenyan businessman recently returned from London, announced his presidential candidacy.

At FORD's inaugural congress on September 4, 1992, Odinga was selected as the party's presidential candidate. However, Shikuku and Matiba supporters boycotted the congress and subsequently broke off to form FORD–Asili (FORD–A, see above). In early April 1993, despite a declaration of support by 51 opposition legislators for Odinga's assumption of the opposition leadership, the assembly speaker recognized FORD–A's Matiba. At the same time, intraparty opposition to Odinga's continued stewardship surfaced, with Kikuyu followers of (then) Deputy Chair Paul MUITE, an Odinga critic and de facto leader of the FORD–K's "young turks," reportedly defecting to the FORD–A and DP, (see above). (Muite subsequently became a founder of Safina, see above.)

In late June 1993 Odinga became leader of the opposition after a FORD–A legislator defected to KANU, and on July 15 he named a shadow cabinet. However, his subsequent efforts to improve relations with the Moi administration split the party, as supporters, led by his son, Raila Odinga, accused the anti-Moi faction aligned with Muite and (then) Secretary General Gitobu Imanyara of seeking to gain control of the party. On September 18 the FORD–K national executive council stripped Imanyara of his post and named Munyua WAIYAKI as his replacement. The following day Muite resigned as deputy chair, and on September 21 Imanyara quit the party, announcing plans to launch a "new democratic opposition movement."

Following Odinga's death on January 20, 1994, (then) Deputy Chair Michael Kijana Wamalwa, a favorite of the late leader's sons, Raila and Oburu ODINGA, was named party chair. In June 1995 Secretary General Waiyaki resigned to help form the United Patriotic Party (UPP, below). Subsequently, a schism developed because of a leadership contest between Wamalwa and Raila Odinga. In December Odinga disregarded a court ruling banning internal party elections by having himself proclaimed chair at meetings in Kisumu and Nairobi (but not in Mombasa, where the police intervened). Wamalwa reacted by announcing that his faction would sponsor grassroots balloting in May and June. Relations between Wamalwa and Odinga sank to a new low in early April 1996 when an extraordinary party congress, convened specifically to settle their leadership dispute, disintegrated into a riot after a party mediator, citing Wamalwa and Odinga's intransigence on procedural disagreements, declared their intraparty electoral contest "null and void" and resigned. Subsequently, on April 15 Wamalwa's supporters dismissed Odinga's claim that he had captured the party leadership. Friction continued throughout the year, culminating in Odinga's announcement in December that he was resigning from the party and joining the NDP. (On March 12 FORD–K officials openly supported a KANU candidate in a by-election contest with Odinga for the seat the latter had vacated when he left the party.)

At a FORD–K national delegates' conference on January 26, 1997, Wamalwa, James ORENGO, and Rachid MZEE were reelected chair, first vice chair, and second vice chair, respectively. Wamalwa was one of four prominent opposition leaders put under house arrest in May for their alleged roles in organizing antigovernment demonstrations. Subsequently, however, Wamalwa's opposition colleagues sharply criticized him after he met with President Moi to declare his intention to establish a dialogue with KANU.

Wamalwa's relations with KANU improved dramatically in 1998, and in October FORD–K legislators helped vote down a nonconfidence motion against the government. On the other hand, the October vote highlighted a split in the party between Wamalwa and a faction led by Orengo, who had tabled the motion. Wamalwa's ambivalent attitude toward KANU and what was considered by many his lackluster leadership style continued to cause dissension within the party, and Orengo attracted considerable publicity. Meanwhile, another anti-Wamalwa figure in the party, George KAPTEN, died under mysterious circumstances in 1999.

FORD–K was heavily involved in 2002 in the formation of a large anti–KANU opposition front, first NAK then the NARC Super Alliance, but Orengo launched his own presidential bid through the SDP (below). Wamalwa was named vice president by President Kibaki in January 2003 but died in August. Musikari Kombo, a Luhya like Wamalwa, became acting chair of the party until he was elected at a subsequent party conference.

After forestalling a challenge to his leadership of the party from Mukhisa Kituyi (who later left FORD–K for NARC–K) in December 2005, Kombo took steps in 2006 to broaden the national appeal of the FORD–K party. In March he opened a party office in the Thika district to build support in the central province. More significantly, Kombo initiated talks with party members to "synergize the FORD family" for the purpose of campaigns and electoral support. Talks with Simeon Nyachae and the FORD–People yielded encouraging results, while negotiations with FORD–A were stymied by FORD–A's own internal divisions (see above). Kombo has also entered a dialogue with DP and NPK leaders to reinvigorate the NARC party organs in the wake of the formal launch of NARC–K and the exodus of cabinet ministers and MPs from NARC.

FORD–K leader Kombo played an important role in the negotiations that established the PNU, and the party joined the PNU coalition as a corporate member. In November 2007 Kipruto arap Kirwa defected from NARC–K, of which he was a vice chair, to join FORD–K. FORD–K won a single seat under its own banner in the December parliamentary election, but a PNU cabinet seat was not allotted to the FORD–K MP.

In 2007 a splinter party, **New FORD–Kenya,** emerged with the support of Soita Shitanda, the housing minister. In 2010 reports indicated that party officials Sammy DIBAYA and Salim BAJABIR led a faction in FORD–K calling for the resignation of Kombo. On March 20, 2011, Moses Wetangula was elected chair of the party at a FORD–K congress. In 2012, FORD–K joined CORD.

In the 2013 general elections, FORD–K secured 5 Senate seats, 9 assembly seats, and 1 governorship.

Leaders: Moses WETANGULA (Chair), John MUNYES (Secretary General), Otieno K'OPIYO (Deputy Secretary General), Jael MBOGO (Organizing Secretary), David SIMIYU.

Kenya African Democratic Union–Asili (KADU-A). KADU-A won one seat in the National Assembly in the December 2007 election. KDAU–A joined CORD in the 2013 balloting and, again, secured 1 seat in the assembly.

Leader: Francis BAYA.

Party of Independent Candidates of Kenya (PICK). One of the earliest fringe parties after the advent of party pluralism, PICK was founded by a Nairobi businessman, John Harun Mwau, who styled himself as the PICK party boss.

PICK candidates won two seats in the December 2007 parliamentary election, and one assembly seat in 2013.

Leaders: G. N. MUSIMI (Chair), F. OLIEWO (Vice Chair), F. NGUGI (Secretary), John Harun MWAU, Clement WAIBARA.

Among the other minor parties that joined CORD was the **Muungano Development Movement Party of Kenya** (MDM), which won 1 assembly seat and 1 governorship in the 2013 elections.

Eagle Alliance. Formed for the 2013 balloting, the Eagle Alliance included the **Kenya National Congress** (KNC), led by S. Kathini Maloba Caines, and the **Party of Action**, led by Raphael Tuju. Peter Kenneth was the group's 2013 presidential candidate. He received 0.6 percent of the vote, while the Alliance secured two seats in the assembly (both held by the KNC).

Leaders: S. Kathini Maloba CAINES, Raphael TUJU, Peter KENNETH (2013 presidential candidate).

Other groupings that competed in the 2013 balloting include the following: the **Federal Party of Kenya** (FPK), which won one Senate seat and one assembly seat; the **Grand National Union** (GNU), formed in March 2012 and led by Mwangi KIUNJURI, which won one governorship in the 2013 elections; the **Maendeleo Democratic Party**, which won one assembly seat; and the **Progressive Party of Kenya** (PPK), which won one assembly seat.

Other Parties and Groups:

Safina. Safina was launched in May 1995 by an opposition group that included Dr. Richard Leakey, a former director of the Kenya Wildlife Service. The group, which applied for registration on June 20, said that it would work with others to establish a viable alternative to KANU. However, a ruling party MP filed a suit in late July to block legalization of the formation on the grounds that its name (translated as "Noah's Arc") was "repugnant to good religious values." The emergence of Leakey (a second-generation white Kenyan) as head of an opposition group reportedly appeared to "unnerve both President Moi and KANU leaders." Among other things, Leakey had been successful in attracting foreign backing for his scientific activities and had served to heighten international awareness of Kenya's domestic turmoil. For its part, the government declared it had no intention of conferring legitimacy on a party "backed by foreigners."

Following his release from prison in December 1996, opposition activist Koigi Wa Wamwere joined Safina and called on the government to recognize the grouping. Official opposition to Safina remained strong, however, and in February 1997 security forces violently thwarted an attempt by party members to convene a meeting. Thereafter, Safina militants were reportedly deeply involved in the organization of antigovernment demonstrations, and at midyear Leakey, Paul Muite, and other party officials joined the NCA's executive wing.

In October 1997 Safina's bid for legalization was again rejected by the government; however, under pressure from moderate opposition leaders, the Moi administration reversed itself, and in November Safina was registered. Although legalized too late to forward a presidential candidate, Safina participated in the December 1997 legislative balloting, capturing three seats.

At Safina's first national convention on September 5, 1998, party delegates elected Farah Maalim interim chair and Mwandawiro MGHANGA secretary general. In addition, the party subsequently chose Josephine Odira SINYO to assume the parliamentary post vacated by Leakey, who had been restored to directorship of the wildlife service. Safina's cohesion subsequently suffered from Leakey's decision to join the KANU administration (see Current issues, above) and from a scandal involving alleged corruption on the part of key leaders.

Safina took part in the PCK negotiations to join forces with the NAK and LDP to form the NARC Super Alliance, but Paul Muite, like Simeon Nyachae of FORD–People, pulled out of NARC almost immediately after NARC refused to institute an electoral college to nominate a single candidate for the presidency. However, Muite has positioned Safina in support of President Kibaki's government by denouncing cabinet members who campaigned against the November 2005 constitutional referendum and by taking the unusually aggressive stance of publicly defending the Kibaki government's raid on *The Standard* newspaper (see Communications, below). Muite described the IMF and World Bank threats to withhold funds as "senseless and uncalled-for fodder for the donors to fight the government."

In September 2007 Safina affiliated with the PNU coalition to contest the parliamentary and presidential elections but never came to a formal agreement for corporate membership. As a result, Safina ran candidates under its own banner in the December parliamentary elections when it put forward candidates in 88 constituencies but secured only five seats in the National Assembly.

Safina announced in August 2008 that it was joining forces with SKS and Saba Saba Asili to form the **Progressive Parties Alliance** (PROPA). The alliance, which also included several youth movements, sought to fill a gap in central Kenya for a party based more on reform and social democratic ideology than on ethnic alliances.

In 2010 party member and member of parliament Abdikadir MOHAMED was chosen to oversee the legislative committee formed to oversee the implementation of the newly approved constitution. In 2011 reports indicated that Muite would run for the national presidency in 2012. In 2012 Safina expelled party member and member of parliament Ephraim MAINA over allegations that he actively supported the presidential bid of Kenyatta of KANU.

Party leader Paul MUITE was the party's 2013 presidential candidate, he received 0.1 percent of the vote in the balloting.

Leaders: Paul MUITE (Chair), Cyprian NYAMWAMU (Secretary General).

Party of National Unity (PNU). Fashioned as an umbrella coalition of parties that supported the reelection of President Kibaki, PNU was organized in September 2007 on the model of the National Rainbow Coalition formed to contest the 2002 election. As a result, some PNU politicians had a direct affiliation with the party, while others maintained their individual affiliations with parties that were corporate members or affiliates of PNU.

The PNU was composed of more than 18 parties, groups, and notables, including the partner party, KANU. Uhuru Kenyatta, KANU's leader, endorsed Kibaki for president, and unlike other member parties in the PNU coalition, he secured an early agreement to run candidates independently of PNU for parliamentary and civic elections under KANU's banner. The major parties, besides KANU, enlisted under PNU were NARC–K, FORD–K (including the splinter group NEW FORD–K), FORD–People, the DP, Safina, Shirikisho Party Kenya (SPK), and Sisi Kwa Sisi (SKS). PNU also included minor parties such as the Social Party for the Advancement of Reforms Kenya (SPARK), Mazingira Green Party of Kenya (MPK), Saba Saba Asili, the Independent Party, and the Agano Party, among others.

PNU ultimately nominated 135 candidates to contest constituencies and made agreements with partner parties running candidates in the same or other constituencies. In the December 2007 election, PNU won 43 seats outright and, via its alliances, had the support of more than 93 seats. With 46 percent of the vote, the ECK declared President Kibaki the winner of the presidential election. In subsequent by-elections in June and September 2008, PNU picked up 3 additional seats. Reports indicated in January 2011 that PNU leaders were endeavoring to transition the coalition into a more formal political party ahead of the 2012 national elections.

In March 2012 Amos Kimunya was elected secretary general of the party. After party vice chair George Saitoti was killed in an air accident in June, Gideon Konchellah was chosen by the PNU executive as his interim replacement. Reports in 2013 indicated that the PNU had entered into an agreement to support the Kenyatta for the presidency and the TNA in the general elections.

Leaders: Mwai KIBAKI (Former President of the Republic), Gideon KONCHELLAH, (Acting Chair), Amos KIMUNYA (Secretary General).

Democratic Party (DP). The DP, which draws support largely from the sizable Kikuyu ethnic group, was formed in January 1992 by a number of former government officials, including Mwai Kibaki, a long-standing ally of President Moi, who had recently resigned from the government and KANU to protest the administration's failure to address widespread official corruption. Kibaki challenged the Moi government on a number of economic issues, especially its continued allocation of funds to inefficient government-owned operations.

At the DP's annual meeting in November 1992 Kibaki's presidential candidacy was unanimously supported; in balloting in late December the DP standard-bearer finished third while party legislative candidates won 23 seats. In early January 1993 the DP agreed to form an electoral coalition with FORD–A and FORD–K, which displayed little effective cohesion in a by-election five months later.

Confronted with the DP's dire financial condition, its main factions agreed to shelve their differences and reelected Kibaki chair at a congress in March 1997. However, a number of party members subsequently signaled their interest in campaigning as the group's standard-bearer in the forthcoming presidential elections. The most noteworthy bid came from Charity Ngilu, a prominent assemblywoman, who joined the SDP (and later formed the NPK) after Kibaki received the group's nomination.

In early 1998 the DP accused propresidential militants of orchestrating the outbreak of ethnic violence in the Rift Valley, alleging that supporters of Kibaki's presidential bid were being targeted. (On January 23 the party had filed suit to have the balloting nullified.) Thereafter, the DP sought to form a multiparty, opposition government-in-waiting; however, subsequent negotiations among opposition leaders quickly fell apart, and in April the DP named a shadow cabinet composed of its own members. In October the DP overwhelmingly supported a nonconfidence motion against the government; however, as many as three of its legislators were alleged to have broken with the party on the issue. Kibaki subsequently continued to reject the assembly's constitutional review process, believing that it unfairly represented the interests of KANU and President Moi.

By 2002, the DP, under Kibaki's direction, played a key role in stitching together the NAC, NAK, and subsequently victorious NARC opposition party alliances to defeat KANU. Kibaki's election as president left him in the dual position of DP chair and NARC party boss. By December 2003 President Kibaki chose to distance himself publicly from any official role in the DP as he battled to dissolve the various parties within NARC in favor of direct NARC membership (see above). The DP, however, did not disband and continues to maintain a formal organization chaired by Kibaki, despite his public statements that the party ceased to exist after the formation of the NAK and despite his calls for DP members to support NARC.

At a June 2005 DP meeting in Nairobi, which was called to revitalize the party, 40 party leaders, who were members of the assembly, failed to attend, including President Kibaki, David Mwiraria, Chris Murungaru, Martha Karua, Peter NDWIGA, and Kiraitu Murungi. The delegates who attended pledged to strengthen the party and avoid its personalization; however, by March 2006 it appeared that their efforts had failed. After announcing the formation of NARC–K, President Kibaki declared that DP "had ceased to exist." The DP's national governing council unanimously voted to remove President Kibaki as its leader and endorsed Rose Waruhiu to act as chair until the National Delegates Council in July 2006 (former ministers and party notables David Mwiraria, Chris Murungaru, and Kiraitu Murungi were suspended from the party in April). Waruhiu maintained that the party would not be dissolved and would field candidates in the 2007 general election either independently or with other political parties. Meanwhile, the party supported Kibaki, NARC, and the Government of National Unity formed when Rail Odinga and the LDP split with the NARC government in 2004.

DP leaders were solidly behind Kibaki's bid for reelection. They also actively engaged in the NARC revival efforts in July 2007 and benefited from the defection of several politicians from the NARC–K and KANU rosters as alliances shifted in the run-up to the elections. The DP later joined Kibaki's PNU as a corporate member in September 2007. DP leaders, however, like leaders of some other PNU corporate affiliate parties, chose to run parliamentary candidates under the party's own banner, despite pressure from PNU notables to stay within the PNU's nominations framework. Several prominent politicians, including Muriuki Karue and Ngenye Kariuki from NARC–K, defected from other PNU parties to join DP during the run-up to the nominations.

In the December 2007 election, the DP ran candidates in 86 constituencies but won only two seats in the National Assembly. None of the PNU cabinet posts were allotted to DP MPs.

In July 2010 Joseph Munyao, who was acting chair, was elected party leader at a meeting of the DP governing council.

Leaders: Joseph MUNYAO (Chair), Chris MURUNGARU (Secretary General), Moses LOONTASATI (Treasurer), Yacob HAJJI (Organizing Secretary).

Sisi Kwa Sisi (SKS). SKS purports to transcend religious barriers by uniting supporters of Islamic Party–Kenya and the Mungiki sect (the party's name is translated as "us among us"). The party won two seats in the 2002 legislative balloting and pledged to work with the NARC coalition to secure political and economic reforms.

In September 2007 the SKS joined the PNU coalition to contest the parliamentary and presidential elections but eventually choose to list its candidates separately in constituencies where it nominated candidates. SKS candidates won two seats in the December 2007 parliamentary election, but none of the PNU cabinet seats were allotted to SKS MPs.

SKS announced in August 2008 that it was joining forces with Safina and Saba Saba Asili to form the **Progressive Parties Alliance**—PROPA.

Leaders: John Rukenya KABUGUA (Chair), Moffat Muia MAITHA, William Gitau KAABOGO.

Mazingira Green Party of Kenya (MPK). In April 2003 the noted environmental and human rights activist and assistant cabinet minister for environment Wangari Maathai formed the Green Party in the mold of Green parties in Europe. In 2004 Dr. Maathai was awarded the 2004 Nobel Peace Prize. She initially resisted invitations to join the NARC or NARC–K groupings because of a desire to see a new generation of leaders and to promote environmental issues.

In 2007 the party joined forces with other parties in President Kibaki's PNU coalition, in part to give Maathai a chance to win a seat in parliament. Running candidates under its own banner, the party secured only one seat in the December 2007 parliamentary election and received no cabinet appointments.

Leaders: Mwangi MAKANGA (Chair), Wangari MAATHAI, Sirus RUTEERE.

Labour Party of Kenya (LPK). Although a founding member of NARC, the LPK controlled no seats in the assembly after the 2002 legislative balloting. The LPK joined the Orange Team in opposing the constitutional referendum and allied itself with the LDP/KANU elements in the ODM in anticipation of the 2007 national elections. The LPK stood to gain 20 percent of the positions in government under the power-sharing scheme devised between the LDP, KANU, and LPK for power sharing if the ODM won the 2007 elections.

As the ODM factional infighting heated up in 2007 over the presidential nomination selection process, party leader Julia Ojiambo allied the LPK with Stephen Kalonzo Musyoka, who subsequently joined the LPK when he broke company with ODM leaders to form the ODM–K in August 2007. Like KANU, the LPK was opposed to the ODM moving toward individual rather than corporate membership.

Leaders: Julia OJIAMBO (Chair), Stephen Kalonzo MUSYOKA (2007 ODM–K presidential candidate).

United Democratic Movement (UDM). The UDM was formed in 1998 under the leadership of Kipruto arap Kirwa, whose organization of an anti-Moi faction within KANU had cost him his post of assistant minister of agriculture in May. In early 1999 the group released a leadership roster, which reportedly included legislators thought to be KANU supporters. (Consequently, President Moi presented a motion that would forbid sitting assembly members to launch new groups.) The Moi administration suppressed UDM's formal registration.

UDM leaders took part in the 2002 negotiations to create the NAK and NARC (see above), and in return Kirwa was named agriculture minister in the NARC administration following the 2002 election. Kirwa formally registered UDM in March 2003. One impetus for the UDM is to provide a party to champion the interests of the Kalenjin ethnic group, according to party Secretary General Stephen Tanis.

In the 2004–2005 NARC party dissolution battles, UDM leaders supported maintaining corporate membership for the parties within NARC. By 2006 the future of UDM was uncertain. Kipruto Rono arap Kirwa (party leader and minister of agriculture) was embroiled in an alleged corruption scandal, and the party's influence at the national level appeared diminished. Moreover, Kirwa and Stephen Tanis allied themselves first with NARC–K and then the PNU after its formation in September 2007 before the elections. Kirwa eventually joined FORD–K, by then affiliated with the PNU, but he failed to win a seat in the National Assembly under that banner.

By the end of the parliamentary balloting, the UDM had secured one seat in the National Assembly and had forged an alliance with the ODM. The lone party MP, Helen Sambili, was named to a cabinet post in the grand coalition that emerged in April 2008. Sambili retained her cabinet post through a series of reshuffles in 2009 and 2010 but was dismissed in March 2012.

In 2012 William Samoei arap RUTO attempted unsuccessfully to take control of the UDM.

Leaders: Nathaniel CHEBELION (Party Leader), Helen Jepkemoi SAMBILI.

Kenya National Democratic Alliance (KENDA). Like the SDP, KENDA's initial policy statements concerned human rights issues, the party calling for, among other things, an end to detention without trial and political imprisonment. Legalized in early 1992, KENDA secured no assembly representation in December 1992, and its presidential candidate, Mukara NG'AND'A, captured only 0.11 percent of the vote.

In 1997 Koigi wa Wamwere campaigned for the presidency under the KENDA banner when his party, Safina, was unable to forward a candidate.

In 2006 KENDA was revived by one of the businessmen implicated in the Goldenberg scandal, Kamlesh Pattni, in a move some critics speculated was a bid to win his election to parliament, boosting his chances for securing immunity from prosecution. Pattni also founded an organization named Hand of Hope to aid unemployed youth in a bid to overcome resistance from some of the party's left-leaning original membership.

KENDA campaigned for the 2007 parliamentary elections as if it were a formal affiliate of PNU, a relationship PNU denied because of Pattni's implication in the Goldenberg scandal. The party won one National Assembly seat. It opposed the 2010 constitution.

Leaders: Kamlesh PATTNI (Chair), Joram KARIUKI (Vice Chair), Bernard KALOVE (Secretary General), Linah KILIMO, Koigi wa WAMWERE (1997 presidential candidate).

National Labor Party (NLP). The NLP has served as a safety valve or "briefcase party" for Kenyan politicians who need a platform for office seeking when other avenues are blocked. In 2005 Joseph Kiliku had open discussion with the LDP's Stephen Kalonzo Musyoka about the latter using the party as a vehicle for his run for the presidency in 2007. (Musyoka eventually won nomination under the ODM–K banner.) Kiliku also sought to use his party, without success, as a platform for a revitalized Third Progressive Force (TPF). Kiliku later joined ODM–K's party summit.

NLP won one seat in the National Assembly in the December 2007 parliamentary election, and the party's MP affiliated with the ODM rather than the ODM–K/PNU alliance. The NLP reportedly joined a coalition of smaller parties ahead of the 2013 balloting.

Leaders: Joseph Kennedy KILIKU (Chair), Walter OSEBE, Daniel Mogaka RAGU.

People's Party of Kenya (PPK). Launched to pursue "radical social democracy" and led by Harun Waweru, the PPK won one seat in the National Assembly in the December 2007 election. The party's MP affiliated with the ODM rather than the ODM–K/PNU alliance. The PPK subsequently lost a June 2010 by-election. The party failed to secure any parliamentary seats in the 2013 balloting.

Leaders: Harun WAWERU (Chair), David MWAURA.

Saba Saba Asili. A splinter party formed in anticipation of the 2007 elections from elements of FORD–Asili, Saba Saba Asili (the name literally means "Seven Seven Original" in Kiswahili) negotiated to join the PNU coalition. Kenneth Matiba sought the party's nomination to run for president in 2007; by early December, however, party leaders urged Matiba to exit the race, citing inadequate financial resources and time to run an effective campaign. None of the party's candidates won a parliamentary constituency, and Matiba drew negligible support in the presidential polling. The party failed to win any seats at the national level in 2013 but did gain representation on local councils.

Leaders: Kenneth MATIBA (2007 presidential candidate), Ngengi MUIGAI (Chair), Mohammed KUSOMA (National Director), Joseph KANGUCHU (Organizing Secretary).

Shirikisho Party of Kenya (SPK). Shirikisho was a little-known regional group that claimed one seat in the 1997 legislative balloting and retained the one seat in the 2002 election. The party draws its support from the Coast Province.

In 2005 allegations of misappropriation of funds granted from the Center for Multiparty Democracy surfaced from former party treasurer Mwakio NDAU. SPK party leader Harry Kombe met in Nairobi with a small number of LDP and KANU assembly members who expressed interest in joining SPK. At the same time, party leaders spurned a plan by the Third Progressive Force to form a new Coast Province party and entertained talks of forming a coalition before the 2007 elections with the LDP and FORD–K representatives.

In July 2007 David MWIRARIA, returning to Kibaki's cabinet after resigning in February 2006 under suspicion of corruption, announced that he was leaving NARC–K to join the SPK. Transport minister Chirau Ali Mwakwere had previously left NARC–K in June to join the SPK (he had been one of the NARC–K vice chairs). Both continued to actively support Kibaki's reelection bid and worked to steer SPK into the Party of National Unity (PNU) coalition backing Kibaki. Chirau Ali Mwakwere won an assembly seat in the 2007 elections under the PNU party label.

The SPK favored greater autonomy for the provinces; SPK leaders pushed the PNU to make concessions in Kibaki's platform on this issue of concern, and some junior party leaders threatened to form a splinter group to advocate for federalism.

Mwakwere was appointed minister of trade in 2010 but was dismissed in a cabinet reshuffle in 2012. The party failed to win any parliamentary seats in 2013.

Leaders: Lina Mkasi BUNI (Chair), Abubakar YUSUF (Secretary General), Kassim JUMA (Organizing Secretary), Chirau Ali MWAKWERE, Harry KOMBE.

Kenyan African Democratic Development Union (KADDU). KADDU is a small party with support in the Luhya districts of Kenya. Party leader Cyrus Jirongo declared in early August 2007 that he was a candidate for president but later pledged his support to the ODM's Raila Odinga, who had named Musalia Mudavadi, a Luhya, his vice president-designate. By early November Jirongo withdrew his support, however, charging the ODM was taking his party's support for granted.

Despite fielding candidates in 97 parliamentary constituencies, the party won one seat in the National Assembly election in December 2007. Because KADDU was not affiliated with any of the parties in the coalition government, however, it is the only party that can be designated the "official opposition." KADDU opposed the 2010 constitution. During the summer of 2011, Jirongo launched a bid for the presidency in 2012. KADDU expelled two party officials in November 2011 for collaborating with other political parties ahead of the 2012 elections.

Leaders: Cyrus JIRONGO (Chair), Amin WALIJI.

Minor groups who put forward candidates or who were referenced in the 2002, 2007, or 2013 election campaigns included the **AGANO Party,** led by David Mwaura WAIHIGA; the **Chama Cha Uma Party** (CCU), led by David Ng'ethe WAWERU (2002 and 2007 presidential candidate); the **Chama Cha Majimbo Na Mwangaza** (CCM), led by Leslie MWACHIRO; the **Islamic Party of Kenya** (IPK), led by Mohammed KHALIFA; the **Kenya Citizens Congress** (KCC); the **Kenya Patriotic Trust Party** (KPTP), led by Joseph KARANI Ngacha (2007 presidential candidate); the **Kenya People's Party** (KPP), led by Pius MUIRU (2007 presidential candidate); the **Kenya Social Congress** (KSC), led by Mathius Ondeyo NYARIBARI; the **Kenya Union of National Alliance for Peace,** led by Wilson Nyakundi Abuga; the **New Aspirations Party of Kenya,** led by Mathew Okwanda; the **Republican Liberty Party** (RLP), led by Zachariah Momanyi Matayo; the **Republican Party of Kenya** (RPK), led by Jeremiah Nixon Kukubo (2007 presidential candidate); the **Social Democratic Party** (SDP), led by James Aggrey ORENGO (2002 presidential candidate); the **Social Party for the Advancement of Reforms Kenya** (SPARK), led by Joseph Owuor NYONG'O; the **United People's Congress,** led by Charles Barongo Nyakeri; the **Workers Congress Party of Kenya,** led by Nazlin Omar RAJPUT (2007 presidential candidate); and the **National Progressive Party** (NPP).

Other groups include the **Alliance for Democracy** (*Muungano wa Ukombozi*); **Chama Cha Mwananchi** (CCM), a party of former political prisoners and government critics, led by Dick KAMAU; the **Generations Alliance Party of Kenya** (GAP–K), formed in January 2006 and led by Gerald Thuita; the **Grand National Union**, led by Mwangi KIUNJURI; the **Independent Party**, led by Kalembe NDILE; the **Kenya National Patriotic Party** (KNPP), led by Salim MWIROTHO; **Labour Party Democracy,** led by Mohamed Ibrahim NOOR; and the **Wakulima Party,** registered in October 2004.

LEGISLATURE

The bicameral **Parliament** was created when the 2010 Constitution added an upper chamber, the 67-member **Senate**, and increased the number of seats in the **National Assembly** to 349 (for the history of the legislature, please see the 2013 *Handbook*).

Senate. The 67-member upper chamber includes 47 senators directly elected, one from each county. In addition, there are 16 women nominated by political parties, based on their proportion of seats in the Senate. Finally, 2 seats are reserved for representatives of youth groups and 2 for representatives of the disabled, all nominated by individual parties based on their proportion of seats. All members serve five-year terms. Following the most recent balloting on March 4, 2013, the seat distribution was as follows: Jubilee, 30 (including the National Alliance, 17 [11 elected, 6 appointed]; United Republican Party, 12 [9, 3]; and the National Rainbow Coalition, 1 [1, 0]); Coalition for Reforms and Democracy, 28 (Orange Democratic Movement, 17 [11, 6]; Forum for the Restoration of Democracy—Kenya, 5 [4, 1]; Wiper Democratic Movement—Kenya, 5 [4, 1]; and the Federal Party of Kenya, 1 [1, 0]); Amani, 6 (including the Kenya African National Union, 3 [2, 1]; and United Democratic Forum, 3 [2, 1]); and the Alliance Party of Kenya, 3 (2, 1).

Speaker: Ekwe ETHURO (ex officio).

National Assembly. The lower chamber consists of 349 members who are elected for five-year terms, including 290 elected from constituencies, 47 seats reserved for women (1 elected from each county), and 12 seats nominated by the parties, based on their proportion of seats won in the most recent balloting. Following the most recent polling on March 4, 2013, most parties belong to or joined one of three coalitions within the National Assembly: Jubilee, the Coalition for Reforms and Democracy, or the Eagle Alliance. As of August 15, 2013, the seat distribution was as follows: Jubilee, 207 (including the National Alliance, 89 [72 elected, 14 women county representatives, 3 nominated]; United Republican Party, 75 [62, 10, 3]; United Democratic Forum [11, 0, 1]; Kenya African National Union, 6 [6, 0, 0]; New Forum for the Restoration of Democracy, 6 [4, 2, 0]; Alliance Party of Kenya, 5 [5, 0, 0]; Forum for the Restoration of Democracy for the People, 4 [4, 0, 0]; National Rainbow Coalition, 3 [3, 0, 0]; Chama Cha Uzalendo [2, 0, 0]; Federal Party of Kenya, 1 [1, 0, 0]; National Rainbow Coalition—Kenya, 1 [1, 0, 0]; People's Democratic Party, 1 [1, 0, 0]; Coalition for Reforms and Democracy, 137 (Orange Democratic Movement, 96 [78, 15, 3]; Wiper Democratic Movement–Kenya, 26 [19, 6, 1]; Forum for the Restoration of Democracy–Kenya, 9 [8, 0, 1]; the Federal Party of Kenya, 2 [2, 0, 0]; Kenya African Democratic Union–Asili, 1 [1, 0, 0]; Muungano Development Movement Party of Kenya, 1 [1, 0, 0]; the Party of Independent Candidates of Kenya 1, [1, 0, 0]); Eagle Alliance, 2 (Kenya National Congress [2, 0, 0]); Maendeleo Democratic Party, 1, 0, 0; independents, 2 (2, 0, 0).

Speaker: Justin MUTURI (ex officio).

CABINET

[as of August 15, 2013]

President	Uhuru Kenyatta (KANU)
Deputy President	William Samoei Arap Rutu (URP)
Cabinet Secretaries	
Agriculture, Livestock, and Fisheries	Felix Koskei
Defense	Rayechelle Omamo [f]
Devolution and Planning	Anne Waiguru [f]
East African Community Affairs, Commerce, and Tourism	Phyllis Kipkingor-Kandie [f]
Education	Jacob Kaimenyi
Energy and Petroleum	Davis Chirchir
Environment, Water, and Natural Resources	Judy Wakhungu [f]
Foreign Affairs	Amina Mohamed (ind.) [f]
Health	James Wainana Macharia
Industrialization and Enterprise Development	Adan Abdulla Mohammed
Information, Communications, and Technology	Fred Okengo Matiangi
Interior and Coordination of National Government	Joseph Ole Lenku
Labor, Social Security, and Services	Samuel Kazungu Kambi (PNU)
Lands, Housing, and Urban Development	Charity Ngilu (NARC) [f]
Mining	Najib Balala (RCP)
National Treasury	Henry Rotich
Sports, Culture, and Arts	Hassan Wario
Transport and Infrastructure	Michael Kamau
Attorney General	Githu Muigai (Ind.)

[f] = female

INTERGOVERNMENTAL REPRESENTATION

Ambassador to the U.S.: Elkanah Odembo ABSALOM.

U.S. Ambassador to Kenya: Robert F. GODEC.

Permanent Representative to the UN: Macharia KAMAU.

IGO Memberships (Non-UN): AfDB, AU, Comesa, CWTH, ICC, IOM, NAM, WTO.

KIRIBATI

Republic of Kiribati
I Kiribati

Political Status: Formerly the Gilbert Islands; became a British protectorate in 1892; annexed as the Gilbert and Ellice Islands Colony in 1915, the Ellice Islands becoming independent as the state of Tuvalu in 1978; present name adopted upon becoming an independent member of the Commonwealth on July 12, 1979.

Area: 313 sq. mi. (811 sq. km).

Population: 103,058 (2010C); 103,248 (2013E—U.S. Census).

Major Urban Center (2005E): BAIRIKI (South Tarawa, 48,000).

Official Language: I-Kiribati (Gilbertese); English is also widely spoken.

Monetary Unit: Australian Dollar (market rate November 1, 2013: 1 Australian dollar = $1.06 US). The British Pound is also in circulation.

President: Anote TONG (*Boutokaan te Koaua*); popularly elected on July 5, 2003, succeeding Teburoro TITO (*Maneaban te Mauri*), whose government had been defeated in a confidence vote on March 28; reelected on October 17, 2007, and January 13, 2012.

Vice President: Teima ONORIO (*Boutokaan te Koaua*); appointed by the president on July 10, 2003, succeeding Beniamina TINGA (*Maneaban te Mauri*); reappointed on October 23, 2007, and on January 19, 2012.

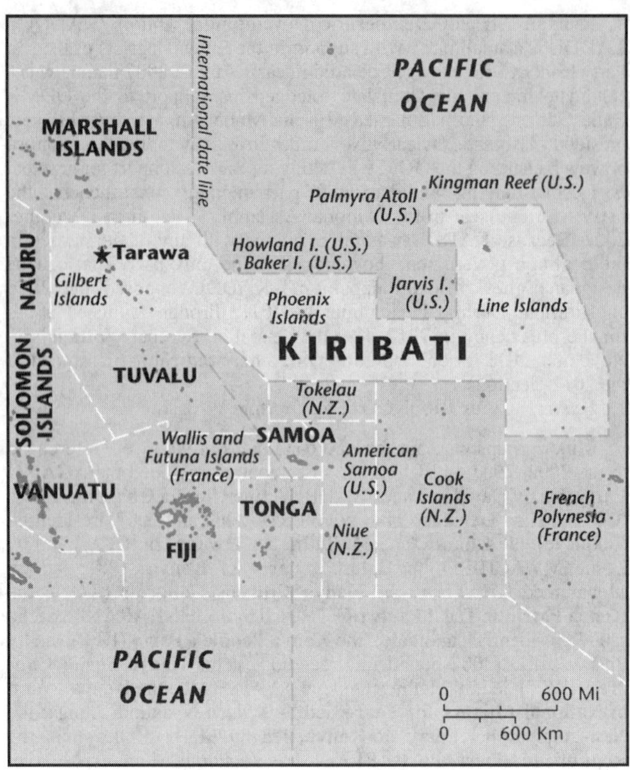

THE COUNTRY

Kiribati consists of Ocean Island (Banaba Island) in the west on the equator and three widely dispersed island groups (comprising 32 atolls and islands) scattered over 1.35 million square miles of the central Pacific Ocean: the Gilbert Islands on the equator; the Phoenix Islands to the southeast; and most of the Line Islands still farther east and both north and south of the equator. The Gilbert group comprises Abaiang, Abemama, Aranuka, Arorae, Beru, Butaritari, Kuria, Maiana, Makin, Marakei, Nicunau, Nonouti, Onotoa, Tabiteuca, Tamana, and Tarawa. The Phoenix group encompasses Birnie, Enderbury, Gardner, Hull, Kanton (formerly Canton), McKean, Phoenix, and Sydney. The Line group embraces Kiritimati (Christmas), Fanning, Malden, Starbuck, Vostock, and Washington, as well as Millennium (formerly Caroline) and Flint, which in 1951 were leased to commercial interests on Tahiti. (The renaming of Caroline in August 1997 was intended to draw attention to the contention that Kiribati, having arbitrarily moved the international date line several hundred miles to the east, was to be the first nation over which the sun would rise on January 1, 2000.) Much of the population resides in South Tarawa, where overcrowding has exacerbated sanitation problems and generated health issues that have contributed to a high child mortality rate. Not all of the islands are inhabited and several attempts at settlement have been abandoned because of drought conditions, with potable water throughout the area often described as being as "precious as gasoline." The country is heavily dependent on imported food since most of the land is unsuitable for agriculture.

Most of the country's national income was traditionally derived from phosphate mining on the most western island, Banaba. By the time of independence, however, the phosphate supply was largely exhausted, and mining ceased at the end of 1979, causing the loss of some 500 jobs. Fishing grounds in the area are said to be among the richest in the world, although the first commercial fishing vessel, built in Japan, was not put into service until 1979. Unemployment is currently estimated as high as 80 percent, with most of the workforce employed by the government due to a paucity of industry.

In early 2008 Kiribati announced that some 72,000 sq. mi. in the Phoenix group had been declared a marine protected area (the world's largest) to ensure its biological diversity and sustainability.

GDP contracted in 2008 and 2009 under the influence of the global economic crisis, but modest growth resumed in 2010, reaching 2.8 percent in 2012. In response to recommendations from the International Monetary Fund (IMF), the government has recently adopted tax reforms to address fiscal imbalances and has pledged to promote the development of marine resources and tourism.

GOVERNMENT AND POLITICS

Political background. The Gilbert and Ellice Islands Colony (which included Ocean Island [Banaba Island], the Gilbert Islands chain, the Phoenix Islands [as of 1937], and the Ellice Islands) was under the jurisdiction of the British High Commissioner for the Western Pacific until 1972, when a governor was appointed from London. In 1975 the Ellice Islands became the separate territory of Tuvalu, which achieved independence in 1978. At a constitutional conference in London in early 1979, the British government refused a request by the Banabans, most of whom had been resettled on Rabi (Rambi) Island in the Fiji group during World War II and had since become Fijian citizens, that Banaba be separated from the Gilberts. Consequently, the independent Kiribati that became a republican member of the Commonwealth on July 12 comprised the Gilberts, Banaba, the Phoenix Islands, and most of the Line Islands. (The United States had claimed sovereignty over the Line Islands but relinquished its claim to all but three [Jarvis Island, Kingman Reef, and Palmyra].)

Upon independence the former chief minister, Ieremia T. TABAI, assumed office as president of the republic, and on July 20 he appointed Teatao TEANNAKI as vice president. Following the first postindependence legislative election of March 26, 1982, Tabai was returned to office in presidential balloting conducted May 4. The government fell, however, on December 10 when the House of Assembly rejected, for the second time in two days, a bill that would have retroactively legitimized 5 percent salary raises for six public officials who, through an oversight, had erroneously benefited from a pay hike granted civil servants earlier in the year. In accordance with Kiribati's somewhat unusual constitutional practice, interim administration was assumed by a three-member Council of State chaired by the chair of the Public Service Commission, Rota ONARIO. Tabai was reelected on February 17, 1983, following legislative balloting on January 12 and 19, and on February 18 he reappointed most members of his previous administration.

On May 12, 1987, following the election of a new House of Assembly on March 12 and 19, Tabai was again reelected, defeating Vice President Teannaki and opposition candidate Teburoro TITO with a 59 percent share of the vote.

With the support of Tabai (who was ineligible for a further term), Teannaki secured the presidency on July 3, 1991, defeating his principal competitor, Roniti TEIWAKI, by a vote margin of less than 5 percent. Teannaki was, however, obliged to resign on May 24, 1994, when the parliamentary opposition, which had accused his administration of financial irregularities, successfully introduced a no-confidence motion. Government authority thereupon passed again to the Council of State, pending a new legislative election and the designation of a successor president. However, a constitutional crisis erupted when one of the council members refused to step down at the expiration of his term on May 28 and was forcibly removed from office by his colleagues. The crisis highlighted a deficiency in Kiribati's basic law, since it was by no means clear that the Council of State possessed the power of self-replenishment. The issue was further complicated by the fact that the country's chief justice was himself a council member, which meant that a legal challenge in the matter would have to be submitted to a temporary judge brought in from Australia or New Zealand.

In balloting held July 21–29, 1994, the incumbent Gilbertese National Progressive Party won only 7 assembly seats as contrasted with 13 for the opposition Christian Democratic Party (subsequently the Christian Democratic Unity Party), which in the wake of the election attracted enough support from independents to capture all four presidential nominations. Thereafter, Teburoro Tito won a decisive 51 percent vote share (half again as much as the runner-up) at a popular election on September 30 and was sworn in as chief executive on October 1. He was elected to a second term on November 27, 1998, easily defeating Dr. Harry TONG and Amberoti NIKORA.

In November 2002 President Tito's legislative grouping, the *Maneaban te Mauri* (MTM) party, lost control to the opposition *Boutokaan te Koaua*—BTK (Supporters of the Truth). However, by early 2003 the BTK was reported to have "fractured," and on February 24 Tito won reelection by narrowly defeating the BTK's Taberannang TIMEON. However, little more than a month later, on March 28, Tito was obliged to resign after failing, in a close vote, to secure approval of a $700,000 supplemental budget.

In the legislative balloting of May 9 and 12, 2003, the MTM secured an initial plurality and appeared subsequently to have achieved a solid majority by the subsequent affiliation of a number of independents. Nonetheless, at the ensuing presidential election of July 5, with President Timeon ineligible after losing his house seat, the BTK's Anote TONG defeated his brother and new MTM standard-bearer, Dr. Harry Tong, by some 1,000 votes. Anote Tong was reelected in controversial balloting on October 17, 2007, following legislative elections on August 22 and 30 in which the BTK secured strong majority support. The BTK and its allies secured a legislative majority again in the October 2011 elections, with the United Coalition Party (*Karikirckean Tei-Kiribati*—KTK*)*, an MTM successor, serving as the main opposition. President Tong was elected to a third consecutive term by gaining 42 percent of the vote in presidential balloting on January 13, 2012. The cabinet named on January 19 included six new members.

Constitution and government. For a small country, Kiribati has a relatively complex constitution (part of the UK Kiribati Independence Order 1979) that includes a number of entrenched provisions designed to safeguard individual and land rights for the Banabans. It provides for an executive president (*beretitenti*) who is elected (for a maximum of three four-year terms) by the House of Assembly and must command the support of a constant legislative majority. Upon passage of a no-confidence motion, the president must immediately resign, transitional executive authority being exercised by a Council of State composed of the chair of the autonomous Public Service Commission, the chief justice, and the speaker of the House pending a legislative dissolution and the holding of a general election. Subsequent to each such election, the House must propose no fewer than three and no more than four candidates for the presidency from its own membership, the final selection being made by nationwide balloting. If the presidency is vacated for reasons other than a loss of confidence, the vice president (*kauoman-ni-beretitenti*), originally appointed by the president from among his cabinet associates, becomes chief executive, subject to legislative confirmation. The cabinet includes the president, vice president, attorney general, and no more than ten other ministers (all drawn from the assembly) and is collectively responsible to the legislature.

Legislative authority is exercised by the unicameral House of Assembly. The judicial system encompasses a Court of Appeal, a High Court, and local magistrates' courts, the last representing the consolidation of former island, lands, and magistrates' courts. There is a right of appeal to the Judicial Committee of the UK Privy Council in regard to the High Court's interpretation of the rights of any Banaban or member of the Rabi Council, which governs the affairs of Rabi Island in Fiji. The nominated Banaban member of Kiribati's House need not be a Kiribati citizen, while all expatriates with ancestors born in Banaba before 1900 may register as electors or stand for election as if resident on the island.

Although Kiribati has generally maintained a positive reputation in regard to press freedom, the *Kiribati Independent* newspaper was temporarily suspended in 2012 after it published a series of articles critical of the government. The newspaper resumed publication in 2013.

Foreign relations. Under a 1979 treaty, the United States agreed to relinquish all claims to territory in the Phoenix and Line island groups except for Jarvis, Kingman Reef, and Palmyra. Included were Canton and Enderbury, previously under joint U.S.-UK administration but from which the British had already withdrawn. The parties also agreed that no military use of the islands by third parties would be permitted without joint consultation and that facilities constructed by the United States on Canton, Enderbury, and Hull islands would not be so used without U.S. approval.

Kiribati became a member of the Commonwealth upon independence, but its international contacts are otherwise quite limited. In March 1984 diplomatic relations (backdated to 1979) were established with Tuvalu, augmenting links established earlier with Australia and the United Kingdom.

Modest developmental assistance has been provided by Australia, Japan, New Zealand, the United Kingdom, the United States, the Asian Development Bank, and the IMF (which Kiribati joined in 1986). A 1985 agreement allowing Russian fishing boats within the archipelago's continental shelf lapsed in October 1986, and Kiribati subsequently enacted legislation to detain crews as well as vessels in cases of poaching within its exclusive economic zone, which Royal New Zealand Air Force planes aid in policing.

In early 1998 it appeared that the future of a Chinese satellite tracking facility in Bonriki in eastern Tarawa might be jeopardized by the transfer of the controlling authority from the People's Republic of China (PRC) Science Commission to the People's Liberation Army. By mid-1999 the issue had become sensitive because of indications that the principal purpose of the facility might be to monitor a missile-defense system under construction by the United States on Kwajalein in the Marshall Islands. Meanwhile, Kiribati was admitted to the United Nations in September, having submitted its first accession request in April.

On November 7, 2003, the Tong administration established diplomatic relations with the Republic of China (Taiwan), saying that it also wished to retain existing relations with the PRC; however, the PRC promptly severed relations. The action was preceded by dismantlement of the satellite tracking station, the withdrawal of Chinese medical personnel, and the termination of PRC funding for the construction of a sports stadium. Subsequently, in August 2004, President Tong accused Beijing of attempting to destabilize his government, although his brother, as opposition leader, stated that he viewed Taiwan as a greater threat to Kiribati than the PRC.

In March 2006 Kiribati received an unrestricted grant of $1 million from Japan. The action came several months after Kiribati had refused an Australian government request to join a campaign to banish "scientific" whaling. In 2010 President Tong repudiated a British newspaper charge that Kiribati had "sold" its vote on the International Whaling Commission to Japan.

Since 2011 President Tong has bucked the opinion of several major regional countries by calling for Fiji's reintegration into regional bodies, citing Kiribati's economic links to Fiji. Meanwhile, he has continued to emphasize strong relations with Taiwan, where Kiribati opened an embassy in 2013.

Current issues. In recent years Kiribati, whose highest point (other than on Banaba) is less than six feet above sea level, has become increasingly concerned about the impact of long-term elevation of the sea level because of global greenhouse emissions. In preparation for the legislative election scheduled for October 2011, Tong solidified his status as "the face of climate change," assisted by a visit to Kiribati by UN Secretary General Ban Ki-Moon, who said he was shocked by the damage already done to Kiribati by the rising sea levels. Following his reelection to a third consecutive term in January 2012, Tong pledged to focus on economic development, one priority being to ensure that Kiribati benefits fully from surrounding rich fishing grounds that are currently exploited by many other nations.

In the first half of 2013 the government announced plans to purchase some 6,000 acres of land in Fiji. President Tong said that the land would initially be used to help provide "food security" for Kiribati, but he also acknowledged that it might someday serve as a place to which climate refugees from Kiribati would relocate.

POLITICAL PARTIES

Traditionally, there were no formally organized parties in Kiribati; instead, ad hoc groups tended to form in response to specific issues or in support of particular individuals. Thus, a grouping known as the Mouth of the Kiribati People (*Wiia I-Kiribati*) was significantly involved in the 1982 defeat of the Tabai government but subsequently became moribund. Prior to the 1991 assembly balloting, the only recognizable party was a Christian People's Party (*Mwaneaba*), organized in August 1985 by a number of Catholic opposition legislators following the failure of a no-confidence motion against President Tabai regarding the Soviet fishing treaty. Prior to the 1991 presidential poll two additional groups emerged: a Gilbertese National Progressive Party (GNPP), launched to support the (ultimately successful) candidacy of Vice President Teatao Teannaki, and a Kiribati United Party (KUP), to further the candidacy of Tewareka TENTOA, whose name was not on the four-man list approved by the assembly. For the 1994 campaign a Protestant-oriented Christian Democratic Party (CDP) was launched in support of Teburoro Tito's successful candidacy, thereafter becoming the nucleus of a Christian Democratic Unity Party (CDUP), which also included the GNPP.

Government and Government-Supportive Groups:

Boutokaan te Koaua—BTK (Supporters of the Truth or Pillars of Truth). Theretofore in opposition, the BTK won the presidency in July 2003, despite failing to obtain a majority in its own right at a legislative poll two months earlier. It was initially reported to have secured 18 seats in the 2007 balloting, but its representation subsequently swelled to a majority of approximately 28 seats after successful independent candidates declared their party affiliations. Although the BTK was officially credited with only a plurality of 15 seats in the 2011 poll, it once again subsequently appeared to secure majority support with the assistance of independents and MKP legislators.

Leaders: Anote TONG (President of the Republic), Ieremia TABAI (Chair).

Maurin Kiribati Party (MKP). The centrist MKP has often been a coalition partner of the BTK since 2003, with the MKP's Nabuti Mwemwenikarawa once serving as minister for finance and economic development. As many as five of the successful candidates in the 2007 legislative poll reportedly were members of the MKP, even though they officially ran as independents. Meanwhile, Mwemwenikarawa finished second in the 2007 presidential elections with approximately one-third of the votes.

The MKP was credited with winning three seats in the 2011 elections. Subsequently, Rimeta BENIAMINA finished third in the January 2012 presidential poll as the MKP candidate. Beniamina had previously been a member of the KTK (below), serving as Leader of the Opposition from 2010 to 2011. Several MKP members subsequently joined the new cabinet formed in January 2012.

Leaders: Banuera BERINA, Nabuti MWEMWENIKARAWA (Former Leader of the Opposition and 2007 presidential candidate).

Opposition Party:

United Coalition Party (*Karikirckean Tei-Kiribati*—KTK). The KTK was formed in August 2010 via the merger of *Maneaban te Mauri*—MTM (Protect the Maneaba) and the Kiribati Independent Party (KIP). Composed of supporters of former president Teburoro Tito, the MTM was the governing party during his administration. Following the party's poor showing (seven seats) in the August 2007 legislative poll, neither of the MTM's main presidential contenders—Dr. Harry Tong (defeated in the 2003 presidential race by his brother, Anote Tong) and Dr. Tetana Taitai—received the necessary endorsement from the House of Assembly to be an official candidate in the October balloting.

The KIP had been formed in late 2007 by former minister of finance and economic development Taanete MAMAU and other members of the House of Assembly. Following the merger of the KIP and the MTM, the KTK became the largest opposition party in terms of legislative representation (12 seats), and the KTK's Rineta Beniamina became the Leader of the Opposition. (Beniamina subsequently aligned with the MKP, above.)

During the 2011 election campaign, the KTK reportedly criticized the BTK government for concentrating too much on climate change at the expense of other issues such as corruption and economic affairs. The KTK was credited with winning 10 seats in the 2011 legislative poll, and Taitai, a former member of the Teburoro Tito's cabinet, finished second in the January 2012 presidential balloting with 35 percent of the vote.

Leaders: Teburoro TITO (Former President of the Republic), Dr. Harry TONG (2003 presidential candidate), Tetana TAITAI (Leader of the Opposition and 2012 presidential candidate).

LEGISLATURE

The unicameral **House of Assembly** (*Maneaba ni Maungatabu*) currently consists of 44 (increased from 40 for the 2007 elections) members elected for four-year terms by majoritarian vote from 23 districts in two-round balloting (if necessary), plus a nominated representative of Banabans resident on the Fijian island of Rabi and the attorney general, ex officio, if he is not an elected member. (If the attorney general is an elected member of the House, the total number of members is 45.) The speaker must be elected by the House from outside its membership and has no voting rights.

Since party affiliations in Kiribati are extremely loose and fluid ("independent" legislators may declare affiliation with a party after elections, and affiliations can be easily changed at other times), legislative election results are difficult to quantify, and reports on party affiliations often vary widely (even in government sources). Following the balloting of October 21 and 28, 2011, the following distribution of elected seats was reported: *Boutokaan te Koaua* (BTK), 15; the United Coalition Party (KTK), 10; the Maurin Kiribati Party (MKP), 3; and independents, 16. A number of the formally independent legislators subsequently aligned with the BTK, and in April 2013 the House Website reported the following distribution of total seats: BTK, 27; KTK, 11; MKP, 5; and independents, 3.

Speaker: Taomati T. IUTA.

CABINET

[as of August 1, 2013]

President	Anote Tong
Vice President	Teima Onorio [f]
Ministers	
Commerce, Industry, and Cooperatives	Pinto Katia
Communication, Transportation, and Tourism Development	Taberannang Timeon
Education, Youth, and Sports	Maere Tekanene [f]
Environment, Lands, and Agricultural Development	Tiarite Kwong
Finance and Economic Development	Tim Murdock
Fisheries and Marine Resources Development	Tinian Reiher
Foreign Affairs and Immigration	Anote Tong
Health and Medical Services	Dr. Kautu Tenaua
Internal and Social Affairs	Teima Onorio [f]
Labor and Human Resource Development	Boutu Bateriki
Line and Phoenix Islands Development	Tawita Temoku

Public Works and Utilities	Kirabuke Teiaua
Attorney General	Tiitabu Taabane

[f] = female

INTERGOVERNMENTAL REPRESENTATION

Kiribati was admitted to the United Nations in September 1999, although it did not open a permanent mission at UN headquarters in New York until 2013. To date Kiribati has not opened an embassy in Washington, D.C.

U.S. Ambassador to Kiribati: Frankie Annette REED (resident in Fiji).

Permanent Representative to the UN: Makurito BAARO.

IGO Memberships (Non-UN): ADB, CWTH, PIF.

KOREA

Chosŏn

Political Status: Politically divided; Democratic People's Republic of Korea under Communist regime established September 9, 1948; Republic of Korea under anti-Communist republican regime established August 15, 1948.

THE COUNTRY

Korea is a mountainous peninsula projecting southeastward from Manchuria between China and Japan. Whether viewed in terms of race, culture, or language, the population is extremely homogeneous. The literacy rate is more than 90 percent. For further details see the separate discussions of the Democratic People's Republic of Korea and the Republic of Korea, which follow.

POLITICAL HISTORY

A semi-independent state associated with China from the seventh century A.D., Korea was annexed by Japan in 1910 and tightly controlled by Tokyo until Japan's defeat in World War II. The northern half of Korea was integrated with the Japanese industrial complex in Manchuria, while the southern half remained largely agricultural. Although the restoration of an independent Korea "in due course" was pledged by U.S. President Franklin Roosevelt, Britain's Prime Minister Winston Churchill, and Nationalist Chinese President Chiang Kai-shek at the Cairo Conference in 1943, the need for prompt arrangements to receive the surrender of Japanese military forces in 1945 led to a division of the country into Soviet (northern) and U.S. (southern) occupation zones along the line of the 38th parallel. Efforts by the two occupying powers to establish a unified Korean provisional government shortly became deadlocked, and the issue of Korea's future was referred to the UN General Assembly on U.S. initiative in 1947. A UN Temporary Commission was set up to facilitate elections and the establishment of a national government but was denied access to the Soviet-controlled zone. UN-observed elections were accordingly held in the southern half of Korea alone in May 1948, and the Republic of Korea (ROK) was formally established on August 15; a separate, Communist-controlled government, the Democratic People's Republic of Korea (DPRK), was established in the North on September 9. The UN General Assembly refused to recognize the latter action and declared the ROK as the lawful government of the nation. Soviet troops withdrew from the DPRK in December 1948, and U.S. forces left the ROK in June 1949.

On June 25, 1950, five months after U.S. Secretary of State Dean Acheson had delineated a Pacific "defense perimeter" that did not include Korea, DPRK troops invaded the ROK in an attempt to unify the peninsula. U.S. forces promptly came to the assistance of the southern regime, and the UN Security Council, meeting without the USSR, called on all member states to aid the ROK. A total of 16 UN members subsequently furnished troops to a UN Unified Command established by the Security Council in July 1950 and headed initially by U.S. Gen. Douglas MacArthur (later by Gens. Matthew B. Ridgway and Mark Clark). The intervention of some 300,000 Chinese Communist "volunteers" on the side of the DPRK in late 1950 produced a military stalemate, and an armistice agreement was eventually signed in the border village of Panmunjom on July 27, 1953, establishing a cease-fire line and a four-kilometer-wide demilitarized zone (DMZ) bisecting Korea near the 38th parallel. Around 1 million Koreans and more than 36,000 American soldiers died in the three-year conflict.

Negotiations in Geneva in 1954 failed to produce a settlement, and relations between the two countries were governed thereafter by the 1953 agreement, under which a Military Armistice Commission representing the former belligerents (including China) continued to meet in Panmunjom. Chinese military forces withdrew from the DPRK in 1958, but UN forces (exclusively American) remain in the South.

Political relations between North and South have alternated between overt hostility and mutual tolerance. Contacts regarding the problem of families separated by the political division of the country began in September 1971 under the auspices of the Red Cross societies of the respective countries. Talks directed toward peaceful reunification were initiated in July 1972 and resulted in the establishment of a North-South Coordinating Committee, which convened in October and continued to meet until August 1973, when negotiations were unilaterally broken off by the DPRK.

Following the North's acceptance of an appeal by ROK President Park Chung Hee to reopen discussions, representatives of the two Koreas met in Panmunjom in February 1979 in preparation for broader negotiations. After three brief sessions the talks ended over differences regarding representation and the level at which future negotiations should be conducted.

In January 1980 Pyongyang and Seoul agreed to a series of working-level talks designed to prepare for a first-ever meeting of their prime ministers. Ten working-level sessions were held during the ensuing eight months without agreement on an agenda for a high-level meeting, and North Korea terminated the discussions in September. A number of social and economic issues were addressed following a resumption of working-level discussions in 1983, with little substantive result, save for a limited number of family reunions conducted in Seoul and Pyongyang under Red Cross auspices in September 1985. Sporadic political-military talks were suspended by the North during annual U.S.–South Korean Team Spirit military exercises.

On January 1, 1989, North Korea's Kim Il Sung called, for the first time (albeit indirectly), for a summit meeting with his South Korean counterpart. The overture was accepted three weeks later by ROK President Roh Tae Woo, but in early February Pyongyang suspended further discussions because of Seoul's refusal to cancel the round of Team Spirit exercises scheduled for March. A year later, Kim extended the initiative, calling for "total openness of both North and South," including the sanctioning of "free and mutual visits." Roh again responded affirmatively and offered to invite North Korean, Chinese, and Soviet observers to scaled-down Team Spirit maneuvers. Pyongyang, however, continued to insist on cancellation of the exercises.

The prospect of a prime ministerial meeting surfaced in mid-1990, following a stunned North Korean reaction to a summit between Soviet President Mikhail Gorbachev and ROK President Roh in San Francisco, but the first-ever chiefs of government meeting in Seoul on September 4–7 ended inconclusively. North Korean Premier Yon Hyong Muk called for an arms control/nonaggression pact that would limit each side to a standing army of 10,000 men and require the withdrawal of U.S. forces; in addition, he demanded the release of South Korean students who had been jailed for traveling illegally to the North, an end to Team Spirit exercises, and a common application for admission to the UN. South Korean Prime Minister Kang Young Hoon aimed at a more gradual cultivation of bilateral relations through a mutual exchange of military information, establishment of a hotline between defense ministers, the conclusion of an economic cooperation agreement, freer travel across the common border, and simultaneous entry into the UN of the two Korean states. Additional sessions were held in October and December 1990, without significant movement.

In May 1991 North Korea abandoned its insistence on common representation at the UN, and on September 17 both Koreas were admitted to the world body. In late October the fourth round of prime ministerial talks were held in Pyongyang, again without notable progress. In contrast, the fifth round in Seoul concluded on December 13–14 with a historic nonaggression pact and an agreement to work toward a nuclear-free Korea. In signing the December accord, which called for formal termination of the 1950–1953 war, the North Korean government for the first time officially recognized its southern counterpart.

Ratifications of the December accords were exchanged during the sixth round of premier-level talks in Pyongyang in February 1992, clearly indicating that Pyongyang had abandoned its long-standing demand for "one Korea" achieved through "liberation of the South." A month later, at the seventh premier-level session, the participants agreed to establish a Joint Nuclear Control Committee, while during the eighth round in mid-September the participants announced agreements on nonaggression, cross-border exchanges, and establishment of a North-South Joint Reconciliation Commission.

Despite these positive developments, relations soon foundered once again, in part over North Korea's refusal to permit inspections by the International Atomic Energy Agency (IAEA) at a number of nuclear sites—a dispute that, during succeeding years, became enmeshed in matters of foreign aid and U.S.-DPRK diplomatic relations (for details, see the Foreign relations section of the DPRK entry). The death of Kim Il Sung in July 1994, shortly before a planned first DPRK-ROK presidential meeting, brought progress to a halt.

In April 1996, after North Korea had threatened to withdraw from the 1953 armistice, U.S. President Bill Clinton and ROK President Kim Young Sam proposed that quadripartite talks, with China as the fourth participant, be initiated in an effort to conclude a definitive peace treaty. The following September Seoul broke off all North-South contacts following the discovery in South Korean waters of an abandoned North Korean submarine, and in July 1997 a military clash in the DMZ further threatened the renewed peace effort. Nevertheless, following a preliminary four-power meeting in August, on December 9–10 representatives of the four met in Geneva, Switzerland, to begin peace negotiations. In March a second four-party session in Geneva descended into procedural wrangling and disagreements over the withdrawal of U.S. troops, but in April, at the DPRK's suggestion, Pyongyang and Seoul held their first ministerial meeting in four years, in Beijing, the purpose being to discuss agricultural aid to the North. The talks ultimately broke down over South Korea's insistence that aid was contingent on North Korea's willingness to discuss family reunification.

In June 1998, for the first time in seven years, officers of the UN Command and the DPRK army held talks in Panmunjom, despite South Korea's capture, the previous day, of a North Korean midget submarine that had become entangled in fishing nets. (Nine bodies were discovered on board when the submarine was opened.) A second, empty five-man sub was found in July.

Four-power talks resumed in October 1998, with subcommittees being created to consider ways to establish a "peace regime" and to reduce peninsular tension. Despite the sinking of yet another suspected DPRK spy vessel in December 1998, the fourth formal four-power session was held in January 1999. The focus of a fifth session, held in April, was humanitarian aid to the North, which had been suffering a devastating famine since 1995. A sixth round in August made little headway, the diplomatic emphasis having shifted toward bilateral negotiations between, on the one hand, the two Koreas and, on the other, North Korea and Washington.

Progress toward improved North-South relations was threatened by a June 15, 1999, naval battle in the Yellow Sea—the first such encounter since the 1953 armistice—that resulted in the sinking of a North Korea gunboat, the death of an estimated 30 North Korean sailors, and additional damage to ships on both sides. Tensions had risen earlier in the month when North Korean vessels began accompanying crab-fishing boats into a buffer zone around the Northern Limit Line (NLL), established at the time of the 1953 armistice. On September 2, 1999, North Korea unilaterally declared an extension of its territorial waters to 40 miles (65 km) south of the NLL, prompting Seoul to announce the following day that it fully intended to defend the disputed area.

Although the North rejected a January 2000 proposal from South Korea's President Kim Dae Jung to foster economic cooperation, a speech delivered by Kim in March in Berlin, Germany, offered massive aid for building the North Korean economy if intergovernmental dialogue resumed. Only a week later secret talks between Seoul and Pyongyang reportedly opened in Beijing, leading to a surprise announcement on April 10 that South Korea's President Kim would meet North Korea's Kim at a first-ever summit. The historic meeting took place June 13–15 in Pyongyang. Noting "the lofty wishes of the Korean people," the two leaders signed an accord that declared their intention to work toward peaceful national unification, authorized family reunions and eventual repatriation of long-term political prisoners, and promoted a "balanced development" of their economies as well as accelerated social, cultural, health, environmental, and sports exchanges.

The foreign ministers of the two Koreas conferred for the first time during the July 2000 forum of the Association of Southeast Asians Nations, held in Bangkok, Thailand. Ministerial-level discussions continued July 29–31 in Seoul and August 29–September 1 in Pyongyang. The latter session concluded with an agreement permitting the ROK and DPRK military establishments to open a dialogue. Both delegations also approved additional family reunion meetings in Mt. Keumgang, a resort just north of the DMZ. Renewals of rail and highway links were also approved. The North-South defense ministers met in late September, with the first working-level military sessions following in November and December. The inaugural meeting of an Inter-Korean Economic Cooperation Promotion Committee convened in December.

Apparently because of the less-than-conciliatory stance of the new U.S. George W. Bush administration, North Korea postponed a fifth round of North-South talks that had been scheduled for March 2001. The session was ultimately held in Seoul on September 15–18 and was followed by a mostly unproductive November 9–14 round in Mt. Keumgang. Objecting to the heightened security instituted in Seoul following the September 11, 2001, terrorist attacks on the United States, Pyongyang delayed the seventh session until August 12–14, 2002. In the interim, another altercation near the NLL had resulted in the sinking of a South Korean patrol boat and casualties on both sides.

Several additional rounds of ministerial-level talks were convened between October 2002 and October 2003, a period that also saw the continuation of family reunions in Mt. Keumgang, the opening of the first road link between North and South in February 2003, and completion of the first rail connection across the DMZ in June 2003. In the same month, groundbreaking occurred for an industrial complex in Kaesong, in the North, to house South Korean manufacturing firms. The first tenant in the industrial park began operations in December 2004.

The North gave way on its demand for bilateral discussions with the Bush administration and agreed to participate in the opening of the six-party nuclear talks in Beijing, held during August 27–29, 2003, involving both the Koreas, China, Japan, Russia, and the United States. (For details of subsequent six-party developments, see the DPRK entry.)

The 14th round of cabinet-level talks, held May 5–7, 2004, was followed by a meeting of senior military leaders on May 26 and by a June 4 agreement to reduce tensions at the DMZ and near the NLL. Such positive developments were more than offset, however, by continuing hostility between Washington and Pyongyang. Following the latter's assertion in October 2002 that it had not abandoned its nuclear weapons program, as it had agreed to do in 1994, fuel oil shipments to the North were halted. Pyongyang then reopened its Yongbyon nuclear facility, ordered the last IAEA inspectors to leave the country, and announced its withdrawal from the Nuclear Non-Proliferation Treaty (NPT).

In August 2004 the North canceled an additional round of North-South cabinet-level talks because 469 North Korean refugees had been flown to South Korea from Vietnam. After a ten-month lapse, working-level discussions, held in Kaesong, resumed on May 16–19, 2005, and on June 22–23 a 15th round of cabinet-level meetings was conducted in Seoul. In addition to further bilateral military talks and a tenth meeting of the Inter-Korean Economic Cooperation Promotion Committee, July saw the restoration of private North-South telephone links, 60 years after they had been severed. The 18th cabinet-level session, held April 21–24, 2006, in Pyongyang, concluded with issuance of an eight-point statement that, among other things, supported joint development of the Han River estuary and of zinc and magnesite mines in the North. The two Koreas also appeared to be moving closer toward resolving a complaint from Seoul that the North continued to hold up to 600 prisoners of war, dating back to the 1950–1953 conflict, as well as nearly 500 abductees. Progress on that and all other fronts came to a halt, however, at the July 11–13 19th session in Pusan, when the North cut the talks short. The walkout occurred because South Korea, disgruntled by recent DPRK missile tests and Pyongyang's withdrawal from the six-party talks, would not discuss additional food and fertilizer aid.

A 20th ministerial session was ultimately held February 27–March 2, 2007, after the North once again rejoined the six-party talks and agreed to dismantle its nuclear weapons program. The talks concluded with announcements that family reunions, suspended since the previous July, would resume, that the Red Cross would be consulted about the missing prisoners of war and abductees, and that long-delayed test runs of two cross-border trains—the first since 1950—would proceed. With considerable fanfare in the South, the rail journeys across the DMZ took place on May 17, following adoption of security arrangements at a meeting of high-level military personnel. Two days later, for the first time since the Korean War, a commercial cargo ship from the North entered a South Korean port.

The next ministerial-level session took place in Seoul from May 29 to June 1, 2007, but ended unfavorably when the ROK refused to release a shipment of food aid until the DPRK acted on its six-party pledge to begin shutting down its nuclear program. Late in the month, the DPRK renewed its commitment to shut down its Yongbyon facility, and on June 26 the South announced that it would resume rice deliveries. The renewed spirit of cooperation led Seoul to repeat a call for a second leadership summit, which the North accepted. The second summit took place in Pyongyang on October 2–4, at the conclusion of which Kim Jong Il and Roh Moo Hyun released a Declaration on the Advancement of South-North Korean Relations, Peace, and Prosperity. Highlights of the declaration included a call to accelerate creation of a peninsular economic bloc, a commitment to work toward conclusion of a Korean War peace treaty and denuclearization, and an agreement to establish a maritime Special Peace and Cooperation Zone. In addition, the Inter-Korean Economic Cooperation Promotion Committee was to be upgraded to a Joint Committee for Inter-Korean Economic Cooperation. Improvements in transportation, communications, infrastructure, agricultural cooperation, and health and medical services were also targeted, and a joint shipbuilding venture was announced. On November 14–16, in the first such meeting since 1992, DPRK Prime Minister Kim Yong Il and ROK Prime Minister Han Duk Soo met in Seoul to advance toward the goals set forth at the October summit.

In the following six months, further progress in North-South relations awaited fulfillment of Pyongyang's commitment to begin dismantling its nuclear facilities and provide an accounting of its weapons programs. Deadlines of December 31, 2007, and then of February 28, 2008, were not met. Meanwhile, South Korea had elected a new president, Lee Myung Bak, who appeared more willing than his immediate predecessors to take the North to task not only for its failure to meet its six-party obligations but also for its human rights record. Bilateral relations were set back once again on July 11 when a South Korean tourist, a member of a group staying at Mt. Keumgang, was shot dead on a beach by North Korean troops, bringing a halt to North-South tourism. Furthermore, in November the North announced that it was suspending rail freight shipment from Kaesong, was cutting nonmilitary phone lines, and would reintroduce stringent border-crossing restrictions. The ostensible precipitant was the continuing distribution by South Korea civic groups of propaganda leaflets sent across the border via helium balloons.

On January 30, 2009, the North stated that it would no longer honor agreements previously concluded with Seoul and that it considered their maritime border accord void. Relations continued to spiral downward following an April 5 rocket launch by the North—Pyongyang identified it as a launch vehicle for a satellite, while most international observers described it as a military test—that provoked criticism from the UN Security Council. Reacting to widespread international condemnation, on April 14 the DPRK announced that it was once again quitting the six-party talks and nullifying all related agreements. On May 15 the North also voided wage and rent agreements governing the Kaesong industrial zone. It then insisted that wages be quadrupled (to about $300 a month per worker) and that the rent for the complex's land be raised from $16 million a year to $500 million.

On May 25, 2009, two days after conducting a second nuclear weapons test and initiating a series of short-range missile launches, Pyongyang withdrew from the 1953 armistice, prompting the South to announce that it would participate in a U.S.-led Proliferation Security Initiative that authorized the interception and inspection of ships suspected of carrying military and other materials forbidden under sanctions regimes. The North indicated that it would regard any such intervention as an act of war.

Less than three months later, Pyongyang once again appeared to be retreating from its hard-line position. The death of former South Korean president Kim Dae Jung, on August 18, 2009, provided an opportunity for the North to send a high-level delegation to the South to pay its respects. The delegation met briefly with President Lee, and within days the two Koreas agreed to resume family reunions in September–October after a two-year lapse. During the same period the North released a handful of detained South Koreans—a Hyundai employee in Kaesong who had criticized the DPRK government and four fishermen who had allegedly strayed into North Korean waters—and indicated a willingness to resume tours to Mt. Keumgang.

The most serious setback to inter-Korean relations in many years occurred on March 26, 2010, when a South Korean corvette, the *Cheonan,* exploded and sank near the NLL, costing the lives of 46 crew members. Seoul was initially cautious in assigning blame for the sinking, but a May 24 report by international experts from Australia, Sweden, the United Kingdom, and the United States as well as South Korea concluded that the ship's destruction was caused by a torpedo fired from a North Korean submarine. However, some military experts claimed that other scenarios could explain the explosion. President Lee announced that, among other measures, his government was cutting all economic ties with the North except for those at the Kaesong industrial park. On May 25 Pyongyang, which vehemently denied any involvement, froze relations with the South, abrogated the nonaggression pact, and threatened other measures, including the expulsion of all South Koreans from Kaesong. On June 15 the North and the South made presentations on the matter to the UN Security Council, which subsequently condemned the attack without assigning blame.

In mid-September 2010, in the first public steps toward renewing the North-South interchange, South Korea stated that it would supply rice and cement to the North to aid recovery efforts following devastating floods. The two Koreas also agreed to resume family reunion visits. Earlier in the month, the DPRK had released the seven-member crew of a South Korean fishing boat that, according to the North, illegally entered its Exclusive Economic Zone in August.

Acting on reports that millions of North Koreans faced malnutrition, in November South Korea authorized the World Health Organization to resume its distribution of South Korean medical assistance to North Korea. In January 2012 South Korea delivered 180 tons of aid to the North and earmarked an additional $465 million for further assistance. But despite promises to the contrary, North Korea tested a long-range missile in April, which brought international condemnation and the suspension of aid shipments.

Typhoon Bolaven struck the Korean Peninsula on August 28, 2012. With a top wind of 145 miles per hour, the typhoon was the strongest storm to hit the Koreas in more than ten years. It dumped more than 27 inches of rain in areas and caused widespread flooding. Bolaven killed 19 in South Korea and 59 in North Korea.

On February 12, North Korea conducted its third nuclear test amid widespread international criticism. On March 7, the UN Security Council enacted additional sanctions on Pyongyang in response to the test. The test severely strained relations with China, prompting Kim Jong Un to pen a personal letter to Chinese president Xi Jingpin in May in an effort to repair ties.

In April 2013, North Korea announced the closure of the Kaesong industrial region. By May, all of the South Korean workers had left the zone, which effectively ceased operations. In July, the officials from both countries announced the industrial region would be reopened.

DEMOCRATIC PEOPLE'S REPUBLIC OF KOREA

Chosŏn Minchu-chui Inmin Konghwa-guk

Political Status: Communist people's republic established on September 9, 1948.

Area: 46,540 sq. mi. (120,538 sq. km).

Population: 24,966,738 (2013E—UN); 24,720,407 (2013E—U.S. Census).

Major Urban Centers (2008C): PYONGYANG (2,581,076 city; 3,255,388 urban area), Namhung (703,610), Chongjin (614,892).

Official Language: Korean.

Monetary Unit: North Korean Won (market rate November 1, 2013: 900 won = $1US). The currency was last revalued in 2009.

Chair of the National Defense Commission: KIM Jong Un; served as de facto head of state from the death of President KIM Jong Il on December 17, 2011, until election to a five-year term by the Supreme People's Assembly on April 13, 2012.

President of the Presidium of the Supreme People's Assembly: KIM Yong Nam; elected to the newly created office by the Supreme People's Assembly on September 5, 1998; reelected on September 3, 2004, and on April 9, 2009.

Premier: PAK Pong Ju; elected by the Supreme People's Assembly on March 31, 2013, succeeding CHOE Yong Rim.

THE COUNTRY

A land of mountains and valleys, the Democratic People's Republic of Korea (DPRK) is located in East Asia, bordering in the north on the People's Republic of China and the Russian Federation and in the south on the Republic of Korea (ROK). Its people are characterized by ethnic and linguistic homogeneity, tracing their origins to the Mongols and the Chinese. Traditionally, Koreans followed Buddhism and Shamanism, but after the establishment of the Communist regime, religion declined as a factor in North Korean life. Preaching Christianity and other religions can be a capital offense. Women constitute an estimated 44 percent of the active labor force and hold 15.6 percent of the seats in the current Supreme People's Assembly (107 of 687).

The DPRK has more plentiful natural resources than the ROK and inherited a substantial industrial base from the Japanese occupation, but the Korean conflict of 1950–1953 destroyed much of the economic infrastructure. The Soviet-type economy was reconstructed at a high rate of growth with substantial Soviet and Chinese aid. More than 90 percent of the economy is socialized, agricultural land and production remain collectivized, and state-owned enterprises continue to produce the vast majority of manufactured goods. The government has permitted farmers and others to retain income from legal "sideline activities," such as kitchen gardens, while a "special economic zone" was established in Rajin-Sonbong in 1991 to facilitate joint ventures with foreigners. In 1998 the government agreed to form a partnership with South Korea's Hyundai to develop scenic Mt. Keumgang on the southeast coast as a tourist resort and to build an industrial park for branches of various South Korean firms. As of January 2013, the industrial complex in Kaesong housed 123 South Korean companies, employed some 53,000 North Koreans, and provided approximately $90 million per year in wages, paid directly to the government of North Korea.

The agricultural sector is dominated by production of rice, maize, and other grains for domestic consumption. Heavy industry includes the manufacture of steel, other metallurgical products, and cement. Ore deposits include coal, iron, gold, silver, magnesite, copper, and lead. Light manufacturing has been of increasing importance since the breakup of the Soviet Union forced economic reorganization, and textiles now constitute a principal source of export earnings. China ranks as North Korea's main trading partner.

Economic data on the DPRK remain difficult to obtain, and those released by the government often are not comparable with those for other countries. According to Pyongyang, the economy suffered drastic declines in the 1990s, with GDP dropping by over 27 percent in 1994 and by more than 18 percent in 1995 and again in 1996. Despite some $1 billion in international food and other aid, as many as 1.5 million people may have died from starvation or related disease from 1995 to 1998.

In 1999 the economy reportedly grew for the first time in a decade, expanding by 6.2 percent. According to South Korea's central bank, growth continued, albeit at a slower pace, through 2005. GDP contracted by 1.1 percent in 2006, before registering 3.7 percent growth in 2007 and 2008, partly because of increased agricultural yields. GDP contracted by 0.9 percent in 2009 and by 0.5 percent in 2010, according to a report by South Korea's Bank of Korea (quoted by Reuters), owing in large part to international sanctions and declines in the agricultural and manufacturing sectors. According to a 2011 UN report, some 6 million people were malnourished and in need of some 434,000 tons of food aid. GDP growth resumed in 2011, rising by 0.8 percent because of strong harvests. GDP grew by 1.3 percent in 2012, as estimated by the Bank of Korea, mainly as a result of international aid in the aftermath of Typhoon Bolaven.

GOVERNMENT AND POLITICS

Political background. A provisional "people's republic" was established in the northern half of Korea under Soviet auspices in February 1946, and the Democratic People's Republic of Korea was formally organized on September 9, 1948, following proclamation of the Republic of Korea in the South. Both the government and the ruling Korean Workers' Party (KWP), which superseded the Communist Party in 1949, were headed by KIM Il Sung, a Soviet-trained Communist.

Suggesting that North Korean political authority might be passing from Kim Il Sung to his son, KIM Jong Il, the younger Kim was appointed to what was one of the country's most powerful posts, chair of the National Defense Commission (NDC), on April 9, 1993. Kim Il Sung died on July 8, 1994, but no action on succession was forthcoming until October 8, 1997, when Kim Jong Il was named KWP general secretary. The state presidency remained vacant.

Uncontested elections to the 687-member Tenth Supreme People's Assembly (SPA) were held on July 26, 1998, with the Central Election Committee. At its first session on September 5 the new legislature, which included 60 generals among its membership, approved a number of constitutional changes (see Constitution and government, below) and reelected Kim Jong Il as NDC chair. Kim was thereby confirmed as de facto head of state, the state presidency having been abolished in deference to the memory of Kim Il Sung, whom the new preamble to the constitution described as the country's "eternal President." On the same day KIM Yong Nam, theretofore foreign minister, was named to the newly created post of president of the Assembly's Presidium, and Vice Premier HONG Song Nam was elevated to the premiership, succeeding KANG Song San, who had served as premier since 1984.

In a surprise statement on April 10, 2000, the two Koreas announced that Kim Jong Il and President Kim Dae Jung of South Korea would hold a summit in Pyongyang in mid-June. The announcement came in the midst of an unprecedented DPRK foreign relations initiative that included conclusion of a new friendship treaty with Russia in February, reestablishment of relations with Australia in May, and an unexpected visit by Kim Jong Il to China in late May—his first trip abroad in 17 years. During the historic June 13–15 summit in Pyongyang, the two Korean leaders called for, among other things, eventual national reunification and economic cooperation (see the preceding Korea entry for details).

In pro forma balloting for the SPA on August 3, 2003, all 687 members were elected unopposed. In its first session on September 3 the new legislature reelected Kim Jong Il as NDC chair and approved the selection of PAK Pong Ju, formerly the chemical industry minister, as premier. Pak was succeeded by KIM Yong Il, theretofore the minister of land and marine transport, on April 11, 2007. No official explanation was offered for Pak's dismissal, although some observers cited his apparent advocacy of a limited incentive-based wage system as part of an effort to raise the standard of living.

Kim Jong Il and South Korean President Roh Moo Hyun met in a second summit in Pyongyang October 2–4, 2007 (see the Korea entry). On November 14–16 Prime Minister Kim met in Seoul with his South Korean counterpart in the first meeting of DPRK-ROK prime ministers in 15 years.

The election of the 12th SPA, initially scheduled for September 2008, was held on March 9, 2009; as in the past, only one KWP-endorsed candidate appeared on each district's ballot. No official reason was advanced for the six-month postponement, although observers attributed the delay to the rumored adverse health of Kim Jong Il, who reportedly suffered a stroke in August 2008. There were additional unconfirmed reports of a second stroke in October. Kim, described as looking frail, appeared at the opening of the new SPA on April 9, at which time he was reelected NDC chair. SPA Presidium Chair Kim Yong Nam and Premier Kim Yong Il were also reelected.

On June 7, 2010, the third session of the SPA approved CHOE Yong Rim, 79, as successor to Premier Kim Yong Il, who had apparently been assigned at least partial blame for a poorly executed and economically disruptive reevaluation of the won (100 old won = 1 new won) on December 1, 2009. Six new vice premiers and three ministers were also named in the cabinet reshuffle.

On December 17, 2011, Kim Jong Il died of a heart attack at the age of 69. He was succeeded by Kim Jong Un, who quickly consolidated power with new appointments to key positions in the military and party (see Current issues, below).

On March 31, 2013, Pak Pong Ju was elected premier by the SPA. A reshuffled cabinet was named on April 2. Meanwhile, the minister of the armed forces was replaced three times between April 2012 and May 2013, as Kim Jong Un reportedly endeavored to solidify his control over the military (see Current issues, below).

Constitution and government. From 1948 to 1972 the DPRK's nominal head of state was the chair of the Presidium of the Supreme People's Assembly. However, the office was of substantially less consequence than that of premier. Under the constitution of December 1972 executive authority was vested in the president of the republic. In addition, a "super cabinet," the Central People's Committee, oversaw operation of the Administration Council, a cabinetlike body headed by the premier.

Constitutional changes adopted on September 5, 1998, by the SPA included abolition of the state presidency. Although the SPA remains the highest state organ, its authority to determine questions of war and peace passed to the ten-member NDC, whose chair now serves as head of state. The Central People's Committee and the Standing Committee were abolished, with most of their duties and powers being assigned to a newly created SPA Presidium that ranks as the "highest organ of state power" between full SPA sessions. The Presidium also assumed responsibility for diplomatic functions, including ratifying and abrogating treaties, that had previously been under the purview of the state presidency; the Presidium's president, the second highest DPRK official, "represents the state" and receives credentials of foreign representatives. The Administration Council was replaced by a smaller Cabinet that not only functions as the SPA's administrative and executive body but also has additional authority for governmental management. The premier, who "represents the government of the DPRK," is assisted by vice premiers. The judicial system is headed by the Central Court and includes a People's Court and local courts. Judges are elected by the SPA.

Additional constitutional changes were made in April 2009. Kim Jong Il was identified as "supreme leader" by virtue of his chairing the NDC, while added emphasis was placed on a "military first" (*songun*) doctrine. According to South Korea's Yonhap news agency, which first reported the changes in September 2009, socialism appeared to have replaced communism as the state's guiding philosophy, and for the first time the human rights of "the workers, peasants, and working intellectuals" were accorded recognition.

Administratively, the DPRK is divided into nine provinces, two directly governed cities (Pyongyang and Rason), and three special administrative regions set up since 2002 to accommodate joint economic ventures with South Korea (Kaesong Industrial Park), China, and Russia (Sinuiju Special Administrative Region and Rajin-Sonbong Economic Special Zone). Smaller units of local government include cities, urban districts, and counties. Each unit has its own people's assembly with a people's committee that, in addition to serving as the "local sovereign power organ" between assembly sessions, functions as the local administrative and executive body.

All news media are censored by the KWP and staffed by KWP-approved personnel. Reporters Without Borders again ranked the DPRK second only to Eritrea as the world's leading violator of press rights in 2013 (178th out of 179 countries). Access to the Internet is very limited, and content is heavily censored.

Foreign relations. The most striking rupture in North-South relations came in October 1983 after a bomb attack in Yangon, Myanmar, that killed four South Korean cabinet ministers. After two captured DPRK army members confessed to having been ordered to attack the South Korean delegation, including President Chun Doo Hwan, Yangon withdrew recognition of the DPRK, and both Seoul and Washington demanded a public apology. Pyongyang, however, persisted in denying any responsibility for the incident.

The country has gone through a number of phases in relations with the Soviet Union/Russian Federation and the People's Republic of China (PRC). The Kim Il Sung regime steadfastly proclaimed a policy of *Juche,* or self-reliance, while depending on both the Soviet Union and the PRC for aid.

In an abrupt reversal of policy, the DPRK in 1990 sought to establish relations with Japan, while demanding that Tokyo apologize for its 35 years of colonial rule and match the $500 million in economic compensation given to South Korea when Tokyo and Seoul normalized relations in 1965. The apology came at the January 30, 1991, launch of normalization talks, but Japan rejected the demand for compensation and the DPRK terminated discussions in 1992.

In April 1992 North Korea reversed a six-year refusal to permit inspection of its nuclear facilities by the International Atomic Energy Agency (IAEA). Although inspectors were permitted to visit some nuclear sites, the government refused to open others and in March 1993 threatened to withdraw from the Nuclear Non-Proliferation Treaty (NPT), to which it had acceded in 1985. On April 1 the IAEA notified the UN Security Council of North Korea's noncompliance and requested a food and fuel embargo. Pyongyang soon called for discussions with Washington to secure an end to the impasse.

In July 1993 U.S.-DPRK negotiators in Geneva concluded an agreement stipulating that Pyongyang would resume talks with the IAEA and Washington would consider aid for the construction of non-military light-water reactors. In August North Korea granted access to five declared sites but not to two others in its Yongbyon nuclear complex. No further progress was registered until February 1994, when the DPRK agreed to unimpeded inspection of all seven sites but denied access to two suspected nuclear waste dumps that could potentially yield a supply of bomb-grade material. In a formal pact concluded on October 21, Washington agreed to extend diplomatic recognition, arrange for financial assistance (estimated at some $4.6 billion) for the construction of two modern nuclear reactors, and supply 500,000 tons of fuel oil a year during the switchover. (Subsequently, it was agreed that South Korea would meet 70 percent of the cost and Japan another 20 percent, with the balance to be provided by the United States and others.) Pyongyang agreed to freeze all of its nuclear activities, provide safe storage for some 8,000 spent nuclear fuel rods, and accept full IAEA inspection after significant progress had been made toward construction of the new facilities. In December, at the conclusion of a two-day meeting in San Francisco, representatives of the United States, South Korea, and Japan agreed to set up a multilateral consortium, named the Korean Peninsula Energy Development Organization (KEDO), to oversee financing of the U.S.-DPRK nuclear accord.

The deadline of April 21, 1995, for finalizing the October 1994 nuclear accord was not met, primarily because of Pyongyang's insistence that the replacement light-water reactors be of U.S. rather than of South Korean manufacture. In June, however, the DPRK accepted a face-saving proviso that the reactors be of "the advanced version of U.S.-origin design and technology." A groundbreaking ceremony was held in the east coast town of Sinpo on August 9, 1997. By then, the European Union had joined the KEDO.

In September 1995 Moscow formally terminated a defense treaty dating from 1961. Pyongyang responded that the treaty had been "as good as nullified" by the collapse of the Soviet Union and welcomed a proposal for a new nonmilitary cooperation agreement with the Russian Federation.

In June 1998 the DPRK suspended a 1997 program under which Japanese-born spouses of Korean men had been allowed to visit their homeland. Earlier, Japan had dismissed the results of an unsuccessful North Korean investigation into the whereabouts of ten or more Japanese who had allegedly been kidnapped in the 1970s and 1980s to teach North Korean agents. Relations with Japan took yet another downturn with the DPRK's August missile launching, which prompted Tokyo to temporarily freeze food aid and development assistance, including its share of KEDO funding. North Korea insisted that the vehicle was a satellite launcher, which U.S. intelligence later acknowledged may have been the case. (Tokyo announced in May 1999 that it would release its KEDO funding.)

Meanwhile, the DPRK continued to deny IAEA inspectors access to some laboratory sites. In August 1998 reports surfaced that U.S. intelligence had discovered yet another underground weapons site. Despite Pyongyang's initial demands for monetary compensation in return for opening the Kumchangri complex, a series of bilateral talks produced in March 1999 a joint statement in which the North Korean regime agreed to provide access to the site beginning in May. U.S. president Bill Clinton's administration subsequently pledged additional food and agricultural aid. An initial inspection of the Kumchangri facilities on May 20–24, 1999, and a repeat inspection a year later revealed that they were incomplete and posed no security threat.

In mid-1999 rumors emerged that North Korea was preparing to test a longer-range version of a missile it had fired on August 31, 1998, over Japan and into the Pacific. Following a visit to Pyongyang by former U.S. secretary of defense William Perry, who reportedly offered additional economic assistance and diplomatic ties if the DPRK showed sufficient restraint in its nuclear weapons and missile programs, Pyongyang in August agreed to suspend further test launches.

On September 17, 1999, Washington announced that it would soon ease the embargo that had been in place since 1953, the principal exception being for military-related goods and technology. A week later Pyongyang formally announced a suspension of ballistic missile testing. Several subsequent negotiating sessions focused on ways of improving relations and on prospects for higher-level discussions.

At a December 1999 meeting in Beijing, representatives of the DPRK and Japan agreed, after a seven-year hiatus, to resume suspended normalization talks.

In February 2000, during a visit to the North Korean capital by the Russian foreign minister Igor Ivanov—the first such visit by a leading Russian official since Moscow had granted diplomatic recognition to South Korea a decade earlier—the two states concluded a friendship treaty.

On June 19, 2000, President Clinton finally lifted economic sanctions against the DPRK. Talks on the missile program resumed in Kuala Lumpur, Malaysia, in July and November but ended with the United States refusing to meet the DPRK's request for $1 billion a year in compensation for ending missile sales. For years the cash-strapped North had been considered the world's leading exporter of rockets and related technology, and in August Kim Jong Il himself had confirmed sales to Iran and Syria. U.S. Secretary of State Madeleine Albright and DPRK Foreign Minister PAEK Nam Sun met for the first time on July 28 during a session of the Association of Southeast Asian Nations in Bangkok, Thailand. On October 23 Albright became the most senior U.S. official ever to visit the North.

The normalization process was set back again in December 2001 when the Japanese coast guard sank a suspected North Korean spy ship in Japan's exclusive economic zone, an act that the North characterized as "brutal piracy."

Relations with the United States deteriorated throughout 2002 in the wake of President Bush identifying the DPRK, along with Iraq and Iran, as part of an "axis of evil." The North also continued to be angered over U.S. insistence on IAEA inspection of all nuclear facilities. On August 7 U.S. officials attended the first pouring of concrete for a nuclear power plant under the 1994 KEDO agreement, but relations deteriorated during the visit in October 3–5 by U.S. Assistant Secretary of State James Kelly to Pyongyang, when the DPRK proclaimed that it had continued its nuclear weapons program in violation of the agreement. On November 15 the KEDO announced that it would suspend future deliveries of heavy fuel oil to the North, pending progress on the nuclear weapons issue.

On September 17, 2002, in an effort to reenergize the diplomatic process, Japanese Prime Minister Junichiro Koizumi traveled to Pyongyang, where, for the first time, the DPRK admitted having abducted Japanese citizens between 1977 and 1983. Kim Jong Il also expressed a willingness to permit full IAEA inspections and to maintain a moratorium on the DPRK's missile testing beyond 2003. In return, Koizumi apologized for Japan's colonial occupation and offered to provide economic assistance following normalization of relations.

In 2003, Pyongyang ordered all IAEA inspectors to leave the country, restarted the Yongbyon nuclear reactor, and in April formally withdrew from the NPT. From August 27 to 29, in an effort to diffuse the crisis, six-party talks involving the two Koreas, the United States, the PRC, Japan, and Russia opened in Beijing, with additional rounds taking place on February 25–27 and June 23–26, 2004. By then, the general consensus was that Pyongyang had sufficient plutonium for up to eight nuclear warheads.

Following a year of political gamesmanship, a fourth six-party round opened in Beijing on July 26, 2005, and continued until a recess on August 7. When the talks resumed on September 13–19, the DPRK indicated its intention to renew participation in both the NPT and the IAEA's safeguards regime, but no additional progress was reported at the opening of the fifth round from November 9 to 11. Less than a month later, the DPRK announced a boycott of further six-party sessions until the United States ended financial sanctions that it had imposed in response to the DPRK's alleged money laundering, smuggling, and counterfeiting of U.S. currency.

Work on the two KEDO reactors was ultimately suspended, and the project was officially terminated in June 2006.Until the nuclear weapons impasse brought the program to a halt, Pyongyang and Washington had regularly discussed the fate of the 8,000 U.S. servicemen still listed as missing in action from the Korean conflict. Since 2000, the remains of more than 200 individuals have been recovered.

On July 5, 2006, North Korea launched seven rockets over the Sea of Japan, one of them a 6,000-kilometer-range *Taepo Dong-2* ballistic missile that failed less than a minute into its flight. On July 15 the UN Security Council passed a resolution condemning the tests, demanding renewal of the ballistic missile test moratorium and North Korea's return to the six-party talks, and strengthening an embargo on the transfer of missile-related technology, materials, and financing. On October 9, in an action that even China branded as "flagrant and brazen," North Korea conducted its first underground nuclear test near Punggye, in the mountainous northeast. The Security Council responded with another condemnatory resolution.

Having captured the world's attention once again, on October 31, 2006, Pyongyang did an about-face, announcing that it was prepared to return to the six-party negotiations, and talks resumed in Beijing on December 18–22. Although the initial session accomplished little, at the next, held on February 8–13, 2007, the North stated that it was prepared to shut down the Yongbyon reactor once again, inventory all nuclear programs, and permit IAEA inspections. In return, the DPRK was to receive 50,000 tons of heavy fuel (with another 950,000 tons to follow after the North closed all its nuclear facilities); both the United States and Japan would reopen normalization talks; and Washington would facilitate the release of $25 million in North Korean assets that had been frozen in a Macao bank as a consequence of U.S. financial sanctions. As a result of the frozen assets, North Korea abruptly ended the opening session of the next round of talks, held on March 19–22. Following the transfer of the funds via a Russian bank in June, the DPRK permitted IAEA inspectors to visit Yongbyon as the first step toward shutting down the nuclear facility. On July 14 the IAEA confirmed that the Yongbyon reactor and other related facilities at the site had been shut down. Pyongyang further agreed that by the end of the year it would disable all facilities at Yongbyon and disclose all its nuclear programs. Although the North began disabling the Yongbyon facility in November, the deadline was not met.

On June 27, 2008, North Korea destroyed the cooling tower at the Yongbyon nuclear facility, a day after delivering to China the much-anticipated accounting of its nuclear weapons program. Two key elements were missing from the declaration, however: details about its existing nuclear bombs and a response to U.S. assertions that Pyongyang had a uranium enrichment program. Nevertheless, the accounting was sufficient to evoke a positive reaction from the other countries in the six-party talks, and President Bush quickly announced that the United States would lift some sanctions and begin the process of removing North Korea from its list of state sponsors of terrorism. Working-level talks between Japan and North Korea also resumed in June, at which time Tokyo agreed to ease sanctions, and Pyongyang agreed, among other things, to reexamine the case of the abducted Japanese.

On July 10–12, 2008, after a nine-month pause, the six-party talks reconvened. Although North Korea complained that fuel oil shipments were lagging behind schedule, it agreed to complete nuclear disablement by October. Meanwhile, on July 11 bilateral relations with South Korea suffered another setback when North Korean guards shot and killed a South Korean tourist who was part of a group visiting Mt. Keumgang.

Progress toward dismantling Yongbyon was subsequently halted again until the United States, on October 11, 2008, removed the DPRK from its list of state sponsors of terrorism. North Korea thereupon agreed to resume tearing down the Yongbyon facility and permit inspections. In November, however, it restricted inspectors from taking soil and other test samples. It also announced its intention to close the border with the South, apparently over continuing dissatisfaction with the conservative South Korean president, Lee Myung Bak. Six-party talks on December 8–11 failed to make progress on verification protocols.

Having announced on January 30, 2009, that it was abrogating agreements previously concluded with Seoul and that it would not honor the NLL that defined their maritime border in the Yellow Sea, the North on April 5 launched another *Taepo Dong*-2 rocket. Pyongyang insisted that the launch carried a communications satellite into orbit, but Western observers saw no evidence of a new satellite and declared the launch an unsuccessful military test, the second and third stages of the rocket having failed to separate. The North responded to broad international condemnation of the launch by announcing on April 14 that it would not tolerate such "unbearable insults" and that it was once again quitting the six-party talks and nullifying all related agreements. As a result, all IAEA inspectors were expelled from Yongbyon, and the North claimed that it was going to resume reprocessing fuel rods. On April 24 the UN Security Council's sanctions committee proposed additional financial and trade penalties. The DPRK conducted a second, larger nuclear weapons test on May 23, which was quickly followed by a series of short-range missile launches and an announcement on May 25 that it was withdrawing from the 1953 armistice. On June 12, responding to the nuclear test, the UN Security Council unanimously voted to tighten sanctions against the North and authorized all UN member states to inspect ships suspected of carrying weapons or nuclear technology to or from the North. In September Pyongyang announced that it was continuing work toward weaponization of plutonium and enrichment of uranium.

Former U.S. president Bill Clinton arrived in Pyongyang on August 4, 2009, in an unannounced private mission to seek the release of two U.S. journalists who had been apprehended in March along the Tumen River border with China. Both were convicted of illegal entry in a closed trial on June 8 and sentenced to 12 years of hard labor, though subsequent reports indicated that they were actually being held at a "guesthouse" in Pyongyang. Following a lengthy meeting with Clinton, Kim Jong Il issued a pardon for the journalists, who left on a private jet with Clinton. Another former U.S. president, Jimmy Carter, undertook a similarly successful humanitarian mission in August 2010, traveling to Pyongyang to secure a pardon for an American who had deliberately entered North Korea in January and was sentenced in April to eight years in prison.

Washington agreed in 2011 to provide North Korea with emergency assistance after the spring floods. Kim Jong Il sent diplomats to meet with their American and South Korean counterparts to discuss the resumption of talks in July 2011, but to no avail.

Spurred by the need for economic assistance during its protracted food crisis, Kim Jong Il deepened trade and diplomatic ties during visits to China in May 2011 and to Russia in August. In September a North Korean copper mine began operation in a joint venture with China, while talks proceeded with Russia on the construction of a natural gas pipeline through North Korea, and construction began on a rail link to Vladivostok.

In October 2011 North Korean citizens working in Libya were banned from returning home, reportedly out of fear that they would spread the news of the revolution that overthrew the regime of Col. Muammar al-Qadhafi and of the other Arab Spring uprisings.

Also in October 2011 U.S. Pentagon officials agreed to resume talks with North Korea for the first time in six years over the issue of recovering the remains of U.S. service members killed in the 1950–1953 war. In November the United States announced that six-party talks would not resume until North Korea halted its nuclear enrichment program.

South Korea charities delivered 180 tons of humanitarian aid to the North in January 2012. North Korea agreed to suspend its nuclear weapons program and ballistic missile tests in exchange for the resumption of U.S. food aid. Despite international condemnation, on April 13, North Korea tested a long-range *Unha*-3 missile, prompting again the suspension of aid. The missile failed shortly after liftoff in an embarrassment to the regime. In May South Korea accused the North of jamming GPS devices on more than 660 commercial air flights (see entry on the Republic of Korea).

In September 2012, Russia announced that it would write off $10 billion of North Korea's $11 billion debt. North Korea tested another *Unha*-3 missile on December 12 (see entry on South Korea). Unlike the April effort, the December launch was successful and prompted a unanimous measure by the UN Security Council condemning the test on January 22, 2013. The UN measure also enacted additional sanctions on North Korea.

In March 2013, North Korea joined Iran and Syria in blocking the adoption of a UN accord to regulate the international arms trade. Meanwhile the UN Human Rights Council voted on March 22 to launch an inquiry into human rights abuses in North Korea.

Current issues. In early June 2009 South Korean media reported that Kim Jong Il, then 67, had named the youngest of his three sons, KIM Jong Un, believed to be 26 at the time, as his successor. Other figures who had recently advanced to the higher ranks of power included Kim Jong Il's brother-in-law, JANG Song Thaek, who was elevated to the NDC's vice chair in June 2010. Jang's promotion coincided with Choe Yong Rim's election as premier by the third session of the 12th SPA. The departure of Kim Yong Il was believed to be a further response to the previous December's currency revaluation, which had reportedly produced a spike in inflation, food shortages, a loss of savings, and unrest. In mid-March news surfaced that PAK Nam Ki, a KWP official responsible for financial policy, had been executed.

In August 2010 the United States increased sanctions against the DPRK, targeting financial networks. An unexpected development was the September 28, 2010, party conference, the first in 44 years, convened to name a new Central Committee, elect new leadership, and bring Kim Jong Un into the party elite. A day before the conference, a series of military promotions were announced, including the appointment of Kim Jong Un (who had no previous military experience) as a four-star general; the promotion of chief of the general staff, RI Yong Ho, from general to vice marshal; and the appointment of Kim Jong Il's sister and close adviser, KIM Kyong Hui, as a general. During the KWP conference Ri was named to the five-member Presidium of the Politburo and joined Kim Jong Un as vice chair of the Central Military Commission. Kim Kyong Hui was also elected to the Politburo, while her husband, Jang Song Thaek, was identified as a member of the Central Military Commission and an alternate member of the Politburo. Hence, in the event of Kim Jong Il's death, Kim Jong Un would have three well-positioned loyalists—Ri, Jang, and Kim Kyong Hui—as mentors. Over the next year Kim Jong Un's transition as his father's official heir apparent was marked by international provocation and purges of potentially antagonistic party officials. On November 23 North Korean artillery fired on the South Korean island of Yeonpyeong, killing four people and further harming North-South relations. Also in November North Korea revealed to a visiting U.S. nuclear scientist an advanced uranium enrichment plant capable of producing weapons-grade uranium, signaling its determination to pursue nuclear weapons despite international sanctions.

Among the numerous purges aimed at eliminating opposition to Kim Jong Un's rise to power, RYU Kuong, a high-ranking intelligence official, was executed in January 2011, and People's Security Minister JU Sang Song was fired in March. By September 23, when the younger Kim appeared prominently with his father at the state visit of Laotian president Choummaly Sayasone, Kim Jong Un's position had been solidified. Underscoring this, state news media in October began referring to him as Gen. Kim Jong Un.

Kim Jong Un succeeded his father after the latter's death in December 2011. However, reports indicated that the new leader's uncle, Jang Song Thaek, and aunt, Kim Kyong Hui, continued to yield considerable power behind the scenes. At the fifth session of the legislature in April 2012, Kim Jong Un was elected chair of the NDC. Vice Marshal KIM Jong GAK was named minister of defense. The appointment was reported to be part of a broader effort to strengthen civilian control over the military. Six other allies of Kim Jong Un were appointed to the NDC, along with three new vice premiers named to the cabinet. Reports in July indicated broad purges of the military as Kim Jong Un consolidated power. Flooding during the summer of 2012 left more than 300 dead and 300,000 homeless and exacerbated widespread malnutrition.

In September 2012, the SPA convened for an unheralded second session during a single year, leading to speculation that the session would be used to introduce economic reforms. However, the SPA only undertook minor legislative business, including the extension of compulsory education from 11 to 12 years.

Relations between Pyongyang and Seoul deteriorated sharply following North Korea's February 2013 nuclear test. In April Pyongyang demanded that all sanctions be lifted as a precondition for any future talks on the country's nuclear program. In July South Korea blamed a series of cyber attacks on government Websites on North Korea. Also in July, Panamanian authorities seized a North Korean vessel carrying military equipment, including missile technology, from Cuba. The crew was arrested after it resisted efforts to search the ship.

On December 13, 2013, Kim Jong Un's uncle, Jang Song Thaek, was executed in a public purge, reportedly the result of a dispute between civilian and senior military leaders.

POLITICAL PARTIES

Dating from 1946, the **Democratic Front for the Reunification of the Fatherland** (DFRF) is an umbrella for the dominant Korean Workers' Party (KWP), two smaller parties, and a number of mass organizations, including the General Federation of Trade Unions of Korea, the Korean Democratic Women's Union, the Kim Il Sung Socialist Youth League, and the Union of Agricultural Working People of Korea. All candidates for elective office must be endorsed by the DFRF. The current chief of the DFRF Secretariat is KIM Wan Su.

Korean Workers' Party—KWP (*Chosŏn No-dong Dang*). Founded in 1949 through merger of the existing Communist Party and the recently established National Party, the KWP controls all political activity in the DPRK through an overlapping of party, executive, and legislative posts. Although party congresses are to meet every five years, the sixth one convened on October 10–14, 1980, nearly a decade after the fifth. Between congresses, a Central Committee acts on its behalf. In turn, the Central Committee names a Politburo. Kim Jong Il was the only remaining member of the five-man Politburo Presidium designated at the 1980 congress, one member having been dismissed and three having died. On October 8, 1997, Kim was named to the additional post of general secretary, an office that had been vacant since Kim Il Sung's death. Other party organs include a Central Military Commission and a Secretariat.

At a party conference on September 28, 2010, a new Central Committee, a 16-member Politburo (plus 15 alternates), and a 19-member Central Military Commission were named, and the conference revised the party charter for the first time since the 1980 congress. The revisions dropped the requirement that a party congress be held every five years, spelled out the duties of party members, redefined the work of party organizations, and provided for a greater party role in the Korean People's Army. After his death, Kim Jong Il in 2011 was named eternal secretary general of the party. In April 2012 Kim Jong Un was elected first secretary of the party, and a number of his allies were appointed to the politburo. Following the February 2013 North Korean nuclear test, the United States enacted new sanctions on members of the KWP politburo.

First Secretary: KIM Jong Un.

Other Members of the Presidium of the Politburo: PAK Pong Ju (Premier), KIM Yong Nam (President, Presidium of the Supreme People's Assembly), V. Mar. CHOE Ryong Hae (Chief of the General Staff).

Other Members of the Politburo: CHOE Thae Bok (Secretary of the Central Committee and Chair of the Supreme People's Assembly), CHOE Ryong-Hae (Vice Chair of the National Defense Commission), KIM Kyong Hui (Director, Light Industry Department of the Central Committee and Kim Jong Il's sister), KIM Kuk Thae (Chair, Control Commission of the Central Committee), KIM Ki Nam (Director, Information of Publicity Department of the Central Committee), PAK To Chun (Secretary for Military Industry), KIM Yong Chun (Former Minister of the People's Armed Forces), YANG Hyong Sop (Vice President, Presidium of the Supreme People's Assembly), KIM Yong Chun (Vice Chair of the National Defense Commission), RI Yong Mu (Vice Chair, National Defense Commission), KANG Sok Ju (Vice Premier), HYON Chol Hae (Director of the General Logistics Bureau of the Korean People's Army).

Alternative Member of the Politburo: KIM Kyok Sik, HYON Yong Chol, CHOE Pu Il, KIM Yang Gon, KIM Pyong Hae, KIM Yong Il, KWAK Pom Gi, MUN Kyong Dok, O KUK Ryol, JU Kyu Chang, KIM Chang Sop, RO Tu Chol, RI Pyong Sam, JO Yon Jun, TAE Jong Su.

Secretariat: CHOE Ryong Hae, CHOE Thae Bok, KIM Ki Nam, KIM Yang Gon, KIM Pyong Hae, KIM Yong Il, MUN Kyong Dok, PAK To Chun, THAE Jong Su, KIM Kyong Hui, KWAK Pom Gi.

Chondoist Chungu Party—CCP (*Chondogyo Chong-u Dang*). Sometimes translated as the Young Friends Party, the CCP was founded in 1946 and descended from a prewar anti-Japanese group of religious (*Chondo,* or Heaven's Way) nationalists. It was purged several times in the 1950s. The Young Friends enjoyed a degree of autonomy until 1958, when it was brought under KWP control.

Leader: RYU Mi Yong (Chair).

Korean Social Democratic Party—KSDP (*Chosŏn Sa-hoi Min-ju Dang*). The KSDP was launched in November 1945 as the Democratic Party, acquiring substantial support in both urban and rural areas prior to the flight of most of its leaders to the south in 1946. The party assumed its current name in 1981 and is allied with the KWP.

Leader: KIM Yong Dae (Chair of Central Committee).

LEGISLATURE

The unicameral **Supreme People's Assembly** (*Choe Go In Min Hoe Ui*) is elected from a single slate of KWP members and party-approved nominees. Although the five-year term of the Ninth Assembly technically expired in 1995, an extended period of mourning for Kim Il Sung was given as the reason for having postponed the election of the 687-member Tenth Assembly until July 26, 1998. The new assembly convened on September 5 to approve constitutional amendments and to elect the state and legislative leaderships. One of the changes to the basic law abolished the assembly's Standing Committee, which had previously conducted the body's business between sessions, and replaced it with a 17-member Presidium. The 12th SPA was elected on March 8, 2009.

President of the Presidium: KIM Yong Nam.

Chair: CHOE Thae Bok.

CABINET

[as of November 15, 2013]

Premier	Pak Pong Ju
Vice Premiers	Thae Jong Su
	Jo Pyong Ju
	Jon Ha Chol
	Kang Nung Su
	Kang Sok Ju
	Kim Rak Hui [f]
	Ri Thae Nam
	Ro Tu Chol
	Ri Chol Man
	Kim In Sik
	Ri Mu Yong
Ministers	
Agriculture	Ri Chol Man
Capital City Construction	Kim In Sik
Chemical Industry	Ri Mu Yong
Coal Industry	Kim Hyong Sik
Commerce	Kim Pong Chol
Construction and Building-Materials Industries	Tong Jong Ho
Culture	Hong Kwang Sun
Education	Tae Hyung Chol
Electric Power Industry	Ho Thaek
Electronics Industry	Kim Jae Seong
Finance	Choe Kwang Jin
Fisheries	Ri Hyuk
Foodstuffs and Daily Necessities Industry	Jo Yong Chol
Foreign Affairs	Pak Ui Chun
Foreign Trade	Ri Ryong Nam
Forestry	Kim Kwang Yong

Labor	Jong Yong Su
Land and Environmental Protection	Kim Kyung Jun
Land and Marine Transport	Ra Tong Hui
Light Industry	An Jong Su
Machine-Building Industry	Jo Pyong Ju
Metal Industry	Kim Thae Bong
Mining Industry	Kang Min Chol
Natural Resources Development	Ri Chun Sam
Oil Industry	Pae Hak Yi
People's Armed Forces	Gen. Jang Jong Nam
People's Security	Gen. Ri Myong Su
Physical Culture and Sports	Ri Jong Moo
Post and Telecommunications	Ryu Yong Sop
Public Health	Choe Chang Sik
Railways	Jon Kil Su
State Construction Control	Pae Tal Jun
State Inspection	Kim Ui Sun
Urban Management	Kang Yong Su
Chair, State Planning Commission	Ro Tu Chol
Director, Central Statistics Bureau	Kim Chang Su
President, Central Bank	Paek Ryong Chon
President, State Academy of Sciences	Pyon Yong Rip
Chief, Cabinet Secretariat	Kim Yong Ho

[f] = female

INTERGOVERNMENTAL REPRESENTATION

At present, there are no diplomatic relations between the United States and the Democratic People's Republic of Korea.

Permanent Representative to the UN: SIN Son Ho.

IGO Memberships (Non-UN): NAM.

REPUBLIC OF KOREA

Taehan-min'guk

Political Status: Independent republic established on August 15, 1948; present constitution approved in a national referendum on October 27, 1987, effective February 25, 1988.

Area: 38,309 sq. mi. (99,221 sq. km).

Population: 49,960,402 (2013E—UN); 48,955,203 (2013—US Census).

Major Urban Centers (2011E—UN): SEOUL (10,038,905), Pusan (3,420,679), Taegu (2,417,943), Inchon (2,675,476), Taejon (1,523,840), Kwangju (1,451,394), Ulsan (1,097,354).

Official Language: Korean.

Monetary Unit: South Korean Won (market rate November 1, 2013: 1063.40 won = $1US).

President: PARK Geun Hye (New Frontier Party); elected on December 19, 2012 and sworn in for a five-year term on February 25, 2013, succeeding LEE Myung Bak (Grand National Party—renamed New Frontier Party in February 2012).

Prime Minister: CHUNG Hong Won (New Frontier Party); nominated by the president on February 8, 2013, and confirmed by the National Assembly on February 26, succeeding KIM Hwang Sik (ind.).

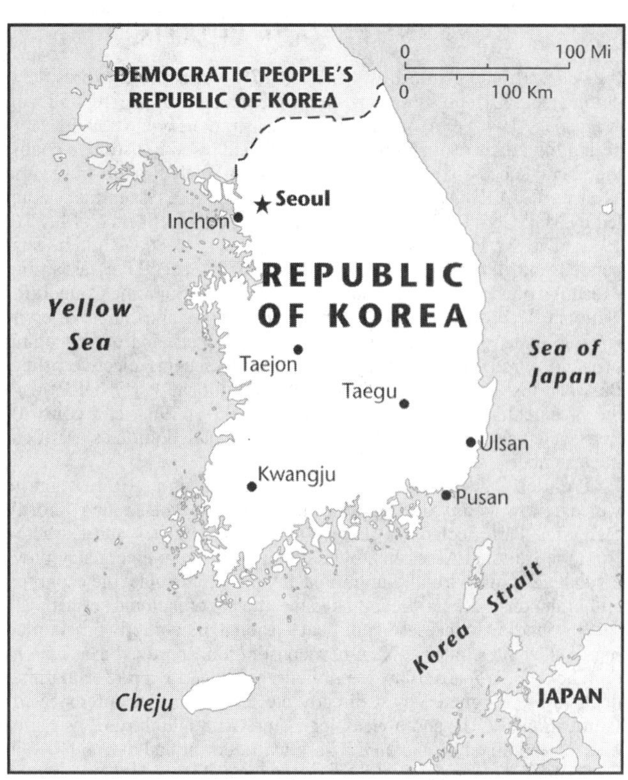

THE COUNTRY

Characterized by mountainous terrain in the north and east and broad plains in the south, the Republic of Korea (ROK) is densely settled. A majority of its population is concentrated in the southern section, although approximately one-quarter are residents of the capital, Seoul, which is located within 30 miles of the demilitarized zone (DMZ) that separates it from the Democratic People's Republic of Korea (DPRK). The people are ethnically homogeneous, tracing their heritage to Mongol and Chinese origins. Buddhism, Shamanism, and Christianity are the important religions; the ROK has one of the largest Christian populations in Asia, numbering in excess of 17 million. Women constitute 42 percent of the active labor force, concentrated in wholesale and retail trade, food and lodging, manufacturing, and education. Women hold 15.7 percent of the seats in the current National Assembly (47 of 300).

Unlike the DPRK, the ROK did not begin the post–World War II period with a substantial industrial base, and postwar growth was cut short by the Korean conflict of 1950–1953. Subsequently, however, industrial expansion was rapid, and by the mid-1970s the agricultural sector (agriculture, fishing, and forestry) had been surpassed by manufacturing as a contributor to GDP. Agriculture now employs 7 percent of the labor force and accounts for under 3 percent of GDP. Farming is devoted primarily to grain production, chiefly rice; ocean fishing, for domestic markets and export, is also important. Industry, which employs 25 percent of workers and contributes 37 percent of GDP, is concentrated in electronics, transport equipment (including ships), machinery, ferrous metals, chemicals, processed foods, and textiles. South Korea's relatively scarce mineral resources include deposits of coal and iron.

During the 1980s South Korea experienced an average annual GDP growth of 9.5 percent, making it one of the world's fastest-growing economies (for more on the economy prior to 1999, please see the 2012 *Handbook*). Far exceeding expectations, the economy recorded growth of 10.9 percent in 1999 and 9.3 percent in 2000, while unemployment rapidly declined. Annual GDP expanded by an average of 4.5 percent in 2001–2008. Following a gain of only 0.3 percent in 2009, economic growth recovered to a robust 6.3 percent in 2010, before slowing to 3.6 percent in 2011 and 2 percent in 2012. According to the IMF, inflation that year was 2.2 percent and the unemployment rate was 3.3 percent. GDP per capita was $23,112. In April 2013, the government announced a $15.3 billion economic stimulus program. Meanwhile, the World Bank rated South Korea 8th out of 185 countries in its 2013 Doing Business survey.

GOVERNMENT AND POLITICS

Political background. Syngman RHEE, a conservative president, dominated ROK politics from the establishment of the republic on August 15, 1948, until student-led demonstrations against ballot tampering forced his resignation in 1960. Plagued by administrative chaos, the liberal successor government of President YUN Po Sun and Prime Minister CHANG Myon was overthrown in a bloodless military coup led by Maj. Gen. PARK Chung Hee and four other officers on May 16, 1961. The National Assembly was dissolved, the constitution suspended, and all political parties disbanded, with General Park assuming executive powers under a military junta called the Supreme Council for National Reconstruction. As a step toward the reestablishment of civilian rule under a revised constitution, General Park and other leading officers retired from the army preparatory to seeking elective office. Park and his newly formed Democratic Republican Party (DRP) won the presidential and legislative elections held in 1963, and constitutional rule was formally restored with Park's inauguration as president in December.

President Park was reelected in 1967 and again in 1971, when he won a narrow victory over opposition candidate KIM Dae Jung. Shortly thereafter, Park declared a state of national emergency and extracted from the National Assembly, over strong opposition, emergency powers that gave him virtually unlimited authority to regulate the economy and limit constitutional freedoms in the interest of national security.

Responding to increased political tension, Park abruptly proclaimed martial law in October 1972. A new constitution, approved in a referendum held under martial-law restrictions, provided for a powerful president, to be designated by a directly elected National Conference for Unification (NCU), and a weak legislature with one-third of its membership appointed by the NCU. Park was reconfirmed by the NCU in December, and a legislative election held in February 1973 completed the nominal return to constitutional government.

Opposition to the so-called *Yushin* (Revitalizing) Constitution of 1972 grew slowly, with the government responding to recurring protests by increasingly repressive measures. Park was returned for a further six-year term in 1978, and the DRP, although failing to capture a plurality of votes in a December election, retained control of the National Assembly.

Following the October 1979 expulsion from the National Assembly of opposition leader KIM Young Sam for having criticized the Park regime in a *New York Times* interview, the entire legislative opposition resigned in protest. At that point student demonstrations, begun in the aftermath of an August labor protest, expanded into riots. Later that month Park and five companions were assassinated at the direction of KIM Jae Kyu, chief of the Korean Central Intelligence Agency (KCIA). Although anticipating military backing for a government takeover, the KCIA's Kim was instead arrested by army authorities within hours of the assassination.

Park was immediately succeeded by the prime minister, CHOI Kyu Hah. He was elected by the NCU in December 1979 to complete Park's term, quickly revoked his predecessor's emergency decrees, and declared an amnesty that freed 1,646 prisoners. Control of the country was, however, largely in the hands of Lt. Gen. CHUN Doo Hwan, head of the Defense Security Command, who had taken control of the armed forces in what amounted to a coup.

A widespread series of labor strikes in April 1980 escalated in May into mass student demonstrations. The government responded by arresting Kim Dae Jung and a number of other opposition leaders, provoking a popular uprising in the southern city of Kwangju. In late May, after heavy fighting and at least 200 deaths, the Kwangju insurrection was suppressed by government forces.

President Choi stepped down in August 1980 and was soon succeeded by Chun Doo Hwan, who had resigned his commission before being elected president by the NCU. A new constitution, approved by a reported majority of 91.6 percent in a referendum, came into effect in October, at which time the existing National Assembly was dissolved and its functions assumed, on an interim basis, by an appointive Legislative Council for National Security. Kim Dae Jung, meanwhile, had been condemned to death for sedition. In January 1981, after worldwide appeals for clemency, his sentence was commuted to life imprisonment. The sentence was further reduced to 20 years in 1982 and eventually suspended.

In January 1981 President Chun rescinded martial law, which had been in effect since the Park assassination, and announced that a presidential election would be held in February, following balloting for an electoral college. Chun's newly formed Democratic Justice Party (DJP) secured 70 percent of the electoral college seats, and he was reinstalled as president in March. In the subsequent National Assembly election, the DJP obtained 151 of 276 seats.

Amid intensifying protests demanding constitutional reform, in June 1987 ROH Tae Woo, who had been formally endorsed by the DJP as its choice to succeed President Chun, reversed policy and unexpectedly announced that virtually all of the opposition's reform demands would be met, including the call for direct presidential election. In July Chun resigned as DJP leader so that he could carry out his remaining official duties from a "supra-partisan position." In a cabinet reshuffle three days later he removed all of the party incumbents. At the end of August a committee of government and opposition representatives reached agreement on the essentials of a new constitution, which was overwhelmingly approved by both the National Assembly and the South Korean voters in October.

Although a unified opposition might have won the December 1987 presidential poll, neither Kim Young Sam nor Kim Dae Jung was willing to defer to the other. As a result, Roh obtained 35.9 percent of the vote, with Kim Young Sam and Kim Dae Jung winning 27.5 percent and 26.5 percent, respectively; KIM Jong Pil, a former prime minister under President Park, ran fourth with 7.9 percent.

The assembly poll of April 1988 gave only a plurality (125 of 299 seats) to the DJP. A preelection agreement to merge opposition forces again failed, with Kim Jong Pil's recently organized New Democratic Republican Party (NDRP) securing the balance of power with 35 seats. In December President Roh dismissed most of the ministers prominently associated with the previous regime.

In a startling political realignment, in February 1990 the DJP merged with Kim Jong Pil's NDRP and Kim Young Sam's Reunification Democratic Party (RDP) to form the Democratic Liberal Party (DLP), which immediately controlled nearly three-fourths of the assembly. In March 1991, despite a major drop in support for the Roh administration's domestic policies, the DLP secured a major political victory by winning more than half the contests in South Korea's first local legislative elections in three decades. It performed even better in voting for provincial and metropolitan assemblies in June, winning nearly two-thirds of the races. However, buffeted by charges of corruption and economic mismanagement, the DLP saw its representation plunge to 49 percent in the National Assembly election of March 1992, although it subsequently attracted enough defectors from other parties to claim a majority. Kim Dae Jung's opposition Democratic Party (DP) increased its strength by nearly one-third, to 97 seats, but the most dramatic showing was the 31 seats won by the Unification National Party (UNP), which had been formed only weeks before by Hyundai tycoon CHUNG Ju Yung.

In the watershed election of December 1992, Kim Young Sam, with a vote share of 42 percent, became the first nonmilitary candidate in three decades to win election as South Korean president. His former opposition colleague, Kim Dae Jung, received 34 percent, while Chung Ju Yung of the United People's Party (the reorganized UNP), drew 16 percent. The day after his inauguration in February 1993, Kim named a regionally dispersed cabinet that excluded former government officials. Earlier in the month Hyundai tycoon Chung had been indicted for using some $63 million in corporate funds for campaign purposes. (Subsequently convicted, he would be granted amnesty in August 1995.)

In March 1995 Kim Jong Pil, having left the DLP, formed the conservative United Liberal Democrats (ULD). In September Kim Dae Jung launched the National Congress for New Politics (NCNP), which immediately became the strongest opposition party by virtue of DP defections. In December, in apparent pursuit of a new image, the DLP changed its name to the New Korea Party (NKP).

The National Assembly election of April 1996 saw the NKP's plurality slip to 139 seats, with the NCNP winning 79 and the ULD, 50. The disintegrating DP was reduced to 15 seats. In August, at the conclusion of South Korea's "trial of the century," former presidents Chun Doo Hwan and Roh Tae Woo were found guilty of mutiny, treason, and corruption during the excesses and illegalities that began with the 1979 coup and extended beyond the 1980 Kwangju suppression. For the more profound crimes Chun was sentenced to death and Roh to 22 and a half years in prison. In December an appellate court commuted Chun's sentence to life imprisonment and reduced Roh's prison term to 17 years.

In the December 1997 presidential election, former dissident Kim Dae Jung, heading an NCNP-ULD coalition, secured a 40.3 percent plurality; his closest competitor, with 38.8 percent, was former prime minister LEE Hoi Chang of the recently formed Grand National Party

(GNP), an amalgamation of the NKP and the DP. Four days later President Kim Young Sam pardoned Chun Doo Hwan and Roh Tae Woo, an action endorsed by his successor but criticized by others as an affront to the prodemocracy movement.

In February 1998 President Kim Dae Jung, as he had agreed to do before the election, nominated the ULD's Kim Jong Pil to be the next prime minister, but the GNP-led assembly rejected the nominee because of his participation in past authoritarian regimes. Undaunted, Kim Dae Jung named Kim Jong Pil as acting prime minister, but the GNP did not relent and approve the appointment until August. By early September defections from the GNP had given the governing coalition a working majority in the National Assembly.

President Kim undertook his first major cabinet reshuffle in May 1999, replacing the majority of his ministers in an effort to reinvigorate his economic reform program. At the same time Kim continued to espouse his "sunshine" policy of peaceful political engagement and economic and cultural cooperation with North Korea, although improving relations were threatened by a June 15 naval battle in the Yellow Sea and North Korea's subsequent unilateral extension of its territorial waters. Kim again reshuffled his cabinet in January 2000, when the ULD's PARK Tae Joon succeeded Prime Minister Kim Jong Pil, who resigned to prepare his party for the upcoming legislative election.

In February 2000 LEE Han Dong, a former GNP faction leader and the newly elected ULD leader, announced that his party would move into opposition because Kim Dae Jung's new Millennium Democratic Party (MDP, successor to the NCNP) had failed to honor its commitments, particularly consideration of constitutional changes that would replace the existing strong presidency with a parliamentary system. The break was less than complete, however, with Prime Minister Park remaining at the head of the cabinet.

On April 10, 2000, three days before the national election, President Kim stunned the opposition by announcing a June summit with North Korean leader Kim Jong Il in Pyongyang. Although the MDP recorded significant gains on April 13, the GNP retained its plurality, a mere 4 seats short of a legislative majority. The ULD suffered major losses, winning only 17 seats, 33 fewer than it had won in 1996.

Prime Minister Park resigned on May 19, 2000, in response to a court ruling that he had accepted bribes while chair of the giant Pohang Iron and Steel and had then evaded taxes. Three days later, President Kim nominated the ULD's Lee Han Dong as Park's successor, unofficially sealing a renewal of the MDP-ULD partnership.

During the historic June 13–15, 2000, summit in Pyongyang, the leaders of the two Koreas called for, among other things, greater economic cooperation and eventual national reunification. On October 13, in recognition of his efforts to promote democracy and human rights and to achieve "peace and reconciliation" with the DPRK, Kim Dae Jung was awarded the 2000 Nobel Peace Prize.

In March 2001 President Kim undertook a major cabinet reshuffle in which the ULD received three portfolios in an effort to cement the MDP-ULD relationship. Shortly thereafter, the small Democratic People's Party (DPP) announced that it would join the coalition, thereby giving the government a slim majority in the National Assembly.

On September 4, 2001, the entire cabinet resigned following passage in the National Assembly of a no-confidence motion against Minister of Unification LIM Dong Won. Joining the GNP in voting for the motion was the ULD, effectively announcing its departure from the government. A revamped cabinet retained Lee Han Dong as prime minister, precipitating his expulsion from the ULD. In National Assembly by-elections a month later, the MDP lost its legislative majority.

With two of his sons under investigation for bribery and tax evasion (they were ultimately convicted, fined, and sentenced to prison), Kim Dae Jung resigned from the MDP on May 6, 2002, as did half a dozen cabinet ministers on the following day. In August the GNP cemented a legislative majority with by-election victories in 11 of 13 contests. On October 5, having rejected two previous nominees, the National Assembly approved former Supreme Court justice KIM Suk Soo as prime minister.

The December 2002 presidential race was made considerably closer in late November when the leading third-party candidate, CHUNG Mong Joon, the head of South Korea's Football Association and a son of the Hyundai founder, left the race in favor of the MDP's ROH Moo Hyun. Although Chung withdrew his support the day before the election, apparently because of policy differences with regard to North Korea, Roh won with 48.9 percent of the vote in a come-from-behind victory over Lee, who received 46.6 percent. On January 22, 2003, President-elect Roh nominated as prime minister GOH Kun, who was approved by the National Assembly on February 26, a day after Roh's inauguration.

The initial months of Roh's presidency were marred by two scandals, one involving the illegal channeling through a Hyundai subsidiary and the Korean Development Bank of some $100–$200 million to the North Korean government to entice its participation in the June 2000 summit, and the other involving alleged insider trading and accounting fraud by the country's leading *chaebols,* including Hyundai, Samsung, and the SK Group. An investigation into the summit scandal led to the June indictment of two former government ministers, LIM Dong Won and PARK Jie Won, both of whom were ultimately found guilty, and the chair of Hyundai, CHUNG Mong Hun, who committed suicide in August.

In September 2003 several dozen reform-minded legislators abandoned the MDP (as did Roh), and in late October they named their new formation the *Uri Dang* (Our Party). In the same month an investigation was launched into charges that prominent members of the MDP and GNP had accepted illegal donations prior to and soon after the 2002 presidential election. On December 4 the National Assembly, in the first such action since 1954, overrode Roh's veto of a bill establishing an independent investigation into the donations. Among those ultimately charged with receiving illegal contributions were leaders in both the GNP and MDP, including a chief aide to President Roh.

On March 12, 2004, following several days of acrimonious debate, the National Assembly, led by the GNP and Roh's former party, the MDP, voted 173–2 to impeach the president for alleged corruption, economic mismanagement, and violation of political neutrality. The last charge involved his having urged voters to support the *Uri* Party in the upcoming general election. Prime Minister Goh assumed the president's duties, pending a decision by the Constitutional Court on Roh's removal from office.

Amid rising public support for Roh, in the April 15, 2004, National Assembly election the *Uri* Party won a majority of 152 seats in the legislature, with the GNP finishing second and the MDP losing representation, from more than 60 seats to 9. On May 14, the Constitutional Court dismissed the corruption and economic mismanagement cases against President Roh. Further, the court ruled that Roh's electioneering violation was insufficient to warrant impeachment. Roh resumed his post and six days later joined the *Uri* Party. On May 24, Prime Minister Goh tendered his resignation, which was accepted on the following day. On June 8 the president nominated the *Uri* Party's LEE Hae Chan as Goh's successor. He was confirmed on June 29.

The cabinet was reshuffled on January 2, 2006. Prime Minister Lee resigned on March 14, after the propriety of his behavior on March 1 was called into question. He had played golf on the same day when a nationwide railway workers' strike began. Deputy Prime Minister HAN Duk Soo (*Uri* Party) headed the government until the confirmation of HAN Myeong Sook (*Uri* Party) on April 19. Han Myeong Sook became the ROK's first woman prime minister.

In furtherance of her presidential aspirations, Han Myeong Sook resigned as prime minister on March 7, 2007, and two days later President Roh nominated as her successor Han Duk Soo, who was confirmed by the National Assembly on April 2.

With the *Uri* Party having dissolved in August 2007, and with most of its members having moved to the new center-liberal United New Democratic Party (UNDP), the December 19 presidential election essentially became a three-way contest. The GNP's Lee Myung Bak secured 48.7 percent of the vote, followed by the UNDP's CHUNG Dong Young with 26.1 percent and former GNP chair Lee Hoi Chang, running as an independent, with 15.1 percent. Turnout was 63.2 percent, a historic low, but the front-runner secured a record margin of victory for a direct presidential election. In January Lee nominated as prime minister HAN Seung Soo, who was confirmed by the National Assembly on February 29, four days after Lee's inauguration.

In the National Assembly election on April 9, 2008, the GNP secured a majority with 153 seats. The United Democratic Party (UDP), formed by merger of the UNDP and the DP in February, finished second, while Lee Hoi Chang's new Liberty Forward Party (LFP) won the third highest number of seats. On May 27, in the wake of corruption charges that reached to members of his extended family, former president Roh Moo Hyun committed suicide. In July the UDP changed its name to the Democratic Party (DP).

By mid-2009, public opinion polls reflected a growing dissatisfaction with President Lee and the GNP, in part because of the failure to reach an accord on a free trade pact with the United States, as well as the adverse impact of the international financial crisis on the economy. In an effort to revive support in advance of local elections in 2010, on

September 3, 2009, Lee named a new prime minister, CHUNG Un Chan, and six new ministers. Chung, the president of Seoul National University, was confirmed by the National Assembly on September 28.

The GNP fared poorly in the June 2, 2010, local elections but won five of eight seats in the National Assembly by-elections on July 28. The following day, Prime Minister Chung expressed his intent to resign (see Current issues, below), and the cabinet was reshuffled. On August 4 President Lee nominated KIM Tae Ho for the post, but the former provincial governor withdrew his name in the wake of corruption allegations. Chung formally resigned on August 10, following ten months of political discord. The minister of foreign affairs resigned on September 6 following allegations of nepotism. On September 16 Lee nominated as prime minister a former Supreme Court justice and the chair of the Board of Audit and Inspection, KIM Hwong Sik. He was confirmed by the legislature on October 1. The defense minister resigned on November 25 after accepting responsibility for engaging in fighting with North Korean forces, who fired on Yeonpyeong Island on November 23 during South Korean military exercises (see Current issues, below). A new defense minister was appointed on November 26. Two ministers were replaced on December 31, 2011.

Minor cabinet reshuffles occurred on May 7, 2011, July 15, and August 30. The knowledge economy minister resigned on September 27 and was replaced on October 26. On December 15 the DP merged with the small Citizens Unity Party to form the Democratic United Party—DUP (*Minju Tonghabdang*). Meanwhile, the GNP recast itself as the New Frontier Party—NFP (*Saenuri Dang*) in February 2012. In legislative elections on April 11, 2012, the NFP maintained a majority in the assembly with 153 seats, while the DUP secured 127 (see Current issues, below).

On December 19, 2012, PARK Geun Hye of the NFP was elected president, defeating MOON Jae In of the DUP. The daughter of former president Park Chung Hee, Park became South Korea's first woman president. CHUNG Hing Won was sworn in as prime minister of an NFP cabinet on March 11, 2013. The legislature refused to take action on two cabinet appointments, leading Park to fill the vacancies by decree on April 17.

Constitution and government. The 1987 constitution (technically the ninth amendment of the country's 1948 basic law) sets forth a variety of guarantees, including freedom of press and assembly, the right of habeas corpus, labor's right to organize and strike, and the prohibition of detention without a court order. In addition, the armed forces are enjoined to observe "political neutrality."

The president, who is directly elected for a single five-year term, appoints a prime minister (subject to legislative confirmation) and, on the prime minister's recommendation, a State Council of 15–30 members from which heads of executive ministries are drawn. Members of the unicameral National Assembly serve four-year terms, are specifically authorized to investigate government affairs, and enjoy complete immunity for activity inside the house. By a two-thirds vote of the membership the assembly may impeach the chief executive, although removal from office requires the concurrence of the Constitutional Court.

The three-tiered judiciary includes at its apex a Supreme Court, with regional appellate high courts and district courts operating at the lower levels. Within the district level are city and county courts and a family court. Justices of the Supreme Court, named by the president and confirmed by the assembly, serve six-year terms. A separate Patent Court was added to the system in 1998, along with the first district-based Administrative Court to handle tax, labor, and similar cases. In addition, a Constitutional Court rules on the constitutionality of legislation, hears petitions on constitutional questions, and also has in its purview impeachments, disputes involving state agencies and local governments, and cases related to the dissolution of political parties.

Administratively, the country is divided into 16 "local authorities": the capital of Seoul and 6 additional metropolitan areas (Inchon, Kwangju, Pusan, Taegu, Taejon, and Ulsan), 8 mainland provinces, and the island province of Cheju. The provinces are divided into counties, cities, towns, and townships. Provincial governors and local executives are directly elected.

Freedom of the press is constitutionally guaranteed. In 2013 Reporters Without Borders ranked the ROK 50th out of 179 countries in freedom of the press.

Foreign relations. Before its admission to the United Nations in September 1991 the ROK maintained a permanent observer at the world organization's New York headquarters and participated in the activities of many of its specialized agencies, but relations with the DPRK and the United States have long been the most sensitive areas of external concern for the ROK. Communication between Seoul and Pyongyang has fluctuated widely in recent years, sporadic talks alternating with hostile exchanges on a variety of issues. Both sides are formally committed to reunification but have adopted differing (and occasionally shifting) positions on the means of achieving it. Low points in relations occurred in October 1983, when North Korean agents killed four South Korean cabinet ministers in a bomb attack in Myanmar, and in November 1987 with the destruction by North Korean agents of a South Korean airliner en route from Bahrain to Seoul. Subsequently, in the wake of global reverses suffered by communist regimes, tensions eased, and in September 1990 a series of talks were launched at the prime ministerial level that culminated in the nonaggression pact of December 1991 (see Korea entry).

In the most serious incursion in nearly three decades, a party of North Korean military personnel and espionage agents came ashore in September 1996 from a submarine that had run aground. Eleven were found dead, 1 was captured alive, and 11 were hunted down and killed by early November, with the loss of 8 South Korean soldiers and 4 civilians. Pyongyang initially rejected South Korean protests at the incursion, which cost the South Korean defense minister his job, but after lengthy discussions with U.S. officials the North Korean government issued a surprisingly contrite apology at the end of December.

Relations with Japan, formally restored in 1965 after 14 years of negotiation, have been constrained by Korean bitterness over the pre-1945 occupation and Tokyo's treatment of resident Koreans. For its part, Japan was long critical of Seoul's record on human rights and then curtailed economic assistance after the abduction of Korean opposition leader Kim Dae Jung from Japan in 1973. A state visit to Japan by Chun Doo Hwan in September 1984, the first by a South Korean president, elicited a ritual apology from Emperor Hirohito for "the unfortunate past between us." President Roh visited Tokyo in May 1990 and again in November 1992, but President Kim canceled a meeting at UN headquarters with Japanese prime minister Tomiichi Murayama in October 1995 after the latter referred to his country's occupation of the Korean peninsula as "legally valid."

Further complicating relations with Tokyo has been the issue of Korean and other "comfort women" forced into unpaid prostitution during World War II by the Japanese military (see Japan entry). Then, in February 1996, a long-standing dispute over sovereignty of an uninhabited small island group in the Sea of Japan (called Tokto by the Koreans, Takeshima by the Japanese, and the Liancourt Rocks by Western navigators) reignited, leading both countries to declare 200-mile exclusive economic zones encompassing the disputed islands. In January 1998 Japan unilaterally terminated a bilateral fishing treaty because of the insular dispute, but eight months later the two governments reached agreement on a new treaty that included a compromise on the issue of fishing zones in the contested area. An October state visit by President Kim Dae Jung to Tokyo reinforced the fisheries pact and also produced a joint statement that included a Japanese expression of "deep remorse and a heartfelt apology" for its 1910–1945 occupation. Historical differences continue to flare up, however, over such matters as the treatment of Korea in Japanese history textbooks.

Normalization of relations with the Soviet Union, long of lesser priority, was severely impaired by the destruction of a civilian Korean airliner in September 1983, after the plane had strayed off course and passed over Soviet missile installations on the Kamchatka peninsula. A meeting between Presidents Roh Tae Woo and Mikhail Gorbachev in San Francisco on June 4, 1990, preceded mutual diplomatic recognition on September 30 and a historic first visit to Moscow by President Roh in December. In August 1992 relations were also normalized with the PRC, and in late September President Roh traveled to Beijing for the first official visit by a South Korean head of state.

Relations with the United States were temporarily strained in the late 1970s not only by the repressive policies of the Park regime but by revelations of widespread Korean influence peddling in U.S. congressional circles. Anti-American sentiment in the ROK, most dramatically symbolized by arson attacks on U.S. cultural centers in Kwangju and Pusan in the early 1980s, came mainly from opposition politicians, students, and religious leaders, who argued that support for President Chun inhibited the emergence of a truly democratic system. In mid-1987, however, Chun's acceptance of constitutional reform was reported to have stemmed in part from strong U.S. diplomatic pressure.

During a brief visit to Washington in July 1999 Kim Dae Jung requested revision of a 1979 agreement with Washington that prevented Seoul from developing surface-to-surface missiles with a maximum range greater than 180 kilometers. Reacting to North Korea's missile program, Kim requested that the limit be extended to 300 kilometers. In January 2001 Seoul announced that it was moving forward on its missile development program, and in January 2002 the Ministry of Defense signed a contract with U.S. manufacturer Lockheed Martin to purchase its Army Tactical Missile System. At the same time, however, Seoul opposed deployment in South Korea of a theater missile defense system, as proposed by the United States.

The withdrawal of U.S. troops from South Korea, initiated in 1990 because of a lessened threat from the Soviet Union, was suspended in October 1992 upon emergence of the North Korean nuclear inspection issue.

A June 2000 DPRK-ROK summit in Pyongyang—the first meeting of the top leaders of the two Koreas—portended a new era of direct North-South bilateral contacts. Since 2003 the ROK has also joined the DPRK, the People's Republic of China (PRC), Japan, Russia, and the United States in intermittent six-party talks aimed at resolving the crisis over the DPRK's nuclear weapons program.

In April 2003 the National Assembly voted to send South Korean troops to provide noncombat assistance in Iraq, a move that the president supported despite differences with Washington over its hardline policy toward North Korea. From 2004 to 2006 ROK troop levels in Iraq reached more than 3,500, thereby making South Korea's the third largest military contingent, after the United States and the United Kingdom. (The last South Korean troops returned home in December 2008.) Meanwhile, Seoul announced that it would remove its military personnel from Afghanistan before the end of 2007.

At the beginning of November 2004, South Korean troops assumed full responsibility for policing the DMZ. Subsequently, it was agreed that wartime control of ROK forces would pass to South Korean commanders in 2012.

In October 2006 the South Korean foreign minister, BAN Ki Moon, was named UN secretary general.

On October 2–4, 2007, President Roh and North Korean leader Kim Il Jong met in the second North-South summit (see the DPRK entry for details), although the occasion was marked by considerably less fanfare than the 2000 summit. In a follow-up meeting, Prime Minister Han welcomed North Korea's prime minister, Kim Yong Il, to Seoul on November 14–16. It was the first meeting of the North-South prime ministers in 15 years.

In 2008–2009, the DPRK, reacting in part to the inauguration of the more conservative Lee Myung Bak administration, announced that it was abrogating the 1953 armistice, declared the six-party process dead, disavowed all military and other agreements with Seoul, conducted a second underground nuclear weapons test and numerous missile tests, and moved to restart its nuclear plant at the Yongbyon nuclear complex (for details, see the DPRK entry).

In April 2008 President Lee Myung Bak traveled to Japan, where he and Prime Minister Yasuo Fukuda agreed to resume talks, after a four-year hiatus, on an economic partnership.

A revised Free Trade Agreement between South Korea and the United States was finalized in December 2010. The original agreement, signed in 2007 under the George W. Bush administration, had never been ratified. In October 2011, the pact was ratified by the U.S. Congress. (The agreement came into force on March 15, 2012.)

In 2011, talks reopened between North and South Korea on the prospect of resuming negotiations on the North's dismantling of its nuclear weapons program. However, six-party talks remained stalled throughout the year. Following the death of North Korean leader Kim Jong Il (see entry on the Democratic People's Republic of Korea), South Korea sent two unofficial delegations to North. Kim Jong Il's death and the succession of his son, KIM Jong Un, did not initially alter relations between the two Koreas.

On January 27, 2012, South Korea delivered 180 tons of flour to the North, with an additional $465 million in aid earmarked for humanitarian assistance. Also in January, South Korea reported that 2,737 North Koreans defected in 2011, an increase of 15 percent over the previous year. In May South Korean officials accused the DPRK of using jamming devices to disrupt the GPS systems of more than 660 flights.

In January 2013, South Korea reported that the number of defections from the North had fallen to 1,508, mainly as a result of increased border tensions between the two states. Following the February nuclear test by North Korea, South Korean and U.S. forces expanded annual joint military exercises in March, including flights by nuclear-capable U.S. bombers over South Korean airspace. On March 24, South Korea and the United States signed the Combined Counter-Provocation Plan, which pledged U.S. military support for Seoul in the event of military provocations short of a full-scale war with Pyongyang. In response, Pyongyang ended participation in a "hotline" connecting the military leadership of the two countries and used to prevent escalations in the DMZ. Nonetheless, in March, President Park Geun Hye announced that South Korea was delinking humanitarian aid to Pyongyang from counter-proliferation efforts. In May 2013, South Korea and Turkey signed a free trade agreement, which came into force immediately.

Current issues. Tensions with North Korea, heightened during President Lee's tenure, have drawn increased attention in recent years. On March 26, 2010, a South Korean corvette, the *Cheonan,* exploded and sank in the Yellow Sea. Seoul was initially cautious in shifting the blame to North Korea, but a May 20 report by an international panel concluded that a torpedo fired from a North Korean submarine had exploded against the hull, killing 46 seamen. North Korea denied responsibility. President Lee immediately announced a trade embargo and a ban on North Korea's use of its shipping channels. Subsequently, South Korea and the United States announced that they would conduct joint naval exercises in response to the sinking. Meanwhile, though Seoul pursued action by the UN Security Council, the world organization condemned the sinking but did not assign blame.

Political turmoil surfaced in mid-2010 when Prime Minister Chung offered to resign in June after failing to gain legislative support to halt the relocation of government offices to Sejong City, an issue that had very nearly blocked his nomination to the post. Failure to win parliamentary approval was seen as a major setback to President Lee's government, coming on top of the GNP's loss of key seats—including in the Sejong City region—in the June 2 local elections. On August 4 President Lee nominated KIM Tae Ho as prime minister, but the former provincial governor withdrew his name in the wake of corruption allegations. Chung formally resigned on August 10, and a new prime minister, Kim Hwong Sik, was confirmed on October 1.

On November 23, 2010, in what was widely described as the most serious incident between the North and the South in many years, North Korean artillery shelled the island of Yeonpyeong in the Yellow Sea, killing four South Koreans and wounding 20, including marines. North Korea said the bombardment was in response to a live-fire exercise, allegedly directed toward the sea, that had been conducted the same day. President Lee in response ordered F-16 jets scrambled over the sea and warned of "enormous retaliation." Most of the island's 1,600 civilians were evacuated along with some 1,000 marines. (They were allowed to return at the end of the month, and the military presence was strengthened.) Military reinforcements were also sent to the other four islands near the disputed NLL in the Yellow Sea. Two days after the incident, South Korea's defense minister resigned after taking responsibility for the attack.

In December 2010 the government forced passage of its $271 billion budget in the assembly in sessions marred by physical fights that broke out between the GNP and the DP, among other opposition legislators, who tried to block the measure. The budget represented a 6 percent increase over the previous year and contained money for President Lee's plan to dredge and alter four rivers, which the DP opposed. Ultimately, 166 lawmakers—including 165 from the GNP—voted for passage.

North-South tensions eased somewhat in 2011 when Seoul agreed to North Korea's proposal in January to hold talks to resolve military issues stemming from the November 2010 attack. In May the government approved additional humanitarian aid totaling $769,000 to the North, after having allowed in March the first aid since the attack. Further aid was approved in July.

In the wake of investigations into alleged corruption on the part of 16 savings banks, resulting in suspension of their operations, in June President Lee called for measures to prevent such activity. Observers said the publicity surrounding the scandal threatened the president's "fair society" campaign and could potentially lead to a lame-duck presidency ahead of the 2012 elections. Exacerbating the situation for the president, one of his former aides was arrested in September on charges of accepting bribes from a lobbyist for one of the banks whose operation was suspended. Around that same time, the head of one of the banks committed suicide. PARK Won Soon, an independent, was elected mayor of Seoul on October 26, 2011, in a surprise defeat for the ruling GNP (Park subsequently joined the DUP in February 2012).

On February 9, 2012, PARK Tee Hai, the speaker of the assembly, resigned following bribery charges related to his campaign to become chair of the GNP. He was replaced by KANG Chang Hee when the new assembly convened in June. Both major parties, the renamed NFP and DUP, faced minor scandals ahead of assembly balloting on April 11. In the elections, the NFP lost 15 seats but maintained a narrow majority.

The DUP gained 46 seats. The newly formed Unified Progressive Party (UPP) placed third with 13 seats.

On September 21, 2012, South Korean naval ships fired warning shots at six North Korean fishing vessels that violated the NLL. A second incident took place the following day. On December 19, Park Geun Hye (NFP) defeated Moon Jae In (DUP) and four independent candidates to become president. Turnout in the balloting was 75.8 percent, a significant increase from the 63.2 percent in the 2007 presidential election.

On October 7, 2012, Seoul and Washington announced an agreement to increase the range of South Korea's ballistic missiles from 300 km (186.4 miles) to 800 km (497.1 miles). The increase in range meant that South Korea could target all of North Korea and areas of China, Japan, and Russia. The deployment was reportedly one of the rationales used by North Korea for the test of a long-range ballistic missile in December in violation of UN restrictions.

The National Assembly approved President Park's first budget on January 1, 2013. The budget cut military spending by $290 million, while raising social and welfare spending and reducing the deficit from 1.1 percent of GDP to an estimated 0.3 percent. On January 30, for the first time, South Korea successfully launched a satellite, becoming just the thirteenth country to do so. In June, WON Sei Hoon, the former head of South Korea's intelligence agency, was arrested on charges that he interfered in the 2012 presidential elections by directing on online "smear" campaign against Moon of the DUP.

POLITICAL PARTIES

In the five years before 1972 South Korea had what was essentially a two-party system of the Democratic Republican Party (DRP), formed in 1963 as an electoral mechanism for the ruling military junta, and the New Democratic Party (NDP), organized in 1967 as a coalition of opposition elements. In the decades that followed, a multiparty political system emerged, marked by frequent turnover of both party names and members, which persisted despite periodic criticism of the "old guard" policies represented by regionalism, close connections to the country's family-owned corporate conglomerates, and corruption scandals. (For more information on party history, see the 2011 *Handbook*.)

Governing Party:

New Frontier Party—NFP (*Saenuri Dang*). The "progressive conservative" NFP was formed in November 1997 as the Grand National Party—GNP (*Hannara Dang*) by merger of the New Korea Party (NKP) and the Democratic Party (DP). It was runner-up to the NCNP/ULD in the December 1997 presidential poll, with candidate Lee Hoi Chang winning 38.7 percent of the vote. In August 1998 most of the party leadership, including President CHO Sun, resigned following the GNP's failure to elect its candidate for speaker of the National Assembly, and by early September 1998 defections had cost the party its legislative majority.

In preparation for the April 2000 assembly election, party leader Lee withheld nominations from a number of GNP legislators who had been associated with former president Kim Young Sam or with the earlier military dictatorship. In February 2000 many of this "old guard" were central to formation of the Democratic People's Party—DPP (*Minkook Dang*), which won 2 seats in April. The GNP won 133 seats, 4 short of a majority, on a 39.0 percent vote share, but subsequent defections from other parties, coupled with by-election victories in October 2001 and August 2002, gave it more than half the seats.

Before the December 2002 presidential election the GNP attempted to win back the support of its most prominent defectors, including members of the DPP, which had participated in the ruling MDP-ULD coalition from April 2001 until the dismissal of DPP legislator Han Seung Soo as foreign minister in January 2002. Han rejoined the GNP in October 2002. A month later Park Geun Hye, daughter of the late Park Chung Hee and a former GNP vice president, also rejoined the party. She had left in early 2002 and in May had formed the short-lived Korean Coalition for the Future (KCF). In the 2002 presidential election Lee Hoi Chang again finished second, with 47 percent of the vote, and he announced his retirement shortly thereafter.

In March 2004 Park Geun Hye replaced the party chair, CHOE Byung Yol, whose leadership had been undermined by the 2002 illegal fund-raising scandal. In the April 2004 National Assembly election the GNP lost its majority, winning 121 seats and less than 36 percent of the party list vote. It had considerable success in subsequent by-elections, however, and by the end of 2005 it had picked up an additional 6 seats. Meanwhile, Park had won election to a full two-year term at the party convention in July 2004. In February 2006 KIM Hak Wan, the only remaining National Assembly member from the United Liberal Democrats (ULD), announced that his party would merge into the GNP before the local elections at the end of May.

On May 20, 2006, while campaigning for local candidates, party leader Park was slashed by a knife-wielding assailant, resulting in perhaps some sympathy votes for the GNP at the polls. On May 31 it won six of seven major mayoral contests and six of nine governorships. In mid-June Park stepped down as chair to pursue the party's endorsement for the national presidency.

Victories in a 2007 by-election raised the party's National Assembly delegation to 128 seats—a plurality, in view of recent defections from the *Uri* Party. On August 20 Lee Myung Bak narrowly won the party's presidential endorsement over Park.

In early November 2007 GNP founder and former candidate Lee Hoi Chang entered the presidential race as a conservative independent, but despite his winning 15.1 percent of the vote at national polls in December, Lee Myung Bak easily won the presidency, with 48.7 percent. The GNP also won 153 seats in the April 2008 National Assembly election.

In July 2008 Park Hee Tae defeated Chung Mong Joon for the party chair. Efforts were already under way to woo back some 30 members of the National Assembly who, as supporters of former chair Park Geun Hye, had left the GNP in a dispute over party endorsements for the April election. The 30 former members had won election either as members of the Park Geun Hye Coalition (also known as the Pro-Park Alliance; see Future Hope Alliance, below) or as independents. About 15 former members ultimately rejoined the GNP.

By mid-2009, despite holding 168 National Assembly seats, the GNP had lost its advantage over the Democrats in public opinion polls. In April by-elections it failed to win any of the five open assembly seats, which contributed to President Lee's decision to appoint a new prime minister and reshuffle the cabinet in September. Party chair Park Hee Tae stepped down to contest a National Assembly by-election in October, and Chung Mong Joon assumed the vacated post.

Following party victories in only 6 of 16 major mayoral and gubernatorial contests in June 2, 2010, Chung Mong Jong and Secretary General CHUNG Byung Kook resigned their leadership posts. On July 14, in a five-way race, Ang Sang Soo, who had been serving as the floor leader in the National Assembly, won election as party chair, defeating Hong Joon Pyo, at a national party convention. The GNP also approved the reintegration of the pro-Park Future Hope Alliance—FHA (*Mirae Himang Yeondae*), which had been formed in 2008 as the Park Geun Hye Coalition—PGHC (*Chinbak Yeondae*) or the Pro-Park Alliance (for more on the FHA, please see the 2012 *Handbook*). In an apparent effort to refresh its image before the 2012 election campaign, Hong was elected to replace Ahn at a national party convention on July 4, 2011.

Internal disputes led to the resignation of Hong Jooh Pyo on December 9, 2011, and his replacement by an Emergency Response Committee, led by Park Geun Hye. In February 2012 the party rebranded itself as the NFP. The NFP maintained its majority in the 2012 assembly balloting, and on May 15, Hwang Woo Yea was elected chair. On August 20, Park was elected by the party as its 2012 presidential candidate. She went on to win the balloting with 51.6 percent of the vote.

Leaders: PARK Geun Hye (President of the Republic), CHUNG Hong Won (Prime Minister), LEE Myung Bak (Former President of the Republic), HWANG Woo Yea (Chair), HONG Jooh Pyo (Former Chair), KIM Moo Sung, KANG Chang Hee (National Assembly Speaker).

Other Parliamentary Parties:

Democratic United Party—DUP (*Minju Tonghabdang*). The current Democratic United Party was formed as the United Democratic Party (UDP) by merger on February 12, 2008, of the United New Democratic Party (UNDP) and the existing Democratic Party (DP, not to be confused with the earlier DP that was involved in forming the GNP in 1997). At the time, the UNDP held 135 seats in the National Assembly, while the DP held only 6. In the April 2008 election the UDP won 81 seats. It then reverted to the "Democratic Party" at a convention in July.

The preexisting DP had been launched by President Kim Dae Jung in January 2000 as the "reformist populist" Millennium Democratic Party—MDP (*Saecheonnyeonminju Dang*), which in the April National Assembly election captured 115 seats and 35.9 percent of the vote, second to the GNP. President Kim subsequently convinced four independent assembly members to join the party's ranks. He resigned the party presidency in November 2001, beset by factional infighting, scandals involving members of his government and his family, and by-election losses in October that cost the MDP its slim legislative majority. Six months later he left the party, as did six cabinet ministers.

In April 2002 Roh Moo Hyun, victor in a series of regional party primaries, emerged as the MDP's 2002 presidential candidate, but his prospects were dimmed by further by-election losses in August. On November 25, however, one of the three leading presidential nominees, Chung Mong Joon of the newly formed NA21, withdrew in favor of Roh, who won the December election with 49 percent of the vote.

Soon afterward, sharp divisions emerged between reform-minded Roh supporters and the party's "old guard." As a consequence, Roh and three dozen members of the National Assembly resigned from the MDP in September 2003. Those departing included the MDP chair, CHYUNG Dai Chul, and another prominent leader, Chung Dong Young, who became chair of the new *Uri* Party. Chyung was among the most prominent politicians subsequently convicted of receiving illegal contributions during 2002–2003.

Following Roh's departure, the MDP joined the opposition and supported Roh's impeachment in March 2004. At the same time, some members of the party strongly objected to readmitting a number of former members who had defected to other parties prior to the 2002 presidential election. Those seeking readmission included SHIN Nak Kyun, who had recently headed the NA21.

The MDP entered the April 2004 National Assembly election holding some 60 seats, but it emerged from the balloting having won only 7 percent of the proportional vote and 9 seats. As a consequence, the party's chair, Chough Soon Hyung, resigned. (He later joined the Liberty Forward Party, below). In August 2005 the MDP dropped "Millennium" from its name and thus became the DP.

The pending merger of this DP and the New Party for Centrist Reform and Alliance (NPCRA) was announced in June 2007, with the resultant party, tentatively named the Centrist United Democratic Party (CUDP), to be launched in July. The NPCRA had been established in early May 2007 by 20 members of the National Assembly who, in opposition to President Roh, had abandoned the *Uri* Party en masse in early February. Leaders included KIM Han Gill, the former *Uri* floor leader in the National Assembly. In announcing formation of the CUDP, Kim and DP leader PARK Sang Cheon attacked efforts by other liberals to form a broader alliance. Remaining members of the *Uri* Party, in turn, attacked the CUDP as a "small-scale alliance" incapable of challenging the GNP.

In early August 2007 a handful of former DP legislators left the CUDP and joined 80 *Uri* defectors in forming the UNDP. Leading figures included former GNP leader Sohn Hak Kyu and former *Uri* Party leader Chung Dong Young, both presidential aspirants. On August 18, 2007, the UNDP absorbed the last members of the *Uri* Party, which had overwhelmingly voted to disband, and thereby became the plurality party in the National Assembly, with 143 seats. (Critics attacked the UNDP as little more than a renamed *Uri* Party.) An effort by the UNDP to unite the center-left prior to the December presidential election failed, however, when the balance of the CUDP refused to accept the UNDP's decision to welcome pro-Roh members from the *Uri* Party. Instead, the remaining CUDP leaders changed the party's designation back to the DP and announced that they would field their own presidential candidate. In mid-October RHEE In Je, who had finished third in the 1997 presidential election as the candidate of his short-lived New Party by the People, won the nomination over several other candidates. (Rhee finished sixth, with 0.7 percent of the vote. In April 2008, having been denied endorsement by the UDP because of his history of defections, he was elected to the National Assembly as an independent.)

The UNDP primary concluded on October 15, 2007, with Chung, having received 44 percent of the vote, elected as the party's presidential nominee. Sohn Hak Kyu finished second, with 34 percent, while President Roh's preferred candidate, former prime minister Lee Hae Chan, garnered only 22 percent of the vote. In the December election Chung finished second, with 26.1 percent of the vote. The election of Sohn as party chair in January 2008 prompted the resignation of Lee Hae Chan from the party.

The decision of the UNDP and the DP to unite as the UDP in February 2008 did not prevent a GNP victory in the April legislative election, at which the merged party won only 25.1 percent of the vote. The party's 2007 presidential candidate, Chung Dong Young, won election as an independent, while former UNDP chair Sohn Hak Kyu announced his retirement from politics after losing his race. At the party's July 2008 national convention, former *Uri* leader Chung Sye Kyun was elected DP chair over CHOO Mi Ae and CHYUNG Dai Chul.

Although the DP's fortunes were buoyed by winning 7 of 16 mayoral and gubernatorial contests in the May 2010 local elections, the party won only 3 of 8 by-elections in July, causing Chung Sye Kyun to submit his resignation as chair.

On October 18, 2011, the national party convention elected Sohn Hak Kyu (back from retirement) as chair. On December 15 the DP merged with the small Citizens Unity Party to create the Democratic United Party (DUP). Former prime minister Han Myeong Sook was elected to lead the new grouping.

In assembly balloting on April 11, 2012, the DUP secured 127 seats. Han Myeong Sook resigned since the party was unable to defeat the ruling NFP. She was replaced on an interim basis, first by MOON Sung Keun, and then, by Park Jie Won. Lee Hae Chan was elected chair on June 9. Moon Jae In was the DUP's 2012 presidential contender. He placed second with 47.8 percent of the vote.

Leaders: LEE Hae Chan (Chair), MOON Jae In (2012 presidential candidate), CHUNG Dong Young (2007 UNDP presidential nominee), PARK Jie Won (Parliamentary Leader), MIKYUNG Lee (Secretary General).

Unified Progressive Party—UPP (*Tonghapjinbodang*). The left-of-center UPP was formed on December 5, 2011 through the merger of the **Democratic Labor Party**—DLP (*Minju Nodong Dang*), the **People's Participation Party**—PPP (*Gukmin Chamyeo Dang*), and a wing of the **New Progressive Party** (see below). The left-wing DLP was organized by labor activists in January 2000, and it campaigned on a platform that included political reform and advocacy of workers' interests. One of the founders, KWON Young Gil, had captured 1.2 percent of the vote in the 1997 presidential race as the candidate of the People's Victory. In a second run for the presidency, Kwon finished third in 2002, with 3.9 percent of the vote. In the April 2004 election, the DLP attracted considerable support from voters who were disaffected with old guard politics, winning 13 percent of the party list vote for a total of eight proportional seats. It also won two district seats. Because the party's constitution prohibits individuals from leading both the party and its parliamentary delegation, Kwon stepped down as DLP president at a party convention in June. His successor, KIM Hye Kyung, resigned after the October 2005 by-elections, at which the DLP failed to retain the seat won in April 2004. In February 2006 MOON Sung Hyun, the interim president, retained the post by defeating CHO Seung Soo in a party runoff. In December 2006 two members of the DLP were among five individuals charged with spying for North Korea.

In September 2007 Kwon Young Gil again won the party's presidential endorsement. In the December presidential poll, he finished fifth with just 3 percent of the vote. As a consequence of the party's poor results, the leadership offered to resign en masse, and party founders Sim and Roh Hoe Chan were named to head an emergency committee, with Sim then becoming interim leader. In February 2008, however, both Sim and Roh, leaders of the party's minority People's Democracy faction, left to form the New Progressive Party (below) when the majority National Liberation faction refused to adopt a proposed reform program that would have altered a pro-Pyongyang stance and expelled party members who had been implicated in spying for the North. In the April National Assembly election, the DLP won five seats.

Meanwhile, the PPP was formed in January 2010 by liberal supporters of former president Roh Moo Hyun, including former unification minister LEE Jae Joung.

In the April 2012 legislative elections, the newly formed UPP placed third, winning thirteen seats. In August, the UPP expelled two members of its assembly delegation in the midst of continuing internal disputes. LEE Jung Hee was the party's 2012 presidential candidate but withdrew from the campaign on December 16 in a reported bid to bolster the electoral chances of DUP candidate Moon Jae In.

Leaders: KANG Ki Kab, YOO Seon Hee.

Liberty Forward Party—LFP (*Jayou Seonjin Dang*). The conservative LFP was established on February 1, 2008, by former GNP leader and presidential candidate Lee Hoi Chang, who had run in December 2007 as an independent and had finished third, with 15 percent of the vote. Formation of the LFP was announced in preparation for the upcoming National Assembly election. A week later, the People First Party (PFP) merged into the LFP, which consequently held a total of eight legislative seats at that time.

The PFP had been formed in October 2005 by the governor of South Chungchong Province, Sim Dae Pyung, and several National Assembly members. At its formal inauguration in January 2006, Sim and assembly independent SHIN Kook Hwan were elected cochairs, while Rhee In Je, who had run for president in 1997 as the candidate of the New Party by the People and had later joined the ULD, was given the responsibility of leading the PFP into the May 2006 local elections. Two other former ULD legislators had also joined the new party, but a merger with the ULD fell through.

In the April 2008 election the new LFP won 18 seats, for third place. It later joined with the liberal Renewal of Korea Party (RKP, below) to form a working group, the Forward and Creative Alliance, in the National Assembly. In June 2008 it was rumored that in an effort to shore up support for his faltering government, President Lee was considering offering the prime minister post to the LFP's SIM Dae Pyung, a former governor of South Chungchong Province. Party chair Lee Hoi Chang, however, dismissed talk of a conservative alliance.

In 2009 Sim briefly left to form a new party but later rejoined the LFP. The LFP secured only five seats in the April 2012 balloting, prompting the resignation of LFP leader SIM Dae Pyung. Rhee In Je was elected chair in May. Also in May, Lee Hoi Chang resigned from the party, reportedly to form a new grouping. In October, the party voted to change its name to the **Forward Unification Party**—FUP (*Seonjin Tongildang*).

Leaders: RHEE In Je (Chair), KIM Nak Seong (Parliamentary Leader).

Other Parties:

Renewal of Korea Party—RKP (*Changjo Hangkuk Dang*). The liberal RKP, which is also commonly called the **Creative Korea Party,** was established at the end of October 2007 and registered in November. Its principal founder, MOON Kook Hyun, a former chief executive of the Yuhan-Kimberley pharmaceutical company, finished fourth in the December presidential contest, with 5.8 percent of the vote. Moon's refusal to align with the UNDP for the election eventually led to a split in the party. In the April 2008 National Assembly election the RKP won only three seats.

Afterward the party became embroiled in a controversy over one of its proportional representatives, LEE Han Jung who was sentenced to two years in prison in September 2008.

In November 2009 Moon and other party leaders resigned in the wake of a Supreme Court ruling that Moon had illegally made profits for the party and had taken kickbacks from a candidate in the 2008 election. Moon received an eight-month suspended sentence and lost his seat in the lower house. The party received less than 1 percent of the vote and no seats in the April 2012 assembly balloting.

Leaders: HAN Myeon Hee (Chair), LEE Young Kyung.

New Progressive Party—NPP (*Jinbo Shin Dang*). The NPP was established in February 2008 by the moderate faction of the DLP (above) headed by Sim Sang Jeung and Roh Hoe Chan following the DLP's rejection of a reform proposal that would have ended the DLP's strong pro-Pyongyang policy. In the April National Assembly election, the NPP failed to win any seats, having narrowly missed the 3 percent threshold for proportional representation.

In April 2009 the party won a by-election after the DLP agreed to back its nominee, CHO Seung Soo, in order to defeat the GNP candidate. The small Socialist Party merged with the NPP in February 2012. The NPP did not win any seats in the 2012 legislative balloting. The party reportedly sought to rebrand itself as a pro-labor grouping in 2013.

Leaders: HONG Sehwa (Chair), KIM Sona, SHIM Jae Ok, KANG Sang Ku, KIM Jongchul.

Korea Vision Party—K Party (*Gungmin Saenggak*). The K Party is a center-right grouping that was established on February 12, 2012. The party sought to draw disaffected conservative voters away from the NFP and the LFP. In the 2012 assembly elections, the K Party won just 1.4 percent of the vote and failed to win any seats.

Leader: PARK Se IL.

A number of small parties were registered for the 2008 and 2012 National Assembly elections: **Arts and Culture Party,** led by KIM Won Young; **Chamjuin Yunhap,** led by KIM Sun Mi; **Christian Love Party** (CLP), led by CHOI Su Hwan; **Citizen's Party,** led by CHOI Yong Ki; **Economic Republican Party,** led by HUH Kyung Young, who had won 0.4 percent of the 2007 presidential vote; **Economy & Unification Party,** led by AHN Dong Uk; **Family Party for Peace and Unity,** led by KWAK Jeong Hwan; **International Green Party,** led by LEE Wae Won and CHEONG Jae Bok; **Korean Society Party,** led by KUM Min, who won 0.1 percent of the 2007 presidential vote; **Liberty Peace Party,** led by LEE Tae Hui; **National Security Party,** led by LEE Geon Gai; **National Unity for Harmony and Advancement,** led by HEO Sul; **Party for Advanced Korea,** led by JANG Suk Chang; **Professional Coalition Party,** led by OH Ho Seok; **Righteous Korea Party,** led by KANG Seung Kyu; **Sinmirae Political Party,** led by KIM Ho Il; **System and Future Party,** led by JI Man Won; and **Unification Korea Party,** led by AHN Kwang Yang.

LEGISLATURE

The present **National Assembly** (*Kuk Hoe*) is a unicameral body of 300 members elected for four-year terms. In the most recent election of April 11, 2012, 246 seats were filled by direct election from single-member constituencies, while 54 were distributed proportionally among those parties winning at least 5 district seats or 3 percent of the party vote. The results (direct/proportional breakdowns in parentheses) were as follows: New Frontier Party (NFP), 152 (127, 25); Democratic United Party (DUP), 127 (106, 21); Unified Progressive Party (UPP), 13 (7, 6); Liberty Forward Party (LFP), 5 (3, 2); independents, 3.

Speaker: KANG Chang Hee.

CABINET

[as of November 15, 2013]

Prime Minister	Chung Hong Won
Ministers	
Culture, Sports, and Tourism	Yoo Jin Ryong
Education, Science, and Technology	Seo Nam Soo
Employment and Labor	Phang Ha Nam
Environment	Yoon Seong Kyu
Food, Agriculture, and Rural Affairs	Lee Dong Phil
Foreign Affairs	Yun Byung Se
Gender Equality, and Family	Cho Yoon Seon
Health and Welfare	Chin Young
Justice	Hwang Kyo Ahn
Land, Infrastructure, and Transport	Suh Seoung Hwan
National Defense	Kim Kwan Jin
Oceans and Fisheries	Yoon Jin Sook
Public Administration and Security	Yoo Jeong Bok
Science, ICT, and Future Planning	Choi Mun Kee
Strategy and Finance	Hyun Oh Seok
Trade, Industry, and Energy	Yoon Sang Jick
Unification	Ryoo Kihl Jae

INTERGOVERNMENTAL REPRESENTATION

Ambassador to the U.S.: CHOI Youngjin.

U.S. Ambassador to Republic of Korea: SUNG Y. Kim.

Permanent Representative to the UN: KIM Sook.

IGO Memberships (Non-UN): ADB, AfDB, APEC, EBRD, G-20, IADB, ICC, IEA, IOM, OECD, WTO.

KOSOVO

Republic of Kosovo
Republika e Kosovës (Albanian)
Republika Kosovo (Serbian)

Note: The decision of the *PHW* editors to devote a separate article to the Republic of Kosovo, despite its ambiguous international status, acknowledges its recognition by 103 countries but does so without prejudice regarding the Republic of Serbia's insistence that Kosovo remains a de jure province of that country. On July 22, 2010, the International Court of Justice issued an advisory opinion that Kosovo's unilateral declaration of independence "did not violate general international law," but the 10–4 decision had no immediate impact on the Kosovo-Serbia dispute.

Political Status: Autonomous district of Kosovo (and Metohija) within the Serbian constituent republic of the communist Federal People's Republic of Yugoslavia (instituted November 29, 1945); autonomous province within the Serbian constituent republic of the Socialist Federal Republic of Yugoslavia (proclaimed April 7, 1963) and then of the Federal Republic of Yugoslavia (proclaimed April 27, 1992); placed under administration of the United Nations Interim Administrative Mission in Kosovo (UNMIK) from June 14, 1999, by authorization of UN Security Council Resolution 1244; autonomous province of the "state union" of Serbia and Montenegro (while remaining under UNMIK administration), which was established February 4, 2003, and then of the independent Republic of Serbia, established June 5, 2006; independence from Serbia unilaterally declared on February 17, 2008, in an action denounced by Serbia, which continues to regard Kosovo and Metohija as an inalienable autonomous province; constitution of the Republic of Kosovo adopted by the Assembly of Kosovo on April 9, 2008, with effect from June 15.

Area: 4,211 sq. mi. (10,908 sq. km).

Population: 1,847,708 (2013E—UN); 1,848,000 (2013E—U.S. Census).

Major Urban Centers (2011): PRIŠTINA (PRISHTINË, 198,000), Prizren (178,000), Peć (Pejë, 96,000), Mitrovica (Mitrovicë, 72,000).

Official Languages: Albanian and Serbian. Bosnian, Roma, and Turkish are official at the municipal level and as otherwise provided by law.

Monetary Unit: Euro (market rate November 1, 2013: 0.74 euro = $1US). The Serbian dinar continues to circulate in areas where the population is mostly ethnically Serb.

President: Atifete JAHJAGA; elected (as a compromise candidate of the Democratic Party of Kosovo, New Kosovo Alliance and Democratic League of Kosovo) in first-round balloting by the National Assembly on April 7, 2011, and sworn in on the same day for a five-year term, succeeding acting president Jakup KRASNIQI. (See Political background, below, for details on the February 2011 presidential election.)

Prime Minister: Hashim THAÇI (Democratic Party of Kosovo); endorsed as prime minister of UNMIK-administered Kosovo by the Assembly of Kosovo and assumed office on January 9, 2008, following the legislative election of November 17, 2007, in succession to Agim ÇEKU (then nonparty); became prime minister of the Republic of Kosovo upon declaration of independence, February 17, 2008; retained office as incumbent following the December 12, 2010, parliamentary election.

THE COUNTRY

The landlocked Republic of Kosovo, bordered by Serbia on the north and northeast, Macedonia on the southeast, Albania on the southwest, and Montenegro on the west, encompasses about 12 percent of Serbia's area before the separation. The terrain is predominantly mountainous and hilly, the principal exception being the Metohija (Dukagjin) basin in the west. The population is an estimated 92 percent ethnic Albanian, with the Serb minority constituting about 5.3 percent; other minorities include Bosniacs, Turks, Roma, Montenegrins, and Croats. Approximately 90 percent of the citizenry profess Islam; the principal minority religions are Serbian Orthodox (7 percent) and Roman Catholic (3 percent).

Long subsidized by the other regions of Yugoslavia, the underdeveloped Kosovar economy suffered in the 1980s from Yugoslavia's economic crisis, then in the 1990s by policies of President Slobodan Milošević, a Serb. Beginning in early 1998 escalating violence in Kosovo led to a renewal of international sanctions against Yugoslavia and then to a bombing campaign authorized by the United Nations Security Council and conducted, primarily against the constituent Republic of Serbia, by the North Atlantic Treaty Organization (NATO) in March–June 1999. Following the cessation of hostilities, a donor conference of over 100 countries and agencies pledged some $2 billion in reconstructive, humanitarian, and administrative assistance for Kosovo.

Under the supervision of the postconflict UN Mission in Kosovo (UNMIK), the Kosovo Trust Agency privatized many state-owned enterprises, a legacy of the Yugoslav socialist era. At present, agriculture contributes about one-fifth of GDP, as does industry, with services accounting for the balance. Leading agricultural products include wheat and other grains, vegetables, and fruits. A significant portion of the countryside remains forested. Industry has traditionally centered on extraction and processing of ores, chiefly lead, silver, and zinc, but in recent decades a lack of investment in equipment and infrastructure has hurt output. Kosovo is believed to have the world's fifth-largest reserves of lignite, and there are also deposits of bauxite, chromium, and other metals. Other important industries are food processing and construction. Leading exports include minerals, processed metals, and scrap metal. In the years immediately before independence was declared, foreign assistance and remittances from Kosovars working abroad amounted to nearly half the GDP. Together, the two continue to account for over one-quarter of GDP. About 45 percent of the population lives in poverty, on under $2 a day.

Following a recessionary period in 2002–2003, Kosovo's GDP grew at an annual average of over 3.9 percent from 2004 to 2011, slowing to 2.1 percent in 2012. High unemployment continued unabated, at about 45 percent in June 2012. For 2013, real GDP growth was projected by the IMF to be about 2.9 percent.

GOVERNMENT AND POLITICS

Political background. Considered their historic homeland by Serbians, what became Kosovo-Metohija was absorbed by the Ottoman Empire in the late 14th century, following the Ottoman victory at the battle of Kosovo Polje. After the Balkan Wars of 1912–1913, Kosovo was included in Serbia and then, from December 1918, the Kingdom of the Serbs, Croats, and Slovenes. Formally renamed Yugoslavia on October 3, 1929, the highly centralized, Serb-dominated monarchy was attacked and occupied by Nazi Germany and Fascist Italy in April 1941. Communist-inspired Partisans, led by Marshal Josip Broz TITO, opposed the occupation with Allied support and assumed power at the end of World War II, establishing a "federal people's republic" that included within the constituent Serbian republic an autonomous district of Kosovo and Metohija, with newly defined borders, in which ethnic Albanians constituted a majority. Although the Autonomous Province of Kosovo and Metohija was granted increased responsibilities under 1963 and 1974 federal constitutions, it remained subservient to the government of the Serbian constituent republic.

Ethnic strife between Serbians and Albanians led members of both ethnic communities to relocate and generated sometimes-violent protests. In July 1989, contrary to the federal constitution, Serbia effectively stripped Kosovo (and Vojvodina) of autonomous status. When the Kosovo Assembly demanded that the province be elevated to republican status within Yugoslavia, Serbia dissolved the legislature. The ethnic Albanian delegates to the assembly nevertheless attempted to declare Kosovo a constituent republic within the Yugoslav federation. Kosovo's autonomous status within Serbia was restored, but the move was insufficient to satisfy Kosovo's ethnic Albanian majority. On October 19, 1991, the Kosovar legislature, citing an independence referendum held the previous month, declared an independent "Republic of Kosovo" that was recognized only by neighboring Albania. Meanwhile, the Yugoslav federation, beset by independence pressures in other constituent republics, was disintegrating: Between June 1991 and March 1992 Croatia, Slovenia, Macedonia, and Bosnia and Herzegovina all declared independence, leaving Montenegro and Serbia as the rump Yugoslavia.

Ethnic Albanians, resisting Serbian attempts to impose political, social, and educational control, established their own underground administration. Elections to the Kosovo Assembly in May 1992, won by the pro-independence Democratic League of Kosovo (*Lidhja Demokratike e Kosovës*—LDK), were condemned as illegal by Belgrade. Nevertheless, on May 25 the LDK leader, Ibrahim RUGOVA, was proclaimed president of the "Republic of Kosovo." The local situation deteriorated in December 1994 when Serbian security forces carried out the most sweeping wave of arrests since 1990 in an effort to eliminate the unauthorized police force created by the ethnic Albanians. Tension intensified further in mid-1995 when the Belgrade government announced that Serb refugees from Croatia's Krajina would be resettled in Kosovo.

As early as 1992 the most militant Kosovar separatists had formed loosely linked guerrilla bands that eventually became the Kosovo Liberation Army—KLA (*Ushtria Çlirimtare e Kosovës*—UÇK). Many of its commanders favored not just separation from Yugoslavia but union in a Greater Albania. Following the murder of four Serbian policemen in February 1998 by KLA members, retaliatory Serb security operations killed over 80 ethnic Albanian villagers. In March some 50,000 protesters demonstrated in Priština, while the United States and the European Union (EU), among others, condemned the excessive use of force and the UN Security Council imposed an arms embargo on Yugoslavia. Despite a series of diplomatic missions to Belgrade and Priština, the Serbian crackdown continued, provoking additional demonstrations and calls by regional neighbors and the international Contact Group on former Yugoslavia (Britain, France, Germany, Russia, and the United States as well as the UN and the EU and, later, Italy) for restraint and the opening of talks on Kosovar autonomy. Later in March, ethnic Albanians, in addition to casting ballots for the shadow "Republic of Kosovo" legislature, reelected the LDK's Ibrahim Rugova as shadow president, although some ethnic Albanian parties boycotted the vote, partly in opposition to Rugova's advocacy of passive resistance in the effort to achieve Kosovar independence.

With daily demonstrations continuing in the province, U.S. diplomats convinced Yugoslav president Milošević and Rugova to meet for the first time in May 1998. Although both sides agreed to initiate weekly talks in Priština, the violence in Kosovo continued to escalate as Serbian army and security forces, sweeping through Kosovar villages, met strong resistance from the rapidly expanding KLA. In June Milošević rejected diplomatic efforts by U.S. negotiator Richard Holbrooke and Russian president Boris Yeltsin, who sought the inclusion of the KLA in negotiations, a cease-fire, and withdrawal of Serbian forces from Kosovo. By then, reports of civilian massacres, torture, and other human rights violations committed by Serbian contingents were regularly surfacing, contributing to the prospect of NATO intervention. In October, facing the threat of imminent NATO air strikes, Milošević agreed to begin withdrawing military and security forces from Kosovo and to allow entry of 2,000 international observers supervised by the Organization for Security and Cooperation in Europe (OSCE). In November, however, Belgrade barred members of the UN's International Criminal Tribunal for the former Yugoslavia (ICTY) from entering Kosovo to investigate allegations of extrajudicial killings.

Although fighting intensified again in mid-December 1998, late in the month both sides accepted a local cease-fire brokered by the head of the OSCE mission. In January 1999, despite renewed threats from NATO, widespread hostilities resumed. The worst atrocity of the conflict to date occurred when Serbian forces executed 45 civilians from the village of Račak.

In February 1999 peace talks between Serbian officials and ethnic Albanians—including KLA representatives—opened in Rambouillet, France. Cosponsored by France and the United States, the negotiations were aimed at winning approval of a proposal by the Contact Group that, while acknowledging Serbian sovereignty in Kosovo, envisaged almost complete administrative autonomy for the province, the withdrawal of all but 1,500 Serbian border troops, the rapid disbanding of the KLA, and formation of a new, ethnically balanced police force. In March the Kosovar delegation signed the pact, but the Serbian delegation continued to reject the presence of NATO peacekeepers.

On March 24, 1999, NATO forces from eight countries initiated Operation Allied Force, the most extensive air campaign in Europe since the close of World War II. In the following weeks allied bombing extended throughout Yugoslavia in an effort to force the Milošević regime to accept the Rambouillet agreement. Serbian forces stepped up a widespread campaign of "ethnic cleansing" that saw the entire Albanian population forced from some cities and villages, creating an immediate refugee crisis at the borders of Albania and Macedonia. By the end of April the refugee exodus was swelling toward 750,000, with additional hundreds of thousands displaced within the province itself.

On May 6, 1999, the Group of Seven (G-7) countries plus Russia (G-8) proposed a peace plan providing for "deployment in Kosovo of effective international civil and security presences" and formation of an interim provincial administration under the UN Security Council. On June 3 President Milošević accepted the terms of an amended peace agreement offered by President Martii Ahtisaari of Finland and Russia's Viktor Chernomyrdin, including the deployment in Kosovo (but not the rest of Serbia) of a UN-sponsored, NATO-dominated peacekeeping contingent (Kosovo Force, or KFOR) expected to number some 50,000 troops. The agreement also called for the complete withdrawal of the Serbian army, police, and paramilitary forces from Kosovo.

On June 10, 1999, NATO suspended its bombing campaign and the UN Security Council adopted Resolution 1244, authorizing international troop deployment and the establishment of an interim civilian administration in Kosovo. The resolution also reaffirmed Yugoslavia's "sovereignty and territorial integrity" but echoed previous calls for "substantial autonomy and meaningful self-administration in Kosovo." Meanwhile, on May 27 the ICTY had indicted President Milošević and four others, including Yugoslavia's interior minister and army chief of staff, for crimes against humanity related to events in Kosovo.

On June 14, 1999, the UN Security Council received a plan for the civil Kosovo administration. The EU would supervise reconstruction, and the OSCE would oversee institution building. Humanitarian and administrative matters would primarily fall in the purview of the Office of the UN High Commissioner for Refugees (UNHCR) and a newly established UN Interim Administration in Kosovo (UNMIK), respectively. On June 20, with the Yugoslav army having completely withdrawn from Kosovo, NATO formally concluded its bombing campaign. On the same day NATO and the KLA signed an agreement providing for KLA demilitarization, although Hashim THAÇI, the KLA leader, refused to renounce the eventual goal of Kosovar independence. Most of the 1 million or more Kosovo Albanian refugees and displaced persons were already returning to their homes, contributing to the collateral flight from the province of ethnic Serbs, many of whom feared reprisals.

In July 1999 UNMIK established a consultative, multiethnic Kosovo Transitional Council (KTC), although the LDK's Rugova initially refused to participate because not all the parties in his shadow government were included. In December UNMIK announced formation of an Interim Administrative Council (IAC) of Rugova, Thaçi, and Rexhep QOSJA of the United Democratic Movement (*Lëvizja Bashimit Demokratike*—LBD); a fourth seat on the IAC was reserved for a representative of the Serb community, which refused to participate. By then, forensic specialists from the ICTY were already exhuming bodies from mass graves in Kosovo. (Late in the year, the Albanian death toll was estimated at 4,000–5,000, considerably less than originally projected.) On April 18, 2000, the Eurocorps, with troop contingents from Germany, Spain, France, Belgium, and Luxembourg, took over control of the Kosovo peacekeeping effort from NATO, but KFOR was encountering increasing difficulty in preventing violent clashes between Albanian and Serb communities.

Municipal elections in Kosovo were held on October 28, 2000, under UNMIK supervision. Participation by ethnic Serbs was minimal. Rugova's LDK finished first, well ahead of Thaçi's recently formed Democratic Party of Kosovo (*Partia Demokratike e Kosovës*—PDK). A new 120-member Assembly of Kosovo was elected on November 17, 2001, with the LDK winning a plurality of 47 seats. Thaçi's PDK finished with 26 seats, and the multiparty Serb Return Coalition (*Koalicija Povratak*—KP) took 22. After opening its first session on December 10 the assembly, with its limited provisional powers, elected a 7-member administrative presidency, but it failed to elect a provincial president. It wasn't until March 4 that Rugova received the two-thirds vote required for election. Under a power-sharing arrangement, Bajram REXHEPI of the PDK was named prime minister.

On February 4, 2003, Serbia and Montenegro dissolved Yugoslavia and established a "state union" with a new Constitutional Charter, under which Kosovo's status remained substantially unchanged.

In the second election for the Kosovar assembly, held October 23, 2004, President Rugova's LDK again finished first, winning 47 seats, followed by Thaçi's PDK with 30. For the most part Kosovo's Serb community boycotted the balloting, with most of the 10 reserved Serb seats being awarded to a Serb List for Kosovo and Metohija (*Srpska Lista za Kosovo i Metohiju*—SLKM) that included members of the KP. On December 3 the newly convened legislature reelected Rugova as president and confirmed a minority government headed by Ramush HARADINAJ of the Alliance for the Future of Kosovo (*Aleanca për Ardhmërinë e Kosovës*—AAK), which had finished third, with 9 seats, in the October legislative election. The selection of Haradinaj, a former KLA commander, caused the Serbian government to withdraw from the first-ever direct talks with Kosovar officials, which had opened in Vienna, Austria, on October 14, 2003.

Haradinaj's tenure as Kosovo's prime minister proved short: On March 8, 2005, he resigned and shortly afterward surrendered to the ICTY to face charges that included crimes against humanity. (His trial, which began in March 2007, concluded in April 2008 with an acquittal.) His successor, the less controversial Bajram KOSUMI, also of the AAK, was confirmed by the legislature on March 23.

Less than a year later, on January 21, 2006, President Rugova died of cancer, which began a series of leadership changes. Nexhat DACI, speaker of the Kosovo Assembly, served as acting president until February 10, when the legislature elected Fatmir SEJDIU of the LDK as president. Prime Minister Kosumi then resigned on March 1, under pressure for stronger leadership during UN-mediated negotiations over Kosovo's future political status. On March 10 President Sejdiu named as prime minister Agim ÇEKU, a former officer in the Croatian Army and more recently a general in the Kosovo Protection Corps.

In February 2006 the UN convened talks in Vienna on Kosovo's future status. Representatives of France, Germany, Italy, Russia, the United Kingdom, and the United States also attended. Serbia's position remained that Kosovo was part of its territory, while Kosovar leaders insisted that the only viable political solution was independence. Progress toward resolution of the political status question was sidetracked immediately by disagreement over more minor issues regarding division of power regionally, and economic, cultural, and religious matters.

On June 3, 2006, Montenegro declared its independence, and the separate Republic of Serbia was proclaimed two days later; UNMIK-administered Kosovo as well as Vojvodina remained autonomous provinces of Serbia. Also in June, Serbia's government unveiled a proposal dubbed "the platform" that offered Kosovo greater autonomy within Serbia for 20 years while preserving Belgrade's control over foreign affairs, borders and customs, monetary policy, protection of Serb religious and cultural matters, and human rights. Kosovo's ethnic Albanian leaders rejected Serbia's proposal outright. The platform also received little support from the parties convened in Vienna.

On March 26, 2007, having stated earlier in the month that he saw no chance of achieving a compromise by the Serbian and Kosovar governments, UN special envoy Martii Ahtisaari submitted to the UN Security Council his plan for Kosovo's "supervised independence." It called for creation of a constitutional commission to draft a basic law that would require approval by two-thirds of the Kosovo Assembly. UNMIK's mandate would expire, but in an arrangement similar to Bosnia and Herzegovina's, an international representative would have veto power over decisions of the Kosovar government.

The Ahtisaari plan paid particular attention to the status of the minority Serb population. (With only a fraction of the estimated 200,000 Serbs who had fled Kosovo since 1999 having returned, ethnic Albanians outnumbered ethnic Serbs by an estimated 1.8 million to 120,000.) Serbs would be granted broad governmental powers in six municipalities, each of which could receive direct aid from Serbia. In addition, Serbs and other minorities would be guaranteed seats in the legislature.

Although the Kosovo Assembly voted its approval of the Ahtisaari plan in early April 2007, Serbia rejected it. Moreover, Russia pledged to use its veto power on the Security Council to derail any plan the Serbian government found unacceptable. Several other regional countries, including Greece and Romania, also expressed reservations. With a December 2007 deadline looming for reaching a final decision, representatives of the Serbian and Kosovar governments, including the presidents and prime ministers of both jurisdictions, met in New York on September 28 for face-to-face discussions. Between then and November 26 five additional negotiating rounds were held either in Belgium or Austria. Serbia's final offer of self-government except in foreign relations, defense, and border control was rejected by Kosovo, the only significant point of agreement being that both would avoid threats and violence.

On November 17, 2007, the PDK won a plurality of 37 seats in an election for the Assembly of Kosovo. The LDK finished second, with 25 seats, a net loss of 22 from its previous total. Six ethnic Serb parties split the 10 seats set aside for Serbs; seven other minority parties won a total of 14 seats. Voter turnout was only 43 percent. On January 9, 2008, the new legislature reelected Fatmir Sejdiu as president and then endorsed Thaçi as prime minister of a coalition cabinet comprising the PDK, the LDK, the ethnic Serb Independent Liberal Party (*Samostalna Liberalna Stranka*—SLS), and the Kosovo Democratic Turkish Party (*Kosova Demokratik Türk Partisi*—KDTP).

On February 17, 2008, addressing the assembly, Prime Minister Thaçi declared Kosovo to be "proud, independent, and free" as a "democratic, multiethnic state moving rapidly toward EU and Euro-Atlantic integration." The declaration of independence was condemned by Serbia. The following day, Albania, France, the United Kingdom, and the United States were among the first countries to recognize Kosovo. On April 9 the assembly adopted a constitution by a vote of 103–0, and it entered into effect on June 15.

On August 15, 2008, Serbia's foreign minister announced that Belgrade would ask the International Court of Justice (ICJ) for an advisory ruling on the legality of Kosovo's unilateral declaration of independence. He added that the current Serbian government would "accept any opinion that comes from the ICJ." In early October the UN General Assembly approved the referral to the court. Following submission of written statements and rebuttals by interested parties, in December 2009 the ICJ began public hearings on the matter. On July 22, 2010, by a vote of 10–4, the ICJ issued an advisory opinion that Kosovo's unilateral declaration of independence "did not violate general international law."

On September 27, 2010, President Fatmir SEJDIU resigned his office following a decision by the Constitutional Court that his continued leadership of the LDK had been unconstitutional. The LDK subsequently left the ruling coalition in October, leaving the minority government vulnerable to a November 2 vote of no confidence and leading to snap elections.

In the December 12, 2010, parliamentary election, the PDK won a plurality of seats (34), with 32.11 percent of the vote. Its nearest competitors were the LDK with 27 seats, *Vetëvendosje* with 14, and the AAK, the **New Kosovo Coalition** (*Koalicioni për Kosovë të Re*—KKR), and the SLS each winning 8 seats. The remaining 17 seats were divided between the 11 minority parties. EU observers noted some irregularities in voting but stated that the process was broadly "calm and orderly." The election also saw much greater participation by ethnic Serb citizens. Whereas in 2008 only 1,000 Serbs voted, in the 2010 elections the total may have been as high as 20,000.

Charges of election fraud were raised by the LDK and AAK, and the Central Electoral Commission ordered revotes in 21 polling stations on January 9, 2011, with the final results being released on January 30. Prime Minister Thaçi was invited to form a government, and he brought the SLS, the **New Kosovo Alliance** (*Aleanca Kosova e*

Re—AKR), which had received all eight seats won by the KKR, and six minority parties into a coalition in February 2011.

The coalition agreements included a provision that Behgjet PACOLLI, leader of the AKR, would be nominated for the presidency. In the indirect February 22 presidential elections conducted by the National Assembly, Pacolli won the third round with 62 votes. However, on March 28, 2011, the Constitutional Court of Kosovo ruled that his election had been unconstitutional as a sufficient parliamentary quorum had not been present in the first two rounds due to a boycott by the opposition. Pacolli resigned on March 30 and was replaced by Jakup KRASNIQI as acting president. A new election was held on April 7, in which the ruling coalition secured an agreement with the LDK to attend the election of a compromise candidate, Atifete JAHJAGA, who won the first round with 80 votes. The agreement included provisions to seek constitutional reforms that would allow for the direct election of the presidency and that Jahjaga would serve a limited, nine-month term. In July 2012, however, the Constitutional Court ruled it unconstitutional to end her mandate early, stipulating the full five years be served.

Constitution and government. Kosovo's constitution identifies the country as a secular state adhering to the principles of religious freedom and freedom of expression except as limited by law "to prevent encouragement or provocation of violence and hostility on grounds of race, nationality, ethnicity, or religion." Apart from a similar limitation, freedom of the media is guaranteed and censorship prohibited. Freedom of association is also protected unless a court determines that an organization or activity threatens constitutional order; violates human rights; or encourages ethnic, national, racial, or religious hatred.

Until the constitution entered into effect on June 15, 2008, Kosovo was administered by UNMIK and "provisional institutions of self-government," which had been established by UNMIK in accordance with a May 15, 2001, Constitutional Framework for Provisional Self-Government. Under the framework, the authority of the presidency to manage foreign relations was limited by a need to set policy "in coordination with" the special representative of the UN secretary general (SRSG). Under the constitution, the president, who is indirectly elected by the national legislature for a five-year term, "represents the unity of the people," represents the country internally and externally, and guarantees the "constitutional functioning" of the republic's institutions. He serves as command in chief of the Kosovo Security Force and, in consultation with the prime minister, may declare a state of emergency. Election of the president requires a two-thirds majority in the assembly, but if no candidate achieves that goal on the first two ballots, the two front-runners proceed to a third ballot in which a simple majority prevails. The 120-member, unicameral Assembly of Kosovo has retained its preexisting structure, which includes 20 seats reserved for ethnic minorities, including 10 Serbs. The assembly sits for a four-year term, subject to early dissolution. The government is headed by a prime minister who commands a majority in the assembly. The cabinet must include minority representation.

The judiciary includes a Supreme Court, district courts, and municipal courts. An independent Constitutional Court serves as "final interpreter" of the constitution. Administratively, Kosovo encompasses 7 districts (*distrikt, rreth*), subdivided into 35 municipalities (*komuna, opština*).

With regard to Kosovo the 2006 Serbian constitution affirms the "equality of all citizens and ethnic communities in Serbia" and adds that Kosovo and Metohija is "an integral part of the territory of Serbia," albeit with "substantial autonomy." On May 11, 2008, Serbia conducted national and municipal elections, including in the mainly northern, Serb-dominated areas of Kosovo. Although UNMIK branded the municipal elections as illegal, on June 28, the anniversary of the 1389 battle of Kosovo Polje, the Serb representatives from 26 municipalities convened in Mitrovica as a 45-member Assembly of the Community of the Municipalities of the Autonomous Province of Kosovo and Metohija, which designated Radovan NIČIĆ as its president (see the 2012 *Handbook* for details).

In 2012 Freedom House described the press in Kosovo as only "partially free" because of financial and political pressures and the inability of a "weak judiciary" to protect press freedoms.

Foreign relations. As of July 1, 2013, Kosovo had been recognized by 103 countries plus Taiwan, an increase of 12 in the preceding 12 months. Twenty-two of the EU's 27 members had granted Kosovo recognition, a notable exception being Spain, which, in view of the decades-old separatist movement in the Basque region, expressed concern that Kosovo's unilateral separation from Serbia would be viewed as a precedent. Of the 15 former Soviet republics, only Estonia, Latvia, and Lithuania have granted recognition. Non-European states doing so included Australia, Canada, Japan, Saudi Arabia, and the United States.

The Kosovar government had indicated at independence that it would quickly seek membership in the UN, but admission requires approval by at least two-thirds (128) of the members—a level unlikely to be achieved in the immediate future. Moreover, Russia, which is not only Serbia's principal European ally but also a target of violent separatist movements in Chechnya and elsewhere in the Caucasus region, refused recognition and stated that, as a permanent member of the Security Council, it would veto Kosovo's membership in the UN unless and until the dispute with Serbia is resolved. China, another country with veto power, also declined to recognize Kosovo. On June 29, 2009, however, Kosovo was formally admitted to the International Monetary Fund and the World Bank Group.

Since December 2006 Kosovo has been a member of the Central European Free Trade Association (CEFTA). The CEFTA agreement had been signed by UNMIK on behalf of Kosovo. Kosovo formally applied to join NATO's Partnership for Peace program on July 11, 2012.

Current issues. The July 2010 ICJ advisory opinion on Kosovo's unilateral declaration of independence had no immediate impact on the Serbia-Kosovo dispute. Serbia, backed by Russia in particular, continued to argue that the unilateral action raised issues of sovereignty and territorial integrity. Serbia's ardent nationalists remained adamant that Kosovo constituted an integral part of their homeland, but other voices focused on two principal issues: negotiating the future status of ethnic Serb areas and restoring the rights of displaced and exiled Serbs. For their part, ardent Kosovo nationalists were not prepared to yield to any arrangement that would diminish Kosovo's territory or grant ethnic Serb communities autonomy.

The UNHCR has reported that between 2000 and 2007 over 17,800 ethnic Serbs and other minorities returned from internal displacement in Kosovo or from exile, but that number pales beside the estimated 210,000 Serbs who had fled the 1999 conflict and its aftermath. Furthermore, in 2008 the UNHCR assisted only about 500 additional refugees in returning, and that number dropped to 220 in 2009. Speaking before the UN Security Council in June 2009, the foreign minister of Serbia, Vuk Jeremić, asserted that a principal reason that many ethnic Serbs were not exercising their right to return was the failure of the Kosovo Property Agency to resolve more than 40,000 claims submitted by ethnic Serbs for illegally seized property. Kosovo's foreign minister, Skender HYSENI, in addition to disputing the UNHCR figures, categorized Jeremić's assertion as "science fiction."

UNMIK, now headed by SRSG Lamberto Zannier, an Italian, continues to maintain a presence in Kosovo, although the nature of the mission has shifted. The EU's economic development "pillar" concluded on June 30, 2008, and was replaced by a civilian crisis management mission, the EU Rule of Law Mission in Kosovo (EULEX), now led by Xavier Bout de Marnhac of France. The focus of the new mission is providing assistance in establishing police, justice, and customs services. The original OSCE assignment, the Democratization and Institution Building Pillar, remains in place under the direction of Austrian diplomat Werner Almhofer. As of November 2012, 5,565 troops from 30 countries remained in Kosovo as part of the KFOR/NATO contingent, led by Gen. Volker Halbauer of Germany.

On February 26, 2009, the ICTY, in its first judgment related to the 1999 Kosovo conflict, convicted five former Yugoslav and Serbian officials of crimes against humanity but acquitted Milan Milutinović, a former Serbian president. Sentences ranged from 15 to 22 years in prison. Other Serbs have been convicted by Serbia's war crimes court, which is also hearing cases in which former KLA members have been accused of victimizing ethnic Serbs. In Kosovo itself, in October 2009 a court panel comprising one Kosovar and two EULEX judges convicted three former KLA members of torture and other criminal offenses committed against ethnic Albanian detainees during 1998–1999. The most prominent defendant, Rrustem MUSTAFA (aka Commander Remi), a PDK representative in the Assembly of Kosovo, received a four-year prison sentence, pending appeal. A 2003 conviction had been overturned by the Supreme Court in 2005.

Meeting in Sarajevo, Bosnia and Herzegovina, on June 2, 2010, representatives of the EU and seven western Balkan states, including both Serbia and Kosovo, conferred on matters related to possible future EU accession. The conference marked the first time since Kosovo's independence declaration that high-ranking Serbian and Kosovar officials sat at the same table. Five months earlier, Kosovo had expelled Goran BOGDANOVIČ, the Serbian minister for Kosovo and Metohija, for being about to engage in "political activities."

Violent clashes in June 2011 between border police and Serbian protestors underscored one of the key problems facing the government in Prishtina. Parallel administrative structures remain in the majority-Serbian region of Mitrovica, working in concert with the Serbian government. Efforts by the government in Prishtina to establish oversight over these structures, as in June, September, October, and November 2011 when it sought to gain control over two border posts, have provoked open resistance. Serbian distrust was underscored by a referendum held in Mitrovica on February 14 and 15, 2012, in which 99.7 percent of those voting rejected the institutions of the Republic of Kosovo.

The issue of corruption was highlighted by a series of indictments by European Union prosecutors. In June 2012 Deputy Prime Minister Bujar BUKOSHI and ten officials from the Ministry of Health were indicted on corruption charges; in August 2012 the head of the anticorruption task force, Special Prosecutor Nazmi MUSTAFI, was indicted along with eight judges. Dino ASANAJ, the head of Kosovo's Agency of Privatization, died in June 2012 in what was officially ruled a suicide, after coming under investigation that he had used his office to solicit bribes.

On April 19, 2013, the governments of Kosovo and Serbia reached a power-sharing agreement regarding Mitrovica. Serb municipalities in the region would adhere to Kosovo's laws, courts, and police systems, and parallel administrative structures funded by Serbia would be dismantled. Serb communities, in return, would gain autonomy over education, cultural life, and health care.

POLITICAL PARTIES

Prior to the declaration of independence from Serbia, ethnic Albanian parties in Kosovo uniformly refused to participate in national elections, and most ethnic Serb parties in Kosovo boycotted Kosovar elections. The parliamentary and local elections held in November 2007 were contested by 25 parties, 2 coalitions, and 36 "citizens' initiatives," including an assortment of Serb parties and initiatives vying for reserved minority seats. With a 5 percent threshold established for proportional representation in the assembly, many of the smaller national parties sought alliances with the principal formations, all of which are on the center-right or right of the political spectrum. In the municipal elections held in November–December 2009, 37 parties, 19 electoral associations, 2 coalitions, and 16 independent candidates ran. The December 2010 elections were contested by 28 parties and citizens' initiatives and 1 coalition.

Government Parties:

Democratic Party of Kosovo (*Partia Demokratike e Kosovës*—PDK). More radical than the moderate Democratic League of Kosovo (LDK, below), the PDK was established as the Party of Democratic Progress in Kosovo (*Partia e Progresit Demokratik të Kosovës*—PPDK) in September–October 1999 by Hashim Thaçi, leader of the Kosovo Liberation Army—KLA (*Ushtria Çlirimtare e Kosovës*—UÇK). The KLA's increasing importance to a Kosovo settlement had been recognized by its participation in the 1999 Rambouillet peace talks, although Adem DEMAÇI, its political spokesperson, argued against attendance and resigned from the KLA leadership. In March a Serbian judge issued an arrest warrant for KLA chief Thaçi, who had been tried in absentia and sentenced to ten years in prison for his activities. Shortly thereafter, the KLA named Thaçi as prime minister of a proposed provisional Kosovar government.

At a PPDK congress in May 2000 the party changed its name to the PDK. In November 2001 it won 26 assembly seats, with Bajram Rexhepi becoming prime minister of Kosovo in March 2002. Following the October 2004 assembly election, in which it again finished second, with 30 seats, the PDK chose to remain outside the governing coalition.

In the November 2007 assembly election the PDK list won 34.3 percent of the vote and thus a plurality of 37 seats. Having recognized that they could not meet the 5 percent threshold for assembly seats, several small parties had signed coalition agreements with the PDK. As a result, Edita TAHIRI, leader of the **Democratic Alternative of Kosovo** (*Aleancë Demokratike të Kosovës*—ADK), and Emrush XHEMAJLI of the **People's Movement of Kosovo** (*Lëvizja Popullore e Kosovës*—LPK) were awarded assembly seats from the PDK list. Tahiri became minister of public administration in a March 2010 cabinet shuffle. Other agreements had been signed with the **Liberal Party of Kosovo** (*Partia Liberale e Kosovës*—PLK), led by Gjergj DEDAJ, who was named a deputy minister in the Thaçi government, and the **Social Democratic Party of Kosovo** (*Partisë Social-Demokratike të Kosovës*—PSDK), then led by Kaqusha JASHARI. In April 2008 the PSDK named former prime minister Agim Çeku as party chair, a post to which he was formally elected in June.

In the December 2010 assembly election the PDK won 32.1 percent of the vote and a plurality of 34 seats. On December 15, a media scandal erupted when a draft report to the Council of Europe was released, alleging that Thaçi had been involved in the smuggling of weapons, drugs, and human organs in 2001. Although the final draft of the report did not accuse Thaçi, but rather a group of close associates, it triggered a storm of domestic controversy and significant negative international attention for the prime minister and for the PDK.

Leaders: Hashim THAÇI (Prime Minister and Chair of the Party), Hajredin KUÇI (Deputy Prime Minister and Vice Chair of the Party), Fatmir LIMAJ (Vice Chair of the Party), Bajram REXHEPI (Minister of Interior Affairs and Vice Chair of the Party), Ramë BUJA (Assembly Leader), Jakup KRASNIQI (Speaker of the Assembly and Secretary General of the Party).

New Kosovo Coalition (*Koalicioni për Kosovë të Re*—KKR). For the December 2010 elections, the New Kosovo Alliance formed an electoral coalition with six smaller parties. These included the **Justice Party** (*Partia e Drejtësisë*), **Social Democratic Party** (*Partia Social Demokrate*), **Pensioners and Disabled Party** (*Partia e Pensionistëve Invalidore*), **Pensioners Party of Kosovo** (*Partia e Pensionistëve të Kosovës*), **Albanian National Democratic Party** (*Partia Nacional Demokratike Shqiptare*), and the **Green Party of Kosovo** (*Partia e të Gjelbërve të Kosovës*). The coalition won eight seats and 7.3 percent of the vote, with all eight seats subsequently going to the AKR.

New Kosovo Alliance (*Aleanca Kosova e Re*—AKR). The AKR was formed in March 2006 by wealthy and controversial businessman Behxhet Pacolli, reputedly Kosovo's richest politician. The conservative party favors laissez-faire capitalism, a secular state, lower taxes, individual freedom and responsibility, and adoption of a presidential system. It won 12.3 percent of the assembly vote and was awarded 13 seats in 2007, for third place.

Leaders: Behxhet PACOLLI (Chair), Ibrahim GASHI, Ibrahim MAKOLLI (Secretary General and Assembly Leader), Mimoza KUSARI-LILA (Vice Chair and Deputy Prime Minister).

Independent Liberal Party (*Samostalna Liberalna Stranka*—SLS). The ethnic Serb SLS was organized in August–September 2006 in Mitrovica under the leadership of Slobodan Petrović. The SLS cast itself as multiethnic in orientation and announced its preference for Kosovo's remaining part of Serbia, but it did not take a hard line on the issue.

In the November 2007 assembly election the SLS won three of the ten seats reserved for Serbs. The party went on to form a floor group in cooperation with other minority parties. It became the sole Serb party to join the government. In the December 2010 elections, the SLS won 2.1 percent of the popular vote and eight seats (including six of those allocated to the Serbian minority).

In May 2013 the board of the SLS reportedly expelled Nenad RAŠIĆ, the minister of labor, over allegations that Rašić had interfered with the party's parliamentary group.

Leaders: Slobodan PETROVIĆ (President), Bojan STOJANOVIĆ (Mayor of Gračanica).

Kosovo Democratic Turkish Party (*Kosova Demokratik Türk Partisi*—KDTP). The KDTP was established in 1990 to represent the ethnic Turkish population. In November 2007 it won three Kosovo Assembly seats, as it had in the previous two elections, and joined the Thaçi government. In July 2010 Mahir Yağcılar was reelected for another two-year term as party chair. In the December 2010 election, the KDTP won 1.2 percent of the popular vote and three seats (including both seats allocated to the Turkish minority).

Leader: Mahir YAĞCILAR (Chair).

Vakat Coalition (*Koalicija "Vakat"*). Vakat was established in June 2004 by three parties: the **Democratic Party of Bosniacs** (*Demokratska Stranka Bošnjaka*—DSB/*Partia Demokratike e Boshnjakëve*), the **Democratic Party Vatan** (*Demokratska Stranka Vatan*—DSV/*Partia Demokratike Vatan*), and the **Bosniac Party of Kosovo** (*Bošnjačka Stranka Kosova*—BSK/*Partia Boshnjake e Kosovës*). The DSB was registered in 2001. Both the DSV and the BSK began as local branches of the Party of Democratic Action (below) and became parties earlier in 2004. In the October Kosovo Assembly election Vakat won three seats. In the 2007 election Vakat again won 3 seats. In the 2010 election, Vakat won 0.8 percent of the popular vote and two seats (including one minority seat).

Leaders: Xhezair MURATI (DSB), Sadik IDRIZI (DSV), Husnija BESKOVIĆ (BSK), Rasim Demiri (Assembly Leader of the 6+ Group).

Serb Democratic Party of Kosovo and Metohija (*Srpska Demokratska Stranka Kosova i Metohije*—SDSKiM). The SDSKiM was organized in June 2005 on the basis of the Citizens' Initiative of Serbia (*Gradjanska Inicijativa Srbija*—GIS). Despite the objections of the Serbian government, the GIS had contested the Serbian set-aside seats in the 2004 Kosovo Assembly election, winning two of them.

In January 2005 party founder Slaviša Petković accepted the post of minister for returns and communities in the Kosovo Council of Ministers. He resigned in November 2006 and was replaced by the SDSKiM's Branislav Grbić, who in July 2007 announced formation of a new ethnic Serbian party, the New Democracy (below). In the November election the SDSKiM won three seats. In the December 2010 election the SDSKiM won one of the Serb-reserved seats.

Leaders: Slaviša PETKOVIĆ, Vladimir TODOROVIĆ.

Ibrahim Rugova List (*Lista Ibrahim Rugova*—LIR). Founded as an independent candidate list in October 2010 by Ukë Rugvoa, son of Ibrahim RUGVOA, and a dissident faction of the LDK. The LIR formed a preelection coalition agreement with the AAK (winning one seat in the November 2010 parliamentary election) but subsequently joined the government.

Leaders: Ukë RUGVOA, Bujar BUKOSHI (Deputy Prime Minister).

In addition, the **Citizens' Initiative of Gora** (*Gradjanska Inicijativa Gore*—GIG), representing the Gorani community and led by Murselj HALILI, claimed the Gorani-reserved seat in the 2010 elections and joined the government coalition. So did the **Ashkali Party for Integration** (*Partia Ashkalinjëve për Integrim*—PAI), winning one minority seat.

Opposition Parties:

Democratic League of Kosovo (*Lidhja Demokratike e Kosovës*—LDK). Founded in 1989 to advocate the creation of an independent, demilitarized republic, it won an overwhelming preponderance of seats in a "constituent republican assembly" for the province in 1992, after which the LDK leader, Ibrahim Rugova, was proclaimed president of a self-declared "Republic of Kosovo." The group boycotted all Yugoslavian and Serbian elections before independence.

Rugova, who consistently advocated nonviolence and a negotiated settlement of the Kosovo issue with Belgrade, was reelected president, with over 90 percent of the vote, in the "Republic" elections of March 1998. Collaterally, the LDK again won most of the seats in the shadow legislature. In the November 2001 election and again in October 2004 the LDK won a leading 47 seats in the Kosovo Assembly, which retained Rugova as president until his death on January 21, 2006. Assembly Speaker Nexhat Daci served as acting president until Fatmir Sejdiu was elected president by the assembly on February 10.

The fallout from Rugova's death led to divisions within the party and the removal of Speaker Nexhat Daci and Deputy Prime Minister Adem Salihaj from leadership posts in early 2006. Daci and Salihaj went on to form the Democratic League of Dardania (LDD, below).

In the November 2007 assembly election the LDK finished second, with 22.6 percent of the vote and 25 seats, a net loss of 22 from its previous total. Two parties in coalition with the LDK were the Christian Democratic Party for Integration (PDKI), a 2007 splinter from the PShDK (below) led by Zef MORINA, and the New Party of Kosovo (*Partisë së Re të Kosovës*—PReK), led by Bujar Bukoshi. Morina and Bukoshi, both of whom received assembly seats, subsequently joined the LDK. In June 2009 the PDKI and the PShDK agreed to reunite.

It took three ballots for the assembly to reelect President Sejdiu in January 2008. On the first two ballots, when he received 62 and 61 votes, respectively, he fell well short of the required two-thirds majority, but on the third, with only a simple majority required, he won with 68.

In February 2010 the Reformist Party ORA (*Partia Reformiste ORA*) merged with the LDK. ORA (Hour or Time) had been established in 2004 by media entrepreneur Veton SURROI. It contested the October 2004 Kosovo Assembly election as the Citizens' List "ORA" (*Lista Qytetarë "ORA"*), winning 6 percent of the vote and seven seats, and was organized as a party in December. In 2007 it won only 4.1 percent of the vote, insufficient for seats, which prompted Surroi to resign the party leadership. In March 2008 Vice Chair Teuta SAHATQIJA was elected as his successor.

Also during 2010, the LDK attracted a number of defectors from the LDD (below), which the LDK has approached about a possible merger.

On November 7 a party congress replaced most of the party leadership, including Fatmir Sejdiu, whose resignation as president of the country had helped break apart the ruling coalition and trigger new elections.

In the December 2010 assembly elections, the LDK took 24.7 percent of the popular vote and 27 seats, emerging as the leading opposition party.

Leaders: Isa MUSTAFA (Chair), Sabri HAMITI (Vice Chair), Lutfi HAZIRI, Ismet BEQIRI (Secretary General).

Movement for Self-Determination (*Lëvizja Vetëvendosje—Vetëvendosje*). *Vetëvendosje* is a nationalist group with antecedents to 2007 but registered as a party by Albin KURTI in 2010. Kurti, a self-described nonviolent activist, had campaigned for Kosovar independence from Serbia but also opposed UNMIK's period of supervision. Following a demonstration in February 2007 that resulted in the deaths of two participants, he was charged with several criminal offenses, including interference with police authorities. Amnesty International and other human rights groups argued that the charges were politically motivated. His 2010 trial was repeatedly postponed because neither he nor his attorney agreed to appear, and his sentencing in June was moot since an earlier detention had exceeded the nine-month sentence he received following conviction on one count.

In the December 2010 elections *Vetëvendosje* took 12.7 percent of the popular vote, winning 14 seats in parliament and emerging as the third most powerful party in the country, eclipsing the AAK.

In March 2011 *Vetëvendosje* absorbed the **New Spirit Party** (*Partia Fryma e Ren*—FER). Founded in October 2010, the FER failed to pass the 5 percent threshold to reach representation in parliament. In June 2011 the combined movement's first general council meeting formally affirmed Kurti as leader.

On January 14, 2012, *Vetëvendosje* organized protests at two border crossings with Serbia, in response to what the party called agreements that "force Kosovo to kneel before Serbia." In resulting clashes with Kosovo police, 47 were reportedly injured and 146 arrested.

Leaders: Albin KURTI (Leader), Shpend AHMETI (First Deputy Leader and Former FER Leader).

Alliance for the Future of Kosovo (*Aleanca për Ardhmërinë e Kosovës*—AAK). The AAK was launched in May 2000 by Ramush Haradinaj, a former KLA commander, as a political alliance that incorporated a number of smaller Kosovar parties, including the Parliamentary Party of Kosovo (*Partyja Parliamentary e Kosovës*—PPK). A conservative party that placed itself ideologically in "the modern European center," the PPK was a principal rival of Ibrahim Rugova's LDK in the early 1990s.

In November 2001 the AAK won eight assembly seats; in 2004 it won nine. Party Chair Haradinaj headed the coalition government formed in December 2004 but resigned in March 2005 to face war crimes charges before the ICTY. He was succeeded by the AAK's Bajram Kosumi, who previously had been a leader of the PPK and the United Democratic Movement (*Lëvizja Bashimit Demokratike*—LBD). Kosumi resigned as prime minister on March 1, 2006.

In the November 2007 assembly election the AAK won ten seats. Its candidate for president, Naim Maloku, finished second in the January 9, 2008, election.

On April 3, 2008, the ICTY acquitted Haradinaj of war crimes.

In the December 2010 elections the AAK took 9.6 percent of the popular vote and twelve seats in parliament, in coalition with the LIR (which received one of the twelve seats).

In 2010 the ICTY ordered a retrial of Haradinaj, but on November 29, 2012, he was again acquitted.

Leaders: Ramush HARADINAJ (Chair), Blerim SHALA (Vice Chair), Ardian GJINI (Assembly Leader), Burim RAMADANI (Secretary General).

New Democratic Initiative of Kosovo (*Iniciativa e Re Demokratike e Kosovës*—IRDK). In the 2004 Kosovo Assembly election the IRDK contested the seats set aside for the Roma, Ashkali, and Egyptian communities. It won two seats. In 2007 it won one and chose to sit with the AAK assembly group; in 2010 it again won one seat and again sat with the AAK group.

Leader: Xhevdet NEZIRAJ (Member of the Assembly).

Other Assembly Parties:

Several minority parties gained representation in parliament but did not formally chose to sit with the government or the opposition, forming the parliamentary group "NG." These included the **United Serbian List** (*Jedinstvena Srpska Lista*—JSL), the **Democratic Ashkali Party of Kosovo** (*Partia Demokratike e Ashkanlive të Kosovës*—PDAK), the **New Democratic Party** (*Nova Demokratska* Stranak—NDS), and the **Bosniak Party of Democratic Action of Kosovo** (*Bošnjačka Stranka Demokratske Akcije Kosova*—BSDAK).

Other Parties Contesting the 2010 Assembly Elections:

Democratic League of Dardania (*Lidhja Demokratike e Dardanisë*—LDD). The center-right LDD, whose name incorporates a historical name for Kosovo, was formed in January 2007 by former assembly speaker Nexhat Daci and other dissidents from the LDK. At its formation the LDD held 7 seats in the assembly. In the November 2007 election the coalition of the LDD and the Albanian Christian Democratic Party of Kosovo (below) won 11 seats.

A May 2010 convention saw Daci instigate a number of leadership changes amid a spate of defections to the LDK.

Leaders: Nexhat DACI (Chair); Besa GAXHERRI, Lulzim ZENELI, Fadil GECI, Drita MALIQI (Vice Chairs); Sejdë TOLAJ (Secretary).

Party of Democratic Action (*Stranka Demokratske Akcije*—SDA/ *Partia e Aksionit Demokratik*). Established in 1990 as a branch of the Yugoslavian SDA, the Kosovo SDA primarily represents the Bosniac community, as do its current counterparts in Bosnia and Herzegovina, Montenegro, and the Sandžak and Preševo regions of Serbia. In the October 2004 Kosovo Assembly election the SDA Kosovo won one seat.

In April 2007 SDA chair Numan Balić, despite his support for independence, opposed the plan put forward by Martii Ahtisaari because, he asserted that it did not adequately address the needs of non-Serb minorities in Kosovo. In the November assembly election he claimed one of the party's two seats.

Leaders: Numan BALIĆ (Chair), Vezira EMRUŠ.

Other eligible parties that failed to win seats in the 2010 assembly election were the **Kosovo Turkish Union** (*Kosova Türk Birliği*—KTB), League of Egyptians of Kosovo (*Lidhja e Egjiptianêve të Kosovës*—LEK), the **Serbian Social Democratic Party** (*Srpska Socijal Demokratska Stranka*—SSDS), the **Serb People's Party** (*Srpska Narodna Stranka*—SNS), the **Montenegrin Democratic Party** (*Crnogorska Demokratska Stranka*—CDS), the **Social Democratic Party of Gora** (*Socialdemokratska Stranka Gora*—SSG), the **Serb Kosovo-Metohija Party** (*Srpska Kosovska-Metohijska Stranka*—SKMS), the **Union of Independent Social Democrats of Kosovo and Metohija** (*Savez Nezavisnih Socijaldemorkata Kosova i Metohije*—SNSKiM), and the **Civic Initiative National Wing** (*Gradjanska Inicijativa Krilo Naroda*—GIKN).

Other Parties:

Albanian Christian Democratic Party of Kosovo (*Partia Shqiptare Demokristiane e Kosovës*—PShDK). Dating from 1990, the PShDK mainly represents Catholic ethnic Albanians in Kosovo but includes some Muslims in its ranks.

After the 2004 Kosovo Assembly election the PShDK was awarded two seats. Shortly thereafter, a major rift resulted in a disputed February 2005 party convention at which a majority faction replaced leader Mark Krasniqi with Tadej RODIQI. The Krasniqi wing subsequently held its own convention. The party remained split thereafter, with the anti-Krasniqi wing ultimately forming the **Christian Democratic Party for Integration** (*Partia Demokristiane për Integrim*—PDKI).

With the November 2007 election approaching, the PShDK announced that it would compete nationally in coalition with the LDD despite a previous association with the LDK. The alliance won 11 seats. After the election, longtime leader Krasniqi, 87, was succeeded by Ton Marku, who was then replaced by Nikë Gjeloshi in 2009, then Ukë Berisha in 2012.

On June 11, 2009, the PShDK and the PDKI signed an agreement on reuniting, with a new leadership and party name to be determined at a future unification congress, but objections on the part of some PShDK leaders delayed implementation.

Leaders: Ukë BERISHA (Chair).

Serb List for Kosovo and Metohija (*Srpska Lista za Kosovo i Metohiju*—SLKM). With the October 2004 Kosovo Assembly election approaching, Oliver Ivanović led formation of the SLKM, which included his own Return Coalition (*Koalicija Povratak*—KP) as well as the national Democratic Party and Serbian Renewal Movement. The Return Coalition had been organized by a group of national Serbian parties prior to the 2001 Kosovo Assembly election on a platform that called for an end to Serbian emigration from Kosovo, the return of those Serbs displaced during the Kosovo conflict, an accounting of those missing, a return of Serbian property, and measures to ensure Serb safety and freedom of movement. The only Serb political group to participate in the November election, it finished third, winning 22 seats.

Because of the low turnout of Serb voters (most Serb parties boycotted the election), the SLKM won only 0.2 percent of the October 2004 vote, but that was sufficient to claim eight of the ten seats reserved for Serbians. At the urging of Serbia's government, the SLKM did not contest the November 2007 elections. Ivanović currently serves as the state secretary of Kosovo and Metohija in Serbia's government.

Leader: Oliver IVANOVIĆ (Chair).

Other eligible parties that participated in the 2007 assembly election were the ethnic Serb **New Democracy** (*Nova Demokratija*—ND), which won one seat; as well as several parties that failed to gain representation, including the **Albanian Republican Party** (*Partia Republikane Shqiptare*—PRS); the **Kosovo Ecological Party** (*Partia Ekologjike e Kosovës*—PEK); the **Justice Party** (*Partia e Drejtësisë*—PD), led by Sylejman ÇERKEZI; the **National Front** (*Balli Kombëtare*—BK); and the **National Movement for the Liberation of Kosovo** (*Lëvizja Kombëtare për Çlirimin e Kosovës*—LKÇK).

LEGISLATURE

The **Assembly of Kosovo** (*Kuvendit të Kosovës/Skupštine Kosova*) comprises 120 representatives, 100 of whom are directly elected on a proportional basis from among those parties winning at least 5 percent of the vote. Ten minority seats are reserved for Serbs; 4 for Ashkali, Roma, and Egyptians; 3 for Bosniacs; 2 for Turks; and 1 for Gorani. All members serve four-year terms.

In the election of December 12, 2010, the Democratic Party of Kosovo won 34 seats; the Democratic League of Kosovo, 27; *Vetëvendosje*, 14; the Alliance for the Future of Kosovo, 11; the New Kosovo Coalition, 8; the Independent Liberal Party, 8 (including 6 seats reserved for Serbians); the Turkish Democratic Party of Kosovo, 1 (plus both seats reserved for Turks); the United Serbian List, 4 (including 3 seats reserved for Serbians; the Vakat Coalition, 2 [including 1 seat reserved for other minorities]); and the Ibrahim Rugova List, 1. The Serb Democratic Party of Kosovo and Metohija won the 1 remaining seat reserved for Serbs. Seven parties split the 7 remaining seats reserved for other minorities, each taking 1: the Democratic Ashkali Party of Kosovo, the New Democratic Party, the Bosniak Party of Democratic Action of Kosovo, the New Democratic Initiative of Kosovo, the Ashkali Party for Integration, the Civic Initiative of Gora, and the United Roma Party of Kosovo.

President: Jakup KRASNIQI.

CABINET

[as of November 15, 2013]

Prime Minister	Hashim Thaçi (PDK)
Deputy Prime Ministers	Behgjet Pacolli (AKR)
	Edita Tahiri (PDK) [f]
	Hajredin Kuçi (PDK)
	Slobodan Petrovic (SLS)
	Bujar Bukoshi (LIR)
	Mimoza Kusari-Lila (AKR) [f]
Ministers	
Agriculture	Blerand Stavileci (PDK)
Culture, Youth, and Sport	Memli Krasniqi (PDK)
Community and Return	Radojica Tomić (SLS)
Education, Science, and Technology	Rame Buja (PDK)
Environment and Spatial Planning	Dardan Gashi (LIR)

Finance	Bedri Hamza (PDK)
Foreign Affairs	Enver Hoxhaj (PDK)
Health	Ferid Agani (PD)
Infrastructure	Fehmi Mujota (PDK)
Integration (EU and NATO)	Vlora Çitaku (PDK) [f]
Interior Affairs	Bajram Rexhepi (PDK)
Justice	Hajredin Kuçi (PDK)
Labor and Social Welfare	Nenad Rašić (ind.)
Local Government	Slobodan Petrovic (SLS)
Public Administration	Mahir Yagcilar (KDTP)
Security Force	Agim Çeku (PSD)
Trade and Industry	Mimoza Kusari-Lila (AKR) [f]

[f] = female

INTERGOVERNMENTAL REPRESENTATION

As of July 1, 2013, the Republic of Kosovo had been recognized by 103 countries plus the Republic of China, or Taiwan. It had not yet applied for UN membership.

Ambassador to the U.S.: Akan ISMAILI.

U.S. Ambassador to Kosovo: Tracey Ann JACOBSON.

KUWAIT

State of Kuwait
Dawlat al-Kuwayt

Political Status: Constitutional hereditary emirate; independent since June 19, 1961, save for occupation by Iraq from August 2, 1990, to February 26, 1991; draft constitution approved by the sovereign on November 1, 1962, and entered into force January 29, 1963.

Area: 6,880 sq. mi. (17,818 sq. km).

Population: 2,213,403 (2005C), including 880,774 Kuwaitis and 1,332,629 non-Kuwaitis (the 2005 figures are not adjusted for underenumeration); the government announced in 2012 that preliminary results from a census conducted in 2011 indicated that total population had reached approximately 3.6 million (35 percent Kuwaitis).

Major Urban Centers (2005E): KUWAIT CITY (32,000), Salmiya (145,000), Hawalli (107,000).

Official Language: Arabic.

Monetary Unit: Dinar (official rate November 1, 2013: 0.28 dinar = $1US).

Sovereign (Emir): Sheikh Sabah al-Ahmad al-Jabir al-SABAH; inaugurated on January 29, 2006, after unanimous confirmation the same day by the National Assembly, following the abdication on January 24 of Sheikh Saad al-Abdallah al-Salim al-SABAH, who was in ill health. Sheikh Saad had become emir on January 15 upon the death of Sheikh Jabir al-Ahmad al-Jabir al-SABAH.

Heir Apparent: Sheikh Nawaf Ahmad al-Jabir al-SABAH; appointed crown prince by his brother, the emir, on February 7, 2006.

Prime Minister: Sheikh Jabir Mubarak al-Hamad al SABAH; appointed by the emir on November 30, 2011, and inaugurated on December 4 to succeed Sheikh Nasir Muhammad al-Ahmad al-SABAH, who had resigned; reappointed following the legislative elections of February 2, 2012; reappointed on July 5, 2012, following annulment of the February elections by the Constitutional Court; reappointed on December 5, 2012, following legislative elections on December 1; reappointed on July 29, 2013, following legislative elections on July 27.

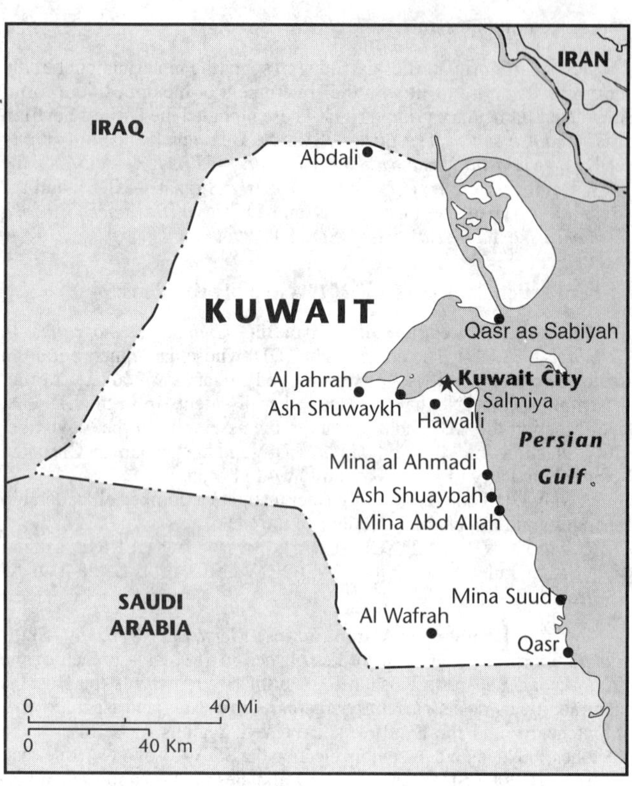

THE COUNTRY

Located near the head of the Persian Gulf, Kuwait is bordered on the north and west by Iraq and on the south by Saudi Arabia. An extremely arid country, Kuwait suffered from an acute shortage of potable water until the 1950s, when the installation of a number of desalination plants alleviated the problem.

About 95 percent of native Kuwaitis, who constitute approximately one-third percent of the country's population, are Muslims; an estimated 70 percent belong to the Sunni sect and the remainder are Shiites. The noncitizen population, upon which the sheikhdom has long depended for a labor pool—about 84 percent of the employed labor force is non-Kuwaiti—is composed chiefly of non-Kuwaiti Arabs, Indians, Pakistanis, and Iranians. Some 50 percent of employed native Kuwaitis work in the public sector. Women make up 22 percent of the employed non-Kuwaiti workforce, compared to 45 percent for their Kuwaiti counterparts, who are concentrated in health care and education. In 2005 women were granted the right to vote and to hold elected office, and in 2009 the first four Kuwaiti women were elected to the National Assembly. There are two women in the current assembly as well as two in the cabinet.

The oil sector was nationalized in 1975, permitting Kuwait to become a highly developed welfare state, providing its citizens with medical, educational, and other services without personal income taxes or related excises. In 2010 Kuwait's petroleum reserves were estimated at 101.5 billion barrels, about 8 percent of proven global reserves. Oil accounts for more than 90 percent of government revenue.

The systematic destruction of the emirate's oil facilities by retreating Iraqi forces in early 1991 precluded a return to preinvasion production until 1993, and the economy continued to suffer lingering effects from the Gulf war for several more years before higher oil prices pushed annual per capita income to approximately $23,000 in the late 1990s. GDP growth averaged about 5.2 percent in 2006–2008, but the global financial crisis resulted in a contraction of more than 7 percent in 2009, owing in large part to a decline in oil prices and a rise in defaults on the part of several of Kuwait's investment companies.

Growth recovered to 2.4 percent in 2010 and 8.3 percent in 2011 in the wake of improvement in the oil sector (expanded production and higher prices), greater government expenditure (including an emiri grant of $3,600 to each citizen), and a supportive fiscal stance on the government's part toward the financial institutions. While commending Kuwait's progress, the International Monetary Fund (IMF) urged further reforms, including programs to better prepare Kuwaitis for private sector jobs and the introduction of a value-added tax and a comprehensive income tax system. The IMF in 2012 also called for invigoration of the state's privatization program, part of a $105 billion, five-year economic development program approved in 2010 but partially stalled by the country's political upheaval. Meanwhile, domestic reformers continued to press for further democratization and strong measures to combat widespread corruption among government officials. GDP grew by more than 6 percent in 2012, but a slowdown was expected for 2013.

GOVERNMENT AND POLITICS

Political background. Kuwait's accession to complete independence in 1961 was preceded by a period of close association with Great Britain that began in the late 19th century when the then semiautonomous Ottoman province sought British protection against foreign invasion and an extension of Turkish control. By treaty in 1899, Kuwait ceded its external sovereignty to Britain in exchange for financial subsidies and defense support, and in 1914 Britain recognized Kuwait as a self-governing state under its protection. Special treaty relations continued until the sheikhdom was made fully independent by agreement with the reigning ruler, Sheikh Abdallah al-Salim al-SABAH on June 19, 1961, at which time Sheikh Abdallah adopted the title of emir. Iraqi claims to Kuwaiti territory were rebuffed shortly afterward by the dispatch of British troops at Kuwait's request and were subsequently reduced to a border dispute. Kuwait and Saudi Arabia shared control of a 2,500-square-mile Neutral Zone until the area was formally partitioned in 1969, with revenues from valuable petroleum deposits in the zone being divided equally by the two states.

On August 29, 1976, the government of Sheikh Jabir al-Ahmad al-SABAH resigned in the wake of alleged "unjust attacks and denunciations against ministers" by members of the National Assembly. Emir Sheikh Sabah al-Salim al-SABAH, who had succeeded Emir Abdallah in 1965, thereupon dissolved the assembly, suspended a constitutional provision that would have required a new election within two months, and instituted severe limitations on freedom of the press. Some observers also attributed the unprecedented measures to the impact of the Lebanese civil war upon Kuwait, which then counted some 270,000 Palestinians among its nonnative population. On September 6 Sheikh Jabir formed a new government that was virtually identical in membership to the old.

Following the death of Sheikh Sabah, Sheikh Jabir became emir on December 31, 1977, and in February 1978 the heir apparent, Sheikh Saad al-Abdallah al-Salim al-SABAH, was named prime minister. There was little political change during the remainder of the decade, despite growing dissatisfaction among some groups, most noticeably Shiite Muslims following the commencement of the Iranian revolution in early 1979.

In the wake of a return to earlier constitutional practices, a nonparty poll for a new National Assembly was held in February 1981. Prime Minister Saad was reappointed following the election, as he was again in March 1985, after a legislative election in February. However, the emir dissolved the assembly in July 1986 in the wake of a series of confrontations between elected and ex officio government members over fiscal and internal security issues. Echoing the events of 1976, the emir postponed new elections and implemented strict press controls.

In 1989 a group of ex-parliamentarians, led by former speaker Ahmad Abd al-Aziz al-SAADOUN, launched a petition drive to revive the 1962 constitution and restore the National Assembly, reportedly gathering over 30,000 signatures by December. The government's response was that it was pursuing a "new form of popular participation" centered on a National Council of 50 elected and 25 appointed members to serve as a surrogate for the former legislature for four years. The opposition nonetheless continued to insist on revival of the earlier body and mounted a largely successful boycott of the National Council election in June, in which all of the contested seats were won by government supporters.

The Iraqi invasion on August 2, 1990 (see Foreign relations, below), resulted in the flight of virtually all members of the country's ruling elite. Upon their return in March 1991 they were confronted by massive physical destruction and widespread demands for meaningful representative government. Opposition leaders vehemently denounced the composition of a new government formed in April as little more than an extension of its predecessor, in which all major posts were held by members of the royal family. The emir, Sheikh Jabir, responded with a promise that elections to a new National Assembly would be held in 1992, and in July the interim National Council was reconvened with orders to discuss and organize the elections. Meanwhile, the regime was buffeted by foreign and domestic criticism of its postwar policies, including the perfunctory trials of alleged Iraqi collaborators and the expulsion of tens of thousands of non-Kuwaiti citizens. Subsequently, the government commuted the death sentences of convicted collaborators, promised defendants the right to a fair trial, and created criminal appeals courts.

In the October 1992 National Assembly election those considered opponents of the government captured a majority of the seats. Sheikh Saad submitted a pro forma postelection resignation but was reappointed by the emir despite objections by the opposition. In a significant concession to the opposition, however, six members of the assembly were named to the new cabinet.

In addition to intensifying Kuwait's "siege mentality," an October 1994 border confrontation with Iraq exacerbated the sheikhdom's budget difficulties, and in 1995 the government announced plans to impose new fees on many public services in an effort to control the deficit. On the political front, attention focused on the conflict between the National Assembly and the government over whether the assembly had the right to review decrees issued during its 1986–1992 hiatus. Legislators also pressed for the prosecution of former officials, most of whom are members of the royal family, on corruption charges. In part, the schism reflected the influence of Islamic fundamentalists within the assembly, 39 of whose 50 elected deputies in 1994 endorsed an effort, subsequently rejected by the government, to make Islamic religious law (sharia) the sole source of Kuwaiti law. Following the assembly election in October 1996, it was reported that 17–22 "solidly progovernment" candidates had won seats with the remainder including an estimated 14–18 representatives from the generally antigovernment Islamist camp.

A substantially reshuffled cabinet was announced in March 1998, but friction continued between the government and the assembly. Consequently, the emir ordered new elections for July 3 (15 months early). Government supporters lost ground to both liberals and Islamists, but the ruling family remained in control of the major ministries in the new cabinet announced on July 11, to the continued disgruntlement of reformers.

Following a reported debate within the ruling family over the makeup of the next government, the new cabinet announced in February 2001 included eight new members and, significantly, oil and finance ministers who were not members of the ruling family. Although aging Prime Minister Saad remained the titular head of government, many of his responsibilities were turned over to the deputy prime minister, Sheikh Sabah al-Ahmad al-Jabir al-SABAH, the brother of the emir.

The assembly elections on July 5, 2003, gave a preponderance of seats to Islamist and progovernment candidates, at the expense of pro-Western liberals. Immediately afterward, Sheikh Sabah was appointed prime minister, replacing the ailing Sheikh Saad (who continued to serve as crown prince and thereby heir apparent to the emirship). On May 16, 2005, belying its predominantly conservative composition, the assembly granted women the right to vote and to stand for elective office, although Islamists succeeded in adding a provision that "females abide by Islamic law." In June, over the objections of Islamist and other conservative lawmakers, Masuma al-MUBARAK was sworn in as the country's first female cabinet minister. Also in 2005, a group of Sunni Muslims formed what they described as Kuwait's first political party, the *Ummah* (Nation) Party, even though formal political parties remained officially illegal (see Political Groups, below).

Upon the death of 79-year-old Sheikh Jabir on January 15, 2006, cabinet ministers immediately proclaimed the crown prince, Sheikh Saad, 75, as the new emir despite his debilitating illnesses. On January 23 the cabinet asked the National Assembly to hold a special session to discuss whether Sheikh Saad was fit to rule—the constitution permitted the transfer of power for health reasons if two-thirds of lawmakers approved—and the following day a letter of abdication from Sheikh Saad was delivered to the legislators. On January 29 the assembly voted unanimously in favor of Prime Minister Sabah, 76, who took the oath of office as emir the same day. The leadership crisis had not only underscored a longtime rivalry between Sheikh Saad and Sheikh Sabah, but also had publicly pitted the two branches of the ruling family, the Jabirs and the Salims, against each other and, ultimately, had upset the tradition of alternating leadership between the two royal branches. On February 7 the emir appointed 65-year-old Sheik Nasir Muhammad al-Ahmad al-SABAH (his nephew) as prime minister and 68-year-old

Sheik Nawaf Ahmad al-Jabir al-SABAH (the emir's brother) as crown prince and heir apparent. The prime minister and the new government were sworn in on February 20. (Sheikh Saad died in 2008.)

In May 2006, 29 opposition members walked out of the assembly when the government rejected their demand that they be allowed to question the prime minister about the government's version of a controversial proposal to reduce the number of electoral districts. Consequently, on May 21 the emir dissolved the National Assembly and called an election for June 29, a year ahead of schedule. Liberal reformists, campaigning on an anticorruption platform, and Islamists reportedly won a total of 33 seats, with the support of many women's groups participating for the first time in elections. On July 17 the new assembly approved the redrawing of 25 electoral districts to create 5 larger ones, making it more difficult for vote-buying to influence elections, according to observers.

Disputes between the government and the assembly prompted cabinet resignations in March 2007 and March 2008, the latter leading to dissolution of the assembly. Islamists were credited with a plurality of 21 seats in early legislative elections on May 17, 2008, with liberals reportedly securing 7 seats. The cabinet resigned in November to prevent lawmakers from questioning the prime minister about his alleged mismanagement of the government and his decision to allow a controversial Iranian Shiite Muslim cleric to enter Kuwait despite a legal ban.

Further accusations against the prime minister led the government to resign on March 16, 2009, again derailing legislators' efforts to question the prime minister, primarily about the government's response to the international financial crisis and what the Islamists alleged was misuse of public funds. Parliamentary debate stalled a proposed stimulus package, which had the backing of the cabinet and the ruling family. Consequently, the emir dissolved the assembly on March 18, thereby paving the way for the $5.2 billion stimulus to be enacted by decree.

The second parliamentary elections within a year were held on May 16, 2009, with Sunni Islamists reportedly declining to 11 seats while liberals, Shiites, and Bedouin independents made noteworthy gains. Although the government appeared to retain majority support, observers noted that Islamist oppositionists were still able to form a significant conservative parliamentary bloc in alliance with tribal members. Sheikh Nasir was designated prime minister for the sixth time on May 20, and on May 29 he named a reshuffled cabinet in which members of the royal family continued to hold the key posts.

Demonstrators were beaten by police and forced to disperse in December 2010 as they joined a protest orchestrated by opposition members of the assembly calling for greater political freedom. Tensions heightened in March 2011 when some 1,000 antigovernment protesters marched outside the main government building in the capital, a demonstration likely spurred by similar, albeit much larger, protests in the region during what was referred to as the Arab Spring.

The entire cabinet resigned on March 31, 2011, this time to avoid assembly demands to question several ministers about their performance. Prime Minister Nasir was reappointed on April 5, and he named a reshuffled government on May 8.

In late September 2011, thousands of antigovernment protesters, including liberals and conservatives, demonstrated in the capital, demanding the resignation of the prime minister and the cabinet as well as the dissolution of the assembly. News reports said that 20 members of parliament, including two who often sided with the government, joined the protests. Several strikes by public employees subsequently compounded difficulties for the government, and tensions boiled over in early November when a group of protesters briefly stormed the assembly, resulting in some 24 arrests. Although the emir ordered the imposition of stricter security measures in the interest of stability, he appeared to bow to public sentiment by accepting the resignation of Prime Minister Nasir on November 28. Sheikh Jabir Mubarak al-Hamad al-SABAH, hitherto a deputy prime minister and minister of defense, took office as prime minister on December 4, but two days later, the emir dissolved the assembly and ordered new elections. A caretaker cabinet was appointed on December 14.

Opposition candidates secured a majority in the early assembly poll on February 2, 2012, and several members of the opposition were reportedly named to the new cabinet inaugurated on February 14 under the continued leadership of Sheikh Jabir. However, discord continued amid corruption allegations against cabinet members as well as opposition parliamentarians. Following the resignation of several ministers, the Constitutional Court on June 20 ruled that the December 2011 decrees dissolving the assembly and ordering new elections were legally flawed and ordered the reinstatement of the legislature elected in 2009. Prime Minister Jabir was reappointed in early July as head of a reshuffled cabinet.

In the wake of continuing public protests, the emir dissolved the assembly on October 7, 2012, and ordered new elections for December 1. Turnout was low because of a boycott by the opposition, which strongly objected to the emir's recent decree changing how voting was to be conducted (see Legislature, below). Although the Constitutional Court in June 2013 rejected the opposition's effort to have the electoral revision overturned, it nevertheless annulled the December 2012 elections because of technical reasons, and new elections were held on July 27. Sheikh Jabir formed a new government on August 4.

Constitution and government. The constitution promulgated in 1962 vests executive power in an emir selected from the Mubarak line of the ruling Sabah family, whose dynasty dates from 1756. The emir rules through an appointed prime minister and Council of Ministers, while legislative authority is shared by the emir and a National Assembly that is subject to dissolution by decree. The judicial system, since its revision in 1959, is based on the Egyptian model and includes a Constitutional Court, courts of the first degree (criminal assize, magistrates,' civil, domestic, and commercial courts), and a Misdemeanors Court of Appeal. The domestic court, which deals with cases involving such personal matters as divorce and inheritance, is divided into separate chambers for members of the Sunni and Shiite sects, with a third chamber for non-Muslims. Civil appeal is to a High Court of Appeal and, in limited cases, to a Court of Cassation. (In May 2012 the emir vetoed a bill passed by the assembly that would have made sharia [Islamic religious law] the "only source" of legislation rather than "a main source" [its current status].)

Although the 1962 constitution theoretically accorded equal rights to men and women, an election law adopted at the same time precluded women from voting or holding elected office. After decades of controversy over the elimination of those proscriptions, the assembly amended the country's election law in 2005, granting women the right to vote in and contest parliamentary and local elections.

Although the Kuwaiti press is generally considered quite free (by standards in the Middle East), self-censorship remains common, and journalists and publications continue to be fined for criticizing members of the royal family and key members of the government. A 2006 law prohibits the jailing of journalists unless they criticize the emir, threaten to overthrow the government, or commit religious offenses. Since 2011 a number of journalists and online activists have been sentenced for offending the emir, although the emir issued a blanket pardon for them in August 2013.

Foreign relations. As a member of the Arab League, Kuwait has closely identified itself with Arab causes and through such agencies as the Kuwait Fund for Arab Economic Development and the Organization of Arab Petroleum Exporting Countries has contributed to the economic development of other Arab countries. In 1967 it launched a program of direct aid to countries experiencing hardship as a result of conflict with Israel. In 1981 Kuwait joined five other regional states in forming the Gulf Cooperation Council (GCC).

Dominating external concerns in the 1980s was the Iran-Iraq war, which curtailed oil exports and generated fear of Iranian expansionism. After a number of attacks on shipping by both participants and a decision by Washington to increase its naval presence in the Gulf, Kuwait, which had previously declined an offer of American tanker escort, proposed in April 1987 that a number of its vessels be transferred to U.S. registry. The reflagging provided enhanced security for oil shipments but was interpreted as solidifying the sheikhdom's pro-Iraqi posture. Diplomatic relations between Kuwait and Iran were eventually restored in November 1988, three months after the Iran-Iraq cease-fire.

Despite Kuwait's support of Iraq during the latter's conflict with Iran, the emirate had long experienced periodic strain with Baghdad. For many decades Iraq had laid intermittent claim to all of Kuwait on the basis of Kuwait's status within the Ottoman province of Basra at the turn of the century. However, the merits of such a case were substantially weakened by an Iraqi agreement in 1963 to respect the independence and sovereignty of its southern neighbor. Unresolved by the 1963 accord was the question of boundary demarcation, in regard to which earlier diplomatic references had been quite vague. Nor was the land boundary the only problem: Iraq had also claimed offshore territory, including, most importantly, Bubiyan Island, which dominated access to the Iraqi port and naval base of Umm Qasr via the Khor Abdallah waterway. The boundary uncertainties also contributed to claims that Kuwait was encroaching on Iraqi oil fields, allegedly by slant drilling, while Baghdad had long complained of the failure of the

Gulf emirates, including Kuwait, to hold to OPEC-mandated oil production quotas.

Iraqi forces invaded Kuwait in early August 1990 and quickly seized control of the entire country, which was formally annexed as Iraq's "19th province." After negotiations failed to yield an Iraqi withdrawal, the UN Security Council in late November authorized the use of "all means necessary" to liberate Kuwait. The U.S.-led operation Desert Storm was launched in mid-January 1991, and the allied ground offensive pushed Iraqi troops out of Kuwait by the end of February.

In June 1991 the Kuwaiti government withdrew its diplomats from Algeria, Jordan, Mauritania, Sudan, Tunisia, and Yemen, saying that it was "reducing" relations with the six countries because of their lack of support during the Gulf crisis. Meanwhile, a ten-year military cooperation agreement authorized the United States to stockpile military equipment and provided its navy with port access; however, the accord did not sanction the permanent stationing of troops.

In February 1992 a UN border commission issued a draft document on delineation of the Kuwait-Iraq border, which included the division of Umm Qasr. Observers described the commission's recommendations as an attempt to punish Iraq for its invasion. On November 23 the UN commission revised the border even further north, giving Kuwait complete control of the naval base as well as additional oil fields in the area, effective January 15, 1993. However, Iraq strongly objected to the decision and sent troops into the disputed territory in early January (ostensibly to retrieve weapons), with friction over the issue contributing to a brief resumption of allied air attacks on Iraqi military targets. Subsequently, Kuwait sought and received Western assurance that the 2,000 American troops still in the emirate would be quickly reinforced if Baghdad maintained a confrontational posture.

In April 1993 George H. W. Bush received an enthusiastic reception on his arrival for a three-day visit to the emirate. Subsequently, there were reports of an Iraqi plot to assassinate the former U.S. president while he was in Kuwait, with 14 people charged in the matter being placed on trial in early June. As the result of what U.S. President Bill Clinton termed "compelling evidence" of Iraqi involvement in such a plot, the United States launched a missile attack against Baghdad in June. (Subsequent reports suggested that the evidence in question was seriously flawed, although a number of Iraqis were among those ultimately convicted in the case.)

In November 1993 Kuwait signed a ten-year defense cooperation agreement with Russia, similar to post–Gulf war pacts with Britain, France, and the United States. A trade and investment agreement with Russia in November 1994 was considered, in part, an outgrowth of Kuwait's announcement several months earlier that it intended to buy some $800 million in Russian armaments.

The specter of another Iraqi incursion was raised in early October 1994 when Iraqi troops were once again deployed near the Kuwaiti border. However, Baghdad retreated quickly from its threatening stance in the face of Western military preparations. Concurrently, Iraq formally recognized Kuwait's sovereignty, including acceptance of the UN's recent demarcation of the border between the two countries. The Kuwaiti government called the recognition "a step in the right direction," although tension remained high, with Kuwait charging that more than 600 of its nationals were still being held as "hostages" in Iraqi jails. Meanwhile, Kuwait agreed to the permanent stationing on its territory of a squadron of U.S. warplanes.

Kuwait remained uncompromising in its anti-Iraq stance in 1997, even though Gulf neighbors Qatar and the United Arab Emirates were promoting the "rehabilitation" within the Arab world of the regime in Baghdad. Consequently, in early 1998 Kuwait was the only Arab state to unequivocally endorse U.S. plans to take military action against Baghdad in the wake of the recent breakdown of UN inspections in Iraq. Additional U.S. troops and warplanes were granted staging rights in Kuwait, with an attack being unleashed on Iraq in December.

The UN Security Council agreed in 2000 that Kuwait ultimately should be awarded $15.9 billion in reparations for the 1990–1991 incursion and occupation. At the Arab League summit in March 2002 Iraq again reportedly agreed to honor Kuwait's independence and territorial integrity, but tensions continued to escalate between Kuwait and Iraq until U.S. forces toppled Saddam Hussein in April 2003. Kuwait backed the creation of a new Iraqi government in 2005.

Relations with Iran deteriorated in 2010 when Kuwaiti officials said they had uncovered an Iranian espionage ring in Kuwait that was allegedly spying on American forces. With regional security issues in mind, Kuwait in late 2011 agreed to a larger U.S. military presence (some 13,500 troops) on its soil as U.S. combat forces withdrew from Iraq. In addition, Kuwait in early 2012 joined Saudi Arabia and the United Arab Emirates in agreeing to increase oil production should Asian countries face shortages from curtailed deliveries resulting from sanctions against Iran. Kuwait also agreed at midyear to purchase an estimated $4.2 billion in U.S.-manufactured missile defense systems.

In July 2013 Kuwait pledged $4 billion in aid to assist the interim government in Egypt following the military's ouster of Egyptian president Morsi.

Current issues. For most of the last decade the principal conflict in domestic politics has been tension between the royal family, which holds virtually all the key ministerial portfolios, and the opposition in the National Assembly, which has repeatedly demanded that the prime minister or other cabinet members submit to questioning. The government has typically responded by resigning, giving the emir the option of installing a reshuffled Council of Ministers, or calling an assembly election. Ministers regularly criticize the assembly—arguably the most powerful legislature in the Gulf region—for its "disabling" interference in government. The opposition, in turn, has argued that the government needs to be more responsive to the wishes of the electorate, a position that has not found many allies within the royal family.

Emboldened by their success in the February 2012 assembly poll, opposition legislators authorized special assembly panels to pursue corruption allegations against cabinet members. Although the government initially pledged to cooperate in such investigations, relations between the government and the legislative opposition remained tumultuous. After the cabinet was buffeted by several resignations, the emir suspended the assembly on June 18 to preclude further questioning of government officials. Ironically, the emir reportedly welcomed the Constitutional Court's ruling two days later (see Political background, above, for details) even though it was based on the premise that the emir's December 2011 decrees had been technically invalid. Some 30,000 protesters subsequently demonstrated in the capital against the annulment of the February elections. In addition to calling for fresh elections soon, the protesters also demanded eventual establishment of a constitutional monarchy under which the ruling family would relinquish significant authority (including appointment of the prime minister and cabinet) to the legislature.

In September 2012 the Constitutional Court overturned new legislation proposed by the government that would have redrawn the boundaries of electoral districts to the perceived disadvantage of the opposition. Shortly thereafter, the emir decreed that henceforth voters would be limited to one vote in assembly balloting (as opposed to the four-vote system used previously). The opposition groups strongly objected to the decree, describing it as designed to stifle their ability to form effective electoral coalitions. Mass protest rallies were subsequently dispersed by forces, and the government prohibited unauthorized gatherings of more than 20 people, prompting critics to warn of a potential "dictatorship."

The opposition presented a united front in boycotting the December 2012 assembly elections to protest the new "one man, one vote" decree, although it was noted that the government's critics had less in common in other policy matters. (The boycotters included Sunni Islamists, youth activists connected via social media, liberals pushing for greater political freedom, and conservative tribal groups concerned primarily with retaining their influence.) Despite what was widely perceived as a heavy-handed approach by the government in dealing with ongoing protests and online criticism, some opposition formations and several main tribal groups elected to participate in the July 2013 assembly poll (the sixth election since 2006). As a result, the new assembly appeared more balanced than the legislatures elected in February 2012 (dominated by the opposition) and December 2012 (heavily progovernment). Prime Minister Jabir called for the opening of a "new page" in relations between the government and the assembly, while emphasizing efforts to implement the many aspects of the 2010 economic development program that had been delayed as a result of the recent political turmoil. Skeptics noted, however, that members of the royal family still held all the major portfolios in the cabinet named in August, and the polarization seemed likely to continue.

POLITICAL GROUPS

Although political parties are not legal in Kuwait, a number of political "groupings," many of them loosely organized, have been permitted to function in public without restriction. The government in mid-2004 indicated that political parties were likely to fully develop at some point, but no specific encouragement has been forthcoming. In addition to the groups discussed below, Kuwait's Bedouin tribes have significant political clout and typically put forward their own candidates, often chosen in unofficial "primaries."

In September 2012 a number of political organizations, labor unions, and youth groups announced the formation of a new opposition umbrella called the **National Front for the Protection of the Constitution**. Founders reportedly included the so-called Majority Bloc of some 34 opposition legislators who had been elected in the February 2012 elections, which were annulled in June. Components of the new front reportedly included members of the PAB, KDF, and ICM. Ahmad al-DYAIN was selected as general coordinator of the front, Dr. Mishari al-MUTAIRI as secretary, and Khalid al-FADHALAH as spokesperson. The front called for new legislative elections, legalization of political parties, and establishment of a full parliamentary system with an independent judiciary.

Islamic Constitutional Movement—ICM (*al-Haraka al-Dusturiya al-Islamiya*—Hadas). A moderate Sunni Muslim organization with ties to the Muslim Brotherhood in other Arab states, such as Egypt and Jordan, the ICM has called for the "adjustment" of all Kuwaiti legislation so as not to "conflict" with sharia (Islamic religious law), while also promoting economic reform. In conjunction with the KDF (below), the ICM led the prodemocracy movement that developed in Kuwait following the expulsion of Iraqi troops in early 1991, with a call for new assembly elections and formation of a more representative cabinet. ICM leaders subsequently stressed that they sought "small steps, not jumps" in liberalization and did not question the authority of the royal family.

The ICM increased its representation from two seats to six in the June 2006 National Assembly election, a change attributed to the group's increased support among women. ICM spokesperson Muhammad Abdullah Hadi al-Olaim was named to the cabinet in the March 2007 reshuffle. The group lost three seats in the 2008 legislative elections, but al-Olaim retained his key cabinet posts in oil, electricity, and water. Al-Olaim was subsequently replaced when the ICM chose not to remain in the government.

The emir's March 2009 decision to dissolve the National Assembly and call an early election was largely prompted by the insistence of several ICM representatives that they be permitted to question the prime minister. The ICM was credited with securing only one seat in the May legislative balloting.

The ICM has supported women's rights as well as Islamization of laws by constitutional means and has called for improved housing, education, and health services. After helping the opposition to make dramatic gains in the February 2012 balloting, the ICM boycotted the December 2012 and July 2013 elections to protest recent electoral law revision. It also strongly opposed the Kuwaiti government's support for the military ouster of Egyptian president Morsi in mid-2013.

Leaders: Muhammad Abdullah Hadi al-OLAIM, Badr al-NASHI (Former Secretary General), Osama al-SHAHEEN (Media Director), Jamaan al-HARBASH (Deputy Secretary General), Nasir al-SANI (Secretary General).

National Democratic Forum (NDF). Led by former assembly member Abdullah al-Naibari, the NDF is considered the backbone of Kuwait's liberals, who have most recently run for the National Assembly as part of a **National Democratic Alliance** (NDA). The secular and progressive NDA (considered close to the country's business class) has been described as a subgroup of the NDF, but it also serves as an umbrella for several other similarly oriented groups, including the KDF (below) and the **National Democratic Movement** (NDM). One of the leading NDA vote-getters in 2009 was Aseel al-AWADHI, one of the first women elected to the assembly.

In 2011 NDF leader Abdullah al-Naibari, a former member of parliament, called for the prime minister to resign and to be replaced with someone from outside the royal family. After boycotting the December 2012 assembly poll, the NDA agreed to participate in the June 2013 balloting, although an NDF faction may have disputed that decision.

Leaders: Abdullah al-NAIBARI, Muhammad al-ABDULJADER (leader of the NDA), Saleh al-MULLA.

Kuwait Democratic Forum—KDF (*al-Minbar al-Dimuqrati al-Kuwayti*). The secularist, center-left KDF was initially described as the best organized of Kuwait's political groupings, with a membership based primarily in urban areas. "Veteran leftist" Ahmad al-KHATIB and other KDF leaders were instrumental in the growth of the prodemocracy movement following the Gulf crisis. Elected to the assembly in 1992, they aligned with Islamic representatives in a campaign to make the royal family "more accountable." The KDF lost its parliamentary representation in the 2003 assembly election. It has recently channeled much of its electoral activity through the NDA (see NDF, above).

Leader: Ahmad al-DYAIN (Secretary General).

Islamic Salafi Alliance—ISA (*al-Tajammu al-Islami al-Salafi*). Descended from the Salafi Movement of Kuwait (*al-Harakat al-Salafiyya al-Kuwait*), the ISA (primarily comprising Wahhabi Sunnis) advocates social reform and a return to "true Islam." The hard-line group conducted a public campaign in 2005 in an effort to thwart the government's extension of voting rights to women. The ISA, which apparently has at least three factions, was credited with securing ten seats in the 2006 assembly balloting but only two in 2009. The ISA fully supported the boycott of the December 2012 assembly elections but was split regarding participation in the June 2013 poll.

Leaders: Khalid al-ISSA, Fuhayd al-HAYLAM, Abdulrahman al-MUTAWA (Secretary General).

National Islamic Alliance (NIA). A leading representative of Kuwaiti Shiites, the NIA is generally described as having close ties to Iran and Hezbollah, although it routinely denies such links. The NIA reportedly derived from the Cultural Social Society (*Jamiyat al-Thaqafah al-Ijtimayah*), established by forces loyal to the Iranian revolution of 1979. Shiite pressure on the Kuwaiti government has been described as less severe than on other neighboring regimes (such as the one in Bahrain), in part because some Shiite leaders in Kuwait participate in the political process while others remain wealthy supporters of the ruling family.

Following episodes of vandalism against Sunni bookstores in January 2008, the NIA publicly condemned the attacks and urged Shiites and Sunnis to present a united front against attempts to stir up sectarian violence. The group was credited with securing one seat in the 2009 election and has participated in all subsequent elections, generally being considered progovernment.

Leaders: Abdul ABDULSAMAD, Hassan JAWHAR, Sheikh Hussain al-MATOUQ (Secretary General).

Justice and Peace Alliance (JPA). A Shiite grouping, the JPA backed several candidates in the 2008, 2009, 2012, and 2013 National Assembly elections.

Leaders: Saleh ASHOUR, Hassan NASEER.

Popular Action Bloc (PAB). Also referenced as the Popular Bloc, this grouping emerged in the early 2000s as a faction of deputies in the National Assembly led by a veteran opposition member, Ahmad al-Saadoun. Later, the PAB, described as populist, centrist, and nationalist in orientation, also functioned as an informal grouping of assembly candidates.

In the May 2008 legislative election the PAB, claimed four seats, and in 2009 it was credited with three. PAB assembly members subsequently remained in the forefront of efforts to question the prime minister and other members of the cabinet in open session. Al-Saadoun was elected speaker of the assembly following the February 2012 elections but lost that position as the result of the subsequent reinstallation of the 2009 legislature. Calling for constitutional change to permit the assembly to appoint the cabinet, the PAB supported the boycotts of the December 2012 and June 2013 assembly elections.

Leaders: Ahmad al-SAADOUN, Musallam al-BARRAK, Khalid al-TAHOUS, Marzouk al-HIBINEI.

***Ummah* Party** (*Hizb al-Ummah*). Formed in January 2005 by former Salafists "to promote pluralism and a multiparty system of government," the *Ummah* (Nation) Party has been described as Kuwait's first true political party. Given that Kuwaiti laws do not provide for political parties, the founders of the group were immediately called in for questioning by police "for violating the public gatherings law." All were acquitted of the violations in May, although party official Hakim al-Mutairi was fined for circulating publications without proper authorization. Three party members said they would run in the 2006 assembly elections, though party leaders ultimately called for a boycott because of potential fraud. In May 2006 the party announced its backing of full political rights for women, becoming the first Sunni Muslim group to do so. The party also called for the removal of all foreign troops from Iraq. A proposal for a draft law permitting the establishment of political parties in Kuwait received the backing of party leaders in July 2007. The party participated in the 2008 parliamentary elections but did not win any seats.

Ummah boycotted the 2009 parliamentary elections, citing lack of progress in political reforms. The group was subsequently described as focusing more on social and governmental issues than on electoral politics per se.

In February 2011, during the time of regional antigovernment uprisings dubbed the Arab Spring, members of *Ummah* demonstrated in Kuwait in solidarity with protesters in Egypt. Reaffirming its call for installation of a full, genuine parliamentary system, *Ummah* boycotted the December 2012 and June 2013 assembly elections.

Leaders: Sajed al-ABDELI, Abdullah al-BARGASH, Awwad al-DHAFIRI, Hakim al-MUTAIRI (Secretary General).

LEGISLATURE

A **National Assembly** (*Majlis al-Ummah*) was organized in 1963 to share legislative authority with the emir, although it was dissolved by decree of the emir from August 1976 to February 1981 and from July 1986 to October 1992. Under the 1962 constitution, the assembly encompasses 50 representatives elected for four-year terms, in addition to ministers who, if not elected members, serve ex officio. (Ministers exercise the same voting rights as elected members.) Since 2005 women have been allowed to participate as candidates and voters in assembly elections. Under a new election law adopted in 2006, 10 representatives are chosen from each of 5 constituencies (previously there had been 2 representatives from each of 25 constituencies). Previously, each voter cast four votes, electing the top ten vote getters in each constituency. However, a controversial emiri decree in October 2012 limited each voter to one vote.

In the wake of continued tension between the assembly and the Council of Ministers, the emir dissolved the assembly on December 6, 2011 and ordered early elections, which were held on February 2, 2012, opposition candidates reportedly retaining a majority. However, the Constitutional Court ruled on June 20 that the December 2011 dissolution decree was invalid. Consequently, the assembly elected in 2009 was reinstated pending new elections, which were held on December 1, 2012, with progovernment candidates winning nearly all the seats in the face of an opposition boycott. However, that balloting was also annulled by the Constitutional Court for technical reasons in June 2013, prompting new elections on July 27, in which some opposition groups agreed to participate. Initial reports indicated that progovernment candidates maintained a slight majority, with tribal candidates securing 24 seats; Shiite candidates, 8; moderate Sunni Islamists, 7; liberals, 3; and others, 8.

Speaker: Marzuq al-GHANIM.

CABINET

[as of September 1, 2013]

Prime Minister	Sheikh Jabir Mubarak al-Hamad al-Sabah
Deputy Prime Ministers	Sheikh Muhammad Khalid al-Hamad al-Sabah
	Lt. Gen. Sheikh Khalid al-Jarrah al-Sabah
	Sheikh Salim Abdulaziz al-Saud al-Sabah
	Mustafa Jasim al-Shamali
Ministers	
Awqaf and Islamic Affairs	Sharida Abdulla Almusharji
Commerce and Industry	Anas Khalid al-Salih
Communications	Issa Ahmad al-Kandari
Defense	Lt. Gen. Sheikh Khalid al-Jarrah al-Sabah
Education	Nayif Falah al-Hajraf
Electricity and Water	Abdulaziz Abdullatif al-Ibrahim
Finance	Sheikh Salim Abdulaziz al-Saud al-Sabah
Foreign Affairs	Sheikh Sabah Khalid al-Hamad al-Sabah
Health	Sheikh Muhammad Abdallah al-Mubarak al-Sabah
Higher Education	Nayif Falah al-Hajraf
Information	Sheikh Salman Sabah Salim al-Hmud al-Sabah
Interior	Sheikh Muhammad Khalid al-Hamad al-Sabah
Justice	Sharida Abdulla Almusharji
Oil	Mustafa Jasim al-Shamali
Public Works	Abdulaziz Abdullatif al-Ibrahim
Social Affairs and Labor	Thikra Ayid al-Rashidi [f]
Ministers of State	
Cabinet Affairs	Sheikh Muhammad Abdallah al-Mubarak al-Sabah
Housing and Municipal Affairs	Salim Muthiba Ahmad al-Uthaynah
National Assembly Affairs	Rula Abdallah Dashti [f]
Planning and Development Affairs	Rula Abdallah Dashti [f]
Youth Affairs	Sheikh Salman Sabah Salim al-Hmud al-Sabah

[f] = female

INTERGOVERNMENTAL REPRESENTATION

Ambassador to the U.S.: Sheikh Salem Abdullah al-Jabir al-SABAH.

U.S. Ambassador to Kuwait: Matthew H. TUELLER.

Permanent Representative to the UN: Mansour Ayyad ALOTAIBI.

IGO Memberships (Non-UN): AfDB, GCC, NAM, OIC, OPEC, WTO.

KYRGYZSTAN

Kyrgyz Republic
Kyrgyz Respublikasy (Kyrgyz)
Respublika Kirgizstan (Russian)

Political Status: Designated autonomous republic of the Russian Soviet Federative Socialist Republic on February 1, 1926; became constituent republic of the Union of Soviet Socialist Republics (USSR) on December 5, 1936; Republic of Kyrgyzstan proclaimed December 13, 1990; independence from the USSR declared by the Kyrgyz Supreme Soviet August 31, 1991; current constitution approved by referendum on June 27, 2010.

Area: 76,640 sq. mi. (198,500 sq. km).

Population: 5,497,403 (2012E—UN); 5,667,822 (2012E—U.S. Census).

Major Urban Center (2009C): BISHKEK (formerly Frunze, 835,300), Osh (258,100).

Official Languages: Kyrgyz, Russian. Kyrgyz is the "state language."

Monetary Unit: Som (market rate November 1, 2013: 48.50 soms = $1US).

President: Almazbek ATAMBAYEV (independent); inaugurated on December 1, 2011, for a six-year term, to succeed Roza OTUNBAYEVA (Social Democratic Party of Kyrgyzstan); following elections on October 30, 2011.

Prime Minister: Zhantoro SATYBALDIEV; confirmed by the legislature on September 5, 2012, succeeding Omurbeck BABANOV (*Republika*) who resigned from office on September 1, 2012.

THE COUNTRY

A mountainous country in eastern Central Asia, Kyrgyzstan is bounded on the northwest by Kazakhstan, on the east by China, on the south by Tajikistan, and on the southwest by Uzbekistan. Approximately

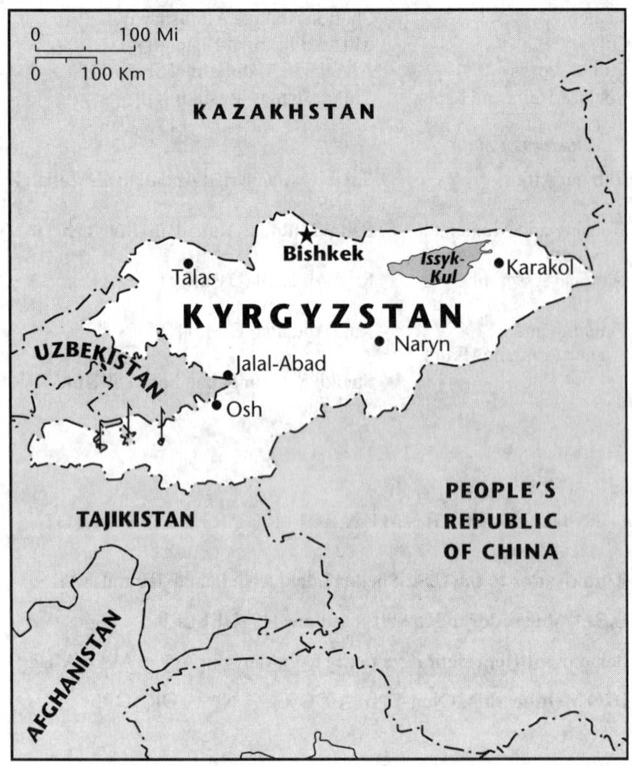

71 percent of the population is Turkic-speaking Kyrgyz, 14 percent Uzbek, and 8 percent Russian, with substantially smaller minorities of other ethnic groups; the dominant religion is Sunni Islam. Women make up about 42 percent of the labor force and 23.3 percent of parliament.

The agricultural sector, which accounts for about 29 percent of GDP and 46 percent of the employed workforce, is now dominated by wheat production. Production of sugar beets, potatoes, and vegetables has also expanded since independence, while livestock and wool output have dropped significantly. Industry contributes about 20 percent of GDP and employs 14 percent of active workers. In 1997 production began at the Kumtor gold mine, which ranks among the ten largest in the world. Other extractable resources include natural gas, petroleum, coal, lead, tungsten, mercury, and uranium. Manufacturing focuses on food processing, metallurgy, clothing and other textiles, and machine building. In addition to gold, leading exports include textiles, metals, mineral products, food products, and machinery. Hydroelectricity is sold primarily to neighboring Kazakhstan and Uzbekistan.

Kyrgyzstan experienced major economic disruptions upon the breakup of the Soviet Union in 1991 (please see the 2012 *Handbook*). Beginning in 1995, however, overall economic growth resumed, and by 1998 the government had privatized the majority of state enterprises, restructured the financial industry, and introduced a liberal trade and capital exchange regime.

Led by a recovery in gold production, GDP expanded by 8.5 percent in 2007 and 7.6 percent in 2008. At the same time, however, soaring prices for imported commodities fueled inflation that reached 25 percent in 2008. The international financial crisis and recession that began in 2009 compounded Kyrgyzstan's economic difficulty by reducing both trade and remittances from workers abroad. Simultaneously, difficulties in the energy and power sector, including a water shortage, coupled with political turmoil and ethnic clashes in 2010, led to a contraction in GDP of 0.5 percent. The economy rebounded by 5.7 percent in 2011 primary fueled by government spending but recessed by approximately –0.9% in 2012 largely based on decreased output and political issues relating to the Kumtor Mine—Kyrgyzstan's largest gold-processing facility. GDP growth in 2013 is estimated at 5.5 percent. GDP per capita was $1,158 in 2012, and the unemployment rate was 7.74 percent.

GOVERNMENT AND POLITICS

Political background. Conquered by Russia between 1855 and 1876, the territory then called Kyrgyzia mounted an unsuccessful revolt against Bolshevik rule before being incorporated into the Russian Soviet Federative Socialist Republic as an autonomous *oblast* (region) in 1924. It was designated an autonomous republic in 1926 and a constituent republic of the Soviet Union in 1936.

As Soviet discipline began to weaken in the late 1980s, Kyrgyzstan became the scene of Central Asia's worst pre-independence ethnic violence, with at least 300 people killed in Kyrgyz-Uzbek clashes in mid-1990. The "Soviet Socialist" component of the republic's name was formally abandoned in December 1990. Independence from the Soviet Union was declared on August 31, 1991, by the Kyrgyz Supreme Soviet, following the failed coup against Soviet president Mikhail Gorbachev in Moscow and a collateral attempt by Soviet authorities to remove the Kyrgyz executive president, Askar AKAYEV.

In October 1990 the Supreme Soviet had elected Akayev from a field of six candidates to the newly created post of president, and a year later he was popularly elected to a five-year presidential term with Feliks KULOV as his running mate. In November 1991 former vice president Nasirdin ISANOV and the current head of the cabinet (de facto prime minister) died in an automobile accident, with Tursunbek CHYNGYSHEV then being designated as his successor.

In December 1993 Vice President Kulov resigned after being accused of complicity in a scheme to embezzle the country's gold reserves. The Chyngyshev government lost a legislative confidence vote over the same issue three days later, after which Apas JUMAGULOV was confirmed as head of a new administration.

In January 1994 voters overwhelmingly backed an economic reform program advanced by President Akayev, but undiminished opposition by former Communists led the president's supporters to threaten a legislative boycott. In September the Jumagulov government resigned but continued in a caretaker capacity. In another referendum in October a large majority of voters approved the abolition of the existing legislature and the creation of a much smaller bicameral body. Elections in February 1995 were contested by over 1,000 candidates, many of them independents but some representing 12 political parties. The voting was largely along clan/ethnic lines, with most of the new deputies being conservative-minded survivors of the Communist-era bureaucracy.

The reappointment of Jumagulov as prime minister in April 1995 signaled President Akayev's intention to pursue his reform program. When conservative elements in the legislature succeeded in September in blocking the president's request for an extension of his mandate to 2001, he called an early presidential election for December and registered a commanding 71.6 percent victory over two other candidates. Moreover, in a referendum in February 1996 Akayev secured 94 percent endorsement for constitutional amendments that substantially increased presidential powers and abolished the post of vice president (which had remained vacant since December 1993).

In March 1998 Prime Minister Jumagulov resigned, ostensibly for health reasons, and he was succeeded the following day by Kubanychbek JUMALIEV, previously head of presidential administration. In September, faced with what he labeled foot-dragging by the conservative Supreme Council on key legislation, such as legalization of private land ownership, President Akayev announced a referendum to restructure the bicameral legislature and reduce its authority in several areas, including budget deliberations. In October some 90 percent of those voting assented.

In December 1998, with the som having depreciated significantly because of the recent Russian economic crisis and Moscow's devaluation of the ruble, the Jumaliev government resigned at the president's request. Jumabek IBRAIMOV, chair of the State Property Fund, succeeded Jumaliev, but Ibraimov died April 1999 and was succeeded on an acting basis by former deputy prime minister Amangeldy MURALIYEV, who had been serving as governor of the Osh *oblast*. Muraliyev was later confirmed as prime minister.

In November 1999 President Akayev announced first-round parliamentary elections for February 20, 2000. The conduct of the balloting drew wide criticism from international observers and the opposition. One of the principal antigovernment leaders, former vice president Feliks Kulov of the recently organized Dignity (*Ar-Namys*) party, lost under highly questionable circumstances at runoff balloting on March 12, and ten days later authorities arrested him for offenses allegedly committed during his 1997–1998 tenure as minister of national security.

A military court acquitted Kulov on August 7, 2000, but the verdict was annulled by a higher court on September 11. Although widely considered a leading opposition candidate in the presidential election scheduled for October 29, Kulov later refused to take a mandatory Kyrgyz language proficiency test and was therefore disqualified, leaving Socialist Party "Fatherland" (*Ata-Meken*) candidate Omurbek TEKEBAYEV as President Akayev's principal opponent. At the election Akayev won 75 percent of the vote against five challengers; Tekebayev finished second, with 14 percent. Kurmanbek BAKIYEV, theretofore a southern governor, was named as prime minister.

On January 22, 2001, the retrial of Feliks Kulov concluded with another guilty verdict, followed by imposition of a seven-year prison sentence. On March 26 Kulov appealed the decision to the Supreme Court, which upheld his conviction and sentence on July 19.

In January 2002 the government arrested Azimbek BEKNAZAROV, an outspoken legislator from the south and a critic of a 1999 Sino-Kyrgyz treaty that had ceded territory to China (see Foreign relations, below). During his trial on charges of having abused his authority while chairing an investigative committee, many of Beknazarov's southern supporters took to the streets, and at a demonstration held March 17–18 in Jalal-Abad's district of Aksy, security forces killed five demonstrators. Although convicted in May and given a short sentence, Beknazarov received amnesty under a bill passed in June.

On May 22, 2002, in the midst of antigovernment protests that condemned not only the prosecution of Beknazarov but also ratification of the border treaty and the government's mishandling of the March demonstrations, Prime Minister Bakiyev and his cabinet resigned. President Akayev immediately appointed Nikolay TANAYEV, first deputy prime minister under Bakiyev, as acting prime minister. Tanayev was confirmed in the post in a permanent capacity on May 30.

On February 2, 2003, three-fourths of those voting approved a constitutional referendum that had been called by the president less than a month before. The changes returned the national legislature to a unicameral Supreme Council, effective as of the election scheduled for 2005, and also called for eliminating all party list (proportional) seats. In a separate question that asked whether Akayev should remain in office until the expiration of his term in late 2005, 79 percent gave him a vote of confidence, despite the previous year's turmoil.

At the election for the new 75-member Supreme Council on February 27 and March 13, 2005, only 6 seats went to members of the opposition, many of whom had been excluded from competing on technical grounds. The release of preliminary results quickly led to peaceful protests, beginning in Osh and Jalal-Abad and spreading elsewhere in the south. On March 21, however, the southern demonstrations turned violent, and protesters began assembling in Bishkek. On March 24 a crowd estimated at 5,000 marched on government offices, looters took to the streets, and President Akayev and his immediate family fled to Russia. On the same day, protesters freed Feliks Kulov from prison and the outgoing bicameral legislature named former prime minister Bakiyev, leader of the multiparty opposition People's Movement of Kyrgyzstan (PMK), as acting president and acting prime minister. On March 25 Bakiyev appointed a new cabinet that included Kulov as minister of security, although Kulov resigned only five days later. Meanwhile, the issue of legislative legitimacy had been resolved in favor of the newly elected Supreme Council. Both houses of the bicameral legislature therefore dissolved themselves on March 28–29.

On April 4, 2005, Askar Akayev, from Moscow, tendered his resignation, which the Supreme Council accepted on April 11. In a presidential election on July 10 Bakiyev won 89.5 percent of the vote against the national ombudsman, Tursunbay BAKIR-UULU, and four other candidates. Kulov, having been appointed first deputy prime minister on May 16, had withdrawn as a presidential candidate after receiving assurances that he would be named to head the next cabinet. Appointed acting prime minister on August 15, Kulov won parliamentary confirmation as prime minister on September 1, although in late September the legislature rejected several ministerial nominees put forward by the Bakiyev-Kulov "tandem." The completed cabinet was finally sworn in on December 20.

Relations between the Bakiyev-Kulov government and the Supreme Council were often antagonistic in the following months, and in early May 2006 the cabinet members submitted their resignations en masse (except for Kulov, who had been urged not to by his colleagues) in response to legislative criticism of most ministers' individual performances. President Bakiyev rejected the resignations but on May 10, bowing to the demands of a growing opposition, announced a number of key changes, including new deputy prime ministers (one of whom was ultimately rejected by the legislature), a new head of presidential administration, and a new chief of the National Security Service.

In April 2006 many key opposition leaders formed the For Reforms (*Za Reformy*) movement in an effort to pressure the government to adopt constitutional reforms that had been promoted during the "Tulip Revolution" of March 2005. In the first week of November street demonstrations in Bishkek succeeded in pressuring Bakiyev and the legislators to approve constitutional changes that reduced the president's powers and called for election of a new 90-seat legislature in which half the seats would be proportionally elected and in which the party with the greatest representation would name the next prime minister.

On December 19, 2006, the Kulov government resigned, reportedly to speed up the holding of a new legislative election. Instead, the resignation threatened to generate a constitutional crisis because no party held sufficient seats in the Supreme Council to name a new prime minister. President Bakiyev responded by threatening to dissolve the legislature unless it restored a number of presidential powers, including designation of a prime minister. On December 30, on a temporary basis, the Supreme Council did as requested. Bakiyev signed the changes into law on January 15, 2007, and quickly named Kulov to form a new administration, but the Supreme Council rejected his selection on January 18 and again on January 25.

On January 29, 2007, Bakiyev named the acting minister of agriculture, Azim ISABEKOV, prime minister, and the legislature concurred. Isabekov's tenure was short, however, and he resigned on March 29 after Bakiyev rejected his decision to fire a number of ministers as a gesture to the opposition. The following day, Bakiyev named opposition moderate Almazbek ATAMBAYEV of the Social Democratic Party of Kyrgyzstan (*Sotsial-demokraticheskaya Partiya Kyrgyzstana*—SDPK) to head a reshuffled cabinet that won approval on April 10.

With the Constitutional Court having ruled on September 17, 2007, that the constitutional changes of November and December 2006 were unconstitutional as they had not been approved by referendum, President Bakiyev called a referendum on further changes (see Constitution and government, below). On October 21, the new edition of the constitution and accompanying changes to the electoral law both officially won 77 percent approval, although there were numerous allegations of polling irregularities. The next day, before promulgating the package of amendments, President Bakiyev dissolved the Supreme Council—a power revoked in the new edition of the constitution. On October 24 the cabinet resigned, as required by the constitution, and parliamentary elections were scheduled for December.

Initially, the Atambayev government remained in place pending the election; however, Atambayev resigned on November 18, 2007, after criticizing President Bakiyev and was replaced as acting prime minister by First Deputy Prime Minister Iskenderbek AIDARALIYEV. Atambayev's resignation was prompted by the perception that Bakiyev was attempting to control both the executive and legislative branches through his part in establishing a new presidential "True Path" Popular Party (*Ak Zhol*).

In the December 16, 2007, election only three parties won seats in the enlarged Supreme Council, where *Ak Zhol* claimed 71 of the 90 seats. The SDPK, the only successful opposition party, won 11. Vote rigging was claimed by other leading opposition parties, including *Ata-Meken,* which finished second in the vote count (8.7 percent) but failed to meet a regional threshold requirement. In its first session, the new legislature elected Igor CHUDINOV (*Ak Zhol*) as prime minister on December 24.

Following a March 2009 ruling by the Constitutional Court that, in accordance with the October 2007 changes to the constitution, a presidential election had to be held before the end of October 2009, the Supreme Council scheduled national voting for July. Six candidates, including the incumbent, appeared on the ballot. Although most of the leading opposition parties, loosely unified in a United People's Movement (UPM), agreed to endorse former prime minister Atambayev as their sole candidate, Temir SARIEV, leader of the *Ak Shumkar* (White Falcon) party, broke from the group and declared his candidacy. On July 23 President Bakiyev won an easy victory, taking 76.4 percent of the vote. Atambayev withdrew on election day, claiming massive voter fraud, but nevertheless finished in second place. On October 21 President Bakiyev approved *Ak Zhol*'s nomination of Daniyar

USENOV as the next prime minister, and on the following day a substantially reorganized cabinet was introduced. Among the changes, the foreign and state security ministries were restructured as agencies that reported directly to the president.

In the following six months public dissatisfaction with Bakiyev's government continued to mount over its perceived authoritarianism, nepotism, corruption, and misuse of state funds. On April 4, amid spreading protests triggered by higher utility prices, a number of opposition leaders, including former presidential candidates Atambayev and Tekebayev, were placed under arrest. By April 5 the increasingly confrontational protests had reached Bishkek, where demonstrators on April 6–7 stormed government buildings and attacked properties owned by the president's family. Security forces, ordered to fire on the crowds, killed at least 17 people, and on April 7 Bakiyev fled from the capital. On the same day, opposition leaders met and formed a provisional government chaired by Roza OTUNBAYEVA, the SDPK leader in the lower house as well as a former foreign minister and ambassador. The provisional government also included Atambayev, Tekebayev, and former defense minister Lt. Gen. Ismail ISAKOV. The death toll from the uprising was reported to be 84.

From his southern home base in Jalal-Abad, Bakiyev refused to resign until April 15, when he departed the country for Kazakhstan and then, five days later, Belarus. Meanwhile, on April 11 Prime Minister Usenov had resigned, and on April 13 Otunbayeva had assumed office as interim head of government. She had already announced that the provisional government would remain in office only for as long as it took to write a new constitution, hold a legislative election, and form a new government. Although some opposition leaders, including Feliks Kulov, advocated retaining a strong presidency, Otunbayeva, Atambayev, and others succeeded in their efforts to prepare a constitutional proposal that, as published on May 21, curtailed the powers of the presidency and granted the legislature greater authority.

On June 10 interethnic violence between Kyrgyz and Uzbeks erupted in Osh and nearby Jalal-Abad, leading to (unofficially) an estimated 400 deaths and the flight from their homes of up to 400,000 Uzbeks, 100,000 of whom crossed the border into Uzbekistan over the next several days. Although comparatively minor clashes had occurred in May, the severity of the renewed violence caused Provisional President Otunbayeva to declare a state of emergency that helped restore order by June 15. Despite widespread property destruction, most Uzbeks had returned to their communities by June 27, when the country's voters went to the polls to endorse or reject, in a single vote, the draft constitution, a law on enactment, and Otunbayeva's interim presidency. With a reported turnout of 72 percent, the referendum passed with 91 percent support, and on July 3, a day after publication of the official results, Otunbayeva was sworn in as interim president for a term to end on December 31, 2011.

The next major step in the transition process was a legislative election held on October 10, 2010, for an expanded 120-seat Supreme Council. Final results, announced on November 1, gave the new nationalist, propresidential Fatherland (*Ata-Jurt*) party 28 seats; the SDPK, 26; A*r-Namys,* 25; Republic (*Respublika*), 23; and the Socialist Party "Fatherland" (*Ata-Meken*), 18. On November 11 President Otunbayeva asked the SDPK chair, Almazbek Atambayev, to open negotiations with the other legislative parties on forming a government that would command a legislative majority. At various times in the following month Atambayev held talks with the leaders of all four parties despite clear ideological differences. On November 30 Atambayev, *Respublika*'s Omurbek BABANOV, and *Ata-Meken*'s Omurbek Tekebayev concluded a coalition agreement that provided for Atambayev to become prime minister and Tekebayev speaker of the Supreme Council, but the deal disintegrated on December 2 when errant *Respublika* legislators failed to back Tekebayev's candidacy and he fell 3 votes short of the 61 needed to elect a speaker.

On December 4, 2010, President Otunbayeva requested that *Respublika*'s Babanov open a new round of coalition negotiations that concluded in mid-December with the announcement of an ideologically diverse three-party coalition encompassing *Ata-Jurt,* the SDPK, and *Respublika.* On December 17 the Supreme Council in quick succession elected *Ata-Jurt*'s Ahmatbek KELDIBEKOV as its speaker and the SDPK's Atambayev as prime minister, with Babanov becoming first deputy prime minister.

On September 23 Babanov temporarily assumed the office of prime minister in order to allow Atambayev to campaign for the presidency (see Current issues, below). Atambayev won the presidential balloting on October 30, with 63.2 percent of the vote, defeating 15 other candidates. His closest challenger was Adahan MADUMAROV (One Kyrgyzstan), who received 14.7 percent of the vote. After the election, Atambayev resumed the prime ministership until he was sworn in as president. He resigned from the SDPK after he assumed the presidency. Babanov was elected prime minister by the legislature on December 23. He formed a coalition cabinet that included the SDPK, *Respublika, Ar-Namys,* and *Ata-Menken.* It was sworn in on December 28.

SDPK, *Ar-Namys,* and *Ata-Meken* formed a new coalition government on September 3, 2012, after the collapse of the previous coalition headed by *Respublika* under Prime Minister Omurbek Babanov in August of 2012. Babanov resigned on September 1 under allegations of corruption and amidst economic turmoil and was unable to form a new coalition government. Zhantoro SATYBALDIYEV was elected prime minister on September 5, 2012, with a margin of 111–2.

Constitution and government. The first post-Communist constitution was introduced on May 5, 1993, but was frequently amended thereafter—for example, in 1999 to introduce a bicameral legislature and then in 2003 to restore a unicameral Supreme Council. Presidential powers tended to increase under amendments approved in 1996 and 1998 but were reduced in November 2006 and then restored a month later. On September 17, 2007, the Constitutional Court threw out the 2006 amendments on the grounds that they should have been submitted to the voters, which led President Bakiyev to call a referendum on additional changes to the constitution as well as a revised electoral law. Held only a month later, on October 21, the referendum reintroduced party list voting, on the basis of a single national constituency.

The constitution of June 2010 transformed Kyrgyzstan into Central Asia's first parliamentary republic, significantly reducing the role of president, expanding the size and role of the Supreme Council, and installing a more powerful prime minister as the head of government. After the current transitional period (through December 2011), the popularly elected president will be restricted to a single six-year term. (Under the new constitution, Roza Otunbayeva is excluded from running for president in 2011.) The president's role is to be largely ceremonial, but the office retains the power to veto most legislation (but not, for example, the budget), subject to a two-thirds override vote in the Supreme Council, and to appoint important judicial, defense, and security officials. The president remains commander in chief but can no longer unilaterally initiate referenda or introduce draft laws. The Supreme Council, expanded to 120 members who are elected by proportional representation and serve terms of five years, can dismiss the president by a two-thirds vote. To avoid the elevation of a single party to near-monopoly status, as happened under Presidents Akayev and Bakiyev, individual parties are limited to a maximum of 65 seats. Together, the Supreme Council and the government, headed by a prime minister who is responsible solely to the legislature, set the direction of domestic and foreign policy. The Supreme Council also has the authority to confirm or reject emergency or wartime decrees issued by the president.

The judicial structure is headed by a Supreme Court that includes a Constitutional Chamber charged with ensuring the constitutionality of executive and legislative acts. The Supreme Court remains the highest organ of civil, criminal, and administrative justice. Enumerated rights include freedom of speech, the press, and assembly, and defamation is no longer a criminal offense.

Administratively, Kyrgyzstan comprises seven regions (*dubans* or *oblasts*)—Batken, Chui, Issyk-Kul, Jalal-Abad, Naryn, Osh, and Talas—plus the cities of Bishkek and Osh. Local and regional assemblies are directly elected. They in turn elect local executives.

In 2013 Reporters Without Borders ranked the country 106th out of 179 countries in freedom of the press.

Foreign relations. Kyrgyzstan became a sovereign member of the Commonwealth of Independent States (CIS) in December 1991. It joined the United Nations in March 1992, with admission to the International Monetary Fund and World Bank following in May and September, respectively. Kyrgyzstan subsequently became a member of the Conference on (later Organization for) Security and Cooperation in Europe (CSCE/OSCE) and, as a predominantly Muslim country, of the Organization of the Islamic Conference. In June 1994 Kyrgyzstan acceded to NATO's Partnership for Peace program, under which Kyrgyz troops have regularly participated in joint military exercises.

In January 1994 Kyrgyzstan became the third member of the Central Asian Economic Union (CAEU), which had been launched by Kazakhstan and Uzbekistan. In February 1995 the CAEU was given a formal ministerial framework, and its role was extended to cover defense, foreign affairs, and social policy. It also began addressing such regional issues as drug-smuggling, the allocation of scarce water resources, and infrastructural development. In July 1998, with Tajikistan having agreed to join, the CAEU adopted the name Central Asian Economic Community, which then became the Central Asian Cooperation Organization (CACO) in March 2002. In January 2006 the CACO merged into another regional grouping, the six-member Eurasian Economic Community (EAEC) of Belarus, Kazakhstan, Kyrgyzstan, Russia, Tajikistan, and Uzbekistan (which suspended its membership in 2008).

Kyrgyzstan also participated in the six-member CIS Collective Security Treaty (with Armenia, Belarus, Kazakhstan, Russia, and Tajikistan), which in 2001 agreed to base a Collective Rapid Reaction Force in Bishkek; in April 2003 the six treaty members reconfigured their association as the Collective Security Treaty Organization (CSTO). The formation of the CSTO was largely a response to concerns about Islamic fundamentalism, terrorism, and drug-trafficking in the region. Earlier, in the mid-1990s, China, Kazakhstan, Kyrgyzstan, Russia, and Tajikistan had begun meeting as the so-called "Shanghai Five," which had as its focus border issues, regional stability, and security concerns involving Islamic militancy. In 2001 Uzbekistan joined the grouping, which redesignated itself as the Shanghai Cooperation Organization (SCO), with a formal SCO charter signed in 2002.

Central Asian summits have repeatedly seen the participants pledge cooperation against terrorism and Islamic extremism. In Kyrgyzstan, the most serious related incidents occurred in 1999 and 2000. In August 1999 a force numbering in the hundreds took 20 or so hostages in Batken. With assistance from Russia and Kazakhstan, the government launched a counteroffensive that ultimately included bombing runs in Tajikistan, to where the insurgents, who were linked to the Islamic Movement of Uzbekistan (see the Uzbekistan entry), had retreated. A negotiated release of the final hostages occurred in October. In August and September 2000 bands of militants, variously numbered from a handful to over 200 according to Kyrgyz officials, reportedly crossed the border from Tajikistan and were met by defense units. Tajik officials denied that the militants had been based in Tajikistan.

In 1999–2000 Uzbekistan began laying land mines along its border with Kyrgyzstan to stop incursions and drug-trafficking. The issue appeared resolved in mid-2004, when Uzbekistan began clearing the mines, which had caused civilian injuries on both sides. Meanwhile, protracted negotiations on delimiting the Uzbek-Kyrgyz border were continuing. Relations were further damaged in 2005 when Kyrgyzstan refused to extradite 29 refugees (out of more than 400) who had fled across the border in May to escape what was widely labeled a massacre of protesters in Uzbekistan's Andizhan region. The definition of this 130-kilometer border is still incomplete, while disputes in the Isfara Valley have delayed completion of delineation with Tajikistan. However, Kyrgyzstan did ratify the Kyrgyz-Kazakh border demarcation treaty on April 11, 2008, following promises of increased imports of subsidized oil and wheat, as well as further foreign investment from Kazakhstan.

Economic difficulties and the allocation of natural resources have also repeatedly contributed to tensions among regional states. During 1999, for example, shipment of natural gas from Uzbekistan to Kyrgyzstan was temporarily discontinued for nonpayment; when deliveries resumed, Tashkent unilaterally raised the price. In June 1999 Kyrgyzstan cut off water supplies to Kazakhstan because the latter had failed to deliver coal shipments as payment. In April 2006 representatives of the regional governments met in Berlin, Germany, in a cooperative effort to conclude an agreement on sharing water and hydroelectricity, two of Kyrgyzstan's principal resources. In exchange, Kyrgyzstan reportedly sought more secure supplies of coal, oil, and natural gas from Kazakhstan and Uzbekistan.

In August 1999 President Akayev signed a Sino-Kyrgyz treaty that ceded to China some 360 square miles of territory. Ratification of the treaty by both houses of the Kyrgyz legislature in May 2002 was met with widespread protests. Final demarcation of the border with China was accomplished in 2004.

President Akayev responded to the September 2001 al-Qaida attacks against the United States and the resultant U.S.-led campaign in Afghanistan by declaring Kyrgyzstan to be a "frontline state" in the war against terrorism, drug-trafficking, and Islamic extremism. Having approved U.S. and NATO use of the Manas airport, in September 2003 Kyrgyzstan reached agreement with Moscow on establishing a Russian air base in nearby Kant. Speaking at the latter facility in August 2004, Foreign Minister Askar AITMATOV characterized Russia as Kyrgyzstan's "main strategic partner."

In July 2006 negotiations concluded on continued U.S. use of the Manas facility, establishing an annual rent of $17.5 million, considerably higher than the previous $2.6 million per year. The presence of U.S. and NATO forces remained controversial, however, and on February 19, 2009, the Supreme Council voted 78–2 to deny U.S. access to the facility, which had been handling up 15,000 troop transfers a month in and out of Afghanistan. Less than a month later, the parliament also voted to close Manas to other countries fighting in the U.S.-led coalition. The status of the base nevertheless remained under discussion, and on June 22 Washington and Bishkek concluded a revised agreement under which Manas would function as a "transit center," with the U.S. paying $60 million annually and also committing $36 million to upgrading the air traffic control system and other infrastructure. The Supreme Council ratified the pact on June 30.

During negotiations with the United States over the Manas air base, Kyrgyzstan was also negotiating additional aid from Russia, which in early 2009 offered investment capital of $1.7 for infrastructure projects as well as over $650 million in the form of direct aid, debt cancellation, and low-interest loans. Despite some media speculation abroad that Russia was interested in gaining access to the Manas air base, Moscow endorsed the "transit center" agreement concluded in June as necessary to the continuing war in Afghanistan. In August, during a CSTO meeting, Moscow and Bishkek agreed that Russia could base its own small "military contingent" in southern Kyrgyzstan, presumably in Osh or Batken. The facility was expected to involve the CSTO's Collective Operational Reaction Forces (CORF). Russia and Kyrgyzstan also agreed to establish a training center for their forces. In addition to its air base in Kant, Russia maintains the Marevo Communications Center of the Russian Navy in the Chui Oblast and a center for testing naval equipment at Lake Issyk-Kul. In exchange for use of the facilities, Russia paid Kyrgyzstan $5 million per year. In the final days of the Bakiyev administration, Kyrgyzstan agreed to consolidate Russian facilities into a single unified base. Meanwhile, in October 2011, Kyrgyzstan agreed to form a free trade area with other members of the CIS.

In February 2012 a dispute over the terms of the initiative to consolidate Russia's military facilities prompted Atambayev to warn that he would force the closure of Moscow's existing bases and the withdrawal of Russian military personnel from the country. Concurrently, the president reaffirmed plans to close U.S. military facilities in the country by 2014. On September 20, 2012, Russia and Kyrgyzstan agreed to extend the Russian military presence in the country until at least 2032.

Tensions continued between Uzbekistan, Kyrgyzstan, and the Uzbek minority population within Kyrgyzstan over border and ethnic disagreements. On January 6, 2013, Uzbek citizens attacked a Kyrgyz border station, capturing and later releasing 34 Kyrgyz citizens. Tensions flared again in June with allegations that Uzbek border guards shot and killed a Kyrgyz citizen in Kyrgyz territory.

Current issues. The autonomous Kyrgyzstan Inquiry Commission issued a report in May 2011 that was highly critical of the interim government's response to ethnic violence that began in April 2010 and charged that government troops participated in attacks on minority groups. The violence displaced more than 411,000 people. Presidential elections were held on October 30. Sixteen candidates qualified for the balloting, which was won by the incumbent prime minister Atambayev and which international observers declared generally free and open (although monitors did criticize government restrictions on press coverage of the campaign and the oversight of voter registration lists). Atambayev's election was the first peace transfer of power since independence from the Soviet Union. Following allegations of financial misconduct, deputies voted on December 12 to replace Ahmatbek Keldibekov (*Ata-Zhurt*), the speaker of the Supreme Council, with Asilbek JEENBEKOV (SDPK).

A ten-day strike by miners at Kumtor in February 2012 was resolved after the government agreed to pay increases and bonuses. The government also initiated a review of environmental problems caused by mining. The work stoppage at the nation's largest gold mine highlighted the dependence of the government on mining for foreign currency. However, the issue over the nationalization of the Kumtor mine has continued to simmer into 2013, with demonstrations in October 2012 leading to the arrest of opposition leaders in the nationalist *Ata Jurt* party. Sadyr JAPAROV, Talant MAMYTOV, and party leader Kamchybek TASHIYEV were sentenced to 18 months in prison in March 2013 for their role in the earlier demonstrations.

By early 2012 and 2013, Kyrgyzstan leaned heavily toward pro-Russian elements and away from Western European influence. With the expected 2013 ascension of Kyrgyzstan into the 2010 formed Customs Union of Belarus, Kazakhstan, and Russia; increased security cooperation and the September 20, 2012, extension of the Russian military presence until at least 2032; and an upswing in both economic aid and debt relief from Russia, the debate over Russian influence was all but decided.

POLITICAL PARTIES

The previously dominant Kyrgyz Communist Party withdrew from the Communist Party of the Soviet Union on August 28, 1991, at which time its property within Kyrgyzstan was nationalized and its funds frozen; three days later it was disbanded. From then until the departure of President Akayev in March 2005, party affiliation did not have a significant impact on government leadership, despite the presence of a vocal opposition.

In January 2004 a number of leading opposition parties—among them the Freedom Party (*Erkindik*), the Party of National Restoration "Banner" (*Asaba*), and the Progressive Democratic Party "Free Kyrgyzstan" (ErK)—established an ideologically diverse electoral bloc, For the People's Power (*Za Vlast Narodna*). The following September, looking toward the 2005 legislative election, the People's Power parties were joined by organizations that included the Party of Communists of Kyrgyzstan (PKK) and New Kyrgyzstan in forming a People's Movement of Kyrgyzstan—PMK (*Narodnoe Dvizhenie Kyrgyzstana*), an electoral alliance that pledged to work for free and fair elections. In November Kurmanbek Bakiyev was elected chair of the PMK.

Earlier, in May 2004, a Civic Union "For Fair Elections" was announced by Dignity (*Ar-Namys*), Socialist Party "Fatherland" (*Ata-Meken*), the Social Democratic Party of Kyrgyzstan (SDPK), and the "Poor and Unprotected" People's Party (*Bei Becharalar;* see SDPK, below), which sought to present a centrist "third force" positioned between strongly progovernment parties and the regime's most vocal opponents. In October 2004, by which time there were at least 40 registered parties, Bakiyev's PMK and For Fair Elections declared that they would join forces. Although the opposition leadership had no expectations that it would win a victory at the February–March 2005 legislative election, the systematic disqualification of opposition candidates, who ended up winning only half a dozen of the 75 seats, directly contributed to the Tulip Revolution of March 24.

In January 2006 a new People's Coalition of Democratic Forces encompassing 7 parties, 2 blocs, and 9 nongovernmental organizations was established to promote constitutional and social reforms, including the adoption of a parliamentary system of government; among the participants were *Ar-Namys, Ata-Meken,* the PKK, and the SDPK. In succeeding months the People's Coalition was increasingly viewed as disenchanted with the Bakiyev-Kulov government, and in April it gave birth to the opposition For Reforms (*Za Reformy*) movement. Following the legislature's rejection in January 2007 of his reappointment as prime minister, Feliks Kulov joined and was subsequently appointed leader of the For Reforms opposition. While For Reforms organized the majority of protests during 2006, it dissolved in March 2007 as leading opposition figures became unwilling to support Kulov, opposing his views on forcing Bakiyev to resign before his term expired.

Meanwhile, a number of Bakiyev supporters, led by Topchubek Turgunaliyev of *Erkindik,* announced a "revival" of the defunct PMK through the formation of the For Political Stability and Unity movement. This was then superseded by the formation of the presidential True Path Popular Party (*Ak Zhol Eldik Partiyasi*) in October 2007, which absorbed many affiliates of For Political Stability and Unity. *Ak Zhol* (*Ak Jol;* also translatable as "White Road" and "Bright Path") was in part an outgrowth of a civic movement, For the Constitution, Reform, and Development, that had been organized a month earlier to promote adoption of constitutional revisions. At its founding congress *Ak Zhol* initially named Bakiyev as its chair, a position he could not hold while serving as president of the republic.

While the number of registered parties increased to 101 in 2007, only 50 officially indicated their intention to contest the December 16 elections. Of these, 22 applied for registration, but 10 failed to meet the requirements, most often because of problems with candidate lists. Three parties—*Ak Zhol,* the SDPK, and the PKK—met the thresholds for winning parliamentary seats. Although *Ata-Meken* easily exceeded the 5 percent national threshold, winning 9.3 percent of the vote and finishing second, it failed to win the minimum of 0.5 percent in each region. (*Ak Zhol* won 47 percent of the vote and 71 parliamentary seats, but disintegrated with Bakiyev's departure in April 2010. Many of its members moved to other parties. For additional details on *Ak Zhol,* see the 2010 *Handbook.*)

In January 2008 some of the leading opposition parties, including *Ak Shumkar, Ata-Meken,* and *Ar-Namys,* joined other organizations in establishing the For Justice Movement—FJM (*Akyikat Ichun*), which named former foreign minister Alikbek JEKSHENKULOV as its coordinator. A broader United People's Movement—UPM (also frequently referred to as the United National Movement or the United Opposition Movement) was formed in December 2008 by a diverse group that included the FJM. It announced on April 20, 2009, that it intended to field a single candidate in the July presidential election. The UPM numbered among its participants White Falcon (*Ak Shumkar*), *Asaba, Ata-Meken,* the Green Party, and the SDPK, although *Ak Shumkar* was expelled in May following its decision to nominate its chair as a candidate for the presidency. The UPM disbanded following Bakiyev's ouster, but its coordinator, Azimbek Beknazarov, subsequently founded a party of the same name.

Kyrgyzstan has well over 100 parties, but many are local or have a limited number of members. Initially, 57 parties indicated their intentions to run in the October 2010 Supreme Council election. Twenty-nine met the deadline for submitting full candidate lists to the election commission.

Governing Coalition:

Social Democratic Party of Kyrgyzstan (*Sotsial-demokraticheskaya Partiya Kyrgyzstana*—SDPK). The SDPK was launched in 1993 with the political endorsement of President Akayev. Supporting the government's reformist, promarket line, it won representation in the 1995 legislative elections and was a leading component of the progovernment Union of Democratic Forces (*Soyuz Demokraticheskikh Sil*—SDS) in 2000. Its chair, Almazbek Atambayev, was a 2000 presidential nominee, winning about 6 percent of the vote, for third place.

In October 2004 the SDPK absorbed the "Poor and Unprotected" People's Party (*El Partiyasi "Bei Becharalar"*). Appealing to intellectuals, the disadvantaged, and students, the leftist, reform-minded *Bei Becharalar* had been registered in December 1995. Its leaders had included Daniyar Usenov, who in 2009–2010 would serve as President Bakiyev's last prime minister, and Melis ESHIMKANOV, who had won about 1 percent of the vote in the 2000 presidential election and was later named head of state-run radio and television.

In the 2007 parliamentary election the SDPK finished second, winning 5.8 percent of the vote and 11 seats. In April 2009 the opposition UPM selected Atambayev as its presidential candidate. Although he withdrew from the contest on Election Day, alleging voter fraud, he finished second, winning 8.4 percent of the vote. Thereafter, he remained a leading opponent of the government and in April 2010, following Bakiyev's ouster, was named first deputy chair of the interim government. He resigned in July to contest the October Supreme Council election, in which the SDPK finished second, with 14.1 percent of the votes cast (7.8 percent of the eligible voters). Also appearing on the SDPK party list was Lt. Gen. Ismail ISAKOV, formerly of the New Kyrgyzstan (below) and the initial minister of defense in the interim government. Atambayev won the presidential balloting in October 2011 and resigned from the party after his inauguration.

Leader: Alay KARASHEV (First Deputy Prime Minister).

Dignity (*Ar-Namys*). *Ar-Namys* was organized in July 1999 by one of Kyrgyzstan's leading oppositionists, former vice president Feliks Kulov, who had resigned as Bishkek mayor in April to protest corruption and antidemocratic tendencies in the Akayev administration. The party quickly emerged as one of Kyrgyzstan's largest.

Because *Ar-Namys* had not existed long enough to offer its own party list for the February 2000 election, it attempted to qualify by joining with the Democratic Movement of Kyrgyzstan (*Demokraticheskoye Dvizhenie Kyrgyzstana*—DDK), which put Kulov at the head of its list. (Founded in 1990, the DDK initially served as an umbrella for various prodemocracy and proindependence groups but was registered as a political party in 1993.) When the DDK list was disqualified, Kulov ran in a single-mandate district, reportedly winning some 40 percent of the vote on February 20 but then, in balloting fraught with accusations of official misconduct, losing in the runoff on March 12. Ten days later, in the context of continuing demonstrations demanding that the election be nullified, he was arrested and charged with abuse of power and other offenses during his tenure as minister of national security in 1997–1998.

Considered a leading opposition candidate for president, Kulov was disqualified in September 2000 when he refused to take the mandatory Kyrgyz language test. Having already announced a preelection alliance with *Ata-Meken* (below), Kulov later agreed to head Omurbek Tekebayev's presidential campaign. In January 2001 and May 2002 he was convicted of various crimes and sentenced to prison. He was nevertheless regarded as a potential contender for the presidency in 2005. Having been freed during the regime-changing demonstrations of March 24, 2005, Kulov later saw his convictions thrown out by the courts. He served as President Bakiyev's first prime minister from 2005 until the Supreme Council rejected his reappointment in January 2007.

Having failed to win a seat in the December 2007 parliamentary election, *Ar-Namys* joined with *Ata-Meken* and others in claiming that the election was marred by vote rigging. While Kulov remained party chair, he accepted a government appointment as coordinator of small- and medium-scale electricity generation programs in May 2008. Following the installation of an interim government in April 2010, he argued for retaining a strong presidency. In the October 2010 election *Ar-Namys* finished third (13.5 percent of the votes cast, 7.6 percent of the eligible voters). In the following days Kulov was frequently mentioned as a possible deputy prime minister, but *Ar-Namys* rejected participation in the various coalitions that were proposed in the subsequent two months. *Ar-Namys* candidate Anarabek KALMATOV received less than 1 percent of the vote in the 2011 presidential balloting.

Leaders: Feliks KULOV (Chair), Gulnara ASYMBEKOVA (Deputy Prime Minister).

Socialist Party "Fatherland" (*Socialisticheskaya Partiya "Ata-Meken"*). The center-left Socialist Party was founded in 1992 by a nationalist faction of the Progressive Democratic Party "Free Kyrgyzstan" (ErK, below). It failed to meet the 5 percent threshold for claiming party list seats in the 2000 Legislative Assembly balloting, although its chair, Omurbek Tekebayev, won election in a single-mandate district and was subsequently elected deputy speaker of the body. Following the disqualification of Feliks Kulov, he became the leading opposition presidential contender for the October 2000 election, at which he finished second, with 14 percent of the vote.

Briefly speaker of the Supreme Council, Tekebayev resigned in February 2006 after criticizing the government's commitment to rapid reform. He was a principal architect of the For Reforms opposition movement that took shape two months later. In the run-up to the December 2007 legislative election, *Ata-Meken* forged an electoral alliance with *Ak Shumkar* (below) that was viewed as the opposition's best opportunity to challenge *Ak Zhol.* Despite winning the second largest proportion of the vote, it failed to gain a seat in the new legislature because it did not meet the 0.5 percent threshold in each of the country's regions. In April 2010 Tekebayev was named a deputy chair of the interim government, but he resigned to run in the October legislative election, in which *Ata-Meken* finished fifth (9.9 percent of the votes cast, 5.5 percent of the eligible voters). In late November Tekebayev agreed to become speaker of the Supreme Council as part of a coalition agreement with the SDPK and *Respublika,* but the arrangement disintegrated on December 2 when errant *Respublika* legislators failed to back Tekebayev's candidacy, and he fell 3 votes short of the 61 needed to elect a speaker. Tekebayev declined to campaign for the presidency in 2011, and the party did not formally endorse any candidate.

Leader: Omurbek TEKEBAYEV (Chair).

Other Parties in the Supreme Council:

Fatherland (*Ata-Jurt, Ata-Zhurt*). Formally called the Idealistic Democratic Political Party "Fatherland" (*Idealisticheskaya Demokraticheskaya Politicheskaya Partiya "Ata-Jurt"*), *Ata-Jurt* was formed in December 2004 in opposition to President Akayev. Its founders included Roza Otunbayeva, who later served as a leader of *Asaba* and then the SDPK (both below). From its base in the Kyrgyz ethnic community in the south, the party is currently strongly nationalistic and has opposed equal rights for ethnic minorities.

In 2010 *Ata-Jurt* opposed the overthrow of President Bakiyev; regarded the results of the June constitutional referendum as a "massive falsification" by the provisional government; and, having won 15.3 percent of the vote (8.5 percent of eligible voters), earned a slim plurality of Supreme Council seats in the October election. The party favors close ties to Russia and the restoration of a strong presidency. Kamchybek Tashiyev was the party's candidate in the 2011 presidential elections. He placed third in the balloting with 14.3 percent of the vote.

Leaders: Kamchybek TASHIYEV (Chair), Ahmatbek KELDIBEKOV (Speaker of the Supreme Council), Myktybek ABDYLDAYEV.

Republic (*Respublika*). Formation of *Respublika* (formally, the Political Party "Republic") was announced in June 2010 by wealthy businessman Omurbek Babanov, who had left the SDPK in 2009 and had briefly served as a deputy prime minister under President Bakiyev. With a nationalist orientation, the party favors close ties to Russia and constitutional changes that would restore a stronger presidency. In the October 2010 legislative election, the party finished fourth, with 12.5 percent of the vote (6.9 percent of eligible voters). Babanov was appointed prime minister of a coalition government in December 2011 but resigned the office on September 1, 2012, after the collapse of his four-party coalition government.

Leader: Omurbek BABANOV (Prime Minister and Chair of the Party).

Other Parties Contesting the 2010 Supreme Council Election:

One Kyrgyzstan (*Butun Kyrgyzstan*). *Butun Kyrgyzstan* (formally, the Political Party "One Kyrgyzstan") was organized in June 2010 under the leadership of Adakhan Madumarov, a former secretary of the Security Council and speaker of parliament. Strongly nationalist and opposed to the diminution of presidential power under the 2010 constitution, the party is strongest in the south.

The results of the October 2010 legislative election were immediately challenged by the sixth-place *Butun Kyrgyzstan.* Final results gave the party 4.6 percent of the eligible voters, below the 5 percent threshold, but initial returns indicated that it had missed representation by less than 0.15 percent. Behind the controversy lay questions regarding the accuracy of the voter rolls being used by the election commission. Madumarov immediately demanded a recount, and the party's supporters organized large demonstrations on its behalf. The five parliamentary parties also supported the call for a recount. Madumarov placed second in the presidential elections in 2011. Reports in 2012 indicated that Madumarov was under investigation for antigovernment activity.

Leaders: Adakhan MADUMAROV, Miroslav NIYAZOV.

White Falcon (*Ak Shumkar*). *Ak Shumkar* (formally, the Political Party "White Falcon") was organized as an opposition parliamentary faction in April 2007. In late October its leaders forged an electoral alliance with *Ata-Meken* to contest the December parliamentary election, but in the run-up to the 2009 presidential election personal differences between the party's chair, Temir Sariev, and the UPM candidate, Almazbek Atambayev, resulted in *Ak Shumkar*'s decision to nominate Sariev, thereby dividing the opposition. As a consequence, the party was expelled from the UPM. Sariev, a founder and initial cochair of the For Justice Movement, finished third in the July election, with 6.4 percent of the vote.

Sariev emerged from the unrest in April 2010 as a deputy chair of the interim government but resigned to lead his party into the October Supreme Council election. *Ak Shumkar* finished seventh (4.7 percent of the votes cast, 2.6 percent of the eligible voters). The party endorsed Atambayev in the 2011 presidential balloting.

Leader: Temir SARIEV (Chair and 2009 presidential candidate).

Contemporary (*Zamandash*). Appealing primarily to migrant workers and their families, *Zamandash* won 3.3 percent of the votes cast (1.8 percent of eligible voters) in the October 2010 election. In July 2008 it leader, Muktarbek Omurakunov, was detained by authorities because of his alleged involvement in an improper procurement contract while press secretary of the State Committee for Migration and Employment.

Leader: Muktarbek OMURAKUNOV.

Political Party "United People's Movement" (*Birikken Eldik Kyymaly*—BEK). Formation of the BEK was announced in July 2010 by Azimbek Beknazarov, a deputy chair of the interim government and previously the coordinator of the opposition's umbrella organization, the United People's Movement. A former prosecutor and former leader of the *Asaba* political party (below), Beknazarov was initially named coordinator of the prosecutor's office and courts in the April 2010 interim government. Unlike most of his colleagues, he remained in the government while his new party contested the October 2010 legislative election, but the BEK captured only 1.1 percent of eligible voters.

Leader: Azimbek BEKNAZAROV.

Green Party of Kyrgyzstan (*Partiya Zelenykh Kyrgyzstana*). Founded in 2006 by Erkin Bulekbayev, the Green Party was a consistent voice in opposition to the Bakiyev government. The party was denied a place on the 2007 parliamentary ballot, and Bulekbayev was jailed for charges ranging from insulting the honor and dignity of the president to fomenting disorder and ethnic hatred during an April 2009 march demanding the expulsion of Kurds.

Following the removal of the Bakiyev government, Bulekbayev was appointed to the initial interim government as chair of the Financial Police Service. In the October Supreme Council election the Greens won under 0.4 percent support from eligible voters. Bulekbayev failed the mandatory language exam for the 2011 presidential balloting and therefore was not a candidate in the election.

Leaders: Erkin BULEKBAYEV, Nargiza ABDYLDAYEV.

Party of Communists of Kyrgyzstan (*Partiya Kommunistov Kyrgyzstana*—PKK). The PKK was launched in June 1992 as the successor to the former ruling Kyrgyz Communist Party, which had been disbanded in August 1991. Registered in September 1992, the party enjoyed significant support in the state bureaucracy. A majority of successful candidates in the February 1995 legislative elections reportedly belonged to or had close ties to the party. PKK leader Absamat MASALIYEV was runner-up in the December 1995 presidential poll, winning 24.4 percent of the vote.

Despite having suffered defections in 1999 to the **Communist Party of Kyrgyzstan**—CPK (*Kommunistov Partiya Kyrgyzstana*), whose dissident leaders had accused Masaliyev of cooperating with ideological enemies and defending corrupt officials, the PKK won a plurality of party list seats (5 of 15) in the 2000 Legislative Assembly election, taking 28 percent of the vote on a platform that included the reconstitution of the Soviet Union. Its contender for president in 2000, Ishak Masaliyev (Absamat's son), failed the mandatory Kyrgyz language test.

In July 2004 longtime party leader Absamat Masaliyev died, and two months later his deputy, Bakytbek BEKBOYEV, was elected his successor, defeating fellow MP Nikolay Baylo. Bekboyev lost the post the following December, partly due to an internal dispute over energy policy, and was replaced by Baylo. Leadership subsequently passed to Ishak Masaliyev, who was reelected to a five-year term as chair in November 2008.

In the December 2007 parliamentary election the PKK barely passed the 5 percent threshold and won eight seats. In the 2009 presidential contest it endorsed President Bakiyev's reelection. In 2010, responding to the renewed violence in the south in May, the PKK called for canceling the constitutional referendum on establishing a parliamentary republic, which it opposed. In late May Masaliyev was detained and then placed under house arrest in connection with allegations that the party had helped orchestrate the May outbreak. Masaliyev termed the investigation politically motivated, but he temporarily stepped down as chair in early August. In October the PKK won the support of less than 0.3 percent of the eligible voters. *Leaders:* Boumairam MAMASEITOVA (Chair), Ishak MASALIYEV, Nikolai BAYLO.

The following 18 parties also contested the October 2010 legislative election, but each won the support of 1.5 percent or less of the eligible voters: the **Liberal-Progressive Party** (*Liberalno-Progressivnaya Partiya*), the **Party of National Government "Bright Future"** (*Ak Sanat*), the **People's Democratic Party of Kyrgyzstan** (*Narodno-Demokraticheskaya Partiya Kyrgyzstana*), the **Political Party "Commonwealth"** (*Sodruzhestvo*), the **Political Party "Gracious People"** (*Aykol El*), the **Political Party "Good Wish"** (*Ak Tilek*), the **Political Party "Homeland Accord"** (*Meken Yntymagy*) (whose 2011 candidate, Temirbek ASANBEKOV, was placed fourth in the presidential balloting), the **Political Party "Independent Kyrgyzstan"** (*Egemen Kyrgyzstan*), the **Political Party "Khanate"** (*Kaganat*), the **Political Party "Live Kyrgyzstan"** (*Jashasyn Kyrgyzstan*), the **Political Party "Party of the Economic Revival of the Kyrgyz Republic"** (*Partiya Ekonomicheskogo Vozrozhdeniya Kyrgyzskoi Respubliki*), the **Political Party "Union. Freedom. Justice. Motherland."** (*Soyuz. Svoboda. Spravedlivost. Rodina,* which in Cyrillic script produces the acronym "U.S.S.R."), the **Political Party "Union of Kyrgyzstan's Peoples"** (*Soyuz Narodov Kyrgyzstana*), the **Political Party "Veterans of the War in Afghanistan and Participants in Other Local Military Conflicts"** (*Veteranov Vojny v Afganistane i Uchastnikov Drugikh Lokalnykh Boevykh Kofliktov*), the **Political Party "Youth Movement of April 7"** (*Molodezhnoe Dvizhenie 7 Aprelya*), the **Republican Party "Justice"** (*Respublikanskaya Partiya "Akiykat"*), the **Republican People's Party of Kyrgyzstan** (*Respublikanskaya Narodnya Partiya Kyrgyzstan*), and the **Republican Social-Political Party "Party of Developers of Kyrgyzstan"** (*Partiya Zastroishchikov Kyrgyzstana*).

Other Parties:

Party of National Restoration "Banner" (*Partiya Natsionalnovo Vozrozhdeniya "Asaba"*). Named with reference to a Kyrgyz military banner, *Asaba* was launched in November 1991 by a nationalist faction of the DDK (see *Ar-Namys*) that supported creation of a sovereign, democratic state and protection of the Kyrgyz economy and political interests. One of its leaders, Azimbek Beknazarov, whose 2002 trial was a precipitating factor in the March riots in the south, was regarded as a possible 2005 presidential contender before *Asaba* and other opposition parties endorsed former prime minister Bakiyev in 2004.

In January 2008, with *Asaba* having failed to win any seats in the December 2007 election, Beknazarov joined in forming a Revolutionary Committee of opposition leaders whose aim was to act in a "very radical manner" to force President Bakiyev's resignation. Beknazarov unexpectedly resigned as the party chair in April 2008 and was succeeded by his deputy, Sovetbek JAMALDINOV. In June 2009 the party elected a new chair, Salmor Dyikanov.

Although *Asaba* supported UPM presidential candidate Atambayev in 2009, the party's Jenishbek NAZARALIEV, a physician, also ran as an independent, but he withdrew on election day and finished last with 0.8 percent of the vote. The party did not compete in the 2010 legislative elections.

Leader: Salmor DYIKANOV (Chair).

Freedom (*Erkindik*). Announced in February 2000 by former members of the Progressive Democratic Party "Free Kyrgyzstan" (ErK, below) who rejected the leadership of Tursunbay Bakir-uulu, *Erkindik* was officially registered in April and held a founding congress a month later, at which time Topchubek Turgunaliyev (previously a founder of ErK) succeeded Adylbek KASYMOV as leader.

In September 2000 Turgunaliyev and seven others were convicted of a 1999 plot to assassinate President Akayev, with Turgunaliyev, labeled the "mastermind" by the government, receiving a 16-year prison sentence. Leading opposition politicians quickly protested the conviction as politically motivated. Akayev later granted a pardon to Turgunaliyev, citing his deteriorating health. In late 2003 Turgunaliyev praised Georgia's "Rose Revolution" and suggested that it might serve as a model for Kyrgyzstan.

A key member of the PMK from 2004 and subsequently a strong supporter of President Bakiyev, Turgunaliyev spearheaded a campaign to dissolve the Supreme Council and hold new legislative elections. In 2007 he helped organize the pro-Bakiyev For Political Stability and Unity movement, but he later joined the opposition. *Erkindik* registered for the December parliamentary election but failed to pass the required thresholds for representation. Turgunaliyev later became a UPM leader, serving as chair of its Committee against Political Persecution. As a consequence of his participation in a protest march following Bakiyev's reelection in July 2009, he was held in jail for 15 days. Following the ouster of Bakiyev, he became a political adviser to Interim President Roza Otunbayeva.

Leader: Topchubek TURGUNALIYEV.

New Kyrgyzstan (*Jany Kyrgyzstan*—JK). Based in southern Osh, the leftist, rural-oriented JK was registered in 1994 as the Agrarian Labor Party of Kyrgyzstan (*Agrarno-Trudovnaya Partiya Kyrgyzstana*—ATPK). Its initial goal was preventing a breakdown in agricultural infrastructure and overcoming what its founders perceived as a crisis in agro-industry. The party's Usen Sydykov, a populist, was disqualified as a parliamentary candidate before the 2000 elections and again in 2002 after having received a near-majority in the first round of a by-election. Sydykov subsequently served as President Bakiyev's head of presidential administration until being transferred in May 2006, although he remained a key presidential adviser.

Ismail Isakov, a former secretary of the Security Council who had resigned in October 2008 because he differed with President Bakiyev on foreign policy matters, lost his position as JK secretary general in December 2008 because he had made overtures to the opposition and supported formation of the UPM. In 2009, although the JK supported Bakiyev's reelection, Isakov announced his intention to run for president (he later withdrew), which led to his expulsion from the party in May.

In July 2010 Usen Sydykov stepped down from the formal party leadership because of a criminal investigation into his activities during the May disturbances in the south.

Leader: Usen SYDYKOV.

Progressive Democratic Party "Free Kyrgyzstan" (*Progressivno-Demokraticheskaya Partiya "Erkin Kyrgyzstan"*—ErK). The ErK (an acronym meaning "will") was founded in 1991 as a splinter group of the Democratic Movement of Kyrgyzstan (DDK) on a platform of moderate nationalism and support for a liberal market economy. It was weakened in 1992 by secession of the more nationalist *Ata-Meken* (above), and its subsequent attempts to build a prodemocracy bloc made little progress.

ErK's founder, Topchubek Turgunaliyev, was campaign manager for Medetkan SHERIMKULOV in the December 1995 presidential election but was arrested (for insulting the incumbent) shortly before the polling, in which Sherimkulov placed last of three candidates. In January 1997, in what his supporters charged was a politically motivated case, Turgunaliyev was convicted of embezzlement during his tenure as rector of Bishkek Humanitarian University. He was released from prison in November 1998 and later joined *Erkindik* (above), which broke from ErK in February 2000.

In April 2000 ErK Chair Tursunbay Bakir-uulu accepted responsibility for the party's failure to win any party list seats at the 2000 national election. He subsequently announced his intention to run for president in October, but he received under 1 percent of the vote. After being elected by the Legislative Assembly in November 2002 to serve as Kyrgyzstan's first ombudsman, Bakir-uulu resigned as ErK's formal leader, although he remained its dominant figure. In July 2005 he finished second in the presidential election, winning 4.0 percent of the vote.

In December 2007 ErK failed to meet the threshold for parliamentary seats, and in 2008 Bakir-uulu lost his bid for a second term as ombudsman. Initially endorsed by the party as its 2009 presidential candidate, he stepped aside upon being named Kyrgyzstan's ambassador to Malaysia. He had also been serving as cochair of Kyrgyzstan's Union of Muslims. For the October 2010 Supreme Council election ErK agreed to participate in an alliance with *Ar-Namys,* as a result of which Bakir-uulu claimed a legislative seat. Bakir-uulu was the party's 2011 presidential candidate. He received less than 1 percent of the vote.

Leaders: Tursunbay BAKIR-UULU, Muradil JANJALBEKOV, Yuruslan ISTANOV.

Banned Organizations:

In November 2003 the Supreme Court banned four Islamic fundamentalist organizations: the **Hizb-ut-Tahrir;** the **East Turkestan Islamic Party** (*Sharq Turkestan Islam Partiyasy*); the **East Turkestan Liberation Organization** (*Sharq Azzat Turkestan*); and the **Islamic Party of Turkestan**, also known as the **Islamic Movement of Uzbekistan** (IMU). In May 2006 a skirmish along the Kyrgyz-Tajik border left at least four dead, allegedly members of the *Hizb-ut-Tahrir* and IMU. Weapons smuggling may have been involved.

LEGISLATURE

The Soviet-era unicameral legislature of 350 members was replaced in 1995 by a bicameral Supreme Council comprising a 70-member (later reduced to 45 members) Assembly of People's Representatives (*El Okuldor Palatasy*) and a 35-member (later increased to 60 members) Legislative Assembly (*Myizan Chygaru Palatasy*). The constitutional referendum of February 2003 endorsed restoration of a unicameral legislature, the **Supreme Council** (*Jogorku Kenesh*), effective from the next election, which was held on February 27, 2005, with runoff balloting on March 13. Most candidates ran as independents. Following the ouster of President Akayev, many members of the former opposition called for throwing out the election results and reseating the bicameral legislature. On March 28–29, 2005, however, the Assembly of People's Representatives and the Legislative Assembly both dissolved in favor of the new Supreme Council, which was organized into deputy groups that typically reflected regional and ethnic biases as well as ideological orientation and party affiliation.

Elections for an expanded 90-seat legislature were held on December 16, 2007, with all seats filled on the basis of national party lists. Party list requirements included 30 percent representation for women, 15 percent for those under age 35, and 15 percent for various ethnic minorities.

Under the 2010 constitution the Supreme Council was increased to 120 seats. Party list requirements regarding women, age, and minorities have been retained, and an unusual restriction was added: no single party can hold more than 65 seats. Moreover, seats are distributed proportionally to those parties attracting at least 5 percent of all eligible voters (not of votes cast) and at least 0.5 percent of eligible voters in each of the country's seven regions and the cities of Bishkek and Osh. The latter provision effectively eliminated regional parties from representation. In addition, there is no provision for independent candidacies. Final results of the October 10, 2010, election were announced on November 1. Fatherland (*Ata-Jurt*) won 28 seats; the Social Democratic Party of Kyrgyzstan, 26; Dignity (*Ar-Namys*), 25; *Respublika*, 23; and the Socialist Party "Fatherland" (*Ata-Meken*), 18.

Speaker: Asilbek JEENBEKOV.

CABINET

[as of September 3, 2013]

Prime Minister	Zhantoro SATYBALDIYEV (SDPK)
First Deputy Prime Minister	Joomart OTORBAEV (*Ata-Meken*)
Vice Prime Minister for Economy and Investments	Tayirbek SARPASHEV (SDPK)
Vice Prime Minister for Social Affairs	Kamila TALIEVA (*Ar-Namys*) [f]
Vice Prime Minister for Security, Law and Order and Border	(Vacant)
Ministers	
Head of Government	Nurkhanbek MOMUNALIEV (SDPK)
Agriculture and Land Reclamation	Chynggysbek UZAKBAEV (*Ar-Namys*)
Culture, Information, and Tourism	Sultan RAYEV (ind.)
Defense	Maj. Gen. Taalaibek OMURALIYEV (ind.)
Economy and Antimonopoly	Temir SARIEV (SDPK)

Education and Science	Kanatbek SADYKOV (SDPK)
Emergency Situations	Kubatbek BORONOV (*Respublika*)
Energy and Industry	Avtandil KALMAMBETOV (ind.)
Finance	Olga LAVROVA (*Ar-Namys*) [f]
Foreign Affairs	Erlan ABDYLDAYEV (ind.)
Health	Dinara SAGYNBAEVA (SDPK) [f]
Internal Affairs	Abdylda SURANCHIYEV (SDPK)
Justice	Almambet SHIKMAMATOV (*Ata-Meken*)
Labor, Migration, and Youth	Alisbek ALYMKULOV (SDPK)
Social Development	Kudaibergen BAZARBAEV (*Ata-Meken*)
State Committee for National Security	Beyshenbay ZHUNUSOV (SDPK)
Transportation and Communications	Kalykbek SULTANOV (*Ata-Meken*)

[f] = female

INTERGOVERNMENTAL REPRESENTATION

Ambassador to the U.S.: Mukhtar DJUMALIEV.

U.S. Ambassador to Kyrgyzstan: Pamela SPRATLEN.

Permanent Representative to the UN: Taalabek KYDYROV.

IGO Memberships (Non-UN): ADB, CIS, EBRD, IOM, OIC, OSCE, WTO.

LAOS

Lao People's Democratic Republic
Sathalanalat Paxathipatai Paxaxôn Lao

Political Status: Fully independent constitutional monarchy proclaimed October 23, 1953; Communist-led people's democratic republic established December 2, 1975; present constitution adopted August 14, 1991.

Area: 91,428 sq. mi. (236,800 sq. km).

Population: 6,408,733 (2012E—UN); 6,695,166 (2013E—U.S. Census).

Major Urban Center (2011E—UN): VIENTIANE (Viangchan, 783,032).

Official Language: Lao (English is considered the business language in government circles).

Monetary Unit: New Kip (market rate November 1, 2013: 7,909.52 new kips = $1US). The Thai baht also circulates.

President: CHOUMMALY SAYASONE (Lao People's Revolutionary Party); elected by the National Assembly for a five-year term on June 8, 2006, to succeed KHAMTAY SIPHANDONE (Lao People's Revolutionary Party); reelected June 15, 2011.

Vice President: BOUNNHANG VORACHIT (Lao People's Revolutionary Party); elected by the National Assembly for a five-year term on June 8, 2006, to succeed CHOUMMALY SAYASONE; reelected June 15, 2011.

Prime Minister: THONGSING THAMMAVONG (Lao People's Revolutionary Party); unanimously approved by the National Assembly on December 23, 2010, to succeed BOUASONE BOUPHAVANH (Lao People's Revolutionary Party) following the latter's resignation.

THE COUNTRY

The wholly landlocked nation of Laos sits between Vietnam and Thailand but also shares borders with Cambodia, China, and Myanmar (Burma). Apart from the Mekong River plains adjacent to Thailand, the country is largely mountainous, with scattered dense forests. The population is divided among three major groups: about 56 percent Lao-Loum (valley Lao), 34 percent Lao-Theung (mountainside Lao), and 9 percent Lao-Soung (mountaintop Lao); the Lao-Theung and Lao-Soung have long protested the disproportionate economic and political influence of the lowland population. Tribal minorities include non-Khmer-speaking groups in the southern uplands and Hmong and Yao in the northern mountains. Although most ethnic Lao, especially the valley Lao, follow Hinayana (Theravada) Buddhism, most of the tribal minorities practice animism. Lao is the official language, while English has supplanted French within government circles. Pali, locally known as *Nang Xu Tham,* a Sanskrit language of Hindu origin, is generally used by priests. About one-third of the population is illiterate. Women constitute 50 percent of the active labor force and hold 25 percent of the seats in the National Assembly.

Laos remains one of Asia's poorest countries. Some 77 percent of the labor force is engaged in agriculture (predominately at the subsistence level), which continues to account for 32 percent of GDP. Rice, the principal food staple, grows on the large majority of the farmed land, while coffee has become an increasingly important export crop; other crops include maize, tobacco, cotton, and citrus fruits. Opium is an important source of illicit income in Hmong hill areas. Industry (including mining, construction, and utilities) accounts for 28 percent of GDP, with services contributing 40 percent. Since 2005 copper has emerged as the leading mining export, followed by gold. There are also deposits of silver, tin zinc, and gemstones as well as large quantities of high-quality iron ore in Xieng Khouang Province. Exports were traditionally dominated by wood products but are now dominated by manufactured garments and electricity, with ongoing efforts to tap the hydroelectric potential of the Mekong basin. Remittances from expatriate Laotians remain a significant income source, as is tourism.

Although the Communist regime that gained power in 1975 instituted strict socialist policies, including the creation of large agricultural cooperatives, in the 1990s it promoted a return to family farming, encouraged private enterprise and foreign investment, privatized nonstrategic state-owned enterprises, and began reorganizing "strategic" companies, including banks and utilities, to compete commercially. Declining exports, a drop in tourism earnings, and lower copper prices led to a 2009 growth rate of about 4.6 percent, down from 7.2 percent in 2008. On January 11, 2011, the first stock exchange in Laos opened. In 2012 GDP growth rose by 8 percent, while GDP per capita increased to $1,445. Inflation that year was 4.3 percent. In June 2013 Laos issued its first government bonds, raising $50 million. The 2013 World Bank's annual Doing Business index ranked Laos 163rd out of 185 countries.

GOVERNMENT AND POLITICS

Political background. Laos became a French protectorate in 1893 and gained limited self-government as an Associated State within the French Union on June 19, 1949. Although the French recognized full Lao sovereignty on October 23, 1953, the Communist-led Vietminh—supported within Laos by the *Pathet Lao* (Land of Lao), the military arm of the Lao Communist movement—mounted a war of "national liberation" in 1954 in conjunction with its operations in Vietnam. Hostilities were ended by the Geneva Accords of 1954, and the last French ties to Laos lapsed in December of that year.

Pro-Western or conservative governments held power from 1954 to 1960, except for a brief interval in 1957–1958 when neutralist Prime Minister SOUVANNA PHOUMA formed a coalition with Prince SOUPHANOUVONG, his half-brother and leader of the pro-Communist Lao Patriotic Front (*Neo Lao Hak Xat*—NLHX). In April 1960 the Lao army, headed by Gen. PHOUMI NOSAVAN, gained control of the government through a fraudulent National Assembly election. A coup in August by a group of neutralist officers under Capt. KONG LE led to the reinstatement of Souvanna Phouma as prime minister, but a countercoup led by General Phoumi brought about the installation four months later of a rightist administration headed by Prince BOUN OUM NA Champassak. In an effort to defuse the fighting and avoid deeper involvement by the great powers, a 14-nation conference was convened in Geneva in May 1961, and the rightists, neutralists, and NLHX eventually agreed to join a coalition government that took office under Souvanna Phouma in June 1962.

Renewed factional feuding nevertheless led to the withdrawal of the NLHX ministers over the next two years and the continuation, with

North Vietnamese support, of the Communist insurgency based in the north. Military encounters between the government and the *Pathet Lao* (formally renamed the Lao People's Liberation Army in 1965) continued thereafter, with the *Pathet Lao* retaining control of the northeast and working closely with North Vietnamese forces concentrated in the area.

Peace talks between the *Pathet Lao* and the Souvanna Phouma government resumed in 1972, and in February 1973 cease-fire proposals put forward by the latter were accepted. A political protocol signed the following September provided for a provisional coalition government and a joint National Political Consultative Council (NPCC) empowered to advise the cabinet. On April 5, 1974, King SAVANG VATTHANA signed a decree appointing the coalition government, thus formalizing the end of a decade of bitter warfare. Prince Souvanna Phouma was redesignated prime minister, while *Pathet Lao* leader Prince Souphanouvong (the "Red Prince") was named president of the NPCC.

In May 1975, following the fall of Cambodia and South Vietnam to Communist insurgents, *Pathet Lao* forces moved into the Laotian capital of Vientiane and began installing their own personnel in government posts while subjecting both military and civilian supporters of the neutralist regime to political "reeducation" sessions. Three months later, on August 23, the formal "liberation" of Vientiane was announced. On December 2, at a People's Congress called by the Lao Patriotic Front, the monarchy was abolished, the 19-month-old coalition government of Prince Souvanna Phouma was terminated, and the Lao People's Democratic Republic (LPDR) was established. Concurrently, Souphanouvong was designated head of state and chair of a newly established Supreme People's Assembly, while KAYSONE PHOMVIHAN, secretary general of the Lao People's Revolutionary Party (LPRP), was named prime minister.

Souphanouvong resigned his state posts after reportedly having suffered a stroke in September 1986; he was succeeded as head of state (on an acting basis) by PHOUMI VONGVICHIT, theretofore a deputy chair of the Council of Ministers. The presidency of the republic was thus separated from the chairpersonship of the assembly.

The government subsequently decentralized economic planning in favor of greater free-market activity. Some degree of political liberalization also ensued, culminating in a Supreme People's Assembly election in March 1989. Although non-LPRP candidates were permitted, all candidates required the advance approval of the Lao Front for National Construction (LFNC).

On August 14, 1991, the assembly unanimously approved the LPDR's first constitution. The basic law provided for a strong presidency, to which ministerial chair Kaysone Phomvihan was elected on August 15, with Gen. KHAMTAY SIPHANDONE as prime minister. Promulgation of the constitution was preceded by a number of legislative measures that provided for a New Economic Mechanism, which sought to reconcile a continued belief in central economic planning with the requirements of a market economy, taking China's recent change of economic course as its model.

President Kaysone died on November 21, 1992. Four days later the renamed National Assembly elected the number three man in the party hierarchy, NOUHAK PHOUMSAVAN, to the presidency, while Prime Minister Khamtay was named on November 24 to succeed Kaysone as party president.

The sixth LPRP congress in March 1996 took a more cautious approach to economic reform while tightening the grip of the military on the country's political structures. Notably, the party removed Deputy Prime Minister KHAMPHOUI KEOBOUALAPHA, a leading proponent of privatization and other market reforms, from both the Politburo and Central Committee. A government reorganization in April included the elevation of Gen. SISAVATH KEOBOUNPHANH, previously minister of agriculture and forestry, to the new post of state vice president.

On February 24, 1998, the newly elected National Assembly designated Prime Minister Khamtay as President Nouhak's successor, moved Vice President Sisavath to the prime ministership, and brought in the LFNC chair, OUDOM KHATTIGNA, as vice president. Oudom died on December 9, 1999, with no successor being named in subsequent months.

The seventh LPRP congress, held March 12–14, 2001, introduced few changes in the aging hierarchy and was followed on March 27 by the National Assembly's election of the outgoing minister of defense and a deputy prime minister, CHOUMMALY SAYASONE, to the vacant vice presidency. The legislature also confirmed the nomination of BOUNNHANG VORACHIT, theretofore the finance minister and a deputy prime minister, to head a new cabinet.

The National Assembly election of February 24, 2002, concluded once again with LPRP candidates winning all but one seat, which went to an independent, the minister of justice. The president, vice president, and prime minister were all retained in office by vote of the new parliament on April 9. In an apparent response to internal security concerns, in October 2003 the National Assembly approved Politburo member BOUASONE BOUPHAVANH to be Laos's fourth deputy prime minister.

The eighth LPRP congress, held March 18–21, 2006, marked the departure of Khamtay Siphandone, 82, from the party leadership and presaged his retirement as president two months later, following the National Assembly election of April 30. His successor in both roles was Choummaly Sayasone, 70, who was elected president at the first session of the new National Assembly on June 8. On the same day, Bounnhang Vorachit was elevated to the vice presidency and Bouasone Bouphavanh was confirmed as prime minister. On December 23, 2010, THONGSING THAMMAVONG, the chair of the National Assembly, was confirmed as prime minister, succeeding Bouasone Bouphavanh, who unexpectedly resigned from office citing "family issues" (see Current issues, below). PANY YATHOTU was subsequently elected as the new chair of the National Assembly. She became the first woman leader of the Laotian legislature.

Constitution and government. The 1991 constitution redefined the country's political and economic systems as well as the rights and duties of citizens, but it preserved a one-party state under the umbrella of the LFNC. The National Assembly, which is elected for a five-year term, names the president for a term of equal duration and approves a cabinet headed by a prime minister whose authority is substantially less than that of the former Council of Ministers chair.

In the wake of the 1975 takeover, judicial functions were assumed by numerous local "people's courts," with a People's Supreme Court subsequently being added. The president of the Supreme Court is chosen by the National Assembly; all other judges are named by the legislature's Standing Committee. The country is divided into 17 provinces (*khoueng*) and the municipality of Vientiane. The state president names provincial governors and the municipal mayor. Provinces are subdivided into districts, each of which has an appointed chief administrator.

All media are tightly controlled by the government or the LPRP. In 2013 Reporters Without Borders ranked Laos 168th out of 179 countries in freedom of the press.

Foreign relations. Laos's neutrality in major power issues ended with the 1975 declaration of the LPDR. In late 1978 Laos strongly supported Soviet-backed Vietnam's ouster of the Pol Pot government in Cambodia, subsequent reports indicating that Laotian troops had joined Vietnamese forces in fighting the regrouped *Khmers Rouges.* Although Laos broke off relations with Beijing over China's incursion into Vietnam in February 1979, it backed the Soviet intervention in Afghanistan ten months later. Relations with China were restored in 1989.

After a lengthy series of skirmishes, Lao-Thai relations hit a nadir in late 1987 when fighting broke out over disputed border territory. A series of high-level talks in late 1990 led to a mutual troop withdrawal from border areas in March 1991. Five months later the two governments concluded a border security and cooperation settlement and agreed to complete the repatriation of some 60,000 Lao refugees from Thailand.

April 1994 saw the inauguration of the first bridge across the lower Mekong River, providing a major road link between Vientiane and northern Thailand and thus giving landlocked Laos easier access to southern Thai ports. A year later Cambodia and Vietnam joined Laos and Thailand in establishing the Mekong River Commission to develop the river basin, and in 1996 Vientiane and Bangkok set up a joint boundary commission to delineate a definitive border. In 2000 Laos joined China, Myanmar, and Thailand in completing a treaty governing navigation on the upper Mekong.

During the Vietnam War, American forces tried to cut off the flow of North Vietnamese troops and supplies passing through Laos and Cambodia into South Vietnam. As part of that effort the U.S. military flew some 580,000 bombing missions over Laos. The United States broke off diplomatic relations with Laos in 1975, and contacts at the ambassadorial level did not resume until 1992.

Recent U.S.-Lao diplomatic activity has addressed two ongoing U.S. concerns: efforts to curtail the narcotics trade and the ongoing search for several hundred U.S. servicemen listed as missing in action in Laos during the Vietnam War. Vientiane's cooperation on these issues in 1995 led to Washington's lifting its 20-year aid embargo, thus making Laos eligible for U.S. assistance and paving the way for further normalization of bilateral relations.

The George W. Bush administration concluded a minor trade agreement with Laos in September 2003 and pledged to pursue reestablishing Normal Trading Relations (NTR) despite congressional criticism of Laos's human rights record, including alleged abuse of prisoners and the Hmong minority (see Current issues, below). NTR status was ultimately approved by both houses of the U.S. Congress in 2004.

In 1992 Laos signaled its desire for greater regional economic and political integration by signing the 1976 Treaty of Amity and Cooperation in Southeast Asia of the Association of Southeast Asian Nations (ASEAN). That move paved the way for ASEAN membership, which was approved in 1997.

In June 2011 Laos and Vietnam signed a series of economic cooperation agreements, including accords on the construction of hydroelectric facilities along the Mekong River. In August Laos and China finalized a number of accords on topics ranging from border security to economic development. In September Laos and Thailand agreed to conduct a survey to better delineate the border between the two countries. Also that month, Laos and Vietnam announced that 2012 would be the "year of Vietnam-Laos friendship and solidarity" and launched new initiatives in economic collaboration and border cooperation, including antismuggling efforts. In December Laos agreed to establish joint border patrols on the Mekong River with China, Myanmar, and Thailand.

In July 2012 Hillary Clinton became the first U.S. secretary of state to visit Laos since 1955. Clinton announced new U.S. support to remove unexploded ordinance from the Vietnam War era and pledged enhanced economic ties. In December the EU announced it would support the Laotian bod to join the World Trade Organization (WTO) and provide $1.2 million in technical assistance to prepare for membership. On February 2, 2013, Laos became the 158th member of the WTO.

In March 2013 Laos and Thailand agreed to increase cooperation on border security to suppress the drug trade and illegal smuggling.

Current issues. On December 28, 2009, Thailand deported over 4,500 Hmong refugees to Laos. Nearly 4,400 of them had been living in the army-run Huai Nam Khao refugee camp in Thailand's Petchabun Province camp, while another 158, whom the Office of the UN High Commissioner for Refugees (UNHCR) had identified as asylum-seekers and who were awaiting resettlement in third countries, had been held at an immigration detention center in Nong Khai. Although Laos insisted that the Hmong would be treated fairly and not prosecuted, international organizations have repeatedly accused the Laotian government of human rights abuses, and even genocide, in its efforts to suppress the Hmong, who may constitute the only remaining significant internal opposition to the Communist regime. Some of the repatriated Hmong may have had historical connections to the U.S. Central Intelligence Agency. Following the Vietnam War, the United States resettled more than 100,000 Hmong (please see the 2013 *Handbook* for more information on U.S. relations with the Hmong).

In July 2010 Foreign Minister and Deputy Prime Minister THONGLOUN SISOULITH became the highest-ranking Laotian official to visit the United States since the LPRP assumed power in 1975. Thongloun met in Washington with U.S. secretary of state Hillary Clinton and signed a civil aviation agreement intended to facilitate trade and tourism.

Because of population increases, the number of seats in the National Assembly was expanded to 132 for the April 30, 2011, elections. Of the 190 candidates who stood for office in the April balloting, only 5 were independents. The rest were members of LPRP. Only one independent secured a seat in the balloting. On December 23 Prime Minister Bouasone Bouphavanh abruptly announced his resignation. Although he cited personal reasons, reports indicated that his removal was the result of an internal power struggle between pro-Chinese members of the LRRP, including Bouasone Bouphavanh, and a pro-Vietnamese faction led by the new prime minister, Thongsing Thammavong.

Major flooding in the summer of 2011 caused by tropical cyclones left 42 dead and more than 430,000 displaced. In November 2012 Laos announced final plans to construct a $3.7 billion dam on the Mekong River. The project met with considerable criticism from ecologists. In addition, at least ten villages will have to be relocated for the project, which will produce electricity primarily for export to Thailand.

Laos faced significant international criticism over the disappearance of noted environmental activist Sombath SOMPHONE who had not been seen or heard from since being detained by police in late December 2012. The United States and other Western powers called for Somphone's release.

POLITICAL PARTIES

In 1979 the Lao Front for National Construction (LFNC) succeeded the Lao Patriotic Front (*Neo Lao Hak Xat*—NLHX) as the umbrella organization for various social as well as political groups committed to national solidarity. The most recent LFNC congress was held in July 2011.

President: PHANH DOUANGCHIT VONGSA.

Leading Party:

Lao People's Revolutionary Party—LPRP (*Phak Pasason Pativat Lao*). Known prior to the Communist seizure of power as the People's Party of Laos (*Phak Pasason Lao*), the LPRP is the Communist core of the LFNC.

The seventh party congress, held March 12–14, 2001, unanimously reelected General Khamtay to another term as LPRP president, expanded the Central Committee from 49 to 53, and added 3 new Politburo members, for a total of 11. With Khamtay having announced his retirement, the eighth congress, held March 18–21, 2006, renamed the office of president as secretary general—its original title until a 1991 change—and elected Choummaly Sayasone to the post. The 498 delegates replaced one-third of the Central Committee, now comprising 55 members, but made only 2 changes in the Politburo, including the addition of its first female, Pany Yathothu, a Hmong. At the ninth congress in March 2011, Choummaly Sayasone was reelected as secretary general, and three members of the Politburo were replaced, including former prime minister Bouasone Bouphavanh. In June, the LPRP signed a memorandum of cooperation with North Korea's sole party, the Korean Worker's Party. In March 2013 the LPRP issued a statement calling for greater cooperation with Vietnam.

Secretary General: Lt. Gen. CHOUMMALY SAYASONE.

Other Members of Politburo: Maj. Gen. ASANG LAOLY (Deputy Prime Minister), THONGSING THAMMAVONG (Prime Minister), BOUNNHANG VORACHIT (Vice President of the LPDR), Maj. Gen. DOUANGCHAY PHICHIT (Minister of National Defense), SOMSAVAT LENGSAVAD (Deputy Prime Minister), THONGLOUN SISOULITH (Minister of Foreign Affairs), PANY YATHOTHU (Chair, National Assembly), BOUNTHONG CHITMANY, BOUNPONE BOUTTANAVONG, PHANKHAM VIPHAVANH.

LEGISLATURE

Under the 1991 constitution the Special People's Assembly was renamed the **National Assembly** (*Sapha Heng Xat*). The most recent election for 132 members (from candidates approved by the Lao Front for National Construction) was held on April 30, 2011. One independent candidate secured a seat, while the Lao People's Revolutionary Party won the other 131.

Chair: PANY YATHOTU.

CABINET

[as of August 15, 2013]

Prime Minister	Thongsing Thammavong
First Deputy Prime Minister	Asang Laoly
Deputy Prime Ministers	Maj. Gen. Douangchai Phichit
	Somsavat Lengsavad
	Thongloun Sisoulith

Ministers

Agriculture and Forestry	Vilayvanh Phomkhe
Communication, Telecommunications, and Post	Hiem Phommachanh
Education and Sports	Phankham Viphavanh
Energy and Mining	Soulivong Daravong
Finance	Phouphet Khamphounvong
Foreign Affairs	Thongloun Sisoulith
Industry and Commerce	Nam Vignaket
Information, Culture, and Tourism	Bosengkham Vongdara
Interior	Khampane Philavong
Justice	Chaleuan Yapaoheu
Labor and Social Welfare	Onchanh Thammavong [f]
National Defense	Maj. Gen. Douangchai Phichit
Natural Resources and Environment	Noulin Sinbandith
Planning and Investment	Somdy Douangdy
Public Health	Eksavang Vongvichit
Public Security	Thongbanh Sengaphone
Public Works and Transportation	Sommath Pholsena
Science and Technology	Boviengkham Vongdara
Prime Minister's Office, Head of Public Administration and Civil Authority	Bounpheng Mounphosay [f]
Prime Minister's Office, Head of Sustainable Development	Kham-Ouane Bouppha
Prime Minister's Office, Head of Water Resources and Environmental Authority	Khempheng Pholsena [f]
Prime Minister's Office	Bouasy Lovansay
	Bounheuang Duangphachanh
	Bountiem Phitsamay
	Douangsavad Souphanouvang
	Onneua Phommachanh
	Saisengli Tengbliachu
Prime Minister's Office, Head of Government Secretariat Committee	Cheuang Sombounkhanh
Prime Minister's Office, Head of National Tourism Authority	Somphong Mongkhonvilay
Prime Minister's Office, Chairperson of National Mekong River Committee	Khamluad Sitlakon
Prime Minister's Office, Head of Cabinet Office	Soubanh Srithirath
President, Committee for Planning and Investment	Sinlavong Khoutphaythoun
President, State Control Commission	Maj. Gen. Asang Laoly
President, Inspection Authority and Chief of Anticorruption Agency	Bounthong Chitmany
Governor, Central Bank	Sampao Phaysith

[f] = female

INTERGOVERNMENTAL REPRESENTATION

Ambassador to the U.S.: Seng SOUKHATHIVONG.

U.S. Ambassador to Laos: Dan CLUNE.

Permanent Representative to the UN: Saleumxay KOMMASITH.

IGO Memberships (Non-UN): ADB, ASEAN, NAM, WTO.

LATVIA

Republic of Latvia
Latvijas Republika

Note: Prime Minister Valdis Dombrovskis (Unity) resigned on November 27, 2013, following the November 21 collapse of a supermarket roof in Riga. Dombrovskis explained that he resigned to accept "political and moral responsibility" for the 54 persons killed in the incident. His surprise departure left President Bērziņš little time to select a replacement before Latvia joins the eurozone on January 1.

Political Status: Absorption of independent state by the Soviet Union on August 5, 1940, repudiated by the Latvian Supreme Council on May 4, 1990; resumption of full sovereignty declared August 21, 1991, and accepted by USSR State Council on September 6.

Area: 24,938 sq. mi. (64,589 sq. km).

Population: 2,037,700 (2013E—UN); 2,178,443 (2013E—U.S. Census).

Major Urban Centers (2013E): RIGA (644,000), Daugavpils (89,000), Liepaja (73,000).

Official Language: Latvian.

Monetary Unit: Lat (official rate November 1, 2013: 0.52 lats = $1US). Following Latvia's accession to the European Union in 2004, the lats was pegged to the euro in January 2005. Latvia adopted the euro as its national currency on January 1, 2014.

President: Andris BĒRZIŅŠ (nonparty); elected by the *Saeima* on June 2, 2011, and sworn in for a four-year term on July 10, 2011, succeeding Vladis ZATLERS (nonparty).

Prime Minister: (*See headnote.*) Valdis DOMBROVSKIS (Unity); renominated by the president on October 19, 2011, and confirmed by the *Saeima* on October 25, 2011; renominated by the president on November 2, 2010, and confirmed by the *Saeima* on November 3; nominated by the president on February 26, 2009, and confirmed by the *Saeima* on March 12 to succeed Ivars GODMANIS (Latvia's First Party and Latvia's Way Union), who had resigned on February 20.

THE COUNTRY

The second-largest of the former Soviet Baltic republics, Latvia is bordered on the north by Estonia, on the east by Russia, on the southeast by Belarus, and on the south by Lithuania. In 2011 an estimated 59.5 percent of the population was Latvian, 27.4 percent Russian, 3.5 percent Belarusian, 2.4 percent Ukrainian, 2.3 percent Polish, and 1.4 percent Lithuanian.

Latvia emerged from World War I in 1918 as an independent country, before being annexed by the USSR in 1940. Since World War II the country has become largely urbanized, with an industrial capacity that includes steel and rolled ferrous metal products. Cattle and dairy farming are the principal agricultural activities. Natural resources include extensive deposits of peat and gypsum, in addition to forests that have long yielded substantial sawn timber output.

The Latvian economy was severely dislocated by the postindependence transition from command to free-market policies, experiencing sharp declines in industrial and agricultural output, as well as food and energy shortages. Between 1990 and 1993 GDP contracted by an estimated 50 percent, inflation averaged nearly 200 percent a year (peaking at 958 percent in 1992), and unemployment rose to 20 percent. There were signs of recovery in 1994, but expansion was impeded in 1995 by a series of bank failures and collateral difficulties in the broader financial sector, which were followed by the implementation in 1997 of a tight monetary policy and other reforms supported by the International Monetary Fund (IMF) and the World Bank.

The Russian financial crisis in the second half of 1998 adversely affected the Latvian economy. However, international confidence in

the economy remained strong. Latvia acceded to the World Trade Organization (WTO) in February 1999 and the European Union (EU) in May 2004, although it was the "poorest" of the 10 new members. By that time, more than 60 percent of Latvia's trade was conducted with EU members.

Persistent inflation compromised Latvia's plans to join the eurozone through the early 2000s. Subsequently, easy credit and buoyant housing prices created unsustainable consumption levels, contributing to a severe recession starting in 2008 in tandem with the global economic downturn. Following contraction of 4.6 percent in 2008, GDP fell in 2009 by an astounding 18 percent, the largest such decline for any country in the world. Stagnant domestic demand and poor employment opportunities continued to impede growth in 2010, but GDP grew 5.5 percent in 2011 and 5.6 percent in 2012. Unemployment is receding more slowly, down from 20 percent in 2010 to 16 percent in 2011, 14.9 percent in 2012, and an estimated at 13.5 percent for 2013—still the highest in the EU.

Political infighting has threatened to interrupt the economic recovery, as governing coalitions have been difficult to create and maintain. The parliament elected in October 2010 quickly collapsed, triggering new parliamentary elections just 11 months later. Ultimately, the same political grouping led the government coalition emerging from the 2011 election, with little interruption of economic policy.

GOVERNMENT AND POLITICS

Political background. Conquered by the Livonian branch of the Teutonic Knights in the 13th century, subjected to Polish domination in the 16th, partly ruled by Sweden in the 17th, and absorbed by Russia in the 18th, Latvia came under Bolshevik control in 1917, prior to German occupation in February 1918. Restored to power after German withdrawal in December, the Bolsheviks were defeated by British naval and German army units in March 1919. A democratic successor regime was recognized by the Soviets in August 1920 under the Treaty of Riga. Following its admittance to the League of Nations in September 1921, Latvia adopted a new constitution in May 1922, but the country succumbed to a military-backed coup by the prime minister, Karlis ULMANIS, in May 1934. Latvia was obliged to conclude a treaty of mutual assistance with the Soviets in October 1939 and was formally incorporated into the USSR on August 5, 1940.

On January 11, 1990, the Latvian Supreme Soviet voted to abolish constitutional clauses according a "leading role" to the Communist Party, and on February 15 it condemned the 1940 annexation in favor of a "free and independent State of Latvia" as part of a restructured Soviet Union. The recently formed Latvian Popular Front secured a clear majority in legislative balloting in March and April, and on May 3 the chair of the Supreme Soviet Presidium, Anatolijs V. GORBUNOVS, became head of state by being elected chair of what was redesignated as the Supreme Council; concurrently, the deputy chair of the Popular Front, Ivars GODMANIS, was named prime minister, in succession to Edvzīns BRESIS.

In a March 3, 1991, referendum, 73.68 percent of the participants voted for independence, which was formally declared on August 21 when hard-liners attempted a coup in Moscow. After securing the crucial endorsement of Russian President Boris Yeltsin, the independence of all three Baltic republics was, in the wake of the failed coup, accepted by the new USSR State Council on September 6.

In elections to a restored Latvian Parliament (*Saeima*) on June 5–6, 1993, the recently organized Latvian Way (*Latvijas Ceļš*—LC) won nearly a third of the votes and a plurality of 36 of 100 seats. On July 7, in the third round of balloting, the *Saeima* elected Guntis ULMANIS of the Latvian Farmers' Union (*Latvijas Zemnieku Savienība*—LZS) as president of the republic, and on July 20 the *Saeima* confirmed the LC's Valdis BĪRKAVS as head of a governmental coalition that included the LZS.

The Bīrkavs government resigned on July 14, 1994, following the withdrawal of the LZS because a promise to impose protectionist duties on food imports had not been kept. After a government proposed by the right-wing Latvian National Conservative Party (*Latvijas Nacionā Konservatā Partija*—LNNK) had been rejected by the *Saeima* on August 18, a new coalition was approved on September 15 under the premiership of Māris GAILIS of the LC.

Elections to the *Saeima* on September 30 and October 1, 1995, produced a fragmented legislature amid greatly reduced LC support, with nine parties winning representation and the 18-seat tally of the centrist Master Democratic Party (*Demokrātiskā Partija Saimnieks*—DPS, or *Saimnieks*) giving it narrow plurality status. A subsequent attempt to form a conservative coalition was voted down by the *Saeima,* which also rebuffed a government proposed by the *Saimnieks* leader, Ziedonis ČEVERS. President Ulmanis then called on a nonparty businessman and former agriculture minister, Andris ŠĶĒLE, who on December 21 obtained parliamentary endorsement (70–24) for a predominantly center-right, eight-party coalition that included the DPS, the LC, and the moderate conservative parties. Least comfortable in the new administration was the Latvian Unity Party (*Latvijas Vienības Partija*—LVP), consisting largely of former Communists, who countered the more reform-minded parties in the ruling coalition. However, the prime minister himself enjoyed considerable public support for his agenda to achieve financial stability and accelerate privatization. Backed by most of the coalition parties, President Ulmanis secured parliamentary election for a second three-year term on June 18, 1996, winning on the first ballot with 53 votes against 25 for Ilga KREITUSE (the *Saeima* speaker and candidate of *Saimnieks*) and a total of 19 for two other candidates.

The increasing assertiveness of the *Saimnieks* as the largest coalition partner subsequently served as a source of instability, as evidenced in late September and early October 1996 by the ouster of Kreituse as *Saeima* speaker (on September 26) and the resignation a week later of her husband, Aivars KREITUSS, as finance minister, amid much internal party acrimony (see Political Parties, below). On October 21, moreover, *Saimnieks* leader Čevers resigned as deputy prime minister, claiming that the prime minister had authoritarian tendencies, his exit leaving the party with only one cabinet representative.

Turmoil continued into 1997 when Šķēle resigned on January 20 over criticism of his choice of a finance minister by President Ulmanis. The latter, however, renominated Šķēle, and the reinstated prime minister formed another diverse coalition of the LC, LNNK, LZS, DPS, and the Fatherland and Freedom Alliance (*Tēvzemei un Brīvībai*—TB) committed to quickening the pace of economic reform. The new cabinet was installed on February 13. However, Šķēle became increasingly at odds with his coalition partners and lost five ministers by mid-1997 to resignations, prompting him to resign again on July 28. The coalition subsequently nominated Economics Minister Guntars KRASTS of the recently merged TB/LNNK to succeed him, the *Saeima* confirming the appointment on July 28.

In April 1998 Krasts dismissed his economics minister, a member of the DPS; the four other DPS ministers immediately quit the coalition, charging the government with responsibility for deteriorating relations with Moscow. In legislative elections on October 3, the newly formed People's Party (*Tautas Partija*—TP), led by popular former prime minister Šķéle, secured a plurality of 24 seats, followed by the LC, 21 seats; the TB/LNNK, 17; and the Popular Harmony Party (*Tautas Saskaņas Partija*—TSP), 16. Meanwhile, in the wake of continued DPS infighting, the former leading legislative party did not win a single seat. Subsequently, nearly two months of negotiations failed to produce an agreement for participation in a new government by the TP, which insisted that Šķéle be named prime minister. Consequently, on November 26 the *Saeima* approved a minority government comprising the LC, TB/LNNK, and the New Party (*Jauna Partija*—JP, which held eight legislative posts) under the leadership of the LC's Vilis KRIŠTOPANS. The coalition as initially constituted appeared extremely fragile, however, and in February 1999 the Latvian Social Democratic Alliance (*Latvijas Sociāldemokratu Apvienāba*—LSDA) was added to the cabinet, its 14 seats giving the government a majority in the *Saeima.*

Seven rounds of voting were required before the *Saeima* was able on June 17, 1999, to agree on Vaira VIKE-FREIBERGA, a well-respected scholar and independent who grew up in Canada, as the next president. Meanwhile, difficulties continued within the government, and on July 4 Prime Minister Krištopans resigned in response to what he called "an atmosphere of distrust" within the coalition. On July 16 the *Saeima* approved a new TP, TB/LNNK, and LC government led by the TP's Šķéle. That coalition also proved restless, however, and Šķéle resigned on April 12, 2000. The president on April 25 named the LC's Andris BĒRZIŅŠ to head a cabinet that, as constituted on May 5, also included the TB/LNNK, TP, and JP. Although the JP formally withdrew from the government in early 2001, two JP ministers retained their posts; they subsequently became members of the new Latvia's First Party (*Latvijas Pirmā Partija*—LPP).

Surprisingly, the LC failed to secure representation in the October 5, 2002, *Saeima* balloting, which was dominated by the recently formed, center-right New Era (*Jaunais Laiks*—JL), the pro-Russian For Human Rights in United Latvia (*Par Cilvē ka Tiesībām Vietnotā Latvijā*—PCTVL), and the TP. The JL leader Einars REPŠE, a former central bank head, was approved on November 7 to head a coalition government comprising the JL, LPP, TB/LNNK, and the new Greens' and Farmers' Union (*Zaļo un Zemnieku Savienība*—ZZS). On June 20, 2003, President Vike-Freiberga was reelected by a vote of 88–6, having won the endorsement of nearly all the major parties.

The LPP withdrew from the government in late January 2004 following a dispute between Prime Minister Repše and Deputy Prime Minister Ainārs ŠLEŠERS of the LPP. Having lost its legislative majority, the government resigned on February 5. Indulis EMSIS of the ZZS was confirmed by the *Saeima* on March 9 to lead a minority government comprising the ZZS, LPP, and TP. It was widely believed that a minority government was approved in order to preclude lengthy negotiations during a time of historic developments for Latvia (which was seeking North Atlantic Treaty Organization [NATO] and EU membership; see Foreign relations, below). The Emsis government resigned on October 25, 2004, after, among other things, the TP voted against the proposed 2005 budget. Aigars KALVĪTIS of the TP (a former economy minister) was approved by the *Saeima* on December 2 to head a majority government comprising the TP, LPP, JL, and ZZS. In April 2006 all JL members of the cabinet resigned after recordings of phone conversations of Transport Minister Ainārs Šlešers were revealed that suggested his possible involvement in a vote-buying scandal in the Jurmala City Council elections. Šlešers was forced to resign, but all other members of the LPP retained their cabinet posts. The JL's abandonment of the government coalition was an early move in preparation for the October 2006 *Saeima* elections.

Despite the scandals and ruptures in the government, the TP and its coalition partners secured a slim majority of 51 seats in the *Saeima* balloting on October 7, 2006, becoming the first sitting administration to be reelected in Latvia's recent history. In order to improve the government's legislative position, Prime Minister Kalvītis invited the TB/LNNK, which had often previously voted with the government, to join the TP, ZZS, and the LPP and LC, which had run in a LPP-LC coalition in the elections, in the new cabinet that was approved by the *Saeima* on November 7. This election was the first for the Russia-oriented Harmony Center (SC) alliance, which came in fourth place with 17 seats but was excluded from the government.

On May 31, 2007, the *Saeima* elected Dr. Valdis ZATLERS, an independent supported by the four government parties, to succeed President Vike-Freiberga, who had served the maximum of two consecutive terms. Zatlers, an orthopedic surgeon with no prior political experience, became a strong advocate on behalf of anticorruption activists in 2007. (For more on that issue and official opposition toward the Corruption Prevention and Combating Bureau [KNAB] between 2007 and 2009, see Current issues in the 2010 *Handbook.*)

Prime Minister Kalvītis announced the resignation of the government, effective December 5, 2007, although the cabinet remained in place in a caretaker capacity. Former prime minister Ivars Godmanis of the LPP-LC (now a formally merged party) succeeded Kalvītis on December 20 as head of a reshuffled cabinet comprising the same parties as in the previous government.

Public anger in 2008–2009 centered on perceived government incompetence as the Latvian economy spiraled downward, precipitating the downfall of the LPP-LC–led government. Much public anger was directed at the so-called oligarchs—powerful businessmen who had become extremely wealthy during the transition to a market economy, possibly by inappropriate deals. Zatlers routinely identified three Latvian politicians as oligarchs: Aivars LEMBERGS of the ZZS, Ainārs Šlešers of the PLL, and Andris ŠKELE of the TP.

In December 2008 the IMF and EU stepped in with rescue loans of $10.5 billion and €1.3 billion, respectively, in December 2008 to prevent the complete breakdown of the Latvian economy. Following protests that evolved into major riots in Riga in January 2009, President Zatlers declared that the government had lost the confidence of the public and that he would allow voters to opt for an early election by referendum unless the government was restructured from within the *Saeima*. The LPP-LC government resigned on February 20, 2009, and was replaced on March 12 by a new JL-led coalition, which included the Civic Union (*Pilsoniskā Savienība*—PS). It also included the TB/LNNK, the ZZS, and the TP, which had been coalition partners in the previous government.

The new government was headed by Prime Minister Valdis DOMBROVSKIS, a former minister of finance in Latvia and member of the European Parliament's Budget Committee. Under the terms of the IMF and EU rescue packages, Dombrovskis had to cut the country's huge government budget deficit—then 12 percent of GDP—by half. He adopted a strategy of "internal devaluation," whereby the budget is balanced by slashing wages instead of devaluing the national currency. Although deficit reduction remained an overall priority for the government, specific cost-cutting measures, such as slashing government salaries by half, were too difficult for some portions of the cabinet, leading to the exit of the TP from government in March 2010. The government then sought the legislative support of the LPP-LC, which agreed to facilitate the business of government but remained officially in opposition.

Regularly scheduled elections held on October 2, 2010, extended the mandate of the JL, which had allied with the PS and the SCP under the Unity (*Vienotiba*) grouping. In addition to the economy, ethnic tensions dominated this campaign as parties lobbied for support by appealing to base voters through identity politics. The SC had won the 2009 local election in Riga, and its candidate, Nils USAKOVS, was now mayor of the capital. Unity's leaders aimed to woo nationalist TB-LNNK voters by implying that the SC would subjugate Latvian national interests to Russia. As a coalition, Unity would collect all of the anti-SC votes into a single bloc. The SC had grown weary of being routinely excluded from ruling coalitions. This perpetual isolation led the SC chair, Jānis URBANOVIČS, to predict that if the party was once again denied a place in the cabinet, there would be a "Bishkek" revolt, referring to the overthrow of the government and ethnic bloodletting in Kyrgyzstan in April 2010. SC placed second in the election, with 29 seats, but it was not invited to join the government. Instead, Unity formed the next government in coalition with the ZZS.

Allegations of corrupt business practices dominated Latvian politics in 2011, prompting early elections in September that year. Acting on his 2009 threat, President Zatlers exercised an obscure presidential power to call a referendum on the dissolution of the *Saeima*. The public, increasingly disgusted with conflicts of interest in public office, endorsed the referendum measure on July 23 with 94 percent of the vote.

Zatlers's term as president was due to end on July 7—between his announcement of the referendum and the actual vote—giving MPs an opportunity to weigh in on the idea of a snap election. On June 2, the *Saeima* elected Andris Bērziņš (53–41), an ally of the ZZS. (see Political Parties, below). The former president formed his own political party, the Zatlers's Reform Party (*Zatlera Reformu Partijaa*—ZRP), that month, adopting an anticorruption platform.

As September approached, relations between the ZZS and Unity deteriorated. The ZZS saw its poll numbers drop noticeably ahead of the parliamentary election, which was increasingly framed as a referendum on corruption and oligarchic interests within the *Saeima*. Unity lost some traction as it competed with the ZRP for center-right votes. Meanwhile, furor over corruption provided an opening for the Harmony Center, which had traditionally been shunned by Latvians. Just before the election, Urbanovičs, head of the SV parliamentary faction, tried to refashion its image as an exclusively Russian party: "We symbolize the ideology of transition from a divided society to an integrated one." Voters weary of both corruption and austerity responded to the party as an alternative to the technocratic Unity and its allies. Leaders even announced they would try to renegotiate the terms of the EU and IMF rescue loans. Responding to this idea, Prime Minister Dombrovski warned voters to return a Unity victory so the government could complete the economic stabilization reforms needed to enter the eurozone. (See Current issues for more.)

Constitution and government. Partially reactivated in 1990 prior to formal independence from the Soviet Union, Latvia's 1922 constitution was fully restored in July 1993, confirming the state as a democratic, parliamentary republic with popular sovereignty exercised through a directly elected parliament (*Saeima*). The 100-member body elects the state president by an absolute majority for a four-year term (amended from three years by the *Saeima* on December 4, 1997), which may be followed by one consecutive renewal. The government, headed by a prime minister, serves at the pleasure of Parliament, which also confirms the appointment of judges; however, the latter may be dismissed only by decision of the Supreme Court, as the highest judicial body.

The Communist Party's press monopoly was outlawed in 1990, and Latvia currently receives fair marks from journalism watchdogs in regard to freedom of the press despite concerns regarding ownership monopolies by vested interests. Reporters Without Borders ranked the country 39th in 2013.

Foreign relations. Soviet recognition of the independence of the three Baltic states on September 6, 1991, paved the way for their admission to the Conference on (later Organization for) Security and Cooperation in Europe (CSCE/OSCE) on September 10 and admission to the United Nations on September 17. Prior to the Soviet action, diplomatic recognition had been extended by a number of governments, including, on September 2, that of the United States, which had never recognized the 1940 annexations. The path toward foreign recognition was eased on September 4 with the passage of legislation providing for the return of foreign property seized after the Soviet takeover. Latvia was admitted to the IMF on May 19, 1992, and to the World Bank on August 9.

Regionally, Latvia concluded a Baltic Economic Cooperation Agreement with Estonia and Lithuania in April 1990. Under the accord, joint ventures were authorized, assuming foreign equity of no more than 50 percent. On September 24, 1991, the three states also reached agreement on a customs union that authorized free trade and visa-free travel among their respective jurisdictions, although implementation of its provisions proceeded very slowly. At the political level, Latvia participated with Estonia and Lithuania to revive cooperation that had existed under the prewar Baltic Council. It was also a founding member of the broader Council of the Baltic Sea States in 1992.

A postindependence objective of securing the withdrawal of Russian troops was complicated by Moscow's intense criticism of alleged discrimination against ethnic Russians in Latvia (see Current issues, below). Western pressure persuaded Moscow to adhere to an August 1994 deadline for withdrawal.

Latvia became a signatory of NATO's Partnership for Peace in February 1994, subsequently reiterating its desire for full membership and also for accession to the EU.

Latvia joined the two other Baltic nations in rejecting Russia's offer of a unilateral security guarantee in 1997. Latvian-Russian relations subsequently remained strained partly because of territorial disputes. Eighteen months of discussion yielded a draft border demarcation agreement, which was approved by the Latvian cabinet in December 1997, but Moscow failed to endorse the accord in an attempt to delay Latvia's accession to the EU and NATO. (A final demarcation treaty was signed in Moscow in March 2007.)

Collaterally, Prime Minister Krasts pressed for quicker economic reform, which was considered a prerequisite to meeting Latvia's top foreign policy objectives of becoming a member of NATO and the EU. On January 16, 1998, the Baltic states and the United States signed a Charter of Partnership, a nonbinding agreement that was seen as supporting the three states' NATO candidacy but not guaranteeing it. Latvia became a member of NATO in March 2004, after having adopted a number of reforms, including increased spending on the military. Latvia supported the U.S. invasion of Iraq in 2003, deploying some 130 troops to support the U.S.-UK–led coalition following the fall of Saddam Hussein. In accordance with NATO obligations, Latvia doubled its troop deployments to Afghanistan after it withdrew from Iraq in 2007. The country's military budget is less than the 2 percent of GDP stipulated by NATO, leading to criticism from Estonia and other members.

Following a national referendum that endorsed accession with a 67 percent "yes" vote in 2003, Latvia joined the EU on May 1, 2004. When the global economic crisis nearly bankrupted Latvia in 2008, the EU, along with the IMF, offered rescue loan packages that required austerity measures designed to reduce the national budget deficit to no more than 3 percent of GDP by 2012, in accordance with the Maastricht criteria. The difficult budget reductions have been effective, and other EU member states, including Ireland and Spain, have begun to study the Latvian model as a possible solution to their own economic woes. The country met the targets imposed by the EU and IMF loans in December 2011 and will join the eurozone in 2014.

In May the Organization for Economic Cooperation and Development (OECD) invited Latvia to begin accession negotiations.

Relations with Russia have been tense since independence and were inflamed in 2008 by Russia's decision to grant ethnic Russian minorities in Latvia and Estonia the right to enter Russia without visas. Latvia and neighboring Estonia predicted that integration would falter in their countries if ethnic Russians could travel to Russia as de facto citizens. They also charged Russia with hypocrisy for pushing the Baltic governments to involve Russians in the political process while subtly undermining the naturalization process. Latvia also strongly protested against Russia's war with Georgia in August 2008. Relations were hardly improved by ZAPAD 2013, a Russian-Belarusian military exercise in September 2013 using a scenario of "preventative occupation" of the Baltic States due to ethnic conflict.

Current issues. Latvia is rebounding from the economic catastrophe that caused rioting in its capital city in 2009. It repaid its IMF loan in January 2013, one year ahead of schedule, and is on track to repay the EU loan by the 2014 deadline. However, the political scene has been highly turbulent in the past two years, with two parliamentary elections in less than one year. Any major shifts in the composition of the government could undermine Latvia's progress. While the EU has praised Latvia's recovery, the IMF has criticized the resulting income gap—the highest in the EU. Money to repay the IMF loan was raised by lowering the guaranteed minimum income level and the income-tax threshold. The growing economic stratification has fueled an exodus of young job seekers—5 percent of the population since 2008—and could exacerbate existing resentment of business tycoons.

In the September 17, 2011, balloting for the *Saeima,* the main Russian-speaking alliance, Harmony Center, placed first, with 28.36 percent of the vote. It was followed by Zatlers's Reform Party, with 20.82 percent of votes, and Unity (now a party led by Prime Minister Valdis Dombrovskis), with 18.83 percent of votes, All for Latvia–LNNK, with 13.88 percent of votes, and the Greens' and Farmers' Union, with 12.22 percent of votes.

Former president Zatlers attempted to create a coalition comprised of his ZRP, Harmony Center, and Unity, but Unity refused to work with the Russian nationalists. Had the deal gone through, it would have been the first time a Russian party had been part of a Latvian government. After several weeks of negotiations, Dombrovskis announced on October 11 the formation of a three-party coalition (Unity, ZRP, and NP) that would control 56 of the 100 seats in the *Saeima*, but exclude Harmony, the largest faction. For the first time, the National Alliance, considered by many to be Latvian nationalist radicals, would be part of the national government. Under the deal, Dombrovskis would be prime minister and Zalters would be speaker of parliament, but after two failed votes, parliament instead reelected the previous speaker, Solvita ABOLTINA of Unity.

On October 19 President Bērziņš invited Dombrovskis to form a government. Parliament approved the three-party coalition on October 25, making Dombrovskis the first Latvian prime minister to serve three consecutive terms. Six members of ZRP, including Klavs OLSTEINS, then dropped out of the party's parliamentary bloc and formed their own independent group. They pledged to support the government, which would lose its majority without them.

Harmony's first-place win put the status of Russians living in Latvia at the political forefront. This longstanding, multidimensional issue is encapsulated in the country's citizenship and language policies. In contrast to Estonia and Lithuania, where they are far less numerous, ethnic

Russians account for more than a quarter of Latvia's overall population, a considerably reduced figure since independence from the USSR in 1991, when more than a third of the population was Russian. During the Soviet era, many Russians arrived in Latvia in accordance with a Kremlin-directed effort to weaken Latvian national identity. They raised families in Latvia and many Russians, especially veterans, decided to remain in the republic after retirement. This influx of Russians, combined with Stalin's deportations of Latvians to Siberia in the 1940s, meant that Latvians risked becoming a minority in their own state. When independence was restored in 1991, Latvians made up almost 52 percent of the population; in 2011 the number still was less than 60 percent.

Tension between the two groups has long been exacerbated by the inability of most Russians to speak Latvian, which is required to become a naturalized citizen. Noncitizens pay taxes but cannot vote or hold government jobs. In addition, some resentment still exists from the long-held perception that ethnic Russians constituted a privileged economic class under communism. Thus, a major question has been the citizenship status of first-generation residents. For example, children born to Russian-speakers in Latvia do not automatically receive Latvian citizenship; their parents must prove that at least one of them has ties to the country that predate World War II.

Harmony Center's victory in the September 2011 parliamentary election has been explained as a protest vote against entrenched business interests, a sign of economic desperation, or a significant shift in social attitudes. The party had long complained that oligarchs controlled the economy and pledged to increase social welfare programs to residents suffering under the economic crisis. Voters weary of the harsh terms for the EU and IMF aid packages may have been desperate enough to consider turning to Moscow for help with fewer strings attached. Subsequent events quickly proved that the ethnic divide in Latvia had not been breached; in fact, it might even be growing wider.

In January the government passed a law requiring balanced state budgets beginning in 2016.

On February 18, 2012, Latvians voted in a referendum that proposed amending the constitution to make Russian a second national language, equivalent to Latvian. The proposed amendment came from the tiny National Bolshevik Party branch in Latvia and predated the parliamentary election. SC took up the cause and campaigned for its passage as a way for the people to protest SC's exclusion from the governing coalition.

The motion was defeated, with votes breaking down almost perfectly along ethnic and linguistic lines: only about 25 percent of the votes cast supported the idea and about 28 percent of the population is Russophone. Public interest was high, with turnout at 70 percent, the largest for any referendum in history and larger than for most parliamentary elections. Many observers suggested that the motion reflected the enduring feeling of exclusion felt by many Russians residing in Latvia. If only the SC had been invited to join the government, Usakovs noted, "I believe people wouldn't really support this referendum." After campaigning against the proposal, Dombrovskis conceded, "What we need to think now is what additional measures could be done on integration and naturalization policies, including more opportunities to study Latvian."

Moscow, busy with its own presidential election in 2012, did not weigh in on the referendum until it was concluded. The Russian Foreign Ministry criticized the accuracy of the results, noting that the 319,000 Russians classified as "noncitizens" were not able to vote. Prime Minister Vladimir Putin, who returned to the presidency in the March vote, took up the issue in a February 27 newspaper article. He blasted Latvia (and Estonia) for citizenship policies that categorized long-time residents as "noncitizens." In addition, Putin denounced the EU for allowing such a category to exist in some of its member states. Russian Foreign Minister Sergei Lavrov also weighed in, calling the term "a disgrace to the European Union."

Also in March, former Prime Minister Einars Repse quit the Unity party. He planned to convert his Latvian Development Association, founded in 2012, into a political party in time for the 2014 parliamentary elections.

Harmony Center dominated the June 1, 2012, local elections, winning a majority in the Riga City Council. The National Alliance placed second (17.9 percent) followed by Unity (14.1 percent). Squabbling, score-settling, and accusations of corruption quickly overshadowed any substantive work in the capital city. Turnout was a low 46 percent. Unofficial, parallel municipal elections were organized by the Non-Citizens Congress (*Nepilsonu Kongress*—NK), a group established in March by Vladimirs Sokholovs, Yuri Alexeyev, and Valery Kamarov. The Congress grew out of an unsuccessful PCTVL attempt to launch a referendum on citizenship in November 2012.

The Unity government achieved its primary goal in June 2013, when Latvia was cleared to join the euro zone on January 1, 2014. However, polls conducted in March showed that two-thirds of Latvian wanted to keep their own currency. Harmony Center has blocked administrative reforms needed to change the currency. The government has declined to hold a referendum on the issue, saying the positive results from the 2003 referendum on joining the EU apply to the common currency as well. Leaders also see adoption of the euro as another step anchoring Latvia to the west, drawing it away from Russia.

In mid-2013 the European Central Bank expressed some concern about the stability of the Latvian banking sector. Many Russian depositors fleeing banks in Cyprus had turned to Latvia; as a result, the rate of non-domicile depositors had passed the 50 percent mark. Latvian officials brushed off the concerns, noting that Latvian banks were better capitalized and regulated than those in Cyprus.

POLITICAL PARTIES

In January 1990 the then Latvian Supreme Soviet revoked the political monopoly of the Latvian Communist Party (*Latvijas Komunistu Partija*—LKP), which was banned on the declaration of independence in August 1991. Having spearheaded the reassertion of national identity, the broadly based Latvian Popular Front spawned a wide array of new and revived parties, with the *Saeima* election of June 1993 being contested by 23 parties or alliances.

Governing Parties:

Unity (*Vienotiba*). Unity began as a coalition of center-right parties formed ahead of the October 2010 elections by New Era (*Jaunais Laiks*—JL), Civic Union (*Pilsoniskā Savienība*—PS), and the Society for Other Politics (*Sabiedrība Citai Politikai*—SCP). The Unity coalition received a plurality of 33 seats following the 2010 election and led the subsequent government in partnership with the ZZS. The three parties agreed to formally merge on August 3, 2011, but won only 20 seats in the September 17 vote, behind Harmony Center and ZRP. Unity refused an invitation from ZRP to enter into a coalition with the Russian-nationalist Harmony Center, instead finding agreement with ZRP and NA. Parliamentary Speaker Solvita ĀBOLTIŅA was elected party chair at the December 2012 party congress.

Leaders: Valdis DOMBROVSKIS (Prime Minister); Solvita ĀBOLTIŅA (Party Chair, Parliamentary Speaker); Dzintars ZAĶIS (Parliamentary Chair); Edvards SMILTĒNS, Lolita ČIGĀNE (Deputy Parliamentary Chairs).

New Era (*Jaunais Laiks*—JL) was launched in February 2002 under the leadership of Einars Repše, the former president of the central bank. Describing itself as "liberal-right," New Era pledged to combat corruption and drug smuggling, support "honest businessmen," and pursue EU and NATO membership. The JL secured a plurality of 26 seats in the October 2002 legislative balloting, and Repše served as prime minister until early 2004, when the coalition dissolved. JL took 16.38 percent of the vote in the 2006 *Saeima* elections, narrowing its share of seats to 18. A JL-led coalition took office on March 12, 2008, following discussions between Valdis Dombrovskis and the president, who nominated Dombrovskis to the position on February 26.

Civic Union (*Pilsoniskā Savienība*—PS). A prominent TB/LNNK dissenter, Ģirts Valdis Kristovskis, led an exodus from that party in February 2008 and founded the PS with JL member Sandra KALNIETE in April. The new party emphasized support for the national anticorruption agency. The PS joined the JL government in March 2009, and it drew the largest number of votes (24.3 percent of the total) in the 2009 EU elections, winning two seats.

Society for Other Politics (*Sabiedrība Citai Politikai*—SCP) was a center-left group formed in 2008 by defections from the People's Party. At that point the SCP had two representatives in the parliament, Aigars STOKENBERGS and Artis PABRIKS.

Reform Party (*Zatlera Reformu Partijaa*—ZRP). The ZRP is a centrist party with an anticorruption, anti-oligarch platform that was founded in July 2011 by former president Vladis Zatlers, days after he lost reelection to the presidency. The party quickly won support in response to growing public intolerance of public corruption. The Zatlers also decried the ethnic divisions in Latvia and pledged to reach out to Russians living in Latvia. The ZRP placed second in the 2011 election, winning 22 seats. Zatlers tried to forge a coalition with Unity and Harmony Center. When that effort was rebuffed by Unity, he agreed to join a coalition with Unity and the National Alliance. Under the deal, Dombrovskis would be prime minister and Zalters would be speaker of parliament, but after two failed votes, parliament instead reelected the previous speaker, Solvita Aboltina of Unity.

Six members of ZRP, including Klavs OLSTEINS, then dropped out of the party parliamentary faction and formed their own independent bloc, leaving the government with only 50 seats. By April 2012 the party appeared to be in disarray, lacking a quorum at its general meeting. The party dropped Zatlers's name in April 2012. In June 2012 Zatlers announced that he had been diagnosed with prostate cancer and a rare disease affecting the blood vessels of the spine. Edmund Demiters was chosen as party chair in July 2013.

Leaders: Edmund DEMITERS (Chair), Vladis ZATLERS (Founder).

National Alliance "All for Latvia"—"For Fatherland and Freedom/LNNK" (*Nacionālā apvienība "Visu Latvijai!"—"Tēvzemei un Brīvībai/LNNK"*—NA-VL-TB/LNNK). Customarily referred to simply as the National Alliance (NA), the party was formed by a merger of For Fatherland and Freedom/LNNK (*Tēvzemei un Brīvībai/LNNK*—TB/LNNK) and All for Latvia (*Visu Latvijai*—VL) in July 2011. Prior to its formal merger, the alliance won eight seats in the 2010 balloting, during which it ran under a joint banner following the Unity umbrella's decision to deny both nationalist parties membership. The platform emphasizes national interests and Latvian culture, which is supported by both classical liberals and conservative nationalists within the party. In 2010 the party unsuccessfully sponsored a referendum to require all schools receiving state funding to teach exclusively in Latvian.

NA won 14 seats in the 2011 parliamentary elections and was invited to join the new government. It performed well in the 2013 municipal elections, winning 12 seats on the Riga City Council.

Leaders: Gaidis BĒRZIŅŠ, Raivis DZINTARS (Co-Chairs).

For Fatherland and Freedom/LNNK (*Tēvzemei un Brīvībai/LNNK*—TB/LNNK). Founded at a joint congress of the TB and the LNNK on June 21, 1997, the TB/LNNK is a right-wing nationalistic formation favoring repatriation of aliens, stringent laws on citizenship, and protection of the purity of the Latvian language, although it maintains a pro-EU and pro-NATO posture.

The TB and the LNNK had been members of the National Bloc (*Nacionālā Bloc*), a parliamentary alliance of conservative parties (including the LZP, LZS, LKDS, and LVP) launched in September 1994. The National Bloc joined the ensuing center-right coalition government and backed the successful reelection bid of President Ulmanis of the LZS in June 1996.

The LNNK had evolved from the Latvian National Independence Movement (*Latvijas Nacionālā Neatkarības Kustība*), which was founded in 1988 and adopted the LNNK rubric in 1994. Ultranationalist and anti-Russian, the LNNK insisted that state benefits should be limited to ethnic Latvians and that no more than 25 percent of non-Latvians should be recognized as citizens. It won 15 seats in 1993 but was somewhat discredited by the far-right agitation of the successful LNNK candidate Joahims ZIGERISTS. On the president's invitation, LNNK attempted to form a right-wing government in August 1994 but was rebuffed by the *Saeima.* For the fall 1995 election the LNNK formed an unlikely alliance with the Latvian Green Party, their joint list winning 8 seats on a 6.3 percent vote share.

The TB was an alliance of several far-right groups that allegedly received support from right-wing extremists in Germany. The TB won 6 seats in 1993, rising to 14 seats in 1995, thus becoming the strongest National Bloc member. After party leader Māris GRĪNBLATS had tried and failed to form a government, the TB agreed to join a center-right coalition headed by a nonparty prime minister.

The TB/LNNK nominated Guntars Krasts, a pragmatic businessman, for prime minister in July 1997, when the Šķēle coalition government unraveled. In August 1998 the party blocked enactment of amendments that would have liberalized the citizenship law and organized a referendum on a more restrictive policy in the general election of October 1998, which was rejected by voters. Also, with 17 seats, the party fared worse in the election than its components did as separate parties in 1995. The TB/LNNK's tally fell to only 7 seats in the 2002 legislative poll, giving it a minority-partner position in the new government. Despite refusing to participate in the coalition formed in 2004, the TB/LNNK worked with the ruling alliance on several issues following New Era's exit from the coalition in April 2006. The TB/LNNK joined the government formed in November 2006 following elections the previous month, in which it secured 8 seats.

A high-profile party dissenter, Ģirts Valdis Kristovskis, exited the party to form the new Civic Union (see Unity in Government Parties, above) in February 2008, apparently prompting a group of subsequent defections from the TB/LNNK. The party secured 7.45 percent of the vote in the European parliamentary voting in 2009, losing three of its four seats. It was placed fifth in the polling.

Following the TB/LNNK's party congress in March 2010, it formed an electoral coalition for the October legislative poll with the VL (below). The coalition stressed its support for "positive nationalism" that upholds Latvian national interests and Latvian culture for all residents of Latvia rather than a nationalism founded on racial intolerance for Russians and other groups.

In July 2011 the party voted to merge with VL, creating the National Alliance.

All for Latvia (*Visu Latvijai*—VL). The VL, a radical nationalist youth organization, was transformed into a political party in January 2006 under the leadership of Raivis Dzintars. Its platform included expelling people who are disloyal to the country and strengthening the role of the Latvian language in society. The VL supported the Estonian government's decision to remove the Bronze Solider (see entry on Estonia) and attempted to initiate debate regarding the removal of its counterpart, the Victory Monument, which commemorates Soviet World War II soldiers in Latvia. During the 2006 parliamentary elections, the VL took 1.48 percent of the vote. The last party congress was held on December 7, 2008, in Riga. The party manifesto argued for the expansion of compulsory instruction in the Latvian language. The party secured 2.81 percent of the vote in the 2009 EU elections.

In 2010 the VL formed an electoral coalition with the TB/LNNK, and in July 2011 the two parties merged as the National Alliance.

Opposition Parties:

Harmony Center (*Saskaņas Centrs*—SC). The name "Harmony Center" has been used for both electoral alliances and parliamentary factions. The composition has changed over time, but they have all been leftist, pro-Russia parties. Formed in July 2005, the SC was an alliance of the Popular Harmony Party (*Tautas Saskaņas Partija*—TSP), the Latvian Socialist Party (*Latvijas Socālistiska Partija*—LSP), and the New Center (*Jaunais Centrs*—JC). (For more information on the TSP and JC, see the 2013 *Handbook.*) Its first chair was Riga city councilor and New Center chair, Sergejs DOLGOPOLOVS. Dolgopolovs, who was expelled from the National Harmony Party in 2004 after a fractious struggle with longtime leader Jānis JURKANS, abdicated the SC chair in favor of the journalist Nils Ušakovs a few months after the alliance's founding. The SC performed well in its electoral debut, taking 14.42 percent of the vote in the 2006 elections and winning 17 seats in the *Saeima.*

The alliance was later challenged in the weeks leading up to the May 2007 presidential elections as outgoing president Vike-Freiberga questioned the leftist SC's loyalty to Latvia in a radio interview. In response, the SC threatened to sue, arguing that the popular president's distrust of the party undermined its presidential candidate, Aivars ENDZIŅŠ.

More moderate than the Russian-speaking PCTVL, the SC favors national unity and free language choice in children's education. The SC opposed proposed cuts to the pensions system and sought to preserve social services during the recession, which earned it a high level of popular support.

In 2009 the TSP, New Center, and the **Social Democratic Party** (*Sociāldemokrātiskā partija*—SDP) regrouped as the **Social Democratic Party "Harmony"** (*Sociāldemokrātiskā Partija "Saskaņa"*—SDPS) under the leadership of Jānis URBANOVIČS. SDPS and LSP ran on the SC ticket and secured 29 seats in the general balloting in 2010. Although the SC received the second highest number of seats, it was accused by other parties of subordinating national interests, with critics objecting to its dialogue with Russia's ruling party, United Russia.

Nevertheless, the SC enjoyed a major surge in public support prior to the snap election in 2011, combining an antiestablishment message with criticism toward the conditions imposed upon Latvia's debts. In response to concerns that the SC would not be included in the next government due to its stance toward Russian occupation, leaders indicated that their view had softened in recent years. While it would not acknowledge ethnic Russians resident in Latvia as occupiers, it was willing to concede that the presence of Soviet authorities in the country after 1945 had been an occupation. The SC also cautioned against including the National Alliance, its Latvian nationalist rival, in the role of supplementary coalition partner in the next government.

SC was the largest vote-getter in the 2011 election, increasing from 29 seats to 31 and benefitting from Unity's plunge from 33 seats to 22. The SC responded favorably to a coalition proposal from ZRP only to have Unity refuse the offer. Instead, Unity assembled a 56-seat coalition that included ZRP and NA but not the SC. It won a majority on the Riga City Council in the June 2013 municipal elections.

Leaders: Nils UŠAKOVS (Chair and Mayor of Riga); Jānis URBANOVIČS (Parliamentary Chair); Alfrēds RUBIKS (Chair, Latvian Socialist Party); Valērijs AGEŠINS, Arturs RUBIKS (Deputy Parliamentary Chairs).

Social Democratic Party "Harmony" (*Sociāldemokrātiskā Partija "Saskaņa"*—SDPS) was established in 2009 by a merger of the TSP, New Center, and the Social Democratic Party (*Sociāldemokrātiskā partija*—SDP), a LSDSP faction led by Egils Rutkovskis. It is the larger half of the Harmony Center alliance, taking 28 of the SC's 31 mandates. In January 2012 SDPS was granted observer status in the Party of European Socialists.

Leader: Jānis URBANOVIČS (Chair).

Latvian Socialist Party (*Latvijas Socālistiska Partija*—LSP). The LSP was launched in 1995 to represent the interests of the non-Latvian population and to urge the adoption of Russian as Latvia's second official language. The LSP's most prominent figure was Alfrēds Rubiks, the former leader of the Latvian Communist Party, who had run on the Equality ticket in June 1993 despite the fact that he was in prison awaiting trial for supporting the failed August 1991 coup on the part of hard-liners in Moscow. Rubiks was elected to the *Saeima,* but the new body rejected his credentials. In July Rubiks was sentenced to eight years of imprisonment for conspiring to overthrow the government in 1991. Nevertheless, he headed the LSP list in the 1995 balloting, in which the party won five seats on a 5.6 percent vote share. Still in prison, Rubiks was also a candidate in the June 1996 presidential contest, receiving five votes in the *Saeima* balloting. He was released from prison in 1997. In 1998 the LSP joined other leftist parties in the For Human Rights in United Latvia (PCTVL) alliance, which enjoyed solid electoral success through 2002. Along with the TSP, the LSP split from the PCTVL in 2003.

Leader: Alfrēds RUBIKS.

Greens' and Farmers' Union (*Zalo un Zemnieku Savienī*—ZZS). The center-right ZZS, a pro-EU, pro-NATO grouping, was formed by a merger of the Latvian Farmers' Union (*Latvijas Zemnieku Savienība*—LZS) and the Latvian Green Party (*Latvijas Zalā Partija*—LZP) ahead of the 2002 legislative poll, in which the ZZS won 12 seats. Former prime minister Vilis KRIŠTOPANS was subsequently described as a leader of the ZZS, as was Ingrīda ŪDRE (formerly of the New Party), who was elected speaker of the *Saeima* in November 2002. A strong coalition partner of the ruling People's Party, the ZZS secured the second-largest vote share in the 2006 *Saeima* elections with 16.7 percent, granting it 18 seats. It remained a partner in the subsequent LPP-LC and JL governments. The ZZS objected to spending cuts that would harm its agricultural constituency in late 2008 and 2009 and was expected to resist the new government's austerity measures in 2009 and 2010. The ZZS won just 3.71 percent of the vote in the 2009 EU polling but assumed a kingmaker role following the 2010 general elections. After securing 22 seats, it joined the Unity-led government. Ties with the senior coalition partner were frayed because of support for the presidential candidacy of Andris Bērziņš against incumbent president Zalters. Gaining only 13 seats, the ZZS lost nearly half of its faction after the 2011 elections, as well as its kingmaker role. The parties plan to field a single candidate list for the European Parliamentary elections in 2014.

Leaders: Andris BĒRZIŅŠ (President of Republic), Raimonds VĒJONIS (Chair).

Latvian Farmers' Union (*Latvijas Zemnieku Savienība*—LZS). The LZS continues the tradition of a similarly named organization founded in 1917 and prominent in the interwar period until banned in 1934. It resumed activity in July 1990. As suggested by its name, it is primarily devoted to defending rural interests, taking a somewhat conservative position on the nationality issue. Having won 12 seats in the 1993 balloting (with 10.6 percent of the vote), the LZS slipped to 8 seats and 6.3 percent in the 1995 election, which it contested in alliance with the LKDS (below, under LZP) and the Democratic Party of Latgale (*Latgales Demokrātiskā Partija*—LDP), the latter based in the underdeveloped eastern region of Latvia. In 1996 former members of the LVP joined the LZS, giving it 13 seats in the Parliament. However, the party failed to win any seats in the election of October 1998. New party leaders were elected in March 2001, with Guntis Ulmanis, former president of the republic and theretofore honorary chair of the LZS, retiring from the party in the fall. Augusts Brigmanis has been party chair since 2002.

Leaders: Augusts BRIGMANIS (Chair), Uldis AUGULIS (Vice Chair), Ingrīda ŪDRE (Former Speaker of the *Saeima*), Artūrs GRAUDIŅŠ (General Secretary).

Latvian Green Party (*Latvijas Zalā Partija*—LZP). Founded in 1990, the LZP endorsed a Green List in the 1993 election, which captured only 1.2 percent of the vote. Despite the party's lack of parliamentary representation, the LZP named a member as the minister of state for environmental protection. The party also obtained representation at the junior level in the center-right government formed in December 1995, having contested the recent election in alliance with the LNNK. The LZP was part of the coalition government formed by Prime Minister Šķēle but was not included initially in the succeeding Krasts coalition. For the June 1998 elections, the LZP joined an electoral alliance with the Latvian Christian Democratic Union (*Latvijas Kristîgi Demokratu Savienîba*—LKDS), but the grouping failed to win any seats. The party's fortunes rose in July 2002 when the LZP party congress voted to merge with the LZS, forming the Greens' and Farmers' Union (ZZS).

Following the collapse of the Repše's government in early 2004, the LZP's Indulis Emsis was named prime minister until December.

Leaders: Gundars DAUDZE (Speaker of the Ninth *Saeima*); Indulis EMSIS (Former Speaker of the Ninth *Saeima* and Former Prime Minister); Viesturs SILENIEKS, Raimonds VĒJONIS (Cochairs).

Other Political Parties That Contested the 2011 Election:

Latvia's First Party and Latvia's Way Union (*Latvijas Pirmās Partijas un Partijas "Latvijas Ceļš" Vēlēšanu Apvienība*—LPP-LC). After failing to win any seats in the *Saeima* in 2002, Latvia's Way (LC) joined forces with Latvia's First Party (LPP) to run on a common ballot for the 2006 elections. While the LPP and the LC held similar positions on economics, the LPP has influenced the bloc's identity as a center-right Christian party.

During the 2006 parliamentary poll, the LPP-LC alliance secured ten seats on an 8.58 percent vote share. A joint congress conducted after elections in November 2006 chose former prime minister Andris Bērziņš of the LC as chair of the party coalition. In a joint conference on August 25, 2007, the LPP-LC officially became a single party, also incorporating two small, previously unknown regional parties, Vidzeme Union and We of Our Region. The LPP-LC was installed as head of a governing coalition under Ivars Godmanis on December 17, 2007, following the resignation of the TP-led government. Prime Minister Godmanis resigned on February 20, 2009, in response to voter frustration with the government's economic management. The LPP-LC placed fourth and maintained its one seat in the European Parliament in the 2009 elections.

In April 2010, LPP-LC joined forces with the People's Party (TP) to form **For a Good Latvia** (*Par labu Latviju*—PLL) after the TP left the cabinet in March and joined the opposition. Both subsets of the party favor probusiness tax policies, including sharp budget cuts. The grouping was briefly known as AS[2], in reference to the names of Ainārs Šlešers and Andris Šķēle, high-profile businessmen who led the LPP-LC and the TP, respectively. Together the alliance won only 8 seats in 2010, down from the 28 they won separately in 2006. Leadership elections in February 2011 appointed Ivar Kalvišķis chair of the umbrella group.

When TP decided not to compete in the snap September 2011 parliamentary election, LPP-LC, changed its name to the **Šlešers Reform Party** (*Šlešera Reformu Partija*—LPP/LC), possibly in response to former president Zatlers's eponymous ZRP, as Zatlers had accused Mr. Šlešers of corruption. The party platform argued that veteran businessmen should be allowed to participate in politics. On election day, the party received just 2.4 percent of the vote and thus failed to gain a seat in the *Saeima*. The party then reverted to its LPP-LC name and disbanded.

For Human Rights in United Latvia (*Par Cilvēka Tiesībām Vienotā Latvijā*—PCTVL). The PCTVL was first referenced in 1998, when the Popular Harmony Party, the LSP, and Equality (*Vienlīdzība*—V) formed an electoral coalition to contest the October balloting to increase their share of votes under the PCTVL rubric. However, the government declined to register the PCTVL, citing what it perceived to be a lack of appropriate endorsement by all the governing bodies of the component parties. Consequently, all the candidates envisioned for the PCTVL ticket were instead presented solely under the TSP banner. One of the main campaign issues for the candidates was pursuit of liberalization of the citizenship and language laws so as to better serve the interests of the Russian-speaking population.

The pro-Moscow PCTVL was permitted to run as a coalition in the 2002 legislative balloting. The alliance's platform endorsed membership in the EU, despite opposition from Equality, but was perceived as ambivalent regarding NATO. Although the PCTVL came in second in the legislative poll with 25 seats on a 19 percent vote share, its pro-Moscow stance on many issues precluded it from participation in subsequent coalitions. The PCTVL split in 2003, when first the TSP and then the LSP exited over programmatic and apparent personal differences. Members of these breakaway parties who still supported the PCTVL registered a new party, BITE (*Brīvā Izvēle Tautu Eiropā,* or Free Choice in People's Europe), which subsequently joined the PCTVL coalition. During the European Parliament elections of 2004, the PCTVL won a seat that was filled by Tatjana Ždanoka. In 2006 the PCTVL took 6.03 percent of the votes, securing 6 seats in the ninth *Saeima.*

Despite a long history of fractures, the affiliated parties of the PCVTL voted in May 2007 to officially merge into a single party and were joined by the Latvian Social Democratic Workers' Party (see LSDSP, below) in January 2009. During the current legislative term, the PCTVL has sought to extend Latvian citizenship to those born in Latvia and foreign residents over 60 years old and grant suffrage to noncitizens. The party was one of the few in government not to sign the economic stabilization program in December 2008. The PCTVL was third, and retained its sole seat, in the European Parliament in the 2009 polling. In 2010 the party nominated its EU representative, Tatjana Ždanoka, as its preferred choice for prime minister ahead of the elections, but it failed to cross the threshold for parliamentary representation. In advance of the 2011 snap election, the party touted increased aid for small- and medium-sized businesses, but it polled only 0.78 percent and was excluded from parliament.

Leaders: Miroslav MITROFANOV, Jakovs PLINERS (Chair), Tatjana ŽDANOKA (Cochair).

Latvian Social Democratic Workers' Party (*Latvijas Socāldemokrātiskā Strādnieku Partija*—LSDSP). Initially formed in 1904 and Latvia's leading party in the 1920s, the LSDSP was relaunched in 1989. However, it secured less than 1 percent of the vote in the 1993 legislative poll. In the 1995 national legislative balloting the LSDSP was part of a "Labor and Justice" coalition that also included the Latvian Democratic Labor Party (*Latvijas Demokrātiskā Darba Partija*—LDDP) and others. The LDDP, formed in April 1990, is a minority breakaway faction of the Latvian Communist Party. In 1995 the LDDP announced (prior to the election) that its name had been changed to the Latvian Social Democratic Party (*Latvijas Socāldemokrātiskā Partija*—LSDP), although the LDDP rubric was still referenced for the legislative balloting, at which the Labor and Justice coalition failed to gain representation on a 4.6 percent vote share. (The LSDP rubric was used consistently following the election.)

The LSDSP, LSDP, and others formed a **Latvian Social Democratic Alliance** (*Latvijas Socāldemokrātu Apvienī*—LSDA) for the 1998 legislative elections, surprising observers by securing 12.8 percent of the vote and 14 seats. In May 1999 the LSDSP and LSDP formally merged, with the LSDSP rubric being retained. The LSDSP lost its legislative representation in the 2002 *Saeima* balloting after securing only 4 percent of the vote, and dropped to a 3.5 percent vote share in the 2006 parliamentary elections. The LSDSP received only 3.8 percent of the vote and no seats in the 2009 European Parliament elections. The party received 0.28 percent of the vote and no seats in the 2011 Latvian parliamentary election.

Leaders: Aivars TIMOFEJEVS (President); Māris PĻAVIŅŠ, Jānis KARAVAIČIKS (Vice Presidents).

Christian Democratic Union (*Kristīgi Demokratu Savienība*—KDS) was established in 1991 and is part of the European Christian Democrat movement. Historically it has formed alliances with other parties ahead of parliamentary elections, including the Latvian Green party in 1998 election, LPP in 2002, and LSDWP in 2006. It contested the 2011 parliamentary elections on its own, but received fewer than 2,000 votes (0.22 percent) and no seats.

Leader: Māra Viktorija ZILGALVE.

A number of other parties registered to compete independently in the 2011 general election. **For a Presidential Republic** (*Par prezidentālu republiku*—PPR), led by Aigara TAUKUĻA, received 0.31 of the votes; the socially liberal **Last Party** (*Pēdējā Partija*—PP) took 0.49 percent; the centrist party **Freedom—Free from Fear, Hatred, and Anger** (*Brīvība. Brīvs no bailēm, naida un dusmām'*—BBBD) with 0.22 percent, and the centrist, family-oriented **Control by the People** (*Tautas kontrole*) rounded out the field with 0.28 percent.

Defunct Parties:

For information on the **People's Party** (*Tautas Partija*—TP), **Free Choice in People's Europe** (*Brīvā Izvēle Tautu Eiropā*—BITE), and **Equality** (*Līdztiesība*), please see the 2013 *Handbook.*

LEGISLATURE

The Latvian **Parliament** (*Saeima*) is a unicameral body of 100 members with a four-year mandate (extended from three years by a constitutional amendment approved on December 4, 1997) elected by universal suffrage for citizens according to proportional representation. (The threshold was increased to 5 percent for individual parties and 7 percent for coalitions in February 1998.) The election of September 17, 2011, resulted in the seats being distributed as follows: Harmony Center, 31; Zatlers's Reform Party, 22; Unity, 20; National Alliance, 14; Greens' and Farmers' Union, 13.

The election was held early as the result of a popular referendum on July 23, 2011. As a result, this parliament will only last for three years, rather than the usual four.

Speaker: Solvita ABOLTINA.

CABINET

[as of November 1, 2013] (*See headnote.*)

Prime Minister	Valdis Dombrovskis (V)
Ministers	
Agriculture	Laimdota Straujuma (V) [f]
Culture	Dace Melbarde (NA) [f]
Defense, Deputy Prime Minister	Artis Pabriks (V)
Economy	Daniels Pavļuts (ZRP)
Education and Science	Vjaceslavs Dombrovskis (ZRP)
Environment and Regional Development	Edmunds Sprūdžs (ZRP)
Finance	Andris Vilks (V)
Foreign Affairs	Edgars Rinkēvičs (ZRP)
Health	Ingrīda Circene (Unity) [f]

Interior	Rihards Kozlovskis (ZRP)
Justice	Baiba Broka (NA)
Transport	Aivis Ronis (Independent)
Welfare	Ilze Viņķele (V) [f]

[f] = female

INTERGOVERNMENTAL REPRESENTATION

Ambassador to the U.S.: Andris RAZĀNS.

U.S. Ambassador to Latvia: Mark A. PEKALA.

Permanent Representative to the UN: Jānis MAŽEIKS.

IGO Memberships (Non-UN): CEUR, EBRD, EIB, EU, ICC, IOM, NATO, OSCE, WTO.

LEBANON

Republic of Lebanon
al-Jumhuriyah al-Lubnaniyah

Political Status: Independent parliamentary republic proclaimed November 26, 1941, with acquisition of de facto autonomy completed upon withdrawal of French troops in December 1946.

Area: 4,036 sq. mi. (10,452 sq. km).

Population: 4,822,000 (2013E—UN); 4,132,000 (2013E—U.S. Census).

Major Urban Centers (2005E): BEIRUT (1,300,000), Tarabulus (Tripoli, 215,000), Saida (Sidon, 151,000), Tyre (120,000).

Official Language: Arabic (French is widely used).

Monetary Unit: Lebanese Pound (market rate November 1, 2013: 1,507.50 pounds = $1US).

President: Gen. Michel SULEIMAN (Maronite Christian, ind.); elected and inaugurated for a six-year term by the National Assembly on May 25, 2008, to succeed Gen. Emile LAHOUD.

Prime Minister: Mohammad Najib MIKATI (ind.); resigned March 23, 2013, remained in caretaker role until new cabinet formed. Tammam SALAM (ind.) named prime minister-designate April 6, 2013.

THE COUNTRY

Lebanon is bounded on the west by the Mediterranean Sea, on the north and east by Syria, and on the south by Israel. A long-standing presumption of roughly equal religious division between Christians and Muslims is no longer valid because of a high birthrate among the latter. (No formal census has been conducted since 1932 for fear that the results might provoke political unrest.) The largest Muslim sects are the Shiites and the Sunni, each traditionally encompassing about one-fifth of the permanent population, although recent estimates place the number of Shiites at approximately 40 percent of the entire population and 70 percent of the Muslim population. The Druze number nearly 200,000, and Christian sects include Maronites, Orthodox Greeks, Greek Catholics, Orthodox Armenians, and Armenian Catholics. An estimated 350,000 Palestinian refugees live in long-standing camps in Lebanon. Women comprise about 30 percent of the paid labor force and are concentrated in lower administrative, commercial, and educational sectors. Though women made substantial ground in Lebanon following the civil war, including the 1996 passage of an antidiscrimination law, gender discrimination continues, especially in the areas of marriage and family law.

The civil war that erupted in 1975 severely damaged Lebanon's economy, leading to the loss of two-thirds of skilled industrial workers and a drop in living standards, which had previously been high relative to other Middle Eastern and developing countries. Continued turmoil into the mid-1980s further decimated Lebanon's industrial and agricultural sectors, while a loss in government income and the value of the once stable Lebanese pound created ballooning budget deficits. The United Nations estimated the war's damage at about $25 billion.

In 2009–2010, the International Monetary Fund (IMF) reported that Lebanon largely eluded the impact of the global economic crisis, as data revealed GDP growth in 2010 of 7.1 percent. The collapse of the Hariri government in 2011 depressed foreign investment and economic activity in general, and the IMF reported 1.5 percent GDP growth. Negative effects from the conflict in Syria kept 2012 GDP growth at 1.5 percent again. The IMF projected GDP growth in 2013 to peak at 2.0 percent, and increase to 4.0 percent in 2014. In 2012 inflation was 6.5 percent and was forecast to rise only slightly to 6.6 percent in 2013. Fiscal debt reached 8.1 percent of GDP in 2012 and was expected to increase to 9.7 percent of GDP in 2013.

Offshore oil and gas deposits discovered in 2013 provided positive economic news, as analysts predicted the deposits could be much larger than those announced by Israel in 2012, and have the potential to make Lebanon the most significant natural gas producer in the Mediterranean.

GOVERNMENT AND POLITICS

Political background. Home to the Phoenicians in the third millennium B.C., Lebanon was later subjected to invasions by the Romans and the Arabs, with Turkish control being established in the 16th century. During the 19th century Mount Lebanon, the core area of what was to become the Lebanese Republic, acquired a special status as a result of European intervention on behalf of various Christian factions. Following the disintegration of the Ottoman Empire after World War I, the country became a French mandate under the League of Nations, France adding to Mount Lebanon areas detached from Syria to enlarge the country's area and its Muslim population. Independence, proclaimed in 1941 and confirmed in an agreement with Free French representatives in 1943, was fully effective after the withdrawal of French troops in 1946, following a series of national uprisings during the tenure of the republic's first president, Bishara al-KHURI. The National

Pact of 1943, an unwritten understanding reflecting the balance of religious groups within the population at that time, provided for a sharing of executive and legislative functions in the ratio of six Christians to five Muslims—an arrangement that helped moderate the impact of Arab nationalism.

In the mid-1960s, Palestinian guerilla groups based in southern Lebanon began launching attacks on Israel, leading to the 1969 Cairo Agreement between Palestine Liberation Organization (PLO) chair Yasir ARAFAT and the Lebanese army. The pact permitted Lebanon to recognize Palestinian action against Israel and placed the military in the position of facilitating movement of commandos across border zones. An increase in the number of cross-border raids generated Israeli reprisals and demands from Christians that the commandos be restrained.

Serious fighting between the Maronite Phalange Party and Palestinian guerrilla groups erupted in Beirut in April 1975 as Muslim nationalists demanded the government identify more closely with Palestinian and other pan-Arab causes. The conflict escalated in 1976 when a group of Muslim army officers attempted a coup against President Suleiman FRANGIEH. A cease-fire lapsed in 1979 as Israel led a cross-border incursion into Lebanon to root out PLO forces. The border clashes sparked the disintegration of Lebanon into a devastating 15-year civil war involving various internal groups backed by private militias and foreign forces represented by Syria and Israel. (See the article in the 2010 *Handbook* for details.)

On October 31, 1992, following the country's first general election in 21 years, Rafiq HARIRI, a wealthy businessman who held dual Lebanese-Saudi citizenship, formed a government that contained representatives of most of the former militias with the conspicuous exception of Hezbollah and the Lebanese Forces Party. Legislative elections were held in 1996, following an assembly-approved constitutional amendment limiting presidents to a single six-year term.

Though politically marginalized, Hezbollah's military capacity increased, and Israeli air raids resumed in 1996 and 1997. The conflict displaced over 400,000 people and caused the deaths of more than 200 Lebanese civilians, many of whom died when Israeli rockets hit a UN Palestinian refugee camp in Qana. In May and June 1998, the first municipal balloting in 35 years took place and included the participation of the Christian parties that had boycotted the previous two elections. On October 15 the National Assembly unanimously elected Gen. Emile LAHOUD, the army chief of staff, as president.

In May 2000, Israeli forces unilaterally withdrew from southern Lebanon, although Hezbollah continued a "resistance" movement to end Israeli occupation of the 25-square kilometer Shebaa Farms in the Golan Heights. Later in 2000, national elections brought Hezbollah into parliament and Rafiq Hariri back to the premiership. Relations between Lahoud and Prime Minister Hariri, never good, deteriorated steadily.

Demonstrating their continuing control of Lebanon, Syrian leaders in 2004 decided to extend Lahoud's term by three years, a move that required amendment of the constitution. Hariri bitterly opposed the extension and subsequently resigned, setting in motion a dramatic series of events leading ultimately to his assassination on February 14, 2005. The assassination of Hariri united citizens across the political spectrum, and more than a million protesters took to the streets of Beirut to demand an end to Syrian military occupation of Lebanon and an international inquiry into the assassination. International pressure and Lebanese protesters obliged Syria to withdraw the last of its forces on April 26, 2005.

A caretaker government led by Prime Minister Najib MIKATI oversaw national elections in June 2005, which produced mixed results. An alliance of anti-Syrian groups, the March 14 Alliance won 72 of parliament's 128 seats, and Fouad SINIORA was named prime minister. Hezbollah increased its parliamentary strength in alliance with Amal, and Lebanon's Maronite community insisted that Lahoud be kept in office as a symbol of Christian political status. Though the assembly called in February 2006 for Lahoud to vacate the presidency, Amal's Michel AOUN rejected the call and reached out to the Shiite community by means of an accord between his Free Patriotic Movement and Hezbollah. Aoun's backing of Lahoud and outreach to Hezbollah signified his recognition of the central role Damascus continued to play in Lebanon.

Lebanon's political leaders agreed in 2006 that the Shebaa Farms were Lebanese lands, irrespective of the June 2000 decision of the United Nations. Some Lebanese leaders believed that Israeli withdrawal from this sliver of land might be the key to Hezbollah's disarmament and the full deployment of the Lebanese Armed Forces to the country's southern border. When Lahoud's presidency ended in November 2007, the National Assembly was deadlocked and unable to elect a new president for six months. A compromise between Hezbollah and the March 14 coalition resulted in the election of General Michel SULEIMAN to the presidency in May 2008.

Legislative elections were held June 2009, and again resulted in a decisive victory for the March 14 Alliance, which won 71 of 128 seats. Saad HARIRI, son of assassinated former prime minister Rafiq Hariri, was appointed prime minister in June. However, Hariri's ability to select a cabinet was stymied by the opposition during five months of negotiations. The defection of Walid JUMBLATT's Progressive Socialist Party from the March 14 Alliance undermined Hariri's strength. Observers noted the new cabinet prevented any one side from controlling the agenda—though the arrangement gave Hezbollah virtual veto power. In December the cabinet adopted a policy granting Hezbollah the right to use arms against Israel, although Christian groups argued that the militia undermined state authority and ran counter to UN resolutions.

In January 2010 the cabinet discussed postponing municipal elections to allow for revisions to the electoral law, though the proposed reforms were too controversial to address. The same year the assembly voted down a bill to lower Lebanon's voting age from 21 to 18, a change that would have favored Hezbollah and Amal since both have larger proportions of young members than Christian parties. In August the worst violence since the 2008 Cedar Revolution broke out in Beirut between Hezbollah and Al-Ahbash, the Association of Islamic Charitable Projects in Lebanon. The strife led to calls for greater control over illegal arms in the country.

The UN's Special Tribunal for Lebanon (STL) investigating the death of Rafiq Hariri began identifying and charging suspects in 2010. Concern over the outcome of the STL investigation caused all of Hezbollah's cabinet members—plus some allies—to resign from the Hariri government in January 2011. After the government's collapse, Hezbollah and its partners in the March 8 Alliance nominated Najib Mikati for prime minister. When Prime Minister Mikati announced his cabinet appointments, members of the March 14 Alliance criticized the new government as an apparatus of Syria.

In July 2010 the STL indicted four men—all Hezbollah members—for the elder Hariri's death. From early 2011 through late 2013, the STL plodded toward an eventual trial. The tribunal decided to try the men in absentia, then fended off defense objections that the entire process was unlawful and that it constituted a violation of human rights.

Domestic politics during 2011 and 2012 was characterized by attacks and recriminations. March 14 opposition members in the assembly forced an unsuccessful no-confidence vote in April 2011. In an effort to resolve political differences, President Suleiman suggested a return to the long-delayed national dialogue process. In a series of sparsely attended meetings in late 2012, the dialogue committee met to discuss a host of controversial issues, though meaningful consensus was not forthcoming.

The status of Syria continued to divide Lebanon in 2011 and 2012: violence continued to flow over the border, causing sectarian tensions and bloodshed inside Lebanon. The city of Tripoli was the site of violent conflicts between Lebanese Alawites and Sunnis, with skirmishes producing death and injury. When Lebanese Shia pilgrims were abducted while in Syria, fears arose that Hezbollah would carry out revenge attacks on Sunnis in Lebanon. Rockets launched from Syria—by both the Syrian Army and rebel groups—landed in Lebanon on multiple occasions, also resulting in death and injury.

In early August 2012 Lebanon experienced a political bombshell involving Syria and former Lebanese information minister Michel SAMAHA. Lebanese security agents detained Samaha with bomb-making material and $170,000 cash that had been transported from Syria. According to officials, Samaha received instructions from a Syrian source to detonate bombs inside Lebanon.

Constitution and government. Lebanon's constitution, promulgated on May 23, 1926, and often amended, established a unitary republic with a president indirectly elected by the legislature, a unicameral legislature elected by universal suffrage, and an independent judiciary. Under the National Pact of 1943, the principal offices of state were divided among members of the different religious communities. The president, traditionally a Maronite Christian, is elected to a six-year term by a two-thirds majority of the legislature, while the prime minister is a Sunni Muslim formally nominated by the president following endorsement by a legislative majority. The speaker is by convention a Shiite Muslim. The Taif accord, incorporated in 1989, provides for an equal number of Christian and Muslim parliamentary deputies. The National Assembly is composed of 128 seats; legislators are elected directly to maximum four-year terms.

Lebanon is administratively divided into six provinces (*muhafazat*), each with a presidentially appointed governor who rules through a Provincial Council. The judicial system is headed by 4 courts of cassation and includes 11 courts of appeal and numerous courts of the first instance. Specialized bodies deal with administrative matters (Council of State) and with the security of the state (Court of Justice) and also include religious courts and a press tribunal.

Starting with a draft law submitted for consideration in 2006, Lebanese leaders have contemplated changing from the current winner-takes-all electoral system to a proportional system for parliamentary elections. In September 2011 the assembly began debating the merits of such a change, with a generally muted response. In December a gathering of academics proposed a single-district, proportional representation system differentiated by sect. This "Orthodox Gathering" proposal received Greek Orthodox, Maronite, Phalange, LFP, and Marada support, but it was rejected by—among others—Interior Minister Marwan CHARBEL. His Ministry put forth a competing reform proposal, approved in August 2012 by the Mikati cabinet, featuring proportional representation across 13 constituencies. Parliament was tasked with determining which—if either—plan would become law (see Current issues below).

For a time, relative to other Middle Eastern countries, the Lebanese press was traditionally free from external controls, but Syrian troops forced suspension of a number of newspapers in December 1976. Following the imposition of formal censorship on January 1, 1977, most suspended newspapers were permitted to resume publication; a number of newspapers and periodicals decided to publish from abroad. Between March and July 1994 the government also banned political broadcasting by private stations. In its 2013 annual index on freedom of the press, Reporters Without Borders ranked Lebanon 101st out of 179 countries—down from 93rd in 2012.

Foreign relations. A member of the United Nations and the Arab League, Lebanon has traditionally pursued a foreign policy reflecting its self-image as a democratic Arab state with a significant Christian population, a country serving as a "bridge" between the West and the Arab world. From 1948 until 1975 the salient characteristics of this approach were good relations with the West (particularly the United States and France), an arm's-length relationship with Arab nationalists and the Palestinian resistance, a cordial (if wary) relationship with Syria, and conflict avoidance with Israel. For nearly 20 years the Lebanese-Israeli frontier was unfenced and quite peaceful, and Lebanon was able to avoid involvement in the Arab-Israeli wars of 1956, 1967, and 1973.

The catastrophic defeat of Arab armies in the June 1967 war and the rise of an independent Palestinian resistance movement posed a new challenge to Lebanon's foreign policy. In 1948 some 100,000 Palestinian refugees had made their way into Lebanon to be housed in UN-run camps. In the late 1960s and early 1970s Palestinian fighters from these camps and from Jordan and Syria began to establish a "state within a state" in southern Lebanon, a largely Shiite area of subsistence farms and poor villages all but neglected by Lebanon's Christian, Sunni, and Druze political elite. The Lebanese government tried simultaneously to appease Palestinian fighters intent on firing into Israel while persuading Israel (through the West) that it harbored no aggressive intent and was itself a victim. Growing Palestinian-Israeli violence exposed deep fissures in Lebanon's body politic, as Muslims and Druze generally sympathized with Palestinian fighters while Christians (especially Maronites) generally resented the Palestinian presence. Lebanon's descent into civil war in 1975 reflected the failure of foreign policy to preserve domestic tranquility in a country lacking consensus on the vital issue of national identity.

Lebanon's reputation for moderation and its tradition of effective participation in the United Nations made it the object of international interest, sympathy, and occasional intervention during its 15-year civil war. UN observers were deployed to the southern part of the country before, during, and after Israel's 1982 invasion. Multinational forces consisting mainly of American and French troops tried to stabilize the country in 1982 and 1983. The UN Secretariat exerted considerable effort in 2000 to confirm the full withdrawal of Israeli forces from Lebanon by actually drawing a line of withdrawal.

In the end, however, Syrian intervention and influence proved decisive. From 1990 to 2005 Syria was Lebanon's suzerain, and Lebanese foreign policy reflected Syria's vital interests. When Syrian interests dictated that the Lebanese government endorse Hezbollah's "resistance" to Israeli occupation—even after the occupation ended in May 2000—the government complied. When Hezbollah and Syria claimed that the Shebaa Farms was actually part of Lebanon and therefore an appropriate object of continued "resistance," the Lebanese government complied.

After Syria dictated the extension of President Emile Lahoud's term of office, the UN Security Council chastened Damascus with Resolution 1559, which called for the withdrawal of foreign forces, free elections, and the disarmament of militias. Undeterred, Lebanon's parliament approved Lahoud's extension, an act triggering Prime Minister Rafiq Hariri's resignation. Hezbollah's decision to join the following cabinet headed by Fouad Siniora indicated that the government would continue to define the party's armed wing as the "Lebanese resistance" rather than a "militia," thereby increasing tensions between Lebanon and the West—particularly the United States.

Lebanon's internal peace was shaken by the 2006 war between Israel and Hezbollah. The Siniora government was powerless to stop Israeli air strikes and deployment of forces into southern Lebanon. Israel was determined to see Hezbollah's military capabilities destroyed despite mounting civilian casualties, which resulted in international outcry and demands for a UN-sponsored ceasefire. In August the UN Security Council adopted Resolution 1701 to end the fighting and force a truce. The United Nations Interim Force in Lebanon (UNIFIL) was expanded and an international peacekeeping mission arrived to help maintain peace.

In autumn 2008 Syria began amassing military forces on its northern border with Lebanon, raising fears in Beirut that Syria intended to invade. Car bombs exploded in northern Lebanese cities in late September, and many believed the attacks were linked to Syrian intelligence agencies. The same year Syria made clear its opposition to Lebanese cooperation with the STL. Nevertheless, Syria formally recognized Lebanon on October 15, 2008. Concurrently, international pressure was brought to bear on Israel to withdraw from the Shebaa Farms as a way to weaken Hezbollah. However, the Israelis argued that Hezbollah's continued militarization was the major issue in its relationship with Lebanon.

Iranian president Mahmoud AHMADINEJAD visited Lebanon in October 2010, receiving an enthusiastic greeting from Hezbollah supporters in Beirut. Meanwhile the United States strongly criticized Syria for its destabilizing influence in Lebanon, claiming that Damascus worked hand in hand with Tehran to keep Hezbollah supplied with increasingly sophisticated weaponry. In addition, the December release of sensitive diplomatic cables between Washington and Beirut exposed contingency plans for the demise of Hezbollah in the wake of another war between the Shiite group and Israel. Leaks also revealed that the Saudis sought the establishment of an Arab coalition army, backed by Western countries that would eradicate Hezbollah from Lebanon.

The crisis in Syria precipitated by President Bashar Assad's violent repression of antigovernment protests spilled over into Lebanon's foreign relations. Lebanese representatives to the UN disassociated themselves from UN Security Council condemnation of Assad. The primary security concern in Lebanon was that civil war in Syria would spill over its border—a threat made manifest by an increasing number of border intrusions through 2013. Despite rational concerns regarding domestic security, Lebanon refused to endorse Arab League condemnation of Syria and maintained a neutral stance—diplomatically referred to as a policy of "disassociation"—vis-à-vis the Assad regime. Despite the government's policy of neutrality, Hezbollah complicated Lebanon's relationship with its neighboring states by openly sending its militiamen to fight in Syria.

UNIFIL convoys were attacked three times during 2011, injuring six Italian soldiers and 10 French peacekeepers. Analysts interpreted the attacks as a threat to Western countries in response to their anti-Assad rhetoric. Nonetheless, the UNIFIL mandate was extended through August 2014. However, in August 2013 Turkey announced the withdrawal of its troops from the mission. Earlier in the year Turkish soldiers serving in UNIFIL had been forced to stay on their bases due to increased threats against them.

In 2012 Iranian officials signed agreements with Beirut for the provision of natural gas via Iraqi and Syrian pipelines. The Iranian ambassador also reiterated Tehran's previous offer to equip the Lebanese army. President Suleiman and other top officials traveled to Tehran in August 2013 to meet Iran's new president Hasan ROWHANI. Together they discussed the cooperative role the two countries could play to increase stability in the region.

In an attempt to isolate Hezbollah, the UnitedStates placed a series of new sanctions on party Secretary General Hasan NASRALLAH in late 2012. U.S. ambassador to the UN, Susan RICE, declared that Hezbollah was part of "Assad's killing machine," while UN Secretary General Ban KI-MOON also condemned Hezbollah's role in Syria. In 2013 U.S. sources revealed Hezbollah and Iran were collaborating on the establishment of a militia network inside of Syria designed to protect Iranian interests there should Assad fall from power.

Russian Deputy Foreign Minister Mikhail BOGDANOV spent considerable time during 2013 meeting with Lebanon's political leaders. Analysts suggested that Bogdanov's goal was to remind Beirut—and the rest of the world—that Moscow considers Lebanon as within its sphere of influence. Bogdanov also was a key member of a December 2012 conference in Beirut attended by ambassadors from Syria, China, and Iran.

The contentious relationship between Lebanon and Israel was strained further by a series of events in 2012 and 2013. In September 2012 Hezbollah threatened retaliation against Israel if it tried to attack Iran. The following month Israeli jets staged mock raids over Southern Lebanon after having shot down an unmanned surveillance aircraft—operated by Hezbollah and manufactured in Iran—over Israeli territory. An August 2013 explosion on the Israel-Lebanon border wounded four Israeli soldiers. UNIFIL reported that the Israelis had crossed the demarcation line into Lebanese territory in violation of UN Resolution 1071. However, since Hezbollah claimed responsibility for the bombing, the Shiite group was judged equally culpable. In late August, a Lebanese militant group with al-Qaida ties, the Abdullah Azzam Brigades, fired several rockets into northern Israel.

Current issues. Two factors continue to exert significant influence over Lebanon: the crisis in Syria and domestic political dysfunction. As the civil war in Syria intensified, sectarian tensions and violence increased in Lebanon. In October 2012 a car bomb in Beirut killed eight people, including the intelligence chief of the country's Internal Security Forces, Wissam al-Hassan. Mr. Hassan played a major role in the arrest of former information minister Michel Samaha, who was charged with plotting terrorist attacks in 2012 on behalf of the Assad regime. Though no group took responsibility for the attack targeting al-Hassan, observers speculated that either Hezbollah or its Syrian allies were probable culprits.

In Tripoli, growing sectarian tension drove both local violence and a call for recruits to fight in Syria. Some Salafist Sunni groups in Tripoli and in other parts of Lebanon became radicalized in response to Hezbollah's military support of Assad, and intelligence reports revealed these groups—such as the Fatah al-Islam movement, the Abdullah Azzam Brigades, and the Ziad Jarrah Brigades—had established links with Syria's Al-Qaida organization, the Al-Nusra Front (*Jabhat al-Nusra*). The Azzam Brigades—an offshoot of the Al-Qaida in Iraq group—took responsibility for attacks on Hezbollah convoys in the Bekaa valley, as well as rockets attacks on northern Israel. A prominent Sunni cleric in Tripoli confirmed that men from his region regularly fought in Syria on behalf of the anti-Assad rebels. This revelation came after public admission by Hezbollah that it had sent—and would continue to send—its militiamen to Syria to fight for Assad.

In what observers feared was an escalation of sectarian animosity, an armed group loyal to Sunni cleric Ahmad al-Assir battled with the Lebanese Armed Forces (LAF) in the city of Sidon during June 2013. Dozens of soldiers and al-Assir's supporters were killed, and hundreds on both sides wounded. July and August bombings in the south Beirut suburb of Dahiya—Hezbollah's stronghold—killed 16 and injured over 300 people. Later in August bombings outside two Tripoli mosques, home of Sunni preachers critical of Syria, killed 42 and wounded over 300 bystanders.

In addition to fanning sectarian discord, the Syrian conflict affected Lebanon directly in the form of border incursions and continued refugee flows. Rockets from Syria landed in Lebanese territory, and Syrian warplanes flew raids over the border, firing missiles at rebel positions. According to UN sources, the number of officially registered Syrian refugees living in Lebanon surpassed 570,000 in August 2013. When taking account of *unregistered* refugees, the total number of Syrians living in Lebanon was estimated at more than 1,000,000.

The inability of Lebanon's political actors to overcome governing obstacles led to the fall of the government of Najib Mikati. The areas of greatest controversy were the consideration of a series of electoral reform proposals, and a decision regarding tenure of the Internal Security Forces' general director, Ashaf RIFI. While Hezbollah preferred that Rifi step down, March 14 Sunnis supported his continued service, seeing him as their best connection to the only branch of Lebanon's military that opposes Hezbollah's right to arms. Tammam SALAM was named prime minister-designate in April. However, his goal to appoint a government of neutral technocrats was thwarted by party interests. In the interim, former Prime Minister Mikati and his cabinet stayed on in their roles as a caretaker government.

Faced with governing paralysis and the growing internal security challenges posed by the crisis in Syria, the Assembly postponed parliamentary elections scheduled for June 2013, extending lawmakers' mandate until November 2014. After the announcement, protesters took to Beirut streets to voice their displeasure with the decision.

POLITICAL PARTIES AND GROUPS

Lebanese parties have traditionally been ethnic and denominational groupings rather than parties in the Western sense, with seats in the National Assembly distributed primarily on a religious rather than on a party basis.

The March 14 Alliance. An alliance of anti-Syrian groups, this bloc was formed after the assassination of Rafiq Hariri and united citizens across the political spectrum to hasten Syria's withdrawal from Lebanon. The legislative elections held in June 2009 resulted in the Alliance winning 71 of 128 seats. Saad Hariri was appointed prime minister, but he needed five months to form a new government. Hariri's longtime ally, Walid Jumblatt, announced in August 2009 that he was leaving the March 14 Alliance to join the president's bloc in the future cabinet, a move that critics said left the alliance weakened and increasingly in the hands of Christian right-wing factions. Even after the withdrawal of Syrian troops in 2005, the alliance had to battle underground Syrian influence while forging official state ties with its neighbor.

The year 2011 brought serious challenges to the March 14 Alliance, as the government of Rafiq Hariri came to an abrupt end when the Hezbollah-led opposition left the cabinet, and President Suleiman named Najib Mikati the new prime minister. Though it took Mikati five months to name a new government, the March 14 Alliance struggled in the role of the opposition. The coalition held, but its image was tarnished when various members pledged to do everything in their power to thwart the new government.

Consideration of proposed reforms to Lebanon's 2008 electoral law caused friction among March 14 parties. While the primary Christian parties, Phalange and the Lebanese Forces Party (LFP), initially supported the Orthodox Gathering proposal, the Future Movement did not because its members feared a loss in electoral clout—primarily to Hezbollah. Trying to heal the rift in the alliance, Phalange and the LFP offered an alternative to the Orthodox plan, though the FM spent too long considering this revision. Later, when contentious negotiation between the LFP and FM produced a hybrid electoral plan upon which both parties agreed, Phalange representatives failed to give their approval to the plan.

Leaders: Saad HARIRI (Former Prime Minister; Future Movement), Fares SOUAID (Secretary General; Lebanese Forces Party).

Future Movement—FM (*Tayyar al-Mustaqbal*). This party was formed by the late Rafiq Hariri after he resigned as prime minister in 1998. To protest the extension of President Lahoud's tenure, this movement became the largest bloc in the March 14 Alliance and is now led by Saad Hariri, the son of the slain prime minister. The FM won 26 seats in the June 2009 legislative elections. Saad Hariri was nominated prime minister, leading an uneasy power-sharing arrangement with the opposition that threatened to gridlock the government. After the collapse of the Hariri government in 2011, the FM attacked Hezbollah harshly: Party official Mustafa ALLOUCH said Hezbollah fit the description of a "terrorist party" and accused it of trying to enforce Islamic law. Critics noted that Future Party representatives showed no support for the anti-Syria demonstrations that took place in its electoral stronghold of Tripoli throughout the spring and summer, instead allowing Lebanon's Salafist groups to become the champion of the beleaguered Syrians.

In 2012 and 2013 Saad Hariri and other FM leaders kept up their attacks on the Syrian regime, which brought them into conflict with the Lebanese parties that continued to support Assad—Hezbollah, the Free Patriotic Movement, and Amal. In May 2012 several FM supporters laid siege to the offices of the Arab Movement party in Beirut. In the melee that ensued, 2 people were killed and more than 20 were injured.

The FM experienced internal dissent in 2013 that resulted in a number of dismissals and resignations. In addition restructuring of the party's organization led to the loss of key regional coordinators. Reports also indicated some FM members left the party to join Salafi-influenced groups.

Leaders: Saad HARIRI, Ahmad HARIRI (Secretary General).

Phalange Party (*al-Kataeb al-Lubnaniyah/Phalanges Libanaises*). Also known as Kataeb, this organization was founded in 1936 by Pierre Gemayel as a militant Maronite organization. The party was deeply involved in provoking the 1975 civil war. Phalangist leader Amin GEMAYEL became president of Lebanon in 1982, following the assassination of his brother, Bashir GEMAYEL. Amin Gemayel went into exile in 1988 at the end of his term, after which the Phalangist movement lost direction and broke into different factions, thus losing its predominant role in the Lebanese political landscape. Amin Gemayel returned to Lebanon in mid-2000 and subsequently accused other leaders of the Phalange Party of being "too cooperative" with Syria. On November 21, 2006, Pierre Amin GEMAYEL, the staunchly anti-Syrian minister for industry and son of former president Amin Gemayel, was assassinated. Supporters claimed that Syria was directly responsible for the death of the younger Gemayel. Despite personal and political hardship, the Phalange Party won five seats in the June 2009 legislative elections.

Phalange advocated limiting Syria's ties to Lebanon's state institutions, as well as de-arming Hezbollah. Meanwhile, Amin Gemayel's son, MP Sami GEMAYEL, emerged as a leading voice in the party. After the Hariri government collapsed in January 2011, Phalange was critical of March 8 Alliance members. In 2012 Gemeyal kept up the Phalangist attack against the Mikati government and called for Lebanon to end all security agreements with Syria. He also suggested that the UN should create a mission similar to UNIFIL tasked with securing the Lebanese-Syrian border. Steadfast in its opposition to the Assad regime, in 2013 Phalange put forth a draft law aimed at incorporating the concept of disassociation from foreign entanglements—understood as neutrality toward Syria—into the preamble of Lebanon's constitution.

Leader: Amin GEMAYEL (Former President).

Lebanese Forces Party—LFP. Organized as a Maronite militia by Bashir GEMAYEL in 1976 and subsequently commanded by Samir GEAGEA, the Lebanese Forces was licensed as a political party in 1991. In March 1994 the party was banned, and a number of members were arrested because of alleged involvement in the February bombing of a Maronite church. On April 21 Geagea was arrested and charged with complicity in the November 1990 assassination of Maronite rival Dany CHAMOUN. In June 1995 Geagea and a codefendant were found guilty and sentenced to death for the 1990 killing, but the sentences were immediately commuted to life imprisonment. Following the 2005 election, the Lebanese parliament passed legislation to release Geagea from prison. In the June 2009 legislative elections, the Lebanese Forces won five seats and obtained the justice ministry in the cabinet reshuffle.

In 2011 Geagea reiterated his party's concern that an armed Hezbollah could invite provocation from Israel—especially if relations between the West and Iran deteriorated. He also identified Hezbollah as an agent of Iran's bidding and suggested that Syria influenced the collapse of Saad Hariri's government. Geagea's life was threatened in April 2012 when gunmen targeted him outside his home in northeast Beirut. A common speculation by political observers was that either the Assad regime or Hezbollah were behind the assassination attempt.

Acting in a foreign policy capacity, Geagea composed an open letter to U.S. President Barack Obama in May 2013 in which he pleaded for direct United States intervention in the Syrian conflict. In the realm of domestic policy, Geagea insisted that Hezbollah be excluded from any government formed by prime minister-designate Salam.

Leader: Samir GEAGEA.

National Liberal Party—NLP (*Hizb al-Ahrar al-Watani/Parti National Libéral*). The NLP, a largely Maronite right-wing grouping founded in 1958, rejected any coalition with Muslim groups with Palestinian involvement. It repeatedly called for the withdrawal of Syrian troops from Lebanon and argued that only a federal system could preserve the country's unity. Periodic clashes between NLP and Phalangist militias culminated in early July 1980 in a major defeat for National Liberal forces. The NLP lost considerable influence in the first decade of the 21st century, despite the return from exile of its leader Dory CHAMOUN in 1998, the older brother of former leader Dany Chamoun, who was assassinated in October 1990. Chamoun was the only NLP representative elected in the June 2009 legislative elections. In 2011 the NLP criticized Hezbollah for exploiting Lebanon's maritime border dispute with Israel (submitted to the UN for arbitration in 2010) in order to justify keeping its military capability.

Leader: Dory CHAMOUN.

Henshag Party. This Armenian party allied with the Future Movement in 1996. It won two seats in the 2009 legislative elections. In 2012 Henshag leaders expressed their distrust of Turkish motives in the Arab Spring, questioning whether Ankara—with its extensive history of denying Armenian rights—was exploiting events of the Arab Spring to suit its own interests. Several Henshag leaders, including Beirut MP Serge TORSARKISSIAN, opposed the Orthodox Gathering electoral reform proposal in 2013 parliamentary deliberations, mainly due to concerns that the plan would deepen the country's sectarian divisions.

Leader: Serge TORSARKISSIAN.

Jamaa al-Islamiya Party. This fundamentalist Sunni group was founded in 1964. It won one seat in the 2009 legislative elections. The party allied with the Future Movement in the 2010 municipal elections in Tripoli. In 2012 party leaders stepped up their criticism of the Mikati government's relationship to Syria, even to the point of asking the government to step down.

Leaders: Imad al-HOUT, Azzam al-AYOUBI (Politburo President).

Ramgavar Party. Also known as the Armenian Democratic Liberal Party, Ramgavar has branches in a number of countries representing the Armenian diaspora. Ramgavar allied with the Future Movement in 1996. It won one seat in the 2009 legislative elections. Ramgavar leader Jean OGASSAPIAN was appointed to the state ministry in the 2009 cabinet reshuffle. In 2012 Ogassapian supported other March 14 allies in calling for the ouster of Syria's diplomatic mission from Lebanon. Rifts between Ramgavar and the Future Movement in 2013 had some observers speculating that the Armenian group would seek alliance with March 8 (see below).

Leader: Jean OGASSAPIAN.

For information on the National Bloc (*al-Kutlah al-Wataniyah/Bloc National*), see the 2010 *Handbook.*

March 8 Alliance. This pro-Syria coalition composed of 13 parties formed in 2005 as an opposition block after the March 14 Alliance came into being. Dominated by Hezbollah, the Alliance transitioned from an opposition to a leadership role when Najib Mikati became prime minister in January 2011. However, the speaker of the National Assembly announced in July 2013 that the alliance had dissolved after the Free Patriotic Movement left the bloc.

Party of God (*Hizb Allah,* commonly rendered *Hezbollah*). Hezbollah, a Shiite group, announced its formation in 1985, stating its goal was to establish an Islamic state in Lebanon. Hezbollah subsequently assumed the major role in the "war of liberation" against Israeli forces in southern Lebanon, widely believed to be financed by Syria and Iran. By 1996, however, Hezbollah had earned significant grassroots support within the Shiite populace because of its network of health and social services. (For information regarding Hezbollah from 1996–2005, see the 2012 *Handbook.*)

The adoption of UN Security Council Resolution 1559, which called for "the disbanding and disarmament of all Lebanese and non-Lebanese militias," put pressure on Hezbollah, particularly after the assassination of Rafiq Hariri. However, Hezbollah performed well in the 2005 parliamentary elections, winning 35 seats as part of a coalition with Amal (see below). In July 2005 Hezbollah agreed to join a government, heading a ministry for the first time.

In May 2008 the pro-U.S. March 14 government issued two directives designed to undermine Hezbollah's military autonomy. In response, Hezbollah took control of West Beirut on May 9. The fighting in Beirut marked the first time Hezbollah had used its military weapons against the Lebanese people. As a result, the popularity of the group fell. A compromise between Hezbollah and the March 14 Alliance led to the election of Gen. Michel Suleiman as president in late May and the creation of a new cabinet in July.

In June 2009 Hezbollah and its allies won 13 seats in the National Assembly. Hezbollah subsequently led the failed effort to reject incoming Prime Minister Saad Hariri's proposed government in September 2009. However, Hezbollah obtained two minor ministries in the new cabinet, agriculture and administrative development.

In recent years, observers say Hezbollah has been trying to reinvent its image from that of a militia to a more conventional political movement, striking a more conciliatory stance with rival political factions. A new party platform, announced in November 2009, did not mention an Islamic state and spoke of "consensual democracy" and coexistence among Lebanon's 18 religious sects. Critics said Hezbollah, whose $100 million budget is supplied largely by Iran, was still a reactionary group.

When all of Hezbollah's ministers abandoned Saad Hariri's cabinet in January 2011—causing the collapse of the government—Hezbollah came under intense criticism from March 14 members, who both organized mass protests calling on Hezbollah to disarm and mounted a campaign of condemnation that significantly prolonged the formation of a new government. However, the most serious challenge to Hezbollah came from the indictments handed down from the STL. Though Hezbollah stymied the ensuing arrest attempt and trial process, observers noted that the party stood to lose both credibility and legitimacy if the accused party members were found guilty of murdering a politician who was well respected in the Shiite community.

Hezbollah also received scorn for its continued support for the Assad regime in Syria. In 2012 party secretary general Hassan Nasrallah welcomed Iran's vice president, Mohammad Reza RAHIMI, on his state visit to Lebanon. Tehran came to the defense of Hezbollah in 2013 when the European Union—acting on U.S. pressure—designated the military wing of the Shiite group a terrorist organization. Prior to the EU's declaration, members of the Gulf Cooperation Council (GCC), led by Saudi Arabia and the UAE, proclaimed Hezbollah a terrorist group.

Leader: Sayyed Hassan NASRALLAH (Secretary General).

Amal (*Amal*). Amal, an acronym for *Afwaj al-Muqawa al-Lubnaniyah* (Groups of the Lebanese Resistance), which also means "hope," was founded by Imam Musa SADR as the militia of the Movement of the Disinherited. Although allied with the Palestinian left during the civil war, Amal subsequently became increasingly militant on behalf of Lebanon's Shiites, many of whom had been forced from their homes in the south, and in support of the Iranian revolution of 1979.

After the 1982 Israeli invasion, several pro-Iranian offshoots of Amal emerged as well-organized guerrilla movements, among them Hezbollah. A "war of words" developed between Amal and Hezbollah prior to the 1996 legislative balloting, and it initially appeared that they would present competing candidates. However, the two groups finally agreed on a joint accord and national list, which secured nearly all the seats in southern Lebanon. Amal leader Nabih BERRI was subsequently reelected speaker of the National Assembly. Amal has been largely disarmed in recent years, as Hezbollah became the primary military opposition to Israeli forces in southern Lebanon. Amal opposed the Syrian withdrawal of 2005. Following the parliamentary elections of 2005, Berri was again elected speaker of the National Assembly. Most of Amal's support today comes from coastal cities in Lebanon's south. Amal joined Hezbollah in the Lebanese cabinet in 2005 and allied itself with Hezbollah and other opposition parties in the legislative elections of June 2009, when it won 13 seats.

In 2011 Amal joined its March 8 Alliance allies in the new government led by Najib Mikati, but not before a report issued by the Lebanese Center for Human Rights accused party members of arresting and torturing suspected Israeli spies.

Leader: Nabih BERRI (President of the Party and Speaker of the National Assembly).

Syrian Socialist Nationalist Party (*Parti Socialiste Nationaliste Syrien*—PSNS). Organized as the Syrian Nationalist Party in 1932 in support of a "Greater Syria" embracing Iraq, Jordan, Lebanon, Syria, and Palestine, the PSNS was considered a rightist group until 1970. Also known as the Syrian People's Party, it was banned from 1962 to 1969 after participating in an attempted coup in December 1961. The party split into factions in the 1970s but reunited by the end of the decade. In 2005 the PSNS allied with Hezbollah in a pro-Syrian bloc, blaming Israel for the assassination of Rafiq Hariri. The PSNS, a Hezbollah ally, maintains in its party platform that Lebanon is a part of Syria. In June 2009 the PSNS won two seats in the legislative elections. After the fall of the Hariri government in 2011, PSNS leader Ali KANSO was appointed minister of state in the Mikati cabinet. In 2012 Kanso visited with Syria's Bashar Assad as part of large delegation of Lebanese political figures. The April 2013 visit by politicians sympathetic to the Assad regime drew condemnation from several March 14 party leaders.

Leader: Ali KANSO.

Free Patriotic Movement—FPM (*Tayyar al-Watani al-Hurr*). The FPM is led by Michel Aoun, former general in the Lebanese Army, who served as the provisional prime minister of one of two governments that contended for power in the final years of the civil war. Most of its leadership and support come from Lebanon's Christian community. Aoun led the FPM from abroad while he was exiled in Paris. He returned to Lebanon in May 2005 to run in the legislative elections held in May and June. The FPM and its allies won 21 seats in the 128-member National Assembly. The party left the March 14 Alliance in 2006 and joined the opposition. The FPM won 19 seats in the June 2009 legislative elections. In September and October 2009 the FPM was a main obstacle in negotiations over incoming Prime Minister Saad Hariri's proposed cabinet.

In 2010 the FPM criticized the Hariri government for many issues, including the legitimacy of the STL and employment rights for Palestinian refugees. As it became part of the Mikati government in 2011, the FPM accused members of the FM of attempting to cause dissension in the Lebanese army after an FM member of parliament characterized army intelligence officers as "armed thugs" who behave like their brutal Syrian counterparts. In 2012 Aoun reiterated his party's support of the Assad regime in Damascus, but observers detected the potential for a rift in the FPM-Hezbollah alliance caused by differing approaches to governance: whereas Aoun agitated for rapid change via political and social polarization, his Hezbollah counterparts reportedly sought a moderate approach. After the dissolution of the March 8 bloc in July 2013, Aoun was courted by former alliance members—notably Hezbollah—as well as parties aligned with March 14. Analysts noted that if Aoun were to spurn Hezbollah the Shiite group would end up severely isolated in national politics.

Leader: Michel AOUN.

Marada Movement. The Marada Movement originated as a militia during the civil war, when it was known as the Marada Brigade. The militia became firmly pro-Syrian in the late 1970s. It was launched as a political party in 2006, when it allied with the pro-Syrian opposition. Its supporters are primarily Christian. The party won four seats in the June 2009 legislative elections. Tensions with the LP party remained high as clashes between the parties in northern Lebanon during the 2010 municipal elections resulted in the deaths of several Marada members. In 2011 Marada's Suleiman FRANJIEH made statements of support for the regime of Bashir Assad, praising the Syrian president's perseverance in the face of adversity promulgated by an "international conspiracy" against him. In July 2012 Franjieh suggested that the Free Syrian Army had established several bases in northern Lebanon, a claim rejected by President Suleiman.

The relationship between Marada and the other March 8 Christian party, FPM, soured during 2013 as the two clashed over the extension of LAF commander Jean Qahwaji's term. Marada member and Defense Minister Fayez Ghosn made the decision, a move steadfastly opposed by Michel Aoun and the FPM.

Leader: Suleiman FRANJIEH.

Progressive Socialist Party—PSP (*al-Hizb al-Taqaddumi al-Ishtiraki/Parti Socialiste Progressif*). Founded in 1948, the PSP is a largely Druze group that advocates a socialist program with nationalist and anti-Western overtones. Relations between former party president Kamal JUMBLATT and President Assad of Syria soured in the 1970s, before the Syrian intervention of April 1976. Jumblatt was assassinated in March 1977, and the party leadership shifted to his son, Walid, who subsequently became a Syrian ally and established close ties with Amal during the Israeli occupation. The alliance ended in early 1987, when the PSP intervened on the side of the PLO. The PSP became steadily more vocal in its opposition to the Syrian presence in Lebanon and opposed the three-year extension for President Lahoud's term given by the assembly.

The PSP allied itself with the March 14 movement after the assassination of Rafiq Hariri and won 11 seats in the June 2009 elections as part of the March 14 bloc. However, Walid Jumblatt announced in August that the PSP would align itself with the president rather than with the March 14 bloc in the incoming government. This substantially reduced the majority won by the March 14 bloc in the June legislative elections and weakened the movement's influence in the incoming cabinet.

In January 2010 the PSP reached a reconciliation agreement with Hezbollah and Amal, concluding the deadly clashes that took place two years before over a government decision to dismantle Hezbollah's telecommunications network. In March, Jumblatt held a reconciliation meeting with President Assad, announcing afterward his desire to "open a new page" with Syria, which he had previously blamed for his father's death. In the aftermath of the Hariri government's collapse in January 2011, the PSP threw its support behind the March 8 Alliance's candidate for prime minister, which tipped the balance in favor of Najib Mikati. However, as the process of appointing a new cabinet dragged on for many months, Jumblatt vehemently criticized his March 8 Alliance allies for putting party interests above governing priorities. By late in the year observers both inside and outside the government speculated that Jumblatt would soon end his party's support for the March 8 Alliance coalition and return to the March 14 Alliance. In 2012 Jumblatt continued to stymy political observers by openly attacking the Syrian regime (including its supporters in Hezbollah) while incongruously continuing his party's relationship with March 8. Jumblatt was perhaps the most critical of all Lebanon's political leaders regarding the proposed electoral law featuring proportional representation. In April 2012 the party elected a new secretary general to replace the retiring Sharif FAYYAD.

Leaders: Walid Kamal JUMBLATT, Zafer NASSER (Secretary General).

Tashnaq Party. The Tashnaq Party, or the Armenian Revolutionary Federation, is the most influential of the three Armenian political parties in Lebanon. The party was founded in 1890 and operates in countries with significant Armenian populations. Before the Lebanese Civil War, the party was aligned with the Phalangist Party; in 2000 the Tashnaq split with Rafiq Hariri and in parliamentary elections that year won only one seat. The Tashnaq boycotted the 2005 elections and lost all seats. Although courted by Saad Hariri in 2009, the Tashnaq joined the pro-Syrian bloc and won two seats in the legislature. Tashnaq successfully obtained the ministry of industry in negotiations over the 2009 cabinet. Politically, it supports President Suleiman and is a parliamentary member of the Reform and Change Bloc headed by FPM leader Michel Aoun.

As a new cabinet was being appointed by Prime Minister Najib Mikati in 2011, parliament member and Tashnaq leader Hagop PAKRADOUNIAN objected to the tradition of reserving certain cabinet positions for certain sects, noting the finance, defense, interior, and justice ministries had rarely—if ever—been led by Armenian ministers. In 2012 Pakradounian noted that though Tashnaq still valued its relationship with the FPM, it had recently allied successfully with March 14 parties such as the LFP, Phalange, and the Future Movement. Pakradounian supported the Orthodox Gathering electoral reform proposal up until its demise in 2013.

Leader: Hagop PAKRADOUNIAN.

Lebanese Democratic Party (*Hizb al-dimuqrati al-lubnani*). The Lebanese Democratic Party was founded by Talal ARSLAN, a Druze, in 2001. It won two seats in the June 2009 legislative elections. In 2010 municipal elections, the LDP allied with the PSP. However, in 2012 Arslan ended the LDP's relationship with the PSP over differences of allegiance to Druze spiritual leader Nasreddine al-GHARIB. However, in 2013 Arslan repaired differences with the PSP's Walid Jumblatt. To show his allegiance to the Syrian government, in February Arslan held private talks with Bashar Assad in Damascus.

Leader: Talal ARSLAN.

Baath Party: The Baath Party was founded in Syria in the 1940s to unify all Arabs in one country. The Lebanese branch remains closely affiliated with the Syrian branch. The Baath Party won two seats in the June 2009 legislative elections. In December 2009, Baath party leader Assem KANSO sided with Hezbollah in legislation allowing the party to maintain arms, calling armed resistance the only way for Lebanon to secure its territory. In 2011 some members of the March 14 Alliance suggested that Lebanon ban the Baath party for its alleged refusal to recognize the sovereignty of Lebanon as an autonomous nation-state and for its allegiance to the Syrian Baath party.

Leader: Assem KANSO.

Other Parties:

Lebanese Communist Party—LCP (*al-Hizb al-Shuyui al-Lubnani/Parti Communiste Libanais*). The LCP was founded in 1924 as the Lebanese People's Party, banned in 1939 by the French Mandate Authority, and legalized in 1970. Although primarily Christian in the first half-century of its existence, the party became predominantly Muslim in the wake of the civil war. Its longtime secretary general, George HRAWI, also served as a vice president of the National Movement. In June 2005 Hrawi, who had left the Communist Party, was assassinated. This made him the third prominent anti-Syrian politician killed that year. In recent years, the LCP has come out in favor of extending the rights of Palestinian refugees, an end to "political sectarianism," and a harder stance against Israel. In the 2009 parliamentary elections, the LCP ran five candidates in five districts and failed to garner any seats.

Leader: Khaled HADADEH (Secretary General).

National Bloc (*al-Kutlah al-Wataniyah/Bloc National*). The National Bloc, a Maronite party formed in 1943, has been opposed to military involvement in politics. In 2008 Carlos Edde called for the disarmament of Hezbollah and reconciliation between all Lebanese factions. The National Bloc won no seats in the 2009 legislative elections.

Leader: Carlos EDDE.

For information on the al-Waad Party, see the 2008 *Handbook.*

Note: For a discussion of Palestinian groups formerly headquartered in Lebanon, see article on the Palestinian Authority/Palestine Liberation Organization.

LEGISLATURE

The former Chamber of Deputies, which in March 1979 changed its name to the **National Assembly** (*Majlis al-Nuwwab*), is a unicameral body elected by universal suffrage for a four-year term (subject to dissolution) through a proportional system based on religious groupings. The National Pact of 1943 specified that the speaker be a Shiite Muslim. The distribution of seats was on the basis of a 6:5 Christian to Muslim ratio until 1990 when, in implementation of a provision of the Taif accord, the total number of seats was raised from 99 to 108, with half assigned to each group. That ratio was maintained in 1996, when the number of seats was increased to 128.

Candidates are not presented as nominees of political parties but on lists supportive of prominent politicians or alliances of political organizations. The March 14 Alliance, an anti-Syrian coalition, polled successfully in the 2009 elections, winning 71 of 128 seats. Hezbollah, Amal, the Free Patriotic Movement, and their allies in the March 8 Alliance won 57 seats. Amal's Nabih Berri was subsequently reelected speaker by the new assembly.

Speaker: Nabih BERRI.

CABINET

The cabinet is traditionally divided into a 15–10–5 structure, granting the majority party 15 ministers, the opposition 10, and the president, 5.

[as of September 1, 2013]

Caretaker Prime Minister	Mohammad Najib Mikati (ind.)
Prime Minister-designate	Tammam Salam (ind.)
Caretaker Deputy Prime Minister	Samir Mokbel (ind.)

Caretaker Ministers

Administrative Development	Mohammed Fneish (Hezbollah)
Agriculture	Husssein Hajj Hassan (Hezbollah)
Culture	Gaby Layyoun (FPM)
Defense	Fayez Ghosn (Marada)
Displaced Persons	Alaa el-Din Terro (PSP)
Economy and Trade	Nicolas Nahhas (ind.)
Education	Hassan Diab (ind.)
Energy and Water	Jibran Basil (FPM)
Environment	Nazem Khoury (ind.)
Finance	Mohammad Safadi (ind.)
Foreign Affairs and Emigrants	Adnan Mansour (Amal)
Industry	Warij Sabonjian (TP)
Information	Walid Daouk (ind.)
Interior and Municipalities	Marwan Charbel (FPM)
Justice	Shakib Cortbawi (FPM)
Labor	Salim Jreissati (FPM)
Public Health	Ali Hassan Khalil (Amal)
Public Works and Transport	Ghazi Aridi (PSP)
Social Affairs	Wael Abu Faour (PSP)
Telecommunications	Nicolas Sehnawi (FPM)
Tourism	Fadi Abboud (FPM)
Youth and Sports	Faysal Karami (March 8)
Minister of State, Parliamentary Affairs	Nicolas Fattoush (ind.)
Ministers of State	Ali Kanso (SSNP)
	Marwan Kheireddine (LDP)
	Ahmad Karami (ind.)
	Panos Manjian (TP)
	Salim Karam (Marada)

INTERGOVERNMENTAL REPRESENTATION

Ambassador to the U.S.: Antoine CHEDID.

U.S. Ambassador to Lebanon: David HALE.

Permanent Representative to the UN: Nawaf SALAM.

IGO Memberships (Non-UN): LAS, NAM, OIC.

LESOTHO

Kingdom of Lesotho

Political Status: Traditional monarchy, independent within the Commonwealth since October 4, 1966.

Area: 11,720 sq. mi. (30,355 sq. km).

Population: 2,231,479 (2012E—UN); 1,936,181 (2013E—U.S. Census).

Major Urban Center (2005E): MASERU (185,000).

Official Languages: English, Sesotho.

Monetary Unit: Loti (official rate November 1, 2013: 10.17 maloti = $1US). The loti is at par with the South African rand, although under a Tripartite Monetary Area agreement concluded between Lesotho, Swaziland, and South Africa on July 1, 1986, the rand has ceased to be legal tender in Lesotho.

Sovereign: King LETSIE III; became king upon the dethronement of his father, King MOSHOESHOE II, on November 6, 1990; voluntarily abdicated upon his father's return to the throne on January 25, 1995; became king again on February 7, 1996, following the death of his father on January 15; took coronation oath on October 31, 1997.

Prime Minister: Thomas THABANE (All Basotho Convention); sworn in on June 8, 2012, following legislative balloting on May 26, 2012; replacing Bethuel Pakalitha MOSISLI (Lesotho Congress for Democracy).

THE COUNTRY

Lesotho, the former British High Commission territory of Basutoland, is a hilly, landlocked enclave within the territory of South Africa. The Basotho people, whose vernacular language is Sesotho, constitute more than 99 percent of the population, which includes small European and Asian minorities. About 80 percent of the population is nominally Christian. The economy is largely based on agriculture and stock raising; diamond mining, which in the late 1970s accounted for more than half of export earnings, was discontinued in 1982 but was resumed in the early 2000s after the discovery of several high-value gems. Lesotho is highly dependent on South Africa, its main trading partner, which employs 80 percent of the country's wage earners and is the principal supplier of energy. Because of the unusual employment pattern, women are primarily responsible for subsistence activities, although they are unable by custom to control household wealth.

Economic growth was stagnant in the early and mid-1980s, partly because of prolonged droughts that depressed agricultural output and compounded problems of unemployment, landlessness, and inflation. However, real GDP growth averaged 6 percent annually from 1987 to 1997, under the influence of an expanding manufacturing sector, a collateral growth in exports, and the economic effect of investment in the massive Lesotho Highlands Water Project (LHWP, see Foreign relations, below). Severe political disruption in 1997 and 1998 (see Political background, below) contributed to a 3.6 percent decline in real GDP in fiscal year April 1998–March 1999. In December 1999 the government, in conjunction with the International Monetary Fund (IMF), announced a new economic recovery program designed to attract foreign investment, diversify the manufacturing base, enhance tourism, privatize state-run enterprises and otherwise promote the private sector, reform tax policy, and overhaul the financial sector. In early 2001 the IMF approved a new three-year assistance package.

The economy was severely compromised in 2001 and 2002 as the result of massive food shortages resulting from drought and soil degradation. Agricultural production subsequently increased, although food shortfalls continued into 2007, and rising food prices contributed to high inflation and burgeoning governmental budget deficits.

Drought hit again in 2007, prompting the UN to appeal for massive international assistance for what it described as the most severe conditions in 30 years. Widespread poverty and the extremely high incidence of HIV/AIDS continued to be major concerns, despite a concerted government effort to address the latter.

Though GDP growth of about 5 percent was recorded in 2008, owing largely to the textile and clothing industry, the economy was hard hit by the global economic downturn, and GDP contracted to 0.9 percent in 2009 as demand for diamonds and textiles declined. Meanwhile, revenue from the South African Customs Union (SACU)—which had accounted for some 60 percent of the country's tax income—decreased significantly, and GDP growth in 2010 improved only marginally to about 1 percent. Driven mainly by the construction and mining sectors, the economy rebounded the next year, with real GDP growth estimated at nearly 6 percent. But the impact of heavy rains and flooding beginning in December 2010 caused widespread loss of life and damage to infrastructure and agriculture, bringing the country to the verge of a food crisis. The cost of recovery and reconstruction, including emergency food imports, was estimated at $88 million, slowing the recovery. Dwindling remittances from laid-off workers in South Africa exacerbated Lesotho's economic troubles.

In March 2011 the IMF, citing progress in structural reforms, approved $9 million in aid as part of a total $61.4 million funding program (later raised to $77.8 million) intended to help offset the sharp decline in SACU revenue. Meanwhile, the government pledged to create more jobs, improve infrastructure, establish high-tech enterprises, and set up a fund to provide training for young entrepreneurs. By December, the combination of shortages and high international commodity prices had driven inflation to 7 percent (from around 3 percent a year before). In light of the government's planned fiscal

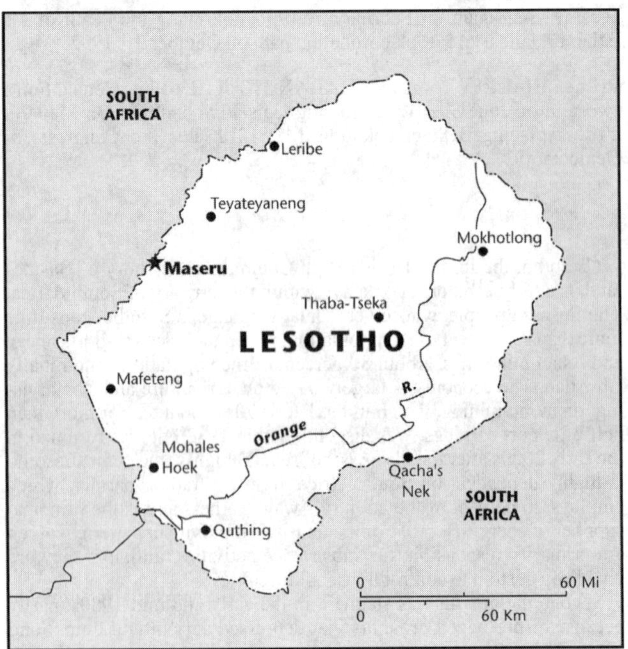

adjustments and an expected recovery in SACU revenues, the IMF projected the overall fiscal position should be in balance by 2013, the first time since the global economic crisis began. GDP grew 4 percent in 2012, while GDP per capita was $1,372. In 2013 the IMF approved the disbursement of $8.7 million to strengthen the economy.

GOVERNMENT AND POLITICS

Political background. United under MOSHOESHOE I in the mid-19th century, Basutoland came under British protection in 1868 and was governed from 1884 by a British high commissioner. A local consultative body, the Basutoland Council, was established as early as 1903, but the decisive move toward nationhood began in the mid-1950s and culminated in the attainment of full independence within the Commonwealth as the Kingdom of Lesotho in 1966. MOSHOESHOE II, the country's paramount chief, became king of the new state, and Chief Leabua JONATHAN, whose Basutoland National Party (BNP) had won a legislative majority in the preindependence election, became prime minister.

A trial of strength between the king and prime minister erupted in 1966 when the former's attempt to gain personal control over both foreign and domestic policy led to rioting by opposition parties; after being briefly confined to his palace, the king agreed to abide by the constitution. Further internal conflict followed the 1970 election, in which the opposition Basotho Congress Party (BCP) appeared to have outpolled the BNP. Voting irregularities were cited to justify the declaration of a state of emergency, a consequent suspension of the constitution, and the jailing of opposition leaders. Subsequently, the detainees were released, and the king, who had gone into exile, returned. The state of emergency was ultimately lifted in July 1973, but, in the wake of a coup attempt in January 1974 against his increasingly unpopular regime, the prime minister introduced new internal security measures (patterned after similar measures in South Africa) that proscribed the transmittal of outside funds to political groups within the country and authorized the jailing of individuals for 60 days without legal assistance. Between 1979 and 1982 numerous armed clashes were reported with the Lesotho Liberation Army (LLA), a guerrilla group affiliated with the outlawed "external" wing of the BCP under Ntsu MOKHEHLE, who claimed from exile that he was Lesotho's true leader on the basis of the election results invalidated in 1970.

In late 1984 the prime minister was mandated by an extraordinary general meeting of the BNP to call for a legislative election, and, with effect from December 31, the king dissolved an interim assembly that had been appointed after the abortive 1970 balloting. Following refusal by the five leading opposition parties to participate in the voting scheduled for September 17 and 18, 1985, Chief Jonathan announced that a formal poll would be unnecessary and declared all the BNP nominees elected unopposed.

On January 20, 1986, the Jonathan regime was toppled in a relatively bloodless coup led by Maj. Gen. Justin M. LEKHANYA, commander in chief of the Lesotho Paramilitary Force (LPF). Among the factors reportedly contributing to the coup were an economic blockade by South Africa (see Foreign relations, below) and power struggles within the BNP and the LPF. A decree issued on the day of the coup conferred executive and legislative powers on the king, who was to act in conjunction with a six-member Military Council and the Council of Ministers. On January 24 the king swore in Lekhanya as chair of the Military Council, with a largely civilian Council of Ministers being installed three days later. In February the king declared an amnesty for political offenders, and in March he banned all political activity pending the establishment of a new constitution. The new government quickly concluded a security pact with Pretoria and began to retreat from the Communist-bloc relations established by Chief Jonathan in the last years of his rule. (Chief Jonathan died in 1987.)

A new crisis erupted in early 1990 following the dismissal and arrest on February 19 of three Military Council members, two of whom were cousins of the king. Moshoeshoe refused to approve the appointment of replacement members and in a publicized letter to Lekhanya demanded an explanation for the arrests. The general responded two days later by declaring that supreme authority would "for the time being" be vested in himself and other members of the council, though the king would remain head of state. On February 22 he announced a major cabinet reshuffle that involved the dismissal of 9 of 18 ministers, including the king's brother, Chief Mathealira SEEISO, from his post as interior minister. On March 5 the council formally validated the action against the monarch, who left the country on March 10 for a "brief sabbatical" in the United Kingdom. The king was dethroned on November 6, and his son, Letsie David SEEISO, was sworn in as King LETSIE III on November 12 after his accession had been approved by an assembly of 22 traditional chiefs.

On April 30, 1991, General Lekhanya was overthrown in a bloodless coup and replaced as chair of the Military Council by Col. Elias Phisoana RAMAEMA. Thereafter, an unsuccessful attempt to depose Ramaema on June 17 led to the arrest of 18 senior military officers, and, in an unrelated action, Lekhanya was placed under house arrest from August 2 to September 17 for allegedly plotting a return to power.

In April 1992 the former king announced that he would be returning to Lesotho in late May, apparently against the wishes of the Military Council. Complicating the situation was a report that King Letsie III was prepared to abdicate in favor of his father. During talks brokered by the Commonwealth secretariat in London in June, it was agreed that Moshoeshoe could return as head of the royal family, but not as monarch, and on July 20 he was accorded a warm reception in Maseru after a two-year absence.

After several postponements, a general election was held on March 27, 1993, in which the previously outlawed BCP swept all 65 National Assembly contests, both General Lekhanya and BNP leader Evaristus SEKHONYANA being among the defeated. Although the results were disputed by the BNP, which subsequently rejected an offer of two nominated Senate seats, Ntsu Mokhehle was installed as head of a BCP government on April 2.

In mid-November 1993 coup rumors were sparked when the government's attempts to fulfill its promise to integrate former LLA soldiers into the Royal Lesotho Defense Force (RLDF) resulted in a confrontation between the latter's senior and junior officers. Furthermore, the RLDF's unwillingness to acquiesce to the new administration was, at least nominally, the catalyst for clashes between rival factions of the RLDF in January 1994. On April 14 dissident soldiers assassinated Deputy Prime Minister Selometsi BAHOLO and seized four other cabinet ministers for four hours in apparent response to government plans to investigate the January violence.

On August 17, 1994, King Letsie announced that he had removed the government of Prime Minister Mokhehle and that the country would be run by an appointed provisional council prior to the scheduling of new elections. The action was immediately challenged by thousands of rock-throwing protesters in a march on the royal palace, while a four-nation summit involving the leaders of Botswana, Zimbabwe, and South Africa was convened in Pretoria late in the month in an effort to resolve the crisis. On September 14 a meeting between the king and Mokhehle yielded an agreement that reinstated the latter and called for the abdication of the former in favor of his deposed father. A bill that provided for the monarchial transfer was approved on November 17, with Moshoeshoe II returning to the throne on January 25, 1995. Paralleling the reaccession of King Moshoeshoe, the more important outcome was his son's agreement to restore democracy, lacking which South Africa had threatened an economic blockade of the landlocked enclave. Subsequently, South Africa's deputy foreign secretary termed the Lesotho settlement "the first success of the Organization of African Unity's regional approach to conflict resolution."

On January 15, 1996, King Moshoeshoe was killed in an automobile accident while returning from a late-night visit to his cattle herds in the royal village of Matsieng, and on February 7 Crown Prince Letsie David ascended the throne for the second time as King Letsie III. The 32-year-old Letsie promised to "abstain from involving the monarchy in any way in politics or with any political parties or groups."

In late 1996 and early 1997 Lesotho's political landscape was dominated by a highly publicized struggle between Prime Minister Mokhehle and Molapo QHOBELA, the leader of the BCP's "modernizing" wing and deputy chief of the party's National Executive Commission (NEC). The NEC denounced Mokhehle's governance and voted to strip Mokhehle of his party leadership posts as the first step in an apparent effort to gain control of the government; however, in mid-April 1997 the High Court reinstated Mokhehle on an interim basis and ordered him to hold intraparty elections by the end of July. On June 7 Mokhehle and 37 BCP legislators defected from the BCP and announced the formation of the Lesotho Congress for Democracy (LCD). Furthermore, Mokhehle asserted that he would continue as prime minister, citing the LCD's control of a majority of the assembly seats. Consequently, on June 11 the BCP suspended its participation in the assembly, asserting that Mokhehle's "coup" was a blatant attempt to avoid the proposed intraparty balloting. In October Mokhehle's deputy, Bethuel Pakalitha MOSISILI, met with Botswanan, South African, and Zimbabwean leaders who had been charged by the Southern African Development Community (SADC) with mediating the political stalemate. Thereafter, dismissing the BCP's continued attacks on its legitimacy, the LCD hosted the official coronation of King Letsie III on October 31.

In early 1998 Prime Minister Mokhehle announced that he would not run for reelection in balloting scheduled for May, citing declining health, and on February 27 the legislature was dissolved in anticipation of the polling. In elections on May 23 approximately 400 candidates from 12 parties vied for posts in the enlarged 80-seat assembly. Although the polling was initially described as "free and fair" by the SADC and Lesotho's Independent Electoral Commission (IEC), the LCD's capture of 78 seats (the BNP being credited with 1, and 1 remaining vacant) was immediately denounced as fraudulent by the opposition, whose subsequent demand for a recount was rejected by the IEC. On May 28 Mosisili was elected prime minister by an LCD intraparty caucus, and on June 4 a new government was sworn in. Nevertheless, opposition calls for an annulment of the elections continued. In late July the Court of Appeals ruled that only the king could annul elections.

On August 4, 1998, opposition demonstrators occupied the grounds outside the royal palace. On August 11 the SADC named a South African judge, Pius Langa to head an international team (referred to thereafter as the Langa Commission) charged with investigating the charges of electoral fraud. Meanwhile, tensions continued to mount at the royal palace, where several people were killed during clashes between the opposition and security forces and progovernment activists. On August 26 the Langa Commission released an interim report in which it accused the IEC of mishandling the vote tallying, and, under pressure from South Africa, the government agreed to a vote recount. However, on September 11, mutinous soldiers arrested more than 20 senior military officials after the dismissal of a military leader with alleged sympathies for the antigovernment demonstrators. Furthermore, the commander of the military, Lt. Gen. Makhula MOSAKENG, was forced to resign at gunpoint. On September 22, South Africa and Botswana, acting under the auspices of the SADC, deployed approximately 800 troops to Maseru at the request of Prime Minister Mosisili, who reportedly feared a coup attempt by the rampaging soldiers. The SADC forces were greeted by stiff resistance from the mutinous soldiers as well as opposition militants and were unable to gain control of Maseru until September 29, by which time dozens of people had been killed and the city severely damaged by looting and burning.

By early October 1998 a majority of the RDLF had returned to the barracks, and between October 2 and 14 the SADC organized government and opposition negotiations that yielded an agreement to create a transitional executive committee that would operate parallel to the government and assist in organizing new elections in 15 to 18 months. The negotiators also agreed to restructure the IEC, draft a new code of conduct for political parties, and create guidelines for equitable access to media outlets for all political groups. Furthermore, it was concluded that Prime Minister Mosisili would remain in office during the transitional phase and that SADC forces would remain for an indefinite period. On December 9 a 24-member Interim Political Authority (IPA) was sworn in, and the following day two opposition party members were elected cochairs of the new body.

SADC peacekeeping forces completed their withdrawal in mid-May 1999, supporters describing the military intervention of the previous year as an "outstanding success." At the same time, the IPA expressed confidence that it would meet its deadline of organizing national elections by mid-2000, when the original IPA mandate was due to expire. Under pressure from international mediators concerned over potential delays, the IPA and the government in December 1999 reached an agreement to hold elections sometime in 2000, with the IPA mandate to be extended indefinitely until balloting was conducted. However, a planned election date in May 2000 was quickly scrapped as the IPA and the government argued over proposed restructuring of the parliament. The IPA and the government subsequently charged each other with attempting to delay the elections, although neutral observers suggested that it was the government that appeared to have the most to gain from such tactics. Plans to conduct the balloting in early 2001 also proved unrealistic in view of disagreement over voter registration and the addition of legislators selected via proportional representation to the assembly.

In legislative balloting on May 25, 2002, the LCD won a new term in office, and on June 11 Mosisili formed an all-LCD cabinet. Four more ministers were announced on July 11.

On April 30, 2005, the nation's first local elections were held, with a government stipulation that one-third of the elected seats be filled by women. Seven opposition parties tried to have the elections postponed, claiming irregularities, which some observers said may have affected voter turnout (reported to be about 30 percent). Though an official breakdown of results was not released, electoral officials announced May 9 that the LCD won "by a large margin," followed by independents, the opposition Basotho National Party (BNP) and the Lesotho People's Congress (LPC), and unspecified smaller parties. Failed elections were reported in 15 districts, attributed to the death of candidates, and new elections were to be scheduled to replace them.

Following the resignation from the LCD of Communications Minister Thomas THABANE and 17 others on October 9, 2006, King Letsie dissolved parliament on November 24 and called for early assembly elections on February 17, 2007. The LCD won a majority in balloting deemed free and fair by some international observers but vehemently contested by opposition parties (see Current issues, below). Prime Minister Mosisili retained his post and was sworn in on February 23. He named a new government on March 2, retaining most of the ministers from the previous government.

Four ministers and an assistant minister were replaced on October 13, 2010, in the first major reshuffle in years. All of the new ministers were LCD members. Following legislative elections on May 26, 2012, Thabane formed a coalition government that includes the ABC, LCD, and the BNP (see Current issues, below).

Constitution and government. Under the 1966 constitution, which was suspended in January 1970, Lesotho was declared to be an independent monarchy with the king functioning as head of state and executive authority being vested in a prime minister and cabinet responsible to the lower house of a bicameral parliament. In April 1973 an interim unicameral body was established, encompassing 22 chiefs and 71 nominated members. A return to bicameralism was voted in 1983, but the bill was never implemented and was voided after the 1986 coup by the Military Council, which announced the vesting of "all executive and legislative powers in HM the King"; the latter action was reversed by the council prior to the exile of Moshoeshoe in March 1990, the new monarch appearing to possess only ceremonial authority.

On July 4, 1991, a National Constituent Assembly approved the draft of a new constitution, which was promulgated following the legislative election of March 1993. The revised basic law restored the bicameral system and returned executive authority to a cabinet headed by a prime minister, without conclusively resolving the issue of the monarch's role. The judicial system consists of a High Court, a Court of Appeal, and subordinate courts (district, judicial commissioners, central, and local). Judges of the High Court and the Court of Appeal are appointed on the advice of the government and its Judicial Service Commission. Local government is based on nine districts, each of which is administered by a commissioner appointed by the central government. In April 1997 the assembly approved a constitutional amendment that established an Independent Electoral Commission.

The constitution guarantees freedom of expression, but there are also criminal defamation laws. Reporters Without Borders ranked Lesotho 81st out of 179 countries in its 2013 report on media freedom.

Foreign relations. Lesotho's foreign policy was long determined less by its membership in the United Nations, the Commonwealth, and the Organization of African Unity (OAU, subsequently the African Union—AU) than by its position as a black enclave within the white-ruled Republic of South Africa. While rejecting the South African doctrine of apartheid and insisting on the maintenance of national sovereignty, the Jonathan government for some years cultivated good relations with Pretoria. Subsequent events, however, led to a noticeable stiffening in Maseru's posture. Following South Africa's establishment of the adjacent Republic of Transkei in October 1976, Lesotho requested a special UN Security Council meeting on the matter, complaining that its border had been effectively closed in an "act of aggression" designed to force recognition of Transkei. Subsequently, South African prime minister Pieter Botha accused Maseru of harboring militants from the African National Congress (ANC) among the approximately 11,000 South African refugees living in Lesotho. Friction over Chief Jonathan's refusal to expel the ANC supporters culminated in South Africa's institution of a crippling economic blockade, ostensibly to block cross-border rebel activity, on January 1, 1986. Pretoria denied charges of complicity in the subsequent overthrow of Chief Jonathan but lifted the border controls one week later when the new military regime flew 60 ANC members to Zimbabwe. The new relationship with South Africa was further demonstrated by the signature in October of a treaty authorizing commencement of the $2 billion Lesotho Highlands Water Project (LHWP), which had been under consideration for more than two decades. The three-phase project, expected to take 25 to 30 years to complete, will divert vast quantities of water to South Africa's arid Transvaal region in return for the payment of substantial royalties. (The project has been the attention of intense scrutiny recently in light of bribery charges against foreign contractors. In May 2002 a former chief executive of the LHWP was sentenced to a lengthy prison term for fraud and accepting bribes, while Canadian, French, and German companies were fined for paying bribes. The first phase of the project was completed in the early 2000s and the second phase began in 2010.)

In an attempt to broaden its international support both regionally and abroad, Lesotho has been an active member of the Southern African Development Coordination Conference (SADCC, subsequently the SADC), a body created in 1980 to lessen members' economic dependence on the then white-ruled regime. However, in view of its vulnerability to South African influence, Maseru, unlike other SADCC governments, did not seek sanctions against Pretoria for its apartheid policies. Rather, on May 21, 1992, the two governments formally established diplomatic relations.

In January 1994 the interwoven nature of relations between Lesotho and South Africa was evidenced by Pretoria's immediate and forceful response to the unrest in Maseru. Although the Commonwealth was subsequently credited with brokering an accord between the combatants, observers cited pressure from a task force created by South African president F.W. de Klerk and other southern African leaders as the reason for the speedy resolution of the dispute. Thereafter, speculation about the possible merger of the two countries continued, with the *Christian Science Monitor* quoting local observers as saying that, if not for the monarchy, Lesotho would be "swallowed up" by South Africa. In 2001 it was reported that relations between the South African government and Lesotho's royal family were strained because of the former's failure to "come clean" on a "massacre" allegedly committed by its paratroopers during the SADC's intervention in 1998. However, relations subsequently improved (apparently influenced by the successful 2002 legislative elections in Lesotho), culminating in a new cooperation protocol through which South Africa agreed to provide economic aid and technical assistance. In 2005 troops from Lesotho were being trained for use in future UN and SADC missions. Late that year, Prime Minister Mosisili visited China amid pledges by both countries for political and economic cooperation.

In 2009 Lesotho asked South Africa to reconsider its overhaul of a program to benefit textile manufacturers, in effect ending an export incentive. Analysts said the decision "puts South Africa on a "collision course" with export-dependent Lesotho.

In November 2012 the Abu Dhabi Fund for Development agreed to provide $21 million to construct the Meolong Dam in Lesotho. The dam was expected to increase access to clean drinking water and help meet the nation's water demands through 2025.

In May 2013 Lesotho signed an agreement with South Africa for a $1.3 billion hydroelectric project. The Lesotho Highlands Water Project would provide electricity to Lesotho and water to South Africa. The project also allowed Lesotho to finalize an accord with Botswana to supply emergency water to that country which was experiencing a significant drought. Lesotho and Rwanda signed a series of bilateral cooperation agreements in May to improve local government and decentralization.

Current issues. Following the king's scheduling of legislative elections in February 2007, the opposition complained they did not have enough time to prepare. Subsequently, the LCD and the All Basotho Convention (ABC), formed in 2006 by former minister Thomas Thabane and 17 other LCD members who lacked confidence in the government, made arrangements with the National Independent Party (NIP) and the Lesotho Workers' Party (LWP) by which the predominant party would contest only the single-member constituencies, while the smaller parties would submit party lists only for compensatory seats. (See the 2012 *Handbook* for more on the dispute over the arrangement and the protests that followed.) In June 2007 a curfew was imposed in the capital in the wake of what the government described as "politically motivated" attacks on the homes of three ministers and against ABC leader Thabane. Shortly thereafter, the government announced that it had thwarted a coup attempt by some members of the military, and a radio journalist was also implicated for allegedly reading on air a letter from a group of soldiers threatening the government. Observers believed the curfew was meant to undermine the "potential political threat" from opposition groups. As tensions increased, the SADC was called upon to resolve the dispute through mediation. Meanwhile, five people, including three members of the military and the radio journalist, were charged with treason in connection with the alleged coup plot.

In late 2007 both the government and Thabane backed the mediation efforts and agreed to meet with the SADC in February 2008. Thabane reiterated that he did not dispute that the LCD had won the most seats, but he claimed that the allocation of seats through proportional representation had been misused since not enough seats were awarded to smaller parties. The matter was subsequently taken to Lesotho's Supreme Court.

On a positive note, international organizations and the United States announced greater financial assistance for Lesotho's efforts to combat HIV/AIDS, and in 2008 China pledged to provide additional medical teams. The number of those infected reportedly had fallen from 31 percent in 2003 to 26 percent in 2008, due in large part to the government's testing program and offers of free counseling and medicine in the past two years.

After the SADC failed to resolve the electoral dispute, the government reportedly was no longer interested in mediation efforts in 2009. With tensions still heightened over the impasse, an attack on the prime minister's home in April was described by the government as a failed assassination attempt.

Electoral reform continued to be a pressing issue in 2010, following a summit in February in which the SADC called for a "road map" for the process of amending Lesotho's constitution and ending electoral disputes. As conditions continued to deteriorate—with low salaries for workers, a lack of water, the collapse of the textile industry, and the disastrous effect of the HIV/AIDS pandemic on the economy—hundreds of people rallied in Maseru in June and delivered a petition to parliament and to the South African High Commission requesting that Lesotho be annexed by South Africa. However, tensions heightened between the two countries around that same time when South Africa, for security reasons in advance of the World Cup games, stopped recognizing the temporary travel documents that workers had used for years to enter and exit the country. (Lesotho had not issued passports for five years.) Meanwhile, the "threat of internal conflict" was cited in a study by the AU, which, while not recommending annexation, did call for economic integration with South Africa. In March parliament passed a controversial land bill, despite a widespread outcry from the public and opposition parties, which boycotted the vote. The bill replaced the long-standing law dating to 1979, significantly decreasing the requirement for shares owned by citizens of Lesotho and increasing the shares foreign entities can own. The new law allows foreign firms to own up to 80 percent of a property, with the remaining 20 percent to be held by citizens of Lesotho.

Previously, a foreign firm could own only a minority share, with 51 percent required to be held by a Lesotho citizen. The government moved to change the law to attract more investment, but opponents claimed it would strip the poor of their only asset. The king signed the bill into law in June. Meanwhile, legislators also approved a measure allowing them to become the only people in the country who can cash in one-quarter of their pensions before they retire.

In October 2010 Prime Minister Mosisili fired five cabinet ministers, the biggest upheaval in government since the LCD gained control in 1997. The reshuffle prompted one of the ousted ministers to resign from the party's executive committee and drew protests from the youth wing of the party.

On a more positive note, the Lesotho government enacted a new law in 2010 providing for free, compulsory education for all children, and for the first time in the country's history, the government began assisting some 5,000 children orphaned by AIDS with a financial grant program.

In late 2010 and early 2011, factionalism plagued several major parties as alliances dissolved and leaders vied for position. Divisions within the LCD carried over into the NIP; the ABC and the LWP severed ties over disputed proportional representation; the coordinator of the Lesotho Opposition Parties Forum resigned due to infighting within the umbrella group; and BNP leader Lekhanya was forced out, and a key member of the party's executive committee resigned (see Political Parties, below).

The IEC's decision in January 2011 to postpone local elections from April to June drew heavy criticism from opposition parties, whose leaders claimed the move was arbitrary and breached an agreement between the opposition and the IEC dating to April 2010 to postpone the polling for one year to allow time for amendments to the local government elections law. According to observers, of particular concern to the opposition was a provision in the law that gave local government ministers the authority to reserve some council seats for women. The IEC, for its part, said more time was needed because the new councils' boundaries had not yet been drawn. In February the opposition was further outraged by a draft bill that would replace the National Assembly Elections Act. The new bill would allow political parties to petition the High Court regarding the allocation of proportional representation seats. The opposition claimed it had again been sidelined and that the draft should have been presented to stakeholders, as all had been agreed upon, before it was presented to parliament. The opposition claimed further that the proposed law would undermine the proportional representation system, leading to political instability. In March the opposition called on the international community to impose sanctions against the country, saying Lesotho did not qualify for assistance because it was "not a democracy."

The run-up to the 2012 election was marked by violent clashes at campaign rallies, assassinations, rumors of a hit squad, and fears of a coup or widespread riots. During an April 27 appearance in Lesotho, Archbishop Desmond Tutu secured pledges from political rivals to respect election results and maintain peace. The elections proceeded peacefully on May 26 and were eventually declared free and fair by international observers. But over several tense days it became clear that no party had secured the necessary 61 seats to govern on its own. The results were announced on May 29, and Thabane told reporters the ABC was negotiating with other parties to form a coalition that would have a majority in parliament. Mosisili submitted his resignation on May 30, but he remained in office until a new prime minister could be sworn in. After an unsuccessful attempt to build his own coalition and remain in power, Mosisili stepped down on June 7, and Thabane was sworn in the following day. This smooth transfer of power was a first for the country, ending fears of another bout of unrest like the one that prompted South Africa's 1998 intervention. International observers hailed it as a success story for democracy on the continent.

In April 2013 Thabane requested the resignation of Michael RAMODIBEDI, the president of the nation's appeals court, following allegations of corruption and judicial infighting with other justices. Ramodibedi refused, and Thabane ordered the justice stripped of a number of his powers and perks. Ramodibedi challenged the actions in court and had his privileges restored after a hearing by South African judges who were brought in to arbitrate the case. Reports in September indicated that the government would seek to impeach Ramodibedi. Meanwhile, in May, the constitutional court upheld the Chieftainship Act, which mandated that only males could inherit any of the 22 traditional chieftaincies in Lesotho.

POLITICAL PARTIES

Political party activity was banned in March 1986 following the January coup that ended nearly 20 years of dominance by the Basotho National Party (BNP). Subsequently, the BNP joined four former opponents (the BCP, UDP, BDA, and CPL) in an informal "Big Five" alliance to demand that the ban be lifted in preparation for a return to civilian government. Ten days after the coup of April 30, 1991, the Military Council announced that party activity could resume as long as it did not degenerate into "divisive politics." However, it was not until nearly two years thereafter that a general election was authorized.

Eleven parties competed individually in the 1998 legislative balloting and were accorded two seats each on the Interim Political Authority (IPA) that was established in late 1998. The UDP and the LLP, which had contested the 1998 election as an alliance, each received one seat on the 24-member IPA.

In May 1999 a number of small parties (the PFD, NPP, NIP, KBP, CDP, CPL, and SDP) announced formation of an anti-LCD grouping called the Khokanyana-Phiri Democratic Alliance. In August another antigovernment grouping, the Setlamo Democratic Alliance, was formalized by the BNP, BCP, MFP, UDP, LLP, and LEP, which had been operating together informally since the beginning of the year.

A new party, the ABC, was launched in 2006 by disaffected LCD members led by former minister Thomas Thabane. The following year, the main opposition parties came together under a grouping called the **Lesotho Opposition Parties Forum** to lobby for fair distribution of proportional representation seats. Majara MOLAPO of the BNP resigned as coordinator of the forum in 2010, citing serious infighting within the group.

Parliamentary Parties:

Lesotho Congress for Democracy (LCD). The LCD was launched by Prime Minister Ntsu Mokhehle, the (then) BCP interim president, on June 7, 1997, one month before the BCP (see below) was scheduled to hold intraparty elections for his post and just two days after a BCP spokesperson had labeled him "permanently incapacitated." Subsequently, Mokhehle cited the LCD's control of a majority of the legislative posts (38 seats) as the basis for his continued control of the government. In early 1998 Bethuel Pakalitha Mosisili, theretofore deputy party leader, was elected to succeed Mokhehle as party leader, the latter declining to run for reelection due to poor health. (Mokhehle died in January 1999.)

Party infighting was reported in 2000, culminating in violence between rival factions in October that precipitated police intervention. Some observers suggested the friction underscored a split between the youthful, possibly more progressive, supporters of Mosisili and a conservative faction led by Shakhana MOKHEHLE, brother of the LCD founder. Subsequently, Mosisili was elected for another five-year term as party leader. Mokhehle was defeated 717–710 in his reelection bid by Sephiri MOTANYANE, described as a close associate of Mosisili's. Prominent LCD leaders, including Deputy Prime Minister Kelebone Maope and several other cabinet members, charged that the elections had been "rigged" and vowed to take the matter to court. Maope's faction left the party in September 2001 to form the Lesotho People's Congress (see below). In April 2005 the LCD won the country's first locally held elections.

In January 2006 Foreign Affairs Minister Monyane MOLELEKI was wounded by gunfire near his home shortly after he had attended a national conference of the LCD, during which tensions reportedly heated up over the accession issue, with Moleleki seen as one of the main contenders for leadership of the party. Another attack in August resulted in the death of a member of parliament. In October cabinet minister Thomas Thabane and 17 other LCD members quit the party to form the ABC (see below), pledging to reduce poverty and improve the economy, among other things. The defections left the LCD without a majority, prompting King Letsie to dissolve parliament and call for early elections. Hours after parliament was dissolved, another attack was reported in the capital at the home of another cabinet minister who was also considered to be vying for LCD leadership. The attack resulted in the death of an aid worker, whose vehicle was reportedly mistaken for that of the minister.

The LCD formed an alliance with the NIP ahead of the 2007 legislative elections. However, it was subsequently reported that eight members of the NIP contravened the arrangement. (In one constituency this reportedly cost the LCD a seat.) Following the election, the

NIP joined other parties in protesting the allocation of seats, claiming that the NIP alliance with the LCD was invalid because NIP leader Anthony MANYELI had rejected it (see NIP, below for details). A court of appeals subsequently upheld the LCD's arrangement with the NIP. However, the Supreme Court dismissed the case in July 2008.

In March 2010 six former members of the LCD's executive committee, led by former LCD secretary general Pashu MOCHESANE, rejoined the party after 10 years. Mochesane, a founding member of the LPC, had tried to bring about reconciliation between the two parties, but the issue of proportional representation proved to be too large an obstacle. During the youth wing conference in August, candidates aligned with Moleleki overwhelmingly won all seats, seen as a boost to the potential return to a leadership position for Moleleki, now minister of Natural Resources.

Infighting and power struggles within the party increased, eventually prompting the cabinet reshuffle in October, observers said. The move was unpopular with the party's youth faction, which staged a demonstration at the palace as the new ministers were sworn in. A leadership conference was called on November 20 to address petitions seeking the ouster of the party's national executive committee. Subsequently, dissidents successfully mounted a legal challenge to the special conference, which they said was against the party's constitution. Rifts within the party deepened in 2011, and some observers said Mpho MALIE, the party's former secretary general, was forming a breakaway party, a claim Malie denied.

Tensions over Mosisili's leadership continued mounting into 2012, with some party members reportedly upset over his desire to unilaterally appoint his own successor. On February 28 Mosisili defected from the LCD to form the new Democratic Congress party, which gained a narrow majority with the support of 45 members of parliament. The move prompted concern among international observers, including UN Secretary General Ban Ki Moon, that a rash of floor crossing might destabilize the electoral process. Rumors of a potential DC-led military coup circulated following a shake up within the army's top ranks and the beefing up of military security around the country. The LCD secured 26 seats in the 2012 election. Party leader Mothejoa METSING was appointed deputy prime minister in the coalition government formed in June 2012.

Leaders: Mothejoa METSING (Deputy Prime Minister and Party Leader), Motloheloa PHOOKO (Deputy), Lebohang NTSLNYL (Treasurer), Keketso RANTSO (Secretary General).

Democratic Congress (DC). Formed by former LCD leader Bethuel Pakalitha MOSISILI in 2012, the new party secured a plurality of 48 seats in the 2012 balloting. Failing to form an alliance, the party became the largest opposition grouping. During the judicial crisis in 2013, the DC was highly critical of Prime Minister Thabane.

Leaders: Bethuel Pakalitha MOSISILI (President of the Party), Monyane MOLELEKI (Deputy), Ralechate MOKOSE (Secretary General), Lebamang MAQALEHA (Chair), Mamphono KHAKETLA (Treasurer), Semano SEKATLE (Deputy Secretary General), Kose MAKOA (Deputy Chair), Malebaka BULANE (Public Relations), Tsoeu MOKERETLA (Deputy Public Relations), Serialong QOO (Publisher).

National Independent Party (NIP). The NIP was formed in late 1984 by a former cabinet member who resigned from the Jonathan government in 1972. In an election manifesto issued in March 1985, the NIP called for establishing diplomatic relations with South Africa and severing links with Communist countries. In mid-1992 it criticized the government for scheduling elections "prematurely" and announced that it would boycott the balloting then scheduled for November. The party failed to win seats in the 2002 assembly elections.

In 2007 the LCD reportedly "went behind the back" of NIP leader Anthony Manyeli to form an alliance with deputy leader Dominic Motikoe over constituency and compensatory polling (see LCD, above). Manyeli, who had rejected the arrangement, joined other parties' leaders in protest after the election, claiming that the parliamentary seats were unfairly allocated. The protesting parties contended that the LCD received more seats than it had legitimately won (through its allegedly invalid arrangement with the NIP) and that some parties did not get the compensatory seats they deserved. The NIP's claim against its alliance with the LCP was ultimately decided in favor of the LCP by a court of appeals, overturning a High Court ruling in favor of Manyeli. However, the Lesotho constitution states that High Court decisions regarding political elections cannot be appealed. Subsequently, the NIP and other parties asked the SADC to review the situation (see Current issues, above).

In April 2009 Motikoe was shot and killed by the husband of a woman with whom Motikoe allegedly had a relationship. Following his death, the Manyeli faction challenged the legality of the executive committee led by Motikoe.

Manyeli, 97, died in 2010. At the time of his death he was facing contempt of court charges stemming from published comments he made about proportional representation, which he believed was unjust.

In April 2011 the party remained deeply divided as some of its members marched on the party headquarters in Maputsoe demanding the dismissal of the secretary general. The protesters, led by member of parliament Thapelo MOKONE, called for new elections to replace the national executive committee, which it claimed had "overstayed" its mandate. The rifts in the party paralleled those within the LCD, with Mokone's NIP faction aligned with the Metsing camp of the LCD, and the NIP faction backing Secretary General Letuka NKOLE supporting Moleleki's wing of the LCD.

The NIP secured two seats in the 2012 election.

Leaders: Serame KHAMPEPE (Chair), Letuka NKOLE (Secretary General).

All Basotho Convention (ABC). Vowing to fight poverty and bring about economic change, former minister Thomas Thabane, once considered a likely successor to Prime Minister Mosisili, formed the ABC in 2006 with 17 LCD dissidents after he resigned from the LCD on October 9. The decline in the LCD majority was seen by observers as the impetus behind King Letsie's decision to dissolve parliament in November in the wake of a possible no-confidence vote and to call early legislative elections in February 2007. The ABC formed an alliance with the LWP in which the ABC supported the LWP in the proportional balloting in the 2007 election, much as the LCD had done with the NIP. Both alliances were criticized for violating the spirit of proportional balloting, prompting numerous protests.

In July 2010 the ABC announced an end to its electoral alliance with the LWP, prompting the LWP to subsequently demand that the ABC give up its proportional representation seats. Under the alliance, the ABC received seven seats and the LWP received three. Following the split, the LWP claimed the seating should be 6–4 in its favor. However, the IEC ruled that the seats cannot be changed. The government refused to recognize Thabane as the official leader of the opposition because he did not have the minimum 25 percent of legislators in the assembly. (The ABC–LWP combined total of 27 seats was three fewer than the minimum required.) The ABC secured 30 seats in the 2012 election. Thabane subsequently formed a coalition government with the LCD and BNP.

Leaders: Thomas THABANE (Prime Minister and President of the Party), Sello Clement MACHAKELA (Deputy President), Molobeli SOULO, Teboho MOHLOMI, Nyane MPHAFI (Secretary General).

Lesotho Workers' Party (LWP). The LWP was formed in August 2001 by left-wing trade unionists and other labor leaders. The party formed a controversial electoral alliance with the ABC in the 2007 legislative elections that dissolved in 2010 (see ABC, above). Some observers blamed increasing factionalism for the split. The LWP secured one seat in the 2012 elections.

Leaders: Billy MACAEFA (Chair), Sello MAPHALLA (Vice Chair).

Alliance of Congress Parties (ACP). The ACP was formed in 2006 by the two parties below and a faction of the BCP, led by Ntsukunyane MPHANYA, in advance of the February 2007 legislative election.

Basutoland African Congress (BAC). The BAC was launched in early 2002 by a breakaway faction of the BCP in a dispute over leadership. BAC founder Molapo Qhobela was suspended from his leadership post in 2003 after he allegedly made unilateral changes to the party's constitution.

Rifts in the party were reported between the Qhobela faction and those favoring BAC leader Khauhelo RALITAPOLE, and in January 2007 a pro-Qhobela faction split off, forming the **Basutoland African National Congress.**

In April 2010 Ralitapole stepped down as BAC leader to make way for "new blood." He was replaced by Paanya PHOOFOLO.

Leaders: Paanya PHOOFOLO (President), Mohopolo MACHELI (Vice President), Sidwell DLANGMANDLA, Kokolia RAMABELE (Spokesperson), Mamapele CHAKELA (Secretary General).

Lesotho People's Congress (LPC). The LPC was established in October 2001 by an LCD breakaway group led by former deputy prime minister Kelebone Maope and former LCD executive committee member Pashu Mochesane. In 2010 Mochesane and five other LPC members rejoined the LCD (above). The LPC secured one seat in the 2012 elections.

Leaders: Kelebone MAOPE (Party Leader), Shakhane MOKHEHLE, Mamoipone PITI (Secretary General).

Basotho Congress Party (BCP). Strongly antiapartheid and pan-Africanist in outlook, the BCP (formerly the Basutoland Congress Party) was split, following the abortive 1970 election, by the defection of (then) deputy leader Gerard P. RAMOREBOLI and several other members, who defied party policy and accepted nominated opposition seats in the interim National Assembly.

Banned in 1970, the main branch of the BCP continued to oppose the Jonathan government, claiming responsibility in the late 1970s for numerous armed attacks on police and BNP-supportive politicians. Concurrently, a Lesotho Liberation Army (LLA) of 500–1,000 operated, under external BCP direction and allegedly with South African support, in the country's northern mountains and from across the border. Despite overtures from the new regime in early 1986, the LLA called for revival of the 1966 constitution as a condition for abandoning antigovernment activity. However, in early 1989 external leader Ntsu Mokhehle returned to Lesotho, along with about 200 BCP supporters, presumably because of Pretoria's satisfaction with the current military government. Meanwhile, although the BCP remained committed to the establishment of a constitutional democracy, the LLA, apparently of no further use to South Africa, was reportedly reduced to a few "rag-tag" dissidents.

Mokhehle and other party members attended the opening of the constituent assembly in June 1990, despite their earlier support of a boycott. Subsequently, the party was rumored to be interested in Lesotho's incorporation into South Africa. Formerly a socialist party, the BCP in its 1993 election manifesto declared its commitment to a mixed economy.

Controversy rocked the BCP in 1996 as the rift between the party's conservative elders and the younger, so-called modernizers widened. At a party congress in March delegates elected a new 12-member National Executive Commission (NEC). In addition, "conservative" Deputy Prime Minister Bethuel Pakalitha Mosisili, a potential Mokhehle successor, secured the party vice presidency, outpolling the incumbent, modernizer Molapo Qhobela. However, Qhobela and his supporters promptly filed suit to have the balloting overturned, alleging that the conservative elders had rigged the elections. Subsequently, in May four prominent modernizer cabinet ministers, including Qhobela and Tseliso MAKHAKHE, were ousted from the government. One week later two other ministers aligned with them quit the cabinet.

In November 1996 the High Court ruled in favor of the Qhobela faction, annulling the March NEC polling and charging the members of the previous NEC with preparing new elections. In fresh balloting for the NEC on January 24, 1997, the modernizers retained their seats, reflecting their reportedly overwhelming numerical dominance within the party. On February 16 the remaining links between the two factions were fractured when the Mokhehle government ignored Qhobela's attempts to mediate an end to a police mutiny and violently squashed the rebellion. The progressives' dismay with Mokhehle was further compounded by testimony at South Africa's Truth and Reconciliation Commission (see separate entry on South Africa) that, according to *Africa Confidential,* appeared to substantiate long-held rumors that Mokhehle and his LLA forces had cooperated with the apartheid-era regime's "death squads." At a BPC meeting on February 28 party delegates voted to remove Mokhehle from the party presidency; however, on April 18 the High Court reversed Mokhehle's ouster, declaring that it violated the BCP's charter and directing Mokhehle to serve as interim president (his term having expired in January) until new party-wide elections could be held.

On June 7, 1997, Mokhehle announced that he and 37 other BCP legislators were leaving the party to form the LCD. On July 27 party delegates elected Qhobela as the BCP's new leader. On December 1 the Khauta KHASU-led Democratic Movement for Reconstruction (DMR) announced that it was disbanding so that its members could rejoin the BCP. (Khasu, former BCP deputy leader Gerard P. Ramoreboli, and Phoka CHAOLANE had been expelled from the BCP in 1992.)

In December 1998 Khauhelo Ralitapole, leader of the BCP's Women's League, was named cochair of the IPA.

Another rift over party leadership developed in 1999 among party officials Tseliso Makhakhe, Sekoala Toloane, and Ntsukunyane Mphanya, who all sought to unseat Qhobela. In early 2001 two different executive committees—one led by Molapo Qhobela, former minister of foreign affairs and heretofore president of the BCP, and the other by Makhakhe, former minister of education—claimed legitimate control of the party. Following a court's decision to accord the pro-Makhakhe faction the legitimate use of the BCP rubric, the pro-Qhobela faction broke away in early 2002 to form the Basutoland African Congress. Makhakhe stepped down from his leadership post in 2002 to give others the opportunity to head the party. For the 2007 legislative elections, Mphanya and his supporters participated in the launching of the ACP. Meanwhile, the BCP proper presented its own candidates and secured one proportional seat.

In August 2010, a BCP member of parliament advocated for state funding of political parties. The BCP secured one seat in the 2012 elections.

Leader: Ntsukunyane MPHANYA.

Basotho National Party (BNP). Organized in 1959 as the Basutoland National Party, the BNP has counted many Christians and chiefs among its members. It traditionally favored free enterprise and cooperation with South Africa while opposing apartheid. In the mid-1970s, however, it began co-opting policies originally advanced by the BCP, including the establishment of relations with Communist states and support for the ANC campaign against Pretoria. Growing internal division was reported in 1985 over who would succeed the aging chief Jonathan as prime minister. One faction was dominated by the paramilitary Youth League, armed and trained by North Korea, which reportedly planned a government takeover. The Youth League was disarmed and officially disbanded in a confrontation with the Lesotho Paramilitary Force on January 15, 1986, prior to the LPF-led coup of January 20. Although the BNP's national chair was named finance minister in the post-Jonathan administration, supporters of Chief Jonathan were barred from political activity. Chief Jonathan was detained briefly after the coup, released, and then placed under house arrest in August along with six BNP supporters for activities allegedly threatening national stability. They were released in September by order of the High Court with an admonition to refrain from political activity. The former prime minister died in April 1987.

On October 18, 1995, BNP leader Evaristus Retselisitsoe Sekhonyana was sentenced to two years' imprisonment or a heavy fine after being convicted of sedition for having urged armed resistance to military units during the August unrest. Sekhonyana assumed a leading role in the interparty negotiations that were held in the aftermath of the September 1998 uprising; however, he died on November 18. At a BNP congress in March 1999, former military leader Justin Metsing Lekhanya was elected as the new party leader. In the 2002 legislative elections the BNP became the second-largest party in the assembly (21 seats) and the main opposition grouping. In 2005 the government rejected a proposal from the BNP to form a government of national unity.

In 2007 the BNP won three seats through proportional representation.

The party was riven by factions in 2010, though Lekhanya survived a no-confidence vote in March. However, the 72-year-old leader was finally forced out by the national executive committee in December, observers citing dwindling poll results during his tenure. Subsequently, Thesele Maseribane was elected party leader over five other candidates at a party congress in March 2011. Maseribane immediately sought to mend the fractured party by inviting the other candidates to join him in unity efforts. However, his election to the post was immediately challenged by Majara Molapo, who earlier had resigned from the party's executive committee. The challenge, which the High Court agreed to consider, underscored a rift in the party's leadership. The party secured five seats in the 2012 election and joined the LCD-led coalition government. Maseribane was appointed minister of gender, youth, and sports in the subsequent cabinet.

Leaders: Thesele MASERIBANE (Minister of Gender, Youth, and Sports, and Party President), Sekhohola MOLELLE (Treasurer), Majara MOLAPO, Ranthomeng MATETE (Secretary General).

Basotho Democratic National Party (BDNP). Founded in November 2006 by former BNP member Thabang Nyeoe, the BDNP stated its commitment to "the creation of a living democracy" in Lesotho. It favors unity through national development rather than under the banner of a single party. The party won one seat in the 2012 balloting.

Leaders: Thabang NYEOE (President), Pelele LETSOELA (Vice Chair), Joang MOLAPO.

Marematlou Freedom Party (MFP). A royalist party, the MFP has long been committed to enlarging the king's authority. In other respects, its position has been somewhere between the BCP and the BNP. An offshoot Marematlou Party (MP), formed in 1965 and led by S. S. MATETE, reemerged with the MFP in 1969. One of its members, Patrick LEHLOENYA, accepted a cabinet post as minister to the prime minister in late 1975, subsequently becoming minister of health and social welfare. The party's (then) president, Bennett Makalo KHAKETLA, was appointed minister of justice and prisons in the cabinet formed after the 1986 coup.

Party leader Vincent Moeketse Malebo and LWP leader Billy Macaefa were scheduled to face trial in mid-2008 on contempt of court charges. The reason for the charges was unclear, and no resolution appears to have been reported.

In early 2011 party leader Malebo slammed the LCD for adopting the controversial Land Bill. Vowing to prevent the government from selling the land to foreigners, Malebo said, "We don't want chaos, but we intend to fight for our legacy because we don't want to be turned into slaves in our own homeland."

The MFP secured one seat in the 2012 elections.

Leaders: Vincent Moeketse MALEBO, Tsitso LEANYA, Seth MAKOTOKO.

The Basotho Batho Democratic Party, formed in 2006 and led by Jeremane RAMATHEBANE, and the Popular Front for Democracy, led by Lekhetho RAKUNE and Thabang KHOLUMO, each secured one seat in the 2007 legislative election. In the 2012 election the BBDP secured one seat and the PFD secured three.

Other Parties That Contested Recent Elections:

The **Lesotho Educational Party,** led by Thabo S. PITSO; the **New Lesotho Freedom Party,** led by Manapo Majara P. KHOABANE; the **Christian Democratic Party,** led by Ernest RAMOKOENA; and the **Social Democratic Party,** described upon its formation in 1998 as a "youth" party under the leadership of Masitise SELESO, also nominated candidates for the 2007 legislative elections.

Other parties that participated in the 2012 balloting (none received more than 0.5 percent of the vote) include: the **African Unity Movement** (AUM); the **White Horse Party**; the **All Democratic Corporation** (ADC); the **Sankatana Social Democratic Party** (SSDP); the **Areka Covenant Front for Development** (ACFD); and **Lekhotla La Mekhoa le Moetto** (LMM).

For more information on the **National Progressive Party** (NPP), the **United Party** (UP), the **Kopanang Basotho Party** (KBP), or the **United Democratic Party** (UDP), please see the 2013 *Handbook*.

LEGISLATURE

The bicameral parliament established under the 1966 constitution was dissolved in the wake of alleged irregularities in the election of January 27, 1970. An interim assembly of 22 chiefs and 71 nominated members, named on April 27, 1973, was dissolved as of December 31, 1984. Subsequent arrangements called for a Senate of 22 chiefs and an assembly of 60 elected and up to 20 nominated members. Since none of the opposition parties nominated candidates for balloting to have been conducted on September 17–18, 1985, Chief Jonathan canceled the poll and declared the BNP candidates elected unopposed. The 1983 Parliament Act, on which the action was based, was voided following the 1986 coup.

At present the **Parliament** is a bicameral body consisting of a nonelective Senate and an elective National Assembly.

Senate. The Senate contains 22 chiefs and 11 nominated members. A restructuring of the Senate (to make the body more "democratic" and "representative") was proposed for consideration by the Interim Political Authority (IPA), established in late 1998. However, little further information on proposed changes has surfaced.

The Senate was renewed on March 9, 2007.

President: Morena Letapata MAKHAOLA.

National Assembly. In the election of May 23, 1998, approximately 400 candidates competed for 80 lower house seats (an increase of 15 since the 1993 polling). The Lesotho Congress for Democracy (LCD) won 78 seats, the Basotho National Party (BNP) secured a sole position, and 1 seat was left vacant. The next election initially was not scheduled until 2003; however, early elections were envisioned as part of the late-1998 agreement negotiated between the government and the opposition following the military intervention of the SADC. After several postponements, balloting was conducted in 2002 for a new assembly, with 80 members elected on a "first-past-the-post" system complemented by 40 members selected by proportional vote.

In the most recent balloting of May 26, 2012, the seat distribution was as follows: the DC, 48 (41 directly elected and 7 proportional seats); ABC, 30 (26 directly-elected and 4 proportional); LCD, 26 (12 directly elected and 14 proportional); BNP, 5 (proportional); PFD, 3 (1 directly elected and 2 proportional); NIP, 2 (proportional); MFP, 1 (proportional); BBDP, 1 (proportional); BCP, 1 (proportional); BDNP, 1 (proportional); LPC, 1 (proportional); LWP, 1 (proportional).

Speaker: Sephiri MOTANYANE.

CABINET

[as of September 15, 2013]

Prime Minister	Thomas Thabane (ABC)
Deputy Prime Minister	Mothejoa Metsing (LCD)
Ministers	
Agriculture and Food Security	Litsoane Simon Litsoane (ABC)
Communications, Science, and Technology	Tseliso Mokhosi (LCD)
Defense and National Security	Thomas Thabane (ABC)
Development Planning	Maboee Moletsane (ABC)
Education and Training	Makabelo Priscilla Mosothoane (LCD) [f]
Employment and Labor	Lebesa Maloi (LCD)
Energy, Meteorology, and Water	Timothy Thahane (LCD)
Finance	Leketekete Victor Ketso (LCD)
Foreign Affairs	Mohlabi Tsekoa (LCD)
Forestry and Land Reclamation	Khotso Matla (LCD)
Gender, Youth, and Sports	Thesele Maseribane (BNP)
Health and Social Welfare	Pinkie Rosemary Manamolela (ABC) [f]
Home Affairs and Public Safety	Joang Molapo (BNP)
Industry, Trade, and Marketing	Temeki Phoenix Tsolo (ABC)
Justice, Human Rights, and Correctional Services	Haae Edward Phoofolo (ABC)
Law and Constitutional Affairs	Haae Edward Phoofolo (ABC)
Local Government and Chieftainship Affairs	Mothejoa Metsing (LCD)
Mining	Tiali Khasu (ABC)
Parliamentary Affairs	Joang Molapo (BNP)
Prime Minister's Office	Molobelo Soulu (ABC)
Public Service	Motloheloa Phooko (LCD)
Public Works and Transport	Keketso Rantso (LCD) [f]
Tourism, Culture, and Environment	Mamahele Radebe (ABC) [f]
Prime Minister's Office	Molobeli Soulo (ABC)
Social Development	Matebatso Doti (ABC) [f]
Deputy Ministers	
Local Government, Chieftainship and Parliamentary Affairs	Selibe Mochoboroane (LCD)
Finance	Matsepo Ramakoae (ABC) [f]
Trade and Industry, Cooperatives and Marketing	Maliehe Prince Maliehe (ABC)

Agriculture	Mahala Molapo (ABC)
Education	Apesi Ratsele (LCD)
Health	Lucia Nthabiseng Makoae (BNP) [f]
Home Affairs	Malebitso Ralebitso (BNP) [f]

[f] = female

INTERGOVERNMENTAL REPRESENTATION

Ambassador to the U.S.: Eliachim Molapi SEBATANE.

U.S. Ambassador to Lesotho: Matthew HARRINGTON (nominated).

Permanent Representative to the UN: Kelebone MAOPE.

IGO Memberships (Non-UN): AfDB, AU, CWTH, IOM NAM, SADC, WTO.

LIBERIA

Republic of Liberia

Political Status: Independent republic established in 1847; under de facto one-party system starting in 1878; martial law imposed on April 25, 1980, following coup of April 12; new constitution approved by national referendum on July 3, 1984 (with full effect from January 6, 1986 [the date of the inauguration of the new president]); constitution effectively voided by rebel action in mid-1990; Interim Government of National Unity (supported militarily by the Economic Community of West African States Monitoring Group) sworn in on November 22, 1990; State Council of Liberian Transitional National Government sworn in on March 7, 1994; new six-member State Council sworn in on September 1, 1995, following cease-fire agreement of August 19; amended version of 1995 cease-fire agreement signed by faction leaders on August 16, 1996, after 1995 accord was rendered moot by an outbreak of violence in April; constitution of 1986 reaffirmed by the National Assembly on August 6, 1997, following presidential and legislative balloting on July 19; transitional government established on October 14, 2003, following settlement of a civil war; new elected government installed on January 16, 2006.

Area: 43,000 sq. mi. (111,369 sq. km).

Population: 4,272,320 (2013E—UN); 3,989,703 (2013E—U.S. Census).

Major Urban Center (2005E): MONROVIA (571,000).

Official Language: English.

Monetary Unit: Liberian Dollar (market rate November 5, 2013: 81 dollars = $1US). The U.S. dollar also circulates.

President: Ellen JOHNSON-SIRLEAF (Unity Party); elected in second-round balloting on November 8, 2005, and inaugurated on January 16, 2006, for a six-year term to succeed the chair of the National Transitional Government, Charles Gyude BRYANT (Liberia Action Party); reelected for another six-year term in second-round balloting on November 8, 2011.

Vice President: Joseph N. BOAKAI (Unity Party); elected in second-round balloting on November 8, 2005, and inaugurated on January 16, 2006, for a term concurrent with that of the president, succeeding the vice chair of the National Transitional Government, Wesley Momo JOHNSON (United People's Party); reelected for another term concurrent with that of the president in second-round balloting on November 8, 2011.

THE COUNTRY

Facing the Atlantic along the western bulge of Africa, Liberia is a country of tropical rain forests and broken plateaus. Established as a haven for freed American slaves, it became an independent republic in 1847, more than a century before its neighbors. A small (3–5 percent of the population) "Americo-Liberian" elite, which traced its descent to the settlers of 1820–1840, subsequently played a significant role in Liberian affairs while being gradually assimilated into the rest of the population, which is currently divided into some 16 principal tribes speaking nearly 30 native languages. An estimated 10 percent of the population is Christian and 10–20 percent Muslim; the remainder practices indigenous religions and traditional customs. Women make up approximately 40 percent of the labor force, mainly in agriculture. Female participation in government, traditionally minimal, has increased significantly since the 1980s; the current president is a woman, and there are 5 women in the cabinet and 13 in the National Assembly.

The Liberian economy was traditionally dependent on exports of iron ore, rubber, and timber, plus smaller quantities of diamonds and coffee. In 1989 iron ore accounted for more than half of export revenue, although the industry employed only 2 percent of the labor force. Industrial development also included diverse smaller enterprises centering on commodities such as processed agricultural goods, cement, plastic explosives, beverages, and refined petroleum. In addition, Liberia provided a "flag of convenience" for about 2,450 ships, or approximately one-fifth of the world's maritime tonnage.

During the decade preceding the collapse of the Doe regime in 1990, a decline in world commodity prices combined with mismanagement of state enterprises to produce a severe fiscal crisis. In response, the government attempted to privatize national industries, mounted an anticorruption campaign, and promoted an agriculture-based "green revolution." Complicating the situation was the suspension of aid in 1986 by the International Monetary Fund (IMF) because of Monrovia's failure to make scheduled payments on its external debt, which exceeded $1.7 billion by mid-1990. Of far greater consequence were the subsequent carnage caused by civil war and the interim government's lack of fiscal resources because of rebel activity. Economic effects included the suspension of iron ore production and the shutting down of many rubber plantations.

The administration installed in mid-1997 pledged to focus its economic rehabilitation efforts on advancement of the private sector and reduction of the high unemployment rate. However, the economy subsequently suffered from the country's increasing international isolation resulting from the government's perceived role in the burgeoning subregional conflict (see Foreign relations, below). Among other things, the unrest led to a UN embargo on diamond sales (integrally related to arms traffic), a halt to many donor-financed development projects, and delays in the government's proposed fiscal reforms.

Intensified internal fighting in 2002 led to a dramatic decline in GDP in 2003 and created severe food and energy shortages and substantial displacement of large segments of the population. In March 2003 the IMF suspended Liberia because of the Taylor administration's failure to pay its dues and repay loans. However, the negotiation of a cease-fire and installation of a national transitional government in the second half of 2003 prompted international donors in February 2004 to pledge $520 million in humanitarian and economic assistance.

Following the 2005 elections, the new administration launched a series of reforms in early 2006. Meanwhile, in exchange for the renewal of foreign aid, donor organizations and states created the Governance and Economic Management Assistance Program (GEMAP), under which international experts were designated to assist members of the new Liberian government. (GEMAP officials were required to countersign all major government expenditures, a condition that generated significant resentment among Liberians.)

In April 2006 the IMF announced that Liberia was one of 11 countries that had qualified for debt relief under the Heavily Indebted Poor Countries initiative. As evidence of the daunting task facing the new government, it was estimated that 50 percent of the population survived on less than $1 per day. In addition, some estimates placed unemployment as high as 80 percent. Acknowledging that significant progress had been achieved by the Johnson-Sirleaf administration but cautioning that annual per capita GDP ($195) remained below prewar levels, the IMF normalized relations with Liberia in 2008 and approved new support.

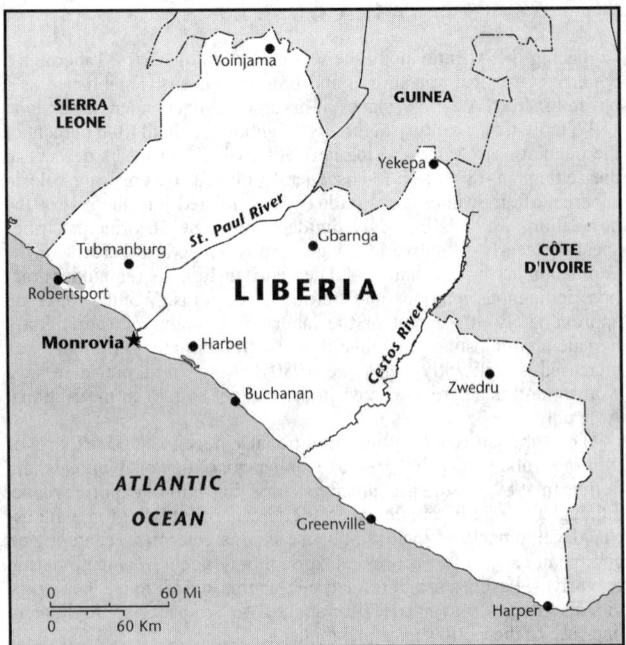

The IMF and the World Bank in June 2010 endorsed a plan providing for $4.6 billion in debt relief for Liberia, and the Paris Club of international creditors soon thereafter approved an additional $1.2 billion write-off. Meanwhile, after suffering from the effects of the global economic downturn in 2009, the economy rebounded to growth of 6 percent in both 2010 and 2011. Significantly, the production of iron ore finally resumed in September 2011, and expansion of rubber plantations continued. Meanwhile, the number of Liberian-flagged ships had grown to more than 4,000, providing the government with some $22 million in annual income.

It was reported in early 2012 that substantial offshore oil deposits had been discovered, attracting the interest of foreign investors already involved in the exploitation of iron ore, palm oil, and timber products. Increased extractive activity contributed to GDP growth of 9 percent in 2012, and the IMF announced new lending to support infrastructure development and social programs.

GOVERNMENT AND POLITICS

Political background. Liberia's political origins stem from a charter granted by the U.S. Congress to the American Colonization Society in 1816 to establish a settlement for freed slaves on the west coast of Africa. The first settlers arrived in 1822 with the financial assistance of U.S. President James Monroe, and in 1847 Liberia declared itself an independent republic under an American-style constitution. During the late 19th and early 20th centuries, such European powers as Britain, France, and Germany became involved in the country's domestic affairs and laid claim to portions of Liberian territory. After World War I, however, American political and economic influence was reestablished, with Firestone assuming operation in 1926 of the world's largest rubber plantation in Harbel.

Relative stability characterized internal politics under the guidance of the True Whig Party (TWP), which ruled continuously for more than a century after coming to power in 1878. Political authority was strongly centralized under the administration of President William V. S. TUBMAN, who was elected in 1944 on a platform calling for the promotion of foreign economic investment and the unification of the country via integration of the Americo-Liberian population and tribal groups. Following Tubman's death in 1971, his successor, William Richard TOLBERT Jr., attempted to maintain Tubman's policies. However, limited economic imagination, insensitivity to popular feeling among indigenous Liberians, and allegations of maladministration and corruption contributed in the late 1970s to growing domestic opposition, including a wave of illegal strikes. Widespread rioting in Monrovia in April 1979 over a proposed increase in the price of rice prompted the Liberian Congress to grant emergency powers to Tolbert, while later in the year municipal elections were postponed and tough labor laws were enacted to end the work stoppages.

Despite legalization in January 1980 of the People's Progressive Party (PPP), the country's first formal opposition in more than two decades, President Tolbert responded to a call for a general strike by PPP leader Gabriel Baccus MATTHEWS in March by asserting that the PPP had planned an "armed insurrection." Matthews and other PPP leaders were arrested, but on April 12, two days before their trial was to begin, a coup led by junior officers overthrew the government of President Tolbert, who was killed along with more than two dozen others. A People's Redemption Council (PRC), chaired by Master Sgt. Samuel Kanyon DOE, was immediately established, and on April 13 the PRC announced a civilian-military cabinet that included Matthews as foreign minister. On April 22, following a series of military trials, a number of former government and TWP officials were publicly executed by firing squad. Three days later, the PRC suspended the constitution and instituted martial law.

In April 1981 the PRC appointed a 25-member commission to draft a new constitution, in keeping with Doe's promise of a return to civilian rule by April 1985. After a number of postponements for the avowed purpose of registering and educating voters, a constitutional referendum was held on July 3, 1984. On July 20 Doe announced that the document had been accepted, and the following day he abolished the PRC and merged its membership with 57 hand-picked civilians to form an Interim National Assembly. Although the new assembly immediately elected him as its president, Doe characterized the status as temporary and announced that he would present himself as a candidate in a national election to be held in October 1985.

Because of restrictions imposed by the government-appointed electoral commission, neither Matthews nor the chair of the constitutional commission, Dr. Amos SAWYER, was allowed to campaign for the presidency in 1985, with their parties also being disqualified from presenting legislative candidates. As a result, three substantially weaker groups challenged Doe's recently launched National Democratic Party of Liberia (NDPL). Amid widespread allegations of electoral fraud and military intimidation, Doe claimed victory in the October 15, 1985, balloting on the basis of a reported 50.9 percent presidential vote share, while the NDPL was awarded 73 of the 90 assembly seats.

In June 1987, as part of an apparent effort to consolidate his power, President Doe dismissed four Supreme Court justices, thereby drawing criticism that he had exceeded his constitutional authority. Three months later the government reported that it had thwarted a coup attempt masterminded by former foreign minister Matthews.

During 1988 the regime continued to crack down on real or imagined opponents. In March, William Gabriel KPOLLEH, president of the Liberian Unification Party (LUP), was charged with leading a coup attempt, and in July Doe's former PRC deputy, J. Nicholas PODIER, was slain in the wake of another alleged overthrow effort (reportedly the ninth since 1980).

In late 1989 a number of villages in the northeastern border region of Nimba County were overrun by a group of about 150 rebels led by Charles Chankay TAYLOR, who five years earlier had escaped from custody in the United States after being charged with the theft of Liberian government funds. In January 1990 the fighting assumed a tribal character, with the rebels (styling themselves the National Patriotic Front of Liberia [NPFL]) attacking members of the president's Krahn ethnic group and government forces retaliating against Nimba's principal tribe, the Gio. By early June what had begun as a seemingly minor insurrection had expanded into a major threat to the Doe regime. After steady progress in a series of engagements with Liberian army units, rebel troops advanced on Monrovia, and by mid-July a "reign of terror" was reported in the capital, with both sides allegedly engaging in atrocities against ethnic opponents and unarmed civilians. Meanwhile, an Independent NPFL (INPFL), which had broken with the Taylor group in February under the leadership of Prince Yormic JOHNSON, emerged as a major "third force" that succeeded in gaining control of central Monrovia on July 23.

With neither the United Nations nor the Organization of African Unity (OAU, subsequently the African Union—AU) taking action to ameliorate the conflict, the Economic Community of West African States (ECOWAS) organized a 4,000-man peacekeeping force styled the ECOWAS Monitoring Group (Ecomog), which arrived in Monrovia on August 25, 1990. The intervention was welcomed by Johnson but was bitterly denounced by Taylor, who insisted that the force had been assembled to avert defeat of the Doe regime by the NPFL.

On September 11, 1990, President Doe was killed by members of the Johnson group as the apparent result of an argument that had broken out during a meeting arranged by Ecomog. Government forces nonetheless continued their defense of the heavily fortified executive mansion under the presidential guard commander, Brig. Gen. David NIMLEY. During the next several days four individuals (Johnson, Taylor, Nimley, and the former constitutional commission chair, Amos Sawyer, who headed an Interim Government of National Unity [IGNU] from exile in Banjul, Gambia) proclaimed themselves president, with the last being recognized, on an interim basis, by ECOWAS on November 22. Six days later the three warring factions within Liberia concluded a cease-fire agreement in Bamako, Mali, and declared their intention to participate in a national conference to establish an interim government. However, Taylor was reported to have signed the accord only because of pressure from his two principal backers, Libya and Burkina Faso.

The suspension of hostilities generally held into 1991, with the three faction leaders (including Gen. Hezekiah BOWEN, who had succeeded Nimley as head of the Armed Forces of Liberia [AFL]), agreeing to meet in Lomé, Togo, on March 15 to pave the way for a transitional regime. At the last moment, however, Taylor refused to attend without the participation of elected representatives from Liberia's 13 counties, all but one of which his forces claimed to control. A compromise structure was eventually agreed upon, providing for a president and two vice presidents (representing the IGNU, NPFL, and INPFL, respectively). However, there was little immediate progress toward implementation of the plan, and Ecomog experienced mounting pressure to move militarily against the obdurate Taylor. On June 30 the stalemate appeared to have been broken in the course of a meeting attended by Taylor, Sawyer, and five West African heads of government in Yamoussoukro, Côte d'Ivoire, that yielded agreement on the establishment of a commission to organize a national election.

Although fighting subsided in July–August 1991, Taylor took no action to disarm his forces as mandated by the Yamoussoukro accord, while Johnson on August 6 announced that the INPFL was withdrawing from the tripartite regime. Faced with Taylor's hostility toward the composition of the Ecomog force, Côte d'Ivoire offered to seek Ecomog's replacement by a UN contingent, but the idea was rejected by Sawyer on August 19. Renewed hostilities thereupon broke out in the form of clashes between NPFL units, which had entered Sierra Leone in support of local dissidents, and Sierra Leonean troops, who were accompanied by a group from former president Doe's Krahn tribe that had styled itself the United Liberation Movement of Liberia for Democracy (Ulimo). Nonetheless, peace talks resumed in Yamoussoukro on September 16 and 17, yielding a new stand-down commitment by the Liberian factions in return for an Ecomog restructuring (primarily in response to NPFL complaints that Ecomog was inappropriately Nigerian-dominated).

A fourth summit in Yamoussoukro on October 29–31, 1991, drew a pledge by the NPFL to withdraw from Sierra Leone, disarm its forces, and relinquish Liberian territory under its control to Ecomog. It was also agreed that a buffer zone would be established between Liberia and Sierra Leone and that the Liberian election would be held within six months. On November 8 Johnson's INPFL announced that it would rejoin the interim government, although Ulimo leader Raleigh SEEKIE repudiated the peace agreement. While additional disagreements, including a refusal by both the NPFL and INPFL to honor new banknotes issued by the Sawyer administration, surfaced by early 1992, a 13-member interim election commission was sworn in on January 13 with instructions to prepare for legislative and presidential balloting in August. A week later, in his annual message to Monrovia's Interim Assembly, President Sawyer offered NPFL leader Taylor the vacant post of vice president in the interim government on the condition that Taylor join in effective implementation of the most recent Yamoussoukro accord. However, no response was reported.

On April 7 and 8, 1992, ECOWAS representatives met in Geneva, Switzerland, with Sawyer, Taylor, the vice president of Nigeria, and the presidents of Burkina Faso, Côte d'Ivoire, and Senegal. The group reaffirmed its support of Yamoussoukro IV, including establishment of the Ecomog buffer zone. On April 14 Taylor renounced the agreement, calling it "unbalanced and unsatisfactory," but on April 29 he reversed himself. On April 30 Ecomog began deployment in border areas theretofore controlled by the NPFL.

In August 1992 heavy fighting broke out between Taylor's NPFL and Ulimo forces, and in September the NPFL accused Ecomog of supporting the NPEL's opponents. In early April Ecomog troops drove Taylor's forces from the strategic port city of Buchanan, and in May the southeastern port of Greenville also fell, confining the NPFL's maritime access to the small town of Harper near the border with Côte d'Ivoire.

On July 25, 1993, in Cotonou, Benin, Liberia's leading combatants (the NPFL, Ulimo, and Ecomog) signed an OAU/UN-brokered peace accord, and on August 1 the lengthy conflict again appeared to end, Taylor advising his followers (prematurely, as it turned out) "to return to your towns and villages and begin to rebuild your lives. The war is over." On August 16 the three factions reached agreement on a transitional Council of State to consist of Bismark KUYON and David KPOMAKPOR (IGNU), Dorothy MUSULENG-COOPER (NPFL), and Dr. Mohamed SHERIFF and Thomas ZIAH (Ulimo). The new council proceeded to elect Kuyon, Musuleng-Cooper, and Sheriff as chair and first and second deputy chairs, respectively. However, a scheduled takeover from the Sawyer government on August 24 was postponed by Kuyon, pending the deployment of a peacekeeping force from throughout Africa to oversee disarmament. One week later Nigeria withdrew its personnel (approximately three-quarters of the force total) from Ecomog, and on September 22 the UN Security Council voted to establish the UN Observer Mission in Liberia (UNOMIL) to ensure implementation of the Cotonou accord. Subsequently, the IGNU designated Philip A. Z. BANKS to succeed Kuyon, while the NPFL named Gen. Isaac MUSA to replace Musuleng-Cooper.

By late 1993 agreement had been reached on the structure of a unified interim assembly and on the allocation of most portfolios in a transitional government. However, it was not until March 7, 1994, that a restructured Council of State with Kpomakpor as chair was formally installed. Following intense bargaining over the distribution of portfolios, the formation was announced of a full Liberian National Transitional Government (LNTG), which first met on May 16. The transitional period was officially dated from the launching of the Council of State, with a six-month mandate to expire on September 7.

On August 4, 1994, NPFL leader Taylor declared that the transitional administration would have no "legal tenure" after September 7, when multiparty elections had been scheduled to take place. He also demanded a cabinet reshuffle, claiming that several key ministers who had been expelled from the NPFL for criticizing his leadership no longer could be counted as representing the NPFL.

On September 7, 1994, Taylor joined AFL leader Bowen and Lt. Gen. Alhaji G. V. KROMAH, the leader of Ulimo's Mandingo-based Muslim faction (Ulimo-M), in a meeting on Lake Volta near Akosombo with Ghana's President Jerry Rawlings and representatives of Ecomog, the OAU, and the UN secretary general. Five days later, an agreement was signed calling for a permanent end to hostilities; continuance until October 10, 1995, of the transitional government, headed by a new five-member Council of State; and the holding of presidential and legislative elections within a year. During the Akosombo meeting, however, the NPFL dissenters, led by Labor Minister Thomas WOEWEIYU, overran the NPFL headquarters in Gbarnga, forcing Taylor to seek temporary refuge in Côte d'Ivoire.

In October 1994 both UNOMIL and Ecomog forces were substantially reduced, prospects for an end to the lengthy Liberian conflict having receded. On November 6 the Ghanaian and Nigerian governments (the largest contributors to Ecomog) convened a "last ditch" meeting in Accra, Ghana, that included, in addition to the signatories of the Akosombo accord, Gen. Roosevelt JOHNSON, leader of Ulimo's Christian-oriented Krahn faction (Ulimo-K); Dr. George E. S. BOLEY, head of the Krahn-based Liberian Peace Council (LPC); François MASSAQUOI, commander of the Lofa Defense Force (LDF); and Woeweiyu, representing the NPFL dissidents. However, the meeting adjourned on November 29 with no agreement on the membership of a reconstituted Council of State.

Despite the failure of the November 1994 talks, follow-up discussions were launched in Accra in December, with the major warring groups (the NPFL, Ulimo-K, Ulimo-M, AFL, LPC, LDF, and the Woeweiyu dissidents [now styled the Central Revolutionary Council–NPFL]) participating. On December 22 agreement was reached on a cessation of hostilities as of December 28 and on a Council of State to include one representative each from the NPFL, Ulimo, the AFL, and the LPC, with a fifth member to be selected by the NPFL and Ulimo from traditional chiefs. It was further agreed that the Council of State would give way to an elected government on January 1, 1996, after multiparty elections on November 1, 1995.

On January 25, 1995, the warring groups agreed to expand the Council of State from five to six members, but they continued to disagree about its composition and adjourned the talks indefinitely on January 31.

Subsequently, on February 6, Ghanaian mediators rejected a Taylor proposal for another five-man council to be chaired by an elderly traditional chief, Tamba TAYLOR (no relation to the NPFL leader), with Charles Taylor as first vice chair, Ulimo-M's Kromah as second vice chair, and the AFL's Bowen as third vice chair. It was not until August 19 that agreement on the makeup of the new council was reached and another cease-fire was declared. The six members inaugurated in Monrovia on September 1 included Charles Taylor, G. V. Kromah, Dr. George E. S. Boley, and three civilians—Chief Tamba Taylor, Oscar QUIAH, and Wilton S. SANKAWULO, a former university professor and newspaper columnist, who was named council chair.

On September 3, 1995, the Council of State announced the formation of a new Transitional Government. However, renewed fighting broke out throughout Monrovia in April 1996, sparked by the attempted arrest of Ulimo-K leader Johnson by NPFL and Ulimo-M fighters. Although Johnson's headquarters were easily taken, he escaped capture, and his forces and Krahn defectors from other factions took up arms throughout the city. By April 9 Johnson and his fighters, with several hundred hostages in tow, had been forced to retreat to their Monrovia barracks; however, systematic looting continued amid anarchic conditions in the capital.

On April 10, 1996, with extremely intense fighting reported around the U.S. embassy (where thousands of Liberian civilians and foreigners were reported to have sought refuge), the United States ordered the deployment of a warship to the Liberian coast to support an evacuation effort begun the previous day. On the same day the warring faction leaders again agreed to a cease-fire; however, it was immediately abandoned after Johnson refused to surrender to Ecomog forces. On April 16 anti-Johnson militiamen laid siege to his base. Three days later another cease-fire was announced, and on April 21 the Ulimo-K released the majority of its hostages. Furthermore, Ecomog commanders reported that they had secured the perimeter of Monrovia in an effort to stanch the flow of arms and fighters. Nevertheless, intense fighting reportedly continued.

At ECOWAS's annual summit in July 1996, its members pledged to organize Liberian elections within nine months. With fighting reported to have subsided, ECOWAS representatives and all of the faction leaders met in mid-August in Abuja, Nigeria, where they agreed to a revised version of the 1995 accord. The faction leaders also unanimously elected Ruth PERRY, a senator during the Doe era, to replace Sankawulo as chair of the Council of State. The cease-fire agreement was highlighted by a proposed schedule for disarmament and demobilization (from November 22, 1996, to January 31, 1997), dissolution of the factions (January 31, 1997), presidential and legislative elections (May 31, 1997), and the inauguration of a new government (June 15, 1997). On August 31 the UNOMIL mandate was extended, and on September 3 Perry was inaugurated, thus becoming the first-ever female African head of state.

Adding muscle to the August 1996 accord, ECOWAS threatened to impose sanctions on "any person or group obstructing the implementation" of the cease-fire agreement. Meanwhile, the United States pledged to finance the anticipated expansion of Ecomog troop strength. Subsequently, amid reports of mass starvation in those areas already cleared of fighters, Ecomog troops began deploying weeks ahead of the scheduled November start of the disarmament process. However, an assassination attempt against Charles Taylor at the presidential palace on October 31 resulted in suspension of Council of State activities and underscored the fragility of the cease-fire. Nevertheless, registration of political parties continued through the end of the year in preparation for the general elections scheduled for May 1997.

In mid-January 1997 the Council of State reconvened for the first time since the attempt on Taylor's life. Meanwhile, Ecomog's Nigerian leadership increased pressure on the former combatants to turn in their arms. Consequently, the disarmament campaign, which had theretofore elicited only a trickle of returns, accelerated to near conclusion by the end of the month, and on February 1 all the armed factions were declared officially dissolved. In mid-February presidential and legislative balloting was scheduled for May 30, and a seven-member electoral commission was established. Two weeks later, Taylor, Kromah, and Boley resigned from the Council of State to begin preparations for the presidential election. In early March, President Perry appointed former information minister Henry ANDREWS as president of the electoral commission, and on April 2 the commission was officially sworn in. Meanwhile, former UN official and international banker Ellen JOHNSON-SIRLEAF emerged as Taylor's primary competition for the presidency in the wake of the splintering of an anti-Taylor coalition, the Alliance of Seven Parties (see introductory text to Political Parties and Groups, below). In addition, 11 others registered as presidential candidates, and at least 13 parties announced their intention to compete for legislative posts. In mid-May the balloting was postponed to July.

In presidential and legislative balloting on July 19, 1997, Taylor and the restyled National Patriotic Party (NPP) overwhelmed their opponents, with Taylor and his vice presidential running mate, Enoch DOGOLEA, capturing approximately 70 percent of the votes and the NPP securing majorities in both the House of Representatives and the Senate. Although some analysts had forecast a tight race between Taylor and Johnson-Sirleaf, Taylor's well-financed campaign, his veiled threats to recommence fighting if he were to lose the elections, and his election-eve apology for his role in the civil war proved too much for Johnson-Sirleaf. She received just 9 percent of the vote, and her Unity Party (UP) was also a distant second in legislative polling. International observers described the balloting as generally fair, but a number of domestic critics characterized it as irreparably tainted by irregularities. On August 2 Taylor and Dogolea were inaugurated, and by mid-month Taylor had finished appointing a predominantly NPP cabinet.

In 1998 President Taylor wielded an increasingly heavy hand in response to domestic criticism, shutting down opposition media outlets, purging dissenters from the government, and, according to critics, covertly supporting violent attacks on opposition foes. In mid-September dozens of people were reportedly killed in Monrovia when presidential forces attempted to arrest Gen. Roosevelt Johnson, who had refused to release his grip on a section of the capital and was suspected of plotting to overthrow the government. During the fighting, Johnson and his entourage fled to the U.S. embassy, where they were allowed to enter only after Taylor's forces attacked and killed two of Johnson's associates and wounded two U.S. personnel. The following day, Johnson, Lt. Gen. Alhaji Kromah (now representing the All-Liberia Coalition Party [ALCOP]), and approximately 20 others were charged with treason. Subsequently, Johnson and Kromah escaped from the country (the former by U.S. helicopter), and neither of the two men, nor half of their codefendants, appeared at the opening of their trial in November. (In April 1999, 13 of the "coup plotters" were sentenced to 10 years in prison.)

At a July 1999 weapons-destruction ceremony, President Taylor declared the end of a "dark chapter" in Liberian history. (More than 200,000 people had died in the civil war.) It soon became clear, however, that many of Taylor's opponents had not given up their fight, as evidenced by guerrilla activity on the part of the Liberians United for Reconciliation and Democracy (LURD) in the northwest. In August 2000 the administration charged a number of opposition figures (many in exile) with treason in connection with ongoing "dissident" activities. However, facing heavy international pressure for both his domestic policies and his role in regional conflicts (particularly involving Sierra Leone), Taylor amnestied many of his opponents and urged them to return to Liberia to assume a role in the political process. Although a fragile peace in Sierra Leone offered some respite for Taylor and other participants in the interlocking regional disputes, the LURD offensive continued into early 2002. Opposition leaders also accused the administration in the first half of 2002 of increasingly repressive (and sometimes violent) measures against dissident voices in the media and elsewhere. In addition, international human rights activists charged Liberian security forces with numerous violations that were seen as contributing to a deteriorating political climate. Meanwhile, additional pressure was applied to the government by another recently launched rebel group, the Movement for Democracy in Liberia (MODEL).

In January 2003 the government announced that new presidential and legislative elections would be held in October. However, LURD/MODEL fighters launched an offensive in February that neared Monrovia in April, causing a mass exodus from the capital and making it clear that normal political activity was an impossibility without a cease-fire.

As the rebels reached Monrovia in June 2003, peace negotiations were launched in Accra, Ghana. On June 17 the Accra accord was signed, calling for withdrawal of the rebels to the north of Monrovia, deployment of an international peacekeeping force, and the resignation of President Taylor in favor of a transitional government. Within days, however, Taylor reneged on his pledge to resign, and the rebels again advanced on Monrovia. Complicating matters for President Taylor was an indictment from the UN-sponsored court in Sierra Leone charging him with 17 counts of crimes against humanity in connection with his alleged role in that nation's recently resolved conflict.

Near the end of July 2003, ECOWAS authorized the deployment of peacekeeping forces under the banner of the ECOWAS Mission in

Liberia (ECOMIL), and some 3,250 ECOMIL troops (mainly from Nigeria) were dispatched to Monrovia in early August. Under intense international pressure, Taylor finally resigned on August 11 and left Liberia for Nigeria. Vice President Moses Zeh BLAH assumed presidential authority on an acting basis, and he quickly negotiated (on August 18) a new cease-fire and a so-called Comprehensive Peace Agreement with the rebels. In accordance with the peace plan, a national transitional government was installed on October 14, with Charles Gyude BRYANT of the Liberia Action Party (LAP) as chair. His cabinet comprised members of the pro-Taylor Government of Liberia (GOL), the LURD, the MODEL, and representatives of civic organizations. At the same time, a 76-member National Transitional Legislative Assembly (NTLA) was installed for a two-year period pending new legislative and presidential elections. Bryant dedicated his administration to the task of bringing Liberia "back from the brink of self-destruction." Priorities included the disarmament (with help from the recently established UN Mission in Liberia [UNMIL]) of the former warring factions and assistance for some 300,000 internal or external refugees (as of November 2004). Sporadic clashes between Muslims and Christians in several areas of the country also contributed to the government's difficulties. In addition, the administration's image was subsequently tarnished by revelations of alleged financial irregularities.

In the first round of presidential balloting on October 11, 2005, George WEAH of the Congress for Democratic Change (CDC) led 22 candidates with 28.3 percent of the vote. Ellen Johnson-Sirleaf of the UP finished second with 19.8 percent. Weah, a former soccer star, ran a populist campaign and enjoyed the support of some elements of the former Taylor regime. However, Johnson-Sirleaf, the former World Bank official who was presented as the candidate who could best restore Liberia's international ties and garner much needed foreign reconstruction aid, handily won the runoff balloting on November 8 with 59.4 percent of the vote. Meanwhile, in the October 11 balloting for the House of Representatives, the CDC led all parties with 15 seats. Since her party did not command a legislative majority, Johnson-Sirleaf (the first democratically elected female leader of a national government in Africa) formed a cabinet that included independents and members of several small parties.

Weah initially alleged fraud surrounding his loss in the second round, although EU and ECOWAS observers described the balloting as generally free and fair and the national election commission dismissed Weah's complaints. Liberian security forces and UN peacekeepers used tear gas and riot batons to disperse protest demonstrations by Weah's supporters shortly after the balloting. However, in order to defuse the situation, Weah later in the month announced he had accepted his defeat and urged his supporters to do likewise.

A South African–style Truth and Reconciliation Commission (TRC) began in October 2006 to gather testimony from victims and alleged war criminals from the earlier conflict. Although the commission suspended its activities in January 2007 due to a lack of funds, the government subsequently announced a broad investigation of former government officials on fraud and corruption charges.

In April 2007 the UN Security Council relaxed the sanctions on the diamond trade in Liberia in exchange for the country becoming a partner in the Kimberley Process, which had been designed to prevent export of "blood diamonds" from conflict areas. Meanwhile, at mid-year, the UNMIL reported that more than 60,000 former fighters had been integrated into job-training programs. However, later in the year the UNMIL reported a "broad range of human rights concerns," particularly in regard to the "decrepit" judicial system.

Much attention in early 2008 focused on the first public hearings on the recently reactivated TRC, although critics described the commission as "toothless" because of its lack of prosecutorial powers. The TRC presented its final report to the legislature in mid-2009, although many analysts described the findings as flawed and representative of the "differing agendas" of the members of the commission. Among the controversial recommendations was a call for President Johnson-Sirleaf to be barred from running for office again because she had for a brief time in 1989 supported Charles Taylor's insurgency. (Johnson-Sirleaf earlier in 2009 had apologized to the TRC for her actions, saying she had been fooled about Taylor's "true intentions.") The legislature suspended action on the TRC's recommendations in September 2009.

The UP led all parties in the legislative elections on October 11, 2011, while Johnson-Sirleaf finished first (with 43.9 percent of the vote) against 15 challengers in the first round of the presidential balloting. Johnson-Sirleaf was credited with 90.7 percent of the second-round vote after the CDC's Winston TUBMAN (who had won 32.7 percent of the vote in the first round) withdrew from the race and called for an electoral boycott.

Constitution and government. The former Liberian constitution, adopted July 26, 1847, was modeled, save in the matter of federalism, after that of the United States. Executive authority was vested in the president, who was limited by a 1975 amendment to a single eight-year term, excluding time spent completing the unexpired term of a predecessor. The bicameral Congress consisted of an 18-member Senate and a 65-member House of Representatives.

The constitution approved in July 1984, with effect from President Doe's inaugural in January 1986, did not differ significantly from its predecessor. Rather than being elected for eight years, the president was restricted to a maximum of two six-year terms. In addition, the legislature was restyled the National Assembly, with the Senate membership being increased to 26 and the House membership being reduced to 64. Suffrage was extended to all adults. The 1984 law also provided for relatively simple registration of political parties, with prohibitions against those considered dangerous to "the free and democratic society of Liberia." Administratively, the country was divided into 9 counties and 5 territories, with lesser units encompassing 30 cities and 145 townships. The number of counties has subsequently increased to 15.

Some of the provisions of the 1984 constitution were superseded by the Comprehensive Peace Agreement of 2003 and the Electoral Reform Act of 2004, which, among other things, established guidelines for elections to a new Senate and House of Representatives (see Legislature, below) and for new presidential/vice-presidential balloting. In mid-2012 President Johnson-Sirleaf created a constitutional review commission to draft proposed basic law revisions regarding a number of issues, including the appointment of an independent electoral commission and the tenure of Supreme Court judges. The president's critics suggested the commission might also consider eliminating the two-term presidential limit.

Freedom of the press has generally been perceived as a genuine component of the nation's democratic transition since 2003, although occasional attacks on journalists by "uncontrolled" members of various groups have been reported. Also, the government was criticized by watchdog organizations for temporarily suspending a number of opposition media outlets prior to the second round of the 2011 presidential election.

Foreign relations. Many of the guiding principles of the OAU originated with President Tubman, who held a prominent position among moderate African leaders dedicated to peaceful change and noninterference in the internal affairs of other countries. President Tolbert was similarly respected in international forums, with the result that the April 1980 coup and his assassination were widely condemned throughout the world.

Liberia's traditional friendship with the United States was reflected both in the extent of U.S. private investment and in the existence of a bilateral defense agreement. Neither proved to be seriously threatened after 1980, despite initial U.S. criticism of the PRC takeover, as the Doe government adopted an essentially pro-Western posture. However, in May 1987 the Soviet embassy, ordered closed by Liberia in 1985, was permitted to reopen in the context of a Liberian overture to the Eastern bloc, while in mid-1989 Doe renewed ties with former close confidant Muammar Qadhafi of Libya.

The core group of rebels led by Charles Taylor in early 1990 was reported to have been given commando training in Burkina Faso and Libya, while the initial point of entry into Nimba appeared to have been from neighboring Côte d'Ivoire. Although the United States maintained formal neutrality in the conflict, it appeared somewhat embarrassed by its support of the Doe regime and suspended trade concessions to Liberia in early May. Concurrently, the United States dispatched a naval flotilla to the region to evacuate American citizens wishing to leave. In March 1991, despite a continued display of reluctance to become involved in Liberian internal affairs, the United States was reported to have worked behind the scenes to persuade the NPFL's Taylor to participate in the roundtable discussions that yielded the abortive cease-fire of May 1991 and the equally ineffective peace agreement of the following October.

In mid-1998 Liberia accused Guinea of attempting to destabilize Liberia through its role in Ecomog. Monrovia's diplomatic offensive against Guinean officials (who denied the charges) coincided with a heightening of tension between the Taylor administration and the Ghanaian and Nigerian governments over Monrovia's alleged support of rebels who were fighting the ECOWAS-backed government of Sierra Leone. In early 1999 the United States declared that it had uncovered evidence of Liberia's support for those rebels, and shortly thereafter Nigeria withdrew its remaining troops from Liberia, asserting that it could no longer maintain a mission there while Monrovia supported attacks against Nigerian troops in Sierra Leone.

An armed incursion from Guinea into northwestern Liberia was reported in April 1999, prompting a state of emergency in Lofa County. Under ECOWAS mediation, a tripartite commission was subsequently formed to attempt to reduce friction in the diamond-rich areas at the conjunction of the borders of Liberia, Guinea, and Sierra Leone. Consequently, a degree of stability ensued, permitting the final Ecomog contingents to leave Liberia in October and the borders to be reopened with Sierra Leone (in October) and Guinea (in February 2000). However, major fighting erupted again in mid-2000 along the border with Guinea, the Liberian government accusing the Guinean government of supporting anti-Taylor elements that had loosely coalesced as the LURD. Skirmishes continued into 2001, exacerbating already extensive refugee problems. Among other things, Liberian refugees in Guinea claimed they were being mistreated by the Guinean military, which in turn argued that the refugees were helping Guinean rebels (see entry on Guinea for additional information). Meanwhile, President Taylor faced growing international pressure for his apparent continued support of the rebel Revolutionary United Front (RUF) in Sierra Leone. The complicated subregional conflict pitted the militaries of Guinea and Sierra Leone, Liberian rebels, and certain tribal groups (notably the Kamajors) from Sierra Leone on one side against the Liberian army and rebel groups from Guinea and Sierra Leone on the other. Much of the fighting involved control of rich mining areas, diamond production permitting various factions to buy armaments for their military campaigns.

In May 2001 the United Nations imposed an embargo on Liberian trade in diamonds and arms and barred senior Liberian officials from international travel as a means of encouraging Taylor's disengagement from the civil war in Sierra Leone. Combined with other pressure (including the suspension of development aid from the European Union [EU]), the UN initiative appeared to have the desired effect in contributing to a tentative resolution of the situation in Sierra Leone (see entry on Sierra Leone for details). However, fighting between the LURD and the Liberian government continued into 2002, relations between Guinea and Liberia remaining tense until a somewhat surprising meeting in late February of the presidents of Liberia, Guinea, and Sierra Leone at which agreement was reached on enhanced border security, repatriation of refugees, and reactivation of the Mano River Union.

The intensification of the civil war in Liberia in late 2002 and early 2003 exacerbated tensions with regional powers as well as with the broader international community. Ghana, Nigeria, and Sierra Leone attempted to mediate a cease-fire as rebel forces moved on Monrovia, while many Western capitals urged President Taylor to resign. (Relations with the United States had deteriorated in late 2002 when evidence emerged that al-Qaida financiers may have been profiting from the Liberian diamond-smuggling trade.)

The UN endorsed the ECOWAS peacekeeping force in early August 2003, but by September ECOMIL had been superseded by UNMIL, which had a force strength of 11,500. In November 2005 the UN expanded the mandate of UNMIL to include the capture of Charles Taylor (then residing in Nigeria) and his transfer to the UN Special Court for Sierra Leone. In December the UN renewed sanctions that prohibited travel for some 60 Liberians who were suspected of involvement in the conflict in Sierra Leone. Meanwhile, the United States supported the continuing efforts to demobilize the militia groups in Liberia in 2005–2006, pledging some $200 million for the effort and providing American military advisors to help train a new security force.

After a lengthy campaign by a range of international bodies, on March 25, 2006, the Nigerian government announced that it would honor a request to extradite Taylor to stand trial before the UN Special Court for Sierra Leone. Taylor escaped on March 28, but he was recaptured the following day. He was subsequently transferred to Monrovia, and then to the Special Court in Freetown, Sierra Leone. Upon Liberian president Johnson-Sirleaf's request, Taylor was later transferred to The Hague to stand trial so that his presence in Sierra Leone did not destabilize the region. (The Special Court was also moved to The Hague for the trial.) Taylor's trial opened in early 2008, and, following several delays, Taylor's lawyers started their defense in mid-2009. Meanwhile, Taylor's son, Charles TAYLOR Jr., was sentenced to 97 years in prison following his conviction in a U.S. court on torture charges similar to those lodged against his father. The younger Taylor, who was born in the United States, was the first person to be tried under a 14-year-old law permitting prosecution of U.S. citizens for torture committed abroad.

Liberia's primary regional concern in 2009 was the situation in Guinea, where unrest emanating from the recent military coup threatened, in the opinion of some analysts, stability throughout the region. Liberian president Johnson-Sirleaf played a prominent leadership role in efforts to implement an agreement in Guinea that would lead to a return to civilian government. Liberia also became intertwined with the conflict in neighboring Côte d'Ivoire in early 2011 as some 100,000 refugees poured over the border into Liberia.

Charles Taylor was convicted by the Special Court in April 2012 of ten counts of aiding and abetting crimes against humanity and other war crimes during the civil war in Sierra Leone, which involved what the court described as "some of the most heinous and brutal crimes ever recorded." Taylor, who said his involvement in Sierra Leone had been solely intended to promote stability in Liberia, was sentenced to 50 years in prison, with his term scheduled to be served in the United Kingdom following the conclusion of the appeals process.

Liberia deployed troops to its border with Côte d'Ivoire in the second half of 2012 to, among other things, combat cross-border banditry and suppress Ivorian rebel activity. As of mid-2013 it was estimated that approximately 60,000 refugees, including supporters of former Ivorian president Gbagbo, remained in Liberia.

Current issues. The opposition strongly criticized President Johnson-Sirleaf in the first half of 2011 for her inattention to the report from the Truth and Reconciliation Commission (TRC, see Political background, above). The perceived ongoing corruption in political and business circles continued as an issue in the campaign for the October elections, and Johnson-Sirleaf's opponents also attacked her for seeking another term despite her earlier pledge to limit herself to one term. However, the president's international reputation remained strong, in part due to recent economic advances. Johnson-Sirleaf also took advantage of the power of incumbency and the inability of the opposition to coalesce behind a single candidate.

On October 7, 2011, it was announced that Johnson-Sirleaf had been awarded the Nobel Peace Prize, her opponents strongly criticizing the timing (four days before national elections) of the announcement as proof of the international community's support for her reelection. Despite heavy pressure from regional leaders to let the electoral process unfold, Winston Tubman of the CDC called for a boycott of the second round, with turnout thereby plummeting to 39 percent. Following her reelection, Johnson-Sirleaf pledged to combat unemployment, particularly for those under 35 (60 percent of the population), to continue the pursuit of national reconciliation, and to promote growth through, among other things, a major road reconstruction project.

In September 2012 the UN Security Council extended the mandate of UNMIL but called for gradual force reduction over the next three years in view of recent progress in Liberia. The Security Council called on UNMIL to focus on combating cross-border drug- and arms-trafficking and to improve the Liberian police force. For her part, President Johnson-Sirleaf described government changes in the first half of 2013 as designed to improve the nation's woeful educational system.

POLITICAL PARTIES AND GROUPS

For more than a century prior to the 1980 coup, an Americo-Liberian elite had dominated Liberia's politics through the True Whig Party (TWP), most of whose leaders were subsequently assassinated or executed.

Upon the PRC's assumption of power in 1980, political party activity was suspended, a ban that was extended in December 1982 to any individual or group "caught making unfavorable speeches and pronouncements against the government." The ban was repealed in July 1984, although only the NDPL, LAP, LUP, and Liberia Liberal Party (LLP) were permitted to contest the election of October 15, 1985.

In anticipation of presidential and legislative elections, the Alliance of Seven Parties was formed in February 1997 by the LAP, LUP, NDPL, TWP, LPP, UP, and UPP. On March 24 the alliance held intraparty primary elections to choose a presidential candidate for the upcoming elections; however, the victory of the LAP's Cletus Wotorson was immediately challenged, and both the UPP and LPP withdrew from the coalition, claiming that the LAP had engaged in fraud and vote buying. With the alliance in disarray, the LPP, LUP, and TWP announced in June that they had switched their allegiance to UP presidential candidate Ellen Johnson-Sirleaf (although the LPP ultimately fielded its own candidate). Likewise, a coalition of the three most prominent Krahn parties—the LPC, NDPL, and the Krahn faction of Ulimo (Ulimo-K)—proved unable to reach agreement on campaign tactics and splintered. Later, one manifestation of efforts to forge an anti-Taylor alliance was the Collaborating Political Parties (CPP), whose members included the ALCOP, LAP, LINU, LPP, NDPL, PDPL, PPP, TWP, UP, UPP, and others.

Government Party:

Unity Party (UP). The UP was formed by Dr. Edward B. KESSELLY, who had served as local government minister in the Tolbert administration and subsequently chaired the PRC's Constituent Advisory Assembly. The party elected one senator and two representatives in the 1985 balloting. In November 1988 Kesselly claimed that the government was attempting to frame him in an effort to squelch his anticorruption protests. (Kesselly died in 1993.)

In April 1997 former finance minister and UN official Ellen Johnson-Sirleaf defected from the LAP and joined the UP to campaign for the presidency. The addition of Johnson-Sirleaf gave the UP newfound prominence and, subsequently, the backing of the TWP, LUP, and a number of LPP members. Despite early polling showing her with a higher popularity rating than Charles Taylor, Johnson-Sirleaf and the UP's poorly financed efforts were ultimately no match for the NPP.

In August 2000 the government issued an arrest warrant for Johnson-Sirleaf for her alleged role in dissident activities in Lofa County. However, she was granted amnesty in July 2001, and she returned to Monrovia in September.

Johnson-Sirleaf was one of the candidates to lead the transitional legislature in 2003, but she failed to gain sufficient support. After she was chosen as the UP's 2005 presidential candidate, a number of prominent members of other parties reportedly defected to the UP in solidarity with her ultimately successful campaign.

In late 2009 "a merger" of the UP with the LAP and LUP was reported, with the LAP's Varney Sherman being named chair of the grouping (sometimes referred to as the New Unity Party), which by that time controlled a plurality of legislative seats

The UP, which had won 8 House seats in 2005, improved to 24 seats in the 2011 balloting and was subsequently viewed as having sufficient allies among other parties and independents to control a legislative majority in support of the new Johnson-Sirleaf administration.

Leaders: Varney SHERMAN (Chair), Ellen JOHNSON-SIRLEAF (President of the Republic), Joseph BOAKAI (Vice President of the Republic), Wilmot PAYE (Secretary General).

Other Legislative Parties:

Congress for Democratic Change (CDC). Formed in 2005 under the leadership of former soccer star George Weah, the CDC is a populist party with broad appeal among Liberia's poor. In the 2005 legislative balloting, it became the largest party in the House with 15 seats.

The CDC splintered in March 2006 when Samuel TWEAH Jr., the chair of the American branch of the party, resigned, along with other leading CDC figures, citing financial irregularities and a dispute over whom the party should have supported for speaker of the House. Further tensions within the party were reported in 2007 when party leaders decided to endorse several LAP candidates in legislative by-elections as part of a collaborative initiative between the parties.

The CDC in mid-2010 presented itself as the driving force behind the formation of an electoral alliance called the Coalition for Democratic Change to contest the 2011 presidential and legislative elections. Other members of the proposed coalition reportedly included Prodem, the LP, NPP, TWP, and, perhaps, a faction of LINU. Although discussions were subsequently reported with other small parties, the coalition failed to solidify completely.

For its 2011 presidential candidate, the CDC chose Winston A. Tubman, a nephew of former Liberian president Tubman. (Winston Tubman had finished fourth in the 2005 race as the candidate of the NDPL before throwing his support behind Weah in the second round. Tubman had also recently been associated with LINU [below].) However, by all accounts the star of the CDC ticket remained Weah, the vice-presidential candidate. Several other parties, most notably the NPP, also backed Tubman, a Harvard-educated lawyer and former diplomat who campaigned on a platform focusing on anticorruption measures and national reconciliation.

The CDC boycotted the second round of the presidential election in November 2011, and several CDC supporters were killed when police opened fire on a protest demonstration shortly before the balloting. Tension subsequently remained high between the CDC and the government, and, in an apparent effort to promote better relations, the administration announced in late 2012 that Weah had been appointed to head a proposed national peace and reconciliation committee.

Leaders: George WEAH (Party President and 2005 presidential candidate), Winston B. TUBMAN (2011 presidential candidate), Geraldine DOE-SHERIFF (Chair), Nathaniel McGILL (Secretary General).

Liberty Party (LP). Formed in 2005, the LP is led by Charles Brumskine, who placed third in the 2005 presidential polling with 13.9 percent of the vote. The LP secured nine seats in the 2005 House elections, making it the second largest party in the chamber.

At a party congress in February 2006, Brumskine announced that he would not stand as the party's presidential candidate in the 2011 elections. Concurrently, a new slate of party leaders was elected, including a new national chair, Israel Akinsanya. However, after the LP failed to negotiate electoral agreements with several other proposed opposition coalitions, Brumskine reversed his earlier position and took another run at the presidency as the LP candidate in 2011. He finished fourth with 5.5 percent of the vote in the first round of balloting and threw his support behind President Johnson-Sirleaf in the second round, despite having previously criticized the administration for a lack of progress in combating poverty.

Leaders: Charles BRUMSKINE (Party President and 2005 and 2011 presidential candidate), Israel AKINSANYA (Chair), Mariah FANIYAH (Secretary General).

National Union for Democratic Progress (NUDP). The NUDP was registered in September 2010 as a vehicle for the presidential candidacy of former warlord Prince Yormic Johnson, who had been elected as a senator in 2005. (Johnson, whose supporters had killed President Doe in 1989, was recommended for prosecution by Liberia's TRC for crimes against humanity. The TRC also included Johnson on the list of those who should be barred from holding public office.) Reportedly attracting the support of "Taylor loyalists" and campaigning on a populist platform, Johnson finished a surprisingly strong third with 11.6 percent of the vote in the first round of the 2011 poll. He subsequently backed President Johnson-Sirleaf in the second round, a decision that apparently rankled several prominent NUDP members.

Leaders: Prince Yormic JOHNSON (2011 presidential candidate), James Laveli SUPUWOOD (2011 vice-presidential candidate), Emmanuel LOMAX (Chair).

National Democratic Coalition (NDC). Upon its formation as an opposition grouping prior to the 2011 election, the NDC included the following parties plus the NP, NDPL, and the small **Labor Party of Liberia** (LPL), led by Joseph WOAH-TEE (2005 presidential candidate). However, the NPP and NDPL subsequently withdrew from the coalition, apparently as the result of a dispute over the selection of a presidential candidate. The NDM's Dew Tuan-Wleh Mayson, who had reportedly helped finance Ellen Johnson-Sirleaf's successful 2005 presidential campaign, secured only 0.5 percent of the vote as the NDC's standard-bearer in the first round of the presidential poll. Meanwhile, it appeared that joint NDC candidates were presented in some legislative seats, while others were contested under the banners of individual NDC components.

Leaders: Dew Tuan-Wleh MAYSON (2011 presidential candidate), Dusty WOLOKOLLIE (2011 vice presidential candidate), Abraham MITCHELL (Secretary General).

New Deal Movement (NDM). The NDM, also referenced as the New Democratic Alternative for Liberia Movement, was launched in 1999 by a number of former LPP members, including George Klay Kieh Jr., a professor who had found his goal of running for president of the republic blocked by senior LPP leaders. The NDM achieved formal party status in mid-2002, and Kieh received 0.5 percent of the vote in the first round of presidential balloting in 2005. The NDM secured three seats in the 2005 legislative poll.

Leaders: George Klay KIEH Jr. (2005 presidential candidate), Dew Tuan-Wleh MAYSON, Henry W. YALLAH (Chair), Moses KWEHAI (Secretary).

Alliance for Peace and Democracy (APD). Formed as a coalition in advance of the October 2005 elections by the two parties below, the APD chose the LPP's Togba-Nah TIPOTEH as its presidential candidate. He placed ninth in the first round of balloting with 2.3 percent of the vote, while the APD secured five seats in the House and three in the Senate in the concurrent legislative balloting.

Leaders: Marcus DAHN (Chair), Jefferson KARMOH (Secretary).

Liberian People's Party (LPP). The LPP was organized by former members of the Movement for Justice in Africa (Moja), whose leader, Togba-Nah Tipoteh, had been dismissed from the cabinet for alleged complicity in a countercoup attempt in August 1981. Moja was a left-nationalist, Pan-Africanist formation organized in 1973 and banned in 1981, at which time Tipoteh went into exile. LPP leader Amos Sawyer, former chair of the PRC's national constitutional commission, was also charged with plotting against the regime in August 1984, although the allegation was widely interpreted as an attempt by General Doe to discredit a leading rival for the presidency in 1985. Reportedly in retaliation for Sawyer's subsequent unwillingness to accept an offer to campaign as General Doe's running mate, an audit was initiated in early 1985 of his financial dealings as constitutional commission chair, thus permitting the electoral commission to deny registration to the LPP. In November 1990 Sawyer was named to head the ECOWAS-supported caretaker government, thereby reportedly earning the disapproval of some LPP stalwarts. Meanwhile, Tipoteh, an avowed supporter of Prince Johnson, returned to Monrovia in mid-1991 to preside over Moja's relaunching as a paramilitary formation styled the Black Berets/Moja, which was later disbanded.

The LPP was significantly fractionalized in regard to the 1997 presidential elections, partly due to the competing presidential ambitions of Sawyer, Tipoteh, and George Klay KIEH Jr., another LPP founder. The party initially intended to back a joint opposition candidate forwarded by the Alliance of Seven Parties. However, following the alliance's nomination of Cletus Wotorson, Tipoteh declared that the alliance's primary had been fraudulent and announced the withdrawal of the LPP from the grouping. Tipoteh then served as the LPP standard-bearer in the presidential balloting, although Sawyer, former LPP chair Dusty WOLOKOLIE, and other prominent LPP members supported various other candidates. Sawyer, Wolokolie, and others were subsequently expelled from the LPP. Meanwhile, Edwin DENNIS-WEAH, a prominent attorney, was selected by the LPP's national committee to succeed James LOGAN as secretary general, Logan reportedly having become disillusioned with the political infighting. For his part, Kieh resigned from the LPP and subsequently helped to form the NDM with a number of other disgruntled former LPP members. Tipoteh later served as the primary spokesperson within Liberia for the LPP (which also has an active branch in the United States), earning a reputation as one of the nation's leading anti-Taylor voices.

While the LPP served as a founding component of the NDC for the 2011 elections, Tipoteh ran for president as the candidate of the FAPL (below).

United People's Party (UPP). A centrist outgrowth of the precoup People's Progressive Party (PPP) and viewed as the most serious threat to the NDPL, the UPP was organized by former PPP leader Gabriel Baccus Matthews, who had been dismissed as foreign minister in November 1981 because of opposition to a pro-U.S. posture by the Doe regime and had left the government again in April 1983 after serving for a year as secretary general of the cabinet. A number of leading officials subsequently quit the party because of the exiled Matthews's unwillingness to join an opposition coalition in March 1986, which induced the government to permit his return from the United States and rescind its proscription of the LAP in late September.

The UPP's Wesley Johnson was chosen as vice chair of the transitional government in 2003.

Leaders: Marcus DAHN (Chair), Wesley JOHNSON.

Liberia Equal Rights Party (LERP). At a party convention in August 2005, delegates elected Joseph Korto as the LERP candidate for the 2005 presidential election. He won 3.3 percent of the vote (seventh place) in the first round of balloting. The LERP supported Ellen Johnson-Sirleaf in the November runoff.

Leader: Joseph KORTO (2005 presidential candidate).

National Patriotic Party (NPP). The NPP is an outgrowth of the rebel group launched by Charles Taylor in Liberia's northeastern region in 1989 that was called the National Patriotic Front of Liberia (NPFL). The NPFL reportedly included a number of former Liberian soldiers who had fled abroad after the 1985 coup attempt. The front succeeded in gaining control of most of Liberia, except for the capital, by mid-1992, although it experienced reverses thereafter (see Political background, above). Charles Taylor received an enthusiastic reception upon his arrival in Monrovia to take a seat on the Council of State in September 1995.

In accordance with the 1996 peace pact, on January 31, 1997, the NPFL's military wing was officially dissolved. On February 1 the interim National Patriotic Association of Liberia (NAPAL) was formed and charged with overseeing the transformation of the NPFL's political wing into a legal political party, and in April the NPP was officially registered. Charles Taylor and the NPP scored easy electoral victories in July 1997, and following his inauguration in August, the new president named a government dominated by NPP stalwarts.

The NPP provided the main base of support for Taylor in the subsequent civil war, although Taylor's actions appeared to undercut popular enthusiasm for the NPP. Following Taylor's departure from Liberia in August 2003, many NPP members reportedly continued to support him, and he reportedly remained in contact with them. However, other NPP stalwarts disassociated themselves from Taylor and joined other parties.

In the first round of the 2005 presidential balloting, the NPP's Roland Massaquoi placed sixth with 4.1 percent of the vote. Meanwhile, Taylor's wife, Jewel HOWARD-TAYLOR, was elected to the Senate.

Charles Taylor was extradited from Nigeria in March 2006 and placed in the custody of the UN's Special Court for Sierra Leone (see Foreign relations, above, for further details).

The NPP was initially reported to have joined the CDC-led Coalition for Democratic Change in 2010 to contest the 2011 elections, although some NPP members had reportedly joined the UP-led administration earlier. In addition, some NPP leaders, including Lewis BROWNE, opted for participation in a newly formed opposition grouping called the Democratic Alliance (DA), which became a core component of the NDC (above) for the 2011 elections. However, Browne (initially referenced as the chair of the NDC) defected to the UP prior to the balloting. Meanwhile, the NPP dropped out of the NDC and threw its support to the CDC's Winston Tubman in the presidential poll. The NPP, which won three seats in both the Senate and the House in 2005, reportedly still enjoyed the loyalty of thousands of supporters (some very wealthy) of Charles Taylor for the 2011 elections. Taylor was convicted of war crimes in 2012 and sentenced to 50 years imprisonment.

Leaders: Charles Chankay (Ghankay/Gankay) TAYLOR (Former President of the Republic, under UN imprisonment), Theophilus C. GOULD (Chair), Cyril ALLEN (Former Chair), Roland MASSAQUOI (2005 presidential candidate), Jewell TAYLOR (Senator), John WHITFIELD (Secretary General).

National Democratic Party of Liberia (NDPL). Essentially a Krahn-based party, the NDPL was formed in August 1984 to support the policies and projected presidential candidacy of General Doe. Amid widespread opposition charges of fraud in the 1985 election, the NDPL, in addition to electing Doe, was awarded an overwhelming majority of seats in both houses of the National Assembly.

NDPL candidate Winston B. Tubman came in fourth in the first round of the 2005 presidential balloting with 9.2 percent of the vote. Two posts in the subsequent Johnson-Sirleaf administration were given to members of the NDPL, and several senior NDPL members reportedly later defected to the UP.

Tubman subsequently left the NDPL in the midst of reported "bickering" and after a period of relative political inactivity, joined the LINU (below) in 2009. After dropping out of the recently formed NDC (above), the NDPL, which had won two Senate seats and one House seat in 2005, ultimately supported President Johnson-Sirleaf in her 2011 reelection effort.

Leaders: Nyandeh SIEH Sr. (Chair), Jackson DOE.

Movement for Progressive Change (MPC). Recently launched by wealthy businessman Simeon Freeman, the MPC campaigned on an anticorruption platform in the 2011 elections. Freeman received 0.5 percent of the vote in the first round of the presidential poll.

Leaders: Simeon FREEMAN (2011 presidential candidate), Saywala KENNEDY (Chair), O'Neil PASSAWE (Secretary).

National Reformation Party (NRP). The NRP was formed by Martin Sheriff in 1996. However, in 2005 Bishop Alfred REEVES was the party's presidential candidate with Sheriff serving as the vice presidential candidate. Reeves, a Christian prelate, and Sheriff, a leading Muslim, campaigned on a platform of religious harmony and a return to morality. Reeves received 0.3 percent of the vote in the first round of balloting, last among the 22 candidates, while the NRP gained one seat in both the House and the Senate in the legislative poll. The NRP supported George Weah in the presidential runoff. Reeves died in 2009.

Leaders: Martin SHERIFF (2005 vice presidential candidate and 1997 presidential candidate), Maximillian T. W. DIABE (Chair), Borbor KROMAH (Secretary).

Liberia Destiny Party (LDP). The LDP, whose 2005 presidential candidate was Nathaniel BARNES, secured one seat in both the Senate and the House in the 2011 legislative balloting.

Leaders: Boimah TAYLOR (Chair), Charles DAVIES (Secretary), Dallas Advertus V. GUEH (Senator).

Liberia Transformation Party (LTP). The LTP was formed prior to the 2011 elections under the leadership of Rev. Kennedy Gbleyah Sandy, who, campaigning on a platform pledging to improve social conditions, finished fifth in the first round of the presidential poll with 1.1 percent of the vote.

Leaders: Rev. Kennedy Gbleyah SANDY (2011 presidential candidate), Alloycious Dennis WOLLOH (2011 vice presidential candidate), A. Marshall DENNIS.

Other Parties That Contested the 2011 Elections:

Freedom Alliance Party of Liberia (FAPL). The FAPL, whose 2005 presidential candidate was Margaret THOMPSON, reportedly nominated T. Q. HARRIS as its initial candidate for the 2011 poll. However, Harris subsequently exited the race (apparently due to fiscal constraints), and the FAPL ultimately nominated former LPP and APD standard-bearer Togba-Nah Tipoteh, who secured 0.6 percent of the vote in the first round of balloting.

All-Liberia Coalition Party (ALCOP). The ALCOP was formed in November 1996 by Ulimo-M leader Lt. Gen. Alhaji Abraham G. V. Kromah, who said that the new party would serve as a vehicle for ethnic Krahns and Mandingos. Although Kromah claimed to have completely disarmed his militants by the end of January 1997, a raid on his headquarters in February unearthed an arms cache, and he was briefly detained.

In September 1998 Kromah was indicted for allegedly plotting a coup against Charles Taylor. Subsequently, Kromah fled the country, and he ignored a summons to appear in court in November. In April 1999 former Ulimo-M members clashed with government forces in northern Liberia; however, the government's allegations that Kromah was behind the incursion from Guinea remained unconfirmed. In August members of the hitherto unknown Joint Forces for the Liberation of Liberia (JFLL), a group reportedly formed by former Ulimo-M members, clashed with security forces and briefly kidnapped foreign aid workers.

Kromah received 7.8 percent of the vote in the first round of the 2005 presidential polling. Although it had secured two House seats and one Senate seat in 2005, the ALCOP was unsuccessful in the 2011 legislative balloting.

Leaders: Ansu DOLLEY (Chair), Lt. Gen. Alhaji Abraham G. V. KROMAH (1997 and 2005 presidential candidate), D. Palmas SAYDEE (Secretary).

Liberia National Union (LINU). The LINU was formed by former vice president of the republic and NDPL executive Harry MONIBA in 1996 as a party for the Lofan and Gbandi peoples. Moniba unsuccessfully contested the 1997 presidential elections as the LINU candidate. Moniba died in 2004, and John Morlu was elected as the party's new leader at a congress in May 2005.

Prior to the 2005 elections the LINU formed a coalition called the United Democratic Alliance (UDA) with the LEDP and RAP (below). Pledging to end corruption and improve social services, Morlu received 1.2 percent of the vote in the first round of the presidential poll, while the UDA secured one House seat in the legislative balloting.

Former presidential candidate Winston B. Tubman, a lawyer and former ambassador, joined the LINU in 2009 and subsequently appeared to attempt to guide the party into the new CDC-led Coalition for Democratic Change. However, factionalization was reported within the LINU over the issue.

Leaders: John MORLU (2005 presidential candidate), Aaron WESSEH (Chair), Billy JOSS (Secretary General).

Grassroots Democratic Party of Liberia (GDPL). Stressing social needs, Gladys G. Y. Beyan of the recently launched GDPL secured 1.1 percent of the vote in first round of the 2011 presidential poll.

Leaders: Gladys G. Y. BEYAN (2011 presidential candidate), Edward G. DESHIELD (2011 vice presidential candidate).

Liberia Reconstruction Party (LRP). Manjerngie Cecilia Ndebe won 0.5 percent of the vote as the LRP's candidate in the first round of the 2011 presidential balloting.

Leaders: Manjerngie Cecilia NDEBE (2011 presidential candidate), Zizi Kolubah ZUBAH (2011 vice presidential candidate).

Victory for Change Party (VCP). Marcus Roland Jones secured 0.4 percent of the vote as the VCP candidate in the first round of the 2011 presidential poll.

Leaders: Marcus Roland JONES (2011 presidential candidate), Emmanuel TULAY (Chair), J. Quiwoe DENNIS (Secretary).

Citizens Unification Party (CUP). Calling for a "new generation of leadership," James Swallah Guseh of the recently formed CUP won 0.4 percent of the vote in the first round of the 2011 presidential poll.

Leaders: James Swallah GUSEN (2011 presidential candidate), Lawrence A. GEORGE (Chair).

Liberian Empowerment Party (LEP). The recently formed LEP presented Rev. Hanniah Zoe as its 2011 presidential candidate. Rev. Zoe, who had run for the presidency in 2005 under the banner of the LEDP (below), campaigned on a platform emphasizing the importance of microlending, securing 0.4 percent of the first-round vote.

Leaders: Rev. Hananiah ZOE (2011 presidential candidate), Richard K. FLOMO (2011 vice presidential candidate).

Progressive People's Party (PPP). Chea Job Cheapoo of the PPP secured 0.3 percent of the vote as the PPP candidate in the first round of the 2011 presidental balloting. Cheapoo, a former minister in the Doe regime, had campaigned for the presidency in 2005 as the candidate of the Liberia National Alliance (LNA), which had included the PPP and the Independent Democratic Party (IDA).

Leaders: Chea Job CHEAPOO (2011 presidential candidate), Jeremiah TARWAY (2011 vice presidential candidate).

Original Congress Party of Liberia (OCPOL). Campaigning on a platform promising economic relief, James Kpa Chelley won 0.3 percent of the vote as the OCPOL candidate in the first round of the 2011 presidential poll.

Leaders: James Kpa CHELLEY (2011 presidential candidate), Evelyn Kou LAH (Chair), Rev. Victor SAYLEE (Secretary).

Union of Liberian Democrats (ULD). Formed in 2005 by Dr. Robert Kpoto, the ULD is a mainly Lofan grouping. In September 2005 senior members of the ULD reportedly broke away to form a new party—the Progressive Independent Movement of the ULD (PIMULD). The PIMULD supported the COTOL and Varney Sherman in the October 2005 elections, and both the ULD and the PIMULD endorsed George Weah in the November runoff. (Kpoto had received just 0.4 percent of the vote in the first round of the presidential poll.) ULD candidate Jonathan A. Mason won 0.2 percent of the vote in the first round of the 2011 presidential poll.

Leaders: Dr. Robert KPOTO (Party Founder and 2005 presidential candidate), Jonathan A. MASON (2011 presidential candidate), George J. TARN (Chair).

Progressive Democratic Party (Prodem). Formed in 2004, Prodem was initially composed mainly of former LURD members, including former LURD leader Sekou Conneh, who was chosen as the party's 2005 presidential candidate. Conneh received only 0.6 percent of the vote in the first round of the presidential election, and the party did not gain any seats in the legislative elections. Following the November presidential runoff, Conneh was prominent in successful efforts to convince George Weah's supporters to accept the decision of the election commission to declare Ellen Johnson-Sirleaf as the victor.

Testifying before the TRC in mid-2008, Conneh denied any wrongdoing during the civil war, despite allegations of atrocities on the part of LURD fighters. Conneh argued he should be considered a hero for having helped to initiate the downfall of Charles Taylor.

Initial reports indicated that Prodem planned to participate in the NDC for the 2011 elections, but the party ultimately presented its own legislative candidates.

Leaders: Sekou CONNEH (2005 presidential candidate), Augustine COLE (Chair), Solomon CHEAPO (Secretary General).

Other small parties that presented legislative candidates in 2011 included the National Social Democratic Party of Liberia (NSDPL) and the Republican Party of Liberia (RPL).

Other Parties That Won Legislative Seats in 2005:

Coalition for the Transformation of Liberia (COTOL). Formed in July 2005 as an electoral coalition by the three parties below and the LAP in preparation for the October presidential and legislative balloting, the COTOL chose the LAP's Varney G. Sherman as its presidential candidate. Sherman placed fifth in the first round of balloting with 7.8 percent of the vote. Most of the COTOL components supported George Weah in the presidential runoff. Meanwhile, the COTOL became the largest Senate grouping with seven seats; it also won eight seats in the House.

Tensions were reported within the COTOL in 2006 as the LAP sought electoral alliances outside of the coalition for upcoming legislative by-elections. The LAP finally withdrew from the COTOL in December, and COTOL appeared moribund when the LUP subsequently joined the LAP in alignment with the UP (see below).

Liberia Unification Party (LUP). Organized in 1984 by Gabriel KPOLLEH, former president of the Monrovia Public School Teachers' Association, the LUP was initially viewed as a potential "Trojan horse" by the NDPL. Kpolleh surprised many observers by backing the LAP-led legislative boycott in 1985, with all four of the party's assembly members refusing to take their seats. In March 1988 the party's leader and deputy leader were arrested on charges of plotting to overthrow the government and were given ten-year prison sentences the following October. Kpolleh was released in 1991 and was later assassinated, although the LUP remained active.

The LUP reportedly merged with the UP in 2009 (see UP, below).

True Whig Party (TWP). Founded in 1868 and Liberia's ruling party until banned in the wake of the 1980 coup, the TWP was revived in 1991. Many members of the TWP defected to either the CDC or the UP prior to the 2005 elections.

Leaders: Peter VUKU (Chair), Othello R. MASON (Secretary General).

People's Democratic Party of Liberia (PDPL). The PDPL was represented by George Toe WASHINGTON in the 1997 presidential balloting. The PDPL broke with the other parties in COTOL and supported Ellen Johnson-Sirleaf in the 2005 presidential runoff.

Liberia Action Party (LAP). The LAP was organized by Tuan WREH, a former supporter and political confidant of General Doe, who was subsequently joined by a number of Tolbert-era officials, including ex–finance minister Ellen Johnson-Sirleaf. In 1985 the LAP emerged as the NDPL's primary challenger following disqualification of the UPP, winning two Senate and eight House seats. However, it decided to boycott legislative proceedings because of the detention of Johnson-Sirleaf and other party leaders for their alleged role in the 1985 coup attempt. In early 1986 Wreh and another LAP member were expelled from the party for agreeing to take their seats in defiance of the boycott. Johnson-Sirleaf, though pardoned in May 1986, fled to the United States claiming her life was in danger after her rearrest in July.

The subsequent naming of an LAP member, David FARHAT, to Doe's cabinet failed to abate the party's antigovernment criticism. The group derided the arrival of U.S. financial experts in early 1988 as a "disgrace to Africa, and Liberia in particular" and in September joined with the UP in condemning the government's banning of student politics. In mid-1989 the leaders of the LAP, UP, and UPP issued a joint communiqué calling on Doe to enact economic and political reforms and return to the tenets of the 1984 constitution. The government responded by dismissing Farhat from his position as finance minister, despite his being credited with increasing budgetary restraint and the repayment of U.S. loans. The LAP's Jackson F. DOE (no relation to the former chief executive) was widely believed to have been the actual winner of the 1985 presidential contest; he was reported in 1990 to have been executed by order of rebel leader Charles Taylor.

At a meeting of the Alliance of Seven Parties in March 1997, the LAP's presidential candidate, Cletus Wotorson, was chosen as the coalition's standard-bearer. However, charges that the primary had been rigged in his favor led to the splintering of the Alliance and prompted the LAP's most prominent member, Ellen Johnson-Sirleaf, to defect to the UP.

In 2003 LAP Chair Charles Gyude BRYANT was chosen as chair of the new transitional government, although he subsequently suspended his party activity to avoid the appearance of favoritism. In December 2006 the LAP announced its departure from the COTOL, but in 2009 the party announced its alignment with the UP and LUP for the 2011 elections (see UP, above).

Other Parties and Groups:

Liberians United for Reconciliation and Democracy (LURD). The LURD claimed responsibility for antigovernment guerrilla activity launched in northwestern Liberia in mid-1999. A number of former Ulimo fighters reportedly participated in the organization of the LURD, and, as had been the case with Ulimo, Krahn-Mandingo infighting was subsequently reported within the new grouping. The Liberian government accused the Guinean government of supplying arms to the LURD, which appeared to include several anti-Taylor factions left over from the Liberian civil war as well as anti-Taylor elements from the complicated conflict in Sierra Leone. The LURD subsequently became the largest anti-Taylor group in Liberia, its fighters ultimately pressuring Taylor to leave the country in August 2003 (see Political background, above, for details).

In January 2004, Aisha CONNEH (the daughter of the president of Guinea and the wife of Sekou Damate Conneh, who had been named chair of the LURD in 1999) reportedly attempted unsuccessfully to gain control of the LURD in cooperation with Chayee DOE (the younger brother of former Liberian president Samuel Doe). Chayee Doe was subsequently killed, while Sekou Conneh was reportedly suspended from the party. The LURD disbanded in late 2004, and many of its members reportedly joined Prodem (above), which chose Sekou Conneh as its 2005 presidential candidate.

Liberia Peace Council (LPC). Organized in 1993, the LPC was a largely Krahn group that engaged in numerous clashes with the NPFL in southeastern Liberia. In January 1996 the LPC was cited by observers as the only faction to have complied with the disarmament provisions of the August 1995 peace accord. However, such claims were subsequently undermined by reports of LPC-NPFL clashes, and in October LPC militants were accused of attempting to assassinate Charles Taylor.

In early 1997 the LPC participated in the Alliance of Seven Parties. However, following the factionalization of the Alliance and breakup of the informal Krahn coalition, the LPC forwarded its chair, Dr. George BOLEY, as its presidential candidate. In early 1999 it was reported that Boley had fled the country in fear of attack by Taylor's security forces. The LPC subsequently disbanded, and many of its members, including Boley, reportedly joined the NDPL.

Movement for Democracy in Liberia (MODEL). Supported primarily by members of the Krahn ethnic group who had previously been core constituents of former president Samuel Doe, MODEL was launched in 2001 and quickly emerged as a major anti-Taylor rebel force during the 2002–2003 civil war. MODEL leader Thomas Yaya NIMELY was named foreign minister under the peace agreement of August 2003. MODEL disbanded in late 2004 under an agreement that also involved the LURD and pro-Taylor groups. Nimely chose not to form a political party, urging his supporters to join existing parties. However, Nimely reportedly continued to employ ex-MODEL fighters at his large ranch near the border with Côte d'Ivoire, and some of them were reportedly implicated in an alleged coup plot by supporters of former president Gbagbo in Côte d'Ivoire in mid-2012. The Liberian government subsequently announced it had issued arrest warrants for a number of ex-MODEL leaders.

United Liberation Movement of Liberia for Democracy (Ulimo). Ulimo was initially a formation drawn primarily from the Krahn tribe of former president Doe. As such, it opposed the granting of concessions to the rebels by ECOWAS and Amos Sawyer's interim government. By 1994 Ulimo had split into two factions: a Krahn-based Christian group (Ulimo-K), led by Gen. Roosevelt Johnson; and a Mandingo-based Muslim group (Ulimo-M), led by Lt. Gen. Alhaji G. V. Kromah. (The former was sometimes referenced as Ulimo-J and the latter confusingly [and incorrectly] as Ulimo-K.)

In early 1996 forces aligned with Johnson fought with Ecomog troops in Tubmanburg after the former refused to comply with the disarmament provisions of the 1995 peace accord. Subsequently, on March 11, 1996, Ulimo-K's Executive Council and military commanders issued a joint statement announcing the dismissal of Johnson as party chair in favor of Brigadier Gen. William KARYEE, citing Johnson's inability to forward the peace process as the reason for his ouster.

Krahn fighters from the AFL and LPC reportedly defected to Ulimo-K during the fighting that ensued after militiamen loyal to the NPFL and Ulimo-M attempted to arrest Johnson on April 6, 1996. Thereafter, amid intense fighting in the capital, Johnson, who continued to be recognized as the faction's de facto leader, was flown to Ghana on May 3 by U.S. helicopters to attend an ECOWAS peace summit then scheduled for May 8.

Under pressure from international observers, on June 11, 1996, Ulimo-K agreed to disarm, and in August a faction spokesperson claimed that the group's militiamen had turned over their weapons to Ecomog troops. Moreover, in late September the two Ulimo factions reportedly agreed to a cessation of their mutual hostilities. However, in early October Ulimo-K fighters agreed to end their armed blockade of the highways leading to Tubmanburg and Cape Mount (where thousands of starving citizens were subsequently discovered) only under pressure from the Council of State and ECOWAS. Meanwhile, Ulimo-M leader Kromah announced his intention to compete in the May 1997 presidential elections as the candidate of the new ALCOP.

Johnson's efforts to form an electoral coalition with the LPC and NDPL failed in early 1997; subsequently, Ulimo-K candidates performed poorly in balloting in July. In August, Johnson was appointed minister of rural development; however, Johnson continued to criticize the Taylor administration, accusing the president in early 1998 of filling the military with former NPFL militiamen. In March, Johnson was the target of what he described as the third recent attempt on his life; concurrently, it was reported that Taylor had removed Johnson from the cabinet with the goal of naming him to an overseas post (ambassador to India). Thereafter, clashes between Ulimo-K militants and presidential forces were reported in neighborhoods controlled by Johnson, and in September an all-out attack by Taylor's troops forced Johnson and his family and close associates to seek refuge in the U.S. embassy, from where they were subsequently airlifted out of the country.

Many members of Ulimo were reportedly involved in the formation of the LURD in 1999. Subsequently, in 2004, Johnson died in exile in Nigeria. Most reports suggested that both Ulimo factions were defunct as of 2005.

LEGISLATURE

The **National Assembly** established by the 1984 constitution was a bicameral body consisting of a Senate and a House of Representatives, both elected by universal adult suffrage. Following the collapse of the Doe administration, the assembly was nominally superseded by interim bodies established by the Sawyer and Taylor regimes. Subsequently, in accordance with the 1993 Cotonou agreement, a 35-member Transitional Legislative Assembly (TLA) composed of representatives of the principal warring factions was inaugurated on March 7, 1994. On July 17, 1997, the TLA approved legislation that limited legislative terms to four years.

Balloting for the Senate and the House of Representatives was held on July 19, 1997, although those bodies ceased to function as a result of the civil war in the early 2000s. Under the terms of a recently completed peace agreement, an appointed 76-member National Transitional Legislative Assembly was established on October 14, 2003. Twelve seats were accorded to the pro-Taylor Government of Liberia, 12 to the Liberians United for Reconciliation and Democracy, 12 to the Movement for Democracy in Liberia, 18 to established political parties, 7 to representatives of civic organizations, and 15 to the nation's counties (1 for each of the 15 counties).

Under the terms of the 2003 peace agreement and the Electoral Reform Law of 2004, new elections were held for both houses of the assembly on October 11, 2005.

Senate. The Senate comprises 30 members (2 from each of the 15 counties) directly elected in a single round of voting. (The top two vote-getters in each county are declared the victors.) According to the guidelines adopted for the 2005 balloting, the first-place finishers in each county were elected for nine-year terms, the second-place finishers for six-year terms. All subsequent elections will be for nine-year terms.

Elections (for nine-year terms) were held for 15 seats on October 11, 2011, with the Unity Party winning 4 seats (for a total of 10); the National Patriotic Party, 4 (6); the Congress for Democratic Change, 2 (3); the Nation for Democratic Progress, 1 (2); the Alliance for Peace and Democracy, 1 (2); the National Democratic Coalition, 1 (1); the Liberia Destiny Party, 1 (1); independents, 1 (3); the National Democratic Party of Liberia, 0 (1); and the Liberty Party, 0 (1).

President: Joseph N. BOAKI (Vice President of Liberia).

President (Pro Tempore): Gbezhongar FINDLEY.

House of Representatives. The lower house comprises 73 directly elected from single-member constituencies in single-round plurality voting for six-year terms. In the balloting on October 11, 2011, the Unity Party won 24 seats; the Congress for Democratic Change, 11; the Liberty Party, 7; the National Union for Democratic Progress, 6; the National Democratic Coalition, 5; the National Patriotic Party, 3; the Alliance for Peace and Democracy, 3; the Movement for Progressive Change, 2; the National Reformation Party, 1; the Liberia Destiny Party, 1; the Liberia Transformation Party, 1; and independents, 9.

Speaker: Jenakai Alex TYLER.

CABINET

[as of August 1, 2013]

President	Ellen Johnson-Sirleaf [f]
Vice President	Joseph N. Boakai
Ministers	
Agriculture	Florence A. Chenoweth [f]
Commerce and Industry	Axel Addy
Defense	Brownie Samukai
Education	Etmonia Tarpeh [f]
Finance	Amara Mohamed Konneh
Foreign Affairs	Augustine Kpehe Ngafuan
Gender and Development	Julia Duncan Cassell [f]
Health and Social Welfare	Dr. Walter Gwenigale
Information, Culture, and Tourism	Lewis G. Browne II
Internal Affairs	Blamoh Nelson
Justice and Attorney General	Christiana Tarr [f]
Labor	Juah Lawson [f]
Lands, Mines, and Energy	Patrick Sendolo
Posts and Telecommunications	Frederick B. Norkeh
Public Works	(Vacant)
Transportation	Tornorlah Varpilah
Youth and Sports	Eugene Lenn Wagbe
Ministers of State	
Presidential Affairs	Vabah Gayflor [f]
Without Portfolio	Conmany B. Wesseh

[f] = female

INTERGOVERNMENTAL REPRESENTATION

Ambassador to the U.S.: Jeremiah Congbeh SULUNTEH.

U.S. Ambassador to Liberia: Deborah Ruth MALAC.

Permanent Representative to the UN: Marjon V. KAMARA.

IGO Memberships (Non-UN): AfDB, AU, ECOWAS, ICC, IOM, NAM.

LIBYA

Republic of Libya
al-Jumhuriyyah al-Libiyah

Political Status: Independent state since December 24, 1951; revolutionary republic declared September 1, 1969; name changed from Libyan Arab Republic to Libyan Arab People's Republic in 1976; present name adopted March 2, 1977; interim draft constitution promulgated on August 3, 2011.

Area: 679,358 sq. mi. (1,759,540 sq. km).

Population: 6,512,765 (2012E—UN); 6,002,347 (2013E—U.S. Census).

Major Urban Centers (2003C): Tripoli (Tarabulus, 1,197,000), Benghazi (Banghazi, 680,000), Misurata (Misratah, 351,000), Sirte (Surt, 162,000). (Many secretariats have reportedly been relocated recently to Sirte—about 400 miles east of Tripoli—and other cities.)

Official Language: Arabic.

Monetary Unit: Dinar (official rate November 1, 2013: 1.23 dinar = $1US).

Prime Minister: Ali ZIDAN (independent), elected on October 14, 2012, to succeed Mustafa Abu SHAGUR (National Front), who had been elected by the General National Congress on September 12, 2012, but failed to win parliamentary approval of his government and lost a vote of no confidence on October 7.

THE COUNTRY

Extending for 910 miles along Africa's northern coast, Libya embraces the former Turkish and Italian provinces of Tripolitania, Cyrenaica, and Fezzan. Some 95 percent of its territory is desert and barren rockland, and cultivation and settlement are largely confined to a narrow coastal strip. Tribal influences remain strong within a population that is predominantly Arab (with a Berber minority) and almost wholly Sunni Muslim. Arabic is the official language, but Italian, English, and French are also spoken. In part due to government efforts to increase the education of females (about 28 percent of whom were reportedly illiterate), women constituted 30 percent of the official labor force in 2011, up from less than 9 percent in the 1980s. Female representation in government continues to be minimal.

Early in the 2000s, leader Muammar al-Qadhafi's perceived resistance to even modest free market reforms constrained foreign investment (for information on Libya's economy prior to 2000, see the 2011 *Handbook*). Economic affairs, particularly in regard to the West, changed dramatically in September 2004 when the United States lifted most of its long-standing unilateral sanctions against Libya. Western companies immediately began to negotiate substantial oil contracts with Tripoli in conjunction with pledges from the Qadhafi regime to enact broad economic policy changes (see Foreign relations and Current issues, below). In 2006 the International Monetary Fund (IMF) praised the government's efforts to ease trade restrictions and to move toward a market economy. The IMF also encouraged Libya to better manage its oil revenue, restructure its public banks, and move forward with structural reforms.

GDP growth has slowed somewhat in recent years, under the influence of lower oil prices and the international economic slowdown, although the non-oil sectors have advanced by 8 percent annually. GDP grew by 4.2 percent in 2010, while inflation was 2.5 percent, and GDP per capita was $9,957. The onset of civil war in 2011 disrupted the country's economy and energy production and led to a significant erosion of GDP. The IMF recognized the National Transitional Council (NTC) as the legitimate government of Libya in September 2011. The IMF and various other international donors pledged $1.1 billion in aid for reconstruction and infrastructure rehabilitation.

With oil production cut to virtually zero, Libya's GDP was estimated to have contracted by 60 percent in 2011. But crude oil output reached 90 percent of preconflict levels by April 2012, boosting economic activity. In order to contend with a legacy of high social inequality, high rates of youth unemployment, and a long record of poor governance and corruption, said the IMF, the government would need to improve the quality of education, rebuild infrastructure, reduce oil dependence, develop an efficient social safety net, and set up a governance framework to promote private sector-led development, job creation, and inclusive growth. With continuing political stabilization in 2012, GDP rose by 104 percent according to the IMF, as the country reversed the losses of 2010–2011. Inflation that year was 6 percent, while GDP per capita was $12,777.

GOVERNMENT AND POLITICS

Political background. Successively ruled by the Phoenicians, Greeks, Romans, Arabs, Spaniards, and others, Libya was under Ottoman Turkish control from the middle of the 16th century to the beginning of the 20th century. It was conquered by Italy in 1911 and 1912 and was ruled as an Italian colony until its occupation by British and French military forces during World War II. In conformity with British wartime pledges and a 1949 decision of the UN General Assembly, Libya became an independent monarchy under Emir Muhammad IDRIS al-Sanussi (King IDRIS I) on December 24, 1951. A constitution promulgated two months earlier prescribed a federal form of government with autonomous rule in the three historic provinces, but provincial autonomy was eliminated and a centralized regime instituted under a constitutional amendment adopted in 1963.

The 1960s witnessed a growing independence in foreign affairs resulting from the financial autonomy generated by rapidly increasing petroleum revenues. This period marked the beginnings of Libyan radicalism in Third World politics and in its posture regarding Arab–Israeli relations. Increasingly, anti-Western sentiments were voiced, especially in regard to externally controlled petroleum companies and the presence of foreign military bases on Libyan soil. The period following the June 1967 Arab–Israeli conflict saw a succession of prime ministers, including the progressive Abd al-Hamid al-BAKKUSH, who took office in October 1967. His reforms alienated conservative leaders, however, and he was replaced in September 1968 by Wanis al-QADHAFI. The following September, while the king was in Turkey for medical treatment, a group of military officers led by Col. Muammar al-QADHAFI seized control of the government and established a revolutionary regime under a military-controlled Revolutionary Command Council (RCC).

After consolidating his control of the RCC, Colonel Qadhafi moved to implement the goals of his regime, which reflected a blend of Islamic behavioral codes, socialism, and radical Arab nationalism. By June

1970 both the British and U.S. military installations had been evacuated, and in July the Italian and Jewish communities were dispossessed and their members forced from the country. In June 1971 an official party, the Arab Socialist Union (ASU), was organized, and in September the Federation of Arab Republics (a union of Egypt, Libya, and Syria) was approved by separate referenda in each country. The federation, while formally constituted at the legislative level in March 1972, became moribund shortly thereafter. Meanwhile, the regime had begun acquiring shares in the country's petroleum industry, resorting to outright nationalization of foreign interests in numerous cases; by March 1976 the government controlled about two-thirds of oil production.

Periodically threatening to resign because of conflicts within the RCC, Colonel Qadhafi turned over his prime-ministerial duties to Maj. Abd al-Salam JALLUD in July 1972 and was in seclusion during the greater part of 1974. In August 1975 Qadhafi's rule was seriously threatened by a coup attempt involving army officers, some two dozen of whom were ultimately executed; a number of drastic antisubversion laws were promptly enacted. In November a quasi-legislative General National Congress (renamed the General People's Congress a year later) was created, while in March 1977 the RCC and the cabinet were abolished in accordance with "the installation of the people's power" under a new structure of government headed by Colonel Qadhafi and the four remaining members of the RCC. The political changes were accompanied by a series of sweeping economic measures, including limitations on savings and consolidation of private shops ("nests of exploitation") into large state supermarkets, which generated middle-class discontent and fueled exile-based opposition activity. The government was further reorganized at a meeting of the General People's Congress in March 1979, Colonel Qadhafi resigning as secretary general (but retaining his designation as revolutionary leader and supreme commander of the armed forces) in favor of Abd al-Ati UBAYDI, who was in turn replaced as secretary general of the General People's Committee (prime minister) by Jadallah Azzuz al-TALHI.

At a congress session in January 1981, Secretary General Ubaydi was succeeded by Muhammad al-Zarruq RAJAB, who, in February 1984, was replaced by Miftah al-Usta UMAR and named to succeed Talhi as secretary general of the General People's Committee. Talhi was returned to the position of nominal head of government in a major ministerial reshuffle announced on March 3, 1986; in a further reshuffle on March 1, 1987, Talhi was replaced by Umar Mustafa al-MUNTASIR.

In October 1990 a government shakeup was undertaken that included the appointment of Abd al-Raziq al-SAWSA to succeed Umar as secretary general of the General People's Congress and Abu Zaid Umar DURDA to succeed Muntasir as head of the General People's Committee. Durda was reappointed in November 1992, while Sawsa was replaced by Zanati Muhammad al-ZANATI. The 1992 reorganization was otherwise most noteworthy for the designation of Muntasir, a moderate who had earlier cultivated a good working relationship with the West, as the equivalent of foreign secretary.

The sanctions imposed by the United Nations in 1992 (see Foreign relations, below) subsequently contributed to what was widely believed to be growing domestic discontent with the regime. Internal difficulties were most sharply illustrated by an apparent coup attempt in early October 1993, reportedly involving thousands of troops at several military locations. Although loyalist forces quashed the revolt in about three days, the government was described as "severely shaken" by the events.

In a cabinet reshuffle on January 29, 1994, Abd al-Majid al-QAUD was named to succeed Durda as secretary general of the General People's Committee. Qaud was succeeded on December 29, 1997, by Muhammad Ahmad al-MANQUSH, who was reappointed along with most other senior ministers in a cabinet reshuffle on December 15, 1998. On March 1, 2000, Manqush was succeeded by Mubarak Abdullah al-SHAMIKH, Colonel Qadhafi concurrently ordering a sharp reduction in the number of ministries in the name of further devolution of power to local "people's" bodies. Shamikh remained in his post during a reshuffle on October 1, 2000, but was replaced in a subsequent reorganization on June 13, 2003, by Shukri Muhammad GHANIM, theretofore the secretary for economy and trade. Ghanim was dismissed in a reorganization on March 5, 2006; he was succeeded by Al-Baghdadi Ali al-MAHMUDI, the former assistant secretary general of the General People's Committee.

Following the renewal of the General People's Congress March 1–4, 2009, an extensive reshuffle of the General People's Committee took place on March 4, 2009, with al-Mahmudi being retained as secretary general and former intelligence chief Mussa KUSSA being named to the foreign liaison post.

In March 2009 the government released two political prisoners who had been sentenced to 12 and 15 years, respectively, in 2007 after they tried to organize a commemorative gathering for protesters who had been killed in clashes with police. Libya also released dozens of other political prisoners (see Libyan Islamic Fighting Group [LIFG] under Political Parties, below). In April, at the urging of the EU, Libya further addressed a major issue of concern dating to 2007 when it ordered stricter supervision of its coastline to combat illegal migration to Europe, particularly Italy (in 2008 Qadhafi had negotiated a "friendship" agreement under which Italy pledged some $5 billion in reparations to Libya over the next 20 years in connection with Italy's colonial rule in the early 1900s).

Antigovernment protests, dubbed the "Arab Spring," which led to the overthrow of regimes in Tunisia and Egypt, spread to Libya in February 2011, when security forces suppressed demonstrators during a series of antiregime protests. Anti-Qadhafi elements united under a broad coalition, the NTC, established in Benghazi on February 27. On March 5 former justice minister Mustafa Abdel JALIL was appointed chair of the NTC. Meanwhile, fighting between the NTC and its allies and pro-Qadhafi forces spread throughout the country. The NTC was aided by the imposition of a UN no-fly zone on March 17 and aerial and missile strikes against the regime by an international coalition that included the United States and European powers (see Foreign relations, below). On March 23 Mahmoud JIBRIL was named chair (prime minister) of the NTC's executive committee. By August the NTC was in control of the majority of the country and had been recognized by most foreign powers as the legitimate government of Libya. However, on August 8 the executive committee was dismissed following the death of NTC military commander Abdul Fatah YOUNIS (see Current issues, below). On October 3 a reshuffled NTC executive committee was appointed. Qadhafi was killed by NTC forces on October 20 (see Current issues, below). On October 22 Jibril resigned as prime minister. Abdurrahim EL-KEIB was appointed to replace him. El-Keib subsequently named a new government on November 22, which was sworn in two days later.

Following balloting in July 2012 for the new General National Congress (GNC), Mustafa Abu SHAGUR was elected prime minister by the legislature. However, the GNC twice rejected Shagur's proposed cabinet and voted him out of office on October 7. The GNC elected Ali ZIDAN prime minister on October 14 and approved his broad-based cabinet on October 30.

Constitution and government. Guided by the ideology of Colonel Qadhafi's *Green Book,* which combines elements of nationalism, Islamic theology, socialism, and populism, Libya was restyled the Great Socialist People's Libyan Arab Jamahiriya in March 1977. The *Jamahiriya* was conceived as a system of direct government through popular organs interspersed throughout Libyan society. A General People's Congress was assisted by a General Secretariat, whose secretary general served as titular head of state, although effective power remained in Colonel Qadhafi's hands since the 1969 coup (for more information on the constitution and government of Libya prior to 2011, see the 2011 *Handbook*). Following the overthrow of the Qadhafi regime, the NTC developed a draft constitution that increased civil liberties and provided for a multiparty presidential democracy. The NTC announced its intention to finalize a permanent constitution and conduct national elections by 2013.

Libya's three provinces are subdivided into ten governorates, with administration based on "Direct People's Authority" as represented in local People's Congresses, People's Committees, Trade Unions, and Vocational Syndicates.

A national electoral law that reserved 136 seats for party lists and 64 constituency seats for independent candidates, with a required alternation between male and female candidates on the party lists, was adopted on January 28, 2012. The ratio was later changed to 120 constituency seats for independent candidates and 80 party list seats.

In 2013 Reporters Without Borders ranked Libya 131st out of 179 countries in its annual index of press freedom. The rating was a significant improvement from 154th the previous year.

Foreign relations. Under the monarchy, Libya tended to adhere to a generally pro-Western posture. Following the 1969 coup its foreign policy was characterized by the advocacy of total war against Israel, a willingness to use petroleum as a political weapon, and a strong commitment to Arab unity that gave rise to numerous failed merger attempts with sister states (Libya, Egypt, Sudan, and Syria in 1969; Libya,

Egypt, and Syria in 1971; Libya and Egypt in 1972; Libya and Tunisia in 1974; Libya and Syria in 1980; Libya and Chad in 1981; Libya and Morocco in 1984).

Libya's position within the Arab world has been marked by an improbable combination of ideological extremism and pragmatic compromise. Following the 1978 Camp David accords, relations were severed with Egypt, both sides fortifying their common border. Thereafter, Tripoli strove to block Cairo's reentry into the Arab fold (extending its condemnation to Jordan following the warming of ties between Jordan and Egypt) and provided support to Syrian-based elements of the Palestinian Liberation Organization (PLO) opposed to Yasir Arafat. Relations with the Mubarak government in Egypt began to warm, however, during a 1989 Arab League meeting and continued to improve with a series of cooperation agreements in 1990 and the opening of the border between the two countries in 1991. By mid-decade, Egypt had become what one correspondent described as Libya's most important potential "bridge to the West," Cairo's supportive stance reflecting the importance of Libya as a provider of jobs for Egyptian workers and the value attached by the Mubarak regime to Colonel Qadhafi's pronounced anti-fundamentalist posture.

Relations with conservative Morocco, broken following Tripoli's 1980 recognition of the Polisario-backed government-in-exile of the Western Sahara, resumed in 1981. Ties with neighboring Tunisia, severely strained during much of the 1980s, advanced dramatically in 1988, the opening of the border between the two countries precipitating a flood of option-starved Libyan consumers to Tunis. Regional relations stabilized even further with the February 1989 formation of the Arab Maghreb Union (AMU), although Colonel Qadhafi remained a source of controversy within the ineffective and largely inactive grouping.

A widespread expression of international concern in the 1980s and 1990s centered on Libyan involvement in Chad. Libya's annexation of the Aozou Strip in the mid-1970s was followed by active participation in the Chadian civil war, largely in opposition to the forces of Hissein Habré, who in 1982 emerged as president of the strife-torn country. By 1983 Libya's active support of the "National Peace Government" loyal to former Chadian president Goukhouni Oueddei (based in the northern Tibesti region) included the deployment of between 3,000 and 5,000 Libyan troops and the provision of air support for Oueddei's attacks on the northern capital of Faya-Largeau. Although consistently denying direct involvement and condemning the use of French troops in 1983 and 1984 as "unjustified intervention," Qadhafi agreed in September 1984 to recall "Libyan support elements" in exchange for a French troop withdrawal. The agreement was hailed as a diplomatic breakthrough for Paris but was greeted with dismay by Habré and ultimately proved to be an embarrassment to the Mitterrand government because of the limited number of Libyan troops actually withdrawn. Subsequently, in March 1987, the militarily superior Qadhafi regime suffered the unexpected humiliation of being decisively defeated by Chadian government forces, which captured the air facility at Quadi Doum, 100 miles northeast of Faya-Largeau, and forced the Libyans to withdraw from all but the Aozou Strip, leaving behind an estimated $1 billion worth of sophisticated weaponry.

In early August 1987, Chadian forces, in a surprise move, captured Aozou, administrative capital of the contested border area, although the town was subsequently retaken by Libya. Skirmishes continued as the Islamic Legion, comprised largely of Lebanese mercenaries, attacked Chadian posts from bases inside Sudan, with Libyan jets supporting counteroffensives in the Aozou Strip. A year later, Libya reportedly had lost 10 percent of its military capability, although it retained most of the disputed territory.

In July 1989 the Organization of African Unity (OAU, subsequently the African Union—AU) sponsored negotiations between President Habré and Colonel Qadhafi, which set the stage for the signing of a peace treaty by the countries' foreign ministers on August 31. The treaty called for immediate troop withdrawal from the disputed territory, exchange of prisoners of war, mutual "noninterference," and continued efforts to reach a permanent settlement. Relations subsequently deteriorated, however, with Habré accusing Libya of supporting Chadian rebels operating from Sudan.

Following the ouster of the Habré regime in December 1990, new Chadian president Idriss Déby announced in early 1991 that a "new era" had begun in relations between Chad and Libya, the belief being widespread that Libya had supplied arms and logistical support (but not personnel) to Déby's victorious rebels. However, Déby subsequently described the Aozou issue as still a "bone of contention" requiring resolution by the International Court of Justice (ICJ). Consequently, in February 1994 the ICJ ruled by a vote of 16–1 that Libya had no rightful claim to the Aozou Strip or any other territory beyond the boundary established in a 1955 treaty between Libya and France. On May 30 the lengthy dispute ended with Libya's withdrawal and a symbolic raising of the Chadian flag. Shortly thereafter, Colonel Qadhafi received President Déby in Tripoli for the signing of a friendship and cooperation treaty.

Relations with the West have been problematic since the 1969 coup and the expulsion, a year later, of British and U.S. military forces. Libya's subsequent involvement in negotiations between Malta and the United Kingdom over British naval facilities on Malta contributed to a further strain in relations with London. In December 1979 the United States closed its embassy in Tripoli after portions of the building were stormed and set afire by pro-Iranian demonstrators, while in May 1981 the Reagan administration ordered Tripoli to shut down its Washington "people's bureau" in response to what it considered escalating international terrorism sponsored by Colonel Qadhafi. Subsequent U.S.–Libyan relations were characterized as "mutual paranoia," with each side accusing the other of assassination plots amid hostility generated by U.S. naval maneuvers in the Gulf of Sirte, which Libya had claimed as an internal sea since 1973.

Simultaneous attacks by Palestinian gunmen on the Rome and Vienna airports on December 27, 1985, brought U.S. accusations of Libyan involvement, which Colonel Qadhafi vehemently denied. In January 1986 President Reagan announced the freezing of all Libyan government assets in U.S. banks, urged Americans working in Libya to depart, banned all U.S. trade with Libya, and ordered a new series of air and sea maneuvers in the Gulf of Sirte. (U.S. officials charged that Libya was harboring members of the Revolutionary Council of Fatah, the radical Palestinian grouping led by Abu Nidal and allegedly behind the 1985 attacks. See entry on the Palestinian Authority/PLO for further details.) Three months later, during the night of April 14, 18 F-111 bombers based in Britain, assisted by carrier-based attack fighters, struck Libyan military targets in Tripoli and Benghazi. The action was prompted by what Washington termed "conclusive evidence," in the form of intercepted cables, that Libya had ordered the bombing of a Berlin discotheque nine days before, in the course of which an off-duty U.S. soldier had been killed. The U.S. administration also claimed to have aborted a planned grenade and machine-gun attack on the American visa office in Paris, for which French authorities ordered the expulsion of two Libyan diplomats.

Tripoli's adoption of a more conciliatory posture during 1988 did not yield relaxation of tension with Washington, which mounted a diplomatic campaign against European chemical companies that were reported to be supplying materials for a chemical weapons plant in Libya. Despite Libyan denial of the charges, reports of U.S. readiness to attack the site were believed to be the catalyst for a military encounter between two U.S. F-14s and two Libyan MiG-23 jets over the Mediterranean Sea on January 4, 1989, which resulted in downing of the Libyan planes. Concern subsequently continued in some Western capitals over the alleged chemical plant (the site of a much-publicized fire in March 1990), as well as Libya's ongoing efforts to develop nuclear weapons. Suspicion also arose over possible Libyan involvement in the bombing of Pan Am Flight 103, which blew up over Lockerbie, Scotland, in December 1988, and the crash of a French DC-10 in Niger near the Chad border in September 1989.

Colonel Qadhafi was described as maintaining an "uncharacteristically low profile" following the August 1990 Iraqi invasion of Kuwait (which he publicly criticized) and the U.S.-led Desert Storm campaign against Iraqi forces in early 1991. However, the respite from the international spotlight proved short-lived as the investigations into the Lockerbie and Niger plane explosions once again focused Western condemnation on Libya.

In October 1991 the French government issued warrants for six Libyans (one of them a brother-in-law of Colonel Qadhafi) in connection with the Niger crash, while American and British authorities announced in mid-November that they had filed charges against two Libyan nationals in connection with the Pan Am bombing. In early December the Arab League Council expressed its "solidarity" with Libya in the Lockerbie matter and called for an inquiry by a joint Arab League–UN committee. Two days later a Libyan judge declared that the two suspects were under house arrest and that Tripoli would be willing to send judicial representatives to Washington, London, and Paris to discuss the alleged acts of terrorism.

On January 21, 1992, the UN Security Council unanimously demanded extradition of the Lockerbie detainees to either Britain or the United States and insisted that Libya aid the French investigation into the Niger crash. Although Libya announced its willingness to cooperate with the latter demand, which involved no extradition request, it refused to turn over the Lockerbie suspects, declaring it would try the men itself. Consequently, the Security Council ordered the imposition of selective sanctions, including restrictions on air traffic and an embargo of shipments of military equipment as of April 15.

On May 14, 1992, in partial compliance with the Security Council, Libya announced that it would sever all links with organizations involved in "international terrorism," admit UN representatives to verify that there were no terrorist training facilities on its soil, and take action to preclude the use of its territory or citizens for terrorist acts. In addition, a special session of the General People's Congress in June agreed that the Lockerbie suspects could be tried in a "fair and just" court in a neutral country as suggested by the Arab League. However, the Security Council reiterated its demand for extradition to the United States or United Kingdom, ordered that the sanctions be continued, and warned that stiffer measures were being considered. After mediation efforts by UN Secretary General Boutros Boutros-Ghali failed to resolve the impasse, the Security Council voted on November 11, 1993, to expand the sanctions by freezing Libya's overseas assets and banning the sales to Libya of certain oil-refining and pipeline equipment. The sanctions were subsequently regularly extended, although the Security Council rejected a U.S. proposal for a total oil embargo.

After more than a year of failed efforts to negotiate a resolution of the Lockerbie impasse, Libya finally agreed in March 1999 to send the two suspects (Abd al-Basset al-MEGRAHI and Lamin Khalifah FHIMAH) to the Netherlands to face a trial under Scottish law before three Scottish judges, though Qadhafi had argued that they be tried in a neutral country. Colonel Qadhafi's acceptance of the plan apparently was predicated on assurances that the trial would not be used to attempt to "undermine" his regime. For their part, Washington and London appeared to compromise on the issue of the trial's location, in part at least, out of recognition that international support for continued sanctions was diminishing. The Security Council announced that the UN sanctions had been suspended as soon as the suspects arrived in the Netherlands on April 5. However, unilateral U.S. sanctions remained in place as long as Libya stayed on Washington's official list of countries perceived to be "state sponsors of terrorism."

An antiterrorism court in Paris convicted in absentia six suspects in the Niger plane crash case, including Abdallah SENOUSSI, Qadhafi's brother-in-law, in March 1999 and issued warrants for their arrest, which could be enforced only if they left Libya. Meanwhile, Colonel Qadhafi had also permitted German investigators to question Libyan intelligence officers concerning the 1986 Berlin disco bombing, although prosecution of the case had been thrown into disarray in 1997 when the main witness apparently recanted his previously incriminating testimony against alleged Libyan operatives. (Four defendants were convicted of the Berlin bombing in October 2001, the court also accepting the prosecution's argument that the Libyan secret service had been involved in planning the attack.)

In July 1999 full diplomatic relations were reestablished with the United Kingdom, which had severed ties after a British policewoman was killed during an anti-Qadhafi demonstration outside the Libyan mission in London. (It had been argued that the policewoman was killed by gunfire directed from the mission at the demonstrators.) Resolution of the dispute included Libya's agreement to cooperate in the investigation and to pay compensation to the victim's family.

The Lockerbie trial opened in May 2000, and on January 31, 2001, Megrahi was convicted of murder in connection with the bombing, the judges having accepted the admittedly circumstantial evidence that he had been at the airport when the bomb was planted and that he was working for Libyan intelligence at the time. Megrahi was sentenced to life in prison, but Fhimah returned to Libya after being acquitted.

Colonel Qadhafi announced in the late 1990s that he was turning his focus away from pan-Arabism and toward pan-Africanism, having described most other Arab states as "defeatist" in dealing with the West and Israel. The quixotic Libyan leader attended his first OAU summit in 20 years in July 1999 to promote his new vision and hosted a special summit in September to address proposed changes in the charter that would permit creation of OAU peacekeeping forces. Subsequently, Qadhafi participated prominently in efforts to resolve the conflicts in Sudan and the Democratic Republic of the Congo and served as a mediator in the war between Eritrea and Ethiopia. However, Libya's image as a potential continental unifier suffered a severe blow in late September 2000 when scores of black African workers died in a series of attacks by Libyans on nonnational workers in a suburb of Tripoli. (Underscoring the continued deterioration of the African initiative, in 2003 Libya recalled its troops from the Central African Republic, a trade agreement with Zimbabwe collapsed, and Qadhafi abolished the ministry for African unity.)

In early 2001 Colonel Qadhafi criticized the conviction of one of the defendants in the Lockerbie trial as politically motivated. However, by that time it was widely accepted that the Libyan government had not supported any terrorist activities or groups in several years and was genuinely interested in reintegration into the global community. Qadhafi had also improved his international image by cooperating extensively with the U.S.-led "war on terrorism," by freeing a number of political prisoners and by indicating a willingness to discuss the proposed payment of compensation to the families of the victims of the Lockerbie bombing.

Qadhafi subsequently continued his drive to improve Libya's international standing, and the initiative appeared to reach critical mass with an August 2003 announcement of final resolution of the Lockerbie affair. Under the carefully crafted language of the settlement, Libya accepted "responsibility for the actions of its officials" and agreed to pay an estimated $10 million (in three installments) to each of the families of the 270 killed in the attack. The UN Security Council formally lifted UN sanctions against Libya in September, permitting payment of the Lockerbie settlements to begin. In January 2004 Libya also agreed to pay a total of $170 million to the families of those killed in the 1989 Niger plane crash. The final piece of the puzzle appeared to be put in place in September 2004 when Libya agreed to pay $35 million to the non-U.S. victims of the 1986 bombing in Berlin.

The Lockerbie bombing returned as a major focus of attention in August 2009 when Abd al-Basset al-Megrahi was released from prison by the Scottish government, ostensibly on compassionate grounds (Megrahi had been diagnosed with cancer and had been given only a few months to live). (See the 2013 *Handbook* for more information on Megrahi.) Megrahi was greeted by a cheering crowd upon his return to Libya, prompting international outrage and casting a shadow over the September celebration of the 40th anniversary of Qadhafi's assumption of power. Meanwhile, human rights organizations, noting that action on the proposed constitution had been shelved indefinitely, described recent improvements in Libya as "limited." Among other things, such issues appeared to contribute to Qadhafi's failure in February 2010 to secure another year at the helm of the AU.

Meanwhile, dramatic progress was also achieved regarding the other long-standing area of intense Western concern—Libya's perceived pursuit of weapons of mass destruction (WMD). In December 2003 the United States and UK announced that after nine months of secret negotiations Qadhafi had agreed to abandon all WMD programs and to permit international inspectors to verify compliance. (Some analysts suggested that the process had been accelerated by the aggressive stance taken by the U.S. Bush administration against Iraq.) Washington announced in February 2004 that it would permit flights to Libya and allow U.S. oil companies to launch talks with Tripoli aimed at further exploitation of oil fields. Many U.S. commercial sanctions were lifted the following April, and in October the European Union (EU) removed its embargo on arms sales to Libya and other economic sanctions. Underscoring the dramatic transformation of the West's perception of Qadhafi, he was visited in 2004 by the British, French, and German heads of state, and a number of U.S. companies were awarded permits in 2005 for oil exploration. However, Libya officially remained on the U.S. list of terrorist-sponsoring states, possibly in part to permit investigation of charges by Saudi Arabia that Crown Prince Abdallah (now king) had been the target of an assassination plot, but Libya and Saudi Arabia reestablished diplomatic relations in late 2005.

In a diplomatic move that observers said was also meant to send a message to Iran and North Korea (both developing nuclear capabilities), the United States restored full relations with Libya on May 15, 2006. The United States also removed Libya from its list of state sponsors of terrorism (the latter requiring congressional approval within 45 days). Some of the families of Lockerbie bombing victims were angered, however, that they had not been notified first and demanded that the U.S. Congress ensure Libya fulfilled its financial commitment to them. (Libya halted its final payment to the families until it was removed from the list of states sponsoring terrorism.) With diplomatic ties restored, further restrictions on American oil companies were lifted, allowing for increased exploration. For its part, Libya opened bidding on its oil reserves to international companies in an effort to boost production over the next ten years and bring in a projected $7 billion.

In July 2007 U.S. President George W. Bush, in a move marking further normalization of relations between the two countries, nominated the first U.S. ambassador to Libya in nearly 35 years. However, several Democrats in the U.S. Congress held up confirmation of the nominee for more than a year pending Libya's full reparations to families of Lockerbie victims.

Relations with France were normalized in July 2007 following Libya's release of five Europeans and one Palestinian, the medics having been imprisoned for eight years after they were found guilty of infecting children with the AIDS virus. The deal to release the medics had been brokered by French President Nicholas Sarkozy and his wife, though Sarkozy initially denied the promise of an arms deal was involved. (In December, however, Sarkozy welcomed Colonel Qadhafi in a full state visit and the two countries signed an arms deal worth nearly $10 billion.) Tripoli's role as a potential peacemaker was further enhanced in 2007 as a result of its having hosted two meetings with rebel groups from the Darfur region of Sudan and an AU-UN summit in September aimed at ending the Darfur conflict.

In January 2008 Libya became a nonpermanent member of the UN Security Council after the U.S. dropped its objections. Libya thus became the sole representative of the Middle East and Africa on the Security Council, a move not entirely welcomed by Saudi Arabia (where the king had alleged an assassination attempt by Qadhafi) and South Africa (whose leader and Qadhafi had a "personal confrontation" at the 2007 AU summit in Ghana). The EU in March made overtures to increase its relations with Tripoli, and later that month President Bush sought congressional approval to exempt Libya from a law that allowed victims of terrorism to seize the U.S. assets of state sponsors of the attacks. With increasing investment by U.S. oil companies in Libya, the Bush administration was concerned that without such a provision, Libya, among other states, would be discouraged from fighting terrorism.

Also in 2008, a federal judge in Washington ruled that the Libyan government and six officials must pay $6 billion in damages to the families of seven U.S. citizens killed in the 1989 Niger crash. (Though Libya had never claimed responsibility, in 2004 it agreed to make reparations of $170 million to the families of 170 victims.) In February 2009 Colonel Qadhafi was installed as chair of the AU, the appointment coinciding with his increasing role of peace broker in connection with conflicts in Sudan, Niger, and Mauritania.

Relations with Switzerland deteriorated in March 2009, when, in an odd diplomatic feud, Libya temporarily disrupted oil deliveries to Switzerland, withdrew $7 billion from Swiss banks, recalled some of its diplomats, and ultimately sued over Swiss allegations that one of Qadhafi's sons, Hannibal, and his wife beat two of their servants at a luxury hotel in Geneva. The younger Qadhafi was arrested and briefly detained before being allowed to return to Libya. Tripoli, however, charged that the action violated international rules of diplomatic relations. (Tensions subsequently escalated when Libya arrested two Swiss businessmen, and Libya's relations with the EU were also compromised before strain subsided in 2010 when Switzerland dropped the charges and the Swiss businessmen were released.)

Following the onset of civil war in February 2011, the UN General Assembly voted to remove Libya from the Human Rights Council, and the Security Council placed an arms embargo on the Qadhafi regime. France recognized the rebel NTC as the legitimate government of Libya on March 10. Two days later the AU endorsed the creation of a no-fly zone over the country in response to reports of atrocities by pro-Qadhafi security forces. On March 17 the Security Council adopted Resolution 1973, which created a no-fly zone over Libya and froze regime assets. A military coalition, including the United States, France, Qatar, the UAE, the UK, and other European powers, launched aerial and missile strikes against regime targets on March 19. The aerial support proved to be decisive, and the allied forces continued to launch attacks against pro-Qadhafi targets into the fall of 2011. A group of 40 nations and international organizations established the Libya Contact Group (LCG) in March 2011 to provide economic, military, and diplomatic support for the TNC. On June 27 the International Criminal Court issued a series of arrest warrants for Qadhafi and members of his family and regime.

Meanwhile, the fighting prompted a wave of more than 100,000 refugees fleeing Libya, including sub-Saharan Africans who had migrated to the country seeking employment. South African president Jacob ZUMA led an unsuccessful AU mediation effort in May 2011. By the summer, most countries, including the United States on July 17, had recognized the TNC as the government of Libya. The UN recognized the TNC on September 21, a decision opposed by Cuba, Venezuela, Iran, and a number of African countries, including South Africa, Kenya and Zimbabwe.

On September 11, 2012, the U.S. embassy in Benghazi was attacked by militants, leading to the death of Ambassador J. Christopher Stevens and three other Americans (see Current issues, below). In October the government announced that Sayf al-Islam AL-QADHAFI, the second son of the former dictator, and Abdullah SENUSSI, the regime's last intelligence head, would be tried in Libya and not extradited for trial by the International Criminal Court at The Hague.

Italy closed its consulate in Benghazi and withdrew diplomatic personnel on January 15, 2013, following an attack on the Italian consul's car in the city. The UN voted in March to ease sanctions on some military equipment and unfreeze some financial assets. An explosion outside the French embassy in Tripoli on April 23 wounded two security guards. In June South Africa announced it would begin returning Libyan assets worth an estimated $1 billion that were invested in the country during the Qadhafi regime.

Current issues. After security forces brutally suppressed antiregime protests on February 15, 2011, fighting between Qadhafi loyalists and opposition forces spread quickly across Libya. A conference of antiregime groups in Benghazi in late February led to the creation of the NTC and the appointment of Jalil as chair of the opposition. Throughout the spring, the better-armed and -equipped Libyan military was able to defeat a series of rebel offensives. However, following the imposition of a UN no-fly zone, international air units, including helicopter gunships, provided vital support to the TNC forces and destroyed regime tanks and armored vehicles. By June rebel forces began to capture key cities. On July 29 the major general of the former regime and then military commander of the NTC, Abdul Fatah Younis, was killed under mysterious circumstances after being detained by rebels for questioning over continuing ties with the Qadhafi regime. The public uproar over responsibility for his death led to the dismissal of the NTC executive committee in August and the appointment of a new body in October.

As the fighting spread, a number of regime officials, including foreign minister Mussa Kussa, resigned, defected, or sought asylum in neighboring states. Most foreign states and organizations, including the UN, recognized the NTC as the legitimate government of Libya by the end of September 2011. By October the NTC had captured most of the country, and Sirte, the last major Qadhafi stronghold, fell on October 20. That day Qadhafi was killed by antiregime forces. Estimates were that roughly 30,000 people were killed in the civil war.

During the first half of 2012, the transition was marked by competing tensions between regional, ethnic, and religious groups. With few visible signs of a functioning government, nothing in the way of economic development, and tribal clashes and occasional gunfights breaking out between rival militias, the NTC's legitimacy was seen as increasingly at stake. In the months leading up to the June 19 elections, militias also threatened central authorities, briefly kidnapping two members of the NTC and attacking the Tripoli headquarters of the interim prime minister.

As disorganized preparations for elections were underway in June, the NTC provoked anger for delaying the vote until July 7. Officials had yet to complete the candidate lists, and voter registration was behind schedule. But observers also noted mounting suspicion that Abdel Jalil and others on the NTC were jockeying to maintain power. Meanwhile, the Supreme Court struck down an eleventh-hour law the NTC pushed through that would make glorifying the era of the former regime a crime. On July 5 the NTC published a decree that changed the role of the General National Congress set to be elected two days later: instead of the congress selecting the 60 members of the Constitutional Convention, these would be elected directly at a national poll to be held at an unspecified date, leaving unclear what the exact role of the congress would be.

The July 7 election went off better than expected, with turnout of about 62 percent and the participation of groups that had formerly threatened to boycott the vote. On August 8 the NTC was dissolved, making the General National Congress the sovereign power in Libya. The next day the National Front Party's Mohammed Yussef MAGARIAF was elected President of the GNC, effectively becoming the acting head of state.

On September 11, 2012, Islamist militants stormed the American Consulate in Benghazi, killing the U.S. ambassador, J. Christopher Stevens, along with three other Americans. Crowds subsequently drove Ansar al-Sharia, the group suspected of being behind the attack, and other militias out from Benghazi. The attack highlighted the need to disarm the country's rogue militias and raised questions abroad about radicalization in Libya. It also figured prominently in the U.S. presidential campaign (see entry on the United States). In October, progovernment militia forces captured the town of Bani Walid, one of the last remaining pro-Qadhafi areas in Libya.

In April 2013 the government approved a measure to bar military tribunals for civilians. The Zidan government negotiated a truce between rival militias in southern Libya. As part of the accord, the groups pledged to surrender their weapons and support the central government. Also in April, a group of women legislators formed the Rally of Women's Voices, an advocacy group that sought to promote gender equality.

On May 28, 2013, Magariaf stepped down as president of the GNC in order to comply with a controversial law that banned those who had served under Qadhafi. Magariaf was succeeded by Nouri ABUSAHMAIN (Independent), who was elected by the GNC on June 25, winning 96 votes to 80 for Al-Sharif AL-WAFI.

Workers went on strike at Libya's two main oil export terminals on July 25, reducing oil exports by 600,000 barrels per day and costing more than $1.6 billion through the end of August. Meanwhile, protestors stormed the al-Kweifiya prison after a Muslim Brotherhood activist was killed. More than 1,000 inmates escaped.

POLITICAL PARTIES

Under the monarchy, all political parties were banned. In 1971 an official government party, the Arab Socialist Union (ASU), was founded with the Egyptian ASU as its model. The formation was designed primarily to serve as a "transmission belt," helping implement government decisions at local levels and serving to channel local concerns upward to the central government; however, there was no public reference to it after 1975. Following the demise of the Qadhafi regime, new political parties emerged.

Political Parties:

National Forces Alliance—NFA (*Tahaalof al-Qiwaa al-Wataniyya*). A coalition of about 60 parties and more than 100 NGOs, the NFA was launched in February 2012 and led by former interim prime minister Mahmoud Jibril. The NFA was a liberal grouping that espoused moderate Islam. The NFA won 39 of the 80 seats chosen on a party list basis. In addition, it was estimated that 25 independents were affiliated with the NFA. Protestors ransacked the NFA headquarters in Tripoli in July 2013.

Leaders: Mahmoud JIBRIL (President), Salaheddin EL BISHARI (Secretary General).

Justice and Construction Party—JCP (*Hizb Al-Adala Wal-Bina*). Formed in March 2012 and backed by the Muslim brotherhood, the JCP won 17 seats, making it the second-largest party. The party was led by Mohamed SAWAN, who spent eight years in prison under the former regime for his ties to the Brotherhood. It endeavored to block the formation of an NFA-led government, following the 2012 balloting.

Leader: Mohamed SAWAN

National Front Party—NFP (*Hizb Al-Jabha Al-Wataniyya*). The party is an offshoot of the National Front for the Salvation of Libya (NFSL), which was formed in Khartoum, Sudan, in 1981, under the banner "Finding the democratic alternative." In September 1986 the Front published a list of 76 regime opponents that it claimed had been assassinated in exile, and in January 1987 it joined with a number of other exile formations in establishing a joint working group during a meeting in Cairo, Egypt. Operating out of Egypt and the United States, the NFSL was in the forefront of efforts to coordinate anti-Qadhafi activity in the first half of the 1990s, including a conference in Washington in late 1993 attended by most of the regime's leading opponents. However, a "statement of principles" of a proposed front was not negotiated.

In early 1994 it was reported that the NFSL had begun to transmit its antiregime radio program, the Voice of the Libyan People, via European Satellite. The program had previously been intermittently broadcast by shortwave radio from neighboring countries. In 1997 the NFSL issued a report alleging that more than 300 Qadhafi opponents had been killed by government operatives abroad or by domestic security forces between 1977 and 1994. In mid-2004 NFSL leaders warned Western leaders that the Qadhafi regime continued to hold political prisoners despite the country's improved international reputation. The NFSL supported the effort to overthrow Qadhafi and the subsequent NTC government. The group was rebranded as a centrist political party after the revolution, and its leader, Mohammed Yussef Magariaf, was elected president of the General National Congress on August 9, 2012. Magariaf resigned as party leader after his election and was succeeded by Mohammed Ali Abdallah.

Leader: Mohammed Ali ABDALLAH (President of the General National Congress).

Other minor parties (each won two seats in the 2012 balloting) include the Union for the Homeland Party, led by Abdurrahman SEWEHLI; the National Centrist Party, led by Ali TARHOUNI, who served as interim oil minister; and the Wadi al-Hayah Party. There were 15 other parties that won a single seat each, and 120 seats were reserved for independents.

LEGISLATURE

The 200-member General National Congress was elected in polling on July 7, 2012 (see Current issues, above).

CABINET

[as of September 15, 2013]

Prime Minister	Ali Zidad
First Deputy Prime Minister	Sadiq Abdulkarim Abdulrahman Karim
Second Deputy Prime Minister	(Vacant)
Third Deputy Prime Minister	Abdussalam al-Mehdi al-Qadi
Ministers	
Agriculture	Ahmed Ali al-Orfi
Communications	Osama Abdurauf Siala
Culture	Habib Mohammed al-Amin
Defense	Abdallah al-Thani
Economy	Mustafa Mohammed Abufunas
Education	Mohammed Hassan Abubaker
Electricity	Ali Mohammed Mihirig
Finance	Alkilani Abdul Kareem Kilani al-Jazi
Foreign Affairs and International Cooperation	Mohamed Imhamid Abdulaziz
Health	Nurideen Abdulhamid Dagman
Higher Education	Ali Muftah Obaid
Housing	Ali Hussein al-Sharif
Industry	Sulaiman Ali al-Lteef al-Fituri
Information	Yousef Mohamed Sherif
Internal Affairs (Acting)	Sadiq Abdulkarim Abdulrahman Karim
Justice	Salah Bashir Abaj Margani
Labor and Retraining	Mohamed Fitouri Ahmed Sualim
Local Government	(Vacant)
Martyrs and the Disappeared	Ali Gadour
Oil	Abdulbari Ali Al Hadi Al-Arusi
Planning	Mahdi Ataher Genia
Religious Affairs	Abdulsalam Mohammed Abusaad
Social Affairs	(Vacant)
Sport and Youth	Abdulsalam Abdullah Guaila
Tourism	Ikram Abdulsalam Bash Imam [f]
Transport	Abdul Qadir Mohamed Ahmed al-Ayib
Water Resources	Alhadi Suleiman Hinshir
Ministers of State	
GNC Affairs	(Vacant)
Wounded	Ramadan Ali Mansour Zarmuh

[f] = female

INTERGOVERNMENTAL REPRESENTATION

Ambassador to the U.S.: Ali Suleiman AUJALI.

U.S. Ambassador to Libya: Deborah K. JONES.

Permanent Representative to the UN: Ibrahim Omar DABBASHI.

IGO Memberships (Non-UN): AfDB, AU, Comesa, IOM, NAM, OIC, OPEC.

LIECHTENSTEIN

Principality of Liechtenstein
Fürstentum Liechtenstein

Political Status: Independent principality constituted in 1719; current constitution promulgated October 5, 1921; established diplomatic association with Switzerland in 1919 and customs and currency association in 1923.

Area: 61.8 sq. mi. (160.475 sq. km).

Population: 36,475 (2013E—Government); 37,009 (2013E—U.S. Census).

Major Urban Centers (2013E): VADUZ (5,236), Schaan (5,853).

Official Language: German (Alemannic).

Monetary Unit: Swiss Franc (market rate November 1, 2013: 0.91 franc = $1US).

Sovereign: Prince HANS-ADAM von und zu Liechtenstein II; assumed the executive authority of the sovereign on August 26, 1984; acceded to the throne at the death of his father, Prince FRANZ JOSEF II, on November 13, 1989. (On August 15, 2004, Prince Hans-Adam turned over most day-to-day governmental responsibility to Hereditary Prince Alois.)

Heir Apparent: Crown Prince ALOIS von und zu Liechtenstein.

Prime Minister (Chief of Government): Adrian HASLER (Progressive Citizens' Party); nominated by the *Langtag* and appointed by Prince Hans-Adam II on March 27, 2013, following the general election of February 3, succeeding Klaus TSCHÜTSCHER (Fatherland Union), who did not seek reelection.

THE COUNTRY

A miniature principality on the upper Rhine between Austria and Switzerland, Liechtenstein has a predominantly Roman Catholic population whose major language, Alemannic, is a German dialect. With a population of only 36,000, the country draws 52 percent of its workforce on cross-border commuters, most of whom work in the service sector.

Once dependent on agriculture, which currently employs less than 2 percent of the population despite the continuing importance of dairying and cattle breeding, Liechtenstein underwent considerable industrialization in the post–World War II era, with an emphasis on metallurgy and light industry. Industry, including dental appliances, electronic monitoring devices, and precision machinery, most of which are exported, principally to Switzerland and the member countries of the European Union (EU), provides 36 percent of GDP. The principality is chiefly known, however, as one of the world's leading "offshore" banking and finance centers; its history of both confidentiality and low tax rates has attracted some 80,000 trust and holding companies, virtually all of which maintain no physical presence in the country. Financial services provide 33 percent of GDP. In recent years external pressure has forced the government to support efforts to end money laundering and the abuse of banking secrecy. Collaterally, the government has attempted to boost tourism and foreign investment in order to improve Liechtenstein's status as a "business center," even offering corporations the chance to "rent" the country for large conferences. On July 1, 2012, voters overwhelmingly rejected a proposal to weaken the power of the reigning prince.

GOVERNMENT AND POLITICS

Political background. The Principality of Liechtenstein, whose origins date back to the 14th century, was established in its present form in 1719. Part of the Holy Roman Empire and after 1815 a member of the German Confederation, it entered into a customs union with Austria in 1852; following the collapse of the confederation in 1866, the principality in 1868 declared permanent neutrality. Formally terminating the association with Austria in 1919, Liechtenstein proceeded to adopt Swiss currency in 1921, and in 1923 entered into a customs union with Switzerland, which continues to administer the principality's customs and provides for its defense and diplomatic representation. Liechtenstein's neutrality was respected in both world wars of the 20th century.

Prior to 1938, the royal family of Liechtenstein lived on estates in Austria and the present-day Czech Republic. Following the Nazi annexation of Austria, the reigning prince took up residence in Vaduz. Unlike other royal houses in Europe, the Liechtenstein family is financially self-sufficient, drawing income from a series of businesses, including banks, wineries, forestry industries, and Texmati rice. Prince HANS-ADAM II has a net worth estimated at $5–7 billion. When faced with the possibility of limits being placed on the prince's personal power in 2003 and 2012, Prince Hans-Adam II threatened to move elsewhere and take his billions with him.

Starting in 1938, the government was a coalition of the Progressive Citizens' Party (*Fortschrittliche Bürgerpartei*—FBP) and the Fatherland Union (*Vaterländische Union*—VU). The environmentalist Free List (*Freie Liste*—FL) won 2 seats in the February 1993 election with 10.4 percent of the vote. However, Prince Hans-Adam II dissolved the *Landtag* in September after Prime Minister Markus BÜCHEL fell victim to a nonconfidence motion brought by his own FBP in protest against his leadership methods. In the ensuing October election the VU secured a majority of 13 seats (with a vote share of 50.1 percent), while the FBP fell back to 11 seats (44.2 percent) and the Free List slipped to 1 seat (8.5 percent). In December the VU's Mario FRICK formed a new coalition administration, with the FBP's Thomas BÜCHEL succeeding him as deputy chief of government. The VU also increased its vote in communal elections in January 1995, winning the mayoralty of Vaduz after nearly 70 years of FBP control.

Landtag elections, moved up nine months, were held in January–February 1997, with the only change in distribution being the loss of one FBP seat to the FL. Although negotiations were expected to produce another coalition cabinet, the FBP announced in March that it was leaving the government, ostensibly to create an "effective opposition." Consequently, Frick formed a new all-VU government.

In the February 2001 election, the opposition FBP won 49.9 percent of the vote and gained 3 additional *Landtag* seats, for a majority of 13. The VU took 41.1 percent, for 11 seats, and the Free List captured 8.8 percent and 1 seat. The new legislature confirmed an all-FBP cabinet and FBP party leader Otmar HASLER as prime minister on April 5.

Prince Hans-Adam II continued promoting a constitutional reform plan designed to strengthen the ruling prince's powers, including giving him the authority to appoint judges with legislative concurrence (rather than the other way around), to dismiss the government or dissolve the *Landtag* without explanation, and to impose emergency rule. Many legislators, in contrast, wanted to limit the monarchy's existing powers, and a minority favored creation of a republic. The prince repeatedly called for his proposed reforms to be put before the voters, while warning that he would go into exile if he lost such a referendum. He even asserted that without the present royal house and its wealth, the principality might have little recourse but to seek a union with either Switzerland or Austria. In a national referendum on March 14 and 16, 2003, voters approved the prince's demands with a 64 percent "yes" vote. The prince's detractors described his vastly enhanced powers as equivalent to "dictatorial" authority, and the Council of Europe threatened to impose sanctions because of the perceived threat to the democratic process. On August 15, 2004, Prince Hans-Adam II transferred most executive power to his son, Hereditary Prince ALOIS, although Prince Hans-Adam II remained monarch and head of state. The transfer partly defused the issue of undue concentration of power in the prince's hands, even though he indicated that he did not expect to abdicate for perhaps 20 years. In 2006 Prince Hans-Adam II turned day-to-day responsibility for the family banking business over to another son, Prince MAXIMILIAN.

The FBP fell to a plurality of 12 seats in the general election of March 11 and 13, 2005, prompting the return of an FBP-VU coalition, again headed by Hasler, on April 21.

In September 2007 the Organization for Economic Cooperation and Development (OECD) again branded Liechtenstein an uncooperative tax haven. Its controversial bank secrecy practices faced additional international challenges in February 2008 when German officials relied on records stolen from the Liechtenstein Group Trust (LGT), a bank owned by the royal family, to pursue hundreds of German citizens suspected of using secretive LGT trusts and foundations to evade taxes. Within weeks, the records were also being used in similar investigations in the United States and United Kingdom. Initial reactions in Liechtenstein were defensive and hostile. However, by summer's end, with parliamentary elections approaching and the secrecy issue threatening the regional economic integration of the principality's high-tech and manufacturing industries, Prince Alois and Prime Minister Hasler announced their readiness to respect international standards regarding financial transparency.

Prime Minister Hasler's FBP mustered only 43.5 percent of the vote in the February 2009 legislative elections. The VU, which won 13 of 25 seats, opted to form another coalition government with the FBP, but nominated their own Klaus TSCHÜTSCHER as prime minister.

At home, criticism of the prince's powers led to political showdowns in 2011 and 2012. First, in September 2011, a referendum was held to decriminalize abortion. A few days before the vote, Prince Alois, a staunch Catholic, announced he would veto the measure if it passed. His declaration effectively sank the proposal before balloting even began, as citizens wondered why they should bother to vote if the outcome was not binding.

The failed abortion referendum led to a referendum for July 1, 2012, on ending the prince's veto power. Ahead of the vote, Prince Hans-Adam II reminded that he had just spent $120 million to restore his family's palace in Vienna saying, "I don't have to live in Liechtenstein." The initiative failed, with less than 24 percent of voters wanting to eliminate the royal prerogative.

Popular attitudes toward the royal family vary, with some residents seeing the prince as the key to the country's stability and prosperity. Others downplay his role in the economy but consider the royal family to be fundamental to the country's identity. As Klaus WANGER, then president of parliament, explained ahead of the 2003 constitutional referendum, "Without the prince, we're nothing."

Constitution and government. Under the constitution adopted October 5, 1921, and amended in 2003 (see above), the monarchy is hereditary in the male line and the sovereign exercises legislative power jointly with a unicameral Diet (*Landtag*), which is elected every four years by direct suffrage under proportional representation, assuming no dissolution. The chief of government (*regierungschef*) is appointed by the sovereign from the majority party or group in the Diet. The government, which is responsible to both the sovereign and the Diet, also includes a deputy chief (*regierungschef-stellvertreter*) and three additional government councilors (*regierungsräte*) elected by the Diet itself. Elections are held in two constituencies (Oberland and Unterland), while administration is based on 11 communes (*gemeinden*). The judicial system consists of civil, criminal, and administrative divisions: the first two include local, Superior, and Supreme Courts, while the third encompasses an Administrative Court of Appeal (for hearing complaints about government officials and actions) and a State Court, both of which consider questions of constitutionality.

Women only gained the right to vote at the national level in 1984, when male voters narrowly endorsed the change, after defeating similar referenda held in 1971 and 1973. Following the 2009 balloting women held 6 of 25 seats in parliament, and 2 of the 5 government ministers were women.

Reporters Without Borders included Liechtenstein in its Index of Press Freedom for the first time in 2013, ranking the principality seventh.

Foreign relations. Liechtenstein maintains an embassy in Bern, Switzerland, but is represented elsewhere by Swiss embassies and consulates through an agreement dating from October 27, 1919. Long a participant in a number of United Nations (UN) specialized agencies, Liechtenstein decided only in December 1989 to seek admission to the UN; the application was approved in 1990. Previously an associate member of the European Free Trade Association (EFTA) because of its customs union with Switzerland, the principality became a full member on May 22, 1991. The country does not have a standing army but is an active participant in the Organization for (formerly Conference on) Security and Cooperation in Europe (OSCE/CSCE).

While not making a formal territorial claim, Liechtenstein in 1992 reopened the question of the extensive lands once owned by the princely family in what was then Czechoslovakia. Ten times the size of Liechtenstein, these hereditary estates had been confiscated in 1919 by the fledgling Czechoslovak Republic, which in 1938, under Axis pressure, had agreed to return half and to pay compensation for the remainder. The agreement was repudiated by the post–World War II Communist regime and the post-communist government in Prague. Liechtenstein's request for a ruling by the International Court of Justice (ICJ) in 2001 was refused in February 2005. Ultimately, the government established diplomatic relations with the Czech Republic in July 2009. The two governments also agreed to set up a commission of historians to examine the confiscated estates.

Switzerland's surprise application in 1992 for membership in the European Community/European Union (EC/EU) caused difficulties for Liechtenstein, which faced the possibility of having to follow suit if it wished to preserve the 1923 customs union between the two states. Of particular concern were proposed labor-mobility rules. Liechtenstein instead favored membership in the proposed European Economic Area (EEA) between the EU and most EFTA countries.

In December 1992, 55.8 percent of Liechtenstein voters endorsed EEA membership, but EEA participation had to be deferred pending renegotiation of the customs union. In April 1995, 55.9 percent of those voting approved the revised arrangement with Switzerland, and Liechtenstein then acceded to the EEA on May 1.

In 2003 Liechtenstein initially refused to approve expansion of the EEA to include the Czech Republic and Slovakia because of the lingering dispute over the post–World War II property agreements. Prince Hans-Adam II subsequently lifted his veto against the proposed EEA expansion on the condition that negotiations to resolve the dispute would be renewed.

In May 2000 the Bank for International Settlements included the principality on its list of offshore facilities having lax supervision, and a month later the independent Financial Action Task Force (FATF) placed Liechtenstein on its list of "noncooperative" jurisdictions in the fight against money laundering. In July the Group of Eight added its criticism of the country's "harmful" tax policies. To safeguard its lucrative financial sector, Liechtenstein stepped up enforcement of existing laws, expanded investigations, and passed new legislation to counter money laundering and better identify account holders shielded by intermediaries and foundations. In 2001 the FATF removed the principality from its blacklist.

In a September 2003 report, the International Monetary Fund found that while Liechtenstein still needed to devote greater resources to monitoring its financial sector, the country "observes a high level of compliance with international standards for anti–money laundering and combating the financing of terrorism."

While Hereditary Prince Alois had defiantly vowed to maintain bank secrecy, by March 2009 the government formally recognized the OECD transparency standards as binding and agreed to implement them. The OECD removed it from the grey list in 2009. The shift followed an agreement with the United States to exchange information on individuals' banking practices upon request, provided Liechtenstein courts deem the request legitimate. The government subsequently reached similar tax information agreements with multiple countries. The government created a special arrangement for British taxpayers, delaying implementation of that 2009 treaty until January 2013. UK citizens can avoid prosecution and additional penalties if they declare accumulated tax arrears from their financial dealings in Liechtenstein. The Liechtenstein Disclosure Facility proved so popular, collecting £64 million in 2011 and £114 million in 2012 that the mechanism was extended through April 2016.

On December 19, 2011, the parliament of Liechtenstein adopted relevant legislation to allow the country to join the EU's Schengen Area, ending border controls between the principality and the rest of Europe.

Current issues. Liechtenstein's reputation as a financial oasis with the world's highest standard of living has suffered as a result of the global economic crisis. Declining revenue forced the adoption of an austerity policy in 2010, when the budget gap equaled 15 percent of expenditure. Cuts equal to $4,000 per person were planned. Prime Minister Klaus TSCHÜTSCHER planned to increase income by expanding into fund management and alternative investments in addition to banking, but his project has not been as lucrative as he had hoped. In April 2013 the deficit was forecast to be €172 million, or 25 percent of the budget. Crown Prince Alois called for reducing government contributions to pension and health insurance funds.

The February 3, 2013, general election shifted the political landscape in Liechtenstein, with a new political grouping taking four seats in the *Landtag*. For the first time in the principality's history, four political parties will be represented in the parliament. The vote was seen as a referendum on the austerity policies imposed by Prime Minister Klaus TSCHÜTSCHER and the VU. The FBP emerged with a plurality in parliament, and the new prime minister, former police chief Adrian HASLER, pledged to resolve the shortfall by cutting public spending. Hasler also has indicated a willingness to discuss automatic bank account information sharing with EU members. First, however, he wants banking clients to have assurances that they will not be fined or imprisoned for avoiding taxes in the past.

POLITICAL PARTIES

Government Parties:

Progressive Citizens' Party (*Fortschrittliche Bürgerpartei*—FBP). Founded in 1918 as the basically conservative Citizens' Party (*Bürgerpartei*) and sometimes identified as the Bourgeois Party, what subsequently became the FBP held a majority of legislative seats from 1928 to 1970 and from 1974 to 1978. Starting in 1938 it participated with the VU (above) in Europe's longest-serving government coalition. After 15 years as the junior coalition partner, it regained seniority in February 1993 under the premiership of Markus Büchel but lost it in the year's second election in October, when the FBP list was headed by Josef BIEDERMANN. Following the 1997 election, in which it won a disappointing 10 seats, the FBP withdrew from the coalition government to sit in opposition. Having won 13 seats at the February 2001 election, the FBP formed a one-party administration in early April. However, after slipping to 12 seats (on a 49 percent vote share) in 2005, it reestablished the coalition with the VU. The coalition continued after the February 2009 election but with the VU in the leadership role, the FBP's vote share having declined to 43.5 percent, good for 11 seats. The FBP's vote share dropped to 40.0 percent and 10 seats in the February 3, 2013, election, giving it a plurality of seats. The party formed a governing coalition with the VU, with Adrian HASLER as prime minister.

Leaders: Adrian HASLER (Prime Minister); Otmar HASLER (Former Prime Minister); Alexander BATLINER (President); Elmar KINDLE, Robert HASSLER (Vice Presidents).

Fatherland Union (*Vaterländische Union*—VU). Considered the more liberal of the two major parties, the VU (sometimes referred to as the Patriotic Union) was formed with substantial working-class support in 1917 as the People's Party (*Volkspartei*), which controlled the government for the decade 1918–1928. Having adopted its present name in 1936, it served as the junior coalition partner of the FBP (below) from 1938 to 1970, when it won a majority of legislative seats. It lost its coalition seniority in 1974, regained it in 1978, lost it in February 1993, and regained it eight months later. It formed its own government in April 1997 after the FBP voluntarily moved into opposition. Following the February 2001 election, the VU declined to reestablish a coalition with the victorious FBP. However, it rejoined the government in April 2005 after securing 10 seats (on a 38 percent vote share) in the March general election. After winning an outright majority of 13 seats on 47.6 percent of the vote in the February 2009 balloting, the VU took the prime leadership position in the new coalition with FBP. The country's financial woes and austerity measures cost the VU in the February 3, 2013, election, where it won only 33.5 percent of the vote and eight seats.

Leaders: Jakub BÜCHEL (President), Thomas ZWIEFELHOFER (Deputy Prime Minister), Klaus TSCHÜTSCHER (Former Prime Minister), Nina PFEIFFER-RITTER (Vice President), Walter HARTMANN (Party Secretary).

Opposition Parties:

"The Independents" (*Die Unabhaengigen*—DU). A self-described "non-party" calling for affordable housing and balancing the budget without raising taxes, "The Independents" registered an upset in the February 2013 general election, emerging as the third-largest party in the *Landtag* by taking votes away from all three incumbent parties. DU secured four seats with a 15.3 percent share. Formed only in 2013, DU is led by Harry QUADERER, a banker and former member of the VU. The DU's other three new MPs include a patent attorney, a communications consultant, and a cross-dressing mechanic.

Leader: Harry QUADERER.

Free List (*Freie Liste*—FL). Less conservative than the traditional parties, the social democratic, environmentalist FL was formed prior to the 1986 election, in which it narrowly failed to secure the 8 percent vote share necessary for parliamentary representation; it again fell short in 1989, in part because 3 percent went to a new Liechtenstein Nonparty List (*Überparteiliche Liste Liechtensteins*—ÜLL). The party finally passed the threshold in the February 1993 balloting, securing 10.4 percent of the vote and two *Landtag* seats. It lost one of those seats the following October, regained it in 1997, and then fell back to a single seat in the February 2001 election before rebounding to three seats (on a 13 percent vote share) in March 2003. After again winning three seats on 13 percent of the vote in the March 2005 balloting, the FL fell back to just one seat with 8.9 percent of the vote in the February 2009 general election. The FL, which campaigned for reducing the prince's veto power, slipped to fourth place after the February 3, 2013, general election, although its 11.1 percent of the vote and three seats were both increases over 2009.

Leader: Wolfgang MARXER (President).

LEGISLATURE

The **Diet** (*Landtag*) is a unicameral body currently consisting of 25 members directly elected for four-year terms (barring dissolution) on the basis of universal suffrage and proportional representation. In the balloting of February 3, 2013, the Progressive Citizens' Party won 10 seats; the Fatherland Union, 8; the Independents, 4; and the Free List, 3.

President: Albert FRICK.

CABINET

[as of November 1, 2013]

Prime Minister	Adrian Hasler (FBP)
Deputy Prime Minister	Thomas Zwiefelhofer (VU)
Ministers	
Cultural Affairs	Aurelia Frick (FBP) [f]

Economic Affairs	Thomas Zwiefelhofer (VU)
Education	Aurelia Frick (FBP) [f]
Environmental Affairs, Land-Use Planning, Agriculture, and Forestry	Marlies Amman-Marxer (VU) [f]
Finance	Adrian Hasler (FBP)
Foreign Affairs	Aurelia Frick (FBP) [f]
General Government Affairs	Adrian Hasler (FBP)
Home Affairs	Thomas Zwiefelhofer (VU)
Justice	Thomas Zwiefelhofer (VU)
Infrastructure	Marlies Amman-Marxer (VU) [f]
Social Affairs	Mauro Pedrazzini (FBP)
Sports	Marlies Amman-Marxer (VU) [f]

[f] = female

INTERGOVERNMENTAL REPRESENTATION

Ambassador to the U.S.: Claudia FRITSCHE.

U.S. Ambassador to Liechtenstein: Donald S. BEYER Jr.

Permanent Representative to the UN: Christian WENAWESER.

IGO Memberships (Non-UN): CEUR, EBRD, EFTA, ICC, OSCE, WTO.

LITHUANIA

Republic of Lithuania
Lietuvos Respublika

Political Status: Independence from Russia declared February 16, 1918; absorption of independent state by the Soviet Union on August 3, 1940, repudiated on March 11, 1990, by the Lithuanian Supreme Council; independence recognized by the USSR State Council on September 6, 1991; current constitution approved by referendum of October 25, 1992.

Area: 25,174 sq. mi. (65,200 sq. km).

Population: 3,423,403 (2012E—UN); 3,515,858 (2013E—U.S.Census).

Major Urban Centers (2010E): VILNIUS (557,126), Kaunas (342,768), Klaipėda (180,282), Šiauliai (123,126), Panevėžys (110,494).

Official Language: Lithuanian.

Monetary Unit: Litas (official rate November 1, 2013: 2.56 litai = $1US). The litas was pegged to the euro as of February 2, 2002. Lithuania joined the European Union in 2004, although the target date for adopting the euro has been pushed back to at least 2013.

President: Dalia GRYBAUSKAITĖ (nonparty); elected in first-round balloting on May 17, 2009, and inaugurated for a five-year term on July 12 to succeed Valdas ADAMKUS (nonparty).

Prime Minister: Algirdas BUTKEVIČIUS (Social Democratic Party); elected by the parliament on November 22, 2012, approved by the president on December 7, and sworn in on December 13 to succeed Andrius KUBILIUS (Homeland Union-Lithuanian Christian Democrats).

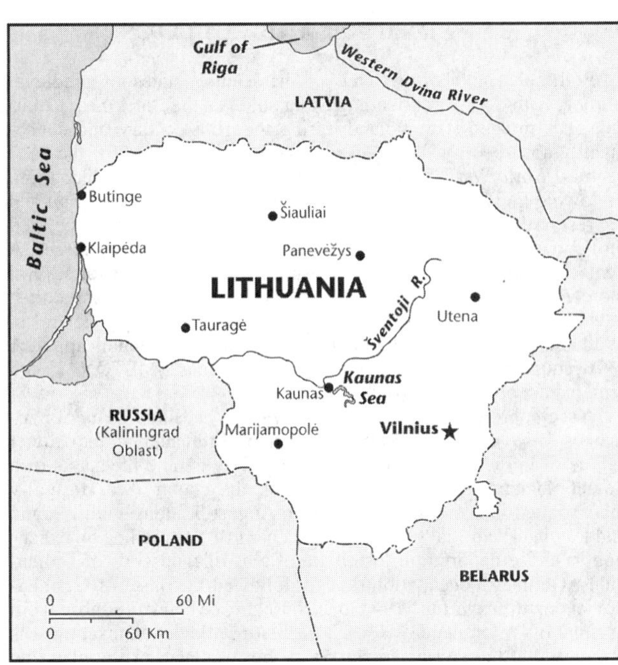

THE COUNTRY

The largest of the former Soviet Baltic republics, Lithuania is bordered on the north by Latvia, on the east by Belarus, on the south by Poland, and on the southwest by the detached Russian region of Kaliningrad. At the 2001 census 83.5 percent of the population was Lithuanian, 6.7 percent Polish, 6.3 percent Russian, and 1.2 percent Belarusan. About 79 percent are Roman Catholic, and 4 percent Russian Orthodox, while 16 percent professed no religion. Women constitute half of the work force and hold 34 seats (24 percent) of the 2012 legislature.

Following World War II the country passed from a largely agricultural to a substantially industrialized country, with a population that was two-thirds urban in 1986. The industrial sector accounts for approximately 27 percent of GDP, with paper, plastics, synthetic fibers, and sulfuric acid being leading products. Services account for 68 percent of GDP, while agriculture contributes only 4 percent. Cattle raising and dairy farming, in addition to grain and sugar beet cultivation, are the principal agricultural activities. Natural resources include forest tracts and relatively extensive peat reserves. Although the majority of exports go to countries in the European Union (EU), Russia is Lithuania's single biggest trading partner.

Economic disruption prompted by political change resulted in a 50 percent fall in GDP between 1990 and 1993, average annual inflation of 200 percent, and an estimated unemployment rate of 15 percent by early 1994. GDP growth had risen to 7.3 percent in 1997 before declining through 1999 as the Russian financial crisis battered Lithuanian exports. With eventual EU accession as a goal, successive governments accelerated structural reforms, including bank privatization, tax rationalization, pension reform, and restructuring of the energy sector. By 2004 conditions had improved sufficiently to permit Lithuania to join the EU. However, inflation postponed the adoption of the euro currency.

GDP growth fell five points to 3.3 percent in 2008 as the mid-decade boom evaporated, and Lithuania suffered the third largest economic contraction (14.8 percent) in the world in 2009. With the impact of the global financial crisis, unemployment more than doubled in 2009 to 13.7 percent. After remaining stagnant in 2010, GDP growth recovered to 5.9 percent, then slowed again. In 2013 GDP saw 3 percent growth, with inflation of 2 percent. Unemployment decreased to 12 percent, down from 17 percent in 2010.

GOVERNMENT AND POLITICS

Political background. One of the leading states of medieval Europe, with domains extending as far south as the Black Sea, Lithuania was merged with Poland during the 16th century and subsequently absorbed by Russia during the Polish partitions of the 18th century. World War I brought with it four years of German occupation. Following the November 1918 armistice, many countries recognized the restoration of Lithuanian independence, which had been declared on February 16 despite the continuing presence of German forces. A democratic government was established in May 1920, but for several more years Lithuania remained beset by Bolshevik, czarist, and Polish interventions, with Vilnius, the capital, being occupied by Poland in 1920 and Kaunas thereupon being declared the provisional capital. A 1926 coup produced the dictatorship of Antanas SMETONA, who remained in power until World War II.

A secret protocol of the German-Soviet "friendship" treaty of September 1939 assigned the greater part of Lithuania to the Soviet sphere of influence; after being compelled to assume the status of a Soviet Socialist Republic in July 1940, the country was formally incorporated into the Soviet Union on August 3, along with Estonia and Latvia. The initial period of Soviet control was marked by executions and the deportation to Siberia of tens of thousands of Lithuanians. German reoccupation quickly followed the onset of German-Soviet hostilities in June 1941, one consequence being the subsequent decimation of Lithuania's Jewish population. Soviet annexation was reimposed at the end of World War II but was never recognized by Britain and the United States.

In elections to the Lithuanian Supreme Soviet in late February and early March 1990, a majority of seats were won by candidates backed by the Lithuanian Reform Movement (*Sąjūdis*), a secessionist formation that cut across ideological lines. On March 11 *Sąjūdis* chair Vytautas LANDSBERGIS defeated Algirdas BRAZAUSKAS, the Communist incumbent chair of the Supreme Soviet Presidium, in balloting for the chair of what was now styled the Supreme Council. Following the election of Landsbergis, the council designated Kazimiera Danutė PRUNSKIENĖ, a *Sąjūdis*-endorsed Communist, to succeed Vytautas SAKALAUSKAS as chair of the Council of Ministers (prime minister). Later the same day, Lithuania became the first Soviet republic to declare its independence by repudiating the 1940 annexation and announcing a Provisional Fundamental Law of the Republic of Lithuania, an action that was immediately rejected by Moscow. In April the Soviet Union imposed an economic blockade on the country, and on June 29, following a meeting of Landsbergis and Prunskienė with President Mikhail Gorbachev in Moscow, the council approved a temporary suspension of its independence declaration. However, subsequent negotiations proved fruitless, and on January 2, 1991, Chair Landsbergis announced an end to the moratorium.

Prime Minister Prunskienė resigned on January 8, 1991, following widespread opposition to price increases that she had authorized. Three days later Soviet army troops moved to occupy key government buildings in Vilnius, precipitating clashes that resulted in the deaths of 14 civilians and 700 injuries. The Lithuanians responded by refusing to participate in the referendum on the Union Treaty on March 17, mounting instead a February 9 poll on independence that elicited a "yes" vote of 90.47 percent. A number of other incidents involving Soviet troops followed, prior to Moscow's acceptance of independence for all three Baltic republics on September 6 in the wake of the failed August coup by hard-liners in Moscow.

Chair Landsbergis attempted to secure sweeping new executive powers in a referendum on May 23, 1992, but a participation rate of less than half of the electorate doomed the proposal. Prime Minister Gediminas VAGNORIUS, who had succeeded Prunskienė following the five-day interim incumbency of Albertas ŠIMINAS, resigned, effective May 28, 1992, in response to left-wing opposition to his reform proposals. However, he continued in office on a caretaker basis until the approval of a new government under Aleksandras ABIŠALA on July 23. In the country's first election since independence, held in two stages on October 25 and November 15, 1992, Lithuanian voters turned away from *Sąjūdis* and awarded a parliamentary majority to the Brazauskas-led Lithuanian Democratic Labor Party (*Lietuvos Demokratinė Darbo Partija*—LDDP), which had been formed in 1990 by the secessionist wing of the Lithuanian Communist Party. In a simultaneous referendum, the electorate gave 78 percent approval to a new constitution. On November 25 Brazauskas was elected chair of Parliament (*Seimas*) and, as such, acting president of the republic. Confirmed in office by direct balloting on February 15, 1993, he named Adolfas ŠLEŽEVIČIUS on March 10 to succeed Abišala as prime minister.

A major political crisis developed in January 1996 over disclosures that the prime minister had withdrawn his personal savings of roughly $34,000 from a Lithuanian bank two days before its operations had been suspended by the central bank because of financial irregularities. Denying any wrongdoing, Šleževičius rejected opposition calls for his resignation and was backed by the LDDP council. However, eroding support among LDDP deputies culminated on February 8 with the *Seimas* approving, by 94 votes to 24, a presidential decree calling for his resignation, whereupon Laurynas Mindaugas STANKEVIČIUS, the minister of administrative reforms and municipal affairs, was named to succeed him. Following the parliamentary endorsement of Stankevičius a week later, a new LDDP government was announced by the president on February 23.

Despite a limited economic upturn in 1996, the LDDP government suffered a comprehensive defeat in legislative elections on October 20 and November 10, retaining only 12 seats out of the 137 filled. In a decisive swing to the right, the Homeland Union (Lithuanian Conservatives) (*Tėvynės Sąjunga* [*Lietuvos Konservatoriai*]—TS[LK]), which had been launched in 1993 as a partial successor to *Sąjūdis,* won an overall majority of 70 seats, while other center-right parties also polled strongly. Meanwhile, in four referenda held on October 20, assorted LDDP proposals for constitutional and electoral reform all failed to obtain majority support.

Negotiations between the TS(LK) and the Lithuanian Christian Democratic Party (*Lietuvos Krikščionių Demokratų Partija*—LKDP) yielded a formal coalition agreement by early December 1996, and on December 10 a new government received legislative endorsement by 87 votes to 21 and was sworn in. Headed by former prime minister Vagnorius, it included 11 additional TS(LK) ministers and 3 from the LKDP, with two portfolios being allocated to the Lithuanian Center Union (*Lietuvos Centro Sąjunga*—LCS).

In March 1997 local elections, the TS(LK) secured 33 percent of the seats, compared to 14 percent for the LDDP. Seven candidates contested the subsequent presidential election, with incumbent Brazauskas having declined to run for reelection. In first-round balloting on December 21, Artūras PAULAUSKAS, a former prosecutor, secured 44.7 percent of the vote, followed by Valdas ADAMKUS with 28 percent and TS(LK) leader Landsbergis with 16 percent. With Landsbergis's support, Adamkus squeaked out a victory in the second round of balloting on January 4, 1998, winning 50.3 percent of the vote. Adamkus, who had worked for Lithuanian independence during four decades in exile in the United States, was inaugurated on February 26. Prime Minister Vagnorius submitted his resignation, but Adamkus subsequently reappointed him to head a reshuffled cabinet that was confirmed by the *Seimas* on March 10.

Vagnorius's reappointment initially appeared to signal continuity in the government's emphasis on economic reform and anticorruption measures. However, over the next year severe discord developed between Adamkus and Vagnorius on several fronts, most notably the president's contention that his office should be accorded greater responsibility in the interest of the "modernization of the state." Adamkus also urged that greater authority be given to elected local officials, accusing the TS(LK) administration of a "Soviet-style" approach to government that imposed policies from the top. Consequently, in mid-April Adamkus announced that he had lost confidence in Vagnorius and urged him and his cabinet to resign. Although the prime minister argued that he was being unfairly vilified for having resisted Adamkus's attempts to "usurp" power, he announced his resignation on April 30 and was replaced on an interim basis by Social Welfare and Labor Minister Irena DEGUTIENĖ. Adamkus then tapped the TS(LK) mayor of Vilnius, Rolandas PAKSAS, who was confirmed as prime minister on May 18, and a new cabinet of TS(LK), LKDP, LCS, and independent ministers was sworn in on June 12. The new administration proved short-lived, however, with Paksas resigning on October 27 because of his opposition to sale of a one-third stake in the country's largest enterprise, the Mažeikiai oil refinery, to U.S.-based Williams International. The ministers of economy and finance also resigned, although the majority of the cabinet as well as President Adamkus supported the arrangement. When Paksas's interim replacement, Degutienė, declined the prime ministership, Adamkus instead nominated Andrius KUBILIUS of the TS(LK), who was confirmed by the *Seimas* on November 3. Five days later the LCS announced that it was leaving the government, although its one minister instead quit the party and remained in the cabinet.

Following a poor showing by the TS(LK) in the March 2000 local election, a group of about a dozen deputies led by former prime minister Vagnorius established a Moderate Conservative faction within the *Seimas,* thereby costing the TS(LK) its majority status. Formation of the Moderate Conservative Union (*Nuosaikiųjų Konservatorių Sąjunga*—NKS) followed in May. In the same month, President Adamkus announced a legislative election for October 8, and the LDDP, the Lithuanian Social Democratic Party (*Lietuvos Socialdemokratų Partija*—LSDP), and two smaller parties agreed to forge an electoral alliance headed by former president Brazauskas. In the October balloting Prime Minister Kubilius's TS(LK) won only 9 seats (down from 70 in 1996), while the A. Brazauskas Social Democratic Coalition (*A. Brazausko Socialdemokratinė Koalicija*—ABSK) won a plurality of proportional seats. Nevertheless, the ABSK parties' overall total of 51 deputies proved insufficient to form a government. President Adamkus then turned to former prime minister Paksas and his four-party "New Policy" (*Naujosios Politikos*) bloc of the Lithuanian Liberal Union (*Lietuvos Liberalų Sąjunga*—LLS), the New Union (Social Liberals) (*Naujoji Sąjunga* [Socialliberalai]—NS[SL]), the LCS, and the Modern Christian Democratic Union (*Moderniųjų Krikščionių Demokratų Sąjunga*—MKDS). Paksas was confirmed for the second time as prime minister on October 26. However, discord over economic policy and privatization brought a quick end to Paksas's tenure. On June 18, 2001, the NS(SL) leader and *Seimas* chair, Artūras Paulauskas, called for him to step down; collaterally, the six NS(SL)-selected cabinet ministers resigned. The prime minister tendered his own resignation two days later, with the LLS minister of the economy, Eugenijus GENTVILAS, then assuming Paksas's duties on an acting basis. The end to Prime Minister Paksas's second brief term in office came about not only because of policy differences between his LLS and Artūras Paulauskas's NS(SL) but also because of the two leaders' political rivalry. On July 3 the *Seimas* confirmed former president Brazauskas as prime minister at the head of a coalition of the LSDP (with which the LDDP had merged in January) and the NS(SL), the new cabinet being announced on July 5.

In first-round presidential balloting on December 22, 2002, President Adamkus led 17 candidates with 35.5 percent of the vote, followed by Paksas (19.7 percent) and Paulauskas (8.3 percent). However, Paksas defeated Adamkus in the runoff election on January 5, 2003, with 54.7 percent of the vote. Prime Minister Brazauskas was reconfirmed on March 6 to head another (only slightly reshuffled) LSDP-NS(SL) coalition government.

In late 2003 President Paksas became embroiled in a controversy concerning his alleged links with a shadowy figure, Yurii BORISOV, a Russian businessman who was reputed to have ties to organized crime. Among other things, it was alleged that Paksas had granted Borisov dual citizenship, despite reported concerns from Lithuanian security services that Borisov might have been involved in smuggling arms. President Paksas's critics charged that Borisov had contributed heavily to Paksas's political finances. After a special legislative committee alleged that Paksas had, in addition to other charges, jeopardized national security, impeachment proceedings were launched in December, resulting in six formal charges against Paksas in February 2004. After Paksas rejected calls for his resignation, the *Seimas* on April 6 found him guilty by large margins of three charges and removed him from office. As mandated by the constitution, Paulauskas (the chair of the *Seimas*) assumed presidential authority on an acting basis. In November a court in Vilnius found Borisov guilty of blackmailing Paksas while Paksas was president.

The first round of a new presidential election was held on June 13, 2004, with Adamkus winning 30.7 percent of the vote, followed by Kazimiera PRUNSKIENĖ of the Union of the Peasants and New Democracy Party (*Valstiečiųir Naujosios Demokratijos Partiju Sąjunga*—VNDPS) with 21.4 percent. (Prunskienė was supported by Paksas after the *Seimas* had ruled that Paksas could not be a candidate.) Adamkus secured the presidency in a second round on June 27 with 52.6 percent of the vote.

Following Lithuania's accession to the EU on May 1, 2004, the recently formed Labor Party (*Darbo Partija*—DP) burst onto the electoral scene with a strong performance in the June 2004 elections for the European Parliament. It continued its ascendancy in the *Seimas* balloting on October 10 and 24, leading all parties with 39 seats. After lengthy negotiations, Prime Minister Brazauskas was reappointed to head a new coalition government (inaugurated on December 14) comprising the DP, LSDP, NS(SL), and VNDPS.

In June 2005 the leader of the Labor Party, Viktor USPASKICH, was dismissed from the post of economy minister after being charged with fraudulent campaign finance practices. In April 2006 the *Seimas* ousted NS(SL) leader Artūras Paulauskas from the office of speaker, accusing him of insufficient efforts to curb abuse of power within the *Seimas.* The speaker's party responded by leaving the government. After President Adamkus expressed no confidence in two DP ministers, Prime Minister Brazauskas resigned as well, saying the coalition could no longer function. Finance Minister Balcytis failed to secure *Seimas* support to extend his acting prime ministership, and President Adamkus nominated Defense Minister Kirkilas to replace him and form a new cabinet. In the ensuing negotiations among the remaining coalition partners, the DP won the vacated cabinet post for social security and labor, while the Lithuanian National Farmers' Union (*Lietuvos Valstiečių Liaudininkų Sąjunga*—LVLS, as the VNDPS had been renamed) won the prestigious foreign affairs ministry. However, the government collapsed in late May when the DP withdrew from the coalition amid severe internal party turmoil. Prime Minister Brazauskas tendered his resignation on June 1, and President Adamkus nominated Finance Minister Zigmantas BALCYTIS as acting prime minister. After Balcytis failed to secure a majority of legislative votes to make the appointment permanent, President Adamkus subsequently tapped Defense Minister Gediminas KIRKILAS, who was confirmed by the *Seimas* on July 4, 2006. A new minority cabinet (comprising the LSDP, LVLS, the Liberal and Center Union, and the recently formed Civil Democracy Party [*Pilietinės Demokratijos Partija*—PDP]) was approved on July 18, with the government subsequently depending upon TS members to honor their agreement not to obstruct the minority government. The NS(SL) rejoined the governing coalition in February 2008, ahead of elections slated for October 12.

Widespread discontent with the rapidly souring economy led to the defeat of the ruling LSDP-led coalition in balloting on October 12 and 16, 2008. The TS-LKD emerged the winner with 45 seats, and composed a government led by Andrius KUBILIUS, including the Lithuanian Republic Liberal Movement (*Lietuvos Respublikos Liberalų Sąjūdis*—LRLS), the Liberal and Center Union, and the recently formed National Revival Party (*Tautos Prisikėlimo Partijos*—TPP) (see Political Parties, below). The inclusion of the TPP reflected the strength of populist sentiment against the establishment parties, and support for the TS-LKD and the TPP was echoed in the June 2009 elections to the European Parliament.

The victory of former EU commissioner Dalia GRYBAUSKAITĖ in the 2009 presidential elections was largely attributed to her reputation as a competent manager who operated above ideological considerations. She won in the first round with 51.7 percent of the vote, convincingly besting her nearest opponent, Algirdas BUTKEVIČIUS of the LSDP, who won 11.9 percent. The president endorsed cuts in pensions and family benefits in an effort to shore up the country's finances, guaranteeing lively debate in the *Seimas.* Grybauskaitė took office on July 12. The conservative government was reappointed by Grybauskaitė and confirmed by the parliament on July 16, 2009, although some incumbent ministers who were viewed as ineffective were dismissed. The president subsequently maintained high approval ratings due to her image as an effective technocrat.

The TS-LKD government was ousted in October 2012 balloting, as a coalition led by the LSDP secured victory. Following a six-week controversy over the integrity of the election, Algirdas Butkevičius was sworn in as prime minister on December 13 (see Current issues, below).

Constitution and government. The 1992 constitution accords primacy, as representing the sovereignty of the people, to a Parliament (*Seimas*) elected for a four-year term, although significant powers, particularly in the sphere of foreign policy, are allocated to the president, who is directly elected for a five-year term. The president appoints the prime minister and, on the latter's nomination, other ministers, all subject to the approval of the *Seimas.* The judicial structure is headed by a Constitutional Court and a Supreme Court, whose judges are selected by the *Seimas* from presidential nominations. Members of district and local courts are appointed by the president.

Government at the local level currently encompasses 10 counties (*apskritys*), which are centrally directed and supervised; 44 rural and 12 urban municipalities, which are self-governing; and 500 neighborhoods. The 56 self-governing units elect local councils, with each council then selecting an executive.

During the Soviet period all media outlets were required to endorse communist ideology. Censorship was abolished in 1989. Lithuania ranked 33rd in the world for press freedom by Reporters Without Borders in 2013.

Foreign relations. Soviet recognition of the independence of the Baltic states on September 6, 1991, paved the way for admission of the three to the Conference on (later Organization for) Security and Cooperation in Europe (CSCE/OSCE) on September 10 and admission to the United Nations on September 17.

Regionally, Lithuania concluded a Baltic Economic Cooperation Agreement with Estonia and Latvia in April 1990. On September 24, 1991, the three states also reached agreement on a customs union that authorized free trade and visa-free travel among their respective jurisdictions, although implementation of its provisions proceeded very slowly. Lithuania was also a founding member of the broader Council of the Baltic Sea States in 1992.

On July 31, 1991, President Landsbergis and Russian President Boris Yeltsin signed an agreement giving Russia rights of transit across Lithuania to its Baltic enclave of Kaliningrad. Subsequently, on February 16, 1992, Landsbergis demanded that former Soviet troops be withdrawn from Kaliningrad on the grounds that their presence had become a "historic anachronism." While firmly rejecting this demand, Russia entered into negotiations on the withdrawal of its troops from Lithuania and agreed to a full withdrawal by August 31, 1993. Under a subsequent economic cooperation agreement, Russia undertook to supply oil, natural gas, and nuclear energy to Lithuania in exchange for agricultural and manufactured goods. In October 1999 the *Seimas* ratified a border treaty that had been negotiated in 1997, but in June 2000 the legislature also passed a resolution seeking compensation for 50 years of Soviet occupation, the cost of which was later estimated at $20 billion. Relations nevertheless remained cordial, with Presidents Adamkus and Vladimir Putin reaching agreement in March 2001 on the status of Kaliningrad and the free movement of the region's residents through Lithuania.

Independent Lithuania moved quickly to reestablish historically close relations with Poland, concluding on January 13, 1992, a joint Declaration on Friendly Relations and Cooperation that included a number of economic and ecological provisions and confirmed the existing border between the two countries. Reciprocal state visits in 1994 and 1995 led to a bilateral accord envisaging that Lithuania would accede to the Central European Free Trade Agreement (CEFTA/Visegrad Group). Lithuania's relations with Moscow-aligned Belarus were more problematic: an economic cooperation agreement concluded on April 2, 1992, included a confirmation of the existing border, but a widely quoted statement by the Belarus defense minister in March had included territorial claims on Lithuania.

A prime ministerial visit to Israel in October 1994 was intended to consolidate a government apology made the previous month for Lithuania's wartime role in the Nazi genocide of European Jewry. The visit followed heated controversy over the decision of the immediate post-Soviet government to exonerate convicted war criminals on the grounds that Soviet-era trials had been coercive and lacking due process. Under international pressure, incoming President Brazauskas had in March 1993 announced a review of pardons issued by the previous government. Tension between Lithuania and Israel again flared when in March 2006 the Vilnius District Court found Nazi collaborator Algimantas DAILIDĖ guilty of genocide but failed to impose any punishment due to the defendant's poor health and old age.

Having joined the Council of Europe in May 1993, Lithuania became a signatory of the North Atlantic Treaty Organization's (NATO) Partnership for Peace in January 1994. Lithuania and the other two Baltic states in July 1995 became the first ex-Soviet republics to sign "Europe" (i.e., association) agreements with the EU, offering the prospect of eventual full membership, for which Lithuania formally applied in December 1995.

Lithuania was not among the three countries invited in July 1997 by NATO to join the alliance in 1999, the process slowed by Russia's strong objections. However, NATO officials announced that they considered Lithuania and the other two Baltic states to be strong candidates for eventual membership. Lithuanian leaders were also disappointed (albeit not surprised) that Lithuania was not included on the list of countries invited in December by the EU to begin membership negotiations in 1998. However, the EU agreed that talks would continue toward Lithuania's inclusion in the "second wave" of expansion. In October 1999 the EU abandoned the second wave concept and then announced in December that Lithuania could proceed with accession negotiations.

The three Baltic states signed the U.S.-Baltic Charter of Partnership on January 16, 1998, in which Washington affirmed the three nations' sovereignty (without making any military commitments), supported the integration of the trio into Western institutions, and approved three bilateral working groups to advance cooperation.

Lithuania was formally invited in November 2002 to join NATO, and the EU issued a similar invitation in December. On May 10 and 11, 2003, 91 percent of Lithuanian voters in a national referendum endorsed joining the EU. Lithuania joined the EU on May 1, 2004, and the *Seimas* ratified the EU's Lisbon Treaty in May 2008. Lithuania continues to support EU expansion and prompted member candidacy for Georgia in 2011. The country's European involvement continued in other ways as it participated in a number of NATO operations, including missions in the Balkans and Afghanistan. The last Lithuanian troops left Iraq at the end of 2008.

President Grybauskaitė, who favors a pragmatic, nonideological foreign policy, has indicated her intention to engage Russia in a measured way. However, Lithuanian relations with its former occupier have been strained since Lithuania's independence and are unlikely to improve substantially, particularly as Russia seeks to maintain Lithuania's dependence on its energy sector. In July 2011 the government announced compliance with EU energy mandates designed to increase competition in the sector, which would ultimately reduce the Russian share of the market. The Russian enclave of Kaliningrad also remains a source of political instability between the two countries. In April 2012 Defense Minister Rasa JUKNEVIČIENĖ criticized Russia's deployment of an antiaircraft system to Kaliningrad as an attempt to challenge Lithuania's NATO-protected airspace. NATO agreed in February to extend its air policing mission over the Baltics until 2018.

Austria's July 2011 decision not to extradite ex-KGB Russian national Mikhail Golovatov, whom Lithuania charges with the deaths of 14 citizens in 1991, strained relations.

Tensions with Poland have mounted due to language rights in both countries. In March 2011 the *Seimas* approved changes to education policy that required that all schools, including those taught in the Polish language, teach Lithuanian history in the Lithuanian language, prompting discussions with Polish Prime Minister Donald Tusk in Vilnius in September 2011. Tensions continued to mount in 2012 when Grybauskaitė refused to attend a meeting with the presidents of the Baltic States and Poland in Warsaw because of the issue of ethnic Poles in Lithuania.

In March 2013 Lithuania signed a cooperation agreement with Rwanda, setting a framework to establish diplomatic relations.

Tensions again flared with Russia in August 2013 when a Lithuanian court ruled to extradite a Russian national suspected of illegal arms smuggling to the United States. In early September, Russia imposed supplementary border checks on passenger and cargo vehicles, apparently to apply pressure as the EU, currently led by Lithuania, competes with Russia to woo Ukraine to join their trade bloc.

Current issues. As the economy declined in 2009, violent protests broke out in the capital. Fiscal policy continued to dominate the government agenda, with entitlement cuts provoking particular opposition in 2010. Public spending was cut by an estimated 30 percent, prompting some coalition deputies to defect from the government in order to improve their electoral prospects. As a result, the coalition was reduced to a minority government by March 2010.

Nevertheless, as economic growth recovered from the 2009 levels, corruption in public office resurfaced as a political issue. In January 2011 the European Court of Human Rights (ECHR) ruled that the impeached former president Rolandas Paksas had been disproportionately punished when he was banned permanently from standing for public office. Although Paksas immediately announced his intention to stand in the 2012 elections, Lithuanian authorities charged that the court's decision could not be implemented without changing the country's constitution. Separately, in March 2011 the erstwhile economy minister, Dainius KREIVYS, responded to presidential pressure to resign following revelations that he had approved the allocation of EU funds for a school renovation project by a company in which his family owned shares.

Corruption continued to be a concern into 2012; a January poll revealed that some 89 percent of Lithuanians consider corruption to be among the country's major problems. In February Interior Minister Raimundas PALAITIS dismissed a deputy minister and the head of the Financial Crimes Investigation Service against Kubilius's will, sparking internal tensions within the TS-LKD coalition. The alliance was on the verge of dissolving when Palaitis bowed to calls for his resignation on March 26. The coalition remained intact for the 2012 parliamentary election.

In May 2012 the LSDP, the DP, and the UTT signed an agreement guaranteeing cooperation between the three leading opposition parties both before and after the election.

Ahead of the October 2012 parliamentary elections, the Lithuanian Constitutional Court ruled in early September that former president Paksas, leader of the UTT, could not run for parliament because the constitution had not yet been revised to reflect the ECHR ruling. Meanwhile, according to Grybauskaitė, the austerity measures would remain in place no matter the outcome of the election. Other economic policies were not as stable, however. The LSDP lead in the polls, with party leader Algirdas Butkevičius pledging to delay the "unrealistic" goal of joining the eurozone by 2014 and sharply criticizing plans for the Visaginas nuclear power plant for its expense. (Butkevičius had initiated the referendum on nuclear power concurrent with October balloting.) Eighteen parties contested the elections held on October 14 and 28. In a vote widely perceived as a rejection of the recent austerity measures, the LSDP won 38 seats, ousting the TS-LKD coalition, which secured 33. Six other parties won representation. The nuclear power measure was rejected, with 62.7 percent voting against the project.

Following the election, President Grybauskaitė vetoed the potential for the DP to join the LSDP-UTT alliance, citing concerns over 27 alleged cases of electoral violations, 18 of which involved the DP. On November 5 the Central Electoral Commission determined that violations committed in multi-mandate races were not significant enough to invalidate the results, except in two single-mandate districts. (By-elections held in March 2013 yielded two more LSDP seats.) On November 10 the constitutional court reaffirmed the decision.

On November 22 parliament elected Butkevičius as prime minister. Following President Grybauskaitė's approval on December 7, Butkevičius and his cabinet were sworn in on December 12.

POLITICAL PARTIES

The constitutional revision of March 11, 1990, effectively revoked the monopoly of the Lithuanian Communist Party (*Lietuvos Komunistų Partija*—LKP). In August 1991 the party itself was banned and its property confiscated, although its secessionist wing had long since withdrawn to form the Lithuanian Democratic Labor Party (LDDP; see LSDP). Legislation was approved in early 1999 for government funds to be allocated to parties demonstrating backing from at least 3 percent of the voters.

Government Parties:

Lithuanian Social Democratic Party (*Lietuvos Socialdemokratų Partija*—LSDP). The present LSDP was established by merger in January 2001 of the existing LSDP and the Lithuanian Democratic Labor Party (*Lietuvos Demokratinė Darbo Partija*—LDDP). Together, they had formed the backbone of the A. Brazauskas Social Democratic Coalition (*A. Brazausko Socialdemokratinė Koalicija*—ABSK), which had been established to present a consolidated list for the proportional component of the October 2000 legislative election. The other ABSK participants were the NDP, VNDPS, and LRS.

The premerger LSDP was formed in 1896 and reestablished in 1989, winning a 5.9 percent vote share in the 1992 balloting. The LDDP was formed in 1990 by a faction of the former Lithuanian Communist Party (LKP) that initially supported Soviet President Gorbachev's reformist program and subsequently endorsed independence for Lithuania. The LDDP scored a surprising victory in the 1992 parliamentary balloting, winning 42.6 percent of the vote on a platform of gradual transition to a market economy; the party's leader, Algirdas Brazauskas, was subsequently confirmed as president. Considerable party turmoil accompanied the government crisis and ouster of Prime Minister Adolfas Šleževičius in early 1996, which led to disastrous returns in the subsequent *Seimas* election: LDDP representation fell to 9.5 percent.

In the October 2000 election the ABSK won a 31 percent vote share. Following the January 2001 LSDP-LDDP merger, Brazauskas had sufficient leverage to form a new administration with the NS(SL) when the latter party's coalition with the LLS dissolved in June. The LSDP presented joint candidates with the NS(SL) in the 2004 legislative balloting, after which Brazauskas continued as prime minister. The NS(SL) left the government in April 2006, and the ruling LSDP/LVLS/DP coalition collapsed due to DP resignations on June 1. Gediminas Kirkilas, then the national defense minister, was nominated by President Adamkus to form a new LSPD-led minority government. Brazauskas subsequently endorsed Kirkilas for the party chair. He was elected to the position during the 2007 party congress. Following the party's third place finish in the October 2008 elections with 25 seats and 11.7 percent of votes, the LSPD profile improved. As the chief opposition party, it benefited because the government faced the brunt of popular anger regarding the economic crisis. The LSDP increased its representation from 2 to 3 seats and its vote share to 18.14 percent in the June 2009 European Parliament elections.

Former Prime Minister Brazauskas died in June 2010. Ahead of the October 2012 elections, the LSPD, led by Algirdas Butkevičius, emerged as a favorite. The party platform was highly critical of the TS-LKD's economic policy, and Butkevičius, in particular, opposed the Visaginas nuclear project because of the expense. In early October, a member of the party was charged with bribery. The LSDP won 38 seats with 18.4 percent of the vote. Subsequently, the LSDP formed a coalition government with the UTT, the LLRA, and, despite President Grybauskaitė's objections, the DP (see below for party entries).

Leaders: Algirdas BUTKEVIČIUS (President and Parliamentary Elder), Vytenis Povilas ANDRIUKAITIS (Vice President), Irena ŠIAULIENĖ (First Deputy Elder), Juozas OLEKAS (Deputy Elder), Gediminas KIRKILAS (Former Prime Minister and Former Chair).

Labor Party (*Darbo Partija*—DP). Formed by ethnic Russian businessman Viktor Uspaskich in 2003, the DP is a populist party that supports increased pensions and higher wages for workers and once touted itself as an alternative to some established parties perceived to be tainted by corruption. After the DP secured 28.44 percent of the vote in *Seimas* elections on October 10, 2004, Uspaskich was named minister of the economy in the government installed in December 2004, though resigned in June 2005 over conflicts between his position and business affairs. Nevertheless, the DP remained in government, winning additional cabinet portfolios in April 2006 when the NS(SL) withdrew from the ruling coalition. In response to aggressive maneuverings by Uspaskich, seven DP party members in the *Seimas* left the party in May 2006 and helped to form the PDP (below).

Allegations of unorthodox accounting and kickbacks to DP legislators as well as lawmakers from other parties led Uspaskich to self-imposed exile in Moscow in May 2006. Upon his return in September 2007, he was arrested and two days later placed under house arrest for six months. His attempt to campaign from home for the 2008 election proved fruitless. In July 2008 a Vilnius court withheld an electoral commission subsidy worth 2.5 million litas due to the allegations regarding the party's financial practices.

The DP continued to be dogged by corruption allegations in 2008 and 2009, and saw its legislative seat share fall to ten after competing in an electoral coalition with the heretofore unknown **Youth Party**. The coalition garnered 9.0 percent of votes. The DP won 8.58 percent of votes in the June 2009 EU balloting, losing four of its five seats. Following an announcement in April 2011, the NS(SL) merged with the DP.

In the October 2012 elections, the DP secured 33 seats and 19.8 percent of the vote. The party was implicated in 18 cases of electoral violations, amid concerns of vote-buying. However, the Constitutional Court ruled in early November that the results were valid, but recommended the replacement of five recently elected DP members. On November 13 parliament rejected the court's proposal.

Leaders: Viktor USPASKICH (Chair), Virtinija BALTRAITIENĖ (Vice President), Sarunas BIRUTIS (Third Vice President).

New Union (Social Liberals) (*Naujoji Sąjunga [Socialliberalai]*—NS[SL]). The left-of-center NS(SL) was established in late April 1998 by Artūras Paulauskas. Prior to the 2000 parliamentary election the NS(SL) joined the LLS, LCS, and MKDS in announcing that after the balloting they would attempt to form a "New Policy" (*Naujosios Politikos*). The coalition foundered in June 2001, however, with Paulauskas calling for Paksas to step down and with all six NS(SL) cabinet ministers resigning. Later in the month Paulauskas negotiated a coalition agreement with the LSDP and joined the new government.

Paulauskas served as interim prime minister during the 2003–2004 impeachment crisis. The NS(SL) later presented joint candidates with the LSDP in the 2004 legislative elections. In 2006 the NS(SL) withdrew from the ruling coalition, but briefly returned with the appointment of Algirdas MONKEVIČIUS aseducation and science minister in June 2008. However, after winning just one seat and 3.6 percent of votes in the October 2008 balloting, the party returned to the opposition. The NS(SL) won 3.37 percent of votes for the European Parliament in 2009.

In April 2011 the party announced that it would merge with the DP notwithstanding their previous policy disagreements in government. A dissenting faction defected to the LCS (below).

For Order and Justice (*Už Tvarka ir Teisinguma*—UTT). The UTT was formed as an electoral coalition of the two groups below in 2004 following President Paksas's removal from office. The coalition was reportedly designed to minimize voter backlash against Paksas's LDP; there was also concern that the LDP might be prevented from presenting its own candidates without a partner. The UTT won 10 seats in the *Seimas* in the October poll on a vote share of 11.4 percent. The UTT alliance performed well in the 2007 local elections and won 12.7 percent votes and 15 seats in the October 2008 election. The party continues to endorse a platform of nationalism, social solidarity, and Christian values, and took 11.92 percent of votes and 2 seats in the European Parliament elections in June 2009.

The UTT continued to play an active oppositional role in 2009 and 2010 and succeeded in securing the removal of the speaker of the *Seimas,* Arūnas Valinskas, in September 2009 (see TPP, below).

In October 2012 balloting, the UTT secured 11 seats with 7.3 percent of the vote, and subsequently entered a coalition with the LSDP.

Leaders: Rolandas PAKSAS (Chair and Former President of the Republic), Valentinas MAZURONIS (First Vice Chair), Almantas PETKUS, Kęstas KOMSKIS (Deputy Parliamentary Elders).

Liberal Democratic Party (*Liberalų Demokratų Partija*—LDP). Formed in March 2002 by former Prime Minister Rolandas Paksas and other LLS defectors, the center-right Liberal Democratic Party pledged to support the business sector and to guarantee "order in the state."

Paksas was elected president of the republic in 2003 but was removed from office in 2004 (see Political background and Current issues for details). The LDP supported the VNDPS candidate in the 2004 presidential poll after Paksas was ruled ineligible to run.

Leaders: Rolandas PAKSAS (Chair, Former Prime Minister, and Former President of the Republic), Valentinas MAZURONIS (First Deputy Chair).

Lithuanian People's Union "For Fair Lithuania" (*Lietuvos Liaudies Sąjunga "Už Teisingą Lietuvą"*—LLS). The LLS was formed in 2000 by Julius Veselka, who ran successfully as a "self-nominated" candidate in the 2000 legislative elections. The LLS won 11 percent of the vote in the 2002 local elections.

Leader: Julius VESELKA.

Lithuanian Poles' Electoral Action (*Lietuvos Lenkų Rinkimų Akcija*—LLRA). The LLRA began as the Lithuanian Polish Union (*Lietuvos Lenkų Sąjunga*—LLS), an ethnic grouping that won four *Seimas* seats in 1992. As the LLRA, it retained only one seat in 1996 but secured two in 2000 and 2004. In the 2008 elections it garnered 4.8 percent of votes and three seats. Following the European parliamentary elections in June 2009, the LLRA joined the European Conservatives and Reformists (ECR) grouping founded with leadership from the British Tories in the European Parliament on June 22. Following proposed revisions to the education policy in 2011, the party was expected to redouble efforts to secure its rights for Polish speakers in Lithuania. In the October 2013 election, the LLRA won 8 seats with 5.8 percent of the vote, and joined the LSDP ruling coalition.

Leaders: Waldemar TOMASZEWSKI (Chair and Member of European Parliament); Zbigniew JEDZIŃSKI, Maria REKŚĆ, Leonard TALMONT (Vice Chairs).

Opposition Parties:

Homeland Union-Lithuanian Christian Democrats (*Tėvynės Sąjunga-Lietuvos Krikščionys Demokratai*—TS-LKD). The TS-LKD was formed as In the Name of Lithuania (*Vardan Lietuvos*—VL) in February 2008 by the TS and LKD as an electoral coalition designed to improve rightist prospects ahead of the October legislative balloting. The parties officially merged in May 2008 and decisively won elections in October that year, taking 19.7 percent of votes and 45 seats, with the social democratic rival, the LSDP, following with 25 seats. The TS-TKD leads the governing coalition with the TPP, LRLS, and LCS and adopted its current name in May 2008. It won a 26.1 percent plurality of votes in the June 2009 European Parliament elections. The party's popularity declined relative to the LSDP from 2010 due to radical cuts in government spending, but the parliamentary speaker, Irena Degutienė, continued to enjoy high public approval ratings. The party suffered a hit in the October 2012 balloting, taking 15 percent of the vote, and reducing its parliamentary seats to 33.

Leaders: Andrius KUBILIUS (Founder, Former Prime Minister and President), Irena DEGUTIENĖ (First Vice President), Rasa JUKNEVICIENE, Agne BILOTAITE, Jurgis RAMZA (Vice Presidents).

Homeland Union (*Tėvynės Sąjunga*—TS). The TS is the current name of the party formerly known as the Homeland Union (Lithuanian Conservatives) (TS [*Lietuvos Konservatoriai*]—TS[LK]), which was launched on May 1, 1993, as a partial successor to the Lithuanian Reform Movement (*Sajūdis*), the party that had spearheaded the independence campaign. Under the leadership of Vytautas Landsbergis, the broadly based Sajūdis was the leading formation in the elections of February and March 1990 but in the face of economic adversity suffered a stinging defeat in 1992, winning only 20.5 percent of the vote. Although the TS(LK) presented itself as a right-of-center party, it indicated that its ranks would be open to former Communists.

Benefiting from the deep unpopularity of the then ruling LDDP, the TS(LK) rose to power in the fall 1996 election with a 30 percent vote share, but Landsbergis finished a disappointing third with 15.7 percent of the vote in the first round of the presidential balloting in December. The TS(LK) renewed its 1996 coalition agreement with the LKDP (see LKD, below) in January 1999; the LCS (below) also remained in the government until departing in November 1999, shortly after the TS(LK)'s Andrius Kubilius had been confirmed as prime minister, in succession to Rolandas Paksas.

Following a poor showing in the March 2000 local election, a group of about a dozen deputies loyal to former TS(LK) prime minister Gediminas Vagnorius established a Moderate Conservative faction within the *Seimas*, thereby costing the TS(LK) its majority status. Formation of the NKS splinter followed. In the October 2000 parliamentary election the TS(LK) won only one constituency seat but won eight more on an 8.6 percent proportional vote share.

In November 2003 the TS(LK) absorbed the LDS (below). In February the party dropped the "Lithuanian Conservatives" from its name and became known simply as the TS. In the October 2004 legislative balloting, the TS won 25 seats, thereby becoming the second-largest grouping in the *Seimas*. After DP deputies resigned from the government in May 2006, the LSPD-led government no longer controlled a legislative majority government without the cooperation of the TS, which remained outside the cabinet. The TS ended its official support for the government in September 2007.

Leaders: Andrius KUBILIUS (Prime Minister, Chair, and 2002 presidential candidate), Vytautas LANDSBERGIS (Former President of the Republic), Rasa JUKNEVIČIENĖ (Deputy Chair), Arvydas VIDŽIŪNAS (General Secretary), Jurgis RAZMA (Parliamentary Elder).

Lithuanian Rightist Union (*Lietuvos Dešiniųjų Sąjunga*—LDS). The LDS was formed in October 2001 by the merger of four small parties, none represented in the current Seimas: the Homeland People's Party (*Tėvynės Liaudies Partija*—TLP), the Independence Party (*Nepriklausombyės Partija*—NP), the Lithuanian Democratic Party (*Lietuvos Demokratų Partija*—LDP), and the Lithuanian Freedom League (*Lietuvos Laisvės Lyga*—LLL).

Leaders: Arūnas ŽEBRIŪNAS (Chair), Laima ANDRIKIENĖ (TLP), Saulius PEČELIŪNAS (LDP), Valentinas ŠAPALAS (NP), Antanas TERLECKAS (LLL).

Lithuanian Christian Democrats (*Lietuvos Krikščionys Demokratai*—LKD). The LKD was formed in May 2001 by merger of the LKDP and the Christian Democratic Union (*Krikščionių Demokratų Sąjunga*—KDS).

The LKDP had been organized in 1989 as the revival of a pre-Soviet party originally formed in 1905. It ran third in the 1992 balloting on a joint list with the Lithuanian Democratic Party (LDP; see LDS, above) and the Lithuanian Union of Political Prisoners and Deportees (LPKTS, below). It won a total of 16 seats, for second place, in 1996 and joined the TS(LK)-led coalition government. In the October 2000 election, however, it secured only 2 seats. A month later the party chair, Zigmas ZINKEVIČIUS, resigned over what he labeled as secret merger negotiations being conducted by the party's board chair, Algirdas SAUDARGAS, with the KDS. A smaller formation, the KDS had won a single parliamentary seat in 1992,

1996, and 2000; its deputy, Kazys Bobelis, had also won 4 percent of the vote in the 1997 presidential balloting. The LKD improved its performance in the 2007 local elections and augmented its influence through its May 2008 merger with the TS.

Leaders: Kazys BOBELIS (2002 and 2004 presidential candidate), Valentinas STUNDYS (Chair), Kazimieras KUZMINSKAS (Deputy Chair).

The Way of Courage (*Drasos Kelias*—DK). The DK is an anti-corruption party founded in 2012 by former judge Nergina VENCK-IENES, who started the political group after her brother was killed after he claimed the judiciary covered up a pedophile ring. In October 2012 it won seven seats with 8 percent of the vote.

Leader: Nergina VENCKIENES (President).

Lithuanian Republic Liberal Movement (*Lietuvos Respublikos Liberalų Sajūdis*—LRLS). Also widely referenced as simply the Liberal Movement, the LRLS was formed in early 2006 after nine LCS legislators rejected the leadership of LCS Chair and Vilnius Mayor Artūras Zoukas.

Despite the failure to present a united liberal ballot in the 2008 elections, the LRLS won 5.7 percent of votes and 11 seats and was included in the cabinet after joining the ruling coalition. The LRLS won 7.16 percent of votes and 1 seat in the 2009 European Parliament balloting.

Support for the LRLS grew through 2010, with the LCS viewed as the party more in need of a liberal merger. However, relations between the two factions remained poor, despite the removal of the divisive Artūra Zoukas from the LCS chair. In October 2012 the LRLS won 8.6 percent of the vote and 10 seats.

Leaders: Eligijus MASIULIS (Chair), Raimondas IMBRASAS (Secretary General).

Lithuanian National Farmers' Union (*Lietuvos Valstiečių Liaudininkų Sąjunga*—LVLS). The LVLS is the name adopted in February 2006 by the Union of the Peasants and New Democracy Parties (*Valstiečiųir Naujosios Demokratijos Partiju Sajunga*—VNDPS). The VNDPS had formed on December 15, 2001, by merger of the Lithuanian Peasants' Party (*Lietuvos Valstiečių Partija*—LVP) and the New Democracy Party (*Naujosios Demokratijos Partija*—NDP), which had formed a joint faction in the *Seimas* following the October 2000 election.

The LVP, which traced its origins to 1905, had been revived as the Lithuanian Peasants' Union (*Lietuvos Valstiečių Sąjunga*—LVS) in 1990 and adopted the LVP designation in 1994. It won one constituency seat in the 1996 parliamentary election, then four in 2000. In March 2001 the party suffered a split when a delegation from Kaunas was not seated at a party congress because two of its leaders had been expelled the previous month for criticizing the leadership of the party chair, Ramūnas Karbauskis. Most of the Kaunas delegation reportedly joined the LSDP in protest. The LVP subsequently helped confirm Prime Minister Brazauskas.

The NDP had been launched as the Lithuanian Women's Party (*Lietuvos Moterų Partija*—LMP) in February 1995 under the leadership of Kazimiera Prunskienė, former head of the Soviet-era Association of Women of Lithuania as well as prime minister in 1990 and 1991. In 1992 the Lithuanian Supreme Court ruled that she had been a conscious collaborator with the KGB, which she denied. The LMP won one seat in the 1996 election, after which it adopted the NDP designation. In 2000 the NDP campaigned as part of the ABSK coalition. It won two single-member constituency seats and one proportional seat but left the coalition shortly thereafter.

In the legislative elections in October 2004, the VNDPS alliance won 6.6 percent of the popular vote and ten seats. Kazimiera Prunskienė, the party's candidate, won 47.4 percent of votes in the second round of presidential elections in June 2004, dipping to 3.9 percent in the first round of presidential elections in May 2009. The party held three parliamentary seats following the 2008 balloting and won 1.83 percent of votes in the 2009 European Parliament elections. In October 2012 balloting, the party was reduced to 1 seat, and received 3.9 percent of the vote.

Leaders: Ramūnas KARBAUSKIS (President), Kazimiera Danutė PRUNSKIENĖ (Honorary Chair and presidential candidate in 2004 and 2009).

Other Parties Contesting the 2012 Election:

Liberal and Center Union (*Liberalųir Centro Sąjunga*—LCS). Formed in March 2003 as an electoral coalition of the three parties below, the LCS is also referred to as the Liberal Centrists. LCS leader Artūra ZOUKAS was reelected as mayor of Vilnius in June 2003, though he later faced allegations that he accepted bribes in exchange for municipal influence. In response, nine LCS legislators rejected Zoukas's leadership and formed the new LRLS (below). The party shares the same abbreviation with the LCS, one of its three founding parties.

The LCS gained 18 seats in the October 2004 legislative elections but saw its representation fall to eight seats and 5.3 percent of votes in the 2008 elections. Following the expulsion of LLS members by the LCS members, the union was in ruins in 2009, despite the exit of the combative former LCS chair, Artūra Zoukas, who did not stand for reelection during the LCS congress on June 27, 2009 (see LCS, below). Both major parties retained an electoral interest in preserving the coalition, although party members charged that the leadership prolonged divisions in order to preserve their positions in the existing hierarchies. The LCS lost both of its seats in the June European parliamentary elections. Its representation in the national parliament appeared increasingly tenuous from 2010, as defections reduced the government majority and threatened to dissolve the party's parliamentary group. In 2011 the LCS merged with the TPP, which had also seen depleted membership (below). The party won 2.1 percent of the vote in October 2012, but no seats.

Leader: Artūras MELIANAS (CHAIR).

Lithuanian Liberal Union (Lietuvos Liberalų Sąjunga—LLS). The founding congress of the moderately right-wing LLS took place in November 1990, but the party failed to win any parliamentary seats in 1992. In 1996 it garnered one. Following a solid performance in the March 1997 local elections, the LLS attempted to position itself as a leader of Lithuanian centrists, broadening its appeal beyond its base in the business community. In December 1999 former Prime Minister Rolandas Paksas, having resigned from the TS(LK), joined the LLS and quickly ascended to the position of party chair.

In the October 2000 election, the party made major gains, winning 17.3 percent of the proportional vote, second only to the ABSK. The LLS then led the New Policy bloc in forming a government under Paksas (see Political background, above), but the coalition dissolved in June 2001 when the NS(SL) parted ways with the LLS. In early September, pressured by the party's governing body, Paksas resigned as party chair. In late December 2001 Paksas and 10 other deputies announced that they intended to leave the LLS. In March the LLS defectors formed the LDP (see UTT, below). The then chair, Eligijus MASIULIS, saw the former chair of the LCS, Artūra Zoukas, as an obstacle to complete the union with the LCS, and he subsequently joined the LRLS, which was formed in 2006.

Progress in reuniting with the LCS seemed more likely with the ascendance of Gintautas BABRAVIČIUS, Zoukas's successor, who was viewed as less divisive. The leadership for the LLS appeared to be vacant following Masiulis's switch to the LRLS.

Lithuanian Center Union (*Lietuvos Centro Sąjunga*—LCS). The LCS originated in 1992 as the Lithuanian Center Movement (*Lietuvos Centro Judėjimas*—LCJ), which contested the 1992 election on a promarket platform and won two *Seimas* seats. Registered as the LCS in 1993, the party went on to win 13 seats in 1996 and then joined the center-right TS(LK) coalition government in December. In the subsequent presidential election it backed Valdas Adamkus.

In November 1999 LCS Chair Romualdas OZOLAS announced that the LCS was breaking with the government; in response, the LCS minister of justice, Gintautas Babravičius, left the party and remained in the cabinet. In the October 2000 election the LCS won only two seats, which led to Ozolas's resignation. As part of the New Policy bloc, it joined the second Paksas government. In June 2009 Gintautas Babravičius, then the deputy mayor of Vilinus, assumed the chairmanship. Babravičius emphasized the strategic advantages of a full merger of the LCS constituent parties.

Modern Christian Democratic Union (*Moderniųjų Krikščionių Demokratų Sąjunga*—MKDS). The constituent congress of the MKDS was held in April 2000 following the decision of the "modern" faction of the LKDP to part ways with the "conservative" faction. The MKDS has now been absorbed into the LCS.

National Revival Party (*Tautos Prisikėlimo Partijos*—TPP). Founded in May 2008 by entertainment producer and personality Arūnas Valinskas, the TPP sought to capitalize on voter apathy toward parliamentary parties and advance a centrist program in support of strategic relationships with Europe and the United States. The TPP announced that it would "seek to have Lithuania become a leader among the Baltic States." The party's first congress lacked the required 1,000 founding members, despite generally positive attitudes toward the party among the public and the support of many Lithuanian celebrities. However, the party filed the required papers with the justice ministry in June 2008, targeting disaffected voters in order to prevent UTT chair Rolandas Paksas from returning to power in a populist revolt. The new party proved remarkably successful in its first balloting in October of that year, securing 15.1 percent of votes, 16 seats, and three cabinet portfolios as a member of the ruling coalition. The TPP chair, Arūnas Valinskas, was named speaker of the *Seimas* and is a noted celebrity, having starred in TV shows for 22 years and organized the first beauty contest for a women's prison in Lithuania, Miss Captivity.

Despite initial momentum, the TPP won only 1 percent of the votes in the June 2009 European Parliament elections, in which 20.9 percent of the Lithuanian electorate voted. That result diminished the chair's political stature, leading to his loss of the speaker's position in September 2009. (The opposition UTT had called for his removal based on allegations that he had met with a gang member, and his own party did not uniformly support him against the motion.) Valinskas subsequently ousted 13 of the 20 TPP parliamentary members from the party in August 2010, calling into question the stability of the government. Internal divisions threatened to dismantle the TPP faction in parliament entirely, as it relied excessively on leaders' personalities and lacked a cohesive political platform. In 2011 the TPP formally merged with the LCS.

Christian Party (Krikščionių Partijos—KPF). Largely composed of conservative TS-LKD and TPP dissidents, who support a platform that favors Christian cultural values, the KPF adopted its current designation early in 2010. (Many KPF members identify themselves as independents.) The party was previously known as One Lithuania, which had not held parliamentary representation immediately following the most recent legislative balloting but was subsequently formed as a legislative faction by TPP defectors after poor TPP results in the 2009 EU elections.

Party leaders had been appointed for regional branches by August 2010, but no national officials had been announced apart from the parliamentary elders. The party was officially relaunched with the merger of the **Christian Conservative Social Union** (*Krikščionių Konservatorių Socialinė Sąjunga*—KKSS), which won 2 percent of the vote in the 2008 legislative balloting, with the LKDP in January 2011.

Leaders: Vidmantas ŽIEMELIS (Parliamentary Elder), Jonas STANEVIČIUS (First Deputy Elder), Albinas PILIPAUSKAS (Spokesperson).

Socialist People's Front (*Socialistinis Liaudies Frontas*—SLF). The SLF launched in February 2010 upon the merger of the **Front Party** (*Frontas Partija*) and the **Lithuanian Socialist Party** (*Lietuvos Socialistu Partija*). The leftist Front Party was founded in May 2008 by Algirdas Paleckis, an LSDP dissident. The new party promoted "milder" redistributive policies and indexed wages and pensions based on inflation, and won 2.37 percent of votes in the June 2009 European Parliament elections, garnering a seat for its chair. In October 2013 the party won 1.21 percent of the vote and no seats.

Leader: Algirdas PALECKIS.

YES (*Tevynes Atgimimas Ir Perspektyva*—TAIP). The TAIP is a center-right party launched in 2011 by Vilnius mayor Artūras ZUOKAS, dedicated to "responsible liberalism."

Leader: Artūras ZUOKAS (President).

"Young Lithuanians," New Nationalists and Political Prisoners Union (*"Jaunosios Lietuvos," Naujųjų Tautininkų ir Politinių Kalinių Sąjunga*—JLNTPKS). Previously known as the Lithuanian National Party "Young Lithuania" (*Lietuvių Nacionalinė Partija "Jaunoji Lietuva"*), the rightist JLNTPKS retained its one parliamentary seat in the October 2000 election, but won no seats in 2004 despite fielding five candidates for single-member districts. The grouping won 1.75 percent of the vote in the 2008 legislative elections and 0.6 percent in 2012.

Leader: Stanislovas BUŠKEVIČIUS (Chair).

Five other parties contested the 2012 elections, all of which received less than 1 percent of the vote: For Lithuania in Lithuania (*Uz Lietuva Lietuvoje*), a four-party coalition led by Birute VALIONYTE; Democratic Labor and Unity Party (*Demokratine Darbo ir Vienybes Partija*—DDVP); Emigrant Party (*Emigrantu Partija*); Republican Party (*Respublikonu Partija*); and the Lithuanian People's Party (*Lietuvos Zmoniu Partija*).

Other Parties:

Civil Democracy Party (*Pilietinės Demokratijos Partija*—PDP). The PDP was formed in mid-2006 by legislators from the DP (who were dissatisfied with the leadership of the DP's former chair, Viktor Uspaskich, and related DP scandals) and the LDP. The party continued to command limited support ahead of the 2008 elections and failed to secure any seats in the October 2008 elections or the June 2009 European Parliament election, in which it won 1.31 percent of votes. The party has since dissolved.

Leader: Algimantas MATULEVIČIUS (President).

Samogitians Party (*Zematis Partija*). Founded to advance the Samogitian dialect for professional, official, and private use, as well as to secure recognition of the Samogitians as a distinct nationality, the party was denied registration due to low support in 2008. The justice ministry also argued that the party's platform, if realized, could lead to federalism by granting official recognition to a regional minority language. The party won 1.23 percent of votes in the 2009 European Parliament balloting.

Party of Trade Unions (*Sąjunga Partija*). Founded in 2008 by former social democrat Kęstutis Juknis, the party registered with the ministry of justice in June of that year, aiming to become the primary political party for Lithuania's trade unions.

Leader: Kęstutis JUKNIS (Founder and Chair).

Other parties contesting recent elections included the **Lithuanian Center Party** (*Lietuvos Centro Partija*—LCP), and the **Lithuanian Russian Union** (*Lietuvos Rusų Sąjunga*—LRS), both of which won less than 1 percent.

(For details on minor parties contesting earlier elections, see the 2008, 2009, and 2010 *Handbooks*.)

LEGISLATURE

The former Supreme Council (*Aukščiausioji Taryba*) was redesignated as the **Parliament** (*Seimas*) on July 7, 1992, with a complement of 141 members, of whom 71 are currently elected from single-member constituencies and 70 are elected from party lists by proportional representation subject to a 5 percent threshold. Under changes enacted in June 1996, voters became entitled, with effect from the fall 1996 election, to record a preference for individual candidates on the party lists.

The election on October 14 and 28, 2012, produced the following totals: the Lithuanian Social Democratic Party secured 38 seats; Homeland Union-Lithuanian Christian Democrats, 33; the Labor Party, 29; the For Order and Justice coalition, 12; the Lithuanian Republic Liberal Movement, 10; Lithuanian Poles' Electoral Action, 8; The Way of Courage, 7; Lithuanian National Farmers' Union, 1; and independents, 3.

Speaker: Vydas GEDVILAS.

CABINET

[as of September 15, 2013]

Prime Minister	Algirdas Butkevicius (LSDP)
Ministers	
Agriculture	Vigilijus Jukna (DP)
Culture	Sarunas Birutis (DP)
Economy	Evaldas Gustas (LSDP)
Education and Science	Dainius Pavalkis (DP)
Energy	Jaroslav Neverovic (LLRA)
Environment	Valentinas Mazuronis (UTT)
Finance	Rimantas Sadzius (LSDP)
Foreign Affairs	Linas Antanas Linkevicius (LSDP)

Health	Vytenis Povilas Andriukaitis (LSDP)
Interior	Dailis Alfonsas Barakauskas (UTT)
Justice	Juozas Bernatonis (LSDP)
National Defense	Juozas Olekas (LSDP)
Social Security and Labor	Algimanta Pabedinskiene (DP) [f]
Transportation and Communication	Rimantas Sinkevicius (LSDP)

[f] = female

INTERGOVERNMENTAL REPRESENTATION

Ambassador to the U.S.: Žygimantas PAVILIONIS.

U.S. Ambassador to Lithuania: Deborah McCARTHY.

Permanent Representative to the UN: Raimonda MURMOKAITĖ.

IGO Memberships (Non-UN): CEUR, EBRD, EIB, EU, ICC, IOM, NATO, OSCE, WTO.

LUXEMBOURG

Grand Duchy of Luxembourg
Grousherzogdem Lëzebuerg (Letzeburgish)
Grand-Duché de Luxembourg (French)
Grossherzogtum Luxemburg (German)

Note: After Prime Minister Jean-Claude Junker announced his resignation on July 11, 2013, early elections were held for the Chamber of Deputies on October 20. The Christian Social People's Party won 23 seats, the Socialist Worker's Party and the Democratic Party each on 13 seats apiece, while the Greens won 6 seats, the Alternative Democratic Reform Party won 3, and the Left won 2. On October 25, Democratic Party leader Xavier Bettel was asked to create a new government in coalition with the Greens and the Socialists. Bettel was sworn in as prime minister on December 4. Both Bettel and his vice prime minister, Socialist Workers' Party head Etienne Schneider are openly gay, raising expectations for social reform.

Political Status: Constitutional monarchy, fully independent since 1867; in economic union with Belgium since 1922.

Area: 998 sq. mi. (2,586 sq. km).

Population: 512,353 (2013E—UN); 514,862 (2013E—U.S. Census).

Major Urban Centers (2013E): LUXEMBOURG-VILLE (Lützelburg, 103,641), Esch-sur-Alzette (31,898).

Official Language: Letzeburgish. As a general rule, French is used for administrative purposes, and German for commerce.

Monetary Unit: Euro (market rate November 1, 2013: 0.74 euro = $1US).

Sovereign: Grand Duke HENRI; ascended to the throne October 7, 2000, on the abdication of his father, Grand Duke JEAN.

Heir Apparent: Prince GUILLAUME, son of the grand duke; proclaimed by the grand duke on December 18, 2000.

President of the Government (Prime Minister): (*See headnote.*) Jean-Claude JUNCKER (Christian Social People's Party); sworn in as the head of a Christian Social–Socialist Workers' coalition by the grand duke on January 20, 1995, succeeding Jacques SANTER (Christian Social People's Party) on the latter's appointment as president of the European Commission; sworn in again on August 7, 1999, following election of June 13 and negotiation of a coalition with the Democratic Party; sworn in for a third term on August 2, 2004, after legislative elections on June 13 and the approval of a revived Christian Social–Socialist Workers' coalition; sworn in for a fourth term on July 23, 2009, after legislative elections on June 7 and approval of another Christian Social–Socialist Workers' coalition.

THE COUNTRY

Located southeast of Belgium between France and Germany, the small, landlocked Grand Duchy of Luxembourg is a predominantly Roman Catholic country whose native inhabitants exhibit an ethnic and cultural blend of French and German elements. Linguistically, both French and German are widely spoken; the local language, Letzeburgish, is a West Frankish dialect. About one-third of the population now consists of immigrants, while a tight labor market has benefited *fortaliers,* cross-border workers from neighboring countries.

Luxembourg is highly industrialized. Iron and steel products have long been mainstays of the economy and still account for nearly one-third of total exports. In the mid-1970s, economic diversification efforts focused on the production of rubber, synthetic fibers, plastics, chemicals, and small metal products. More recently, the government has encouraged high-tech sectors, including satellite services, broadband access, and e-commerce. Luxembourg also became an international financial center, which accounted for 28 percent of GDP, one-third of tax revenue, and 20 percent of the workforce in 2012. Stock transactions, insurance, and reinsurance have also become of major importance, and Luxembourg-based firms were managing €2.5 trillion in assets in early 2013. Women held 12 of 60 seats in the Chamber of Deputies following the 2009 election. Four of the current 15 government ministers are women, occupying 8 of 28 ministries. Agriculture, which occupies only 2 percent of the labor force, consists primarily of small farms devoted to livestock raising, although viticulture is also of some prominence. Trade is largely oriented toward Luxembourg's neighbors and fellow participants in the Benelux Economic Union and the European Union (EU, formerly the European Community—EC).

Until recently, Luxembourg typically enjoyed one of the lowest budget deficits in the EU (approximately 1 percent of GDP) and one of the lowest unemployment rates. After a downturn in 2005, the economy returned to its robust state until the global financial turmoil of 2008 pulled it into a recession. Real GDP growth fell to 0 percent in 2008 and declined by 3.4 percent in 2009, marking Luxembourg's worst economic performance in 30 years. (For more information on the economy prior to 2008, please see the 2013 *Handbook*.) Unemployment grew to 7.8 percent in 2011, up from 6.0 percent in 2010 but dropped to 6.0 percent in 2012. The economy continued to register positive—if slight—growth, at 0.1 percent GDP in 2012, down from 3.0 percent in 2011. In April 2013 the head of the European Central Bank warned that Luxembourg's oversized banking sector make it highly exposed to the expanding euro debt crisis and suggested that it might face a financial crisis similar to that of Cyprus.

GOVERNMENT AND POLITICS

Political background. For centuries Luxembourg was dominated and occupied by foreign powers, until the Congress of Vienna in 1815 declared it a grand duchy subject to the king of the Netherlands. On Belgium's secession from the Netherlands in 1830, the greater part of Luxembourg went with it (today constituting the Belgian province of the same name); the remainder was recognized as an autonomous neutral state in 1867 and came under the present ruling house of Nassau-Weilbourg in 1890, when the link with the Netherlands was formally severed. An economic union with Belgium was established in 1922, but Luxembourg retains its independent political institutions under a constitution dating from 1868.

Since World War II political power has been exercised by a series of coalition governments in which the Christian Social People's Party (*Chrëschtlech Sozial Vollekspartei*—CSV) has traditionally been the dominant element. For 15 years beginning in 1959, the government was led by Pierre WERNER, who formed coalitions with both the Socialist Workers' Party of Luxembourg (*Lëtzebuergesch Sozialistesch Arbechterpartei*—LSAP) and the Democratic Party (*Demokratesch Partei*—DP). A month after the 1974 election, however, the latter two formed a new government under DP leader Gaston THORN. After the 1979 election a fairly lengthy period of intraparty negotiation resulted in the formation of a CSV-DP government and the return of Werner as prime minister.

Following the 1984 election, in which the CSV remained the largest party but the LSAP registered the greatest gain, a new round of negotiations led to a revived center-left CSV-LSAP coalition under former finance minister Jacques SANTER. In the 1989 poll, the three leading parties lost three seats each, with Santer forming a new bipartisan government after the CSV had retained its plurality in the Chamber of Deputies.

Economic policy questions dominated the campaigning for the 1994 national elections, which produced only marginal shifts in the party balance. A month later, in July, Prime Minister Santer was unexpectedly named the compromise choice to take over the European Commission presidency in January 1995. His successor as prime minister was another CSV finance minister, Jean-Claude JUNCKER.

In the June 1999 election both governing parties suffered losses, enabling the DP to negotiate an agreement with the CSV that brought it into the government for the first time in 15 years.

On October 7, 2000, Grand Duke JEAN, who had reigned since his mother's abdication in 1964, stepped aside in favor of his son, Grand Duke HENRI. In preparation for his accession, Henri had been designated as his father's "lieutenant-representative" in 1998. In December 2000 he followed tradition and named his eldest son, Prince GUILLAUME, as heir apparent.

The grand duke's political role is primarily ceremonial. In February 2008 parliament passed a bill legalizing euthanasia and assisted suicide for the terminally ill, putting Luxembourg's stance in line with Belgium and Netherlands. The bill was subsequently vetoed by the grand duke, but the Chamber nullified the veto and, in December 2008, approved a constitutional amendment removing the grand duke's veto power.

Juncker and the CSV have dominated politics in the 21st century. The CSV decisively won the June 13, 2004, legislative elections with 24 of the 60 available seats, and Juncker announced a new coalition government with the LSAP on July 31. In the June 7, 2009, balloting the CSV won a 26-seat plurality and, after a month of negotiations, formed another coalition government with the LSAP, sworn in on July 23 with Juncker again as prime minister. Juncker's victory was attributed to his adept handling of the country's financial affairs and his efforts to resolve the controversy over the grand duchy's bank secrecy laws by agreeing to assist foreign authorities in pursuing tax evaders. His impeccable reputation was severely damaged by a scandal with the national intelligence agency in late 2012 (see Current issues, below).

On October 20, 2012, Heir Apparent Grand Duke Guillaume married Countess Stéphanie de Lannoy at the Cathedrale de Notre-Dame in Luxembourg-Ville.

Juncker reshuffled his cabinet in April 2013, when Minister of Justice Francois Biltgen resigned to join the European Union Court of Justice and Marie Josée Jacobs retired.

Constitution and government. Luxembourg's 1868 constitution has been repeatedly revised to incorporate democratic reforms, to eliminate the former status of "perpetual neutrality," and to permit devolution of sovereignty to international institutions. Executive authority is exercised on behalf of the grand duke by the prime minister and the cabinet, who are appointed by the sovereign but are responsible to the legislature. Legislative authority rests primarily with the elected Chamber of Deputies, although until 2008 the grand duke could veto laws. A nonelective Council of State serves as an advisory body to the Chamber. Deputies are elected on a proportional basis from four electoral constituencies (north, center, south, and east).

The judicial system is headed by the Superior Court of Justice and includes a Court of Assizes for serious criminal offenses, district courts, and justices of the peace. There are also administrative and special social courts and, since 1996, a Constitutional Court. Judges are appointed for life by the grand duke. The country is divided into 3 districts, 12 cantons, and 116 communes. The districts function as links between the central and local governments and are headed by commissioners appointed by the central government.

All news media are privately owned and free from censorship, and Luxembourg was ranked fourth by Reporters Without Borders in 2013.

Foreign relations. Luxembourg's former neutral status was abandoned after the German occupation of World War II. The country was a founding member of the United Nations (UN) and a leader in the postwar consolidation of the West through its membership in Benelux, the North Atlantic Treaty Organization (NATO), the EC/EU, and other multilateral organizations. Relations with Belgium have long been close.

Luxembourg enjoys a prominent role in EU affairs. The secretariat of the European Parliament is located in the country, as is the EU Court of Justice and EU Court of Auditors. Prime Minister Juncker chaired the Eurogroup, comprised of all eurozone ministers of finance, from its creation in 2005 until January 2013, when he stepped aside, citing exhaustion. Yves MERSCH, former Luxembourg Central Bank chief, was appointed to the six-member governing board of the European Central Bank in July 2012.

In 1992 the Chamber of Deputies overwhelmingly approved the EU's Maastricht Treaty. During negotiations of the EU's Treaty of Nice in 2000, Luxembourg joined other small EU states in trying to retain their long-standing level of influence and power in view of planned EU expansion. Prime Minister Juncker, who assumed the six-month presidency of the EU's European Council in January 2005, put his political career on the line by announcing that he would resign as prime minister if voters did not approve the proposed EU constitution. The July 10 national referendum on the question produced a 56.5 percent "yes" vote, making Luxembourg one of the few countries in which a direct popular vote approved the controversial EU initiative.

Luxembourg has continued to support both NATO and the development of an autonomous European security and defense identity. The Juncker government approved NATO expansion at the 2002 Prague summit. Meanwhile, Luxembourg provided a 180-person reconnaissance unit as part of the European Rapid Reaction Force operations in Bosnia, Kosovo, and Afghanistan. Drawing on its telecommunications industry, Luxembourg has developed "emergency.lu," a mobile satellite communications platform available for use to relief workers during humanitarian crises. It has also supported increased European cooperation on defense-industrial issues, including the design and production of military aircraft and major arms systems. While Luxembourg strongly opposed the U.S./UK-led invasion of Iraq in 2003, it has not opposed bidding on U.S. military contracts. The U.S. military currently uses imagery provided by satellite companies based in Luxembourg to guide drone attacks in Afghanistan and Pakistan.

Luxembourg faced challenges in the early 2000s regarding how its financial sector operated. Within the EU, the United Kingdom and France were particularly vocal in fighting for full information exchange between national tax authorities as the best means of stopping tax evasion on savings income, whereas Luxembourg argued that maintaining its banking secrecy was a necessity to avoid flight of investment accounts to offshore facilities. In January 2001 Luxembourgian banks began withholding taxes on investments from U.S. sources. In 2003 Luxembourg reached a compromise agreement with the EU under which a withholding tax would be phased in at 15 percent in 2004, rising to 35 percent by 2010. Luxembourg, together with Austria and Switzerland, agreed in March 2009 to loosen secrecy laws and cooperate with foreign tax authorities.

Current issues. Yielding to international pressure, the Juncker government agreed to substantial changes in the country's financial practices in April 2013. First, Juncker announced that Luxembourg would begin automatically sharing account information with U.S. (but not EU) tax authorities on January 1, 2015. The move constituted a major policy shift regarding bank secrecy. The government also withdrew its May 15, 2012, objections to allowing the EU to begin debate on revising a savings account tax agreement involving Switzerland, Liechtenstein, Monaco, Andorra, and San Marino. Once a new treaty is reached with those five countries, Luxembourg will likely consider automatic data sharing within the EU framework. Second, after consistently resisting requests for value-added tax (VAT) reforms that would bring it in line with other EU members, Juncker announced that the country would raise its VAT on January 1, 2015. He did not mention a specific rate, only an intention to remain the lowest in the EU. Analysts believe the new level will likely be 16 or 17 percent, slightly about the current 15 percent VAT, to avoid an exodus of the large telecom and electronic commerce industries, such as Apple Computer and Amazon.com that have their European headquarters in Luxembourg and contribute some €300 million ($225 million) annually to government coffers. Effective January 1, 2012, Luxembourg slashed the VAT on e-books from 15 percent to 3 percent, triggering a lawsuit by the European Court of Justice.

The Juncker government is working to protect other vital economic sectors as well. In July 2012 Finance Minister Etienne SCHNEIDER announced that Luxembourg, France, and Belgium would launch a joint effort to prevent steel giant ArcelorMittel, the largest private employer in Luxembourg, from closing additional facilities in Europe. The European Union also warned the company to not go through with its planned layoffs. In February 2013 EU investigators traced the horsemeat found in frozen lasagnas sold in Europe to a Luxembourg-based factory, potentially damaging the country's food service sector.

Juncker's government was rocked by scandal in late 2012 when RTL television and radio revealed that the former head of the SREL intelligence service, Marco MILLE, had secretly taped a conversation with the prime minister in January 2007. Further investigation uncovered numerous instances of illegal wire tapping of politicians and journalists between 2007 and 2009 as well as possible official links to bomb attacks in the 1980s. Juncker's popularity dropped from 85 percent in April 2012 to 73 percent in April 2013, behind Luxembourg Ville Mayor Xavier BETTEL (DP). In June Minister Juncker was called to testify before the parliamentary committee regarding lax oversight of the SREL. Juncker survived a no confidence vote called by the Greens and DP, the country's first in 150 years.

On July 10, 2013, the parliamentary investigatory committee held Juncker responsible for the SREL's actions, suggesting he was too involved in Eurogroup activities to adequately supervise the secret service. Juncker replied, "The intelligence service was not my top priority." All opposition parties plus the LSAP voted to approve the report. Juncker submitted his resignation to Grande Duke Henri on July 11 and requested elections in October, eight months early.

POLITICAL PARTIES

With an electoral system based on proportional representation, for decades Luxembourg has been ruled by coalition governments headed by the Christian Social People's Party or the Democratic Party allied with each other or with the Socialist Workers' Party.

Government Parties:

Christian Social People's Party (*Chrëschtlech Sozial Vollekspartei*—CSV/*Parti Chrétien Social*—PCS). Formed in 1914, Luxembourg's strongest single party traditionally drew its main support from farmers, Catholic laborers, and moderate conservatives. Often identified as a Christian Democratic grouping, the CSV endorses a centrist position that includes support for the monarchy, progressive labor legislation, assistance to farmers and small business owners, church-state cooperation, and an internationalist foreign policy. The dominant partner in most postwar coalitions, the CSV most recently won 38.0 percent of the vote and 26 seats in the June 7, 2009, election. Jean-Claude Juncker, who has served as prime minister since 1995 (making him Europe's longest-serving leader), subsequently formed another coalition government with the LSAP.

Leaders: Jean-Claude JUNCKER (Prime Minister); Michel WOLTER (President); Octavie MODERT, Claude WISELER (Vice Presidents), Gilles Roth (Head of Parliamentary Group).

Socialist Workers' Party of Luxembourg (*Lëtzebuergesch Sozialistesch Arbechterpartei*—LSAP/*Parti Ouvrier Socialiste Luxembourgeois*—POSL). Founded in 1902, the LSAP draws its major support from urban lower- and lower-middle-class voters, particularly those affiliated with trade unions. It advocates extension of the present system of social legislation and social insurance, and supports European integration, NATO, and the UN. In 1971 a conservative wing split off to form the Social Democratic Party, which was dissolved in 1983.

After 15 years of government partnership with the CSV, in 1999 the LSAP finished third in the balloting and returned to opposition as Prime Minister Juncker established a center-right government with the second place DP. Following the election of June 13, 2004, the LSAP was again invited to form a coalition government with the CSV. The coalition was renewed following the 2009 balloting, in which the LSAP won 21.6 percent of the vote and 13 seats. Etienne SCHNEIDER, minister of economy and foreign trade, will head the LSAP list for the 2013 parliamentary election.

Leaders: Alex BODRY (President); Jean ASSELBORN (Minister of Foreign Affairs); Michèle DIEDERICH, Georges ENGEL (Vice Presidents); Yves CRUCHTEN (Secretary General).

Opposition Parties:

Democratic Party (*Demokratesch Partei*—DP/*Parti Démocratique*—PD). The DP includes both conservatives and moderates and draws support from professional, business, white-collar, and artisan groups. Also referred to as the Liberals, the party is committed to free enterprise, although it favors certain forms of progressive social legislation. It is mildly anticlerical and strongly pro-NATO. It participated in the Werner government prior to the 1984 election, after which it went into opposition. It won 11 Chamber seats in 1989 and 12 in 1994. Having moved ahead of the Socialist Workers' Party in the June 1999 election, winning 15 seats, the DP negotiated a coalition agreement with the CSV. In the June 13, 2004, elections the DP fell to 16.1 percent of the vote and 10 seats, and it declined further in the 2009 balloting to 15.0 percent of the vote and 9 seats. Popular Luxembourg-Ville mayor Xavier BETTEL was chosen to lead the DP at the February 2013 party congress.

Leaders: Xavier BETTEL (President); M. Charles GOERENS (First Vice President); Claudia MONTI, Maggy NAGEL (Vice Presidents); Claude MEISCH (Head of Parliamentary Group); Fernand ETGEN (Secretary General).

Alternative Democratic Reform Party (*Alternativ Demokratesch Reformpartei/Parti Réformiste d'Alternative Démocratique*—ADR). This party was initially organized in 1957 as the Five-Sixths Action Committee (*Aktiounskomitee "5/6-Pensioun fir Jidfereen"*), the name referencing its support for an across-the-board introduction in the private sector of pensions worth five-sixths of final salary (the level then operative for public employees). In November 1992 it adopted the name Action Committee for Democracy and Pension Justice (*Aktiounskomitee fir Demokratie a Rentengerechtegkeet—ADR/Comité d'Action pour la Démocratie et la Justice Sociale*—CADJS). After winning five Chamber seats in 1994, seven in 1999, and five in 2004, the party in 2006 changed its name again (to the current form) in an apparent attempt to foster a broader position in mainstream politics. The ADR won four seats on 8.1 percent of the vote in the 2009 balloting. Party President Fernand KARTHEISER, elected in March 2012, resigned in December 2012 following in-fighting over the party's platform. In June 2013 Kartheiser was revealed to have been a spy for both the United States and USSR in the 1980s.

Leaders: Jean SCHOOS (President); Carlo KIRSCH, Michèle RETTER, Roy REDING, Marceline GOERGEN (Vice Presidents); Liliana MIRANDA (Secretary General).

The Greens (*Déi Gréng/Les Verts*). Organized at a June 1983 congress as the Green Alternative (*Gréng Alternativ Partei/Parti Vert-Alternatif*), The Greens won two legislative seats in 1984 but in 1986 suffered a major split. The party again won two seats in 1989 and then added three more in 1994 before reuniting with the Green Ecological Initiative List (*Gréng Lëscht Ekologesch Initiativ*—GLEI) in 1995. Its current program advocates environmental protection, democracy, social justice, human rights, and similar causes. In the June 1999 election it won five seats in the Chamber of Deputies, and it won seven seats in 2004 and 2009.

Leaders: François BAUSCH (Parliamentary Group President); Christian KMIOTEK, Sam Tanson (Copresidents).

The Left (*Déi Lénk/La Gauche*). The constituent congress of The Left took place on January 30, 1999, culminating efforts to overcome previous cleavages and organize political forces to the left of the social democratic DP and The Greens. Participants included the KPL (below), DP dissidents, trade unionists, and members of other small left-wing parties, including the Revolutionary Socialist Party (*Parti Socialiste Révolutionnaire*—PSR) and the New Left (*Neue Linke/Nouvelle Gauche*—MNG). In the legislative election of June 1999 the new grouping won one seat in the Chamber of Deputies. In local balloting in Esch-sur-Alzette in April 2000, The Left finished third, with 12.8 percent of the vote, enabling it to join a majority coalition with the DP and The Greens. The Left's André HOFFMAN resigned his seat in the Chamber of Deputies to join Esch-sur-Alzette's council of aldermen, with the KPL's Aloyse BISDORFF thereupon succeeding him in the national legislature. Bisdorff was subsequently succeeded by Serge URBANY. The Left received 1.9 percent of the vote in the June 2004 elections but won no seats. Its vote percentage rose to 3.3 in the 2009 balloting, resulting in The Left winning one seat.

The Left has no formal leadership positions; the organization's first ordinary congress in May 2000 elected a 45-member *Nationale Koordination/Coordination Nationale,* which subsequently selected an 11-member *Koordinationsbüro/Bureau de Coordination.*

Other Parties Contesting the 2009 Legislative Elections:

Communist Party of Luxembourg (*Kommunistesch Partei vu Lëtzebuerg*—KPL/*Parti Communiste Luxembourgeois*—PCL). Established in 1921, the historically pro-Soviet KPL draws its main support from urban and industrial workers and some intellectuals. It advocates full nationalization of the economy and was the only Western European Communist party to approve the Soviet invasion of Czechoslovakia in 1968. The KPL suffered a loss of three of its five parliamentary seats in the 1979 election, retaining the two that remained in 1984. Its longtime leader, René URBANY, died in 1990, and the party lost its sole remaining Chamber seat in 1994. Many Communist Party officials joined The Left party after the 1994 elections, and the KPL decided not to contest the elections. The KPL received only 0.9 percent of the vote in the 2004 legislative poll and 1.5 percent in 2009.

Leader: Ali RUCKERT (President).

Citizens' List (*Biergerlëscht/Liste des Citoyens*). Formed in early 2009 in anticipation of the June elections, Citizens' List displayed a decidedly single-issue focus on increased pension rights. The party placed two candidates on the 2009 ballot. One was Aly Jaerling, a former ADR member of parliament who left the ADR in 2006 to sit as an independent in protest over the ADR's decision to broaden its issue focus beyond pensions and in objection to the ADR's nationalist appeals. The other was Jean Ersfeld, former leader of the now defunct FPL (see below). Neither candidate was elected, as the Citizens' List won only 0.8 percent of the vote.

Leader: Aly JAERLING.

Other Parties:

Party for Integral Democracy (*Partei fir Integral Demokratie—PID*). Formed in June 2013 by former ADR politician Jean COLOMBERA to give ordinary people a voice in politics.

Free Party of Luxembourg (*Frai Partei Lëtzebuerg*—FPL). Led by Jean ERSFELD, the FPL received 0.12 percent of the vote in the June 2004 elections. However, it did not field candidates in 2009 and is now defunct.

LEGISLATURE

Legislative responsibility is centered in the elected Chamber of Deputies, but the appointive Council of State retains some vestigial legislative functions.

Council of State (*Der Staatsrat/Conseil d'État*). The council consists of 21 members appointed for life; 7 are appointed directly by the grand duke, while the others are appointed by him on proposal of the council itself or of the Chamber of Deputies.

President: Georges SCHROEDER.

Chamber of Deputies (*Chamber vum Deputéirten/Châmbre des Députés*). The Chamber currently consists of 60 deputies elected for five-year terms (subject to dissolution) by direct universal suffrage on the basis of proportional representation.

In the June 7, 2009, elections the Christian Social People's Party won 26 seats; the Socialist Workers' Party of Luxembourg, 13; the Democratic Party, 9; the Greens, 7; the Alternative Democratic Reform Party, 4; and The Left, 1.

President: Laurent MOSAR.

CABINET

[as of June 21, 2013]

Prime Minister and Minister of State	Jean-Claude Juncker (CSV)
Vice Prime Minister	Jean Asselborn (LSAP)
Ministers	
Agriculture, Viticulture, and Rural Development	Romain Schneider (LSAP)
Civil Service and Administrative Reform	François Biltgen (CSV)
Cooperation and Humanitarian Affairs	Marc Spautz (CSV)
Culture	Octavie Modert (CSV) [f]
Defense	Jean-Marie Halsdorf (CSV)
Economy and Foreign Trade	Etienne Schneider (LSAP)
Equality of Opportunity	Françoise Hetto-Gaasch (CSV) [f]
Family and Integration	Marc Spautz (CSV)
Finance	Luc Frieden (CSV)
Foreign Affairs	Jean Asselborn (LSAP)
Health	Mars Di Bartolomeo (LSAP)
Higher Education and Research	Martine Hansen (CSV) [f]
Housing	Marco Schank (CSV)
Interior and Territorial Planning	Jean-Marie Halsdorf (CSV)
Justice	François Biltgen (CSV)
Middle Classes, Tourism, and Equality	Françoise Hetto-Gaasch (CSV) [f]
National Education and Professional Training	Mady Delvaux-Stehres (LSAP) [f]
Religious Affairs	Octavie Modert (CSV) [f]
Social Security	Mars Di Bartolomeo (LSAP)
Sports	Romain Schneider (LSAP)
Sustainable Development and Infrastructure	Claude Wiseler (CSV)
Treasury	Jean-Claude Juncker (CSV)
Work, Employment, and Immigration	Nicolas Schmit (LSAP)
Ministers Delegate	
Administrative Simplification	Octavie Modert (CSV) [f]
Communications and Media	Luc Frieden (CSV)
Parliamentary Relations	Marc Spautz (CSV)

[f] = female

INTERGOVERNMENTAL REPRESENTATION

Ambassador to the U.S.: Jean-Louis WOLZFELD.

U.S. Ambassador to Luxembourg: Robert A. MANDELL.

Permanent Representative to the UN: Sylvie LUCAS.

IGO Memberships (Non-UN): ADB, CEUR, EBRD, EIB, EU, ICC, IEA, IOM, NATO, OECD, OSCE, WTO.

MACEDONIA

Republic of Macedonia
Republika Makedonija

Note: The country was admitted to the United Nations in April 1993 as "The former Yugoslav Republic of Macedonia," although international usage of this title (particularly in regard to capitalization) has varied, with the abbreviation FYROM sometimes being invoked. As of 2013 no resolution had been achieved in the dispute with Greece over use of "Macedonia" in the country's official name.

Political Status: Former constituent republic of the Socialist Federal Republic of Yugoslavia; independence proclaimed under constitution of November 17, 1991, on the basis of a referendum conducted September 8.

Area: 9,928 sq. mi. (25,713 sq. km).

Population: 2,113,180 (2012E—UN); 2,087,000 (2013E—U.S. Census).

Major Urban Center (2009E): SKOPJE (529,051).

Official Languages: Macedonian, Albanian. Macedonian, with a Cyrillic alphabet, is further designated as the official language for international relations. Albanian, with a Latin alphabet, became an official language under a 2001 constitutional revision that authorized that status for any language spoken by at least 20 percent of the population. Moreover, in local jurisdictions other languages used by at least 20 percent of the citizens are considered official. (Local authorities may also permit additional languages to be used in public interactions with the government.)

Monetary Unit: New Macedonian Denar (market rate November 1, 2013: 44.67 denars = $1US).

President: Gjorge IVANOV (Internal Macedonian Revolutionary Organization–Democratic Party for Macedonian National Unity); directly elected in second-round balloting on April 5, 2009, and sworn in for a five-year term on May 12, succeeding Branko CRVENKOVSKI (Social Democratic Union of Macedonia).

Chair of the Council of Ministers (Prime Minister): Nikola GRUEVSKI (Internal Macedonian Revolutionary Organization–Democratic Party for Macedonian National Unity); approved by the Assembly and sworn into office on August 26, 2006, following the election of July 5 and 19, succeeding Vlado BUČKOVSKI (Social Democratic Union of Macedonia); formed new government on July 29, 2011, following the early legislative elections in June.

THE COUNTRY

The former Yugoslavian component of historical Macedonia is a landlocked country bordered on the east by Bulgaria, on the north by Serbia and Montenegro, on the west by Albania, and on the south by Greece. According to the 2002 census, 64.2 percent of the population is ethnic Macedonian and 25.2 percent ethnic Albanian, with Turks, Roma, Serbs, Bosniaks, Vlachs, and others forming smaller groups. Most of the Macedonian majority supports the Macedonian Orthodox (Christian) Church; the Albanians are predominantly Muslim. Demography contributes to the ethnic tensions within the country. The higher birthrate among the ethnic Albanian, Turkish, and Roma communities is frequently cited by ethnic Macedonian nationalist politicians as eroding the nature of the state as the homeland of the "Macedonian people." Equally important is the depopulation of the countryside; two-thirds of Macedonian towns and villages continue to see long-term population decline because of internal migration, primarily to Skopje. The perception that rural areas are underfunded has contributed, in part, to past ethnic conflict.

Agriculture accounted for about 11 percent of GDP and roughly 17 percent of employment in 2012, the principal crops being fruits, vegetables, grains, and tobacco. The industrial sector, contributing about 26 percent of GDP and 26 percent of employment, principally exports iron and steel, footwear and clothing, nonferrous metals, tobacco products, and beverages (especially wine). Women constitute 40 percent of the labor force. Extractable resources include lignite, copper, lead, and zinc. Germany, Greece, Bulgaria, and Italy are Macedonia's leading trading partners.

The poorest of the former Yugoslav republics, Macedonia was economically distressed in the postindependence period by regional conflict and the disruption of established trading links with neighboring countries. Industrial and agricultural production declined sharply, yielding GDP contraction of about one-third in 1990–1993, during which inflation averaged 600 percent per year and unemployment rose to 40 percent. Beginning in 1994 the government initiated a structural reform program suggested by the International Monetary Fund (IMF) and World Bank; initiatives included liberalization of trade regulations, modernization of customs procedures, privatization of state-run enterprises, and reform of the financial sector. Macedonia gained membership in the World Trade Organization (WTO) in 2003 and the Central European Free Trade Association (CEFTA) in 2006.

Severe difficulties have continued since independence, however, including a dearth of foreign investment, continued high unemployment, and increasing poverty (nearly one-quarter of the population lives below the poverty line). The ethnic Albanian Muslim minority has been disproportionally affected by economic problems, generating additional resentment in a segment of the population already embittered over perceived "second class" treatment.

The European Union (EU) formally declared Macedonia as a candidate for EU membership in December 2005, but among other things, EU accession appeared dependent on a resolution of the name dispute with Greece (see Current issues, below). The effects of the global economic crisis produced GDP contraction of 2.4 percent in 2009 and 1.3 percent growth in 2010. In addition, corruption remained a problem (Transparency International in 2006 had rated Macedonia among the most corrupt countries in Europe), while official unemployment in mid-2013 surpassed 30 percent, one of the highest rates in Europe. (The rate was almost 54 percent for those under 25 years of age.) GDP growth was 3 percent in 2011 but 0 percent in 2012 due to the ongoing eurozone crisis. The IMF estimates 2 percent growth in 2013.

GOVERNMENT AND POLITICS

Political background. Greater geographic Macedonia was contested between rival Balkan empires until its incorporation into the Ottoman Empire. Ottoman rule lasted five centuries prior to the Second Balkan War and the Treaty of Bucharest of 1913, which divided most of the territory between Greece and Serbia, the respective portions being known as Aegean (or Greek) Macedonia and Vardar Macedonia. A much smaller portion (Pirin Macedonia) was awarded to Bulgaria. After World War I Vardar Macedonia (South Serbia) became part of the Kingdom of the Serbs, Croats, and Slovenes, later renamed Yugoslavia in October 1929. In 1944 it was accorded the status of a constituent republic of the communist-ruled federal Yugoslavia.

Following Belgrade's endorsement of a multiparty system in early 1990, Vladimir MITKOV of the newly styled League of Communists of Macedonia–Party of Democratic Change (*Sojuz na Komunistite na Makedonija–Partija za Demokratska Preobrazba*—SKM-PDP) was named president of the republic's State Presidency, pending a general election. The balloting for a 120-member Assembly, conducted in three stages on November 11 and 25 and December 9, was marked by ethnic tension between the Macedonian and Albanian communities and yielded an inconclusive outcome: the opposition Internal Macedonian Revolutionary Organization–Democratic Party for Macedonian National Unity (*Vnatrešno Makedonska Revolucionerna Organizacija–Demokratska Partija za Makedonsko Nacionalno Edinstvo*—VMRO-DPMNE) won a plurality of 37 seats, compared with 31 for the second-place SKM-PDP, and a total of 25 for two Albanian groups. As a result of the stand-off, Kiro GLIGOROV of the SKM-PDP (subsequently the Social Democratic Union of Macedonia [*Socijaldemokratski Sojuz na Makedonija*—SDSM]) was named to succeed Mitkov as president.

On January 25, 1991, the Assembly unanimously adopted a declaration of sovereignty that asserted a right of self-determination, including secession from Yugoslavia. On September 8, 75 percent of the republic's registered voters (with most Albanians abstaining) participated in a referendum that endorsed independence by an overwhelming margin. On November 17 the Assembly approved a new constitution, and on December 24 Macedonia joined Bosnia and Herzegovina, Croatia, and Slovenia in seeking recognition from the European Community (EC, subsequently the EU). The ethnic Albanians reacted in January 1992 with a 99.9 percent vote in favor of territorial and political autonomy for the Albanian-majority regions in western Macedonia. While Belgrade tacitly recognized Macedonian autonomy by handing over border posts to Macedonian army units in March and withdrawing its own military forces from the republic, most foreign governments withheld recognition because of Greek protests over the country's name (see Foreign relations, below).

A mid-1992 cabinet crisis resulted in the formation of a new coalition headed by Branko CRVENKOVSKI of the SDSM and including the Party for Democratic Prosperity (*Partija za Demokratski Prosperite/Partia për Prosperitet Demokratik*—PDP/PPD), a primarily ethnic Albanian party. The new government introduced short-term emergency economic measures, including devaluations of the denar in October and December. Meanwhile, in light of an influx of some 60,000 refugees from the war in Bosnia and Herzegovina, the Assembly in October approved a 15-year residency requirement for Macedonian citizenship, which was modified to eight years in 2003.

The prime importance attached by the government to securing full international recognition helped to ensure the survival of the disparate ruling coalition, which had been mandated to cement national unity. Nevertheless, underlying tensions between the ethnic Macedonian and ethnic Albanian communities surfaced in 1993 amid accusations of Albanian separatism, and in early 1994 the PDP/PPD split into moderate and nationalist factions, the latter joining the opposition.

In the October 1994 presidential election Gligorov secured easy reelection as the candidate of an SDSM-led alliance, winning 78.4 percent of the valid votes cast (52.4 percent of the total electorate), against 21.6 percent for the nominee of the VMRO-DPMNE, Ljubčo GEORGIEVSKI. In the two-stage legislative election the SDSM-led alliance won 95 of the 120 seats and then opted to maintain the coalition with the PDP/PPD under the continued premiership of Crvenkovski. The opposition parties claimed that both the presidential and legislative elections had been riddled with fraud, a view that received some support from international observers.

On October 3, 1995, President Gligorov suffered serious injuries in a bomb attack on his car in Skopje that resulted in two fatalities (for details, see the 2012 *Handbook*).

In a major cabinet reshuffle in February 1996, Prime Minister Crvenkovski dropped the LPM from the ruling coalition. An LPM attempt in April to force an early election was easily rebuffed, given the government's comfortable parliamentary majority, the SDSM's position being reinforced when it won a plurality of council seats as well as mayoralties in the municipal elections in late 1996.

In February 1997 an estimated 3,000 ethnic Macedonian students protested against a law permitting the Albanian language to be used in teaching at Skopje University's teacher college, reflecting nationalistic sentiment that the government should not yield to perceived separatism on the part of ethnic Albanians. In March the EU formally expressed concern over rising ethnic tensions. Rioting, resulting in 3 deaths, 100 wounded, and 500 arrests, erupted in July in Gostivar over the right to fly the Albanian flag at municipal buildings in ethnic Albanian areas.

The problems of ethnic Albanians in Kosovo subsequently spilled over into Macedonia, including a series of car bomb explosions in January and February 1998 that were disputably claimed by the Kosovo Liberation Army—KLA (*Ushtria Çlirimtare e Kosovës*—UÇK). The leaders of several ethnic Albanian parties were charged in mid-March with violating (during a pro-Kosovo rally) Macedonian laws limiting the display of Albanian nationalist symbols. In addition, the mayors of Tetovo and Gostivar were imprisoned for flying the Albanian flag over municipal buildings. In response, the PDP and the Democratic Party of Albanians (*Demokratska Partija na Albancite*—DPA/*Partia Demokratike Shqiptare*—PDSh—DPA/PDSh), under the leadership of longtime Albanian nationalist Arben XHAFERI, threatened to withdraw from governmental institutions.

The legislative election in October–November 1998 gave a majority of 62 seats to the VMRO-DPMNE and its electoral partner, the newly formed, probusiness **Democratic Alternative** (*Demokratska Alternativa*—DA). A governmental crisis was averted after the election, when Prime Minister–designate Georgievski negotiated a coalition agreement that included the DPA/PDSh, theretofore perceived as a more militant segment of the Albanian population than the more mainstream PDP/PPD. Georgievski's new VMRO-DPMNE-DA-DPA/PDSh government pledged to further integrate Albanians into Macedonian institutions and society as a whole. Pardons were granted for several Albanian figures charged with political crimes, including the mayors of Tetovo and Gostivar.

In presidential balloting to replace the retiring Gligorov, the VMRO-DPMNE candidate, Boris TRAJKOVSKI, captured 52.9 percent of the second-round vote in November 1999, outdistancing the SDSM's Tito Petkovski, who had finished first in the initial round. Trajkovski's victory came with the support of the DA and the DPA/PDSh, both of which had fielded their own candidates in the first round. Official confirmation of Trajkovski's victory was delayed, however, when the Supreme Court ordered that a revote be held in selected precincts because of ballot stuffing and other irregularities. The results of the reballoting proved nearly identical to the previous totals, and Trajkovski was inaugurated on December 15.

In February 2001 fighting erupted in Tanusevçi, on the border with Kosovo, precipitated by members of the Albanian National Liberation Army—NLA (*Ushtrisë Çlirimtare Kombëtare*—UÇK) led by Ali AHMETI. By mid-March fighting had spread to the Tetovo area, leading the UN Security Council to pass a unanimous resolution condemning "extremist violence" as "a threat to the security and stability of the wider region." In April the DPA and PDP, both having condemned the NLA, began discussions with the government on possible constitutional changes that would address the status of ethnic Albanians. In May the Assembly, by a vote of 104–1, approved formation of a national unity government that, in addition to the three parties in the previous Georgievski administration, included the SDSM, the PDP, the Internal Macedonian Revolutionary Organization–True Macedonian Reform Option (*Vnatrešno Makedonska Revolucionerna Organizacija–Vistinska Makedonska Reformska Opcija*—VMRO-VMRO), and the Liberal-Democratic Party (*Liberalno-Demokratska Partija*—LDP), which incorporated elements of the LPM. Fighting nevertheless escalated in succeeding weeks, and as of June some 65,000 ethnic Albanians had fled to Kosovo to escape the conflict.

A Western-brokered peace agreement (the Ohrid Framework Agreement) was achieved on August 13, 2001. Two weeks later NLA members began surrendering their arms to a 3,500-member NATO force, "Operation Essential Harvest," which had entered the country at the request of President Trajkovski and which transitioned to "Operation Amber Fox" in September to oversee the implementation of the Ohrid Agreement. On September 6 the Assembly formally approved the peace accords. The pact called in part for constitutional revisions that would excise the privileged status accorded the Macedonian majority and grant official status to other languages with a native-speaking population of at least 20 percent, effectively making Albanian a second official language. An amnesty bill regarding the 2001 conflict passed in March 2002, and a series of language laws won approval in June, the Assembly finally enacting a package of related constitutional amendments on November 16. Five days later, declaring that the national unity government had achieved its aim of restoring domestic stability, the SDSM and LDP resigned from the administration, which was quickly joined by the New Democracy Party (*Nova Demokratija*—ND).

In the parliamentary election of September 15, 2002, former prime minister Branko Crvenkovski's SDSM led a ten-party alliance, the Coalition for Macedonia Together (*Koalicija za Makedonija Zaedno—Koalicija* ZMZ), to a near-majority of 60 seats in the 120-seat *Sobranje*. Prime Minister Georgievski's VMRO-DPMNE and its principal ally, the LPM, managed to win only 33 seats. The Democratic Union for Integration (*Demokratska Unija za Integracija/Bashkimit Demokratik për Integrim*—DUI/BDI), chaired by former Albanian National Liberation Army leader Ali Ahmeti, won 16 seats and joined a new Crvenkovski coalition government, which was confirmed by the *Sobranje* and took office on November 1.

On February 26, 2004, President Trajkovski and six of his staff members were killed in a plane crash near Mostar in Bosnia and Herzegovina. In the first round of elections to choose Trajkovski's successor on April 14, Prime Minister Crvenkovski of the SDSM and Sasko KEDEV of the VMRO-DPMNE advanced, leaving behind two ethnic Albanian candidates. Crvenkovski won the April 28 runoff with 62.7 percent of the vote and was sworn in as president on May 12, Assembly Speaker Ljubčo JORDANOVSKI having served in the interim as acting president. Interior Minister Hari KOSTOV succeeded Crvenkovski as prime minister and was sworn in on June 2. On November 15, however, Kostov resigned in protest against corruption and nepotism within the coalition. He was replaced by Vlado BUČKOVSKI, who also took over as SDSM chair. On December 17 the Assembly approved Bučkovski's coalition government, which included the DUI/BDI.

Parliamentary elections were held on July 5 and July 19, 2006, in balloting judged generally free and fair, although the process was marred by outbreaks of violence and allegations of electoral irregularities. The VMRO-DPMNE, leading a broad coalition, won 45 seats, defeating rival coalitions led by the SDSM and DUI/BDI. Negotiations between the VMRO-DPMNE's Nikola GRUEVSKI, the prospective prime minister, quickly brought the New Social Democratic Party (*Nova Socijal Demokratska Partija*—NSDP), the SPM, and the LPM into government. However, the search to find a partner from the country's three ethnic Albanian parties proved more protracted. Following unsuccessful negotiations with the DUI/BDI and PDP/PPD, an agreement was made with the DPA/PDSh. The cabinet was inaugurated on August 26 following approval by the *Sobranje* on the same day.

Prime Minister Gruevski's inclusion of the DPA/PDSh in the ensuing government deepened rifts among the political parties representing ethnic Albanians. Outbreaks of ethnic and political violence were subsequently reported, including a rocket-powered grenade attack on the central building of the government in August 2007. The key provisions of the Ohrid accords continued to be implemented, but only slowly and with some opposition among ethnic Macedonians. Among other things, certain elements within the Albanian community expressed a preference for union with Kosovo, and former members of the NLA called for a referendum to allow the village of Tanusevci (one of the flash points of the 2001 war) to accede to Kosovo. Subsequent police raids seized small but significant caches of weapons reportedly held by NLA splinter groups.

In 2007 both the SDSM and DUI/BDI coalitions broke apart, leading to broader support for the government with the PDP/PDD and several smaller parties joining the ruling coalition. Nevertheless, the government was unable to secure sufficient legislative support to enact economic reforms and proposals regarding the ethnic Albanian minority. The government faced an additional setback in April 2008 when Greece vetoed the expected offer of NATO membership for Macedonia, citing the continued name dispute. The VMRO-DPMNE and allied parties consequently voted for an early election in 2008, hoping for a "mandate" to enact change.

The June 2, 2008, Assembly elections were tarnished by outbreaks of violence and voting irregularities. Much of the conflict was between supporters of the DPA/PDSh and DUI/BDI (see the 2012 *Handbook*). Irregularities at some stations led to the State Electoral Commission invalidating the results in several districts, where revotes were held on June 15. Following new problems in that round, a third round was held in some districts on June 29. The VMRO-DPMNE secured a decisive victory, with its coalition winning an outright majority with 63 seats. Prime Minister Gruevski subsequently formed a new government with the DUI/BDI that was also supported by the Party for a European Future (*Partija za Evropska Idnina*—PEI). As a result, the government was backed by 82 legislators, more than the two-thirds necessary to enact constitutional reforms.

Gjorge IVANOV of the VMRO-DPMNE finished first among seven candidates in the first round of presidential balloting on March 22, 2009, with 35.0 percent of the vote, followed by the SDSM's Ljubomir FRČKOSKI with 20.5 percent. Ivanov won the runoff with Frčkoski on April 5 with 63.1 percent of the vote.

In January 2011 the SDSM, its coalition allies, and the ND boycotted parliament in protest against what, according to them, were measures to put the "media under the direct control of the democracy." Gruevski responded in February 2011 by calling for new elections. Following negotiations in March over changes to the electoral law (which included the inclusion of three new seats for Macedonians living abroad), parliament was dissolved on April 14.

The June 5, 2011, election was judged generally free, fair, and without incident. The coalition led by the VMRO-DPMNE won 56 seats, defeating rival coalitions led by the SDSM and DUI/BDI, although the SDSM significantly increased its position in parliament. Negotiations to retain the DUI/BDI proceeded smoothly, and a restructured cabinet was approved by the *Sobranje* on July 28.

Constitution and government. The constitution proclaimed in November 1991 defines Macedonia as a state based on citizenship, not ethnicity, and specifically rules out any territorial claims on neighboring countries. The Albanian minority, however, asserted that the preamble and dozens of provisions of the basic law accorded privileged status to the ethnic and religious Macedonian majority. This perception contributed to the violent events of 2001 and led to enactment of a series of corrective amendments later that year. The principal changes were a revised preamble referring to nonethnic Macedonian communities as citizens; a requirement that certain legislation obtain minority group approval as well as passage by the full legislature (a "double majority"); provision for additional official languages in areas where native speakers constitute 20 percent of the population; and proportional representation of ethnic Albanians in the Constitutional Court, public administration, and security forces.

The constitution provides for a directly elected president serving a five-year term as head of state and a cabinet, headed by a prime minister, owing responsibility to a unicameral national Assembly (*Sobranje*). The Assembly is elected for a four-year term by a combination of majority and proportional voting. Ultimate judicial authority is vested in a Supreme Court, with a Constitutional Court adjudicating constitutional issues.

In 2002 the Assembly approved legislation providing for the devolution of greater authority to local government, effectively granting a measure of self-rule to ethnic Albanian regions. In other measures to integrate ethnic Albanians into national life, legislators passed a controversial law granting status as a state university to the underground Albanian-language university in Tetovo. A new citizenship law passed in 2003 enabled foreign nationals to qualify for citizenship after 8 rather than 15 years of legal residence.

In 2004 the Assembly passed a redistricting law cutting the number of administrative districts from 123 to 84, in 16 of which Albanians claimed a majority. The law, which was in accordance with the 2001 Ohrid peace accords, gave local authorities greater powers in regional planning, finance, and health care. The measure was opposed by many ethnic Macedonians, who feared that redistricting could lead to partition of the country along ethnic lines, but a November referendum to annul the legislation was boycotted by many parties and groups and therefore failed by nearly half to obtain the necessary 50 percent participation rate. Further proposals advanced by Gruevski in 2007 to reform the electoral system by adding 13 guaranteed seats for non-Albanian ethnic minorities and émigré Macedonians living abroad have been stalled by opposition in parliament. Three seats for émigré Macedonian citizens in North America, Europe, and Asia/Australia were added in 2011, a significant overrepresentation of their numbers.

Freedom of the press is protected by the constitution. In 2012 Freedom House ranked Macedonia as "partly free," noting self-censorship of the media in the face of political pressure. In 2013 Reporters Without Borders ranked the Macedonian government's respect for freedom of the press in 116th place, a fall of more than 20 places from the previous year.

Foreign relations. Recognition of Macedonia by the EC/EU was stalled by the insistence of Greece that recognition be conditioned on Macedonia's changing its name. Greece based its position on historical considerations, including the fact that its own northernmost province is also named Macedonia. Thus, the EC/EU foreign ministers declared at a meeting in May 1992 that the community was "willing to recognize Macedonia as a sovereign and independent state within its existing borders and under a name that can be accepted by all parties concerned."

On December 11, 1992, the UN Security Council authorized the dispatch of some 700 UN peacekeeping troops and military observers to the Macedonia-Serbia/Kosovo border in an effort to prevent the fighting in Bosnia and Herzegovina from spreading to the south. Although the Clinton administration in the United States had consistently refused to commit ground forces to the Bosnian theater, it committed an eventual 500-strong U.S. contingent to join the UN Preventive Deployment Force (UNPREDEP) in Macedonia. The force's mandate was renewed at six-month intervals thereafter, with its size increasing to 1,150 by November 1996.

Disagreements with Greece, including the nomenclature dispute, continued throughout the 1990s. After the Skopje government formally applied for UN membership on January 7, 1993, a partial Greek concession permitted the new state to join the UN in April as "The former Yugoslav Republic of Macedonia." Under the compromise, a definitive name as well as a related dispute over the use of Alexander the Great's Star of Vergina symbol on the Macedonian flag would have to be negotiated.

Strains with Greece were aggravated by the return to power of a socialist government in Athens in October 1993. Greek Prime Minister Andreas Papandreou was incensed by the decision of the leading EU states in December to recognize Macedonia, and on February 16, 1994, after Washington had extended recognition, Athens imposed a controversial partial trade embargo on Macedonia, cutting the landlocked republic off from the northern Greek port of Salonika (Thessaloniki), its main import-export channel, for all goods except food and medicine.

UN and U.S. mediation brought Macedonia's dispute with Greece to partial resolution on September 13, 1995, when the respective foreign ministers initialed an agreement in New York covering border definition, revision of the Macedonian constitution to exclude any hint of territorial claims, and a new Macedonian flag. Following ratification by the Macedonian Assembly, the accord was formally signed in Skopje on October 15, whereupon Greece lifted its trade embargo. In light of the accommodation with Greece, Macedonia was admitted to full membership in the Organization for Security and Cooperation in Europe (OSCE) on October 12, 1995, and to the Council of Europe a week later. Despite the 1995 agreement, the Greek government has continued to strongly oppose the name "Republic of Macedonia."

Moves by the Skopje government to counter a developing Belgrade-Athens axis on Balkan matters included the cultivation of relations with Bulgaria, which had recognized Macedonia in January 1992, and with Turkey. Relations with Bulgaria were complicated by the widespread view in Bulgaria that Macedonians are really Bulgarians (and their language a variant of Bulgarian); while Bulgaria had recognized Macedonia, it had not recognized Macedonian nationality. Although several bilateral accords have been signed, extending to Bulgaria's provision of military aid for the Macedonian army, the Bulgarian government continues to deny aspects of ethnic Macedonian identity, language, and history. (See the 2013 *Handbook* for details.) This was underscored on July 24, 2006, when Bulgarian Minister of Foreign Affairs Ivailo Kalfin noted that "aggression towards the Bulgarian nation or history on behalf of the Macedonian authorities" might limit Bulgaria's support for Macedonian membership in the EU following its own accession on January 1, 2007.

The Belgrade-Athens axis and Serb claims on Macedonian territory militated against a natural alignment between the Macedonians and the Serbs, despite widespread sympathy within Macedonia for Serbia in the Yugoslav conflicts. The NATO bombing campaign launched against Yugoslavia in March–June 1999 precipitated the temporary flight of more than 250,000 ethnic Albanians into Macedonia from Kosovo. Most ethnic Macedonians, concerned over the broader regional implications of greater autonomy for the Albanian Kosovars, reportedly opposed the NATO action, while ethnic Albanians in Macedonia called upon the government to provide their confreres with massive assistance. In addition, some ethnic Albanians in Macedonia indicated they might join the KLA in combating Serbian forces, raising the specter of a spillover of the conflict into Macedonia. However, the DPA/PDSh's Xhaferi successfully appealed for calm among ethnic Albanians in Macedonia, while the government dutifully accepted the temporary deployment of some 12,000 NATO forces in Macedonia as part of the peacekeeping force proposed for Kosovo.

In view of the Kosovo conflict, most UN members had wanted UNPREDEP to continue to function, but China vetoed a further extension of the mission beyond February 28, 1999. The decision appeared directly related, despite Beijing's denials, to Skopje's establishment of relations with Taiwan in January, an action that caused China to sever ties to Macedonia. Some members of the Georgievski government had argued that recognition of Taiwan would produce a much-needed inflow of foreign investment, on top of foreign aid, from the island, but the results did not meet expectations. Skopje renewed diplomatic ties with Beijing on June 18, 2001, as a consequence of which Taiwan immediately broke relations with Macedonia.

In early 2001 Macedonia indicated that it would no longer pursue new diplomatic ties to countries that refused to recognize the country's designation as the "Republic of Macedonia." (The United States officially recognized Macedonia by its constitutional name, the Republic of Macedonia, in 2004.) Meanwhile, negotiations with Athens over the name issue continued, even while economic ties between the neighbors moved forward. In November 1999, for example, Greece and Macedonia concluded an agreement on construction of a $90 million oil pipeline between Thessaloniki and Skopje, while in April 2000 the National Bank of Greece was one of three foreign investors to purchase Macedonia's largest bank from the government. In May 2002 the Greek and Macedonian defense ministers concluded a military cooperation agreement. (Military ties with the West were subsequently further strengthened by Macedonia's contribution of 40 soldiers to the U.S.-led force in Iraq and 140 troops to the NATO mission in Afghanistan.)

Macedonia formally submitted its application for EU membership in 2004. EU concern was raised when the OSCE criticized the conduct of the March 2005 local elections, but the European Commission deemed Macedonia a "worthy candidate" in November, and the EU summit granted official candidate status in December. However, substantive negotiations for admission were delayed due to the dispute between Greece and Macedonia over the latter's name. In December 2006 the name dispute was exacerbated when Skopje airport was named "Aleksandar Makedonski Airport," resulting in protests from the Greek government and a rebuke from the EU.

During 2000–2007 more than 75,000 Macedonian citizens applied for Bulgarian passports (including former prime minister Ljubčo Georgievski, who was granted Bulgarian citizenship). As a result, accusations arose in Macedonia that the Bulgarian government was attempting an assimilation policy that would lead to Macedonia's "suicide."

The unilateral declaration of independence by Kosovo in February 2008 and subsequent recognition by the United States and majority of EU members were met with caution in Macedonia, but on October 9, 2008, Macedonia formally recognized Kosovo's independence.

The name dispute with Greece took center stage once more in April 2008, when Macedonia's bid to join NATO was formally vetoed by Greece pending the resolution of the issue. The Greek government warned that it would similarly oppose any EU application by Macedonia while the question remained open. The resulting public anger among ethnic Macedonians was widely credited by domestic media as one factor in the VMRO-DPMNE's electoral victory in 2008. (Prime Minister Gruevski had promised not to "trade off" changing the state's name for NATO and EU admission.)

In November 2008 Macedonia filed a complaint with the International Court of Justice arguing that Greek actions to block Macedonian membership in the EU and NATO were contrary to the 1995 interim agreement between the two countries. Tensions were increased further by the Gruevski government's decision to name the country's north-south highway after Alexander the Great, to name the main soccer stadium in Skopje after Phillip II of Macedonia, and to commission a statue of Alexander to be placed in the main square of Skopje.

Negotiations between Macedonia and Greece continued in 2010 over the potential compromise name of "Republic of Northern Macedonia." On February 27, 2011, Foreign Minister Antonio MILOSOSKI announced that Macedonia would be willing to open negotiations that the name be resolved as "Republic of Macedonia (Skopje)," as suggested by UN mediators, but only if approved by a general referendum.

While resolving the naming issue would aid Macedonia's accession to the EU, the European Commission warned that reforms in the judiciary and public administration, greater media freedom, and anticorruption efforts all require additional progress.

In December 2011 the International Court of Justice found that Greek efforts to block Macedonia's admission to NATO violated the UN-sponsored agreement of 1995. The court did not impose penalties, however, and in April 2012 NATO reiterated that Macedonian membership could only come with a solution to the name issue.

Little progress was reported on resolving the dispute, and actions by both sides continued to keep tensions high. In May 2012 the Macedonian government unveiled a 42-foot (13-meter) statue of Philip II, father of Alexander the Great, in Skopje; in June Greek customs officials placed FYROM stickers on the license plates of Macedonian-registered cars crossing the border, obscuring the abbreviation MK (for Macedonia).

Current issues. The EU indicated that open, free, and peaceful presidential elections in 2009 would be a precondition for progress to continue regarding EU membership for Macedonia. Those conditions were largely met, although turnout declined from over 1 million voters in the first round to 750,000 in the second round, largely reflecting a boycott by ethnic Albanian voters. Collaterally, the domestic media and Albanian political leaders reported rising ethnic tensions, in part stemming from divisions along ethnic lines regarding the continuing dispute with Greece, which was seen as hindering Macedonia's chances to join the EU and NATO. (A Gallup poll released in February 2009 showed that a majority of both ethnic Macedonian and ethnic Albanian citizens considered membership in the EU desirable. However, if such membership required changing the name of the state, only 3 percent of ethnic Macedonians said they would agree, compared to 69 percent of ethnic Albanians.) On October 14, 2009, the European Commission recommended that membership negotiations be opened with Macedonia, while urging Gruevski's government to resolve the name issue with Greece.

The name conflict was complicated by the unveiling in February 2010 of the controversial "Skopje 2014" town plan, which called for rebuilding the city center. Ethnic Albanian leaders protested the proposed incorporation of an Orthodox cathedral but not a mosque in the project; opposition leaders criticized the estimated cost (200 million euros); and the Greek government objected to the proposed centerpiece, a statue of Alexander the Great that would stand roughly 72 feet (22 meters) tall.

In April 2010 Greece suggested its most recent compromise name, "Northern Macedonia," which Gruevski rejected. Meanwhile, the Greek government continued to insist it would approve Macedonia's accession to the EU and NATO only after the name dispute is resolved.

A series of scandals emerged in September 2010 concerning the lustration process, intended to provide information on secret agents and informers of the Yugoslav-era security services. Among other things, leaders of the opposition charged the VMRO-DPMNE with using the Lustration Commission as a means of harassing political rivals.

Criticism was raised in 2011 by domestic journalists and by international groups that the Gruevski government had acted to restrict or silence critical media outlets. In January 2011 the government acted to freeze the accounts of several media outlets due to claims of overdue taxes, including A1 television, the largest private broadcaster in the country. On July 3 three daily newspapers were closed on similar allegations of overdue taxes.

In 2012, tensions were raised by ethnic clashes following the killing of two ethnic Albanians by an off-duty police officer in February and the shooting of five ethnic Macedonian fishermen in April. In September the DUI/BDI blocked a bill providing benefits for families of deceased soldiers and veterans of the 2001 conflict unless these were extended to the NLA. As the year drew to a close, politicians were struggling to agree on a budget for 2013, leading to street protests and the ejection from the Assembly of SDSM members for brawling in the chamber. In response, the SDSM boycotted the Assembly into March 2013 and threatened to also boycott upcoming local elections. The boycott, among other issues, was cited by the EU enlargement commissioner as a factor in the decision to postpone negotiations over Macedonia's candidacy. The February appointment of Talat XHAFERI, an ethnic Albanian commander in the NLA during the 2001 fighting, as minister of defense triggered a series of ethnic riots. On July 1, 2013, former prime minister Bučkovski was sentenced to three years in jail for corruption, stemming from a 2001 case involving the procurement of spare parts for tanks during his tenure as minister of defense.

Leaders of the VMRO-DPMNE and DUI/BDI publicly clashed in July 2013 over the continued failure to obtain a start date for accession negotiations with the EU. Lack of progress on the name dispute was reportedly linked to Macedonia's failure to advance its EU accession status, leading Gruevski to suggest bilateral talks with Greece in July.

POLITICAL PARTIES

For four and a half decades after World War II, the only authorized political party in Yugoslavia was the Communist Party, which was redesignated in 1952 as the League of Communists of Yugoslavia (in Serbo-Croatian, *Savez Kumunista Jugoslavija*—SKJ). In 1989 non-Communist groups began to emerge in the republics, and in early 1990 the SKJ approved the introduction of a multiparty system, thereby triggering its own demise. In Macedonia the party's local branch, the League of Communists of Macedonia (*Sojuz na Komunistite na Makedonija*—SKM), had been succeeded by the SKM-PDP in 1989 (see SDSM, below).

Nearly three dozen parties offered candidates for the 1998, 2002, 2006, 2008, and 2011 elections, on their own, in coalitions, or both.

Government and Government-Supportive Parties:

Coalition Internal Macedonian Revolutionary Organization–Democratic Party for Macedonian National Unity (*Koalicija Vnatrešno Makedonska Revolucionerna Organizacija–Demokratska Partija za Makedonsko Nacionalno Edinstvo—Koalicija* VMRO-DPMNE). While officially registered under this name, the domestic media often uses **Coalition for a Better Macedonia** (*Koalicija za Podobra Makedonija*—KzPM) as it represents a continuation of the 19-party electoral list by that name established for the 2008 legislative election. The KzPM was, in turn, the continuation of the 2006 VMRO-DPMNE–led "National Unity" coalition. Both 2006 and 2008 lists were frequently referred to as the "VMRO-DPMNE coalition" in the local media, while the 2011 list similarly was frequently referred to as the KzPM.

The 2011 coalition included a number of small ethnic parties, many of which had been part of the 2008 coalition but previously had supported the opposition in 2006. Their joining the KzPM in 2008 reflected Prime Minister Gruevski's interest in reforming the parliament by adding dedicated seats for ethnic minorities.

Smaller coalition members in 2011 that were allocated one seat each in parliament included the **Democratic Party of Turks in Macedonia** (*Partija za Dviženje na Turcite vo Makedonija*—PDTM), the **Democratic Party of Serbs in Macedonia** (*Demokratska Partija na Srbite vo Makedonija*—DPSM), the **Union of Roma in Macedonia** (*Sojuz na Romite na Makedonija*—SRM), the **Internal Macedonian Revolutionary Organization-Macedonian** (*Vnatrešno Makedonska Revolucionerna Organizacija-Macedonska*—VMRO-*Makedonska*), and the **Party for Democratic Action of Macedonia** (*Stranka na Demokratska Akcija na Makedonija*—SDA). Coalition members that did not receive representation included the **United Party for Emancipation** (*Obedineta Partija za Emancipacija*—OPE), the **Party of Justice** (*Partija na Pravata*), the **Party for Integration of the Roma** (*Partija za Integracija na Romite*—PIR), the **Democratic Party of the Bosniaks** (*Bošnjačka Demokratska Partija*—BDP), the **People's Movement of Macedonia** (*Narodno Dviženje za Makedonija*—NDM), the **New Liberal Party** (*Nova Liberalna Partija*—NLP), the **Party of Vlachs in Macedonia** (*Partija na Vlasite od Makedonija*—PVM), the **Democratic Forces of the Roma** (*Demokratski Sili na Romite*—DSR), the **Permanent Macedonian Radical Unification** (*Trajno Makedonsko Radikalno Obedinuvanje*—TMRO), the **Internal Macedonian Revolutionary Organization–Democratic Party** (*Vnatrešno Makedonska Revolucionerna Organizacija–Demokratska Partija*—VMRO-DP), the **Internal Macedonian Revolutionary Organization–United** (*Vnatrešno Makedonska Revolucionerna Organizacija–Demokratska Partija–Obedinena*—VMRO-Ob), the **Macedonian Alliance** (*Makedonska Alijansa*—MA), and the **Homeland Macedonian Organization for Radical Reconstruction–Vardar–Egej–Pirin** (*Tatkovinska Makedonska Organizacija na Radikalna Obnova–Vardar–Egej–Pirin*—TMORO-VEP).

Internal Macedonian Revolutionary Organization–Democratic Party for Macedonian National Unity (*Vnatrešno Makedonska Revolucionerna Organizacija–Demokratska Partija za Makedonsko Nacionalno Edinstvo*—VMRO-DPMNE). The VMRO is named after a historic group (founded in 1893) that fought for independence from the Ottoman Empire. The DPMNE, launched by Macedonian migrant workers in Sweden, merged with the VMRO in June 1990.

The VMRO-DPMNE, with significant support within the ethnic Macedonian population, strongly endorsed a revival of Macedonian cultural identity, its nationalistic stance being broadly perceived as anti-Albanian and right-wing, despite the group's description of itself as representing the "democratic center." The party won a plurality of 39 seats in the 1990 Assembly, subsequently serving as the main opposition to the Communist-led government. The VMRO-DPMNE's presidential candidate in 1994, Ljubčo Georgievski, gained 21.6 percent of the vote against the SDSM's Kiro Gligorov. However, the VMRO-DPMNE boycotted the second round of the 1994 legislative balloting, alleging fraud in the first round, in which it had been credited with no seats.

The VMRO-DPMNE competed for many of the single-member district seats in the 1998 legislative balloting in an alliance with the DA called "For Changes." It emerged from that balloting with 49 seats, having led all parties in the proportional contest with 28.1 percent of the vote. By that time, the VMRO-DPMNE appeared to have substantially moderated its platform, presenting itself as dedicated to "reconciliation and progress." Nevertheless, it was still a surprise when Georgievski invited the DPA, a hard-line ethnic Albanian grouping, to join his new government. Georgievski was reelected president of the party at a May 1999 congress.

The VMRO-DPMNE presidential candidate, Boris Trajkovski, won the 1999 election over the SDSM candidate, taking 52.9 percent of the vote in second-round balloting on November 14. He had finished second, with 20.6 percent, in the first round two weeks earlier, when the DA and DPA had offered their own candidates. In the September–October 2000 local elections, a VMRO-DPMNE/DA alliance won the majority of mayoralties.

The government's legislative majority was briefly threatened in November 2000 when the DA left the governing coalition, but Georgievski quickly announced the inclusion of the LPM, which, with added independent support, permitted the administration to remain in power.

The party did poorly in the 2002 legislative elections, winning less than 25 percent of the vote. The poor showing, and the rise of Nikola Gruevski to leadership of the party, resulted in July 2004 in supporters of Georgievski leaving the VMRO-DPMNE to form the VMRO-NP (below) and others to form the short-lived **Democratic Republican Union for Macedonia** (*Demokratski Republički Sojuz za Makedonija*—DRUM).

The split by much of the party's conservative wing effectively moved the VMRO-DPMNE closer to the political center. The VMRO-DPMNE led a coalition with some 13 other (mostly smaller) parties for the 2006 Assembly balloting, winning 38 seats (out of a total of 45 for the coalition). Success has allowed the VMRO-DPMNE to subsequently absorb eight smaller political parties, including the **League for Democracy** (*Liga za Demokratija*), the **Internal Macedonian Revolutionary Organization–True Macedonian Reform Option** (*Vnatrešno-Makedonska Revolucionerna Organizacija–Vistinska Makedonska Reformska Opcija*—VMRO-VMRO), the DRUM, and the **Agricultural People's Party of Macedonia** (*Zemjodelska Narodna Partija na Makedonia*—ZNPM).

Following the 2006 elections, the VMRO-DPMNE's reform agenda was stymied by opposition in parliament. As a result, in April 2008 it led government parties in calling for early elections.

Following the 2011 election, VMRO-DPMNE received 47 seats from the coalition's total and continued to lead the ruling government.

Leaders: Nikola GRUEVSKI (President of the Party and Chair of the Council of Ministers); Gjorge IVANOV (President of the Republic); Trajko SLAVESKI, Gordana JANKULOVSKA (Vice Presidents of the Party); Kiril BOZHINOVSKI (General Secretary).

Socialist Party of Macedonia (*Socijalistička Partija na Makedonija*—SPM). Formerly called the Socialist League–Socialist Party of Macedonia (*Socijalistički Sojuz–Socijalistička Partija na Makedonija*—SS-SPM), the SPM is the successor to the local branch of the former **Socialist League of the Working People of Yugoslavia** (in Serbo-Croatian, *Socijalistički Savez Radnog Narodna Jugoslavija*—SSRNJ). Following the death of Kiro POPOVSKI, Ljubisav Ivanov-Dzingo was elected SPM leader in May 1996.

In the wake of the collapse of the SM in 1996, the SPM contested the proportional seats and some of the single-member district seats in the 1998 Assembly balloting in coalition with the **Party for the Total Emancipation of Roma in Macedonia** (*Partija za Celosna Emancipacija na Romite vo Makedonija*—PCERM) and the **Democratic Progressive Party of the Roma in Macedonia** (*Demokratska Progresivna Partija na Romite od Makedonija*—DPPRM) as well as some smaller ethnic parties. The SPM won one constituency seat, but the coalition, the Movement for Cultural Tolerance and Civic Cooperation, won only 4.7 percent of the proportional vote and therefore no proportional seats. For the 2000 local elections the SPM entered an SDSM-led alliance.

The SPM retained its single seat in the 2002 Assembly poll. Subsequently, in December 2003, it announced the formation of a coalition called the Third Way that also included the DA and the Democratic Union (below). The SPM joined the VMRO-DPMNE's electoral bloc in 2006, winning three seats in parliament and entering the coalition government. It retained these seats in 2011.

Leaders: Ljubisav IVANOV-DZINGO (President), Blagoje FILIPOVSKI.

Democratic Union (*Demokratski Sojuz*—DS). The DS was founded on March 25, 2000, by former minister of the interior Pavle Trajanov. Identifying itself as a "law and order" party, its program emphasizes the rule of law, the territorial integrity of Macedonia, and an "effective campaign against organized crime, corruption, and drugs." It entered into a coalition with the Socialist Party of Macedonia in 2005 and then joined the SPM in coalition with the VMRO-DPMNE. In the 2011 elections it took one seat in parliament as part of the coalition.

Leader: Pavle TRAJANOV (President).

Democratic Renewal of Macedonia (*Demokraticka Obnova na Makedonija*—DOM). The DOM was founded in November 2005 by former LDP member Liljana Popovska. The DOM's platform calls for "sustainable development" and the promotion of tourism and environmental protection, and the party self-identifies as a Green party.

Leader: Liljana POPOVSKA (President).

Democratic Union for Integration (*Demokratska Unija za Integracija/Bashkimit Demokratik për Integrim*—DUI/BDI). The DUI/BDI was formed in June 2002 by Ali Ahmeti, the former head of the Albanian National Liberation Army—NLA (*Ushtrisë Çlirimtare Kombëtare*—UÇK), which had been dissolved in late September 2001 as a consequence of the August peace accord with the government. The principal focus of the DUI/BDI, according to its chair, was the full implementation of the provisions of the Ohrid accords.

In 2003 the BUI/BDI merged with the **National Democratic Party** (*Nacionala Demokratska Partija/Partisë Demokratike Kombëtar*—NDP/PDK), another Albanian party led by Kastriot HAXHIREXHA and comprising former members of the NLA. However, some NDP/PDK members denounced Haxhirexha for having abandoned the NDP/PDK's "pursuit of federalism." Claiming "no common interest" with the DUI/BDI, the rump NDP/PDK elected new leaders, including Basri HALITI as chair. Some reports of the 2006 elections referenced both the DUI/BDI–NDP/PDK and the "rump" NDP/PDK presenting their own candidates, indicating that the split between NDP/PDK factions continued. (See the entry in the 2011 *Handbook* for details.)

In the 2006 parliamentary elections the DUI/BDI led an electoral bloc that included the PDP/PPD and the **Democratic League of Bosnians** (*Demokratska Liga na Bošnjacite/Demokratski Savez Bošnjaka*—DLB/DSB). The DUI/BDI won 14 seats, establishing it as the strongest ethnic Albanian party in parliament. Although the VMRO-DPMNE initially approached it with regards to joining the government, it ultimately chose DPA/PDSh as a partner. The DUI/BDI responded with protests, roadblocks, and mass rallies. The conflict between VMRO-DPMNE and DUI/BDI, which claimed that the government was failing to uphold the Ohrid accords, led to a lengthy boycott of parliament by the latter from January 26 through August 2007, precipitating a political crisis. In May 2007 Menduh Thaçi threatened to remove the DPA/PDSh from the government coalition if the VMRO-DPMNE reached a political agreement with the DUI/BDI, reflecting continued rivalry and conflict between ethnic Albanian political parties. In July 2007 Fazli VELIU, a member of the DUI parliamentary group and one of the founders of the National Liberation Army, suggested that renewed military struggle was a possibility if Kosovo failed to receive independence and ethnic Albanians failed to receive equality within Macedonia. The DUI/BDI leadership subsequently criticized Veliu's statement that "thousands" of ethnic Albanians in Macedonia were ready to take up arms to defend Kosovo.

In the 2008 Assembly election the party took 18 parliamentary seats, strengthening its position as the leading ethnic Albanian party. After negotiations with both the DPA/PDSh and DUI/BDI, the VMRO-DPMNE (which possessed sufficient legislative strength to rule alone) brought the latter into the ruling coalition government, even though previous disagreements between the two parties (particularly over the recognition of Kosovo) remained unresolved. In response to reports of rising ethnic Albanian frustration in 2009, the DUI/BDI urged its coalition partners in the ruling government to find a compromise with Greece over the name dispute by the end of the year. The DUI/BDI still defended the Ohrid Agreement as resolving key minority demands, though the party suggested that implementation might be hastened.

The DUI/BDI's Agron Buxhaku won 7.5 percent of the vote in the first round of the 2009 presidential poll.

In October 2010 allegations were made based on files reportedly leaked from the Lustration Commission that several leading DUI/BDI members had served as informers or agents for the Yugoslav-era security services.

In the June 2011 election the DUI/BDI led a coalition with the DLB/DSB. The coalition won 10.2 percent of the vote and 15 seats, of which the DUI/BDI received 14 and the DLB/DSB received 1.

Leaders: Ali AHMETI (Chair), Agron BUXHAKU (2009 presidential candidate), Abdilaqim ADEMI (Secretary General).

Other Parliamentary Parties:

Social Democratic Union of Macedonia Coalition (*Socijaldemokratski Sojuz na Makedonija Koalicija*—SDSM *Koalicija*). Officially registered with the election authorities under this name, this was a continuation of the 2008 **Sun–Coalition for Europe** (*Sonce–Koalicija za Evropa*) and the 2002 and 2006 **Coalition for Macedonia Together** (*Koalicija Za Makedonija Zaedno—Koalicija* ZMZ), the **Union of Tito's Left Forces** (*Sojuz na Titovi Levi Sili*—STLS), and the **Party of Free Democrats** (*Partija na Slobodni Demokrati*—PSD). The LDP was an integral part of the coalition in the 2002, 2006, and 2008 elections, but left it to run independently in 2011.

In addition to the parties below, the SDSM coalition included three smaller parties that gained one seat after the coalition's seats were distributed: the **Party for the Total Emancipation of Roma in Macedonia** (*Partija za Celosna Emancipacija na Romite vo Makedonija*—PCERM), the **Movement of National Unity of Turks in Macedonia** (*Dvizhenje za Nacionalno Edinstvo na Turcite vo Makedonija*—DNETM), and the **Serbian Progressive Party in Macedonia** (*Srpska Napredna Stranka vo Makedonija*—SNSM). Smaller parties that did not gain representation included the **New Alternative** (*Nova Alternativa*—NA), the **Democratic Union of Vlachs from Macedonia** (*Demokratski Sojuz na Vlasite ot Makedonija*—DSVM), the **Party of Pensioners of the Republic of Macedonia** (*Partija na Penzionerite na Republika Makedonija*—PPRM), the **Party for Movement of the Turks in Macedonia** (*Partija za Dvizhenje na Turtsite vo Makedonija*—PDTM), and the **Sandzak League** (*Sanjačka Liga*—SL).

The coalition won 32.8 percent of the popular vote and 42 seats in the 2011 Assembly balloting, substantially increasing the strength of the opposition.

Social Democratic Union of Macedonia (*Socijaldemokratski Sojuz na Makedonija*—SDSM). The SDSM was the name adopted in 1991 by the League of Communists of Macedonia–Party of Democratic Change (*Sojuz na Komunistite na Makedonija–Partija za Demokratska Preobrazba*—SKM-PDP), which had been launched in 1989 as successor to the SKM. Although the SKM-PDP had run second to the VMRO-DPMNE in the 1990 legislative poll, its nominee, Kiro Gligorov, was subsequently designated president of the republican presidency.

The SDSM was the largest component of the Union of Macedonia (*Sojuz na Makedonija*—SM), an electoral alliance formed for the 1994 presidential and legislative balloting by the SDSM, SPM, and LPM, the three non-Albanian parties of the post-1992 government. The SM supported the SDSM's Gligorov in his successful bid for a second presidential term in 1994, and the SM secured 95 seats (58 for the SDSM) in the controversial concurrent legislative poll, with the SDSM's Branko CRVENKOVSKI remaining as prime minister of the subsequent SM-led government. However, friction developed within the SM, leading to the departure of the LPM from the government in a February 1996 reshuffle. The SM was subsequently described as having collapsed, and minimal cooperation between the SDSM and the SPM was reported in the 1998 legislative elections, from which the SDSM emerged with only 27 seats. (One of the seats credited to the SDSM was won in coalition with the Social Democratic Party of Macedonia [SDPM], which had won a seat in 1994.)

In the 1999 presidential contest the SDSM candidate, former Assembly speaker Tito Petkovski, finished first in the first round, with 32.7 percent of the vote, but lost in the November runoff to the governing coalition's candidate. In May 2000 the SDSM and the LDP concluded a cooperation agreement for the upcoming local elections and the next general election. The League for Democracy soon joined the alliance, and all three immediately called for new elections. An SDSM-led rally in Skopje in mid-May attracted 40,000 people, who heard Crvenkovski charge the government with corruption, failure to raise the standard of living, and an inability to fulfill its election promises. However, a year later the SDSM agreed to join a national unity government, although it withdrew in November 2001, noting that the unity government had accomplished its immediate goal of achieving domestic stability.

In 2004 Crvenkovski was elected president of the republic as the candidate of the *Koalicija* ZMZ. The coalition was renewed for the 2006 Assembly election, at which the SDSM won 23 of the coalition's 32 seats. The defeat resulted in an internal shake-up within the party, with party leader Vlado Bučkovski being removed after losing a no-confidence vote and with Crvenkovski sidelined within the party. In the November 2006 party elections Radmila Sekerinska became the first female leader of a major Macedonian political party since independence.

Following the announcement in April 2008 of early elections, the SDSM organized the *Sonce* coalition, pledging to achieve NATO membership and begin the first steps in EU accession talks by the end of the year. *Sonce*'s poor performance in the June 2008 elections led Sekerinska (and other senior party members) to announce their resignations from their posts in July. Although a temporary party leadership was appointed, Crvenkovski's role was strengthened and he resumed leadership of the party after finishing his presidential term in May 2009.

In the June 2011 election, the SDSM received 29 seats from the coalition's total.

Despite an electoral alliance with the NSDP, VMRO-NP, OM, and LDP in the 2013 local elections, SDSM won only 4 of 80 municipal mayoral races. Crvenkovski resigned as party president, with Zoran ZAEV elected at a party congress on June 2, 2013.

Leaders: Zoran ZAEV (President), Branko CRVENKOVSKI (Former President of the Republic), Ljubomir FRČKOSKI (2009 presidential candidate), Andrej PETROV (Secretary), Frosina REMENSKI (Vice President).

New Social Democratic Party (*Nova Socijal Demokratsčka Partija*—NSDP). The NSDP was formed in November 2005 by former members of the SDSM who sought a more centrist social democratic party. Its party platform is broadly pro-Western and technocratic, stressing Macedonian membership in the EU, improved relations with the United States, investment in "information and communication technology," and the need for economic development. In the 2006 legislative elections the party won seven seats and was subsequently invited to join the government, assuming the ministries of both defense and the economy. In 2008 the party joined the opposition prior to the elections, taking three seats in parliament. In the 2011 Assembly election, the party received four seats from the coalition's total.

Leader: Tamara BAARA (President).

Party for a European Future (*Partija za Evropska Idnina*—PEI). The PEI is a centrist party that advocates deeper integration with NATO and the EU. The party was formed in March 2006 by Fijat Canoski. In 2006 and 2008 it won a single seat in parliament. Although it did not receive a cabinet position following the 2008 balloting, the PEI pledged legislative support for the government. It moved to the opposition prior to the 2011 election and received three seats. However, in mid-June the PEI moved to form its own opposition bloc in parliament independent of the SDSM-led coalition.

Leader: Fijat CANOSKI.

Liberal Party of Macedonia (*Liberalna Partija na Makedonija*—LPM). The LPM was organized initially as the Alliance of Reform Forces of Macedonia (*Sojuz na Reformskite Sili na Makedonija*—SRSM), an affiliate of the federal Alliance of Yugoslav Reform Forces (in Serbo-Croatian, *Savez Reformskih Snaga Jugoslavije*—SRSJ). In the 1990 balloting it was allied in some areas with the Young Democratic and Progressive Party (in Serbo-Croatian, *Mlas Demokratska Progresivna Partija*—MDPS), which it later absorbed, adopting the name Reform Forces of Macedonia–Liberal

Party (*Reformskite Sili na Makedonija–Liberalna Partija*—RSM-LP) in 1992. Using the shorter LPM rubric, the party won 29 seats in the 1994 election as part of the Union of Macedonia (SM; see under SDSM, above) and continued to be a component of the ruling coalition. However, growing friction with the dominant SDSM culminated in ejection of the LPM from the coalition in February 1996, whereupon party leader Stojan Andov resigned as speaker of the legislature and committed the LPM to vigorous opposition. A 1997 merger with the Democratic Party of Macedonia (DPM) to form the Liberal-Democratic Party (LDP) ended in 2000, when the LPM reemerged as a separate organization. In November 2000 the revived party joined the governing coalition led by the VMRO-DPMNE. The LPM participated in the electoral bloc led by the VMRO-DPMNE for the 2006 Assembly poll, winning two seats in parliament and subsequently participating in government. In 2008 it moved to join the opposition, stating dissatisfaction with the government's progress in obtaining NATO and EU membership. In the 2011 election, it received a single seat as part of the coalition.

Leaders: Ivon VELIČKOVSKI (President), Ristanka LALČEVSKA (Vice President).

Democratic Party of Albanians (*Demokratska Partija na Albancite/Partisë Demokratike Shqiptare*—DPA/PDSh). The DPA/PDSh was formed in mid-1997 by the merger of the Party for Democratic Prosperity of Albanians in Macedonia (*Partija za Demokratski Prosperitet na Albancite vo Makedonija*—PDPA) and the People's Democratic Party (*Narodna Demokratska Partija*—NDP). The NDP was an ethnic Albanian grouping that resulted from a split between the moderate majority of the ethnic Albanian Party for Democratic Prosperity and an antigovernment minority, led by Ilijaz Halimi, at a congress of the parent party in February 1994. The NDP became the largest nongovernment party after the October–November elections, at which it won four seats, but lost that status when the LPM joined the opposition in February 1996.

The PDPA had been launched in April 1995 as another breakaway from the PDP by a group opposed to the parent party's participation in the government coalition. Its leader was Arben Xhaferi, a spokesperson for the militant Albanian population who had spent many years in the separatist movement in Kosovo before establishing a base in Tetovo in western Macedonia and being elected as an independent to the Macedonian legislature.

The government allegedly refused to recognize the DPA/PDSh after its formation in 1997 on the grounds that the grouping supported unconstitutional demands on behalf of the Albanians. In fact, official government reports on the 1998 legislative election referenced the grouping as the PDPA/NDP, which contested the balloting in partial alliance with the PDP. Following the election, the use of the DPA/PDSh title appeared to gain the government's sanction, particularly after the DPA/PDSh, which had won 11 legislative seats, agreed to join the subsequent VMRO-DPMNE-led coalition government. Xhaferi, described by the *Christian Science Monitor* as the "flint" that could "set Macedonia afire," called his accord with the VMRO-DPMNE's Ljubčo Georgievski "a small miracle." The DPA/PDSh was not officially registered under that name until July 2002.

Following its entrance into the government, the DPA/PDSh appeared to moderate its course, although Deputy Chair Menduh Thaçi remained one of the more hard-line advocates for Albanian rights. In the 1999 presidential election the party's candidate, Muharem NEXIPI, finished fourth, with 14.8 percent of the vote; in the second round, the DPA/PDSh threw its support to the successful VMRO-DPMNE candidate. The DPA/PDSh won 7 seats in the 2002 Assembly poll, but from April 2005 through January 2006 the delegates boycotted parliamentary sessions in protest of "manipulated results" in the 2005 local elections. In the 2006 parliamentary elections the DPA/PDSh ran independently, winning 11 seats. After failing to reach an agreement with the DUI/BDI, the VMRO-DPMNE negotiated for the DPA/PDSh's entrance into the government.

There were reports during the 2008 Assembly election of violence between members of the DPA/PDSh and the DUI/BDI and of serious electoral irregularities in several districts with a majority of ethnic Albanians. The DPA/PDSh rejected the results of the second round of voting on June 15 but accepted the third round, while accusing the DUI/BDI of fostering division and violence within the Albanian community. Meanwhile, merger discussions with the PDP/PPD proved unsuccessful, although PDP/PPD leader Abduljhadi Vejseli and a significant faction of the PDP/PPD joined the DPA/PDSh (see PDP/PPD below for details).

The DPA/PDSh's Mirushe Hoxha won 3.1 percent of the vote in the first round of presidential balloting in 2009.

In the 2011 Assembly election DPA/PDSh won 5.9 percent of the popular vote and eight seats.

Leaders: Menduh THAÇI (Chair), Imer ALIU (Vice President), Mirushe HOXHA (2009 presidential candidate), Metin IZETI.

National Democratic Renewal (*Nacionalna Demokratska Prerodba/Rilindja Demokratike Kombëtare*—NDP/RDK). The NDP/RDK was founded in March 2011 on a platform of Albanian minority rights. Its founder, Rufi Osmani, had previously served a prison term for his role in the 1997 dispute over the flying of the Albanian flag in front of municipal buildings in the town of Gostivar.

In the June 2011 election, the NDR/RDK won 2.7 percent of the popular vote and two seats in parliament.

Leader: Rufi OSMANI (Chair).

Other Parties That Contested the 2011 Legislative Elections:

Internal Macedonian Revolutionary Organization–People's Party (*Vnatrešno Makedonska Revolucionerna Organizacija–Narodna Partija*—VMRO-NP). The VMRO-NP was formed in Skopje in July 2004 by supporters of former VMRO-DPMNE chair and prime minister Ljubčo GEORGIEVSKI. The VMRO-NP is a conservative party whose platform closely resembles the VMRO-DPMNE. In the 2006 parliamentary elections it won six seats, but three members of parliament subsequently left the party. Georgievski took Bulgarian citizenship in 2006, resigned as party president in 2007 (though retaining an honorary position as "party leader"), and subsequently entered Bulgarian politics as a mayoral candidate for Blagoevgrad. In May 2008 the state election commission revoked the party's candidate list, citing that the group missed submission deadlines. In the 2011 election, the party took 2.5 percent of the popular vote but failed to pass the threshold for representation.

In February 2012 party president Marjan DODEVSKI resigned and led a faction that joined the VMRO-DPMNE, with Georgievski taking over active leadership.

Leader: Ljubčo GEORGIEVSKI (President).

New Democracy (*Nova Demokratija/Demokracia e Re*—ND/DR). The ND/DR was formed in September 2008 as a new party representing Albanian interests by Imer SELMANI, former vice president of the DPA/PDSh, and other DPA/PDSh members (including a number of legislators) who cited policy differences with the DPA/PDSh leadership for their defection. Selmani won 15 percent of the vote in the first round of the 2009 presidential election, finishing ahead of the candidates from rival ethnic Albanian parties. The ND/DR was subsequently reported to have five legislators within its membership. In the 2011 election the party took 1.8 percent of the vote, failing to pass the threshold to gain representation.

Leaders: Imer SELMANI (Chair and 2009 presidential candidate), Sulejman RUSHITI.

United for Macedonia (*Obedineti za Makedonija*—OM). The conservative OM was founded in May 2009 by Ljube BOŠKOSKI. A former VMRO-DPMNE figure and interior minister, Boškoski was tried by the International Criminal Tribunal for the former Yugoslavia for possible involvement as minister in the attacks on ethnic Albanians during the 2001 conflict. He was acquitted on all charges and returned to found the OM in May 2009.

In June 2011, one day after the Assembly election, Boškoski was arrested, allegedly for improper campaign financing. OM has charged that the accused the allegations were politically motivated by a ruling government seeking to silence a conservative rival. In November 2011 Boškoski was sentenced to seven years in prison, the sentence later reduced on appeal to five years.

Leader: Ljube BOŠKOSKI.

Liberal-Democratic Party (*Liberalno-Demokratska Partija*—LDP). The centrist LDP was formed in January 1997 by what proved to be a temporary merger of the LPM (above) and the Democratic Party of Macedonia (*Demokratska Partija Makedonija*—DPM). The DPM had been registered in July 1993 under the leadership of a Communist-era prime minister but unexpectedly failed to have much impact in the 1994 balloting. When the DPM and LPM merged as the LDP, the DPM's Petar Gošev became leader of the new formation.

The LDP won only four seats in the 1998 legislative poll, securing 7.0 percent in the proportional balloting; Gošev resigned as chair in January 1999 in view of that poor electoral performance. In 2000 the LPM was reestablished as a separate party, taking with it three of the four LDP parliamentary deputies. In May 2000 the LDP joined the SDSM in an electoral alliance for the September local elections and the 2002 Assembly election.

The LDP's participation in the *Koalicija* ZKM contributed to the coalition's success in the 2004 presidential election. In 2006 the party won five seats in parliament. The coalition's poor showing led, in 2007, to party leader Risto PENOV's resignation, the election of Jovan MANASIEVSKI as party president, and a decision for the party to leave the *Koalicija* ZKM, positioning the party for an independent bid in the expected 2010 elections. The 2008 early elections, however, saw the party remain in coalition with its previous partners. It received four seats in parliament.

The LDP's Nano Ruzin won 4.1 percent of the vote in the first round of the 2009 presidential balloting.

After the party failed to secure any seats in the 2011 elections, Manasievski resigned as party leader.

Leaders: Andrej ZHERNOVSKI (President), Nano RUZIN (2009 presidential candidate), Petar GOŠEV.

Party for Democratic Prosperity (*Partija za Demokratski Prosperite/Partia për Prosperitet Demokratik*—PDP/PPD). The PDP/PPD was one of the principal vehicles for supporting ethnic Albanian interests in Macedonia after its May 1990 launch. Subsequent to the 1990 election (in which it won 25 seats), it absorbed a smaller party with the same abbreviation, the Popular Democratic Party of Ilijaz Halimi.

The PDP/PPD was riven by splits between the progovernment moderates and antigovernment nationalists in February 1994 and April 1995 and the respective breakaway of the NDP and the PDPA (for both, see DPA, above). Having lost ground in the October–November 1994 Assembly balloting, the PDP/PPD continued as a government party.

The PDP/PPD contested the 1998 legislative balloting in partial coalition with the DPA/PDSh (PDPA/NDP), securing 14 seats. However, the PDP/PPD subsequently moved into opposition, while the DPA/PDSH joined the new VMRO-DPMNE–led cabinet. Following the poor showing of the party's 1999 presidential candidate, Muhamed HALILI, who finished sixth with 4.2 percent of the vote, the party leadership was replaced virtually en masse in April 2000, President Abdurahman HALITI giving way to Imer IMERI (Ymer YMERI). Although the party competed in the first round of the local elections in 2000, it pulled out of the second round, alleging major irregularities.

With the departure of the DA from the government in November 2000, Imeri apparently agreed to support the opposition in its bid to replace the Georgievski coalition, but he changed his mind when several of the party's Assembly members objected. Subsequent talks with the DPA/PDSh's Xhaferi and the VMRO-DPMNE about joining the government broke down in late December, in part because a hard-line faction demanded that the proposed private Albanian-language university in Tetovo be a state institution and that use of the Albanian language be permitted in the National Assembly—demands that the government was not prepared to accept at that time. Early in 2001 speculation rose that the PDP/PPD and the DPA/PDSh might merge, but that was before the outbreak of hostilities between militant Albanians and the government. International pressure reportedly led the PDP/PPD to join the May 2001 national unity administration.

In May 2002 Haliti returned to the party presidency following Imeri's resignation for health reasons. The PDP/PPD won two seats in the 2002 Assembly poll.

In the 2006 legislative elections the party ran in an electoral bloc with the DUI/BDI, winning three seats. The DUI/BDI's conflict with the VMRO-DPMNE resulted in a boycott of parliament in 2007 by both the DUI/BDI and PDP/PPD. Fears that the PDP/PPD was becoming marginalized prompted it to break its coalition in May 2007. On June 12 the PDP/PPD formally entered the government, where it attempted to moderate relations between the VMRO-DPMNE and the DUI/BDI.

The PDP/PPD performed poorly in the June 2, 2008, legislative elections, taking less than 1 percent of the vote and no seats. Party leader Abduljhadi Vejseli consequently proposed a full merger with the DPA/PDSh, and PDP/PPD members were encouraged to vote for the DPA/PDSh in the revotes held on June 15 and June 29. However, the merger proposal provoked a backlash within the PDP/PPD that prompted Vejseli to leave the party and join the DPA/PDSh.

Sefedin Haruni was appointed president of the PDP/PPD in August 2008 and confirmed at a party congress in December. In June 2009 Haruni joined other Albanian political figures (including Hisni SHAQIRI, a former prominent parliamentarian and current leader of the NDU/BDK, below) in calling for extensive constitutional changes to Macedonia beyond those laid out in the Ohrid Framework. Among other things, they proposed the creation of a "bi-national" state under a federal structure.

In the June 2011 election the erosion of support for the PDP/PDD continued, polling in 17th place out of 18 parties and coalitions. In 2012 Sefedin HARUNI reportedly stepped down as chair of the party after the Lustration Commission had reported him to be an informer for the Yugoslav secret police before 1989.

In March 2013 there were reports in domestic media that the PDP/PDD would be reregistered and hold a party congress to elect leaders.

Minor parties participating in the 2011 election include the political party **Dignity** (*Dostoinostvo*), the **Democratic Union of Albanians** (*Demokratska Unija na Albancite/Bashkimi Demokratik Shqiptar*—DUA/BDSh), the **Party of United Democrats of Macedonia** (*Partija na Obedineti Demokrati na Makedonija*—PODEM), the **Social Democratic Union** (*Socialdemokratska Unija*—SDU), the **Social Democratic Party of Macedonia** (*Socijaldemokratska Partija na Makedonija*—SDPM), the **Democratic Right** (*Demokratska Desnica*—DD), the **National Democratic Union** (*Nacionalna Demokratska Unija/ Bashkimi Demokratik Kombëtar*—NDU/BDK), and the **European Party of Macedonia** (*Evropska Partija na Makedonija*—EPM). None of these parties was able to obtain even 1 percent of the total vote.

LEGISLATURE

The present **Macedonian Assembly** (*Sobranje*) is a directly elected unicameral body of 123 members, elected for a four-year term through proportional representation from six electoral districts, each with 20 seats. In 2011, 3 seats were added to represent Macedonian citizens resident in Europe, North America, and Asia/Australia. Prior to 2002, 85 of the legislators were directly elected in two-round (if necessary) majoritarian balloting in single-member districts; the other 35 were elected on a nationwide proportional basis, with seats distributed to parties winning at least 5 percent of the national vote.

Following the early election of June 5, 2011, the seat distribution was as follows: the Coalition VMRO-DPMNE, 56 (the Internal Macedonian Revolutionary Organization–Democratic Party for Macedonian National Unity, 47; the Socialist Party of Macedonia, 3; the Democratic Union, 1; the Democratic Party of Serbs in Macedonia, 1; the Democratic Party of Turks in Macedonia, 1; the Party of Democratic Action of Macedonia, 1; the Union of Roma in Macedonia, 1; and the Internal Macedonian Revolutionary Organization-Macedonia, 1); the Coalition SDSM, 42 (the Social Democratic Union of Macedonia, 29; the New Social Democratic Party, 4; the Party for a European Future, 3; the Movement of National Unity of Turks in Macedonia, 1; the Serbian Progressive Party, 1; the Party for Total Emancipation of Romania, 1; the New Alternative, 1; the Liberal Party of Macedonia, 1; and non-party candidates, 2); the Democratic Union for Integration, 15 (of which its coalition partner the Democratic League of Bosnians received 1); the Democratic Party of Albanians, 8; and the National Democratic Revival, 2.

Speaker: Trajko VELJANOSKI.

CABINET

[as of November 15, 2013]

Prime Minister	Nikola Gruevski (VMRO-DPMNE)
Deputy Prime Minister	Zoran Stavreski (VMRO-DPMNE)
Deputy Prime Minister (Economy)	Vladimir Peshevski (VMRO-DPMNE)
Deputy Prime Minister (European Affairs)	Fatmir Besimi (DUI/BDI)
Deputy Prime Minister (Ohrid Agreement Implementation)	Musa Xhaferi (DUI/BDI)
Ministers	
Agriculture, Forestry, and Water Supply	Ljupčo Dimovski (SPM)

Culture	Elizabeta Kančevska Milevska (VMRO-DPMNE) [f]
Defense	Talat Xhaferi (DUI/BDI)
Economy	Valon Saraqini (DUI/BDI)
Education and Science	Spiro Ristovski (VMRO-DPMNE)
Environment and Physical Planning	Abdulakim Ademi (DUI/BDI)
Finance	Zoran Stavreski (VMRO-DPMNE)
Foreign Affairs	Nikola Popovski (VMRO-DPMNE)
Health	Nikola Todorov (VMRO-DPMNE)
Information Society	Ivo Ivanovksi (VMRO-DPMNE)
Internal Affairs	Gordana Jankulovska (VMRO-DPMNE) [f]
Justice	Blerim Bexheti (DUI/BDI)
Labor and Social Policy	Dime Spasov (VMRO-DPMNE)
Local Self-Government	Tahir Hani (DUI/BDI)
Transport and Communications	Mile Janakieski (VMRO-DPMNE)
Without Portfolio	Nezhdet Mustafa (OPE)
Without Portfolio	Hadi Neziri (PDTM)
Without Portfolio (Responsible for Attracting Foreign Investment)	Vele Samak (ind.)
Without Portfolio (Responsible for Attracting Foreign Investment)	Bill Pavleski (ind.)
Without Portfolio (Responsible for Attracting Foreign Investment)	Jerry Naumoff (ind.)

[f] = female

INTERGOVERNMENTAL REPRESENTATION

Ambassador to the U.S.: Zoran JOLEVSKI.

U.S. Ambassador to Macedonia: Paul WOHLERS.

Permanent Representative to the UN: Pajo AVIROVIKJ.

IGO Memberships (Non-UN): CEUR, EBRD, ICC, OSCE, WTO.

MADAGASCAR

Republic of Madagascar
Repoblikan'i Madagasikara (Malagasy)
République de Madagascar (French)

Note: In presidential runoff elections on December 20, 2013, Hery Rajaonarimampianina won 53.5 percent of the vote, defeating his opponent Jean Louis Robinson. Robinson filed complaints with the electoral court claiming the vote was rigged. Results of concurrently held legislative elections were not available as of January 7, 2014.

Political Status: Established as the Malagasy Republic within the French Community in 1958; became independent June 26, 1960; military regime established May 18, 1972; name of Democratic Republic of Madagascar and single-party system adopted in new constitution and Socialist Revolutionary Charter approved by national referendum on December 21, 1975; present name adopted in the new constitution of the Third Republic (codifying multiparty activity first authorized by presidential decree of March 1990) that was approved by national referendum on August 19, 1992, but was subsequently the subject of extensive political conflict; federal system established by constitutional amendments approved by national referendum on March 15, 1998, and promulgated on April 8; federal system restructured by constitutional amendments passed by referendum on April 4, 2007, and promulgated April 28; transitional government following a coup on March 17, 2009; new constitution approved by referendum on November 17, 2010.

Area: 226,657 sq. mi. (587,041 sq. km).

Population: 22,029,861 (2012E—UN); 22,599,000 (2013E—U.S. Census).

Major Urban Center (2005E): ANTANANARIVO (1,581,000).

Official Languages: Malagasy, French, English.

Monetary Unit: Ariary (official rate November 1, 2013: 2,187.94 ariarys = $1US). The ariary replaced the Madagasy Franc in mid-2003.

President: (*See headnote.*) Andry RAJOELINA (Young Malagasies Determined); installed as president of the High Authority of the Transition on March 21, 2009, after his predecessor, Marc RAVALOMANANA (I Love Madagascar) surrendered power to a military directorate on March 17.

Prime Minister: Omer BERIZIKY; assumed office October 28, 2011, after being named prime minister by President Rajoelina following the resignation of Col. Albert Camille VITAL on October 17.

THE COUNTRY

The Republic of Madagascar, consisting of the large island of Madagascar and five small island dependencies, is situated in the Indian Ocean off the southeast coast of Africa. The island is renowned for its biodiversity and its treasure trove of unique plant and animal species. Although the population includes some 18 distinct ethnic groups, the main division is between the Asian Mérina people (the largest ethnic group [26 percent of the population]) of the central plateau and the sub-Saharan peoples of the coastal regions (*côtiers*). The Malagasy language is of Malayo-Polynesian origin, yet reflects African, Arabic, and European influences. The nonindigenous population includes some 30,000 Comorans and smaller groups of French, Indians, Pakistanis, and Chinese. Women constitute more than 45 percent of the labor force, performing the bulk of subsistence activity. However, due largely to matriarchal elements in precolonial Malagasy culture, females are significantly better represented in government and urban managerial occupations than their mainland counterparts.

Agriculture, forestry, and fishing account for more than one-fourth of Madagascar's gross domestic product (GDP) but employ more than four-fifths of the labor force, the majority at a subsistence level. Leading export crops are coffee, cloves, and vanilla, while industry is concentrated in food processing (notably seafood) and textiles. Mineral resources include deposits of graphite, nickel, chromium, and gemstones (particularly sapphires), in addition to undeveloped reserves of bauxite, iron, titanium, and petroleum.

In the 1970s much of the country's economic base, formerly dominated by foreign businesses, was nationalized by a strongly socialist regime. However, in the face of mounting external debt, worsening trade deficits, and capital flight, the administration in 1980 abandoned its formal commitment to socialism and called for assistance from the International Monetary Fund (IMF), the World Bank, and U.S. and European donors. In addition, budget austerity, currency devaluations, and measures to reduce food imports by boosting agricultural production were introduced. Although foreign creditors applauded such actions, no measurable economic progress was subsequently achieved, with economic reforms aggravating the decline of living standards in urban areas.

In the early 1990s a series of economic reforms, including deregulation and the privatization of some state-run industries, was instituted following suspension from the IMF and a series of austerity measures placed upon the country. These measures led to a period of sustained growth in the late 1990s, but the country suffered a series of economic shocks in the early 2000s. The lingering effects of three cyclones in early 2000 and weak export prices made the economy a key issue in the controversial 2001 presidential campaign (see Political background, below).

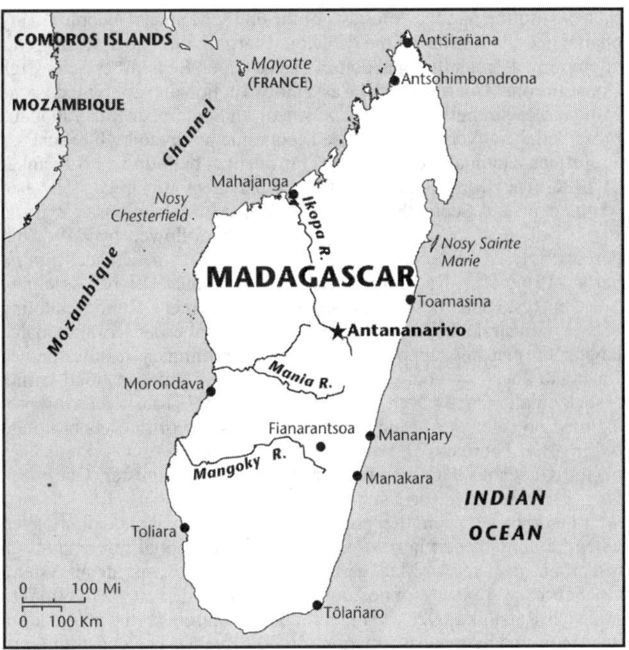

In 2002 the GDP steeply declined and inflation spiked as a result of violence and uncertainty associated with the contested presidential election. The new administration subsequently enjoyed consistent international support, in part because of its measures to support economic liberalization, encourage foreign investment, and eliminate corruption. In 2003 the economy began to recover with the introduction of a new currency, the ariary. The country's accession in May 2006 to the Southern African Development Community (SADC) was expected to expand regional trade opportunities. Beginning in 2007, the nation's mining sector began expanding due to the discovery of nickel, copper, and platinum deposits and the development of chromite and ilmenite mines.

As in 2002, Madagascar's protracted political crisis of 2009–2010 resulted in a significant drop in foreign investment, development aid, and revenue from tourism. Government services such as sanitation were halted for long periods amid the uncertainty of the transition. Meanwhile a severe drought in the south, several major cyclones, and the steep increase in food prices contributed to a humanitarian emergency in 2009. The additional impact of the global financial crisis, which reduced demand for exports such as vanilla, resulted in GDP contraction of 4.1 percent in 2009, according to the IMF. The agrarian sector subsequently rebounded with above-average rice harvests, but the tourism industry remained in decline and international development aid, accounting for roughly 40 percent of government expenditures, remained frozen. A sharp increase in illegal rosewood logging threatened the island's protected forests, according to environmental groups (see Current issues, below). GDP grew by 0.4 percent in 2010, and growth slowly continued into the new decade, with GDP gaining 1.8 percent in 2011 and 1.9 percent in 2012. Madagascar remains one of the world's poorest countries, however, ranking sixth in the world for malnutrition. Worsening conditions prompted the World Bank to award $167 million in emergency assistance in December 2012, though warning the package did not indicate the "normalization" of relations. The United Nations (UN) ranked Madagascar 151st out of 185 countries in its 2013 Human Development Index. In 2013 GDP grew by 2.6 percent, with inflation of 7 percent.

GOVERNMENT AND POLITICS

Political background. During the 18th century and most of the 19th century, Madagascar was dominated by the Mérina people of the plateau. However, after a brief period of British influence, the French gained control and by 1896 had destroyed the Mérina monarchy. Renamed the Malagasy Republic, it became an autonomous state within the French Community in 1958 and gained full independence on June 26, 1960, under the presidency of Philibert TSIRANANA, a *côtier* who governed with the support of the Social Democratic Party (*Parti Social Démocrate*—PSD).

Tsiranana's coastal-dominated government ultimately proved unable to deal with a variety of problems, including ethnic conflict stemming from Mérina opposition to the government's pro-French policies. In addition, economic reverses led to a revolt in 1971 by peasants in Tulear Province, while students, dissatisfied with their job prospects in a stagnating economy, mounted a rebellion in early 1972. Having acknowledged his growing inability to rule in May, Tsiranana abdicated his duties as head of state and chief of government in favor of Maj. Gen. Gabriel RAMANANTSOA, a Mérina, who was confirmed for a five-year term by a referendum held October 8.

An attempted coup by dissident *côtier* officers led to Ramanantsoa's resignation on February 5, 1975; his successor, Col. Richard RATSIMANDRAVA, a Mérina, was assassinated six days later, with Brig. Gen. Gilles ANDRIAMAHAZO assuming the leadership of a Military Directorate. Cdr. Didier RATSIRAKA in turn succeeded Andriamahazo on June 15. Subsequently, on December 21, 1975, voters approved a Socialist Revolutionary Charter and a new constitution that called for the establishment of a National Front for the Defense of the Malagasy Socialist Revolution (*Front National pour la Défense de la Révolution Socialiste Malgache*—FNDR) as an overarching political formation. The voters also designated Ratsiraka, a *côtier*, for a seven-year term as president of the newly styled Democratic Republic of Madagascar; thereby he continued his role as chair of a Supreme Revolutionary Council (*Conseil Suprême de la Revolution*—CSR) that had been established in 1972.

The new Ratsiraka government formed on January 11, 1976, was designed to reflect a regional balance of both military and civilian elements. The government was reconstituted on August 20 following the accidental death of Prime Minister Joël RAKOTOMALALA on July 30 and his replacement by Justin RAKOTONIAINA on August 12. Local elections, the first since the constitutional revision, began in March 1977 and were dominated by the Vanguard of the Malagasy Revolution (*Antoky'ny Revolosiona Malagasy*—Arema), established by Ratsiraka a year earlier as the main FNDR component. Arema members also filled 112 of the 137 positions on the FNDR's single list of National Assembly candidates, which was approved by a reported 90 percent of voters on June 30. Ratsiraka subsequently appointed a new cabinet, headed by Prime Minister Lt. Col. Désiré RAKOTOARIJAONA.

President Ratsiraka was popularly reelected to a seven-year term on November 7, 1982, by a four-to-one margin over Monja JAONA of the National Movement for the Independence of Madagascar (*Mouvement National pour l'Indépendqnce de Madagascar*—Monima). Assembly elections scheduled for 1982 were postponed until August 23, 1983, at which time more than 500 candidates from FNDR-affiliated groups were allowed on the ballot. Arema secured 117 seats on the basis of a 65 percent vote share.

On February 12, 1988, Lt. Col. Victor RAMAHATRA (theretofore minister of public works) was named to succeed Colonel Rakotoarijaona as prime minister. With the FNDR increasingly unable to maintain control of its constituent groups, the scheduled 1988 assembly elections were postponed, ostensibly to permit their being held simultaneously with presidential balloting in November 1989. However, under powers granted by a constitutional amendment approved by the assembly in December 1988, Ratsiraka moved the presidential election up to March 12, 1989. Aided by disunity within the opposition, which fielded three candidates, Ratsiraka was reelected to another term, albeit with a reduced majority (63 percent) and with waning support in Antananarivo and other urban areas. Arema had little trouble maintaining its large majority in assembly balloting on May 28.

After the government thwarted a coup attempt in Antananarivo in July 1989, party leaders became increasingly critical of the administration's policies. In early 1990 President Ratsiraka issued a decree that abolished mandatory participation in the FNDR as of March 1. A number of new parties immediately emerged, six of which joined with the Christian Council of Churches of Madagascar (*Fikambanan'ny Fiangonana Kristiana Malagasy*—FFKM) in sponsoring a National Meeting for a New Constitution on May 23. Ten days earlier, three people had been killed and some two-dozen injured in a coup attempt by the Republican Committee for Public Safety (*Comité Républican pour le Salut Publique*). Thereafter, highly publicized FFKM-opposition party conferences held August 16–19 and December 5–9 demanded abolition of the CSR, the formation of an all-party transitional government, and the convening of a constituent assembly to define the institutions of a Third Republic. Ratsiraka announced in January 1991 that he had asked the government to present a series of proposals to the assembly to bring the constitution into closer conformity with the "national and international context."

On July 28, 1991, following seven weeks of strikes and demonstrations in Antananarivo by the opposition Living Forces (*Forces Vives/ Hery Velona*) group, Ratsiraka dissolved the government and announced that he would call for constitutional reform by the end of the year. On August 8 he appointed as prime minister the mayor of Antananarivo, Guy Willy RAZANAMASY, who, after being granted extensive executive powers, proclaimed a desire to lead his country "down the tortuous and difficult road to democracy." However, an interim government announced by Razanamasy on August 26 included no representatives from the FFKM or *Hery Velona,* which was composed of 16 political parties. As a result, the opposition launched a general strike and organized a protest rally in the capital of some 300,000 persons, bringing economic life to a sudden halt. In the wake of Ratsiraka's loss of control, Dr. Albert ZAFY, the leader of *Hery Velona*, set up a shadow government, proclaiming himself as the prime minister and the *Haute Autorité*, a political body composed of the parties in the *Hery Velona*, as the national assembly.

In the wake of continued unrest, Ratsiraka and Razanamasy agreed on October 29, 1991, to the formation of a new unity government that would include representatives of opposition formations, religious groups, and the armed forces. In addition, both the CSR and the assembly transferred their functions to the transitional High State Authority (*Haute Autorité d'État*—HAE) and a Committee for Economic and Social Recovery (*Comité pour le Redressement Économique et Social*—CRES). On October 31 Ratsiraka and the *Hery Velona* signed the Panorama Convention, which established a transitional government. The terms of the convention left Ratsiraka as president but transferred most of his powers to the HAE and CRES, promising a new constitution, which would be submitted to a popular referendum by the end of the year. Zafy was named HAE president on November 23, and Rakotonirina and Andriamanjato became cochairs of the CRES. The result was a quadripartite distribution of power involving the prime minister, the HAE president, the CRES chairs, and the increasingly marginalized president of the republic. A 1,400-member National Forum met March 22–29, 1992, to draw up the new constitution, which was approved by referendum on August 19.

Zafy received 45.2 percent of the vote against seven other candidates in first-round presidential balloting on November 25, 1992. In a runoff against Ratsiraka on February 10, 1993, Zafy defeated the incumbent president by a two-to-one margin. Subsequent legislative balloting on June 16, 1993, gave Zafy supporters a majority of 75 of 138 seats on a 55 percent vote share. The new assembly approved Francisque RAVONY as prime minister on August 9.

By mid-1995 the president and prime minister were at odds, with Zafy accusing Ravony of having impoverished the country through maladministration of its structural adjustment program. However, Zafy was unable to mount sufficient legislative support to secure Ravony's removal from office. As a result of the impasse, the two leaders arrived at an unusual compromise whereby Ravony would receive long-sought authorization to name a new cabinet (implemented on August 18, with the exclusion of Zafy supporters), while a constitutional referendum would be held to give the president opportunity to appoint a new prime minister.

Despite complaints of a return to authoritarianism, Zafy won a 63 percent "yes" vote in the referendum of September 17, 1995, and on October 30 he appointed Emmanuel RAKOTOVAHINY to succeed Ravony, who had resigned on October 13. Rakotovahiny's cabinet, appointed on November 10, was dominated by members of Zafy's UNDD. The ongoing controversy over economic policy came to a head in early May 1996 when IMF director Michel Camdessus, during a visit to Antananarivo, announced that the government as constituted was not suitable to negotiate new agreements with the IMF and World Bank. Consequently, on May 17, the assembly passed a motion of no-confidence in the government by a vote of 109–15. Although Rakotovahiny challenged the constitutionality of the vote, he submitted his resignation on May 20, and on May 28 Zafy appointed Norbert RATSIRAHONANA, chief judge of the High Constitutional Court, as the new prime minister. The cabinet announced by Ratsirahonana on June 5 was again comprised primarily of UNDD members.

The executive/legislative conflict culminated on July 26, 1996, in a 99–39 assembly vote to remove Zafy from office on grounds that he had violated his oath of office by taking numerous actions contrary to the constitution and the "interests of the entire Malagasy people." Zafy challenged the legality of the decision, charging that the assembly was attempting a "constitutional coup." However, on September 5 the High Constitutional Court upheld the assembly's action and appointed Prime Minister Ratsirahonana interim president. In September Ratsirahonana presented the government's revised economic policy to IMF officials.

Fifteen candidates contested the presidential balloting on November 3, 1996. The front-runner was former president Ratsiraka (who had returned in late September from 18 months of self-imposed exile in Paris), with 36.6 percent of the vote. He was followed by Zafy, 23.4 percent; Herizo RAZAFIMAHALEO (head of the Leader–*Fanilo* party), 15 percent; Ratsirahonana, 10 percent; and National Assembly Speaker Rev. Richard ANDRIAMANJATO, 5 percent. Runoff balloting between Ratsiraka and Zafy took place on December 29, Razafimahaleo having thrown his support to the former. Preliminary results showed Ratsiraka ahead by about 30,000 votes, but Zafy alleged fraud during vote tabulation. However, on January 30, 1997, Ratsiraka was proclaimed president by virtue of a 51 percent share of the second-round polling. On February 21 Ratsiraka named Pascal RAKOTOMAVO, a business executive and Arema official, as prime minister. One week later Rakotomavo formed a new multiparty government.

Relations between the president and his opponents plummeted when he announced plans to organize a constitutional referendum on his proposal to return Madagascar to its pre-1995 provincial system. On February 4, 1998, opposition legislators failed in their effort to impeach Ratsiraka over the matter, and on March 15 the referendum was approved by a narrow margin (50.96 percent). The constitution of the Third Republic entered into force on April 8, providing for a federal system comprising six provincial governments. At the same time, opponents of Ratsiraka accused him of attempting to consolidate power in a "presidential regime." (Under the new constitution the president could name the prime minister and other members of government without reference to the assembly and could dissolve the assembly without any provision for an automatic subsequent election. Whereas previously representative groups nominated 30 senators for appointment by the president, the president could appoint the senators without them having to be nominated by groups. The amendments also left largely to presidential interpretation the relationship between the central and provincial governments.)

In legislative balloting on May 17, 1998, Arema captured 63 seats. The next largest bloc of seats, 32, went to a group of independent, but predominantly propresidential, candidates. On July 6 a power struggle between Prime Minister Rakotomavo and Deputy Prime Minister Rajaonarivelo culminated in the resignation from the government of the latter along with 17 other ministers. Unable to govern and constitutionally obligated to resign following assembly elections, Rakotomavo left office on July 22. The following day the president appointed Tantely René Gabrio ANDRIANARIVO, an Arema stalwart and former deputy prime minister, to replace Rakotomavo. On July 31 a new government was named in which Arema controlled all the key portfolios, underscoring the extent to which President Ratsiraka and Arema had secured political control. On the other hand, the administration's economic recovery program continued to falter, with its halting privatization efforts and apparent unwillingness to adhere to international reform prescriptions undermining its chances of securing much needed financial aid.

The opposition remained disorganized, as evidenced by Arema's successes in the first provincial government elections on December 3, 2000, in which Arema won a majority in all provinces except Antananarivo, and in the first Senate election on March 18, 2001, in which Arema secured 49 of the 60 elected seats. However, a number of smaller parties subsequently endorsed the presidential candidacy of Marc RAVALOMANANA, the supermarket magnate and mayor of Antananarivo who had gained strong support among the middle class with his promises to spur economic growth.

There were six candidates in the presidential election on December 16, 2001, and balloting produced highly controversial and destabilizing results. The government reported that no candidate had secured 50 percent of the votes and that a runoff was required between President Ratsiraka (officially credited with 41 percent of the first-round votes) and Ravalomanana, who had been credited with a front-running 46 percent. However, Ravalomanana, supported by the I Love Madagascar (*Tiako I Madagasikara*—TIM) party, claimed he had in fact won nearly 52 percent of first-round votes, setting the stage for massive political turmoil in early 2002. Ravalomanana's supporters poured into the streets of the capital in late January to protest the government's ruling that a second round of balloting was required. International observers concluded that massive tampering had occurred in the initial official tabulations.

As demonstrations continued, Ravalomanana declared himself president on February 22, 2002, and began installation of his own cabinet under the leadership of Jacques SYLLA. Ratsiraka responded by declaring a national state of emergency on the same day and martial law on February 28. Ravalomanana ignored the declaration of martial law, forming a government without resistance from the army or the security forces. On March 4 the pro-Ratsiraka governors of the five provinces declared that they were autonomous from Antananarivo and established their "capital" in Ratsiraka's home town of Toamasina with the support of five of the six provinces' governors. The army then split its support between the rival candidates. Conditions deteriorated in March as groups loyal to the two parallel governments clashed violently in Antananarivo, control of which was ultimately gained by Ravalomanana's forces, while many of his supporters were arrested, tortured, or killed in the provinces. Negotiations in Senegal in April pointed toward a compromise settlement. However, on April 16 the administrative chamber of the Supreme Court declared the initial published results of the December 16 voting void and ordered a recount, which, as reported by the High Constitutional Court, showed that Ravalomanana had won a first-round majority of 51.5 percent. Ravalomanana was formally inaugurated on May 6, becoming the first elected Mérina president. He subsequently sent the army to regain control of the provinces, replacing provincial governors with special presidential delegates. Ratsiraka refused to accept the legitimacy of that situation and continued to fight it. However, the United States officially recognized Ravalomanana as president of Madagascar on June 26, and similar action by France on July 3 sealed the fate of Ratsiraka, who left the country on July 5 for eventual exile in France.

On June 18, 2002, President Ravalomanana reappointed Sylla as prime minister. Hopes for reconciliation were dashed when the new cabinet excluded Ratsiraka's supporters, with the exception of one Arema minister. In the next month, President Ravalomanana used his power to appoint 30 senators, but Arema retained a majority in the Senate. Early legislative elections, observed for the first time by foreign monitors, were held on December 15, 2002, with Ravalomanana's TIM party winning a majority of 103 seats in the 160-seat assembly. The Patriot Front, an electoral alliance supporting Ravalomanana, gained an additional 22 seats, while Arema's representation declined to 3 seats. Significantly, 23 deputies were elected as independents. Sylla was reappointed prime minister on January 12, 2003.

In August 2003 Ratsiraka and two former Central Bank officials were tried and sentenced in absentia to ten years hard labor for allegedly embezzling $8.25 million from the bank during the crisis. The former Arema prime minister and the secretary-general of the party also received sentences in 2003.

In early 2004 there was a major cabinet reshuffle to incorporate leaders of other parties, and Ravalomanana released some prisoners convicted of crimes committed during the political crisis of 2002. Ravalomanana managed to neutralize the challenges to his reelection. Pierrot RAJAONARIVELO, the exiled Arema leader, was twice barred from entering the country to register his candidacy before the official deadline. The president was easily reelected on December 3, 2006 and subsequently appointed Gen. Charles RABEMANANJARA as prime minister, marking the first time in Madagascar's post-independence history that Mérina highlanders filled both the presidential and prime ministerial offices.

The TIM then expanded its majority in the assembly to 106 out of 127 seats in balloting on September 23, 2007. The national opposition parties managed to capture only 1 seat in the lower house, with the remainder going to independents. Since the former ruling party Arema remained in disarray, Madagascar's opposition parties had become small, fragmented, and driven by personalities. The only significant electoral setback for the TIM during this period came when Andry RAJOELINA defeated the TIM candidate to become mayor of Antananarivo on December 12, 2007. The opposition fared badly in the Senate balloting of April 20, 2008, when TIM swept every seat.

By 2008, President Ravalomanana came under increasing criticism for corruption and authoritarianism. The president, a wealthy businessman, appeared to use the authority of the office to enhance the interests of his Tiko company. His most unpopular initiative was to lease 3 million acres (1.3 million hectares) of arable land to the South Korean company Daewoo, which planned to practice export-oriented agriculture. When the negotiations became public in November 2008, critics questioned the appropriateness of such a sizable giveaway to a foreign company at a time of economic crisis and widespread food insecurity.

The mayor of Antananarivo, Andry RAJOELINA, capitalized on the president's floundering popularity. The former disc jockey and owner of the Vivo radio and television stations galvanized popular discontent, just as Ravalomanana himself had as mayor of the capital. In December, Vivo TV aired an interview with Didier Ratsiraka, in which the exiled former leader called for open revolt against the government. Ravalomanana reacted by shutting down the TV station on December 13. For the next three months, protests took place in the capital almost daily. More than 40 people were killed on January 26, 2009, as security forces opened fire on rioting crowds. With his opposition movement, Young Malagasies Determined (*Tanora malaGasy Vonona*—TGV), demonstrating relentlessly against the Ravalomanana regime, Rajoelina demanded the president's resignation on January 31, and proclaimed that he would henceforth lead the nation. Ravalomanana in turn used his prerogative to sack the mayor on February 3. Undaunted, Rajoelina announced on February 7 that he had asked Monja ROINDEFO of the Monima party to become prime minister of a transitional government. That day the presidential guard killed more than 20 protesters.

As the showdown continued, the army grew unwilling to put down the ongoing demonstrations. In March 2009 mutinying soldiers ousted the defense minister and army chief of staff, and a coup appeared imminent. Rajoelina demanded the president's arrest on March 14. Soldiers loyal to the opposition occupied a presidential palace and the central bank building on March 16. The following day, Ravalomanana announced that he was stepping down, dissolving the government, and transferring power to a self-chosen group of four senior military officials. The officers, however, declined to become a ruling directorate and instead invited Rajoelina to form a transitional government. The High Constitutional Court approved the transfer of power on March 18. On March 19 Rajoelina announced he was nullifying the government's land agreement with Daewoo. Rajoelina was sworn in as head of state on March 21, in a ceremony notable for the absence of invited foreign dignitaries. The new leader committed to elections within two years. On March 31 he named 44 members to the High Authority of the Transition (HAT), with himself as its president. The transitional body was made up of representatives of numerous political parties and most of the country's geographical regions; its precise function remained ambiguous. On November 17, 2010, a new constitution was overwhelmingly approved in a referendum, with 70.5 percent of the vote in favor. The new basic law lowered the minimum age to be president to 35, thereby legalizing Rajoelina's tenure as chief executive. Col. Albert Camille VITAL was named prime minister of a new unity government on December 20.

On March 26, 2011, a new unity government was announced by the HAT. Vital was reappointed prime minister. However, the major opposition parties boycotted the new cabinet, prompting new negotiations to end the political stalemate. Following the passage of an agreement between the various opposing factions to bring about a united government, Prime Minister Vital and his entire government resigned on October 28, and he was replaced by Omer BERIZIKY. Beriziky appointed a new cabinet composed of supporters of both the current and former governments. (See Current issues, below.)

The first presidential balloting since the 2009 political crisis was held on October 25, 2013 (see Current issues, below).

Constitution and government. Under the 2010 constitution, the president is directly elected for a five-year term, renewable twice, by runoff between the two leading contenders if such is needed to secure a majority. Cabinet leadership is assigned to a prime minister, responsible to the legislature but now appointed by the president (from a legislative list) and subject to dismissal by the president. The bicameral Parliament consists of a Senate of both indirectly elected and presidential appointees and a National Assembly of deputies directly elected by proportional representation. While the president can dissolve the assembly, it retains the power to pass a motion of censure requiring the prime minister and the cabinet to step down.

In 1995 Madagascar's former six provinces were replaced by 28 regions. The former 111 prefectures (*fivondronana*) were replaced by 148 departments and the former 1,252 subprefectures (*firaisana*) by 1,400 communes, of which 45 were urban.

The constitutional amendments of 1998 reversed the changes incorporated in 1995, restoring a federal system with six semiautonomous provinces. The amended document also included provisions for the establishment of regional and communal districts; however, as of mid-2010 no further progress toward their creation had been reported.

Authority over regional representatives and budget allocations was centralized in the national government under President Ravalomanana.

A package of constitutional amendments was approved by referendum on April 4, 2007. These revisions again abolished the six provinces, replacing them with 22 regions. In addition, the constitution recognized English as an official language, alongside Malagasy and French; allowed the president to legislate by decree in national emergencies; and upheld President Ravalomanana's economic policy, the Madagascar Action Plan (MAP).

Under Madagascar's constitution at the time, the president must be no less than 40 years of age, and thus Rajoelina was not legally entitled to hold the office until 2014. After some delays, a new constitution, containing mostly minor revisions from the 2007 text, was approved on November 17, 2010. The major change was a reduction in the minimum age to be president.

Media censorship in Madagascar was formally lifted in March 1989. Madagascar's Communication Code of 1990 provided further liberalization but made defamation and insult punishable by up to six months in prison. In its 2013 annual index of press freedom, Reporters Without Borders ranked Madagascar 88th out of 179 countries.

Foreign relations. During the Tsiranana administration, Madagascar retained close economic, defense, and cultural ties with France. In 1973, however, the Ramanantsoa government renegotiated all cooperation agreements with the former colonial power, withdrew from the Franc Zone, and terminated its membership in the francophone Common African and Malagasy Organization.

Subsequently, there was a drift toward the West. Ambassadorial links with Washington were restored in November 1980 after a lapse of more than four years. Aid agreements were negotiated with the United States, France, Japan, and a number of Scandinavian countries, although ties were also maintained with the Soviet Union and China.

In a dramatic policy reversal in mid-1990, economic and air links were established with South Africa as President Ratsiraka, heralding President F.W. de Klerk's "courageous" efforts to reverse apartheid laws, sought Pretoria's aid in developing Madagascar's mineral and tourism industries. In September 1998 Ratsiraka attended an international conference in Durban, thus becoming the first Malagasy head of state to visit South Africa. Subsequent regional negotiations focused on Madagascar candidacy for SADC membership (achieved in 2005).

Following the disputed presidential election of 2001, several countries terminated diplomatic relations with Madagascar and the country was suspended from meetings of the African Union (AU) for over a year. In June 2002 the Ravalomanana government was recognized by the United States; France and Senegal followed suit one month later, and the administration gradually established substantial international support. During a January 2007 visit, a high European Union (EU) official confirmed the union's support for Madagascar. The introduction of English as an official language underscored the nation's closer relations with English-speaking countries, especially the United States.

Meanwhile regional Asian influence became more apparent. In June 2008 the president met with foreign donors, including China and India, to showcase the nation's economic growth and secure aid for poverty reduction efforts. The prospective leasing of 3 million acres (1.3 million hectares) of agricultural land to the South Korean company Daewoo helped inflame the protest movement that unseated President Ravalomanana in March 2009.

The international community condemned the unconstitutional transfer of power to Andry Rajeolina. The AU suspended Madagascar on March 20, and foreign diplomats boycotted Rajeolina's inauguration as head of the transition authority the following day. No state recognized the new regime. Several nations suspended nonhumanitarian foreign aid, and the United States halted development funding through the Millennium Challenge Corporation (see Current issues, below). Mediated negotiations between four political groupings, led by the UN, AU, and SADC, broke down in May. In June the SADC appointed Joaquim Chissano, former president of Mozambique, to mediate a new round of talks, which yielded a tentative agreement on August 9. The transitional government's failure to implement this agreement, however, meant that development aid continued to be withheld in 2010. The nation's duty-free trade status with the United States, provided by the African Growth and Opportunity Act, was suspended in January 2010, leading to the reported loss of 50,000 jobs in textiles, formerly Madagascar's leading export industry.

Ahead of presidential elections initially slated for July 24, 2013, Madagascar came under intense international pressures. Three controversial candidates, including Rajoelina, drew calls for withdrawal from international observers and prompted the EU to suspend funding for printing the presidential ballots. A June meeting of the International Contact Group on Madagascar (ICG-M), which includes representatives from the AU, UN, SADC, and others, produced a seven-point electoral reform plan (see Current issues, below). On August 6, the EU threatened sanctions if the plan was not implemented within two weeks.

Current issues. The transfer of power in March 2009 and ongoing political crisis have had a deleterious impact on the nation's economy. The international community roundly condemned the coup, and foreign development aid, which constituted more than 40 percent of the government's budget, was frozen.

After Ravalomanana surrendered power and went into exile in South Africa, the UN, AU, and SADC convened crisis talks between four main parties in Malagasy politics: the Rajoelina and Ravalomanana camps as well as representatives of former leaders Didier Ratsiraka and Albert Zafy. The negotiations appeared close to an agreement on a consensual transition leading to all-party elections, but Ratsiraka, demanding amnesty for his supporters accused of crimes during the 2002 crisis, walked out on May 23 and the talks broke down. On June 3 a court sentenced Ravalomanana in absentia to four years in jail on corruption charges for the president's 2008 purchase of a $60 million presidential jet. On August 9 negotiations hosted by Mozambican president Joaquim Chissano between Rajoelina, Ravalomanana, Ratsiraka, and Zafy resulted in an agreement that called for elections within 15 months, a general amnesty, and the creation of government of national unity led by an agreed-upon prime minister and three deputy prime ministers. However, the three former presidents subsequently rejected Rajoelina's effort to develop a new unity government in September. After further negotiations, on November 13 Eugene Mangalaza was inaugurated as the new "consensus" prime minister, and two "copresidents" (representing the Ravalomanana and Zafy camps) were appointed later in the month. However, Rajoelina refused to participate in negotiations for the national unity cabinet. On December 18 Rajoelina declared the power-sharing agreement void, dismissed the two copresidents, and unilaterally appointed Col. Vital Albert Camille as prime minister, prompting widespread international criticism. For reneging on his prior agreements, the African Union imposed sanctions on Rajoelina, along with his ministers and the members of the HAT, in March 2010.

In May Rajoelina unilaterally announced a timetable for elections and declared that he would not stand for election as president. On August 8 former president Ravalomanana was sentenced in absentia to life imprisonment with hard labor for ordering the presidential guard to fire on demonstrators in the capital on February 7, 2009.

In Antananarivo on August 13, Rajoelina announced that he had entered into an agreement with 99 political parties and civic associations to lead the nation out of its political impasse, boasting that the pact was reached without international mediation. "No one can any longer criticize the path we have taken as unilateralist," Rajoelina stated. Ravalomanana, Zafy, and Ratsiraka spurned the agreement, though other members of the former presidents' parties (the TIM, CRN, and AREMA) did affix their names to the accord.

The agreement, signed in Ivato, called for the convening of a national conference, to be followed by a referendum on a proposed constitution on November 17, 2010. Legislative and presidential elections were scheduled for March 16 and May 4, 2011, respectively. Rajoelina vowed not to participate in the presidential balloting, but until the assumption of office by the new president, Rajoelina continued to serve as president of the transition, and a prime minister of his choosing would lead the government. He named the members of a bicameral transition parliament.

Negotiations under the auspices of the SADC resulted in a road map agreement on September 17, 2011, to resolve the crisis. Rajoelina and former presidents Ravalomanana and Zafy, along with the leaders of six other parties, signed the agreement, which called for the creation of a bicameral transitional legislature, future elections, and the appointment of representatives of the former presidents as copresidents. Ex-president Didier Ratsiraka opposed the accord. In October members of the transitional legislature were appointed (see Legislature, below).

Under the road map agreement of September, the Madagascar transitional government was required to establish a new government of national unity by November 1. This stipulation resulted in the resignation of Albert Camille Vital and his cabinet on October 28 and the appointment of Omer Beriziky as new prime minister by President Rajoelina. Beriziky appointed a new cabinet on November 21. Per the terms of the national unity agreement signed in September, the new cabinet appoint by Beriziky included supporters of Rajoelina,

Ravalomanana, and Zafy. Despite the move toward unity, one of the newly appointed supporters of Ravalomanana resigned after three days. Instead of appointing a new minister, Prime Minister Berizikiy added the portfolio to the responsibilities of Vice Premier Herivelona ANDRIANAINARIVELO.

Under immense pressure from foreign governments, President Rajoelina met with exiled, former president Marc Ravalomanana in late July 2012 to come up with an agreement for how to resolve the crisis and hold free elections. While no consensus was reached at the first meeting, Rajoelina and Ravalomanana continued their meetings for several weeks. Ultimately, they resolved few of their differences, but through mediation of the SADC, a timetable was reached to allow the return of Ravalomanana to Madagascar by mid-October.

In February 2012 the Independent National Election Commission of the transition (CENIT) was established to oversee elections of a new government.

In April 2013 former first lady Lalao Ravalomanana received the presidential nomination of the former president's party Ravalomanana Movement (*Mouvance Ravalomanana*), leading Rajoelina to rescind his previous nonparticipation pledge and throw his hat in. Lalao Ravalomanana, Rajoelina, and former president Didier Ratsiraka were all included on the 41-candidate list approved by CENIT on May 3, drawing sharp criticism from abroad (see Foreign relations, above). In June the polls were postponed from the original date of July 24 to August 23.

In order to comply with an internationally recommended seven-point plan, CENIT was restructured in August. Eight presidential candidates, including Lalao Ravalomanana, Rajoelina, and Ratsiraka, were disqualified, and on August 22, polling was further postponed until October 25, with runoff presidential and concurrent parliamentary balloting slated for December 20. Subsequently the Ravalomanana Movement backed Jean Louis Robinson of the Avana Party.

Observers from the EU and SADC hailed October 25 balloting, in which 33 candidates contested, as free and fair. A runoff election was scheduled for December 20, 2013.

POLITICAL PARTIES AND GROUPS

While Madagascar has long featured multiple parties, they were required under the 1975 constitution to function as components of a national front (see Arema, below). The requirement was rescinded under a decree that became effective on March 1, 1990, restoring a multiparty system. For details on the principal electoral alliances formed before 2009, see the entry in the 2009 *Handbook*.

Government Party:

Young Malagasies Determined (*Tanora malaGasy Vonona*—TGV). This group began in 2007 as a vehicle for Andry Rajoelina' campaign for mayor of Antananarivo. His party's acronym, TGV—which also alludes to the French high-speed train—was soon applied as a moniker for Rajoelina himself, capturing his relentless determination and the rapidity of his ascent. Rajoelina defeated an experienced TIM politician for the mayoralty of the capital, and shortly mounted a challenge to Ravalomanana himself. The president temporarily shut down Rajoelina's Vivo TV station in December 2008, after it aired an incendiary interview with the exiled former president Didier Ratsiraka. The incident raised Rajoelina's profile and catalyzed the street protest movement that ultimately brought Ravalomanana down. The TGV demonstrations, complete with pop music and a festival atmosphere, attracted a large number of youthful supporters. Considering that roughly half of Madagascar's population is under the age of 21, Rajoelina's successful courtship of urban youth gave him a substantial amount of leverage.

The TGV political association was relatively slow to develop the trappings and formal infrastructure of a traditional party. The ministers Rajoelina selected for his provisional government mostly belonged to other parties or were independents. Rajoelina vowed not to compete in the presidential elections that would inaugurate Madagascar's Fourth Republic; however he entered the 2013 presidential race in April. Following his disqualification in August (see Current issues, above), the TGV officially backed Edgar RAZAFINDRAVAHY, though many party members supported former finance minister Hery RAJAONARIMAMPIANINA or former prime minister Camille Vital.

Leaders: Andry RAJOELINA (President of the High Authority of the Transition), Lanto RAKOTOMAVO (National Secretary).

Space for Concerted Political Action (*Escopol Espace Politique*—Escopol). Escopol was founded in 2010 as a coalition of the signatories of the August 2010 Ivato Agreement (see Current issues, above). Under the formation of the transitional parliament, Escopol was awarded 18 of 90 seats in the upper house, the High Council of Transition (CST), and 62 of 256 seats in the lower house, the Transitional Congress (CT). Escopol is the largest party in the CT. In August 2011 the members of Escopol signed its Republican Pact, solidifying its ideological commitment to resolving the Madagascar crisis.

Leader: Benjamina Ramanantsoa RAMARCEL (Coordinator General).

Union of Democrats and Republicans for Change (*Union des Democrates et Republicains pour le Changement*—UDR-C). The UDR-C is a coalition party formed in 2010, following the Ivato Agreement, by a group of supporters for transition president Andry Rajoelina. While the UDR-C organizations were signatories of the Ivato Agreement, the UDR-C is an opposing party of Escopol, but it retained its seats in the government by virtue of backing Rajoelina. The UDR-C was awarded 25 of 90 seats in the CST and 29 of 256 seats in the CT. Following the declaration of UDR-C president Jean LAHINIRIKO that he would contest the 2013 presidential election with the PSDUM (below), the party backed Andry Rajoelina.

Leader: Julien REBOZA (President).

Other Parties and Groups:

I Love Madagascar (*Tiaho I Madagasikara*—TIM). A "political association," TIM was formed to support the presidential campaign of Marc Ravalomanana, the businessman who had been elected mayor of Antananarivo in 1999 as an independent. Ravalomanana's candidacy was also endorsed by numerous other parties, including the AVI, RPSD, PMDM/MFM, and *Grad-Iloafo.* TIM became a formal party in mid-2002 and became the majority party in the assembly following the 2002 legislative elections, when it received 34.3 percent of the vote and 103 seats.

In 2005 an internal power struggle emerged within the TIM, and Prime Minister Jacques Sylla failed to be reelected as the party's secretary general at a congress in January 2005. A rift between Ravalomanana and then assembly speaker Jean Lahiniriko in 2006 moved to the forefront of party friction. Lahiniriko, who had become increasingly critical of the government, was sacked as speaker of the National Assembly in May 2006, having faced criticism for praising Iran's nuclear program. Lahiniriko was also ejected from the TIM. He formed a new party in February 2007 (see below).

By 2008 the party had achieved complete political dominance, controlling the national legislature and local politics. However, the rising protests against President Ravalomanana unraveled the party's control over Malagasy politics, and after the incidents of January 26 and February 7, 2009, in which security forces killed scores of demonstrators, the momentum decisively shifted to Andry Rajoelina and his TGV movement. Shortly after attaining power in March, Rajoelina dissolved the legislature and took over the office of the prime minister, effectively wiping out what remained of the TIM's power base in the national government.

Representatives of the TIM, now referred to in the press as "the Ravalomanana faction," participated in the internationally mediated four-party negotiations throughout 2009. The goal of restoring the former president to power—the objective of his "legalist" supporters in the TIM—grew more remote after Ravalomanana was sentenced in absentia on corruption charges in June, and three former officials in the TIM government were accused of responsibility for a bomb attack in the capital in July. In August 2010 the former president was given a life sentence on murder charges for his role in the killings of February 7, 2009.

The August 2010 Ivato accord (see Current issues, above) widened a split within the TIM. Ravalomanana and the top TIM leaders denounced these initiatives as unilateralist, but a former TIM deputy, Raharinaivo Andrianantoandro, endorsed the agreement. In October Andrianantoandro was elected president of the Congress of the Transition. Officials close to Ravalomanana disputed Andrianantoandro's claim that a majority of regional TIM leaders supported his nomination as deputy president of the party. Former first lady Neny Lalao Ravalomanana returned from exile in March 2013 and became the party's presidential candidate. Following her disqualification in August, the TIM backed Jean Louis ROBINSON.

Leaders: Marc RAVALOMANANA (Former President of the Republic), Yvan RANDRIASANDRATRINIONY (President of the Party and Former President of the Senate), Fetison ANDRIANIRINA

(Lead negotiator), Raharinaivo ANDRIANANTOANDRO (President of the Congress of the Transition), Ivohasina RAZAFIMAHEFA (Secretary General).

Leader–*Fanilo*. Launched in 1993 by a group of self-styled "nonpoliticians," Leader–*Fanilo* opposed President Zafy in the September 1995 referendum and expelled Trade and Tourism Minister Henri RAKOTONIRAINY for accepting cabinet reappointment two months later.

Party leader Herizo Razafimahaleo finished third in the first round of the 1996 presidential balloting with 15 percent of the vote and fourth in 2001 with 4.2 percent. (Three Leader–*Fanilo* cabinet members resigned from the government in early October 2001 after Razafimahaleo announced his intention to campaign for the presidency.) Razafimahaleo's 2006 presidential campaign emphasized the lack of separation between President Ravalomanana's company, Tiko, and TIM. Razafimahaleo finished fourth in the balloting with 9.05 percent of the vote.

Leader-*Fanilo* was the only nationally organized party, apart from the TIM, to win an assembly seat in the 2007 balloting, when Jonah Parfait Prezaly was elected. On July 25, 2008, the opposition party suffered a significant loss with the death of Herizo Razafimahaleo. He was succeeded as president by historian Manassé Esoavelomandroso, theretofore the party's secretary general. Rajoelina named Prezaly to the High Authority of the Transition in March 2009. Leader-*Fanilo* opposed the efforts of SADC to isolate Madagascar's transitional government and strongly supported the multiparty agreement of August 2010. Omer BERIZIKY of Leader-*Fanilo* became prime minister in 2011.

Ahead of the 2013 election, Leader-*Fanilo* initially backed Camille Vital, though reportedly switched to support Hery Rajaonarimampianina in September.

Leaders: Jean Max RAKOTOMAMONJY (President), Omer BERIZIKY (Transitional Prime Minister).

Rally for Socialism and Democracy (*Rassemblement pour le Socialisme et la Démocratie*—RPSD). The RPSD is the current incarnation of the Social Democratic Party (*Parti Social Démocrate*—PSD) that was legalized in March 1990 as a revival of the party originally formed in 1957 by Philibert Tsiranana. (The group is still frequently referenced under the PSD rubric.) Although initially sympathetic to the Ratsiraka government, in the second half of 1990 the party moved into opposition. The party's prestige was bolstered by the addition of former MFM leaders Franck Ramarosaona and Evariste Marson in 1990 and 1992, respectively. The RPSD supported Albert Zafy in the second presidential round (after a bid by Marson had failed in the first) and went into opposition after the June 1993 assembly poll. Jean Eugène Voninahitsy, RPSD secretary general and vice president of the National Assembly, received 2.79 percent of the vote in the first round of the 1996 presidential election.

The RPSD won 11 assembly seats in May 1998, and thereafter reportedly joined Arema's legislative alliance. In late 2000, however, relations between Arema and the RPSD were strained when Voninahitsy was arrested on charges of insulting the head of state and "putting out false information." Earlier, he had criticized Ratsiraka for purchases made by the state. The RPSD left Arema's legislative faction and supported opposition candidate Marc Ravalomanana in the 2001 presidential campaign. Disaffected members left the RPSD to join the Patriotic Front (FP) prior to the 2002 assembly elections. The RPSD allied itself with the TIM in the election and secured 5 seats in the polling.

In 2003 RPSD dissidents led by former secretary general Voninahitsy left the party to form a new group, the New RPSD or **RPSD-Nouveau** (RPSD-*Vaovao*), which was active in the anti-Ravalomanana protests of October 2005. Voninahitsy was subsequently convicted of corruption and sentenced to two years in jail in December 2005. He was expected to run in the 2006 presidential race but was arrested on additional charges in February 2006 and received a four-year jail sentence, which was upheld by an appeals court in June 2008. The RPSD did not field a candidate in the 2006 presidential election, but a former RPSD leader, Philippe TSIRANANA, son of former president Philibert Tsiranana, stood as an independent. The RPSD-Nouveau expressed disapproval of the constitutional reforms approved by referendum in 2007. Marson was appointed to the High Authority of the Transition on March 31, 2009, as was Pelops Ariane VONINAHITSY, the wife of Jean Eugène Voninahitsy. Husband and wife both became members of the Parliament of the Transition in October 2010.

Leaders: Evariste MARSON (President), Jean Eugène VONINAHITSY.

One Should Be Judged By One's Works (*Asa Vita no Ifampitsanara*—AVI). In May 1998 the AVI won 14 assembly seats as a moderate opposition party under the leadership of former prime minister and interim president Norbert Ratsirahonana. Subsequently, however, the AVI joined the Arema-led propresidential legislative alliance. In the 2001 presidential campaign, Ratsirahonana withdrew his candidacy in late October and endorsed Marc Ravalomanana. In 2002 the AVI joined Ravalomanana's first government as part of the now-defunct pro-Ravalomanana Patriot Front (*Firaisankinam-Pirenenai*—FP) formed in conjunction with former RPSD members. The FP secured 20 of the coalition's 22 seats in that year's legislative elections. In late 2003 the AVI began to distance itself from the president and joined the opposition group the **Parliamentary Solidarity for Democracy and National Union** (*Solidarité des Parlementaires pour la Défense de la Démocratie et de l'Unité National*—SPDUN), which it left in March 2006. Ratsirahonana formally split from the president in October 2006, claiming Ravalomanana had become a dictator, and entered that year's presidential election as the AVI candidate, winning 4.2 percent of the vote. The poor showing weakened the party's position among the opposition. Ratsirahonana was a major supporter of Andry Rajoelina's struggle to unseat Ravalomanana, standing by the new leader's side as he assumed power on March 17, 2009, and arguing his claim before the High Constitutional Court. He was subsequently named to the High Authority of the Transition and was perceived as one of Rajoelina's most influential counselors.

Leader: Norbert RATSIRAHONANA (Secretary General).

Militant Party for the Development of Madagascar (*Parti Militant pour le Développement de Madagascar*—MDM/MFM). The MDM/MFM is a successor name for the Movement for Proletarian Power (*Mouvement pour le Pouvoir Prolétarien/Mpitolona ho'amin'ny Fanjakan'ny Madinika*—MFM) formed in 1972 by student radicals who helped to overthrow President Tsiranana. Although it continues to be referenced by its earlier Malagasy initials, the party adopted its current name at a 1990 party congress.

The MFM initially opposed the Ratsiraka government and remained outside the FNDR framework until 1977. The group won three assembly seats in 1983 and seven in 1989. Party leader Manandafy Rakotonirina placed second in the 1989 presidential balloting with 19 percent of the vote. As an opposition party, the MFM was part of the movement that forced Ratsiraka from power in 1991. The party completed a conversion from Marxism to liberalism in the 1990s, supporting the establishment of a market economy and a Western-style multiparty system.

MFM leader Rakotonirina, who stood as a first-round presidential contender in 1992, supported Albert Zafy in the second round. Following the legislative poll of June 1993, the MFM went into opposition. It supported prime minister and interim president Norbert Ratsirahonana in the 1996 presidential balloting but reportedly swung back over to the government camp following the May 1998 legislative elections. The MFM supported opposition candidate Marc Ravalomanana in the 2001 presidential campaign, and Rakotonirina was influential in Ravalomanana's controversial decision to declare victory and take to the streets after the first round of voting. Rakotonirina later became a special adviser to President Ravalomanana. In the 2002 elections the MFM won two seats in the National Assembly.

Despite its initial closeness to Ravalomanana, the MFM subsequently shifted to the opposition, joining the SPDUN (from which it withdrew in March 2006) and. The party declared unconstitutional Ravalomanana's decision to move the presidential election date to December 2006. As an independent candidate in that election, Rakotonirina won 0.33 percent of the vote. The MFM won no seats in the 2007 legislative voting.

On April 20, 2009, while in exile in Johannesburg, Ravalomanana declared MFM's Rakotonirina his nominee to be Madagascar's next prime minister. Rakotonirina released a partial list of ministers for a prospective legalist government on April 28. but was arrested at an Antananarivo hotel by a militia loyal to Rajoelina. The 70-year-old Rakotonirina was incarcerated at Mantasoa but later released to allow him to participate in August's four-party talks in Maputo. He received a two-year suspended sentence.

Leaders: Razafimahatratra PAULÉON, Ramarosonarivo JEANSON, Manandafy RAKOTONIRINA.

Vanguard of the Malagasy Revolution (*Avant-Garde de la Révolution Malgache/Antoky'ny Revolosiona Malagasy*—Arema). Arema was organized by Didier Ratsiraka in 1976 and subsequently served as the nucleus of the National Front for the Defense of the Malagasy Socialist Revolution (*Front National pour la Défense de la Révolution Socialiste Malgache*—FNDR), which was renamed the Militant Movement for Malagasy Socialism (*Mouvement Militant pour le Socialisme Malgache*—MMSM) in mid-1990. The 1975 constitution provided for organization of the FNDR as the country's overarching political entity, with a variety of "revolutionary associations" permitted to participate in elections as FNDR components. However, three FNDR members (the MFM, Vonjy, and Monima) initiated joint antigovernment activity, beginning in early 1987, and contested the 1989 presidential and legislative elections as the equivalent of opposition formations, thus dissolving the FNDR's political monopoly.

After losing the 1992 presidential election, Ratsiraka eventually moved to Paris, France. He remained a force in Malagasy politics, regularly criticizing the Zafy administration and what he described as the nation's political "chaos." In 1993 he formed the Vanguard for Economic and Social Recovery (*Avant-Garde pour le Redressement Économique et Social*—ARES) as a successor to Arema; however, his supporters and media groups continue to use the Arema acronym and earlier title.

Ratsiraka regained the presidency in February 1997. On November 29 of that year, at Arema's first party congress since taking power, Deputy Prime Minister Pierrot Rajaonarivelo was elected to the secretary general's post vacated by Ratsiraka. The party also reportedly adopted the Malagasy title, *Andry sy Riana Enti-Manavotra an'i Madagasikara,* or Supporting Pillar and Structure for the Salvation of Madagascar; however, the Arema acronym remained in common use.

In legislative balloting in May 1998 Arema and its allies secured an overwhelming mandate (its forces reportedly controlled approximately 90 percent of the assembly seats). Meanwhile, intraparty relations between Rajaonarivelo and Prime Minister Rakotomavo reached a nadir on July 6 when Rajaonarivelo and 17 of his ministerial allies withdrew from the cabinet, thereby paralyzing the government and effectively destroying Rakotomavo's chances for reappointment.

Following the violence surrounding the 2001 presidential election, Arema lost substantial public support. Ratsiraka and other senior Arema figures, including Secretary General Pierrot Rajaonarivelo, went into exile in France. In the legislative balloting in 2002, Arema secured only three seats, and it boycotted local elections in 2003. In 2003 Rajaonarivelo was sentenced in absentia to five years in prison on several charges involving his alleged abuse of office while deputy prime minister. His sentence was reduced to three years in 2005.

Arema was significantly weakened in 2006 by internal divisions over whether to support Pierrot Rajaonarivelo's presidential candidacy and whether to advocate the revision of the electoral code, with those supporting the status quo arguing that the code had been instituted by Didier Ratsiraka and therefore should be accepted. Reports subsequently indicated a growing split in the party, with one faction loyal to the exiled leadership and a second group (led by Assistant Secretary General Pierre RAHARIJOANA) eager to distance itself from the exiles.

In 2006 Rajaonarivelo called upon the government to issue an amnesty to potential candidates, such as himself, whose sentences would otherwise preclude them from participating in the upcoming presidential poll. Rajaonarivelo, considered Ravalomanana's main opponent, officially announced his candidacy for the presidential election in May. However, he was convicted in absentia of embezzlement of public funds in August and sentenced to 15 years of hard labor and barred from holding office. Rajaonarivelo twice attempted to return to Madagascar to register his candidacy, but the Malagasy authorities blocked his return and the High Constitutional Court denied his candidacy. Arema then announced that it would boycott the election. In 2007 Arema was divided, with factions supporting each of the two exiled leaders, Ratsiraka and Rajaonarivelo. The pro-Ratsiraka contingent challenged the standing of the interim national secretary, Pierre Houlder RAMAHOLIMASY. Arema won no seats in the 2007 legislative election.

Ratsiraka was instrumental in sparking the crisis that resulted in the overthrow of Ravalomanana. His televised interview calling for insurrection against the government led to the shutdown of Rajoelina's Viva television network in December 2008. Rajoelina, who had received early financial backing from Rajaonarivelo for his business enterprises, was perceived by numerous analysts as a front for the exiled Arema leaders. Arema initially supported the coup, but Ratsiraka later condemned it. Rajoelina named Ramaholimasy to the High Authority of the Transition. Rajaonarivelo returned from exile in April 2009, stating that he hoped to foster national reconciliation. But Ratsiraka himself, still exiled and in frail health, led the Arema delegation in the UN-mediated four-party talks on the crisis. The admiral clearly signaled his intention to resume command of the party, pushing Rajaonarivelo aside. The negotiations led to two failed provisional power-sharing agreements in 2009.

Ratsiraka, returning from exile in April 2013, stood for president but was disqualified in August (see Current issues, above).

Leaders: Adm. Didier RATSIRAKA (Former President of the Republic), Pierre Houlder RAMAHOLIMASY (Interim National Secretary).

National Reconciliation Committee (*Comité pour la Réconciliation Nationale*—CRN). The CRN was launched in 2002 by former president Albert Zafy and other prominent former officials in an attempt to foster a solution to the "post-election crisis," pitting the supporters of former president Ratsiraka against the supporters of President Ravalomanana.

Zafy had led the National Union for Development and Democracy (*Union Nationale pour le Développement et la Démocratie*—UNDD), a party originally organized in 1955 and revived by Zafy in 1998. The UNDD stridently denounced "corruption" under the Ratsiraka regime. In 1990 Zafy organized the Living Forces coalition (*Forces Vives/Hery Velona*), an alliance of 16 opposition parties, trade unions, and religious groups, whose agitation prompted the dissolution of the Ratsiraka government in 1991. This grouping was sometimes referred to as the Living Forces Rasalama Coalition (*Cartel Hery Velona Rasalama*—Cartel HVR). Zafy was then named to head the High State Authority under the Provisional Government and elected president in 1993. UNDD members came to dominate the cabinet in 1995 and 1996, until Zafy was impeached in September 1996. Prior to presidential balloting in 1996, a number of parties disavowed their *Forces Vives* membership, and Zafy lost narrowly to Ratsiraka in the second-round balloting.

In legislative balloting in May 1998, what remained of the pro-Zafy grouping competed under the banner of the recently established **Action, Truth, Development, and Harmony** (*Asa Fahamarianana Fampandrosoana Arinda*—AFFA). Six AFFA candidates, including Zafy, were elected. The AFFA supported Zafy in the 2001 presidential election but failed to gain any seats for itself in the 2002 legislative balloting.

Zafy and the CRN never formally recognized the legitimacy of Marc Ravalomanana's presidency and advocated for a transitional regime to govern before new elections were held lest the problems of 2001–2002 be repeated. At the national conference in June 2005, the CRN advocated creating a "parallel government." In December 2006 Zafy's property was raided by the police as part of the government's investigation of General Fidy's alleged November coup attempt; the police sought to locate and arrest Zafy.

Despite Ravalomanana's reelection, the CRN continued to press for a national reconciliation. Zafy traveled to Paris in July 2007 for a series of closed meetings with ex-president Ratsiraka and other former officials.

Zafy took part in the negotiations mediated by the UN and the AU after the March 2009 coup. The former president advocated for an inclusive, consensual basis for a democratic transition, calling for a truth and reconciliation commission based on the South African model. He rebuked Rajoelina in December for reneging on agreements the transition leader had made with the three former presidents. The CRN was not among the 99 parties to endorse the election timetable outlined in Ivato in August 2010.

Leaders: Dr. Albert ZAFY (Former President of the Republic), Emmanuel RAKOTOVAHINY (Chairperson and Former Prime Minister).

National Movement for the Independence of Madagascar/ Madagascar for the Malagasy Party (*Mouvement National pour l'Indépendance de Madagascar/Madagasikara Otronin'ny Malagasy*—Monima). A left-wing nationalist party based in the south, Monima (also called *Monima Ka Miviombio*—Monima K) withdrew from the National Front FNDR in 1977, charging it had been the victim of electoral fraud. Its longtime leader, Monja JAONA, was under house arrest from November 1980 to March 1982, at which time he brought the group back into the FNDR and was appointed to the Supreme Revolutionary Council (CSR). He joined the 1982 presidential election as Commander Ratsiraka's only competitor, winning almost 20 percent of the vote. That December he was again placed under house arrest for activities "likely to bring about the fall of the country." He was released in mid-August 1983, after undertaking a hunger strike, and returned to the legislature as one of Monima's two representatives. Jaona won 3 percent in the 1989 presidential balloting and became Monima's sole assembly representative. Monima's deputy general secretary, René RANAIVOSOA, resigned from the party in June 1990, following a dispute with Jaona, and established the **Democratic Party for Madagascar Development** (*Parti Démocratique pour le Développement de Madagascar*—PDDM/ADFM).

In March 1992 Jaona was seriously wounded during a pro-Ratsiraka demonstration. Monima's influence decreased after Jaona's death. The party reportedly endorsed President Ratsiraka's reelection bid and did not support Ravalomanana in the 2002 crisis. In the 2002 and 2007 assembly balloting, Monima won no seats. Jaona's son, Monja ROINDEFO Zafitsimilavo, stood as an independent in the 2006 presidential election and came in last.

Andry Rajeolina announced that Roindefo would serve as prime minister of his transitional administration on February 7, 2009. Roindefo's position became official in March, after Rajeolina was installed as leader. Monima defended the legality of the transfer of power, asserting that it was supported by popular demand. In June, the party spoke out against the involvement of the SADC in mediation efforts, and opposed extending amnesty to either Ravalomanana or Ratsiraka. Rajoelina sacked Roindefo on October 9 following an internationally mediated power sharing agreement with three former presidents. Roindefo refused to accept his replacement by Eugene Mangalaza and continued to refer to himself as the nation's legal prime minister a year later, even in the absence of political support.

Roindefo contested the October 2013 presidential election.

Leaders: Monja ROINDEFO (Chair), Gabriel RABEARIMANANA (Secretary General), Bruno Raharivelo TOMPSON (Director).

Socialist and Democratic Party for the Union of Madagascar (*Parti Socialiste et Démocratique pour l'Union à Madagascar*—PSDUM). This party was launched on February 3, 2007, by Jean LAHINIRIKO, speaker of the National Assembly from 2003 to 2006. During a visit to Iran in April 2006, Lahiniriko congratulated the Tehran government on the success of its nuclear program. His comment was not meant to represent official state policy; nevertheless, some of his fellow legislators accused him of treason. Lahiniriko was removed from office and expelled from the ruling TIM party. He then vowed to challenge incumbent Marc Ravalomanana for the presidency. Running as an independent, he finished second with 11.65 percent in the December 2006 vote, carrying his home province of Toliara. As he launched his new party, he warned that "a programmed return of dictatorship" was threatening Madagascar. He ran as a PSDUM candidate for assembly in September 2007 and was soundly defeated by the TIM candidate, although he disputed the returns.

Lahiniriko declared his support for Rajoelina just before the demonstrations of January 26, 2009. Lahiniriko and another party leader, former government minister Julien Reboza, were named to the High Authority of the Transition on March 31. Lahiniriko contested the October 2013 presidential elections.

Leader: Jean LAHINIRIKO (2013 presidential candidate and Former Speaker of the Assembly).

Three newer parties fielded candidates in the 2006 presidential election: **Union** (*Tambatra*), whose candidate, Pety RAKOTONIAINA, was sentenced in October 2007 to five years in prison for stealing state-owned cars, but pardoned by Rajoelina in March 2009; **Our Madagascar** (*Madagasikarantsika*), boasting the first female presidential candidate, Elia RAVELOMANANTSOA; and **Good Governance Madagascar** (*Fihavanantsika*), supporting Daniel RAJAKOBA. Other minor parties include the **Fihaonana Confédération des Societés pour le Développement**, led by Guy Willy Razanamasy; the Republican Party of Madagascar (PRM), led by Roger Ralison; and the pro-Arema party, the Malagasy **Tonga Saina** (MTS). Roland RATSIRAKA (the nephew of the former president, the mayor of Toamasina, and a leader of the MTS) ran as an independent candidate in the 2006 presidential election and came in third with 10.09 percent of the votes, only to be jailed on charges of embezzlement in April 2007. He was released with a deferred sentence after six months and installed in 2009 as a vice president of the HAT.

For more information on the Congress Party for Madagascar **Independence–Renewal** (*Parti du Congès* de *l'Indépendance de Madagascar–Renouveau*—AKFM-*Fanavaozana*), see the 2008 *Handbook*.

LEGISLATURE

The 1992 constitution provides for a bicameral **Parliament** (*Parlement*) consisting of a Senate and a National Assembly. Both houses were suspended immediately following the coup of March 17, 2009. A transitional legislature was convened on October 13, 2011, to remain in place until new elections for the Senate and National Assembly were conducted in 2013. The upper chamber, the Higher Transition Council (*Conseil Supérieur de la Transition*—CST), had 90 appointed members. The lower chamber, the Congress of Transition (*Congrès de la Transition*—CT), included 256 members. Rasolosoa DOLIN was elected president of the CST and Raharinaivo Andrianantoandro, president of the CT.

Senate (*Sénat*). Prior to the constitutional amendments of April 2008, the Senate had 60 elected members (10 representing each of the six provinces) and 30 appointed members. Arema won 49 of the 60 elected seats in the balloting of March 18, 2001, and President Ratsiraka made appointments the following month. After taking power in 2002, President Ravalomanana used his constitutional power to replace the appointed senators, mostly with members of his new I Love Madagascar party.

As of 2008, Madagascar's upper house has 33 members: 22 (1 from each region) are elected by electoral colleges composed of regional and municipal officials, and 11 are appointed by the president. The term of office is six years. In legislative elections held on April 20, 2008, I Love Madagascar received all the elective seats. Results of elections held on December 20, 2013, were not available as of press time.

National Assembly (*Assemblée Nationale*). The lower house encompasses 127 members, who are directly elected by proportional representation for five-year terms. President Ravalomanana dissolved the assembly in July 2007, claiming that its composition did not represent the national makeup following the constitutional reforms approved by referendum on April 4, 2007. The results of the balloting on September 23, 2007, were as follows: I Love Madagascar, 106 seats; Leader–*Fanilo,* 1 seat; independents, 20. Results of elections held on December 20, 2013, were not available as of press time.

CABINET

[as of November 1, 2013] (*See headnote.*)

Prime Minister	Omar Beriziky
Vice Premier	Julien Reboza
Vice Premier	Pierrot Botozaza
Ministers	
Agriculture	Rolland Ravatomango
Armed Forces	Gen. Andre Lucien Rakotoarimasy
Budget and Finance	Lantoniaina Rasoloelison
Civil Service, Labor, and Social Laws	Marcel Bernard (acting)
Commerce	Olga Ramalason [f]
Communication	Harry Laurent Rahajason
Culture	Elisa Razafitombo Alibena [f]
Decentralization and Urban Planning	Herivelona Andrianainarivelo
Economy and Industry	Pierrot Botozaza
Energy	Nestor Razafindroriaka
Environment and Forests	Joseph Randriamiharisoa
Fisheries and Marine Resources	Sylvainn Manoriky
Foreign Affairs	Jacques Andriantiana (acting)
Higher Education	Etienne Hilaire Razafindehibe
Hydrocarbons	Marcel Bernard
Interior	Florent Rakotoarisoa
Internal Security	Pol. Gen. Arsene Rakotondrazaka
Justice and Keeper of the Seals	Christine Razanamahasoa [f]
Livestock	Ihanta Randriamandranto [f]
Mines	Daniella Tolotrandry Rajo Randrianfeno [f]
National Education	Regis Manoro
Population and Social Affairs	Olga Vaomalala [f]
Posts, Telecommunications, and New Technology	Ny Hasina Andriamanjato

Promotion of Crafts	Elisa Razafitombo Alibena [f]
Public Health	Johanita Ndahimananjara [f]
Public Works and Meteorology	Col. Botomanovatsara
Relations with Institutions	Víctor Manantsoa
Sports	Gerard Botralahy
Technical Education and Professional Training	Jean André Ndremanjary
Tourism	Jean Max Rakotomamonjy
Transport	Benjamina Ramarcel Ramanantsoa
Water	Johanita Ndahimananjara (acting) [f]
Youth and Leisure	Jacques Andriantiana
Secretary of State	
Gendarmerie (Mounted Police)	Gen. Thierry Randrianazary

[f] = female

INTERGOVERNMENTAL REPRESENTATION

Ambassador to the U.S.: Jocelyn Bertin RADIFERA.

U.S. Ambassador to Madagascar: Eric WONG (interim).

Permanent Representative to the UN: Zina ANDRIANARIV ELO-RAZAFY.

IGO Memberships (Non-UN): AfDB, AU, Comesa, ICC, IOM, NAM, SADC, WTO.

MALAWI

Republic of Malawi

Political Status: Independent member of the Commonwealth since 1964; republic under one-party presidential rule established July 6, 1966; constitution amended on June 22, 1993, to provide for multiparty activity following national referendum of June 15; new constitution enacted provisionally as of May 16, 1994, and adopted permanently (as amended) on May 18, 1995.

Area: 45,747 sq. mi. (118,484 sq. km).

Population: 15,936,806 (2012E—UN); 16,777,547 (2013E—U.S. Census).

Major Urban Centers (2011E—UN): LILONGWE (669,021), Blantyre (661,444), Mzuzu (107,345).

Official Language: English. (Chichewa is classified as a national language.)

Monetary Unit: Kwacha (market rate November 1, 2013: 394.43 kwacha = $1US).

President: Joyce BANDA (People's Party); sworn in on April 7, 2012, to succeed Bingu wa MUTHARIKA (Democratic Progressive Party) who died in office on April 5 (see Government and politics, below), after he was popularly reelected on May 19, 2009, and inaugurated for a second five-year term on May 22.

First Vice President: Khumbo Hastings KACHALI (People's Party); sworn in on April 13, 2012, to succeed Joyce BANDA (People's Party) who assumed the presidency on April 7 after being popularly reelected on May 19, 2009, and inaugurated for a five-year term on May 22.

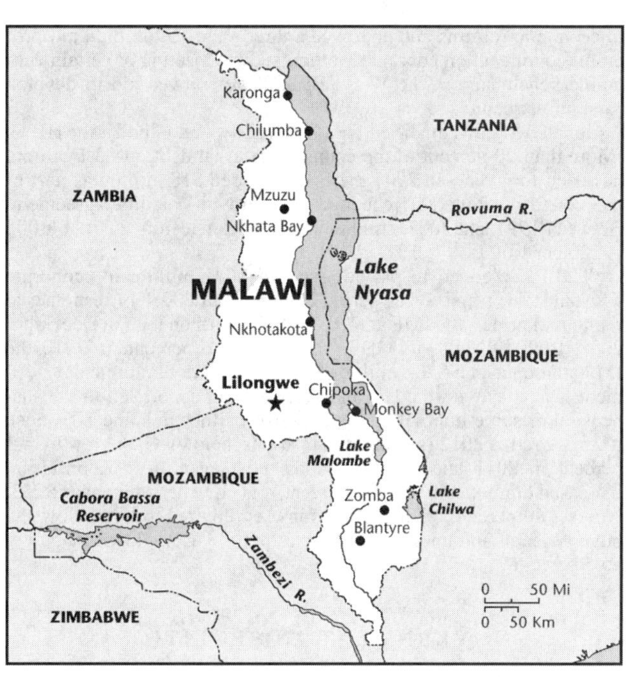

Second Vice President: Vacant following the resignation of Chakufwa CHIHANA (Alliance for Democracy) on February 24, 2004.

THE COUNTRY

Malawi, the former British protectorate of Nyasaland, is a landlocked southeastern African nation bordering the western side of 360-mile-long Lake Malawi (formerly Lake Nyasa). The country's name is a contemporary spelling of "Maravi," which historically referenced the interrelated Bantu peoples who inhabit the area. The main tribal groups are the Chewas, the Nyanja, and the Tumbuka. It is estimated that 83 percent of the population is Christian and 13 percent Muslim, with the remainder, except for a very small Hindu population, adhering to traditional African beliefs. A small non-African segment of the population includes Europeans and Asians. Three-quarters of adult females are subsistence agricultural workers, while the number of households headed by women has increased in recent years as men have relocated to pursue cash-crop labor. Following the 2009 elections, women held 43 of 193 seats (23.3 percent) in the parliament. In 2013 women held 9 of 26 cabinet ministries, one of the highest proportions in the region.

About 90 percent of the population is engaged in agriculture, the most important cash crops being tobacco, tea, peanuts, sugar, and cotton. Agriculture accounts for 31 percent of the nation's GDP and 80 percent of export revenues. Development efforts have focused on integrated rural production, diversification in light industry (particularly agriprocessing and import substitution), and improved transportation facilities.

Real GDP growth fell to 1.7 percent in 2000, with inflation steadying at 45 percent (for an overview of the economy prior to 2000, see the 2011 *Handbook*). In 2001 GDP declined by 4.1 percent, before posting a small recovery in 2002 and growing by 4.4 percent in 2003. In addition, inflation was brought down to 10 percent in 2003.

In 2000 Malawi was approved for $1 billion in debt reduction under the World Bank's Heavily Indebted Poor Countries (HIPC) initiative, and the International Monetary Fund (IMF) provided a $65 million loan for poverty reduction. However, excessive government spending, corruption, and the slow pace of economic reforms led international donors, including the World Bank, IMF, United States, and European Union (EU), to suspend some economic aid during 2001–2002, although humanitarian assistance continued in light of Malawi's worsening food crisis (caused by drought in some areas and severe flooding in others). Meanwhile, the EU resumed full economic and development aid, including support for ports, hydroelectric facilities, and direct financial contributions to limit the government's deficit. In April 2006 the IMF reported that the new government had made progress in regard to economic reforms and approved a three-year, $59 million aid program (contingent on continued reform and the meeting of certain economic benchmarks). The World Bank also approved aid to develop rural infrastructure.

In 2006 Malawi qualified for additional debt relief under the HIPC. (More than 90 percent of the country's external debt, or $3.1 billion, has been forgiven.) In 2007 the IMF provided $18 million as part of the country's Poverty Reduction and Growth Facility agreement. Between 1997 and 2007, child mortality rates fell from 221 per 1,000 to 120 per 1,000.

The EU pledged to provide Malawi $677 million in economic assistance over a six-year period beginning in 2008. In response to rising fuel prices, the IMF agreed to a $77.1 million loan in December 2008. In 2010 Malawi's GDP growth was 6.6 percent. In 2010 the IMF announced an $80.1 million loan to promote economic development. Disputes with the UK and other foreign donors led to the suspension of some international aid in 2011, although some assistance was restored in 2012 (see Foreign relations, below). GDP grew by 4.3 percent in 2011 and 1.9 percent the next year. In 2012 inflation increased dramatically to 21.3 percent, and GDP per capita was $253. At least 60 percent of the population was reported to live below the poverty level, and unofficial estimates put the unemployment rate at 45.5 percent.

GOVERNMENT AND POLITICS

Political background. Under British rule since 1891, the Nyasaland protectorate was joined with Northern and Southern Rhodesia in 1953 to form the Federation of Rhodesia and Nyasaland. Internal opposition to the federation proved so vigorous that a state of emergency was declared, with nationalist leaders H. B. M. CHIPEMBERE, Kanyama CHIUME, and Hastings Kamuzu BANDA being imprisoned. They were released upon the attainment of internal self-government on February 1, 1963, and dissolution of the federation at the end of that year. Nyasaland became a fully independent member of the Common wealth under the name of Malawi on July 6, 1964, and a republic two years later, with Prime Minister Banda being installed as the country's president.

The early years of the Banda presidency were marked by conservative policies, including the retention of white civil service personnel and the maintenance of good relations with South Africa. Younger, more radical leaders soon became disenchanted, and in 1965 a minor insurrection was led by Chipembere, while a second, led by Yatuta CHISIZA, took place in 1967. Both were easily contained, however, and Banda became entrenched as the nation's political leader.

In March 1983 Dr. Attati MPAKATI of the Socialist League of Malawi (one of the two principal exile groups) was assassinated in Zimbabwe. In May, Orton CHIRWA, the former leader of the other main exile organization (the Malawi Freedom Movement—Mafremo) was found guilty of treason and was sentenced to death. (Chirwa had been jailed, along with his wife and son, since December 1981.) Subsequent appeals in December 1983 and February 1984 were denied, and Chirwa, who claimed that he and his family had been abducted from Zambia to permit their arrest, became an object of international human rights attention. Bowing to the pressure, Banda commuted the sentence to life imprisonment in June 1984. (Chirwa died in 1992 under unclear circumstances.)

In an apparent response to pressure from international aid donors, President Banda instructed the National Assembly in December 1991 to "make a final decision" on unipartyism, albeit prefacing his call for debate by commending the "successes" of his Malawi Congress Party (MCP), which had voted for a continuation of the existing system only three months before. Thus, despite the country's first mass protests against MCP rule in May 1992, no opposition groups were permitted to present candidates in legislative balloting on June 26–27. Somewhat unexpectedly, given another MCP vote against pluralism on October 2, President Banda on October 18 announced plans for a national referendum to decide Malawi's future political structure. On June 15, 1993, 63.5 percent of those participating voted in favor of a multiparty system.

On October 13, 1993, 11 days after Banda underwent emergency brain surgery, the office of the president announced the formation of a three-member Presidential Council, thus rejecting the opposition's call for a "neutral" president to rule in Banda's absence. The council was comprised of the MCP's recently appointed secretary general, Stephen Gwandanguluwe CHAKUAMBA Phiri, as well as MCP stalwarts John TEMBO and Robson CHIRWA. Nevertheless, preparations for the May 1994 multiparty balloting continued, with the assembly approving constitutional amendments reforming the electoral process and presidency (see Constitution and government, below) and authorizing the formation of two transitional bodies: the National Consultative Council (NCC) and the National Executive Council (NEC), charged with electoral preparation and oversight.

In early December 1993 the Presidential Council ordered the disarmament of the Malawi Young Pioneers (MYP), an MCP-affiliated paramilitary group whose recent killing of two regular army soldiers had exacerbated tensions between the two armed forces. The ensuing crackdown, resulting in 32 deaths and the reported flight of 1,000 pioneers to Mozambique, was denounced by the NCC, which accused the Presidential Council of having "lost control." Consequently, on December 7 a still visibly ailing Banda dissolved the Presidential Council and reassumed presidential powers. Shortly thereafter, Banda appointed a new defense minister, Maj. Gen. Wilfred John MPONERA, who, on January 7, 1994, announced the completion of MYP disarmament.

In the country's first multiparty election on May 17, 1994, voters decisively rejected bids by Banda and two other presidential candidates in favor of Bakili MULUZI of the United Democratic Front (UDF). In simultaneous legislative balloting, the UDF also led the field, although it fell short of a majority by five seats. Four days after his inauguration on May 21, President Muluzi announced a coalition government in which two minor parties—the Malawi National Democratic Party (MNDP) and the United Front for Multiparty Democracy (UFMD)—were allocated one portfolio each.

On July 21, 1994, the MCP and the Alliance for Democracy (Aford) announced the formation of a shadow government that included Banda's former second in command, John Tembo, as finance minister. However, the MCP-Aford pact was effectively terminated when Aford president Chakufwa CHIHANA accepted an appointment by Muluzi as second vice president designate and three other Aford members joined an expanded cabinet on September 24. Constitutional revision was required to accommodate Chihana's appointment (see Constitution and government, below).

In response to domestic and international criticism of the size of his cabinet, Muluzi reshuffled it and reduced its size from 35 to 32 members on July 16, 1995. A more significant change occurred on July 27, when the UDF and Aford announced that they had signed an agreement to form a coalition government. However, in December relations between the two groups cooled when Aford leader Chihana accused the government of "lacking transparency" and failing to combat corruption.

On December 23, 1995, former president Banda and his five codefendants were acquitted of all charges relating to the murder of "reformist" politicians in 1983 (see MCP in Political Parties and Groups, below). Shortly thereafter, Banda apologized for the "pain and suffering" that had occurred while he was in office. However, he continued to deny personal responsibility, instead blaming "selfish individuals" in his government. Meanwhile, the new UDF-led government continued to press inquiries into a wide range of abuses that were alleged to have taken place under Banda's rule. Ultimately, although official scrutiny remained leveled at some of Banda's former confidants, investigative fervor in general dissipated substantially upon Banda's death on November 25.

On May 2, 1996, Chihana resigned from the government, saying that he wanted to concentrate on his party responsibilities. Six Aford cabinet ministers refused to comply with Chihana's demand that they resign from the government as well, and they declared themselves "independents." In response, Aford and the MCP suspended their participation in the assembly, accusing the UDF of attempting to secure a legislative majority by "poaching" their representatives as cabinet ministers. Assembly activity subsequently remained blocked (the UDF proving unable to muster a quorum) until April 1997, when Aford and the MCP ended their boycott after President Muluzi agreed to pursue constitutional amendments that would "prevent political horse trading and chicanery." However, the matter was not resolved on July 24, when Muluzi appointed a new cabinet that still included Aford representatives against the wishes of Aford leaders.

On June 15, 1999, President Muluzi was reelected to a second five-year term with 51.37 percent of the vote, compared to 44.3 percent for runner-up Chakuamba, the joint MCP/Aford candidate. (Aford's Chihana had served as Chakuamba's vice presidential running mate.) In concurrent legislative polling the UDF secured a plurality of 93 of 193 seats. The opposition accused the government of numerous irregularities, including manipulation of the media and the voter registration process as well as vote rigging. The losing candidates also argued that a runoff should have been held because Muluzi's vote total had not surpassed the level of 50 percent of the registered voters. Although the international community generally accepted the balloting as free and fair and the courts in Malawi upheld the results, Chakufwa Chihana of Aford, the MCP/Aford vice presidential candidate, called for a campaign of civil disobedience to protest the government's actions. Muluzi's critics also challenged the cabinet he appointed on July 1 for containing too many ministers (21 of 36) from the southern part of the country, the UDF stronghold.

Corruption charges prompted the appointment of new cabinets in March and November 2000. Meanwhile severe intraparty infighting continued to hamper both the MCP and Aford, as evidenced by their poor showing in the November 2000 local elections, which were dominated by the UDF, albeit in the context of a low voter turnout. Muluzi's second term was marked by a bitter dispute over proposed constitutional changes to allow a president to seek a third term. The initial proposal failed to gain the needed two-thirds majority in the assembly in 2002, and a second effort in the legislature was rebuffed in 2003. The UDF attempted to have the measure brought to the public in a national referendum. However, it became clear that the constitutional amendment would fail because of widespread opposition, and the referendum request was withdrawn. Muluzi subsequently announced that he would not seek a third term. Instead he handpicked his successor, economist Bingu wa MUTHARIKA, who had run as a presidential candidate in 1999 for the defunct United Party (UP).

Presidential polling in 2004 was delayed by two days as a result of complaints by opposition parties that some 1 million voters, including many of their supporters, had been purged from the list of eligible voters. However, the High Court accepted the government's explanation that only double registrations and ineligible voters had been eliminated from the rolls.

In January 2004 a coalition of seven small parties, calling itself *Mgwirizano* (Unity), was launched to present Chakuamba as a joint presidential candidate. However, President Mutharika was reelected in balloting on May 20 with 35.9 percent of the vote, compared to 27.1 percent for Tembo (the MCP candidate) and 25.7 percent for Chakuamba. In concurrent legislative balloting, the MCP secured 60 seats, followed by the UDF with 49. Opposition parties and candidates challenged the legitimacy of the polling. However, Chakuamba withdrew his objections and accepted the post of minister of agriculture in the new Mutharika government, which also included the UDF, the National Democratic Alliance, the *Mgwirizano* coalition, and independents. Many independent legislators agreed to support the UDF in the assembly, some 23 of them subsequently joining the UDF. Additional realignments occurred after a dispute within the UDF prompted Mutharika to form a new party (see Current issues, below). As part of his anti-corruption campaign, the president dismissed 35 senior government officials between 2004 and 2006.

Mutharika announced a new economic plan in 2007 designed to enhance the country's agricultural sector through new investments in technology and infrastructure. Tensions between the president and individual government ministers led to four cabinet reshuffles in the period 2004–2008, with Mutharika assuming the portfolios of minister of agriculture and food security, and of education, science, and technology.

On May 16, 2009, the president dissolved the cabinet ahead of national elections. In the presidential elections on May 19, Mutharika was reelected with 66.4 percent of the vote. Tembo placed second with 30.3 percent. Five other minor party candidates received less than 1 percent each in polling that was criticized by some domestic and foreign monitors (see Current issues, below). In legislative balloting held on the same day, the DPP won an outright majority in the assembly with 113 seats. A new cabinet was appointed on June 15. Only eight ministers were retained from the previous cabinet. Mutharika's brother Peter was appointed minister of justice and constitutional affairs and the president retained the portfolio of agriculture and food security. Islamic groups protested the new cabinet because it included only two Muslims, as opposed to the seven in the previous government.

The president carried out a major cabinet reshuffle on August 9, 2010. He relinquished the portfolio of agriculture and food safety, and his brother moved to the ministry of education, science, and technology. As part of the reshuffle, Mutharika named his wife Callista CHIMOMBO as "first lady" in charge of the ministry of maternal, infant and child health. Reports indicated that Mutharika's replacement of some ministers was part of an effort to reflect greater tribal and clan diversity in the government.

In January 2011 Mutharika assumed the portfolio of the defense minister. Following the deadly protests in July, Mutharika dismissed the cabinet and declared that the government would be run from the president's office (see Current issues, below). A new cabinet was named on September 7.

On April 5, 2012, Mutharika died of a heart attack. Vice President Joyce BANDA (People's Party—PP) was sworn in as interim president on April 7 (see Current issues, below). She named a new coalition cabinet on April 26. The cabinet was reshuffled on December 6, 2012, and again in July 2013.

Constitution and government. The constitution of July 6, 1966, established a one-party system under which the MCP was accorded a political monopoly and its leader extensive powers as head of state, head of government, and commander in chief. Originally elected to a five-year presidential term by the National Assembly in 1966, Hastings Banda was designated president for life in 1971.

Following approval of a multiparty system in a national referendum on June 15, 1993, the assembly on June 22 amended the basic law to permit the registration of parties beyond the MCP. In November further revision abolished the life presidency and repealed the requirement that presidential candidates be MCP members. Following the return of ailing President Banda to active status in early December, an additional amendment was enacted to provide for an acting president in case of the president's incapacitation.

A new constitution (proposed by a National Constitutional Conference) was approved by the assembly on May 16, 1994, and entered into effect provisionally for one year on May 18. The new basic law incorporated the 1993 amendments, while also providing for a new Constitutional Committee and a Human Rights Commission. It also authorized the eventual creation of a second legislative body (the Senate) no sooner than 1999. However, in January 2001, much to the consternation of opposition parties and some civic organizations, the assembly revised the basic law to eliminate reference to the proposed Senate. The government argued that the creation of the Senate would have burdened the country's fragile economy, but opponents claimed that the administration was in reality primarily concerned that the new body would have had the power to impeach the president. Following review and refinement by the Constitutional Conference, the new constitution was once again approved by the assembly and promulgated as a permanent document on May 18, 1995. One of the amendments approved by the assembly in November 1994 provided for a presidentially appointed second vice president. The first vice president is elected as a running mate to the president and assumes the presidency if that office becomes vacant. The president is not required to designate a second vice president, but any such appointment must be made outside the president's political party.

The 1995 constitution provided for a Western-style judicial system, including a Supreme Court of Appeal, a High Court, and magistrates' courts. No mention is made of the so-called traditional courts (headed by local chiefs), which had been restored in 1970. For administrative purposes Malawi is divided into 3 regions, and 28 districts, which are headed by regional ministers and district commissioners, respectively.

Most newspapers are privately owned and operated. Constitutional amendments in the 1990s eased press restrictions but censorship remains a problem; two journalists were arrested in 2005 after publishing a story in which they suggested that the president was afraid of ghosts and had moved out of the presidential mansion because he believed it to be haunted. In the 2007 budget, opposition members of parliament managed to reduce funding of the state broadcasting companies to a symbolic one kwacha because of claims that the media had become organs of the government. The Malawi Electoral Commission criticized the state radio and television station for failing to provide equal access to all parties during the 2009 balloting. In January 2011 Mutharika approved a highly restrictive press law that gave the information minister the authority to censor any content judged "contrary to the public interest." In its 2012 ratings of global press freedom, Reporters Without Borders ranked Malawi 75th out of 179 countries, a rise from 146th the previous year. The dramatic increase was attributed to the removal of a range of press restrictions by the Banda government.

Foreign relations. Malawi under President Banda's leadership sought to combine African nationalism with multiracialism at home and a strongly pro-Western and anticommunist position in world affairs. Citing economic necessity, Malawi was one of the few black African states to maintain uninterrupted relations with white-ruled South Africa. A consequence of the linkage was a September 1986 meeting in Blantyre, during which the leaders of Mozambique, Zambia, and Zimbabwe reportedly warned Banda to change his policies, particularly concerning alleged Malawian support for Renamo rebels in Mozambique. Banda, while denying the allegations, nevertheless quickly concluded a joint defense and security pact with Mozambique. The government also reaffirmed its commitment to an effort by the Southern African Development Coordination Conference (SADCC, subsequently the Southern African Development Community—SADC) to reduce dependence on South African trade routes. To that end, Malawi in 1987 agreed to increase shipments through Tanzania, with which it had established diplomatic ties in 1985 despite long-standing complaints of Tanzanian aid to Banda's opponents. Relations with Zambia had also been strained by Malawi's claim to Zambian territory in the vicinity of their common border.

In 1994 the new Muluzi administration moved quickly to strengthen regional ties, the president traveling to Zimbabwe, Zambia, and Botswana. In addition, Malawi and Mozambique created a joint commission to locate and repatriate former rebels located in the opposite state. Malawi also endeavored to improve relations and security ties with the United States. In June 2003 five suspected al-Qaida terrorists were turned over to U.S. custody.

President Mutharika's anticorruption campaign won international praise from European states, the United States, and international organizations such as the IMF and the World Bank. As a result, donors increased aid and assistance to the government, Malawi receiving about $60 million annually in U.S. economic aid in 2005 and 2006. Concurrently, Malawi's exports to the United States increased dramatically through the African Growth and Opportunity Act (AGOA), which eliminated U.S. tariffs on more than two-thirds of Malawian exports.

Following record maize harvests in 2006 and 2007, the government purchased excess crops from farmers to donate to Swaziland and Lesotho following a widespread drought. Malawi also increased sales of maize to Zimbabwe to record levels—400,000 tons per year. The two countries signed an economic cooperation agreement in May 2006, despite international criticism that closer ties undermined efforts to democratize Zimbabwe.

Relations between Malawi and China were strained in 2006 after Malawi refused an invitation to participate in a 2006 conference called by China in an effort to convince a group of African countries to break off diplomatic and economic relations with Taiwan. Instead of accepting the Chinese overtures, Malawi, Burkina Faso, Gambia, São Tomé and Principe, and Swaziland signed a joint declaration of support in 2007 for Taiwan. Among other things, Taiwan since 2002 has provided financial and technical support to Malawi for a number of programs designed to improve education and health care, including an initiative to combat the spread of HIV/AIDS.

However, in January 2008 Malawi announced the suspension of diplomatic relations with Taiwan and the initiation of new ties with China. China subsequently pledged $287 million in new economic aid for Malawi. Chinese officials also promised new infrastructure assistance. The new relationship was expected to be especially beneficial to Malawi's tobacco sector, the largest in Africa, because China accounted for one-third of worldwide tobacco. In May Malawi and Zambia agreed on a joint electrification program whereby Malawi would provide power to remote areas along the border of the two countries. Malawi agreed to deploy 50 police officers to the Darfur region of Sudan as part of the UN–African Union (AU) peacekeeping force and pledged an additional 800 troops. In September Malawi withdrew recognition of the Polisario Front government in the Western Sahara and instead called for a negotiated settlement over the disputed region.

In 2009 foreign minister Yang Jiechi became the first senior Chinese official to visit Malawi and he announced a $90 million loan for economic development during the trip.

In January 2010 Malawi and India signed four new bilateral trade agreements. Trade between India and Malawi has increased 100 percent since 2003. In February Mutharika was elected as the new leader of the AU. A number of foreign governments protested the trial and conviction of two Malawians for homosexuality (see Current issues, below).

The Millennium Challenge Corporation (MCC) announced in January 2011 that it would provide $350 million to Malawi for infrastructure projects. However, after countries such as Germany announced the reduction of aid because of the newly enacted press restrictions (see Current issues, below) and the criminalization of homosexuality, the MCC first delayed signing the agreement until April and then froze payments in July. Meanwhile, in April a diplomatic cable written by the British high commissioner to Malawi, Fergus Cochrane-Dyet, was printed by the Malawian newspaper the *Weekend Nation.* The note was critical of Mutharika and led to the expulsion of Cochrane-Dyet. The British retaliated and expelled the Malawian representative to London, Flossie Gomile CHIDYAONGA. The UK subsequently froze $122.8 million in aid for Malawi in July following reports of human rights violations by the government (see Current issues, below).

In September 2012 Malawi and the UK reestablished diplomatic ties. Meanwhile, after the inauguration of Banda in April, donors, including the UK, the United States, and the World Bank restored most aid to the country. In October Banda requested that the AU arbitrate Malawi's maritime border dispute with Tanzania over Lake Malawi (Lake Nyasa). Subsequent bilateral negotiations launched in November failed and were superseded in March 2013 by talks under the auspices of the Forum for Former African Heads of State and Government. Also in October 2012 the United States announced it would provide $105 million to Malawi for economic and social development, including funds to upgrade health care facilities and services.

Malawi agreed in March 2013 to contribute troops to a UN peacekeeping force in the Democratic Republic of the Congo (see entry on the DRC).

Current issues. Following the 2004 elections, new president Mutharika launched a broad anticorruption campaign that earned praise (and additional aid) from donors such as the EU and the United States. However, the initiative generated a rift between Mutharika and former president Muluzi, some of whose close allies (including several UDF leaders) were arrested on corruption charges. (Critics of Mutharika accused him of using the new anticorruption bureau as a personal political tool.) Consequently, supporters in the assembly of Muluzi (who remained leader of the UDF after leaving the presidency) began to block legislation presented by the Mutharika administration. The conflict culminated in the president's decision in February 2005 to quit the UDF and form a new Democratic Progressive Party (DPP), which attracted a number of Mutharika's supporters within the UDF and other parties and prompted significant legislative realignment.

In March 2005 the UDF and MCP attempted without success to impeach Mutharika for inappropriate use of government funds. At the same time, it was reported that the government was contemplating an investigation of former president Muluzi's alleged acquisition of millions of dollars during his presidential tenure. Relations between the executive and legislative branches deteriorated further when Mutharika moved his offices into the new assembly building, forcing the assembly to return to its old headquarters. Opposition parties (led by the UDF) again attempted to start impeachment proceedings against the president in June, and, in apparent retaliation, Mutharika removed the UDF's Cassim CHILUMPHA from his cabinet post, although Chilumpha remained vice president. Collaterally, Mutharika announced a cabinet reshuffle that raised the number of ministers from 27 to 33 so that he could include some of his independent supporters.

The assembly formally approved the start of impeachment proceedings in mid-October 2005, but the High Court ordered them stopped after pro-Mutharika demonstrations deteriorated into "riots" in which opposition legislators were reportedly attacked. In any event, it had been widely expected that the impeachment motion would not have garnered the two-thirds assembly vote required for success. In addition, analysts suggested that much of the population considered the impeachment initiative a waste of time and resources, particularly in view of the nation's severe food crisis. Among other things, the assembly's blockage of the administration's proposed budget compromised the distribution of emergency food supplies. (The budget had also called for a pay raise of more than 350 percent for the president.)

The government conducted another string of arrests in November 2005 as part of its anticorruption campaign. Among those charged were two legislators who had led the recent impeachment drive and Vice President Chilumpha. However, the High Court ruled that Chilumpha could not be brought up on criminal charges while serving as vice president. In February 2006 Mutharika attempted to dismiss Chilumpha for "undermining the government," but the High Court declared the president lacked the constitutional authority for such a move. At the end of April, Chilumpha and some 12 others (including senior members of the UDF) were arrested on treason charges, the administration accusing them of having plotted the assassination of Mutharika. The charges against most of those arrested were quickly dropped, but Chilumpha remained under house arrest along with two codefendants. Meanwhile, former president Muluzi was arrested on corruption charges in July, but he was released the following day after all charges were dismissed.

The restrictions on Vice President Chilumpha's house arrest were gradually relaxed as his trial began in January 2007. (The case proceeded slowly and continued into the fall because of repeated motions and challenges by the defense.) Meanwhile, the crackdown on the UDF continued, as three party officials were arrested on charges of treason in January.

In June 2007 the Supreme Court upheld the article in the constitution that declared that any member of parliament who switched parties could be expelled and forced to stand for office in a by-election. Opposition members of parliament initially blocked debate on the government's proposed budget in an effort to force the by-elections. A compromise was finally reached in September that allowed passage of the budget in return for subsequent legislative debate on the management of new polling for by-elections.

In February 2008 opposition parties boycotted the opening of the assembly and insisted that debate over by-elections be the first priority of the parliament. Only 6 of the 105 opposition deputies attended the opening of the legislature. In May the government arrested a number of opposition figures, including former president Muluzi, on charges that they were plotting a coup. Also charged were former senior military leaders and the secretary general of the UDF, Kennedy MAKWANGWALA. Opposition leaders decried the arrests as part of an intimidation campaign ahead of presidential and legislative elections scheduled for 2009. All were subsequently released on bail. Also in May, Mutharika initiated the parliamentary budgetary session despite the ongoing opposition boycott. Meanwhile, the government announced a 17 percent increase in pay for civil servants in an effort to prevent a general strike. The UDF nominated Muluzi as its presidential candidate at a party congress in May, although concerns were raised over his eligibility because presidents were limited to two consecutive terms. Muluzi and his supporters contended that the wording of the constitution allowed more than two terms as long as they were not consecutive. The nation's constitutional court ruled that Muluzi was ineligible, leaving the UDF without a candidate in the presidential balloting (see Political Parties, below).

In the presidential and legislative balloting, concerns were raised over potential fraud. Protests were also lodged to the electoral commission over the use of state media to support the ruling Mutharika and the ruling DPP. However, most domestic and foreign observers asserted that the balloting was generally free and fair. The polling marked the first time in Malawi that a woman, Loveness Gondwe of the New Rainbow Coalition (see Political parties, below), ran for the presidency. Although Gondwe did not win, Joyce Banda of the DPP became the country's first female vice president.

The construction of a new presidential palace for Mutharika in the midst of economic uncertainties prompted protest and threats of parliamentary investigations. In May two Malawians were convicted of homosexuality and sentenced to 14 years in prison. The United States and a number of other countries protested the sentences. In addition, some foreign donors reportedly threatened to suspend aid payments unless the case was reexamined. In September a corruption trial began for former president Muluzi on charges from 2005.

Security forces brutally suppressed protests against rising fuel and energy costs on July 20, 2011. At least 19 people were killed and more than 250 arrested (see Political Parties and Groups, below). Two days after the demonstrations, Mutharika replaced the head of the Malawian army in an effort to ease tensions. Additional protests scheduled for August 17 were cancelled following an agreement between opposition leaders and the government to launch a national dialogue. On August 19 Mutharika dismissed the cabinet, ostensibly in response to the government's crackdown on the demonstrators. Opposition groups and critics charged that the action was designed to consolidate the president's power. Meanwhile, Banda formed a new political grouping, the People's Party (PP) (see Political Parties and Groups, below).

Mutharika died on April 5, and DPP loyalists sought to conceal his death, even reportedly flying the president's body to South Africa and asserting that he was undergoing medical treatment, in an effort to prevent Banda from assuming the presidency. However, Banda secured the support of the military and was sworn on April 7. She subsequently named a new cabinet that was purged of Mutharika loyalists, including the former president's brother and wife. Following Banda's inauguration, up to 45 members of the parliament attempted to switch parties and join the PP. However, as Malawian law requires a member of parliament to resign and stand in a by-election when changing parties, the majority remained formally in their original groupings but supported the government.

In March 2013, ten current and former government officials were arrested on suspicion of plotting a coup in the aftermath of Mutharika's death by keeping Banda from taking office. Among those arrested where Arthur MUTHARIKA, the dead president's brother and a former foreign minister. Strong harvests in the summer of 2013 increased government revenues and allowed an increase in farm aid to the poor. In June Anastasia MSOSA became the first woman chief justice of Malawi's judiciary.

POLITICAL PARTIES AND GROUPS

For nearly three decades prior to the 1993 national referendum, the Malawi Congress Party (MCP) was the only authorized political group, and it exercised complete control of the government. On June 29, 1993, the constitution was amended to allow for multiparty activity, and on August 17 the government announced that the first groups had been authorized to function as legal parties.

Legislative Parties:

Democratic Progressive Party (DPP). The DPP was launched in February 2005 by President Bingu wa Mutharika and other UDF dissidents who opposed UDF president Muluzi. Disaffected members of other parties and a number of independents also joined the DDP, which as of mid-2006 was credited with controlling some 74 assembly seats. DPP Vice President Gwanda Chakuamba was dismissed from the cabinet and expelled from the party in September 2005 after he strongly criticized President Mutharika. Ralph KASAMBARA was dismissed as attorney general in 2006 and left the party to form the **Congress for Democrats** (CODE). Chakuamba's successor as party vice president, Uladi MUSSA, was also dismissed in January 2007 on charges that he was attempting to launch a new political party. Mussa was replaced by the party's Secretary General Heatherwick Ntaba.

Mutharika was reelected president of the republic in May 2009 during elections in which the DPP secured 113 seats and an outright majority in the assembly. Reports indicated that factions emerged within the party over a possible successor to Mutharika, who was constitutionally prevented from seeking another term as president in 2014. After Vice President Joyce BANDA refused to support Mutharika's brother and hand-picked successor, Peter Mutharika's bid to be the DPP candidate in 2014, she and a number of her supporters were dismissed from the DPP. Banda went on to form a new entity, the **People's Party** (see below).

The government's suppression of protests in July 2011 created divisions within the party and led to the expulsion of several prominent party leaders, including Henry Dama PHOYA, who was reported to be organizing a new political grouping to challenge the DPP. Peter Mutharika succeeded his brother as party leader after the latter's death on April 5, 2012. In October DPP Secretary General Elias Wakuda KAANGA defected to the PP.

DPP First Vice President Goodall Edward GONDWE was arrested along with other DPP members and government officials on coup charges related to the 2012 attempt to prevent Banda from assuming the presidency. In April Mutharika defeated Parliamentary Speaker Henry CHIMUNTHU to be reelected party president.

Leaders: Peter MUTHARIKA (President), Goodall Edward GONDWE (First Vice President), Elias Wakuda KAANGA (Secretary General).

United Democratic Front (UDF). The UDF was founded in April 1992 by former MCP officials who operated clandestinely until October, when they announced their intention to campaign for a multiparty democracy. A party congress on December 30, 1993, chose UDF chair Bakili Muluzi to be the UDF's presidential candidate. Meanwhile, the UDF leaders were embarrassed by allegations, attributed to the MCP, that they had engaged in anti-opposition activities while MCP members.

Muluzi defeated incumbent president Banda and two other candidates in March 1994 with a 47.3 percent plurality of the vote. In the legislative balloting the UDF won a plurality of 84 of 177 seats. Muluzi was reelected with 51.37 percent of the vote in 1999, while the UDF increased its legislative plurality to 93 out of 193 seats in 1999.

Beginning in 2000, the party suffered serious internal divisions, leading to the formation of the anti-Muluzi NDA (below). In 2003, dissident members of the UDF left the party to form a new entity, the People's Progressive Movement (PPM), led by former UDF party vice president Aleke Banda. In the 2004 legislative elections the UDF lost its plurality and became the second-largest party (49 seats) in the assembly behind the MCP.

Following the 2004 presidential election, a leadership struggle emerged between Muluzi, who remained party president, and his hand-picked successor as Malawi's president, Bingu wa Mutharika. Among other things, Muluzi's supporters objected to elements of the broad anticorruption efforts by Mutharika, who in February 2005 left the UDF to form the DPP (above).

The UDF led the subsequent effort to impeach President Mutharika, although its legislative representation had reportedly fallen to 30 by mid-2006 due to defections to the DPP. In addition, many UDF leaders faced corruption charges pressed by the Mutharika administration (see Current issues, above). Muluzi announced in March 2007 that he intended to be the UDF candidate for the presidency in 2009, and he won the party's nomination at a convention in April 2008. The subsequent ruling by the constitutional court that Muluzi was ineligible to run led many UDF supporters to back MCP candidate John Tembo (see below). In the legislative balloting the UDF secured 17 seats. Many party members blamed the UDF's poor performance on Muluzi's failed presidential effort. In December 2009 Muluzi announced his retirement from politics. Friday JUMBE was chosen as interim leader of the MCP to replace Muluzi. In September 2010 a dissident faction of the UDF, calling itself the UDF Task Force for Change, attempted unsuccessfully to force Jumbe to resign. Muluzi's son Atupele MULUZI was appointed minister of Development Planning and Cooperation in 2012. In October the younger Muluzi was elected party president. He subsequently lost his cabinet post in a cabinet reshuffle.

Leaders: Atupele MULUZI (President), Gerald MPONDA (Secretary General).

Malawi Congress Party (MCP). The MCP is a continuation of the Nyasaland African Congress (NAC), which was formed in 1959 under the leadership of President H. Kamuzu Banda. Overtly pro-Western and dedicated to multiracialism and internal development, the party was frequently criticized for being excessively conservative. It held all legislative seats prior to the multiparty poll of May 1994, when it ran second in both the presidential and legislative races.

On August 25, 1994, Banda retired from politics although he retained the title of MCP president for life. The 1994 vice presidential candidate, Stephen Chakuamba, assumed leadership of the party. Thereafter, in early 1995, the party was shaken by the arrests of Banda, John Tembo (longtime Banda associate and MCP leader), and others for alleged involvement in the killing 12 years earlier of Dick MATENJE and several other MCP cabinet ministers. At the time of his death, Matenje had headed an increasingly popular reform wing within the party that had clashed with Tembo and his supporters. Banda, Tembo, and their codefendants in the murder trial were acquitted on all charges in December. Related charges against Cecilia KADZAMIRA, Banda's longtime companion who had been the country's "official hostess" during the latter part of the Banda regime, had been dismissed prior to trial on technical grounds. However, the government continued to press the case by appealing the verdict to the High Court, which ultimately upheld the acquittal. Meanwhile, Tembo and Kadzamira were arrested in September 1996 on charges of conspiracy to commit murder in connection with an alleged plot to assassinate cabinet members in 1995. They were quickly released on bail, and it was subsequently unclear if the case would be pursued. Similar ambiguity existed regarding fraud charges against Tembo and Kadzamira stemming from alleged malfeasance during the accumulation of the vast Banda "economic empire." Banda himself had been the focus of a corruption investigation in early 1997, but the case was dropped later in the year when it became apparent that the former president had little time to live.

Conflict between Banda's supporters and MCP "reformists" continued through 1997, with the latter clearly gaining the ascendancy at the party convention in July. In a surprisingly decisive vote of 406–109, Tembo was defeated in the race for MCP president by Chakuamba, who immediately declared his intention to run for president of the republic in 1999, insisting that the MCP should merge with Aford (below) to present the strongest possible challenge to the UDF. However, the proposed merger was shelved in the wake of objections from MCP veterans, including Tembo, who had been elected unopposed as MCP vice president.

In intraparty polling in January 1999, Chakuamba defeated Tembo in a contest to decide who would be the MCP's standard-bearer in mid-year presidential balloting. Subsequently, Chakuamba rejected suggestions that he choose Tembo as his running mate and named Aford's Chakufwa Chihana to his campaign ticket. On February 8 an electoral alliance for the presidential race between the two parties was officially inaugurated. Meanwhile, pro-Tembo activists staged demonstrations to protest what they (and reportedly Tembo) considered an affront. The MCP/Aford ticket finished second (with 44.3 percent of the vote) in the June presidential ballot, while the MCP secured 66 seats (on 33.82 percent of the vote) in the legislative poll. Meanwhile, tension between Chakuamba and Tembo continued, and in late May Tembo called upon Chakuamba to step down as party leader. In early June, Chakuamba called for an MCP boycott of the opening session of parliament, but his request was ignored and he was given a one-year suspension from the house (later voided by the High Court). On June 24 Speaker Sam Mpasu endorsed Tembo as new leader of the opposition in parliament, a decision that was subsequently challenged by Chakuamba.

The MCP infighting continued unabated into 2000, and the rival factions held separate conventions in August at which Chakuamba and Tembo were each declared party chair. However, the following summer the High Court nullified the parallel conventions. Meanwhile, the Chakuamba faction, which announced it had expelled Tembo and his supporters from the party, pursued ties with the NDA, the newly formed antigovernment grouping, while the Tembo faction was perceived as cooperating more and more with the administration. Chakuamba subsequently joined the Republican Party (below) in December 2003. The MCP became the largest party in the assembly after the 2004 elections, but Tembo lost his presidential bid. MCP Secretary General Kate KAINGA-KALULUMA joined the new Mutharika government and subsequently left the MCP to join the DPP. Subsequently, the MCP cooperated with the UDF's attempt to impeach President Mutharika, although internal MCP dissension was reported regarding that and other issues. (A dissident faction led by Respicius DZANJALIMODZI reportedly challenged Tembo's supporters for party supremacy.)

In 2007 Tembo rejected a proposal from the UDF to rally behind a single candidate in the 2009 presidential elections. Under the proposal, Tembo would have run as the vice presidential candidate with Muluzi as the presidential contender. Dissatisfied with Tembo's leadership, former party vice president Nicholas DAUSI and at least 60 MCP members and elected officials left the party in 2008 to join the DPP.

During the 2009 elections the MCP campaigned on a pledge to implement a universal subsidy for all farmers. Tembo placed second in the presidential balloting and the MCP became the second largest party in the legislature with 27 seats, although it lost more than half its former seats. After the balloting many MCP officials who criticized Tembo, including party spokesperson Ishmael Chafukira, who had called for the presidential candidate's resignation, were removed from their positions. In November, Ephraim Adele KAYEMBE of the MCP was elected leader of the opposition in parliament after a rule change that allowed the entire legislature to vote for the opposition leader (Kayembe won because of votes from the DPP). However, Tembo successfully challenged the election in court on the grounds that only opposition parties should be allowed to participate in selecting the opposition leader. Tembo subsequently replaced Kayembe in June. Following protests in July 21, the government accused the MCP of inciting violence. The MCP continued to be the largest opposition party after Banda became president in April 2012.

In August 2013 Lazarus CHAKWERA was elected MCP president, while Chriss DAZA was elected secretary general.

Leaders: Lazarus CHAKWERA (President), Chriss DAZA (General Secretary).

Alliance for Democracy (Aford). Aford was launched in Lilongwe on September 21, 1992, by trade union leader and prodemocracy advocate Chakufwa Chihana, who at the time of the group's founding was awaiting trial on sedition charges. The grouping was led by a 13-member interim committee that included civil servants, academics, and businesspeople. Although Aford described itself as "not a party but a pressure group," the government on November 7 declared membership in the group illegal. In late December many of its members were arrested during demonstrations ignited by the sentencing of Chihana to three years imprisonment.

In March 1993 a spokesperson for the Zimbabwean-based Malawi Freedom Movement (Mafremo) announced that the group had dissolved and had merged with Aford. (Mafremo, in the wake of the 1981 arrest and imprisonment of its leader, Orton CHIRWA, had been relatively inactive until an early 1987 attack on a police station near the Tanzanian border that was attributed to the group's military wing, the Malawi National Liberation Army. Although initially based in Dares

Salaam, Mafremo had subsequently been reported to have secured Zimbabwean support through the efforts of a new leader, Dr. Edward YAPWANTHA, who was expelled from Zimbabwe in mid-1990, apparently as a result of improved Malawian-Zimbabwean relations.)

In mid-1994 Chihana, who had been granted a sentence reduction and released two days before the multiparty referendum, pressed President Banda to resign in favor of an MCP-UDF-Aford transitional government. In August Aford turned back a merger bid from another opposition party—the Congress for the Second Republic (CSR)—asserting an interest in the CSR's then exiled leader, Kanyama CHUIME, but not the party.

Following its third-place showing in the 1994 assembly balloting, Aford declined an invitation to participate in a government coalition with the UDF, which was five seats short of a legislative majority. On June 20 Aford signed a memorandum of understanding with the MCP, in which the two groups committed themselves to preservation of "the endangered national unity and security of the country." However, in September Chihana joined the Muluzi government as second vice president designate, while three other Aford members accepted cabinet posts. Although Chihana rejected reports that the party was defecting to the UDF, in January 1995 Aford announced the dissolution of its alliance with the MCP.

Relations between the UDF and Aford deteriorated over the next year, and on May 2, 1996, Chihana, who had criticized the UDF on several points in December 1995, resigned from the second vice presidency, ostensibly to devote more time to party affairs. In June it was reported that an Aford national congress had voted to withdraw from the government coalition and had ordered its members in the cabinet to resign their posts. However, most of the ministers refused to leave the government, and it was reported that at least six members of the Aford executive council rejected the decision to separate from the coalition with the UDF. In response, Chihana called for the ouster of the "renegade" members. The issue remained clouded throughout 1997 as the new cabinet announced in July included not only the previous Aford ministers but also several other Aford members. Meanwhile, at the party's annual congress in December, Aford delegates voted against a merger with the MCP that had been advocated by many within the Chihana camp.

In June 1998 two Aford legislators, Joseph MSEKAWANTHU and Edward MUSYANI, declared their independence from the party, charging that the party's dictatorial" leadership policies had marginalized them. In October Aford officially acknowledged having decided to compete for the presidency on a joint ticket with the MCP, and in February 1999 Chihana agreed to campaign for the vice presidency on a ticket led by MCP leader Chakuamba. Aford was credited with 10.52 percent of the vote and 29 seats in the June 1999 assembly balloting.

Intraparty fighting continued in 2000–2001 over issues such as the future of the alliance with the MCP and whether the party should cooperate with the government. The Chihana faction was reportedly in favor of continuing an antigovernment stance, another wing pressed to form a national unity government with the UDF. Aford won only six seats in the 2004 elections and supported the subsequent Mutharika government after Chihana was appointed minister of agriculture and food security, a post he left in February 2005. Four of Aford's legislators reportedly defected to the DPP in 2005. In June 2006 Chihana died in South Africa; he was succeeded as party leader by Chipimpha Mughogho. At a party conference in December, Aford officials voted to expel members who did not support Mughogho as Aford leader. In October 2007 Dindi Gowa NYASULU was elected president of Aford at a congress that was marred by the death of 26 Aford delegates who perished in a bus accident on the way to the convention.

Nyasulu was the Aford presidential candidate in the 2009 balloting. He placed last among the six contenders with less than 1 percent of the vote. In the concurrent assembly polling, Aford secured only one seat. Aford received one cabinet post in the Banda government appointed in April 2012. Godfrey SHAWA became Aford's president following the resignation of Nyasulu in November 2012 (Nyasulu died of natural causes on December 11).

Leaders: Godfrey SHAWA (President), Khwauli MSISKA (Secretary General).

Malawi Forum for Unity and Development (MAFUNDE). MAFUNDE was formed in 2002 under the leadership of George MNESA to fight corruption and end food shortages. The party failed to gain seats in the 2004 balloting, but it secured one seat in the 2009 assembly election. MAFUNDE led protests in April 2011 over the expulsion of the British high commissioner to Malawi.

Leaders: George MNESA, Levison GAMIZA (Secretary General).

Maravi People's Party (MPP). Formed in 2007, the MPP initially opposed Mutharika and the DPP. When MPP secretary general and party cofounder Paul Maulidi attempted to form an electoral alliance with the ruling DPP, he was ousted from the party and replaced by Yusuf Haudi (Maulidi subsequently joined the DPP). The MPP gained one seat in the 2009 assembly elections. After the elections, the MPP announced it would support Mutharika and the DPP. Party leader Uladi Mussi defected to the PP in 2012, and reports that year indicated that the MPP was defunct.

Leaders: Uladi MUSSI (President), Yusuf HAUDI (Acting Secretary General).

People's Party (PP). Formed by then vice president Joyce Banda in September 2011, the PP attracted dissidents from a range of parties, including former vice president Cassim Chilumpha of the UDF. Following the death of president Mutharika in April 2012, Banda became president of Malawi and named a coalition cabinet that included members of the PP and other legislative parties. In August Banda was reelected party chair, as was General Secretary Henry CHIBWANA. Chilumpha was elected second vice president.

Leaders: Joyce BANDA (President of the Republic and Party Chair), Khumbo Hastings KACHALI (Vice President of the Republic), Henry CHIBWANA (Secretary General).

Other Parties That Contested the 2009 Legislative Election:

Republican Party (RP). The RP was formed in 2004 by Gwanda Chakuamba, Stanley Masauli, and other opponents of John Tembo from the MCP. Using the RP as the nucleus of the anti-Muluzi coalition *Mgwirizano,* Chakuamba placed third in the 2004 presidential balloting with 25.7 percent of the vote. He subsequently joined the government as minister of agriculture and food security. In the legislative elections, the RP became the third largest party with 15 seats.

In March 2005 Chakuamba resigned from the RP, along with a number of RP members, to join the new DPP. Chakuamba initially announced the dissolution of the RP, but the RP's executive council rejected the proposed "merger" with the DPP. Following his dismissal from the government and the DPP in September, Chakuamba attempted to reassert control over the RP. However, he was formally expelled from the RP in October, and he subsequently announced the formation of the **New Republican Party** (NRP). The NRP supported Muluzi of the UDF in the 2009 presidential elections but was subsequently described as defunct.

In the 2009 elections Stanley Masauli was the RP presidential candidate, but he received less than 1 percent of the vote. The RP failed to secure any seats in the concurrent assembly elections.

Leaders: Anastansia MSOSA (Party Chair), Stanley MASAULI (2009 Presidential Candidate).

People's Progressive Movement (PPM). Formed in 2003 by former UDF vice president Aleke Banda and other UDF members opposed to their party's Muluzi faction, the PPM joined the *Mgwirizano* coalition for the 2004 elections, gaining six seats in the assembly. Party member and former vice president of the republic John MALEWEZI ran as a presidential candidate for the PPM in 2004, placing fifth with just 2.5 percent of the vote. In 2005 a number of PPM members joined the DPP, although the PPM retained its status as an independent party. The party endorsed Mutharika in the 2009 presidential balloting. Party founder Banda died on April 9, 2010. The PPM was active in the protests and demonstrations in July 2011. KATSONGA would reportedly be the PPM candidate in the 2014 presidential elections.

Leader: Mark KATSONGA (Party Leader).

Other parties that contested the May 2009 legislative elections included the **People's Transformation Party** (Petra), which gained one seat in the 2004 balloting, but failed to gain any representation in 2009 and whose presidential candidate Kamuzu CHIBAMBO placed third; the **National Unity Party** (NUP), formed in 2005 and led by Harry CHIUME; the **Pamodzi Freedom Party** (PFP), established in 2002 and led by Rainsford NDIWO; **Congress for Democracy** (CODE), led by Ralph KASAMBARA; the **Congress for National Unity** (CONU), led by Bishop Daniel NKHUMBWE and the **United Democratic Party** (UDP), formed in 2005 by Kenedy Solomon KALAMBO.

For information on the **National Democratic Alliance** (NDA), see the 2009 *Handbook.* For information on the **Movement for Genuine Democratic Change** (MGODE), the **Malawi Democratic Party** (MDP), the **New Congress for Democracy** (NCD), and the **New Republican Party** (NRP), see the 2010 *Handbook.* For information on the **New Rainbow Coalition** (NARC) and the **Mgwirizano** (Unity) coalition, please see the 2013 *Handbook.*

LEGISLATURE

Members of the unicameral **National Assembly** normally sit for five-year terms. From 1978 through 1992 candidates had to be approved by the MCP. The first multiparty balloting was held on May 17, 1994, for an enlarged body of 177 members. The number of legislators was increased to 193 for the balloting of July 15, 1999. In legislative balloting on May 19, 2009, the Democratic Progressive Party secured 113 seats; the Malawi Congress Party, 27; the United Democratic Front, 17; Alliance for Democracy, 1; Malawi Forum for Unity and Development, 1; the Malawi People's Party, 1; and independents, 38. One seat was not filled during the balloting.

Speaker: Henry CHIMUNTHU BANDA.

CABINET

[as of August 15, 2013]

President	Joyce Banda (PP)
Vice President	Khumbo Hastings Kachali (PP)
Second Vice President	(Vacant)
Ministers	
Agriculture and Food Security	James Munthali
Civil Service Administration, Disaster Management, Nutrition, HIV and AIDS Management, and the Greenbelt Initiative	Joyce Banda (PP)
Defense	Ken Edward Kandodo (DPP)
Disability and Elderly Affairs	Reen Kachere [f]
Economic Planning and Development	Ralph Pachalo Jooma
Education, Science, and Technology	Eunice Kazembe [f]
Energy	Ibrahim Matola
Environment and Climate Change	Halima Daudi [f]
Finance	Ken Lipenga
Foreign Affairs and International Cooperation	Ephraim Mganda Chiume
Gender, Children, and Social Welfare	Anita Kalinde (PP) [f]
Health	Catherine Gotani Hara [f]
Home Affairs and Internal Security	Uladi Mussa (PP)
Industry and Trade	Sosten Gwengwe
Information	Moses Kalonga Shawa Kunkuyu
Justice and Constitutional Affairs	Ralph Kasambara (CODE)
Labor	Eunice Makangala [f]
Lands, Housing, and Surveys	Henry Duncan Phoya (PP)
Local Government and Rural Development	Grace Zinenani Maseko [f]
Mining	John Frances Bande
National Relief and Disaster Management, National Public Events Office, Central Government Stores, and the Department of Printing Services	Khumbo Hastings Kachali (PP)
Tourism and Culture	Rachel Patience Mazombwe Zulu [f]
Transport and Public Works	Mohammed Sidik Mia
Water Development and Irrigation	Brown Mpinganjira
Youth and Sports	Enoch Chakufwa Chihana (Aford)

[f] = female

INTERGOVERNMENTAL REPRESENTATION

Ambassador to the U.S.: Steven Dick Tennyson MATENJE.

U.S. Ambassador to Malawi: Jeanine JACKSON.

Permanent Representative to the UN: Charles Peter MSOSA.

IGO Memberships (Non-UN): AfDB, AU, Comesa, CWTH, ICC, NAM, SADC, WTO.

MALAYSIA

Political Status: Independent Federation of Malaya within the Commonwealth established August 31, 1957; Malaysia established September 16, 1963, with the addition of Sarawak, Sabah, and Singapore (which withdrew in August 1965).

Area: 127,316 sq. mi. (329,749 sq. km), encompassing Peninsular Malaysia, 50,806 sq. mi. (131,588 sq. km); Sarawak, 48,050 sq. mi. (124,450 sq. km); Sabah, 28,460 sq. mi. (73,711 sq. km).

Population: 29,494,074 (2012E—UN); 29,628,392 (2013E—U.S. Census).

Major Urban Centers (2011E—UN): KUALA LUMPUR (1,644,783), Kelang (Klang, 375,566), Ipoh (505,434). The new administrative capital, Putrajaya, is 25 miles south of Kuala Lumpur.

Official Language: Bahasa Malaysia.

Monetary Unit: Malaysian ringgit (market rate November 1, 2013: 3.19 ringgit = $1US).

Paramount Ruler: Sultan ABDUL HALIM al-Muadzam Shah (Sovereign of Kedah); elected for a five-year term on October 30, 2011, by the Conference of Rulers; sworn in on December 13 and formally installed on April 11, 2012, succeeding Sultan MIZAN Zainal Abidin ibni al-Mahum Sultan Mahmud al-Muftaki Billah Shah (Sovereign of Terengganu).

Deputy Paramount Ruler: Sultan MUHAMMAD V (Sovereign of Kelatan); elected on October 30, 2011, and sworn in on December 13 for a term concurrent with that of the paramount ruler, succeeding Sultan ABDUL HALIM al-Muadzam Shah (Sovereign of Kedah).

Prime Minister: Mohamad NAJIB Abdul Razak (United Malays National Organization); appointed on April 3, 2009, and sworn in the same day to succeed ABDULLAH bin Ahmad Badawi (United Malays National Organization), who had resigned on April 2; formed new government on April 9; sworn in for second term on May 6, 2013; and formed a new government on May 15.

THE COUNTRY

Situated partly on the Malay Peninsula and partly on the island of Borneo, Malaysia consists of 11 states of the former Federation of Malaya (Peninsular or West Malaysia) plus the states of Sarawak and Sabah (East Malaysia). Thailand and Singapore are the mainland's northern and southern neighbors, respectively, while Sarawak and Sabah share a common border with the Indonesian province of Kalimantan. The multiracial population is comprised predominantly of Malays (50 percent), followed by Chinese (24 percent), non-Malay

tribals (11 percent), and Indians and Pakistanis (7 percent). Although the Malay-based Bahasa Malaysia is the official language, English, Tamil, and several Chinese dialects are widely spoken. Islam is the state religion, but the freedom to profess other faiths is constitutionally guaranteed. Minority religious groups include Buddhists (19 percent), Christians (9 percent), and Hindus (6 percent). The status of women is largely determined by ethnic group and location, urban Malay women being better educated than their rural counterparts. Overall, women comprise 36 percent of the active workforce, concentrated in services and manufacturing. Following the May 2013 balloting, women held 22 of 222 seats (10.4 percent) in the House of Representatives and 15 of 70 seats in the Senate (29.4 percent).

Malaysia continues to be the world's principal supplier of palm oil and a significant source of its other traditional exports, rubber and tin, but these and other commodity exports, including petroleum, liquefied natural gas, and timber, have been superseded in importance by manufactures—chiefly semiconductors and electrical equipment and appliances, which together account for about 50 percent of export earnings. Agriculture and fishing contribute only about 10 percent of GDP and employ 14 percent of the labor force, while industry accounts for 46 percent of GDP and 29 percent of jobs.

GDP growth in 2002–2008 averaged 5.7 percent annually, but in 2009 GDP growth contracted by 1.7 percent, owing in large part to a sharp decline in exports as a result of the global economic crisis (for more on the Malaysian economy prior to 2002, please see the 2012 *Handbook*). Restrictions on foreign participation in the economy were loosened in 2009, as were percentage requirements for Malays in most public employment. The economy rebounded in 2010 with a 10-year-high growth of 7.2 percent. Annual GDP growth moderated at 5.1 percent in 2011 and 5.6 percent in 2012. That year inflation was 1.7 percent and unemployment was 3 percent. GDP per capita was $10,304. In 2013 the World Bank ranked Malaysia 12th out of 185 countries, between Finland and Sweden, in its annual ease of conducting business report.

GOVERNMENT AND POLITICS

Political background. Malaysia came into existence as a member of the Commonwealth on September 16, 1963, through merger of the already independent Federation of Malaya with the self-governing state of Singapore and the British Crown Colonies of Sarawak and Sabah. The Malay states, organized by the British in the 19th century, had achieved sovereign status in 1957, following the suppression of a long-standing communist insurgency. Tunku ABDUL RAHMAN, head of the United Malays National Organization (UMNO) and subsequently of the Alliance Party, became Malaya's first prime minister and continued in that capacity after the formation of Malaysia. Singapore, with its predominantly Chinese population, had been ruled as a separate British colony that became internally self-governing in 1959 under the leadership of LEE Kuan Yew of the People's Action Party (PAP). Its inclusion in Malaysia was terminated in August 1965, primarily because the PAP's attempt to extend its influence beyond the confines of Singapore was viewed as a threat to Malay dominance of the federation.

In May 1969 racial riots in Kuala Lumpur led to a declaration of national emergency. A nine-member National Operations Council was given full powers to quell the disturbances. Parliamentary government was not fully restored until February 1971. Meanwhile, communist guerrillas, relatively quiescent since 1960, had begun returning from sanctuaries across the Malaysian-Thai border, and by early 1974 they were once again posing a serious threat to domestic security. In the context of a vigorous campaign against the insurgents, an August election resulted in an impressive victory for Prime Minister ABDUL RAZAK bin Hussein's newly styled National Front (*Barisan Nasional*—BN) coalition of ethnic and regional parties.

In January 1976 Abdul Razak died and was succeeded by the deputy prime minister, HUSSEIN bin Onn, who was also designated chair of the BN. Under Hussein's leadership the front retained overwhelming control of the federal House of Representatives in an early election in July 1978. In May 1981 Hussein announced that for health reasons he would not stand for reelection as UMNO president, and he was succeeded in June by the party's deputy president, MAHATHIR bin Mohamad, who formed a new government following his designation as prime minister in July.

In early elections in 1982 and 1986 the BN continued to win easy victories. In early 1987, however, a major crisis surfaced within UMNO as it prepared for a triennial leadership poll in April. Accusing Mahathir of tolerating corruption, mismanagement, and extravagant spending, Deputy Prime Minister MUSA bin Hital joined with a number of other prominent UMNO figures in supporting the candidacy of Trade and Industry Minister Tengku RAZALEIGH Hamzah for the party presidency. After an intensely fought campaign, Mahathir narrowly defeated Razaleigh, with Abdul GHAFFAR bin Baba outpacing Musa by an even closer margin for the deputy presidency. The party thereupon divided into two factions, a "Team A" headed by the prime minister and a dissident "Team B."

In February 1988 Peninsular Malaysia's High Court ruled that UMNO was an illegal entity under the country's Societies Act because members of 30 unregistered branches had participated in the April 1987 balloting. Former prime ministers Abdul Rahman and Hussein bin Onn, on behalf of the Team B dissidents, thereupon filed for recognition of a new party (UMNO-Malaysia) but were rebuffed by the Registrar of Societies on the grounds that the High Court order had not yet become effective. Mahathir, applying on February 13 (the date of deregistration), was granted permission to begin the process of legalizing a government-supportive "new" UMNO (UMNO-*Baru*). Subsequently, the government secured legislation authorizing the transfer of UMNO assets to UMNO-*Baru* and also saw enacted a series of constitutional amendments rescinding the right of the High Court to interpret acts of Parliament.

The prime minister subsequently invited Razaleigh and Musa to join UMNO-*Baru*. While both dissidents initially rejected the offer, their somewhat uneasy alliance collapsed in January 1989, when Musa rejoined the government formation. Razaleigh subsequently announced that the successor to Team B, *Semangat '46* (Spirit of '46, after the year of UMNO's founding), had formed a coalition with the opposition *Parti Islam* (Pas) that, with the addition of two smaller formations, was registered in May as the Muslim Unity Movement (*Angkatan Perpaduan Ummah*—APU). Although the APU secured only 53 of 180 seats in the federal parliamentary election of October 1990, at the state level the opposition won control in Kelantan and ousted UMNO's chief minister in Penang.

In November 1993 Finance Minister ANWAR Ibrahim emerged as Prime Minister Mahathir's most likely successor by replacing Ghaffar bin Baba as UMNO deputy president. In December Mahathir followed tradition by naming Anwar deputy prime minister.

In parliamentary elections in April 1995 the BN scored a landslide victory, capturing 162 of 192 seats. In addition, front parties won overwhelming majorities in 10 of the 11 contested state assemblies. A year later the governing alliance in Kelantan between Pas and *Semangat '46* collapsed, Razaleigh Hamzah having announced in May his intention to return to UMNO. Shortly thereafter the fundamentalist Pas, which still held a legislative majority in Kelantan, was forced by the federal government to suspend a plan to introduce a harsh Islamic criminal code similar to the one imposed by the Taliban in Afghanistan.

In the second half of 1997, differences between Mahathir and his deputy began to surface in their approaches to the regional financial crisis that was drawing Malaysia into its grasp. Mahathir, an economic nationalist, attributed the crisis to foreign-currency traders and speculators, who were abetting international institutions and foreign powers that wanted to "recolonize" the country. In contrast, Anwar, a proponent of the global marketplace, responded to the crisis by introducing a series of austerity and financial reform measures, including a relaxation of racial quota laws to allow the country's Chinese and Indian minorities greater participation in Malay-dominated companies. In September 1998 Mahathir dismissed Anwar from the cabinet, and later he removed him as deputy president of UMNO. Anwar quickly opened a campaign against Mahathir under the banner of *reformasi,* the call for political reform that had accompanied President Suharto's resignation in Indonesia earlier in the year. Mahathir then stated that he had removed Anwar because of "moral misconduct," alluding to widely circulated rumors that Anwar had engaged in both homosexual and heterosexual liaisons.

On September 20, 1998, addressing a crowd variously estimated at between 30,000 and 50,000—the country's largest opposition rally in three decades—Anwar called for Mahathir to resign. Later that day he was arrested under the Internal Security Act (ISA) (for subsequent information on the ISA, see Current issues, below). By late October 1998 Anwar faced five counts of sodomy as well as five of corruption for using his office to interfere with official investigations into his activities. In April 1999 Anwar was convicted of corruption and sentenced to six years (later reduced to four years) in prison. The verdict sparked renewed rioting by Anwar's supporters. In August 2000 the High Court in Kuala Lumpur convicted Anwar of sodomy and pronounced an additional nine-year prison sentence.

In June 1999 the principal opposition parties had announced that they would join forces. The resultant Alternative Front (*Barisan Alternatif*—BA) included Pas, the Democratic Action Party (DAP), the small Malaysian People's Party (*Parti Rakyat Malaysia*—PRM), and the new National Justice Party (*Parti Keadilan Nasional*—PKN), which had been formed in early April by Anwar's wife, Wan AZIZAH Wan Ismail, an eye surgeon and political novice.

In late November 1999 the BN won more than enough seats to maintain its two-thirds majority in the House of Representatives. Mahathir took the oath of office for his fifth term in December, after which he named Deputy Prime Minister ABDULLAH bin Ahmad Badawi as his preferred successor to head UMNO upon his eventual retirement.

On October 31, 2003, Prime Minister Mahathir handed the prime ministership over to Abdullah Badawi, who took a cautious approach to ministerial changes until confirming his support at the polls in an early election held March 21, 2004. The BN captured 198 of 219 seats in an expanded House of Representatives, while Pas saw its numbers diminish to 7.

In September 2004 with his sodomy conviction having been overturned on final appeal, Anwar Ibrahim was released from prison. Under the terms of his 1999 corruption sentence, he remained barred from holding public office until 2008. As an adviser to the People's Justice Party (*Parti Keadilan Rakyat*—PKR), of which his wife Wan Azizah was president, Anwar helped unify the opposition ahead of the 2008 general election. In voting on March 8, the opposition People's Front (later changed to People's Alliance [*Pakatan Rakyat*—PR]) claimed 82 seats in the House of Representatives, depriving the governing BN of a two-thirds majority for the first time since 1969, and won control of five state governments (although defections later returned one to the BN).

Under increasing pressure by the governing party to leave office early, Abdullah resigned as prime minister on April 2, 2009. The BN's Mohamad NAJIB Abdul Razak was designated prime minister on April 3 and six days later named a reshuffled cabinet.

The cabinet was reshuffled on June 1, 2010. Opposition leader Anwar Ibrahim was again brought to trial in 2011 on sex abuse charges stemming from an alleged incident in 2008. He adamantly proclaimed his innocence in court, declaring that the accusations were motivated by the prime minister's desire to send him into "political oblivion." Prime Minister Najib, for his part, said the trial was not politically motivated. Anwar Ibrahim was acquitted on January 9, 2012.

Sultan ABDUL HALIM al-Muadzam Shah, sovereign of Kedah and former deputy paramount ruler, was elected for a five-year term as paramount ruler on October 30, 2011, becoming the first person to hold the post twice and, at 83, the oldest person to hold the office. He was sworn in on December 13.

In legislative balloting on May 5, 2013, the BN coalition maintained its majority, and Najib was reappointed prime minister (see Current issues, below). He formed a new coalition government on May 15.

Constitution and government. The constitution of Malaysia is based on that of the former Federation of Malaya, as amended to accommodate the special interests of Sarawak and Sabah, which joined in 1963. It established a federal system of government under an elective constitutional monarchy. The administration of the 13 states (11 in the west, 2 in the east) is carried out by rulers or governors acting on the advice of State Executive Councils. Each state has its own constitution and a unicameral State Assembly that shares legislative powers with the federal Parliament. The supreme head of the federation is the paramount ruler (*Yang di-Pertuan Agong*), who exercises the powers of a constitutional monarch in a parliamentary democracy. He and the deputy paramount ruler (*Timbalan Yang di-Pertuan Agong*) are chosen for five-year terms by and from among the nine hereditary rulers of the Malay states, who, along with the heads of state of Malacca, Penang, Sabah, and Sarawak, constitute the Conference of Rulers (*Majlis Raja Raja*). In 1993, with the reluctant agreement of the rulers, constitutional amendments were enacted that curbed royal legal immunities; a further restriction in 1994 ended the paramount ruler's authority to block legislation.

Executive power is vested in a prime minister and cabinet responsible to a bicameral legislature consisting of a partially appointed Senate with few real powers and a directly elected House of Representatives. Ultimate judicial authority is vested in a Federal Court (formerly called the Supreme Court); Peninsular and East Malaysia have separate high courts. An intermediary Court of Appeal was established by constitutional amendment in 1994. The pattern of local government varies to some extent from state to state.

The federal government has authority over such matters as external affairs, defense, internal security, justice (except Islamic and native law), federal citizenship, finance, commerce, industry, communications, and transportation. Sarawak and Sabah, however, enjoy guarantees of autonomy with regard to immigration, civil service, and customs matters.

Journalists are subject to arrest under the Official Secrets Act, and Sedition Act, and the home minister is empowered "at any time by notification in writing" to alter a newspaper license. Self-censorship as well as official censorship is common. Party newspapers of the PKR and Pas were banned two weeks before legislative by-elections in March 2009, but Prime Minister Najib lifted the bans on April 3, his first day in office. In 2013 Reporters Without Borders ranked Malaysia 145th in freedom of the press out of 179 countries.

Foreign relations. From the early 1960s, Malaysia was a staunch advocate of regional cooperation among the non-Communist states of Southeast Asia, and it has been an active member of the Association of Southeast Asian Nations (ASEAN) since the organization's inception in 1967. Although threatened by leftist insurgency in the first two decades of independence, Malaysia committed itself to a nonaligned posture. At the same time, it maintained links with Western powers, Britain, Australia, and New Zealand all pledging to defend the nation's sovereignty and assisting Malaysia against Indonesia's armed "confrontation" policy of 1963–1966. Britain, Australia, New Zealand, Malaysia, and Singapore are further linked through the Five Power Defense Arrangement (for more on Malaysia's foreign affairs prior to the 1980s, please see the 2013 *Handbook*).

In February 1982 Malaysia became the first neighboring state to recognize Indonesia's archipelagic method of defining territorial seas by means of lines drawn between the outermost extensions of outlying islands. In return, Indonesia agreed to respect Malaysian maritime rights between its peninsular and Borneo territories, and in 1984 the two countries concluded a joint security agreement that strengthened a 1972 accord. In January 1994 talks between Malaysia and Indonesia ended without resolution of conflicting claims to two islands, Sipadan and Ligitan, off the east coast of Borneo, although the two sides agreed to settle the dispute in accordance with principles of international law. In December 2002 the International Court of Justice (ICJ) awarded both islands to Malaysia, but since then access to surrounding waters in the Sulawesi Sea has become a persistent irritant.

In January 1998 Jakarta received assurances that Indonesians holding valid temporary work permits in Malaysia would be exempt from a recently announced "Operation Go Away," the expulsion of tens of thousands of mainly illegal foreign workers who had been welcomed during Malaysia's economic boom. A large percentage of illegal workers were Indonesian, however, and the Mahathir government moved quickly to begin deporting them. The most violent incident occurred on March 26 at the Seminyeh repatriation camp, where rioting claimed nine lives. Subsequently, several dozen members of Indonesia's Acehnese minority, fearing reprisals related to a decades-old separatist conflict in Aceh district, sought asylum by breaking into a handful of foreign missions in Kuala Lumpur. Although Brunei, French, and Swiss officials quickly permitted Malaysian authorities to remove the Acehnese, in August some 20 who had sought refuge at the U.S. embassy and the offices of the UN High Commissioner for Refugees were granted asylum by Denmark and Norway. In 2004–2005 Malaysia's threatened expulsion of up to 1.5 million illegal immigrant workers, most of them Indonesian, again drew protests from Jakarta. In late May 2005 Malaysia, faced with an unexpected labor shortage, reversed the policy. In 2009, however, Indonesia placed a temporary ban on the hiring of Indonesians for domestic work in Malaysia. The announcement came in the wake of reported abuses by Malaysian employers.

Relations with Singapore, which were cool following Singapore's withdrawal from the Federation of Malaya in August 1965, improved in subsequent years. In April 1998 the two states agreed to submit to the ICJ competing claims to the islet of Pulau Batu Putih (Pedra Branca) off the coast of Johor. In September 2001 Malaysia and Singapore agreed to settle differences over such matters as water supplies to Singapore and the use of Malaysian airspace by Singapore's aircraft. Little additional progress was achieved through 2003, however, because Singapore sought to resolve open issues as a package. In December 2004 the two countries launched new talks, which also focused on releasing Malaysian workers' pension funds held by Singapore and on building a bridge to replace the outdated causeway that connects Singapore to the mainland. In April 2006, however, Malaysia scrapped plans for the bridge, construction of which Singapore continued to link to restoration of full airspace rights as well as to a 20-year commitment from Malaysia for 1 billion cubic meters of sand for reclamation. On May 23, 2008, the ICJ found that sovereignty over Pulau Batu Putih had passed to Singapore.

Relations with China have been particularly strong in recent years, despite competing claims to the Spratly Islands. Both sides have endorsed a code of conduct for all claimants. Regionally, Malaysia under Mahathir advanced the idea of a broad East Asian Economic Community, to include the ASEAN countries plus China, Japan, and South Korea, and in 2005 hosted the first East Asian summit.

Following Prime Minister Najib's appointment in 2009, relations with the United States warmed, and in May U.S. secretary of state Hillary Clinton declared that relations between the two countries were excellent, with cooperation in security matters as well as trade and investment. Najib's April 2010 visit to the United States included discussions with President Barack Obama.

In July 2011 the Malaysian government and the Vatican agreed to establish diplomatic ties following a meeting between Pope Benedict XVI and the prime minister. Talks leading to the diplomatic agreement had been going on for years, as the Malaysian government aimed to reassure Christians, who have long complained of discrimination or marginalization.

In February 2012 Malaysia deported Saudi journalist Hamza KASHGARI to his home country to face charges of blasphemy. Kashgari fled to Malaysia after posting remarks on social media that were deemed insulting to the prophet Muhammad. The deportation led to both domestic and international protests. Also in February, Malaysian police arrested an Iranian wanted in Thailand for participation in a failed terrorist attack on the Israeli embassy in Bangkok. In May a court in the United Kingdom opened an inquiry into a 1948 massacre in which 24 ethnic Chinese Malaysians were shot by British troops. However in September a British appeals court issued an injunction stopping the inquiry. The incident had long been a source of tension between the two countries. In December Malaysia announced it would recruit up to 100,000 Bangladeshis to work on plantations. Malaysia had previously stopped using Bangladeshi labor in 2009.

In January 2013 Malaysia and South Korea signed an extradition treaty. Also in January the Malaysian-Australian free trade agreement came into effect. In February a group of some 200 Filipino militia fighters, calling itself the Royal Army of the Sulu Sultanate, landed in Sabah. Fighting between the group and Malaysian security forces left 68 dead (see entry on the Philippines). More than 4,000 ethnic Filipinos left the region and returned to the Philippines during the strife.

Current issues. In 2009 Prime Minister Najib began to modify Malaysia's racially based Bumiputra Policy, which was conceived in the 1970s to help reduce ethnic tensions. Non-Malays increasingly opposed the policy, which gave preferential treatment to Malays in many areas, including education, housing, and employment. The policy also required a 30 percent Bumiputra stake in foreign-owned companies. Prime Minister Najib abolished the latter.

Reform efforts continued in 2010, when subsidies were cut for sugar, fuel, and natural gas as part of his New Economic Model. However, the administration did not loosen other strict laws. Police cracked down on a cartoonist whose latest book allegedly poked fun at the prime minister and his wife; a blogger was sued for making fun of the national electricity corporation; and the license renewals of several opposition newspapers were rejected. Meanwhile, religious tensions also heightened following the firebombing of three churches amid controversy over the use of the word *Allah*. Muslims contend that the use of "Allah" is exclusive to Islam and were angered after a court rejected a ban on the use of "Allah" in non-Muslim literature. The prime minister condemned the attacks; meanwhile, the government appealed the verdict.

Further government crackdowns came in 2011, most notably during a July 9 rally by some 10,000 demonstrators calling for electoral reform, specifically longer campaign periods and an end to vote buying ahead of upcoming elections. The rally in Kuala Lumpur was broken up by the police, who used tear gas on the demonstrators, 500 of whom were arrested, including Ibrahim. Some 31 activists, including members of the Socialist Party of Malaysia (*Parti Sosialis Malaysia*—PSM), had been arrested ahead of the rally, allegedly for promoting a communist ideology and thus "waging war against the king." In the wake of the protest, the prime minister announced the formation of a new parliamentary committee, comprising government and opposition representatives, to review ways to make the electoral process more democratic. In September Prime Minister Najib called for what was described as the biggest overhaul to national security measures in decades, including plans to abolish the law that allows detention of suspects without a trial. Late in the year the prime minister rejected the proposal to hold a general election in 2011. The next polls are due in 2013.

In April 2012 the ISA was replaced by a new security law. The new measure ended the power of the police to hold suspects indefinitely, but security forces were still allowed to detain individuals for up to 28 days without charging them. In December the high court ruled that 2,036 hectares of land that the government had reserved for ethnic Malays belonged to the indigenous Orang Asli community. The decision was reported as a major victory for indigenous peoples.

The BN won 133 seats in the May 5, 2013, legislative balloting, securing a reduced majority in the House. The opposition PR launched street protests, declaring the balloting to be fraudulent. The PR also launched a campaign to challenge the results in 25 constituencies. By August the PR had lost a succession of those challenges and been fined $45,788 for each losing challenge.

POLITICAL PARTIES

Malaysia's political system has long been dominated by the National Front (BN) coalition. Numerous opposition coalitions have formed, but until 2008, none had ever posed a meaningful threat to the UMNO-led alliance.

In September 1998, following the ouster and arrest of Anwar Ibrahim, two loose opposition coalitions emerged: the Coalition for a People's Democracy (*Gagasan Demokrasi Rakyat*), chaired by TIAN Chua, and the People's Justice Movement (*Gerakan Keadilan Rakyat—Gerak*), chaired by Fadzil NOR of Pas. The two shared overlapping memberships that encompassed various social and reform organizations as well as several political parties. Out of this organizing came the Alternative Front (*Barisan Alternatif*—BA), an ideologically incongruous grouping that won 42 seats in the November 1999 election. With the Democratic Action Party (DAP) having withdrawn from the BA in 2001, the coalition won only 7 seats in the March 2004 general election. The People's Alliance (*Pakatan Rakyat*—PR) emerged as the successor to the BA prior to the 2008 balloting.

Government Coalition:

National Front (*Barisan Nasional*—BN). Malaysia's leading formation since its launching in 1973, the BN is a coalition of parties representing the country's leading ethnic groups. The nucleus of an earlier coalition, organized in 1952 as the Alliance Party, was Tunku Abdul Rahman's United Malays National Organization (UMNO). With the establishment of Malaysia, the alliance was augmented by similar coalitions in Sarawak and Sabah. By September 1996 the BN controlled 12 of the country's 13 state assemblies, the sole exception being Kelantan's.

Although the number of member parties has varied somewhat over the years, the BN long held a two-thirds legislative majority until 2008, when a strong showing by the opposition brought it to within 30 seats of controlling the House of Representatives. At the same time, the BN lost control of several state governments, although a subsequent realignment in the Perak legislature enabled the BN to replace the PR government. As of 2013 the BN controlled 10 of 13 states. In the May 2013 balloting, the BN secured 133 seats, with 40.4 percent of the vote. It also won 330 of 576 state assembly seats.

Leaders: Mohamad NAJIB Abdul Razak (Prime Minister), Tengku Adnan MANSOR (Secretary General).

United Malays National Organization—UMNO (*Pertubuhan Kebangsaan Melayu Bersatu*). The leading component of the BN, UMNO has long supported the interests of the numerically predominant Malays while acknowledging the right of all Malaysians, irrespective of racial origins, to participate in the political, social, and economic life of the nation. Party officials are selected by indirect election every three years.

In April 1987 Prime Minister Mahathir bin Mohamad retained the presidency by a paper-thin margin after an unprecedented internal contest. The intraparty struggle culminated in deregistration of the original party in February 1988, in the wake of which the pro-Mahathir faction organized the "new" UMNO (UMNO-*Baru*). The dissidents, led by Tengku Razaleigh Hamzah, were denied an opportunity to regroup as UMNO-Malaysia. In 1989 Mahathir launched a partially successful campaign to woo back the dissidents. The party dropped "*Baru*" and restored its original name in 1997.

In the November 1999 federal election UMNO won 71 seats, 17 fewer than in 1995, which analysts attributed to a loss of support among Malay backers of Anwar Ibrahim, who had been ousted as deputy president in September 1998. In December, having already announced that he was serving his final term as prime minister, Mahathir named Deputy Prime Minister Abdullah Badawi as his successor.

In May 2001 the People's Justice Movement (*Angkatan Keadilan Rakyat*—Akar) overwhelmingly voted to disband and join UMNO. Akar, formed in 1989 by former members of the Sabah United Party (PBS), had participated in the BN since 1991.

With Mahathir having stepped down from party and government posts in October 2003, Abdullah Badawi led UMNO to victory at the polls in March 2004, when the party won 110 lower house seats. Mahathir subsequently denounced the policies of his successor and briefly quit the party in the wake of the BN's setbacks in the 2008 balloting, hoping to create pressure on Abdullah to resign. Abdullah responded in July by announcing that Deputy Prime Minister Najib Razak would succeed him in June 2010. However, facing increasing pressure from party members, Abdullah resigned in 2009. At the party's congress in March, Najib was unanimously elected party president, and a week later, he was sworn in as Malaysia's sixth prime minister. Najib pledged to reform the party, which was widely acknowledged to be in danger of losing its dominance.

In August 2010 the UMNO Supreme Council accepted the **Malaysian Indian Muslim Congress** (*Parti Kongres Indian Muslim Malaysia*—Kimma), led by Syed Ibrahim KADER, as an affiliate, thereby granting Kimma privileges that include observer status at the UMNO annual assembly and access to alliances with other BN parties. Kimma, founded in 1977 as a means of uniting Malaysia's Indian Muslims, had repeatedly sought BN membership.

In July 2011 Tengku Razaleigh Hamzah formed the nonpartisan Movement for Independence Trust (*Amanah*) and invited members of the UMNO and the opposition to join, in what observers described as an attempt to position himself as a third force ahead of national elections. In August 2012 the party reportedly launched an effort to reintegrate some splinter parties and groups that had been formed by former UMNO members. The UMNO increased its seats in the House in the 2013 balloting, from 79 to 88, and Najib was reappointed prime minister of a MUNO-dominated coalition cabinet.

Leaders: Mohamad NAJIB Abdul Razak (Prime Minister and President of the Party), MUHYIDDIN Mohamed Yasin (Deputy Prime Minister and Deputy President of the Party), Ahmad ZAHID Hamidi, HISHAMMUDDIN Hussein (Vice President), Mohammad SHAFIE Apdal (Vice President), Tengku Adnan MANSOR (Secretary General).

Malaysian Chinese Association—MCA (*Persatuan China Malaysia*). The MCA supports the interests of the Chinese community but is committed to "moderation" and the maintenance of interracial goodwill and harmony. More conservative than the Chinese opposition DAP, it has participated in the governing alliance continuously since 1982.

For over a decade the MCA's representation in the lower house of Parliament had been stable at around 30 seats, but it dropped to 15 after the March 2008 election. Taking responsibility for the poor showing, party president ONG Ka Ting declined to seek reelection. At the party congress in October, Transport Minister Ong Tee Keat (no relation) won the party presidency, and NG Yen Yen, the minister of tourism, became the first female vice president of a major BN party. Ong announced a plan to revive grassroots participation in the party and assess the performance of party leaders, but his leadership soon came under attack, culminating in a three-way contest for the presidency in March 2010. Ong Tee Keat and former president Ong Ka Ting were defeated by Deputy President Chua Soi Lek, and in June Ong Tee Keat was dropped from the cabinet.

The party only won seven House seats in the 2013 legislative balloting and received no posts in the subsequent coalition government.

Leaders: CHUA Soik Lek (President), LIOW Tiong Lai (Deputy President), KONG Cho Ha (Secretary General).

United Traditional Bumiputra Party (*Parti Pesaka Bumiputra Bersatu*—PBB). Founded in 1983, the PBB traces its origins to the Sarawak Alliance of *Bumiputra,* a mixed ethnic party; *Pesaka,* a Dayak and Malay party; and the Sarawak Chinese Association. The PBB won a plurality of 19 seats in the 1983 Sarawak state assembly election and subsequently formed a coalition government with the Sarawak Native People's Party (PBDS; see the PRS, below) and the SUPP (below). This coalition, dominated by the PBB, has controlled Sarawak's government ever since, with PBB president Abdul Taib Mahmud serving continuously as the state's chief minister.

In 2004 the party won 11 seats in the House of Representatives, and in 2008 it added 3 more. In May 2006 the party won all 35 seats it contested in the state assembly elections. The PBB won state balloting in 2012, and Taib was reelected chief minister. In the 2013 House balloting, the PBB won 14 seats and 35 of 71 seats in the Sarawak state assembly.

Leaders: Abdul TAIB Mahmud (Chief Minister of Sarawak and President of the Party), ABANG Johari Tun Abang Openg (Deputy President), Alfred JABU Anak Numpang (Deputy President), AWANG Tengah Ali Hasan, Douglas UGGAH Embas.

Sarawak People's Party (*Party Rakyat Sarawak*—PRS). Registered in October 2005, the PRS traces its origin to a leadership dispute that split the now-defunct Sarawak Native People's Party (*Parti Bansa Dayak Sarawak*—PBDS), which had been organized in 1983 by a number of legislators from the Sarawak National Party (SNAP, below) who wished to affiliate with a purely ethnic Dayak party. The new formation was accepted as a National Front partner in 1984. In the 1999 and 2004 national elections it won six seats, but it was deregistered in October 2004 because of a protracted leadership dispute precipitated by the retirement of longtime party leader and cabinet member Leo MOGGIE anak Irok.

The new PRS was already being organized under SIDI Munan when the PBDS was deregistered. As expected, the PBDS faction loyal to James Masing joined the new party, with Masing being named president shortly thereafter. In June 2005 the PRS was accepted into the BN.

In January 2006 the PRS and another National Front party, the SPDP (below), announced their intention to merge, but discussions were ultimately postponed, first because of the May 2006 state election, in which the PRS won eight of the nine seats it contested, and then because of a leadership dispute within the PRS. Masing was reelected president at a conference in December 2006, while Larry

SNG Wei Shien claimed leadership of a faction loyal to former deputy president SNG Chee Hua, his father. Masing expelled Sng from the party in April 2008, a month after the PRS won six lower house seats. The split appeared to have driven many former PRS members into the ranks of the opposition PKR.

The PRS won six House seats in the 2013 national elections and received one post in the subsequent coalition government.

Leader: James Jemut MASING (President).

Sarawak United People's Party—SUPP (*Parti Bersatu Rakyat Sarawak*). The SUPP was organized in 1959 as a left-wing Sarawak party. Although the SUPP began as a Chinese ethnic party, it has since become one of Malaysia's most ethnically diverse parties. In November 1999 it won eight seats in the House of Representatives. That number dropped to six in the 2004 and 2008 national elections.

At the state level, in May 2006 it won 11 legislative seats, unexpectedly losing 8 of those it contested as part of the National Front. In 2011 Peter CHIN Fah Kui was elected PRS leader. In 2013 the SUPP won one House seat and six seats in the Sarawak state assembly. It received one post in the UMNO-led coalition government.

Leader: Peter CHIN Fah Kui (President).

Sarawak Progressive Democratic Party—SPDP (*Parti Demokratik Maju Sarawak*). The SPDP was established in November 2002 following a leadership crisis in the Sarawak National Party (SNAP, below) that led to SNAP's deregistration. Several months before, William MAWAN had been elected president of SNAP, but a competing SNAP faction had refused to accept the decision. Within days of SNAP's deregistration, Mawan announced formation of the multiracial SPDP, which was soon accepted into the BN as SNAP's replacement.

In the 2004 and 2008 general elections the SPDP won four seats. In June 2008 the SPDP and PRS agreed to merge, but grassroots opposition to the plan, and Anwar Ibrahim's challenge to the sitting government, slowed the process. In 2009 the party was trying to form new branches outside Sarawak, in West Malaysia, although internal disputes continued to cause difficulties. The SPDP won six seats in the 2011 Sarawak elections. In the 2013 national elections, the SPDP won four House seats.

Leaders: William MAWAN Ikom (President), Nelson BALANG (Secretary General).

United Pasok Momogun Kadazandusun Murut Organization—UPKO (*Pertubuhan Pasok Momogan Kadazandusun Murut Bersatu*). Reviving the name of a Sabah party from the 1960s, a congress of the Sabah Democratic Party (*Parti Demokratik Sabah*—PDS) voted in 1999 to adopt the UPKO designation. The PDS had been organized in 1994 by withdrawal from the PBS of a group of dissidents led by Deputy President Bernard DOMPOK. The original UPKO had been established by the 1964 merger of the *Pasok Momogun* party and the United National Kadazan Organization (UNKO), but the party dissolved in 1967.

Intended to unite the majority Kadazandusun community and the Murut population of Sabah, the current UPKO subsequently indicated its willingness to discuss mergers not only with other Sabah-based BN parties but also with the PBS. UPKO won four lower house seats at the 2004 and 2008 general elections. The party has been active on immigration and citizenship issues. In 2009 party leader Dompok was appointed minister of agricultural development and commodities. In balloting for the House in 2013, the UPKO secured three seats, and Ewon EBIN was appointed minister of science, technology, and innovation.

Leaders: Bernard DOMPOK (President), Wilfred BUMBURING (Deputy President).

Malaysian Indian Congress—MIC (*Kongresi India Malaysia*). The leading representative of the Indian community in Malaysia, the MIC was founded in 1946 and joined the alliance in 1955. S. Samy VELLU first won the party presidency in 1979. In March 2009 he was reelected to an 11th term, but in September 2010 he announced his retirement and identified his preferred successor as Deputy President G. PALANIVEL.

The MIC won seven House seats in the 1995, 1999, and March 2004 elections, but its parliamentary representation dropped to three in the 2008 vote. The Hindu Rights Action Force (Hindraf; see below), a nongovernment group banned by the home ministry in 2008, has posed a challenge to the MIC's leadership among Malaysia's Indian population. Vellu resigned in January 2011. The MIC secured four seats in the 2013 House elections, and Palanivel was appointed minister of natural resources and environment.

Leaders: G. PALANIVEL (President), S. K. DEVAMANY, M. SARAVANAN (Vice President), S. SUBRAMANIAM (Vice President), T. RAJAGOPALU (Secretary-General).

Sabah United Party (*Parti Bersatu Sabah*—PBS). A predominantly Kadazan party with a Roman Catholic leader, the PBS was founded by defectors from the now-moribund Sabah People's Union (*Bersatu Rakyat Jelata Sabah*—Berjaya) in 1985. Appealing to urban, middle-class voters disaffected with the Berjaya-led government, it won a majority of state assembly seats in April. Having been admitted to the BN in 1986, in 1988 the PBS announced a "loose alliance" with fellow BN member *Gerakan.*

The PBS retained control of the Sabah assembly in a state general election in July 1990, but less than a week before the federal legislative poll of October 1990 it withdrew from the BN and went into opposition. In what some viewed as an act of political retaliation, the party president, Joseph PAIRIN Kitingan, was arrested by federal authorities in early 1991. His conviction on corruption charges resulted in a fine of approximately $4,600.

In 1993 the PBS attracted almost half of the state assembly contingent of the United Sabah National Organization (USNO), immediately prior to that party's long-envisaged merger with UMNO. In an early state election in 1994 the PBS obtained a plurality of seats but because of subsequent defections was obliged to yield to a BN administration. It won only 17 of 48 seats in the 1999 state election and then lost 2 to defections.

The PBS was readmitted to the BN in January 2002, and in the March 2004 election won 4 seats in the federal House of Representatives and 13 in the Sabah legislature. It currently has 4 federal MPs but no posts in the coalition government.

Leaders: Joseph PAIRIN Kitingan (President), Henrynus AMIN (Secretary General).

Malaysian People's Movement Party (*Parti Gerakan Rakyat Malaysia*). Based in Pulau Pinang (Penang), *Gerakan* is a social democratic party that has attracted many intellectual supporters, especially in the Chinese community. It was organized in 1968 by TAN Chee Khoon, who left the party after the 1969 election to form the now-defunct Social Justice Party (*Parti Keadilan Masyaraka*—Pekemas). The party was weakened by a leadership dispute in 1988 that saw numerous members defect to the MCA and two of its vice presidents resign.

In April 2007 Lim Keng Yaik retired after 26 years of party leadership. Former Penang chief minister KOH Tsu Koon, initially the acting president, was elected president at the party's 2008 congress. Koh called for the party to reinvent itself after its poor showing in the 2008 election, when its lower house membership fell from 10 seats to 2. That year the party also lost control of the state government in Penang, which it had led for nearly four decades.

With the party's power diminishing, several prominent members quit, and some members advocated pulling out of the BN coalition. In the 2013 national elections, the party won one seat in the House.

Leaders: KOH Tsu Koon (President), CHANG Ko Youn (Deputy President), TENG Chang Yeow (Secretary General).

United Sabah People's Party (*Parti Bersatu Rakyat Sabah*—PBRS). The PBRS was launched in 1994 by Joseph KURUP, theretofore secretary general of the PBS. In the 1999 national election Kurup came within a few hundred votes of unseating PBS President Joseph Pairin Kitingan. In 2002 a leadership dispute ended with a decision by the Registrar of Societies that Kurup was the legitimate president. His challenger, Jeffrey Kitingan, was then expelled by the party. (He joined the PKR in October 2006.)

In the 2008 election, Kurup won the party's only seat in parliament, running unopposed after an officer rejected the nomination papers of PKR candidate Danny Anthony ANDIPAI. Subsequently, Malaysia's Election Court declared the vote void, but on March 13, 2009, a federal court upheld Kurup's election. In 2013 the PBRS won one House seat.

Leaders: Joseph KURUP (President), Ellron ANGIN (Deputy President).

Liberal Democratic Party—LDP (*Parti Liberal Demokratik*). A Chinese-dominated party based in Sabah, the LDP formed in 1989 and joined the BN in 1991. In 1999, under the leadership of its first president, CHONG Kah Kiat, it captured one seat in the House of Representatives; it lost the seat in 2004, but V. K. LIEW won it back in 2008. Liew was appointed a deputy minister in April 2009. The LDP secured only 0.1 percent of the vote in the 2013 national elections and no seats in the House.

Leader: Vui Keong LIEW (President).

People's Progressive Party of Malaysia—PPP (*Parti Kemajuan Rakyat Malaysia*). Centered in Ipoh, where there is a heavy concentration of Chinese, the multiracial, left-wing PPP was organized in 1955. In 1996 the Registrar of Societies approved a new constitution for the party, which thereupon adopted the name *Parti Progressif Penduduk Malaysia (Baru),* or PPP (New). However, a four-year-old dispute over the party leadership continued. In September 1999 the High Court annulled the presidency of M. KAYVEAS, who had been elected in 1993, and threw out the 1996 constitutional changes, at which time the party reverted to its original name. Kayveas quickly obtained a stay from the Court of Appeal, which confirmed him as president in November. Kayveas was reelected president in September 2005.

The PPP won one seat in parliament in the 2004 general election but none in 2008. In May 2009 the party expelled a member of its supreme council for corruption. The party failed to secure any seats in the 2013 balloting.

Leader: M. KAYVEAS (President).

Parliamentary Opposition:

People's Alliance (*Pakatan Rakyat*—PR). The Democratic Action Party (DAP), Pan-Malaysian Islamic Party (Pas), and People's Justice Party (PKR), along with the Malaysian People's Party (PRM; see below under PKR), organized the Alternative Front (*Barisan Alternatif*—BA) in 1999. The BA put forth Anwar Ibrahim as a candidate for prime minister in that year's election, although the former Mahathir deputy was incarcerated after his corruption conviction. The DAP withdrew from the BA in September 2001 because of opposition to Pas's Islamic agenda, and in the 2004 national election the BA won only seven seats.

On April 1, 2008, following their successful cooperation in the March elections, the leaders of the DAP, Pas, and PKR announced that they would solidify their relationship under the PR banner. By agreeing not to compete with each other, the three won control of 5 of Malaysia's 13 state assemblies (in Kedah, Kelantan, Penang, Perak, and Selangor) and had ended the BN's two-thirds majority in the House of Representatives. Despite their ideological differences, the three parties agree on the nation's need for transparent and egalitarian governance.

ANWAR Ibrahim reentered Parliament on August 28, 2008, and took over leadership of the PKR and the PR from his wife, Dr. Wan Azizah Wan Ismail. At first, Anwar set out to engineer enough defections from the BN to allow the PR to capture the government. That plan failed, but the coalition demonstrated increasing strength in 2009 by winning two of three by-elections on April 7.

In February 2010 the Federal Court brought an end to a year-long constitutional crisis in Perak, ruling that defections by MPs from the PR had legitimately permitted the BN to take over the state government. Two months later, the Sarawak National Party (SNAP) joined the PR.

In the 2013 national elections, the PR won a majority of the vote, 50.9 percent, but only 89 seats. The coalition also won 244 of 576 state assemblies. The PR subsequently unsuccessfully challenged a number of the election results.

Leaders: ANWAR Ibrahim, LIM Kit Siang, Abdul HADI Awang.

Democratic Action Party—DAP (*Parti Tindakan Demokratik*). A predominantly Chinese, democratic socialist party, the DAP is a 1965 offshoot of the ruling People's Action Party (PAP) of Singapore.

In 1987 a number of DAP politicians, including parliamentary opposition leader LIM Kit Siang, were arrested and held without trial for "provoking racial tensions." In 1989 Lim was released from jail and the party agreed to cooperate with the APU in upcoming elections, although refusing to join the coalition because of its Muslim orientation. The DAP went on to win 20 seats in the House of Representatives in 1990 but saw its representation plummet to 9 in 1995.

In August 1998 LIM Guan Eng, deputy secretary general of the party and son of Lim Kit Siang, was sentenced to prison on charges of sedition relating to a political pamphlet he had written. An effort by the elder Lim to mount support for his son led critics to charge the secretary general with nepotism and dictatorial actions. Lim responded by suspending the party's vice chair, treasurer, and publicity secretary, all of whom subsequently helped found the MDP (below).

Lim Guan Eng was released from prison in August 1999. Three months later, as part of the Alternative Front, the DAP won only 10 seats in the national election, although it remained the leading legislative opponent of various BN parties in a majority of states. The elder Lim resigned as party secretary general—a post he had held for three decades—but he was immediately named party chair.

In September 2001 objecting to Pas's call for establishing an Islamic state, the DAP withdrew from the BA. In the March 2004 election, the DAP kept its distance from Pas and went on to win 12 seats, thereby becoming the leading opposition party once again. At a party congress in September Lim Kit Siang stepped down as chair. Lim Guan Eng was elected secretary general.

The DAP returned to cooperating with Pas and the PKR in the 2008 voting, winning 28 lower house seats. In September, Lim Kit Siang called on Prime Minister Abdullah to convene a special session of Parliament to vote on a no-confidence measure. A DAP parliamentarian, Teresa KOK, along with a journalist and a popular blogger, were arrested on September 12 under the ISA. The party called the arrests politically motivated and demanded the abolition of the ISA. In March 2009 DAP national chair Karpal SINGH was charged with sedition; he in turn accused the government of using the sedition laws selectively against political opponents. In 2010 the charges were dismissed, but the dismissal was reversed in 2012.

In the 2013 national elections, the DAP secured 38 seats in the House.

Leaders: Karpal SINGH (Chair), LIM Kit Siang, TAN Seng Giaw (Deputy Chair), LIM Guan Eng (Secretary General).

Pan-Malaysian Islamic Party (*Parti Islam SeMalaysia*—Pas). An Islamic party with a strong rural base, Pas participated in the governing coalition in 1973–1977 but since then has been in opposition. Pas has governed Kelantan State continuously since 1990. It increased its federal legislative representation from 7 to 27 seats in 1999, rising to lead the opposition and also capturing Terengganu State.

Pas membership is open only to Muslims, and the party prohibits women candidates at the state and federal levels. Officially, the party seeks the establishment of an Islamic state, but its leaders have stated that should it win control of the federal government and introduce Islamic law, non-Muslims could be tried in accordance with the country's current secular legal system. In Kelantan, non-Muslims are exempt from some of the strictest aspects of sharia (Islamic) law.

In June 2002 the party's president, the moderate Fadzil Mohamad NOR, died. His immediate successor, Abdul Hadi Awang, a more radical Islamist and longtime supporter of Afghanistan's ousted Taliban regime, announced in July that Islamic law would be strictly enforced in Terengganu State, where he served as chief minister until Pas was ousted in the March 2004 state election. Nationally, it saw its lower house representation plummet to six seats. A loss in a state by-election in December 2005 reduced the party's majority in the Kelantan assembly to a single seat.

Party elections held in June 2005 were notable for the success of more moderate politicians. Although Abdul HADI Awang had no challengers, the new deputy president and all three vice presidents were regarded as reformers. The party election of June 2007 reconfirmed the ascendancy of the "young Turks," led by Deputy President Nasaruddin Mat Isa, although the presidency was again uncontested.

In 2008 Pas won control of the state of Kedah, expanded its majority in Kelantan, and joined coalition governments in two other states with its People's Alliance partners. In an effort to broaden the party's base, Pas toned down its rhetoric about imposing Islamic law and pledged to uphold social equality and freedom of religion. Its relative success at attracting Chinese and Indian support with a more moderate image reflected the shifts in the country's racial and political dynamics.

Hadi Awang was reelected to his post, again uncontested, in May 2009. Internal debates reflected a division between party moderates committed to the PR and conservatives open to cooperation with UMNO. The party won 21 House seats in the 2013 balloting.

Leaders: Abdul HADI Awang (President), NIK ABDUL AZIZ Nik Mat (Spiritual Leader of Pas), NASARUDDIN Mat Isa (Deputy President), Mustafa ALI (Secretary General).

People's Justice Party (*Parti Keadilan Rakyat*—PKR). The PKR resulted from the August 2003 merger of the National Justice Party (*Parti Keadilan Nasional*—PKN) and the Malaysian People's Party (*Parti Rakyat Malaysia*—PRM).

Announced in April 1999 by Wan Azizah Wan Ismail as a centrist, multiracial formation, the PKN was organized by supporters of Anwar Ibrahim in an effort to unite anti-Mahathir forces. The party was largely an outgrowth of the nonparty Movement for Social Justice (*Pergerakan Keadilan Sosial*—Adil), which had been announced by Wan Azizah the previous December as a vehicle for reform. Anwar indicated from prison that he would not officially join the party. As part of the BA, *Keadilan* won five lower house seats in November 1999. It unexpectedly picked up a sixth, at the BN's expense, in a November 2000 by-election.

Formerly the Malaysian People's Socialist Party (*Parti Sosialis Rakyat Malaysia*—PSRM), the PRM was a left-leaning party that never held legislative seats. Its former leader, KASSIM Ahmad, was arrested in 1976 on suspicion of having engaged in communist activities and was not released until 1981. Another leader, Syed Husin Ali, was similarly detained without trial under the country's Internal Security Act from 1974 until 1980. In 1989 the party changed its name back to its pre-1970 title as part of an effort to assume a more moderate position.

In July 2002 the PRM and *Keadilan* signed a memorandum of understanding to merge as the PKR, which was accomplished in August 2003. At the party's fourth congress, held in May 2007, Wan AZIZAH was reelected president. Anwar Ibrahim, concerned that his election might result in the party's deregistration, decided not to run.

Meanwhile, the PKR's representation ballooned to 31 in the March 2008 election, making it the second strongest party in the House of Representatives. Wan Azizah resigned her seat on July 31 to allow her husband to run in a by-election, which he won handily on August 28, 2008. He subsequently took over leadership of the PKR and the PR from his wife.

In May 2009, in what the party termed "an unprecedented move for a political party in Malaysia," the PKR announced the adoption of direct "one-member, one-vote" election of all party officials. Wan Azizah became surrogate party leader while her husband faced trial on sexual abuse charges (see Current issues, above). In 2013 the PKR secured 30 seats in the House elections.

Leaders: Wan AZIZAH Wan Ismail, ANWAR Ibrahim, SYED HUSIN Ali, TIAN Chua, Saifuddin NASUTION Ismail (Secretary General).

Socialist Party of Malaysia (*Parti Sosialis Malaysia*—PSM). The leftist PSM was formed in 1998 but was denied registration by the government, which viewed it as a threat to national security, until after the 2008 election. At that time the PSM claimed a seat in the lower house, its representative having been elected as a PKR candidate. At the party's congress in June 2010, the PSM decided that it would not join the PR but would commit itself to "close cooperation," including campaigning with or participating in an electoral pact with the opposition alliance for the next election. The party failed to secure any seats in the 2013 balloting.

Leaders: NASIR Hashim (Chair), S. ARUTCHELVAN (Secretary General).

Other Parties:

Sabah Progressive Party—SAPP (*Parti Maju Sabah*). Formally registered in 1994, the SAPP is a Chinese formation that was admitted to the BN after splitting from the PBS. It won two seats in the 1999 balloting. In September 2002 one of the seats was vacated when the Election Commission found the party's president guilty of corrupt electoral practices. In March 2008 the SAPP won two seats in the House of Representatives.

Party president YONG Teck Lee threatened in June 2008 to file a no-confidence motion against Prime Minister Abdullah Ahmad Badawi. The motion did not go forward, but on September 17, SAPP withdrew from the BN to become an independent party. Deputy president Raymond TAN, who was also deputy chief minister of Sabah, subsequently quit the party and later joined *Gerakan.* The party failed to win any seats in the 2013 federal parliament balloting.

Leaders: YONG Teck Lee (President), LIEW Teck Chan, Eric Enchin MAJIMBUN (Deputy Presidents), Richard YONG We Kong (Secretary General).

Indian Progressive Front—IPF (*Barisan Kemajuan India SeMalaysia*). The IPF was launched in 1990 by M.G. PANDITHAN, who had been an MIC vice president until ousted by Samy Vellu. The IPF supported the BN for the 1999 and 2004 elections. Although the MIC opposed the party's inclusion in the front, Vellu and Pandithan reconciled in April 2007.

Pandithan died in May 2008, and his wife, Jayashree PANDITHAN, took over as party leader. However, after the Registrar of Societies nullified her election in February 2009, the IPF was riven by factions. Prime Minister Abdullah Badawi attempted to heal the divide, dangling a potential offer to join the BN if the party reconciled. In June 2010 M. SAMBATHAN was elected president. The party did not win any seats in the 2013 House elections.

Leaders: M. SAMBATHAN (President), M. GEORGE (Deputy President), K. VELAYUTHAN (Secretary General).

Malaysia Makkal Sakthi Party (MMSP). Established in 2009 under the leadership of R.S. Thanenthiran, formerly the national coordinator of the Hindu Rights Action Force (Hindraf), the MMSP represents a division within the Hindraf movement. The Registrar of Societies approved the new party on May 11, less than two months after it had applied. Thanenthiran said the new party would remain independent of the BN and the PR for the time being but would be willing to join whichever coalition could satisfy the aspirations of Malaysia's Indian community.

In late 2009 the MMSP became embroiled in a leadership dispute that saw competing factions loyal to Thanenthiran and Deputy President A. VATHEMURTHY both claiming control. In September 2010 the dissident group convened what it called an emergency general meeting that named the party's initial secretary general, Kannan RAMASAMY, as president. In October the Thanenthiran forces, with support from the BN, held an annual general meeting at which it continued to claim legitimacy. The party now reportedly supports the BN.

Leaders: R. S. THANENTHIRAN (President), U. THAMOTHARAN (Deputy President).

Sarawak National Party—SNAP (*Parti Kebangsaan Sarawak*). Long a leading Sarawak party, SNAP ran in the 1974 federal election as an opposition party, capturing nine seats in the lower house. Supported largely by the Iban population of Sarawak, it joined the BN at both the state and federal levels in 1976.

On November 5, 2002, SNAP was formally deregistered because of a leadership dispute in which the party's deputy president, Peter TINGGOM Karmarau, had challenged its longtime president, James WONG Kim Ming. In August an extraordinary party meeting had elected William Mawan Ikom as successor to Wong, who refused to accept what he termed a "coup d'état." Within days of the deregistration, which Wong planned to challenge, Mawan announced formation of the Sarawak Progressive Democratic Party (SPDP).

The deregistration was suspended by the Court of Appeal in April 2003, permitting SNAP to compete in the March 2004 national election. SNAP won only one state seat in 2006, and in 2008 it contested six lower house seats. In April 2010, as part of an effort to revitalize the party, SNAP joined the opposition PR. However it withdrew in May 2012. In January 2013 the party was officially deregistered and subsequently reported as defunct.

There are numerous other small parties, including The **Malaysian Justice Movement** (*Parti Angkatan Keadilan Insan Malaysia*—AKIM), launched in 1995 by a number of *Semangat '46* and Pas dissidents and led by Hanafi MAMAT; the **Malaysian Punjabi Party** (*Parti Punjabi Malaysia*), led by Sushel KAUR, the only woman to head a Malaysian party; the **State Reform Party**—Star (*Parti Reformasi Negeri*), led by former SNAP vice president, PATAU Rubis; and the **Malaysian Workers' Party** (*Parti Pekerja-Pekerja Malaysia*), which dates from 1978.

Sabah opposition parties include the **Sabah People's Unity Front** (*Parti Barisan Rakyat Sabah*—Bersekutu), led by Barman ANGKAP; the **Sabah People's United Democratic Party** (*Parti Demokratik Setiasehati Kuasa Rakyat Bersatu Sabah*—Setia); and the **United Pasok Nunkragang National Organization** (*Pertubuhan Kebangsaan Pasok Nunkragang Bersatu*—Pasok).

There are numerous parties within the Indian community. They include, in addition to the MIC, the IPF, and the MMSP, the **Malaysian Indian United Party** (MIUP), founded in 2007 and led by S. NALLAKARUPAN, and the **Malaysian Indian Democratic Action**

Front (Mindraf), established in 2009 by the former journalist Manuel LOPEZ. The **Parti Cinta Malaysia,** whose leaders include Huan Cheng GUAN and Gabriel Adit DEMONG, was formed in 2009. In 2010 P. UTHAYAKUMAR, a legal adviser to Hindraf (Hindu Rights Action Force, below), established the **Human Rights Party** (HRP). The **Parti Ekonomi Sarawak Bersatu** (PERSB) was formed by a group of plantation owners.

Illegal Organization:

Hindu Rights Action Force—Hindraf (*Barisan Bertindak Hak-Hak Hindu*). This union of nongovernmental organizations, formed to advocate for the rights of Malaysia's Indian community, captured the nation's attention in November 2007. The group held a massive rally in Kuala Lumpur, without obtaining a government permit, to protest against social and economic discrimination against Indians and the destruction of Hindu temples. Police arrested more than 200 people, and five leaders were later detained without charges for more than a year. Party leader P. WAYTHAMOORTHY's six-year-old daughter was reportedly among those arrested. The unusual street demonstration galvanized Malaysia's ethnic minorities and played a significant role in the loss of support for the BN in the 2008 polling. The home minister declared Hindraf an illegal organization in October 2008. Prime Minister Najib freed the five detained leaders during his first month in office in 2009.

In 2011 the party held a rally to protest the government's requirement that the school curriculum include a book Hindraf considers to be racist. More than 100 arrests were made at the demonstration, which the authorities declared illegal. In August 2012 Waythamoorthy returned to Malaysia after a four-year absence. In August 2013 Waythamoorthy was appointed a deputy minister in the prime minister's office in the UMNO-led government.

Leader: P. WAYTHAMOORTHY (Chair).

Radical Islamic Group:

Malaysian Mujahideen Group (*Kumpulan Mujahideen Malaysia*—KMM). The shadowy KMM, which advocates Malaysia's conversion to an Islamic state, was apparently organized in 1998 as the Malaysian Militant Group (*Kumpulan Militan Malaysia*). It is regarded as an affiliate of the Indonesian-based terrorist group *Jemaah Islamiah.*

A number of alleged KMM members have been jailed under Malaysia's security law, which permits detention without trial. In many cases the KMM detainees have been Pas members, including NIK ADLI Nik Abdul Aziz Nik Mat, son of the chief minister of Kelantan, who was held from August 2001 until October 2006.

In 2011 KMM leader Zulkifli bin Hir, who allegedly fought alongside Osama bin Laden, was on the most wanted terrorists list of the U.S. Federal Bureau of Investigation for alleged crimes in Indonesia, Malaysia, and the Philippines. Reports in 2012 indicated that Zulkifli was in hiding in the southern Philippines.

Leader: ZULKIFLI bin Hir.

LEGISLATURE

The federal **Parliament** (*Parliamen Malaysia*) is a bicameral body consisting of a Senate and a House of Representatives.

Senate (*Dewan Negara*). The upper chamber comprises 70 members: 44 appointed by the paramount ruler (including 2 senators from the Federal Territory of Kuala Lumpur and 1 each from Labuan and Putrajaya) and 2 selected by each of the 13 state legislatures. Members serve once-renewable three-year terms. The Senate is never dissolved, new elections being held by the appropriate state legislative assembly as often as there are vacancies among the elected members. As of May 21, 2013, the National Front held 56 seats (United Malays National Organization, 30; Malaysian Chinese Association, 10; Malaysian Indian Congress, 6; United Traditional Bumiputra Party, 3; Malaysian People's Movement Party, 2; People's Progressive Party, 1; Sarawak United People's Party, 2; United *Pasok Momogun Kadazandusun Murut* Organization, 1; Sarawak Progressive Democratic Party, 1; Sarawak People's Party, 1); People's Alliance, 8 (Pan-Malaysian Islamic Party, 3; People's Justice Movement, 3; Democratic Action Party, 2). There were six vacancies.

President: Abu ZAHAR Ujang.

House of Representatives (*Dewan Rakyat*). The lower house currently has 222 elected members. The term of the House is five years, subject to dissolution. Elections are by universal adult suffrage, but the voting is weighted in favor of the predominantly Malay rural areas, with some urban (mainly Chinese) constituencies having three to four times as many voters as their rural counterparts.

In the most recent election of May 5, 2013, the National Front (BN) won 133 seats (United Malays National Organization, 88; United Traditional Bumiputra Party, 14; Malaysian Chinese Association, 7; Sarawak People's Party, 6; Malaysian Indian Congress, 4; Sabah United Party, 4; Sarawak Progressive Democratic Party, 4; United *Pasok Momogun Kadazandusun Murut* Organization, 3; Malaysian People's Movement Party, 1; Sarawak United People's Party, 1; and United Sabah People's Party, 1). The opposition People's Front won 89 seats, distributed as follows: Democratic Action Party, 38; People's Justice Party, 30; and Pan-Malaysian Islamic Party, 21.

Speaker: PANDIKAR Amin Mulia.

CABINET

[as of September 1, 2013]

Prime Minister	Mohamed Najib Abdul Razak (UMNO)
Deputy Prime Minister	Muhyiddin Mohamed Yasin (UMNO)
Ministers	
Agriculture	Ismail Sabri Yaakob (UMNO)
Communication and Multimedia	Ahmed Shabery bin Cheek (UMNO)
Defense	Hishammuddin Hussein (UMNO)
Domestic Trade and Consumer Affairs	Hasan bin Malek (UMNO)
Education and Higher Education	Muhyiddin Mohamed Yasin (UMNO)
Education and Higher Education, Second Ministry	Idris bin Jusoh (UMNO)
Energy, Green Technology, and Water	Maximus Johnity Ongkili (PBB)
Federal Territories	Tengku Adnan Tengku Mansor (BN)
Finance	Mohamed Najib Abdul Razak (UMNO)
Finance, Second Ministry	Ahmad Husni Hanadzlan (UMNO)
Foreign Affairs	Anifah Aman (UMNO)
Health	S. Subramaniam (MIC)
Home Affairs and Internal Security	Ahmad Zahid bin Hamidi (UMNO)
Human Resources	Richard Riot Anak Jaem (SUPP)
International Trade and Industry	Mustapha Mohamed (UMNO)
Natural Resources and Environment	G. Palanivel (MIC)
Plantation Industries and Commodities	Douglas Uggah Embas (PBB)
Prime Minister's Office, without Portfolio	Joseph Kurup (UMNO)
Prime Minister's Office, without Portfolio	Jamil Khir Baharom (UMNO)
Prime Minister's Office, without Portfolio	Abdul Wahid bin Omar (ind.)
Prime Minister's Office, without Portfolio	Idris Jala (ind.)
Prime Minister's Office, without Portfolio	Joseph Entulu Anak Belaun (ind.)
Prime Minister's Office, without Portfolio	Paul Low Seng Kwan (ind.)
Prime Minister's Office, without Portfolio	Nancy Shukri (PRS) [f]
Rural and Regional Development	Mohamed Shafie Haji Apdal (UMNO)

Science, Technology, and Innovation	Ewon Ebin (UPKO)
Tourism and Culture	Mohamed Nazri bin Abdul Aziz (UMNO)
Transport (Acting)	Hishammuddin Hussein (UMNO)
Urban Welfare, Housing, and Local Government	Abdul Rhaman Dahlan (UMNO)
Women, Family, and Community Development	Rohani Abdul Karim (UMNO)
Works	Fadillah Yusof (UMNO)
Youth and Sports	Khairy Jamaluddin abu Baker (UMNO)

[f] = female

INTERGOVERNMENTAL REPRESENTATION

Ambassador to the U.S.: Othman HASHIM.

U.S. Ambassador to Malaysia: Paul W. JONES.

Permanent Representative to the UN: Hussein HANIFF.

IGO Memberships (Non-UN): ADB, APEC, ASEAN, CWTH, NAM, OIC, WTO.

MALDIVES

Republic of Maldives
Dhivehi Jumhuriyah

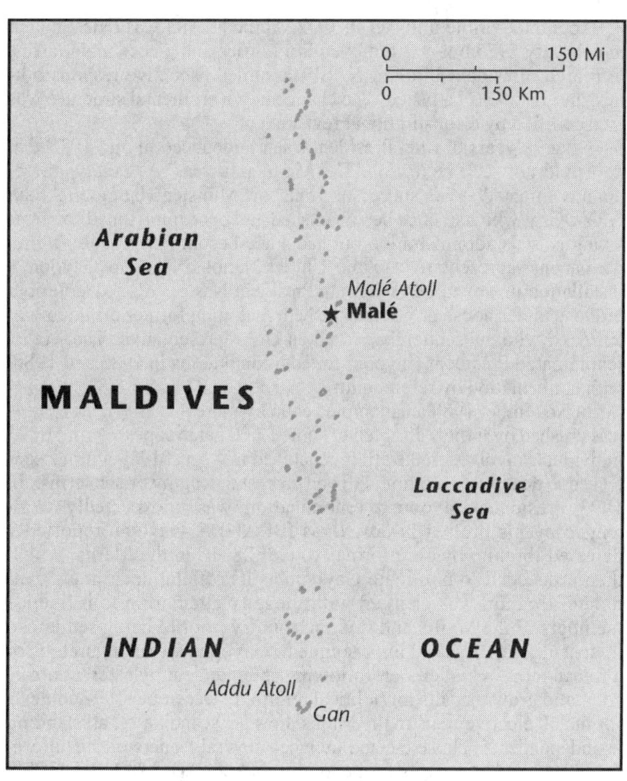

Political Status: Former British protectorate; independent since July 26, 1965; sultanate replaced by republican regime November 11, 1968; present constitution promulgated August 7, 2008.

Area: 115 sq. mi. (298 sq. km).

Population: 326,718 (2012E—UN); 393,988 (2013E—U.S. Census).

Major Urban Center (2011E): MALÉ (132,000).

Official Language: Dhivehi.

Monetary Unit: Maldivian Rufiyaa (market rate November 1, 2013: 15.39 rufiyaa = $1US).

President: Abdullah YAMEEN Abdul Gayoom (Progressive Party of the Maldives); sworn in on November 17, 2013 following the runoff election of November 16, succeeding Mohammed WAHEED Hassan Manik (National Unity Party), who assumed office on February 7, 2012.

Vice President: Mohamed JAMEEL Ahmed (Progressive Party of the Maldives); appointed on November 17, 2013, to succeed Mohamed Waheed DEEN (independent) who was appointed by the president on February 8, 2012.

THE COUNTRY

The Republic of Maldives is a 500-mile-long chain of small, low-lying coral islands in the Indian Ocean, southwest of India's tip. Grouped into 20 atoll clusters, the more than 1,200 islands (only about 200 are inhabited) have vegetation ranging from scrub to dense tropical forest. The population displays mixed Sinhalese, Dravidian, and Arab traits. The official language, Dhivehi, is related to Sinhalese. Islam is the state religion, most of the population belonging to the Sunni sect. Women make up 42 percent of the active labor force, but only 5 were elected to the 77-seat national legislature in 2009.

The economy was traditionally dependent on fishing, which continues to lead the islands' exports but agriculture and fishing now account for only 5.6 percent of GDP and 11 percent of employment. In recent years fishing has been surpassed in importance by a booming tourism sector, which accounts for 28 percent of GDP. Manufacturing, which contributes about 16.9 percent of GDP and employs 23 percent of the active labor force, is limited, the most important products being canned fish and garments. Cottage industries and handicraft production are also significant sources of employment and income. The government dominates most economic activity, but private sector participation has been increasingly encouraged.

The economy was hit severely by the December 2004 Indian Ocean tsunami. About 100 people died, and damage to infrastructure and housing was estimated at $375 million—about half the country's GDP that year. Fourteen islands suffered what the International Monetary Fund (IMF) labeled "virtually complete destruction"; 3 of the 14 were abandoned. Consequently, according to the IMF, the economy contracted by 8.7 percent in 2005 though recovered to see growth of 19.6 percent the following year. Recovery continued over the next two years, though with the impact of the global financial crisis, contracted by 3.6 percent in 2009. With considerable IMF loan assistance, GDP grew by 7 percent in 2010 and 2011. In response to pressure from the IMF in 2011, the Maldives agreed to allow its currency to float in a 20 percent range above or below 12.85 rufiyaa per $1 (the rufiyaa had been pegged at a fixed rate of 12.8 rufiyaa per $1). In 2013 growth slowed to 3.8 percent. Inflation was 5.8 percent, down from an 11.3 percent peak in 2011.

GOVERNMENT AND POLITICS

Political background. Subjected to a brief period of Portuguese domination in the 16th century, the Maldives came under British influence in 1796 and was declared a British protectorate in 1887. Internal self-government was instituted in 1960, and full independence was achieved on July 26, 1965, following negotiations with the United Kingdom covering economic assistance and the retention of a British air facility on southern Gan Island. The centuries-old Maldivian sultanate, which had been temporarily replaced by a republican form of government in 1953–1954, was then reinstated until 1968, when the Maldives again became a republic following a national referendum.

Appointed prime minister in 1972, Ahmed ZAKI was redesignated in February 1975 but was removed from office and placed under arrest in March. President Ibrahim NASIR assumed executive responsibilities, and Zaki was banished. The change in governmental structure was then codified by a constitutional revision.

After 21 years of rule, President Nasir announced in mid-1978 that he would not seek reelection. The Majlis (Citizens' Assembly) thereupon nominated as his successor Transport Minister Maumoon Abdul GAYOOM, who had once been banished and once imprisoned for criticizing Nasir's administration but had since become the country's first permanent representative to the United Nations. Prior to Gayoom's installation in November, outgoing President Nasir pardoned a number of those under house arrest or banished, including former prime minister Zaki, who subsequently served as UN representative. The Majlis renominated President Gayoom for additional terms in 1983 and 1988, with confirmation by referendum.

In November 1988 an attempted coup by more than 400 mercenaries was crushed by India's dispatch of some 1,600 paratroopers. A trial of 73 individuals involved in the affair concluded in August 1989 with 17 sentenced to death (later commuted) and the rest to lengthy prison terms. In 1993 President Gayoom's renomination was unexpectedly challenged by his brother-in-law, Ilyas IBRAHIM. Gayoom reportedly defeated Ibrahim by an informal vote of 28–18 in the Majlis, which then proceeded to nominate Gayoom as its official unanimous candidate. Ibrahim was charged with illegally attempting to influence members of the Majlis and fled the country prior to being sentenced in absentia to 15 years' imprisonment. Gayoom was inaugurated for a fourth term in November, following endorsement by referendum.

Amid growing calls for political reform, in December 1994 contests for the 40 elective seats in the Majlis drew 229 candidates, all standing as independents. Those elected included several leaders of the "proreform" movement, notably former ministers Abdulla KAMALUDHEEN and Ahmed MUJUTABA.

Ilyas Ibrahim returned to house arrest in 1996 but was released in 1997, his case apparently having influenced the way presidential balloting in the legislature was to be conducted under a new constitution that was promulgated on January 1, 1998. Although four others sought the presidential nomination during secret balloting in the legislature in September 1998, President Gayoom received a unanimous endorsement. Following confirmation by referendum, he took the oath of office for a fifth term in November. The new cabinet introduced by President Gayoom included his erstwhile adversary Ilyas Ibrahim as well as Abdulla Kamaludheen.

The People's Majlis election of November 1999 saw a nearly 50 percent turnover in the elected membership. A total of 129 independent candidates contested the election.

In 2003 President Gayoom won unanimous endorsement for a sixth term. He was confirmed by 90.3 percent of the voters on October 17 and sworn in on November 11.

On August 13, 2004, the president declared a state of emergency following demonstrations demanding the release of political prisoners, some of whom had been detained since protesting the deaths of several prisoners at the hands of security personnel in September 2003. When the state of emergency was lifted on October 10, 2004, nearly 80 of the 185 who had been arrested in August were still being held.

Legislative elections to the 50-seat People's Majlis, originally scheduled for December 31, 2004, but postponed because of the Indian Ocean tsunami, were held on January 22, 2005. Although all candidates were required to run as independents, reform advocates performed strongly. Those endorsed by the Maldivian Democratic Party (MDP), an opposition party then based in Sri Lanka, captured 18 of the 42 elective seats.

On May 28, 2004, voters cast ballots for a partially elected People's Special Majlis that was assigned the task of drafting another new constitution. Political parties were legalized on June 2, 2005. The MDP quickly registered and immediately became the principal opposition to President Gayoom's newly organized *Dhivehi Rayyithunge* Party (DRP).

In August 2005 more than 130 demonstrators were arrested, including the MDP chair, Mohamed NASHEED (familiarly called Anni), who had returned from exile in April. Nasheed faced charges of terrorism and sedition. In October Jennifer LATHEEF, daughter of exiled MDP founder Mohamed LATHEEF, was convicted of inciting a riot in September 2003 and sentenced to ten years in prison. In August 2006, however, Jennifer Latheef was released from house arrest, as was Nasheed in September. The releases came in the context of "Westminster House" talks, chaired by the United Kingdom's high commissioner to the Maldives, between the government and the opposition.

On August 18, 2007, some 62 percent of voters in a national referendum supported maintaining a strong presidency, while the balance favored a parliamentary system. After four years of work, the People's Special Majlis approved a new constitution on June 26, 2008, and on August 7 it was signed by the president. The day before, Gayoom had pardoned a number of prisoners, including others who had been convicted of terrorism in connection with the September 2003 unrest.

Voting in the country's first multiparty presidential election, held October 8, 2008, Maldivians gave a plurality of 40.3 percent to the incumbent, President Gayoom, and 24.9 percent to the second-place finisher, the MDP's Mohamed Nasheed. Finishing third was former attorney general and independent candidate Hassan SAEED of the New Maldives movement. In the resultant two-way runoff on October 29, Nasheed won 53.7 percent of the vote to Gayoom's 45.3 percent. Inaugurated on November 11, along with Vice President Mohammed WAHEED Hassan Manik of the National Unity Party (NUP), President Nasheed named a multiparty cabinet. The peaceful transfer of power won wide international praise.

The country's first multiparty legislative election, for an expanded 77-seat People's Majlis, was held on May 9, 2009. The DRP won a leading 28 seats, while its ally, the People's Alliance (PA), won 7. The president's MDP took 26 seats, with independents claiming most of the balance.

On December 9, 2010, the Supreme Court ruled that cabinet appointees who had not been confirmed by the opposition-controlled legislature could not remain in office. The ruling arose from a dispute between the executive and legislative branches over President Mohamed Nasheed's decision, five months earlier, to reappoint the members of his cabinet en masse following their June 29 resignations. On December 11 Nasheed announced a reshuffled cabinet in which a number of portfolios were assigned on an acting basis. By August 2011 the parliament had approved replacements for the ministers who had resigned.

Following widespread protests and rioting, on February 7, 2012, President Mohamed Nasheed resigned amid a mutiny by security forces (see Current issues, below). Vice President Waheed was sworn in as interim president on the same day. A new coalition government was named in stages, beginning February 8.

Former president Nasheed secured a clear victory as MDP candidate in the first round of 2013 presidential elections on September 7, the results of which were subsequently annulled by the Supreme Court. Abdulla Yameen of the Progressive Party of the Maldives (PPM) secured the presidency in the second round of a new election in November (see Current issues, below).

Constitution and government. Following adoption of a republican constitution in 1968, the Maldivian government combined constitutional rule with de facto control by members of a small hereditary elite. The 1998 basic law, which was drafted over a 17-year period by a Citizens' Special Majlis, provided for a unicameral legislature controlled by an elected majority. The legislature nominated the president for a five-year term, with confirmation required by popular referendum. The 1998 constitution also provided for a People's Special Majlis (previously the Citizens' Special Majlis) to draft or amend a constitution. Either the president or the legislature, the People's Majlis, could convene a People's Special Majlis, whose membership included the 50 members of the legislature, an additional 42 elected members, 8 presidential appointees, and the members of the cabinet.

The new constitution approved by the People's Special Majlis in June 2008 and signed by President Gayoom in August retains a strong presidential system but reduces some powers and limits the president to two terms in office. It provides for a two-way runoff should no presidential candidate achieve 50 percent of the vote in a first round. A president must be the child of Maldivian citizens and must practice the Sunni branch of Islam. Cabinet ministers are named by the president but must receive legislative endorsement. The People's Majlis, now wholly elected using a first-past-the-post system, was expanded from 50 to 77 seats.

The 2008 constitution also enumerates a broad range of human rights, including freedom of speech, assembly, and association, and provides for the separation of executive, legislative, and judicial powers. The judicial system encompasses a Supreme Court, a High Court, and trial courts. Independent bodies are to be established for human rights, defense, police, elections, and corruption investigations. The constitution prohibits ministers from having private businesses, one immediate consequence being that four cabinet members tendered their resignations on August 6, 2008.

The current constitution includes no provision for a People's Special Majlis. Constitutional amendments require the assent of three-fourth of the full People's Majlis and the signature of the president, although the legislature may call for a referendum if the president does not assent to a change.

There are 20 atoll-based administrative divisions. The capital constitutes a separate, centrally administered district. In the past, each atoll was governed by a presidentially appointed atoll chief (*verin*), who was advised by an elected committee. Under the 2008 constitution, all divisions are to be "administered decentrally." As authorized by law, the president may create constituencies, posts, and councils, with the members of all councils to be elected democratically. Each council may then elect a president and vice president to serve as administrative officers for the jurisdiction.

Freedom of the press is protected. In 2013 the media group Reporters Without Borders ranked the Maldives 103rd in media freedom, a decline from 73rd in 2011, reflecting threats and attacks on journalists around the time of President Nasheed's controversial resignation.

Foreign relations. An active participant in the Nonaligned Movement, the Republic of Maldives has long sought to have the Indian Ocean declared a "Zone of Peace," with foreign (particularly nuclear) military forces permanently banned from the area. Thus, despite the adverse impact on an already depressed economy, the government welcomed the withdrawal of the British Royal Air Force from Gan Island in 1976 and rejected a subsequent Soviet bid to establish a base there. The republic became a "special member" of the Commonwealth in July 1982 and a full member in June 1985. It continues to claim some 62,000 square miles (160,000 square kilometers) of the British Indian Ocean Territory.

Maldives is a founding member of the South Asian Association for Regional Cooperation (SAARC). The Gayoom government took an active role addressing global warming. In November 2009 Maldives hosted the first meeting of the 11-member Climate Vulnerable Forum (V-11).

India remains the Maldives's closest international partner and the only country with which Malé has a defense cooperation agreement. In 2010 the two governments negotiated a pact on combating terrorism and subsequently expanded antipiracy cooperation. China and the Maldives signed an economic cooperation agreement in August 2010.

In January 2012 the Maldives and Burkina Faso established diplomatic ties. Following the February coup (see Current issues, below), the Commonwealth suspended the Maldives from its ministerial action group and dispatched a fact finding mission that was critical of the transfer of power. In September Waheed announced that the entire Maldives would become a marine reserve by 2017.

The Supreme Court's halt of the presidential runoff election in September drew criticism from the United Nations, the Commonwealth, the United States, and a host of other international observers (see Current issues, below).

Current issues. On June 29, 2010, the entire cabinet resigned. On the same day two leading opposition lawmakers, Gasim IBRAHIM of the Republican Party (*Jumhooree* Party) and Abdulla YAMEEN of the People's Alliance (PA), were placed under house arrest while being investigated for allegedly bribing other lawmakers to vote against the government. On July 11 the Supreme Court ordered their release. Four days earlier, Nasheed had reinstated the cabinet, an action that DRP leaders questioned on constitutional grounds. A reshuffled cabinet was appointed and subsequently approved in increments through August 2011.

Islam is the official religion in Maldives. Recently, a number of legislators have called for stricter adherence to fundamentalist precepts, though the government has stuck to a policy of "moderate Islam." New regulations in 2010 prohibited proselytizing and non-Islamic preaching and introduced a licensing plan to restrain radical Islamic clerics.

In local elections in February 2011, the MDP won majorities in most urban councils, while the DRP secured majorities in the rural areas. On May 1 an antigovernment protest erupted in violence after security forces used tear gas to break up the demonstration that involved approximately 5,000 people. In July the Gayoom faction of the DRP (known as the Z-DRP; see Political Parties, below) formed a parliamentary coalition with the Republican Party (*Jumhooree* Party—JP), the Maldives National Party (*Dhivehi Qaumee Party*—DQP), and the People's Alliance (PA) (see Political Parties, below) to oppose the MDP government.

On January 17, 2012, Nasheed ordered the arrest of the chief justice of nation's criminal court, Abdulla MOHAMED, for blocking corruption investigations after the latter released a leading government critic. The arrest prompted widespread protests and criticism by government members and opponents, including Vice President Waheed. On February 7 Nasheed resigned, reportedly at gunpoint, as police and military units mutinied. Pro-Nasheed demonstrators took to the streets in running battles with police that left 50 injured, 90 in jail, and 18 police stations burned. Meanwhile, Waheed took office, forming a unity cabinet that included all of the country's main parties except the MDP. In response to international criticism of the transfer of power, Waheed created a national commission of inquiry on the coup.

Four candidates contested the September 2013 presidential elections. Former president Nasheed, as MDP candidate, was the clear leader with 45.5 percent of the vote. Abdulla Yameen, half brother of former president Gayoom, running for the Progressive Party of the Maldives (PPM), placed second with 25.4 percent of the vote, a hair ahead of Gasim Ibrahim, of a JP-led coalition, with 24.1 percent. Meanwhile incumbent Mohamed Waheed placed fourth with just 5.1 percent. Gasim, whose third-place finish precluded his participation in the runoff set for September 28, accused the election commission of fraud and called for the results to be annulled despite positive reports from numerous international electoral observers. On September 23 the Supreme Court suspended runoff balloting until the claims could be investigated, and subsequently annulled the results. Mass protests, led by the MDP, broke out.

A second election scheduled for October 19 was suspended on the grounds that Gasim and Yameen had failed to approve the voter register. After the candidates came to an agreement in early November, polling was held on November 9, in which Nasheed was the clear leader with 46.9 percent of the vote. As no candidate secured the necessary 50 percent, Nasheed and the runner-up, Yameen, proceeded to run-off balloting on November 16. Yameen won with 51.3 percent of the vote, while Nasheed secured 48.6 percent. Yameen was sworn in the following day.

POLITICAL PARTIES

On June 2, 2005, at President Gayoom's request, the People's Majlis unanimously passed a reform allowing the registration of political parties, which had long been banned in Maldives. In May 2008 a National Unity Alliance (NUA) of five opposition groups—the Maldivian Democratic Party (MDP), the Islamic Democratic Party (IDP), the Social Liberal Party (SLP), the *Adhaalath* Party, and the New Maldives (NM)—failed to agree on selection of a single opposition candidate to compete against President Gayoom in the upcoming presidential election. The NUA had been organized in 2007, in part to press for an interim government before new elections. In mid-2008 the Maldivian National Congress (MNC) became the NUA's sixth member. The cabinet sworn in on November 12 included five parties plus the NM movement (subsequently the *Dhivehi Qaumee* Party—DQP), but the DQP and the *Jumhooree* Party later left the coalition.

In the May 2009 legislative election, 13 parties had been registered. Eleven offered candidates, and 5 won seats.

With the ratification of new regulations under the Political Party Act in March 2013, 11 parties were dissolved for failing to have the requisite membership of 10,000, reducing the number of registered parties to 5. In September the Supreme Court reduced the membership requirement to 3,000, enabling more parties to qualify for registration.

Governing Coalition:

Progressive Party of the Maldives (PPM) was formed in September 2011 by former president Gayoom and defectors from the Z-DRP faction of the DRP. The PPM joined the February 2012 unity cabinet and received two portfolios. Abdulla Yameen, Gayoom's half-brother and former leader of the PA, contested the September 2013 elections on the PPM ticket, placing second in the first round with 25.4 percent of the vote. The NUP subsequently endorsed Yameen for the September 28 runoff election (see Current issues, above).

Leaders: Abdullah YAMEEN Abdul Gayoom (President of the Republic), Mohamed JAMEEL Ahmed (Vice President of the Republic), Maumoon Abdul GAYOOM (Party Chair and Former President of the Republic).

National Unity Party—NUP (*Gaumee Itthihaad*). Former education minister Mohamed Waheed Hassan launched the NUP, sometimes referenced in English as the National Alliance Party (NAP), in mid-2008. Initially the party's presidential candidate, Waheed formed an alliance with the MDP and became Mohamed Nasheed's running mate for the October election. In the May 2009 legislative election the NUP won only 0.3 percent of the vote and no seats.

In May 2010 the NUP's Mohamed RASHEED was dismissed as minister of economic development by President Nasheed. Members of the MDP leadership then called for the NUP to be dismissed from the governing coalition for being uncooperative, but Nasheed instead expressed his continuing confidence in Waheed's counsel. Following the resignation of Nasheed in February 2012, Waheed became president of the Maldives and formed a unity cabinet.

Following controversy over whether the NUP fulfilled the new regulation to have membership of at least 10,000, Waheed contested the September 2013 election as an independent. The incumbent suffered a resounding defeat, placing fourth with just 5.1 percent of the vote. Subsequently, he announced the NUP's support for the **Progressive Party of the Maldives** (see PPM, below).

Leaders: Mohamed WAHEED Hassan Manik (Party President and former President of the Republic), Ahmed THAUFEEQ (Secretary General).

Maldive People's Party (*Dhivehi Rayyithunge Party*—DRP). Registered shortly after the legalization of parties, the DRP was established by President Gayoom. Its members included the cabinet and the government-supportive members of the People's Majlis and the People's Special Majlis. The party held its first congress April 19–21, 2006, at which time Gayoom was formally elected party chair by a vote of 887–33 over reform activist Ali SHAFEEQ.

A number of more youthful party leaders, including Ahmed Shaheed, Mohamed Jameel, and Hassan Saeed, headed a proreform "New Maldives" caucus that initially claimed the support of President Gayoom. A more conservative faction was led by Ilyas Ibrahim and Ahmed Thasmeen. The resignations from the cabinet in August 2007 of Shaheed, Jameel, and Saeed came amid accusations that the president was hindering democratic reform. In late October Saeed left the DRP and declared his intention to seek the presidency in 2008 (see the DQP, below). President Gayoom won the party's endorsement for reelection but lost an October runoff in which he took 45.3 percent of the vote. In the May 2009 People's Majlis election the DRP won a slim plurality of seats (28) despite receiving fewer votes—24.6 percent of the total—than the MDP.

In January 2010 Umar NASEER, 2008 presidential candidate for the Islamic Democratic Party (IDP), announced we would join the DRP shortly after the IDP dissolved.

Gayoom's January 2010 announcement that he would not seek reelection was seen as a step toward party unification; however, tensions mounted following Thasmeen's election to party chair. The former president created a faction within the party, the Z-DRP, which subsequently formed an opposition coalition within parliament. In September 2011 Gayoom formed the PPM.

Thasmeen stood as running mate of incumbent President Waheed, of the NUP, in the first round of presidential balloting in September 2013. Following a fourth-place finish, the DRP backed the MDP for the runoff.

Leaders: Ahmed THASMEEN Ali (Leader and 2013 vice presidential candidate), Ibrahim SHAREEF (Deputy Leader), Abdul RASHEED Nafiz (Secretary General).

People's Alliance (PA) Organized by Abdulla Yameen, a half-brother of former president Gayoom, the PA endorsed Gayoom for reelection in 2008 and then ran in the May 2009 People's Majlis election as a partner of the DRP, winning 5.0 percent of the vote and 7 seats.

In June 2010 Yameen was detained following accusations that he had been involved in attempted bribery of fellow legislators. The Supreme Court ordered his release from house arrest in July, although authorities continued to pursue allegations of bribery and treason. Yameen subsequently left and defected to the PPM.

Republican Party (*Jumhooree* Party—JP). The JP was founded in May 2008 by Ahmed Nashid, an associate of former finance minister Gasim Ibrahim, reputedly the country's wealthiest businessman. Ibrahim, who resigned from the cabinet and the DRP in mid-July, joined the JP in August and was quickly named its presidential candidate. By then, the JP had reportedly become the largest opposition party in the People's Majlis, with nine seats.

Ibrahim finished fourth in the 2008 presidential election, winning 15.2 percent of the vote as the candidate of the Republican Coalition, which also included *Adhaalath* and the Maldivian National Congress (MNC, below). Ibrahim and two others joined the cabinet. Ibrahim resigned in December 2008, however, and in May 2009 Fathimath Diyana SAEED was dismissed by President Nasheed for criticizing the government. The JP threatened court action against the MDP for failing to fulfill their coalition agreement.

In the May 2009 People's Majlis election the JP won one seat. On June 29, 2010, Ibrahim, now aligned with the opposition, was arrested as part of a bribery investigation. He was released in July after the Supreme Court determined that his detention was unwarranted. Following the 2012 resignation of president Nasheed, the JP became part of the unity government and received one cabinet post.

Ibrahim contested the September 2013 election, with the support of a coalition of the JP, the Maldives National Party (see DQP, below), and *Adhaalath*. He placed third with 24.1 percent of the vote, on the heels of Yameen of the PPM. Ibrahim challenged the results, accusing the electoral commission of negligence and staging party protests (see Current issues, above).

Leader: Gasim IBRAHIM (2013 presidential candidate).

Maldives National Party (*Dhivehi Qaumee Party*—DQP). The DQP originated in the New Maldives (NM) movement, which was formed by former attorney general Hassan Saeed and former foreign minister Ahmed SHAHEED, both of whom had resigned from the government in August 2007 and had criticized President Gayoom for delaying democratic reforms. Mohamed Latheef, an MDP founder, joined upon returning from exile in January 2007.

In 2008 Saeed sought the presidency as an independent and finished third, with 16.7 percent of the vote, in the first round. Shaheed, his running mate, was subsequently reappointed as foreign minister by President Nasheed, and Saeed became an adviser to Nasheed. After only 100 days in office, however, Saeed resigned because, he claimed, the new president was not heeding his advice.

In May 2009 the newly registered DQP won 3.5 percent of the national vote and two seats in the People's Majlis. In October it withdrew from the government, charging the MDP with not consulting its coalition partners and with failing to improve governance. In response, Shaheed announced that he was joining the MDP. In 2011 the DQP joined the Z-DRP-led opposition grouping, and in 2012 it joined the NUP-led unity cabinet. Ahead of the 2013 presidential elections, the DQP joined the JP-led coalition fronted by Gasim Ibrahim.

Leaders: Hassan SAEED (Chair and 2008 presidential candidate), Mohamed JAMEEL, Abdulla AMEEN (Secretary General).

Justice Party (*Adhaalath* Party). The Justice Party, registered in August 2005, is Islamic in orientation, including Muslim clerics and scholars among its membership. Some members have called for adoption of strict sharia law and the death penalty for Muslims who convert to other religions. The party endorsed Gasim Ibrahim of the JP for president in 2008 but in July 2009 signed a coalition agreement with the MDP for the next local council elections. In May the party had won less than 1 percent of the vote and no People's Majlis seats. Sheikh Imran Abdulla was elected party leader in July 2011. *Adhaalath* joined the NUP-led unity government in February 2012. In 2013 *Adhaalath* again backed Ibrahim for president.

Leaders: Sheikh Imran ABDULLA (President), Mohamed MUIZZU, Mohamed Shaheem ALI Saeed.

Parliamentary Opposition:

Maldivian Democratic Party (MDP). Efforts to establish a legal MDP date back to 2001, when the government refused to register it. As a result, the MDP was based in Colombo, Sri Lanka, from 2003 until officially registered in the Maldives in June 2005. The Majlis elected in 1999 reportedly included 7 MDP supporters; 18 representatives elected in January 2005 had run with MDP endorsements. Following legalization of political parties, the center-right MDP assumed leadership of the parliamentary opposition. In May 2006 the party president, Ibrahim ISMAIL, resigned over tactical issues.

In November 2006 officials arrested 100 MDP members and supporters, ostensibly to avert a violent demonstration, and later charged acting MDP president Ibrahim Hussein ZAKI with treason for voicing support for protesting fishermen. The charge was later downgraded to committing "enmity, contempt, and disharmony." In April 2007 the MDP was fined, not for the first time, for holding illegal gatherings, this time to welcome home Majlis member Mariya Ahmed DIDI, who in March had received an International Woman of Courage Award from the U.S. State Department for her advocacy of women's rights.

In June 2007 former attorney general Mohamed MUNAVVAR was elected chair. In a presidential primary, Mohamed Nasheed (Anni) defeated Munavvar and Moosa "Reeko" Manik. Nasheed secured 24.9 percent of the first-round 2008 presidential vote for second place and defeated the incumbent president with 53.7 percent in the second round.

In the May 2009 legislative election the MDP finished second, with 26 seats, despite claiming a plurality of votes, 30.8 percent. As of September 2010, the MDP held a plurality of 32 seats but was still outnumbered by the combined opposition. In March 2011 former party leader Munavvar established a new party, the **Maldives Reform Party** (MRP).

In February 2012 Nasheed was forced to resign amid public protests, as well as pressure from security forces. The MDP subsequently rejected an invitation to join a unity government.

Nasheed, with running mate Mustafa LUTFI, contested the September 2013 presidential election, emerging the clear leader in the first round of voting with 45.5 but failing to pass the 50 percent mark. Following the JP's call for annulment of the election, the MDP offered a "truce" with *Adhaalath*, which was rejected. Party supporters protested the postponing of the runoff election (see Current issues, above).

Leaders: Moosa MANIK (Chair and Parliamentary Leader), Mohamed NASHEED (Former President of the Republic and 2013 presidential candidate).

Other Parties:

Other parties include the following: the **National Alliance** (NA), led by Mohamed WAHEED and formed in 2008; the **Maldivian Labor Party** (MLP), established in 2008 as the Poverty Alleviating Party; and the **Maldivian National Congress** (MNC), chaired by Mohamed NAEEM, which won less than 0.1 percent of the vote in 2009.

For more information on the **Maldivian Social Democratic Party** (MSDP) and the **People's Party** (PP), see the 2011 *Handbook.* For more information on the **Social Liberal Party** (SLP), please see the 2012 *Handbook.*

LEGISLATURE

Prior to adoption of the 2008 constitution, the Maldivian **People's Majlis** was a unicameral body of 50 members: 8 appointed by the president and 42 popularly elected as independents. The country's first multiparty election, for a 77-seat People's Majlis, was held May 9, 2009, with revoting in one district on July 11. The results were as follows: *Dhivehi Rayyithunge* Party, 28 seats; Maldivian Democratic Party, 26; People's Alliance, 7; *Dhivehi Qaumee* Party, 2; Republican Party, 1; independents, 13. Representatives, all of whom are now elected from districts drawn on the basis of population, serve five-year terms.

Speaker: Abdulla SHAHID.

CABINET

[as of November 23, 2013]

President	Abdulla Yameen Abdul Gayoom (PPM)
Vice President	Mohamed Jameel Ahmed (PPM)
Ministers	
Defense and National Security	Col. Mohamed Nazim (ind.)
Economic Development	Mohamed Saeed (JP)
Education	Aishath Shiham (PPM)
Environment and Energy	Thoriq Ibrahim
Finance and Treasury	Abdulla Jihad (ind.)
Fisheries and Agriculture	Mohamed Shainee (PPM)
Foreign Affairs	Dunya Maumoon (PPM) [f]
Health and Gender	Mariyam Shakeela [f]
Home Affairs	Umar Naseer (PPM)
Housing and Infrastructure	Mohamed Muizzu (JP)
Islamic Affairs	Mohamed Shaheem Ali Saeed (JP)
Tourism	Ahmed Adheeb abdul Gafoor (ind.)
Transport and Communication	Ameen Ibrahim (JP)
Youth and Sports	Mohamed Maleeh Jamal
Attorney General	Uz Mohamed Anil

[f] = female

INTERGOVERNMENTAL REPRESENTATION

Ambassador to the U.S.: Ahmed SAREER.

U.S. Ambassador to the Maldives: Michele J. SISON (resident in Sri Lanka).

Permanent Representative to the UN: Ahmed SAREER.

IGO Memberships (Non-UN): ADB, CWTH, ICC, NAM, OIC, SAARC, WTO.

MALI

Republic of Mali
République du Mali

Note: According to preliminary results of the November–December 2013 balloting for the National Assembly, President Ibrahim Keïta's Rally for Mali (RPM) was credited with winning a plurality of 66 of 147 seats. RPM allies (including the Alliance for Democracy in Mali/Pan African Party for Liberty, Solidarity, and Justice [16 seats]) reportedly secured enough seats to provide Keïta with a comfortable legislative majority. The leading opposition party was the Union for the Republic and Democracy, which was credited with 17 seats. Although turnout was low, the balloting was generally peaceful and was deemed "acceptable" by international observers.

Political Status: Independent republic proclaimed September 22, 1960; military regime established November 19, 1968; civilian rule reestablished under constitution approved in 1974 and promulgated June 19, 1979; 1974 constitution suspended on March 26, 1991, and replaced by interim Fundamental Act on March 31; multiparty constitution drafted by National Conference in July–August 1991, approved by popular referendum on January 12, and formally proclaimed on February 14, 1992; military regime briefly established by coup of March 21–22, 2012, followed by installation of a transitional government pending new presidential and legislative elections; permanent government inaugurated in September 2013 following presidential elections.

Area: 478,764 sq. mi. (1,240,000 sq. km).

Population: 15,287,331 (2013E—UN); 15,968,882 (2013E—U.S. Census).

Major Urban Center (2005E): BAMAKO (1,995,000).

Official Language: French. Bambara, Fulfuldé, Songhai, and Tamasaq are also commonly spoken.

Monetary Unit: CFA franc (official rate November 1, 2013: 486.52 CFA francs = $1US). The CFA franc, previously pegged to the French franc, is now permanently pegged to the euro at 655.957 CFA francs = 1 euro.

President: Ibrahim Boubacar KEÏTA (Rally for Mali); elected in second-round balloting on August 11, 2013, and inaugurated on September 4 for a five-year term in succession to Interim President Dioncounda TRAORÉ (Alliance for Democracy in Mali/Party for Liberty, Solidarity, and Justice).

Prime Minister: Oumar Tatam LY (nonparty); appointed by the president on September 5, 2013, to succeed Interim Prime Minister Django SISSOKO; formed new government on September 8, 2013.

THE COUNTRY

Of predominantly desert and semidesert terrain, landlocked Mali stretches northward into the Sahara from the upper basin of the Niger and Senegal rivers. The country's lifeline is the Niger River, which flows northeastward past Bamako, Ségou, and Timbuktu in Mali and then southeastward through Niger and Nigeria to the Gulf of Guinea. Mali's overwhelmingly Muslim population falls into several distinct ethnic groups, including the Bambara and other southern peoples, who

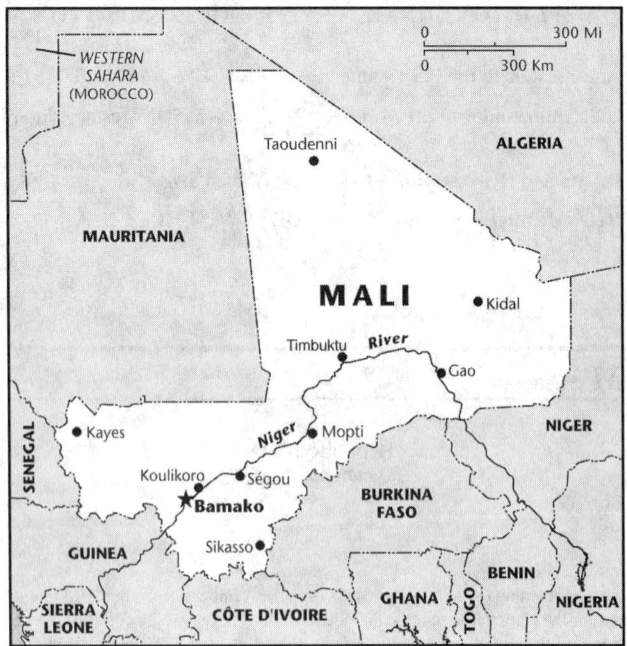

are mostly farmers. The Peul, or Fulani, as well as the Tuaregs (who are Berbers) pursue a primarily nomadic and pastoral existence on the fringes of the Sahara. Women constitute only about 15 percent of the formal workforce, and female involvement in politics has traditionally been minimal. However, in 2010 women won 15 seats in parliament, or 10.2 percent of the total, and in April 2011 the country's first woman prime minister was appointed.

Approximately 80 percent of the economically active population is dependent on agriculture and fishing, with cotton, peanuts, and livestock being the leading sources of foreign exchange. Although the country was once dubbed the potential "breadbasket of Africa," Mali's food output has periodically been severely depressed by droughts, locust infestations, and land mismanagement. Industrial activity is concentrated in agro-processing, some enterprises having been privatized as part of an overall retreat from state dominance of the economy. Extraction of minerals such as uranium, bauxite, ferronickel, phosphates, and gold, while drawing the interest of international investors, has been hindered by inadequate transport and power facilities. Although some progress toward economic reconstruction has been registered with assistance from a variety of foreign sources, Mali remains one of the world's poorest countries.

The International Monetary Fund (IMF) approved an immediate disbursement of funds in March 1994 to help dampen economic and social turmoil generated by devaluation of the CFA franc two months earlier. Subsequently, the Fund urged an increased pace of privatization, harmonization of investment regulations and business laws, and greater efficiency in collection of tax revenues, in part to permit increased social spending.

Record gold and agricultural production in the early 2000s helped maintain strong economic growth, which averaged 5 percent annually in 2000–2004. In 2006 the World Bank approved additional debt relief and provided other credits to support agriculture as well as poverty-reduction efforts, and the United States provided $461 million for infrastructure improvement. Subsequently, the government granted oil exploration licenses to two foreign companies in exchange for a commitment from the companies to invest more than $11 million in the Malian economy over a four-year period.

GDP grew by 4.5 percent in 2009, 5.5 percent in 2010, and 5.4 percent in 2011 as good harvests helped Mali avoid contagion from the global economic downturn. The IMF approved new lending in December 2011, although disbursements were subsequently compromised by a coup in March 2012. Further undercut by a temporary rebel takeover in the north, real GDP fell by 0.4 percent in 2012. However the return to an elected civilian government in the second half of 2013 appeared to lay the foundation for the resumption of normal economic activity, including aid transfers.

GOVERNMENT AND POLITICS

Political background. Mali, the former French colony of Soudan, takes its name from a medieval African kingdom whose capital was located near the present capital city of Bamako. As a part of French West Africa, Soudan took part in the general process of post–World War II decolonization and became a self-governing member state of the French Community in 1958. Full independence within the community was achieved on June 20, 1960, in association with Senegal, with which Soudan had joined in January 1959 to form a union known as the Federation of Mali. However, Senegal seceded from the federation on August 20, 1960, and on September 22 Mali proclaimed itself an independent republic and withdrew from the French Community.

Mali's government, led by President Modibo KEITA of the Soudanese Union/African Democratic Rally (*Union Soudanaise/ Rassemblement Démocratique Africain*—US/RDA), gradually developed into a leftist, one-party dictatorship with a strongly collectivist policy at home and close ties to the Soviet bloc and the People's Republic of China. In late 1968 the Keita regime was ousted in a bloodless coup d'état led by Lt. Moussa TRAORÉ and Capt. Yoro DIAKITÉ under the auspices of a Military Committee of National Liberation (*Comité Militaire de Libération Nationale*—CMLN).

The new military regime began to reverse the economic policies of the Keita government and pledged that civil and political rights would soon be restored. However, further centralization of the military command took place in 1972 following the trial and imprisonment of Captain Diakité and two associates for allegedly plotting another coup. Overthrow attempts were also reported in 1976 and 1978, the latter involving a reputed pro-Soviet faction of the CMLN that opposed a projected return to civilian rule under a constitution approved in 1974.

After a five-year period of transitional rule by the CMLN, civilian government was formally restored on June 19, 1979, when General Traoré was elected, unopposed, to a five-year term as president and prime minister. Earlier, in March, the Malian People's Democratic Union (*Union Démocratique du Peuple Malien*—UDPM) had been formally constituted as the country's sole political party. In 1982 the presidential term was increased to six years, resulting in the reelection of Traoré coincident with pro forma legislative balloting on June 9, 1985. Three days earlier the president had carried out a cabinet reshuffle that included the designation of Dr. Mamadou DEMBELE as prime minister. The latter office was abolished in the course of a further cabinet shakeup on June 6, 1988, that preceded assembly renewal on June 26.

Widespread opposition to harsh conditions under the Traoré regime erupted into rioting in Bamako and other towns in January–March 1991 amid mounting demands for the introduction of a multiparty system. On March 26 Traoré was ousted by an army group under the leadership of Lt. Col. Amadou Toumani TOURÉ, who formed a 17-member Council of National Reconciliation (*Conseil de la Réconciliation Nationale*—CRN). On March 30 the CRN joined with anti-Traoré political leaders in establishing a Transitional Committee for the Salvation of the People (*Comité de Transition pour le Salut du Peuple*—CTSP), comprised of 10 military and 15 civilian members. On April 2 the CTSP announced the appointment of Soumana SACKO, a highly respected senior official of the UN Development Program, as prime minister. The cabinet that was announced two days later consisted largely of "unknown" technocrats, although military officers were awarded a number of key portfolios.

On April 5, 1991, the CTSP authorized the formation of political parties and declared its intention to rule for a nine-month period ending with a constitutional referendum and multiparty elections. However, Traoré supporters were subsequently purged from the government and military, and, following a foiled attempt to liberate the imprisoned former president in June, a coup attempt by the then territorial administration minister, Maj. Lamine DIABIRA, failed in mid-July.

At a National Conference on July 29–August 14, 1991, charged by the CTSP with the founding of a "third republic" based on "legality and freedom," 1,000 delegates from 42 parties and 100 associations drafted a new constitution, which the government pledged to put to a referendum on December 1 in anticipation of multiparty elections in early 1992. However, in November the government extended the transition period to March 26, 1992, citing difficulties in establishing an electoral system and the inability to guarantee safe polling sites for voters in the north, where Tuareg insurgents had long been active.

On January 12, 1992, the new proposed constitution was approved by 98.35 percent of referendum participants. One week later the Alliance for Democracy in Mali (*Alliance pour la Démocratie au Mali*—Adema) won a majority of seats in municipal balloting. Both polls, as well as legislative balloting in February–March, were marred by low voter turnout, coupled with allegations of electoral fraud and inappropriate CTSP support for Adema. In addition, a number of parties protested a reported CTSP decision to assign Tuareg groups uncontested legislative seats as an outgrowth of a National Peace Pact concluded with the rebels on March 25. Nonetheless, after a one-month postponement, Adema leader Alpha Oumar KONARÉ led eight competitors in first-round presidential balloting on April 12 and went on to defeat Tréoulé Mamadou KONATÉ by a 40 percent margin in the runoff two weeks later. On June 8 Younoussi TOURÉ, a former Central Bank president, was named to succeed Sacko as prime minister.

On May 18, 1993, the Supreme Court upheld death sentences that had been passed on former President Traoré and three associates for causing the "premeditated murder" of 106 persons during prodemocracy riots in the capital in March 1991. Meanwhile, an escalation of student demonstrations, which had commenced seven months earlier, yielded arson attacks on a number of public installations, including the National Assembly building. On April 9, in response to the unrest, President Konaré announced the resignation of the Touré government and appointed Defense Minister Abdoulaye Sekou SOW to head a new administration.

Citing austerity concerns, Prime Minister Sow downsized his fledgling cabinet on November 7; however, Adema membership in the reshuffled, technocratic government grew as its members replaced three nonparty ministers. In December the government confirmed reports that an imprisoned former Traoré aide, Lt. Col. Oumar DIALLO, and five others had been charged with plotting to "topple democratic institutions" and "dispose" of anyone opposed to Diallo's release.

On February 2, 1994, Sow became the second consecutive prime minister to resign amid student protests over government spending decisions. Collaterally, Sow, like his predecessor, argued that Adema members had undermined his premiership. Two days later President Konaré named an Adema member, Ibrahim Boubacar KEÏTA, as the new prime minister. On February 6 the cabinet was thrown into disarray when ministers from the National Congress for Democratic Initiative (*Congrès National d'Initiative Démocratique*—CNID) and the Rally for Democracy and Progress (*Rassemblement pour la Démocratie et le Progrès*—RDP) resigned, with CNID leader Mountaga TALL accusing the administration of having "marginalized" non-Adema ministers. Subsequently, the government named by Keïta on February 7 included only 16 members—11 from Adema and 5 from minor parties.

The military conflict between the government and Tuaregs appeared to end in June 1995 when the last active rebel group, the Arab Islamic Front of the Azawad, halted its guerrilla campaign and announced its interest in peace negotiations. In November the government announced that approximately 20,000 Tuareg refugees had returned from exile in Mauritania, and by February 1996 more than 3,000 former rebels had reportedly been integrated into the armed forces.

The first of two rounds of new assembly balloting was held on April 13, 1997; however, the polling was marred by reported gross irregularities, including a shortage of balloting papers. Consequently, on April 25 the Constitutional Court annulled the first-round results and postponed the second round indefinitely. At the same time, the court ordered that preparations for presidential polling continue, despite opposition threats to boycott such balloting if it preceded the assembly elections.

In presidential balloting on May 11, 1997, Konaré garnered 95.9 percent of the vote, overwhelming his sole opponent, Mamadou Maribatourou DIABY of the small Unity, Development, and Progress Party (*Parti pour l'Unité, le Développement, et le Progrès*—PUDP). Eight other opposition candidates boycotted the polling, which was marked by a low voter turnout and antigovernment demonstrations. Subsequently, in two rounds of legislative balloting on July 20 and August 3, Adema candidates also easily dominated an electoral field depleted by an opposition boycott. On September 13 Konaré reappointed Prime Minister Keïta, who rejected opposition calls for a "unity" government and named a cabinet on September 16 that was dominated by propresidential parties and moderate opposition groups.

President Konaré made a number of conciliatory gestures to his opponents in the second half of 1997, including releasing opposition members arrested during the violent unrest that surrounded the May–August polling and reducing the death sentences of former president Traoré and his associates to life imprisonment. The president's pledge to convene an all-inclusive national forum gained momentum in mid-April 1998, when a broad range of opposition groups responded positively to a conciliatory proposal brokered by former U.S. president Jimmy Carter. However, on April 20 hard-line opposition groups in the Collective of Opposition Political Parties (*Coordination des Partis Politiques de l'Opposition*—COPPO) refused to attend a government-sponsored summit, asserting that the government representatives lacked legitimacy and vowing to boycott the upcoming local elections and launch a civil disobedience campaign.

In municipal balloting on June 21, 1998, Adema candidates captured an overwhelming number of mayoral and local council posts. In August the government announced that further local polling, then tentatively scheduled for November, would be postponed in the hopes of avoiding an opposition boycott. The Konaré administration reportedly remained intent on convincing opposition hard-liners to participate in future polling, since their previous boycotts had undermined the credibility of Mali's democratization and decentralization efforts. In January 1999 the government convened an internationally monitored national forum to garner input from Malian political leaders on the electoral process. However, only four of the parties aligned with the so-called radical opposition attended, and COPPO again urged its supporters not to vote in the May 2 and June 5, 1999, balloting, in which Adema secured about 60 percent of the seats on local councils.

Prime Minister Keïta resigned on February 14, 2000, and was succeeded the following day by Mande SIDIBÉ, one of President Konaré's economic advisors. The cabinet announced on February 21 included 15 new ministers. Keïta's resignation was seen in some quarters as designed to permit him to concentrate on an anticipated campaign to succeed Konaré in 2002. (The president had earlier announced he would not attempt to circumvent the two-term limit, despite encouragement from his supporters to seek reelection.) At midyear COPPO leaders announced plans to present a coalition opposition candidate in the campaign. Subsequently, former president Amadou Touré resigned from his army post in September 2001 as required by law to be able to run for the presidency.

Forty parties signed a "pact of good conduct" in January 2001 in preparation for the 2002 balloting. However, late in the year President Konaré suspended plans for a referendum on new electoral laws that had been approved by the assembly in mid-2000 based on recommendations from the 1999 national forum. In February 2002 the assembly adopted new electoral legislation that did not require a referendum, paving the way for first-round presidential balloting in late April and legislative elections in July. Most parties agreed to participate in the polls.

Prime Minister Sidibé resigned on March 18, 2002, to contest the upcoming presidential election. He was succeeded by former president Modibo Keïta. In the first round of balloting on April 28, Amadou Touré, backed by a number of parties, finished first among more than 20 candidates. He was elected president on May 12 by securing about 64 percent of the vote in a runoff against Soumaïla CISSÉ of Adema. Touré appointed Mohamed Ag AMANI (nonparty) as the new prime minister on June 9; on June 15 a new "national unity" cabinet, including members of a number of parties as well as independents, was named. One of President Touré's first acts was to pardon former President Traoré in an attempt to promote national unity and reconciliation.

In controversial assembly balloting on July 14 and 28, 2002, Hope 2002 (*Espoir 2002*)—an alliance of parties upset over the conduct of the first round of the presidential poll—won 66 seats, followed by the Alliance for the Republic and Democracy (a coalition that included Adema and others), with 51 seats, and Alternation and Change (a coalition of parties that had supported Touré in the presidential balloting), with 10.

In by-elections on October 20, 2002, Adema won all 8 seats being contested and became the largest single party in the assembly with 53 seats. Hope 2002, with 66 seats, combined with 19 presidential-supportive deputies to create a stable presidential majority within the legislature.

Local elections on May 30, 2003, were relatively free of the problems that had surrounded the 2002 presidential and assembly elections. In part due to a government campaign to encourage voting, turnout was high, and more than 20 parties won seats, with Hope 2002 securing a majority of the mayoral posts.

Prime Minister Amani resigned on April 28, 2004, and he was replaced by former transport minister Ousmane Issoufi MAÏGA (nonparty), who formed a new cabinet on May 2.

Tuareg rebels renewed their fight against the government by launching attacks on several cities and military bases in the north in early May 2006, prompting renewed Algerian-mediated negotiations that led to a July accord under which the Tuaregs agreed to cease their militancy and to drop their demand for autonomy. In return the government promised to invest in major development programs in the north. A second pact in February 2007 endorsed Tuareg disarmament and integration of former rebels into the Malian military. However some Tuaregs remained disaffected, and the situation was complicated by the influx into the region of militants from the Algerian-based al-Qaida in the Islamic Maghred (AQIM, see the article on Algeria for additional information).

As the candidate of the new Alliance for Democracy and Progress (*Alliance pour la Démocratie et le Progrès*—ADP), President Touré was reelected to a second term in the first round of balloting on April 29, 2007, with 68 percent of the vote. Former prime minister Ibrahim Keïta of the recently formed Front for Democracy and the Republic (*Front pour la Démocratie et las République*—FDR) finished second with 19 percent. Opposition parties condemned the balloting as fraudulent, but international observers generally described the poll as free and fair. Touré subsequently reappointed Prime Minister Maïga and most of the incumbent cabinet ministers. The ADP also dominated the two-round assembly balloting in July, capturing 113 seats. Maïga resigned from the prime minister's post on September 27 and was replaced the next day by Modibo SIDIBÉ, a nonparty technocrat.

President Touré reshuffled the cabinet on April 9, 2009, reappointing Sidibé and moving several of the prime minister's political allies into key cabinet positions.

In the second half of 2009 the Tuaregs and other ethnic groups in the north who had been involved in sporadic fighting among themselves agreed to establish a permanent intercommunity political structure to resolve their differences peacefully. Under government pressure, the groups also reportedly endorsed the campaign against the AQIM, whose highly publicized kidnappings of Westerners had compromised the region's important tourism sector.

In September 2010 President Touré announced that he did not intend to pursue another term in 2012, which would have required constitutional revision of the current two-term presidential limit. Analysts subsequently described Prime Minister Sidibé as the front-runner for the post, and he resigned on March 30, 2011, in order to campaign for the presidency. Independent political figure Cissé Mariam Kaïdama SIDIBÉ (no relation) was named as the country's first female head of government on April 3.

In the face of intensifying Tuareg rebellion in the north, components of the Malian military perpetrated an essentially bloodless coup on March 21–22, 2012, under the leadership of Capt. Amadou Hayo SANOGO, who announced the formation of a National Committee for the Recovery of Democracy and the Restoration of the State (*Comité National pour le Redressement pour la Démocratie et la Restauration de l'État*—CNRDRE) to govern the country (under his leadership) indefinitely pending new elections. However, facing severe sanctions from its neighbors in the Economic Community of West African States (ECOWAS), the junta in early April agreed to a specific framework for the beginning of the return to civilian government, and under an agreement negotiated with ECOWAS, Dioncounda TRAORÉ, the speaker of the assembly, was appointed interim president of the republic. Traoré, who as speaker was constitutionally authorized to become president if the sitting president became unable to perform the duties of the office, was inaugurated (as endorsed by the Constitutional Court) on April 8 after President Touré submitted his resignation. It was also reported that Captain Sanogo had announced his resignation as self-appointed head of state. On April 17 Traoré appointed Cheick Modibo DIARRA, the grandson of former president Moussa Traoré, as interim prime minister. The cabinet named by Diarra on April 24 included three members of the junta, which retained significant de facto authority. Again reportedly reacting to ECOWAS pressure, Sanogo at the end of May agreed to the extension of Interim President Traoré's term for a year (the initial appointment had been for only 40 days). In August Interim Prime Minister Diarra appointed what he described as a national unity government, although military influence remained apparent. Meanwhile Islamist militants had joined and, to some extent, co-opted the rebellion in the north, gaining ascendancy in a number of important towns and attracting intense attention from regional and Western governments concerned over the spread of jihadism.

On December 11, 2012, the military leaders forced Prime Minister Diarra to resign, along with his cabinet. Interim President Traoré appointed Django SISSOKO, the former head of the prime minister's office as prime minister the next day, and a reshuffled cabinet was named on December 15.

Following a French-led military ouster of the Islamist militants in the north in early 2013 and the subsequent restoration (for the most part) of Malian government control there, the first round of presidential elections was held on July 28, 2013. Former prime minister Ibrahim Keïta, the candidate of his Rally for Mali (*Rassemblement pour le Mali*—RPM), led 27 candidates with 39.8 percent of the vote, and he defeated Soumaïla Cissé of the URD in the August 11 runoff with a vote share of 77.6 percent. Following his inauguration in September, Keïta named Oumar Tatam LY, an economist and former regional bank officer, as the new prime minister.

Constitution and government. The constitution adopted at independence was abrogated by the military in November 1968. A new constitution was approved by referendum on June 2, 1974, but did not enter into force until June 19, 1979. The constitution drafted by the National Conference of July 29–August 14, 1991, and approved by referendum on January 12, 1992, replaced the interim *Acte Fondamental* that the CTSP had promulgated in April 1991 following abrogation of the 1974 document. The new basic law includes an extensive bill of individual rights, a charter for political parties, guarantees of trade union and press freedoms, and separation of executive, legislative, and judicial powers. A directly elected president, who may serve no more than two five-year terms, appoints a prime minister and other cabinet members, who are, however, responsible to a popularly elected unicameral National Assembly. The judicial system is headed by a Supreme Court, which is divided into judicial, administrative, and fiscal sections. There is also a nine-member Constitutional Court, while a High Court of Justice is empowered to hear cases of treason.

Mali is administratively divided into eight regions, the eighth being created in May 1991 by the halving of a northern region as a concession to Tuareg separatists. The regions, headed by appointed governors, are subdivided into 46 districts (*cercles*) and 282 counties (*arrondissements*), also administered by appointed officials. Most municipalities have elected councils, which have been given increased authority in connection with recent decentralization program efforts.

The military junta that assumed control in March 2012 immediately announced it was suspending the constitution and "dissolving" all national institutions, but the de facto constitutional effect of the coup ultimately appeared negligible in view of the plan (which included the restoration of the constitution) that was quickly adopted for new presidential and legislative elections in 2013. (Constitutional amendments had been scheduled for a national referendum in conjunction with the presidential elections that had been scheduled, prior to the coup, for April 2012. The revisions, which had been heavily promoted by President Touré [ousted by the coup], had among other things, called for the formation of an upper house [Senate] in the national legislature and installation of an independent electoral commission. Other provisions appeared designed to strengthen presidential authority. The proposals were subsequently shelved.)

Mali has long been considered an African exemplar of respect for freedom of the press. However, conditions deteriorated following the March 2012 coup as a number of journalists were attacked in both the south and north.

Foreign relations. Reflecting a commitment to "dynamic nonalignment," Mali improved its relations with France, Britain, the United States, and other Western nations under General Traoré. It also cultivated links to China and the former Soviet Union.

For two decades Mali was locked in a dispute with Burkina Faso (formerly Upper Volta) over ownership of the 100-mile long, 12-mile wide Agacher strip between the two countries. The controversy triggered a number of military encounters, including a four-day battle in December 1985.

Some 2,500 Malian workers were expelled from Libya in 1985 as part of the Qadhafi regime's drive to reduce its dependence on foreign labor. Subsequently, Mali charged Libya with supporting Tuareg insurgents in northern Mali. (Relations between the two countries had previously cooled due to Libya's involvement in the Chadian civil war.)

The dispute with Burkina Faso was finally settled by a ruling in late 1986 from the International Court of Justice that divided the disputed territory into roughly equal parts, with the border being defined in accordance with traditional patterns of nomadic passage. Border tensions with Mauritania were similarly resolved by a border demarcation agreement in May 1988.

In January 1991 the Algerian government mediated a truce between the Malian government and moderate Tuareg party leaders. International diplomatic efforts were subsequently credited with generating agreements among Algeria, Mali, and Niger in 1992, which resulted in the repatriation of thousands of Tuaregs from Algeria in August 1993. Negotiations between Mali and Algeria in February 1995 yielded an accord on border security issues.

Relations with Côte d'Ivoire were strained following a coup attempt in that country in January 2001. Ivorian authorities reportedly unofficially implied that Mali and Burkina Faso had backed the overthrow effort, and many Malians living in Côte d'Ivoire at the time were attacked when the armed rebellion began in 2002.

The growing presence of foreign Islamic extremists, mainly from Pakistan and Afghanistan, prompted the Malian government in 2004 to seek international counterterrorism aid, prompting U.S. military advisers to initiate an antiterrorism training program for the Malian armed forces. The United States had earlier sponsored military training exercises in Mali and provided equipment and financial aid for Malian security efforts.

The Malian government also gave permission for U.S. special operations units to undertake antiterrorism missions in the north of the country, where Algerian militants had reportedly established a presence. The United States subsequently announced it would use its Malian base as a headquarters for regional antiterrorism efforts. Algeria also assisted the Malian government and Tuareg rebels to reach another peace deal after a mutiny in the northeastern region of Kidal in July 2006.

Mali signed a broad economic accord with China in 2006. In return for increased exports of cotton from Mali to China, China agreed to expand investment in Mali's agriculture, tourism, and telecommunications sectors.

In September 2009 military leaders from Algeria, Mali, Mauritania, and Niger announced plans for joint initiatives against terrorism and cross-border crime in the region. The antiterrorism plan was primarily aimed at the activities of the Algerian-based Al-Qaida in the Islamic Maghreb (AQIM), which had recently expanded its activities to sparsely populated northern Mali (see section on the AQIM in the article on Algeria for additional information). In an apparently related development, the United States in October announced it would give Mali $4.5 in military equipment and provide counterterrorism training for Malian security forces. In the first half of 2010 regional neighbors criticized the Malian government for being too lax in regard to the battle with the AQIM, especially after several AQIM hostages were released in Mali after ransoms were apparently paid by European countries for their nationals. Subsequently, President Touré reportedly strengthened his resolve to confront the AQIM, and in September Mali permitted Mauritanian troops to enter Malian territory in pursuit of the Islamic militants. Mali also pledged troops for the regional command headquarters being established in Algeria to combat terrorism.

Following the death of al-Qaida leader Osama bin Laden in May 2011, the AQIM called for attacks on pro-Western targets, prompting warnings about travel to Mali by Western countries. Meanwhile, Mali, Algeria, Mauritania, and Niger invited representatives from the United States and the EU to a regional conference in Algiers to coordinate the anti-AQIM strategy. By 2011 it was estimated that there were 200–300 AQIM fighters in Mali.

The international community strongly condemned the March 2012 coup in Mali, having previously promoted the country as one of Africa's strongest and most stable democracies. Regional neighbors aligned in ECOWAS adopted a particularly hard line and pressured the Malian junta into quickly accepting a plan for the full return of civilian government within a year. Subsequently, the world's focus turned to the chaotic conditions in northern Mali where the rapidly rising influence of Islamic militants posed a threat to neighboring countries as well as the broader international community. Responses included joint Algerian/Mauritanian airstrikes against jihadists near the border between the two countries and a decision by the EU to send a team to Niger to assist local forces in combating terrorism and criminal activity such as drug trafficking.

Current issues. In late 2011 Tuareg restiveness in the north intensified into an uprising, led by the National Movement for the Liberation of the Azawad (*Mouvement National pour la Libération de l'Azawad*—MNLA), a recently formed rebel group that reportedly included Tuareg fighters returning from Libya, where they had fought alongside Muammar Qadhafi's security forces. (For additional details about events in the north, see Northern Groups under Political Parties and Groups, below.) In early February 2012 demonstrations were held in Bamako to protest the government's perceived ineffectiveness to quell the revolt and attendant violence. (It was estimated that some 130,000 people had been displaced by that time.)

The military leaders who seized power in March 2012 took a number of government officials into temporary custody and announced that they would restore civilian rule after order had been restored in the north. However, ECOWAS immediately closed the borders to Mali and froze Malian assets in ECOWAS member states in an effort to force Captain Sanogo and the CNRDRE to endorse a specific (and short) transitional timetable. The United States and other countries concurrently suspended foreign aid payments. Most observers concluded that Sanogo had hoped to be named interim president, but he and the CNRDRE moved to the background under the ECOWAS plan, which restored at least a veneer of constitutionality to affairs via the elevation of assembly speaker Traoré to the interim presidency. The accord provided amnesty for all members of the junta and authorized the lifting of the ECOWAS sanctions. For his part, President Touré, who had gone into hiding after the putsch, submitted his resignation for the sake of his "love for Mali," and all the officials that had been detained in March were released. Meanwhile, reports surfaced that the coup had resonated positively with those segments of the population upset by high prices and perceived systemic corruption in the government, although several conflicts were reported between Touré loyalists in the military and the putschists.

By mid-2012 Islamic jihadists had surpassed the MNLA in significance in the north, where the harsh imposition of sharia (Islamic religious law) by the Islamists had reportedly appalled some of the Tuareg population. In September the Traoré/Diarra administration called upon the UN Security Council to approve the proposed deployment of an ECOWAS force to combat the northern rebels. However Captain Sanogo opposed international intervention, insisting that the Malian army was up to the task and that policy difference was reportedly the reason for the forced resignation of Prime Minister Diarra in early December. (The new prime minister, Sissoko, had earned a reputation for a collaborative style during his previous government service.)

Fighters from *Ansar Dine*, one of the recently emergent Islamist groups in the north, unexpectedly began to move toward the south in early January 2013. In response, France, which for many months had advocated military intervention, immediately launched air strikes against rebel positions in the north, followed by a ground assault that had largely routed the militants by mid-February. (Malian and Chadian forces also participated in the offensive, while a number of Western nations contributed indirect support.) At midyear a new UN peacekeeping force began to assume a wide range of responsibilities, while international donors pledged $4.1 billion in reconstruction aid.

The international community broadly welcomed the decisive victory by former prime minister Keïta in the July–August 2013 presidential elections. Immediate concerns for Keïta and the government of the new prime minister, Ly, included stabilization in the north (sporadic bomb attacks on the part of the jihadists continued) and preparations for the national legislative elections scheduled for late November.

POLITICAL PARTIES AND GROUPS

The only authorized party prior to the March 1991 coup was the Malian People's Democratic Union (*Union Démocratique du Peuple Malien*—UDPM), but it was dissolved in the wake of President Traoré's ouster. Public demonstrations that preceded the 1991 coup were orchestrated by a number of groups (including Adema), which were linked in a Coordination Committee of Democratic Associations and Organizations (CCADO), which joined the CRN in forming the CTSP on March 30, after which both it and the CRN were dissolved. On April 5 the CTSP authorized the formation of political parties, and by late 1991 approximately 50 formations, many with links to pre-1968 political personalities or groups, had applied for legal status, though only 27 parties presented legislative candidates in 1992.

For the 2007 presidential and legislative elections, more than 40 parties came together to form the ADP (below) to support Touré's reelection. (For comprehensive information on a number of opposition coalitions from 1992 to 2002, see the 2012 *Handbook*.)

The following party structure reflects the results of the 2007 legislative elections, successful candidates in that balloting having had their terms of offices extended in June 2012 until new elections were held in the wake of the March 2012 coup. A number of parties formed electoral pacts in the run-up to the new assembly balloting scheduled for late 2013.

Legislative Parties:

Alliance for Democracy and Progress (*Alliance pour la Démocratie et le Progrès*—ADP). Formed to support the incumbent Amadou Toumani Touré in the 2007 presidential election, the ADP included more than 40 parties. Touré won the April poll, and the ADP won a strong majority (113 seats) in the July legislative elections. After being overthrown in the March 2012 coup, Touré was granted asylum in Senegal, from where in August 2013 he congratulated Ibrahim Keïta on his victory in the new Malian presidential elections.

Leaders: Dioncounda TRAORÉ (Adema), Mountaga TALL (CNID).

Alliance for Democracy in Mali/Pan African Party for Liberty, Solidarity, and Justice (*Alliance pour la Démocratie au Mali/Parti Pan-Africain pour la Solidarité et la Justice*—Adema/PASJ). A principal organizer of anti-Traoré demonstrations and subsequently among those groups represented in the CTSP, Adema registered for legal status in April 1991. Adema candidates won substantial majorities in the 1992 local and National Assembly elections, and the party also captured the presidency on April 26 with a 70 percent second-round vote share for Alpha Oumar Konaré.

At the party's July 1993 congress dissident members released a manifesto calling for the "appointment to positions of responsibility [within the party]... of competent men and women of integrity" and the "destruction of the old state apparatus." Subsequently former prime ministers Younoussi Touré and Abdoulaye Sow cited subversive activities by "radical" elements within Adema as among their reasons for resigning from the party. Observers attributed the intraparty friction to a conflict between members identifying with the former prime ministers and favoring integration of non-Adema political groups into the government and a smaller faction advocating Adema's unilateral rule.

At a party congress on September 25–27, 1994, founding member Mohamed Lamine Traoré lost the party chair in an action spearheaded by Prime Minister Ibrahim Boubacar Keïta, who had hinted at dramatic party changes at his investiture. Subsequently, Traoré, Secretary General Mohamedoun DICKO, and a number of other senior members resigned from the party; two months later the dissidents launched MIRIA (below).

Although Konaré reportedly emerged from the 1999 congress heralding the health of his party, continued factionalization was subsequently reported between Keïta's supporters and his critics, led by Secretary General Ali Nouhoun DIALLO. Despite such opposition, Keïta was reelected as party chair in October. He resigned from all his party duties, however, in October 2000 in reaction to the advances registered by the "reformist" wing. Keïta then launched his own formation, the RPM (below). In March 2002, in a bitterly contested party election, Adema chose Soumaïla Cissé over former Prime Minister Mandé Sidibé to be the party's presidential candidate. However, Cissé was defeated in the second round of the presidential poll. Subsequently, Adema's parliamentary majority was reduced from 128 seats to 53 in legislative balloting, although the party remained the largest single group in the assembly. The electoral decline led to infighting within the party, and Cissé led a group of dissident members in the formation of a new rival party, the URD (below).

In 2006 former defense minister Soumaylou Boubèye Maïga announced he intended to seek Adema's nomination for the 2007 presidential election. However, Adema subsequently was instrumental in the formation of the ADP, which endorsed President Touré. Maïga consequently ran in the election as the leader of a small grouping, Convergence 2007, and was endorsed by the "rival" FDR (see below). In the 2007 legislative balloting, Adema won 51 of the ADP's 113 seats and became the largest party in the assembly. Party leader Dioncounda Traoré was subsequently elected president of the assembly.

The Adema/PASJ candidates were the top winners in the April 2009 municipal elections, securing a majority in all regions and four out of six communes in Bamako. Party president Traoré was named the Adema/PASJ candidate for the presidential elections that were scheduled for April 2012 but were not held due to the coup in March. Traoré, a former cabinet minister described as a "consensus builder," was subsequently appointed interim president of the republic because of his position prior to the coup of speaker of the assembly. As a condition for ECOWAS's endorsement of Traoré's appointment, he was declared ineligible to run for president in 2013. Consequently Adema/PASJ nominated Dramane Dembélé, an engineering professor described as one of Traoré's protégées. Dembélé finished third in the first round of balloting with 9.71 percent of the vote.

Leaders: Dioncounda TRAORÉ (Former Interim President of the Republic and President of the Party), Alpha Oumar KONARÉ (Former President of the Republic), Dramane DEMBÉLÉ (2013 presidential candidate), Abdel Karim KONATÉ (Secretary General of the National Bureau).

Union for the Republic and Democracy (*Union pour la République et la Démocratie*—URD). Launched in 2003 by former members of Adema who supported former presidential candidate Soumaïla CISSÉ, the URD is a centrist party that supports secularism and economic reforms. As part of the ADP, the URD won 34 seats in the 2007 legislative election. URD candidates won the second largest number of seats in the April 2009 municipal elections. Cissé, a regional bank official, was scheduled to be the URD candidate for president again in 2012. Following the March 2013 coup, Cissé was a prominent member of the Rejection Front (*Front du Refus*), a group of parties strongly opposed to the coup. Cissé finished second in the first round of presidential balloting in July 2013 with 19.70 percent of the vote and only improved to 22.39 percent in the August runoff, despite endorsements from several of the candidates eliminated in the first round.

Leaders: Soumaïla CISSÉ (Founder and 2013 presidential candidate), Younoussi TOURÉ (President), Lassana KONÉ (Secretary General).

Union for Democracy and Development (*Union pour la Démocratie et le Développement*—UDD). Running on a platform calling for "security, good citizenship, and clean streets," the UDD, whose founder, Moussa Balla COULIBALY, was an official in the Traoré government, won 62 seats in the 1992 municipal elections.

In 1999 it was reported that the Socialist Party for Progress and Development had merged into the UDD. In late 2001 Coulibaly was nominated as the UDD's presidential candidate for the 2002 presidential contest. He was eliminated in the first round, and the UDD supported Soumaïla Cissé of Adema in the second round. Despite his age, the 77-year-old Coulibaly was expected to be the UDD candidate in the eventually aborted 2012 presidential balloting.

Leaders: Moussa Balla COULIBALY (Chair and 2002 presidential candidate), Tiéman Hubert COULIBALY.

National Congress for Democratic Initiative (*Congrès National d'Initiative Démocratique*—CNID). Launched in 1990 as the National Committee for Democratic Initiative (*Comité National d'Initiative Démocratique*), the CNID was included in the April 1991 formation of the CTSP in recognition of its role in the overthrow of the Traoré regime. In 1992 the party, supported by a predominantly youthful constituency, secured 96 municipal and 9 National Assembly seats. Mountaga TALL, the party's 35-year-old presidential candidate, finished third in the first round of the 1992 presidential balloting, with 11.41 percent of the vote.

In March 1995, on the eve of the party's first conference, a group of dissidents reacted to the expulsion of ten governing committee members by holding a rival conference of the "true" CNID (see Parena, below).

In 1998 the CNID emerged as one of the most prominent of the radical opposition groups, organizing boycotts of the June elections and allegedly attempting to interfere with polling. However, the group's stance toward the government reportedly softened in 2000 and 2001, and the CNID participated in presidential and legislative balloting in 2002. Tall finished fifth as the CNID's candidate in the first round of the presidential poll with 3.75 percent of the vote. Meanwhile, the CNID joined Hope 2002 for the legislative poll, reportedly securing 13 of that coalition's seats.

The CNID's representation was reduced to seven seats following the 2007 assembly elections, in which it participated in the ADP. The party subsequently suffered from a rift among its senior leadership over party activities in Bamako.

CNID Chair Mountaga Tall was named as the party's candidate for the 2012 presidential poll, although he supported the March 2012 coup that blocked that election. He received 1.54 percent of the vote in the first round of the 2013 presidential balloting, apparently running formally as an independent.

Leaders: Mountaga TALL (Chair), Fanta Mantchini DIARRA (Senior Deputy), N'Diaye BAH (Secretary General).

Sudanese Union/African Democratic Rally (*Union Soudanaise/ Rassemblement Démocratique Africain*—US/RDA). The Malian wing of the RDA was formed in the aftermath of an RDA convention in Bamako in 1946. Supported by a rural constituency, the group came to power with the formation of Modibo Keïta's post-independence government in 1960 but went underground following his ouster in 1968.

At a special congress in January 1992, the US/RDA split over the selection of a presidential candidate. Members initially selected Tréoulé Mamadou KONATÉ, the son of an RDA founder and an advocate of purging "Stalinism" from the party, but the party leadership ultimately repudiated the action, nominating instead former UN official Baba Hakib HAIDARA. Subsequently, both stood as candidates, with Konaté finishing second in the first round of balloting but securing only 30 percent of the second-round vote in a contest with Alpha Oumar Konaré. In October 1995 Konaté was killed in a car crash.

The US/RDA supported former president Amadou Touré's presidential campaign in 2002. It reportedly won three seats in the 2002 legislative balloting as part of the Alliance for Alternation and Change (*Alliance pour l'Alternance et le Changement*—ACC), a grouping of some 28 parties. In the 2007 balloting the US/RDA secured one of the ADP's seats.

Leader: Mamadou Bachir GOLOGO (President).

Patriotic Movement for Renewal (*Mouvement Patriotique pour le Renouveau*—MPR). The MPR, which described itself as a descendant of the UDPM, was legalized in January 1995. Because of its ties to former President Traoré, the party was reportedly widely denigrated until 1997, when it assumed a prominent role in the opposition camp. Following the splintering of the US/RDA in mid-1998, one observer described the MPR as the most "stable" of the moderate opposition groups.

The MPR was described by *Africa Confidential* in 1999 as being "openly aligned" with the imprisoned Traoré but committed to the pursuit of "national reconciliation." Indeed, in 2000 the group decided to participate in presidential and legislative elections in 2002, nominating Choguel MAÏG for president. Maïga received 2.71 percent of the vote in the first round, and the MPR joined Hope 2002 for the subsequent legislative balloting. The MPR secured eight of the ADP's seats in the 2007 balloting, and the MPR supported the reelection of President Touré that year. Maïga finished seventh in the first round of the 2013 presidential election with 2.36 percent of the vote.

Leader: Choguel Kokalla MAÏGA (President and 2002 and 2013 presidential candidate).

Other minor parties in the ADP included the **Democratic Bloc for African Integration** (*Bloc Démocratique pour l'Intégration Africaine*—BDIA), a liberal party formed in 1993 under the leadership of Youssouf TRAORÉ that won three seats in the 2002 assembly elections and one in 2007; the **Alternation Bloc for Renewal, Integration, and African Cooperation** (*Bloc des Alternances pour la Renaissance, l'Intégration, et la Coopération Afrique*—BARICA, two seats in 2007), formed in 2004; the **Movement for African Independence, Renewal, and Integration** (*Mouvement pour l'Indépendence, la Renaissance, et l'Intégration Africaine*—MIRIA, two seats in 2007), established by dissident members of Adema, including Mohamed Lamine TRAORÉ; the **National Rally for Democracy** (*Rassemblement National pour la Démocratie*—RND, one seat in 2007), established in 1997 and led by Abdoulaye Garba TAPO; the **Solidarity and Progress Party** (*Parti de la Solidarité et du Progrès*—PSP, two seats in 2007); and the liberal **Citizens' Party for Renewal** (*Parti Citoyen pour le Renouveau*—PCR, one seat in 2007), formed in July 2005. (Ousmane Ben TRAORÉ of the PCR won 0.53 percent of the vote in the first round of the 2013 presidential election.)

Front for Democracy and the Republic (*Front pour la Démocratie et la République*—FDR). The FDR was formed by some 16 parties in advance of the 2007 elections to oppose the reelection of President Touré. Former defense minister and Adema member Soumaylou Boubèye Maïga and RPM leader Ibrahim Boubacar Keita were the main forces behind the creation of the new coalition. Four of the FDR members (including the small, newly formed Convergence 2007, led by MAÏGA) presented their own candidates in the first round of the 2007 presidential poll in an unsuccessful effort to force a runoff election. The FDR opposed the March 2012 coup, but an FDR member joined the National Unity government named in August.

Leaders: Ibrahim Boubacar KEÏTA, Tiéblé DRAMÉ, Soumaylou Boubèye MAÏGA, Mamadou SANGARÉ (2007 presidential candidates).

Rally for Mali (*Rassemblement pour le Mali*—RPM). Launched initially in February 2001 as "Alternative 2000," the RPM was a breakaway faction from Adema supportive of former Prime Minister Ibrahim Keïta, who left Adema in October 2000 and placed third in the first round of the 2002 vote with 21 percent of the vote. The RPM gained 46 seats in the 2002 legislative balloting as part of Hope 2002, and in September Keïta was elected president of the assembly. However, he resigned from that post in 2007 to run for president again, placing second in the first round with 19 percent of the vote. The RPM secured 11 of the FDR's 15 seats in the 2007 assembly elections.

Several key members of the RPM broke away from the party in January 2008 to form the base of a new Malian political formation, the FDM/MNJ (see below). In July 2011 the RPM chose Keïta as its candidate for the 2012 presidential balloting, which was precluded by the March 2012 coup. Keïta formally opposed the coup, but he was not subsequently subjected to mistreatment (as other leading anti-coup political figures were). Keïta, supported by some 15 other small political parties, finished first in the first round of the 2013 presidential poll with 39.79 percent of the vote, and won the runoff with 77.61 percent.

Leaders: Ibrahim Boubacar KEÏTA (President of the Republic), Bocary TRETA (Secretary General).

Front for Mali's Development (*Front pour le Développement du Mali–Mali Niéta Jekulu*—FDM/MNJ). Created in January 2008, the FDM/MNJ included a number of former RPM members. The group described itself as a response to poor governance under President Touré, who party leaders accused of violating the spirit of the 1991 coup d'état that ousted Gen. Traoré from power.

Leader: Harouna SISSOKO (President).

Party for National Renaissance (*Parti pour la Renaissance Nationale*—Parena). Parena was officially launched in September 1995 after its founders, CNID dissidents Capt. Yoro Diakité and Tiéblé DRAMÉ, lost their five-month legal battle for control of the CNID. A number of Parena leaders were former or current Konaré government ministers, a status reflected in the signing of the Parena-Adema cooperation pact in February 1996. Parena participated in the cabinet announced in 1997 but declined to accept any posts in the February 2000 government. Meanwhile, Diakité was reported to have formed a new party.

In 2001 Parena distanced itself from Adema, and Dramé became Parena's presidential candidate in 2002, finishing fourth in the first round of balloting with 4 percent of the vote. Parena reportedly won one of the ACC seats in the 2002 legislative poll. Dramé again was the party's candidate in the 2007 presidential poll, in which he placed third with 3 percent of the vote in the first round. Parena was credited with 4 of the 15 assembly seats won by the FDR in 2007. In April 2011 Parena agreed to support the governing coalition.

Dramé, who had helped to negotiate the June 2013 tentative peace agreement between the government and northern Tuaregs, initially was presented as Parena's candidate for the July presidential poll. However he withdrew his candidacy in mid-July on the grounds that the balloting was being inappropriately rushed.

Leaders: Tiéblé DRAMÉ (2002 and 2007 presidential candidate and Party President), Amidou DIABATE (Secretary General).

Democratic and Social Convention (*Convention Démocratique Sociale*—CDS). The self-styled "centrist" CDS was launched by Mamadou Bakary SANGARÉ in 1996. Unlike its moderate opposition party peers, the CDS chose not to join the government named in September 1997. Sangaré received 2.21 percent of the vote in the first round of presidential balloting in 2002. The CDS joined the FDR in 2007, and Sangaré ran as one of the four presidential candidates from the coalition, finishing fifth in the first round of balloting. He secured 1.08 percent of the vote in the first round of the 2013 presidential election.

Leader: Mamadou Bakary SANGARÉ (2007 presidential candidate).

African Solidarity for Democracy and Independence (*Solidarité Africaine pour la Démocratie et l'Indépendence*—SADI). Established in 2002 prior to the presidential elections, the SADI presented Oumar

MARIKO as its presidential candidate. He received less than 1 percent of the vote in the first-round balloting. In the subsequent legislative elections, the SADI won six seats. Mariko was also the party's candidate in 2007 and placed fourth in the first round of balloting with 2.7 percent of the vote. SADI legislative candidates won four seats in the July 2007 elections. The SADI rejected an invitation to join the new government appointed in April 2011, and the party opposed the 2011 constitutional reforms.

The SADI was described as providing political backing for the junta responsible for the March 2012 coup, Mariko having reportedly routinely criticized the Touré administration in the past for co-opting potential opponents through government favors. Mariko finished sixth in the first round of the 2013 presidential elections with 2.57 percent of the vote.

Leaders: Cheick Oumar SISSOKO (Chair), Oumar MARIKO (President and 2002, 2007, and 2013 presidential candidate).

Other Groups:

Party for Economic Development and Solidarity (*Parti pour le Développement Économique et la Solidarité*—PDES). Formed in mid-2010 by a number of cabinet ministers and members of the progovernment Citizen Movement (*Mouvement Citoyen*—MC), the PDES was considered a vehicle for extending the influence of President Touré, who was constitutionally precluded from seeking another term in 2012. (The MC had arisen in 2002 as an informal association of Touré supporters from a variety of political parties and civic organizations.) It was not immediately clear what relationship the PDES would eventually develop with the various components of the ADP, although analysts suggested the new party might challenge Adema's longstanding domination of Malian political affairs. PDES leaders, who included Lobbo Traoré TOURÉ (the president's wife), pledged to support President Touré's recent efforts to promote transparency in governmental affairs.

Following President Touré's overthrow in March 2012, the PDES reportedly fragmented. Jeamille BITTAR, initially a member of the PDES, ran for president of the republic in 2013, possibly as an independent. He secured 1.77 percent of the first-round vote.

Leader: Hamed Diané SÉMÉGA.

Alternative Forces for Renewal and Emergence (*Forces Alternatives pour le Renouveau et l'Émergence*—FARE). The FARE was formed to support the 2013 presidential candidacy of Modibo SIDIBÉ, who had resigned as prime minister in 2011 with the expectation that he would be elected to succeed President Touré. Following the March 2012 coup that overthrew Touré, Sidibé was arrested and briefly held in detention, with his home reportedly being looted. Also supported by the Convergence for a New Political Division (comprising numerous associations and political formations), Sidibé finished fourth in the first round of the 2013 presidential balloting with 4.97 percent of the vote. He endorsed Soumaïla Cissé of the URD in the second round, following through with a preelection pact among anti-coup parties that they would support the top vote getter from among their ranks.

Leaders: Alou KEÏTA (chair), Modibo SIDIBÉ (2013 presidential candidate).

Convergence for the Development of Mali (*Convergence pour le Développement du Mali*—CODEM). CODEM was formed in May 2008 by five national legislators, including Housseini GUINDO, who finished fifth in the first round of the 2013 presidential poll with 4.75 percent of the vote. He endorsed Ibrahim Keïta in the second round.

Leader: Housseini GUINDO.

Alliance for Democracy and Peace–Maliba (*Alliance pour la Démocratie et la Paix–Maliba*—ADP–Maliba). Recently formed under the leadership of gold mine owner Aliou Boubacar DIALLO, the ADP-Maliba ("Greater Mali") ultimately supported the RPM's Ibrahim Keïta in the 2013 presidential poll.

Leaders: Aliou Boubacar DIALLO, Amadou THIAM (Secretary General).

In the 2007 presidential election, Sidibé Aminata DIALLO was the candidate of the **Movement for Environmental Education and Sustainable Development** (*Rassemblement pour l'Éducation Environnementale et le Développement Durableé*—REDD), while Madiassa MAGUIRAGA was the candidate of the **Popular Party for Progress** (*Parti Populaire pour le Progrès*—PPP). Both candidates received less than 1 percent of the vote in the first round of balloting. (Diallo was Mali's first female presidential candidate.)

Mamadou Maribatourou Diaby, the incumbent's sole challenger in the 1997 presidential balloting, was a member of the **Unity, Development, and Progress Party** (*Parti pour l'Unité, le Développement, et le Progrès*—PUDP). (Diaby also ran unsuccessfully for the presidency in 2002.)

In 2011 the **African Convergence for Renewal** was launched under the leadership of Cheick Bougadary TRAORÉ, the son of former president Moussa Traoré. Bougadary Traoré, who had been living in the United States since 1991, returned to Mali to run for president in 2012. He won 0.31 percent of the vote in the first round of the 2013 presidential balloting. Another new party formed in 2011 was the **Rally for the Development of Mali** (*Rasemblement pour le Développement du Mali*—RPDM), which nominated Cheick Modibo Diarra, an astrophysicist and president of Microsoft Africa, as its candidate for the 2012 presidential election. After that balloting was postponed by the March 2012 coup, Diarra was named interim prime minister in April. After being forced out of that position in December 2012, Diarra won 2.14 percent of the vote in the first round of the 2013 presidential election.

Following the March 2012 military takeover, coup supporters reportedly coalesced initially as the Coordination of Patriotic Organizations of Mali (*Coordination des Organisations Patriotiques du Mali*—Copam), while anti-coup groupings formed the United Front for the Protection of Democracy and the Republic (*Front Uni pour la Sauvegarde de la Démocratie et de la République*), led by Adema member Kasssoum TAPO. (In addition to Adema, other parties and groups that objected to the coup reportedly included the URD, MPR, UDD, PSP, and FDR.)

(For information on additional minor parties that were active in the 1990s and early 2000s, see the 2012 *Handbook.*)

Other parties presenting candidates in the 2013 presidential election included the **Alliance Chato 2013**, whose candidate, Aïchata Alassane HAÏDARA (a former union activist), received 0.75 percent of the first-round vote; the **National Convention for African Solidarity**, whose candidate, former prime minister Soumana Sacko, won 0.90 percent; the **Party for the Civic and Patriotic**, a new party whose candidate, Niankoro Yeah SAMAKE, won 0.58 percent; and **Change** (*Yelema*), whose president, Moussa MARA, won 1.53 percent and was named to the September 2013 cabinet. Also named to that cabinet was former Adema leader Soumeylou Boubèye MAÏGRA, who had recently helped to form the **Alliance for Solidarity in Mali–Convergence of Patriotic Forces**.

Northern Groups:

National Movement for the Liberation of the Azawad (*Mouvement National pour la Libération de l'Azawad*—MNLA). Launched in the fall of 2011 by Tuareg rebels (many of whom had recently returned from Libya where they had served in the security forces of Muammar Qadhafi), the MNLA subsequently attacked Malian forces in the north at an increasing rate. Although some MNLA leaders advocated independence for northern Mali, other MNLA components called for autonomy rather than full independence. MNLA support included that of the National Movement for the Azawad (*Mouvement National pour l'Azawad*—MNA), which had been formed in 2010 by exiled Tuareg activists and the National Front for the Liberation of the Azawad (*Front National pour la Libération de l'Azawad*—FNLA), described as a secular Arab militia. (*Azawad* is derived from a Berber word that has historically referenced a Tuareg-populated region covering parts of Mali and several neighboring countries.)

The MNLA assumed control of a number of northern towns by defeating Malian army units in early 2012, and in April declared the "independent state of *Azawad*." However, the MNLA's dominance was soon challenged by the Islamist *Ansar Dine* (see below). The two groups surprisingly announced an alliance in May to govern an "Islamic Republic" in northern Mali. However, the alliance quickly collapsed because of the conflicting ideologies and goals of the two groups. (The MNLA, primarily comprising secular, French-speaking Tuaregs, reportedly chafed at *Ansar Dine*'s planned "Arabization" of the region and imposition of sharia.)

After losing the area it had previously controlled to *Ansar Dine* and another Islamist group (MUJAO, see below), the MNLA indicated its interest in being part of any future political settlement in the north. Following the rout of Islamist forces by French-led troops in early

2013, the MNLA reassumed control of the important northern city of Kidal. However, under a June cease-fire agreement with the government, the MNLA subsequently ceded control of the city.

Leaders: Col. Mohamed AG NAJEM (Chief of Staff), Hama AG SID'AHMED (Spokesperson), Bilal AG ACHERIF (Secretary General).

Ansar Dine (Defenders of the Faith). Launched at the end of 2011, the militant Islamist *Ansar Dine*, comprising both Arabs (the majority) and some Tuaregs, reportedly had ties to the Algeria-based Al-Qaida in the Islamic Maghreb (see Current issues, above, and the article on Algeria for additional information on the AQIM). *Ansar Dine* made significant military strides in northern Mali in the first half of 2012, for a brief time in a sketchy alliance with the MNLA (see MNLA, above, for details). Iyad Ag GHALI, a Tuareg described as a "veteran rebel leader" who had recently turned to "radical Islam," said that *Ansar Dine*'s primary goal was the imposition of sharia in northern Mali. However, other components of the group, while likewise committed to sharia, also appeared to favor independence for the region. Its forces having reportedly been augmented by former MNLA fighters, *Ansar Dine* by September controlled large areas of northern Mali, including the important towns of Kidal and Timbuktu. Meanwhile, the precise relationship between *Ansar Dine* and the AQIM (and, for that matter, the MUJAO [the other prominent Islamist group in the region]) remained unclear.

Although *Ansar Dine* in late 2012 reportedly agreed to peace talks with the government, its forces launched an offensive toward the south in January 2013, prompting the French-led campaign that ultimately forced most of the Islamist militants to abandon the territory they had controlled in the north.

Leader: Iyad AG GHALI.

Movement for Oneness and Jihad in West Africa (*Mouvement pour l'Unicité et le Jihad en Afrique de l'Ouest*—MUJAO). The jihadist MUJAO first surfaced in 2011, its forces reportedly augmented in July by militant Islamists from Algeria. The MUJAO appeared to have links with the AQIM, to which some observers attributed the "professionalism" displayed by the MUJAO fighters when they defeated the MNLA for control of the northern city of Gao in July 2012. Most of the MUJAO's membership was considered non-Malian and therefore unlikely to be approached by southern leaders regarding a possible political (rather than military) settlement. The MUJAO/AQIM fighters seized control of several other northern towns in late 2012, but they were pushed out by the French-led campaign in early 2013. Apparently continuing to operate from secluded mountainous regions in Mali and neighboring countries, the MUJAO claimed responsibility for several subsequent attacks throughout the year.

Leaders: Ould Mohamed KHEIROU, Sultan Ould BADI, Abu Walid SAHRAOUI.

Previously, the major Tuareg political organization was the **Alliance for Democracy and Change** (*Alliance pour la Démocratie et le Changement*—ADC), most of whose members endorsed, at least in principle, the Algerian-mediated peace plan of 2006 between Tuaregs and the Malian government. However, some Tuaregs subsequently continued their antigovernment activities. Although the ADC signed a disarmament accord in early 2009, the Tuareg Alliance of Northern Mali (*Alliance Tuareg Nord-Mali*—ATNM) led by Ibrahim AG BAHANDA, rejected that agreement. Following a government offensive against his forces in February 2009, Ag Bahanda fled to Algeria, from where he expressed interest in returning to peace negotiations. Although the Malian government declined direct talks with Ag Bahanda, it negotiated a reconciliation agreement in the second half of the year with the Tuareg community and other ethnic groups in northern Mali. However Turaeg leaders subsequently continued to criticize the government for its perceived failure to follow through on its development pledges for the north.

In early 2013 the formation of the **Islamic Movement of Azawad** (*Mouvement Islamique de l'Azawad*—MIA) was announced under the leadership of Alghabass AG INTALLAH, the son of the traditional leader of the dominant Tuareg clan. The MIA rejected ties with the AQIM and MUJAO and pledged to pursue a negotiated settlement with the government regarding limited autonomy for the north.

LEGISLATURE

Following the March 1991 coup, the UDPM-dominated legislature was dissolved, with its powers being assigned to the CTSP. The current **National Assembly** (*Assemblée Nationale*) contains 147 members serving (subject to dissolution) five-year terms. Legislators are directly elected in two-round balloting (as necessary) from 125 constituencies. Following balloting on July 1 and 22, 2007, the Alliance for Democracy and Progress held 113 seats (the Alliance for Democracy in Mali/Pan African Party for Liberty, Solidarity, and Justice, 51; the Union for the Republic and Democracy, 34; the Patriotic Movement for Renewal, 8; the National Congress for Democratic Initiative, 7; the Union for Democracy and Development, 3; the Alternation Bloc for Renewal, Integration, and African Cooperation, 2; the Solidarity and Progress Party, 2; the Movement for African Independence, Renewal, and Integration, 2; the Democratic Bloc for African Integration, 1; the National Rally for Democracy, 1; the Citizens' Party for Renewal, 1; and the Soudanese Union/African Democratic Rally, 1); the Front for Democracy and the Republic, 15 (the Rally for Mali, 11; the Party for National Renaissance, 4); African Solidarity for Democracy and Independence, 4; and independents, 15. The next election was scheduled for July 1, 2012, but was canceled because of the March coup. In June the assembly voted to extend the term of office of the current members until the completion (tentatively scheduled for April 2013) of the recently negotiated transitional period. Although new elections were tentatively scheduled for April 2013, they were subsequently postponed several times, most recently until November 24, 2013 (first round) and December 15 (second round). (*See headnote.*)

President (Interim): Younoussi TRAORÉ.

CABINET

[as of October 31, 2013]

Prime Minister	Oumar Tatam Ly
Ministers	
Civil Service	Bocar Moussa Diarra
Commerce	Abdel Karim Konaté (Adema/PASJ)
Communications and New Information Technology	Jean Marie Sangaré
Culture	Bruno Maïga
Defense and Veterans	Soumeylou Boubèye Maïga
Economy and Finance	Bouaré Fily Sissoko [f]
Employment and Professional Training	Mahamane Baby
Energy and Water	Mamadou Frankaly Keïta
Environment and Sanitation	Ousmane Ag Rhissa (RPM)
Equipment and Transportation	Col. Abdoulaye Koumaré
Foreign Affairs and International Cooperation	Zahabi Ould Sidi Mohamed
Handicrafts and Tourism	Berthé Aissata Bengaly [f]
Health and Public Hygiene	Ousmane Koné (RPM)
Higher Education and Scientific Research	Moustapha Dicko
Housing	Mohammed Diarra
Industry and Mining	Boubou Cissé
Justice and Keeper of the Seals	Mohamed Ali Bathily
Labor and Social and Humanitarian Affairs	Hamadoun Konaté
Malians Abroad	Abdramane Sylla (RPM)
National Education	Togola Jacqueline Nana [f]
National Reconciliation and Development of the Regions of the North	Cheikh Oumar Diarrah
Planning	Cheikna Seydi Ahamadi Diawara
Promotion of Women, Children, and the Family	Sangaré Oumou Ba (RPM) [f]
Rural Development	Bokary Tereta
Security	Sada Samaké
State Property and Land Affairs	Tiéman Hubert Coulibaly

Territorial Administration	Gen. Moussa Sinko Coulibaly
Urban Affairs	Moussa Mara
Youth and Sports	Mamadou Gaoussou Diarra
Ministers Delegate	
Ministry of Economy and Finance (in Charge of Budget)	Madani Touré
Ministry of Economy and Finance (in Charge of the Promotion of Investment and the Private Sector)	Moustapha Ben Barka
Ministry of Rural Development (in Charge of Livestock, Fisheries, and Food Security)	Nango Dembélé
Ministry of Territorial Administration (in Charge of Decentralization)	Malick Alhousseini
Ministry of Territorial Administration (in Charge of Religious Affairs)	Tiero Amadou Omar Hass Diallo

[f] = female

INTERGOVERNMENTAL REPRESENTATION

Ambassador to the U.S.: Al Maamoun Baba Lamine KEÏTA.

U.S. Ambassador to Mali: Mary Beth LEONARD.

Permanent Representative to the UN: Oumar DAOU.

IGO Memberships (Non-UN): AfDB, AU, ECOWAS, ICC, IOM, NAM, OIC, WTO.

MALTA

Republic of Malta
Repubblika ta' Malta

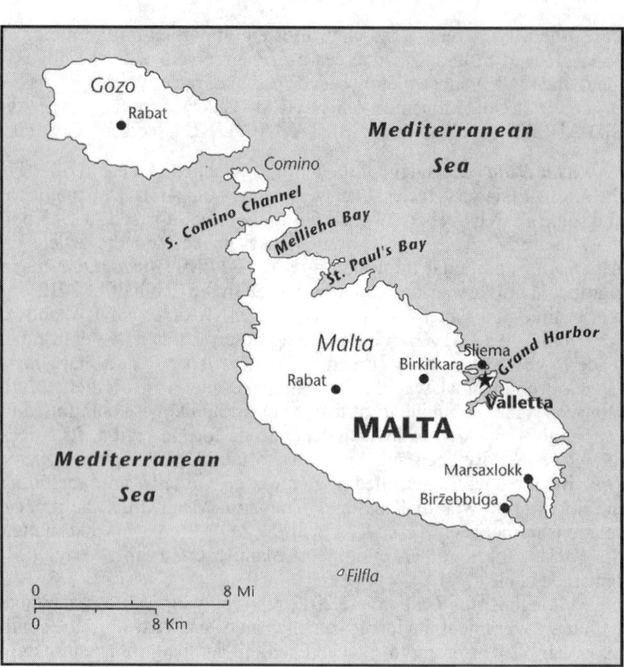

Political Status: Became independent within the Commonwealth on September 21, 1964; republic declared by constitutional amendment on December 13, 1974.

Area: 122 sq. mi. (316 sq. km).

Population: 417,520 (2013E—UN); 411,277 (2013E—U.S. Census).

Major Urban Centers (2011E): VALLETTA (5,784), Birkirkara (21,533), Sliema (13,511).

Official Languages: Maltese, English; Italian is also widely spoken.

Monetary Unit: Euro (market rate November 1, 2013: 0.74 euro = $1US). The euro became Malta's official currency on January 1, 2008, at a fixed rate of 1 euro = 0.4293 Maltese lira.

President: George ABELA (Malta Labour Party); elected on April 1, 2009, to a five-year term by the House of Representatives and sworn in on April 4, succeeding Edward (Eddie) FRENCH ADAMI (Nationalist Party). (Presidents resign from their parties upon election.)

Prime Minister: Joseph MUSCAT (Malta Labour Party); sworn in on March 11, 2013, to replace Lawrence GONZI (Nationalist Party), following the legislative election of March 9.

THE COUNTRY

Strategically located in the central Mediterranean some 60 miles south of Sicily, Malta comprises the two main islands of Malta and Gozo in addition to the small island of Comino. The population is predominantly of Carthaginian and Phoenician descent and of mixed Arab-Italian cultural traditions. The indigenous language, Maltese, is of Semitic origin. Roman Catholicism is the state religion, but other faiths are permitted.

Malta has few natural resources, and its terrain is not well adapted to agriculture. Services comprise 80 percent of GDP, followed by industry (17 percent) and agriculture (2 percent). Historically, the country has been dependent upon British military installations and expenditures, but today it focuses on tourism and shipping. Tourism reached record high levels in 2011, and the country has become a global leader in the online gaming industry. A 2011 European Commission report found that gaming accounted for 7.82 percent of Malta's GDP in 2008. (For details on the Malta economy in the 1970s and 1980s, see the 2012 *Handbook.*)

Malta joined the European Union (EU) in 2004 and adopted the euro at the start of 2008. Compared with other European nations, Malta weathered the global recession well. GDP declined by 2.1 percent in 2009, but it recovered and grew by 2.3 percent in 2010 and 2.1 percent in 2011, but only 0.8 percent in 2012. Unemployment has remained stable, averaging 6.5 percent.

GOVERNMENT AND POLITICS

Political background. Malta has a long history of conquest and rule by foreign powers. It first came under British control in 1800, possession being formalized by the Treaty of Paris in 1814, and its strategic importance being enhanced by the opening of the Suez Canal in 1869. Ruled by a military governor throughout the 19th century, it experienced an unsuccessful period of internal autonomy immediately following World War I. Autonomy was abolished in 1933, and Malta reverted to its former status as a Crown Colony. A more successful attempt at internal self-government was initiated in 1947, after Malta had been awarded the George Cross by Britain for its resistance to Axis air assaults during World War II. In 1956 the islanders voted three to one in favor of full integration with Britain, as proposed by the ruling Malta Labour Party (MLP), led by Dominic (Dom) MINTOFF. However, British reservations, combined with a change of government in Malta, resulted in the submission in 1962 of a formal request for independence within the Commonwealth by Prime Minister Giorgio

BORG OLIVIER of the Nationalist Party (*Partit Nazzjonalista*—PN), who led the islands to full sovereignty on September 21, 1964. The first post-independence change of government came in the 1971 election, which returned the MLP and Mintoff to power. Disenchanted with the British connection, Mintoff led Malta to republican status within the Commonwealth in December 1974.

The MLP retained its legislative majority in the elections of 1976 and 1981. The results of the 1981 poll were challenged by the opposition PN, which had won a slim majority of the popular vote and which, after being rebuffed in an appeal for electoral reform, instituted a boycott of parliamentary proceedings. In a countermove to the boycott, Prime Minister Mintoff declared the 31 Nationalist-held seats vacant in April 1982, with the PN subsequently refusing to make by-election nominations. In March 1983, however, PN leader Edward FENECH ADAMI agreed to resume parliamentary activity on the basis of a commitment from Mintoff to discuss changes in the electoral law.

The interparty talks were suspended in July 1983 in the wake of increasingly violent antigovernment activity and the adoption of a legislative measure that prohibited the charging of fees by private schools and indirectly authorized the confiscation of upwards of 75 percent of the assets of the Maltese Catholic Church. During 1984 the conflict erupted into a major confrontation between church and state, with the Catholic hierarchy ordering the closure of all schools under its jurisdiction—half the island's total—in September. The schools reopened two months later, with Vatican officials agreeing in April 1985 to the introduction of free education over a three-year period in return for government assurances of noninterference in teaching and participation in a joint commission to discuss remaining church-state issues, including those regarding church property.

Meanwhile, in December 1984 Mintoff had stepped down as prime minister in favor of Karmenu MIFSUD BONNICI. The church-state dispute was officially resolved in July 1986, while in January 1987 both the MLP and the PN supported constitutional changes that included modification of the electoral law to ensure that a party winning a majority of the popular vote would have a parliamentary majority.

In the bitterly contested 1987 election, Labour, as in 1981, won 34 of 65 legislative seats, but, after 16 years in office, lost control of the government because the PN had obtained a popular majority and was therefore awarded additional seats. Thus, PN leader Fenech Adami became prime minister. Earlier in the year, at the conclusion of her five-year term, President Agatha BARBARA had yielded her office, on an acting basis, to the Speaker of the House of Representatives, Paul XUEREB. Xuereb retained the position from February 1987 until the House elected the PN's Dr. Vincent TABONE as his successor in April 1989.

In the election of February 1992 the PN won 34 legislative seats with a vote share of 51.8 percent, while the MLP obtained 31 seats with 46.5 percent. Five days later, Fenech Adami formed a new government in which all senior ministers were retained. In 1994 former PN leader Ugo MIFSUD BONNICI was sworn in as Malta's fifth president.

In March 1995 Fenech Adami brought in a younger generation of ministers as part of a strategy to retain power in the next general election. However, the prime minister's decision to call an early election for October 1996 proved a miscalculation. Labour unexpectedly outpolled the PN 50.7 to 47.8 percent in fiercely contested balloting that drew a record turnout of 97 percent. Although the PN won 34 elective seats to Labour's 31, the 1987 constitutional amendment entitled Labour to 4 additional seats, handing it a parliamentary majority. The new Labour government was sworn in under the premiership of Alfred SANT, a Harvard-educated former physicist. Fulfilling one of its major domestic campaign promises, the Sant government in July 1997 abolished the country's 15 percent value-added tax (VAT), which had been introduced in 1995.

The government's single-seat majority evaporated when former prime minister Mintoff, Sant's aging MLP predecessor, deserted the party on two votes relating to a development project in Mintoff's district. Plagued by resignations, bitter attacks from Mintoff, and dissatisfaction within the MLP over Sant's failure to follow traditional patronage policies and his perceived drift to the right, the prime minister called an election for September 1998, three years early. The PN emerged with 35 seats to the MLP's 30, permitting the PN's Fenech Adami to return as prime minister. In March 1999, voting along straight party lines, the House of Representatives elected as president the PN's Guido DE MARCO, until then the deputy prime minister and foreign minister.

Membership in the EU became one of the main priorities of Fenech Adami's government. In response to criticism from the anti-EU MLP, Fenech Adami called a nonbinding referendum on EU membership for March 8, 2003. Although those voting endorsed membership by 53.65 to 46.35 percent, Sant and other MLP leaders argued that the closeness of the vote, when combined with the 9 percent of the eligible voters who did not cast a ballot, meant that the majority of Maltese opposed accession. In response, Fenech Adami called for elections on April 12, 2003, just four days before Malta was to sign the accession treaty, to affirm support for membership. Turnout was 96.2 percent. The PN received 51.8 percent of the vote and 35 seats, while the MLP won 47.5 percent and 30 seats. Malta signed the EU accession treaty on April 16 and formally entered the EU a year later, on May 1, 2004.

Having decided to seek the presidency, Fenech Adami resigned as prime minister on March 23, 2004. He was replaced by Lawrence GONZI (PN), who reshuffled and expanded the cabinet, sworn in on the same day as Fenech Adami's resignation. Fenech Adami, elected president by the House of Representatives on March 29, was sworn into office on April 4.

European parliamentary elections on June 12, 2004, showed that EU membership remained a contentious issue. Each of the major parties ran a full slate of candidates, and there were a number of fringe and independent candidates as well. The MLP, which ran a Euro-skeptic campaign, outpolled the ruling PN, while the small pro-EU green-oriented Democratic Alternative (*Alternattiva Demokratika*—AD) gained no seats but had its highest electoral vote in history at 9.3 percent. The MLP received 48.4 percent of the vote and three seats, and the PN secured 39.8 percent and two seats.

During the campaign for the March 8, 2008, legislative elections, Prime Minister Gonzi's PN ruled out the possibility of forming a coalition with the AD. The election contest thereby became a debate principally between the PN and MLP, despite increased public attention on immigration issues and the emergence of two new political parties (the National Action and Empire Europe) with strong anti-immigrant positions. The PN outpolled the MLP by a slim margin in the national vote, but it won only 31 seats, based on the results within the voting districts. As in 1987, the PN was awarded 4 more seats, giving it a 35–34 majority. President Adami subsequently reappointed Gonzi as prime minister, and Gonzi was sworn in on March 11. His cabinet was approved and sworn in the following day.

After lengthy negotiations, an agreement was announced in July by the PN and MLP to cooperate through a new special committee in the House of Representatives designed to facilitate compromise on outstanding issues. The accord was considered a victory for the MLP, which had long complained of being left out of the decision-making process during the last 20 years of PN rule. Prime Minister Gonzi's government also reached across the aisle and nominated George ABELA of the MLP for president. The House of Representatives unanimously approved Abela on the same day, and he was sworn in on April 4.

The MLP won four seats in the June 2009 balloting for the European Parliament, while the PN won two. Prime Minister Gonzi struggled to hold onto his one-seat parliamentary majority due to party defections in 2011 and 2012. Backbencher Franco DEBONO frequently clashed with Gonzi and threatened to withhold his vote on key legislation. (See Current Issues, below.)

Constitution and government. The 1964 constitution established Malta as an independent parliamentary monarchy within the Commonwealth, with executive power exercised by a prime minister and cabinet, both appointed by the governor general but chosen from and responsible to parliament. By constitutional amendment, the country became a republic on December 13, 1974, with an indirectly elected president of Maltese nationality replacing the British monarch as de jure head of state. The president serves a five-year term, as does the prime minister, subject to the retention of a legislative majority. The parliament consists of a unicameral House of Representatives elected on the basis of proportional representation every five years, assuming no prior dissolution. Under an amendment adopted in February 1987, the party winning a majority of the popular vote is awarded additional House seats, if needed to secure a legislative majority.

The judicial system encompasses a Constitutional Court, a Court of Appeal, a Criminal Court of Appeal, and lower courts. The president appoints the judges for the Constitutional Court and the Court of Appeal. There was little established local government in Malta until 1993, when a Local Councils Act (subsequently amended) was passed. In 2001 provisions for local councils were incorporated into the constitution. At present, there are 68 directly elected local councils, 54 on the island of Malta and 14 on Gozo.

Reporters Without Borders ranked Malta 45th out of 179 countries in its 2013 Index of Press Freedom. Many print and broadcast outlets are owned by political parties, unions, or the Catholic Church.

Foreign relations. After independence, Maltese foreign policy centered primarily on the country's relationship with Great Britain and thus with the North Atlantic Treaty Organization (NATO). A ten-year Mutual Defense and Assistance Agreement, signed in 1964, was abrogated in 1971 by the Mintoff government. Under a new seven-year agreement, concluded in 1972 after months of negotiation, the rental payments for use of military facilities by Britain were tripled. Early in 1973 Mintoff reopened the issue, asking additional payment to compensate for devaluation of the British pound, but he settled for a token adjustment pending British withdrawal from the facilities in March 1979. Rebuffed in an effort to obtain a quadripartite guarantee of Maltese neutrality and a five-year budgetary subsidy from France, Italy, Algeria, and Libya, the Mintoff government turned to Libya. During ceremonies marking the British departure, the Libyan leader, Col. Muammar al-Qadhafi, promised "unlimited" support. In the course of the following year, however, the relationship cooled because of overlapping claims to offshore oil rights, and in September 1980 an agreement was concluded with Italy whereby Rome guaranteed Malta's future neutrality and promised a combination of loans and subsidies totaling $95 million over a five-year period. In 1981 Malta also signed neutrality agreements with Algeria, France, and the Soviet Union.

In December 1984 Prime Minister Mintoff announced that the defense and aid agreement with Italy would be permitted to lapse in favor of a new alignment with Libya, which would undertake to train Maltese forces to withstand "threats or acts of aggression." Six months later the maritime issue was resolved, the International Court of Justice establishing a boundary 18 nautical miles north of a line equidistant between the two countries.

In March 1986 Prime Minister Karmenu Mifsud Bonnici met with Colonel Qadhafi in Tripoli in what was described as an effort to ease the confrontation between Libya and the United States in the Gulf of Sidra. In August the Maltese leader stated that his government had warned Libya of the approach of "unidentified planes" prior to the April attack by U.S. aircraft on Tripoli and Benghazi, although there was no indication that Libyan authorities had acted on the information.

Upon assuming office in May 1987, Prime Minister Fenech Adami indicated that the military clauses of the 1984 agreement with Libya would not be renewed, although all other commitments would be continued. Cooperation between the two countries at the political and economic levels was reaffirmed in 1988, with Libya renewing its $38 million oil supply pact with Malta late in the year.

A member of the United Nations, the Conference on (later Organization for) Security and Cooperation in Europe (CSCE/OSCE), and a number of other international organizations, Malta concluded an association agreement with the European Community (EC) in 1970 and in July 1990 applied for full membership. The government's perseverance in the face of initial reservations in Brussels was rewarded by a decision of the EU summit in Essen in December 1994 that Malta would be included in the next round of enlargement negotiations.

While maintaining its neutrality, Malta also joined NATO's Partnership for Peace (PfP) program in April 1995. Following Labour's victory at the polls in October 1996, Prime Minister Sant suspended participation, contending that Malta could best promote regional stability by a policy of neutrality that was neither anti-European nor anti-American. He also made it clear that Malta would continue to observe UN sanctions imposed on Tripoli over the Lockerbie affair, while expressing the hope that the sanctions would soon be lifted.

Almost immediately following his victory in the snap election of September 1998, Prime Minister Fenech Adami accelerated Malta's pursuit of EU membership. In February 1999, following Malta's reintroduction of the VAT, the European Commission recommended that accession talks with Malta start later in the year. In 2000–2002 the government continued its efforts to bring the Maltese economy in line with EU standards, sparking further attacks from the MLP, which argued that EU accession would freeze crucial foreign investment, decimate Malta's manufacturing and agricultural sectors, and raise administrative costs. Malta signed the EU accession treaty in 2003 and joined the EU on May 1, 2004. Although the MLP had opposed Maltese inclusion in the EU, it joined the PN in supporting accession to the eurozone in 2008 with the expectation that adopting the euro would increase tourism and foreign investment.

Following the PN's victory in March 2008, Malta reactivated its PfP membership in April. Officials noted that the country had been unable to participate in training exercises that would help its own armed forces and had been barred from attending EU–NATO meetings. In September 2011 MLP leader Joseph MUSCAT said that a future Labour government would not reverse that decision but complained that the decision was made before the new parliament convened.

Relations with the EU were damaged in 2012 when PN politician John DALLI resigned as EU commissioner for health and consumer policy. An internal investigation by the EU accused Dalli of influence peddling, specifically, telling a Swedish tobacco firm that he could arrange for exemptions from EU laws. Dalli resigned and was replaced by Deputy Prime Minister and Foreign Minister Tonio BORG, also of the PN. Dalli later asked the European Court of Justice to annul his resignation and award him compensation, saying he had been forced to resign by EC president José Manuel Barroso.

CURRENT ISSUES

Current issues. Malta's strategic location has meant that it is often the intercepting country for illegal immigrants from Africa, many attempting to make their way through Malta to the European mainland. Between 2002 and 2013, 16,617 migrants arrived in Malta, most from Somalia, Eritrea, and Libya. In July 2009 the EU launched a two-year €2 million pilot project, European Relocation Malta (Eurema), that provided financial assistance for EU member states that would resettle asylum seekers from Malta. While Germany agreed to accept over 100 persons, other states will only consider between five and ten refugees.

The Maltese government closely monitored the 2011 civil war in Libya and cut ties with Colonel Qadhafi shortly before his regime collapsed. Thousands of refugees from Libya sought asylum in Malta—2,000 on April 30, 2011, alone—prompting the EU to extend Eurema for at least one more year. Malta helped evacuate 12,000 citizens from 89 different countries from Libya in February 2011, and the World Health Organization based its Libyan relief operations in Malta.

In July 2011 the Maltese legislature passed a law that made divorce legal under certain conditions, following a nonbinding referendum on the issue in which 53 percent of the voters supported the measure. This significant shift among the strongly Roman Catholic population opened government consideration of other social issues, including same-sex marriage and in-vitro fertilization.

Debono backed a June 4, 2012, Labour no-confidence vote on Home Affairs Minister Carmelo MIFSUD BONNICI due to deficiencies with the police and other services in his portfolio.

Gonzi's economic policies came under fire from several directions. While the International Monetary Fund (IMF) predicted GDP growth in 2012, the European Commission questioned the optimism of Gonzi's 2012 budget and asked for spending cuts worth €40 million. Labour seized this request as an opportunity to loudly condemn Gonzi's plan to build a new €80 million parliament building.

On December 10 PN backbencher Debono withdrew his support for the 2013 budget, particularly a plan to outsource Malta's public bus service to a Germany company. The defection triggered the dissolution of parliament. In elections held on March 9, 2013, the PN lost control of parliament, polling 43.34 percent of the vote, good for 30 seats. After 15 years in opposition, the Labour Party returned to power with 54.83 percent of the vote and 39 seats, the largest vote share since 1955. MLP leader Joseph Muscat was sworn in as prime minister and vowed to fulfill his platform of promoting economic growth, fighting corruption, and reducing energy costs by 25 percent.

The auditor general released a scathing report in July 2013 regarding the amateurish management of the Enemalta fuel procurement committee from 2008 through 2010. Executives stood accused of taking kickbacks and price-fixing. Few policy documents existed, and meeting minutes were often "handwritten and undecipherable." Austin GATT, the PN appointee responsible for Enemalta, blithely announced that he was "not interested" in the findings.

The number of migrants intercepted or rescued by Maltese forces increased in mid-2013. The government tried to push back a ship carrying 45 migrants from Libya in July. A three-day standoff between Malta and Italy ensued in August, when Malta refused entry to a tanker carrying 102 migrants rescued in the waters near Libya. Italy eventually accepted the migrants. On October 3 a ship carrying 500 migrants from Africa capsized near Lampedusa Island, and more than 300 perished. A boat carrying 250 migrants from Syria sank on October 11, prompting Muscat to warn that the Mediterranean is being turned into a cemetery. He appealed to the EU to formulate a common strategy regarding immigration.

POLITICAL PARTIES

Government Party:

Malta Labour Party—MLP (*Partit Laburista*). In power from 1971 to 1987, the MLP advocated a socialist and "progressive" policy, including anticolonialism in international affairs, a neutralist foreign policy, and emphasis on Malta's role as "a bridge of peace between Europe and the Arab world." The party has periodically complained of intrusion by the Catholic Church into political and economic affairs.

In the election of December 1981 the MLP's vote share fell to 49.1 percent from 51.2 percent in 1976 but without loss of its three-seat majority in the House of Representatives; its vote share fell further, to 48.8 percent, in 1987 when it moved into opposition, and continued its decline, to 46.5 percent, in 1992, prompting former prime minister Karmenu Mifsud Bonnici to announce his retirement as party leader. His successor, Alfred Sant, initiated a modernization of the party's organization and policies while maintaining the MLP's commitment to neutrality and opposition to EU accession. Labour returned to power in 1996, winning 50.7 percent of the popular vote but was ousted when it secured only 47 percent in September 1998. In the 2003 elections the MLP received 47.5 percent of the vote and 30 seats. As a result of the election, Sant resigned as party leader, but he was subsequently reelected to the post. Sant resigned again following the March 2008 legislative poll, in which the MLP had won a majority of seats (34) but finished second (with 48.8 percent of the votes) to the PN as far as the total vote was concerned. Sant was succeeded as MLP leader by Joseph Muscat, a 34-year-old member of the European Parliament, who won the June 6 party leadership election on the second ballot. In January 2009 Prime Minister Gonzi announced his government would nominate MLP member George Abela for the Maltese presidency. Abela officially resigned from the party to pave the way for his accession to the post on April 1.

The MLP scored a resounding victory in the June 2009 balloting in Malta for the European Parliament by securing 55 percent of the vote, compared to 40 percent for the PN and only 2.3 percent for the AD. Most analysts attributed the MLP's surge to dissatisfaction among the populace over rising unemployment and steady increases in the cost of living. The MLP also led in concurrent balloting for one-third of the nation's local councils.

The MLP regained control of parliament in elections held March 9, 2013, taking 39 seats and 54.83 percent of the vote.

Leaders: Joseph MUSCAT (Prime Minister of Malta and Party Leader); Louis GRECH (Deputy Prime Minister of Malta and Deputy Party Leader); Toni ABELA (Deputy Leader); Daniel MICALLEF (President); Lydia ABELA (Executive Secretary).

Opposition Party:

Nationalist Party (*Partit Nazzjonalista*—PN). Advocating the retention of Roman Catholic and European principles, the PN brought Malta to independence. It formerly supported alignment with NATO and membership in the EC, but because of a constitutional pact with Labour, in February 1987 it adopted a neutral foreign policy. The party obtained 50.9 percent of the vote in the 1981 election without, however, winning control of the legislature. In the 1987 balloting it again obtained only a minority of elective seats but under the February constitutional amendment was permitted to form a government because of its popular majority.

The Nationalists retained power in the 1992 election but were unexpectedly defeated in 1996, when their share of the popular vote slipped from 51.8 to 47.8 percent. The PN returned to power in the election of September 1998 with a vote share of 51.8 percent. In the April 2003 elections, the PN won 51.8 percent and 35 seats. In March 2004 Edward Fenech Adami, theretofore the prime minister, was elected president, and PN Vice Chair Lawrence Gonzi became prime minister.

Although the PN finished second in seat totals to the MLP in the 2008 legislative poll, it secured a plurality of the nationwide votes (49.3 percent) and was therefore awarded additional seats to give it a slim parliamentary majority and continued governmental control.

Internal bickering eclipsed policymaking in 2011 and 2012, and on July 12, 2012, the PN executive committee announced that three current members of parliament (MPs), Jeffrey PULLICINO ORLANDO, Franco DEBONO, and Jesmond MUGLIETT, would not be on the PN list for the next parliamentary election because they had "voted with the opposition" twice in June (for details see the 2013 *Handbook*). Debono's refusal to support the budget led to the collapse of the Gonzi government in December 2012. The party dropped from 35 seats to 30 following the parliamentary election of March 9, 2013, and lost control of the government after 15 years in power. Gonzi immediately resigned as party chair. Simon BUSUTTIL, a lawyer and member of the European Parliament, was elected deputy party chair when Tonio BORG resigned in late 2012. Busuttil beat three opponents to become party chair in May 2013.

After the election, the PN was discovered to be on the brink of bankruptcy. The party and its affiliated media holdings were at least €8 million in debt. Over half of the staff was laid off, and plans were made to sell off property and real estate belonging to the party. Angry party members accused Gonzi of fiscal mismanagement.

Leaders: Simon BUSUTTIL (Chair), Lawrence GONZI (Former Prime Minister), Mario DE MARCO (Deputy Chair), Chris SAID (Secretary General).

Other Parties That Contested the 2013 Legislative Election:

Democratic Alternative (*Alternattiva Demokratika*—AD). An ecologically oriented grouping launched in 1989, the AD, also referenced as the Maltese Green Party, ran a distant third in the 1992 balloting, securing no legislative seats on a vote share of 1.7 percent. It was again unsuccessful in 1996, when its vote share slipped to 1.5 percent, and in September 1998, when it won 1.2 percent of the vote. In the 2003 elections the AD received only 0.7 percent of the vote, and, after the AD won only 1.3 percent in 2008, Harry VASSALO resigned as party leader. The AD collected 5,506 votes in 2013 (1.8 percent). Michael BRIGUGLIO subsequently declined to seek another term as party leader.

Leaders: Arnold CASSOLA (Chair), Carmel CACOPARDO (Deputy Chair), Ralph CASSAR (Secretary General).

For information on the defunct **National Action** (*Azzjoni Nazzjonali*—AN) party, please see the 2013 *Handbook*.

LEGISLATURE

The **House of Representatives** (*Il-Kamra Tad-Deputati*) consists of 65 elective members returned for a five-year term (subject to dissolution) on the basis of proportional representation applied in 13 electoral districts. The constitution requires that the party obtaining the highest number of votes nationwide must also end up with a legislative majority, assuming only two parties win seats. Consequently, if a party wins the nationwide vote but trails in seats awarded in the district results, it is given enough additional seats to reach a majority.

In the most recent election, held March 9, 2013, the Malta Labour Party (MLP) secured a majority with 39 seats, winning a majority in 23 of 35 electoral districts. The Nationalist Party (PN) won only 26 seats, but it was awarded 4 additional seats because of its share of first-preference votes.

Speaker: Angelo FARRUGIA.

CABINET

[as of October 15, 2013]

Prime Minister	Joseph Muscat
Deputy Prime Minister	Louis Grech
Ministers	
Economy, Investment, and Small Business	Christian Cardona
Education and Employment	Evarist Bartolo
Energy and Conservation of Water	Konrad Mizzi
European Affairs and Implementation of the Electoral Manifesto	Louis Grech
Family and Social Solidarity	Marie-Louise Coleiro Preca [f]
Finance	Edward Scicluna
Foreign Affairs	George Vella

Gozo Island	Anton Refalo
Health	Godfrey Farrugia
Home Affairs and National Security	Emanuel Mallia
Social Dialogue, Consumer Affairs, and Civil Liberties	Helena Dalli [f]
Sustainable Development, Environment, and Climate Change	Leo Brincat
Tourism	Karmenu Vella
Transport and Infrastructure	Joe Mizzi

[f] = female

INTERGOVERNMENTAL REPRESENTATION

Ambassador to the U.S.: Marisa Maria Louise MISCALLEF.

U.S. Ambassador to Malta: Gina ABERCROMBIE-WINSTANELY.

Permanent Representative to the UN: Christopher GRIMA.

IGO Memberships (Non-UN): CEUR, CWTH, EBRD, EIB, EU, ICC, IOM, OSCE, WTO.

MARSHALL ISLANDS

Republic of the Marshall Islands

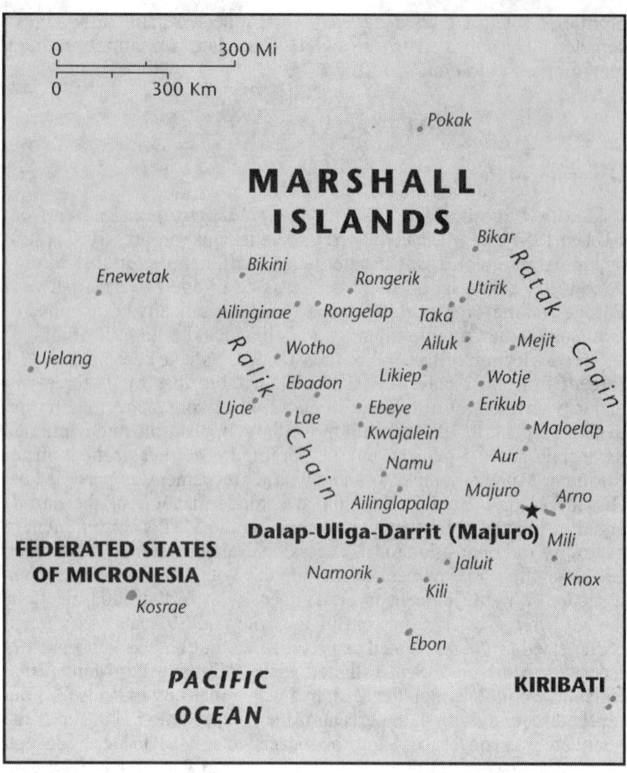

Political Status: Sovereign state in free association with the United States (which retains authority with regard to defense) since October 21, 1986.

Area: 70 sq. mi. (181 sq. km).

Population: 53,158 (2011E—UN); 69,747 (2013E—U.S. Census). (It is estimated that more than 20,000 of the Marshellese citizens reside in the United States.)

Major Urban Center (2005E): DALAP-ULIGA-DARRIT (Majuro Atoll; 26,000).

Official Languages: Marshallese. English is also widely spoken.

Monetary Unit: U.S. Dollar (see the entry on United States for principal exchange rates).

President: Christopher J. LOEAK (Our Islands); elected by the House of Representatives following the legislative elections on November 21, 2011, and inaugurated (along with his new cabinet) on January 17, 2012, to succeed Jurelang ZEDKAIA.

THE COUNTRY

The Republic of the Marshall Islands (RMI) consists of a double chain of coral atolls and islands (comprising 29 atolls, 5 single islands, and more than 850 reefs) within the Pacific region known as Micronesia, some 2,000 miles southwest of Hawaii. The two chains are about 80 miles apart, the eastern (which includes the capital, Majuro) being known as the Rataks ("Sunrise") Chain and the western (which includes Bikini, Eniwetak, and Kwajalein) being known as the Ralik ("Sunset") Chain. More than 90 percent of the inhabitants are indigenous Marshallese. Christianity is the principal religion, with adherents of Roman Catholicism the most numerous. Copra products have long dominated exports, although a decline in copra oil prices in the early 1980s led to a severe trade imbalance. The sale of fishing licenses and income from fishing-related services now make up a significant portion of external earnings. Financial assistance from the United States (currently at about $80 million annually, approximately 60 percent of the RMI budget) is a crucial component of government revenue for a country whose GDP declined by nearly 25 percent in 1995–2001, with debt servicing equaling about 40 percent of budget outlays and far exceeding export earnings. For a number of years the unemployment rate has been relatively unchanged at around 30 percent; nearly half of those in the salaried work force are employed by the government. The government has recently asked for additional international aid to combat the so-called lifestyle diseases that have become prevalent.

In late 2007 the Organization for Economic Cooperation and Development (OECD) removed the Marshalls from the watch list of "uncooperative" tax havens after the government pledged to improve the transparency of its accounts. However it was subsequently placed on an OECD's "gray list," members of which must negotiate tax information exchange agreements with a minimum of 12 countries to be moved onto the OECD's "white list." Although the RMI does not license offshore financial activity (a primary focus of OECD attention), it has attracted scrutiny in regard to its large nonresident corporate registry and flag of convenience ship registry, both of which can be used for tax evasion purposes. The RMI was also strongly criticized for poor safety standards affiliated with its ship registry (at approximately 2,500 vessels the third largest in the world) in 2010, when it was learned that the Deepwater Horizon oil rig, which exploded in the Gulf of Mexico in April 2010, was registered in the RMI.

According to the International Monetary Fund (IMF), GDP rebounded to 5.6 percent growth in fiscal year 2010 after contracting the previous two years under the influence of the global financial crisis. However growth declined to 0.8 percent in fiscal year 2011.

In the wake of a continuing investigation of government employees allegedly involved in fraud in regard to U.S. grants, the United States in March 2012 added the RMI to its "concern list" regarding money laundering. In a possibly related vein, several months later France put the RMI on the French blacklist of uncooperative nations regarding tax matters.

The IMF in late 2012 called upon the RMI government to reduce subsidies to state-owned enterprises, reform the public employee pension system, and revamp the tax code in the interest of promoting the budgetary self-reliance that will be required when the grant component of the current Compact of Association with the United States expires in 2023.

GOVERNMENT AND POLITICS

Political background. Purchased by Germany from Spain in 1899, the Marshalls were seized in 1914 by Japan and retained as part of the mandate awarded by the League of Nations in 1920. The islands were occupied by U.S. forces near the end of World War II and (along with the Caroline and Northern Mariana islands) became part of the U.S. Trust Territory of the Pacific in 1947. In 1965 a Congress of Micronesia was established, with the Marshalls electing 4 of the 21 members of the Congress's House of Representatives. Subsequently the Marshall Islands district drafted its own constitution, which came into effect on May 1, 1979. Three years later the RMI concluded a Compact of Free Association with the United States, which was declared to be in effect on October 21, 1986, following ratification by the U.S. Congress and final approval by the RMI government. Under the Compact, the RMI became a fully sovereign state, save with regard to defense, which was to remain a U.S. responsibility for at least a 15-year period (see below for information on extension of the Compact); the RMI was also obligated to "consult" with Washington regarding major foreign policy matters.

The islands' first president was Amata KABUA, who assumed office on May 1, 1979, and was subsequently reelected to four successive four-year terms. He died on December 20, 1996, while undergoing medical treatment in Honolulu. Minister of Transportation Kunio D. LEMARI was named acting president pending legislative designation of a successor. In balloting within the House of Representatives (*Nitijela*) on January 14, 1997, Imata KABUA (a cousin of Amata KABUA and a minister without portfolio in the previous government) was elected to fulfill the remainder of Amata Kabua's term.

In the legislative poll of November 15, 1999, the United Democratic Party (UDP) won a first-ever majority for an opposition group, and on January 3, 2000, the UDP named Kessai H. NOTE, theretofore *Nitijela* speaker, to succeed Imata Kabua as president. (Note was the first commoner to be elected president.)

On November 1, 2002, after several rounds of negotiations, the U.S.'s George W. Bush administration and the Note government initialed a new 20-year Compact of Association. However the RMI voiced reservations with regard to specific monetary figures pending completion of negotiations governing future use by the United States of the defense facilities on Kwajalein (a major contributor to the RMI economy). That issue was resolved in early 2003 when the United States agreed on a five-year lease renewal for the Kwajalein missile range, which had been renamed the Ronald Reagan Missile Defense Test Site in 2001. Consequently the new compact was signed in May, providing for some $960 million in grants through 2023 and an annual U.S. contribution of $7 million toward a trust fund, which was scheduled to provide budgetary support after the conclusion of the grant component. The new compact also preserved the right of citizens to enter, reside, and work in the United States without visas.

On November 17, 2003, the UDP secured a 20-seat majority in the *Nitijela,* and on January 4, 2004, President Note won reelection by a 20–9 House vote over Justin DeBRUM. Subsequently in 2005 concern was expressed in the RMI that the trust fund established under the Compact of Free Association with the United States might not be sufficient to finance government services following the scheduled cessation of grants in 2023.

The Our Islands (*Ailon Kein* Ad—AKA) grouping and its allies (primarily the United People's Party [UPP]) won a majority of seats in the November 19, 2007, balloting for the *Nitijela*. Consequently, Note's bid for a third term was rejected on January 7, 2008, by the *Nitijela,* which elected its speaker, Litokwa TOMEING of the UPP, as Note's successor. However, Tomeing was obliged to vacate the presidency by the country's first successful nonconfidence vote on October 21, 2009. Five days later, the AKA's Jurelang ZEDKAIA was elected president by a two-vote margin over Note. (See Current issues and Political Groups, below.)

President Zedkaia and his supporters (now reportedly aligned as the Our Government [*Kein Eo Am*—KEA] political grouping) were unable to gain a legislative majority in the November 21, 2011, balloting for the House of Representatives. Consequently, with the support of Note's UDP and independents, Christopher J. LOEAK of the rump AKA was elected president by a vote of 21–11 in the *Nitijela* on January 2, 2012.

Constitution and government. The 1979 constitution provides for a bicameral parliament whose popularly elected lower house, the *Nitijela,* performs most legislative functions. The 33-member *Nitijela* selects from its own ranks an executive president, who serves for the duration of the four-year parliamentary term, assuming the retention of parliamentary support. The upper house is a council of 12 traditional chiefs who make recommendations with regard to customary law and practice. Municipalities are governed by elected magistrates and councils, while villages follow traditional forms of rule.

The judicial system encompasses a Supreme Court (comprising three part-time justices resident in the United States); a High Court, which presides over District and Community Courts; and a Traditional Rights Court, which deals primarily with land and customary title disputes. The latter, inactive for many years, was revived in mid-2010 with a number of new government appointments.

The RMI is highly ranked in regard to press freedom.

Foreign relations. The effective degree of the RMI's autonomy in foreign affairs is not entirely clear. In early 1987 the *Nitijela* debated whether to endorse the Treaty of Rarotonga, which called for the establishment of a South Pacific Nuclear Free Zone. However, unlike the Federated States of Micronesia (see separate entry), the RMI decided not to take action in the matter after a Washington official had termed adherence "inappropriate" given the U.S. obligation under the Compact to defend the Marshalls, coupled with the U.S. decision not to sign the document.

In December 1990 the UN Security Council formally abrogated the U.S. Trusteeship in respect to the Marshall Islands, the Federated States of Micronesia, and the Commonwealth of the Northern Marianas, and in September 1991 both the FSM and the Marshalls were admitted to the United Nations. In May 1992 the Marshalls became the 161st member of the IMF and the 157th member of the World Bank. Regionally, the RMI belongs to the Asian Development Bank, the Pacific Community, and the Pacific Islands Forum.

Following independence, the Marshalls joined a number of Pacific neighbors in attempting to attract investors by the sale of passports to Asians. By mid-1996 the practice was officially suspended in the wake of complaints by allegedly disadvantaged Marshallese businesses and objections by the U.S. State Department on the impact of such sales on the Compact provision granting islanders the right of entry into the United States. Because of the problem, Washington initiated a policy late in the year of denying entry to passport holders whose places of birth were other than the Marshalls.

In November 1998 the Marshalls established diplomatic relations with Taiwan, hoping thereby to attract both trade and investment. Already linked to the People's Republic of China (PRC), the RMI government hoped that a "two-Chinas" policy might be possible; however, the PRC, saying that the Marshalls "must correct their mistake," severed relations three weeks later.

In April 2006 the RMI government supported a lawsuit by residents of Bikini against the United States for nonpayment of approximately $560 million of a 2000 award and $150 million of a 2001 award by the Marshall Islands Nuclear Claims Tribunal (NCT). The NCT had been allocated $150 million by the 1986 compact to pay for claims associated with the 67 tests of nuclear weapons conducted by the United States from1946–1958. Following the disbursement of the original funds, no money was available to cover the new awards. (In April 2010 the U.S. Supreme Court rejected a petition from the RMI plaintiffs to review a lower court decision that the 1986 payments were final and that no additional funds were legally required.)

In recent years, the Marshalls has joined a number of its low-lying neighbors in warning of the consequences of an anticipated rise in sea levels because of global warming. It demonstrated its concern by participating in the global meeting on climate change in Copenhagen in late 2009. Subsequently, however, it complained that very little of the $45 billion pledged at the meeting had been given to the Marshall Islands and other low-lying countries that needed it.

The new government installed in 2012 complained that the RMI was losing development assistance because of its close alignment with the United States in the UN. Among other things, RMI officials said they had lost aid from Arab states because of the RMI's adherence to the U.S. stance on UN votes concerning Israel. The RMI also continued to press the United States for additional compensation in regard to the Nuclear Claims Tribunal. In that vein, a special UN rapporteur concluded in 2013 that "durable solutions" to the dislocation of the island inhabitants by the U.S. nuclear tests have not yet been found.

Current issues. In early 2008 residents of Kwajalein Atoll temporarily rejected extension of a land-use agreement with the U.S. Defense Department for the Reagan test site, insisting that they be given $19 million in annual rent rather than the $15 million offered by the

Pentagon. The dispute prompted a split between President Tomeing, who favored conciliatory talks with Washington over the issue, and his influential foreign minister, Tony DeBRUM, who, as a legislator from Kwajalein, called for a confrontational posture. Faced with the potential loss of a confidence vote, Tomeing expelled DeBrum from the cabinet in February 2009 and took the unusual approach of bringing five opposition members into a drastically reshuffled cabinet. As a result of the complicated dispute, Tomeing was ousted by a nonconfidence vote of 17–15 in the House of Representatives on October 21, as several AKA legislators supported his ouster. Following his election on October 26, President Zedkaia announced a cabinet that retained most of the previous members.

The Kwajalein dispute was finally resolved in May 2011, when the landowners accepted the initial offer of $15 million per year, bolstered by an escrow account that had grown to an additional $32 million. The agreement provided for 50 more years of U.S. use of the missile range.

The run-up to the November 2011 legislative poll was complicated by an apparent split within the AKA and the emergence of the new pro-Zedkaia KEA. President Zedkaia and his supporters pledged to continue recent government economic initiatives and to protect islanders' access to the United States in the face of proposed new restrictions. (Several members of the U.S. Congress had recently called for limitations to be imposed on the visa-free system because of the increasing expenses being borne by U.S. states in assisting RMI immigrants.) Meanwhile, the rump AKA (at that point the leading opposition group) called for improved educational services and intensified cooperation between the government and the business sector. Following the election of Christopher Loeak, a traditional chief and longtime senator, as the nation's new president in January 2012, Zedkaia promised that he and his allies would cooperate with the new administration, which included Tony DeBrum as an influential assistant to the president.

A state of emergency was declared in May 2013 in the wake of a severe prolonged drought that RMI officials characterized as symptomatic of the problems presented by climate change, which the RMI argued threatens low-lying countries with "oblivion" unless high-emitting, developed countries adopt drastic measures to curb global warming.

POLITICAL GROUPS

Traditionally there have been no formal parties in the Marshalls. In the 1991 legislative balloting, however, an Our Islands "presidential caucus" chaired by Amata Kabua defeated a Ralik-Ratak Democratic Party organized by Tony DeBrum, a former Kabua protégé. Several other groups have also recently emerged, although their structures and formal memberships remain amorphous and fluid.

Our Islands (*Ailon Kein Ad*—AKA). An outgrowth of the earlier Our Islands caucus, the AKA was formally launched in 2002. It contested the November 2007 legislative elections in coalition with the **United People's Party** (UPP), a conservative grouping to which Litokwa Tomeing of the UDP (below) had recently defected. After several successful independent legislative candidates announced their support for the AKA/UPP coalition, Tomeing, a traditional chief, was elected president of the republic in January 2008. However, following a split between Tomeing and influential AKA leader Tony DeBrum in 2008–2009 (see Current issues, above), many AKA legislators supported the nonconfidence motion that ousted Tomeing in October 2009. Tomeing's successor, Jurelang Zedkaia, was also referenced as a member of the AKA, but shortly before the 2011 legislative balloting, Tomeing and his supporters reportedly launched a new grouping (see KEA, below). The rump AKA (for a short time considered an opposition grouping following the formation of the KEA) was credited by some sources with securing approximately 11 legislative seats in the November poll. The AKA subsequently reached an agreement with the UDP that led to the election of the AKA's Christopher Loeak in January 2012 as president of the republic.

Leaders: Christopher LOEAK (President of the Republic), Michael KABUA, Tony DeBRUM.

United Democratic Party (UDP). The main opposition grouping prior to the legislative poll of November 1999, the UDP supported the successful presidential candidacy of Kessai Note in 2000 and his reelection in 2004. The UDP was credited with controlling 13–15 seats following the 2007 balloting for the House of Representatives.

In January 2008 Note lost his bid for a third presidential term by a vote of 18–15 in the *Nitijela* to Litokwa Tomeing, a protégé of Note's who had left the UDP to join the UPP (see AKA, above) shortly before the 2007 legislative poll. After Tomeing was deposed by a nonconfidence vote in October 2009, Note reportedly attempted to secure enough parliamentary support for his own candidacy to return to the presidency. When that effort failed, some of the UDP legislators reportedly endorsed the successful candidacy of the AKA's Jurelang Zedkaia, although Note's relationship with the Zedkaia administration subsequently remained distant.

Note and his UDP supporters reportedly secured control of approximately five seats in the November 2011 legislative poll and subsequently formed an anti-Zedkaia alliance with the rump AKA in support of the successful presidential candidacy of the AKA's Christopher Loeak in January 2012. Consequently, Note allies were appointed to several key positions in the new cabinet.

Leaders: Kessai H. NOTE (Former President of the Republic), Donald F. CAPELLE (Speaker of the House of Representatives).

Our Government (*Kien Eo Am*—KEA). The KEA was reportedly formed in October 2011 by supporters of President Zedkaia and other legislators and cabinet members (including Alvin Jacklick, then speaker of the House of Representatives) who had apparently separated from the AKA. Initial reports credited the KEA and its supporters with gaining control of approximately 15 seats (including seats for Zedkaia and Jacklick) in the House of Representatives in the November poll, but Zedkaia earned only 11 (out of 32) votes in his unsuccessful bid to retain the presidency in January 2012. It was subsequently unclear if the KEA would continue to function as a political grouping.

Leaders: Jurelang ZEDKAIA (Former President of the Republic), Alvin JACKLICK (Former Speaker of the House of Representatives), Litowka TOMEING (Former President of the Republic).

LEGISLATURE

Technically, a bicameral system prevails, although only the lower house, the *Nitijela,* engages in normal legislative activity.

Council of Chiefs (Council of *Iroij*). The council is composed of 12 traditional leaders who tender advice on matters affecting customary law and practice.

Chair: Iroij Kotak LOEAK.

House of Representatives (*Nitijela*). The *Nitijela* comprises 33 members (called senators) directly elected on a majoritarian basis for four-year terms from 24 electoral districts (19 single-member, 5 multi-member). Initial reports on the most recent balloting on November 21, 2011, credited Our Government and other allies of incumbent president Jurelang Zedkaia with controlling approximately 15 seats; the revamped Our Islands and its allies, 11; the United Democratic Party, 5; and independents, 2. (Affiliations with political groupings are very loose, and election results should be considered imprecise.)

Speaker: Donald F. CAPELLE.

CABINET

[as of August 1, 2013]

President	Christopher J. Loeak
Ministers	
Assistance to the President	Tony A. DeBrum
Education	Hilda C. Heine [f]
Finance	Denis P. Momotaro
Foreign Affairs	Phillip H. Muller
Health	David Kabua
Internal Affairs	Wilbur Heine
Justice	Thomas Heine
Public Works	Hiroshi Yamamura
Resources and Development	Michael Konelios
Transportation and Communications	Rien Morris

[f] = female

INTERGOVERNMENTAL REPRESENTATION

Ambassador to the U.S.: Charles Rudolf PAUL.

U.S. Ambassador to the Marshall Islands: Thomas Hart ARMBRUSTER.

Permanent Representative to the UN: Amatlain Elizabeth KABUA.

IGO Memberships (Non-UN): ADB, ICC, PIF.

MAURITANIA

Islamic Republic of Mauritania
al-Jumhuriyah al-Islamiyah al-Muritaniyah

Note: Mauritania held the first round of parliamentary elections on November 23, 2013, and a second round on December 21. The elections solidified the position of the ruling Union for the Republic party (UPR), earning them 75 seats in the 146-seat National Assembly. UPR Coalition partners took an additional 34 seats. The opposition largely boycotted the elections; however, the Islamic opposition party National Rally for Reform and Development participated, earning 12 seats for a total of 16 in the National Assembly. The election, postponed since October 2011, was largely peaceful despite opposition claims of fraud.

Political Status: Independent republic since November 28, 1960; 1961 constitution suspended by the Military Committee for National Recovery on July 20, 1978; present constitution, providing for multiparty civilian government, approved by referendum July 12, 1991; constitution suspended by the High Council of State following bloodless coup on August 6, 2008; multiparty civilian government restored following presidential election on July 18, 2009.

Area: 397,953 sq. mi. (1,030,700 sq. km).

Population: 3,629,960 (2012E—UN); 3,437,610 (2013E—U.S. Census).

Major Urban Center (2011E—UN): NOUAKCHOTT (846,871). In recent years the population of Nouakchott has grown rapidly, as many former nomads have taken up permanent residence in the capital since the 1970s.

Official Language: Arabic. (Three languages of the Black African community—Poular, Soninke, and Wolof—are constitutionally designated as national languages. French, an official language until 1991, is still widely spoken, particularly in the commercial sector. In addition, in 1999 the government designated French as the "language for science and technical subjects" in Mauritanian schools.)

Monetary Unit: Ouguiya (official rate November 1, 2013: 299.54 ouguiyas = $1US).

President: Gen. Mohamed Ould ABDELAZIZ (Union for the Republic), elected for a five-year term in multiparty balloting on July 18, 2009, to succeed Interim President Ba Mamadou MBARÉ, who had acceded from Senate president on April 15 following Abdelaziz's resignation the same day as chair of the High Council of State; inaugurated on August 5, 2009.

Prime Minister: Moulaye Ould Mohamed LAGHDAF, appointed by the chair of the High Council of State on August 14, 2008, to succeed Yahya Ould Ahmed el-WAGHF (National Pact for Development and Democracy), who was ousted in the bloodless coup on August 6; named new government on August 31; reinstated with new transitional government on June 26, 2009; reappointed by the president on August 6, 2009, and formed new government on August 11.

THE COUNTRY

Situated on the western bulge of Africa, Mauritania is a sparsely populated, predominantly desert country, overwhelmingly Muslim and, except in the south, Arabic in language. The dominant Beydane (Arabic for "white") Moors, descendants of northern Arabs and Berbers, have been estimated as constituting one-third of the population, with an equal number of Haratines (mixed-race descendants of black slaves) having adopted Berber customs. Black Africans, the most important tribal groups of which are the Toucouleur, the Fulani, the Sarakole, and the Wolof, are concentrated in the rich alluvial farming lands of the Senegal River valley. They have recently claimed to account for a much larger population share than is officially acknowledged, their case being supported by the government's refusal to release pertinent portions of the last two censuses. Racial tension, exacerbated by government "arabization" efforts, has contributed to internal unrest and conflict with several neighboring nations. Further complicating matters has been the de facto continuation of slavery, officially banned in 1980 but still reportedly encompassing an estimated 100,000–400,000 Haratines and blacks in servitude to Arab masters.

Before 1970 nearly all of the northern population was engaged in nomadic cattle raising, but the proportion had shrunk to less than one-quarter by 1986. Prolonged droughts, desertification, the loss of herds, and a devastating locust attack in 2004 that destroyed about half of the country's crops, have driven more Mauritanians to urban areas, where many depend on foreign relief aid. Many Mauritanians seek their livelihood in other countries.

The country's first deep water port, financed by China, opened near Nouakchott in 1986. Mauritania's coastal waters are among the richest fishing grounds in the world and generate more than half of its foreign exchange, although the region is also routinely fished by foreign trawlers.

To secure aid from international donors, the government initiated numerous economic reforms, including privatization of state-owned enterprises, promotion of free market activity, and currency devaluation. The government also endorsed political liberalization, although genuine progress in that regard has been minimal, while international lenders called for measures to address the unequal distribution of wealth. More than 50 percent of the population lives in poverty, and the social services sector is considered grossly inadequate.

In 2002 the International Monetary Fund (IMF) and the World Bank announced debt relief of $1.1 billion for Mauritania. In 2003 exploratory tests indicated the presence of offshore oil fields, prompting investments from international oil companies. Annual GDP growth remained stable at an average of 5.2 percent in 2003–2005. Further, following the military coup in August 2005 and the transitional government's reforms, there was a significant decline in inflation. The exportation of crude oil began in 2006, with daily production reportedly averaging 54,000 barrels per day, contributing to robust annual growth of about 10 percent. Growth contracted to 3.7 percent in 2008, and then dipped to –1 percent in 2009, owing in large part to a decrease in donor revenue due to a perceived lack of progress in restoring democracy after the August 2008 coup, followed by the global financial crisis, which had a negative impact on food and fuel prices. Additionally, iron and oil prices declined sharply, key investors pulled out of plans to privatize the country's largest mining company, and the government instituted price controls on food and fuel. Following the multiparty presidential election in 2009, the World Bank restored some $14 million to improve infrastructure. GDP growth expanded to 4.6 percent in 2010. On another positive note, the IMF agreed to contribute $118 million through 2012 to support development for the poorest segment of the population, while the government began instituting reforms in the energy sector and efforts to bolster the non-oil sector. Despite robust annual GDP growth averaging 5.6 percent for 2011–2012, the IMF noted that high unemployment and widespread poverty remained "serious challenges." On the heels of a 2011 drought, a rebound in agricultural production and a pickup in the building and public works sector drove strong economic recovery in 2012, as GDP grew by 6.4 percent, while inflation declined to 4.9 percent. GDP per capita was $1,157. Citing widespread corruption and poor infrastructure, the World Bank rated Mauritania as 167th out of 185 countries in its 2013 annual Doing Business survey.

GOVERNMENT AND POLITICS

Political background. Under nominal French administration from the turn of the century, Mauritania became a French colony in 1920, but de facto control was not established until 1934. It became an autonomous republic within the French Community in 1958 and an independent "Islamic Republic" on November 28, 1960. President Moktar OULD DADDAH (died October 14, 2003), who led the country to independence, established a one-party regime with predominantly Moorish backing and endorsed a policy of moderate socialism at home combined with nonalignment abroad. Opposition to his 18-year presidency was periodically voiced by northern groups seeking union with Morocco, inhabitants of the predominantly black south who feared Arab domination, and leftist elements in both student and trade union organizations.

Under an agreement concluded in November 1975 by Mauritania, Morocco, and Spain, the Ould Daddah regime assumed control of the southern third of Western (Spanish) Sahara on February 28, 1976, coincident with the withdrawal of Spanish forces and Morocco's occupation of the northern two-thirds (see map and discussion under entry for Morocco). However, an inability to contain Algerian-supported insurgents in the annexed territory contributed to the president's ouster in a bloodless coup on July 10, 1978, and the installation of Lt. Col. Mustapha OULD SALEK as head of state by a newly formed Military Committee for National Recovery (*Comité Militaire de Recouvrement National*—CMRN). Ould Salek, arguing that the struggle against the insurgents had "nearly destroyed" the Mauritanian economy, indicated that his government would be willing to withdraw from Tiris El-Gharbia (the Mauritanian sector of Western Sahara) if a settlement acceptable to Morocco, Algeria, and the insurgents could be found. However, the overture was rejected by Morocco, and in October the Algerian-backed Popular Front for the Liberation of Saguia el Hamra and Rio de Oro (Polisario) announced that the insurgency would cease only if Mauritania were to withdraw from the sector and recognize Polisario's government in exile, the Saharan Arab Democratic Republic (SADR).

In March 1979 Ould Salek reiterated his government's desire to extricate itself from the conflict but dismissed several CMRN members known to favor direct talks with Polisario. Subsequently, on April 6 he dissolved the CMRN in favor of a new Military Committee for National Salvation (*Comité Militaire de Salut National*—CMSN) and relinquished the office of prime minister to Lt. Col. Ahmed OULD BOUCEIF, who was immediately hailed as effective leader of the Nouakchott regime. On May 27, however, Ould Bouceif was killed in an airplane crash and was succeeded (following the interim incumbency of Lt. Col. Ahmed Salem OULD SIDI) by Lt. Col. Mohamed Khouna OULD HAIDALLA on May 31.

President Ould Salek was forced to resign on June 3, and the CMSN named Lt. Col. Mohamed Mahmoud Ould Ahmed LOULY as his replacement. Colonel Louly immediately declared his commitment to a cessation of hostilities and on August 5, after three days of talks in Algiers, concluded a peace agreement with Polisario representatives. While the pact did not entail recognition of the SADR, Mauritania formally renounced all claims to Tiris El-Gharbia and subsequently withdrew its troops from the territory, which was thereupon occupied by Moroccan forces and renamed Oued Eddahab.

On January 4, 1980, President Louly was replaced by Col. Ould Haidalla, who also continued to serve as chief of government. The following December Ould Haidalla announced that, as a first step toward restoration of democratic institutions, his largely military administration would be replaced by a civilian government headed by Sid Ahmad OULD BNEIJARA. Only one army officer was named to the cabinet announced on December 15, while the CMSN published a draft constitution four days later that proposed establishment of a multiparty system.

The move toward civilianization was abruptly halted on March 16, 1981, as the result of an attempted coup by a group of officers (who were allegedly backed by Morocco), and Prime Minister Ould Bneijara was replaced on April 26 by the army chief of staff, Col. Maaouya Ould Sidahmed TAYA. A further coup attempt, involving an effort to abduct President Ould Haidalla at Nouakchott airport on February 6, 1982, resulted in the arrest of Ould Bneijara and former president Ould Salek, both of whom were sentenced to ten-year prison terms by a special tribunal on March 5.

On March 8, 1984, in a major leadership reshuffle, Taya returned to his former military post, and the president reclaimed the prime ministry, to which was added the defense portfolio. The following December Ould Haidalla was ousted in a bloodless coup led by Colonel Taya, who assumed the titles of president, prime minister, and chair of the CMSN.

Amid increasingly vocal black opposition to Moorish domination, Colonel Taya announced plans in mid-1986 for a gradual return to democratic rule (see Constitution and government, below), and local councils were elected in the country's regional capitals in December. However, north-south friction persisted, with 3 Toucouleur officers being executed and some 40 others imprisoned for involvement in an alleged coup attempt in October 1987.

Although the Taya regime was subsequently charged with systematic repression of opponents, particularly southerners, elections were held for councils in the principal townships and rural districts in January 1988 and 1989, respectively. New elections to all the municipal councils, originally planned for late 1989 but postponed because of a violent dispute with Senegal (see Foreign relations, below), were held in December 1990. Meanwhile, racial tension remained high because of reports that security forces had imprisoned thousands of black army officers and government officials, several hundred of whom had allegedly been executed or tortured to death. Although the government claimed that the arrests had been made in connection with a coup plot, opponents charged that the regime was merely intensifying an already virulent antiblack campaign.

On April 15, 1991, Colonel Taya surprised observers by announcing that a referendum would be held soon on a new constitution, followed by multiparty presidential and legislative elections. The draft constitution was released on June 10 by the CMSN, approved by nearly 98 percent of voters in a national referendum on July 12, and formally entered into effect on July 21. Four days later the CMSN adopted legislation on the legalization of political parties, six of which were quickly recognized, including the regime-supportive Democratic and Social Republican Party (*Parti Républicain Démocratique et Social*—PRDS). On June 29 Colonel Taya declared a general amnesty for detainees held on state security charges, thereby somewhat mollifying black hostility.

In presidential balloting on January 24, 1992, Colonel Taya, as the PRDS nominee, was credited with winning 63 percent of the vote; his principal challenger, Ahmed OULD DADDAH, received 33 percent. Ould Daddah, the previously exiled brother of former president Moktar Ould Daddah, was supported by a number of the new political parties, including the influential Union of Democratic Forces (*Union des Forces Démocratiques*—UFD), which challenged the accuracy of the official election results.

On February 10, 1992, five opposition parties requested postponement of National Assembly elections scheduled for March 6 and 13 to avoid a repetition of what they claimed had been massive fraud in the presidential poll. Their appeal rejected, 6 of the 14 opposition groups, including the UFD, boycotted the balloting, in which the PRDS won an overwhelming majority of seats on a turnout of little more than a third of the electorate.

In indirect senatorial balloting on April 3 and 10, 1992, the participants were further reduced to the PRDS and the small Avante-Guard Party (*Parti Avant-Garde*—PAG). The PAG received none of the available seats, as contrasted with 36 for the PRDS and 17 for independents.

On April 18, following Colonel Taya's inauguration as president, Taya yielded the office of prime minister to a young technocrat, Sidi Mohamed OULD BOUBACAR, who announced the formation of a new government on April 20.

In 1994 the government party won control of 172 of the 208 municipal councils (as compared to 19 for independents and 17 for the UFD), prompting opposition charges of extensive electoral fraud. The opposition also questioned the results of the April Senate replenishment, in which the PRDS won 16 of 17 seats. In September it was reported that President Taya had dropped his military title in pursuit of a more civilian image. At the same time, the government launched a crackdown on Islamic "agitators," fundamentalists having reportedly gained converts by providing much-needed social services in urban areas.

Taya dismissed Ould Boubacar on January 2, 1996, replacing him with Cheikh el Avia Ould Mohamed KHOUNA. The December 12, 1997, elections won President Taya another six-year term, with an official 90 percent of the vote, and named Mohamed Lemine Ould GUIG, an academician, as prime minister. The UFD and several other opposition parties boycotted the balloting in objection to the regime's failure to establish an independent electoral commission, among other things. Despite growing opposition, President Taya's PRDS maintained a firm grip on power, winning a majority of seats in the 1996 and 2001 National Assembly elections.

The Mauritanian cabinet underwent more than a dozen reshufflings between June 1997 and May 2003, prompting concerns about the stability of the government. On June 7, 2003, those concerns were validated when rebels stormed the presidential palace in a coup attempt that led to two days of fighting in the capital. After regaining power on June 9, President Taya began a crackdown on the Muslim extremists he blamed for the uprising. On July 7, 2003, Taya appointed Sighair OULD MBARECK as prime minister, replacing Khouna. Ould Mbareck was the first former slave to hold the position.

Four months later Taya was elected to his third term. His principal challenger, former president Ould Haidalla, who had assembled a coalition of prominent Islamists, Arab nationals, and reformers, won 18.7 percent of the vote. Ould Haidalla and several of his supporters were arrested and detained on the day before the election, then released, only to be arrested and released again the next day. International monitors were not permitted to observe the elections, which were labeled fraudulent by Taya's opponents.

In August and September 2004 government officials announced discovery of two more coup attempts, allegedly organized by former army officers Saleh OULD HANENA and Mohamed Cheikhna. Officials accused Libya and Burkina Faso of arming and financing the coup, charges the two countries denied.

In February 2005 Ould Haidalla was acquitted on charges relating to the 2003 and 2004 attempted coups. Four soldiers were found guilty and sentenced to life in prison. A bloodless coup was staged on August 3, 2005, when Taya was in Saudi Arabia attending the funeral of King Fahd. A group of security and army officers led by Col. Ely Ould Mohamed VALL established themselves as the ruling Military Council for Justice and Democracy (MCJD) with Vall as head of state. On August 5 the parliament was dissolved. Mbareck resigned as prime minister on August 7 and was immediately replaced by Ould Boubacar, ambassador to France, who resigned from the former ruling PRDS party on August 9. A new cabinet, described as consisting primarily of technocrats, was announced on August 10.

In keeping with their promise of a quick return to a civilian government, the leaders of the junta presented constitutional amendments in a national referendum in June 2006 that provided for new legislative and presidential elections. Balloting for the National Assembly was held on November 19 and December 3, while senate elections were held on January 21 and February 4, 2007. Many of the successful candidates in both houses were technically independents (see Current issues, below, for details), although a coalition of opponents of the Taya regime called the Coalition of Forces of Democratic Change (*Coalition des Forces des Changement Démocratique*—CFCD) secured 38 seats in assembly elections. Women held 18 percent of seats in the assembly and 16 percent of seats in the senate, close to the junta's goal of 20 percent participation by women.

Of the 20 candidates in first-round presidential balloting on March 11, 2007, only 8 ran under the banner of political parties. Sidi Mohamed Ould Cheikh ABDALLAHI ran as an independent, though he was considered by many to be representing the MCJD. However, among his backers was Gen. Mohamed Ould ABDELAZIZ, who had participated in the 2005 military coup that ousted Taya. Abdallahi won with 53 percent of the vote in a runoff election on March 25 (with the support of half of the first-round candidates), defeating Ahmed Ould Daddah of the Rally of Democratic Forces (*Rassemblement des Forces Démocratiques*—RFD), who garnered 47 percent. Abdallahi was sworn in on April 19, and on April 20 he appointed as prime minister Zeine Ould ZEIDANE, the former head of the Central Bank who had finished third in the first round of presidential balloting. The new government formed on April 28 reportedly was made up largely of technocrats and at least four members of the Popular Progressive Alliance (*Alliance Populaire et Progressive*—APP).

In January 2008 independents and supporters of Abdallahi from small political parties formed the National Pact for Development and Democracy (*Pacte National pour le Développment et le Démocratie*—PNDD), which subsequently became the governing party. On May 6, 2008, Abdallahi replaced Zeidance as prime minister, appointing the PNDD's Yahya Ould Ahmed el-WAGHF, and on May 11 el-Waghf reshuffled the cabinet. Though dominated by the PNDD, the cabinet included for the first time a small number of opposition party representatives as well as the National Rally for Reform and Development (*Rassemblement Nationale pour la Réforme* et *le Développement*—RNRD), described as a moderate Islamist party. El-Waghf resigned along with the entire cabinet on July 3 in advance of a proposed no-confidence vote by parliament, but he was immediately reappointed by the president. A new, expanded cabinet, consisting entirely of PNDD members, was named on July 15.

On August 6, 2008, Abdallahi was deposed in a bloodless coup led by Gen. Abdelaziz, the head of the Presidential Guard, who formed an 11-member High Council of State. Abdallahi, el-Waghf, and the minister of the interior were arrested (all of whom were subsequently released). On August 14 Abdelaziz appointed Moulaye Ould Mohamed LAGHDAF, a diplomat, as prime minister. Laghdaf formed a new government on August 31, retaining four ministers from the previous government. On April 15, 2009, Ba Mamadou MBARÉ, the president of the Senate, became interim head of government, following the resignation of Abdelaziz, who stepped down to contest the presidential elections that had been set for June 6. Abdelaziz and his supporters subsequently formed a new party, styled as the Union for the Republic (*Union pour la République*—UPR), comprising pro-junta parliamentarians, including many from the former governing PNDD. Opposition parties threatened to boycott the balloting amid claims that junta leaders had ensured Abdelaziz's election, since all candidates approved by the Constitutional Court were reportedly pro-junta. Mediation by Senegalese officials in mid-July ended a series of street protests by the opposition coalition National Front for the Defense of Democracy (*Avant National pour la Défense de la Démocratie*—FNDD) and averted a boycott, with both sides agreeing on a new election date of July 18, and a provision for the formal resignation of Abdallahi. Abdallahi officially resigned on June 27, one day after naming a transitional unity government with Laghdaf as prime minister. The new government retained 13 ministers and added 13 ministers from the opposition.

In presidential balloting on July 18, 2009, Abdelaziz secured 52.6 percent of the vote to defeat nine other candidates. Speaker of parliament and APP leader Massaoud Ould Boulkheir, running as the candidate of the FNDD, finished a distant second, with 16.3 percent. The RFD's Ahmed Ould Daddah, who had backed Abdallahi in the 2007 election, was third, with 13.7 percent. None of the remaining candidates received more than 4.8 percent of the vote. Though the opposition immediately lodged complaints of vote rigging, international observers declared the elections free and fair. Prime Minister Laghdaf was reappointed on August 6, and his new government, formed on August 11, was comprised chiefly of Abdelaziz loyalists from the new UPR. Notable among cabinet members was Naha Mint MOUKNASS, president of the Union for Democracy and Progress (*Union pour la Démocratie et le Progrès*—UDP). Mouknass, who previously had strong ties to the Taya regime, was tapped as Mauritania's first female foreign minister. In the Senate replenishment on November 8 and 15, the UPR and its allies won 14 of the 18 seats. The RNRD, previously aligned with the FNDD, formed a parliamentary alliance with the UPR after the opposition failed to win the 3 seats required to form its own parliamentary group.

President Abdelaziz reshuffled the cabinet on March 31, 2010, and three ministers were dismissed on December 16.

The cabinet was reshuffled on February 12, 2011, and Foreign Affairs Minister Naha Mint Mouknass resigned on March 23 and was replaced by the minister of defense, with other changes following (see Current issues, below). The cabinet underwent another minor reshuffle in April 2013.

Constitution and government. The constitution of May 23, 1961, which had replaced Mauritania's former parliamentary-type government with a one-party presidential system, was formally suspended by the CMRN on July 20, 1978. A Constitutional Charter issued by the Military Committee confirmed the dissolution of the National Assembly and the Mauritanian People's Party (*Parti du Peuple Mauritanien*—PPM) and authorized the installation of the committee's chair as head of state until such time as "new democratic institutions are established."

In December 1980 the CMSN published a constitutional proposal that was to have been submitted to a referendum in 1981. However, no balloting was held prior to the coup of December 1984. Subsequently, Colonel Taya indicated that the military would prepare for a return to democracy through a program called the Structure for the Education of the Masses that would involve the election of councilors at the local level to advise the government on measures to improve literacy, social integration, and labor productivity. In the series of municipal elections conducted in 1986–1990, voters chose from multiple lists of candidates approved by the government, although no formal political party activity was permitted.

The 1991 constitution declared Mauritania to be an "Islamic Arab and African republic," guaranteed "freedom of association, thought, and expression," and conferred strong executive powers on the president, including the authority to appoint the prime minister. Directly elected by universal suffrage in two-round voting, the president was allowed to serve an unlimited number of six-year terms. The new basic law also established a bicameral legislature (comprising a directly elected National Assembly and an indirectly elected Senate), as well as constitutional, economic and social, and Islamic councils.

The legal system traditionally reflected a combination of French and Islamic codes, with the judiciary encompassing a Supreme Court; a High Court of Justice; courts of first instance; and civil, labor, and military courts. In June 1978 a commission was appointed to revise the system according to Islamic precepts, and in March 1980, a month after the replacement of "modern" codes by Islamic law (sharia), the CMSN established an Islamic Court consisting of a Muslim magistrate, two councilors, and two *ulemas* (interpreters of the Koran). Earlier, in October 1978, a special Court of State Security had been created. The 1991 constitution provided for an independent judiciary, with sharia serving as the "single source of law."

The Military Council for Justice and Democracy (MCJD), formed by the leaders of the August 2005 coup, maintained the 1991 constitution, supplementing it with a military council "charter" that stipulated the MCJD held power over the executive and legislative branches, dissolved the parliament, and gave the MCJD advisory power over the Constitutional Council. Constitutional amendments proposed by the transitional government were approved by 97 percent of voters in a June 25, 2006, limiting a president to two terms of five years each and setting a maximum age limit of 75 for a president, among other things.

The constitution was suspended by the military junta's High Council of State following the bloodless coup in August 2008. Constitutional order was restored after multiparty elections on July 18, 2009.

For administrative purposes the country is divided into 12 regions, plus the capital district of Nouakchott, and 32 departments; in addition, 208 urban and rural districts (areas populated by at least 500 inhabitants) were created in October 1988.

Freedom of the press is constitutionally guaranteed. In 2013 the media group Reporters Without Borders ranked Mauritania 67th out of 179 countries. In June 2013 Khira Mint CHEIKHANY became the first woman to head Mauritania's state television.

Foreign relations. Mauritania has combined nonalignment in world affairs with membership in such groups as the Arab League (since 1973) and, as of 1989, the Arab Maghreb Union (AMU). Following independence, economic and cultural cooperation with France continued on the basis of agreements first negotiated in 1961 and renegotiated in 1973 to exclude special arrangements in monetary and military affairs. As a consequence, French military advisers were recalled and Mauritania withdrew from the Franc Zone, establishing its own currency. In late 1979 a limited number of French troops returned to ensure Mauritania's territorial integrity following Nouakchott's withdrawal from Western Sahara and the annexation of its sector by Morocco.

Mauritania's settlement with the Polisario Front was followed by restoration of diplomatic relations with Algeria, which had been severed upon Algiers' recognition of the Saharan Arab Democratic Republic (SADR) in 1976. During 1980–1982 Nouakchott maintained formal neutrality in Polisario's continuing confrontation with Morocco, withholding formal recognition of the SADR but criticizing Rabat's military efforts to retain control of the entire Western Sahara. In 1983 Colonel Ould Haidalla concluded a Maghreb Fraternity and Cooperation Treaty with Algeria and Tunisia that was implicitly directed against Rabat and Tripoli. On the other hand, declaring that the conflict in the Western Sahara had "poisoned the atmosphere," Colonel Taya subsequently attempted to return Mauritania to its traditional posture of regional neutralism. While still maintaining its "moral support" for the SADR, which it officially recognized in 1984, the Taya regime normalized relations with Morocco and Libya, thereby balancing growing ties with Algeria that included the signing of a border demarcation agreement in April 1986.

Relations with Senegal were tense after an April 1989 incident when violence erupted between villagers along the border, provoking race riots in both nations' capitals that reportedly caused the death of nearly 500 people and injury to more than 1,000. During the ensuing months an estimated 170,000–240,000 Mauritanian expatriates fled Senegal, while Mauritania reportedly expelled 70,000 Senegalese and 40,000 of its own black residents. Mauritania and Senegal severed diplomatic relations in August, with each country accusing the other of instigating further violence. Although the countries restored ties in April 1992 and the border was partially reopened the following November, tension continued as black Mauritanians charged they were being prevented from returning to Mauritania, and Senegal attributed widespread "banditry" along the border to the refugee situation. Despite several flare-ups, relations between the two countries improved after Senegal's president Abdoulaye Wade expressed his support for the Taya regime, following the 2003 coup attempt in Mauritania, and extradited a suspected coup plotter to Mauritania.

Mauritania has also had strained relations with Mali, whose black-dominated Traoré regime accused Nouakchott in the late 1980s of supporting antigovernment activity among its ethnically Berber Tuareg population. Following the resolution of the Tuareg situation in the mid-1990s, relations with Mali warmed.

Mauritania attracted an unusual amount of international attention because of its support for Iraq in the 1990–1991 Gulf crisis, causing Western donors to sharply curtail aid to Nouakchott. However, assistance was subsequently restored, apparently reflecting Western support for the Taya regime's strong antifundamentalist posture. The government distanced itself from Iraq, expelling Baghdad's ambassador in October 1995 amid reports of a coup plot among "pro-Baathist" elements. Among other things, the policy shift contributed to improved relations with Gulf Arab states.

In November 1995 Nouakchott announced plans to open an "interest" office in Tel Aviv as part of what was expected to be eventual restoration of full relations with Israel. The action was condemned by some hard-line Arab states, including Libya, which recalled its ambassador and discontinued all aid to Mauritania. However, Tunisian mediation in early 1997 helped restore relations between Mauritania and Tripoli. In late 1999 the Taya government completed the foreign policy reversal started in mid-decade by severing relations with Iraq and becoming only the third Arab state (after Egypt and Jordan) to establish full diplomatic relations with Israel.

French officials have been critical of Mauritania's human rights record, but relations between the two countries improved after France offered support to the Taya regime following the 2003 coup attempt.

The government has cooperated with the United States in several counterterrorism training programs beginning in 2003. Such programs target al-Qaida–affiliated groups operating in Mauritania and several neighboring countries. In a major decision, Mauritania announced in December that it was withdrawing from the Economic Community of West African States (ECOWAS); analysts suggested that Nouakchott had grown increasingly concerned over the possibility that the non-Francophone countries in ECOWAS would adopt a common currency to the detriment of the ouguiya. Subsequently, the Taya administration declared that it would focus on affairs in northern Africa, particularly through the proposed rejuvenation of the Arab Maghreb Union, rather than on its relations with its southern neighbors. (As a result, Nouakchott was described in 2000 as having informally accepted the premise that the Western Sahara would remain a province of Morocco.)

Regional tensions increased in August and September 2004 after President Taya accused Libya and Burkina Faso of arming renegade soldiers allegedly preparing to topple the Taya regime in two separate coup attempts. Both countries denied the accusations.

Following the August 2005 coup, Colonel Vall pledged to maintain Mauritania's relations with Israel. The African Union (AU) suspended

Mauritania's membership the day after the coup but readmitted the country on April 10, 2007, following democratic elections.

In November 2007 Mauritania, Senegal, and the United Nations High Commissioner for Refugees (UNHCR) signed a tripartite agreement to initiate the return of thousands of black Mauritanian refugees.

After the bloodless coup in 2008, Algeria and Nigeria condemned the military takeover, while Libya expressed its support for the junta. Morocco and Senegal were reported to have "shown understanding," while a French minister canceled a planned visit in October after the junta refused to release the deposed president from house arrest. Relations were mended in late 2009, as France renewed cooperation with Mauritania in counterterrorism efforts, and the European Union (EU) restored aid that had been frozen in the aftermath of the coup. Algeria, Mali, Niger, and the United States also provided counterterrorism support in late 2009.

Mauritania and Israel severed ties in 2009 over the issue of Israel's recent retaliatory attacks against Palestinians in the Gaza Strip. Mauritania withdrew its ambassador from Israel, and Israel closed its embassy in Nouakchott on March 6 after the junta asked the ambassador to leave. Iran then stepped in to expand its ties with Mauritania, and in January 2010 President Abdelaziz made an official visit to Tehran.

Relations with Mali were strained in February 2010 when Mauritania withdrew its ambassador in the wake of Mali's agreement to a demand by al-Qaida in the Islamic Maghreb that it release four al-Qaida members in exchange for a French hostage. Meanwhile, France and Spain provided weapons and training for the Mauritanian army to further enhance its counterterrorism operations, and NATO pledged to back Mauritania in its fight against terrorism at its borders.

In August 2012 Mauritania agreed to provide troops to a 45,000-member rapid reaction military force, along with Algeria, Burkina Faso, and Niger, to fight Islamist militants in the region. In September Malian troops killed 16 Islamic clerics, including 9 Mauritanians, prompting denunciations by the Abdelaziz government. Human rights groups protested the election of Mauritania to the vice president's position on the UN Human Rights Council because of the continuation of slavery in the country.

In January 2013 China announced it would provide $260 million for development projects in Mauritania. Mauritania deployed 1,800 troops as part of an AU-led military force in Mali (see entry on Mali) in April. In addition, Mauritania allowed French forces to use the country to support its military operations in Mali. Meanwhile the fighting in Mali was reported to have produced more than 100,000 refugees who fled to Mauritania. Also in April Mauritania and Morocco signed 17 economic, cultural, and educational cooperation agreements. In August Mauritania and Niger finalized a defense cooperation accord.

Current issues. Domestic discontent, spurred by rising food prices and allegations of corruption against President Sidi Mohamed Ould Cheikh Abdallahi and his wife, stirred unrest throughout early 2008. Abdallahi, who is Muslim, was criticized for using public money to build a mosque at the presidential compound, for seeking dialogue with Islamists allegedly linked to an al-Qaida affiliate in North Africa, and for releasing some Islamist prisoners. In addition, the administration was criticized for not representing the majority parties in parliament. In May Abdallahi replaced the government, naming Yahya Ould Ahmed el-Waghf, leader of the newly formed governing party PNDD, as prime minister and installing several ministers from the former Taya regime, as well as some opposition parties in the reshuffled cabinet. The RFD refused to participate in a unity government, party leader Ahmed Ould Daddah claiming that the opposition parties had essentially been invited to sign on to the president's political program. Within months, el-Waghf found himself facing the prospect of a no-confidence vote in parliament, initiated by disaffected PNDD members who opposed the new government appointments. El-Waghf resigned in July, along with the entire cabinet, but he was immediately reappointed by the president. The new cabinet, named within two weeks, comprised only members of the PNDD. Disaffection with Abdallahi and his perceived ineptitude in curbing high food prices, coupled with allegations of corruption against him, ultimately led 48 members of the PNDD to resign on August 4. Two days later, Abdallahi fired several members of his elite Presidential Guard, including its head, General Abdelaziz, who had backed Abdallahi in his bid for the presidency. Hours after the security staff were dismissed, Abdelaziz staged a bloodless coup, with soldiers surrounding the palace. Abdallahi, el-Waghf, and the interior minister were immediately placed under arrest. State-run radio and television were shut down, and the country was returned to military rule. Police dispersed, without violence, throngs of citizens outside the palace, and Abdelaziz took over as chair of an 11-member High Council of State. Despite Abdelaziz's pledge that he would hold elections at some unspecified date, the African Union (AU), the EU, the UN, and the United States immediately condemned the coup and called for a return to constitutional rule. Further, the United States announced it was suspending aid, and Mauritania's biggest bilateral donor, the French Agency for Development, suspended all non-emergency funding.

The interior minister and the former prime minister were released on August 11, 2008, but Abdallahi remained in custody. The following day the junta authorized laws granting its members the right to rule until such time as a presidential election could be organized. Mohamed Lemine Ould Guig, a former prime minister in the Taya regime, was named secretary general of the High Council of State. Two days later Abdelaziz named Moulaye Ould Mohamed Laghdaf as prime minister. Observers noted his choice of a former ambassador for prime minister and his anti-Islamist stance, not only in direct opposition to former president Abdallahi's inclinations, but also as elements that would appeal to the West, and the United States in particular. However, Washington refused to recognize the military government.

Laghdaf's new cabinet retained four key ministers—defense, justice, economy, and finance—and all ministers were reported to be from parties that supported the coup, including the RFD and the Islamist RNRD party led by Mohamed Jemil Ould Mansour. Meanwhile, members of the PNDD, APP, and UFP, as well as some civil societies, formed the opposition alliance FNDD in protest of the coup. The coup appeared to have the support of the majority of members of parliament, as more than two-thirds from both chambers signed a declaration praising the junta.

On September 2, 2008, the assembly named a council to try Abdallahi on charges of corruption and obstructing parliament. (An attempt by parliament before the coup to hold a special session to conduct the corruption probe had been blocked by Abdallahi.) The former president's supporters claimed that the allegations were a front that gave the military leaders an excuse to stage the coup. The assembly also launched an investigation of Abdallahi's wife, who was accused of stealing public funds. Meanwhile, it was reported that another former coup leader and associate of Abdelaziz, Col. Vall, had returned to Mauritania on September 1.

Turmoil continued on another front in 2008 as al-Qaida in the Islamic Maghreb denounced the coup and called for a "holy war" in Mauritania, claiming the junta leaders had been acting in concert with the "infidels" of Israel, the United States, and France. On September 15 al-Qaida militants killed 12 Mauritanian soldiers in what news reports said was an attempt by the terrorist group to avenge the coup. That same day the National Assembly voted to hold elections within 12 to 14 months. Meanwhile, General Abdelaziz vowed to crack down on al-Qaida.

In mid-September 2008 General Abdelaziz rejected an ultimatum by the AU that Mauritania restore constitutional order by October 6 and reinstate President Abdallahi or else face sanctions. A "democratic convention" scheduled for December was boycotted by the opposition, the FNDD saying that participation would be the equivalent of recognizing the junta. In January 2009 the junta announced that a presidential election would be held on June 6, Abdelaziz having announced earlier that he would not be a candidate. Meanwhile, Abdallahi, who had been released from custody—reportedly to avert EU sanctions—said he would accept the outcome of a new election only if the army abdicated authority and constitutional order was restored. Mass demonstrations protesting his release were reported, with Abdallahi claiming that the rallies were arranged by the junta, while some observers said public opinion was mixed.

The junta formed an independent electoral commission in March 2009 to supervise the upcoming presidential election. Further, Abdelaziz stepped down on April 15 in order to be eligible to contest the election, though earlier he had said he would not run. The following day Senate president Ba Mamadou Mbaré moved into the position of interim head of government. Abdelaziz officially announced his presidential candidacy, as did Kane Hamidou Baba, who withdrew as vice president of the RFD in a rift over his support for the junta, and former prime minister Sighair Ould Mbareck, who ran as an independent. Opposition parties, under the umbrella FNDD, threatened to boycott the balloting, claiming that all the candidates were pro-junta. During pro-Abdallahi demonstrations in advance of the election, hundreds of protesters were reportedly beaten by police. The elections, originally scheduled for June, were postponed while efforts were under way to persuade opposition parties to participate. Subsequently, as tensions increased, Senegalese president Abdoulaye Wade helped avert a political crisis by mediating talks in Dakar between junta leaders and the chairs of the FNDD and the RFD. In early June an agreement was reached not only on a new election date of July 18, but also on the formation of a transitional unity government, with Laghdaf retained as prime minister and a cabinet that included equal numbers of opposition and government ministers. On June 27 Abdallahi, in accordance with the agreement reached in Senegal, officially resigned as president. At the end of the month, the AU dropped its sanctions against Mauritania, citing the junta's efforts to restore democracy. Meanwhile, former coup leader Col. Vall announced his candidacy. Vall, a cousin and former ally of Abdelaziz, condemned the most recent coup, saying it was "wrong and there was no reason for it." A month before the election, assembly speaker Massaoud Ould Boulkheir announced his candidacy under the banner of the opposition FNDD; a few days later, Mohamed Jemil Ould Mansour of the RNRD announced his candidacy, reportedly becoming the first Islamist to run for president. Other parties, including new ones formed ahead of the election, subsequently named candidates, bringing the field to ten. Colonel Vall ran as an independent, as did former prime minister Ould Mbareck. General Abdelaziz, for his part, campaigned under the banner of the UPR as "the candidate of the poor," pledging to lower food and fuel prices and provide greater access to health care. Meanwhile, three weeks before the election, al-Qaida of the Islamic Maghreb (AQIM) claimed responsibility for the killing of an American aid worker in Nouakchott, as observers began warning of Mauritania's becoming a "hotbed" for al-Qaida and jihadists. Nevertheless, there was no violence during the election, which General Abdelaziz won handily. Despite accusations of fraud from opposition candidates, and the resignation a few days later of the head of the electoral commission (who cited concerns about the validity of the results but lacked sufficient evidence to pursue them), General Abdelaziz's victory stood. Subsequently, the constitutional court confirmed the outcome. The new government formed by Prime Minister Laghdaf was comprised chiefly of presidential loyalists.

Domestic tensions heightened at the end of December, as thousands of people protested price hikes and the new government's "dictatorial policies." The protesters rallied under the umbrella of a new opposition coalition, the Coordination of Forces of Democratic Opposition (*Coordination des Forces Démocratique*—CFOD [see Political Parties, below]). In January 2010 the CFOD boycotted a government-sponsored political forum to discuss constitutional revisions and other democratic reforms. CFOD member parties claimed they had not been consulted in advance of the conference.

Domestic concerns soon focused on terrorism, as in early 2010 parliament drafted new legislation that would authorize wiretapping, eliminate the statute of limitations for terrorist acts, and tighten citizenship requirements. Subsequently the constitutional court struck down ten of the law's provisions, including those that allowed for the tapping of phone calls and emails, unrestricted home searches, and the incarceration of minors. Some analysts said the ruling underscored the court's independence from the executive and judicial authorities in the struggle toward a more democratic government. A law was adopted in June granting special conditions for AQIM militants who turned themselves into authorities. The measure was endorsed by the CFOD on the basis that it would encourage youths who had "gone astray" to return to moderate Islamic practices.

With legislative elections scheduled for October 1, 2011, in January the CFOD began efforts, driven by RFD leader Daddah and UFP president Mohammed Ould MAALOUD, to present a "formidable challenge" to the presidential party. The PNDD, however, agreed to work with the ruling party. Subsequently, civil unrest, which had begun in the Middle East and North Africa, prompted proreform demonstrations in Nouakchott against rising prices and security policies. The RNRD had urged government officials to take action to avoid unrest ahead of the protests that included HATEM and the UPSD, among other small parties. Another protest, which took place over two days in February in a town southeast of the capital, was halted by the police, and several people were arrested. A resurgence on the terrorism front occurred in February, when government forces killed AQIM militants linked to a suicide bomb plot, and Mali extradited an AQIM fighter suspected in another failed suicide bomb attack. Domestically, calls for reform increased, particularly among young people, as many formed a movement called February 25 Youth, defined more by social networking than by a political agenda. Their demands included the resignation of the prime minister, establishment of a coalition government of technocrats, and abolition of the Senate, among other things. They also had the support of other civil groups, including trade unions. Meanwhile, as unrest spread throughout North Africa and the Middle East, Mauritania's foreign minister, Naha Mint Mouknass, was dismissed in March, reportedly because of her close ties with Libyan leader Muammar Qadhafi, whose regime was under attack by rebels within the country. Mauritanian authorities subsequently seized land they had sold to Libya to build a hotel and called for a halt to the violence, much of it perpetrated by Qadhafi against the civilian population. Prime Minister Laghdaf, prompted in part by pressure from the RNRD, called on the youth movement to submit their demands and appoint a representative with whom the government could negotiate. Opposition parties scored another concession when elections scheduled for April 24 to renew one-third of the Senate were postponed indefinitely after the CFOD requested it. The coalition claimed that conditions did not exist for holding free and fair elections, alleging bribery of voters by the ruling party and use of state resources for partisan gain.

In May 2011 President Abdelaziz supported an initiative urged by rights groups to find the remains and mark the graves of black Mauritanians who disappeared during civil unrest since independence in 1960. In July, in the run-up to municipal and legislative elections scheduled for October, the government began revising the electoral rolls, though some observers said the lists did not include 200,000 refugees, mainly black Mauritanians, who had returned from Senegal and lacked proper identification. Subsequently, the UFP and the RFD said they would boycott the elections. Meanwhile, the RNRD said it would join the CFOD, but the APP dropped out, claiming too many differences with other member parties. On a positive note, the opposition coalition in July approved the president's national dialogue document, which included a recommendation for review of the electoral process and was aimed at promoting further talks between the president and the opposition.

In an October 20, 2011, statement, military officials claimed to have destroyed "enemy elements who were preparing to launch an attack on our territory." The next day the al-Akhbar news agency quoted a military source saying that a purported senior AQIM commander was killed in the attack, which consisted of an air force strike on camps near the Malian border.

In March 2012 Abdullah Senussi, chief of Libyan intelligence services under Qadhafi, was arrested at Nouakchott airport after flying in from Morocco with a fake passport and disguised as a Tuareg chieftain. In September authorities bowed to Libyan demands for his extradition in what was seen as a blow to the International Criminal Court, which wanted to try him for crimes against humanity.

On March 6, 2012, the legislature adopted constitutional amendments reinforcing its powers, prohibiting coups, and criminalizing slavery. But the next week the CFOD opposition organized antigovernment protests in the capital, demanding long-delayed legislative elections. On March 15 Abdelaziz rejected the possibility of talks with the CFOD.

A new seven-member national electoral authority was created on June 13. The basis for the National Independent Electoral Commission had been established in an October deal the government signed with four opposition parties, but which the CFOD refused to recognize.

On June 20, 2012, Al-Jazeera reported that CFOD members announced the creation of Struggle, a women's alliance opposed to Abdelaziz. The same day government officials named Ahmed El Hacen Ould CHEIKH Mohamedou Hamed as the new president of the Higher Islamic Council, a state body that advises the government on Islamic precepts as they relate to legislation.

On October 13, 2012, Abdelaziz was slightly wounded when troops opened fire on his presidential convoy. Officially the shooting was an accident, but reports indicate that it may have been an abortive coup attempt.

On January 11, 2013, former interim president and current Senate President Mbaré died of natural causes in Paris. In March the government established an agency to aid former slaves in their integration into society and to combat household slavery, reportedly still common throughout the country. Throughout much of 2011 and 2012 officials continuously postponed scheduled elections. The government set November 23 as the date for national assembly elections and 2014 for presidential polling. (*See headnote.*)

POLITICAL PARTIES

Mauritania became a one-party state in 1964, when the Mauritanian People's Party (*Parti du Peuple Mauritanien*—PPM/*Hizb al-Shah al-Muritani*) was assigned legal supremacy over all governmental organs. The PPM was dissolved following the coup of July 1978. Although partisan activity was not permitted, some candidates in municipal elections in 1986–1990 were linked to various informal groups.

The constitution approved in July 1991 guaranteed "freedom of association," and subsequent legislation established regulations for the legalization of political parties. Groups based on race or region were proscribed, while Islamic organizations were declared ineligible for registration on the ground that Islam belonged to "all the people" and could not be "claimed" by electoral bodies.

In view of the near-total dominance of the Democratic and Social Republican Party (PRDS) in national and municipal elections, legislation was adopted in late 2000 providing for a degree of proportional representation in the 2001 assembly balloting and concurrent local polls. It was also announced that all parties securing at least 1 percent of the votes in the municipal elections would receive government financing (based on their total vote) and that "equal access" to the state-controlled media would be provided to opposition parties (for a history of party developments between the 2005 and 2008 coups, see the 2012 *Handbook*).

Following the bloodless coup of 2008, the PNDD, APP, and UFP, as well as some civil societies, formed an alliance under the rubric National Front for the Defense of Democracy (*Avant National pour la Défense de la Démocratie*—FNDD) in opposition to the coup. It later included the RNRD, but that party dropped out after its leader was defeated in the 2009 presidential election.

Following a large rally in December 2009 to protest the Abdelaziz government, nine parties formed the Coordination of Forces of Democratic Opposition (*Coordination des Forces Démocratique*—CFOD) to promote democratic principles. The coalition, chaired by Massaoud Ould Boulkheir, included the UFP, the Alternative, the APP, the RFD, the PLEJ, and the PNDD, and three minor parties. Another opposition grouping, reportedly open only to parties represented in parliament, was formed about the same time by the RFD's Ahmed Ould Daddah. The CFOD was said by Boulkheir to be open to all parties.

Governing Party:

Union for the Republic (*Union pour la République*—UPR). General Abdelaziz and members of parliament who supported the 2008 coup and the subsequent ruling High Council of State formed the UPR in April 2009 in the run-up to the presidential election. Many of the parliamentarians were from the former governing PNDD (below). In May 2009 it was widely reported that 83 of 151 legislators had joined the new party. Shortly thereafter, some 50 members of the RFD reportedly defected to the UPR after their party's vice president, Kane Hamidou Baba, announced his support for the junta. Abdelaziz resigned as head of state and as chair of the party in order to contest the presidential election. The party subsequently elected former defense minister Mohamed Mahmoud Ould Mohamed Lemine as chair in August. Following opposition calls for Abdelaziz to step down in September 2012, the UPR launched a concerted media campaign to discredit the opposition.

Leaders: Gen. Mohamed Ould ABDELAZIZ (President of the Republic), Mohamed Mahmoud Ould Mohamed LEMINE (Chair), Omar Ould MAATALA (Vice President), Ba COUMBA (Vice President), Saleh Ould DEHMACH, Abah Ould SIDATI, Ali Ould Ahmed SALEM (Secretary General).

Other Legislative Parties:

National Pact for Development and Democracy (*Pacte National pour le Développment et le Démocratie*—PNDD). The governing party during the term of former president Sidi Mohamed Ould Cheikh Abdallahi, the PNDD was established in January 2008 over the strident objections of the opposition and smaller parties. The PNDD (also referenced as the PNDD-ADIL) named Yahya Ould Ahmed el-Waghf as chair, since the country's constitution prohibits a president from heading a political party. The party was seen as supporting Abdallahi's move to consolidate government authority in the executive and legislative branches (the PNDD was reported to have held a majority of seats in parliament and all of the cabinet posts under Abdallahi's tenure as president). Among its founders were political activists and some members of the RDU who had backed President Abdallahi and his programs. El-Waghf, for his part, served as secretary general of the presidency in the Abdallahi administration. In May 2008 he was appointed prime minister.

In mid-2008 some 40 party dissidents called for a no-confidence vote against Prime Minister el-Waghf, criticizing him for not representing the will of the electorate by including opposition members and others formerly aligned with the Taya regime in the government. Among those who resigned was the party's secretary general, Mohamed Lemine Ould ABOYE. Just prior to the coup in August, some 48 PNDD parliamentarians resigned in the wake of mounting criticism of Adballahi. The disaffected party members objected to the cabinet reshuffle in May, owing to the number of Taya loyalists, and accused the president of corruption. Those who resigned, including one of the party's leaders, Sidi Mohamed Ould MAHAM (who was elected to the Supreme Court a month after the coup), said they intended to form a new political group (subsequently, the UPR, above). As a result, the PNDD lost its legislative majority, though it remained the single largest party in parliament. Shortly after General Abdelaziz seized control as head of state and announced that a presidential election would be held, another 26 pro-coup PNDD members resigned.

However, other PNDD members, led by Boidiel Ould Houmeid, were among the organizers of the FNDD, formed to give voice to those groups that opposed the August 2008 coup. After the junta installed itself, several members of the PNDD were arrested, and el-Waghf was imprisoned for six months. His release in June 2009 was among the conditions set forth by the opposition during negotiations in Senegal in May (see Current issues, above). In December the PNDD was among nine parties that formed the opposition CFOD. In early 2011 it was reported that the PNDD had agreed to work with the ruling party.

Leaders: Yahya Ould Ahmed el-WAGHF (Chair and Former Prime Minister), Sidi Mohamed Ould Cheikh ABDALLAHI (Former President of the Republic), Boidiel Ould HOUMEID, Yahya Ould ABDELGHAHAR, Mohamed Mahmoud Ould DAHMANE (Deputy Secretary General).

Rally of Democratic Forces (*Rassemblement des Forces Démocratiques*—RFD). The RFD was formed in 2001 by former members of the Union of Democratic Forces (*Union des Forces Démocratiques*—UFD), which had been legalized in October 1991 under the leadership of Hadrami Ould KHATTRY and had originally encompassed a number of diverse opposition groups whose desire to oust the Taya regime appeared to be their only common bond. Widely viewed as the strongest opposition formation at that time, the UFD supported Ahmed Ould Daddah, half-brother of former Mauritanian president Moktar Ould Daddah, in the January 1992 presidential election while spearheading the subsequent legislative boycotts. In May 1992 it was announced that the supporters of Ahmed Ould Daddah had been incorporated into the union, which was reported thereupon to have adopted the name of Union of Democratic Forces–New Era (*Union des Forces Démocratiques–Ere Nouvelle*—UFD-EN). However, news reports often continued to use the original name when referencing the group.

The party remained highly critical of the government; Ahmed Ould Daddah, who was elected UFD president in June 1992, charged that official harassment was impeding "normal" party activity. After Ould Daddah was reconfirmed as leader in early 1993, several prominent members left the party and formed the UDP. More serious were the announced defections in June 1994 of two of the union's most important components, *El-Hor,* which formed the Action for Change and the Movement of Independent Democrats (*Mouvement des Démocrates Indépendants*—MDI), which joined the PRDS.

The UFD was one of only two opposition parties (the UDP being the other) to contest the municipal elections in early 1994, gaining a majority in 17 of the country's 208 local councils. It boycotted the 1992 legislative poll but obtained one senate seat in 1994. The UFD competed unsuccessfully in the first round of 1996 legislative balloting but boycotted the second round, charging that the government had tampered with voting lists to excise supporters of the opposition.

In October 2000 the government banned the UFD-EN, accusing the party of inciting violence in connection with pro-Palestinian street demonstrations. Supporters subsequently launched the RFD, which won three assembly seats in the 2001 legislative balloting and control of four districts in municipal polls. Ahmed Ould Daddah was unanimously elected as president of the RFD in January 2002.

In April 2002 the RFD won one seat in partial Senate elections, the first of Taya's radical opposition ever to do so. A year later, in May 2003, a senior RFD member was arrested in the wake of the U.S.-led attack on Iraq and subsequent crackdown on Mauritanian Islamic groups. That same month the government appointed a close associate of Ahmed Ould Daddah, Abdellahi Ould Souleimana Ould CHEIKH SIDYA, to a cabinet position in an apparent attempt to gain some RFD support.

In 2004 Ahmed Ould Daddah was charged with helping to finance the opposition Knights of Change (see below), a movement in exile that reportedly advocated the armed overthrow of the Taya government. Daddah was later acquitted.

The RFD refused to join the new government of Prime Minister el-Waghf in May 2008, and in July the party further indicated its unhappiness with the current administration by aligning itself with those in parliament who proposed a no-confidence vote against the prime minister, prompting his resignation. (The president reappointed el-Waghf, and the no-confidence vote was never held.)

Though the RFD initially supported the 2008 junta, it later announced that it would boycott the upcoming presidential election, calling it a "masquerade," and the RFD aligned itself with the opposition grouping FNDD. However, the RFD subsequently agreed to participate in the election, following a compromise agreement between junta leaders and political parties. Party vice president Kane Hamidou Baba resigned, along with some 50 other dissidents, after declaring support for the junta. Subsequently, Baba announced his bid for the presidency without the backing of the RFD, which instead endorsed Ould Daddah, now allied with the FNDD. Ould Daddah, with 13.6 percent of the vote, finished a distant third to General Abdelaziz. Baba, who was deputy speaker of parliament, ran as an independent and received just 1.5 percent of the vote.

The RFD joined the opposition coalition CFOD in 2009, pledging to support a challenge to the president and his party in the upcoming elections. In mid-2011, the party announced its plans to boycott municipal and legislative elections scheduled for October. In August 2013 the RFD announced that, if Abdelaziz did not resign, the party would boycott legislative elections in October.

Leaders: Ahmed OULD DADDAH (President of the Party and 1992, 2003, 2007, and 2009 presidential candidate), Mohamed Ould BOILIL.

Republican Democratic Party for Renovation (*Parti Républicain Démocratique Rénové*—PRDR). This party is a successor to the Democratic and Social Republican Party (*Parti Républicain Démocratique et Social*—PRDS). The PRDS was launched in support of President Taya by a longtime associate, Cheikh Sid Ahmed Ould BABA, who resigned from the cabinet and military in mid-1991 to concentrate on party politics. As the PRDS nominee, Taya won the January 1992 presidential poll by a substantial margin, and the PRDS assumed essentially unchallenged political control by winning large majorities in the subsequent elections for the National Assembly and the Senate, which were boycotted by most opposition groups. The party also dominated the municipal and senate balloting of early 1994.

In March 1995 the PRDS absorbed the MDI, led by Bechir el-HASSEN, which had left the UFD (above) in June 1994.

The party won 70 of 79 seats in the 1996 legislative balloting on its own right and also had the support of the seven independent legislators (some of whom were former PRDS members) and the RDU representative in the assembly. Taya was reelected as party leader in November 1999. The PRDS won 64 of 81 seats in the assembly in the 2001 balloting and 15 of 18 open seats in the April 2004 partial senate elections. In 2003 President Taya won his third term in office.

Following the August 3, 2005, coup, Colonel Vall named PRDS member Sidi Mohamed Ould Boubacar as prime minister, and Boubacar quit the party on August 9. The PRDS initially objected to the junta, calling on its members to support the former regime. However, a few days later it reportedly reversed itself and gave approval to the ruling MCJD. Support for Taya, widely reported to be a repressive leader who imprisoned dissidents, particularly Islamists, had waned over the years, and his policy of engagement with Israel angered Arab nationalists, observers said. On September 19 the party took the further step of abolishing the chair that Taya had held for 15 years. In October the party held an extraordinary congress and reportedly changed its name to the Republican Democratic Party for Renovation. However, the actions of the congress were canceled in November by a Mauritanian court, which also ordered the party's assets seized pending the outcome of a dispute within the party over whether an audit should have been conducted during the congress. Further turmoil was evidenced when the party's Islamist wing, led by Abdou MAHAM, severed its ties the same month, reportedly to join the Rally for Democracy and Unity (*Rassemblement pour la Démocratie et l'Unité*—RDU). On November 25 the PRDS elected Ethmane Ould Cheikh Abou Ali Maali, Mauritania's ambassador to Kuwait, as president. The party further distanced itself from Taya by announcing its opposition to the diplomatic ties with Israel that the former president had established. In the 2006 parliamentary elections the party won seven seats.

The party supported the 2008 coup, and Maali was appointed to the transitional unity government in mid-2009. He retained his cabinet post following the 2009 presidential election and the pursuant cabinet reshuffle but was subsequently dismissed from the government.

Leaders: Ethmane Ould Cheikh Abou Ali MAALI (President and 2007 presidential candidate), Cheikh El Avia Ould Mohamed KHOUNA (Former Prime Minister), Rachid Ould SALEH (Former Speaker of the National Assembly), Sidi Mohamed Ould Mohamed VALL (Secretary General).

Rally for Democracy and Unity (*Rassemblement pour la Démocratie et l'Unité*—RDU). Led by the mayor of Atar who had served as a cabinet minister under Mauritania's first president, the RDU supported President Taya in the January 1992 presidential campaign, but, after winning one seat in the first round of the March assembly election, broke with the government and boycotted the second round, as well as the subsequent senate race. However, as of the 1996 legislative elections, in which it retained its seat, the RDU was once again described as allied with the PRDS, and the RDU leader was named an adviser to the president in the government announced in December 1998. In the 2004 Senate elections, the RDU won one seat.

The RDU, which had been critical of the 2005 coup, soon reversed its position and supported the military junta, saying it hoped the junta could return stability to the country and lead Mauritania to democracy. In August the RDU announced it would boycott legislative balloting scheduled for October.

Leader: Ahmed Moktar Sidi BABA.

Union for Democracy and Progress (*Union pour la Démocratie et le Progrès*—UDP). The UDP was legalized in June 1993, its ranks including prominent ex-UFD members, some of whom had also served in the administration of Mauritania's first president, Moktar Ould Daddah. UDP leaders pledged to work toward "restoration of national unity," which, in contrast to government policy, appeared to be aimed at conciliation with black Mauritanians. However, despite its professed multiracial stance, the UDP more recently has been described as continuing, for the most part, to represent conservative Moorish interests.

The UDP participated in the 1994 municipal balloting, although it did not gain control of any of the 19 local boards for which it offered candidates, party leaders reportedly having encouraged supporters to vote for whichever opposition candidate had the best chance of defeating the PRDS candidate. Said to be suffering from internal dissension, the UDP won no seats in the 1996 legislative poll. When UDP leader Hamdi OULD MOUKNASS was appointed as a presidential adviser in December 1997, the UDP moved into a position as a government-supportive party. At the same time, some party members had reportedly aligned with the FPO, the recently organized leading opposition coalition.

Hamdi Ould Mouknass died in September 1999 and was succeeded as UDP president in May 2000 by his daughter, Naha Mint Mouknass, who thereby became one of two female party leaders in the Arab world. She was also named a presidential adviser, reaffirming the rump UDP's ties to the government.

In August 2009 Mouknass was named Mauritania's first female foreign minister. In November the party won one seat in the partial Senate elections.

Leaders: Naha Mint MOUKNASS (President), Sheikh Saad Bouh CAMARA, Ahmed OULD MENAYA (Secretary General).

Union of Progressive Forces (*Union des Forces Progressives*—UFP). Formed by former members of the UFD (above), the UFP, whose leadership includes former Marxists, called for dialogue with the PRDS in order to "improve the political atmosphere." The new party won three seats in the 2001 assembly balloting. In 2003 the UFP supported Ould Haidalla for president and joined other opposition groups in complaining of fraud following the Taya victory. The party considered boycotting the 2004 Senate elections but ultimately participated with two nominees. Both lost, one by a narrow margin, to PRDS candidates. In 2005 the party demanded the return of Mauritanian exiles and an end to slavery in the country, precepts it pushed for in the transitional program following the August coup.

Party chair Mohammed Ould Maaloud received 4.08 percent of the vote in the first round in the 2007 presidential election; he supported Ould Daddah in the second round.

The UFP opposed the August 2008 coup, and Maaloud became a leader of the opposition grouping FNDD.

In 2009 the party joined the opposition grouping styled the CFOD. In July 2011 the UFP said it would boycott elections set to take place in October. In August 2013 the UFP announced it would boycott local and regional balloting scheduled for November.

Leaders: Mohammed Ould MAALOUD (Party Chair and 2007 presidential candidate), Kadiata Malick DIALLO (Vice Chair), Mohamed Moustafa Ould BEDREDINE.

Popular Front (*Front Populaire*—FP). The FP, formerly referenced as the Popular and Democratic Front (*Front Populaire et Démocratique*—FPD), is led by former minister Mohamed Lemine Chbih Ould Cheikh Malainine, who finished second (with 7 percent of the vote) as an independent candidate in the December 1997 presidential polling. Malainine, a Muslim spiritual leader, was elected chair of the FP at its first congress in April 1998.

In early 2001 Malainine announced that the FPD would participate in the October legislative balloting, eliciting criticism from the UFD-EN. Despite Malainine's apparently conciliatory gesture toward the government, he was arrested in April on charges of conspiring with Libya to commit acts of terrorism and sentenced to five years in prison (he was released after having served two-and-a-half years). Amnesty International described Malainine as a "prisoner of conscience" and charged that his arrest was merely an attempt to "stifle" the opposition. The sentence was also strongly condemned by other opposition parties. In October 2002 the FP formed, with the Cavaliers for Change and RFD, the United Opposition Framework (UOF), which sought dialogue on democratic reform between the government and opposition groups.

In July 2006 in the run-up to legislative elections, FP leader Malainine helped form the CFCD. In the first round of the 2007 presidential election, he ran as an independent, finishing with less than 1 percent of the vote.

Leaders: Mohamed Lemine Chbih Ould Cheikh MALAININE (Party President and 2007 presidential candidate), Mohamed Fadel SIDIYA, Badi Ould IBNOU.

Popular Progressive Alliance (*Alliance Populaire et Progressive*—APP). A number of APP members were arrested in early 1997 on "conspiracy" charges emanating from the group's allegedly "pro-Libyan" tendencies. The APP boycotted the 2001 elections. On August 1, 2004, Massaoud Ould Boulkheir, the former leader of the dissolved Action for Change, was elected president of the APP, replacing Mohamed El-Hafedh Ould Ismail. That same month the party won two seats in the partial senate elections. In the first round of the 2007 presidential election, Boulkheir placed fourth with 9.8 percent of the vote and pledged to support the new president (despite his ties with the CFCD, led by Ahmed Ould Daddah).

The party was among several that called on the government in 2007 to sever ties with Israel.

The APP opposed the 2008 bloodless coup, and in 2009 Boulkheir ran for president as the candidate of the FNDD. He agreed to support the RFD's Ould Daddah if a second round of voting was held. That proved not to be the case, as Ould Daddah finished third, and Boulkheir himself finished a distant second with 16.3 percent of the vote. The APP subsequently joined the opposition grouping CFOD. In July 2011 the APP withdrew from the coalition, citing differences with other member parties.

Leaders: Massaoud Ould BOULKHEIR (Chair, Speaker of the Assembly, and 2007 and 2009 presidential candidate), El Khalil Ould TEYIB (Vice Chair), Mohamed Lamine Ould el-NATI.

Mauritanian Party of Union and Change (*Parti Mauritanien pour l'Union et le Changement*—HATEM). This party originated in 2003 as a military organization referenced as the **Knights of Change** (*Umat*), led by former army colonel Saleh Ould Hanena. The Knights had staged several failed coup attempts against President Taya, and Hanena was accused of being the mastermind behind the 2003 plot. In February 2005 Hanena was sentenced to life imprisonment, but he was released by the new junta later that year.

The group became a political party in 2006 and changed its name to HATEM. In the first round of the 2007 presidential election, Hanena won 7.65 percent of the vote. He and his Islamist supporters backed Ould Daddah for president in the second round. The party, along with the APP and El Sawab, among others, urged the new government to break diplomatic ties with Israel.

Following the 2008 coup, HATEM was among the first parties to support the junta. Subsequently, in January 2009, some 57 senior party members resigned to form a prodemocracy group, the **Patriotic Sphere of Influence**. The group was reportedly dissatisfied with HATEM's leadership. In the July presidential election party leader Hanena received 1.3 percent of the vote.

In 2010 the HATEM members of the legislature, lacking the three-seat threshold for a parliamentary group, were seated as independents. In 2011 HATEM joined the CFOD. Following his wounding in October 2012, HATEM called for Abdelaziz to step down, asserting that the president was physically unable to perform his duties.

Leader: Saleh Ould HANENA (2007 and 2009 presidential candidate).

National Rally for Reform and Development (*Rassemblement Nationale pour la Réforme* et *le Développement*—RNRD). A moderate Islamist party, the RNRD, also referenced as *Tawassoul*, gained legal status in 2007. Among its leaders is Zainab bint Dadeh, a former Baath party member. More recently, the party is described as one that promotes "democratic Islam." In May 2008 the party accepted a cabinet post in the government of Prime Minister Yahya Ould Ahmed el-Waghf. Following the August coup, the party joined the opposition FNDD coalition in 2009. After his defeat in the 2009 presidential election, party leader Mohamed Mansour dropped out of the FNDD, and in the wake of the opposition's failure to win any seats in the Senate replenishment in November (the RNRD blaming corruption), the party joined a legislative alliance with the governing UPR.

In mid-2011 the RNRD agreed to join the opposition coalition CFOD.

Leaders: Mohamed Jemil Ould MANSOUR (Chair and 2009 presidential candidate), Zainab bint DADEH, Ahmed Ould WEDIA.

Alternative (*El Badil*). The Alternative was founded in 2006 and chaired by Mohamed Yahdi Ould Moctar HACEN, a former interior minister in the Abdhallahi government. The party was reported to be the main party supporting the 2008 coup. Hacen, secretary general of the former ruling PRDS and formerly a close ally of President Abdallahi, left the government before the coup. In 2009 he was nominated as the Alternative's presidential candidate, but he did not run. In March the party organized a forum with 10 political parties to try to begin a dialogue between supporters of Abdallahi and those backing General Abdelaziz.

Leaders: Mohamed Yahdi Ould Moctar HACEN (Chair), Mamadou LY (Vice President).

Other parliamentary parties are the **National Rally for Democracy, Liberty, and Equality** and the **Democratic Renovation Party**.

Other Parties That Contested Recent Elections:

El Sawab ("The Correct," "The Right Track"). El Sawab, formed in May 2004 by politicians close to former head of state Mohamed Khouna Ould Haidalla, said it had an "original" society program. The party, which was officially recognized in July 2004, opposed Taya's regime. It was described in 2008 as a Baathist party that opposed Mauritania's support for Israel and called on the media to "expose the Zionists" in Mauritania.

Leaders: Abdelsalam Ould HOURMA (Chair), Mohamed Ould GUELMA.

Party for Democratic Convergence (PCD). Many Mauritanians refer to the PCD as "Haidalla's friends," referring to former president Mohamed Khouna Ould Haidalla, but the Arabic initials, formed in May 2004, reveal another allegiance: they spell El Hamd, literally, "praise to God." The PCD is composed of a wide range of groups that were persecuted under the Taya regime, including many black Mauritanians, Islamic radicals, and those who supported the 2003 coup attempt. The vice president of the group, former Nouakchott mayor Mohamed Jemil Ould MANSOUR, an accused Islamic radical, was arrested in 2003 but escaped from prison during the coup attempt and fled to Belgium. There Mansour helped found the **Mauritanian Forum for Reform and Democracy**, along with other political exiles from the 2003 coup. Upon returning to Mauritania, Mansour was arrested again and then released.

Ould Haidalla, who had challenged Taya in the November 2003 presidential election, was arrested two days after the election, and in December he was convicted of plotting a coup against Taya. Ould Haidalla, who denied the charges, received a suspended sentence. In 2005 he was acquitted on charges relating to attempted coups in 2003 and 2004. Also in 2005 the ruling junta refused to recognize the PCD because it contended the party advocated the monopoly of Islam in politics. Party leaders denied it had Islamist links, despite having religious leaders among its members. In the first round of the 2007 presidential election, party leader Isselmou Ould Moustapha was officially credited with 0.24 percent of the vote. It was unclear why he appeared on the ballot under the PCD banner since the PCD had been banned. In the same election, Ould Haidalla ran as an independent, receiving 1.73 percent of the vote in the first round.

Leaders: Isselmou Ould MOUSTAPHA (2007 presidential candidate), Mohamed Khouna OULD HAIDALLA (2003 presidential candidate).

National Union for Democracy and Development (*Union Nationale pour la Démocratie et le Développement*—UNDD). Formed by Sen. Tidjane Koita after he left the AC in 1997, the UNDD has been described as the "moderate opposition" and a proponent of dialogue between the PRDS and the more strident antiregime groups. None of the UNDD's candidates was successful in the 2001 assembly balloting. Social justice and national unity are listed as key party goals.

Leader: Tidjane KOITA.

Mauritanian Renewal Party (*Parti Mauritanien pour le Renouvellement*—PMR). Shortly after legalization of the PMR, also referenced as the **Mauritanian Party for Renewal and Concord** (PMRC), in mid-September 1991, its leaders charged that inappropriate links had been formed between the PRDS and long-standing national and municipal leaders, placing other groups at a disadvantage in forthcoming elections. The PMR, however, won one seat in the 1992 legislative balloting. In the 1997 presidential balloting, PMR leader Moulaye al-Hassan OULD JEYDID finished third with less than 1 percent of the vote.

In April 2001 the government announced the recognition of a new party also named the Mauritanian Renewal Party, led by Atiq OULD ATTIA.

In 2007 leaders Ould Jeydid and Rajel dit Rachit MOUSTAPHA each received less than 1 percent of the vote as presidential candidates representing the PMRC and the PMR, respectively. The relationship between the two parties was unclear. The party failed to win seats in the 2009 partial Senate elections.

Alliance for Justice and Democracy (*Alliance pour la Justice et la Démocratie*—AJD)—**Movement for Renovation** (*Mouvement pour la Rénové*—MR). The AJD was formed in 2000 by Massoud Ould Boulkheir, former leader of the outlawed Action for Change, and other AC dissidents. The AJD was officially recognized in 2001. It opposed the Taya regime on the issue of recognition of Israel, the AJD urging the government to cut all ties with Israel, and it appealed for a fair resolution to the problems of Mauritanian refugees in Senegal. Boulkheir was the AJD's presidential candidate in 2003.

The AJD boycotted the 2006 constitutional referendum, saying the proposed amendments did not adequately address the issue of slavery, among other things.

According to the *Africa Research Bulletin*, a leading figure in FLAM (see below), Ba Mamadou BOCAR, was elected AJD vice president in August 2007. The party was subsequently referenced as having merged with the MR and as having "integrated" FLAM—Renovation (see below). It was unclear what the latter association meant.

Ibrahima Moctar Sarr, a journalist, ran as an independent in the 2007 presidential balloting, receiving just under 8 percent of the vote; he supported Ould Daddah in the second round. In the 2009 presidential election, Sarr received 4.6 percent of the vote.

Leaders: Ibrahima Moctar SARR (President and 2007, 2008, and 2009 presidential candidate), Kebe ABDOULAYE, Alpha DIALLO, Cisse Amadou CHEIKH (Secretary General).

Party for Liberty, Equality, and Justice (*Parti pour la Liberté, l'Egalité, et la Justice*—PLEJ). The PLEJ was founded in 1991 by Ba Mamadou Alassane, a former ambassador and cabinet minister who was among the first Black Africans to head a political party in Mauritania. The PLEJ's main concerns are the return of Mauritanian refugees from Senegal and the elimination of racism in Mauritania. In 1997 party member Kane Amadou Moctar was one of four candidates who challenged Taya in the presidential election.

In the first round of the 2007 presidential election, Alassane received less than 1 percent of the vote; he supported Ould Daddah in the second round. The party opposed the 2008 coup.

Leaders: Ba Mamadou ALASSANE (Chair and 2007 presidential candidate), Daouda MBAGNIGA.

Other parties and groups that participated in recent elections include the **Third Generation** (*Parti de la Troisienne Generation*—PTG), led by Lebat OULD JEH; the **Social Democratic Party,** formed in 2005 by Mohamed Salek Ould DIDAH; the **Rally for Mauritania,** formed in 2005 by Cheikh Ould HORMA; the **Mauritanian Party for the Defense of the Environment** (*Parti Mauritanien pour la Défense de l'Environment*—PMDE), also known as the Green Party, established in 2003 by Mohamed Ould DELLAHI; the **Mauritanian Party of Liberal Democrats** (*Parti Mauritanien des Libéraux Democrates*—PMLD), led by Moustapha Ould LEMRABOTT; the **Socialist and Democratic Popular Union** (*Union Populaire Socialiste et Démocratique*—UPSD); the **Union of the Democratic Center** (*Union du Centre Démocratique*—UCD); and the **Party of Labor and National Unity** (*Parti du Travail et de l'Unité Nationale*—PTUN), led by Ali Bouna Ould OUENINA and Mohamed Ould EL BAH.

Other Parties and Groups:

African Liberation Forces of Mauritania (*Forces de Libération Africaine de Mauritanie*—FLAM). Organized in 1983 in opposition to what were perceived as repressive policies toward blacks, FLAM was believed responsible for an "Oppressed Black" manifesto that in 1986 was widely distributed within Mauritania and at the nonaligned summit in Zimbabwe. Based partly in Dakar, Senegal, the group also condemned reprisals against blacks by the Taya regime following an alleged coup attempt in 1987. Many FLAM supporters were reported to be among those who fled or were expelled to Senegal in 1989. Subsequently engaged in guerrilla activity, FLAM leaders announced in July 1991 that they were suspending "armed struggle" in response to the government's general amnesty and promulgation of a new Mauritanian constitution. FLAM endorsed Ahmed Ould Daddah in the January 1992 presidential election, after which it renewed its antigovernment military campaign near the Senegalese border. Leaders of the group stated in early 1995 that they were neither secessionists nor terrorists, reiterating their support for the establishment of a federal system that would ensure an appropriate level of black representation in government while protecting the rights of blacks throughout Mauritanian society. In early 2001 the FLAM called upon the international community to exert pressure on the Mauritanian government to address the issue of black refugees remaining in Senegal and Mali as the result of the 1989 exodus.

The group, along with the Patriotic Alliance and other anti-Taya organizations, again pledged to give up its armed struggle following the 2005 coup.

In February 2006 a breakaway group formed under the rubric **FLAM—Renovation,** reportedly planning to join in the political process in Mauritania, though it was unclear how it intended to do so (see AJD-MR, above). The breakaway group, issuing a report from Senegal, called on the government to address the refugee issue.

FLAM had called for a boycott of the constitutional referendum in 2006 and criticized the approved amendments on the grounds that they did not adequately address the issue of slavery, among other things. According to FLAM's Web site, the group has never participated in an election in Mauritania because FLAM's "standard conditions," including issues like human rights, slavery, and refugees, have not been met. In June 2007 a group of Mauritanian expatriates living in New York filed a suit against Taya, alleging torture and other human rights violations. The suit included claims by two black Mauritanians that they were among the victims of "ethnic cleansing" under the Taya regime.

In November 2007 following the signing of a tripartite agreement by Mauritania, Senegal, and the UNHCR to allow for the return of thousands of black Mauritanian refugees, FLAM raised concerns about the country's ability to handle the influx.

Despite the adoption in 2007 of a law making slavery illegal in Mauritania, black Mauritanians were still allegedly being persecuted. In early 2011 it was reported that the antislavery campaigner Biram Dah ABEID remained in custody since December 2010, charged with assaulting two police officers. FLAM and other groups claimed he was being harassed because of his antislavery campaign. FLAM opposed Mauritania's troop deployment to Mali in 2013.

Leader: Samba THIAM (President).

Patriotic Alliance (a.k.a. Democratic Alliance). Several Mauritanian political groups created the Patriotic Alliance on July 10, 2004. It is allegedly affiliated with Ould Haidalla and those responsible for the failed 2003 coup. In February 2005 Senegal deported a leader of the Patriotic Alliance, Ely Ould SNEIBA, to Mali. Sneiba later was convicted in absentia by a Mauritanian court and sentenced to five years for his role in the coup attempt. In July 2005 Sneiba was granted political asylum in Belgium.

In 1994 security forces accused a number of previously unknown extremist organizations, including **Call to Islam** and the **Mauritanian Islamic Movement** (*Hasim*) of conspiring to overthrow the government. As part of its antiterrorism efforts, backed by the United States, the Mauritanian government in October 2004 arrested three leaders of the

Mauritanian Islamic Movement—Mohamed El-Hacen Ould DEDOW, Moctar Ould Mohamed MOUSSA, and Mohamed Jemil Ould Mansour—on charges of subversion. Mansour, who was later listed as the leader of the **Centrist Reformers**, described as moderate Islamists, has been named as among the leaders of several parties or groups.

Among 18 new parties licensed by the government in August 2007 were the **Work and Equality Party**; the **Mauritanian Hope Party**, founded by women and led by Tahi bint LAHBIB, it aims to have women make up half of its membership; the **Conservative Party**; the **Alternation and Consultation Party**; and the **Coalition for Democracy in Mauritania**. Also licensed was the **Movement for Direct Democracy** (MDD), led by Omar Ould RABAH. The MDD was banned in 2005, but its members aligned themselves with the CFCD prior to the 2006 assembly elections. The MDD was described as reformist rather than Islamist, in accordance with the political parties law, although it was reported to be an offshoot of the Muslim Brotherhood (see Mauritanian Islamic Movement, above).

Additional parties include the **Democratic and Social Union** (*Union Démocratique et Sociale*—UDS), which was led by Isselmou Ould HANEFI and boycotted the 2006 parliamentary elections; the **National Party for Unity and Democracy** (*Parti National pour l'Unité et la Démocratie*—PNUD); the **Mauritanian Liberal Democrats,** led by Mustapha OULD LEMBRABET; the **Mauritanian Labor Party,** led by Mohamed Hafid OULD DENNA; the **Democratic Alliance,** led by Mohamed Ould Taleb OTHMAN; the **National Renaissance Party** (*Parti de la Renaissance Nationale*—PRN), led by Mohamed Ould Abdellaki Ould EYYE; the **National Pact** (*Pacte National*—PN), led by former PRDS member Mohamed Abdallah OULD KHARCY; the **Popular Initiatives Rally**, which supported the 2008 junta, led by Mohamed SALEM; and the **National Union for Democratic Alternative**. In November 2008 the **Union of Democratic Youth** was formed under the leadership of Jeddou Ould AHMAD, with a platform of anti-terrorism. It was licensed in April 2009, along with 11 others—the first parties to be approved by the junta. In addition to the governing UPR (above), the newly licensed parties are: the **Mauritanian Authenticity Party**; the **Party for Peace and Democratic Progress**; **Mauritanian National Congress**; **Mauritanian Loyalty Party**; **League of Mauritanians for the Homeland**; **Rally of National Youth**; **Democratic Choice**; **Wellbeing Party**; **Union of Social Forces**; and **Mauritanian People's Rally**.

LEGISLATURE

The 1991 constitution provides for a bicameral legislature consisting of an indirectly chosen Senate and a popularly elected National Assembly. The parliament was dissolved by the Military Council for Justice and Democracy following the August 3, 2005, coup. Constitutional amendments approved in a public referendum on June 25, 2006, included provisions for restoring the **Parliament**.

Senate (*Majlis al-Shuyukh*). The Senate is renewed by thirds every two years for six-year terms, with 53 of its 56 members selected by the country's mayors and municipal councilors and three seats representing Mauritanians abroad chosen by the elected senators.

In the election on January 21 and February 4, 2007, the seat distribution was as follows: independents, 34; the Rally of Democratic Forces (RFD), 5; the Republican Democratic Party for Renovation, 3; the Coalition of Forces of Democratic Change, 3; the Mauritanian Party of Union and Change (HATEM), 2; the Union of Progressive Forces (UFP), 1; the RFD/UFP, 1; the RFD/Independents, 1; the HATEM/Independents, 1; the Union for Democracy (UDP) and Progress/Independents, 1; and the People's Progressive Alliance /Independents, 1.

In partial elections on November 8 and November 15, 2009, for one-third of the members, or 17 seats, the Union for the Republic won a total of 13 seats; independents, 2; the National Rally for Reform and Development, 1; and the UDP, 1. (Parties that win fewer than 3 seats sit as independents unless they join an alliance.)

President: Vacant.

National Assembly (*Majlis al-Watani*). In 2006 the size of the assembly was increased from 81 to 95 seats, 14 of which are elected nationally in proportional balloting on a party basis and 81 of which are elected in 45 regional constituencies. The mixed voting system is majoritarian in single-member and 2-seat constituencies, with proportional representation in constituencies of 3 or more seats. All members are elected for five-year terms.

In the balloting on November 19 and December 3, 2006, the seat distribution was as follows: the Coalition of Forces of Democratic Change, 38 (the Rally of Democratic Forces [RFD], 15; the Union of Progressive Forces [UFP], 8; the Popular Progressive Alliance, 5; the Mauritanian Party of Union and Change [HATEM], 2; the HATEM/APP, 2; the RFD/UFP, 2; the Democratic Renovation Party, 2; the Popular Front, 1; the Socialist and Democratic Popular Union, 1); the Republican Democratic Party for Renovation, 7; the Rally for Democracy and Unity, 3; the Union for Democracy and Progress, 3; the Union of the Democratic Center, 1; the Alternative, 1; the National Rally for Democracy, Liberty, and Equality, 1; independents, 41.

Many members of the legislature reportedly joined the new National Pact for Development (PNDD), formed in March 2007. Before the bloodless coup on August 6, 2008, the PNDD was said to have held 50 of the assembly's 95 seats, but it was unclear which groups had aligned themselves with the governing party.

Speaker: Massaoud Ould BOULKHEIR.

CABINET

[as of September 2, 2013]

Prime Minister	Moulaye Ould Mohamed Laghdaf
Ministers	
Communications and Relations with Parliament	Mohamed Ould Horma
Culture, Youth, and Sport (Acting)	Aicha Mint Michel Verges [f]
Defense	Ahmed Ould Idey Ould Mohamed Radhi
Economic Affairs and Development	Sidi Ould Tah
Energy and Oil	Wane Ibrahima Lamine
Equipment and Transport	Yahya Hademine
Finance	Amedi Camara
Fisheries and Maritime Economy	Ghdafina Ould Eyih
Foreign Affairs and Cooperation	Hamadi Ould Hamadi
Health	Cheikh el Moctar Ould Horma Ould Babana
Housing and Town and Country Planning	Ismael Ould Bedde Ould Cheikh Sidiya
Industry and Mines	Mohamed Abdallahi Could Oudaa
Interior and Decentralization	Mohamed Ould Boilil
Islamic Affairs and Religious Education	Ahmed Ould Neini
Justice	Abidine Ould El Khaire
Public Sector and Modernization	Maty Mint Hamadi [f]
Rural Development	Brahim Ould Mbareck Ould Mohamed El Moctar
Secretary General of the Government	Mohamed Ould Mohamedou
Secretary General to the Presidency	Adama Sy
Social Affairs, Children, and Families	Aicha Mint Michel Verges [f]
Trade, Industry, Handicrafts, and Tourism	Bamba Ould Dermane
Water Resources and Sanitation	Mohamed Lemine Ould Aboye
Ministers of State	
National Education, Higher Education, and Scientific Research	Ahmed Ould Baya
Ministers Delegate	
Minister Delegate to the Prime Minister in Charge of Environment and Sustainable Development	Ba Housseinou Hamady
Minister Delegate to Minister of State in Charge of National Education, Higher Education, and Scientific Research	Oumar Ould Maatalla

Minister Delegate to the Prime Minister in Charge of Employment, Professional Training, and New Technology	Mohamed Ould Khouna
Minister Delegate to the Minister of State for National Education; in Charge of Basic Education	Hamed Ould Hamouny

[f] = female

INTERGOVERNMENTAL REPRESENTATION

Ambassador to the U.S.: Mohamed Lemine HAYCEN.

U.S. Ambassador to Mauritania: Larry ANDRE (nominated).

Permanent Representative to the UN: Jiddou JIDDOU (Chargé d'affaires).

IGO Memberships (Non–United Nations): AfDB, AU, IOM, LAS, NAM, OIC, WTO.

MAURITIUS

Republic of Mauritius

Political Status: Constitutional monarchy under multiparty parliamentary system established upon independence within the Commonwealth on March 12, 1968; became a republic on March 12, 1992.

Area: 790 sq. mi. (2,045 sq. km).

Population: 1,332,432 (2012E—UN); 1,322,238 (2013E—U.S. Census).

Major Urban Centers (2011E—UN): PORT LOUIS (148,638), Beau Bassin/Rose Hill (110,687), Vacoas-Phoenix (108,186).

Official Language: English (French is also used, while Creole is the lingua franca and Hindi the most widely spoken).

Monetary Unit: Mauritian rupee (official rate November 1, 2013: 30.50 rupees = $1US).

President: Rajkeswur PURRYAG (Mauritius Labour Party); elected by the National Assembly on July 20, 2012, for a five-year term, to succeed acting president Monique Ohsan BELLEPEAU after Sir Anerood JUGNAUTH (Mauritian Socialist Movement) resigned on March 31, 2012.

Vice President: Monique Ohsan BELLEPEAU (Mauritius Labour Party) was elected by the National Assembly on November 11, 2010, and was sworn in on November 13, for a term concurrent with the remainder of the president's, to succeed Angidi Verriah CHETTIAR (Mauritius Labour Party), who died in office on September 15.

Prime Minister: Navin RAMGOOLAM (Mauritius Labour Party); named prime minister on July 5, 2005, in succession to Paul Raymond BÉRENGER (Mauritian Militant Movement) following legislative election of July 3; reappointed following legislative elections on May 5, 2010, and sworn in on May 11.

THE COUNTRY

The island of Mauritius, once known as Ile de France, is situated 500 miles east of Madagascar, in the southwestern Indian Ocean (see map, below); Rodrigues Island, the Agalega Islands, and the Cardagos Carajos Shoals (St. Brandon Islands) also are national territory. (Mauritius also claims Diego Garcia and other islands in the Chagos Archipelago, currently controlled by the United Kingdom as part of the British Indian Ocean Territory [see Foreign relations, below, for details].) The diversity of contemporary Mauritian society is a reflection of its history as a colonial sugar plantation. African slave laborers were imported initially, and they were followed by the migration of Indians (who now constitute two-thirds of the population), Chinese, French, and English. Religious affiliations include Hinduism, to which 48 percent of the population adheres; Christianity (predominantly Roman Catholicism), 24 percent; and Islam, 17 percent. Women are significantly engaged in subsistence agriculture, although they comprise only 32 percent of the paid labor force. Thirteen women were elected to the National Assembly in 2010 (18.8 percent of the total deputies). Women held the vice presidency and two cabinet posts in 2013 and 26.2 percent of local elected posts.

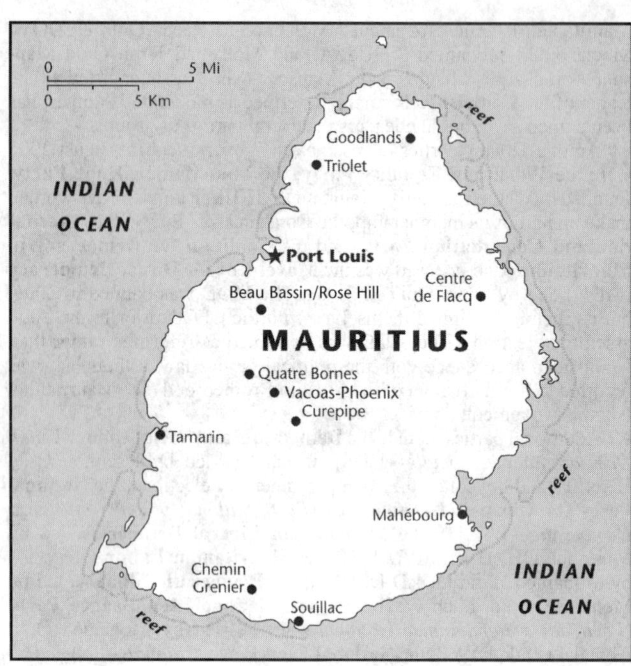

The overall strong economic performance in the 1990s led some experts to reference a "Mauritian miracle" and to describe the country as a case study in the successful management of a developing country that pursued investor-friendly policies. (For more on the history of the economy, see the 2013 *Handbook.*)

GDP growth averaged 4.18 between 2000 and 2008, while inflation averaged 6.3 percent. Unemployment during this period peaked at 10.2 percent in 2004, before declining to 7.3 percent by 2009. Reforms lowered average tariffs from 19.9 percent in 2001 to just 6.6 percent in 2007, while the financial services sector, valued at $35.86 billion, continued to draw foreign investment. The country's main trading partners were the United Kingdom, India, France, and China. Meanwhile, in 2008 China announced the construction of a $730 million industrial park on the island, the largest direct foreign investment to date. The global economic crisis slowed the economy in late 2008 and early 2009; however, GDP grew by 4 percent in 2010, while inflation remained low at 2.9 percent, and unemployment was 7.5 percent.

Growth for 2011 was estimated at 3.8 percent, while GDP growth slowed to 3.3 percent in 2012 because of a slowdown in sugar production as well as the impact of the European debt crisis on tourism and demand for exports such as textiles. In 2012 inflation rose by 3.9 percent, while unemployment was 8 percent. A 2013 World Bank report ranked Mauritius 19th out of 185 countries, and best in Africa, for ease in conducting business. That year, according to the IMF, real per-capita income increased to $9,306—one of the highest levels in Africa.

GOVERNMENT AND POLITICS

Political background. Because of its location, Mauritius had strategic importance during the age of European exploration and expansion, and the Dutch, French, and English successively occupied the island. France ruled Mauritius from 1710 to 1810, when Britain assumed control to protect its shipping during the Napoleonic wars. Political evolution began as early as 1831 under a constitution that provided for a Council of Government, but the franchise was largely restricted until after World War II. The postwar era also witnessed the introduction of political parties and increased participation in local government.

An election under a system of internal parliamentary democracy initiated in 1967 revealed a majority preference for full independence, which was granted by Britain on March 12, 1968, with Sir Seewoosagur RAMGOOLAM of the Independence Party (IP) as prime minister. A state of emergency, occasioned by an outbreak of severe communal strife between Muslims and Creoles, was lifted in 1970, although new disorder brought its reimposition from December 1971 to March 1978.

Under constitutional arrangements agreed upon in 1969, the mandate of the existing Legislative Assembly was extended by four years. In the election of December 20, 1976, the radical Mauritian Militant Movement (*Mouvement Militant Mauricien*—MMM), led by Anerood JUGNAUTH and Paul BÉRENGER, won a plurality of legislative seats, but the IP and the Mauritian Social Democratic Party (*Parti Mauricien Social-Démocrate*—PMSD) formed a coalition that retained Prime Minister Ramgoolam in office with a slim majority. In the country's second postindependence balloting on June 11, 1982, the incumbent parties lost all of their directly elective seats, Jugnauth proceeding to form an MMM-dominated government on June 15.

In the wake of a government crisis in March 1983, which yielded the resignation of 12 ministers, including Bérenger, and the repudiation of the prime minister by his own party, Jugnauth and his supporters regrouped as the Mauritian Socialist Movement (*Mouvement Socialiste Mauricien*—MSM) and, in alliance with Ramgoolam's Mauritius Labour Party (MLP) wing of the IP and the PMSD, won a decisive legislative majority in a new election held August 21.

In February 1984 Ramgoolam's successor as MLP leader, Sir Satcam BOOLELL, was relieved of his post as minister of economic planning, whereupon the MLP voted to terminate its support of the MSM. However, 11 Labour deputies, under the leadership of Beergoonath GHURBURRUN, refused to follow Boolell into opposition and remained in the government alliance (initially as the Mauritian Workers' Movement—MWM and later as the Mauritian Labour Rally—RTM).

In municipal council balloting on December 8, 1985, the opposition MMM won 57.2 percent of the vote, decisively defeating the coalition parties, who captured only 36.8 percent, while the MLP was a distant third with 5.4 percent. Although insisting that the MMM victory represented a rejection of Jugnauth's policies, Bérenger did not immediately call for the government to resign. However, such an appeal was made in the wake of a major scandal at the end of the month, which stemmed from the arrest on drug charges of four coalition members at Amsterdam's Schipol Airport. Subsequently, the MLP agreed to reconcile with the MSM, and Boolell was awarded three portfolios and the post of second deputy prime minister in a cabinet reorganization August 8, 1986.

At an early election on August 30, 1987, called largely because of favorable economic conditions, a reconstituted Jugnauth coalition consisting of the MSM, the MLP, the RTM (subsequently absorbed by the MSM), the PMSD, and the Rodriguan People's Organization (*Organisation du Peuple Rodriguais*—OPR) retained power by capturing 41 of 62 elective legislative seats. In August 1988, however, the PMSD, whose leader, Sir Gaëtan DUVAL, had frequently been at odds with the coalition mainstream in domestic and foreign policy, withdrew from the government, forcing Jugnauth to form a new cabinet whose assembly support had fallen to a majority of 10. Two months later the largely urban-based coalition suspended participation in municipal balloting to avoid the embarrassment of a major defeat, with the MMM (allied with several small parties) winning all of the seats in a two-way contest with the PMSD.

In an effort to strengthen his parliamentary position, Jugnauth in July 1990 concluded an electoral pact with the opposition MMM. However, the move angered a number of his fellow MSM ministers, as well as MLP leader Boolell. In August, after the government narrowly failed to secure the 75 percent approval necessary to make the country a republic within the Commonwealth, Jugnauth dismissed the dissident ministers and announced that he would continue as head of a minority administration with the parliamentary support of the MMM. A month later the MMM formally joined the government, with its president, Dr. Prem NABABSINGH, named deputy prime minister.

At an early election on September 15, 1991, the governing alliance won 59 of 62 legislative seats, far in excess of the 75 percent required to implement a change to republican status, which was approved by the Legislative Assembly on December 10, with effect from March 12, 1992. By agreement between the coalition's leading parties, Sir Veerasamy RINGADOO, who had been appointed governor general in January 1986, was designated nonexecutive president of the new republic for three months; he was succeeded on June 30 by the MMM's Cassam UTEEM.

In a cabinet reshuffle on August 18, 1993, Bérenger, who had been openly critical of government policies, was ousted as foreign minister. Two months later he was removed as MMM secretary general by the party's Political Bureau, which named Jean-Claude DE L'ESTRAC as his successor. However, the action was reversed on October 23 by the MMM Central Committee, which proceeded to name a new, pro-Bérenger party leadership. On November 16 Bérenger crossed the aisle to sit with the opposition, although he formally rejected the opposition leadership on the grounds that he had no electoral mandate for such a role. A year later Bérenger and De L'Estrac resigned as MPs; only the former regained his seat in by-elections in January 1995.

After the MLP had in January 1995 rebuffed Prime Minister Jugnauth's offer of power sharing, the PMSD agreed in early February to join the coalition, which then encompassed the MSM, MTD, OPR, and the Mauritian Militant Renaissance, despite opposition from a number of leading PMSD members, with a cabinet realignment following on February 13. An early election was then called after Jugnauth had failed to secure passage of a constitutional amendment to introduce a variety of languages (Hindi, Urdu, Tamil, Marathi, Telegu, Chinese, and Arabic) into the educational curriculum. The Creole opposition strongly opposed the amendment, which also provoked the withdrawal not only of the recently appointed PMSD members but also of the OPR representative, thus effectively shrinking the government coalition.

In an outcome not dissimilar to Prime Minister Jugnauth's 1982 electoral victory, an opposition MLP-MMM alliance swept the legislative balloting of December 20, 1995, with the MLP's Dr. Navin RAMGOOLAM, son of former prime minister Sir Seewoosagur Ramgoolam, forming a new government on December 31. It consisted of 13 MLP ministers, 9 MMM ministers (including Bérenger as deputy prime minister and foreign minister), and 1 OPR representative at the junior ministerial level. However, Bérenger was dismissed from the cabinet on June 20, 1997, and most of the other MMM ministers resigned their posts in protest. After reportedly failing to convince the PMSD to participate in the government, Ramgoolam on July 2 formed a new cabinet, which included only MLP ministers except for 1 OPR member and 1 independent (Dr. Ahmed Rashid BEEBEEJAUN, who had recently left the MMM rather than give up his portfolio for land transport, shipping, and public safety). Meanwhile, President Uteem was reappointed to another term, although his relationship with the MMM (which had promoted his initial appointment) remained unclear. Ramgoolam reshuffled his cabinet on October 25, 1998, reportedly to enhance the role of young MLP legislators in the government after an alliance formed between Bérenger's MMM and Jugnauth's MSM. The prime minister also attempted to shore up his control by including the recently formed Xavier Duval Mauritian Party (PMXD) in a cabinet reshuffle on September 26, 1999.

The Ramgoolam administration was buffeted by the resignation of several top officials tainted by scandal in 1999, as well as by drought-induced economic decline. Consequently, in August 2000 the prime minister felt compelled to dissolve the National Assembly and call for new elections in September, four months early. The MSM and MMM quickly concluded an unbeatable electoral alliance, based on an agreement that former prime minister Jugnauth would reassume the reins of government for three years, with Bérenger serving as prime minister the following two years. The new administration appeared to have the support of the private sector, notably the sugar companies and the Catholic Church.

However, in the legislative balloting on September 11, 2000, the MSM-MMM electoral coalition soundly trounced the MLP-PMXD alliance, securing 54 of the 62 elected seats. Consequently, Jugnauth returned as prime minister on September 17 to lead with Bérenger a MSM-MMM coalition government, which required Jugnauth to resign after three years and Bérenger to assume the premiership.

On February 15, 2002, President Uteem resigned after he refused to approve an antiterrorism law recently passed by the National Assembly. (Uteem argued that the new legislation could undermine national sovereignty in the name of U.S. security concerns.) He was replaced by Vice President Angidi Verriah Chettiar, who resigned on February 18 after he also refused to sign the bill into law. In accordance with the constitution, Chief Justice Arriranga PILLAY replaced Chettiar as the interim president on February 18 and subsequently signed the controversial legislation. On February 25 the National Assembly elected Karl Auguste OFFMANN and Raouf BUNDHUN as the president and vice president, respectively.

On September 29, 2002, the OPR won 10 of 18 seats in the new Rodrigues Regional Assembly, while the Rodrigues Movement won the remaining 8 seats.

Although many observers doubted the MSM-MMM "marriage" of 2000 would survive, Bérenger assumed the premiership on October 1, 2003, and Jugnauth took the largely ceremonial presidency on October 7. Bérenger, a Creole, became the nation's first non-Hindu prime minister. The most noteworthy of Bérenger's subsequent cabinet changes was the appointment of Pravind Kumar JUGNAUTH (the son of Anerood Jugnauth) as deputy prime minister and finance minister.

At balloting for 62 elected members of the National Assembly on July 3, 2005, the Social Alliance (led by the MLP) won 38 seats, while the alliance of the MSM and the MMM won 22 and the OPR won 2. Prime Minister Bérenger resigned on July 5 and was succeeded the same day by MLP leader Navin Ramgoolam, who formed a new cabinet comprising (for the most part) the parties that had formed the Social Alliance. The Social Alliance also swept municipal balloting in October, winning 122 of 124 seats in five towns, including all 30 seats in the capital, Port Louis. It also won the majority of mayoral contests.

In regional balloting in December 2006, the Rodriguan Movement (*Mouvement Rodriguais*—MR) gained a majority in the Regional Assembly after two decades of dominance of island politics by the Rodriguan People's Organization (*Organisation du Peuple Rodriguais*—OPR).

Although new presidential balloting was technically due in 2007, the government postponed the election until 2008, arguing that President Jugnauth was entitled to a full five-year term. The MSM appeared comfortable with that decision but strongly objected to the MLP's insistence that new vice-presidential elections should proceed as scheduled in 2007. Nevertheless, Prime Minister Ramgoolam nominated former vice president Chettiar to the post in August 2007, and the appointment was endorsed by the MLP-dominated assembly. In September former prime minister Paul Bérenger of the MMM was appointed opposition leader in the assembly, following the resignation of Nando Bodha of the MSM (see Political Parties, below).

Ramgoolam dismissed the foreign minister in March 2008 after the minister publicly criticized the coalition government. The prime minster then took over the foreign ministry portfolio, but carried out a major cabinet reshuffle on September 13 in which four new ministers were appointed and thirteen ministers had their portfolios altered. The cabinet continued to be dominated by the MLP and the reshuffle was reportedly an effort to improve the government's popularity ahead of the 2010 legislative balloting. On September 19 Jugnauth was unanimously reelected president by the assembly in balloting that had been postponed for a year.

Prior to the assembly elections, Ramgoolan formed a new electoral coalition, the Alliance of the Future (*Alliance de L'Avenir*), that included the MLP, MSM, and the PMSD (see Current issues, below). The coalition secured a comfortable majority with 45 seats. The rival Alliance of the Heart (*Alliance du Coeur*) which included the MMM, the Mauritian Socialist Party (*Parti Socialiste Mauricien*—PSM), and the National Union (*Union Nationale*), received 20. Ramgoolan was reappointed prime minister of a reshuffled cabinet that was sworn into office on May 11. The new cabinet also included 14 members from the MLP, 7 from the MSM, 2 from the PMSD, and 1 from the MR, which had not been part of the electoral coalition.

Monique Ohsan BELLEPEAU (MLP) was elected vice president by the National Assembly on November 11, 2010, to replace Angidi Verriah Chettiar, who died in office on September 15. She was the first female vice president of the country.

Ramgoolan dismissed Health Minister Santi Bai HANOOMANJEE (MSM) on July 26, 2011, following her arrest on corruption charges. That day, all MSM members of the cabinet resigned. They were replaced on August 7 by officials from other parties in the governing coalition.

Constitution and government. The Mauritius Independence Order of 1968, as amended the following year by the Constitution of Mauritius (Amendment) Act, provided for a unicameral system of parliamentary government with executive authority exercised by a prime minister appointed by the governor general (as the representative of the Crown) from among the majority members of the Legislative Assembly. In December 1991 the assembly approved a change to republican status as of March 12, 1992, with an essentially titular president, appointed by the assembly to a five-year term, replacing the queen as head of state. The change also included creation of an indirectly elective vice presidency. The legislature (known under the present basic law as the National Assembly) includes a Speaker, 60 representatives directly elected from three-member districts on the main island, plus 2 from Rodrigues, and the attorney general, if not an elected member. In addition, up to 8 "best loser" seats may be awarded on the basis of party or ethnic underrepresentation as indicated by shares of total vote and total population, respectively. Judicial authority, based on both French and British precedents, is exercised by a Supreme Court, four of whose five judges (excluding the chief justice) preside additionally over Appeal, Intermediate, District, and Industrial court proceedings. There are also inferior courts and a Court of Assizes. In conformity with the practice of a number of other small republican members of the Commonwealth, final appeal continues to be to the Judicial Committee of the Privy Council in London.

Nine districts constitute the principal administrative divisions, with separate administrative structures governing the Mauritian dependencies. The Agalega and Cargados Carajos islands are ruled directly from Port Louis, while Rodrigues Island has a central government under a resident commissioner. On the main island, municipal and town councils are elected in urban areas and district and village councils in rural areas.

In 1991 a Rodrigues Local Council, comprising 21 members appointed by the minister for Rodriguan affairs, was established to exercise a degree of autonomy on Rodrigues. However, its mandate expired in 1996 amid political infighting concerning the issue. Subsequently, in November 2001, the National Assembly authorized creation of an elected Rodrigues Regional Assembly (see Legislature, below). In addition to enjoying the same authority as that of local bodies on the main island, the new Regional Assembly was empowered to propose bills to the National Assembly and to oversee development projects and otherwise administer internal initiatives.

The traditionally free Mauritian press was subject to censorship under the state of emergency imposed in 1971, but restrictions were lifted on May 1, 1976. Radio and television are under the semipublic control of the government-appointed Independent Broadcasting Authority. In its 2013 report, Reporters Without Borders asserted that press freedoms in Mauritius were similar to those in Western, developed countries and ranked Mauritius 62nd out of 179 countries in freedom of the press.

As of September 2012, Ramgoolam was expected to push an electoral reform bill, following the December 2011 publication of the Carcassone Report, which contained recommendations for reform from constitutional experts—most significantly, reducing the number of constituencies and major political parties. The hope is to reduce the need for coalition governments, which were thought to be prone to breaking down before reaching their full term and to lead to destabilizing defections.

Foreign relations. Mauritius maintains diplomatic relations with most major foreign governments. One principal external issue has been the status of Diego Garcia Island, which was considered a Mauritian dependency until 1965, when London transferred administration of the Chagos Archipelago to the British Indian Ocean Territory (BIOT). The following year, Britain concluded an agreement with the United States whereby the latter obtained use of the island for 50 years. Following independence in 1968 Mauritius pressed its claim to Diego Garcia, while international attention was drawn to the issue in 1980 when Washington announced that it intended to make the island the chief U.S. naval and air base in the Indian Ocean. In July the Organization of African Unity unanimously backed Port Louis's claim, but efforts by Prime Minister Ramgoolam to garner support from the UK government were rebuffed.

In July 1982 Britain agreed to pay $4 million in compensation for its 1965–1973 relocation of families from the Chagos islands to Mauritius. In accepting the payment, Port Louis reversed its position in regard to Diego Garcia and insisted that existence of the U.S. base violated a 1967 commitment by the United Kingdom (denied by London) that the island would not be used for military purposes (for more on the dispute between 1989 and 2000, see the 2012 *Handbook*). In October 2000 the British High Court ruled that some 2,000 inhabitants of Diego Garcia and other islands of the Chagos Archipelago had been "unlawfully removed" to Mauritius prior to independence, possibly opening the way for the return of Chagossians to all of the islands in question except, notably, Diego Garcia. Suits have been filed for substantial UK and U.S. financial support for the proposed return, while Mauritius has continued to press its claim to sovereignty over the islands. In 2004 lawyers representing the Chagossians petitioned Queen Elizabeth to permit the Chagossians to return to the Chagos Archipelago and to compensate them further for the UK's previous "unlawful actions." The petition also requested that the UK rebuild the infrastructure on the islands to permit the resumption of fishing and agriculture. In 2006 the UK High Court ruled in favor of the return of the Chagossians. The ruling was appealed by the UK Foreign Office, but the Court of Appeal affirmed the original decision. Chagossians were allowed to return to any of some 65 islands in the archipelago, but not Diego Garcia. Since many of the Chagossians had assimilated well in Mauritius, it was expected that only a small number would actually return to the islands, which had been uninhabited for more than 30 years.

Many years earlier, in June 1980, the Ramgoolam government had announced that it was amending the country's constitution to encompass the French-held island of Tromelin, located some 350 miles to the north of Mauritius, thus reaffirming a claim that Paris had formally rejected in 1976. In December 1989 the Jugnauth administration announced that it would seek a ruling on Tromelin from the General Assembly's Committee on Decolonization. Six months later French President François Mitterrand, during a tour of the Indian Ocean region, agreed to Franco-Mauritian discussions on the future of the island, although its status remained unchanged as of 2010.

Mauritius is a member of the Indian Ocean Commission (IOC). In February 1995 it hosted a ministerial meeting to form a regional economic bloc, the Indian Ocean Rim Association for Regional Cooperation (IOR-ARC), which first met in Mauritius in March 1997. In August 1995 Mauritius became a member of the Southern African Development Community (SADC). It is also a member of the Common Market for Eastern and Southern Africa (Comesa). Mauritius is pushing for trade expansion through the IOR-ARC because it finds the IOC and Comesa ineffective.

In an effort to overcome reductions in EU subsidies for Mauritian exports of sugar and textiles, the Ramgoolam government signed the U.S.-Mauritian Trade and Investment Framework in September 2006. The accord reduced tariffs on trade between the two countries and led to a rise in Mauritian exports to the United States, with total trade between the two countries at $237 million in 2007. Meanwhile, the government signed an interim trade agreement with the EU in December 2007. Also in December, Mauritius and India signed a 30-point antiterrorism agreement, which focused on efforts to curtail financial support for illegal organizations and activities.

In appreciation for continued Chinese investment, in March 2008 business leaders chartered the Mauritian Council for the Promotion of Peaceful Reunification of China to support unification of China and Taiwan. In May Mauritius donated $300,000 for the victims of the earthquake in southwest China. Nonetheless, there were tensions over China's growing influence (see Current issues). In July the two countries signed a series of bilateral economic agreements. In August Mauritius opposed the SADC Gender Protocol which set, among other goals, a requirement that women comprise 50 percent of all government posts and elected offices by 2015. Mauritian delegates argued that the protocol would require the country's constitution to be changed and replace existing equal rights measures with quota systems.

During a February 2009 visit to Mauritius, Chinese president Jintao Hu announced that his country would invest $260 million to expand the country's main airport. The following year, China committed to invest more than $700 million in a special economic zone in Mauritius.

Mauritius and the Seychelles met before the UN in August to defend rival claims for an extended maritime boundary. Both countries indicated they would accept whatever ruling the UN put forth. Mauritius and the Seychelles also agreed to increase naval cooperation to combat piracy and terrorism in the Indian Ocean. In September Mauritius hosted an anti-piracy conference of regional and international leaders to coordinate strategies to reduce piracy in the Indian Ocean. At the meeting, Mauritius offered to try pirates seized off of Somalia. In December Mauritius announced that it would challenge British plans to create a marine sanctuary in the disputed Chagos islands. Also in December Mauritius and Bangladesh agreed on a memorandum of understanding to increase the number of Bangladeshi workers in the islands (in 2011 there were an estimated 11,500 Bangladeshi workers in Mauritius). The following year, Mauritius began negotiations to allow as many as 30,000 Ugandans to work in the country.

In 2011 a dispute over a 30-year-old treaty on taxation between Mauritius and India strained relations between the two countries. The agreement allowed Indian companies to avoid some taxes if they routed investments through Mauritius. India sought to renegotiate the accord, through which it lost an estimated $600 million a year. Through eight rounds of talks since 2006, Mauritian officials had refused to substantially alter the arrangement, despite warnings from the IMF that the end of the treaty would significantly erode the Mauritian economy.

In June 2012 a new deal was announced with the UK under which pirates the Royal Navy picked up at sea could be transferred to Mauritius for prosecution.

In January 2013 a tribunal of the UN Convention on the Law of the Sea (UNCLOS) agreed to review a Mauritian challenge to the British transfer of the Chagos Islands to the BIOT. Mauritius and the Maldives announced the formation of a joint economic commission in March, an initiative that was part of the broader effort to increase regional economic collaboration. Also in March Mauritius and India agreed to increase security cooperation, including the expansion of existing training programs. India further agreed to provide aircraft parts and equipment in a subsequent agreement. Meanwhile the IMF established the Africa Training Institute in Mauritius. The institute may train up to 200 economic and finance officials per year. The EU granted Mauritius $1.72 million to enhance regional cooperation in July.

Current issues. The 2010 assembly campaign highlighted continuing ethnic divisions in Mauritius, with Ramgoolan and the Alliance of the Future drawing support from the majority South Asian community, while Bérenger and the Alliance of the Heart secured the backing of most Creoles and made a concerted effort to gain the votes of the Muslim community. The main issue in the balloting was the economy, and voters rewarded Ramgoolan's pragmatic approach to economic policy that allowed Mauritius to maintain growth, despite the global slowdown. Ramgoolan also brought the MSM into his coalition, further bolstering his appeal. The prime minister's new alliance won the May balloting with an expanded majority.

Health Minister Hanoomanjee (MSM) was arrested in July 2011 on charges that she had illegally awarded a government contract to the son-in-law of President Jugnauth. Ramgoolan dismissed her from the cabinet. Hanoomanjee's supporters claimed that the arrest and removal from office were politically motivated and designed to undermine the MSM and the president. On July 26 all of the MSM members of the cabinet resigned in protest, and the party left the governing coalition. This reduced the coalition's majority in the parliament to three seats (36 to 33).

After several weeks of political crisis in early 2012, Jugnauth resigned his post as president on March 31, ending a standoff triggered by Paul Bérenger's announcement of a new MSM-MMM opposition alliance that would be headed by Jugnauth. Ramgoolan reportedly told Jugnauth to either deny the statement or else to resign. Jugnauth has plans to run for prime minister in the 2015 elections, and the MSSM-MMM alliance, which replicates the one he had previously fronted and won the office of prime minister with in 2000, was said to be working to topple the government. Vice President Monique Ohsan Bellepeau took over as acting president. Rajkeswur PURRYAG, a former president of the National Assembly, was elected the new president at a special parliamentary session on July 21 and sworn in the next day. Razack PEEROO was subsequently elected speaker of the Assembly. In February 2013 Peeroo was elected speaker of the SADC's parliamentary forum.

Local elections in 2012 were the first to be held under a quota system in which one-third of a party's candidates had to be women. In the balloting, the MMM/MSM won majorities on three councils, including Port Louis, while the MLP/PMSD won one council, Vacoas-Phoenix. The final council was divided, with seven councilors each for the MMM/MSM and the MLP/PMSD and one seat for the small Mauritian Social Democratic Movement (*Mouvement Mauricien Sociale Démocrate*—MMSD).

In March 2013 Ramgoolam announced his support for electoral reforms, including the elimination of the system whereby the ethnicity and religion of candidates was listed on ballots. Opposition leaders have also endorsed the reforms. On March 30 severe flooding devastated Port Louis. More than 6 inches of rain fell in less than an hour, killing 11 and causing widespread damage.

POLITICAL PARTIES

More than 60 political parties have contested the recent Mauritian elections but because most of the groups are leftist in orientation, ideological differences tend to be blurred, with recurrent cleavages based largely on pragmatic considerations.

Government and Government-Supportive Parties:

Mauritius Labour Party (MLP). A Hindu-based party, the MLP (also referenced as the Workers' Party [*Parti des Travailleurs*—PTr]), under the leadership of Seewoosagur Ramgoolam, joined the country's other leading Indian group, the Muslim Action Committee (CAM), in forming the Independence Party (IP) prior to the 1976 election. Collectively, the MLP and the CAM won an overwhelming majority of 47 legislative seats in the 1967 preindependence balloting, whereas the IP retained only 28 in 1976 and lost all but 2 in 1982 (both awarded to the MLP on a "best loser" basis). A condition of the MLP joining the 1983 government alliance was said to be the designation of Ramgoolam as president upon the country's becoming a republic; following failure of a republic bill in December 1983, the longtime MLP leader was named governor general.

In February 1984, after MLP leader Sir Satcam Boolell was relieved of his post as minister of planning and economic development, the party went into opposition. It reentered the government in August 1986, with Boolell as second deputy prime minister. In September 1990 the MLP again moved into opposition, Seewoosagur Ramgoolam's son, Navin, succeeding Boolell as party leader and assuming the post of leader of the opposition. On the basis of a preelectoral accord with the MMM's Paul Bérenger, the younger Ramgoolam became prime minister following the MLP-MMM victory in December 1995. The MLP-MMM coalition dissolved in mid-1997 with Ramgoolam subsequently remaining the head of an all-MLP (with the exception of one OPR minister) cabinet. At that point the MLP was described as holding a majority of 35–37 seats in the assembly. With the MMM aligning with the MSM for the September 2000 assembly balloting, the MLP was left with only the PMXD and several small parties as electoral partners, their coalition securing 36.6 percent of the vote but only 6 of the 62 elected seats.

The Rally for Reform (*Rassemblement pour la Réforme*—RPR) joined the MLP prior to the 2005 legislative elections. The RPR was launched in August 1996 by a dissident faction of the MSM led by Rama Sithanen (a former finance minister) and Sheila Bappoo (who had briefly been MSM secretary general). It formed an alliance with the PMSD for the October 1996 municipal elections, the combined list polling some 25 percent of the vote. In the September 2000 assembly balloting, the RPR was aligned with the MLP-PMXD coalition. Its leaders, Rama SITHANEN and Sheila BAPPOO, both subsequently gained cabinet posts in the MLP-led government after the 2005 elections.

The Social Democratic Movement (*Movement Social-Démocrate*—MSD) joined the MLP ahead of the 2010 balloting. The MSD was formed in March 2005 by four MSM legislators (including two who had recently resigned from the cabinet) to protest the proposed continuation of the MSM-MMM electoral alliance. The new party joined the Social Alliance for the July legislative balloting and integrated with MLP for the May 2010 balloting. MSD leaders Anil Kumar BAICHOO and Mookhesswur CHOONEE both received cabinet posts in the MLP government.

For the 2005 assembly elections, the MLP led a Social Alliance (Alliance Social) that included the new MSD, the PMXD, the MR, and the MMSN. In 2006 former vice president Angidi Verriah Chettiar was chosen as the honorary president of the party. He was subsequently appointed vice president of the republic in 2007. Chettiar died in office in 2010.

Ahead of the 2010 assembly elections, the MLP formed the Alliance for the Future, which included the MSM, and the PMSD. The coalition won the election with 49.3 percent of the vote, and Ramgoolan was reappointed prime minister. On November 11, 2011, Monique Ohsan BELLEPEAU was elected vice president of Mauritius. In local balloting in 2012, the MLP formed an electoral coalition with the PMSD.

Leaders: Dr. Navin RAMGOOLAM (Prime Minister and Leader of the Party), Monique Ohsan BELLEPEAU (Vice President of the Republic), Ahmed Rashid BEEBEEJAUN (Deputy Prime Minister and Deputy Party Leader), Patrick ASSIRVADEN (Chair), Lormus BUNDHOO (Secretary General).

Rodriguan Movement (*Mouvement Rodriguais*—MR). A regional rival of the OPR favoring U.S.-style federalism rather than separation, the MR was awarded two "best loser" seats following both the 1995 and 2000 legislative polls. Following the defection of two OPR deputies and the loss of that party's majority in the Regional Assembly in 2006, MR member Johnson ROUSSETY was appointed chief commissioner of the island. The MR subsequently won a majority in the 2006 regional elections, and Roussety was reappointed.

In the 2010 legislative balloting the MR secured two seats. It subsequently joined the MLP-led government, and was given one ministry in the coalition government. The MR won 8 of 21 seats in the 2012 Rodriguan regional assembly balloting.

Leaders: Johnson ROUSSETY (Chief Commissioner of Rodrigues), Nicolas VON MALLY (Party Leader).

Mauritian Social Democratic Party (*Parti Mauricien Social-Démocrate*—PMSD). Composed chiefly of Franco-Mauritian landowners and middle-class Creoles, the PMSD initially opposed independence but subsequently accepted it as a fait accompli. Antisocialist at home and anticommunist in foreign affairs, it has long been distinguished for its Francophile stance. The party was part of the Ramgoolam government coalition until 1973, when it went into opposition.

The party was awarded 1 "best loser" seat following the 1991 election. In January 1994 Sir Gaëtan Duval, the leader of the PMSD, failed in an attempt to persuade Prime Minister Jugnauth to form a common front to block the threatened electoral alliance between the MLP and the MMM. At a party congress on May 22 he turned the leadership over to his son, Xavier Luc Duval, under whom the PMSD retreated visibly from its theretofore rightist posture. The party joined the MSM-led coalition in February 1995, with the younger Duval being given the industry and tourism portfolios; however, the move was opposed by the PMSD Central Committee, which in April called on Duval to resign from the government (a move which he undertook only in October for a quite different reason—his opposition to the proposed language amendment). The episode reflected a growing rift between the two Duvals, with Sir Gaëtan subsequently withdrawing from the PMSD to form the Gaëtan Duval Party (*Parti Gaëtan Duval*—PGD). As the PGD candidate he reentered the assembly on a "best loser" basis after the December elections. Because the PMSD had failed to gain representation, the elder Duval effectively resumed its leadership until his death in May 1996, when his seat in the legislature passed to his brother, Hervé Duval. It was reported that Prime Minister Ramgoolam had approached Hervé Duval with a proposal to join the government in late June 1997 following the split in the MLP-MMM coalition. However, the PMSD leader decided to align instead with the MMM in the short-lived National Alliance opposition grouping, a decision that apparently exacerbated Duval's differences with Charles Gaëtan Xavier Luc DUVAL, who subsequently formed his own grouping, the Xavier Duval Mauritian Party (*Parti Mauricien Xavier Duval*—PMXD). Following his split with his uncle, Xavier Luc Duval was elected to the National Assembly in a by-election on September 19, 1999, on a MLP-PMXD ticket. He was subsequently named minister of industry, commerce, corporate affairs, and financial services in the new MLP-led cabinet announced on September 26, and the party ran in alliance with the MLP in the September 2000 legislative poll, Duval securing one of the "best loser" seats in the assembly following that poll. In the 2000 balloting the PMSD was described as associated with the coalition led by the MSM and MMM. (Hervé Duval's supporters have also been referenced as the *Vrai Bleus* [True Blues].) The party joined the MSM-MMM electoral coalition for the 2005 assembly balloting. When the MLP's Navin Ramgoolam became prime minister in 2005, he named Xavier Luc Duval one of his three deputy prime ministers (a position that was subsequently retitled vice-prime minister in 2008).

In September 2006 the PMSD switched its support to the governing MLP-led coalition, reportedly in hopes of gaining a cabinet post. Charles Gaëtan Xavier Luc Duval subsequently reintegrated with the PMSD prior to the 2010 balloting, and the PMSD joined the MLP-led electoral coalition for the balloting and in the subsequent MLP-led coalition government. Duval's domestic popularity increased dramatically following his selection in 2012 as African Minister of Finance by *African Leadership Magazine*.

Leaders: Charles Gaëtan Xavier Luc DUVAL (Vice Prime Minister and President of the Party), Clifford EMPEIGNE.

Opposition Parties:

Mauritian Socialist Movement (*Mouvement Socialiste Mauricien*—MSM). The MSM was organized initially on April 8, 1983, as the Militant Socialist Movement (*Mouvement Socialiste Militant*) by Prime Minister Jugnauth following his expulsion, in late March, from the MMM. Prior to the 1983 election, the MSM, with the MLP, the PMSD, and the OPR, formed a coalition that secured a clear majority of legislative seats. In February 1984 the MLP withdrew from the alliance, although a number of its deputies remained loyal to the government.

The MSM secured 26 of the 41 elective seats won in August 1987 by the reconstituted five-party alliance, from which the PMSD withdrew a year later. The MLP again moved into opposition following an electoral agreement between the MSM and MMM in July 1990, with the new MSM-led alliance winning 59 of the 62 elective seats in September 1991. In a disastrous loss in December 1995, all of the MSM deputies, including Jugnauth, lost their seats. However, the MSM formed a coalition with the MMM for the snap legislative elections in September 2000 and secured 54 of the elected seats with 51.7 percent of the vote.

Pravind Kumar Jugnauth succeeded his father as leader of the MSM in April 2003. In 2004 he called for retention of the MSM-MMM electoral alliance in the 2005 assembly balloting, prompting several prominent MSM members to quit the party to form the new MSD (above). Tensions grew within the MSM-MMM coalition in March 2008 over the MSM's demand that should the coalition win the next election, the new prime minister would be the younger Jugnauth, the current MSM party chair. In the 2010 balloting the MSM joined the MLP-led Alliance of the Future. Pravind Jugnauth was subsequently appointed vice prime minister in the MLP-led government. The MSM withdrew from the governing coalition in July 2011 after the dismissal of MSM health minister Santi Bai Hanoomanjee on corruption charges. In 2012 the party was reportedly seeking to change its mainly Hindu image by reaching out to disaffected Creole politicians from the MLP.

After resigning from the presidency on March 31 to return to party politics in an alliance between the MSM and the MMM, Anerood Jugnauth surprised the MMM leadership by announcing on April 2 that he would be merely an observer of negotiations between the parties, leaving his son Pravind in charge. But the MMM leadership insisted that, if the alliance wins the election, Anerood Jugnauth himself would become prime minister for three years, before handing the position over to Bérenger. At a meeting three days later, Pravind Jugnauth reportedly acquiesced.

The MSM and the MMM formed an electoral coalition for the 2012 local balloting.

Leaders: Sir Anerood JUGNAUTH (Former President of the Republic), Pravind Kumar JUGNAUTH (Chair of the Party), Nando BODHA (Secretary General).

Mauritian Militant Movement (*Mouvement Militant Mauricien*—MMM). The leadership of the MMM was detained during the 1971 disturbances because of its "confrontational politics," which, unlike that of other Mauritian parties, was intended to cut across ethnic-communal lines. Following the 1976 election, the party's leadership strength was only 2 seats short of a majority; in 1982, campaigning in alliance with the Mauritian Socialist Party, it obtained an absolute majority of 42 seats.

In March 1983, 12 members of the MMM government of Anerood Jugnauth, led by Finance Minister Paul Bérenger, resigned in disagreement over economic policy and because they and their supporters believed that Creole should be designated the national language. Immediately thereafter, Jugnauth was expelled and proceeded to form the MSM (above), which, with its allies, achieved a decisive victory in the August 21 election.

Prior to the 1987 balloting, Bérenger, long viewed as a Marxist, characterized himself as a "democratic socialist." However, he was unsuccessful in securing an assembly seat on either a direct or "best loser" basis. The party itself campaigned as the leading component of a Union for the Future alliance, which included two minor groups, the **Democratic Workers' Movement** (*Mouvement des Travaillistes Démocrates*—MTD), then led by Anil Kumar BAICHOO and later by Sanjeet TEELOCK; and the **Socialist Workers' Front** (*Front des Travailleurs Socialistes*—FTS). On July 17, 1990, the MMM concluded an electoral accord with the MSM and MTD and formally entered the Jugnauth government on September 26.

In October 1993 Bérenger was briefly ousted as MMM secretary general, but he was returned to office by the party's Central Committee, which proceeded to expel the anti-Bérenger majority of Political Bureau members, including Prem Nababsingh and Dharmanand Goopt FOKEER, theretofore MMM president and chair, respectively, who remained members of the Jugnauth administration. In April 1994 Bérenger concluded an electoral pact with Navin Ramgoolam of the MLP under which, in the event of a coalition victory, Ramgoolam was to become prime minister and Bérenger his deputy. Two months later Nababsingh and his supporters formally left the MMM to organize the Mauritian Militant Renaissance.

Bérenger resigned his parliamentary seat on November 29, 1994, after having charged the MSM of manipulating the 1991 election, despite having been a government minister at the time. He regained his MP status in a by-election in January 1995 and became deputy prime minister and foreign minister as a result of the MLP-MMM victory in December 1995. However, Bérenger was relieved of his cabinet posts in June 1997, and the MMM moved into opposition when all but one of the party's nine other ministers resigned from the government.

In August 1997 Bérenger spearheaded the organization of a National Alliance (*Alliance Nationale*—AN) in an apparent attempt to improve his chances of securing the top governmental post in the next election. In addition to the MMM, the AN comprised the PMSD, the RPR, and the MMSM. However, the grouping did poorly in an April 1998 by-election (the AN candidate finished third with 16 percent of the vote), and a correspondent for the *Indian Ocean Newsletter* described the AN as "having been shot at dawn." Bérenger subsequently joined with Jugnauth in late 1998 to announce a MMM-MSM "federation" that would present joint candidates in the next general election and share governmental responsibility in the event of success. The federation was formally established in January 1999, and, as expected, Bérenger assumed a deputy post in the coalition with the understanding that he would be named to a similar rank in a Jugnauth-headed government. Following the landslide victory of the MSM-MMM coalition in the September 2000 balloting, Bérenger was named deputy prime minister, with the understanding that he would succeed Jugnauth as prime minister in three years. Bérenger also negotiated a similar proposed arrangement with Pravind Jugnauth of the MSM prior to the 2005 balloting.

On April 8, 2006, Bérenger resigned his position as leader of the opposition in the assembly because relations between the MMM and the MSM had deteriorated following the MMM-MSM coalition's defeat in the 2005 elections.

In May 2007 the MMM launched a campaign to attract younger, professional voters after a new Central Committee was elected. The effort was part of a larger initiative to remake the image of the party in advance of upcoming local and national elections. In September Bérenger was appointed leader of the opposition in the assembly. Reports indicated that the MMM and the MSM were unable to form a coalition because of the demand by the MSM's that party leader Pravind Jugnauth be prime minister, if a MMM-MSM coalition won the next election. In November 2008 Bérenger launched an initiative to reform the Mauritian electoral system by adopting a proportional system of representation.

The MMM formed the Alliance of the Heart prior to the 2010 balloting, which included the MMSM and the UN. The coalition was placed second in the balloting, losing to an MLP-led grouping. Bérenger led efforts to force MSM health minister Santi Bai Hanoomanjee to resign in 2011. The MMM has since formed an alliance with the MSM (see Current issues, above).

In January 2013 MMM party leader Alan GANOO became the official leader of the opposition in the Assembly.

Leaders: Paul BÉRENGER (Opposition Leader and Former Prime Minister), Premnath RAMNAH (Former Speaker of the National Assembly), Alan GANOO (Party President), Rajesh BHAGWAN (General Secretary), Jaya Krishna CUTTAREE (Deputy Party Leader).

Mauritian Militant Socialist Movement (MMSM). The MMSM is a radical Hindu group led by former agriculture minister Madun DULLO. It participated in the MLP-PMXD electoral alliance in the September 2000 assembly poll and the MLP-led Social Alliance in 2005. Dullo was dismissed as foreign minister in March 2008, and reports indicated that the MMSM would withdraw its support from the coalition government. The MMSM joined the MMM-led electoral coalition for the 2010 assembly balloting. However, MMSM member of parliament Eric GUIMBEAU left the parliament and became an independent in 2010 before forming the **Mauritian Social Democratic Movement** (*Mouvement Mauricien Sociale Démocrate*—MMSD).

Leader: Madun DULLO.

Rodriguan People's Organization (*Organisation du Peuple Rodriguais*—OPR). The OPR captured the two Rodrigues Island seats in the 1982 and 1983 balloting and, having earlier indicated that it would support the MSM-Labour alliance, was assigned one cabinet post in the Jugnauth government of August 1983; it retained the post after the ensuing two elections. The OPR again won Rodrigues's two elective parliamentary seats in 1995, despite its affiliation with the Jugnauth administration. It joined the resultant MLP-led government, although its customary full ministerial responsibility for Rodrigues affairs was downgraded to junior level under the prime minister. The OPR regained the full cabinet authority for Rodrigues affairs in the new government announced in July 1997. The party again secured the two elective seats from Rodrigues in the 2000 and 2005 legislative polls.

In 2006 two OPR deputies in the Regional Assembly defected to the opposition **Rodriguan Movement** (*Mouvement Rodriguais*—MR), which gave the MR a majority in the assembly and forced Louis Serge Claire to resign as chief commissioner. Clair subsequently became the leader of the opposition in the assembly, and the OPR remained in opposition following regional elections in 2006. The MR secured 8 seats after the February 2012 election; the OPR secured 11; the Rodrigues Patriotic Front (RPF) secured 2 seats.

Leaders: Louis Serge CLAIR (Former Rodrigues Island Minister, Leader of the Opposition in the Regional Assembly and Leader of the Party), Jean Alex NANCY (Secretary).

Mauritian Solidarity Front (*Front Solidarite Mauriciene*—FSM), formed as the **Party of God** (*Hizbullah*), the Islamic party obtained one assembly seat as a "best loser" in the December 1995 election. (Some subsequent reports referenced the seat as belonging to the **Mauritian Liberal Movement** [*Mouvement Libéral Mauricien*—MLM], described as *Hizbullah*'s "ally.") Party leader Cehl MEEAH was held for three years on murder charges before being released in 2003. The party led an effort to replace the "best loser" system with one based on ethnic representation. In 2005 the FSM adopted its current name. The party secured one seat in the 2010 assembly balloting. In 2010 media reports indicated an increasing radicalization of the MSF.

Leader: Cehl MEEAH.

The small **National Union** (*Union Nationale*) joined the MMM-led Alliance of the Heart in the 2010 balloting, but did not gain any seats of its own.

Other Parties and Groupings:

Green Party (*Les Verts*). The Green Party was reportedly aligned with the MSM-MMM electoral coalition in the September 2000 legislative balloting, and party leader Sylvio Louis MICHEL was named minister of fisheries in the new cabinet. For the 2005 balloting, the party joined the MLP-led electoral alliance, but failed to gain any seats, nor did it secure representation following the 2010 balloting.

Leader: Sylvio Louis MICHEL.

Republican Movement (*Mouvement Républicain*—MR). The MR was founded on the eve of the October 1996 municipal balloting, in which its leader, Rama VALAYDEN, won a local council seat. Valayden had presented himself as an heir to the policies pursued by the late Sir Gaëtan Duval of the PMSD. The MR aligned with the MSM-MMM coalition in the September 2000 balloting, one MR member reportedly securing a seat as an alliance candidate. In May 2001 the MR decided to end its support for the government, and subsequent press reports referred to the MR as an "opposition party." The MR participated in the MLP-led Social Alliance in 2005, and Rama Valayden was named attorney general and minister of justice and human rights in the new Ramgoolam government. In 2006 the MR's Mirella CHAUVIN was elected mayor of Beau Bassin/Rose Hill, the second largest city in Mauritius. The MR negotiated with the MLP on an electoral alliance for the 2010 balloting, but did not join the Alliance of the Future and failed to gain any seats in the balloting. In 2010 Chauvin was appointed ambassador to Australia. In 2011 MR leader Valayden led an initiative to publicize the plight of sex workers in Mauritius.

Leaders: Rama VALAYDEN, Sada ETWAROO, Mirella CHAUVIN.

Mauritian Socialist Party (*Parti Socialiste Mauricien*—PSM). The original PSM was formed in 1979 by the withdrawal from the MLP of a group of dissidents led by Harish BOODHOO. It was dissolved in May 1983 by absorption into the MSM, and Boodhoo was named deputy prime minister. In January 1986 Boodhoo resigned his government post in the wake of a disagreement with Prime Minister Jugnauth over drug policy, and he withdrew from the assembly the following November. Subsequently, he mounted an opposition campaign in his newspaper, *Le Socialiste,* and in June 1988 announced the PSM's revival. Boodhoo was aligned with the MSM-MMM alliance for the September 2000 balloting. However, the PSM apparently withdrew its support for the government in early 2002, and Boodhoo subsequently attempted to forge an opposition coalition. In the 2005 elections, many PSM members supported the MSM. The PSM did not gain any seats in the 2010 assembly balloting or the 2012 local elections.

Leader: Harish BOODHOO.

In addition, there are two far-left organizations that remain active: **The Struggle** (*Lalit*), led by Lindsey COLLEN, and the **Socialist Workers' Party** (*Parti Socialiste Ouvriére*—PSO), whose secretary general is Didier EDMOND. In 2005 *Lalit* called for the United States to close its military base on Diego Garcia and for all of the Chagos Archipelago to be returned to Mauritian sovereignty.

Other parties participating in the 2000, 2005, or 2010 assembly elections were the **Agricultural Planting Movement** (*Mouvement Planteur Agricole*—MPA); **Authentic Mauritian Movement** (*Mouvement Authentique Mauricien*—MAM); **Liberal Action Party** (*Parti Action Libéral*—PAL); **Mauritian Democracy** (*Démocratie Mauricienne*—DM); **Mauritian Democratic Movement** (*Mouvement Démocratique Mauricien*—MDM); **Mauritius Party Rights** (MPR); **National Democratic Movement** (*Mouvement Démocratique National*—MDN); **NouvoLizur,** a grouping led by former cabinet minister Joceline MINERVE which, among other things, supports "Chagossian rights"; **Party of the Mauritian People** (*Parti du Peuple Mauricien*—PPM); **Socialist Workers Movement** (*Mouvement Travailliste Socialiste*—MTS); **Tamil Council** (TC); **Mauritian Union** (*Union Mauricienne*—UM); **Muslim Action Committee** (*Comité d'Action Musulman*—CAM); **National Mauritian Movement** (*Mouvement National Mauricien*—MNM); and **Resistance and Alternative**.

LEGISLATURE

The Mauritian **National Assembly** is a unicameral body containing 62 elected deputies (3 from each of the 20 constituencies on the main island and 2 from Rodrigues Island), plus up to 8 appointed from the list of unsuccessful candidates under a "best loser" system designed to provide "balanced" ethnic and political representation. The legislative term is five years, subject to dissolution. In the National Assembly elections held on May 5, 2010, the Alliance of the Future (led by the Mauritius Labor Party) won 41 of the 60 elected seats from the main island; 18 going to the Alliance of the Heart, a coalition led by the Mauritian Militant Movement, and the final seat taken by the Mauritian Solidarity Front. The Rodriguan Movement (MR) won the 2 elected seats on Rodrigues Island. In the subsequent "best loser" distribution of appointed seats for the assembly, the Alliance of the Future was accorded 4 additional seats; the Alliance of the Heart, 2; and the Rodriguan People's Organization, 1.

Speaker: Abdool Razack PEEROO.

Rodrigues Regional Assembly. As authorized by a constitutional amendment approved by the National Assembly in November 2001, the Rodrigues Regional Assembly comprises 18 members, 12 elected from six constituencies on a first-past-the-post system and 6 elected on a proportional basis. To comply with formulas governing the proportional allocation of seats, 3 extra seats were given to the RPO after balloting on February 5, 2012. The RPO secured 11 seats, the MR secured 8 seats, and the RPF secured 2 seats.

Chair: Joseph Chenlye LAMVOHEE.

CABINET

[as of August 15, 2013]

Prime Minister	Navinchandra Ramgoolam (MLP)
Deputy Prime Ministers	Ahmed Rashid Beebeejaun (MLP)
Vice Prime Ministers	Charles Gaëtan Xavier Luc Duval (PMXD)
	Anil Kumar Bachoo (MLP)
Ministers	
Agro-Industries, Food Protection and Security	Satya Faugoo (MLP)
Art and Culture	Mookhesswur Choonee (MLP)
Business, Enterprise, Cooperatives, and Cooperatives	Jangbahadoorsing Iswurdeo Mola Roopchand Seetaram
Civil Service Affairs and Administrative Reforms	Sutyadeo Moutia (MLP)
Defense and Home Affairs	Navinchandra Ramgoolam (MLP)
Education, Culture and Human Resources	Vasant Kumar Bunwaree (MLP)
Energy and Public Affairs	Ahmed Rashid Beebeejaun (MLP)

Environment and National Development	Devanand Virahsawmy (MLP)
Finance and Economic Development	Charles Gaëtan Xavier Luc Duval (PMXD)
Fisheries	Louis Joseph von Mally (MR)
Foreign Affairs, International Trade, and Regional Cooperation	Arvin Boolell (MLP)
Health and Quality of Life	Lormus Bundhoo
Housing and Lands	Abu Twalib Kasenally (MLP)
Industry, Commerce, and Consumer Protection	Abd-al-Cader Sayed-Hossen (MLP)
Information Technology and Telecommunications	Tassarajen Pillay Chedumbrum
Island of Rodrigues	Navinchandra Ramgoolam (MLP)
Justice and Human Rights; Attorney-General	Yatindra Nath Varma (MLP)
Labor, Industrial Relations, and Employment	Shakeel Ahmed Yousef Abdul Razack Mohamed (MLP)
Local Government and Outer Islands	Louis-Hervé Aimée (MLP)
Public Infrastructure, National Development, Land Transport, and Shipping	Anil Kumar Bachoo (MLP)
Social Integration and Economic Empowerment	Surendra Dayal (MLP)
Social Security, National Solidarity, Senior Citizen Welfare, and Reform Institutions	Sheilabai Bappoo (MLP) [f]
Tertiary Education, Science, Research, and Technology	Rajeshwar Jeetah (MLP)
Tourism, Leisure, and External Communications	John Michaël Tzoun Sao Yeung Sik Yuen (PMSD)
Women's Rights, Child Development, and Family Welfare	Maria Francesca Mireille Martin (MLP) [f]
Youth and Sports	Satyaprakash Ritoo (MLP)

[f] = female

INTERGOVERNMENTAL REPRESENTATION

Ambassador to the U.S.: Somduth SOBORUN.

U.S. Ambassador to Mauritius: Shari VILLAROSA.

Permanent Representative to the UN: Milan Jaya Nyamrajsingh MEETARBHAN.

IGO Memberships (Non-UN): AfDB, AU, Comesa, CWTH, ICC, IOM, NAM, SADC, WTO.

MEXICO

United Mexican States
Estados Unidos Mexicanos

Political Status: Independence originally proclaimed 1810; present federal constitution adopted February 5, 1917.

Area: 761,600 sq. mi. (1,972,544 sq. km).

Population: 117,812,936 (2012E—UN); 116,220,947 (2013E—U.S. Census).

Major Urban Centers (2010E): MEXICO CITY (Federal District, 8,851,000), Guadalajara (4,435,000), Tijuana (1,751,000), Ciudad Juárez (1,332,000), León (1,610,000), Monterrey (4,090,000), Chihuahua (853,000), Acapulco (863,000), Mexicali (937,000), Veracruz (81,000).

Official Language: Spanish.

Monetary Unit: New Peso (market rate November 1, 2013: 13.08 pesos = $1US).

President: Enrique PEÑA Nieto (Institutional Revolutionary Party); elected July 1, 2012, and sworn in for a six-year term, along with a new government, on December 1, succeeding Felipe CALDERÓN Hinojosa (National Action Party).

THE COUNTRY

Extending southeastward from the U.S. border to the jungles of Yucatán and Guatemala, Mexico ranks third in size and second in population among North American countries and holds comparable rank among the countries of Latin America. Its varied terrain encompasses low-lying coastal jungles, a broad central plateau framed by high mountain ranges, and large tracts of desert territory in the north. The people are mainly of mixed Indian and Spanish (*mestizo*) descent, with minority groups of pure Indians and Caucasians. Despite the predominance of Roman Catholicism, constitutional separation of church and state has prevailed since 1857, with links to the Vatican in abeyance until 1992 (see Foreign relations, below). About one-seventh of the population is still engaged in agriculture, which now contributes less than 5 percent of GDP. In 2000 women constituted 37 percent of the nonagricultural labor force, concentrated mainly in trade, manufacturing, and domestic service; in the export-oriented border factories (*maquiladoras*), the majority of the workforce is female.

Industrialization has been rapid since World War II, but its benefits have been unevenly distributed, and much of the rural population remains substantially unaffected. The economy grew robustly through the 1970s and then fell into deep recession, with unserviceable foreign debt, massive capital flight, widespread unemployment, and rampant inflation. Successive International Monetary Fund (IMF) interventions slowed the decline in 1983–1984, but by mid-1986, in the wake of a disastrous earthquake in Mexico City the preceding September and a collapse in oil prices, crisis conditions had returned, stabilizing by 1989.

Mexico's economy was transformed by passage of the North American Free Trade Agreement (NAFTA), which went into effect on January 1, 1994, severely weakening the agricultural sector and accelerating the growth of the *maquiladoras.* That December the country was engulfed by a fiscal crisis that prompted a $50 billion U.S.-led rescue package in January 1995. GDP contracted in 1995 but rebounded well for the remainder of the decade until stalling again in early 2001, in large part because of weakness in the U.S. economy but also because of a decline in *maquiladora* activity as the result of Chinese competition. The economy recovered in the next several years, annual GDP growth averaging 3.5 percent in 2003–2007, owing in large part to the country's flexible exchange rate and robust policies, according to the IMF.

During the global financial crisis beginning in 2008, Mexico's "resiliency was severely tested," according to the IMF, particularly as the currency depreciated—the peso fell 25 percent against the U.S. dollar in 2009. In addition, an outbreak of swine flu hit Mexico in midyear, and manufacturing exports declined. The IMF granted Mexico a flexible credit line of some $47 billion in April.

The economy shrunk nearly 7 percent in 2009, the government reporting it as the worst contraction in 30 years. However, with prompt intervention, growth resumed rapidly by early 2010, rebounding to 5.4 percent; the exchange rate recovered; and economic stability returned. Fund managers granted another $48 billion credit line and commended Mexican authorities for instituting tax reform measures to offset losses from declining oil production. Strong annual growth continued in 2011, with GDP of 4.5 percent, owing in large part to domestic demand, "benign" inflation, and increased foreign investment. GDP grew 4.5 percent in 2011 and 3.9 percent in 2012, while unemployment dipped

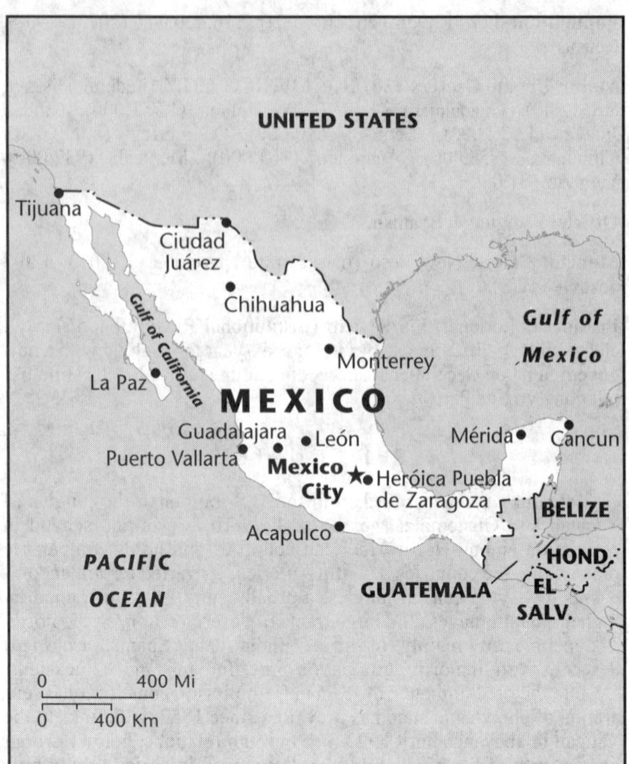

from 5.2 percent in 2011 to 4.8 percent in 2012. Unemployment had returned to more than 5 percent by early 2013 and was up to 5.3 percent in September 2013.

GOVERNMENT AND POLITICS

Political background. The territory that is now Mexico was conquered by Spain in the 16th century. Mexico proclaimed its independence in 1810 and the establishment of a republic in 1822. The country was ruled by Gen. Antonio López de SANTA ANNA from 1833 to 1855, a period that encompassed the declaration of Texan independence in 1836 and war with the United States from 1846 to 1848. Archduke MAXIMILIAN of Austria, installed as emperor of Mexico by Napoleon III in 1865, was deposed and executed by Benito JUAREZ in 1867. The dominant figure during the latter years of the 19th century was Gen. Porfirio DÍAZ, who served as president from 1877 to 1910.

Modern Mexican history dates from the Revolution of 1910, which shattered an outmoded social and political system and cleared the way for a generally progressive republican regime whose foundations were laid in 1917. From 1928 political life was dominated by a nationwide grouping known since 1946 as the Institutional Revolutionary Party (*Partido Revolucionario Institucional*—PRI), which purported to carry forward the work of the 1917 constitution.

Luis ECHEVERRÍA Alvarez, who assumed the presidency in 1970, sought to overcome inequitable distribution of income, widespread alienation and unrest, scattered urban and rural violence, and a visible erosion in the prestige, if not the power, of the PRI. Echeverría's efforts were opposed both by the right, because of a feeling that the traditional favoritism shown to business interests was waning, and by the left, because of a conviction that the reform was a sham.

In the presidential election of July 4, 1976, Finance Minister José LÓPEZ Portillo, running as the PRI candidate, obtained 94.4 percent of the popular vote against a group of independents, no opposition party having presented an endorsed candidate. Soon after his inauguration on December 1, the new chief executive introduced a far-reaching program of political reform that resulted in three previously unrecognized parties, including the Mexican Communist Party, being conditionally legalized prior to the legislative election of July 1979, after which all three were granted seats in the Chamber of Deputies according to their vote totals.

A left-wing coalition, the Unified Socialist Party of Mexico (*Partido Socialista Unificado de México*—PSUM), formed in November 1981 by the Communists and four smaller parties, failed to gain ground against the entrenched PRI in the July 1982 balloting. The ruling party captured all but one elective congressional seat and saw its presidential candidate, former minister of programming and budget, Miguel de la MADRID Hurtado, win 74.4 percent of the vote in a field of seven nominees. During the ensuing four years the PRI was buffeted by an unprecedented, if minor, set of electoral losses to the rightist National Action Party (*Partido Acción Nacional*—PAN). In the lower house election of July 1985 PAN won nine elective seats, while in a supplementary distribution under proportional representation the leftist parties gained substantially more seats than in 1982.

At a congress in October 1987 the PRI ratified the selection of former planning and budget minister Carlos SALINAS de Gortari as its 1988 presidential candidate. Although seemingly assured of victory, Salinas was credited with a bare 50.4 percent vote share in the balloting of July 6, 1988. His three competitors, Cuauhtémoc CÁRDENAS Solórzano of the leftist National Democratic Front (*Frente Democrático Nacional*—FDN), PAN's Manuel CLOUTHIER, and Rosario IBARRA de la Piedra of the far-left Revolutionary Workers' Party (*Partido Revolucionario de los Trabajadores*—PRT), immediately brought charges of widespread fraud, which in September were rejected by the Congress sitting as an electoral college to review the results.

In the legislative and gubernatorial elections of August 18, 1991, the PRI won 31 of 32 available Senate seats and 290 of 300 directly contested Chamber seats. It was also declared the winner in all six state governorship contests, although two of the victors were forced to withdraw because of manifest voting irregularities. Subsequent gubernatorial, state, and municipal elections in 1992–1993 showed a pattern of eroding PRI support, occasional opposition successes, frequent violence, and continual opposition charges of fraudulent electoral practice. Following disclosures that the PRI had received large financial donations from the beneficiaries of privatization, party chair Genaro BORREGO Estrada in March 1993 announced a limit on individual contributions; later that month he was removed from office by President Salinas. The president, seeking to respond to domestic and international criticism of Mexican political practice, then initiated other PRI leadership changes and introduced electoral reform measures that were approved by Congress in September (see Constitution and government, below). Meanwhile, the government had come under strong censure for its unconvincing response to the killing on May 25 of the archbishop of Guadalajara, Cardinal Juan Jesús POSADAS Ocambo, who was caught in an apparent shootout between rival drug gangs at the city's airport.

In November 1993 the PRI leadership endorsed Luis Donaldo COLOSIO Murrieta, the social development secretary and a Salinas loyalist, as the party's presidential candidate for the 1994 election. However, a state of crisis generated by the eruption of a major insurgency in the southern state of Chiapas in January 1994 was compounded by the assassination of Colosio in the northern border city of Tijuana on March 23. The replacement PRI candidate, Ernesto ZEDILLO Ponce de Léon (another Salinas loyalist but regarded as more conservative than Colosio), was duly elected president on August 21, but with the PRI's lowest-ever share of the popular vote, while simultaneous congressional elections yielded significant gains for opposition parties. Even more ominous for the PRI was a near sweep by PAN of executive and legislative races in the state of Jalisco on February 12, 1995, and the party's capture of the Guanajuato governorship on May 28. Meanwhile, the assassination of PRI secretary general José Francisco RUIZ Massieu on September 28, 1994 prompted an ever-widening inquiry into possible linkage with the Colosio killing and speculation as to ties between political figures and drug traffickers. On February 28, 1995, Raúl SALINAS de Gortari, the former president's older brother, was arrested for allegedly masterminding the Ruiz Massieu killing. (For more on the case, see the 2012 *Handbook*.)

In August 1995 the PAN retained control of Baja California (where the PRI in 1988 had experienced its first state-level defeat), its third victory of the year out of four such contests. By mid-November both the PAN and the leftist Democratic Revolutionary Party (*Partido de la Revolución Democrática*—PRD) had substantially increased their local representation, although the PRI succeeded in retaining the governorship of Michoacán, a PRD stronghold. The ruling party was subsequently embarrassed in the state of Guerrero, whose governor, Rubén FIGUEROA Alcocer, was obliged to resign on March 12, 1996, after being accused of attempting to cover up a police massacre of 17 opposition peasants. Meanwhile, PAN had pulled out of electoral reform talks with the PRI, although the PRD, which had earlier withdrawn from the discussion, returned to the negotiating table, paving the way for a tentative agreement on April 15 by parties holding 70 percent of the federal legislative seats.

Meanwhile, the outbreak of insurgent activity in the southernmost state of Chiapas continued under the direction of an indigenous formation styling itself the Zapatista National Liberation Army (*Ejército Zapatista de Liberación Nacional*—EZLN). Led by a charismatic *mestizo* using the alias "Subcomandante Marcos," the group issued a "Declaration of the Lacandona Jungle" that sought redress from "a dictatorship of more than 70 years."

On January 1, 1996, the Zapatistas announced the creation of a Zapatista National Liberation Front (*Frente Zapatista de Liberación Nacional*—FZLN), characterized as "a new political force with its base in the EZLN" that would work for the "transforming of Mexico." A month later the government and the EZLN reached agreement on a draft charter expanding the rights of Indians, thus clearing the way for a peace accord. However, the pact was threatened in late May, when the Zapatistas declared a "red alert" in areas under their control because of alleged military provocations by the government. The rebels again withdrew from the peace process but agreed on June 10 to return following the release of two high-ranking Zapatista leaders who had been captured in February. Meanwhile, an even more radical Popular Revolutionary Army (*Ejército Popular Revolucionario*—EPR) had emerged in the southern state of Guerrero. With no apparent links to the EZLN, EPR guerrillas mounted an attack on police and military installations in four Mexican states on August 28 that left 13 dead and 23 wounded.

By late 1996, the government also faced continued erosion in its political strength in the rest of the country. The PAN and the PRD both made significant inroads against PRI dominance in elections held in the states of Coahuila and México, winning a number of mayoralties. In addition, public opinion polls indicated that the PRI faced a genuine challenge in retaining its legislative majority in the national elections scheduled for mid-1997 and could also lose the concurrent first-ever direct balloting for mayor of Mexico City (considered the second-most influential office in the country). On July 6, 1997, the PRI retained only 238 of 500 lower house seats and yielded the Mexico City mayoralty to the PRD's Cárdenas Solórzano.

Following the election, the PRD, PAN, and two smaller legislative groups, the Labor Party (*Partido del Trabajo*—PT) and the Mexican Green Ecologist Party (*Partido Verde Ecologista de México*—PVEM), formed a working majority to constrain the PRI's theretofore unchallenged domination of the lower house, particularly in regard to the allocation of committee chairs. While the right-wing PAN subsequently insisted that its participation in the alliance was tactical, not strategic, it joined with the other opposition members in a semiformal *Grupo de los Cuatro* in mid-October.

On December 22, 1997, a band of gunmen, reportedly PRI adherents, attacked a small village in Chiapas, killing 45 Indians, including 15 children. President Zedillo branded the attack as "a cruel, absurd, and unacceptable criminal act." Subsequent contacts with the EZLN were distinctly uneven. Despite a number of peace initiatives by both federal and state authorities, talks stalled, and on June 8 Bishop Samuel RUIZ, resigned as the head of Conai, the negotiation commission, which declared its dissolution the same day. However, on October 18 the EZLN announced that it would return to the bargaining table, albeit only to attend talks involving a parliamentary Commission of Concord and Pacification (*Comisión de Concordia y Pacificación*—Cocopa), originally set up parallel to Conai, that had no executive representation.

The PRI closed out 1998 with a record of seven victories in ten governors' races, thus reversing a three-year decline that had cast doubt on its electoral appeal. In a verdict handed down on January 21, 1999, Raúl Salinas was convicted of ordering the 1994 Ruiz Massieu assassination and sentenced to 50 years' imprisonment (subsequently reduced to 27.5 years). In February state elections the PRI held three additional governorships but lost Baja California Sur to the PRD, while in March about 90 percent of the 3 million voters participating in the Indian rights plebiscite voiced support for the Zapatista program, including explicit constitutional recognition of Indian rights.

The election of July 2, 2000, was a watershed event in Mexican political history. Although consistently trailing in the public opinion polls, Vicente FOX Quesada of the right-wing PAN, in a coalition with a number of smaller parties called Alliance for Change, succeeded in defeating the PRI nominee, Francisco LABASTIDA Ochoa, 43–36 percent. In the 500-member Chamber of Deputies, the Alliance for Change won a substantial plurality of 223 seats, and in the 128-member Senate the PRI's former majority of 77 seats was reduced to a plurality of 60, with the Alliance for Change gaining a close second at 51. The PRD, heading a six-member Alliance for Mexico City, retained control of the capital, electing Andrés Manuel LÓPEZ Obrador to the office from which Cárdenas had resigned to run for the presidency.

In late April 2001 the government passed an Indigenous Rights Bill that authorized constitutional changes prohibiting discrimination based on race, religion, or gender. It also permitted election of indigenous officials by standard electoral practices; guaranteed the right to preserve Indian languages and cultures; and offered indigenous peoples preferential use of natural resources. Though Fox had offered concessions to the Zapatistas, including the closure of military bases in Chiapas, the EZLN and its supporters had traveled en masse to Mexico City in March, rallying some 200,000 people from diverse groups to lobby for the EZLN's preconditions. Meanwhile, some Indian groups opposed the bill because of last-minute changes that altered the conditions of autonomy. Ultimately, the EZLN refused to resume peace talks with the government. In late 2003 the group declared political autonomy in 30 of its indigenous municipalities.

The 2003 general congressional balloting yielded significant changes in the political landscape. The PAN representation plummeted, while that of the PRI rose to just short of a majority. The biggest surprise, however, was the success of the PRD in nearly doubling its representation from 52 to 95, enhancing López Obrador's presidential prospects.

Though López Obrador was the front-runner during much of the 2006 presidential campaign, he lost to the PAN's Felipe CALDERÓN Hinojosa by just 0.5 percent of the vote in controversial balloting on July 2. López Obrador demanded a national recount, alleging widespread election irregularities. He and his allies staged massive protests in Mexico City, and though the rallies lost popular support over time, López Obrador continued to dispute the outcome of the election. After a partial recount in August, the Federal Electoral Court certified the results and declared Calderón president-elect on September 5. He was inaugurated along with a new cabinet on December 1 while López Obrador led a massive march along the central avenue of the city. In concurrent parliamentary elections, the PAN won a plurality in both the Senate and the Chamber of Deputies.

In 2009 President Calderón dispatched 45,000 troops and 30,000 federal police to cities hard-hit by drug-related violence. In February drug gangs killed an army general assigned to head the police in Cancún, engaged in a prolonged firefight with the army in Chihuahua, and forced the resignation of the police chief in Ciudad Juárez, where more than 6,000 people were killed in 2008. The troops replaced corrupt, ineffective, or overwhelmed local police. Among the cartels fighting for control of the region were the Arellano FÉLIX or Tijuana organization; *Los Aztecas,* headed by Arturo GALLEGOS Castrellón; the Sinaloa cartel, which included the factions of Joaquín "El Chapo" GUZMÁN and the BELTRÁN LEYVA brothers; the Gulf cartel, also known as *Las Zetas* or *La Compañía;* and the Michoacán-based *La Familia.* Meanwhile, the Sinaloa cartel's Guzmán appeared in *Forbes* magazine's list of the richest people in the world, his fortunes owing to cocaine trafficking. He was also cited for allegedly being responsible for "thousands of murders."

In the July 5, 2009, midterm balloting for the Chamber of Deputies, the PRI secured 237 seats, an increase of 133 compared with 2006. The PAN was second with 143 seats, a loss of 63 seats compared with the previous election.

By September 2009, drug-related killings, reported at nearly 6,000, had surpassed the total for all of 2008. Observers said the government crackdown helped fuel the rise in homicides, as drug cartels were broken up and infighting occurred. Late in the year the government's security woes were compounded by economic issues, as 20,000 demonstrators, led by members of the electrical workers union, rallied in a symbolic "taking of Mexico City" demonstration to protest President Calderón's having seized a large central power plant in October, liquidating its assets, and firing all 45,000 workers. The government's move was meant to dissolve the union, whose members had been a leading force in organizing protests against the president's economic policies, including his effort to privatize the power industry, observers said.

The drug war continued to take its toll in 2010. In March three people connected with the U.S. consulate in Ciudad Juárez were killed. Calderón maintained that the increasing bloodshed demonstrated that the cartels had become desperate. It was reported that the majority of firearms used by the drug gangs were manufactured in or imported from the United States, according to U.S. and Mexican authorities (see Foreign relations, below). Government figures for the year showed that violent crime associated with drug cartels had resulted in 15,273 deaths, an increase of 59 percent compared with 2009.

A minor cabinet reshuffle occurred on March 10, 2010. On July 14, following a dispute between the president and Interior Minister Fernando GÓMEZ MONT, the minister resigned in protest of Calderón's overtures to the PRD to form an alliance against the PRI, and he also quit the PAN. The cabinet, including a new economy minister, comprised members of the PAN, the military, and independents.

In the run-up to the July 4, 2010, gubernatorial elections, several candidates were assassinated, including the front-running PRI candidate for governor of Tamaulipas. President Calderón blamed the drug cartels for the killings. As tensions heightened, the PAN, PRD, PT, and Convergence parties asked the electoral coalition to take the unusual step of monitoring the state elections. Meanwhile, the PRD was losing electoral traction due to infighting. Subsequently, though the PRI made overall gains in the elections, it lost control of the politically important states of Oaxaca, Sinaloa, and Puebla, where it was defeated by the faction known as the anti-PRI alliance. The upsets were the PRI's first gubernatorial defeats in those three states in decades.

Narcotrafficking-related deaths and kidnappings continued to increase during Calderón's tenure in office. A significant step was achieved in November 2010, when the leader of the *Los Aztecas,* Gallegos Castrellón, was arrested. Castrellón claimed his gang was responsible for 80 percent of the killings in Ciudad Juárez. He also claimed responsibility for killing two U.S. consulate employees in March and for a massacre at a teenager's party in January. By year's end the United States had tripled the amount of money it spent annually (to $34 million a year) on the training of Mexican military and police officers.

Violence surged in 2011, as 38 people were killed in the first week of January, ahead of the gubernatorial race in Guerrero. Three mayors were assassinated in January, and in February a U.S. customs and immigration agent was shot and killed and another was wounded when their vehicle was attacked in the state of San Luis Potosi. Four days later, 18 people were killed in another state, prompting President Calderón to create four new army battalions. In April 145 bodies were discovered in mass graves in Tamaulipas state, and 13 bodies were found later that month at another site, all of the deaths allegedly linked to the *Las Zetas* cartel. Benjamin Arellano Félix, a leader of the Tijuana drug cartel and allegedly one of the major cocaine suppliers to the United States, was extradited on charges of trafficking cocaine into California. In another key arrest, Sinaloa leader Martin BELTRÁN was detained in May, as well as 11 members of *La Familia*. José de Jesús MÉNDEZ Vargas, the alleged leader of *La Familia,* was arrested in June. On June 16 some 33 people were killed within 24 hours in Monterrey.

A Supreme Court ruling in July 2011, hailed by human rights groups, ordered that soldiers on domestic security duty and accused of human rights violations be tried in civilian, not military, courts. The high court also ruled that all judges in Mexico are required to ensure that rulings meet universal human rights standards in accordance with the Mexican constitution.

Drug-related killings escalated in July and August in various states, with 97 deaths reported in two days in July. In August Miguel Angel NEVAREZ, accused of killing three people affiliated with the U.S. Consulate in Ciudad Juárez, was extradited to the United States on charges of conspiracy, murder, and carrying federal firearms.

An attack on a major casino in Monterrey on August 26 that killed 52 people prompted Calderón to dispatch 1,500 federal agents, in addition to the 4,000 soldiers deployed there. He also declared three days of national mourning in response to the massacre. Five men, all suspected *Las Zetas* members, were arrested on August 30. Meanwhile, a video showing the brother of Monterrey's mayor and a municipal official receiving alleged "protection" payments at a casino days before the attack prompted calls by the PAN for the mayor to step down to avoid accusations of interference with the investigation. The mayor, an ally of President Calderón, refused to resign.

Constitution and government. Under its frequently amended constitution of February 5, 1917, Mexico is a federal republic consisting of 31 states (each with its own constitution, elected governor, and legislative chamber) plus a Federal District, whose chief executive (formerly appointed, but elected as of 1997) is advised by 365 elected councilors. The president is directly elected for a single six-year term. Since 2000 only one, rather than both, parents of presidential contenders must be native-born Mexicans. There is no vice president. Mexico has no constitutionally defined line of succession should the president resign or become incapacitated; in that event, the Congress chooses the next president by secret ballot.

The bicameral Congress, consisting of an elected Senate and Chamber of Deputies (both under a mixed direct and proportional system), was long confined by the party system to a secondary role in the determination of national policy; at present, however, with different parties controlling the legislative and executive branches, its influence has drastically increased. The judicial system is headed by a 21-member Supreme Court, which has four divisions: administrative, civil, labor, and penal. The justices of the Supreme Court are appointed for life by the president with the approval of the Senate. Lower courts include collegiate and single-judge circuit courts, district courts, and jury courts. The basis of local government is the municipality (*municipio*).

State and Capital	*Area (sq. mi.)*	*Population (2010E)*
Aguascalientes (Aguascalientes)	2,112	1,185,000
Baja California Norte (Mexicali)	26,997	3,155,000
Baja California Sur (La Paz)	28,369	637,000
Campeche (Campeche)	19,619	822,000
Chiapas (Tuxtla Gutiérrez)	28,653	4,797,000
Chihuahua (Chihuahua)	94,571	3,406,000
Coahuila (Saltillo)	57,908	2,748,000
Colima (Colima)	2,004	651,000
Durango (Durango)	47,560	1,633,000
Guanajuato (Guanajuato)	11,773	5,486,000
Guerrero (Chilpancingo)	24,819	3,389,000
Hidalgo (Pachuca)	8,036	2,665,000
Jalisco (Guadalajara)	30,535	7,350,000
México (Toluca)	8,245	15,176,000
Michoacán (Morelia)	23,138	4,351,000
Morelos (Cuernavaca)	1,911	1,777,000
Nayarit (Tepic)	10,417	1,085,000
Nuevo León (Monterrey)	24,792	4,653,000
Oaxaca (Oaxaca)	36,275	3,802,000
Puebla (Puebla)	13,090	5,580,000
Querétaro (Querétaro)	4,421	1,828,000
Quintana Roo (Chetumal)	19,387	1,326,000
San Luis Potosí (San Luis Potosí)	24,351	2,586,000
Sinaloa (Culiacán)	22,486	2,768,000
Sonora (Hermosillo)	70,291	2,662,000
Tabasco (Villa Hermosa)	9,756	2,239,000
Tamaulipas (Ciudad Victoria)	30,650	3,269,000
Tlaxcala (Tlaxcala)	1,511	1,170,000
Veracruz-Llave (Veracruz)	27,683	7,643,000
Yucatán (Mérida)	14,827	1,956,000
Zacatecas (Zacatecas)	28,283	1,491,000
Federal District		
Ciudad de México	579	8,792,000

Reporters Without Borders ranked Mexico 153rd out of 179 countries in its 2013 Index of Press Freedom. Six journalists were killed in Mexico in 2012, and censorship was evident during coverage of the national elections.

Foreign relations. A founding member of the United Nations, the Organization of American States (OAS), and related organizations, Mexico has generally adhered to an independent foreign policy based on the principles of nonintervention and self-determination. One of the initiators of the 1967 Treaty for the Prohibition of Nuclear Weapons in Latin America (Treaty of Tlatelolco), it is the only non–South American member of the Latin American Integration Association (ALADI) and the only OAS state to have continually maintained formal relations with Cuba. In return, Mexico was the only major Latin American country for which Castro refused to train guerrillas.

Under President de la Madrid the country continued to exercise a leadership role in the region, despite a diminution of influence because of its economic difficulties. In the 1980s, as a participant in the Contadora Group, which also included Colombia, Panama, and Venezuela as original members, Mexico took the group's agenda for regional peace to both South America and the United States. U.S. military policy in Central America continued to be a major source of strain in the traditionally cordial relationship between Mexico and its northern neighbor.

In 1988–1989 the United States pledged to support Mexico's efforts to enact economic reforms and negotiate a debt reduction agreement. Meanwhile, U.S.-Mexico commercial relations continued to expand; in November 1989 the leaders of the two nations signed a trade accord, and in September 1990 Mexico, in a dramatic reversal of its traditional posture, formally requested the opening of free trade talks. Thereafter, Canada, which had concluded a free trade agreement with the United States in December 1989, was invited to participate in the discussions, which commenced in mid-1991 and concluded with agreement on the precedent-shattering NAFTA on August 11–12, 1992.

In a historic move, Mexico and the Vatican reestablished diplomatic relations in September 1992—for the first time in well over a century since President Juarez confiscated all church property. The renewal of ties followed President Salinas's unprecedented audience with Pope John Paul II the previous year and revisions in July to sections of the constitution dating to 1917 that had denied legal status to the Roman Catholic Church and to other religious groups.

NAFTA was ratified by the Mexican Congress in December 1993 (coming into effect on January 1, 1994) following agreement months earlier on some contentious labor and environmental subclauses. In late 1993 Mexico joined with Colombia and Venezuela (the so-called Group of Three) in a regional trade pact intended to create an economic market encompassing some 145 million people.

Counternarcotics policy has been a continuing subject of cooperation and contention between the United States and Mexico. In 1997, during a period of increased U.S. assistance in combating the drugs trade, the head of Mexico's antidrug agency, Gen. Jesús GONZÁLEZ Rebollo, was arrested on charges of collusion with traffickers. In the wake of the U.S. action, opposition legislators charged the Zedillo administration with sacrificing Mexican interests to Washington's agenda. Further fueling the controversy was the charge by a high-ranking U.S. Drug Enforcement Agency official in mid-1997 that Colombian drug activities had been "eclipsed" by those of the Mexican cartels.

In December 2000 the Mexican Senate ratified a free trade agreement with Guatemala, Honduras, and El Salvador that had been concluded six months earlier.

Despite a decline in U.S.-Mexico cooperation in countering drug trafficking, President Fox was the first foreign leader President George W. Bush traveled to meet, in February 2001. Fox's subsequent trip to Washington in early September marked the first state visit under President Bush. Following the September 11 terrorist attacks in the United States, however, relations with Mexico became a much lower priority for the Bush administration. Relations with the United States grew more distant after President Fox refused to back U.S. policy in Iraq and opposed as "inadequate" most overtures by President Bush on resolving the status of Mexican nationals in the United States (who were said to account for approximately 60 percent of all illegal immigrants).

Mexico and Venezuela severed diplomatic ties in November 2005 after President Hugo Chavez accused President Fox of being "a puppy" of U.S. president Bush, and Fox demanded an immediate apology. The withdrawal of their respective ambassadors highlighted the two countries' differences over trade relations with the United States.

In 2007, at the conclusion of a five-country tour of Latin America, President Bush pledged to push Congress to approve a comprehensive immigration reform package to increase efforts to stem the demand for illegal drugs in the United States, as well as to restrict supplies from Latin America and combat arms trafficking from the United States to Mexico and Central America.

In July 2007 Argentina's president, Néstor Kirchner, and his wife Cristina Fernández (the president-elect) visited Mexico to sign agreements enhancing trade, and encouraged Mexico to apply for full membership in Mercosur, the South American customs union of which Mexico is an associate member. Mexico also began a dialogue to repair relations with Venezuela and Cuba.

In June 2008 the Mérida Initiative, a framework for U.S. counterdrug assistance worth $1.4 billion over three years benefiting Mexico, the Dominican Republic, Haiti, and the countries of Central America, was signed into law.

An increase in drug-related crime near the U.S.-Mexico border, including an October 11, 2008, grenade and gunfire attack on the U.S. consulate in Monterrey, revived Mexico as a top concern of U.S. policymakers. Numerous U.S. administration officials visited Mexico between October 2008 and August 2009, including a visit by President Barack Obama, to discuss law enforcement and cooperation on security.

U.S.-Mexican security cooperation was enhanced in 2009 when the Mexican Navy participated in its first joint exercise with the United States. The U.S. Congress subsequently approved an additional $420 million for Mexican security in June, well beyond the $66 million the Obama administration had requested.

Relations between Mexico and Honduras were restored in August 2010. Mexico had withdrawn its ambassador from Tegucigalpa following the coup that ousted President Manuel Zelaya in June 2009.

Formal negotiations on a strategic bilateral accord with Brazil began in November 2010.

In April 2010 violence related to drug trafficking in the area of the U.S.-Mexico border had escalated to the point that the U.S. government began issuing travel advisories for northern Mexico. Around the same time, the Mexican government warned its population about entering the American state of Arizona due to increased arrests under that state's new immigration law. Tensions increased significantly as a result of the fallout from Operation Fast and Furious, a U.S. initiative in 2009–2010 aimed at curbing the flow of arms to drug traffickers and other criminals in Mexico. Following the death by shooting of a U.S. Border Patrol agent in late 2010, reportedly by use of a weapon linked to Fast and Furious, controversy over the program and cross-border tensions heightened, and a U.S. congressional investigation determined that lax management had allowed weapons to fall into the hands of criminals.

In February 2012 the two countries signed the U.S.-Mexico Transboundary Hydrocarbons Agreement, which will facilitate joint exploration of offshore oil and gas reserves in the western Gulf of Mexico.

President Peña Nieto hosted visits from U.S. President Barack Obama in May 2013 and Chinese President Xi Jinping in June.

Current issues. As he entered the last year of his presidency, Calderón's tactics against drug-related crime continued to come under fire. The military units he deployed in high crime areas were criticized for excessive force, brutality, and human rights violations. In November 2011 activists reported President Calderón and top administration officials to the International Criminal Court (ICC) for alleged war crimes in the fight against the drug cartels. Human Rights Watch issued a similar indictment of the Calderón government the same month, adding that "virtually none" of these alleged torture and extrajudicial killings were "being adequately investigated."

On July 1, 2012, Mexico held elections for the president, both chambers of the Union Congress, and governors. Slow economic growth and the bloody drug wars topped the political agenda. Over 50,000 people were murdered in drug-gang violence during Calderón's presidency, including 16,000 in 2011, and the body count grew during in the final days of the campaign. Fourteen mutilated corpses were found in a parked truck in Ciudad Mante on June 22 and another 14 in the same city on June 23.

The PRI swept the elections, winning the presidency and pluralities in both the Senate and the Chamber of Deputies. In alliance with PVEN, the PRI has a majority in the Chamber and was just two votes shy of a majority in the Senate. The party also controlled 21 of Mexico's 32 states. After 12 years of PAN rule, the PRI again dominated the Mexican political scene.

In the presidential race, Enrique Peña Nieto (PRI) received 38.2 percent of the vote, followed by Andrés Manuel López Obrador (PRD) with 31.6 percent. Josefina Vázquez Mota (PAN), the first woman to head the slate of a major party, finished third, with 25.4 percent, followed by Gabriel QUADRI (Panal) with 2.3 percent. Peña Nieto, the 46-year-old former governor of the state of Mexico, campaigned on a platform that presented him as the "new generation" of the PRI. He promised to spur economic growth, cut crime, and open the state oil company *Petroleos Mexicanos* (Pemex) to private investment.

López Obrador finished the 2012 election much as he had the 2006 presidential race: in second place by a very slim margin. He had contested the results of the 2006 race but pledged to accept the results in 2012 whether he won or lost. However he quickly reneged on that promise. At his insistence, the Mexican electoral authority retabulated the results from 50 percent of the polling stations, confirmed their original vote count, and certified Peña Nieto as the winner on August 31. López Obrador organized a rally in Mexico City on September 9, during which he announced that he would not recognize a Peña Nieto presidency and that he was leaving the PRD to form a new political movement.

The recount did not satisfy all voters. Anti-PRI groups joined López Obrador in accusing Peña Nieto of buying votes with store gift cards and biased media coverage. Hackers took over a dozen government websites on September 16, Mexican Independence Day, calling Peña Nieto an "imposed president." The attacks have been linked to "#YoSoy132," a social-media based student movement that criticized media coverage of Peña in the last weeks of the campaign.

The outgoing Congress approved a bipartisan labor reform package on November 2012 that better regulated temporary and part-time workers and offered improved protections to women and child laborers. While the PRI and PAN approved of the package, the PRD and many unions did not.

Peña Nieto was sworn in on December 1 and announced an ambitious reform agenda. His program consists of five broad "pillars": reducing violence, combating poverty, boosting economic growth, reforming education, and fostering social responsibility. Peña Nieto plans to pay for new programs, such as social security, by raising the top income tax rate, taxing capital gains, and expanding value-added taxes to food and medications. On December 10 he also announced a 5 percent pay cut for all mid- and upper-level civil servants. He also opened the telecommunications sector to foreign investment.

His most ambitious income program is opening PEMEX to outside investors, which will require a constitutional amendment—and support from two-thirds of Congress. To this end, he announced a Pact for Mexico on December 2 in which the opposition PAN and PRD pledged to support legislation to implement the five pillars. Shortly thereafter, Congress passed legislation that transferred control of the national school system from the National Union of Education Workers (*Sindicato Nacional de Trabajadores de la Educación*—SNTC) to the federal government. The PAN praised the reform as the "first visible achievement" of the Pact for Mexico.

On January 31 an explosion ripped through the PEMEX office tower in downtown Mexico City, killing 37 people and injuring more than 100. It was later determined to be the result of a gas buildup, not a bomb.

In a major crackdown on corruption, Elba Esther GORDILLO Morales, head of SNTC, was arrested on February 27 and charged with embezzling $150 million. Gordillo had previously been secretary general of the PRI before launching Panal.

Mexican officials arrested several high-profile drug lords, including a dozen members of *La Familia Michoacana* in January, Jonathan "The Ghost" SALAS of the Sinaloa cartel in February, and "Z-40," Miguel Angel TREVIÑO Morales, the leader of *Las Zetas* drug cartel, in July.

Local elections in 900 municipalities were held on July 7, and PRI candidates won roughly half of the contested seats. The run-up to the votes was marred by violence; 12 candidates were assassinated, and many more dropped out. The attacks undermined the progress the new government had registered against violent crime and shook the unity of the act.

Thanks in part due to the pact, Peña Nieto had a remarkable honeymoon, pushing through significant policy changes at a rapid pace, especially compared to the gridlock of the Calderón years. But the pact was starting to fray before the president introduced a constitutional amendment to open up Pemex in August. It was too radical for the PRD but did not go far enough for the PAN. Meanwhile, Lopez Obrador seized the issue for his latest populist crusade. In September teachers staged regular protests against educational reforms.

POLITICAL PARTIES

Mexican politics for more than seven decades after the late 1920s featured the dominance of a single party, the Institutional Revolutionary Party (PRI), which enjoyed virtually unchallenged control of the presidency, the Congress, and state governments. The situation changed dramatically, however, when the PRI lost the election of July 2, 2000. After a dozen years in the opposition, the PRI returned to power in 2012, albeit by a very small margin.

Parties must now capture a mandated minimum of 2 percent of the total vote in a national election to maintain their registrations. Seven parties qualified for the 2012 national elections. In January 2013 11 groups applied to the Federal Electoral Institute (*Instituto Federal Electoral*—IFE) for new party recognition.

Government Party:

Institutional Revolutionary Party (*Partido Revolucionario Institucional*—PRI). Founded in 1929 as the National Revolutionary Party (*Partido Nacional Revolucionario*—PNR) and redesignated in 1938 as the Mexican Revolutionary Party (*Partido de la Revolución Mexicana*—PRM), the PRI took its present name in 1946. As a union of local and state groups with roots in the revolutionary period, it was gradually established with a broad popular base and retains a tripartite organization based on three distinct sectors (labor, agrarian, and "popular"), although in 1978 it was officially designated as a "workers' party." While the PRI's general outlook may be characterized as moderately left-wing, its membership includes a variety of factions and outlooks. Since the early 1980s controversies surrounding electoral outcomes have led to internal turmoil, which in late 1986 resulted in the formation of the Democratic Current (*Corriente Democrática*—CD) faction under the leadership of Cuauhtémoc Cárdenas Solórzano and former party president Porfiro MUÑOZ LEDO, which called for more openness in PRI affairs, including the abolition of secrecy (*tapadismo*) in the selection of presidential candidates. In June 1987, five months after a shake-up in which half of the party's 30-member Executive Committee was replaced, the PRI withdrew recognition of the CD and in 1988 Cárdenas accepted the presidential nomination of the National Democratic Front (FDN; see under PRD, below), prior to organizing the PRD.

The precipitous decline of the PRI's presidential vote (94.4 percent in 1976, 71.0 in 1982, 50.4 in 1988), coupled with diminished congressional representation, prompted Carlos Salinas in the wake of the 1988 campaign to pledge thorough reform of the party apparatus, which Secretary General Manuel CAMACHO Solís characterized as being ridden by "bureaucratization, autocracy, [and] corruption." The issue intensified in the wake of charges that the central government had provided upward of $10 million to finance the PRI's unsuccessful Baja California Norte gubernatorial campaign in 1989. Thus, during the party's 14th National Assembly in Mexico City in September 1990, Salinas persuaded the delegates to adopt a series of measures that included direct and secret balloting for most leadership posts and the selection of a presidential candidate by a democratically elected convention rather than by the outgoing chief executive.

In March 1993 controversy over donations to the PRI from newly privatized enterprises led to the appointment as party chair of Fernando ORTIZ Arana, who dismissed six of the seven PRI Executive Committee members. Notwithstanding the 1990 assembly decisions, the PRI's first 1994 presidential candidate, Luis Donaldo Colosio Murrieta, was effectively chosen by Salinas, as was Ernesto ZEDILLO Ponce de León, following Colosio's assassination in March 1994. This continuance of the so-called *destape* ("unveiling") tradition of nomination by the presidential incumbent was condemned by the PRI's Democracy 2000 (*Democracia 2000*) faction but did not prevent Zedillo from being elected in August, albeit with a record low share (48.8 percent) of the popular vote. On September 28 the PRI's newly appointed secretary general, José Francisco Ruiz Massieu, was assassinated in Mexico City. A little over a year later, on October 13, 1995, a disaffected Camacho Solís, who had been passed over as the PRI's 1994 presidential nominee, quit the party to work for "real political change."

In the election of July 6, 1997, the PRI for the first time lost control of the Chamber of Deputies and also failed to capture the newly elective mayoralty of Mexico City. On March 17, 1999, the party's president, Mariano PALACIOS Alcocer, and its secretary general, Carlos ROJAS Gutiérrez, both resigned, ostensibly to reduce the role of the party hierarchy in selecting its 2000 presidential candidate. Earlier, President Zedillo had announced that he would break tradition by not designating his successor, proposing instead an open primary in fall 1999.

Following Vicente Fox's stunning defeat of Francisco LABASTIDA Ochoa on July 2, 2000, Dulce María SAURI Riancho, who had been appointed in November 1999 as party president, submitted her resignation, but she was persuaded to stay on pending the designation of a successor. In the next year the PRI lost several governorships, and by November 2001 it held only 17 of 31. Meanwhile, it was facing an internal leadership struggle pitting its traditionalists (dubbed the *dinosaurios* by opponents and the media) against a reform-oriented wing (the *técnicos*). An open election for the PRI presidency was held in February 2002, with Roberto MADRAZO Pintado, a former Tabasco governor, narrowly defeating Beatriz PAREDES Rangel, then president of the Chamber of Deputies.

A serious intraparty row erupted in late 2003 between Madrazo and the party's secretary general, Elba Esther GORDILLO. As a result of the dispute, Gordillo lost her post as bloc leader in the Chamber of Deputies and subsequently withdrew to launch her own formation, the New Alliance Party (below).

The PRI contested the 2006 election in a coalition with the PVEM (below) styled the Alliance for Mexico (*Alianza por México*). Since Madrazo's third-place finish in that election, the PRI has been a principal beneficiary of the decline in support for President Calderón's PAN, securing a number of governorships. The PRI generally cooperated with the president on major initiatives in 2008. Of particular note was the PRI's support of private company participation in off-shore drilling.

With voters turning away from the PAN, and the PRD riven by infighting, the PRI was the overwhelming winner of the midterm election on July 5, 2009. With 36.7 percent of the vote, the party saw its representation in the Chamber of Deputies more than double, and it also gained a plurality in the Senate.

The party remained resurgent in the July 2010 state elections, winning 9 of 12 gubernatorial races, though it lost three long-held key statehouses to a coalition of the PAN, the PRD, and other left-wing parties in an anti-PRI alliance. In September the PRI gained the presidency of both houses of Congress. Enrique Peña Nieto, the youthful governor of the state of México, as well as former party president Beatriz Paredes Rangel and Senate leader Manlio Fabio Beltrones, were seen as likely contenders to be the party's standard bearer in the 2012 presidential election.

In October 2010 the PRI put forth its own labor reform proposal in direct counterpoint to the measures proposed by the labor secretary, which were viewed as hostile to workers. Party leader Humberto MOREIRA Valdés resigned in December 2011, following controversy over the budget deficit of Coahuila state when he was governor.

The PRI formed an electoral alliances with the PVEM, "Committed to Mexico," for the 2012 elections. Enrique Peña Nieto won the 2012 presidential poll, leading the party to take control of both chambers of the Union Congress, with 52 senators and 212 deputies.

Leaders: Enrique PEÑA Nieto (President of Mexico), César CAMACHO Quiroz (President), Antonio Emilio GAMBOA Patrón, Manlio Fabio BELTRONES, Aracelly Ivonne ORTEGA Pacheco (Secretary General).

Mexican Green Ecologist Party (*Partido Verde Ecologista de México*—PVEM). An outgrowth of the National Ecologist Alliance (*Alianza Ecologista Nacional*), Mexico's Greens initially adopted the name Green Ecologist Party (PVE) upon formally entering the political arena in 1987. Having failed to obtain registration in time for the 1988 election, the PVE participated in the FDN. A dispute over the party name led to its registration as the Ecologist Party of Mexico (PEM) for the 1991 election, but the party narrowly failed to secure the minimum necessary to gain full legal status. It assumed its present name in 1993.

PVEM founder Jorge GONZÁLEZ Torres received 0.9 percent of the vote in the August 1994 presidential poll, and the party failed to win congressional representation. However, it won 6 Chamber seats in 1997, on a vote share of 4 percent. The party went on to secure 5 Senate and 15 Chamber seats as an ally of PAN in 2000, although its leadership had come under fire from like-minded groups for abandoning environmental issues in its pursuit of electoral success. It won 2 additional lower house seats in 2003 but in early 2004 became entangled in a bribery scandal stemming from a tape-recorded solicitation of Jorge Emilio González Martínez, the son of Gonzáles Torres and current party president. In 2008 the party made advocacy of the death penalty, especially for kidnappers, a signature issue, which caused the European Green Party to withdraw its recognition of the PVEM as a "green" party.

The PVEM contested the 2006 election in a coalition with the PRI styled the Alliance for Mexico (*Alianza por México*). The party won 17 seats in the Chamber of Deputies and 4 in the Senate. It maintained this alliance for the 2009 legislative elections, winning 21 seats in the Chamber of Deputies.

In the 2010 gubernatorial elections, the PVEM's alliances with the PRI in seven states helped the PRI gain its overall total of nine governorships.

The PRI and PVEM formed a new coalition for 2012, "Committed to Mexico." PVEM candidates won 9 seats in the Senate and 29 in the Chamber of Deputies.

Leaders: Arturo ESCOBAR Vega (President of the Party), Jorge Emilio GONZÁLEZ Martínez (1994 presidential candidate), Jorge LEGORRETA Ordorica (Executive Secretary).

Other Legislative Parties:

National Action Party (*Partido Acción Nacional*—PAN). Founded in 1939 and dependent on urban middle-class support, the long-time leading opposition party has an essentially conservative, proclerical, and probusiness orientation, and favors limitations on the government's economic role. It has traditionally been strongest in the north and west of the country. Largely because of fragmentation within the leftist opposition, PAN was, until recently, the main beneficiary of erosion in PRI support. In 1982, despite losing all but 1 of its directly elective Chamber seats, the party's proportional representation rose from 39 to 54, with party spokespeople claiming that they had been denied a number of victories as the result of PRI electoral fraud. Similar claims were made after the 1985 election, in which PAN gained 9 directly elective Chamber seats and a number of mayoralties, and was widely acknowledged to have gained the majority of votes in two gubernatorial races awarded to the PRI. The party ran third in both the presidential and legislative balloting of July 1988.

On July 2, 1989, Ernesto RUFFO Appel, PAN's Baja California Norte gubernatorial candidate, captured the party's first governorship. In November 1990 PAN again accused the PRI of fraud after it had secured landslide victories in state and local balloting.

The party secured its first Senate seat in the August 1991 balloting, despite a drop in Chamber representation from 101 to 99. The most startling development, however, was in the Guanajuato gubernatorial race, in which the official victor, a PRI hard-liner, was induced to defer to the interim incumbency of PAN's Carlos MEDINA Plascencia. The party registered another notable gain by winning the state governorship of Chihuahua in July 1992. However, a number of influential party dissidents insisted that the victories were achieved through a policy of rapprochement with the PRI and vowed to respond to the *"salinista"* drift by formation of a breakaway party.

In the August 1994 presidential balloting the PAN candidate, Diego FERNÁNDEZ de Cevallos, came in second with 25.9 percent of the popular vote, while PAN representation in the Chamber rose to 119 seats and in the enlarged Senate to 25. Far more impressive was the stunning defeat inflicted on the PRI in Jalisco on February 13, 1995, with PAN capturing the governor's office, the Guadalajara mayoralty, and an overwhelming majority of state legislative seats. In mid-March Secretary General Felipe Calderón Hinojosa defeated Ruffo Appel in a contest to succeed Carlos CASTILLO Peraza as party president. Calderón Hinojosa was succeeded on March 6, 1999, by Luis BRAVO Mena.

PAN contested the 2000 election in a coalition with the Mexican Green Ecologist Party (PVEM, below), styled the Alliance for Change (*Alianza por el Cambio*), which won the presidency and a plurality of 223 seats in the Chamber of Deputies. In the following year the party won several additional governorships, a number of which were lost in 2004.

In July 2006 Calderón Hinojosa, a member of the party's conservative wing, defeated the PRD's López Obrador for the presidency by a narrow margin of 35.9–35.4 percent. PAN also became the largest party in both the Senate and the Chamber of Deputies.

Despite the party's electoral success, tension arose between Calderón and party president Manuel ESPINO Barrientos, who pushed for Mexican membership in the Christian Democratic Organization of the Americas (*Organización Demócrata Cristiana de América*), of which he was also president. The poor showing of PAN in the local elections following the 2006 presidential elections prompted Espino to step down. He was replaced on December 9, 2007, by a loyalist, Germán MARTÍNEZ Cázares.

In the July 5, 2009, midterm elections, the party finished second, more than 8 points behind the PRI, and its representation in the Chamber of Deputies dropped from 206 to 143 members. The party won only 1 of 6 state governorship contests; of the 5 losses, 2 were in states that had previously had PAN governors. Martínez quit the party presidency shortly after the elections. On August 11 the party chose President Calderón's former private secretary, César NAVA, as its new president.

The PAN crossed ideological lines in an unusual alliance with the PRD and other left-wing parties against the PRI in the gubernatorial elections on July 4, 2010. The anti-PRI alliance prompted Interior Secretary Fernando Gómez Mont, who had reportedly promised PRI leaders that no such left-right partnership would occur, to quit the party. After the strategy was vindicated by coalition victories in the key states of Oaxaca, Sinaloa, and Puebla, Gómez Mont resigned from the government. In December Senator Gustavo MADERO Muñoz was elected party president. On July 21 electoral regulators ruled that President Calderón had violated the article of the constitution that prohibits presidents and governors from participating in election campaigns. The ruling referred to a televised speech by the president in June in which he voiced support for the anti-PRI alliance.

The party chose Josefina VÁZQUEZ MOTA, leader of the PAN delegation in the Chamber of Deputies, as its 2012 presidential candidate. With a later start than other presidential contenders, she finished in third place with 25.4 percent of the vote. PAN dropped from 52 to 38 Senate seats and 114 deputies, down from 147 in 2009. PAN joined President Piña Nieto's Pact for Mexico alliance in December 2012.

Leaders: Felipe CALDERÓN Hinojosa (Former President of Mexico), Gustavo MADERO Muñoz (President of the Party), César NAVA, Vicente FOX Quesada (Former President of Mexico), Josefina VÁZQUEZ MOTA.

Democratic Revolutionary Party (*Partido de la Revolución Democrática*—PRD). The PRD was launched in 1988 by Cuauhtémoc Cárdenas Solórzano, who had previously led the dissident Democratic Current (CD) within the PRI and had placed second in the July presidential balloting as standard-bearer of the National Democratic Front (*Frente Democrático Nacional*—FDN) coalition. Other participants in the FDN included the PVE (see PVEM), PARM, and PPS (below), the Social Democratic Party (*Partido Social Demócrata*—PSD), the Movement Toward Socialism (*Movimiento al Socialismo*—MAS), and the Mexican Socialist Party (*Partido Mexicano Socialista*—PMS).

The PMS had been launched in March 1987 by merger of Mexico's two principal leftist groups, the Unified Socialist Party of Mexico (*Partido Socialista Unificado de México*—PSUM) and the Mexican Workers' Party (*Partido Mexicano de los Trabajadores*—PMT), and three smaller formations. Recognized by the Soviet Union as the country's official Communist Party, the PSUM dated from the November 1981 merger of the Mexican Communist Party (*Partido Comunista Mexicano*—PCM) with four smaller groups. (The PCM, formed in 1919, was accorded legal recognition from 1932 to 1942 and was thereafter semi-clandestine until returned, conditionally, to legal status in 1978.)

Following the 1987 launch of the PMS, discussions with the FDN during the latter half of the year failed to yield agreement on a joint candidate for the 1988 presidential election. As a result, the PMS nominated Herberto CASTILLO of the PMT. It was not until early June 1988 that Castillo withdrew in favor of the FDN's Cuauhtémoc Cárdenas, who a month later narrowly lost to the PRI's Carlos Salinas in a widely disputed election. Formation of the PRD as a unified party followed, with a variety of additional political and social organizations joining the CD, PMS, and MAS.

The newly formed PRD's July 1989 loss to the PRI in the Michoacán gubernatorial balloting was widely viewed as the result of fraudulent vote tallying. Subsequently, PRD members occupied municipal buildings and commandeered public roads, leading to clashes with PRI adherents and government forces that continued into 1990. Meanwhile, the party, which had been denied legalization on a national basis in June, sought international assistance in investigating the alleged political assassination of some 60 of its members since 1988.

In November 1990, defying a new law criminalizing false fraud accusations, the PRD claimed that the PRI had employed "all known forms of violating the vote" in capturing elections in México and Hidalgo states. The PRD's México state vote fell from 1.2 million for Cárdenas alone in 1988 to 200,000 for all PRD candidates in 1990. Meanwhile, observers described the January 1991 resignation of a PRD leader, Jorge ALCOCER, who accused Cárdenas of being "authoritarian and intolerant," as symptomatic of the dissension that had wracked the party since the 1988 balloting. In the August 1994 presidential balloting Cárdenas came in third with 16.6 percent of the popular vote, while PRD representation in the Chamber rose to 71 seats and in the enlarged Senate to 8 seats.

In June 1996 the PRD became the first Mexican party not only to place selection of its leadership in the direct vote of its members but also to confer the franchise on all registered voters who opted to join on polling day. Andrés Manuel López Obrador, PRD leader in Tabasco, defeated two other candidates for the party presidency in July.

At the election of July 6, 1997, the PRD placed second in the Chamber of Deputies, with 125 seats, while Cárdenas became the first elected mayor of Mexico City. In February 1999 the PRD claimed its third governorship, winning Baja California Sur from the PRI.

For the 2000 election Cárdenas resigned his mayoralty for a renewed presidential bid, but he ran a distant third as head of the Alliance for Mexico (*Alianza por México*), which included the Labor Party, Convergence for Democracy, Nationalist Society Party, and Social Alliance Party.

The PRD, which had been supportive of the Fox regime, severed its links with the federal government in early 2004 because of its conviction that the administration had been orchestrating charges of corruption in the capital to damage the presidential prospects of its popular incumbent mayor, López Obrador. Following massive demonstrations in support of López Obrador, President Fox in April 2005 suspended charges against the mayor.

For the 2006 campaign, the PRD formed a grouping with the PT and the Convergence Party (below), styled the **Coalition for the Good of All** (*Coalición por el Bien de Todos*). Despite López Obrador's narrow defeat by the PAN's Calderón Hinojosa in the disputed 2006 presidential elections, the PRD became the second largest party in the Chamber of Deputies with 25 percent of the seats. The party subsequently split over how to respond to Calderón's victory, as radicals supported López Obrador's street protests and his creation of a "legitimate" government, while moderates were willing to engage the government. The divisions were evident in the March 16, 2008, elections for PRD president, which pitted Jesús ORTEGA of the moderate New Left (*Nueva Izquierda*) against Alejandro ENCINAS, who supported López Obrador. With 70 percent of the ballots counted and accusations of fraud from both sides, the party annulled the election after missing several deadlines for releasing the results. Finally, on November 12, 2008, the national elections tribunal ruled in favor of Ortega.

In December 2008 the PRD's national congress decided not to form alliances with other parties for the 2009 midterm elections, effectively dissolving the Coalition for the Good of All. In party primaries on March 15, New Left candidates generally fared worse than supporters of López Obrador. For his part, López Obrador campaigned against moderate PRD candidates in some districts, openly supporting candidates from the Labor Party and the Convergence Party. On July 5, 2009, the divided party finished a distant third with 12.2 percent of the vote; its representation in the lower house of Congress fell from 126 to 71 seats.

The PRD's unusual alliance with the PAN for the July 2010 local elections succeeded in defeating incumbent PRI governors in Oaxaca and two other key states. PRD leaders disagreed over whether to reprise the strategy in 2011 against Enrique Peña Nieto, governor of the state of México and PRI presidential hopeful. Mexico City mayor Marcelo EBRARD and the moderates supported the left-right coalition, while López Obrador opposed such a move. The conflict revealed the early jockeying among aspirants for the next presidential race. Ultimately, López Obrador, 59, won the bid as the candidate of the left. Ebrard accepted the results, which left him in a position to handpick his successor as mayor, observers said. López Obrador finished second in the presidential race, with 31.6 percent, and publically questioned the validity of the voting process. The PRD picked up 32 deputies, increasing its delegation from 72 to 104, but lost 4 Senate seats, dropping from 26 to 22. On September 9, 2012, López Obrador announced that he was leaving the PRD to form a new political movement.

PRD joined President Piña Nieto's Pact for Mexico alliance in December 2012. Carlos NAVARRETE Ruiz resigned from his post as Mexico City's secretary of labor in October 2013 in order to seek the presidency of the PRD.

Leaders: Jesus ZAMBRANO Grijalva (President), Miguel Angel MANCERA (Mayor of Mexico City), Alejandro ENCINAS, Carlos NAVARRETE Ruiz, Alejandro SÁNCHEZ Camacho (Secretary General).

Labor Party (*Partido del Trabajo*—PT). A moderate leftist formation founded in 1990 by a number of organizations, the PT won 1.2 percent of the vote in the 1991 congressional poll. In the August 1994 presidential contest Cecilia SOTO González fought a vigorous campaign that drew support away from the more established PRD and gave her 2.7 percent of the national vote. Ten PT candidates were elected to the Chamber of Deputies in 1994, 7 in 1997, 8 in 2000, and 6 in 2003.

In 2006 the PT joined the Convergence Party (below) and the Coalition for the Good of All. Andrés Manuel López Obrador, the PRD's 2006 presidential candidate, campaigned on behalf of some PT candidates, some of whom had been close advisors during his candidacy and his tenure as Mexico City mayor.

In the July 2009 balloting for the Chamber of Deputies, the party won 13 seats. In July 2012 Labor received 5 Senate seats and 15 in the Chamber of Deputies.

Leader: María Guadalupe RODRÍGUEZ Martínez (National Coordinator).

New Alliance Party (*Partido Nueva Alianza*—Panal). Panal was launched in 2005 by former PRI secretary general Elba Esther Gordillo, leader of the National Education Workers' Syndicate (*Sindicato Nacional de Trabajadores de la Educación*—SNTE), the largest labor union in Latin America and the driving force behind civil disturbances in Oaxaca in 2006.

In 2006 the party won nine seats in the Chamber of Deputies and one Senate seat. Panal retained its nine seats in the Chamber of Deputies in the 2009 elections. Gabriel Quadri represented Panal in the 2012 presidential race, finishing a distant fourth with 2.3 percent of the vote. The party retained its single Senate seat and took ten seats in the Chamber of Deputies.

Party founder Elba Esther Gordillo was arrested for embezzlement in February 2013 (see above), triggering a crisis within the party, as her daughter, Mónica T. ARRIOLA Gordillo, had recently become Panal's secretary general. She resigned from that post in September.

Leader: Luis CASTRO Obregón (President).

Citizens' Movement (*Movimiento Ciudadano*). Established in 1999 as the Convergence for Democracy (*Convergencia por la Democracia*—CD), the democratic party was led by former Veracruz governor Dante Delgado and other PRI dissidents. In the 2000 federal election it participated in the Alliance for Mexico, and as a result, secured one Senate seat and two Chamber seats.

In 2002 the party voted to adopt the shortened form of its name, Convergence (*Convergencia*). It won five seats in the Chamber of Deputies in 2003.

In 2006 the party participated in the Coalition for the Good of All with the PT and PRD, fielding the PRD's Andrés López Obrador as its presidential candidate. It won 17 seats in the Chamber of Deputies and 5 in the Senate. Subsequently, the coalition dissolved.

In the 2009 balloting for the Chamber of Deputies, the party won six seats in the Chamber of Deputies on a vote share of 2.4 percent, barely exceeding the 2 percent threshold required to maintain its legal status.

In the 2010 state elections the party allied with the leftist PRD and PT in Oaxaca, where Convergence member Gabino CUÉ Monteagudo was elected governor.

On July 31, 2011, the party modified its name to **Citizens' Movement** (*Movimiento Ciudadano*). The following year, it went from 6 seats in the Chamber of Deputies to 16, but dropped from 6 senators to 1.

Leaders: Luis WALTON Aburto (President), Dante DELGADO Rannauro (Coordinator), Jesús Armando LOPEZ VELARDE CAMPA (Secretary General).

Other Parties and Groups:

(For more information on minor or defunct parties, see the 2008, 2009, and 2013 editions of the *Handbook.*)

Paramilitary Groups:

Zapatista National Liberation Army (*Ejército Zapatista de Liberación Nacional*—EZLN). Initial accounts of the January 1994 uprising in Chiapas (see Political background, above) suggested that the rebels numbered upward of 1,000 men seeking economic relief for Mexico's "dispensable" indigenous groups. Ideologically, the EZLN was unique in neither invoking traditional Marxist jargon nor attempting to seize national power. In early 1996 the group announced the launching of a "sister organization," the **Zapatista National Liberation Front** (*Frente Zapatista de Liberación Nacional*—FZLN), which was not a "formal" political party and did not contest elections.

A march by EZLN leaders to Mexico City in February–March 2001 culminated in a controversial invitation to address the Congress of Deputies on March 28. The EZLN urged passage of the Indigenous Rights Bill, although the Zapatistas ultimately rejected the version of the bill that was passed in late April as offering insufficient autonomy and land rights. As a consequence, the EZLN refused to negotiate with the Fox government.

In 2005 the group's spokesperson, known as "Subcomandante Marcos," declared that the group was entering mainstream politics; he was subsequently appointed coleader of a Chiapas "good government" municipal board. In 2006 he led a tour of Mexican cities to generate popular support ahead of the elections.

The EZLN seeks indigenous control over land and resources, most recently via lobbying efforts on the Internet. It has been less active nationally in recent years, though it remains an intact movement and a political force in several municipalities of Chiapas, relying on its skillful use of the media to garner support around the world.

In February 2011 Subcomandante Marcos wrote a lengthy critique, styled as a communiqué, on Mexico's drug war.

Leader: Subcomandante MARCOS.

Popular Revolutionary Army (*Ejército Popular Revolucionario*—EPR). The EPR was apparently launched in 1994 as a coalition of a dozen-odd minor leftist factions allied with the peasant-based Revolutionary Workers' Party and Clandestine Popular Union–Party of the Poor (*Partido Revolucionario Obrerista y Clandestino de Unión Popular–Partido de los Pobres*—PROCUP-PDLP). PROCUP was founded in the 1970s by radicals under the leadership of Oaxaca University rector Felipe MARTÍNEZ Soriano, who has been imprisoned since 1990 for involvement in the killing of two security guards at a Mexican newspaper office. The PDLP, dating from 1967, was a largely moribund clandestine formation before being revived by merger with PROCUP. In 1991 PROCUP claimed responsibility for a series of bombings of the Mexico City offices of a number of international corporations and was charged in 1994 with the kidnapping of Alfred Harp Helu, the chair of Mexico's largest bank, for whose release his family paid a $30 million ransom.

During 1996 the EPR was reported to have killed 26 soldiers or police officers while extending its activities into more than half of Mexico's 31 states. At a secret press conference in August 1996 it announced formation of a 14-organization **Popular Democratic Revolutionary Party** (*Partido Democrático Popular Revolucionario*—PDPR) that would serve as its political wing. Three months earlier the PROCUP-PDLP reportedly had dissolved.

Relatively quiescent after 1997, the EPR resurfaced in May 2002 when it appeared responsible for the killing of two police officers 95 miles east of Acapulco. In 2004 President Fox indicated that the group was still active, while media reports suggested that it had spawned a number of splinter formations, particularly in the south. Between July and September 2007 the EPR claimed responsibility for massive bombings of natural gas pipelines, which resulted in thousands of people being evacuated and cost millions in damage to the economy. The group has carried out few armed actions since 2007, but it issues periodic political statements, including a 2009 endorsement of a small movement urging voters in the midterm elections to turn in blank ballots. A yearlong effort at mediation between the EPR and the government ended in April 2009 due to lack of progress. It supported striking teachers in 2013.

In June 2013 a group called the **People's Revolutionary Army** (*Ejército Revolucionario del Pueblo—ERP*) announced it had broken away from the EPR because the latter group had strayed too far from its Marxist-Leninist roots. The EPR responded that the alleged rebels had never been part of the older group.

Popular Insurgent Revolutionary Army (*Ejército Revolucionario Insurgente Popular*—ERIP). The formation of the ERIP was announced in November 1996 by a group claiming to represent "peasants, Indians, workers, and businesspeople." The ERIP, which called for the resignation of the Zedillo administration and the convening of a national congress to draft a new constitution, said it would operate in northern and central Mexico as a "complement" to the southern-based EZLN and EPR.

Zeta Killers (*Mata Zetas*). In the summer of 2011 a group calling itself the Zeta Killers began posting videos online portraying themselves as an organized paramilitary force bent on destroying the Zetas drug ring in Veracruz. The government dismissed the claims, calling the videos a new tactic among rival drug gangs.

(For more information on guerilla groups, see the 2008 and 2009 editions of the *Handbook.*)

LEGISLATURE

The **Union Congress** (*Congreso de la Unión*) consists of a Senate and a Chamber of Deputies, both elected by popular vote. When Congress is not in session, limited legislative functions are performed by a Permanent Committee of 18 senators and 19 deputies elected by their respective houses. Legislators cannot serve consecutive terms.

Senate (*Cámara de Senadores*). The upper chamber contains 128 members, the number having been doubled with the election, for six-year terms, of 96 senators in 1994. In 1997, 32 senators were elected for three-year terms. In 2000 all 128 seats were renewed for the first time, half by majority vote in each state and the Federal District, one-quarter by assignment to the leading minority candidate in each of the 32 jurisdictions, and one-quarter by national proportional representation.

Following the most recent election on July 1, 2012, the seat distribution was as follows: the Institutional Revolutionary Party, 52; National Action Party, 38 seats; Democratic Revolutionary Party, 22; Mexican Green Ecologist Party, 9; Labor Party, 5; Citizens' Movement, 1; and New Alliance Party, 1.

President: Raúl CERVANTES Andrade.

Chamber of Deputies (*Cámara de Diputados*). The lower chamber presently contains 500 members elected for three-year terms, including 200 seats distributed on a proportional basis among parties winning more than 2 percent of the vote nationwide.

Following the most recent election on July 1, 2012, the seat distribution was as follows: the Institutional Revolutionary Party, 212 seats; National Action Party, 114; Democratic Revolutionary Party, 104; Mexican Green Ecologist Party, 29; Labor Party, 15; and New Alliance, 10.

President: Ricardo ANAYA Cortés.

CABINET

[as of October 15, 2013]

President	Enrique Peña Nieto
Secretaries	
Agrarian Reform	Jorge Carlos Ramirez Marín
Agriculture, Livestock, Rural Development, Fisheries, and Food	Enrique Martínez y Martínez
Attorney General	Jesús Murillo Káram
Communications and Transport	Gerardo Ruiz Esparza
Economy	Ildefonso Guajardo Villarreal
Energy	Pedro Joaquín Coldwell
Environment and Natural Resources	Juan José Guerra Abud
Finance and Public Credit	Luis Videgaray Caso
Foreign Affairs	José Antonio Meade Kuribreña
Health	Mercedes Juan López [f]
Interior	Miguel Angel Osorio Chong
Labor and Social Welfare	Jesús Alfonso Navarrete Prida
National Defense	Salvador Ciefuegos Zepeda
Navy	Vidal Francisco Soberón Sanz
Public Education	Emilio Chuayffet Chemor
Public Safety	Manuel Mondragón y Kalb
Social Development	Rosario Robles Berlanga [f]
Tourism	Claudia Ruiz Massieu Salinas [f]

[f] = female

INTERGOVERNMENTAL REPRESENTATION

Ambassador to the U.S.: Eduardo MEDINA MORA Icaza.

U.S. Ambassador to Mexico: E. Anthony WAYNE.

Permanent Representative to the UN: Jorge Mario MONTAÑO Y MARTÍNEZ.

IGO Memberships (Non-UN): APEC, EBRD, G-20, IADB, ICC, IOM, OAS, OECD, WTO.

FEDERATED STATES OF MICRONESIA

Political Status: Sovereign state in free association with the United States (which retains authority with regard to defense) since October 21, 1986.

Land Area: 271 sq. mi. (701 sq. km).

Population: 112,981 (2013E—UN); 106,104 (2013E—U.S.). (It is estimated that nearly 50,000 FSM citizens reside in the United States.)

Major Urban Centers (2005E): PALIKIR (Pohnpei, 6,600), Weno (Chuuk, 12,300), Kitti (Pohnpei, 6,800), Nett (Pohnpei, 6,300), Kolonia (Pohnpei, 5,000).

Official Language: English. The principal native languages are Kosrean, Pohnpeian, Trukese, and Yapese.

Monetary Unit: U.S. Dollar (see the entry on United States for principal exchange rates).

President: Emanuel (Manny) MORI; elected by the Congress on May 11, 2007, and sworn in on the same day for a four-year term, succeeding Joseph J. URUSEMAL; reelected for a second four-year term on May 11, 2011, following the legislative elections on March 8.

Vice President: Alik L. ALIK; elected by the Congress on May 11, 2007, and sworn in on the same day for a term concurrent with that of the president, succeeding Redley KILLION; reelected on May 11, 2011.

THE COUNTRY

The Federated States of Micronesia (FSM), with the Republic of Palau at its western extremity, comprises the archipelago of the Caroline Islands, some 300 miles to the east of the Philippines. The constituent states are the island groups (from west to east) of Yap, Chuuk (formerly Truk), Pohnpei (formerly Ponape), and Kosrae, each of which has its own indigenous language, with English as the official language of the Federation. Most inhabitants of the more than 600 islands are of either Micronesian or Polynesian extraction. Roman Catholicism predominates among the largely Christian population. Subsistence farming and fishing are the principal economic activities, with tourism of increasing importance. More than half of the taxpaying wage earners are government employees, with most of the remainder dependent on spending by either government or government workers. The paucity of job prospects has heightened emigration to the United States, where visas are not required for FSM citizens under the provisions of the Compact of Free Association with the United States.

The International Monetary Fund (IMF) has warned that "achieving long-term economic stability has become more challenging" for the FSM, considering that Compact assistance (approximately $90 million in 2009) was scheduled to decline by $800,000 annually until 2023 (when grants were slated to end).

Growth was estimated by the IMF to have fallen from 3.1 percent in 2010 to 1.4 percent in 2011 and 2012 as the private sector (responsible for only 25 percent of GDP) remained sluggish. In consonance with IMF recommendations, the government is pursuing tax reforms designed to enhance revenue while also emphasizing private-sector growth, particularly in regard to fisheries and tourism. In addition, the FSM has recently launched an offshore corporate registry.

GOVERNMENT AND POLITICS

Political background. Purchased by Germany from Spain in 1899, the Carolines were seized in 1914 by Japan and retained as part of the mandate awarded by the League of Nations to Japan in 1920. The islands were occupied by U.S. forces in World War II and (along with the Marshall and Northern Mariana islands) became part of the U.S. Trust Territory of the Pacific in 1947. In 1965 a Congress of Micronesia was established, with the Carolines electing 14 of the 21 members of its House of Representatives. Following acceptance of a 1975 covenant

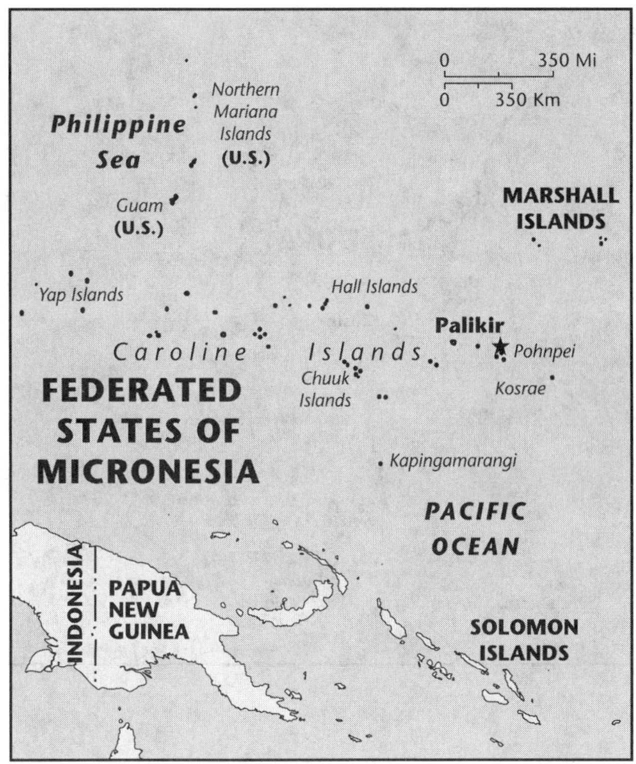

authorizing creation of the Commonwealth of the Northern Mariana Islands, the remaining components of the Trust Territory were regrouped into six districts, four of which in July 1978 approved a constitution of the FSM that became effective on May 10, 1979. In October 1982 the FSM concluded a 15-year Compact of Free Association with the United States, which was declared to be in effect on November 3, 1986, following ratification by the U.S. Congress and final approval by the FSM government. Under the Compact (and its 2003 successor) the FSM is a sovereign entity, save with regard to defense; the FSM is also obligated to "consult" with Washington on major foreign policy matters.

On May 15, 1987, John R. HAGLELGAM was sworn in as the FSM's second president, succeeding Tosiwo NAKAYAMA. Haglelgam was unable to stand for a second term because of his failure to secure reelection to the FSM Congress on March 5, 1991, and on May 11 Bailey OLTER, formerly vice president under Nakayama, was elected as Haglelgam's successor. Olter was elected to a second term on May 11, 1995.

In November 1996 the Congress ruled that President Olter, who had recently suffered a stroke, was unable to fulfill his responsibilities and directed Vice President Jacob NENA to serve as acting president. Subsequently, it was determined that Olter would be unable to return to office, and on May 8, 1997, Nena was formally installed for the balance of his four-year mandate. Olter died in February 1999.

On May 12, 1999, Vice President Leo A. FALCAM was elected to the presidency by the Congress, all 14 members of whom had been returned to office in nationwide balloting on March 2. However, both President Falcam and former president Nena lost their seats at the full legislative replenishment of March 4, 2003, and on May 10 the Congress elected Joseph J. URUSEMAL as chief executive.

Following a two-year extension of the 1986 Compact, a successor was signed on May 1, 2003, and approved by the U.S. Congress in November. The document provided for 20 more years of direct U.S. financial support in the form of annual grants (starting at about $77 million and decreasing by $800,000 annually until 2023) to subsidize the government's budget as well as $16 million annually for a trust fund to support the government after 2023. (The nonfinancial elements of the treaty have no expiration date.)

President Urusemal failed in a reelection bid after the congressional election of March 6, 2007. Emanuel (Manny) MORI, a longtime critic of the current compact, was named to replace him on May 11. Mori was reelected on May 11, 2011.

Constitution and government. The 1979 constitution provides for a unicameral Congress of 14 members, referred to as senators. The president and vice president, who serve four-year terms, are selected by the Congress from among the four-year senators, the vacated seats being refilled by special election. The individual states have elected governors and legislatures, the latter encompassing a bicameral body of 38 members for Chuuk (a 10-member Senate and a 28-member House of Representatives) and unicameral bodies of 27, 14, and 10 members, respectively, for Pohnpei, Kosrae, and Yap. The state officials serve for four years (legislative terms on Chuuk and Pohnpei are staggered). Municipalities are governed by elected magistrates and councils, while villages follow traditional forms of rule.

State	*Area (sq. mi.)*	*Population (2007E)*
Chuuk	45.6	53,900
Kosrae	42.3	8,100
Pohnpei	132.4	35,500
Yap	46.7	11,400

In late 2000 local voters overwhelmingly endorsed creation of a fifth state, Faichuk, encompassing eight islands (with a population of about 20,000) that currently constitute part of Chuuk. In addition, sentiment has mounted for a constitutional amendment that would provide for direct election of the president and vice president. However, no action had been taken in either matter by mid-2013.

Foreign relations. In December 1990 the UN Security Council formally abrogated the U.S. Trusteeship with respect to the FSM, the Northern Marianas, and the Marshall Islands, and in September 1991 both the Marshalls and the FSM were admitted to the United Nations. In June 1993 the FSM was admitted to the IMF and the World Bank. The FSM is also a member of the Asian Development Bank, the Pacific Community, and the Pacific Islands Forum.

As in the case with the Marshall Islands, FSM's political autonomy is seemingly constricted by the U.S. retention of authority in defense matters and its right of "consultation" in foreign affairs. Nevertheless, the FSM parted company with both Majuro and Washington in endorsing the Treaty of Rarotonga that called for the establishment of a South Pacific Nuclear Free Zone.

Current issues. At present, the overwhelming concern is Micronesia's fate in the course of global warming. Insisting that his country is "on the verge of drowning" because of atolls being less than a meter above sea level, President Mori has joined with other island leaders in addressing the issue at the United Nations and elsewhere.

Although reports surfaced of intense backroom maneuvering on the matter, President Mori was ultimately reelected in May 2011 without opposition in the formal vote in Congress. Mori subsequently announced that his administration would focus on foreign investment, development in the private sector, climate change negotiations, and completion of infrastructure projects funded through the compact.

In 2012 the IMF warned that it currently appeared that the Compact Trust Fund would fall significantly short of the money it would need to support the FSM budget following the scheduled expiration of compact grants in 2023. Calling for greater attention to education and policies designed to promote the private sector, President Mori in 2013 proposed the convening of a constitutional convention to address, among other things, the "conflicting mandates" of the states and the federal government, which Mori characterized as hampering decisive economic action. He also proposed creation of a regional airline to serve the FSM, Palau, and Marshall Islands.

POLITICAL PARTIES

There are, at present, no formal parties in the FSM, political activity tending to center on regional (state) alignments.

LEGISLATURE

The FSM **Congress** is a 14-member body, 4 of whose members are elected on a statewide basis (1 from each state) for four-year terms, while 10 (5 from Chuuk, 3 from Pohnpei, and 1 each from Kosrae and Yap) are selected for two-year terms in first-past-the-post voting in single-member districts delineated on a population basis.

Balloting for all 14 seats was held on March 8, 2011. In a referendum held at the same time, voters rejected a proposed amendment that would have made all legislative terms of four years' duration. Elections for the 10 two-year seats were most recently held on March 5, 2013.

Speaker: Dohsis HALBERT.

CABINET

[as of August 1, 2013]

President	Emanuel (Manny) Mori
Vice President	Alik L. Alik
Secretaries	
Education	Rufino Mauricio
Finance and Administration	Kensley Ikosia
Foreign Affairs	Lorin S. Robert
Health and Social Services	Dr. Vita Akapito Skilling [f]
Justice	April Dawn Skilling
Resources and Development	Marion Henry
Transportation, Communication, and Infrastructure	Francis I. Itimai

[f] = female

INTERGOVERNMENTAL REPRESENTATION

Ambassador to the U.S.: Asterio R. TAKESY.

U.S. Ambassador to the Federated States of Micronesia: Dorothea-Maria ROSEN.

Permanent Representative to the UN: Jane J. CHIGIYAL.

IGO Memberships (Non-UN): ADB, PIF.

MOLDOVA

Republic of Moldova
Republica Moldova

Political Status: Formerly the Moldavian Soviet Socialist Republic, a constituent republic of the Union of Soviet Socialist Republics; declared independence as the Republic of Moldova on August 27, 1991; became sovereign member of the Commonwealth of Independent States on December 21, 1991; new constitution approved on July 28, 1994, and entered into force on August 27.

Area: 13,000 sq. mi. (33,670 sq. km).

Population: 3,599,249 (2012E—UN); 3,619,925 (2013E—U.S. Census).

Major Urban Centers (2013E): CHIŞINĂU (formerly Kishinev, 672,000), Tiraspol (158,000), Bălți (145,000), Tighina (94,000).

Official Language: Moldovan.

Monetary Unit: Moldovan leu (official rate November 1, 2013: 12.89 leu = $1US).

President: Nicolae TIMOFTI (ind.); sworn in for a four-year term on March 23, 2012, and assumed office on the same day, replacing Marian LUPU (Democratic Party); named acting president (due to his position as speaker of Parliament) by Parliament on December 30, 2010.

Prime Minister: Iurie LEANCĂ (Liberal Democratic Party of Moldova); appointed acting prime minister on April 25, 2013, following the ruling of the Constitutional Court of Moldova against the renomination of Vladimir FILAT, who had resigned on March 8 after losing a vote of nonconfidence in parliament on March 5. Leancă was then nominated by President Timofti on May 15 and approved with his cabinet on May 30, 2013.

THE COUNTRY

Located in Eastern Europe, Moldova is bordered on the north, east, and south by Ukraine and on the west by Romania. The breakaway region of Transnistria (Transdniestria) lies between the Dnestr (Nistru) River and Ukraine. The 2004 census recorded the country as 78 percent Moldovan (compared to 64 percent in 1989, the last census to include Transnistria); 8 percent Ukrainian (14 percent); 6 percent Russian (13 percent); 4 percent Gagauz (4 percent), a Turkic people of Christian Orthodox faith; and 2 percent Bulgarian (2 percent).

A mild climate and fertile soil permit the cultivation of a wide variety of crops, including grains, sugar beets, fruits, and vegetables, with food processing being the leading industry. Metalworking and the manufacture of electrical equipment are also of importance. Excluding Transnistria, agriculture contributes approximately 13 percent of GDP and approximately 28 percent of employment, while industry accounts for 20 percent of GDP and 13 percent of employment. Principal exports are foodstuffs, beverages (notably wine), and tobacco. Romania was the leading trade partner in 2012, followed by Russia, Ukraine, Italy, and Germany.

Political and economic transition in the decade after 1989 yielded the largest decline in GDP in Eastern Europe, a fall of approximately 70 percent from the 1990 level. Inflation reached a high of 2,200 percent in 1992 before gradually falling to 115 percent in 1994. The economy was further shaken by the Russian financial crisis of 1998, the leu losing almost half its value in a single day in November, creating the most severe currency crisis since independence. The economy recovered in 2000, and late in the year the International Monetary Fund (IMF) and World Bank approved a new civil code (adopted in 2002) favoring free-market principles.

In January 2006 Russian energy giant Gazprom temporarily cut off natural gas deliveries to Moldova—which is almost completely dependent on its neighbors for energy—and doubled the price of gas. In March the Russian government banned imports of Moldovan wine, citing health and quality issues. The wine ban was particularly painful because, previously, Moldovan wine sales approached 15 percent of GNP, and it exported approximately 80 percent of its wine to Russia. (See the 2012 *Handbook* for details.)

Although the IMF expressed concern with the lack of structural reform, in 2006 it released a statement in which it noted, "Moldova's European aspirations have provided much-needed momentum to the authorities' structural reform efforts and commitment to combat corruption." The World Bank reported in 2006 that "GDP growth is no longer reducing poverty," particularly rural poverty. Roughly half the population lives off subsistence farming. Those who do produce a surplus have difficulty getting it to market, as the country's road network is deficient and agricultural purchase prices are low. Moreover, with an average wage of only about $129 per month, Moldova reportedly has the lowest standard of living in Europe. Inflation has remained high, averaging 16.6 percent annually from 1995 to 2008. One clear result of the economic difficulties is that 600,000 Moldovans (one in four adults) have left the country to look for work, principally in Russia and Italy. Remittances from workers abroad amounted to an estimated $950 million in 2007, accounting for over 35 percent of GDP.

In the first half of 2009 remittances fell by approximately 30 percent under the effects of the global financial crisis. That decline and a corresponding drop in consumer demand contributed to a 25 percent contraction in the manufacturing and construction sectors, although agriculture remained steady. GDP plummeted by 6.5 percent for the year, but growth averaged 6.9 percent in 2010 and 6.8 percent in 2011 in part due to an increase in remittances. GDP growth contracted by 0.8 percent in 2012, but the IMF predicts growth by 4 percent in 2013.

GOVERNMENT AND POLITICS

Political background. Historical Moldova lay between the frontiers of the Russian, Habsburg, and Ottoman empires and was the object of numerous invasions and territorial realignments, including incorporation in Greater Romania from 1918 to 1940. Present-day Moldova encompasses the territory of the pre-1940 Moldavian Autonomous Soviet Socialist Republic, which was located within Ukraine and which was joined to all but the northern and southern portions of Bessarabia upon detachment of the latter from Romania in 1940. With its redrawn borders, the redefined Moldavian SSR became a constituent republic of the Soviet Union.

On July 29, 1989, Mircea SNEGUR was elected chair of the Presidium of the republican Supreme Soviet. Although a member of the Politburo of the Communist Party of Moldova (*Partidul Comunist din Moldova*—PCM), he subsequently endorsed the nationalist demands of the Popular Front of Moldova (*Frontul Popular din Moldova*—FPM), which had been launched earlier in the year. The language law of 1989 asserted a "Moldo-Romanian" identity, and in 1990 the Moldovan flag was adapted from the Romanian tricolor.

On August 19, 1990, the Turkic-speaking Gagauz minority in the southern part of the country responded to the prospect of union with Romania by announcing the formation of a "Republic of Gagauzia." On September 2 the Slavic majority in the eastern Dnestr valley followed suit, proclaiming a "Pridnestrovskian Moldavian Soviet Socialist Republic" (changing to Pridnestrovskian Moldavian Republic [*Pridnestrovskaia Moldavskaia Respublika*] in 1991, commonly called either Transnistria or Transdniestria in English). The Supreme Soviet thereupon went into emergency session, naming Snegur to the new post of executive president on September 3 and empowering him to introduce direct rule "in regions not obeying the constitution." Despite continued unrest, including a pitched battle between police and secessionist militia at a bridge over the Dnestr River on November 2, the situation eased late in the year after political intervention by Soviet President Mikhail Gorbachev.

On August 22, 1991, in the wake of the failed Moscow coup against Gorbachev, PCM First Secretary Grigory YEREMEY resigned from the Politburo of the Communist Party of the Soviet Union (CPSU), and on August 23 President Snegur, who had opposed the Moscow hardliners, effectively banned the PCM. On August 27 Moldova declared its independence and two days later established diplomatic relations with Romania. In October 1991 the leading pro-unification FPM faction came out in opposition to Snegur and called for a boycott of the presidential election set for December 8. Snegur was nevertheless reelected as the sole candidate in a turnout officially given as 82.9 percent, this time drawing his main political support from the pro-independence Agrarian Democratic Party of Moldova (*Partidul Democrat Agrar din Moldova*—PDAM).

In March 1992 ethnic conflict again erupted. Igor SMIRNOV, the president of Transnistria, called for mobilization of all men between ages 18 and 45. Concurrently, his deputy, Aleksandr KARAMAN, insisted that the only viable solution would be a confederal republic in which Moldovans, Russians, and Gagauz would have separate, autonomous territories. For his part, President Snegur offered special economic status to the Transnister region but rejected the concept of a separate republic. Local Red Army units stationed in the region intervened for Transnistria, escalating the conflict from September 1991 to July 1992. In July 1992 a cease-fire was signed and Russian Federation troops entered the region to act as monitors for the agreement.

Initial enthusiasm in Moldova and Romania for unification faded quickly, with public opinion polls in Moldova showing that no more than 10 percent of the population supported union. On January 7 President Snegur called for a referendum on unification to be held, appealing for strengthened Moldovan independence. The referendum split pro- and anti-unionist deputies, the referendum call ultimately being defeated by one vote. On August 3 Snegur was granted decree powers for the ensuing year to facilitate economic reforms, and in February 1994 his administration indicated that it sought accommodation with Transnistria on the basis of substantial autonomy for the region, including its own legislative body and the use of distinctive political symbols.

The parliamentary election of February 27, 1994, yielded an overall majority for the PDAM and was followed on March 6 by a referendum in which a reported 95.4 percent of participants voted for maintaining Moldova's separation from both Romania and Russia. A further national unity government under the continued premiership of the PDAM's Andrey SANGHELI obtained legislative approval on April 5, its first major act being the introduction of a new devolutionary constitution in August, effectively removing union with Romania as an option, except as a long-term aspiration.

Fortified by an IMF loan, the Moldovan government in March 1995 embarked on a major privatization program to dispose of some 1,500 state enterprises. However, resistance to privatization remained prevalent within the state bureaucracy, while opposition parties forecast an outbreak of widespread corruption. Principally because of such opposition within the PDAM, President Snegur in July launched the Party of Rebirth and Conciliation of Moldova (*Partidul Renaşterii şi Concilierii din Moldova*—PRCM).

Although Prime Minister Sangheli was able to announce on August 1, 1995, that the five-year Gagauz conflict was over (see Constitution and government, below), the Transnister problem remained more intractable. On December 24 a referendum in Transnister yielded an 82.7 percent majority in favor of a draft independence constitution and of separate membership in the Commonwealth of Independent States (CIS). However, on January 19, 1996, President Snegur secured the signatures of his Russian and Ukrainian counterparts on a joint statement asserting that the Transnister region was part of Moldova but should have special status. Further talks between Snegur and Smirnov culminated in an agreement on June 17 defining the region as "a state-territorial formation in the form of a republic within Moldova's internationally recognized borders." This tortuous wording appeared to satisfy both sides' core demands, although detailed implementation and ratification were expected to be difficult processes.

On the domestic political front, President Snegur launched his campaign for reelection in November 1996. A key feature of his platform was that Moldova should move to a more presidential form of government, particularly in respect to authority to appoint and dismiss ministers. The president faced obstruction from the opposition-dominated Parliament, which in February voted down a presidential proposal to change "Moldovan" to "Romanian" as the constitutional descriptor of the official language.

Backed by a PRCM-initiated "Civic Movement," Snegur headed the poll in the first round of presidential elections held on November 17, 1996, winning 38.7 percent of the vote against eight other candidates. In second place, with 27.7 percent, came Petru LUCINSCHI, the parliamentary speaker and unofficial PDAM candidate. Enlivened by a phone-tapping scandal and PDAM allegations that the president's supporters were attempting to rig the outcome, the second round of voting on December 1 featured a runoff between Snegur and Lucinschi, with the latter receiving the formal endorsement not only of the PDAM but also of the Party of Communists of the Republic of Moldova (*Partidul Comuniştilor din Republica Moldova*—PCRM). The outcome was a decisive victory for Lucinschi, who obtained 54 percent of the vote. After Lucinschi was inaugurated on January 15, 1997, he nominated Ion CIUBUC, an economist, to succeed Sangheli. The new prime minister pledged that his administration would focus on economic reforms.

Balloting for a new Parliament was held on March 22, 1998, with the PCRM winning a plurality of 40 seats, followed by the pro-Snegur Democratic Convention of Moldova (*Convenţia Democrată din Moldova*—CDM) with 26 seats, the pro-Lucinschi bloc For a Democratic and Prosperous Moldova (*Pentru o Moldovă Democratică și Prosperă*—PMDP) with 24 seats, and the Party of Democratic Forces (*Partidul Forțelor Democratice*—PFD) with 11 seats. A center-right coalition consisting of the CDM, PMDP, and PFD, called the Alliance for Democracy and Reforms (*Alianța pentru Democrație și Reforme*—ADR), formed a new government on April 21, with Ciubuc as premier. A growing economic crisis, however, led to Ciubuc's resignation on February 1, 1999. A new cabinet under Ion STURZA was approved on March 12, but it fell on November 9, when the Christian Democrats (*Frontul Popular Creștin Democrat*—FPCD), PCRM, and a handful of independents passed a vote of no confidence in the government's economic policies. (See the 2012 *Handbook* for details.)

A struggle between the president and the legislature ensued, with the latter rejecting two nominees for prime minister and Lucinschi not even submitting the name of his third choice when it became apparent that Parliament would again reject the cabinet. With the president having vowed to dissolve the legislature if it turned down another nominee, on December 21 Parliament approved a largely nonparty government led by Dumitru BRAGHIȘ, theretofore deputy minister for the economy and reform.

What remained of the former governing alliance, the ADR, broke apart in April 2000 when the principal component of the PMDP, Parliament Speaker Dumitru DIACOV's Movement for a Democratic and Prosperous Moldova (*Mișcarea o Moldovă Democratică și Prosperă*—MMDP), announced its reconfiguration as the Democratic Party of Moldova (*Partidul Democrat din Moldova*—PDM) and its independence from President Lucinschi and his efforts to strengthen the presidency through constitutional amendment. The struggle over Moldova's system of government took a different direction in July, when Parliament, overriding Lucinschi's vehement veto, overwhelmingly passed constitutional changes that included indirect election of the president by the legislature. A corresponding election law promulgated in October mandated that a presidential candidate would need a three-fifths majority to secure a victory.

In December 2000 neither the PCRM's Vladimir VORONIN nor Pavel BARBALAT, chair of the Constitutional Court, succeeded in marshaling the 61 votes required to win the presidency. Barbalat, who was backed by Diacov's PDM, Snegur's CDM, and the Christian Democrats, repeatedly failed to break 40 votes, while Voronin came no closer than 59 (in a third ballot on December 6). A center-right parliamentary boycott prevented a quorum and thus a fourth ballot on December 21, and on December 26 the Constitutional Court ruled that President Lucinschi had the "right and duty" to order new elections. Accordingly, he dissolved Parliament on January 12, 2001, in preparation for a general election. On February 25 the PCRM won a clear majority of 71 seats on a 50.7 percent vote share. The only other formations to win seats were the new Braghiș Alliance (19 seats, 13.3 percent) and the Christian Democrats (11 seats, 8.3 percent). The PCRM landslide ensured the election of Voronin as Moldova's next president on April 4 and also gave it enough seats to amend the constitution unilaterally. On April 19 Parliament endorsed a new cabinet headed by Vasile TARLEV, a political independent.

In July 2004 the separatists in Transnistria raised tensions by shutting down schools in the region that taught Moldovan in the Latin script. Consequently Voronin broke off negotiations. In early August the separatists blocked rail lines between Transnistria and Moldova, and they subsequently announced that they were mobilizing reserves for the "Transnister Army." Smirnov collaterally declared that Transnistria" is marching on the road to setting up an independent, sovereign state." In October Russia stated that it would not leave Transnistria until the issue was resolved.

In the March 6, 2005, parliamentary elections, the PCRM failed to win a majority but, with 56 seats, remained the plurality party. Since the PCRM did not win the 61 seats required to elect a president, a successful opposition boycott of the subsequent presidential election would have meant, after two failed ballots, new parliamentary elections. Ultimately, however, enough members of the Democratic Moldova Bloc (*Blocul Electoral "Moldova Democrată"*—BMD) voted for Voronin for him to be reelected on the second ballot. Prime Minister Tarlev formed a new government later in April and indicated that he would trim the government's staff size by 70 percent.

Despite initial overtures to opposition parties, relations between the PCRM-led government and opposition parties worsened through 2005–2007. On October 13, 2005, in a strictly partisan vote, PCRM members of Parliament removed the immunity of three opposition members prior to charging them with abuse of office. In response, the Our Moldova Alliance (*Alianța Moldova Noastră*—AMN), the main opposition party, on November 24 joined the Social Liberal Party (*Partidul Social-Liberal*—PSL) in calling (unsuccessfully) for the impeachment of President Voronin, charging him with "breaking laws, flouting a ruling of the European Court of Human Rights, offending the Romany ethnic minority with epithets used in relation to the opposition, and promoting his own candidate to the post of Chișinău mayor."

Legislation proposed by the Moldovan government in the spring of 2005 reportedly would have given Transnistria autonomous status within the Moldovan Republic, although banking, armed forces, customs, and foreign policy would have remained under Moldovan authority. This initiative did not progress significantly, and the government—with the support of the United States and the European Union (EU)—increased pressure on the separatists by gaining the agreement of Ukraine in March 2006 to refuse exports from Transnistria unless they were approved by the Moldovan customs. The separatist government, whose finances derive primarily from those exports, responded by instituting a blockade of train traffic at the border, which continued to be subject to transit disputes involving Russia as well as Moldova and Ukraine.

Local elections in 2007 (held in 2006 in autonomous Gagauzia) resulted in political setbacks for the PCRM, amid what the U.S. embassy termed "intimidation of candidates, unequal access to and coverage in the media for all parties, misuse of administrative resources, reports of improper campaigning near voting stations, government bias in favor of ruling-party candidates, and irregularities in voter lists." Particularly symbolic was the loss of the mayoral race in Chișinău to the Liberal Party (*Partidul Liberal*—PL) candidate, Dorin CHIRTOACĂ. Although the PDM and AMN saw only modest gains in the district elections, many of the smaller opposition political parties saw significant gains or obtained district seats for the first time, with nearly 30 percent of district seats held by members of the smaller parties or by independents. The Tarlev government subsequently became increasingly unpopular due to its problems in implementing economic and political reforms. Consequently, Tarlev stepped down as prime minister on March 19, 2008, stating the need for "new individuals" to lead the country. Deputy Prime Minister Zinaida GRECIANÎI subsequently became Moldova's first female prime minister.

The PCRM won 60 seats in the April 5, 2009, legislative balloting, leaving it 1 shy of the 61 seats (a three-fifths majority) needed to elect a president on its own. Consequently, balloting in Parliament on May 20 and June 3 failed to elect a president, necessitating a new legislative poll on July 29 at which the PCRM declined to 48 seats, compared to 53 seats for the opposition (the PDM, AMN, PL, and the recently formed Liberal Democratic Party of Moldova [*Partidului Liberal Democrat din Moldova*—PLDM]), which coalesced as the Alliance for European Integration (*Alianța Pentru Integrare Europenă*—APIE) and pledged to form a new government.

President Voronin resigned effective September 11, 2009, and he was succeeded in an acting capacity by the PL's Mihai GHIMPU, who had recently been elected speaker of Parliament. At the request of the APIE, Ghimpu on September 17 nominated PLDM leader Vladimir FILAT to form a new government, which, as approved with 53 votes in Parliament on September 25, included members of the four APIE parties. However, Marian LUPU, the presidential candidate of APIE, failed to gain the 61 votes needed for election in ballots in the Parliament on November 10 and December 7, 2009. Consequently, acting president Ghimpu remained in the post (see Current issues, below, for subsequent developments).

The PCRM again took the lead in the November 28, 2010, parliamentary election, winning 42 seats, compared with a combined 59 for APIE (now comprising the PLDM, PDM, and PL). Again due to the inability to indirectly elect a president, the new speaker of Parliament, Lupu, became acting president.

Local elections in 2011 broadly confirmed the existing political deadlock, although the larger political parties dominated the results, with the PCRM and APIE taking approximately 97 percent of all district seats. Chirtoacă was reelected as mayor of Chișinău in a tight race that saw him emerging as winner of the PCRM candidate by a margin of roughly 1 percent of all votes cast.

Transnistria held presidential elections in 2011; the Russian government notably withdrew its past support for Igor Smirnov, the president since 1990, and backed Anatoliy KAMINSKI of Renewal (*Obnovleniye*). The first round, on December 11, included three party candidates and three independent candidates. Yevgeny SHEVCHUK (ind.) received 38.6 percent of the vote and Kaminski (Renewal) 26.3, and both advanced to the second round; Smirnov placed third with 24.7

percent. In the second round, Shevchuk was elected with 73.9 percent over Kaminski, who obtained 19.7 percent of the vote.

In February 2011 the Moldovan Constitutional Court ruled that Parliament could schedule new elections given the "unique legal situation" of the lengthy acting presidency. Parliament subsequently called for a new presidential election, initially for November 18; when no candidates registered for that election, a second election was scheduled for December 16. Marian LUPU was the only registered candidate. But as in 2009 and 2010, the ruling coalition was unable to win the necessary super-majority, obtaining 58 of the 61 votes needed, the PCRM having boycotted the voting. This second failed election should have resulted in early parliamentary elections in 2013; but on January 12, 2012, the Constitutional Court ruled that the December 16 balloting was unconstitutional, as some legislators had revealed their secret ballots to the media, and thus the attempt was nullified. A third round of voting was therefore permitted and held on March 16, 2012. Nicolae TIMOFTI (ind.) was elected with 62 votes when three former PCRM legislators who had previously defected to small socialist parties agreed to support him. This ended a period of 917 days during which Moldova lacked a president-elect.

Conflicts within the governing coalition (see Current events, below) led the PCRM and PDM to support a nonconfidence motion on March 5, 2013; Filat resigned effective March 8. President Timofti renominated Filat as prime minister on April 10, but the Constitutional Court on April 22 blocked the nomination due to the ongoing corruption investigations against members of his former cabinet. Reportedly fearing early elections in which polls predicted the PCRM would gain seats, the PDM and PL agreed in May to form a coalition government under Iurie LEANCĂ of the PLDM. The PCRM boycotted the vote to approve the new cabinet, calling instead for early elections.

Constitution and government. The 1994 constitution, replacing the 1977 Soviet-era text, described Moldova as a "presidential, parliamentary republic" based on political pluralism and "the preservation, development, and expression of ethnic and linguistic identity." Executive power continues to be vested in a president, who was directly elected until constitutional changes passed in July 2000 (over President Lucinschi's veto) transformed the country into a "parliamentary republic" and led to passage in September–October of a law establishing procedures for indirect election by the unicameral Parliament. (A three-fifths majority is required for a president to be elected. After two failed ballots, new legislative elections must be held, although only two legislative elections can be held in a single calendar year.) The president nominates the prime minister, subject to approval by the Parliament, which is elected for a four-year term. Passage of a nonconfidence motion in the Parliament forces the resignation of the Council of Ministers. Other constitutional clauses proclaim Moldova's permanent neutrality and proscribe the stationing of foreign troops on the national territory.

The 1994 constitution authorized "special status" for both the Gagauz region in the south and the Transnister region, where separatist activity had broken out in 1990. Statutes providing broad autonomy to Gagauz-Yeri (Gagauzia, *Găgăuzia*) went into effect in February 1995, with referendums the following month to determine which villages wished to be part of the special region. Subsequently, direct elections for a 35-member regional People's Assembly were held in May–June, as was the direct election of a regional executive leader (*bashkan*), who was authorized to carry out quasi-presidential responsibilities.

Meanwhile, the status of Transnistria remained unresolved. In December 1995 Transnistrians overwhelmingly endorsed an independence constitution, and in December 2006, 97 percent voted in a referendum to seek independence. In May 1997, however, the Moldovan and Transnister leaders, meeting in Moscow, agreed to participate in a single state, although the dynamics of the region's "special status" remained to be defined. In Kyiv, Ukraine, in July 1999 Smirnov and Lucinschi signed a declaration on normalizing relations that committed both sides to a single "economic, judicial, and social sphere within Moldova's existing borders." Nevertheless, subsequent claims by Transnistria that Chişinău ignored its needs and opinions soon led to a renewal of demands for independence. At present, a strong president who also serves as prime minister leads Transnistria's government; under changes introduced in 2000, a 43-member, unicameral Parliament replaced a bicameral legislature.

In January 2003 the government approved new legislation replacing 9 provinces and 2 autonomous regions introduced in 1999 with a structure that now encompasses 32 districts, 3 municipalities (Tighina and Bălţi as well as the capital), the Autonomous Territorial Unit of Gagauzia, and Transnistria. Local administrative units include communes and cities.

Although the constitution guarantees freedom of the press, onerous control was exercised by the PCRM prior to the 2009 ouster of President Voronin (see the 2010 *Handbook* for details). Conditions have subsequently reportedly improved in Moldova proper, which Reporters Without Borders ranked in 2013 as 55th in the world in respect for press freedoms, but censorship remains heavy in Russian-dominated Transnistria.

Foreign relations. Moldova's first international action following independence in 1991 was to establish diplomatic relations with Romania. On March 2 Moldova was admitted to the UN and on April 27 was formally offered membership in the IMF and World Bank. It also joined the Conference on (later Organization for) Security and Cooperation in Europe (CSCE/OSCE).

Possible union with Romania was placed on the agenda by the creation of a parliamentary-level National Council of Reunification in late 1991, but a growing preference in Moldova for independence meant that by mid-1993 reunification had ceased to be a practical political option. However, spurred by Romania's eagerness to join the North Atlantic Treaty Organization (NATO) and settle border issues, Moldova and Romania agreed in April 1997 to resume talks on a basic treaty, which was finally initialed on April 28, 2000, by the countries' foreign ministers. Despite years of further negotiation, the treaty remained unsigned, in part because Romania has refused to accept references to a separate Moldovan language.

On March 16, 1994, during a visit to Brussels for talks with officials from NATO and the EU, President Snegur signed NATO's Partnership for Peace, while the Moldovan Parliament on April 8 finally ratified membership in the CIS and its economic union. Although Moldovan participation in CIS military or monetary integration was ruled out, the CIS ratification indicated cautious alignment with Moscow, with the aim in particular of securing the long-sought departure of the Russian Fourteenth Army from Transnistria.

In July 1995 Moldova became the first CIS member to be admitted to the Council of Europe. In 1997 the government announced its support for negotiations with the EU toward associate membership, perhaps leading eventually to full membership. Regionally, in October 1997 Moldova joined Georgia, Ukraine, and Azerbaijan in forming the GUAM group.

Moldova subsequently made efforts to reach beyond purely regional issues. In September 2003, for example, it began participating in post-war security operations in Iraq at the invitation of the U.S. government. In addition, in January 2004 Moldova agreed to participate in UN peacekeeping operations, subsequently contributing soldiers to missions in Liberia, Côte D'Ivoire, Sudan, and Georgia.

In recent years Moldova's foreign relations have directly reflected its internal conflicts to an unusual degree. With large ethnic populations who identify with Romania and Russia, relations with those two countries have been at the forefront of Moldovan foreign policy. Relations with Romania were strained over suggestions by Moldovan President Voronin that "greater" Moldova included the Romanian province of Moldova. Romanian President Ion Iliescu in January 2004, called the idea "a falsification of historical reality and an expression of revisionist inclinations."

Not coincidentally, Moldova's relations with Russia have often been the inverse of its relations with Romania. While Voronin (a former KBG officer) was considered pro-Russian when he first took office, he gradually adopted more anti-Russian positions, largely as a result of the conflict in Transnistria. In April 2004 Voronin emphasized that Moldova's relations with Russia were still good, with only the Transnister issue being a problem. But Russia has repeatedly declined to sign a "Declaration on Stability and Security for the Republic of Moldova" sought by Voronin. Russia maintains that such a guarantee of Moldovan sovereignty would be possible only if Moldova guaranteed a peaceful settlement of the Transnister issue.

Moldova's desire for integration with the EU received a setback on March 10, 2004, when Ivan Borisavljevic, the European Commission's envoy to Moldova, said that there were serious obstacles on the road to accession, including the Transnistria conflict, corruption, poverty, and lack of genuine reforms. In February 2005 Moldova signed an "action plan" with the European Union (EU) to bring the country closer to EU standards. The action plan involved a wide range of political, economic, and judicial reforms.

Relations with Russia worsened in January 2006, when Russia cut off supplies of natural gas to Moldova after the latter declined to accept a 100 percent increase in prices. In mid-January, the two countries agreed on a less dramatic increase in prices. In March, however, the Russian government banned the import of wine from Moldova and Georgia, purportedly for health reasons. In fact, most analysts characterize Russia's move as retaliation for Moldova's and Georgia's position opposing Russia's entry into the World Trade Organization (WTO) until Russia stops supporting separatists in those two countries and removes troops from their territory. Relations improved in 2007 as both the Moldovan and international media reported rumors of feelers by both Moldova and Russia to resolve the Transnister problem.

Romania's accession to the EU on January 1, 2007, raised new issues with Moldova. Romanian President Traian Băsescu has urged Moldovan admission to the EU and offered Romanian assistance toward this goal. He stated in June 2007 that this would effectively "bring the Romanian people together under the umbrella of the European Union." Voronin, however, had declared in December 2006 that Romanian offers of assistance were "interference in the domestic affairs of a sovereign state." An agreement to open new Romanian consulates in the Moldovan towns of Bălți and Cahul was reversed in March 2007 by the Moldovan foreign ministry, which complained that Romania had released inflated figures regarding Moldovans seeking Romanian citizenship. Relations worsened in December 2007 with the expulsion of two Romanian diplomats and when Voronin and Romanian officials traded accusations over the continued delay in ratifying the basic treaty and border treaty between the two states. In July 2008 relations improved when it was announced that the Romanian consulate in Cahul would open in exchange for a Moldovan consulate in Iasi.

In March 2008 Moldovan media reported that the crucial issue in obtaining Russian support to resolve the Transnistrian conflict was Moscow's requirement for a formal repudiation of any future Moldovan membership in NATO. Voronin met with Smirnov in April 2008 for the first time in seven years, agreeing on further talks to "gradually" resolve the conflict. In the wake of the Russian-Georgian war of mid-2008, however, Smirnov in September called instead for Transnistria's formal independence and expressed confidence that Russia would support the "120,000 Russian citizens" living in Transnistria.

The pro-Western coalition government installed in September 2009 set further integration with the EU as one of its chief priorities in foreign affairs. Meanwhile, acting president Mihai Ghimpu, while acknowledging past personal convictions for a union with Romania, stressed that unification was not a goal for the new government. In response, Russian far-right political leader Vladimir Zhirinovsky called for immediate Russian recognition of the independence of Transnistria, a statement widely interpreted in Moldova as suggesting possible Russian opposition to continued EU expansion in the region. Romanian former foreign minister Adrian Cioroianu suggested that the Moldovan government effectively ignore the status of Transnistria while pursuing other aspects of European integration, this statement in turn seen as evidence of continued Romanian desire for unification.

In 2009 Romania modified its citizenship laws to allow foreigners to apply for naturalization if their grandparent or great-grandparent held Romanian citizenship. Roughly 17,000 Moldovans gained Romanian citizenship in this fashion in January–July 2010, and the Romanian government said that 800,000 applications remained pending. This policy was criticized by many political party leaders in Western Europe, who feared that hundreds of thousands of Moldovans might enter the EU workforce through a "loophole" if Romania is successful in its plan to join the Schengen Accord, which would allow visa-free travel for Romanian passport holders to the 25 EU countries.

The stalled negotiations between Romania and Moldova over the basic treaty were partially resolved with an April 2010 bilateral "strategic partnership" agreement pledging cooperation and a November 2010 border treaty. In May 2011 Romanian Foreign Minister Teodor Baconschi referred to the basic treaty as an "obsolete" concept.

Moldova and the EU concluded negotiations in June 2013 for a free trade agreement to be signed in November 2013 and come into force in 2014.

Current issues. The status of the Transnister region has been a major focus of attention since independence. Chișinău has insisted that the region remain an integral part of Moldova, while Transnister leaders have fluctuated between demanding outright independence and proposing a confederal system that would grant the region autonomy. The presence of Russian troops in the region has complicated the issue (see Foreign relations, above).

Protesters (estimated at 15,000 in Chișinău alone) took to the streets throughout Moldova after the results of the April 2009 legislative elections were announced, claiming fraud on the part of the ruling PCRM. Demonstrators broke through police lines in the capital, and part of the Parliament building and the office of the president were burned. Several hundred protesters were injured in the subsequent police crackdown, and at least three died in custody.

The problems following the April 2009 elections appeared to undercut support for the PCRM in the July reballoting, especially after PCRM leader Marian Lupu defected, along with a number of other legislators, to the PDM. Eight years of communist rule came to an end with the installation of the APIE government in September under Vladimir Filat, a prominent businessman who pledged to pursue further integration with the EU, strengthen ties with Romania, and seek to replace Russian troops in Transnistria with international peacekeepers. In response, Transnistrian leader Smirnov announced plans to expand his region's armed forces.

After the July 2009 elections the new Parliament was unable to elect a president of the republic in November or December, as the PCRM boycotted the proceedings, thereby preventing Lupu, the APIE candidate, from securing the two-thirds majority required for election. Deadlock ensued, since no further presidential balloting could be held until after new legislative elections, which were constitutionally proscribed until at least July 2010 (one year from the last election). For many, permanent resolution of the problem required revision of the constitution to provide for direct popular election of the president. Despite fierce opposition from the PCRM, a referendum to that effect was held on September 5, 2010. Although 87.5 percent of those voting supported the change, the results of the initiative were declared invalid because turnout had been only 31 percent (33 percent was required). Consequently, acting president Ghimpu, in accordance with instructions from the Constitutional Court, dissolved Parliament on September 28 and new elections were scheduled for November 28.

Meanwhile, Moldovan leaders pursued "constructive dialogue" with Transnistria leaders. The continued presence of Russian soldiers in the region, however, was seen as a continued violation of Moldova's neutral status. Tensions increased when Transnistrian leader Smirnov in February 2010 invited Russia to base missiles in Transnistria in response to Romania's agreement to host elements of a U.S. antimissile system.

A referendum was held on September 5, 2010, proposing two constitutional amendments: the direct election of the presidency and officially changing the name of the official language from "Moldovan" to "Romanian." Although 87.8 percent of those voting approved of the measures, voter turnout was only 30.3 percent, short of the 33.3 percent of eligible voters required to validate the election. When the December 28, 2010, legislative elections saw both the PCRM and the APIE fail to win the three-fifths of Parliament seats necessary to elect a president, Parliament again elected a speaker, who then assumed the role of acting president. The Constitutional Court, however, ruled in February 2011 that the inability to elect a president does not require a new, immediate round of parliamentary elections. Negotiations to amend or reform the electoral process for the presidency continued into 2012.

On July 13, 2012, Parliament banned the use of communist symbols, prompting protests by the PCRM and concerns in the domestic media that relations with Transnister would grow further estranged.

Domestic media reported that the breakdown between PLDM and PDM was motivated at least in part by efforts by Filat to displace the PDM's control over the state's anticorruption institutions. In January 2013 Filat requested that Prosecutor General Valeriu ZUBCO resign following the latter's involvement in a fatal hunting accident in December 2012. Filat had previously sought Zubco's removal, leading to charges by the PDM that the resignation was politically motivated; the PLDM countercharged that investigations launched in January by the National Anti-Corruption Center against cabinet ministers from the party were an attempt at revenge. On February 13 Filat publicly accused his coalition partners of corruption (notably naming PDM Vice Chair Vlad PLAHOTNIUC) and declared that the AMIE coalition agreement would need to be renegotiated. In March the PCRM introduced a nonconfidence motion that passed with assistance by the PDM (the PL having stated it would abstain in the vote). Filat was renominated as prime minister by President Trimofti, but the Constitutional Court rejected the nomination, which Filat has stated was instigated by the PDM. Filat led the PLDM to join the PCRM in voting to dismiss Parliamentary Speaker Marian Lupu.

Although a new coalition agreement was established in May, local analysts speculated that it is unlikely to resolve the constant power struggle between the leaders of the parties in the AMIE.

POLITICAL PARTIES

Since independence, Moldovan parties have frequently formed electoral blocs to contest parliamentary elections, but none have lasted more than one national election cycle. (See the 2011 *Handbook* for details.) Moldova's unusually high bar for representation in Parliament (see Legislature, below, for details) helped encourage the formation of electoral blocs. In July 2003 the AMN was formed by merger of the Social Democratic Alliance (ASD), successor to the Braghiş Alliance; the Liberal Party (PL); and the Alliance of Independents (AI). In May 2004 the three primary center-left opposition parties—the AMN, the Democratic Party of Moldova (PDM), and the Social Liberal Party (PSL)—announced the formation of the Democratic Moldova Bloc (BMD). By January 2005, however, two months before the next legislative election, cracks were already showing in the alliance. Three members of the former Braghiş Alliance announced they were running on the Party of Communists (PCRM) list. The following October, 30 senior members of the AMN, including former prime minister Braghiş, left the party to form a new Party of Social Democracy (PDS).

Nine parties, 2 electoral blocs, and 12 independent candidates contested the March 2005 parliamentary elections, with only the PCRM, BMD, and Christian Democratic People's Party (PPCD) meeting the threshold for representation. Twelve parties and 5 independent candidates contested the April 2009 parliamentary election (recent electoral law changes having barred bloc participation), with the PCRM, the PLDM, AMN, and PL meeting the threshold. Following the failure by Parliament to elect a president, 8 parties contested the new elections in July, with the PCRM, PLDM, AMN, PL, and ADM meeting the threshold. The PLDM, AMN, PL, and ADM subsequently formed a ruling government as the Alliance for European Integration (*Alianţa Pentru Integrare Europenă*—APIE). Early elections held in December 2010 saw 20 parties and 19 independent candidates compete, with only the PCRM, PLDM, PDM, and PL meeting the threshold. Of the 16 remaining parties, the **European Action Movement** (MAE) (since merged with the PL) took more than 1 percent of the vote.

The APIE ruling government (now minus the ADM) thus continued in power.

Government Parties:

Liberal Democratic Party of Moldova (*Partidului Liberal Democrat din Moldova*—PLDM). The PLDM was founded in December 2007 by Vladimir Filat, a legislator who had left the PDM in September 2007, citing differences with the party leadership. In April 2008 the PLDM began a petition drive to change presidential elections to uninominal, direct elections, thereby confronting the PCRM and emerging as the most vocal opposition party. In the April 2009 elections the PLDM took 12.4 percent of the vote and won 15 seats. In the July balloting the PDLM gained 18 seats on a vote share of 16.6 percent. In the November 2010 election the PLDM took 29.4 percent of the vote and won 32 seats.

On March 22, 2011, the PLDM signed an agreement to merge with the **Our Moldova Alliance** (*Alianţa Moldova Noastră*—AMN). The AMN was formed in July 2003 by the joining of three parties and was cochaired by former prime minister Dumitru Braghiş. (See this entry in the 2010 *Handbook* for an expanded history of the AMN.) Braghiş would leave in 2005 to found the Party of Social Democracy of Moldova (see below). The AMN formed the core of the center-left Electoral Bloc "Democratic Moldova" (*Blocul Electoral "Moldova Democrată"*—BMD) in the 2005 parliamentary elections. The AMN won 9.8 percent of the vote and 11 seats in the April 2009 legislative elections but declined to a 7.4 percent vote share and 7 seats in the July balloting.

Leaders: Vladimir FILAT (President), Iurie LEANCĂ (Prime Minister and First Vice President of the Party).

Democratic Party of Moldova (*Partidul Democrat din Moldova*—PDM). The PDM was established in April 2000 as successor to the movement "For a Democratic and Prosperous Moldova" (*Mişcarea "Pentru o Moldovă Democraticăşi Prosperă"*—MMDP). The centrist movement had been formed in February 1997 to promote the policies of President Lucinschi. Its leader, Dumitru Diacov, the former deputy speaker of the Parliament, had left the PDAM along with a group of other legislators in a policy dispute over support for the government.

In October 1999 the decision of four members of the MMDP's legislative delegation to sit as independents cost the government of Prime Minister Sturza its majority.

The formation of the PDM marked Speaker of Parliament Diacov's formal split with President Lucinschi, Diacov having strongly argued against the adoption of a presidential form of government. In 2001, running independently, the PDM failed to win any seats in Parliament. In the 2005 election the PDM won eight seats as a component of the BMD.

In February 2008 the PDM and the **Social Liberal Party** (*Partidul Social-Liberal*—PSL) announced a merger intended to create a unified opposition party to the PCRM. The PSL was formed in May 2001 under the leadership of Oleg Serebrian. In December 2002 it absorbed the Party of Democratic Forces (*Partidul Forţelor Democratice*—PFD), whose chair, Valeriu MATEI, had finished fifth in the first round of the 1996 presidential election. The center-right PSL favored domestic political reform and integration with the EU. It won three parliamentary seats in 2005.

In the April 2009 elections the PDM won only approximately 3 percent of the vote. However, the party's fortunes were transformed in June, following the dissolution of Parliament and announcement of new elections. Marian Lupu, a prominent member of the PCRM, left that party after stating that "reform from within was not possible." Lupu subsequently joined the PDM as de facto leader, bringing with him about a dozen sitting members of the PCRM parliamentary delegation and a substantial electoral base. Consequently, the PDM won 13 seats in the July balloting on a vote share of 12.5 percent. Subsequently, Lupu became the presidential candidate of the APIE for the balloting scheduled for late October, but he failed to gain the position when the APIE could not muster the required 61 votes.

In February 2010 as much as two-thirds of the membership of the Social Democratic Party (see below) reportedly left that party to join the PDM, which Lupu welcomed as a "consolidation" of the center-left.

In the December 2010 election the PDM took 12.7 percent of the vote and won 15 seats. Lupu was elected the same month as the speaker of parliament but was dismissed from the position on April 25, 2013 (see Current events, above).

Leaders: Marian LUPU (Chair), Dumitru DIACOV (Former Chair), Vlad PLAHOTNIUC (First Vice Chair), Oleg SEREBRIAN (Former Chair of the PSL).

Liberal Party (*Partidul Liberal*—PL). The PL (which should not be confused with the party of the same name that joined in forming the AMN in 2003; see above) was established in 1993 as the center-right Party of Reform (*Partidul Reformei*—PR), which changed its name to the PL in April 2005. The PL supports national unity, withdrawal of Russian forces, and integration into Western institutions.

The PR won 2.4 percent of the vote in the 1994 parliamentary election and 0.5 percent in 1998. In 2001 it joined the National Romanian Party (*Partidul Naţional Român*—PNR) in the Electoral Bloc "Faith and Justice" (*Blocul Electoral "Credinţaşi Dreptate"*—BECD), which won 0.7 percent. It did not compete in 2005. In June 2007 the PL's Dorin Chirtoacă, 28, unexpectedly won election as mayor in Chişinău.

In the April 2009 elections the PL emerged as a significant political force, taking 13.1 percent of the vote and winning 15 seats. In the July balloting it again secured 15 seats (on a vote share of 14.7 percent).

In the November 2010 elections, the PL took almost 10 percent of the vote and won 12 seats.

In March 2011 the **"European Action" Social-Political Movement** (*Mişcarea Social-Politică "Acţiunea Europeana"*—MAE) merged with the PL. Founded in 2007, the MAE officially called for Moldovan integration into the EU. In the April 2009 election the MAE's candidate list won only 1.0 percent of the vote, and 1.2 percent of the vote in the December 2010 election.

Following the February 2013 cabinet crisis, some members of the PL reportedly formed a reform faction critical of party chair Mihai GHIMPU's leadership.

Leaders: Mihai GHIMPU (Chair); Dorin CHIRTOACĂ, Anatol ŞALARU (Vice Presidents).

Opposition Party:

Party of Communists of the Republic of Moldova (*Partidul Comuniştilor din Republica Moldova*—PCRM). The PCRM is a successor to the Soviet-era Communist Party of Moldova (*Partidul Comunist din Moldova*—PCM). The latter was suspended in August 1991 but achieved legal status in September 1994 as the PCRM even though many former Communists had by then opted for the Socialist Party of Moldova (PSM, below). The party was not legalized until after the 1994 legislative balloting, but it subsequently attracted defectors from other parties.

In 1996 the PCRM sought to build an alliance of "patriotic popular forces" for the fall presidential election, in which party leader Vladimir Voronin finished third in the first round with 10.3 percent of the vote. The PCRM then backed the successful second-round candidacy of Petru Lucinschi and was awarded two ministries in the new government of Ion Ciubuc.

During the legislative campaign of late 1997 and early 1998 the PCRM called for the "rebirth of a socialist society," in which a "pluralist economy" would be supported by a "strengthened" state sector. Party leaders also expressed support for renewed linkage of the sovereign republics that had emerged following the breakup of the Soviet Union as well as close political and military ties with Russia. The PCRM led all parties in the March 1998 balloting with 30 percent of the vote, which earned it a plurality of 40 seats, including 9 non-PCRM supporters.

For the 1999 local elections it spearheaded formation of a Communist, Agrarian, and Socialist Bloc (*Blocul Comuniştilor, Agrarienilorşi Socialiştilor*—BCAS) that also finished first in total district and local council seats. Participants included the PDAM and the Party of Socialists (PSRM, below). In the 2001 election the PCRM won 71 seats, enabling it to elect its chair as president.

The PCRM did not fare as well in the 2005 parliamentary elections, winning only 56 seats. Lacking enough votes to ensure the reelection of Voronin as president, and threatened with a boycott of the presidential election by opposition parties, the PCRM reached out to members of the Democratic Moldova Bloc to gain enough votes to ensure Voronin's reelection. The 2007 local elections saw the PCRM weaken further, slipping from holding 615 district council seats nationwide to 465. Most notably, in Chişinău the PCRM lost the mayoral election. In 2008, however, the party and local coalition allies secured over a third of the seats for the People's Assembly in the autonomous region of Gagauzia, interpreted in the domestic press as arresting the party's decline.

The PCRM won 49.5 percent of the vote and 60 seats in the April 2009 parliamentary elections, falling one seat short of the three-fifths majority necessary to elect a president on its own. In the July balloting the PCRM declined to 44.7 percent of the vote and 48 seats, prompting Voronin's resignation from the presidency and the party's move into opposition status.

In the November 2010 elections, the PCRM won 39.3 percent of the vote and 42 seats in Parliament, again winning a plurality but isolated from the other parties in Parliament and thus not invited to form a government. Its position was weakened in November 2011 when a group of three MPs, including Igor DODON, PSRM leader Veronica ABRAMCIUC (of the PSRM, but who obtained her seat as a candidate on the PCRM list) and former prime minister Zinalda GRECEANII defected from the party and subsequently joined the PSRM. All voted for Timofti in the March 2012 elections, breaking the deadlock over the presidency.

Leaders: Vladimir VORONIN (Chair of the Party and Former President of the Republic), Maria POSTOICO (Parliamentary Leader), Marc TKACIUK (Secretary, PCRM Central Committee).

Other Parties That Contested the 2010 Legislative Election:

People's Democratic Party of Moldova (*Partidul Popular Democrat din Moldova*—PPDM). Registered as the **Humanist Party of Moldova** (*Partidul Umanist din Moldova*—PUM) in February 2006. The party ran in the local elections of 2007 on a conservative platform that stressed the restoration of "human dignity," with attention to social morals, faith, and economic conditions in the country. The PUM did not register for the April 2009 elections, instead negotiating with the UCM for PUM members to be included on the UCM candidate list. The March 27, 2011, party congress adopted the present name.

Leader: Valeriu PASAT (Chair).

Christian Democratic People's Party (*Partidul Popular Creştin Democrat*—PPCD). A pro-Romanian party, the PPCD was known until December 1999 as the Christian Democratic People's Front (*Frontal Popular Creştin Democrat*—FPCD). The FPCD was a February 1992 continuation of the former Popular Front of Moldova (*Frontul Popular din Moldova*—FPM), which was formed in 1989 and became the dominant political group following the eclipse of the Communist Party of Moldova in mid-1991. The FPCD won nine parliamentary seats on a vote share of 7.3 percent in the February 1994 election, subsequently reiterating its commitment to eventual union with Romania.

The FPCD broke with the CDM alliance in March 1999 when it boycotted the confidence vote that installed the Sturza government. The FPCD insisted on four portfolios in the government instead of the two it was offered and, as a result, received none. In November it voted with the Communists against the Sturza government, and in December it supported the Braghiş cabinet.

At a December 1999 party congress the renamed PPCD deleted from its manifesto an insistence on Romanian national unity and instead called for Moldovan integration within Europe. In June 2000 the party's vice chair, Valentin DOLGANIUC, and a group of supporters resigned, accusing the party chair of creating an "atmosphere of intolerance and dictatorship" and of abandoning the party's principals through an alliance with the PCRM. Roşca subsequently commented that he viewed eventual unification with Romania as inevitable. The PPCD won 11 parliamentary seats in February 2001.

With the PCRM growing increasingly critical of Russia, the PPCD continued to move closer to the ruling party. Roşca even indicated in April 2005 that he would consider joining the cabinet. This led some party members to join other opposition parties, including, in December 2006, former party vice president Sergiu BURCA, who left for the PSL. After the 2005 elections PPCD seats in Parliament remained at 11; however, several deputies subsequently re-registered as independents.

The PPCD took 3.0 percent of the vote in the April 2009 elections and declined to 1.9 percent in July.

Leaders: Victor CIOBANU (President), Busila RADU (Vice President), Dinu ŢURCANU (Secretary General).

National Liberal Party (*Partidul Naţional Liberal*—PNL). The party was founded in 2006 to revive its namesake party of 1993, which in turn was an attempt to resurrect the traditions of the historical Romanian party of 1875–1947. The party platform supports classical liberal principles, integration into the EU and NATO, and unification with Romania.

Leader: Vitalia PAVLICENCO (President).

Social Democratic Party (*Partidul Social Democrat*—PSD). This party was previously known as the Social Democratic Party of Moldova (*Partidul Social-Democrat din Moldova*—PSDM), one of many Moldovan parties to claim a social democratic orientation following independence. The PSDM contested the 1994 election as the core component of the Social Democratic Electoral Bloc (*Blocul Social-Democrat*—BSD), which secured 3.7 percent of the votes, barely missing the 4 percent threshold for parliamentary representation. In 1997 the party suffered a major split, when a wing supporting President Lucinschi separated and formed the United Social Democratic Party of Moldova (*Partidul Social-Democrat Unit din Moldova*—PSDUM) in conjunction with four other groups. In the 1998 election the PSDM, running on its own, won 1.9 percent of the vote, while the electoral alliance of the PSDUM and two other organizations received 1.3 percent. The PSDM subsequently reunited, and in 2001 it won 2.5 percent of the vote.

Prior to the March 2005 elections, the PSDM accused the ruling PCRM of illegally and unethically controlling the Central Election Commission and the country's media to block access by opposition parties. The commission rejected the PSDM charges. Running without an electoral bloc in 2005, the PSDM marginally improved its showing, earning 2.9 percent of the vote.

In June 2008 the PSDM merged with the Party of Social Democracy of Moldova (*Partidul Democraţiei Sociale din Moldova*—PDSM). Founded on April 15, 2006, and led by former prime minister Dumitru Braghiş, the PDSM was formed by disgruntled former members of Our Moldova Alliance. It adopted a social democratic agenda and advocated strong partnerships with the Russian Federation, the United States, and the EU. The party also called for closer relations with Romania and an ultimate withdrawal from the CIS. The PDSM's strong showing in the 2007 district elections left it the fourth-largest opposition party, albeit considerably behind the PDM, AMN, and PPCD.

Upon the 2008 merger of the PSDM and PDSM, the new grouping, which subsequently drew away a faction of the UCM (below) as well, was renamed the PSD, with Braghiş assuming leadership of the new party. In the April 2009 elections the PSD received 3.7 percent of the vote, failing to pass the threshold. In June the leadership of the PSD and UCM announced that the parties would merge by the end of 2009, calling for other centrist parties to join as well. The PSD won 1.9 percent of the vote in the July legislative poll. Following the failure of the party to gain parliamentary seats, Braghiş stepped down as party leader. In a party congress in April 2010, Braghiş stood as a candidate for party leadership but was defeated by Victor Şelin. (A number of PSD members had reportedly joined the PDM earlier in the year.)

Leaders: Victor ŞELIN (Chair), Sergiu COROPCEANU (Secretary General).

Republican Party of Moldova (*Partidul Republican din Moldova*—PRM). Established in 1999 under Ion CURTEAN, the PRM joined the PSRM in the *"Edinstvo"* electoral bloc for the 2001 parliamentary election. It won only 0.04 percent of the vote in 2005 and 0.09 percent of the vote in April 2009.

Leaders: Andrei STRATAN (Chair), Ion CURTEAN.

Conservative Party (*Partidul Conservator*—PC). Founded in 2006, the PC called for decentralization of governmental authority. It won 0.29 percent of the vote in the April 2009 elections.

Leader: Natalia NIRCA (Chair).

Party "Moldova United" (*Partidul "Moldova Unită–Edinaya Moldova"*—PMUEM). Originally founded in 2005 as the **Party of Spiritual Development "United Moldova"** (*Partidul Dezvoltării Spirituale" Moldova Unită*—PDSMU), the PDSMU called for, among other things, greater inclusiveness for women. In the April 2009 elections it won 0.22 percent of the vote. It did not formally contest the July balloting but encouraged party members to support the PSD. In February 2010 a party congress elected a new leadership and renamed the party as the PMUEM.

Leader: Vladimir ŢURCAN (Chair).

Ecologist Party of Moldova "Green Alliance" (*Partidul Ecologist "Alianţa Verde" din Moldova*—PEAVM). The PEAVM, which had participated in the 2007 elections on its own, ultimately withdrew from the April 2009 balloting, calling upon its supporters to vote for the PLDM. The PEAVM officially returned to the electoral arena for the July balloting, in which it won 0.4 percent of the vote.

Leader: Vladimir BRAGA (President).

Republican Popular Party (*Partidul Popular Republican*—PPR). Founded in 1999 as the Peasants' Christian Democratic Party (*Partidul Ţărănesc Creştin Democrat din Moldova*—PŢCDM), the party changed its name at a party conference in May 2005 to the PPR. The party runs on a platform of improving conditions for the peasants of Moldova, in part through subsidized government loans. More specifically, it has called for a new Parliament of 51 members, each elected individually; for popular election of the president; and for a dramatic reduction in the size of government by cutting the number of ministries down to 6 at most.

The PŢCDM collected 1.4 percent of the vote in 2005. The PPR did not compete in 2009 but stated its support for the UCM.

Leader: Nicolae ANDRONIC (Chair).

Socio-Political Republican Movement "Equality" (*Mişcarea Social-Politică Republicană "Ravnopravie"*—MSPRR). A far-left party, the MSPRR advocates closer relations with Russia and Ukraine, seeks introduction of Russian as an official language, and opposes reunification with Romania. The party won 2.83 percent of the vote in the 2005 parliamentary elections (up from 0.4 percent in 2001), failing to win any seats.

In late 2008 talks were launched with the leadership of the UCM over a potential merger, but no accord was reached. However, the MSPRR in early 2009 announced its support for the UCM in the upcoming legislative 2009 elections, creating friction within the party that led to the ouster of Chair Valerii Klimenko in March. Some party members maintained that Klimenko remained the legal chair, however, and by early 2010 he had apparently regained control over the party.

Leader: Valerii KLIMENKO (Chair).

For Nation and Country Party (*Partidul Pentru Neamşi Tară*—PPNT). Founded in 2007 on a platform that stressed "social-liberal" values, modernization, and economic reform. It supported AMN in the 2009 elections but ran independently in November 2010.

Leader: Nicolae UŢICA (President).

Labour Party (*Partidul Muncii*—PM). The party was founded in 1999 as the Labor Union "Motherland" (*Uniunea Mundi "Patria-Rodina"*—UMPR) with a charter that called for the creation of a "social state" providing dignity and opportunity for all citizens. In 2007 the UMPR merged with an organization of Moldovans abroad, the *Asociaţia" Patria-Moldova"* to form **Motherland-Moldova** (*Patria-Moldova*—PM). The combined movement dissolved in 2009, and the UMPR subsequently changed its name to the Labour Party.

Leader: Gheorghe SIMA (President).

Patriots of Moldova (*Partidul "Patrioţii Moldovei"*—PPM). Founded in 2010, the PPM platform emphasizes independence from Romania, a distinctive national and linguistic character to Moldovans, and stronger relations with Ukraine.

Leader: Mihail GARBUZ (President).

Roma Social-Political Movement of the Republic of Moldova (*Mişcarea social-politică a Romilor din Republica Moldova*—MRRM). Often referred to as the Roma Movement of Moldova in the domestic press, the MRRM was founded in 2010 on a platform that promotes both the values of Roma culture in Moldova and that the Roma are an "integral part" of the Moldovan people within a multiethnic framework.

Leader: Vasile DRANGOI (President).

Other Parties:

Centrist Union of Moldova (*Uniunea Centristă din Moldova*—UCM). Founded in 2000 on a platform that called for adherence to the rule of law and creation of a civil society, it won one parliamentary seat in 2001 as part of the Braghiş Alliance but took only 0.8 percent of the vote in 2005. For the April 2009 elections, the UCM included members of the PLD and PUM on the UCM candidate list in an effort to combine the parties' support and pass the threshold into Parliament without violating the recent ban on electoral blocs. However, the UCM list secured only 2.8 percent of the vote. It did not contest the November 2010 election but did enter the 2011 local elections.

Leader: Mihai PETRACHE (Chair).

Party of Law and Justice (*Partidul Legiişi Dreptăţii*—PLD). The PLD began in 1998 as the Party of Social and Economic Justice (*Partidul Dreptăţii Social-Economice din Moldova*—PDSEM). The party received less than 2 percent of the vote in 1998.

With Gen. Nicolae Alexei as its new leader, the PDSEM ran in the 2005 elections on a platform advocating European integration, closer relations with Romania, and popular election of the president. The party failed to improve on its previous performance, winning only 1.7 percent of the vote. The PLD did not register for the 2009 or 2010 legislative elections but did enter the 2011 local elections.

Leader: Gen. Nicolae ALEXEI.

Electoral Bloc "Motherland" (*Blocul Electoral "Patria-Rodina"*—BEPR). The BEPR was formed in January 2005 by two left-wing parties: the Party of Moldovan Socialists (PSRM) and the Socialist Party of Moldova (PSM). The bloc advocated closer relations with Russia, self-determination for Transnistria, and elimination of the office of president. It opposed accession to the EU and closer relations with the West. The bloc earned only 4.97 percent of the vote in parliamentary elections in 2005, well below the threshold for representation.

Leader: Boris MURAVSCHII.

Party of Socialists of the Republic of Moldova "Patria-Rodina" (*Partidul Socialiştilor din Republica Moldova*—PSRM). The PSRM was organized in 1997 by former PSM members. The party won only 0.6 percent of the national vote in the 1998 parliamentary election. For the February 2001 election it joined the Republican Party of Moldova (PRM, above) and the Party of Progressive Forces of Moldova (*Partidul Forţelor Progresiste din Moldova*—PFPM) in forming the Unity Electoral Bloc (*Blocul Electoral "Edinstvo"*). In January 2005 it formed the Electoral Bloc "Motherland" (*Blocul Electoral "Patria-Rodina"*—BEPR) with the PSM (below).

For the 2007 local elections PSRM joined forces with the Social Movement *"Ravnopravie"* (MSPRR, above) in the Electoral Bloc *"Patria-Rodina-Ravnopravie."* In the 2009 and 2010 parliamentary elections, it supported the PCRM. In November 2011, however, it broke with the PCRM.

Leaders: Igor DODON (Chair), Veronica ABRAMCIUC (Honorary Chair).

Socialist Party of Moldova (*Partidul Socialist din Moldova*—PSM). Established in 1992 by former members of the proscribed Communist Party (PCM), the pro-Russian PSM ran for Parliament in 1994 as part of the PSMUE electoral bloc, winning 28 seats on a 21.8 percent vote share. The resultant Socialist Union (*Unitatea Socialistă*) parliamentary faction then aligned with the dominant PCRM. In 1996, however, the PSM fell into disarray over the presidential election, in which most of the leadership backed Prime Minister Sangheli but others preferred Petru Lucinschi. With a number of deputies having deserted the party and formed the PSRM, the four-party Socialist Union list won only 1.8 percent of the vote in 1998. In the 1999 local elections the PSM, running independently, fared no better. In 2001 the party joined the Braghiş Alliance.

In the 2007 local elections the PSM ran on its own in a limited number of city and village council races. The party leader, Victor Morev, was eventually accused of having illegally sold state property while mayor of Balti, and he reportedly fled the country to Russia.

Leader: Victor MOREV (Chair).

Other registered parties include the **Movement of Professionals "Hope"** (*Mişcarea Profesioniştilor "Speranţa-Nadezhda"*); the **Party for the Union of Moldova** (*Partidul Politic pentru Unirea Moldovei*); the **Social-Political Movement "New Force"** (*Mişcarea social-politică "Forţă Nouă"*); the **Green Ecologist Political Party** (*Partidul Politic Partidul Verde Ecologist*); the **New Historical Option Party** (*Partidul Politic Noua Opţiune Istorică*); the **European Action Movement** (*Partidul Mişcarea "Acţiunea Europeană"*); the **"Our Home–Moldova" Party** (*Partidul politic "Casa Noastră–Moldova"*); the **Popular Anti-Mafia Movement** (*Partidul politic Mişcarea Populară Antimafie*); the **Popular Party of the Republic of Moldova** (*Partidul Politic Partidul Popular din Republica Moldova*); the **Democracy at Home Party** (*Partidul Politic "Democraţia Acasă"*); the **Popular Socialist Party of Moldova** (*Partidul Popular Socialist din Moldova*); the **Party of Regions of Moldova** (*Partidul Regiunilor din Moldova*); the **Democratic Action Party** (*Partidul Acţiunea Democratică*); the **Renaissance Party** (*Partidul Politic Partidul Renaştere*); and the **People's Force Party** (*Partidul Politic Partidul Forţa*).

Transnistrian Parties:

Renewal (*Obnovleniye*). Established in 2000 as a nongovernmental organization, Renewal competed in the 2000 and 2005 Transnistrian parliamentary elections before becoming officially registered as a party in 2006. Having won 7 seats in 2000 (when most of the victors were officially nonpartisan, although supportive of President Smirnov), Renewal became the majority party in December 2005, winning 23 seats and gaining additional support from allied parties, which won 6 more. Probusiness in orientation, it has campaigned for full independence from Moldova; political reform, including adoption of a parliamentary rather than presidential system; and integration with Europe. In 2011 Russia supported Anatoly Kaminsky's campaign for the presidency; he won 26.3 percent of the vote in the first round and 19.7 percent in the second.

Leaders: Anatoly KAMINSKY (Chair and Speaker of Parliament), Mikhail BURLA.

Republic (*Respublika*). Long the center of power in Transnistria, Republic began as a social association and emerged as the government party under the leadership of Igor Smirnov and Grigori MARACUTSA, Transnistria's president and parliamentary speaker, respectively. In the December 2005 election, however, Republic won only 13 seats, losing its majority status, after which Maracutsa was replaced as speaker.

Leaders: Gen. Aleksandr KOROLYOV, Vladimir RILYAKOV.

Breakthrough (*Proriv*). Founded in 2005 as a youth movement but registered as a political party in 2006, the party supports continued independence and closer relationships with Russia and Ukraine.

Leaders: Aleksandr GORELOVSKIY (President), Dmitry SOIN.

Transnistria's political party system is becoming increasingly complex, with more than half a dozen new parties registering in 2006–2007 alone. Some are closely associated with particular business interests. Among the more prominent of the current parties are the **Patriotic Party of Pridnestrovie,** chaired by Oleg SMIRNOV, son of the former president; the **Social Democratic Party of Pridnestrovie,** which, led by Aleksandr RADCHENKO, is the principal advocate of full union with Moldova; and the **Pridnestrovie Communist Party**. Several other parties have close ties to established parties in Russia.

LEGISLATURE

In May 1991 the unicameral Supreme Soviet was redesignated as the **Parliament** (*Parlamentul*), which is elected for a four-year term by proportional representation from a single nationwide district. There are currently 101 members. Previously, the thresholds to gain representation were 6 percent for individual parties, 9 percent for two-party coalitions, and 12 percent for three-party blocs. Changes to the electoral code in 2008 banned coalitions, although some parties circumvented the ban in the April 2009 elections by having candidates from several parties run on the list of one of the parties. The thresholds were changed prior to the July 2009 balloting to 3 percent for independents and 5 percent for parties. A May 2013 law restored the threshold for parties to 6 percent.

Following the November 28, 2010, elections, the seats were distributed as follows: the Party of Communists of the Republic of Moldova (PCRM), 42; the Liberal Democratic Party of Moldova (PLDM), 32; the Democratic Party of Moldova (PDM), 15; and the Liberal Party (PL), 12.

Speaker: Igor CORMAN.

CABINET

[as of August 1, 2013]

Prime Minister	Iurie Leancă (PLDM)
Deputy Prime Ministers	Valeriu Lazăr (PDM)
	Natalia Gherman (PLDM) [f]
	Mihai Moldovanu (PL)
Deputy Prime Minister for Territorial Re-Integration Affairs	Eugen Carpov (ind.)
Deputy Prime Minister for Social Affairs	Tatiana Poting (PL) [f]
Ministers	
Agriculture and Processing Industry	Vasile Bumacov (PLDM)
Construction and Regional Development	Marcel Răducan (PDM)
Culture	Monica Babuc (PDM) [f]
Defense	Vitalie Marinuţa (PL)
Economy	Valeriu Lazăr (PDM)
Education	Maia Sandu (PLDM) [f]
Environment	Gheorghe Şalaru (PL)
External Affairs and European Integration	Natalia Gherman (PLDM) [f]
Finance	Veaceslav Negruţă (PLDM)
Health	Andrei Usatîi (PLDM)
Information Technology and Communications	Pavel Filip (PDM)
Internal Affairs	Dorin Recean (PLDM)
Justice	Oleg Efrim (PLDM)
Labor, Social Protection, Family, and Children	Valentina Buliga (PDM) [f]
Transport and Roads	Vasile Botnari (PDM)
Youth and Sports	Octavian Bodisteanu (PL)

[f] = female

INTERGOVERNMENTAL REPRESENTATION

Ambassador to the U.S.: Igor MUNTEANU.

U.S. Ambassador to Moldova: William MOSER.

Permanent Representative to the UN: Vlad LUPAN.

IGO Memberships (Non-UN): CEUR, CIS, EBRD, ICC, IOM, OSCE, WTO.

MONACO

Principality of Monaco
Principauté de Monaco

Political Status: Independent principality founded in the 13th century; constitutional monarchy since 1911; present constitution promulgated December 17, 1962 (amended in April 2002).

Area: 0.70 sq. mi. (1.81 sq. km).

Population: 30,500 (2013E—U.S. Census).

Major Urban Center (2005E): MONACO-VILLE (1,100).

Official Language: French.

Monetary Unit: Euro (market rate November 1, 2013: 0.74 euro = $1US). Although not a member of the European Union (EU), Monaco was authorized by the EU to adopt the euro as its official currency and mint a limited supply of Monégasque euro coins.

Sovereign: Prince ALBERT II; acceded to the throne April 6, 2005, following the death of his father, Prince RAINIER III; formally installed in two-part process on July 12 and November 19, 2005.

Heiress Presumptive: Princess CAROLINE Louise Marguerite Grimaldi, elder sister of the sovereign.

Minister of State: Michel ROGER; assumed office March 29, 2010, following nomination by the sovereign to succeed Jean-Paul PROUST, who had resigned due to poor health.

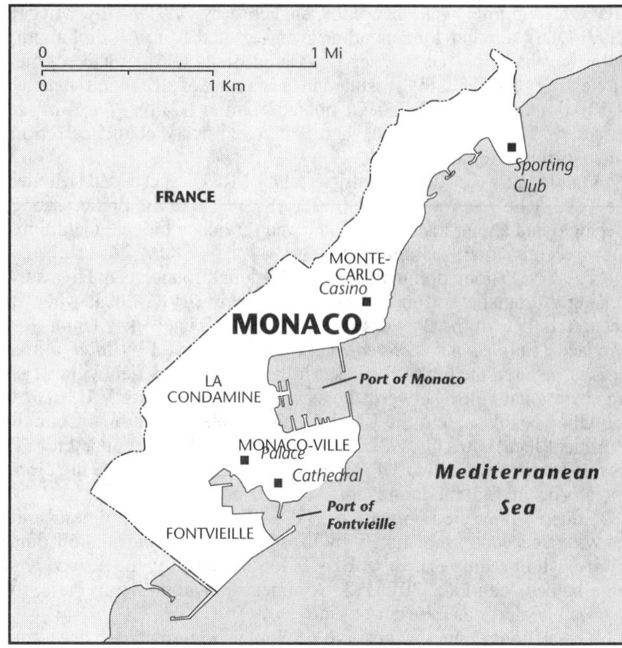

THE COUNTRY

A tiny but celebrated enclave on the Mediterranean coast nine miles from Nice, Monaco is surrounded on three sides by France. The principality is divided into four districts: Monaco-Ville (the capital, built on a rocky promontory about 200 feet above sea level), Monte Carlo (the tourist quarter), La Condamine (the business district around the port), and Fontvieille (the industrial district). A majority of the citizenry is of foreign origin, primarily French or Italian. Monégasques constitute approximately 19 percent of the population and speak their own language, a combination of French and Italian. Roman Catholicism is the state religion, and French is the official language, although other European languages are also spoken.

The principality's main sources of income are tourism, import-export trade, financial services, corporate and indirect taxes, and corporate research centers. Shipping is increasingly important, while gambling now accounts for no more than 4 percent of the country's income. In 2011 service industries accounted for 90 percent of GDP, and light industry, such as plastics, pharmaceuticals, glass, precision instruments, and cosmetics yielded about 10 percent of the GDP. Customs, postal services, telecommunications, and banking are governed by an economic union with France established in 1956.

Concerted land reclamation efforts begun in the 1960s succeeded in expanding the principality's total area by some 25 percent in the following 40 years, with some of the new acreage sold for private development consistent with the government's urban master plan. A new convention center, the Grimaldi Forum, opened in 2000 as part of a more recent effort to attract such business-related activities as conferences and seminars. In 2009 the national tourist bureau launched Concept URI, a campaign to attract "ultra-rich individuals" from India, Brazil, and Russia.

In general, the principality's economic status reflects that of France and, indirectly, the European Union (EU). Monaco is also directly dependent on the French labor force; each business day an estimated 40,000 French workers cross the border, more than doubling the population. Per capita income is understood to be one of the highest in the world, and there is virtually no unemployment.

A period of stagnation in the mid-1990s was followed by significant recovery and sustained growth from 1997 until the global economy crisis in 2008. GDP declined by 11.45 percent in 2009 but rebounded with a 2.47 percent increase in 2010. Growth continued at 5.1 percent in 2011 and 6.6 percent in 2012. The local economy was affected by the banking transparency rules imposed by the Organization for Economic Cooperation and Development (OECD) as local banks could no longer count on funds from dubious sources.

GOVERNMENT AND POLITICS

Political background. Ruled by the Grimaldi family since 1297, the Principality of Monaco has maintained its separate identity in close association with France, under whose protection it was placed in 1861. A 1918 treaty stipulated that Monégasque policy had to conform with French political, military, naval, and economic interests. A further treaty of July 17, 1919, provided for Monaco's conversion to an autonomous state under French guidance should the reigning prince die without leaving a male heir. New conventions redefining the French-Monégasque relationship were signed in 1963 in response to the principality's status as a tax refuge, and the earlier treaties were superseded in 2005 (see Foreign relations, below, for details).

In the 1960s Prince RAINIER III, who had acceded to the throne in 1949, embarked on a three-year struggle with shipping magnate Aristotle S. Onassis for control of the *Société des Bains de Mer* (SBM), a corporation that owns the Monte Carlo Casino, main hotels, clubs, restaurants, and considerable Monégasque real estate. Monaco gained control of the company in 1967 by buying out Onassis's majority shareholdings.

World attention focused briefly on the principality again in 1982, following the death of Princess GRACE (the former American actress Grace Kelly) as the result of an automobile accident in the Côte d'Azur region. Subsequently, the passing of the princess was viewed as representing a fiscal as well as personal loss for Monégasques, whose economy, based in large part on tourism, had recently stagnated, with income from both real estate and gambling receding sharply over previous years. Other income sources include the annual Formula One Grand Prix, which brings in some $120 million, while the country's thriving contemporary art community is becoming a significant tourist draw.

Elections to the National Council in January 1993 appeared to mark a movement toward more competitive politics, although groupings remained electoral lists rather than parties as such. In December 1994 Paul DIJOUD (a former French ambassador to Mexico) was sworn in as Monaco's minister of state (chief minister) in succession to Jacques

DUPONT. Dijoud was succeeded on February 3, 1997, by Michel LÉVÊQUE, another long-standing member of the French diplomatic corps who had most recently served as ambassador to Algeria. Elections on February 1 and 8, 1998, resulted in the capture of all council seats by the list of the National and Democratic Union (*Union Nationale et Démocratique*—UND), which had dominated every council election since its formation in 1962.

On January 1, 2000, Patrick LECLERCQ succeeded Michel Lévêque, who had retired as minister of state. Like his predecessors, Leclercq had a long history of diplomatic service to France, including, most recently, as ambassador to Spain.

The UND's long domination of the National Council came to a surprisingly dramatic end in the balloting of February 6, 2003, when it secured only 3 of the 24 seats in the National Council. The Union for Monaco (*Union pour Monaco*—UPM) list, presented by three allied parties, secured the other 21 seats. The balloting was widely viewed as a generational battle between the "young lion," Stéphane VALÉRI of the UPM coalition, and the UND's longtime leader, National Council President Jean-Louis CAMPORA, who had served in the council for 30 years. The overwhelming UPM victory was also attributed to the electorate's desire for "modernization."

Prince Rainer died on April 6, 2005, after an extended illness, and he was succeeded immediately by his son, ALBERT Alexandre Louis Pierre, who became Prince ALBERT II. Subsequently, the new sovereign named Jean-Paul PROUST, a former chief of police in Paris, to succeed Leclercq as minister of state.

The nation's ongoing positive economic performance helped the governing UPM secure 53 percent of the vote and 21 seats in the February 3, 2008, elections, compared to 40 percent for the UND-led Rally and Issues for Monaco and 7 percent for Monaco Together.

Jean-Paul Proust resigned as minister of state in March 2010 because of illness (he died on April 7). He was succeeded on March 29 by Michel ROGER, a French jurist, who was one of the seven members of the Monaco Supreme Court. His appointment disappointed some Monégasques who had hoped that Prince Albert would appoint a native of Monaco this time.

On July 2, 2011, Prince Albert married his longtime companion, Charlene WITTSTOCK, 34, a former South African swimming champion. Monégasques welcomed the news as a necessary first step to producing a legitimate heir.

Constitution and government. As amended in 2002, the 1962 constitution (replacing the one of 1911) vests executive power in the hereditary prince or princess, grants universal suffrage, outlaws capital punishment, and guarantees the rights of association and trade unionism. The sovereign rules in conjunction with a minister of state, who is assisted by a cabinet (Council of Government), whose members, like the minister of state and all other palace personnel, are appointed by the sovereign

Traditionally, the legislature (the National Council) has had few powers, although the 2002 constitutional amendments authorized the council to review budgets, introduce members' private bills, and ratify certain treaties and other international agreements. Advice on constitutional, treaty, and other matters may be offered by a 7-member Crown Council, while a 12-member State Council advises the sovereign in such areas as legislation, regulations, and law and order.

Municipal affairs in the four *quartiers* are conducted by a 15-member elected Communal Council (*Conseil Communal*), with the mayor of Monaco-Ville presiding. The judiciary includes a Supreme Court of five full and two deputy members, all named by the sovereign on the basis of nominations by the National Council and other institutions. In addition, a Review Court considers appeals based on alleged violations of law. At lower levels there are a district court, a labor court, a court of the first instance, and a court of appeals. The majority of judges are French nationals.

The 2002 amendments in part focused on succession to the throne, an issue that had come to the forefront because Prince Albert (Prince Rainier's son) had never married and thereby had no legitimate male heirs. (He later acknowledged two illegitimate children, but they are precluded from the line of succession.) Under the 2002 revisions, which technically entered into effect upon French ratification in 2005 of a 2002 treaty (see Foreign relations, below), the long-standing principle of male primogeniture was modified to permit succession by a female sibling and her descendants in the event a reigning sovereign leaves no direct, legitimate male heir.

Given Monaco's small population and its location, most residents depend on French mass media for much of their information. A law on freedom of the media was passed in July 2005.

Foreign relations. Monaco's foreign relations were traditionally controlled by France, based on treaties from the early 1900s (see Political background, above, for details). However, those treaties were superseded by a new "Treaty adapting and confirming relations of friendship and co-operation between the French Republic and the Principality of Monaco," which was signed in Paris on October 24, 2002, and ratified by France on October 13, 2005. Most significantly, the new treaty ended Monaco's subservience to French policy, replacing it with the principle of sovereign equality in the context of historically "close and privileged relations." Furthermore, a new "Convention to adapt and develop administrative co-operation between the French Republic and the Principality," signed in November 2005 as a replacement for a 1930 convention, gave preference in senior government and civil service appointments to Monégasques. Consultation with Paris on major appointments remains the rule, but such senior positions as minister of state are no longer filled on a pro forma basis by French nationals. The principality participates indirectly in the EU by virtue of its customs union with France but has no plans to become a member. Prior to joining the United Nations (UN) in 1993, it maintained a Permanent Observer's office at UN headquarters in New York and had long belonged to a number of UN specialized agencies. The treaty also allowed other countries to accredit ambassadors to Monaco, rather than considering the principality to be a branch of the French government. The United States and Monaco upgraded from consular to full diplomatic relations in December 2006.

In 1994 Monaco signed an agreement with France providing for coordinated action against money laundering and requiring Monégasque banks and other institutions to report dubious financial transactions to the authorities. However, dissatisfaction with Monaco's progress in this regard surfaced in 1998 when young reformist judges alleged that the old guard was being lax in its prosecution. Consequently, overruling Prince Rainier, Paris appointed new prosecutors and chief judges. Stung by criticism (*Le Monde* characterized Monaco as a "refuge for cheats"), the government released a report in January 1999 denying that inappropriate activity was prevalent in the principality and attacking the "myth" of Monaco as a "superficial playground." In part, the report was seen as a component of the government's campaign to gain membership in the Council of Europe, which at first reportedly considered Monaco as neither fully sovereign nor sufficiently democratic. In October 2004, in consideration of the 2002 treaty revisions, an ongoing legal reform process, and the successful conduct of the 2003 legislative election under a new election law, Monaco was admitted to the Council of Europe.

Pressure on the principality increased in February 2008 after German officials bribed a bank official in Liechtenstein to release private bank records, which exposed many German nationals who were evading taxes. Monaco's practices fell under more scrutiny because Liechtenstein, in addition to Monaco, was among those cited by the Organization for Economic Cooperation and Development as retaining harmful tax policies. In March 2009 Monaco bowed to international pressure and agreed to follow OECD regulations on tax evasion. In return, the principality was removed from the "black list" and placed on a "gray list," pending implementation of reforms. It was removed from the list altogether in 2010.

By 2011 Monaco had signed agreements with 24 countries to exchange tax information. The banks in Monaco are under the watchful eye of the *Banque de France,* as well as the *Service d'Information et de Controle sur les Ciruits Financiers,* the French authority that monitors money laundering, terrorist financing, and corruption. Michel Roger, the minister of state, declared, "Today if you've got dirty money, Monaco is not the place to put it."

In March 2012, however, the Council of Europe's Group of States against Corruption (GRECO) criticized Monaco's efforts in revising its criminal code, noting that anticorruption laws still did not apply to senior government officials or to many foreign nationals.

Monaco has no income tax. When France's President François Hollande imposed a 75 percent tax on individuals making over €1 million per year, as promised in 2012, many French millionaires moved to Monaco. One unintended beneficiary was the national soccer team, which offered large, tax-free salaries to French team players.

Current issues. Prince Albert has continued his father's focus on expanding its economy, with shipping and cruise-ship tourism in particular showing strong growth prior to the global financial crisis that began in 2008. Albert also established a new department for external affairs, underscoring the need for the principality to keep pace with the fast-changing European landscape. In that context, Monaco began systematically (but slowly) reviewing and adopting some 200 Council of Europe conventions in an effort to cement its broader ties to Europe. The conventions, which cover legal, social, economic, institutional, and diplomatic concerns, also necessitated reform of many domestic laws and codes.

In 2006 the principality requested bids on a new, ten-year land reclamation project that would add 25 acres and possibly 4,000 residents to Monaco. However, environmentalists alleged that the expansion could extensively damage the ecosystem, and Prince Albert suspended the project in December 2008, pending a review of the environmental impact.

The Prince Albert II of Monaco Foundation was established in June 2006 to address climate change, biodiversity, and water shortages. The principality has funded research and sponsored international conferences on whaling, deforestation, and sustainable fishing. In March 2010 Monaco made a proposal to the 175-nation Convention on International Trade in Endangered Species to ban commercial trade in Atlantic bluefin-tuna fishing until the population level of the fish recovers. While most of the EU supported the ban, the proposal was voted down, with Japan playing a major role in marshaling opposition to it.

In January 2011, in response to the dismal GDP numbers for 2010, the prince appointed three new cabinet members, José BADIA for foreign affairs; Marie-Pierre GRAMAGLIA for public works, environment, and urban affairs; and Marco PICCININI for finance and the economy. As Monaco's former ambassador to India and China, Piccinini worked to attract banks and people from emerging countries, while improving banking transparency overall.

Along with banking reform, the government introduced new regulations on political funding. The July 2, 2012, Law on Campaign Finance established a €400,000 limit for each candidate and required candidates to submit an expense report to the Audit Committee within two months in order to receive reimbursement. (Candidates who pass a 5 percent threshold can be compensated for 25 percent of their expenses.)

Piccinini resigned in October to return to the private sector. Jean CASTELLINI, who had served in the cabinet in 2006–2007, was appointed minister of finance and economy.

The National Council election on February 13, 2013, gave a new alliance, Horizon Monaco (*Horizon Monaco*—HM), 20 of the 24 seats. Union for Monaco (*Union pour Monaco*—UPM), which had controlled the legislature since 2003, won only three seats. The remaining seat went to Renaissance, a new party representing workers from SBM. The country's main employer had registered a 40 percent drop in revenue since 2008, and employees feared possible layoffs or wage cuts.

In May bidding opened on a new land reclamation project that would increase the principality by 3 percent and include a 30–40 berth port. With an estimated €1 billion price tag, the reclamation project sets rigorous standards for sustainability and ecological soundness.

On June 18 the Venice Commission of the OSCE issued a sharply critical report on the balance of power in Monaco. It noted that the prince has ultimate control over executive, legislative, and judicial branches, while the National Council has little input on the composition of government or laws. "Monaco is not a parliamentary monarchy," the report concluded. "The Venice Commission strongly urges Monaco to adopt a new law on the independent functioning and organization of the National Council." Monegasque political leaders denounced the report for failing to consider the country's unique circumstances.

POLITICAL PARTIES

Although a party system is slowly developing, at present there is no political party law distinguishing parties from other associations. Nor is there public funding of parties except for small reimbursements to help cover election expenses. As explained by a 2007 report by the Monitoring Committee of the Council of Europe: "The primary function of a party in the Principality is not to attain power and thus enter government... but only to contribute to the management of the State's affairs whilst permanently seeking a compromise between the will of the Prince and the expectations of Monégasques as represented by the National Council."

In the absence of formal political parties, Monaco's politics were until recently dominated for nearly four decades by the **National and Democratic Union** (*Union Nationale et Démocratique*—UND). Formed in 1962 through the merger of the National Union of Independents (*Union Nationale des Indépendants*) and the National Democratic Entente (*Entente Nationale Démocratique*), the UND won all 18 National Council seats in the elections of 1968, 1978, 1983, and 1988. In 1993, when the UND captured 15 seats, it was sometimes informally referenced as the Campora List (*Liste Campora*), reflecting the leadership of Jean-Louis Campora, who was elected president of the new council to succeed long-term UND leader Jean-Charles REY. Two seats were also won in 1993 by the Médecin List (*Liste Médecin*), led by Jean-Louis MÉDECIN, the former mayor of Monaco-Ville. The UND list was credited with winning all the seats in the 1998 elections in competition with lists from the **National Union for the Future of Monaco** (*Union Nationale pour l'Avenir de Monaco*—UNAM) and the **Rally for the Monégasque Family** (*Rassemblement de la Famille Monégasque*—RFM).

In 2003 the UNAM, the **Promotion of the Monégasque Family** (*Promotion de la Famille Monégasque*—PFM, as the RFM had been renamed), and the **Union for the Principality** (*Union pour la Principauté*—UP) combined forces under an opposition Union for Monaco (*Union pour Monaco*—UPM) list. Led by former UND member Stéphane Valéri, now of the UP, the UPM won 21 of 24 seats, with the balance going to the UND list of the Rally for Monaco (*Rassemblement pour Monaco*—RPM).

In January 2006 the PFM, led by René GIORDANO, left the UPM. Also during 2006 UND councilor Christine PASQUIER-CIULLA formed her own **Monégasque Party** (*Parti Monégasque*—PM), while in September former UNAM vice chair Claude BOISSON and the UP's Vincent PALMARO established the **Principality, Ethics, and Progress** (*Principauté, Éthique, et Progrès*—PEP) party.

On February 3, 2008, the UPM, now comprising only the UP and the UNAM, repeated its 2003 win, securing 21 seats as Valéri urged voters to support the "evolution" of UPM programs. The conservative coalition called the Rally and Issues for Monaco (*Rassemblement et Enjeux pour Monaco*—REM), consisting of the RPM (led by Guy MAGNAN) and the **Values and Issues** (*Valeurs & Enjeux*) party (led by Laurent NOUVION) won 3 seats. A third coalition (Monaco Together [*Monaco Ensemble*—ME]), which included the PFM, **Monégasque Synergy** (*Synergie Monegasque*—SM), and the **Association of Non-Attached Monégasques** (*Association des Nom Inscrits Monégasques*—NIM), also took part in the election but won no seats with only about 7 percent of the vote. The PM did not participate in the election because it did not have a slate of at least 13 candidates as required by law. The PEP candidates ran under the banner of the RPM.

Three electoral alliances contested the February 13, 2013, election. **Horizon Monaco** (*Horizon Monaco*—HM) won a landslide victory, taking 20 seats in the National Council. Founded by Laurent Nouvion in September 2012, HM included members of REM, SM, and UP. The incumbent UPM took only three seats, while **Renaissance** (*Renaissance*), a new party founded in November 2012 to represent employees of SBN, captured one seat.

LEGISLATURE

The **National Council** (*Conseil National*) is a 24-seat unicameral body elected via direct universal suffrage for a five-year term. Councilors are elected from one multimember national constituency, and voters can vote for up to 24 candidates. Sixteen seats are filled by the top vote-getters, with the balance then being chosen by proportional representation from those lists receiving at least 5 percent of the vote. (The proportional element was introduced in 2002 at the request of the Council of Europe.) In the most recent election on February 13, 2013, the seat distribution was as follows: Monaco Horizon, 20; Union for Monaco, 3; and Renaissance, 1. The next elections are scheduled for 2018.

President: Laurent NOUVION.

CABINET

[as of August 25, 2013]

Minister of State	Michel Roger
Councilors	
Finance and Economy	Jean Castellini
Foreign Affairs	Franck José Badia
Health and Social Affairs	Stéphane Valéri
Interior	Paul Masseron
Public Works, Environment, and Urban Affairs	Marie-Pierre Gramaglia [f]

[f] = female

INTERGOVERNMENTAL REPRESENTATION

Monaco maintains consuls general in Washington and New York, while the U.S. consul general in Nice, France, also services U.S. interests in Monaco.

Ambassador to the U.S.: Gilles Alexandre NOGHÈS.

U.S. Ambassador to Monaco: Charles H. RIVKIN (resident in Paris).

Permanent Representative to the UN: Isabelle F. PICCO.

IGO Memberships (Non-UN): CEUR, OSCE.

MONGOLIA

Monggol Ulus

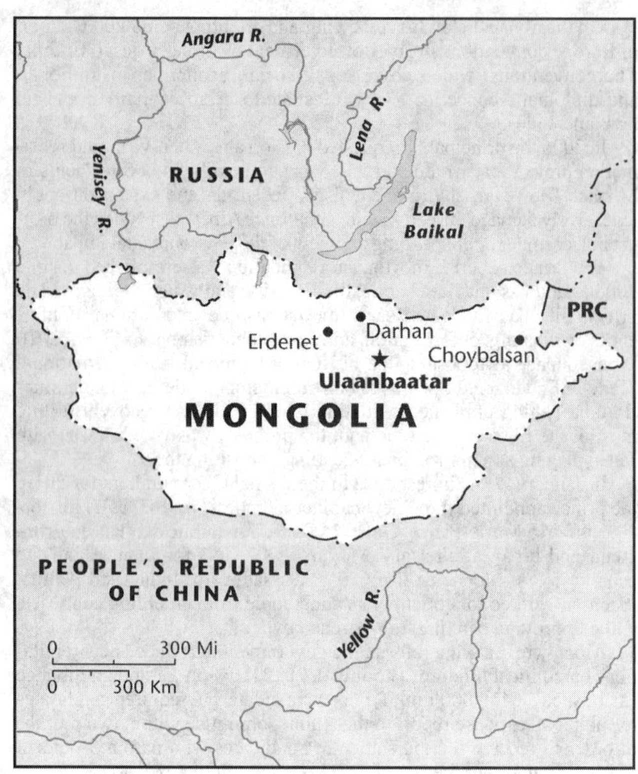

Political Status: Independent since 1921; Communist People's Republic established November 26, 1924; multi-party system introduced by constitutional amendment of May 11, 1990; current constitution adopted January 13, 1992, in effect from February 12.

Area: 604,247 sq. mi. (1,565,000 sq. km).

Population: 2,863,495 (2012E—UN); 3,226,516 (2013E—U.S. Census).

Major Urban Centers (2010C): ULAANBAATAR (Ulan Bator, 1,089,358), Erdenet (83,379), Darkhan (74,738).

Monetary Unit: Tugrik (market rate November 1, 2013: 1,684.39 tugriks = $1US).

Official Language: Khalkha Mongol.

President: Tsakhiagiyn ELBEGDORJ (Democratic Party), popularly elected for a four-year term on May 24, 2009, and sworn in on June 18, succeeding Nambaryn ENKHBAYAR (Mongolian People's Revolutionary Party); reelected on June 26, 2013.

Prime Minister: Norovyn ALTANKHUYAG (Democratic Party); nominated by the president on July 16, 2012, and confirmed by the State Great Hural on August 8, succeeding Sukhbaatar BATBOLD (Mongolian People's Party).

THE COUNTRY

Traditionally known as Outer Mongolia (i.e., that portion of historic Mongolia lying north of the Gobi Desert), the present country of Mongolia occupies a vast area of steppe, mountain, and desert between the Russian Federation on the north and the People's Republic of China on the south. Khalkha Mongols make up 82 percent of the population. The remainder are other Mongol groups (often speaking their own dialects); Turkic-speaking peoples; and Chinese, Russian, and Tungusic minorities. Lamaist Buddhism is the prevalent faith, practiced by an estimated 40 percent of the population, even though its leadership was largely wiped out by antireligious activity in 1937–1939. Islam is practiced by the small Kazakh minority (4 percent), and there are also small numbers of Christians and shamanists. Some 51 percent of the active labor force is female. Women constitute 14.9 percent of the legislators elected in 2012, a dramatic increase from 2008 when they made up 4 percent of the legislature.

The Mongolian economy was traditionally pastoral, and agriculture, especially animal husbandry, continues to employ 34 percent of the active labor force. In addition, a significant proportion of the rural population is engaged in nonwage and subsistence level agriculture. The industrial sector is largely driven by ore extraction and processing, chiefly of copper and gold. One of the world's largest copper-molybdenum facilities is located in Erdenet, while initial production at the massive Oyu Tolgoi copper-gold mine was expected to begin in 2013 (see Current issues, below). Other mineral resources include uranium, fluorspar, coal, tungsten, and recently discovered petroleum. Mineral production has typically accounted for 60–67 percent of export earnings. Manufacturing is largely devoted to processing agricultural products into such goods as cashmere and textiles, the second most important export product. More than 33 percent of the population lives below the poverty line.

The breakup of the Soviet Union precipitated a severe economic crisis in the first half of the 1990s. As Mongolia began privatizing state-owned enterprises, financial assistance from the West and international institutions helped support an economic recovery. In 2007, as world prices for copper and gold rose and livestock production recovered, GDP growth reached 10.2 percent, and in 2008 Mongolia registered an 8.9 percent gain. In 2009, however, in the context of the global financial crisis, exports and commodity prices fell, contributing to a loss in GDP of 1.0 percent. With copper prices recovering, and with international assistance from the International Monetary Fund (IMF) and elsewhere, Mongolia experienced a dramatic turnaround in 2010 when GDP grew by 6.3 percent. In 2011 GDP grew by 17.3 percent and 12.3 percent the next year. In 2012 inflation grew by 15 percent, while unemployment was 6.8 percent. GDP per capita was $3,673. In 2013 the World Bank ranked Mongolia 76th out of 185 countries in its annual Doing Business survey.

GOVERNMENT AND POLITICS

Political background. The home of such legendary figures as Genghis Khan and Tamerlane, Mongolia fell under Chinese control in the 17th century and continued under Chinese suzerainty for over 200 years. The fall of the Manchu dynasty resulted in a brief period of independence from 1911 until 1919, when Chinese hegemony was reestablished. Two years later Mongolian revolutionary leaders Sukhe BATOR and Horloogiyn CHOYBALSAN (Khorloin CHOIBALSAN) defeated the Chinese with Soviet assistance and established permanent independence.

Initially, a constitutional monarchy was created under Jebtsun Damba KHUTUKHTU, but following his death in 1924 the Mongolian People's Party (founded in 1921) was renamed the Mongolian People's Revolutionary Party (MPRP) (in 2010, it reverted to MPP), and the Mongolian People's Republic was proclaimed as the first Communist state outside the Soviet Union. Rightist influences, including a major revolt in 1932, were suppressed, and Choybalsan gained the ascendancy in 1934–1939, after which he continued to dominate both party and government until his death in 1952.

Yumjaagiyn TSEDENBAL was named chair of the Council of Ministers in 1952 and, after a two-year period of apparent political eclipse, succeeded Dashiyn DAMBA as MPRP first secretary in 1958. In addition, in 1974 he was named chair of the Presidium of the People's Great Hural. In 1984 Tsedenbal was relieved of his government and party posts, reportedly because of failing health, with Jambyn BATMÖNH being named MPRP secretary general. Upon designation as Presidium chair in December, Batmönh relinquished the chair of the Council of Ministers to Dumajiyn SODNOM. Both were reconfirmed following the 19th MPRP Congress in 1986.

In obvious response to political change in Eastern Europe, the regime in December 1989 permitted the organization of an opposition Mongolian Democratic Union (MDU), and additional opposition groups emerged; starting in February 1990 some 300 MDU adherents organized the Mongolian Democratic Party (MDP).

At an MPRP Central Committee plenum in March 1990 the entire Politburo was replaced, with Gombojavyn OCHIRBAT succeeding Batmönh as party leader, Punsalmaagiyn OCHIRBAT (no relation to the party leader) succeeding Batmönh as head of state, and Sharavyn GUNGAADORJ replacing Sodnom as chair of the Council of Ministers.

In May 1990 the Great Hural approved constitutional amendments that formally abandoned the one-party system and provided for a proportionally elected standing body (Little Hural) to complement the existing legislature. At the ensuing election in July–August the MPRP won approximately four-fifths of the seats in the Great Hural and nearly two-thirds of those in the Little Hural, but a three-party opposition Coalition of Democratic Forces also won representation. A week later Dashiyn BYAMBASUREN succeeded Gungaadorj as chief of government (now termed prime minister) and on the following day named a "coalition" government that did not, however, include representatives of the MDP.

In June 1992, under a new constitution, an election for a reinstituted unicameral legislature saw the MPRP capturing 71 of 76 seats even though opposition parties won 40 percent of the vote. In July the Great Hural elected a free-market economist, Puntsagiyn JASRAY, as prime minister, and in August an all-MPRP administration was announced.

In April 1993 a special MPRP congress refused to nominate President Ochirbat for reelection, selecting instead Lodongiyn TUDEV, editor of the party newspaper *Ünen*. As a result, Ochirbat agreed to stand as joint candidate of the MSDP and the Mongolian National Democratic Party (MNDP), and in June he retained the presidency, winning 57.8 percent of the vote.

Elections in June 1996 marked the end of more than seven decades of communist rule. A recently organized Democratic Union (DU), led by the MNDP and the MSDP, defeated the MPRP by an unexpected two-to-one margin. Thirty days later the coalition's leader, Mendsaikhan ENKHSAIKHAN, formed a new government. However, the MPRP quickly regained a dominant position in the provincial and municipal elections of October. Moreover, the MPRP's Natsagiyn BAGABANDI overwhelmed incumbent president Ochirbat, the DU nominee, by 60.8 percent to 29.8 percent in the May 1997 presidential election.

In January 1998 the Great Hural approved a measure that would permit its members to serve concurrently as government ministers. In April the governing organs of the MNDP and MSDP both recommended that the DU chair, Tsakhiagiyn ELBEGDORJ of the MNDP, assume the prime ministership, leading Prime Minister Enkhsaikhan to tender his resignation. A week later, the Great Hural endorsed Elbegdorj by a vote of 61–5. For more than a month, however, parliamentary infighting led to rejection of several ministerial nominees, with the cabinet that was ultimately assembled consisting entirely of legislators.

In late May 1998 the MPRP precipitated a parliamentary crisis when its delegation began a boycott of the Great Hural following approval (subsequently rescinded) of a merger involving the bankrupt public Renovation Bank with a private bank. With the legislative process paralyzed by the boycott, in July the Great Hural passed a no-confidence motion 42–33, and as a consequence the prime minister resigned three months after taking office.

The DU leadership and the MPRP's Bagabandi were soon at loggerheads. The president repeatedly rejected the coalition's nominee for prime minister, Davaadorgjiyn GANBOLD of the MNDP, while the Great Hural rejected the DU nominee Rinchinnyamiin AMARJARGAL. Before the end of the month the president had rejected two additional nominees, while on October 2 the country was deeply shaken when an apparent MNDP compromise candidate, Sanjaasürengiyn ZORIG, who had been a principal leader of the prodemocracy movement in 1989–1990, was killed in his home. The political stalemate continued, with Ganbold again being rejected by the president for a seventh time, and the DU refusing to nominate any of six potential candidates deemed acceptable by Bagabandi.

On November 24, 1998, the Constitutional Court ruled for the second time in less than a month that the constitution prohibited members of the Great Hural from serving as prime minister or in the cabinet. The decision helped break the impasse, and on December 9, having received the imprimatur of both the DU and the president, Janlav NARANTSATSRALT, the mayor of Ulaanbaatar, was easily confirmed as prime minister. The Great Hural nevertheless rejected the majority of his initial cabinet nominees and withheld approval of the final four until January 1999.

Barely six months later, Narantsatsralt was accused of jeopardizing national interests in a letter he had sent, without prior ministerial consultation, to a Russian official regarding terms for the sale of Russia's share in the Erdenet copper-molybdenum joint venture. Having lost a legislative no-confidence vote 41–22 on July 23, Narantsatsralt resigned the following day. On July 30 the State Great Hural gave swift approval, this time, to President Bagabandi's prime ministerial nominee, Amarjargal, who resigned from the legislature and immediately won confirmation by a vote of 50–2. The cabinet approved on September 2 was substantially unchanged.

In the general election of July 2, 2000, the MPRP swept back into power, capturing 72 of the 76 seats in the State Great Hural. The sole MNDP seat was won by former prime minister Narantsatsralt, while the MSDP won none. Nambaryn ENKHBAYAR, chair of the MPRP and a member of the State Great Hural, was confirmed as prime minister on July 26, and an MPRP cabinet won legislative approval on August 9. The legitimacy of Enkhbayar's appointment was ultimately resolved in May 2001, when President Bagabandi accepted constitutional amendments permitting legislators to serve as cabinet members.

President Bagabandi won a second term in the election of May 20, 2001, taking 58 percent of the vote. His chief opponent was Radnaasümbereliyn GONCHIGDORJ, of the Democratic Party (DP), which had been formed the preceding December by merger of the MNDP, the MSDP, and three smaller parties.

In 2003 the DP and the Motherland–Mongolian Democratic New Socialist Party (M-MDNSP), led by gold magnate Badarch ERDENEBAT, formed the Motherland Democratic Coalition (MDC), which was joined by the Civil Will Republican Party (CWRP) in March 2004. In the June 27 parliamentary election the MDC won 34 seats, only 2 less than the governing MPRP. With neither group able to claim a majority in the legislature, protracted negotiations on forming a new government ensued. On August 13, 2004, the legislators unanimously elected the outgoing prime minister, Nambaryn Enkhbayar, as chair of the State Great Hural, and on August 20 former prime minister Tsakhiagiyn Elbegdorj of the DP/MDC was again appointed prime minister. It took another month for the MPRP and MDC to reach agreement on an equal division of cabinet posts, with a "Grand Coalition Government" subsequently sworn in on September 28. However, in December the M-MDNSP withdrew from the MDC, which soon led to the dissolution of the coalition and to the dismissal in February 2005 of the two M-MDNSP ministers.

With President Bagabandi prohibited from seeking a third term, the MPRP nominated Nambaryn Enkhbayar as its presidential candidate in the May 22, 2005, election. Enkhbayar won with 53.4 percent of the vote, defeating former prime minister Mendsaikhan Enkhsaikhan of the DP (19.7 percent) and three other candidates.

On January 11, 2006, all ten MPRP ministers resigned from the coalition cabinet, and two days later the State Great Hural voted to dissolve the government. Four key votes in favor of dissolution were cast by members of the DP, including Enkhsaikhan, former prime minister Janlav Narantsatsralt, and Mishig SONOMPIL. An effort by the MPRP to forge a "national unity" government was rejected by the DP, though Enkhsaikhan, Narantsatsralt, and Sonompil all accepted posts in the new cabinet of MPRP chair Miyegombo ENKHBOLD, who was confirmed as prime minister by the legislature on January 25. The three maverick ministers were expelled from the DP and formed the National New Party (NNP). Also joining the coalition government were the Motherland Party (formerly the MDNSP), the Republican Party (RP), and the People's Party (PP).

On November 5, 2007, Prime Minister Enkhbold resigned after he was ousted as MPRP party chair in October in favor of the incumbent secretary general, Sanj BAYAR. On November 22 the State Great Hural confirmed Bayar as prime minister, and he appointed a coalition cabinet including members of the Civil Will Party (CWP, formerly the CWRP), the NNP, and the RP.

In the aftermath of the legislative elections on June 29, 2008, DP leaders questioned the integrity of the vote, prompting a violent demonstration in Ulaanbaatar on July 1 that resulted in five deaths, the burning of the MPRP's headquarters, several hundred arrests, and a four-day state of emergency declared by President Enkhbayar. Official election results announced on July 14 gave the MPRP a majority, with ten seats unassigned pending recounts. Nine days later 25 of 27 DP deputies walked out of the opening session of the State Great Hural, making a quorum impossible and preventing new members from being sworn in. While the legislature was blocked, a group of MPRP and DP members acted as an interim government by consulting on urgent national affairs. After Prime Minister Bayar agreed to invite the DP into a coalition government, the DP legislators ended their walkout on August 28. Bayar was reappointed as prime minister on September 11 and named a new MPRP-DP government that received the Hural's approval on September 19.

In the presidential election on May 24, 2009, DP leader and former prime minister Tsakhiagiyn Elbegdorj, who also had the backing of the CWP and the Mongolian Green Party (MGP), defeated the incumbent Enkhbayar on a narrow vote share of 51 percent. Elbegdorj, the first non-MPRP president in the country's history, was sworn in for a four-year term on June 18.

Prime Minister Bayar, citing ill health, resigned from office on October 25, 2009. Four days later, the State Great Hural confirmed Minister of Foreign Affairs Sukhbaatar Batbold (MPRP) as his successor.

In legislative elections on June 28, 2012, the DP secured a plurality with 31 seats, followed by the MPP with 25 seats. DP chair Norovyn ALTANKHUYAG became prime minister on August 8. He named a DP-led coalition cabinet that included members of the DP, the new Justice Coalition (see Parties and Groups, below), and the newly merged Civil Will–Green Party. The government was approved by the legislature on August 20.

On June 26, 2013, Elbegdorj was reelected, securing 50.9 percent of the vote to 42. 5 percent for Badmaanyambuugiin BAT-ERDENE (MPP) and 6.6 percent for Natsag UDVAL (MPRP). Elbegdorj was sworn in on July 10.

Constitution and government. The constitution adopted in 1960 left intact the guiding role of the MPRP, whose highly centralized leadership also dominated the state administration. The national legislature (People's Great Hural) was identified as the supreme organ of government, with the chair of its Presidium serving as head of state. Constitutional changes approved in 1990 included renunciation of the "guiding role" of the MPRP in favor of a multiparty system, conversion of the Presidium chair into a state presidency, and the creation of a vice presidency. Selected by the Great Hural, the vice president was to serve as ex officio chair of a new standing assembly (Little Hural).

The current constitution, adopted on January 13, 1992, returned legislative power to a single chamber, known as the State Great Hural, whose 76 members are elected by universal suffrage for four-year terms. The powers of the State Great Hural include appointing and dismissing the prime minister and other administrative officials. A popularly elected president serves as head of state for a four-year term; should no presidential candidate receive a majority of the votes cast, a two-way runoff is held. The president can veto legislative decisions (subject to override by a two-thirds majority), nominates the prime minister in consultation with the largest legislative party, and serves as commander-in-chief of the armed forces. A Supreme Court sits at the apex of the judicial system, while a Constitutional Court is charged with ensuring the "strict observance" of the basic law and with resolving constitutional disputes.

Mongolia is divided into 21 provinces (*aymguud* or *aimags*), each subdivided into counties and *baghs,* plus the capital city of Ulaanbaatar, subdivided into districts and *horoos.* At the provincial and capital level the prime minister appoints governors (*dzasag darga*) nominated by elected hurals. Each county (*soum*) and district (*khoron*) also elects a hural, while "General Meetings of Citizens" function at the lowest administrative tier. A local governor is nominated by each subdivision's legislative body and appointed by the governor of the next highest level.

The constitution guarantees freedom of the press and the right "to seek and receive information." However, journalists can be prosecuted for disclosing state secrets. The central government's leading newspapers were privatized in 1999. A 2005 law ordered the conversion of state-run broadcast outlets into public service companies. In 2013 Reporters Without Borders ranked Mongolia 98th out of 179 countries in freedom of the press.

Foreign relations. Mongolia attempted to take a neutral stance in the early period of the Sino-Soviet dispute, but subsequently aligned with the Soviet Union, in part because of an inherited fear of Chinese hegemony and in part because of a dependence on Soviet military, economic, and cultural assistance. A member of the UN since 1961, it became a full member of the Soviet-dominated Council for Mutual Economic Assistance (CMEA) in 1962 and signed a treaty of friendship and mutual assistance with the Soviet Union in 1966. Relations with China began to thaw in 1985; a consular treaty signed the following year was the first since 1949.

In March 1989 Moscow announced that it would begin withdrawing its reported 50,000 troops from Mongolia, a process completed in September 1992. President Ochirbat visited Russia in January 1993 for talks with President Boris Yeltsin that yielded a treaty of friendship and cooperation, under which the two countries agreed to refrain from entering into military-political alliances aimed against each other.

Mongolia signed a friendship and cooperation treaty with China in 1994 (replacing a 1962 predecessor) during an official visit by Chinese premier Li Peng. Earlier that year Mongolia, China, and Russia had signed a tripartite pact defining their border junctures. China is Mongolia's largest foreign investor and receives roughly 70 percent of Mongolian exports. At the same time, Mongolia has become increasingly wary of China's growing economic power, which already dominates Mongolia's cashmere industry.

Since the Cold War ended, Mongolian foreign policy has been based on carefully balanced relations with Russia and China as well as "third neighbors," including the Western powers. Diplomatic relations with the United States were not established until 1987. In January 1991 President Ochirbat became the first Mongolian head of state to travel to the United States, where he met with President George H. W. Bush and signed a bilateral trade agreement. The nation was soon admitted into the Asian Development Bank along with the World Bank and the IMF. More recently, Mongolia has frequently been in accord with Washington on foreign policy matters, including the "war on terrorism."

In the mid-2000s Mongolian troops joined coalition forces in Iraq following the U.S.-led invasion in 2003, and Mongolia also deployed some military trainers to Afghanistan. Visits in 2005 by U.S. secretary of defense Donald Rumsfeld and President George W. Bush (the first sitting U.S. chief executive to do so) marked a significant shift in relations.

In 2008 enhanced economic cooperation between Mongolia and Russia was evidenced by Mongolia's importing almost all of its oil from Russia. In March 2009 Russian Prime Minister Vladimir Putin offered $300 million in credits to Mongolia's agriculture industry. In May the two nations agreed to develop a rail network extending to the Oyu Tolgoi and Tavan Tolgoi mines. Under the deal, Russian firms would receive licenses to mine both sites.

In October 2011 Germany and Mongolia signed a series of economic agreements to allow German companies to extract rare earth materials. In response to the growing number of foreign corporations operating in Mongolia, the legislature passed a measure in May 2012 that limited foreign ownership of mining firms to 49 percent for all companies worth at least $75 million.

In March 2013 Mongolia and Japan announced plans for a free trade agreement. In May Mongolia and Canada signed a defense cooperation agreement that expanded exchanges and training exercises between the two militaries. Also in May, during a state visit by Thai Prime Minister Yingluck Shinawatra, Mongolia and Thailand finalized an agreement designed to double trade between the two countries by 2017.

Current issues. In the 2009 presidential election, Tsakhiagiyn Elbegdorj drew much of his electoral strength from young and urban voters. He was aided by the support of small parties, including the CWP and MGP. In the polling on May 24, Elbegdorj won with 51 percent of the vote. Enkhbayar conceded defeat immediately, relieving concerns about a repeat of the 2008 postelection violence. When Elbegdorj was sworn in on June 18, he became the first head of state in Mongolia's history as an independent nation who did not belong to the MPRP.

The main domestic issues facing the new administration in 2009 were the development of the nation's mineral resources and the equitable distribution of profits from mineral extraction. The Oyu Tolgoi (Turquoise Hill) copper-gold deposit, among the world's richest, was expected to create thousands of jobs and add 30 percent or more to Mongolia's GDP when fully operational. However, a final deal had been held up in the State Great Hural for several years as lawmakers debated how to determine the government's share of the project. During the presidential campaign, both the DP and the MPRP pledged a proportion of mining profits to the Mongolian people. The DP proposed that dividends be paid annually to citizens. President Elbegdorj opposed taking an equity stake in Oyu Tolgoi, preferring to leave the industry in private hands, but in July DP lawmakers proposed a 34 percent stake for the government, as the State Great Hural was under great pressure to conclude a deal swiftly.

In August 2009 a special session of parliament overwhelmingly approved terms for the Oyu Tolgoi investment agreement, granting the government a 34 percent stake in the project, which is to be developed by Canada's Ivanhoe Mines and Australia's Rio Tinto, and repealing a 68 percent windfall profits tax. In September the finance minister announced that the government would create a sovereign wealth fund from its share of the revenues from Oyu Tolgoi. Government and industry representatives signed the agreement on October 6 in Ulaanbaatar. Nevertheless, the $5 billion project—the largest in Mongolian history—remained controversial. In April 2010 more than 5,000 demonstrators, reportedly mostly rural dwellers and the urban poor, protested over the profit distribution.

The projected expansion of the Tavan Tolgoi coal mine, with the world's largest deposit of coking coal for steel production, received parliamentary approval in August 2011 to offer new contracts to foreign firms. The bidding process in particular proved controversial in the domestic media.

In January 2012 the DP withdrew from the MPP-led governing coalition ahead of national and local elections. The DP won the June balloting for the State Great Hural and formed a coalition government. Meanwhile, in August former president Enkhbayar was convicted on corruption charges and sentenced to four years in prison.

In October 2012 reports indicated that the government again launched negotiations to revise the Oyu Tolgoi contract with Rio Tinto. Also in October the falcon was named as the country's national bird (Mongolia is home to more than 6,800 falcons or about 45 percent of the world total). The designation was part of an effort to protect the raptor.

In January 2013 Mongolia conducted its first sovereign bond, raising $1.5 billion or 15 percent of GDP.

POLITICAL PARTIES

On March 23, 1990, the People's Great Hural ended the monopoly held by the Mongolian People's Revolutionary Party (MPRP), and other parties quickly formed. By 2000 Mongolia had 24 registered parties.

Prior to the provincial and local elections held in October 2000, a significant coalescence of forces occurred. The principal opponents of the MPRP, which had been returned to power three months earlier, were a six-party Coalition of Democratic Forces (the "Big Six"), led by the Mongolian National Democratic Party (MNDP) and the Mongolian Social Democratic Party (MSDP), and another eight-party grouping led by the Civil Will Party (CWP) and the Mongolian Republican Party (MRP). In December 2000 the MNDP and MSDP led the formation of a new Democratic Party (DP).

In June 2003 the DP and the Motherland–Mongolian Democratic New Socialist Party (M-MDNSP) announced formation of the Motherland Democratic Coalition—MDC (*Ekh Oron Ardchilsan Evsel*), as a consequence of which the MPRP faced a unified front of the major opposition parties in the June 2004 election. The MDC won 44.7 percent of the national vote and emerged with sufficient seats to demand a role in the new government. In December 2004 the M-MDNSP (renamed Motherland in 2005) withdrew from the MDC, which disbanded.

Twelve parties and one coalition were registered for the June 2008 State Great Hural election, which, under a new proportional representation system with a 5 percent threshold, was dominated by the MPRP and the DP. In 2009, given that only parliamentary parties may nominate candidates for the state presidency, the presidential race was a contest between MPRP and DP contenders, as the only other parties in the State Great Hural, the CWP and the MGP, decided to back the DP's Elbegdorj rather than risk splitting the opposition.

Government Parties:

Democratic Party—DP (*Ardchilsan Nam*). The DP was formed on December 6, 2000, by the merger of six parties and groups: the Mongolian National Democratic Party (MNDP), which dated from the 1992 merger of four opposition parties, including the Mongolian Democratic Party (MDP) of Sanjaasürengiyn Zorig; the Mongolian Social Democratic Party (MSDP), which ultimately broke away and reregistered as a separate party in January 2005 (see below); the Mongolian Democratic Party (MDP), which traced its roots to Zorig's earlier MDP and which had been formed in January 2000 by disaffected members of the MNDP; the Mongolian Democratic Renewal Party (MDRP), which was founded in 1994 and participated in the "Big Six" coalition for the October 2000 provincial and local elections; the Mongolian Religious Democratic Party (MRDP), a Buddhist party that was established in 1990 and later participated in the DU coalition; and a faction of the Mongolian Traditional United Party—MTUP (*Mongolyn Ulamjlaliin Negdsen Nam*).

The DP's founding chair was the MNDP's Dambyn DORLIGJAV, a former minister of defense. The party's 2001 presidential candidate, former MSDP chair Radnaasümbereliyn Gonchigdorj, finished second, with 36.6 percent of the vote. In the June 2004 State Great Hural election the DP won 26 of the MDC's 35 seats. The MDC and the MPRP then formed a coalition government led by the DP's Tsakhiagiyn ELBEGDORJ. In December the DP's national committee voted to overhaul the party's leadership and replace former prime minister Mendsaikhan Enkhsaikhan with Gonchigdorj. Enkhsaikhan nevertheless remained the party's 2005 candidate for president, finishing second with 19.7 percent of the vote. In February 2006 Enkhsaikhan, former prime minister Janlav Narantsatsralt, and Mishig Sonompil were dismissed from the party after casting deciding votes against the Elbegdorj government and then accepting cabinet posts in the new MPRP government.

At the party congress on March 30–April 1, 2006, former prime minister Elbegdorj was elected chair over Erdeniin BAT-UUL and two other candidates. In November 2007 the DP was the sole parliamentary party to oppose the designation of the MPRP's Bayar as prime minister.

Following the 2008 election for the State Great Hural, Elbegdorj challenged the results and accused the MPRP of stealing the election. For weeks, a walkout by all but two of the party's legislators blocked the seating of a new parliament. However, while the legislature remained in limbo, members of the MPRP and DP worked as a de facto interim government, and the DP subsequently joined a new government with the MPRP in November.

Nonovyn Altankhuyag was elected party chair in 2008, Elbegdorj having stepped down in August. Elbegdorj subsequently was tapped as the party's flag bearer for the 2009 presidential election. He became the first Mongolian president from a party other than the MPRP.

The DP won balloting for the State Great Hural, securing 31 seats. Altankhuyag was appointed prime minister and named a coalition government that included all of the legislative parties except for the MPP. In May 2013 at a party congress, Elbegdorj was unanimously renominated as the DP's presidential candidate. He was subsequently reelected president in June.

Leaders: Tsakhiagiyn ELBEGDORJ (President of the Republic), Nonovyn ALTANKHUYAG (Prime Minister and Chair of the Party), T. OYUNDARI (General Secretary).

Civil Will—Green Party—CW-GP (*Irgenii Zorig—Nogoon Nam*). The center-left CW-GP was formed by a merger of the Civil Will Party—CWP (*Irgenii Zorig* Nam) and the Mongolian Green Party—MGP (*Mongol Nogoon Nam*) in March 2012. Sanjaasuren OYUN of the CWP was elected as the groupings first chair. The centrist CWP was registered in March 2000 under the leadership of Oyun, sister of the slain MNDP activist and cabinet member Sanjaasürengiyn Zorig. The CWP campaigned in coalition with the MGP for the July 2000 legislative election, with Oyun winning its only seat.

In September 2000 Oyun was elected chair of an eight-party opposition coalition to contest the October 2000 provincial and local elections. Participants included the Mongolian Republican Party (MRP), the Mongolian Liberal Democratic Party (MLDP), the Mongolian Civil Democratic New Liberal Party, and the Party for Mongolia (PM), which was established by Luvsandambyn DASHNYAM in 1998 and which agreed to join the CWP in December 2000. For the 2001 presidential election the CWP nominated Dashnyam, who captured only 3.5 percent of the vote.

In February 2002 the CWP and the MRP merged to form the Civil Will Republican Party—CWRP (*Irgenii Zorig Najramdakh Bügd Nam*), but they separated in December 2003 (see the RP, below), although the CWRP retained "Republican" in its name when it reregistered in April 2004. It then entered the national election campaign as part of the MDC, winning two State Great Hural seats. In January 2006 the party reestablished itself as the CWP.

Despite the objections of some members, in 2007 the party decided to join the MPRP-led coalition government. Oyun accepted the post of foreign minister under Prime Minister Bayar. She won the party's only seat in the 2008 parliamentary election. In the 2009 presidential election, the CWP supported Elbegdorj, Oyun expressing hope that he would help reconcile the nation's partisan divide.

The MGP was organized in 1990 as the political arm of the Mongolian Alliance of Greens. It competed as part of the DU in 1996 but failed to win any seats. For the July 2000 election it was allied with the CWP, but for the October provincial and local elections, the MGP participated in the six-party Coalition of Democratic Forces. Unlike its fellow coalition members, however, it later announced that its agenda prevented it from joining in the DP merger. In 2001 the MGP supported the presidential candidacy of the DP's Gonchigdorj. It ran six unsuccessful candidates for the State Great Hural in 2004.

In the 2008 elections for the State Great Hural, the MGP ran as part of the **Civil Alliance** (*Irgenii Evsel*), and its leader, Dangaasuren ENKHBAT, was declared the winner of a seat in Bayangol after a lengthy investigation of the vote. He quickly formed a Green Group in the State Great Hural to advocate for ecological approaches to the mining industry. In 2009 the Green Party supported the DP's Tsakhiagiyn Elbegdorj for president.

The CW-GP secured two seats in the 2012 parliamentary elections and joined the DP-led coalition government with Oyun appointed as minister of the environment. The CW-GP endorsed Elbegdorj of the DP in the 2013 presidential election.

Leader: Sanjaasuren OYUN.

Justice Coalition—JC (*Shudarga Yos Evsel*). The JC was an electoral coalition between the newly formed **Mongolian People's Revolutionary Front**—MPRP (*Mongol Ardiin Khuvsgalt Nam*) and the small **Mongolian National Democratic Party** (MNDP). The MPRP was formed by former president Nambaryn Enkhbayar in 2011 with dissidents from the MPP. The MNDP was established as the **National New Party**—NNP (*Ündesnii Shine Nam*) by Janlav NARANTSATSRALT and Mendsaikhan Enkhsaikhan following their expulsion from the DP for joining the MPRP government in February 2006. Narantsatsralt died in November 2007. In September 2011 the NNP voted to change its name to the Mongolian National Democratic Party.

The JC secured 11 seats in the 2012 legislative balloting and was given three portfolios in the subsequent DP-led coalition government.

The MPRP nominated Natsag UDVAL as its presidential candidate. Although she placed third, Udval was the first woman presidential candidate in Mongolia. Meanwhile the MNDP supported the DP's Elbegdorj in the balloting, creating tensions within the coalition.

Leaders: Nambaryn ENKHBAYAR (Former President of the Republic and MPRP Chair), Dendev TERBISHDAGVA (Deputy Prime Minister), Mendsaikhan ENKHSAIKHAN (MNDP Chair), Natsagiin UDVAL (Minister of Health and 2013 presidential candidate).

Opposition Party:

Mongolian People's Party—MPP (*Mongol Ardyn Nam*). Initially founded as the MPP in 1921, the party was renamed the Mongolian People's Revolutionary Party—MPRP (*Mongol Ardyn Khuv'sgalt Nam*) in 1924, before reverting to its original name in 2010. Organized along typical communist lines for nearly seven decades, its tightly centralized structure was nominally subject to party congresses meeting at five-year intervals (for more on the party's history, please see the 2013 *Handbook*).

In 1993 the party's presidential candidate, Lodongiyn Tudev, editor of the party newspaper, lost to the incumbent, Punsalmaagiyn Ochirbat, who had maintained nominal MPRP membership despite being denied renomination and running as a joint candidate of the MNDP and MSDP. In a further setback, the MPRP's legislative representation plummeted to 25 seats in the 1996 election, a loss of 46 from its 1992 total. In 1997, however, the party's chair, Natsagiyn Bagabandi, won a landslide presidential victory, defeating President Ochirbat, who had formally resigned from the party to run as the DU candidate.

In 1999 a contemporary Mongolian People's Party (MPP), founded in 1991, merged with the MPRP, although a number of party dissidents continued to claim the MPP name.

In the July 2000 general election the MPRP won 72 of 76 seats in the State Great Hural, after which the party chair, Nambaryn Enkhbayar, won easy confirmation as prime minister. In local elections in October, the MPRP controlled all 21 provincial legislatures.

In June 2004 the party won 46.5 percent of the national vote but lost half its seats in the State Great Hural. Shy of a legislative majority, the MPRP courted the three parliamentary independents but was unsuccessful and therefore entered into negotiations with the opposition MDC for a coalition government. Ultimately, Prime Minister Enkhbayar agreed to step down and was elected chair of the legislature.

In May 2005 Enkhbayar was elected president, succeeding Bagabandi. A month later, following Enkhbayar's mandatory resignation as party chair, the MPRP elected Miyegombo Enkhbold, mayor of Ulaanbaatar, as his successor. Enkhbold became prime minister in January 2006 after ten MPRP ministers resigned from the Elbegdorj government, forcing its collapse. A wave of public protest followed, as the formerly communist MPRP stood accused of undermining democracy.

In June 2007 the MPRP's Tsend NYAMDORJ resigned as chair of the State Great Hural shortly after the Constitutional Court ruled that he had acted unconstitutionally in amending laws. At the party's congress in October, the secretary general, Sanj Bayar, successfully challenged Enkhbold for the party chair, winning 57 percent of the votes. As a consequence, Enkhbold resigned as prime minister and was succeeded by Bayar.

On July 1, 2008, the MPRP won a majority in legislative elections, but following accusations of vote fraud, an angry throng set fire to the MPRP headquarters in the capital. In the 2009 presidential election the MPRP was defeated for the first time since popular elections for that office began in 1990. President Enkhbayar's loss to the DP's Tsakhiagiyn Elbegdorj led to internal criticism of the party's strategy and turnover of its local leadership. Some younger party members sought to open the party to new reformist leadership and wider debate of strategy and policy. The party also considered adopting the name Mongolian Democratic Development Party but ultimately decided against a change.

On April 8, 2010, former prime minister Sanj BAYAR resigned as chair of the party and nominated in his place the current prime minister, Sukhbaatar Batbold, who easily won election.

In November 2010 the party was renamed the MPP. However, Enkhbayar disagreed with the decision and led a faction of the MPP into schism, founding a new organization, the new Mongolian People's Revolutionary Party (MPRP). After the MPP placed second in legislative balloting in June 2012, Batbold resigned as party leader and was replaced by Ulziisaikhan Enkhtuvshin.

The MPP nominated nationally famous wrestler Badmaanyambuugin BAT-ERDENE as its 2013 presidential candidate. He placed second in the polling.

Leaders: Ulziisaikhan ENKHTUVSHIN (Chair), Ukhnaa KHURELSUKH (General Secretary).

Other Parties:

Mongolian Social Democratic Party—MSDP (*Mongolyn Sotsial Ardchilsan Nam*). The MSDP called at its inaugural congress in March 1990 for a just and humane society patterned on the values espoused by social democratic parties in the West. The party's legislative representation fell from 7 (overall) in 1990 to 1 in 1992, but it won 12 State Great Hural seats in 1996 as part of the DU. One of its leaders, Radnaasümbereliyn Gonchigdorj, served as state vice president and chair of the State Great Hural before running as a DP candidate for president. The party lost all its State Great Hural seats in the July 2000 election and in September agreed to merge with the MNDP. The DP resulted in December.

In December 2004, however, objecting to DP policies, the MSDP separated from the DP. It was reregistered as a separate party on January 20, 2005, although the DP protested the restoration of the party's name. The MSDP held a party congress in March 2008 but did not field candidates in the elections for the State Great Hural. It failed to win seats in the 2012 balloting.

Leaders: Adyagiin GANBAATAR (Chair), Ts. SAIKHANBILEG (Secretary General).

Motherland Party (*Ekh Oron Nam*). Motherland began as the Mongolian Democratic New Socialist Party (*Mongoliin Ardchilsan Shine Sotsialist Nam*—MDNSP). The MDNSP was organized in 1998 under the auspices of Badarch Erdenebat, the wealthy director general of the Erel Company. The new formation quickly attracted defectors from other parties, including the MPRP.

In mid-1999 the MDNSP and the Mongolian Workers' Party (*Mongolyn Ajilchny Nam*—MWP) announced formation of a leftist Motherland coalition. Although the MWP offered its own candidates in the July 2000 election, Erdenebat ran under the banner of the Motherland-MDNSP (M-MDNSP), winning the organization's sole seat.

The M-MDNSP supported President Bagabandi's 2001 reelection but in June 2004 ran as part of the MDC, from which it withdrew at the end of December, in part because of Erdenebat's presidential aspirations. He served as minister of defense in the Elbegdorj cabinet until February 2005 and finished fourth, with 11.4 percent of the vote, in the May presidential election as candidate of Motherland, as the party had been renamed in January. Erdenebat served in the Enkhbold cabinet of 2006–2007 but lost his seat in parliament in the 2008 election. The party failed to secure any seats in the 2012 legislative elections. The party supported Elbegdorj of the DP in the 2013 presidential elections.

Leader: Badarch ERDENEBAT (Chair).

Republican Party—RP (*Bügd Najramdahk Nam*). The RP traces its origins to the 1992 launching of the Mongolian Capitalists' Party, which changed its name to the Mongolian Republican Party (MRP) in 1997.

In early 2002 the MRP merged with the CWP (above) to form the Civil Will Republican Party (CWRP), but the MRP reemerged as the RP in December 2003 because of its leaders' opposition to contesting the 2004 national election in alliance with the DP. Longtime leader Bazarsadiin Jargalsaikhan won the party's only seat in that polling.

In May 2005 Jargalsaikhan won 13.9 percent of the vote in the presidential election. He joined the Enkhbold coalition cabinet in January 2006 as minister of industry and commerce but left in February 2007 because of discontent with mining law reforms. He lost his Hural seat in the 2008 election. The RP endorsed Elbegdorj in the 2013 presidential balloting.

Leader: Bazarsadiin JARGALSAIKHAN.

For more information on the **Civil Movement Party** (CMP), please see the 2012 *Handbook.*

LEGISLATURE

State Great Hural (*Ulsyn Ikh Khural*). The 76 members of the Great Hural are popularly elected for four-year terms. In the election on June 28, 2012, Mongolia introduced a mixed system in which 48 seats were elected by majority vote in single-member districts and the remaining 28 elected through a proportional voting system based on party lists, with parties winning at least 5 percent of the national vote being awarded seats. Twenty percent of a party's candidates must be women. Following the June 28, 2012, elections, the seat distribution was as follows: the Democratic Party (DP), 31; Mongolian People's Party (MPP), 25; Justice Coalition (JC), 11; Civil Will—Green Party (CW-GP), 2; independents, 3; and four vacancies awaiting new voting.

Chair: Zandaakhuugiin ENKHBOLD.

CABINET

[as of August 15, 2013]

Prime Minister	Norovyn Altankhuyag (DP)
Deputy Prime Minister	Dendev Terbishdagva (MPRP)
Ministers	
Construction and Urban Development	Tsevelmaa Bayarsaikhan (DP)
Culture, Sport, and Tourism	Tsedevdamba Oyungerel (DP) [f]
Defense	Dashdemberel Bat-Erdene (DP)
Economic Development	Nyamjav Batbayar (DP)
Education and Science	Luvsannyam Gantumur (DP)
Energy	Mishig Sonompil (ind.)
Environment	Sanjaasuren Oyun (CW-GP) [f]
Finance	Chultem Ulaan (MPRP)
Foreign Affairs	Luvsanvandan Bold (DP)
Health	Natsag Udval (MPRP)
Industry and Agriculture	Khaltmaa Battulga (DP)
Justice and Home Affairs	Khishigdemberel Temuujin (DP)
Labor	Yadamsuren Sanjmyatav (DP)
Mining	Davaajav Gankhuyag (DP)
Population and Social Welfare	Sodnomzundui Erdene (DP)
Roads and Transportation	Amarjargal Gansukh (DP)
Chief of Government Secretariat	Chimed Saikhanbileg (DP)

[f] = female

INTERGOVERNMENTAL REPRESENTATION

Ambassador to the U.S.: Khasbazar BEKHBAT.

U.S. Ambassador to Mongolia: Piper CAMPBELL.

Permanent Representative to the UN: Od OCH.

IGO Memberships (Non-UN): ADB, EBRD, ICC, IOM, NAM, SCO, WTO.

MONTENEGRO

Republic of Montenegro
Republika Crna Gora

Political Status: An autonomous principality formally independent of the Ottoman Empire in 1878; declared a kingdom in 1910; incorporated as part of the Kingdom of the Serbs, Croats, and Slovenes, which was constituted as an independent monarchy on December 1, 1918, and formally renamed Yugoslavia on October 3, 1929; constituent republic of the communist Federal People's Republic of Yugoslavia instituted November 29, 1945, and then of the Socialist Federal Republic of Yugoslavia proclaimed April 7, 1963; constituent republic, along with Serbia, of the Federal Republic of Yugoslavia proclaimed April 27, 1992, and of the "state union" of Serbia and Montenegro established February 4, 2003, under new Constitutional Charter; Republic of Montenegro established June 3, 2006, following an independence referendum on May 21; new constitution adopted by the legislature (sitting as a Constituent Assembly) on October 19, 2007, and promulgated October 22.

Area: 5,333 sq. mi. (13,812 sq. km).

Population: 648,675 (2012E—UN); 653,000 (2013E—U.S. Census).

Major Urban Centers (2011C): PODGORICA (formerly Titograd, 156,000).

Official Languages: Montenegrin; however, in areas established by national minorities, their languages (Albanian, Bosnian, Croatian, Serbian) are also accorded official status.

Monetary Unit: Euro (market rate November 1, 2013: 0.74 euro = $1US). The euro has been legal tender in Montenegro since January 1, 2002.

President: Filip VUJANOVIĆ (Democratic Party of Socialists of Montenegro); served as Montenegrin prime minister 1998–2002; elected chair of the Montenegrin Assembly on November 5, 2002, following the legislative election of October 20, and thus became acting president upon the resignation of President Milo DJUKANOVIĆ on November 25; elected president for a five-year term on May 11, 2003, and inaugurated June 13; reelected president in the first postindependence presidential election on April 6, 2008, and inaugurated on May 20; reelected again on April 7, 2013, and inaugurated on May 20.

Prime Minister: Milo DJUKANOVIĆ (Democratic Party of Socialists of Montenegro); nominated by the president on November 9, 2012 and confirmed by the legislature on December 4, succeeding Igor LUKŠIĆ (Democratic Party of Socialists of Montenegro).

THE COUNTRY

Montenegro is a Balkan republic, mostly mountainous, with a 180-mile coastline along the Adriatic Sea. The terrain, part of the Karst Plateau, is renowned for its rugged scenery. The country is bordered by Albania to the south, Serbia and Kosovo to the east, and Bosnia and Herzegovina to the north. Per the results of the 2011 census, Montenegrins constitute 45 percent of the population, Serbs 28.7 percent, Bosniaks 8.7 percent, Albanians 4.9 percent, and various other

ethnic groups (e.g., Croats and Roma) the remainder. Such categories obscure the complicated nature of identity, however, since ethnicity and "mother tongue" notably diverged on the census, particularly along the Montenegrin-Serbian divide (37 percent registering Montenegrin as their native language, 42.9 percent Serbian). Eastern Orthodox Christianity predominates, although there is a large Muslim minority (19.1 percent), a legacy of the Ottoman Empire.

Industrial production, which was badly damaged by the United Nations (UN) economic sanctions imposed against Yugoslavia in the 1990s, is concentrated in hydroelectricity generation; the extraction and processing of raw materials, especially bauxite, and also coal, lumber, and salt; and production of aluminum and steel. Processing of tobacco and food is also a major manufacturing activity. The industrial sector as a whole comprises 11 percent of GDP and employs approximately 21 percent of the total workforce, compared to 88 percent of GDP and 73 percent of employment for services. Only about 14 percent of the total area of the country is suitable for cultivation so that agriculture employs 6 percent of the workforce and contributes 1 percent to GDP. Tourism, concentrated along the Adriatic coastline, has been targeted for expansion.

Following independence, GDP grew at an annual rate of 7.6 percent from 2005 through 2008. Challenges include rebuilding neglected infrastructure, curbing public-sector corruption, boosting private-sector employment, and suppressing the enormous black-market sector that developed during the period of sanctions. Foreign investment, particularly in finance and tourism, has grown since independence, and in 2007 Montenegro had the third highest investment per capita ratio in Europe. The international financial crisis of 2008–2009 led to GDP contraction of 5.7 percent in 2009, fueled in part by the decline of the foreign-owned Kombinat Aluminijuma Podgorica aluminum processing facility, which in 2008 had accounted for 15 percent of the country's GDP. The economy had rebounded to 2.5 percent annual growth in 2010 and 2011. Economic development has addressed the widespread unemployment of the 1990s, although the official unemployment rate in June 2013 reached 13.1 percent. GDP growth slowed to 0.03 percent in 2012, but the International Monetary Fund (IMF) estimates 1.2 percent growth in 2013.

GOVERNMENT AND POLITICS

Political background. Following centuries of struggle against the Ottoman Empire, an autonomous Montenegrin principality emerged over the 16th and 18th centuries. As with Serbia, in the 19th century Montenegro broke all but nominal ties to the Ottomans, finally achieving formal independence in 1878. The newly independent state was both an ally and rival to Serbia, with Prince (later, King) NIKOLA I himself hoping to unify Serbian-inhabited lands. Montenegro's incorporation on December 1, 1918, into the Kingdom of the Serbs, Croats, and Slovenes under the Serbian House of Karadjordjević led to a brief civil war. Montenegro was initially a constituent part of the kingdom, was later incorporated into the Banovina of Zeta in 1929 as part of King ALEKSANDAR'S efforts to reduce inter-ethnic identities, then became a constituent republic of the Federal People's Republic of Yugoslavia in 1945 (see the Political background in the Serbia entry for details). As with other republics, Montenegro gained greater autonomy in the federal constitution of 1963 and following the death of Marshal Josip Broz TITO in 1980.

Economic ills set off a series of events that led to the dissolution of greater Yugoslavia into the independent states of Croatia, Slovenia, Bosnia and Herzegovina, and Macedonia, with only Serbia and Montenegro remaining in a diminished federation. In February 1992 Serbia and Montenegro agreed to join in upholding "the principles of a common state which would be a continuation of Yugoslavia." In April a rump Federal Assembly adopted the constitution of a new Federal Republic of Yugoslavia (FRY).

In 1996 the Democratic Party of Socialists of Montenegro (*Demokratska Partija Socijalista Crne Gore*—DPS) achieved a majority in elections for the separate Montenegrin Assembly. On July 15, 1997, Slobodan MILOŠEVIĆ, constitutionally barred from running for a third term as president of Serbia, was elected unopposed as the Yugoslav federal president. However, he continued to face electoral threats to his power. Montenegrin Prime Minister Milo DJUKANOVIĆ led a faction of the DPS against Milošević's local allies, culminating in Djukanović's victory over Bulatović in the second round of the 1997 presidential elections (see the entry in the 2011 *Handbook*).

The new president took office on January 13, 1998, despite violent protests by Bulatović supporters. Through mediation by Yugoslav Prime Minister Radoje KONTIĆ (a Montenegrin), on January 21 the demonstrators agreed to settle for early legislative elections in May 1998. A transitional government under the leadership of the DPS's Filip VUJANOVIĆ was appointed on February 4. It included 17 ministers from Djukanović's DPS faction, 7 from the opposition, and 4 independents; the Bulatović faction of the DPS as well as the pro-independence Liberal Alliance of Montenegro (*Liberalni Savez Crne Gore*—LSCG) refused to participate.

On May 19, 1998, former Montenegrin president Bulatović was named prime minister of Yugoslavia. On May 31, however, Montenegrin voters awarded 49.5 percent of the vote and a majority of seats in the Montenegrin Assembly to President Djukanović's For a Better Life electoral coalition, while Bulatović's recently organized Socialist People's Party of Montenegro (*Socijalistička Narodna Partija Crne Gore*—SNP) claimed 36 percent of the vote and emerged as the leading opposition party. Montenegro's interim prime minister, Vujanović, was reappointed on July 16 to head a government encompassing the three coalition partners: the DPS, the People's Party (*Narodna Stranka*—NS), and the Social Democratic Party of Montenegro (*Socijaldemokratska Partija Crne Gore*—SDP).

In 1999 Montenegrin president Djukanović continued his efforts to distance his administration from federal policies in regard to Kosovo, particularly "ethnic cleansing" of ethnic Albanians, which had precipitated military action by the United States and other North Atlantic Treaty Organization (NATO) countries (see the Serbia entry for details). Even though Montenegro was not exempt from the NATO air campaign, and despite rumors that the Serbian military was preparing to depose him, on April 21 Djukanović rejected orders that the Montenegrin police be placed under the command of the FRY army. Djukanović accused Milošević of using "the pretext of the defense of the country" to displace the civil government. Later, the republican government proposed replacing the federal republic with a looser association in which Montenegro would set its own foreign and military policy and establish independent currency controls.

In July 2000 Milošević's allies pushed through the Federal Assembly constitutional changes designed to maintain his hold on power. The changes included directly electing the president, permitting the incumbent to serve two additional four-year terms, and putting organization of elections under the FRY instead of the individual republics. Although the Montenegrin Assembly described the changes as "illegal" and "a gross violation of the constitutional rights of the Republic of Montenegro," the legislators rejected a proposal for an immediate referendum on Montenegrin independence. In late July Milošević called elections for September, even though his presidential term would not expire until July 2001. The governing coalition in Montenegro quickly announced that it would boycott the balloting. The federal election of September 24 was followed by two weeks of turmoil that concluded with the demise of the Milošević regime and the inauguration on October 7 of Vojislav KOŠTUNICA.

On December 28, 2000, the NS withdrew from Montenegro's governing coalition in opposition to further movement toward independence. Four months later, President Djukanović entered the Montenegrin Assembly election of April 22, 2001, banking on a strong vote for separation from Serbia, but his DPS-SDP alliance failed to achieve more than a slight plurality against a coalition of the SNP, the NS, and the Serbian People's Party (*Srpska Narodna Stranka*—SNS). Three seats short of a majority, Djukanović turned to the Liberal Alliance, which agreed to extend external support to a new Vujanović cabinet, but the government's minority status soon forced the president to backtrack on plans for an immediate independence referendum.

On March 14, 2002, the governments of the Federal Republic of Yugoslavia and its two constituent republics announced an "agreement in principle" that would bring the history of Yugoslavia as such to an end, with its replacement by a "state union" to be called Serbia and Montenegro. Over the objections of parties that wanted a separate and independent Serbia, the Serbian legislature ratified the accord 149–79 on April 9. The same day, the Montenegrin legislature voted in favor of the agreement 58–11, despite strong opposition from the SDP and the previously government-supportive LSCG, both of which favored Montenegrin independence. Four SDP-affiliated ministers quickly resigned from the Montenegrin cabinet, and on April 19 Prime Minister Vujanović submitted his resignation, announcing that his government no longer commanded a legislative majority. At President Djukanović's request, Vujanović attempted to fashion another government, but he was unable to do so, and in July the president called for an early legislative election. Meanwhile, on May 31 both chambers of the Federal Assembly had approved the state union agreement by wide margins.

The Montenegrin Assembly election of October 20, 2002, saw a list headed by the DPS win 39 of 75 seats, compared to 30 for an opposition coalition. Following the election, caretaker Prime Minister Vujanović was elected speaker of the Montenegrin legislature. On November 25 Milo Djukanović resigned as president of Montenegro, and a day later Speaker Vujanović, in his new capacity as acting president, nominated Djukanović for the prime ministership (the office he had previously held from 1991 to 1998). Vujanović then ran in the Montenegrin presidential election of December 22. Although he won an overwhelming majority, an opposition boycott held the turnout under 50 percent, invalidating the results and forcing a similarly unsuccessful revote on February 9, 2003. In response, the Montenegrin Assembly eliminated the 50 percent requirement, and on May 11 Vujanović was elected president with 63 percent of the vote. Meanwhile, on January 8 Djukanović had been confirmed as prime minister.

On January 27 and 29, 2003, the Serbian and then the Montenegrin assemblies approved the Constitutional Charter for the state union of Serbia and Montenegro. The Federal Assembly concurred on February 4 (by votes of 26–7 in the upper chamber and 84–31 in the lower), thereby excising Yugoslavia from the political map. Under the charter a new state union assembly was elected by and from among the members of the FRY, Serbian, and Montenegrin legislatures, and the new assembly in turn elected the DPS's MAROVIĆ, the only candidate, as state union president and chair of the Council of Ministers on March 7.

Under their 2003 European Union (EU)-backed state union agreement, both Serbia and Montenegro had the right to vote on the question of independence in three years. On May 21, 2006, by a vote of 55.5 percent to 44.5 percent (half a percentage point above the EU threshold for approval), Montenegrins chose independence. Two weeks later, on June 3, the Montenegrin Assembly declared independence. On June 5, although many Serbians were unhappy with what they viewed as an abrupt divorce, the Serbian National Assembly declared Serbia to be the independent successor state to the state union, as had been agreed upon under the charter, and thereby extinguished the last remnants of the former Yugoslavia.

Opposition parties in Montenegro seized on cultural anxieties raised by the slim pro-independence margin. For example, petition drives demanding dual Montenegrin-Serbian citizenship sprang up soon after the votes were counted. Meanwhile, the pro-independence Bosniak and Albanian leadership was dismayed that the Constitutional Court had struck down the Minority Rights Act, which guaranteed seats in the assembly to minority groups based on their proportion in the population, even if they fell below the usual electoral threshold. The act had been passed just ten days before the referendum, after these leaders had made the bill a condition for their support of independence.

In the Montenegrin election of September 10, 2006, a coalition led by the DPS and SDP won a majority of 41 seats in the expanded 81-seat Montenegrin legislature. A multiparty opposition Serbian List, headed by the SNS, won 12 seats, while another ethnic Serbian coalition led by the SNP won 11. The new Movement for Change (*Pokret za Promjene*—PzP) also won 11 seats. On October 3 President Vujanović revealed that Prime Minister Djukanović had decided not to seek reappointment as prime minister, although he would remain at the helm of the DPS. A day later, Vujanović asked the minister of justice, Željko ŠTURANOVIĆ, to form a new government, and on November 10 the legislature confirmed the revamped Council of Ministers.

The closeness of the September 2006 assembly election left the legislature sharply divided on a number of hot-button issues for the minority communities, especially the Serb population. Their concerns, as reflected in the process of drafting a new constitution, included whether minority representation should be guaranteed not only in the legislature but also in the government bureaucracy and agencies, how much autonomy minorities would be accorded with respect to education and cultural matters, and whether Serbian should remain the official language. Disputes also raged over state symbols, including the national coat-of-arms, the national anthem, and the design of the flag.

In early April 2007 the assembly, after a week of heated debate, adopted a constitutional draft that included alternatives proposed by minority representatives, and a period of "public debate" ensued. By August, however, neither the government majority nor the opposition appeared willing to compromise on the remaining issues. Apart from the concerns of the ethnic minority parties, the largest opposition party, the PzP, demanded that the government agree to a snap election upon adoption of the constitution. The DPS-SDP refused, but in the end the PzP and the BS voiced support for the proposed constitution, which, with 55 votes in favor and 21 against, achieved the two-thirds tally needed for passage. Most ethnic Albanian representatives abstained, while the Serbs voted in opposition.

On January 31, 2008, Prime Minister Šturanović resigned, citing health issues, and on February 20 President Vujanović once again nominated Milo Djukanović, who won confirmation on February 29. On April 6 Vujanović was reelected for another term in the first presidential elections since independence. In the first round of voting, Vujanović (51.9 percent of the vote) won an absolute majority over the Serb List candidate Andrija MANDIĆ (19.6 percent), PzP candidate Nebojša MEDOJEVIĆ (16.6 percent), and SNP candidate Srdjan MILIĆ (11.9 percent). Vujanović was inaugurated for his second term on May 21, 2008.

In January 2009 Prime Minister Djukanović proposed early elections although the sitting parliament had a year of its term remaining. Djukanović argued that new elections would provide a four-year mandate for a government to negotiate EU membership. The parliament voted for dissolution by a thin majority, the opposition arguing that the government hoped to use early elections to avoid voter retaliation for slowing economic growth.

In the parliamentary election of March 29, 2009, the Coalition for a European Montenegro (*Koalicija za Evropska Crna Gora*—KzECG) of the DPS, SDP, BS, and Croat Civic Initiative (*Hrvatska Gradjanska Inicijativa*—HGI) won 48 out of 81 seats; they were subsequently joined in forming a government by the Democratic Union of Albanians (*Demokratska Unija Albanaca*—DUA/*Unioni Demokratih i Shqiptarëve*—UDSh), a small Albanian political party with 1 seat. The SNP led the opposition with 16 seats, while the New Serb Democracy (*Nova Srpska Demokracija*—NSD) won 8 and the PzP won 5, with the remaining 3 seats being split between small Albanian political parties. Djukanović was reconfirmed as prime minister on June 10.

A new electoral law (see Constitution and government, below) was passed in 2011, responding to the Constitutional Court's 2006 decision on the Minority Rights Act. The new law reserved five seats for minority parties but in a way interpreted by local analysts as reducing the influence of the ethnic Albanian minority.

On July 26, 2012, the ruling coalition voted to dissolve parliament. The government justified early elections by stressing the need to create a new government to respond to the challenges of EU accession. Local analysts have suggested it was timed to take place before unpopular austerity measures could diminish the popularity of the DPS.

In the parliamentary election of October 14, 2012, the KZECG, now comprised of the DPS, SDP, and the Liberal Party of Montenegro (*Liberalna Partija Crne Gore*—LPCG) won 39 out of 81 seats. They formed a government with the support of ethnic minority parties: the BS, with 3 seats, and the single seats each held by the HGI, Albanian Coalition (*Albanska Koalicija/Koalicioni Shqiptare*—AK/KS), and the New Democratic Force (*Nova Demokratska Snaga/Forca e Re Demokratike*—FORCA). The Democratic Front (*Demokratski front*—DF), a coalition including the NSD and PzP, led the opposition with 20 seats, the SNP won 9, and the newly formed Positive Montenegro (*Pozitivna Crna Gora*—PCG) won 7.

Vujanović's candidacy for a third term in the 2013 presidential elections was controversial because the constitution mandates a two-term limit. In February the SDP sided with the opposition and lodged a court challenge in the Constitutional Court. The court, however, ruled that the constitutional limit applies only to terms after the election of 2008. On April 7 Vujanović was reelected on the first round, with 51.2 percent of the vote, over the joint opposition candidate, Miodrag LEKIĆ (48.8 percent). The opposition had appealed the results several times, but the Constitutional Court rejected the final appeals.

Constitution and government. At independence, Montenegrins had yet to craft a process for drafting and approving a new constitution for the republic. A parliamentary drafting committee, assisted by the OSCE, succeeded in enumerating a variety of basic rights, such as freedom of speech, press, assembly, and association as well as presumption of innocence and the right to a fair and public trial. The committee also laid out a governmental structure based on the division of powers among executive, legislative, and judicial branches, complete with a system of checks and balances. The new basic law was approved by the assembly, sitting as a Constituent Assembly, on October 19, 2007, and promulgated on October 22.

Under the constitution the president is elected for a five-year term. The term of the unicameral assembly, subject to early dissolution, is four years, with a 3 percent threshold to gain representation. Until 2011 the minority Albanian community was guaranteed representation with five seats allocated to a separate minority bloc. The electoral law was amended in September 2011, however. Five seats are now allocated for Albanian, Bosnian, and Croat minority parties. If no party for a given minority reaches the threshold of 3 percent, the threshold is reduced to 0.7 percent (except for the Croat minority, at 0.4 percent). Up to three seats per ethnic group may be gained through such lowered thresholds.

The government is headed by a prime minister nominated by the president and confirmed by the legislature. The judiciary includes a Constitutional Court and a Supreme Court. Local government is based on 21 municipalities.

Reporters Without Borders ranks Montenegro as 113th worldwide in 2013 in respect to press freedom. Threats of violence, arson, and the use of libel suits to intimidate the press have been reported by local journalists, and several physical attacks were reported in 2013.

Foreign relations. As a constituent republic of the Federal Republic of Yugoslavia in the 1990s and then of the state union, Montenegro suffered from the international sanctions imposed because of the policies of the Slobodan Milošević era (see the Serbia entry). Following the defeat of Milošević in 2000, the new Yugoslav government moved broadly to reestablish its international linkages. FRY was formally reintegrated into the UN on November 1 and into the Organization for Security and Cooperation in Europe (OSCE) on November 27. In April 2003 it joined the Council of Europe, and two months later it applied for membership in NATO's Partnership for Peace (PfP) program.

Just days after the declaration of independence, President Vujanović sent a letter to the UN seeking membership for Montenegro. The United States, the EU and its member nations, Russia, China, and many other governments quickly recognized Montenegrin independence shortly thereafter. The UN admitted Montenegro as its 192nd member on June 28, 2006, not long after Montenegro became the 56th member of the OSCE. It has subsequently been admitted to the International Monetary Fund, the World Bank, and other UN-related organizations, and in May 2007 it became the newest member of the Council of Europe. Two months earlier, Montenegro and the EU initialed a Stabilization and Association Agreement, regarded as the first step toward eventual EU membership. The Montenegrin government joined NATO's Partnership for Peace (PfP) program in December 2006 and applied for NATO membership on November 5, 2008. It formally began the EU integration process by applying for membership on December 15, 2008.

Despite both historical ties to Serbia and divided domestic popular opinion, the Montenegrin government recognized the independence of Kosovo on October 9, 2008. Serbia subsequently expelled the Montenegrin ambassador to Belgrade, with relations sinking to their lowest level since Montenegrin independence. Negotiations regarding dual citizenship, begun in October 2008, were one casualty of weakened relations, with talks continuing into 2009 with no resolution. The large number of Slavic Montenegrins identifying themselves as ethnically Serbian makes the issue particularly sensitive for the DPS.

A Membership Action Plan was signed with NATO in December 2009, outlining the formal steps the country must take to join the alliance. In March 2010 Montenegro deployed soldiers for the NATO mission in Afghanistan, currently a force of 27 as of June 2013. The contribution sparked domestic opposition, but the government defended the policy as a demonstration of its commitment to NATO.

On May 1, 2010, Montenegro became an associate member of the EU. On December 17, 2010, Montenegro was granted candidate status in the EU. On October 12, 2011, the European Commission recommended that accession negotiations should be opened, while highlighting the need for further reform to combat corruption and organized crime. On April 29, 2012, Montenegro was admitted to the World Trade Organization (WTO). Accession negotiations with the EU opened on June 29, 2012.

Current issues. Milo Djukanović continues to be reviled by many opponents, who have labeled him as corrupt (Italian officials have accused him of tobacco smuggling) and tyrannical. Nevertheless, as the acknowledged architect of Montenegrin independence, he remains the country's most prominent politician internationally.

Questions of symbolism continue to play a role in politics. The 2007 constitution made Montenegrin the official language of the country. Polls in that year showed that over 50 percent of the country preferred to refer to the language as Serbian, a position backed by the pro-union opposition. In June 2008 the SPD proposed that the capital be moved to the historic royal capital of Cetinje (recognized as such within the 2007 constitution), a move criticized by the SNS. In June 2009 a new Montenegrin Latin alphabet was announced as standard, replacing the existing Serbian Latin and Cyrillic alphabets; in July, a new official standard for the language was announced.

In August 2010 the government announced a new action plan to combat corruption, but opposition parties, domestic NGOs, and foreign observers criticized the plan as lacking clear goals and as having been devised without public input. The European Commission noted in November 2010 that "organized crime remains a problem" and that "corruption... constitutes a particularly serious problem."

On December 21, 2011, Djukanović resigned, stating that he had achieved his goals of creating a stable Montenegro and initiating accession into NATO and the EU. Despite having been in high office since the early 1990s, Djukanović is only in his 40s, and he may well play a key a role in advancing Montenegro's integration into the European community.

On December 21 former deputy minister Svetozar Marović resigned for personal reasons. The subsequent arrest of his brother and local officials in the town of Budva on charges of fraud and embezzlement fueled domestic media speculation about influence trading by DPS leaders.

In May 2012 there were reports of financial irregularities and corruption at Prva Banka Crne Gore, a bank owned by the Djukanović family, reigniting criticism that Milo Djukanović had used his government position for self-enrichment.

POLITICAL PARTIES

In Montenegro, the Democratic Party of Socialists of Montenegro (DPS), successor to the League of Communists of Montenegro, has headed the government since the party's formation in the early 1990s, usually in alliance with the smaller Social Democratic Party of Montenegro (SDP). Other parties have proliferated, with 38 registered in 2009. Both the DPS and opposition parties have frequently turned to the use of coalitions.

For the October 2012 parliamentary election, five coalitions and eight individual parties offered candidate lists.

Government Parties:

Coalition for a European Montenegro (*Koalicija za Evropski Crna Gora*—KzECG). The KzECG is the latest variation in a series of coalitions led by the DPS starting in 1998, initially as an anti-Milošević grouping. In 2009 the coalition included the DPS, HGI, BS, and SDP. In the March 2009 elections the KzECG won 51.9 percent of the vote and 48 seats (47 in the national proportional vote, and 1 of the seats elected by the ethnic Albanian minority), securing a majority in parliament. In 2012 the minority parties chose to run independently, and the coalition included the DPS, SDP, and the LPCG. In the October 2012 elections, the KzECG won 46.3 percent of the vote and 39 seats.

Democratic Party of Socialists of Montenegro (*Demokratska Partija Socijalista Crne Gore*—DPS). The DPS is the successor to the League of Communists of Montenegro. In December 1992 it retained a majority in the Montenegrin legislative poll with 44 percent of the vote and finished fourth in the federal lower house. In November 1996 it increased its federal representation and maintained its majority at the republican level, winning 45 seats. Historically very close to Slobodan Milošević, the party suffered from intense internal squabbling as increasingly anti-Milošević Prime Minister Milo Djukanović narrowly beat Momir Bulatović in the 1997 Montenegrin presidential election and ousted him from the party leadership. The party split in January 1998, with the Bulatović faction forming the SNP (below).

In May 1998 the DPS won 30 of the For a Better Life (*Da Živimo Bolje*—DŽB) coalition's 42 legislative seats. Despite overtures from the anti-Milošević Democratic Opposition of Serbia alliance, the DPS chose to boycott the September 2000 federal elections, a major tactical error that left the anti-independence SNP in unchallenged control of the Montenegrin delegation to the federal Chamber of Citizens. In the April 2001 Montenegrin Assembly election the DPS-led Victory Is Montenegro–Milo Djukanović Democratic Coalition (*Pobjeda Je Crne Gore–Demokratska Koalicija Milo Djukanović*) coalition finished first, with 36 seats and 42 percent of the vote, but required the external support of the Liberal Alliance (see LPCG, below) to organize a government.

At the October 2002 republican election the DPS won 30 of the 39 seats (and 48 percent of the vote) won by the Democratic List for European Montenegro–Milo Djukanović (*Demokratska Lista za Evropsku Crnu Goru–Milo Djukanović*). An effort in late 2002 by President Djukanović and Prime Minister Filip Vujanović to, in effect, exchange jobs was finally accomplished in 2003. The DPS also held the office of state union president and was the leading Montenegrin party in the state union assembly, although it fully intended to lead Montenegro to independence.

The DPS introduced the independence referendum legislation in the assembly. After the Constitutional Court ruled the Minority Rights Act unconstitutional, the DPS leadership offered guaranteed slots in the assembly to several of the minority parties provided they join the DPS in an election coalition. It also promised to pursue legislation or a constitutional provision to undo the court ruling and reinstate the guaranteed legislative seats for ethnic minority parties.

In the September 2006 parliamentary election the DPS led the Coalition for a European Montenegro–Milo Djukanović (*Koalicija za Evropsku Crnu Goru–Milo Djukanović*), which also included the SDP and the Croat Civic Initiative, to a slim majority of 41 seats. In April 2008 the DPS candidate for the presidency, Filip Vujanović, was reelected in the first round with almost 52 percent of the vote, surprising analysts who had predicted two rounds of elections. In March 2009 the DPS won 35 seats as part of the Coalition for a European Montenegro list.

In early elections on October 14, 2012, the DPS won 30 seats again as part of the KzECG list. Djukanović accepted a new term as prime minister, while in the April 2013 presidential elections, DPS candidate Filip Vujanović was reelected to a third term with 51.2 percent of the vote.

Leaders: Milo DJUKANOVIĆ (President of the Party and Prime Minister), Filip VUJANOVIĆ (President of the Republic and Vice President of the Party), Željko ŠTURANOVIĆ (Vice President), Igor LUKŠIĆ (Vice President of the Party and Former Prime Minister), Svetozar MAROVIĆ (Vice President), Miodrag RADUNOVIĆ.

Social Democratic Party of Montenegro (*Socijaldemokratska Partija Crne Gore*—SDP). Dating from the 1992 merger of three parties (two social democratic and one communist), the SDP was strongly pro-independence. It won one federal parliamentary seat in 1996. In the May 1998 Montenegrin legislative election, it won five seats as part of the For a Better Life coalition and joined the resultant government. It boycotted the 2000 federal election but again ran in coalition with the DPS in the April 2001 Montenegrin election. In October Ranko Krivokapić was elected party president, succeeding Žarko RAKČEVIĆ. In October 2002 the SDP won nine Montenegrin Assembly seats as part of the Democratic List. The SDP was once again in coalition with the DPS in 2006, both for the independence referendum and the September parliamentary election, at which it won seven seats. In the March 2009 elections the SDP won nine seats as part of the Coalition for a European Montenegro list; in the October 14, 2012 elections, the SDP again in the KzECG coalition won eight seats.

Leaders: Ranko KRIVOKAPIĆ (President of the Party and of the Montenegrin Assembly); Ivan BRAJOVIĆ, Vujica LAZOVIĆ, Rifat RASTODER, Rasko KONJEVIĆ (Vice Presidents).

Liberal Party of Montenegro (*Liberalna Partija Crne Gore*—LPCG). The LPCG was established on October 31, 2004, under the leadership of Miodrag Živković, the former chair of the Liberal Alliance of Montenegro (*Liberalni Savez Crne Gore*—LSCG), following his expulsion from the LSCG in September.

Established in 1990 as a strong supporter of independence for Montenegro, the LSCG won 13 seats in the 1992 republican elections but failed to approach that total in subsequent contests. It won 6 seats in the April 2001 assembly election, after which it supported formation of a minority DPS-SDP government. Only a year later, however, it withdrew its support over objections to formation of the state union. In the resultant October 2002 Montenegrin election its representation fell to 4 seats, even though it had made major gains in municipal elections. In the May 2003 three-way republican presidential contest, Živković finished second, with 30 percent of the vote.

In 2004 the party split, largely over the issue of independence, leading to the Liberal Alliance chair's expulsion in September. On March 24, 2005, delegates to an extraordinary conference of the LSCG voted to end the Liberal Alliance party's existence. Longtime party leader Slavko PEROVIĆ condemned Montenegro's intelligentsia and opposition for abandoning their mission, and attacked the Djukanović regime as "mafia-ridden."

With the LSCG now defunct, LPCG leader Živković set his new party in support of independence but continued opposition to the alleged criminality and abuse of power by the Djukanović regime. (In July 2004 he had been found guilty of libeling the prime minister with salacious accusations.) It ran in alliance with the BS in 2006, winning only one seat.

For the 2009 elections the LPCG formed an electoral alliance with the **Democratic Center** (*Demokratskog Centra*—DC), the **For a Different Montenegro Coalition** (*Za Drugačiju Crnu Goru*—ZDCG). The ZDCG took 2.71 percent of the vote in the March 29, 2009, elections, failing to pass the threshold.

For the October 14, 2012, elections, the LPCG joined in coalition with the DPS and SDP, securing one seat.

Leaders: Andrija POPOVIĆ (Chair), Miodrag ŽIVKOVIĆ.

Bosniak Party (*Bošnjačka Stranka*—BS). The BS was established in February 2006 by merger of the Bosniak Muslim Alliance, the International Democratic Union, the Bosniak Democratic Alternative, and the Party of National Equality. With the independence referendum looming, the BS was seen as a vehicle for negotiating with both sides to achieve the most favorable terms for the Bosniak minority, which was split on the issue, in part because the Bosniak communities in the Sandžak region straddle the border between Serbia and Montenegro. In the end, the party chair, Rafet Husović, supported independence.

Afterwards, the BS rejected an overture by the DPS to join its coalition for the September 2006 parliamentary election and instead formed a coalition with the Liberal Party, the Liberals and Bosniak Party–"Correct in the Past, Right in the Future" (*Liberali i Bošnjačka Stranka–"Ispravni u Prošlosti, Pravi za Budnućnost"*), which won three seats.

Although not officially a party leader, the Sandžak politician Harun HADŽIĆ has been closely linked to the BS.

In the March 2009 elections, the BS won three seats as part of the KzECG list.

The BS ran independently in the October 14, 2012, elections, securing three seats with 4.2 percent of the vote.

Leaders: Rafet HUSOVIĆ (President and Minister without Portfolio), Suljo MUSTAFIĆ (Leader of Assembly Delegation).

New Democratic Force (*Nova Demokratska Snaga/Forca e Re Demokratike*—FORCA). FORCA was founded in October 2005 as a local ethnic Albanian political party in the coastal town of Ulcinj. FORCA subsequently expanded into other municipalities with a substantial ethnic Albanian minority. In the September 2006 parliamentary elections FORCA won 0.7 percent of the vote and no seats. In the March 29, 2009, elections, it won 1.9 percent of the vote and one of the seats elected by the ethnic Albanian minority.

For the October 14, 2012, elections, FORCA formed a coalition, the Force for Unity (*Forca za jedinstvo/Forca për Bashkim*—FzJ/FpB), with two smaller groups, the **Civic Initiative-Tuzi** and **Civil Movement "Perspective."** The coalition secured one of the minority seats, with 1.5 percent of the nationwide vote.

Leader: Nazif CUNGU (Chair).

Croat Civic Initiative (*Hrvatska Gradjanska Inicijativa*—HGI). The HGI was organized in 2002 prior to the October municipal elections in Tivat, in which it won four seats. The first Croat party to officially function in Montenegro since before World War II, it named Dalibor BURIĆ its first chair. It supported the independence referendum in 2006 and then in August agreed to join in the coalition formed by the DPS and SDP for the legislative election. It won one seat. Again competing with a DPS-led coalition in the March 2009 elections, the HGI won one seat as part of the coalition's list. In the October 14, 2012, elections it ran independently, securing one of the minority seats with 0.4 percent of the national vote.

Leader: Marija VUČINOVIĆ (President).

Albanian Coalition (*Albanska Koalicija/Koalicioni Shqiptare*—AK/KS). The AK/KS coalition includes the **Democratic Alliance in Montenegro** (*Demokratski Savez u Crnoj Gori/Lidhja Demokratike në Mal të Zi*—DSCG/LDMZ), the **Albanian Alternative** (*Albanska Alternativa/Alternativa Shqiptare*—AL/AS), and the **Democratic Party** (*Demokratska partija/Partia Demokratike*—DP/PD).

The DSCG and AL/AS each won a single parliamentary seat in the September 2006 parliamentary elections. For the March 2009 elections, the two parties formed the **Albanian List** (*Albanski List/Lista Shqiptare*—AL/LS), a coalition that won 0.9 percent of the national vote and secured a single seat in parliament from those elected by the ethnic Albanian minority.

Conflicting reports in 2011 and 2012 suggested the DP/PD had either merged or entered into an alliance with the **Albanian Coalition–Perspective** (*Albanska Koalicija–Perspektiva/Koalicioni Shqiptar–Perspektiva*—AKP/KSP), a party founded in 2009 by dissident factions from several other parties and that had received 0.8 percent of the vote in the March 2009 elections, securing one of the minority seats in parliament.

In the October 14, 2012, elections, the AK/KS won one of the minority seats with 1.1 percent of the national vote.

Leader: Fatnur GJEKA (Chair).

Opposition Parties:

Democratic Front (*Demokratski front*—DF). Formed in July 2012 as an alliance of the opposition, the DF has a program that focuses on overturning the "authoritarian" rule of the DPS but also calls for anti-corruption reform, investigations into the privatization process, and the creation of a lustration commission. The DF includes the NSD, PzP and DSJ, and several small civic groups. In the October 14, 2012, elections, the DF secured 20 seats with 23.2 percent of the vote. Independent candidates affiliated with the DF but not with constituent parties were elected to six of those seats.

For the April 7, 2013, presidential elections, the DF along with the New Serb Democracy, Socialist People's Party, and Positive Montenegro joined to support the candidacy of Miodrag LEKIĆ as an independent opposition candidate. (Lekić, although president of the DF, was not a member of any of its constituent parties.)

Leader: Miodrag LEKIĆ (President).

New Serb Democracy (*Nova Srpska Demokratija*—NSD). The NSD was formed in January 2009 as a merger between the Serbian People's Party (*Srpska Narodna Stranka*—SNS) and the People's Socialist Party of Montenegro (*Narodna Socijalistička Stranka Crne Gore*—NSS).

The Serbian People's Party was registered as a party in March 1998 by a dissident faction of the NS (below). Although the party supported the Milošević regime through the Kosovo crisis, some local party leaders refused to support the federal president's reelection in 2000. A party congress in February 2001 elected former NS leader Božidar Bojović as chair, succeeding Zelidrag NIKČEVIĆ. In October 2002 the SNS won six seats in the Montenegrin legislature. A year later Bojović was replaced by current leader Andrija Mandić and quickly formed the DSS.

The SNS joined the pro-union coalition in opposition to the 2006 independence referendum. Postreferendum news accounts alleged that SNS party members attributed the success of the referendum vote to the support of ethnic minority voters and therefore demonstrated increased hostility toward ethnic minorities, especially Bosniaks, in Serb-dominated areas.

After independence, SNS leaders positioned the party to advocate for policies aimed at protecting the status of Serbs in Montenegro. The SNS launched a petition drive advocating dual Serbian citizenship for Montenegrin Serbs, and party leaders publicly called for measures to preserve cultural autonomy and proportional representation in political institutions for Serbs. It parted ways with a key ally, the SNP, prior to the September 2006 election and instead headed the Serbian List–Andrija Mandić (*Srpska Lista–Andrija Mandić*), which included another frequent ally, the Montenegrin branch of the Serbian Radical Party (see SSR, below), as well as the Democratic Party of Unity (DSJ, below), the NSS, and a nongovernmental organization, the Serb National Council (*Srpsko Naradno Veće*—SNV). The SNS won 8 of the list's 12 seats, with each of the other four organizations in the coalition claiming 1. Mandić was reelected president in December 2006. As PzP president, he has endorsed strongly pro-Serbian policies, including opposition to the 2007 constitution (for formally changing the national language to Montenegrin from Serbian) and organizing rallies against any Montenegrin recognition of Kosovo's independence. Mandić himself has taken dual Montenegrin and Serbian citizenship. In the 2008 presidential elections the SNS-led Serbian List nominated Mandić as a common candidate, taking second place with almost a fifth of the vote. Following the government's decision to recognize an independent Kosovo in October 2008, the SNS led the Serbian List in a boycott of parliamentary functions.

The NSS was established in February 2001 by supporters of former FRY prime minister Momir Bulatović following his ouster from the SNP. The party failed to attract significant support in the April 2001 Montenegrin Assembly election, capturing less than 3 percent of the vote and therefore winning no seats. In 2002 it ran as a component of the Patriotic Coalition for Yugoslavia (*Patriotska Koalicija za Jugoslavia*—PK), which also included the Serbia-based Yugoslav United Left and Serbian Radical Party, but again failed to meet the 3 percent threshold. In 2006, as a component of the Serbian List, the NSS won one parliamentary seat.

The unified NSD won 9.2 percent of the vote in March 2009, securing eight seats.

In the October 14, 2012, elections, the NSD received eight seats from the coalition's total.

Leaders: Andrija MANDIĆ (President); Goran DANILOVIĆ (Deputy President); Emilo LABUDOVIĆ, Slaven RADULOVIĆ, Strahinja BULAJIĆ (Vice Presidents).

Movement for Change (*Pokret za Promjene*—PzP). The PzP began as a nongovernmental organization, the Group for Change (*Grupa za Promjene*—GzP), which was a significant participant in public discourse from its founding in 2002. Modeled on Serbia's G17 Plus think tank of economists, the GzP focused in part on ending corruption in the public sector, which it attributed primarily to the dominance of the DPS under Milo Djukanović. Its principal leaders, Executive Director Nebojša Medojević and Chair Svetozar JOVIĆEVIĆ, ranked among Montenegro's most respected public figures in the period leading up to independence. Many of its members appeared to support independence, but the GzP itself did not take a stand on the referendum.

Registered as a party in July 2006, the PzP surprised most observers by winning 11 legislative seats in September. As part of the opposition, it has frequently been allied with the leading Serbian parties, although it supported adoption of the 2007 constitution. Medojević, the party's candidate in the 2008 presidential elections, took third place with almost 17 percent of the vote in the first round. In the March 2009 elections the party took approximately 6 percent of the vote and 5 seats.

In the October 14, 2012, elections, the PzP received five seats from the coalition's total.

Leaders: Nebojša MEDOJEVIĆ (Chair); Branko RADULOVIĆ, Dušanka TUŠUP, Zoran MARSENIĆ (Deputy Chairs).

Democratic Party of Unity (*Demokratska Stranka Jedinstva—DSJ*). The DSJ is a new party registered in mid-2006 by Zoran ŽIŽIĆ, who was previously vice chair of the SNP. Žižić left the SNP when that party declined to join the Serbian List coalition in the run-up to the September 10 polls. Failing to reach a coalition accord with the SNP or the Serbian List, the DSJ did not enter the March 2009 elections. In the October 14, 2012, elections, the DSJ received a single seat from the coalition's total.

Leader: Zoran ŽIŽIĆ (Chair).

Socialist People's Party of Montenegro (*Socijalistička Narodna Partija Crne Gore*—SNP). The SNP was formed in early 1998 by Momir Bulatović following his rupture with the DPS. It held its first congress in March 1998. In the republican election of May 1998 the party came in second, with 29 seats.

Under FRY Prime Minister Bulatović, the party maintained strict support for Slobodan Milošević through the September 2000 election. Because the governing Montenegrin coalition boycotted the balloting, the SNP virtually swept the Montenegrin polls, winning 19 of the republic's 20 upper house seats and 28 seats in the lower house. With Bulatović having resigned the federal prime ministership following Milošević's concession, the party's vice chair, Zoran ŽIŽIĆ, was selected as his successor by newly installed President Koštunica in late October.

The chair passed from Momir Bulatović to an opponent, Predrag BULATOVIĆ (no relation), at a party congress in February 2001, after which the SNP formed the Together for Yugoslavia (*Zajedno za Jugoslaviju*) alliance with the SNS (see above) and the NS (see below) to contest the April Montenegrin legislative election, subsequently winning 30 seats with 38 percent of the vote. Following the June 2001 extradition to The Hague of Milošević to stand trial before the International Criminal Tribunal for the former Yugoslavia (ICTY), Prime Minister Žižić resigned in protest, but he was succeeded in mid-July by another SNP member, Dragiša Pešić, who remained in office until FRY was replaced by the state union. In the 2002 republican election the party won 19 of the 30 seats claimed by the Together for Changes coalition.

The SNP joined the other opposition parties in street protests against the DPS-SDP government throughout 2004 and the boycott of parliament in the same year. The SNP also spearheaded the pro-union coalition in opposition to the 2006 independence referendum. After the vote for independence, Predrag Bulatović steered the party toward a pragmatic "constructive dialogue" on postindependence platform issues, especially the need for a draft constitution, support for more democratic institutions, and engagement with the path toward European integration.

Negotiations toward a pre-election coalition with the other opposition parties were complicated by charges by SNP leaders of "poaching" tactics by the other opposition parties, especially the SNS, directed at SNP voters. In the end, the SNP and SNS formed separate coalitions, with the SNP leading the **SNP-NS-DSS Koalicija,** which won 11 parliamentary seats, 8 of them by the SNP. As a result of the poor showing, Bulatović resigned as chair in October. At the party's Fifth Congress, held in late November, Srdjan Milić defeated Dragiša Pešić and Borislav GLOBAREVIĆ for the leadership. Three deputy chairs were named in January 2007. Milić, nominated by the party for the 2008 presidential election, took almost 12 percent of the vote in the first round, placing fourth.

In the March 29, 2009, elections the SNP won 16.83 percent of the vote, for 16 seats in parliament.

In May 2010 the SNP led, along with the PzP and NSD, a broad coalition of 12 opposition parties to oppose the DPS in municipal elections. The coalition won only 2 of the 14 municipalities, highlighting the continued weakness of the opposition.

The SNP entered negotiations with the DF (see above) regarding an electoral coalition but was unable to secure an agreement on the future allocation of seats. In response, a dissident faction of the party left to join the DF.

In the October 14, 2012, elections, the SNP secured nine seats with 11.2 percent of the vote.

Leaders: Srdjan MILIĆ (Chair); Milorad BAKIĆ, Vasilije LALOŠEVIĆ, Neven GOŠOVIĆ, Radoman GOGIĆ (Deputy Chairs).

Positive Montenegro (*Pozitivna Crna Gora*—PCG). The PCG was founded as a self-described "center-left" party in May 2012, advocating socioeconomic issues, anticorruption reform, and socially responsible environmental policies.

In the October 14, 2012, elections, the PCG secured seven seats with 8.4 percent of the vote.

Leaders: Darko PAJOVIĆ (President), Goran TUPONJA (Secretary General).

Other Parties That Contested the 2012 Elections:

Serbian Unity (*Srpska sloga*—SS). An electoral coalition formed in August 2012 for the October parliamentary elections and included the People's Party, the **Serbian Homeland Party** (*Otadžbinska srpska stranka*—OSS), the **Democratic Center of Boka** (*Demokratski Centar* Boke—DCB), the Montenegrin chapter of the **Serbian Radical Party** (*Srpska radikalna stranka*—SRS), and the **Serbian List** (*Srpska lista*—SL), a new party founded in January 2012.

In the October 14, 2012, elections, the SS won 1.5 percent of the vote, failing to pass the threshold.

People's Party (*Narodna Stranka*—NS). Historically an intensely pan-Serbian formation, the NS supported the maintenance of Montenegro's ties with Serbia. It won 14 seats and 13 percent of the vote in the December 1992 Montenegrin election. In November 1996 an NS coalition with the Liberal Alliance (see LPCG, below) called the People's Accord (*Narodna Sloga*) won 19 seats in the Montenegrin legislature as well as 8 federal seats. In March 1997 differences over continuing support for the coalition led supporters of the party's vice chair, Božidar Bojović, to attempt expulsion of the president, Novak KILIBARDA, who was moving closer toward accepting Montenegrin independence. Kilibarda's NS joined the DPS in forming the For a Better Life coalition shortly before the May 1998 Montenegrin election, in which it won 7 seats. In the same month the Bojović faction registered a new pro-Belgrade party, the SNS. Kilibarda joined the governing Montenegrin coalition as a deputy prime minister.

In March 2000, rejecting Kilibarda's pro-independence stance, the NS replaced him with Dragan ŠOĆ, the Montenegrin minister of justice. On December 28, objecting to the latest independence moves by President Djukanović, the NS left the governing coalition and subsequently allied itself with the SNP for the April 2001 election. (Kilibarda, meanwhile, had established the **People's Accord of Montenegro** [*Narodna Sloga Crne Gore*—NSCG], which has not played a notable role in Montenegrin politics.) In October 2002 it won five assembly seats as part of the Together for Changes coalition.

After independence, the NS leaders rebuffed SNS proposals for a Serbian List in favor of working to preserve the broader pro-union coalition with the SNP and DSS. In the September 2006 election the NS won 2 of the SNP-NS-DSS Coalition's 11 seats and then formed a 3-member parliamentary floor group with the DSS representative.

In February 2009 the NS formed an electoral alliance with the DSS, the **People's Coalition** (*Narodjačka Koalicija*—NK) but then failed to draw in the SNP or NSD. In the March 29, 2009, elections the NK took 2.9 percent of the vote, failing to pass the threshold.

Leader: Predrag POPOVIĆ (Chair).

Serbian National Alliance (*Srpski Nacionalni Savez*—SNS). The DSS formed this electoral alliance of Serbian parties in September 2012, along with the SSR and the **Serbian National Council** (*Srpskog narodno veće*—SNV). In the October 14, 2012, elections the SNS won 0.9 percent of the vote, failing to pass the threshold.

Democratic Serbian Party (*Demokratska Srpska Stranka*—DSS). This Montenegrin-based version of Serbia's DSS was launched by former NS and SNS party leader Božidar Bojović in December 2003. The DSS joined the opposition parties' street protests against the DPS-SDP government throughout 2004. The DSS also joined the pro-union coalition in opposition to the 2006 independence referendum. After the referendum DSS leaders rebuffed calls from the SNS for a Serbian list to contest the 2006 parliamentary elections, advocating instead for preservation of the larger pro-union coalition of parties.

Leaders: Ranko KADIĆ (Chair), Božidar BOJOVIĆ.

Party of Serb Radicals (*Stranka Srpskih Radikala*—SSR). The SSR began as the Montenegrin branch of Serbia's Serbian Radical Party (*Srpska Radikalna Stranka*—SRS), which was founded in February 1991 by Vojislav Šešelj, the radical pan-Serbian leader being tried by the ICTY for crimes against humanity.

The Montenegrin SRS joined the Serbian List in the run-up to the 2006 election and came away with one seat. In December it adopted its current name because the inclusion of Šešelj's name in the party's formal title violated Montenegro's law on political parties. Although legally independent of Serbia's SRS, the SSR leadership has stated that in all other respects they are the same. Confusingly, a party named the SRS registered in 2012 as part of the Serbian Unity coalition (see above).

In the March 2009 elections, the SSR headed a new **Serb National List** (*Srpska Nacionalna Lista*—SNL) coalition, with the SNV and a faction of the SNS. The coalition received 1.3 percent of the vote, failing to pass the threshold.

Leaders: Duško SEKULIĆ (Chair), Bojan STRUNJAŠ.

Democratic Union of Albanians (*Demokratska Unija Albanaca*—DUA/*Unioni Demokratih i Shqiptarëve*—UDSh). In the 2002 legislative election the DUA ran as the Democratic Coalition "Albanians Together" (*"Albanci Zajedno"*), which won two seats reserved for the Albanian community. The coalition included two other ethnic Albanian parties, the DSCG and the Party for Democratic Prosperity (both discussed below). In April 2001 the three had run independently, with the DUA and the DSCG each winning one seat.

In 2006 the DUA supported independence but chose to run alone in the parliamentary election, in which it won one seat and then joined the governing coalition. In the March 2009, elections the DUA again ran alone, winning 1.5 percent of the vote and one of the seats in parliament reserved for election by the ethnic Albanian minority.

In the October 2012 election, the DUA won 0.8 percent of the vote, failing to pass the threshold.

Leaders: Mehmed ZENKA (President), Ferhat DINOŠA (Honorary President).

Together (*Zajedno*). This coalition included the **Party of Pensioners and Disabled People of Montenegro** (*Stranka Penzionera i Invalida Crne Gore*) and the **Yugoslav Communist Party of Montenegro** (*Jugoslovenska Komunistička Partija Crne Gore*—JKPCG). In September 2009 the JKPCG merged with the **Montenegrin Communists** (*Crnogorski Komunisti*).

The coalition won 0.4 percent of the vote, failing to pass the threshold.

Albanian Youth Alliance (*Albanska omladinska alijansa/Aleanca Rinore e Shqiptarëve*—AOA/ARS). A newly founded citizen's initiative, the AOA/ARS received 0.2 percent of the vote, failing to pass the threshold.

Leader: Anton LULGJURAJ.

LEGISLATURE

Assembly of the Republic of Montenegro (*Skupština Republike Crne Gore*). The 81 members of the assembly (sometimes referred to as parliament) are elected to four-year terms by proportional representation. Parties must meet a 3 percent threshold to qualify for 76 national seats; the Albanian minority elects 5 other representatives. Results for the election of October 14, 2012, were as follows: Coalition for a European Montenegro, 39 seats (Democratic Party of Socialists of Montenegro, 30; Social Democratic Party, 8; Liberal Party of Montenegro, 1); Democratic Front, 20 (New Serb Democracy, 8; Movement for Changes, 5; Democratic Party of Unity, 1; independent, 6); Socialist People's Party of Montenegro, 9; Positive Montenegro, 7; Bosniak Party, 3; New Democratic Force, 1; Albanian Coalition, 1; and Croat Civic Initiative, 1.

President: Ranko KRIVOKAPIĆ.

CABINET

[as of August 1, 2013]

Prime Minister	Milo Djukanović (DPS)
Deputy Prime Minister for the Political System	Duško Marković (DPS)
Deputy Prime Minister for European Integration	Igor Lukšić (DPS)
Deputy Prime Minister for Economic Policy	Vujica Lazović (SDP)
Deputy Prime Minister for Regional Development	Rafet Husović (BS)
Ministers	
Agriculture	Petar Ivanović (Ind.)
Culture	Branislav Mićunović (DPS)
Defense	Milica Pejanović-Djurišić (DPS)
Economy	Vladimir Kavarić (DPS)
Education and Sport	Slovljub Stjepović (DPS)
Finance	Radoje Zugić (DPS)
Foreign Affairs	Igor Lukšić (DPS)
Health	Miodrag Radunović (DPS)
Human and Minority Rights	Suad Numanović (DPS)
Information Society and Telecommunications	Vujica Lazović (SDP)
Interior	Rasko Konjević (SDP)
Justice	Duško Marković (DPS)
Labor and Social Welfare	Suad Numanović (DPS)
Science	Sanja Vlahović (DPS) [f]
Sustainable Development and Tourism	Branimir Gvozdenović (DPS)
Transportation and Maritime Affairs	Ivan Brajović (SDP)
Without Portfolio	Marija Vučinović (HGI) [f]

[f] = female

INTERGOVERNMENTAL REPRESENTATION

Ambassador to the U.S.: Srdjan DARMANOVIĆ.

U.S. Ambassador to Montenegro: Sue K. BROWN.

Permanent Representative to the UN: Milorad ŠĆEPANOVIĆ.

IGO Memberships (Non-UN): EBRD, ICC, IOM, OSCE, WTO.

MOROCCO

Kingdom of Morocco
al-Mamlakat al-Maghribiyah

Political Status: Independent since March 2, 1956; constitutional monarchy established in 1962; present constitution approved by referendum on July 1, 2011.

Area: 274,461 sq. mi. (710,850 sq. km), including approximately 97,343 sq. mi. (252,120 sq. km) of Western Sahara, two-thirds of which was annexed in February 1976 and the remaining one-third claimed upon Mauritanian withdrawal in August 1979.

Population: 32,873,714 (2012E—UN); 32,649,130 (2013E—U.S. Census).

Major Urban Centers (2007E—UN): RABAT (1,654,000), Casablanca (2,995,000), Fez (1,026,000), Marrakesh (1,126,000), Oujda (489,000).

Official Languages: Arabic and Tamazight.

Monetary Unit: Dirham (official rate November 1, 2013: 8.31 dirhams = $1US).

Sovereign: King MOHAMED VI became king on July 23, 1999, following the death of his father, HASSAN II.

Heir to the Throne: Crown Prince MOULAY HASSAN.

Prime Minister: Abdelillah BENKIRANE (PJD), appointed on November 29, 2011, replacing Abbas EL FASSI (Istiqlal).

THE COUNTRY

Located at the northwest corner of Africa, Morocco combines a long Atlantic coastline and Mediterranean frontage facing Gibraltar and southern Spain. Bounded by Algeria on the northeast and (following annexation of the former Spanish Sahara) by Mauritania on the south, the country is topographically divided into a rich agricultural plain in the northwest and an infertile mountain and plateau region in the east that gradually falls into the Sahara in the south and southwest. The population is approximately two-thirds Arab and one-third Berber, with small French and Spanish minorities. Islam is the state religion, most of the population adhering to the Sunni sect and following the Maliki school. Arabic is the language of the majority, most others speaking one or more dialects of Berber; Spanish is common in the northern regions and French among the educated elite. Women comprise 35 percent of the paid labor force, concentrated mainly in textile manufacture and domestic service; overall, one-third of the female population is engaged in unpaid family labor on agricultural estates. Increasing numbers of women from upper-income brackets have participated in local and national elections, but have obtained minimal representation. In the 2009 local elections women gained just over 3,400 seats as the result of legislation that guaranteed women a minimum of 12 percent of the total seats. This was an increase in representation of 250 percent over the 2003 balloting. Following the 2011 parliamentary elections, women held 6 of 270 seats in the upper chamber (2.2 percent) and 67 of 395 seats in the lower chamber (17 percent). Past abuses of human rights, including the disappearance of dissenters, have diminished. The status of women in Moroccan society has been officially reformed, with the legal age for marriage raised from 15 to 18 and polygamy virtually outlawed.

The agricultural sector employs approximately 45 percent of the population; important crops include cereals and grains, oilseeds, nuts, and citrus fruits. One of the world's leading exporters of phosphates, Morocco also has important deposits of lead, iron, cobalt, zinc, manganese, and silver; overall, mining accounts for about 45 percent of export receipts. The industrial sector emphasizes import substitution (textiles, chemicals, cement, plastics, machinery), while tourism and fishing are also major sources of income. Trade is strongly oriented toward France, whose economic influence has remained substantial. Since the early 1980s the economy has suffered from periodic droughts, declining world demand for phosphates, rapid urbanization, and high population growth. Unemployment remains a problem, with youth and talent seeking opportunity in Europe. Continued dependence on the agricultural sector of the economy remains a problem.

Living conditions remain low by regional standards, and wealth is poorly distributed. However, with its low inflation rate and cheap labor pool, Morocco is considered by some as a potential target for substantial investment by developed (particularly European) countries. To encourage such interest, the government continues to privatize many state-run enterprises, address the high (44.9 percent) illiteracy rate, and reform the stock market, tax system, and banking sector. However, the pace of reform remains somewhat sluggish.

A more costly wage structure and higher oil subsidies contributed to a rapidly rising budget deficit and a concurrent drop in the GDP growth rate to 1.2 percent in 2005. However, a 2004 free trade agreement with the United States (see Foreign relations, below) took effect in January 2006, improving prospects for increased direct foreign investment. Concurrently, Morocco's decision to allow private purchase of shares in the largest state-owned bank and the state telecommunications company further enhanced the climate for foreign capital. A widespread drought in 2007 hindered grain production that year and the following one.

Although in 2008 the agricultural sector recovered from the droughts of previous years, the worldwide economic crisis constrained growth as remittances from Moroccans living abroad declined by 9.7 percent, while exports were down 34 percent and imports fell by 23 percent. Nonetheless, GDP grew by 3.6 percent in 2010 and 5 percent in 2011. In August 2011 the European Union (EU) granted Morocco €185 million to support economic development and antipoverty programs. GDP grew by 5 percent in 2012, while inflation remained low at 1.3 percent. Meanwhile unemployment was 8.8 percent, and GDP per capita was $3,041. In 2012 the International Monetary Fund (IMF) provided Morocco a $6.2 billion line of credit in exchange for a pledge to reduce a range of consumer subsidies. In 2013 the World Bank ranked Morocco 97th out of 185 countries in its annual Doing Business survey, second only to Tunisia among the Maghreb states.

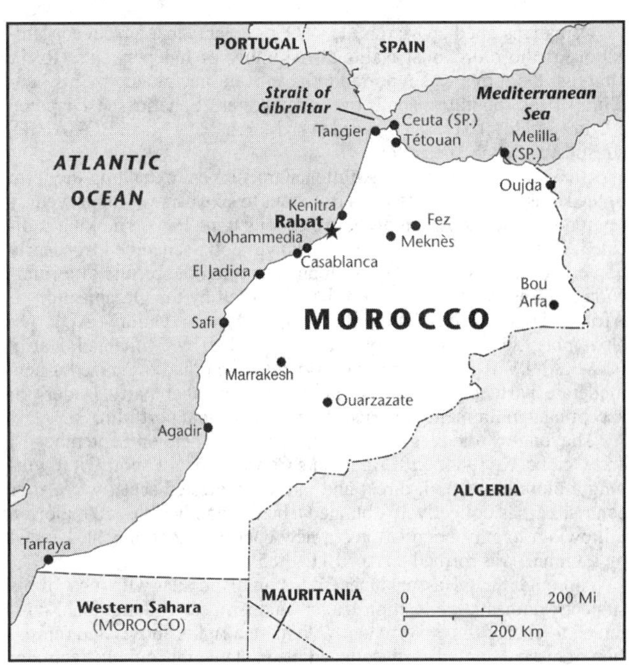

GOVERNMENT AND POLITICS

Political background. Originally inhabited by Berbers, Morocco was successively conquered by the Phoenicians, Carthaginians, Romans, Byzantines, and Arabs. From 1912 to 1956 the country was subjected to de facto French and Spanish control, but the internal authority of the sultan was nominally respected. Under pressure by Moroccan nationalists, the French and Spanish relinquished their protectorates, and the country was reunified under Sultan MOHAMED V in 1956. Tangier, which had been under international administration since 1923, was ceded by Spain in 1969.

King Mohamed V tried to convert the hereditary sultanate into a modern constitutional monarchy but died before the process was complete. It remained for his son, King HASSAN II, to implement his father's goal in a constitution adopted in December 1962. However, dissatisfaction with economic conditions and the social policy of the regime led to rioting at Casablanca in March 1965, and three months later the king assumed legislative and executive powers.

In June 1967 the king relinquished the post of prime minister, but the continued hostility of student and other elements led to frequent governmental changes. A new constitution, approved in July 1970, provided for a partial resumption of parliamentary government, a strengthening of royal powers, and a limited role for political parties. Despite the opposition of major political groups, trade unions, and student organizations, an election for a new unicameral House of Representatives was held in August 1970, yielding a progovernment majority. However, the king's failure to unify the country behind his programs was dramatically illustrated by abortive military revolts in 1971 and 1972.

A new constitution was overwhelmingly approved by popular referendum in March 1972, but the parties refused to enter the government because of the monarch's reluctance to schedule legislative elections. After numerous delays, elections to communal and municipal councils were finally held in November 1976, to provincial and prefectural assemblies in January 1977, and to a reconstituted national House of Representatives in June 1977. On October 10 the leading parties agreed to participate in a "National Unity" cabinet headed by Ahmed OSMAN as prime minister.

Osman resigned on March 21, 1979, ostensibly to oversee reorganization of the proroyalist National Assembly of Independents (RNI), although the move was reported to have been precipitated by his handling of the lengthy dispute over the Western Sahara (see Disputed Territory, below). He was succeeded on March 22 by Maati BOUABID, a respected Casablanca attorney.

On May 30, 1980, a constitutional amendment extending the term of the House of Representatives from four to six years was approved by referendum, thus postponing new elections until 1983. The king indicated in June 1983 that the legislative poll, scheduled for early September, would be further postponed pending the results of a referendum in the Western Sahara to be sponsored by the Organization of African Unity (OAU, subsequently the African Union—AU). On November 30 a new "unity" cabinet headed by Mohamed Karim LAMRANI was announced, with Bouabid, who had organized a new moderate party eight months earlier, joining other party leaders in accepting appointment as ministers of state without portfolio.

The long-awaited legislative poll was finally held on September 14 and October 2, 1984, with Bouabid's Constitutional Union (UC) winning a plurality of both direct and indirectly elected seats, while four centrist parties collectively obtained a better than two-to-one majority. Following lengthy negotiations, a new coalition government, headed by Lamrani, was formed on April 11, 1985.

Although King Hassan appeared to remain popular with most of his subjects, domestic opposition leaders and Amnesty International continued to charge the government with human rights abuses and repression of dissent, including the alleged illegal detention and mistreatment of numerous leftists and Islamic extremists arrested in 1985 and 1986. On September 30, 1986, the king appointed Dr. Azzedine LARAKI, former national education minister, as prime minister, following Lamrani's resignation for health reasons.

Attributed in large measure to improvements in the economy, calm ensued, with domestic and international attention focusing primarily on the Western Sahara. Thus, a national referendum on December 1, 1989, overwhelmingly approved the king's proposal to postpone legislative elections due in 1990, ostensibly to permit participation by Western Saharans following a self-determination vote in the disputed territory.

In mid-1992, amid indications that the referendum might be delayed indefinitely or even abandoned, the government announced that forthcoming local and national elections would include the residents of Western Sahara as participants. On August 11 King Hassan reappointed Lamrani as prime minister and announced a "transitional cabinet" to serve until a postelection cabinet could be established under new constitutional provisions (see Constitution and government, below).

The basic law revisions were approved on September 4, 1992, by a national referendum, which the government hailed as a significant step in its ongoing democratization program. Widespread disbelief greeted the government's claim that 97.5 percent of the electorate had participated and that a 99.9 percent "yes" vote had been registered.

In balloting for directly elective house seats, delayed until June 25, 1993, the newly established Democratic Bloc (*Koutla*), a coalition of center-left opposition groups led by the old-guard *Istiqlal* party and the Socialist Union of Popular Forces (USFP), secured 99 seats. They won only 15 more in the September 17 voting in electoral colleges made up of local officials, trade unionists, and representatives of professional associations. Meanwhile, the National Entente (*Wifaq*), a group of center-right royalist parties, increased its representation from 116 in the first round of balloting to 195 after the second. The Democratic Bloc subsequently charged that the indirect election encompassed widespread fraud, an allegation that received some support from international observers.

Although King Hassan rejected the Democratic Bloc's demand that the results of the indirect poll be overturned, he did propose that the bloc participate in the formation of a new cabinet, the first of what the king envisioned as a series of alternating left-right governments. The offer was declined because of the monarch's insistence that he retain the right to appoint the prime minister and maintain de facto control of the foreign, justice, and interior portfolios. Consequently, Lamrani formed a new nonparty government on November 11.

With his poor health again cited as the official reason for the change, Lamrani was succeeded on May 25, 1994, by former foreign minister Abdellatif FILALI, a longtime close adviser to the king. On June 7 Filali presented the monarch with a ministerial list unchanged from that of his predecessor, while King Hassan continued to seek Democratic Bloc leadership of a new coalition government. The negotiations eventually collapsed in early 1995, in part because of the king's wish that Driss BASRI, long-term minister of state for interior and information, remain in the cabinet. The opposition parties had objected to Basri's influence for many years, charging that he had sanctioned human rights abuses and tolerated electoral fraud. Nonetheless, Basri retained the interior post on February 28 when Filali's new government, including 20 members of the National Entente, was announced.

Despite his failure to draw the leftist parties into the government, the king continued to pursue additional democratization, particularly regarding the proposed creation of an upper house of the legislature that, theoretically, would redistribute authority away from the monarchy to a certain degree. The king's proposal was affirmed by a reported 99.56 percent "yes" vote in a national referendum on September 13, 1996, most opposition parties having endorsed the amendment (see Constitution and government, below, for details).

Local elections were held on June 13, 1997, with seats being distributed along a wide spectrum of parties and no particular political dominance being apparent. Such was also the case with the November 14 balloting for a new House of Representatives as the *Koutla, Wifaq,* and a bloc of centrist parties each won about one-third of the seats. On the other hand, the indirect elections to the new House of Councilors revealed a decided tilt toward the *Wifaq,* not a surprising result considering its long-standing progovernment stance.

Continuing to pursue an alternating left-right series of governments, King Hassan was subsequently able to finally persuade the Democratic Bloc to assume cabinet control, and on February 4, 1998, he appointed Abderrahmane YOUSSOUFI of the USFP (which had won the most seats in the House of Representatives) as the next prime minister. As formed on March 14, the new cabinet included representatives from seven parties, although the King's supporters (most notably Basri) remained in several key posts.

King Hassan, whose health had been a concern since 1995, died of a heart attack on July 23, 1999; Crown Prince SIDI MOHAMED succeeded his father immediately, the official ceremony marking his enthronement as King MOHAMED VI being held on July 30. Shortly thereafter, Driss Basri, who was nicknamed "The Butcher" by human rights activists and had presided over a period of government crackdowns on the opposition, was dismissed as minister of the interior and moved to Paris. The new king confirmed his support for Prime Minister Youssoufi and his government. The cabinet was reshuffled on September 6, 2000, with Youssoufi retaining the top post, but the new king replaced him with an independent, Driss JETTOU, in 2002.

Palace officials were concerned by the rise of radical Islamists who have been spurred on by the Iraq War. Several suicide attacks on one day in early 2003 in Casablanca killed more than 40 people. Some 2,000 Moroccans were convicted of the bombings, with several given death sentences and others long prison terms. A new antiterrorism law was swiftly passed amid concerns in the media that increased powers of detention and surveillance would erode the gains in human rights.

In 2005 a Moroccan truth commission—formally called the Equity and Reconciliation Commission (IER)—released its final report on alleged human rights abuses during the reign of King Hassan. The commission, described as the first of its kind in the Arab world, had been set up in January 2004. The commission reported that between independence in 1956 and the end of Hassan's rule in 1999, nearly 600 people were killed and that opposition activists were systematically suppressed, with numerous instances of torture and disappearances. Many prodemocracy activists, including the Moroccan Association for Human Rights, criticized the panel for its policy of withholding the names of those found responsible for the abuses and for not recommending prosecution of the perpetrators. The hearings were televised throughout the country, an event unprecedented in the region.

Parliamentary elections in September 2007 maintained a conservative government. After a record low turnout of 37 percent, the party *Istiqlal,* a member of the Democratic Bloc, took control. Abbass EL FASSI was appointed prime minister on September 19, 2007, and on October 15 formed a cabinet that reflected the king's desire for a moderately conservative, reformist government.

Prior to local balloting in June 2009 the newly formed Party of Authenticity and Modernity (PAM), which included a number of members of the House of Representatives who had defected from other parties, announced it would join the opposition (see Political parties, below). PAM placed first in the local elections, followed by *Istiqlal* in the contest to select more than 28,000 local councilors. During the balloting, Fatima Zahra Mansouri of the PAM became the first woman elected mayor of a major city, Marrakech, and only the second woman ever elected to lead a city in Morocco. Women won 12 percent of the seats in the balloting. In July there was a minor cabinet reshuffle which brought the Popular Movement (MP) into the government and expanded the number of ministers from the USFP and the RNI. The reshuffle was undertaken in order to maintain the government's majority in the legislature following the defection of deputies to PAM. As a result, the government had the support of 200 of the 325 deputies in the House. In regional balloting in September, the PAM won the chairpersonship of four of the eight regions. In indirect elections for one-third of the upper chamber in parliament, the PAM won 22 of 90 seats, followed by *Istiqlal* with 17 and the MP with 11.

There was a minor cabinet reshuffle in January 2010. That same month, the king created the Advisory Committee on Regionalization to develop recommendations to reform regional governments.

Following prodemocracy protests (see Current issues, below), the king appointed a committee to draft a new constitution in March 2011. The new basic law was approved by referendum on July 1 with 98.5 percent of the vote in favor (although some opposition groups boycotted the voting).

Early elections were held on November 25, 2011, and the PJD won a majority (see Current issues, below). PJD leader Abdelillah BENKIRANE formed a coalition government on January 3, 2012. *Istiqlal* withdrew from the government on July 8, 2013, and its ministers resigned from the cabinet on July 22 (see Current issues, below).

Constitution and government. Morocco is a constitutional monarchy, the crown being hereditary and normally transmitted to the king's eldest son, who acts on the advice of a Regency Council if he accedes before age 20. The 2011 constitution reduces the monarch's authority. However, the king remains the commander in chief of the armed forces and has the power to declare a state of emergency, veto legislation, and initiate constitutional amendments. The king appoints the prime minister from the largest party in the legislature. Meanwhile, the prime minister has the power to appoint the cabinet and dissolve the assembly. The House of Representatives initiates legislation and confidence motions and launches investigations. The 2011 constitution also guaranteed freedom of expression and equality for men and women.

All members of the House of Representatives are now elected directly. Included in the new legislature's expanded authority is the power to censure the government and to dismiss cabinet members, although such decisions can still be overridden by the king. The upper house (House of Councilors) is elected indirectly from various local government bodies, professional associations, and employer and worker organizations.

The judicial system is headed by a Supreme Court (*Al-Makama al-Ulia*) and includes courts of appeal, regional tribunals, magistrates' courts, labor tribunals, and a special court to deal with corruption. All judges are appointed by the king on the advice of the Supreme Council of the Judiciary. The 2011 constitution established the judiciary as an independent branch of the government.

The country is currently divided into 49 provinces and prefectures (including four provinces in the Western Sahara), with further division into municipalities, autonomous centers, and rural communes. The king appoints all provincial governors, who are responsible to him. In addition, the basic law changes of September 1996 provided for 16 regional councils, with some members elected directly and others representing various professional organizations.

Moroccan newspapers have a reputation for being highly partisan and outspoken, although those incurring the displeasure of the state face reprisal, such as forced suspension, and government control has at times been highly restrictive. Following the enthronement of the reform-minded King Mohamed VI in 1999, the government somewhat relaxed its grip on the print media. However, domestic and international journalists' organizations criticized a libel law adopted in April 2002, accusing the government of eroding civil and press liberties by making it easier to file libel suits. In May 2006 Human Rights Watch issued a report critical of tightening controls on the press, citing recent harassment of independent news weeklies that had questioned government policies. Meanwhile, the government continued to arrest journalists for articles critical of the king. In October 2010 Morocco banned Al-Jazeera from broadcasting from Morocco after the Arab-language station carried reports critical of the kingdom's actions in the Western Sahara. In its 2013 annual index of freedom of the press, Reporters Without Borders ranked Morocco 136th out of 178 countries.

Foreign relations. A member of the UN and the Arab League, Morocco has been chosen on many occasions as a site for Arab and African Islamic conferences at all levels. It has generally adhered to a nonaligned policy, combining good relations with the West with support for African and especially Arab nationalism. Morocco has long courted economic ties with the European Union (EU, formerly the European Community—EC), although its request for EC membership was politely rebuffed in 1987 on geographic grounds. An association agreement was negotiated in 1995 and signed in 1996 with the EU, which reportedly had begun to perceive the kingdom as the linchpin of a European campaign to expand trade with North Africa. Morocco also joined the EU's European Neighborhood Policy and in this context developed an Action Plan, finalized in July 2005, which defined mutual priorities and objectives in the areas of political, economic, commercial, justice, security, and cultural cooperation. These objectives included negotiating an agreement on liberalized trade, pursuing legislative reform, applying human rights provisions, managing migration flows more effectively, and signing a readmission agreement with the EU and developing the energy sector. The action plan also called for an enhanced dialogue on combating terrorism.

In July 2008 France launched a new initiative, the Union for the Mediterranean, a regional group of European, Middle Eastern, and North African countries that gave Morocco a leading role. In addition, the Moroccan government has long been interested in formalizing its relationship to the EU as an advanced status partner, which would allow Moroccans greater access to EU labor markets. France strongly supported Morocco's bid and promoted its application.

Relations with the United States have been friendly, with U.S. administrations viewing Morocco as a conservative counter to northern Africa's more radical regimes. An agreement was signed in mid-1982 that sanctioned, subject to veto, the use of Moroccan air bases by U.S. forces in emergency situations. Periodic joint military exercises have since been conducted, with Washington serving as a prime supplier of equipment for Rabat's campaign in the Western Sahara. In 2004 the United States and Morocco signed a free trade agreement that went into effect in 2006. As a result, exports from Morocco to the United States increased from $445.8 million in 2005 to $878.5 million in 2008, while imports rose from $480.8 million to $1.44 billion. Morocco is a signatory to the U.S.-led Trans-Sahara Counterterrorism Initiative, a seven-year program worth $500 million, and the United States continues to view Morocco as a key ally in combating terrorism.

During early 1991 Rabat faced a delicate situation in regard to the Iraqi invasion of Kuwait the previous August. Many Arab capitals were critical of King Hassan for contributing 1,700 Moroccan troops to the U.S.-led Desert Shield deployment in Saudi Arabia and other Gulf states; domestic sentiment also appeared to be strongly tilted against Washington. However, the king defused the issue by permitting a huge pro-Iraq demonstration in the capital in early February and by expressing his personal sympathy for the Iraqi people during the Gulf war. His middle-of-the-road approach was widely applauded both at home and abroad.

Morocco's role in regional affairs has been complicated by a variety of issues. Relations with Algeria and Mauritania have been marred by territorial disputes (until 1970, Morocco claimed all of Mauritania's territory). The early 1970s brought cooperation with the two neighboring states in an effort to present a unified front against the retention by Spain of phosphate-rich Spanish Sahara, but by 1975 Morocco and Mauritania were ranged against Algeria on the issue. In an agreement reached in Madrid on November 14, 1975, Spain agreed to withdraw in favor of Morocco and Mauritania, who proceeded to occupy their assigned sectors (see map) on February 28, 1976, despite resistance from the Polisario Front, an Algerian-backed group that had proclaimed the establishment of an independent Saharan Arab Democratic Republic (SADR). Following Mauritanian renunciation of all claims to the territory in a peace accord with Polisario on August 5, 1979, Moroccan forces entered the southern sector, claiming it, too, as a Moroccan province.

Relations with Algeria were formally resumed in May 1988 prior to an Arab summit in Algiers on the uprising in the Israeli-occupied territories. The stage was thus set for diplomatic activity, which in the wake of first-ever talks between King Hassan and Polisario representatives in early 1989 appeared to offer the strongest possibility in more than a decade for settlement of the Western Sahara problem. Although little progress was achieved over the next seven years on a proposed UN-sponsored self-determination vote, a new UN mediation effort in 1997 rekindled hopes for a settlement (see Disputed Territory, below). Relations with Algeria improved further following the 1999 election of the new Algerian president, Abdelaziz Bouteflika, who suggested that bilateral affairs be handled independently of the conflict in the Western Sahara. Nevertheless, tensions between the two states persisted and the border remained closed from 1994. However, this rivalry does not prevent the two states from cooperating on common strategic concerns, such as security, including extradition of terrorist suspects and energy. In July 2008 Algerian officials announced that they would export electricity to Spain through a Moroccan pipeline and would be an energy provider to Morocco in emergencies. Long strained ties with Libya (which had been accused of complicity in several plots to overthrow the monarchy) began to improve with a state visit by Muammar Qadhafi to Rabat in mid-1983. The process of rapprochement culminated in a treaty of projected union signed by the two leaders at Oujda on August 13, 1984. An inaugural meeting of a joint parliamentary assembly was held in Rabat in July 1985, and commissions were set up to discuss political, military, economic, cultural, and technical cooperation. By February 1989, cordial relations paved the way for a summit in Marrakesh, during which Qadhafi joined other North African leaders in proclaiming the Arab Maghreb Union.

Morocco's attitude toward Israel has been markedly more moderate than that of many Arab states, in part because more than 500,000 Jews of Moroccan ancestry live in Israel. King Hassan was known to relish his conciliatory potential in the Middle East peace process and was believed to have assisted in the negotiations leading up to the Israeli/PLO agreement of September 1993. Israeli Prime Minister Yitzhak Rabin made a surprise visit to Rabat on his return from the historic signing in Washington, his talks with King Hassan being heralded as an important step toward the establishment of formal diplomatic relations between the two countries.

In late 2001 relations between Morocco and Spain were strained by disagreements over illegal immigration, fishing rights, and smuggling. In July 2002 the countries were involved in a brief military standoff over an uninhabited islet (called Perejil by Spain, Leila by Morocco, and claimed by both) off the coast of Ceuta. With U.S., EU, and Egyptian mediation, the two sides agreed to withdraw their troops from the islet and begin cooperating on various issues. The March 2004 bombings in Madrid, which were partly perpetrated by Moroccan immigrants, encouraged the states to coordinate security policy and exchange counterterrorism intelligence. Tensions eased dramatically when Spain's conservative government was replaced by the Spanish Socialist Workers Party in March 2004, but the relationship is still fragile. When Spain's King Juan Carlos visited Ceuta in November 2007, Morocco protested by recalling its ambassador from Spain.

In March 2009 Morocco broke off diplomatic relations with Iran, following statements by an Iranian official critical of Bahrain. The remarks prompted widespread outrage among Sunnis. The severance followed the recall of the Moroccan envoy to Iran in February because of that country's criticism of Morocco and reports in Rabat of Iranians endeavoring to undermine the monarchy. Also in March, Morocco expelled four foreign missionaries on the grounds they were illegally attempting to convert Muslims to Christianity.

Morocco withdrew from Libya's fortieth anniversary celebrations in September 2009 in protest over the appearance of Polisario leader Mohamed Abd al-Azziz (see Disputed territories, below). However, the following month the two countries signed a range of bilateral economic agreements to expand cooperation in tourism, air travel, and various industries.

An agreement to expand economic cooperation between Morocco and Poland was signed during a visit by El Fassi to Poland in January 2010. In March the first EU-Morocco summit was held in Granada, Spain, to discuss closer economic and political collaboration. Moroccan activists periodically blockaded food shipments to the Spanish enclave of Melilla to protest reported instances of abuse by Spanish border guards through the summer of 2010. The king and Spanish prime minister met in September and pledged to reduce tensions. In December 2010 representatives from Morocco, Polisario, Algeria, and Mauritania resumed negotiations on the Western Sahara, the first direct talks since 2008.

In June 2011 a raid by Moroccans to secure a water reservoir that supplied water to Melilla led to protests from the Spanish government.

In the spring of 2012, high-level meetings with Algerian diplomats raised hopes the two countries might reopen their borders, reflecting a thaw in relations that some observers attributed to the need of both governments to deliver reforms. In October Spain and Morocco signed a series of confidence-building measures to improve cultural ties and economic cooperation.

Saudi Arabia provided Morocco $400 million in February 2013 for development projects. In March the EU announced it would begin negotiations with Morocco on a free trade agreement. During a state visit to Morocco by French President François Hollande in April, a series of bilateral economic agreements were signed. Also in April Canada announced it would provide up to $500 million to Morocco for infrastructure projects that utilized Canadian firms. In June the United Arab Emirates (UAE) agreed to provide Morocco with $1.25 billion to promote sustainable economic development. The next month Morocco and the EU finalized a new four-year fishing agreement to allow European vessels to fish in Moroccan waters in exchange for a $53 million annual subsidy.

Current issues. In January 2007 the militant Algerian organization *Groupe Salafiste pour la Predication et Combat* (GSPC) became al-Qaida in the Islamic Maghreb (AQIM), suggesting potential regionwide cooperation among militant groups. Since then, the government has made several high-profile preventive arrests, reporting in July 2008 that it had found 55 terrorist cells since 2003. One such alleged cell included the Islamist political party the Civilized Alternative (*Al-Badil al-Hadari*). In February 2008 officials arrested 32 members of the group including leader Mustapha Mouatassime and revoked its legal status for suspected ties to clandestine extremist groups, including al-Qaida.

In March 2009 the government initiated a broad campaign against what it described as subversives, including homosexuals and Shiite Muslims. A number of Shiite schools were closed, while dozens of known Shiites were arrested, as were at least 20 homosexuals. Reports indicated that the campaign was a response to calls in several newspapers for greater tolerance for Shiites and homosexuals.

Throughout February and March 2011, there were widespread prodemocracy demonstrations in Marrakesh and other major cities. The protests were led by a loose coalition known as the February 20 Movement. On April 28, 2011, a bomb killed 16 and injured more than 20 in Marrakesh. Also in April the king pardoned 96 political prisoners and reduced the sentences of 80 others. A new constitution that reduced the power of the king was overwhelmingly approved by a referendum in July. Despite the new constitution, antigovernment protests continued through the summer.

On October 28, 2012, Moroccan national Adil el-ATMANI was sentenced to death for his role in the bombing of a Marrakesh café that killed 17 people in April. Hakim DAH received a life sentence, and six others received two- to four-year sentences.

On November 25, 2011, early elections were held for the House of Representatives, which had been increased from 325 to 395 members (with 305 coming from party lists and the remaining 90 from national lists, two-thirds of which were reserved for women). The Justice and Development Party (PJD) secured a plurality with 107 seats, followed by the Independence Party, 60, and the National Assembly of Independents, 52. The turnout was 45.4 percent. On November 29, PJD leader Benkirane was named prime minister. On December 16 Benkirane signed a charter with *Istiqlal*, the Popular Movement, and the Party for Progress and Socialism for a coalition government that would command 217 of the 395 seats in the House of Representatives. On December 19 the new House elected *Istiqlal*'s Karim GHALLAB as its speaker.

On January 3 the king appointed a government under Benkirane as prime minister, who declared that his priorities would be eradication of shanty towns around cities and abject rural poverty.

Government representatives met with leaders from the Polisario Front for talks in New York on March 14, one month after Polisario leader Mohamed ABDELAZIZ warned that armed struggle might be resumed. The talks failed to make headway.

Later that month the government announced it had joined a defamation lawsuit filed by Moroccans in Austria against the Freedom Party of Austria over an election poster that featured the slogan, "Love your native country rather than thieves from Morocco." On April 1 the party announced it would remove the posters. The next day the government announced that Thami Najim, a Danish national of Moroccan heritage, had been detained on charges of plotting to overthrow the Moroccan government. On April 24 the UN Security Council extended the mandate of the UN Mission for the Referendum in Western Sahara (MINURSO) until April 30, 2013, calling on both parties to continue negotiations. The next month, however, Morocco's government spokesman blamed UN envoy Christopher Ross for the lack of progress in negotiations, accusing him of bias and calling for his replacement.

On May 5, 2012, authorities announced they had broken up a "terrorist network" with ties to AQIM. On May 27, tens of thousands took part in a trade union rally in Casablanca, accusing Benkirane of failing to deliver promised reforms. On October 6 more than 2,300 judges held a demonstration at the main appeals court in Rabat, demanding that promised judicial reforms be implemented. On October 17 stone carvings in the Atlas Mountains, estimated to be more than 8,000 years old, were destroyed by Islamic militants who claimed the pagan artifacts were "idolatrous."

On July 9, 2013, *Istiqlal* withdrew from the governing coalition and the government. The party announced it sought to force Benkirane's resignation. Meanwhile the prime minister accused the Islamist party of attempting to sabotage reforms. In August reports indicated that the RNI agreed to join the government, thereby preserving the coalition and forestalling the need for early elections.

POLITICAL PARTIES

Governing Coalition:

Justice and Development Party (*Parti de la Justice et du Développement*—PJD). The PJD was formerly known as the **Popular Constitutional and Democratic Movement** (*Mouvement Populaire Constitutionnel et Démocratique*—MPCD). The MPCD was a splinter from the Popular Movement. It won 3 legislative seats in 1977 and none in 1984 or 1993. In June 1996 the moribund MPCD was rejuvenated by its merger with an unrecognized Islamist grouping known as **Reform and Renewal** (*Islah wa al-Tajdid*), led by Abdelillah Benkirane. The Islamists were allocated 3 of the MPCD's secretariat seats, and Benkirane was generally acknowledged as the party's primary leader. He announced that his supporters had relinquished their "revolutionary ideas" and were now committed to "Islam, the constitutional monarchy, and nonviolence." The party won 9 seats in the House of Representatives in 1997, while Benkirane was successful in a by-election on April 30, 1999. The PJD has gained popularity, taking 42 seats in the House of Representatives in 2002, having won in most districts where it was permitted to run a candidate. In local elections in 2003, it scaled back the candidates it presented, with new leader Saad Eddine OTHMANI explaining that the party did not want to scare off foreign investors with high-profile wins.

The PJD was expected to make major gains in the 2007 parliamentary elections, and many viewed the party as a test case for an Islamist parliamentary victory. While the party fielded candidates in just 50 constituencies in 2002, the PJD campaigned in 94 constituencies in the September elections. Although the party won the largest share of the vote, it took only 46 legislative seats—6 fewer than *Istiqlal.* Despite its status as the second largest party, the PJD was not included in the governing coalition.

In July 2008 the party membership chose Abdelillah Benkirane, a well-known moderate and former leader of the Reform and Renewal party, as its new secretary general. Benkirane, who supports the monarchy, aimed to turn the party away from an overtly religious agenda.

The PJD came in sixth in local balloting in the June 2009 elections and secured only 5.5 percent of the seats, although the party did well in urban areas where it gained 16 percent of the posts. In June 2010 the leader of the PJD in parliament resigned over what he described as the "marginalization" of the legislature. The PJD supported ratification of the new constitution in the 2011 referendum.

In the 2011 elections, the party won by a considerable margin the largest share of votes, securing 107 seats in the new House. Benkirane was appointed prime minister in November 2011.

Reports indicated internal divisions within the party after the PJD leadership decided to not adopt an official position on the 2013 Egyptian coup (see entry on Egypt).

Leader: Abdelillah BENKIRANE (Prime Minister and Secretary General of the Party).

Popular Movement (*Mouvement Populaire*—MP). Organized in 1958 as a monarchist party of Berber mountaineers, the MP was legally recognized in 1959. The MP was a major participant in government coalitions of the early 1960s. It secured the second-largest number of legislative seats in the election of June 1977 and was third ranked after the 1984 and 1993 elections. In October 1986 an extraordinary party congress voted to remove the MP's founder, Mahjoubi AHERDANE, from the post of secretary general, replacing him with Mohand LAENSER. Aherdane subsequently formed a new Berber party (see MNP, below). It is known to be loyal to the monarchy and still draws its support base from rural Berber areas. In the 2002 elections the MP won 27 seats and Laenser was named minister of agriculture. In 2006 the MP absorbed the **Popular National Movement** (*Mouvement National Populaire*—MNP) and the **Democratic Union** (*Union Démocratique*—UD), a center-leaning Berber party led by Bouazza IKKEN. In the 2007 elections the MP won 41 seats and became the third largest party in the House of Representatives. The MP won 2,213 seats in local council elections in June 2009. It joined the government following a cabinet reshuffle in July in which Laenser was appointed a minister of state without portfolio. The MP placed third in indirect elections for the House of Councilors with 11 seats. In the 2011 elections the party came in sixth, securing 32 seats. In 2012 Laenser was appointed interior minister.

Leader: Mohand LAENSER (Interior Minister and Secretary General).

Party of Progress and Socialism (*Parti du Progrès et du Socialisme*—PPS). The PPS is the successor to the **Moroccan Communist Party** (*Parti Communiste Marocain*), which was banned in 1952; the **Party of Liberation and Socialism** (*Parti de la Libération et du Socialisme*), which was banned in 1969; and the **Party of Progress and Socialism** (*Parti du Progrès et du Socialisme*—PPS), which obtained legal status in 1974. The single PPS representative in the 1977 chamber, Ali YATA, was the first communist to win election to a Moroccan legislature. The fourth national congress, held in July 1987 in Casablanca, although strongly supportive of the government's position on the Western Sahara, criticized the administration's recent decisions to privatize some state enterprises and implement other economic liberalization measures required by the International Monetary Fund. However, by mid-1991 the PPS was reported to be fully converted to *perestroika,* a stance that had apparently earned the party additional support within the Moroccan middle class. In late 1993 Yata unsuccessfully urged his Democratic Bloc partners to compromise with King Hassan in formation of a new government.

Ali Yata, who had been reelected to his post of PRP secretary general in mid-1995, died in August 1997 after being struck by a car. Ismail Alaoui was elected as the new secretary general. In March 2002 the PPS and the PSD (above) announced that they had launched the **Socialist Alliance** (*Alliance Socialiste*) and that they were planning to cooperate in the legislative poll in September. In that election the PPS collected only 11 seats. The PPS won 1,102 seats in local balloting in June 2009. It also secured 2 seats in the upper chamber of the parliament in the October balloting. In April 2011 the PPS announced that it had established a formal relationship with the Communist Party of China. In the 2011 elections the party secured 18 seats. It joined the PJD-led government and received four cabinet posts.

Leaders: Nabil BENABDELLAH (Secretary General), Ismail ALAOUI.

National Assembly of Independents (*Rassemblement National des Indépendants*—RNI). The RNI was launched at a Constitutive Congress held October 6–9, 1978. Although branded by a left-wing spokesperson as a "king's party," it claimed to hold the allegiance of 141 of 264 deputies in the 1977 chamber. Subsequent defections and other disagreements, both internal and with the king, resulted in the party's designation as the "official" opposition in late 1981. It won 61 house seats in 1984, thereafter returning to a posture of solid support for the king and the government. RNI leader Ahmed Osman, a former prime minister and former president of the House of Representatives, is one of the country's best-known politicians and is also the son-in-law of the former king. Previously affiliated with the National Entente, the RNI participated (as did the MNP) in the November 1997 elections as an unaligned "centrist" party (winning 46 seats) and subsequently agreed to join the *Koutla*-led coalition government named in early 1998. In 2002 RNI won 41 seats. RNI sustained few losses in the 2007 elections and emerged with 39 seats.

In April 2007 Ahmed Osman was ousted by younger members who organized an extraordinary congress and demanded a successor be found. In May 2007 Mustafa MANSOUI was elected as the new president after Ahmed Osman agreed not to nominate himself again. Mansouri became the speaker of the House of Representatives in October 2007.

The RNI placed third in local balloting in June 2009 with 4,112 seats, or 14 percent of all positions. It was fifth in the indirect balloting for the upper chamber of the parliament with 9 seats. The RNI endorsed the 2011 constitution. In the 2011 elections RNI finished third, securing 52 seats.

Following the withdrawal of *Istiqlal* from the PJD-led government, the RNI's national committee voted on August 2, 2013, to join the governing coalition.

Leaders: Mustafa MANSOURI (Chair), Salaheddine MEZOUAR.

Other Parties:

Independence Party (*Parti de l'Istiqlal, or Istiqlal*—PI). Founded in 1943, *Istiqlal* provided most of the nation's leadership before independence. It split in 1959, and its members were relieved of governmental responsibilities in 1963. Once a firm supporter of the throne, the party now displays a reformist attitude and only supports the king on selected issues. Stressing the need for better standards of living and equal rights for all Moroccans, it has challenged the government regarding alleged human rights abuses. In July 1970 *Istiqlal* formed a National Front with the UNFP (see below) but ran alone in the election of June 1977, when it emerged as the then-leading party. It suffered heavy losses in both the 1983 municipal elections and the 1984 legislative balloting.

In May 1990 *Istiqlal* joined the USFP, the PPS, and the OADP (all described below) in supporting an unsuccessful censure motion that charged the government with "economic incompetence" and the pursuit of "antipopular" and "antisocial" policies. In November 1991 *Istiqlal* announced the formation of a "common front" with the USFP to work toward "establishment of true democracy," and the two parties presented a joint list in 1993, with *Istiqlal*'s 118 candidates securing 43 seats in the direct *Majlis* poll. *Istiqlal* was the leading party in the June 1997 local elections but fell to fifth place in the November house balloting. In the 2007 elections, *Istiqlal* won 52 seats, more than any other party. Its secretary general, Abbas El Fassi, was named prime minister in September 2007.

The party placed second in local balloting in June 2009 and secured 5,292 seats, or 19 percent of total, on local and regional councils. It also placed second in balloting for one-third of the seats in the upper chamber of the parliament, with 17, in October. The party led efforts to enact the new constitution in the 2011 referendum. In the 2011 elections, the party finished second, securing 60 seats. At the party conference on September 24, 2012, Hamid CHABAT, a former mechanic, was elected as the party's secretary general, narrowly beating rival Abdelouahed al-FASSI, son of party founder Allal Fassi. Observers described Chabat's meritocratic rise as evidence of a newly emergent democratic trend in a party whose leadership was traditionally chosen by a small cast of senior leaders.

At a party congress in May 2013, 870 of 976 delegates voted for *Istiqlal* to withdraw from its coalition with the PJD and join the opposition. Party member Mohamed EL OUAFA, the minister of education, refused to resign from the cabinet.

Leaders: Hamid CHABAT (Secretary General), Hachmi EL FILALI, Abou Bakr KADIRI, Abdelkrim GHALLAB, Mohamed BOUCETTA, M'hamed DOUIRI (Presidential Council).

Socialist Union of Popular Forces (*Union Socialiste des Forces Populaire*—USFP). The USFP was organized in September 1974 by the UNFP-Rabat Section (see UNFP, below), which had disassociated itself from the Casablanca Section in July 1972 and was accused by the government of involvement in a Libyan-aided plot to overthrow King Hassan in March 1973. The USFP subsequently called for political democratization, nationalization of major industries, thorough reform of the nation's social and administrative structures, and the cessation of what it believed to be human rights abuses by the government. It secured the third-largest number of legislative seats in the election of June 1977 but withdrew from the House in October 1981 in protest at the extension of the parliamentary term. A year later it announced that it would return for the duration of the session ending in May 1983 so that it could participate in the forthcoming electoral campaigns. The majority of nearly 100 political prisoners released during July–August 1980 were USFP members, most of whom had been incarcerated for alleged antigovernment activities in 1973–1977.

After 52 of its 104 candidates (the USFP also supported 118 *Istiqlal* candidates) won seats in the June 1993 *Majlis* balloting, the union was reportedly divided on whether to accept King Hassan's offer to participate in a coalition government, the dispute ultimately being resolved in favor of the rejectionists. Subsequently, the USFP was awarded only four additional house seats in the September indirect elections. First Secretary Abderrahmane Youssoufi resigned his post and departed for France in protest over "irregularities" surrounding the process. The party also continued to denounce the "harassment" of prominent USFP member Noubir EL-AMAOUI, secretary general of the **Democratic Confederation of Labor** (*Confédération Démocratique du Travail*), who had recently served 14 months in prison for "insulting and slandering" the government in a magazine interview.

Youssoufi returned from his self-imposed exile in April 1995, apparently in response to overtures from King Hassan, who was again attempting to persuade leftist parties to join a coalition government. Although observers suggested that the USFP would soon "redefine" the party platform and possibly select new leaders, a July 1996 congress simply reconfirmed the current political bureau. Meanwhile, one USFP faction was reportedly attempting to "re-radicalize" the party under the direction of Mohamed BASRI, a longtime influential opposition leader. In June 1995 Basri returned from 28 years in exile, during which he had been sentenced (in absentia) to death three times.

The USFP was the leading party in the November 1997 house balloting, securing 57 seats and distancing itself somewhat from its *Koutla* partner *Istiqlal* (32), with which it had been considered of comparable strength. Subsequently, the 74-year-old Youssoufi (once again being referenced as the USFP first secretary) was named by King Hassan to lead a new coalition government, although many younger USFP members reportedly opposed the party's participation. Internal dissent continued, as some radical members charged Youssoufi and the party administration with acting timidly in government and failing to push for further reforms in state institutions. Demands for a leadership change were reportedly voiced in the party congress in March 2001, especially by younger members and those associated with labor unions. However, Youssoufi managed to retain his post, prompting some members to leave the party to form the **National Ittihadi Congress** (CNI, below). USFP was the leading party in the 2002 elections, winning 50 seats. In 2003 Youssoufi resigned, and Mohamed EL YAZGHI took over as first secretary. In 2005 the **Socialist Democratic Party** (*Parti Socialiste et Démocratique*—PSD), which had won 6 seats in the 2002 balloting, merged with the USFP. USFP came in with the largest losses in the 2007 elections; it won only 38 seats, down from 50 seats in 2007. In December of 2007, El Yazghi resigned his party leadership post following disagreements over the 2008 budget. Abdelwahed Radi and Fathallah OUALALOU ran for first secretary, and Radi was elected at a party congress in November 2008.

In local balloting in June 2009 the USFP won 3,266 seats, or 11.6 percent of the total, while in balloting for the House of Councilors, the party placed fourth with 10 seats. Radi urged USFP supporters to vote "yes" in the 2011 constitutional referendum. In the 2011 elections the party came in fifth, securing 39 seats. At a party congress in December 2012, Driss LACHGAR was elected first secretary.

Leaders: Driss LACHGAR (First Secretary), Amina OUCHELH.

Party of Authenticity and Modernity (*Parti Authenticité et Modernité*—PAM). PAM was formed in August 2008 by Fouad El Himma, a childhood friend of Mohamed VI who had previously led another coalition, the **Movement for All Democrats** (*Mouvement pour tous les Démocrates*—MTD). PAM was created by a merger of five smaller parties: Alliance of Freedom (ADL), the Citizens' Initiatives for Development (ICD), the Covenant Party (Al Ahd), the Environment and Development Party (PED), and the National Democratic Party (PND). Its stated purpose is to limit the fragmentation of the Moroccan political environment and prevent the rise of Islamist parties.

In January 2009 the PND (see below) withdrew from the PAM after the party failed to win any seats in by-elections the previous September. PAM joined the opposition prior to the June local elections, reportedly as a means to demonstrate its independence from the monarchy. The grouping placed first in the balloting and secured 21.5 percent of the seats. It then won control of four of the eight regions in regional balloting in September. By the end of 2009 some 89 deputies in the House of Representatives had switched their allegiance to PAM, making the party the largest in the chamber. PAM secretary general Mohammed Cheikh BIADILLAH was elected speaker of the House of Councilors in October after balloting for one-third of the seats in the chamber in which PAM placed first with 22 seats. In the 2011 elections PAM formed an alliance with seven other parties of different political leanings and finished fourth, securing 47 seats.

Following the withdrawal of *Istiqlal* from the PJD-led government in 2013, the PAM rebuffed an offer to join the governing coalition.

Leader: Mustapha BAKKOURY (President).

Alliance of Freedom (*Alliance des Libertés*—ADL). The ADL was created in 2002 by Ali Bel Haj as a moderate, reformist party. It went on to win four seats in the legislative balloting that year. The ADL only secured one seat in the 2007 elections.
Leader: Ali BEL HAJ.

Citizens' Initiatives for Development (*Initiatives Citoyennes pour le Développement*—ICD). The ICD was formed in 2002 by defectors from the MNP (see below).
Leader: Mohammed BENHAMMOU.

Covenant Party (*Parti Al Ahd*), The Covenant Party was established in 2002 by former members of the MP and the MNP. The party listed its candidates with the PND (below) in the 2007 elections to win a collective 14 seats in the legislature.
Leader: Najib EL OUAZZANI.

Party of Environment and Development (*Parti de l'Environnement et du Développement*—PED). PED is a progressive party founded in 2002 to promote sustainable development and environmental preservation. The party won two legislative seats in 2002 and five in 2007. It also secured four seats in the House of Councilors in 2009.
Leader: Ahmed AL ALAMI.

National Democratic Party (*Parti National Démocrate*—PND). The PND was founded as the Democratic Independents (*Indépendants Démocrates*—ID) in April 1981 by 59 former RNI deputies in the House of Representatives. At the party's first congress on June 11–13, 1982, its secretary general, Mohamed Arsalane al-JADIDI, affirmed the PND's loyalty to the monarchy while castigating the RNI for not providing an effective counterweight to the "old" parties. In the 2007 elections, the party ran its candidates with the Covenant Party (see below). Together they won 14 legislative seats. The PND was one of the founding parties of the PAM in 2008, but then withdrew in January 2009 over leadership issues.
Leaders: Abdallah KADIRI, Thami KHYARI (Secretary General).

Constitutional Union (*Union Constitutionelle*—UC). Founded in 1983 by Maati Bouabid, UC is a moderate party that emphasizes economic self-sufficiency. Said to have royal support, the party won 83 house seats in 1984. UC's representation fell to 54 seats in 1993, although it retained a slim plurality and one of its members was elected president of the new house. Bouabid died in November 1996, exacerbating problems within a party described as already in disarray. UC was the second leading party in the November 1997 house balloting, winning 50 seats, but dropped to 16 in 2002. In the 2007 elections UC won 27 seats. In the June 2009 local elections the UC won 1,307 seats. The UC gained 1 seat in the House of Councilors in the October 2010 balloting for one-third of the chamber. It was staunchly supportive of the 2011 constitutional reforms. Reports in 2013 indicated that the UC had participated in discussions to join the PJD-led governing coalition.
Leader: Mohamed ABIED (Secretary General).

Democratic Forces Front (*Front des Forces Démocratiques*—FFD). Launched in 1997 by PRP dissidents, the FFD won nine seats in the November house balloting, and its leader was named to the March 1998 cabinet. In 2007 the party again won nine seats. It has endeavored unsuccessfully to enact legislation to abolish the death penalty in Morocco. The FFD secured one seat in the upper chamber of parliament following the 2010 balloting.
Leader: Thami KHYARI (National Secretary).

Democratic and Social Movement (*Mouvement Démocratique et Social*—MDS). Launched in June 1996 (as the National Democratic and Social Movement) by MNP dissidents, the right-wing Berber MDS is led by a former policeman. The party held seven seats following the 2002 balloting for the House of Representatives. The party had nine seats after the 2007 elections. The MDS opposed the expansion of the UN mission in the Sahara in 2013.
Leader: Mahmoud ARCHANE (Secretary General).

Unified Socialist Party (*Parti Socialiste Unifié*—PSU). This party has had several incarnations, initially as the Organization of Democratic and Popular Action (*Organisation de l'Action Démocratique et Populaire*—OADP). Claiming a following of former members of the USFP and PPS, the OADP was organized in May 1983. It obtained one seat in 1984 balloting and two seats in 1993. A new 74-member Central Committee was elected at the third OADP congress, held November 5–6, 1994, in Casablanca.

The OADP was one of the few major parties to oppose the king's constitutional initiatives of 1996, some of its members subsequently splitting off to form the PSD (see above) because of the issue. The OADP won four seats in the November 1997 *Majlis* elections. Although the OADP was a member of the ruling Democratic Bloc, it was not listed as having any members in the March 1998 cabinet. OADP sources defined the group's stance as one of "critical" support of the coalition government. In 2002 it merged with other groups to form the United Socialist Left (*Gauche Socialiste Unifiée*—GSU).

In 2005 GSU reformed to create PSU. In the 2007 elections it ran in electoral coalition with the **Party of the Democratic Socialist Avant-Garde** (*Parti de l'Avant-Garde Démocratique Socialiste*—PADS) and the National Congress Party, collectively winning six seats.
Leader: NABILA MOUNIB (Secretary General).

National Congress Party (*Congrès National Ittihadi*—CNI). The CNI was founded in 2001 by USFP dissidents.
Leader: Abdesalam EL AZIZ (Secretary General).

Party of the Democratic Socialist Avant-Garde (*Parti de l'Avant-Garde Démocratique Socialiste*—PADS). Formed by USFD dissidents in 1991, PADS boycotted the 1997 elections on the ground that its members had been harassed by the government. In 2007 PADS formed a union with the National Congress Party (see above) and the Unified Socialist Party (see above) and took six seats in the legislature.
Leader: Ahmed BENJELLOUNE.

Workers' Party (*Parti Travailliste*). This left-wing party was established in May 2006. It was set up by trade unionists and old militants from the USFP. Among its founders was Abdelkrim Benatiq, who was close to the former prime minister, Abderrahman Youssoufi. The Workers' Party won five legislative seats in the 2007 election. The party supported adoption of the 2011 constitution.
Leader: Abdelkrim BENATIQ (Secretary General).

Other Parties and Groups:

Other parties, a number of which won seats in 2002, 2006, and 2007 include the **Action Party** (*Parti de l'Action*—PA), led by Mohammed EL IDRISSI; the small but longstanding **Democratic Party for Independence** (*Parti Démocratique pour l'Indépendance* or *Parti de la Choura et de l'Istiqlal,* or *Choura*—PDI), led by Abdelwahed MAACH; the **Moroccan Liberal Party** (*Parti Marocain Libéral*—PML), led by Mohammed ZIANE; the **Moroccan Union for Democracy** (*Union Marocaine pour la Démocratie*—UMD), led by Abdellah AZMANI; the **National Ittihadi Congress** (*Congrès National Ittihadi*—CNI), a breakaway group from the USFP led by Abdelmajid BOUZOUBAA; the **National Party for Unity and Solidarity** (*Parti National pour l'Unité et la Solidarité*—PNUS), led by Muhammad ASMAR; the **Party of Citizens' Forces** (*Parti des Forces Citoyennes*—PFC), led by Abderrahim LAHJOUJI; the **Party of Reform and Development** (*Parti de la Réforme et du Développement*—PRD), led by former RNI member Abderrahmane EL KOHEN; the **Party of Renewal and Equity** (*Parti du Renouveau et de l'Equité*—PRE), led by Chakir ACHEHBAR; the **Renaissance and Virtue Party** (*Parti de la Renaissance et de la Vertu*), an Islamist party set up in December 2005 by a former member of the PJD, led by Mohamed KHALIDI; and the **Social Center Party** (*Parti du Centre Social*—PCS), led by Lachen MADIH.

For more information on the **Popular National Movement** (*Mouvement National Populaire*—MNP) and groups active through the 1990s, see the 2008 *Handbook.*

Clandestine Groups:

Justice and Welfare (*Adl wa-al-Ihsan*). The country's leading radical Islamist organization, *Adl wa-al-Ihsan* was formed in 1980. Although denied legal party status in 1981, it was informally tolerated until a mid-1989 crackdown, during which its founder, Sheikh Abd Assalam Yassine, was placed under house arrest and other members were imprisoned. The government formally outlawed the group in January 1990; two months later, five of its most prominent members were given two-year prison terms, and Yassine's house detention was extended, touching off large-scale street disturbances in Rabat. Although the other detainees were released in early 1992, Yassine remained under house arrest, with King Hassan describing extremism as a threat to Moroccan stability. An estimated 100 members of *Adl wa-al-Ihsan* were reportedly among the prisoners pardoned in mid-1994, although Yassine was pointedly not among them. He was finally released from house arrest in December 1995 but was soon thereafter placed under "police protection" for apparently having criticized the government too strenuously. (Among Yassine's transgressions, in the eyes of the government, was his failure to acknowledge King Hassan as the nation's supreme religious leader.) His house arrest prompted protest demonstrations in 1998 by his supporters, whom the government also charged with responsibility for recent protests among university students and a mass demonstration in late December 1998 protesting U.S.–UK air strikes against Iraq. Although the group remained proscribed, Yassine was released from house arrest in May 2000. Based on Yassine's rejection of violence, the government tolerated the group's activities. However, in May 2006 the government arrested hundreds of *Adl wa-al-Ihsan* members across the country, apparently in reaction to rumors that the party had planned an uprising. Those rounded up were later freed, but party members claimed that materials such as computers and books had been seized from party offices.

Subsequently the authorities continued to put pressure on the party. In July 2006 *Adl wa-al-Ihsan* member Hayat Bouida was allegedly abducted and tortured for three hours by six intelligence agents in Safi, a city 300 kilometers south of Casablanca. In May 2007 she was stabbed by two intelligence agents in front of her house. In March 2008 more than 20 members of the group were arrested and several were prosecuted. In July 2009 8 members of the group were arrested for illegal activities. By 2010 authorities estimated that there were approximately 200,000 members of *Adl wa-al-Ihsani* throughout Morocco. In June 2010 seven officials of the group were arrested for belonging to an illegal group. The group was one of the leading organizers of antiregime protests in February and March 2011. It opposed the 2011 constitution, asserting that it did not do enough to reform the government and it called for an end to electoral quotas for women. In 2013 reports indicated that *Adl wa-al-Ihsan* rebuffed a government offer to register the grouping as a political party.

Leaders: Sheikh Abdessalam YASSINE, Fathallah ARSLANE (Spokesperson).

LEGISLATURE

The constitutional amendments of September 1996 provided for a bicameral **Parliament** (*Barlaman*) comprising an indirectly elected House of Councilors and a directly elected House of Representatives. Previously, the legislature had consisted of a unicameral House of Representatives, two-thirds of whose members were directly elected with the remainder being selected by an electoral college of government, professional, and labor representatives.

House of Councilors (*Majlis al-Mustasharin*). The upper house consists of 270 members indirectly elected for nine-year terms (one-third of the house is renewed every three years) by local councils, regional councils, and professional organizations. In the election to renew one-third of the house on October 3, 2010, the Authenticity and Modernity Party won 22 seats; Independence Party, 17; Popular Movement, 22; the Socialist Union of Popular Forces, 10; National Assembly of Independents, 9; Party of Environment and Development, 4; the Constitutional Union, 3; Party of Progress and Socialism, 2; Party of Citizens' Forces, 1; Democratic Forces Front, 1; Moroccan Liberal Party, 1; and various labor organizations, 9.

Speaker: Mohammed Cheikh BIADILLAH.

House of Representatives (*Majlis al-Nawwab*). The lower house has 395 members directly elected on a proportional basis for five-year terms. Following legislative elections on November 25, 2011, the distribution of seats was the following: Party of Justice and Development, 107; Independence Party (*Istiqlal*), 60; National Assembly of Independents, 52; Authenticity and Modernity party (PAM), 47; Socialist Union of Popular Forces, 39; Popular Movement, 32; Constitutional Union, 23; Party of Progress and Socialism, 18; Workers' Party, 4; Renewal and Equity Party, 2; Democratic and Social Movement, 2; Party of Environment and Development, 2; Democratic Oath (SD), 2; Democratic Forces Front, 1; Action Party, 1; Union and Democracy Party (PUD), 1; Party of Liberty and Social Justice (PLJS), 1; Green Left Party (PGV), 1.

Speaker: Karim GHELLAB.

CABINET

[as of August 15, 2013]

Prime Minister	Abdelilah Benkirane (PJD)
Minister of State	Abdellah Baha (PJD)
Ministers	
Agriculture, Rural Development, and Marine Fisheries	Aziz Akhenouch (ind.)
Communication, Spokesperson of the Government	Mustapha El Khalfi (PJD)
Culture	Mohamed Amine Sbihi (PPS)
Education	Mohamed el Ouafa (*Istiqlal*)
Employment and Vocational Training	Abdelouahed Souhail (PPS)
Energy, Mining, Water, and Environment	(Vacant)
Equipment and Transport	Aziz Rabbah (PJD)
Finance and Economy (Acting)	Aziz Akhennouch (ind.)
Foreign Affairs and Cooperation	Saad-Eddine El Othmani (PJD)
General Secretary of the Government	Driss Dahak (ind.)
Habous (Religious Endowments) and Islamic Affairs	Ahmed Toufiq (ind.)
Handicrafts	(Vacant)
Health	El Hossein El Ouardi (PPS)
Housing and Urban Planning	Nabil Benabdellah (PPS)
Industry, Trade, and New Technologies	Abdelkader Aamara (PJD)
Interior	Mohand Laenser (MP)
Justice	Mustafa Ramid (PJD)
National Education, Higher Education, Staff, Training, and Scientific Research	Lahcen Daoudi (PJD)
Relations with Parliament	Lahbib Choubani (PJD)
Social Development, the Family, and Solidarity	Bassima Hakkaoui (PJD) [f]
Tourism, Handicrafts, and Social Economy	Lahcen Haddad (MP)
Youth and Sports	Mohamed Ouzzine (MP)
Ministers Delegate (Ministries)	
Moroccans Living Abroad	(Vacant)
Foreign Affairs and Cooperation	(Vacant)
General Affairs and Governance	Mohamed Najib Boulif (PJD)
National Defense	Abdellatif Loudiyi (ind.)
Civil Service and the Modernization of the Administration	Abdeladim El Guerrouj (MP)
Economy and Finance in Charge of the Budget	Idriss Azami Al Idrissi (PJD)
Interior	Charki Draiss (ind.)

[f] = female

INTERGOVERNMENTAL REPRESENTATION

Ambassador to the U.S.: Mohammed Rachad BOUHLAL.

U.S. Ambassador to Morocco: Dwight BUSH, Sr. (nominated).

Permanent Representative to the UN: Mohammed LOULICHKI.

IGO Memberships (Non-UN): AfDB, EBRD, IOM, LAS, NAM, OIC, WTO.

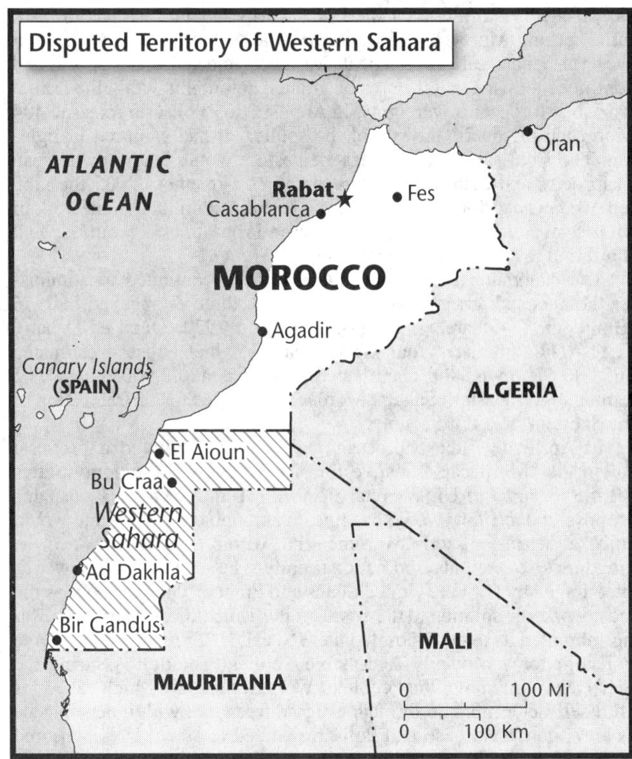

DISPUTED TERRITORY

Western Sahara. The region known since 1976 as Western Sahara was annexed by Spain in two stages: the coastal area in 1884 and the interior in 1934. In 1957, the year after Morocco attained full independence, Rabat renewed a claim to the territory, sending irregulars to attack inland positions. In 1958, however, French and Spanish troops succeeded in quelling the attacks, with Madrid formally uniting Saguia el Hamra and Rio de Oro, the two historical components of the territory, as the province of Spanish Sahara. Mauritanian independence in 1960 led to territorial claims by Nouakchott, with the situation being further complicated in 1963 by the discovery of one of the world's richest phosphate deposits at Bu Craa. During the next dozen years, Morocco attempted to pressure Spain into relinquishing its claim through a combination of diplomatic initiatives (the UN first called for a referendum on self-determination for the Sahrawi people in 1966), direct support for guerrilla groups, and a legal challenge in the International Court of Justice (ICJ).

Increasing insurgency led Spain in May 1975 to announce that it intended to withdraw from Spanish Sahara. In November King Hassan ordered some 300,000 unarmed Moroccans, in what became known as the Green March, to enter the territory. Although Spain strongly objected to the action, a tripartite agreement with Morocco and Mauritania was concluded in Madrid on November 14. As a result, Spanish Sahara ceased to be a province of Spain at the end of the year; Spanish troops withdrew shortly thereafter, and Morocco and Mauritania assumed responsibility for Western Sahara on February 28, 1976. On April 14 Rabat and Nouakchott reached an agreement under which Morocco claimed the northern two-thirds of the region and Mauritania claimed the southern one-third.

Opposition to the partition was led by the Popular Front for the Liberation of Saguia el Hamra and Rio de Oro (Polisario, see below), which in February 1976 formally proclaimed a government-in-exile of the Sahrawi Arab Democratic Republic (SADR), headed by Mohamed Lamine OULD AHMED as prime minister. Whereas Polisario had originally been based in Mauritania, its political leadership was subsequently relocated to Algeria, with its guerrilla units, recruited largely from nomadic tribes indigenous to the region, establishing secure bases there. Neither Rabat nor Nouakchott wished to precipitate a wider conflict by operating on Algerian soil, which permitted Polisario to concentrate militarily against the weaker of the two occupying regimes and thus to aid in the overthrow of Mauritania's Moktar Ould Daddah in July 1978. On August 5, 1979, Mauritania concluded a peace agreement with Polisario in Algiers, but Morocco responded by annexing the southern third of Western Sahara. Meanwhile, Polisario launched its first raids into Morocco, while continuing a diplomatic offensive that by the end of 1980 had resulted in some 45 countries according recognition to the SADR.

At an OAU Council of Ministers meeting in Addis Ababa, Ethiopia, on February 22, 1982, a SADR delegation was, for the first time, seated, following a controversial ruling by the organization's secretary general that provoked a walkout by 18 member states, including Morocco. For the same reason, a quorum could not be declared for the next scheduled Council of Ministers meeting in Tripoli, Libya, on July 26, or for the 19th OAU summit, which was to have convened in Tripoli on August 5. An attempt to reconvene both meetings in November, following the "voluntary and temporary" withdrawal of the SADR, also failed because of the Western Sahara impasse, coupled with disagreement over the composition of a delegation from Chad. Another "temporary" withdrawal of the SADR allowed the OAU to convene the long-delayed summit in Addis Ababa in May 1983 at which it was decided to oversee a referendum in the region by the end of the year. Morocco's refusal to meet directly with Polisario representatives forced postponement of the poll, while the 1984 Treaty of Oujda with Libya effectively reduced support for the front's military forces. Subsequently, Moroccan soldiers crossed briefly into Algerian soil in "pursuit" of guerrillas, while extending the area under Moroccan control by 4,000 square miles. The seating of a SADR delegation at the twentieth OAU summit in November 1985 and the election of Polisario Secretary General Mohamed Abd al-AZZIZ as an OAU vice president prompted Morocco's withdrawal from the organization.

At the sixth triennial Polisario congress, held in "liberated territory" in December 1985, Abd al-Azziz was reelected secretary general; he subsequently appointed a new 13-member SADR government that included himself as president, with Ould Ahmed continuing as prime minister. The following May a series of "proximity talks" involving Moroccan and Polisario representatives concluded at UN headquarters in New York with no discernible change in the territorial impasse. Subsequently, Rabat began construction of more than 1,200 miles of fortified sand walls that forced the rebels back toward the Algerian and Mauritanian borders. Polisario, while conceding little likelihood of victory by its 30,000 fighters over an estimated 120,000 to 140,000 Moroccan soldiers, nonetheless continued its attacks, hoping that the economic strain of a "war of attrition" would induce King Hassan to enter into direct negotiations—a position endorsed by a 98–0 vote of the forty-first UN General Assembly. The UN also offered to administer the Western Sahara on an interim basis pending a popular referendum, but Rabat insisted that its forces remain in place. In 1987 the SADR reported an assassination attempt against Abd al-Azziz, alleging Moroccan complicity. Rabat denied the allegation and suggested that SADR dissidents may have been responsible.

Following the resumption of relations between Rabat and Algiers in May 1988, which some observers attributed in part to diminishing Algerian support for Polisario, progress appeared to be developing toward a negotiated settlement of the militarily stalemated conflict. On August 30, shortly after a new SADR government had been announced with Mahfoud Ali BEIBA taking over as prime minister, both sides announced their "conditional" endorsement of a UN-sponsored peace plan that called for a cease-fire and introduction of a UN peacekeeping force to oversee the long-discussed self-determination referendum. However, agreement was lacking on the qualifications of those who would be permitted to participate in the referendum and whether Moroccan troops would remain in the area prior to the vote. Underlining the fragility of the negotiations, Polisario launched one of its largest attacks in September before calling a cease-fire on December 30, pending face-to-face talks with King Hassan in January 1989. Although the talks eventually broke down, the cease-fire continued throughout most of the year as UN Secretary General Javier Pérez de Cuéllar attempted to mediate an agreement on referendum details. However, Polisario, accusing Rabat of delaying tactics, initiated a series of attacks in October, subsequent fighting being described as some of the most intense to date in the conflict. Another temporary truce was implemented in March 1990, and in June the UN Security Council formally authorized creation of a Western Saharan mission to supervise the proposed referendum. However, it was not until April 29, 1991, that the Security Council endorsed direct UN sponsorship of the poll, with the General Assembly approving a budget of $180 million, plus $34 million in voluntary contributions, for a UN Mission for the Referendum in Western Sahara (referenced by its French acronym, MINURSO). The mission's charge included the identification of bona fide inhabitants of the territory, the assembly of a voting list, the establishment of polling stations, and supervision of the balloting itself. The plan appeared to be in jeopardy when fierce fighting broke out in August between Moroccan and Polisario forces prior to the proposed deployment of MINURSO peacekeeping troops; however, both sides honored the UN's formal cease-fire date of September 6.

By early 1992 the broader dimensions of the Western Sahara conflict had significantly changed. The collapse of the Soviet Union and heightened internal problems for Polisario's principal backers, Algeria and Libya, created financial and supply problems for the rebels. At midyear it was estimated that more than 1,000 rank and file had joined a number of dissident leaders in defecting to Morocco. Meanwhile, Morocco had moved tens of thousands of settlers into the disputed territory, thereby diluting potential electoral support for Polisario. In addition, the proposed self-determination referendum, which the UN had planned to conduct in February, had been postponed indefinitely over the issue of voter eligibility, Polisario leaders charging that UN representatives had compromised their impartiality through secret dealings with Rabat. An unprecedented meeting, brokered by the UN at El Aaién between Moroccan and Polisario representatives, ended on July 19, 1993, without substantial progress. The main difficulty lay in a dispute about voting lists, Polisario insisting they should be based on a census taken in 1974 and Morocco arguing that they should be enlarged to include the names of some 100,000 individuals subsequently settling in the territory.

A second round of face-to-face talks, scheduled for October 1993, was cancelled at the last moment when Polisario objected to the presence of recent defectors from the front on the Moroccan negotiating team. Although the prospects for agreement on electoral eligibility were regarded as slight, MINURSO began identifying voters in June 1994 with the hope that balloting could be conducted in October 1995. Registration proceeded slowly, however, and UN officials in early 1995 protested that the Moroccan government was interfering in their operations. In April, UN Secretary General Boutros Boutros-Ghali reluctantly postponed the referendum again, sentiment reportedly growing within the UN Security Council to withdraw MINURSO if genuine progress was not achieved shortly.

In May 1996 the Security Council ordered a reduction in MINURSO personnel, UN officials declaring an impasse in the voter identification dispute and observers suggesting that hostilities could easily break out once again. However, face-to-face contacts between Polisario and Moroccan officials resumed in September, but no genuine progress ensued. It was reported that only 60,000 potential voters had been approved, with the cases of some 150,000 other "applicants" remaining unresolved at the end of the year.

New UN Secretary General Kofi Annan made the relaunching of the UN initiative in Morocco one of his priorities in early 1997 and in the spring appointed former U.S. Secretary of State James Baker as his personal envoy on the matter. Baker's mediation led to face-to-face talks between Polisario and representatives of the Moroccan government in the summer, culminating in the announcement of a "breakthrough" in September. Essentially, the two sides agreed to revive the 1991 plan with the goal of conducting the self-determination referendum in December 1998. They also accepted UN "supervision" in the region pending the referendum and agreed to the repatriation of refugees under the auspices of the UN High Commissioner for Refugees. MINURSO resumed the identification of voters in December 1997; however, the process subsequently again bogged down, with most observers concluding that the Moroccan government bore primary responsibility for the foot-dragging. Annan launched what he said would be his final push for a resolution in early 1999, calling for the resumption of voter registration at midyear leading up to a referendum by the end of July 2000.

In September 1999 several pro-independence riots in Western Sahara were suppressed by what some saw as an overreaction by the police, who beat and arrested scores of demonstrators. The heavy-handedness of the security forces reportedly strengthened the resolve of King Mohamed VI to oust the "old guard" of the Moroccan regime, especially Interior Minister Driss Basri. Although the new king later espoused a more flexible stance toward the Western Sahara issue, UN special envoy Baker noted in April 2000 that he remained pessimistic about the prospects of a resolution of the conflict, citing Morocco's insistence that Moroccan settlers in Western Sahara be eligible in the proposed referendum. In September 2001 Polisario rejected Baker's proposal to grant the Western Sahara political autonomy rather than hold an independence referendum. Recent interest in oil drilling in the region reportedly further complicated the matter. In November 2002 King Mohamed described the notion of a self-determination referendum as "obsolete." In mid-2004 the UN Security Council adopted a resolution urging Morocco and Polisario to accept the UN plan to grant Western Sahara self-government. Morocco rejected the proposal and continued to insist that the area be granted autonomy within the framework of Moroccan sovereignty. In August 2005 Polisario released 404 Moroccan prisoners, the last of the soldiers it had captured in fighting. The front said it hoped that the gesture would lead to Moroccan reciprocity and then a peace settlement. In November 2005 the king renewed his call for autonomy for the region within the "framework of Moroccan sovereignty," but the Polisario Front quickly rebuffed what it referred to as the king's "intransigence."

The stalemate lasted into 2006. Morocco continued to administer the annexed territory as four provinces: three established in 1976 (Boujdour, Es-Smara, El-Aaiún) and one in 1979 (Oued ed-Dahab). The SADR administers four Algerian camps, which house an estimated 165,000 Sahrawis, and claims to represent some 83,000 others who remain in the Western Sahara. Morocco has called for the relocation of the Sahrawis to a third country.

In April 2007 the Moroccan government submitted a proposal called the "Moroccan Initiative for Negotiating an Autonomy Status for the Sahara," to UN Secretary General, Ban Ki-Moon. Under this proposal the territory would become an autonomous region and would enjoy a measure of self-government but within the framework of the kingdom's sovereignty and national unity. The idea of autonomy was encouraged by both the United States and France, who viewed it as the most workable solution to the crisis. At the same time, however, Polisario submitted its own proposal to the UN, called "Proposal of the Frente Polisario for a Mutually Acceptable Political Solution Assuring the Self-Determination of the People of Western Sahara," which called for "full self-determination through a free referendum with independence as an option." Morocco and Polisario agreed to attend UN-sponsored talks in June 2007, a groundbreaking development given that this was the first time in ten years that the two sides had sat down at the same table. In 2008 the UN envoy was quoted saying that independence was not an option for the Western Sahara, a comment that had the Polisario Front and the Algerian government crying foul. In April 2008 the UN renewed its mission in the region for another year, and the stalemate that had persisted in the last three attempts at negotiation between the parties continued. In August 2009 Morocco resumed informal negotiations with the Polisario Front under UN sponsorship. However, Algeria subsequently accused Morocco of responsibility for delaying the resumption of official talks. On October 7, 2010, the Polisario Front's top police officer, Mustapha Salma SIDI MOULOUD, was arrested after he made public comments supportive of a Moroccan compromise autonomy plan for the region. In November a raid by Moroccan security forces killed 12 in the disputed area around Laayoune. The raid was in response to rioting in October. In June 2011 a Moroccan judge ordered the release of 37 people who had been arrested during the incident. Reports in 2013 indicated that Islamist militants from Mali had established bases in the Western Sahara. In February 2013 Morocco sentenced 25 human rights activists to varying prison terms for their participation in a November 2010 protest. The sentences were widely condemned by the international community.

Sahrawi Front:

Popular Front for the Liberation of Saguia el Hamra and Rio de Oro (*Frente Popular para la Liberación de Saguia el Hamra y Rio de Oro*—Polisario). Established in 1973 to win independence for Spanish (subsequently Western) Sahara, the Polisario Front was initially based in Mauritania, but since the mid-1970s its political leadership has operated from Algeria. In consonance with recent developments throughout the world, the once strongly socialist Polisario currently promises to institute a market economy in "the future Sahrawi state," except in regard to mineral reserves (which would remain state property). The front also supports "eventual" multipartyism, its 1991 congress, held in Tindouf, Algeria, pledging to draft a "democratic and pluralistic" constitution to present for a national referendum should the proposed self-determination vote in the Western Sahara go in Polisario's favor. In other activity, the Congress reelected longtime leader Mohamed Abd al-Azziz as secretary general of the front and thereby president of the SADR. However, in August 1992 the defection to Morocco of the SADR foreign minister, Brahim HAKIM, served to point out the increasingly tenuous position of the rebel movement. Subsequently, a new SADR government in exile announced in September 1993 was most noteworthy for the appointment of hard-liner Brahim GHALI as defense minister.

In 1995 Polisario reportedly was still threatening to resume hostilities if the UN plan collapsed. However, it was widely believed that the front's military capacity had by then diminished to about 6,000 soldiers.

The Ninth Polisario Congress, held August 20–27, 1995, reelected Abd al-Azziz as secretary general and urged the international community to pressure the Moroccan government regarding its perceived stonewalling. In September a new SADR government was announced under the leadership of Mahfoud Ali Larous Beiba, a former SADR health minister. On October 12 the first session of a SADR National Assembly was convened in Tindouf, its 101 members having been elected via secret ballot at local and regional "conferences." A new SADR government was named on January 21, 1998, although Beiba remained as prime minister and a number of incumbents were reappointed. Beiba was succeeded in 1999 by Bouchraya Hamoudi Bayoun, who was in turn succeeded in 2003 by Abdelkader Taleb Oumar.

In the summer and fall of 2005, many Sahrawis had begun referring to their campaign against Morocco as an "*intifada,*" and Abd al-Azziz called for assistance from South Africa's Nelson Mandela and U.S. President George W. Bush in resolving the Western Sahara standoff.

In 2008 SADR announced that it sought bids for offshore oil exploration, but it received little foreign interest because of concerns over the long-term legal status of any contracts.

In August 2010 Antigua and Barbuda, Grenada, Saint Kitts and Nevis, and St. Lucia withdrew their recognition of SADR after a Moroccan diplomatic effort. In June 2011 Polisario attempted unsuccessfully to block an EU-Moroccan fisheries agreement. Meanwhile, in July Morocco and Polisario conducted a series of informal negotiations in New York under the auspices of the UN. Polisario denied reports in 2013 that its youth wing had connections with Al-Qaeda in the Islamic Maghreb (AQMI).

Secretary General: Mohamed Abd al-AZZIZ (President of the SADR).
Prime Minister of the SADR: Abdelkader Taleb OUMAR.

MOZAMBIQUE

Republic of Mozambique
República de Moçambique

Political Status: Former Portuguese dependency; became independent as the People's Republic of Mozambique on June 25, 1975; present name adopted in constitution that came into effect on November 30, 1990.

Area: 309,494 sq. mi. (801,590 sq. km).

Population: 25,182,220 (2013E—UN); 24,096,669 (2013E—U.S. Census).

Major Urban Center (2005E): MAPUTO (1,122,000).

Official Language: Portuguese (a number of African languages are also spoken).

Monetary Unit: Metical (market rate November 1, 2013: 29.80 meticals = $1US). The "new metical" was introduced in 2006 at the rate of 1 new metical = 1,000 old meticals.

President: Armando Emilio GUEBUZA (Mozambique Liberation Front); elected on December 1–2, 2004, and inaugurated on February 2, 2005, to succeed Joaquim Alberto CHISSANO (Mozambique Liberation Front); reelected on October 28, 2009, and inaugurated on January 14, 2010.

Prime Minister: Alberto Clementino VAQUINA (Mozambique Liberation Front); appointed by the president on October 8, 2012, to succeed Aires Bonifacio ALI (Mozambique Liberation Front), who resigned the same day.

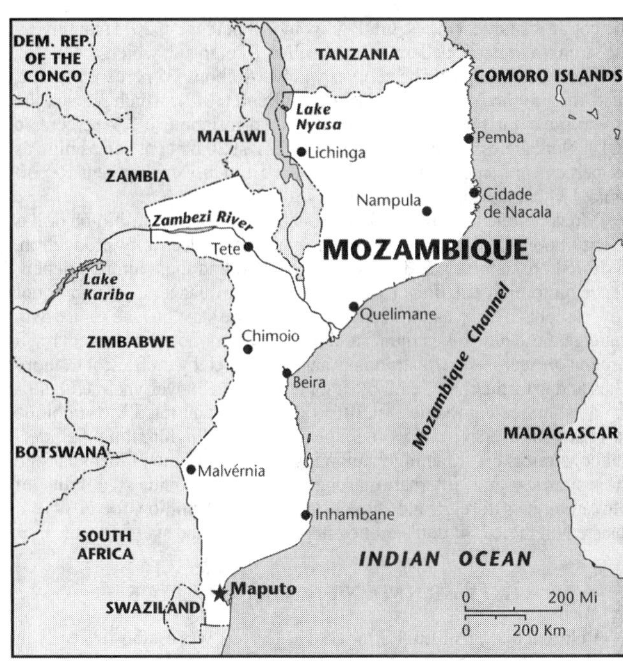

THE COUNTRY

Mozambique lies on the southeast coast of Africa, its contiguous neighbors being Tanzania on the north; Malawi and Zambia on the northwest; and Zimbabwe, South Africa, and Swaziland on the west and south. Mozambique's varied terrain comprises coastal lowlands, central plateaus, and mountains along the western frontier. The country is bisected by the Zambezi River, which flows southeastward from the Zambia-Zimbabwe border. The population, while primarily of Bantu stock, is divided into several dozen tribal groups, most speaking distinct local languages or dialects. About 55 percent of the population is Christian, and approximately 18 percent is Muslim, while about one-quarter of the population practices traditional religions. Women constitute 48 percent of the labor force, primarily in the agricultural sector; there are a number of female ministers in the current cabinet and 98 members of the assembly are women (39.2 percent).

Agriculture remains the mainstay of the economy, employing two-thirds of the workforce and providing the principal cultivated exports: cashew nuts, cotton, sugar, and tea. Seafood is also an important export. Following independence, agricultural output declined—particularly in production of sugar and cotton as well as of such minerals as coal and copper—as the government introduced pervasive state control and the Portuguese community, which possessed most of the country's technical and managerial expertise, left the country. In the early 1980s, however, the government began to encourage limited private ownership, foreign investment, and the development of family-owned and operated farms. For the most part, industry has been limited to processing agricultural commodities, although significant deposits of natural gas, as well as bauxite, iron, manganese, tantalite, uranium, and other ores, await exploitation.

Mozambique remained among the lowest-ranked nations regarding development, and poverty was widespread, much of the population living in small villages lacking electricity or running water (for information on Mozambique's economy prior to 2000, see the 2011 *Handbook*). Nonetheless, fueled by foreign aid, from 2000 through 2010, GDP grew an average of 7.9 percent per year, while inflation averaged 10.5 percent.

In 2008 the government announced a $3 billion effort, funded mainly by foreign investments, to develop Mozambique as a tourist destination. Through 2008, the World Bank provided $60 million annually for 17 infrastructure projects. Meanwhile, Portugal cancelled Mozambique's $390 million debt, while Ireland pledged $290 million over a four-year period for poverty reduction. The 2008–2009 global economic downturn slowed GDP growth slightly as foreign investment was reduced, but higher agricultural output offset the economic decline. In June 2009 the European Commission agreed to provide $598 million in aid to Mozambique, while the World Bank and other donors pledged $446 million to improve health care. In October 2010 the World Bank announced it would provide $143 million to expand water and sewage systems in the country's largest cities. GDP grew by 7.3 percent in 2011, mainly on the strength of expanded exports as well as foreign aid, which accounted for 15 percent of GDP. The economy grew by about 7.5 percent in 2012, according to the International Monetary Fund (IMF), which praised the government for policies that brought down inflation to 2.1 percent in 2012. Nonetheless, unemployment was almost 20 percent and as high as 60 percent in some areas. The 2013 UN Human Development Report ranked Mozambique as 185th out of 186 countries.

Mozambique is considered to be on the verge of a multi-billion dollar energy boom—in hydropower, coal mining and electricity production, and offshore natural gas deposits—that could end the country's dependence on foreign aid, drastically reducing the influence of foreign donor governments. But questions remain whether the state has the capacity to manage these new investments and prevent corruption. Investments will depend on access to infrastructure that is regulated by inefficient monopolies and is further hampered by labor constraints in overwhelmed building and service companies. In 2013 the World Bank rated Mozambique as 146th out of 185 in its Doing Business survey, highlighting the internal constraints on attracting foreign investment. In June of that year, the 19 countries and international agencies that provide the bulk of Mozambique's foreign aid agreed to give $580 million for 2014 but insisted on increased transparency in government and state industries.

GOVERNMENT AND POLITICS

Political background. Portuguese hegemony was established early in the 16th century, when Mozambican coastal settlements became ports of call for traders from the Far East. However, it was not until the Berlin Congress of 1884–1885 that Portuguese supremacy was formally acknowledged by the European powers. In 1952 the colony of Mozambique became an Overseas Province and, as such, was constitutionally incorporated into Portugal. In 1964 armed resistance to Portuguese rule was initiated by the Mozambique Liberation Front (*Frente de Libertação de Moçambique*—Frelimo), led by Dr. Eduardo MONDLANE until his assassination by Portuguese agents in 1969. Following Mondlane's death, Samora MACHEL and Marcelino DOS SANTOS overcame a bid for control by Frelimo Vice President Uriah SIMANGO and were installed as the movement's president and vice president, respectively. After the 1974 coup in Lisbon, negotiations in Lusaka, Zambia, called for the formation of a new government composed of Frelimo and Portuguese elements and for complete independence in mid-1975. The agreement was challenged by leaders of the white minority, who attempted to establish a white provisional government under right-wing leadership. After the collapse of this rebellion on September 10, 1974, most of the territory's 250,000 whites migrated to Portugal or South Africa.

On June 25, 1975, Mozambique became an independent "people's republic," with Machel assuming the presidency. Elections of Frelimo-sponsored candidates to local, district, provincial, and national assemblies were held during September–December 1977. In an apparent easing of its commitment to Marxist centralism, the government took steps in the early 1980s to separate government and party cadres. However, a government reorganization in March 1986 reestablished party domination, with the Council of Ministers being divided into three sections, each directed by a senior member of the Frelimo Political Bureau.

On July 26, 1986, Mário Fernandes da Graça MACHUNGO, an economist who had overseen recent liberalization of the economy, was sworn in as prime minister, a newly created post designed to permit President Machel to concentrate on defense of the regime against the Mozambique National Resistance (*Resistência Nacional Moçambicana*—Renamo), which had grown from a relatively isolated opponent to an insurgent force operating in all ten provinces. Machel, who had remained a widely respected leader despite the country's myriad problems, died in a plane crash on October 19 and was succeeded on November 6 by his longtime associate, Foreign Affairs Minister Joaquim Alberto CHISSANO. Chissano extended the economic liberalization policies initiated by his predecessor, overtures to the West for emergency and development aid generally being well received. However, domestic progress remained severely constrained by the ongoing civil war.

Frelimo abandoned its commitment to Marxism-Leninism in July 1989. A year later, direct talks with Renamo representatives were launched in Rome, Italy. On November 2, 1990, following extensive National Assembly debate, a new, pluralistic constitution was adopted. Subsequently, a tenuous cease-fire negotiated with Renamo on December 1 broke down, the rebels withdrawing from the Rome talks. The talks resumed in May 1991, and five months later the rebels agreed to halt armed activity, to drop demands for a UN transitional government, and to recognize the government's authority. For its part, the government agreed to procedures by which Renamo could function as a political party following a formal cease-fire.

After several weeks of deadlock in the ninth round of the Rome talks, the parties finally agreed on a protocol, which was signed March 12, 1992. It provided for election to the Assembly of the Republic by proportional representation; the holding of simultaneous legislative and presidential balloting; the formation of a National Electoral Commission, one-third of whose members would be named by Renamo; and government assistance to Renamo in establishing itself as a political grouping in every provincial capital. After another delay, the round continued with a June 10 agreement on the formation of a unified, nonpartisan army; the specifics of a cease-fire; and transitory arrangements before the general election. On August 5 Chissano and Renamo leader Gen. Afonso DHLAKAMA held their first ever face-to-face meeting, and on August 7 they reached an accord on a cease-fire and electoral preparations. Subsequently, despite reports of Renamo intransigence and an increasingly restive national army, Chissano and the rebel leader signed a peace treaty in Rome on October 4, ending the 16-year conflict. Included in the treaty were provisions for a cease-fire, multiparty elections within a year, the establishment of a 30,000-member army drawn equally from the existing forces, a political amnesty, and Western-financed repatriation of refugees. Five days later the assembly approved the treaty and the launching of the UN's Operation in Mozambique (*Operação des Naões Unidas em Moçambique*—ONUMOZ), a peacekeeping force with responsibility for disarming both combatants, integrating troops into the new armed forces, organizing elections, and securing trade routes.

In April 1993 the UN Security Council voiced "serious concern" over implementation of the October 1992 accord because of a shortfall in funds for deployment of peacekeeping troops and the withdrawal of Renamo members from the cease-fire and control commissions established under the treaty. Renamo subsequently indicated that it would not return to the commissions until a number of logistical problems had been resolved and some $15 million to support its political activities had been received.

On June 3, 1993, the commissions resumed meeting, and on June 21 the disarmament program was launched. Two months later the Joint Commission for the Formation of the Mozambique Defense Armed Forces announced that it had reached agreement on creation of the inclusive Mozambique Defense Armed Forces. In addition, an August 27–September 3 meeting between Chissano and Dhlakama, their first since 1992, yielded an accord on territorial administration, following Renamo's retreat from insistence that it be given jurisdiction over the provinces it controlled. At a further meeting on October 16–20 the two agreed on the establishment of a 20-member electoral commission (to be composed of ten government appointees, seven Renamo officials, and three from other opposition parties). Thereafter, the peace process continued to advance as the government and Renamo settled electoral law differences and formally agreed to a demobilization plan that would commence on November 30 and continue for six months.

By mid-January 1994 over 50 percent of the rebels were reported to have arrived at demobilization sites. By contrast, the government was widely criticized for a compliance level of only 19 percent. Nonetheless, President Chissano, responding to a Security Council call for a transfer of power to democratically elected officials by the end of November, announced that the country's first multiparty balloting would take place on October 27–28.

At the long-deferred balloting (extended by one day to October 29), President Chissano was a clear victor, polling 53.7 percent of the vote, compared to 33.7 percent for his principal opponent, Renamo's Dhlakama. While the legislative outcome was much closer (129–112), no opposition members were named to the government subsequently formed under former foreign minister Pascoal Manuel MOCUMBI.

Under pressure from the opposition and international donors to broaden its definition of what constituted a viable polling district, the assembly, with Renamo support, approved a constitutional amendment in November 1996 that provided for the establishment of a local government electoral system wherein communities with a functioning administration and a "reasonable" local tax base would participate in polling. In early 1997 Renamo reversed itself, threatening to stalemate the assembly and boycott elections if the scope of the polling was not expanded. Nevertheless, in March 1997 the assembly approved the creation of a nine-member, bipartisan national elections commission, which it charged with preparing for balloting. In June it was announced that elections would be held in 23 cities and 10 towns (1 in each of the provinces) in December, one year after originally scheduled. Balloting was subsequently postponed until May 1998 and, once again, in March 1998 to June 30.

In April 1998 the partners in the Coordinating Council of the Opposition formally announced their intention to boycott the local polling, citing the government's unwillingness to allow their representatives to participate in the commission that was investigating alleged electoral roll fraud. The opposition's subsequent efforts to garner support for their boycott plans appeared to have succeeded dramatically, as on June 30 less than 20 percent of the electorate was reported to have participated in the balloting. In the immediate aftermath of the elections, during which Frelimo candidates easily overwhelmed a field of independent competitors, the opposition declared the polling "null and void" and threatened to launch a civil disobedience campaign if the results were upheld. Subsequently, however, the Renamo-led opposition announced that it would not hinder the efforts of the newly elected officials, asserting that it was turning its attention to preparing for general elections in 1999.

Chissano once again defeated Dhlakama (52.3–47.7 percent) in the presidential poll conducted on December 3–5, 1999, while Frelimo won 133 seats in the concurrent assembly balloting, compared to 117 seats for Renamo and its recently formed opposition alliance called the Renamo/Electoral Union (Renamo/*União Electoral*—Renamo/UE). After the Supreme Court rejected a Renamo/UE call for nullification of the results, Chissano was sworn in for another five-year term on January 15, 2000. Two days later he reappointed Mocumbi to head a new all-Frelimo cabinet, which was described as bringing "fresh blood" into the government while retaining the "tested core" of the previous administration.

Tension between the government and the opposition rose significantly in November 2000, when more than 40 people were killed during countrywide protest demonstrations called by Renamo. Although it was later announced that the Chissano and Dhlakama had agreed to form consultative "working committees," and the government pledged to consider Renamo's preferences in appointing governors in the disputed provinces, the exact form of this accommodation remained unclear. Dhlakama also shied away from formally recognizing the president, acknowledging only that Chissano "was *de facto* governing the country." Analysts noted that Dhlakama's subsequently muted rhetoric could be attributed in part to problems he was facing within his own party (see Renamo under Political Parties, below).

In February 2003 Renamo announced that it would run alone in upcoming municipal elections, thereby leading ten other opposition parties to form a new electoral coalition—the Movement for Change and Good Governance (*Movimento para a Mudança e Boa Governação*—MBG)—to oppose Frelimo and Renamo. In the municipal elections held on November 19, 2003, Frelimo won 28 mayoral posts and a majority of council posts in 29 municipalities, while Renamo won 5 mayor's races and council majorities in 4 municipalities (its best showing in municipal elections since multiparty elections were implemented). Although there was low voter turnout (estimated at 24.2 percent) and Renamo complained of irregularities, monitors from the European Union (EU) judged the elections free and fair, and the Constitutional Council confirmed the results in January 2004.

On February 19, 2004, former World Bank economist and Finance Minister Luisa Dias DIOGO was appointed prime minister. (Mocumbi had earlier announced his plans to retire from the premiership to take a UN job.) Diogo became the country's first female prime minister. Analysts suggested that she was appointed ahead of presidential and legislative elections in an effort to reinvigorate Frelimo and demonstrate a commitment by the party to economic reform.

Chissano having announced in 2001 that he would not seek reelection in 2004, Frelimo chose Armando GUEBUZA as its presidential candidate. In balloting on December 1–2, Guebuza won 63.74 percent of the vote. His closest rival was Dhlakama, who received 31.72 percent of the vote. In concurrent legislative balloting, Frelimo won 62.03 percent of the vote and 160 seats, while Renamo won 29.73 percent and 90 seats. None of the other 23 parties received more than 2 percent of the vote. Both the presidential and legislative elections were heavily criticized by the opposition and international observers. Renamo protested to the Constitutional Council, and its deputies initially refused to take their seats in the assembly. Nonetheless, on January 20, 2005, the council certified the results. Diogo was reappointed as prime minister on February 3, and she subsequently formed a new cabinet of Frelimo appointees.

During the 2004 presidential campaign, divisions within Frelimo emerged between the supporters of Armando Guebuza (the Frelimo candidate) and Chissano. The new cabinet appointed following Guebuza's victory contained many new members and appeared to represent an attempt by the new president to break with Frelimo's "old guard." In addition to purging many "*Chissanoistas*" from their former posts throughout government ranks, Guebuza also launched a broad anticorruption initiative that often focused on members of the former administration. (Guebuza described the "remoralization" of government as his top priority.) Tensions between Frelimo and Renamo also remained high, although Dhlakama (who continued to refuse to accept the validity of the 2004 election results) agreed to take his seat on the new Council of State in December 2005. Underscoring the ongoing friction, a bipartisan assembly commission, established in 2005 to propose electoral law reforms, disbanded in April 2006 without reaching agreement.

In March 2007 Guebuza conducted two cabinet reshuffles in an effort to improve the government's popularity. In particular, Guebuza replaced his brother-in-law, Defense Minister Gen. (Ret.) Tobias DAI, who had been heavily criticized following an explosion at a military facility. The president named as Transport and Communications minister Paulo ZUCULA, whose management of relief efforts following heavy flooding in January and February was widely acclaimed.

In local and regional elections in November 2008, Frelimo won 42 of the 43 mayoral contests and secured majorities on all 43 municipal councils. Renamo protested the results, which were judged as generally free and fair by both domestic and international observers. The constitutional court rejected the challenge and certified the results.

Presidential, legislative, and provincial elections were held on October 28, 2009. Many opposition candidates and parties were barred from participation, and both domestic and international observers criticized the conduct of the polling. Guebuza was reelected with 75 percent of the vote, Dhlakama placed second with 16 percent, and Daviz Simango of the Democratic Movement of Mozambique (*Movimento Democrático de Moçambique*—MDM) secured 8.6 percent. In the assembly balloting, Frelimo increased its majority from 160 to 191 seats. Renamo placed second with 51 seats, and the MDM gained 8. In the provincial balloting, Frelimo secured 703 seats; Renamo, 83; the MDM, 24; and the Party for Peace, Democracy, and Development (*Partido para a Paz, Democracia, e Desenvolvimento*—PPDD), 2. After he was inaugurated, Guebuza appointed a largely reshuffled cabinet and named Aires Bonifacio ALI, then minister of education and culture, as prime minister. In October Ali conducted a minor cabinet reshuffle, replacing four ministers.

In May opposition parties in the assembly held a brief boycott as the legislature began to consider amendments to the country's constitution. In August the assembly and the cabinet approved a new austerity measure designed to reduce Mozambique's growing budget deficit, which rose to 5.4 percent of the GDP in 2010. Previous efforts to reduce government spending had resulted in riots and demonstrations.

In April 2008 Amnesty International issued a report that criticized the Mozambican police for excessive force and extrajudicial killings. Continuing internal strife among the opposition parties was instrumental in Frelimo's sweep of the 2009 presidential, legislative, and provincial balloting. In the polling, Guebuza was reelected with 75 percent of the vote, and Frelimo increased its majority in the assembly and among the provincial councils. MDM and Renamo candidates were banned by the election commission in many districts or faced restrictions on campaigning, and six candidates from smaller parties were banned from running for the presidency. International observers criticized the balloting for irregularities. Renamo rejected the results and called for new balloting. In response, some international donor states cut aid to the government.

Ali was dismissed as prime minister on October 8, 2012, and was immediately replaced by Alberto Clementino VAQUINA (see Current issues, below). Guebuza concurrently conducted a minor cabinet reshuffle.

Constitution and government. The 1975 constitution characterized the People's Republic of Mozambique as a "popular democratic state" while reserving for Frelimo "the directing power of the state and society," with decisions taken by party organs to be regarded as binding on all government officials. A subsequent constitution, adopted in August 1978, set as a national objective "the construction of the material and ideological bases for a socialist society." The president of Frelimo served as president of the republic and chief of the armed forces, while an indirectly elected People's Assembly was designated as the "supreme organ of state power."

The basic law approved by the assembly in November 1990 contained no reference to Frelimo or leadership of the working class, while "People's" was dropped from the state name. It provided for a popularly elected president serving a maximum of two five-year terms. The Council of Ministers continued to be headed by a presidentially appointed prime minister, with national legislators selected on a proportional basis in multiparty balloting. In addition to freedom of association and of the press, the new document guaranteed various human and civil rights, including the right to private property and the right to strike. A Supreme Court heads an independent judiciary.

A number of constitutional amendments were approved by the Assembly of the Republic in November 2004, although most of the basic elements of the 1990 text remained intact. (The president continued to hold the power to appoint the prime minister, cabinet ministers, and provincial governors.) The amendments reaffirmed the authority of the Constitutional Council (established in 2003) to rule on the constitutionality of legislation and to validate election results. Other changes provided for an Ombudsman (appointed by a two-third's majority in the assembly) to investigate allegations of misconduct by state officials, for the election of provincial assemblies (beginning in 2008), and for the establishment of an advisory Council of State (comprised of automatic members [such as former presidents, former assembly presidents, and the runner-up in the most recent presidential election], as well as members appointed by the president and the assembly). Although the new council was given no formal decision-making authority, the president was required to consult with the council on a broad range of matters, including the conduct of elections. The basic law revisions also removed the president's immunity from prosecution by authorizing impeachment by a vote of two-thirds of the assembly.

The governors of the country's ten provinces are appointed by the president, who may annul the decisions of provincial, district, and local assemblies. The city of Maputo (which has provincial status) is under the administrative direction of a City Council chair. Legislation in 2006 provided for the creation of elected assemblies for the ten provinces, the size of the assemblies to be determined by population. In 2008 the number of municipalities with elected mayors and assemblies was increased from 33 to 43.

After having maintained strict control of the media since independence, the government in 1990 permitted substantial press liberalization. In late 1991 a press law was ratified, giving existing publications six months to reregister in accordance with new provisions, including revised ownership rules. Reporters Without Borders ranked Mozambique as 73rd out of 179 countries in their 2013 Press Freedom Index, a considerable improvement from 2010 when the country ranked 135th out of 178 states.

Foreign relations. Avowedly Marxist in orientation until mid-1989, the Frelimo government was for many years the beneficiary of substantial economic, technical, and security support from the Soviet Union, Cuba, East Germany, and other Moscow-line states. However, links with the West began to increase in 1979. The UK and Brazil extended credit, and in 1982 Portugal resumed relations that had ceased in 1977 as a result of the nationalization of Portuguese holdings. Relations with the United States, troubled since 1977 by charges of human rights abuses, reached a nadir in 1981 with the expulsion of all U.S. embassy personnel for alleged espionage. Relations were reestablished in July 1983, and President Machel made a state visit to Washington in September 1985, securing economic aid and exploring the possibility of military assistance. President Chissano was similarly received in March 1990 by President George H. W. Bush, who promised an unspecified amount of U.S. aid for reconstruction and development. Meanwhile, in 1984 Mozambique had been admitted to the IMF and World Bank, signifying a desire on Maputo's part to become a more active participant in the world economy.

Despite its prominence as one of the Front-Line States committed to majority rule in southern Africa, Mozambique maintained economic links to white-dominated South Africa as a matter of "realistic policy," with some 40,000 Mozambicans employed in South African mines and considerable revenue derived from cooperation in transport and hydroelectric power. However, relations were severely strained by South African support for the Renamo insurgents in the 1980s. In a 1984 nonaggression pact, the "Nkomati Accord," South Africa agreed to stop aiding Renamo in return for Mozambique's pledge not to support the African National Congress (ANC) in its guerrilla campaign against the South African minority government. The accord proved ineffective, however, as growing rebel activity fostered Mozambican suspicion of continued destabilization attempts by its white-ruled neighbor. In August 1987 the two countries agreed that the pact should be reactivated, prompting an unprecedented meeting between President Chissano and South African President Botha in September 1988, at which Botha again promised not to support the insurgents. In 1990 President Chissano announced that he was convinced that the new government in Pretoria had indeed halted its support of Renamo and that the two countries could now concentrate on economic cooperation.

The civil war also dominated Maputo's relations elsewhere in the region. The Zimbabwean government, declaring "If Mozambique falls, we fall," sent an estimated 10,000 troops to combat the Renamo rebels, particularly in the transport corridor to Beira, which played a central role in the Front-Line States' effort to reduce dependence on South African trade routes. In December 1986 Tanzanian President Mwinyi also agreed to make troops available to Mozambique, as did Malawi following a dispute over alleged Renamo bases within its borders (see Malawi article). In 1992 Zimbabwean president Robert Mugabe, along with Italian officials, played a major role in brokering the peace accord that was signed in Rome in October.

By early 1993 approximately 1.7 million Mozambicans had taken refuge in neighboring countries, Malawi housing 1.1 million. On June 12 Mozambique and the UN High Commission for Refugees (UNHCR) formally inaugurated a repatriation operation (beginning with exiles in Zimbabwe), which observers described as the largest ever in Africa, and by August 19 Mozambique had signed repatriation agreements with Malawi, Swaziland, and Zambia. The repatriation program was formally terminated on November 21, 1995, at which time the UNHCR announced that more than 1 million refugees had returned home.

The most surprising foreign policy development of 1995 was Mozambique's admission to the Commonwealth as the group's 53rd member. Its entry on a unique and special case basis had been urged by its anglophone neighbors as a means of enhancing regional trade, most importantly in cashew nuts, which critics insisted was effectively controlled by Indian and Pakistani interests.

In 1996 Mozambique negotiated security agreements with Malawi, Swaziland, and Zimbabwe in an effort to squelch the border violence attributed to *Chimwenje,* a shadowy grouping of Zimbabwean dissidents who were allegedly led and trained by former Renamo militiamen from bases along their shared borders (for more information on *Chimwenje,* see article on Zimbabwe). Meanwhile, following approximately a year of negotiations, Mozambique signed an agreement with South Africa in May that provided South African farmers with access to Mozambican agricultural land. The deal was opposed by both Renamo leaders and Frelimo activists, who charged that "exporting white farmers to Mozambique" was favored by South Africa's ANC as a means of freeing up land for black settlement. At the same time, South Africa and Mozambique inaugurated the Maputo Corridor Development Project with the aim of redeveloping the trade route between Johannesburg and Maputo and refurbishing the latter's harbor. In 2002 the government initiated a program to resettle white farmers from Zimbabwe whose land had been expropriated.

Relations between Mozambique and the United States have improved in the 2000s. In 2002 Chissano, along with the leaders of Botswana and Angola, met with U.S. President George W. Bush in Washington, D.C., in a summit on development of the region. Mozambique is part of the U.S. Africa Growth and Opportunity Act (AGOA) that offers preferential trade opportunities to African states. Relations with European states also remained strong, with both France and Russia agreeing in 2002 to cancel portions of Mozambique's debt. Meanwhile the EU increased direct annual aid to Mozambique to $131 million per year through 2007.

In 2002 and 2003 Mozambique conducted a series of cooperative military exercises with Portugal. (The two countries also have an agreement whereby soldiers from Mozambique are trained in Portugal.) Although the relationship between the two countries subsequently remained essentially strong, friction developed in 2005 over the proposed takeover by Mozambique of a hydroelectric plant on the Zambesi River for which the Portuguese government held 85 percent financial responsibility. New President Guebuza refused to accept the amount of back debt that Portugal demanded be paid by Mozambique prior to the transfer of ownership, and, although a tentative agreement was announced in late 2005, it was not implemented until Mozambique paid Portugal $700 million in November 2007. Meanwhile, the Guebuza administration reached out to a broad range of other potential donors for assistance, achieving success most notably with China, Germany, and India. China agreed in 2007 to give Mozambique $2.5 million in military equipment and to provide training for Mozambican military officers annually at Chinese military academies.

In 2007 South Africa decided to reopen an investigation into the 1986 death of President Machel because of suspicions that the apartheid regime had been involved in the plane crash that had killed the Mozambique leader. Meanwhile, a South African soldier was killed along with five Mozambicans in June while participating in a joint operation to destroy mines and leftover military ordnance from Mozambique's civil war.

Political violence against Zimbabweans in South Africa led more than 10,000 refugees to flee to refugee camps in Mozambique in May 2008. In December Mozambique and China signed an agreement to increase military cooperation and collaboration. Meanwhile, China granted Mozambique $1.5 million to upgrade its military equipment.

Mozambique and Portugal signed an agreement in February 2009 to expand cooperation in the areas of law enforcement and criminal justice. Also in February Mozambique and India signed two new economic agreements and India granted Mozambique a $25 million line of credit to improve industry and infrastructure. A further accord, to increase cooperation in economic development, was signed in September 2010 between the two countries. In December 2010 diplomatic cables released by WikiLeaks revealed the increasing concern of the United States over the rise in drug trafficking in Mozambique. The documents also highlighted connections between the drug trade and some Frelimo officials. In June the United States listed prominent Mozambican businessman Mahamed Bachir SULEMAN as an international drug kingpin and requested assistance from the government in investigating him.

The UK announced in April 2011 that it would provide $538 million over four years to improve health and education in Mozambique. In June Mozambique and South Africa signed an agreement to cooperate on antipiracy measures, including joint naval patrols and intelligence collaboration. The Frelimo government announced in August that it would not ratify the ICC treaty until further study had been undertaken. Critics charged that government officials were afraid that they would be charged by the ICC for recent incidents, including the response to the September 2010 riots.

Mozambique and Zambia finalized an agreement to demarcate most of their mutual borders in August 2012 after a year's negotiations. Several disputed areas remained with both countries pledging further talks. In September China announced that it would provide $25 million in poverty-reduction assistance to Mozambique. This was in addition to $500 million in economic aid already pledged over a five-year period. In December Zimbabwe deployed more than 1,000 troops along the border with Mozambique in response to reported incursions by Renamo rebels.

In January 2013 Spain announced that it would be forced to cut aid to Mozambique as a result of financial pressures. The following month Mozambique and Thailand signed an accord to expand trade and commerce between the two nations. South Africa announced in May that it would increase border security with Mozambique following an increase in poaching of rhinos (see entry on South Africa). In June Mozambique and Japan signed an accord to promote investment. The agreement was the first of its kind between Japan and a sub-Saharan African country.

Current issues. After the government announced a 30 percent decrease in subsidies for food and energy, rioting swept through the country for three days in September 2010, leaving 13 dead and causing more than $3 million in damages. The government subsequently altered its plan and left most subsidies in place.

The government announced an increase in minimum wages for all economic sectors in April 2011, with some professions securing a 52 percent salary increase. Concurrently, Prime Minister Ali promulgated a new plan to reduce fuel and food subsidies.

In August 2011 Afonso Dhlakama announced Renamo was setting up new military barracks, ostensibly in response to Frelimo violations of the demobilization clause of the peace accord, and threatened to set up a parallel government. In November a commission was launched to update the constitution, which critics said Guebuza might use to secure a third term. Renamo refused to fill its 6 of 17 seats on the commission.

Several Frelimo mayors resigned in the run-up to December 7 by-elections, amid reports that the party was afraid of losing future elections following anticorruption protests in some towns. Renamo boycotted the polls, saying that no free voting would happen under a Frelimo government. The outcome of the mayoral elections in the three northern cities saw the Frelimo candidate defeated by the MDM's Manuel de ARAUJO in the city of Quelimane, bolstering the sense that MDM might overtake Renamo as the main opposition party. In subsequent months a leaked report from the national police on why Frelimo lost the election created a stir, describing how an elite police force raided MDM property without warrants and how officials otherwise obstructed opposition staff and candidates.

By late 2012 proposals for anticorruption laws demanded by foreign aid donors were bogged down by procedural issues as officials labored to put off action until after the 2014 elections. These include conflict of interest reforms that could reportedly jeopardize legislators' lucrative business interests. At a Frelimo party congress in September, Ali lost his seat on Frelimo's governing committee (see Political parties, below). Guebuza responded by dismissing the prime minister and replacing him with Alberto VAQUINO, a popular governor who was elected to the Frelimo executive.

Flooding in Maputo and southern areas of Mozambique killed 55 and displaced more than 169,000 in January 2013. In April clashes between opposition groups and security forces in the Sofala left seven dead and more than a score injured. Meanwhile Renamo officials threatened to boycott municipal elections in protest of new electoral laws that the party claimed inappropriately favored Frelimo (see Political parties, below). Renewed fighting between Renamo and government forces continued into June. The passage of new measures on conflicts of interest led to the resignation of more than 30 Frelimo parliamentarians and party officials in May. The new law banned public servants from collecting both their government salary and pay from private or state firms.

POLITICAL PARTIES

For its first 15 years of independence Mozambique was a one-party state in which the Mozambique Liberation Front (Frelimo) was constitutionally empowered to guide the operations of government at all levels. However, a constitutional revision in October 1990 guaranteed freedom of association, with subsequent legislation establishing the criteria for party legalization. Some 19 parties or alliances contested the 2009 legislative elections, while 12 more had their candidate lists rejected by the electoral commission.

Government Party:

Mozambique Liberation Front (*Frente de Libertação de Moçambique*—Frelimo). Founded in 1962 by the union of three nationalist parties and led by Dr. Eduardo Mondlane until his death in 1969, Frelimo engaged in armed resistance to Portuguese rule from 1964 to 1974, when agreement on independence was reached. At its third national congress in 1977, the front was designated a Marxist-Leninist party (directed by a Central Committee, a Political Bureau, and a Secretariat), but at the fourth party congress in 1983 economic philosophy began to shift toward the encouragement of free-market activity. Following the death of Samora Machel in October 1986, the Central Committee designated his longtime associate, Joaquim Alberto Chissano, as its political leader.

Frelimo retreated even further from Marxist doctrine at the group's fifth congress in 1989. The party opened its membership to many formerly excluded groups, such as private property owners, the business community, Christians, Muslims, and traditionalists. The congress also called for a negotiated settlement with Renamo, bureaucratic reform, and emphasis on family farming rather than state agriculture.

Although President Chissano easily defeated Renamo's Afonso Dhlakama in the 1994 election, Frelimo as a party performed much more poorly, barely securing a majority of legislative seats. On a regional basis the results were quite mixed, the party substantially outpolling Renamo in the south, while being decisively defeated in the center and trailing marginally in the north.

In what was described as a break with "old guard" leadership, five of the Frelimo Central Committee's six members were replaced on July 24, 1995, and Manuel Tome was appointed as the party's new secretary general. In spite of these changes, corruption charges continued to dog the party. Observers attributed Frelimo's subsequent endorsement of a proposal to limit the geographic scope of municipal elections to weak support beyond its southern base. Challenged only by small opposition groups and independent candidates, Frelimo dominated balloting for local posts in June 1998. It secured 48.5 percent of the vote and 133 seats in the December 1999 legislative balloting.

During a party congress in June 2002, Chissano was reelected as Frelimo chair. However, former parliamentary leader Armando Guebuza was elected as the new secretary general and the party's 2004 presidential candidate despite the fact that Chissano had supported Herder MUTEIA for the post. Guebuza was elected president in the 2004 balloting, and Frelimo increased its seats in the assembly to 160. Significant friction was subsequently reported between President Guebuza and former members of the Chissano administration.

Guebuza further consolidated his control over Frelimo at a party congress in November 2006. His close supporters gained dominance of the 160-member party central commission and the 17-member political commission, the main decision-making body of Frelimo. Meanwhile, Guebuza loyalist Filipe Paunde was elected general secretary of the party. A party congress in July 2008 chose candidates to compete in municipal and regional elections. Reports indicated that the majority of candidates were Guebuza supporters. In September Guebuza was chosen as Frelimo's presidential candidate for the 2009 balloting at a party contest where the incumbent ran unopposed. Guebuza was reelected in the October 2009 balloting and Frelimo increased its seats in the assembly to 191. In January Guebuza replaced prime minister Luisa Dais DIOGO, who was seen as a possible successor to the president and the leader of the Chissano wing of the party, with Aires Bonifacio Ali, a close Guebuza ally. Tensions within the party led to the resignation of three Frelimo mayors in August 2011. Reports indicated that the trio were members of the Chissano wing of the party who were ousted to make way for pro-Guebuza candidates ahead of the 2013 balloting.

By December 2011, with Guebuza's futile efforts to change the constitution to allow a third term, contenders were reportedly jockeying to succeed him. There is also said to be growing resentment within the party against a group of Guebuza's associates and their families who have benefited financially from his tenure and were accelerating the accumulation of wealth in advance of his departure. Guebuza was reelected as party leader at the September 23–29, 2012, party congress. However Ali lost his position on the 17-member of the political committee in what was seen as a defeat for Guebuza, who was subsequently forced to dismiss the prime minister. Alberto Clementino VAQUINA, a close Guebuza ally, became prime minister.

Leaders: Armando GUEBUZA (President of the Republic and Secretary General), Alberto Clementino VAQUINA (Prime Minister), Joaquim Alberto CHISSANO (Former President of the Republic and Honorary Party President), Verónica Nataniel MACAMO (President of the Assembly), Filipe PAUNDE (General Secretary), Margarida TALAPA (Parliamentary Leader), Edson MACUACUA (Party Spokesperson).

Opposition Parties:

Mozambique National Resistance—MNR (*Resistência Nacional Moçambicana*—Renamo). Also known as the *Movimento Nacional da Resistência de Moçambique* (MNRM) and as the André Group, after its late founder, André Matade MATSANGAI, Renamo was formed in the early 1970s primarily as an intelligence network within Mozambique for the white Rhodesian government of Ian Smith. Following Rhodesia's transition to majority rule as "Zimbabwe" in 1980, Renamo developed into a widespread anti-Frelimo insurgency, relying on financial support from Portuguese expatriates and, until the early 1990s, substantial military aid from South Africa. The 20,000-member Renamo army, comprising Portuguese and other mercenaries, Frelimo defectors, and numerous recruits from the Shona-speaking Ndau ethnic group, operated mainly in rural areas, where it interdicted transport corridors and sabotaged food production. Widely condemned for terrorist tactics, including indiscriminate killing and mutilation of civilians, Renamo, although largely stalemating the government militarily, generally failed to gain external recognition. In an apparent attempt to foster its nationalist image, Renamo launched an "Africanization" program in 1987 that included replacements for white Portuguese at its Lisbon-based headquarters. Further image-building took place at the 1989 Renamo congress, which revamped the movement's internal bodies. The congress also declared that Renamo was no longer intent on overthrowing the government but was seeking instead a peace settlement under which it could participate as a recognized "political force" in free elections resulting from constitutional revision. However, the Renamo leadership appeared disconcerted when, in 1990, the government agreed to hold such elections. Thereafter, despite a December 1, 1990, cease-fire, Renamo's military activities continued, thus supporting a widely held view that apart from its advocacy of a multiparty system the group lacked a political agenda.

When rebel strikes coincided with the reopening of peace talks in March and May 1991, there was speculation that party president Gen. Afonso Dhlakama had lost control over some of his forces. Thereafter, in negotiations with the government in Rome, Renamo, weakened by dwindling finances and pressed by South Africa, the UK, and the United States to negotiate seriously, signed the first of a series of concessionary protocols. By mid-1992 it was apparent that the lengthy rebellion was drawing to a close.

While Dhlakama failed in his bid to win the presidency from Chissano in December 1994, the results of the legislative poll left Renamo only marginally second to Frelimo. In May 1995 President Chissano stated that, while Dhlakama could not be styled leader of the opposition (because he was not an elected member of the People's Assembly), he would be accorded "dignified status."

Although Renamo's legislative initiatives were blocked in the Frelimo-controlled assembly in 1995–1996, observers credited Dhlakama with continuing to enhance both the group's and his own political viability. In November 1996 Renamo legislators reportedly gave unanimous support to a constitutional amendment altering local election laws. In early 1997, however, the party reversed itself, threatening to boycott upcoming balloting unless the 1996 bill was repealed. Amid escalating tensions, the party organized nationwide antigovernment demonstrations in May 1997.

Although Renamo officials publicly insisted that they had no interest in returning to an armed struggle, arson attacks and disruption of the water supply were reported in July 1997. Subsequently, Dhlakama denounced the government's use of force to suppress the unrest.

Citing the need for the party to be "more flexible," Dhlakama forced the ouster of Secretary General Jose de CASTRO and Assistant Secretary General Albino FAIFE in January 1998. João Alexandre was subsequently named to Castro's former post.

In mid-1999, the **Mozambique National Resistance/Electoral Union** (*Resistência Nacional Moçambicana/União Electoral*—Renamo/UE) was formed. The Renamo/UE electoral alliance secured 38.8 percent of the vote and 117 seats in the December legislative balloting, a surprisingly good result in the opinion of most analysts after what was generally viewed as a minimalist campaign that lacked a coherent platform. Collaterally, Renamo/UE presidential candidate Afonso Dhlakama won 47.7 percent of the votes in the presidential balloting in 1999.

A split was reported in 2000 between those Renamo members, including a number of legislators, who appeared to be interested in negotiating a settlement with Frelimo, and those led by Dhlakama, who at midyear were still refusing to accept the results of the December 1999 legislative and presidential elections. In September 2000 the party's former legislative leader, Raul DOMINGOS, was expelled for "having collaborated with Frelimo" and for "corruption" during secret talks he allegedly held with the government. (Some analysts noted that Domingos had previously been seen as a possible successor to Dhlakama.)

Despite facing increasing dissent within the party, Dhlakama nevertheless was reelected as Renamo's president in November 2001. At a subsequent party congress, a ten-member political committee was created as a means to decentralize party leadership and broaden the party's appeal. Renamo contested municipal elections independently in 2003, but revived the Renamo/UE alliance in the 2004 presidential elections. The alliance was hurt by the defection of Renamo members to form the Party for Peace, Development, and Democracy (see below) and the loss of Unamo (see below). Dhlakama again ran as the party's candidate, receiving 31.74 percent of the vote. The Renamo-led electoral alliance won 29.73 percent of the vote in the concurrent legislative elections, its representation declining from 117 to 90 seats in the assembly. Renamo deputies initially boycotted the assembly to protest perceived irregularities in the polling, but, after the Constitutional Council upheld the results, the deputies were seated in January 2005.

A number of regional and local Renamo leaders reportedly defected to Frelimo in 2006. Partially in response to losses within the party, the senior Renamo leadership decided to contest upcoming regional and local elections without its coalition partners in an effort to gain greater representation at the provincial and municipal levels. In July 2007 the Renamo/UE electoral alliance ended. Some members of the grouping subsequently formed a new coalition, the **Electoral Union Coalition** (*Coligação União Eleitoral*—UE) (see below). Nonetheless, the member parties pledged to continue political cooperation in opposition to Frelimo. Prior to the 2008 local elections party leaders decided against allowing Daviz Simango, the popular mayor of Beira, from seeking reelection. Simango led a mass defection from Renamo. Reports indicated that at least ten Renamo deputies in the assembly resigned from the party. Simango campaigned as an independent and won another term and subsequently launched a new party, the **Mozambique Democratic Movement** (*Movimento Democrático de Moçambique*—MDM).

Led by Sebastiao JANOTA and Saimon MUTERO, a group of Renamo dissidents formed a splinter group, the Renamo National Salvation Junta (*Junta Nacional de Salvação da Renamo*—JNSR) in 2008. The JNSR reportedly sought to replace Dhlakama and institute a number of party reforms, including greater financial transparency and openness in internal Renamo elections. Dhlakama was chosen as Renamo's candidate for the 2009 presidential balloting. He placed second with 16.41 percent of the vote. Renamo had its worst electoral performance in flawed legislative balloting, dropping to 51 seats in the assembly.

In July 2011 Dhlakama publicly renounced violence and pledged not to engage in armed struggle in the future. However, the following month, Renamo began constructing "barracks" for former rebels in areas that had been Renamo strongholds. Opposition to a new electoral law in April 2013 led to renewed clashes between Renamo and government forces. Reports indicated that as many as 300 Renamo members were arrested that month. Meanwhile the party pledged to both boycott and disrupt the 2013 municipal polling.

Leaders: Gen. Afonso Macacho Marceta DHLAKAMA (President), Ossufo QUITINE (Legislative Leader), Fernando MAZANGA (Spokesperson), João ALEXANDRE (Former Secretary General), Ossufo MOMAD (Secretary General).

Mozambique Democratic Movement (*Movimento Democrático de Moçambique*—MDM). The MDM was formed in 2009 by former Renamo members led by Daviz SIMANGO. Simango was elected mayor of Beira as an independent in 2008. The MDM drew support from independents and former opposition members. Reports indicated that at least four Renamo deputies in the assembly had defected to the MDM. Simango was the MDM presidential candidate for 2009 and placed third in the balloting with 8.59 percent of the vote. The MDM received 3.93 percent of the vote in the assembly balloting and secured eight seats. In April 2011 MDM secretary general Ismael MUSSA resigned. He was replaced by Bernabé Nkomo. At a party congress in December 2012, Simango was reelected MDM president.

Leaders: Daviz SIMANGO, Bernabé NKOMO (Secretary General).

Other Groups That Contested the 2009 Legislative Elections:

Democratic Alliance of Veterans for Development (*Aliança Democrática de Antigos Combatentes para o Desenvolvimento*—ADACD). In June 2008 four small parties announced the creation of the ADACD electoral alliance to compete in future municipal and legislative elections. The ADACD included the **Mozambique People's Progress Party** (*Partido de Progresso do Povo Moçambicano*—PPPM), the **Democratic Congress Party** (*Partido do Congresso Democrático*—Pacode), the **Mozambique Socialist Party** (*Partido Socialista de Moçambique*—PSM), and the **Union for Reconciliation** (*Partido da União para a Reconciliação*—PUR). ADACD was led by PSM general secretary Joao da Rosa Likalamba, and it pledged to support the Frelimo candidate in the 2009 presidential election. The ADACD failed to qualify for the 2008 municipal elections. It ran in the 2009 assembly elections but received less than 1 percent of the vote. The party was reported to be defunct in 2013.

Leader: Joao da Rosa LIKALAMBA (Chair).

Party for Peace, Democracy, and Development (*Partido para a Paz, Democracia, e Desenvolvimento*—PPDD). Formed in 2003 by disaffected members of Renamo, including Raul Domingos, the PPDD is a liberal party that promotes nonpartisanship in public administration. At the first party congress on October 4, 2003, Domingos was nominated to run for the presidency in 2004. He placed third in the balloting with 2.73 percent of the vote. The PPDD also came in third in the concurrent legislative elections with 2 percent of the vote. Most analysts believe that the PPDD pulled votes away from Renamo. The party hoped to continue to build its base through provincial and municipal elections in 2008 and then challenge Renamo as the main opposition party. In 2008 the ruling Senegalese Democratic Party (PDS) pledged to provide monetary and technical assistance to the PPDD in the 2008 local elections and the 2009 legislative balloting. The PPDD participated in the 2008 municipal balloting, placing third, behind Frelimo and Renamo, in overall votes. Following the local elections, Domingos reportedly offered to merge the PPDD with Renamo if Afonso Dhlakama resigned as leader of Renamo. The PPDD failed to secure any seats in the 2009 balloting for the national legislature, but it gained two seats in the concurrent provincial assembly elections. Reports in 2013 indicated that the PPDD had agreed to cooperate in future elections with Renamo.

Leader: Raul DOMINGOS.

Green Party of Mozambique (PVM). Formed in 1997, the PVM (also known as *Os Verdes* [The Greens]) split into two factions prior to the 1999 elections, one supportive of membership in Renamo/UE and the other committed to an independent campaign. In 2004 the independent faction gained 0.33 percent in legislative elections, and in 2009, it secured 0.50 percent in the assembly polling.

Leader: Armando Bruno João SAPEMBE.

Other minor parties that participated in the 2009 assembly balloting but failed to gain seats included the **Party for Liberty and Development** (*Partido de Liberdade e Desenvolvimento*—PLD), formed in June 2009 and led by Caetano SABINDE; the **Party of Freedom and Solidarity** (*Partido de Solidariedade e Liberdade*), formed in 2004 and led by Carlos Inácio COELHO; the **National Reconciliation Party** (PARENA), led by André José BALATE; the **Mozambique Independents Alliance** (*Aliança Independente de Moçambique*—ALIMO), led by Khalid Hussein SIDET; the **Ecological Party–Land Movement** (*Partido Ecologista–Movimento da Terra*), led by João Pedro MASSANGO; the **Party of Union for Mundança** (*Partido de União para Mundança*—UM); **Patriotic Movement for Democracy** (*Movimento Patriótico para Democracia*—MPD), created in 2009 by Matias Dianhane BANZE; the **Union of Mozambican Democrats–Popular Party** (*União dos Democratas de Moçambique–Partido Popular*—UDM-PT), led by José Ricardo VIANA; the **National Party of Workers and Peasants** (*Partido Nacional dos Operários e Camponeses*—PANAOC); the **Popular Democratic Party** (*Partido Popular Democrático*—PPD); the **Electoral Union Coalition** (*Coligação União Eleitoral*—UE); the **Labor Party** (*Partido Trabalhista*—PT), led by Miguel MABOTE; and the **Social Democratic Reconciliation Party** (*Partido de Reconciliação Democrática Social*—PRDS).

Other Parties and Groups:

Independent Party of Mozambique (*Partido Independente de Moçambique*—Pimo). Described as a "thinly disguised Islamic party," Pimo won 1.23 percent of the legislative vote in 1994 and 0.71 percent in 1999. Pimo leader Yaqub SIBINDE attempted to run for president in 1999, but his nomination was declared invalid by the Supreme Court. In 2003 Pimo won three posts in municipal elections in predominately Islamic areas. In 2004 Sibinde ran for the presidency and received 0.91 percent of the vote. In the concurrent legislative elections, Pimo received 0.59 percent of the vote. In 2006 Sibinde was reported to have formed an opposition alliance of 18 minor parties called the **Constructive Opposition Bloc**. Besides Pimo, other members of the bloc included the PT and Panamo. Pimo gained one council seat in the 2008 municipal elections but failed to register candidates for the 2009 assembly elections. Pimo led an unsuccessful effort in 2011 to reform electoral practices ahead of balloting in 2013. In 2012 Sibinde was appointed a special advisor to the government on Islamic affairs.

Leaders: Yaqub Neves Salomão SIBINDE, Magalhaes IBRAMURGY (General Secretary).

Social, Liberal, and Democratic Party (*Partido Social, Liberal e Democrático*—PSLD). The PSLD was formed by former Palmo leader Casimiro Nhamithambo, who complained of the parent group "lacking democracy." The PSLD, also referenced by the initials SOL, was a founding member in early 1999 of the Mozambican Opposition Union (*União Moçambicana da Oposição*—UMO), which its supporters hoped would serve as an electoral front for as many as a dozen parties. Nhamithambo initially served as the UMO secretary general, but he resigned from that post later in the year as the result of friction with Wehia RIPUA, the leader of another UMO component, the **Mozambique Democratic Party** (*Partido Democrático de Mocambique*—Pademo). Although Nhamithambo announced at that time that the PSLD would remain in UMO despite the dispute, the PSLD ultimately contested the December 2000 legislative poll on its own, winning 2.02 percent of the vote. (Only three groups finally ran under the UMO banner: Pademo, the **Democratic Congress Party** [*Partido do Congresso Democrático*—Pacode], and the **Democratic Party for the Reconciliation of Mozambique**. Meanwhile, UMO supported Renamo's Afonso Dhlakama in the presidential race after Ripua's candidacy was disallowed due to faulty nomination papers.) In 2004 the PSLD won 0.46 percent of the legislative vote, but its candidate list was rejected by the electoral commission prior to the 2009 elections.

Leader: Casimiro Miguel NHAMITHAMBO.

Democratic Union (*União Democrática*—UD). UD was formed in 1994 as a coalition of the **National Democratic Party** (*Partido Nacional Democrático*—Panade), the **Liberal Democratic Party of Mozambique** (*Partido Liberal Democrático de Moçambique*—Palmo), and the **National Party of Mozambique** (*Partido Nacional de Moçambique*—Panamo), led by Marcos Juma and Chabane ASSANE. It secured 5.15 percent of the vote in the December legislative poll, thereby gaining nine seats and becoming only the third party, behind Frelimo and Renamo, to gain representation. (Earlier editions of the *Handbook* incorrectly assigned those seats to the Democratic Union of Mozambique [*União Democrática de Moçambique*—Udemo], a former separatist group in northern Mozambique.) However, Palmo left UD in mid-1999, and the rump coalition of Panade and Panamo managed only 1.48 percent of the vote (and consequently no seats) in the December balloting. UD only received 0.34 percent of the vote in the 2004 legislative elections. Juma reportedly led Panamo to join the Constructive Opposition Bloc in 2006. The UD did not participate in the 2008 municipal elections, and its candidates were rejected by the electoral commission for the 2009 legislative balloting. Reports in 2013 indicated that the UD was defunct.

Leaders: José Chicuarra MASSINGA, Marcos JUMA.

Liberal Democratic Party of Mozambique (*Partido Liberal Democrático de Moçambique*—Palmo). Reportedly seeking legal recognition in late 1990, Palmo criticized the nonindigenous population for "controlling" the economy to the detriment of "original" (black) Mozambicans. At the party's first congress on May 6–11, 1991, Martins Bilal won a hotly contested presidential contest over Dr. António Palange. Consequently, another prominent leader, Casimiro Miguel Nhamithambo, resigned from the party, criticizing it for "lacking democracy" and launching a breakaway group (PSLD, above).

In July 1998 a dispute between Bilal and Palange split Palmo. In November Palange was formally expelled and subsequently launched his own formation (CDU, below).

Palmo had filled five of the nine legislative seats won by UD in 1994. However, it split from UD in August 1999, securing 2.47 percent of the vote and no seats in the December poll. In balloting in 2004, Palmo received 0.30 percent of the vote. Palmo did not field candidates in the 2008 municipal balloting.

Leaders: Martins Luis BILAL (Chair), Antonio MUEDO (Secretary General).

National Democratic Party (*Partido Nacional Democrático*—Panade). Panade was launched in late 1992 by José Massinga, a former foreign ministry official who was discharged in 1979 for alleged links to the U.S. intelligence network. The party's platform, based on "Christian values and human dignity," reportedly mirrored the teachings of activist Catholic bishops in central Mozambique. The group was legalized in 1993.

Leader: José Chicuarra MASSINGA.

Social Broadening Party of Mozambique (*Partido de Ampliação Social de Moçambique*—Pasomo). Pasomo won 0.05 percent of the legislative vote in 1999 and 0.52 percent in 2004. It did not qualify for the 2009 assembly balloting. Ahead of local balloting in 2013, Pasomo called for more state funding for minor parties.

Leader: Helder Francisco CAMPIRA.

United National Coalition of the Opposition (*Coligação União Nacional de Oposição*—UNO). In 2008 the **Liberal Front** (*Frente Liberal*—FL) and PARENA formed the **National Democratic Alliance** (*Alianca Nacional Democrática*—AND) to compete in the municipal elections. AND also included two other small parties, the **Democratic Reconciliation Party** (*Partido de Reconcilliação Democrática*—PAREDE), led by Joaquina Joaquim NOTICO, and the **Independent Social-Democratic Party** (PASDI). The coalition was reshuffled and reformed ahead of the 2009 balloting as the UNO and included PAREDE, PASDI, and the **Mozambican Social Democratic Party** (*Partido Moçambicano da Social Democracia*—PMSD).

Mozambican Social Democratic Party (*Partido Moçambicano da Social Democracia*—PMSD). The PMSD was launched as political heir to the Mozambican Nationalist Movement (*Movimento Nacionalista Moçambicana*—Monamo) at the conclusion of Monamo's first congress in May 1992. Monamo had been founded in 1979 by exiled former Frelimo members led by Máximo Dias, who in 1973–1974 had attempted to persuade the Lisbon government to negotiate with the insurgents. In the late 1980s Monamo merged with the West German–based Mozambique National Independent Committee (*Comité Nacional Independente de Moçambique*—Conimo) to form the Mozambican Political Union (*União Política Moçambicana*—Upomo). In 1989 the group called for an immediate cease-fire under UN auspices, the departure of foreign troops, and the holding of national elections. Upomo operated until adoption of the 1990 constitution, after which Dias returned to Mozambique and Monamo reportedly decided to seek legal party status on its own. (Despite the formal change of name in 1992, the Monamo acronym continues in use.)

In 2006 Dias reportedly threatened to leave the Renamo/UE coalition because of the dominance of Renamo. In July 2007 Dias announced that he intended to dissolve Monamo/PMSD and create a new humanitarian nongovernmental organization. However, Monamo/PMSD contested the 2008 local balloting, led by Dias, and subsequently formed the UNO ahead of the legislative balloting.

Leader: Dr. Máximo Diogo José DIAS (Secretary General).

Patriotic Action Front (*Frente de Acção Patriótica*—FAP). Founded in 1991, FAP was a proponent in 1992 of delaying multiparty elections and naming a two-year transitional government. Ahead of the 2008 municipal elections, FAP announced it would not run any of its own members, and would support the Renamo candidates.

Leaders: José Carlos PALAÇO (President), Raulda CONCEIÇÃO (Secretary General).

United Front of Mozambique–Democratic Convergence Party (*Frente Unida de Moçambique–Partido de Convergência Democrática*—Fumo-PCD). Linked to Germany's Christian Democrats, Fumo-PCD held its inaugural congress in Maputo in January 1993. The party secured 1.39 percent of the legislative votes in 1994. It joined the Renamo/UE in 1999 despite the objection of Fumo-PCD founder Domingos Arouca, who resigned from the party's presidency in protest. A June 2000 Fumo-PCD congress offered Arouca the position of "honorary president," but he angrily refused the post. The death of Arouca on January 3, 2009, at age 80, reportedly enhanced party president Jose Samo GUDO's control over Fumo-PCD. Fumo-PCD did not run any candidates in the 2008 local elections.

Leaders: Jose Samo GUDO (President), Pedro LOFORTE (Secretary General).

Mozambican National Union (*União Nacional Moçambicana*—Unamo). Reportedly then in control of three battalions of rebel fighters in Zambezia province, Unamo was formed in 1987 by a Renamo breakaway faction. Subsequently, some of its leaders appeared to be operating from Malawi, while others established an office in Lisbon. Political leaders returned from exile in 1990 in anticipation of Unamo being recognized as a legal party, spokespersons indicating it would participate in upcoming legislative contests but would endorse President Chissano in his reelection bid.

In 1992 Unamo was the first opposition party granted legal status. However, in August party president Carlos Alexandre Reis was imprisoned for financial crimes for which he had been convicted and sentenced in absentia seven years earlier.

In April 1994 Unamo was alleged to be financing Rombezia, an armed group in northern Mozambique led by Manuel ROCHA and Octavio CUSTODIO, which was descended from the African National Union of Rombezia (União Nacional Africana da Rombezia—UNAR). UNAR was believed to have been formed by the Portuguese secret police in the 1960s to promote an independent state in the Rovuma and Zambezia provinces (which gave the grouping its name).

Unamo secured only 0.73 percent of the vote in the 1994 legislative balloting and subsequently announced it was forming the extraparliamentary United Salvation Front (Frente Unida de Salvação—FUS) with the PSLD, PT, Pacode, Pimo, the Mozambique People's Progress Party (PPPM), and the Democratic Renewal Party (PRD). However, in 1999 Unamo chose to participate in the Renamo/UE, while the other FUS members either ran alone or joined different coalitions. In 2004, however, Unamo joined the electoral coalition, the Movement for Change and Good Governance (Movimento para a Mudança e Boa Governação—MGB), while Reis ran as the Unamo candidate for the presidency. He received 0.9 percent of the vote. In the 2008 local elections, Unamo secured one council seat. It appealed the election results, alleging fraud, but Unamo's bid for new balloting was rejected by the constitutional court.

Leaders: Carlos Alexandre REIS (President), Florencia João Da SILVA (Secretary General).

For more information on the **National Convention Party** (*Partido de Convenção Nacional*—PCN) or the **United Democratic Front** (*Frente Democrática Unida*—FDU), see the 2011 *Handbook.*

Other minor parties that were registered at the time of the 2009 assembly elections included the **Progressive Unity Party** (*Partido de União Progressista*—PUP), led by Pedro LANGA; the **Democratic Conservative Party** (*Partido Conservador Democrático*—PCD), formed in 2004 and led by Gonçalvos MAGAGULE; the **United Party for Democratic Freedom** (*Partido Unido de Moçambique e de Liberdade Democrática*—PUMILD), formed in 2007 and led by Leonardo Francisco CUMBE; the **Mozambique People's Progress Party** (*Partido de Progresso do Povo Moçambicano*—PPPM); the **Congress of United Democrats** (*Congresso dos Democratas Unios*—CDU), formed in January 2002 by António PALANGE following his expulsion from Palmo; the **African Conservative Party** (*Partido*

Africano Conservador—PAC), created in 2003 and led by Alexandre PANONE; the **Party of All Mozambican Nationalists** (*Partido de Todos os Nativos Moçambicanos*—Partonamo); the **National Democratic Party of Mozambique** (*Partido Democrático Nacional de Moçambique*—PDNM); and the **United Democratic Front** (*Frente Democrática Unida*—UDF), established in 1995 and led by Janerio Mariano PORDINA.

Minor parties that competed in the 2008 municipal balloting included the **Group for Democracy in Beira** (*Grupo para a Democracia de Beira*—GDB), an independent local grouping in Beria, which won seven council seats in the 2008 balloting; the **Natives and Residents of Manhica** (*Naturais e Residentes da Vila da Mahiça*—NATURMA); **Together for the City** (*Juntos pela Cidade*—JPC), a regional grouping that ran only in Maputo; the **Group for Change in Marromeu** (*Grupo para Mundança de Marromeu*—GMM), active only in Marromeu; and the **Organization of Independent Candidates of Nacala** (*Organização dos Candidatos Independentes de Nacala*—OCINA).

LEGISLATURE

A **People's Assembly** (*Assembleia Popular*), consisting of Frelimo's then 57-member Central Committee, was accorded legislative status in an uncontested election in December 1977. The body was increased to 210 members in April 1983 by the addition of government ministers and vice ministers, provincial governors, representatives of the military and of each province, and ten other citizens. While its term was not constitutionally specified, the original mandate was set by law at five years. The lengthy poll eventually conducted in August–December 1986 was for 250 deputies, indirectly elected by provincial assemblies from a list of 299 candidates presented by Frelimo. The name of the body was changed to the Assembly of the Republic in the 1990 constitution, which also provided for future elections to be conducted by direct universal suffrage on a multiparty basis.

Assembly of the Republic (*Assembleia da República*). The current legislature is a unicameral body of 250 members elected on a proportional basis for five-year terms. Parties must secure 5 percent of the vote on a nationwide basis to gain representation. In the balloting of October 28, 2009, the Mozambique Liberation Front won 191 seats; the Mozambique National Resistance/Electoral Union, 51; and the Democratic Movement of Mozambique, 8.

President: Verónica Nataniel MACAMO.

CABINET

[as of November 15, 2013]

Prime Minister	Alberto Clementino Vaquina
Ministers	
Agriculture and Rural Development	José Pacheo
Culture	Armando Artur João
Development and Planning	Aiuba Cuereneia
Education	Augusto Luis Jone
Energy	Salvador Namburete
Environmental Coordination	Alcinda de Abreu [f]
Finance	Manuel Chang
Fisheries	Victor Borges
Foreign Affairs and Cooperation	Oldemiro Baloi
Health	Alexandre Lourenço Jaime Manguele
Industry and Commerce	Armando Inroga
Interior	Ricardo Alberto Mondlane
Justice	Maria Benvida Levy [f]
Labor	Helena Taipo [f]
Mineral Resources	Esperanca Bias [f]
National Defense	Felipe Jacinto Nyusi
President's Office with Responsibility for Parliamentary Affairs	Adelaide Amurane [f]
President's Office with Responsibility for Social Affairs	Feliciano Salomao Gundana
President's Office	Antonio Sumbana
Public Service	Vitoria Diogo [f]
Public Works and Housing	Cadmiel Muthemba
Science and Technology	Luis Augusto Pelembe
State Administration	Carmelita Namashalua [f]
Tourism	Carvalho Muaria
Transport and Communications	Paulo Zucula
War Veterans' Affairs	Mateus Oscar Kida
Women and Social Action Coordination	Iolanda Cintura [f]
Youth and Sports	Fernando Sumbana Júnior

[f] = female

Note: All of the above are members of the Mozambique Liberation Front.

INTERGOVERNMENTAL REPRESENTATION

Ambassador to the U.S.: Amelia Matos SUMBANA.

U.S. Ambassador to Mozambique: Douglas GRIFFITHS.

Permanent Representative to the UN: António GUMENDE.

IGO Memberships (Non-UN): AfDB, AU, NAM, OIC, SADC, WTO.

MYANMAR (BURMA)

Republic of the Union of Myanmar
Pyihtaungsu Thamada Myanmar Naingngandaw

Political Status: Independent republic established January 4, 1948; military-backed regime instituted March 2, 1962; one-party constitution of January 4, 1974, abrogated upon direct assumption of power by the military on September 18, 1988, at which time the words "Socialist Republic" (*Socialist Thamada*) were dropped from the country's official name; official title in English changed from Union of Burma to Union of Myanmar on May 27, 1989; new republican constitution ratified through referendum of May 10 and 24, 2008, and promulgated May 29.

Area: 261,789 sq. mi. (678,033 sq. km).

Population: 49,517,233 (2013E—UN); 55,167,330 (2013E—U.S. Census).

Major Urban Centers (2007E): NAYPYIDAW (NAY PYI TAW, 420,000); Yangon (Rangoon, 4,090,000), Mandalay (960,000). In November 2005 the military regime began moving government offices to the vicinity of Pyinmana, 320 miles north of Yangon, the former capital. The newly built capital was officially designated Naypyidaw on March 27, 2006. City population estimates vary widely.

Official Language: Myanmar (Burmese).

Monetary Unit: Kyat (official rate November 1, 2013: 971.97 kyats = $1US). Exchange rate quoted here is set by the Myanmar government; black market rates can vary significantly.

President: Lt. Gen. (Ret.) THEIN SEIN (Union Solidarity and Development Party); elected by the Electoral College on February 4, 2011, and sworn in for a five-year term on March 30, following implementation of a new constitution that combined the offices of president and prime minister; previously appointed acting prime minister on May 18, 2007, due to medical incapacity of Prime Minister Lt. Gen. SOE WIN; confirmed as prime minister on October 24, following the death of Soe Win on October 12.

First Vice President: Adm. (Ret.) NYAN Tun; elected by the parliament on August 15, 2012, to replace Gen. (Ret.) TIN AUNG MYINT OO (Union Solidarity and Development Party), who resigned on May 3.

Second Vice President: SAI Mauk Kham (Union Solidarity and Development Party); elected by the Electoral College on February 4, 2011, and sworn in on March 30 for a term concurrent with that of the president.

THE COUNTRY

Myanmar, the largest country on the Southeast Asian mainland, has an extensive coastline running along the Bay of Bengal and the Andaman Sea. It shares a land border with Bangladesh and India in the west, China in the north, and Laos and Thailand in the east. Dominating the topography are tropical rain forests, plains, and mountains that rim the frontiers of the east, west, and north. Nearly three-quarters of the population is concentrated in the Irrawaddy (Ayeyawady) basin in the south.

More than 70 percent of the country's inhabitants are Burman. Karens (Kayins, about 7 percent) are dispersed over southern and eastern Myanmar, while Shans (9 percent), Thai in origin, are localized on the eastern plateau; Chins, Kachins, Mons, and Rakhines (Arakanese), totaling about 1 million, are found in the north and northeast. In addition, about 400,000 Chinese and 120,000 Indians and Bangladeshi are concentrated primarily in the urban areas. The various ethnic groups speak many languages and dialects, but the official Myanmar (Burmese), which is related to Tibeto-Chinese, is spoken by the vast majority. About 90 percent of the population professes Theravada Buddhism, the state religion; minority religions include Islam (4 percent), Christianity (4 percent), Hinduism (3 percent), and animism. Women make up an estimated 46 percent of the active labor force. Female representation in the military-dominated government is rare. Following the 2010 elections, women held 26 seats in the House of Representatives (6 percent) and 4 seats in the House of Nationalities (1.8 percent).

Although the country is rich in largely unexploited mineral resources (including hydrocarbons, silver, zinc, copper, lead, nickel, antimony, tin, and tungsten), its economy is heavily dependent on agriculture, which accounts for 44 percent of GDP and employs nearly two-thirds of the labor force. Teak and other hardwoods, and pulses and beans are among the major exports, and agriprocessing remains the leading industry, although production of textiles and garments has become more important as a source of export earnings. Production of natural gas from offshore fields is expanding; base metals, ores, and gemstones also contribute to national income. On the whole, the industrial sector contributes about 20 percent of GDP. There is also a thriving trade in opium, grown primarily in the "Golden Triangle" at the border juncture with Laos and Thailand, and in methamphetamines.

On May 3, 2008, Cyclone Nargis hit Myanmar's Irrawaddy region. By May 15 the UN estimated the number of severely affected people to be between 1.6 million and 2.5 million. In late June Myanmar raised the death toll to 84,500, with another 53,800 missing. A subsequent report from the Association of Southeast Asian Nations (ASEAN) put the cost of reconstruction and relief at $1 billion. Despite international criticism of the junta's response to the disaster, which initially included denying visas to foreign aid workers, the UN reported on July 10 that a total of 50 countries had pledged around $175 million to support relief, recovery, and rehabilitation efforts, with the United Kingdom and United States the largest donors.

In 2011 GDP grew by 5.5 percent and 6.3 percent in 2012 as economic reforms led to increased foreign investment and industrial production. Two major new natural gas production fields, which would double energy exports, were expected to be operational in 2014. In 2012 inflation rose by 5.1 percent. Unemployment was estimated to be 5.4 percent, and GDP per capita was $843.

GOVERNMENT AND POLITICS

Political background. Modern Burma was incorporated into British India as a result of the Anglo-Burmese wars of 1824–1886 but in 1937 was separated from India and granted limited self-government. During World War II Japan occupied the country and gave it nominal independence under a puppet regime led by anti-British nationalists, who subsequently transferred their loyalties to the Allied war effort.

The Anti-Fascist People's Freedom League (AFPFL), a coalition of nationalist forces, emerged as the principal political organization in 1945. Under the AFPFL, various groups and regions joined to form the Union of Burma, which gained full independence from the British in January 1948 and for a decade maintained a parliamentary democracy that was headed for most of that period by Prime Minister U NU. In May 1958 the AFPFL dissolved into factional groups, precipitating a political crisis that, four months later, forced Nu to resign in favor of a caretaker government headed by Gen. NE WIN, commander-in-chief of the armed forces.

The Nu faction of the AFPFL returned to power under the name of the Union Party in elections in 1960. However, problems involving internal security, national unity, and economic development led Ne Win to mount a coup d'état in March 1962, after which a Revolutionary Council of senior army officers ran the government. A Burma Socialist Program Party (BSPP) was launched by the council the following July. In January 1974, after 12 years of army rule, the Ne Win government adopted a new constitution and revived the legislature as a single-chambered People's Assembly.

In February 1977 Prime Minister SEIN WIN was among those denied reelection to the party's Central Committee. In March a new cabinet was organized with MAUNG MAUNG KHA as prime minister, and a new People's Assembly was elected in January 1978.

At the BSPP's fourth congress in August 1981, Ne Win announced his intention to resign as president while retaining his post as party chair. Following a legislative election in October, the assembly approved San Yu as his successor. Serious student-led disturbances erupted in the capital in 1988, leading to an extraordinary BSPP congress that concluded with both Ne Win and San Yu resigning from the party leadership. In July the People's Assembly named the new BSPP chair, SEIN LWIN, to succeed San Yu as state president, while Maung Maung Kha stepped down as prime minister in favor of TUN TIN. Student leaders thereupon mounted a campaign to press for President Sein Lwin's resignation, which culminated in a popular outpouring of more than 100,000 demonstrators in Yangon. Shortly thereafter, Sein Lwin was replaced as both president and party chair by the attorney general, Dr. MAUNG MAUNG. Like his predecessors, Maung Maung was a longtime associate of Ne Win.

On September 18, 1988, the military again seized power. The president was relieved, and army commander, Gen. SAW MAUNG, assumed the chair of a new State Law and Order Restoration Council (SLORC). The Defense Service Intelligence director, Brig. Gen. KHIN NYUNT, assumed the post of SLORC first secretary. On September 21

Saw Maung became prime minister, presiding over a new cabinet composed, with one exception, of military figures. Although few restrictions were placed on the formation of opposition parties, many of their supporters were severely repressed, and all public gatherings of more than four individuals were banned.

The February 1989 electoral campaign for a new People's Assembly was largely a contest between the government's National Unity Party (NUP, successor to the BSPP) and the National League for Democracy (NLD), led by AUNG SAN SUU KYI, the daughter of the "founder of modern Burma," AUNG SAN, who had been assassinated in 1947 on the eve of independence. On May 27, 1990, voters awarded a massive victory to the NLD, which secured more than 80 percent of the seats. Humiliated by the NUP's showing, 2.1 percent of the seats, the SLORC leadership refused to let the assembly convene and began systematic delegalization of opposition parties.

In October 1991 Aung San Suu Kyi was awarded the Nobel Peace Prize, which focused world attention on the repressive policies of the SLORC and triggered a wave of domestic demonstrations on behalf of the opposition leader, who had been held in detention since July 1989. The government responded by shutting down universities, arresting numerous protestors, and mounting a dry-season campaign against dissident minorities, especially Karen insurgents on the Thai border.

In April 1992 Saw Maung, who was reported to be in poor mental health, was succeeded as prime minister and SLORC chair by Gen. THAN SHWE. In May the SLORC announced that a "coordination meeting" would be convened to pave the way for a National Convention to draft a new constitution. Most opposition groups were excluded from the preparatory process for the convention, which opened in January 1993. In July 1995 Aung San Suu Kyi was freed, but in November the NLD delegation (only 86 members out of 703) pulled out of the National Convention, insisting that the body had displayed scant interest in democratic reform. In March 1996 the convention began what would turn out to be an eight-year hiatus.

In advance of a planned NLD congress in May 1996, the government arrested some 260 party members, limiting the number of attendees to 18. Some 500–800 NLD supporters were arrested when they attempted to hold another congress at Suu Kyi's house in September. In early December weeklong demonstrations in Yangon and Mandalay prompted the government to close the universities once again and reimpose Suu Kyi's house arrest. In late September 1997 the NLD held its first authorized congress since 1995, with Suu Kyi in attendance, but the event had no appreciable effect on the government's underlying strategy of arresting and imprisoning NLD activists.

During the mid-1990s the SLORC had mounted a series of successful attacks on longtime insurgents. In January 1995 the military captured Manerplaw, the headquarters of the rebel Karen National Union (KNU), which was followed by the fall of the KNU's last stronghold in Kawmoora, on the Thai border. In March Gen. BO MYA resigned as commander of the Karen National Army (KNA), although continuing as chair of the KNU. Also in March, the Karenni National Progressive Party (KNPP) abandoned its armed struggle, leading SLORC officials to claim that 14 of 16 rebel groups had now laid down their arms. Most of the remaining military opposition came from the Mong Tai Army (MTA) of Shan drug warlord KHUN SA. Eight months later Khun Sa announced his "retirement" as MTA chief, and in January 1996 his troops began their formal surrender. In April the government announced that Khun Sa would neither be tried for his crimes nor extradited to the United States to face charges of drug trafficking. In early 1997 negotiations between the regime and the KNU collapsed, and government forces immediately launched a lengthy offensive against the remaining rebel bases, forcing thousands of refugees to flee into Thailand.

On November 15, 1997, the SLORC was dissolved and immediately replaced by the "permanent" State Peace and Development Council (SPDC), which thereupon announced a cabinet reshuffling. Subsequently, Khin Nyunt ordered the detention of a number of former cabinet officials and their supporters on corruption charges.

Although the SPDC approved an NLD party congress held in May 1998 at Aung San Suu Kyi's residence, the military blocked attempts by the NLD leader to visit supporters outside the capital. In September Suu Kyi and nine other activists carried out a threat to initiate a "People's Parliament." Calling themselves the Committee Representing Elected Lawmakers, they declared all junta laws and proclamations invalid, demanded the release of all political prisoners, and stated their intention to act as a parliament until the Constituent Assembly elected in 1990 was allowed to meet. Meanwhile, the SPDC continued what had become its biggest crackdown against the opposition since early in the decade. By October nearly 900 NLD members had been detained. In August–September 2000 Aung San Suu Kyi twice tried to venture outside Yangon but was again prevented from doing so.

In November 2001 the government hierarchy underwent its most significant changes since the formation of the SPDC four years earlier. SPDC Secretary WIN MYINT was dismissed, as were the three deputy prime ministers. Several additional cabinet changes were announced, and 10 of 12 regional military commanders were reassigned. Although the SPDC did not explain its actions, observers concluded that the changes had served to strengthen the hands of Than Shwe and SPDC vice chair Sr. Gen. MAUNG AYE.

During the same period a UN special envoy to Myanmar, Malaysian diplomat Razali Ismail, was attempting to facilitate prisoner releases and discussions between the opposition and the SPDC. The military regime had begun releasing detained NLD members, but at the end of the year an estimated 1,500 political prisoners continued in custody. On May 6, 2002, Suu Kyi was unconditionally released from house arrest.

Two months earlier, in March 2002, the SPDC had reported the discovery of a planned coup led by Ne Win's son-in-law AYE ZAW WIN. Ne Win and his daughter SANDAR WIN, wife of the alleged ringleader, were placed under house arrest. In September Aye Zaw Win and his three sons were sentenced to hang for treason. (Although the Supreme Court confirmed the sentences in August 2003, executions, in deference to the country's Buddhist heritage, are rarely carried out.) Ne Win, age 91, died in December 2002.

On May 30, 2003, a convoy carrying Aung San Suu Kyi and supporters was attacked near Mandalay. The attack, reportedly by a mob of up to 2,000, was orchestrated by the government-supportive Union Solidarity and Development Association (USDA). Shortly after, the NLD leader was placed in "protective custody" until transferred to her home on September 26. The regime's actions provoked widespread international outrage.

On August 25, 2003, the SPDC announced a major cabinet reshuffle that saw Than Shwe turn over the prime ministership to Khin Nyunt, who was replaced as SPDC first secretary by the former second secretary, Lt. Gen. SOE WIN. Five days later the new prime minister announced that the long-adjourned National Convention would reconvene as the first element of a "seven-step road map" to democracy that would also include a referendum on a new constitution, legislative elections, and the selection of state leaders by the resultant People's Assembly.

The National Convention reconvened on May 17, 2004, with SPDC second secretary Lt. Gen. THEIN SEIN as chair. The 1,088 delegates included representatives of political parties, ethnic groups ("national races"), workers, farmers, the intelligentsia, and state service personnel, plus "invited delegates" from state "Special Regions" and former insurgent groups that had "exchanged arms for peace." Conspicuously absent were NLD representatives, who refused to participate until the regime released Aung San Suu Kyi and NLD vice chair TIN OO from house arrest.

On October 19, 2004, Prime Minister Khin Nyunt was "permitted to retire" and reportedly placed under house arrest. Soe Win assumed the cabinet leadership, and Thein Sein was elevated to SPDC first secretary. The SPDC began another major reorganization of the military command structure as well as a purge of the military intelligence apparatus, previously headed by Khin Nyunt, who was convicted of corruption and bribery in July 2005.

In late 2006 the KNU demanded that the military halt an offensive in the east that had brought an end to a two-year-old de facto cease-fire and had reportedly displaced 10,000 Karens. (In March the Norwegian Refugee Council had estimated that Myanmar had 540,000 internally displaced people, the largest number of any country in Asia.) The government justified its offensive against the KNU and other ethnic groups as a response to a number of small bomb blasts, which were also blamed on exile groups. The most serious incident occurred on May 7, 2005, in the capital; according to official sources, three bombs killed 19 people and injured 150.

On May 18, 2007, with Soe Win undergoing medical treatment, Thein Sein became acting prime minister. He officially succeeded the deceased Soe Win on October 24, when the SPDC also announced the appointment of Lt. Gen. TIN AUNG MYINT OO as SPDC first secretary.

On August 15, 2007, the SPDC announced major price hikes for fuels, triggering a series of protests led initially by the 88 Generation Students group. As September approached, Buddhist monks increasingly took control of what gradually became the first public uprising against the government since 1988. Antigovernment protests spread across the urban landscape, with some 100,000 people demonstrating. On September 25 the SPDC imposed a curfew, outlawed gatherings of more than five people, and sent troops and the police into the streets to quell demonstrations. USDA-organized militias—the *Swan-ar Shin* (Masters of Force)—also clashed with the protesters. Between September 26 and 28, the government reported the deaths of 10 demonstrators and the arrest of some 2,100. The country's principal Internet service provider was shut down, as were all cellular telephone networks. By September 30, with government forces having raided and cordoned off several monasteries in Yangon, the protest movement had succumbed.

Efforts by UN under-secretary general for political affairs Ibrahim Gambari to bring the government and the opposition to the negotiating table met with scant success until late October 2007. The curfew and ban on assembly were lifted on October 20, and within a week a government representative had met with Aung San Suu Kyi. On November 8 Gambari released a statement on behalf of Suu Kyi, who indicated she was "ready to cooperate with the government in order to make this process of dialogue a success." Nevertheless, no progress was made during a series of meetings between the government and Suu Kyi.

Although Suu Kyi's annually renewed house arrest technically expired in May 2009, at that time she was being held at Insein Prison in Yangon since being formally charged earlier in the month with harboring for two days an uninvited American who had swum to her lakeside home. Suu Kyi was convicted on August 11 and sentenced to three years in prison, but Gen. Than Shwe commuted the sentence to another 18 months under house arrest.

Meanwhile, the government pushed forward with its "Road Map for Democracy." Between July 18 and September 3, 2007, a final National Convention session completed "basic principles" for a new constitution. A 54-member, government-appointed State Constitution Drafting Commission then produced a complete text that was published on April 9, 2008, approved by 92 percent of those voting in a referendum on May 10 and 24, and promulgated by the SPDC on May 29. Under the Referendum Law for the Approval of the Draft Constitution, anybody who publicly critiqued the referendum faced a fine and a three-year prison sentence.

On August 13, 2010, the SPDC announced that it had set November 7 as the date for nationwide parliamentary elections. Several dozen new or reorganized political parties had already been registered, the most prominent of the progovernment parties being the USDA-backed Union Solidarity and Development Party (USDP), headed by Prime Minister Thein Sein. As required under the new constitution, he and several dozen other government ministers and SPDC members resigned their military commissions to run for office. Among the prodemocracy parties, the NLD, faced with having to expel Suu Kyi in order to register, instead chose forced dissolution, although some senior members rejected the NLD's call for an election boycott and registered as the National Democratic Force (NDF).

In the November 2010 elections, the USDP secured 259 of the 330 elective seats in the People's Assembly, 129 of the 168 elective seats in the National Assembly, and a large majority of seats in the 14 state and regional parliaments. The leading opposition group, the Shan Nationalities Democratic Party (SNDP), won 18 seats in the lower house, where the NDF came away with only 8. Even before the official results were announced, however, world attention turned to the release of Aung San Suu Kyi on November 13, at the expiration of her most recent period of house arrest.

Thein Sein was elected president by the Electoral College on February 4, 2011. He subsequently named a new cabinet, which was approved by the assembly and sworn in on March 30. The SPDC was abolished that day (see Current issues, below). The cabinet was reshuffled in August 2011.

The NLD won 38 of 39 seats in by-elections in April 2012 (see Current issues, below). The vacancies were created when elected members resigned their seats to take government posts. First vice president TIN AUNG MYINT OO, regarded as a hardliner, resigned on May 3. He was replaced by Adm. (Ret.) NYAN Tun, a reformer, who was elected on August 16. A cabinet reshuffle began on August 29 and ended September 4. Thirteen ministries were involved in the reshuffle in which conservative ministers were replaced by reformers.

On March 20, 2013, the Union Parliament voted to create a commission to recommend revisions to the constitution, including the removal of the mandate that 25 percent of seats of the legislature be reserved for the military and prohibitions against foreign spouses or children for presidential candidates (a clause created to prevent Suu Ki, whose husband was a British citizen, from running for the presidency).

Constitution and government. The 1974 constitution was adopted with the stated objective of making Burma a "Socialist Republic" under one-party rule. It provided for a unicameral People's Assembly as the supreme organ of state authority and for a State Council comprising 14 representatives from the country's major political subdivisions plus 15 additional members (including the prime minister) elected from the assembly. The State Council and its chair, who was also state president, served four-year terms, concurrent with that of the assembly. The prime minister was designated by the Council of Ministers, which was elected by the assembly from its own membership, following nomination by the State Council. All of these institutions were abolished upon direct assumption of power by the military in September 1988.

A new constitution was promulgated on May 29, 2008, following passage with 92 percent voter support, according to the SPDC. In addition to creating a republic, the constitution provides for a multiparty political system, the election of a bicameral Union Parliament, the indirect election of a president, and establishment of an independent judiciary. It also ensures a "national political leadership role" for the military, which it recognizes as the ultimate protector of the constitution and accords "the right to independently administer and adjudicate all affairs of the armed forces." In both houses of the Union Parliament and in the country's 14 state and regional assemblies, 25 percent of the seats are reserved for military designees.

The president is elected by members of the Union Parliament sitting as a tripartite Electoral College comprising (1) representatives of the states and divisions, with an equal number from each; (2) representatives elected from township constituencies on the basis of population; and (3) members of the defense services. The three groups each select a vice president, with the one who then receives the most votes from the full Electoral College assuming the executive presidency for a five-year term; the other two vice presidents serve a concurrent term. The president may be impeached for treason, breach of the constitution, misconduct, or "inefficient discharge of duties." Impeachment requires support by two-thirds of the full membership of both parliamentary houses.

With the concurrence of the Union Parliament, which can only reject the nominees for cause, the president is empowered to name government ministers and the justices of the supreme court. The president also names the commander-in-chief of the defense services, with the "proposal and approval" of the National Defense and Security Council (NDSC). The 11-member NDSC comprises the president and the 2 vice presidents; the speakers of the upper and lower houses; the commander-in-chief and his deputy; the minister of foreign affairs; and the ministers of defense, home affairs, and border affairs, all three of whom must be army officers. Thus, the military holds at least six seats on the NDSC. In the event of a national emergency, the president turns authority over to the commander-in-chief, who may rule with full presidential, legislative, and judicial powers and may suspend the rights of citizens. Following termination of the emergency, the NDSC is responsible for running the government until the conclusion of new elections, which must be held within six months.

The Supreme Court sits at the apex of the judiciary, followed by a system of high courts in the states and regions, courts of self-administered zones and divisions, and district and township courts. The constitution also provides for separate courts-martial to adjudicate defense service personnel. A Constitutional Tribunal is responsible for interpreting the constitution, reviewing the constitutionality of legislation, reviewing the actions of executive authorities, and resolving constitutional disputes between jurisdictions. Constitutional amendment requires 75 percent support from the Union Parliament, with the added proviso that amendments to specified sections of the basic law must then receive the assent of half of all eligible voters in a referendum.

Local government is based primarily on seven states (Chin, Kachin, Kayah, Kayin, Mon, Rakhine, Shan) and seven regions (Ayeyawady, Bago, Magway, Mandalay, Sagaing, Tanintharyi, Yangon), plus the Union Territory of Naypyidaw. The states and regions (previously called divisions) are divided into townships, which are subdivided into urban wards and village tracts. The 2008 constitution also recognizes five "self-administered zones" (Danu, Kokang, Naga, Palaung, and Pa-O) and one "self-administered division" (Wa), each comprising specified townships within a particular state or region. Each state and region elects an assembly. The executive is headed by a chief minister, who is nominated by the president and approved by the respective legislature. The union territory is directly administered by the president.

Government control of the media has loosened. In December 2012 the government announced that privately owned newspapers would be allowed for the first time in 50 years, starting in April 2013. Also, on January 16, 2013, the law forbidding criticism of the military was repealed. In 2013 Reporters Without Borders ranked Myanmar 151st out of 179 countries in freedom of the press, a rise from 169th the previous year.

Foreign relations. Nonalignment was the cornerstone of Burmese foreign policy from 1948 through the end of the Cold War in the early 1990s, and until quite recently the country's participation in most intergovernmental organizations, including the UN and its specialized agencies, was marginal. In 1979 Burma announced its withdrawal from the Nonaligned Movement. In 1992, however, it rejoined the existing group. In 1997 Myanmar was admitted to ASEAN, partly in an effort by neighboring states to foster "constructive engagement" with the SPDC.

In 1949 Burma became the first noncommunist country to recognize the People's Republic of China. The two signed a Treaty of Friendship and Mutual Nonaggression in 1960, following settlement of a long-standing border dispute. By 1967, however, leftist terrorism, aimed at instituting a Chinese-style "Cultural Revolution," led to a severe deterioration in Sino-Burmese relations that lasted into the next decade.

Relations with Bangladesh worsened in mid-1978 because of an exodus from Burma of some 200,000 Rohingya Muslims who, according to Dhaka, had been subjected to an "extermination campaign." Later, it appeared that Muslim leaders had encouraged the flight in part to publicize their desire to establish the Rakhine (Arakan) region as an Islamic state; meanwhile, the number of refugees living in makeshift camps on the Bangladeshi side of the border had reportedly risen to more than 260,000 by March 1992. Repatriations began in September 1992; however, many Rohingyas were reluctant to return, while some of those who did were reported to be members of a terrorist Rohingya Solidarity Organization (*Kalarzo*) that was responsible for the killing of 16 Myanmar troops in May 1994. By September 1995 most refugees had been repatriated, although more than 20,000 remained in Bangladesh as of early 1998. Myanmar subsequently announced it would guarantee the safety of any additional voluntary returnees. In January 2000 Yangon rejected reentry for some 14,000 refugees, whom it claimed were not Myanmar, but in April 2004 the two governments agreed that the remaining Rohingyas would be repatriated. Nevertheless, most have refused to leave or have not received authorization from Myanmar. In June 2010 the Bangladeshi government stated that it would approach "international bodies" for assistance in the absence of a bilateral resolution.

A dispute between Bangladesh and Myanmar over territorial boundaries in the Bay of Bengal also persists. Dating back to 1974, the dispute has taken on added significance because of possible oil and natural gas deposits under the sea. In October 2009 Bangladesh stated that it was prepared to resolve the issue through compulsory arbitration under the UN Convention on the Law of the Sea (UNCLOS).

In October 1994 Myanmar concluded a friendship pact with Thailand, but relations have remained cool. Insurgent refugee camps are still located on Thai soil, and Myanmar military forces have repeatedly crossed the border in pursuit of guerrillas. In October 1999 Thai authorities freed the five Myanmar perpetrators of a hostage incident at the Myanmar embassy in Bangkok, leading an angered SPDC to close the Thai-Myanmar border until late November. In contrast, in January 2000 Thailand earned the SPDC's praise for a swift, response when a small Kayinni group called God's Army took some 700 hostages at a hospital near the border (see Political parties and groupings, below). In June 2001, four months after a cross-border clash led to a series of bilateral meetings, Myanmar and Thai leaders agreed to resolve border issues and to jointly fight drug production and smuggling. Difficulties continued into 2002, however, and the border was closed from May to October. In July 2003 the Thai government announced plans to relocate all Myanmar dissidents to refugee camps near the border. Largely as a result of the decades-old conflict with the KNU, some 400,000 Karens lived in refugee camps across the border in Thailand. (According to the Office of the UN High Commissioner for Refugees, between 2005 and 2008 some 30,000 Myanmar refugees were resettled from Thai camps, 21,500 of them in the United States.) In November 2010, immediately after Myanmar's national election, fighting between Karen insurgents and the government forces led an estimated 20,000 additional Myanmar refugees to flee across the border into Thailand, although as the violence diminished in the following days, they began returning to their homes.

In April 1997 the United States announced the imposition of economic sanctions against Myanmar, largely because of its repression of prodemocracy advocates. In 1998 the United States and Japan approved a grant of $3.8 million to the UN Drug Control Program to help eliminate opium poppy cultivation in Myanmar, but Washington continued its ten-year-old policy of refusing to make direct grants to the Yangon regime. In April 2000 the European Union (EU) announced that it was freezing assets of Myanmar officials in addition to increasing sanctions.

Following the protests of 2007, further sanctions were applied by both the United States and the EU. On May 1, 2008, the U.S. Treasury froze the assets of state-owned firms in Myanmar, adding to the sanctions of October 2007 in which the Treasury froze the financial assets of members of the military regime. The EU added a ban on imports of timber, gemstones, and precious metals in response to the military junta's crackdown on prodemocracy groups.

In mid-2000 the SPDC was condemned, not for the first time, by the International Labor Organization (ILO) for using forced labor and was also accused at an international conference in Nepal of having more child soldiers—at least 50,000, according to a Save the Children spokesperson—than any other country in the world. On November 16 the ILO, for the first time in its 81-year history, urged its members to impose sanctions against a country. In March 2002, in an effort to diffuse continuing criticism, the government signed an agreement permitting the ILO to monitor compliance through a new liaison office in Yangon. An action plan drawn up in May 2003 by ILO representatives and the government remained largely unimplemented, and in June 2005 the ILO once again called for sanctions. In February 2007 the government agreed not to act against individuals who bring complaints of forced labor before the ILO. Since then, the ILO has convened a series of meetings with government personnel to raise awareness of the issue. A 2010 report submitted to the ILO accused the junta of forcing Rohingyas and others in Arakan State to erect a fence along the border with Bangladesh.

On September 29, 2006, for the first time in its history, the UN Security Council discussed human rights and internal developments in Myanmar. On January 12, 2007, however, Russia and China vetoed a Security Council resolution that called on the SPDC to release political prisoners, permit free expression and political activity, and end human rights violations and military action against ethnic minorities. The resolution had been sponsored by the United States and the United Kingdom. In June 2007 the International Committee of the Red Cross added its voice to those condemning the SPDC for human rights abuses.

On June 26–27, 2009, Ibrahim Gambari visited Myanmar for the eighth time in his capacity as special representative of the UN secretary general. In general, his visits focused on democratization. On July 3–4 UN secretary general Ban Ki Moon paid a second visit to Myanmar—his first had come in the wake of Cyclone Nargis in 2008—at which time Sr. Gen. Than Shwe promised that the planned 2010 elections would be free and fair. The secretary general was not permitted to meet with Aung San Suu Kyi.

Renewed fighting in November 2010 in the northeast of Myanmar between ethnic Karens and government forces created an estimated 30,000 refugees, who fled into Thailand (see Current issues, below). In April 2011 the EU temporarily suspended some travel and economic sanctions against officials of the Myanmar government as an incentive for further democratization. In November Hilary Clinton became the first U.S. secretary of state to visit Myanmar since 1955.

In March 2012 the International Tribunal for the Law of the Sea ruled in favor of Bangladesh in a dispute with Myanmar over maritime claims in the Bay of Bengal, around St. Martin's Island.

In April 2012 Australia and the EU eased economic sanctions on Myanmar, after the election of Aung San Suu Kyi to the assembly (see Current issues, below). The prime minister of the United Kingdom, David Cameron, became the first Western leader to visit Myanmar since 1962. The following month the United States also relaxed trade sanctions and named its first ambassador to Myanmar since 1990. A succession of foreign leaders visited Myanmar, including President Barack Obama in November. Some nations offered new economic and development assistance: Japan agreed to write off $3.7 billion in debt, while Australia pledged to double its aid to $104 million per year. In November 2012, the World Bank announced it would lend to Myanmar for the first time since the 1980s. Meanwhile in 2012 the United States appointed its first ambassador to Myanmar since 1990.

In January 2013 the Asian Development Bank resumed operations in Myanmar with a 30-year, $512 million loan. In May Japan announced it would forgive Myanmar's remaining $1.7 billion in debt and provide a new $504 million economic development loan during a visit to Naypyitaw by Prime Minister Shinzo Abe, the first by a Japanese leader in 36 years. In June Coca-Cola announced a $200 investment in Myanmar and the resumption of production in the country after more than 60 years. Meanwhile Myanmar and the United States finalized a trade treaty in May as President Sein became the first Myanmar leader to visit the White House since 1966.

Current issues. The August 2009 conviction of Aung San Suu Kyi for harboring American John Yettaw was interpreted by international observers as a means of preventing her involvement in the 2010 elections. Yettaw, sentenced to a seven-year prison term for illegally visiting Suu Kyi, was released on August 15. In September U.S. secretary of state Hillary Clinton nevertheless announced that the Obama administration was in fact ready to engage in direct talks with the SPDC, but without weakening sanctions. Suu Kyi reportedly supported the policy change. In November 2009 President Obama and Prime Minister Thein Sein met during a U.S.-ASEAN summit, marking the first time that a U.S. president and a junta leader had direct contact.

With the constitution reserving 25 percent of the seats in all legislative bodies for military appointees, and with the national party scene dominated by former senior officers in the progovernment USDP, the election results for the bicameral Union Parliament were a foregone conclusion. The USDP was the only party with sufficient resources to run in virtually all districts, and there were innumerable reports of vote buying, stuffed ballot boxes, voter intimidation, and other irregularities. Opposition parties were hampered by a lack of finances, domination of the state-controlled media by the SPDC and the USDP, and organizational impediments. Foreign journalists and international monitors were not permitted to observe the elections.

In the week after the elections, attention increasingly turned toward Aung San Suu Kyi's residence in anticipation of the expiration of her latest period of house arrest. On November 13 crowds gathered in front of her house even before the announcement that she had been freed. Her release gave an immediate boost to prodemocracy advocates, and she wasted no time in championing their cause, delivering public addresses and media interviews in which she called for relegalizing the NLD and for peacefully pressuring the junta to open negotiations. The government stated that it would continue to register new political parties but gave no indication that it would expand the limited range of discussions its representatives had conducted with Suu Kyi during her confinement.

An estimated 2,200 political prisoners remained incarcerated in 2010. The SPDC periodically granted amnesty to thousands of prisoners—9,000 in September 2008, 7,100 in September 2009—but relatively few of them fall into the category of political prisoners. Moreover, courts throughout the country continue to convict dissidents and sentence them to decades-long prison terms for crimes that most other countries would consider noninfractions or, at worst, minor offenses, such as drawing cartoons critical of SPDC members or breaching "public order." Among those currently serving sentences of more than 60 years are leaders of the September 2007 protests, including MIN KO NAING of the 88 Generation Students and ASHIN GAMBIRA of the Alliance of All Burmese Buddhist Monks.

During 2009 the SPDC continued a three-year military offensive against the KNU. There have been recent reports of offenses against ethnic Chinese in northeastern Kokang, and a report by Human Rights Watch in January called attention to the plight of the Chin minority, adjacent to India, where army abuses were described as including forced labor, summary executions, torture, food shortages, and sexual exploitation. In April–May 2009 the junta approached a number of cease-fire groups with a proposal calling for them to operate as elements of a Border Guard Force (BGF) under the command of the army. Although a number of the cease-fire groups accepted the plan, others refused, concerned that the junta's intention was to neutralize them.

On March 30, 2011, the SPDC was officially abolished. However, former SPDC chair Than Shwe and other senior members of the group were appointed to a new body, the State Supreme Council. Reports described the council as an extra-constitutional grouping created to preserve the influence of the military within the government.

In June 2011 the construction of the $3.6 billion Myitsone Dam across the Irrawaddy River prompted a new round of fighting with the Karen Independence Organization (KIO) and other Karen groups. The KIO opposed the project because it would dislocate several thousand Karens. The strife displaced an estimated 15,000 civilians. On September 30, 2011, Thein Sein ordered an end to the construction in an effort to end the fighting. Fighting in the region in 2012 led the UN to suspend aid operations in northern Kachin.

On September 6, 2011, the government established a human rights commission to investigate complaints against the government. The following month, legislation was enacted to legalize trade unions for the first time since 1962. Concurrently, the government announced the release of more than 6,350 prisoners, including 220 political detainees.

Aung San Suu Kyi ended her boycott of elections and won a seat in the Assembly in by-elections on April 1, 2012. Her election prompted foreign governments to restore ties and assistance to the country. In June a state of emergency was declared in Rakhine (Arakan) state, following protracted sectarian violence between Buddhists and Muslims that left 78 dead and created more than 90,000 internally displaced persons. Also in June, the military announced the end to Myanmar's small nuclear program, which critics charged was designed to produce atomic weapons.

Following a ruling in March 2012 that limited the power of the legislature to investigate government agencies or ministers, the Union Parliament voted to impeach the constitutional court. The nine justices of the court subsequently resigned on September 6.

In January 2013 a 1988 law banning public gatherings of more than four people without a permit was repealed. On March 20, sectarian strife broke out between Buddhists and Muslims in Mandalay. The violence left more than 100 dead and prompted the deployment of military troops to restore order. More than 10,000 Muslims were resettled into camps, ostensibly for their safety. The UN and international rights groups called on the government to end the violence and reduce anti-Muslim discrimination. The government announced the release of 93 political prisoners in April. In June, despite ongoing negotiations, renewed fighting broke out between the KIO and government forces. Approximately 60,000 ethnic Kachins were displaced by the violence.

POLITICAL PARTIES AND GROUPS

Following the 1962 coup, political parties continued to exist until March 1964, when the Revolutionary Council banned all but its own Burma Socialist Program Party (BSPP). During this period the Beijing-oriented Burmese Communist Party (BCP), which had been in open rebellion since 1948, and at least a score of ethnic insurgent groups continued to oppose the government. Following the September 1988 coup, the government rescinded the party ban, and the BSPP reorganized as the National Unity Party (NUP). By then, the BCP had diminished in importance. Ethnic opposition groups, in contrast, continued to control considerable territory, especially in the north and east.

The 2008 constitution provides for the formation of political parties within a "genuine and discipline-flourishing multiparty democratic system" (Chapter X). Party registrations may be revoked for receiving foreign assistance, abusing religion, or "directly or indirectly contacting or abetting" terrorists or insurgent groups in armed rebellion against the state. Members of the military are among those excluded from party membership. Under the Political Parties Registration Law, parties that did not seek reregistration were automatically dissolved. These included the NLD and the SNLD.

Competing in the November 2010 elections were 37 parties, about two-thirds of them based in ethnic communities. Many parties contested no more than a handful of seats at the national level, partly because of financial limitations, including having to pay a fee of 500,000 kyats (about $500) per candidate.

Parties in the Union Parliament:

Union Solidarity and Development Party (USDP). Registered in June 2010, the USDP sprang from the Union Solidarity and Development Association (USDA), a junta-supportive mass organization founded in 1993 and described by the *Far Eastern Economic Review* in 1998 as a more inclusive "quasi-political party established under the guise of a community-assistance organization." In May 2003 the USDA was accused of organizing the attack against Aung San Suu Kyi's motorcade, and it was subsequently used to suppress, sometimes violently, other antijunta activities. Sometimes referred to by the derogatory *Kyant Phut* (translatable as "monitor lizard" or, roughly, "stupid reptile"), the USDA had a reputed membership of some 23 million when it was dissolved in July 2010 in favor of the USDP, to which its assets were transferred. Most of the Thein Sein cabinet and many members of the SPDC joined the USDP after relinquishing their military commissions.

Before the November 2010 election it was widely expected that the USDP would win 80 percent of the elective seats in the new Union Parliament, and it nearly equaled that forecast, taking 79.7 percent and 259 seats in the People's Assembly, and 76.8 percent and 129 seats in the National Assembly. It also won a large majority of seats in the state and regional parliaments. In 2013 Thein Sein announced that he would not seek reelection. Subsequently the speaker of the House of Representatives, Shwe MANN, a prominent reformer, declared his intention to be the USDP's 2015 presidential candidate.

Leaders: Lt. Gen. (Ret.) THEIN SEIN (President of the Republic and USDP Chair), Adm. (Ret.) NYAN Tun (First Vice President of the Republic).

Shan Nationalities Democratic Party (SNDP). The prodemocracy SNDP is the successor to the Shan Nationalities League for Democracy (SNLD), which opposed the 2008 constitution, decided not to seek registration, and was dissolved by the election commission in September 2010. The SNLD (see under Dissolved Parties, below) had finished second in the 1990 Constituent Assembly election as an ally of the NLD. The SNDP's first chair, Ai Pao, was the SNLP's secretary general.

Registered in May 2010, the SNDP, which is widely known as the White Tiger Party from its party emblem, focused its attention on winning Union Parliament seats in Shan State. In the lower house it finished second to the USDP overall, winning 5.5 percent of the vote and 18 seats. In the upper house it was less successful, taking 1.8 percent of the vote and winning 3 seats. It won an additional seat in the upper house in by-elections in April 2012. Meanwhile, party leader Khun Htun Oo was released in January 2012 after being imprisoned since 2005. In December 2012, reports indicated that the SNDP sought to create an electoral alliance with other Shan parties ahead of the 2015 balloting.

Leaders: KHUN HTUN OO (Chair), SAI NYUNT LWIN (General Secretary).

National Unity Party—NUP (*Taingyintha Silonenyinyutye* Party). An outgrowth of the former BSPP, the NUP was launched in September 1988. Unlike the practice under BSPP rule, members of the armed forces were specifically excluded from membership. The party won only 10 of 485 available seats in the Constituent Assembly election of May 1990.

The government-supportive NUP, reregistered in April 2010, is backed by business interests. Its chair is a former deputy commander in chief of the armed forces. In the 2010 balloting, it won 3.7 percent of the vote and 12 seats in the People's Assembly, plus 3.0 percent and 5 seats in the National Assembly. The NUP ran 23 candidates in the April 2012 by-elections but failed to secure any seats.

Leaders: TUN YI (Chair), THAN TIN and KHIN MAUNG GYI (General Secretaries), HAN SHWE (Spokesperson).

Rakhine Nationalities Development Party (RNDP). Officially registered in June 2010, the RNDP is a prodemocracy formation in the western state of Rakhine (Arakan). During the subsequent legislative election campaign it complained of harassment and other forms of intimidation by USDP members. Its general secretary was vice chair of the Arakan League for Democracy (ALD) when it won 11 seats in the 1990 Constituent Assembly. (Led by AYE THAR AUNG, who also served as secretary of the Committee Representing the People's Parliament, the ALD chose not to run in 2010.)

In the November 2010 elections the RNDP won 2.8 percent of the lower house vote, for nine seats, and 4.2 percent in the upper house, for seven seats, second to the USDP. Following violence in Rakhine in 2012, party leader Aye Maung participated in government-sponsored peace negotiations, although reports alleged that the RNDP was complicit in the strife.

Leaders: AYE MAUNG (Chair), TIN WIN (Vice Chair).

National Democratic Force (NDF). The NDF was registered in July 2010 by former members of the dissolved NLD's Central Executive Committee who objected to Aung San Suu Kyi's call to boycott the upcoming national elections. One of the leading prodemocracy parties to participate in the November election, the NDF put forward about 150 candidates for the Union Parliament. It won 2.5 percent of the vote and eight seats in the lower house, and 2.4 percent and four seats in the upper. In 2013 the NDF announced its support for constitutional changes that would allow Aung San Suu Kyi of the NLD to seek the presidency in 2015.

Leaders: THAN NYEIN (Chair), TIN AUNG AUNG (Vice Chair), KHIN MAUNG SWE, THEIN NYUNT (Spokesperson), SEIN WIN (Secretary).

All Mon Region Democracy Party (AMRDP). Campaigning on behalf of the Mon people in eastern Myanmar, the AMRDP was registered in May 2010. With the New Mon State Party (NMSP), a cease-fire group, having decided to boycott the November elections, the AMRDP was the only ethnic Mon party to compete. It won three seats (0.9 percent of the vote) in the People's Assembly but four seats (2.4 percent) in the National Assembly. In September 2012 the AMRDP agreed to merge with the small Mon Democracy Party (MDP); however, reports in 2013 indicated tensions between the two groupings had prevented the finalization of the merger.

Leaders: NGWE THEIN (Chair), HLA AUNG (Vice Chair).

Pa-O National Organization (PNO). The PNO, representing the Pa-O ethnic minority in the Pa-O Self-Administered Zone of Shan State, was registered in May 2010. Formed from one of the cease-fire groups and elements of the Union Pa-O National Organization, which had contested the 1990 election but was formally dissolved in September 2010 for failing to register, the PNO received at least tacit government support. It won three uncontested People's Assembly seats as well as one uncontested seat in the National Assembly.

Leaders: AUNG KHAM HTI (Chair), KHUN SAN LWIN, MAI OHN KAING (Secretary General).

Chin National Party (CNP). Officially registered in May 2010, the CNP campaigned on behalf of the Chin people, calling for increased self-determination, economic development, and an end to arbitrary arrests and forced labor. The Union Election Commission censored part of the party's election manifest, including a call for religious freedom and the teaching of the Chin language.

In the November 2010 polling the CNP won 0.6 percent of the vote and two seats in the lower house, and 1.2 percent of the vote and two seats in the upper house. In June 2013 the CNP was reported to have merged with the Chin Progressive Party (see below).

Leaders: ZAM CIIN PAU (Chair), CHAN HAY (Vice Chair), CEU BIK THAWNG (Secretary General).

Chin Progressive Party (CPP). Based in Chin State and Sagaing Division, the CPP registered in May 2010. Its leadership includes a number of former government workers as well as businessmen. Its goals include advancing economic development and the rights and cultural identity of ethnic Chin. It won two seats in the People's Assembly (0.6 percent of the vote) but four in the National Assembly (2.4 percent). In 2013 the CPP was reported to have merged with the CNP in order to contest the 2015 elections.

Leaders: NOE THANG KUP (Chair), LAEL HTAN (Secretary).

Phalon-Sawaw Democratic Party (PSDP). Based in Kayin State and targeting ethnic Kayins, the PSDP registered in May 2010. Its election manifesto championed human rights, international peace, national unity, and overcoming oppression. The PSDP won two seats in the lower house and three in the upper in the November election.

Leaders: KHIN MAUNG MYINT (Chair), AUNG KYAW NAING (Vice Chair), KYI LIN (Secretary).

Wa Democratic Party (WDP). Registration of the WDP was approved in July 2010. Based in Shan State, the party has ties to the USDP. Its chair won a seat in the 1990 Constituent Assembly election as an NUP candidate. In November 2010 the WDP won two seats in the People's Assembly and one in the National Assembly. In 2013 the WDP refused to participate in an all-Shan state conference called by the SNLD.

Leaders: KHUN TUN LU (Chair), HSAI PAUNG NAP (General Secretary).

Inn National Development Party (INDP). Registration of the INDP was approved in June 2010. It ran in only one Shan State township, where the Intha ethnic group is centered. During the campaign the party accused SPDC officials of forcing civil servants to cast early ballots. The INDP won one seat in the People's Assembly.

Leaders: WIN MYINT (Chair), AUNG KYI WIN.

Kayin People's Party (KPP). Founded in 2001 and reregistered in May 2010, the KPP is led by Tun Aung Myint, a former naval commander, and Saw Simon Tha, a physician and peace negotiator who has been involved in discussions between the junta and Karen insurgents, including the Karen National Union (KNU, below). The party sought an alliance with the USDP before the November elections, when it won one seat in each house of the Union Parliament. KPP official Aloti SINGHA was arrested in February 2013 for allegedly harboring two KLO militants.

Leaders: TUN AUNG MYINT (Chair), SAW SIMON THA (First Vice Chair), SAW SAY WAH (General Secretary).

Taaung (Palaung) National Party (TNP). The TNP, which was registered in May 2010, represents the Taaung (Palaung) ethnic group based primarily in Shan State. Its chair served as leader of the Palaung State Liberation Army, which accepted a cease-fire with the junta in the early 1990s. At that time a Palaung Self-Administered Zone was established. In November 2010 the TNP claimed one seat in each house of the Parliament and four in the state parliament, all of them uncontested.

Leaders: AIK MONE (Chair), TIN MAUNG, MAI OHN KAING (General Secretary).

Unity and Democracy Party of Kachin State (UDPKS). Registered in August 2010, the projunta UDPKS was formed by a number of USDA members with connections to the military government. It won one seat in each house of the Union Parliament in November.

Leaders: KHET HTEIN NAN (Chair), KHIN MAUNG LATT and AYE KYAW (Vice Chairs).

Kayin State Democracy and Development Party (KSDDP). The KSDDP was established by former members of cease-fire groups allied with the junta. Some of its members had reportedly belonged to the Democratic Karen Buddhist Association and the Karen Peace Force, both of which were splinters from the KNU (below). The new party was registered in August 2010 and won one seat in the upper house in November.

Leader: HTOO KYAW (Chair).

National League for Democracy (NLD). Registered as a political party in September 1988, the NLD was an outgrowth of the Democracy and Peace (Interim) League (DPIL), which had been formed by a number of leading dissidents a month earlier. Its founding president, AUNG GYI, withdrew to form the Union National Democratic Party (UNDP) after having called, unsuccessfully, for the expulsion from the DPIL of a number of alleged communists. (The UNDP was deregistered in 1992.)

Following her return to Myanmar in April 1988, the party's first general secretary, Aung San Suu Kyi, became the regime's most vocal and effective critic. Both she and fellow NLD leader Tin Oo were arrested in July 1989 and declared ineligible to compete in the May 1990 balloting, which produced an overwhelming victory for the NLD, tacitly allied with some 21 ethnic-based regional parties. The NLD's two other principal leaders, KYI MAUNG and CHIT KHAING, were arrested in September 1990.

In April 1991 the SLORC announced that the NLD's Central Committee had been "invalidated," thus technically removing the four leaders from their party positions. Kyi Maung and Tin Oo were released from prison in March 1995, while Suu Kyi was freed from house arrest in July. Kyi Maung left the NLD in 1997, reportedly because of a dispute with Suu Kyi.

In July 1997 SLORC leader Khin Nyunt met with NLD chair AUNG SHWE, and on September 27–28 NLD delegates were permitted to hold the group's first congress with Suu Kyi in attendance in two years. An authorized NLD Congress on May 27–28, 1998, at her residence was attended by 400 party members. In the following months, however, in response to the NLD's threat to call a "People's Parliament," the regime began a series of crackdowns against the party that included hundreds of detentions, closure of many local offices, and forced resignations. In all, tens of thousands of party members may have been forced to resign in 1998–1999. Suu Kyi was again placed under de facto house arrest from September 2000 until May 2002.

On May 30, 2003, following a violent attack on an NLD motorcade by government supporters, Suu Kyi was taken into "protective custody." An unclear number of NLD members—initial reports indicated 4, but some subsequent accounts said 60 or more—were killed by the mob. Suu Kyi's house arrest resumed on September 26. On April 13, 2004, Aung Shwe and Secretary General U LWIN were released, leaving Suu Kyi and Tin Oo as the only senior NLD members in detention. A month later the NLD refused to participate in the reconvened National Convention until both were freed.

As part of a wider amnesty for 9,000 prisoners, described by Amnesty International as mostly drug dealers and petty criminals, WIN TIN, one of the founders of the NLD, was released from prison in September 2008 along with several other NLD members. Described as Myanmar's longest-serving political prisoner, Win Tin had been incarcerated since 1989. Several dozen NLD members were among the 7,000 prisoners released in September 2009.

The 2008 constitution includes as a condition for presidential eligibility that a candidate as well as the individual's parents, spouse, and natural children and their spouses cannot owe allegiance to a foreign country. Because Suu Kyi's late husband, Michael Aris, was British, she is excluded from seeking the office. At the time of the constitutional referendum, both she and Tin Oo remained under house arrest. Suu Kyi's was not renewed in May 2009, but at the time she was being held in a prison after being charged with having harbored in her home an uninvited American. In August she was convicted, but a three-year prison sentence was commuted to another 18 months of house arrest. She lost all appeals of the verdict. Tin Oo was released from house arrest on February 13, 2010.

In April 2009 the NLD indicated that it would participate in the 2010 elections but only if the SPDC released all political prisoners, amended the 2008 constitution to meet democratic standards, and agreed to let the international community supervise the elections. It failed to reregister in 2010 and was therefore dissolved, although some members of the Central Executive Committee, rejecting Suu Kyi's call for an election boycott, organized the NDF. Shortly after her release from house arrest on November 13, Suu Kyi appealed against the party's dissolution to the Supreme Court. The high court rejected Suu Kyi's appeal on January 28, 2011. In December the NLD was reregistered as a political party.

Suu Kyi ended her electoral boycott and ran for office in the April 2012 by-elections. In the balloting, the NLD won 38 of 39 seats in the assembly and 4 of 5 seats in the upper chamber. Suu Kyi's reentry into politics paved the way for the easing of international sanctions on the country.

In March 2013 the NLD held its first national conference. Suu Kyi was reelected unanimously as NLD leader by the party's central committee.

Leaders: AUNG SAN SUU KYI (Chair), TIN OO (Vice Chair).

Other Parties Contesting the November 2010 Elections:

Democratic Party Myanmar (DPM). Registered in May 2010, the DPM descends from the Democratic Party that was established by THU WAI in 1988 and that contested the 1990 election. In September 2009 MYA THAN THAN NU, daughter of the country's last elected prime minister, U Nu, and Nay Yee Ba Swe, daughter of former prime minister BA SWE (1956–1957), announced that they would organize a new Democratic Party to contest the legislative election scheduled for 2010. They were joined by CHO CHO KYAW NYEIN, daughter of former deputy prime minister KYAW NYEIN. The "three princesses," as they have been familiarly labeled, had all served time in prison or lived in exile.

The DPM, which alleged campaign and voting irregularities by the SPDC and the USDP, failed in its bid for seats in the Union Parliament but won three at the state/regional level. In December 2012 the DPM proposed the creation of a federal system similar to that of the United States.

Leaders: THU WAI (Chair); MYA THAN THAN NU, NAY YEE BA SWE, and CHO CHO KYAW NYEIN (Joint Secretaries).

Lahu National Development Party (LNDP). Based in the Lahu tribe of eastern Shan State, the LNDP is one of the few extant parties that competed in 1990 and later participated in the National Convention. Government supportive, it condemned the NLD's announcement of the People's Parliament in 1998. It reregistered in April 2010 and won one state parliamentary seat in November.

Leaders: KYAR HAR SHE (Chair), YAW THAT (Vice Chair).

88 Generation Student Youths (Union of Myanmar) (88GSY). The junta-supportive 88GSY, despite its name, bears no connection to the dissident 88 Generation Students movement. It is closely connected to another party, the **Union of Myanmar Federation of National Politics** (UMFNP), both of which were officially registered in May 2010. The 88GSY won one seat at the state/division level in November, while the UMFNP won none.

Leaders: YE TUN (Chair), SAN OO (General Secretary).

Ethnic National Development Party (ENDP). Representing the Mara people in Chin State, the ENDP won one state-level parliamentary seat in November 2010.

Leaders: PU HIPA (President), VAN CING (Vice President).

Kokang Democracy and Unity Party (KDUP). The KDUP, founded in 1988 and based in Shan State, competed in the 1990 election, subsequently participated in the National Convention, and was reregistered in May 2010. It represents ethnic Chinese in the self-administered Kokang zone. It failed to win any seats in the November 2010 elections.

Leaders: LO Xingguang (Chair), YAN KYIN KAN (Vice Chair).

Mro National Solidarity Organization (MNSO). Also known as the **Khami National Solidarity Organization,** the government-supportive MNSO is based in Rakhine and Chin states and claims to represent the interests of the Mro (Khami) ethnic group. It contested the 1990 Constituent Assembly election, winning one seat, and reregistered in April 2010. It won no seats in the November elections.

Leaders: SAN THAR AUNG (Chair), KYAW TUN KHAING (Vice Chair).

National Democratic Party for Development (NDPD). Despite being targeted by USDP members, the NDPD won two seats in the Rakhine state parliament in November 2010. The NDPD was highly critical of the government response to strife in Rakhine and claimed that casualty figures were substantially higher than official reports.

Leader: MAUNG MAUNG NI (Chair).

The following parties also ran for seats in the November 2010 elections but were unsuccessful: the **Democracy and Peace Party** (DPP), the **Kaman National Progressive Party** (KNPP), the **Kayin National Party** (KNP), the **Khami National Development Party** (KNDP), the **Modern People Party** (MPP), the **National Development and Peace Party** (NDPP), the **National Political Alliances League** (NPAL), the **Peace and Diversity Party** (PDP), the **Rakhine State National Force of Myanmar** (RSNF), the **United Democratic Party** (UnitedDP), the **Union Democratic Party** (UnionDP), the **Wa National Unity Party** (WNUP), and the **Wuntharnu NLD–Union of Myanmar** (WNLD).

Dissolved Parties:

Shan Nationalities League for Democracy (SNLD). Established in 1988, the SNLD won 23 seats in the 1990 Constituent Assembly balloting, second only to the NLD. Its leader, KHUN TUN OO, was a key opposition figure both in Shan State and on the national scene, where he participated in the "People's Parliament" and conferred repeatedly with UN and EU representatives. The SNLD refused to participate when the National Convention reconvened in May 2004.

In February 2005 Tun Oo and SAI SAW AUNG, the party's secretary, were among nearly a dozen individuals charged with treason, insurrection, and other offenses. In November Tun Oo was convicted and sentenced to spend the rest of his life in prison. Eight others also received lengthy sentences. The SNLD and NLD made a joint call for a "no" vote in the 2008 referendum on the new constitution and denounced the result.

In September 2010 the election commission announced that the following parties were dissolved: the **Shan State Kokang Democratic Party;** the **Union Pa-O National Organization,** based in west-central Shan State; and the **Wa National Development Party.** At the same time, the following five parties, which had previously been registered, were dissolved for failing to submit complete candidate lists by the deadline: the **Mro National Party,** the **Myanmar Democracy Congress,** the **Myanmar New Social Party,** the **Regional Development Party (Pyay),** and the **Union Karen League.** Earlier, in July, the government had ruled the **Kachin State Progressive Party** ineligible for registration because of links to the Kachin Independence Organization (KIO), a cease-fire group that had rejected participation in the border guard force proposal.

Dissident Groups:

88 Generation Students. Named after the 1988 uprising organized by the group's leaders, many 88 Generation members have been subjected to lengthy prison terms, and human rights groups have catalogued a number of claims of torture. The unofficial leader of the group is Min Ko Naing (Paw U Tun), who has won numerous human-rights awards for his nonviolent campaign for democracy. He was arrested in 1989 and was released in November 2004 after 15 years in prison. Along with four other key members, he was detained again in September 2006. In January 2007 all five were released, without explanation.

The 88 Generation Students was directly involved in organizing the 2007 protests. Dozens, including Min Ko Naing, were arrested as a consequence and in November 2008 were convicted in various courts and sentenced to as much as 65 years in prison for incitement and "disturbing public tranquility." Min Ko Naing and other Generation 88 leaders were released in January 2012 as part of a government amnesty. In 2013 KO KO GYI of Generation 88 was appointed to a government committee reviewing the status of political prisoners.

Leaders: MIN KO NAING, KO MYA AYE, NILAR THEIN, THIN THIN.

Alliance of All Burmese Buddhist Monks (AABBM). The AABBM, which has termed the military an "enemy of the people," was a prime mover behind the September 2007 prodemocracy demonstrations. Its leader, Ashin Gambira, was sentenced in November 2008 to 12 years in prison for offenses that included insulting religion and committing "crimes against the peace." He was later convicted of additional offenses, with 56 years being added to his prison term, but was released in January 2012.

Leader: Ashin GAMBIRA.

Cease-Fire Groups:

United Wa State Party (UWSP). The UWSP and the associated United Wa State Army (UWSA), founded in 1989 after Wa elements separated from the Communist Party of Burma, are reputedly the country's leading producer of opium, heroin, and methamphetamines. Reportedly numbering as many as 25,000, with another 10,000 in associated village militias, the UWSA has operated with considerable autonomy within the Golden Triangle area of Shan State, even before negotiating a cease-fire agreement with the junta. A leading ally is the smaller **National Democratic Alliance Army** (NDAA). Although the UWSP/UWSA leader, Bao Yuxiang, has asserted that poppy cultivation has been eliminated in the area under UWSA control, in November 2008 the U.S. State Department described the UWSA as the "largest and most powerful drug trafficking organization in Southeast Asia."

The UWSA has repeatedly rejected inclusion in the junta's Border Guard Force, and in November 2010 the UWSP refused to allow elections to take place in the area under its control. Reports in June 2012 indicated that negotiations between the UWSA and the government were underway whereby the militia would be incorporated into the nation's security forces. Reports in 2013 indicated that the UWSA had purchased missiles and other weaponry from China.

Leader: BAO YUXIANG (PAU YU CHANG).

Cease-fire groups that have agreed to become part of the Border Guard Force (BGF) include the **Kachin Defense Force,** a splinter from the KIO's Kachin Independence Army (KIA); the **Karen Peace Force,** which split from the KNU in 1997; the **Karenni National People's Liberation Front,** a 1978 splinter from the KNPP; and the **New Democratic Army–Kachin,** which left the KIA in 1989. In August 2009 junta troops overran the **Myanmar National Democratic Alliance Army** (MNDAA) after the group rejected becoming part of the BGF, with the altercation resulting in the flight of some 37,000 Kokang refugees to China. The MNDAA, which separated from the Communist Party of Burma in 1989, has been replaced by a more compliant **Kokang Region Provisional Leading Committee**.

In addition to the UWSA and the NDAA, cease-fire groups that have rejected the government's BGF proposal include the **Kachin Independence Organization** (KIO), the **Karen National Liberation Army Peace Council,** the **New Mon State Party** (NMSP), the **Shan State Army–North** (SSA-N).

Insurgent Groups:

During the first half of the 1990s the military regime eliminated or arranged cease-fires with most of the country's longtime military insurgents, although negotiations with several groups subsequently broke down. (For a more complete accounting of insurgent groups active prior to 1995, see the 1993 and 1994–1995 editions of the *Handbook.*)

Karen National Union (KNU). With origins dating back to 1947, the KNU and its military wing, the **Karen National Liberation Army** (KNLA), was one of the more effective minority-based insurgent groups. The KNU declared a unilateral cease-fire in March 1995, following the loss of its Manerplaw headquarters in January and its base in Kawmoora a month later. In early 1997, however, talks between the KNU and the government broke down, with government troops quickly renewing their campaign against remaining KNU bases. At a ten-day party congress held in late January 2000, Bo Mya stepped down as KNU chair in favor of the party's former secretary general, SAW BA THEIN SIEN, who advocated for a political solution to the conflict.

A fringe KNU group, God's Army, took 700 hostages at a hospital in Ratchaburi, Thailand, in January 2000, demanding an end to an anti-Karen offensive in the Thai-Myanmar border region. All 10 hostage-takers died in an assault by Thai forces a day later. Dating from 1997 and probably numbering no more than 150 men, the cultlike God's Army was ostensibly led by 12-year-old twins, Johnny and Luther HTOO. It apparently disbanded in October 2000, with the Htoo brothers being granted asylum in Thailand in January 2001.

At a congress held November 18–December 8, 2004, Bo Mya, reportedly in poor health, was replaced as vice chair but remained in charge of defense. A cease-fire came to an end after Khin Nyunt's removal from office in October 2004.

In May 2006 a renewed government offensive against KNU supporters drew widespread international criticism as well as calls for a new cease-fire and renewed negotiations. Bo Mya died on December 24, 2006. In February 2007 a KNU splinter led by HTAIN MAUNG signed a peace agreement with the government, and two months later reports surfaced of a major military defeat for the KNU.

On February 17, 2008, Secretary General PADOH MAHN SHA of the KNU was shot dead in his home. Thai police reported the assailants were Karen, although government culpability was suspected. In late 2008 the KNU elected its vice chair, Tamla Baw, as chair and his daughter, Zipporah SEIN, as secretary general.

Of the various groups that have split from the KNU, the most significant is the **Democratic Karen Buddhist Organization** (DKBO), which separated from the largely Christian KNU in 1994. With the support of government forces, the DKBO's military wing, the **Democratic Karen Buddhist Army** (DKBA), spearheaded several assaults in 1997–1998 on KNU refugee camps in Thailand. The KNU responded in March 1998 by attacking DKBA bases in Myanmar. As the **Democratic Karen/Kayin Buddhist Association,** the group was invited by the government to participate in the reconvened National Convention in 2004. More recently, a brigade of the DKBA led by SAW LAH PWE refused to function as a border guard force under the military, severed its association with the parent organization, and renewed armed attacks against junta forces. The first talks between the KNU and the DKBO since the 1994 split were reportedly held in October 1999. The rebellious faction, which was directly involved in the 2010 postelection fighting in Shan State that led to the temporary flight of some 20,000 refugees into Thailand, has reportedly joined forces with the KNLA in some areas. On April 7, 2012, the KNU and the government signed a 13-point peace plan. In December Gen. MUTU SAE POE was elected KNU chair, with former secretary general Zipporah Sein selected as vice chair.

Leaders: Gen. MUTU SAE POE (Chair), Zipporah SEIN (Vice Chair), SAW KWE HTOO (Secretary General).

Karenni National Progressive Party (KNPP). With a predominantly Kayinni membership, the KNPP was established in the mid-1950s. It concluded an agreement with the SLORC in March 1995 but in mid-1996 took up arms again and remained in active opposition in 2004, although two splinter groups, the Kayinni National Progressive Party Dragon Group and the Kayinni National Progressive Party (Hoya Splinter), had concluded cease-fire agreements with the SPDC and, on that basis, were invited to send delegates to the reconvened National Convention.

The KNPP held cease-fire discussions with the government in 2007 but failed to reach an agreement. In June 2007 it sponsored a meeting of ethnic groups that were still engaged in armed resistance. Among the attendees were the KNU and the Shan State Army–South (below). In the run-up to and in the aftermath of the November 2010 national election, the KNPP's military commander, Bee Htoo, asserted that half a dozen insurgent groups that rejected the 2008 constitution were in the process of forming an alliance to continue armed opposition to the government. Other participants included the KNU, the antijunta wing of the KIO, the NMSP, and the SSA-N.

Another cease-fire agreement was signed between the KNU and the government in March 2012, with a more formal accord finalized in June 2013. The new agreement included plans for demining and the resettlement of displaced Kayinnis.

Leaders: KHU HTE BU PEH, BEE HTOO (Commander of the Karenni Army).

Shan State Army–South (SSA-S). Dating from 1964, the Shan State Army established the Shan State Progressive Party (subsequently the Shan State Peacekeeping Council) in 1972, although the two later separated. In April 1998 Amnesty International, in a report quickly ridiculed by the SPDC, accused the Myanmar army of torturing or killing hundreds of Shans and forcing at least 300,000 to flee their homes in 1996–1997 as part of its effort to cut off support for the SSA. Although the SSA-North concluded a peace agreement with the SPDC, the SSA-South remained in militant opposition to the government.

During 2005 two cease-fire groups, the Shan State National Army (SSNA) and the Shan State Nationalities People's Liberation Organization (SNPLO) announced that they had ended their cooperation with the government and were joining the SSA insurgency. By the end of 2005, however, the SSNA had surrendered, as did the SNPLO in August 2008.

The SPDC declared the SSA-S to be a terrorist organization in August 2006. In mid-2009 there was considerably speculation that the SPDC, having achieved measurable gains in a recent offensive against ethnic Karens, was planning to launch a campaign against the SSA-S before the end of the year. Similar speculation followed the November 2010 national election.

A cease-fire was signed in January 2012. In June 2013 SSA commander Col. YAWD SERK urged other ethnic minorities to reach similar cease-fire accords with the government.

Leaders: Col. YAWD SERK (Commander), SAI LAO HSENG.

Among the other groups reputedly engaged in drug manufacture and trafficking is the **Shan United Revolutionary Party,** an offshoot of the Mong Tai Army that rejected the latter's surrender to government forces. In July 2008 a group calling itself the **Vigorous Burmese Student Warriors** (VBSW) claimed responsibility for a bomb that exploded outside a Yangon office of the USDA; it also claimed responsibility for a bomb in April 2010 that killed ten people.

Exile Groups:

A number of exile opposition groups currently function. Most supported the **National Coalition Government of the Union of Burma** (NCGUB), a shadow government that was established in 1991 but dissolved itself in 2012.

All Burma Student Democratic Front (ABSDF). The ABSDF was founded in 1988 by disaffected students. In March 1998 the Yangon regime accused the ABSDF of organizing a plot to assassinate government leaders and bomb government buildings and foreign embassies. The ABSDF denied the charge, responding that it had decided in 1997 to abandon armed conflict in favor of "nonviolent, political defiance." Earlier, ABSDF leader KO AUNG TUN was imprisoned for 15 years for writing a history of the Burmese student movement.

In September 2009 the ABSDF joined the 88 Generation Students and the All-Burma Monks' Alliance in a statement urging the junta to end its assaults against ethnic minority groups. In 2012 the ABSDF issued a formal apology for its role in political killings and torture in the 1990s. In September prominent ABSDF members, including former leader MOE THEE ZUN, returned to Myanmar. In May 2013 the government launched a new round of negotiations with the ABSDF.

Leaders: THAN KE (Chair), MYO WIN (Vice Chair), Sonny MAHINDER (General Secretary).

Other exile groups include the **Democratic Party for a New Society,** the **People's Defense Front,** the **Burma Women's Union,** and the **Network for Democracy and Development**. In February 2004 they joined with the ABSDF and a number of other groups to organize an umbrella **Democratic Alliance of Burma**. Additional formations include the **National Council of the Union of Burma** (NCUB), the **Federation of Trade Unions Burma** (FTUB), the **National League for Democracy–Liberated Areas** (NLD-LA), and the **U.S. Campaign for Burma**.

LEGISLATURE

The former People's Assembly (*Pyithu Hluttaw*), elected in November 1985, was abolished by the military government on September 18, 1988. In the election of May 27, 1990, 93 parties competed for 485 of 492 seats in a new Constituent Assembly (polling being barred in 7 constituencies for security reasons). The National

League for Democracy won an overwhelming majority of 392 seats, compared to 10 for the government-backed National Unity Party. The military junta never permitted the assembly to convene. The 2008 constitution provides for a bicameral legislature, the **Union Parliament** (*Pyidaungsu Hluttaw*), in which all members serve five-year terms. Among those excluded from candidacy are civil servants, members of religious orders, employees of state-owned companies, and those who have criminal records.

House of Nationalities (*Amyotha Hluttaw*). The upper house comprises 224 members. The seven states and seven regions are equally represented by 12 directly elected members each, with an additional 56 seats (25 percent) reserved for members of the military, chosen by the commander in chief. In the election of November 7, 2010, the Union Solidarity and Development Party won 129 seats; Rakhine Nationalities Progressive Party, 7; National Unity Party, 5; All Mon Region Democracy Party, 4, Chin Progressive Party, 4; National Democratic Force, 4; Phalon-Sawaw Democratic Party, 3; Shan Nationalities Democratic Party, 3; Chin National Party, 2; Kayin National Party, Kayin People's Party, Pa-O National Organization, Taaung (Palaung) National Party, Unity and Democracy Party of Kayin State, and Wa Democratic Party, 1 each; independents, 1.

Speaker: KHIN Aung Myint.

House of Representatives (*Pyithu Hluttaw*). The lower house comprises 440 members, of whom 330 are directly elected from township-based districts according to population; 110 seats (25 percent) are reserved for military appointees. The election of November 7, 2010, produced the following results: Union Solidarity and Development Party, 259 seats; Shan Nationalities Democratic Party, 18; National Unity Party, 12; Rakhine Nationalities Progressive Party, 9; National Democratic Force, 8; All Mon Region Democracy Party, 3; Pa-O National Organization, 3; Chin National Party, 2; Chin Progressive Party, 2; Phalon-Sawaw Democratic Party, 2; Wa Democratic Party 2; Inn National Development Party, Kayin People's Party, Taaung (Palaung) National Party, and Unity and Democracy Party of Kachin State, 1 each; independents, 1. The security situation prevented voting in a handful of districts.

Speaker: SHWE MANN.

CABINET

[as of November 15, 2013]

President	Lt. Gen. (Ret.) Thein Sein
First Vice President	Adm. (Ret.) Nyan Tun
Second Vice President	Sai Mauk Kham

Ministers

Agriculture and Irrigation	Myint Hlaing
Attorney General	Tun Shin
Auditor General	Lt. Gen (Ret.) Thein Htaik
Border Affairs	Maj. Gen. (Ret.) Htet Naing Win
Commerce	Win Myint
Communications, Posts, and Telegraphs	Lt. Gen. (Ret.) Myat Hein
Construction	Kyaw Lwin
Cooperatives	Brig. Gen. (Ret.) Kyaw Hsan
Culture	Aye Myint Kyu
Cyclone Relief and Resettlement	Myat Ohn Khin [f]
Defense	Gen. Wai Lwin
Education	Mya Aye
Electric Power	Khin Maung Soe
Energy	Maj. Gen. (Ret.) Zayar Aung
Environmental Conservation and Forestry	Win Tun
Finance and Revenue	Win Shein
Foreign Affairs	Gen. (Ret.) Wunna Maung Lwin
Health	Pe Thet Khin
Home Affairs	Lt. Gen. (Ret.) Ko Ko
Hotels and Tourism	Htay Aung
Industry	Maung Myint
Immigration and Population	Brig. Gen. (Ret.) Khin Yi
Information	Aung Kyi
Labor and Welfare	Brig. Gen. (Ret.) Aye Mint
Livestock and Fisheries	Brig. Gen. (Ret.) Ohn Myint
Mines	Myint Aung
National Planning and Economic Development	Kan Zaw
Office of the President	Col. (Ret.) Thein Nyunt
Office of the President	Maj. Gen. (Ret.) Soe Mang
Office of the President, Finance	Gen. (Ret.) Hla Htun
Office of the President, Economic Planning	Brig. Gen. (Ret.) Tin Naing Thein
Office of the President, National Reconciliation	Gen. (Ret.) Aung Min
Office of the President, Industry	Lt. Gen. (Ret.) Soe Thein
Rail Transport	Brig. Gen. (Ret.) Than Htay
Religious Affairs	Brig. Gen. (Ret.) San Sint
Science and Technology	Ko Ko Oo
Sports	Tint Hsan
Transport	Col. (Ret.) Nyan Tun Aung

Armed Forces Commander in Chief	Vice Sr. Gen. Min Aung Hlaing
Joint Chief of Staff of the Armed Forces	Lt. Gen. Min Aung Hlaing

[f] = female

INTERGOVERNMENTAL REPRESENTATION

Ambassador to the U.S.: Than SWE.

U.S. Ambassador to Myanmar (Burma): Derek J. MITCHELL.

Permanent Representative to the UN: U Kyaw TIN.

IGO Memberships (Non-UN): ADB, ASEAN, NAM, WTO.

NAMIBIA

Republic of Namibia

Political Status: Former German territory assigned to South Africa under League of Nations mandate in 1920; declared to be a United Nations responsibility by General Assembly resolution adopted October 27, 1966 (resolution not recognized by South Africa); subject to tripartite (Angolan-Cuban-South African) agreement concluded on December 22, 1988, providing for implementation from April 1, 1989, of Security Council Resolution 435 of 1978 (leading to UN-supervised elections on November 1 and independence thereafter); independence declared on March 21, 1990.

Area: 318,259 sq. mi. (824,292 sq. km).

Population: 2,421,126 (2013E—UN); 2,182,852 (2013E—U.S. Census). Both area and population figures include data for Walvis Bay (see Political background and Foreign relations, below).

Major Urban Center (2009E—U.S.): WINDHOEK (342,000).

Official Language: English.

Monetary Unit: Namibian Dollar (official rate November 1, 2013: 10.17 dollars = $1US). Introduced on September 13, 1993, the Namibian dollar is at par with the South African rand, which is also legal tender in Namibia.

President: Hifikepunye POHAMBA (South West Africa People's Organization of Namibia); popularly elected on November 15–16, 2004, and inaugurated for a five-year term on March 21, 2005, to succeed Samuel (Sam) Daniel Shafilshuna NUJOMA (South West Africa People's Organization of Namibia); reelected for another five-year term on November 27–28, 2009; inaugurated on March 21, 2010, and named a new government the same day.

Prime Minister: Hage GEINGOB (South West Africa People's Organization of Namibia); appointed by the president and sworn in on December 4, 2012, to succeed Nahas ANGULA (South West Africa People's Organization of Namibia), following the latter's resignation that day.

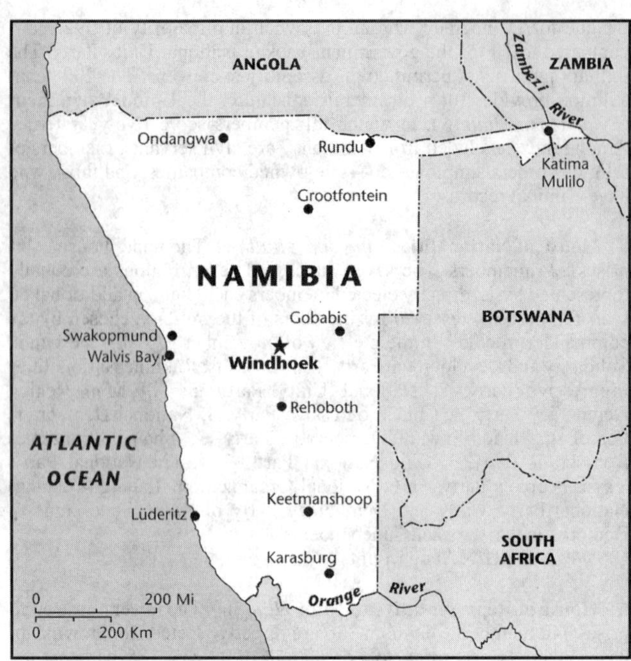

THE COUNTRY

Bordered on the north by Angola and Zambia, on the east by Botswana, on the southeast and south by South Africa, and on the west by the Atlantic Ocean, Namibia consists of a high plateau bounded by the uninhabited Namib Desert along the Atlantic coast, with more desert land in the interior. The inhabitants are of diversified origins, although the Ovambo constitute by far the largest ethnic group (approximately 50 percent of the population). A substantial exodus has reduced the white population, traditionally engaged in commercial farming and ranching, fish processing, and mineral exploitation, from approximately 12 percent to 6 percent. Other groups include the Kavango, the Herero, the Damara, the Nama, and those classified as "coloured." Although women continue to face a variety of discrimination in the economic and social sectors, strides have been made in politics. Women hold 19 of 78 seats in the lower house of parliament (24.4 percent), and 7 of 26 seats in the upper house (26.9 percent), as well as 5 cabinet posts.

The country is one of the world's largest producers of diamonds, which yield about half of export earnings, and uranium; copper, lead, zinc, tin, and other minerals are also available in extractable quantities. These resources yielded substantial economic growth during the 1970s; subsequently, falling mineral prices, extended periods of drought, and internal insecurity caused a severe recession, marked by 40–50 percent unemployment, 13–16 percent inflation, and severe budgetary problems. In July 1990 international donors committed $200 million to help offset a $270 million fiscal shortfall caused by South Africa's withdrawal from the economy. GDP growth averaged 5 percent annually in 1990–1993 and 3 percent annually in 1994–1999. Economic policies have focused on further exploitation of the country's rich fisheries, export manufacturing, promotion of private investment, and programs designed to ameliorate the severe maldistribution of wealth and continuing high unemployment rate. A 2002 agreement to allow Namibian craft to fish in South African territorial waters further expanded the sector.

Steady economic growth continued in the early 2000s, with GDP increasing by an average of 3–4 percent annually. Significantly, inflation fell to 5 percent by 2004 (from 8.8 percent in 1997) after the Bank of Namibia cut interest rates from 12.75 percent to 5 percent over a four-year period.

International firms have invested $800 million in the development of natural gas fields. Long-term plans are to use the fields to produce electricity for export to surrounding states, including South Africa. In an effort to reduce unemployment and poverty, the government launched a controversial land redistribution program in 2004 in order to increase farm ownership among black Namibians. (For details on land redistribution, see the 2011 *Handbook.*) Despite the economic challenges of an unemployment rate exceeding 20 percent and widespread poverty, real GDP growth averaged 4.2 percent in 2005–2007. While overall economic performance remained strong and debt declined, growth was insufficient to create new jobs. The International Monetary Fund (IMF) in 2007, while commending Namibia's overall economic progress, emphasized the need for authorities to develop the non-mining sector to help reduce poverty. The prevalence of HIV/AIDS, affecting an estimated 20 percent of the population, continued to be a major concern, though the outlook improved somewhat with the government's development of a strategy to address the disease. The IMF also cited progress in the implementation of education reforms, financial assistance to farmers in the wake of a major drought, and the establishment of an anticorruption commission. Economic growth contracted to an annual average of 1.5 percent over 2008–2009, owing in large part to a downturn in the mining sector as a consequence of the global financial crisis. Inflation fell from nearly 11 percent in 2008 to about 5 percent in 2010. The IMF noted that the banking sector in particular withstood well the adverse effects of the financial crisis. GDP grew by 6.6 percent in 2010 as the economy made a strong recovery, spurred by an increase in mineral exports, especially diamonds and uranium, and growth in domestic demand. In 2011 GDP growth slowed to an estimated 4.8 percent amid severe flooding in the north and a weaker global economy.

The IMF estimated that GDP grew by 4 percent in 2012, and 4.2 percent in 2013, while inflation was 6.7 percent and 5.9 percent, respectively. Poverty remains significant with the UN estimating that approximately 55.8 percent of the population lives on less than $2 per day. In its 2013 Human Development Index, the UN ranked Namibia 128th out of 186 countries, one place below Vietnam and one place above Nicaragua. Meanwhile, continued concerns over corruption and government inefficiency led the World Bank to rank Namibia 89th out of 185 countries, a dramatic drop from 2006 when the country was rated 39th.

GOVERNMENT AND POLITICS

Political background. South West Africa came under German control in the 1880s, except for a small enclave at Walvis Bay, which had been annexed by the United Kingdom in 1878 and subsequently became a part of South Africa. Having occupied the whole of South West Africa during World War I, South Africa was granted a mandate in 1920 to govern the area under authority of the League of Nations. Declining to place the territory under the UN trusteeship system after World War II, South Africa asked the UN General Assembly in 1946 for permission to annex it; following denial of the request, Pretoria continued its rule on the strength of the original mandate.

Although the international status of the territory and the supervisory authority of the United Nations were repeatedly affirmed in advisory opinions of the International Court of Justice (ICJ), the court in 1966 declined on technical grounds to rule upon a formal complaint by Ethiopia and Liberia against South Africa's conduct in the territory. The UN General Assembly then terminated the mandate in a resolution of October 27, 1966, declaring that South Africa had failed to fulfill its obligations. A further resolution on May 19, 1967, established an 11-member UN Council for South West Africa, assisted by a UN commissioner, to administer the territory until independence (originally set for June 1968) and to prepare for the drafting of a constitution, the holding of an election, and the establishment of responsible government. The council was, however, refused entry by the South African government, which contended that termination of the mandate was invalid. South Africa subsequently disregarded a number of Security Council resolutions to relinquish the territory, including a unanimous resolution of December 1974 that gave it five months to initiate withdrawal from Namibia (the official name adopted on December 16, 1968, by the General Assembly).

Beginning in the mid-1960s, South Africa attempted to group the black population into a number of self-administering tribal homelands ("Bantustans"), in accordance with the so-called Odendaal Report of 1964. Ovamboland, the first functioning Bantustan, was established in October 1968, but its legitimacy was rejected by the UN Security Council. Fully implemented, the partition plan would have left approximately 88,000 whites as the largest ethnic group in two-thirds of the territory, with some 675,000 black inhabitants confined to the remaining third.

Both the Organization of African Unity (OAU, subsequently the African Union—AU) and the South West Africa People's Organization (SWAPO) consistently pressed for full and unconditional self-determination for Namibia. In May 1975, however, Prime Minister John Vorster of South Africa stated that while his government was prepared to "exchange ideas" with UN and OAU representatives, it was not willing to accede to the demand that it "acknowledge SWAPO as the sole representative of the Namibian people and enter into independence negotiations with the organization."

On September 1, 1975, the South African government convened a constitutional conference in Turnhalle, Windhoek, on the future of the territory. SWAPO and other independence groups boycotted the conference and organized demonstrations against it. As a result, the Ovambos, with approximately half of the territory's population, were represented by only 15 of 135 delegates. At the second session of the conference, held in March 1976, Chief Clemens KAPUUO, then leader of the Herero-based National United Democratic Organization, presented a draft constitution that called for a bicameral legislature encompassing a northern chamber of representatives from Bantu areas and a southern chamber that would include representatives from the coloured and white groups. During the third session of the conference in August, a plan was advanced for the creation of a multiracial interim government to prepare Namibia for independence by December 31, 1978. Despite continued opposition from SWAPO, the conference's constitution committee unanimously approved a resolution on December 3 that called for establishment of an interim government.

A draft constitution calling for representation of the territory's 11 major racial and ethnic groups was approved by the Turnhalle delegates on March 9, 1977, and was subsequently endorsed by 95 percent of the white voters in a referendum on May 17. However, it continued to be opposed by SWAPO as well as by a group of diplomats representing the five Western members of the UN Security Council (Canada, France, the Federal Republic of Germany, the United Kingdom, and the United States). The Western delegation visited Windhoek on May 7–10 and subsequently engaged in talks with South African Prime Minister Vorster in Cape Town, in the course of which it indicated that the Turnhalle formula was unacceptable because it was "predominantly ethnic, lacked neutrality, and appeared to prejudice the outcome of free elections." The group added, however, that the appointment of an administrator general by the South African government would not be opposed insofar as it gave promise of contributing to "an internationally acceptable solution to the Namibia question." For his part, Vorster, prior to the appointment of Marthinus T. STEYN as administrator general on July 6, agreed to abandon the Turnhalle proposal for an interim government, accept the appointment of a UN representative to ensure the impartiality of the constituent election in 1978, and initiate a withdrawal of South African troops to be completed by the time of independence. He insisted, however, that the South African government had no intention of abandoning its jurisdiction over Walvis Bay and certain islands off the South West African coast. (Governed as part of South Africa until 1922, when it was assigned to South West Africa for administrative purposes, Walvis Bay was reincorporated into South Africa's Cape Province in August 1977.)

During November and December 1977 representatives of the diplomatic group engaged in inconclusive discussions with leaders of SWAPO and of the black African "Front-Line States" (Angola, Botswana, Mozambique, Tanzania, and Zambia). The main problem concerned South African security forces within Namibia, SWAPO asserting that their continued presence would influence the outcome of the projected election despite a UN presence. Nonetheless, Administrator General Steyn moved energetically to dismantle the territory's apartheid system, including abolition of the pass laws and the Mixed Marriages Act, in preparation for the 1978 balloting.

On March 27, 1978, Chief Kapuuo, who had assumed the presidency of the Democratic Turnhalle Alliance (DTA, see Political Parties, below), was shot and killed by unknown assailants on the outskirts of Windhoek. The assassination removed from the scene the best-known tribal figure apart from SWAPO leader Sam NUJOMA, who denied that his group had been involved. Three days later the Western nations presented Prime Minister Vorster with revised proposals calling for a cease-fire between SWAPO guerrillas and the 18,000 South African troops in the territory. The latter force would be expected to gradually decrease to 1,500, with UN troops being positioned to maintain order in preparation for Constituent Assembly balloting. South Africa accepted the plan on April 25 after receiving assurances that the status of Walvis Bay would not be addressed until after the election, that the reduction of its military presence would be linked to "a complete cessation of hostilities," and that some of its troops might be permitted to remain after the election if the assembly so requested. On July 12 SWAPO agreed to the Western plan, which had also been endorsed by the Front-Line States. The UN Security Council approved the plan on July 27, but Pretoria reacted bitterly to an accompanying resolution calling for the early "reintegration" of Walvis Bay into South West Africa and subsequently announced that its own final approval would be deferred. In early September South African Foreign Minister P. W. Botha denounced the size of the proposed UN military force for the territory, and two weeks later he indicated that his government had reversed itself and would proceed with an election of its own before the end of the year. Undaunted, the Security Council on September 29 approved Resolution 435, which called for the formation of a 7,500-member UN Transitional Assistance Group (UNTAG) to oversee free and fair elections, while declaring "null and void" any unilateral action by "the illegal administration in Namibia in relation to the electoral process." Administrator General Steyn nonetheless proceeded to schedule balloting for a Constituent Assembly, which on December 4–8, without SWAPO participation, gave the DTA 41 of 50 seats.

In May 1979 the South African government agreed to the Constituent Assembly's request that the body be reconstituted as a National Assembly, although without authority to alter the status of the territory. Collaterally, conflict between SWAPO guerrilla forces and South African troops intensified, the latter carrying out a number of preemptive raids on SWAPO bases in Angola and Zambia. By midyear negotiations between UN and South African representatives had not resumed. In an effort to break the deadlock, Angolan President António Agostinho Neto, a few weeks before his death in September, proposed the creation of a 60-mile-wide demilitarized zone along the Angolan-Namibian border to prevent incursions from either side. He also pledged that Angola would welcome a UN civilian presence to ensure that any guerrillas not wishing to return to Namibia to participate in an all-party election would be confined to their bases.

Although Pretoria agreed to "the concept" of a demilitarized zone, discussions during 1980 failed to yield agreement, and on November 24 UN Secretary General Kurt Waldheim called for a meeting in Geneva in January 1981 to discuss all "practical proposals" that might break the lengthy impasse. Earlier, DTA spokesperson had urged repeal of the General Assembly's 1973 recognition of SWAPO, arguing that the root of the problem lay in the fact that "the UN is required to play a neutral role in respect of implementation but at the same time is the most ardent protagonist of SWAPO."

During 1981–1982 units of both the South West Africa Territorial Force (SWATF) and the South African Defence Force (SADF) conducted numerous "search and destroy" raids into Angola, Pretoria insisting that the withdrawal of Cuban troops from the latter country was a necessary precondition of its own withdrawal from Namibia and the implementation of a UN-supervised election. Thus, Prime Minister Botha declared at a Transvaal National Party congress in September 1982 that his government would never accede to Namibian independence unless "unequivocal agreement [could] first be reached" on the linkage issue. Subsequently, an Angolan spokesperson indicated that a partial withdrawal of Cuban forces was possible if Pretoria would agree to reduce the size of its military presence to 1,500 troops and discontinue incursions into his country. The overture prompted a secret but inconclusive series of talks between Angolan and South African ministerial delegations on the island of Sal in Cape Verde in early December, the South African foreign minister subsequently asserting that responsibility for a Cuban withdrawal was "the task of the Americans."

In November 1983 a Multi-Party Conference (MPC) of seven internal groups, including the DTA, was launched in Windhoek in an effort to overcome the standoff. Although the "Windhoek Declaration of Basic Principles" that was issued on February 24, 1984, did little more than reaffirm the essentials of the earlier UN plan, South African Prime Minister Botha announced in March that his government would be willing to enter into negotiations with all relevant parties to the dispute, including the Angolan government and UNITA, the Angolan rebel movement that enjoyed de facto SADF support. However, the overture was rejected by SWAPO on the ground that only Namibian factions should be involved in independence discussions. Collaterally, Angola offered to participate as an observer at direct negotiations between SWAPO and Pretoria. Two months later Zambian President Kenneth Kaunda and South West African Administrator General Willem VAN NIEKERK jointly chaired a meeting in Lusaka that was attended by representatives of South Africa, SWAPO, and the MPC, while a meeting between van Niekerk and SWAPO president Nujoma was held in Cape Verde on July 25. Although unprecedented, the bilateral discussions also proved abortive, as did subsequent talks involving Washington, Luanda, SWAPO and/or Pretoria.

After lengthy discussion with the MPC, on June 17, 1985, Pretoria installed a Transitional Government of National Unity (TGNU), with a cabinet, 62-member legislature, and Constitutional Council of representatives from the MPC parties. Having largely excluded Ovambos, the new administration was estimated to command the support of perhaps 16 percent of the population and was further limited by Pretoria's retention of veto power over its decisions; not surprisingly, international support for the action was virtually nonexistent. While the TGNU's "interim" nature was stressed by Pretoria, which mandated a formal constitution within 18 months, stalled negotiations with Angola and continued SWAPO activity provoked South African intimations that the arrangement could lead to a permanent "regional alternative to independence."

In early 1986 Pretoria proposed that independence commence August 1, again contingent upon withdrawal of the Cubans from Angola. The renewed linkage stipulation, termed by the United Nations as "extraneous," prompted both Angola and SWAPO to reject the plan as nothing more than a "public relations exercise." In September a UN General Assembly Special Session on Namibia strongly condemned South Africa for effectively blocking implementation of the UN plan for Namibian independence and called for the imposition of mandatory sanctions against Pretoria; however, U.S. and UK vetoes precluded the passage of such resolutions by the Security Council.

During 1987 South Africa continued to seek Western recognition of the TGNU as a means of resolving the Namibian question. However, even within the TGNU, differences emerged regarding a draft constitution and the related question of new elections to second-tier legislative bodies.

In 1988 the long drawn-out dispute moved toward resolution. A series of U.S.-mediated negotiations among Angolan, Cuban, and South African representatives that commenced in London in May and continued in Cairo, New York, Geneva, and Brazzaville (Republic of the Congo) concluded at UN headquarters on December 22 with the signing of an accord that linked South African acceptance of Resolution 435/78 to the phased withdrawal, over a 30-month period, of Cuban troops from Angola. The agreement provided that the resolution would go into effect on April 1, 1989, with deployment of UNTAG (approximately 7,100 individuals from 22 countries). As ratified by the Security Council on February 16, the timetable further provided that South African troop strength would be reduced to 1,500 by July 1, followed by the election of a constituent assembly on November 1 and formal independence for the territory by April 1990.

Ten groups were registered to contest the slightly deferred Constituent Assembly election of November 7–11, 1989, with SWAPO winning 41 of 72 seats and the DTA winning 21. On February 16, 1990, the assembly elected Nujoma to the presidency of the new republic. He was sworn in by UN Secretary General Pérez de Cuéllar during independence ceremonies on March 21, with Hage GEINGOB installed as prime minister of a 20-member cabinet.

In July 1993 Namibia and South Africa agreed to joint administration of Rooikop Airport at Walvis Bay, and on August 18 South African President F. W. de Klerk announced that his government had agreed to relinquish its claim to the port. The actual withdrawal on March 1, 1994, was hailed as completing the process of Namibian independence.

On July 18, 1994, Windhoek's already battered economic record was dealt a further blow when the auditor general released a report criticizing the Nujoma government for widespread financial mismanagement and accusing three ministries of criminal fraud. However, on December 6, one day before Namibia's first presidential and legislative elections since independence, South African President Nelson Mandela announced his country's plans to forgive Namibia's $190 million debt. Thereafter, propelled by Mandela's timely largesse and SWAPO's enduring image as the party of independence, President Nujoma and SWAPO legislative candidates easily outpaced the opposition in balloting on December 7–8, capturing approximately 76 percent of the presidential vote and 53 assembly seats. Nujoma's sole competitor, Mishake MUYONGO of the renamed DTA of Namibia (who received 23 percent of the vote), cited SWAPO's dominance in the north and declared that the elections left Namibia divided along ethnic lines. Although SWAPO captured the two-thirds assembly majority necessary to amend the constitution, Nujoma had announced earlier that any proposed changes would be submitted to popular referendum. SWAPO gained control of 27 of 45 local councils in the February 1998 balloting, followed by the DTA of Namibia with 9.

On October 16, 1998, the SWAPO-dominated National Assembly approved a constitutional amendment that granted President Nujoma the opportunity to compete for a third presidential term and increased the powers of the office. On October 30 the assembly voted against a DTA of Namibia proposal to hold a popular referendum on the bill, despite its earlier pledges to the contrary, and on November 19 the National Council also passed the third-term amendment, leaving final approval to Nujoma, who signed the bill into law in 1999. Despite continued opposition objections to the constitutional revamping, Nujoma was easily reelected for a third term in balloting on November 30–December 1, 1999, securing 76.8 percent of the vote, while SWAPO maintained its assembly dominance in concurrent legislative balloting. In late March 1999 Nujoma slightly reshuffled his government, appointing several prolabor deputy ministers in what observers described as an apparent attempt to counter the formation of a new party, the Congress of Democrats (CoD), by Ben ULENGA, a former independence fighter and trade unionist who had recently left SWAPO as the result of his opposition to the third term for Nujoma. The CoD, which called for an anticorruption drive among public officials and for the withdrawal of Namibian troops from the Democratic Republic of the Congo (DRC), was expected by some observers to offer SWAPO its first genuine electoral challenge. However, SWAPO easily maintained more than enough seats to permit constitutional revision at will.

Although President Nujoma volunteered in April 2001 to seek a fourth term if he believed that popular will favored such a decision, late in the year he announced that he had ruled out another term. Meanwhile, tension was reported between Nujoma and Prime Minister Geingob, resulting in the appointment of Theo-Ben GURIRAB to the premiership in August 2002. (Geingob declined Nujoma's offer of another cabinet post.)

In May 2004 a SWAPO party convention nominated Hifikepunye POHAMBA (the minister of lands, resettlement, and rehabilitation) as the party's presidential candidate in the November elections. Pohamba was challenged by six other candidates, including Ben Ulenga of the CoD. Pohamba received 76.3 percent of the vote in the November 15–16, 2004, elections, with his closest rival being Ulenga with 7.34 percent. None of the other candidates received more than 5.2 percent. In the concurrent legislative elections, SWAPO maintained its dominance, winning 55 of the 72 seats. Following the elections, a new cabinet composed of SWAPO members was chosen, with Nahas ANGULA, the former minister of higher education, training, and employment creation, as prime minister. Although the elections were initially described as free and fair by foreign observers, opposition groups took the electoral commission of Namibia to court over alleged irregularities. The charges were prompted by the discovery of uncounted ballots that had been removed from polling places. A recount in March 2005 confirmed the SWAPO victory, although opposition parties gained a small number of additional votes. In October 2006 a new ministry for veterans affairs was created. The cabinet was reshuffled on April 8, 2008, and was again dominated by SWAPO members.

President Pohamba defeated 11 challengers in balloting on November 27–28, 2010, securing 75.25 percent of the vote. SWAPO also won 54 of the 72 directly elected seats in concurrent legislative elections. The SWAPO breakaway Rally for Democracy and Progress (RDP) was a distant second in both polls, with party leader Hidipo HAMUTENYA garnering 10.91 percent of the presidential vote, and the RDP winning eight assembly seats. Nevertheless, the relatively young RDP gained representation in the assembly for the first time. Nine opposition parties immediately criticized the results, which were announced six days after the poll, alleging irregularities with voter rolls and electoral procedures. The parties mounted a court challenge, which the high court dismissed on March 5, 2010, saying the applications were improperly presented to the court. The RDP members of parliament subsequently refused to attend the swearing-in ceremony and assume their seats. Pohamba and his new all-SWAPO cabinet were sworn in on March 21, with Angula again designated as prime minister.

On December 4, 2012, former prime minister Geingob was again named to that post in a major cabinet reshuffle that included the transfer of incumbent prime minister Angula to the defense portfolio (see Current issues, below). Also, Minister of Trade Calle SCHLETTWEIN became the first white cabinet minister since independence.

Constitution and government. On February 9, 1990, the Constituent Assembly approved a liberal democratic constitution that became effective at independence on March 21. The document provides for a multiparty republic with an executive president, selected initially by majority vote of the legislature (but by direct election thereafter) for a maximum of two five-year terms. (An amendment was approved in 1998 to permit incumbent President Nujoma to serve a third term, although the two-term limit will still exist for future presidents.) The bicameral legislature encompasses a National Assembly elected by proportional representation for a five-year term and a largely advisory National Council consisting of two members from each geographic region who are elected by regional councils for six-year terms. A Council of Traditional Leaders advises the president on the utilization and control of communal land. Provision is made for an independent judiciary, empowered to enforce a comprehensive and unamendable bill of rights, considered to be the centerpiece of the document. Capital punishment and detention without trial are outlawed. The basic law also calls for a strong affirmative action program. Freedom of the press is guaranteed. In 2013 Reporters Without Borders ranked Namibia as 19th out of 179 countries in press freedom, the highest ranking for an African country.

Regional and local units of elective government, delineated on a purely geographical basis, are to function "without any reference to the race, colour, or ethnic origin" of their inhabitants.

Foreign relations. At independence Namibia became the 50th member of the Commonwealth and shortly thereafter the 160th member of the United Nations. For economic reasons, it was deemed necessary to continue trading with South Africa; at the same time it viewed continuance of Pretoria's apartheid policies as precluding the establishment of normal diplomatic relations. Thus South Africa was permitted to maintain a mission in Windhoek that did not have the status of a full-fledged embassy.

In September 1990 it was reported that discussions (South Africa rejected the term "negotiations") had begun on the future status of South African–controlled Walvis Bay, title to which was claimed in both countries' constitutions. The talks continued in March 1991 without yielding agreement, Pretoria indicating that the only concession it would consider would be some form of joint administration of the enclave, but in November the two governments agreed to establish an interim joint administration committee. On August 21, 1992, the Walvis Bay Joint Administrative Body was formally launched. Meanwhile, neither government retreated from its territorial claim, with South Africa insisting that it would withhold a final decision until after it had formed a postapartheid government. However, on August 16, 1993, in a major decision of the multiparty forum convened to decide on the future of South Africa, the South African government delegation agreed under pressure from the African National Congress and other participants to transfer the Walvis Bay enclave to Namibia. South Africa, however, refused in November 2000 to continue negotiations with Namibia on the precise position of the Orange River border between the two countries. In 2006 the two countries agreed to a draft plan for the use of water from the river, though agreement on the exact boundary had not been reached as of mid-2012.

A seemingly less consequential dispute with a neighboring country has turned on the status of Sedudu, a small island in the middle of the Chobe River along the southern border of Namibia's Caprivi Strip. The island had been assumed to be part of Botswana until 1992, when Namibia advanced a claim that yielded a number of armed skirmishes in the area. Following an unsuccessful mediation attempt by President Robert Mugabe of Zimbabwe, the two nations agreed in early 1995 to forward the dispute to the ICJ. On December 15, 1999, the ICJ ruled in favor of Botswana regarding Sedudu, and Namibia announced that it would accept the decision.

In an effort to end illegal trading across its border with Angola (which had been closed since September 1994), Windhoek ordered troops to fire at vehicles attempting to cross the frontier in 1995. Encountering continued insecurity along the border, Namibian authorities decided in September to create a "control unit" in support of defense and police efforts to monitor contraband traffic. On the other hand, a meeting between Namibian and Angolan officials in March 1996 was described as "positive," and in April Namibia welcomed the arrival of UN troops in southeastern Angola, suggesting that when the peacekeepers had established themselves, the border might be reopened. (The border was reopened in 1999.) In July 1997 an international human rights group accused the Nujoma administration of being responsible for the disappearance of over 1,700 Angolans since the 1994 crackdown.

In August 1998 President Nujoma confirmed that Namibian forces had been sent to the Democratic Republic of the Congo at the request of the DRC's president, Laurent Kabila, to fight Rwandan-backed rebels. While effectively acknowledging domestic critics' assertions that his office had acted unilaterally, Nujoma attributed his decision to join Angola and Zimbabwe in aiding the DRC to the "spirit of Pan-Africanism, brotherhood and international solidarity." Thereafter, in late October the DRC rebellion topped the agenda of Nujoma's summit with South African President Mandela. The latter had been a critic of involving the forces of the members of the Southern African Development Community (SADC) in the violence. The country's involvement with the conflict in DRC was widely criticized by the Namibian opposition during 1999 and 2000. Following the assassination of Kabila in 2001, Namibian troops were withdrawn under the auspices of a UN agreement.

In February 2001 Namibia joined Angola and Zambia in the establishment of a tripartite mechanism aimed at improving security along their mutual borders, Windhoek having continued to provide the Angolan government with military support in the campaign against UNITA. After the cease-fire agreement between the Angolan government and UNITA (see entry on Angola), the Namibian government began repatriating Angolan refugees, with 20,000 returned by the end of 2003.

In 2001 descendants of Hereros killed by the Germans during their occupation of the country filed a suit in the United States against the German government, seeking \$2 billion in reparations. Although the suit was dismissed in 2004, Germany formally apologized for the role played by its colonial officials in the 1904–1907 Herero uprising against German rule. Germany also remained a leading Namibian donor.

Relations between Namibia and Brazil increased significantly during Nujoma's tenure as president. Brazilian companies were contracted to explore the edges of Namibia's continental shelf in order to determine the country's formal oceanic boundaries. In addition, under the terms of the 2002 Naval Cooperation Agreement, Brazil provided assistance to construct a naval port at Walvis Bay and to train Namibian naval officers in return for the purchase of Brazilian-built vessels for the Namibian navy. Namibia has also developed closer military ties with Russia. A 2001 bilateral military accord called for Russian technical and military assistance and the eventual purchase of Russian-built MiG fighters.

In late 2005, following President Pohamba's visit to Beijing, relations with China were enhanced as the two countries signed extradition and trade agreements, and China pledged continued economic and social assistance to Namibia. In 2006 Namibia and Zimbabwe signed extradition treaties to assist each other in legal and criminal matters.

Russian officials visited Namibia in 2007, resulting in discussions on a joint venture to produce and sell uranium to meet future needs in the development of nuclear power plants. North Korea also engaged in closer relations with Namibia, owing in part to the latter's uranium stores. (Namibia was the fifth-largest producer in the world). In March 2008 Kim Yom Nam, North Korea's second-most senior leader, attended the inauguration in Windhoek of the new presidential residence, built by North Korea at a cost of $125 million.

Relations with Germany deteriorated in 2010 when Namibia accused two political foundations reportedly linked to Germany's ruling party of seeking "regime change" after they clandestinely monitored Namibia's November 2009 elections and subsequently made reports critical of the elections. Nevertheless, Germany committed $168 million in development aid for 2011 and 2012, with a further $9.5 million in 2013. Namibia declined to recognize Libya's National Transitional Council or renew diplomatic relations pending democratic elections in Libya. In December, Namibia declined a request by the SADC to provide troops for a multilateral peacekeeping force created in response to renewed fighting in the DRC.

In March 2013 the EU informed Namibia that it needed to conclude negotiations on an Economic Partnership Agreement (EPA) within 18 months or lose duty-free incentives with the Union. Namibia had refused to sign a draft EPA, arguing that it was economically disadvantageous. In May the government rejected a request from the DRC to establish fishing quotas in order to protect domestic fisheries in that country.

Current issues. Accusations of fraud and illegal practices were frequently exchanged between members of SWAPO and dissidents who broke away from the governing party to form the Rally for Democracy and Progress (RDP) in 2008. The former senior SWAPO members were reviled by the party, which purged its central committee of anyone whose name appeared on a list linked to the RDP (see Political Parties and Groups, below). Collaterally, in a move described as ushering in a new era in SWAPO's history, longtime SWAPO leader Sam Nujoma handed over party leadership to President Pohamba and lined up the president's likely successor by bringing former prime minister Hage Geingob back into the leadership fold as vice president of the party. Subsequently, attention in 2008 turned to the presidential and assembly elections in 2009; SWAPO initiated its campaign in April, stating its intention to increase its parliamentary seats from 55 to 71. A month earlier the elections commissioner and three of his top officials were suspended, critics claiming that now that the director was an impartial administrator, SWAPO had him removed. The elections director subsequently was reported to have joined the RDP. The dismissals led to the postponement of a local by-election that was deemed to be of special importance to SWAPO in one of its first contests against members of the breakaway RDP; however SWAPO members secured all but one of the seats in the thrice-postponed by-election.

In December 2008 President Pohamba approved a 24 percent salary increase for all political office-holders, and in early 2009 he granted pay increases for civil servants, a move that was seen by some analysts as a "stimulus" to the economy during the global financial downturn. In March President Pohamba received SWAPO's bid to stand for reelection as president of the republic.

Meanwhile, widespread flooding over four months in early 2009 affected more than 200,000 people, with 102 reported dead and 82,000 in need of food aid due to the huge loss of crop land and livestock, particularly in the north. The government estimated it would need $240 million to clean up after the disaster, and the UN sought urgent funds to help flood victims.

As the 2009 elections drew near, more than a dozen parties signed up to contest the assembly poll, and 12 candidates were on the slate for the presidency. Only three opposition parties campaigned nationally—the RDP, DTA, and Congress of Democrats (CoD). Domestic attention was focused on the downturn in the economy, due in large part to a decline in diamond sales; in the political arena the RDP claimed that some 300 SWAPO members had threatened violence to keep the party from campaigning in one constituency. SWAPO, for its part, claimed harassment of its supporters by the RDP. Meanwhile, the CoD was reportedly riven by infighting, its leader having left to start the All People's Party (APP) a year earlier. About a month before the elections, the RDP and the CoP asked the state-owned broadcasting company to provide equal air time to all parties, a request that was met with the broadcaster's immediate cancellation of all free campaign air time. Subsequently, it was reported that SWAPO had garnered 82 percent of broadcast coverage, while the opposition's was 4 percent. Following Pohamba and SWAPO's landslide victory on November 27–28, nine opposition parties challenged the results in court, primarily citing irregularities with the electoral register, though observers generally considered the polling to be free and fair.

As soon as Pohamba and his new government were sworn in on March 21, 2010, jockeying began among potential candidates for the 2014 elections, prompted by the president's appointment of Utoni NUJOMA, son of the country's first president Sam Nujoma, as minister for foreign affairs, reportedly in response to pressure from the elder Nujoma and his SWAPO allies. Already, pundits were pointing to former prime minister and SWAPO vice president Geingob and Deputy Prime Minister Hausiku as his likely rivals.

After the court's rejection of the opposition's legal challenge in March 2010, the RDP members of parliament began a boycott that lasted until October 2010, when the Supreme Court overturned its earlier ruling and agreed to hear the case. In the wake of the ruling, SWAPO and the electoral commission were ordered to pay $146,000 in appeal costs, in addition to the opposition's legal costs. The same two judges who had originally dismissed the appeal on technical grounds were to decide the case; the RDP raised no objection. The ruling party was overwhelmingly successful in local and regional elections on November 26 and 27, winning 92 percent of the constituencies. The RDP was a distant second.

The legal challenges to the 2009 presidential elections were dismissed by the high court in February 2011 in a ruling that found "insufficient evidence to prove irregularities." In March the president declared a state of emergency in the wake of what he described as the worst flooding in the country's history. Aid organizations estimated that nearly 38,000 people were displaced.

The demise of Libya's Muammar al-Qadhafi alarmed Namibian leaders, and Defense Minister Charles NAMOLOH justified an increase in military expenditure in April 2011 by pointing out that Namibia, with its high inequality, could also be roiled by unrest.

Corruption continues to be a major issue. A long awaited trial for fraud against seven defendants with ties to senior members of SWAPO was delayed in June 2011, pending a ruling from the Supreme Court on a related constitutional challenge.

On March 28, 2012, Frans GOAGOSEB announced the dissolution of the Namibia Democratic Movement for Change (NDMC) party, which he founded in 2002 (the party received 0.53 percent of the vote in the 2004 legislative poll and 0.22 percent in the 2009 presidential election). In November, in order to overcome a budget deficit estimated to be $558.1 million, or 4.4 percent of GDP, the government for the first time offered bonds on the Johannesburg Stock Exchange. On December 4 Geingob was again appointed prime minister in a move that signaled he would be SWAPO's presidential candidate in 2014.

In May 2013 Pohamba recalled the nation's ambassadors and high commissioners and conducted a broad reshuffle of the nation's foreign service, including the appointment of a number of new diplomats. Also in May, Pohamba declared a nationwide emergency in response to a widespread drought.

POLITICAL PARTIES AND GROUPS

Government Party:

South West Africa People's Organization of Namibia—SWAPO. Consisting mainly of Ovambos and formerly known as the Ovambo People's Organization, SWAPO was the largest and most active South West African nationalist group and was recognized prior to independence by the United Nations as the "authentic representative of the Namibian people." Founded in 1958, it issued a call for independence in 1966 and subsequently initiated guerrilla activity in the north with the support of the OAU Liberation Committee. Further operations were conducted by the party's military wing, the People's Liberation Army of Namibia (PLAN), from bases in southern Angola. A legal "internal wing" engaged in political activity within Namibia, although it was the target of arrests and other forms of intimidation by police and South African military forces. SWAPO's co-founder, Andimba TOIVO JA TOIVO, was released from 16 years' imprisonment on March 1, 1984, and was immediately elected to the organization's newly created post of secretary general. In February 1988, at what was described as the largest such meeting in the movement's history, 130 delegates representing about 30 branches of SWAPO's internal wing reaffirmed their "unwavering confidence" in the exiled leadership of Sam Nujoma and their willingness to conclude a cease-fire in accordance with implementation of the UN independence plan. Nujoma returned to Namibia for the first time since 1960 on September 14, 1989, and was elected president of the new republic by the Constituent Assembly on February 16, 1990.

At a party congress in December 1991, the first since the group's inception, delegates reelected Nujoma and Rev. Hendrik Witbooi party president and vice president, respectively, while Moses GAROËB captured the secretary generalship from Toivo ja Toivo. The congress also elected a new Central Committee (enlarged from 38 to 67 members) and adopted a revised constitution, expunging references to the PLAN and changing descriptions of the group from a "liberation movement" to a "mass political party."

In presidential and legislative balloting in December 1994 President Nujoma and SWAPO legislative candidates captured approximately 70 percent of the vote. However, some internal friction was subsequently reported between Nujoma loyalists and the party's "pragmatists" over Nujoma's allegedly heavy-handed direction of party affairs. Thereafter, in what observers described as a possible shift of power to the group's younger leaders, in April 1996 Deputy Minister of Foreign Affairs Netumbo NANDI-NDAITWAH was named party secretary general. She replaced Garoëb, who had resigned days earlier.

In May 1997, at SWAPO's second congress since independence, party delegates adopted a resolution supporting amendment of the constitution to allow Nujoma a third presidential term. In addition, SWAPO Vice President Witbooi retained his post, staving off a challenge by Prime Minister Hage Gottfried Geingob, while cabinet member and Nujoma confidante Hifikepunye Pohamba was elected secretary general.

On the eve of the extraordinary party congress of August 29–30, 1998, Ben Ulenga, Namibia's high commissioner to Britain and a SWAPO central committeeman, resigned from his overseas post to protest the plans to allow Nujoma a third term as well as the deployment of Namibian troops in the DRC. Ulenga's public denouncement of the Nujoma amendment, the first by a ranking SWAPO member, colored the late August proceedings, at which the congress rebuffed calls from party dissidents for a debate on the issue and formally approved the proposed bill. In November the party voted to suspend Ulenga, who had recently led "like-minded" colleagues in the formation of a self-described bipartisan grouping. (In early 1999 Ulenga launched the Congress of Democrats, below.)

Meanwhile, in regional council balloting in December 1998 SWAPO easily won the majority of the posts in polling marked by low voter turnout. In the legislative election in November–December 1999 the party got 76.1 percent of the vote and won 55 seats in the National Assembly, and Nujoma was reelected president with 76.8 percent of the vote.

At the August 2002 congress, the party's politburo underwent a significant change. Some analysts noted that new prime minister Theo-Ben Gurirab, new SWAPO vice president Hifikepunye Pohamba, and new secretary general Ngarikutuke Tjiriange were among the possible successors to Nujoma, who had announced in late 2001 that he would not seek a fourth presidential term.

In May 2004 Pohamba was chosen as Nujoma's successor at a party conference. Nujoma was reelected as party president for a three-year term. SWAPO was successful in the November legislative elections; Gurirab subsequently was elected speaker of the assembly, and Nahas Angula was appointed prime minister.

Party infighting erupted in 2005 after SWAPO secretary and deputy works minister Paulas KAPIA was accused in a scandal involving state funds (the opposition claimed Nujoma was involved as well; he denied the allegations). Kapia resigned his government post and his assembly seat, and was suspended from the party. Some observers suggested that it was President Pohamba who had forced the resignation of Kapia, a Nujoma protégé; subsequently, Nujoma returned Kapia to the party payroll. The rift between "Nujomaists" and backers of former foreign minister Hidipo Hamutenya, who took over Kapia's assembly seat, deepened after Jesaya NYAMU, a leading party member for some 40 years (and loyal to Hamutenya), was dismissed from the party in late 2005 for alleged "serious misconduct." The vote to oust him reportedly divided the party between backers of Nujoma and Hamutenya, with some observers speculating that Hamutenya might throw his support to Pohamba in an effort to remove Nujoma from the party presidency.

Nujoma retained party leadership in 2006, despite accusations by some party officials that the elections were fraudulent. Tensions increased in 2007, the rival factions now including those who backed Pohamba, in addition to supporters of Nujoma and Hamutenya. Because of the fractured party and lack of support from many cabinet ministers still loyal to Nujoma, observers said Pohamba was unable to lead the country effectively. Pohamba's uncertain status in the party contributed to the postponement of the next congress from midyear to November 2007. By the time the congress convened, however, Nujoma had decided to give up his party position after decades at the helm and to withdraw from active politics, thus handing off control to Pohamba (and to a slate of party officers tapped by Nujoma). The congress was also notable for the absence of party cofounder Toivo ja Toivo from the party's central committee, along with other high-ranking party members. (Though Toivo ja Toiva had been rumored at the time to have joined a new party started by Hamutenya and other dissidents—the Rally for Democracy and Progress—he denied it.) Reportedly, the list of breakaway RDP members had somehow been supplied to SWAPO, resulting in a great deal of acrimony toward the dissidents and the purge of the party's central committee in a scheme engineered by Nujoma to reward SWAPO loyalists. Collaterally, the startup of the RDP (see below) coincided with the election of the new SWAPO slate, including former prime minister Hage Geingob as the party's vice president. Pohamba was elected as party president, with Geingob, a political moderate, described as the likely successor to Pohamba as Namibia's president. (Geingob subsequently was given a ministerial post in 2008.) The party also elected its first female secretary general, justice minister Pendukeni Iivula-Ithana.

In the run-up to a by-election in the newly incorporated town of Omuthiya in early 2008, Pohamba called for a boycott of businesses owned by RDP members. SWAPO also postponed the by-election for several months, reportedly to fend off an initial electoral victory for the RDP, but also due to the dismissal of the elections commissioner over unspecified irregularities. SWAPO ultimately won the poll with a reported 90 percent of the vote.

In 2008 the elections director, Philemon KANIME, who had been a member of SWAPO for nearly 50 years, was suspended from his job (and subsequently not reappointed) after he had been accused of illegally registering the new RDP (below). Kanime then joined the RDP.

In 2009 SWAPO denied allegations of violence against the APP (below). In February the party suspended three members who were allegedly involved with the RDP. In March the party nominated President Pohamba as its standard-bearer in the November presidential elections, despite what were described as "behind the scenes" attempts to oust him. SWAPO won a landslide victory, claiming 75 percent of votes in both the legislative and presidential polls.

In March 2011 the central committee pledged that whoever was elected vice president at the party congress, regardless of tribe or gender, would become its flagbearer in the 2014 presidential election. Party officials said Pohamba would continue to head SWAPO. However, questions arose whether he would be able to complete his term after he suffered a mild stroke in July 2011. Changes to the party branch structure barred new branches from voting for delegates to the elective congress, which prompted nearly half of the 310 delegates at a November 2011 Women's Council conference in Caprivi to boycott the vote for a new regional executive. Jockeying and infighting increased through 2012, prompting Pohamba to appoint a commission to investigate the use of smear tactics. At a SWAPO congress in December, Pohamba was reelected party president. Geingob was again elected party vice president, and subsequently appointed prime minister, thereby confirming his place as Pohamba's successor.

In May 2013, in an apparent effort to unify bolster support for Geingob, 10 allies of the prime minister were elevated to SWAPO's party secretariat to replace supporters of Geingob's main rivals, Pendukeni Iivula-Ithana and Jerry EKANDJO.

Leaders: Hifikepunye POHAMBA (President of the Republic and Party President), Hage GEINGOB (Former Prime Minister and Party Vice President), Theo-Ben GURIRAB (Speaker of the National Assembly), Rev. Hendrik WITBOOI, Nangolo MBUMBA (Deputy Secretary General), Pendukeni IIVULA-ITHANA (Secretary General).

Other Legislative Parties:

Rally for Democracy and Progress—RDP. One of three parties formed within months of each other in the run-up to the 2009 elections, the RDP was established on November 17, 2007, as a result of rifts within SWAPO. Former senior SWAPO members, including Hidipo Hamutenya and Jesaya Nyamu, both former ministers, and Kandi Hehova, a former chair of SWAPO's National Council, launched the party with pledges to eradicate poverty and unemployment and improve health and education services, areas in which they believed SWAPO had failed to make significant progress. They denied some analysts' description of RDP as a tribal party.

Another factor that observers said led to the formation of the new party was Hamutenya's dismissal from his ministerial post following his having contested the SWAPO presidency in 2004 against Pohamba. Hamutenya had been a SWAPO loyalist for 46 years, having served on SWAPO's central committee for 30 years.

In its first electoral test in a local by-election in April 2008, the party fared poorly; SWAPO won overwhelmingly. Another by-election in the new town of Omuthiya, which had been scheduled for February 2008, was postponed until late April, observers saying that SWAPO was trying to postpone a likely RDP victory. SWAPO did not want the RDP to win in its first contest (see SWAPO, above). Following a large RDP rally in July, the by-election was postponed again until September, the RDP winning only one seat while SWAPO won the remaining six. Observers described the defeat as a serious blow to the RDP, since most of its leaders are from Omuthiya and its surrounding regions. Subsequently, the RDP, alleging "political anarchy," called on the government to resign and hold early elections. Violence broke out in another constituency in November, when hundreds of SWAPO supporters allegedly prevented the RDP from holding a rally and several reportedly were beaten.

At the party's congress in December 2008, former foreign minister Hidipo Hamutenya, who had been dismissed by President Nujoma in 2004, was elected party president. As flagbearer in the 2009 presidential election, he placed a distant second with 10.91 percent of the vote. Though the party was widely regarded as SWAPO's biggest challenger and won the second-highest number of assembly seats (eight) to become the official opposition, it significantly trailed SWAPO's representation.

In April 2010 the party joined the general public outcry against a proposed 35 percent increase in electricity rates. In late 2010 the **Republican Party** (RP), led by member of parliament and 2004 and 2009 presidential candidate Henk MUDGE, announced it would merge with the RDP. Mudge gave up his assembly seat and his party fully in 2011 to complete the merger.

Reports in May 2013 indicated that the RDP had run out of funds and was unable to pay party staff.

Leaders: Hidipo HAMUTENYA (President and 2009 presidential candidate), Steve BEZULDENHOUT (Vice Chair), Kandi HEHOVA, Jeremiah NAMBINGA (Information Secretary), Jesaya NYAMU (Secretary General).

Republican Party—RP. Originally part of the DTA, the RP was reestablished as an independent party in 2003 under the leadership of Henk Mudge, the son of Dirk MUDGE, the leader of the former Republican Party within the DTA. The conservative RP won 1.9 percent of the vote in the 2004 elections and gained a seat in the assembly for the first time. In addition, the younger Mudge ran as a presidential candidate; he came in fifth with 1.95 percent of the vote. Secretary General Carola ENGELBRECHT was dismissed in 2005 for allegedly discussing the party's internal affairs in public.

Joseph KAUANDENGE, formerly of the Namibia Democratic Movement of Change (DMC) and Namibia Movement for Independent Candidates (NMIC) (below), was reported in 2005 to be an adviser to RP president Henk Mudge.

In October 2008 the party claimed that four of its members, including Vice Chair Clara Gowases, were illegally arrested for distributing flyers urging voters to boycott an upcoming regional by-election. The party members were released after a few hours. The party subsequently boycotted the by-election.

In the 2009 assembly election the party won one seat; Henk Mudge received 1.16 percent of the vote in concurrent presidential balloting. He resigned his assembly seat and gave up the party presidency officially in 2011 to join the RDP. Though the parties were said to have merged, Clara Gowases replaced Mudge in the assembly and ascended to chair of the party.

Leaders: Clara GOWASES (Chair), Cap GAESEB (Acting Secretary General).

DTA of Namibia. The grouping known as the Democratic Turnhalle Alliance (DTA) until adoption of the abbreviated form in November 1991 was launched in the wake of the Turnhalle Conference as a multiracial coalition of European, coloured, and African groups. Advocating a constitutional arrangement that would provide for equal ethnic representation, the DTA obtained an overwhelming majority (41 of 50 seats) in the Constituent Assembly balloting of December 4–8, 1978, and was instrumental in organizing the Multi-Party Conference in 1983. Its core formations were the white-based Republican Party (RP), organized in October 1977 by dissident members of the then-dominant South West Africa National Party (SWANP), and the Herero-based National United Democratic Organization (NUDO), which had long advocated a federal solution as a means of opposing SWAPO domination. (For a list of other groups participating in the formation of the DTA, see the 1999 *Handbook.*)

At a Central Committee meeting on November 30, 1991, DTA officials announced the transformation of the coalition into an integrated political party. The committee also reelected the party leaders to permanent positions, adopted a new constitution, and announced that the group would thenceforth be known as the DTA of Namibia.

An intraparty chasm between former RP leader Dirk Mudge and a faction led by party president Mishake MUYONGO and information secretary Andrew MATJILA widened in the wake of the DTA of Namibia's poor showing in regional and local council elections in November–December 1992. At a central committee meeting in February 1993, the Muyongo faction pressed Mudge to resign, arguing that his former ties to South Africa had contributed to the party's loss of electoral support from all but small-town whites and the Herero and Caprivi communities. In April Mudge announced that he would be vacating his parliamentary seat, insisting that he had made the decision for purely personal reasons and would retain the DTA of Namibia chair. In mid-1994 Matjila broke with the party, and less than a year later Mudge resigned his party post and bowed out of politics. Thereafter, in balloting in December, Muyongo secured only 23 percent of the presidential vote, while the party's parliamentary representation fell to 15 seats, the DTA of Namibia claiming that there had been widespread voting irregularities.

On August 25, 1998, the DTA of Namibia's Executive Committee suspended Muyongo from the party presidency and named Vice President Katuutire Kaura interim party leader after Muyongo called for the secession of the Caprivi Strip region from Namibia. Muyongo subsequently assumed control of the militant Caprivi Liberation Movement (see CLF, under Illegal Groups, below).

The legislative elections on November 30–December 1, 1999, proved nearly disastrous for the DTA of Namibia as the party secured less than half the seats it had won in 1994, winning only 9.5 percent of the vote and seven seats in the National Assembly. In the presidential election, Kaura received 9.6 percent of the vote. In early April 2000 the DTA of Namibia and the UDF formed an opposition coalition when the negotiations with the CoD broke down.

The DTA of Namibia won four seats in the 2004 legislative elections while its presidential candidate, again Kaura, placed third with 5.2 percent of the vote. The defections of DTA of Namibia members to the RP and NUDO hurt the party most in the December Regional Council elections, where voters split among the three parties, giving SWAPO its greatest success ever in such balloting. The DTA of Namibia secured two seats in the 2004 legislative balloting.

In 2005 Katuutire Kaura was elected party president, and Alois Gende won the post of secretary general over McHenry Venaani, 27, who had also challenged Kaura for the party presidency. Early in 2007 the DTA proposed a "grand coalition" of opposition parties, a notion that did not interest the RP, CoD or NUDO.

Venaani, a member of parliament, announced in March 2008 that he would not contest any party office at the central committee meeting to be held later in the year, citing his desire to keep the party unified. Rifts had begun to develop after constituents in the Kavango region called for Kaura to step down and expressed their support for Venaani. Two months earlier, party stalwart Rudolf KAMBURONA resigned from the DTA after 32 years, saying he wanted to concentrate on farming, rejecting speculation that he was going to join the RDP (below). Meanwhile, observers noted growing dissatisfaction within the party with Kaura's leadership. Nevertheless, Kaura was reelected along with other party leaders at the DTA congress in November 2008, the only surprise being the election of Venaani as secretary general, according to observers.

In January 2009 some tribal members claimed that the government had refused drought aid to tribe members who belonged to parties other than SWAPO. The government denied the allegations. Venaani also demanded that the agencies that distributed the food stop claiming that the relief came directly from SWAPO. In the November elections the party won two assembly seats. Presidential candidate Kaura came in a distant third with 2.98 percent of the vote. In 2012 Kaura announced he would not seek reelection as party leader in 2013.

In June 2013 the DTA called for the creation of an opposition coalition ahead of the 2014 national elections.

Leaders: Katuutire KAURA (President and 2004 and 2009 presidential candidate), Philemon MOONGO (Vice President), McHenry VENAANI (Secretary General).

United Democratic Front—UDF. The UDF is led by Justus Garoëb, longtime head of the **Damara Council,** which withdrew from the MPC in March 1984; chair of the group was Reggie DIERGAARDT, leader of the **Labour Party,** a largely coloured group that was expelled from the DTA in 1982 but participated in the MPC subsequent to its November 1983 meeting. Two small leftist groups were also Front members: the **Communist Party of Namibia** (CPN) and the Trotskyist **Workers' Revolutionary Party** (WRP). (For more information on the WRP, see the 2013 *Handbook.*) The UDF ran a distant third in the November 1989 election, winning four assembly seats. In balloting during November–December 1992 the party was unable to lessen the gap between itself and the two major parties, capturing only 1 of 13 regional council seats.

In a November 1993 action opposed by other clan chiefs, UDF president Garoëb was enthroned as the king of Damara. Thereafter, observers attributed Garoëb's failure to participate in the December 1994 presidential balloting, despite a pledge to the contrary, to the UDF's poor financial condition. Meanwhile, the party, securing only 2 percent of the vote, lost two of its 4 assembly seats.

In late 1998 a UDF spokesperson denounced SWAPO's legislative efforts to grant Nujoma a third term. The UDF won two seats in the 1999 National Assembly election, while Garoëb secured 3 percent of the vote in the presidential poll.

In the 2004 presidential balloting Garoëb gained 3.8 percent of the vote, and the UDF won three seats in the assembly.

The UDF, along with several other opposition parties, was unsuccessful in calling for postponement of by-elections in one constituency in 2008 because of alleged irregularities.

In 2009 the party won two assembly seats; Garoëb placed fifth in presidential balloting with 2.37 percent of the vote. In February 2013 Garoëb announced he would not seek reelection as UDF leader at the party's September congress.

Leaders: Justus GAROËB (King of Damara, President of the Party, and 2004 and 2009 presidential candidate), Eric BIWA (Chair), Dudu MURORUA (Secretary General).

All People's Party—APP. Licensed on January 22, 2008, the APP was established ahead of the 2009 elections by former minister and former CoD secretary general Ignatius Shixwameni and his brother, Herbert Shixwameni, following the former's leadership dispute with CoD president Ben Ulenga. Other members were said to be defectors from SWAPO, DTA, and NUDO, with the party's stronghold in the northern Kavango region. The stated goals were to unite a broad, national base in a "truly democratic party" and to fight to wipe out poverty, unemployment, and inequality. If successful in presidential elections, the leaders pledged to set up a welfare state, providing free education and access to decent housing.

The party's first rally, held in March 2008, was reported to be a "huge success," with thousands attending in the Kavango region.

In the 2009 elections the party secured one assembly seat; Shixwameni won 1.23 percent in the presidential poll.

Party leader Shixwameni in June 2011 called for an end to corruption in government and for equitable distribution of wealth while making his intentions known as a potential candidate for the 2014 presidential election. Shixwameni was reelected party president at an APP congress in May 2013. Fifteen of the 31 members elected to the party's central committee were women.

Leaders: Ignatius SHIXWAMENI (Party President and 2009 presidential candidate), Madala NAUYOMA (Vice President), Mariska BRENDEL (Secretary General).

Congress of Democrats—CoD. The CoD was launched in March 1999 by former SWAPO stalwart Ben Ulenga, who had been suspended by SWAPO in 1998 after he criticized efforts to permit President Nujoma to run for a third term and had formed a grouping styled Forum for the Future. Included in the CoD's platform were calls for a smaller cabinet and the withdrawal of Namibian troops from the DRC. The CoD won 9.9 percent of the votes in the legislative elections held on November 30–December 1, 1999. It won seven seats in the National Assembly and became the official parliamentary opposition, supplanting the DTA of Namibia. Ulenga received 10.5 percent of the vote in the presidential election.

The CoD lost support in the 2004 elections; Ulenga only received 7.34 percent of the presidential vote while the party fell to five seats. Factionalism within the party was reported in 2007, with some members continuing to call for new leadership following failed party elections in May. The election was declared void due to fraud and other irregularities (Ulenga defeated his challenger by 14 votes). Though Ulenga said he would step down based on what had happened during the party election, he apparently retained the leadership post amid the discord. Ignatius Shixwameni, leader of the main faction within the CoD and the party's secretary general, formed a splinter group that broke away in late 2007 and became the basis for the new All People's Party.

Kala GERTZE, one of the CoD's founding members and its secretary general from 2004–2007, died from asthma in March 2008. Infighting continued through July 2008, despite a High Court ruling that the party hold a congress in five months. The court subsequently ruled that if the two factions could not agree on a chairperson to oversee the party's elections, the Law Society of Namibia would appoint a candidate. Ultimately, Ulenga retained his post as party president, defeating Nora SCHIMMING-CHASE, a faction leader and the party's former vice president, in balloting at a party congress in November. Elma Dienda, an assembly member who reportedly was a Schimming-Chase supporter, was elected party treasurer.

In 2009 the party secured one assembly seat; presidential candidate Ulenga received 0.72 percent of the vote. In December 2012 the CoD announced that it would delay a party congress scheduled for November 2013 to early 2014.

Leaders: Ben ULENGA (President and 2004 and 2009 presidential candidate), Elma DIENDA (Treasurer), Gretchen BOOIS (Deputy Secretary General), Tsudao GURIRAB (Secretary General).

National Unity Democratic Organization—NUDO. Led by the Herero High Chief, Kuaima Riruako, former members of NUDO left the DTA of Namibia (and his seat in parliament) in 2003 to reestablish their Herero-based party. In the 2004 elections, NUDO secured 4.79 percent of the vote and three seats in the assembly. Riruako came in third with 5.2 percent of the vote in the presidential poll. Party leader Chief Kuaima Riruako resigned his National Assembly seat on February 1, 2008, saying he wanted to "focus his energies on other matters," including recruiting more supporters for NUDO across the country. He retained his post as party chair.

In January 2009 a youth leader in the party called on the government to make an early announcement of the dates of the presidential and legislative elections, rather than waiting until the customary two months ahead of time, to give candidates and parties time to adequately prepare. The party won two assembly seats in November; Riruako placed fourth in concurrent presidential balloting with 2.92 percent of the vote.

Leaders: Chief Kuaima RIRUAKO (Party Chair and 2004 and 2009 presidential candidate), Tumbee TJOMBE (Vice President), Asser MBAI (Secretary General).

South West Africa National Union—SWANU. Formerly coordinating many of its activities with SWAPO's internal wing, the Herero-supported SWANU joined with the Damara Council and a number of smaller groups to form a multiracial coalition in support of the Western "contact group" solution to the Namibian problem. SWANU's president, Moses KATJIOUNGUA, participated in the 1983 MPC meeting and in September 1984 was reported to have been replaced as party leader by Kuzeeko Kangueehi, who indicated that the group would leave the MPC, with a view to possibly merge with SWAPO. In October, on the other hand, Katjioungua was again identified as holding the presidency, with Kangueehi described as the leader of a dissident faction (subsequently styled SWANU-Left). The incumbent's anti-SWAPO orientation was reflected by his inclusion in the "national unity" cabinet of 1985. A founding member of the Democratic Coalition of Namibia (DCN), SWANU abruptly dropped out of the grouping in November 1994 while Katjioungua stayed within the

DCN. SWANU formed an electoral alliance with the **Workers' Revolutionary Party** (below), which received less than 0.5 percent of the vote in the legislative election on November 30–December 1, 1999.

SWANU secured less than 1 percent of the vote in the 2004 legislative elections.

At the party's congress in November 2007, Usutuaije Maamberua, a former finance secretary, was elected party president. In recent years the party has been campaigning for reparations from Germany for alleged atrocities committed under German rule more than 100 years ago, similar to reparations paid to Jewish people who suffered at the hands of the Nazis.

In advance of the 2009 parliamentary elections, SWANU presented its ten-point platform in February, calling for a "socialist, transformationist, revolutionary approach" to government. The party won one seat; in the concurrent presidential election, flagbearer Maamberua won 0.37 percent of the vote.

In 2013 Maamberua rejected calls from within the party for a new SWANU congress (the last all-party meeting was scheduled for 2009, but was also cancelled).

Leaders: Usutuaije MAAMBERUA (President and 2009 presidential candidate), Dr. Rihupisa KANDANDO (National Chair), Kuzeeko KANGUEEHI, Hitjevi Gerson VEII, Tangeni IYAMBO (Secretary General).

Other Parties That Contested the 2009 Elections:

Monitor Action Group—MAG. A conservative, predominantly white grouping, the MAG won one assembly seat in December 1994. The MAG received 0.7 percent of the vote in the legislative election on November 30–December 1, 1999, and won one seat in the National Assembly.

In the 2004 polls Jacobus Pretorius received 1.2 percent of the presidential vote, while the party retained its single seat in the assembly.

The MAG did not field a presidential candidate in 2009, nor did it receive enough votes to gain a seat in the assembly. In June MAG chair and former presidential candidate Pretorius announced his retirement from politics.

Leaders: Gernot SCHAAF (Interim Chair), Jurgie VILJOEN.

Democratic Party of Namibia—DPN. Formed in July 2008 by Solomon Dawid Isaacs, a former SWAMU member who lived in exile from the 1960s to 1978, the party's stated mission is to address the marginalization of minority groups, particularly in the south. Isaacs said the DPN supports equal distribution of wealth and redistribution of land or "regaining" ancestral lands.

Presidential candidate Isaacs won 0.23 percent of the vote in the 2009 election. The party did not field candidates in the assembly election, but continued to contest local balloting.

Leader: Solomon Dawid ISAACS (Interim Chair and 2009 presidential candidate).

Other Parties and Groups:

Federal Convention of Namibia—FCN. Strongly opposed to the UN independence plan, the FCN was organized by J. G. A. (Hans) DIERGAARDT, a former minister of local government and leader of the **Rehoboth Free Democratic Party** (*Rehoboth Bevryder Demokratiese Party*—RBDP). The RBDP was an outgrowth of the former Rehoboth Liberation Front (RLF), which endorsed the partition of Namibia along ethnic lines and obtained one assembly seat in 1978 as representative of part of the Baster community, composed of Afrikaans-speaking people with European customs. The RFDP was an original member of the MPC but in 1987 joined the SWANP in opposing the draft constitution endorsed by other transitional government members. However, following the Constituent Assembly election in 1989, in which the party secured one seat, FCN members subsequently participated on the team that drafted the new constitution.

In 1994 the FCN chose former Women's Party (WP) leader Hileni LATVIO as its presidential candidate; however, Latvio failed to register her candidacy by the appropriate date and was denied an extension. The FCN won less than 0.5 percent of the vote in the 1999 legislative elections and won no seats. Diergaardt, party chair, died in 1998 at age 70.

Namibia Movement for Independent Candidates—NMIC. The NMIC was launched in July 1997 on a platform stressing the need to incorporate Namibian youths into the political process. In September 1998 NMIC became affiliated with the DTA of Namibia (above). Party leader Joseph Kauandenge subsequently had a leading role in several parties, most recently in the DMC and RP (above).

Illegal Groups:

Caprivi Liberation Front—CLF. Formed in 1994, the CLF has sought autonomy or independence for the Caprivi Strip, a narrow portion of northern Namibia that juts about 250 miles into central Africa, touching the borders of Angola, Botswana, Zambia, and Zimbabwe. The strip, theretofore part of the British protectorate of Bechuanaland (subsequently Botswana), was ceded to Germany, colonial ruler of South West Africa, in 1890 as part of a land swap that included Britain's assumption of control in Zanzibar. The region is part of the former ancestral kingdom of Barotseland, which also included portions of Zambia, Botswana, and Zimbabwe. In the 1970s and 1980s the strip was used by South African forces as a base for military activities against independence fighters in Namibia as well as against the Angolan government.

In 1998 the Namibian government reported that a security sweep had uncovered training bases in Caprivi for the CLF-affiliated Caprivi Liberation Army (CLA). Several thousand Caprivians subsequently fled to Botswana, including Mishake Muyongo, the CLF/CLA leader who been dismissed from both SWAPO and the DTA of Namibia for his secessionist sentiments. In early August 1999 a small group of alleged CLA members attacked security locations in the town of Katima Mulilo, the fighting leaving at least 16 dead. The insurgents were quickly routed, but the Namibian government declared a state of emergency in the region for three weeks and implemented what critics described as a heavy-handed crackdown that allegedly included the abuse of detainees. Among the factors reportedly fueling antigovernment sentiment among Caprivians (primarily from the Lozi ethnic group) is the political and economic dominance of Ovambos in Namibia.

In August 2007 ten men, all Namibian citizens, including CLF leader Mishake Muyongo, were found guilty of high treason in the 1999 attempt to overthrow the government in the Caprivi region and establish a separate state. The men were among alleged CLA members who crossed the border into Angola in 1998 to obtain arms, returning to CLA training camps in northern Namibia, according to the government. All of the men, claiming they were not Namibian, refused to recognize the court's authority. They were sentenced to prison terms ranging from 30 to 32 years, and all ten appealed their convictions. (Two other men accused in the same case were acquitted in June 2007.) In February 2009, police arrested Albius Moto LISELI, who they claimed was an associate of Muyongo and a participant in the insurgency. He was also charged with high treason. Another leader in the secessionist movement, John MABUKU, who had fled with Muyongo, died in exile in Botswana in 2008.

In June 2012 prime minister Angula offered to relaunch negotiations with Muyongo if the latter renounced his call for secession. However, the CLF leader rejected the overture and repeated his call for talks under the auspices of the UN.

Leader: Mishake MUYONGO (under asylum in Denmark).

United Democratic Party—UDP. The UDP (with the CLA as its military wing) was founded in 1985 by Mishake Muyongo. The UDP, subsequently led by Crispin Matongo following his resignation from the CoD, was affiliated with the DTA until 1999. Matongo, who had been banned from Namibia, returned in 1990 and served as the country's prison commissioner for six years. After his retirement in 1996 he became chair of the UDP, which shared the CLF's goal of self-rule for the Caprivi Strip. In 2006 Matongo, a cousin of Muyongo, tried to revive the UDP. However, in September the government declared the UDP illegal and banned it from holding any meetings in the country.

Leader: Crispin MATONGO.

LEGISLATURE

The Namibian **Parliament** consists of an indirectly elected National Council and a National Assembly whose voting members are directly elected.

National Council. The largely advisory upper house is a 26-member body containing 2 members from each of 13 regional councils; the term of office is six years. The national body launched its first session on May 11, 1993, following regional and local elections on November 29–December 4, 1992 After SWAPO gained control of 12 of the 13 regional councils in balloting on November 30–December 1, 2004, the distribution of seats in the National Council was as follows: South West Africa People's Organization of Namibia, 24; the Democratic Turnhalle Alliance of Namibia, 1; and the United Democratic Front, 1.

President: Asser Kuveri KAPERE.

National Assembly. The 72 members of the current lower house were initially elected on November 7–11, 1989, to the Namibian Constituent Assembly, which at independence assumed the functions of an ordinary legislature with a five-year mandate. Following the most recent balloting of November 27–28, 2009, the distribution of seats was as follows: the South West Africa People's Organization of Namibia, 54; Rally for Democracy and Progress, 8; Democratic Turnhalle Alliance of Namibia, 2; National Unity Democratic Organization, 2; United Democratic Front, 2; All People's Party, 1; Republican Party, 1; Congress of Democrats, 1; and South West Africa National Union, 1. In addition to the elected members, up to 6 nonvoting members may be named by the president.

Speaker: Dr. Theo-Ben GURIRAB.

CABINET

[as of November 15, 2013]

Prime Minister	Hage Geingob
Deputy Prime Minister	Marco Hausiku
Ministers	
Agriculture, Water, and Rural Development	John Mutorwa
Attorney General	Albert Kawana
Defense	Nahas Gideon Angula
Education	David Namwandi
Environment and Tourism	Uahekua Herunga
Finance	Saara Kuugongelwa-Amadhila [f]
Fisheries and Marine Resources	Bernard Esau
Foreign Affairs	Netumbo Nandi-Ndaitwah [f]
Health and Social Services	Richard Kamwi
Home Affairs and Immigration	Pendukeni Iivula-Ithana [f]
Information and Communication Technology	Joel Kaapanda
Justice	Utoni Nujoma
Labor	Doreen Sioka [f]
Lands, Resettlement, and Rehabilitation	Alpheus Naruseb
Mines and Energy	Isak Katali
Presidential Affairs	Albert Kawana
Regional and Local Government and Housing	Maj. Gen. (Ret.) Charles Namoloh
Safety and Security	Immanuel Ngatjizeko
Trade and Industry	Calle Schlettwein
Veterans Affairs	Nickey Iyambo
Women's Affairs and Child Welfare	Rosalia Nghidinwa [f]
Works and Transport	Errki Nghimtina
Youth, Sport, and Culture	Jerry Ekandjo

[f] = female

Note: All ministers are members of SWAPO.

INTERGOVERNMENTAL REPRESENTATION

Ambassador to the U.S.: Martin ANDJABA.

U.S. Ambassador to Namibia: Wanda NESBITT.

Permanent Representative to the UN: Wilfried EMVULA.

IGO Memberships (Non-UN): AfDB, AU, Comesa, CWTH, NAM, SADC, WTO.

NAURU

Republic of Nauru
Naoero

Political Status: Independent republic since January 31, 1968; special membership in the Commonwealth changed to full membership on May 1, 1999.

Area: 8.2 sq. mi. (21.3 sq. km).

Population: 10,086 (2011C); 9,434 (2013E—U.S. Census).

Major Urban Centers: None; the Domaneab ("meeting place of the people"), which is the site of the Nauru Local Government Council, is located in Uaboe District, while government offices are located in Yaren District.

Official Languages: Nauruan. English is widely spoken and is used for most governmental and commercial purposes.

Monetary Unit: Australian Dollar (market rate November 1, 2013: 1.06 Australian dollar = $1 US).

President: Baron WAQA; elected by Parliament on June 11, 2013, following legislative elections on June 8 and inaugurated the same day to succeed Sprent DABWIDO.

THE COUNTRY

An isolated coral island in the west-central Pacific, Nauru is located just south of the equator between the Marshall Islands and Solomon Islands. The present population consists of approximately 60 percent indigenous Nauruans (a mixture of Micronesian, Melanesian, and Polynesian stocks), 25 percent other Pacific islanders, 8 percent Chinese, and 7 percent Caucasians (primarily from Australia). Habitation is mainly confined to a fertile strip of land ringing a central plateau composed of very high-grade phosphate deposits. For several decades this mineral wealth yielded one of the world's highest per capita incomes, which, however, declined from a peak of over $17,000 in 1975 to, by some estimates, less than $3,000 in 2007.

Income from the government-owned Nauru Phosphate Company was intended to provide an investment fund against the time when the phosphate deposits would be exhausted. However, the economy fell into crisis in the second half of the 1990s as the phosphate deposits began to be depleted and the phosphate trust assets were squandered in a series of failed investments. To compensate, Nauru turned to offshore banking accounts, which, however, led to accusations by the Organization for Economic Cooperation and Development (OECD) and others that Nauru had become a center for tax evasion and money laundering. (Russian deposits alone amounted to $70 billion, according to the U.S. Treasury Department.)

Parliament passed an anti–money laundering bill in August 2001, but Nauru remained on the OECD's uncooperative list because of little concrete action against an estimated 400 shell banks. In March 2003 offshore banking was outlawed in Nauru, but the action failed to dispel recurrent charges of corruption that yielded an average of two executive turnovers a year in the period 1999–2004. It was not until May 2008 that the OECD indicated partial acceptance of the anticorruption effort by withdrawing two of its reporting and compliance conditions.

In 2011 a state-sponsored company in Nauru received one of the first contracts issued by the International Seabed Authority for mineral exploration in the deep sea. In mid-2012 the government announced that it believed that phosphate production ($59 million for the fiscal year ending in July 2012) could actually begin to expand again soon. Significant revenue was also anticipated from the controversial detention centers opened on Nauru by Australia to process asylum seekers (see Political background and Current issues, below). However, Nauru continued to struggle with a number of long-term issues, including high unemployment (as much as 40 percent according to some estimates), the threat of inundation from global warming, and a lack of arable land that has necessitated reliance on imports for 90 percent of the island's food.

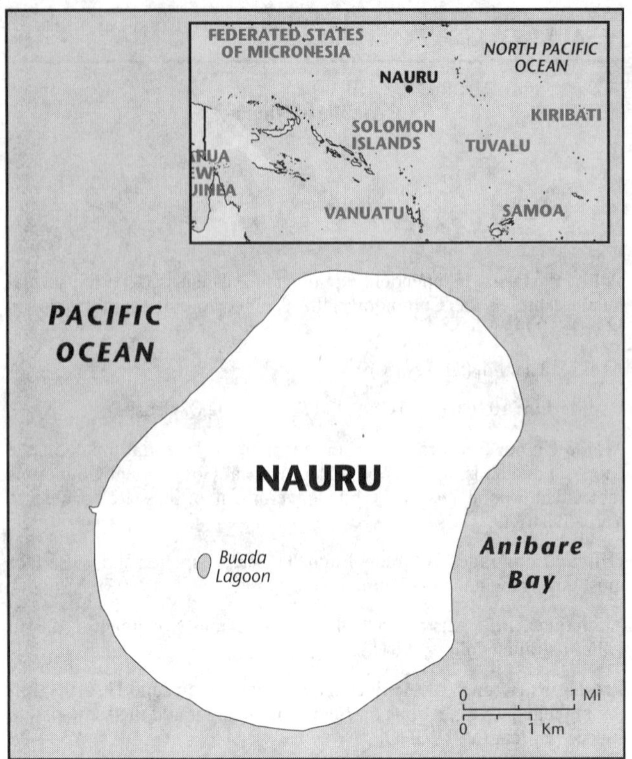

GOVERNMENT AND POLITICS

Political background. A former German colony, Nauru became a British League of Nations mandate in 1919, with Australia as the administering power. The Japanese occupied the island during World War II and transported most of the inhabitants to Truk, where fewer than two-thirds survived the hardships of forced labor. In 1947 Nauru was made a UN Trust Territory under joint administration of the United Kingdom, Australia, and New Zealand, with Australia again serving as de facto administering authority. Local self-government was gradually accelerated, and in 1966 elections were held for members of a Legislative Council that held jurisdiction over all matters except defense, external affairs, and the phosphate industry. Pursuant to that council's request for full independence, Australia adopted the Nauru Independence Act in November 1967, and the trusteeship agreement was formally terminated by the United Nations, effective January 31, 1968. The arrangements for independence were negotiated by a delegation led by Hammer DeROBURT, who had been head chief of Nauru since 1956 and who became the new republic's first president by legislative designation on May 18, 1968.

President DeRoburt, reelected in 1971 and 1973, was replaced by Bernard DOWIYOGO following a legislative election in December 1976.

Although reconfirmed following a parliamentary election in November 1977, President Dowiyogo resigned in January 1978 because of a deadlock over budgetary legislation. He was immediately reelected but resigned again in mid-April after the opposition had blocked passage of a bill dealing with phosphate royalties. Dowiyogo was succeeded by Lagumot HARRIS, who in turn resigned on May 11 because of an impasse on an appropriations bill. Harris was succeeded, on the same day, by former president DeRoburt, apparently as the result of a temporary defection by an opposition representative.

President DeRoburt was reelected in 1980 and 1983, but he was forced to yield office temporarily to Kennan Ranibok ADEANG during a ten-day loss of his parliamentary majority in October 1986 and for a four-day period in the wake of an election on December 6. DeRoburt was sworn in for a ninth term on January 27, 1987, following redesignation by a new parliament elected three days earlier.

President DeRoburt again fell victim to a no-confidence vote on August 17, 1989, Kenas AROI being designated his successor. However, Aroi was obliged to resign on December 12 to seek medical treatment in Australia, and Dowiyogo returned for a third time as chief executive.

Legislative balloting on November 15, 1992, yielded a standoff between supporters of President Dowiyogo and Beraro DETUDAMO, a protégé of former president DeRoburt, who had died on July 15. After intense negotiations, Dowiyogo succeeded in forging a ten-member coalition of the nominally independent members.

On November 22, 1995, following a legislative poll the day before, Parliament reelected former president Lagumot Harris over Dowiyogo by a 9–8 vote. However, Dowiyogo was reappointed by Parliament on November 7, 1996, only to be ousted himself on November 26 in favor of Adeang, who in turn lost a confidence motion soon thereafter, prompting the appointment of Reuben KUN as acting president. Following new legislative elections on February 8, 1997, Kinza CLODUMAR, a former finance minister, was named president on February 12. He was ousted by a no-confidence vote on June 17, 1998, and was succeeded by Dowiyogo, who assumed office for a fifth term. Dowiyogo himself lost a no-confidence motion on April 27, 1999, and was succeeded by René HARRIS, a member of Parliament since 1977 and former head of Nauru's national phosphate corporation.

President Harris was reelected following legislative balloting on April 8, 2000, but he was obliged to resign on April 19 because of factional differences, with Dowiyogo being returned to office on April 20. Dowiyogo's sixth term in office ended with passage of a no-confidence motion on March 30, 2001, at which time René Harris resumed the presidency.

President Harris was defeated in a no-confidence vote on January 8, 2003, with Dowiyogo sworn in as his successor the following day. However, the Nauru Supreme Court (sitting in Australia) ruled that the vote for Dowiyogo was invalid because it had been called without the presence of Harris and his ministers. With the Harris group in attendance, the vote was split 9–9. Following a period of confusion that included Harris's return to the presidency for one day, Dowiyogo defeated Clodumar on a 9–8 vote and was reinvested on January 20. However, Dowiyogo died after undergoing heart surgery in Washington, D.C., on March 20, and he was succeeded on an acting basis by Derog GIOURA.

Another general election was held on May 3, 2003, and on May 29 Ludwig SCOTTY was installed as president. On August 8 Scotty was ousted and replaced by Harris; however, on June 22, 2004, Harris was in turn replaced by Scotty. On October 1, Scotty dissolved Parliament, and in the ensuing general election on October 23 he was accorded a new majority that permitted his reinvestiture. Scotty was again reconfirmed on August 28, 2007, following an early legislative poll on August 24, but he lost a no-confidence vote on December 18 and was succeeded the following day by Marcus STEPHEN.

President Stephen, after declaring a state of emergency because of a parliamentary impasse, survived a snap election on April 26, 2008, and was reinvested on April 28. The standoff continued through 2009, leading to a bizarre sequence of events in 2010. Stephen survived a no-confidence vote on February 18, then attempted to secure passage of a constitutional amendment that, inter alia, would have provided for a popularly elected chief executive. Failing to obtain the bill's approval (see Constitution and government, below), Stephen called for an election on April 24, which yielded no change in parliamentary representation. On May 13, a new speaker, Godfrey THOMA, was named, after which the president proposed the creation of a 19th legislative seat to avoid a repeat of the earlier impasse. The effort failed, however, and Thoma resigned. Two legislators crossed the aisle on June 1 to elect Dominic TABUNA as Thoma's successor. However, Tabuna himself stepped down on June 3, and another election was held on June 19 that yielded one new legislator.

On July 7, 2010, the president extended the state of emergency. Two days earlier, Aloysius AMWAN had been named speaker after securing a pledge from Stephen that he would stand down. Instead, the president, in an action ultimately securing judicial approval, removed Amwan from office, and on August 2 Stephen extended the state of emergency for another 21 days. On November 1, former president Ludwig Scotty accepted designation as speaker, thus eliminating the parliamentary deadlock by restoring the government's slim majority, and Stephen was again confirmed as president.

President Stephen resigned on November 10, 2011. Frederick PITCHER, who had resigned from Stephen's cabinet earlier in the year but had remained a government supporter, was elected president the same day by a vote of 9–8 in Parliament. However, Pitcher lost a confidence vote five days later and was succeeded by Sprent DABWIDO, who was elected by the usual 9–8 vote after he switched his allegiance to the opposition. Dabwido appointed a number of opposition legislators to his new cabinet with the stated hope of achieving the constitutional reform deemed critical in establishing political stability. That concept failed, however, and on June 11, 2012, Dabwido dismissed the cabinet and brought former president Stephen and several of Stephen's former cabinet members back into the government. Dabwido was succeeded on June 11, 2013, by Baron WAQA following legislative elections that were held on June 8 in the wake of a complicated constitutional wrangle (see Current issues, below).

Constitution and government. Nauru's constitution, adopted by an elected Constitutional Convention on January 29, 1968, and amended on May 17 of the same year, provides for a republic whose president combines the functions of head of state and chief of government. The unicameral Parliament selects the president (for a three-year term) from among its membership; the president in turn appoints a number of legislators to serve as a cabinet that is responsible to Parliament and is obligated to resign as a body in the event of a no-confidence vote.

The island is administratively divided into 14 districts, which are regrouped into 8 districts for electoral purposes. An elected Local Government Council of nine members (one of whom is designated Head Chief) shares administrative responsibilities with Parliament. The court system is headed by a Supreme Court.

In April 2007 voters went to the polls to elect members of a constitutional convention to debate the findings of an independent Commission on Constitutional Review appointed a year earlier to assess the country's 39-year-old basic law. In its report, the commission recommended that the president be popularly elected, that the legislative speaker not be a member of Parliament, that a Public Service Commission be established, that an independent director of audit be appointed, that judicial appeals to the High Court of Australia be abolished, and that the language in the basic law regarding human rights be expanded. After acceptance by the convention, the recommendations were unanimously approved by Parliament in August 2009. However, some of the proposed changes (most notably the one concerning the election of the president) required endorsement in a national referendum, and voters rejected them with a 67 percent "no" vote on February 27, 2010.

A constitutional reform package was narrowly rejected by Parliament in June 2012, but the government pledged to pursue the proposed changes as individual pieces of legislation. Consequently, in July the Parliament agreed to increase the number of legislators to 19 in order to resolve a problem associated with the provision that the speaker (chosen from the members of Parliament) votes only in case of a tie vote among the other legislators. (Prior to the membership expansion, in a Parliament divided politically on a 9–9 basis, the side electing the speaker paradoxically fell into minority status.)

Nauru has generally received a satisfactory rating regarding freedom of the press, although complaints were lodged against the government in 2013 for alleged interference in reporting on controversial issues.

Foreign relations. Relations with the Commonwealth were initially defined by an agreement announced on November 29, 1968, whereby Nauru became a "special member" entitled to full participation in the organization's activities, except meetings of the heads of government. Nauru also maintains formal diplomatic relations with about a dozen foreign governments, primarily through representatives accredited to Australia and Fiji. Long a member of the UN Economic and Social Commission for Asia and the Pacific and of the South Pacific Forum (SPF, now the Pacific Islands Forum), Nauru acceded in August 1982 to the South Pacific Regional Trade Agreement, under which Australia and New Zealand had agreed to permit the duty-free entry of a wide variety of goods from SPF member countries. Its principal international tie, however, has been with the Commonwealth (in which Nauru was accorded full membership in 1999).

In January 1992 Nauru joined with sister island nations Kiribati and Tuvalu, and the New Zealand dependencies of the Cook Islands and Niue, to form a Small Island States (SIS) grouping to address a number of common concerns, including global warming, the negotiation of fishing rights in their 200-mile Exclusive Economic Zones (EEZs), and the possibility of renting airspace to planes overflying their countries.

During 1995 Nauru adopted the hardest line of all regional countries in opposing France's decision to resume nuclear testing at Mururoa Atoll in September. Among other things, President Dowiyogo, who had previously supported New Zealand's World Court bid to stop the tests, traveled to Paris with other regional leaders in an unsuccessful effort to secure cancellation.

In January 1998, on the 30th anniversary of Nauru's independence, President Clodumar announced that the country would apply for membership in the United Nations. A formal request was issued in April 1999 with admittance to the world body in September.

In July 2002 Nauru and the Republic of China (Taiwan) ended two decades of diplomatic relations as the Harris government and the People's Republic of China (PRC) agreed to establish formal ties. The Harris administration, attempting to justify its about-face, cited the alleged interference of a Taiwanese envoy in a recent parliamentary by-election, although most observers attributed the shift to an expectation that Beijing would provide substantially more economic aid than Taipei.

Subsequently, Nauru entered into a series of agreements with Australia for the detention of large numbers of "boat people" whom Canberra did not wish to admit as refugees. The arrangements, part of Australia's "Pacific Solution" for migrants, were not intended to be permanent, and in late 2003 a group of detainees staged a hunger strike to press consideration of their claim by Canberra. The strike was called off in early 2004, after Australia agreed to review their cases and New Zealand said it would accept some of the refugees on humanitarian grounds. Subsequently, in another decision with broad economic implications, the Scotty administration in Nauru resumed relations with Taiwan in 2005, arguing that the PRC had provided little aid since 2002.

Australia closed the detention center on Nauru in 2007, thereby negatively affecting Nauru's economy, which had benefited from payments of an estimated A$100 million over a six-year period. As a result, Canberra agreed to fund a limited resumption of phosphate mining and provide A$29 million in developmental assistance for fiscal 2009.

In late 2009 Nauru, apparently at Russia's request, became one of the few countries to formally recognize the independence of the Georgian breakaway republics of Abkhazia and South Ossetia. Reports subsequently surfaced that Russia had agreed to give Nauru $50 million for infrastructure improvement. Nauru's reputation for "checkbook diplomacy" was also underscored by allegations that government ministers and legislators were continuing to receive substantial monthly payments from Taiwan.

In the second half of 2011 discussion took place over the possible reopening of the Australian detention center in Nauru. In September possibly to facilitate such a decision, Nauru became a party to the UN Convention on Refugees, which, among other things, sets minimum standards that would have to be met at the reopened center. (Activists argued that the earlier experience in Nauru had been "a disaster" marked by rampant human rights abuses.) Australia and Nauru concluded an agreement in mid-2012 to reestablish a "processing center" on Nauru for the asylum seekers, as the Australian government adopted the policy that none of the boat people would be allowed to settle in Australia. By mid-2013 two centers (housing some 400 asylum seekers) were being operated on Nauru (in addition to similar operations in Papua New Guinea), and a third was being planned.

Current issues. President Stephen's resignation in November 2011 was reportedly prompted by a looming nonconfidence motion being promoted by opposition legislator David ADEANG, who reportedly questioned Stephen's interactions with foreign phosphate dealers. However, new president Pitcher described the criticism of Stephen as unwarranted and retained Stephen in his cabinet. Consequently, Adeang quickly announced his opposition to Pitcher, who was forced out after only five days in office. Adeang was included in the cabinet subsequently named by new president Dabwido, who said he had joined the opposition in the hope of getting legislation approved that would eliminate the nation's "revolving-door presidency." That goal remained as elusive as ever, however, and Dabwido realigned with Stephen and his supporters in June 2012.

President Dabwido dismissed two of his six cabinet ministers in early 2013, and two others resigned, leaving the Parliament fractionalized and the government ineffective. Consequently, Dabwido asked Speaker Ludwig Scotty to dissolve Parliament and set a date for early elections. Scotty, also citing "unruly" behavior on the part of some legislators, ordered the dissolution on April 1, refusing to permit debate on the matter. The lack of debate proved significant as opposition legislators demanded the opportunity to present a no-confidence motion against the Dabwido administration rather than proceed directly to elections. Based on their appeal, the Supreme Court overturned the initial dissolution decree and another announced by Scotty in mid-March. Godfrey THOMA was elected as the new speaker in April, and in May he reluctantly ordered another dissolution in the face of a continued boycott of proceedings by pro-Dabwido legislators. Thoma initially set the new elections for June 22, but on May 27 President Dabwido declared a state of emergency, arguing that the proposed date would compromise access to budget funds. Setting a new election for June 8, he also decreed a temporary ban on constitutional rulings from the Supreme Court and dismissed the speaker.

Seven of the 19 successful candidates in the June 8, 2013, legislative balloting were new to Parliament, suggesting potential relief from the country's longstanding political gridlock. Similar hopes were expressed when Baron Waqa, a former education minister, was subsequently elected president by a vote of 13–5. Waqa called for better communication between the government and the populace, particularly in regard to the Australian detention centers (see Foreign relations, above). That issue attracted even greater attention when asylum seekers at one of the centers rioted at the end of July (causing an estimated $60 million in damage), and reports circulated that some of the asylum seekers might eventually be permitted to settle in Nauru despite apparent popular opposition to such a policy.

POLITICAL PARTIES

Until 1976 there were no political parties in Nauru. Following the election of December 1976 at least half of the new Parliament claimed membership in the Nauru Party, a loosely structured group led by Bernard Dowiyogo and consisting primarily of younger Nauruans opposed to some of President DeRoburt's policies. The grouping won 9 of 18 seats in the election of November 1977 but became moribund thereafter.

Following the election of January 1987, it was reported that eight members of Parliament had joined an opposition Nauru Democratic Party under the leadership of former president Kennan Adeang. A subsequent report indicated that Dowiyogo's supporters had formed a Democratic Party, with supporters of former president Lagumot Harris having launched another Nauru Party. None, however, developed into effective organizations.

In 2001 a Nauru First (*Naoero Amo*) party was organized by a group of activists, including David ADEANG, Dr. Kieren KEKE, and Marlene MOSES, in opposition to both the Dowiyogo and René Harris camps. A second new formation, the Center Party, also emerged under the leadership of former president Kinza Clodumar. However, neither group appears to have been referenced recently.

LEGISLATURE

The unicameral **Parliament** comprises 19 members (raised from 18 in 2012) directly elected in eight districts for a three-year term, subject to dissolution. Voting is compulsory for those over 20 years of age. The speaker only votes in case of a tie vote among the other legislators. The most recent election was on June 8, 2013.

Speaker: Ludwig SCOTTY.

CABINET

[as of August 1, 2013]

President	Baron Waqa
Ministers	
Assistant to the President	David Adeang
Climate Change	Baron Waqa
Commerce, Industry, and Environment	Aaron Cook
Education	Charmaine Scotty [f]
Finance and Sustainable Development	David Adeang
Fisheries	Valdon Dowiyogo
Foreign Affairs and Trade	Baron Waqa
Health	Valdon Dowiyogo
Home Affairs	Charmaine Scotty [f]
Justice	David Adeang
Land Management	Charmaine Scotty [f]
Nauru Rehabilitation Corporation	Aaron Cook
Nauru Royalties Trust	Shadlog Bernicke
Nauru Utilities Corporation	Shadlog Bernicke
Phosphate	Aaron Cook
Police and Emergency Services	Baron Waqa
Public Service	Baron Waqa
Sports	Valdon Dowiyogo
Telecommunications	Shadlog Bernicke

[f] = female

INTERGOVERNMENTAL REPRESENTATION

Ambassador to the U.S. and Permanent Representative to the UN: Marlene MOSES.

U.S. Ambassador to Nauru: Frankie Annette REED (resident in Fiji).

IGO Memberships (Non-UN): ADB, CWTH, ICC, PIF.

NEPAL

Federal Democratic Republic of Nepal
Sanghiya Loktantrik Ganatantra Nepal

Note: Elections for the Constituent Assembly were held on November 19, 2013. The Nepali Congress won 196 of 601 seats, followed by the Communist Party of Nepal (Unified Marxist-Leninist) with 175. As of January 7, 2014, the Nepali Congress was in discussions to form a new government..

Political Status: Independent monarchy established 1769; limited constitutional system promulgated December 16, 1962; constitutional monarchy proclaimed under constitution of November 9, 1990; interim constitution promulgated January 15, 2007, changing country's official name from Kingdom of Nepal to State of Nepal; monarchy formally ended and federal democratic republic proclaimed May 28, 2008, by a Constituent Assembly.

Area: 54,362 sq. mi. (140,797 sq. km).

Population: 31,164,915 (2012E—UN); 30,430,267 (2013E—U.S. Census).

Major Urban Center (2010E): KATHMANDU (990,000).

Official Language: Nepali.

Monetary Unit: Nepalese Rupee (market rate November 1, 2013: 99.15 rupees = $1US).

President: Ram Baran YADAV (Nepali Congress); elected by the Constituent Assembly on July 21, 2008, and sworn in on July 23, following the abolition of the monarchy on May 28, and the abdication of King GYANENDRA on June 11.

Vice President: Paramananda JHA (Madhesi People's Rights Forum Nepal), elected by the Constituent Assembly on July 19, 2008, and sworn in on July 23.

Prime Minister: Khil Raj REGMI, sworn in as leader of the interim election council on March 14, 2013; succeeding Baburam BHATTARAI (Unified Communist Party of Nepal [Maoist]); elected prime minister by the Constituent Assembly on August 28, 2011.

THE COUNTRY

Landlocked between India and Tibet in the central Himalayas, Nepal encompasses three distinct geographic zones: a southern plain known as the Terai, a central hill region with many rivers and valleys, and a northern section dominated by the Himalaya Mountains. The country is inhabited by more than 50 tribes, who fall into two main ethnic groupings, Mongolian and Indo-Aryan. The majority of the population, particularly in the south, is Hindu in religion and linked in culture to India. The northern region, adjoining Tibet, is mainly Buddhist, but throughout the country Hindu and Buddhist practices have intermingled with each other and with shamanism. In 2008

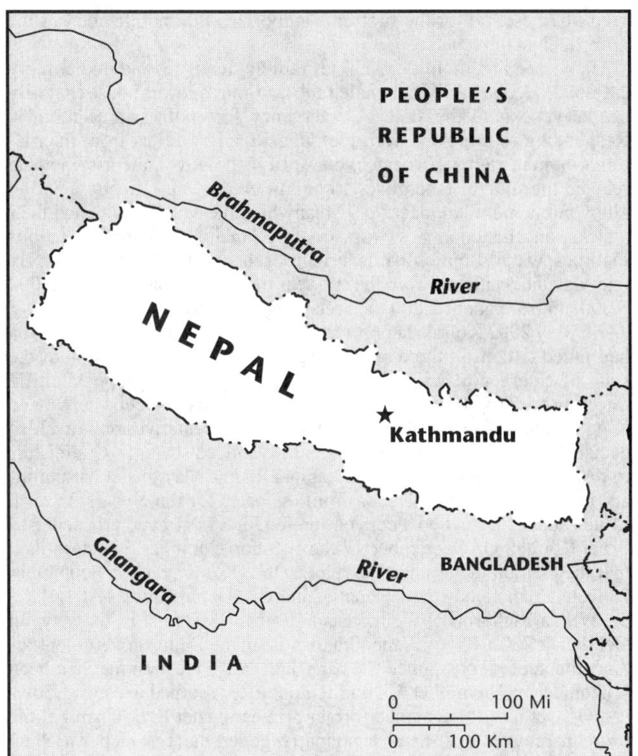

women constituted 45 percent of the active labor force, mostly in agriculture; however, female participation in government has been minimal, although after the 2008 balloting, women constituted 33.2 percent of the members of the national legislature.

With gross national income per capita of approximately $524 in 2010 and with 50 percent illiteracy (higher for females), Nepal is considered one of the world's least developed nations. Moreover, Nepal suffers from a severely unequal distribution of wealth: according to some estimates, average income in the "hill country" is less than 10 percent that of the capital region.

Agriculture continues to employ 75 percent of the labor force and to account for about 35 percent of GDP. Industry, which contributes 16 percent of GDP, is oriented toward processed foods and other nondurable consumer goods, industrial development being hindered by rudimentary communication and transportation facilities. Natural resources include timber (despite extensive deforestation in some areas), mica, and coal, while there is increasing emphasis on the export potential of hydropower. At present, leading exports include woolen carpets, ready-made clothing, and such agricultural products as pulses, jute, and grain. Another significant source of foreign exchange is remittances from Nepalese employed abroad.

Annual GDP growth averaged about 3 percent in 2003–2007. After GDP growth rose to 6.1 percent in 2008 on the strength of a good growing season, more tourism, and the end of a decade-old Maoist insurgency, the rate of growth slipped to 4.4 percent in 2009, largely due to a decline in exports and a deceleration in remittances due to the global economic downturn. Growth hovered for the following years. In 2013 GDP increased at a rate of 3.0 percent and inflation was 9.6 percent.

GOVERNMENT AND POLITICS

Political background. Founded in 1769 by the Gurkha ruler Prithvi NARAYAN Shah as a kingdom comprising 46 previously sovereign principalities, Nepal was ruled by Narayan's descendants until the 1840s, when the Rana family established an autocratic system that, under hereditary prime ministers, lasted until 1951. A revolution in 1950, inspired in part by India's independence, restored the power of King TRIBHUVAN Bir Bikram Shah Dev and initiated a period of quasi-constitutional rule that continued after 1955 under the auspices of Tribhuvan's son, King MAHENDRA Bir Bikram Shah Dev.

A democratic constitution promulgated in 1959 paved the way for an election that brought to power the socialist-inclined Nepali Congress (NC) under Biseswar Prasad KOIRALA. In December 1960, however, the king charged the new government with misuse of power, dismissed and jailed its leaders, suspended the constitution, banned political parties, and assumed personal authority. A new constitution promulgated in 1962 and amended in 1967 established a tiered *panchayat* (assembly) system of representative bodies that was held to be more in keeping with Nepal's traditions. The nonparty system encountered persistent opposition, despite reconciliation efforts that included Koirala's release from detention.

King BIRENDRA Bir Bikram Shah Dev, who succeeded to the throne in 1972, accorded high priority to economic development but encountered difficulty in combining monarchial rule with pressures for political liberalization. In 1979, after prolonged demonstrations, King Birendra announced that a referendum would be held to determine whether the nation favored revision of the *panchayat* structure or its replacement by a multiparty system. In May 1980 Nepalese voters rejected reintroduction of a party system, and in December the king proclaimed a number of constitutional changes, including direct, nonparty election to the National Assembly.

In the wake of economic distress caused by the March 1989 lapse of crucial trade and transit treaties with India (see Foreign relations, below), the banned NC called for dissolution of the government. The NC and seven communist groups joined in February 1990 to form a Movement for the Restoration of Democracy that sought multiparty elections and an end to the *panchayat* system. In April King Birendra reluctantly agreed to the appointment of the NC president, Krishna Prasad BHATTARAI, to head an interim cabinet. In May the king declared an amnesty for all political prisoners (most of whom had campaigned for party legalization). Shortly thereafter, he approved the government's nominees to a Constitutional Recommendation Commission and in September accepted the commission's draft of a new basic law, formally promulgated on November 9.

On May 12, 1991, in the country's first multiparty general election since 1959, the NC won control of the new House of Representatives, although Bhattarai lost his seat. As a result, the party's strongly anticommunist general secretary, Girija Prasad KOIRALA (brother of the former prime minister), was named to head a new administration. In July 1994 Koirala submitted his resignation.

In the election held in November 1994 the Communist Party of Nepal (Unified Marxist-Leninist)—CPN (UML) won a plurality of 88 seats in the 205-member lower house, and its leader, Man Mohan ADHIKARI, was sworn in as prime minister. In June 1995, however, the NC tabled a no-confidence motion that the National Democratic Party (*Rastriya Prajatantra* Party—RPP), theretofore a crucial CPN (UML) ally, announced it would support. Two days later, at Adhikari's request, the king dissolved the National Assembly. The action was protested by the NC, the rightist RPP, and the royalist Nepali Goodwill Party (*Nepal Sadbhavana* Party—NSP), which collectively held 106 legislative seats. In August the Supreme Court ruled the action unconstitutional, and the prime minister resigned following rejection of a confidence motion in September. The NC's Sher Bahadur DEUBA then formed the country's first coalition administration, encompassing the NC, RPP, and NSP.

The Deuba coalition government remained vulnerable to potential shifting alliances, especially among the RPP ministers, and the prime minister resigned in March 1997, after losing a confidence motion by two votes. The king invited former prime minister Lokendra Bahadur CHAND (1983–1986, 1990) of the RPP to form a new government, which included the CPN (UML), RPP, and NSP. Following local elections in May, elements within the RPP as well as opposition parties charged the victorious CPN (UML) with having committed election fraud and other irregularities. By late September the RPP had split into factions led by Chand and former prime minister Surya Bahadur THAPA (1963–1964, 1965–1969, 1979–1983). When Chand lost a confidence motion in October, he resigned, and Thapa became prime minister for the fourth time, naming a new government that included the RPP and NSP. The NC subsequently joined the cabinet in another reshuffle, but the coalition remained unstable, and in January 1998 Thapa asked the king to dissolve the parliament and call new elections. The CPN (UML) and the Chand faction of the RPP objected and instead called for a special legislative session to consider a no-confidence motion. As a result, the RPP expelled the Chand group, which immediately formed a "New RPP." Meanwhile, the king had referred the issue to the Supreme Court, which in February recommended convening the House of Representatives. On February 20 the government survived a no-confidence motion by only three votes. In April, Prime Minister Thapa resigned in accordance with a power-sharing arrangement with the NC.

Former NC prime minister G. P. Koirala was sworn in on April 15, 1998, as the head of a three-person minority government, the NC being the plurality party in the House following a March split in the CPN (UML). The latter party had lost more than half its MPs to a new Communist Party of Nepal (Marxist-Leninist)—CPN (ML) in a dispute over the water-sharing treaty concluded with India in 1996. On April 18 Koirala secured a confidence vote and three days later introduced an expanded cabinet.

A cabinet reshuffle in August 1998 marked formation of an NC-led coalition with the new CPN (ML), which had demanded in return for its support review of the 1950 Indo-Nepal Peace and Friendship Treaty; withdrawal of Indian troops from the disputed Kalapani border area, where they had been posted since the 1962 Sino-Indian war; and repatriation to Bhutan of the nearly 100,000 Bhutanese refugees of Nepali descent who had been sheltered in camps in southeast Nepal since 1990 (see Foreign relations, below). In December, charging that the NC had failed to honor its commitment, the CPN (ML) withdrew from the government, prompting Prime Minister Koirala to recommend that the lower house be dissolved. The NC and the CPN (UML) then agreed to form an interim, pre-election government—Nepal's sixth in four years—that was sworn in with the additional participation of the NSP. The interim administration won a confidence vote in January 1999, and a day later the king dissolved the House of Representatives and announced that a general election would be held in May.

With the left split by the CPN (UML)–CPN (ML) rupture, and with Prime Minister Koirala having announced that he would step aside in favor of his longtime intraparty rival, former prime minister K. P. Bhattarai, the NC swept to victory in the May 3 and 17, 1999, election. The election had been conducted in two phases to ensure adequate security in the western and central regions, site of a Maoist "People's War" insurgency, which largely relied on support from the illiterate, impoverished peasantry in the hinterlands. With the NC having won a majority of 111 seats in the lower house, Bhattarai was sworn in as prime minister on May 31. Nevertheless, internecine warfare continued between NC President Koirala and Prime Minister Bhattarai, even though the two septuagenarians had committed to preparing a "younger generation" of leaders. On March 16, 2000, one day before a scheduled vote by the NC parliamentarians would have ousted him from office, Bhattarai announced to the lower house that he would submit his resignation to the king. On March 18 Koirala easily defeated former prime minister Deuba in the NC's first-ever open leadership election, and on March 20 the king appointed him prime minister for the fourth time.

In February 2001 Koirala included members of Deuba's NC faction in a reshuffled cabinet, but after two months of parliamentary boycotts and disruptions led by the opposition CPN (UML), King Birendra prorogued both houses of the legislature on April 5.

On June 1, 2001, Nepal experienced an unprecedented trauma when Crown Prince DIPENDRA Bikram Shah Dev killed most of the royal family, including King Birendra and Queen AISHWARYA, with an automatic weapon during a family get-together at the palace. Eight died immediately and two others, including Dipendra, who had shot himself, succumbed on June 4. Upon the death of Dipendra, who had been proclaimed king on June 2 despite his comatose state, Prince Regent GYANENDRA Bir Bikram Shah Dev, brother of King Birendra, ascended to the throne. The massacre had apparently originated in the late king and queen's persistent rejection of Dipendra's choice of a bride, whose ancestry they found wanting.

With the kingdom barely recovered from the June tragedy, Prime Minister Koirala resigned on July 19, 2001, having proved unable to quell the Maoist insurgency and to overcome corruption allegations. On July 22 King Gyanendra named the new NC leader, former prime minister Deuba, to head a new government that was sworn in four days later. Upon nomination, Prime Minister Deuba had identified resolving the insurgency as his highest priority, and on July 23 he declared a cease-fire with the rebels. By mid-August Deuba had announced an ambitious series of reforms, including a land redistribution plan to aid the poor (and undercut rural support for the Maoists), a proposal to make discrimination against Dalits (untouchables) a crime, establishment of a National Women's Commission to pursue gender equality, and forward movement on the previous administration's anticorruption bill. The measures, particularly land reform, drew opposition from within his party.

The opening of talks between the Communist Party of Nepal (Maoist) and the government on August 30, 2001, was preceded by mutual prisoner releases, but the two sides failed to make progress before a third round of talks collapsed on November 13. Shortly thereafter the Maoists broke the cease-fire, and on November 26 the king declared a state of emergency; promulgated a Terrorist and Disruptive Activities Ordinance, which defined terrorism and suspended many civil liberties; and for the first time authorized full mobilization of the army against the rebels.

In succeeding months casualties rapidly mounted, and on February 21, 2002, Deuba easily marshaled the two-thirds lower house majority needed to extend the state of emergency for another three months. Responding to criticism from the opposition as well as from international human rights advocates, on April 4 the government somewhat relaxed the state of emergency to permit greater press freedom and to allow public political meetings. Meanwhile, the Maoists widened their attacks on the country's infrastructure, including communications facilities, water supplies, dams, bridges, schools, and health clinics. By late May the death toll from the six-year insurgency had risen to 4,000–5,000, up from about 1,800 the preceding October.

In May 2002 Koirala supporters within the NC, charging that Deuba had failed to consult them before requesting a second extension of the state of emergency, prepared to join the parliamentary opposition in rejecting the proposal. Facing defeat, Prime Minister Deuba convinced King Gyanendra to dissolve the House of Representatives on May 22, a decision that was attacked by most parties and led several NC ministers to resign from Deuba's caretaker cabinet. In late May the NC disciplinary committee expelled Deuba from the party for three years. In turn, Deuba supporters called a convention for June 16–19 and proceeded to expel Koirala. On September 17 the Election Commission determined that the Koirala faction had the right to the NC title, and on September 23 Deuba registered a new Nepali Congress (Democratic)—NC(D).

With a backdrop of the increasingly intense Maoist insurgency, on October 4, 2002, King Gyanendra dismissed the Deuba government for "incompetence," postponed the early legislative election that had been scheduled for November 13, and temporarily assumed executive powers. On October 11 he named former prime minister L. B. Chand of the promonarchy RPP to head a nonparty government, which was then expanded in mid-November. After negotiations with the CPN (Maoist)—CPN-M broke down, Prime Minister Chand resigned on May 30, 2003.

On June 4, 2003, the king named as prime minister the RPP's S. B. Thapa (his fifth term) after rejecting the candidate of a five-party opposition Joint People's Movement (JPM), Madhav Kumar NEPAL, the CPN (UML)'s general secretary. Like its predecessor, the all-RPP cabinet introduced on June 1 was denounced as illegitimate by the NC, the CPN (UML), and the other JPM parties, who accused the king of undermining multiparty democracy through "regression." Many in the opposition advocated recalling the dismissed House of Representatives—although there was no constitutional provision for doing so—as well as forming an all-party government.

A third round of peace talks on August 17–19, 2003, made no significant progress as the Maoists continued to insist that a constituent assembly be elected to draft a new constitution. On August 27 the CPN-M leader, Pushpa Kamal DAHAL (Comrade PRACHANDA), issued a statement announcing an end to both the talks and the cease-fire, and in succeeding months the violence escalated once again as the insurgents demonstrated their ability to attack throughout the country. The CPN-M also continued its efforts to organize administrative machinery in the districts it claimed to control.

On May 7, 2004, Prime Minister Thapa resigned. On June 2 the king reappointed former prime minister Deuba—the country's 14th prime minister in 14 years. Shortly thereafter, the CPN (UML), contending that opposition-supported antigovernment street demonstrations were no longer "meaningful," withdrew from the JPM. On July 5 the Deuba cabinet was expanded to include the CPN (UML), the RPP, and the NSP, in addition to Deuba's NC(D).

At the beginning of 2005 the government remained in disarray. The NC had joined the CPN (UML) in calling for creation of a republic, while other parties had decided to support the Maoists' demand for election of a constituent assembly and their inclusion in an interim government. On February 1 King Gyanendra dismissed the Deuba government, reintroduced a state of emergency, placed many political leaders under house arrest, ordered the army into the streets of the capital, and suspended press and other freedoms. Having vowed to "restore peace and effective democracy in this country within the next three years," on February 2 he named a cabinet of loyalists under his leadership. Although the state of emergency was lifted on April 29, 2005, a number of civil restrictions remained in effect. The cabinet was expanded on July 15 by the addition of several other loyalists.

On May 8, 2005, the country's leading opposition parties announced formation of a "Seven-Party Alliance" (SPA), adopting a roadmap to the restoration of democracy that included reinstating the dissolved House of Representatives and forming a unity government. Participating in the SPA were the NC; the NC(D); the CPN (UML); the NSP (Anandi Devi), an NSP splinter formed in 2003; People's Front Nepal (*Janamorcha Nepal*—JMN); the Nepal Workers' and Peasants' Party (NWPP); and the United Left Front (ULF), at that time a five-party grouping of small communist parties. Together, the SPA parties had held all but about a dozen of the 205 seats in the dissolved House of Representatives.

Responding to prodemocracy overtures from the SPA, on September 3, 2005, the Maoists' Prachanda announced a three-month unilateral cease-fire. Subsequent talks between the SPA and the Maoists led to a November 22 announcement of a 12-point agreement designed to end the king's "autocracy" and move toward election of a constituent assembly. The cease-fire was extended on December 2 but ended on January 2, 2006, because of lack of response by the government.

Municipal elections on February 8, 2006, were boycotted by the SPA, while Maoist threats against candidates and voters contributed to a low turnout. With the Maoists in control of an estimated three-fourths of the countryside and with the roads into Kathmandu again blockaded, the SPA began a general strike on April 6. In the wake of public protests, King Gyanendra on April 24 announced that he would reinstate the House of Representatives and asked the SPA to assume responsibility "for taking the nation on the path to national unity and prosperity, while ensuring permanent peace and safeguarding multiparty democracy." On April 26 the SPA nominated veteran NC leader G. P. Koirala for prime minister, the same day the Maoists announced another cease-fire. The House of Representatives convened on April 28. Two days later, the House unanimously approved a resolution endorsing formation of a constituent assembly.

On May 18, 2006, the House of Representatives assumed all legislative powers; stripped most governmental rights and responsibilities from the king, including his role as commander in chief; and delegated executive authority to a Council of Ministers responsible to the House. In their first face-to-face meeting, held June 16, 2006, Prime Minister Koirala and Comrade Prachanda, joined by other Maoist negotiators and representatives of the SPA, concluded an agreement that called for implementing the November 2005 agreement and a cease-fire code of conduct that had been signed on May 26. The new agreement expressed a commitment to "democratic norms and values" and provided for the immediate drafting of an interim constitution, to be followed by formation of an interim government in which the CPN-M would participate. On November 28 the government and the CPN-M signed, along with a UN representative, a tripartite agreement calling for the Nepalese Army to return to barracks, for the 30,000–40,000 soldiers of the Maoist People's Liberation Army to be confined to several camps, and for a comparable number of arms from each side to be locked away under UN supervision. In all, more than 16,000 people died during the 1996–2006 Maoist insurgency, nearly half of them civilians, with another 1,200 listed as missing and over 70,000 displaced by the fighting. During the last years of the conflict, casualties and reports of human-rights violations by both sides escalated, and difficulties persisted even after the peace accord.

Following protracted negotiations, a draft interim constitution was approved by the SPA and the CPN-M in December 2006 and promulgated on January 15, 2007, by the House of Representatives. The legislature was immediately superseded by a unicameral Interim Legislature-Parliament of 330 members, including 83 representatives of the CPN-M. An Interim Council of Ministers, including Maoists, assumed office on April 1.

An election for a Constituent Assembly to draft a new constitution was set for November 22, 2007, having been postponed from June. However, on September 18 the Maoists resigned from the government over the issue of abolishing the monarchy, and their continuing demands for the declaration of a republic in advance of the referendum contributed to a further postponement of the polling. They subsequently rejoined the government in December, and on December 23, the CPN-M and the government parties signed an agreement that included support for establishing a federal democratic republic at the first meeting of the Constituent Assembly, once its 601 members were chosen. Meanwhile, five small royalist parties formed the United Inclusive Front to oppose the republican trend, and former prime minister Thapa of the RPP campaigned in favor of retaining the monarchy.

The elections to the Constituent Assembly were finally held on April 10, 2008, with the elections commission estimating voter turnout of 60 percent. Both first-past-the-post and proportional representation systems were employed, with the CPN-M winning the most seats (220). On May 28 the assembly voted 560–4 to abolish the monarchy and declared Nepal a federal democratic republic. King Gyanendra confirmed on June 2 that he would abdicate, and he left the palace on June 11. On June 26 Prime Minister Koirala resigned, effective upon the election of a president. On July 19 the assembly elected Paramananda JHA of the Madhesi People's Rights Forum (*Madheshi Janadhikar* Forum—MJF) as vice president, and two days later it chose Ram Baran YADAV (NC) as president. Yadav then asked the CPN-M to form a government, and Pushpa Kamal Dahal was named prime minister on August 18.

Dahal's brief tenure ended in May 2009 in the wake of turmoil over the reintegration of the Maoist People's Liberation Army (PLA), resulting in Dahal's firing the army chief of staff, Gen. Rookmangud KATAWAL, on May 3. On the same day, however, President Yadav overruled Dahal, who resigned on May 4. The Maoists, demanding that the assembly debate the president's action, subsequently obstructed parliament with walkouts and heckling, and slowed the economy with strikes and other demonstrations. With the Maoists boycotting the session, on May 23 the assembly elected Madhav Kumar Nepal of the CPN (UML) as prime minister of a coalition government that also included the NC and the newly formed Madhesi People's Rights Forum (*Madheshi Janadhikar* Forum [Democratic]—MJF-L) as its principal components. Prime Minister Nepal gradually filled out his new government with ministers from additional parties. Meanwhile, the CPN-M merged with smaller parties to create a new grouping, the United Communist Party of Nepal (Maoist)—UCPN-M (see Political Parties, below).

Faced with continuing obstruction by the Maoists, on May 28, 2010, the assembly extended by a year its own term as well as the deadlines for integrating the PLA and completing a new constitution. On June 30 Prime Minister Nepal resigned to make way for a consensus government, but he and his cabinet remained in place pending election of a new prime minister.

After seven months of negotiations, on February 3, 2011, Jhala Nath KHANAL (CPN [UML]) was elected prime minister and sworn into office three days later. However, tensions between Khanal and the UCPN-M, the largest party in the legislature, led to the latter's resignation on August 14. On August 28 Baburam Bhattarai (UCPN-M) was elected prime minister. He formed a coalition government that included the UCPN-M, the newly formed coalition, and the United Democratic Madhesi Front (UDMF). Meanwhile, the Constituent Assembly again extended its term on August 29.

On May 27, 2012, the Constituent Assembly dissolved when the deadline to draft the new Constitution passed. Prime Minister Bhattarai called for elections on November 21, but none were held. President Yadav repeatedly called on party leaders to establish an interim government, which was finally achieved in March when the four largest parties, the UCPN-M, UDMF, NC, and CPN (UML), agreed to appoint chief Justice Khil Raj REGMI leader of a nonpartisan election government (see Current issues, below).

Constitution and government. The *panchayat* system in operation prior to the May 1980 referendum provided for a hierarchically arranged parallel series of assemblies and councils encompassing four different levels: village (*gaun*) and town (*nagar*), district (*jilla*), zone (*anchal*), and national (*Rastriya Panchayat*). The members of the village and town assemblies were directly elected, members of the other bodies being indirectly elected by bodies directly below them in the hierarchy. The constitutional changes introduced in December 1980 provided for direct, rather than indirect, election to a nonpartisan National Assembly; designation of the prime minister by the assembly, rather than by the king; and parliamentary responsibility of cabinet members.

Under the 1990 constitution the remaining vestiges of the *panchayat* system were abandoned in favor of multiparty parliamentary government, with the king's role substantially curtailed. Executive powers were exercised jointly by the king and a Council of Ministers, the latter headed by a prime minister who, although named by the king, had to command a majority in the popularly elected lower house of Parliament, the House of Representatives. An upper chamber, the National Assembly, contained both indirectly elected and nominated members. The constitution could be amended by a two-thirds majority of the lower house, save for entrenched provisions dealing with such matters as human rights, the basic structure of the governmental system, and the rights of parties. Treaties and other major state agreements required approval by a two-thirds majority of both houses in joint session. The judicial hierarchy encompassed district courts, appellate courts, and a Supreme Court with powers of constitutional review.

The May 18, 2006, proclamation by the House of Representatives, which stripped King Gyanendra of his rights and powers, specified that the House was "sovereign... until another constitutional arrangement is made." Executive authority was delegated to the Council of Ministers, which was responsible to the House. The House also assumed full authority over the Nepalese Army (renamed from Royal Nepal Army), made the king's property and income subject to taxation, and declared Nepal to be a secular state. Further, the proclamation declared that the 1990 constitution and prevailing laws "shall be nullified to the extent of inconsistency" with the proclamation. An additional measure passed on June 10 specifically stripped the king of the veto and of his power to sign legislation into law.

The 167-article interim constitution adopted in January 2007 enumerated a wide range of "fundamental rights," including those of free expression, assembly, and equal protection. It endowed the Council of Ministers with executive authority and stated that "no power regarding the governance of the country shall be vested in the king," but it stopped short of naming the prime minister as head of state. The interim constitution also established a unicameral Interim Legislature-Parliament pending election of a Constituent Assembly tasked with determining the fate of the monarchy and drafting a permanent constitution. The existing judicial system was left in place. Amending the interim constitution required a two-thirds vote of the legislature, which in late December 2007 passed an amendment endorsing establishment of a federal republic. The Constituent Assembly, at its inaugural session on May 28, 2008, formally created the republic, abolishing the monarchy entirely after 239 years.

The Fifth Amendment to the interim constitution was approved by the Council of Ministers on June 25, 2008, and adopted by the Constituent Assembly on July 13. This provision allows for the formation of a government through a simple majority vote of the Constituent Assembly. It creates a national president and vice president, although their powers are not specified, executive power being vested in the prime minister. According to the amendment, the president, vice president, prime minister, and Constituent Assembly chair and vice chair are to be selected on the basis of a political understanding; however, if such understanding cannot be reached, they can be elected by a simple majority vote in the assembly. A Constituent Assembly majority is required to remove a prime minister from office through a no-confidence vote. The amendment also stipulates that the leader of the opposition shall be a member of the Constitutional Council, which is responsible for recommending appointees to key posts.

The 1990 constitution endorsed freedom of the press, most importantly by outlawing prior censorship, although on occasion the government attempted to restrict independent media from disseminating news it considered sensationalist or unverified. More severe restrictions accompanied recent states of emergency, and journalists were detained under antiterrorism ordinances and acts. During the Maoist insurgency a significant number were tortured or killed, either by the police and the military for supporting the Maoist cause or by Maoists for spying or other alleged offenses. The 2007 interim constitution lists freedom to publish and broadcast as a fundamental right, subject to "reasonable restrictions on any act which may undermine the sovereignty and integrity of Nepal or which may endanger the harmonious relations subsisting among the peoples of various castes, tribes or communities, or on any act of sedition, defamation, contempt of court or incitement to an offence; or on any act which may be contrary to decent public behavior or morality." Dozens of journalists were threatened or attacked in 2012 by political groups unhappy with coverage leading up to the May 27 constitution vote (see Current issues, below). In 2013 Reporters Without Borders ranked Nepal 118th out of 179 countries in freedom of the press.

Administratively, Nepal is divided into 5 development regions, 14 zones, 75 districts, nearly 4,000 villages, and 36 municipalities. Among the issues the Constituent Assembly must negotiate is the structure of a federal system for the nation, including the number of states or provinces, the borders between them, their relationship to the nation's ethnic composition, and their degree of autonomy.

Foreign relations. Although historically influenced by Britain and subsequently by India, Nepal has endeavored to strengthen its independence, particularly after India's annexation of the adjacent state of Sikkim in 1975. Thus, Kathmandu adopted a policy of nonalignment and has sought a balance in regional relations. Nepalese leaders have moved to involve not only India and China, but also Bangladesh, Bhutan, and Pakistan in cooperative endeavors, with primary emphasis on water resource development.

In November 1979 a major issue in relations with China was apparently resolved when an agreement defining Nepal's northern frontier was signed, seen as a model for settling border disputes China had with India and Bhutan.

In 1989 Nepal and India reached an impasse over trade and transit agreements upon which the Nepalese economy was highly dependent. Factors influencing India's reluctance to renew the treaties included recent Nepalese arms purchases from China, the levying of a 55 percent tariff on Indian goods, and the enactment of legislation requiring non-Nepalese to obtain work permits. The agreements were revived following an announcement by Prime Minister Bhattarai in 1990 that his government had postponed receipt of the latest Chinese arms shipment "to accommodate Indian sensitivities on [the] issue." Additional agreements covering trade, transit, border control, agriculture, and cultural exchanges were signed in December 1991.

In January 1996 the Nepalese and Indian foreign ministers signed an agreement in Kathmandu calling for a joint hydroelectric project in the Mahakali River basin. The $5 billion undertaking was bitterly opposed by a faction of the CPN (UML). The Indo-Nepal Mahakali Integrated Development Treaty was ratified in September.

In the 1990s successive governments expressed concern about an influx of ethnic Nepalese from nearby Bhutan. Although some claimed to be descendants of 19th-century settlers, Bhutanese authorities insisted that most had relocated to Bhutan in the 1980s and were illegal immigrants. After preliminary talks in October 1993, an agreement was reached in April 1994 on how to categorize the more than 90,000 Bhutanese of Nepalese origin stranded in eastern Nepal. However, subsequent bilateral talks failed to resolve the dispute, despite international pressure mounted to address the plight of the refugees living in UN-run camps. As of April 2013 nearly 80,000 had been resettled from the camps, the majority in the United States. (For additional details, see the entry on Bhutan in this edition of the *Handbook.*)

On January 23, 2007, the UN Security Council established a UN Mission in Nepal (UNMIN) to help maintain the cease-fire, monitor sequestration of arms by the Maoists and the Nepalese Army, and oversee the Constituent Assembly election. The UNMIN mandate was repeatedly extended but expired on January 15, 2011. The UCPN-M sought to extend the mission but was blocked in the Constituent Assembly by opposition from the CPN (UML) and the NC, which both supported an immediate cessation of UNMIN.

In June 2011 the UN declared Nepal landmine free following an extensive, five-year international campaign that destroyed more than 8,000 landmines that had been deployed during the Maoist insurgency.

In September 2012 the United States removed the Unified Communist Party of Nepal (Maoist) from its list of terrorist organizations, noting that the party had abandoned its militant past and was taking steps toward reconciliation.

Current issues. On May 3, 2012, Bhattarai's cabinet resigned after the leaders of the major political parties decided to form a new government under national consensus toward the goal of completing a new constitution by the May 27 deadline, a process hindered by failure to agree on the number, boundaries, and names of the country's states. The new national unity government, which included representatives from the country's major parties except the CPN (UML), the unity government failed to meet the deadline, and the legislature was disbanded upon the expiration of their term at midnight on May 27, without option for term extension. Nepal plunged into legal uncertainty, which Bhattarai tried to remedy by calling for elections to be held on November 22. Opposition political leaders meanwhile denounced the move as a power grab.

The UCPN-M ruling party split on June 19 when hard-line party member Mohan BAIDYA Kiran left to form the new Nepal Communist Party (Maoist—NCP-M). Thirty-three members of the UCPN-M defected to the NCP-M on August 25.

In late July Nepal's Election Commission announced confirmed that the country lacked the legal framework to hold legitimate elections on November 21, the date named by Bhattarai, although the elections were not officially postponed until November 20, after the CPN (UML) and the NC refused to take part in polling organized under Maoist leadership. President Yadav called for leaders of the parties to form a unity government by November 29, a deadline twice extended and ultimately unheeded.

Progress came in February 2013, when leaders of the UCPN-M, NC, CPN-UML, and UDMF began negotiating a plan for Chief Justice Khil Raj Regmi to lead a nonpartisan interim government until elections could be held. Talks were temporarily derailed when the UCPN-M demanded that amnesty for past crimes by Maoists be included in the agreement. In a marathon 13-hour session on March 13, the parties agreed to an 11-point pact, addressing the composition of a truth and reconciliation commission and integration of Maoist fighters into the national army, paving way for Regmi to take office on March 14, leading an 11-member cabinet, with the expectation that elections would be held by June 21 (viewed to be ambitious, given that the leading parties had not yet settled on a legal framework). His term ends upon the election of a new government, or in December 2013. The formation of the interim government generated significant opposition, some arguing it to be unconstitutional because it violated separation of powers. Led by the CPN-M, 22 parties protested Regmi's inauguration.

In mid-March the UCPN-M, NC, CPN-UML, and UDMF formed a "high level political committee," chaired on a one-month rotational basis by each party chief. The coalition was highly criticized from the outside as well as from within; in April CPN-UML member Pradip GYANWALI criticized the committee for unconstitutionally ruling the country and shutting other parties out.

Three months after taking office, the Regmi government announced in June that Constituent Assembly elections would take place on November 19, after the promulgation of an amendment removing the stipulation that parties must secure 1 percent of the vote to win a seat in the proportional representation system, a step reportedly taken to ensure all parties' participation in writing the constitution. Three parties—the CPN-M, the Federal Socialist Party Nepal, and the Madhesi Janaadhikar Forum–Nepal—vocally refused to participate in the election in protest of the installation of the Regmi government. By June the election commission reported that 11.7 million of an estimated 15.4 million eligible voters had already registered. (*See headnote.*)

POLITICAL PARTIES

Political formations were banned by royal decree in 1960, although de facto party affiliations continued. The 1990 constitution prohibited restrictions on political parties. At the time of the 1999 election, there were 101 recognized parties, of which 30 offered candidates. Only 6 parties captured 3 percent or more of the vote, a requirement for designation as a "national party."

In May 2003, seven months after King Gyanendra had dissolved the House of Representatives, with no new election in sight, the Nepali Congress (NC), the Communist Party of Nepal (Unified Marxist-Leninist)—CPN (UML), the Nepali Goodwill Party (Anandi Devi), the Nepal Workers' and Peasants' Party (NWPP), and the People's Front Nepal (JMN) formed an opposition Joint People's Movement (JPM) that won the support of half a dozen other parties. In June 2004 the CPN (UML) left the JPM, and in July it joined a multiparty cabinet that excluded the remaining JPM members. The king's assumption of power in February 2005 led directly to the May 8 formation of the Seven-Party Alliance (SPA) of the original five JPM parties, the NC (Democratic), and the United Left Front of smaller communist parties. The subsequent decision of the king to recall the 1999 House of Representatives put the SPA in power and began the road toward bringing the Communist Party of Nepal (Maoist)—CPN-M into the interim government and electing a Constituent Assembly.

A total of 62 parties applied to the Election Commission for formal recognition prior to the assembly election. By late July 2007 about 40 had been registered and assigned election symbols. A total of 25 parties won seats in the Constituent Assembly, including several new parties.

Government Parties:

Unified Communist Party of Nepal (Maoist)—UCPN-M. Established in 1994 by a breakaway faction of the CPN (Unity Center), in 1996 the CPN-M launched the "People's War" insurgency, which continued and intensified for ten years. In August 2000 the Maoists announced that they had formed a People's Liberation Army (PLA). They also set up a United People's Revolutionary Council as a quasi-central government for the areas under its control.

Despite having rejected previous government overtures, in early 2000 the Maoists indicated they would be willing to open discussions related to a 32-point list of demands. At the first round of peace talks with the Deuba government on August 30, 2001, the Maoist representative Krishna Bahadur Mahara pressed for an end to the monarchy, the formation of an interim government, the establishment of a constituent assembly to draft a new constitution, and the release of all Maoist prisoners. No significant progress was made, and the insurgents abruptly ended a four-month-old cease-fire in November. A January–August 2003 cease-fire and the resultant peace talks also came to nothing, as the Maoists continued their insistence on elections for a constituent assembly. In the following 18 months the insurgency expanded its reach and its tactics, initiating general strikes and, on more than one occasion, blockading Kathmandu.

With opposition to King Gyanendra's "autocratic monarchy" mounting, secret talks between the CPN-M and the SPA began even before a unilateral Maoist cease-fire in September 2005. Further discussions then led to the November 2005 12-point plan for restoring democracy and bringing the CPN-M into the political mainstream. In early May 2006 one of the first measures of the new Koirala government was to end the party's proscription.

The June 16, 2006, eight-point agreement with the new government, accomplished following the first face-to-face meeting between Prime Minister Koirala and Prachanda, granted the Maoists much of what they had been seeking, including the election of a constituent assembly in the near future and a role in an interim government, while committing them to dissolving the rural governments they had formed and to permitting international supervision of their army and weapons prior to the election. A comprehensive peace agreement followed in November, ahead of the promulgation of the interim constitution on January 15, 2007. The CPN-M, effecting a transformation from a guerrilla army to a political party, joined the Interim Legislature-Parliament with 83 seats. In September 2007 the CPN-M withdrew its four ministers from the government, rejoining after securing a commitment from the Council of Ministers to support establishment of a republic.

The Maoists took first place in the election on April 10, 2008, securing 220 of the assembly's 575 elected seats. On August 15 the assembly elected Pushpa Kamal Dahal to the office of prime minister.

In January 2009 the CPN-M merged with the Communist Party of Nepal (Unity Center *Mashal*)—CPN (UCM). (For a history of the latter party, see the People's Front Nepal, below.) Renaming itself the Unified Communist Party of Nepal (Maoist), the party formally renounced the "Prachandapath"—the leader's adaptation of Maoist principles to Nepalese conditions—as its guiding doctrine.

The party advocated for the integration into Nepal's army of its nearly 20,000 PLA combatants, who were confined to temporary quarters under UN monitoring. When President Yadav overturned Prime Minister Dahal's dismissal of the army chief of staff on May 3, 2009, Dahal claimed the move exceeded the president's constitutional authority and threatened civilian control of the military. He resigned the following day, and the party shifted to the opposition, launching intense protests. Maoist partisans stormed the Constituent Assembly on May 18 and boycotted the election for a new prime minister. Following Prime Minister Nepal's resignation at the end of June 2010, Dahal again stepped forward as a candidate for prime minister, but neither he nor anyone else was able to muster the necessary two-thirds support, and Dahal, under increasing criticism for questionable financial dealings, withdrew from consideration on September 26, after seven ballots.

Meanwhile, within the party, former party leader Matrika YADAV in 2009 rejected Dahal's deviation from the revolutionary path and organized a splinter party that adopted the UCPN-M's former name, the **Communist Party of Nepal (Maoist)**. Mani THAPA formed the **Revolutionary Communist Party of Nepal**—RCPN. In November 2010, in the context of an ongoing party plenum, the hard-liner Mohan BAIDYA Kiran called for a renewal of the people's revolt, while Baburam Bhattarai advocated moderation. Both viewed Dahal as dictatorial and questioned his integrity. Bhattarai was elected prime minister in August 2011, after Dahal agreed to withdraw from balloting in the Constituent Assembly. The party split in June 2012, as the dissenting faction formed the **Communist Party of Nepal (Maoist)** (below).

In February 2013 Bhattarai agreed to resign as prime minister to make way for Chief Justice Regmi to lead the interim government, a decision backed by the party. In March the UCPN-M joined the NC, CPN-UML, and UDMF in forming the High Level Political Committee (HLPC). Both decisions spurred dissent within the party, with many concerned about the constitutionality of Regmi's government, and the exclusion of smaller parties from the committee.

Leaders: Baburam BHATTARAI (Prime Minister and Vice Chair), Pushpa Kamal DAHAL (a.k.a. Comrade PRACHANDA; Chair and Former Prime Minister), Nanda Kishor PUN (Commander, PLA).

Communist Party of Nepal (Maoist)—CPN-M. Former UCPN-M member and communist hard-liner Baidya led a dissenting faction of the ruling Maoist party to form the CPN-M in June 2012. Baidya asserted that the party had strayed from its roots by accepting a parliamentary system and the integration of the military. In August, 33

UCPN-M members publicly defected to the fledgling party, but stayed loyal to Bhattarai. The parties diverged in March 2013 when Baidya led 22 parties in protest against the installation of the Regmi government. In June the CPN-M led a 33-party alliance in agreeing to boycott the November elections, complaining that the big parties had shut them out of the process. In July Baidya said that he would consider working with the former king ahead of the November election.

Leaders: Mohan BAIDYA Kiran (Chair), Netra Bikram CHANDRA (Secretary).

Madhesi People's Rights Forum (*Madheshi Janadhikar* Forum—MJF). The MJF began in 1997 as a civic organization advocating for the rights of the Madhesis—the indigenous people who make up the majority in Nepal's southern plain—to self-determination. The MJF organized an uprising and general strike in January 2007, in protest against the interim constitution, which they said ignored the interests of the marginalized groups. The situation in the Terai escalated into violence that claimed roughly 50 lives.

In August 2007, despite some factional opposition, the MJF signed an agreement with the government on 22 points. Later, the MJF declared that the government had failed to fulfill the terms of the agreement and called for militant protests around November 22, the scheduled date for the Constituent Assembly election. A second wave of violence arose in the Terai in February 2008.

After the uprising, the government agreed to several of the UDMF's demands, including the creation of an autonomous Madhesi state. The UDMF parties were also allowed to register for the Constituent Assembly election, although the deadline had passed. In its first electoral contest the MJF won 52 seats, making it the fourth largest party in the assembly, and it then joined the government led by the Maoists. Party leader Upendra Yadav was named foreign minister.

Following Prime Minister Dahal's resignation in May 2009, the incoming prime minister Nepal offered the deputy prime minister position to Bijaya Kumar Gachchhadar, the leader of the MJF parliamentary group, without the approval of the MJF executive committee. This led to a bitter division, resulting in the expulsion of Gachchhadar and six others. Gachchhadar, however, claimed the support of the majority of the party's lawmakers. His faction continued to participate in the government and later received additional ministerial portfolios (see MJF-L, above). Yadav accused the leaders of the CPN (UML) and NC of intentionally provoking a split in the MJF and joined the opposition. In February 2008 the MJF and its breakaway factions joined with the Sadbhavana Party—SP and the Terai Madhesh Democratic Party (*Tarai Madhesh Loktantrik* Party—TMLP) (below) to form the **United Democratic Madhesi Front**—UDMF, which negotiated an agreement to join the UCPN-M government.

After movements in summer 2013 toward a unification of Madhesi parties, Yadav pulled the MJF out of negotiations with the TMLP (below), noting that an alliance of Madhes parties should be policy based.

Leader: Upendra YADAV (Chair).

Madhesi People's Rights Forum (Democratic) (*Madheshi Janadhikar* Forum [*Loktantrik*]—MJF-L). Formed by a fissure in the indigenous MJF (below), the MJF-L was established in mid-2009 after Bijaya Kumar Gachchhadar had accepted the position of deputy prime minister under Madhav Kumar Nepal. The MJF leadership had asked Nepal not to appoint any party member without their formal approval. Gachchhadar, who had previously belonged to the NC and then the NC(D), refused to decline the high office and claimed leadership of the party, asserting that a majority of MJF Constituent Assembly members supported him. He and the other dissidents, who included 28 members of the Constituent Assembly, then formed the MJF-L. The MJF-L joined the UCPN-M coalition government in August 2011. Gachchhadar was reappointed deputy prime minister. In July 2012 central committee member Sanjay SHAH defected to join the Sadbhavana Party (below).

Leader: Bijaya Kumar GACHCHHADAR (Chair).

Rastriya Madhes Samajwadi Party. Formed in June 2012 by senior Madhesi leader Sharad Singh Bhandari, the RMS is a splinter group of the MJF-L. Nine party leaders, including Bhandari, were expelled by Deputy Prime Minister Gachchhadar when they refused to support the decision to back Bhattari's call for November 22 elections. In February 2013 Bhandari backed the interim government, arguing for it to remain nonpartisan.

Leader: Sharad Singh BHANDARI (Chair).

Madhesi People's Rights Forum (Republic) (*Madhesi Janadhikar* Forum [*Ganatantrik*]—MJF-G). Formed in May 2011 by Jayaprakash Prasad Gupta, the MJF-G was an offshoot of the MJF. The MJF-G agreed to join the UCPN-M government in August 2011, and party leader Gupta was made minister of information and communication.

Leader: Raj Kishore YADAV (Chair).

Terai Madhesh Democratic Party (*Tarai Madhesh Loktantrik* Party—TMLP). An ethnic and regional party founded in 2008 by former NC leader Mahanta Thakur, the TMLP demands, with the *Sadbhavana* Party—SP (below) and the Madhesi People's Rights Forum—MJF, that Madhesis be granted an autonomous province and that Madhesis and all ethnic groups be given proportional representation in all state organizations. In February 2008 the TMLP joined with the MJF and the SP to form the UDMF.

The party came in fifth in the Constituent Assembly voting, winning 20 seats. It joined the government for the first time in June 2009.

Ahead of the elections expected in November 2013, in June, Thakur urged Madhesi parties to unite in a single alliance. In late July the SP sought unification with the UDMF.

Leader: Mahanta THAKUR (Chair).

Sadbhavana Party (SP). The SP separated from the Nepal Goodwill Party (*Anandi Devi*)—NSP-A (below) in 2007, and in February 2008 it joined the MJF and the TMLP to form the United Democratic Madhesi Front (UDMF).

The SP's leader, Rajendra Mahato, had been general secretary of NSP-A and a cabinet minister. Mahato announced his resignation from the interim parliament on January 19, 2008, accusing the government of ignoring the demands of the Madhesis. He was elected to the Constituent Assembly along with eight others from his party, and he was appointed minister of commerce in the Dahal cabinet. On May 3, 2009, the party withdrew from the Maoist-led government to protest the firing of the army chief of staff.

The party initially chose not to join Prime Minister Nepal's government due to disagreement over how many and which portfolios it would be assigned, but in July 2009 Mahato joined the cabinet. Additional SP members were appointed to the government in September. The SP joined the 2011 UCPN-M government. Meanwhile, reports indicated the emergence of a breakaway faction of the party, calling itself the Federal Sadbhavana Party—FSP. A leader of the FSP, Anil Kumar Jha, was appointed minister of industry in the 2011 government. In January 2012 a faction of the party broke off to form the Rastriya Sadbhavana Party (below).

In July 2013 amid calls for unity among Madhesi parties in the November election, the SP sent a letter seeking unification with the UDMF.

Leaders: Rajendra MAHATO (Chair), Manish SUMAN (General Secretary).

Rastriya Sadbhavana Party (RSP). Gauri Mahato and Ram Naresh Yadav, two lawmakers from the SP, defected in January 2012 to form the RSP. They accused party leader Mahato of nepotism and revenge politics.

Leaders: Gauri MAHATO, Ram Naresh YADAV.

Other Legislative Parties:

Communist Party of Nepal (Unified Marxist-Leninist)—CPN (UML) (*Nepala Kamyunishta Parti* [*Ekikrit Marksbadi ra Leninbadi*]). Sometimes referred to as the United (or Unified) Communist Party of Nepal (UCPN), the CPN (UML) was formed in 1991 by the merger of two factions of the Communist Party of Nepal: the CPN (Marxist) and the CPN (M-L). In April 1990 the CPN (Marxist) and the CPN (ML) had joined with five other leftist formations, three pro-Soviet CPN factions, a pro-Chinese group, and the Nepal Workers' and Peasants' Party (below), in a United Leftist Front (ULF) in support of the restoration of democracy. This diverse grouping became moribund prior to the 1991 poll.

In May 1991 Man Mohan Adhikari was elected head of the CPN (UML) parliamentary group and, therefore, leader of the opposition. Following the November 1994 election, he was sworn in as prime minister of Nepal's first communist government, but he was obliged to resign after losing a no-confidence vote in September 1995. The CPN (UML) subsequently participated in the coalition government formed by Prime Minister Chand in March 1997, before joining that of Prime Minister Koirala in December 1998.

In March 1998 more than half the CPN (UML) legislators reorganized under the former CPN (ML) title to protest the 1996 water-sharing agreement with India. In February 2002 the bulk of the CPN (ML) members rejoined the parent party, although a faction remained independent as the "reconstituted" CPN (ML)—see below.

In April 1999 former prime minister Adhikari, the party's candidate for prime minister in the upcoming election, died. In the May election the CPN (UML) won 71 seats, down from the 88 it had claimed in 1994. In early 2001 the CPN (UML) was largely responsible for the legislative boycotts and disruptions that led the king to prorogue both houses of parliament in April.

The party's former general secretary, Madhav Kumar Nepal, was the principal organizer of the JPM in 2003. Having left the JPM following Prime Minister Deuba's reappointment, in July 2004 the CPN (UML) joined an expanded, four-party cabinet, in which Bharat Mohan Adhikari served as deputy prime minister until the entire government was dismissed on February 1, 2005.

The party won the third highest number of seats in the Constituent Assembly election in April 2008, splitting the left-wing vote with the Maoists and other communist groupings. Jhalanath Khanal was elected party chair at a convention in February 2009, defeating K. P. Oli. The party left the Maoist-led government in May after Prime Minister Dahal, the Maoist leader, dismissed the army chief of staff without consulting the other government parties. When Dahal resigned, the CPN (UML) was invited to form a new government. M. K. Nepal was elected prime minister, and party members assumed several key ministries. The party subsequently was divided in its stance toward the Maoists, but in June 2010 Nepal offered his resignation to facilitate the formation of a consensus government. Khanal was elected prime minister in February 2011 but resigned that August, and the CPN (UML) joined the opposition.

In December 2012 the CPN (UML) joined calls from other opposition parties for the resignation of Prime Minister Bhattarai. Though initially split over the proposal for a Regmi-led interim government, the party eventually threw its support behind the measure on March 13, 2013. Days later, the party joined the three other largest parties in forming the HLPC (see Current issues, above).

Leaders: Madhav Kumar NEPAL (Former Prime Minister); Jhalanath KHANAL (Chair and Former Prime Minister); Ishwar POKHAREL (General Secretary), Bishnu Poudel (Party Secretary).

Nepali Congress—NC. Founded in 1947, the NC long sought abolition of the *panchayat* system and defied the regime by holding a national convention in Kathmandu in 1985, after which it launched a civil disobedience movement (satyagraha) to press for the release of political prisoners and for party legalization. Following the widespread popular agitation that began in February 1990, NC president K. P. Bhattarai was asked to head a coalition government pending nationwide balloting in May 1991. Although the NC won 110 of 205 seats in the house in 1991, Bhattarai failed to secure reelection and hence was obliged to yield the office of prime minister to G. P. Koirala, who served until 1994. Sher Bahadur Deuba served as prime minister in a coalition government from 1995 to 1997. Koirala returned as prime minister in April 1998, although his cabinet provoked considerable intraparty controversy over the inclusion of what some members considered "corrupt" ministers who had served in previous administrations.

During the parliamentary campaign of 1999 Koirala stepped aside in favor of Bhattarai, who returned as prime minister when the NC, on a 38 percent vote share, won a clear majority of 111 seats in the House of Representatives. Conflict between Bhattarai and supporters of Koirala, who had retained the party presidency, continued, forcing Bhattarai to resign on March 16, 2000. Meeting two days later for the party's first open leadership election, the parliamentarians, as expected, selected Koirala as their leader by a 69–43 vote over Deuba. Accordingly, King Birendra redesignated Koirala as prime minister on March 20.

Leadership disputes within the NC continued to simmer. On August 8, 2000, Koirala dismissed the minister of water resources, Khum Bahadur KHADKA, for demanding that Koirala step aside as party president. Although Koirala beat back another challenge by Deuba's supporters at a party convention in January 2001, he had to resign as prime minister on July 19. Deuba then defeated Secretary General Sushil Koirala, 72–40, for the party leadership and was designated by the king to be prime minister.

The stark division between the Koirala and Deuba factions persisted, culminating in the May 2002 decision by the NC disciplinary committee to expel Deuba for failing to consult the party before seeking parliamentary extension of the country's state of emergency. Deuba's supporters then expelled Koirala at a "general convention" in June 16–19. Deuba to registered his faction as the Nepali Congress (Democratic)—NC(D), following a decision by the Election Commission that the Koirala faction held ownership of the name "Nepali Congress," taking 40 of the NC lower house representatives with him.

In the months following the king's October 2002 decisions to dissolve the House of Representatives and replace Prime Minister Deuba with the National Democratic Party's L. B. Chand, the NC joined the CPN (UML) and other, smaller parties in challenging the constitutionality of the moves. The NC was the prime mover in the formation of the JPM in April–May 2003 and of the SPA two years later. The NC(D) also joined the SPA. Deuba had been reappointed prime minister for the third time in June 2004, only to be dismissed once again on February 1, 2005, placed under house arrest, and convicted by a corruption commission. However, he was released in February 2006 and went on to regain leadership of the NC(D) parliamentary delegation.

With election of a Constituent Assembly in the offing, the NC and the NC(D) reunited on September 25, 2007. A collateral decision to support a republican form of government led former prime minister Bhattarai to resign from the party. The NC won 110 of 601 Constituent Assembly seats in April 2008, reflecting a decline from the party's historic levels of popular support, especially in the Terai region of southern Nepal. The party joined the coalition government headed by Madhav Kumar Nepal in May 2009. Koirala angered some in the party by nominating his daughter Sujata KOIRALA for the post of foreign minister. In June, in a contested election for leader of the party's parliamentary group, Ram Chandra Poudel defeated former prime minister Deuba. G. P. Koirala died on March 20, 2010, at the age of 86.

The party's 12th general convention, held in September 2010, marked a continuation of the struggle between the Koirala and Deuba factions. In the election for party president, Sushil Koirala defeated Deuba and a third candidate, Bhim Bahadur TAMANG, by a vote of 1,652–1,317–78. The Deuba faction also opposed the party's continuing support for its prime ministerial candidate, Ram Chandra Poudel.

In March 2013 Koirala put the party's support behind the interim government, later noting that it was in the interest of the country. The party joined the HLPC. A split between Koirala and Deuba, apparently resolved in February 2012 when the factions shared the task of appointing chiefs of sister organizations, resurfaced. Though the leaders worked to mend the rift, Deuba supporters bristled over party appointments by Koirala in May.

Leaders: Ram Baran YADAV (President of Nepal), Ram Sushil KOIRALA (President), Girija Sher Bahadur DEUBA (Former Prime Minister), Ram Chandra POUDEL (Chief Secretary).

National Democratic Party (*Rastriya Prajatantra* Party—RPP). A monarchist party comprising largely former *panchayat* members and supporters, the RPP was formed in 1992 by the merger of two groups (both calling themselves the National Democratic Party), one led by S. B. Thapa and the other led by L. B. Chand. The unified RPP won 20 legislative seats in the 1994 election. It joined the government as a member of the NC-led coalition in September 1995, but factionalism within the RPP contributed to the government's instability. The demise of the coalition in March 1997 led to Chand's designation as prime minister in a CPN (UML)-RPP-NSP cabinet, which survived less than seven months before being replaced by an RPP-NSP (and subsequently NC) government under Thapa. In January 1998 the RPP expelled former prime minister Chand and nine supporters for threatening to back a no-confidence vote against Prime Minister Thapa, who had asked the king to dissolve the House of Representatives. The rebel group quickly formed a "New RPP," commonly called the RPP (Chand).

The RPP won 11 percent of the vote and 11 seats in the May 1999 election, while the RPP (Chand) claimed a meager 3 percent and no seats. The Thapa and Chand groups then reunified in January 2000. After the dismissal of the Deuba government in October 2002, the king reappointed former prime minister Chand to that office, but Chand resigned in May 2003 and was in turn replaced by former prime minister Thapa. The change further widened the rift between the Chand and Thapa factions in the party, and in December 2003 the RPP called for Thapa's resignation for undermining multiparty democracy. Thapa ultimately resigned in May 2004.

By late 2004 the rupture within the RPP appeared complete. Although Chand and the party's president, P. S. Rana, were continuing their efforts to hold the party together, Thapa had stated his intention to form a new party, which was launched in March 2005 as the *Rastriya Janshakti* Party—RJP (below). The departure of Thapa's supporters did not, however, end the factionalism within the RPP. In September the

RPP announced that it would support the "prodemocracy agitation" led by the SPA, but in December half a dozen RPP members were in the reshuffled cabinet announced by the king. In January 2006 President Rana ousted ten members of the party's central committee, including six cabinet ministers. The royalist dissidents ultimately formed the RPP (Nepal)—see below.

With nine seats, the RPP became the largest opposition party in the Interim Legislature-Parliament. Party divisions, as well as the RPP's opposition to ending the monarchy, weakened its showing in the Constituent Assembly balloting; the party won eight seats. It subsequently joined the government in June 2009.

Leaders: Pashupati Shumsher RANA (Chair), Lokendra Bahadur CHAND (Leader and Former Prime Minister), Deepak BOHARA, Parshu Ram KHAPUNG, and Dhurba Bahadur PRADHAN (General Secretaries).

Communist Party of Nepal (Marxist-Leninist)—CPN (ML). On March 5, 1998, 46 of the CPN (UML)'s 89 house members, led by former deputy prime minister Bamdev Gautam and others, left the parent grouping and formed the CPN (ML). The split occurred primarily because of the dissidents' opposition to the water-sharing arrangements in the 1996 Indo-Nepal Mahakali Integrated Development Treaty. Describing the new formation as a party of the progressive left, its leaders voiced support for nationalism and democracy while labeling the United States imperialist and India a "regional hegemonist."

The CPN (ML) joined the NC in the government of August–December 1998; its departure over policy differences guaranteed the administration's collapse. Despite winning 7 percent of the vote in May 1999, the party failed to capture any lower house seats. In August 2001 the CPN (ML) and the CPN (UML) agreed to discuss reunification, although the February 2002 decision to proceed with it was rejected by some CPN (ML) leaders. They then restructured the party, which was sometimes referred to as the CPN (ML)-Reorganized or CPN (ML)-Reconstituted.

At a party convention in January 2007, a rift developed in the CPN (ML) central committee, with a faction led by Rishi Kattel subsequently helping to start a new party, the CPN (Unified)—see below.

The CPN (ML) formed the ULF with other CPN splinters and joined the Seven-Party Alliance in the Koirala government. Contesting independently for the Constituent Assembly in 2008, it won eight seats.

In August 2010 Jagat Bahadur BOGATI, objecting in part to General Secretary C. P. Mainali's decision not to support the Maoist's Dahal for prime minister, led a group of dissidents, including four Constituent Assembly members, to form a new party, the **Communist Party of Nepal (Marxist-Leninist-Samajwadi)**—CPN-ML (*Samajwadi*).

In July 2013 CPN (ML) leaders met with the HLPC over concerns about the distribution of citizenship certificates. The CPN (ML) plans to contest in the November 2013 election.

Leaders: Chandra Prakash MAINALI (General Secretary), N. P. ACHARYA, Damber SHRESTHA.

Communist Party of Nepal (United)—CPN (United). The CPN (United) traces its origin to the pro-Moscow branch of the original CPN, which was launched in 1949 but suffered repeated fractures beginning in 1982. In 1991 the CPN (Democratic), led by Bishnu Bahadur MANANDHAR; the CPN (Varma) of K. N. VARMA; and the CPN (Amatya), led by Tulsi Lal AMATYA, formed a unified party, the CPN (United). In December 1993 Amatya broke from the CPN (United) and led his faction into the CPN (UML).

In 1998 the party formed a United Marxist Front (UMF) with the small CPN (Marxist), led by Prabhu Narayan CHAUDHARI. In 2001 the Varma faction joined the CPN (UML).

Although the CPN (United) and the CPN (Marxist) merged in September 2005, the party split in late 2006. The CPN (United) was reestablished in 2007 under the leadership of Chandra Dev Joshi. As part of the ULF, it joined the governing Seven-Party Alliance, but in 2008 the ULF was dissolved.

The CPN (United) won seats for five members in the Constituent Assembly. Party leader Ganesh Shah was given a ministry portfolio in the Maoist-led government. The party boycotted the election of a new prime minister in May 2009, but in July T. P. Sharma was appointed to Prime Minister Nepal's cabinet. The CPN (United) did not join the 2011 UCPN-M government. In February 2013 Joshi joined the chorus of opposition leaders calling for the resignation of Prime Minister Bhattarai.

Leaders: Chandra Dev JOSHI (President), Thakur Prasad SHARMA (Former Minister of Environment, Science, and Technology).

Socialist Democratic People's Party (*Samajwadi Prajatantrik Janata* Party—SPJP). Formed in 2003, the leftist SPJP won one seat in the Constituent Assembly election. It joined Prime Minister Nepal's government in July 2009 but was not part of the UCPN-M government formed in August 2011.

Leader: Prem Bahadur SINGH.

National People's Force Party (*Rastriya Janshakti* Party—RJP). The RJP was launched in March 2005 by former prime minister S. B. Thapa, whose long and complicated history of rivalry with former prime minister L. B. Chand over control of the RPP culminated in his decision to form a new party. Although a royalist, in May 2006 Thapa, arguing in favor of "political stability," backed the legislative proclamation that stripped King Gyanendra of his powers. Subsequently, the RJP and RPP began discussions on reunification, although the RJP registered separately for the Constituent Assembly election, in which it won three seats. S. B. Thapa had been included in the RPP's delegation to the Interim Legislature-Parliament.

In September 2009 the RJP joined Prime Minister Nepal's government in a junior capacity, but the party declined to join the August 2011 UCPN-M government.

The RJP plans to contest in the elections planned for November 2013.

Leaders: Surya Bahadur THAPA (President), Prakash Chandra LOHANI (Vice President).

People's Front Nepal (*Janamorcha Nepal*—JMN). The JMN began as the electoral front for the Communist Party of Nepal (Unity Center *Mashal*)—CPN (UCM), the formation of which was announced in April 2002 by the leaders of the CPN (Unity Center) and the CPN (*Mashal*). Both parties traced their origins to the pro-Chinese CPN (Fourth Congress), which had been founded in India in 1974 but from which several *Mashal* (Torch) groups emerged in the 1980s. The CPN (Unity Center) was formed in 1990 from the merger of a CPN (Fourth Congress) rump, two *Mashal* factions, and the Nepal Proletarian Labor Organization.

During the 1990s both the CPN (Unity Center) and the CPN (*Mashal*) established electoral fronts. In 1991 the Unity Center's United People's Front/Nepal (*Samyukta Janmorcha Nepal*—SJN) won nine seats in the House election. In 1994 the party split, one faction forming the radical CPN (Maoist), which took with it an allied SJN faction. The rump SJN won no seats in the 1994 election but took one in May 1999, on a 1 percent vote share. Meanwhile, the CPN (*Mashal*), after boycotting the 1991 election, formed the National People's Front (*Rastriya Janamorcha*—RJM) for electoral purposes, although its two successful candidates in 1994 technically ran as independents. Thereafter, the majority of the CPN (*Mashal*) leadership chose to remain in conventional politics and opposed the Maoist rebellion. In the May 1999 election the RJM won five seats despite capturing only 1 percent of the vote.

The April 2002 decision to form the CPN (UCM) was followed in July by an announcement that the SJN and the RJM would also merge as the JMN. In 2006 the JMN became a member of the governing Seven-Party Alliance, a move that the CPN (UCM) rejected. The JMN (KC), led by Chitra Bahadur K. C., left the SPA and registered in 2007 as the reconstituted *Rastriya Janamorcha* (RJM, below). Another JMN faction, the JMN (Ale), led by Chitra Bahadur Ale, later joined in forming the CPN (Unified), also discussed below. A third JMN group, led by Amik SERCHAN, retained the JMN designation, remaining part of the SPA and, in April 2008, winning seven seats in the Constituent Assembly. In August 2008, however, Serchan's support for the election of President Yadav led to his ouster, with Lilamani POKHAREL becoming acting chair.

In January 2009 the CPN (UCM), led by General Secretary Narayan Kaji SHRESTHA, merged with the CPN (Maoist) to form the UCPN-M. Shrestha, Serchan, and Pokharel were all named to the UCPN-M Secretariat. Opponents of the merger then reconstituted the JMN.

In November 2012 the JMN joined 14 opposition parties in calling for the resignation of Prime Minister Bhattarai.

Leaders: Dan Bahadur BISHWOKARMA (Chair), Man Bahadur SINGH, Bharat DAHAL, Sadhya Bahadur BHANDARI (General Secretary).

Nepal Goodwill Party (Anandi Devi) (*Nepali Sadbhavana* Party [Anandi Devi]—NSP [Anandi Devi] or NSP-A). The Nepal Goodwill Party was formed in the mid-1980s to promote the interests of the Madhesi inhabitants of the Terai. It sought redelineation of the southern constituencies on the basis of population and the granting of citizenship to all persons settled in Nepal before adoption of the 1990 constitution. The NSP won three House seats in 1994 after winning none in 1991 and was awarded one portfolio in the Deuba government of September 1995. In December 1998 the NSP entered the NC-CPN (UML) coalition administration as a junior partner. In the May 1999 election the NSP won five seats on a 3 percent vote share.

In January 2002 the party's founder and longtime president, Gajendra Narayan SINGH, died. Differences subsequently emerged over who should fill party posts. At a divisive national convention in March 2003 one faction supported Singh's widow, Anandi Devi SINGH, for the presidency, while another backed the acting president, Deputy Prime Minister Badri Prasad MANDAL. As a consequence, the party split. In April 2004 the Supreme Court upheld an August 2003 Election Commission decision that awarded the NSP title to the Mandal faction, with the other faction becoming the NSP (Anandi Devi). The latter helped form the opposition JPM in 2003 and was among the first of Nepal's mainstream parties to call for election of a constituent assembly as a means of resolving the Maoist insurgency.

In June 2007 the NSP and the NSP (Anandi Devi) reunited, retaining the latter designation, but a faction led by cabinet minister Rajendra Mahato sought recognition as a separate party. In September the Election Commission denied the request, prompting Mahato to resign from the party and the government. He and his supporters nevertheless remained active in the Terai agitation and continued to use the NSP designation until renaming their splinter the Sadbhavana Party (SP, above), allied with the Madhesi People's Rights Forum (MJF, above).

The party won only two seats in the 2008 Constituent Assembly election, after which factional disputes led to the apparent removal of an ailing Anandi Devi as chair by Shyam Sundar Gupta, a move rejected by the Sarita Giri faction. The party withdrew from the Maoist-led government in February 2009, after which the internal conflict intensified. The Gupta faction was recognized in May 2010 by the election commission, prompting Giri and Vice Chair Kushi Lal MANDAL to petition the Supreme Court for a stay. In July Giri charged Gupta and the party's secretary general, Yashwant Kumar SINGH, a nephew of Anandi Devi, with having abducted the honorary chair. The Giri faction supported the August 2011 UCPN-M government, and Giri became minister of labor and transportation.

In June 2013 the Supreme Court settled the leadership issue, ruling that Giri is the chair of the party.

Leader: Sarita GIRI (Chair).

National Democratic Party (Nepal) (*Rastriya Prajatantra* Party [Nepal]—RPP [Nepal]). The RPP (Nepal) began as a faction of the RPP (above) that approved participating in King Gyanendra's government after the king deposed the democratic government in 2005. In January 2007 it absorbed two other small parties: the *Rastriya Prajatantra* Party (*Rastrabadi*), or RPP (Nationalist), led by Rajeshwor DEVKOTA, itself an earlier splinter from the RPP; and the *Nepal Bidwat Parishad,* led by Jit Bahadur ARJEL.

At the inaugural session of the Constituent Assembly on May 28, 2008, the RPP (Nepal)'s four members cast the only votes against forming a republic. The right-wing party continued to favor popular referendums on restoring the monarchy and on whether Nepal should be a secular or a Hindu state.

In July 2013 ahead of the polling scheduled for November, Thapa hinted at the possibility of an alliance with the CPN-M.

Leader: Kamal THAPA.

National People's Front (*Rastriya Janamorcha*—RJM). The RJM began as electoral front of the CPN (*Mashal*) in the 1990s. It merged with the political front of another CPN splinter in 2002 to form the People's Front Nepal (*Janamorcha Nepal*—JMN, above). After the JMN joined the governing Seven-Party Alliance in 2006, Chita Bahadur K. C. led a faction out of the party and reclaimed the name of the RJM. The party held three seats in the Interim Legislature-Parliament and won four seats in the 2008 Constituent Assembly. The current **CPN (*Mashal*)** is led by Mohan Bikram SINGH.

The RJM was the first party in the Constituent Assembly to oppose any type of federal structure for the Nepalese republic. The party maintains that federalism, especially if enacted along ethnic or caste lines, could lead to the disintegration of national unity. Instead, the party advocates decentralization within the existing unitary system.

In July 2010 the party expelled its general secretary, Dilaram ACHARYA, for breaking party discipline. Acharya thereupon announced the formation of **Rastriya Janamorcha (Nepal)**—RJM-N.

In May 2013 the RJM joined other fringe parties in calling for citizenship reform, and for removal of the provision requiring parties to demonstrate they have 10,000 voters.

Leader: Chitra BAHADUR K. C. (Chair).

Nepal Workers' and Peasants' Party—NWPP (Nepal *Majdoor Kisan* Party). An advocate for the poor and working people, the NWPP began as a Maoist formation but currently advocates nonalignment and a mixed economy. Most of the party's support lies in its stronghold in the Bhaktapur area. It doubled its lower house strength from two to four seats in 1994 but won only 1 in May 1999. The NWPP was a member of the Seven-Party Alliance but declined an invitation to join the government. It agreed to sign the December 2007 23-point agreement with the Maoists despite objections. It won four seats in the 2008 Constituent Assembly election.

In February 2009 the party proposed that Nepal's 14 existing zones become separate states in a federal structure with a president as head of state and government. It opposed federalism based on castes or ethnic communities.

Leader: Narayan Man BIJUKCHHE ("Rohit").

National People's Liberation Party (*Rastriya Janamukti* Party). An ethnically based party founded in 1990 by the indigenous leaders M. S. Thapa and Gore Bahadur KHAPANGI, the party favors a federal system based on autonomous ethnic federal units. The party won two seats in the 2008 Constituent Assembly balloting.

Leaders: Malwat Singh THAPA (Chair), Bayan Singh RAI (General Secretary).

Communist Party of Nepal (Unified)—CPN (Unified). Formed in 2007, the CPN (Unified) brought together three splinter groups from other communist organizations: the Chitra Bahadur ALE wing of the JMN, the Rishi KATTEL wing of the CPN (ML), and the faction of the CPN (Marxist-Leninist-Maoist Center) led by Sitaram TAMANG. The new party assumed the two seats in the Interim Legislature-Parliament that had been assigned to the JMN (Ale) and subsequently won two seats in the Constituent Assembly. In April 2010 a faction led by Navaraj SUBEDI joined the UCPN-M.

Leaders: Ram Singh SHRIS, Mohan BIKRAM (General Secretary).

Nepali People's Party (*Nepali Janata Dal*—NJD). The NJD was formed in 1995, intending to work for the emancipation of Dalits, Janjatis, and other disadvantaged groups in Nepalese society, including women. The party won two Constituent Assembly seats in 2008. Supporting the contention that President Yadav exceeded his authority by overturning the move to fire the army chief of staff, the NJD boycotted the election of a new prime minister in May 2009.

Leaders: Hari Charan SHAH (Chair), Kabi Raj TIMILSINA (Vice Chair).

Federal National Democratic Forum (*Sanghiya Loktantrik Rastriya Manch*—SLRM). The SLRM, first registered in early 2008, is an umbrella organization of state councils and other groups, some of them armed, representing Nepal's indigenous ethnic groups, or Janjati, such as the Limbus. Reflecting its ethnic base, the party advocates self-determination, a federal system based on autonomous regions, and proportional representation of diverse populations in government. The party won two seats in the Constituent Assembly.

Leaders: Kumar LINGDEN (Chair), Khagendra MAKHIM (General Secretary).

In addition, the following parties each won one Constituent Assembly seat: **Nepal Democratic Socialist Party** (*Nepal Loktantrik Samajbadi Dal*), represented by Laxmilal CHAUDHARY; **Dalit Janjati Party**, representing Dalits and other marginalized peoples, led by Bishwendra PASAWAN; **Nepal Family Party** (*Nepal Parivar Dal*), a utopian socialist party that envisions Nepal as one family, represented by Eknath DHAKAL; **Nepa National Party** (*Nepa Rastriya* Party), an ethnonationalist party supporting the linguistic and cultural rights of the Newar community, represented by Buddha Ratna MANANDHAR; and **Chure Bhawar National Unity Party Nepal** (*Chure Bhawar Rastriya Ekta* Party *Nepal*), the front of a regional defense organization, led by Keshab MAINALI.

Ethnic Organizations:

In the past, indigenous and other ethnic organizations played little part in national politics per se, but the success of the Maoist insurgency in

2006 and the subsequent adoption of an interim constitution generated demands from many, including the MJF, for federalism, self-determination, and ethnic autonomy.

A principal instigator of the insurgency in the Terai that began in January 2007 was an offshoot of the CPN (Maoist), the **Janatantrik Terai Mukti Morcha** (JTMM), which sought an independent Terai. The group has several armed and active wings. Another group, the **Khumbuwan National Front** (*Khumbuwan Rastriya Morcha*—KRM), representing the Limbu population in the east, also left the CPN (Maoist), with which it had been associated for a number of years. The **Tharu Kalyankari Sabha** (TKS) sought autonomy for the Tharu people.

In the wake of the unrest in the Terai, a nonpartisan umbrella organization representing 54 indigenous groups (Janjatis), the **Nepal Federation of Indigenous Nationalities** (NFIN), chaired by Pasang SHERPA, opened discussions with the government. Its demands included use of a strictly proportional voting system for the Constituent Assembly. On August 30, 2007, the MJF and the government announced a 22-point agreement that included provision for a federal constitutional structure, but the nature of that federalism remains highly contentious.

LEGISLATURE

The 1990 constitution provided for a bicameral Parliament (*Sansad*) consisting of a permanent upper house, the National Assembly (*Rastriya Sabha*), of 60 indirectly elected and appointed members, and a 205-member directly elected House of Representatives (*Pratinidhi Sabha*) with a five-year mandate. The proclamation of sovereignty by the House of Representatives on May 18, 2006, effectively suspended the National Assembly's governmental role. The lower house was dissolved by the king on May 22, 2002, and reinstated on April 28, 2006.

When the House promulgated the interim constitution on January 15, 2007, both houses of Parliament "automatically cease[d] to subsist." At the same time, a 330-member Interim Legislature-Parliament came into existence, encompassing a combination of 209 legislators from the previous Parliament—excluded were the king's nominees and those who had supported his assumption of power—plus party nominees. The three largest parties—the Nepali Congress, the Communist Party of Nepal (Unified Marxist-Leninist), and the Communist Party of Nepal (Maoist)—held roughly the same number of seats. Nine other parties were represented, including the Nepali Congress (Democratic), which reunited with the Nepali Congress in September.

As called for in the interim constitution, the tenure of the Interim Legislature-Parliament came to an end upon formation of the **Constituent Assembly**. In addition to drafting a new constitution, the assembly was to act as a unicameral legislature for two years, but in May 2010 the mandate was extended to May 2011. The assembly has 601 members: 240 directly elected in districts, through the "first-past-the-post" method; 335 elected by proportional representation on the basis of party lists; and 26 named by the Council of Ministers to represent indigenous and marginalized groups.

In the election on April 10, 2008, for 575 seats, the seat distribution was as follows: the Communist Party of Nepal (Maoist), 220; Nepali Congress, 110; Communist Party of Nepal (Unified Marxist-Leninist), 103; Madhesi People's Rights Forum (MJF), 52; Terai Madhesh Democratic Party, 20; *Sadbhavana* Party, 9; National Democratic Party, 8; Communist Party of Nepal (Marxist-Leninist), 8; People's Front Nepal, 7; Communist Party of Nepal (United), 5; National Democratic Party (Nepal), 4; National People's Front, 4; Nepal Workers' and Peasants' Party, 4; National People's Force Party, 3; National People's Liberation Party, 2; Communist Party of Nepal (Unified), 2; Nepal Goodwill Party (Anandi Devi), 2; Nepali People's Party, 2; Federal National Democratic Forum, 2; *Chure Bhawar* National Unity Party Nepal, Dalit Janjati Party, Nepa National Party, Nepal Family Party, Nepal Democratic Socialist Party, and Socialist Democratic Peoples' Party, 1 each; independents, 2.

The 26 seats appointed by the Council of Ministers were distributed as follows: the Communist Party of Nepal (Maoist), 9; Nepali Congress, 5; Communist Party of Nepal (Unified Marxist-Leninist), 5; Madhesi People's Rights Forum, 2; Communist Party of Nepal (Marxist-Leninist), Nepal Workers' and Peasants' Party, People's Front Nepal, *Sadbhavana* Party, and Terai Madhesh Democratic Party, 1 each.

In January 2009 the Communist Party of Nepal (Maoist) merged with a smaller Communist party and thereupon adopted a new name, the Unified Communist Party of Nepal (Maoist). The most significant postelection change in the makeup of the assembly occurred with the mid-2009 split in the MJF, which saw 28 of its representatives join the new Madhesi People's Rights Forum (Democratic). In August 2010 the Communist Party of Nepal (Marxist-Leninist-*Samajwadi*) separated from the Communist Party of Nepal (Marxist-Leninist), which thereby lost 4 seats.

The Constituent Assembly dissolved on May 27, 2012, after the body failed to meet the deadline to draft a new constitution. In June 2013 the interim government led by Prime Minister Regmi announced that elections would take place on November 19 (see Current issues, above, and headnote).

CABINET

[as of November 12, 2013]

Prime Minister	Khil Raj Regmi
Ministers	
Agriculture Development; Forest and Soil Conservation	Tek Bahadur Thapa Gharti
Culture, Tourism, and Civil Aviation; Youth and Sports; Peace and Reconstruction	Ram Kumar Shrestha
Defense	Khil Raj Regmi
Education; Information and Communication; General Administration	Madhave Paudel
Environment, Science, and Technology; Energy; Irrigation	Uma Kanta Jha
Federal Affairs and Local Development; Health and Population	Biddhyadhar Mallik
Finance; Industry; Commerce and Supplies	Shankar Koirala
Foreign Affairs; Home Affairs	Madhav Prasad Ghimire
Labor and Employment; Law and Justice	Hari Prasad Neupane
Physical Infrastructure; Transport and Urban Development	Chabi Lal Panta
Women, Children, and Social Welfare; Land Reform and Management	Riddhi Baba Pradhan [f]

[f] = female

INTERGOVERNMENTAL REPRESENTATION

Ambassador to the U.S.: Shankar Prasad SHARMA.

U.S. Ambassador to Nepal: Peter W. BODDE.

Permanent Representative to the UN: Durga Prasad BHATTARAI.

IGO Memberships (Non-UN): ADB, IOM, NAM, SAARC, WTO.

NETHERLANDS

Kingdom of the Netherlands
Koninkrijk der Nederlanden

Political Status: Constitutional monarchy established 1814; under multiparty parliamentary system.

Area: 13,103 sq. mi. (33,936 sq. km).

Population: 16,730,348 (2013E—UN); 16,805,037 (2013E—U.S. Census).

Major Urban Centers (2013E): AMSTERDAM (799,000), Rotterdam (616,000), The Hague (seat of government, 506,000), Utrecht (322,000), Eindhoven (218,000).

Official Language: Dutch.

Monetary Unit: Euro (market rate November 1, 2013: 0.74 euro = $1US).

Sovereign: King WILLEM-ALEXANDER; ascended the throne April 30, 2013, upon the abdication of his mother, Queen BEATRIX Wilhelmina Armgard.

Heir Apparent: CATHARINA-AMALIA, Princess of Orange.

Prime Minister: Mark RUTTE (People's Party for Freedom and Democracy); reelected and sworn in as head of a two-party minority coalition on November 5, 2012, following the general election of September 12; first sworn in as head of a two-party minority coalition on October 14, 2010, following the general election of June 9, 2010, succeeding Jan Peter BALKENENDE (Christian Democratic Appeal).

THE COUNTRY

Facing the North Sea between Belgium and Germany, the Netherlands (often called "Holland," from the name of one of its principal provinces) is noted for the dikes, canals, and reclaimed polder lands providing constant reminder that two-fifths of the country's land area lies below sea level. The largely homogeneous, Germanic population is divided principally between Catholics (31 percent) and Protestants (21 percent), with 40 percent declaring no religious affiliation. In 2011 women constituted 58 percent of the labor force, concentrated in the services sector; women currently occupy about one-third of the seats in each parliamentary chamber, chair both chambers, and head 5 of 13 ministries.

The Netherlands experienced rapid industrialization after World War II, although the industrial sector is now limited to approximately 22 percent of the labor force as compared with 74 percent in the services sector. The traditionally important agricultural sector employs fewer than 4 percent but is characterized by highly efficient methods of production, which are amply rewarded by the common agricultural policy of the European Union (EU, formerly the European Community—EC), of which the Netherlands was a founding member. Leading agricultural products include potatoes, vegetables, sugar beets, wheat, and pork. Since there are few natural resources except large natural gas deposits, most nonagricultural activity involves the processing of imported raw materials. Refined petroleum, chemicals, steel, textiles, and ships constitute the bulk of industrial output. Principal exports include machinery and transport equipment, chemicals and petroleum products, and food.

In the early 1980s the economy was stagnating under the influence of persistently high budget deficits necessitated, in part, by the nation's extensive welfare system. However, a labor/business pact in 1982 established the basis for significant governmental cost-cutting, private-sector promotion, wage moderation, and more flexible employment regulations. As a result, the economy grew steadily, rising from an average of 1.9 percent in the late 1980s to 4.1 percent in 1998. The Netherlands easily met the economic criteria required to participate in the EU's new Economic and Monetary Union (EMU) on January 1, 1999.

However, the budget surplus of the late 1990s (which had permitted tax reduction) was replaced by a deficit that reached 3.25 percent of GDP in 2004, thereby creating difficulty for the administration regarding EMU fiscal guidelines. The economy began a recovery in 2004, only to fall into recession in the second quarter of 2008 as a result of the global financial crisis, to which Netherlands was particularly vulnerable because of its robust financial sector and international connections. A slow and fragile economic recovery began in 2010 with GDP growing by 1.8 percent, driven mostly by exports, yet unemployment climbed to 4.5 percent. GDP grew 1.6 percent in 2011, but dropped 0.9 percent in 2012. Unemployment was 5.2 percent in 2011 and 5.3 percent in 2012. Youth continue to have disproportionately higher levels: 10 percent among native Dutch youth and 29 percent for immigrants in July 2012.

GOVERNMENT AND POLITICS

Political background. Having declared independence from Spain in 1581 at the time of the Counter Reformation, the United Provinces of the Netherlands were ruled by hereditary *stadhouders* (governors) of the House of Orange until the present constitutional monarchy was established under the same house at the close of the Napoleonic period. Queen JULIANA, who had succeeded her mother, WILHELMINA, in 1948, abdicated in favor of her daughter BEATRIX in April 1980.

Following World War II the Netherlands was governed by a succession of coalition governments in which the large Catholic People's Party (*Katholieke Volkspartif*—KVP) typically played a pivotal role prior to its merger into the more inclusive Christian Democratic Appeal (*Christen-Democratisch Appèl*—CDA) in 1980. Coalitions between the KVP and the Labor Party (*Partij van de Arbeid*—PvdA) were the rule until 1958, when the latter went into opposition, the KVP continuing to govern in alliance with smaller parties of generally moderate outlook. A center-right coalition headed by Petrus J. S. DE JONG assumed office in April 1967 and was followed by an expanded center-right government formed under Barend W. BIESHEUVEL in 1971.

The inability of the Biesheuvel government to cope with pressing economic problems led to its early demise in July 1972 and to an election four months later. A 163-day interregnum then ensued before a PvdA-led government organized in May 1973 by Johannes (Joop) M. DEN UYL emerged as the first Dutch administration dominated by the political left. It survived until March 1977, when it collapsed in the wake of a bitter dispute between PvdA and CDA leaders over compensation for expropriated land. After another extended interregnum (the longest in the nation's history), Andreas A. M. VAN AGT succeeded in organizing a government of his CDA and the People's Party for Freedom and Democracy (*Volkspartif voor Vrijheid en Democratie*—VVD) in late December.

In the election of May 1981 the center-right coalition lost its legislative majority and was replaced by a grouping that included the CDA, PvdA, and center-left Democrats 66 (*Democraten 66*—D66), with van Agt continuing as prime minister. The comfortable legislative majority thus achieved was offset by sharp differences over both defense and economic policy, and the new government collapsed in May 1982. The principal result of balloting in September was a loss of 11 seats by the D66 and a gain of 10 by the VVD. Ruud F. M. LUBBERS was installed as head of another center-right government in November following his succession to the CDA leadership in October. Contrary to opinion poll predictions, the CDA won a plurality in the lower house election of May 1986, Lubbers being returned as head of a new center-right government in July.

Lubbers was forced to resign on May 2, 1989, following coalition disagreement over funding for an ambitious environmental plan, although he remained in office in a caretaker's capacity pending new elections. Because of its perceived antienvironmental posture, the VVD's parliamentary representation dropped from 27 to 22 seats in the balloting on September 6, with the PvdA becoming the CDA's partner in a new center-left administration sworn in on November 7 under Lubbers's leadership. His continuation in office was made possible by a commitment to the PvdA to increase antipollution and social welfare expenditures, financed largely by the imposition of a "carbon dioxide" tax on business firms and a freeze on defense spending in 1991. While the subsequent course of events in Eastern Europe permitted an actual cutback in projected military expenses, the overall economic situation deteriorated.

The May 1994 general election marked the withdrawal from Dutch politics of Prime Minister Lubbers, who failed to gain the presidency of the European Commission in June. (The U.S. government vetoed his candidacy for the post of secretary general of the North American Treaty Organization [NATO] in 1995, but Lubbers was named to head the UN Office of the High Commissioner for Refugees in 2000.) The CDA campaign in 1994 was headed by Elco BRINKMAN, party leader in the Second Chamber. With Lubbers's departure, the CDA suffered its worst-ever defeat, losing a third of its support. The PvdA also lost ground, but it replaced the CDA as the largest parliamentary party, while substantial gains were registered by the VVD and D66. Far-right and far-left parties also gained seats, and two new pensioners' movements made their chamber debuts. In light of the new parliamentary arithmetic, the outcome of lengthy postelection negotiations was, as expected, the formation in August 1994 of a three-party coalition of the PvdA, VVD, and D66, with Willem (Wim) KOK becoming the first Labor prime minister since 1977.

With the government having received wide international praise for the "Dutch model" of sustained economic growth, substantial job creation, and an effective social services sector, the PvdA and the VVD improved their positions in the May 6, 1998, Second Chamber elections, although the D66 slipped significantly. The new government announced by Kok on August 3 comprised six ministers each from the PvdA and the VVD and three from the D66, with the coalition controlling 97 of the 150 seats in the *Tweede Kamer.*

On May 19, 1999, the cabinet resigned following the defeat by one vote in the *Eerste Kamer* of a bill sponsored by the D66 that would have permitted national "corrective referendums" to veto certain economic and social legislative decisions. However, on June 2 the three parties agreed to resume the coalition and to back a revised "consultative referendum" bill under which referendum results would not be binding.

Although the three-party governing coalition flirted with collapse in May 1999, two years of relative stability followed.

At the same time, the Netherlands attracted international attention frequently in the past, for legalizing controversial social practices. In 2001 it became the world's first country to permit same-sex marriages, and in 2002 a law legalizing euthanasia entered into effect. The Dutch euthanasia law made headlines again in February 2012, when Prince Johan Friso suffered a severe brain injury while skiing in Austria. He remains on life support with little hope of recovery at a London hospital, a situation criticized by Dutch euthanasia advocates.

On August 26, 2001, Prime Minister Kok confirmed that he would not seek reelection, so the party turned to its parliamentary leader, Ad MELKERT, to lead it into the 2002 elections. Kok and his cabinet resigned on April 16, 2002, in response to a report that criticized the Dutch military for failing to prevent the July 1995 massacre at the Bosnian "safe haven" of Srebrenica. The government continued to serve in a caretaker capacity until the May general election.

Events prior to the May 15, 2002, balloting for the *Tweede Kamer* were dominated by the sudden emergence of the flamboyant Pim FORTUYN, whose promotion of a populist mix of liberal policies (such as the improvement of public services) and rightist positions (such as heavy curbs on immigration and restrictions on rights for ethnic minorities) had struck a chord within a Dutch population increasingly concerned over deteriorating economic conditions and rising crime. Following Fortuyn's assassination on May 6 by an animal rights and environmental activist, consideration was given to postponing the balloting. However, all the major party leaders consented to proceeding as scheduled. The List Pim Fortuyn (*Lijst Pim Fortuyn*—LPF) won 26 seats and joined the CDA (43 seats) and VVD (24 seats) in a center-right coalition government installed on July 22 under the leadership of Jan Peter BALKENENDE of the CDA.

The coalition government resigned on October 16, 2002, as a result of differences over the proposed expansion of the EU, a power struggle within the LPF, and increasing economic difficulties, which prompted early elections on January 22, 2003, at which the CDA again achieved a slim plurality (44 seats versus 42 for the PvdA). The CDA initially sought to form a coalition with the PvdA, but negotiations fell apart due primarily to personal animosity between the leaders of the parties.

A CDA/VVD/D66 coalition was announced on May 27, with Balkenende retaining the premiership and promising a crackdown on drug trafficking and other crimes. Although the LPF seat total fell to 8 in the January balloting and the party lost its cabinet status, some of its proposals regarding immigration and crime had become official government policy. Prime Minister Balkenende's administration also tried to combat a burgeoning fiscal crisis through proposed liberalization of labor regulations and reductions in longstanding welfare and pension benefits.

The intertwined issues of immigration and rising anti-Muslim sentiment moved dramatically to the forefront again in November 2004 when Theo van GOGH, a filmmaker who had recently released a movie that focused on Islam's treatment of women, was assassinated, allegedly by an Islamic radical. Numerous anti-Muslim disturbances broke out in the wake of the murder, further threatening the Netherlands' reputation for tolerance. In early 2005 the government announced that stricter qualifications would be imposed on potential immigrants regarding their knowledge of the nation's history and culture. Concurrently, an extensive campaign to combat terrorism was launched, and a number of alleged Islamic militants were either arrested or deported. The immigration and terrorism issues were widely believed to have been major factors in the 61.5 percent "no" vote registered by the Dutch electorate in a national referendum in June on the question of whether the proposed new EU constitution should be approved. (The government and most major parties had called for a "yes" vote.)

In May 2006 Immigration and Integration Minister Rita Verdonk of the VVD announced that she was considering revoking the citizenship of Ayaan HIRSI ALI, a member of the legislature and an immigrant from Somalia, for having allegedly lied on her application for asylum. After public uproar, the government ultimately decided to allow Hirsi Ali to retain her Dutch citizenship, though she had already resigned her legislative seat and accepted a job at the American Enterprise Institute, a conservative think tank in the United States. The D66 party, the smallest member of the governing coalition, demanded the resignation of Verdonk in exchange for its continuing participation in the government. Verdonk was also under fire from D66 for her proposals to require Dutch to be the only language spoken in the streets of Holland. When Verdonk refused to resign, the D66 on June 29 left the coalition; Prime Minister Balkenende consequently announced the resignation of his government and set the stage for new elections to be held approximately a year early. Former Prime Minister Ruud Lubbers was called on to negotiate a new government, and within a week an interim minority government comprising the CDA and VVD was installed to begin work on the 2007 budget.

Although many analysts had predicted a major defeat for the CDA, the party lost only 3 of its seats in the November 22, 2006, *Tweede Kamer* balloting, while the PvdA lost 9 of its seats. Most electoral gains were registered on the extremes, as the extreme-left Socialist Party (*Socialistische Party*—SP) won 25 seats (up from 9 in 2003) and new extreme right-wing Party for Freedom (*Party voor de Vrijheid*—PVV) won 9 seats. The PVV was led by Geert WILDERS, who continued the anti-immigrant, anti-Islam beliefs espoused by the late Fortuyn (see Current issues, below). After more than two months of negotiations, Balkenende was able to construct a broad-spectrum coalition government comprising the CDA, PvdA, and the Christian Union (*ChristenUnie*—CU), which was installed on February 22, 2007.

The PVV continued to rise in popularity, stunning many analysts by finishing second in the European Parliament elections in June 2009 with 17 percent of the vote. Although the CDA led all parties in that balloting with 19 percent of the vote, the three-party governing coalition lost 6 of the 16 seats it had previously held.

The Balkenende government fell on February 20, 2010, after the PvdA pulled out of the three-party coalition over the government's extension of the Dutch mission in Afghanistan. The governing coalition had previously agreed that Dutch troops would be withdrawn from the Afghan province of Uruzgan in 2010; however, Prime Minister Balkenende opted to consider further extension of the mission after receiving a request by NATO in early 2010. (While Afghanistan was the proximate reason for the PvdA's withdrawal, the PvdA and CDA were also divided over the government's plans to adopt strict fiscal austerity measures and to increase the retirement age.) On February 21 Balkenende stated that his caretaker CDA-CU government had no authority to accept NATO's request for an extension and, consequently, that troops would be removed on schedule in August 2010. Left without a governing majority, the CDA and the CU formed a minority caretaker government and scheduled a new election for June 9.

Domestic issues dominated the 2010 electoral campaign, especially the growing deficit. The VVD campaigned on a package of tough deficit-cutting measures and restrictions on the entry of non-EU migrants into the Netherlands, while the PVV appealed to anti-immigrant sentiments and popular discontent with the major parties. The PvdA hoped to attract voters on the liberal side of the immigration issue, and in March the party chose Job COHEN, the former mayor of Amsterdam and a well-known supporter of multiculturalism, as its new leader.

In voting on June 9, 2010, the VVD became the largest party in the legislature with 31 of the 150 seats. Under Cohen's leadership, the PvdA performed better than expected, finishing second with 30 seats. The PVV became the third-largest party with 25 seats, a gain of 16. The big loser was the CDA, which fell from first to fourth largest. While the Socialist Party won only 15 seats, down from 25, the Green Left and the D66 both saw their vote and seat shares increase, each winning 10 seats.

In view of preelection speculation that the PVV would hold enough seats to influence the formation of the next governing coalition, discussion about including the PVV in government had begun during the campaign. Many of PVV leader Wilders's xenophobic policy proposals, such as a tax on headscarves worn by Muslim women and a ban on the Koran, were thought to be too extreme to warrant serious consideration by the other parties, although no party expressly ruled out forming a coalition with the PVV. In the early weeks of the electoral campaign, Wilders announced that he was willing to compromise on any issue except his opposition to an increase in the retirement age. After the ballots were counted, Wilders announced that he would be willing to compromise even on the retirement issue.

Coalition negotiations focused principally on whether the PVV would participate in government, play a critical but subsidiary role as a government-supportive party, or be excluded entirely. Combined, the VVD and CDA controlled only 52 of the legislature's 150 seats. With the support of the 24 PVV legislators, the three parties would control a bare majority of 76 seats putting the PVV in a critical, if not pivotal, position.

After four months of negotiations, in late September 2010 Rutte proposed that the VVD and CDA form a two-party minority government, with a supporting role for the PVV. The agreement secured unanimous approval from VVD and PVV legislators, but CDA legislators forced the party leadership to put the PVV's proposed role to a vote in their party congress, which ultimately acquiesced to the coalition arrangement in October.

The Rutte government primarily focused on bringing the national deficit below the 3 percent of GDP EU threshold through budget cuts and other austerity measures. The new government also proposed to reduce the size of the legislature and the number of governmental ministries, ostensibly to cut government costs, and to increase the retirement age. Meanwhile, proposals on immigration, demonstrating the PVV's influence, included restrictions on non-EU migrants, a tightening of asylum measures, a ban on headscarves for political and judicial officials, and a general ban on the full-length Islamic burka.

In a preemptive attempt to ensure that his fragile majority could weather potential stormy periods, Prime Minister Rutte also agreed not to liberalize Sunday shopping hours, as his party had planned, in order to secure implicit support from the two legislators from the right-wing Political Reformed Party (*Staatkundig Gereformeerde Partij*—SGP). The government collapsed in April 2012, triggering elections in September (see Current issues, below).

Constitution and government. Originally adopted in 1814–1815, the Netherlands' constitution has been progressively amended to incorporate the features of a modern democratic welfare state in which the sovereign exercises strictly limited powers. Under a special Statute of December 29, 1954, the Kingdom of the Netherlands was described as including not only the Netherlands proper but also the fully autonomous overseas territories of the Netherlands Antilles and Suriname, the latter ultimately becoming independent in 1975. On January 1, 1986, the island of Aruba formally withdrew from the Antilles federation, becoming a separate, self-governing member of the kingdom.

Political power centers in the parliament, or States General (*Staten Generaal*), consisting of an indirectly elected First Chamber (*Eerste Kamer*) and a more powerful, directly elected Second Chamber (*Tweede Kamer*). Either or both chambers may be dissolved by the sovereign prior to the holding of a new election. Executive authority is vested in a Council of Ministers (*Ministerraad*) appointed by the sovereign but responsible to the States General. An advisory Council of State (*Raad van State*), comprised of the queen and crown prince plus a number of councillors appointed by the queen upon nomination by the Second Chamber, is consulted by the executive on legislative and administrative policy. The judicial system is headed by a Supreme Court and includes five courts of appeal, 19 district courts, and 62 cantonal courts.

For administrative purposes the Netherlands is divided into 12 provinces, the most recent, Flevoland, having been created on January 1, 1986, from land formed under the more than half-century-old Zuider Zee reclamation project. Each province has its own elected council, which elects an executive, and a sovereign commissioner appointed by the queen. At the local level there are approximately 640 municipalities, each with a council that designates aldermen to share executive responsibilities with a crown-appointed burgomaster.

Under the arrangements providing for the dissolution of the Netherlands Antilles in October 2010, the islands of Bonaire, Saba, and St. Eustatius became "special municipalities" within the Netherlands. The islands were expected to retain their elected Island Councils.

Newspapers are free from censorship and published by independent commercial establishments, with strict separation between managerial and editorial boards. Reports Without Borders ranked the Netherlands 2nd of 179 countries in its 2013 Index of Press Freedom.

Foreign relations. Officially neutral before World War II, the Netherlands reversed its foreign policy as a result of the German occupation of 1940–1945 and became an active participant in the subsequent evolution of the Western community through the Benelux Union, NATO, the Western European Union, the EC/EU, and other West European and Atlantic organizations. A founding member of the UN, the Netherlands also belongs to all of the UN's specialized agencies. The country's principal foreign policy problems in the postwar period stemmed from the 1945–1949 transition to independence of the Netherlands East Indies (Indonesia); Jakarta's formal annexation in 1969 of West New Guinea (Irian Jaya); and continued pressure, including numerous acts of terrorism, by South Moluccan expatriates seeking Dutch aid in the effort to separate their homeland from Indonesia.

In late 1979 the Dutch reluctantly acceded to the wishes of their NATO allies and agreed to modernize and expand their nuclear arsenal, but officials indicated that they would postpone local deployment of 48 cruise missiles in the hope that a meaningful arms control agreement with the Soviet bloc could be negotiated. In the absence of such an agreement, a treaty with the United States authorizing deployment of the missiles by mid-1989 was finally ratified by the Netherlands in February 1986. However, preparations for installation of the missiles were suspended prior to the signing of the U.S.-Soviet intermediate-range nuclear force treaty in December 1987 and were formally terminated upon acceptance of the treaty by the States General in March 1988.

On December 15, 1992, the States General completed its ratification of the EC's Maastricht Treaty on economic and political union. However, the Netherlands' enthusiasm for European integration did not extend to participation in the "Eurocorps" military force inaugurated by France and Germany in 1992. Instead, the Netherlands on March 30, 1994, signed an agreement with Germany providing for the creation of a 30,000-strong Dutch-German joint force that would be fully integrated into NATO and open to other NATO members. The new joint force was formally inaugurated in August 1995, with staff headquarters in Münster, Germany.

Amsterdam took offense in November 1995 when the U.S. government vetoed the candidacy of former prime minister Ruud Lubbers for the post of NATO secretary general, reportedly because of Lubbers's record of concern about German dominance in Europe. Nevertheless, the Netherlands, which had previously committed troops to peacekeeping efforts in Bosnia, assigned 2,100 troops to the NATO-commanded International Force (IFOR) under the Dayton peace accords. The Kok administration was also a solid supporter of NATO action against Yugoslavia in early 1999.

The Hague is home to the International Court of Justice and the UN-sponsored International Criminal Tribunals for the former Yugoslavia and Rwanda (see the discussion under the UN Security Council). A Dutch air base also served as the trial site for two Libyans accused of the 1988 bombing of Pan Am Flight 103 over Lockerbie, Scotland; the Dutch government had permitted the base to be regarded as Scottish territory for the duration of the trial, which concluded with one guilty verdict and one acquittal in early 2001.

Although the Netherlands had contributed naval resources to the U.S.-led UN coalition in the 1991 Gulf War, support for the U.S./UK-led invasion of Iraq in 2003 was tepid (at best) in many quarters. Although the government initially deployed 1,700 troops to the Iraqi campaign, those forces were withdrawn in 2005. However, in February 2006 the Dutch parliament bowed to entreaties of U.S. and NATO officials and agreed to send up to 1,700 troops to Afghanistan as part of a NATO reconstruction mission. Those troops were withdrawn at the end of the mission in August 2010.

Dutch voters took a dramatic step back from European integration when a larger-than-expected 61.5 percent of voters rejected the EU constitution in a referendum in June 2006. Prime Minister Balkenende's government had conducted a campaign in favor of the treaty, and Balkenende subsequently announced that any future consideration was to take place in the legislature rather than by referendum. The government announced approval of the treaty in July 2008 after both houses of parliament provided large majorities voting in support.

In January 2011 the government sent 545 Dutch personnel and four F-16 fighter jets to Afghanistan but only after Green Left party leaders extracted a written guarantee from the Afghan government that Dutch-trained personnel would not be used in military action.

On August 7, 2012, Dutch diplomat Maurits R. Jochems was appointed NATO senior civilian representative in Afghanistan. At NATO's request, in December the Netherlands and Germany deployed Patriot missiles around two Turkish cities to protect against a possible attack by Syria.

In January, Finance Minister Jeroen DIJSSELBLOEM was named chairman of the Eurogroup, the association of all EU finance members, replacing Luxembourg's Jean-Claude Juncker.

Royal Dutch Shell signed a production agreement with the Ukrainian government in January 2013 to develop the Yuzivska gas field in eastern Ukraine. The company was forced to suspend its Arctic drilling program in February 2013, however, after one of its ships ran around off the Alaskan coast. The incident was the latest in a series of expensive mishaps in the first major effort to tap potentially lucrative Arctic oil deposits. The United States will not allow Shell to resume without new safety measures.

The Ministry of Foreign Trade and Development Cooperation shifted its foreign aid program in early 2013, moving to support Dutch investments in foreign countries rather than awarding cash grants. For example, in April, the Dutch government gave Tanzania $164 million to help construct a new airport terminal using a Dutch construction company.

Foreign Minister Frans TIMMERMANS concluded an agreement with Venezuela in June that will provide greater economic cooperation between the two countries. Venezuela is the closest neighbor of Aruba, Curaçao, and St. Maarten. In August Timmermans unveiled a list of 54 policy areas that the Netherlands wanted to remain under national, not EU, purview.

Current issues. In March and April 2012, the government spent seven weeks trying to adopt a budget that would cut €16 billion and bring the budget deficit below 3 percent of GDP, the EU target. Possible solutions on the table included higher taxes, raising the retirement age from 65 to 67, and charging for prescription medications. Consumer spending continued to contract, as homeowners struggled to pay down mortgages.

On April 21 the far-right wing Party for Freedom (PVV), refusing to raise the retirement age, withdrew its support from the government. Wilders dramatically declared, "We won't let our pensioners suffer for the Brussels dictators." Unable to create a new coalition, Prime Minister Rutte submitted his resignation on April 23, triggering new elections. Rutte and Finance Minister Jan KEES DE JAEGER (CDA) quickly put together a five-party coalition (VVD, CDA, D66, CU, GL) to serve as a caretaker government and to pass a budget by April 27, 2012. The PVV was left on the sidelines, as Wilders launched a book tour in the United States. While on tour, Wilders called on the Netherlands to leave the EU, saying, "Europe is the worst thing that ever happened to us."

The Dutch parliament ratified the establishment of the European Stability Mechanism (ESM) in April. The Netherlands would be the fifth-largest donor, contributing €700 billion to bail out struggling members of the eurozone. Wilders filed suit, asking a Dutch court to overturn the parliamentary vote so that the new parliament due to be elected in September would take up the issue. A court rejected his argument on June 1.

Snap parliamentary elections were held on September 12, 2012. Although most observers predicted a fragmented outcome, voters went with two longstanding centrist, pro-Europe parties. Prime Minister Mark Rutte's Party for Freedom (VVD) finished first, with 41 seats, followed closely by Labor (PvdA) with 38. Voters rejected the anti-Europe rhetoric of the PVV, which won only 15 seats, down from 24. The new VVD-PvdA government was sworn in on November 5, after reaching an agreement to cut €16 billion in government spending. However, it almost immediately collapsed as rank-and-file Liberals objected to a proposal to index health care premiums to income.

Racial and ethnic tensions flared in January, when a group of ethnic Moroccan youth beat a white, European soccer coach to death in Almere, a working-class suburb of Amsterdam.

The government nationalized SNS Reaal on February 1, injecting €3.7 billion to keep the bank solvent and prevent it from further damaging the national financial system.

Following the precedent of her mother and grandmother, on January 28 Queen Beatrix announced her intention to abdicate the throne in favor of her eldest son. King Willem-Alexander was inaugurated on April 30.

In March, the government announced that an additional €4 billion in austerity cuts were needed, as revised estimates put the budget deficit for 2013 at 3.3 percent of GDP. However, the ruling coalition faced stiff opposition to the proposal, especially in the Senate, where it did not have a majority. D66 demanded the reinstatement of €200 million in education spending, while the CU insisted the government abandon plans to make illegal immigration a criminal offense. In April the government announced it had reached a "social accord" with labor that would postpone difficult decisions on spending cuts until the fall and changes to unemployment benefits until 2016.

By August, the Dutch economy had contracted for six consecutive quarters, unemployment had grown to 6.8 percent, and the country was poised to miss the 3 percent deficit limit in 2014. EU officials ordered an additional €6 billion in spending cuts and taxes increases, which led labor unions to pull out of the social accord. Voters, weary of continued austerity, began to turn away from the ruling parties and the PVV's favorability ratings rose.

In his first annual address to parliament, King Willem-Alexander on September 17 announced that the Dutch welfare model was no longer viable and that in the new "participatory society," citizens would have to assume more responsibility for their healthcare, pensions, and other social benefits.

POLITICAL PARTIES

The growth of the Dutch multiparty system, which emerged from the tendency of political parties to reflect the interests of particular religious and economic groups, has been reinforced by the use of proportional representation. Twenty-one parties contested the 2012 *Tweede Kamer* elections; 11 won seats.

Government Parties:

People's Party for Freedom and Democracy (*Volkspartij voor Vrijheid en Democratie*—VVD). The forerunners of the VVD included the prewar Liberal State and Liberal Democratic parties. Organized in 1948, the party drew its major support from upper-class businesspeople and middle-class, white-collar workers. Although it accepted social welfare measures, the VVD was conservative in outlook and strongly favored free enterprise and separation of church and state.

The party lost ground in both the 1986 and 1989 elections, on the latter occasion going into opposition for the first time since 1982. In the May 1994 balloting, however, the VVD advanced from 14.6 to 19.9 percent of the vote and then entered into a governing coalition with the PvdA and D66 in August. The VVD struck a popular chord with its tough line on immigration and asylum seekers, overtaking the CDA as the strongest party in provincial elections in March 1995. The VVD's Second Chamber seat total rose from 31 to 38 in the May 1998 poll (based on 25 percent of the vote), although it fell to second place behind the CDA in the provincial elections of March 1999. The rise of the LPF (below) cost the VVD in the May 2002 general election, at which VVD representation fell to 23 seats.

Jozias van AARTSEN became party leader when the VVD joined the coalition government in July 2002 and former party leader Garrit ZALM left the post to become minister of finance. Van Aartsen resigned his position after the party performed poorly in the municipal elections of March 2006, and Mark Rutte was elected new party leader on May 31, defeating Immigration and Integration Minister Rita Verdonk for the post.

Verdonk was at the center of the controversy that brought down the government in late June 2006, as the D66 left in protest over her actions in the Hirsi Ali affair (see Political background, above). Although the VVD remained a partner in the interim minority government that followed, the November election saw the VVD vote share drop to 14.7 percent and its seat total to fall to 22, a loss of 6. Verdonk stirred another government crisis in December 2006, and when she continued to press her anti-immigrant criticisms of the VVD, the party expelled her in September 2007. Rather than resign her parliamentary seat, she decided to sit as an independent and subsequently formed a new political group called Proud of the Netherlands (see below).

In the 2010 legislative balloting the VVD for the first time became the largest party in the *Tweede Kamer,* winning 31 seats on 20.5 percent of the vote. The party campaigned on a program of tough fiscal austerity measures and immigration restrictions. Under the continuing leadership of Mark Rutte, the VVD entered into a minority government coalition with the CDA, with pledged support from the PVV.

Following the collapse of the government in April 2012 over EU-mandated budget cuts, Rutte remained as caretaker prime minister and led his party to the September parliamentary election on a platform pledging to cut more government social security, health care, and aid funding. The VVD won 41 seats on a 26.58 percent vote share, and Ruute formed a majority government with the Labor Party.

Leaders: Mark RUTTE (Prime Minister), Halbe ZIJLSTRA (Parliamentary Chair), Benk KORTHALS (President), Wiet DE BRUIJN (Vice President), Robert REIBESTEIN (Second Vice President), Lucie WIGBOLDUS (General Secretary).

Labor Party (*Partij van de Arbeid*—PvdA). The Labor Party was formed in 1946 by a union of the former Socialist Democratic Workers' Party with left-wing Liberals and progressive Catholics and Protestants. It favored democratic socialism and was a strong supporter of the UN and European integration. The party program stressed the importance of equality of economic benefits, greater consultation in decision making, and reduced defense spending. In October 1977, against the advice of its leadership, the party's national congress voted in favor of the establishment of a republican form of government for the Netherlands. During the same period, the PvdA strongly opposed both nuclear power generation and the deployment of cruise missiles. Subsequent policy considerations focused on employment; strengthening social security, health care, and education; transport infrastructure; and debt reduction.

In the May 1994 general election, the PvdA slipped from 31.9 to 24.0 percent of the vote but overtook the CDA as the largest Second Chamber party with 37 seats. It won 45 seats (on a 29 percent vote share) in May 1998. The PvdA's seat total slipped badly to 23 in the May 2002 balloting for the *Tweede Kamer,* but the party rebounded to 42 seats in January 2003, making it the second largest party in the country.

In municipal elections in March 2006, the PvdA showed a sharp increase in support, raising its share of the vote by 7.6 percent to 23.4 percent from the 2002 elections. Some analysts predicted that the PvdA would be the main beneficiary of the resignation in June 2006 of the Balkenende government, since recent opinion polls projected that the PvdA would win the largest share of parliamentary seats if a snap election were held. Those forecasts proved premature, however. With the economy rebounding and the CDA losing only 3 seats in the November election, the PvdA lost 9 seats. However, its 33-seat total kept it as the second largest party in the parliament, which was enough to make it the most viable partner for the CDA in the new government.

In February 2010 the PvdA withdrew from government in opposition to Prime Minister Balkenende's agreement to extend the Dutch mission in Afghanistan beyond previously agreed upon terms, prompting a call for new elections in June. Job Cohen, the former mayor of Amsterdam, was selected to lead the PvdA in the election campaign. Running on a platform of multiculturalism and opposition to other parties' plans for strong austerity measures, the PvdA held its position as the second-largest party in the *Tweede Kamer,* winning 30 seats on 19.6 percent of the vote. The party's policy disagreements with the other major parties led Cohen to give only fleeting consideration to reaching an agreement to have the PvdA participate in a new government. PvdA lost considerable popular support while out of the government and did not have a strategy for dealing with the far-right PVV. Cohen resigned on February 20, 2012.

A PvdA party congress elected Diederik Samsom as chair of the parliamentary group on March 21, 2012. He opted not to join the five-party caretaker government and argued that the 3 percent deficit target would disproportionately hit Labor's constituents. The PvdA finished second in the September election, winning 38 seats with 24.84 percent of votes. Samsom agreed to be the junior partner in a majority government with the VVD.

Leaders: Diederik SAMSOM (Party Leader), Hans SPEKMAN (Party Chair), Lodewijk ASSCHER (Deputy Prime Minister).

Opposition Parties:

Party for Freedom (*Party voor de Vrijheid*—PVV). The PVV grew out of a one-man faction in the *Tweede Kamer* in 2004 by Geert Wilders, who had resigned from the VVD in a dispute with party leaders over Turkey's possible entry into the EU but had refused to resign his legislative seat. Wilders subsequently continued to promote anti-immigration policies and other right-wing causes. For the 2006 legislative poll, the Euro-skeptic PVV presented itself as a free-market, low-tax party and an advocate of conformity to Judeo-Christian cultural traditions. The PVV surprised observers by securing nine seats in the *Tweede Kamer* on a vote share of 5.9 percent.

Wilders burst onto the political scene by focusing on immigration issues, especially with respect to Muslims. *Fitna*, his 2008 short film portrays the Koran as a source of violence and terrorism. After Dutch television refused to air the film, Wilders released it on the Internet, leading to the closing of the Dutch embassy in Afghanistan and calls for boycotts of Dutch products. The film drew little reaction from Dutch Muslims, but the government put Wilders on trial for inciting hatred and discrimination against Muslims. (Wilders was acquitted of all charges in June 2011.)

Even though the PVV had called for the European Parliament to be dissolved, the party presented candidates for the elections to that body for the first time in June 2009. In a surprising outcome, the PVV finished second in that balloting with 17 percent of the vote, securing 4 of 25 seats. Wilders' hate speech trial began in January 2010 but was aborted in the autumn (after Wilders successfully pressed a charge of judicial bias) and scheduled for retrial. The final court verdict was announced in June 2011 and cleared Wilders of all charges against him. The court concluded that while Wilders's remarks were "insulting," they were protected under the country's freedom of speech laws and were aimed mostly at Islam as a religion rather than the Muslim population.

With concerns over immigration on the rise, the Wilders-led PVV surpassed expectations by becoming the third-largest party in the *Tweede Kamer* in the June 2010 poll, winning 24 seats on 15.5 percent of the vote. Holding a significant share of the seats, Wilders made it clear that he would be willing to compromise on his policy positions in order to be part of a government arrangement. In October the PVV entered into a government-supportive role with the minority VVD-CDA coalition through an agreement that contained policy plans aimed at restricting immigration and tightening integration policies, including a ban on the Islamic burka.

In April 2012 Wilders and the PVV brought down the ruling VVD/CDA coalition by refusing to vote budget cuts needed to meet EU-imposed fiscal targets. Instead, Wilders advocated quitting the EU and readopting the guilder as its own currency.

Members of the PVV parliamentary faction have complained about a perceived lack of democracy within the party. Between April and July 2012, three PVV MPs quit, calling Wilders a dictator. Hero BRINKMAN formed his own political party (see below), while Wim KORTENOEVEN and Marcial HERNANDEZ tweeted their resignations as Wilders unveiled the PVV campaign platform ("Out of the morass, out of the euro, out of the EU!") during a press conference. The PVV dropped from 24 seats to 15 in the September parliamentary elections, but its popularity revived in early 2013. Wilders announced plans to create an anti-Europe bloc for the 2014 European Parliamentary elections with France's National Front and Italy's Lega Nord, among others.

Leaders: Geert WILDERS (Chair and Parliamentary Chair), Fleur AGEMA (Parliamentary Vice Chair), Martin BOSMA (Group Secretary).

Socialist Party (*Socialistische Partij*—SP). The left-wing SP increased its vote share from 0.4 percent in 1989 to 1.3 percent in the May 1994 Second Chamber poll, returning two deputies. In preparation for the May 1998 elections, party leaders argued that there was "too much poverty" in the country and criticized a perceived widening of the gap between the rich and poor. It won 3.5 percent of the votes, for five seats. The SP also offered a progressive agenda, in contrast to the LPF, for the 2002 and 2003 elections for the *Tweede Kamer,* securing nine seats both times. In 2005 the SP opposed the proposed new EU constitution.

The SP won 5.7 percent of the votes in the March 2006 municipal elections (more than doubling its number of seats). In the 2006 *Tweede Kamer* election the SP won 25 seats, a gain of 16, making it the third largest party in that chamber. The party dropped to fifth largest following the June 2010 general election, at which it won 15 seats on 9.8 percent of the vote.

The SP was leading public opinion polls going into the September 2012 parliamentary elections, and it was projected to take 32 seats. However, on election day the SP secured only 15 seats with a 9.65 share of the vote, finishing fourth overall.

Leaders: Emile ROEMER (Parliamentary Chair), Jan MARIJNISSEN (Chair); Hans van HEIJNINGEN (General Secretary).

Christian Democratic Appeal (*Christen-Democratisch Appèl*—CDA). Party organization in the Netherlands has long embraced a distinction between confessional and secular parties, although the former experienced a gradual erosion in electoral support. Partly in an effort to counter the anticonfessional trend, the CDA was organized in December 1976 as an unprecedented alliance of the Catholic People's Party (*Katholieke Volkspartij*—KVP) and two Protestant groups, the Anti-Revolutionary Party (*Anti-Revolutionaire Partij*—ARP) and the Christian Historical Union (*Christelijk-Historische Unie*—CHU). The KVP was founded in 1945 as a centrist party supported primarily by Roman Catholic businesspeople, farmers, and some workers. It endorsed many social welfare programs while favoring close cooperation between spiritual and secular forces in the community. The ARP, founded in 1879, was the nation's oldest political organization, drawing its principal strength from Calvinist businesspeople, white-collar workers, and farmers. The CHU was formed in 1908 by a dissident faction of the ARP. Traditionally more centrist than the parent party, it shared the ARP's Calvinist outlook.

The three constituent parties, which had presented joint lists at the May 1977 parliamentary election, agreed in October 1980 to merge into a unified political grouping. Led by Ruud Lubbers, the CDA obtained a plurality of legislative seats in both 1986 and 1989, aligning itself with the Liberals on the earlier occasion and with Labor on the latter. Under the new leadership of Elco Brinkman for the May 1994 poll, the CDA lost a third of its support (falling from 35.3 to 22.2 percent of the vote) and was reduced to the status of second strongest Second Chamber party. Brinkman resigned as CDA leader in August.

A period of "uncertainty and wrangling" developed within the CDA in the wake of the 1994 electoral decline, the right wing appearing to gain ascendancy in 1997 with selection of Jaap de HOOP SCHEFFER as new party leader. In the May 1998 Second Chamber balloting, the CDA slipped to 29 seats (down from 34) on a vote share of 18.4 percent, although it rebounded strongly to finish first in the March 1999 provincial elections and, thus, in selection of the new First Chamber two months later. De Hoop Scheffer resigned as parliamentary leader in September 2001, citing inadequate support from the party. He was succeeded by Jan Peter Balkenende.

Positioning itself as a "reasoned choice" between the radically conservative LPF (below) and the social-democratic PvdA, the CDA led all parties by securing 43 seats in the May 2002 election to the *Tweede Kamer.* Balkenende subsequently formed a coalition government with the LPF and VVD, but the government collapsed three months later due to divisions within the LPF. Balkenende formed another coalition (this time with the VVD and the D66) following the January 2003 general election, in which the CDA again finished first with 44 seats.

In municipal elections in March 2006, the CDA showed a moderate loss of support, winning 16.9 percent of the vote, a drop of 3.4 percent over the 2002 elections, apparently as a result of an underperforming economy and unpopular pension and health care reforms.

After the June 29, 2006, cabinet crisis and the installation of a minority interim government of the CDA and VVD on July 7, new elections were held in November. The CDA won 26.5 percent of the vote and 41 seats. Balkenende formed a new government in coalition with PvdA and CU in February 2007. Following the break-up of the governing coalition in February 2010, the CDA suffered its worst-ever results (only 21 seats on a vote share of 13.6 percent) in the June elections. Balkenende resigned as CDA leader immediately after the balloting and was replaced by Maxime Verhagen on June 10.

Negotiations over a new government formation became prolonged as CDA legislators debated whether and how to align with a VVD-led administration that would grant a influential role to the right-wing PVV. The CDA leadership left the decision to approve a VVD-CDA minority government with pledged support from the PVV to its party congress. The congress approved the initiative on a 68 percent vote in favor (a smaller majority than expected), and the CDA became the junior government party on October 14. Verhagen asked to be removed from the CDA list for the September 2012 election, citing the need for a break from politics.

The CDA plummeted from junior government partner to fifth place in the September 2012 elections, dropping from 21 seats to only 13 on an 8.51 vote share.

Leaders: Ruth PEETOM (Party Chair), Sybrand VAN HAERSMA BUMA (Parliamentary Chair), Mijam STERK (Parliamentary Vice Chair).

Democrats 66 (*Democraten 66*—D66). Formed in 1966 as a left-of-center party, the D66 favored the dropping of proportional representation and the direct election of the prime minister. Its stand on other domestic and foreign policy questions was similar to that of the PvdA. It changed its name from Democrats '66 to Democrats 66 in 1986. The party's lower house representation rose from nine seats in 1986 to 12 in 1989, the latter figure being doubled in 1994 on a vote share of 15.5 percent.

In May 1999 the D66 caused the near collapse of the government when its proposal for "corrective referendums" (to override certain parliamentary decisions) was defeated by one vote in the upper house. The matter was resolved in early June when the D66 accepted a compromise that opened the way for nonbinding referendums.

The D66's representation fell to seven seats in the May 2002 Second Chamber balloting, down from 14 in 1998. Although the party secured only six seats in the January 2003 election, the D66 became something of a "kingmaker" when it provided the necessary legislative majority for the new coalition government led by the CDA and the VVD.

The D66 withdrew its support for the Balkenende coalition government in June 2006, resulting in the collapse of the government. The immediate cause of the party's withdrawal was the failure of the VVD's Rita Verdonk to resign as immigration minister (see Current issues for details), but the party also objected to the Balkenende government's support for sending additional Dutch troops to Afghanistan.

The D66's electoral decline continued in the 2006 legislative poll, in which it won only three seats on a 2.0 percent vote share. However, the party rebounded to win ten seats on 7.0 percent of the vote in the June 2010 general elections.

The party won a dozen seats—a gain of two—in September 2012 with its platform promoting job growth, sound public finances, education, and an end to stagnation.

Leaders: Alexander PECHTOLD (Parliamentary Chair), Ingrid van ENGELSHOVEN (Chair), Woulter KOOLMEES (Vice Chair).

Christian Union (*ChristenUnie*—CU). The Christian Union dates from January 2000, when the Reformational Political Federation (*Reformatorische Politieke Federatie*—RPF) and the Reformed Political Union (*Gereformeerd Politiek Verbond*—GPV) agreed to unify. Appealing to both Calvinists and interdenominational Christians, the RPF had been formed in 1975; it obtained two Second Chamber seats in 1981 and 1982, one in 1986 and 1989, and three in 1994 and 1998. Established in 1948, the more conservative, Calvinist GPV long supported a strong defense policy and the Atlantic alliance but opposed any subordination to a supranational governmental body. It won two Second Chamber seats in each of the last three general elections prior to the launching of the CU.

Following the merger, the Christian Union controlled four seats in the First Chamber and five seats in the Second Chamber. The GPV and RPF factions in the Second Chamber formally merged in March 2001. The Christian Union won three seats in the *Tweede Kamer* in 2002 as well as 2003. After winning nearly 4 percent of the vote and six seats in the *Tweede Kamer* in November 2006, the CU joined the Balkenende-led governing coalition. The CU stayed on as a partner in the caretaker government after the PvdA withdrew from the coalition in February 2010. The CU thereafter won five seats on 3.2 percent of the vote in the June balloting but did not retain a position in government. It similarly secured five seats on 3.13 percent of the vote in September 2012. Long-time chair Peter BLOKHUIS retired in 2012.

Leaders: Arie SLOB (Chair), Bert GROEN (Vice Chair), Esmé WIEGMAN-VAN MEPPELEN SCHEPPINK (Group Secretary).

Green Left (*GroenLinks*—GL). The GL was organized as an electoral coalition prior to the 1989 balloting by the Evangelical People's Party (*Evangelische Volkspartij*—EVP), the Radical Political Party (*Politieke Partij Radikalen*—PPR), the Pacifist Socialist Party (*Pacifistisch Socialistische Partij*—PSP), and the Netherlands Communist Party (*Communistische Partij van Nederland*—CPN). It became a permanent party in 1991, when each of its constituent groups voted to disband. The party seeks to establish a country that is sustainable and socially minded.

The GL more than doubled its previous representation when it won 11 *Tweede Kamer* seats on a 7.3 percent vote share in 1998. After the GL won 10 seats in the 2002 elections, its representation fell to 8 seats in 2003 and 7 in 2006. The GL's seat share increased to 10, on 6.7 percent of the vote, in the June 2010 balloting, but it dropped back to 4 seats, on 2.33 percent of the vote, in September 2012. The party elected a new slate of leaders in March 2013, ahead of the 2014 European parliamentary elections.

Leaders: Bram VAN OJIK (Parliamentary Chair), Rik GRASHOFF (Chair).

Political Reformed Party (*Staatkundig Gereformeerde Partij*—SGP). Dating from 1918, the SGP is an extreme right-wing Calvinist party that bases its political and social outlook on its own interpretation of the Bible. It advocates strong legal enforcement, including the use of the death penalty, and is against supranational government, which it feels opens society to corrupting influences. Since 1993 women have been banned from active membership.

The SGP retained its existing three Second Chamber seats in the 1989 election but slipped to two in May 1994 before rebounding to three in 1998. It frequently cooperated with the GPV and RPF (see Christian Union), including presentation of joint lists for European Parliament balloting. The SGP won two seats in the *Tweede Kamer* in 2002, 2003, 2006, and 2010 (on 1.7 percent of the vote in the latter). It picked up a third seat in 2012, with 2.09 percent of the vote.

Leaders: C. G. (Kees) van der STAAIJ (Parliamentary Chair), Adrie VAN HETEREN (Chair).

Party for the Animals (*Party voor de Dieren*—PvdD). Founded in 2002 as an advocate for animal rights, the party won 0.5 percent of the *Tweede Kamer* vote in 2003. However, it secured two seats in the Second Chamber in 2006 (on a vote share of 1.8 percent), thus becoming the first party principally devoted to animal welfare to gain entry into parliament. The party retained its two seats in the June 2010 election, on 1.3 percent of the vote, and again in September 2012 on 1.93 percent of the vote.

Leader: Marianne THIEME (Chair).

50Plus Party (*50 Plus Partij*). 50Plus was established in 2009 to advocate for pension reform, including cost of living increases, tax rates, rent freezes, and retirement age. The party calls upon the government to create a cabinet-level post for senior citizens affairs. The president of 50Plus is Jan Nagel, who served in the Dutch Senate for six years as a member of the PvdA. The party has a hotline that provides advice to patients whose prescriptions are not covered under current insurance programs. 50Plus has one seat in the Senate (held by Nagel) and nine provincial office holders. It entered the *Tweed Kamer* in September 2012, winning two seats on 1.88 percent of the vote.

Leaders: Jan NAGEL (President), Henk KROL (Vice President).

Other Parties That Contested the 2012 Elections:

Democratic Political Turning Point (*Het Demokratisch Politiek Keerpunt*—DPK) formed by the June 2012 merger of Hero Brinkman's Independent Citizen's Party and the Rita Verdonk's Proud of the Netherlands Party (TON). Brinkman had been a member of the extremist PVV and won a parliamentary seat in 2010 as an independent. He resigned from the PVV on March 20, 2012, complaining that the party structure was not democratic. Verdonk, the minister of immigration and integration from 2003 to 2006, set up her own party in 2010 after losing a bid to lead the VVD to Mark Rutte.

Leaders: Hero BRINKMAN (Chair), Rita VERDONK.

Nine other parties and lists contested the 2012 elections to the *Tweede Kamer* unsuccessfully. They were the **Pirate Party** (*Piratenpartij*—PiratenP), led by Dirk POOT (0.3 percent); the **Party for Human and Spirit** (*Partij voor Mens en Spirit*—MenS), led by Lea MANDERS (0.2 percent of the vote); **Sovereign Independent Pioneers** (*Soeverein Onafhankelijke Pioniers Nederland*—SOPN), led by Johan OLDENKAMP (0.1 percent); **Party of the Future** (*Partij van de Toekomst*—PvdT), Johan VLEMMIX (0.1 percent); **Libertarian Party** (*Libertarische Partij*—LP), led by Toine MANDERS (4,163 votes); **Netherlands Local** (*Nederland Lokaal*—NL), led by Ton SCHIJVENAARS (2,842 votes); **Liberal Democratic Party** (*Liberaal Democratische Partij*—LibDem), founded by Samuel VAN TUYLL VAN SEROOSKERKEN (2,126 votes); **Anti-Europe Party** (*Anti Europa Partij*—AeuP), led by Arnold REINTEN (2,013 votes); and the **Political Party NXD** (Politieke Partij NXD) of Anil SAMLAL (62 votes).

The Greens (*De Groenen*). Founded in 1983 as a federation of local parties, the conservative Greens won 1 upper House seat in 1995 on an independent list and retained it in May 1999. Although the party failed to capture any upper or lower House seats in 2003, it remained active at the local level.

Leader: Paul FRERIKS (Chair).

In 2004 Paul van BUITENEN (a former member of the European Commission) launched **Transparent Europe,** which secured two seats in the June 2004 balloting for the European Parliament on an antifraud and antiwaste platform. (For a list of other small parties that were active in the 1990s and/or early 2000s, see the 2007 *Handbook.*)

LEGISLATURE

The **States General** (*Staten Generaal*) is a bicameral body consisting of an indirectly elected First Chamber and a directly elected Second Chamber.

First Chamber (*Eerste Kamer*). The 75 members of the upper house are indirectly elected by the country's 12 provincial councils for four-year terms. Following the provincial balloting of March 2, 2011, elections to the First Chamber on May 23 gave the People's Party for Freedom and Democracy 16 seats; the Labor Party, 14; the Christian Democratic Appeal, 11; the Freedom Party, 10; the Socialist Party, 8; the Democrats 66, 5; The Green Left, 5; the Christian Union, 2; the Political Reformed Party, 1; the 50 Plus Party, 1; the Party for the Animals, 1; and the Independent Senate Group, 1.

President: Ankie BROEKER-KNOL.

Second Chamber (*Tweede Kamer*). The lower house consists of 150 members directly elected (in a single nationwide district under a pure proportional representation system) for four years, subject to dissolution and, under certain circumstances, term extension. The threshold for a party or list to secure representation is 0.67 percent of the national vote. Following the most recent election of September 12, 2012, the People's Party for Freedom and Democracy held 41 seats; the Labor Party, 38; the Party for Freedom, 15; the Socialist Party, 15; the Christian Democratic Appeal, 13; the Democrats 66, 12; the Christian Union, 5; the Green Left, 4; the Political Reformed Party, 3; the Party for the Animals, 2; and the 50Plus Party, 2.

Chair: Anouchka VAN MITTENBERG.

CABINET

[as of September 14, 2013]

Prime Minister	Mark Rutte (VVD)
Deputy Prime Minister	Lodewijk Asscher (PvdA)
Ministers	
Defense	Jeanine Hennis-Plasschaert (VVD) [f]
Economic Affairs	Henk Kamp (VVD)
Education, Culture, and Science	Jet Bussemaker (PvdA) [f]
Finance	Jeroen Dijsselbloem (PvdA)
Foreign Affairs	Frans Timmermans (PvdA)
Foreign Trade and Development Cooperation	Lilianne Ploumen (PvdA) [f]
General Affairs	Mark Rutte (VVD)
Health, Welfare, and Sport	Edith Schippers (VVD) [f]
Housing and the Central Government Sector	Stef Blok (VVD)

Infrastructure and the Environment	Melanie Schultz van Haegen-Mass Geesteranus (VVD) [f]
Interior and Kingdom Relations	Ronald Plasterk (PvdA)
Security and Justice	Ivo Opstelten (VVD)
Social Affairs and Employment	Lodewijk Asscher (PvdA)

[f] = female

INTERGOVERNMENTAL REPRESENTATION

Ambassador to the U.S.: Rudolf BEKINK.

U.S. Ambassador to the Netherlands: Tim BROAS.

Permanent Representative to the UN: Karel VAN OOSTEROM.

IGO Memberships (Non-UN): ADB, AfDB, CEUR, EBRD, EIB, EU, IADB, IEA, ICC, IOM, NATO, OECD, OSCE, WTO.

RELATED TERRITORIES

The bulk of the Netherlands' overseas empire disappeared with the accession of Indonesia to independence after World War II and the latter's subsequent acquisition of West New Guinea (Irian Jaya). Remaining under the Dutch Crown were the two Western Hemisphere territories of Netherlands Antilles and Suriname, the latter of which became independent on November 25, 1975. As of January 1, 1986, the island of Aruba was politically detached from the Antilles federation, joining it as an internally self-governing territory. In September 2010 the Netherlands and Netherlands Antilles signed a final declaration that Curaçao and St. Maarten would become autonomous entities (like Aruba) within the Kingdom of the Netherlands with Bonaire, St. Eustatius, and Saba (the other components of the Netherlands Antilles), becoming special municipalities within the Netherlands proper. The new arrangements went into effect on October 10, 2010.

ARUBA

Political Status: Formerly part of the Netherlands Antilles; became autonomous in internal affairs on January 1, 1986.

Area: 74.5 sq. mi. (193 sq. km).

Population: 110,227 (2012E—UN); 107,635 (2012E—U.S. Census).

Major Urban Center (2005E): ORANJESTAD (30,000).

Official Language: Dutch. English, Spanish, and Papiamento (an Antillean hybrid of mainly Portuguese and Spanish that is common to the Leeward Islands) are also spoken.

Monetary Unit: Aruban Guilder (official rate November 1, 2013: 1.79 guilders = $1US). The guilder (also called the florin) is at par with the Netherlands Antilles guilder, which is pegged to the U.S. dollar.

Sovereign: Queen BEATRIX Wilhelmina Armgard.

Governor: Fredis J. (Freddy) REFUNJOL; invested on May 7, 2004, succeeding Olindo KOOLMAN.

Prime Minister: Michael (Mike) Godfried EMAN (Aruban People's Party); sworn in on October 30, 2009, following legislative election of September 24, succeeding Nelson Orlando ODUBER (People's Electoral Movement, *Movimento Electoral di Pueblo*—MEP); reelected on September 27, 2013.

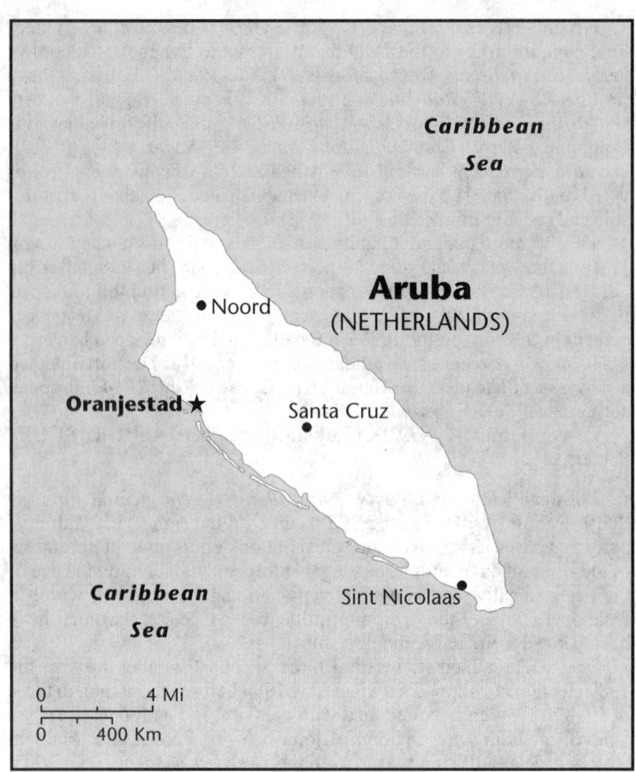

THE COUNTRY

Aruba is a Caribbean island situated approximately 16 miles off the northeast coast of Venezuela and 50 miles west of Curaçao. Like other former Dutch dependencies in the area, its population is largely of mixed African ancestry, with minorities of Carib Indian and European extraction. Roman Catholicism is the dominant religion. Tourism is presently of primary economic importance, making up 78 percent of the GDP in 2010. The island's only oil refinery, which ceased operations in March 2012, was a significant source of income (see Current issues, below). The tourism sector was adversely affected by the September 2001 terrorist assaults on the United States, which contributed to a 4 percent decline in GDP for the year, as well as by negative publicity after the disappearance of American teenager Natalee Holloway in May 2005. From 2006 to 2008 a recovery in tourism, along with what the International Monetary Fund (IMF) defined as "robust" activity in the construction and utility sectors, contributed to an economic rebound. However, the impact of the recent global economic crisis was severe; the IMF estimated a cumulative GDP contraction of 15 percent in 2009 and 2010. After suffering another dip in late 2012, growth of 2 percent was expected in 2013.

GOVERNMENT AND POLITICS

Political background. Like Curaçao and Bonaire, Aruba became a Dutch possession in 1634 and remained so, save for a brief period of British control during the Napoleonic wars, until participating in constitutional equality with the Netherlands as part of the Netherlands Antilles in 1954.

However, a majority of the islanders disliked what was perceived as both political and economic domination by Curaçao and entered into lengthy discussions with Dutch authorities that resulted in the achievement of formal parity with the Netherlands and Netherlands Antilles, under the Dutch crown, on January 1, 1986. Upon the assumption of domestic autonomy, the assets and liabilities of Aruba and the five remaining members of the federation were divided in the ratio 30–70, Aruba agreeing to retain economic and political links to the Netherlands Antilles at the ministerial level for a ten-year period. (Full independence was initially projected for 1996 but tentative agreement was reached in July 1990 for the island to maintain its existing status indefinitely rather than move on to independence. References to the 1996 independence date were removed from the related constitutional documents completely in April 1995.)

Pre-autonomy balloting on November 22, 1985, yielded victory for a four-party coalition headed by John Hendrik Albert (Henny) EMAN of the center-right Aruba People's Party (AVP) over the MEP, then led by "the architect of Aruba's transition to... eventual independence," Gilberto (Betico) CROES. Following the election of January 7, 1989, a three-party government was formed, led by the MEP's Nelson ODUBER. The coalition continued in office after the election of January 8, 1993. Oduber resigned on April 17, 1994, after disagreements with his coalition partners. Eman headed a new government coalition that included the small Aruban Liberal Organization (OLA) following a general election on July 29.

The legislature was dissolved on September 15, 1997, in the wake of a dispute between the AVP and its coalition partner. A general election on December 12 failed to resolve the impasse, the parliamentary distribution remaining unchanged. Subsequent negotiations continued until April 16, 1998, when the former coalition partners reached agreement on a new government.

The AVP/OLA government again collapsed in June 2001 when the two OLA members resigned after voicing objections to the AVP's plan to convert the tourism ministry into a semiprivate agency. Early elections were therefore held on September 28, with the MEP winning a majority of 12 seats, setting the stage for the return of MEP leader Oduber to the prime minister's post on October 30. Oduber remained in office following the election of September 23, 2005, at which the MEP retained control with 11 seats. On the basis of a 12-seat AVP victory in the most recent election of September 8, 2009, Michael (Mike) EMAN, the youngest brother of former prime minister Henny Eman, was named to form a new government. In June 2010 the chair of Parliament, Rendolf LEE (AVP), announced his retirement during a parliamentary meeting, citing lack of respect from his party.

Seven parties contested the September 27, 2013, elections. The AVP, led by Eman, won 13 seats with 58 percent of the vote, a solid victory over the MEP's 7 seats, with 30 percent of the vote.

Constitution and government. The Dutch sovereign is titular head of state and is represented in Aruba by an appointed governor. Domestic affairs are the responsibility of the prime minister and other members of the Council of Ministers, appointed with the advice and approval of a unicameral *Staten* (legislature) of 21 deputies. Control of foreign affairs and defense is vested in the Council of Ministers in The Hague, with the Department of Foreign Affairs in Aruba working in conjunction with the Ministry of Foreign Affairs in The Hague. Similarly, an Aruban minister plenipotentiary sits as a voting member of the Council of Ministers on matters affecting the island. Judicial authority is exercised by a local court of first instance, with appeal to a joint Court of Appeal of the Netherlands Antilles and Aruba, and ultimate appeal to the Supreme Court of the Netherlands in The Hague.

Current issues. In March 2012 Valero closed its oil refinery on the island because of high costs. The refinery was a major player in the country's economy; when Valero temporarily shut down the refinery in 2009 over a tax issue, Aruba's economy dramatically contracted, and unemployment rose to 11 percent. An unidentified bidder made a $350 million nonbinding bid for the facility in May, and sources close to the negotiation said the anonymous company was PetroChina. In September, Valero unveiled plans to convert the refinery to a products terminal.

In July the government approved plans to construct the island's second wind farm.

POLITICAL PARTIES

Parliamentary Parties:

Aruban People's Party (*Arubaanse Volkspartij*—AVP/*Partido di Pueplo Arubano*—PPA). Like the MEP, the AVP advocated separation of Aruba from the Netherlands Antilles. A member of the Christian Democrat International, it formed a coalition government that included the PPA and AND (below) after the 1985 balloting but was forced into opposition in 1989. Though its vote share exceeded that of the MEP in 1993, they tied with 9 seats each. It formed a new government in coalition with the OLA (below) after the 1994 election, which was revived in May 1998 but fell in June 2001. In the September election it won 6 *Staten* seats, adding 2 more in 2005. It returned to power with a majority of 12 seats in 2009, and added a seat in 2013 balloting.

Leader: Michael (Mike) Godfried EMAN (Party Leader).

People's Electoral Movement (*Movimiento Electoral di Pueblo*—MEP). Founded in 1971 and a member of the Socialist International, the MEP was in the forefront of the struggle for self-government. It won a plurality of 10 *Staten* seats in 1989. Two were lost in 1993, but the MEP was able to form a governing coalition with the AND and PPA (below) prior to the withdrawal of both in April 1994. In 2001 the MEP won 12 seats, 1 of which was lost in 2005. It fell to a minority of 8 seats in 2009. In July 2011 a major party leader, Booshi WEVER, announced his resignation from the party leadership because of a lack of confidence in the party's political leader, Nelson Oduber. The MEP won 7 seats in September 2013 balloting.

Leader: Nelson Orlando ODUBER (Party Leader).

Real Democracy (*Democracia Real*—DR). Launched in 2004, the DR failed to secure legislative representation in 2005 but won one seat in 2009. With 8 percent of the vote, the DR maintained its single seat in 2013 balloting.

Leader: Andin BIKKER (Party Leader).

Other Parties:

Aruban Patriotic Party (*Arubaanse Patriottische Partij*—APP/*Partido Patriótico Arubano*—PPA). Organized in 1949, the PPA is a social-democratic group that has opposed full independence for the island. It won two parliamentary seats in 2001 but lost both in 2005, and again was unsuccessful in 2013.

Leader: Benedict (Benny) Jocelyn Montgomery NISBETT.

Network of Eternal Democracy (*Red Eternal Democratico*—RED). The RED won one seat in the 2005 election, but lost in 2009. It contested unsuccessfully in 2013.

Leader: Armando (Rudy) LAMPE.

Also contesting the 2013 elections were the **United Christians Reinforcing Aruba's Potential** (*Cristiannan Uni Reforzando Potencial*—CURPA); the **Independent Social Movement/Aruban Liberal Organization** (Organisatie Liberaal Arubaanse/*Organisacion Liberal Arubano/Organisashion pa Liberashou di Aruba*—OLA) led by Glenbert François CROES; and the **Aruban Patriotic Movement** (*Movimento Patriotico Arubana*—MPA), led by Monica ARENDS-KOCK, who has been described as Aruba's first female party leader.

Other parties include the **National Democratic Action** (*Acción Democratico Nacional*—AND), led by Pedro Charro KELLY; the **Aruban Democratic Alliance** (*Aliansa Democratico Arubano*—ADA), led by Robert Frederick WEVER; and the **Concentration for the Liberation of Aruba** (*Conscientisacion y Liberacion Arubano*—CLA), led by Mariano Duvert BLUME.

LEGISLATURE

The unicameral **States** (*Staten*) consists of 21 members elected for four-year terms, subject to dissolution. In the most recent balloting, held on September 27, 2013, the Aruban People's Party won 13 seats; the People's Electoral Movement, 7; Real Democracy, 1.

Chair: Paul CROES.

CABINET

[as of September 1, 2013]

Prime Minister	Michael Godfried Eman
Ministers	
Economic Affairs, Social Affairs and Culture	Michelle Hooyboer-Winklaar [f]
Finance, Communications, Utilities, and Energy	Mike Eric de Meza
General Affairs	Michael Godfried Eman
Integration, Infrastructure, and Environment	Oslin Benito Sevinger
Justice and Education	Arthur Lawrence Dowers
Public Health and Sports	Richard Wayne Milton Visser
Tourism, Transportation, and Labor	Otmar Enrique Oduber
Minister Plenipotentiary in the Hague	Edwin Bibiana Abath
Minister Plenipotentiary in Washington, D.C.	Jocelyne Croes [f]

[f] = female

INTERGOVERNMENTAL REPRESENTATION

Foreign relations are for the most part conducted through the Netherlands Ministry of Foreign Affairs in The Hague, although there is a Minister Plenipotentiary in the Netherlands Embassy in Washington, D.C., and the United States maintains a Consulate General's Office in Curaçao that also serves Aruba.

CURAÇAO

Country of Curaçao
Land Curaçao (Dutch)
Pais Kòrsou (Papiamento)

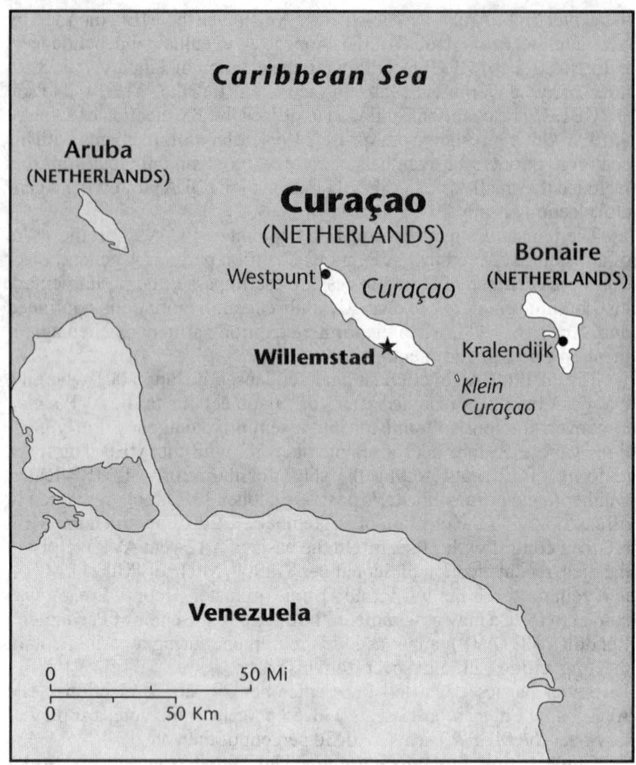

Political Status: Former Dutch dependency; from 1948 a component of the Netherlands Antilles, which became autonomous in internal affairs, under charter of the Kingdom of the Netherlands, effective December 29, 1954; achieved separate autonomous status in internal affairs upon dissolution of the Netherlands Antilles on October 10, 2010.

Area: 171 sq. mi. (444 sq. km).

Population: 148,000 (2010E—UN), 146,836 (2013E—U.S. Census).

Major Urban Center (2005E): WILLEMSTAD (urban area, 76,000).

Official Languages: Dutch, English, and Papiamento (an Antillean hybrid, principally of Portuguese and Spanish).

Monetary Unit: Netherlands Antilles Guilder (official rate November 1, 2013: 1.79 guilders = $1US). The guilder is pegged to the U.S. dollar. A new Caribbean guilder, likewise pegged to the dollar, is to be introduced jointly by St. Maarten and Curaçao in January 2012.

Sovereign: King WILLEM-ALEXANDER.

Governor: Lucille GEORGE-WOUT; nominated by the Council of Ministers of Curaçao in August 2013, appointed by the Netherlands Council of Ministers on November 1; sworn in by the king on November 4, 2013, effective November 8; succeeding Dr. Fritz M. de los SANTOS GOEDGEDRAG, who resigned on November 24, 2012, due to health issues.

Prime Minister: Ivar ASJES (Sovereign People), sworn in as prime minister on June 7, 2013; succeeding Daniel HODGE (Restructured Antilles Party), who served as prime minister of a transitional government from December 31, 2012, until the formation of the new cabinet on June 7, 2013.

THE COUNTRY

Only 40 miles off the coast of Venezuela in the southern arc of the Lesser Antilles, the Caribbean island of Curaçao lies east of Aruba and west of Bonaire. The Country of Curaçao also includes the small, uninhabited island of Little Curaçao. Approximately 85 percent of the population is of mixed African ancestry, the remainder being of Carib Indian and European derivation. Roman Catholicism is professed by 85 percent of the population, which also includes various Protestant denominations and a small Jewish population. (Curaçao is home to the oldest continuous Jewish congregation in the Americas, dating from 1651.) Some 85 percent of the population speaks Papiamento, but many also speak English, Spanish, or Dutch.

The economy was initially dependent on salt refining and, given the island's superior deepwater ports, trade (including the slave trade). Since 1920 the principal industry has been petroleum refining and transshipment, followed by tourism and offshore finance in later decades. Agriculture, accounting for only 1 percent of GDP, is restrained by poor soil and little rainfall. Services provide 85 percent of GDP and employ the large majority of the labor force. Since the 2009 international financial crisis, when GDP declined by 0.2 percent, Curaçao has struggled. In 2011 the economy contracted by 0.6 percent, and GDP remained stagnant in 2012. In 2011 unemployment remained at about 12 percent. (For more on the economy, see Current issues below.)

GOVERNMENT AND POLITICS

Political background. Sighted by the Spanish in 1499 and claimed by the Dutch in 1634, Curaçao subsequently served as the region's principal slave-trading port. From the late 17th century until the Dutch firmly established ownership in 1815, possession of the island was frequently contested by Britain and France as well as the Netherlands. In 1828 Curaçao became part of the Dutch West Indies, along with the South American territory of Dutch Guiana, the nearby islands of Aruba and Bonaire, and the northern Leeward Islands of St. Eustatius and Saba plus the southern third of St. Maarten (the northern two-thirds, St. Martin, is a French possession). Having been administered for over a century as a colonial dependency, in 1954 the six island jurisdictions, known collectively since 1948 as the Netherlands Antilles, were granted constitutional equality with the Netherlands and Suriname (the former Dutch Guiana) as an autonomous component of the Kingdom of the Netherlands. In 1975 Suriname achieved full independence, and in 1986 Aruba became a separate, largely autonomous "country" within the kingdom.

Given the geographical range of the Netherlands Antilles, political differences were largely island-based, necessitating highly unstable coalition governments that rival parties from the most populous islands, Aruba and Curaçao, tended to dominate. Aruba's departure on January 1, 1986, resulted in an Antillean legislature, the States (*Staten*), in which Curaçao was assigned 14 of the 22 seats, compared to 3 for St. Maarten, 3 for Bonaire, and 1 each for St. Eustatius and Saba. Thus, the Curaçao-based rival New Antilles Movement (*Movimentu Antiá Nobo*—MAN), National People's Party (*Partido Nashonal di Pueblo*—PNP), Workers' Liberation Front (*Frente Obrero de Liberashon*—FOL), and (from 1994) Restructured Antilles Party (*Partido Antiá Restrukturá*—PAR) became the leading parties in a series of coalition governments that also included various smaller parties from the other, less-populous Antilles jurisdictions. The same parties also dominated Curaçao's local legislature, the 21-member Island Council.

In the November 1985 election for the Netherlands Antilles *Staten,* Maria LIBERIA-PETERS of the PNP, the Antilles's first female prime minister, was defeated in an election held in preparation for Aruba's departure on January 1, with former prime minister Dominico MARTINA (MAN) then forming a new administration. Between

December 1987 and March 1988, however, Martina lost the backing of the 3 representatives from St. Maarten and another from Curaçao's FOL, and he was forced from office in favor of Liberia-Peters, who returned in May as head of a new coalition that claimed the support of 13 of 22 *Staten* members.

In a referendum on November 19, 1993, 73 percent of Curaçao voters rejected a government-backed proposal that the island seek special autonomy status similar to that of Aruba; 8 percent favored incorporation into the Netherlands and only 1 percent endorsed full independence. Two of the PNP's non-Curaçao partners thereupon withdrew from the government coalition, forcing Liberia-Peters's resignation. The PNP justice minister, Susanne CAMELIA-RÖMER, took over as acting prime minister, and in late December she was succeeded by the PNP's Alejandro Felippe PAULA, a professor of sociology at the University of the Netherlands Antilles, pending a general election in February 1994. At the polls, the recently organized PAR, led by Miguel POURIER, secured an eight-member plurality of *Staten* seats and in late March formed a broad-based coalition government.

Although the PAR maintained a plurality in the *Staten* election of January 1998, it lost four of its eight seats on a vote share that fell from nearly 40 percent to less than 19 percent. Pourier was invited by the governor to form a new government but was unable to attract the necessary support from the ten other groups that had secured legislative representation. Consequently, while Pourier and his government continued in a caretaker capacity, lengthy negotiations were launched on a variety of alternatives, which in June yielded a six-party coalition headed by the PNP's Camelia-Römer.

The Camelia-Römer government collapsed in October 1999 amid a dispute concerning a national recovery plan that would have entailed substantial civil service cuts, and Pourier formed a new coalition government in November. Benefiting from continued economic difficulties, the FOL led all groups in the *Staten* election of January 18, 2002, winning five seats. However, the FOL was excluded from the six-party cabinet that was finally installed on June 3 under the leadership of the PAR's Etienne YS.

The absence of the FOL from the Netherlands Antilles government became more of an issue following the Curaçao Island Council election of April 2003, when the FOL won 8 of the 21 seats. In May 2003 Prime Minister Ys resigned to permit the formation of a new Netherlands Antilles government that would include the FOL. Because the FOL leader, Anthony GODETT, was under indictment for corruption, the FOL's Bernhard KOMPROE assumed office as acting prime minister on July 22, and on August 11 Mirna LUISA-GODETT, Anthony Godett's sister, was in turn sworn in as Komproe's successor.

In December 2003 Anthony Godett was convicted of forgery, bribery, and money laundering and sentenced to prison. Two of the FOL's partners thereupon withdrew from the government, leaving the coalition temporarily without a majority in the *Staten;* however, the coalition was strengthened shortly thereafter with the addition of parties from Bonaire and St. Maarten. On April 6, 2004, the government again collapsed when the PNP refused to continue with Komproe as justice minister. Luisa-Godett resigned, with the PAR's Etienne Ys returning as prime minister on June 3.

In contrast to the results of the 1993 referendum, on April 8, 2005, 68 percent of Curaçao's voters endorsed autonomous status for the island within the Kingdom of the Netherlands. As a result, on November 26 the five constituent islands and the kingdom's government agreed that the Netherlands Antilles would dissolve by July 2007, with Curaçao and St. Maarten (whose voters had expressed support for autonomy in a 2000 referendum) achieving "country" status, like Aruba, and with Bonaire, Saba, and St. Eustatius becoming "Kingdom Islands" (*Koninkrijkseilanden*) with the status of special municipalities within the Netherlands proper.

In November 2006, however, Curaçao's Island Council voted to reject the 2005 agreement, under which The Hague would retain control of defense, foreign policy, and law enforcement. As a result, the date for its implementation was put back to December 15, 2008, to permit reevaluation of the objectionable provisions. The other four islands appeared, in general, to be satisfied with the proposed restructuring.

Meanwhile, in the Netherlands Antilles *Staten* election of January 27, 2006, the PAR had won five seats and the MAN, three, with the PAR's Emily DE JONGH-ELHAGE being sworn in as prime minister on March 26. On April 20, 2007, the two parties again finished first and second, respectively, in an election for Curaçao's Island Council, with the PAR winning seven seats and the MAN, five.

In late 2007 the Dutch government expressed doubt that the deadline for constitutional changes for Curaçao and St. Maarten autonomy could be met, and in April 2008 The Hague formally declared that it was no longer realistic. Although agreement on division of the islands' assets and liabilities was reportedly near, a new target of early 2010 was advanced, coincident with expiration of the Antillean legislative term. On May 15, 2009, Curaçao voters narrowly approved a nonbinding referendum acquiescing to the retention of substantial economic control by The Hague in return for Dutch assumption of a major portion of Curaçao's foreign debt, thus clearing the way for political autonomy in 2010.

Further delays in implementing the planned dissolution of the Netherlands Antilles necessitated a final election for its *Staten.* In balloting on January 22, 2010, nine parties divided the 22 seats, with the PAR adding 1 to its 2006 tally, for a total of 6. Of the other successful Curaçao parties, a three-party Change List (*Lista di Kambio*), headed by the MAN, won 5 seats, while the Sovereign People (*Pueblo Soberano*) took 2 and the PNP, 1. Prime Minister de Jongh-Elhage, with support from other islands, then succeeded in forging another multiparty coalition whose principal task became clearing the way for the dissolution of the Netherlands Antilles.

In a temporary setback for autonomy advocates, on June 19, 2010, Curaçao's Island Council failed to muster the two-thirds vote needed to approve a constitution for the Country of Curaçao. Under the kingdom charter, this necessitated a new council election before a second vote, in which a simple majority would prevail. On the weekend of June 26–27 the governor dissolved the council and called for an election, which was held on August 27. The PAR won eight seats, while the newly organized Movement for the Future of Curaçao (*Movementu Futuro Kòrsou*—MFK) won five; the Sovereign People (*Pueblo Soberano*—PS), four; the MAN, two; the FOL, one; and the PNP, one. In a quick series of actions on September 4, the leader of the MFK, Gerrit SCHOTTE, completed a coalition agreement with the PS and MAN, the new Island Council convened and approved the constitution by a 15–6 vote, and the legislators appointed a new Executive Council to serve until dissolution of the Netherlands Antilles.

On October 10, 2010, the Country of Curaçao came into existence. The Island Council automatically became the new *Staten* of Curaçao, and Gerrit SCHOTTE took office as Curaçao's first prime minister, heading an MFK-PS-MAN Council of Ministers. After the MFK lost its majority when a minister left the party, Schotte dissolved parliament on August 3, 2012, and called for early elections in October. Later in August, 12 parliamentarians petitioned Governor Frits GOEDGEDRAG to form an interim cabinet. Goedgedrag bowed to pressure in September and appointed former Lieutenant Governor Stanley BETRIAN to create a temporary government.

The PS won a narrow majority in balloting on October 19, and after several months of negotiations, established a coalition government with the PAIS and the PNP. Daniel HODGE of the PS took office on December 31 as leader of a transitional government. He dissolved his cabinet three months later on March 27, 2013. On June 7, PS-leader Ivar ASJES was sworn in as prime minister. (For more on the recent elections, see Current issues below.)

Constitution and government. Under the 2010 constitution the Dutch sovereign, the titular head of state, is represented in Curaçao by an appointed governor. Domestic affairs are the responsibility of the prime minister and other members of the Council of Ministers, appointed with the advice and approval of the unicameral legislature, the States of Curaçao (*Staten van Curaçao*). Elections to the *Staten* are held every four years, subject to dissolution. A Council of Advice, whose members are appointed by government decree, reviews proposed legislation and administrative orders and may offer advice to the government. The constitution also provides for an ombudsperson. Control of foreign affairs and defense remains vested in the Council of Ministers in The Hague, where a minister plenipotentiary from Curaçao advises on matters relevant to Curaçao. Judicial authority is exercised by a Court of First Instance and by a Common Court (for Aruba, Curaçao, St. Maarten, and the special municipalities of Bonaire, St. Eustatius, and Saba), whose members are appointed by the queen. Ultimate appeal is to the Supreme Court of the Netherlands in The Hague. The constitution may be amended by a two-thirds vote of the Curaçao legislature, subject to the subsequent approval of the Dutch government.

Current issues. In elections on October 19, 2012, the PS won five seats with 22.7 percent of the vote, narrowly defeating the leading MFK, which also won five seats but with 21.2 percent. After attempts to negotiate a coalition government, former prime minister and MFK leader Gerrit Schotte withdrew his party, effectively halting efforts to form the new leadership. After several weeks of negotiations with other parties, a PS-led coalition secured 11 of 21 seats in the assembly with the PAIS, the PNP, and former PAR-member Glenn SULVARAN. On December 31 Daniel Hodge was sworn in as prime minister, followed by his cabinet on January 2, 2013, to serve for a transitional period of three to six months. On March 27, 2013, Prime Minister Hodge and his cabinet resigned, citing that his leadership was intended to be short-term. Newly appointed PS leader Ivar Asjes assumed the office of prime minister on June 7, 2013, on the same day the new cabinet was sworn in.

Four days after the general election, Governor Goedgedrag submitted his resignation, effective November 24, 2012, because of health problems related to a heart condition. Adele Van der PLUIJM-VREDE served on an acting basis for almost a year. The Council of Ministers nominated Lucille GEORGE-WOUT to fill the position in August 2013. She was approved by the Netherlands Council of Ministers on November 1, sworn in by the king on November 4, and installed on November 8, becoming the first woman to hold the post.

Helmin WIELS, the leader of the PS, was shot dead on May 5, 2013. Wiels had been a major player in forming the leading coalition. It was unclear whether his assassination was politically motivated or linked to his outspoken opposition to organized crime.

Meanwhile, Curaçao's economic situation has worsened. In December 2012, the Dutch government expressed its concern for Curaçao's public finances. A budget shortfall of $176 million is expected for 2013 and predicted to increase to $236.5 million by 2015.

POLITICAL PARTIES

Even after the departure of Aruba from the Netherlands Antilles in 1986, no single Curaçao-based party held a majority in either the Netherlands Antilles *Staten* or the Island Council in Curaçao, necessitating a series of coalitions at both levels that were not always stable. A total of eight parties contested the October 2013 elections, with six winning seats.

Governing Coalition:

Sovereign People (*Pueblo Soberano*—PS). Founded in 2006 as a left-of-center, progressive party, the pro-independence PS won one seat in Curaçao's Island Council election of April 2007, two in the Netherlands Antilles *Staten* election of January 2010, and four in the August 2010 Island Council election. Its representatives voted against the Curaçao draft constitution, but the party agreed to join the MFK-led government in September 2010. The PS has called for an end to U.S. military use of an air base on the island. The PS secured a narrow majority with 22.6 percent and five seats in polling on October 19, 2012.

Following the murder of party president and founder Helmin Wiels on May 5, 2013, internal tensions emerged within the party, with members of the parliamentary party calling for the committee members to step down. On May 15 Ivar Asjes assumed party leadership.

Leaders: Ivar ASJES (Party President), Melvin Cijntje (Chair).

Social Progress and Innovation Party (*Partido Adelanto i Inovashon Soshul*—PAIS). The PAIS was registered in 2010 by Alex Rosario, a former PNP member and finance official. The PAIS won 3 percent of the Curaçao Island Council vote and no seats in August 2010. In October 2012, the PAIS secured four seats and 17.7 percent of the vote.

Leader: Alex ROSARIO (Political Leader).

National People's Party (*Partido Nashonal di Pueblo*—PNP/ *Nationale Volkspartij*). The right-of-center PNP served as the core of the governing coalition in the Netherlands Antilles from 1988 to 1993. Its leader, Maria Liberia-Peters, was obliged to step down as prime minister as a result of the November 1993 referendum result, and its *Staten* representation dropped from seven to three seats in February 1994, before rising to four in January 1998. In May 1998–November 1999 Susanne Camelia-Römer headed the Antilles government. The PNP secured three seats in 2002, one of which was lost in 2006. In January 2010 the PNP won only one seat. It also claimed one seat, on 6 percent of the vote, in the August 2010 Curaçao Island Council election, a loss of one seat from 2007. In the October 2012 elections, the PNP secured one seat and 5.9 percent of the vote.

Leaders: Humphrey DAVELAAR (Party Leader), Gisette SEFERINA (Chair).

Other Parliamentary Parties:

Movement for the Future of Curaçao (*Movementu Futuro Kòrsou*—MFK). The MFK was organized by Gerrit Schotte in July 2010. He had previously been affiliated with the FOL (below) and had also been a founder of the Patriotic Movement of Curaçao (*Movementu Patriotiko Kòrsou*—MPK). In August 2010, in its first electoral contest, the MFK won 21 percent of the vote and five seats in Curaçao's Island Council, after which Schotte negotiated a coalition agreement with the PS (above) and MAN (below). In late September he was asked by the governor of Curaçao to form the Country of Curaçao's first Council of Ministers, which took office on October 10.

The MFK lost power in the October 2012 elections, coming in second with 21.2 percent of the vote and winning five seats.

Leaders: Gerrit SCHOTTE (Former Prime Minister and Party Leader), Dean ROZIER (Chair).

Restructured Antilles Party (*Partido Antiá Restrukturá*—PAR). The PAR is a social-Christian formation launched in the wake of the November 1993 referendum. It became the leading party of the Netherlands Antilles government coalition formed after the 1994 election, in which it won 8 of 22 *Staten* seats. It was reduced to a minority of 4 seats in 1998 and secured the same number in 2002, with 1 additional seat added in 2006, at which time it became the plurality party and headed a multiparty governing coalition under Prime Minister Emily de Jongh-Elhage. The PAR picked up an additional *Staten* seat in January 2010, thereby retaining its plurality in the final Netherlands Antilles *Staten*.

In Curaçao's Island Council, the PAR finished second to the FOL in the May 2003 election, when it won 5 of 21 seats, but claimed a plurality of 7 seats in the April 2007 election and 8 in August 2010 (with 30 percent of the vote). Despite obtaining a plurality of votes, the PAR became the main party of the opposition after the creation of an MFK-led coalition.

In balloting of October 19, 2012, the PAR secured 4 seats and 19.7 percent of the vote. After the party withdrew from coalition negotiations with the PS, member Glenn SULVARAN severed ties with the PAR to independently join the leading coalition.

Leader: Emily DE JONGH-ELHAGE (Political Leader).

New Antilles Movement (*Movishon Antiá Nobo/Movimentu Antiyas Nobo*—MAN). The MAN is a left-of-center member of the Socialist International that served as the core of the Dominico Martina administrations of 1982–1984 and 1985–1988 in the Netherlands Antilles, although holding only four *Staten* seats on the latter occasion. Its representation in the *Staten* dropped to two seats in 1990, both of which were retained in 1994 and 1998. The party failed to gain representation in 2002 but won three seats in 2006, and in January 2010 it led the three-party **Change List** (*Lista di Kambio*), which also included the **Upwards Curaçao** (*Forsa Kòrsou*), led by Nelson NAVARRO, and **Not One Step Back** (*Niun Paso Atras*), led by Carlos MONK. The Change List came in second, with five *Staten* seats.

As for recent Curaçao Island Council elections, the MAN finished with 19 percent of the vote and five seats in April 2007 but in August 2010 saw its support drop to 9 percent and two seats. It was awarded two ministerial posts in the Schotte cabinet. Member Eugene CLEOPA left the party in September 2012 but retained his seat in parliament. In the October 2012 election, the MAN won two seats and 19.7 percent of the vote.

Leader: Hensley KOEIMAN (Party President).

Other Parties:

Workers' Liberation Front of 30 May (*Frente Obrero di Liberashon 30 di Mei*—FOL). A Marxist group, the FOL entered the 1990 Netherlands Antilles election in coalition with the Independent Social (*Soshal Independiente*—SI), which had been formed in 1986 by a group of PNP dissidents. The two groups also presented joint candidates in the January 1998 balloting (as the Social Independence–Workers' Liberation Front—SIFOL), winning two seats. The FOL left the Netherlands Antilles government coalition in mid-2001 as a result of tension between FOL leader Anthony Godett and the administration regarding budget cuts. The FOL was the top vote-getter in the 2002 Antilles election, winning five legislative seats on a vote share of 23 percent, but Godett was precluded from installation as prime minister because of his indictment (and later conviction) for bribery, fraud, and money laundering. In September 2005 the High Court in The Hague upheld a 15-month prison sentence for Godett.

An Antilles government under Godett's sister, Mirna Luisa-Godett, fell in the wake of Godett's conviction, and in 2006 the FOL won only two *Staten* seats. In 2010 the FOL lost both Netherlands Antilles *Staten* seats and one of its Curaçao Island Council seats.

In the 2012 elections, 29 FOL candidates contested, but the party did not secure any seats. Godett subsequently resigned from party leadership.

Democrat Laboral. In the October 2012 general election, the Labor Party Popular Crusade (PLKP) and the Democratic Party–Curaçao (DP) (both below) combined. Twenty-nine candidates ran, winning 1.3 percent of the vote and no seats.

Labor Party Popular Crusade (*Partido Laboral Krusada Popular*—PLKP). A trade union–based group launched in 1997, the PLKP won three seats in the 1998 Netherlands Antilles legislative election. It joined the subsequent cabinet led by the PNP's Susanne Camelia-Römer but withdrew in 1999 and was not included in the PAR-led cabinet of November 1999. The PLKP rejoined the government in June 2002, having secured 12.1 percent of the vote and two seats in the January legislative poll; it lost both seats in 2006. Although it held three Curaçao Island Council seats after the May 2003 election, the PLKP was later weakened by a split that produced the Social Labor Movement (*Movementu Social Laboral*—MSL), and in the 2007 election it failed to retain council representation.

The PLKP won only 1 percent of the Curaçao Island Council vote in August 2010.

Leader: Errol GOELOE (Party Leader).

Democratic Party–Curaçao (*Partido Democraat—DP*). Prior to the 1985 election the DP was primarily Curaçao-based, with a Dutch-speaking branch on Bonaire and English-speaking branches on St. Maarten and St. Eustatius. In 2010 it won no seats in either the January Netherlands Antilles vote or the August Curaçao Island Council vote. In the latter, it won 4 percent of the vote.

Leader: Norberto RIBERIO (Political Leader).

LEGISLATURE

The unicameral **States of Curaçao** (*Staten van Curaçao*) consists of 21 members elected by proportional representation for four-year terms, subject to dissolution. In the election held October 19, 2012, for the Curaçao Island Council, the PS won 5 seats; the Movement for the Future of Curaçao (MFK), 5; the PAIS, 4; the PAR, 4; the New Antilles Movement (MAN), 2; and the National People's Party (PNP), 1.

Chair: Mike FRANCO.

CABINET

[as of November 21, 2013]

Prime Minister	Ivar Asjes (PS)
Ministers	
Economic Development	Stanley Palm (PAIS)
Education, Science, Culture and Sports	Ivar Asjes (PS) (acting)
Finance	Jose Jardim (Ind.)
General Affairs	Ivar Asjes (PS)
Government Policy, Planning, and Services	Etienne van der Horst (PAIS)
Justice	Nelson Navarro (PAIS)
Public Health, Environment, and Nature	Bernard Whiteman (PS)
Social Development, Labor, and Welfare	Jeanne Francisca (PS) [f]
Traffic, Transport, and Urban Planning	Earl Balborda (PNP)
Minister Plenipotentiary to The Hague	Marvelyne Wiels (PS) [f]

[f] = female

INTERGOVERNMENTAL REPRESENTATION

Foreign relations are for the most part conducted through the Dutch Ministry of Foreign Affairs in The Hague, although the United States maintains a Consulate General's Office in Curaçao.

ST. MAARTEN

Country of Saint Maarten
Land Sint Maarten

Political Status: Former Dutch dependency; from 1948 a component of the Netherlands Antilles, which became autonomous in internal affairs, under charter of the Kingdom of the Netherlands, effective December 29, 1954; achieved separate autonomous status in internal affairs upon dissolution of the Netherlands Antilles on October 10, 2010.

Area: 13.1 sq. mi. (34 sq. km).

Population: 43,000 (2010E—UN), 39,689 (2013E—U.S. Census).

Major Urban Center (2010E): PHILIPSBURG (1,228), Lower Prince's Quarters (8,123).

Official Languages: Dutch and English.

Monetary Unit: Netherlands Antilles Guilder (official rate November 1, 2013: 1.79 guilders = $1US). The guilder is pegged to the U.S. dollar. A new Caribbean guilder, likewise pegged to the dollar, is to be introduced jointly by St. Maarten and Curaçao in January 2012.

Sovereign: King WILLEM-ALEXANDER.

Governor: Eugene HOLIDAY; nominated by the St. Maarten Executive Council in June 2010 and approved by the Netherlands Council of Ministers on September 7; sworn in by the queen for a six-year term on September 30, 2010, effective October 10.

Prime Minister: Sarah WESCOT-WILLIAMS (Democratic Party of St. Maarten); named prime minister–designate by coalition agreement concluded on September 23, 2010, following the general election of September 17, and took the oath of office on October 10.

THE COUNTRY

Located 160 miles east of the island of Puerto Rico in the Leeward Islands of the Lesser Antilles, between the British overseas territory of Anguilla to the north and the French overseas collectivity of St. Barthelemy to the southeast, St. Maarten occupies the southern third of a small Caribbean island that is shared by the French overseas collectivity of St. Martin. About two-thirds of the population, which is of mixed African, Carib Indian, and European ancestry, speak English; less than 5 percent speak Dutch. Roman Catholicism and Protestantism are the principal religions. The economy was traditionally dependent on the export of salt, the only significant onshore natural resource. However, salt production declined by the mid-20th century, after which tourism became increasingly important. Only 10 percent of the land is arable, and most farming is at the subsistence level, despite some earlier plantation production of sugarcane.

Tourism currently accounts for over 80 percent of GDP and employment, with small-scale industry contributing another 15 percent. Remittances from abroad are another significant source of island income. Growth fell to 1.6 percent in 2008 as the international financial crisis adversely affected the tourist trade, marking the beginning of a period of stagnation. According to the Sint Maarten Department of Economic Affairs, the economy contracted by 1.5 percent in 2011, and again by –0.2 percent the following year, before climbing to 1.6 percent in 2013. After peaking at 12 percent in 2011, unemployment fell slightly to 11.3 percent in 2013.

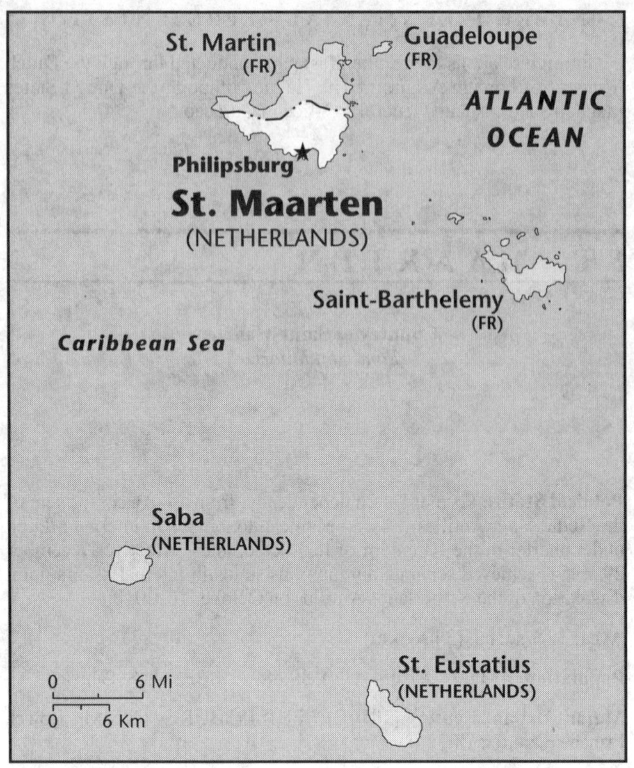

GOVERNMENT AND POLITICS

Political background. Discovered by the Spanish at the time of Christopher Columbus, the island of St. Martin/St. Maarten saw its first French settlers arrive in 1628, and they were soon joined by the Dutch, who in 1634 proclaimed the Leeward Islands as possessions. A brief period of Spanish occupation followed. In 1648 the French and Dutch concluded the Treaty of Mt. Concordia, which divided the island between them, although it took another two centuries for the arrangement to be firmly established. In 1828 St. Maarten became part of the Dutch West Indies, along with the nearby islands of St. Eustatius and Saba; the islands of Aruba, Bonaire, and Curaçao in the southern arc of the Lesser Antilles; and the South American territory of Dutch Guiana. Having been administered for over a century as a colonial dependency, in 1954 the six island colonies, known collectively since 1948 as the Netherlands Antilles, were granted constitutional equality with the Netherlands and Suriname (the former Dutch Guiana) as an autonomous component of the Kingdom of the Netherlands. In 1975 Suriname achieved full independence, and in 1986 Aruba became a separate, largely autonomous "country" within the kingdom.

Given the geographical range of the Netherlands Antilles, political differences were largely island-based, necessitating highly unstable coalition governments that rival parties from the most populous islands, Aruba and Curaçao, tended to dominate. Aruba's departure on January 1, 1986, resulted in an Antillean legislature, the States (*Staten*), in which Curaçao was assigned 14 of the 22 seats, compared to 3 for St. Maarten, 3 for Bonaire, and 1 each for St. Eustatius and Saba. Thus, the Curaçao-based rival New Antilles Movement (*Movimentu Antiá Nobo*—MAN), National People's Party (*Partido Nashonal di Pueblo*—PNP), Workers' Liberation Front (*Fronte Obrero de Liberashon*—FOL), and (from 1994) Restructured Antilles Party (*Partido Antiá Restrukturá*—PAR) became the leading parties in a series of coalition governments that at various times also included the St. Maarten-based Democratic Party of St. Maarten (*Democratische Partij Sint Maarten*—DP-StM or DP) and the Sint Maarten People's Alliance (SPA). In 2002 the SPA and the National Progressive Party (NPA) formed the National Alliance (NA), led by William MARLIN, which won 1 *Staten* seat in 2002 and 2 in 2006.

On the island of St. Maarten itself, from 1954 local politics were long dominated by the DP's Claude WATHEY, an outspoken advocate for independence who in 1992 strongly objected when the Netherlands, citing concerns over illegal immigration and the smuggling of arms and drugs, imposed stricter financial supervision on the island. In 1993 a criminal investigation into these matters implicated Wathey and several other prominent island figures. Wathey, although charged in 1994 with corruption and criminal conspiracy, was ultimately convicted only of perjury.

In a referendum on October 14, 1994, voters on St. Maarten indicated a preference (by 59 percent of the vote) for remaining within the Netherlands Antilles. Another 32 percent of the voters preferred becoming an autonomous "country" within the Dutch kingdom, while only a few backed the other two options, namely closer ties to the Netherlands or independence.

From 1994 until 1999, the DP's leading role on St. Maarten was challenged by the SPA, which led to a series of unstable administrations. In the Island Council election of May 1999, however, the DP, now led by Sarah WESCOT-WILLIAMS, won 7 of the 11 seats.

A referendum held June 23, 2000, revealed a marked shift in public sentiment from the 1994 referendum, with some 70 percent of the voters supporting withdrawal from the Netherlands Antilles in favor of greater autonomy. In April 2005 Curaçao's voters registered similar sentiments, and on November 26, 2005, the five constituent islands and the kingdom's government agreed that the Netherlands Antilles would dissolve by July 2007, with Curaçao and St. Maarten achieving autonomous country status, like Aruba, and with Bonaire, Saba, and St. Eustatius becoming municipalities within the Netherlands proper.

Mainly because of objections from Curaçao's Island Council regarding The Hague's retaining control of defense, foreign policy, and law enforcement, implementation of the dissolution was delayed beyond 2007. In April 2008 the Dutch government formally declared that even the new deadline of December 15, 2008, could not be met. Although agreement on division of the islands' assets and liabilities was reportedly near, a new target of early 2010 was advanced, coincident with expiration of the Antillean legislative term.

In May 2003 the DP had retained six seats on the St. Maarten's Island Council, to four for the NA and one for the People's Progressive Party. In April 2007 the election split gave the DP six seats and the NA five, but in November 2008 the DP lost its one-seat majority when Labor Commissioner Louie LAVEIST resigned from the St. Maarten Executive Council and left the party after being charged with corruption. Laveist retained his Island Council seat, however, which left the DP and NA with five seats each. Following Laveist's May 2009 conviction for bribery, forgery, and fraud (which the Common Court of Justice of Aruba and the Netherlands Antilles later overturned), he resigned from the Island Council. Subsequent efforts by the DP and NA to form a joint national government failed when the DP objected to the NA's demands that it be accorded a majority of Executive Council posts and that the NA's Marlin be named head of that council. In June the NA gained the support of Theo HEYLIGER, a member of the Island Council who until then had belonged to the DP, and formed a new government headed by Marlin.

Delays in implementing the planned January 2010 dissolution of the Netherlands Antilles necessitated a final election for its *Staten.* In balloting held on January 22, 2010, the NA won all three seats from St. Maarten—the first time since the 1960s that the DP had failed to claim at least one seat—and then gave its support to the incumbent prime minister, Emily de Jongh-Elhage of Curaçao's PAR, in her successful effort to forge a multiparty coalition.

On July 21, 2010, the St. Maarten Island Council adopted a constitution that would enter into force upon dissolution of the Netherlands Antilles, and on September 17 the island's voters cast ballots for a 15-member States of St. Maarten (successor to the Island Council) that would convene on October 10, 2010, the new date for dissolution. The NA won a plurality of 7 seats in the September poll, with Theo Heyliger's new United People's (UP) party taking 6 and the DP being reduced to 2.

On September 23, 2010, the UP and the DP concluded a governing accord that awarded the DP the prime ministership and one additional cabinet post. DP party leader Sarah Wescot-Williams took her oath of office as prime minister, heading a seven-member UP-DP cabinet, on October 10, when the island officially became the Country of St. Maarten.

The UP-DP coalition lost its legislative majority in April 2012 when two independent members of parliament formed a new legislative bloc with a member of the UP and signed an agreement with the NA. The government resigned on May 8 and Wescot-Williams formed a new coalition government, with the NA and DP. The NA's William Marlin became deputy prime minister. The second Wescot-Williams cabinet was installed on May 21.

A third government under Wescot-Williams was formed on June 14, 2013, a month after another shift in legislative power returned leadership to a UP-DP coalition (see Current issues, below).

Constitution and government. Under the 2010 constitution, the Dutch sovereign, the titular head of state, is represented in St. Maarten by an appointed governor. Domestic affairs are the responsibility of the prime minister and other members of the Council of Ministers (direct institutional successor to the island's Executive Council), which is appointed with the advice and approval of the unicameral legislature, the States of St. Maarten (*Staten van Sint Maarten*). Elections to the *Staten* are held every four years, subject to dissolution. A Council of Advice, whose members are appointed by government decree, reviews proposed legislation and administrative orders and may offer advice to the government. The constitution also provides for an ombudsperson and a General Audit Chamber. Control of foreign affairs and defense remains vested in the Council of Ministers in The Hague, where a minister plenipotentiary from St. Maarten advises on matters relevant to St. Maarten. Judicial authority is exercised by a Court of First Instance and by a Common Court (for Aruba, Curaçao, St. Maarten, and the special municipalities of Bonaire, St. Eustatius, and Saba), whose members are appointed by the queen. Ultimate appeal is to the Supreme Court of the Netherlands in The Hague. In addition, St. Maarten has a Constitutional Court to examine the constitutionality of legislation and government actions. The constitution may be amended by a two-thirds vote of the St. Maarten legislature, subject to the subsequent approval of the Dutch government. Freedom of expression is constitutionally protected.

Dutch Prime Minister Mark Ruute visited St. Maarten in July 2013 and instructed Governor Holiday to investigate corruption allegations against the government. Prime Minister Wescot-Williams denounced the move as outside intrusion but invited Transparency International to review the situation.

Current issues. In July 2011 St. Maarten made a request for associate membership in the Caribbean Community (Caricom). The application was officially under review in February 2012. As of mid-2013, no decision has been made as to the eligibility for the states of the dissolved Netherlands Antilles.

On May 4, 2013, one independent and two DP parliamentarians withdrew their support from the ruling NA-DP coalition, causing the collapse of the second Wescot-Williams cabinet. The defectors cited dissatisfaction with the way issues have been addressed within the coalition, which became apparent in April when a faction of DP parliamentarians voted against a motion for a $100 million Department of Justice complex supported by Justice Minister Roland DUNCAN. Three days later, five NA ministers, led by Vice Prime Minister Marlin, submitted a concept national decree to Governor Holiday calling for an early election to be held on July 26. Wescot-Williams dismissed the demands, instead negotiating a new UP-DP-Independent coalition. The new cabinet took office on June 14.

POLITICAL PARTIES

Since 1990 politics on St. Maarten has largely been a contest between the dominant Democratic Party of St. Maarten (DP) and the National Alliance (NA) or its predecessor, the Sint Maarten Political Alliance (SPA), despite the frequent presence of short-lived smaller parties. That balance was upended in September 2010 by the United People's (UP) party, which in its first election finished second to the NA and left the DP a distant third.

Governing Parties:

Democratic Party of St. Maarten (*Democratische Partij Sint Maarten*—DP-StM or DP). The DP began in the mid-1980s as an English-speaking branch of the Democratic Party–Curaçao (*Democratische Partij–Curaçao*). Under the leadership of Claude Wathey, who supported independence, the DP dominated island politics into the 1990s. Another DP leader, Louis C. GUMBS, resigned from the government and the party in 1991 to stand for an Island Council seat as a candidate of the Progressive Democratic Party (PDP), which had recently been launched by a group of DP dissidents. The party lost one of its two *Staten* seats in 1994, its leadership passing thereafter from Wathey to Sarah Wescot-Williams (formerly of the PDP). Wathey died in 1998.

The DP's representation in the Netherlands Antilles legislature fell from 2 seats in 2002 to 1 in 2006, but it nevertheless remained the leading party in the St. Maarten Island Council, winning 7 of 11 seats in 1999, 6 in 2003, and 6 in 2007. In January 2010, however, it failed to win any seats in the Netherlands Antilles election, and in September it took only 2 of 15 seats in the new St. Maarten *Staten*. An accord with the UP brought DP leader Wescot-Williams into office as the Country of St. Maarten's first prime minister. The DP-UP coalition lost its majority in 2012, leading Wescot-Williams to negotiate a new coalition with the NA. In 2013, after another parliamentary power shift, the DP-NA leadership dissolved and the DP remained in power by establishing a new coalition with the UP.

Leaders: Sarah WESCOT-WILLIAMS (Prime Minister and Party Leader), Michael FERRIER (President), Roy MARLIN (Parliamentary Faction Leader).

United Peoples (UP). The UP party was launched in late July 2010 by former DP member Theo Heyliger, who had most recently served as a commissioner (member of the island's Executive Council) in an alliance with the NA. The new party's platform emphasized unity, fighting crime, creating jobs, and investing in youth and their education. In late July, Gracita ARRINDELL, theretofore the leader of the PPA (below), announced her resignation from that party and her collateral decision to join the UP.

In the September 2010 election the UP won 6 of 15 seats in the new *Staten,* after which it formed a coalition government with the DP (2 seats). In 2012 the DP-UP coalition lost power when the UP's Romaine Laville left the party to form a bloc with the NA. The UP returned to power in June 2013 when a new governing coalition was formed.

Leaders: Theodore HEYLIGER (Party Leader), Sylvia MEYERS (Parliamentary Faction Leader).

Opposition Party:

National Alliance (NA). The NA traces its origins to the Sint Maarten Patriotic Movement (SPM), which was formed in 1979, initially as a loose grouping in opposition to the DP, and evolved into the Sint Maarten Patriotic Alliance (SPA) in 1990. In the 1990 Netherlands Antilles *Staten* poll the SPM captured one of the three seats theretofore held by the DP. In the 1991 Island Council election the SPA doubled its representation from two of nine seats to four, after which it formed an island government in coalition with the recently organized Progressive Democratic Party (PDP) of DP dissidents. That government collapsed in August, however, when the PDP withdrew and formed a coalition with the DP. The SPA increased its Netherlands Antilles *Staten* representation to two seats in 1994, one of which was lost in 1998. For the 2002 Netherlands Antilles election the SPA joined with the National Progressive Party (NPP) to form the NA, which secured one seat under the leadership of William Marlin.

In May 2003 the NA won 4 Island Council seats, and it increased its total to 5 of 11 in April 2007. In June 2009, following the DP's loss of its Island Council majority, the NA formed its first island government in ten years through the support of Louie Laveist, a DP representative who had become an independent. In November 2009 the party held its first formal congress.

The final Netherlands Antilles parliamentary election, held in January 2010, saw the NA win all 3 seats from St. Maarten. It won a plurality of 7 seats in the new 15-member St. Maarten *Staten* in September, but a UP-DP coalition, with 8 seats, formed the Country of St. Maarten's first government. In April 2012 the NA regained a legislative majority and formed a coalition with the DP and three independent members of parliament, however the party returned to the backbench in May 2013 when a new DP-led coalition came to power.

Leaders: William MARLIN (President and Former Deputy Prime Minister), George PANTOPHLET (Parliamentary Faction Leader).

Other Parties:

Concordia Political Alliance (CPA). The CPA was launched on August 15, 2010, by Jeffrey Richardson, who had previously run for office as a DP candidate. The party champions native St. Maarteners, whose interests and concerns, Richardson claimed, have been ignored by the other parties. He cited youth unemployment, the absence of a recreational center, and inadequate housing as contributing to the high crime rate. In the September Island Council election Richardson was the CPA's only candidate, winning 1 percent of the vote.

Leader: Jeffrey RICHARDSON (Party Leader and Founder).

People's Progressive Alliance (PPA). The PPA was formed in January 2003 by Don HUGHES, with Gracita Arrindell as its first leader. It was represented in the Island Council from 2003 to 2007 and ran unsuccessfully in the Netherlands Antilles election of January 2010. Following Arrindell's decision in July 2010 to join the new UP, the party was widely expected to dissolve. It did not compete in the September 2010 Island Council election.

Leader: Donald HUGHES.

LEGISLATURE

The unicameral **States of St. Maarten** (*Staten van Sint Maarten*) consists of 15 members (often styled senators) elected by proportional representation for four-year terms, subject to dissolution. In the election on September 17, 2010, for the final St. Maarten Island Council, the National Alliance (NA) won 7 seats; the United People, 6; and the Democratic Party of St. Maarten (DP), 2. The members of the Island Council were sworn in as senators of the *Staten* on October 10, 2010, upon the dissolution of the Netherlands Antilles. After a shift in power in 2012 and a subsequent reshuffle in 2013, the leading coalition comprises of the DP with 2 seats, the UP, with 5, and an independent. The minority includes the NA, 5 seats, and 2 independent seats.

President: Gracita ARRINDELL.

CABINET

[as of November 21, 2013]

Prime Minister	Sarah Wescot-Williams (DP) [f]
Deputy Prime Minister	Dennis L. Richardson (UP)
Ministers	
Education, Culture, Youth, and Sports Affairs	Patricia Lourens-Philip (UP) [f]
Finance	Martin Hassink (UP)
General Affairs	Sarah Wescot-Williams (DP) [f]
Health, Social Development, and Labor	Cornelius De Weever (DP)
Housing and Spatial Planning, Environment and Infrastructure	Maurice Lake (UP)
Justice	Dennis L. Richardson (UP)
Tourism, Economic Affairs, Transport, and Telecommunications	Ted Richardson (DP)
Minister Plenipotentiary to The Hague	Mathias Voges (DP)

[f] = female

INTERGOVERNMENTAL REPRESENTATION

Foreign relations are for the most part conducted through the Dutch Ministry of Foreign Affairs in The Hague. St. Maarten is represented by attachés in various Dutch embassies and consulates, including those in Cuba, Dominican Republic, Trinidad and Tobago, Venezuela, and the United States (Washington, D.C., and Miami, Florida).

NEW ZEALAND

Aotearoa

Political Status: Constitutional democracy with Queen Elizabeth II as titular head of state; formally independent since 1947.

Area: 104,454 sq. mi. (270,534 sq. km).

Population: 4,619,036 (2012E—UN); 4,327,944 (2012E—U.S. Census); 4,495,721 (2013E—N.Z. Statistics).

Major Urban Centers (2012E): WELLINGTON (202,200), Auckland (1,397,300; conurbation 1,507,700), Christchurch (348,200), Hamilton (148,200), Dunedin (126,900).

Official Languages: English, Maori.

Monetary Unit: New Zealand Dollar (market rate November 1, 2013: 1.22 dollars = $1US).

Sovereign: Queen ELIZABETH II.

Governor General: General Sir Jerry MATAPARAI, named by Queen Elizabeth II on March 7, 2011, to succeed Sir Anand SATYANAND, effective August 31.

Prime Minister: John Phillip KEY (National Party), named by the governor general to form a new government following the parliamentary election of November 8, 2008, and sworn in on November 19.

THE COUNTRY

Located approximately 1,200 miles southeast of Australia in the southern Pacific Ocean, New Zealand is the most physically isolated of the world's economically developed countries. The two main islands (North Island and South Island), separated by the Cook Strait, extend nearly 1,000 miles on a northeast-southwest axis. They exhibit considerable topographical diversity, ranging from fertile plains to high mountains, but enjoy for the most part a relatively temperate climate. The 2006 census found that the majority of the population (77 percent) was of European extraction, and the Maori, descendants of the original Polynesian settlers, constituted almost 15 percent of the total. Smaller ethnic groups included Asians (9 percent) and Pacific island peoples (7 percent). The Anglican, Roman Catholic, and Presbyterian churches predominate. Women constituted over 46 percent of the active labor force, primarily in wholesale and retail trade, health and social work, and education. Female representation in the House of Representatives (parliament) elected in November 2011 totaled 38 out of 122 MPs.

The service sector is the largest contributor to the GDP, just over 70 percent in 2011, employing 74 percent of the workforce. Although the agricultural sector employs less than 10 percent of the labor force, it remains the basis of the country's wealth. Dairy products, meat, forest products, fish, fruits and vegetables, wine, and wool provide over half of New Zealand's merchandise export earnings. The manufacturing sector employs 19 percent of the workforce and contributes a quarter of the GDP, with processing of foods, wood and paper products, aluminum, and chemicals ranking among the leading industries. Exports of machinery, transport and marine equipment, chemical products, and metals have become important earners. Since the mid-1970s, efforts have focused on the exploitation of natural gas, oil, coal, and lignite deposits, as well as hydroelectric capacity, and in 2013 crude oil constituted the fourth most valuable export by value. Top trading partners are Australia, China, the United States, Japan, South Korea and Great Britain. In the 1990s tourism surpassed dairy exports to emerge as New Zealand's single most valuable source of foreign exchange.

From 1999 through 2004 GDP growth averaged about 4 percent annually, but a downturn in primary production and overseas earnings and a weakening of housing, finance, and retail markets dragged the economy into recession and the GDP shrank by 1.7 percent in 2009. Two devastating earthquakes in Christchurch, freezing weather during the lambing season in Southland, floods and droughts slowed recovery despite high overseas earnings for commodities. The International Monetary Fund (IMF) forecast a GDP growth of 2.7 percent in 2013, easing to 2.6 percent in 2014. Net foreign debt remained high at 79 percent of GDP.

GOVERNMENT AND POLITICS

Political background. New Zealand's link to Europe began with a landfall by the Dutch mariner Abel Tasman in 1642, but settlement by the English did not begin until the 18th century. In 1840 British sovereignty was formally accepted by Maori chieftains, who signed the Treaty of Waitangi. Recurrent disputes between the settlers and the Maori were not resolved, however, until the defeat of the latter in the land wars of the 1860s. Granted self-government in 1852 and dominion status in 1907, New Zealand became an independent member of the Commonwealth upon accession to the Statute of Westminster in 1947.

Through the mid-20th century both of the main political parties, National and Labour, endorsed a protected economy and extensive

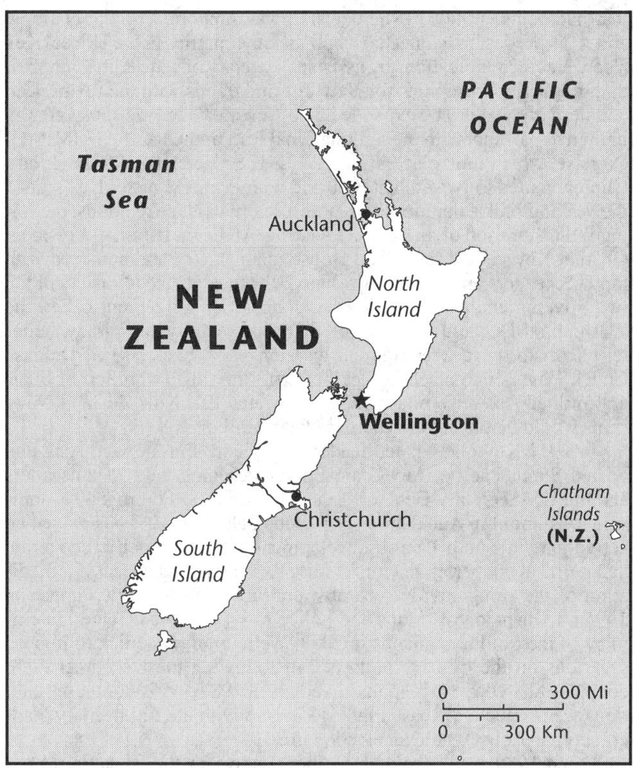

programs of social welfare. The more conservative National Party, which was in power from 1960 to 1972 under the leadership of Keith J. HOLYOAKE and then John R. MARSHALL, was succeeded in government by the Labour Party in 1972, led by Norman E. KIRK and, upon Kirk's death in August 1974, by Wallace E. ROWLING. Labour was succeeded in turn by National, led by Robert MULDOON, in 1975. Thereafter, the two major parties alternated in power: Labour in 1984, National in 1990, Labour in 1999, and National in 2008, albeit each needing the support of minor parties. The adoption of a proportional representation electoral system, first employed in the 1996 election, enabled smaller parties, disadvantaged by the traditional first-past-the-post system, to win seats, and NZ First, Alliance, Green, ACT, Maori, United NZ, and Progressive candidates subsequently took their places in the House. (See the 2010 *Handbook* for details.)

Following the election of 1999, Labour Party leader Helen CLARK, New Zealand's first elected woman prime minister, was sworn in on December 10 at the head of a minority government. Alliance leader James (Jim) ANDERTON negotiated with Clark a novel coalition agreement permitting "public differentiation between the parties in speech and vote" when they disagreed and was rewarded with the deputy prime ministership. This established a formula employed by subsequent minority governments, allowing Labour to govern following the elections of 2002 and 2005 and National to govern after the elections of 2008 and 2011 although neither party achieved a majority of seats.

Controversy had erupted in 2004 over a bill that would ensure state ownership of New Zealand's shorelines. The legislation, the Foreshore and Seabed Bill, was adamantly opposed by most Maori leaders, who viewed it as truncating tribal rights. Despite opposition by the National, United Future, and Maori parties, the Foreshore and Seabed Bill was enacted into law in November. (For more on opposition to the bill, see Maori party, below, and also the 2011 *Handbook*.)

Uninspiring leadership, alleged contact with a religious sect, and admitted marital infidelity by Don BRASJ hampered the National Party until a new leader, John Phillip KEY, was chosen in November 2006, whereupon National began a steady rise in the polls. By 2008 economic issues (jobs, taxes, property values) rose to the top of the list of public worries. The economy in 2006 and 2007 had grown on the strength of high agricultural export earnings and a strong dollar, but it turned downward in 2008 as energy and food import prices rose, the dollar and property values weakened, credit tightened, and financial institutions declared bankruptcy, with thousands of investors losing their savings. Labour was widely blamed despite its prudent financial management, accumulation of a budget surplus, and partial repayment of overseas debt.

Two contentious issues of 2007–2008 were "anti-smacking" legislation (an amendment to the Crimes Act) and the Emissions Trading Act. The anti-smacking legislation was criticized for criminalizing parents who employed corporal punishment of any kind. The bill was a concession by Labour in return for support by the Greens and was roundly condemned by parties of the right and members of fundamentalist religious groups. A citizens' petition led by the new Kiwi Party and supported by fundamentalist churches succeeded by August 2008 in obtaining over 320,000 signatures to compel a referendum. The following August, 88 percent of voters condemned the law. Key refused to repeal the law but recommended that the police and courts "interpret it sensibly," and few prosecutions have resulted.

The Emissions Trading Act, promoted by Clark to make New Zealand an international leader in reducing greenhouse gas emissions, was opposed by National, ACT, United Future, and the Maori Party on grounds of its cost and marginal effectiveness. Labour persuaded the Greens and NZ First to support the bill by making concessions, such as subsidizing home insulation and clean energy technology research and giving households a rebate to cover higher electricity charges. The new National government postponed implementation of the Emissions Trading Act to soften its economic impact until the recession eased.

In the general election of November 8, 2008, the National Party won 44.9 percent of the popular vote and 58 seats in the House of Representatives, followed by Labour's 34.0 percent and 43 seats, thus neither commanding a majority of seats. The third-ranked party, the Greens, won 6.7 percent of the vote and 9 seats, but these seats, combined with Labor's 43 seats, failed to outnumber National's 58 seats. In the end, ACT New Zealand (5 seats), the Maori Party (5 seats), and United Future New Zealand (1 seat) pledged their support in confidence and budget votes to a National-led minority government. The new government led by Prime Minister John Key was sworn in on November 19 and comprised 23 ministers in the cabinet, all National MPs, and 8 ministers outside the cabinet, including 3 from National, 2 from ACT, 2 from Maori, and 1 from United Future. On election night Helen Clark announced her resignation as party leader. Phil GOFF was subsequently chosen by Labour as Clark's successor, thereby becoming leader of the opposition in the House. Clark resigned her Mount Albert parliamentary seat in April 2009 to take up the post of administrator of the United Nations Development Program. Winston PETERS, Clark's erstwhile minister of foreign affairs, was embroiled in a secret campaign donations exposé and lost his seat, as did all his NZ First Party colleagues.

In June 2010 the government reached an agreement with the Maori Party to repeal the Foreshore and Seabed Act, which was accomplished on April 1, 2011. Its replacement, the Marine and Coastal Area (Takutai Moana) Act, restored Maori tribal authorities' rights to appeal to the courts to secure customary rights and resources but did not permit the sale of land covered by customary title or deny public access to it.

In response to the worldwide recession, the Labour-led government had guaranteed bank and savings institution deposits in October 2008, and the National-led government inherited this commitment. In August 2010 the government transferred NZ$1.6 billion to the receivers of South Canterbury Finance, a major firm that had failed in July, to cover its depositors. Unlike counterparts in Australia and the United States, the new National-led government in its 2009 through 2013 budgets declined to initiate an economic stimulus package, choosing instead to accelerate infrastructure projects and implement promised tax cuts, and to make up the deficit by borrowing from abroad. However, on October 1, 2010, alongside income tax reductions and pension increases, National hiked the goods and services tax (GST) from 12.5 percent to 15 percent.

Public criticism of abuse by parliamentarians of their housing and travel allowances erupted in mid-2009 and continued into 2010 driven by media exposés, obliging several MPs, including leaders of the National, ACT, and Green parties, to repay excess claims and inducing the prime minister to counsel his ministers to exercise spending restraint. Allegations that National MP Pansy WONG had used her travel privileges to further her husband's business interests in China led to her resignation from parliament in December. She was followed in March 2012 by Nick SMITH who as accident compensation minister intervened improperly in a friend's case. Peter DUNN, leader of National's coalition partner United Future, lost his revenue portfolio in 2013 for allegedly leaking information to a journalist. John BANKS, leader of the ACT, another coalition partner, resigned his portfolios in October to stand trial for alleged electoral fraud. Both continued to support the government in Parliament.

Constitution and government. New Zealand's political system, historically patterned on the British model, has no consolidated written constitution. As in other Commonwealth states that have retained allegiance to the queen, the monarch is represented by a governor general, now a New Zealand citizen, who performs the largely ceremonial functions of chief of state. The only legally recognized executive body is the Executive Council, which includes the governor general and all government ministers. De facto executive authority is vested in the cabinet, headed by the prime minister, under a system of parliamentary responsibility. The national legislature, the House of Representatives, popularly referred to as Parliament, is elected through a combination of single-seat local constituencies and a nation-wide party list. Some constituency seats (currently seven) are filled from a separate electoral roll on which Maori may choose to be registered. The judicial system is headed by a High Court, a Court of Appeal, and the Supreme Court, with district courts and justices of the peace functioning at lower levels.

Local administration is based on 16 regions. Four (Nelson City, Gisborne, Tasman, and Marlborough) are defined as unitary authorities, whereas the other 12 are subdivided into 57 districts and 16 cities. In addition, the remote, sparsely populated Chatham Islands, some 500 miles east of Christchurch, have unitary status. Each local unit is governed by an elected council headed by a chair or mayor, and advised by elected community boards in some urban areas.

Constitutional change appeared imminent when Prime Minister Clark said in February 2002 that New Zealand would "inevitably" become a republic. A step in that direction was taken in October 2003 when the House of Representatives, over opposition by National, passed a bill ending the right of final legal appeal to the Privy Council in London and creating a national Supreme Court, which began hearing cases in July 2004. The government also discontinued awarding knighthoods to meritorious citizens, opting instead for nonmonarchical honors. National upon assuming office in 2008 reinstated royal honors, and subsequently, republicanism faded as a political issue.

Foreign relations. New Zealand has traditionally maintained preferential trading and defense relations with its nearest neighbor, Australia, and has supported collective security through the United Nations, the ANZUS treaty with Australia and the United States, and the Five Power Defense Arrangements with Australia, Malaysia, Singapore, and the United Kingdom. Wellington has also engaged in regional security consultations in the Association of Southeast Asian Nations Regional Forum (ARF). New Zealand is an active member of the Commonwealth (of which former foreign minister Don McKINNON was secretary general from 2000 to 2008), and of the Pacific Islands Forum, having hosted its inaugural meeting in Auckland in 1971 and a 40th anniversary meeting in 2011.

In February 1985 the Labour government led by David LANGE refused entry to a U.S. Navy warship alleged to be capable of carrying nuclear weapons. Wishing to deter similar ship visit bans by other allies, the Ronald Reagan administration discontinued bilateral exercises, intelligence sharing, and cabinet-level diplomatic intercourse. In June 1987 New Zealand's Parliament approved a Nuclear Free Zone, Disarmament, and Arms Control Act that legally prohibited the entry of nuclear-armed or nuclear-powered ships into New Zealand waters, whereupon Secretary of State George Schultz suspended U.S. security commitments and declared ANZUS "inoperative" with respect to New Zealand. A decade of cool relations followed.

In September 1999 U.S. president Bill Clinton, to prepare for the UN-backed peacekeeping mission in East Timor, to which New Zealand committed some 800 troops, announced that the U.S. ban on military exercises with New Zealand would be waived for this and other multilateral operations. In 2001 the Clark government strongly endorsed the U.S.-led "war on terrorism" and dispatched troops to Afghanistan in support of the U.S.-led Operation Enduring Freedom. In March 2002 Prime Minister Clark was invited to meet with U.S. president George W. Bush, the first consultation with a Labour leader since the mid-1980s. The Clark government refused to participate in the 2003 invasion of Iraq, but troop contributions to Afghanistan, counterterrorism patrols in the Persian Gulf, assistance in negotiations with North Korea, and participation in the U.S.-led Proliferation Security Initiative earned goodwill in Washington. Secretary of State Condoleezza Rice paid an official visit in July 2008, signaling that the unresolved nuclear ship disagreement would no longer impede high-level relations.

Following two meetings with President Obama, Key in August 2009 announced the deployment of 70 Special Air Service combat troops to Afghanistan in addition to the 140 NZ Defence Force personnel and civilian specialists serving as a Provincial Reconstruction Team that had begun in 2003. The decision was supported by the National and ACT parties but contested by all the other parties in the House. Key also welcomed indications by assistant secretary of state Kurt Campbell that training opportunities for New Zealand troops with their American counterparts were to be expanded, and New Zealand was subsequently invited to participate in the multinational Rim of the Pacific (RIMPAC) exercise, which took place in July 2012. U.S. secretary of state Hillary Clinton visited in November 2010 and with Prime Minister Key signed the Wellington Declaration, signaling a return of close relations, including full restoration of intelligence sharing. At the invitation of President Obama, Key visited the White House in July 2011 and confered with top U.S. leaders and officials. In June 2012 the defence ministers of the two governments signed a defence cooperation agreement called the Washington Declaration covering maritime security, antipiracy, counter-terrorism, peacekeeping, and disaster relief. Secretary of Defense Chuck Hagel announced in October 2013 the full restoration of bilateral military exercise relations and indicated that New Zealand Navy ships would be welcome to berth in Pearl Harbor.

In 2011 Key also visited leaders in Britain, Europe, and Asia and hosted South Pacific, American, European Union, and Asian leaders and the UN Secretary General at the Pacific Island Forum's 40th-anniversary summit in Auckland in September. New Zealand has played an active part in South Pacific development and Asia-Pacific economic and political cooperation, with its initiatives including successful mediation of the Bougainville separatist conflict in Papua New Guinea in 1996 and dispatch of troops and police to support the elected government of the Solomon Islands in 2003. Wellington was quick to impose sanctions on the military junta of Fiji following the December 2006 coup, as it had done in response to coups in 1987 and 2000; these sanctions were selectively eased in 2013 in step with the Fiji military leader's preparations to hold an election in 2014.

Since 1989 New Zealand has been active in the 21-nation Asia-Pacific Economic Cooperation (APEC) forum, and from 2006 New Zealand has participated in the East Asian Summit meetings, which proponents hope will evolve into a 16-nation Asia-wide trade liberalization pact. Starting in 2000 New Zealand diplomats negotiated free-trade agreements with Singapore, then with Chile and Brunei, which culminated in July 2005 with the signing of the Trans-Pacific Strategic Economic Partnership Agreement (TPPA or P-4). New Zealand's free trade negotiations with China came to fruition in the New Zealand–China Free Trade Agreement signed April 7, 2008, China's first with a developed country. China in 2010 became New Zealand's second most valuable trade partner. Free trade agreements with Malaysia and Hong Kong and with the Association of Southeast Asian Nations (ASEAN) followed, and negotiations or studies with South Korea, India, the Gulf Cooperation Council, and Russia were undertaken, and a free trade agreement with Taiwan was signed in July 2013. In 2013 negotiations for a 121-member Trans Pacific Partnership (TPP) trade agreement including New Zealand, the United States, Canada, Australia, and eight Asian and Latin American governments progressed, with completion forecast for 2014.

The Defence White Paper issued in November 2010 reaffirmed New Zealand's commitment to the defense of Australia and the Pacific islands; security cooperation with the United States, Britain, Singapore, and Malaysia; and peacekeeping under United Nations auspices. Peacekeeping commitments in Solomon Islands, Timor-Leste, and Afghanistan were concluded in 2013 but 590 Defence Force personnel remained deployed abroad in 21 peacekeeping and other missions in 16 countries, including those on the frigate *HMNZS Te Mana* attached to a U.S.-led international counter-piracy force.

Current issues. As the 2011 election approached, political issues dividing the parties included representation of Maori and other ethnic minorities in the decision-making processes of the Auckland "super-city," legislation on the legal drinking age and sentencing and parole of violent offenders, the financing of facilities for the 2011 Rugby World Cup, approval of sales of dairy farms to China-based corporations, and concessions for off-shore oil and gas drilling. National's proposal to sell minority shareholdings in four energy companies and Air New Zealand attracted opposition from the public and all other parties save ACT and United Future. The November 26 election was marked by a record low voter turnout of 68.8 percent. National won 47.3 percent of the vote and 59 seats in the House but fell short of an outright majority, so entered into supply and confidence agreement with ACT and United Future (1 MP each) and the Maori Party (3 MPs) to form a minority government, similar to the previous three years. An accompanying referendum on the electoral system saw 57.8 percent of voters opting to retain the MMP system, which was reviewed in 2012 without significant change.

Controversy over the government's asset sale plans continued in 2013. The Maori Council asserted traditional ownership rights over watercourses, briefly holding up the sale of hydro-power company shares. The government's issue of Mighty River Power shares to the public went ahead in May and those of Meridian Energy in October. Despite the success of a Green Party petition opposing asset sales triggering a referendum in December, the government sold Air New Zealand shares in November. Meanwhile, a Shanghai firm's bid to buy a set of dairy farms was opposed by the Labour Party and temporarily held up by court action by a New Zealand bidder, and the Labour Party proposed setting limits on foreign purchases of residential properties; neither initiative succeeded. Other controversies included the following: Maori and environmentalists' objections to exploration of offshore sites for oil and gas wells and proposals to facilitate oil extraction by injection of water at high pressure, called "fracking"; the government's recasting of its target for greenhouse gas emissions reduction from 10 percent to 5 percent; and bills in parliament to detain mass asylum seekers (passed in June 2013), legalize same-sex marriages (passed in August), augment the surveillance powers of the Government Communications Security Bureau (passed in August), extend paid parental leave, raise the retirement age, and restrict welfare. Relations with Australia were disturbed by the inability of long-term New Zealand residents and tax payers in Australia to obtain welfare benefits. The combat deaths of five soldiers in Afghanistan, and allegations of violations of international law by Special Air Service personnel, stimulated adverse media and public comment and the prime minister brought forward the end date of the Provincial Reconstruction Team's deployment from September to April 2013 but kept 27 soldiers in Afghanistan on training and liaison duties. He also travelled to Asia, Europe, and New York to promote New Zealand's bid in October 2014 for election to a nonpermanent seat on the UN Security Council. Mid-2013 opinion surveys showed continued support for the National Party over the Labour Party by 10 percent, and for John Key as preferred prime minister over the leader of the opposition, David SHEARER, precipitating the latter's resignation in August and replacement by David CUNLIFF.

POLITICAL PARTIES

A two-party system has long characterized New Zealand politics, with conservative and liberal policies offered by the National and Labour parties, respectively. Differences between the two narrowed considerably after World War II, and even more so with the initiation of policies by the Labour Party after its election in 1984 that introduced liberalization and deregulation reforms similar to those advocated by the National Party, thus attenuating New Zealand's long-standing protectionist and welfare state policies.

The potential for smaller parties to form and play a significant role in politics was enhanced by the adoption in the 1996 election of a mixed member proportional representation system (MMP) similar to Germany's. In the general election in November 2011 13 parties offered party lists (down from 19 in 2008), of which 5 won no seats, 3 won a single seat, and 5 won 3 or more seats.

Governing Coalition:

New Zealand National Party (National Party). Founded in 1936 as a union of the earlier Reform and Liberal Parties, the National Party controlled the government from 1960 to 1972, 1975 to 1984, 1990 to 1999, and 2008 to the present. A party of the center-right drawing its strength from well-off rural and suburban areas, National was traditionally committed to the support of personal initiative, private enterprise, and minimum government regulation. However, the distinction between right and left blurred as Labour shifted to free-market policies, and the 1975–1984 National government led by Sir Robert Muldoon endorsed selective state intervention in the economy, including subsidies for farmers.

While National won a landslide victory over Labour in 1990, Bolger's young populist colleague Winston Peters overtook him in popularity, and the two became rivals. Bolger dismissed Peters as Maori affairs minister in late 1991 for alleged disloyalty and a year later excluded him from the party's parliamentary caucus. Peters responded by resigning his seat and humiliated the government by winning a by-election under the banner of his newly established NZ First Party.

The National Party won a bare majority of 50 of the 99 legislative seats in the 1993 balloting, but the defection of Ross MEURANT in September 1994 to form the Right of Centre Party eliminated this margin, obliging Bolger to form a coalition with the new party. In the 1996 election National won a plurality of 44 out of 120 seats, sufficient for it to form a coalition government with NZ First, with Peters as deputy prime minister. In November 1997 Bolger was supplanted as party leader by Jenny SHIPLEY, the leader of the party's right wing, who was named prime minister in December, the first woman to achieve this office.

NZ First left the coalition in August 1998, but Shipley survived until the November 1999 election, which National lost to Labour. Shipley resigned her party leadership post in October 2001 and was succeeded by Bill ENGLISH, a former minister of health, who was then ousted in November 2003 by Don Brash, a former governor of the Reserve Bank of New Zealand who had joined the party only three years before. In the July 2002 election the party's list vote share plummeted to 20.9 percent, with only 27 seats won, a record low. In November 2006 Brash, whose leadership was tarnished by public gaffes, marital infidelity, and alleged links to a secretive right-wing Christian organization, resigned as party leader and was succeeded by former international currency trader John Key.

The November 8, 2008, election produced a plurality for National of 58 seats with 44.33 percent of the total vote and enabled Key to form a coalition government. Despite resignations in 2009 and 2010 by National MPs Richard WORTH and Pansy Wong for alleged misconduct, and in the face of the economic recession, John Key's vigorous response to the South Canterbury Finance collapse and the Christchurch earthquakes and his cordial meetings with President Obama contributed to Key's personal popularity and helped win National 47.3 percent of the vote and a record 59 seats in the November election despite a campaign marked by few divisive issues and a record low voter turnout.

Leaders: John KEY (Party Leader and Prime Minister), Bill ENGLISH (Deputy Leader and Deputy Prime Minister), Peter GOODFELLOW (President), Greg HAMILTON (General Manager).

Maori Party. Tariana TURIA, a former Labour MP and associate minister for Maori affairs, established the Maori Party in June 2004. She had left Labour in May to protest the government's Foreshore and Seabed Bill, which she saw as a betrayal of Maori customary rights. Under the new banner of the Maori Party, Turia won a parliamentary by-election for her old seat in July, taking some 90 percent of the vote.

Partly as a consequence of the demise of its rivals *Mana Maori Motuhake* (Maori Self-Determination) and the *Mana Maori* Movement, the Maori Party won four Maori-roll seats in the 2005 election.

In the November 2008 election the Maori Party contested all seven Maori seats (and a number of general seats besides) and succeeded in winning five of them with 2.39 percent of the total vote. To build a governing coalition, National offered Turia and her co-leader Pita SHARPLES ministerial portfolios (outside cabinet) and pledged to review Labour's Foreshore and Seabed Act. Turia and Sharples protested Prime Minister Key's June 2010 proposal to repeal the act and at the same time curb certain Maori customary rights, but they were persuaded to continue supporting the National-led government until the next election. In August Maori Party MP Hone HARAWIRA provoked criticism for announcing his disapproval of his children's dating *pakeha* (people of European decent). In September Harawira threatened to vote against the Marine and Coastal Area (Takutai Moana) Bill negotiated by his party with the National-led government. Facing criticism from Turia and Sharples, he resigned from the party in February 2011, resigned from parliament in May, formed a new party called Mana in June, and on June 25 won the subsequent by-election in the Te Tai Tokerau electorate, defeating the Maori Party and Labour Party challengers. Rahui KATENE lost the Te Tai Tonga seat to the Labour challenger, reducing the Maori Party to 3 MPs. Turia and Sharples pledged to support a National-led minority government and were given the portfolios (outside cabinet) of Disability Issues and Maori Affairs, respectively. Both indicated they would stand down after the 2014 election, and drafted Te Ururoa Flavell as the next Maori Party leader.

Leaders: Tariana TURIA and Te Ururoa FLAVELL(Coleaders); Pem BIRD (President); Helen LEAHY (National Secretary).

ACT New Zealand (ACT). Founded in 1994 as the political arm of the Association of Consumers and Taxpayers, ACT advocates tax reduction, welfare reform, school choice, health care reform, and termination of Waitangi Tribunal claims. One of the party's founders, Sir Roger DOUGLAS, was a former Labour finance minister and the architect of the deregulatory and free-market reforms introduced in 1985.

The party won eight seats in the 1996 election and nine in the 1999 election and provided crucial confidence votes to Prime Minister Shipley's minority government. In 2002 ACT retained its nine seats on the basis of a 7.1 percent share of the party list vote.

But with public support for ACT falling below 3 percent, Richard PREBBLE stepped down as party leader in April 2004 and Rodney HIDE won a four-way battle for the leadership. In September 2005 the party won only 1.5 percent of the party list vote but thanks to Hide's constituency victory ACT was eligible for one list seat, which was taken by Heather ROY. Sir Roger Douglas contested the 2008 election as a list candidate, ranked third behind Hide and Roy; he was elected but not awarded a ministerial portfolio because of Prime Minister Key's adamant refusal to work with him. Hide and Roy were awarded portfolios (outside cabinet) in the new National-led government. In August 2010 Roy, critical of Hide's leadership, was dismissed as deputy leader by the ACT caucus and was replaced by John Boscawen.

Former National Party leader Don Brash successfully seized the leadership of ACT in April 2011 and then named former Auckland mayor John Banks to contest the Eden electorate in place of Rodney Hide, who was voted out of the leadership and resigned from parliament after the 2011 election. All sitting ACT MPs subsequently declined to stand in the 2011 election. ACT's popularity thereupon sank and by election night November 26 stood at 1.1 percent, with only Banks winning his constituency seat. Brash then resigned as leader, deputy leader John Boscawen foreshadowed his retirement at the next election, and Banks began negotiations to support a National-led government in supply and confidence, for which he was rewarded with the portfolios of Regulatory Reform and Small Business, both outside cabinet. In October 2013 Banks resigned his portfolios to stand trial for alleged electoral fraud during his 2010 Auckland mayoral bid.

Leaders: John BANKS (Leader), John BOSCAWEN (Party President), Barbara ASTILL (Vice President),Garry MALLETT (Party Secretary).

United Future New Zealand (United Future). United Future was formed in 2000 by the merger of United New Zealand (United NZ) and Future New Zealand (Future NZ). (See the 2010 *Handbook* for background details on these parties.)

In its first national election in July 2002, United Future won eight House seats and agreed to support Helen Clark's Labour-Progressive coalition. In 2005 the party won only three seats, but these proved crucial in Labour's effort to remain in power, as a consequence of which Dunne was awarded the post of minister of revenue.

In the 2008 election Dunne again won his electorate seat, but he was the sole surviving MP for United Future. Nevertheless, he was kept on by Prime Minister Key as minister of revenue (outside cabinet). United Future's popularity remained low, registering just 0.6 percent in the November 2011 election, but Dunne retained his constituency seat and was reinstated as minister for revenue in the new National-led government. The Electoral Commission deregistered United Future on May 31, 2013, for insufficient membership; although the party was reregistered on August 13, Dunn lost his revenue portfolio to National's Tod McCLAY.

Leaders: Peter DUNNE (Party Leader and Minister of Revenue), Judy TURNER (Deputy Leader), Robin GUNSTON (Party president), Ronald GARROD (Secretary).

Other Parties in Parliament:

New Zealand Labour Party (Labour Party). Founded in 1916 and in power 1935–1949, 1957–1960, 1972–1975, and 1984–1990, the Labour Party initiated much of the legislation that created the New Zealand welfare state. However, in a radical policy shift compelled by international economic changes, the post-1984 Labour administration of David Lange introduced free-market policies, including privatization of state enterprises, deregulation of commercial activities, and elimination of subsidies. The party nonetheless maintained its traditional antimilitary and antinuclear postures and in 1985 prohibited a visit by a U.S. warship, precipitating a curtailment of bilateral defense relations by Washington. Labour was reelected in 1987 but in 1989 the increasingly unpopular Lange resigned in favor of Geoffrey PALMER, who was in turn succeeded by Michael (Mike) MOORE in 1990. The party's legislative representation fell to an all-time low of 28 seats in the 1990 election, but it staged a recovery to 45 seats out of 99 in 1993.

In December 1993 a Labour caucus ousted Moore in favor of his deputy, Helen Clark, a leader of the party's left wing. In the 1994 and 1996 elections Labour lost seats and remained in opposition. Labour recovered in the 1999 election, taking 38.7 percent of the list vote and gaining 49 seats. Clark negotiated a coalition with the Alliance (10 seats) and secured support on crucial votes from the Greens, and thus became New Zealand's first elected woman prime minister.

The collapse of the Alliance led to an early election in July 2002, in which Labour retained its plurality, winning 52 seats (including all 7 Maori roll seats) on the strength of 45 percent of the electorate votes and 41 percent of the party list votes. Clark then negotiated a coalition with the former Alliance leader Jim Anderton's new Progressives and a cooperation agreement with United Future that assured her new government a working majority. In late 2004 Labour lost the 7 Maori members, who left to form a new Maori Party (see above). In September 2005, although its electorate vote dropped to 40 percent, Labour won a plurality of 50 seats, just ahead of the rival Nationals, formed another coalition with Jim Anderton's Progressives, and gained sufficient support from United Future and New Zealand First to form a minority government.

Labour contested the election of November 2008 with a new front bench and relatively unknown candidates, winning only 33.99 percent of the vote and 43 seats. On election night as the result became clear, Helen Clark unexpectedly announced her retirement as Labour leader. She subsequently retired from Parliament to head the United Nations Development Program. The party's nomination for her seat went to David Shearer, a former UN official who had served in Iraq. Shearer won the by-election of June 13, 2009, with 63.31 percent of the vote.

In March 2009 Phil Goff was unanimously chosen to lead the party and Annette KING became his deputy. Party president Mike WILLIAMS stepped down and union secretary Andrew LITTLE was elected in his place; he was succeeded in 2010 by Moira Coatsworth. In mid-2010 Labour's Shane JONES was demoted from his shadow ministership as a result of parliamentary allowance spending abuses, and in October Chris CARTER was expelled from the Labour Party for undermining Phil Goff's leadership. A promising young MP, Darren HUGHES, resigned from Parliament in March 2011 following allegations of sexual misconduct. By August Labour's popularity sagged to 30 percent in polls, and Phil Goff's desirability as preferred prime minister declined to 12 percent. The November election found Labour's vote reduced to 27.5 percent and Parliamentary seats to 34, whereupon Goff and King offered their resignations as leader and deputy, and the Labour caucus elected David Shearer and Grant ROBERTSON in their place. In 2012 and 2013 neither the party nor the leader polled well, and in August 2013 Shearer resigned, to be replaced by David CUNLIFF. David PARKER was chosed as deputy leader and shadow finance minister. The leadership change boosted Labour's popularity from 30 percent to 35 percent in late 2013.

Leaders: David CUNLIFF (Party Leader and Leader of the Opposition), David PARKER (Deputy Party Leader), Moira COATSWORTH (President), Tim BARNETT (General Secretary).

Green Party of Aotearoa (Greens). Founded in 1972 as the New Zealand Values Party, the country's left-oriented environmental party adopted its present name in 1988. In addition to environmental and conservation concerns, it advocates disarmament, pacifism, and devolution of power to the people and opposes free trade agreements. In 1991 the Greens entered an alliance with New Labour and other small groups, which gained three legislative seats in the 1996 balloting.

In the 1999 election the Greens, contesting independently, won seven seats in the House. Because the Labour-Alliance coalition failed to gain a majority, the incoming Clark minority government appealed for Green support, which it got for crucial votes, although a formal cooperation agreement was never concluded.

In the 2002 election the Green seats rose to nine, but Prime Minister Clark rejected their demand for a blanket moratorium on genetically modified organisms, so the Greens went into opposition. In September 2005 the Greens won six seats and again, while remaining outside the new Labour-led minority government, agreed not to oppose it on confidence votes, enabling Clark to remain prime minister.

The Greens surged to 6.7 percent in the November election, winning nine seats and placing third behind National and Labour and well ahead of ACT. Labour's attempt to build a new coalition failed, and the Greens moved to the opposition benches again. The Greens' most popular activist, Jeanette FITZSIMONS, retired from coleadership in June 2009, and the party chose Metiria TUREI as the new coleader. Russel Norman replaced the late Rod DONALD as the male coleader. On election night November 26, 2011, the Greens attracted 11.0 percent of the party vote to send 14 list members to Parliament despite winning no constituency seats. The party's popularity rose to 12 percent in 2013.

Leaders: Russel NORMAN and Metiria TUREI (Coleaders); Georgina MORRISON and Pete HUGGINS (Coconveners); Sarah HELM (General Manager); Jon FIELD (General Secretary).

New Zealand First Party (NZ First). The right-wing populist NZ First was launched in July 1993 by the flamboyant former Maori affairs minister, Winston Peters, who had been ejected from the National Party caucus earlier in the year. Forcing a by-election by resigning from the House, he retained his seat with a massive 11,000-vote majority in the Tauranga electorate and subsequently attracted much public approval for his allegations of corruption in the Cook Islands (see Related Territories, below). NZ First won only 2 seats in the 1993 election but improved to 17 seats (including all 5 Maori roll seats) in the 1996 election, enabling Peters to negotiate a coalition agreement with the National Party whereby he was named deputy prime minister and treasurer. However, his rapid elevation generated opposition within National Party ranks.

On August 14, 1998, a day after calling Prime Minister Shipley "devious" and "untrustworthy" on the floor of the House, Peters was sacked and NZ First moved into opposition. Several members subsequently formed the short-lived *Mauri* Pacific (Spirit of the Pacific) party, which failed to win any House seats in 1999 and was dissolved in 2001. NZ First failed to reach the 5 percent threshold in the 1999 national election, but Peters retained his Tauranga seat (by 63 votes), and this enabled NZ First to claim four additional party list seats.

In the 2002 election NZ First appealed to anticrime, anti-immigration, and anti-Maori sentiments and took 10.4 percent of the party list vote, to surge to 13 House seats, but the party remained in opposition. In the 2005 election the party declined to only 7 list seats on a 5.7 percent vote share and Peters lost his Tauranga seat to a National candidate. But Peters, elected on the party list, then negotiated a "supply and confidence agreement" with Labour that made him minister of foreign affairs, although he remained outside cabinet and able to criticize the government. Subsequent allegations that he had accepted secret donations from wealthy business interests damaged his credibility, and in August 2008 Prime Minister Clark suspended him as minister of foreign affairs. Parliament passed a motion of censure three weeks later. Peters was ultimately cleared by the Serious Fraud Office, but meanwhile, NZ First had slumped in the polls and won only 4.07 percent of the vote. Furthermore, Peters lost his constituency race, so the party was excluded from the new parliament altogether. The party continued to attract a small but loyal following Peters' return to campaigning in the 2011 election run-up revived it; despite winning no constituencies NZ First garnered 6.8 percent of the party vote and sent 8 MPs to Parliament. Peters declined to enter into negotiations with either National or Labour, opting again to position his party on the opposition benches.

Leaders: Winston PETERS (Leader), Ken GARDENER (President), Anne MARTIN (Secretary).

Mana Party. Registered on June 24, 2011, by Hone Harawira, following his resignation from the Maori Party, the party championed the redressing of Maori grievances. It objected particularly to the compromises made by the Maori Party in the Marine and Coastal Area (Takutai Moana) Act. Its leader forced a by-election by resigning from parliament and then successfully contested the Te Tai Tokerau seat against Labour and Maori Party rivals and returned to parliament on the opposition benches. Despite attracting high-profile personalities John MINTO and Sue BRADFORD as members, it remained a one-person ethnic protest party, gaining only 1.0 percent of the party vote in the November 2011 election despite Harawira's constituency victory.

Leaders: Hone HARAWIRA (Leader), Gerard HEHIR (Party Secretary).

Other Parties:

Conservative Party. Launched in July 2011, the Conservative Party is led by Auckland property developer Colin Craig. It espouses lower taxes, minimum government, strict law enforcement and sentencing of convicted persons, opposition to asset sales and the Emission Trading Act, and family and Christian values. In the 2011 election it fielded a full slate of 60 candidates and garnered 2.8 percent of the party vote but failed to reach the 5 percent threshold or win the Rodney seat contested by Craig and won no parliamentary seats. Opinion surveys in 2013 showed its popularity declining to less than 1 percent.

Leaders: Colin CRAIG (Leader), Christine RANKIN (Chief Executive Officer), Kevin STITT (National Administrator), Nathaniel HESLOP (Party Secretary).

The Alliance. The Alliance was launched in 1991 as a coalition of five parties—the NewLabour Party, the *Mana Motuhake,* the New Zealand Democratic Party, the Green Party of Aotearoa, and the Liberal Party—on a platform calling for preservation of the welfare state and an end to the free-market policies of the two major parties. It won 2 seats in 1993 and in the 1996 campaign won 13 seats. However, in late 1997 the Greens left the Alliance and in early 1998 the Liberal Party dissolved.

Nevertheless in the November 1999 election the Alliance captured ten seats and worked out a power-sharing arrangement with Labour that permitted separate stances on issues affecting the "distinctive political identity" of each party. The new Labour-led cabinet included four Alliance ministers and a fifth minister for consumer affairs and customs outside cabinet. However, in 2002 a sharp division between the Alliance caucus and the party leadership headed by Matt McCARTEN led to the expulsion of Anderton and six other MPs who had supported the government's decision to participate in U.S.-led military operations in Afghanistan.

In the July 2002 election, called early because of the split, the Alliance was ousted from the House, having won only 1.3 percent of the party list vote. In December 2002 *Mana Motuhake* formally left the Alliance and dissolved in 2005. In subsequent elections the Alliance won 0.07 percent of the vote in 2005, 0.08 percent in 2008, and 0.05 percent in 2011 and no seats.

Leaders: Kay MURRAY (Coleader and Treasurer), Kevin CAMPBELL (Coleader), Tom DOWIE (President), Andrew MCKENZIE (General Secretary).

Jim Anderton's Progressive Party (Progressives). When divisions over defense policy and relations with the United States split the Alliance coalition party in April–May 2002, its former leader and the sitting deputy prime minister organized his own "Jim Anderton's Progressive Coalition," which was registered as a party by the Electoral Commission in June 2002. In the July 2002 election the Progressive Coalition attracted only 1.7 percent of the party list vote but claimed one additional proportional seat on the strength of Anderton's constituency seat victory. Anderton retained his agriculture and other ministerial portfolios, but not his position as deputy prime minister, in the new Clark minority government.

In April 2004 the Progressive Coalition was formally reregistered as the Progressive Party, adopting its current name in July 2005. In the 2005 election Anderton retained his seat, but the party's 1.2 percent party list vote did not entitle it to another seat. In the 2008 election Anderton again won his electorate seat, but his party garnered only 0.91 percent of the vote, and Anderton moved to the opposition seats with Labour and the Greens. In October 2010 Anderton ran unsuccessfully for the mayoralty of Christchurch and then retired from Parliament after the 2011 election. His party did not contest that poll and was deregistered on March 9, 2012.

Leaders: Jim ANDERTON (Leader), Matt ROBSON (Deputy Leader), Phil CLEARWATER (General Secretary).

New Zealand Democratic Party for Social Credit (Democrats for Social Credit). Established in May 1953 as the Social Credit Political League, the party campaigned largely on a platform that promoted economic sovereignty, small business, worker shareholding and participation in management, tax and banking reform, public ownership of utilities, and introduction of a "Universal Basic Income." Social Credit subsequently proposed a defense posture of "armed neutrality" and a nuclear-free zone.

Leader Bruce BEETHAM held a seat in the House from 1978 until 1987, but his party secured no representation for a decade until winning two seats as part of the Alliance in 1996. It retained both in 1999. When the Alliance split in 2002, the party joined Jim Anderton's Progressive Coalition but won no seats in the July 2002 House election. At a party conference three months later the party opted to separate from the Progressives.

The party adopted its present name in July 2005 but won only 0.1 percent of the party list vote that year, 0.05 percent of the vote in 2008, and 0.08 percent in 2011. It holds no seats.

Leaders: Stephanie de RUYTER (Leader), John PEMBERTON (Deputy Leader), David WILSON (President), Katherine RANSOM (Vice President), Roxanne HANSEN (Secretary).

The following parties contested the 2008 or 2011 election without success, and nine were subsequently deregistered. The **Kiwi Party** (registered February 15, 2008; Larry BALDOCK, leader; Gordon COPELAND, president; Simonne DYER, secretary), which successfully led the petition initiative to force the August 21, 2009, referendum on the "anti-smacking" bill, won 0.54 percent. It did not contest the 2011 election and was deregistered on February 8, 2012. The **Aotearoa Legalize Cannabis Party** (Michael APPLEBY, leader; Michael BRITNELL, deputy leader; Kevin O'CONNELL, president; Irinka BRITNELL, secretary) won 0.41 percent in 2008 and 0.52 percent in 2011. The **Libertarianz** (Richard MCGRATH, leader; Sean FITZPATRICK, deputy leader; Craig MILMINE, president; Robert PALMER, secretary), a radical minimum-government party founded in 1996, won 0.05 percent of the vote in 2008 and 0.07 percent in 2011. The **Workers Party of New Zealand** (registered October 3, 2008; Philip FERGUSON, national organiser; Daphna WHITMORE, national secretary), which won 0.04 percent, is a descendent of numerous small leftist parties, most recently the **Anti-Capitalist Alliance** (2002–2006); it was deregistered in May 2011. The **New Citizen Party**, aspiring to represent recent Asian migrants, was registered on November 25, 2010, with Kevin LIU as party secretary but did not contest the 2011 election and was deregistered on February 29, 2012.The **Bill and Ben Party** (registered July 29, 2008; Ben BOYCE and Jamie LINEHAM, co-leaders; Andrew ROBINSON, secretary), a "joke party" led by two TV satirists, won 0.56 percent of the vote in 2008; it was deregistered in April 2010. The **Family Party** (registered December 17, 2007; Richard LEWIS, leader; Paul ADAMS, deputy leader; Elias KANARIS, president; Anne WILLIAMSON, secretary), which won 0.35 percent of the vote, descended from two fundamentalist parties, the **New Zealand Family Rights Protection Party** (registered March 2005 and deregistered September 2007) and **Destiny New Zealand** (registered July 2003 and deregistered in October 2007); it was deregistered in April 2010. The **New Zealand Pacific Party** (Philip FIELD, leader; Ropeti GAFA, interim secretary) won 0.37 percent; it was deregistered in August 2010. The **RAM–Residents Action Movement** (Grant BROOKES, chair; Elaine BLADE, vice chair; Elliott BLADE, secretary) won 0.02 percent; it was deregistered in April 2010. The **Republic of New Zealand Party** (Kerry BEVIN, leader; Richard NIGHTINGALE, secretary), which won 0.01 percent, was registered in July 2005 and deregistered on June 30, 2009. The **New World Order Party**, founded in 2006 and registered in May 2008 (Nathan Lee COUPER, President and Secretary), was deregistered in June 2011. The Electoral Commission registered the logo of an aspiring party,**Thrive New Zealand**, which promotes citizens' referenda and direct democracy, on August 28, 2013; full registration is pending.

LEGISLATURE

The former bicameral General Assembly of New Zealand became a unicameral body in 1950 with the abolition of its upper chamber, the Legislative Council. Now called the **House of Representatives** (although delegates are referred to as members of parliament, or MPs), the body currently consists of 120 members elected by universal suffrage for a three-year term, subject to dissolution. Under a partially proportional system (mixed member proportional, or MMP) introduced in 1996, 69 members are elected from single-member constituencies by majority vote (including 7 elected by voters on a separate Maori electoral roll) and at least 51 from party lists to ensure proportional representation for those parties winning at least one constituency or obtaining at least 5 percent of the national vote.

In the election of September 17, 2005, the new Maori Party won 1 more electorate seat than would otherwise have been awarded on the basis of the party list vote. Under New Zealand's complicated MMP electoral system, this "overhang" seat meant that for the length of its term the house had 121 seats (69 electorate seats and 52 party list seats). The 2008 election produced an "overhang" of 2 Maori seats and a house of 122 members. These were distributed as follows: National Party, 58 (constituency seats 41, party list seats 17); Labour Party, 43 (21, 22); Green Party of Aotearoa, 9 (0, 9); ACT New Zealand, 5 (1, 4); Maori Party, 5 (5, 0); Jim Anderton's Progressive Party, 1 (1, 0), United Future New Zealand, 1 (1, 0). The October 2010 expulsion of Chris Carter reduced the Labour caucus to 42, the June 2011 resignation of Hone Harawira to win a by-election seat under the Mana Party label reduced the Maori Party caucus to 4, and the July resignation from the house of John CARTER to become High Commissioner to Cook Islands reduced the National caucus to 57 and the number of legislative seats to 121.

The election of November 26 returned the following parties to the House: National 59 (constituency seats 40, list seats 19); Labour 34 (23, 11); Green 14 (0, 8); NZ First 8 (0, 8); Maori 3 (3, 0); Act 1 (1, 0); Mana 1 (1,0); United Future 1 (1, 0). The Maori Party's three constituency victories with only 1.3 percent of party vote produced an "overhang" of 2 and a House of 122 seats.

Speaker: David CARTER.

CABINET

[as of November 1, 2013]

Prime Minister, Tourism, Ministerial Services, NZ Security Intelligence Service, Government Communications Security Bureau	John Key
Deputy Prime Minister, Finance	Bill English
Ministers in Cabinet	
Attorney General, Treaty of Waitangi Negotiations, Arts, Culture and Heritage	Christopher Findlayson
Canterbury Earthquake Recovery, Transport, Earthquake Commission	Gerry Brownlee
Commerce, Consumer Affairs, Broadcasting	Craig Foss
Conservation, Housing	Nick Smith
Defense, State Services	Jonathan Coleman
Economic Development, Science and Innovation, Tertiary Education, Skills and Employment	Steven Joyce
Education, Pacific Island Affairs	Hekia Parata [f]
Energy and Resources, Labour	Simon Bridges
Environment, Communications, and Information Technology	Amy Adams [f]
Food Safety, Civil Defence, Youth Affairs	Nikki Kaye [f]
Foreign Affairs, Sport and Recreation	Murray McCully
Health, State Owned Enterprises	Tony Ryall
Internal Affairs, Local Government	Chris Tremain
Justice, Accident Compensation Corporation, Ethnic Affairs	Judith Collins [f]
Police, Corrections	Anne Tolley [f]
Primary Industries, Racing	Nathan Guy
Social Development	Paula Bennett [f]
Trade, Climate Change Issues	Tim Groser
Ministers Outside Cabinet	
Building and Construction, Customs, Land Information, Statistics	Maurice Williamson
Community and Voluntary Sector, Senior Citizens, Women's Affairs	Jo Goodhew [f]
Courts	Chester Borrows
Immigration, Veterans' Affairs	Michael Woodhouse
Revenue	Tod McClay
Support Party Ministers	
Maori Affairs	Dr. Pita Sharples (Maori Party)
Whanau Ora, Disability Issues	Tariana Turia (Maori Party) [f]

[f] = female

Note: Unless otherwise noted, all ministers belong to the National Party.

INTERGOVERNMENTAL REPRESENTATION

Ambassador to the U.S.: Mike MOORE.

U.S. Ambassador to New Zealand: Mark D. GILBERT (nominated).

Permanent Representative to the UN: Jim McLAY.

IGO Memberships (Non-UN): ADB, APEC, CWTH, ICC, IEA, IOM, OECD, PIF, WTO.

RELATED TERRITORIES

New Zealand has links to two self-governing territories in free association, the Cook Islands and Niue, and administers two dependent territories, Tokelau and Ross Dependency.

Cook Islands. Located some 1,700 miles northeast of New Zealand and administered by that country from 1901 to 1965, Cook Islands is now a self-governing political entity recognizing Queen Elizabeth II, (represented by New Zealand's governor general) as its sovereign and constitutionally linked in free association with New Zealand. The islands have a land area of 90 square miles (234 sq. km) and are divided between a smaller, poorer, northern group and a larger, more fertile, southern group. The most populous island, Rarotonga, is the site of the capital, Avarua. The islands' total resident population of 12,000 (2010E) consists almost entirely of Polynesians who are New Zealand citizens. In 2006, 58,011 Cook Islanders resided in New Zealand, with another 15,000 in Australia, and their remittances are a significant source of income for the territory. Exports include fish, pearls, tropical fruits, and handicrafts, while tourism is the source of over 75 percent of foreign earnings. Offshore banking and the sale of fishing licenses to foreign ships also contribute income. Future prospects include mining of undersea mineral nodules. Cook Islands annually receives more than $20 million from an integrated New Zealand and Australia development cooperation program, supplemented by project and relief aid from Japan, France, the European Union, China, and the Asian Development Bank (ADB).

In June 2000 the Cook Islands was named by the Organization for Economic Cooperation and Development (OECD) as 1 of 35 uncooperative tax havens and by the international Financial Action Task Force on Money Laundering (FATF) as 1 of 15 noncooperative countries and territories. In 2002 the Cook government undertook remedial action and in 2005 was removed from the FATF list, having satisfied demands for tighter controls.

Self-government with an elected Legislative Assembly (commonly called the Parliament) and a premier (prime minister, since 1981) elected by the Parliament was instituted in 1965, with New Zealand obligated by legislation to assist in external and defense affairs when requested. A hereditary House of Ariki, with up to 15 members, serves as an upper legislative chamber, advising on customary matters and land use. In 2004 Parliament voted to drop the seat for voters overseas, reduce the size of the legislature to 24, and shorten the legislative term from five to four years.

Over the past 30 years political power has swung between the **Cook Islands Party** (CIP), which dates from 1965, and the **Democratic Party** (DP), founded in 1971 and named the Democratic Alliance Party (DAP) until 2003, often entailing coalition governments (for details, see the 2010 *Handbook*). The political landscape stabilized in 2004 when, following formation of a new grouping called *Demo Tumu* (subsequently renamed Cook Islands First) by defectors from the CIP and the DP, Jim MARURAI was elected prime minister. Marurai shored up his leadership by including CIP and DP leaders in his cabinet. After losing his majority in Parliament in 2006, he called a snap election that concluded with the DP holding 15 seats; the CIP, 8; and a CIP-aligned independent, 1. Marurai was reinstated as prime minister, with Terepai MAOATE as his deputy and Wilkie RASMUSSEN as minister of foreign affairs. The CIP's Tom MASTERS became leader of the opposition.

In a cabinet reshuffle in November 2009 Marurai sacked Maoate, brought in Robert WIGMORE as deputy prime minister and foreign minister, and moved Rasmussen to the finance portfolio. In July 2010 Marurai, facing serious opposition from the CIP, held on as prime minister by refusing to convene Parliament except for a session to pass the budget. The election of November 17 brought the CIP to power with 44.5 percent of the vote and 16 seats to the DP's 8 seats. Henry PUNA, leader of the CIP since 2006, became prime minister, and Mapu TAIA, DP, became speaker of Parliament. In 2012 senior politician Norman GEORGE resigned from the CIP to re-join the DP and challenged the constitutionality of the Electoral Amendment Act 2007 preventing parliamentarians from changing parties, and in August 2013 Minister of Marine Resources Teina BISHOP stood down amid allegations of fraudulent practices regarding granting of fishing licenses to Chinese-flagged boats.

Internationally, the Cook Islands is a member of the Pacific Community, the Smaller Island States subgroup (with Kiribati, Nauru, Niue, and Tuvalu) within the Pacific Islands Forum, various UN agencies, and the ADB, and is engaged in negotiations to augment the Pacific Agreement on Closer Economic Relations that includes Australia, New Zealand, and the Forum governments. In 2009 Marurai and Prime Minister John Key announced completion of a tax information exchange agreement, further dispelling lingering allegations of tax evasion. A similar agreement was negotiated with Australia. Cook Islands in April petitioned the UN Commission on the Limits of the Continental Shelf (CLCS) to extend its Exclusive Economic Zone by 400,000 sq. km, and in July 2011, the Minister for Minerals and Natural Resources Tom Masters announced plans to begin issuing deep-sea mining exploration licenses in 2013. This was followed in June 2012 by legislation under the Cook Islands Seabed Mining Act 2009 establishing Cook Island jurisdiction over resources in its EEZ and in August by an agreement with neighboring Kiribati, Niue, and Tokelau demarcating their respective maritime boundaries. The budget for 2012–2013 foreshadowed a surplus made possible by new taxes on imported tobacco and beverages and tourism activities and foreign grants and loans of NZ$48 million, including NZ$4 million from China. The ratio of debt to GDP was forecast to rise to 33 percent in 2013–2014 reflecting borrowing from the ADB and China for infrastructural improvements. New Zealand's aid in the period 2013–2015 included NZ$12 million annually for economic growth and infrastructure, NZ$4 million for health and education, and NZ$1.6 million for governance improvement, a projected three-year total of NZ$57 million. Australia contributed another NZ$5 million annually. In 2013 New Zealand and China commenced a joint water reticulation project, a first for both governments.

New Zealand High Commissioner: John CARTER.
Prime Minister: Henry PUNA.
Queen's Representative: Sir Frederick Tutu GOODWIN.

Niue. An island of 100 square miles (259 sq. km), Niue is the largest and westernmost of the Cook Islands but has been administered separately since 1903. The territory obtained self-government in 1974, with a premier heading a 4-member cabinet and a Legislative Assembly (*Fono*) of 20 members, 6 elected from a common roll and 14 chosen by villages, serving three-year terms. It is now a self-governing political entity recognizing Queen Elizabeth II, represented by New Zealand's governor general, as its sovereign and is constitutionally linked in free association with New Zealand. Niueans have New Zealand citizenship, and New Zealand is obligated by legislation to assist Niue with foreign affairs and defense when requested. The capital is Alofi.

Niue's resident population has declined almost continuously from 5,194 in 1966 to 1,740 in 2006 and an estimated 1,300 in 2013. According to the 2006 census, 22,473 Niueans resided in New Zealand, and their overseas remittances constitute a major source of the island's income. Other economic resources include annual budgetary and project aid from New Zealand, loans from international agencies, and export sales of noni juice, fish, taro, honey, and vanilla. A small tourism industry attracted some 3,500 tourists in 2007, but numbers remain low due to limited hotel facilities and airline flights. Arrivals are also affected by the threat of cyclones. Recent efforts to increase the island's income have included leasing its telephone area code for sex-related and other services, selling its postal code ("NU") for Internet domain addresses, and investigating prospects for commercial fishing. Internationally, Niue participates in the Pacific Community, the Smaller Island States subgroup (with the Cook Islands, Kiribati, Nauru, and Tuvalu) within the Pacific Islands Forum, the UN Educational, Scientific, and Cultural Organization (UNESCO), the World Health Organization (WHO), and the UN Food and Agricultural Organization and has economic and trade agreements with New Zealand, Australia, the European Union, and the other Pacific islands.

Niue's first and longest-serving premier Sir Robert R. REX died in December 1992, and a Legislative Assembly election in February 1993 brought Frank LUI to the premiership. The period 1994–2004 saw a divided assembly and a series of inconclusive no-confidence motions as the Niue People's Party (NPP) disintegrated. (See the 2010 *Handbook* for details.)

In June 2002 the legislature repealed a controversial 1994 act that had permitted the licensing of offshore banks. Never as lucrative as hoped, this banking legislation had contributed to Niue's designation in 2000 by the international FATF as noncompliant in fighting money laundering. Collaterally, the OECD had labeled Niue as 1 of 35 jurisdictions considered to be an uncooperative tax haven. By the end of 2002 Niue had taken sufficient corrective actions to warrant removal from both lists.

With the NPP having dissolved in 2003, all candidates in the election of 2005 ran as independents. Veteran politician Young VIVIAN retained the premiership. In early March 2007 he easily survived a no-confidence motion, 12–7, despite a financial crisis that had necessitated a cut in civil service pay as well as other major spending reductions. Following the June 2008 general election, Toke TALAGI secured 14 assembly votes to Vivian's 5 to take the premiership. The May 2011 election produced a similar result, with Talagi gaining 11 votes to 8 for challenger Togia SIONEHOLO.

To increase fiscal security, the governments of Niue, New Zealand, and Australia in 2006 established a Niue International Trust Fund, which is now valued at nearly NZ$40. In 2009 Talagi hosted a visit by Prime Minister John Key, at which time he urged speedier release of NZ$2 million earmarked for tourism development under the 2004 Halavaka Agreement, criticized micromanagement of aid by Wellington, and hinted that he was prepared to talk with China, with which Niue had established diplomatic relations in 2008, if New Zealand did not look after the island's needs. In 2010 the two governments agreed on a five-year aid plan under which New Zealand was to provide nearly NZ$20 million per year for tourism and infrastructure development and administrative capacity building. The aid allocation for 2013 was NZ$13.5 million. Meanwhile, China in January 2011 made a grant of NZ$1.5 million to finance purchase of 25 tractors and in August undertook discussions to provide solar panels to be funded by New Zealand aid. In April 2012 Niue ratified the Comprehensive Nuclear Test Ban Treaty, and in June Premier Tolagi announced plans to issue licenses to foreign firms to explore for gold and copper.

New Zealand High Commissioner: Mark BLUMSKY.

Premier: Toke TALAGI.

Tokelau. A group of three atolls (Atafu, Fakaofo, and Nukunonu) north of Samoa with an area of 4 square miles (10.4 sq. km), the Tokelaus were originally claimed by the United States in the Guano Islands Act 1856, but the claim was never acted on. The atolls were subsequently administered by Great Britain and, from 1923, New Zealand, and were included within New Zealand's territorial boundaries by legislation enacted in 1948. The United States ceded claims to the three main atolls in 1979 but incorporated Swain's Island (Olohega) into American Samoa, creating the potential for dispute if Tokelau becomes independent in the future. The islands have limited economic viability, the principal income sources being annual budget and project aid from New Zealand; remittances from Tokelauans working overseas; the export of coconut, copra, and tuna; the sale of stamps, handicrafts, and souvenir coins; and the sale of fishing licenses to foreign fleets. In 2004 an International Trust Fund for Tokelau was established in 2004, which is now valued at over NZ$70 million. Tokelau has a resident population of 1,449 (2007E), while 6,819 Tokelauans reside in New Zealand (2006C) and others in Sydney, Samoa, and Hawaii.

Tokelau is now a non-self-governing territory of New Zealand and remains on the agenda of the UN Special Committee on Decolonization. In UN-supervised referenda in 2006 and 2007 Tokelauans rejected the option of independence, with many anxious that New Zealand would not sustain its present financial commitment and extension of citizenship if Tokelau became independent. Consequently Tokelauans remain New Zealand citizens, use the New Zealand dollar as their currency, and rely on New Zealand for the conduct of their foreign affairs and defense. Tokelau is a member of the Pacific Community Secretariat, an observer in the Pacific Island Forum, and an associate member of the WHO and UNESCO.

Each of the atolls elects for a three-year term a *faipule,* whose duties include executive and judicial responsibilities. As each atoll's highest elected official, the *faipule* advises the territory's New Zealand–appointed administrator, who represents the crown and is responsible to New Zealand's Ministry of Foreign Affairs and Trade. Each atoll also has a Council of Elders (*Taupulega*) and an elected mayor (*pulenuku*), and together the *faipule* and the mayors constitute the Council for the Ongoing Government. The government is chaired for a one-year term by the *Ulu-O-Tokelau,* the titular head of the territory, which rotates among the three *faipule.* The 23 members of the *Fono,* which includes the *faipule* and the *pulenuku,* are elected for three-year terms, most recently in January 2008. In April 2010 the *faipule,* led by Foua TOLOA on behalf of the *Fono,* declared Tokelau's exclusive economic zone waters as a whale sanctuary, the 11th to be so declared in the Pacific.

The election of January 2011 resulted in replacement of two of the three *faipule* and installation of new members in the *Fono*. New Zealand aid for 2013 was estimated at NZ$20 million, supplemented by technical exchanges, telecommunications assistance, information sharing, maritime surveillance, and visits by Navy ships whose personnel contribute small scale health and construction projects. In 2012 New Zealand initiated a NZ$9 million solar panel project to make Tokelau the first nation entirely powered by solar power, eliminating a NZ$1 million diesel fuel import bill and in 2013 carried out a project to conserve fresh water.

Administrator: Jonathan KINGS

Faipule (Titular Heads of *Tokelau's* three atolls)*:* Foua TOLOA (Fakaofo), Kelisiano KALOLO (Atafu), Salesio LUI (Nukunonu).

Ross Dependency. A large, wedge-shaped portion of the Antarctic Continent, the Ross Dependency extends from 160 degrees east to 150 degrees west longitude and has an estimated area of 160,000 square miles (414,400 sq. km). It includes the Ross Ice Shelf, the Balleny Islands, and Scott Island. Although the Ross Dependency has been administered by New Zealand since 1923, the Antarctic Treaty of 1959 puts New Zealand's claim, as well as all other states' claims, in abeyance. Nevertheless, New Zealand criminal law and conservation laws and other legislation are recognized as valid in the territory, which in 1977 was extended 200 nautical miles into the Southern Ocean by the Territorial Sea and Exclusive Economic Zone Act. A permit is required from the Ministry of Foreign Affairs and Trade to visit the territory or from the Ministry of Fisheries to conduct fishing activities. In accordance with the Antarctica (Environmental Protection) Act 1994, mineral prospecting and mining is prohibited. The territory, in accordance with the Antarctic Treaty, is a conventional and nuclear-weapons-free zone.

New Zealand maintains a permanent scientific research station in the territory called Scott Base, serviced by Royal New Zealand Air Force aircraft, and cooperates with the U.S. National Science Foundation, which maintains the McMurdo scientific station nearby. New Zealand designates senior staff at Scott Base as officers of the government, empowering them to administer New Zealand law in the dependency. Any person born in the Ross Dependency becomes a New Zealand citizen. Since 1988, in an effort to stop illegal fishing in the Ross Sea, surveillance of the area has been exercised by patrols undertaken periodically by air force planes and navy vessels, in coordination with similar surveillance by Australian planes and ships. The 2002 Statement of Strategic Interest stressed New Zealand's environmental stewardship of the region. The November 2010 Defence White Paper echoed warnings by conservationists in calling attention to the vulnerability of the Antarctic landmass and seas to unscrupulous resource exploitation. The July and October 2013 meetings of the Commission for the Conservation of Antarctic Marine Living Resources considered a joint New Zealand–United States proposal to establish a 2.27 million square kilometer marine protected area in the Ross Sea but failed to reach a decision because of Russian objections.

NICARAGUA

Republic of Nicaragua
República de Nicaragua

Political Status: Independence originally proclaimed 1821; separate republic established 1838; provisional junta installed July 19, 1979; present constitution adopted November 19, 1986, in effect from January 9, 1987.

Area: 50,193 sq. mi. (130,000 sq. km).

Population: 6,071,045 (2013E—UN); 5,788,531 (2013E—U.S. Census).

Major Urban Center (2009E): MANAGUA (985,143).

Official Language: Spanish.

Monetary Unit: Córdoba Oro (principal rate November 1, 2013: 25.15 córdobas = $1US).

President: José Daniel ORTEGA Saavedra (Sandinista National Liberation Front); served as president 1985–1990; reelected on November 5, 2006, and inaugurated for a five-year term on January 10, 2007, succeeding Enrique BOLAÑOS Geyer (Grand Liberal Union); reelected on November 6, 2011, and inaugurated on January 10, 2012, for an unprecedented third term.

Vice President: Omar HALLESLEVENS Acevedo (Sandinista National Liberation Front); elected on November 6, 2011, and inaugurated, for a term concurrent with that of the president on January 10, 2012, succeeding Jaime MORALES Carazo (Sandinista National Liberation Front).

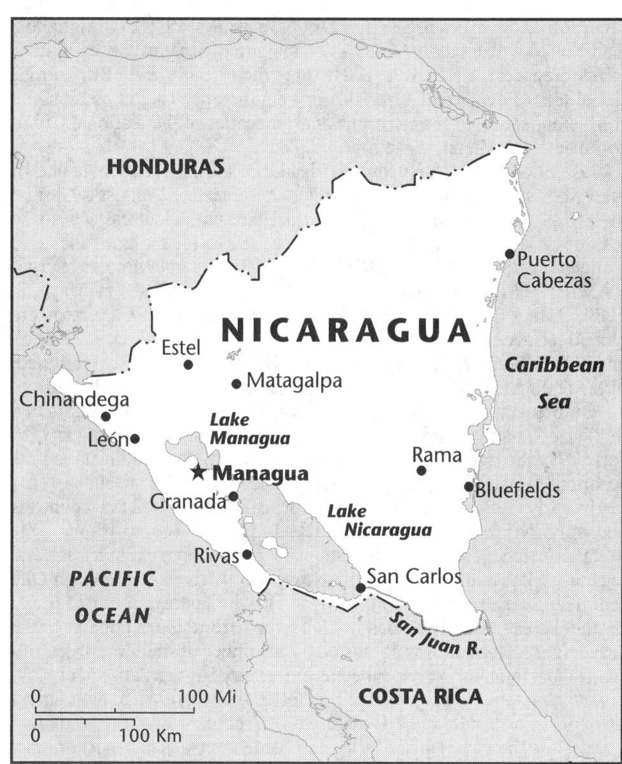

THE COUNTRY

Bounded by Honduras on the north and west and by Costa Rica on the south, Nicaragua is the largest but, apart from Belize, the least densely populated of the seven Central American states. Its numerous mountains are interspersed with extensive lowlands that make it a potential site for an interoceanic canal. The population is predominantly (69 percent) mestizo (mixed Indian and European), with smaller groups of whites (17 percent), blacks (9 percent), and Indians (5 percent). Although freedom of worship is constitutionally recognized, 58.5 percent of the inhabitants adhere to Roman Catholicism, followed by 21.6 percent who are Evangelical.

There were approximately 3 million people in the Nicaraguan labor force as of 2013. Women comprise about 47 percent of the labor force and are concentrated in domestic service, teaching, and market vending; in recent years, female participation has greatly increased, particularly in agriculture (under the Sandinista regime women also constituted 40 percent of the armed forces and nearly half of the civil militia). Women are also well represented in the cabinet.

Services account for 56.8 percent of Nicaragua's GDP, followed by industry at 25.9 percent and agriculture at 17.3 percent. Agricultural exports, however, account for about 75 percent of the country's export revenue; the biggest single export being coffee, worth $342 million in 2010, most of which was exported to the United States. The UN Food and Agriculture Organization (FAO) commended Nicaragua in April 2013 for reducing the undernourished citizens from 55.1 percent in 1990 and 20.1 percent in 2010. The extraction of mineral resources (including silver, gold, lead, gypsum, and zinc) is also important.

The Nicaraguan economy has been battered by numerous natural and human-inflicted disasters in the past decades, including a disastrous earthquake that struck Managua in December 1972. The final phase of the anti-Somoza rebellion in 1978–1979 also severely disrupted development, as did the U.S. economic blockade of the Sandinista regime and support of the antigovernment rebels throughout the 1980s, which together culminated in a more than 12 percent contraction of the country's economy in 1988.

Economic recovery in the 1990s was halted by Hurricane Mitch in October 1998, which left more than 4,000 people dead and destroyed or damaged about 36,000 homes. Hurricane Felix, on September 4, 2007, destroyed or damaged more than 19,000 homes. While social indicators had improved over the previous two decades, 42.5 percent of the population lived at or below the poverty line in 2009.

The economy contracted as a result of the global economic downturn, but budgetary reforms and reductions in spending helped GDP grow 4.5 percent in 2010, 4.7 percent in 2011, and 5.2 percent in 2012. Unemployment has steadily dropped from 8.2 percent in 2009 to 7.4 percent in 2012. Remittances added $1.014 billion in 2011, mostly from Nicaraguan residents in the United States and Costa Rica. Venezuela provides cheap oil to Nicaragua, as well as about $500 million annually through the Bolivarian Alliance for the Americas programs. Much of this money comes from Venezuela and is used for social programs administered through Ortega's office and therefore not tracked through Nicaragua's official budget sheet. Venezuelan aid accounted for 6 percent of GNP in 2011.

A priority of the Ortega government has been to increase access to electricity, which it claims has expanded from 53 percent of the country in 2006 to 67 percent in 2011, and reduce Nicaragua's dependence on foreign oil, which accounts for almost 70 percent of energy production. Foreign direct investment in the country doubled from 2010 to 2011 to $1 billion and jumped to $1.28 billion in 2012.

GOVERNMENT AND POLITICS

Political background. Nicaraguan politics following the country's liberation from Spanish rule in 1821 was long dominated by a power struggle between leaders of the Liberal and Conservative parties, punctuated by periods of U.S. intervention, which was virtually continuous during 1912–1925 and 1927–1933. A Liberal Party victory in a U.S.-supervised election in 1928 paved the way for the assumption of power by Gen. Anastasio SOMOZA García, who ruled the country as president from 1937 until his assassination in September 1956.

Political power remained in the hands of the Somoza family under the Liberal Party presidencies of Luis SOMOZA Debayle, the dictator's elder son (1956–1963); René SCHICK Gutiérrez (1963–1966); Lorenzo GUERRERO Gutiérrez (1966–1967); and Gen. Anastasio SOMOZA Debayle (1967–1972), the younger son of the late dictator. Constitutionally barred from a second term, Somoza Debayle arranged an interim collegial executive (consisting of two members of the Liberal Party and one member of the Conservative Party) that oversaw the promulgation of a new constitution and administered the nation until the election of September 1, 1974, when he was formally returned to office by an overwhelming margin.

The stability of the Somoza regime was shaken by the Sandinista National Liberation Front (*Frente Sandinista de Liberación Nacional*—FSLN or Sandinistas), which launched a series of coordinated attacks throughout the country in October 1977 in an effort to instigate a general uprising. While the immediate effort failed, far more serious disturbances erupted in 1978, including occupation of the National Palace in Managua by FSLN rebels on August 22 and a major escalation of the insurgency in early September. During the first half of 1979 the tide turned decisively in favor of the Sandinistas, who by the end of June controlled most of the major towns as well as the slum district of the capital. Despite 12 days of intense bombardment of FSLN positions within Managua, government forces were unable to regain the initiative, and on July 17 General Somoza left the country after resigning in favor of an interim president, Dr. Francisco URCUYO Maliaños. Confronted with a bid by Urcuyo to remain in office until the expiration of his predecessor's term in 1981, three members of the FSLN provisional junta flew from Costa Rica to León on July 18 and, amid some confusion, accepted the unconditional surrender of the National Guard commander in Managua the following day.

Daniel ORTEGA Saavedra, the leader of the five-man junta and of the FSLN's nine-member Directorate, announced in August 1980 that the FSLN would remain in power until 1985, with electoral activity to resume in 1984. In addition to Ortega, the original junta included Violeta Barrios de CHAMORRO, Moisés HASSAN Morales, Sergio RAMÍREZ Mercado, and Alfonso ROBELO Callejas. On May 18, 1980, Rafael CORDOVA Rivas and Arturo José CRUZ Porras were named to succeed Chamorro and Robelo, who had resigned on April 19 and 22, respectively. On March 4, 1981, Hassan and Cruz also resigned, Ortega being named coordinator of the remaining three-member group.

On September 17, 1980, former president Somoza was assassinated in a bazooka attack on his limousine in central Asunción, Paraguay. (In early 1999 the former chief of state security during the Sandinista regime reportedly acknowledged his agency's responsibility for the attack.)

In early 1984, under diplomatic pressure from Western countries and military pressure from U.S.-backed insurgent (contra) forces, the junta adjusted its electoral timetable to permit both presidential and legislative balloting the following November. Although attempts by the regime to reach procedural agreement with the opposition failed (most of the latter's larger parties withdrawing from the campaign), the November 4 election was contested by a number of small non-Sandinista groups. In balloting described as exemplary by international observers (who nonetheless objected to preelection censorship and harassment of opposition candidates), Ortega won 67 percent of the presidential vote, while the FSLN gained a similar percentage of seats in a National Constituent Assembly, which approved a new basic law on November 19, 1986.

After extensive negotiations, a preliminary peace agreement for the region, based in part on proposals advanced by President Oscar Arias Sánchez of Costa Rica, was approved by the five Central American chief executives in Guatemala, on August 7, 1987. In accordance with the agreement, talks between the Sandinista government and contra leaders were initiated in January 1988 that failed to yield a definitive cease-fire agreement, although most of the rebel forces had quit Nicaragua for Honduras by mid-August because of a failure to secure further military aid from the United States. Subsequently, the Central American presidents, during a meeting in El Salvador, on February 13–14, 1989, agreed on a program of Nicaraguan electoral reform that would permit opposition parties unimpeded access to nationwide balloting no later than February 25, 1990, while the U.S. Congress in mid-April approved a $49.7 million package of nonlethal aid for the contras over the ensuing 10 months.

Although public opinion polls had suggested that the FSLN enjoyed a substantial lead in the 1990 elections, Chamorro, heading a National Opposition Union (UNO) coalition, defeated Ortega by a 15 percent margin in the February presidential poll, with the UNO capturing 51 of 92 assembly seats. Following her inauguration in April, President Chamorro was confronted with a perilously weak economy reeling from numerous clashes between peasants who had benefited from the Sandinista land policies and demobilized contras pressing for promised land and monetary compensation. Chamorro responded by naming a number of influential contras to government positions, while retaining her predecessor's brother, Cdr. (thereafter Gen.) Humberto ORTEGA Saavedra as chief of the armed forces. These actions, in addition to continuance of a social pact (*concertación*) with the FSLN led Vice President Virgilio GODOY Reyes' conservative UNO bloc to adopt a posture of de facto opposition. The complexity of the new alignment was evidenced by the January 1991 balloting for president of the National Assembly (*Asamblea Nacional*): former contra leader and presidential adviser Alfredo CESAR Aguirre, with the backing of both Sandinista and moderate UNO members, defeated incumbent Míriam ARGUELLO Morales, a conservative hard-liner from the UNO party supported by Godoy.

On January 9, 1993, a cabinet reshuffle was announced that for the first time awarded a portfolio (tourism) to a Sandinista, while a new assembly, dominated by Sandinistas and the ex-UNO Center Group, was convened, which proceeded to elect Gustavo TABLADA Zelaya, a former communist, as its presiding officer. By now the breach between Chamorro and her former coalition supporters was such that some UNO leaders called for shortening her term of office, and in late February General Ortega charged Vice President Godoy and former assembly president César with encouraging a resurgence of contra activity in the north to create sufficient unrest to cause the government's collapse. The UNO hardliners responded by organizing a series of mass demonstrations against the president's "cogovernment" with her former adversaries.

Following an abortive effort by Chamorro to launch a national dialogue on the issues dividing the country, a remarkable series of tit-for-tat military actions erupted. On July 21–22, 1993, nearly 50 people were killed when a group of 150 demobilized contras, known as recompas, seized control of the northern town of Estelí, plundering three local banks before being routed by government troops. On August 19 right-wing recontras took 42 hostages in an attack on another northern town, El Zúngana; in retaliation a recompa unit stormed the Managua offices of the UNO, taking captive an equal number of individuals, including Godoy and César. All of the hostages were released within days, following intervention by the Organization of American States (OAS).

On September 2, 1993, President Chamorro angered her FSLN supporters by announcing that General Ortega would be removed as military chief in 1994; the pledge did not, however, mollify her UNO critics, who called for his immediate dismissal. During the following week General Ortega and Vice President Godoy held two private meetings that led to an unprecedented series of talks between FSLN and UNO representatives in October and November on proposals for constitutional reform.

By early 1994 a new legislative majority had emerged in the form of a working alliance between the FSLN, the Center Group, and the Christian Democratic Union (UDC), which advanced the process of constitutional revision by lifting a requirement that amendments be approved by two successive assembly sessions. Subsequently, General Ortega, in response to continuing pressure to step down, indicated that he would not do so until a new military statute had been enacted that placed nomination to his office in the hands of a Military Council (*Consejo Militar*). On May 18 President Chamorro stated that Ortega would retire on February 21, 1995. The announcement came one day before submitting to the assembly her proposals for military reform, which did not call for subordination of the military to civilian control and did not provide for a ministry of defense.

Meanwhile, the FSLN had encountered an identity crisis because of General Ortega's continuing governmental role. Ortega was seen as moving to the right in a possible bid to gain the presidency in 1996. This led to the formation of a centrist faction within the FSLN National Directorate that, while distancing itself from a hard-line leftist minority, sought "a basic reordering of the economy" along genuinely social-democratic lines. Disarray within the Sandinista leadership was also seen in a growing cleavage between Ortega and the party's relatively moderate legislative leader, former vice president Sergio Ramírez. Significantly, one of the constitutional reforms endorsed by Ramírez would restrict a president to a single term, which would deny the former chief executive an opportunity to vindicate himself for his 1989 loss to Chamorro. Ortega subsequently repositioned himself to the left of his party's mainstream, urging opposition to economic restructuring and occasionally endorsing violence to oppose privatization by the Chamorro administration. His new hard-line posture won the day at an extraordinary FSLN congress in May 1994 and secured the dismissal of Ramírez as FSLN legislative leader in September. However, Ortega was unable to prevent the election of another moderate, Dora María TÉLLEZ, as Ramírez's assembly bloc successor.

On September 2, 1994, a new military code was approved that limited the armed forces chief to a single five-year term and prohibited appointment of relatives of the president to the post. On the other hand, the military would continue to nominate its commander. Subsequently, the Military Council proposed Maj. Gen. Joaquín CUADRA Lacayo to succeed Gen. Humberto Ortega on February 21, 1995.

In November 1994 the National Assembly approved a lengthy series of constitutional amendments (see Constitution and government, below), significantly altering the distribution of power between the executive and legislative branches in favor of the latter. The changes were strongly opposed by President Chamorro and by the orthodox wing of the Sandinistas, which supported a new effort by Míriam Argüello to recapture the assembly presidency in January 1995. Argüello was, however, unable to deny reelection to the reformist Luis Humberto GUZMÁN, and on February 17 the assembly published the constitutional revisions after Chamorro had refused to do so. The conflict intensified further on April 6, when the legislature named 5 new Supreme Court justices (2 to replace members whose terms had expired and 3 to expand the size of the Court from 9 to 12 under a provision of the amended basic law). On May 8, following presidential repudiation of the appointments, the court, without ruling on the substance of the constitutional changes, declared the amendments null and void in the absence of executive promulgation. However, on June 15, in the wake of mediation by Cardinal Miguel OBANDO y Bravo, then the archbishop of Managua, the lengthy impasse was broken with Chamorro's acceptance of the constitutional reform package, which was promulgated on July 4. An agreement on the new Supreme Court justices followed on July 21.

By early 1995 campaigning for the 1996 election by Nicaragua's more than two dozen parties was effectively under way. One of the leading candidates, Presidency Minister Antonio LACAYO Oyanguren, indicated that he might divorce his wife, Cristiana CHAMORRO, so as to comply with the new constitutional requirement that blood and marriage relatives serving heads of state be disqualified. Other likely contenders were Daniel Ortega and Sergio Ramírez of the deeply divided FSLN and, on the right, Managua Mayor Arnaldo ALEMÁN Lacayo, representing the largely reunited Liberals. On December 6, 1995, legislative passage of a new general election law included a provision for a presidential runoff if no candidate gained at least 45 percent of the vote.

On July 6, 1996, the Supreme Electoral Council (*Consejo Supremo Electoral*—CSE) formally declared Antonio Lacayo ineligible for the presidency; the council also disqualified Alvaro ROBELO of the conservative Nicaraguan Alliance (AN) and Edén PASTORA Gómez of the Democratic Action Party (PAD) for having acquired, respectively, Italian and Costa Rican citizenship.

In the balloting of October 10, 1996, Alemán Lacayo emerged as the clear victor in the presidential race, although the FSLN insisted that his official tally of 51 percent was fraudulently inflated. The legislative outcome was far less simple, as Alemán's Liberal coalition was held to a plurality of 42 seats, while the runner-up FSLN gained 36.

With Alemán ineligible for reelection in 2001, Enrique BOLAÑOS Geyer, who had resigned as vice president in October 2000 to qualify as a presidential candidate, won the Constitutionalist Liberal Party (*Partido Liberal Constitucionalista*—PLC) nomination and garnered 56.1 percent of the vote to defeat Daniel Ortega in the FSLN leader's third nationwide effort on November 4. Alemán supporters subsequently secured his election as president of the National Assembly, a post that he was obliged to relinquish on September 19, 2002, amid mounting evidence of corruption during his tenure as chief executive. On December 7, 2003, Alemán was convicted of fraud, money laundering, and the theft of state funds and received a 20-year sentence.

In late 2003 Alemán, who continued as Liberal leader despite his imprisonment, joined forces with Ortega, thus splitting the party into pro- and anti-Bolaños factions. The president responded by forming a new party, the Grand Liberal Union (GUL), which joined with five minor groups in an **Alliance for the Republic** (*Alianza por la República*—APRE) to contest the November 2004 municipal elections.

The FSLN swept the November 7, 2004, local balloting, winning more than 90 of 152 mayoralties, including 15 of 17 capitals, on a 45 percent vote share. The PLC won 41 mayoralties and only 1 capital, while the APRE took 5 mayoralties and 1 capital. Following the election, the FSLN and PLC concluded a power-sharing pact under which the two would alternate the presidency, beginning with whomever won the next election, with guarantees to the other of a share of high-level government positions.

Ortega made a comeback in his fourth bid for the presidency on November 5, 2006, with 38 percent of the vote. Eduardo MONTEALEGRE of the **Nicaraguan Liberal Alliance** (*Alianza Liberal Nicaragüense*—ALN) placed second, with 28.3 percent, followed by the PLC's José RIZO with 27.1 percent. In concurrent legislative balloting, the FSLN secured a plurality of 38 seats, followed by the PLC and the ALN. The cabinet was reshuffled on January 10, 2007.

Political infighting and tensions dominated the government in 2007, when the PLC and the ALN formed an electoral alliance in July, in direct opposition to a similar effort between the FSLN and the PLC. However, the PLC-ALN alliance fell apart ahead of the 2008 municipal elections because the PLC refused to break with the FSLN. This resulted in a rift in the ALN, with the party dismissing Montealegre, who formed his own party, Let's Go with Eduardo (*Vamos con Eduardo*—VCE), which aligned with the PLC, the small Independent Liberal Party (*Partido Liberal Independiente*—PLI), and the Central American Unity Party (*Partido Unidad de Central America*—PUCA). The rift healed in time for the PLC to name Montealegre as its candidate for mayor of Managua in the November 2008 municipal elections. Montealegre lost that election amid allegations of fraud and vote-rigging, and a recount, which was not monitored by outside observers, also drew heavy criticism. The results gave a narrow victory (51.3 percent) to world boxing champion and FSLN candidate Alex ARGÜELLO, who unexpectedly died in 2009 at age 38.

Meanwhile, the principal opposition parties in the National Assembly staged several walkouts in 2008 to protest Ortega's governing style. Opponents called their coalition the "Block against the Dictatorship" and criticized Ortega's increasingly hostile reaction toward the United States and excessively close ties to Venezuela and Iran. The Civil Society Coordinating Committee, composed of numerous nongovernmental organizations, demonstrated against Ortega on July 17, 2008, the first major protest since he took office. The FSLN responded two days later, on the 29th anniversary of the Sandinista revolution, with a progovernment demonstration by tens of thousands of people, including the presidents of Venezuela and Paraguay.

High food prices continued to be a major challenge in 2009, as poverty affected thousands more Nicaraguans. The government sought international donor aid and initiated a Zero Hunger Program in March in efforts to mitigate effects from the global financial crisis. Meanwhile, President Ortega proposed constitutional reforms that included, among other things, the elimination of presidential term limits and the possibility of a recall referendum on elected officials.

Facing insurmountable opposition from the PLC, Ortega took his proposed term-limit revision to the judiciary. On October 19, 2009, the CSJ lifted the constitution's ban that prevented a president from serving two consecutive terms in office. Many observers called the decision illegal, saying that only the legislature was invested with the power to strike down the prohibition. Both supporters and opponents of the Ortega administration took to the streets of Managua on November 21 in mass protests over Ortega's initiative.

On January 9, 2010, Ortega again appeared to challenge the constitutional separation of powers by promulgating a decree that extended the mandates of sitting judicial and election officials who were scheduled to be replaced but for whom replacements had not been approved by the deadlocked legislature. Ortega unilaterally continued the terms of 25 officials, saying that he did not want to see a power vacuum form.

Opposition legislators with the PLC, the ALN, the Sandinista Renovation Movement (*Movimiento de Renovación Sandinista*—MRS), and the VCE boycotted the legislature in protest over Ortega's decree to extend terms for a number of officials, preventing it from convening. However, observers said the opposition was unable to muster a unified front due to interference by influential former president and PLC leader Arnoldo Alemán, who held a decade-old power-sharing pact with Ortega. In April 2010 the CSJ president, a PLC ally, refused to recognize two magistrates (aligned with the FSLN) who had attempted to retain their expiring positions in accordance with Ortega's decree. Later that month the opposition tried to convene the assembly after the nearly two-month boycott in order to overturn the decree. However, they were stopped by hundreds of Ortega supporters blocking access to the capitol building. Legislators then attempted to convene the assembly at a hotel but were attacked with rocks and fireworks, which injured three PLC politicians. The next day FSLN supporters held 18 opposition party members hostage and set two vehicles on fire. Ortega endorsed the violence as a "simple, legitimate expression of the people." A number of civil society groups, the OAS, and the United States voiced strong concerns over the violence and erosion of the political process in Nicaragua. The congress convened on April 22 under heavy police protection but did not open debate on the decree, instead ratifying two uncontroversial international loans.

On June 28, 2010, at least nine people were injured when FSLN supporters joined police to storm the mayor's office in the opposition-held central Nicaraguan city of Boaco. The group ejected the mayor, who voiced opposition to Ortega's reelection bid and who was aligned with Eduardo Montealegre's opposition VCE. The CSE validated the ejection by installing a new mayor. The move was the fifth removal of mayors who did not support Ortega's bid for another term as president and, combined with the alleged skullduggery of the 2008 municipal elections, pointed to an offensive campaign by the president against local governments.

Following maneuvering in August 2010 that left a majority of CSJ magistrates allied with the FSLN, the court ruled in September that Ortega's January decree to continue the mandates of judiciary officials was legal. The CSJ then ruled that Ortega's push to end presidential term limits, which was endorsed in October 2009 by the CSJ's constitutional chamber, was also legal on the grounds that the ban on running for office consecutively was an infringement of human rights against the president. In September Ortega ordered a reprinting of the constitution that included his January decree. The opposition protested, arguing that the printing amounted to a change in the constitution and thus required a two-thirds majority vote in the assembly. On September 22 the opposition—the PLC, the ALN, the MRS, and the VCE—began an indefinite boycott of the legislature in protest. The new version of the constitution was approved in the assembly on October 5 in what opposition leaders characterized as an illegal vote.

Constitution and government. The constitution approved by a National Constituent Assembly in November 1986 provided for a president, vice president, and National Assembly elected for six-year terms (later changed to five-year terms, concurrent with that of the president). The assembly contains 90 members directly elected by proportional balloting in regional districts, with additional seats for unsuccessful presidential candidates securing a minimum number of votes. The assembly may be expanded in accordance with population growth, while its acts may be vetoed, in whole or in part, by the president within 15 days of their approval. The judiciary encompasses a Supreme Court of at least seven judges elected for six-year terms by the National Assembly, in addition to appellate and municipal courts.

The country is divided into 15 departments and two largely indigenous, self-governing areas, the North Atlantic Autonomous Region (RAAN) and the South Atlantic Autonomous Region (RAAS). Municipalities are governed by elected councils.

On November 24, 1994, the assembly approved a series of constitutional amendments that provided for increased legislative authority vis-à-vis the president, whose term was reduced from six years to five, with a ban on relatives of a serving president standing for the office. In addition, both the president and National Assembly were authorized to introduce tax measures and to share responsibility for appointing Supreme Court justices, the comptroller general, and the president and vice president of the national bank. Other provisions guaranteed the rights of primary and secondary education and free health care for all citizens, provided greater independence for the judiciary, increased civilian control over the military, eliminated conscription, and recognized the rights of indigenous populations on both the east and west coasts.

In late January 2000 President Alemán signed into law another round of constitutional changes, including a reduction from 45 to 35 percent in the vote share required for presidential election; legislative life tenure for himself, with a two-thirds vote required for removal of immunity from prosecution; the appointment of five permanent members of the State Comptroller's Office from a list approved by the president and the assembly; an increase in the number of Supreme Court justices to 16 from 12; an increase in the membership of the Supreme Electoral Council to seven from five; and the deregistration of political parties securing less than 4 percent of the vote. In addition, President Alemán advocated holding a constitutional assembly election in place of the presidential poll scheduled for 2001, but he failed to secure sufficient legislative support for the proposal.

In late 2004 the National Assembly approved a new package of constitutional reforms that included legislative ratification of ministerial and ambassadorial appointments and lowered to a simple majority (from two-thirds) the vote needed to overturn a presidential veto. The package was struck down by the Central American Court of Justice on March 29, 2005, on the ground that it should have been submitted to a constituent assembly. However, Nicaragua's Supreme Court of Justice (CSJ) approved the changes on March 30, arguing that the regional court lacked jurisdiction because of a protocol approved by the Central American presidents in December that banned it from intervening in intrapower disputes in member states.

Beginning in 2009, President Ortega began calling for the abolition of the constitutional ban on presidential term limits and for a measure designed to wrest control of some legislative power from the National Assembly, where his FSLN held a minority of seats (see Current issues, below). Two actions drew the most attention: a CSJ ruling that abolished the ban on a president running for office for two consecutive terms and Ortega's decree that the expiring terms of judicial and electoral officials be extended in the face of legislative gridlock on new appointments (see Currents issues, below).

The Somoza regime severely constricted the media, while the subsequent Sandinista government also suspended several publications. Acceding to opposition demands, a press law stipulating that all printed matter must reflect "legitimate concern for the defense of the conquests of the revolution" was rescinded before President Ortega's departure from office in 1990. Reporters Without Borders described the relationship between the current Ortega administration and the privately owned press as "conflictual," resulting in a number of reported incidents of government attempts to pressure journalists. In 2013 Nicaragua was listed as 78th out of 179 countries in the Reporters Without Borders annual ranking of press freedom.

Foreign relations. The conservative and generally pro-U.S. outlook of the Somoza regime was reflected in a favorable attitude toward North American investment and a strongly pro-Western, anti-communist position in the UN, OAS, and other international bodies. The United States, for its part, did not publicly call for the resignation of General Somoza until June 20, 1979, and subsequently appealed for an OAS peacekeeping presence to ensure that a successor government would include moderate representatives from what it deemed acceptable to "all major elements of Nicaraguan society." Although the idea was rejected by both the OAS and the FSLN, the United States played a key role in the events leading to Somoza's departure, and the administration of President Jimmy Carter extended reconstruction aid to the new Managua government in October 1980. By contrast, President Ronald Reagan was deeply committed to support of the largely Honduran-based rebel contras, despite a conspicuous lack of enthusiasm for such a policy by many U.S. members of Congress.

Regional attitudes toward the contra insurgency were mixed, most South American countries professing neutrality, although Managua-Quito relations were broken in 1985 after then Ecuadorian president Febres Cordero called Nicaragua "a bonfire in Central America." Subsequently, members of the Contadora Group (Colombia, Mexico, Panama, and Venezuela) and the Lima Group (Argentina, Brazil, Peru, and Uruguay) met intermittently with Central American leaders in an effort to broker the conflict, although neither bloc directly influenced the accords of August 1987 and February 1989.

In April 1991 President Chamorro became the first Nicaraguan head of state in more than 50 years to make an official visit to Washington, D.C., where she was warmly received and addressed a joint session of the U.S. Congress. In sharp contrast, an August 1992 report issued by a top aide of U.S. senator Jesse Helms charged the Chamorro government with being controlled by "communists, terrorists, thugs, robbers and assassins" and recommended the discontinuance of aid to Nicaragua pending a number of changes, including the replacement of all Sandinista army and police personnel by former contras and the return of properties belonging to Nicaraguans living in the United States (many of whom were supporters of the former Somoza regime).

Regionally, Nicaragua called in May 1991 for deferment on formal admission to the new Central American Parliament (*Parlamento Centroamericano*—Parlacen) on the ground that it lacked the resources for an early referendum on the matter. In October 1992 Nicaraguan authorities accused Costa Rica of contaminating the San Juan River by sanctioning the use of highly toxic pesticides on its banana plantations. A month later, in the first such meeting since the end of the Sandinista-contra war, General Ortega traveled to Honduras, where he conferred with his counterpart, Gen. Luis Alonso Discua Elvir, on collaborative efforts to limit the use of their countries "for illegal drug, arms, cattle, or fish trafficking."

During a summit meeting in Managua on April 22, 1993, Nicaragua joined its three northern neighbors (El Salvador, Guatemala, and Honduras), which had previously undertaken a *Triángulo Norte* free trade initiative, in launching the *Grupo América Central 4* (AC-4), which was viewed as paving the way for a free trade zone throughout the isthmus. The process was further advanced during a five-member regional summit in Guatemala City on October 27–29, 1993, following inauguration of the headquarters of the Central American Integration System (SICA, under the Central American Common Market—CACM).

A long-dormant territorial dispute with Colombia was rekindled in April 1995 with Nicaragua's seizure of two Colombian fishing vessels and the alleged violation of its airspace by three Colombian aircraft. At issue was Nicaragua's 1980 revocation of a 1928 treaty, by which Nicaragua, under reported U.S. pressure, ceded ownership of certain Caribbean islands to its neighbor in compensation for construction of the interoceanic canal through Panama.

In November 1995 Nicaragua and Costa Rica agreed to regularize the status of 50,000 Nicaraguans working illegally in Costa Rica. Under the accord, the workers would be given special Nicaraguan passports, while work permits would be issued by Costa Rican authorities once worker employment had been certified.

Relations with Honduras, complicated during the 1980s by the presence of several thousand mainly former Somoza supporters, exiled in Honduran border camps, were exacerbated in early 1995 by the eruption of a "shrimp war" in the Gulf of Fonseca. Tensions were reignited in May and August 1997 following the Nicaraguan navy's seizure of numerous Honduran fishing boats that had reportedly strayed into Nicaraguan waters.

In August 1998 Nicaragua rescinded an agreement that had been concluded only a month earlier with Costa Rica for free navigation, including police patrols, along the San Juan River because of opposition claims that Nicaragua had ceded sovereignty to its neighbor. The dispute was temporarily abated by a new agreement in mid-2000 that restored Costa Rica's right to the patrols as long as Nicaragua received prior notification of their movements. However, in 2005 Costa Rica filed suit at the International Court of Justice (ICJ) against Nicaragua for a judgment on Costa Rica's navigational rights on the San Juan River (see below for subsequent developments).

A crisis with Honduras erupted in November 1999, following ratification by the Honduran legislature of a 1986 maritime border treaty with Colombia that involved 50,000 square miles of coastal waters, portions of which were alleged to have been forcibly ceded to Colombia during the U.S. occupation of Nicaragua in the 1920s. In reprisal, Nicaragua imposed a 35 percent duty on all goods imported from Honduras. In June 2001 the two countries accepted an OAS-brokered pact that allowed OAS observers to monitor activities along both land and marine borders. However, friction continued into 2002, with periodic seizures of Honduran boats in alleged Nicaraguan waters and Nicaragua authorizing oil prospecting in the region. In March 2003 the Nicaraguan assembly suspended the 35-percent tariff.

Relations with the United States warmed in 2004 when President Bolaños announced that all surface-to-air missiles remaining in Nicaragua from its conflict with U.S.-backed rebels would be destroyed. He destroyed about 1,000 of the missiles. (In 2008 President Ortega refused to destroy all of the missiles, despite ongoing pressure from the United States.)

In 2005 Nicaragua, Costa Rica, El Salvador, Guatemala, Honduras, and the Dominican Republic signed a wide-ranging free trade agreement known as CAFTA-DR with the United States. In 2006 Ortega signed a treaty incorporating Nicaragua into the Bolivarian Alternative for the Americas (ALBA), Venezuelan President Hugo Chávez's alternative to U.S.-led free trade agreements. Nicaragua and Venezuela signed a number of other accords, including one that canceled Nicaragua's $38 million debt with Venezuela and one that allowed Venezuela to build a $2.5 billion oil refinery in Nicaragua. Ortega also reestablished relations with Cuba and Iran.

Nicaragua and Costa Rica in recent years have disputed a 170-square-mile strip of poorly demarcated swampland on the southern shore of Lake Nicaragua. The 5,000 impoverished residents of the area have rejected the claims of both governments, seeking instead an independent "Republic of Airrecú." Tensions with Costa Rica heightened in June 2008, when Costa Rica rejected a request from Nicaragua that it halt development of an open-pit gold mine several miles from the San Juan River.

Relations with the United States cooled through mid-2008, as President Ortega criticized a loan from the U.S. Agency for International Development (USAID) to 16 nongovernmental organizations to promote citizen participation in the November municipal elections.

In the midst of a regional dispute in March 2008 prompted by a Colombian raid inside Ecuador against guerilla fighters, Nicaragua briefly suspended diplomatic relations with Colombia.

In mid-2009 Nicaragua, like most of its neighbors, supported ousted Honduran president Manuel Zelaya and his efforts to negotiate his return to power from Nicaragua. Nicaragua further refused to allow the use of its airspace by de facto Honduran leader Roberto Micheletti. The presence of Zelaya in Nicaragua spurred tensions between the FSLN and its opponents, and threatened long-standing bilateral agreements between Nicaragua and Honduras.

Relations with the United States and the European Union deteriorated in mid-2009 amid accusations of fraud regarding municipal elections, resulting in both major donors indefinitely suspending millions of dollars in aid to Nicaragua. Washington eliminated a $64 million development aid program following the less than free and fair 2010 regional elections.

In July 2009 the ICJ released its judgment on the case brought before it by Costa Rica in 2005 pertaining to navigation rights on the San Juan River. In a decision that offered partial victories to both sides, the court ruled that Costa Rica had commercial navigation rights on the river but that Nicaragua could require that Costa Rican vessels stop at Nicaraguan border posts. Although the court ruled that the river belonged entirely to Nicaragua, it also stated that official Costa Rican vessels could use the river "in specific situations" to provide essential services to its citizens but not for police functions or to move border personnel between posts.

The Ortega administration's dredging project on a section of the San Juan River, which began in October 2010, brought Nicaragua back into conflict with Costa Rica over their respective border demarcations. Both sides said they would appeal to the OAS, the UN Security Council, and the ICJ. In December Costa Rican president Laura Chinchilla announced the deployment of more police to the border area and said relations between the two countries had fallen "to a minimum."

Relations with Washington cooled again in early 2011, when the state department cables released by WikiLeaks revealed activities by the U.S. Chamber of Commerce, a nongovernmental group that promotes American corporate interests, in support of Ortega's opponents in recent years. On April 8 the state department criticized Nicaragua in its annual human rights report, charging the government with corruption and harassment of media and nongovernmental groups. At a July rally celebrating the 50th anniversary of the FSLN, Ortega proposed a referendum to enable citizens to decide whether to seek compensation from the United States for its "dirty war" against the Sandinistas during the 1980s. The International Court of Justice in The Hague had ruled in favor of the suit in 1986, but the United States ignored the ruling by the UN court, which it does not recognize.

The ICJ ruled in Nicaragua's favor on November 19, 2012, granting it 75,000 square kilometers of the Caribbean Sea previously claimed by Colombia. Nicaragua's plans to prospect for oil in the region could threaten the Seaflower biosphere reserve. The map change could cause a surge in drug trafficking, as Nicaragua does not have adequate naval capacity to fully patrol the area. In September 2013 Ortega asked the ICJ to formally demarcate the maritime border between Nicaragua and Colombia and to extend Nicaragua's claim by 150 nautical miles.

Current issues. The Supreme Court endorsed Ortega's bid for an unprecedented third term as president, and on November 6, 2011, Ortega defeated Fabio GADEA (Independent Liberal Party) and Arnoldo Alemán (Constitutionalist Liberal Party). However, some of the president's closest allies appeared uncomfortable with his disregard for the constitution. Vice President Morales declined to stay on for Ortega's third term, a move regarded as indicating his disapproval. Instead, Ortega selected Omar HALLESLEVENS Acevedo as his running mate, raising some concerns that he might again turn to the military to enforce his rule.

In simultaneous parliamentary elections, the FSLN increased its existing majority, capturing a commanding 63 seats. The PLI won 27 seats, while the PLC garnered only 2. Monitors from the Organization of American States reported many irregularities.

The new parliament began its term on January 10, 2012. With the additional seats picked up in November, the FSLN had a supermajority in the National Assembly, so dissenting voices from opposition parties can easily be squelched. The opposition MPs unanimously voted against Ortega's 2012 budget, for example, but it still easily passed. With municipal elections scheduled for November, in May the National Assembly tripled the number of municipal councilors from 2,178 to 6,534.

In June 2012 the U.S. indicated its displeasure with the 2011 polls by refusing to issue a fiscal transparency waiver and withholding $3 million of development funding. However, Washington did extend the more important ($1.4 billion) waiver regarding seizures of property in Nicaragua owned by U.S. citizens, much to the relief of the Nicaraguan government.

Ortega has not moved to replace the holdover appointees on the Supreme Court and CSE now that his third term has been secured. Opposition groups wonder if he is keeping them on standby to on day appoint him president for life.

The CSE made questionable calls about which parties qualified for the municipal elections. The UDC, now an independent party that has attracted disillusioned FSLN members, was disqualified; with the CSE announcing the UDC had valid candidates in only 73 percent of municipalities, below the 80 percent threshold. Yet APRE, which mustered less than 10,000 votes in 2011, was declared valid in 98 percent of municipalities. The PCN and ALN also had astonishingly high registration levels. Some analysts suggested that Ortega was using Somoza's *zancudismo* (bloodsucker) strategy—a collection of "fake" opposition parties to create the appearance of democracy.

In November 4 municipal elections, the Sandinistas won about 75 percent of the vote, increases its control from 109 municipalities to 134 out of a total 153 and sparking charges of fraud by opposition parties.

The PLI won 13 races, followed by the regional party Yátama (3), PLC (2), and Liberal Alliance (1). The Organization of American States expressed support for the elections, but the U.S. State Department issued a statement expressing concern with voting irregularities. Three people were killed in clashes between Sandinistas and the opposition. The PLI and PLC appealed the results in 5 races but were rebuffed by the CSE.

Members of the FSLN marches have staged several protests in 2012, upset that the party apparatus, headed by Ortega's wife, Rosario MURILLO, selected local candidates without consulting them. Murillo has transformed the image of the FSLN and her husband by using the party network to solve local problems, often working one-on-one with citizens having difficulty with the government bureaucracy. The president may use his increasing powers to help his wife run for president in 2016.

Murillo launched a signature program, "Vivir Bonito" (Live Nicely) in March. The campaign seeks to create a civil society by encouraging citizens to be orderly and patriotic, to respect authority, and to volunteer in their communities. In the first phase, teachers are to issue report cards on the behavior of their students' parents on these performance standards. Critics decried the program as an invasion of privacy, and 20 percent of teachers boycotted weekend training sessions.

With the prolonged illness and March 2013 death of Venezuelan patron Hugo Chávez, Ortega's focus has been on securing alternative sources of funding. An extended credit facility agreement with the International Monetary Fund (IMF) expired in December 2011 and had not been renewed as of mid-2013. Russia also continues to provide assistance, including military equipment, training, and counter-narcotics operations. The Russian General Staff Chief Colonel-General Valery Gerasimov paid an official three-day visit to Nicaragua in April.

In May Ortega confirmed that in September 2012 he had granted a 99-year concession to the Hong Kong Nicaragua Development (HKND) company for an ambitious $40 billion project to build a canal to connect the Atlantic and Pacific Oceans through Nicaragua. The waterway project, which would be twice the size of the Panama Canal, also includes a high-speech railroad, airports, and an oil pipeline. The shadowy HKND, believed to be a front for the Chinese government, was granted a range of tax breaks and exemptions from labor laws. The news upset local investors, neighboring countries, and environmental groups.

In July the CSE stripped Augustin JARQUIN Anaya of his parliamentary seat when he joined the Nicaraguan Democratic Bench (*La Bancada Democrática Nicaragüense*—BND), a faction started by the PLI. The CSE controversially ruled that seats are won by parties—in this case, the UDC—not individuals. Many observers denounced the decision as a tactic to undermine the formation of new parties and alliances.

POLITICAL PARTIES AND GROUPS

Historically, the Liberal and Conservative parties dominated Nicaraguan politics in what was essentially a two-party system. During most of the Somoza era (1936–1974), the heir to the liberal tradition, the Nationalist Liberal Party (*Partido Liberal Nacionalista de Nicaragua*—PLN), enjoyed a monopoly of power, while in mid-1978 the Nicaraguan Conservative Party (*Partido Conservador Nicaragüense*—PCN) joined other opposition groups in a Broad Opposition Front (*Frente Amplio de Oposición*—FAO) that called for the president's resignation and the creation of a government of national unity. Following the Sandinista victory, the principal internal groupings were the FSLN-led Patriotic Front for the Revolution (*Frente Patriótico para la Revolución*—FPR) and a series of opposition center-right coalitions. (For details on the principal electoral alliances formed before the 2011 election, see the 2010 *Handbook.*)

Following the FSLN's landslide victories in 2011 and 2012, opposition groups began intensive discussions about creating a united opposition party ahead of the March 2014 elections for the assemblies in the North and South Atlantic Autonomous Regions (which were postponed in November 2012) and especially in time for presidential and legislative elections in 2016. Several parties split over whether or not to embrace this strategy.

In August 2013 leaders of the **Independent Liberal Party** (*Partido Liberal Independiente*—PLI), **Sandinista Renewal Movement** (*Movimiento de Renovación Sandinista*—MRS), and **Constitutionalist Liberal Party** (*Partido Liberal Constitucionalista*—PLC) created the **United for the Republic** (UNIR) coalition.

Government Party:

Sandinista National Liberation Front (*Frente Sandinista de Liberación Nacional*—FSLN). The FSLN was established in 1961 as a Castroite guerrilla group named after Augusto César Sandino, a prominent rebel during the U.S. occupation of the 1920s. The FSLN displayed a remarkable capacity for survival, despite numerous eradication campaigns during the later years of the Somoza regime, in the course of which much of its original leadership was killed. In 1975 it split into three factions: two small Marxist groupings, the Protracted People's War (*Guerra Popular Prolongada*—GPP), and the Proletarian Tendency (*Tendencia Proletaria*), and a larger, less extreme Third Party (*Terceristas*), a nonideological, anti-Somoza formation supported by peasants, students, and upper-class intellectuals. The three groups coordinated their activities during the 1978 offensive and were equally represented in the nine-member Joint National Directorate. Although the July 1979 junta was largely *tercerista*-dominated, the subsequent withdrawal of a number of moderates yielded a more distinctly leftist thrust to the party leadership, hard-liner Bayardo ARCE reportedly characterizing the November 1984 balloting as "a bother." In an August 1985 reorganization of the Directorate, its Political Commission was replaced by a five-member Executive Commission, chaired by Daniel Ortega, with Arce as his deputy.

Following the unexpected Sandinista defeat in February 1990, Ortega pledged to "obey the popular mandate" and participated in the inauguration of Violeta Barrios de Chamorro on April 25. In conformity with a postelectoral agreement precluding the holding of party office by military personnel, his brother Gen. Humberto Ortega withdrew as a member of the FSLN Executive after being named the armed forces commander by the new president.

The 581 delegates to the first FSLN congress on July 19–21, 1991, reaffirmed the Front's commitment to socialism, while confessing to a variety of mistakes during its period of rule. Former president Ortega was elected to the new post of general secretary, while seven former *comandantes* of the previous leadership were elected to a new nine-member National Directorate that also included former Nicaraguan vice president Sergio Ramírez Mercado.

A pronounced intraparty split emerged before an extraordinary FSLN congress on May 20–22, 1994, the reflection primarily of an "orthodox" faction headed by Ortega and a moderate "renewalist" faction headed by Ramírez, with party treasurer Henry RUIZ Hernández leading an avowedly centrist unity grouping. The Ortega faction emerged victorious, gaining eight seats on an expanded Directorate, against four for the renewalists and three for the centrists. However, public opinion polls had shown Ramírez to be much stronger than Ortega as a potential presidential candidate.

Ramírez served in the National Assembly as Ortega's alternate; thus, in September 1994, the former president was able to oust him as legislative bloc leader by reclaiming the seat. However the FSLN delegation proceeded to elect a moderate, Dora María Téllez, as its new leader rather than Ortega, thus formalizing a cleavage between the Front's legislative members and its National Directorate. In early 1995 Ramírez, Téllez, and approximately three-quarters of the Sandinista legislative delegation withdrew from the FSLN to form the MRS (below).

In November 1995 Ortega surprised observers by announcing that he would seek his party's nomination for reelection to the post that he had lost to Chamorro five-and-a-half years earlier. In the October 1996 balloting he lost to the AL's Alemán Lacayo by more than 13 percent of the popular vote.

Ortega was reelected FSLN general secretary at a party congress in May 1998, and on January 21, 2001, defeated two other candidates, Alejandro MARTINEZ Cuenca and Víctor HUGO Tinoco, for the party's 2001 presidential endorsement.

Defeated in his third presidential bid on November 4, 2001, Ortega nonetheless retained leadership of the FSLN at its third congress in March 2002, during which the group's 205-member assembly was supplanted by a 40-member Board of Directors headed by an 8-member Executive Commission. The move was seen as concentrating power among Ortega supporters, thus limiting intraparty dissent.

In late 2004 the FSLN concluded a power-sharing pact with the PLC (see Political background, above). However, the prospect of an FSLN victory in the 2006 balloting was seemingly diminished by the expulsion from the party in February 2005 of Ortega's leading rival, former Managua mayor Herty Lewites, who had been leading Ortega in the opinion polls (see MRS, below).

His critics notwithstanding, Ortega was returned to the presidency after a 16-year hiatus on November 6, 2006. Ortega's close win and the FSLN's plurality in the National Assembly have forced the FSLN to continue its agreement, commonly referred to as "the pact," with the PLC. In the 2008 municipal elections the party was accused of widespread fraud which resulted in successful bids for more than 40 mayoral seats.

In October 2009 the Supreme Court revoked a constitutional ban on the reelection of incumbent presidents and of those who have served two terms, opening the way for Ortega to run for president again. On February 26, 2011, the FSLN nominated Ortega as its candidate in the November 6, 2011, presidential elections. Dissident Sandinistas, denouncing Ortega for what they called a power grab, promptly declared February 26 a day of "shame and rage." On March 18 Ortega announced that his running mate for the vice presidency would be Gen. (Ret.) Omar HALLESLEVENS Acevedo. Ortega easily won a third term with 62.46 percent of the vote, while the party received a supermajority of 63 seats in the National Assembly. The party won 134 of the 153 municipal seats contested in November 2012.

Leaders: Daniel ORTEGA Saavedra (President of the Republic and General Secretary of the Party), Jacinto SUÁREZ (Deputy General Secretary).

Other Legislative Parties:

Independent Liberal Party (*Partido Liberal Independiente*—PLI). Organized in 1944 by a non-*somocista* group calling for a return to the traditional principles of the PLN, the PLI participated in the Broad Opposition Front before the 1979 coup. Subsequently led by postcoup labor minister Virgilio Godoy Reyes, it was a member of the Patriotic Front, but following *Coordinadora*'s withdrawal, it became the most vocal opposition formation of the 1984 campaign. The party was a founding member of the UNO in 1989, Godoy Reyes becoming its most conspicuous leader. Having endorsed Godoy Reyes as its 1996 presidential candidate, the PLI was the only Liberal group not to have joined the ALN before the October poll. The PLI entered into an alliance with the PLC and Let's Go with Eduardo, the movement formed by Eduardo Montealegre, in November 2008, but failed to win any seats. For the 2011 election, the PLI formed an alliance, **Nicaraguan Unity for Hope** (*Unidad Nicaragüense por la Esperanza*—UNE), with the MRS, the **Citizens' Action Party** (*Partido Acción Ciudadana*—PAC), and the **Coastal Unity Movement** (*Movimiento de Unidad Costeña*—PAC) around the presidential candidacy of Fabio GADEA Mantilla, who finished second to Ortega, with 31 percent of the vote. The PLI also finished second, behind the FSLN, with 26 seats. It won 13 municipal seats in November 2012.

Leaders: Indalecio RODRIGUEZ (President), Roberto SÁNCHEZ Cordero (General Secretary).

Constitutionalist Liberal Party (*Partido Liberal Constitucionalista*—PLC). The PLC originated in 1968 as a spin-off of the Somoza-era PLN. It was subsequently affiliated with the UNO and in 1996 constituted the core of the AL.

Although retaining the presidency and securing a majority of legislative seats in 2001, the party became deeply divided between supporters of President Bolaños and former president Alemán, as a result of which Bolaños launched a separate grouping, the Grand Liberal Union (GUL) in early 2004.

Following his imprisonment in late 2003, Alemán delegated the party presidency to his wife, María Fernánda Flores. Reacting to the move, three members of the party directorate, including National Secretary René HERRERA, resigned in protest.

In January 2005 Eduardo Montealegre Rivas (see ALN, below) was expelled from the party for refusing to resign his cabinet post as secretary to the presidency after President Bolaños had endorsed corruption proceedings against his predecessor.

The PLC's José RIZO placed third in the 2006 presidential balloting with 27.1 percent of the vote. In concurrent legislative elections, the PLC won 25 seats, the second-largest number behind the FSLN.

The party supported the FSLN on key issues in 2008 but formed an alliance with several small parties to field candidates in the 2008 municipal elections. The PLC endorsed Montealegre's candidacy for the mayorship of Managua after he lost a leadership battle in the ALN.

In January 2009 the Supreme Court overturned former president Alemán's conviction on charges of fraud, money laundering, and corruption. (Alemán had been sentenced to 20 years in prison in December 2003 for stealing more than $35 million of state money for personal use.) Alemán ran as the party's presidential candidate in 2011, with support from the Conservative Party of Nicaragua and the Indigenous Multiethnic Party (see below), receiving 5.91 percent of the vote. The PLC received 6.44 percent of the vote and two legislative seats in the 2011 election. It also won two municipal seats in November 2012.

Leaders: Maria HAYDEE Osuna (Chair), Miguel ROSALES (Secretary General).

Other Parties That Contested the 2011 Elections:

The **Nicaraguan Liberal Alliance** (*Alianza Liberal Nicaragüense*—ALN) and **Alliance for the Republic** (*Alianza por la República*—APRE) both fielded candidates for the 2011 elections but won less than 1 percent of the vote. Their leaders have moved on to other political groupings, and the two alliances appear defunct. For details on their past, see the 2013 *Handbook*.

Other Parties:

Sandinista Renewal Movement (*Movimiento de Renovación Sandinista*—MRS). The MRS was launched in January 1995 by former Sandinista legislative leader Sergio RAMÍREZ Mercado and the renewalist majority of the FSLN National Assembly delegation. Members of the MRS strongly opposed Chamorro's efforts to secure an enhanced role for the presidency in the 1995 constitutional reforms. Ramírez Mercado, the party's 1996 presidential candidate, subsequently withdrew from an active role in partisan politics and was highly critical of a 2001 electoral alliance with the FSLN. In early 2006 the MRS announced FSLN dissident Herty LEWITES as its candidate for the upcoming presidential election. However, Lewites, considered one of the top three presidential contenders, died in early July.

Since December 2006 the MRS has been in alliance with the PSN, the **Autonomous Women's Movement** (*El Movimiento Autónomo de Mujeres*—MAM), and the **CREA Movement** (*El Movimiento CREA*). The MRS was barred from running in the 2008 elections after the Supreme Electoral Council revoked its registration in June 2008 on a technicality.

The MRS joined the PLI to form an alliance around the candidacy of Fabio Gadea for the 2011 presidential poll (see below).

Leaders: Ana Margarita VIJIL Gurdián (President), Víctor Hugo TINOCO (Vice President).

Conservative Party of Nicaragua (*Partido Conservador de Nicaragua*—PCN). Formed in emulation of Nicaragua's historic Conservative Party, the current PCN resulted from a 1992 merger of the Democratic Conservative Party (*Partido Conservador Demócrata*—PCD) with two smaller formations, the Conservative Social Party (*Partido Social Conservador*—PSC) and the Conservative Party of Labor (*Partido Conservador Laborista*—PCL).

Launched in 1979 by supporters of the traditional PCN, the PCD had long been deeply divided, with one of its leaders, Rafael Cordova Rives, joining the junta in May 1980 while most others were in exile. The party was a surprising first runner-up in the 1984 balloting, winning 14 legislative seats and a 14 percent vote share for its presidential candidate; rent by further defection, including formation of the PANC, the party secured no representation in 1990 but won 3 seats on a fifth-place finish in 1996.

The Conservatives, who have undergone several changes in their top leadership, including the February 2001 resignation of Pedro SOLORZANO Castillo as president, saw their poll numbers diminish in the run-up to the November 2001 elections when their presidential nominee, Noel VIDAURRE Argüello, and his running mate, Carlos TUNNERMAN Bernheim, withdrew on July 18 because of policy differences with other party leaders. Earlier in the year, the PCN's initial choice for the vice presidency, former defense minister José Antonio ALVARADO, had withdrawn because of continuing controversy over his citizenship. On July 31 the party announced a new ticket headed by Alberto Saborío Morales, whose standing in the polls fell below 5 percent in September. He won only 1.4 percent of the vote on November 4, while the party's legislative representation dropped from three to two.

For the 2006 campaign, the PCN joined in supporting the presidential candidacy of PLC dissident Eduardo Montealegre Rivas under a grouping styled the Liberal Nicaraguan–Conservative Party Alliance (*Alianza Liberal Nicaragüense–Partido Conservador*—ALN-PC). The PCN lost its registration as a valid party in June 2008 for failing to meet the threshold for candidates in municipal elections. It formed an electoral alliance with the PLC and the Indigenous Multiethnic Party in support of Arnoldo Alemán for the 2011 presidential election.

Leaders: Alejandro César BOLAÑOS Davis (President), Alfredo AGUIRRE (Vice President), Alzalea AVILES (Honorary President).

Christian Democratic Union (*Unión Demócrata Cristiana*—UDC). The UDC was formed in early 1993 by merger of two former UNO members, the Social Christian Popular Party (*Partido Popular Social Cristiano*—PPSC) and the Democratic Party of National Confidence (*Partido Democrático de Confianza Nacional*—PDCN), both of which had been formed (in 1976 and 1988, respectively) by dissidents from the PSCN. The UDC joined with the FSLN in a new coalition, United Nicaragua Triumphs (*Unidad Nicaragua Triunfa*—UNT), to contest the 2008 municipal elections, but separated from the FSLN in 2012 so that Augustín Jarquin Anaya could run for mayor of Managua in 2012 against an FSLN candidate. Instead, the party was controversially disqualified over registration regulations.

Leader: Augustín JARQUIN Anaya.

There are a number of small indigenously-based political parties in the Atlantic Coast region, including: **Misatán**, a pro-Sandinista Indian movement led by Rufino LUCAS WILFRED; the northern-based **Yátama**, a member of the FSLN's electoral coalition for the 2008 municipal elections, and a former contra group led by Brooklyn RIVERA Bryan, who was named by President Chamorro as cabinet-level head of a new Institute for the Development of the Autonomous Regions of the Caribbean Coast; the right-wing **Coastal Democratic Alliance**, led by RAAS coordinator Alvin GUTHRIE; the **Multiethnic Indigenous Party** (*Partido Indigenista Multiétnico*—PIM), led by Carla WHITE Hodgson; the **Central American Unity Party** (*Partido Unionista Centroamericano*—PUCA); the **Multiethnic Party for Caribbean Coastal Unity** (PAMUC); the **Union of Nicaraguan Coastal Indians** (KISAN), led by Roger GERMAN; the **Coastal Authentic Autonomy Movement**; and the Corn Island–based **Island Youth Movement**. The PAMUC and the PIM were disqualified by the Supreme Electoral Council in June 2008 for failing to field candidates in at least 80 percent of electoral districts.

For a list of groups active prior to the 2006 elections, see the 2006 *Handbook.*

LEGISLATURE

The previously bicameral Congress (*Congreso*) was dissolved following installation of the provisional junta in July 1979. A 47-member Council of State (*Consejo de Estado*), representing various Sandinista, labor, and other organizations, was sworn in May 4, 1980, to serve in a quasi-legislative capacity.

Under the constitution promulgated in 1987 and amended in 1994, the **National Assembly** (*Asamblea Nacional*) was established, with 90 members popularly elected for five-year terms on a proportional representation basis from party lists, 20 from a nationwide constituency and 70 from multi-member constituencies. Two additional seats are reserved for the outgoing president of the republic and the second-place finisher in the most recent election.

After the most recent election on November 6, 2011, the seat distribution was as follows: the Sandinista National Liberation Front, 62; Liberal Independent Party, 26; and Constitutionalist Liberal Party, 2. (One seat was reserved for 2011 runner-up presidential candidate Fabio Gadea Mantilla of the PLI. One seat is also reserved for the outgoing president, but since President Ortega was reelected, the seat was given to his deputy, Jaime Rene Morales of the FSLN.)

President: René NÚÑEZ Téllez.

CABINET

[as of September 21, 2013]

President	Daniel Ortega Saavedra
Vice President	Moises Omar Halleslevens Acevedo
Ministers	
Agriculture and Forestry	Ariel Bucardo Rocha
Development, Industry, and Commerce	Orlando Solórzano Delgadillo
Education, Culture, and Sports	Miriam Raudez [f]
Energy	Emilio Rappaccioli
Environment and Natural Resources	Juana Argeñal Sandoval [f]
Family	Marcia Ramirez Mercado [f]
Finance and Public Credit	Alberto José Guevara Obregón
Foreign Affairs	Samuel Santos López
Governance	Ana Isabel Morales Mazún [f]
Health	Sonia Castro González [f]
Interior	Ana Isabel Morales Mazún [f]
Labor	Jeannette Chávez Gómez [f]
Secretary General of Defense	Ruth Esperanza Tapia Roa [f]
Tourism	Mayra Salinas [f]
Transportation and Infrastructure	Pablo Fernández Martínez Espinosa

[f] = female

INTERGOVERNMENTAL REPRESENTATION

Ambassador to the U.S.: Francisco Obadiah CAMPBELL Hooker.

U.S. Ambassador to Nicaragua: Phyllis M. POWERS.

Permanent Representative to the UN: María RUBIALES DE CHAMORRO.

IGO Memberships (Non-UN): IADB, IOM, NAM, OAS, WTO.

NIGER

Republic of Niger
République du Niger

Political Status: Former French dependency; independence declared August 3, 1960; military regime established April 15, 1974; constitution of September 1989, providing for single-party military/civilian government, suspended on August 4, 1991, by a National Consultative Conference that had declared itself a sovereign body on July 30; multiparty constitution of December 27, 1992, suspended by military coup on January 27, 1996; new constitution adopted on May 22, 1996, following approval by national referendum on May 12; constitution suspended by the military-based National Reconciliation Council on April 11, 1999; new multiparty constitution providing for return of civilian government approved by national referendum on July 18, 1999, and promulgated on August 9; new constitution approved by national referendum on August 4, 2009, suspended by military coup on February 18, 2010; new constitution providing for return of civilian government approved by national referendum on October 31, 2010.

Area: 489,189 sq. mi. (1,267,000 sq. km).

Population: 16,667,531 (2012E—UN); 16,899,327 (2013E—U.S. Census).

Major Urban Center (2011E—UN): NIAMEY (707,951).

Official Language: French.

Monetary Unit: CFA Franc (official rate November 1, 2013: 486.52 CFA francs = $1US). The CFA franc, formerly pegged to the French franc, is now permanently pegged to the euro at 655.975 CFA francs = 1 euro.

President: Mahamadou ISSOUFOU (Nigerien Party for Democracy and Socialism–*Tarayya*), elected for a five-year term in runoff balloting on March 12, 2011, and sworn in on April 7 to succeed Lt. Gen. Salou

DIJBO (Council for the Restoration of Democracy) who led military coup on February 18, 2010, that ousted President Mamadou TANDJA (National Movement for a Developing Society–Victory).

Prime Minister: Brigi RAFINI (Nigerien Party for Democracy and Socialism–*Tarayya*), appointed by the president on April 7 to succeed Mahamadou DANDA.

THE COUNTRY

A vast landlocked country on the southern border of the Sahara, Niger is largely desert in the north and arable savanna in the more populous southland, which extends from the Niger River to Lake Chad. The population includes numerous tribes of two main ethnic groups: Sudanese Negroes and Hamites. About 75 percent of the population is classified as Sudanese Negro, with Hausa being the predominant subgroup (56 percent); Hamites, found in the north, include the nomadic Tuareg, Toubou, and Peulh subgroups. The population is largely (85 percent) Muslim, with smaller groups of animists and Christians. While French is the official language, Hausa is the language of trade and commerce and is constitutionally classified, along with Arabic and five other tribal languages, as a "national" language. Women constitute a minority of the labor force, excluding unpaid family workers. Following balloting in 2011, women held 15 of 113 seats in the Assembly (13.3 percent).

Agriculture and stock raising occupy 90 percent of the work force, the chief products being millet and sorghum for domestic consumption and peanuts, vegetables, and live cattle for export. The country's major exports are cotton and uranium, of which Niger is one of the world's top five producers. Coal, phosphates, iron ore, gold, and petroleum have also been discovered, but their exploitation awaits development of a more adequate transportation and communication infrastructure. Niger's economy declined in the 1980s, with agriculture suffering from both floods and drought. Also, a decrease during the decade in uranium demand contributed to a severe trade imbalance and mounting foreign debt. The introduction of austerity measures, while generating substantial social unrest, yielded assistance from the International Monetary Fund (IMF) and debt rescheduling from the Paris Club. In June 1996 the IMF approved a new three-year loan to facilitate further structural adjustments.

The government's economic policies in 1996–1998, which focused on privatization of state-run enterprises, were described as "broadly satisfactory," with GDP growth rising from 2.8 percent in 1997 to 10.4 percent in 1998. However, political turmoil and an eight-month imposition of military rule following the assassination of President Maïnassara halted economic progress, as some external financing was frozen and domestic arrears (including the payment of civil service salaries) accumulated. GDP, which had contracted by 0.6 percent in 1999, grew by an average of about 1.5 percent per year between 2001 and 2003 in view of returned support from the IMF and World Bank, which endorsed the new government's commitment to structural reform and financial transparency. Drought and widespread devastation by locusts in 2004 weakened the economy and resulted in a lack of trade and subsequent GDP growth of less than 1 percent. Because of progress the country made in economic reforms, however, the IMF provided substantial debt relief at the end of 2005, noting that Niger remains one of the poorest countries in the world. Though annual GDP growth contracted from 6.8 percent to 3.2 percent in 2007, the IMF noted strong performance in the mining sector and stable growth in the agriculture sector. The United States approved $1.4 million in poverty reduction assistance in 2007, and additional international debt relief was reported by the IMF to be "yielding results," particularly in health and education services and in the rural sector. Annual GDP growth averaged 3.5 percent in 2008–2009, owing in large part to greater mining production and an increase in investments in mining, oil, and infrastructure, as well as a strong yield in the agriculture sector. Also in 2009, the IMF approved an additional $15 million in poverty reduction funds for Niger.

In the wake of the political crisis and coup in 2010, coupled with poor agricultural performance and flooding that contributed to famine, Niger withstood the economic shocks with support from the IMF. The European Union also was prepared to resume aid. The IMF noted that the economic reforms following the coup focused on transparency in public finance management. GDP growth of about 5 percent was recorded in 2011; annual growth of 8.5 percent was forecast for 2012. Fund managers cited factors including foreign investment in

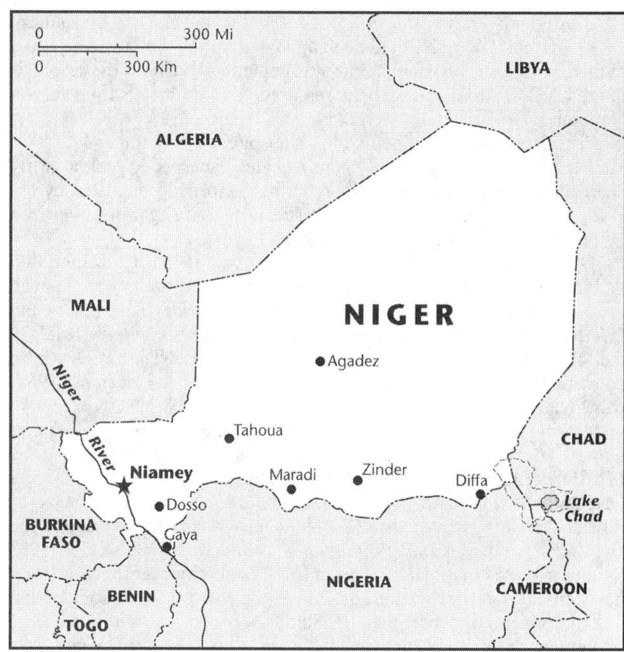

infrastructure and $112 million from the United States for improved food security and to help bolster uranium mining. The World Bank also gave Niger $110 million to finance two water and sanitation projects.

Growth slowed through the second half of 2011, owing to a decline in agricultural production under less-than-average rainfall in the Sahel. Consequently, according to the IMF, growth was estimated at only 1.5 percent (down from a projected 4 percent). As almost half of the population might be affected by food shortages, the government requested donor support for food aid programs. In 2012 GDP grew by 11.2 percent, while inflation rose by a low 0.5 percent. GDP per capita that year was $408. For 2013, the government announced a balanced budget.

GOVERNMENT AND POLITICS

Political background. An object of centuries-old contention among different African peoples, Niger was first exposed to French contact in the late 19th century. Military conquest of the area began prior to 1900 but, because of stiff resistance, was not completed until 1922, when Niger became a French colony. Political evolution began under a constitution granted by France in 1946, with Niger becoming a self-governing republic within the French Community in 1958 and attaining full independence in August 1960. Although its membership in the community subsequently lapsed, Niger has retained close economic and political ties with its former colonial ruler.

The banning of the Marxist-oriented *Sawaba* (Freedom) Party in 1959 converted Niger into a one-party state under the Niger Progressive Party (*Parti Progressiste Nigérien*—PPN), headed by President Hamani DIORI, a member of the Djerma tribe. Thereafter, Djibo BAKARY led *Sawaba* elements to continue their opposition activity from abroad, with terrorist incursions in 1964 and 1965 that included an attempt on the president's life. The Diori government, carefully balanced to represent ethnic and regional groupings, was reelected in 1965 and 1970 by overwhelming majorities but proved incapable of coping with the effects of the prolonged Sahelian drought of 1968–1974. As a result, Diori was overthrown on April 15, 1974, by a military coup led by Gen. Seyni KOUNTCHÉ and Maj. Sani Souna SIDO, who then established themselves as president and vice president, respectively, of a Supreme Military Council (*Conseil Militaire Suprême*—CMS). On August 2, 1975, Kountché announced that Sido and a number of others, including Bakary, had been arrested for attempting to organize a second coup.

A National Development Council (*Conseil National pour le Développement*—CND), initially established in July 1974 with an appointive membership, was assigned quasi-leadership status in August

1983, following indirect election of 150 delegates. Earlier, on January 24, Oumarou MAMANE had been appointed to the newly created post of prime minister; on August 3 he was named president of the reconstituted CND. Hamid ALGABID replaced him as prime minister on November 14.

President Kountché died in a Paris hospital on November 10, 1987, after a lengthy illness. He was immediately succeeded by the army chief of staff, Col. Ali SAIBOU. After being formally invested by the CMS on November 14, the new president named Algabid to head an otherwise substantially new government.

On August 2, 1988, following a July 15 cabinet reorganization that included the return of Mamane as prime minister, Saibou announced the formation of a National Movement for a Developing Society (*Mouvement National pour une Société de Développement*—MNSD) as the "final step in normalization of Niger's politics." The CND, whose constituent functions had been reaffirmed by Saibou in December 1987, was given the task of further defining the role of the MNSD.

Adding to the complexity of the restructuring process was General Saibou's declaration on January 1, 1989, that the initial congress of the MNSD would elect the membership of a Supreme Council of National Orientation (*Conseil Suprême de la Orientation Nationale*—CSON) to replace the CMS, while the CND would become an advisory Economic and Social Council (*Conseil Economique et Social*—CES). On May 17 Saibou was elected president of the CSON, thereby becoming, under a new constitution approved in September, the sole candidate for election as head of state on December 10. Saibou was credited with more than 99 percent of the votes, as was the single list of 93 MNSD candidates concurrently elected to the new National Assembly.

The post of prime minister was eliminated upon the formation of a new government on December 20, 1989. However, it was reestablished in a March 2, 1990, reshuffle precipitated by student-government confrontations in Niamey; Aliou MAHAMIDOU, a government industrial executive, was named to the position. Three months later, the CSON committed itself to "political pluralism," and in mid-November, after encountering further dissatisfaction with his policies, Saibou announced that a National Consultative Conference would convene to consider constitutional reform.

The conference opened on July 29, 1991, with delegates from 24 political groups and 69 mass organizations in attendance. After declaring its sovereignty and electing André SALIFOU as chair, the conference suspended the constitution on August 9 and transferred all but ceremonial presidential powers from Saibou to Salifou. It was decided at the time that Prime Minister Mahamidou would remain in office. However, on November 1, in the wake of an inquiry into the May 1990 massacre of Tuareg nomads by government troops, Amadou CHEIFFOU was named to succeed Mahamidou for a 15-month transition to multiparty balloting scheduled for January 31, 1993. On November 2 the conference appointed a 15-member High Council of the Republic (*Haut Conseil de la République*—HCR), chaired by Salifou, to serve as a constituent assembly and provisional legislature for the duration of the transitional period. The following day the conference voted to disband the HCR in favor of another form of transitional government.

Cheiffou announced the creation of a transitional government on November 4, 1991, which was then dissolved on March 23, 1992, in the wake of a failed military coup on February 28; a new cabinet was named on March 27. In early July Cheiffou survived a nonconfidence motion triggered by a mid-June decision to recognize Taiwan in exchange for an economic aid package, an arrangement that the HCR branded as contravening National Conference resolutions. The split between Cheiffou and the HCR proved short-lived, as the two agreed at an August 7 meeting to reconcile their differences. Meanwhile, preparations for a constitutional referendum and multiparty election proceeded haltingly. The new constitution was finally approved on December 26 by 89 percent of referendum voters, despite observations that the polling was marred by irregularities.

In late December 1992 the government admitted it had lost control over troops assigned to the northeastern Tuareg region where the insurgent Front for the Liberation of Air and Azaouad (*Front de Libération de l'Aïr et l'Azaouad*—FLAA) had resumed activity, further complicating the transitional process. Seven months earlier, the government had responded to the FLAA capture of some 28 military personnel and two officials of the recently restyled National Movement for a Developing Society-Victory (*Mouvement National pour une Societé de Développement-Nassara*—MNSD-*Nassara*) by giving the army control of security in the region, a decision criticized by local Tuareg officials as equivalent to imposing a state of emergency. Frustrated by the rebels' unwillingness to release their prisoners, the army, apparently without government approval, arrested 186 alleged FLAA rebels and supporters, including a number of prominent Tuareg members of the transitional administration. Tuareg officials denounced a subsequent soldiers-for-civilians exchange offer and appealed to the UN for assistance. A Niamey offer to create a "forum for national reconciliation" in November was rebuffed by the Tuaregs, who questioned the government's ability to provide for their safety.

Following a National Assembly election on February 14, 1993, the MNSD-*Nassara,* with a plurality of 29 seats, appeared likely to form a coalition with one or more of its competitors, as a means of retaining control of the government. However, two days later, nine opposition parties, decrying the possibility of MNSD-*Nassara* controlling 50 assembly seats and continuing its rule, formed a majoritarian Alliance of Forces of Change (AFC). In the first round of presidential balloting on February 27 MNSD-*Nassara* candidate Mamadou TANDJA led the eight-candidate field with 34.22 percent of the vote, followed by Mahamane OUSMANE of the Democratic and Social Convention-*Rahama* (*Convention Démocrate et Sociale-Rahama*—CDS-*Rahama*), with 26.59 percent. However, in the second round on March 27, Ousmane was able to surpass Tandja with 54.42 percent of the vote, thanks to solid AFC backing; he was sworn in for a five-year term on April 16. The next day Mahamadou ISSOUFOU, leader of the Nigerien Party for Democracy and Socialism–*Tarayya* (PNDS-*Tarayya*), was appointed prime minister. Issoufou named a cabinet on May 23.

In early 1994 opposition legislators launched a boycott against the assembly, but all 33 were arrested for advocating civil disobedience following violent antigovernment demonstrations on April 16–17. Among those incarcerated for their roles in the unrest were Tandja and the leaders of two theretofore AFC parties, André Salifou of the Union of Democratic Patriots and Progressives–*Chamoua* (UPDP-*Chamoua*) and Issoufou ASSOUMANE of the Democratic Union of Progressive Forces–*Sawaba* (UDFP-*Sawaba*). Their defection lent credence to reports of discord within the AFC, apparently stemming from the president's poorly received efforts to seize Mahamadou Issoufou's prime ministerial powers.

The AFC lost its assembly majority on September 25, 1994, when the PNDS-*Tarayya* broke with the coalition, complaining it had been marginalized by the CDS-*Rahama.* Prime Minister Issoufou resigned on September 28, and Ousmane named CDS-*Rahama* cabinet minister Abdoulaye SOULEY as the new head of government the same day. However, on October 16, two days after the MNDS-*Nassara* and PNDS-*Tarayya* had successfully orchestrated an assembly nonconfidence vote, the 11-day-old Souley government was forced to dissolve. The following day Ousmane reappointed Souley, who proffered the same cabinet. A second nonconfidence vote ensued and, faced with the choice of appointing a prime minister from the new parliamentary majority or dissolving the National Assembly and holding a new legislative election, Ousmane chose the latter.

On January 9, 1995, three days before the election, the MNSD-*Nassara* coalition threatened a boycott due to alleged voter registration fraud and the assassination of an opposition candidate, Seydou Dan DJOUMA. Nevertheless, the coalition participated in the poll and captured 43 legislative seats; AFC-affiliated groups secured the remaining 40. Ousmane ignored MNSD-*Nassara*'s request that he name Hama AMADOU as prime minister, despite the party's assembly majority, and instead appointed another MNSD-*Nassara* member, Amadou Boubacar CISSÉ, on February 8. Two days later the MNSD-*Nassara* expelled Cissé, and on February 20 the assembly voted to censure the new prime minister. The following day Ousmane dismissed Cissé and appointed Amadou, who subsequently formed a cabinet drawn from supporters of the new governing coalition.

Despite differences within the Tuareg leadership, a final peace accord was signed on April 25, 1995. On June 12, the National Assembly unanimously decided to grant full amnesty to all participants of the civil war. Meanwhile, political turmoil continued in Niamey as the AFC, which had earlier accused the MNSD-*Nassara* and its partners of "monstrous irregularities" during the January polling, criticized Prime Minister Amadou's new government for failing to represent "half of the population." Ousmane refused Amadou's call for a cabinet meeting on July 6, in an apparent attempt to avert a vote on his own non-cabinet appointments. Amadou contended that Ousmane lacked the authority to name government officials and responded by ordering riot police to prevent Ousmane-appointed administrators from entering their offices. Despite subsequent negotiations, Amadou dismissed the officials in question on August 1; however, a Niamey court immediately reinstated them. On August 4 the prime minister held a cabinet meeting without Ousmane, who promptly declared all cabinet decisions "null and void."

In early October 1995 opposition parliamentarians aligned with Ousmane declared that the prime minister had deliberately violated the constitution by convening the cabinet without presidential approval and called for his censure. However, their attempt to pass a nonconfidence motion on October 8 failed (in part because some members boycotted the vote to protest the absence of the assembly speaker). In November international mediators met with the president and prime minister in what was described as a successful attempt to end the constitutional impasse, although the question of who controlled government appointments remained unresolved.

On January 27, 1996, at least ten people were killed in a military coup directed by Army Chief of Staff Col. Ibrahim Baré MAÏNASSARA, who claimed that he had acted to end the "absurd, irrational, and personalized crisis" gripping the Nigerien government. Following seizure of the presidential palace and assembly building, Maïnassara announced the "dismissal" of the president and prime minister (both of whom had been arrested), the dissolution of the assembly, suspension of political party activity, and his own installation as chair of the National Salvation Council (*Conseil pour le Salut National*—CSN), an 11-member military body organized to govern until a civilian government could be reestablished. On January 30 the CSN designated Boukari ADJI, vice governor of the Central Bank of West African States (BCEAO), as prime minister.

In February 1996 Maïnassara appointed a 100-member Committee of Wisemen to act as an advisory council and a 32-member Coordinating Committee for the Democratic Renewal to supervise the restoration of a democratic government and draft a new constitution. At a meeting chaired by Maïnassara on February 12, Ousmane and Amadou publicly acknowledged the "constitutional problems" that had prompted the coup and endorsed the CSN's early governing efforts.

On February 17, 1996, the CSN announced a timetable for the return to a democratically elected government, which called for a constitutional referendum in September and presidential and legislative elections by the end of the year. However, under pressure from France, which on March 6 became the first international donor to renew ties with the junta, the CSN released a revised timetable that moved the schedule up by three months. On March 27 the regime established a transitional legislature, the National Forum for Democratic Renewal, consisting of members from the Committee of Wisemen and the Coordinating Committee, as well as former National Assemblymen. The National Forum met for the first time on April 1 and six days later it approved a draft constitution that included provisions for a second legislative body (a Senate), as well as a government wherein the prime minister would be accountable to the president. On April 19 the National Forum released yet another transitional timetable, rescheduling the constitutional referendum to May 12, presidential balloting to July 7, and legislative elections to September 22.

The constitutional referendum was approved on May 12, 1996, by 92 percent of the voters—though the election was poorly attended. Maïnassara revoked the ban on political parties May 19, and lifted the state of emergency four days later.

In balloting July 7–8, 1996, Brig. Gen. Maïnassara (who was promoted on May 14) captured the presidency, securing 52 percent of the vote, according to government figures. However, the election was marred by the junta's termination of the Independent National Electoral Commission (CENI) on the second day of voting and installation of a National Electoral Commission (CNE) filled with Maïnassara's supporters. Dismissing the regime's claim that it had dissolved the CENI to end the "corruption" of ballots by opposition activists, Maïnassara's top three challengers (former president Ousmane, MNSD-*Nassara* chair Mamadou Tandja, and former National Assembly president Mahamadou Issoufou) filed a petition to have the results overturned. (Ousmane had been credited with 19.75 percent of the vote, Tandja 15.65 percent, and Issoufou 7.6 percent. The fifth candidate, Moumouni DJERMAKOYE of the Nigerien Alliance for Democracy and Progress-*Zaman Lahiya* (*Alliance Nigérienne pour la Démocratie et le Progrès-Zaman Lahiya*—ANDP-*Zaman Lahiya*), secured 4.77 of the vote; he did not formally contest the results.) The Supreme Court officially validated Maïnassara's electoral victory July 21, and on August 23 the new president named a cabinet, again led by Prime Minister Adji, which included no military officials.

Following his inauguration on August 7, 1996, President Maïnassara attempted to negotiate an agreement that would prompt angry opposition groups to participate in upcoming legislative elections. Among other things, he dissolved the CNE on August 30 and announced the formation of a new electoral commission. However, the opposition, most of which coalesced in September as the Front for the Restoration and Defense of Democracy (*Front pour la Restauration et la Défense de la Démocratie*—FRDD), demanded that the members of the CENI be reappointed and that other measures be taken to ensure fair elections. Unconvinced of the regime's democratic intentions, the FRDD ultimately boycotted the balloting for a new National Assembly held on November 23, paving the way for the National Union of Independents for Democratic Renewal (UNIRD), which had recently been established by supporters of resident Maïnassara, to win 59 of the 83 seats. Declaring the transition to civilian government complete, Maïnassara dissolved the CSN on December 12. On December 21 he appointed a new government, headed, ironically, by Amadou Cissé, whose attempted appointment to the premiership in February 1995 had triggered the constitutional crisis leading up to the January 1996 coup.

Antigovernment sentiment culminated in large-scale demonstrations in the capital in early January 1997. Maïnassara responded with a crackdown that resulted in the arrest of the FRDD leaders; however, the detainees were released after ten days, regional leaders having apparently persuaded the president to adopt a less harsh approach.

On March 31, 1997, Maïnassara dissolved the Cissé government in response to the opposition's agreement to set aside its preconditions for entering into negotiations (i.e. dissolution of the assembly and organization of fresh elections) and accept cabinet postings. However, talks between the two sides quickly broke down, and no opposition members were included in the government named on June 13. The opposition rejected subsequent government entreaties, and unrest was reported throughout the country. Consequently, on November 24 Maïnassara again dismissed the Cissé government, accusing it of "incompetency" and failing to ease political tensions.

On November 27, 1997, Ibrahim Assane MAYAKI was named to replace Cissé, and on December 1 a new government was appointed. Despite Maïnassara's pledge to include opposition figures in the new cabinet, only one minister, Tuareg leader Rhissa ag BOULA, came from outside the pro-presidential coalition of parties. Moreover, a number of Cissé ministers were reappointed.

Opposition candidates captured a majority of the contested seats in local, municipal, and regional balloting on February 7, 1999. Heightened government-opposition tension was consequently reported in Niamey after the Supreme Court (acting, according to the opposition, under pressure from the administration) ordered extensive repolling in early April.

On April 9, 1999, President Maïnassara was assassinated at the Niamey airport upon returning from a trip to Mecca, reportedly by members of the presidential guard. Troops immediately took control of the capital, and Prime Minister Mayaki dissolved the assembly, suspended political party activities, and asserted that he and his cabinet would continue governing until a "unity" government was formed. After two days of uncertainty, however, junior army officers announced on April 11 that they had assumed power and formed a National Reconciliation Council (*Conseil de Réconciliation Nationale*—CRN), whose chair, Maj. Daouda Malam WANKÉ (theretofore commander of the presidential guard), was also named head of state. The junta suspended the constitution and formally dissolved the government and Supreme Court. In addition, the results of the February elections were annulled. At the same time, the military announced a nine-month transitional plan that would culminate in the inauguration of an elected president. On April 16, 1999, the CRN named an interim government that included Wanké as the head of government, Mayaki in a diminished prime ministerial role, and a number of FRDD ministers.

A new constitution, designed, among other things, to resolve the presidential/prime-ministerial power-sharing confusion of the early to mid-1990s, was approved by 90 percent of the vote in a national referendum on July 18, 1999, although turnout was estimated at only 32 percent. Seven candidates ran in the presidential election on October 17, and in runoff balloting on November 24 Mamadou Tandja of MNSD-*Nassara* defeated Mahamdou Issoufou of PNDS-*Tarayya*, 60 percent to 40 percent. The MNSD-*Nassara* also secured a plurality in new assembly balloting on November 24, and in coalition with the CDS-*Rahama* controlled a comfortable majority of 55 legislative seats. Tandja was inaugurated on December 22 and, upon the recommendation of the assembly, named fellow party member Hama Amadou as prime minister on December 31. In addition to the MNSD-*Nassara* and CDS-*Rahama*, the new cabinet announced on January 5, 2000, included representatives of two small, nonlegislative parties—the Union of Popular Forces for Democracy and Progress-*Sawaba* (*Union des Forces Populaires pour la Démocratie et le Progrès-Sawaba*—UFPDP-*Sawaba*) and the Party for National Unity and Development-*Salama* (*Parti pour l'Unité Nationale et la Développement-Salama*—PUND-*Salama*)—as well as two leaders of former Tuareg rebel organizations. However, in a reshuffle on September 17, 2001, the ministers from the UFPDP-*Sawaba* and PUND-*Salama* were dropped from the cabinet.

The country's first municipal elections, postponed from May 4, 2004, were successfully held on July 24, 2004, with councilors elected to represent 206 communities.

Tandja was reelected in 2004, after winning the first round of balloting on November 16 and easily defeating Issoufou in second-round balloting on December 4 with 65.5 percent of the vote. He named a new cabinet on December 30, which included five women and retained Amadou as prime minister. The assembly, also elected on December 4, seated seven members from a new party formed earlier in the year by former transitional leader Cheiffou: the Rally for Social Democracy-*Gaskiya* (*Rassemblement pour Sociale Democrate*—RSD-*Gaskiya*). In the wake of the dismissal of two cabinet ministers in 2006 in connection with a corruption scandal, the parliament backed a no-confidence vote on May 31, 2007, that dissolved the government and forced the resignation of Prime Minister Amadou on June 1. President Tandja's appointment of equipment minister Seini OUMAROU as prime minister on June 3 was initially rejected by the parliament, and the opposition refused to participate in a proposed unity government. However, Oumarou was sworn in on June 7 and a new government was installed on June 9, comprising members of the MNSD-*Nassara,* the CDS-*Rahama,* and the Democratic Rally of the People–Jamaa (*Rassemblement Démocratique du Peuple–Jamaa*—RDP-*Jamaa*). The cabinet included eight women and a former Tuareg rebel leader, Issad KATO.

In 2008 the president extended a state of emergency that had been effect since August 2007 in response to the continuing conflict with Taureg rebels in the north. The measure enhanced the powers of the armed forces in the region. In May 2009 a presidential decree extended the state of emergency for another three months.

The cabinet was reshuffled on May 14, 2009, when the president dismissed ministers from two parties that opposed his plan for a constitutional referendum—the RDP-*Jamaa* and the ANDP-*Zaman Lahiya*—and replaced them with members of the MNSD. He also replaced the justice minister without explanation. On May 26 the president dissolved parliament following a Constitutional Court ruling the previous day rejecting his proposal for a referendum that, if approved, would change the constitution to allow him to seek a third five-year term. In June the president dissolved the Constitutional Court and assumed emergency powers, announcing that the referendum would be held on August 4. The new constitution, which removed presidential term limits, was approved by voters (see Constitution and government, below). Opposition parties protested and later announced they would boycott National Assembly elections scheduled for October. On August 19 the government stepped down to allow the president to name a new government, but he reappointed all members the same day. On September 24 Prime Minister Oumarou resigned to seek election to parliament (he returned to the post following the poll). Interior Minister Albadé ABOUBA served as interim prime minister.

In controversial parliamentary balloting on October 20, 2009, the MNSD-*Nassara* secured a majority, winning 76 of 113 seats, and for the first time, independents won representation. One seat was subsequently annulled. Months of political turmoil followed, and on February 18, 2010, soldiers led by Lt. Gen. Salou DJIBO stormed the presidential residence in a violent coup and assumed power. Djibo, the head of the Council for the Restoration of Democracy (*Conseil Suprême pour la Restauration de la Democratie*—CSRD), on February 19 suspended the constitution and dissolved parliament. Former president Tandja and many of his ministers were detained under house arrest. On February 23, Djibo named a new prime minister, Mahamadou DANDA, who had served as a minister in the transitional government following the 1999 coup. On March 1 Djibo formed a transitional government comprising 20 members, primarily technocrats, as well as five military officers. Five women were also given portfolios. The cabinet was reshuffled on October 10. Following an alleged October 22 coup attempt, four officers were arrested. A national referendum on a new constitution to restore civilian governance was approved by 93.5 percent of voters on October 31. In December Tandja was charged with misappropriation of state funds and moved to a prison near Niamey, ignoring an ECOWAS ruling that had ordered his release a month earlier.

The junta moved forward with plans for civilian rule by paving the way for multiparty presidential and parliamentary elections on January 31, 2011, despite protests from opposition party leaders, who claimed there were problems with the voter rolls and sought a postponement. The PNDS-*Tarayya* secured a plurality of seats, followed by strong showings by the MNSD-*Nassara* and the newly formed Nigerien Democratic Movement for an African Federation—*Lumana* (*Mouvement Démocratique Nigérien pour une Fédération Africaine-Lumana*—MODEN-*Lumana* FA/Niger) of Hama Amadou. Five other parties won representation, and four women secured seats. In the first round of presidential balloting, former Tandja opponent Mahamadou ISSOUFOU of the PNDS-*Tarayya* was the top vote getter among the ten candidates but fell short of the threshold to avoid a runoff with former prime minister Oumarou of the MNSD-*Nassara.* Ahead of the March 12 presidential runoff, Issoufou formed alliances with several other candidates, most notably Amadou, whose MODEN-*Lumana* FA/Niger had won a third of the seats in municipal elections on January 8. Issoufou handily defeated Omarou in the runoff with 58 percent of the vote. He was sworn in on April 7 and the same day, in what was viewed as a significant effort toward reconciliation, appointed a Taureg, Brigi RAFINI as prime minister. Over the years, Rafini, a former government minister, had been a member of several parties, including the RDP-*Jamaa,* of which he was a founder, before joining the PNDS-*Tarayya*. A new government, dominated by the PNDS-*Tarayya* but including members of the parties that had supported Issoufou in the runoff and six women, was appointed on April 21. Former prime minister and presidential challenger Amadou Cissé and CDS-*Rahama* dissident Abdou LABO were appointed as two of the three ministers of state. Omarou was invited to join the government, but he declined.

On August 13, 2013, Issoufou reshuffled the cabinet, bringing in members of the opposition to form a unity government.

Constitution and government. In January 1984 President Kountché created a National Charter Commission, largely comprised of CND members, to develop a constitutional framework that was ultimately endorsed in a national referendum on June 14, 1987. On December 17 of the same year, General Saibou announced the formation of a national "reflection committee" to finalize guidelines for the new basic law, which was approved by popular referendum on September 24, 1989. Capping the government structure was the CSON, whose 67 civilian and military members (14 serving as a National Executive Bureau) were elected by the MNSD and whose president became sole candidate for election to the presidency of the republic. The 1989 document, which also provided for a National Assembly of 93 MNSD-approved members and for a judiciary headed by a presidentially appointed Supreme Court, was suspended by the National Conference on August 9, 1991.

By mid-1992 the presidency had been reduced to an essentially symbolic institution, as true executive power was exercised by the prime minister who until early 1993 answered to a quasi-legislative High Council of the Republic (HCR). One of the functions of the HCR was to oversee the drafting of the new basic law, which was approved by national referendum on December 27, 1993. The document provided for a directly elected president to serve a once-renewable five-year term. A presidentially nominated prime minister is responsible to a unicameral National Assembly whose members are also elected for five-year terms.

Upon its ascension to power in early 1996 the CSN military regime suspended the 1993 document and appointed a commission to draft a new charter. The new constitution, which was approved by national referendum on May 12, 1996, featured an executive branch headed by a powerful president, thus clearly distinguishing itself from its predecessors. Meanwhile, in early June the regime created a ten-member High Court of Justice and granted it sole authority to prosecute the president and government members.

The 1996 basic law was suspended by the CRN on April 11, 1999, and an interim Consultative Council (*Conseil Consultative*—CC) was appointed in May by the new military head of state, Maj. Daouda Malam Wanké, to draft yet another constitution. As approved in a national referendum on July 18, the new basic law accorded strong power to the president to prevent a reoccurrence of the difficulties experienced in interpreting the 1993 document with regard to the authority of the prime minister versus the president.

A new constitution was promulgated on August 18, 2009, following a referendum on August 4 that was approved by 92.5 percent of voters. The new charter granted the president an extension beyond his second five-year term (ending in December 2009) and the right to seek unlimited reelection. Following the coup of February 18, 2010, the constitution was suspended. A new constitution limiting the presidential mandate to two five-year terms and granting amnesty to coup leaders was approved by voters on October 31 and signed by head of state Lt. Gen. Salou Djibo on November 25, following validation by the Constitutional Court a day earlier. The charter was promulgated on November 30. The new constitution guaranteed freedom of the press. In 2013 the media watchdog group ranked Niger 43rd out of 179 countries.

Foreign relations. Prior to the 1974 coup Niger pursued a moderate line in foreign affairs, avoiding involvement in East-West issues and generally maintaining friendly relations with neighboring states. The Kountché government established diplomatic links with a number of communist states, including China and the Soviet Union, and adopted a conservative posture in regional affairs, including a diplomatic rupture with Libya from January 1981 to March 1982. Tripoli was periodically charged thereafter with backing anti-Niamey forces, including those involved in a late 1983 coup attempt and northern Tuareg rebel activity in 1985 and 1990. However, a bilateral security agreement in December 1990 eased tensions between Niger and Libya.

Niamey's relations with neighboring Algeria and Mali have been complicated since October 1991 by the resurgence of militant Tuareg activities across their shared borders. In March 1992 a meeting between Prime Minister Cheiffou and Tuareg officials in Algeria yielded a two-week truce. However, the truce was allowed to lapse, and in February 1993 Nigerien and Malian troops clashed, after reportedly mistaking each other for Tuareg units. The January 1996 military coup in Niger drew condemnation from both regional and international observers, with France, the European Union, and the United States suspending aid payments. Although Paris resumed cooperation in March 1996, Washington reiterated its stance following the controversial July presidential elections.

A number of regional and other international capitals condemned the military takeover in April 1999; France, for example, promptly broke off its relations with Niger and suspended all aid. Such pressure was considered influential in the subsequent quick return to civilian rule, after which normal international relations were reestablished and external financial assistance was resumed.

In May 2000 a long-standing dispute between Niger and Benin over ownership of Lete Island and a number of smaller islands in the Niger River resurfaced. After mediation by the Organization of African Unity (OAU, subsequently the African Union—AU) failed to produce successful border delineation, the case was submitted to the International Court of Justice (ICJ). In 2005 the ICJ ruled that 16 of the 25 disputed islands, including Lete, belonged to Niger. In 2007 Niger officially took ownership of Lete Island. In 2007 Benin officially took possession of nine other islands it was awarded by the ICJ's ruling.

Longtime tensions between Niger and Burkina Faso escalated in 2007, each accusing the other's security forces of crossing the border to rob villagers. Local officials called for a jointly controlled buffer zone, and the two countries agreed to ask the ICJ to mediate the dispute.

Relations with France were strained in 2007 following the deportation of a French journalist from Niger after his imprisonment for filming a documentary on Tuareg rebels. Questions about the role of French uranium-mining company Areva also played a part in the deterioration of ties with France (see Current issues, below).

China, meanwhile, maintained warm relations with Niger in 2007, the former having opened what was described as a "vast new embassy" in Niamey and having secured a number of uranium prospecting licenses. In September 2007 President Tandja and officials of the Chinese Communist Party met in Niger and agreed to foster cooperation between the two governments; they signed an oil production agreement in 2008. In 2009 China loaned Niger $95 million for a uranium mining project owned in partnership between the two countries.

During the political crisis in President Tandja's government in 2009, ECOWAS offered the government and the opposition a "road map" for resolving differences. Despite objections by ECOWAS, Tandja followed through with plans for a controversial constitutional referendum in August. ECOWAS immediately suspended Niger after the national poll.

Following the February 2010 coup, ECOWAS condemned the junta's action as an unconstitutional "ascension to power."

Seven foreign nationals, including five from France, all of whom worked for French companies, were kidnapped near a northern Nigerien mining town in September 2010. The French government subsequently deployed military personnel, aircraft, and weapons to help find the hostages. Al-Qaida in the Islamic Maghreb (AQIM) claimed responsibility for the abductions. Three of the hostages were released in February 2011, and French president Nicolas Sarkozy thanked the authorities in Niger for their efforts in the matter. In a separate incident reported in February, a French Niger national was executed by his kidnappers after he was abducted in January. Around the same time, the U.S. Peace Corps withdrew its volunteers from the country, citing security concerns, marking the first time the agency had ceased operations there since 1962.

In April 2011 Niger called for donor aid to help some 59,000 Africans—many of them Nigeriens—who fled the Libyan civil war.

In August 2012 Niger joined Algeria, Burkina Faso, and Mauritania in the creation of a 45,000 member "hot pursuit" force to combat terrorism and cross-border incursions. Officials from China and Niger announced in September a loan offer of $1.1 billion for infrastructure projects, including airport terminals, a light rail line for the capital, and improving the country's internet capability.

Reports in January 2013 indicated that Niger had granted the United States permission to establish a drone base in the country. In addition, Niger agreed to contribute 675 troops to the AU-led intervention force in Mali. The International Court of Justice ruled in April on a border dispute between Niger and Burkina Faso. The ruling finalized the border along 380 km (236 miles). In August Niger and Mauritania signed a defense cooperation accord.

Current issues. A corruption scandal involving two ministers accused of embezzling more than $1 million in 2006 led to a parliamentary vote of no confidence on May 31, 2007, based on delegates' allegations of Prime Minister Amadou's complicity. After the prime minister resigned on June 1, parliament submitted a list of three nominees for his successor to President Tandja, who selected Seini Oumarou. The new government named on June 9 reportedly did not include any members of the opposition. The immediate issue of concern in the wake of the government shake-up was the renewed violence in the north by a new Tuareg rebel group, the Movement of Nigeriens for Justice (*Mouvement des Nigériens pour la Justice*—MNJ), which had emerged in February 2007 (see Rebel Groups, below). In June the government moved 4,000 troops to the northern region to confront the rebels, who were demanding that the government use more of the country's uranium profits to improve the living conditions in the north and that the president fulfill the terms of the 1995 peace agreement.

The conflict escalated throughout 2007 and 2008, with reports of landmines laid by rebels and accusations against a French-owned uranium mining company, Areva, of fomenting instability in the north—seen as a means of discouraging other international companies from vying for a stake in the lucrative mining industry—and similar claims against Libya's president Muammar al-Qadhafi, who had offered to mediate the dispute. Additionally, international human rights groups reported that the government had carried out illegal executions, torture, and revenge attacks against Tuareg rebels, all of which the administration denied. Meanwhile, President Tandja was facing growing unrest among the populace due to food shortages and a lack of jobs. In November the president renewed the state of emergency for another three months.

Fighting continued in 2008, but President Tandja steadfastly refused to acknowledge the rebels, who were now said to have widened their base of support to include the Toubou and some Tuaregs from neighboring Mali. Meanwhile, international human rights groups reported that a crisis was developing, as some 20,000 people had been displaced by the fighting. In June the rebels kidnapped four French employees of a nuclear power company, releasing them days later. The rebels announced that their reason for such actions was to pressure the governments of Niger and France to enter negotiations to end the conflict. That same month, news reports surfaced that MNJ leader Acharif had been killed by government forces.

Political turmoil heightened in 2008 following the arrest in June of former prime minister Hama Amadou on corruption charges. Widely viewed as President Tandja's likely successor, Amadou denied that he had embezzled state funds, claiming he was being targeted to prevent him from seeking the presidency in 2009. Amadou was removed as party leader of the MNSD as a consequence of the corruption charges and his subsequent imprisonment. Amadou was released after ten months, in April 2009, and he left Niger to seek medical treatment.

In the run-up to the 2009 elections, scheduled for November-December, President Tandja said he would not seek a third term (which would require a constitutional amendment), but he changed his mind in early May. With several parties voicing their opposition to Tandja's proposed constitutional revision allowing him to seek a third term, the president removed several cabinet members whose parties objected to the referendum. Days later the Constitutional Court, having taken up the issue after it was referred by parliament, ruled that the president "cannot undertake to change the constitution without violating his oath of office." The next day, Tandja dissolved parliament, a move that meant he could avoid having to appear before the High Court of Justice on charges of high treason, observers said. The high court judge, Moumouni Adamou DJERMAKOYE of the pro-government ANDP-*Zaman Lahiya*, had recently warned that the proposed referendum would divide the country. The president's plan drew international protests as well, the United States calling the proposed referendum "a setback for democracy," and the Economic Community of West African States (ECOWAS) threatening sanctions. Tandja, however, rejected the criticism and defied the Constitutional Court and the National Assembly by going forward with plans for the referendum, scheduled for August 4. In June protesters led by Mahamadou Issoufou of the PNDS-*Tarayya* announced they would defy the government ban on demonstrations. Subsequently, more than 230 parties and groups under the umbrella Front for Defense of Democracy (FDD) held a series of protests to counter what they claimed was the president's plan to "install absolute power." On June 26 the president dissolved the government and assumed emergency powers. Several days later he dissolved the Constitutional Court and suspended a television station that aired opposition views. On July 3 the president appointed a new Constitutional Court, which was widely criticized; ten days later the country's attorneys went on strike in protest. Following a controversial referendum in August, in which nearly 93 percent of voters approved constitutional amendments that removed presidential term limits, ECOWAS offered to help negotiate a resolution to the political crisis that ensued, recommending a power-sharing arrangement. Meanwhile, Issoufou was arrested, charged with misappropriation of funds, and released on bail. He left the country on October 29, the day controversial parliamentary elections were held, but he returned the following day, saying he would cooperate with the judiciary. In results announced in early November, the MNSD regained the majority it had lost in 2004. ECOWAS immediately suspended Niger for not postponing the poll. Domestic dissent continued over the president's enhanced authority, the unrest exacerbated by famine and a lack of progress toward a resolution proposed by ECOWAS. On a positive note, late in the year Taureg rebels in Niger and in neighboring Mali agreed to disarm as a result of peace talks brokered by Libyan leader Muammar al-Qadhafi.

"So chaotic and tense" had the last year been, according to *Africa Research Bulletin,* some 10,000 opposition demonstrators protested in Niamey on February 14, 2010. Four days later, in what was described as an "audacious daylight attack," soldiers stormed the presidential palace, engaged in a four-hour gun battle in which ten people were killed, and overthrew the government. President Tandja and his cabinet were arrested, the constitution was suspended, and parliament was dissolved by the junta, styled as the Council for the Restoration of Democracy—CSRD. The action was immediately condemned by the AU, France, and the UN, while the United States issued more vague comments urging "a speedy return to democracy." Junta leader Lt. Gen. Salou Djibo subsequently appointed Mahamadou Danda as interim prime minister and on March 1 named a transitional government dominated by technocrats. Meanwhile, though some ministers were released from custody, Tandja and his key officials remained under house arrest on the grounds of the presidential compound. The junta announced that it would hold elections following a transitional period, and that its members, along with police, customs officers, and others, would not be allowed to participate. Further, governors, district administrators, and tribal chiefs were banned from participating in political activity. On March 12 Djibo appointed military officers as governors of seven of the eight regions, replacing civilians in the posts. In response to international pressure, Djibo met with representatives of political parties and civil societies to discuss a scheme for successful political transition. Subsequently, he formed a Consultative Council from a cross-section of society to assist in the transition, naming as its head Marou AMADOU, the former president of a civil association, United Front for the Safety of Democracy (FUSAD), which had opposed Tandja's constitutional reform in 2009. (Marou Amadou had been arrested repeatedly during the Tandja regime for his opposition stance.) While the coup was reported to have the approval of a majority of the populace, Djibo, for his part, requested that the public refrain from demonstrations of support in order to "maintain a spirit of neutrality." Meanwhile, that same month former prime minister and former MNSD stalwart Hama Amadou returned from exile in France and formed a new political party, the MODEN-*Lumana* FA/Niger (see Political Parties, below).

In April 2010 the junta announced a schedule for returning to civilian rule, with presidential elections set for December 26, and a second round, if needed, on January 26, 2011, with democracy to be restored by March 1, 2011. In May the junta acknowledged the alarming food shortage in the country (20 percent of the population reportedly had food for only ten days), something former president Tandja had refused to do. Junta leaders also vowed to clean up corruption as reports surfaced of alleged kickbacks to Tandja's allies in exchange for mining contracts. In early October two high-ranking junta members were arrested for an alleged plot to overthrow Djibo when he was out of the country in September. Another military officer was fired from the cabinet. No reason was given. Progress was made toward restoring civilian rule after a new constitution was overwhelmingly approved in a national referendum on October 31and subsequently validated by the Constitutional Court and signed by Djibo. The new charter limits the presidential mandate to two five-year terms and grants amnesty to those involved in the February coup. The junta announced a new schedule for ending the transitional period, with parliamentary and presidential elections now set for January 31, 2011, and a second round of presidential balloting, if needed, on March 12, 2011, with a new president to be inaugurated on April 6. On November 8 the ECOWAS court ruled that Tandja should be released from what it deemed was illegal detention and urged junta leaders to respect its decision. A group of opposition parties issued a statement calling for Tandja to remain in custody and be charged with high treason. The junta rejected the ECOWAS court's ruling and called for Tandja to be charged with high treason. In December the State Court lifted Tandja's presidential immunity, and he was charged with misappropriating $1 million in state funds. He was then transferred from house arrest to a prison near Niamey and was scheduled to stand trial in May 2011.

The junta rejected a demand by nine of the ten presidential candidates that the election be postponed due to their concerns about complaints lodged against the national electoral commission. Meanwhile, four of the presidential candidates—Issoufou, Mahamane Ousmane of the CDS-*Rahama*, Amadou Cissé, now of the Union for Democracy and the Republic-*Tabbat* (UDR-*Tabbat*), and Hama Amadou—had formed an electoral alliance, styled as the Coordination of Democratic Forces for the Republic (*Coordination des Forces pour la Démocratie et la République*—CFDR). However, shortly before the election, another coalition was formed, including two candidates who switched allegiance (Amadou and Ousmane) to join the National Reconciliation Alliance against Issoufou. Following the latter's success in the first round of balloting, Amadou threw his new party's support behind the PNDS-*Tarayya* candidate. The PNDS fell short of a majority in concurrent legislative balloting, but Issoufou handily defeated Oumarou in second-round voting on March 12. After naming a Taureg as his prime minister, Issoufou made further conciliatory moves by offering Oumarou a ministerial post (which the MNSD leader turned down) and by including presidential challengers Mahamane Ousmane and Amadou Cissé, as well as CDS-*Rahama* dissident Abdou Labo in his new government. The cabinet also included members of the UDR-*Tabbat*, which had endorsed his candidacy. Marou Amadou, a key opponent of Tandja's constitutional reforms in 2009, was appointed minister of justice. One of the new president's first acts was to bestow the country's highest award upon coup leader Lieutenant General Djibo. Issoufou pledged to provide water and help improve the agriculture sector, to waive school fees for children up to age 16, and to provide an additional 2,500 classrooms and teachers, among other things.

In a move that seemed to take many observers by surprise, the country's appeals court in May 2011 dismissed all corruption charges against Tandja and ordered his release from prison. The decision was based on the law that prohibits Niger from trying a head of state after he has left office, which observers said was meant to prevent politically motivated cases from being brought against deposed leaders. Upon his release, the former president was greeted by thousands of cheering supporters.

In 2011–2012 the situation in Niger was strained by the arrival of groups displaced by neighboring conflicts: some 200,000 Nigerian migrant workers passing from Libya through Agadez; several hundred men carrying weapons procured in Libya en route to Mali; and at least

20,000 refugees fleeing the instability in Mali. The government feared events could inspire an uprising from its own Tuareg population.

In a national broadcast on Aug. 9, 2011, Issoufou announced that ten people had been arrested for their involvement in a failed coup attempt scheduled for July 12–13.

In September 2011 Saadi Qadhafi, the son of Libya's ex-ruler, turned up in the northern town of Agadez in a convoy, prompting accusations of Niger's complicity from Libya's National Transitional Council. Issoufou's decision to grant him asylum the next month, which some observers attributed to a sense of personal obligation stemming from Qadhafi's funding of his past campaigns, further angered the NTC. In February Saadi was placed under de facto house arrest after he caused a diplomatic headache for his host by announcing in a phone call interview with Al Arabiya news channel that he was in touch with insurgents in Libya and claiming there would be a new rebellion against the NTC.

Fourteen people were killed and 13 arrested on November 6 when troops engaged a convoy of gunmen outside the northern town of Assamaka near the borders with Algeria and Mali. Local sources reported the gunmen included Libyans and Tuaregs from Mali, likely Qadhafi loyalists fleeing the conflict. Also in November, five aid workers who had been kidnapped by an Islamic group, the Movement for Oneness and Jihad in West Africa (MUJAO), were freed during a military operation. A sixth hostage was killed during rescue.

On May 23, 2013, attacks on a uranium complex and a military base left 35 dead. The strikes were blamed on AQIM. The following month, militants staged a jail break that freed 22, including several prominent AQIM leaders.

POLITICAL PARTIES

Political parties were not permitted in Niger during the more than 13 years of the Kountché regime. The National Movement for a Developing Society (MNSD, below) was established as a government formation in 1988, and some 15 parties received provisional recognition in the five months following President Saibou's November 1990 acceptance of a multiparty system. All party activity was suspended in the wake of the January 1996 coup, but the ban was soon lifted on May 19. However, the new standards guiding party formations and activities were described as restrictive. Nevertheless, numerous coalitions were formed in 1996–1998, though alliances continued changing. Most notably, the once powerful Alliance of Forces of Change (*Alliance des Forces de Changement*—AFC) appeared to have collapsed by the late 1990s. (For further information on the AFC, see p. 680 of the 1998 *Handbook.*)

Political party activity was suspended immediately following the April 1999 military takeover; however, within days of President Maïnassara's death the leading opposition groups announced their intention to cooperate with the military junta, and the suspension was lifted.

In March 2000 the PNDS-*Tarayya,* RDP-*Jamaa,* ANDP-*Zaman Lahiya,* and a number of smaller parties formed a loose antigovernment coalition called the Coordination of Democratic Forces (*Coordination des Forces Démocratiques*—CFD). In response the MNDS-*Nassara* and several allies, including the CDS-*Rahama,* announced the creation of an Alliance of Democratic Forces (*Alliance des Forces Démocratiques*—AFD) in July. The ANDP-*Zaman Lahia* joined the AFD coalition on July 8, 2002.

Prior to the 2004 legislative elections, the PNDS-*Tarayya* formed electoral coalitions with several parties: the PPN/RDA and the PNA-*Al Ouma;* the UNI/UDR-*Tabbat;* and the PPN/RDA.

Government and Government-Supportive Parties:

Nigerien Party for Democracy and Socialism-Tarayya (*Parti Nigerien pour la Démocratie et le Socialism-Tarayya*—PNDS-*Tarayya*). In the legislative election of February 1993 the PNDS-*Tarayya,* then affiliated with the AFC, won 13 seats. Having gained only a 16 percent vote share in the first round of 1993 presidential balloting, party leader and presidential candidate Mahamadou Issoufou was eliminated from the runoff election; he was subsequently named prime minister.

On September 25, 1994, the PNDS-*Tarayya* withdrew from the AFC, claiming that it had been "betrayed" by its coalition partners, and three days later Issoufou resigned his prime ministerial post. In mid-October the PNDS-*Tarayya* joined with the MNSD-*Nassara* in a successful no-confidence motion against the Souley government. In the January 1995 legislative poll the party won 12 seats; Issoufou was then elected National Assembly president. He captured 7.6 percent of the vote as the party's standard bearer in the July 1996 presidential elections. He fared significantly better in 1999, finishing second in the first round with 22.8 percent of the vote before losing the runoff with 40.1 percent. Once aligned with the MNSD-*Nassara* and the CDR-*Rahama* in the FRDD, the PNDS-*Tarayya* competed against those parties in the 1999 legislative balloting in alliance with the RDP-*Jamaa* and ANDP-*Zaman Lahiya.*

Issoufou faced a runoff with incumbent President Tandja in 2004, after winning 24.6 percent of the vote in first-round balloting. In the second round Tandja handily defeated his rival with 65.5 percent of the vote. However, the PNDS-*Tarayya* ran in coalition with a number of small parties and won 17 seats in the 2004 legislative election (see Legislature, below).

In 2007 the party's secretary general, Alou Bozari, joined numerous parties in the northern region in calling for an immediate cease-fire between government troops and Tuareg rebels.

The party opposed the president's constitutional referendum in 2009 and organized a massive, peaceful protest in May that included civil rights groups, trade unions, students, and supporters of former prime minister Amadou. Issoufou was arrested in October on charges of misappropriation of funds. He left the country but then returned the day after parliamentary elections and vowed to cooperate with the authorities. Following the 2010 coup that ousted Tandja, the PNDS nominated Issoufou as its flagbearer for the 2011 presidential election. The PNDS won 34 seats in the concurrent parliamentary election. Issoufou stepped down as party president after his election, in keeping with the requirement that the head of state not be involved in party politics. Party vice president Mohamed Bazoum, who assumed the leadership position, was appointed minister of state for foreign affairs in the new government. The party's secretary of state, Foumakoye Gado, was appointed minister of mines, and then minister of petroleum and energy.

Leaders: Mohamed BAZOUM (Acting President), Kalla ANKOURAO, Hassoumi MASSAOUDOU (Deputy Secretary General), Foumakoye GADO (Secretary General).

Democratic Rally of the People–Jamaa (*Rassemblement Démocratique du Peuple–Jamaa*—RDP-*Jamaa*). The RDP-*Jamaa* held its inaugural congress on August 14–19, 1997, and was the party of then-President Maïnassara. Thereafter, the party emerged as the leader of a loose coalition of parties that supported the president. At local and municipal polling in early 1999, the RDP-*Jamaa* reportedly captured the largest number of seats; however, the military junta that came to power in April nullified the balloting.

Intraparty fighting erupted over the choice of a 1999 presidential nominee, leading former Prime Minister Amadou Boubacar Cissé and his supporters to leave the party. Meanwhile, Hamid Algabid of the RDP-*Jamaa* won 10.9 percent of the vote in the first round of presidential balloting and supported Mahamadou Issoufou of the PNDS-*Tarayya* in the second round. In the first round of presidential elections in 2004, Algabid won only 4.9 percent of the vote, finishing in last place. He supported Tandja in the second round. The party won only six seats in the assembly elections of 2004.

Disagreements within the party led to the departure of Secretary General Abdourahamane SEYDOU in 2008.

The party opposed the president's proposed constitutional referendum early in 2009 unless it also included a measure that would abolish amnesty for those who had been involved in the assassination of President Maïnassara, but in midyear it unexpectedly dropped the conditional demand and supported the referendum.

The party won seven seats in the October 2009 assembly elections.

In the first round of presidential balloting in 2011 the RDP-*Jamaa* backed the MNSD-*Nassara*'s Seini Oumarou, but it joined several other parties in supporting Issoufou over Oumarou in the second round. In the National Assembly elections the RDP-*Jamaa* won seven seats.

Leader: Hamid ALGABID (Chair and 1999 and 2004 presidential candidate).

Democratic and Social Convention-Rahama (*Convention Démocrate et Sociale-Rahama*—CDS-*Rahama*). In the legislative balloting of February 1993 CDS-*Rahama* captured 22 seats, the most by any opposition party. Its candidate Mahamane Ousmane who had finished second in the first round of balloting, captured the presidency with 54.42 percent of the vote in the second round of presidential balloting on March 27. In January 1995 the party increased its assembly representation to 24 seats. Ousmane was ousted from office in the January 1996 coup; his bid to regain the presidency in the July balloting fell short as he came in second (at least according to government tallies) with 19.75 percent of the vote. He finished a close third in the first round of presidential balloting in 1999 with 22.5 percent of the vote. The CDS-*Rahama* subsequently threw its support behind Mamadou Tandja of the MNSD-*Nassara* for the second round. In the 2004 presidential balloting Ousmane was again third in the first round of voting and again threw his support behind Tandja in the second round. CDS-*Rahama* won 22 seats in the assembly balloting of 2004.

Though the party had been supportive of President Tandja, in 2009 it opposed his plan for a constitutional referendum, saying Niger's "political and institutional stability" would be threatened. The CDS-*Rahama* agreed with the court ruling that the referendum was unconstitutional. Further, party leader Mahamane Ousmane had been speaker of the assembly when Tandja dissolved parliament in May. In June the party withdrew its eight ministers from the government in protest and subsequently formed an opposition coalition styled the **Movement for Defense and Democracy** (*Mouvement pour le défense et le démocratie*—MDD) with five minor parties.

The party failed to win seats in the October 2009 parliamentary election.

In 2011 Ousmane finished fourth in the presidential balloting with 8.4 percent of the vote. The party won three seats in the concurrent parliamentary election and dissident Abdou Labo, who went against the party and backed Issoufou in the presidential runoff, was appointed to the new government. In August 2013 Labo was appointed minister of state.

Leaders: Mahamane OUSMANE (Former Speaker of the National Assembly and Former President of the Republic, President of the Party), Nabram ISSOUFOU, Maïdagi ALLAMBEY.

Nigerien Democratic Movement for an African Federation-Lumana (*Mouvement Démocratique Nigérien pour une Fédération Africaine-Lumana*—MODEN-*Lumana* FA/Niger). Founded in early 2010 by Hama Amadou, the embattled former MNSD-*Nassara* chair who was imprisoned in 2008 and former prime minister in the Ousmane government in 1995, the MODEN party's motto is liberty, justice, and progress. The party nominated Amadou in November as its flagbearer in the 2011 presidential election. Ahead of the election in January, MODEN was among the three parties that formed the umbrella Alliance for National Reconciliation to support whichever party's candidate reached the second round. Following Amadou's third-place showing in the first round with just under 20 percent of the vote, MODEN, citing its commitment to the political and institutional stability of the country, changed course and backed Issoufou in the second round. The party won the third highest number of seats—23—in the 2011 parliamentary election, and in April Amadou was elected speaker of the National Assembly. In spring 2012 a scandal followed Lumana MP, Zakou DJIBO, and seven other MPs suspected of embezzling $3 million. Citing the importance of Lumana's support for the governing coalition, observers said Issoufou appeared politically hamstrung, unwilling to lift Djibo's parliamentary immunity and so open to criticism from the opposition, which took the case to the Constitutional Court and threatened to accuse Issoufou of perjury. In August 2013 the party suspended its involvement in the coalition government, asserting that the number of cabinet posts it held were "inadequate."

Leaders: Hama AMADOU (President of the Party, Speaker of the National Assembly, and 2011 presidential candidate), Salissou Mamadou HABI (Vice President), Noma OUMAROU (Second Vice President), Almoustapha CISSÉ (Treasurer), Ali GAZAGAZA (Deputy Secretary General), Omar Hamidou TCHIANA (Secretary General).

Union for Democracy and the Republic-Tabbat (UDR-*Tabbat*), founded in 1999 by former prime minister and 2011 presidential candidate Amadou Boubacar CISSÈ, formerly of the RDP-*Jamaa*. The UDR-*Tabbat* won six seats in the 2011 parliamentary elections, and Cisse was appointed one of three ministers of state in the new government.

Leader: Amadou Boubacar CISSÈ.

Other Legislative Parties:

National Movement for a Developing Society-Victory (*Mouvement National pour une Societé de Développement-Nassara*—MNSD-*Nassara*). General Saibou announced the formation of the MNSD on August 2, 1988. Rejecting calls for a multiparty system, he claimed that the new group would allow for the "plural expression of opinions and ideological sensibilities," while paving the way for the normalization of politics in Niger.

General Saibou was reelected MNSD chair at a party congress on March 12–18, 1991, during which a transition to multipartism was formally endorsed. The military also announced its withdrawal from politics, and the MNSD added the Hausa word *Nassara* (Victory) to its name. On July 12, just as the party prepared to enter the competitive arena, Saibou resigned his chairmanship, citing a need to serve in a nonpartisan capacity.

In legislative balloting on February 14, 1993, the MNSD-*Nassara* secured 29 seats, 7 more than its nearest competitor; however, the subsequent formation of the AFC coalition relegated the then ruling party to minority status. Accusing the new group of procedural irregularities, the MNSD-*Nassara* refused to promote a candidate for the National Assembly presidency in April; thereafter, it spearheaded numerous protests against the government's alleged "constitutional violations." In October ten party members were sentenced to prison for engaging in violent clashes with security forces, and in March 1994 Mamadou Tandja, the MNSD-*Nassara*'s leader and former 1993 presidential candidate, was arrested for his alleged role in an antigovernment demonstration in Niamey.

The MNSD-*Nassara* again captured 29 seats in legislative balloting in January 1995, thus retaining its position as the dominant partner in the parliamentary coalition it had led since late 1994. Tandja secured 15.65 percent of the vote during presidential balloting in July 1996. Tandja and his fellow PNDS-*Tarayya* and CDS-*Rahama* presidential competitors (below) subsequently sought to have the elections nullified, claiming "massive fraud," but the Supreme Court promptly dismissed their petitions.

In September 1996 the MNSD-*Nassara* joined the PNDS-*Tarayya,* CDS-*Rahama,* and several other small groups in launching the **Front for the Restoration and Defense of Democracy** (*Front pour la Restauration et la Défense de la Démocratie*—FRDD), which immediately became the primary opposition to the Maïnassara regime. The leaders of the front demanded the restoration of the "original" Independent National Commission (CENI), equal access to the media, and supervision of the balloting by the Organization of African Unity and/or the United Nations as preconditions for FRDD participation in the upcoming national elections. Despite some apparent compromise on the part of the government, the FRDD ultimately called for a boycott of the legislative balloting.

Following prodemocracy demonstrations in Niamey in early January 1997, the leaders of the three main FRDD components were arrested and reportedly threatened with prosecution by a tribunal especially created for that purpose by President Maïnassara. However, the party leaders and 60 other detainees were released ten days later, and they immediately urged the resumption of antigovernment demonstrations.

Each of three main FRDD components presented its own presidential candidate in the first round of balloting in 1999, and Mamadou Tandja led with 32.3 percent. Due in part to the support of former president Mahamane Ousmane of the CDS-*Rahama,* Tandja was elected with 59.9 percent of the vote in the second round. For the November 1999 legislative balloting the MNSD-*Nassara* was portrayed as still aligned with the CDS-*Rahama* but no longer with the PNDS-*Tarayya.*

Tandja again took the lead in the presidential elections of 2004, taking 40.7 percent of the vote in the first round of balloting on November 16. He retained his post in the second round of balloting on December 4 with a resounding victory (65.5 percent of the vote) by striking alliances with ANDP-*Zaman Lahiya* candidate Moumouni Djermakoye (who was fifth in the first-round balloting) and Amadou Cheiffou of the Rally for Social Democracy-*Gaskiya,* who ran as an independent (fourth in the first round), and gaining the support of the CDS's Ousmane, who garnered just 24.6 percent of votes in the first round, and Hamid Algabid of the Democratic Rally of the People-*Jamaa* (sixth place in the first round). The MNSD-*Nassara* captured 47 legislative seats, a gain of 9 from the previous elections, though it failed to gain an absolute majority of the expanded 113-member assembly (see Legislature, below). The legislative election coincided with the second round of presidential elections on December 4.

In 2008 former prime minister and party chair Hama Amadou was arrested on charges of corruption and subsequently imprisoned, galvanizing his supporters in the party and creating a rift with the backers of President Tandja. The Amadou faction, who viewed him as Tandja's likely successor, also denounced the violence that they alleged had been used against them. Meanwhile, tensions were exacerbated when, at a special congress in February 2009, Amadou was replaced as party chair by Prime Minister Oumarou after Tandja pushed forth a constitutional referendum in an effort to allow him to run for a third term in balloting at the end of the year. (Amadou's backers opposed the proposal.) Shortly thereafter, eight members, including five assembly members—all Amadou supporters—were expelled from the party. The party then named five replacement assembly deputies.

In the 2009 elections the MNSD won 76 assembly seats.

Following the February 2010 coup, party secretary general Albadé Abouba, along with other high-ranking government members, was detained. Though other ministers were quickly released, Abouba, who was a minister at the time of the coup, was kept under house arrest. Despite repeated party protests, junta leaders said he would not be released. Former party secretary general Salissou Mamadou HABI left the MNSD in March 2010 to join Hama Amadou's MODEN-*Lumana* FA/Niger (below).

The party won 25 seats in the January 2011 parliamentary elections. Abouba was released on March 4 after 379 days in detention with no charges having been brought against him. On March 12, Oumarou, who was backed by the Alliance for National Reconciliation, lost to Issoufou by 16 percentage points in the second-round presidential balloting.

In August 2013 members of MNSD joined the unity government. Abouba was appointed a minister of state, and party members were given three other ministries. However, the MNSD subsequently announced it would boycott the government.

Leaders: Seini OUMAROU (Former Prime Minister and Party Chair, 2011 presidential candidate), Albadé ABOUBA (Secretary General).

Nigerien Alliance for Democracy and Progress-Zaman Lahiya (*Alliance Nigérienne pour la Démocratie et le Progrès-Zaman Lahiya*—ANDP-*Zaman Lahiya*). On August 28, 1992, ANDP-*Zaman Lahiya* vice president Birgi RAFFINI, a former Saibou government official, was arrested during an army crackdown on suspected FLAA rebels and sympathizers. He was released in early 1993, and his party won 11 seats in legislative balloting that February. ANDP-*Zaman Lahiya*'s candidate, Moumouni Adamou Djermakoye, secured only 15 percent of the vote in the first round of presidential balloting, but his support for the CDS-*Rahama*'s Ousmane was described as pivotal to Ousmane's presidential victory. In April Djermakoye was named National Assembly president. The party's legislative representation fell to 9 seats in January 1995.

In the July 1996 presidential balloting Djermakoye received only 4.77 percent of the vote, finishing last in the five-candidate field. The ANDP-*Zaman Lahiya* was the only major party not to boycott the November 1996 elections, in which it secured eight seats.

In 1998 the ANDP-*Zaman Lahiya* joined the PUND-*Salama* and the PNA (see below) to form a pro-Maïnassara group called the Alliance of Democratic Social Forces (*Alliance des Forces Démocratiques et Sociales*—AFDS). Djermakoye won 7.7 percent of the votes in the first round of presidential balloting in 1999 and endorsed Mahamadou Issoufou of the PNDS-*Tarayya* in the second round. The ANDP-*Zaman Lahiya* agreed to join the progovernment Alliance of Democratic Forces in 2002.

In 2004 presidential candidate Djermakoye received only 6.1 percent of the vote in the first round of balloting, the fifth of six candidates. Since his party belonged to the ruling coalition, his support in the second round likely went to Tandja. ANDP-*Zaman Lahiya* won five seats in the assembly election of 2004.

Despite his support for the president in the past, Djermakoye warned in 2009 that the country "will be split in two" if the president's proposed constitutional referendum were approved. Djermakoye died as he was about to address an opposition rally in June.

The party failed to win seats in the October 2009 parliamentary election. In January 2010 a divided party elected Kindo HAMANI as its interim leader. However, a former MNSD member, Amadou BAGNOU, appeared on television a day later, claiming to be the party's president. In July, Moussa Moumouni Djermakoye, brother of the deceased party leader, was elected party president. He subsequently represented the party in the 2011 presidential election, in which he finished sixth in the first round, with 4 percent of the vote. He backed Issoufou in the second round. The party won eight seats in the 2011 parliamentary election.

Leader: Moussa Moumouni DJERMAKOYE (President and 2011 presidential candidate).

Other legislative parties, include the **Union of Independent Nigeriens** (UNI), led by Amadou Djibo ALI.

Other Parties That Contested the 2011 Elections:

Rally for Social Democracy-Gaskiya (*Rassemblement pour Sociale Democrate-Gaskiya*—RSD-*Gaskiya*). The RSD-*Gaskiya* split off from CDS in January 2004. Amadou Cheiffou, a former transitional prime minister from 1991 to 1993 and party founder, ran as an independent presidential candidate in 2004, receiving only 6.3 percent of the vote in the first round of balloting. However, the new party did win seven seats in the assembly and subsequent representation in the cabinet of President Tandje.

In 2009 the RSD-*Gaskiya* was one of only a few parties that supported President Tandja's plan for a constitutional referendum with the aim of ending presidential term limits. The party won 15 seats in the October assembly elections.

Leaders: Amadou CHEIFFOU (Former Prime Minister and 2004 presidential candidate), Mahamadou Ali TCHÉMOGO (Secretary General).

Another party that participated in the 2011 elections was the **Alliance for Democratic Renewal** (*Alliance pour le Renouveau Démocratique-Adaltchi-Mutunchi*—ARD-*Adaltchi-Mutunchi*), led by presidential candidate Issoufou Ousmane OUBANDAWAKI.

Other Parties:

Niger Party for Self-Management (*Parti Nigérien pour l'Autogestion-Al Ouma*—PNA-*Al Ouma*). Former CDS vice chair Sanoussi Jackou formed the PNA in early 1997. It supported Mamadou Tandja in the 1999 presidential balloting despite its previous affiliation with the AFDS. Chair Jackou received a four-month suspended prison sentence in May 2002 after he was accused of slander and inciting racial hatred. In January 2005 he was released after serving a one-month prison sentence for insulting an ethnic group during a radio broadcast.

In the 2004 legislative elections the PNA was allied in various coalitions along with PNDS-*Tarayya*.

Ahead of the 2009 elections the party participated in protests organized by the umbrella Front for Defense of Democracy (FDD) against President Tandja's constitutional referendum. The party contested the October parliamentary elections alone and won one seat.

Leader: Sanoussi JACKOU.

Nigerien Democratic Front-Mutunci (*Front Démocratique Nigerien-Mutunci*—FDN-*Mutunci*). The launching of the FDN-*Mutunci* in late January 1995 represented a redefinition of the Nigerien Progressive Party (*Parti Progressiste Nigerien*—PPN), which had previously operated as the local section of the African Democratic Rally (*Rassemblement Démocratique Africaine*—RDA) under the PPN/RDA rubric. The new name was adopted shortly after the group withdrew from the AFC, as it was being increasingly dominated by CDS-*Rahama*. The platform advanced by the FDN-*Mutunci* calls for the "preservation" of Niger's sovereignty and the "strengthening of national cohesion." The party won one seat in the January 1995 balloting and none in November 1996.

Ide OUMAROU was elected chair of FDN-*Mutunci* at a party congress in October 1998. Thereafter, he announced that the group (still widely referred to as the PPN/RDA) would align itself with parties supporting President Maïnassara. It ran in coalition with smaller parties for the 2004 assembly elections (see Legislature, below).

Former party chair Ide Oumarou died in February 2002. At the time of his death he had been vying with RDA leader Abdoulaye Hamani DIORI, son of the country's first president, to be chair of the party. In 2004 the PPN/RDA contested the assembly elections in separate alliances with the PNDS-*Tarayya* and with the PNDS-*Tarayya* and the PNA-*Al Ouma*.

Diori opposed President Tandja's attempt to extend his term by amending the constitution prior to the 2010 coup, and in the 2011 presidential election, Diori backed Issoufou. On April 7 he was appointed as special counsel to the president in the new government, but he died at age 65 on April 25.

Leaders: Dan Dicko DANKOLODO (Former Chair), Oumarou Garba YOUSSOUFOU (1993 presidential candidate), Léopold KAZIENDE.

Union of Popular Forces for Democracy and Progress–Sawaba (*Union des Forces Populaires pour la Démocratie et le Progrès–Sawaba*—UFPDP-*Sawaba*). The UFPDP-*Sawaba* is an offshoot of the UDN-*Sawaba*. It was led by Djibo Bakary, a 74-year-old former prime minister and former opponent of President Diori, from May 1957 to December 1958. He was unanimously elected party president in February 1992. Running on a platform calling for national unity and increased dialogue with the Tuareg rebels, Bakary captured 1.68 percent of the presidential vote in February 1993. The party lost both of its former legislative seats in January 1995 and was equally unsuccessful in the November 1996 balloting. Bakary died in 1998.

The UFPDP-*Sawaba* supported Mamadou Tandja in the 1999 presidential poll and was rewarded with a cabinet seat in the January 2000 government. However, the UFPDP-*Sawaba* minister, Issoufou Assoumane, was not reappointed in the September 2001 reshuffle; he formed a new political party in 2001 called the **Union of Nigerien Democrats and Socialists** (*Union des démocrates et socialistes nigériens*—UDSN-*Talaka*), which in 2009 opposed President Tandja's plans to hold a constitutinal referendum.

Union for Democracy and Social Progress–Amana *(Union pour la Démocratie et le Progrès Social–Amana*—UDPS-*Amana*). On August 28, 1992, (then) UDPS-*Amana* leader Akoli Daouel was imprisoned during the army's crackdown on suspected Tuareg dissidents. He was released in 1993 and later joined the PUND-*Salama*.

A deadly grenade attack on a UDPS-*Amana* meeting at Agades in October 1994 was blamed on Tuaregs angered by ongoing negotiations with the government. Thereafter, in the legislative balloting of January 1995, the party doubled its parliamentary representation to two seats.

Although technically an opposition grouping, the UDPS-*Amana* was awarded a cabinet portfolio by Prime Minister Amadou in February 1995. However, under pressure from opposition allies, who termed the appointment "regrettable," the minister was expelled from the party. The UDPS-*Amana* won three seats in the November 1996 assembly elections. Rhissa ag Boula, formerly with the ORA, joined the UDPS-*Amana* in August 2005. President Tandja met with Boula a few times in 2006 to discuss ways to prevent the Tuareg uprisings in neighboring Mali from spilling over into Niger. In a televised debate in 2007 Rhissa ag Boula expressed concerns over what he described as the "increasing anti-Tuareg xenophobia" and the government's failures to follow through on all aspects of the 1995 peace agreement.

Though he had been involved in the peace process in 2009, Rhissa ag Boula rejoined an MNJ faction abroad, known as the **Front of Forces for Rectification** (*Front des forces de redressement*—FFR). He was arrested and imprisoned by the junta upon his return to Niger following the February 2010 coup.

Leaders: Almoctar ICHA, Mohamed ABDULLAHI, Mohamed MOUSSAL, Rhissa ag BOULA.

Other parties were the **Rally of Nigerien Patriots-*Al Kalami***, founded in May 2009 by Ousmane Issoufou OUBANDAWAKI; the **Workers' Movement Party-*Albarka***—PMT-*Albarka*, led by Abdoulkarim MAMALO; and the **Revolutionary-Social Democracy** party (*Mouvement Socio-Révolutionnaire pour la Démocratie-Damana*—MSRD-*Damana*), led by Ibrahima Saidou MAIGA.

For a listing of minor parties dating to the early 2000s, see earlier editions of the *Handbook*. For more information on the **Nigerien Social Democratic Party–Alheri** (*Parti Social Démocrate du Niger–Alhéri*—PSDN-*Alhéri*), the **Front for the Liberation of Tamoust** (*Front pour la Libération de Tamoust*—FLT), and the **Party for National Unity and Development–Salama** (*Parti pour l'Unité Nationale et la Développement–Salama*—PUND-*Salama*), see the 2013 *Handbook*.

Former Rebel Groups:

Organization of the Armed Resistance (*Organisation de la Résistance Armée*—ORA). ORA emerged in March 1995 upon the temporary demise of the CRA when the FLAA withdrew from the coalition (see below). Successful implementation of a final peace agreement, signed by Rhissa ag Boula on behalf of the ORA on April 25, 1995, was viewed as depending on the resolution of differences between the FLAA and CRA chair Mano Dayak. In June the ORA denounced the inclusion of the so-called "self-defense" groups in the proposed amnesty, arguing that the groups were responsible for attacks on Tuareg civilians.

At the end of 1996 the FPLS and the ARLN reportedly left ORA to join the new UFRA (below) in an attempt to "rationalize" the Tuareg leadership situation. At that point it was not clear if Boula's FLAA would maintain the ORA structure, as FLAA appeared to be the dominant, and perhaps only, component in the ORA. Furthermore, the FLAA also appeared to have distanced itself from the 1995 accord. Such concerns were at least temporarily eased in September 1996 when the ORA reportedly integrated a number of its fighters into the government's newly formed "peacekeeping detachment." (In 1998 the ORA and the CRA turned in their weapons when parliament granted amnesty to the rebel groups in March.) In 1997 Boula was named to the Mayaki government. He remained in the new governments announced in January 2000 and September 2001, but was dismissed from his post as tourism minister in the Tandja government on February 13, 2004. Boula was then arrested and jailed for his alleged involvement in the assassination of a militant member of the ruling party, MNSD-*Nassara,* in January (see FLAA, below). He was released in March 2005, allegedly after his brother, rebel leader Mohamed ag Boula (see below), claimed he would not release four kidnapped soldiers until his brother was freed. (The hostages returned home in February 2005 after Libya helped secure their release.) Rhissa ag Boula left the ORA in August 2005 and became a leader of the UDPS-*Amana*; he was reported to be living in exile in France. In 2008 he was sentenced to death in absentia by a Nigerien court for the alleged assassination plot dating to 2004. (See Union for Democracy and Social Progress-*Amana*, above.)

Leader: Attaher ABDOULMOUMINE.

Popular Front for the Liberation of the Sahara (*Front Populaire pour la Libération de la Sahara*—FPLS). The FPLS was launched on January 28, 1994, by Mohamed Anako and Issad Kato, who pledged to cooperate with existing Tuareg groups. In April 1999, Anako was reportedly appointed minister without portfolio and special adviser to head of state Maj. Daouda Wanké, a move some observers said was meant to avert further violence following Wanké's ascension after the assassination of President Maïnassara. Issad Kato, who had reestablished relations with the government, was named animal resources minister in 2007. Mohamed Anako in 2007 headed the Nigerien Commission for Peace, which called for dialogue with the Tuareg rebels, and was said to be an adviser to President Tandja.

Coordination of Armed Resistance (*Coordination de la Résistance Armée*—CRA). Originally formed in January 1994 by the FLAA, FPLS, ARLN, and FLT (below), the CRA met in Tenere in early February to elect an executive bureau and draft a platform calling for the creation of an autonomous Tuareg territory and Tuareg representation in the armed forces, government, and National Assembly. The coalition participated in talks with the government in Ouagadougou, Burkina Faso, in late February and in Paris in June, which ultimately resulted in a preliminary peace accord on October 9.

The CRA splintered in March 1995 following a disagreement between FLAA leader Boula and CRA chair Mano Dayak over the latter's approach to renewed peace negotiations. Immediately thereafter, Boula reorganized the CRA members, including the Dayak-led FLT, under the ORA banner; however, in June the FLT withdrew from the coalition. In July Dayak announced that he had revived the CRA; he would no longer respect the peace agreement and further negotiations would have to include his new Toubou and Arab allies (below).

In October 1995 FLT militants were accused of violating the peace accord; however, Dayak continued to negotiate with the government, and CRA officials pledged to proceed with peace talks following his death in a plane crash in December. Thereafter, at a summit of the leaders of the Tuareg and Toubou fronts in Kawar on March 8, 1996, the CRA agreed to recognize the 1995 peace accord and joined the others in declaring a unilateral cease-fire as a sign of support for the military regime. Consequently, the junta offered to include the CRA in its "application" of the treaty, and the group signed the accord on April 2.

A split between the CRA and the ORA was reported in November 1996, with the emergence of the new UFRA. Included in the "new" CRA were a number of Toubou and Arab autonomous movements based in the southeast who had complained of being ignored by the peace process.

Leaders: Mohamed AOUTCHEKI Kriska (FLT), Mohammed AKOTE.

Democratic Renewal Front (*Front Démocratique pour le Renouvellement*—FDR). The FDR surfaced in May 1994 in the Lake Chad region under the leadership of Cpl. Ahmed Mohammed, a Nigerien who had served in the Libyan army. A militant group of members from the Arab Choa, Toubou, and Kanouri ethnic groups (who Mohammed claimed had been excluded from the greater Tuareg movement), the FDR professed dedication to "conducting the political and military battle" necessary to bring about the "annihilation" of the present governing system. The FDR's platform also advocated the division of Niger into federal states with boundaries conforming to "geographical and social reality."

In the first half of 1995 the FDR's clashes with government and Tuareg forces reportedly left over 40 people dead. At the same time, the group called attempts to implement the April 1995 peace accord the "facade of democracy" and urged Niamey to recognize their demands for autonomy. FDR/government clashes continued throughout 1996 and 1997.

In August 1998 the FDR signed a peace accord with the government, and party spokesperson Issa Lamine was named to the cabinet in January 2000.

Leaders: Cpl. Ahmed MOHAMMED, Mamane KODELAMI Ali, Goukouni ZENE, Issa LAMINE (Spokesperson).

Rebel Groups:

Armed Revolutionary Forces of the Sahara (*Forces Armées Révolutionnaires de la Sahara*—FARS). The primarily Toubou and Arab FARS gained international attention in February 1997 for kidnapping a Canadian aid worker and three Nigerien security officials in an effort to dramatize demands for an inquiry into the death of 14 FARS fighters in a clash with government forces the month before. Following peaceful resolution of that crisis, the FARS signed a cease-fire agreement with the government in June; however, that accord proved short-lived, and the FARS was subsequently reported to have formed an alliance with the UFRA before the latter grouping disarmed in 1998. In September 2001 the government launched a major crackdown that, among other things, resulted in the death of a FARS leader, Chahayi BARKAYE. In an effort to establish peace, France agreed to help finance the reintegration of some 250 FARS rebels into the northern region of Bilma.

FARS reemerged in 2006 when the group kidnapped and later released 11 tourists in protest against what the group claimed was the ongoing marginalization of the Toubous.

Leaders: Barka OUARDOUGOU, Boubacar Mohamed SOGOMA.

Movement of Nigeriens for Justice (*Mouvement des Nigériens pour la Justice*—MNJ). The Tuareg rebel group was not widely known until after it launched an attack against an army post near the northern town of Iferouane in February 2007. Following a series of attacks over the next several months against army installations, uranium mining sites, Red Cross convoys, and a northern airport, for which the MNJ claimed responsibility, the government refused to acknowledge the group's existence, instead blaming "bandits" and "drug traffickers." The MNJ accused the government of not upholding the tenets of the 1995 peace agreement with the Tuaregs, and called for more economic development in the north, including more equitable distribution of uranium profits; greater representation of Tuaregs in the government, the army, and the police; and government recognition of the MNJ (see Current issues, above). The MNJ reported in mid-2007 that some 700 army deserters had joined its group, including one high-ranking officer. It also claimed to have drawn support from Arabs, Fulani, and Toubou, as well as Tuaregs in Mali, the latter forming a group called the Niger-Mali Tuareg Alliance. In 2008 MNJ leaders stepped up their attacks, including strikes against uranium and oil interests. In June it was reported that MNJ vice president Mohamed Acharif had been killed by Nigerien soldiers. Throughout the year, the group continued to engage in fighting with government forces, but in September the rebels agreed to lay down their arms in a peace deal negotiated by Libya's leader Muammar al-Qadhafi.

Leaders: Agali ag ALAMBO (President), Moktar ROMAN (Spokesperson).

LEGISLATURE

The unicameral **National Assembly** (*Assemblée Nationale*) was enlarged from 83 to 113 members in 2003, based on an increase of nearly 3 million in the country's population between 1998 and 2001. Members are directly elected for five-year terms: 105 from 8 multi-member constituencies using a proportional representation system, and the remainder from single-member constituencies using a first-past-the-post system.

The assembly elected in January 1995 was dissolved by the National Salvation Council on January 27, 1996, and replaced on March 27 by a 600-member transitional body known as the National Forum for Democratic Renewal, which included former assemblymen as well as members of various advisory groups supportive of the new military regime. Balloting for a new assembly was held on November 23, though it was boycotted by most major opposition groups.

On April 10, 1999, Prime Minister Mayaki suspended the assembly in the wake of the assassination of President Maïnassara. Balloting to refill the body was held on November 24, 1999.

In balloting on October 20, 2009, the National Movement for a Developing Society–Victory won an overwhelming majority of seats. Parliament was dissolved following the military coup of February 18, 2010. The new constitution promulgated in November restored a unicameral parliament.

Following the most recent election on January 31, 2011, the seat distribution was as follows: Nigerien Party for Democracy and Socialism—*Tarayya,* 34; National Movement for a Developing Society—Victory, 25; Nigerien Democratic Movement for an African Federation—*Lumana,* 23; Nigerien Alliance for Democracy and Progress—*Zaman Lahiya,* 8; Democratic Rally of the People—*Jamaa,* 7; Union for Democracy and the Republic—*Tabbat,* 6; Democratic and Social Convention—*Rahama,* 3; and Union of Independent Nigeriens, 1. Six seats were nullified due to irregularities.

Speaker: Hama AMADOU.

CABINET

[as of August 15, 2013]

President	Mahamadou Issoufou
Prime Minister	Brigi Rafini
Council of Ministers	
Civil Service and Administrative Reform	Laoulai Chaibou
Commerce and Promotion of the Private Sector	Alma Oumarou (MNSD)
Communications, Information Technology in Charge of Relations with Institutions	Yahouza Salissou
Culture, Arts, and Leisure	Oumane Abdou
Employment, Labor, and Social Security	Salissou Ada
Environment, Urban Health, and Sustainable Development	Ada Cheiffou
Equipment	Ibrahim Nomaou
Finance	Gilles Bayet
Government Spokesman	Marou Amadou
Handicrafts and Tourism	Hadiza Oumarou Tchani [f]
Higher Education and Scientific Research	Soumana Sanda (MODEN-*Lumana* FA/Niger)
Interior, Public Security, Decentralization, and Religious and Customary Affairs	Massaoudou Hassoumi
Justice and Keeper of the Seals	Marou Amadou
Land Management and Community Development	Mamane Sani Mallam Mamane (MODEN-*Lumana* FA/Niger)
Livestock	Mahamane Elhadj Ousmane
Petroleum and Energy	Foumakoye Gado (PNDS-*Tarayya*)
National Defense	Karidjo Mahamadou
National Education, Literacy, and Promotion of National Languages	Ali Mariama Elhadj Ibrahim [f]
Office of the President	Saidou Sidibé
Professional Education and Employment	Chaibou Dan Ina
Population, Promotion of Women and Protection of Children	Maikibi Kadidiatou Dan Dobi [f]
Posts, Telecommunications, and the Digital Economy	Abdou Mani
Public Health	Manou Aghali (MODEN-*Lumana* FA/Niger)
Secondary Education	Beity Aichatou Habibou Oumani [f]

Transport	Saley Seydou
Urban Affairs, Housing, and Sanitation	Habi Mahamane Salissou (MNSD)
Water and the Environment	Wassalké Boukary (MNSD)
Youth, Sports, and Culture	Abdoulkarim Dan Mallam
Ministers of State	
Agriculture	Abdou Labo (CDS-*Rahama*)
Foreign Affairs, Cooperation, African Integration, and Niger Citizens Abroad	Mohamed Bazoum (PNDS-*Tarayya*)
Mines and Industrial Development	Omar Hamidou Tchiana
Planning, Land Management, and Community Development	Amadou Boubacar Cissé
Presidency	Alabadé Abouba (MNSD)

[f] = female

INTERGOVERNMENTAL REPRESENTATION

Ambassador to the U.S.: Maman Sambo SIDIKOU.

U.S. Ambassador to Niger: Bisa WILLIAMS.

Permanent Representative to the UN: Baboucar BOUREIMA.

IGO Memberships (Non-UN): AfDB, AU, ECOWAS, IOM, NAM, OIC, WTO.

NIGERIA

Federal Republic of Nigeria

Political Status: Independent member of the Commonwealth since 1960; republic established in 1963; civilian government suspended as the result of military coups in January and July 1966; executive presidential system established under constitution effective October 1, 1979; under military rule following successive coups of December 31, 1983, and August 27, 1985; constitution of Third Republic promulgated May 3, 1989; existing state organs dissolved following military takeover of November 17, 1993; 1979 constitution restored and Provisional Ruling Council established on November 21, 1993; current constitution entered into effect May 29, 1999, with installation of new civilian government.

Area: 356,667 sq. mi. (923,768 sq. km).

Population: 167,273,730 (2012E—UN); 174,507,539 (2013E—U.S. Census).

Major Urban Centers (2006C): ABUJA (776,298), Lagos (7,937,932), Kano (2,163,225), Ibadan (1,338,659), Port Harcourt (1,382,592), Benin City (1,147,188), Kaduna (760,084).

Official Language: English (the leading indigenous languages are Hausa, Igbo, and Yoruba).

Monetary Unit: Naira (official rate November 1, 2013: 158.73 naira = $1US).

President: Goodluck JONATHAN (People's Democratic Party); appointed acting president on February 9, 2010; sworn in as president on May 6 to serve out the remainder of the term of Umaru Musa YAR'ADUA (People's Democratic Party), who died in office on May 5; elected on April 16, 2011, and sworn in for a four-year-term on May 29.

Vice President: Namadi SAMBO (People's Democratic Party); appointed on May 13, 2010, and sworn in on May 19 to succeed Goodluck JONATHAN (People's Democratic Party) who was appointed president on May 6; reelected for a term concurrent with that of the president on April 16, 2011.

THE COUNTRY

The most populous country in Africa and one of the most richly endowed in natural resources, Nigeria extends from the inner corner of the Gulf of Guinea to the border of Niger in the north and to Lake Chad in the northeast. Included within its boundaries is the northern section of the former United Nations Trust Territory of British Cameroons, whose inhabitants voted to join Nigeria in a UN–sponsored plebiscite in 1961. Nigeria's topography ranges from swampy lowland along the coast, through tropical rain forest and open plateau country, to semidesert conditions in the far north. The ethnic pattern is similarly varied, with tribal groups speaking more than 250 languages. The Hausa, Fulani, and other Islamic peoples in the north; the mixed Christian and Islamic Yoruba in the west; and the predominantly Christian Ibo in the east are the most populous groups. Nearly half the population is Muslim, with 40 percent Christian and the remainder adhering to traditional religious practices. Numerous traditional rulers retain considerable influence, particularly in rural areas. Women are responsible for the bulk of subsistence farming, and their participation in the paid work force (about 36 percent) is concentrated in sales and crafts. Following the 2011 legislative elections, women held 24 out of 352 seats (6.8 percent) in the House of Representatives and 7 out of 109 (6.4 percent) in the Senate.

Nigeria's natural resources include petroleum and natural gas, hydroelectric power, and commercially exploitable deposits of tin, coal, and columbite. Oil production of 2.5–2.7 million barrels per day accounts for an estimated 95 percent of exports and provides 80 percent of the government's revenue; some 60–90 percent of Nigerian crude, considered ideal for gasoline production, is exported to the United States. The leading cash crops are cocoa, peanuts, palm products, and cotton, with timber and fish also important.

High oil prices provided significant additional resources in 2004–2005 for the government, which, among other things, established a $6 billion "emergency fund" (for an overview of the Nigerian economy prior to 2004, see the 2013 *Handbook*). Late in the year, the Paris Club of creditor nations accepted an agreement under which Nigeria could fulfill its obligation to them by paying only $12 billion of the $30 billion owed. In April 2006 Nigeria made its final payment to the Paris Club.

GDP rose by an average of 11 percent per year between 2000 and 2008 (primarily as a result of higher oil prices and significant growth in the non-oil sector), while inflation averaged 12.3 percent and unemployment 20 percent. A modest increase in foreign investment also contributed to the improved economic outlook, as did significant advances in the telecommunication and financial sectors. However, intensified antigovernment activity in the oil-rich Niger Delta subsequently continued to constrain oil production, while most analysts concluded that corruption remained entrenched throughout all levels of government and business, hampering efforts to reduce the 70 percent poverty level. In 2008 the government began to implement IMF-recommended reforms to the banking and fuel sectors. In 2009 Nigeria conducted an audit of the nation's 24 major banks and found 10 were significantly undercapitalized, prompting the central bank to put more than $6 billion into the institutions to keep them solvent (see Current issues, below). In May 2010 the World Bank agreed to loan Nigeria $915 million for infrastructure improvements, while a $23 billion oil investment deal to build new refineries was finalized between Nigeria and China. In 2012 GDP rose by 6.3 percent and inflation increased by 12.2 percent. Estimates were that the unemployment rate exceeded 22 percent. GDP per capita was $1,555 that year. In 2012 Nigeria announced an ambitious program to expand oil production to 4 million barrels per day (see Current issues, below). However, reports indicated in 2013 that as much as 400,000 barrels per day were lost to theft or waste and that as much as $100 billion in oil revenues had been illicitly diverted since 2002. In its 2013 Doing Business survey, the World Bank ranked Nigeria 131st out of 185 countries in terms of conducting commerce.

GOVERNMENT AND POLITICS

Political background. Brought under British control during the 19th century, Nigeria was organized as a British colony and protectorate

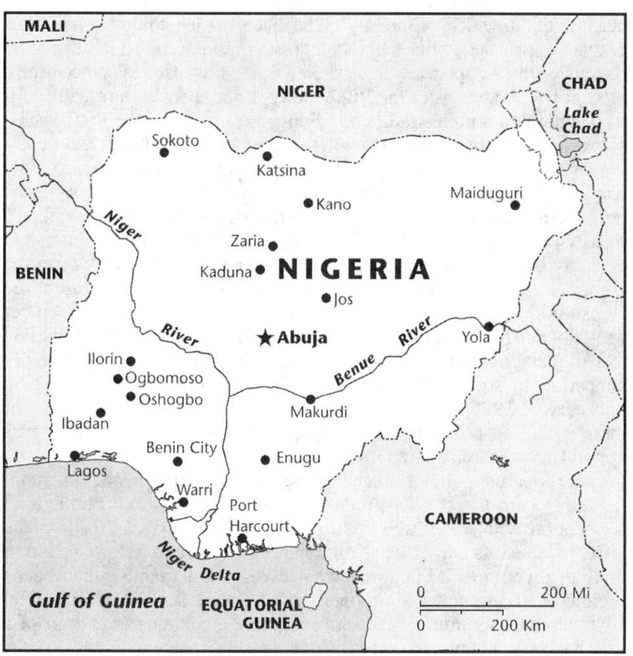

in 1914, became a self-governing federation in 1954, and achieved independence within the Commonwealth on October 1, 1960. Under the guidance of its first prime minister, Sir Abubaker Tafawa BALEWA, Nigeria became a republic three years later, with the former governor general, Dr. Nnamdi AZIKIWE of the Ibo tribe, as president. The original federation consisted of three regions (northern, western, and eastern); a fourth region (the midwestern) was created in 1963.

Independent Nigeria experienced underlying tensions resulting from ethnic, religious, and regional cleavages. Weakened by strife and tainted by corruption, the federal government was overthrown on January 15, 1966, in a coup that cost the lives of Prime Minister Balewa and other northern political leaders and resulted in the establishment of a Supreme Military Council (SMC) headed by Maj. Gen. Johnson T. U. AGUIYI-IRONSI, the Ibo commander of the army. Resentment on the part of northern Muslims toward the predominantly Ibo leadership and its subsequent attempt to establish a unitary state resulted on July 29 in a second coup, led by a northerner, Col. (later Gen.) Yakubu GOWON. Events surrounding the first coup had already raised ethnic hostility to the boiling point, and thousands of Ibo who had settled in the north were massacred before and after the second coup, while hundreds of thousands began a mass flight back to their homeland at the urging of eastern leaders.

Subsequent plans for a constitutional revision that would calm Ibo apprehensions while preserving the unity of the country were blocked by the refusal of the Eastern Region's military governor, Lt. Col. Odumegwu OJUKWU, to accept anything less than complete regional autonomy. Attempts at conciliation having failed, Colonel Gowon, as head of the federal military government, announced his assumption of emergency powers and the reorganization of Nigeria's four regions into 12 states on May 28, 1967. Intended to equalize treatment of various areas and ethnic groups throughout the country, the move was also designed to increase the influence of the Eastern Region's non-Ibo inhabitants. The Eastern Region responded on May 30 by declaring independence as the Republic of Biafra, with Ojukwu as head of state. Refusing to recognize the secession, the federal government initiated hostilities against Biafra on July 6. Peace plans were subsequently proposed by London, the Commonwealth, and the Organization of African Unity (OAU, subsequently the African Union—AU). However, Ojukwu rejected them repeatedly on the ground that they failed to guarantee Biafra's future as a "sovereign and independent state." Limited external support, mainly from France, began to arrive in late 1968 and enabled Biafra to continue fighting despite the loss of most non-Ibo territory, massive casualties, and a growing threat of mass starvation. A series of military defeats in late 1969 and early 1970 finally resulted in surrender of the rebel forces on January 15, 1970.

The immediate postwar period was one of remarkable reconciliation, as General Gowon moved to reintegrate Ibo elements into Nigerian life. Not only were Ibo brought back into the civil service and the military, but the federal government also launched a major reconstruction of the devastated eastern area. Normal political life remained suspended, however, and on July 29, 1975, while Gowon was attending an OAU meeting in Kampala, Uganda, his government was overthrown in a bloodless coup led by Brig. (later Gen.) Murtala Ramat MUHAMMAD. In October the SMC charged a 50-member committee with drafting a new constitution that would embrace an "executive presidential system."

General Muhammad was assassinated on February 13, 1976, during an abortive coup apparently provoked by his campaign to wipe out widespread government corruption. He was succeeded as head of state and chair of the SMC by Lt. Gen. (later Gen.) Olusegun OBASANJO, who had been chief of staff of the armed forces since the 1975 coup.

A National Constituent Assembly met in 1977 to consider the constitution proposed by the committee established two years earlier. The assembly endorsed a draft on June 5, 1978, although the SMC made a number of changes before the new basic law was promulgated on September 21, at which time Nigeria's 12-year-old state of emergency was terminated and the ban on political parties was lifted.

Elections were contested in mid-1979 by five parties that had been approved by the Federal Electoral Commission (Fedeco) as being sufficiently national in representation. Balloting commenced on July 7 for the election of federal senators and continued, on successive weekends, with the election of federal representatives, state legislators, and state governors, culminating on August 11 with the election of Alhaji Shehu SHAGARI and Dr. Alex EKWUEME of the National Party of Nigeria (NPN) as federal president and vice president, respectively. Following judicial resolution of a complaint that the NPN candidates had not obtained a required 25 percent of the vote in 13 of the 19 states, the two leaders were inaugurated on October 1.

By 1983 public confidence in the civilian regime had waned in the face of sharply diminished oil income, massive government overspending, and widespread evidence of official corruption. Nonetheless, the personally popular Shagari easily won reelection in the presidential balloting of August 4. Subsequent rounds of the five-week election process, marred by evidence of electoral fraud and by rioting in Oyo and Ondo states, left the ruling NPN in control of 13 state houses, 13 governorships, and both houses of the National Constituent Assembly. However, the economy continued to decline after the balloting, with an austerity budget adopted in November further deepening public discontent. On December 31 a group of senior military officers (most of whom had served under Obasanjo) seized power. On January 3, 1984, Maj. Gen. Muhammadu BUHARI, formerly Obasanjo's oil minister, was sworn in as chair of a new SMC, which launched a "war against indiscipline," reintroduced the death penalty, and established several special tribunals that moved vigorously in convicting numerous individuals, including leading politicians, of embezzlement and other offenses.

In the wake of increasing political repression and a steadily worsening economy, Major General Buhari and his armed forces chief of staff, Maj. Gen. Tunde IDIAGBON, were deposed by senior members of the SMC on August 27, 1985. The ensuing administration, headed by Maj. Gen. (later Gen.) Ibrahim BABANGIDA as chair of a new Armed Forces Ruling Council (AFRC), abolished a number of decrees limiting press freedom, released numerous political detainees, and initially adopted a more open style of government that included the solicitation of public opinion on future political development. However, there was a countercoup attempt late in the year by a group of disgruntled officers, several of whom were executed in March 1986.

In September 1987 the Babangida regime announced a five-year transition to civilian government, including the promulgation of a new constitution, lifting of the ban on political parties in 1989, gubernatorial and state legislative elections in 1990, and federal legislative and presidential elections in 1992. To guard against tribal and religious fractionalization, the AFRC adopted the recommendation of a university-dominated "Political Bureau" that only two political parties be sanctioned. Late in 1987 Babangida announced that most former and current leaders, including himself and the rest of the AFRC, would be barred from running in forthcoming elections. Local nonparty elections were held on December 12, 1987; however, many of the results from that poll were invalidated, and further balloting was conducted on March 26, 1988.

In May 1989 General Babangida lifted the ban on party politics, calling on parties to register with the National Electoral Commission (NEC) and announcing details of a draft constitution that had been presented to him in April by the National Constituent Assembly. Although more than 50 parties were reportedly interested in securing recognition, a short enrollment period and a complex application process limited the number of actual petitioners to 13, 6 of which were subsequently recommended to the AFRC for further reduction to 2. However, on October 7, amid reports of the arrest of members of "illegal" parties, Babangida cited "factionalism" and "failing marks" on preregistration examinations as reasons for dissolving all 13 parties and substituting in their place the regime-sponsored Social Democratic Party (SDP) and National Republican Convention (NRC).

In January 1990 General Babangida canceled state visits to Italy and the United States in the wake of widespread unrest provoked by a December 29 reshuffle of senior military and civilian officials. The tension culminated in a coup attempt on April 22 in Lagos by middle-ranked army officers, with at least 30 persons being killed in heavy fighting. On August 30 General Babangida announced another extensive cabinet reshuffle and the appointment of Vice Admiral Augustus AIKHOMU to the newly created position of vice president of the republic. Shortly thereafter, in furtherance of General Babangida's plan to "demilitarize" politics, Aikhomu and a number of other senior government leaders retired from military service, while ten military state governors were replaced by civilian deputies pending the upcoming gubernatorial elections. Meanwhile, organization of the SDP and NRC continued under stringent government supervision, with two-party local elections being held on December 8.

Neither of the parties secured a clear advantage in the 1990 local poll or in gubernatorial and state assembly elections in December 1991, although the SDP won control of both the Senate and House of Representatives in National Constituent Assembly balloting on July 4, 1992. Party presidential primaries (on August 7 and again on September 12, 19, and 26) were invalidated on grounds of widespread irregularities, with presidential balloting originally slated for December 5 being rescheduled to June 1993. Concurrently, General Babangida announced that the AFRC would be replaced by a National Defense and Security Council (NDSC) and that the existing Council of Ministers would be abolished in favor of a civilian Transitional Council to pave the way for the planned installation of a new government in August 1993. On December 15, 1992, Chief Ernest Adegunle SHONEKAN was named to chair the Transitional Council, which, along with the NDSC, was formally installed on January 4, 1993.

The long-delayed presidential balloting was held on June 12, 1993, with the SDP candidate, reputed billionaire Moshood Kashimawo Olawale ("MKO") ABIOLA, appearing to be the winner over the NRC's Bashir Othma TOFA. However, on June 16 the NEC bowed to a court order restraining it from announcing the outcome. The two parties thereupon agreed to form an interim coalition government if General Babangida would authorize a return to civilian rule by the previously agreed upon date of August 27. The general's response being negative, serious rioting erupted in Lagos on July 5, followed by the announcement that a new election, from which the earlier candidates would be excluded, would take place on July 31. Not surprisingly, this plan was scuttled, with Babangida naming Shonekan as head of an Interim National Government (ING) before stepping down as president on August 26. On September 19 the NEC announced that new presidential and local elections would be held on February 19, 1994. However, on November 10 the Federal High Court unexpectedly pronounced the ING unconstitutional, and on November 17 Shonekan resigned in favor of a new military administration headed by Defense Minister Sani Abacha, who had long been viewed as the "power behind the throne" of both the Babangida and Shonekan governments. Subsequently, Abacha formally dissolved both the ING and the National Constituent Assembly, banned the SDP and NRC, and, on November 24, announced the formation of a Provisional Ruling Council (PRC) comprising senior military figures and several members of a new cabinet-level Federal Executive Council (FEC).

On April 22, 1994, the Abacha regime outlined the first phase of a political transition program that called for the convening of a constitutional conference to prepare a draft basic law for approval by the PRC. Elections were held nationwide in May to select the conference participants, although the balloting was boycotted by a number of prodemocracy groups as well as organizations representing southern interests. On June 22, 1994, Moshood Abiola, who, based on the 1993 poll, had declared himself president 11 days earlier, emerged from hiding to address a rally in Lagos; he was arrested the following day for treason. On June 27 General Abacha opened a National Constitutional Conference (NCC), which was promptly adjourned for two weeks because of "logistical problems." Subsequently a large number of strikes erupted to protest Abiola's arrest and resumption of the NCC. The most serious of the stoppages was by the oil unions, whose resistance crumbled in late August after the PRC had replaced their leaders with military-appointed administrators. On September 6, 1994, the PRC issued several new decrees that restricted the media and precluded legal challenges to action taken by the regime in regard to "the maintenance of law and order." Further underscoring the regime's hard-line approach, the new 25-member PRC formed on September 27 contained only military officers, even though 4 of the 11 members on the previous council had been civilians. Meanwhile, NCC sessions continued, and in October the conference gave its preliminary endorsement to a draft constitution (see Constitution and government, below). In addition, the NCC in December formally notified the military that the conference expected the transition to a civilian government to be accomplished by January 1, 1996. Initially appearing to support that schedule, the PRC dissolved the FEC on February 8, 1995, so that members of the council could "prepare for their upcoming political careers." However, the new FEC, which was appointed on March 20, reportedly favored an extension of military control, the apparent policy change being attributed to turbulence surrounding the recent arrest of a group of military officers and civilians in connection with an alleged coup plot. Consequently, on April 25 the NCC reversed its earlier decision regarding the deadline for a return to civilian government and approved a new resolution granting the Abacha regime what amounted to an open-ended tenure. As a result, the final NCC report, submitted to Abacha on June 27, contained the draft of a new basic law but no proposed timetable for its implementation.

The international criticism prompted by the apparent retrenchment on democratization (see Current issues in the Nigeria entry in the 2007 *Handbook* for details) intensified sharply when minority rights activist Kenule SARO-WIWA and other members of the Movement for the Survival of the Ogoni People (MOSOP) were hung on November 10, 1995, soon after their conviction on what were perceived outside the government to be highly dubious murder charges. However, the regime angrily rejected what it termed external meddling in its domestic affairs and refused to reevaluate its proposed timetable, which called for the government to turn authority over to an elected civilian government on October 1, 1998.

Consequently, Nigeria entered 1996 regarded internationally as a "pariah state," and developments over the next year did little to alter that situation. The government refused to permit Commonwealth representatives into the country until November and, even then, blocked access to prisoners such as former president Obasanjo (jailed since March 1995 on what most analysts considered spurious coup plot charges) and Mobiola. In addition, following a fact-finding mission to Nigeria in March, the UN Human Rights Committee accused the government, already considered one of the most repressive in Nigeria's history, of a wide range of abuses.

Local elections were held on March 16, 1996, although political parties remained proscribed. The campaign period was limited to only five days, and balloting was conducted by having voters line up behind their preferred candidate, a practice long criticized by prodemocracy activists. Facing ongoing internal and external pressure, the government in June issued regulations for the proposed legalization of a limited number of political parties, five of which were recognized in September, although the initiative elicited only scorn from prodemocracy groups. Six new states were established on October 1, and the government announced that 183 additional municipalities would be created for the next local elections, with balloting to be conducted on a limited multiparty basis.

Two bomb attacks in Lagos killed several soldiers and wounded more than 30 other people in January and February 1997; no groups claimed responsibility. The government subsequently intensified its crackdown on opposition groups, among other things charging Nobel Prize winner Wole SOYINKA (in self-imposed exile) and 14 other dissidents with treason in March. Spokespersons for the regime linked several subsequent attacks to the National Democratic Coalition (NADECO), although impartial observers strongly questioned any such connection and suggested the government was merely attempting to silence some of its more effective critics. Harassment was also reported of journalists who questioned the regime. New local elections were held on March 15, 1997, followed by balloting for state assemblies on December 6. Meanwhile, on November 17 President Abacha announced that the cabinet had been dissolved, a number of incumbent senior ministers being left out of the new government appointed on December 18.

In national legislative elections on April 25, 1998, the United Nigeria Congress Party (UNCP) reportedly captured the majority of the seats. Voter turnout was described as scant (as little as 10 percent in some areas), with many Nigerians apparently heeding the opposition's call for a boycott of the contest. Meanwhile, Abacha was reportedly named as the candidate of all the legal parties for the upcoming presidential election. On June 8 Abacha died of an apparent heart attack, and the following day Gen. Abdulsalam ABUBAKAR was sworn in as his replacement. Opposition militants derided Abubakar's inaugural pledge to adhere to his predecessor's transitional program, and in mid-June government troops forcibly broke up an opposition demonstration. Thereafter, Abubakar approved the release of dozens of political prisoners, and in early July UN Secretary General Kofi Annan announced that the regime was preparing to release all political prisoners, including Abiola, who had reportedly agreed to relinquish his claim to the presidency. However, on July 7 (the eve of his release) Abiola fell ill during a meeting with a high-level U.S. mission and died. On July 8 General Abubakar dissolved the five legal parties as well as the government that had been named by General Abacha. Two weeks later Abubakar called for the creation of an "unfettered" democracy and announced that he would soon release all political prisoners and allow the free formation of political parties. To that end, in early August the regime appointed a 14-member electoral commission, the Independent National Electoral Commission (INEC), which it charged with overseeing a transitional schedule expected to culminate in the return to civilian rule in May 1999. On August 21 Abubakar named a new cabinet, which included only five holdovers from the Abacha government. Four days later, the INEC released an electoral timetable calling for local elections in December, gubernatorial polling in January 1999, and legislative and presidential balloting on February 20 and 27, respectively. Twenty-five political groups applied for provisional legal status between August 27 and September 5, and nine were subsequently registered. However, in local elections in December only three of those parties—the People's Democratic Party (PDP), the All People's Party (APP), and the Alliance for Democracy (AD)—secured the minimum vote tally (at least 5 percent in 24 of the 36 states) required to maintain their legal status and continue on to the next electoral stages. The PDP, under the leadership of General Obasanjo, led all parties in the local balloting with approximately 60 percent of the vote.

In gubernatorial elections held January 9–30, 1999, the PDP once again overwhelmed its competitors, capturing 21 of the 36 state houses (unrest in the state of Bayelsa had forced officials to postpone balloting there from January 9 to January 30). Seeking to prevent further PDP domination, the APP and AD subsequently announced their intention to form an electoral alliance and forward a joint candidate for president. On February 5 the INEC ruled that such an alliance would be illegal; however, faced with an APP/AD threat to boycott further elections, the commission subsequently reversed itself, although it precluded the two groups from using a single symbol on ballot papers.

The PDP won approximately two-thirds of the seats in both the Senate and House of Representatives in poorly attended legislative polling on February 20, 1999. In presidential balloting on February 27, General Obasanjo completed the sweep for the PDP, capturing 62.8 percent of the vote and easily defeating Samuel Oluyemisi ("Olu") FALAE, the APP/AD candidate. International observers asserted that the elections "generally" reflected the "will of the people" but refused to describe them as free and fair because both sides appeared to have tried to rig the balloting. Obasanjo was sworn in on May 29, and on the same day the new constitution (signed by General Abubakar on May 5) also came into effect. On June 28 Obasanjo swore in a new 47-member cabinet, claiming the large size was necessary to represent Nigeria's ethnic and regional diversity. The government included representatives from all 36 states as well as ministers from all three registered parties.

The incoming Obasanjo administration and PDP-dominated legislature confronted economic, political, and social problems of immense proportions in 1999. Among the most pressing issues awaiting the new government were violent political and social unrest in the economically critical oil-producing regions, a decayed infrastructure, and a treasury depleted by corruption. As a first step in his anticorruption program, Obasanjo in June expelled 60 senior military officers and suspended all contracts negotiated by the Abacha government.

Ethnic tensions in the oil-producing Niger Delta escalated throughout the fall of 1999, resulting in the deployment of 2,000 government troops to the state of Bayelsa. Political discord increased significantly in June 2001 when religious and ethnic conflict between Christians and Muslims in the northern state of Bauchi left 1,000 dead. Another 1,000 were killed in continuing violence in the region before the end of the year. One area of dispute involved Muslim efforts to implement sharia (Islamic religious law) in the region. (A dozen northern states instituted sharia, despite opposition from the federal government.) In addition, a series of general strikes by oil workers threatened to disrupt production.

The registration of political parties having begun in 2002, multiparty legislative and presidential elections were held on April 12, 2003. The PDP again won a commanding majority in both the House of Representatives and the Senate, its strongest opposition coming from the All Nigeria People's Party (ANPP), the successor to the APP. Gubernatorial races were also held on April 19, and the PDP secured 29 of the 36 governorships. In addition, the PDP also won about two-thirds of the total seats in the state assemblies in elections held May 3.

President Obasanjo was reelected with 62 percent of the vote in balloting on April 19, 2003, that was contested by 20 candidates. His closest rival was former SMC chair Buhari, with 32 percent; no other candidate received more than 3.5 percent of the vote. Buhari challenged the results, but the federal Court of Appeal ruled in favor of Obasanjo, who was inaugurated on May 29. However, it was not until July 17 that Obasanjo was able to form a new federal government.

President Obasanjo's second term was initially marked by efforts at economic reform and a broad range of anticorruption campaigns, but strikes and other problems in the petroleum sector continued to constrain the government's efforts. On May 18, 2004, because of the escalating violence between Christians and Muslims in the region, Obasanjo declared a state of emergency for Plateau State and ordered the federal government to take control from the state governor and assembly, the first time that the federal government had taken over a state since 1962. A similar state of emergency was also declared in Ekiti in October 2006.

The government convened a National Political Reforms Conference (NPRC) in February 2005 in an effort to ease tensions among the regions. After contentious debate, the conference in April issued a report that called for increased oil revenues to be allocated to southern and eastern regions and rejected the proposed revision of the constitution to permit Obasanjo to run for a third term. The latter issue was permanently put to rest in May 2006 when the Senate blocked an amendment presented by supporters of a third term. (Obasanjo agreed to abide by that ruling.)

The other dominant issue in late 2005 and early 2006 was sustained severe discord in the oil-rich Niger Delta region. Two groups—the Niger Delta's People's Volunteer Force (NDPVF) and the Movement for the Emancipation of the Niger Delta (MEND)—claimed responsibility for a number of attacks on pipelines and kidnappings designed to disrupt production. Their goals were greater autonomy for the region and compensation for environmental damage done by oil companies in the state of Bayelsa. In June 2006 MEND declared a "cease-fire" after a Nigerian court ordered Shell (the country's largest oil producer) to pay $1.5 billion for environmental "reparations." However, MEND conducted new attacks in August. In response to the continued unrest, federal security forces launched an offensive in the region that led to more than 100 arrests but did not substantially reduce the level of violence.

A political feud between President Obasanjo and Vice President Atiku ABUBAKAR over control of the PDP led the president in September 2006 to ask the Senate to impeach Abubakar on corruption charges. The High Court in November blocked the impeachment effort, thereby apparently permitting Abubakar to become a candidate for the 2007 presidential election. However, the PDP subsequently nominated Umar YAR'ADUA, a relative unknown within the party, fueling speculation that Obasanjo had orchestrated the nomination. (Abubakar subsequently left the PDP to stand as the candidate of a new small party called the Action Congress of Nigeria [ACN].)

In January 2007 President Obasanjo announced a major cabinet reshuffle in which a number of ministries were eliminated. The initiative was presented as a means of streamlining the government and reducing corruption, with a view toward enhancing the ruling party's domestic approval in advance of the 2007 elections.

The PDP dominated the elections for governorships and state assemblies on April 14, 2007, as well as the federal balloting for the Senate and House of Representatives on April 21. Also on April 21, Umaru Musa Yar'Adua, nominated by the PDP after efforts to revise the constitution to permit President Obasanjo to run for a third term were blocked, handily won the presidential poll, securing more than 70 percent of the vote. International and domestic observers strongly criticized the elections for fraud at the local, state, and national levels. The courts subsequently ordered new balloting for a number of offices, but a special tribunal in February 2008 upheld the presidential results.

Following Yar'Adua's inauguration on May 29, 2007, the new president formed what he described as a new "government of national unity" on July 26. Although dominated by the PDP, the new cabinet was noteworthy for the inclusion of independents and members of the ANNP and several other new small parties.

The new government's first year in office was marked by an anti-corruption campaign that snared a number of officials from the Obasanjo administration. Yar'Adua initiated a major cabinet reshuffle in October 2008 and finalized the new government in December. Another, minor, reshuffle occurred in July 2009, as part of a broader anti-corruption campaign by the government that included a program to spend more than $2 billion to reform the federal security forces (see Current issues, below). Yar'Adua left Nigeria for medical treatment in Saudi Arabia for a heart condition on November 23. He remained hospitalized out of the country until February of the next year.

On February 9 the Assembly enacted legislation that made Vice President Goodluck JONATHAN acting president in light of Yar'Adua's continuing medical problems. Jonathan appointed a new cabinet on April 6. Yar'Adua died on May 5, and Jonathan was sworn in as president the following day to complete the remainder of the former president's term (see Current issues, below). The governor of Kaduna, Namadi SAMBO of the PDP, was appointed vice president.

Jonathan was elected for a full term in the first round of presidential balloting on April 16, 2011. In legislative balloting that began on April 9 the PDP maintained a commanding majority in the Senate, with 71 seats, followed by the Action Congress of Nigeria (ACN) with 18 seats (no other party secured more than 8 seats). In the House of Representatives the PDP secured a reduced majority with 202 seats, followed by the CAN, 66 seats, and the CPC, 35 (see Current issues, below). The PDP also won 18 of the 26 gubernatorial elections. Jonathan finalized a new government on July 14.

In March 2012 five gubernatorial elections were held after the Supreme Court ruled in January that the terms of the governors had expired in 2011. All of the governors had been originally elected in 2007 but were forced to compete in new elections in 2008 because of irregularities in the balloting. All of the governors were members of the PDP. Four were reelected. The fifth stood down, but another PDP candidate won the balloting. The president conducted a minor cabinet reshuffle on May 24. Another minor reshuffle occurred on October 31. On February 4, 2013, the minister for power was replaced, and Kabiru Saminu TURAKI was appointed a minister in the office of the presidency and tasked to oversee the government response to rising Islamic extremism (see Current issues, below).

Constitution and government. In February 1976, it was announced that the 12 states created in 1967 would be expanded to 19 to alleviate the domination of subunits by traditional ethnic and religious groups. A centrally located area of some 3,000 square miles was also designated as a federal capital territory, with the federal administration to be transferred (a process declared completed in late 1991) from Lagos to the new capital of Abuja. New states were progressively added, bringing the total to 36 (see the 2013 *Handbook* for more information). In 1996 it was also announced that 183 new municipalities would be established, bringing the total to 776.

Region (Pre-1967)	*State (1967)*	*State (1987)*	*State and Capital (1996)*
Northern	Benue Plateau	Benue	Benue (Makurdi)
			Kogi (Lokoja) †*
		Plateau	Plateau (Jos)
			Nassatawa (Lafia) ‡
	Kano	Kano	Kano (Kano)
			Jigawa (Dutse) †
	Kwara	Kwara	Kwara (Ilorin)
	North-Central	Kaduna	Kaduna (Kaduna)
		Katsina	Katsina (Katsina)
	North-Eastern	Bauchi	Bauchi (Bauchi)
			Gombe (Gombe) ‡
		Borno	Borno (Maiduguri)
			Yobe (Damaturu) †
		Gongola	Adamawa (Yola) †
			Taraba (Jalingo) †
	North-Western	Niger	Niger (Minna)
		Sokoto	Sokoto (Sokoto)
			Kebbi (Birnin Kebbi) ‡
			Zamfara (Gusau) ‡
Eastern	East-Central	Anambra	Anambra (Akwa)
			Enugu (Enugu) †
		Imo	Imo (Owerri)
			Abia (Umuahia) †
			Eboniyi (Abakaliki) ‡**
	Rivers	Rivers	Rivers (Port Harcourt)
			Bayelsa (Yenagoa) ‡
	South-Eastern	Cross River	Cross River (Calabar)
		Akwa Ibom	Akwa Ibom (Uyo)
Mid-Western	Mid-Western	Bendel	Delta (Asaba) †
			Edo (Benin) †
Western	Lagos	Lagos	Lagos (Ikeja)
	Western	Ogun	Ogun (Abeokuta)
		Ondo	Ondo (Akure)
			Ekiti (Ado-Ekiti) ‡
		Oyo	Oyo (Ibadan)
			Osun (Oshogbo) †

Notes: † created in 1991; ‡ created in 1996; *also includes territory from Kwara; **also includes territory from Enugu.

The 1979 constitution established a U.S.-style federal system with powers divided among three federal branches (executive, legislative, and judicial) and between federal and state governments. Executive authority at the national level was vested in a president and vice president who ran on a joint ticket and served four-year terms. To be declared the victor on a first ballot, a presidential candidate was required to win a plurality of the national popular vote and at least one-quarter of the vote in two-thirds of the (then) 19 states. Legislative power was invested in a bicameral National Assembly comprising a 95-member Senate and a 449-member House of Representatives.

Upon assuming power on December 31, 1983, the Supreme Military Council (SMC) suspended those portions of the constitution "relating to all elective and appointive offices and representative institutions." A constitutional modification decree issued in January 1984 established a Federal Military Government encompassing the SMC; a National Council of States, headed by the chair of the SMC and including the military governors of the 19 states, the chief of staff of the armed forces, the inspector-general of police, and the attorney general; and a cabinet-level Federal Executive Council (FEC). The decree also provided for state executive councils headed by the military governors. Following the coup of August 1985, the SMC was renamed the Armed Forces Ruling Council (AFRC), and the FEC was renamed the National Council of Ministers. The chair of the AFRC was empowered to serve as both the head of state and chief executive. However, responsibility for "civilian political affairs" was delegated to a chief of general staff. Following the AFRC's announcement in September 1987 of a five-year schedule for return to civilian government, a 46-member Constitution Review Committee was created to prepare a revision of the 1979 basic law.

In May 1988 a 567-member Constituent Assembly was established to complete the work of the Constitution Review Committee. The most controversial issue faced by the assembly was the proposed institution of sharia, which was not favored by Muslim president Babangida or the Christian population. Unable to reach agreement, the assembly provided two separate and divergent submissions on the matter, which the president stated the AFRC would review in the context of "the national interest."

The draft constitution of the "Third Republic," presented to the AFRC by the Constituent Assembly in April 1989, mirrored the 1979 basic law with the notable addition of anticorruption measures and extension of the presidential term to six years. The document took no position on sharia, as Babangida claimed the issue would constrain debate on other provisions and should be addressed separately at a future time. The existing judiciary was left largely intact, although it was enjoined from challenging or interpreting "this or any other decree" of the AFRC.

A new National Assembly was elected on July 4, 1992, and convened on December 5. Presidential balloting was, however, deferred until June 12, 1993, with a return to constitutional government scheduled for the following August 27. In the meantime, a Transitional

Council, with a chair as nominal head of government, was designated to serve in a quasi-executive capacity. The system nonetheless remained tutelary, since both legislative and executive actions were subject to review by the president and the military-civilian National Defense and Security Council (NDSC). Coincident with President Babangida's resignation in 1993, the Transitional Council was abolished, not in favor of a constitutional government but of an Interim National Government (ING), which was in turn superseded by the Provisional Ruling Council (PRC)/Federal Executive Council (FEC) in November.

The 369 participants in the constitutional conference that convened on June 27, 1994, had been selected in widely boycotted balloting on May 23 and 28 from a list of PRC-approved candidates. The conference's recommendations were formally submitted to the PRC on June 27, 1995, and the provisions in the new proposed basic law called for a presidency that would rotate between the north and the south, the election of three vice presidents, the creation of several new states, and the installation of a transition civilian government pending new national elections. However, many of the 1995 document's provisions were not included in the draft charter released by the Abubakar regime for comments in September 1998. The new draft more resembled the 1979 constitution, providing for a strong, executive president responsible for nominating a cabinet subject to senate approval. At the state level, power was vested in a popularly elected governor and the state legislature. In early 1999 the regime announced that it had agreed on details of the new constitution, which was promulgated into law in May. The 1999 document codified a federal system comprising 36 states and the federal capital territory. The states were divided into 776 local government districts and municipalities. The term of office for the president and the two-house legislature (both elected by universal suffrage) was set at four years, renewable only once for the president.

Prior to the scheduled 2011 elections, the Assembly approved a constitutional change in October 2010 that required national elections to be held between 30 and 150 days prior to the May inauguration date (see Current issues, below).

Nigerian journalists have been significantly affected by the violence that pervades political life, suffering, according to watchdog organizations, beatings and arrests at the hands of local, regional, and national officials who operate for the most part with impunity. "Abusive judicial procedures" are also often initiated against journalists for articles that have irked authorities, according to Reporters Without Borders, which has characterized the State Security Service as a "press freedom predator." The group ranked Nigeria 115th out of 179 countries in terms of freedom of the press in 2013.

Foreign relations. As a member of the United Nations, the Commonwealth, and the OAU following independence, Nigeria adhered to a policy of nonalignment, opposition to colonialism, and support for liberation movements in all white-dominated African territories (for more information on the history of Nigerian Foreign relations, please see the 2012 *Handbook*). At the regional level, Nigeria was the prime mover in negotiations leading to the establishment in 1975 of the Economic Community of West African States (ECOWAS) and spearheaded the ECOWAS military and political involvement in Liberia in 1990 and Sierra Leone in 1998.

Benin and Cameroon have challenged Nigerian territorial claims along the Benin-Nigeria border and in offshore waters, respectively. In 1989 President Babangida sought to repair relations that had been strained by expulsion of illegal aliens by the Shagira regime, primarily by providing Benin with financial assistance. Cameroon and Nigeria continued to assert rival claims to the Bakassi Peninsula, several deaths having been reported during military clashes in 1994 in that oil-rich region. Briefs in the case were submitted to the International Court of Justice (ICJ) during the first half of 1995, but tension stemming from the dispute subsequently remained high. Seeking to repair relations even as legal wrangling over the region continued, president-elect Obasanjo visited Cameroon in early 1999.

In 2002 the ICJ ruled in favor of Cameroon in the border dispute. The governments of both Cameroon and Nigeria subsequently entered into the UN-brokered talks to implement the decision. By 2003 Nigeria had turned over more than 30 small villages to Cameroon in exchange for control of a small area. A second round of territorial exchange occurred in July 2004, and diplomatic relations were also restored between the two countries. However, in September the Obasanjo administration refused to participate in a third round of land exchange, which led to a new UN mediation effort (see entry on Cameroon). (In 2006 Obasanjo signed a UN-brokered agreement regarding a final settlement.)

Relations with Benin were also strengthened in the early 2000s. Joint border patrols were initiated in 2002 between the two states, which subsequently agreed to redraw their borders. Three areas claimed by Nigeria were turned over to Nigeria in return for its release of seven areas claimed by Benin. In addition, in May 2003 Nigeria and Benin agreed, along with Ghana and Togo, to the construction of a 1,000-kilometer pipeline to transship oil. In 2006 Obasanjo signed a UN-brokered agreement regarding a final settlement.

Relations between Nigeria and the United Kingdom, weakened by the flight to Britain of a number of political associates of former president Shagari, were formally suspended in mid-1984, when British police arrested a Nigerian diplomat and expelled two others for the attempted kidnapping of former transport minister Umaru DIKKO, who was under indictment in Nigeria for diversion of public funds. Full relations with the United Kingdom resumed in February 1986, with Dikko being denied asylum in early 1989.

Despite Nigeria's admission to full membership in the Organization of the Islamic Conference (OIC) in 1986, intense Christian opposition prompted the country to formally repudiate its links to the conference in 1991, although the OIC continued to list Nigeria as one of its members. Muslims objected strenuously to the 1991 reversal of an 18-year lapse in relations with Israel, although the Babangida regime two years earlier had recognized the Palestinian claim to statehood.

In February 1998 Nigerian troops were at the vanguard of the ECOWAS Monitoring Group (Ecomog) that invaded Freetown, Sierra Leone, in an effort to restore to power the democratically elected government of Ahmed Tejan Kabbah. (Kabbah had been forced into exile in the aftermath of the military coup [see entry on Sierra Leone for further details].)

In 2003 Liberian leader Charles Taylor accepted a Nigerian proposal whereby he received asylum in Nigeria in exchange for surrendering power. Taylor left Liberia for Nigeria in August 2003 and settled in Calabar. Nigeria then contributed 1,500 troops to the UN-sponsored peacekeeping mission to Liberia in October 2003.

The new civilian regime installed in 1999 received much international praise for its attempt to eliminate widespread corruption and its commitment to democratic practices. Among other things, the United States restored military ties and announced that Nigeria would receive $10 million in military aid. In addition, a U.S.-Nigerian committee was established in 2005 to address regional security issues as well as to combat violence in Nigeria's oil-producing areas.

In March former Liberian leader Taylor tried to flee from Nigeria when it became apparent that President Obasanjo planned to extradite him. However, Taylor was captured and turned over to a special UN court for trial on charges of having committed war crimes. In June Nigeria withdrew its citizens from the Bakassi Peninsula as part of an additional UN-sponsored border agreement with Cameroon. Nigeria also relocated 13 villages located along its border with Niger to move them from disputed territory. In November Nigeria finalized an agreement under which South Korea agreed to spend $10 billion on Nigerian railways in return for preferential treatment in regard to future oil contracts. In February 2007 Nigeria, Benin, and Togo signed an agreement to increase security and economic cooperation, in part through the proposed creation of a three-state common market.

Nigeria formally handed over the Bakassi Peninsula to Cameroon in August 2008, although the Nigerian government acknowledged it was "painful" to acquiesce to the transfer. (Some 100,000 of the approximately 300,000 residents on the peninsula [most of whom consider themselves Nigerian] had reportedly already relocated to Nigeria proper.) Nigerian officials were more sanguine about the recent demarcation of the maritime border with Cameroon, under which the two countries agreed to work together to develop what were expected to be rich offshore oilfields.

In May 2009 the U.S. firm Halliburton revealed that it had paid several million dollars in bribes to Nigerian officials in exchange for energy contracts worth more than $6 billion. The revelations prompted the government to establish investigations in several large agreements with foreign firms. Nigeria and Russia signed a joint agreement in June, worth $2.5 billion, to expand Nigeria's gas production capabilities. Also in June, China and Nigeria finalized a broad accord to improve the quality and safety of products imported from China. In July the EU pledged more than $110 million in development aid to the Niger Delta. In November the EU and Nigeria agreed to a $1 billion accord to promote development in the Niger Delta and to fund peace-building measures. On November 20 a Swiss court ordered more than $350 million in assets owned by the son of former president Abacha seized as part of an ongoing investigation into corruption that had already returned more than $700 million to Nigeria. In August 2010 the Nigerian government filed suit against U.S. energy company Halliburton for bribes paid to Nigerian officials between 1996 and 2005.

On August 25, 2011, a car bomb exploded at the UN office in Lagos, killing 18 and wounding more than 60. The attack was blamed on a new Islamic extremist group, *Boko Haram* (see Current issues, below). Also in August, a British court ordered the Anglo-Dutch oil firm Shell to establish a $410 billion trust fund to compensate the Ogoni people for environmental damage from oil spills.

Continuing unrest (see Current issues, below) in northern Nigeria in December 2011 prompted Jonathan to close the borders with Niger and Chad after evidence revealed that militants were launching attacks from bases in the two countries. On March 8, 2012, British and Nigerian special operations forces attempted to rescue a British and an Italian hostage who had been abducted by *Boko Haram.* Both hostages were killed in the raid. In response to increased *Boko Haram* attacks, the United States announced new intelligence and security cooperation with the Nigerian government. Relations between Nigeria and the UK were reported to have become strained after the Nigerian Senate passed a measure that criminalized gay marriage. Also in 2012, Nigeria and China announced a joint venture to construct three new refineries in Lagos.

Relations between Nigeria and Saudi Arabia deteriorated sharply in September 2012 when Saudi officials deported more than 600 Nigerian women pilgrims for travelling without "a male guardian." In response, Nigeria cancelled flights to Saudi Arabia and argued that an existing bilateral agreement exempted its citizens from the rule. On September 5 Nigerian naval forces rescued a hijacked oil freighter off the coast of Lagos.

Nigeria deployed 900 troops to Mali in January 2013 as part of an ECOWAS force, the African International Support Missions to Mali (AFISMA) (see entry on Mali). AFISMA was commanded by a Nigerian general. The intervention in Mali followed growing reports that *Boko Haram* fighters had established bases there. In April seven French hostages were released by *Boko Haram,* reportedly in exchange for a $3.15 million ransom. The French government denied any ransom had been paid. Also in April, Nigeria and Austria signed an accord to promote investment between the nations. The next month, Nigeria and Cuba signed a treaty to expand sports cooperation between the two countries.

Current issues. A 2009 government offensive against MEND fighters left hundreds dead, including civilians, and led MEND to launch retaliatory strikes against oil facilities. On June 8, 2009, Royal Dutch Shell consented to pay $15.5 million to people along the Niger delta to settle court cases brought against the energy giant. Also in June, Yar'Adua announced an amnesty program and 60-day ceasefire for MEND fighters (see Political parties, below). Meanwhile fighting in July between government forces and an Islamic militant group alternatively known as *Al Sunna Wal Jamma* or *Boko Haram* left more than 700 dead and thousands displaced. Police captured group's leader Mohammad Yusuf, who subsequently died in custody. Audits in August revealed widespread corruption in the financial sector and led the Central Bank to replace the heads of five of the nation's largest banks. The investigations were in response to bad loans and other problems that caused the Nigerian stock market to lose 65 percent of its value between March 2008 and March 2009. In response, the Central Bank allocated more than $6 billion to shore up the banking sector.

Yar'Adua fell ill in November 2009 because of a heart condition and never fully recovered. He died on May 5, 2010. Vice President Goodluck Jonathan was appointed to replace the ailing chief executive. Jonathan dismissed the cabinet on March 17 and appointed a new government the following month. Reports indicated that the new cabinet had been purged of Yar'Adua loyalists. Jonathan was inaugurated to serve the remainder of Yar'Adua's term on May 6. Reports that Jonathan, a southern Christian, would seek reelection, prompted protests and condemnation among northern Muslims since within the PDP the presidency unofficially rotated between the six regions of the country, and Yar'Adua was a northern Muslim. Also in May, police in the UAE arrested former Delta governor James IBORI who was wanted for corruption and embezzlement. The arrest was reportedly part of a broader anticorruption campaign by Jonathan (Ibori subsequently pled guilty to ten counts of corruption and was sentenced to 13 years imprisonment).

Renewed fighting in 2010 in Jos left more than 600 dead. Meanwhile, in March, MEND announced an end to a cease-fire followed by two car bombings in Warri. Jonathan dismissed the head of the election commission in April because of charges related to fraud during the 2007 elections. Bombings in Abuja on October 1, 2010, the national independence day holiday, killed 12 and were widely blamed on MEND.

Presidential and legislative elections scheduled for January 2011 were postponed until April following negotiations between the national electoral commission and political parties. The change required a constitutional amendment, approved on October 28, 2010, which reduced the amount of time between balloting and the inauguration of officials.

In late 2010 *Boko Haram* launched a campaign of bombings and assassinations against the government and Christian targets. Described as the "Nigerian Taliban," the group was reported to have established ties with al-Qaida. Attacks in the northern areas of the country led to the deployment of more than 400 security personnel in October 2010. In June 2011 a series of *Boko Haram* attacks killed more than 50 Nigerians.

In national elections on April 16, 2011, Jonathan was elected president with 58.9 percent of the vote. His closest rival was Buhari with 32 percent (no other candidate received more than 6 percent of the vote). In balloting on April 9 and 26, 2011, the PDP secured majorities in both houses of the legislature in balloting that domestic and international observers described as among the freest and fairest in recent Nigerian history. The northern areas of the country were wracked by postelection violence as supporters of Buhari and other opposition candidates rejected the results and protested what they perceived to be Jonathan's violation of the unofficial rotation of the presidency between the north and south. More than 500 were killed in the strife, which led to the deployment of additional security forces and curfews in five states. In October, three former governors were arrested on charges of embezzling more than $615 million while in office. In November, 65 people were killed in a series of coordinated bombings by *Boko Haram.*

On January 20, 2012, *Boko Haram* militants killed 185 people in Kano. Also in January Jonathan announced that the government would end a popular fuel subsidy, asserting that Nigeria could no longer afford the costs of the program. The announcement prompted widespread protests and a partial reversal of the order, which reduced the subsidy by 50 percent. By June attacks on energy production facilities by MEND and *Boko Haram* had reduced oil output to 2.7 million barrels per day, far below the government's goal of 3.7 million barrels per day for 2012. Meanwhile, severe flooding—said to be the worst in 50 years—killed more than 300 people and displaced more than two million people.

More than 800 people were killed in *Boko Haram* attacks between 2012 and 2013. Meanwhile, there was a growing number of civilian casualties as fighting between the extremist group and security forces intensified. The government launched an investigation into the deaths of 228 people who were killed during an anti-*Boko Haram* operation in Baga in April, 2013. Meanwhile, government efforts to negotiate with the group were rebuffed. By the summer of 2013, the conflict had produced an estimated 20,000 internally displaced persons. Jonathan declared states of emergency in the northern states of Adamawa, Borno, and Yobe and dispatched additional military troops.

An explosion and fire at a refinery on June 19, 2013, at Bodo forced Shell to stop operations and cut production by 150,000 barrels per day. Company officials blamed the accident on efforts to steal oil, while community leaders blamed Shell. A simmering political feud between Jonathan and the governor of Rivers State, Rotimi AMAECHI (PDP), erupted in July, when rival backers of the two leaders fought each other in Port Harcourt, prompting the deployment of security forces. Amaechi has emerged as the most visible opponent to Jonathan's reelection efforts within the PDP.

POLITICAL PARTIES AND GROUPS

In June 1995 General Abacha announced that the ban on "political activity" had been lifted, although "rallies and campaigns" remained restricted and other constraints continued as a consequence of the country's severe political turmoil (see the 2011 *Handbook* for information on political parties prior to 1995). In April 1998 all 5 current legal parties nominated Abacha to be their presidential candidate in balloting then scheduled for August. However, following Abacha's death in June, his successor, General Abubakar, dissolved the 5 parties and called on political associations to register with the newly created Independent National Electoral Commission (INEC). Between August 27 and September 9, 25 political groups applied to the INEC for provisional legal status. Only 9 of the applicants met the baseline qualifications, including maintaining functional offices in 24 states. In local elections in December only 3 of those groups—the People's Democratic Party (PDP), the All People's Party (APP), and the Alliance for Democracy

(AD)—secured the voting tally necessary to maintain their legal status and move on to legislative and presidential elections. The other 6 groups were reportedly deregistered. Three new parties—the National Democratic Party (NDP), the United Nigeria People's Party (UNPP), and All Progressive Grand Alliance (APGA)—were registered in June 2002, and by 2010 some 50 parties had been legalized. Propresidential parties created an electoral alliance, the Patriotic Electoral Alliance of Nigeria (PEAN), ahead of the planned 2011 balloting. Members of PEAN included a number of small parties, such as Accord, the Nigerian People's Congress, and the Advanced Congress of Democrats (ACD). PEAN supported incumbent president Jonathan's election bid.

Legislative Parties:

People's Democratic Party (PDP). The PDP was formed in Lagos in August 1998 as an umbrella for more than 60 organizations, including many from the so-called Group of 34, which registered among its leaders traditional chiefs, businesspeople, academicians, and a strong contingent of retired generals. Alex EKWUEME, a former national vice president, and Jerry GANA emerged from the PDP's inaugural meetings as the group's chair and second in command, respectively. The party presented a platform that reflected its broad political base, advocating the "guided" deregulation of the economy, respect for human rights, and improved funding for health care and education.

In late October 1998 Gen. Olesegun Obasanjo, the military head of state between 1976 and 1979, joined the PDP. With Obasanjo at the helm, the party subsequently swept local and gubernatorial elections, won a majority in the assembly, and in February 1999 captured the national presidency.

In January 2003 the PDP elected Obasanjo as its presidential candidate for the upcoming elections, which he won with 62 percent of the vote. The PDP also retained its majorities in the federal Senate and House of Representatives and among state governors and state assemblies.

A feud developed in 2005 between President Obasanjo and Vice President Atiku Abubakar over the proposed constitutional amendment to permit Obasanjo to seek a third term (see Current issues, above). The split also appeared to reflect the schism between the party's founding members ("concerned elders") led by Abubakar and the "progressive faction" led by Obasanjo. A party congress elected Ahmadu ALI as the PDP chair, and Obasanjo's supporters blamed Ali for the defeat of the constitutional amendment that would have allowed Obasanjo a third term. Subsequently, a PDP faction led by Solomon LAR declared itself the real leadership of the party and sued for access to the PDP assets.

Abubakar was suspended from the PDP in September 2006 for "antiparty activities," and he subsequently joined the new Action Congress of Nigeria (below). In December a PDP congress chose Umaru Yar'Adua as its presidential candidate. He easily secured the presidency (with more than 70 percent of the vote) in the April 2007 balloting, while the PDP also dominated the federal legislative polls and secured 27 of 36 state governorships.

Although Yar'Adua had been characterized as Obasanjo's handpicked successor, significant infighting was subsequently reported between supporters of the two leaders, particularly because the new government's anticorruption campaign focused on many officials from Obasanjo's administration. Obasanjo backed Sam EGWU to be the new PDP leader, but Egwu was defeated for the post by Vincent Ogbulafor at the PDP convention in March 2008. Ogbulafor, a former PDP general secretary, was considered a compromise candidate who reportedly faced a difficult task in reunifying the party. Between 2007 and 2009, a number of members of the All Nigeria People's Party defected to the PDP, including two sitting governors, Aliyu Mahmud SHINKAFI of Zamfara and Isa YUGUDA of Bauchi.

Jonathan declared his intent to seek the party's nomination for the January 2011 presidential race. He was challenged by former president Ibrahim Babangida and former vice president Atiku Abubakar. A bitter internal dispute emerged within the PDP over the selection of delegates to the party's nominating convention, with Jonathan and his supporters arguing that current office holders be allowed to serve as delegates, while Babangida's adherents opposed the change. As a result, primaries planned for October 2010 were postponed until January 14, 2011. Jonathan won the PDP primary and was victorious in the general election, winning a full term in balloting on April 16. Meanwhile, the PDP secured reduced majorities in the house and Senate in legislative polling.

At a party congress on March 24, 2012, Alhaji Bamangar Tukur, a close ally of Jonathon, was elected party chair. Meanwhile, in April Obasanjo resigned as chair of the PDP board of trustees. In June 2013, Tukur survived an effort among the PDP's executive committee to replace him.

Leaders: Goodluck JONATHAN (President of the Republic), Namadi SAMBO (Vice President of the Republic), Gen. Olesegun OBASANJO (Former Chair of the PDP Board of Trustees and Former President of the Republic), Alhaji Bamangar TUKUR (Chair), Olagunsoye OYINLOLA (General Secretary).

All Progressives Congress (APC). The APC was formed in February 2013 by a merger of four opposition parties, the **Congress for Progressive Change** (CPC), the **Action Congress of Nigeria** (CAN), and the **All Nigeria People's Party** (ANPP). The new grouping described itself as a progressive socialist party, and Bisi Akande of the ACN was elected its first chair.

Leader: Bisi AKANDE (Chair).

Congress for Progressive Change (CPC). The mainly Muslim, centrist CPC was formed in 2009 by supporters of former general Muhammadu Buhari. The party's main strength is in the north. Many of the original CPC leadership consisted of former members of the ANPP. In 2010 Buhari formally left the ANPP and joined the CPC. Buhari was the party's 2011 presidential candidate. He was placed second in the balloting with 32 percent of the vote, while the CPC was placed third in the Senate and house balloting. The party also secured one governorship. Reports in 2013 indicated that Buhari would be the APC candidate for the presidency in 2015.

Leaders: Muhammadu BUHARI (2011 presidential candidate), Tony MOMOH (Chair), Buba GALADIMA (Secretary General).

All Nigeria People's Party (ANPP). The ANPP is a successor to the All People's Party (APP), a center-right grouping established in September 1998 by some 14 Ibo and Hausa-Fulani political associations. Within the APP's ranks were some former members of the five parties dissolved in July 1998, as well as so many associates of former president Abacha that APP detractors derisively labeled the group the "Abacha's People's Party." The APP forwarded its own candidates for local, gubernatorial, and national legislative balloting in late 1998 and early 1999, capturing one-quarter of the governorships and representation in both assembly bodies. On the other hand, prior to the 1999 presidential balloting, the APP formed an electoral alliance with the AD (below). After the AD's standard-bearer, Samuel Oluyemisi Falae, outpolled the APP's proposed candidate, Ogbonnaya Onu, in intra-alliance balloting, the APP backed Falae's presidential bid.

Membership in the APP having initially come largely from the northern region, the party in 2000 claimed to have reorganized in an attempt to widen membership to the southeast, with particular focus on the Igbo tribe. As part of the APP's reorganization, the party set up a monitoring mechanism to ensure that the party's elected officials lived up to the party platform, which included support for the implementation of sharia in northern states.

In May 2002 the APP announced its intention to change its name to the ANPP in anticipation of a planned merger with the then-unrecognized UNPP (below). However, both parties subsequently suffered internal factionalization over the proposed merger, with one APP faction demanding retention of the party's original rubric. In November a special APP national convention ratified the name change, although only a portion of the UNPP membership joined the group.

In the 2003 elections Muhammadu Buhari ran as the ANPP's presidential candidate and received 32 percent of the vote. In the legislative elections, the ANPP secured 96 seats in the House and 27 in the Senate, making it the largest opposition party. Buhari finished second in the April 2007 presidential poll with 18.7 percent of the vote, while the ANPP won 22 seats in the Senate, 64 seats in the House of Representatives, and 5 state governorships. Following the elections, two members of the ANPP joined the new national unity government, although ANPP leaders continued to refer to the party as a member of the opposition, and Buhari pressed for an annulment of the presidential poll.

In 2009 an internal struggle divided that party as a faction loyal to Buhari sought to replace party chair Edwin Ume-Ezeoke with former governor Abubakar AUDU, ahead of the 2011 elections. Buhari and a number of his supporters resigned from the party in January 2010 to join the CPC. At a party congress in September 2010, Ogbonnaya Onu was elected ANPP chair. ANPP presidential candidate Ibrahim Sherarau was placed fourth in the balloting with 2.4 percent of the vote in the 2011 elections. Meanwhile, the party ANPP won three governorships, 7 Senate seats, and 25 seats in the House. On June 26, 2012, the chair of the ANPP in the Rivers State, Julius NWAOFU, was assassinated. Through 2013, *Boko Haram* conducted a series of attacks on ANPP officials.

Leaders: Ogbonnaya ONU (Chair), Lawan Shettima ALI (National Secretary), Ibrahim SHERARAU (2011 presidential candidate).

Action Congress of Nigeria (ACN). The party was originally formed as the Action Congress (AC) in 2006 by dissidents from the AD, Justice Party, ACD, and other smaller parties. Vice President of the Republic and former PDP member Atiku Abubakar was the 2007 AC candidate for the presidency, having left the PDP. He placed third in the balloting with 7.25 percent of the vote. On the eve of the April election, an AC gubernatorial candidate, Femi PEDRO, defected and joined the Labour Party, along with a number of other AC members. The AC went on to win 1 governorship, 6 seats in the Senate, and 32 seats in the House of Representatives, making it the third largest party in both chambers. The AC was subsequently invited to join the PDP national unity government but declined, leading to the resignation of the party's national secretary, Bashir DALHATU, who had strenuously supported participation. In 2010 the AC changed its name to the Action Congress of Nigeria (ACN).

The ACN won three governorships in the 2011 elections. It was second in the legislative balloting, while the party's presidential candidate, Nuhu RIBADU, was placed third in the presidential election, with 5.4 percent of the vote. ACN opposition to the 2013 state of emergency in northern Nigeria divided the party.

Leaders: Bisi AKANDE Hassan ZURMI (Chair), Lawal SHUAIBU (National Secretary), Atiku ABUBAKAR (Former Vice President of the Republic and 2007 presidential candidate).

Accord. Formed in 2006 by Ikra Bilbis, a former member of the PDP, Accord maintained close ties with the PDP, and President Obasanjo appointed Bilbis to a cabinet post in 2006. Accord supported PDP candidate Yar'Adua in the 2007 presidential election. Reports in 2009 indicated that many members of Accord joined the PDP. Accord won five seats in the 2011 House elections.

Leaders: Muhammad Lawal MALADO (Chair), Suleiman ISI-YAKU (National Secretary).

All Progressive Grand Alliance (APGA). Launched in April 2002, the APGA is led by a prominent chief of the southern Igbo ethnic group, Chekwas Okorie. However, its founders criticized those who branded the APGA as an "Igbo party," arguing instead that it intended to represent "all the marginalized people of Nigeria." Okorie came in third in presidential balloting in 2003 with 3.29 percent of the vote. The party also gained two seats in the house but none in the Senate in 2003.

A faction of the party led by Chief Victor Umeh claimed to be the legitimate leader of the APGA in 2005–2006, and the INEC recognized the claim in 2007. However, Okorie challenged the INEC decision in the courts, but his suit was rejected in 2008. The APGA won one governorship in 2007. At a gathering in 2009, Okorie's faction reelected him as chair and expelled Umeh, along with Governor Peter Obi. However, the faction led by Umeh and Obi refused to recognize the authority of the convention, and Umeh was ultimately recognized by the national election commission as the party leader.

The APGA won one governorship in the 2011 balloting and six seats in the House. Reports in 2012 indicated that continued infighting between Umeh and Obi led to a significant decline in APGA membership. Although the APGA was part of the negotiations to form the APC, the party ultimately rejected the merger.

Leaders: Chief Victor UMEH (Chair), Sani SHINKAFI (National Secretary), Peter OBI.

Other parties that secured representation in the legislature in the 2011 balloting included the **Democratic People's Party** (DPP), which had been formed in 2006 by dissidents from the ANPP, led by Jeremiah USENI, and which secured two seats in the house and one in the Senate, and the **People's Party of Nigeria** (PPN), led by Abiodun ODU-SANYA, which won two seats in the house.

Other Parties That Contested the 2011 Elections:

Progressive People's Alliance (PPA). The PPA was formed in 2003, and the party's candidate—Orji Uzor KALU (a former PDP member)—won the gubernatorial election in Abia that year. Kalu served until 2007 but was indicted after he left office on charges of corruption. In 2007 the PPA won the gubernatorial elections in Abia and Imo. After the 2007 legislative elections the PPA joined the PDP-led national unity government. In 2009 the governor and deputy governor of Imo, both members of the PPA, defected to the PDP, leading the PPA to launch a legal challenge against the right of the former members to remain in office. The PPA failed to secure any seats in the 2011 legislative elections. In June 2013 the PPA voted to change its name to the All Progressive People Alliance (APPA).

Leaders: Sam NKIRE (Chair), Peter Ojonugwa AMEH (National Secretary).

United Nigeria People's Party (UNPP). The UNPP is a successor to the United Nigeria Democratic Party (UNDP), which was launched in August 2001 by, among others, former members of the PDP and supporters of former president Babangida. The UNDP changed its name to the UNPP in May 2002 to avoid confusion with the UN Development Program (also UNDP). The UNPP subsequently was splintered by a proposed merger with the APP; although some UNPP members joined the new ANPP, a rump UNPP continued to operate. Jim NWOBODO, the UNPP candidate in the 2003 presidential poll, secured 0.43 percent of the vote. In the concurrent legislative balloting, the UNPP secured 2.72 percent of the vote in the Senate (but no seats) and 2.8 percent of the vote and two seats in the house.

In 2006 it was reported that many members of the UNPP had defected to the newly formed Movement for Restoration and Defense of Democracy (MRDD, below). The UNPP did not secure any seats in the 2011 legislative balloting. In 2012 former deputy governor and UNPP official Alhaji Musa Adebayo AYENI won, and a number of supporters defected to the ACN. The UNPP was deregistered by the national election commission in December 2012.

Leaders: Mallem Salek JAMBO (Chair), Ukeje NWOKEFORO (National Secretary).

People's Redemption Party (PRP). The PRP was formed in 2002 under the leadership of Balarabe Musa, who was also the party's unsuccessful presidential candidate in 2003. The PRP won one seat in the House in 2003 but failed to gain representation in 2007. The PRP launched a series of efforts to form an electoral coalition with parties such as the PPA ahead of the 2011 elections, but it declined to join the PEAN. The PRP failed to secure any seats in the 2011 House or Senate elections. In 2012 the PRP filed suit with the electoral commission over government plans to deregister the party because of a lack of electoral success and the low number of candidates it fielded. Reports in 2013 indicated that the party was defunct.

Leaders: Balarabe MUSA (Chair), Dr. Ngozi OKAFOR (National Secretary).

Advanced Congress of Democrats (ACD). The ACD was formed in April 2005 to oppose President Obasanjo's bid for a third presidential term. The party attracted a number of elected officials at the state and national level, including members of the House and Senate, as well as senior PDP figures, including a former chair of the PDP, Audu OGBEH. The party mainly comprises northerners and is essentially an anti-PDP formation. After Obasanjo announced that he would not stand for a third term, the party announced a progressive platform that emphasized honesty in politics. The ACD reportedly attracted members from other parties, principally the AD, but failed to gain representation in the 2007 federal elections. The ACD announced in 2010 that it would support incumbent president Jonathan of the PDP in the 2011 elections. It ran only four candidates in the 2011 house balloting and failed to secure any seats. The ACD announced in April 2013 that it was forming an opposition coalition ahead of the 2015 balloting.

Leaders: Yusuf BUBA (Chair), Kenneth KALU (National Secretary), Lawal KAITA (Former Governor of Kaduna), Ghali Umar NA'ABA (Former President of the House of Representatives).

The parties participating in the 2011 elections included, among others (all received less than 1 percent of the vote and no representation in the legislature) the **People's Salvation Party** (PSP), created in 2002 and led by Lawal MAITURARE; the **National Conscience Party** (NCP), formed in October 1994 by Gani FAWEHINMI, an attorney and political activist who was arrested in mid-1995, and currently led by Osagie OBAYUWANA; the **Justice Party** (JP), led by former NADECO member Ralph OBIOHA; the **Movement for Democracy**

and Justice (MDJ), led by J. O. OSULA; the **People's Mandate Party** (PMP), led by Edward OPARAOJI and 2011 presidential candidate, Nwadike CHIKEZIE; the **New Nigeria Peoples' Party** (NNPP), chaired by B. O. ANIEBONAM; the **United Democratic Party** (UDP), formed in 1998 and led by Umaru DIKKO; the **Democratic Party Alliance** (DPA), a "progressive" party formed in November 2006 by Ulu FALAYE; the **Nigeria People's Congress** (NPC), led by Ngozi EMIONA and Brimmy Asekharuagbom OLAGHERE (2007 presidential candidate); the **African Democratic Congress** (ADC), formed in 2006 by Chief Okewo OSUI, which ran Peter NWANGWU as its 2011 presidential candidate; the **Fresh Democrats,** established in 2006 under the leadership of Chris Okotie (2007 and 2011 presidential candidate); the **People's Progressive Party** (PPP), led by 2011 presidential candidate Lawson Igboanugo AROH; the **People for Democratic Change** (PDC), led by 2011 presidential contender Mahmud WAZIRI; and the **Mega-Progressive People's Party** (MPPP), who ran Rasheed SHITTA-BEY as its 2011 presidential candidate.

For information on the **Movement for Restoration and Defense of Democracy** (MRDD) and the **National Democratic Party** (NDP), please see the 2012 *Handbook*.

Other Groups:

National Democratic Coalition (NADECO). Organized in May 1994 by a group of former politicians, retired military officers, and human rights activists, NADECO demanded that the Abacha regime yield to an interim government led by Moshood Abiola, the apparent winner in the aborted 1993 presidential election. As in the case of other prominent antigovernment figures, several NADECO leaders were temporarily detained, including the revered 87-year-old ex-governor of Ondo, Michael AJASIN. NADECO unsuccessfully supported a People's Progressive Party for recognition in 1996, and Ajasin angrily denounced the failure of the regime to legalize opposition groupings.

Wole Soyinka, the prominent exiled critic of the government who was involved in the reported formation of several external groups (see the National Liberation Council of Nigeria in the 2007 *Handbook*), was identified as a NADECO leader in 1997. Soyinka (in absentia) and other NADECO supporters were charged with treason in March 1997 for their antiregime activities. In early May 1998 NADECO's secretary general, Ayo Opadokum, was among 20 opposition activists arrested when a rally in Ibadan turned violent.

Beginning in mid-1998 the Abubakar regime released a number of opposition figures and was reportedly preparing to release Moshood Abiola when Abiola died. In October Soyinka, who had been a leading advocate for Abiola's release, returned from exile, where most recently he had been calling for the formation of a South African–style human rights tribunal to investigate the alleged abuses of Nigeria's military regimes. Subsequently, NADECO Chair Ndubuisi Kanu stated that the organization would resume its role as unofficial opposition, although it would not assume the status of political party. In 2009 a NADECO convention endorsed a call for a new constitution that emphasized regional autonomy. In September 2010 Soyinka reportedly formed a new political party, the **Democratic Front for a People's Federation** (DFPF). In 2012 Kanu called on Jonathan to engage in a national dialogue to end sectarian violence.

Leaders: Commodore Ndubuisi KANU (Chair), Bolaji AKINYEMI, Wole SOYINKA, Ayo OPADOKUM (Secretary General).

Movement for the Survival of the Ogoni People (MOSOP). MOSOP pressed the government for years on the rights of the indigenous Ogoni ethnic group in oil-rich southwestern Nigeria. Having previously suggested that a self-determination referendum would be appropriate, MOSOP has more recently concentrated on forcing the government to share the oil wealth more equitably with the local population.

Kenule SARO-WIWA (a well-known author, minority rights activist, and longtime MOSOP leader) was arrested in 1994 on murder charges involving the death of four progovernment Ogoni leaders. Saro-Wiwa vehemently denied the charges, calling them a blatant attempt by the Abacha regime to silence his criticism. Most internal and external observers remained extremely skeptical of Saro-Wiwa's guilt, and Western and African capitals urged his release. However, Saro-Wiwa and eight others were found guilty by a special military tribunal in late October 1996 and, following ratification of the sentences by the PRC, were hanged on November 10. The executions prompted an international outcry that contributed significantly to the government's sustained isolation in 1996–1998. MOSOP subsequently attempted to change the constitution so that the presidency would rotate on a regional basis. In 2009 MOSOP was divided by a leadership crisis in which one faction supported Ledum Mitee and another Goodluck DIIGBO, following a December 2008 congress in which Mitee was reelected chair. In 2011 the rivalry between Mitee and Diigbo was reported to have split the grouping. In 2013 MOSOP organized demonstrations in Bori to protest the government's failure to implement UN environmental recommendations.

Leader: Ledum MITEE.

Movement for the Actualization of the Sovereign State of Biafra (MASSOB). An Ibo group formed by lawyer and activist Ralph Uwazurike in 1999, MASSOB advocates the secession of Biafra and is opposed to the introduction of sharia in northern states. In October 2005 Uwazurike and 6 members of MASSOB were arrested on charges of treason and organizing an illegal organization. In 2009 MASSOB announced that after years of boycotting elections, it would participate in regional balloting in 2010 and support APGA candidates. In July 2010, 68 members of MASSOB were arrested for illegal demonstrations. In 2013 ten MASSOB members were arrested following clashes with police in Nnobi.

Leader: Ralph UWAZURIKE.

O'odua People's Congress (OPC). The OPC is a militant organization that advocates secession for the Yoruba ethnic group. It was allegedly behind a November 1999 dispute between Yoruba and Hausa merchants in the Lagos market that killed dozens. In addition, the OPC was blamed for several attacks in early 2000, including the murder of a Banga police officer. Some members of the OPC reportedly support the spread of sharia in northern states in the hope that the issue will further divide the country and thereby make Yoruba secession easier to obtain. Attacks by OPC members in October 2008 left six dead and more than a score injured. Seven members of the OPC were arrested in November 2010 for arms smuggling.

Movement for the Emancipation of the Niger Delta (MEND), which emerged in early 2006 when it conducted a series of attacks on oil production facilities. MEND was subsequently believed responsible for the kidnapping of a number of foreign oil workers. It demanded compensation from foreign oil companies for environmental damage done in the Niger Delta as well as more equitable distribution of oil revenue to the Delta inhabitants. MEND reportedly finances its operations through large-scale bunkering of oil.

In May 2007 MEND announced a cease-fire after new president Yar'Adua pledged to develop a revenue-sharing plan and to accord greater autonomy to the Niger Delta. The reconciliation was reportedly facilitated by new vice president Jonathan, who, like many MEND members, is a member of the Ijaw ethnic group. Although federal military forces were deployed into the region to confront other rebel forces, the MEND cease-fire appeared to hold into September. However, MEND subsequently resumed its attacks on oil facilities and kidnapping of oil workers after MEND leader Henry OKAH (who reportedly also uses the nom de guerre of Jomo Gbomo) was arrested in Angola on gun-running charges and was extradited to Nigeria to face trial for treason, terrorism, and arms smuggling. (A Nigerian court in May 2008 ruled that Okah's trial would be conducted in secret.) After a series of deadly incidents, MEND, reportedly interested in improving its image and differentiating itself from the numerous militias (described by some as "criminal gangs") operating in the Delta, announced another cease-fire in late June. However, hostilities erupted again in September, rebel attacks on deepwater oil platforms (previously considered safe) having prompted significant production shutdowns. In spite of a two-month government amnesty program in April 2009, MEND launched a series of new attacks on oil facilities and pipelines in the region causing more than $60 million in damage and reducing oil output by 20 percent. In July Okah accepted a government pardon and was freed from custody and went into exile in South Africa. Meanwhile, a new rebel leader, Government EKPEMUPOLO ("Tompolo"), emerged as one of the main MEND leaders and was the subject of a government manhunt and offensive through the summer before also accepting the amnesty in October, along with other MEND leaders Victor Ben

EBIKABOWEI, Ateke TOM, and Farah DAGOGO. Following the October 2010 Abuja bombings, Okah was arrested in South Africa. In November 2010 MEND kidnapped seven foreign oil workers in Akwa Ibom state. Meanwhile, in March 2011 MEND and the Nigerian government launched a new round of negotiations. On February 5, 2012, MEND destroyed an oil pipeline in Bayelsa.

Okah was convicted of terrorism in South Africa in January 2013 and sentenced to 24 years in prison. The conviction sparked a new wave of MEND attacks, including a strike that killed 12 police officers in Azuzama in April.

Boko Haram. Formally known as the Congregation and People Committed to the Propagation of the Prophet's Teachings and Jihad, *Boko Haram* (loosely translated as "Western education is sinful") was established in Northern Nigeria in 2001 by Mohammed YUSUF to spread sharia. It subsequently evolved into an Islamic terrorist organization. Estimates are that the conflict between *Boko Haram* and the Nigerian government killed more than 10,000 since 2001. Western intelligence agencies have linked *Boko Haram* with other extremist groups, including al-Qaida in the Islamic Maghreb. The group was consistently rejected efforts by the government to negotiate. Members of *Boko Haram* broke away in January 2012 to form another militant group, the **Vanguard for the Protection of Muslims in Black Lands** (*Ansaru*), led by Abu Usmatul AL-ANSARI. The new grouping was reportedly critical of *Boko Haram* for its attacks on Muslims.

In October 2012 top *Boko Haram* commander Shuaibu Mohammed BAMA was captured by security forces. After a state of emergency was declared in northern Nigerian states in May 2013, reports indicated that many *Boko Haram* fighters had fled into Mali.

Leader: Abubakar SHEKAU.

For more information on the **People's Democratic Congress** (PDC), the **People's Liberation Party** (PLP), the **Liberal Democrats** (LD), **Movement for National Reconciliation,** the **National Democratic Movement** (NDM), the **New Democratic Party** (NDP), the **Nigerian People's Movement,** the **United Action for Democracy** (UAD), the **South-South Liberation Movement,** the **Ijaw Youth Organization,** the **Federated Niger Delta Izon Communities** (FNDIC), the **Rivers' States Coalition,** and the **Niger Delta's People's Volunteer Force** (NDPVF), see the 2011 *Handbook.*

For information on the **Arewa People's Congress** (APC), the **United Democratic Forum** (UDF), the **Alliance for Democracy** (AD), the **Eastern Mandate Union,** the **National Democratic Movement** (NDM), the **Northern Elders' Forum,** the **United Democratic Congress,** the **Fourth Dimension,** the **National Solidarity Party** (NSP), and the **Social Democratic Mega-Party** (SDMP), please see the 2012 *Handbook.*

LEGISLATURE

The **National Assembly,** encompassing a Senate and a House of Representatives, was dissolved in December 1983. It was revived under the 1989 constitution, with an election of members to four-year terms in both houses on July 4, 1992. However, the new body did not convene until December 5 and was again dissolved in the wake of the November 1993 coup, with new elections held on April 25, 1998.

Senate. The upper chamber consists of 109 seats: 3 from each state and 1 from the Federal Capital Territory of Abuja. Members serve four-year terms. Following the balloting of April 9 and 26, 2011, the seats were distributed as follows: People's Democratic Party, 71; Action Congress of Nigeria, 18; All Nigeria People's Party, 7; Congress for Progress Change, 7; Labour Party, 4; All Progressive Grand Alliance, 1; and Democratic People's Party, 1.

President: David MARK.

House of Representatives. The lower house consists of 360 seats, with the number of seats per state being apportioned on the basis of population. Members serve four-year terms. Following the balloting of April 9 and 26, 2011, the seats were distributed as follows: People's Democratic Party, 202; Action Congress of Nigeria, 66; Congress for Progressive Change, 35; All Nigeria People's Party, 25; Labour Party, 8; All Progressive Grand Alliance, 6; Accord, 5; Democratic People's Party, 2; People's Party of Nigeria, 2; and the remaining 9 seats to be decided in by-elections.

President: Aminu TAMBUWAL.

CABINET

[as of August 15, 2013]

President	Goodluck Jonathan
Vice President	Namadi Sambo
Federal Executive Councilors	
Agriculture and Natural Resources	Akinwunmi Ayo Adesina
Aviation	Stella Oduah-Ogiemwoyi [f]
Communication Technology	Omobola Johnson Olubusola [f]
Communications and Information	Labaran Maku
Culture and Tourism	Edem Duke
Defense (Acting)	Erelu Olusola Obada [f]
Education	Rugayyatu Rufa'i [f]
Environment	Hadiza Ibrahim Mailafa [f]
Federal Capital Territory	Bala Muhammad
Finance	Ngozi Okonjo-Iweala [f]
Foreign Affairs	Olugbenga Ashiru
Health	Christian Otu Onyebuchi
Internal Affairs	Abba Moro
Justice and Attorney General	Mohammed Bello Adoke
Labor	Chukwuemeka Ngozichineke Wogu
Lands, Housing and Urban Development	Ama Pepple [f]
Mines and Steel Development	Musa Mohammed Sada
National Planning	Shamsudeen Usman
Niger Delta Region	Peter Godsay Orubebe
Petroleum	Diezani Alison-Madueke [f]
Police Affairs	Capt. (ret.) Caleb Olubolade
Power	Chinedu Nebo
Presidency	Kabiru Tanimu Turaki
Science and Technology	Ita Okon Bassey Ewa
Sports	Bolaji Abdullahi
Trade	Olusegun Aganga
Transport	Idris Umar
Water Resources	Sarah Reng Ochekpe [f]
Women Affairs	Zainab Maina [f]
Works and Housing	Mike Onolememen
Youth Development	Inuwa Abdullkadir
Ministers of State	
Agriculture and Natural Resources	Bukar Tijani
Defense	Erelu Olusola Obada [f]
Education	Nyesom Wike
Federal Capital Territory	Olajumoke Akinjide [f]
Finance	Yerima Lawal Ngama [f]
Foreign Affairs	Viola Onwuliri [f] Nuruddeen Mohammed
Health	Vacant
Niger Delta Affairs	Darius Dickson Ishaku
Power	Zainab Ibrahim Kuchi [f]
Trade and Investment	Samuel Ioraer Ortom
Works and Housing	Bashir Yugudu

[f] = female

INTERGOVERNMENTAL REPRESENTATION

Ambassador to the U.S.: Adebowale Ibidapo ADEFUYE.

U.S. Ambassador to Nigeria: James ENTWHISTLE.

Permanent Representative to the UN: U. Joy OGWU.

IGO Memberships (Non-UN): AfDB, AU, CWTH, ECOWAS, ICC, IOM, NAM, OPEC, WTO.

NORWAY

Kingdom of Norway
Kongeriket Norge

Political Status: Constitutional monarchy established in 1905; under multiparty parliamentary system.

Area: 149,282 sq. mi. (386,641 sq. km), including Svalbard and Jan Mayen (see Related Territories).

Population: 4,953,088 (2013E—UN); 4,722, 701 (2013E—U.S. Census).

Major Urban Centers (2013E): OSLO (623,966), Bergen (267,950), Trondheim (179,692), Stavanger (129,191).

Official Language: Norwegian.

Monetary Unit: Krone (official rate November 1, 2013: 5.97 kroner = $1US).

Sovereign: King HARALD V; succeeded to the throne January 17, 1991, upon the death of his father, King OLAV V.

Heir to the Throne: Crown Prince HAAKON Magnus, son of the king.

Prime Minister: Erna SOLBERG (Conservative Party); appointed by the king on October 16, 2013, succeeding Jens STOLTENBERG (Norwegian Labor Party), who had submitted his resignation on the same day, following the election of September 9.

THE COUNTRY

A land of fjords and rugged mountains bisected by the Arctic Circle, Norway is the fifth-largest country in Western Europe but the second-lowest in population density, after Iceland. In addition to borders with its two Scandinavian neighbors, Sweden and Finland, Norway has also had a common border in the far north with the Soviet Union/Russia since 1944. Three-fourths of the land area is unsuitable for cultivation or habitation, and the population, homogeneous except for asylum-seekers and foreign workers, is heavily concentrated in the southern sector and along the Atlantic seaboard. For generations, the population was homogeneous except for a small Sámi (Lapp) minority of approximately 40,000 in the north. Immigrants from developing countries have flocked to Norway in recent years and now make up almost 15 percent of the population—double that number in Oslo. For historical reasons the Norwegian language exists in two forms: the Danish-inspired *Bokmål* as well as *Nynorsk,* a traditional spoken tongue with a comparatively recent written form; in addition, the Sámi speak their own language, a member of the Finno-Ugrian group. The state-supported Evangelical Lutheran Church commands the allegiance of 78 percent of the population, although a recent survey concluded that only 10 percent of those members attend religious services or other church-related activities more than once a month.

Women constitute 47 percent of the active labor force, concentrated in the health and social services sector, wholesale and retail trade, and education. Just under 40 percent of the national legislators elected in 2009 were women, and no Norwegian government has been formed since 1986 with less than 40 percent women. Both the World Economic Forum and the United Nations (UN) Development Program rank Norway second in terms of economic and political gender equality. In 2013 parliament passed legislation to include women in military conscription.

The Norwegian merchant fleet is one of the world's ten largest (by country of owner) and, prior to the discovery of North Sea oil, was the country's leading foreign-exchange earner. Norway continues to export considerable amounts of such traditional commodities as fish and forest products, although the agricultural sector as a whole now contributes only 1 percent of GDP. Norway was the world's second-largest exporter of natural gas and seventh-largest crude oil exporter, and the country has Western Europe's largest petroleum reserves, located in the Norwegian and Barents Seas as well as the North Sea. In addition, the development of hydroelectric power in recent decades has made Norway one of the largest exporters of aluminum and nitrogen products in Western Europe. Since exports and foreign services, including shipping, account for roughly 40 percent of the GNP, the economy is heavily influenced by fluctuations in the world market. Oil and natural gas production have made Norway one of the world's most affluent countries, but production peaked in 2004 and new reserves must be found.

Norway has felt few direct effects of the global financial crisis or eurozone crisis, thanks to injecting a large fiscal stimulus and buoyancy in the hydrocarbon sector. GDP growth was 0.7 in 2010 and 1.7 percent for 2011, and 3.0 percent for 2012. Norway has one of the lowest unemployment rates in Europe, ranging from 3.2 percent to 3.6 percent for 2009–2012. Norway offered a $9.2 billion loan to the International Monetary Fund (IMF) in April 2012 to be used in global economic stability programs.

GOVERNMENT AND POLITICS

Political background. Although independent in its early period, Norway came under Danish rule in 1380. A period of de facto independence began in January 1814 but ended nine months later, when the legislature (*Storting*) accepted the Swedish monarch as king of Norway. Norway remained a territory under the Swedish Crown until 1905, when the union was peacefully dissolved and the Norwegians elected a sovereign from the Danish royal house. Though Norway avoided involvement in World War I, it was occupied from 1940 to 1945 by Nazi Germany, which sponsored the infamous puppet regime of Vidkun QUISLING, while the legitimate government functioned in exile in London.

Norway's first postwar election continued the prewar ascendancy of the Norwegian Labor Party (*Det Norske Arbeiderparti*—DNA), and a government was formed in 1945 under Prime Minister Einar GERHARDSEN. Labor continued in the majority until 1961 and then maintained a minority government until 1965, when a coalition of nonsocialist parties took control under Per BORTEN, leader of the Center Party (*Senterpartiet*—Sp). The Borten government was forced to resign in 1971, following disclosure that the prime minister had deliberately leaked information on negotiations for entering the European Community (EC, later the European Union—EU). A Labor government under Trygve BRATTELI subsequently came to power but was forced from office in September 1972, when EC membership was rejected in a national referendum by 53.5 to 46.5 percent of participants. However, when a coalition government under Lars KORVALD of the Christian People's Party (*Kristelig Folkeparti*—KrF) failed to win the September 1973 general election, Bratteli returned as head of a minority government. Upon stepping down, Bratteli was succeeded in January 1976 by Labor's Odvar NORDLI. In the election of September 1977, Labor and its ally, the Socialist Left Party (*Sosialistisk Venstreparti*—SV), obtained a combined majority of one seat over four nonsocialist parties, enabling Nordli to continue in office.

Prime Minister Nordli resigned for health reasons in February 1981 and was succeeded by Gro Harlem BRUNDTLAND, the country's first female chief executive. However, in September her first minority government fell in the wake of a 10-seat loss at the polls by Labor, and in October Kåre WILLOCH formed a minority administration led by the Conservative Party (*Høyre*) with the legislative support of the KrF and the Sp. Responding to the recessionary effects of Willoch's economic policies, voters nearly unseated the government in September 1985; the three ruling parties obtained a total of 78 seats, as opposed to 77 for Labor and the SV, making the 2 seats won by the right-wing Progress Party (*Fremskrittspartiet*—Frp) key to the balance of power.

In April 1986 the Willoch government lost a confidence vote on a proposed gas tax increase when the anti-tax Frp voted with the opposition. In the first change in power without an intervening election in 23 years, Brundtland returned as head of another minority Labor administration. In the parliamentary poll of September 1989 the Labor and Conservative parties both lost ground, with the Conservatives, under Jan P. SYSE, forming a new minority administration in coalition with the KrF and Sp. The resignation of the Syse government in late 1990 was forced by the Center Party's objection to the proposed signing of a European Economic Area (EEA) agreement (see entry on the European Free Trade Association—EFTA) that would have necessitated revision of Norwegian laws restricting foreign ownership of industrial and financial institutions.

The Center Party agreed to support Labor's return to power under Brundtland in December, when she pledged to prioritize domestic control over natural resources and economic activities. Norway signed the EEA Treaty in May 1992, after securing additional clauses designed to meet its concerns.

Controversy over Norway's renewed application for EC/EU membership, approved by the *Storting* in November 1992, dominated the general election of September 1993. The Labor and Conservative Parties favored accession (although the former was deeply divided over the issue), whereas the Center, Socialist Left, Christian People's, and Progress Parties were opposed. The results were far from definitive: Labor and the Center Party gained seats, while the other parties lost ground. Brundtland subsequently formed another Labor minority government, although the anti-EU parties had sufficient collective strength to deny the government the three-quarters majority required for approval of formal accession. Thus, the question was put to a referendum at which voters had to weigh whether accession provisions had sufficiently resolved questions regarding such key issues as the future of Norway's oil and gas reserves, access to Norway's fisheries, and safeguards for Norwegian farmers (among the most heavily subsidized in the world). On November 28, 1994, the Norwegian electorate again rejected EU membership, this time by a margin of 52.2 to 47.8 percent. Having acknowledged the outcome as a major defeat, Prime Minister Brundtland decided to negotiate appropriate changes to the EEA Treaty that would continue to apply to Norway as a non-EU member.

Brundtland stepped down in October 1996, and Labor entered the September 1997 election under the leadership of Thorbjørn JAGLAND, who had promised during the campaign to resign if his party polled less than the 36.9 percent of the vote it had received in 1993. Although Labor won 65 seats, compared to 25 each for the KrF and the Frp and 23 for the Conservatives, Jagland narrowly missed his self-imposed target and submitted his resignation in October. KrF leader Kjell Magne BONDEVIK subsequently formed a new minority government (42 seats) comprised of the KrF, the Sp, and the Liberal Party (*Venstre*–V). Bondevik submitted his resignation in March 2000 after losing a vote of confidence triggered by the government's objections to proposed construction of two gas-fired power stations. Labor's Jens STOLTENBERG was subsequently named head of an all-Labor, minority government.

The election of September 10, 2001, saw Labor narrowly retain its plurality, but with only 43 seats—its worst election returns in nearly a century. As a result, Kjell Bondevik returned to office at the head of a center-right minority coalition of the KrF, the Conservatives, and the Liberals. Controlling only 62 of the *Storting*'s 165 seats, the government required external support from the Frp, which had won 26 seats in the election.

The Labor Party's promise to increase welfare spending and reverse the tax reforms and other conservative policies initiated by prime minister Bondevik resonated with voters and led to a dramatic victory for Labor in the September 12, 2005, election. Labor captured 61 seats and in partnership with the Socialist Left (15 seats) and Center (11 seats) parties established a red-green majority of 87 seats. The election also saw the populist Progress Party become the principal opposition by outpolling the Conservatives, 38 seats to 23.

Reinstalled on October 17, 2005, as head of Norway's first majority government in two decades, Jens Stoltenberg drew upon the country's immense oil wealth to increase spending on education, health, and welfare, and in general to swing the domestic agenda to the left. The government rejected calls for another referendum on EU membership despite public opinion polls that indicated approximately 50 percent support for accession. Given the wide range of views among coalition members, some analysts questioned how long the three-party government coalition would survive. That concern was reinforced by the September 2007 municipal and county elections. Although Labor improved on its 2003 performance and the Center Party basically held even, the Socialist Left took a drubbing, losing nearly half its support. The Frp's vote share also dropped from 22 percent in the 2005 national election to under 18 percent in the 2007 balloting, while the Conservatives staged a comeback, climbing from 14 to 19 percent.

In June 2007 the *Storting* approved a major consolidation within the domestic oil industry—Statoil's purchase of the oil and gas operations of Norsk Hydro, the petroleum and aluminum giant, for $30 billion. The state now owns a 67 percent interest in the world's largest offshore oil producer.

The economy and immigration dominated the run-up to the September 15, 2009, parliamentary election. The Stoltenberg government increased public spending by temporarily exceeding the 4 percent ceiling on using the country's oil revenues. The main challenge to the government came from the Frp, which campaigned on a platform calling for tax cuts, privatization, and tighter immigration controls. Although the election results marked a new electoral high for the Frp in votes and seats, center-right parties declared they would not join a Frp-led coalition. Instead, the relatively stable economy, coupled with Stoltenberg's personal popularity, resulted in an increase of 3 seats for the DNA. The red-green DNA-led coalition claimed 86 of the 169 seats, marking the first time in 16 years that an incumbent government won reelection and the first time since 1969 that a government maintained a majority after an election.

In the 2013 election, a conservative four-party coalition won control of the *Stortinget* (Parliament), with 96 of its 169 seats. Conservative party leader Erna SOLBERG formed a minority government with the Progress Party. Stotenberg's Labor Party won 55 seats and 73 total for his coalition.

Constitution and government. The Eidsvold Convention, one of the oldest written constitutions in Europe, was adopted by Norway on May 17, 1814. Executive power is exercised on behalf of the sovereign by a Council of State (*Statsråd*), which is headed by a prime minister and is responsible to the *Storting*. Should the cabinet resign on a vote of no confidence, the chair of the party holding the largest number of seats (exclusive of the defeated party) is asked to form a new government.

The members of the *Storting* are elected by universal suffrage and proportional representation for four-year terms. There are no by-elections, and the body is not subject to dissolution. Until October 1, 2009, the *Storting* operated as a modified bicameral assembly by electing one-fourth of its members to serve as an upper chamber (*Lagting*), while the remainder served as a lower chamber (*Odelsting*). Legislative proposals were considered separately by the two, but most other matters were dealt with by the *Storting* as a whole. The division proved largely meaningless in recent years as the party division in the chambers was the same, and legislation approved by the *Odelsting* was routinely rubber-stamped by the *Lagting*. In February 2007 the *Storting* approved a constitutional amendment, by a vote of 159–1, to dissolve the *Lagting* following the 2009 election.

The judicial system consists of district courts (*tingrett*), courts of appeal (*lagmannsrettene*), and a Supreme Court of Justice (*Høyesterett*). Judges are appointed by the king on advice from the Ministry of Justice. In addition to the regular courts, there are three special judicial institutions: a High Court of the Realm (*Riksrett*), consisting of the members of the Supreme Court and lay justices, which adjudicates charges against senior government officials; a Labor Relations Court (*Arbeidsretten*), which handles all matters concerning relations between employer and employee in both private and public sectors; and, in each community, a Conciliation Council (*Forliksråd*), to which most civil disputes are brought prior to formal legal action.

Local government is based on 19 counties (*fylker*), with Oslo, the capital, serving as one of the counties; in each county, the central government is represented by an appointed governor (*fylkesmann*). The

County Council (*Fylkestinget*), which elects a board and a chair, is the representative institution at the county level. The basic units of local government are urban municipalities and rural communes, each of which is administered by an elected council (*Kommunestyre*), a board, and a mayor.

In 1987, following nearly a decade of agitation by the country's then approximately 20,000 Laplanders, agreement was reached on the establishment of a Sámi Parliament (*Sámediggi*) as replacement for the former Norwegian Sámi Council, which had been viewed as an inadequate defender of Sámi interests. The 43-member legislature has been granted authority in certain areas, such as the future of the Sámi language, the preservation of Sámi culture, and the determination of land use in Sámi-populated areas. It also has advisory functions in such areas as regional control of natural resources. Elections are held in tandem with balloting for the *Storting*.

Freedom of the press is constitutionally guaranteed. As in many other countries, media ownership has become more concentrated, which prompted the *Storting* to enact checks in 1998. Norway was ranked 3rd out of 179 countries in terms of media freedom by Reporters Without Borders in 2013.

Foreign relations. A founding member of the UN and the homeland of its first secretary general, Trygve LIE, Norway was also one of the original members of the North Atlantic Treaty Organization (NATO) and has been a leader in Western cooperation through such organizations as the Council of Europe and the Organization for Economic Cooperation and Development. Norway participated in the establishment of EFTA but, in national referendums held in 1972 and 1994, rejected membership in the EC/EU. Regional cooperation, mainly through the Nordic Council and the Nordic Council of Ministers, has also been a major element in its foreign policy.

A long-standing concern has been a dispute with what is now the Russian Federation regarding ocean-bed claims in the Barents Sea. At issue is a 60,000-square-mile area of potentially oil-rich continental shelf claimed by Norway on the basis of a median line between each country's territorial coasts and by its neighbor on the basis of a sector line extending northward from a point just east of their mainland border. A collateral disagreement has centered on fishing rights in a southern "grey zone" of the disputed area, where 200-mile limits overlap. A 1977 provisional agreement governing joint fishing in an area slightly larger than the "grey zone" proper has subsequently been renewed on an annual basis pending resolution of the larger controversy.

In 1992 Norway attracted international criticism by withdrawing from the International Whaling Commission (IWC) rather than accept an IWC ban on commercial whaling; a month later it joined with Iceland, the Faroe Islands, and Greenland to establish the pro-whaling North Atlantic Marine Mammals Commission. In 1993 foreign disapproval grew when Norwegian vessels resumed commercial whaling despite U.S. threats of trade sanctions and EU warnings that whaling was incompatible with membership.

Seeking to promote peaceful regional cooperation in the post-Soviet era, Norway became a founding member of the ten-nation Council of the Baltic Sea States in 1992 and also joined the Barents Euro-Arctic Council set up in 1993 by the five Nordic countries and Russia and the Arctic Council established in 1996 with the five Nordic countries plus Finland, Iceland, and Sweden as members. Meanwhile, Norway had not only endorsed the EEA Treaty but had also, in 1992, accepted associate membership of the Western European Union (WEU), thereby seeking to demonstrate the pro-European axis of its foreign policy. Norway has also actively promoted peace in the wider international sphere, most dramatically through its participation in the negotiations that concluded with the 1993 Oslo Accord between Israel and the Palestinians.

Norway became enmeshed in an acrimonious fisheries dispute with Iceland in 1994, arising mainly from the latter's determination to fish in the waters around the Norwegian Svalbard islands. In November 1997 Norway concluded an agreement with Iceland and Denmark (on behalf of Greenland) establishing fishing limits in the region. Fishing issues periodically resurface, with Norway typically letting the EU take the lead in negotiations with Reykjavík.

Norway's commitment to NATO has included deploying troops in peacekeeping operations in Bosnia, Kosovo, and Afghanistan. Although Norway initially pledged $74 million to aid the reconstruction of Iraq and sent 150 troops to support peacekeeping efforts there, Prime Minister Bondevik described the Iraq war as "regrettable and sad." Prime Minister Stoltenberg recalled the remaining contingent of Norwegian troops from Iraq shortly after winning the September 2005 parliamentary election. Norwegian peacekeepers left Afghanistan in late 2012.

Norway irritated the United States and some of its European neighbors with the passage of an ethical code for investments by the country's Government Pension Fund. By law, the fund, pooled from more than $300 billion in oil exports, must be invested outside Norway. The ethical code requires investments to be made only in "socially responsible" companies. From the beginning, such U.S. companies as General Dynamics, Boeing, Lockheed Martin, and Northrop Grumman were blacklisted.

Tensions between Russia and Norway increased as a result of Moscow's decision in October 2006 to forbid Norway, along with other countries, from developing Russia's natural gas fields in the Barents Sea. Norway's Statoil took a 24 percent stake in Russia's Shtokman field, one of the world's largest, but it pulled out of the project in August 2012 and wrote off its $335 million investment. At a meeting in Greenland in May 2008, Norway and Russia joined Canada, Denmark, and the United States in agreeing to use existing international laws to resolve Arctic disputes. In November 2010 Norway joined the other seven members of the Arctic Council in the signing of the Council's first binding international treaty, which established a permanent secretariat in Tromso, Norway. After 40 years of intransigence, Norway and Russia arrived at a provisional agreement on the Arctic maritime border in 2010, granting a nearly 50–50 split of the disputed area. The agreement was finalized in a treaty signed September 15, 2011. Now Norway plans to begin prospecting the southeastern Barents region.

Norway's attempt to become the first European country to forge a bilateral trade agreement with China was dealt a blow when the Nobel committee awarded the Nobel Peace Prize to Chinese dissident Liu Xiao Bo. China subsequently cancelled a series of trade talks and block salmon shipments, despite the Norwegian government's insistence that it had no influence on the committee's decision. Beijing appeared still upset in June 2012, refusing to issue a visa to former prime minister Kjell Magne Bondevik in June 2012 so that the ordained minister could attend a meeting of the World Council of Churches.

Current issues. Stoltenberg's second term was clouded by two terrorist attacks against Norwegians. First, on July 22, 2011, a bomb exploded in downtown Oslo, killing 8 and damaging government buildings, and 68 people were shot to death at a youth camp run by the ruling DNA. Anders Behring Breivik, a Norwegian citizen, far-right extremist, and former member of the Progress Party, admitted to being the perpetrator of both attacks. Breivik released a 1,500-page manifesto that railed against a Muslim "demographic jihad" threatening Norway's national identity. Breivik received the maximum prison sentence in August 2012.

Public anger about the slow response to the attacks initially focused on Justice Minister Knut Storberget and security services chief Janne Kristiansen, leading them to resign in November 2011 and January 2012, respectively. Political fallout from the Breivik attack began in the September 2011 local elections. The far-right Progress Party dropped from 18 percent to 11 percent of the vote, while the DNA's showing rose from 29.6 percent in 2007 to 31.6 percent. Public opinion switched, however, on August 13, 2012, when the government-appointed independent commission investigating the attacks released its findings. The scathing report determined that the attacks could have been prevented, cited numerous lapses in security and communications, and blamed the high death toll on incompetence. Many Norwegians called for Stoltenberg's resignation.

Amid declining popularity of the Norwegian Labor Party and increasing calls for his resignation, Stoltenberg shuffled his cabinet in September 2012. He changed the ministers of labor and social inclusion, health, defense, foreign affairs, and culture. Hadia TAJIK, the new minister of culture, became both the youngest and the first Muslim to serve in the Norwegian Cabinet. The Center and SV reshuffled their ministers earlier in the year.

Second, on January 16, 2013, Islamist militants attacked a gas processing plant in Algeria, killing dozens, including five Norwegian Statoil employees. The insurgents were believed to have entered Mali from Algeria. Defense Minister Anne-Grete STRØM-ERICHSEN (DNA) announced on June 4 that Norway would contribute 25 troops to the UN peacekeeping mission in Mali. The news came as a surprise, as the SV, DNA's pacifist junior partner, had been vehemently against any involvement.

Stoltenberg has taken a hard-line stance toward the domestic petroleum industry. Aware of their sector's importance, oil and gas workers struck for higher wages in 2012, the government responded with a lockout and binding arbitration. Norway's oil wages are 69 percent above the EU average, driving up wages across the board and undermining competitiveness. To appease Center's agricultural constituents, the government imposed higher tariffs on beef (200 percent), lamb (429 percent), and hard cheese (277 percent) in November 2012, sparking protests from Denmark and Sweden.

Stoltenberg's government tightened Norway's immigration regulations in January 2012, cracking down on individuals whose requests for asylum had been denied. In a widely condemned move, the prime minister ordered the deportation of more than 1,000 Ethiopians, including 450 children born and raised in Norway. Many of the Ethiopians had actively worked to expose crimes committed by the incumbent Ethiopian regime and faced likely imprisonment and possible torture upon their return. Other ethnic groups were also frightened by the policy shift, with one Sri Lankan immigrant immolating herself and her 20-month-old son in protest. On July 12, 2013, the European Court of Human Rights ruled against Stoltenberg, saying the practice of returning child asylum-seekers was illegal.

Anti-immigration forces turned their attention to the Roma people living in Norway, with members of the Conservative and Progressive parties calling for a ban on begging. In July 2012 Jenny KLINGLE, from the red-green coalition's Center Party, blamed the Roma for rising crime. The Progress Party seeks to reduce immigration, especially by Muslims, while the Conservatives see immigration as providing needed labor while emphasizing their need to assimilate into Norwegian society.

Parliamentary elections were held on September 9, 2013. No prime minister has won three consecutive elections in Norway's history, and Stoltenberg did not change that statistic.

Top issues in the race included health care, education, and immigration, with parties differing over how best to use the country's oil revenue fund. Stoltenberg's coalition fractured ahead of the election over how to balance industrialization and environmental concerns. Distancing itself from Labor, the Center Party's 2013 congress ended with calls for Norway to leave the Schengen area and the European Economic Area. The Conservatives stressed improving competitiveness through education, innovation, and privatizing some health care services.

Voters in 12 municipalities, about 250,000 residents, were able to vote online. A coalition of 4 conservative parties, led by Erna Solberg (nicknamed "Iron Erna" in an allusion to Britain's Margaret Thatcher), won 96 seats in the *Stortinget*, comfortably exceeding the 85 needed for a majority. Solberg's Conservatives won 48 seats, followed by the Progress Party with 29, the Christian Democrats with 10, and the Liberals with 9. The populist Progress Party has never been in government before, and even with its toned-down anti-immigration rhetoric, the Christian Democrats and Liberals were reluctant to join a coalition that included them. On September 30 Solberg announced she was forming a minority government with the Progress Party, winning its support after agreeing to halt Arctic oil exploration and to tighten asylum policies.

POLITICAL PARTIES

Government Parties:

Conservative Party (*Høyre*—H). The oldest of the contemporary Norwegian parties (founded in 1884), the *Høyre* (literally "Right") advocates a "modern, progressive conservatism" emphasizing private investment, elimination of government control in the semipublic industries, lower taxes, and a revised tax structure that would benefit business. It has long favored a strong defense policy.

Although the party's parliamentary representation declined from 50 seats in 1985 to 37 in 1989, it succeeded in forming a short-lived minority coalition administration under Jan Syse—the party's sole prime minister Kåre Willoch left office in 1986. In the September 1993 election the pro-EU Conservatives slumped from 37 seats to 28. Subsequent moves by some Conservative branches to establish local alliances with the populist Progress Party caused considerable internal dissension, as the national leadership frequently gave parliamentary backing to the minority Labor government, particularly on budgetary matters. In 1997 the party decline continued as it won only 23 seats. In 2001 it resurged, winning 38 seats, but its chair, Jan PETERSEN, yielded to KrF insistence that Kjell Bondevik be prime minister of any KrF-Conservative-Liberal government.

Although the party captured only 23 seats in the 2005 election, in 2006 it opted to maintain its leadership, reelecting Erna Solberg as chair. Solberg pledged to refocus the party on the September 2007 municipal and county elections, in which it won 19 percent of the vote. The Conservative vote share rebounded to 17.2 percent in 2009, increasing the party's seat total from 23 to 30, but still 11 seats behind the Frp. Perhaps out of frustration among conservatives in the electorate over the inability to elect a Center-right government, public opinion polling a month after the election showed the Conservatives pulling ahead of the Frp for the first time in several years.

Campaigning on a platform of lower taxes, economic diversification, and privatization, Solberg led the Conservatives to victory in 2013, winning 48 seats—placing it second behind Labor—but head of a four-party coalition that secured a majority of 96 seats. Solberg formed a minority government with the Progress Party.

Leaders: Erna SOLBERG (Chair), Jan Tore SANNER (First Vice Chair), Bent HØIE (Second Vice Chair), Lars Arne RYSSDAL (Secretary General).

Progress Party (*Fremskrittspartiet*—Frp). A libertarian group founded by Anders LANGE in 1974, the anti-EU Progress Party was known until 1977 as Anders Lange's Party for a Strong Reduction in Taxes, Rates, and Public Intervention (*Anders Langes Parti til Sterk Nedsettelse av Skatter, Avgifter, og Offentlige Inngrep*). Although it lost 2 of its 4 seats in the 1985 balloting, the Frp was subsequently invited to join the ruling coalition to offset the Conservatives' losses. Declining to do so, the party held a subsequent balance of power in the *Storting* and provided the crucial votes needed to defeat the Willoch government in April 1986. In the 1989 parliamentary poll the Frp emerged as the third largest party, with 22 *Storting* seats, but in 1993 it suffered a major reverse, winning only 10. In 1997 the Frp regained its strength by winning 25 seats and a 15.3 percent share of the vote, second only to Labour. The Frp has favored dismantling the welfare state and has opposed subsidies to such sectors as fishing and agriculture. It takes a restrictive stand on immigration issues and favors tough anti-crime measures.

Less than a year before the September 2001 election, polls showed the Frp as the country's most popular party, but that changed in February 2001 when party members, including its second most influential leader, Terje SÖVIKNES, were implicated in a sex scandal. Meanwhile, the party was also being torn by sharp differences between its more moderate elements, on the one hand, and its more overtly fascistic and racist wing, on the other. In the end, the party registered a modest loss in vote share, to 14.7 percent, and won 26 seats. Carl I. HAGEN, the chair since 1978, extended the party's conditional support to the new Bondevik three-party coalition, thereby enabling it to take office in October.

Entering the September 2005 election, the Frp positioned itself as an outside party and campaigned both in defense of a strong welfare state and for radical tax cuts. It was rewarded with 22 percent of the vote and 38 seats, supplanting the Conservatives as the leading opposition party. In May 2006 Siv Jensen—the first woman to lead the party—was elected chair. Under her leadership the party has moved closer to the Conservative Party and taken an increasingly hard line against immigrants, especially Muslim immigrants.

In the September 2007 local elections the Frp registered a modest improvement over its 2003 totals, winning about 18 percent of the vote, below its 2005 vote share and a percentage point behind the Conservatives. The Frp continued to make electoral progress in the September 2009 balloting, increasing its vote share to a best-ever 22.9 percent and winning 41 seats. The party's popularity dropped initially following the in the wake of Anders Behring Breivik's murder spree in 2011 (Breivik, who had once been a member of the Frp, attacked the Labor Party because he believed that its promotion of multiculturalism had allowed a Muslim "demographic jihad" threatening Norway's national identity), but it recovered and finished third in the 2013 parliamentary election, winning 29 seats. It entered government for the first time in coalition with the Conservative Party.

Leaders: Siv JENSEN (Chair, Head of Parliamentary Group), Per SANDBERG (First Vice Chair), Ketil Solvik OLSEN (Second Vice Chair), Finn Egil HOLM (Secretary General).

Other Parliamentary Parties:

Norwegian Labor Party (*Det Norske Arbeiderparti*—DNA). Organized in 1887, Labor has been the strongest party in Norway since 1927. Its program of democratic socialism resembles those of other Scandinavian Social Democratic parties. Its longest-serving post–World War II prime ministers have been Einar Gerhardsen, who served three times (for a total of over 17 years), between 1945 and 1965, and Gro Harlem Brundtland, who also served three times (for some 10 years), between 1981 and 1996.

In June 1994 a special Labor conference decided by a 2–1 majority to back EU accession in the November referendum, although substantial rank-and-file Labor opposition to membership contributed to the eventual "no" vote. When Brundtland decided to retire as prime minister in 1996, she handed over leadership to Thorbjørn Jagland. During this period, despite its close links to labor unions, the party leadership seemed open to finding private sector solutions for the problems of the welfare state, alienating some of its more left-wing supporters. Labor also remained a firm backer of NATO.

Jagland resigned as prime minister after the 1997 legislative election. Even though Labor had won a plurality of 65 seats, it fell short of his prediction. Labor's vote share declined in municipal balloting in September 1999 and February 2000, but the fall of the Bondevik coalition government in March 2000 led to formation of a Labor minority government under Jens Stoltenberg. After Labor won a dismal 43 *Storting* seats in the September 2001 election, Stoltenberg resigned as prime minister and became party chair, replacing Jagland, in November 2002.

Building on positive results in the September 2003 local elections, Stoltenberg negotiated a red-green alliance with the Center and Socialist Left Parties that, led by Labor's 61 seats at the September 2005 election, permitted Stoltenberg to reclaim the office of prime minister. In the September 2007 local elections Labor increased its vote share over 2003 by about 2 percent, to 30 percent of the total. Even more impressive was Labor's 35.4 percent vote share in the September 2009 general election. Its 64 seats allowed the Stoltenberg-headed, Labor-led coalition to continue its majority status. Labor dropped 9 seats in 2013 and lost control of the *Stortinget.* Stoltenberg tendered his resignation on October 14, after completing the 2014 budget.

Leaders: Jens STOLTENBERG (Former Prime Minister and Party Leader), Helga PEDERSEN (Deputy Leader), Raymond JOHANSEN (General Secretary), Signe BRUDESET (International Secretary).

Christian People's Party (*Kristelig Folkeparti*—KrF or KFp). Also known as the Christian Democratic Party, the KrF was created in 1933 with the primary objective of maintaining the principles of Christianity in public life. In addition to support for most Conservative policies, the KrF's agenda subsequently centered on introduction of anti-abortion legislation and increased trade with developing countries. In the 1989 election its legislative strength dropped from 16 to 14 seats, falling further by 1 seat in 1993, when it campaigned against EU membership. The party nearly doubled its representation in September 1997, going up to 25 seats. Joining with the Liberal and Center Parties to form a minority coalition government in October, the KrF was permitted to select the new prime minister—former deputy prime minister and foreign affairs minister Kjell Bondevik—because it held the largest deputy bloc of the three. Bondevik resigned as prime minister in March 2000 following defeat of a government bill in the *Storting.* Although the party finished with only 22 seats after the September 2001 election, Bondevik returned to the prime ministership. Following a poor performance by the KrF in the September 2003 local elections, Valgerd Svarstad HAUGLAND resigned after nearly nine years as KrF chair; she was succeeded in 2004 by Health Minister Dagfinn Høybråten, a strong opponent of EU membership.

Under Bondevik, Norway enjoyed strong economic growth, with personal incomes rising and the stock market almost tripling. Moreover, inflation remained largely in check while interest rates declined sharply. Despite these gains, Bondevik's insistence on a conservative fiscal policy and tax cuts seemed out of step with the general public, which favored higher levels of public sector spending. In 2005 the KrF won less than 7 percent of the votes cast and only 11 seats. Bondevik announced his retirement from politics shortly after the election. In the September 2009 parliamentary balloting the KrF vote share fell back to 5.5 percent (good for 10 seats), its worst showing since shortly after the party was formed in the 1930s. It polled a similar 5.6 percent in 2013, again taking 10 seats.

Leaders: Knut Arild HAREIDE (Chair); Dagun ERIKSEN, Bjørg Tysdal MOE (Deputy Chairs); Hans Olaf SYVERSEN (Parliamentary Leader); Knut JAHR (Secretary General), Andreas Haug LØLAND (International Secretary).

Center Party (*Senterpartiet*—Sp). Formed in 1920 to promote the interests of agriculture and forestry, the Sp was originally known as the Agrarian Party. In the late 1980s it began to take steps to broaden its appeal, changing its name, stressing ecological issues, and advocating reduced workdays for families with small children. Not surprisingly, it also championed the post-1975 government policy of bringing farmers' incomes up to the level of industrial workers, although it remained conservative on some economic, social, and religious matters.

Campaigning on a strongly anti-EU ticket, the Sp made major gains in the September 1993 election, increasing its representation from 11 to 32 seats. In the new *Storting* the Sp often backed the minority Labor government, although in June 1996 the party issued a joint statement with Christian People's and Liberal Parties envisaging a nonsocialist coalition after the 1997 election. In 1997, the Sp dropped back to 11 seats, although its vision of a center-liberal coalition government became a reality the following month.

Anne Enger LAHNSTEIN, Sp chair for 16 years, resigned her party post (but not her cabinet position) in March 1999 and was succeeded by Odd Roger ENOKSEN. In the 2001 election the party won ten *Storting* seats, remaining in opposition. Åslaug HAGA assumed the party's leadership in 2005 and entered into the red-green alliance with the Labor and Center Parties. By doing so, she further moved the party to a centrist position, supporting, for example, oil production in the Barents Sea (under strict environmental standards) and further participation in the global markets. Some members of the party charged that Haga abandoned farmers and the party's traditional agricultural values. In the September 2007 local elections the Sp won about 8 percent of the total vote, as it had in 2003.

After receiving fierce criticism over allegations that she had obtained illegal building permits for her family's homes, Haga resigned her party leadership and ministerial positions in mid-June 2008. She was replaced on a temporary basis by Deputy Leader Lars Peder Brekk until the party elected Liv Signe Navarsete as its new leader in September. Under Navarsete's leadership the Sp held onto its 11 seats (on a vote share of 6.2 percent) in the September 2009 election, which allowed it to continue as a junior partner in the Labor-led majority coalition, despite misgivings about Labor's intention to keep open the possibility of more off-shore oil exploration. The party dropped from 11 seats to 10 in the 2013 election.

Leaders: Liv Signe NAVARSETE (Party Leader), Ola Borten MOE (Deputy Leader), Trygue Magnus Slagsvold VEDUM (Parliamentary Leader), Knut OLSEN (Secretary General).

Liberal Party (*Venstre*—V). Formed in 1884, the Liberal Party (*venstre* means "left"), like the Sp, currently stresses ecological issues, while in economic policy it stands between the Conservative and Labor Parties. Having suffered defections to splinter groups, the Liberals lost their two remaining parliamentary seats in 1985. In June 1988 the Liberal People's Party (*Det Liberale Folkepartiet*—DLF), which had been formed in 1972 by Liberal dissidents who favored Norway's entrance into the EC and had lost its only parliamentary seat in 1977, rejoined the parent party. After failing to regain *Storting* representation in 1989, the Liberals won 1 seat in 1993 and took 6 seats in 1997, joining the subsequent KrF-led coalition government until its dissolution in March 2000. *Venstre* won only 2 seats in 2001 but again joined Prime Minister Bondevik's governing coalition. In the September 2005 elections the party made its best showing since 1972, winning almost 6 percent of the vote and capturing 10 seats, but the success was short-lived. Ahead of the September 2009 parliamentary election, leader Lars SPONHEIM ruled out his party's participation in any government that included the Progressives, possibly undermining a center-right coalition. The party won only 3.9 percent of the vote and 2 seats. Sponheim resigned after the election, and Trine Skei Grade, one of the party's two parliamentarians, was elected party leader in April 2010. *Venstre* won 9 seats in 2013 as part of Erna Solberg's conservative coalition.

Leaders: Trine Skei GRADE (Leader); Ola ELVESTUEN, Terje BREVIK (Deputy Leaders).

Socialist Left Party (*Sosialistisk Venstreparti*—SV). Organized prior to the 1973 election as the Socialist Electoral Association (*Sosialistisk Valgforbund*), the SV was until late 1975 a coalition of the Norwegian Communist Party (below), the Socialist People's Party (*Sosialistisk Folkeparti*—SF), and the Democratic Socialist/Labor Movement Information Committee against Norwegian Membership in the Common Market (*Demokratiske Sosialister/Arbeiderbevegelsens Informasjonskomite mot Norsk Medlemskap i EF*—DS/AIK). At a congress held in Trondheim in March 1975, the members of the coalition committed themselves to the formation of the new party, although dissolution of the constituent parties was not mandatory until the end of 1976. In November 1975 the Communist Party decided against dissolution, and in the September 1977 election the SV, damaged in August when two of its deputies leaked a secret parliamentary report on defense negotiations with the United States, retained only 2 of the 16 seats formerly held by the Socialist alliance. The party nonetheless provided the Nordli government with the crucial support needed to maintain a slim parliamentary majority prior to the 1981 balloting, in which it won 2 additional seats. In 1989 the party raised its parliamentary representation from 6 to 17 seats before slipping back to 13 in 1993.

The SV campaigned against EU accession in the November 1994 referendum. In April 1996 SV leader Erik SOLHEIM accused Labor and its Center parliamentary allies of "Americanizing" Norway by a combination of tax cuts for the rich and welfare benefit cuts for the poor. The SV faltered in the 1997 election, dropping from 13 seats to 9. It has toned down its anti-NATO rhetoric in recent years and is now a strong advocate for Norway's "international responsibilities," including foreign aid. The SV more than doubled its representation in the September 2001 election, winning 23 seats.

Looking to build upon its 2001 success, the SV continued to move toward more centrist positions and joined Labor and the Center Party to form the red-green alliance in the September 2005 election. As a requirement for joining the alliance, the SV agreed to set aside its long-standing demand that Norway withdraw from NATO and muted much of its anti-U.S. rhetoric. However, it retained only 15 seats. In 2006–2007 the SV grew more critical of the government's environmental policies and the country's continuing presence in Afghanistan. In the September 2007 local elections the SV won only 6 percent of the vote, about half of its 2003 share. Its electoral fortunes also fell in the 2009 parliamentary balloting, in which it won only 6.2 percent of the vote and 11 seats. The SV subsequently kept its minor coalition partner role in government, but only after agreeing to the Labor Party positions on tightening restrictions on asylum seekers and keeping open the possibility of more off-shore oil exploration. Long-time party leader Kristin HALVORSEN stepped down as party chair on March 10, 2012. She was succeeded by Audun Lysbakken, the former minister of children, equality, and social inclusion. Lysbakken had resigned that post just five days earlier amid charges of channeling public funds to charity groups linked to him, but he was the only candidate for the job. The party dropped from 11 seats to 7 in the 2013 elections.

Leaders: Audun LYSBAKKEN (Party Chair), Bård Vegar SOLHJELL (Deputy Chair, Parliamentary Leader), Inga Marte THORKILDSEN (Deputy Chair), Silje Schei TVEITDAL (Secretary General), Lene Aure HANSEN (International Secretary).

Environment Party The Greens (*Miljøpartiet De Grønne*—MDG). Norway's Green Party was established in 1988 by consolidating many local movements. It advocates a "caring society in ecological balance" and is especially concerned with the environmental impact of Norway's petroleum industry. The party received only 0.3 percent of the vote in 2009, its first run for the *Stortinget*, but won representation in 18 city councils in 2011, including Oslo, Bergen, Trondheim, and Stavanger. It won its first national seat in 2013, with 2.8 percent of the vote.

Spokespersons: Hanna MARCUSSEN, Harald A. NISSEN.

Other Parties Contesting the 2013 Elections:

Red (*Rødt*). Red was formed in March 2007 by merger of the Red Electoral Alliance (*Rød Valgallianse*—RV) and the Workers' Communist Party (*Arbeidernes Kommunistparti*—AKP). The RV had been formed in 1973 as an electoral front for the Maoist AKP but subsequently grew to include a substantial number of self-described "independent socialists." Prior to the 1989 elections the RV joined with the Norwegian Communist Party (NKP, above) in the FMS. Returning to a separate status, in 1993 the RV won 1.1 percent of the vote and one *Storting* seat, which it lost in 1997. In 2005 the RV won only 1.2 percent of the vote and again failed to capture any seats. Torstein Dahle was reelected party president in 2005 and then leader of the newly formed Red. He was able to lead the party to a slight increase in vote support in the September 2009 balloting, but the RV's 1.4 percent of the vote entitled it to no seats. It dropped to 1.1 percent in 2013.

Leaders: Bjønar MOXNES (Leader); Marie Sneve MARTINUSSEN, Marielle LERAAND (Deputy Leaders); Mari ELFRING (Secretary).

The only other parties to achieve at least 0.1 percent in 2013 were the **The Christians** (*De Kristne*), with 0.6 percent; the **Pensioners' Party** (*Pensjonistpartiet*—Pp), 0.4 percent; the **Pirate Party of Norway** (*Piratpartiet Norge*), 0.3 percent; the **Coastal Party** (*Kystpartiet*), **Coastal Party** (*Kystpartiet*). (*Demokratene i Norge*) and the **Christian Unity Party** (*Kristent Samlingsparth*), each polled 0.1 percent.

Norwegian Communist Party (*Norges Kommunistiske Parti*—NKP). The NKP held 11 *Storting* seats in 1945 but lost all of them by 1961. In March 1975 it participated in the initial formation of the Socialist Left Party, but the following November it voted at an extraordinary congress against its own dissolution. Prior to the 1989 election it joined with the Red Electoral Alliance (see Red, above) to form the Local List for Environment and Solidarity (*Fylkeslistene for Miljø og Solidaritet*—FMS), which failed to secure representation. The party chose not to contest the 1993 election and obtained only 0.1 percent of the vote or less in 1997, 2001, 2005, and 2009. It received 611 votes in 2013.

Leader: Svend Haakon JACOBSEN (Leader).

LEGISLATURE

The ***Stortinget*** (also frequently rendered as *Storting*) is a unicameral parliament whose members are elected to four-year terms by universal suffrage and party-list proportional representation from 19 multimember (3 to 16 seats each) constituencies (corresponding to the 19 counties). (Of the 169 members, 150 are elected based solely on results within each constituency. The other 19 sears [one in each constituency] serve as "top up" or compensatory seats and are distributed according to nationwide vote percentages for parties.) From 1814 through mid-2009 it divided itself for certain purposes into two chambers by electing one-fourth of its members to an upper chamber (*Lagting*), while the remaining members constituted a lower chamber (*Odelsting*). Each *ting* named its own president; the president of the *Storting* served for the duration of its term, and the presidents of the two chambers were chosen annually. The *Lagting* sat for the last time in June 2009, and the dual chamber structure was officially dissolved on October 1.

In the most recent election on September 9, 2013, the Norwegian Labor Party won 55 seats; the Conservative Party, 48; the Progress Party, 29; the Christian People's Party, 10; the Center Party, 10; the Liberal Party, 9; the Socialist Left Party, 7; and the Greens, 1.

President of the Storting: Dag Terje ANDERSEN.

CABINET

[as of November 22, 2013]

Prime Minister	Erna Solberg (H) [f]
Ministers	
Agriculture and Food	Sylvi Listhaug (Frp)
Children, Equality, and Social Inclusion	Solveig Horne (Frp) [f]
Culture and Church Affairs	Thorhild Widvey (H) [f]
Defense	Ine Marie Eriksen Søreide (H) [f]
Education, Research, and Higher Education	Torbjørn Røe Isaksen (H)
Environment	Kristine Sundtoft (H) [f]
Finance	Siv Jensen (Frp) [f]
Fisheries and Coastal Affairs	Elisabeth Aspaker (H) [f]
Foreign Affairs	Børge Brende (H)
Health and Care Services	Bent Høie (H)
Justice and Public Security	Anders Anundsen (Frp)
Labor and Social Affairs	Robert Eriksson (Frp)
Local Government and Regional Development	Jan Tore Sanner (H)
Office of the Prime Minister and EU Affairs	Vidar Helgesen (H)
Petroleum and Energy	Tord Lien (Frp)
Trade and Industry	Monica Mæland (H) [f]
Transport and Communications	Ketil Solvik-Olsen (Frp)

[f] = female

INTERGOVERNMENTAL REPRESENTATION

Ambassador to the U.S.: Wegger Christian STROMMEN.

U.S. Ambassador to Norway: George TSUNIS (nominated).

Permanent Representative to the UN: Geir O. PEDERSEN.

IGO Memberships (Non-UN): ADB, AfDB, CEUR, EBRD, EFTA, IADB, ICC, IEA, IOM, NATO, OECD, OSCE, WTO.

RELATED TERRITORIES

Norway's principal overseas territories are the islands of the Svalbard group and Jan Mayen, both of which are legally incorporated into the Norwegian state. In addition, Norway has two dependencies in southern waters, Bouvet Island and Peter I Island, and claims a sector of Antarctica.

Svalbard. Svalbard is the group name given to all the islands in the Arctic Ocean between 74° and 81° north latitude and 10° and 35° east longitude, Spitzbergen being the most important island in the group. Svalbard has a land area of 23,957 square miles (62,049 sq. km); its resident population is approximately 2,600 (2006E), of whom some 1,600 are Norwegians, most of the remainder being Russians.

The islands were placed under Norwegian sovereignty by the 1920 Svalbard Treaty, the 39 signatories of which are entitled to exploit Svalbard's natural resources, although only Norwegian and Soviet/Russian companies have done so. Coal mining is the major activity in the area; oil and gas exploration began in the late 1980s. In 1993 the government and four Norwegian universities established at the largest settlement, Longyearbyen, the University Center in Svalbard, which hosts domestic and international researchers and students. More recently, tourism has been gaining in importance.

In 2007 construction began on the Svalbard International Seed Vault on Spitzbergen. The vault, positioned 120 meters inside a mountain, will store seeds from all known varieties of food crops as protection against their loss.

Governor: Odd Olsen INGERØ.

Jan Mayen. Jan Mayen is an island of 144 square miles (373 sq. km) located in the Norwegian Sea, 555 nautical miles from Tromsø. It was incorporated as part of the Kingdom of Norway in 1930. A meteorological station was established on the island during World War II, with navigational and radio facilities added thereafter. There are no permanent inhabitants.

Bouvet Island (*Bouvetøya*). Located in the South Atlantic, Bouvet Island has an area of 22 square miles (58 sq. km) and is uninhabited. It became a Norwegian dependency in 1930 and was declared to be a nature reserve in 1971.

Peter I Island (*Peter I Øy*). Situated some 250 miles off the Antarctic continent in the Bellingshausen Sea, Peter I Island has an area of 96 square miles (249 sq. km) and became a Norwegian dependency in 1933. It is uninhabited.

Queen Maud Land (*Dronning Maud Land*). The Norwegian-claimed sector of Antarctica, Queen Maud Land, extends from 20° west longitude to 45° east longitude. Its legal status has been placed in suspense under terms of the 1959 Antarctic Treaty.

OMAN

Sultanate of Oman
Sultanat Uman

Political Status: Independent sultanate recognized December 20, 1951; present regime instituted July 23, 1970; new "basic law" decreed on November 6, 1996.

Area: 119,500 sq. mi. (309,500 sq. km).

Population: 2,918,335 (2012E—UN); 3,154,134 (2013E—U.S. Census).

Major Urban Center (2005E): MUSCAT (urban area, 640,000).

Official Language: Arabic.

Monetary Unit: Oman Rial (official rate November 1, 2013: 0.39 rial = $1US).

Head of State and Government: Sultan Qabus ibn Said Al SAID; assumed power July 23, 1970, in a coup d'état that deposed his father, Sultan Said ibn Taymur Al SAID.

THE COUNTRY

The Sultanate of Oman (known prior to August 1970 as Muscat and Oman), which occupies the southeast portion of the Arabian Peninsula and a number of offshore islands, is bounded by the United Arab Emirates on the northwest, Saudi Arabia on the west, and Yemen on the extreme southwest. A small, noncontiguous area at the tip of the Musandam Peninsula extends northward into the Strait of Hormuz, through which much of the world's ocean-shipped oil passes. Although the Omani population is predominantly Arab (divided into an estimated 200 tribes), small communities of Iranians, Baluchis, Indians, East Africans, and Pakistanis are also found. Ibadhi Muslims constitute up to 75 percent of the population; most of the remainder are Wahhabis of the Sunni branch, although there is a small Shiite population. In addition to Arabic, English, Farsi, and Urdu, several Indian dialects are spoken.

Prior to 1970 the Sultanate was an isolated, essentially medieval state without roads, electricity, or significant educational and health facilities; social behavior was dictated by a repressive and reclusive sultan. However, following his overthrow in 1970, the country underwent rapid modernization, fueled by soaring oil revenue. Oman currently provides free medical facilities, housing assistance for most of its citizens, and schooling, with a 97 percent enrollment rate for primary school aged children in 2011, according to the World Bank. Economic growth has been concentrated in the coastal cities with an accompanying construction boom relying on a large foreign workforce. However, under a government program designed to reduce migration to urban areas, services have been extended to most of the vast rural interior. Growing access to education (more than 40 percent of Omani students are female) has reduced the once high illiteracy rate among women. Women have visible roles in both private and public sectors in part because of the relatively moderate (in regional terms) stance of the sultan.

Although much of the labor force works in agriculture, most food must be imported; dates, nuts, limes, and fish are exported. Cattle are bred extensively in the southern province of Dhofar, and Omani camels are prized throughout Arabia. Since petroleum production began in 1967, the Sultanate has become heavily dependent on oil revenue, which, at a production rate of more than 700,000 barrels per day, accounts for more than 70 percent of government revenue and 40 percent of GDP. However, liquefied natural gas continues to be a rapidly growing segment of the economy. In a further effort to offset the nation's dependence on oil, the government has launched a program of economic diversification, intended to encourage foreign investment, promote small-scale private industry, and enhance the fledgling tourism sector. Recent initiatives include changes in investment law to permit Omani companies to be owned by non-nationals. The government of Oman has undertaken a number of large infrastructure projects, including the construction of the giant maritime trans-shipment terminal at the port of Mina Raysut, and development of gas exports.

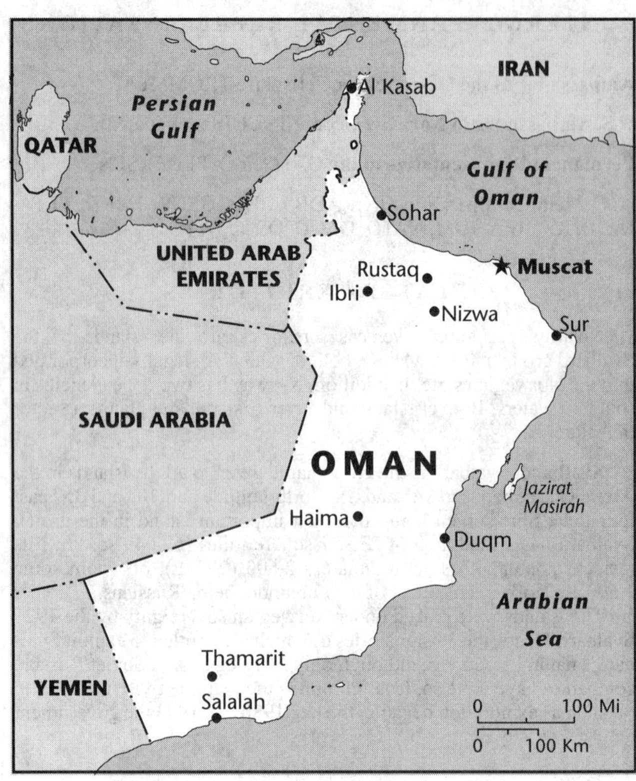

Annual GDP growth averaged 5.4 percent in 2004–2007. The International Monetary Fund (IMF) in recent years has commended Oman's sound economic policies, including diversification and the reduction of public debt. These policies, in combination with high crude oil prices, rising consumption and investment, and increasing non-oil revenue, have contributed to the positive economic forecast. Oman's decision in 2008 to continue its monetary peg to the U.S. dollar rather than join a monetary union with the Gulf Cooperation Council (GCC) was commended by fund managers, though they acknowledged that the peg was among the chief reasons for rising inflation in the sultanate. In February the sultan ordered pay raises of as much as 43 percent for public sector workers and an increase in food subsidies to help offset rising prices for housing and commodities. In the wake of the global economic crisis in 2009, the government said it would increase spending by 11 percent to help offset declining oil revenues, and efforts were undertaken to reduce an unemployment rate of 9 percent by expanding job training, particularly for youth. Annual GDP growth remained robust, averaging 4.4 percent from 2008 to 2011, even as oil reserves (and output) declined. The estimated real GDP growth rate for 2013 was 4.2 percent. Increases in tourism, direct foreign investment, oil prices, and public spending helped bolster the economy, which IMF managers said had weathered the global economic crisis well. Inflation was 2.9 percent. In December 2012, the unemployment rate was 5.4 percent, according to the Ministry of Manpower.

GOVERNMENT AND POLITICS

Political background. Conquered by the Portuguese in 1508, the Omanis successfully revolted in 1650 and subsequently extended their domain as far south as Zanzibar. A brief period of Iranian intrusion (1741–1743) was followed in 1798 by the establishment of a treaty of friendship with Great Britain; thereafter, the British played a protective role, although formally recognizing the Sultanate's independence in 1951.

Oman is home of the Ibadhi sect, centered in Nazwa, which evolved from the egalitarian Kharijite movement of early Islam. During much of the twentieth century, Omani politics centered on an intrasect rivalry between imams, who controlled the interior, and sultans of the Said dynasty, who ruled over the coastal cities of Muscat and Muttrah, although the Treaty of Sib, concluded in 1920, acknowledged the nation's indivisibility. On the death of the incumbent imam in 1954, Sultan Said ibn Taymur Al SAID attempted, without success, to secure election as his successor. However, revolts against the sultan by the new imam's followers were ended with British help in 1959, thus cementing the sultan's authority over the entire country. The foreign presence having become the subject of a number of UN debates, the remaining British bases were closed in 1977, although a number of British officers remained attached to the Omani armed forces.

The conservative and isolationist Sultan Said was ousted on July 23, 1970, by his son, Qabus ibn Said Al SAID. The former sultan fled to London, where he died in 1972. Qabus, whose takeover was supported by the British, soon began efforts to modernize the country, but his request for cooperation from rebel groups who had opposed his father evoked little positive response. In 1971–1972 two left-wing guerrilla groups merged to form the Popular Front for the Liberation of Oman and the Arabian Gulf (renamed in July 1974 as the Popular Front for the Liberation of Oman—PFLO), which continued resistance to the sultan's regime, primarily from bases in the (then) People's Democratic Republic of Yemen (South Yemen). Qabus maintained his superiority with military assistance from Saudi Arabia, Jordan, Iran, and Pakistan, and in December 1975 he asserted that the rebellion had been crushed, and a formal cease-fire was announced in March 1976.

Although the sultan subsequently stated his desire to introduce democratic reforms, a Consultative Assembly established in 1981 consisted entirely of appointed members, and Oman remained for all practical purposes an absolute monarchy. In November 1990 the sultan announced plans for a Consultative Council of regional representatives in an effort to provide for more citizen participation.

On November 6, 1996, Sultan Qabus issued "The Basic Law of the Sultanate of Oman," the nation's first quasi-constitutional document. Although it confirmed the final authority of the sultan in all government matters, it also codified the responsibilities of the Council of Ministers and provided for a second consultative body, the Council of State (see Legislature, below). Subsequently, following preliminary balloting for a new Consultative Council on October 16, 1997, Sultan Qabus reshuffled his cabinet on December 16, designating several "young technocrats" as new ministers.

New elections to the Consultative Council were held on September 14, 2000, successful candidates for the first time not being subject to approval by the sultan. The Omani government continued to pursue "quiet progress" toward political liberalization by mandating that 30 percent of the electors in the electoral college be women. As it turned out, only two women candidates were successful then and in the elections of October 4, 2003, the first time that all citizens could participate. Members were elected to four-year terms in the first balloting open to all citizens.

In the October 27, 2007, Consultative Council elections, no women won seats, and the two women who had held seats were not reelected, marking the first time in many years that the assembly was without female representation. The cabinet was reshuffled on September 9, 2007, and the manpower minister was replaced in September 2008. The minister of health was replaced in March 2010.

Beginning with protests in Tunisia in December 2010, the so-called Arab Spring uprisings spread quickly throughout North Africa and the Middle East, erupting in Oman in late February, driven by high unemployment and a large underage population, more than half of which is under age 30. On the second day of demonstrations in the port town of Sohar, police shot and killed two protesters. Sultan Qabus responded quickly, reshuffling the cabinet, granting pay raises to civil servants, pledging to create 50,000 public sector jobs, and ceding some lawmaking powers to the Consultative Council. Though demonstrations continued in various parts of the country with activists calling for democratic reforms and an end to corruption, the protests were generally much smaller in number than in other countries in the region. Sultan Qabus, for his part, authorized a $2.6 billion social spending package, including financial assistance to military and civil service employees and an increase in the minimum wage. Amnesty International published a report on March 31, 2011, lambasting Omani authorities for their treatment of protesters. Protests continued into April, and clashes left a total of five people dead.

Minor changes to the cabinet were made on February 27, 2011, in response to the protests, while a major reshuffle occurred on March 7.

Constitution and government. Lagging behind most other Arab states in this regard, Oman until recently had no constitution or other fundamental law, absolute power resting with the sultan, who ruled by decree. However, on November 6, 1996, Sultan Qabus issued "The Basic Law of the Sultanate of Oman," formally confirming the government's status as a hereditary Sultanate—an "independent, Arab, Islamic, fully sovereign state" for which sharia (Islamic religious law) is the "basis for legislation." Total authority for the issuance of legislation remains with the sultan, designated as head of state and commander in chief of the armed forces. The "ruling family council" is authorized to appoint a successor should the position of sultan become vacant. The sultan rules with the assistance of a Council of Ministers, whose members he appoints. The first woman was appointed to the cabinet in 2004. The sultan may appoint a prime minister but is not so required. Consultation is also provided by the Oman Council, comprising a new Council of State and the Consultative Council (see Legislature, below). The basic law can be revised only by decree of the sultan. Among other things, the basic law provides for freedom of opinion, expression, and association "within the limits of the law."

The sultanate fell 24 places to 141st on the 2013 annual press freedom index by Reporters Without Borders, reflecting a crackdown on bloggers. At least 50 were prosecuted for cyber-crime in 2012, and the trend continued into the following year when a blogger was arrested for Facebook posts in May, and an author sentenced to prison in June for selling books on the 2011 protests.

The judicial system is also based on sharia and is administered by judges (*qadis*) appointed by the minister of justice. Appeals are heard in Muscat. In remote areas the law is based on tribal custom. Administratively, the country is divided into nine regions in the north and one province in the south (Dhofar). Governors (*walis*) posted in the country's 59 *wilayahs* (administrative districts) work largely through tribal authorities and are responsible for maintaining local security, settling minor disputes, and collecting taxes. In December 2012 municipal council elections were held for the first time (see Current issues, below).

Foreign relations. Reversing the isolationist policy of his father, Sultan Qabus has fostered diplomatic relations with most Arab and industrialized countries. Britain has been deeply involved in Omani affairs since 1798, while the United States and the Sultanate signed their first treaty of friendship and navigation in 1833. In recent years Japan has also become a major trading partner. Diplomatic relations were established with the People's Republic of China in 1978 and with the Soviet Union in September 1985. In June 1989, the Sultanate signed a military cooperation agreement with France.

Despite its importance as an oil-producing state, Oman is not a member of either the Organization of Petroleum Exporting Countries (OPEC) or the Organization of Arab Petroleum Exporting Countries (OAPEC). However, since the late 1980s it has cooperated with OPEC regarding production quotas.

Relations with the more radical Arab states, already cool, were not improved by Sultan Qabus's endorsement of the Egyptian-Israeli peace treaty of March 1979. However, Oman broke off relations with Israel in the wake of the intifada. Long-standing tension with the (then) People's Democratic Republic of Yemen, occasioned largely by that country's support of the sultan's opponents in Dhofar, moderated substantially at an October 1982 "reconciliation" summit, which was followed by an exchange of ambassadors in late 1983. After a cooperation pact in October 1988, Oman concluded a formal border agreement with the Republic of Yemen in 1997.

In June 1980, after statements by Sultan Qabus opposing what he viewed as Soviet efforts to destabilize the Middle East, Muscat granted the United States access to Omani air and naval facilities in return for economic and security assistance. Oman has remained a U.S. military base since.

Sultan Qabus strongly supported the Saudi decision to invite U.S. forces to defend the Gulf in the wake of Iraq's invasion of Kuwait in August 1990, and Oman subsequently contributed troops to Operation Desert Storm.

Oman's already warm relations with Washington further improved after the September 11, 2001, terrorist attacks in the United States. Oman and Saudi Arabia issued a joint statement calling for greater cooperation in combating terrorism, and Oman was later described as highly cooperative in the U.S.-led "war on terrorism." In 2006, the United States signed a free trade agreement with Oman.

With an eye to regional long-term stability, the sultan favors stronger ties with Iran, as well as the moderate Arab position of a peace settlement with Israel and an independent Palestinian state. Oman considers Iran's nuclear power an asset to the region inasmuch as there is a peaceful application of the technology. In March 2008 U.S. Vice President Dick Cheney visited Oman to discuss Iran's nuclear program, an issue of heightened international concern and of particular significance for Oman, given its "guardianship" with Iran over the Strait of Hormuz.

In January 2009 Oman, along with several other Arab nations, sent tons of food and medical supplies to Gaza during the fighting between Israel and Hamas (see entry on Palestinian Authority/Palestine Liberation Organization for details). In February Oman and Russia discussed expanding bilateral ties. The relationship with India strengthened in 2010 with announcements of a joint investment fund of $100 million, a higher education initiative, and a joint military exercise planned for 2011.

Oman was among several nations that did not attend the 2010 Arab League summit in Libya, observers citing objections to remarks made earlier at the UN by Libyan leader Muammar al-Qadhafi, among other issues. Late in the year Oman and Pakistan agreed to boost economic ties.

Immigration issues received attention in 2010 when in May the government agreed to take back deported Bangladeshi workers who could prove that they did not violate immigration law. The action came after a meeting between the sultan and the Bangladeshi ambassador in the wake of reports that Oman had recently deported some 10,000 Bangladeshi, 17,000 Pakistani, and 26,000 Indian workers.

The arrest of seven Omani fishermen by an Irani navy vessel in Iranian waters in May 2012 strained relations between the countries. The Omani embassy in Tehran arranged for their release.

In May 2012 Oman ordered its embassy staff to leave Sana'a, the capital of Yemen, due to death threats from an unknown group related to the continuing civil conflict in that country. The Omani embassy was not closed, however.

In December 2012 India moved to sign a mutual cooperation treaty with Qatar to ensure collaboration in prevention, investigation, and prosecution of crime, and the subsequent judicial process.

In February, Nepal announced plans to open an embassy in Oman. The following month, Oman moved to improve bilateral ties with Turkey and Uzbekistan and established relations with Bangladesh.

Current issues. In response to the Arab Spring uprisings, Qabus in September called for Consultative Council elections to be held on October 15, 2011. For the first time, candidates were allowed to conduct advertising campaigns on billboards, posters, banners, and in newspapers. Voter registration was reported to be at an all-time high of more than 522,000 citizens, and voter turnout was 76 percent.

Popular unrest resurged in the spring of 2012 after contract workers of Petroleum Development Oman went on what the Omani government regarded as an illegal strike for higher wages in May. Three men were arrested after going to an oilfield to show solidarity with the strikers. The government dismissed 400 PDO workers, but they were later reinstated.

The government responded with renewed efforts to improve social programs and government transparency.

In December 2012 local municipal elections were held for the first time. Some 1,475 candidates contested the 192 seats on 61 councils. Of the 46 women who ran, 4 were elected. Though largely symbolic because the council has no executive powers, the elections were seen as a step toward democracy.

Foreign workers, estimated to be 40 percent of the population, and poor private sector job opportunities contribute to the unemployment rate, which stood at 24.4 percent in 2010. Half of those employed by the private sector between 2006 and 2011 were dismissed or left their jobs. In an effort to combat unemployment and make private sector jobs more attractive, the sultan issued a decree effective July 2013 for the minimum wage to rise by 60 percent (the second increase in as many years) and for a reduction of foreign workers to 33 percent of the population.

POLITICAL PARTIES

There are no political parties in Oman. Most opposition elements previously were represented by the Popular Front for the Liberation of Oman (PFLO), although there has been no reference to PFLO activity for many years. (See the 1999 edition of the *Handbook* for a history of the PFLO.)

LEGISLATURE

The basic law decreed by the sultan in November 1996 provided for a consultative **Oman Council,** consisting of a new, appointed Council of State and the existing Consultative Council.

Council of State (*Majlis al-Dawlah*). Considered roughly the equivalent of an upper house in a bicameral legislature, the Council of State was expected to debate policy issues at the request of the sultan, although the extent of its authority and its relationship to the Consultative Council remained unclear. On December 16, 1997, Sultan Qabus appointed 41 members (including four women) from among prominent regional figures to the first Council of State. In 2006 the council had 59 members, 9 of whom were women, all serving four-year terms. On November 4, 2007, a total of 70 members, including 14 women, were appointed by royal decree. Following Consultative Council elections in October 2011, the sultan appointed 15 women to the council.

President: Yahya bin Mafouz al-MUNTHERI.

Consultative Council (*Majlis al-Shura*). The former Consultative Assembly, established in 1981, was replaced on December 21, 1991, by the Consultative Council, an advisory body appointed by the sultan (or his designee) from candidates presented by local "dignitaries" and "people of valued opinion and experience." The council is authorized to propose legislation to the government but has no formal lawmaking role. The initial council consisted of 59 regular members (one from each *wilayah*) and a speaker who served three-year terms. In 1994 the council was expanded to 80 regular members (two from each *wilayah* with a population over 30,000 and one from each of the other *wilayahs*) and a president. For the first time women were allowed to stand as candidates (albeit only from six constituencies in or around Muscat), and two women were among those seated at the new council's inaugural session on December 26, 1994. The council was expanded to 82 members in 1997, and women from all of Oman were allowed to stand as candidates and participate in the preliminary balloting for the new council on October 16. An "electoral college" of 51,000 people (all approved by the government, primarily based on literacy requirements) elected 164 potential council members from among 736 candidates (also all approved by the government). Final selections were made in December by the sultan, who had essentially been presented with 2 candidates from which to choose for each seat.

On October 4, 2003, an expanded council of 83 members was elected to serve a four-year term. This was the first ballot open to all citizens. The president of the council, appointed by the sultan, serves as the 84th member. In the balloting on October 27, 2007, those elected were reported by the government to have strong tribal connections or were prominent businesspeople. None of the 21 women who contested were elected. In the elections of October 15, 2011, there were 1,133 candidates, including 77 women, and voting generally lined up with tribal loyalties. Those elected included 3 activists from the prodemocracy movement and 1 woman. Khalid al-Mawali was elected chair of the council on October 29, the first time the chair had been elected and not appointed by Sultan Said.

President: Khalid al-MAWALI.

CABINET

[as of November 12, 2013]

Prime Minister	Sultan Qabus ibn Said al-Said
Deputy Prime Minister for Cabinet Affairs	Said Fahd ibn Mahmud al-Said
Secretary General of the Cabinet	Sheikh al-Fadhl bin Muhammad bin Amed al-Harthy
Ministers	
Agriculture and Fisheries	Fuad bin Jaafar bin Muhammad al-Sajwani
Civil Service	Sheikh Khalid bin Omar bin Said al-Marhoon
Commerce and Industry	Ali ibn Masoud ibn Ali Sunaidy
Defense	Said Badr ibn Saud al-Busaidi
Diwan of Royal Court	Said Khalid ibn Hilal al-Busaidi
Education	Madeeha bint Ahmed bin Nassir al-Shibaniyah [f]

Environment and Climate Affairs	Sheikh Muhammad bin Salim bin Said al-Toobi
Finance	Darwish bin Ismaeel bin Ali al-Balushi
Foreign Affairs	Yusuf ibn Alawi ibn Abdallah
Health	Dr. Ahmed bin Muhammad bin Obaid al-Saeedi
Heritage and Culture	Haitham bin Tariq al-Said
Higher Education	Rawya bint Saud al-Busaidi [f]
Housing	Saif al-Shabibi
Information	Dr. Abdulmunim ibn Mansour bin Said al-Hasani
Interior	Said Hamud bin Faisal al-Busaidi
Justice	Abdulmalik ibn Abdallah ibn Ali al-Khalili
Legal Affairs	Abdullah bin Muhammad bin Said al-Saeedi
Manpower	Abdullah bin Nasser bin Abdullah al-Bakri
Palace Office Affairs	Lt. Gen. Sultan bin Muhammad al-Nuamani
Personal Representative of the Sultan	Said Thuwainy bin Shihab al-Said
Petroleum and Gas	Dr. Muhammad ibn Hamad al-Rumhi
Regional Municipalities and Water	Ahmed bin Abdullah bin Muhammad al-Shuhi
Religious Trusts (*Awqaf*) and Islamic Affairs	Abdullah ibn Muhammad al-Salimi
Social Development	Muhammad bin Said bin Saif al-Kalbani
Sports	Saad ibn Muhammad ibn Said al Mardhouf al-Saadi
Tourism	Ahmed ibn Nasser ibn Hamad al-Mehrzi
Transportation and Communications	Ahmed bin Muhammad bin Salim al-Futaisi
Ministers of State	
Governor of the Capital	Sayyid Saud bin Hilal bin Hamad al-Busaidi
Governor of Dhofar	Said Muhammad ibn Sultan ibn Hamud al-Busaidi

[f] = female

INTERGOVERNMENTAL REPRESENTATION

Ambassador to the U.S.: Hunaina Sultan al-MUGHAIRY.

U.S. Ambassador to Oman: Greta HOLTZ.

Permanent Representative to the UN: Lyutha al-MUGHAIRY.

IGO Memberships (Non-UN): GCC, LAS, NAM, OIC, WTO.

PAKISTAN

Islamic Republic of Pakistan
Islami Jamhuria-e-Pakistan

Political Status: Formally became independent on August 14, 1947; republic established on March 23, 1956; national territory confined to former West Pakistan with de facto independence of Bangladesh (former East Pakistan) on December 16, 1971; independence of Bangladesh formally recognized on February 22, 1974; martial law regime instituted following military coup of July 5, 1977; modified version of 1973 constitution introduced on March 2, 1985; martial law officially lifted December 30, 1985; constitution suspended and state of emergency imposed on October 14, 1999, following military coup of October 12; constitution restored on November 16, 2002, as amended by Legal Framework Order (LFO) promulgated on August 21; 17th constitutional amendment, containing many of the LFO provisions, approved by Parliament on December 29–30, 2003, and signed by the president on December 31; LFO abolished by passage of the 18th constitutional amendment in Parliament and 1973 constitution restored on April 15, 2010.

Area: 310,402 sq. mi. (803,943 sq. km), excluding Jammu and Kashmir, of which approximately 32,200 sq. mi. (83,400 sq. km) are presently administered by Pakistan.

Population: 184,405,126 (2013E—UN); 193,238,868 (2013E—U.S. Census).

Major Urban Centers (2005E): ISLAMABAD (974,000), Karachi (11,767,000), Lahore (6,317,000), Faisalabad (2,514,000), Rawalpindi (1,778,000), Gujranwala (1,460,000), Multan (1,436,000), Hyderabad (1,374,000), Peshawar (1,241,000).

National Language: Urdu. The 1973 constitution identified Urdu as the "national language" but added that "arrangements shall be made for its being used for official and other purposes within fifteen years from the commencing day." In the meantime, English "may be used for official purposes." As of 2011 the clause requiring adoption of Urdu as an official language had not yet been implemented. Each province may also identify and promote its own "provincial language," and all have done so.

Monetary Unit: Pakistani Rupee (market rate November 1, 2013: 106.90 rupees = $1US).

President: Mamnoon HUSSAIN (Pakistan Muslim League–Nawaz); elected for a five-year term by combined votes of Parliament and the four provincial assemblies on July 30, 2013, and sworn in on September 9, succeeding Asif Ali ZARDARI (Pakistan People's Party).

Prime Minister: Muhammad Nawaz SHARIF (Pakistan Muslim League–Nawaz); elected by the National Assembly on June 5, 2013; succeeding acting prime minister Mir Hazar Khan KHOSO (independent) who had been sworn in on March 25.

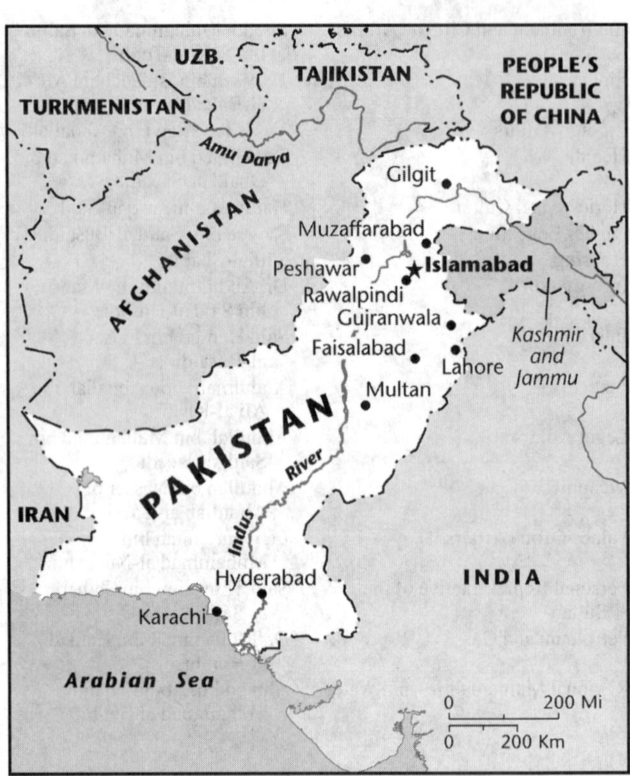

THE COUNTRY

Located in the northwest of the Indian subcontinent, Pakistan extends from the Arabian Sea a thousand miles northward across eastern plains to the Hindu Kush and the foothills of the Himalayas. The racial stock is primarily Aryan, with traces of Dravidian. The dominant language is Punjabi (50 percent), followed by Pushtu, Sindhi, Saraiki, Urdu, Gujarati, and Baluchi. English is widely spoken in business and government. Islam, the state religion, is professed by over 95 percent of the people; Christians and Hindus constitute most of the balance. Women make up only 21 percent of the active labor force, but many others participate in unpaid agricultural work. In addition, women are often engaged in home-based or cottage industries. Female participation in government has been constrained by Islamic precepts in the past, although Benazir BHUTTO was the Muslim world's first woman prime minister (1988–1990, 1993–1996). Only about half the adult population is literate—less in the case of women.

Much of the country consists of mountains and deserts, but some of the most fertile and best-irrigated land in the subcontinent is provided by the Indus River system. Agriculture continues to employ more than 45 percent of the active labor force, the principal crops being cotton, wheat, rice, sugarcane, and maize. In addition, the western province of Baluchistan supplies a rich crop of fruits and dates. The agricultural sector contributes about 22 percent of GDP, while industry accounts for 23.6 percent of GDP and just under 20 percent of employment. Though it is not heavily endowed in mineral resources, the country extracts petroleum, natural gas, iron, limestone, rock salt, gypsum, and coal. Manufacturing includes production of cotton and other textile yarns and fabrics, clothing and accessories, cement, and sugar and other foodstuffs. Pakistan's exports also include fruits, seafood, carpets, and handicrafts.

In 2000, the newly installed government privatized nonstrategic, state-owned enterprises, improving tax collection, and cutting nonessential spending as components of an economic program partly designed to secure additional assistance from the International Monetary Fund. Fueled in large part by some $5.5 billion in U.S. aid since late 2001, growth peaked mid-decade at 7.7 percent before dropping to 2.0 percent in 2008 and 2009 in response to global economic conditions. Inflation surged to 20.8 percent in 2009 in response to rising commodity prices. In November 2008, the International Monetary Fund (IMF) approved $7.6 billion in stabilization funding, which was raised in August 2009 to $11.3 billion. The country also saw a large inflow of foreign aid to counter and rebuild from the catastrophic flooding it experienced in 2010, with promised international funding totaling more than $4 billion as of September that year. Aid from the United States, a crucial donor, was cut by $800 million following the death of Osama bin Laden in Pakistan in May 2011 (see Foreign relations, below). In 2010 GDP expanded by 4.8 percent, while inflation grew by 10.1 percent. The economy expanded by 3 percent in 2011, while inflation accelerated to 13.6 percent. In 2012, GDP grew by 3.7 percent, and the inflation rate moderated slightly to 11 percent. GDP per capita that year was $1,2961. In December 2012, the World Bank announced a $5.5 billion aid program for Pakistan.

GOVERNMENT AND POLITICS

Political background. Subjected to strong Islamic influences from the 7th century onward, the area that comprises the present state of Pakistan and former East Pakistan (now Bangladesh) became part of British India during the 18th and 19th centuries and contained most of India's Muslim population. First articulated in the early 1930s, the idea of a separate Muslim state was endorsed in 1940 by the All-India Muslim League, the major Muslim political party. After the league swept the 1946–1947 election, the British accepted partition and Parliament passed the Indian Independence Act, which incorporated the principle of a separate Pakistan. Transfer of power occurred on August 14, 1947, with the new state formally coming into existence at the stroke of midnight, August 15. Mohammad Ali JINNAH, head of the All-India Muslim League, became independent Pakistan's first governor general.

India's Muslim-majority provinces and princely states were given the option of remaining in India or joining Pakistan. Sindh, Khyber Pakhtunkhwa (formerly the North-West Frontier Province [NWFP] until it was renamed in 2010), Baluchistan, and three-fifths of the Punjab accordingly combined to form what became West Pakistan, while a part of Assam and two-thirds of Bengal became East Pakistan. The Hindu maharaja of the predominantly Muslim state of Jammu and Kashmir subsequently acceded to India, but Pakistan challenged the action by sending troops into the territory; resultant fighting between Indian and Pakistani forces was halted by a UN cease-fire on January 1, 1949, leaving Pakistan in control of territory west and north of the cease-fire line. Communal rioting and population movements stemming from partition caused further embitterment between the two countries.

In March 1956, the tie to the British Crown was broken with implementation of a republican constitution, under which Iskander Ali MIRZA served as Pakistan's first president. In October 1958, however, Mirza abrogated the constitution, declared martial law, dismissed the national and provincial governments, and dissolved all political parties. Field Marshal Mohammad Ayub KHAN, appointed supreme commander of the armed forces and chief martial law administrator, took over the presidency from Mirza and was confirmed in office by a national referendum of "basic democrats" in February 1960.

Constitutional government, under a presidential system based on indirect election, was restored in June 1962, with Ayub Khan continuing to rule until March 1969, when, in the context of mounting political and economic disorder, he resigned. Gen. Agha Mohammad Yahya KHAN, army commander in chief, thereupon assumed authority as chief martial law administrator, suspended the constitution, dismissed the national and provincial assemblies, and took office as president.

Normal political activity resumed in 1970, the major unresolved issue being East Pakistani complaints of underrepresentation in the central government and an inadequate share of central revenues. In preparing for the nation's first direct election on the basis of universal suffrage (ultimately held in December 1970 and January 1971), efforts were made to assuage the long-standing political discontent in the more populous East Pakistan by allotting it majority representation in the new assembly, rather than, as in the previous legislature, mere parity with West Pakistan. Of the 300 seats up for direct election (162 from East Pakistan, 138 from West Pakistan), Sheikh Mujibur RAHMAN's East Pakistani Awami League won 160 and the Pakistan People's Party (PPP), 82.

After repeated postponements of the assembly opening, originally scheduled to take place in Dacca (East Pakistan) in March 1971, the government banned the Awami League and announced in August the disqualification of 79 of its representatives. By-elections to the vacated seats, scheduled for December, were prevented by the outbreak of war between Pakistan and India in late November and the occupation of East Pakistan by Bengali guerrilla and Indian military forces. Following the surrender of some 90,000 of its troops, Pakistan on December 17 agreed to a cease-fire on the western front. Yahya Khan stepped down as president three days later and was replaced by Zulfikar Ali BHUTTO as president and chief martial law administrator. In July 1972 President Bhutto and India's prime minister, Indira Gandhi, met in Simla, India, and agreed to negotiate outstanding differences. As a result, all occupied areas along the western border were exchanged, except in Kashmir, where a new Line of Control (LoC) was drawn. In July 1973 the National Assembly granted Bhutto the authority to recognize Bangladesh, and in August a new constitution was adopted. The speaker of the assembly, Fazal Elahi CHAUDHRY, was elected president of Pakistan, and Bhutto was designated prime minister.

PAKISTAN

A general election held in March 1977 resulted in an overwhelming victory for the ruling PPP; however, the opposition Pakistan National Alliance (PNA) denounced the returns as fraudulent and initiated a series of strikes and demonstrations that led to outbreaks of violence throughout the country. Faced with impending civil war, the army mounted a coup on July 5 that resulted in the arrest of many leading politicians, including Prime Minister Bhutto, and the imposition of martial law under Gen. Mohammad ZIA ul-Haq. Shortly after President Chaudhry's term expired in August 1978, General Zia assumed the presidency, announcing that he would yield to a regularly elected successor following a legislative election in 1979.

In April 1979, despite worldwide appeals for clemency, former prime minister Bhutto was hanged. Riots immediately erupted in most of the country's urban areas, and PNA representatives withdrew from the government. Later in the year, Zia postponed elections, banned all forms of party activity, and imposed strict censorship on the communications media.

An interim constitution promulgated in March 1981 provided for the eventual restoration of representative institutions "in conformity with Islam," while the formation the same year of the PPP-led Movement for the Restoration of Democracy (MRD) created a force against both the regime and right-wing Islamic parties. In late 1984 the president announced a referendum on an "Islamization" program, endorsement of which would also grant him an additional five-year presidential term. In the wake of an MRD call for a referendum boycott, the size of the turnout was hotly disputed, estimates ranging from as low as 15 percent to as high as 65 percent. Nevertheless, citing an overwhelming margin of approval, Zia scheduled parliamentary elections on a nonparty basis for February 1985. Despite another opposition call for a boycott, five incumbent ministers and a number of others associated with the martial law regime lost their bids for parliamentary seats. As a result, the president dissolved the cabinet and designated Mohammad Khan JUNEJO, of the center-right Pakistan Muslim League (PML), as the country's first prime minister in eight years. In the absence of legal parties, the assembly divided into two camps—a government-supportive Official Parliamentary Group (OPG) and an opposition Independent Parliamentary Group (IPG).

In October 1985, the assembly approved a political parties law despite objections by President Zia, who continued to view a multiparty system as "un-Islamic." Dissent immediately ensued within the MRD; some components—including the PML and the moderate *Jamaat-e-Islami,* which controlled the OPG and IPG, respectively—announced their intention to register, while others termed the entire exercise fraudulent and continued to press for fresh elections under a fully restored 1973 constitution. Without responding to the pressure, Zia proceeded with the scheduled termination of martial law on December 30.

In what was dubbed a "constitutional coup," in May 1988 President Zia abruptly dismissed the Junejo government because of alleged corruption. He also dissolved the National Assembly, the provincial assemblies, and local governments. In June he appointed a PML-dominated caretaker administration headed by himself and in July announced that "free, fair, and independent" elections to the national and provincial assemblies would be held on November 16 and 19, respectively.

On August 17, 1988, General Zia, the U.S. ambassador, and a number of senior military officers were killed in a plane crash in southeastern Punjab. Immediately afterward the Senate chair, Ghulam Ishaq KHAN, was sworn in as acting president and announced the formation of a caretaker Emergency National Council to rule the country pending the November elections. The PPP secured a substantial plurality in the National Assembly poll but achieved only second place in three of the four provincial elections. Nonetheless, in what some viewed as a political "deal," on December 1, Ishaq Khan formally appointed as prime minister Benazir BHUTTO, daughter of the executed prime minister, and was himself elected to a five-year term as president on December 12.

By 1990, relations between the president and the prime minister became increasingly strained. Accusing her government of corruption, abuse of power, and various other unconstitutional and illegal acts, President Khan dismissed Bhutto on August 6, 1990, appointing as her interim successor Ghulam Mustafa JATOI, leader of the Islamic Democratic Alliance (IDA), a somewhat disparate coalition of conservative anti-Bhutto groups that had been organized two years earlier. Two months later the PPP was decisively defeated in national and provincial elections, including a loss in its traditional stronghold of Sindh. On November 6 the IDA's Mohammad Nawaz SHARIF was sworn in as Pakistan's first Punjabi prime minister.

On April 18, 1993, in the wake of a failed effort by Nawaz Sharif to curtail the president's constitutional power, Ishaq Khan dismissed the Sharif government, naming Balkh Sher MAZARI, a dissident member of Sharif's PML, as acting prime minister. In May, however, the Supreme Court reinstated Sharif, thereby canceling a general election that had been scheduled for July. The action failed to resolve the widening split within the PML, and on July 18, following intervention by the recently appointed army chief of staff, Gen. Abdul WAHEED, both the president and prime minister stepped down. Ishaq Khan was succeeded, on an acting basis, by Senate chair Wasim SAJJAD. A relatively unknown former World Bank vice president, Moeenuddin Ahmad QURESHI, succeeded Nawaz Sharif.

Nawaz Sharif attempted to regain power as leader of the PML's largest faction, the PML-Nawaz (PML-N). Although the PML-N outpolled the PPP 41–38 percent in the National Assembly election of October 1993, the latter gained a plurality of seats (86, as opposed to 72 for Sharif supporters), and Bhutto was returned to office. In electoral college balloting for president in November, the PPP's Sardar Farooq Ahmad Khan LEGHARI defeated the acting incumbent.

In July 1996, in the wake of increased tension with India over Kashmir and heightened domestic unrest on the part of Islamic fundamentalists and activists of the *Muhajir Qaumi* Movement (MQM), 13 opposition parties announced an alliance to topple Bhutto. On July 31 the prime minister greatly enlarged her cabinet. Among 14 new appointees was her controversial husband, Asif Ali ZARDARI, who, in his first ministerial assignment, was named to head an investment portfolio. In September the prime minister's estranged brother, Murtaza BHUTTO, was one of seven breakaway PPP faction members killed in a gunfight outside Murtaza's Karachi home.

Citing evidence of corruption, intimidation of the judiciary, misdirection of the economy, and failure to maintain law and order, President Leghari on November 5, 1996, dismissed Prime Minister Bhutto, naming Malek Meraj KHALID, a former legislative speaker and long-estranged Bhutto confidant, as her successor in a caretaker capacity pending election of a new National Assembly in February 1997. In the interim, President Leghari announced formation of a Council for Defense and National Security (CDNS) comprising himself, the prime minister, several cabinet ministers, and the heads of the branches of the armed forces.

Voter turnout was low for the February 1997 legislative election, in which the PML-N swept to power by securing 134 of the 207 seats, compared to 19 seats for Bhutto's PPP. The PML-N subsequently invited a number of smaller parties to join the governing coalition, giving it more than the two-thirds majority required for constitutional amendment. Following the installation of a new cabinet on February 26, Prime Minister Sharif quickly oversaw the abolition of the CDNS and directed constitutional revision that, among other things, removed the president's authority to dismiss the prime minister and assembly at will and to appoint military leaders.

In the wake of renewed violence in Karachi (much of it perpetrated by rival MQM factions) as well as conflict between minority Shiite and majority Sunni Muslim militants in Punjab, a new antiterrorism bill was adopted in August 1997, granting sweeping new powers to security forces and establishing special courts to try terrorism cases. The collateral usurpation of judicial power exacerbated tension between the government and the judiciary. On December 2, calling Sharif an "elected dictator," Leghari resigned rather than comply with the prime minister's order to swear in a new acting chief justice. On December 31 a Sharif ally, Mohammad Rafiq TARAR, was elected president by an overwhelming majority of electors.

There was an upsurge in religious, ethnic, and political violence through 1998. In August, the Sharif administration's failure to contain the violence led the principal MQM faction to withdraw its support for the government, which in February had already lost a leading ally when the Awami National Party (ANP) left the cabinet because of the prime minister's reluctance to endorse renaming the NWFP as Pakhtoonkhwa (Land of the Pakhtoon). Demands for greater provincial autonomy also continued to gather momentum in Khyber Pakhtunkhwa and elsewhere.

To the surprise of many observers, on October 7, 1998, Gen. Jehangir KARAMAT, chair of the joint chiefs of staff, resigned, two days after calling for greater military participation in the government and criticizing the prime minister for his administration's economic shortcomings and its inability to stem domestic disorder. On April 9, 1999, Prime Minister Sharif named Karamat's replacement as army chief of staff, Gen. Pervez MUSHARRAF.

In May 1999, India discovered that militant Islamic separatists backed by Pakistani forces had crossed the LoC into Kargil. India gained the upper hand after two months of clashes. Military forces withdrew in July, but sporadic fighting continued as the government's perceived retreat was widely denounced within Pakistan, particularly by Islamic groups.

On October 12, 1999, while attending a conference in Sri Lanka, General Musharraf was alerted by supporters within the army that Sharif was replacing him. Musharraf immediately flew back to Pakistan on a commercial flight, but, on the prime minister's order, his plane was denied permission to land in Karachi, whereupon the army moved in and secured the airport. At the same time, the military arrested Sharif and his cabinet. On October 14 Musharraf proclaimed a state of emergency (but not martial law), suspended the constitution, and named himself "chief executive" of Pakistan. President Tarar continued in office. On October 25 the chief executive named the initial civilian members of a governing National Security Council (NSC), which also included, ex officio, the naval and air force chiefs. President Tarar swore in the civilian members of the NSC and a nonparty cabinet on November 6.

Ruling unanimously on May 12, 2000, the Supreme Court legitimized the October 1999 coup as justified and necessary to end political corruption and lawlessness, despite being "extra-constitutional." It also ruled that democratic national and provincial assembly elections should be held no later than October 2002. On August 15 the NSC was reconstituted to include four civilian ministers, and the cabinet was expanded.

On April 6, 2000, an antiterrorism court sentenced Nawaz Sharif to life imprisonment following his conviction for hijacking and terrorism in connection with his refusal to let General Musharraf's plane land. The terrorism conviction was ultimately overturned on appeal, and on December 10 Musharraf granted a pardon to Nawaz Sharif, who flew into exile.

On June 20, 2001, General Musharraf dismissed President Tarar, assumed the presidency himself, dissolved both houses of Parliament, and also disbanded all provincial legislatures. In an apparent effort to legitimize his standing, General Musharraf called an April 30, 2002, referendum in which voters were asked to extend his presidency for another five years, to support economic reforms as well as a crackdown on Islamic extremists. Although 97.7 percent of those casting ballots reportedly voted "yes," the referendum was replete with irregularities, and the outcome was rejected by the boycotting Alliance for the Restoration of Democracy (ARD), an umbrella grouping of more than a dozen opposition parties, including the PPP and the PML-N.

In August–December 2001, searching for domestic stability as well as increased international legitimacy following the September 11 al-Qaida attacks on the United States, Musharraf began freezing assets and detaining the leaders of militant Islamic groups. On January 12, 2002, in what was widely regarded as a landmark speech, Musharraf rejected the "intolerance and hatred" of extreme sectarianism; banned a number of militant Islamic political parties and groups (see Banned and Other Extremist Organizations, below); stated that all fundamentalist Islamic schools (madrasas) would be brought under government supervision to ensure that they adopted adequate educational goals; and called for creation of a modern, progressive Islamic society based on the "true teachings of Islam."

On August 21, 2002, President Musharraf promulgated a controversial Legal Framework Order (LFO) that incorporated 29 constitutional amendments, including the creation of a permanent NSC to institutionalize a governmental role for the military leadership. The LFO also enlarged both houses of Parliament and gave the president sweeping powers, including the right to dismiss the cabinet, dissolve the National Assembly, appoint provincial governors if he saw fit, name Supreme Court judges, and unilaterally increase his term of office.

An election for the 272 directly elective seats in Pakistan's reconfigured, 342-seat National Assembly took place on October 10, 2002, with the Musharraf-supportive *Qaid-i-Azam* faction of the PML (PML-Q) finishing ahead of the newly registered PPP Parliamentarians (PPPP) and the *Muttahida Majlis-e-Amal* (MMA), an Islamic coalition. Most international observers regarded the electoral process as seriously deficient in meeting democratic standards. When the 60 seats reserved for women and 10 seats reserved for religious minorities were distributed at the end of the month, the PML-Q held a plurality of 118 seats, followed by the PPPP with 81 and the MMA with 60.

In simultaneous provincial assembly elections, the PML-Q won in Punjab and the MMA assumed control in Khyber Pakhtunkhwa (formerly known as the NWFP), with the two parties forming coalition administrations in Baluchistan and, in conjunction with smaller parties, in Sindh. Immediately upon assuming power in Khyber Pakhtunkhwa, the MMA government announced that it would impose Islamic law in the province. Efforts by Musharraf and the United States to track down al-Qaida terrorist network members and the deposed Taliban regime in neighboring Afghanistan were set back by the MMA's success in Khyber Pakhtunkhwa. The MMA opposed both Islamabad's participation in the U.S.-led "war on terrorism" and the consequent presence of U.S. forces on Pakistani soil.

At the central level, over the next several weeks the PML-Q and PPPP jockeyed for MMA support in an effort to establish a governing coalition, but neither succeeded. The process culminated on November 21, 2002, when the National Assembly confirmed Zafarullah Khan JAMALI of the PML-Q as prime minister after he secured the backing of several small parties and ten dissenters within the PPPP, who organized as the PPP-Patriots. Runner-up in the voting was the MMA's Fazlur RAHMAN, followed by the PPPP's Shah Mahmood QURESHI.

During the following year the National Assembly was unable to overcome the obstructive tactics of LFO opponents, including the PPPP and MMA, who also demanded that President Musharraf resign as chief of the army staff. Indirect elections to the Senate were held on February 25 and 27, 2003, with the PML-Q again attaining a plurality, but the opposition parties extended their LFO protest into a Senate boycott. The stalemate over the LFO was not resolved until late December, when Musharraf announced an agreement with the MMA under which he would step down as army chief by December 2004, submit to a vote of confidence by Parliament, and permit review by the Supreme Court of any presidential decision to dissolve the National Assembly. In addition, it was agreed that the NSC would be established by legislative act, not by constitutional amendment. With the deadlock broken, on December 29 the National Assembly voted, 248–0, to incorporate most LFO provisions as the 17th amendment to the constitution, although the PPPP and the PML-N walked out of the session. By a vote of 72–0 the Senate approved the amendment the following day. On January 1, 2004, Musharraf received a vote of confidence from both houses, 191–0 in the assembly (the MMA abstaining and ARD boycotting), and 56–1 in the Senate, as well as from the provincial assemblies. A bill establishing a 13-member NSC, to include the chiefs of the army, navy, and air force, was signed into law by the president on April 19.

On June 26, 2004, Prime Minister Jamali resigned under pressure from President Musharraf. Chaudhry Shujaat HUSSAIN, leader of the largely reunited PML (minus the PML-N), was confirmed as an interim successor on June 29 and sworn in on June 30. He was expected to serve until Finance Minister Shaukat AZIZ won a National Assembly seat, thereby making him eligible for designation as prime minister. Following a by-election victory on August 18, Aziz won assembly approval as prime minister on August 28 and assumed office on August 29.

On November 30, 2004, Mohammadmian SOOMRO, chair of the Senate and acting president during a trip abroad by General Musharraf, signed into law a bill permitting Musharraf to continue as both army chief of staff and president. The new law, which proponents justified as necessary to maintain stability in the face of terrorism and subversion, was attacked by the MMA as a betrayal of its December 2003 pact with Musharraf.

On May 14, 2006, meeting in London, former prime ministers Benazir Bhutto and Nawaz Sharif signed a Charter of Democracy, which decried "the erosion of the federation's unity" and "the military's subordination of all state institutions." The charter called for repealing the LFO and the 17th constitutional amendment, establishing a Federal Constitutional Court to resolve constitutional issues, providing for minority representation in the Senate, releasing all political prisoners and permitting the return of political exiles, installing neutral caretaker governments prior to national elections, and creating a Defense Cabinet Committee (in place of the NSC) that would exert control over the military and its nuclear capability.

In September 2006, the government concluded an agreement with tribal leaders in the Federally Administered Tribal Area (FATA) of North Waziristan that tacitly acknowledged the failure of the military and security agencies to bring the region under its control despite years of efforts. In effect, the government turned control of the agency over to tribal leaders. Modeled on a pact that Musharraf had concluded in February 2005 in South Waziristan, the agreement called for Islamabad to withdraw an estimated 70,000 troops, release prisoners, and provide amnesty to Taliban and tribal militants, in return for which the tribal leaders agreed to end attacks against army and law enforcement personnel, to prevent the Taliban from launching attacks into Afghanistan, and to expel foreigners who failed to honor the agreement.

On March 8, 2007, President Musharraf set off a political firestorm by suspending Chief Justice Iftikhar Mohammed CHAUDHRY on grounds of misconduct and abuse of authority. With the presidential term set to expire in November, Musharraf apparently perceived Chaudhry as an obstacle to his reelection. Musharraf wanted the sitting national and provincial legislators—the same ones who had confirmed him in January 2004—to authorize another term, and without his first stepping down as army chief. The opposition, arguing that any such procedure would be antidemocratic and unconstitutional, pledged to appeal to the Supreme Court, which, under Chaudhry, had previously demonstrated its independence. In response to Chaudhry's dismissal, dozens of judges tendered their resignations, while the opposition and the legal establishment condemned the action as an attack on judicial independence. The crisis widened on May 12–13, when members of the government-supportive MQM clashed with Chaudhry supporters in the streets of Karachi, leaving more than 40 people dead. On July 20 Chaudhry was reinstated by the Supreme Court, which unanimously ruled Musharraf's action illegal.

Less than a week earlier, tribal militants in North Waziristan, responding to the storming by security forces of Islamabad's Red Mosque (*Lal Masjid*), canceled the September 2006 agreement with the government. The Red Mosque assault concluded a July 3–11, 2007, siege that had been precipitated by clashes with militant students, who for six months had been aggressively promoting Islamization in the capital, sometimes by attacking noncompliant civilians. Following unsuccessful negotiations with the students and their clerical mentors, military personnel cleared the mosque and adjacent madrasas in a prolonged assault that cost more than 100 lives. Among those killed in the fighting was the radical cleric Abdul Rashid GHAZI. Although President Musharraf's decision to storm the mosque won considerable praise in the West and from domestic secularists, Islamists increased suicide bombings, ambushes, and other attacks.

On August 23, 2007, the Supreme Court ruled that former prime minister Nawaz Sharif could not be prevented "from returning to his motherland." Nevertheless, when he flew into Islamabad on September 10, the government detained him at the airport and within hours deported him to Saudi Arabia. Four days later, Benazir Bhutto, in the context of negotiations with Musharraf on power-sharing arrangements, announced that she planned to return to Pakistan in October.

With Chief Justice Chaudhry having recused himself, the Supreme Court ruled 6–3 on September 28, 2007, that President Musharraf could stand for reelection while still serving as army chief. Although Musharraf had stated that, should he win reelection, he would resign from the military before inauguration, most of the opposition declared that it would boycott the presidential voting. On October 6 an electoral college of Parliament and the four provincial assemblies reelected Musharraf to a five-year term by a margin of 671–8 against token opposition from a former judge, Wajihuadin AHMAD. A day earlier, however, the Supreme Court had announced that the results could not be declared official until it had ruled on opposition challenges.

Although power-sharing discussions with former prime minister Bhutto remained incomplete, on October 5, 2007, Musharraf promulgated a National Reconciliation Ordinance (NRO) that quashed corruption charges—including 11, involving some $1.5 billion, against Bhutto and her husband, Asif Ali Zardari—targeting politicians for illegalities allegedly committed during 1986–1999. On October 18 Bhutto ended eight years in exile, returning to Karachi. The triumphal occasion turned grim, however, when suicide bombers attacked her motorcade from the airport, killing 145 and wounding more than 200 others.

On November 3, 2007, citing the need to combat rising Islamic extremism, Musharraf, in his capacity as chief of the army staff, suspended the constitution and declared a state of emergency. Chief Justice Chaudhry was immediately dismissed, while most of his fellow justices resigned or refused to take a new oath under a provisional constitutional order. The emergency declaration provoked demonstrations by many of those associated with the July protests. More than 5,000 activists were temporarily jailed in the following days, and Bhutto was twice placed under house arrest.

On November 16, 2007, a day after the completion of the 2002–2007 legislative term, Musharraf swore in a caretaker government headed by Senate Chair Mohammadmian Soomro, an ally. On November 22 the Supreme Court, now packed with Musharraf supporters, dismissed the last of four opposition petitions challenging Musharraf's reelection, which paved the way for his stepping down as chief of the army staff on November 28 and his taking the presidential oath of office as a civilian on November 29. Shortly before, he had designated Gen. Ashfaq KAYANI, a former head of the Inter-Services Intelligence (ISI) agency, as his military successor.

On November 25, 2007, opposition demands for restoration of the constitution had been further strengthened by the successful return to Pakistan of Nawaz Sharif, following intervention on his behalf by the king of Saudi Arabia. Nevertheless, it appeared unlikely that the courts would lift the prohibition against his directly participating in the legislative election that had been scheduled for January 8, 2008.

Former prime minister Benazir Bhutto was assassinated by Islamist extremists while leaving a campaign rally in Rawalpindi on December

27, 2007. Shortly after, her 19-year-old son, Bilawal Bhutto ZARDARI, a college student in the United Kingdom, was named titular head of the PPP, while her husband, Asif Ali Zardari, was given responsibility for running day-to-day party operations. On January 2, 2008, citing the violent disturbances that had followed Bhutto's death, the Pakistan Election Commission briefly postponed the National Assembly election. The PPP, the PML-N, and other opposition parties objected to the decision. (A UN commission investigating Bhutto's assassination concluded in April 2010 that her death could have been prevented if authorities had provided the proper level of security.)

Voters went to the polls instead on February 18, 2008, and gave the PPP (still technically running as the PPPP) a plurality of 124 seats. The PML-N finished second, with 91 seats, while the PML-Q (officially listed on the ballot simply as the PML) came in a distant third, with 54 seats. On March 25 a PPP vice chair, Syed Yousaf Raza GILANI, was sworn in as prime minister of a multiparty government led by the PPP and PML-N. One provision of their coalition agreement called for reinstating the dismissed judges, but the government's failure to do so led Nawaz Sharif to announce the withdrawal of the PML-N ministers on May 12.

Facing pending impeachment over allegedly unconstitutional acts, including the 1999 coup and the November 2007 state of emergency, President Musharraf resigned on August 18, 2008. A week later Nawaz Sharif took the PML-N into opposition because the PPP had not reinstated 63 dismissed judges and had proposed Zardari, rather than a nonpartisan, as Musharraf's successor. Most parties nevertheless coalesced around Zardari, who was elected president on September 6 with 482 of 700 possible electoral college votes. Zardari took the oath of office on September 9. On November 3 Prime Minister Gilani not only filled the cabinet posts that had been vacated by the PML-N withdrawal but announced one of the largest cabinets in the country's history, which was further expanded when the MQM joined the government in January 2009.

Meanwhile, in the wake of the Red Mosque siege in July 2007 and the failed peace agreements in North and South Waziristan, a dozen or more militant Islamic groups came together under the framework of the *Tehrik-e-Taliban* Pakistan (TTP), led by Baitullah MEHSUD. Although the TTP operated throughout the FATA and Khyber Pakhtunkhwa, in 2008 the Swat valley in Khyber Pakhtunkhwa's Malakand division emerged as a focus of militant activity. In an effort to disrupt the government and inculcate strict adherence to Islamic law, the TTP executed dozens of opponents and alleged government collaborators, destroyed more than 180 schools (most of which had been educating girls), and by early 2009 controlled up to 90 percent of the valley. On February 13 the Khyber Pakhtunkhwa government and the leader of the pro-Taliban *Tehrik-e-Nifaz-e-Shariat-e-Muhammadi* (TNSM), cleric Sufi MOHAMMED, signed an agreement on adoption of sharia throughout Malakand that was approved by the National Assembly and then signed into law by President Zardari on April 13, despite protests from the MQM. By then, up to 1,500 people, many of them bystanders, had been killed in the conflict.

On March 17, 2009, the Gilani government reinstated Chief Justice Chaudhry, four other Supreme Court judges, and six provincial high court judges. The move, spurred by a Karachi-to-Islamabad protest caravan by lawyers and other activists, was seen as a victory for Nawaz Sharif. Furthermore, on May 26 the Supreme Court overturned a February ruling that, citing earlier criminal convictions, had barred Nawaz Sharif from seeking office and had forced his brother, Mohammad Shahbaz SHARIF, to step down temporarily as chief minister of Punjab.

By May 2009 it had become apparent that the February peace agreement in Khyber Pakhtunkhwa was illusory, as the TTP, led locally by Maulana FAZULLAH, a son-in-law of Sufi Mohammad, continued to extend its reach beyond Swat. As a consequence, the Pakistani military, which was already fighting for control in the FATA's Bajaur Agency and elsewhere, launched a concerted effort to end the Taliban threat in Malakand. By late June most of Swat had been secured and impressive gains had been registered in other districts, in part with the cooperation of local militias. The military undertook a long-anticipated ground campaign against the TTP in South Waziristan in October 2009.

In September 2010, the Supreme Court reopened corruption cases against high-level politicians, including President Zardari, after a December 2009 ruling declared a 2007 general immunity from prosecution instituted by former president Musharraf was unconstitutional (see Constitution and government, below). The high court's call joined with growing government pressure for Swiss authorities to reopen money-laundering cases against Zardari that had been suspended in 2008 because of the immunity order. The Swiss cases involved an alleged $12 million in bribes paid to Zardari and his late wife Benazir Bhutto by companies to win contracts in Pakistan throughout the 1990s. The allegations led to calls for his removal from office. Musharraf, living in self-imposed exile in London, announced in September that he would soon launch a new party called the All Pakistan Muslim League to contest the general election in 2013 (see Current issues, below).

The cabinet was reshuffled and expanded in April 2012. On April 26, the high court convicted Gilani of contempt of court for failing to pursue prosecution of Zardari (Gilani argued in vain that the president was immune from prosecution). On June 19, the court ruled that Gilani's conviction made him ineligible to serve in the legislature and, therefore, to be prime minister. Three days later, Zardari named Makhdoom SHAHABUDDIN as prime minister, but the appointee was arrested over alleged drug trafficking, leading to speculation that the courts and the military were endeavoring to end the PPP government. On June 22, Water and Power Minister Raja Pervaiz ASHRAF was designated prime minister and confirmed the same day. A reshuffled cabinet was approved on June 26.

Ashraf's PPP-led government was the first civilian government in Pakistani history to complete its full term and turn over power. In accordance with the constitution, the assembly was dissolved on March 16, 2013, in preparation for new elections. Mir Hazar Khan KHOSO (independent) was sworn in along with a caretaker government on March 25. The PML-N won a plurality in the May 11 assembly balloting and, with allied parties, was able to secure a majority in the chamber (see Current issues, below). On June 5, Nawaz Sharif was elected prime minister and formed a mainly PML-N cabinet two days later. Mamnoon HUSSAIN (PML-N) was subsequently elected president by the parliament and was sworn in on September 9.

Constitution and government. Between 1947 and 1973, Pakistan adopted three permanent and four interim constitutions. In August 1973 a presidential system introduced by Ayub Khan was replaced by a parliamentary form of government. Following General Zia's assumption of power in 1977, a series of martial law decrees and an interim constitution promulgated in March 1981 progressively increased the powers of the president, as did various revisions accompanying official restoration of the 1973 document in March 1985. Constitutional changes introduced in April 1997 revoked major provisions of the 1985 revisions, reducing the president to little more than a figurehead.

On October 15, 1999, General Musharraf, who had suspended the constitution and assumed the title of chief executive the previous day, issued Provisional Constitution Order No. 1 of 1999, which specified that Pakistan would continue to be governed, "as nearly as may be," in accordance with the constitution. The order also restricted the president to acting on the advice of the chief executive and mandated the continued functioning of the existing court system, with the proviso that no court could act against the chief executive, his orders, or his appointees. The order left intact all fundamental constitutional rights, such as freedom of the press, not in conflict with the state of emergency.

The LFO instituted by General Musharraf in August 2002, effective from October 12, incorporated 29 constitutional changes, enhancing presidential power, enlarging both houses of Parliament, and creating as a permanent body a civilian-military National Security Council (NSC). The LFO also disqualified convicted criminals from running for the legislature, thereby ensuring that neither Benazir Bhutto nor Nawaz Sharif could stand in the October 2002 election. Opposition to promulgation of the LFO ultimately led to a December 2003 compromise under which most of the LFO provisions were enacted as the 17th amendment to the constitution. The NSC provision was removed, however, and enacted by law in April 2004.

In November 2006, the Khyber Pakhtunkhwa legislature passed an Islamic accountability law, but President Musharraf successfully petitioned the Supreme Court for a stay. In August, the court had thrown out 20 subsections of a previous law authorizing clerics to oversee media content and social behavior, including interactions between the sexes. The central government had argued that the law overstepped constitutional bounds. A collateral debate focused on a national Protection of Women Bill, which was ultimately signed into law on December 1 despite fierce opposition from all but the most moderate Islamic organizations. Under the new law rape cases were assigned to civil rather than religious courts and for the first time permitted conviction on the basis of forensic and circumstantial evidence rather than on the testimony of male witnesses.

A number of ordinances brought into being in 2007 under former president Musharraf expired in November 2009, including presidential control of Pakistan's nuclear weapons arsenal, which subsequently transferred to the authority of the prime minister. Musharraf's NRO, which granted amnesty to late prime minister Benazir Bhutto, her husband and current president Zardari, and nearly 8,000 other officials who faced prosecution for corruption, also expired without extension. The Supreme Court ruled in December that the NRO was unconstitutional and ordered corruption cases voided by the ordinance, including those against Zardari, be reopened. The corruption charges involved many members of the PPP, including several cabinet ministers. The attorney general resigned in April 2010, citing obstruction of criminal investigations into the corruption cases.

In April 2010, the federal legislature passed a bill that restored the 1973 constitution and repealed former president Musharraf's 2003 LFO. On April 15 the Senate unanimously passed the 18th constitutional amendment bill, which contained 102 clauses, after earlier unanimous passage of the bill in the National Assembly on April 8. The changes transferred power from the president to the prime minister to dismiss the National Assembly and to name the armed services chiefs and the elections commissioner, while also empowering an independent commission to appoint judges. The bill gave the prime minister and provincial chief ministers the power to dissolve provincial assemblies, and eliminated the two-term-limit imposed on the prime minister. Reinstatement of the old governing laws rescinded most of the powers that had been accumulated in the office of the presidency and left the position largely ceremonial. One clause also renamed the NWFP as the Khyber Pakhtunkhwa, doing away with a vestige of British colonial rule. The portion of the amendment that created the commission to appoint judges was challenged in the Supreme Court on grounds that it impeded judicial independence.

The current constitution mandates that the president, who serves a five-year term, is chosen by vote of Parliament and the four provincial assemblies sitting jointly as an electoral college. The bicameral Parliament includes an indirectly elected Senate and a popularly elected National Assembly; the latter includes reserved seats for women and religious minorities, and it has sole jurisdiction over money bills. Sitting in joint session, Parliament may by a simple majority enact bills that have been returned to it by the president. The prime minister, who must be a member of the National Assembly, may be removed by a majority vote of the house's total membership; the president may be removed by a two-thirds vote of the full Parliament.

The judicial system includes a Supreme Court, a Federal Shariat Court to examine the conformity of laws with Islam, high courts in each of the four provinces (Baluchistan, North-West Frontier, Punjab, and Sindh), and a number of antiterrorism courts authorized by legislation in 1997. The assembly approved measures in 1991 that called for formal appeal to the Koran as the country's supreme law and mandated the death penalty for blasphemy.

Centrally appointed governors head provincial administrations. Each province also has an elected Provincial Assembly and a Council of Ministers led by the prime minister, the latter named by the governor. Central appointees govern the Federal Capital Territory and the Federally Administered Tribal Areas (FATA), which are located between Khyber Pakhtunkhwa and Afghanistan. The seven FATA agencies, roughly from north to south, are Bajaur, Mahmand, Khyber, Orakzai, Kurram, North Waziristan, and South Waziristan. Pakistan also administers parts of disputed Kashmir, and in 2009, Gilgit-Baltistan was granted self-governance (see Related Territories, below).

A Federal Legislative List defines the exclusive authority of the center; there also is a Concurrent Legislative List, with residual authority assigned to the provinces. To safeguard provincial rights, a Council of Common Interests is mandated, comprising the chief ministers of the four provinces plus four federal ministers.

Pakistan is one of the most dangerous countries in the world for journalists. The constitution guarantees press freedom, but formal censorship has been imposed during periods of martial law and states of emergency. The imposition of sharia law in the Swat Valley and other areas of the country had a significant impact on press freedom. The country was ranked 159th out of 179 countries in the 2013 press freedom index by Reporters Without Borders.

Foreign relations. Relations between India and Pakistan reflect a centuries-old rivalry based on mutual suspicion between Hindus and Muslims. Widespread communal rioting and competing claims to Jammu and Kashmir accompanied the British withdrawal in 1947. Relations improved in 1960 with an agreement on joint use of the waters of the Indus River basin, but continuing conflict over Kashmir and the Rann of Kutch on the Indian Ocean involved the two countries in armed hostilities in 1965, followed by a withdrawal to previous positions, in conformity with the Tashkent Agreement negotiated with Soviet assistance in January 1966. After another period of somewhat improved relations, the internal crisis in East Pakistan, accompanied by India's open support of the Bengali cause, led to further hostilities in 1971.

Following recognition by Pakistan of independent Bangladesh, bilateral negotiations with India were renewed, and a number of major issues were resolved by the return of prisoners of war, a mutual withdrawal from occupied territory, and the demarcation of a new LoC in Kashmir. Further steps toward normalization were partially offset by Pakistani concern over India's detonation of a nuclear device in May 1974, and formal diplomatic ties were not resumed until July 1976.

A rapprochement followed General Zia's death in August 1988 but abruptly ended in early 1990 as Kashmir became the scene of escalating violence on the part of Muslim separatists. By April thousands of residents had fled to Pakistan from the Indian-controlled Kashmir valley.

On April 6, 1998, Pakistan test fired its first domestically produced medium-range surface-to-surface missile, which provoked immediate criticism from India's recently installed Vajpayee administration. Then on May 11 and 13 India exploded five nuclear weapons in underground testing, prompting Pakistan to respond on May 28 and 30 with six nuclear tests of its own. The international community quickly condemned the tests, and a number of countries imposed economic sanctions against both governments. Shortly after, however, Prime Ministers Sharif and Vajpayee adopted less belligerent stances, meeting during the July session of the South Asian Association for Regional Cooperation (SAARC) in Colombo, Sri Lanka, and again in September in New York, where they announced renewed talks on Kashmir and other matters.

Although the Kashmir talks produced no tangible results, the prime ministers met again in February 1999 in Lahore. The resulting Lahore Declaration included pledges by both administrations to reduce the possibility of accidental nuclear war.

On October 1, 1999, militants carried out an assault on the state assembly building in Srinagar, the summer capital of the Indian State of Jammu and Kashmir, resulting in nearly 40 deaths. Charging that Pakistan had failed to stop terrorist infiltrators, India ordered additional troops to Kashmir, with Pakistan responding in kind. On December 13 terrorists attacked India's Parliament, leaving 14 dead, including the terrorists, and by May 2002, when three gunmen stormed a Kashmiri army base and left nearly three dozen dead, India and Pakistan had a combined million troops or more stationed along the LoC. Diplomatic intervention, led by the United States, ultimately helped to diffuse the immediate situation.

When Prime Minister Vajpayee called on April 18, 2003, for "open dialogue" with Pakistan, Islamabad announced its willingness to cooperate, which led to a mutual deepening of diplomatic relations. On November 26 the two governments instituted a cease-fire, the first in 14 years, between Pakistani and Indian forces in the disputed border region. The cease-fire was followed by an announcement at the January 4–6, 2004, SAARC session that the two governments would undertake "composite talks" on bilateral issues, and in late June 2005 Prime Minister Aziz described the peace process as "irreversible." Nevertheless, scant progress was made in the following six years, in large part because of terrorist attacks within India by Islamist groups with Pakistani connections (see Current issues, below). The most dramatic recent instance occurred on November 26–29, 2008, when a ten-person assault team attacked predetermined targets in Mumbai, leaving 163 people dead and another 300 hurt. All of the assailants, including the lone survivor, Ajmal Amir AMIN (Ajmal Kasab), were ultimately shown to have Pakistani addresses. On February 12, 2009, Islamabad admitted that "some part of the conspiracy" had been planned in Pakistan. Attention focused on the *Lashkar-i-Taiba* (LiT), whose chief of operations, Zaki-ur-Rehman LAKHVI, was alleged to be the mastermind behind the Mumbai attack. On November 19 a special antiterrorism court indicted Lakhvi and six others. (On May 3, 2010, Amin was found guilty for his part in the Mumbai shootings and sentenced to death by an Indian special court.)

Relations with Bangladesh have improved considerably in recent years, although no formula has yet been found for relocating some 300,000 Biharis, most of whom have been living in over 100 camps in the former East Pakistan since the 1972 breakup. An agreement in August 1992 led to the airlifting of an initial contingent to Lahore in early 1993, but the Bhutto government suspended the program later in the year. Although Pakistan recommitted itself in early 1998 to resettling the Biharis, no substantive move toward that goal had been achieved by May 2008, when the Bangladeshi High Court approved offering citizenship to some 150,000 Biharis who were minors in 1971 as well as all those born since then.

Although Pakistan and Afghanistan had long been at odds over the latter's commitment to the creation of an independent Pushtunistan out of a major part of Pakistan's NWFP, Islamabad reacted strongly to the Soviet invasion of its neighbor in 1979, providing Muslim rebel groups (mujahidin) with weapons and supplies for continued operations against the Soviet-backed regime. Support for the rebels occasionally provoked bombing raids in the area of Peshawar, the Khyber Pakhtunkhwa capital, and the presence of more than 3.5 million Afghan refugees proved economically burdensome.

Following the Soviet departure, which was completed in early 1989, Pakistan supported the installation of an interim coalition government in Kabul. Kabul later accused Islamabad of supporting the fundamentalist Taliban militia, which Pakistan recognized as Afghanistan's government shortly after it took power in September 1996.

Following the U.S.-led ouster of the Taliban in 2001, relations with Kabul have been complicated by the fact that Islamic fundamentalists, having been permitted to establish education and training camps in the Peshawar area during the Afghan revolution, became increasingly active within Pakistan itself, particularly in FATA and Khyber Pakhtunkhwa as well as within the divided Kashmir. Relations with Afghanistan were frayed from early 2006, when President Hamid Karzai accused Pakistan of failing to secure Pakistan's side of the border and of not curbing Pakistani-based al-Qaida and Taliban militants.

Pakistan and Iran signed a $7.6 billion deal in March 2010 to build a natural gas pipeline from Iran to Baluchistan and Sindh provinces. The pipeline was expected to become operational in 2015, and it was expected to significantly relieve Pakistan's power shortages. Analysts also viewed engagement with Iran, despite its potential to increase regional instability, as a means to develop Pakistani influence in the region.

U.S.–Pakistani relations have been dominated by counterterrorism since the mid-1990s. In February 1995, the government permitted U.S. agents to join in the apprehension of Ramzi Ahmed YOUSEF, the suspected mastermind of the 1993 World Trade Center bombing in New York, and then approved his prompt extradition. Following the September 11, 2001, assaults on the United States, relations with the new U.S. administration were significantly strengthened by Pakistan's assistance in fighting al-Qaida and the Taliban. In early 2002 the Musharraf regime reacted swiftly to the murder of the American journalist Daniel Pearl in Pakistan. The principal suspect, Ahmad Omar SHAIKH, a UK national, was captured in February and later sentenced to death. Despite Pakistan's decision not to back the 2003 U.S. invasion of Iraq, the Bush administration continued to praise and support Musharraf. Not even a public admission in February 2004 by Abdul Qadeer KHAN, the former head of Pakistan's nuclear weapons program, that he had passed nuclear secrets to Iran, Libya, and North Korea damaged the U.S.-Pakistani relationship. Musharraf immediately pardoned Khan, a national hero, without protest from Washington. (The International Atomic Energy Agency subsequently speculated that Khan's revelations were merely the "tip of the iceberg" in an operation that also involved the sale of nuclear components in a number of countries.) In March, U.S. Secretary of State Colin Powell, making his fourth visit to Pakistan, announced that Pakistan was regarded as a "major non-NATO ally," and a week later U.S. President Bush lifted the few remaining sanctions imposed after the 1998 nuclear tests and the 1999 coup. Pakistan has handed over hundreds of suspected al-Qaida operatives. Additionally, its armed forces have also launched major offensives against tribal Islamists, al-Qaida, and Taliban elements in Khyber Pakhtunkhwa and especially in FATA. The central government regained control of the Swat Valley following an offensive in 2009, though the slow distribution of aid money hampered subsequent progress.

In March 2009, the administration of U.S. President Barack Obama acknowledged that stemming the flow of militants back and forth across the Afghan-Pakistani border required Pakistan's active participation. As an incentive, President Obama proposed a five-year civilian aid package of $7.5 billion. When the U.S. Congress passed the aid bill in October, however, it met fierce criticism from some Pakistanis, who claimed that it would permit U.S. interference in Pakistan's civilian and military affairs. The bill requires the secretary of state to certify that Pakistan is participating in counterterrorism, maintaining civilian authority over the military, safeguarding its nuclear arsenal, and meeting international nonproliferation standards.

Relations deteriorated, however, following the discovery in May 2011 that Osama bin Laden had been hiding for years in a compound that was at walking distance from an elite Pakistani military academy in Abbottabad. After his death on May 20, the U.S. authorities openly questioned whether Pakistan was both willing and capable of cooperating with counterterrorism efforts. Despite the embarrassment for the military, much of the scrutiny focused on the Inter-Services Intelligence (ISI), which has long been viewed as holding an ambivalent position toward militant groups. The ISI remains deeply suspicious of India and thus has been known to police local and regional militants only haphazardly, allowing them some support in the event that they are needed to respond to a hypothetical attack by India. Although the United States had accepted this partial cooperation for years, it suspended $800 million, or one-third, of its military aid to Pakistan in July 2011.

U.S. Secretary of State Hillary Clinton visited Pakistan in October 2011 and called for a new "partnership" between the two countries. She also revealed that the ISI had facilitated negotiations between the United States and the terrorist Haqqani network (see entry on Afghanistan). Meanwhile, on October 24, Pakistan was elected for a two-year term on the UN Security Council.

In November 2011, Pakistan's ambassador to the United States, Hussain HAQQANI, was forced to resign after allegations surfaced that he sought U.S. assistance in curbing the power of the Pakistani military. Tensions with the United States increased dramatically following a U.S. air strike on November 26 that killed 24 Pakistani soldiers along the Afghan border. In response to the incident, Pakistan closed North Atlantic Treaty Organization (NATO) supply lines into Afghanistan. Pakistan also ordered the withdrawal of U.S. forces from the Shamsi airbase in Baluchistan.

In April 2012, Pakistan deported to Saudi Arabia three of bin Laden's widows and 11 of his children. In June, after 45 days of negotiations, U.S. diplomats left Pakistan with no resolution to the dispute over the closure of NATO supply routes through Pakistan. Meanwhile, U.S. drone strikes continued including three in June that killed 27, including 16 suspected militants. In October, Kabul accused Islamabad of violating a bilateral transport treaty by denying or delaying cargo bound for Afghanistan. Pakistan denied the allegations.

In January 2013, a series of skirmishes and artillery exchanges across the LoC left three Pakistani and two Indian soldiers dead. Reports indicated that tension had increased dramatically after India built two new military bunkers in a disputed area. By month's end Pakistani and Indian military officials had launched negotiations to forestall additional fighting. On March 11, 2013, the presidents of Pakistan and Iran attended the ceremonial opening of a gas pipeline from Iran. The pipeline was seen as a diplomatic snub to the United States, which endeavored to block its construction.

In August 2013 Pakistan approved the Convention on the Transfer of Sentenced Prisoners. The accord allowed the EU and the United States to extradite convicted prisoners back to Pakistan.

Current issues. A January 2010 report found 3,021 civilians had been killed in Pakistan in 2009 and 7,334 had been injured over the course of 2,586 terrorist, sectarian, and insurgent attacks. The numbers killed rose 48 percent over the previous year. The report said the total of dead rose to more than 12,000 in 2009 if those killed in military action or U.S. drone attacks were included. The killings continued into 2011.

This situation is further complicated by tacit support for selected rebel groups by the ISI and sympathizers within the military. This issue is muted in Pakistan, as several journalists have been pressured to self-censor following apparent assassinations of colleagues who were critical towards the security apparatus. Security in Karachi, Pakistan's most important port city and the center of commercial and industrial operations, has been particularly affected. Rival criminal organizations claiming affiliation with Pakistan's opposing political parties, including the PPP, the MQM, and the ANP, have contributed to increasing violence, with over 300 people killed in gang-related violence in July 2011 alone. Violence increased after the crackdown in the FATA from October 2009, which upset the city's ethnic balance as migrating Pashtuns from the Afghan border areas, commonly represented by the ANP, reduced the proportion of the dominant Mujhairs, who are affiliated with the MQM. The PPP, which is associated with Sindhi people, along with the ANP, have attempted to reduce the influence of the MQM in the city. Local critics posited in late 2011 that the NRO had enabled corrupt officials to continue governing, notwithstanding their inability to secure the country's eroding semblance of order (see PPP, Political Parties and Groups, below).

The MQM left the coalition in June 2011. The grouping refused to agree to delay elections in Karachi in a bid to increase the number of PPP seats at its expense. Campaigning has increased across the country, with voters in the FATA hailing amendments to the Victorian-era Frontier

Crimes Regulations (FCR), which outlawed the mass arrest of entire tribes or appropriation of business in retaliation for the act of a single individual. The FCR had previously been used by local governments to deter would-be rivals from campaigning. Flooding in August and September killed more than 430 and affected an estimated 5 million. On December 6 Zardari traveled to the United Arab Emirates (UAE) for medical treatment following what was described as a "minor heart attack."

In Senate elections on March 2, 2012, the PPP won 19 of 54 seats, followed by the PML-N, 14, and the ANP, 12. The election was seen as a strong popular endorsement of the PPP. A government offensive in the FATA in April resulted in more than 250,000 internally displaced persons who fled to other provinces. On April 20, an airliner crashed near Karachi, killing all 127 aboard. In May, Shakil AFRIDI, who had assisted the United States in locating bin Laden, was arrested, tried, convicted, and sentenced to 33 years in prison. The conviction was protested by the United States. In September, protests swept across the region against the movie *The Innocence of Muslims,* which ridiculed Islam and the Prophet Muhammad. At least 25 were killed in clashes with security forces.

On October 9, 2012, Malala YOUSAFZAI, a schoolgirl who had risen to prominence as an education activist, was shot by Taliban militants in an assassination attempt. The attack was met by international condemnation and sparked a significant domestic backlash against the Taliban in Pakistan. Yousafzai was flown to the United Kingdom for treatment and recovery. Meanwhile, massive flooding in four provinces killed 422, destroyed some 275,000 homes, and affected more than 4.5 million people. In December, the government and international health groups suspended a polio vaccine program after suspected Taliban militants killed eight healthcare workers.

The government of Baluchistan was dismissed on January 13, 2013, following massive demonstrations in protest of rising sectarian violence in the province. Two bombings on January 10 killed 86 and wounded more than 100. On January 15, the Supreme Court issued arrest warrants for Prime Minister Ashraf and 15 other officials on corruption charges. However, Ashraf was not arrested and denounced the charges as politically motivated to undermine the PPP ahead of future assembly balloting.

Musharraf returned to Pakistan in March 2013 in an effort to relaunch his political career through a new grouping, the All Pakistan Muslim League. However, on April 16, a court rejected his political candidacy for the assembly. Three days later, the former ruler was placed under house arrest while he awaited trial on treason and other charges. A major military offensive against the Taliban in the Tirah Valley in April killed more than 100 militants and displaced over 43,000. A major earthquake on April 16, in Baluchistan, killed 36, injured over 300, and left more than 19,000 homeless.

In assembly balloting on May 11, 2013, PML-N and its allies fell six votes short of a majority but were able to form a coalition with support from 19 independents. Nawaz Sharif was subsequently elected prime minister by the assembly. In August, the coalition was bolstered when the JUI-F joined the government.

POLITICAL PARTIES AND GROUPS

Political activity has often been restricted in independent Pakistan. Banned in 1958, parties were permitted to resume activity in 1962. The Pakistan Muslim League (PML), successor to Mohammad Ali Jinnah's All-India Muslim League, continued its dominance during Ayub Khan's tenure. The election of December 1970 provided a major impetus to the reemergence of parties. The PML's supremacy ended with the rise of Zulfikar Ali Bhutto's Pakistan People's Party (PPP) in West Pakistan and the Awami League in East Pakistan (now Bangladesh). In the election of March 1977, the PPP faced a coalition of opposition parties organized as the Pakistan National Alliance (PNA). In October 1979 all formal party activity was again proscribed.

In February 1981 nine parties agreed to form a joint Movement for the Restoration of Democracy (MRD), of which the most important component was the PPP under the leadership of Begum Nusrat Bhutto and her daughter, Benazir Bhutto. The composition of the alliance changed several times thereafter, although it remained the largest opposition grouping for the balance of the Zia era. (For an overview of party politics from 1980 to 2008, please see the 2011 *Handbook.*)

Prior to the February 2008 election, Pakistan had 110 registered parties and coalitions. Most of the APDM parties chose to boycott the February 2008 election, the most notable exception being the PML-N. In all, 46 parties contested the election. In the 2013 assembly balloting, 111 parties participated in the balloting.

Government Parties:

Pakistan Muslim League (Nawaz)—PML-N. Under the leadership of former Punjab chief minister and then prime minister Mohammad Nawaz Sharif, the PML-N emerged from the PML-Junejo Group in 1993 and quickly established itself as the dominant PML grouping. In 1997 the PML-N won a parliamentary majority under Nawaz Sharif. Following the October 1999 coup, the PML-N established a 15-member Coordination Committee to consider party reorganization. It did not, however, call for the immediate restoration of the Sharif government, having concluded that directly confronting the military would be inadvisable.

As a condition of his release from prison in December 2000, Sharif agreed to abandon politics for at least two decades, although he continued to exert considerable influence from exile. In May 2004 his brother, Shahbaz, having received a favorable ruling from the Supreme Court on his right to return, attempted to end his four-year exile but was immediately ushered back out of the country by officials.

At the October 2002 National Assembly election, the PML-N ran as part of ARD, winning 19 seats. A year later the party's acting president, Javed Hashmi, was arrested for distributing a letter, allegedly written by army officers, that was critical of President Musharraf. Despite widespread expressions of outrage from ARD and other elements of the opposition, Hashmi was convicted in April 2004 of treason, mutiny, and forgery. In August, he was put forward as the opposition candidate for prime minister.

In August 2007, Hashmi was freed on bail by the Supreme Court after nearly four years' incarceration. Late in the same month, the justices also ruled that Nawaz Sharif could return from exile, but his attempt to do so on September 10 was thwarted by the government, which ordered him detained at the airport, served him an arrest warrant for corruption and money laundering, and immediately deported him to Saudi Arabia. Nawaz Sharif returned again on November 25, following the intervention of Saudi Arabia's king, and was greeted by thousands of supporters.

In the February 2008 National Assembly election, PML-N candidates won 91 seats, the vast majority from Punjab. Nawaz Sharif was prevented from running by earlier corruption convictions. Afterward, the PML-N formed a governing coalition with the PPP, but it withdrew its ministers in May, primarily because of differences with the PPP over reinstatement of the Supreme Court justices and other judges that had been dismissed by President Musharraf. The PML-N joined the opposition in August that year. Its candidate for president, Saeeduzzaman SIDDIQUI, finished second in September 2008.

The PML-N placed second in Senate balloting in March 2012, gaining 8 seats, for a total of 14. In 2012, Hashmi defected to the **Pakistan *Tehreek-e-Insaf*** (see below). In the 2013 assembly elections, the party secured 166 seats, and Nawar Sharif was elected prime minister of a coalition government.

Leaders: Mohammad Nawaz SHARIF (Prime Minister and Party Leader), Mamnoon HUSSAIN (President of the Republic); Raja ZAFAR-UL-HAQ (Chair), Iqbal Zafar JHAGRA (Secretary General).

Jamiat-Ulema-e-Islam Fazlur Rahman Group (JUI-F). The *Jamiat-Ulema-e-Islam* (Assembly of Islamic Clergy) was founded in 1950 as a progressive formation committed to constitutional government guided by Sunni Islamic principles. In 1988 the JUI's Darkhwasty Group withdrew from the IDA to reunite with the parent formation, although a faction headed by Maulana Sami ul-Haq remained within the government coalition until November 1991. Factionalization subsequently remained a problem, with Sami ul-Haq heading one group, the JUI-S (below), and Fazlur Rahman heading another, the JUI-F. The latter, which won two National Assembly seats from Baluchistan in 1997, emerged as the dominant faction. Fazlur Rahman supported Afghanistan's Taliban and, following the 1999 coup, condemned ousted prime minister Sharif's "lust for unlimited powers." He was placed under house arrest in October 2001, at the opening of the U.S.-led military campaign in Afghanistan.

In the 2002 National Assembly election, the JUI-F claimed the most MMA seats. The *Muttahida Majlis-e-Amal* (United Council for Action), organized in June 2001 by the JUI-F and five other Islamic parties, campaigned on a platform that included restoration of the constitution, creation of an Islamic state, and resolution of the Kashmir issue through negotiation. All of the constituent parties opposed General Musharraf's decision to join the U.S.-led "war on terrorism" and to permit U.S. forces to operate from Pakistani soil. Having won 60 seats in the National Assembly, the MMA was courted by both the PML-Q and the PPPP (with which it had little in common ideologically) to form a coalition government, but it rejected both. Its firm opposition to the

2002 Legal Framework Order was largely responsible for the yearlong stalemate in the National Assembly, until an agreement was reached with President Musharraf in December 2003.

Although the MMA was chaired from its inception by the moderate Maulana Shah Ahmad Noorani Siddiqui of the JUP (below) until his death in December 2003, the leaders of the two largest member parties—the JUI-F's Fazlur Rahman and Qazi Hussain Ahmad of the JIP (below)—exerted more influence. One contentious issue was the JIP's objections to participation in President Musharraf's National Security Council. As leader of the opposition, the JUI-F's Fazlur Rahman held a seat on the council, as did JUI-F member Akram Khan Durrani, who was at that time the chief minister of Khyber Pakhtunkhwa.

In July 2007, the MMA participated in the anti-Musharraf All Parties Conference and joined in forming the APDM, but the alliance subsequently split over whether to boycott the February 2008 election. The JUI-F chose to contest the election, in which it ran under the MMA banner, taking 2.2 percent of the vote, winning 7 seats, and then joining the PPP-led government. At the same time, however, it was soundly defeated in the Khyber Pakhtunkhwa legislative election, winning only 14 of 124 seats. Following the 2009 Senate election, it held 10 seats in the upper house. In April 2012, the JUI-F began a boycott of parliamentary committees over a disagreement with the PPP about the suspension of NATO's supply routes through Pakistan.

The party secured 15 seats in the 2013 assembly balloting and joined the governing coalition in August. The party was given one cabinet post in the PML-N-led government.

Leaders: Maulana Fazlur RAHMAN, Akram Khan DURRANI (Minister of Communications and Former Chief Minister of NWFP), Hafiz Hussein AHMAD.

Pakistan Muslim League (Functional)—PML-F. The PML-F was established by longtime PML leader Pir Sahib Pagaro, who broke from the PML in mid-1992. In 2002, the PML-F won five National Assembly seats and one in the Senate.

Although Pagaro initially appeared willing to participate in the reunification of the various PML parties with the dominant PML-Q in 2004, he soon retreated from that position. In 2005, the largely reunited PML indicated that it regarded the PML-F as a separate, allied party. In February 2008 the PML-F won five National Assembly seats, and two months later Pagaro indicated that he was considering unification with the PML-Q. Nevertheless, in November 2008, the PML-F joined the cabinet.

Jehangir Khan Tareen, an erstwhile party parliamentary leader, announced the possible launch of a new "party of the clean" in September 2011. The new party would focus on uniting electable, ethical politicians opposed to the corruption of establishment parties. In October 2012, the PML-F announced that it would not participate in an electoral alliance with the PPP in future balloting. Instead, the grouping joined the PML-N in an electoral alliance for the 2013 assembly elections and won six seats. The PML-F was given one cabinet seat in the subsequent PNL-N-led cabinet.

Leaders: Pir Sahib PAGARA, Haji Khuda Bux RAJAR (Minister of Narcotics), Jehangir Khan TAREEN.

Other Parties Represented in the National Assembly:

Pakistan People's Party (PPP). An Islamic socialist party founded in 1967 by Zulfikar Ali Bhutto, the PPP held a majority of seats in the National Assembly truncated by the independence of Bangladesh in 1971. Officially credited with winning 155 of 200 assembly seats in the election of March 1977, it was the primary target of a postcoup decree in October that banned all groups whose ideology could be construed as prejudicial to national security.

Bhutto was executed in April 1979, the party leadership being assumed by his widow and daughter Benazir, both of whom, after being under house arrest for several years, went into exile in London. After having briefly returned to Pakistan in July 1985 to preside over the burial of her brother, Shahnawaz, Benazir Bhutto again returned in April 1986. The PPP won a sizable plurality (92 of 205 contested seats) in the National Assembly election of November 1988, and Bhutto became prime minister. She remained in office until dismissed in August 1990. The party's legislative strength was then cut by more than half in the October general election (for which it joined with a number of smaller groups to campaign as the People's Democratic Alliance—PDA). It regained its plurality in 1993, with Ms. Bhutto being reinstalled as prime minister.

In December 1993, the PPP's Executive Council ousted Prime Minister Bhutto's mother, Begum Nusrat BHUTTO, as party cochair. The action was the product of estrangement between the two over the political role of Benazir's brother, Murtaza Bhutto, who had returned from exile in November to take up a seat in the Sindh provincial legislature. In March 1995 he announced the formation of a breakaway faction of the PPP, but he died in a firefight with gunmen in September 1996. Following the ouster of Prime Minister Bhutto in November, her husband, Asif Ali Zardari, was charged with complicity in the killing. Meanwhile, Benazir Bhutto was meeting with leaders of smaller opposition parties, which ultimately led to the formation of the PAI alliance in February 1998.

Earlier, at the end of 1996, allegations about the death of Murtaza Bhutto led his widow, Ghinwa BHUTTO, to form the **Pakistan People's Party (Shaheed Bhutto)** or PPP-SB to challenge Benazir Bhutto's hold on the party. The subsequent national legislative campaign in early 1997 contained an added element of personal hostility between the two women, although both suffered disastrous defeats in the election.

During 1998–1999 new corruption allegations or charges were repeatedly brought against Benazir Bhutto and her husband. Bhutto's political viability suffered a major blow in April 1999 when a Lahore court sentenced her and her husband to five years in prison, disqualified them from public office for five years, and fined them $8.6 million for corruption and abuse of power. Bhutto asserted from England that she would appeal the conviction to the Supreme Court, which in April 2001 threw out the decision and ordered a retrial because of apparent government involvement in the verdict.

In March 1999, the party leadership elected the former prime minister chair for life, a decision reiterated by a party convention in September 2000 in defiance of the government's August announcement that convicted criminals could not hold party offices. Bhutto remained in self-imposed exile, the Musharraf regime having refused to lift outstanding arrest warrants.

To get around a proscription against the electoral participation of any party having a convicted criminal as an officeholder, the PPP organized the legally separate **Pakistan People's Party Parliamentarians** (PPPP) in August 2002. Two months after its formation, the PPPP won 81 National Assembly seats, but in November it suffered the defection of 10 representatives who supported the installation of the Jamali government. (The move was possible because the antidefection clause of the constitution remained suspended.) The defectors then organized under Rao Sikander IQBAL as the Pakistan People's Party (Patriots), which merged with the PPP (Sherpao), a 1999 splinter (see the separate write-up, below), in June 2004. The new organization was then registered by the Election Commission as the "official" PPP. Bhutto's PPP immediately appealed the Election Commission's decision on the grounds that use of the PPP name by another party would deceive and defraud the electorate. Iqbal and his supporters joined the PML-Q before the 2008 general election, for which the PPP (Sherpao) was separately registered.

On July 27, 2007, President Musharraf and Benazir Bhutto met in Abu Dhabi in the context of ongoing discussions between the government and her representatives on a power-sharing arrangement. Bhutto returned to Pakistan on October 18, following Musharraf's promulgation of the NRO that freed her from prosecution, but the imposition in November of a state of emergency resulted in her calling, while under house arrest, for Musharraf's resignation. Following Bhutto's assassination on December 27, she was succeeded as party chair by a teenaged son, Bilawal, with Asif Zardari handling the party's day-to-day affairs.

In the February 2008 election, the PPP, running as the still-registered PPPP, won 30.6 percent of the vote and a plurality of 124 seats. (Zardari was prevented from running by earlier corruption convictions.) It then forged a coalition agreement with the PML-N and several smaller parties, after which the PPP vice chair, Yousaf Raza Gilani, was elected as prime minister. Following President Musharraf's August resignation, Zardari emerged as the leading candidate for the presidency, even though the PML-N had withdrawn from the coalition. Zardari was elected president on September 6. In the March 2009 election for one-half of the Senate, the PPP claimed nearly half the seats and thereby surpassed the PML-Q as the plurality party in the upper house.

In March 2010, the Supreme Court demanded the chairman of the National Accountability Bureau reopen hundreds of corruption cases, many involving PPP officials that were stopped by Musharraf's 2007 NRO (see Political background, above). In 2011, the PPP was also criticized for deteriorating public security, notably in the Sindh province and its increasingly turbulent capital, Karachi. The minister for Sindh, Dr. Zulfiqar MIRZA, a senior PPP member, resigned from all of his government posts in August 2011. He accused his own party of failing to take adequate measures to stem the violence. Also in 2011, PPP Executive Committee Member Shah Memood QURESHI left the PPP to join the **Pakistan Tehrik-e-Insaaf** (PTI). Following the dismissal of Gilani as prime minister in June, PPP member Raja Pervaiz ASHRAF succeeded him. At a party congress in January 2013, Makhdoom Amin Fahim was elected party president, and Ashraf was elected secretary general. In the 2013 balloting, the PPP secured a disappointing 42 seats but remained the majority party in Azad Kashmir, Gilgit-Baltistan, and Sindh.

Leaders: Bilawal Zardari BHUTTO (Chair), Makhdoom Amin FAHIM (Party President), Asif Ali ZARDARI (Former President of Pakistan and Cochair of the PPP), Raja Pervaiz ASHRAF (Former Prime minister and Secretary General), Syed Yousaf Raza GILANI (Former Prime Minister and PPP Vice Chair).

Pakistan Movement for Justice (Pakistan *Tehreek-e-Insaf*-PTI). The PTI is a centrist grouping founded by popular cricket captain Imran Khan in 1996. It gained one seat in the assembly elections in 2002 but boycotted the 2008 polling. The party surprised pundits in the 2013 balloting by placing second in the election with 16. 9 percent of the vote, and third in seats with 35. The party also formed a coalition government to govern Khyber Pakhtunkhwa province.

Leaders: Imran KHAN (Chair), Javed HASHMI (President), Jenhangir Khan TAREEN (Secretary General).

Muttahida Qaumi Movement (MQM). Organized in 1981 as the *Muhajir* National Movement, at that time the MQM (Nationalist People's Movement) was primarily concerned with the rights of post-partition migrants to Pakistan, whom it wanted to see recognized as constituting a "fifth nationality." Originally backed by Zia ul-Haq as a counter to Zulfikar Bhutto's Sindh-based PPP, the party became the third largest National Assembly grouping, with 13 seats, after the 1988 election. It was subsequently allied, at different times, with both the PPP and the PML.

The assassination of party chair Azim Ahmad TARIQ in May 1993 exacerbated a violent cleavage that had emerged within the group the year before, the principal leaders being Altaf Hussain (MQM-Altaf), who is now a citizen of the United Kingdom, and Afaq Ahmed of the MQM-*Haqiqi* (below). Although the party boycotted the National Assembly election in 1993, it was runner-up to the PPP in the Sindh provincial elections. In 1994 Altaf Hussain and two of his senior associates were sentenced in absentia to 27-year prison terms for terrorism, but in 1997 the convictions were quashed.

In February 1997, the MQM-Altaf, under the banner of the **Haq Parast Group,** won 12 National Assembly seats, all from Sindh, and thereafter entered a governing alliance with the PML-N at both provincial and national levels. Also in 1997 the party changed its name from *Muhajir* to *Muttahida* to indicate that its interests had broadened to encompass Pakistanis in general rather than only the Muslim migrants from India.

In August 1998, the MQM announced its intention to withdraw from the governing coalitions, in part because the Nawaz Sharif administration had not done enough to stem the increasingly violent clashes in Karachi between the MQM-Altaf and the MQM-*Haqiqi,* the latter functioning primarily as a collection of urban street fighters. When Islamabad responded to the violence by dismissing the Sindh provincial government and imposing federal rule, Altaf Hussain loyalists accused the Nawaz Sharif government of trying to take away the party's power base. In 1999, a number of party leaders broke with Hussain and threatened to form a separate party unless he adopted a stronger stance toward autonomy for Sindh.

In the 2002 National Assembly election, the MQM won 17 seats, after which it joined the Jamali government. In July 2006, however, it threatened to pull its ministers from the cabinet and to leave the Sindh government because President Musharraf would not fire the Sindh chief minister. The crisis was resolved a week later, and the MQM remained in the government.

In the February 2008 election, the MQM-Altaf won 7.4 percent of the vote and a total of 25 National Assembly seats. The MQM did not immediately join the Gilani cabinet, reportedly because the party demanded more posts than were offered. It eventually joined the government in January 2009 and June 2011.

In 2010 and 2011, party supporters in Karachi were involved in political violence against ethnic Pashtuns and the ANP. Raza HAIDER, an MQM leader and lawmaker in the Sindh Assembly, was gunned down in Karachi in a drive-by shooting that was part of the violence that left at least 37 people dead in August. In October 2011, the MQM announced it would join the PPP-led government, but later rejected the coalition agreement. In the 2013 assembly balloting, the MQM won 23 seats.

Leaders: Altaf HUSSAIN (President), Babar GHAURI (Parliamentary Leader of the Party).

Pakistan Muslim League (PML-Q). Officially registered in 2004 as the PML, the current party continues to be interchangeably identified as the **Pakistan Muslim League–Qaid-i-Azam** ("Father of the Nation," a reference to Mohammad Ali Jinnah) or PML-Q.

The complicated history of the PML began in 1962 when it was launched as successor to the pre-independence All-India Muslim League. Long riven by essentially personalist factions, it split over participation in the February 1985 election. A Chatta Group, led by Kawaja KHAIRUDDIN, joined the MRD's boycott call, while the mainstream, led by Pir Sahib PAGARO, participated in the election "under protest" and won 27 seats. Mohammad Khan Junejo, a longtime party member, became prime minister.

The PML split again in August 1988, with an army-supported faction of Zia loyalists (the PML-Fida) emerging under Fida Mohammad KHAN. The party reunited as a component of the IDA prior to the November balloting, in which the IDA routed the PPP, Mohammad Nawaz Sharif of the PML thereupon being named prime minister. Pagaro formed his own party, the PML-Functional (see PML-F, above), in mid-1992.

In May 1993, two months after Junejo's death, the Junejo group split into a majority (Nawaz or PML-N) faction headed by Nawaz Sharif and a rump (Junejo or PML-J) faction led by Hamid Nasir CHATTA. The latter joined the Bhutto government following the October 1993 election, while the PML-N became the core of the parliamentary opposition.

Following the elections of February 1997 in which it won a majority of the assembly seats, the PML-N took power. The party remained prone to factionalism, however, with the PML-J and a Qasim Group (PML-Qasim) joining the opposition PAI alliance upon its formation in 1998. Following the October 1999 coup, another faction, the PML-Q, was formed with the tacit support of the military and became the party most closely associated with President Musharraf.

Entering the 2002 election, the PML-Q was allied with the National Alliance (NA) in the Grand National Alliance. The PML-N ran as part of the ARD. The PML-J, although still separate, appeared to be drawing closer to the PML-Q. Also running independently were the PML-F; the PML–Zia ul-Haq (PML-Z), which had been formed by the son of the late president in August 2002; and the PML-Jinnah, which had been established in 1998 following a factional dispute within the PML-J. Electoral results gave the PML-Q 118 seats; the PML-F, 5; the PML-J, 3; and the PML-Z, 1.

With the PML-Q in the ascendancy, holding a plurality of seats in both houses of parliament and dominating the government, efforts to unite the PML factions gathered strength in 2003, leading to the announcement in May 2004 of a "united PML," excluding only the PML-N. In August, however, objecting in particular to the leadership of Chaudhry Shujaat Hussain, Pir Sahib Pagaro declared that he intended to restore the PML-F's separate standing.

Days after the formation of the "united PML," the NA parties, which had won 16 seats in the October 2002 election, announced that they were merging with the PML. (One of the founding NA parties, the Sindh National Front, had already withdrawn from the alliance.) The Sindh Democratic Alliance (SDA), led by Arbab Ghulam RAHIM (chief minister of Sindh since June 2004), had been launched in September–October 2001 and had already established a working relationship at the provincial level with the PML-Q. The Millat Party (MP) had been launched in August 1998 by former president Sardar Farooq Ahmad Khan Leghari. There was, however, opposition to the merger within the other NA parties. In the end, the National People's Party (see NPP, below) and the National Awami Party (see the ANP, above) retained separate identities.

In mid-June 2004, the election commission approved the merger of the PML-F, PML-J, PML-Jinnah, PML-Z, and SDA into the PML-Q and the redesignation of the latter as, simply, the PML, although the PML-Q designation is still commonly used (in part, to distinguish it from the PML-N). Formal incorporation of the MP followed.

In 2005, vocal opposition surfaced to the continued leadership of the party president, Shujaat Hussain, and to the prominent role of the

Punjab chief minister, Chaudhry Pervez ELAHI, who allegedly ignored the recommendations of National Assembly representatives in choosing candidates for local council elections. The "forward bloc" dissident group, numbering about 30 members of the National Assembly, was led by Mian Riaz Hussain PIRZADA, Farooq Amjad MIR, and Mazhan QURESHI. In May 2006, President Musharraf, looking toward the next general election, asked Shujaat Hussain to form a dispute resolution board to resolve the differences. Nevertheless, Pirzada, in particular, continued to object to many of President Musharraf's decisions, including the dismissal of the Supreme Court judges and the imposition of a state of emergency in November 2007.

In the February 2008 National Assembly election, the PML finished third, with 23 percent of the vote and a total of 54 seats. Those defeated for reelection included Shujaat Hussain. In March, the PML candidate for prime minister, Pervez Elahi, finished a distant second, with 42 votes. In May former senior vice president Manzoor Ahmad WATTOO (previously leader of the PML-Jinnah) joined the PPP.

At the same time, dissatisfaction with the continued dominance of Shujaat Hussein and Pervez Elahi led a group of dissidents to form a **Like-Minded Bloc** within the PML. In October 2008, the bloc called for new party elections, charging that Shujaat Hussain failed to consult with the party's executive and working committees and that his failure of leadership had left the PML out of the Baluchistan provincial government despite its having won a legislative plurality. With Shujaat Hussain virtually guaranteed reelection, the bloc then boycotted the July 2009 party election. Two months later, it announced its own leadership as Hamid Nasir Chatta, chair; Salim SAIFULLAH, president; and Humayan Akhtar KHAN, secretary general.

On June 25, 2012, PML-Q leader Chaudhry Pervaiz Elahi was appointed deputy prime minister. In the 2013 assembly balloting, the PML-Q secured two seats.

Leaders: Chaudhry Shujaat HUSSAIN (President), Chaudhry Pervaiz ELAHI (Former Deputy Prime Minister), Wasim SAJJAD (Leader of the Opposition in the Senate), Aleem ADIL Sheikh (Chair), Mushahid HUSSAIN Syed (2008 presidential candidate and Secretary General).

Awami National Party (ANP). The ANP was formed in July 1986 by four left-of-center groups: the National Democratic Party (NDP), a group of Pakistan National Party (PNP) dissidents led by Latif AFRIDI, elements of the *Awami Tehrik* (PAT, below), and the *Mazdoor Kissan* Party (MKP). As originally constituted under the direction of Pushtoon leader Khan Abdul WALI KHAN, the ANP was unusual in that each of its constituent groups drew its primary support from a different province.

The NDP had been organized in 1975 upon proscription of the National Awami Party, a remnant of the National Awami Party of Bangladesh that, under the leadership of Wali Khan, was allegedly involved in terrorist activity aimed at secession of Baluchistan and Khyber Pakhtunkhwa. A founding component of the PNA, the NDP withdrew in 1978, and in 1979 a group of dissidents left to form the PNP.

The ANP won three assembly seats in October 1993 and ten seats—all from Khyber Pakhtunkhwa—in February 1997. A year later the ANP terminated its alliance with the governing PML-N because of the latter's refusal to support the redesignation of the NWFP as Khyber Pakhtunkhwa, the area's precolonial name. Later in 1998 the ANP was a prime mover in formation of the PONM opposition alliance, but it parted ways in 1999 with what it considered the PONM's unrealistic goals for national reconfiguration.

The ANP failed to win representation in the National Assembly election of 2002 but won two Senate seats in February 2003. The party's founder, Khan Abdul Wali Khan, died in January 2006.

In June 2006, the central party leadership endorsed the Charter of Democracy proposed by former prime ministers Bhutto and Nawaz Sharif. In the same month, the National Awami Party (NAP), a 2000 offshoot led by Arbab Ayub JAN and Sharif KHATTAK, reunited with the parent party.

In February 2008, the ANP won 13 National Assembly seats and also won control of the Khyber Pakhtunkhwa legislature. It then joined the PPP, PML-N, and JUI-F in forming a central government. In March 2009 it won 5 Senate seats, for a total of 6.

A prominent NWFP legislator, Alamzeb KHAN, was killed by a roadside bomb in Peshawar in February 2009, and party supporters engaged in violent confrontations with supporters of MQM in Karachi throughout 2011. In Senate elections in March 2012, the ANP placed third, raising its representation to 12. In the 2013 assembly balloting, the ANP only won one seat.

Leaders: Asfandyar WALI KHAN (President), Haji Muhammad ADIL (Senior Vice President), Zahir Khan OCH (First Deputy Vice President), Bushra GOHAR (Second Deputy Vice President).

Jamaat-e-Islami Pakistan (JIP). Organized in 1941, the *Jamaat-e-Islami* (Islamic Assembly) is a right-wing fundamentalist group that has called for an Islamic state based on a national rather than a purely communalistic consensus. The group participated in formation of the IDA in 1988 but withdrew in 1992, in part because the coalition had failed to implement a promised Islamization program. In 1993 it was instrumental in launching a Pakistan Islamic Front (PIF), which won only three seats in the October legislative poll. Although the JIP held no national legislative seats following the 1997 election, it remained politically influential. It welcomed the October 1999 coup but called for setting up a caretaker civilian government.

One of the two largest parties in the MMA, the JIP increasingly differed with the JUI-F (above) after the 2002 general election, threatening the MMA's effectiveness. One contentious issue was the JIP's objections to the JUI-F's participation in President Musharraf's National Security Council. In 2008 the JIP boycotted the general election.

In March 2009, the JIP elected its secretary general, Syed Munawwar Hassan, to a five-year term as chair.

Officially a branch of the *Jamiat-e-Islami* in Pakistan but so independent that it might well be considered a separate movement, the **Jammu and Kashmir Jamiat-e-Islami** was active in electoral politics by 1970 and even participated to a limited degree in Indian *Lok Sabha* and provincial elections. In 1997 the party denied that it was the political wing of the militant *Hizb-ul-Mujaheddin,* and in October, 40 of its members challenged the militant campaign as not contributing to the goal of an independent Kashmir.

In the 2012 Senate elections, the JIP lost its representation in the upper chamber. In the 2013 assembly polling, the party secured four seats.

Leaders: Syed Munawwar HASSAN (Chair), Qazi Hussain AHMAD (Former Chair), Liaqat BALOCH (Secretary General).

Baluchistan National Party–Awami (BNP-A). One of several rival political formations in Baluchistan, the BNP was formed by the 1997 merger of the Baluchistan National Movement (Mengal Group) and the Pakistan National Party of Mir Ghaus Baksh Bizenjo. It won three National Assembly seats that year and initially backed the Nawaz Sharif government, but it later withdrew its support. The party soon split into factions. In the 2002 National Assembly election the BNP-Mengal (below) won one seat; in the 2003 Senate election the BNP-Mengal and the BNP-A each won one. Also in 2003, another BNP faction led by Abdul HAYEE Baloch joined in forming the National Party (NP, below).

In the February 2008, National Assembly election, the BNP-A won one seat. In July it won a second Senate seat in a by-election necessitated by the resignation of the BNP-Mengal senator. The BNP-A joined the government in November 2008 and added a third Senate seat in 2009.

The BNP-A called upon the government to deploy troops to troubled cities, including Karachi, in response to the ethnically motivated killings of Baloch people in 2011. In a separate development the party dismissed Sen. Muhammad Ali Rind in response to his conviction for electoral fraud in August that year. In September 2012, local party official Jihadul Islam ZIA was killed in a bomb attack in Jessore. In the 2013 assembly elections, the BNP-A secured one seat.

Leader: Syed Ehsan SHAH (President).

Pakhtoonkhwa Milli Awami Party (PkMAP). Drawing its support mainly from the Pakhtoon ethnic group in Khyber Pakhtunkhwa, the PkMAP has campaigned for greater regional autonomy. It elected three National Assembly members in 1993 but none in 1997. In 1998 it participated in formation of the PONM opposition alliance.

In the 2002 National Assembly election, the PkMAP won one seat; in 2003 it won two Senate seats, picking up a third in 2006. The party's chair, Mahmood Khan Achakzai, was elected president of the PONM in June 2006 and then became convener of the APDM. He has used that platform to demand a separate province for Pukhtuns. After the March 2009 Senate election, the PkMAP held only one seat in the upper house, which it lost after the 2012 balloting. In the 2013 general elections, the PkMAP won four seats in the assembly.

Leaders: Mahmood Khan ACHAKZAI (Chair), Sen. Abdul Rahim Khan MANDOKHEL.

National People's Party (NPP). The NPP was formed in 1986 by a group of PPP moderates led by former Sindh chief minister Ghulam Mustafa Jatoi, who accused Benazir Bhutto of "authoritarian tendencies" prior to being removed as provincial PPP president. Jatoi served as interim prime minister following the dismissal of Bhutto in 1990. The NPP entered the first Sharif government coalition but was expelled in 1992 because of alleged collusion with the PPP. The NPP turned to the PPP (Shaheed Bhutto) for an electoral alliance in 1997, winning one seat.

The NPP became a founding member of the National Alliance in May 2002. Two years later, following the announcement that some alliance parties were merging with the PML, Ghulam Mustafa Jatoi stated that although the party's parliamentary group may have decided to join the PML, he had not. The NPP has since maintained its independence and won one National Assembly seat in 2008. Jatoi died in November 2009. The party won three seats in the 2013 assembly balloting.

Leader: Asif JATOI.

Qaumi Watan Party (QWP). The QWP was initially formed as the **Pakistan People's Party (Sherpao)**—PPP(S). It was established by Aftab Ahmad Khan Sherpao following Benazir Bhutto's 1999 decision to dismiss him as PPP senior vice president for breaking party discipline over political developments involving the Khyber Pakhtunkhwa government. In the 2002 general election, the PPP (Sherpao) won two seats in the Senate and two in the National Assembly. A June 2004 merger with the progovernment PPP (Patriots) resulted in a decision by the Election Commission to assign the unified party the PPP designation—Benazir Bhutto's PPP had been deregistered—but the issue of who held title to the name became moot after Bhutto's return to Pakistan in 2007 and the decision of the PPP (Patriots) leaders to join the PML-Q.

In April and again in December 2007, Aftab Sherpao was the apparent intended target of suicide bombings that killed a total of some 80 people. The PPP(S) ran independently in the 2008 National Assembly election, retaining one assembly seat. It secured one seat in the 2013 assembly elections.

Leader: Aftab Ahmad Khan SHERPAO.

National Party (NP). The NP was formed in 2003 by merger of the leading faction of the **Baluchistan National Movement** (BNM), led by Abdul Hayee Baloch, and the **Baluchistan National Democratic Party** (BNDP), led by Hasil Bizenjo and Sardar Sanaullah ZEHRI. Competing primarily against supporters of the BNP, the NP has had little electoral success at the national level. It currently holds two Senate seats.

As a member of the APDM, the NP chose to boycott the February 2008 National Assembly election, but Senior Vice President Zehri objected, formed a **National Party Parliamentarians** (NPP) group, and won a seat in the Baluchistan Assembly.

In April 2009, Ghulam Muhammad BALOCH, president of the BNM and secretary general of the eight-party **Baluchistan National Front** (BNF), was killed along with another BNM leader and the head of the **Baloch Republican Party** (BRP), Sher Mohammad BALOCH. The execution-style deaths led to rioting and antigovernment demonstrations in Baluchistan, although it was unclear who was responsible for the murders.

The NP announced in 2012 that it would contest future assembly elections and not repeat its 2008 boycott. It won one assembly seat in 2013.

Leaders: Abdul HAYEE Baloch, Sen. Abdul MALIK (President), Sen. Mir Hasil BIZENJO (Secretary General).

The following parties secured one seat in the assembly (all received less than one percent of the vote): the **Pakistan Muslim League-Zia ul-Haq** (PML-Z), led by Ijaz ul-HAQ; **Awami Muslim League**, founded in 2008 and led by Sheikh Rashid AHMED; **Awami Jamhuri Ittehad Pakistan**; **All Pakistan National Muslim League**, founded by former president Perez MUSHARRAFF; and the **Baluchistan National Party–Mengal** (BNP-M), led by Araullah MENGAL.

Other Parties:

Jamiat Ulema-e-Pakistan (JUP). Founded in 1968, the JUP (Assembly of Pakistani Clergy) is a popular Islamic group that withdrew from the PNA in 1978. Its president, Maulana Shah Ahmed NOORANI, was among those failing to secure an assembly slot in 1988; its secretary general, Maulana Abdul Sattar Khan NIAZI, quit the Nawaz Sharif cabinet in 1991 after being criticized by the prime minister for not supporting government policies on the Gulf war against Iraq. The party subsequently split into four factions, including those led by Noorani and Niazi. Niazi died in May 2001 and Noorani, in December 2003.

In May 2006, the JUP (Niazi), which supported the ARD, indicated that it would sign the Charter of Democracy that had been drafted by former prime ministers Bhutto and Nawaz Sharif. In March 2008 the president of the JUP (Noorani), Muhammad Anas Noorani, announced that he was stepping down. His successor, Abu al-Khair Zubair, later led an unsuccessful effort to reconcile the leaders of the JUI-F and JIP in the hope of revitalizing the MMA.

In May 2009, the JUP joined in forming the **Sunni Ittehad Council** (SIC), a group of eight moderate Sunni parties that strongly opposed the Taliban but also called for the withdrawal of U.S. forces from Afghanistan and an end to missile attacks from unmanned drones. The JUP's Fazal Kareem was named SIC chair. Another SIC founder, cleric and religious scholar Sarfraz Ahmed NAEEMI, was assassinated by a Taliban suicide bomber in June. Another former JUP official, Maulana SALIMULLAH, was killed in May 2011.

The JUP organized protests in September 2012 against the anti-Islamic film *The Innocence of Muslims*.

Leaders: Abu al-Khair Muhammad ZUBAIR (President, JUP-Noorani), Muhammad Anas NOORANI (JUP-Noorani), Pir Syed Anis HAIDER Shah (President, JUP-Niazi), Muhammad Fazal KAREEM (President, JUP-FK), Saleem Ullah KHAN (President, JUP-*Nifaz-i-Shariat*).

Jamhoori Watan Party (JWP). A successor to the Baluchistan National Alliance (BNA), the JWP (Republican National Party) is active at both provincial and national levels. The JWP, which was formed in 1990 by Nawab Akbar BUGTI, won two seats from Baluchistan in the 1997 National Assembly election and as of early 1999 held five Senate seats.

The death of the JWP's prominent founder in an August 2006 military operation precipitated widespread rioting, and the first anniversary of his death was observed by a general strike across Baluchistan. By then, the party had split into two factions, the more radical of which was led by a grandson of Akbar Bugti, Baramdagh BUGTI, who is also a leader of the separatist Baluchistan Republican Army.

The JWP boycotted the 2008 National Assembly election. In August 2011 the party supported a general strike in observance of the fifth anniversary of the death of Baloch leader Nawab Akbar BUGTI. Bugti's grandson was killed in violence in Karachi in 2011. In 2012, Bugti called for the creation of a broad opposition coalition.

Leaders: Nawabzada Talal Akbar BUGTI (President), Sen. Shahid Hassan BUGTI, Shah Zain BUGTI.

Markazi Jamiat-e-Ahle Hadith (MJAH). A militant Sunni group with a number of factions, the MJAH has close ties to former prime minister Nawaz Sharif. Originally a component of the MMA, it withdrew when the latter decided to function as an electoral alliance for the 2002 National Assembly election, although it later returned. The leader of the most prominent faction, Sajid Mir, was reelected in 2009 to a Punjab seat in the Senate with the endorsement of the PML-N.

Leader: Sajid MIR.

Among the more than 100 parties that participated in the 2013 balloting were (all received less than 0.5 percent of the vote): the **Bahawalpur National Awami Party,** formed in 2010 by Nawab Salahuddin ABBASI; **Sindh United Party**, led by Syed Jalal Mahmood SHAH; **Movement for the Protection of Pakistan** (*Tehreek-e-Tahaffuz-e-Pakistan*-TTP), led by Abdul Qadeer KHAN; **Pakistan Muslim League-J**; the **Awami Jamhuri Ittehad Pakistan,** led by Shahram KHAN; the **Pakistan National Muslim League**; and the **Sunni Ittehad Council.**

For further information on the **Awami Qiadat Party** (AQP), **Jamiat-Ulema-e-Islam Sami ul-Haq Group** (JUI-S), **Khaksar Tehrik, Muhajir Qaumi Movement–Haqiqi** (MQM-*Haqiqi*), **Pakistan Awami Tehrik** (PAT), the **Pakistan Democratic Party** (PDP), the **Sindh National Front** (SNF), and **Tehrik-e-Istiqlal Pakistan** please see the 2009 *Handbook.*

Banned and Other Extremist Organizations:

Tehrik-e-Taliban Pakistan (TTP). The TTP is an umbrella for radical groups that support strict adherence to sharia, oppose the presence of Western forces in Afghanistan, and have conducted attacks directed against the Pakistani military, police, and civilian government. Although Afghanistan's Taliban government had adherents and supporters in Pakistan's FATA and NWFP even before the United States launched its attack on Afghanistan in October 2001, the TTP as it currently functions probably dates from late 2007, when Baitullah Mehsud convinced a dozen or so jihadist and Islamist organizations to accept a degree of central coordination. Based in South Waziristan, Mehsud's home base, the TTP is directly linked to **al-Qaida** (see the entry on

Afghanistan). Al-Qaida was banned by Pakistan in 2003, as was the TTP in August 2008.

With Mehsud as its most vocal presence, the TTP quickly extended its reach in the FATA, but its greatest impact occurred in Khyber Pakhtunkhwa's Swat valley, where its violent actions included bombings, assassinations, and the burning of girls' schools. In an effort to end the violence, in February 2009 the Khyber Pakhtunkhwa government agreed to the adoption of sharia in the Malakand division. The central government accepted the pact in April, by which time the TTP was reportedly already establishing its own sharia courts. In June militia leader Qari ZAINUDDIN, who had broken from Mehsud in 2008 and later rejected the use of suicide bombers, was assassinated. By then, the government, responding to continuing TTP violence, had already discarded the February pact and was engaged in a new military offensive.

Meanwhile, in March 2009, the United States had placed a $5 million bounty on Mehsud, who was described as a "key al-Qaida facilitator" and who was believed to have directed the assassination of former prime minister Bhutto. On August 5 a missile launched from an unmanned NATO drone mortally wounded Mehsud, who succumbed later in the month and was succeeded by Hakimullah Mehsud and Waliur Rehman. Hakimullah is believed to have close ties to *Sipah-i-Sahaba* (SSP) and *Lashkar-i-Jhangvi* (LiJ) (below) as well as al-Qaida.

Maulana FAZLULLAH, a son-in-law of Sufi Muhammad of the TNSM (below) and a leader of the TTP in Swat, was arrested in early September 2009 during the continuing military offensive. The Pakistani government later announced a $5 million bounty for information leading to the capture or death of Hakimullah. On October 17, the government sent some 30,000 troops on a military offensive into the FATA against the TTP after weeks of bombing militant strongholds by the air force. The group retaliated with violence in cities around Pakistan. On December 28 a TTP suicide bomber attacked a Shia Muslim procession in Karachi, killing more than 40, injuring 100, and setting off riots and widespread arson in the city. Hakimullah Mehsud and another TTP commander were thought to have died of their injuries after one of two U.S. drone aircraft missile strikes in January. In April 2010 the TTP took responsibility for a heavily armed attack against the U.S. consulate in Peshawar. Hakimullah showed up in a video in May threatening that TTP militants would soon strike within the United States hours after the group claimed responsibility for a failed car-bombing of New York City's Times Square. In May Afghan police claimed Fazlullah had been killed as he led 500 Pakistani Taliban in fighting in Nuristan Province. It became clear to Pakistani government officials that the offensive against the TTP served only to disperse militants from the FATA around the country, and by July 2010 the TTP were returning to that area, the Swat Valley, and also making inroads in eastern Punjab province.

In September that year, the U.S. government added the TTP to its list of foreign terrorist organizations and offered a bounty of $5 million for the capture of Hakimullah and Rehman. The same month the TTP carried out a series of 3 suicide attacks in Lahore, killing more than 30 and injuring hundreds more. The attacks were aimed at the city's Shi'ite population and triggered riots as citizens vented frustration at the city's security forces, who had been unable to stem a dozen such attacks that had occurred in Lahore since March. The TTP claimed responsibility for a subsequent attack on a bus carrying students from an exclusive English-language school near Peshawar in September 2011.

TTP strikes in February 2012, including suicide attacks, killed more than 100. Security forces reported the deaths of 50 TTP militants in fighting during the same period. On April 15, a TTP attack on a prison in Bannu freed more than 380 prisoners, including more than 20 militants.

In an effort to support Afghan negotiations with the Taliban, on December 31 Pakistan released four senior members of the Afghan Taliban. Reports in 2013 indicated that the Pakistani Taliban was shifting focus to concentrate on the war in Afghanistan.

Leaders: Hakimullah MEHSUD, Waliur REHMAN, Maulvi OMAR.

Lashkar-i-Taiba (LiT). LiT (Army of the Pure) was established in 1993 by Hafiz Muhammad Sayeed and Zafar IQBAL as the military wing of an above-ground religious group, the *Markaz ad-Dawa Wal Irshad* (Center for Religious Learning and Propagation), which was formed in 1986 to organize Pakistani Sunni militants participating in the Afghan revolution. The *Markaz* was officially dissolved in December 2001 and all its assets transferred to the new **Jamaat-ud-Dawa**—JuD (Party for Religious Propagation) in an effort to avoid proscription. The LiT was banned by Pakistan in January 2002. The JuD was placed on a "watch list" by the Pakistani government in November 2003 and banned in December 2008 because of links to terrorists who had carried out attacks in Mumbai, India, a month earlier.

The LiT, which may be the largest Pakistan-based militant group seeking separation of Jammu and Kashmir from India, with bases in Azad Kashmir and near the LoC, has claimed responsibility for and been implicated in innumerable attacks within Kashmir and elsewhere. Following a series of transport blasts that killed several hundred people in Mumbai, India, in July 2006, the Indian government placed suspicion on LiT, which denied involvement. LiT has also been active in a number of other conflict areas, including Bosnia and Herzegovina, Chechnya, Iraq, and Southeast Asia.

Following a massive earthquake that struck Khyber Pakhtunkhwa and Azad Kashmir on October 8, 2005, several reports from the stricken region particularly credited the rescue and recovery work performed by the LiT and JuD.

The LiT chief of operations, Zaki-ur-Rehman Lakhvi, has been described as the mastermind of the November 2008 Mumbai assault, which was carried out by Pakistani nationals linked to the LiT. In December Lakhvi, Sayeed, and dozens of other leaders of the LiT and the JuD were detained, but in June 2009 the Lahore High Court ordered Sayeed's release from house arrest on the grounds that his detention was without constitutional grounds. In October the court dismissed the case. Lakhvi and six others were indicted by an antiterrorism court on November 25.

In an effort to circumvent its proscription, the JuD has reportedly reorganized as the **Tehrik-e-Tahafuz Qibla Awal** (Movement for the Safeguarding of the First Center of Prayer).

In April 2012, the United States offered a $10 million reward for the capture of Sayeed. Reports in September 2013 indicated the central government was investigating the transfer of provincial funds to support the LiT's nonmilitary activities.

Leaders: Hafiz Mohammed SAYEED, Zaki-ur-Rehman LAKHVI (Chief of Operations), Haji Muhammad ASHRAF (Chief of Finance).

Sipah-i-Sahaba (SiS). The SiS (Guardians of the Friends of the Prophet) is a militant Sunni group founded in 1982 as a JUI breakaway by Maulana Haq Nawaz JHANGVI, who was later murdered. It has close connections to the extremist **Lashkar-i-Jhangvi** (LiJ) and the equally militant TNSM (below), both of which have been involved in sectarian bloodshed.

In February 2000, the SiS announced that it was prepared to give nearly 100,000 workers to Masood Azhar's newly organized JMMT (below) to aid in holy war (jihad). Both were banned in January 2002, as the LiJ had been in August 2001. The LiJ's leader, Riaz BASRA, was killed by Indian police in May 2002. Another leader, Asif RAMZI, who had been linked to the kidnapping and murder of American journalist Daniel Pearl, was killed in a bomb explosion in December 2002. ATTAULLAH, an alleged LiJ leader, was sentenced to death in September 2003. Another alleged LiJ member was also sentenced to death in June 2005 for his involvement in the bombing of Shia mosques that killed 45 in May 2004.

In October 2003, SiS leader Muhammad Azam TARIQ, who had won election to the National Assembly a year earlier as an independent while still in prison, was assassinated, allegedly by members of the Shiite TJP (see TiP, below). Earlier, the SiS had been renamed the **Millat-i-Islamia Pakistan** (MIP) to circumvent a government ban, but the MIP was then proscribed in November 2003. The United States has placed both SiS and the LiJ on its list of terrorist organizations; both have direct links to al-Qaida, and LiJ was thought to have linked up with the TTJ in February 2010. Dr. Khalid Nawaz FAROOQI, a prominent member, died from injuries sustained in an attack in September 2011. More than 200 SiS members were arrested during protests in September 2012 during protests against the film *The Innocence of Muslims.*

Leaders: Maulana Muhammad Ahmad LUDHIANVI, Ghulam Mustafa JADOON, Abid PARACHA, Ibrahim QASIMI.

Tehrik-e-Nifaz-e-Shariat-e-Mohammadi (TNSM). The TNSM (Mohammedan Movement for the Enforcement of Islamic Law), a fundamentalist group established in 1992 by Sufi Muhammad, was blamed by the government for the deaths of 11 persons in May 1994 and of 10 more the following November as the result of tribal demands in the northern Malakand division for the introduction of Islamic law. The TNSM responded to the August 1998 U.S. missile attack against terrorist camps in Afghanistan by organizing a rally in Peshawar at which it threatened to lay siege to U.S. property and kidnap Americans. In response to the 2001 onset of U.S.-led efforts to oust al-Qaida and the Taliban from Afghanistan, the TNSM helped recruit thousands of activists to fight the Western forces. The TNSM was then banned in January 2002.

After six years in prison, Sufi Muhammad was released in April 2008, which also saw the TNSM and the recently installed ANP-led NWFP government reach a peace agreement. A further agreement in February 2009 permitted the application of sharia in Malakand division, including Swat. The agreement was signed by President Zardari on April 13, after adoption by National Assembly. Nevertheless, continuing militant activity in the region led in May to a renewed effort by the Pakistani military to recover control of Malakand, with Sufi Muhammad and his three sons detained in July. The group continued to plan attacks in 2011. In September 2012, the government was forced to drop terrorism cases against Sufi Muhammad and a dozen TNSM figures. Nineteen other charges against Sufi Muhammad remained, with 13 ongoing in August 2013.
Leader: Sufi MUHAMMAD.

Other proscribed organizations include **Harkat-ul-Mujaheddin al-Alami** (HMA); **Islami Tehrik-i-Pakistan** (TiP), led by Allama Sajid Ali NAQVI and Abdul Jalil NAQVI; **Jaish-e-Muhammad Mujaheddin-e-Tanzeem** (JMMT or JeM), led Maulana Masood AZHAR and Abdul RAUF; **Baluchistan National Army** (BLA), led by Brahamdagh Khan BUGTI; **Lashkar-e-Islam** (LeI), formed in 2004 by Munir SHAKIRA; and **Ansar-ul-Islam** (AuI), established by Saifullah SAIFI.

Banned groups based in the Khyber and Bajaur agencies of the FATA have links to the TTP but have frequently clashed with each other. In April 2008 the LeI branch in Bajaur Agency, led by Wali REHMAN, reportedly changed its name to **Jaish-e-Islami,** while Mengal Bagh stated in August 2009 that he had renamed the LeI as the **Tehrik Lashkar-e-Islam**. Pakistan has also banned the **Al Akhtar Trust** and the **Al Rasheed Trust,** both based in Karachi and involved in financing terrorist groups, as well as the **Hizb-ut-Tahrir**.

LEGISLATURE

The **Parliament** (*Majlis-e-Shoora*), also known as the Federal Legislature, is a bicameral body consisting of the president, an indirectly elected Senate, and a directly elected National Assembly. Both were suspended by proclamation of Chief Executive Musharraf on October 15, 1999, and dissolved by him on June 20, 2001. Elections to expanded lower and upper houses were held in October 2002 and February 2003, respectively.

Senate. The current upper house comprises 100 members: 22 elected by each of the four provincial legislatures (14 general seats, 4 reserved for women, and 4 reserved for technocrats/*ulema*), plus 8 from the Federally Administered Tribal Areas (FATA) and 4 from the Federal Capital (2 general, 1 woman, 1 technocrat/*aalim*). FATA and Federal Capital senators are chosen by the National Assembly members of their respective jurisdictions. Senatorial terms are six years, with one-half of the body retiring every three years, although the election of February 24 and 27, 2003, was for the full, reconfigured house. The most recent election was held March 2, 2012, for 54 seats. After the election, the Pakistan People's Party Parliamentarians held 41 seats; Pakistan Muslim League–Nawaz, 14; Awami National Party, 12; *Jamiat-Ulema-e-Islam* Fazlur Rahman Group, 7; *Muttahida Qaumi* Movement, 7; Baluchistan National Party–Awami, 4; Pakistan Muslim League-*Qaid-i-Azam*, 4; Pakistan Muslim League, Pakistan Muslim League–Functional, and National Party, 1 each; independents, 12.
Chair: Syed Nayyer Hussain BOKHARI.

National Assembly. Serving a five-year term, subject to premature dissolution, the current National Assembly has 342 seats: 272 directly elected in single-member constituencies; 60 seats reserved for women, distributed proportionally according to party seats won in provincial assemblies; and 10 seats designated for members of religious minorities (4 Christian; 4 Hindu; 1 Sikh, Buddhist, or Parsi; 1 Qadiani), distributed proportionally to parties based on the directly elected National Assembly seat totals. The most recent election for the directly elected seats took place on May 11, 2013. The final results were as follows: the Pakistan Muslim League–Nawaz won 166 seats (126 directly elected, 34 seats reserved for women, 6 seats reserved for minorities); the Pakistan People's Party Parliamentarians, 42 (33, 8, 1); Pakistan Movement for Justice, 35 (28, 6, 1); *Muttahida Qaumi* Movement, 23 (18, 4, 1); *Jamiat-Ulema-e-Islam* Fazlur Rahman Group, 15 (11, 3, 1); Pakistan Muslim League–Functional, 6 (5, 1, 0); *Jamiat-Ulema-e-Islam*, 4 (3, 1, 0); *Pakhtoonkhwa Milli* Awami Party, 4 (3, 1, 0); National People's Party, 3 (2, 1, 0); Pakistan Muslim League, 2 (2, 0, 0); Pakistan Muslim League-Z, Awami Muslim League, *Awami Jamhuri Ittehad Pakistan,* Awami National Party, Baluchistan National Party—Awami, All Pakistan Muslim League, *Qaumi Watan*, National Party each secured 1 directly elected seat; independents, 27. Nine elections were scheduled to be redone. All 10 representatives elected from FATA are categorized as independents, but in the past the majority have supported Islamic parties.
Speaker: Saradr Ayaz SADIQ.

CABINET

[as of September 15, 2013]

Prime Minister	Muhammad Nawaz Sharif
Federal Ministers	
Agriculture	Sikandar Bosan
Communications	Akram Khan Durrani (JUI-F)
Defense	Muhammad Nawaz Sharif
Defense Production	Tanveer Hussain
Finance, Revenue, Planning and Development, Economic Affairs and Statistics	Mohammad Ishaq Dar
Industry and Production	Ghulam Murtaza Khan Jatoi
Information, Broadcasting, and National Heritage	Pervez Rashid
Inter-Provincial Coordination	Riaz Hussain Pirzada
Interior and Narcotics Control	Nisar Ali Khan
Kashmir Affairs and Gilgit-Baltistan	Muhammad Barjees Tahir
Law, Justice and Parliamentary Affairs	Muhammad Nawaz Sharif
National Food Security and Research	Sikandar Hayat Bosan
Overseas Pakistanis	Sadaruddin Shah Rashdi (PML-F)
Petroleum and Natural Resources	Khagan Abbasi
Planning and Development	Ahsan Iqbal
Ports and Shipping	Kamran Micheal
Railways	Saad Rafiq
Religious Affairs and Inter-Faith Harmony	Sardar Muhaamd Yousef
Science and Technology	Zahid Hamid
States and Frontier Regions	Gen. (ret.) Abdul Qadir Baloch
Water and Power	Mohammad Asif
Ministers of State	
Education, Training, and Standards in Higher Education	Muhammad Baligh Ur Rehman
Housing and Works	Usman Ibrahim
Information Technology and Telecommunications	Anusha Rahman Ahmad Khan [f]
National Health Services, Regulation, and Coordination	Saira Afzal Tarar [f]
Parliamentary Affairs	Aftab Ahmad
Petroleum and Natural Resources	Jam Kamal Khan
Privatization	Khurram Dastagir
Railways	Abdul Hakeem Baloch
Religious Affairs and Inter-Faith Harmony	Muhammad Amin Ul-Hasant
Water and Power	Abid Ser Ali

[f] = female

Note: Except where noted all are members of the PML-N.

INTERGOVERNMENTAL REPRESENTATION

Ambassador to the U.S.: Sherry REHMAN.

U.S. Ambassador to Pakistan: Richard OLSON.

Permanent Representative to the UN: Masood KHAN.

IGO Memberships (Non-UN): ADB, IOM, NAM, OIC, SAARC, SCO, WTO.

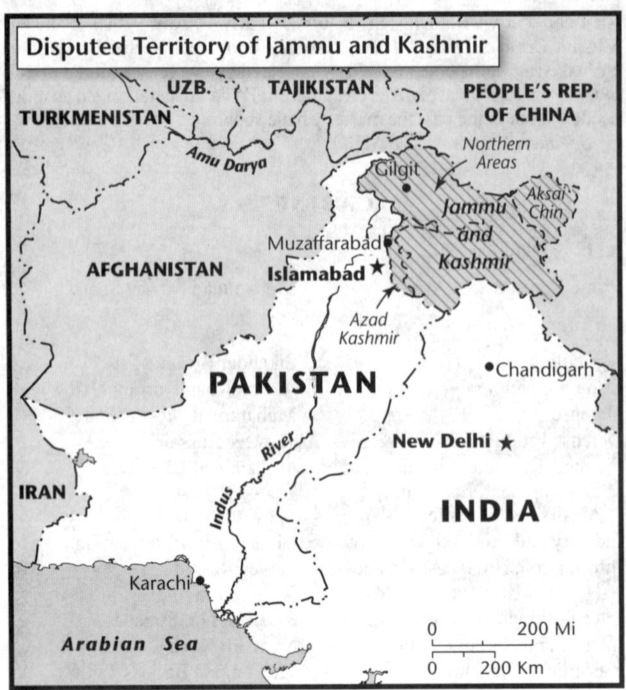

RELATED TERRITORIES

The precise status of predominantly Muslim Jammu and Kashmir has remained unresolved since the 1949 cease-fire, which divided the territory into Indian- and Pakistani-administered sectors. While India has claimed the entire area as a state of the Indian Union, Pakistan has never regarded the portion under its control as an integral part of Pakistan. Rather, it has administered Azad Kashmir and the Gilgit-Baltistan (known as the Northern Areas until September 2009) as de facto dependencies for whose defense and foreign affairs it is responsible.

Azad Kashmir. Formally called Azad (Free) Jammu and Kashmir, the smaller (4,200 sq. mi.) but more populous (estimated at 3,623,000 in 2006) of the Jammu and Kashmir regions administered by Pakistan is a narrow strip of territory lying along the northeastern border adjacent to Rawalpindi and Islamabad. It is divided into eight districts (Bagh, Bhimber, Kotli, Mirpur, Muzaffarabad, Neelum, Poonch, and Sudhnoti). Muzaffarabad City serves as the territory's capital. An Interim Constitution Act of 1974 provided for a Legislative Assembly, now comprising 49 members—41 directly elected plus 5 women and single representatives for technocrats, overseas Kashmiris, and *mashaikh* (Muslim spiritual leaders), all named by those directly elected. The principal executive body is the Azad Kashmir Council, which is chaired by the prime minister of Pakistan and also includes the president of Azad Kashmir as vice chair, the prime minister of Azad Kashmir or his designee, six members elected by the Legislative Assembly, and five federal ministers.

In the June 1996 Legislative Assembly election, the governing **All Jammu and Kashmir Muslim Conference** (also known simply as the Muslim Conference—MC) suffered an unprecedented drubbing by candidates from the Azad Kashmir affiliate of the PPP, and on July 30 Sultan MAHMOOD CHAUDHRY, president of the Azad Kashmir PPP, was sworn in as prime minister, replacing the MC's Sardar Abdul QAYYUM Khan. Except for a brief period in 1990, the MC had been in power for 13 years. On August 12, President Sikander HAYAT Khan, also of the MC, lost a no-confidence motion in the assembly, in which the PPP now controlled more than three-fourths of the seats. On August 25, Mohammad IBRAHIM Khan was sworn in as his successor. The transition marked the fourth time the octogenarian Ibrahim had assumed the presidency.

The MC turned the tables on the PPP in the July 5, 2001, election, winning 25 out of 40 directly elected seats to the PPP's 8 and then picking up 5 more of the reserved seats. The PPP ended up with a total of 9 seats and the PML, 8. When the new legislature convened, Sikander Hayat defeated the incumbent by a vote of 30–17 and thereby returned as prime minister.

Seventeen parties contested the legislative election of July 11, 2006, in which the MC won 22 of 41 elective seats (after a revote in one district) and quickly gained the support of several independents. The PPP Azad Kashmir, led by Sahibzada Ishaq ZAFAR, won 7 seats; a PML alliance, 4; the MQM, 2; and Sardar Khalid IBRAHIM Khan's **Jammu and Kashmir People's Party,** 1. Immediately after the election the MMA, which had fielded a large slate of unsuccessful candidates, led a chorus of opposition parties in accusing the central government of vote-rigging, particularly in refugee camps set up in the wake of a devastating October 8, 2005, earthquake, which affected some 2,800 villages in Azad Kashmir and Khyber Pakhtunkhwa, killed more than 73,000 people, and left 3.3 million homeless. On July 22 the MC added 6 of the 8 reserved seats to its total, with the others going to the PPP and the JUI.

With Sikander Hayat having chosen not to seek reelection to the Legislative Assembly, the MC proposed Sardar ATTIQUE AHMED Khan, son of Sardar Abdul Qayyum, as prime minister, and he was sworn in on July 24, 2006. Three days later, the new legislature elected the MC's Raja Zulqarnain Khan as president by a vote of 40–8 over the PPP Azad Kashmir candidate, Sardar QAMAR-U-ZAMAN.

A September 2006 report by Human Rights Watch labeled the Azad Kashmir government a "façade" dominated by Islamabad, the military, and the intelligence services. The report further alleged that free expression has been routinely curtailed and torture allowed. Open advocates of Kashmiri independence are not allowed to seek public office and often face persecution.

In the following two years a split within the MC widened. An anti-Attique Ahmed faction, the Forward Bloc, accused the prime minister of nepotism, mismanagement, malfeasance, and a lack of transparency. On January 6, 2009, a combination of the Forward Bloc, led by Raja FAROOQ HAIDER Khan, and the opposition passed a no-confidence motion against Attique Ahmed and endorsed as his successor Sardar Muhammad YAQOOB Khan, who had been elected in 2006 as an independent. The rift in the MC was subsequently repaired, however, and on October 14 Yaqoob Khan resigned rather than face a no-confidence vote in the Legislative Assembly. On October 22 Farooq Haider, by a vote of 29–19, defeated Yaqoob Khan and was sworn in as prime minister. Yaqoob Khan had been backed by a four-party alliance of the Azad Kashmir PPP, the MQM, Sultan Mahmood Chaudhry's **Jammu and Kashmir People's Muslim League,** and a so-called Friends Group of dissident MC members. In 2011, Chaudhry Abdul MAJID (PPP) was elected prime minister of Azad Kashmir.

An avalanche in the northernmost area of the region killed 124 Pakistani soldiers and 15 civilians on April 7, 2012.

President: Raja ZULQARNAIN Khan.

Prime Minister: Chaudhry Abdul MAJID.

Gilgit-Baltistan. Gilgit-Baltistan, which was called the Northern Areas from 1970 until September 2009, encompasses approximately 28,000 square miles, with a population (2006E) of 970,000. The region has served as the principal conduit for supplying troops and matériel to the Line of Control, facing Indian Kashmir. Pakistan's overland route to China, the Karakoram Highway, also traverses the region, which currently comprises seven districts: Astore, Diamir, Ghanche, Ghizar, Gilgit, Hunza-Nagar, and Skardu. Approximately half the population is Shiite, with the other half divided between Sunnis and Ismailis. The region has frequently seen outbreaks of sectarian violence involving Sunni and Shiite groups.

In May 1999, Pakistan's Supreme Court ruled that the Northern Areas Legal Framework Order 1994, under which Islamabad had introduced a number of governmental reforms, failed to provide adequate institutions and safeguards to residents of the Northern Areas. The court said that residents were entitled to full constitutional rights, including an elected legislature and an independent judiciary, and it gave the government six months to institute the changes. In early October the Sharif administration announced that party-based elections would be held on November 3 for a Northern Areas Legislative Council having the same powers as provincial assemblies. The announcement marked a significant departure in that the government had previously argued that no permanent institutions could be established until the fate of the entire Jammu and Kashmir was determined through a UN-sponsored plebiscite.

Although the October 1999 military coup in Islamabad intervened, the November election took place as scheduled. Of the leading parties, the PML won 6 seats (5 more than it had previously held); the PPP, 6; and the *Tehrik-e-Jafariya-e-Pakistan* (TJP), 6. Voter turnout was very low, which analysts attributed in part to the council's severely limited role. After the 5 seats reserved for women were finally filled nearly nine months later, a PML-TJP alliance controlled 19 of the 29 seats.

As a result, the PML's Sahib KHAN was elected speaker of the council and the TJP's Fida Muhammad NASHAD became deputy chief executive, second in the governmental hierarchy to the federal minister for Kashmir and the Northern Areas.

At the Northern Areas Legislative Council election of October 12, 2004, the PML-Q and PPP Parliamentarians (PPPP) each won 6 of the 24 directly elective seats, and the PML-N won 2, the balance being claimed by independents, 8 of whom then aligned with the PML-Q. When the 12 reserved seats (including 6 for women), all chosen by the elected members, were finally filled on March 22, 2006, the PML-Q picked up 10 of them, with independents claiming the remaining 2. The PPPP immediately protested that the election had been rigged and argued that seats should have been assigned on a proportional basis.

In October 2007, President Musharraf announced a Northern Areas reform package that called for creation of a seventh district (Hunza-Nagar); conversion of the Northern Areas Legislative Council to the Northern Areas Legislative Assembly (NALA), to be chaired by the minister of Kashmir and Northern Areas affairs; and elevation of the office of deputy chief executive to that of chief executive. A new chief executive, Ghazanfar ALI KHAN (PPP), with enhanced administrative powers, was sworn in on January 4, 2008.

Following the national legislative election held in February 2008, members of the PML-Q–dominated NALA expressed concern that the assembly would be dissolved prematurely by the central government, which was now controlled by the PPP and PML-N. In April they were assured by Minister Qazar Zaman Kaira that the NALA would be permitted to complete its term.

On September 7, 2009, President Zardari signed the Gilgit-Baltistan (Empowerment and Self-Government) Order 2009, which had been passed by Parliament in late August. The order, in addition to changing the region's name, provided for a level of autonomy comparable to that of Azad Kashmir, which prompted some Kashmiri activists to charge that Islamabad was making Gilgit-Baltistan a de facto province of Pakistan. Under the order, Islamabad's principal representative is a governor appointed by the president of Pakistan on the advice of the prime minister. The territory's Legislative Assembly comprises 33 members—24 directly elected plus 9 named to reserved seats (6 women and 3 professionals). A chief minister and his cabinet is responsible to the Legislative Assembly, which has significantly expanded powers. An executive Gilgit-Baltistan Council is chaired by the prime minister of Pakistan, with the governor as vice chair. Also sitting on the council are the chief minister of Gilgit-Baltistan, 6 members elected from the Legislative Assembly, and 6 representatives of the central government (ministers or members of Parliament). A Supreme Appellate Court is to sit at the apex of the independent judicial system.

The first election for the new Legislative Assembly was held on November 12, 2009. The PPP was initially credited with winning 11 seats; the PML-N, 2; the PML-Q, 2; the JUI-F, 1; the MQM, 1, and independents, 4. (Polling in one district was postponed due to the death of a candidate, and disruptions at some polling stations in two other districts necessitated partial revotes.) The PML-N and other parties immediately rejected the results as the product of irregularities and of favoritism on the part of the acting governor, PPP minister Qamar Zaman Qaira. A group of NGOs monitoring the elections found widespread irregularities and flaws in the election procedures. By late November, however, the PPP claimed the support of 17 legislators, including 3 of the independents and the JUI-F member, and anticipated gaining additional seats when the 9 nonelected members were chosen. The PPP's nominee for chief minister, party chair Syed Mehdi Shah, was confirmed by the full Legislative Assembly on December 12.

Among the groups attacking the 2009 Gilgit-Baltistan Order was the **Balawaristan National Front** (BNF), chaired by Abdul Hamid KHAN. The BNF has called for self-rule and elections to a constituent assembly that would then draft a constitution.

On March 23, 2010, Dr. Shama Khalid was sworn in to office as the first governor of Gilgit-Baltistan after being selected by President Zardari. Khalid, was also the country's first female governor. She died in office from cancer on September 15, 2010, and was replaced by acting governor Wazir BAIG (PPP) and then Pir Karam Ali Shah in January 2011.

In April 2012, after a grenade attack killed 14 Sunnis, sectarian violence spread through the region, prompting the deployment of government security units.

Governor: Pir Karam Ali SHAH (PPP).

Chief Minister: Syed Mehdi SHAH (PPP).

PALAU

Republic of Palau
Belu'u era Belau

Political Status: Former U.S. Trust Territory; became sovereign state in free association with the United States on October 1, 1994.

Land Area: 178 sq. mi. (461 sq. km).

Population: 21,108 (2013E—U.S. Census). Approximately 6,000 residents are nonnationals.

Major Urban Center (2005C): Koror (10,743), MELEKEOK (250). Melekeok, located on the largely undeveloped northern island of Babeldaob, replaced Koror as Palau's capital in October 2006.

Official Languages: English, Palauan.

Monetary Unit: U.S. Dollar (see U.S. article for principal exchange rates).

President: Thomas (Tommy) REMENGESAU Jr. (nonparty); elected on November 6, 2012, and inaugurated for a four-year term on January 17, 2013, succeeding Johnson TORIBIONG (nonparty).

Vice President: Antonio (Tony) BELLS; elected on November 6, 2012, for a term concurrent with that of the president, succeeding Kerai MARIUR (nonparty).

THE COUNTRY

Palau encompasses a chain of more than 200 Pacific islands and islets at the western extremity of the Carolines, some 720 miles southwest of Guam and 500 miles east of the Philippines. The population in 2012 was approximately 72 percent Palauan, 15 percent Filipino, 5 percent Chinese, and the remainder divided among smaller groups. Both Palauan and English are spoken, and Roman Catholicism is the principal religion. The climate is tropical with quite heavy rainfall. Fishing and tourism are the leading economic sectors, with the United States pledging approximately $650 million in aid over a 15-year period as part of a trusteeship settlement that became effective on October 1, 1994. Because of the aid, Palau's nominal GDP grew by 24.3 percent in fiscal year 1994–1995 but declined sharply thereafter. From 2000 to 2008, GDP growth registered about 2.2 percent annually.

GDP contracted by 4.6 percent in 2009, before posting a slight gain, 0.3 percent, in 2010. However, a surge in tourist arrivals initiated a strong recovery in 2011, with a GDP growth of 5.8 percent. Rising fuel and food prices drove annual inflation up by 6 percent in 2012. The International Monetary Fund (IMF) reported that GDP grew by 4 percent in 2012. GDP per capita was $11,164 in 2013. Of longer-term consequence, however, the IMF has also expressed concern about the fiscal adjustment that will be required when U.S. grant assistance ends in 2024 (see Current issues, below).

GOVERNMENT AND POLITICS

Political background. Purchased by Germany from Spain in 1889, the Palau group was among the insular territories seized by Japan in 1914 and retained as part of the mandate awarded by the League of Nations in 1920. The islands were occupied by U.S. forces near the end of World War II and became part of the U.S. Trust Territory of the Pacific in 1947. A republican constitution was adopted by referendum in October 1979, and on January 1, 1981, Haruo I. REMELIK was inaugurated as the country's first president. On November 30, 1984, Remelik was elected to a second four-year term on a platform that called for early implementation of a 1980 Compact of Free Association with the United States. Remelik was assassinated on June 30, 1985, and in a special election on August 28 Lazarus SALII defeated Acting President Alfonso OITERONG in balloting for Remelik's successor.

The Palauan Compact, including provision for substantial U.S. aid, required that the republic provide facilities for U.S. conventional and

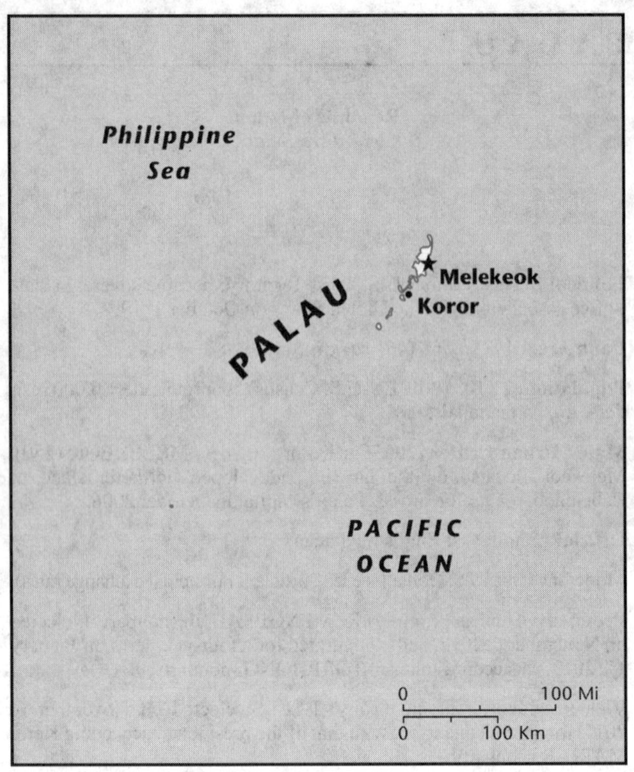

nuclear forces. After failed attempts to pass the Palauan Compact because of the controversial nuclear weapons clause, President Salii, who had received assurances that Washington would not "use, test, store, or dispose of nuclear, toxic, chemical, gas, or biological weapons on the islands," suggested that only a simple majority was needed for approval of the compact. His position was challenged by the islands' ranking chief, who obtained a favorable appellate ruling by the Palauan Supreme Court on September 17.

After two more failed attempts to pass the compact in December 1986 and June 1987, a referendum on amending the constitution to suspend the applicability of its antinuclear clause to the compact was held on August 4, which resulted in 71 percent approval, with majorities in 14 of the 16 states. The vote was hailed by the government, which contended that amending (as distinguished from overriding a constitutional proscription) required only a simple majority overall, coupled with majorities in at least 12 states. The constitutional issue seemingly having been resolved, a sixth plebiscite (yielding 73 percent approval) was held on August 21, with the Palauan legislature voting on August 27 to approve the compact. On April 22, acting on a refiled opposition suit, the islands' Supreme Court trial division ruled that the August 4 referendum was invalid.

On August 20, 1988, President Salii was found dead in his office from an apparently self-inflicted gunshot wound, and Vice President Thomas REMENGESAU was subsequently sworn in to serve for the rest of the year, pending the results of November's regularly scheduled presidential election. Shortly thereafter, the appellate division of the Supreme Court upheld the April decision invalidating the 1987 compact voting. While ruling that a special referendum on constitutional revision could be called at any time, the court declared that the proposed amendment must first be approved by 75 percent majorities in both houses of parliament or be requested by a petition signed by at least 25 percent of the electorate.

In balloting on November 2 Ngiratkel ETPISON, who appeared to enjoy the backing of many former Salii supporters, was elected president from among seven candidates. After another failed vote in 1990, the issue was referred back to Washington with a demand to reduce the length of the compact, but this was rejected by President George H. W. Bush. President Etpison thereupon called for a threshold vote on July 13 but was again rebuffed by the court, which ruled that prior congressional approval was required. In August the legislators responded by placing the matter on the ballot for the general election of November 4.

For the 1992 presidential balloting, Etpison was defeated in a primary that resulted from abandonment of the earlier first-past-the-post system, and on November 3 the incumbent vice president, Kuniwo NAKAMURA, defeated Johnson TORIBIONG by a slim 50.7 percent majority. More important, the amendment to reduce the threshold required to alter the antinuclear provision of the constitution was approved by the voters. This cleared the way for approval of the compact by 64 percent of the participants on November 9, 1993. In September 1994 the Palauan Supreme Court dismissed an appeal challenging the validity of the 1993 vote, and on October 1, 1994, independence was formally proclaimed. (For more on the process by which the Palauan Compact was passed, see the 2011 *Handbook*.)

Benefiting from an economic upswing based on the infusion of U.S. compact funds, in addition to a "look north" policy that had attracted significant Japanese, Filipino, and Taiwanese investment, President Nakamura won reelection on November 6, 1996, easily defeating the mayor of Koror, Paramount Chief Ibedul Yutaka GIBBONS, by a 2–1 margin.

In voting on November 7, 2000, Vice President Tommy REMENGESAU Jr. was elected president, defeating Sen. Peter SUGIYAMA. Running separately, Sen. Sandra PIERANTOZZI defeated her nephew, Alan REID, for the vice presidency even though Reid had been endorsed by outgoing President Nakamura.

President Remengesau was accorded a second term in the election of November 2, 2004, although Vice President Pierantozzi was defeated by Elias Camsek CHIN. The vice-presidential outcome led to a constitutional amendment (approved in 2004) that the president and vice president thereafter be elected as a team.

On November 4, 2008, Johnson Toribiong defeated Chin with a presidential vote share of 51.2 percent.

In November 2009 former president Remengesau was found guilty of violating Palau's fiscal disclosure law and was assessed a fine of $156,000 on December 28.

Remengesau won presidential balloting on November 6, 2012, with 58 percent of the vote to Toribiong's 42 percent. The campaign focused on management of the trust (see Current issues, below). Antonio (Tony) Bells was concurrently elected vice president.

Constitution and government. Under the Compact of Free Association, Palau is a fully sovereign state, save with regard to defense, which was to remain a U.S. responsibility for at least a 15-year period; it was also obligated to "consult" with Washington regarding major foreign policy matters. For the first decade of independence, its constitution provided for a president and vice president elected on separate tickets for four-year terms after having been selected (since 1992) by primaries replacing a first-past-the-post system. This was replaced in 2004 by a requirement that the two offices be filled on a single ticket. The bicameral National Congress consists of a Senate currently composed of 14 members elected on a population basis (9 from Koror, 4 from the northern islands, 1 from the southern islands), and a House of Delegates, encompassing one representative from each of the republic's 16 states (a proposal to abandon bicameralism in favor of a unicameral legislature was rejected by voters in 2004). There is also a 16-member Council of Chiefs to advise the government on matters of tribal laws and customs. The judicial system consists of a Supreme Court (including both Trial and Appellate Divisions), a National Court, and a Court of Common Pleas. In late 2007 a Senate bill was introduced that would create a court to deal with land, property, and other issues governed by traditional principles.

Each of the states (Aimeliik, Airai, Angaur, Kayangel, Koror, Melekeok, Ngaraard, Ngardmau, Ngaremlengui, Ngatpang, Ngchesar, Ngerchelong, Ngiwal, Peleliu, Sonsorol, and Tobi) elects its own governor and legislature. Palauans, on a per capita basis, have been termed "the most governed people on earth."

In addition to the measures referenced above, three constitutional amendments were approved in 2004: the holding of dual U.S.-Palau citizenship, a limitation of three four-year terms for legislators, and a cap on congressional salaries. In addition to the amendments passed in 2004, a second constitutional convention was held in 2005. During the convention, some 24 changes to the constitution were approved. Among these changes were establishing the joint election of president and vice president, setting a specific date for the inauguration of new members of Congress, and a constitutional ban on same-sex marriage. These changes were approved by the citizens of Palau in 2008 in a referendum held concurrently with the state's general elections.

Foreign relations. Palau was admitted to the United Nations on December 15, 1994. It participates in the Pacific Islands Forum and a number of other intergovernmental organizations. Following independence, the government opened embassies in Tokyo and Washington. In 2004, on the other hand, President announced that Palau was withdrawing from the G-77 group of developing countries (which it had joined two years before) on the grounds that it had been ineffective in lobbying on environmental issues, such as global warming.

In 1999 diplomatic relations were established with Taiwan, a linkage that critics subsequently urged the Remengesau administration to abandon in favor of ties with the People's Republic of China. (For more on relations with Taiwan, see the 2012 *Handbook*.)

The establishment of diplomatic relations with Russia in late 2006 was followed by an upsurge in tourists that prompted an increase in Russian-speaking staff by resort owners.

In April 2012, relations with China were strained after Palau marine police killed a Chinese fisherman suspected of illegal fishing and arrested 25 others.

In December 2012, Palau voted against observer status for the Palestinian Authority in the UN (see entry on Palestine). In June 2013, Palau and Tuvalu became the first Pacific countries to sign the UN Small Arms Treaty (see entry on the UN).

Current issues. In February 2009, with the value of Palau's Trust Fund having lost approximately 40 percent of its value because of the U.S. recession, President Toribiong called for renegotiation of the compact's funding provisions. Ironically, while the existing compact yielded $13 million in annual subsidies and grants, Washington was reported to have offered up to $200 million in long-term financial assistance if Koror would accept 17 Chinese Muslims detained at Guantánamo Bay. While many of the detainees rejected the transfer, 6 arrived in Palau in November 2009. Although officials denied any connection, a one-year extension of U.S. financial assistance was negotiated for October 2009–October 2010.

On the 15th anniversary of the Palauan Compact in September 2009, a review was established in accordance with the initial compact. The United States reached an agreement with Palau in September 2010 to extend aid in the amount of $250 million to the country until 2024. The agreement was signed by both sides (it remained unapproved by the U.S. Senate as of July 2013). Also in September, Palau became the first nation to ban commercial shark fishing in its waters.

Despite having begun the process of reviewing the Compact of Free Association and having secured an agreement for continued financial aid, in May 2011, Palau overdrew its financial aid from the United States. The United States had placed a $5 million borrowing limit on the island's U.S.-funded trust fund until the approval of the aid agreement by the U.S. Congress. Palau had withdrawn $7 million from the fund, causing the U.S. Department of the Interior to demand that Palau repay the $2 million excess.

With the compact still awaiting approval from the U.S. Congress, the United States extended more than $13 million in aid to Palau for 2012.

In March 2012, five senators filed two lawsuits against Toribiong, charging him with personal liability for the $2 million in overspending and alleging that he misused $500,000 in U.S. funding for the resettlement of the Chinese Muslim detainees, half of which was used to renovate a building owned by his relative for their housing.

In March 2013, Remengesau introduced legislation to ban commercial fishing in Palau's 200-nautical mile marine exclusive economic zone. In 2013, audits indicated that the trust had been overdrawn again in 2012, by $2 million, leading to delays in the release of $13.2 million in U.S. aid.

POLITICAL PARTIES

Traditionally there were no formal parties in Palau. However, an antinuclear **Coalition for Open, Honest, and Just Government** emerged to oppose the Compact of Free Association, which was defended by a Ta Belau Party, led by Kuniwo Nakamura. Subsequently, a **Palau National Party** was launched by (then) opposition leader Johnson Toribiong. However, there is no indication that any of them currently exists.

LEGISLATURE

The **Palau National Congress** (*Olbiil Era Kelulau,* which translates literally as "House of Whispered Decisions") is a bicameral body, both of whose chambers have four-year mandates (there is a three-term limit). Balloting was last held on November 6, 2012.

Senate. The upper house currently consists of 13 members, selected in a nationwide election.
President: Camsek CHIN.

House of Delegates. The lower house contains 16 members, one from each of Palau's states.
Speaker: Sabino ANASTACIO.

CABINET

[as of November 12, 2013]

President	Thomas Remengesau Jr.
Vice President	Antonio (Tony) Bells
Ministers	
Attorney General	Victoria Roe [f]
Community and Cultural Affairs	Baklai Temengil [f]
Education	Andrew Tabelual
Finance	Elbuchel Sadang
Health	Greg Ngirmang
Justice	Antonio (Tony) Bells
Natural Resources, Environment, and Tourism	Fleming Umiich Sengebau
Public Infrastructure, Industries, and Commerce	Charles Obichang
State	William (Billy) Kuartei

[f] = female

INTERGOVERNMENTAL REPRESENTATION

Ambassador to the U.S.: Hersey KYOTA.

U.S. Ambassador to Palau: Amy Jane HYATT (nominated).

Permanent Representative to the UN: Caleb OTTO.

IGO Memberships (Non-UN): ADB, PIF.

PANAMA

Republic of Panama
República de Panamá

Political Status: Became independent of Spain as part of Colombia (New Granada) in 1819; independent republic proclaimed on November 3, 1903; present constitution, adopted on September 13, 1972, substantially revised on April 24, 1983.

Area: 29,208 sq. mi. (75,650 sq. km).

Population: 3,672,384 (2012E—UN); 3,559,408 (2013E—U.S. Census).

Major Urban Centers (2010E): PANAMA (also known as Panama City, 894,565), San Miguelito (373,703).

Official Language: Spanish.

Monetary Unit: Balboa (official rate November 1, 2013: 1.00 balboa = $1US). The balboa is at par with the U.S. dollar, which is also acceptable as legal tender.

President: Ricardo MARTINELLI Berrocal (Democratic Change Party); elected on May 3, 2009, and inaugurated on July 1 for a five-year term, succeeding Martín TORRIJOS Espino (Democratic Revolutionary Party).

Vice President: Juan Carlos VARELA (Pro-Panamanian Party); elected on May 3, 2009, and inaugurated on July 1 for a term concurrent with that of the president, succeeding Samuel Lewis NAVARRO (Democratic Revolutionary Party).

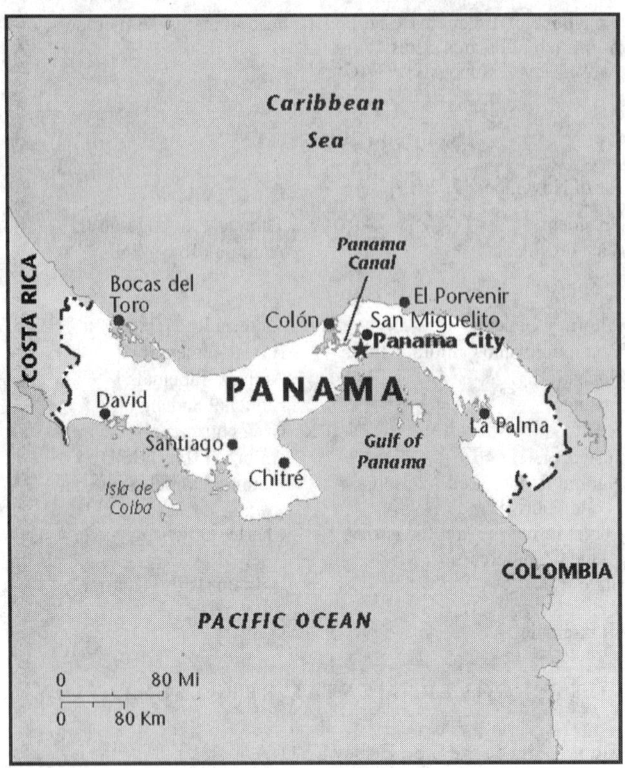

THE COUNTRY

Situated on the predominantly mountainous isthmus that links North and South America, Panama has the second-smallest population of any Latin American country but ranks comparatively high in per capita wealth and social amenities, due mainly to the economic stimulus imparted by the Panama Canal, the interoceanic canal built in 1904–1914 that cuts across the country's midsection. Population density is not high, although nearly one-fourth of the people live in Panama City and Colón. About 70 percent of the populace is of mixed Caucasian, Indian, and African descent; pure Caucasian is estimated at 9 percent and pure African at 14 percent, the balance being of Indian ancestry and other origins. Roman Catholicism is professed by approximately 85 percent of the people, but other faiths are permitted. In 2011, women constituted 37 percent of the workforce; female participation in government has traditionally been minimal, although the president in 1999–2004 was a woman (the first in the nation's history). In 2013, 3 of the 15 cabinet ministers were women. Law 22, passed on July 14, 1997, required that 30 percent of candidates nominated by parties be women. There were 6 women in the 71-member National Assembly elected in 2009.

Panama's shipping fleet is the largest in the world by virtue of flag-of-convenience registrations. It is also one of the world's most important centers of entrepôt activity, its economy being heavily dependent on international commerce and transit trade. Since 1970, when a new banking law went into effect, it has become a leading Spanish-language and offshore banking center. The service sector now accounts for 80 percent of GDP and employs almost 74 percent of the workforce. Bananas remain the most important export, followed by shrimp and other seafood, clothing, sugar, and coffee.

Economic performance was mixed throughout the 1990s but began a steady march upward beginning in 2002. Economic expansion produced a GDP growth rate of 12.1 percent in 2007, a high not seen in decades. Panama's economy outpaced that of its regional counterparts, owing in large part to the country having one of the highest rates of direct foreign investment in Latin America.

GDP expansion continued to be strong at 10.1 percent in 2008 but fell to 3.2 percent in 2009 as unemployment rose to 6.9 percent, reflecting the trade decrease of the global financial downturn. However, International Monetary Fund (IMF) managers said the country's banking system had "weathered the global financial crisis relatively well," and inflation decreased from a two-and-a-half-decade high of 8.8 percent in 2008 to 2.4 percent in 2009. In 2010, the IMF forecast that Panama's economy would post the fastest expansion in Central America through at least 2015, spurred by the robust services sector and the economic injection caused by upgrading the Panama Canal. After posting consistent growth of 11 percent in 2011 and 2012, GDP expansion slowed slightly to 9 percent in 2013, which the IMF attributed as a typical decline because of decreased capital spending. Inflation fell to 5.2 percent, and unemployment remained steady at 4.2 percent.

GOVERNMENT AND POLITICS

Political background. After renouncing Spanish rule in 1821, Panama remained a part of Colombia until 1903, when a U.S.-supported revolt resulted in the proclamation of an independent republic. Shortly thereafter, Panama and the United States signed a treaty in which the latter guaranteed the independence of Panama while obtaining "in perpetuity" the use, occupation, and control of a zone for the construction, operation, and protection of an interoceanic canal. Panama also received a down payment of $10 million and subsequent annual payments of $250,000.

In the absence of strongly rooted political institutions, governmental authority was exercised in the ensuing decades by a few leading families engaged in shifting alliances and cliques. Following World War II, however, Panamanian politics were increasingly dominated by nationalist discontent inspired by U.S. control of the canal and the exclusive jurisdiction exercised by the United States in the Canal Zone. Despite increases in U.S. annuity payments and piecemeal efforts to meet Panamanian complaints, serious riots within the zone in January 1964 yielded a temporary rupture in diplomatic relations with Washington. Following their restoration in April, the two countries agreed to renegotiate the treaty relationship, but progress was impeded by internal unrest in Panama as well as by political opposition within the United States.

In early 1968 the outgoing president, Marco A. ROBLES, became involved in a major constitutional conflict with the National Assembly over his attempt to designate an administrative candidate, David SAMUDIO, for the presidential election of May 12. Samudio was defeated in the voting by Arnulfo ARIAS Madrid, a veteran politician who had already been twice elected and twice deposed (in 1941 and 1951). Inaugurated for the third time on October 1, Arias initiated a shake-up of the National Guard, a body that served both as an army and police force, and guard officers who felt threatened by his policies again overthrew him on October 11–12. Col. José María PINILLA and Col. Bolívar URRUTIA Parilla were installed at the head of a Provisional Junta Government, which suspended vital parts of the constitution and normal political processes, promised a cleanup of political life, and indicated that a new election would be held without military participation in 1970. Real power, however, was exercised by the high command of the National Guard under the leadership of then colonel Omar TORRIJOS Herrera and Col. Boris N. MARTÍNEZ, his chief of staff. Martínez was relieved of his command and exiled in February 1969, leaving Torrijos in undisputed control of the military. In December 1969 Pinilla and Urrutia attempted to purge Torrijos; they failed, however, and were subsequently replaced by two civilians, Demetrio Rasilio LAKAS Bahas and Arturo SUCRE Pereira, as president and vice president. On July 15, 1975, Sucre resigned for health reasons and was succeeded by Gerardo GONZÁLEZ Vernaza, the former minister of agricultural and livestock development.

Politics in the wake of the 1968 coup focused primarily on two issues: renegotiation of the Canal Zone treaty and the long-promised reactivation of normal political processes. Nationalist sentiments put increasing pressure on the United States to relinquish control over the Canal Zone, while a partial return to normalcy occurred in 1972 with the nonpartisan election of an Assembly of Community Representatives. The assembly's primary function was to legitimize existing arrangements, and one of its first acts was the formal designation of General Torrijos as "Supreme Leader of the Panamanian Revolution."

Following a legislative election on August 6, 1978, General Torrijos announced that he would withdraw as head of government and would refrain from seeking the presidency for the 1978–1984 term. On October 11 the National Assembly designated two of his supporters, Arístides ROYO and Ricardo de la ESPRIELLA, as president and vice president, respectively.

During 1979 political parties were authorized to apply for official recognition, although the leading opposition party and a number of smaller groups refused to participate in balloting on September 28, 1980, to elect one-third of an expanded Legislative Council (theretofore primarily identifiable as a nonsessional committee of the National Assembly).

General Torrijos was killed in a plane crash on July 31, 1981 and, on August 1, was succeeded as National Guard commander by Col. Florencio

FLORES Aguilar. On March 3, 1982, Colonel Flores retired in favor of Gen. Rubén Darío PAREDES, who was widely regarded as a leading presidential contender and who was due to retire from the military on September 11. Under pressure from Paredes, President Royo resigned on July 30, allegedly for health reasons, in favor of Vice President de la Espriella, who reaffirmed an earlier pledge that "clean and honest" elections would be held in 1984. On September 6 it was announced that Paredes had acceded to requests from the president and the military high command to remain in his post beyond the mandated retirement date.

On April 24, 1983, a series of constitutional amendments (see below) were approved in a national referendum, paving the way for a return to full civilian rule, and on August 12 General Paredes retired as military commander in favor of Gen. Manuel Antonio NORIEGA Morena to accept presidential nomination by the *torrijista* Democratic Revolutionary Party (*Partido Revolucionario Democrático*—PRD). Because of widespread opposition to his candidacy, he was, however, forced to step down as PRD standard-bearer in September.

On February 13, 1984, following designation of Nicolás ARDITO Barletta as the nominee of a PRD-backed electoral coalition called the National Democratic Union (*Unión Nacional Democrática*—Unade), President de la Espriella was obliged to resign in a second "constitutional coup." Vice President Jorge ILLUECA, who was identified with more leftist elements within the PRD, succeeded him.

On May 6, 1984, Panama conducted its first direct presidential balloting in 15 years. From a field of seven candidates, Unade's Ardito Barletta narrowly defeated former president Arias Madrid amid outbreaks of violence and allegations of vote-rigging. The new chief executive assumed office on October 11, pledging to alleviate the country's ailing economy, expose corruption, and keep the military out of politics. The legislative election, held concurrently with the presidential poll, also yielded victory for the six-party Unade coalition, which took 40 of the 67 National Assembly seats.

In the second such action in 18 months, Ardito Barletta resigned on September 27, 1985, being succeeded the following day by First Vice President Eric Arturo DELVALLE Henríquez. The move was reportedly dictated by General Noriega, who had warned a month earlier that the country's political situation was "out of control and anarchic." During his year in office, Ardito had drawn criticism for a series of economic austerity measures, although the more proximate cause of his downfall appeared to be an effort by the military to deflect attention from the "Spadafora scandal," involving the death of former health minister Hugo SPADAFORA, whose decapitated body had been found near the Costa Rican border on September 14. After leaving the government in 1978, Spadafora had joined the *sandinista* forces opposing Nicaraguan dictator Anastasio Somoza but subsequently shifted his allegiance to the *contra* group led by Edén Pastora. Spadafora had publicly accused General Noriega of involvement in the drug trade, and opposition groups charged that the president's resignation had been forced in the wake of a decision to appoint an independent investigative committee to examine the circumstances surrounding the murder.

In June 1986, the *New York Times* published a series of reports that charged General Noriega with electoral fraud, money-laundering, drug trafficking, clandestine arms trading, and the sale of high-technology equipment to Cuba. Noriega vehemently denied the charges and insisted that they were part of a campaign aimed at blocking Panama's assumption of control of the Panama Canal in the year 1999. A year later, in apparent retaliation for his forced retirement as military chief of staff, Col. Roberto DÍAZ Herrera issued a barrage of accusations in support of the *Times* reports, also charging his superior with complicity in the 1981 death of General Torrijos. Popular unrest was fanned by the National Antimilitarist Crusade (*Cruzada Civilista Nacional*—CCN), a newly formed middle-class group with opposition party and church support. In July Vice President Roderick ESQUIVEL joined in an opposition call for an independent commission to investigate Díaz's claims. Although Díaz issued a retraction late in the year, a U.S. federal grand jury handed down indictments on February 4, 1988, charging Noriega and 14 others with drug trafficking. On February 25 President Delvalle, who had previously supported Noriega, announced his intention to dismiss the general, but the following day, based on the grounds that he had exceeded his constitutional authority, he was himself dismissed by the National Assembly, which named Education Minister Manuel SOLIS Palma as his acting successor. Delvalle, whom the United States and a number of Latin American countries continued to recognize as chief executive, escaped from house arrest, went into hiding, and announced that he would continue to struggle against the Noriega "puppet regime." Subsequently, Panamanian assets in U.S. banks were frozen, further exacerbating a financial crisis stemming from the fact that the U.S. dollar was, for all practical purposes, the only circulating currency. On March 16 Noriega's forces put down a coup attempt by midlevel dissident officers, while a general strike called by the CCN five days later collapsed following the arrest of numerous opposition leaders and journalists on March 29.

Despite internal political resistance and continued economic pressure by the United States, Noriega clung to power during the ensuing year, amid preparations for national elections on May 7, 1989, in which, contrary to expectations, the general did not run. In the wake of the balloting, despite evidence of massive government fraud, it became clear that the regime's nominee, Carlos DUQUE Jaén, had been substantially outpolled by the opposition candidate, Guillermo ENDARA Galimany (Arias Madrid having died the previous August), and on May 10 the Electoral Commission nullified the results because of "obstruction by foreigners" and a "lack of voting sheets [that] made it impossible to proclaim winners."

On September 1, 1989, when Delvalle's term would have ended, Francisco RODRÍGUEZ, a longtime associate of General Noriega, was sworn in as president after designation by the Council of State, a body composed of senior military and civilian officials. Little more than a month later, on October 3 Noriega put down a violent coup attempt led by Maj. Moisés GIROLDI Vega, who, with a number of fellow conspirators, was summarily executed. On December 15 a revived National Assembly of Community Representatives elevated Noriega to the all-inclusive title conferred earlier on General Torrijos and accorded him sweeping powers to deal with what was termed "a state of war" with the United States. Washington responded on December 20 with U.S. troops attacking Panamanian Defense Forces in Panama City and elsewhere, forcing Noriega to take refuge in the Vatican Embassy, from which he voluntarily emerged on January 3, 1990. Immediately taken into custody, he was flown to the United States for trial on drug trafficking and other charges for which he was ultimately convicted on April 9, 1992. Meanwhile, on December 21, 1989, Guillermo Endara, head of the four-party Democratic Alliance of Civil Opposition (*Alianza Democrática de Oposición Civilista*—ADOC) that included the Christian Democratic Party (*Partido Demócrata Cristiano*—PDC), the National Republican Liberal Movement (*Movimento Liberal Republicano Nacional*—Molirena), the Authentic Liberal Party (*Partido Liberal Autenico*—PLA), and his Arnulfist Party (*Partido Arnufista*—PA), had been declared the winner of the May 7 election and was formally invested as Panamanian president. Concurrently, the PDC's Ricardo ARIAS Calderón and Molirena's Guillermo FORD Boyd were reconfirmed as first and second vice presidents, respectively.

Throughout 1991, President Endara's political influence eroded dramatically. In April Vice President Arias and four other PDC ministers left the government after being charged by Endara with a variety of hostile acts, including the operation of a domestic spy operation with the help of former Noriega supporters. Subsequently, Arias (who retained his elective post) branded the government's increasingly unpopular austerity measures as "senseless," although he refused to endorse a plebiscite on continuance of the Endara presidency on the grounds that it would "weaken the democratic process." On September 1, the PLA's Arnulfo ESCALONA lost a bid for the assembly presidency to fellow PLA member Marco AMEGLIO, who had aligned himself with the opposition. However, the most embarrassing reversal for Endara came on September 30, when Mireya MOSCOSO de Gruber, the widow of former President Arias Madrid, defeated Endara's candidate, Francisco ARTOLA, for the presidency of the PA.

The election of May 8, 1994, was largely a contest between a United People (*Pueblo Unido*) coalition of the PRD plus two minor parties, and a similar three-party Democratic Alliance (*Alianza Democrática*) led by the PA. In the presidential race the PRD's Ernesto PÉREZ Balladares defeated the PA's Moscoso by an unexpectedly close vote margin of 3.7 percent, while the PRD won a plurality of 31 assembly seats to the PA's 15. The new president's cabinet, sworn in with Pérez on September 1, was PRD-dominated but included a number of independents and opposition figures in accordance with a campaign pledge to form a coalition administration.

With President Pérez excluded from seeking a second term, Martín TORRIJOS Espino, Gen. Omar Torrijos's son, won a PRD presidential primary on October 25, 1998, but he was defeated on May 2, 1999, by Moscoso at the head of an *Arnulfista*-led populist coalition that included Molirena, the National Renovation Movement (*Movimiento de Renovación Nacional*—Morena), and the recently registered Democratic Change (*Cambio Democrático*—CD). The PA-led alliance failed, however, to capture a majority in simultaneous balloting for the assembly, in which the PRD-led New Nation coalition won 41 seats. Thus, Moscoso courted additional support from the PDC and two erstwhile New Nation organizations, the Solidarity Party (*Partido Solidaridad*—PS) and the National Liberal Party (*Partido Liberal Nacional*—PLN). By her September 1 inauguration she had cobbled together a working parliamentary majority of 1 seat, but it lasted only until August 2000, when the PRD and the PDC (subsequently renamed the Popular Party) agreed to cooperate in the assembly. With the further addition of two PS legislators, the opposition controlled 38 seats by September 2001.

The PRD's Martín Torrijos was elected president with 47.4 percent of the votes on May 2, 2004. The PRD-led New Nation also secured a substantial legislative majority, while the PRD won control of most municipalities (including the country's five largest) and an overwhelming majority of communal assemblies. The most surprising result of the presidential poll was the second-place finish (30.9 percent) by the PS candidate, former president Endara, who had left the PA in the wake of Moscoso's ascendancy. By contrast, the PA candidate, José Miguel ALEMÁN, captured only 16.4 percent of the vote. Following constitutional revisions approved in 2004 that abolished the post of second vice president (see Constitution and government, below), the PRD's Rubén AROSEMENA was the last to hold the post. He subsequently was named minister of the presidency.

Despite the strong GDP growth in 2007, the economy, particularly the rising cost of living, remained the primary concern of Panamanians in the final year of President Torrijos's tenure, as well as the most prominent issue of the subsequent presidential campaign. In the run-up to the 2009 elections, President Torrijos reshuffled the cabinet in May 2008, as ministers resigned in advance of presidential and legislative balloting, and others were dismissed because of involvement in a scandal. Meanwhile, three days before the May 3, 2009, presidential elections, the Supreme Court overturned rules barring independent candidates from running.

In December 2008, the Alliance for Change (*Alianza por el Cambio*—AC) coalition began forming around businessman Ricardo MARTINELLI, a CD member, when the Molirena party broke from a brief alliance with the PP, whose candidate, Juan Carlos VARELA, was struggling in the polls. On January 28, 2009, Martinelli struck an agreement allowing the PP to join the broad opposition coalition, which was then given the AC name, and PP candidate Varela became Martinelli's running mate. Meanwhile, the PRD government was enjoying relatively high approval ratings, though Martinelli dominated the issue of crime, which polling showed to be a rapidly growing domestic concern. Observers said the government's failure to curb crime and improve the economy, along with the controversial security measures, worked to Martinelli's advantage. A proposal by Martinelli for a $1 billion subway system to help relieve traffic congestion was also well received.

On May 3, Martinelli won a landslide victory, becoming the first presidential candidate in modern Panamanian history to win an absolute majority of the votes (59.97). His closest challenger was the PRD's Balbina HERRERA, with 37.7 percent. Former president Guillermo Endara of the Moral Vanguard of the Homeland (*Vanguardia Moral de la Patria*—VM), won just 2.3 percent. In concurrent legislative elections, the AC won a majority of seats, while the PRD lost 15 seats. The PRD also lost the mayorship of Panama City to the Pro-Panamanian Party (*Partido Panameñista*—PP), though it won 62 of 75 mayoralties and more than half of municipal council seats nationwide in 2009.

President Martinelli named a new government, dominated by CD and PP members, on May 10, 2009. The new government drew heavily from the business community and members of the AC coalition. Figuring most prominently were the PP's Varela as foreign minister in addition to his post as vice president; banker Alberto VALLARINO, whom Varela had defeated for the PP presidential nomination in 2008, as minister of economy and finance; and José Raúl MULINO of the small Patriotic Union Party (*Partido Unión Patriótica*—PUP) as interior and justice minister.

In January 2010, former leader Manuel Noriega's appeal against extradition from the United States to France, where he had been convicted in absentia in 1999 on money-laundering charges, was denied. Noriega was sent to France in April after Secretary of State Hillary Clinton approved the extradition. A new trial in France in June led to a seven-year sentence on money-laundering charges. In December 2011, Noriega returned to Panama to serve the rest of his sentence.

On May 24, 2010, Vice President Juan Carlos delivered a formal apology on behalf of the state for crimes committed under the military dictatorship era of 1968–1989. It was Panama's first formal recognition of crimes committed under military rule.

Following the dissolution of the AC in 2011, the CD secured a parliamentary majority, as 17 members defected to the CD since the 2009 elections. Prompted by a corruption scandal, Martinelli conducted a cabinet reshuffle in August 2012 (see Current issues, below).

Constitution and government. The constitutional arrangements of 1972 called for executive authority to be vested in a president and vice president designated by a popularly elected Assembly of Community Representatives for terms concurrent with the latter's six-year span. Under a series of amendments approved by national referendum on April 24, 1983, the 1972 document was substantially revised. The major changes included direct election of the president for a five-year term, the creation of a second vice presidency, a ban on political activity by members of the National Guard, and abolition of the National Assembly of Community Representatives in favor of a more compact National Assembly (see Legislature, below). Under an earlier amendment introduced by General Paredes in October 1982, provincial governors and mayors, all theretofore presidential appointees, were made subject to popular election.

Headed by a nine-member Supreme Court, the judicial system embraces Superior District tribunals and Circuit and Municipal courts. The country is divided into nine provinces and one special (Indian) territory, the smallest administrative units, *corregimientos,* forming the basis of the electoral system.

The Technical Judicial Police supplemented a Public Force that encompassed the National Police, National Air Service, and National Maritime Service in early 1991. In 1992 the National Assembly endorsed the constitutional abolition of an armed defense force, an action that was reversed by popular referendum on November 15, but revived by President Endara in August 1994 and accorded formal ratification by the post-Endara assembly on October 4.

A package of constitutional reforms backed by President-elect Torrijos was approved by the legislature in mid-2004. Among the changes were a two-month limit on the transitional period between governments; establishment of a Constituent Assembly to consider constitutional revisions; reduction of the National Assembly from 78 to 71 seats; and abolition of the position of second vice-president.

On March 31, 2010, the parliament approved the reorganization of the Ministry of Interior and Justice into two separate entities: the Ministry of the Interior and the Ministry of Public Safety.

The constitution of Panama guarantees freedom of speech and of the press without censorship, but adds "there exist legal responsibilities when one of these media launch attacks against people's reputation or honor, or against social security or public order." A revised penal code passed in 2007 abolished "gag laws" that had made it a criminal offense to defame or libel state officials. Panama fell from 55th (in 2009) to 111th out of 179 countries in the 2013 Reporters Without Borders press freedom index, because of a number of recent incidents, such as in 2011 when two Spanish journalists were expelled from the country.

Foreign relations. Panama is a member of the United Nations and many of its specialized agencies, as well as of the Organization of American States (OAS) and other regional bodies. Though not a member of the now-moribund Organization of Central American States (ODECA), Panama was active in some of the organization's affiliated institutions and participated in a number of regional peace initiatives in the 1980s sponsored by the Contadora Group, of which it was a founding member. However, the government, expressing an interest in joining the North American free trade agreement (FTA), in the early 1990s did not pursue economic integration with its Central American neighbors with enthusiasm.

The country's principal external problems have traditionally centered on the Canal Zone and its complex and sensitive relationship with the United States because of the latter's presence in the zone (see Panama Canal Zone, below). This relationship, which eased on conclusion of the canal treaties, was again strained in 1987 as the administration of Ronald Reagan committed itself to the support of Noriega's domestic opponents—a policy complicated by evidence that the general had previously been associated with the U.S. Central Intelligence Agency (CIA) in a variety of clandestine operations. The United States refused to recognize the appointment of Solís Palma as acting president in February 1988 or of Rodríguez in September 1989 and intervened militarily to oust Noriega the following December (see Political background, above). Subsequently, the United States strongly supported the reconstruction efforts of the Endara administration, although the U.S. aid package of $420 million was estimated to be substantially less than half of the loss attributable to the invasion. As a result, an OAS body, the Inter-American Human Rights Commission (IAHRC), agreed in October 1993 to look into compensation claims of $1.2 billion advanced by 285 Panamanian families. However, the action was complicated by the fact that the United States, while a member of the OAS, had not ratified the IAHRC accord and hence remained technically outside its jurisdiction.

During 1996, Panama became increasingly concerned about an influx of Colombians, including left-wing guerrillas and right-wing paramilitaries, in the remote Darién region. In mid-July troops were dispatched to curb unrest in the area, which had been infiltrated by Colombian rebels and drug traffickers in addition to serving as a sanctuary for refugees.

In August 2004, Cuba and Venezuela broke off relations with Panama after outgoing President Moscoso pardoned four men convicted of plotting to assassinate Cuba's president, Fidel Castro, because the men (one of whom had been convicted of counterrevolutionary activity and escaped from prison in Venezuela) would be executed if they were extradited. Subsequently, President Torrijos said that that he disagreed with his predecessor's action, and relations with Cuba were restored.

The September 2007 release of former dictator Manuel Noriega caused disagreement between the United States and Panama. Panama wanted him returned as a prisoner of war, while Washington, believing that he would be accorded light treatment in his homeland, preferred extradition to France, where Noriega had been convicted of a number of criminal offenses. Ultimately, it was decided that Noriega would remain in a U.S. prison until all appeal routes had been exhausted. That year, the United States and Panama signed a Trade Promotion Agreement (TPA), which the Panamanian government immediately approved, but the measure was held up by the U.S. Congress. Meanwhile, Panama established bilateral FTAs with Chile, Costa Rica, and Honduras.

In June 2008, the U.S. Congress approved $4 million for Panama's police as part of a security agreement between the United States and Mexico, known as the Mérida Initiative, to fight crime and drug trafficking in the region.

Relations with Cuba were enhanced in January 2009, when the two signed a trade agreement that would more than double Panama's exports to Cuba. In March, President Torrijos traveled to Guatemala to sign another agreement in an effort to cushion both countries from the global economic slowdown and to fight drugs and crime. A Guatemala–Panama FTA was implemented in June.

Canada and Panama completed negotiations for an FTA in August 2009. Signed in May 2010, along with compacts on labor cooperation and environmental protection, but in 2012 the agreement stalled in Canadian Parliament.

Ties between Panama and its southern neighbor Colombia grew stronger with the 2009 election of Martinelli, who shared similar right-wing ideology to Colombian president Alvaro Uribe and his successor Juan Manuel Santos. In January 2010 the countries revealed a new military alliance to combat drug trafficking and the paramilitary Revolutionary Armed Forces of Colombia (*Fuerzas Armadas Revolucionarias de Colombia*—FARC). The FARC had been pushed onto Panamanian soil with the Colombian government's successful plan to push the group to its own periphery. But the relationship with Colombia came under strain when in late 2010 the Panamanian government granted asylum to a former director of the Colombian intelligence service who had fled the country after being named a suspect in a wiretapping scandal. The Santos administration reacted angrily both for not being made aware of the asylum request when it was made and for the Panamanians granting it. Observers speculated that asylum was given as a personal favor by Martinelli to the former Colombian president Alvaro Uribe. Both countries played down the diplomatic row and focused attention on the joint fight against the FARC. By late 2010, Panamanian authorities claimed at least eight alleged members of the group had been killed on their soil.

Panama submitted a formal request to withdraw from the Central American Parliament (Parlacen), a regional legislative body dedicated to fostering cooperation among its members. In October 2010, the Central American Court of Justice ruled that Panama could not legally withdraw from Parlacen without approval from the regional body's other member states. Panama rejected the ruling, arguing that the court did not have jurisdiction over the country's membership because the Panamanian legislature never ratified Parlacen's founding documents. In November the country formally withdrew from Parlacen.

Panama and the United States signed a tax information exchange agreement (TIEA) in April 2011 to improve information sharing between the two countries, a necessary step before the U.S. Congress would ratify the FTA that had been held up since 2007. Panama was removed from the Organization for Economic Cooperation and Development's list of tax havens in July, after it signed a TIEA with France, bringing the total number of such agreements it had signed with other countries to 12, the minimum international standard. The U.S. Congress passed the Panama–U.S. FTA on October 12, 2011.

In July 2012, after "months of negotiations," Martinelli formally recognized the Taiwanese ambassador, seven months after the latter took up his post—reportedly in retaliation for a meeting that took place between Vice President Varela and Taiwan's foreign minister, which inspired accusations that Taiwan was meddling in Panama's affairs.

Originally set to take effect on October 1, 2012, the Panama-U.S. FTA was postponed until October 31 awaiting ratification of amendments to the agreement by the Panamanian parliament. A December clash between the FARC and Panama's National Border Service left one insurgent dead and resulted in seven arrests.

In July 2013, Panamanian authorities seized a North Korean–flagged ship found to be carrying 25 containers of Cuban obsolete military hardware, including fighter aircrafts, anti-aircraft systems, and missiles, which Havana said were being sent for repair. In August, North Korea appealed to Panama for a bilateral settlement of the issue. Though Panama was pursuing charges against the 35-member crew for endangering collective Panamanian security by failing to declare the weapons, the foreign ministry made clear that the matter would be handled by the United Nations. Later that month, the foreign ministry quoted an unpublished UN report that the ship was an "undoubted violation" of the arms embargo on North Korea.

Current issues. Increasing crime rates, drug trafficking, and violent conflicts near the Colombian border became major domestic concerns in 2008, leading to a change of police commissioners. The legislature in June voted to give President Torrijos two months to rule by decree on security matters. Subsequently, the president's orders created new agencies for air and naval service, border security, national defense, and intelligence. Critics argued that the new bodies—especially the border-security force—would too closely resemble Panama's army, abolished under a 1995 constitutional amendment. President Torrijos submitted approval of these new security measures to the legislature, which quickly approved them.

Thousands of indigenous citizens organized by the National Mobilization of Indigenous, Peasants and People (*Movilización Nacional, Indígena, Campesina y Popular*) protested in September and October 2009 for more rights and against government policies allowing development on indigenous lands.

In November 2009, the recently elected Martinelli administration began efforts to meet international tax standards to change Panama's image as an international tax haven. With the promise of a U.S.–Panama FTA in the balance, the government signed the first of 12 accords with other countries to increase tax transparency, improve the sharing of fiscal information, and end double taxation. The efforts combined with domestic tax reforms to push Panama's credit rating higher into an investment-grade bracket.

Panama, a growing transit point for the distribution of cocaine and heroin, opened the first of 11 new air and sea bases in December 2009 to combat organized crime. Panamanian intelligence said there were more than 2,000 hideouts along the country's coast that served as shipment transit points. The country's overall crime situation also worsened, which led the Martinelli government to launch a raft of new security laws including reducing the age of criminal responsibility to 12 years old, increasing the maximum prison sentence, and bolstering recruitment into the police forces. The country, traditionally one of the safest in the region, saw a dramatic surge in its homicide rate to 23.2 per 100,000 in 2009.

President Martinelli was also criticized in December 2009 when he appointed two close allies as Supreme Court justices. Although the constitution allows the president to make the appointment, which must then be ratified by congress, opposition legislators protested that the process leads to a politicized judiciary and renewed previous calls for constitutional reform.

In March 2010, about 10,000 protestors around the country took to the street against a value-added tax increase of 2 percent and education reforms put in place by the Martinelli administration. Some 200 protesters were arrested in violent clashes with the police. The administration also pushed through other reforms that abolished 30 taxes, reduced the tax rate for a segment of the population, and updated the fiscal code.

Martinelli, who was elected on a pro-business platform, forced through legislation in June 2010 that weakened environmental and labor regulations. These changes sparked deadly protests from labor groups, civil society, and the opposition, and the government eventually repealed the laws.

Panama's attorney general, a close Martinelli ally, resigned from his post in December 2010 because of allegations by the U.S. Drug Enforcement Agency that his office had been infiltrated by an organized crime network. Though cases of corruption continued to loom large in the country throughout the year, efforts by the national police to combat 2009's surge in homicides appeared to have taken hold by the end of the year, with total deaths falling year on year. A new attorney general, meanwhile, was appointed in January 2011.

The government again repealed laws it had recently enacted in March 2011, after changes to mining laws in February prompted violent nationwide protests that left several protesters dead. The approved and then quashed laws would have opened Panama's mining industry to foreign government investment. Indigenous and environmental protesters said the change would put more land under exploitation, including ancestral territory held sacred by indigenous groups. Both highly unpopular and eventually repealed laws gave new talking points to the corruption-wracked and floundering opposition PRD, which backed the indigenous groups, and the umbrella leftist and labor group National Front for the Defense of Social and Economic Rights (*Frente Nacional por la Defensa de los Derechos Economicos y Sociales Panama*—Frenadeso), which moved to register as a political party in 2011. The nascent party was calling itself the Broad Front for Democracy (*El Frente Amplio por la Democracia*—FAD) as it began collecting voter signatures in late August (see Political parties, below).

Shifts within political parties and within the AC coalition turned into a political crisis in mid-2011 (see Political Parties, below). The PRD—hit by corruption allegations and looming criminal investigations—went into a freefall that included massive losses to party membership and defections from its congressional delegation to other parties, primarily the CD. Earlier, the PUP had voted to merge with the CD, while Molirena's leadership signaled it would also fold into the ruling party. The realignment helped the ambitions of Martinelli's CD both within its own coalition and to build majorities with other parties to enact its legislative agenda. But the PP, led by Vice President Varela, moved farther apart from the CD on presidential election proposals such as immediate reelection and holding runoffs, and the coalition all but disintegrated as of late August. At the same time, Martinelli claimed that Varela, who was also Panama's foreign minister, was spending too much time on his 2014 candidacy and fired him from that post on August 30. Fellow PP finance and housing ministers resigned in solidarity on August 31.

In September 2011, opposition lawmakers said they would challenge a bill, passed by Congress, replacing Panama's previous electoral system with a two-stage one, providing for a presidential run-off if a presidential candidate received less than 50 percent of votes. Critics said the bill was unconstitutional.

In June 2012, Martinelli announced plans to sell government shares in state-owned telecom companies, which the opposition claimed would be used to fund a reelection bid—forbidden under the present constitution. Martinelli withdrew the proposal after Congress was briefly suspended to reduce tensions between opposition and progovernment legislators, street protests drew thousands. Faced with declining popularity, in February 2012, Martinelli signed a statement committing not to seek reelection in 2014.

At the Summit of the Americas in Cartagena in April 2012, Martinelli was among a number of Latin American leaders to criticize the United States about its war on drugs strategy by favoring decriminalization.

Following the political crisis of 2011, the CD secured a majority in the National Assembly, gaining 17 additional seats since the 2009 elections (see Political Parties, below). However, corruption scandals continued to mar Martinelli. In July 2012, one of his closest advisers, Minister of the Presidency Demetrioc Papadimitriu, resigned over his role in a corrupt land titling deal. Martinelli conducted a cabinet reshuffle in August, replacing five ministers.

In September, the parliament approved a controversial electoral reform package with a 40 to 22 majority. The legislation, which allows for independent candidates but does not introduce a cap on campaign funding, prompted street protests. Deadly protests erupted on October 19 against controversial legislation that allowed the sale of public land plots from the Colón free trade zone to private parties, with protesters afraid the law would cut jobs and run them out of the area. A week later, parliament repealed the law, marking the fourth time Martinelli backtracked immediately after rushing through legislation.

POLITICAL PARTIES

Eight parties were legally recognized in 2009. Seven of them organized into two coalitions. The Alliance for Change (AC), which backed Ricardo Martinelli, included Democratic Change (CD), the Pro-Panamanian Party (PP), the Nationalist Republican Liberal Movement (Molirena), and the Patriotic Union Party (PUP). A Country for Everyone, which backed Balbina Herrera, included the Democratic Revolutionary Party (PRD), Popular Party, and Liberal Party (PL).

Government Parties:

Alliance for Change (*Alianza por el Cambio*—AC). The AC was formed in January 2009 after the PP became the fourth—and largest—party to support Martinelli. The coalition's parties share a 42-seat majority in the legislature. The alliance was damaged in 2009 when several members, including Martinelli's cousin, were implicated in corruption scandals. It came under further stress when the CD proposed a bill in January 2011 that would allow the president to stand for reelection. The PP had previously agreed to support the CD's Martinelli in 2009 in return for the PP heading up the AC coalition ticket in the 2014 elections. The bill was defeated in the committee. The two parties pulled farther apart because of Martinelli's continuing quest to amend election laws so that political contests would include runoffs.

But defections to the CD by legislators from other parties, particularly the PRD, caused the fragile coalition's numbers to swell. Then, in March the PUP voted to merge with the CD. The relative strengths of the CD and PP within the AC switched with the defections and merger, and so did the dynamics of power, with the CD no longer reliant on the PP to wield a majority for legislative action. As a result, the CD reneged on agreements with the PP and installed a CD politician as the president of the National Assembly, a seat that was supposed to be rotated between the two parties. In 2011, the two parties began a search for separate presidential candidates to run in the 2014 elections. The coalition dissolved in September 2011.

Democratic Change (*Cambio Democrático*—CD). The CD was initially registered in 1998 as a breakaway group from the PRD, its main campaign opposing corruption. Initially it ran as the Democratic Party, winning two legislative seats in 1999 as a minor party in the coalition, along with the PP and Molirena, that supported President Moscoso. As the CD, it won three seats in 2004.

In 2009, the CD won 17 seats, making it the third-largest vote-getter in the country, and its leader, Ricardo Martinelli, secured the presidency of the republic. The party's membership increased by 20 percent with the popularity of the new president by the end of 2009. The party's legislative delegation attracted a number of defectors subsequent to the elections, and by October 2011, the party had 36 seats in total, giving it an absolute majority in the National Assembly.

In July 2011, the Panamanian electoral authorities approved the incorporation of the small **Patriotic Union Party** (*Partido Unión Patriótica*—PUP) into the CD. The PUP, founded in 2006 as a result of a merger of the PLN and the PS, won 6.4 percent of the vote and four seats in the 2009 elections. (For more on the PUP, see the 2013 *Handbook*.) In March 2011, the PUP voted to be incorporated within the CD, which brought the CD's voter rolls up to more than 380,000 members, an increase of more than three times over the party's size in 2008, and as of June 2012, it had more than 473,000 members.

A heated campaign for the 2014 presidential candidacy culminated on May 13, 2013, when former housing minister José Domingo Arias secured 67.5 percent of the vote. His opponent, Romulo ROUX, who had received the backing of the extinct PUP, accepted defeat and put his support behind Arias.

Leaders: Ricardo MARTINELLI Berrocal (President of the Republic and President of the Party), José Domingo ARIAS (2014 presidential candidate), Ruben DARIO Campos (Vice President of the Party), Giacomo TAMBURELLI, Soul CUTS (Secretaries General).

Pro-Panamanian Party (*Partido Panameñista*—PP). The PP is the rubric adopted in 1995 by the Arnulfist Party (*Partido Arnulfista*—PA), which was legalized in 1990. The PA originated from the mainstream of the Authentic Panamanian Party (*Partido Panameñista Auténtico*—PPA), itself an outgrowth of the original *Partido Panameñista* that supported the three abortive presidencies of Arnulfo Arias Madrid. Following Arias's death in August 1988, the PPA split into factions, a minority headed by Hildebrando Nicosia seeking to achieve a "national union" with the Noriega-backed regime.

For the 1994 elections, the PA formed a Democratic Alliance (*Alianza Democrática*) with two minor parties, the Authentic Liberal Party (*Partido Liberal Auténtico*—PLA) and the Independent

Democratic Union (*Unión Democrática Independiente*—UDI). The PA won 15 of the alliance's 20 legislative seats, while its presidential candidate, Mireya Moscoso de Gruber, finished a close second. (The PLA and the UDI were subsequently deregistered for failing to obtain at least a 5 percent vote share in the legislative balloting.)

In mid-1996, the PA formed a "strategic alliance" with Molirena, Morena, and the PDC to oppose what they termed was the government's lack of leadership. In September 1996 Mireya Moscoso de Gruber, the widow of former president Arias, was reelected president of the party. In 1997 the PA, Molirena, the PDC, and Morena grouping was expanded to include the PRC, the Gloria Young faction of *Papá Egoró,* and the PNP in a National Front for the Defense of Democracy (*Frente Nacional por la Defensa de Democracia*—FNDD) to oppose a reelection bid by President Peréz Balladares. PA president Moscoso de Gruber won the national presidency in 1999, but her party's candidate, José Miguel ALEMAN, ran a poor third in 2004.

In January 2005, the party dropped its PA designation in favor of the historical PP label. In March, Moscoso de Gruber was forced to resign as the PP's leader, ostensibly because of the party's poor showing in the 2004 balloting but also in the wake of corruption charges having recently been brought against her.

The PP nominated Juan Carlos Varela as its presidential candidate for 2009. Varela had fallen out with the party in the late 1990s after he ran the losing primary campaign of Alberto VALLARINO Clément against Moscoso. However, Varela returned to the party in 2003 and defeated Vallarino for the party's nod in the upcoming election. In January 2009 Varela, trailing in the polls, threw his support behind the CD's Martinelli and subsequently became Martinelli's running mate and vice president of Panama when the coalition won. The PP won 21 seats in the legislature with 23.4 percent of votes but subsequently lost 1 seat to a defection as of September 2011 and several others to the CD. After it became clear that the AC would be splitting, the PP leadership in mid-2011 began asserting that the party would become a voice of strong opposition to the CD, saying that Martinelli had mismanaged and created instability in the country. In March 2013, Varela secured the 2014 presidential nomination with 99 percent of the vote; however, just one quarter of party members voted in the primary, a high level of abstention interpreted as lack of enthusiasm within the party, and detractors began an effort to collect signatures to remove Varela, calling his candidacy "very weak."

Leaders: Juan Carlos VARELA (Vice President of the Republic, 2014 presidential candidate, and President of the Party), Alcibiades VÁSQUEZ (Secretary General and 2014 vice presidential candidate), Alberto VALLARINO Clément (Vice President).

Nationalist Republican Liberal Movement (*Movimiento Liberal Republicano Nacionalista*—Molirena). Molirena is a relatively small conservative grouping that was legally recognized in 1981. Its legislative representation increased from 14 to 16 as a result of the partial election of January 27, 1991, but fell to 5 in 1994 and to 3 in 1999. It won 4 seats as a member of the *Visión* coalition in 2004.

In the run-up to the 2009 elections, Molirena endorsed the PP's Juan Carlos Varela for president, but backed off in late December 2008 when Varela lagged in polls. Molirena subsequently endorsed Ricardo Martinelli in January 2009, shortly before the PP itself followed suit. In the 2009 elections, the party won 3.4 percent of the vote and two seats in the legislature, but one seat was lost to defection in September 2011. As an imminent AC split became apparent in 2011, Molirena's leadership moved for a merge with the CD, following suit with the PUP. However, election authorities rejected the first vote in July 2011 because it was not done by secret ballot; subsequently, a split emerged within the party between the founders, who did not support a merge, and the leadership. Morilena, an ally of Martinelli's CD, has been absorbing former members of the PP following the AC split, and its total membership reached 100,000 in May 2012.

In February 2013, party president Sergio González announced that Molirena would not hold primary elections and would support the CD's 2014 presidential candidate. Tensions with the party's founders continued, and in May, the leadership began removal proceedings against party founder Olimpo SÁEZ, alleging he collaborated with organizations opposed to the party. He was expelled in August.

Leaders: Sergio GONZÁLEZ Ruiz (President), Guillermo QUIJANO, Rubén DARÍO Carles, Gisela CHUNG (Founders of the Party).

Other Legislative Parties:

A Country for Everyone (*Un País para Todos*). This coalition of the PRD, Popular Party, and PL resembles President Torrijos's earlier PRD-dominated coalition, New Nation (*Nueva Nación*). New Nation, also referenced as New Motherland (*Patria Nueva*—PN), was launched prior to the 1999 elections by the PRD, PS, PLN, and elements of the Motherland Movement (*Movimiento Papá Egoró*—MPE). (For additional information on the MPE, which lost its registration in 1999, see the 2008 *Handbook.*) The alliance won a majority (41 seats) in the Legislative Assembly in 1999 but failed to capture the presidency. As reconstituted for the 2004 balloting, New Nation included the PRD and the Popular Party; it won 42 legislative seats (41 for the PRD and 1 for the Popular Party). Defectors from other parties reportedly gave the PRD-led alliance control of 46 seats as of 2008.

The coalition supported the PRD's Balbina Herrera in the May 2009 presidential election, and subsequently a PRD member was given a cabinet appointment. In concurrent legislative elections, the coalition won 27 seats, but a number of defections, amid allegations of corruption and threatened criminal prosecution within the PRD, caused its total representation to fall to 20 as of September 2011.

Democratic Revolutionary Party (*Partido Revolucionario Democrático*—PRD). The PRD was initially a left-of-center *torrijista* group organized as a government-supportive party in 1978. It obtained 10 of 19 elective seats in the 1980 Legislative Council balloting.

In May 1982 the PRD secretary-general, Gerardo González Vernaza, was replaced by Dr. Ernesto Pérez Balladares, a former financial adviser to General Torrijos. In November Pérez Balladares resigned in the wake of a dispute between left- and right-wing factions within the party, subsequent speculation being that General Rubén Paredes, commander of the National Guard, would be the country's 1984 presidential candidate. Paredes announced as a candidate in mid-1983 before accepting retirement from military service, and was reported to have been nominated by the party in August. In the face of opposition to his candidacy, he announced his withdrawal from politics in September but later ran as a nominee of the National People's Party (*Partido Nacionalista Popular*—PNP), which was deregistered in late 1984. The PRD named Nicolás Ardito Barletta, then World Bank regional vice president for Latin America, as its candidate after formation of the progovernment Unade coalition in February 1984. Elected chief executive in May 1984, Ardito Barletta resigned on September 27, 1985, and was succeeded by First Vice President Eric Delvalle, who was himself dismissed by the National Assembly in February 1988.

In early 1990, a new group of PRD leaders emerged, distancing themselves from Noriega, praising the country's commitment to democracy, and offering themselves as a "loyal opposition" to the Endara regime, which it nonetheless characterized as being responsible for the U.S. invasion. As the party's nominee in 1994, Pérez Balladares captured the presidency on a 33.2 percent vote share, while the PRD won a plurality of 31 legislative seats at the head of a United People (*Pueblo Unido*) coalition that also included the Republican Liberal Party (*Partido Liberal Republicano*—Libre) and the right-wing Labor Party (*Partido Laborista*—Pala), both of which were later deregistered for failing to meet a 5 percent vote threshold.

In primary balloting on October 25, 1998, the PRD named Martín Torrijos Espino, the son of Gen. Omar Torrijos, as its presidential standard-bearer in 1999. However, he gained only 38 percent of the popular vote in losing by a seven-point margin to Mireya Moscoso on May 2, 1999. Torrijos returned as the PRD candidate in 2004, winning the presidency by a substantial margin. The party won a majority of the legislature with 41 seats.

In 2008 the PRD nominated Balbina Herrera, a former mayor of San Miguelito, as its 2009 presidential candidate in a closely fought primary victory over Juan Carlos Navarro, the mayor of Panama City. Herrera ran as a left-of-center candidate, promising more social expenditure and denying any ties to the bloc of elected leftist governments led by Venezuela. Herrera's campaign was damaged by a 2009 statement by a jailed Colombian pyramid-scheme manager and accused money-launderer that he had contributed $3 million to Herrera's campaign and another $3 million to that of the PRD's Panama City mayoral candidate, Roberto VELÁSQUEZ. The remarks were said to have contributed to both candidates' failed bids for office. She finished second behind Ricardo Martinelli with 37.7 percent of votes. The PRD was the largest single vote-getter in the legislative elections, with 34.6 percent of all votes. The party won 26 seats, 15 less than it won in 2004.

On October 5, 2009, the PRD's national executive committee resigned en masse to "renovate and rejuvenate" the party after its defeat in the elections. Fighting between party members and corruption scandals were blamed for the PRD's poor showing. Declining membership was another consequence of the party's internal crisis; the almost 635,000 constituents on 2009 voter rolls slid to 464,000 by June 2011. The threat of criminal prosecutions over corruption and the decreasing public support for the party caused seven legislators to abandon the PRD's ranks and join other parties as of September 2011. Meanwhile, the PRD sought to use the disintegration of the ruling AC coalition to improve on its own bad situation, saying the country should focus on the recent outbreaks of dengue fever and the rising cost of food.

In August 2012, Juan Carlos Navarro was elected secretary general in a landslide against incumbent Mitchel DOENS at a party conference. Beating 17 other candidates, Navarro secured the party's nomination for 2014 presidential candidate with 94 percent of the vote by internal balloting in March 2013. He has called for creation of a Ministry of Indigenous Affairs and pledged to ease tensions with organized labor and indigenous leaders. Polls in mid-2013 found he held a narrow but consistent lead over the CD's Arias.

Leaders: Francisco Sánchez CÁRDENAS (President of the Party), Juan Carlos NAVARRO (Secretary General and 2014 presidential candidate), Martín TORRIJOS Espino (Former President of the Republic).

Popular Party (*Partido Popular*). The Popular Party adopted its current name in 2001, having previously been called the Christian Democratic Party (*Partido Demócrata Cristiano*—PDC). In what its leadership termed a "training exercise," the PDC participated in the 1980 balloting, winning two council seats. Named a vice-presidential candidate in 1984, PDC leader Ricardo Arias Calderón was viewed as a likely successor to Arias Madrid as principal spokesperson for the opposition and was ADOC vice-presidential candidate in 1989.

Possessing a plurality within the assembly, the PDC was estranged from its coalition partners in September 1990, when the latter joined with the opposition PRD to reject its nominees for chamber officials; despite the rebuff, the party stayed within ADOC until April 1991, when its ministerial delegation was ousted by President Endara for displaying "disloyalty and arrogance." In a move that was seen as reflecting a desire to distance himself from President Endara in the run-up to the 1994 election, Arias Calderón resigned as first vice president of the republic in December 1992. The party secured only one assembly seat in 1994.

With Alberto Vallarino, a prominent banker who had run in the 1994 presidential race again serving as its standard-bearer, the PDC contested the May 1999 elections in an Opposition Action (*Acción Opositora*) coalition that included the Civil Renovation Party (*Partido Renovación Civilista*—PRC), which secured one of the group's five seats, and the Liberal Party (*Partido Liberal*—PL) and Popular Nationalist Party (*Partido Nacionalista Popular*—PNP), neither of which won representation.

As the junior partner in Torrijos's 2004 New Nation coalition, the Popular Party obtained one assembly seat. In 2008 the party announced that it intended to remain in the coalition for the 2009 elections. Again, it won one assembly seat with 2.6 percent of the vote.

In August 2013, the Popular Party voted to form an electoral alliance with the PP in support of Vice President Varela for the 2014 presidential election. Meanwhile, Aníbal CULIOLIS led Popular Party members who did not support the alliance to form a faction called the **Movement for Panama Greens and Independents** (*Movimiento Verdes e Independientes por Panamá*).

Leaders: Milton COHEN-HENRÍQUEZ Sasso (President of the Party), Teresita de Jesus YANIZ (Vice President), José RAMOS (Secretary General).

Liberal Party (*Partido Liberal*—PL). The PL was the smallest member of the coalition headed by the PRD. The PL negotiated an alliance with the Popular Party to secure membership in the PRD-led coalition in 2009. With less than 1 percent of votes, it failed to win any legislative seats and was wiped out under Panama's election laws, which required that each party reach a minimum percentage of the total votes cast.

Leaders: Joaquin FRANCO III (President), Venus CARDENAS (Vice President), Augusto AROSEMENA (Secretary General).

Other Party That Contested the 2009 Elections:

Moral Vanguard of the Homeland (*Vanguardia Moral de la Patria*—VM). The VM was a center-right party founded in November 2007 by former President Guillermo Endara after he broke with the PS. (He ran under the PS flag in the 2004 presidential election, finishing second to Torrijos with 30.9 percent of votes.) The VM did not participate in a coalition in 2009, and it failed to win a legislative seat. Former president Endara won 2.3 percent of the vote in the presidential election, finishing a distant third. Endara died on September 28, 2009, at the age of 73. The party failed to meet the required minimum percentage of total votes cast and was dissolved by the election authorities.

Leaders: Guillermo ENDARA Galimany (President of the Party and 2009 presidential candidate), Menalco SOLIS (First Vice President), Ana Mae DIAZ de Endara (Secretary General).

Other Groups:

Alternative Grassroots Party (*Partido Alternativa Popular*—PAP). The PAP is a center-left party that was registered in August 2007 to compete in the 2009 election. However, its registration remained under review by the Electoral Tribunal, preventing it from participating in the 2009 poll, and in January 2011 the authorities stripped the PAP of recognition as a party in formation.

Leaders: Raúl GONZÁLEZ (Sub-Secretary), Olmedo Ernesto BELUCHE Velasquez (Secretary General).

Broad Front for Democracy (*El Frente Amplio por la Democracia*—FAD). Born from the umbrella leftist and labor group National Front for the Defense of Social and Economic Rights (*Frente Nacional por la Defensa de los Derechos Economicos y Sociales Panama*—Frenadeso), the FAD began collecting signatures to register as a political party in August 2011. In June 2013, the party was officially recognized by the Electoral Tribunal and in August held its first congress and announced its participation in the 2014 general election.

Leader: Ignacio IRIBERRI (Chair).

LEGISLATURE

Before 1984 the Panamanian legislature consisted of an elected 505-member National Assembly of Community Representatives (*Asamblea Nacional de Representantes de Corregimientos*), which met on average only one month a year, and a de facto upper house, the National Legislative Council (*Consejo Nacional de Legislación*), consisting of 19 elected members and 37 appointed from the assembly. Under a constitutional revision approved in April 1983, the *Asamblea Nacional* was abolished, while the council was converted into a smaller, fully elected Legislative Assembly. **National Assembly** (*Asamblea Nacional*). The present assembly consists of 71 members elected for five-year terms. The number of seats was reduced from 78 as part of a 2004 constitutional reform.

Following the most recent election on May 3, 2009, the distribution of seats was as follows: Alliance for Change, 42 (Pro-Panamanian Party, 21; Democratic Change, 15; Patriotic Union, 4; Nationalist Republican Liberal Movement, 2); A Country for Everyone, 27 (Democratic Revolutionary Party, 26; Popular Party, 1); and independents, 2.

A number of defections, the dissolution of a coalition, and a party merger occurred subsequent to the elections. The distribution of seats as of September 1, 2012, was as follows: Democratic Change, 37; Pro-Panamanian Party, 12; A Country for Everyone, 20 (Democratic Revolutionary Party, 16; Popular Party, 1); and Nationalist Republican Liberal Movement, 4.

President: Sergio GALVEZ.

CABINET

[as of August 27, 2013]

President	Ricardo Martinelli Berrocal (CD)
Vice President	Juan Carlos Varela (PP)
Ministers	
Agricultural Development	Oscar Osorio (CD)
Canal Affairs	Roberto Roy (CD)
Commerce and Industry	Ricardo Quijano (CD)
Economy and Finance	Frank de Lima (CD)
Education	Lucy Molinar (CD) [f]
Foreign Relations	Fernando Nunez Fabrega
Health	Javier Diaz (CD)
Housing	Jasmina Pimentel (CD) [f]
Interior	Jorge Ricardo Fabrega (CD)
Labor and Social Welfare	Alma Lorena Cortés Aguilar (CD) [f]
Micro, Small and Medium-Sized Business	(Vacant)
Presidency	Roberto Henriquez (CD)
Public Safety	José Raúl Mulino (PUP)
Public Works	Jaime Ford
Social Development	Guillermo Antonio Ferrufino Benítez (CD)
Tourism	Salomon Shamah Zuchin (ind.)

[f] = female

INTERGOVERNMENTAL REPRESENTATION

Ambassador to the U.S.: Mario Ernesto JARAMILLO Castillo.

U.S. Ambassador to Panama: Jonathan D. FARRAR.

Permanent Representative to the UN: Pablo Antonio THALASSINÓS.

IGO Memberships (Non-UN): IADB, ICC, IOM, NAM, OAS, WTO.

PANAMA CANAL ZONE

Bisecting Panama in a southwesterly direction from the Atlantic to the Pacific, the Canal Zone served historically for the protection of the interoceanic waterway completed by the United States in 1914. Occupation, use, and control of a 553-square-mile area extending about five miles on either side of the canal were granted to the United States in perpetuity by Panama in a treaty concluded in 1903. Following nationalist riots within the zone in 1964, the two countries in 1967 negotiated a new draft treaty that would have replaced the 1903 accord, recognized Panamanian sovereignty in the zone, and enabled Panama to participate in the management of the canal. In 1970, however, following a change in government, Panama declared the draft to be unacceptable. After further extended negotiations, U.S. and Panamanian representatives reached agreement on an amended accord that was incorporated into two treaties signed in Washington, D.C., on September 7, 1977. Endorsed by Panama in a plebiscite on October 23, the treaties were barely approved by the U.S. Senate on March 16 and April 18, 1978. U.S. president Jimmy Carter subsequently exchanged documents of ratification during a state visit to Panama on June 16.

The first treaty provided for a phased assumption of control of the canal and the Canal Zone by Panama, beginning six months after ratification and concluding in the year 2000. Panama would assume general territorial jurisdiction, although until December 31, 1999, the United States would maintain control of all installations needed to operate and defend the canal. Until 1990 the canal administrator would be American, while his deputy would be Panamanian; from 1990 to 1999, the administrator would be Panamanian, with an American deputy.

The second treaty declared that "the canal, as an international transit waterway, shall be permanently neutral." It also provided that "tolls and other charges... shall be just, reasonable and equitable" and that "vessels of war and auxiliary vessels of all nations shall at all times be entitled to transit the canal, irrespective of their internal operation, means of propulsion, origin, destination, or armament."

Implementation of the treaties was delayed because of a U.S. Senate stipulation that ratification would not be deemed complete until the passage of enabling legislation by the Congress or until March 31, 1979, whichever came first. Thus it was not until October 1, 1979, that the American flag was lowered within the Canal Zone and administrative authority for the canal formally transferred to a binational Panama Canal Commission.

In early 1980, despite a significant increase in revenue accruing to Panama under the new arrangement, President Royo formally complained to the United States about a "unilateral" provision of the enabling legislation that effectively brought the commission under the control of the U.S. Defense Department. Subsequently, in the wake of an assessment that the existing facility, which was unable to offer transit to vessels in excess of 75,000 tons, would be obsolete by the year 2000, Royo and a group of high-level advisers visited Japan to discuss the possibility of Japanese involvement in the building of a new sea-level waterway.

During a meeting in Panama City in December 1982, the feasibility of a new waterway was further discussed by Panamanian, Japanese, and U.S. representatives. Earlier, a 9.8 percent increase in canal tolls had been agreed on to offset an anticipated shortfall of up to $5 million a month after the opening of a new trans-isthmian oil pipeline.

In mid-1984 the canal again became the focus for anti-U.S. sentiment, following U.S. reluctance to provide a major portion of the $400 to $600 million needed to widen the waterway on the grounds that it would be unlikely to recover its investment before full reversion in the year 2000. Late in the year, however, the United States and Japan agreed to a four-year program to consider canal improvements, not excluding the possibility of constructing a new facility to accommodate ships of up to 300,000 tons.

In June 1986, a tripartite commission, composed of Panamanian, Japanese, and U.S. representatives, began a projected four-year study on the feasibility of measures to upgrade or augment the existing facility, including improved pipeline, highway, and rail transport across the isthmus. The commission was also charged with undertaking an analysis of world shipping requirements in the 21st century and drafting recommendations on U.S.-Panamanian relations on expiration of the present canal treaties.

In July 1988, Panama refused to send delegates to a scheduled Canal Commission board meeting because of U.S. economic pressure against the Noriega regime and the U.S. rejection of representatives appointed by the Solis Palma administration. However, the problems were resolved by the overthrow of Noriega in December 1989 and the longtime Panamanian deputy administrator, Fernando Manfredo BERNAL became acting administrator on January 1, 1990. On April 30, during a visit by President Endara to Washington, D.C., President George H. W. Bush endorsed the appointment for a regular term of Gilberto GUARDIA Fábrega, who was formally approved by the U.S. Senate on September 11. Meanwhile, doubts arose as to the Panamanian government's ability to administer and defend the canal after December 31, 1999, then Government and Justice Minister Ricardo Arias Calderón having conceded in August that "a military defense [of the waterway] similar to the proportions of the United States is outside the practical and economic scope of Panama."

In early 1993, the Panamanian Legislative Assembly approved the establishment of an autonomous Interoceanic Region Authority (*Autoridad de la Regón Interoceánica*—ARI) to administer canal-related property acquired from the United States under the 1977 treaties. However, its future was clouded in late 1994 by a proposed constitutional amendment that would create a new Panama Canal Authority (*Autoridad del Canal de Panama*—ACP). Critics charged that the move was linked to a proposal before the U.S. Senate authorizing the formation of a corporation to administer the canal as a private undertaking.

In early September 1995, the U.S. Armed Forces' Southern Command said it would withdraw from the country and turn over two of its bases, Fort Davis and Fort Gulik, to the government of Panama. Shortly after, President Balladares met with President Bill Clinton in Washington, D.C., to discuss "maintaining some degree of U.S. military presence after the year 2000." A month later an opinion poll indicated that 86 percent of Panamanians wanted at least some bases to remain under U.S. control. On September 25, 1997, the U.S. Southern Command quit Panama, leaving five of eight bases for Panama (two more bases were relinquished in 1998). During 1998 labor unions expressed concern over the imminent privatization of canal services and attendant job losses after the U.S. pullout. Opinion polls indicated that nearly three-quarters of Panamanians supported the continued presence of the U.S. military. But the United States formally handed over administration of the canal to Panama in December 1999 after it vacated the last U.S. installation, Howard Air Force Base. The canal administrator later announced that technical proposals for constructing a new set of locks to accommodate ships up to 150,000 tons would be presented by the ACP to a canal advisory group representing 12 of the waterway's principal users. While the cost of the upgrade was estimated at $3 to $6 billion, experts insisted that demand would outstrip the existing system's capacity by 2010.

By mid-2003, estimates of canal expansion costs had risen to $4 to $8 billion, with no decision as to which of several options might be adopted. The most viable, large-scale widening of the facility was bitterly opposed by *campesinos* on both shores, while funding sources were far from clear.

In April 2006, the government announced its intention to invest $5.25 billion, obtained largely from increased toll charges, in an eight-year project to expand the canal and construct a new set of locks 40 percent wider and 60 percent longer than the existing locks. The undertaking, approved in a national referendum on October 22, 2006, was officially launched on September 3, 2007, and was expected to be completed by 2014. Once complete the expansion was expected to double the tonnage of cargo that could pass through the canal every year to 600 million tons.

Three international consortia submitted bids in March 2009 for the largest single construction project, the $3.2 billion design and construction of two new locks.

The ACP reported annual totals for fiscal year 2008–2009 that were largely untouched by the global economic downturn. It awarded the last of four major excavation contracts in January 2010, and as of June around 100 contracts had been awarded for the expansion project. In July 700 workers, who were employed with the consortium that won the largest contract to build two new locks, went on a week-long strike, demanding a repeal of new labor and environmental regulations pushed through by the Martinelli government (see Current issues, above).

As of November 2010, the canal authority had awarded contracts totaling $4.2 billion. Cargo tonnage moving through the canal in 2011 was estimated to be more than 15 million tons above what was predicted at the start of the fiscal year, and this prompted the ACP to release a record fiscal 2012 budget of nearly $293 million.

Engineer Jorge Luis Quijano assumed administration over the canal in September 2012. In February 2013, the canal expansion reached the halfway point, signifying that the inauguration date would likely be postponed from October 2014 until April 2015 (a result of a seven-month delay in cement pouring in 2011). The delay does not make a proposed canal project in Nicaragua any more likely. (For more on the proposed Nicaraguan canal, see the Nicaragua entry.)

In July 2013, Panamanian authorities halted a North Korean ship found to be carrying Cuban weapons (see Foreign relations, above).

Panama Authority Chair: Roberto ROY.

Panama Canal Administrator: Jorge Luis QUIJANO.

PAPUA NEW GUINEA

Independent State of Papua New Guinea

Gau Hedinarai ai Papua-Matamata Guinea (Hari-Motu)

Independen Stet bilong Papua Niugini (Tok Pisin)

Note: The literal translation of *Gau Hedinarai* is "entity of the people," hence the official title in Hari-Motu could be "Republic of Papua New Guinea."

Political Status: Former Australian-administered territory; achieved internal self-government on December 1, 1973, and full independence within the Commonwealth on September 16, 1975, under constitution of August 15.

Area: 178,259 sq. mi. (461,691 sq. km).

Population: 7,192,017 (2012E—UN); 7,059,653 (2011E—PNG Census).

Major Urban Centers (2009E): PORT MORESBY (metropolitan area, 254,158), Lae (78,038), Mt Hagen (27,789).

Official Languages: English, Tok Pisin, Hari-Motu.

Monetary Unit: Kina (market rate November 1, 2013: 2.61 kina = $1US).

Sovereign: Queen ELIZABETH II.

Governor General: Sir Michael OGIO; elected by the National Parliament on January 14, 2011, sworn in on January 25, and installed for a six-year term after formal appointment by the Queen on April 26, succeeding Sir Paulias MATANE, who served from 2004 until December 10, 2010, with Jeffrey NAPE serving as acting governor general in the interim.

Prime Minister: Peter O'NEILL (People's National Congress); elected by parliament and sworn in by the governor general on August 2, 2011, and elected by parliament and sworn in for a second term on August 3, 2012, succeeding Sir Michael SOMARE (National Alliance Party), who served from September 1975 to March 1980, from August 1982 to November 1985, and from August 2004 to December 13, 2010. Sam ABAL served as acting prime minister in the interim.

THE COUNTRY

Situated between Australia and the Equator in the southwest Pacific, Papua New Guinea (PNG) consists of the eastern half of the island of New Guinea and numerous adjacent islands, including those of the Bismarck Archipelago as well as part of the Solomon group. It shares its only land border with the Indonesian province of Papua. The indigenous inhabitants, mainly of Melanesian ethnic origin, comprise over 1,000 tribes that speak more than 700 languages, of which English and two pidgins, Tok Pisin and Hari-Motu, have become lingua franca and accorded official status. Although animism and traditional beliefs are widespread among the predominantly rural population, Christianity, encouraged by foreign missionaries, is the dominant formal religion, with Protestant denominations in the majority. While females are reported to constitute more than 40 percent of the labor force, most are engaged in subsistence agriculture, and make up only 30 percent of the wage sector. Female representation in formal elected bodies is minimal, but women's councils are active at both the national and provincial levels, and enjoy social status and government recognition and funding.

Much of the country's terrain consists of dense tropical forests and inland mountain ranges separated by grassland valleys. The climate is monsoonal. Roughly 70 percent of the population relies on subsistence farming and hunting and lives in primitive conditions, although some rural modernization has been achieved with government support; only 20 percent of the labor force is employed in the formal sector. PNG is rich in natural resources and exports of gold, copper, and oil comprised nearly 70 percent of foreign earnings in 2013, with agricultural, forestry and fisheries products comprising the balance; natural gas exports are expected to go on stream in 2014. Australia is the principal trading partner, followed by Japan, China, and Malaysia.

Real economic growth, according to the World Bank, averaged 5 percent during 1990–1996. However, falling mineral prices, lagging private investment, sagging demand from Asia, the aftermath of the Bougainville insurrection, a prolonged drought, and three severe tsunamis drove the economy down for half a decade. Rising commodity prices and energy exports brought the GDP growth rate up to a peak of 8.9 percent in 2008, after which it eased to 6.0 percent in 2009. The International Monetary Fund (IMF) forecasts growth at 4.4 percent in 2013 rising to 5.6 percent in 2014. Inflation ran at 6.5 percent in 2013. Distribution of wealth is uneven, unemployment remains high at as much as 80 percent in urban areas, the population below the poverty line was 28 percent in 2009, and malnutrition and hunger have been reported. The United Nations Development Program (UNDP) in 2012 ranked PNG 156th out of 185 countries on the Human Development Index. Government corruption, urban crime, and tribal vendettas have combined to discourage international investment, entrepreneurialism, and tourism despite the attractiveness of the country's natural wealth.

GOVERNMENT AND POLITICS

Political background. Sighted in 1526 by a Portuguese navigator who gave it the name Papua ("woolly haired"), the island of New Guinea was colonized over the centuries by a succession of European and Asian nations, including Portugal, Netherlands, Great Britain, Germany, and Japan. Indonesia, the most recent colonizer, retains the western half, now designated the provinces of Papua and West Papua. In 1906 the British New Guinea southern sector of the eastern half, renamed the Territory of Papua, was transferred to Australia. Northeast New Guinea, formerly a German colony, was assigned to Australia as a League of Nations mandate in 1920. Parts of both sectors were occupied by Japanese forces from 1942 to 1945, after which Australia reassumed control. Australia unified the northern and southern sectors administratively prior to granting independence to Papua New Guinea in 1975.

Representative government was initiated by the election of a House of Assembly in 1964, and in 1968 the Administrator's Executive Council admitted a majority of assembly members. The territory achieved independence on September 16, 1975, and the former chief minister Michael T. SOMARE assumed the office of prime minister. Somare was immediately confronted by a unilateral declaration of independence by secessionist leaders of a "Republic of the North Solomons" in the island province of Bougainville. They were aggrieved by unequal revenue sharing of the proceeds from the Panguna copper mine, but were pacified by a revised formula and the granting of substantial autonomy to the provincial government in August 1976.

After the nation's first postindependence election for the National Parliament in June-July 1977, Somare's Papua and Niugini Union Pati (Pangu), the People's Progress Party (PPP), and a number of independents formed a coalition government with Somare confirmed as prime minister. But in March 1980 the Somare government, now including the United Party (UP), collapsed in the face of a no-confidence vote led by the PPP. A new coalition led by Sir Julius CHAN governed for two years, but in August 1982 Somare returned as prime minister for a further three years. His coalition was weakened by the withdrawal of Deputy Prime Minister Paias WINGTI, who then, in November 1985, defeated Somare in a vote of no confidence and became prime minister, serving three years. He was replaced in June 1988 by Rabbie NAMALIU (Pangu), who led the country at the head of a succession of coalition governments for the following 14 years. The election of June 1992 produced a new coalition led by Wingti, but in 1994 the Supreme Court ordered a new election that led to a PPP-Pangu coalition under Sir Julius Chan, who assumed the prime ministership. (For details, see the 2010 *Handbook*.)

In May 1989, the Bougainville copper mine suspended operations in the face of sabotage by local landowners frustrated at the lack of compensation for despoliation of their lands and rivers. A full-scale secessionist movement broke out in midyear, led by the Bougainville Revolutionary Army (BRA) under the leadership of a former land surveyor, Francis ONA, who on May 17, 1990, declared Bougainville's independence. Mediation aboard a Royal New Zealand Navy ship led to the "Endeavor Accord," signed by Somare and Joseph KABUI, whereby PNG lifted its air and naval blockade, restored communications and other essential services, and pledged that the PNG Defense Force (PNGDF) would not return to the island. Despite the Declaration on Peace, Reconciliation and Rehabilitation in January 1991 and establishment of a Bougainville Interim Government (BIG) followed by a Bougainville Transitional Government (BTG) in 1995, a PNGDF invasion rekindled BRA guerilla skirmishes.

Prime Minister Bill SKATE's negotiations with the Bougainville rebels yielded a new truce in October 1997, stabilized by a Truce Monitoring Group led by New Zealand with Australian, Fijian, Tongan, and Vanuatu support. A peace treaty followed on January 23, 1998, as did a series of agreements to implement Bougainville's political autonomy and consider eventual independence for the island. Despite ongoing political turmoil and legal disputes, an election for a Bougainville People's Congress (BPC) was held in May 1999. In August 2001 agreement was reached to create an interim provincial government with an autonomous police force. Subsequently a Bougainville Constituent Assembly approved a draft constitution, and on January 14, 2005, power was formally handed over to Governor John MOMIS. In May–June 2005 Bougainville conducted a peaceful election that brought Kabui to the presidency, backed by his Bougainville People's Congress Party (BPCP) with a majority of legislative seats. The legislative elections of June–July 2007 saw 77 of the 109 parliamentary seats change hands and the rival National Alliance Party win a plurality with 27 seats. President Kabui died on June 7, 2008, and was succeeded pro tem by his vice president, John TABINAMAN. In December James TANIS was elected as the interim president, taking office on January 6, 2009.

Meanwhile, in Port Moresby Prime Minister Chan's secret contract with Sandline International to deploy mercenary soldiers to quell the Bougainville insurgency led to his defeat in parliament in July 1997, and Port Moresby mayor Bill Skate was chosen as his successor. Skate survived protests, defections, and no-confidence votes for two years by skillful cabinet reshuffles and by enlisting the support of members of the newly organized United Resources Party (URP). He was succeeded in 1999 by the PDM leader, Sir Mekere MORAUTA, who presided for a further four years despite intermittent challenges and political turmoil.

The election of June 2002 yielded a plurality of 20 parliamentary seats for NA (below), and Somare was designated prime minister a third time in August. Somare named a broad coalition administration that, after a reshuffle in 2003, encompassed the NA, Melanesian Alliance Party (MAP), Pangu, People's Action Party (PAP), People's Labour Party (PLP), People's National Congress (PNC), Papua New Guinea National Party (PNGNP), PPP, UP, and URP. Somare continued as prime minister after the election of June-July 2007 at the head of a similar coalition augmented by the Melanesian Labour Party (MLP).

Somare unexpectedly adjourned parliament on July 29, 2009. His action was precipitated by the desertion from the governing coalition of 14 members of parliament (MPs) who accused his government of bribery, threats, and dictatorship. Somare's 13-party coalition was further shaken by the sacking of the corrections minister in January 2010 following a series of prison breakouts, the resignation of the attorney general, the departure from the coalition of the Melanesian Liberal Party in May, and the rejection by the Supreme Court in June of a law prohibiting MPs from changing political parties. Somare buttressed his leadership by enlarging the cabinet from 28 members to 31 and, in April, sought to curb the powers of the Ombudsman to oversee the activities of MPs. Parliament's outlawing in June of third-party lawsuits against resource projects, thus lifting a restraining order on the controversial Ramu nickel mine, and its failure to resolve landowners' demands for compensation for land earmarked for the giant ExxonMobile LNG project, triggered public accusations of official collusion with foreign economic interests.

Somare's leadership came under further pressure in July when three of his ministers, Beldan NAMAH, Charles ABEL, and Ano PALA, announced their support for an opposition motion of no confidence. Before the vote could be taken, Speaker Jeffery NAPE on July 20 adjourned parliament for three months, and Somare on July 23 reshuffled his cabinet and appointed eight new ministers to shore up his leadership. However, confronted by charges of tax evasion and other illegal activity, Somare resigned on December 13, 2010, surrendering the prime ministership to Sam ABAL. He was found guilty on April 4, 2011, of tax evasion and electoral funding irregularities and suspended from parliament for two weeks; he announced his retirement on June 30. On July 4, Somare's son Arthur, minister for state enterprises and regarded as a contender for the prime ministership, was suspended from office.

Prime Minister Abal's erratic leadership, including his summary dismissal of his foreign minister and treasury minister, led to his suspension from the National Alliance party in July, and on August 2, he was defeated in parliament by former treasurer Peter O'Neill, who was elected prime minister by a vote of 70–24. The new prime minister appointed a cabinet representing 5 political parties and 21 independents. The new government announced reform measures, including the sale of a controversial government executive aircraft, investigation of alleged corruption in the National Planning Department, and initiatives to raise the minimum wage and give ownership of subsurface minerals to traditional landowners.

On December 12, 2011, the Supreme Court ruled O'Neill's August election invalid, whereupon Governor General Ogio announced that Somare was still prime minister and swore him in. O'Neil, backed by parliament, refused to step aside, and on December 19, Governor General Ogio reversed himself and declared O'Neill was still the prime minister. Somare, having named a new cabinet, police chief, and army chief, vowed to fight for reinstatement. In January 2012, retired colonel Yaura SASA staged an abortive mutiny and declared his support for Somare but surrendered after a week and was arrested; his followers were granted amnesty on January 30. O'Neill resumed his leadership as prime minister, but on May 21, the Supreme Court ruled that Somare was still legally prime minister. O'Neill disputed the court's authority to make a decision on political leadership and took his case to parliament, where he was again elected as the prime minister on May 30, whereupon he called a general election.

Constitution and government. Under the 1975 constitution, which can be amended by a two-thirds legislative majority, executive functions are performed by a National Executive Council that includes a governor general, nominated by the council itself to represent the Crown for a six-year term; a prime minister, appointed by the governor general on advice of the legislature; and other ministers who are designated on advice of the prime minister and must total no fewer than six and no more than one-quarter the number of legislators. The unicameral National Parliament normally sits for a five-year term, dissolution not being mandated in the wake of a no-confidence vote (which can be called by 10 percent of the members) if an alternative prime minister (previously designated by the leader of the opposition) succeeds in securing a majority. The judicial system encompasses a Supreme Court that acts as the final court of appeal, a National Court, and lesser courts (currently including district, local, warden, and children's courts) as established by the legislature.

A 1977 initiative to decentralize government into 19 provinces was abandoned under a 1995 constitutional amendment that also provided for a regional assembly member from each province to become governor. In July 2009 the National Parliament approved the upgrading of two regions, Hela and Jiwaka, to the status of provinces, bringing the total number to 21. At the subprovincial level there are approximately 145 local government councils and community governments.

In July 2013, the O'Neill cabinet proposed two amendments to the constitution to specify the length of annual parliamentary sittings—40 days minimum—and to stiffen requirements for a motion of no confidence in the government—three months' notice and signatures by one-third of parliamentarians.

The island of Bougainville, formerly called the North Solomons Province, achieved its current status of Autonomous Bougainville Government (ABG) on January 14, 2005, with its own constitution; an elected legislature and president; taxing, judiciary, and policing power; and an independent budget. External security and foreign policy are shared with Port Moresby, and since 2010 the ABG has consulted with the central government in a Joint Supervisory Body regarding a referendum on possible independence, whose date is yet to be negotiated.

Foreign relations. Two issues have shaped PNG's foreign policies since independence: sensitive relations with Indonesia stemming from the status of Irian Jaya (formerly West New Guinea, now the provinces of Papua and West Papua) and negotiations with Australia regarding demarcation of a maritime boundary through the Torres Strait and a host of security concerns.

Though the PNG government officially supported Jakarta's jurisdiction in Irian Jaya, and concluded a Status of Forces Agreement in January 1992, relations were disturbed by advocates of a "free Papua" who called on the United Nations to review the allegedly manipulated 1969 plebiscite that served as the basis of Indonesia's annexation of the mineral-rich territory. More than 10,000 refugees have entered PNG from the Indonesian side since 1983, fleeing violence and alleging persecution by Indonesian authorities. PNG's maintenance of border refugee camps was denounced by Jakarta, who suspected that they were sources of aid for rebels of the Free Papua Movement, now part of a recently organized umbrella organization, the West Papua National Coalition for Liberation. Closure of the camps in 2002 to ease tensions with Indonesia led to new squatter camps springing up, and PNG's attempts to repatriate rebels have not stemmed the influx. In May 2008 PNG blocked a move in the Melanesian Spearhead Group (see below) to grant observer status to the Papuan separatists, and in March 2009 it announced the creation of a civilian Border Development Authority with a budget of $28 million to bring order to the border region. Nevertheless, armed clashes in Papua and border incursions by Indonesian forces in pursuit of rebels, most recently by a platoon of troops in July 2008 and a police officer in June 2009, and PNG's refusal in June 2011to extradite rebels to Indonesia, continued to disturb PNG-Indonesia relations and retard tourism and cross-border economic activity. Working relations were restored by a visit in March 2010 by Indonesia's president, during which Somare reaffirmed PNG's recognition of Papua and West Papua as integral parts of Indonesia and the two leaders signed agreements on improved defense cooperation, double taxation relief, and agricultural cooperation. Eleven further agreements—on cooperation in labor, tourism, sport, education, air transport, mining, and energy—and an extradition treaty were concluded in June 2013 during a visit by Prime Minister Peter O'Neill to Jakarta.

Shortly after independence from Australia, the PNG government attempted to negotiate a boundary in the Torres Strait based on the equidistance principle. Canberra objected that this would remove the Torres Strait islands from Queensland state's jurisdiction. In a treaty concluded in 1985 the two governments compromised on a complex formula involving (1) an exclusive economic zone (EEZ) seabed line running south of a number of islands and reefs that would nevertheless remain Australian territories, and (2) a protected zone to which citizens of each country would have access. In 2008 the two governments agreed to extend a moratorium on drilling in the strait to protect its ecosystem.

Australia continues to be a crucial partner, not only as PNG's principal trading partner but also as the largest source of aid and technical assistance. Canberra's 2013–2014 Partnership for Development aid package, totaling A$507 million, focuses on health, HIV/AIDS, education, transport, and law and justice. Prime ministers and ministers meet regularly in the Australia–Papua New Guinea Ministerial Forum. Australian-listed investors include Oil Search Ltd, Lihir Gold Ltd (major shareholder Rio Tinto), Highlands Pacific Ltd., Coca Cola Amatil, Campbell Australia Ltd., and Nestle Australia.

In response to security concerns, Australia has provided extensive training, equipment, and weapons to the PNGDF and the police. The secondment of Australian defense and police officers, however, has provoked nationalist opposition by Port Moresby officials, as has Canberra's "Pacific Policy" of deflecting intercepted Middle East "boat people" to Manus Island for refugee processing. The Manus camp was closed in 2008, but Prime Minister O'Neill in August 2012 accepted Australia's request to reopen it and on July 19, 2013, despite criticism by the UN High Commission for Refugees, the International Organization for Migration, and Australian human rights groups, signed the Regional Resettlement Arrangement between Australia and PNG formalising the transfer of intercepted asylum seekers to Manus for processing and possible permanent resettlement in PNG. This and other agreements were encompassed in an omnibus PNG-Australia Partnership declared by the two prime ministers on May 10.

After independence PNG conducted an uneasy relationship with the governments of both the People's Republic of China (PRC) and the Republic of China (ROC) on Taiwan, initially granting formal diplomatic recognition to the PRC but also hosting a trade office sponsored by Taiwan's ROC government. In 2008 Beijing approved PNG as a "Chinese industrial zone," reflecting China's status as a significant investor in mining ventures. Prime Minister Somare visited Beijing in April 2009 and military chief Commodore Peter HAU in June reaffirmed PNG's commitment to its military exchange program with China, which has emerged as PNG's second most valuable trading partner and a growing source of investment and aid. Visits by potential investors from Shanghai followed in 2009 and 2010.. In November 2009 PNG signed three bilateral agreements gaining, among other things, a concessional loan facility with the China Exim Bank worth $123 million, and in October 2010 PNG signed an agreement with the Shenyang Corporation for International Economic and Technical Cooperation (SCIETC) to construct a Pacific Marine Industrial Zone in Madang valued at $79 million.

Ethnic rioting broke out in Lae in May 2009, directed against Chinese shops and Chinese nickel miners for alleged unfair prices and discrimination in favor of Chinese workers in violation of PNG employment law. A previous attack on Chinese took place in August 2008 at the Ramu Nico nickel mine, and another occurred in July 2009 at Popondetta, an oil palm-growing center, inducing the Chinese embassy to express "grave concern" about the safety of Chinese nationals and businesses. China's rising purchases of PNG hardwoods became controversial following revelations by international environmentalists of rapid and often illegal deforestation allegedly conducted by unscrupulous Chinese and Malaysian entrepreneurs with the connivance of corrupt PNG officials.

Relations with the neighboring Solomon Islands became tense upon the outbreak of the uprising on Bougainville in 1989 because the rebellious province is closer geographically and ethnically to the Solomon Islands than to the PNG mainland. In late 1991 Honiara's provincial affairs minister called for Bougainville's independence or its merger with the Solomons, and Solomon Islanders were reported to be smuggling supplies to the beleaguered Bougainvilleans in defiance of the PNG blockade. The peace agreement with the Bougainville leaders eased tensions between Port Moresby and Honiara, and in July 2003 the Solomon Islands National Parliament approved the participation of PNG personnel in the Regional Assistance Mission to Solomon Islands (RAMSI) to restore law and order in the wake of interethnic violence. In May 2009 PNG joined with the Solomon Islands and Federated States of Micronesia to submit to the United Nations a joint claim to the Ontong Java continental shelf, which would extend their economic zones into a pocket currently regarded as international waters. Port Moresby and Honiara also cooperated, with other Pacific island states, in initiatives to curb bottom trawling and tuna poaching in their adjoining EEZ waters.

As a member of the Pacific Islands Forum (PIF), PNG has championed self-determination for French Overseas Territories, particularly New Caledonia. In 1985 PNG joined with Solomon Islands, Vanuatu, and Fiji in the "Melanesian Spearhead Group," a caucus within the PIF to coordinate policy on regional issues with a view to possible formation of a Melanesian free trade zone. In 2009 PNG and other Spearhead members publicly supported Vanuatu's claim to Matthew and Hunter islands, two rocky outcrops north of New Caledonia claimed also by France. In 2012, PNG and its neighbours established a Melanesian Spearhead Group Police Formed Unit to promote regional security and engage in peacekeeping activities abroad.

PNG also participates in Association of Southeast Asian Nations (ASEAN) meetings as an observer, having acceded to ASEAN's 1976 Treaty of Amity and Cooperation in December 1987, and aspires to full memberhip.

Relations with the United States have been continuous but not always harmonious since independence in 1975. A dispute over tuna fishing rights was settled by negotiation in 1987 of the U.S.–Pacific Islands Multilateral Fisheries Treaty. While bilateral trade volume is small, U.S. aid is substantial, directed to health (particularly to combat HIV/AIDS), education (particularly of women), rural development (particularly food and forestry), and the training of civil servants, police, and PNGDF military personnel. U.S. based energy and mineral consortia led by ExxonMobile and Rio Tinto have made major investments. Secretary of State Hillary Clinton visited PNG in November 2010, pledged closer partnership, and announced new aid initiatives, and United States Agency for International Development (USAID) opened a Pacific Regional Office in Port Moresby in October 2011. In 2012, a dispute arose over payment for access to PNG and neighboring waters by U.S. tuna boats.

From independence PNG has maintained diplomatic, trade, and aid relations with leading European governments, particularly the United Kingdom and Germany, from which it receives aid. In December 2007 it entered into an interim Economic Partnership Agreement (EPA) with the European Union, expanding on PNG participation in the prior Lomé and Cotonou agreements between the EU and more than 75 African, Caribbean, and Pacific (ACP) countries. The EPA, finalized on July 30, 2009, grants PNG fish exports continued preferential access to the European market and facilitates EU aid projects.

Current issues. The 2012 election took place June 23–July 17 with 3,435 candidates in 46 political parties contesting 111 National Parliament seats. Ninety-five candidates from 21 parties and 16 independents won seats. Prime Minister Peter O'Neill on August 9 named 33 ministers representing 9 political parties and 1 independent to his new cabinet.

PNG's central government budget for 2013 forecast expenditures of a record 10.8 billion kina and included allocations for free education and hospital care as well as funding for transport and road infrastructure. Revenues, buoyed in 2011 by rising international prices of gold, copper, and gas and by investments anticipating the massive ExxonMobil LNG project, declined sharply in 2012 as world commodity prices sagged. Treasurer Don POLYE in July 2013 reported that the tax take had fallen by over 5 percent and that the budget deficit could reach 7.2 percent of GDP by year's end.

Corruption in government continued to retard economic development. In 2012, Transparency International ranked PNG 150th out of 176 countries. In August Prime Minister O'Neill took steps to set up an Independent Commission Against Corruption and provide more funding for the Task Force Sweep anticorruption unit. Despite PNG's establishment of a national human rights commission in 2010, the U.S. State Department in 2013 identified several categories of persistent human rights violations, including police abuse of detainees, poor prison conditions, infringement of privacy rights, discrimination against women, and ineffective enforcement of labor laws, and placed PNG in the bottom tier of its annual human trafficking classification alongside Sudan and Zimbabwe. The O'Neill government responded by passing the People Smuggling and Trafficking in Persons Act in July 2013. Parliament in February 2012 declined to pass a bill to establish 22 seats reserved for women. Only 3 women were elected to the current parliament, but Prime Minister O'Neill appointed 1, Loujaya TONI, to the new cabinet. Nevertheless PNG remained in the top quarter of 179 countries assessed by Reporters Without Borders in 2013 by gaining a 41st ranking for press freedom.

In May 2010, veteran leader John Momis won the presidential election for the autonomous Bougainville government. Sworn in on June 15, he declared his three priorities to be improving governance, sequestering weapons, and attracting foreign investment. Port Moresby in April 2011 announced a 500 million kina ($39 million) five-year grant to Bougainville for roads, health, education, and law and order reform, but ABG minister for finance Albert PENGHU in July 2013 complained that 188 million kina earmarked for Bougainville were being withheld by the central government. Meanwhile, despite national government leaders' denial of the legal competence of the ABG to make agreements with foreign firms, Bougainville officials began exploratory talks with Bougainville Copper Limited and other firms to encourage resumption of mining and palm oil planting. In June 2013 landowners in Wakunai, Panguna, and Kieta declared their support for reopening the mine, but the secessionist Me'ekamui Movement, led by Philip MIRIORI, declared it would oppose any deals until Bougainville achieved full independence.

POLITICAL PARTIES

At the time of the July 2012 election, the Integrity of Political Parties and Candidates Commission listed 46 parties registered by the Registrar of Parties of which 21 secured one or more seats. It also listed 26 deregistered parties.

Government Parties:

People's National Congress (PNC). Launched in early 1993 by a group of independent MPs, the original PNC merged in April 1998 with the Christian Century Party (CCP) and a number of smaller formations to form the **PNG First Party** (PNGFP) led by Prime Minister Skate. In June 1999, the PNGFP split; 22 PNG First MPs remained with the restored PNC, and 11 moved to the revived National Party (see PNGNP, below). By mid-2001, the party held only about half a dozen seats in parliament and then won only three seats in 2002. It secured three ministerial portfolios in the new Somare government, but all were ousted in May 2004.

The PNC fortunes declined further when Skate was expelled from the party in early 2005 and party (and opposition) leader Peter O'Neill was arrested in August 2005 on charges of misappropriating funds. The PNC won four legislative seats in 2007 and joined the Somare government with one cabinet post—public service—going to O'Neill. O'Neill was elected prime minister in July 2011 and again in August 2012, his party having won a plurality of 27 seats in the election. Twelve other PNC members were appointed to the new cabinet.

Leaders: Peter O'NEILL (Prime Minister), Simon KORAWA (President), Jonathan OATA (Secretary General).

Triumph Heritage Empowerment Party (THE). Founded January 23, 2012, by Don Polye and members of the Polye faction that broke away from the National Alliance Party (below), THE espouses Christian and family values, environmental sustainability, multiculturalism, better working conditions, and a moderate foreign policy. THE won 10.8 percent of the vote in the 2012 parliamentary election and entered into coalition with PNC, gaining four portfolios in the O'Neill cabinet.

Leaders: Don POLYE (Leader and Treasury Minister), Douglas TOMURIESA (President), James KIELE (General Secretary).

National Alliance Party (NA). NA was founded by Bernard NAROKOBI in 1995 on an anticorruption platform. Michael Somare, who had been associated with the People's National Alliance (PNA), the Bougainville-based Melanesian Alliance Party (MAP), the Movement for Greater Autonomy (MGA), and the People's Action Party (PAP), soon became its leading member and prime minister and secured the inclusion of the NA in every subsequent cabinet. The traditional NA leadership balance of four deputy prime ministers, one each for Papua, the Madang-Sepic region, the highlands, and the islands, was disrupted by Somare's numerous patronage appointments, with Polye and other highlanders emerging stronger.

Somare's temporary departure from office in December 2010 in the face of accusations of financial irregularities and his subsequent absence for medical treatment brought Sam Abal to party leadership. But, Abal's assertive style split the NA party between the Abal and Polye factions, induced the party's national executive to suspend his membership, and led parliament to vote him out of power in July 2011, whereupon Abal became leader of an opposition faction of the NA. Polye subsequently left to found the Triumph Heritage Empowerment Party (above), and Patrick PRUAITCH was chosen as the new party leader. In August 2012, three NA members, Pruaitch, Jim SIMATAB, and Kerenga KUA, were invited into the new O'Neill cabinet.

Leaders: Patrick PRUAITCH (Leader), Simon KAIWI (President), Joyce GRANT (General Secretary).

United Resources Party (URP). Organized in early December 1997 by defectors from other parties, URP advocated a greater voice for resource owners and resource-rich provinces. After its launching, it joined, then withdrew from, the Skate administration. In December 1999, the party leaders extended their support to the Morauta government. Peter IPATAS, governor of Enga Province, defected to the PDM in April 2001. The URP won five seats in 2007 and seven in 2012,, joining the governing coalition in each case. URP members in the O'Neill cabinet include Steven KAMA, Fabian POK, and William DUMA.

Leaders: William DUMA (Minister of Petroleum and Energy), Ken YAPANE (President), Peter KOIM (Secretary General).

People's Party (PP). The party was founded in 2006 by the governor of Enga Province since 1997, Peter Ipatas, a member of the PDM until 2005 and then briefly of the NA. The PP is based in PNG's most rugged inland province and represents the interests of the central highlands. It won 3 of the 109 seats in the election of 2007. In July 2010, veteran politician John PUNDARI, previously a member of the Advance PNG and PDM parties and who served in 1999–2001 as house speaker, minister of foreign affairs, and deputy prime minister, was appointed minister for mining in the expanded Somare cabinet. The party won 6 seats in the 2012 parliamentary election, and members Pundari and Davies STEVEN were invited into the O'Neill cabinet.

Leaders: John PUNDARI, Davies STEVEN (Leaders), Douglas IVARATO (President), Willie PALMERS (Secretary General).

People's Progress Party (PPP). The PPP was formed in 1976 and alternated between government participation and opposition for the next ten years. Sir Julius Chan led the party to victory in 1985 and became prime minister but moved to the opposition benches from July 1988 to June 1992 until rejoining the government under Paius Wingti. In 1993, PPP withdrew from the governing coalition with the PDM and revived its earlier alliance with Pangu, whereupon Chan returned as prime minister. Although PPP members continued in the Skate cabinet after the election of 1997, Chan lost his seat. The PPP withdrew from the Skate administration in October 1998, joined the Morauta government in July 1999, but suffered party leader Michael NALI's dismissal as trade and industry minister in November 2000. In 2001, Sir Julius rejoined the party leadership in preparation for the 2002 general election. The party won nine seats and joined the Somare administration but went into opposition when Chan failed in the challenge to Somare in 2007. The PPP won six parliamentary seats in 2012, and Byron CHAN and Ben MICAH were invited into the O'Neill cabinet.

Leaders: Sir Julius CHAN (Member of Parliament, Former Prime Minister), Byron CHAN (Minister of Mining), Brown SINAMOI (President), Philip KUWIMB (Secretary General).

People's Democratic Movement (PDM). The PDM was organized by former Deputy Prime Minister Paias Wingti, who broke with Pangu in March 1985. PDM formed a government in November and Wingti remained in office following the 1987 election but was defeated in a nonconfidence vote on July 4, 1988. Wingti returned in July 1992 as head of a coalition government that included the PPP. However, the PPP withdrew in August 1994 and Wingti lost the prime ministership, but during the next eight years, led by Bill Skate, then Mekere Morauta, the PDM participated in shifting governing coalitions. In May 2000 most of the **Advance PNG Party** (APNGP) was absorbed by the PDM, which thereupon claimed a majority in the national legislature. After the 2007 election, the PDM joined the National Alliance coalition government and party leader Michael Ogio was rewarded with the ministry of higher education, research, science and technology. On July 29, 2008, PDM MP John BOITO moved to the opposition benches in protest over the adjournment of parliament for four months. Ogio was elected PNG's governor general on January 14, 2011. In August 2012, Boito was appointed minister of internal security in the new O'Neill cabinet.

Leaders: Geoffrey BULL (President), Ezekiel PAWAI (Secretary General).

United Party (UP). UP is a highlands-based party organized in 1969. It was opposed to early independence. It entered the government in coalition with Pangu in November 1978. After March 1980 many of its members joined the Chan majority. After losses in the balloting of June 1982, it rejoined forces with the Pangu-led government but returned to opposition in April 1985.

The UP won only two legislative seats at the 1997 election but subsequently saw its delegation swell to more than a dozen. Prime Minister Morauta brought the UP into his coalition, but by May 2001 its ministers had been dismissed and defections had claimed most of its MPs. It won three seats in 2002, one of which was lost in 2007. The UP subsequently joined the Somare-led government, and leader Bob DADAE was given the defense portfolio. The party won only one seat in the 2012 election, but Rimbink PATO was offered a portfolio in the O'Neill cabinet.

Leaders: Chris KOPYOTO (President), Mathew TASO (Secretary General), Rimbink PATO (Minister of Foreign Affairs and Immigration).

Social Democratic Party (SDP). The SDP was launched on February 27, 2010, under the label United Democratic Front until July. It was led by Powes PARKOP, governor of the National Capital District, whose platform includes a campaign against corruption and elite power politics. SDP won three seats in the 2012 election, and Justin TKATCHENKO was awarded the portfolio of sports and Pacific games in the O'Neill cabinet.

Leaders: Wesley SANARUP (President), David Dom KUA (Secretary General), Powes PARKOP (NCD Governor).

Papua New Guinea Party (PNGP). Sir Mekere Morauta formed the PNGP in 2003 after being ousted as leader of the PDM after losing the 2002 election. Three of PNGP's members, though not Morauta himself, joined the Somare government in May 2004. The PNGP won eight seats in the 2007 election to become the second largest party in parliament, and Morauta was elected leader of the opposition. For his role in helping unseat Acting Prime Minister Abel, Morauta was given the portfolio of state enterprises in the O'Neill cabinet in August 2011 and was appointed minster for state enterprises in the August 2012 O'Neill cabinet, his party having won eight seats in parliament. Belden Namah, deputy prime minister in the 2011 O'Neill cabinet, was dropped from the August 2012 O'Neill cabinet whereupon he joined Pangu (below) and became Leader of the Opposition.

Leaders: Philip ELEDUME (President), Tom KUKHANG (General Secretary), Sir Mekere MORAUTA (Former Prime Minister now Minister for State Enterprises).

Indigenous People's Party (IPP). A new party registered in 2012 and based in Lae, IPP champions PNG's ethnic minorities. Party leader Loujaya TONI is one of only three female members of parliament and the only female in the current cabinet.

Leaders: John TEKWIE (President), Augustine SASAKING (General Secretary), Loujaya TONI (Minister for Religion, Youth, and Community Development).

Opposition Parties:

Papua and Niugini Union Pati (Pangu). The urban-based Pangu was organized in 1967 to represent the pro-independence movement. It was the senior component of the National Coalition that secured the largest number of legislative seats in the 1977 election. It moved into opposition following parliamentary defeat of the Somare government in March 1980 but returned to power after the election of June 1982 and the redesignation of Somare as prime minister in August. Despite Somare's ouster and Wingti's defection, the party secured a plurality of 26 assembly seats in the election of November 1987. Pangu suffered the worst defeat of the 1992 balloting, losing half of its 30 sitting members. Pangu returned to government in 1994 in a coalition with the PPP and other parties, with Sir Julius Chan, then Bill Skate, as prime minister. It joined the Morauta government in September 1999 and continued as part of the Somare administration after the 2002 and 2007 elections. Leader Andrew KUMBAKOR was awarded the housing and urban development portfolio after the 2007 election, and Philemon EMBEL was subsequently appointed minister for sport and constitutional matters. Pangu leaders Ken FEARWEATHER and Waka GOI were appointed ministers in the O'Neill cabinet in August 2011 but dropped from the August 2012 cabinet, which contained no Pangu members, the party having won only one seat in the 2012 election.

Leaders: Bendan NAMAH (Leader of the Opposition), Milo TIMINI (President), Morris DOGIMAI (Secretary General).

Melanesian Liberal Party (MLP). The MLP was formed in early 2007 by Dr. Allan MARAT and, in the June–July 2007 election, won two seats. Marat joined Somare's NA-led coalition government and was awarded the justice portfolio. In May 2010, Marat publicly disagreed with government policy and was dismissed by Somare, whereupon the MLP party went into opposition. The MLP won two seats in the 2012 election.

Leaders: Lui POE (President), Gabriel BUAKIA (Secretary General), Alan MARAT (Member of Parliament and Former Prime Minister).

Other Opposition Parties in Parliament:

Coalition for Reform, 2 seats; People's Movement for Change, 2; People's United Assembly Party, 2; New Generation Party, 1; Our Development Party, 1; PNG Constitutional Democratic Party, 1; PNG Country Party, 1; Stars Alliance, 1; United Party, 1.

Parties Winning No Seats in 2012:

Melanesian Alliance Party (MAP). Led by Dame Carol Kidu, the MAP (not to be confused with the earlier Bougainville-based MAP of Fr. John Momis) appealed to the urban women's vote. In the 2007 election it returned a single MP, Dame Kidu, the only woman in parliament, who joined Somare's coalition government as minister of community development, religion, and sports. It won no portfolios in the August 2011 O'Neill cabinet and no seats in the 2012 election.

Leaders: Dame Carol KIDU (Leader), Simon EYORK (President), Nick KLAPAT (Secretary General).

People's Action Party (PAP). PAP was formed on December 4, 1986, by the then forestry minister Ted DIRO as a right-of-center party. After a hiatus, Diro returned to the cabinet as minister without portfolio in April 1988. PAP's founding president, Vincent ERI, was named governor general in early 1990. Diro was convicted of corruption in September 1991, and the new PAP leader, Akoka DOI, failed to be reelected in 1992. The PAP was accorded five cabinet posts in the 2002 Somare government. In the 2007 election the party won six seats and was awarded two ministerial posts: correctional services for Tony AIMO and fisheries and marine resources for Ben SEMRI. Aimo, held responsible for several prison breakouts, was dropped from the government in January 2010 but in May was reinstated by Somare to shore up the governing coalition; he and his party colleagues were excluded from the O'Neill government that was formed in August 2011 and won no seats in the 2012 election.

Leaders: Mark SARONG (President), Simon BOLE (Secretary General).

People's Labor Party (PLP). Launched in 2001 by Peter YAMA, the PLP won five parliamentary seats in 2002 and held the housing portfolio in the Somare administration until January 2004. The party won only two seats in the 2007 election and joined the opposition coalition led by Sir Mekere Morauta (PNGP) but won no seats in the 2012 election.

Leaders: Thomas TULIN (President), Michael KONDAI (Secretary General).

Rural Development Party (RDP). Winning three seats in the 2007 election, this party's base of support lies to the east of the capital, in Milne Bay and Manus, where its leader served as provincial governor. RDP joined the government when Moses MALADINA was appointed minister of state for constitutional matters by Somare in July 2010. Malanda was invited into the August 2011 O'Neill cabinet. In 2012, the RDP won no seats and no portfolios.

Leaders: John ROBIN (President), Bafike KONRUI (Secretary General), Moses MALADINA (former Minister for Implementation and Rural Development).

Other Parties Without Seats in Parliament:

Christian Democratic Party, Kingdom First Party, League for Democracy Party, Mama Papa Graun Pati, Mapai Levites Party, National Conservative Party, National Front Party, New Dawn Transformation Party, Pan Melanesian Congress Party, PNG Greens Party, PNG National Party, People's Action Party, People's First Party, People's Freedom Party, People's Heritage Party, People's Labour Party, People's Resource Awareness Party, PNG Labour Party, PNG Conservative Party, PNG Country Party, PNG Destiny Party, PNG New Vision Party, Republican Party, Rural Development Party, and Transform PNG Party.

Bougainville Parties:

Bougainville parties include the **Bougainville Independence Movement** (BIM), formed in April 2005 by current leader James TANIS, former president of autonomous Bougainville, and supported by former rebel leader Francis Ona; the **Bougainville Labour Party** (BLP), led by lawyer Thomas TAMUSIO; the **Bougainville People's Congress Party** (BPCP), led by provincial president Joseph Kabui until his death in 2008; and the **New Bougainville Party** (NBP), founded in April 2005 by former island governor and current provincial president John Momis and now led by Ezekiel MASATT. A shadowy group based on remnants of the Panguna Landowners' Association and the Bougainville Revolutionary Army, called variously **Original Me'ekumi, Me'ekamui Tribal Nation, Me'ekumi Defence Force or Me'ekumi Government of Unity,** led by Philip Miriori, asserted itself in 2011 but was not recognized by either the Bougainville or the national government. (For further details on inactive political parties, see the 2011 *Handbook.*)

LEGISLATURE

The unicameral **National Parliament** was called the House of Assembly (*Bese Taubadadia Hegogo*) before independence. It currently consists of 111 members (90 from open and 21 from provincial electorates) elected to five-year terms by universal adult suffrage. Traditionally, candidates were not obligated to declare party affiliation, and postelectoral realignments were common; however, controversial legislation passed in December 2000 required future candidates to declare their affiliations and then, if elected, to maintain them or face expulsion. In 2007 the limited preferential voting system was employed for the first time, replacing the first-past-the-post system.

The following was the distribution of seats after the balloting of June 23–July 17, 2012: People's National Congress Party, 27 seats; Independents, 16; Triumph Heritage Empowerment Party, 12; PNG

Party, 8; National Alliance, 7; United Resources Party, 7; People's Progress Party, 6; People's Party, 6; Social Democrat Party, 3; People's Movement for Change, 2; People's United Assembly Party, 2; People's Democratic Movement, 2; Coalition for Reform, 2; Melanesian Liberal Party, 2; New Generation Party, 2; Indigenous People's Party, 1; Our Development Party, 1; Pangu Party, 1; PNG Constitutional Democratic Party, 1; PNG Country Party, 1; Stars Alliance, 1; United Party, 1.

Speaker: Theodore Zibang ZURECNUOC.

CABINET

[as of August 1, 2013]

Prime Minister	Peter O'Neill (PNC)
Deputy Prime Minister	Leo Deon (THE)
Ministers	
Agriculture and Livestock	Tommy Tomscoll (PDMP)
Autonomous Regions	Steven Kama (URP)
Civil Aviation	Davies Steven (PP)
Communication and Information Technology	Jimmy Miringtoro (PNC)
Correctional Services	Jim Simatab (NAP)
Defense	Fabian Pok (URP)
Education	Paru Aihi (PNC)
Environment and Conservation	John Pundari (PP)
Finance	James Marape (PNC)
Fisheries and Marine Resources	Mao Zeming (PNC)
Foreign Affairs and Immigration	Rimbink Pato (UP)
Forest and Climate Change	Patrick Pruaitch (NAP)
Health and HIV-AIDS	Michael Malabag (PNC)
Higher Education, Research, Science, and Technology	Don Polye (THE) (acting)
Housing and Urban Development	Paul Isikiel (PNC)
Intergovernmental Relations	Leo Dion (THE)
Internal Security	John Boito (PDM)
Justice, Attorney General	Kerenga Kua (NAP)
Labor and Industrial Relations	Mark Maipakai (THE)
Lands and Physical Planning	Benny Allan (PNC)
Mining	Byron Chan (PPP)
National Planning	Charles Abel (PNC)
Petroleum and Energy	William Duma (URP)
Police	Peter O'Neill (PNC) (acting)
Public Enterprise and State Investment	Ben Micah (PPP)
Public Service	Puka Temu (ODP)
Religion, Youth, and Community Development	Loujaya Toni (MLP) [f]
Sports and Pacific Games	Justin Tkatchenko (SDP)
State Enterprises	Mekere Morauta (PNGP)
Tourism, Arts and Culture	Boka Kondra (PNC)
Trade, Commerce and Industry	Richard Maru (I)
Transport	Ano Pala (PNC)
Treasury	Don Polye (THE)
Works and Implementation	Francis Awesa (PNC)

[f] = female

INTERGOVERNMENTAL REPRESENTATION

Ambassador to the U.S.: Evan Jeremy PAKI.

U.S. Ambassador to Papua New Guinea: Walter NORTH.

Permanent Representative to the UN: Robert Guba AISI.

IGO Memberships (Non-UN): ADB, APEC, CWTH, MSG, PIF, WTO.

PARAGUAY

Republic of Paraguay
República del Paraguay (Spanish)
Tetã Paraguái (Guaraní)

Political Status: Independent since 1811; under presidential rule established in 1844; present constitution promulgated on June 20, 1992.

Area: 157,047 sq. mi. (406,752 sq. km).

Population: 6,749,234 (2012E—UN); 6,623,252 (2013E—U.S. Census).

Major Urban Centers (2008E): ASUNCIÓN (518,792).

Official Languages: Spanish, Guaraní.

Monetary Unit: Guaraní (market rate November 1, 2013: 4,427.13 guaraníes = $1US).

President: Horacio CARTES (National Republican Association–Colorado Party); elected on April 21, 2013, and sworn in on August 15, 2013, succeeding Luis Federico FRANCO Gómez (Patriotic Alliance for Change/Authentic Radical Liberal Party).

Vice President: Juan AFARA Marques (National Republican Association–Colorado Party); elected on April 21, 2013, and sworn in on August 15, 2013, succeeding Oscar Amancio DENIS (Authentic Radical Liberal Party).

THE COUNTRY

A landlocked, semitropical country wedged between Argentina, Bolivia, and Brazil, the Republic of Paraguay takes its name from the river that divides the fertile grasslands of the east ("Oriental") from the drier, less hospitable Chaco region of the west ("Occidental"). The population is 95 percent *mestizo,* mainly of Spanish and Indian origin, although successive waves of immigration have brought settlers from all parts of the globe, including Japan and Korea. Spanish is the official language; however, 90 percent of the population also speaks Guaraní, the language of most of the indigenous inhabitants. Approximately 89 percent of the population adheres to Roman Catholicism, the established religion, while about 7 percent practices other forms of Christianity. Women constitute 40 percent of the labor force, concentrated primarily in the informal sector, manufacturing, and domestic service. Women have played a greater role in politics in recent years, but remain a minority in that sphere.

With 77 percent of the land owned by 1 percent of the population and without an adequate transportation network, Paraguayan development has long been impeded. Agriculture and cattle-raising constitute the basis of the economy; soybeans, beef, cotton, and vegetable oils are the main exports. Industry is largely confined to processing agricultural, animal, and timber products, but there is a small consumer-goods industry. The government is presently embarked on exploitation of the vast hydroelectric potential of the Paraná river. The Itaipú Dam, the world's second largest and jointly constructed with Brazil, was opened in November 1982. The Yacyretá Dam, the globe's twelfth biggest and developed together with Argentina, entered full operation in 1998. As a result, Paraguay is now one of the world's leading exporters of electricity.

Paraguay is one of the world's most unequal societies in terms of income distribution. Inequities in the distribution of land, education, and wealth have fueled ongoing tensions and a climate of social mistrust. More than one-third of the Paraguayan labor force has either been unemployed or under-employed in the last decade. In 2010 one out of five Paraguayans lived in extreme poverty, while 35 percent of the population lived below the national poverty line. Health coverage in Paraguay remains one of the poorest in the Western Hemisphere. Though illiteracy has dropped to 5.4 percent of the adult population, functional illiteracy remains high. Among neighboring countries, only Bolivia's per capita GDP of $1,973 was below that of Paraguay's at $2,860 in 2010.

Paraguay's GDP rose by an average of 2.8 percent from 2000–2008, and inflation averaged 8.8 percent (for an overview of Paraguay's economy prior to 2000, see the 2011 *Handbook*). A 2008 stimulus package, combined with increased social spending, created a government deficit of 2.5 percent of GDP, following a surplus equal to 2.6 percent of GDP the previous year. In September 2009 Paraguay announced that it would offer foreign bonds for the first time in its history in an effort to attract $200 million in foreign investment (foreign investment accounted for only 1.6 percent of GDP in 2008). In 2009, the World Bank approved $600 million in grants and loans to Paraguay to mitigate the impact of the economic downturn. In addition, the IADB provided loans and credits worth more than $1.45 billion to modernize the country's transport and sanitation sector and to shore up the social security system. Mainly as a result of the global recession, GDP declined by 4 percent in 2009, while unemployment rose to 6.4 percent, although inflation declined to 2.6 percent. The following year, the influx of aid and the largest soy crop in the country's history led to a spectacular GDP growth of 13.1 percent. GDP shrank by 1.2 percent in 2012, due largely to a drought that devastated soybean production. The IMF projected a strong recovery of 11 percent in 2013, with inflation at 3.6 percent and unemployment at 5.4 percent.

GOVERNMENT AND POLITICS

Political background. Paraguay gained independence from Spain in 1811 but was slow to assume the contours of a modern state. Its initial years of independence were marked by a succession of strong, authoritarian leaders, the most famous of whom was José Gaspar RODRIGUEZ de Francia. Known as "El Supremo," Rodriguez ruled Paraguay from 1814 until 1840, during which time he sought to isolate the country from the outside world by expelling foreigners and cutting off communications. In 1865–1870 Paraguay fought the combined forces of Argentina, Brazil, and Uruguay in the War of the Triple Alliance, which claimed the lives of approximately half of the country's population and the vast majority of its males. From 1880 to 1904 the country was ruled by a series of Colorado Party (*Partido Colorado*—PC) presidents, while the Liberals ruled for most of the period from 1904 to 1940. A three-year war against Bolivia over the Chaco territory ended in 1935, with Paraguay winning the greater part of the disputed region.

For more than half a century two men dominated the political scene: the dictatorial Gen. Higinio MORÍNIGO (1940–1947) and the equally authoritarian Gen. Alfredo STROESSNER, who came to power in 1954 through a military coup against President Federico CHÁVEZ. Initially elected to fill the balance of Chávez's unexpired term, Stroessner was subsequently reelected to successive five-year terms, the last on February 14, 1988. Stroessner was overthrown on February 3, 1989, in a coup led by Gen. Andrés RODRIGUEZ Pedotti, who was elected on May 1 to serve the balance of the existing presidential term. In simultaneous balloting, the Colorados retained their existing majorities in both houses of Congress.

At municipal balloting on May 26, 1991, the Colorados lost the race for the Asunción mayorship to the labor-backed Asunción for All (*Asunción para Todos*), while their traditional liberal opponents won in 43 other municipalities. The faction-ridden ruling party recovered to win 122 of 198 National Constituent Assembly seats on December 1. After six months of extensive debate, the assembly produced the draft of a new basic law, which became effective on its acceptance by the president on June 22, 1992.

Despite a heated challenge for the 1993 Colorado presidential nomination from Dr. Luis María ARGAÑA, Juan Carlos WASMOSY was named the party's standard-bearer at a convention in February, amid serious charges of fraud. The Colorado Party won pluralities in both houses of Congress in the May 9 presidential election with overt military support and widespread use of state resources to finance its campaign.

In early 1995, a rift developed between President Wasmosy and the self-styled military "strongman," Gen. Lino César OVIEDO Silva. In mid-May Oviedo was induced to join Wasmosy in an agreement with the congressional opposition that provided for the "temporary suspension" of party memberships held by army and police personnel.

In late April 1996, General Oviedo resigned from the army for violating a constitutional ban on its members' involvement in politics. Prior to his departure, though, the general threatened to bring down the Wasmosy government. The coup attempt, however, was thwarted as a result of intense international pressure and divisions within the military. Oviedo's subsequent appointment to head the Ministry of Defense was canceled soon thereafter amid strong congressional and street opposition. Oviedo went on to form his own Colorado Party faction (see Political Parties, below).

On September 7, 1997, Oviedo outpaced Argaña and Wasmosy's candidate, Finance Minister Carlos Alberto FACETTI, to win the Colorado presidential primary, with nearly 37 percent of the vote, close to Argaña's 35 percent and well above Facetti's 22 percent. Oviedo's victory triggered fears within the political and military establishment, which prompted an alliance between Wasmosy and Argaña aimed at stopping the former general's presidential bid. Oviedo's victory was challenged in the courts following *argañista* complaints of fraud.

On October 3, Wasmosy ordered Oviedo's disciplinary arrest under military law for "insults" leveled against the president, including the charge that he was a "thief." Wasmosy's efforts to postpone the May 10, 1998, presidential elections were rebuffed at various times by the political opposition and leading foreign ambassadors, notably between December 1997 and March 1998.

On December 12, Oviedo turned himself in to serve the 30-day sentence ordered by the president. Although Oviedo on December 29 became the legally recognized Colorado standard-bearer, a special military tribunal ordered that his incarceration continue indefinitely, pending further investigation of the abortive 1996 coup.

On April 17, 1998, the Supreme Court upheld a second sentence of ten years imposed on Oviedo in March, and his registration as Colorado standard-bearer was nullified the next day. His vice-presidential running mate, Raúl CUBAS Grau, was subsequently named his successor and went on to defeat opposition candidate Domingo LAÍNO in presidential balloting on May 10.

Three days after taking power, Cubas ordered Oviedo's release on a legal technicality. The measure elicited great controversy. Under an alliance of *argañistas,* with the opposition PLRA and the National Encounter Party (PEN), the National Congress challenged Cubas's decision in the courts.

On December 2, 1998, the Supreme Court annulled Cubas's release of Oviedo and ordered that the former general be returned to jail. However, Cubas issued a statement two days later rejecting the court's decision. The court, again unsuccessfully, directed Cubas to order Oviedo back to jail in February 1999, and Congress held preliminary discussions on impeachment proceedings. Although some observers initially believed Cubas might survive a congressional vote, the political landscape was dramatically altered on March 23 when Argaña was shot to death in Asunción by a professional hit squad. Suspicion of possible involvement immediately fell on Oviedo, and demonstrators poured into the streets of the capital to demand the president's resignation. After four days of protest in front of the National Congress, seven antigovernment demonstrators were killed by *oviedista* sniper fire and more than 150 protestors were wounded. The massacre took place while demonstrators were protecting the Congress from Oviedo supporters bent on blocking impeachment proceedings against Cubas.

Under intense international pressure, Cubas resigned on March 28, 1999, only hours before the Senate's final vote on his removal. He was succeeded within hours by Luis GONZÁLEZ Macchi, the *argañista* president of the Senate. On March 30 González Macchi appointed a "national unity" government, which included two members each from the PLRA and PEN. Meanwhile, Oviedo fled to Argentina and Cubas to Brazil. In late April the Supreme Court ruled that González Macchi was entitled to serve out the remainder of Cubas's term (until 2003) and directed that a new vice president be elected later in the year, a decision later postponed by the Supreme Electoral Court until August 13, 2000.

Subsequently, the Colorados indicated that they would contest the poll, despite a national unity agreement that the post be awarded to the opposition. As a result, the PLRA withdrew from the ruling coalition in February 2000, depriving the government of its legislative majority. González Macchi suppressed a botched-up coup attempt by Oviedo stalwarts in May 2000, an event that prompted Oviedo's arrest by Brazilian authorities the following month.

Liberal candidate Julio César FRANCO narrowly bested the Colorado nominee, Félix ARGAÑA (son of the former vice president), in the August balloting. President González Macchi's tenure was beset with corruption scandals, which prompted the PLRA to launch several efforts to impeach González Macchi, the last of which failed by a handful of votes in the Senate in February 2003.

Paraguayan domestic politics were largely determined by the *oviedistas* and rivals jostling for access to presidential power amid allegations of corruption and conspiracy. In 2002 the *oviedistas* withdrew from the PC, with Oviedo announcing from Brazil, where he was then under detention, that he intended to return to Paraguay and seek the presidency in 2003. Meanwhile, opposition pressure against President González Macchi continued, fueled in part by the filing in April of formal charges against him for the diversion of about $16 million in public funds into a U.S. bank account. In addition to having immunity from prosecution while in office, the president retained enough support in the Chamber of Deputies to prevent the two-thirds vote needed to impeach him. Over the next six months, however, a series of sometimes violent antigovernment, anticorruption demonstrations took place, with supporters of González Macchi insisting that they were orchestrated by Oviedo and Vice President Franco. (In 2006, González Macchi was sentenced to eight years in prison; the ruling, though, was overturned later by the Court of Appeals.)

In the election of April 27, 2003, Nicanor DUARTE Frutos of the Colorado Party was elected president with 38.3 percent of the vote. The Colorados secured only pluralities in the Senate (16 of 45 seats) and the Chamber of Deputies (37 of 80 seats). Following his inauguration, President Duarte enjoyed initial popularity, stemming in part from his opposition to the privatization of state-owned enterprises and support for land reform. On August 15, 2003, President Duarte reached an agreement with the opposition to change six members of the Supreme Court. The Duarte administration stabilized Paraguay's rocky economy after reaching a stand-by agreement with the International Monetary Fund in December 2003, and initiated various administrative and tax reforms to increase public revenue. Duarte's reformist impetus, however, began to lose traction in 2004 in the face of mounting social discontent and conflict in the countryside. That year, landless peasants occupied 74 large properties, leading to 1,156 arrests among rural activists and the murder of five landless peasants.

Disenchantment with the Duarte administration increased after 2005. A series of high-profile kidnappings and street murders in early 2005 triggered extensive concern over public security issues. The May resignation of Duarte's independent and well-reputed finance minister signaled the political limits of Duarte's promise to modernize and clean up the Paraguayan state.

In February 2006, President Duarte resumed formal leadership of the Colorados, arguing that a constitutional ban on his holding any office other than the presidency applied only to governmental posts. Concurrently, however, he indicated that he would seek a Constitutional Court ruling validating the action. In the meantime, he delegated interim leadership of the party to José Alberto ALDERETE. Three months earlier Duarte had appealed for constitutional reform in a move widely interpreted as clearing the way for a reelection bid by revoking the one-term limitation. His congressional critics, led by the PLRA, responded with a threat of impeachment, but they clearly lacked the required two-thirds majority in both chambers. A poll taken in late 2006 showed that only 23 percent of the population had a positive view of President Duarte, a sharp drop from the 61 percent rating in late 2003. In May 2007 Duarte, facing pressure even within the Colorado Party, announced that he had given up on his effort to challenge the one-term limitation.

With Duarte out of the race, Oviedo, who had returned to Paraguay in late June 2004, fixated on the presidency. Upon his return, he was held in a military prison to serve the sentence issued in early 1998 for his April 1996 coup attempt. He was released on parole in early September 2007, as result of a Supreme Court decision that was widely perceived to have been engineered by Duarte, in hopes of splitting the broad anti-Colorado coalition formed in support of a presidential bid by Fernando LUGO, a progressive Catholic bishop. On October 31 the Supreme Court annulled Oviedo's sentence for the 1996 coup attempt, which allowed him to launch his own presidential candidacy through the National Union of Ethical Citizens (*Unión Nacional de Ciudadanos Éticos*—UNACE).

Meanwhile, Duarte decided to support Blanca OVELAR de Duarte, his minister of education and culture, rebuffing Vice President Luis CASTIGLIONI Soria and the Colorado Party president Alderete, who both expected his endorsement. Castiglioni and Alderete went on to form their own movements to bid for the Colorado presidential slot.

In December 2007, Ovelar defeated Castiglioni for the Colorado nomination by less than 5,000 votes. Castiglioni and his supporters refused to recognize Ovelar's victory. However, the Colorado Party proclaimed Ovelar its standard-bearer in January 2008; she thereby became the first woman to head the presidential ticket of a major party.

Meanwhile, Lugo had become the opposition's main hope for defeating the ruling Colorado Party, after serving as the main speaker at an anti-Duarte demonstration attended by 40,000 people in late March 2006. Lugo helped to forge a broad coalition in September 2007 called the Patriotic Alliance for Change (*Alianza Patriotica para el Cambio*—APC) and, after resigning from the priesthood (the constitution forbids religious leaders from holding political office), defeated five other candidates (including Oviedo and Ovelar of the Colorado Party) in the presidential election of April 20, 2008. The results in the concurrent congressional and gubernatorial elections were essentially split, although the Colorado Party remained small pluralities in both legislative chambers.

On April 16, 2009, Lugo conducted a minor cabinet reshuffle and replaced four ministers in an effort to enhance the popularity of the government following an inability to enact promised reforms because of legislative resistance. Later that month he reached outside of the APC and chose Hector LACOGNATA of the Beloved Homeland Party (*Partido Patria Querida*—PPQ) to replace the foreign minister, who had resigned, in an effort to broaden his support within the Congress. He also supported the election of Miguel CARRIZOSA Galiano of the PPQ as president of the Senate. However, the effort led to the withdrawal of the PLRA from the APC (see Political Parties, below). The PLRA did maintain its three cabinet positions and continued to support the government.

In municipal elections on November 7, 2010, the Colorado Party secured 139 of the country's 238 municipalities. The party won the mayorship of the national capital and those of the capitals of 14 of Paraguay's 17 departments. The victory was seen as a major defeat for Lugo and the APC.

On June 22, 2012, the Senate voted to impeach President Lugo. Vice President Luis Federico FRANCO was immediately sworn in as president. Elections proceeded on schedule on April 21, 2013. In the wake of Lugo's impeachment, leftist parties fell into disarray, paving the way for political newcomer Horacio CARTES of the Colorado Party to win a decisive victory and for the party to secure majorities in both legislative houses. (For more on Lugo's impeachment and the 2013 election, see Current issues, below.)

Constitution and government. The 1992 constitution established an important break from the 1967 constitution. While maintaining the country's presidential system and a two-chamber legislature, the current constitution upholds basic democratic guarantees of association and expression, and improved the rights of women and indigenous people. The legislative branch was strengthened and various provisions were included to enhance judicial independence, including a Council of Magistrates responsible for screening nominations to the Supreme Court and appointing judges to the appellate and lower courts.

The new constitution introduced the post of vice president, to be elected along with the president by simple plurality (thus denying the opposition an opportunity to join forces in a runoff), and limited the president to a single five-year term. In a rebuff to the military, the constitutional assembly prohibited the chief executive from transferring his or her powers as commander-in-chief to another and instituted elections for the governors and council members of the country's departments. Strong guarantees for private property rights were established at the expense of constitutional provisions in favor of land reform.

For administrative purposes Paraguay is divided into 17 departments (exclusive of the capital), which are subdivided into a total of 230 municipalities.

The judicial system encompasses justices of the peace, courts of the first instance, appellate courts, and, at the apex, the Supreme Court of Justice. Despite significant reforms undertaken after 1995, including the overhaul of all judges, public opinion continues to view the judiciary as a corrupt institution.

Newspapers did not enjoy complete freedom of the press, and a number ceased publication during the Stroessner era. Freedom of the press is constitutionally guaranteed, but it is common for reporters to be threatened, both legally and violently. Reporters Without Borders ranked Paraguay 91st out of 179 countries in its 2013 press freedom index.

Foreign relations. A member of the United Nations, the Organization of American States, the Latin American Integration Association, and other regional organizations, Paraguay traditionally maintained a strongly anti-leftist foreign policy, including a suspension of relations with Nicaragua in 1980 following the assassination in Asunción of former Nicaraguan president Anastasio Somoza Debayle. Paraguay began to soften its approach to foreign policy with the reestablishment of diplomatic ties with Cuba in 1996.

Relations with neighboring regimes have been relatively cordial. In March 1991 Paraguay joined Brazil, Argentina, and Uruguay to establish the Southern Cone Common Market (*Mercado Común del Cono Sur*—Mercosur). Periodic disagreements with Brazil and Argentina over hydroelectric issues have flared. At the Itaipú Dam, an unfair pricing system has provoked repeated demands by successive governments to renegotiate the 1973 Itaipú treaty with Brazil.

Relations with the United States improved after Stroessner's demise. Prior to this, Paraguay had been a close ally during the Cold War, but repeated human rights violations and allegations of high-level Paraguayan involvement in narcotics trafficking strained relations between both countries, especially after 1977. The United States government played an influential role in preventing a coup against General Oviedo in 1996, and thereafter began to press Paraguay to curb illicit economic practices, notably in the realm of intellectual property violations and drug trafficking.

Following September 11, 2001, the shared border of Paraguay, Brazil, and Argentina became a leading point of concern for United States policymakers, who viewed the area as a haven for money laundering, arms and drug trafficking, and Islamist militants. In response, the United States provided Paraguay with technical assistance, equipment, and training to strengthen counternarcotics operations and to assist in developing legislation to counter money laundering and terrorism. In July 2003 the U.S. government suspended all military aid to Paraguay as a result of the country's refusal to grant immunity to U.S. citizens in legal cases involving the International Court of Justice in The Hague. Enhanced democratic stability in Paraguay and closer relations with neighboring leftist governments reduced the traditional influence exercised by the United States in Paraguayan foreign policy. In 2004 Paraguay was one of twelve nations to join the newly-created Union of South American Nations (*Unión de Naciones Suramericanas*—UNASUR), designed to bring together MERCOSUR and the Andean Community. However, the Congress failed to ratify the organization's treaty.

In July 2009, Paraguay and Brazil signed an accord that settled a long-running dispute over the operations of the bilateral Itaipu hydroelectric plant. Under the agreement, Brazil agreed to pay higher fees for the electricity produced by the plant and to cover the costs of the construction of new transmission lines. In August 2010, the government had to withdraw a bill supporting Venezuelan membership in MERCOSUR after opposition parties mustered the votes to defeat the measure. Opposition to Venezuelan membership was led by Vice President Luis Federico Franco Gómez, creating a dispute with Lugo, who campaigned heavily in favor of extending membership. All members of the organization except Paraguay and Brazil, had already approved Venezuela's entry into the trade bloc.

Meanwhile, Paraguay rejected participation in the U.S.-sponsored military program New Horizons 2010, which offered training and equipment to countries in the region. In September Paraguay joined with other South American nations to create the Bank of the South (*Banco del Sur*) in an effort to reduce the influence of institutions such as the IMF and the World Bank.

In a sign of improving cooperation with the United States in counternarcotics efforts, Paraguay extradited three Lebanese nationals to the United States to face drug-trafficking charges in February 2011. In May the Brazilian legislature approved the increase in payments for energy from the Itaipú Dam from $120 million per year to $360 million. A visit by the Iranian foreign minister in August led to increased economic ties between the two nations. In August, the Congress officially approved the UNASUR treaty, and membership was finalized when the president signed on in September.

Paraguayan authorities began meetings with Brazilian officials in November 2011 to develop a program to fight organized crime and corruption, along with joint security operations along the border between the two countries.

The impeachment of Lugo in June 2012 strained relations throughout the region; Mercosur and UNASUR suspended Paraguay, and several Latin American countries withdrew their ambassadors. Tension ran particularly high with Venezuela, which had cut off oil shipments following Lugo's impeachment, and in October Venezuela expelled all Paraguayan diplomats. In November Paraguay's foreign ministry stated that the country would not facilitate electoral observers from neighboring countries but ultimately agreed to a mission from UNASUR. In April 2013, president-elect Cartes signaled his interest in joining the Pacific Alliance, the regional trade bloc formed in June 2012.

Current issues. In April 2010, Congress enacted legislation allowing the government to declare a state of emergency in five departments as part of a broader effort to suppress the Paraguayan People's Army (*Ejército del Pueblo Paraguayo*—EPP), which was behind a series of high-profile murders and kidnappings. On July 29, EPP leader Severiano MARTINEZ was killed in fighting with security forces.

The Senate rejected a petition to hold a referendum on whether Lugo could seek a second term in July 2011 (supporters had collected 30,000 signatures petitioning for a referendum), ending any possibility that Lugo could stand for reelection.

In June 2012, a dispute broke out between police forces and landless farmers over an attempt by authorities to remove some 150 farmers from part of a privately owned estate. Advocates for the farmers asserted that the land should have been part of an agrarian reform program, pointing to Lugo's unfulfilled campaign promise to enact reform to serve Paraguay's 87,000 landless farm families. Lugo ordered the army to intervene on June 15 and, in the ensuing clashes, 6 police officers and 11 farmers were killed. The interior minister and the chief of police resigned.

Opponents of Lugo seized upon the incident, and the lower chamber of Paraguay's Congress voted to impeach the president less than a week later. The following day, on June 22, the Senate held a public impeachment trial, spearheaded by the majority Colorado Party, which accused Lugo of malfeasance. Lugo, who was given two hours to present a defense, did not attend, sending lawyers instead to ask for 18 days so he could prepare his case. The request was dismissed and the Senate voted 39–4 in favor of the impeachment. Vice President Franco was subsequently sworn in as president, and the power transfer was widely denounced as a parliamentary coup.

Lugo initially accepted the ouster but reversed his position shortly afterward, vowing to form a popular movement to regain power. He formed a parallel cabinet and, in September, received the official support of the PDC.

The electoral court announced in August 2012 that elections would be held on April 21, 2013. Eleven presidential candidates contested. In December, the Colorado Party confirmed Horacio Cartes, a tobacco magnate who was investigated by the United States in 2000 for drug trafficking, as the nominee, the PLRA selected Efrain ALEGRE, and in January, Lino OVIEDO of UNACE launched his campaign. UNACE was jolted on February 2 when Oviedo died in a helicopter crash. Instead of selecting a new candidate, UNACE and the PLRA opened discussions on forming an alliance. Initial efforts were abandoned, reportedly because of complex electoral laws, but in April, UNACE agreed to promote Alegre. The election focused on issues including job creation and infrastructure spending. Cartes won decisively, securing 48.5 percent of the vote; Alegre followed with 39 percent. The Colorado Party retained its majority in both legislative chambers, securing 45 seats in the lower house and 19 in the senate; the PLRA followed, with 26 seats and 13 seats, respectively.

Cartes was inaugurated on August 15, 2013, at which time he named his cabinet.

POLITICAL PARTIES

Paraguay's two traditional political organizations were the now-divided Liberal Party, which was last in power in 1940, and the National Republican Association (Colorado Party), which dominated the political scene from 1947 and sponsored the successive presidential candidacies of Gen. Alfredo Stroessner. In addition to these two traditional parties, Paraguay has a number of smaller, independent parties and political movements, ranging from right to left positions on the political spectrum.

Government Parties:

National Republican Association–Colorado Party (*Asociación Nacional Republicana–Partido Colorado*—ANR-PC). Formed in 1887, the mainstream of the Colorado Party has long been conservative in outlook and consistently supported General Stroessner for more than three decades. The party has, however, been subject to factionalism (for a discussion of its shifting "currents" before 1991, see the 1990 *Handbook*).

During the run-up to municipal elections in May 1991, the principal internal groupings were three *tradicionalista* alignments: the highly conservative *Tradicionalistas Autónomos,* led by then acting party president Dr. Luis María Argaña; the moderately liberal *Movimiento Tradicionalista Democrático,* led by Blás RIQUELME; and the centrist *Tradicionalismo Renovador,* led by Angel Roberto SEIFART. Following the municipal balloting the *democráticos* and the *renovadors* joined forces as the *Tradicionalismo Renovador Democrático* (Trardem), which commanded a majority at an extraordinary party convention on July 15–19. Subsequently, Trardem and the *autónomos* ran joint lists in Colorado balloting on October 6 to pick candidates for the forthcoming Constituent Assembly elections, winning all of the contests.

Other party factions included the *Frente Democrático* (FD), led by Waldino Ramón LOVERA; the strongly renewalist *Coloradismo Democrático* (Codem), led by Miguel Angel GONZALEZ Casabianca; and the youthful *Nueva Generación* (NG), led by Enrique RIERA Jr. In 1993 a Colorado dissident, Leandro PRIETO Yegros, attempted to campaign for the presidency under the banner of a Progressive Social Movement (*Movimiento Social Progresista*—MSP), but the electoral tribunal rejected his candidacy.

At a Colorado convention in February 1993 the military-backed Juan Carlos Wasmosy defeated Argaña for the party's presidential nomination. Following the election, Argaña's faction, now styled the Colorado Reconciliation Movement (*Movimiento Reconciliación Colorada*—MRC), held a majority of the party's seats in the Chamber of Deputies and formed a legislative bloc with the PLRA and PEN. In late 1994, after three generals had accused Wasmosy of intraparty vote rigging, *argañistas* formally challenged the validity of the president's incumbency by calling for his impeachment. (For more information on the alliance formed between the *argañistas* and *oviedistas* in early 1995, see the 2008 *Handbook.*)

In May 1996, following his forced retirement from the army, Oviedo launched a PC faction styled the National Union of Ethical Colorados (*Unión Nacional de Colorados Éticos*—UNACE, below). Meanwhile, in an April 28 election for the party leadership, Argaña secured an easy victory of 55 percent over Seifart (35 percent) and Riquelme (8 percent).

Despite his status as a coup suspect (see Political background, above), General Oviedo was elected Colorado presidential candidate in September 1997, with runner-up Argaña accusing his opponent of fraud. Following Oviedo's preclusion from the 1998 presidential poll by the Supreme Court, he was replaced as the Colorado standard-bearer by Raúl Cubas Grau, previously the vice-presidential candidate and a close ally of Oviedo. Argaña became the vice-presidential candidate. Despite the success of the Colorado ticket, intense conflict subsequently persisted between the *argañistas* and the Cubas/Oviedo faction, In mid-March, the *oviedistas* took control of the Colorado headquarters in Asunción after the *argañistas* had postponed the scheduled election of new party leaders. Shortly thereafter, Argaña was assassinated, leading to the ouster of President Cubas and elevation of Luis González Macchi, an Argaña supporter, to the national presidency. González was succeeded by Nicanor Duarte Frutos in April 2003. Duarte, Argaña's running mate in the 1997 Colorado presidential primaries, became the Colorado standard-bearer after defeating Osvaldo DOMINGUEZ Dibb, who contested the result of the December 22, 2002, primaries. The Colorado Party went on to win the April 27 presidential contest by a 13 percent advantage over the PLRA.

In a February 19, 2006 internal party election Duarte was challenged again by Dibb, but Duarte won convincingly. Alfredo Stroessner died in Brazil on August 16 of that year. His grandson, Alfredo (Goli) DOMINGUEZ Stroessner, who prefers to be known as Alfredo STROESSNER, assumed leadership of the *neostronista* faction.

Duarte's exploration of a possible constitutional change to permit him to run for another presidential term caused further turmoil in the party. Vice President Luis Alberto Castiglioni in particular criticized Duarte and announced plans to seek the party's presidential nomination himself. In May Duarte withdrew his name from consideration and backed Education and Finance Minister Blanca Ovelar de Duarte for the nomination. Castiglioni, supported within the party by the Colorado Vanguard Movement (*Movimiento Vanguardia Colorado*—MVC), resigned as vice president in early October to contest the 2008 elections but lost a close primary vote to Ovelar in December. Castiglioni and his supporters described the vote as fraudulent and did not subsequently support the Colorado ticket with enthusiasm. When Ovelar finished second in the April 2008 presidential poll with 30.72 percent of the vote, Castiglioni promised to launch a "true" Colorado Party and demanded immediate leadership elections. However, competing claims for the party's presidency remained in a legal imbroglio through November. The party was also reportedly split by a decision by Duarte's backers to provide legislative support for the new Lugo government. (The Castiglioni camp declined Lugo's offer.) Meanwhile, Duarte, to his consternation, was seated (because of his status as a past president) as a nonvoting member of the Senate, despite the fact that he had been elected as a regular member in the April balloting.) Duarte, maintaining that his Senate bid had been approved by the Supreme Election Tribunal, appealed to the Supreme Court, which ruled in November 2011 that he was entitled to be seated.

The ANR-PC played a leading role in the June 2012 impeachment of President Lugo. Businessman and political newcomer Hugo Cartes secured the party's presidential nomination in December with 59.6 percent of the vote, a solid victory over runner-up Javier Zacaría IRÚN. Cartes won a decisive victory in April 2013, with 48.5 percent of the vote. The party retained majorities in both legislative houses.

Leaders: Hugo CARTES (President of the Republic), Lilian SAMANIEGO (Party President), Nicanor DUARTE Frutos (Former President of the Republic and Leader of the *Movimiento Progresista Colorado*), Luis Alberto CASTIGLIONI (Former Vice President of the Republic and Leader of the MVC).

Other Legislative Parties:

Authentic Radical Liberal Party (*Partido Liberal Radical Auténtico*—PLRA). Paraguay's historical **Liberal Party** (*Partido Liberal*—PL) was founded in 1887 and legally proscribed in 1942. The party was legally reestablished in 1961, but most of its members left in the same year to form the **Radical Liberal Party** (*Partido Liberal Radical*—PLR). In 1977, a majority of PL and PLR members withdrew from their organizations to form the **Unified Liberal Party** (*Partido Liberal Unificado*—PLU). The government, however, refused to legalize the new grouping, continuing instead to recognize a rump of the PLR. The PLRA was formed in 1978 by a group of center-left PLU dissidents, many of whom had been subjected to police harassment after the 1978 election. (For PLRA history between 1978 and 1996, see the 2013 *Handbook.*)

In November 1996, the PLRA's Martín BURT, running with the support of PEN (below), was elected mayor of Asunción. He subsequently heralded that outcome as an example of how cooperation between the two leading opposition parties might defeat the Colorados in 1998, and in August 1997, the PLRA joined with PEN in a **Democratic Alliance** (*Alianza Democrática*—AD) to contest the general election of May 1998. The PLRA was awarded two seats in the national unity government installed in March 1999. It withdrew from the González administration on February 6, 2000. In March 2002, the party's president, Miguel Abdón SAGUIER, was ousted in favor of legislator Oscar Denis.

Having won the vice presidency in August 2000, Julio César Franco resigned the office in October 2002 to meet a legal requirement that presidential candidates vacate their governmental positions six months before the scheduled balloting. The PLRA attempted to form an opposition Power Front 2003 (*Frente Poder 2003*) and subsequently attempted alliances with the *oviedista* Unace (see below) and Pedro Fadul's PPQ (see below). Obliged to run alone, the PLRA finished second in both the presidential and the legislative races.

In October 2005, longtime party icon Domingo Laíno and a number of others were temporarily expelled from the PLRA for actions that appeared to make them de facto allies of the ruling Colorados.

After leading the formation of the CN in 2006, the PLRA in January 2007 announced plans for PLRA president Frederico FRANCO (the brother of Julio César Franco) to serve as the PLRA's nominee in what it hoped would be a multiparty primary to determine the opposition's presidential candidate for 2008. However, in a very close vote, the PLRA in June endorsed Fernando Lugo, who agreed to allow the PLRA to select his running mate. In a very close primary election for the vice-presidential slot in December, Franco defeated Sen. Carlos MATEO Balmelli, who initially rejected the slim victory but, after a simmering dispute, agreed to endorse Franco's candidacy. However, the party remained factionalized. Some components complained that the party was not sufficiently represented in Lugo's government. After he became vice president, Franco stepped aside as party leader, and Antonio Gustavo CARDOZA became acting PLRA leader.

The PLRA left the APC in 2009 over frustration with Lugo's efforts to reach out to the opposition Colorados and the PPQ. In June 2011, following a cabinet reshuffle, members of the PLRA called for Lugo's resignation. Franco assumed the presidency upon the ouster of Lugo in June 2012 and subsequently announced that he would step aside after the April 2013 elections.

Ahead of the 2013 presidential election, the PLRA officially allied with the PDP in April 2012 and the PEN in October. In a December primary election, Efraín Alegre secured the party nomination for presidency. Following the February death of UNACE presidential candidate Lino Oviedo, the PLRA attempted to form an alliance. Though discussions were abandoned in February, in early April, UNACE agreed to promote Alegre.

In April 21 balloting, Alegre came in second with 39 percent of the vote. The PLRA won 26 seats in the lower house and 13 in the Senate.

Leaders: Efraían ALEGRE (2013 presidential candidate), Federico FRANCO Gómez (Former President of the Republic), Sen. Blas Antonio LLANO Ramos (President of the Party).

Progressive Democratic Party (*Partido Democrata Progresista*—PDP). The PDP was founded by dissident members of the PPS in 2007. Party leader Rafael Augusto Filizzola Serra served as interior minister in the Lugo government but was dismissed in June 2011 after Lugo charged that the minister's presidential aspirations interfered with his official duties. The PDP subsequently left the FG. In April 2012, the PDP and the PLRA formalized their alliance, paving the way for Filizzola to take the vice presidential slot on the Alegre ticket. The PDP secured three Senate seats in April 2013 balloting.

Leader: Rafael Augusto FILIZZOLA Serra (PDP President and 2013 vice presidential candidate).

National Encounter Party (*Partido Encuentro Nacional*—PEN). PEN was organized in mid-1992 as a somewhat loose alignment of supporters of independent presidential candidate Guillermo Caballero Vargas, who consistently led in the public opinion polls until the eve of the 1993 balloting. The group, which included elements of the PRF and PDC as well as Carlos Filizzola's CPT (see PPS, above), won eight seats in each legislative house and subsequently entered into an opposition pact with the Liberals, which was reaffirmed for Asunción's mayoral contest in November 1996. In the latter balloting, PEN agreed to support the PLRA candidate after public opinion polls showed him ahead of the other contenders. PEN accepted two cabinet posts in the national unity government installed in March 1999. A week earlier Filizzola had lost the party presidency to Eúclides ACEVEDO. PEN's Diego Abente BRUN ran a distant fifth in the 2003 presidential race, while none of the party's candidates won congressional representation.

In April 2012, party president Fernando Camacho announced his candidacy for the FG presidential nomination. However, in October, the PEN formalized a split with the FG and threw support behind the Alegre-Filizzola ticket. The PEN won two Chamber seats and one Senate seat in the April 2013 balloting.

Leaders: Fernando CAMACHO (President), Guillermo Caballero VARGAS.

Guasú Front (Frente Guasú—FG). The FG was formed in March 2010 when the **Patriotic Alliance for Change** (*Alianza Patriotica para el Cambio*—APC), led by then-president Fernando Lugo, entered an alliance with the **Unitary Space–People's Congress** (*Espacio Unitario-Congreso Popular*—EU-CP), a movement created by leftist leaders in June 2009. The APC is an outgrowth of the National Concertation (*Concertación Nacional*—CN), a broad coalition formed in September 2006 with the aim of ending the Colorado Party's 60-year dominance of Paraguayan politics. The CN comprised the PLRA, PPS, PEN, PPQ, and UNACE, as well as additional leftist and civil organizations. (For more on the CN, see the 2013 *Handbook.*)

Dissension within the CN emerged in early 2007 over the question of how to pick a candidate for the 2008 presidential elections, resulting in the eventual withdrawal of the UNACE and PPQ (the second and third largest parties in the opposition camp) in September, after the PRLA and five smaller parties (the PPS, PEN, PDC, PRF, and the **Socialist Party** [*Partido Socialista*—PS]) had named Lugo as presidential nominee.

The APC was launched on September 18, 2007, by the PRLA, PPS, PEN, PDP, PRF, PDC, PPT, the **Broad Front** (*Frente Amplio*—FA), and other groups, including the influential social movement **Social and Popular Bloc** (*Bloque Social y Popular*). Lugo, whose concern for the impoverished peasantry had earned him the nickname "Red Bishop," was elected president of the republic under the APC rubric with 40.82 percent of the vote in the April 2008 election. The APC component parties presented their own candidates in the concurrent congressional balloting, although several lists (from which two candidates were successful) were presented under the APC designation. In July 2009, the PLRA officially withdrew from the APC. Efforts to change the constitution to allow Lugo to seek a second term further divided members of the APC.

Meanwhile, the EU-CP launched in June 2009 under the leadership of *campesino* leader Elvio BENÍTEZ as a progressive alternative to challenge the traditional parties. The movement united some 19 small leftist parties, including the **Paraguayan Communist Party** (*Partido Communista Paraguayo*—PCP), the **Popular Socialist Convergence Party** (*Partido Convergencia Popular Socialista*—PCPS), and the **Popular Patriotic Movement** (*Movimiento Patriótico y Popular*—MPP).

In March 2010, Lugo's APC and the EU-CP officially merged under the FG banner.

Following Lugo's impeachment in June 2012, the former president was appointed leader of the FG coalition with unanimous support. A rift formed within the party the following month when Mario FERREIRO, who had announced his candidacy for the 2013 presidential race, did not secure the FG nomination and formed a new coalition, taking the PDC and several other parties with him (see Avanza País, below). In January 2013, the coalition confirmed Aníbal CARRILLO as presidential candidate. In April 21 balloting, Carrillo secured 3.5 percent of the vote. The FG won five Senate seats and one Chamber seat.

Leader: Fernando LUGO (Former President of the Republic).

Country in Solidarity Party (*Partido País Solidario*—PPS). The PPS was formed in 2001 by Carlos Filizzola, who had led PEN from its formation until losing a leadership election in March 1999. Earlier, he had headed the Asunción for Everybody (*Asunción para Todos*—APT), winning the capital's mayoralty in 1991, and then the Constitution for Everybody (*Constitución para Todos*—CPT), which ran third, with 11 percent of the vote, in the Constituent Assembly balloting in December 1991. A joint secretary of the labor confederation *Central Unitaria de Trabajadores,* he had been imprisoned several times by the Stroessner regime for supporting peasant land seizures. Filizzola lost the Asunción mayoral election of November 2001 despite PLRA support. The party won two Senate and two Chamber seats in 2003. However, it suffered a split in 2007 (which led to the creation of the PDP, below) and retained only one Senate seat in 2008. The PPS was a leading force in an unsuccessful petition for a referendum to abolish the one-term presidential limit.

Leader: Carlos FILIZZOLA (President).

Popular Tekojoja Party (*Partido Popular Tekojojá*—PPT). The PPT was established in December 2006 by left-wing social and political activists in support of Fernando Lugo's presidential candidacy. Party leader Aníbal CARRILLO Iramain accepted a government post in the ministry of health as part of the Lugo government, but resigned in 2009 and was replaced by Esperanza MARTINEZ, who left office when Franco became president. Carrillo won the FG presidential nomination in January 2013 internal balloting.

Leader: Aníbal CARRILLO Iramain (President).

Forward Country (*Avanza País*—AP). The AP formed in October 2012 when Mario Ferreira led a splinter group of six left-wing parties off former president Lugo's FG. The **Movement Towards Socialism Party** (*Partido del Movimiento al Socialismo*—P-MAS, led by Camilo SOARES), one of the founding members of the APC, joined the new movement. In April 2013 balloting, Ferreira came in third place in the presidential race, securing 6.2 percent of the vote. The alliance won two seats in both legislative houses.

Leader: Mario FERREIRA (2013 presidential candidate).

Christian Democratic Party (*Partido Demócrata Cristiano*—PDC). The PDC, which was refused recognition by the Electoral Commission from 1971 through 1988, is the furthest left of the non-Communist groupings and one of the smallest of Paraguay's political parties. The party won only 1 percent of the vote in 1989. It secured one Constituent Assembly seat in 1991, none thereafter.

In September 2012, the Paraguayan PDC released a statement that the party, with the support of parallel groups in other Latin American countries, does not recognize the incumbent Paraguayan government.

Leader: Alba Cristaldo ESPINOLA (President).

Other members of the AP include the small leftist **February Revolutionary Party** (*Partido Revolucionario Febrerista*—PRF) (see the 2011 *Handbook* for more information on the PRF); the **Democratic Unity for Victory Movement** (*Movimiento Unidad Democrática para la Victoria*—MUDV); the **April 20 Political Movement** (*Movimiento Político 20 de Abril*—M-20A, a pro-Lugo movement created in 2010 and led by Miguel LOPEZ PERITO); and the **Paraguay Tekopyahú Party** (*Partido Paraguay Tekopyahú*—PPT).

National Union of Ethical Citizens (*Unión Nacional de Ciudadanos Éticos*—UNACE). The present UNACE (sometimes identified as the UNACE Party, or PUNACE) began as the ANR-PC's *Unión Nacional de Colorados Éticos* faction, which Lino Oviedo had launched in 1996. In March 2002, while under arrest in Brazil, Oviedo announced that he intended to sever his faction's links to the Colorados, return to Paraguay, and establish a new party as a vehicle for a presidential bid in 2003. However, the Supreme Court invalidated any candidacy by the general. His surrogate, Sen. Guillermo Sánchez Guffanti, received 13.5 percent of the popular vote. In September 2007 Oviedo was released from prison. The Supreme Court subsequently annulled his sentence for the April 2006 coup attempt, allowing him to present a presidential bid in April 2008, in which he obtained 21.98 percent of the vote.

Oviedo launched his campaign for the April 2013 presidential election in January. Weeks later, on February 2, he was killed in a helicopter crash. Soon thereafter, UNACE opened discussions with the PLRA over forming a possible alliance, which subsequently dissolved. In early April, the parties reached an agreement to promote PLRA presidential candidate Efraín Alegre. Nonetheless, Lino Oviedo Sanchez, who assumed the UNACE nomination after the death of his uncle and namesake, received 0.8 percent of the vote on April 21. UNACE secured two Senate and two Chamber seats.

Leaders: Lino OVIEDO Sanchez (2013 presidential candidate), Gen. (Ret.) Lino César OVIEDO Silva (2008 presidential candidate).

Beloved Homeland Party (*Partido Patria Querida*—PPQ). The PPQ was launched in early 2002 by Catholic businessman Pedro Fadul Niella, who launched an anticorruption campaign for the 2003 elections, in which he received 21.3 percent of the presidential vote, while the PPQ won nine seats in the Chamber of Deputies and seven in the Senate. Fadul subsequently initiated the abortive call for President Duarte's impeachment in November 2005.

The PPQ broke away from the CN, the broad anti-Colorado coalition, in July 2007 after Fernando Lugo agreed to have a PLRA running mate and the CN's proposed primary system was eliminated. Fadul subsequently ran as the PPQ presidential candidate in 2008, but he won only 2.37 percent of the votes. The PPQ won four Senate seats and three in the Chamber of Deputies, one of which was belonged to Orlando PENNER Drksen of the **Departmental Alliance of Boquerón** (*Alianza Departamental de Boquerón*—ADB), a regional political movement comprising the PPQ, PEN, and PLRA.

The PPC selected Miguel Carrizosa as 2013 presidential candidate in September 2011. Sebastian Acha assumed party leadership in internal elections in December 2012. Carrizosa won 1.2 percent of the vote in April 2013, and the party secured one Chamber seat.

Leaders: Miguel CARRIZOSA (2013 presidential candidate), Sebastian ACHA (Party Chair).

Chaqueña Passion Alliance (*Alianza Pasión Chaqueña*). The Chaqueña Passion Alliance secured one seat in the Chamber of Deputies in April 2013 balloting.

Other Parties Contesting the 2013 Elections:

Minor political parties and movements that participated in the 2013 elections, individually or as part of coalitions, included the **Paraguayan Humanist Party** (*Partido Humanista Paraguayo*—PHP), whose presidential candidate Roberto FERREIRA won 0.19 percent of the vote; the **Kuña Pyrenda Movement** (*Movimiento Kuña Pyrenda*—MKP), whose presidential candidate, Lilian SOTO, won 0.17 percent; the **Workers' Party** (*Partido de los Trabajadores*—PT), whose presidential candidate, Eduardo ARCE, won 0.13 percent; the **White Party** (*Partido Blanco*), whose presidential candidate, Ricardo ALMADA, won 0.12 percent; the **Free Homeland Party** (*Partido Patria Libre*—PPL), whose presidential candidate Atanasio GALEANO, won 0.11 percent of the vote; the **Youth Party** (*Partido de la Juventud*); the **Independent Constitutionalist Movement** (*Independiente Constitucionalista en Alianza*); and the **Civic Awakening Movement** (*Movimiento Depertar Ciudadano*).

LEGISLATURE

The bicameral **National Congress** (*Congreso Nacional*) currently consists of a Senate and a Chamber of Deputies, both elected concurrently with the president for five-year terms.

Senate (*Cámara de Senadores*). The upper house comprises 45 members who are directly elected via party-list proportional balloting in one nationwide constituency, plus former presidents of the republic, who serve as senators for life but without voting power. In the most recent election of April 21, 2013, the Colorado Party won 19 seats; the Authentic Radical Liberal Party, 13; the Guasú Front, 5; the Progressive Democratic Party, 3; the Forward Country, 2; National Union of Ethical Citizens, 2; and the National Encounter Party, 1.

President: Jorge OVIEDO Matto.

Chamber of Deputies (*Cámara de Diputados*). The lower house comprises 80 members who are directly elected via party-list proportional balloting in 18 multimember constituencies (the country's 17 departments plus the capital). Following the most recent election of April 21, 2013, election officials listed the following distribution of seats: the Colorado Party, 45; the Authentic Radical Liberal Party, 26; the National Union of Ethical Citizens, 2; the Forward Country, 2; the National Encounter Party, 2; the Beloved Homeland Movement, 1; the Guasú Front, 1; and the Pasión Chaqueña Alliance, 1.

President: Juan Bartolomé RAMÍREZ.

CABINET

[as of August 13, 2013]

President	Horacio Cartes
Vice President	Juan Afara Marques
Ministers	
Agriculture and Livestock	Jorege Gattini
Education	Marta Lafuente [f]
Finance	Germán Rojas
Foreign Relations	Eladio Loizaga

Health	Antonio Barrios
Industry and Trade	Gustavo Leite
Interior	Francisco de Vargas
Justice and Labor	Shelia Abed [f]
National Defense	Bernardino Soto Estigarribia
Public Works and Communications	Ramón Giménez
Women's Affairs	Ana María Baiardi [f]

[f] = female

Note: All ministers belong to the Colorado Party.

INTERGOVERNMENTAL REPRESENTATION

Ambassador to the U.S.: Fernando Antonio PFANNL Caballero.

U.S. Ambassador to Paraguay: James H. THESSIN.

Permanent Representative to the UN: José Antonio DOS SANTOS.

IGO Memberships (Non-UN): IADB, IOM, Mercosur, OAS, WTO.

PERU

Republic of Peru
República del Perú

Political Status: Independent republic proclaimed 1821; military rule imposed on October 3, 1968; constitutional government restored on July 28, 1980; national emergency declared in wake of army-backed "presidential coup" on April 5, 1992; present constitution effective from December 29, 1993.

Area: 496,222 sq. mi. (1,285,216 sq. km).

Population: 30,086,277 (2012E—UN); 29,849,303 (2012E—U.S. Census).

Major Urban Center (2011E): LIMA (metropolitan area, 9,130,000).

Official Languages: Spanish, Quechua.

Monetary Unit: New Sol (market rate November 1, 2013: 2.78 new sols = $1US).

President: Ollanta Moisés HUMALA Tasso (Peruvian Nationalist Party); elected in runoff balloting on June 5, 2011, and sworn in on July 28, to succeed Alan GARCÍA Perez (Peruvian Aprista Party).

First Vice President: Marisol ESPINOZA (Peruvian Nationalist Party); elected on June 5, 2011, and sworn in on July 28 for a term concurrent with that of the president, to succeed Luis GIAMPETRI Rojas (Peruvian Aprista Party).

Second Vice President: Vacant, as of November 1, 2013, following resignation of Omar CHEHADE (Peruvian Nationalist Party) on January 16, 2012; elected on June 5, 2011, and sworn in on July 28.

President of the Council of Ministers (Prime Minister): Juan Fedérico JIMÉNEZ Mayor (Independent), appointed by the president and sworn in on July 23, 2012, succeeding Oscar VALDÉS (Independent).

THE COUNTRY

The third-largest country in South America and the second after Chile in the length of its Pacific coastline, Peru comprises three distinct geographical areas: a narrow coastal plain; the high sierra of the Andes; and an inland area of wooded foothills, tropical rain forests, and lowlands that includes the headwaters of the Amazon River. While it contains only 30 percent of the population, the coastal area is the commercial and industrial center. Roman Catholicism is the state religion, and Spanish has traditionally been the official language, although Quechua (recognized as an official language in 1975) and Aymará are commonly spoken by Peruvian Indians. Of Inca descent, Indians constitute 46 percent of the population but remain largely unintegrated with the white (10 percent) and *mestizo* (44 percent) groups. Women constitute approximately 45 percent of the labor force, primarily in agriculture, with smaller groups in domestic service and the informal trading sector; female participation in government is minimal, save at the national level, where women constituted 28 of the 120 legislators elected in 2011. After a reshuffle in 2013, women held half the offices in the 18-member cabinet.

The Peruvian economy depends heavily on the extraction of rich and varied mineral resources, the most important being copper, silver, zinc, lead, and iron. Petroleum, which was discovered in the country's northeastern jungle region in 1971, is being extensively exploited. The agricultural sector employs approximately 40 percent of the labor force and embraces three main types of activity: commercial agriculture, subsistence agriculture, and fishing. The most important legal commodities are coffee, cotton, sugar, fish, and fishmeal, with coca production the major component of the underground economy.

Like most of its neighbors, Peru faced economic adversity in the 1980s, and in August 1985 the International Monetary Fund (IMF) declared the government ineligible for further credit after it had embarked on a somewhat unorthodox recovery program (see Political background, below). Peru suffered a major contraction in 1989, with GDP growth dropping to a historic low of –13.4 percent. Overall, GDP rose from 1990 to 2000 at an average of 3.2 percent per year, although widespread poverty showed little improvement. From 2001 to 2008 it marched upward at an average rate of 5.9 percent before the global economic crisis caused expansion to slow to a 0.9 percent crawl in 2009. Inflation held within the single-digit range since falling there in 1997, and the unemployment rate averaged 8.7 percent from 1999 to 2009. The government in 2009 spent $3 billion in savings from accumulated commodities revenue to launch a stimulus plan that helped the economy avoid a hard landing from the global economic downturn. Peru's GDP growth rebounded after the lull in 2009, averaging 7 percent from 2010 through 2012. GDP grew by 6.3 percent in 2013, with inflation of 2.1 percent. Unemployment held steady at 6.75 percent.

GOVERNMENT AND POLITICS

Political background. The heartland of the Inca empire conquered by Francisco Pizarro in the 16th century, Peru held a preeminent place in the Spanish colonial system until its liberation by José de SAN MARTIN and Simón BOLIVAR in 1821–1824. Its subsequent history has been marked by frequent alternations of constitutional civilian and extra constitutional military rule.

The civilian government of José Luis BUSTAMANTE, elected in 1945, was overthrown in 1948 by Gen. Manuel A. ODRIA, who held the presidency until 1956. Manuel PRADO y Ugarteche, elected in 1956 with the backing of the left-of-center American Popular Revolutionary Alliance (APRA), presided over a democratic regime that lasted until 1962, when a new military coup blocked the choice of *Aprista* leader Víctor Raúl HAYA DE LA TORRE as president. An election in 1963 restored constitutional government under Fernando BELAÚNDE Terry of the Popular Action (AP) party. With the support of the now defunct Christian Democratic Party (PDC), Belaúnde, although hampered by an opposition-controlled Congress and an economic crisis at the end of 1967, implemented economic and social reforms. Faced with dwindling political support, his government was ousted in October 1968 in a bloodless coup led by Div. Gen. Juan VELASCO Alvarado, who assumed the presidency, dissolved the Congress, and formed a military-dominated leftist administration committed to a participatory, cooperative-based model that was known after mid-1974 as the Inca Plan. Formally titled the Plan of the Revolutionary Government of the Armed Forces, it aimed at a "Social Proprietorship" (*Propiedad Social*) in which virtually all enterprises—industrial, commercial, and agricultural—would be either state- or worker-owned and would be managed collectively.

Amid growing evidence of discontent within the armed forces, Velasco Alvarado was overthrown in August 1975 by Div. Gen. Francisco MORALES BERMÚDEZ Cerruti, who had served as prime minister since the preceding February and initially pledged to continue his predecessor's policies in a "second phase of the revolution" that would make the Inca reforms "irreversible." Despite the existence of well-entrenched rightist sentiment within the military, Div. Gen. Oscar VARGAS Prieto, who had succeeded Morales Bermúdez as prime minister in September 1975, was replaced in January 1976 by a leftist, Gen. Jorge FERNÁNDEZ Maldonado, who was put forward as a figure capable of maintaining the policies of the revolution in the midst of growing economic difficulty. Under the new administration, Peru's National Planning Institute (INP) prepared a replacement for the Inca Plan known as the *Plan Túpac Amaru.* The document was, however, considered too radical by rightist elements. Its principal authors were deported as part of a move to clear the INP of "left-wing infiltrators," and Fernández Maldonado was replaced in July 1976 by the conservative Gen. Guillermo ARBULÚ Galliani, following the declaration of a state of emergency to cope with rioting occasioned by a series of austerity measures.

Gen. Oscar MOLINA Pallochia was designated to succeed Arbulú Galliani after the latter's retirement in January 1978, while on June 18, in Peru's first nationwide balloting in 15 years, a 100-member Constituent Assembly was elected to draft a new constitution. The assembly completed its work in July 1979, paving the way for presidential and congressional elections in May 1980, at which Belaúnde Terry's AP scored an impressive victory.

By 1985, economic conditions had plummeted, yielding massive inflation, underemployment estimated to encompass 60 percent of the workforce, and negative per capita GDP growth. As a result, the AP was decisively defeated in the election of April 14, Javier ALVA Orlandini running fourth behind APRA's Alan GARCÍA Pérez; Alfonso BARRANTES Lingán, the popular Marxist mayor of Lima; and Luis BEDOYA Reyes, of the recently organized Democratic Convergence (Conde). APRA fell marginally short of a majority in the presidential poll, but second-round balloting was avoided by Barrantes's withdrawal, and García was sworn in on July 28 as, at age 36, the youngest chief executive in Latin America.

In May 1986, the García administration reversed an earlier position and agreed to pay IMF arrears, but after unilaterally rolling over repayment of approximately $940 million in short-term debt, the country was cut off from further access to IMF resources. Concurrently, intense negotiations were launched with the country's more than 270 foreign creditor banks to secure 15- to 20-year refinancing on the basis of a medium-term economic program intended to reduce the country's dependence on food imports and restructure Peruvian industry, in a manner reminiscent of the Inca Plan, toward basic needs and vertical integration. The audacious effort was buoyed by short-term evidence of recovery. Aided by the upswing, APRA secured an unprecedented 53 percent of the vote at municipal elections in November 1986, winning 18 of 24 departmental capitals.

By mid-1987, the recovery had run its course, with increased inflationary pressure and a visible slackening of the 8.5 percent GDP growth registered in 1986. On June 29 García's second vice president, Luis ALVA Castro, who had served additionally as prime minister, resigned the latter post in the wake of a well-publicized rivalry with the president, leaving economic policy in the hands of the chief executive and a group styled "the bold ones" (*los audaces*), who in late July announced that the state would assume control of the country's financial system. Although bitterly condemned by the affected institutions and their right-wing political supporters, a somewhat modified version of the initial expropriation bill was promulgated in October. The action was followed by a return to triple-digit inflation, and in mid-December the government announced a currency devaluation of 39.4 percent.

During 1988, virtually all efforts by President García to reverse the country's plunge into fiscal chaos proved fruitless. An attempt at midyear to formulate an agreement (*concertación*) between business and labor (and subsequently with rightist and leftist political opponents) elicited scant response, and in September the administration introduced a "shock program" that included a 100 percent currency devaluation, a 100–200 percent increase in food prices, and a 120-day price freeze in the wake of a 150 percent increase in the minimum wage. However, the inflationary surge continued, necessitating a further 50 percent devaluation and the appointment in December of the government's fifth finance minister in less than four years. On several occasions there was evidence of García's desire to abandon the presidency, including indications that he might not be adverse to military intervention—a prospect that the armed forces, with no apparent solution to the nation's problems within their grasp, seemed unwilling to implement.

Events continued on an erratic course during 1989. The leftist alliance virtually collapsed, with the popularity of the fledgling right-wing contender, novelist Mario VARGAS Llosa, far outdistancing that of the leftist alliance's leading aspirant, Barrantes Lingán, by early May. Despite a clear lead in opinion polls for most of the year-long campaign, Vargas Llosa failed to gain a majority in presidential balloting on April 8, 1990, and was defeated in a runoff on June 10 by a late entrant, Alberto Keinya FUJIMORI, of the recently organized Change 90 (*Cambio 90*) movement.

Assuming office on July 28, 1990, Fujimori startled both domestic and foreign observers by a series of initiatives that were at once wide-ranging and controversial. He installed a supporter of Vargas Llosa, Juan Carlos HURTADO Miller, as both prime minister and finance minister, and embarked on an austerity program that was not only at variance with his campaign promises, but more severe than that advocated by his opponent. His cabinet included two active-duty army officers (appointed after the virtually unprecedented cashiering of both the air force and navy commanders), three left-wingers (one of whom resigned in late October), and a number of independents. He instituted corruption proceedings against 700 members of the judiciary, discharged 350 police officers, and publicly disagreed with the United States on antidrug policy (insisting on free-market enticement of farmers away from coca production rather than crop eradication). By mid-November, his audacity had reaped visible benefits: the army appeared to be a staunch ally; triple-digit monthly inflation had eased dramatically; a near-empty treasury had been replenished with reserves of about $500 million; payment on portions of the foreign debt had been resumed; and in his attitude toward the church and judiciary, Fujimori, according to a *Washington Post* report, had "taken positions that [struck] a chord in a society long disenchanted with institutional failures."

In April 1991, the Shining Path (*Sendero Luminoso*), a guerrilla organization, launched a new wave of attacks, and Fujimori felt obliged to replace his interior minister, Gen. Adolfo ALVARADO, whose anti-insurgency policies had drawn increasing criticism. Concurrently, the administration announced that it planned a fourfold increase in the number of its rural self-defense patrols (*rondas campesinas*) while moving to establish similar units in urban areas (*rondas urbanes civiles*). In June 1991 Congress granted the president emergency powers to deal with the escalating guerrilla activity as well as drug-related terrorism, and in July Fujimori felt obliged to reverse himself and conclude an antidrug accord with the United States.

On April 5, 1992, after what appeared to have been extensive consultation with the military, Fujimori seized extraconstitutional power in a dramatic self-coup (*autogolpe*). Announcing the formation of an Emergency Government of National Reconstruction, the president dissolved Congress, launched a reorganization of the judicial and penal systems, and declared that he would take "drastic action" against both the *Sendero Luminoso* and drug traffickers.

In response to the coup, a number of senior officials resigned, with Education Minister Oscar DE LA PUENTE Raygada being named prime minister. On November 13 three retired army generals who had served in the military household of the García administration mounted an unsuccessful attempt to overthrow Fujimori and hand over the presidency to First Vice President Máximo SAN ROMÁN Caceras.

With most major opposition groups as nonparticipants, Fujimori supporters captured a majority of seats in balloting on November 22, 1992, for a Democratic Constituent Congress (CCD), which was charged with drafting a new constitution. Earlier, the president had indicated that the CCD would not be superseded by a democratically constituted successor in April 1993 as initially announced, but would remain in office for the duration of his term (that is, to mid-1995). Municipal elections (postponed from October 1992) were, however, held on February 7, 1993, with both the regime and the traditional parties losing ground to locally based independent movements.

Meanwhile, on September 12, 1992, Peru's most celebrated outlaw, *Sendero Luminoso* leader Manuel Abimael GUZMÁN Reinoso, was captured in Lima after a 12-year national search. On October 17 five other members of the organization's Central Committee were also apprehended, offering hope that the antirebel campaign might be drawing to a conclusion.

Approval of the new constitution in December 1993 made it possible for Fujimori to present himself as a candidate for reelection in 1995. Given the success of his economic policies, he appeared to be an odds-on favorite before indications in early 1994 that Javier PÉREZ de Cuéllar might oppose him. Initially, polls showed the former UN secretary general leading Fujimori, but by not announcing his candidacy until late August, Pérez de Cuéllar gradually fell behind by about 15 percentage points.

With an ease that reportedly surprised the incumbent himself, Fujimori won nearly two-thirds of the valid votes in presidential balloting on April 9, 1995. Equally surprising was the showing of his ruling coalition (*Cambio 90–Nueva Mayoría*), which won 67 of 120 congressional seats with 51.5 percent of the vote, humbling the leading "traditional" parties, none of whom surpassed the 5 percent threshold needed to retain legal registration.

Growing concern about Peru's economic future, stemming in part from a proposed privatization of the state oil company, *Petroperú,* led to a decline in the president's popularity to 60 percent by late February 1996. On May 31 *Petroperú* was formally put up for sale, with the president's rating reportedly dropping to less than 56 percent shortly thereafter. Nevertheless, the Congress on August 23 paved the way for Fujimori to stand for a third term by voting, after a heated debate, that his initial incumbency was excluded from an existing two-term limit since it began under the previous constitution.

On December 17, 1996, about 25 members of the Túpac Amaru Revolutionary Movement (MRTA, below) stormed a reception at the Japanese embassy in Lima, taking nearly 600 guests prisoner. In the course of intense negotiations all but 83 were released by the end of the month. However, Fujimori rejected concessions in the form of economic policy changes and the release and safe passage out of the country of imprisoned MRTA members. As a result, the siege continued for 126 days, the longest in Latin American history, ending with an assault on the complex by Peruvian commandos April 22, 1997, during which all of the rebels were killed. In the wake of the crisis Fujimori's popularity, which had crested at 70 percent, plummeted to a low of 27 percent, in part because of a move by the government-controlled Congress to dismiss three members of the Constitutional Tribunal who had voted against the president's bid to seek a third term; by midyear his popularity had declined even further because of unsubstantiated charges that Fujimori had been born in Japan, rather than in Peru, as had long been alleged.

On June 4, 1998, Alberto PANDOLFI Arbulú resigned as prime minister and, somewhat surprisingly, was succeeded by Javier VALLE Riestra, a prominent defender of human rights who had publicly opposed Fujimori's reelection. Punctuated by clashes with military and governmental hard-liners, Valle Riestra's tenure lasted only two months, his predecessor, Pandolfi Arbulú, being reinvested as prime minister on August 21. Pandolfi Arbulú resigned again, on January 4, 1999, and Víctor JOY WAY Rojas, the president of Congress and a trusted Fujimori lieutenant, was named his successor. The cabinet resigned en masse on April 14 after the new labor and social promotion minister charged that corruption was rife in the customs system. Many of the ministers were reappointed the following day, although the one who made the accusations and four of his "technocrat" colleagues did not return. On October 8 Joy Way stepped down as prime minister to stand for reelection to Congress and was succeeded by Alberto BUSTAMANTE Belaúnde.

In late December 1999, the National Election Board accepted Fujimori's argument that he was not bound by the two-term limit because he had assumed office before adoption of the current constitution. In mid-March 2000, despite remarkable polling gains, the leading opposition candidate, Alejandro TOLEDO Manrique, threatened to withdraw from presidential contention because of anticipated fraud. However, he remained in the race and at first-round balloting on April 8 was officially credited with a vote share of 40.3 percent, as contrasted with 49.8 for the incumbent. Unable to secure postponement of the run-off scheduled for May 28, Toledo pulled out, urging his followers to abstain. The appeal was only partially successful: Fujimori won 50.3 percent in the "uncontested" second poll and Toledo 16.2 percent, with 32.5 percent of the ballots nullified.

The concluding months of 2000 yielded a remarkable turnabout in Peruvian politics. On September 16 a videotape surfaced that allegedly showed Fujimori's intelligence chief, Vladimiro MONTESINOS, offering a bribe to an opposition member of Congress. Two days later, Fujimori announced that he would call for a new presidential poll, at which he would not stand as a candidate. Collaterally, defections from Fujimori's Peru 2000 coalition cost him his legislative majority. On September 25, Montesinos flew to Panama, and on October 12 the government ordered that the National Intelligence Service be disbanded. On November 20 Fujimori, who had taken up residence in Japan, tendered his resignation. However, the Congress countered with a declaration that the office was vacant because the president had become "morally unfit." Meanwhile, both the first and second vice presidents had resigned, and on November 22 the recently installed congressional president, Valentín PANIAGUA Corazo, was sworn in as interim chief executive. On November 23 a new cabinet took office with Javier Pérez de Cuéllar as prime minister.

In the first-round presidential poll of April 8, 2001, Toledo again failed to secure a majority but went on to defeat former president Alan García Pérez by a narrow margin (53.1 to 46.9 percent) in a runoff on June 3. Subsequently, he named Roberto DAÑINO to head a cabinet composed, with one exception, of members from his Peru Possible grouping, which had won a plurality of 45 legislative seats in April. On July 12, 2002, with the government ministers divided over privatization policy, Toledo shuffled the cabinet, replacing Dañino with Luis SOLARI de la Fuente. Solari lasted until June 2003, after widespread public disturbances in the wake of a teachers' strike had led Toledo to proclaim a state of emergency. Beatrix MERINO Lucero succeeded him. Merino, a highly popular and seemingly incorruptible tax lawyer, held office for only six months before succumbing to a whisper campaign that involved rumors of influence peddling as well as supposed homosexuality. Carlos FERRERO Costa took her seat on December 15. Ferrero, after having served as president of Congress, became Toledo's fourth prime minister in 30 months. Ferrero resigned on August 11, 2005, in the wake of ordinances by two regional governors legalizing coca cultivation, and was succeeded by Economy Minister Pedro Pablo KUCZYNSKI.

The Toledo presidency was characterized by relative social peace and higher economic growth rates than Peru had seen since the 1970s. The president, however, consistently rated among Latin America's least popular; Toledo spent many of his years in office with an approval rating at or below 20 percent. The president's inner circle was hit by corruption allegations, while poll respondents generally regarded Toledo as lacking a work ethic and being unaware of voters' priorities. Leading the list of these concerns were corruption, steadily rising crime rates, and frustration with the unequal distribution of wealth generated by recent economic growth.

Discontent was plainly visible in the 2006 presidential campaign. The candidate who most closely identified herself with Toledo's policies, conservative one-time front-runner Lourdes FLORES Nano, finished third in first-round balloting on April 9. The first-round winner was Ollanta HUMALA, an intensely nationalistic retired army officer, who led the field with 30.6 percent of the vote. Former president García, leading a new party, the Peruvian Aprista Party (*Partido Aprista*

Peruano—PAP), defeated Humala 44.5–55.4 percent in a runoff on June 4. Humala's Union for Peru (UPP) won a plurality (45 of 120) of legislative seats.

Five months later, on November 19, 2006, the PAP was trounced in municipal and regional elections, winning only 2 (down from 12) of the country's 25 regional governments. PAP also failed to unseat Lima Mayor Luis CASTAÑEDO Lossio of the National Unity (*Unidad Nacional*—UN) coalition. The only consolation PAP could take from the voting was that no other party fared better, including Humala's UPP/Peru Nationalist Party (PNP), which failed to win a single regional presidency. "Independent" candidates, many of them powerful local political bosses, won 20 of the regional presidencies, along with 112 of 195 provinces.

The return of Alan García to the Peruvian presidency in 2006 was surprising in view of the disastrous outcome of his previous incumbency. Equally surprising was the emergence of Ollanta Humala as his principal rival. Humala, who sought to emulate the success of Evo Morales, his ethnically based Bolivian counterpart, had difficulty in distancing himself from the shadow of Hugo Chávez, while García's victory would not have been possible without the support of the third-ranked contender, Lourdes Flores. Overall, García won only 9 departments, compared to his opponent's share of 15, although most of the latter were in the less densely populated, impoverished, central and southern highlands, where Humala had hoped to launch his "great transformation."

Significantly, Keiko Fujimori, the daughter of the former president, won election to Congress in 2006, winning more votes than any other candidate. Even as the ex-president neared an extradition decision in Santiago, García's Aprista bloc entered into what some regarded to be an unofficial alliance with pro-Fujimori political movements. Fujimori's Alliance for the Future Party was the only one to join in García's failed attempt, in late 2006 and early 2007, to institute the death penalty in terrorism cases. President García's dependence on the pro-Fujimori bloc to advance his legislative agenda opened him to charges of insufficiently supporting Fujimori's prosecution for human rights crimes. Opposition politicians speculated in July that García had granted Fujimori a "golden jail" in exchange for his legislative bloc's support for PAP legislator Javier VELÁSQUEZ Quesquen's candidacy for president of the Congress.

In April 2007, García chose a hard-line response to disputes with coca farmers in the highlands, who had organized strikes and blockades to protest the forcible eradication of their crops. With much of the chamber abstaining on April 26, 2007, the Congress gave the president the authority to rule by decree on issues relating to drug trafficking, terrorism, and organized crime. Human rights defenders assailed the decrees, which included a prohibition on local officials participating in strikes and an automatic pardon for security personnel who injure or kill strikers while "fulfilling their duty."

On August 15, 2007, an 8.0 magnitude earthquake devastated a region in southern Peru centered on the city of Pisco, killing more than 500 people. President García received high marks for his personal, highly visible response to the disaster, though many voiced discontent at the confused, improvised nature of the rescue and rebuilding efforts he led.

The Fujimori trial dominated the country's political discourse during 2008. In December 2007, Fujimori was sentenced to six years in prison for illegally ordering the search and seizure of his shadowy former intelligence chief, Vladimiro Montesinos. He then went on to face human rights charges, beginning with two massacres committed by a government death squad in the early 1990s.

As the findings of a groundbreaking 2003 truth commission report continued to reverberate, human rights were a major topic of debate in 2007 and 2008. Human rights defenders argued that the PAP and pro-Fujimori political blocs wished to remove Peru from the Inter-American Human Rights Court, a body of the Organization of American States (OAS) that, on two occasions, has required the Peruvian government to pay damages to the relatives of massacred *Sendero Luminoso* guerrillas and sympathizers. In May 2008, Vice President Luis GIAMPETRI Rojas called publicly for Peru's withdrawal from the court. The PAP and pro-Fujimori blocs also collaborated in late 2006 on controversial legislation that placed strict regulations on the financing and activities of nongovernmental organizations (NGOs). In May 2008, after APRODEH, one of Peru's main human rights groups, recommended that the European Union (EU) remove the nearly defunct MRTA guerrillas from its list of international terrorist groups, President García called APRODEH "traitors to the country" and ordered an investigation of its financing. That month, media reports alleged that the government had set up an intelligence group *Comando Canela* to infiltrate nongovernmental human rights defender groups and others engaged in social protest.

During his first year in office, García's approval ratings consistently hovered around 50 percent, but by July 2008, they had fallen to 26 percent. Economic growth and reduced poverty levels helped the president, though good economic news was far scarcer in the impoverished regions where Humala was popular. Inflation, which was expected to reach 7 percent in 2008, was an increasing concern as higher food and fuel prices disproportionately impacted the poor. Public security became a principal complaint as citizen concerns increased about worsening crime, particularly by drug-related organizations, prompting the García government to give the armed forces a greater internal crime-fighting role. Meanwhile, remnants of *Sendero Luminoso* and other narco-criminal gangs were responsible for sporadic acts of violence in the countryside, including ambushes that killed police and officials involved in coca leaf regulation in December 2006 and April 2007 as well as an attack on a rural police station in November 2007. About 42 Peruvian antinarcotics police or coca eradicators were killed from January 2007 to July 2009.

On May 13, 2008, President García created a new cabinet-level environment ministry and named Antonio BRACK Egg to head it.

In October, a scandal emerged from the revelation of audiotapes documenting a top state oil-licensing official and a PAP politician discussing plans to steer contracts to a Norwegian petroleum company in exchange for bribes. On October 9, the entire cabinet tendered its resignation over the matter. García's new prime minister, leftist politician Yehude SIMON Munaro of the Peruvian Humanist Movement Party (*Partido Movimiento Humanista Peruano*—PMHP), assembled a new cabinet on October 14, keeping ten of the ministers and replacing six.

The cabinet underwent another major reshuffle on July 11, 2009, following the violent outcome of indigenous protests. Simon was replaced by the president of Congress, Javier VELÁSQUEZ Quesquén of the PAP, who retained nine ministers and replaced seven.

As García's term neared its end in the April 2011 presidential and congressional elections, his approval ratings dropped to 11 percent in some districts—the lowest in his cohort of South American leaders. Though his work saving and shoring up the Peruvian economy brought plaudits from world leaders and international organizations, at home he dealt with anger over the handling of indigenous and worker protests that led to killings in the street, natural gas supply insecurity that led to Lima running out of liquefied petroleum gas in July 2010, increasing *Sendero* attacks against the military, and more cocaine production under his watch that brought pressure from foreign governments and the UN (see Current events, below).

The president of the council of ministers Velásquez resigned on September 13, 2010. Minister of Education José Antonio CHANG Escobedo was named the new president of a reshuffled council on September 14. Chang resigned on March 18, 2011, and was replaced by Justice Minister Rosario FERNÁNDEZ Figueroa the following day.

Prior to the national elections in April 2011, five main electoral coalitions emerged. Humala's PNP joined with four other left-wing parties to create the Peru Wins Alliance (*Alianza Gana Perú*). Keiko FUJIMORI, daughter of the former president, formed a center-right coalition, Force 2011 (*Fuerza 2011*), which included the National Renewal (*Renovación Nacional*—Renovación). The other electoral alliances included the National Solidarity Alliance (*Alianza Solidaridad Nacional*), led by former Lima mayor Luís CASTAÑADA Lossio; Alliance for the Great Change (*Alianza por el Gran Cambio*), under former prime minister Kuczynski; and the centrist Peru Possible (*Perú Posible*), which supported the presidential candidacy of former president Toledo.

In legislative balloting on April 10, 2011, the Peru Wins Alliance won a plurality with 47 seats. After no candidate received more than half the total votes in the concurrent presidential balloting on April 10, a runoff election was held on June 5 between the two front-runners, Humala and Keiko Fujimori. In one of the most highly polarized and contested elections in Peruvian history, Humala won with 51.5 percent of the vote to Fujimori's 48.5 percent. Humala was sworn in on July 28 for a five-year term. He appointed political independent Salomón LERNER Ghitis as prime minister of a PNP-dominated cabinet, which was sworn in on July 28.

The first year of Humala's presidency was fraught with problems. Lerner unexpectedly resigned in December 2011 over his mishandling of a mining dispute. Interior Minister Oscar VALDÉS took the post, only to step down in July 2012, prompting a cabinet reshuffle in which 10 out of 19 ministers were replaced. The post is currently held by Juan JIMÉNEZ Mayor, who previously served as minister of justice, while the post of second vice president remains vacant as of mid-2013 (see Current issues, below). In July 2013, a series of unrelated resignations led to a minor renewal of Humala's cabinet.

Constitution and government. On December 29, 1993, the "Fujimori constitution," which had been approved by a slim 52.2 percent in an October 31 referendum, came into effect. The principal departures from its 1979 predecessor were supersession of the former bicameral legislature by a unicameral body and the lifting of a ban on presidential reelection. (Although the new basic law provided for only one five-year renewal, it was subsequently argued that Fujimori's incumbency could extend to 2005, as his previous election was under the old constitution.) In addition, the president's authority was significantly enhanced, including the redesignation of control over military appointments as an executive rather than a legislative prerogative. The death penalty was restored for convicted terrorists, although assumed not to be applicable to persons currently incarcerated, while a number of social amenities were abolished, including free university education and a right to job security.

In April 2003, Congress overwhelmingly endorsed restoration of the country's two-chamber legislature, composed of a 150-member lower house and a 50-member Senate. It was argued that the lower chamber would cater to the interests of the various departments and the upper would focus on issues of national concern. The action was never implemented; in 2005 Toledo tried to restore the Senate but lacked the necessary two-thirds majority. In mid-2007, the legislature's constitutional committee approved a proposal to leave the lower house at 120 members and add a 50-member Senate. This proposal failed to pass.

The country's judicial system is headed by a Supreme Court and includes 18 district courts in addition to a nine-member Constitutional Court and a National Council for the judiciary. In March 1987 President García promulgated legislation that divided the country's 25 departments into 12 regions, each with an assembly of provincial mayors, popularly elected representatives, and delegates of various institutions.

In September 2009, the Congress approved a bill to increase the number of seats in the legislature from 120 to 130, effective after the next election in 2011. The constitutional change was approved by a two-thirds majority of legislators, meaning a referendum on the matter was unnecessary. The reform was brought forward to decrease the high number of citizens being represented by each representative.

The press is primarily privately owned. There are reports of intimidation against journalists, including violence against journalists reporting on the mining protests in the first half of 2012. In its 2011–2012 annual index of press freedom, Reporters Without Borders ranked Peru 105th out of 179 countries.

Foreign relations. Peruvian foreign policy stresses protection of its sovereignty and its natural resources. After the 1968 coup the military government expanded contacts with Communist countries, including the Soviet Union, the People's Republic of China, and Cuba. Its relations with neighboring states, though troubled at times by frequent regime changes, are generally equable, apart from a traditional suspicion of Chile and a long-standing border dispute with Ecuador that yielded overt conflict in January–February 1981 and a renewed flare-up in late January 1995 when its neighbor charged Peru with "launching a massive offensive." Peru claimed that Argentina illegally sold arms to Ecuador in the second dispute, damaging relations between the two for decades. The more recent fighting gave way to a cease-fire on February 13, after a Peruvian announcement that it had recaptured the last Ecuadorian outpost on its territory, and to another on March 1, following a brief, but intense, resumption of fighting. On July 26 the two countries agreed to demilitarize more than 200 square miles of the disputed territory, while President Fujimori attended a Rio Group (*Grupo de Rio*) summit in Quito, Ecuador, in September, during which he surprised observers by extending an unofficial invitation to Ecuadorian President Sixto Durán-Ballén to visit Peru.

A seemingly more definitive event was an agreement reached in Rio de Janeiro on January 19, 1998, on a timetable for a peace treaty. The accord called for the establishment of four commissions dealing with major aspects of the controversy, including one centering on the thorniest issue: border demarcation. The lengthy dispute was formally settled with a "global and definitive" accord signed by Fujimori and his Ecuadorian counterpart in Brasília on October 26, 1998. While the disputed territory was awarded to Peru, control (but not sovereignty) of the principal town of Tiwintza, in addition to a corridor from the border, was assigned to Ecuador, which was also granted free navigation along the Amazon and the right to establish two port facilities within Peruvian territory. Provision was also made for link-up between the two countries' electrical grids and oil pipelines. On June 1, 2007, President García met Ecuador's President Rafael Correa in the northern Peruvian town of Tumbes. García said that Peru had "no territorial or maritime claim to make with Ecuador," and Correa described relations as the "best... in the history of the two countries." The two countries' foreign and defense ministers met in February 2008, signing accords establishing a binational confidence-building and security commission. In November 2012, Ecuador and Peru signed a maritime border treaty addressing their claims to the Gulf of Guayaquil, paving the way for bilateral exploration of hydrocarbon deposits.

Long-standing differences with Chile were largely resolved in November 1999 during a state visit by Fujimori to Santiago (the first by a Peruvian leader since the war of the Pacific in 1879–1883). However, a new flare-up occurred in early 2004 with the killing by Chilean marines of a Peruvian national after Chile had heightened border security against illegal immigrants seeking Chilean employment. Lima became frustrated in 2005 by its inability to secure the extradition of former president Fujimori, who had been arrested in Chile in November 2005 after his return from Japan to seek the Peruvian presidency. Under house arrest, Fujimori's fate was determined by Chile's Supreme Court, which heard his case in August 2007 and extradited him to Peru on September 22, based on 7 of the original 13 charges. Relations chilled further in November 2005, when the Peruvian Congress passed a bill claiming sovereignty over 15,000 square miles of Pacific waters controlled by Chile. Peru presented its arguments over the maritime border dispute before the International Court of Justice (ICJ) in The Hague in March 2009, and Chile responded in March 2010. The court began deliberation in 2012 but as of late 2013 no verdict had been issued.

Peru's relations with Venezuela have been troubled since the 2006 presidential campaign, when Venezuelan President Hugo Chávez was widely accused of interference in internal affairs with his vocal endorsements of Humala. Opponents alleged that Humala's campaign was receiving financial support from Caracas, which he denied. The two countries recalled their ambassadors in April 2006, only to restore them in March 2007. Peruvian sensitivity to perceived Venezuelan meddling has remained high, however. Strong concerns have been raised about health care programs and the opening of offices of the Venezuelan-supported ALBA movement (Bolivarian Alternative for Latin America) in several regions of Peru. An investigative commission established in 2008 to investigate the financing of so-called "ALBA houses" released a strongly worded report in March 2009 recommending that the 148 existing "ALBA houses" be closed, characterizing them as a tool of foreign political infiltration. However, the step was not taken, because of support for the program in Peru's provinces and to the political fallout of June indigenous protests that ended in violence.

Relations with neighboring Bolivia worsened in 2008, as Presidents Alán García and Evo Morales—a close ally of Venezuela's Chávez—traded periodic criticisms and insults. Though the substance tended to be disagreements over free trade and Venezuelan influence, the bickering reached its nadir in June, when Morales said García was "very fat and not very anti-imperialist." Peru briefly recalled its ambassador from Bolivia.

Relations with the United States had been strained by recurrent controversies over the expropriation of U.S. businesses, the seizure of U.S. fishing boats accused of violating Peru's territorial waters, and the degree of U.S. involvement in combating the narcotics trade. In April 2001, a Peruvian jet downed a civilian aircraft carrying U.S. missionaries, killing a woman and her infant daughter, after a CIA-contracted surveillance plane had mistakenly identified it as engaged in drug smuggling. International attention had been drawn to the case of a U.S. journalist, Lori Berenson, who was convicted in 1996 of aiding the MRTA guerrillas. Initially sentenced to prison by a secret military court, Berenson was reconvicted by a civilian court in June 2001, with an appeal rejected by the Supreme Court in February 2002. Relations with the United States were jarred in August 2003 when the U.S. Export-Import Bank refused, on environmental grounds, to issue loan guarantees for a controversial trans-Amazon natural gas pipeline; however, in September the Inter-American Development Bank, with the U.S. representative abstaining, approved a loan package for the project, which was then 70 percent completed.

Peru remains the world's second-largest producer, after Colombia, of coca, the plant used to make cocaine. Police estimate that a large number of small narcotrafficking organizations, most with ties to Mexican, Colombian, and Brazilian cartels, operate in Peru. Though U.S. and UN measurements have found coca cultivation in Peru to have increased by about one-third since 1999, Washington has generally praised Lima's commitment to eradication and interdiction. In May 2007, in part to placate the U.S. government, President García fired his agriculture minister, Juan José SALAZAR, who had taken a conciliatory attitude toward the country's organized coca growers' organizations who wished to see assistance in marketing the leaf for legal purposes.

President García courted the favor of the U.S. government. He traveled to the United States on several occasions to urge the Democratic Party leadership in the U.S. Congress to ratify a free trade agreement (FTA) that President George W. Bush and the Toledo government signed in April 2006. The agreement was ratified in December 2007, after passing the House by a 285–132 vote and the Senate by a 77–18 vote.

García's government sought tighter trade ties with Brazil, with a May 2008 agreement for petrochemical investments and a September 2008 offer from García to set up "a sort of bilateral free trade agreement." Peru's trade push continued with the November 2008 hosting, in Lima, of the fifteenth meeting of the 21-member Asia-Pacific Economic Forum (APEC). During his stay in Lima, Chinese president Hu Jintao signed ten accords for new investment in Peru. An FTA between the two was signed in Beijing in April 2009 and went into effect in March 2010.

Peru's relations with Venezuela and Bolivia remained poor in 2009. Manuel Rosales, President Hugo Chávez's main opponent in Venezuela's 2006 presidential elections, took up residence in Lima in April 2009. Peru gave asylum in May 2009 to a top minister of the Bolivian Gonzalo Sánchez de Lozada government in power from 2002 until 2003. A month later, after Bolivian president Evo Morales expressed solidarity with indigenous protesters clashing with Peruvian police and accused the government of "genocide," the García government recalled its ambassador from La Paz.

Relations with Chile reached a new low in November 2009 after the arrest by Peruvian authorities of a Peruvian air-force officer whom the government accused of spying for Chile. A Peruvian court put out an arrest order for two Chilean military officers for paying the Peruvian officer to reveal sensitive information. Peruvian officials reprimanded Chile, which denied the spying charge. Also in November, President García sent envoys to neighboring countries to boost his proposal that the 12 member nations of the Union of South American Nations (Unasur) cut military spending by 3 percent and arms purchases by 15 percent and create a regional peacekeeping force. The savings would be used to cut poverty and fight global warming. The president came under criticism on the seeming incongruence between his arms de-escalation and his 2010 budget, which included a 27 percent increase in defense spending over 2009.

In March 2010, Peru received Argentine president Cristina Fernández Kirchner on the first official state visit by that country's chief executive in 16 years. Kirchner came to repair relations that were damaged during Peru's 1995 border war with Ecuador. The two presidents signed a number of bilateral trade agreements.

Brazil and Peru drew closer in June 2010 when the two countries' presidents signed bilateral cooperation agreements covering science and technology, border integration, agricultural production, and water resources.

In June 2012, Peru and Colombia signed a FTA with the EU, which was ratified by the European Parliament in December. As tariffs are gradually eliminated on products and services, GDP is expected to increase by at least 1 percent.

Current issues. Social protests were frequent in 2008, including agrarian demonstrations in February, violent protests in a southern mining region in June, an anti–free-trade general strike on July 9, and a large-scale mobilization of indigenous groups in August. García government officials accused the pro-Humala political opposition of instigating the disturbances to destabilize the country. The indigenous mobilizations protested natural resource decrees that would have allowed indigenous reserves to sell concessions to foreign energy companies, an issue that the August 2008 repeal of two of the decrees failed to resolve.

On April 7, 2009, Peru's Supreme Court convicted 70-year-old former president Alberto Fujimori and sentenced him to 25 years in prison for his role in two massacres carried out by the Grupo Colina death squad, among other abuses. His conviction, plus a subsequent July conviction on corruption charges, left the pro-Fujimori political current with an uncertain future.

On May 16, 2009, President García declared a 30-day state of emergency in several Amazon-basin provinces, sending the armed forces to help the police deal with a growing wave of indigenous groups' protests, which had begun a month earlier and had grown to include about 30,000 people blockading roads, rivers, and pipelines. The protesters were opposing additional decrees, among a number that President García had issued in 2007, shortly before U.S. ratification of the countries' free-trade agreement, to ease foreign investment in such sectors as energy, mining, and forestry. Violence erupted in Bagua, Amazonas, on June 5, as clashes between indigenous protesters and police claimed at least 33 lives, 24 of them police officers.' Indigenous leaders claimed that their death toll was higher and that police had fired on them from helicopters. The Congress sought a censure vote on June 30 against Prime Minister Simon and Interior Minister Mercedes CABANILLAS for their handling of the matter; the vote failed only because 11 pro-Humala legislators were under suspension for their earlier role in a raucous protest in the Congress in support of the indigenous cause. While they survived the censure vote, Simon, Cabanillas, and several other cabinet ministers were drummed out less than two weeks later, amid a cabinet shakeup that saw Simon replaced with Congressional president Velásquez of the PAP, and Cabanillas replaced with independent politician Octavio SALAZAR. Salazar became the García government's fourth interior minister in a twelve-month period.

In September 2009, the government created a commission to investigate events surrounding May's indigenous uprising in Bagua with the aim of creating a consensual plan of development for the region and reconciling the indigenous population with the government. On September 30 seven-and-a-half years were added on to former president Alberto Fujimori's prison sentence when he was found guilty of wire-tapping the phones of journalists, businesspeople, and politicians; bribing 12 legislators to get them to join his Peru 2000 alliance; and bribing members of the news media for favorable coverage.

The commission set up to report on the Bagua violence released its report in January 2010, which said the government had misjudged animosity to the opening of the region to private investment. Indigenous rights umbrella group Interethnic Association for the Development of the Peruvian Rainforest (*Asociación Interétnica de Desarrollo de la Selva Peruana*—AIDESEP), which was one of the organizers of the protests and whose members sat on the commission, said the report had failed to investigate the incident deeply enough. In February the government, under pressure from AIDESEP, indefinitely suspended a company's exploratory mining activities in the Amazon region to avert more confrontation. In May Congress approved a law that required the government to consult indigenous communities on state business that affects their lands and traditions. The same month authorities arrested and charged Alberto PIZANGO Chota, the leader of AIDESEP, for fomenting the June 2009 violence between indigenous protestors and authorities.

Two drug reports released in 2010 criticized Peru's efforts to control cocaine coming out of the country, which in 2009 was the world's second largest producer of coca and its drug derivative. U.S. government and UN analyses found that Peru had seized fewer drugs in 2009 than in 2008, cocaine-manufacturing potential had increased, and coca acreage had expanded by 45 percent over the decade.

The specter of the deadly Bagua protests reappeared in April 2010 when two separate groups blocked the Pan-American Highway in southern Peru in protest to changes in mining laws and a proposed copper mine. Thousands of informal miners in Arequipa protested new mining exclusion zones and a prohibition on unregulated gold panning and river dredging. Five protestors were killed in clashes with police. Another protest occurred in the same department over a major copper mining project. Both protests ended after the government agreed to include local citizens in decisions concerning the region.

The Peru Wins Alliance won the legislative balloting on April 10, 2011, but failed to gain an absolute majority in the Congress. Discussions to form a governing coalition with former president Toledo's Peru Possible Alliance fell apart in July. However, a subsequent Peru Wins Alliance government included some members of Peru Possible. Ten candidates contested the concurrent presidential balloting on April 10. No candidate won an absolute majority, and Humala (Peru Wins) and Keiko Fujimori (Force 2011) advanced to runoff balloting on June 5. Humala narrowly won the polling and was sworn in on July 28. He appointed a cabinet dominated by moderates in an effort to assuage fears that he would implement a radical, antimarket economic and social agenda that would scare off foreign investment.

A wave of resignations in late 2011 brought turnover within the government. On December 5, Second Vice President Omar CHEHADE's seat in the Congress was suspended by a vote of the legislature. Facing corruption accusations, Chehade refused to resign the vice presidency despite increasing pressure by the legislature and calls by the president to leave office. The crisis highlighted the inability of the president to remove either of the vice presidents. Five days later, Prime Minister Salomón Lerner Ghitis resigned over the government's mishandling of a mining dispute. Humala appointed Minister of the Interior Oscar Valdés in his place and reshuffled the cabinet at that time. Chehade finally caved to pressure the following month, handing in his resignation from the vice presidency on January 17, 2012, but he retained his seat in Congress. As of September 2013, the second vice presidency remains vacant.

In February, the Peruvian government confirmed the capture of Florindo Flores, known as "Comrade Artemio," the last member of the Shining Path's central committee who had not yet been killed or imprisoned. Two months later, Humala declared the Shining Path "defeated" upon the capture of Freddy Arenas, known as Braulio, the leader in the Alto Huallaga Valley. The blow proved not to be fatal to the remnants of the organization, however. Later that month, Shining Path rebels captured several gas workers in Cusco (reports varied from 30 to 36 captives). In response, the government deployed 1,500 troops, the largest military action against the Shining Path since the 1990s. Between April and May, the group killed nine Peruvian police officers. Estimated to be about 500 people strong, the group was nowhere near as large as it was at its peak; however, the resurgence of activity was surprising to many who considered it near extinction. Meanwhile, the Maoist group's political arm, Movadef, also began to reemerge, with reports that rallies were held in poor neighborhoods and on university campuses in September. The government blocked the group from registering as a political party in an effort to prevent its growth.

In May 2012, Humala declared a state of emergency after eight days of protests over Xstrata's proposed expansion of the Tintaya copper mine in Cusco. Two people were killed and at least 50, including 30 police officers, were injured in the clash. Shortly after the 30-day state of emergency in Cusco ended in June, conflict erupted over the $4.8 billion Conga gold mine in Cajamarca, with locals protesting that the mine would contaminate the water. On July 3, the government declared a state of emergency in the region, the second use of the measure in just five weeks. Five civilians were killed as the protests escalated.

Following the government's crackdown on the demonstrations, several prominent members of Congress called for Prime Minister Valdés' resignation, arguing that he should have encouraged mediation rather than force. On July 23, Valdés stepped down as part of the second cabinet reshuffle in the first year of Humala's presidency. Juan Jiménez was appointed in his place.

In October 2012, Alberto Fujimori, currently serving a 25-year sentence for corruption and human rights violations, filed a petition for amnesty on humanitarian grounds because of poor health. Humala rejected the request in June 2013, in line with a recommendation by a presidential commission, noting that the illness is not terminal. The decision led to greater political tension with the main opposition party Fuerza Popular (formerly Fuerza 2011), led by Keiko FUJIMORI.

Humala announced in January 2013 the establishment of a new body to combat high-level political corruption, comprising the president of national congress, cabinet heads, and judicial leaders.

In July 2013, Shining Path founder Florindo FLORES was sentenced to life in prison. The following month, three rebels were killed by security forces.

On July 17, Congress appointed an ombudsman, six members to the Constitutional Court, and three new Central Reserve Bank directors, all candidates selected by the leading congressional parties. The vote stirred controversy, attracting criticism for threatening the political independence of the institutions. Several thousand marched in protest, and on July 24, Congress rescinded the appointments.

POLITICAL PARTIES AND GROUPS

Most of the political parties active before the 1968 coup were of comparatively recent vintage, the principal exception being the Peruvian affiliate of APRA (PAP, below), which was alternately outlawed and legalized beginning in the early 1930s. While failing to capture the presidency until 1985, it contributed to the success of other candidates and was the nucleus of a powerful opposition coalition that controlled both houses of Congress during Belaúnde's 1963–1968 presidency.

During the decade after 1968, the status of the parties fluctuated, many being permitted a semilegal existence while denied an opportunity to engage in electoral activity. Most, except those of the extreme left, were allowed to register before the Constituent Assembly election of June 1978, with further relaxation occurring before the presidential and legislative balloting of May 1980, in which 20 groups participated. By contrast, only 9 groups presented candidates in 1985, with the PAP, the IU, the Democratic Convergence, and the AP collectively capturing 96.9 percent of the valid votes.

Virtually all of the major opposition parties either boycotted or failed to qualify for the Democratic Constituent Congress election of November 22, 1992, at which the regime-supportive C-90–NM won a majority of seats, with the remainder scattered among 8 other parties. Subsequent elections were contested by an average of more than 20 parties or party coalitions.

Presidential Party:

Peru Wins Alliance (*Alianza Gana Perú*). Formed in 2010 to support the presidential candidacy of Ollanta Humala, the left-wing Peru Wins Alliance was the successor of the Nationalist Union Party for Peru (*Partido Nacionalista Unión por el Perú*—PNUP). The PNUP was launched by Humala in late 2005 as a coalition of the UPP and PNP. Thereafter, it was frequently referenced as the UPP or the UPP/PNP rather than the PNUP, as the two parties maintained distinct identities. The coalition was the largest vote-getter in the 2006 legislative elections, with 21.2 percent of valid votes. Internal dissent caused two new parties, the Popular Bloc (*Bloque Popular*—BP) and Democratic Commitment (*Compromiso Democrático*—CD), to splinter from the UPP in 2008. In 2010 Humala formed the Peru Wins Alliance with the PNP and four other left-wing parties. During the 2011 campaign Humala offered reassurances that his presidency would not be extremist, in an effort to attract more moderate voters. In balloting on April 10 the Peru Wins Alliance secured congressional 47 seats. After none of the presidential candidates secured a majority, Humala won the presidency with a bare majority of 51.5 percent in a June 5 runoff election. Though negotiations to gain an absolute majority by forming an alliance with Peru Possible dissolved, several Peru Possible members were appointed in the Peru Wins Alliance government.

A trilateral effort to unite with Peru Possible and Popular Force to elect the Constitutional Court in July 2013 (see Current issues, above) dissolved, casting the relationship with Peru Possible into question.

Leader: Lt. Col. (Ret.) Ollanta HUMALA Tasso (President of the Republic).

Peru Nationalist Party (*Partido Nacionalista Peruano*—PNP). The PNP is the political arm of the Etnocacerista Movement (*Movimiento Etnocacerista*—ME), founded by former army major Antauro HUMALA, Ollanta Humala's younger brother, who participated in an abortive uprising against former president Fujimori. The ME is an openly racist, antiwhite formation, claiming to reflect the Incan moral code of Marshal Andrés CACERES, a hero of the 19th-century war with Chile. The PNP has grown distant from the UPP, which has been more moderate in its opposition to the García government. In mid-2009 the PNP had 23 seats in the Congress, making it the largest party in the bloc supporting Ollanta Humala. In September 2009 the PNP legislators were alone in opposing the expansion of the Congress from 120 members to 130, arguing that it would lead to more inefficiency and unnecessary expense.

Leader: Ollanta HUMALA Tasso (President of the Republic).

Socialist Party of Peru (*Partido Socialista del Perú*—PSP). The PSP is a left-wing party organized in 1979. It ran in 1995 under the Opening for a National Development–Socialist Party (*Apertura para el Desarrollo Nacional–Partido Socialista*) list but won only 0.3 percent of the legislative vote.

During the 1990s, PSP leader Javier Diez Canseco was a vigorous opponent of the Fujimori regime and, as a member of Congress, participated in investigations of alleged human rights violations by members of both the Shining Path and the Peruvian Armed Forces. The PSP joined the Peru Win Alliance ahead of the 2011 balloting.

Leaders: Javier DIEZ Canseco (2006 presidential candidate), Julio Sergio CASTRO Gomez, Aída García NARANJO Morales (Secretary General).

Other parties in the Peru Wins Alliance include the **Peruvian Communist Party** (*Partido Comunista Peruano*—PCP), the **Revolutionary Socialist Party** (*Partido Socialista Revolucionario*—PSR), and the **Political Movement Socialist Voice** (*Movimiento Politico Voz Socialista*).

Other Legislative Parties:

Popular Force (*Fuerza Popular*). The right-wing Force 2011 was formed in 2010 to support the presidential candidacy of Keiko Fujimori, the daughter of the former president. Force 2011 was the successor to the **Alliance for the Future** (*Alianza por el Futuro*—AF). The AF was formed in 2005 as a coalition of the two pro-Fujimori groups below, in anticipation that the former president's attempt to reenter the country and seek reelection as head of his party (see *Sí Cumple,* below) would be denied. With 13.1 percent of all votes cast, the group finished fourth and won 13 legislative seats in 2006, including 1 by Keiko Fujimori, who received more votes than any other single legislative candidate. Alberto Fujimori's extradition and trial was an uncomfortable topic for Peruvian politicians, whose agendas at times required support from the AF congressional bloc. In July 2008, *Fujimorista* support proved crucial to the election of the PAP's Javier Velásquez to the presidency of the Congress; opposition figures alleged that the vote coincided with a relaxing of the conditions of Fujimori's imprisonment. Leading legislator Keiko Fujimori declared her intention in 2008 to fuse the pro-Fujimori parties into a single entity, Fuerza 2011, to compete in the 2011 presidential and congressional elections. Keiko Fujimori was selected as the alliance's presidential candidate for the 2011 election. Her platform featured her intent to pardon her father if elected. She also advocated bolstering foreign investment and a transparent tax system. She was placed second in the presidential balloting, while Force 2011 was placed second in the legislative polling and secured 37 seats in the Congress.

In January 2013, Fujimori announced the party would be renamed Popular Force.

Leaders: Keiko FUJIMORI (Party Leader and 2011 presidential candidate), Martha Gladys CHÁVEZ Cossio (2005 presidential candidate), Santiago FUJIMORI (*Sí Cumple*).

New Majority (*Nueva Mayoría*—NM). The NM was launched in 1992 by a group of independents who presented a joint list with *Cambio 90* for the 1992 and 1995 polls, participated in the *Perú 2000* coalition, and remained allied with C90 in 2001. By 2006 the C90 designation had given way to NM.

Leader: Martha Gladys CHÁVEZ Cossio (2005 presidential candidate).

He Delivers *(Sí Cumple*). *Sí Cumple* was founded by former president Alberto Fujimori in 1998 as *Vamos Vecino* (Let's Go Neighbor), adopting its current name in 2005. In 2000 the party joined with C90 and the NM in a Peru 2000 Alliance to support Fujimori's reelection. In 2005 the group again joined with C90 and NM in *Aliaga Sí Cumple,* but the action was rejected by the National Jury of Elections and the other two groups contesting the 2006 poll as the Alliance for the Future (see above).

Leaders: Alberto FUJIMORI (Former President of the Republic, imprisoned), Absalón VASQUEZ, Carlos ORELLANA Quintanilla (Secretary General).

National Renewal (*Renovación Nacional*—Renovación). This rightist party was founded by Rafael Rey in 1992. It formed part of the UN coalition in the 2001 and 2006 elections. It split with UN later in 2006 and spent two years as part of the Parliamentary Alliance (above) until it joined the newly formed GANA in 2008. Rey has served in the García government as minister of production, ambassador to Italy (briefly in 2009), and minister of defense. Rey was one of Fujimori's vice-presidential candidates in 2011.

Leader: Rafael REY (President and 2011 vice-presidential candidate).

Peru Possible (*Perú Posible*). The Peru Possible Alliance was formed prior to the 2011 national elections by the members of the **Parliamentary Alliance** (*Alianza Parliamentaria—Alianza*), which was the successor of the Center Front (*Frente del Centro*—FC). The FC was formed before the 2006 election as a coalition of the AP (Popular Action), *Somos Perú,* and the CNI (*Coordinadora Nacional de Independientes*). Its candidates received 7.1 percent of the votes cast in the 2006 legislative elections, finishing fifth and winning 5 seats. Following the election, it was joined by the two legislators from President Toledo's Peru Possible party, making a total of 7 seats. The coalition also included *Renovación* between 2006 and 2008. As a temporary electoral alliance, the FC was formally dissolved after the 2006 elections and replaced by Peru Possible. Toledo was the alliance's 2011 presidential candidate; he was placed third in the balloting. Meanwhile, the alliance secured 21 seats in the legislative elections. Efforts to create a parliamentary alliance with the Peru Wins Alliance after the 2011 election were abandoned. Following controversy over the appointment of the Constitutional Court (see Current issues, above), five party members defected in July 2013 and formed the **Regional Union** (*Unión Regional*—below).

Leaders: Alejandro TOLEDO (2011 presidential candidate), Drago Guillermo KISIC Wagner, Victor Andrés GARCÍA Belaúnde.

Popular Action (*Acción Popular*—AP). Founded by Fernando Belaúnde TERRY in 1956, the moderately rightist AP captured the presidency in 1963 and served as the government party until the 1968 coup. Democratic, nationalist, and dedicated to the extension of social services, AP sought to mobilize public energies for development on Peru's terms. After the 1968 coup, the party split, a mainstream faction remaining loyal to Belaúnde and another, headed by former vice president Edgardo SEONE Corrales, collaborating with the military junta. Belaúnde was returned to office in the 1980 election, winning 45.4 percent of the votes cast, while the AP captured 98 of 180 Chamber seats and 26 of 60 seats in the Senate. However, in a massive voter reversal, the party won only one provincial city in the municipal elections in November 1983 and ran fourth in the 1985 balloting, obtaining only 10 Chamber and 5 Senate seats. The party supported Vargas LLOSA for the presidency in 1990 as a member of the Democratic Front. A shadow of its former self, the AP won only 4 congressional seats in 1995, while its presidential candidate, Raúl Diez CANSECO, drew a vote share of 1.6 percent. In April 2000 AP presidential candidate, Víctor Andrés García Belaúnde, secured a minuscule 0.4 percent of the vote, while the party's legislative representation dropped to 3 seats. It won an equal number in 2001. Former leader Terry died in June 2002. AP candidates accounted for 4 of the 5 seats won by the FC coalition in the 2006 legislative elections.

Leader: Victor Andrés GARCÍA Belaúnde (President).

Peru Possible (*Perú Posible*). *Perú Posible* leader Alejandro Toledo entered the 1995 presidential race as organizer of a group styled Possible Nation (*País Posible*), which joined with the **Democratic Coordination** (*Coordinadora Democrática*—Code) in an alignment registered as *Code–País Posible.* The renamed formation was credited with a second-place legislative finish (29 seats) in 2000, Toledo himself withdrawing from the presidential runoff of May 28 because of anticipated fraud. He secured a 53.1 percent victory in the second-round balloting on June 3, 2001. A group of *Perú Posible* dissidents subsequently organized as **Peru Now** (*Perú Ahora*). Running without a coalition, the party fared poorly in the 2006 elections; it decided not to field a presidential candidate, and its candidates for the legislature received only 4.1 percent of the votes cast, finishing sixth and winning only 2 seats. The party made a similarly poor showing in the 2006 municipal and regional elections. Toledo ran as the party's presidential candidate in the 2011 election. After he came in third in the presidential elections, Toledo supported Humala of the Peru Wins Alliance in the runoff balloting.

Leaders: Juan SHEPUT (Party Leader), David WAISMAN (Former Second Vice President of the Republic), Alejandro TOLEDO Manrique (Former President of the Republic, and 2011 presidential candidate), Luis SOLARI de la Fuente (Former Prime Minister).

We Are Peru (*Somos Perú*). *Somos Perú* is an outgrowth of the *Somos Lima* movement, organized by former independent Alberto Andrade Carmona after his capture of the Lima mayorship in November 1995. The party's supporters include some former members of the defunct right-wing Solidarity and Democracy (*Solidaridad y Democracia*—Sode), which had been led by Javier SILVA Ruete. In early 1999 Andrade led in public opinion polls for the 2000 presidential election but dropped to a distant third in the balloting of April 2000. For the 2001 presidential poll it joined with the CD in supporting the candidacy of Jorge SANTISTEVAN de Noriega. Andrade is the only We Are Peru member of Peru's Congress.

In March 2013, Fernando Andrade, brother of the late party founder, was elected party president, after Alberto Andrade's wife was kept off the ballot by a controversial technicality.

Leaders: Fernando ANDRADE (Party President), Alberto ANDRADE Carmona (2000 presidential candidate).

Alliance for the Great Change (*Alianza Por El Gran Cambio*). The alliance was established in 2010 to support the presidential campaign of former prime minister Pedro Pablo Kuczynski. Kuczynski was placed fourth in the balloting, while the alliance secured 12 seats. Following divisions within the alliance over the election of officers for the Constitutional Court, five Congress members defected, marking the departure of the **National Restoration** (*Restauracion Nacional*—RN) and the **Humanist Party** (*Partido Humanista*). Left with seven seats, the alliance regrouped under the banner **PPC-APP**, led by Alberto Beingolea.

Leaders: Alberto BEINGOLEA (Party President), Pedro Pablo KUCZYNSKI (2011 presidential candidate).

Christian People's Party (*Partido Popular Cristiano*—PPC). The PPC was formed in the wake of the split in the now defunct PDC in 1967, with Luis Bedoya Reyes leading a conservative faction out of the parent group. The party was runner-up to the PAP in the Constituent Assembly election of June 1978 and was placed third in the 1980 presidential and legislative races, after which it joined the Belaúnde government by accepting two ministerial appointments. For the 1985 balloting it formed an alliance with Townsend Ezcurra's MBH (Hayista Bases Movement), styled the Democratic Convergence (*Convergencia Democrática*—Conde), which secured 7 Senate and 12 Chamber seats. It participated in the 1990 campaign as a member of Fredemo, which won a plurality of one-third in each house of Congress. Initially endorsing its secretary general for the 1995 presidential race, it subsequently backed the UPP's Pérez de Cuéllar. In the congressional poll it won only 3 seats, none of which was retained in 2000.

For the 2001 campaign, it served as the core of the UN coalition, which included the PSN (National Solidarity Party), RN (National Restoration), and *Renovación*. The UN secured 15 congressional seats, while its leader, Lourdes Flores Nano, placed third in the presidential race. Led by Flores, the PPC again participated in the UN coalition in 2006, with Flores finishing third in the first round of presidential voting despite leading in the pre-election polls. With 15.3 percent of the vote and 17 congressional seats, the UN finished third.

Antero Flores, a top PPC leader who frequently jockeyed for position with Lourdes Flores, became the García government's defense minister in a December 2007 cabinet shake-up. Flores served in this position until July 2009. The UN political bloc effectively disbanded in August 2008, with Flores citing ideological differences with the PSN and its leader, Lima mayor Luis CASTAÑEDA, whom she accused of being too accommodating to the García government. The UN continues to exist in name as a legislative grouping of PPC members and a handful of independent legislators, totaling 13 seats in the Congress. The party selected Flores to be its presidential candidate for the 2011 election, but owing to a weak showing in polls, she withdrew. Two legislators defected from the party in August 2013.

Leaders: Raúl CASTRO Stagnaro (President of the Party), Rafael YAMASHIRO Oré (Secretary General).

Alliance for Progress (*Alianza para el Progreso*—APP). Established in 2001 by César Acuña Peralta, the APP joined.

Leader: César ACUÑA Peralta.

Regional Union (*Unión Regional*). The Regional Union parliamentary bloc formed in July 2013 with three defectors from the Alliance for the Great Change and five from Peru Possible.

National Restoration (*Restauracion Nacional*—RN). The RN is a small formation led by evangelicals. It won two legislative seats in 2006, finishing seventh with 4.0 percent of the votes cast. After a poor showing in the 2006 local elections—in which most of the party's few winning candidates were not from an evangelical background—the party expelled its leader Humberto Lay Sun in early 2007. Later in the year, however, Lay reestablished himself as the party's leader. It joined the Alliance for the Great Change in 2010; however, in July 2013, Lay withdrew the RN from the Alliance and joined the Regional Union, reportedly to focus on the political work within the party.

Leader: Humberto LAY SUN.

Humanist Party (*Partido Humanista*). The Humanist Party's leader and sole legislator Yehude Simon defected from the Alliance for the Great Change in 2013, citing ideological differences. Despite offers from the Peru Wins Alliance to create an alliance, the Humanist Party opted to remain independent.

Leader: Yehude SIMON.

National Solidarity Alliance (*Alianza Solidaridad Nacional*). The National Solidarity Alliance is a center-right grouping that was created in 2010. The alliance's 2011 presidential candidate was former Lima mayor Luís Castañeda Lossio. The alliance gained nine seats in the 2011 elections. After he was eliminated from the run-off balloting, Castañada endorsed Keiko Fujimori of Force 2011. Enrique WONG defected from the Alliance for the Great Change in July 2013, joining the NSA.

Leader: Luís CASTAÑEDA Lossio (2011 presidential candidate).

National Solidarity Party (*Partido de Solidaridad Nacional*—PSN). Formally registered in early 1999, the PSN served in 2000 as the vehicle for the presidential campaign of Luís Castañeda Lossio, former head of the social security system. During the 2001 campaign Castañeda withdrew in favor of the UN's Flores Nano. In October 2005 Castañeda announced he would not contend for the position in 2006; shortly thereafter, he was reelected as mayor of Lima. Flores Nano split with the PSN in 2008, accusing Castañeda of supporting the García government in exchange for central government funding of municipal projects in Lima. The popular Castañeda initially led the field of 2011 presidential candidates in polls but was placed fifth in the balloting.

Leaders: Luís CASTAÑEDA Lossio (President of the Party, Former Mayor of Lima, and 2000 and 2011 presidential candidate), Jose LUNA Gálvez (Secretary General).

Union for Peru (*Unión por el Perú*—UPP). The UPP was formed as a campaign vehicle for Javier Pérez de Cuéllar following the announcement by the former UN secretary general on August 18, 1994, that he would stand for the presidency in 1995. The UPP candidate ran a distant second to Fujimori, with 21.8 percent of the vote. Though the UPP secured just 0.3 percent in the presidential election of April 2000, Pérez de Cuéllar was named prime minister in the Paniagua administration of November 2000.

Pérez de Cuéllar withdrew from the party following the designation of Humala as its 2006 standard bearer. The UPP received the largest percentage of voting in the 2006 legislative elections, with 21.2 percent of the total valid votes cast.

Leaders: Eduardo ESPINOZA Ramos (President), Aldo Vladimiro ESTRADA Choque (First Vice President), José VEGA Antonio (Secretary General).

Change 90 (*Cambio 90*—C90). *Cambio 90* was organized before the 1990 campaign as a political vehicle for Alberto Fujimori. While Fujimori secured a majority of the second-round presidential votes, C90 ran third in both upper and lower house legislative contests. Before the 1992 election, it formed a coalition with the *Nueva Mayoría* (below), which won a 55 percent majority of CCD seats on a vote share of 38 percent. In 1995 Fujimori was reelected with 64.3 percent of the vote, while the ruling coalition decimated the traditional parties by securing 51.4 percent of the valid ballots. For the 2000 balloting C90 headed a coalition styled *Perú 2000,* which included *Vamos Vecino* (under *Sí Cumple,* below), and was credited with winning 52 of 120 congressional seats. It was reduced to 3 seats in 2001. By the 2006 elections C90 had largely given way to the *Nueva Mayoría* among the pro-Fujimori bloc. The remaining C90 members refused to endorse Keiko Fujimori and instead joined the National Solidarity Alliance.

The small **Always Together** (*Siempre Unidos*) also joined the alliance.

Peruvian Aprista Party (*Partido Aprista Peruano*—PAP). The PAP was launched in 1930 as the Peruvian affiliate of the regionwide American Popular Revolutionary Alliance (*Alianza Popular Revolucionaria Americana*—APRA), formed six years earlier in Mexico. APRA was initially a radical left-wing movement that attracted substantial mass support. Its Peruvian branch (also frequently referenced as APRA) was not legalized until 1945. Subsequently, it mellowed into a mildly left-of-center, middle-class grouping with a strong labor base. Despite long-standing antagonism between the PAP and the military, its principal figure, Víctor Raúl Haya de la Torre, was permitted to return from exile in 1969 and was designated president of the Constituent Assembly after the party had won a substantial plurality in the election of June 18, 1978. Following his death in August 1979, Armando VILLANUEVA del Campo assumed party leadership. Decisively defeated in the 1980 balloting, the party subsequently split into a left-wing faction headed by Villanueva and a right-wing faction headed by second vice-presidential candidate Andrés TOWNSEND Ezcurra, who was formally expelled from the party in January 1981 and later formed the Hayista Bases Movement (*Movimiento de Bases Hayista*—MBH).

While he remained an influential party figure, Villanueva's control of the organization ended in 1983, with the rise of Alan García Pérez, a centrist, who in 1985 became the first Aprista leader to assume the presidency of the republic. His widespread popularity was viewed as the principal reason for the party's unprecedented sweep of municipal elections in November 1986. Unable to resolve the country's burgeoning economic problems, García suffered a dramatic loss in popular support during 1988 and resigned the party presidency at a congress in late December, with the office itself being abolished. The delegates then voted to install his rival, former prime minister Luis Alva Castro, as general secretary. Alva Castro placed third in the 1990 presidential race.

Following the 1992 coup, former president García was granted political asylum in Colombia, which in early 1993 rejected a request by the Fujimori government that he be extradited to face charges of personal enrichment while in office. Shortly thereafter, the Aprista leadership stripped García of his position as secretary general, granting him the honorary title of "secretary general in exile." It then proceeded to name a tripartite interim secretariat consisting of an *alanista,* former prime minister Villanueva; a García opponent, Alva Castro; and an "equidistant" chair, Luis Alberto SÁNCHEZ Sánchez. This did not satisfy the more radical *Generación en Marcha* "renewalist" and *Nueva Generación* leaders, who pressed for a party plenum to elect new officials.

In November 1993, García announced that he had applied for Colombian citizenship, and in August 1994, resigned, after a secret Cayman Islands bank account in the name of a fugitive businessman to whom he was linked was discovered. However, Agustin MANTILLA Campos, elected secretary general in August 1994, and Mercedes Cabanillas, the party's 1995 standard-bearer, were both *alanistas.*

By plunging to less than 5 percent of the vote in April 1995, the party faced the loss of its registration and the humiliating need to collect 100,000 signatures in support of relegalization. It responded by appointing Germán PARRA Herrera as head of an "action command" charged with reorganizing the party. He later resigned in October, claiming that other party members were refusing to recognize the gravity of the crisis. The party leadership subsequently reverted to Alva Castro, assisted by a political commission.

In early 2001, the Supreme Court revoked a sentence for corruption that had been passed against García in absentia, saying that the statute of limitations had run its course. The former president subsequently returned for a reelection bid, losing to Alejandro Toledo Manrique of Peru Possible (below) in the second-round poll of June 3.

At the first-round presidential poll of April 19, 2006, García placed second with a 24.3 percent vote share but went on to defeat Ollanta Humala of the UPP (below) in a runoff on June 4. The PAP received the second-largest vote percentage in the 2006 legislative elections, with 20.6 percent of the total valid votes cast, only 0.6 percentage points behind the UPP. Its legislators hold 36 congressional seats. The PAP fared poorly in November 2006 municipal and regional elections, but the party maintained the presidency of Peru's Congress in 2007–2009, with support from the pro-Fujimori Alliance for the Future and Humala's UPP. A string of high-profile corruption scandals in 2010 involving members of PAP, including the party's two cosecretaries general, brought into doubt its prospects for local and regional elections in 2010 and national balloting in 2011. President Garcia had not yet settled on a potential successor to be the party's presidential candidate as of the latter half of 2010, but his prime minister, Javier Velásquez Quesquén, resigned on September 13 and became the PAP's vice-presidential candidate. Mercedes ARAÓZ Fernández was chosen as the PAP's presidential candidate. She withdrew from the campaign on January 17, citing lack of support in opinion polls.

Leaders: Alan Gabriel Ludwig GARCÍA Pérez (Former President of the Republic and President of the Party), Jorge Alfonso Alejandro DEL CASTILLO Gálvez (Former Prime Minister and Secretary General), Ángel Javier VELÁSQUEZ Quesquén (Former Prime Minister and President of Political Committee).

Other Parties Contesting the 2011 Election:

Other parties that participated in the 2011 national elections included the following (unless noted otherwise, the parties received less than 1 percent of the vote): **Radical Change** (*Cambio Radical*), which received 2.7 percent of the vote in the legislative balloting; the **Fonavist Party** (*Fonavistas Des Perú*), which secured 1.3 percent of the vote; the **Forward Party** (*Partido Politico Adelante*); the **Decentralist Party Social Force** (*Partido Decentralista Fuerza Social*); the **National Force Party** (*Partido Fuerza Nacional*); the **National Awakening Party** (*Partido Despertar Nacional*); and the **Justice, Technology, Ecology Party** (*Justicia, Tenologia, Ecologia*), whose presidential candidate, Humberto PINAZO, was placed sixth in the 2011 presidential balloting.

Other Parties:

National Coordination of Independents (*Coordinadora Nacional de Independientes*—CNI). The CNI, a grouping of independents organized before the 2006 elections, ran as part of the Center Front coalition (see *Alianza,* above). The CNI failed to elect any of its candidates to Peru's Congress in 2006. In January 2010 former prime minister Pedro Pablo KUCZYNSKI announced that he was considering running in the 2011 presidential election under the CNI banner, but instead, he ran as the candidate for the Alliance for the Great Change.

Leaders: Drago Guillermo KISIC Wagner, Gonzálo AGUIRRE Arriz.

Independent Moralizing Front (*Frente Independiente Moralizador*—FIM). The FIM was launched before the 1995 election by Luis Fernando Olivera Vega, a former investigator for the state prosecutor's office who had pursued a six-year crusade to bring former president Alan García to trial for alleged misdeeds while in office. The party won 6 congressional seats in 1995, 9 in 2000, and 11 in 2001. Olivera finished fourth, with 9.9 percent of the vote, in the 2001 presidential balloting. The party briefly endorsed Peru Possible candidates in 2006, then chose to run its own candidates. Olivera ultimately dropped out of the presidential balloting to focus on the legislative campaign. Neither he nor other FIM candidates won any seats.

Leader: Luis Fernando OLIVERA Vega (2001 presidential candidate).

Decentralizing Coalition (*Concertación Decentralista*—CD). The center-left CD was formed before the 2006 election as a coalition of the **Party for Social Democracy–Compromise Peru** (*Partido por la Democracia Social–Compromiso Perú*) and the **Peruvian Humanist Movement Party** (*Partido Movimiento Humanista Peruano*—PMHP). The party has since been inactive.

Leader: Susana María del Carmen VILLARÁN de la Puente (President and 2006 presidential candidate).

Democratic Force (*Fuerza Democrática*—FA). The FA was launched in 1998 to compete at the municipal level. It won a small number of local positions in 2006, mainly in Peru's remote Amazon basin region.

Leader: Alberto BOREA.

Popular Agricultural Front of Peru (*Frente Popular Agrícola del Perú*—Frepap). In the 1995 election Frepap was known as the Peruvian Agricultural and Popular Front (*Frente Agrícola y Popular del Perú*—FAPP). It won two congressional seats in 2000 and none in 2001 or 2006.

Leader: Alfredo GÁLVEZ (2006 presidential candidate).

Country Project (*Proyecto Pais*—PP). The PP is a "law and order" group founded in 1998 by Marco Antonio Arrunategui Cevallos.

Leader: Marco Antonio ARRUNATEGUI Cevallos (2001 and 2006 presidential candidate).

Andean Renaissance (*Renacimiento Andino*—RA). The RA was launched in 2001 by Ciro Alfredo Gálvez Herrera, who won less than 1 percent of the vote that year. It withdrew from the 2006 presidential election to avoid drawing support from Lourdes Flores.

Leader: Ciro Alfredo GÁLVEZ Herrera (2001 and 2006 presidential candidate).

Popular Bloc (*Bloque Popular*—BP). On August 6, 2008, after a series of disagreements with the UPP, particularly over leading UPP members' support of PAP legislators to serve as president of the Congress, a group of eight more radical legislators split from the party and declared themselves the Patriotic Peruvian Unity—Popular Bloc.

Leader: Antonio LEÓN (Spokesperson).

Democratic Commitment (*Compromiso Democrático*—CD). Twelve days after the BP split from the UPP, another group of three UPP legislators followed suit, citing similar disagreements, and formed the CD.

Leader: Washington ZEBALLOS Gámez (Coordinator).

Also participating in the 2006 poll were the **National Justice Party** (*Partido Justicia Nacional*—PJN), led by Jamie SALINAS; **Advance the Country—Social Integration Party** (*Avanza País—Partido de Integración Social*—AP-PIS), led by Ulisés HUMALA, Ollanta Humala's brother; the **New Left Movement** (*Movimiento Nueva Izquierdo*—MNI), led by Alberto MORENO; the **With Force Peru** (*Con Fuerza Perú*—CFP), led by Pedro KOECHLIN Von Stein; **Peru Now** (*Perú Ahora*), led by Luis GUERRERO Figueroa; the **Democratic Reconstruction** (*Reconstrucción Democrática*—RD); the **Peruvian Resurgence** (*Resurgimiento Peruano*—RP); the **And It's Called Peru** (*Y se llama Perú*); and the **Let's Make Progress Peru** (*Progresemos Perú*—PP).

Land and Liberty (*Tierra y Libertad*—TL) is a new leftwing movement founded on June 30, 2009, in the wake of clashes with indigenous protesters (see Current issues, above), by Catholic priest Marco ARANA and Pedro FRANCKE. Arana launched an unsuccessful campaign for the 2011 presidential race on his foundation of liberation theology, arguing for environmental rights and social justice.

Leaders: Marco ARANA, Pedro FRANCKE.

Guerrilla and Terrorist Organizations:

Shining Path (*Sendero Luminoso*). The *Sendero Luminoso* (also translated as Luminous Path) originated at Ayacucho University as a small Maoist group led by a former philosophy instructor Dr. Manuel Abimael Guzmán Reinoso. During 1980 it was involved in a number of bombings in Lima, Ayacucho, Cuzco, and other provincial towns in southern Peru, causing property damage only. About 170 of its followers were arrested in October 1980 and January 1981, but most were freed in a daring raid on the Ayacucho police barracks in March 1982. Thereafter, guerrilla activity in the region intensified, including the assassination of a number of local officials and alleged police informants. While the insurgency appeared to remain localized (apart from sporadic terrorist attacks in Lima), the government felt obliged to order a major sweep through the affected provinces by 1,500 military and police units at the end of the year. Subsequently, the rebellion showed no sign of diminishing, despite the imposition of military rule in the departments of Ayacucho, Apurímac, Huancavelica, Huánuco, and part of San Martín. By late 1987 more than 10,000 deaths, on both sides, had been reported since the insurgency began, and the organization, estimated to encompass at least 3,000 members, had become increasingly active in urban areas. Its reputed second-in-command, Osman MOROTE Barrionuevo, was captured by Lima police in June 1988 and subsequently sentenced to 15 years' imprisonment. The insurgency intensified during 1989 as the nation's economy approached collapse; however, its adherents were surprisingly unsuccessful in a campaign to limit participation at municipal elections in November. Guzmán himself was captured in Lima on September 12, 1992, and sentenced by a secret military tribunal to life imprisonment, while his principal deputy, Edmundo Daniel Cox Beauzeville, was apprehended in August 1993.

In January 1994, it was reported that *Sendero Luminoso* had split into two factions, one loyal to the imprisoned Guzmán and another, styled the **Red Path** (*Sendero Rojo*), committed to continuing the rebellion under the leadership of Oscar Ramírez Durand (a.k.a. "Camarada Feliciano"). By March, however, nearly 4,100 alleged *senderistas* had surrendered under a 1992 "Repentance Law," while a number of Ramírez's lieutenants were apprehended during the ensuing three months. By midyear, while 66 of the country's 155 provinces remained under a state of emergency, guerrilla activity was reported to be confined largely to three areas: some marginal districts of the capital, the highlands of Lima department, and the Huallaga valley jungle region. In August 1997 *Sendero Luminoso* guerrillas captured about 30 oil workers in a remote jungle area 200 miles east of Lima; two days later the hostages were released after their French-based employer sent supplies of food, medicine, and clothing. The deputy leader of *Sendero Rojo,* Pedro Domingo QUINTEROS Ayllón (a.k.a. "Camarada Luis"), was captured in April 1998, while the senior military leader, Juan Carlos RIOS, was arrested in December, by which time the grouping was described as "largely impotent" as the result of the government's campaign. Ramírez Durand, the formation's last major leader, was captured in July 1999 and sentenced to life imprisonment.

Bomb attacks in March 2002, preceding a visit to Lima by U.S. President Bush, were attributed to a *Sendero Luminoso* faction. From mid-2003, *Sendero* activity was reported by apparently drastically depleted guerrilla units.

In November 2004, a retrial of Guzmán and his lieutenants was launched, after a constitutional tribunal had overturned their original convictions on the grounds that they should have been tried in a civilian rather than a military court. However, the proceedings collapsed when two of the three presiding judges stepped down because of involvement in earlier rulings, with a second retrial opening in Lima in September 2005. On October 13, 2006, Guzmán and several lieutenants were sentenced to life in prison for "aggravated terrorism."

Sendero activity continued at a low but significant level in 2007 and 2008, including two ambushes that took the lives of police and civilian coca-regulation authorities as well as a November 2007 attack that destroyed a police station in Apurímac. Most analysts believed the group had less than 500 members and depended almost entirely on the cocaine trade, both by protecting narcotraffickers and by engaging in the business directly.

Sendero activity increased significantly in 2008, particularly in the Upper Huallaga and Apurimac and Ene Valley (VRAE) regions, with military casualties totaling 25, the largest figure since the early 1990s. The group's VRAE faction, led by "Comrade JOSÉ," is called the Principal Regional Committee and rejects both founder Guzmán and any possibility of negotiation. "Comrade ARTEMIO," the Sendero leader in the Upper Huallaga and a member of the group since the 1980s, made periodic offers of negotiation—the most recent in a December 2008 radio interview—which the García government rejected.

On September 3, 2009, the group attacked and downed an air-force helicopter (responding to an ambush that wounded three soldiers earlier that day) in the central highlands Junín region, killing three troops and wounding five others. *Sendero* killed more than 40 members of the military and police in 2009, leading to a warning that it was increasing its firepower and capabilities.

The group had been in the process of transforming from a primarily drug-trafficking organization to one that participated in Peru's electoral process, analysts said in 2010. *Sendero* leaders confirmed that the group intended to compete in municipal and regional elections in 2010 and 2011's national balloting. The decade-long shift included targeting only the police and military for violence. In September 2011 military units were deployed in the Vrae region following fresh *Sendero* attacks. Just three months into his presidency, Humala declared a state of emergency in five provinces. In February 2012, Peruvian troops captured Comrade Artemio, the last remaining member of the central committee who had not been arrested or killed. He was sentenced to life in prison in July 2013. The following month, three rebels were killed by security forces.

Leaders: "Comrade JOSÉ" (Principal Regional Committee), "Comrade ARTEMIO" (imprisoned), "Comrade Miriam" Elena IPARRAGUIRRE (imprisoned), Manuel Abimael GUZMÁN Reinoso (imprisoned), Edmundo Daniel COX Beauzeville (imprisoned), Margie Evelyn CLAVO Peralta (imprisoned), Oscar RAMÍREZ Durand (*Sendero Rojo,* imprisoned).

See the 2010 *Handbook* for information on the now defunct **Túpac Amaru Revolutionary Movement** (*Movimiento Revolucionario Túpac Amaru*—MRTA).

LEGISLATURE

The bicameral Congress (*Congreso*), established under the 1979 constitution, encompassed a Senate and a Chamber of Deputies, both elected for five-year terms by universal adult suffrage. The Congress elected in 1990 was declared by President Fujimori to have been dissolved, as of April 6, 1992. In its place a unicameral Democratic Constituent Congress (*Congreso Constituyente Democrático*—CCD) was established, elections to which were conducted on November 22, 1992. The CCD gave way, in turn, to a new unicameral Congress elected on April 9, 1995. Subsequent elections were held on April 9, 2000; on April 8, 2001 (following a premature dissolution); on April 9, 2006; and on April 10, 2011.

Congress (*Congreso*). The Congress had 120 members, who, before 2001, were selected by proportional vote from a single national list but now represent geographic constituencies. Ahead of the 2011 elections, the number of seats was increased to 130.

Following the most recent elections on April 10, 2011, the seat distribution was as follows: Peru Wins, 47 seats; Force 2011, 37; Possible Peru, 21; Alliance for Great Change, 12; National Solidarity Alliance, 9; and Peruvian Aprista Party, 4. Following party shifts in July and August 2013, seat distribution was as follows: Peru Wins, 47; Popular Force, 37; Possible Peru, 16; National Solidarity Alliance, 10; Regional Union, 8; PPC-APP, 7; Peruvian Aprista Party, 4; Humanist Party, 1.

President: Fredy OTÁROLA.

CABINET

[as of August 29, 2013]

President of Council of Ministers	Juan José Jiménez
Ministers	
Agriculture	Milton Von Hesse La Serna
Commerce and Tourism	Magali Silva [f]
Culture	Diana Alvarez Calderon [f]
Defense	Pedro Cateriano Bellido
Economy and Finance	Luis Miguel Castilla Rubio
Education	Patricia Salas O'Brien [f]
Energy and Mines	Jorge Humberto Merino Tafur
Environment	Manuel Gerardo Pedro Pulgar-Vidal
Foreign Relations	Eda Rivas [f]
Health	Midori Musme de Habich Rospigliosi [f]
Housing, Construction, and Sanitation	René Cornejo Diaz
Interior	Wilfredo Pedraza Sierra
Justice	Daniel Figallo
Labor and Employment	Teresa Nancy Laos Caceres [f]
Production (Fisheries and Industry)	Gladys Triveno Chan Jan [f]
Social Development and Inclusion	Monica Rubio Garcia [f]
Transport and Communications	Carlos Paredes Rodríguez
Women's Affairs and Social Development	Ana Jara Velasquez [f]

[f] = female

INTERGOVERNMENTAL REPRESENTATION

Ambassador to the U.S.: Harold Forsyth MEJIA.

U.S. Ambassador to Peru: Brian NICHOLS (nominated).

Permanent Representative to the UN: Alexis AQUINO.

IGO Memberships (Non-UN): APEC, IADB, ICC, IOM, Mercosur, NAM, OAS, WTO.

PHILIPPINES

Republic of the Philippines
Republika ng Pilipinas

Political Status: Independent republic since July 4, 1946; currently under constitution adopted by referendum of February 2, 1987, effective from February 11.

Area: 115,830 sq. mi. (300,000 sq. km).

Population: 96,912,186 (2012E—UN); 105,720,644 (2013E—U.S. Census).

Major Urban Centers (2011E—UN): MANILA (de facto capital, 1,660,714), QUEZON CITY (designated capital, 2,679,450), Caloocan City (1,381,610), Davao (1,366,153), Cebu (799,762).

Official Languages: Pilipino and English.

Monetary Unit: Philippine Peso (market rate November 1, 2013: 43.44 pesos = $1US).

President: Benigno S. AQUINO III (Liberal Party); popularly elected on May 10, 2010, and inaugurated on June 30 for a six-year term; succeeding Gloria MACAPAGAL-ARROYO (*Lakas Kampi* Christian Muslim Democrats).

Vice President: Jejomar C. BINAY (Filipino Democratic Party–Laban); elected for a six-year term on May 10, 2010, and sworn in on June 30, succeeding Noli DE CASTRO (*Lakas Kampi* Christian Muslim Democrats).

THE COUNTRY

Strategically located along the southeast rim of Asia, the Philippine archipelago embraces over 7,000 islands stretching in a north-south direction for over 1,000 miles. The largest and most important of the islands are Luzon in the north and sparsely populated Mindanao in the south. The inhabitants, predominantly of Malay stock, are 83 percent Roman Catholic, although a politically significant Muslim minority (5 percent) is concentrated in the south. The country is not linguistically unified; English and Spanish are used concurrently with local languages and dialects, although Pilipino, based on the Tagalog spoken in the Manila area, has been promoted as a national language. Women, who constitute about 38 percent of the active labor force, have been prominent in journalism and politics. Women made up 22.9 percent of the representatives in the lower house of Congress, following the May 2010 elections, and 25 percent of the Senate (following the May 2013 balloting).

Rice for domestic consumption and wood, sugar, and coconut products for export were traditionally mainstays of the economy. Although agriculture continues to employ about 35 percent of the labor force, it now accounts for only 15 percent of GDP, compared to about 30 percent for industry and 55 percent for services. Well over half of the country's exports by value are electronics; garments, other manufactures, minerals and mineral products, coconut products, sugar cane, and bananas also rank among the leading exports. The mining industry has benefited from investment in recent years. Remittances from as many as ten million overseas workers (over one quarter of the country's labor force) are a leading source of foreign exchange. The Philippines had significant GDP growth through the 2000s. However, poverty and income inequality remain persistent problems, creating an instability exacerbated by rising food prices during the global financial crisis of 2008–09. Despite rising remittance inflows, domestic consumption fell sharply in 2009. The Philippine economy grew by just 1.1 percent in 2009 but rose by 7.6 percent in 2010, 3.9 percent in 2011, and 6.5 percent in 2012 due to increasing investor confidence and a recovery in the global economy. According to the IMF, inflation in 2012 was 3.1 percent, while unemployment was 7 percent. GDP per capita that year was $2,614. In 2013, the World Bank ranked the Philippines 138th out of 179 countries in its annual Doing Business survey, a ranking far below neighboring states, such as Singapore (1), Malaysia (12), or even Vietnam (99), mainly because of widespread corruption.

GOVERNMENT AND POLITICS

Political background. Claimed for Spain by Ferdinand Magellan in 1521 and ruled by that country until occupied by the United States during the Spanish-American War of 1898, the Philippines became a self-governing commonwealth under U.S. tutelage in 1935 and gained independence on July 4, 1946. Manuel ROXAS, first president of the new republic (1946–1948), took office during the onset of an armed uprising by Communist-led Hukbalahap guerrillas in central Luzon that continued under his successor, the Liberal Elpidio QUIRINO (1948–1953). Quirino's secretary of national defense, Ramon MAGSAYSAY, initiated an effective program of military action and rural rehabilitation designed to pacify the Huks, and he was able to complete this process after his election to the presidency on the

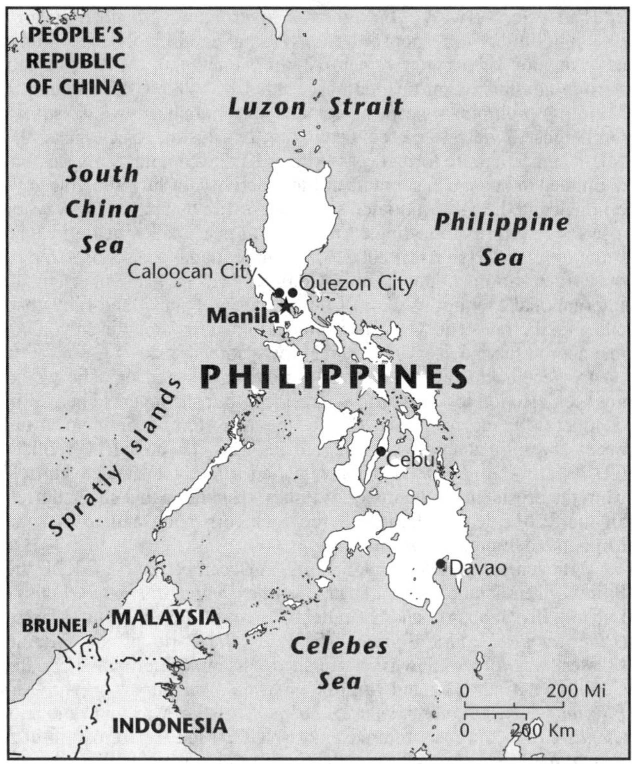

Nacionalista Party ticket in 1953. Magsaysay also dealt strongly with bureaucratic corruption and did much to restore popular faith in government, but his accidental death in 1957 led to a loss of reformist momentum and a revival of corruption under his *Nacionalista* successor, Carlos P. GARCIA (1957–1961). Efforts toward economic and social reform were renewed by Liberal President Diosdado MACAPAGAL (1961–1965).

The election, under *Nacionalista* auspices, of former Liberal leader Ferdinand E. MARCOS in 1965 was accompanied by pledges of support for the reform movement, but discontent with prevailing conditions of poverty, unemployment, inflation, and corruption fostered a climate of violence that included the activities of the Maoist New People's Army (NPA), which was founded in 1969, and a persistent struggle between Muslim elements and government forces on Mindanao and in Sulu Province. In some areas Muslims sought to drive out Christian settlers from the north, but as antigovernment activities expanded under the direction of the Moro National Liberation Front (MNLF), Muslim leaders increasingly called for regional autonomy or outright independence.

In the midst of a rapidly deteriorating political situation, a Constitutional Convention began work on a new constitution in July 1971, but its deliberations were curtailed by a declaration of martial law in September 1972. Strict censorship immediately followed, as did widespread arrests of suspected subversives and political opponents of the regime, most notably Liberal Party (LP) leader Benigno S. AQUINO Jr. The new constitution, which provided for a parliamentary form of government, was declared ratified in January 1973; concurrently, Marcos assumed the additional post of prime minister and announced that the selection of an interim National Assembly called for by the constitution would be deferred.

Following talks in early 1975 between representatives of the Philippine government and the MNLF, the Muslims dropped their demand for partition of the republic, while the government agreed to an integration of rebel units into the Philippine armed forces. President Marcos ordered a suspension of military operations in the south in late 1976, following a cease-fire agreement signed in Tripoli, Libya, with representatives of the moderate MNLF faction. In accordance with the agreement, a referendum was held in April 1977 on the establishment of an autonomous Muslim region. Most Muslims boycotted the polls, however, and the proposal was defeated by an overwhelming majority of those participating. Meanwhile, in 1973 the Communist Party of the Philippines–Marxist-Leninist (CPP) and its military wing, the NPA, had joined with other leftist Marcos opponents to organize a National Democratic Front (NDF).

Amid charges of widespread voting irregularity, particularly in the Manila area, the interim National Assembly was elected in April 1978. The president's recently organized New Society Movement (*Kilusan Bagong Lipunan*—KBL) was officially credited with winning 151 of 165 elective seats.

Martial law was lifted in January 1981, prior to the April adoption by plebiscite of a series of constitutional changes that included direct presidential election. In nationwide balloting in June Marcos was overwhelmingly reelected to a six-year term.

In the first full election to a unicameral National Assembly in May 1984, opposition candidates claimed approximately one-third of the seats. Despite the lifting of martial law, the Marcos regime continued to rule by decree. Opposition feeling had already been inflamed by the assassination of Benigno Aquino upon his return from the United States in August 1983, which precipitated 18 months of often violent antiregime demonstrations. In October 1984 a government commission of inquiry concluded that ultimate responsibility for Aquino's death lay with the armed forces chief of staff, Gen. Fabian VER, who was thereupon temporarily suspended from his duties. (In December 1985, having been acquitted of conspiracy in the assassination, he was reinstated.)

A year later, in the face of mounting support for Corazon AQUINO as political surrogate for her slain husband, Marcos announced that a premature presidential election would be held in early 1986 to "restore confidence" in his administration. Mrs. Aquino filed as the sole opposition candidate for the presidency, with Salvador H. LAUREL as her running mate. The election in February was conducted amid allegations by both opposition leaders and foreign observers of manifest government fraud; Aquino was named the victor by an independent citizens' watchdog group, while official figures attesting to the president's reelection were accepted by the National Assembly. With both candidates thus claiming victory, Aquino called for an expanded program of strikes, boycotts, and civil disobedience to "bring down the usurper."

The turning point came on February 22, 1986, when Defense Secretary Juan Ponce ENRILE and Lt. Gen. Fidel V. RAMOS, the leader of an anticorruption campaign within the military, declared their allegiance to Aquino. Ramos quickly joined troops loyal to him at Camp Crame, the national police headquarters. In response to an appeal from Cardinal Jaime SIN to protect the rebels, the base was surrounded by thousands of Philippine citizens in what became known as the first "People Power" rally. Subsequently, much of the media passed to opposition control, while the military, including the palace guard, experienced mass defections. On February 26, a day after the swearing in of both presidential claimants, Marcos and his immediate entourage departed for exile in Hawaii.

In March 1986 the new chief executive dissolved the National Assembly by suspending the 1973 constitution, presenting in its place an interim document "under which our battered nation can shelter."

In February 1987, more than 80 percent of those voting approved a new U.S.-style constitution, under which President Aquino and Vice President Laurel would remain in office until 1992. In the subsequent congressional election, Aquino supporters won more than 80 percent of 200 directly elective seats in the House of Representatives and defeated opposition candidates in 22 of 24 Senate races.

The Aquino government survived six coup attempts, the most serious of which erupted in December 1989, with the seizure by rebel troops of two military installations in Manila followed by an air attack on the presidential palace. Despite U.S. air support of the government, the insurgency was not completely crushed for ten days, in the course of which 119 persons died and more than 600 were wounded.

Seven candidates vied for the presidency in May 1992, with Aquino-endorsed Fidel Ramos turning back strong challenges by political newcomer Miriam DEFENSOR-SANTIAGO and conservative businessman Eduardo COJUANGCO of the National People's Coalition (NPC). Ramos's People Power–National Union of Christian Democrats (*Lakas*-NUCD) emerged as the principal victor in the May 1995 legislative poll, winning approximately two-thirds of the lower house seats.

In September 1992, the MNLF had rejected an offer of amnesty until the government implemented its 1976 pledge to sanction the creation of semiautonomous political structures for the Mindanao region. In November 1993 the two sides concluded a three-month truce agreement, which was followed by the signing of a cease-fire in January 1994 and a formal peace agreement in September 1996. That month, the MNLF's Nur MISUARI was elected unopposed as governor of the Autonomous Region of Muslim Mindanao (ARMM), encompassing the four provinces—Sulu, the Tawi Tawi island group, and the mainland provinces of Maguindanao and Lanao del Sur—then controlled by the MNLF. Meanwhile, 7,500 of the MNLF's 16,000-member military would be incorporated into the national army and police. The peace agreement was immediately rejected by the more militant Moro Islamic Liberation Front (MILF) and by hard-line MNLF splinters.

Political developments in 1997 were dominated by preparations for the 1998 presidential election. In June a Supreme Court decision scuttled a campaign by a group of President Ramos's supporters to amend the constitution so that he could run for a second term. Also in June, Vice President Joseph E. ESTRADA, a former film actor and the leading contender for the presidency, formed a three-party electoral coalition called the Struggle for the Nationalist Filipino Masses (*Laban ng Makabayang Masang Pilipino*—LAMMP), which included his own Party of the Filipino Masses (*Partido ng Masang Pilipino*—PMP), the NPC, and the Democratic Filipino Struggle (*Laban ng Demokratikong Pilipino*—LDP). In December Estrada selected the LDP's Edgardo ANGARA as his running mate. Estrada won the May 11, 1998, presidential election with 39.9 percent of the vote in a field of ten candidates, with Gloria MACAPAGAL-ARROYO, backed by Ramos's *Lakas*-NUCD, easily winning the vice presidency over Angara. The LAMMP electoral coalition, which later merged to become the Party of the Philippine Masses (*Lapian ng Masang Pilipino*—LAMP), also swept to victory in the House of Representatives and won a majority of the open seats in the Senate. Estrada thus held a firm base of support in the Congress despite opposition from most of the business community and the Catholic hierarchy, which called him morally unfit for office.

A year into his term Estrada's popularity dropped dramatically in response to his ultimately unsuccessful effort to introduce constitutional changes that would have opened the economy to increased foreign investment. His administration was further damaged by allegations of corruption, cronyism, and mismanagement. In October 2000 Luis SINGSON, governor of Ilocos Sur, charged that he had transmitted to President Estrada some $8.6 million in illegal gambling payoffs and another $2.8 million in provincial tobacco taxes. On October 12 Vice President Macapagal-Arroyo resigned from the cabinet amid opposition calls for Estrada to resign. By the end of the month the vice president was at the front of a "united opposition" that included most of the opposition political parties, led by *Lakas*-NUCD.

On November 4, 2000, a rally organized by Cardinal Sin drew tens of thousands of anti-Estrada demonstrators into the streets of Manila. Proclaiming his innocence, Estrada asked the House to move quickly on an impeachment complaint that had been introduced in October. On November 13, arguing that more than one-third of the House membership had signed the impeachment complaint, Speaker of the House Manuel VILLAR Jr. ordered, without a formal committee vote or a floor debate, that the articles of impeachment be forwarded to the Senate for trial.

The Senate trial opened on December 7, 2000, but adjourned on January 17, 2001, a day after the Senate voted 11–10 not to admit evidence proving, according to the prosecution, that Estrada held secret bank accounts under aliases. In response, the Senate president and the House prosecutors resigned, an estimated 500,000 people took to Manila's streets in "People Power II" demonstrations, most of the cabinet joined the opposition, and the police and military withdrew their support from Estrada. On January 19 the Supreme Court, acting extraconstitutionally, ruled the presidency vacant, and Estrada abandoned the presidential palace, although he refused to resign. Macapagal-Arroyo took the oath of office as president on January 20.

On April 25, 2001, Estrada was arrested and charged with economic plunder, his immunity from prosecution having been lifted by the Supreme Court. At that time a unanimous court had also confirmed the legitimacy of the Macapagal-Arroyo presidency, asserting that Estrada "by his acts and statements" had resigned. In legislative elections held on May 14, Macapagal-Arroyo's *Lakas*-NUCD and its immediate allies won a plurality in the House of Representatives.

Upon taking office Macapagal-Arroyo had moved quickly to open discussions with Communist and Muslim insurgents, with mixed results. Since 1992 the Communist-led NDF had engaged in a series of on-again, off-again talks with successive administrations, but without resolving the conflict, which was estimated to have cost 40,000–50,000 lives since the late 1960s. Negotiations were renewed in April 2001 in Oslo, Norway, but in June the government suspended the process indefinitely in response to the NPA's alleged involvement in the assassination of a congressman. At the same time, the Macapagal-Arroyo administration opened peace talks with the MILF in June in Tripoli. A preliminary peace agreement was announced two days later. On August 7, despite the condemnation of Muslim rejectionists, the MILF signed a more formal cease-fire in Kuala Lumpur, Malaysia, but continued to engage in sporadic military activity. In July 2003 the government and the MILF initiated a new cease-fire that paved the way for a series of informal meetings. More formal peace talks, held in Kuala Lumpur, resumed in April 2005. Meanwhile, under the sponsorship of the Organization of the Islamic Conference (OIC), members of an International Monitoring Team from Malaysia, Brunei, and Libya had taken up their posts in Mindanao. (Japan joined the group in July 2006, in a nonmilitary advisory role, and Norway joined in 2010.)

In December 2002, Macapagal-Arroyo had stated that she would not seek election to a full term as president, but she reversed herself in October 2003, asserting that she needed a full term to implement the necessary political and economic reforms. Her vice president, Teofisto GUINGONA of *Lakas*-NUCD, who had already distanced himself from the president on a number of issues, responded that she had been an ineffective leader, failing to root out corruption and to end the Muslim rebellion in the south.

With general elections approaching, in December 2003 the LDP, the Filipino Democratic Party–Laban (*Partido Demokratikong Pilipinos–Laban*—PDP-Laban), and Estrada's Force of the Filipino Masses (*Puwersa ng Masang Pilipino*—PMP, as the Party of the Filipino Masses was now known) established an opposition alliance, the Coalition of the United Filipinos (*Koalisyon ng Nagkakaisang Pilipino*—KNP). A month later the *Lakas*–Christian Muslim Democrats (*Lakas*-CMD, the reconfigured *Lakas*-NUCD) led the formation of a second major electoral alliance, the Coalition for Truth and Experience for the Future (*Koalisyon ng Katapatan at Karanasan sa Kinabukasan*—K4), which also included the NPC, the LP, and several smaller parties.

In the presidential election on May 20, 2004, Macapagal-Arroyo won 40 percent of the vote against four other candidates, chiefly the KNP's Fernando POE Jr., a film actor and friend of former president Estrada. Poe won 35.5 percent of the vote. The vice presidency was won by former news anchor Sen. Noli DE CASTRO of the *Lakas*-CMD, who defeated another former news anchor, the KNP's Sen. Loren LEGARDA. In congressional contests the K4 parties won 7 of the 12 contested Senate seats and a clear majority in the House of Representatives. Although Poe and his supporters, claiming fraud, refused to accept the presidential results, a joint session of Congress officially named Macapagal-Arroyo the winner on June 24, and she was sworn in on June 30.

On February 11–14, 2004, Manila and the NDF had reopened peace talks in Oslo, and additional rounds were held in March–April and June. An August session was canceled by the NDF, however, in part because the government had not attempted to convince the United States, Canada, Australia, and the European Union (EU) to remove the NDF, CPP, and NPA from their lists of foreign terrorist organizations.

In July 2005, President Macapagal-Arroyo included in her annual State of the Nation address to Congress a constitutional reform proposal that called for replacing the existing "dysfunctional" presidential system with a unicameral parliamentary form of government headed by a prime minister. Such a "charter change" could be implemented by an elected constitutional convention or by Congress's sitting as a constituent assembly. The Senate's opposition to forming a constituent assembly led the government to begin circulating a "people's initiative" petition that, with sufficient signatures (from at least 12 percent of the voters, including a minimum of 3 percent in each congressional district) could have put the charter change proposal to the voters in a referendum. In October, however, a divided Supreme Court ruled that a plebiscite could not be employed to make such major constitutional revisions. The charter change initiative was shelved but remained high on Macapagal-Arroyo's agenda.

On July 8–11, 2005, a dozen cabinet members and senior aides resigned and called for President Macapagal-Arroyo to do likewise over allegations of vote-rigging during the 2004 presidential election (during the vote count she had spoken with an election official) and illegal gambling payoffs to members of her immediate family. The president refused to step down and told her opponents to "take your grievances to Congress," where they could pursue impeachment. On July 20 a formal impeachment motion was introduced in the House of Representatives, where the removal effort split the LP. On August 31 the House's Justice Committee rejected the complaint 48–4, and a week later, with 79 votes needed to pursue impeachment, only 51 House members voted against accepting the committee report.

Opposition to the president nevertheless persisted, and on February 24, 2006, she declared a state of emergency in response to the discovery of an alleged coup plot by elements of the armed forces. The state of emergency was lifted on March 3, four days after charges were filed against 16 individuals. On August 24 another effort to impeach the president, citing abuse of her authority and other offenses, was ended by a 173–32 vote of the House.

The May 14, 2007, election for the House of Representatives and half the Senate saw *Lakas*-CMD and its allies, including Kampi and the NPC, win a convincing majority in the lower house. Control of the Senate swung to the opposition, now led by the LP and the NP, but candidates backed by the progovernment caucus won election as Senate president and majority leader.

On September 12, 2007, former president Estrada was convicted of plunder and sentenced to life in prison. Not long after, however, the government initiated talks with Estrada on a conditional pardon, which was granted by Macapagal-Arroyo on October 26.

The nation's two strongest parties, *Lakas*-CMD and Kampi, agreed to merge in June 2008, and the formal merger was completed on May 28, 2009. The new *Lakas* Kampi CMD, the nation's largest party by far, appeared poised to make a strong run in the 2010 elections, but the party was wracked by internal divisions and its presidential candidate, former defense minister Gilbert TEODORO, never entered the top tier. Sen. Benigno AQUINO III of the LP, the only son of Benigno and Corazon Aquino, won a decisive victory in the polling on May 10, 2010, and formed a majority coalition in the new parliament. By August 2012, the secretaries of foreign affairs and transportation and communications had been replaced. The secretary of the interior and local government died in a plane crash on August 18, 2012, and was replaced on an interim basis by the cabinet's executive secretary.

In legislative elections on May 13, 2013, the LP won a plurality in the House, followed by the NPC (see Current issues, below). Meanwhile, pro-presidential parties secured an absolute majority in elections for one half of the Senate seats.

Constitution and government. The basic law approved on February 2, 1987, supplanting the "Freedom Constitution" of March 1986, contains broad civil rights guarantees, denies the military any form of political activity save voting, prohibits abortion, authorizes local autonomy for Muslim-dominated areas, calls for a "nuclear-free" policy (save where the national interest dictates otherwise), and requires legislative concurrence for the leasing of Filipino territory to foreign powers.

In April 2006 the Supreme Court declared unconstitutional a "calibrated preemptive response" (CPR) policy introduced "in lieu of maximum tolerance" toward rallies and public demonstrations. In its ruling the court stated that the CPR "has no place in our legal firmament and must be struck down as a darkness that shrouds freedom. It merely confuses our people and is used by some police agents to justify abuses." In the same decision the court also rejected a "no permit, no rally" policy but added that local governments could restrict permitless demonstrations to designated "freedom parks." The court further stated that officials could deny permits "only on the ground of clear and present danger to public order, public safety, public convenience, public morals or public health."

The constitution provides for a directly elected president serving a single six-year term in conjunction with a separately elected vice president; a bicameral Congress consisting of a Senate and a House of Representatives (with senators and representatives who may serve no more than two and three terms, respectively); and an independent judiciary headed by a Supreme Court. The president is specifically enjoined from imposing martial law for more than a 60-day period without legislative approval. The House of Representatives may impeach the chief executive if one-third of its membership concurs, with a two-thirds vote of the Senate then needed for conviction.

Administratively, the country encompasses 17 regions, 82 provinces, over 130 cities, 1,500 municipalities, and nearly 42,000 local authorities (*barangays*). In November 1975 an enlarged Metropolitan Manila was created by merging the city with 16 surrounding communities, including the official capital, Quezon City. The new metropolis, with a total population of more than 5 million, is governed by a Metropolitan Manila Commission. The Autonomous Region of Muslim Mindanao (ARMM) currently includes the provinces of Basilan, Lanao del Sur, Maguindanao, Sulu, and Tawi Tawi, plus Marawi City. An agreement negotiated with Muslim rebels to expand the "ancestral domain" of Philippine Muslims was struck down by the Supreme Court in October 2008 (see Current issues, below).

Freedom of the press is guaranteed by the constitution, but in the wake of the February 2006 state of emergency the government, in an effort to reduce the incidence of negative news reports about its activities, employed pressure tactics that included, according to the *International Herald Tribune,* "warnings, watch lists, surveillance, court cases, harassment lawsuits and threats of arrest on charges of sedition." Moreover, the Communist and Islamic insurgencies have contributed to a climate of violence that has made the Philippines the second deadliest country for journalists, after Iraq. In 2013, Reporters Without Borders ranked the Philippines 147th out of 179 countries in freedom of the press.

Foreign relations. After independence Philippine foreign policy was based on strong opposition to communism, close alliance with the United States, and active participation in the United Nations and its related agencies. The Philippines also joined various regional organizations, such as the Association of Southeast Asian Nations (ASEAN) and the Asian Development Bank (ADB). After the Vietnam War, however, uncertainty about the U.S. role in Southeast Asia spurred greater independence in foreign policy, and diplomatic and trade relations were established with several Communist states, including the People's Republic of China, the Soviet Union, and Vietnam.

A major issue for Corazon Aquino's government concerned U.S. financial assistance during the remaining years of the 1947 treaty that provided for U.S. use of six military installations, including Clark Air Base and Subic Bay Naval Station, the two largest U.S. overseas installations. Following the eruption of Mount Pinatubo in June 1991, however, the U.S. Defense Department announced that, because of the magnitude of cleanup costs, no attempt would be made to reopen Clark, which had been engulfed in volcanic ash. Negotiations to extend the Subic Bay lease ultimately broke down, with formal "disestablishment" being proclaimed in September 1992.

In January 1998, despite nationalist and leftist opposition, Manila and Washington signed a controversial Visiting Forces Agreement (VFA) that would permit large-scale joint military exercises, allow U.S. warships in Philippine waters, and accord legal standing to visiting U.S. forces. The Philippine Senate approved the pact in May 1999, prompting the formal withdrawal of the Communist NDF from peace negotiations with the government. The first joint military exercises under the VFA were held in February 2000. In November 2002, in the context of the U.S.-led "war on terrorism," the two governments signed a Mutual Logistics Support Agreement, which permits the United States to position communications and other nonlethal equipment in the Philippines. In March 2003, during a visit by President Macapagal-Arroyo to Washington, U.S. President George W. Bush declared the Philippines to be a "major non-NATO ally." These ties were reaffirmed in August 2009 when Macapagal-Arroyo met with U.S. president Barack Obama at the White House.

In February 1994, at the conclusion of the first U.S. court case involving alleged human rights violations in another country, a federal jury in Honolulu, Hawaii, ordered the estate of the late President Marcos to pay damages of some $2.5 billion to thousands of individuals said to have suffered under his rule. To settle the claim, in February 1999 the Marcos family agreed to pay $150 million to some 10,000 victims. In July 2004 the Hawaii district court ordered $40 million in hidden assets to be paid out, but Manila appealed the decision on the grounds that "all decisions on ill-gotten wealth lie within the sovereign prerogative of the Philippines." In May 2006 a U.S. appeals court backed the Hawaii court's decision. In 1998 the Swiss Supreme Court had rejected a final appeal by Marcos family representatives that would have prevented the return to the Philippine government of $590 million from the former president's Swiss bank accounts.

Relations between Manila and its ASEAN partners have typically been stable. Nevertheless, a vexing regional issue concerns competing claims to the Spratly Islands in the South China Sea, which sit astride vital shipping lanes, support a major fishing industry, and may contain significant oil and natural gas deposits. In addition to the Philippines, the claimants include China, Taiwan, and three other members of ASEAN (Brunei, Malaysia, and Vietnam). Since 1995 China and the Philippines have had numerous clashes over fishing rights and construction on various reefs and shoals. In March 1999 the Chinese and Philippine foreign ministers, conferring in Manila, agreed to "exercise joint restraint" in the Spratlys, although China continued to oppose a Philippine proposal for international mediation. Altercations also occurred with Malaysia and Vietnam in 1999. A visit by President

Estrada to China in May 2000 concluded with both countries repeating their intentions to settle the dispute peacefully. In September 2004 the Philippine and Chinese state oil companies announced that they would jointly conduct a seismic study to determine if oil and natural gas are present in the Spratlys. In March 2005 they and Vietnam's counterpart agreed to a tripartite Joint Marine Seismic Undertaking. The Philippines codified its territorial claims, including its claim to the Spratly Islands, by approving "baselines" legislation in March 2009. China protested the law and sent a military patrol boat into the area days later. As the diplomatic issue heated up following an ASEAN regional forum in 2010, some Filipino commentators urged the state to make its military presence in the region more credible to back up its policy concerning the South China Sea.

Over the past decade, Malaysia has helped broker peace talks between the Philippine government and the MILF, leading to the Memorandum of Agreement on Ancestral Domain that was invalidated by the Supreme Court in October 2008 (see Current issues, below). On April 24, 2012, the Philippine government and MILF signed a new ten-point peace plan following talks in Malaysia (see Current issues, below).

In January 2012, the United States and the Philippines launched negotiations on increased defense ties, including the possible restoration of U.S. military bases in the Philippines. In April, a Philippine naval vessel stopped two Chinese fishing vessels in the disputed waters on the Scarborough Shoal. China dispatched two patrol ships to the area, while the Philippines deployed another vessel. A standoff ensued until June 18, when both nations withdrew their naval units ostensibly because of the onset of typhoon season. China and the Philippines both continued to assert sovereignty over the area. In September, in a symbolic measure, the Philippines renamed areas of the South China Sea as the West Philippine Sea.

In January 2013, the Philippines announced it would refer its maritime dispute with China over the Spratly Islands for international arbitration under the UN Convention on the Law of the Sea. On January 31, the United States issued an apology to the Philippines for the wreck of a U.S. naval minesweeper that ran aground in the Tubbataha Reefs Natural Park, a UN-world heritage site. The United States also announced it would dismantle the ship. However, in April, the United States refused to pay a $1.4 million fine for the incident. Meanwhile, a Chinese fishing vessel ran aground on the reefs on April 8, and the crew was charged with poaching after officials discovered 10 tons of endangered scaly anteater meat aboard.

Fighting broke out between approximately 200 members of a Filipino militia group, the Royal Army of the Sulu Sultanate, and Malaysian security forces in Saban, Malaysia, in March 2013. At least 90 were killed in the violence, which prompted the Malaysian government to deploy some 5,000 soldiers to disperse the Filipinos. Reports indicated that more than 4,000 ethnic Filipinos who lived in Saban fled back to the Philippines to avoid reprisals. Philippine President Aquino condemned the violence but maintained a claim to the territory.

Current issues. On August 1, 2009, former president Corazon Aquino died. More than 200,000 people lined the streets of Manila to glimpse her casket before it was laid to rest beside the grave of her husband, Benigno Aquino Jr. The funeral electrified the opposition. In a country whose politics are dominated by dynastic families, the outpouring of love for the departed "Cory" Aquino transformed into a movement to draft her son, Benigno Aquino III, for the presidency. Aquino, a backbench LP senator with a relatively low profile, wavered at first, but after Sen. Manuel ROXAS II, already nominated as the LP's candidate, withdrew from the race on September 1, "Noynoy" Aquino announced his candidacy eight days later, with Roxas as his running mate.

Political violence overshadowed the election season, especially in the southern provinces. On November 23 in Maguindanao, a group of armed men loyal to the province's ruling family set upon the friends and family of a rival candidate, killing 57 people, including several dozen journalists, and burying them collectively using a backhoe owned by the local government. The family's patriarch, Andal AMPATUAN Sr., and his son Andal AMPATUAN Jr., mayor of Datu Unsay, were indicted for their roles in the massacre. The incident brought to light the magnitude of intimidation and violence inflicted by the private armies of political families, some of whom, such as the Ampatuans, were allied with President Macapagal-Arroyo.

Noynoy Aquino campaigned on his family's legacy and an anticorruption platform. The issue of corruption worked to Aquino's advantage, since his two principal rivals, former House speaker Manuel Villar of the NP and former president Estrada of the PMP (who had defied a condition of his 2007 pardon by running for office again), were both alleged to have enriched themselves illicitly while in power. In addition, the Philippines introduced nationwide computerized voting in the 2010 general election. Relatively few glitches marred the May 10, 2010, balloting. Aquino won handily with 42 percent of the vote to Estrada's 26.3 percent and Villar's 15.4 percent. Jejomar BINAY of PDP-Laban narrowly defeated Roxas for the vice presidency. In August 2011, it was announced that former president, and now member of Congress, Macapagal-Arroyo had been barred from traveling abroad due to pending corruption charges. She faced "plunder charges" as she allegedly illegally misused hundreds of millions of pesos (tens of millions of dollars) of government funds to fund her election campaign. These charges carried a maximum of 40 years in prison. Additionally, she faced separate charges that she did not remit $1.7 million in taxes on the sale of a government lot. There were also allegations that she used $17 million of state fertilizer funds for her 2004 reelection campaign. Macapagal-Arroyo's spokesperson claimed the charges were politically motivated.

Earlier, and in a related development, General Angelo Tomas REYES, who was chief of staff of the Armed Forces of the Philippines from 2000 to 2001 and held more than one cabinet position, including the post of secretary of defense, committed suicide on February 8, 2011. Many viewed that tragic event as a result of the drive against corruption by the government, which affected the career of many Filipino politicians, including General Reyes.

In his first executive order following his inauguration on June 30, President Aquino established a truth commission to investigate and "bring necessary closure to allegations of official wrongdoing and impunity" during the prior administration. Former president Macapagal-Arroyo and her supporters accused Aquino of a "vendetta" and vowed to go to the Supreme Court to stop the commission. Legal advocates hoped to extend the scope of the commission's inquiry beyond corruption to allegations of human rights abuses.

On the island of Mindanao, the October 2008 Supreme Court decision nullifying the government's negotiated agreement with the MILF created a serious setback in the peace process. On July 16 of that year the administration announced that it had reached a peace agreement with the MILF, after three years of talks brokered by Malaysia. The Memorandum of Agreement on Ancestral Domain (MOA-AD) would create an autonomous Muslim homeland much larger than the current Autonomous Region in Muslim Mindanao (ARMM). Fearing that the pact would lead the separatists to declare an independent state, several Philippine politicians brought suit. On August 4, one day before the scheduled signing ceremony in Kuala Lumpur, the Supreme Court issued a temporary restraining order against accession to the MOA-AD. Several violent raids by MILF fighters followed; citing these incidents, the Macapagal-Arroyo administration backed away from the agreement, amid sharp criticism for failing to consult with lawmakers during the negotiations. In an 8–7 decision, on October 14 the court ruled that the administration had exceeded its constitutional authority by negotiating the document in full knowledge that it would require amending the constitution.

Numerous clashes in the succeeding months resulted in hundreds of deaths and more than a half million refugees. Despite a loss of confidence, both sides prepared to resume talks. The president ordered a suspension of military operations in July 2009, days before her final State of the Nation address, and MILF swiftly followed suit. Administration officials said the government aimed to finalize peace agreements with both the Muslim MILF rebels and the Communist forces of the NDF before the end of Macapagal-Arroyo's term, but the president was unable to meet either of these goals.

On August 4, 2011, MILF chairperson Al-Haj MURAD Ebrahim and President Benigno Aquino had a meeting at Narita, Japan, to discuss self-determination for Bangsamoro. Meanwhile, on November 18, Macapagal-Arroyo was arrested for electoral fraud. In February, she pleaded not guilty to the charges. Typhoon Washi hit Mindanao on December 16–18. The storm killed 1,249, with more than 60,000 left homeless.

The government and MILF signed a peace accord on April 24, 2012, in Malaysia. The agreement endorsed the creation of a new political body to replace the ARMM and offer greater autonomy to the region. Nonetheless, sporadic fighting continued between government forces and MILF. A further ceasefire was signed in October. Meanwhile, on May 29, the Senate voted to impeach Supreme Court Chief Justice Renato CORONA for failing to disclose $2.4 million in assets. The Senate failed to convict the chief justice on concurrent charges that he obstructed efforts to prosecute Macapagal-Arroyo.

On July 30, 2012, Typhoon Saola hit the island of Luzon, killing 50. A week later, tropical storm Haiku again devastated Luzon, killing at least 65 and leaving more than 646,000 homeless.

In April 2013, MILF accused security forces of carrying out a series of attacks, but the government asserted that the strikes had been aimed at the Abu Sayyaf Group. The LP won House elections on May 13, securing 112 seats, followed by the NPC with 43, and the newly formed National Unity Party, 24. The LP also won the majority of governorships, securing 38 of the country's 80, compared to the NPC's 13 and the NP's 10, among others. Although the government reported that the elections were relatively peaceful, 46 people were killed in election-related violence.

In November 2013, Super Typhoon Haiyan struck the Philippines with an estimated loss of life of more than 4,000 and an estimated population of over four million displaced. The typhoon struck the agricultural heartland of the Philippines but spared most of the industrial base. The aftermath of the event resulted in widespread looting and violence; the government response was criticized for failing to deliver humanitarian aid and security in a timely manner. As of January 2014, it was estimated that only nine percent of Typhoon Haiyan victims had received support for rebuilding. With over 4 million estimated displaced, the relief effort is expected to continue for years.

POLITICAL PARTIES AND GROUPS

From 1946 until the imposition of martial law by Ferdinand Marcos in 1972, political control oscillated between the *Nacionalista* Party (NP), founded in 1907, and the Liberal Party (LP), organized by slightly left-of-center elements that split from the *Nacionalistas* in 1946. Since martial law was lifted in 1978, Filipino parties have tended to form loose and shifting coalitions around electoral campaigns. Some parties and coalitions jointly endorse legislative candidates with other national parties or with small local or regional parties. Party platforms and ideologies are relatively loose and it is common for politicians to switch parties, sometimes during campaign season. Parties often contain members belonging to both the pro-administration and opposition blocs in Congress. In addition, the party-list system guarantees significant parliamentary representation for minority constituencies.

In the period leading up to the 2010 general election, President Macapagal-Arroyo revamped the Filipino political landscape by orchestrating the formal merger of the ruling *Lakas*-CMD and Kampi parties to create the nation's largest party. No major coalition formed among the opposition as parties jockeyed for position in the presidential and legislative races. Shortly before the May 10 balloting, the *Nacionalista* Party (NP) and Nationalist People's Coalition (NPC), whose presidential and vice-presidential candidates, respectively, were running mates, announced an electoral alliance. However, the Supreme Court upheld a lawsuit by the Liberal Party (LP), claiming that the NP and NPC had missed the filing deadline with the Commission on Elections (COMELEC) by several months, nullifying the coalition.

For details on the principal electoral alliances formed prior to the most recent campaign, see the entry in the 2010 *Handbook*.

Presidential Party:

Liberal Party (LP). The LP was organized in 1946 by a group of centrist *Nacionalista* dissidents. Formerly a member of Unido, its congressional delegation after the 1987 election encompassed 8 senators and 42 representatives. Subsequently, it divided into a pro-Aquino mainstream faction headed by Jovito SALONGA and a more rightist group headed by Eva KALAW.

Manila mayor Alfredo LIM was the party's 1998 "law-and-order candidate" for president and ran with the endorsement of former president Corazon Aquino. Lim won only 8.7 percent of the vote, and the LP captured 14 House seats. The party subsequently entered a "strategic" coalition with the LAMP. In January 2000 Lim joined the Estrada cabinet.

Although the LP was also divided over the Estrada impeachment question, most of the party leadership ended up calling for the president's resignation. The LP won 21 lower house seats in May 2001. It supported President Macapagal-Arroyo's reelection in 2004 and participated in the K4, winning more than two dozen seats in the House of Representatives, as well as 2 in the Senate.

The 2005 presidential impeachment battle effectively split the LP. In March 2006 a faction led by Manila mayor Jose ATIENZA, supporting Macapagal-Arroyo, ousted Senate president Franklin Drilon as party leader, but the Drilon faction met shortly thereafter and expelled Atienza and cabinet member Michael DEFENSOR. Drilon subsequently asked the Commission on Elections to decide the issue. In July Drilon stepped down as Senate president. On November 26, the party's Executive Council appointed Manuel ROXAS II as party president. In April 2007, the Supreme Court sided with the Drilon faction. In the May election the party won 23 House seats to lead the opposition and retained 4 Senate seats.

Senator Manuel Roxas II at first appeared set to become the party's standard-bearer in the 2010 presidential election, but the death of Corazon Aquino on August 1, 2009, caused a shift in the political winds, sparking a public clamor for Benigno Aquino III to enter the race. Roxas withdrew his previously declared candidacy to make way for his Senate colleague. "Noynoy" Aquino accepted the challenge days later, taking Roxas as his running mate and vowing to restore clean government to the nation. As the campaign got underway, several prominent leaders bolted their parties to join the Aquino campaign, including Sen. Francis "Chiz" ESCUDERO (from the NPC) and former Quezon City mayor Feliciano "Sonny" BELMONTE Jr. (from *Lakas* Kampi CMD). Aquino vaulted ahead of his rivals and marched to a decisive victory in the presidential race; Roxas narrowly lost the vice presidential contest to Jejomar Binay. The LP made dramatic gains in the House of Representatives, becoming the second largest party behind *Lakas* Kampi CMD, and entering a majority coalition with other parties (including many lawmakers from *Lakas*) to elect Belmonte as speaker. In June 2012, Sarangani Governor Miguel Rene DOMINGUEZ defected from *Lakas* and joined the Liberal Party.

In the May 2013 national elections, the LP became the largest party in the House. In concurrent local balloting, the LP won 33.4 percent of the vote and pluralities or majorities of seats on 45 percent of the provincial boards.

Leaders: Benigno C. AQUINO III (President of the Republic and Executive Vice President of the party), Sen. Franklin DRILON (Chair), Manuel ROXAS II (Minister of the Interior and Local Government), Joseph Emilio ABAYA (Secretary General).

Other National Congressional Parties:

Lakas Kampi Christian Muslim Democrats (*Lakas-Kabalikat ng Malayang Pilipino ng Kristiyano at Muslim Demokrata—Lakas Kampi* CMD). Two of the largest Filipino parties, *Lakas*—CMD and Kampi, completed a merger in 2009. *Lakas*-CMD traces its origin to the People Power Party (*Partido Lakas ng Tao*—PPP) that was founded by presidential hopeful Fidel Ramos in January 1992, two months after he had left the dominant LDP because of its decision to designate Ramon Mitra as its nominee. In early February the formation was redesignated as EDSA-LDP (EDSA being an acronym for Epifanio de los Santo Avenue, the location of the first "People Power" rally in 1986). Subsequently, *Lakas ng EDSA* (EDSA Power) joined in a coalition with the National Union of Christian Democrats (NUCD), led by Raul MANGLAPUS, who had previously led the pre-1972 Christian Socialist Movement.

While *Lakas*-NUCD won only 51 of 201 lower house seats in the 1992 election, its ranks were subsequently swelled by defections from other parliamentary groups, including, most notably, the LDP. In mid-1994, by contrast, it lost a number of House supporters, most prominently its majority leader, Ronaldo Zamora. It captured an overwhelming majority of House seats in 1995. In June 1997 the Supreme Court ruled that Ramos could not run for reelection, and in December he backed Jose de Venecia, Speaker of the House of Representatives.

To enhance his party's chances at the polls, Ramos engineered an electoral alliance with the moderate United Muslim Democratic Party (UMDP) of Mindanao and with the Alliance of Free Filipinos (*Kabalikat ng Malayang Pilipino*—Kampi), which had been organized in 1997 by Jose Cojuangco and others to support the presidential aspirations of Gloria Macapagal-Arroyo, daughter of former president Diosdado Macapagal. Although opinion polls indicated that Macapagal-Arroyo was running second only to Joseph Estrada among presidential contenders, she agreed to unite Kampi with *Lakas*-NUCD and to serve as de Venecia's running mate.

In May 1998, de Venecia finished second, with 15.9 percent of the presidential vote, while Macapagal-Arroyo won the vice presidency with a 47 percent share and subsequently agreed to join the cabinet as secretary of social welfare and development. Following her victory, Kampi remained in existence, although most of its members were also affiliated with *Lakas*-NUCD. Although the *Lakas*-NUCD won 5 Senate seats and 50 House seats, its effectiveness as the leading opposition party was soon weakened by defections to President Estrada's LAMP.

The situation was reversed following Estrada's departure from office in January 2001, and the *Lakas*-NUCD emerged from the May 2001 election with a plurality of some 85 seats (including those won by *Lakas* candidates with other endorsements).

President Macapagal-Arroyo was named chair of the party in June 2002, at which time she proposed adopting a new, consolidated name. Accordingly, in October the party leadership approved the change to *Lakas*-CMD.

In October 2003, Macapagal-Arroyo reversed a 2002 decision not to seek election to a full term in 2004, which resulted in the departure from the party of Vice President Teofisto Guingona, who had been *Lakas*-CMD's president. In the May 2004 balloting Macapagal-Arroyo won a full term, with 40 percent of the vote, against four other contenders. At the same time, the party and its K4 allies (including Kampi) captured sufficient seats to maintain a government majority in the Senate and swept to an easy victory in the House of Representatives. The K4's apparent unity subsequently suffered a significant setback in the House, however, when several dozen members, dissatisfied with the House leadership and the divvying up of key committee assignments, declared allegiance to a revitalized Kampi.

In May 2007, *Lakas*-CMD won a plurality of seats in the House of Representatives and, in partnership with second-place finisher Kampi, the NPC, and others, held a majority. De Venecia was ousted from his position as House Speaker on January 28, 2008, and from the party presidency on March 10. Prospero Nograles succeeded him in both posts.

A formal agreement on the merger of *Lakas*-CMD and Kampi was signed in Davao City on June 18, 2008, and announced by President Macapagal-Arroyo. The process of integrating the nation's two largest parties on the regional level was completed at a ceremony in Manila on May 28, 2009. The merger left *Lakas* Kampi CMD with a majority in the House of Representatives and control of more than half the nation's governorships. The party claimed more than five million members.

At a party convention in Manila on November 19, 2009, Lakas Kampi CMD nominated the former defense minister Gilbert TEODORO as its 2010 presidential bet. President Macapagal-Arroyo surrendered the party chair to the youthful Teodoro, who had departed from the NPC the previous July to join *Lakas*. However, the party was losing far more members through defections than it was gaining.

In late March 2010, Teodoro surprised onlookers by resigning as chair of the party, claiming a need to set aside administrative duties in order to concentrate on his own lagging campaign. Observers noted disarray in the nation's dominant party, especially at the local and regional levels, where candidates were complaining of insufficient support from the party apparatus. Interim party chair Amelita VILLAROSA had to fend off questions about the imminent disintegration of Lakas, especially when House Speaker Prospero NOGRALES announced he was leaving the party in April. (Nograles changed his mind the next day.)

Lakas led all parties in the 2010 general election, winning 93 House seats, but defections and internal divisions made the party weaker than those numbers suggested. In a party caucus shortly following the election, outgoing president Macapagal-Arroyo, who had won her race to enter Congress from Pampanga, assumed the party presidency once again. A sizable majority of the *Lakas* delegation declared support for the incoming administration, allowing the LP to elect former *Lakas* stalwart Feliciano "Sonny" Belmonte as speaker. Subsequently, a large number of *Lakas* representatives defected to other parties, including the LP, or joined a new grouping, the National Unity Party (NUP) (see below).

In February 2013, Ferdinand Martin Romualdez succeeded Macapagal-Arroyo as party leader. Following the May balloting, there were calls within the party for Romualdez to resign after *Lakas* only secured 14 seats in the House balloting, a decline of 4 from the previous election.

Leaders: Ferdinand Martin ROMUALDEZ (President), Ramon REVILLA Jr. (Chair of the Party), Arthur DEFENSOR (Executive Vice President), Fidel V. RAMOS, Gloria MACAPAGAL-ARROYO (Chairs Emeritus).

Nationalist People's Coalition (NPC). The NPC was formed prior to the 1992 balloting by right-wing elements of both the Liberal and *Nacionalista* parties under the leadership of President Aquino's estranged cousin and former Marcos business confidant, Eduardo Cojuangco. Although Cojuangco finished third in the 1992 presidential poll, NPC candidate Joseph Estrada won the vice presidency on a 33 percent vote share.

The NPC remained in opposition during the Ramos presidency, joining LAMMP upon its formation in June 1997. In December, however, NPC President Ernesto Maceda was ousted as Senate president and, blaming Estrada and LDP leader Edgardo Angara, apparently sidetracked a planned formal merger of the three LAMMP parties.

The NPC remained allied with President Estrada until his departure from office in January 2001, after which it agreed to cooperate with President Macapagal-Arroyo's administration. In the May 2001 lower house election the NPC finished second to *Lakas*-NUCD.

As the 2004 elections approached, the NPC was divided over support for Macapagal-Arroyo's reelection bid. As a result, some members supported her principal opponent, Fernando Poe Jr., and ran for Congress as participants in the opposition KNP alliance, while the majority participated in the K4 alliance. In the election the NPC won over 50 House seats. In 2007 it finished third, but with only 28 seats.

Senator Francis "Chiz" Escudero, expected to run for president in 2010, quit the NPC in October 2009 and declined to run as an independent. His Senate colleague Loren Legarda, Poe's running mate in the 2004 election, declared her candidacy first for the top job, then shifted course toward the vice president's office. Legarda, a former anchorwoman known for her environmental advocacy, became the running mate of Sen. Manuel VILLAR of the NP. The rival LP brought a successful suit to stop the NP and NPC from formalizing their uneasy coalition. The NPC secured 29 House seats in the 2010 polling and added several more through defections from other parties. The party joined the majority bloc in Congress with the promise of holding onto several committee chairpersonships and campaigned with the LP in the 2013 Senate elections. The NPC placed second in the 2013 House balloting with 43 seats and third in local government balloting, with 100 of the 926 council seats up for election.

Leaders: Faustino DY Jr. (Chair), Frisco SAN JUAN (President), Michael John DUAVLT (Secretary-General), Eduardo COJUANGCO (Chair Emeritus).

Nacionalista Party (NP). Essentially the right wing of the Philippines' oldest party (formed in 1907), the *Nacionalistas* had been reduced by 1988 to a relatively minor formation within the Grand Alliance for Democracy (GAD), which had been organized by former defense minister Juan Ponce Enrile, prior to the 1987 congressional election as an anti-Aquino and anticommunist formation. The GAD also included the now-defunct Mindanao Alliance and the Philippine Democratic Socialist Party (PDSP, above). In February 1990 Enrile was arrested on charges of involvement in the December 1989 coup attempt, but the Supreme Court subsequently ordered the more serious charges reduced, and Enrile quickly returned to politics.

As the party's 1992 presidential candidate, Vice President Salvador Laurel ran eighth with a vote share of only 3.4 percent. In 1998 Enrile, who had been expelled from the party by Laurel in 1991, ran for president as an independent, capturing 1.4 percent of the vote. For the 1998 elections the NP was allied with the *Lakas*-NUCD and subsequently supported the removal of President Estrada.

Although allied with *Lakas*-CMD in 2004's K4 alliance, the NP ran in 2007 as part of the GO. It won ten House seats and held four Senate seats. However, its leader, Manuel Villar Jr., was subsequently able to retain the role of Senate president only because he received the support of the pro-Macapagal-Arroyo senators. He later lost their backing and ceded the Senate presidency to Juan Ponce Enrile in November 2008. The Senate's ethics committee investigated and finally cleared Villar of corruption charges in 2009, after accusations that he had directed extra government funds to a road project traversing his own property.

Despite the scandal, Villar topped polls as the 2010 presidential race got underway and outspent his opponents in the campaign's early months, but he was unable to stop the meteoric rise of Benigno Aquino III. Villar chose the NPC's Loren Legarda as his running mate. Villar finished a distant third in the balloting. In the general election, the NP gained 12 House seats.

In balloting in 2013, the NPC won 17 seats in the House, 6 governorships, and 106 seats on regional councils.

Leaders: Sen. Manuel VILLAR Jr. (President of the Party), Sen. Alan Peter CAYETANO (Secretary General).

United Nationalist Alliance (UNA). The UNA was an electoral coalition formed in 2012 by the PMP and the PDP-Laban. A number of smaller or regional parties joined the grouping before the 2013 national elections. In the May balloting. World-famous boxer Manny PACQUIAO was reelected to Congress as a representative from

Sarangani; his **People's Champ Movement** was part of the UNA. The UNA secured 5 Senate seats, 8 seats in the House, 4 governorships, and 47 seats on local councils.

Leaders: Jejomar BINAY (President), Joseph ESTRADA (Chair)

Force of the Filipino Masses (*Puwersa ng Masang Pilipino*—PMP). The PMP was founded as the Party of the Filipino Masses (*Partido ng Masang Pilipino*—PMP) in the early 1990s by Joseph Estrada, a former Liberal, to support his presidential aspirations. He ran as the vice presidential candidate of the NPC in 1992, but by 1998 the rejuvenated PMP claimed 5 million members and Estrada was elected. The PMP was virtually eliminated as an electoral force in the May 2001 election, although Estrada's wife, Luisa EJERCITO-ESTRADA, won election to the Senate as a PnM candidate.

With his trial ongoing, former president Estrada continued to hold sway over the PMP (now known as the Force of the Filipino Masses) as the 2004 elections approached. In December 2003 the PMP joined in formation with the KNP and supported presidential aspirant Fernando Poe Jr. After the May 2004 balloting the PMP claimed several House seats, while Estrada's son Jose joined his mother in the Senate. According to reports, in September 2004 the former president rejected a proposal by LDP opposition leader Edgardo Angara to merge the PMP into the LDP.

In August 2005, Juan Ponce Enrile, the chair of the party, took the unorthodox step of joining the majority in the Senate. Enrile stated at the time that former president Estrada had approved the move. In 2007 the PMP won four House seats. Shortly thereafter, Enrile and Jose Estrada were criticized by much of the opposition for joining the pro-Macapagal-Arroyo senators in supporting the NP's Manuel Villar Jr. for Senate president. The mayor of Manila, Alfredo Lim, was appointed party president in 2007, but removed from the position in August 2008.

As the 2010 presidential race heated up, Estrada repeatedly stated that he was willing to offer himself as a candidate if the opposition could not unite behind a single contender. It became increasingly clear that the former president, known in headlines as "Erap," intended to seek the office again, even though his pledge not to do so had been instrumental in obtaining his 2007 pardon. Estrada declared his candidacy, with the PMP's backing, in October 2009. The Commission on Elections (COMELEC) dismissed three petitions filed to prevent his candidacy. The former movie star proved to have enduring popularity, finishing second in the 2010 balloting with 26 percent of the vote. His running mate, Jejomar BINAY of PDP-Laban, won the vice presidency. The PMP won five House seats in 2010 and retained its two Senate seats, with Enrile winning a second term as Senate president. Ahead of the 2013 Senate elections, the PMP joined with the PDP-Laban to form the United Nationalist Alliance (UNA). Estrada was selected as the chair of the UNA.

Leaders: Joseph ESTRADA (Chair of the Party and Former President of the Republic), Sen. Juan Ponce ENRILE, Sen. Jose "Jinggoy" ESTRADA.

Filipino Democratic Party–Laban (*Partido Demokratikong Pilipinas–Lakas ng Bayan*—PDP-Laban). The current PDP-Laban constitutes the branch of the original PDP-Laban that refused to join in formation of the LDP (see above) in 1988. In 2004 it won two lower house seats as a component of the KNP alliance. In 2005–2006 party leader Aquilino Pimentel Jr. was one of the more outspoken voices demanding President Macapagal-Arroyo's resignation.

In the 2007 election, the PDP-Laban won three House seats. Two PDP-Laban members entered the 2010 presidential contest: Jejomar "Jojo" Binay, mayor of Makati, and Senator Ana Consuelo "Jamby" Madrigal. The latter, a wealthy senator, left the party to run as an independent. Binay switched to the vice presidential race, as running mate of the PMP's Joseph Estrada. Binay's victory brought hopes for a revival of the party to its former heights during the Corazon Aquino era. The PDP-Laban joined with the PMP in the UNA. Binay was selected as the president of the UNA.

Leaders: Jejomar BINAY (Vice President of the republic), Aquilino PIMENTEL Jr. (Former Senate Minority Leader), Aquilino PIMENTEL III (Secretary-General), Teodoro LOCSIN Jr.

Democratic Filipino Struggle (*Laban ng Demokratikong Pilipino*—LDP). Formally established in September 1988, the LDP constituted a merger of the Filipino Democratic Party–Laban (*Partido Demokratikong Pilipinas–Lakas ng Bayan*—PDP-Laban) and the People's Struggle (*Lakas ng Bansa*). The PDP, launched in 1982 by former members of the Mindanao Alliance, had joined with the People's Power (*Lakas ng Bayan*—Laban), nominally led by Benigno Aquino Jr. until his death in August 1983, to form the PDP-Laban. (Part of the PDP-Laban formation, led by Aquilino Pimentel, refused to enter the LDP and maintains a separate identity—see below.) The People's Struggle had been formed in 1987 by a nephew of Corazon Aquino.

Following the May 1995 election, at which the LDP was nominally allied with *Lakas*-NUCD, the LDP split, Edgardo ANGARA, the LDP chair, going into opposition after being ousted as Senate president in favor of Neptali GONZALES, also of the LDP. As a result, elements of the LDP ended up on both sides of the political aisle. In May 1996, however, the LDP severed its remaining coalition links. Five months later Gonzales, a strong supporter of President Ramos, was himself removed as Senate leader.

The LDP won 22 House seats (1 in coalition with the NPC) in the May 2001 election. Earlier in the year a faction known as the "Conscience Bloc" abandoned the party because of its support for pro-Estrada candidates. Most of the dissenters ultimately joined the *Lakas*-NUCD.

In 2004, the party was divided over the presidential contest, with supporters of party leader Edgardo Angara constituting the backbone of the KNP and backing its nominee, actor Fernando Poe Jr., who finished second, with 36.5 percent of the vote. A smaller LDP faction headed by Agapito "Butz" AQUINO supported the candidacy of Sen. Panfilo LACSON, who finished third, with 10.9 percent of the vote. (Poe died on December 14, 2004, three days after suffering a stroke.)

Angara reaffirmed his control of the party at a March 2005 national congress. Senator Angara won reelection in 2007 and the LDP took three House seats. Angara and his son, Juan Edgardo Angara, a House member from the Aurora district, were the only party members elected to Congress in 2010. The party endorsed the vice-presidential bid of the NPC's Loren Legarda.

In the 2013 elections, the LDP won 1 Senate seat, 2 House seats, and 4 spots on provincial councils.

Leaders: Sen. Edgardo ANGARA (Chair), Juan Edgardo ANGARA (Secretary General).

National Unity Party (*Partido Ng Pambansang Pagkakaisa*—NUP). The NUP was formed by disaffected members of *Lakas*-CMD in 2011. The Populist Party was split in the 2013 elections, with the party formally supporting the LP, but a large number of members reportedly backing the UNA. In the 2013 balloting, the NUP secured 24 seats in the House, 8 governorships, and 73 seats on local councils.

Leaders: Pablo GARCIA (Chair), Rodolfo ANTONIO (President).

New Society Movement (*Kilusan Bagong Lipunan*—KBL). Organized in 1978 as a pro-Marcos formation, the KBL was utilized by the former president's widow, Imelda MARCOS, for her own presidential bid in 1992. Initially considered a major threat to the other contenders, Marcos captured only 10.3 percent of the vote for a fifth-place finish.

In April 1998, trailing in the polls with only a 2 percent share, Marcos withdrew from the upcoming presidential election "to save the Filipino people from the ultimate injustice of a bloody election." In 2001, 2004, and 2007 the party won one seat in the House of Representatives.

Congressman Ferdinand "Bongbong" Marcos Jr. won the *Nacionalista* Party endorsement for his 2010 senatorial bid. The NP and KBL formed a brief alliance that was dissolved in December 2009, but Marcos remained on the NP senatorial slate and won a seat in the upper house. His mother, Imelda, ran for the House on the KBL line and won with 80 percent of the vote, while his sister Imee R. MARCOS, who joined the NP in 2009, was elected governor of Ilocos Norte province. Marcos retained her seat in the House in the 2013 balloting.

Leaders: Imelda MARCOS (Member of the House), Vicente MILLORA.

People's Reform Party (PRP). The PRP was the nominal party vehicle for the 1992 presidential bid of political independent Miriam Defensor-Santiago, who campaigned with sufficient vigor on an anti-corruption platform to gain a 19.7 percent vote share as runner-up to Fidel Ramos. Senator Defensor-Santiago proved less successful in 1998, winning only 3.0 percent of the presidential vote. She was one of President Estrada's strongest Senate supporters before and after his November 2000 impeachment. In May 2001 she lost her reelection bid.

Defensor-Santiago was expected to seek another Senate term in 2004 as an opposition candidate, but she ultimately gained the endorsement of the government-supportive K4. After winning, she had a falling out with the *Lakas*-CMD and declared herself an independent. Later, however, she repaired relations with the administration and spoke in favor of constitutional reform. One of the most colorful politicians in the Philippines, Defensor-Santiago, was reelected in 2010 with the third-highest vote total among Senate candidates and reelected again in 2013.

Leader: Sen. Miriam DEFENSOR-SANTIAGO.

Other National Parties:

Bagumbayan-Volunteers for a New Philippines (*Bagumbayan-*VNP). This party began as a volunteer advocacy group in Olongapo in the early 1990s, as the U.S. prepared to depart from the Subic Bay naval station. The community organized to convert the base for civic purposes. Richard Gordon, who led the effort as mayor of Olongapo, later became a cabinet officer and was elected to the Senate as an independent in 2004. The Bagumbayan movement launched a political party in April 2009, intending to support a Gordon presidential campaign to transform the nation. Bayani FERNANDO, former head of the Metropolitan Manila Development Authority, became Gordon's running mate after failing to win Lakas Kampi CMD's presidential nomination. Gordon finished sixth in the balloting with 1.4 percent of the vote; Fernando ran fourth at 2.9 percent.

Leaders: Richard GORDON (Chair), Leon B. HERRERA (President).

Party for Democratic Reform—Lapjang Manggagawa (*Partido para sa Demokratikong Reporma-Lapjang Manggagawa*—Reporma-LM). This party came about in 1998 to support the presidential tandem of Renato DE VILLA and running mate Oscar ORBOS, both former cabinet officials. The party won one House seat in the 2001 and 2004 elections. Congressman Antonio DIAZ of Zambales, a former LP member, was reelected on the Reporma-LM ticket in 2010. The party did not win any seats in the 2013 balloting.

Leaders: Hermogenes EBDANE Jr. (Chairperson), Jose Malvar VILLEGAS Jr. (President).

Other Parties Winning Seats in 2010 or 2013:

The Philippines has many small local or regional parties that are sometimes affiliated with the more established national parties. In 2013 single House seats were also won by candidates from the **United Negros Alliance** (UNA), the **Shield and Fellowship for Kapampangans**; the **Party of Change for Palawan** (PPP); and the **Centrist Democratic Party of the Philippines** (CDP). The **New People Power Party of Nueva Ecija** (*Lapiang Bagong Lakas ng Nueva Ecija*—BALANE) won one seat with the joint endorsement of the NPC.

Abante, based in Nueva Viscaya, and **Alayon**, of Cebu, in partnership with the NP, and the **Sarangani Reconciliation and Reformation Organization** (SARRO) and both of whom had also been endorsed by *Lakas*-CMD. The **Progressive Movement for Development of Initiatives** (PROMDI), founded by former Cebu governor and 1998 presidential candidate Emilio OSMEÑA, won one seat with the joint endorsement of *Lakas* and another Cebu party, the **Bando Osmeño–Pundok Kauswagan** (BO-PK). Another candidate endorsed by both the BO-PK and *Lakas* won a second seat from Cebu City. The **Navoteno** party of Navotas won a seat in coalition with the PMP, as did the **Partido Magdiwang** of former San Juan mayor Joseph Victor EJERCITO, the son of former president Estrada.

Akbayan! Citizens' Action Party (*Akbayan*). *Akbayan* was formed in January 1998 as an electoral coalition of various leftist groups, including splinters from the Communist Party of the Philippines (CPP, below) and the KRMR (see under PMP, below). In the May 1998 election it won one party-list seat. In May 2001 it again won sufficient support for one seat, while in 2004 it captured 6.7 percent of the vote and was awarded three seats. In 2007 it held one seat, but gained another in April 2009 following the Supreme Court's party-list reallocation (see Legislature, below). Walden BELLO, an academic and well-known globalization critic, joined the lower house and won a full term in 2010. Bello made headlines in August 2010 for uttering a scathing indictment on the House floor of former president Macapagal-Arroyo for alleged corruption. Allies of the former president filed an ethics complaint against the left-wing lawmaker. In 2013, the party won two seats in the House.

Leaders: Risa HONTIVEROS-BARAQUEL, Walden BELLO (Members of the House of Representatives).

Bayan Muna Party. The leftist *Bayan Muna* (People First), which descends from the Communist-affiliated New Nationalist Alliance (*Bagong Alyansang Makabayan*—Bayan), was the most successful of the party-list groups in 2001 and 2004, winning three House seats in both elections. In 2004 the government charged that it and two associated party-list organizations—the **Gabriela Women's Party** (GWP), led by Liza LARGOLA-MAZA, and the *Anakpawis* (Toiling Masses), previously led by the late Crispin BELTRAN—had channeled money to Communists. Party leader Satur Ocampo has also been associated with the NDF (below).

Among those arrested in connection with the alleged coup plot against Macapagal-Arroyo in February 2006 were the six party-list members from *Bayan Muna, Anakpawis,* and the GWP. The six, minus Beltran, who had already been arrested, initially sought sanctuary in the House complex, Batasan, and were therefore dubbed the "Batasan 5." In July 2007 the Supreme Court dismissed the charges against all six. *Bayan Muna,* Anakpawis, and the GWP formed the core of a new progressive coalition, Makabayan, which ran a slate of Senate candidates in 2010. *Bayan Muna* won two party-list House seats in 2010.

Leaders: Satur OCAMPO, Teodoro CASIÑO Jr.

For a complete list of the groups that won party-list seats in the House of Representatives in 2013, see the Legislature section, below. (For more information on the **Philippine Democratic Socialist Party** [*Partido Demokratiko Sosyalista ng Pilipinas*—PDSP], please see the 2013 *Handbook.*)

Communist Groups:

National Democratic Front (NDF). The NDF was launched by the Communist Party of the Philippines (CPP) in April 1973 in an effort to unite Communist, labor, and Christian opponents of the Marcos regime, which declared it illegal. It encompasses more than a dozen "revolutionary allied organizations," most prominently the CPP and the CPP's military wing, the New People's Army (NPA). After decades of fighting and multiple failed ceasefires, on March 16, 1998, in The Hague, representatives from the government and the NDF signed a Comprehensive Agreement on Respect for Human Rights and International Humanitarian Law (CARHRIHL). (For more information on the history of the NDF, please see the 2013 *Handbook.*)

In July 2006, responding to President Macapagal-Arroyo's directive that the police join with the armed forces to pursue all-out war against the NPA, NDF leader Luis Jalandoni called for renewed peace talks. With military operations against the NPA continuing, in October 2007 the government indicated that a cease-fire would have to be established before peace talks could resume. NDF leaders expressed willingness to reopen talks, accusing the government of closing the door to further negotiations by imposing preconditions such as disarmament and demobilization.

In May 2009, the government announced the expected resumption of peace talks with the rebels. Under a restored security agreement, NDF negotiator Luis Jalandoni briefly returned from exile in July. Two detained rebel "consultants" were freed in August, but the delay in releasing more threatened to scuttle the revival of the peace process. Peace negotiations resumed in September 2012 but were suspended in February 2013 by the government citing a lack of progress.

Leaders: Luis JALANDONI (Chair of the NDF Negotiating Panel), Fidel AGCAOILI (Spokesperson for Negotiating Panel), Jose Maria SISON (Political Consultant).

Communist Party of the Philippines–Marxist-Leninist (CPP-ML or CPP). The CPP was launched as a Maoist formation in 1968, with the **New People's Army** (NPA) established as its military wing in early 1969. Between 1986 and 1991, many of its leaders were captured by government forces, including NPA commander Romulo KINTANAR, who was released in 1992, abandoned the guerrilla movement, and was assassinated in January 2003. Jose Maria Sison (who reportedly uses the pseudonym Armando Liwanag) was reelected party chair at a Central Committee meeting in September 1992, although he had been an exile in the Netherlands since his release by the Aquino government in 1986. A number of splinter groups subsequently left the CPP (see below).

The NPA numbers some 5,000 rural-based guerrillas, down from a peak of 25,000 in 1987; it is strongest in northeast and central Luzon, in the Samar provinces of the Visayas, and in southern Mindanao, although at various times it has undertaken insurgent activity in well over three-quarters of the country's provinces. In March 1999 the NPA announced that it had established an alliance with the MILF (below). In October 2002 the government declared the CPP to be a terrorist organization.

In 2004, hard-liners attacked Sison for supporting electoral candidates through a number of party-list organizations, including the *Bayan Muna* Party. In the 2010 election campaign, a coalition of leftist party-list groups ran two Senate candidates on the *Nacionalista* Party slate; they were defeated. Some press reports suggested a growing divide between the exiled Sison and hardline leaders Benito and Wilma Tiamzon.

Meanwhile, the NPA and government forces continued to clash. President Macapagal-Arroyo vowed to defeat the NPA by the end of her term in 2010. While the military fell short of this goal, it claimed it had reduced the NPA to a small "spent force" in several regions. Skirmishes and ambushes continued after the Aquino administration took office. In September 2012, an NPA grenade attack in Davao City injured 47 at a circus. In August 2013, Philippine security forces captured a major NPA camp in Northern Samar.

Leaders: Jose Maria SISON (Chair, in exile), Benito E. TIAMZON (Vice Chair), Wilma TIAMZON (Secretary General), Gregorio ROSAL (Spokesperson).

Please see the 2013 *Handbook* for more information on other recently active Communist splinter parties including: the **Marxist-Leninist Party of the Philippines** (MLPP); the **Metro Manila Rizal Regional Party Committee;** and the **Revolutionary Worker's Party–Mindanao** (*Rebolusyonaryong Partido ng Manggagawa–Mindanao*—RPM-M). For more information on the **Filipino Workers' Party** (*Partido ng Manggagawang Pilipino*—PMP), see the 2009 *Handbook.* For information on the **Revolutionary Workers' Party–Philippines** (*Rebolusyonaryong Partido ng Manggagawa–Pilipinas*—RPMP), please see the 2012 *Handbook.*

Southern-Based Muslim Groups:

Moro National Liberation Front (MNLF). In separatist rebellion since 1974 on behalf of Mindanao's Muslim communities, the MNLF split in 1975 into Libyan- and Egyptian-backed factions, the latter subsequently calling itself the Moro Islamic Liberation Front (MILF, below). Originally the stronger of the two guerrilla armies, MNLF forces had dwindled by 1986 to one-third their original size, and in early 1987 the MNLF leader, Nur Misuari, tentatively agreed to drop his demands for an independent southern state in favor of autonomy. A January 1994 cease-fire and a subsequent peace agreement directly led to Misuari's election as governor of the Autonomous Region of Muslim Mindanao (ARMM) on September 9, 1996, although hard-line MNLF splinters and the MILF rejected the arrangement.

In April 2001, the MNLF Central Committee voted to remove Misuari as chair, citing a lack of progress during his tenure as governor of the ARMM. He was replaced by a "Council of 15" but refused to acknowledge the decision. In August the government named the MNLF general secretary, Muslimin Sema, to replace him as head of the Southern Philippines Council for Peace and Development (SPCPD), and in October he was derecognized by the OIC. On November 19 Misuari loyalists broke the MNLF's five-year-old cease-fire in a series of attacks on Jolo Island. Arrested on November 24 while attempting to enter Malaysia, Misuari was later extradited to the Philippines to face charges of rebellion. On November 26 the MNLF's Parouk Hussin was elected to succeed Misuari as ARMM governor.

In February 2006, the MNLF elected Nur Misuari to return as chair (despite his continuing detention), only to remove him again from that position in April 2008. In June 2009, the MNLF declared it would boycott the upcoming ARMM elections to demonstrate its dissatisfaction with the implementation of the 1996 peace accord. On April 20, 2010, in Tripoli, following talks facilitated by the OIC, the MNLF and the Philippine government signed a Memorandum of Understanding on implementation of the 1996 peace agreement. The memorandum called for the creation of the Bangsamoro Development Assistance Fund, instituted the previous month by President Macapagal-Arroyo through an executive order, with an initial disbursement of 100 million pesos. Reports in 2013 indicated that factions within the MNLF were preparing to declare full independence.

Leaders: Nur MISUARI (Chair), Muslimin SEMA (Central Committee Chairperson and Mayor of Cotabato City), Nur MISUARI (Former Chair), Abdul SAHRIN (Secretary General), Parouk HUSSIN.

Moro Islamic Liberation Front (MILF). The MILF was launched as a fundamentalist faction within the MNLF, with Hashim Salamat, a Cairo-trained *ulema* (Islamic religious leader), as deputy to Nur Misuari. It split from the parent group in 1978, adopting the MILF name in 1980. Estimates of the size of its military wing, the **Bangsamoro Islamic Armed Forces**, vary widely, from a Philippine government assessment of 10,000 to an MILF claim of 120,000.

In opposing the September 1996 peace agreement, the MILF indicated that it would settle for nothing less than full independence for Muslim-dominated areas.

In December 1997, MILF leader Salamat returned from 20 years of exile in Libya, and in March 1998 the government and the MILF reached agreement on setting up a quick-response team to prevent future altercations from escalating. In March 1999 Hashim Salamat and the MNLF's Nur Misuari reportedly conferred for the first time in 21 years.

Intermittent formal peace talks, interrupted by suspensions and punctuated by continuing hostilities, continued into 2000. In August the MILF indefinitely suspended talks following a series of military defeats, including the loss of its headquarters at Camp Abubaker in July. Salamat responded by calling for a *jihad* (holy war) against the government and insisted that any further peace talks should take place abroad, in a Muslim country. Negotiations in Tripoli in June 2001 quickly led to a peace pact that was formalized in Kuala Lumpur in August. At the same time, the MILF and the MNLF concluded a "framework of unity" agreement.

Although the MILF condemned the subsequent participation of U.S. troops in the *Balikatan* military exercises, in a meeting with government representatives in Putrajaya, Malaysia, in May 2002 it agreed to assist in eliminating such criminal activities as kidnapping for ransom. The MILF also accepted responsibility for distributing funds to be provided by Manila as reparations for damages attributable to the 2000 military campaign in Mindanao.

In March 2003, the MILF and the Communist NPA announced a "tactical" alliance that stopped short of actual military cooperation. Later in the same month, the MILF agreed to resume peace negotiations with the government, but continuing military activity by the MILF led the Macapagal-Arroyo administration to cancel talks and to reject a cease-fire offer. On June 23 MILF Chair Salamat stated that the MILF renounced terrorism and denied any terrorist links, despite numerous reports that members of the regional *Jemaah Islamiah* (JI) network had infiltrated the MILF. Salamat's statement undoubtedly contributed to the government's decision to reverse itself and accept a cease-fire from July 19. Although it was not made public until August 5, 2003, Hashim Salamat died suddenly on July 13, 2003, and was soon succeeded by the vice chair for military affairs, Murad Ebrahim.

A series of informal meetings concluded in February 2004 with an announcement that formal peace talks would open in Kuala Lumpur. That year Manila complied with two MILF preconditions: the dropping of charges against MILF members for a series of bombings near Davao Airport and government withdrawal from a captured MILF complex in Buliok. October witnessed the deployment of some 50 Malaysian troops, the core of an International Monitoring Team offered by members of the OIC. Exploratory peace talks resumed in April–June 2005.

Negotiations with the government resulted in a Memorandum of Understanding on Ancestral Domain (MOA-AD), announced on July 16, 2008. The Philippine Supreme Court declared the agreement unconstitutional on October 14, and MILF responded by going on an offensive that led to nearly a half-million displaced people on Mindanao. The government declared a unilateral ceasefire in July 2009, and the MILF agreed to return to the negotiating table (see Current issues). The Macapagal-Arroyo administration was unable to arrive at a new agreement with the MILF before leaving office. On May 3, 2012, Aleem Abdul Azis MIMBANTAS, a MILF cofounder and the organization's current vice chair for military operations, died of a heart attack. Reports in July 2013 indicated renewed fighting between MILF and the MNLF in North Cotabato. The strife displaced more than 2,000 villagers.

Leaders: Al-Haj MURAD Ebrahim (Chair), Ghazali JAAFAR (Vice Chair for Political Affairs), Mohaqher IQBAL, Jun MANTAWIL (Head, Peace Panel Secretariat), Muhammad AMEEN (Chairperson, Central Committee Secretariat).

Abu Sayyaf. The most radical of the fundamentalist Muslim insurgent groups, *Abu Sayyaf* (Bearers of the Sword) has continued its activities despite an August 1994 announcement by Manila that the rebels, including their leader, Brahama SALI, had been "annihilated." Although the MILF had earlier condemned the group as a terrorist organization at odds with the precepts of Islam, *Abu Sayyaf* reportedly agreed in September 1996 to operate under MILF command in opposition to the government's accord with the MNLF. In December 1998 the authorities announced that *Abu Sayyaf*'s leader, Abdurajak Abubakar

JANJALANI, had been killed by government forces. In contrast to the MILF, *Abu Sayyaf* is believed to number no more than a few hundred guerrillas.

After more than a year of relative quiescence, *Abu Sayyaf* dramatically resurfaced in March–April 2000 with the kidnapping of more than 50 Philippine hostages on the southern island of Basilan and more than 20 others from the Malaysian resort island of Sipadan, off the Borneo coast. Half a dozen of the Basilan hostages were reportedly executed. Most of the Sipadan hostages were ultimately ransomed for some $17.5 million, in part through the intercession of Libya. In 2001 *Abu Sayyaf* renewed its kidnapping activities, abducting dozens of people and beheading a number of them.

In May 2002, the United States offered a $5 million reward leading to the apprehension of five *Abu Sayyaf* leaders; the Philippine government already had in place its own bounty program, which had contributed in July 2001 to the capture of a principal leader, Najmi SABDULA ("Commander Global"). In December 2003, another *Abu Sayyaf* commander, Ghalib ANDANG ("Commander Robot"), was captured by government forces. The United States, noting the organization's apparent links to the Indonesian-based JI as well as al-Qaida, added *Abu Sayyaf* to its list of foreign terrorist organizations.

Through 2004, *Abu Sayyaf* continued its tactics, including deadly bombings, which most often centered on Zamboanga, a Mindanao port on the Basilan Strait, but which also included the February 2004 bombing of a Manila ferry that cost over 100 lives. In August 2004 a Basilan court sentenced 17 members to death for the 2002 kidnappings.

A failed prison break on March 14–15, 2005, resulted in over two dozen deaths. Those killed included Najmi Sabdula and Ghalib Andang. Since then, *Abu Sayyaf* has continued its bombings and kidnappings, although none on the scale evidenced earlier. At the same time, the Philippine military has stepped up its attacks, aided by intelligence data from U.S. military personnel. In September 2006 *Abu Sayyaf*'s leader, Khaddafy JANJALANI, was killed, as was another commander, Abu SULAIMAN, in January 2007. Five months later the Philippine military announced that Yasser Igasan had succeeded Janjalani. In June 2008, the group kidnapped well-known television journalist Ces Drilon and her crew, releasing them nine days later. Kidnappings, beheadings, and attacks by Abu Sayyaf and military efforts to capture the militants were ongoing through 2013. For instance, an Abu Sayyaf attack in August 2013 killed one soldier and seven militants in Basilan.

Leader: Yasser IGASAN.

Please see the 2013 *Handbook* for more information on the **Rajah Solaiman Movement** (RSM) and the so-called **Pentagon Group.**

LEGISLATURE

The 1987 constitution provides for a bicameral **Congress of the Philippines,** encompassing a Senate and a House of Representatives.

Senate. The upper house consists of 24 at-large members who may serve no more than two six-year terms. Half of the body is elected every three years; voters may cast as many votes as there are seats to be filled.

Because of the upper house's small size, senators are often elected less by party affiliation than by personal following. (At the 2004 election, for example, the victors included three film actors with no significant political experience.) In the most recent election, held May 13, 2013, the *Nacionalista* Party (NP) won 3 seats; United Nationalist Alliance (UNA), 3; the Liberal Party (LP), 1; Nationalist People's Coalition (NPC), 1; Democratic Filipino Struggle (LDP), 1; Filipino Democratic Party–Laban (PDP-Laban), 1; and independents, 2.

Following the 2012 election the party breakdown for the Senate was as follows: UNA, 5; NP, 5; LP, 4: NPC, 2; *Lakas Kampi* CMD, 2; LDP, 1; PDP-Laban, 1; People's Reform Party, 1; independents, 3.

President: Franklin DRILON.

House of Representatives. The lower house includes a maximum of 292 members, of whom the majority are directly elected from legislative districts. A maximum of 20 percent of the members are elected via "a party-list system of registered national, regional, and sectoral parties or organizations." Each voter may cast a ballot for both a district representative and a party-list group. For each party-list seat, an organization must receive at least 2 percent of the total party-list votes cast, but no group may exceed three seats. (For 2013 the Commission on Elections accredited 150 party-list organizations.) In April 2009, a Philippine Supreme Court decision (*Banat vs. Comelec*) changed the formula for allocating party-list seats in the House, mandating that the maximum number of party-list representatives be seated. All representatives serve for three years, with no member to be reelected more than twice.

The most recent election was held May 13, 2013. As in the past, a number of winning candidates ran with more than one party endorsement. The following totals are based in part on information from the House itself. Of the 234 district seats, the Liberal Party (LP) won 112; the Nationalist People's Coalition (NPC), 43; the National Unity Party (NUP), 24; the National Party (NP), 17; *Lakas Kampi* Christian Muslim Democrats (*Lakas Kampi* CMD), 14; the United Nationalist Alliance (UNA), 10; the Democratic Filipino Struggle (LDP), 2; Shield and Fellowship for Kapampangans, 1; First Cry of *Nueva Ecija*—Party of Change, 1: the United Negros Alliance, 1; the Party of Change for Palawan (PPP), 1; the New Society Movement (KBL), 1; the Centrist Democratic Party of the Philippines (CDP), 1: and independents, 6.

In the May 2013 elections, 32 parties and other organizations were awarded a total of 58 party-list seats, giving the House a total membership (counting district and party-list seats) of 292. Party-list seats were secured by the *Buhay Hayaang Yumabong* (*Buhay*), which gained three seats, while each of the following won two seats: the *Bayan Muna* Party; Akbayan! Citizens' Action Party; *Ako Bicol*; *Abono*; Gabriela Women's Party; Cooperative NATCCO Network Party (Coop-NATCCO); 1st Consumers Alliance for Rural Energy: Advocacy for Teacher Empowerment Through Action, Cooperation and Harmony Towards Educational Reforms (A TEACHER); OKW Family Club; Agricultural Sectoral Alliance of the Philippines, Inc. (AGAP); Citizens' Battle Against Corruption (CIBAC); and *Magdalo Para Sa Pilipino—Magdalo*: and *An Waray*. Each of the following won one seat *Abante Mindanao*—ABAMIN; Alliance of Concerned Teachers; Luzon Farmers Party (Butil); *Anak Mindanao—Amin*; Advocacy for Social Empowerment and Nation Building Through Easing Poverty—*Kalinga*; Anti-Crime and Terrorism Community Involvement and Support—ACT-CIS; LPG Marketers Association—LPGMA; Youth Against Corruption and Poverty (YACAP); *Agri-Agra na Reproma Para Sa Magsasaka Pilipinas Movement—AGRI; Alyansa ng mga Batayang Sektor* (ABS); *Ang Partido Ng Mga Pilipinong Marino—ANGKLA*; Democratic Independent Workers' Association (DIWA); *Kabataan; Anakpawis; Alay Buhay; Ang Asosasyon Sang Mangunuma Nga Bisaya-Owa Mangunguma—AAMBIS-OWA*; Social Amelioration and Genuine Intervention on Poverty—SAGIP; Alliance of Volunteer Educators (AVE); *Agbiag! Timpuyog Ilokano*; Adhikaing Tinataguyod Ng Kooperatiba—ATING Koop; BANAT and AHAPO Coalition; *Abakada-Guro; Ang Mata'y Aalagaan* (AMA); *Ang Nars*; Ang National Coalition of Indigenous Peoples Action. Four seats remained undecided after the balloting.

Speaker: Feliciano "Sonny" BELMONTE Jr.

CABINET

[as of November 12, 2013]

President	Benigno Aquino (LP)
Vice President	Jejomar Binay (PDP-Laban)
Secretaries	
Executive Secretary	Paquito Ochoa Jr.
Chief of Staff	Julia Abad [f]
Agrarian Reform	Virgilio De Los Reyes
Agriculture	Proceso Alcala (LP)
Budget and Management	Florencio Abad (LP)
Education	Armin Luistro
Energy	Jose Rene Almendras
Environment and Natural Resources	Ramon Paje (LP)
Finance	Cesar Purisima (LP)
Foreign Affairs	Albert del Rosario
Health	Enrique Ona
Interior and Local Government	Manuel Roxas II.
Justice	Leila De Lima [f]
Labor and Employment	Rosalinda Baldoz [f]
National Defense	Voltaire Gazmin

National Economic Development Authority	Cayetano Paderanga Jr.
Public Works and Highways	Rogelio Singson
Science and Technology	Mario Montejo
Social Welfare and Development	Corazon Soliman [f]
Tourism	Ramon Jimenez Jr.
Trade and Industry	Gregory Domingo
Transportation and Communications	Joseph Emilio Abaya
Chair, Housing and Urban Development Coordinating Council	Jejomar Binay (PDP-Laban)
Governor, Central Bank of the Philippines	Amando Tetangco Jr.

[f] = female

INTERGOVERNMENTAL REPRESENTATION

Ambassador to the U.S.: Jose CUISIA Jr.

U.S. Ambassador to the Philippines: Philip GOLDBERG.

Permanent Representative to the UN: Libran N. CABACTULAN.

IGO Memberships (Non-UN): ADB, APEC, ASEAN, IOM, ICC, NAM, WTO.

POLAND

Polish Republic
Rzeczypospolita Polska

Political Status: Independent state reconstituted 1918; Communist-ruled People's Republic established 1947; constitution of July 22, 1952, substantially revised in accordance with intraparty agreement of April 5, 1989, with further amendments on December 29, including name change to Polish Republic; new interim "small" constitution introduced December 8, 1992; permanent "large" constitution approved by national referendum on May 25, 1997, effective October 17, 1997.

Area: 120,725 sq. mi. (312,677 sq. km).

Population: 38,538,447 (2013E—UN); 38,383, 809 (2013E—U.S. Census).

Major Urban Centers (2013E): WARSAW (1,716,000), Kraków (758,000), Łódź (719,000), Wrocław (631,000), Poznań (551,000), Gdańsk (460,000), Szczecin (409,000).

Official Language: Polish.

Monetary Unit: Złoty (market rate November 1, 2013: 3.11 złotys = $1US). After Poland joined the European Union in May 2004, the Polish government announced that it hoped to adopt the euro as Poland's national currency by 2007. However, the target date was subsequently pushed back.

President: Bronisław KOMOROWSKI (elected as a member of Civic Platform); elected in special balloting on July 4, 2010, to succeed Lech KACZYŃSKI (elected as a member of Law and Justice), who was killed in a plane crash on April 10. (Presidents are constitutionally required to resign their party affiliations upon inauguration.)

Prime Minister: Donald TUSK (Civic Platform); nominated to a second term as prime minister by the president on November 8, 2011, following the legislative elections of October 9 and inaugurated (along with his new cabinet) on November 16.

THE COUNTRY

A land of plains, rivers, and forests, Poland has been troubled throughout its history by a lack of firm natural boundaries to demarcate its territory from that of powerful neighbors of both East and West. Its present borders reflect major post–World War II adjustments that involved the loss of some 70,000 square miles of former Polish territory to the former Soviet Union and the acquisition of some 40,000 square miles of previously German territory along the country's northern and western frontiers, the latter accompanied by the expulsion of most ethnic Germans and resettlement of the area by Poles. These changes, following the Nazi liquidation of most of Poland's prewar Jewish population, left the country 96 percent Polish in ethnic composition and 90 percent Roman Catholic in religious faith.

Poland's economy underwent dramatic changes in the years after World War II, including a large-scale shift of the workforce into the industrial sector. A resource base that included coal, copper, and natural gas deposits contributed to significant expansion in the fertilizer, petrochemical, machinery, electronic, and shipbuilding industries, placing Poland among the world's dozen leading industrial nations. Attempts to collectivize agriculture proved largely unsuccessful, with 80 percent of cultivated land remaining in private hands, and the lack of agricultural modernization contributed to periodic agricultural shortages, which in turn, contributed to consumer unrest. The communist government sought Western loans to finance industrial improvements but often could not keep up with payments, allowing interest to accumulate at $1 billion each year.

On October 22, 1978, Cardinal Karol WOJTYŁA, archbishop of Kraków, was invested as the 264th pope of the Roman Catholic Church. The first Pole ever selected for the office, Pope JOHN PAUL II was regarded as a politically astute advocate of church independence who had worked successfully within the strictures of a Communist regime. During a June 2–10, 1979, visit by the pope to his homeland, he was greeted by crowds estimated at 6 million. In 1980, Polish Primate Cardinal Stefan WYSZYŃSKI played a key role in moderating the policies of the country's newly formed free labor unions while helping persuade the Communist leadership to grant them official recognition. Cardinal Wyszyński died on May 28, 1981, and he was succeeded as primate on July 7 by Archbishop Józef GLEMP, whose efforts to emulate his predecessor were interrupted by the imposition of martial law on December 13. The result was a worsening in church–state relations that continued until May 1989, when the Polish *Sejm* voted to extend legal recognition to the church for the first time since 1944. Two months later, Poland and the Holy See established diplomatic relations.

In 1987, after the external debt had risen to more than $39 billion, the United States agreed to provide assistance in loan consolidation and rescheduling with the "Paris Club" of Western creditors. The action came after Polish officials had approved limited economic and political liberalization. Far more drastic revision from late 1988 included an end to price controls, the privatization of many state-owned companies, and a variety of other measures intended to introduce a market economy. Limited political reforms were introduced in 1988, eventually leading to round-table discussions between the government and Solidarity. Over a matter of months, the two sides negotiated open elections for a new, multiparty government in July 1989. The political and economic transitions were difficult; gross domestic product (GDP) contracted nearly 20 percent, and annual inflation hit 120 percent in 1991–1992, prior to the resumption of growth in 1993. Inflation averaged approximately 5 percent annually in 1998–2004, while unemployment rose steadily from a low of about 10 percent in 1998 to a high of 20 percent in 2003–2004.

Poland was the largest of the ten new members to join the European Union (EU) in May 2004, and a year later much of the country was reportedly content with the EU developments to date. Farmers, initially concerned that subsidies in other EU countries would undercut Polish productivity, reported increased exports.

Poland was the only country in the EU to register consistent economic growth during the 2008–2012 financial crisis, averaging 3.52 percent, primarily because its large domestic market made it less dependent on exports than some of its neighbors. Poland has a large number of small businesses (2.3 million) that have helped support the domestic economy, but 55 percent of its exports go to EU member states. The government also took steps to maintain confidence by such measures as strengthening household deposit insurance, obtaining a $20.5 billion precautionary loan from the IMF, and increasing fiscal

stimulus to the economy. Inflation averaged 3.5 percent, while unemployment hovered around 9.2 percent. The fiscal debt rose to 7.8 percent of GDP in 2010 but shrunk to 5.2 percent in 2011, and 3.5 percent in 2012, slightly above EU limits.

GOVERNMENT AND POLITICS

Political background. Tracing its origins as a Christian nation to 966 A.D., Poland became an influential kingdom in late medieval and early modern times, functioning as an elective monarchy until its liquidation by Austria, Prussia, and Russia in the successive partitions of 1772, 1793, and 1795. Its reemergence as an independent republic at the close of World War I was followed in 1926 by the establishment of a military dictatorship headed initially by Marshal Józef PIŁSUDSKI. The first direct victim of Nazi aggression in World War II, Poland was jointly occupied by Germany and the USSR, coming under full German control with the outbreak of German-Soviet hostilities in June 1941.

After the end of the war in 1945, a Communist-controlled "Polish Committee of National Liberation," established under Soviet auspices in Lublin in 1944, merged with a splinter group of the anti-Communist Polish government-in-exile in London to form a Provisional Government of National Unity. The new government was headed by Polish Socialist Party (*Polska Partia Socjalistyczna*—PPS) leader Edward OSÓBKA-MORAWSKI, with Władysław GOMUŁKA, head of the (Communist) Polish Workers' Party (*Polska Partia Robotnicza*—PPR), and Stanisław MIKOŁAJCZYK, chair of the Polish Peasants' Party (*Partia Stronnictwo Ludowe*—PSL), as vice premiers. Communist tactics in liberated Poland prevented the holding of free elections as envisaged at the Yalta Conference in February 1945. Instead, the election that was ultimately held in 1947 represented the final step in the establishment of control by the PPR, which forced the PPS into a 1948 merger as the Polish United Workers' Party (*Polska Zjednoczona Partia Robotnicza*—PZPR).

Poland's Communist regime was thereafter subjected to periodic crises resulting from far-ranging political and economic problems, accompanied by subservience to Moscow and the use of Stalinist methods to consolidate the regime. In 1948 Gomułka was accused of "rightist and nationalist deviations," which led to his replacement by Bolesław BIERUT and his subsequent imprisonment (1951–1954). By 1956, however, post-Stalin liberalization was generating political turmoil, precipitated by the sudden death of Bierut in Moscow and "bread and freedom" riots in Poznań, and Gomułka returned to the leadership of the PZPR as the symbol of a "Polish path to socialism." The new regime initially yielded a measure of political stability, but by the mid-1960s Gomułka was confronted with growing dissent among intellectuals in addition to factional rivalry within the party leadership. As a result, Gomułka-inspired anti-Semitic and anti-intellectual campaigns were mounted in 1967–1968, yielding the mass emigration of some 18,000 Polish Jews (out of an estimated 25,000) by 1971. Drastic price increases caused a serious outbreak of workers' riots in December 1970, which, although primarily economic in nature, provoked a political crisis that led to the replacement of Gomułka as PZPR first secretary by Edward GIEREK.

Following a parliamentary election on March 23, 1980, a new austerity program was announced that called for a reduction in imports, improved industrial efficiency, and the gradual withdrawal of food subsidies. Workers responded by demanding wage adjustments and calling strikes, which by August had assumed an overtly political character, with employees demanding that they be allowed to establish "workers' committees" to replace the PZPR-dominated, government-controlled official trade unions. Among those marshaling support for the strikers was the Committee for Social Self-Defense (*Komitet Samoobrony Społeczej*—KSS), the largest of a number of recently established dissident groups.

On August 14, 1980, the 17,000 workers at the Lenin Shipyard in Gdańsk struck, occupied the grounds, and issued a list of demands that included the right to organize independent unions. Three days later, workers from a score of industries in the area of the Baltic port presented an expanded list of 16 demands that called for recognition of the right of all workers to strike, abolition of censorship, and release of political prisoners. In an emergency session also held on August 17, the PZPR Politburo agreed to open negotiations with the strikers, eventually consenting to meet with delegates of the Gdańsk interfactory committee headed by Lech WAŁĘSA, a former shipyard worker who had helped organize the 1970 demonstrations. On August 30, strike settlements were completed and the *Sejm* approved the 21-point Gdańsk Agreement, which was signed by Wałęsa and the government on August 31. While recognizing the position of the PZPR as the "leading force" in society, the unprecedented document stated, "It has been found necessary to call up new, self-governing trade unions which would become authentic representatives of the working class."

Although most workers along the Baltic coast returned to their jobs on September 1, 1980, strikes continued to break out in other areas, particularly the coal- and copper-mining region of Silesia, and on September 6, First Secretary Gierek resigned in favor of Stanisław KANIA. On September 15, the government announced registration procedures for independent unions to file with the Warsaw provincial court. Three days later, 250 representatives of new labor groups established a "National Committee of Solidarity" (*Solidarność*) in Gdańsk with Wałęsa as chair, and on September 24 the organization applied for registration as the Independent Self-Governing Trade Union Solidarity. The court objected, however, to its proposed governing statutes, particularly the absence of any specific reference to the PZPR as the country's leading political force. Not until November 10—two days before a threatened strike by Solidarity—did the Supreme Court, ruling in the union's favor, remove amendments imposed by the lower court, the union accepting as an annex a statement of the party's role. By December some 40 free trade unions had been registered, while on January 1, 1981, the official Central Council of Trade Unions was dissolved.

The unprecedented events of 1980 yielded sharp cleavages between Wałęsa and radical elements within Solidarity and between moderate and hard-line factions of the PZPR. Fueled by the success of the registration campaign, labor unrest increased further in early 1981, accompanied by appeals from the private agricultural sector for recognition of a "Rural Solidarity." Amid growing indications of concern by other Eastern-bloc states, the minister of defense, Gen. Wojciech JARUZELSKI, was appointed chair of the Council of Ministers on February 11. Initially welcomed in his new role by most Poles, including the moderate Solidarity leadership, Jaruzelski attempted to initiate a dialogue with nonparty groups and introduced a ten-point economic program designed to promote recovery and counter "false anarchistic paths contrary to socialism." The situation again worsened following a resumption of government action against dissident groups, although the Independent Self-Governing Trade Union for Private Farmers–Solidarity (Rural Solidarity), which claimed between 2.5 and 3.5 million members, was officially registered on May 12.

At a delayed extraordinary PZPR congress that convened on July 14, 1981, in Warsaw, more than 93 percent of those attending were new delegates selected in unprecedented secret balloting at the local level.

As a consequence, very few renominations were entered for outgoing Central Committee members, while only four former members were reelected to the Politburo. Stanisław Kania was, however, retained as first secretary in the first secret, multicandidate balloting for the office in PZPR history.

Despite evidence of government displeasure at its increasingly political posture, Solidarity held its first national congress in Gdańsk on September 5–10 and September 25–October 7, 1981. After reelecting Wałęsa as its chair, the union approved numerous resolutions, including a call for wide-ranging changes in the structure of trade-union activity. First Secretary Kania resigned at the conclusion of a PZPR Central Committee plenary session on October 18 and was immediately replaced by General Jaruzelski, who on October 28, made a number of changes in the membership of both the Politburo and Secretariat. Collaterally, Jaruzelski moved to expand the role of the army in maintaining public order.

During the remaining weeks of 1981 relations between the government and Solidarity progressively worsened. On December 11 the union announced that it would conduct a national referendum on January 15, 1982, that was expected to yield an expression of no confidence in the Jaruzelski regime. The government responded by arresting most of the Solidarity leadership, including Wałęsa. On December 13 the Council of State declared martial law under a Military Committee for National Salvation headed by Jaruzelski. The committee effectively banned all organized nongovernmental activity except for religious observances and established summary trial courts for those charged with violation of martial law regulations.

On October 8, 1982, the *Sejm* approved legislation that formally dissolved all existing trade unions and set guidelines for new government-controlled organizations to replace them. The measures were widely condemned by the Catholic Church and other groups, and Solidarity's underground leadership called for a nationwide protest strike on November 10. However, the appeal yielded only limited public support, and Wałęsa was released from detention two days later. On December 18, the *Sejm* suspended (but did not lift) martial law.

On July 21, 1983, State Council Chair Henryk JABŁOŃSKY announced the formal lifting of martial law and the dissolution of the Military Committee for National Salvation. Four months later a National Defense Committee, chaired by General Jaruzelski, was vested with overall responsibility for both defense and state security.

Following *Sejm* elections in October 1985, General Jaruzelski succeeded the aging Jabłońsky as head of state, relinquishing the chair of the Council of Ministers to Zbigniew MESSNER, who entered office as part of a major realignment that substantially increased the government's technocratic thrust. Jaruzelski was reelected PZPR first secretary at the party's tenth congress in mid-1986, during which nearly three-quarters of the Central Committee's incumbents were replaced.

In October 1987, Jaruzelski presented to the PZPR Central Committee a number of proposed economic and political reforms that far outstripped Mikhail Gorbachev's "restructuring" agenda for the Soviet Union. Central to their implementation, however, was a strict austerity program that included massive price increases and was bitterly opposed by the outlawed Solidarity leadership. Even though voters rejected the proposals in a remarkable referendum on November 29, the government indicated that it would proceed with their implementation, albeit at a slower pace than had originally been contemplated.

New work stoppages erupted in Kraków in late April 1988 and quickly spread to other cities, including Gdańsk, before being quelled by security forces. On August 22 emergency measures were formally invoked to put down a further wave of strikes, and six days later the PZPR Central Committee approved a plan for broad-based talks to address the country's economic and social ills. Although the government stated that "illegal organizations" would be excluded from such discussions, a series of meetings were held between Solidarity leader Wałęsa and Interior Minister Czesław KISZCZAK. On September 19, however, the Messner government resigned after being castigated by both party and official trade union leaders for economic mismanagement. Mieczysław RAKOWSKI, a leading author of the March 1981 economic program, was named prime minister on September 26.

In the wake of further party leadership changes on December 21, 1988, which included the removal of six Politburo hard-liners, a new round of discussions with representatives of the still-outlawed Solidarity was launched on February 6, 1989. The talks resulted in the signing on April 5 of three comprehensive agreements providing for the legalization of Solidarity and its rural counterpart; political reforms that included the right of free speech and association, democratic election to state bodies, and judicial independence; and economic liberalization. The accords paved the way for parliamentary balloting on June 4 and 18, at which Solidarity captured all of the 161 non-reserved seats in the 460-member *Sejm* and 99 of 100 seats in the newly established Senate.

On July 25, 1989, six days after General Jaruzelski was elected president of the republic by the barest of legislative margins, Solidarity rebuffed his effort to secure a PZPR-dominated "grand coalition" government. On August 2, the *Sejm* approved Jaruzelski's choice of General Kiszczak to succeed Rakowski as prime minister; however, opposition agreement on a cabinet proved lacking, and Kiszczak was forced to step down in favor of Solidarity's Tadeusz MAZOWIECKI, who succeeded in forming a four-party administration on September 12 that included only four Communists (although the PZPR was, by prior agreement, awarded both the interior and defense portfolios).

On December 29, 1989, the *Sejm* approved a number of constitutional amendments, including a change in the country name from "People's Republic of Poland" to "Polish Republic," termination of the Communist Party's "leading role" in state and society, and deletion of the requirement that Poland must have a "socialist economic system." Subsequently, on January 29, 1990, formal Communist involvement in Polish politics ended when the PZPR voted to disband in favor of a new entity to be known as Social Democracy of the Republic of Poland (*Socjaldemokracja Rzeczypospolitej Polskiej*—SdRP).

In the face of widespread opposition to his status as a holdover from the Communist era, President Jaruzelski on September 19, 1990, proposed a series of constitutional amendments that would permit him to resign in favor of a popularly elected successor. At first-round balloting on November 25 Wałęsa led a field of six candidates with a 40 percent vote share; in the second round on December 9, he defeated émigré businessman Stanisław TYMIŃSKI by a near three-to-one margin, and he was sworn in for a five-year term on December 22. On January 4, 1991, the president's nominee, Jan Krzysztof BIELECKI, won parliamentary approval as prime minister, with the *Sejm* formally endorsing his ministerial slate on January 12.

In June 1991, amid mounting opposition to government economic policy, President Wałęsa twice vetoed bills calling for a form of proportional representation that he insisted would weaken Parliament by admitting a multiplicity of parties, but he was eventually defeated by legislative override on June 28. As predicted, the ensuing poll of October 27 yielded a severely fragmented lower house, with the Democratic Union (*Unia Demokratyczna*—UD) winning the most seats but no party securing more than 13 percent of the vote. A lengthy period of consultation followed, during which Wałęsa offered to serve as his own prime minister. Unable to secure the reappointment of Bielecki, the president was ultimately obliged to settle on a critic of his free-market strategy, Jan OLSZEWSKI, who narrowly succeeded in forming a government on December 23. Four days earlier Wałęsa had been forced to withdraw a group of proposed constitutional amendments that would have given him authority to appoint and dismiss ministers and to veto parliamentary no-confidence motions, while authorizing a simple rather than a two-thirds *Sejm* majority to enact legislation.

The government was weakened in May 1992 by the successive resignations of the economy and defense ministers, the latter in the wake of allegations he had made concerning the military's involvement in politics. Far more contentious, however, was legislative authorization on May 28 to release secret police files of individuals who had reportedly collaborated with the Communist regime. The action had long been sought by the right-of-center Olszewski government but had been resisted as a violation of human rights by the center-left parties, which insisted that many of the dossiers had been deliberately falsified by departing members of the security forces. Olszewski's subsequent publication of a list of alleged collaborators generated widespread outrage, not least from President Wałęsa, who publicly called for the prime minister's dismissal, and on June 5 the *Sejm* approved a no-confidence motion by an overwhelming margin.

On June 6, 1992, the *Sejm* endorsed Waldemar PAWLAK, the relatively obscure leader of the PSL, as new prime minister. However, Pawlak was unable, during the ensuing month, to muster sufficient parliamentary support to form a government and was obliged to resign. On July 6 the UD's Hanna SUCHOCKA was confirmed as Poland's first female prime minister, and five days later she secured *Sejm* approval of a new coalition administration, which included seven parties with ministerial posts and several others pledged to give it parliamentary support. Committed to speedier transition to a market economy, Suchocka's government relaunched the privatization program and secured the reactivation of International Monetary Fund (IMF) credit facilities that had been suspended since 1991. However, Suchocka's austerity policies, including a firm stand against striking coal miners and rail workers, incurred widespread opposition from Solidarity deputies, and on May 28, 1993, her government fell by one vote over a continued tight budget. President Wałęsa responded by refusing to accept the prime minister's resignation, asking Suchocka to remain in office on a caretaker basis pending a new election.

The balloting of September 19, 1993, yielded a pronounced swing to the left, with the SdRP-dominated Democratic Left Alliance (*SojuszLewicy Democratycznej*—SLD) winning 37 percent of the legislative seats and the PSL winning 29 percent. Five weeks later, on October 26, the two groups formed a coalition government headed by the PSL's Pawlak.

Conflict between the presidency and the ruling coalition intensified in October 1994, when the government rejected President Wałęsa's dismissal of the defense minister and the legislature voted by a large majority to urge the president to cease interfering in the democratic process. Wałęsa responded by denouncing the Pawlak government and calling for stronger presidential powers; the controversial defense minister was forced out the following month. The crisis deepened in January 1995 amid various policy differences between the president and his government, which culminated in Pawlak's resignation on February 7, after the president had threatened parliamentary dissolution. Collateral strains between the two coalition parties were resolved sufficiently to enable the SLD's Józef OLEKSY, a Communist-era minister, to be sworn in on March 6 as prime minister of a continued SLD-PSL coalition, albeit with half of its members new appointees.

Despite the relative failure of a 1993 effort to form a "presidential" party styled the Nonparty Bloc in Support of Reform (*Bezpartyjny Blok Wspierania Reform*—BBWR), Wałęsa in April 1995 confirmed his candidacy for a second presidential term. His main opponents were Aleksander KWAŚNIEWSKI of the SLD/SdRP, Jacek KUROŃ of the center-right Freedom Union (*Unia Wolnósci*—UW), and former prime ministers Olszewski and Pawlak. In the first round of balloting on November 5 Kwaśniewski took a narrow lead, with 35.1 percent against 33.1 percent for Wałęsa. In the runoff contest on November 19, Kwaśniewski won 51.7 percent to 48.3 percent for Wałęsa, even though most of the other first-round candidates and center-right parties had thrown their support behind Wałęsa.

Sworn in on December 22, 1995, Kwaśniewski quickly lost his prime minister, Oleksy, who resigned on January 24, 1996, over allegations (later dismissed) that he had passed information to the Soviet, later Russian, intelligence service. He was replaced on February 8 by Włodzimierz CIMOSZEWICZ of the SLD, heading a further coalition of the SLD and PSL that included six independents.

In preparation for the 1997 legislative elections Solidarity in June 1996 began organizing small center-right parties into the Solidarity Electoral Action (*Akcja Wyborcza Solidarność*—AWS), which ultimately became a coalition of some 36 parties and groups. Despite President Kwaśniewski's popularity and four years of economic growth, the AWS won 201 seats against 164 for the SLD in the balloting on September 21, 1997. The AWS's success was attributed to its alignment with the Catholic Church and its appeal to lingering resentment against the ex-Communists. After protracted negotiations, the AWS signed a coalition agreement with the UW on October 20 and formed a new government on October 31, with Jerzy BUZEK of the leading AWS party, the Social Movement-Solidarity Electoral Action (*Ruch Społeczny-Akija Wyborcza Solidarność*—RS-AWS), as prime minister.

In 1998 and early 1999, Warsaw's imminent entry into the North Atlantic Treaty Organization (NATO) and its preparations for accession to the EU had far-reaching effects on both foreign and domestic policies. With Poland about to become the eastern front line of NATO and the EU, Warsaw was under pressure to tighten its eastern borders, which increased tension with Belarus and raised concerns in Ukraine. Warsaw sought to reassure its former Soviet bloc neighbors and held talks to improve relations with Germany, with whom it hoped to tie up lingering postwar issues, particularly compensation for deported Poles used by the Nazi regime as slave laborers. Poland formally entered NATO on March 12, 1999.

On the domestic front, reforms designed to prepare for EU accession created labor unrest with political fallout. Privatization plans and other reforms, some of which raised the prospects of huge job losses, caused strikes in the coal mining, steel, railway, and defense industries. In trying to curb subsidies and protectionist tariffs, the government alienated farmers, who, under the leadership of radical unionist Andrzej LEPPER of the Self-Defense of the Polish Republic (*Samoobrona Rzeczypospolitej Polskiej*), blocked roads throughout the nation in a series of disruptive protests, the most serious of which began in December 1998 and extended into 1999. At the beginning of 1999 the government was also confronted by opposition to a series of health care reforms, introduction of which led to physician resignations, more strikes, and public confusion. The crisis in health care also contributed to a potential rift in the governing coalition, but the AWS managed to mollify its junior partner, the UW, in late January, in part by dismissing a deputy health minister. The UW nevertheless continued to criticize its senior partner for what it saw as half-hearted pursuit of free-market policies, particularly privatization. Meanwhile, public opinion polls registered increasing dissatisfaction with the AWS and growing support for the leftist SLD.

Policy and leadership differences within the government continued to cause persistent internal friction, and on October 11, 1999, in an effort to stabilize the situation, the AWS and the UW signed a renegotiated coalition agreement. Nevertheless, on June 6, 2000, objecting to Buzek's continuation as prime minister as well as to the inability of the AWS to exert discipline over its disparate components, the UW formally withdrew. The move left the AWS in charge of a minority government, although it continued to receive regular UW support in Parliament and survived until the legislative term ended in 2001.

On October 8, 2000, President Kwaśniewski won reelection with 53.9 percent of the vote against 11 other active candidates. Second place (17.3 percent) went to an independent, Andrzej OLECHOWSKI, who had previously been associated with the AWS, while Solidarity's Marian KRZAKLEWSKI, despite AWS backing, finished third (15.6 percent). Former president Wałęsa managed only 1 percent of the vote, finishing seventh.

In December 2000 Solidarity announced that it was withdrawing from active politics and turned over to Prime Minister Buzek's RS-AWS its voting rights in the AWS, which was rapidly disintegrating as its various leaders and parties sought to position themselves as the best center-right alternative to the SLD for upcoming parliamentary elections. In the *Sejm* and Senate elections on September 23, 2001, a coalition of the SLD and the much smaller Union of Labor (*Unia Pracy*—UP) claimed a plurality of 216 seats in the lower house and an overwhelming majority in the upper, while Buzek's new coalition, the Solidarity Electoral Action of the Right (*Akcja Wyborcza Solidarność Prawicy*—AWSP), failed to meet the 8 percent coalition threshold for *Sejm* representation. The UW also lost all representation in the *Sejm* as three new formations—the Civic Platform (*Platforma Obywatelska*—PO), with 65 seats; Law and Justice (*Prawo i Sprawieliwość*—PiS), with 44; and the League of Polish Families (*Liga Polskich Rodzin*—LPR), with 38—split much of the center-right vote. Andrzej Lepper's populist *Samoobrona* entered the *Sejm,* finishing third, with 53 seats.

On October 9, 2001, the SLD/UP completed a coalition agreement with the rural PSL that permitted the SLD's Leszek MILLER, an electrician who had risen through the ranks of the PZPR and the SdRP, to become prime minister of an SLD-dominated cabinet on October 19, concurrent with the opening of the new parliamentary session.

In early March 2003 the PSL left the governing coalition following a disagreement with the SLD over a tax initiative. The government was therefore left with a minority of only 212 seats (of 460) in the *Sejm,* a situation that was only partially eased by addition of the newly formed, but now-defunct, Peasant Democratic Party (*Partia Ludowe Democratyczna*—PLD) to the coalition from late March until January 2004. The government remained stressed on several fronts, and Miller announced his resignation on May 2, 2004, only one day after Poland had acceded to the EU. President Kwaśniewski immediately designated "technocrat" Marek BELKA of the SLD to succeed Miller, but Belka lost a confirmation vote on May 14 in the *Sejm,* which was then constitutionally permitted to present its own candidate. When the *Sejm* failed to act in that regard, the president reappointed Belka on June 11, and he and his SLD/UP cabinet were confirmed by the *Sejm* on June 24. Marek Belka was immediately regarded as, at best, a caretaker leader of a dying government, a perception underscored by the poor performance of the SLD and UP in the June European Parliament balloting.

In the legislative elections on September 25, 2005, the PiS led all parties by securing 155 seats in the *Sejm,* followed by the PO with 133 seats and *Samoobrona* with 56. The SLD was relegated to fourth place with 55 seats. Given the recent wave of scandals, the dramatic decline of the SLD was not unexpected. However, the plurality achieved by the rightist PiS surprised observers across Europe. On September 27, the PiS named Kazimierz MARCINKIEWICZ as its choice for prime minister and sought to form a coalition government with the PO.

The first round of presidential elections was held on October 9, 2005, with a field of 12 candidates. Donald TUSK of the PO won 36.33 percent of the vote, followed by Lech KACZYŃSKI of the PiS with 33.10 percent. In the runoff on October 23, 2005, Kaczyński bested Tusk 54.04 percent to 45.96 percent to gain the presidency.

President Kwásniewski on October 24, 2005, formally designated Marcinkiewicz to form a new government. However, the PiS/PO talks collapsed, and Marcinkiewicz was sworn in as head of a minority PiS government on October 31, depending on the support of two diverse "fringe parties"—*Samoobrona* and the LPR—to maintain a legislative majority. On November 10 the government won a vote of confidence in the 460-seat *Sejm* with 272 votes, thanks to support from *Samoobrona* and the LPR. The PiS ascendancy was completed with Kaczyński's inauguration on December 23. Subsequently, in a May 5, 2006, reshuffle, the LPR and *Samoobrona* formally joined the government, their leaders being named deputy ministers. However, following a series of disputes between Prime Minister Marcinkiewicz and President Kaczyński and his twin brother Jarosław KACZYŃSKI (the chair of the PiS) over privatization and the campaign to remove former Communists from all levels of government, Marcinkiewicz resigned on July 10. President Kaczyński immediately named his brother as prime minister–designate, and Jarosław Kaczyński was sworn in as prime minister on July 14 to head an essentially unchanged cabinet. The PiS/LPR/*Samoobrona* government won a vote of confidence in the *Sejm* on July 19 with 240 votes.

The gap between the goals of PiS and its coalition partners widened throughout 2006–2007, particularly as the Kaczyński brothers began to pursue their policies of lustration, fiscal discipline, and anticorruption more vigorously, dismissing *Samoobrona* Chair Andrzej Lepper on two occasions. *Samoobrona* was also compromised by the findings of the Central Anti-Corruption Bureau (*Centralne Biuro Antykorupcyjne*—CBA), an institution whose formation was promised in the PiS campaign platform. Critics later alleged that the CBA had focused primarily on political rivals of the ruling party. As one of its conditions for allowing allies to remain in government during the crisis of July 2007, the PiS insisted that junior coalition partners refrain from investigating the controversial agency. The combination of demands for unconditional compliance with the PiS, or "loyalty conditions," and a lack of promised evidence regarding the charges against Lepper precipitated *Samoobrona*'s break with the government. The coalition crisis endured for several weeks, prompting a PiS meeting with its rival, the center-right PO, in August, after which early elections were scheduled for the fall, two years ahead of schedule.

Snap legislative elections on October 21, 2007, resulted in a pronounced victory for the PO, whose chair, Donald Tusk, formed a centrist government on November 16 comprising the PO and the PSL. In the *Sejm,* the PO won 209 seats, and its coalition partner, the PSL, won 31. The Law and Justice party took 166, while the Left and Democrats garnered only 53. In the Senate, the PO obtained a clear majority, winning 60 of the 100 seats. The PiS took 39, and 1 seat went to an independent.

The decisive victory for the europhile PO in the 2007 legislative poll neutralized Prime Minister Kaczyński's bid to strengthen his power. Turnout was one of the largest in history, and the PO surge was attributed in part to its support among young voters. By 2008, Prime Minister Tusk was ranked in public opinion polls as Poland's most trusted politician, while his rival Lech Kaczyński was among the least trusted. However, restricted spending remained necessary to reduce the deficit, which threatened to damage his popularity and his alliance with the PSL. Energy problems also provided cause for concern. Poland has the largest coal reserves in the EU and generates 95 percent of its electricity from coal. However, stringent EU carbon emission standards would raise electricity rates astronomically if Poland were forced to conform to them. Consequently, Poland in 2009 announced plans to build a nuclear energy plant.

The PO received a vote of confidence from the Polish electorate in elections for the European Parliament that were held on June 7, 2009, winning 44.4 percent of the vote and obtaining 25 seats. Jerzy Buzek, a PO member, was subsequently elected president of the European Parliament, becoming the first Eastern European to hold that office.

The plane crash of April 10, 2010, that killed 96 people (many from the Polish political elite) represented one of the most devastating political catastrophes any country has ever faced. In addition to President Lech Kaczyński and his wife, 18 members of parliament, including 3 deputy speakers, died. Also among the victims were Sławomir SKRZYPEK, the president of the National Bank of Poland; Franciszek GĄGOR, chief of the general staff of the Polish Armed Forces; Vice Admiral Andrzej KARWETA, the commander in chief of the Polish Navy; and a host of other dignitaries. The plane was on its way to Smolensk, Russia, to attend a memorial service marking the massacre of around 22,000 Polish nationals by Soviet authorities in 1940. The event was to be a milestone in Polish–Russian relations, as the Soviets had once blamed the atrocity on the Nazis, and Russia had not acknowledged Soviet responsibility until 1990. The offices of the victims of the crash were subsequently filled with calm deliberation, and the accident precipitated neither a national nor an international crisis in spite of the many conspiracy theories that arose after the tragedy.

The early presidential election of June–July 2010 was widely viewed as a referendum on the PO's performance, and PO candidate Bronisław Komorowski, the speaker of the *Sejm,* was expected to secure an easy victory. However, the election results were closer than expected because Komorowski proved to be a poor campaigner and Jarosław Kaczyński a surprisingly good one. Nevertheless, with Komorowski's ultimate success, the PO held control of both the executive and legislative branches of government. Its victory was expected to mean closer ties with its partners in the EU as well as with Russia.

In July, Poland took over as president of the EU, a position that rotates every six months, and Tusk gave a rousing speech, praising the EU as the best place on earth to live and disparaging euroskeptics. His ability to handle his role in a dispassionate way and still argue for policies that were favorable to his own country would test his political ability.

Constitution and government. The constitutional changes of April 1989 provided for a bicameral legislature that incorporated the existing 460-member *Sejm* as its lower chamber and added a 100-member upper chamber (Senate). For the June 1989 balloting it was specified that all of the Senate seats would be free and contested, while 65 percent (299) of the lower house seats would be reserved for the PZPR and its allies (35 on a noncontested "National List" basis). All seats at subsequent elections were to be open and contested. Initially, the combined houses were empowered to elect a state president for a six-year term; however, constitutional changes prior to the December 1990 poll provided for a popularly elected president serving a five-year term. A new "small" constitution became effective on December 8, 1992, having been signed by President Wałęsa on November 17. It redefined the powers of, and relations between, the legislature, presidency, and government. A new "large" constitution, including a charter of liberties and human rights, was approved by a popular referendum on May 25, 1997, by a vote of 56.8 percent.

Parliament sits for a four-year term, save that the *Sejm* may dissolve itself (and by such action end the Senate term) by a two-thirds majority, assuming a quorum of at least 50 percent. The president has widespread authority in foreign and defense matters, with decrees in other areas requiring countersignature by a prime minister who is nominated by the president but must be confirmed by the *Sejm.* The prime minister appoints other ministers, while the president names military leaders and high-level judges. The president may veto legislation but can be overridden by a three-fifths majority of the lower house. There is a Constitutional Tribunal, whose members are appointed by the *Sejm,* while the regular judiciary has three tiers: regional courts, provincial courts, and a Supreme Court.

As a result of constitutional and administrative reforms in 1975, the number of provinces (voivodships, or *województwa*) was increased from 22 to 49. However, in July 1998, following a contentious debate over boundaries, Parliament reduced the number to 16 (4 more than the government initially proposed). The reduction was part of a package of administrative reforms that also created a "middle tier" of 65 cities and 308 districts (*powiats*) and, in furtherance of decentralization, assigned authority for regional economic development to the voivodships. At the local level, there are nearly 2,500 communes (*gminas*). The prime minister appoints provincial governors (*wojewodowie*); provincial assemblies as well as executives and legislative organs at the lower levels are elected.

Although the leading organs were under government control, the Polish press for most of the Communist era was livelier than in other East European countries, the regime making little effort to halt publication of "uncensored" (*samizdat*) publications, many of which were openly distributed prior to the imposition of martial law in late 1981, when strict censorship was imposed. Many state-controlled newspapers and magazines were privatized following the collapse of the Communist regime, and freedom of the press was subsequently protected for the most part. Reporters Without Borders ranked Poland 22nd out of 173 for 2013, despite criticism of a penal code provision that criminalizes defamation.

Foreign relations. During most of the postwar era, Polish foreign policy supported the stationing of Soviet troops in Poland as well as Polish participation in the Warsaw Pact and the Council for Mutual Economic Assistance. The events of the first half of 1980 elicited harsh criticism from the Soviet Union, Czechoslovakia, and East Germany while prompting expressions of concern in the West that the Warsaw Pact might intervene militarily, as it had in Hungary in 1956 and in Czechoslovakia in 1968. Predictably, the Soviet Union and most Eastern-bloc countries endorsed the Polish government's crackdown of December 1981. Western disapproval was alleviated by the lifting of martial law in mid-1983, and Washington withdrew its opposition to Polish membership in the IMF at the end of 1984, facilitating the country's admission to that agency and its sister institution, the World Bank, in June 1986.

In February 1990, Prime Minister Mazowiecki traveled to Moscow for talks with President Gorbachev, reiterating Polish concern that a newly unified Germany might attempt to reclaim land ceded to Poland after World War II. These fears were allayed by the outcome of "two-plus-four" talks between the two Germanys and World War II's victorious powers in July, which yielded a treaty between Bonn and Warsaw on November 14 that confirmed Poland's western border at the Oder and Neisse rivers. Poland's other major foreign policy concern was alleviated when the last Russian military contingent withdrew on September 17, 1993.

On May 21–23, 1992, during President Wałęsa's first visit to Moscow, a friendship and cooperation treaty was concluded that subsequently generated widespread resentment in Poland for its failure to address the issue of Russian responsibility for Stalinist atrocities during World War II. In October this source of strain was reduced when Moscow, bringing to an end over 50 years of false denials, admitted that the former Communist regime had ordered the execution of some 26,000 captured Polish army personnel in Katyn forest in 1940.

On November 2, 1992, Poland's National Defense Committee adopted a new policy based on the assumption that Poland had no natural enemies and no territorial claims on neighboring states. Longer-term security was seen as lying in a Euro-Atlantic system involving Polish membership in NATO. The main thrust of Polish foreign policy, however, was toward membership in the European Community (EC, subsequently the EU). To this end, Poland helped establish a series of new, transitional international groupings of postcommunist countries, including the Central European Free Trade Area (CEFTA) treaty with Czechoslovakia and Hungary in 1991 and the Central European Initiative (CEI).

Having joined NATO's Partnership for Peace in February 1994, Poland on April 8 followed Hungary's lead in formally applying for admission to the EU. A month later, on May 9, it was one of nine former Communist states to become an "associate partner" of the Western European Union (WEU). Despite the Western thrust, which included a warm reception for U.S. President Clinton during an address to the *Sejm* on July 7, Poland also sought improved relations with Russia and the other members of the Commonwealth of Independent States (CIS). The motivation for the latter was largely economic: relatively stiff tariffs had generated a deficit in trade with the EU countries, whereas Poland had previously maintained a trade surplus with the Soviet Union. In December 1997 EU leaders agreed to open entry negotiations with Poland and five other nations, and the first formal talks were held in November 1998.

Under an agreement signed in Paris on July 11, 1996, Poland became the third ex-Communist state (after the Czech Republic and Hungary) to gain full membership in the Organization for Economic Cooperation and Development (OECD). The signing coincided with the end of an official visit to the United States by President Kwaśniewski, during which he received assurances of U.S. support for Poland's accession to NATO. Meanwhile, Poland had assigned 700 troops to the NATO-commanded International Force (IFOR) deployed in Bosnia under the Dayton peace agreements. At the Madrid summit meeting in July 1997, NATO leaders invited Poland and two other former Warsaw Pact nations (the Czech Republic and Hungary) to join the alliance. They became members on March 12, 1999, at ceremonies celebrating NATO's 50th anniversary in Independence, Missouri.

Poland was one of the more supportive countries of the U.S./UK-led invasion of Iraq in early 2003, lending some 2,400 troops to the campaign. In April 2003, Prime Minister Miller endorsed a plan for Poland to buy 48 U.S. fighter planes for an estimated $3.5 billion as part of a 15-year military upgrade program. Prime Minister Donald Tusk ended the mission to Iraq in October 2008, which had dwindled to 900 troops largely involved in training and humanitarian work.

On June 7–8, 2003, Polish voters endorsed their country's proposed accession to the EU by a 58.9 percent "yes" vote in a national referendum. Poland joined nine other states as new EU members on May 1, 2004.

Tensions rose between Germany and Poland in late 2004 over the issue of reparations from World War II and its aftermath. Representatives of Germans who had been deported from former German territory in 1945–1946 after the territory was incorporated into Poland renewed their campaign for compensation in 2004. In return, Poland threatened to seek reparations from Germany for damage inflicted during the war.

The PiS minority cabinet and the subsequent PiS-led coalition that emerged from the 2005 elections adopted a nationalistic, euroskeptic approach toward foreign policy. Among other things, other European countries reportedly objected to the new Polish administration's blockage of cross-border takeovers of Polish state-run enterprises slated for privatization. In addition, the EU specifically noted Poland in a resolution condemning perceived growing racism and ultranationalism throughout the continent. Of particular concern to the EU was the inclusion of the LPR in the Polish cabinet in 2006. The Polish legislature, in turn, issued a counter-resolution condemning the EU resolution.

Relations with the EU worsened during Germany's subsequent presidency of the EU, as the PiS coalition argued against reduced voting representation for Poland in a treaty meant to replace the EU constitution rejected by French and Dutch voters in 2005. Prime Minister Kaczyński famously asserted in a June 2007 radio interview that Poland's population-based representation would be greater if its people had not been decimated by Germany and Russia during World War II. Poland's government also charged that Germany was undermining European energy security by cooperating with Russia in the construction of a Baltic pipeline.

Following his election in October 2007, Prime Minister Donald Tusk adopted a more europhilic stance, meeting with Angela Merkel in Berlin in December 2007 and hosting a one-day summit with Nicolas Sarkozy in Warsaw in May 2008. In December 2007, he visited EU headquarters in Brussels and declared his will to "defend European interests." Poland and Sweden launched an Eastern Partnership in 2009, a regional association under EU auspices that would work to bring Ukraine, Moldova, Georgia, Armenia, and Azerbaijan into a closer relationship with the EU. Tusk, however, declined to sign the EU Charter of Fundamental Rights, noting that it could compel Poland to recognize the claims of Germans forced from their homes following postwar border changes and because of its stance on gay rights and other social issues that he considered antithetical to Poland's more conservative public opinion. President Kaczyński remained opposed to the EU and refused to sign the ratification of the Lisbon Treaty, which had passed both houses of parliament in April.

Since the political ascendancy of the PO, Prime Minister Tusk has made a concerted effort to forge closer relations with all of Poland's neighbors. In 2009, Poland and Ukraine signed an agreement to make border crossings easier for people living near the frontier. The two countries jointly hosted the European soccer championship in June 2012. Warsaw is also mentoring Kyiv in its bid for EU membership.

In September 2009, the Obama administration reversed a George W. Bush administration plan to deploy a missile shield in Poland. The decision was popular among the Polish public, but Foreign Minister Radosław SIKORSKI commented that the action created a "credibility problem" for the United States. Sikorski's criticism resonated with the U.S. government, and in October, it was announced that Poland could still host U.S. missiles, although not ones that could be converted to offensive nuclear weapons or otherwise pose a threat to Russia. That announcement was followed in December with an agreement to place mobile Patriot missiles and 100–150 U.S. soldiers at Morag, Poland, which is about 35 miles from the Russian base at Kaliningrad. Russia complained that it could not understand the necessity "to create the impression as if Poland is bracing itself against Russia." The troops and missiles arrived in Poland in May 2010, and Russia replied by deploying an antiaircraft missile installation to Kaliningrad.

The presence of Polish troops in Afghanistan was an issue in the 2010 presidential election. Komorowski argued that Poland's deployment of 2,500 soldiers achieved nothing and squandered funds that Poland needed to modernize its military. In July, Foreign Minister Radosław Sikorski visited Afghanistan and stated, "We would like to withdraw our brigade at the end of 2012 and possibly continue to support Afghans in some other form." In 2011, Poland declined to participate in the NATO alliance against Libya, although it was willing to send humanitarian aid. It claimed that its pilots were not yet trained well enough in flying F-16s to contribute effectively and it would be prohibitively expensive.

The April 2010 plane crash in Russia that killed so many Polish officials briefly improved relations with Russia. Prime Minister Putin was extremely compassionate, bringing roses to the crash site and accompanying the body of President Kaczyński back to Warsaw. Russia also declared a national day of mourning to honor the dead. A week after the misfortune Russian television showed the Polish film *Katyn* to a national audience, most of which were unfamiliar with the Soviet atrocity and the related ongoing anger among Poles. The warming trend cooled in January 2011, when the official Russian report attributed the crash to an error of the Polish pilots, who were under pressure to land in unsafe conditions. In July, the Polish report gave some responsibility for the crash to the Russian air traffic controllers but ascribed most of the blame to Polish officials and procedures. Polish minister of defense Bogdan KLICH resigned after the report was issued because his department trained the pilots.

In May 2011 President Obama visited Poland at the end of a six-day trip to Europe. He praised Poland as a democratic model for the emerging Arab states and supported legislation that would make it easier for Poles to obtain visas to the United States. He also promised that the Poles would not suffer from his reset of U.S. relations with Russia, endorsing an agreement, which was signed in June, to station U.S. air force personnel and planes in Poland to train Polish pilots. However, in May 2012, Obama mistakenly used the phrase "Polish death camps" when speaking of Nazi camps located in Poland. The gaffe outraged many Poles, despite Obama's quick apology.

In 2011 Poland's relations with Western Europe, especially Germany, were positive. Tusk, who spoke fluent German, had a warm relationship with Merkel. At their meeting in Warsaw in June Merkel promised that if the Nord Stream pipeline caused problems of access to Polish Baltic ports, Germany would bury them deeper. Tusk noted that trade between German and Poland was 1 billion euros greater than trade between Russia and Germany. Both countries decided not to engage in military activity in Libya. In June 2011, Tusk also met with Sarkozy in Paris, where the French president promised to support Poland during its EU presidency and vowed not to interfere with Poland's shale gas extraction, although the practice has been banned by the French parliament.

Poland held the rotating presidency of the EU for the second half of 2011, but as it does not use the euro, Warsaw was left out of many critical negotiations about the economic crisis.

Relations with Lithuania became strained due to a decision to drop Polish-language classes in Lithuanian schools and limit the use of Polish in public areas. Warsaw insists that would deprive Lithuania's Polish ethnic group of a basic right. The new Lithuanian government elected in October 2012 was more amenable to Polish language use.

Poland sent 20 troops to Mali in April 2013 as part of an EU training mission. Meanwhile, Warsaw anticipated withdrawing its troops from Afghanistan in 2014. The Polish military base in Ghazni province will be renovated for use as a geology and mining university.

Current issues. On October 9, 2011, Poland held elections for both the Senate and the *Sejm,* the upper and lower houses of parliament. The ruling coalition, consisting of the dominant Civic Platform (*Platforma Obywatelska*—PO) and the Polish Peasants' Party (*Partia Stronnictwo Ludowe*—PSL), made history by becoming the first government to win reelection since the fall of communism in 1989. Prime Minister Donald Tusk returned to office by stressing that Poland was the only European nation not to fall into recession during the ongoing global economic crisis and that Poland needed continuity in order to continue growing. The PO won 207 seats in the *Sejm,* and the PSL won 28 seats, for a coalition total of 235 (51 percent) of the 460 seats. The PO won 63 of the 100 seats in the Senate. Discouragingly, turnout was only 48.92 percent.

The Law and Justice Party (*Prawo i Sprawieliwość*—PiS) of former prime minister Jarosław Kaczyński won 157 seats in the *Sejm,* down 8 from the previous election. The success of the new party Palikot's Movement was a surprise. It won 40 seats in the *Sejm,* taking third place. It was headed by a charismatic vodka entrepreneur, Janusz Palikot, who ran an anticlerical campaign, supporting abortion on demand, homosexual civil unions, and legalizing marijuana. He appealed to young people and the supporters of the Democratic Left Alliance (*SojuszLewicy Democratycznej*—SLD), which won only 27 seats in this election, down dramatically from the 55 it had won in 2007.

Unlike his EU neighbors, Tusk did not have to face voters after imposing a tough austerity package onto an already suffering population. Instead, he initiated a series of reforms to trim government expenditure and encourage growth. In May, the *Sejm* voted to raise the retirement age from 60 for women and 65 for men to 67 years for both, deferring pension costs. Solidarity activists responded by barring the gates of the *Sejm*, so MPs could not exit the building. Tusk also planned to deregulate some 200 professions, such as cab drivers, with the goal of creating 100,000 jobs. Current cabbies did not take the news well, blocking the streets of Warsaw in a protest in May. Tusk also planned to invest in infrastructure projects, including railways, road construction, power plants, and shale-gas exploration. Responding to Palikot's constituents, Tusk addressed family and social issues, such as insurance coverage for fertility treatments, longer maternity leave, and cheaper preschool. Both Tusk and Palikot introduced laws on civil partnerships, and both were rejected by the *Sejm*.

Revelations that Poland allowed the United States to use its territory as a venue for incarcerating and interrogating terror suspects from 2001 to 2004 have sparked controversy. The current government has launched an investigation into this decision, and on January 10, 2012, former interior minister and secret services chief Zbigniew SIEMIATKOWSKI was indicted for false imprisonment. Poland is the first EU member state to indict an official in this matter, and the case may expand.

Poland's economy slowed to a standstill in 2013, as its neighbors tightened their belts and passed on purchasing Polish exports. Economists predicted a recession, rising unemployment, and growing budget deficits, as slowing sales would cut into tax revenue. Companies began to lay off workers, as unemployment rose above 14 percent. The popularity of both Tusk and the PO fell, although they survived a no confidence vote called by PiS in February. With elections on the horizon—the European parliament in 2014 and the *Sejm* in 2015—Tusk took steps to improve his standing with voters. The government also requested an additional IMF line of credit for $33.8 billion. In February, Finance Minister Jacek Vincent ROSTOWSKI (PO) was promoted to deputy prime minister, signaling Tusk's focus on the economy.

The question of whether Poland should join the eurozone dominated political discussion in 2013. The country should have fulfilled all of the Maastricht criteria and been eligible to adopt the euro in 2015. The *Sejm* endorsed the EU Fiscal Compact by a vote of 282 to 155 on February 20, which President Komorowski ratified on February 28. The PiS asked the constitutional tribunal to review the matter, arguing that approval needed a two-thirds majority to give budgetary control to an external power. However, eurozone nonmembers are not bound by the compact, they merely are allowed to participate in eurozone discussions.

All parties agree that a constitutional amendment must be enacted before Poland joins the eurozone, as Article 227 gives the National Bank of Poland exclusive control over printing and regulating the national currency. Tusk and the PO favored changing the constitution immediately, so that "When the eurozone resolves its problems we should be ready to join it." However, the PO-PSL government did not have the two-thirds majority in the Sejm needed to pass a constitutional amendment. The PiS insisted on a popular referendum on when to change currency before any constitutional amendment. In March Tusk offered a compromise to the PiS, agreeing to a referendum if the PiS in return for the party's backing to change the constitution.

Given the financial crisis within the eurozone since 2008, many Poles question the logic of abandoning their own currency. They fear prices will rise or that the zone will collapse from bailing out Greece, Cyprus, and other members. Public opinion polls in 2013 showed that two-thirds of Poles oppose the euro. Kaczyński and the PiS accused Tusk of using the euro issue to distract voters from urgent budget matters.

With the PO and PiS dominating politics for the past decade, smaller political parties began to explore alliances ahead of the upcoming elections. The PSL, the PO's junior partner in the past two governments, elected a new chairman, Janusz PIECHOCIŃSKI, who began to construct a center-right group with Poland Comes First (PJN). In February, former president Aleksander Kwaśniewski created a new center-left political movement, Europa Plus, to end the recent dominance of the PO and PiS. Former SLD member Ryszard KALISZ launched Poland—Everyone's Home (*Polska—Dom Wszystkich*) in April. By June, Palikot, Kaliz, the PD, SDPL, and Union of Labor had all joined Europa Plus.

Fallout from the Smolensk airplane crash continued in 2013, three years after the tragedy (see Government and Politics, above). Conspiracy theories continue to blame the Polish government for the crash, especially after traces of explosives were found in the ruins. Russia has not returned the wreckage of the plane. The bodies of some victims were discovered to have been mixed up before burial.

In the wake of the March cancellation of the United States's missile defense system in Europe, Foreign Minister Sikorski announced that Poland would create its own link in the NATO air-defense system for $43.3 billion. But as the economy slowed, the Defense Ministry slashed spending for 2014 by 10 percent.

Spring 2013 saw several adjustments in the cabinet. Tusk sacked Treasury Minister Mikolaj BUDZANOWSKI in April for failing to disclose a pipeline expansion deal with Russia's Gazprom. Justice Minister Jarosław GOWIN was fired on April 29 for suggesting that Polish fertility clinics were selling embryos. By June, popular support for the PO dropped to 27 percent, behind the PiS at 30 percent. Support for the PSL sunk below the 5 percent threshold for entering the *Sejm*. Gowin challenged Tusk in the PO's August 2013 leadership election but failed to unseat the prime minister; Tusk received 79.4 percent of the vote, compared to Gowin's 20.4.

POLITICAL PARTIES AND GROUPS

Postcommunist Poland's first fully democratic election in October 1991 unleashed a profusion of parties and groupings of all conceivable orientations, several tracing their origins from the Solidarity movement. Of the more than 100 parties active in 1991, no fewer than 29 parties won representation in the 460-seat *Sejm,* none with more than 13 percent of the vote. The scene thereafter was one of constant flux in party allegiance and identity, particularly on the center-right of the political spectrum. Because of a new minimum vote threshold, only seven groups secured parliamentary representation in September 1993. As of mid-1995, however, a total of 275 distinct political parties had achieved official registration.

During the second half of the 1990s the division in Polish politics was most clearly represented by the leftist coalition, the Democratic Left Alliance, of President Aleksander Kwaśniewski, who had been elected in 1995, and the center-right Solidarity Electoral Action (*Akcja Wyborcza Solidarność*—AWS) coalition, which was launched in 1996 under the leadership of Solidarity in preparation for the 1997 legislative balloting. Among the other major participants in the AWS were the Conservative Peasant Party, the now-defunct Christian National Union, the Center Alliance, and the Christian Democratic Party. In all, more than 30 (mostly small) parties and groups joined the AWS, which won 33.8 percent of the vote at the 1997 legislative elections and secured a plurality of 201 seats in the *Sejm*. Its two most visible figures were Solidarity Chair Marian Krzaklewski and the new prime minister, Jerzy Buzek.

Despite its electoral success in 1997, the AWS failed to cohere into a unified party, in part because many of the constituent organizations did not want to merge into a larger grouping that they perceived as dominated by trade unionists. Only about half of the legislators elected under the banner of the AWS coalition joined a new Solidarity-backed party, the Social Movement–Solidarity Electoral Action (see Social Movement, below), upon its formation in December 1997.

The third-place finish of Krzaklewski in the 2000 presidential race accelerated the disintegration of the unwieldy AWS, although Prime Minister Buzek managed to remain in office through the full parliamentary term. At the September 2001 legislative election, Buzek's new coalition, the Solidarity Electoral Action of the Right, failed to meet the threshold for representation in the *Sejm,* and the SLD, in coalition with the Union of Labor, easily outdistanced a handful of recently formed, post-AWS formations—chiefly, the Civic Platform (PO), Law and Justice (PiS), and the League of Polish Families. Thus, the presidency, the National Assembly, and the Council of Ministers were dominated by the heirs of Poland's Communist past, while the heirs of the Solidarity movement were scattered among a variety of center and right parties.

The 2005 elections brought a substantial change to Polish party politics, with the significant diminution of the electoral strength of the political left and the ascension of the right side of the party system. However, the presence of populist partners in the subsequent coalition government, combined with a series of contested corruption investigations, undermined the PiS goal of establishing a dominant Christian-democratic movement. This did not entirely unravel the center-right, as support remained steady for the business-friendly PO, which performed well in the 2006 regional elections, won a strong plurality in the early elections of October 2007, and went on to form a new two-party coalition government with the small Polish People's Party. The PO was victorious in the October 2011 parliamentary elections, becoming the first postcommunist government to win reelection.

Government Parties:

Civic Platform (*Platforma Obywatelska*—PO). The PO was organized in January 2001 at the initiative of three prominent politicians: former presidential candidate Andrzej Olechowski, who, running as an independent, had finished second in the 2000 poll with 17 percent of the vote; Donald Tusk, formerly of the Freedom Union (UW, below); and former AWS leader and *Sejm* Speaker Maciej PŁAŻYŃSKI. The new formation's liberal, free-market orientation soon attracted other disparate elements, including much of the previously AWS-supportive Conservative Peasant Party (see SKL-RNP, below) and the extreme right-wing Realpolitik Union (UPR). (For additional information on the UPR, see the 2007 *Handbook.*) For the 2001 Senate campaign, the PO joined the Solidarity Electoral Action of the Right (AWSP), the UW, and Law and Justice (PiS, below) in a **Senate Bloc 2001** (*Bloc Senat 2001*) in an unsuccessful effort to prevent the SLD from gaining a majority. In the concurrent *Sejm* election the PO finished second, with 12.7 percent of the vote and 65 seats, although a number of deputies elected on its list, including eight from the SKL, chose to sit in the lower house as members of other parliamentary groups.

The PO, which had entered the 2001 elections as a "group of voters," was registered as a political party in March 2002. In April 2003, PO Chair Maciej Płażyński resigned to protest the centrist party's failure to adopt his rightist policies. The PO led all parties in the balloting for the Polish seats in the European Parliament in June 2004.

In the 2005 parliamentary elections, the PO won the second largest block of seats with 133, more than doubling the 65 seats that it won in 2001. Initially, the party was thought to be in a position to partner with the PiS to form the government, but talks collapsed.

The PO's candidate, Donald Tusk, came in first in the first round of presidential polling in October 2005 but lost to the PiS candidate in the second round. Enjoying a strong 27.2 percent vote share in the 2006 regional elections, the Civic Platform secured the coveted mayoralty of Warsaw and was rated the most popular party in several public opinion polls, despite being in opposition. After a meeting with the PiS in August 2006, the PO announced support for early elections, pledging to work with the government to pass critical EU legislation before the next poll.

Early parliamentary elections in October 2007 yielded a substantial plurality for the PO in the *Sejm* (on a 41.5 percent vote share) and a three-fifths majority in the Senate. In spite of difficult economic conditions the party did extremely well in the elections for the European parliament in June 2009, gaining 44.4 percent of the vote and half of the 50 seats allotted to Poland. In order to show its commitment to Europe, a PO candidate, who subsequently won a seat in Gdańsk, debated two of his rivals in English. On July 3, 2010, Tomasz Tomczykiewicz was elected head of the PO's parliamentary caucus, replacing Grzegorz Schetyna, who was elected speaker of the *Sejm*.

In November 2010 the PO did very well in local elections, winning 222 seats in regional assemblies. The PiS was second with 141 seats. The party also was the top vote getter in the October 9, 2011, parliamentary election. With 39.18 percent of the vote, the PO received 207 seats in the *Sejm* and 63 in the Senate, down slightly from 209 and 60 in 2007. To shore up his position, Tusk moved elections for party chair from 2014 to August 2013, which he won by a healthy margin (see Current issues, above).

Leaders: Donald TUSK (Prime Minister and Party Chair), Grzegorz SCHETYNA (First Vice President of the Party), Hanna GRONKIEWICZ-WALTZ (Vice President of the Party), Ewa KOPACZ (Vice President of the Party and Marshal of the *Sejm*), Radoslaw SIKORSKI (Vice President of the Party and Minister of Foreign Affairs).

Polish Peasants' Party (*Polskie Stronnictwo Ludowe*—PSL). The original PSL was organized in 1945 by Stanisław Mikołajczyk after the leadership of the traditional Peasant Party (Stronnictwo Ludowe—SL), founded in 1895, had opted for close cooperation with the postwar Communist regime. In November 1949, following Mikołajczyk's repudiation by leftist members, the two groups merged as the United Peasants' Party (Zjednoczone Stronnictwo Ludowe—ZSL), which became part of the Communist-dominated FJN.

In August 1989, a group of rural activists met in Warsaw to revive the PSL on the basis of its 1946 program. (Party leaders subsequently insisted that the Polish name of the party should more appropriately be translated as Polish People's Party, a usage that has recently gained wide acceptance.) In September, the ZSL was awarded four portfolios in the Solidarity-led coalition government, and in November the ZSL reorganized into two parties, the PSL-Rebirth (PSL-*Odrodzenie*—PSL-O) and the PSL-*Wilnanóv* (PSL-W). Six months later, the present PSL emerged from a unification congress of the PSL-O, part of the PSL-W, and some members of the PSL-*Solidarność,* which had been formed by former Rural Solidarity members in 1989. The party was nevertheless weakened by continuing controversy between ex-ZSL activists and those who sought to have them purged. The PSL's principal support came from small farmers who opposed the introduction of large-scale agricultural enterprises on the U.S. model.

At the 1991 election, the PSL was the core of a Peasant Coalition (*Sojusz Programowy*) that won 48 *Sejm* seats. Running alone, it secured 132 seats in 1993 and formed a governing coalition with the SLD. Amid frequent strains between the coalition parties, the PSL deputy president was dismissed as chair of the *Sejm*'s privatization committee in November 1994 on the grounds that he had tried to block or slow down the sell-off of state enterprises.

The PSL lost considerable ground in the 1997 balloting, dropping from 132 seats to 27 on a 7.3 percent vote share. Party leader Jarosław Kalinowski finished fourth, with 6.0 percent of the vote, in the 2000 presidential election. In September 2001 the party won 9.0 percent of the *Sejm* vote, for 42 seats, as a result of which it negotiated a governing coalition with the larger SLD/UP alliance. However, Prime Minister Miller of the SLD forced the PSL to leave the government in April 2003 after the PSL voted against its coalition partners on a contentious road tax measure.

The PSL secured only 25 seats in the 2005 *Sejm* balloting (on a vote share of 6.96 percent), but it won 13.2 percent of the vote in the 2006 regional elections. After securing 8.9 percent of the vote in the October 2007 *Sejm* balloting, the PSL moved into a surprisingly strong government position, as its 31 seats were necessary to provide the PO-led coalition cabinet with a legislative majority. Party leader Waldemar Pawlak, who is also deputy prime minister and minister of the economy, has been a good partner, but the party's performance in the 2009 European Parliament elections, where it won only 7 percent of the vote and 3 seats, weakened its position in the coalition. Pawlak ran in the first round of the 2010 presidential elections, but he garnered only 1.75 percent of the vote. Yet in local elections in 2010 the party won 93 seats, coming in third behind the PO and PiS. The party came in fourth in the 2011 elections, with 8.36 percent of the vote. It lost three seats in the *Sejm* (from 31 to 28) but secured two seats in the Senate after having nonce since 2007. The PO and PSL again formed the governing coalition. On November 17, 2012, Janusz Piechociński upset Pawlak, 547 votes to 530, to become party chair. Pawlak immediately resigned from the cabinet.

Leaders: Janusz PIECHOCINSKI (Deputy Prime Minister, Minister of the Economy, and Party Chair), Jan BURY (Vice Chair), Jolanta FEDAK (Vice Chair), Ewa KIERZKOWSKA (Vice Chair and Secretary of State at the Chancellery of the Prime Minister), Marek SAWICKI (Vice Chair).

Opposition Parties:

Law and Justice (*Prawo i Sprawiedliwość*—PiS). Drawn primarily from conservative elements of the Christian National Union (ZChN, below), the SKL, and the Republican League (*Liga Republikańska*—LR) of Mariusz KAMIŃSKI, the PiS was organized in March 2001 under the leadership of Jarosław Kaczyński, a former editor of *Tygodnik Solidarność* (*Solidarity Weekly*) and a longtime supporter of Lech Wałęsa. In its Christian-democratic orientation the PiS resembled an earlier Kaczyński formation, the now-defunct Center Alliance (*Porozumienie Centrum*—PC; see SKL-RNP, below), which had been organized in 1991 and had then formed the core of a Center Citizens' Alliance (*Porozumienie Obywatelskie Centrum*—POC) that secured 44 *Sejm* seats the following October. In January 1998 Kaczyński resigned after eight years as PC chair because of the party's decision to remain in the AWS.

Registered as a party in June 2001, the PiS gained additional support through the presence of Kaczyński's twin brother, Lech Kaczyński, who had served in the minority AWS government following the departure of the UW but had been dismissed in July 2001 because of a disagreement with Prime Minister Buzek over the handling of a fraud investigation. Lech Kaczyński, a former justice minister, brought to the party his reputation as an anticorruption, anticrime campaigner as well as one of Poland's most popular politicians. At the September 2001 elections the PiS won 44 seats in the *Sejm,* based on 9.5 percent of the vote.

In April 2002, the PiS and the Alliance of the Right (*Przymierze Prawicy*—PP) announced their pending merger. The PP (not to be confused with the Polish Agreement [PP], below, under the LPR) had been established in March 2001 by Minister of Culture Kazimierz UJAZDOWSKI and former members of the AWS-affiliated SKL and ZChN, including the latter's ex-chair, Marian PIŁKA. Ujazdowski, a close ally of Lech Kaczyński, had headed the Conservative Coalition (*Koalicja Konserwatywna*—KK) before its merger with the SKL in early 1999. In July 2001 he resigned from the Buzek cabinet to protest Kaczyński's sacking.

The PiS consistently opposed the economic policies of the Miller administration, and the Kaczyński brothers regularly accused government officials of corruption. That stance appeared to resonate with the public, which accorded the PiS a third-place finish in the June 2004 balloting for the European Parliament.

The PiS's share of seats in the *Sejm* increased from 44 in 2001 to 155 in the 2005 elections. The party also won the presidency and a plurality of seats in the Senate. The PiS subsequently formed an unsteady coalition with two populist parties, *Samoobrona* and the LPR, hoping to establish a leading Christian-democratic conservative party by co-opting smaller factions. While the PiS performed well in regional assembly elections in 2006, taking 25.1 percent of total votes, it was eclipsed by the PO, which also took the mayoralty of Warsaw from PiS control. The PiS-led coalition faced a succession of crises in 2007, as public support flowed from *Samoobrona* and the LPR to the PO. Dwindling poll numbers were exacerbated by seemingly excessive PiS-led corruption investigations of government officials, which in July 2007 resulted in the president's controversial dismissals of several cabinet ministers, including Andrzej Lepper, the agricultural minister and *Samoobrona* chair. Following a breakdown in negotiations toward continuing the current coalition, PiS leaders asserted that the *Sejm* might be dissolved and early elections held. The final blow to the coalition appeared to come with the dismissal of Interior Minister Janusz KACZMAREK on August 8 for alleged leaks that purportedly undermined ongoing investigations of Lepper. The PiS subsequently agreed with the PO to hold snap elections in the fall. Despite having hoped for a renewed mandate, the PiS was ousted from power following the October 21 poll, in which it finished second to the PO with 166 seats on a 32.1 percent vote share. Nevertheless, President Kaczyński indicated that he intended to utilize the leverage left to him in his position, exerting some control over defense, economic, and foreign affairs through his veto power. The party spent most of 2008 on the defensive but sent a representative (an invited guest) to the U.S. Democratic National Convention in Denver, with hopes of learning campaign techniques that could be applied in Poland. The PiS came in second to the PO in the European Parliament elections that were held in June 2009, electing 15 members, who plan to group with conservatives from 7 other countries to form a conservative coalition.

In January 2010, the PiS suffered a further setback when seven of its members in the *Sejm* bolted from the party to form a short-lived new party called **Poland Plus** (see the 2013 *Handbook* for details). Subsequently, the plane crash in April that took the life of President Kaczyński and the failure of his brother to beat the PO candidate in the special presidential election meant that the party lost the right to veto legislation.

The PiS performed poorly in the November 2010 regional elections, winning 81 seats less than the PO, and dissatisfaction within its ranks became open. Seven members who were unhappy with the party's leadership left to form a new party, **Poland Comes First** (see below). Kaczyński has criticized the Tusk administration for its handling of the plane crash that killed his brother and promised to make it an issue during the campaign.

PiS placed second in the October 9, 2011, parliamentary elections, with 29.89 percent of the vote. It received 157 seats in the *Sejm*, down from 166 in 2007, and 31 in the Senate, down from 39 in 2007. Seventeen influential party members blamed the disappointing results—a sixth consecutive loss—on Kaczyński's leadership style and ultimately left the PiS to form a new party, **United Poland** (see below).

Leaders: Jarosław KACZYŃSKI (Former Prime Minister and President of the Party), Mariusz KAMINSKI, Adam LIPIŃSKI, Beato SZYDLO (Vice Presidents of the Party).

United Poland (*Solidarna Polska*—SP). Following the PiS loss in the October 9, 2011, parliamentary election, Deputy Chair Zbigniew Ziobro accused Kaczyński of having a controlling style that damaged the party. Ziobro, a member of the European Parliament and former minister of justice in Poland, and PiS strategist, formed a new parliamentary political bloc, United Poland. Sixteen MPs and 1 senator took up his cause when Ziobro and 2 other MEPs were expelled from the PiS on November 4. By spring, the SP had 20 MPs, 2 senators, and 4 MEPs, who turned it into a formal political party on March 24, 2012. Members elected Ziobro as the party chair and announced a platform that favored taxing wealthy individuals and large businesses, banning abortion and euthanasia, and opposing nuclear power. They did not, however, rule out a future coalition with the PiS, describing the two groups as the "two lungs" of Polish conservative politics.

Leaders: Zbigniew ZIOBRO (Chair), Jacek KURSKI, Beata KEMPA (Deputy Chairs).

Palikot's Movement (*Ruch Palikota*—RP). Palikot's Movement was founded as a progressive, anticlerical party by Janus Palikot, a flamboyant entrepreneur and defector from the PO. The RP platform supported abortion on demand, homosexual civil unions, and the legalizing of marijuana. It placed a surprising third, taking 10 percent of the vote and 40 seats in the Sejm. It did not participate in the Senate race. Slawomir Kopycinski, elected to the Sejm on the SLD list, later changed his affiliation to RP.

Leader: Janusz PALIKOT (Chair).

Democratic Left Alliance (*Sojusz Lewicy Democratycznej*—SLD). The SLD was launched prior to the 1991 election as a coalition of the Social Democracy of the Republic of Poland (*Socjaldemokracja Rzeczypospolitej Polskiej*—SdRP) and the previously Communist-dominated All Poland Trade Unions Alliance (*Ogólnopolskie Porozumienie Związków Zawodowych*—OPZZ). The SdRP had been established on January 29, 1990, upon formal dissolution of the Polish United Workers' Party (*Polska Zjednoczona Partia Robotnicza*—PZPR). Formed in 1948 by merger of the (Communist) Polish Workers' Party (*Polska Partia Robotnicza*—PPR) and the Polish Socialist Party (*Polska Partia Socjalistyczna*—PPS), the PZPR claimed approximately 3 million members prior to the events of 1980–1981, as a result of which enrollment declined by nearly 800,000.

At the December 1990 presidential poll, the candidate backed by the SdRP, Włodzimierz CIMOSZEWICZ, placed fourth, with 9.2 percent of the vote; by contrast, the SLD was runner-up in the 1991 *Sejm* balloting and then became the largest *Sejm* formation in 1993 by increasing its representation from 60 to 171. Announced in May 1995, the presidential candidacy of SLD/SdRP leader Aleksander Kwaśniewski was subsequently endorsed by some 30 parties and groups, sufficient to yield a comfortable three-point margin of victory for him in the second round of the November balloting. Although the SLD improved its vote share from 1993, it actually won fewer seats (164) in 1997, when it was unable to withstand the pro–Catholic Church, anti-Communist campaign of the AWS. However, following the local elections of October 1998, the SLD controlled 9 of the nation's 16 provinces, having won a vote share of 32 percent.

Józef Oleksy became SdRP chair in January 1996, after Kwaśniewski won the 1995 presidential election. After the 1997 election the party chose Leszek Miller to replace Oleksy, who had not run for reelection. Miller's easy victory over Wiesław KACZMAREK, a former economics minister, was considered a blow to reformers who wanted further distance from the party's Communist origins.

The SLD was transformed into a political party announced in April 1999, after which the SdRP dissolved, and in July Miller formally took over the leadership of the SLD. Two other coalition partners, the Polish Socialist Party (PPS) and the Movement of Polish Working People (RLP), chose to remain distinct from the new party. All three parties endorsed President Kwaśniewski for reelection in 2000, and on October 8 he claimed a first-round victory against 11 other candidates, winning 53.9 percent of the vote.

In preparation for the September 2001 parliamentary elections the SLD and the Union of Labor (UP, below) forged an electoral coalition (*Koalicja Sojuszu Lewicky Demokratycznej i Unii Pracy*) that captured 41 percent of the national vote and 216 seats, 15 short of a majority. Miller thereupon negotiated a coalition with the Polish Peasants' Party (PSL) and became prime minister. The SLD/UP coalition had even greater success in the majoritarian Senate contest, winning 75 of 100 seats. However, the SLD's popularity subsequently declined amid discontent in some quarters over government austerity measures and disputes among government coalition parties. Miller resigned as SLD president in March 2004, although one of his close allies, Krzysztof JANIK, was elected to succeed him. Miller also resigned as prime minister on May 2, his replacement, Marek Belka, only achieving confirmation as a caretaker prime minister until the 2005 parliamentary balloting after pledging to undo some of the economic measures adopted by the Miller administration. The SLD (weakened by the defection of a group of legislators in March) managed only a fifth-place finish (again in alliance with the UP) in the June 2004 elections to the European Parliament. Subsequently, Janik was defeated in December in his bid for reelection as SLD leader by former prime minister Oleksy, although Oleksy came under intense scrutiny regarding allegations concerning his activities during Communist rule. The SLD was repudiated at the ballot box in 2005 when it saw its number of seats in the *Sejm* drop to 55. Oleksy was replaced as party leader by Wojciech OLEJNICZAK on May 29, 2005. The party regrouped in 2006 as part of an electoral coalition with the SDPL, UP, and PD, sharing in the collective 14.2 percent of votes taken by the coalition in the November regional elections. Along with the PiS, the SLD had its financial records for the previous cycle rejected by the State Election Commission due to the party having apparently accepted campaign donations in violation of electoral law. Its disappointing showing in the 2007 election caused the replacement of Olejniczak as party leader by Grzegorz NAPIERALSKI on May 31, 2008, but their popularity has continued to decline. Party member Marek Siwiec was elected as a vice president of the last European parliament.

The SLD won only seven seats in the 2009 EU elections in which the SLD ran in a coalition with UP. Napieralski came in a distant third (13.7 percent) behind the PiS and PO candidates in the first round of the June 2010 presidential election. He had been chosen to represent the party in April after Jerzy SZMAJDZIŃSKI was killed in the plane crash of April 10. In the local elections of November 2010 the SLD came fourth, trailing the PO, the PiS, and the PSL. Napieralski again led the party in the October 2011 elections, where it ran a list of younger candidates in the hope of appealing to youth. When the party won only 27 seats in the *Sejm*, Napieralski was sacked. Miller was brought back as party chair.

Leaders: Leszek MILLER (Chair, former prime minister), Leszek ALEKSANDRAK, Paulina PIECHNA-WIĘCKIEWICZ, Joanna SENYSZYN (Vice Chairs).

German Minority of Lower Silesia (*Mniejszość Niemiecka Slaska Opolskiego*—MNSO). Representing ethnic Germans in western and northern Poland, the MNSO list won seven seats in the October 1991 balloting, four of which were retained in 1993. It won two seats in 1997, 2001, and 2005 under rules that exempt national minority parties from the 5 percent threshold. (Both deputies were from the largest German association—the German Social and Cultural Society of Opole Silesia [*Towarzystwo Spoleczno–Kulturalne Niemcówna Slasku Opolskim*—TSKN].) Ethnic rights issues having apparently faded in relevance following the recent adoption of EU legislation guaranteeing minority rights; the party won one seat in the 2007 *Sejm* balloting on a 0.2 percent vote share. The German minority's former representative to the *Sejm*—Henryk KROLL—who had been elected to the *Sejm* five times between 1991 and 2005, was elected in 2009 to the European Parliament as a representative of the German minority in Poland. The party won a single seat in the *Sejm* in October 2011.

Leader: Ryszard GALLA (Chair and Parliamentary Leader).

Other Parties That Contested the 2011 Elections:

Self-Defense of the Polish Republic Party (*Partia Samoobrona Rzeczypospolitej Polskiej*). Popularly known as *Samoobrona,* this party has its base in the agrarian trade union of the same name. Formed in 1993, the union encompassed about half a million mostly rural members, although the much smaller party initially also attracted a high percentage of businesspersons disaffected from the rest of the political establishment. Generally regarded as the most militant of Poland's three principal farmers' unions, *Samoobrona* did not become a significant parliamentary force until the 2001 national election, at which the party won 10.2 percent of the vote and 53 seats in the *Sejm.* Following *Samoobrona* success at the polls in 2001, Andrzej Lepper was named vice marshal of the lower house, but he was removed from the post in late November, partly as a consequence of provocative statements made against other national figures. On January 25, 2002, the house revoked his parliamentary immunity, and five days later he was fined by an appeals court for defamatory statements made against President Kwaśniewski and others in 1999. In February 2002 Lepper was charged with seven additional counts of slander. However, the charges appeared to enhance Lepper's popularity.

In 2006, *Samoobrona* (whose support fell to 5.6 percent of the vote in the 2006 regional elections) joined the PiS and the LPR to form a coalition government, with Lepper named deputy prime minister. Lepper was subsequently dismissed in July 2007 in the face of corruption allegations. *Samoobrona* demanded elaboration of the charges brought against its chair, arguing that they were designed to encourage *Samoobrona* legislators to defect and join the PiS.

Samoobrona and the LPR in July 2007 announced formation of an electoral alliance called the League and Self-Defense (*Liga i Samoobrona*—LiS) in preparation for possible early elections. The LiS pledged to challenge Poland's adoption of the new EU treaty proposed in 2007, rejecting the "loyalty conditions" endorsed by the PiS as necessary to preserve the coalition. The alliance did not last long, and both parties eventually decided to contest the October balloting on their own and the LiS was disbanded. Samoobrona secured only 1.5 percent in the 2007 *Sejm* elections and did not win a seat. Its performance in the 2009 elections for the European parliament was equally unimpressive, winning only 1.46 percent of the vote and no seats. The party's chair Andrzej Lepper ran in the first round of the presidential elections in 2010, but obtained only 1.3 percent of the vote. On August 4, 2011, Lepper was found hanging in his office, an apparent suicide. It was blamed on financial troubles and his conviction for soliciting sex in exchange for a job in the party. The party received less than 10,000 votes in October 2011. Andrzej PROCHON was elected party chair in March 2012, then replaced by Lech Kuropatwinski in August 2012.

Leader: Lech KUROPATWINSKI (Chair).

Congress of the New Right (*Kongres Nowej Prawwicy*—KNP) is a free market, euroskeptic party that was founded in March 2011 by Janusz Ryszard Korwin-Mikke, a libertarian conservative who received 2.5 percent of the vote in the first round of the presidential poll. It represents a merger of the UPR and WIP. The party secured 35,169 votes in October 2011, or 1.06 percent of those cast.

Leader: Janusz Ryszard KORWIN-MIKKE.

Poland Comes First (*Polska jest Najważniejsz*—PJN). Founded by disgruntled members of PiS, including 4 former PP members, PJN counted 18 MPs and 1 senator ahead of the October 2011 parliamentary election. However, key members switched affiliation before election day. The most high-profile defector was Chair Joanna KLUZIK-ROSTKOWSKA, who went over to the PO. The center-right party received 2.19 percent of the votes in October 2011 and failed to cross the threshold for seats. The PJN was considering an alliance with the PSL for the 2014 European elections.

Leader: Pawel KOWAL (President).

Polish Labor Party/August 80 (*Polska Partia Pracy-Sierpien 80*—PPP). The **Polish Labor Party** emerged for the 2007 *Sejm* elections, where it received 0.8 percent of votes. It did no better in the European parliamentary elections of 2009 when it also took 0.7 percent of the vote under the leadership of Bogusław Zbigniew ZIĘTEK. Ziętek ran for president in 2010, receiving 0.2 percent of the vote in the first round. The party polled 0.55 percent in the 2011 parliamentary election. Chair Bogusław Zbigniew Zietik resigned in April 2013, and the PPP joined Europa Plus.

Leader: Bogusław Zbigniew ZIĘTEK.

Republic Right Party (*Prawica Rzeczypospolitej*—PRP). The Republic Right Party is an antiabortion party that won 1.95 percent of the vote in the 2009 EU elections. In 2010, it ran Marek JUREK, a former speaker of the *Sejm,* as its candidate in the presidential elections. He received 1 percent of the vote in the first round. The party ran for the *Sejm* in October 2011 and received 35,169 votes for 0.24 percent.

Leader: Marek JUREK.

Other Parties:

Union of Labor (*Unia Pracy*—UP). Known as Labor Solidarity (*Solidarność Pracy*—SP) in 1991, when it won 4 *Sejm* seats as a left-wing faction of the original Solidarity movement, the UP captured 41 seats in 1993. With a 4.7 percent vote share in 1997, the UP failed to meet the 5 percent threshold and thus retained no seats. Key members, who include representatives of the Belarusan minority, subsequently were reported to have joined the UW (see below) early in 1998. The UP was part of the Social Alliance in the October 1998 local elections.

Having lost most of its initial Solidarity members, the UP concluded an electoral coalition with the SLD for the 2001 legislative contests and, following the alliance's success at the polls, joined the new administration under Prime Minister Miller. Izabela JARUGA-NOWACKA was elected president of the UP at an April 2004 party congress, and she joined the new government formed by the SLD's Marek Belka in May as a deputy prime minister. The UP again presented joint candidates with the SLD in the June 2004 balloting for the European Parliament.

Even running in coalition with the SDPL, the UP was unable to win a seat in the 2005 elections, after having won 16 in the 2001 contests. However, cooperation within the LiD improved the UP's prospects, and the UP coordinated platform issues such as health policy in advance of the October 2007 elections, but not a single UP candidate was elected. In 2008, the UP and the SLD signed an agreement to cooperate in attempting to collaborate to achieve a left-wing political agenda, and they ran together as a coalition in the 2009 elections for the European Parliament, gaining 12.3 percent of the vote and 7 seats.

Going into the 2011 parliamentary election, the UP had acquired three members in the *Sejm* in spite of its failure to win a seat in the 2007 election. Two members of the SDPL splinter group defected to the UP in 2009, and one of the UP's members took the oath of office as a legislator in May to succeed an SLD legislator who was killed in the plane crash of April. The two former SDPL members, however, again defected this time from the UP to the PO in May 2011. The UP unsuccessfully ran one candidate under the SDL banner in the October elections.

Leaders: Waldemar WITKOWSKI (President), Adam GIEREK (Vice President for International Affairs), Arkadiusz HORONZIAK, Jan LUS, Catherine MATUSZEWSKA (Vice Presidents).

Democratic Party (*Partia Demokratyczna*—PD). A promarket, pro-European grouping hoping to attract centrist support, the PD was launched in the first half of 2005 by Jerzy Hausner (former SLD deputy prime minister) and Władysław Frasyniuk of the UW. Hausner had recently quit the SLD after his proposal to cut the federal budget had been rejected.

The PD took 2.5 percent of the vote in the 2005 parliamentary elections before joining the LiD umbrella for the 2007 balloting, when it gained 3 of the LiD's 53 seats. The PD ran in coalition with the SDPL and the Greens in the 2009 elections for the European Parliament, but the coalition gained only 2.4 percent of the vote. The PD supported the PO's Bronisław Komorowski in both rounds of the 2010 presidential elections. (The PD should not be confused with the long-standing party of the same name; see SD, below.) They did not participate in the October 2011 elections.

Leaders: Andrzej CELINSKI (Chair), Elizabeth BINCZYCKA (Vice Chair).

Polish Social Democracy Party (*Socjaldemokracja Polska*—SDPL). The SDPL was formed in March 2004 by Marek Borowski (a former speaker of the Sejm) and some 22 other SLD deputies seeking to distance themselves from the administration of Prime Minister Miller. Although the SDPL declined formal coalition status in the government formed by the SLD's Marek Belka in June 2004, an SDPL member was named minister of health, and the SDPL pledged to support the caretaker government in the legislature until the 2005 elections.

In 2005, the SDPL ran in coalition with the UP and failed to gain seats in the legislature. The SDLP continued to garner low returns with a 3.9 percent vote share in the 2006 regional elections. It competed in the 2007 election as part of the LiD coalition, securing 10 of the LiD's 53 seats.

Eight of the SDPL's legislators subsequently broke with the SLD and in 2009 formed their own parliamentary caucus, calling itself Social Democracy of Poland–New Left (*Socjaldemoracja Polska-Nowa Lewica*—SDPL-NL). However, the splinter group subsequently collapsed; consequently, several SDPL legislators formed an independent parliamentary caucus, while others either caucused with the Left or remained unattached. The SDPL competed in the 2009 elections for the European Parliament in a coalition with the PD and the Greens but failed to gain a seat. The party's vice chair and spokesperson Arkadius Kasznia ran under the PO list in the October 2011 elections, but he did not win a seat. It has joined the Europa Plus alliance for the 2014 European election.

Leaders: Wojciech FILEMONOWICZ (Chair), Arkadiusz KASZNIA (Vice Chair).

League of Polish Families (*Liga Polskich Rodzin*—LPR). Initially formed as a "group of voters," the LPR brought together an assortment of nationalist, predominantly anti-EU and Catholic groups, many of them associated with *Radio Maryja.* Registered as a party on May 30, 2001, the LPR was headed by Antoni MACIERWICZ, a former interior minister whose efforts to expose former Communist collaborators contributed to the fall of the Olszewski government in 1992. In February 1993, Macierewicz launched the now-defunct right-wing Christian National Movement–Polish Action (*Ruch Chrześcijańsko-Narodowe–Akcja Polska*—RChN-AP), and in 1995, he participated in the formation of the now-defunct Movement for the Reconstruction of Poland (ROP). He broke from the ROP in late 1997 and established the Catholic National Movement for the Reconstruction of Poland, which in May 1998 shortened its name to the Catholic National Movement (*Ruch Katolicko-Narodowy*—RKN) and then joined the AWS. Another LPR founder, Jan ŁOPUSZAŃSKI of the Polish Agreement (*Porozumienie Polskie*—PP) had won 0.8 percent of the vote in the 2000 presidential race.

For the 2001 legislative elections, the LPR list included not only members of the PP but also members of the National Party (*Stronnictwo Narodowe*—SN) and the ROP. The SN dated from the December 1999 merger of Bogusław KOWALSKI'S National Democratic Party (*Stronnictwo Narodowo Demokratyczne*—SND) and an existing SN. In the 2000 presidential election campaign, the SN had been a leading supporter of Gen. Tadeusz WILESKI, who won 0.2 percent of the vote.

In September 2001, the LPR won 9 percent of the vote and 38 seats in the *Sejm.* Within six months, however, significant differences had emerged within the parliamentary delegation, pitting Macierewicz's supporters against a larger group headed by Roman Giertych. In April 2002, Macierewicz and Jan Łopuszański both reportedly resigned from the party Presidium, and Macierewicz and four other disaffected LPR deputies subsequently resumed coordination under the RKN rubric. Macierewicz served as one of the main opponents to EU membership in the run-up to the 2003 referendum on the issue.

The LPR became part of the government in May 2006, but popular support for the party dwindled, as evidenced by its 4.7 percent vote share in regional elections later that year. Influential Catholic media owner Father Tadeusz RYDZYK publicly urged the coalition to continue, as LPR voters had been wooed away by the PiS's increasingly conservative stance, dampening the LPR's prospects for the next election cycle. Nevertheless, LPR Chair Giertych resigned his position as national education minister in July 2007, with *Samoobrona* and the LPR subsequently announcing plans (eventually aborted) to present candidates on a common LiS ballot in the next parliamentary poll.

Damaged by public discontent with the ruling party and a tumultuous summer, as well as isolated xenophobic incidents involving LPR members, support for the party dipped to 1.3 percent in the October 2007 parliamentary balloting. Giertych announced that he would resign as chair following the party's loss of parliamentary representation. In 2009, their candidates ran as members of the Libertas party in the European parliamentary elections. None were elected.

Leaders: Witold BAŁAŻAK (Chair of Party), Maciej GIERTYCH (Chair of Political Council).

Polish Peasant Party, aka Conservative-Peasant Party–New Poland Movement (*Stronnictwo Konserwatywno-Ludowe*–Ruch *Nowej Polski*—SKL-RNP). The SKL-RNP was established in January 2002 by merger of the SKL and the Polish Party of Christian Democrats (*Porozumienie Polskich Chrześcijańskich Demokratów*—PPChD).

Founded in January 1997, the SKL united two small right-wing parties, the Conservative Party (*Partia Konserwatywna*—PK), which had been launched in December 1992 by amalgamation of the Forum of the Democratic Right (*Forum Prawicy Demokratycznej*—FPD) the Peasant-Christian Alliance (*Stronnictwo Ludowo-Chrześcijańskie*—SLCh), and others. The SKL's founding members included ex-ministers Jan Maria ROKITA and Bronisław KOMOROWSKI and elements of the Christian Democratic Labor Party (*Chrześcijańska Demokracja Stronnictwo Pracy*—ChDSP). (For additional information on the ChDSP, see the 2007 *Handbook.*) At the SKL party congress in late February 1998, two groups joined the SKL: the Party of Republicans (Partia Republikanów—PR), led by Jerzy EYSYMONTT, and the Integrative Initiative (*Inicjatywa Integracyjna*—II) faction of the Center Alliance (*Porozumienie Centrum*—PC), led by Wojciech DOBRZYŃSKI. In February 1999, the Conservative Coalition (*Koalicja Konserwatywna*—KK) of Kazimierz Ujazdowski also joined the SKL.

In September 1999, what remained of the Center Alliance, which dated from 1991, and the Christian Democratic Party (*Partia Chrześcijańskich Demokratów*—PChD) announced their merger as the PPChD under Antoni TOKARCZUK, previously the PC chair. Also joining the new formation were former members of an assortment of other small parties that had participated in the AWS. These included the 100 Movement (*Ruch 100*), which had been founded by former foreign minister Andrzej Olechowski, now of the PO; the Polish Peasants' Party–Peasant Alliance (*Polskie Stronnictwo Ludowe–Porozumienie Ludowe*—PSL-PL); and the Movement for the Republic (*Ruch dla Rzeczypospolitej*—RdR), which traced its origins to the 1992 formation of the Christian Democratic Forum (*Forum Chrześcijańsko-Demokratyczne*—FChD) by supporters of ousted prime minister Jan Olszewski. In April 2001, the PPChD added to its ranks the Electoral Solidarity (*Solidarni w Wyborach*—SwW) of Jerzy GWIŻDŻ, a long-time ally of former president Lech Wałęsa. Later in the same month, the PPChD aligned itself with Prime Minister Buzek's efforts to reshape the AWS. The failure of Buzek's AWSP coalition at the September 2001 poll ultimately led the PPChD to seek a stronger alliance, which led to the 2002 merger with the SKL.

In March 2001, the SKL announced that it would leave the government and enter the Civic Platform (PO) in preparation for the September 2001 legislative elections. Following the balloting, however, a number of deputies who had been elected on the PO list established themselves as a separate SKL parliamentary group. In January 2002, the party split over the question of the PO affiliation. One faction, led by Jan Maria Rokita, opted to remain with the PO, and another, led by Artur BALAZS, instead approved the merger with the PPChD and the creation of the SKL-RNP. The latter was subsequently largely absorbed into the PiS but found its position there increasingly awkward, unsuccessfully pressuring the PiS-led coalition to tighten abortion laws in early 2007. In August 2007, the SKL-RNP reformed itself and now uses the simpler name of Polish Peasant Party (*Stronnictwo Konserwatywno-Ludowe*—SKL). In policy, it remains closely tied to the PO, and it supported Bronisław Komorowski in the 2010 presidential elections. At a party congress that was held on June 18, 2011, however, the party decided to work closely with the new party PJN, but that party collapsed before election day. Instead, party leader Marek Zagorski unsuccessfully ran for a seat under the PiS banner.

Leader: Marek ZAGORSKI (Chair).

Polish Socialist Party (*Polska Partia Socjalistyczna*—PPS). Founded in 1892, the PPS went underground during World War II and provided Poland's first postwar prime minister. Although only a small faction was pro-Communist, the party was formally merged with the Communist PPR in 1948 to form the PZPR. The party was revived in 1987 and, in March 1990, sponsored a congress of non-Communist leftists. Weakened by internal strife, the PPS failed to secure *Sejm* representation in 1991 or 1993. In February 1996, the two main PPS factions unified under the leadership of 82-year-old Jan MULAK. He was unanimously replaced by Piotr IKONOWICZ at a party congress in April 1998. Although it had been a member of the SLD coalition, in 1999, the PPS did not enter the new SLD party. Ikonowicz won only 0.2 percent of the vote in the 2000 presidential election. In 2003, Ikonowicz formed a new party (see New Left, below), and he was succeeded as PPS chair by Andrzej ZIEMSKI, who pledged to "moderate" the PPS to appeal to a broader range of voters. The PPS ran on a common ballot with the Polish Pensioners' Party and the Center-Left of the Republic of Poland for European parliamentary elections in 2003 and 2004. Members of the PPS were invited in 2007 to join the new LiD, which remains a group far from the mainstream of Polish politics. In 2010, it made a point of neither running its own candidate nor endorsing any other candidates in the presidential elections, nor did it participate in the 2011 parliamentary election.

Leaders: Boguslaw GORSKI (President), Gregory ILNICKI, Lukasz SZYMANSKI (Vice Presidents).

Democratic Party (*Stronnictwo Demokratyczne*—SD). Recruiting its members predominantly from among professional and intellectual ranks, the SD was founded in 1939 as a non-Marxist group and was a Front party during the Communist era. In mid-1989, the party abandoned its alliance with the Communists and, in September, accepted three portfolios in the Solidarity-led Mazowiecki government. Thereafter, it was seemingly unable to decide what its political profile should be, securing only one *Sejm* seat in the 1991 balloting and none in 1993 or 1997. In 2001, the SD ran in conjunction with the SLD. In June 2002, at the party's 20th congress, delegates replaced Jan KLIMEK as party chair, citing the party's weak performance under his leadership. (The SD should not be confused with the PD [above] that was launched in early 2005.) In the European parliamentary elections of 2002, the SD garnered only 0.27 percent of the vote. In 2005, it formed a coalition with the SDPL but attained only 0.17 percent of the vote. In 2009, the SD formed a coalition with the Greens and the SDPL called Agreement for the Future, which gained 2.4 percent of the vote in elections for the European Parliament. The SD ran former finance minister Andrzej OLECHOWSKI in the first round of the 2010 presidential elections. He obtained only 1.4 percent of the vote, however, and both Olechowski and party chair Pawel Piskorski supported Bronisław Komorowski, the PO candidate, in the second round. Piskorski has been in trouble with the law on a number of issues, including forging documents regarding antiques and artworks stolen before 1945. He was briefly removed from office by the regional court in Warsaw, but then he was reinstated in March 2011, although the forgery charges still loomed. The party did not to run an independent list of candidates in the October 2011 elections.

Leader: Pawel PISKORSKI (Chair).

The Left and Democrats (*Lewica i Demokraci*—LiD). Hoping to take advantage of instability within the PiS-led government coalition, former president Aleksander Kwaśniewski announced the formation of the LiD, a center-left coalition, in September 2006. It consisted of the **Democratic Left Alliance** (*Sojusz Lewicy Democratycznej*—SLD), the **Polish Social Democracy Party** (Socjaldemokracja Polska—SDPL), the **Democratic Party** (*Partia Demokratyczna*—PD, and the **Union of Labor** (*Unia Pracy*—UP). The alliance aimed to create an alternative to the PiS in the upcoming early elections and reportedly approached the PO about the possibility of creating a common ballot. Kwaśniewski, who was credited with modernizing social democracy in Poland, opposed the Kaczyński ambition of purging former communists from government. The LiD received 13.15 percent of votes in the 2007 Sejm elections, giving it 53 seats out of 460. The LiD coalition was formally dissolved after the election, but a coalition of 43 legislators (comprising members of the SLD and UP and former members of the SDPL) formed a parliamentary caucus called simply the Left (Lewica).

In preparation for the 2005 general election, a number of new parties emerged, including the **Center Party** (*Centrum*), a pro-EU grouping that received 0.19 percent of votes in that election and supported the PO in the 2007 election under the leadership of Dr. Zbigniew RELIGA, an internationally renowned heart surgeon; and the **New Left** (*Nowa Lewica*—NL), a left-wing "anticapitalist" grouping established in 2003 by former PPS leader Piotr IKONOWICZ, which held demonstrations against the missile shield in August 2008.

Other parties participating in the 2005 *Sejm* balloting included the **Polish National Party** (*Polska Partia Narodowa*—PPN), led by nationalist and xenophobe Leszek BUBEL, with 0.3 percent of votes; the **National Civic Coalition** (*Ogólnopolska Koalicja Obywatelska*—OKO), a collection of 140 social organizations and unions, with 0.1 percent of votes; the **Polish Dignity and Work Confederation** (*Polska Konfederacja-Godność i Praca*—PKGiP), with 0.07 percent of votes; the **Labor Party** (*Stronnictwa Pracy*—RS), with 0.01 percent of votes; and **Social Rescuers** (*Społeczni Ratownicy*—SR), a party in favor of expanded welfare benefits, with 0.01 percent of votes.

New parties participating in the 2007 *Sejm* elections included the **Women's Party** (*Komitet Wyborczy Partii Kobiet*—PK), which gained only 0.3 percent of the vote and subsequently did not compete in the 2009 elections for the European parliament.

The pan-European Libertas party, which was started by Irishman Declan GANLEY in 2009, presented candidates in Poland for the 2009 European parliamentary elections. In Poland, it consisted of 3 members of the Libertas party, 57 independent candidates, and 67 members from six other parties. These consisted of **Forward Poland** (*Naprzód Polsko*—NP, **Polish People's Party "Piast"** (*Polskie Stronnictwo Ludowe "Piast"*—PSL Piast, **Party of Regions** (*Partia Regionów*—PR), **League of Polish Families** (*Liga Polskich Rodzin*—LPR), **National Polish Organization-Polish League** (*Organizacja Narodu Polskiego-Liga Polska*—ONP-LP), and the **Christian National Union** (*Zjednoczenie Chrześcijańsko-Narodowe*—ZChN). Libertas, which was organized in opposition to the Lisbon Treaty, gained only 1.1 percent of the vote and no seats. The **Greens 2004** (*Zieloni 2004*), a member of the European Green Party, was first registered in 2004. It ran in the 2009 European parliamentary elections in the coalition Agreement for the Future with the SD and SDPL. Another party that participating in the 2009 EU elections included the **Republic Right Party** (*Prawica Rzeczypospolitej*—PRP), an antiabortion party that won 1.95 percent of the vote. The right-wing **Realpolitik Union** (*Unia Polityki Realnej*—UPR) won 1.1 percent of the vote in the 2009 European Parliament balloting.

For more information on the **Peasant Democratic Party** (*Partia Ludowe Democratyczna*—PLD), the **Movement for the Reconstruction of Poland** (*Ruch Odbudowy Polski*—ROP), and smaller parties active during the 2005 balloting, see the 2008 *Handbook*.

The 2010 presidential election saw the rise of the **Liberty and Rule of Law Party** (*Wolność i Praworządność*—WIP), which was founded by Janusz KORWIN-MIKKE, Meanwhile, a hero of the original Solidarity movement—Kornel MORAWIECKI—ran as a candidate of a party that he founded in 1982 called **Fighting Solidarity** (*Solidarność Walcząca*—SW). He received 0.1 percent of the vote in the first round of balloting.

(For information on the defunct parties—**Social Movement, Christian National Union, Freedom Union,** and the **Christian Democratic Party of the Third Republic**—see the 2011 *Handbook.*)

LEGISLATURE

Under Communist rule, the 460 members of the *Sejm* (Diet or Parliament) were elected via direct universal suffrage from candidate lists strictly controlled by the Front of National Unity and its successor, the Patriotic Movement for National Rebirth. Following extensive government/Solidarity negotiations, a bicameral legislature was established in 1989 that incorporated the existing *Sejm* and added a 100-member Senate, each serving four-year terms, subject to dissolution. Only a portion of the *Sejm* seats were open to opposition candidates in the 1989 balloting, although subsequent elections have been conducted on a fully open basis. As codified in the 1997 constitution, when sitting together, the *Sejm* and the Senate constitute the **National Assembly** (*Zgromadzenie Narodowe*).

Senate (*Senat*). The upper house comprises 100 members elected under a majoritarian system from 40 multimember constituencies. The Senate cannot initiate legislation but has the power of veto over the *Sejm,* which the latter can overturn only by a two-thirds majority. Following the most recent election of October 9, 2011, the distribution of seats was as follows: Civic Platform, 63; Law and Justice, 31; independent, 4; and Polish People's Party, 2. Two senators from Law and Justice joined the breakaway United Poland party when it formed in March 2012.

Speaker: Bogdan Michał BORUSEWICZ.

Sejm. The lower house comprises 460 members elected from 41 multimember constituencies under a proportional system (revised in 2001) in which parties (save for national minority groups) must gain 5 percent of the vote and coalitions need 8 percent to qualify for lower house seats. The distribution following the election of October 9, 2011, was as follows: Civic Platform, 207; Law and Justice (PiS), 157; Palikot Movement, 40; the Polish Peasants' Party, 28; Democratic Left Alliance (SLD), 27; and the German Minority of Lower Silesia, 1. By November 30, when the United Poland group (later party) split from the PiS, the seat distribution shifted as follows: Civic Platform, 207; PiS, 137; Palikot Movement, 41; SLD, 26; United Poland, 18; and independent, 3.

Marshal: Ewa KOPACZ.

CABINET

[as of August 21, 2013]

Prime Minister	Donald Tusk (PO)
Deputy Prime Minister	Janusz Piechociński (PSL)
Deputy Prime Minister	Jacek Vincent-Rostowski (PO)

Ministers

Agriculture and Rural Development	Stanisław Kalemba (PSL)
Culture and National Heritage	Bogdan Zdrojewski (PO)
Economy	Janusz Piechociński (PSL)
Environment	Martin Korolec (PO)
Finance	Jacek Vincent-Rostowski (PO)
Foreign Affairs	Radosław Sikorski (PO)
Health	Bartosz Arlukowicz (PO)
Interior and Administration	Bartłomiej Sienkiewicz (ind.)
Justice	Marek Biernacki (PO)
Labor and Social Policy	Władysław Kosiniak-Kamysz (PSL) [f]
National Defense	Tomasz Siemoniak (PO)
National Education	Krystyna Szumlias (PO) [f]
Public Administration and Digitalization	Michał Boni (PO)
Regional Development	Elżbieta Bieńkowska (PO) [f]
Science and Higher Education	Barbara Kudrycka (PO) [f]
Sports and Tourism	Joanna Mucha (PO) [f]
Transport, Construction, and Maritime Economy	Slawomir Nowak (PO)
Treasury	Wlodzimierz Karpinski (PO)

[f] = female

INTERGOVERNMENTAL REPRESENTATION

Ambassador to the U.S: Ryszard Marian SCHNEPF.

U.S. Ambassador to Poland: Stephen MULL.

Permanent Representative to the UN: Ryszard Stanisław SARKOWICZ.

IGO Memberships (Non-UN): CEUR, EBRD, EIB, EU, ICC, IEA, IOM, NATO, OECD, OSCE, WTO.

PORTUGAL

Portuguese Republic
República Portuguesa

Political Status: Independent republic proclaimed on October 5, 1910; corporative constitution of March 19, 1933, suspended following military coup of April 25, 1974; present constitution promulgated on April 2, 1976, with effect from April 25.

Area: 35,553 sq. mi. (92,082 sq. km).

Population: 10,542,398 (2013E—UN); 10,799,270 (2013E—U.S. Census).

Major Urban Centers (2013E): LISBON (548,000), Porto (Oporto, 238,000).

Official Language: Portuguese.

Monetary Unit: Euro (market rate November 1, 2013: 0.74 euro = $1US).

President: Aníbal CAVACO SILVA (Social Democratic Party); popularly elected on January 22, 2006, and sworn in for a five-year term on March 9, succeeding Jorge SAMPAIO (Socialist Party); reelected on January 23, 2011.

Prime Minister: Pedro Passos COELHO (Social Democratic Party); designated by the president following legislative elections on June 5, 2011, and sworn in along with a new government on June 21 to succeed José SÓCRATES (Socialist Party).

THE COUNTRY

Known in antiquity as Lusitania, Portugal overlooks the Atlantic along the western face of the Iberian Peninsula, while including politically the Azores and the Madeira Islands in the Atlantic. Mainland Portugal is divided by the Tagus River into a mountainous northern section and a southern section of rolling plains whose geography and climate are akin to those of northern Africa. The population, a blend of ancient Celtic, Iberian, Latin, Teutonic, and Moorish elements, with a recent admixture of African and other immigrants, is culturally homogeneous and almost wholly affiliated with the Roman Catholic Church, which traditionally exercised commanding social and political influence. Portuguese, the official language, is spoken by virtually all of the population. Women comprise 44 percent of the official labor force, concentrated in agriculture and domestic service; female representation in government and politics—despite the participation of a few prominent women, including former prime minister Maria de Lourdes PINTASILGO—averages less than 10 percent. Although the legislature recently rejected a mandate that women be allotted 25 percent of all posts in the Portuguese Assembly as well as in the Portuguese delegation to the European Parliament, all of the major parties volunteered to observe the proposed quota. (As of 2011, women held 26.5 percent of seats in the national legislature.)

The economy, one of the least modernized in Europe, retains a somewhat paternalistic structure characterized by limited social services and per capita GDP of $20,700 in 2013. Although agriculture accounts for about 42 percent of the land area, it contributes only 2.4 percent of GDP. Industry, consisting primarily of small manufacturing firms, employs some 28.5 percent of the labor force and contributes 23 percent of GDP. Exports include machinery and tools as well as such traditional goods as textiles, clothing, fish products, cork, and olive oil, of which Portugal is one of the world's largest producers. The European Union (EU) accounts for three-quarters of Portugal's imports and exports. The service sector, including tourism and retail, has become Portugal's largest employer. The government has successfully recruited investment into renewable energy industries in an effort to offset Portugal's dependence on foreign sources of oil and natural gas. The government plan called for Portugal to produce more than 60 percent of its electricity from renewable sources by 2020, far more than the EU target of 20 percent. Already home to Europe's largest onshore wind farm, Portugal's first floating offshore wind turbine began producing electricity in 2012.

By 2008, falling demand for goods and services, including a 20.8 percent decrease in exports, pushed Portugal's economy into negative economic growth (for an overview of the economy prior to 2008, see the 2013 *Handbook*). In 2009, GDP declined by 2.9 percent, while inflation was –0.9 percent. Unemployment rose to 9.5 percent and the government deficit rose sharply to 9.4 percent of GDP, prompting warnings from the EU and International Monetary Fund (IMF) and the implementation of an austerity plan. Lisbon requested a debt bailout in 2011, as the country slid into a recession. GDP declined by 1.5 percent in 2011 and a further 3.3 percent in 2012. Inflation rose 3.6 percent in 2011 and 3.2 percent in 2012, while unemployment was 12.7 percent and 14.4 percent, respectively. The World Bank ranked Portugal 30th of 183 countries in its 2012 Doing Business survey.

GOVERNMENT AND POLITICS

Political background. As one of the great European monarchies of late medieval and early modern times, Portugal initiated the age of discovery and colonization and acquired a far-flung colonial empire that was one of the last to be abandoned. Interrupted by a period of Spanish rule from 1580 to 1640, the Portuguese monarchy endured until 1910, when a bloodless revolution initiated a republican era marked by chronic instability and recurrent violence. A military revolt in 1926 prepared the way for the presidency of Marshal António CARMONA (1926–1951) and the assumption of governmental authority by António de Oliveira SALAZAR, an economics professor who became finance minister in 1928 and served as prime minister from 1932 until his replacement because of illness in 1968. Salazar, mistrustful of democratic and socialist ideologies and influenced by Italian fascism, established economic and political stability, and in 1933 he introduced a "corporative" constitution designed to serve as the basis of a new Portuguese State (*Estado Novo*). With the support of the Catholic Church, the army, and his National Union, the only authorized political

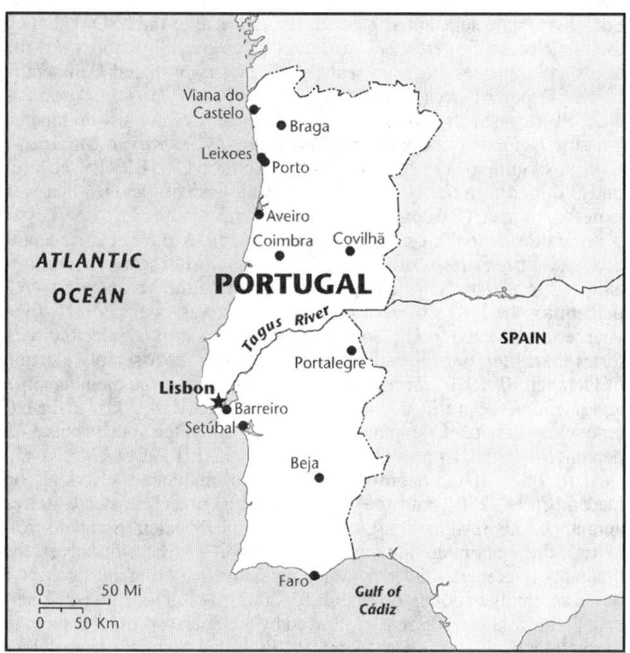

movement, Salazar completely dominated Portuguese political life and reduced the presidency to an auxiliary institution.

The later years of Salazar's regime were marked by rising, though largely ineffectual, domestic discontent and growing restiveness in the Overseas Territories. Elections were frequently boycotted by the opposition, and direct presidential elections were eliminated following a vigorous but unsuccessful opposition campaign by Gen. Humberto DELGADO in 1958. Overseas, the provinces of Goa, Damão, and Diu were seized by India in 1961; in the same year, a revolt broke out in Angola, while independence movements became active in Portuguese Guinea in 1962 and in Mozambique in 1964. Attempts to suppress the insurrections resulted in severe economic strain as well as increasing political isolation and repeated condemnation by the United Nations (UN).

The crisis created by Salazar's nearly fatal illness in September 1968 was alleviated by the selection of Marcello CAETANO, a close associate, as the new prime minister. Although he permitted a measure of cautious liberalization, including some relaxation of secret police activity and the return from exile of the Socialist Party (*Partido Socialista*—PS) leader Mário SOARES, Caetano preserved the main outlines of Salazar's policy both in metropolitan Portugal and overseas.

Prior to the parliamentary election of October 1969, opposition parties were legalized, but they were again outlawed after a campaign in which the official National Union won all 130 seats in the National Assembly. The atmosphere of repression eased again after the adoption in 1971 of constitutional legislation expanding the power of the enlarged National Assembly, granting limited autonomy to the Overseas Territories, abolishing press censorship, and permitting religious freedom. Nevertheless, in the legislative election of October 1973 the ruling Popular National Action (successor to the National Union) won all 150 seats, including 34 representing the Overseas Territories.

In a bloodless coup on April 24, 1974, a group of mainly left-wing military officers calling themselves the Armed Forces Movement (*Movimento das Forças Armadas*—MFA) seized power, ending more than 40 years of civilian dictatorship. The president and prime minister were arrested and flown to Brazil, where they were granted political asylum. The leader of the "Junta of National Salvation," Gen. António Sebastião Ribeiro de SPÍNOLA, assumed the presidency, and on May 15 a center-left cabinet was sworn in with Adelino de PALMA CARLOS as prime minister. After a dispute with the reconstituted Council of State as to the extent of his powers, Palma Carlos resigned on July 9 and was replaced by Gen. Vasco dos Santos GONÇALVES, whose administration recognized the right of the Overseas Territories to "self-determination" and independence. On September 30 General Spínola also resigned, leaving power in the hands of leftist military officers and civilians. The new president, Gen. Francisco da COSTA GOMES, subsequently reappointed General Gonçalves as prime minister.

In May 1974, Costa Gomes declared that the new government was prepared to offer a cease-fire in Angola, Mozambique, and Portuguese Guinea, with the guerrilla organizations being permitted to organize political parties and participate in democratic elections. As a result of the initiative, negotiations were undertaken that led to the independence of Guinea-Bissau (formerly Portuguese Guinea) in September and independence for Mozambique, São Tomé and Principe, and Cape Verde the following year. Although negotiations with Angolan leaders were complicated by the presence of a sizable white minority and by the existence of three major insurgent groups, the formation of a united front by the insurgents opened the way for independence. The front subsequently collapsed, but Portugal withdrew from Angola on the agreed date of November 11, 1975.

On March 11, 1975, right-wing military elements, reportedly acting at the instigation of former president Spínola, attempted to overthrow the government. When the coup failed, General Spínola flew to Brazil, and the Junta of National Salvation was dissolved in favor of a Supreme Revolutionary Council (SRC). The latter, sworn in by President Costa Gomes on March 17, was given full executive and legislative powers for the purpose of "directing and executing the revolutionary program in Portugal." One-third of the cabinet announced on March 25 was comprised of military officers, in addition to representatives of the main political parties.

In a Constituent Assembly election on April 25, 1975, the Socialists received 38 percent of the total vote, compared with 26 percent for the Popular Democrats and less than 13 percent for the Communists. The first session of the assembly was convened on June 2, with the Socialists holding 116 of the 250 seats. Despite their commanding legislative strength, the Socialists and Popular Democrats subsequently announced their intention to resign from the government, in part because of a Communist takeover of the Socialist newspaper *República,* and on July 31 a new, essentially nonparty cabinet was formed. However, increasing opposition to Communist influence led, on August 29, to the resignation of Prime Minister Gonçalves and the appointment of Adm. José Baptista Pinheiro de AZEVEDO as head of a new cabinet (the sixth since the 1974 coup) comprising representatives of the three leading parties, as well as of the Armed Forces Movement.

In mid-November 1975 a Communist-led labor union general strike in Lisbon was followed on November 26 by an uprising of leftist military units that was crushed by loyalist troops. Although the SRC had previously rebuked Azevedo for his conduct during the strike, the coup's failure was seen as a major defeat for the Communists, and in mid-December, following designation of a new army chief of staff, the council ordered a major reorganization of the armed forces, emphasizing military discipline and the exclusion of the military from party politics.

The new constitution came into effect on April 25, 1976, and an election to the Assembly of the Republic was held the same day. The Socialists remained the largest party but again failed to win an absolute majority. On June 27 Gen. António dos Santos Ramalho EANES, a nonparty candidate supported by the Socialists, Popular Democrats, and Social Democrats, was elected to a five-year term as president. The election was a further setback for the Communists, whose candidate, Octávio PATO, finished third, behind far-left candidate Maj. Otelo SARAIVA DE CARVALHO. Three weeks later, on July 16, Soares was invested as prime minister, heading a Socialist minority government that was, however, endorsed by the other two parties in the presidential election coalition.

Having lost a crucial assembly vote on an economic austerity plan, Soares was forced to resign on December 8, 1977, though he was subsequently able to return as head of a governmental coalition with the conservative Social Democratic Center (*Centro Democrático Social*—CDS) on January 30, 1978. On July 27, however, President Eanes dismissed Soares after the CDS ministers had resigned over disagreements on agricultural and health policies, leaving the Socialists without a working legislative majority. His successor, Alfredo NOBRE DA COSTA, was in turn forced to resign on September 14 following legislative rejection of an essentially nonparty program. A new government, largely composed of independents, was eventually confirmed on November 22 with Dr. Carlos Alberto da MOTA PINTO, a former member of the Social Democratic Party (*Partido Social Democrata*—PSD, the renamed Popular Democratic Party), as prime minister.

Having witnessed assembly rejection of his proposed budget on three occasions since March, Prime Minister Mota Pinto resigned on June 6, 1979. On July 19, Maria de Lourdes Pintasilgo, a member of several previous post-1974 governments, was named to head a caretaker, nonparty government, pending an early legislative election. The balloting of December 2 confirmed Portugal's move toward the extremes of the political spectrum. Francisco SÁ CARNEIRO, a conservative Social Democrat who in July had formed a Democratic Alliance (*Aliança Democrática*—AD) with the Center Democrats, Monarchists, and disaffected Socialists, led his electoral coalition to a clear majority and was named on December 29 to organize a new government—the 12th since 1974—that was sworn in on January 3, 1980. The Alliance was returned to office with an increased majority at the second legislative election within a year on October 5, 1980.

Prime Minister Sá Carneiro was killed in a plane crash on December 4 and was succeeded as PSD leader and prime minister by Dr. Francisco Pinto BALSEMÃO, who proceeded to organize a new AD cabinet that was sworn in on January 5, 1981. Balsemão continued as head of a reorganized administration on September 1, 1982, prior to resigning on December 19, 1982.

In a general election on April 25, 1983, the Socialists obtained a substantial plurality, enabling Soares to form a cabinet of nine Socialists, seven Social Democrats, and one independent that assumed office on June 9. However, severe economic difficulties eroded the popularity of the Socialists, while the coalition partners disagreed on the extent of proposed austerity measures. On June 4, 1985, PSD parliamentary leader Aníbal CAVACO SILVA announced his party's withdrawal from the government, although agreeing to a postponement until the signature on June 12 of Portugal's entry accord with the EC. Two days later, Soares was named to head a caretaker administration pending a new election, while declaring himself a candidate for the forthcoming presidential poll.

The October 6, 1985, legislative balloting dealt a serious blow to the Socialists, whose representation was cut nearly in half. The largest vote share, 30 percent, went to the PSD, and Cavaco Silva formed a minority government based on his party's assembly plurality on November 6. The PSD's preferred presidential candidate, the Christian Democrat Diogo FREITAS DO AMARAL, captured nearly half the vote in the initial presidential balloting on January 23, 1986, out of a field of four candidates; however, an unusual coalition of the Socialists, the pro-Eanes Democratic Renewal Party (*Partido Renovador Democrático*—PRD), and the Communist-led United People's Alliance (*Aliança Povo Unido*—APU) succeeded in electing Soares, the remaining center-left candidate, with 51 percent of the vote in the February 16 runoff. Soares, the first civilian head of state in 60 years, was sworn in as Eanes's successor on March 9.

President Soares dissolved the assembly on April 28, 1987, following the April 3 defeat of the Cavaco Silva government on a censure motion that had charged the administration with mismanagement of the economy. In elections on July 19, the Social Democrats became the first party in 13 years to win an absolute majority of legislative seats. The incumbent prime minister returned to office on August 17 as head of an all-PSD government. Following his reconfirmation, Cavaco Silva moved to privatize state-owned firms and to reverse a number of post-1974 measures aimed at agricultural collectivization. In November 1988, the two leading parties reached agreement on constitutional changes that would strip the basic law of its Marxist elements, reduce the number of legislative deputies, permit the holding of binding national referenda, and accelerate the privatization process.

On January 13, 1991, President Soares gained easy election to a second five-year term on a 70.4 percent vote share. The PSD retained its majority in legislative balloting on October 6 and Cavaco Silva remained in office as head of a slightly modified administration.

With most economic indicators positive or stable, the government took the escudo into the broad band of the EC's exchange rate mechanism (ERM) on April 6, 1992. Five months later it was thrown off course by the European monetary crisis, which led to devaluations of the escudo by 6 percent in November and by 7 percent in May 1993. Deepening economic recession and assorted political problems resulted in a sharp decline in the government's standing, accompanied by an upsurge of "cohabitation" tensions between the president and the prime minister. In December the Socialists outpolled the PSD in local elections, winning their highest-ever share of a nationwide vote.

Recession and rising unemployment increased the government's unpopularity and led Cavaco Silva to resign as PSD leader but not as prime minister, in January 1995. In balloting on October 1, the Socialists made substantial gains at the expense of the PSD, although their 112-seat tally left them just short of an overall majority. Of the two smaller parties that won seats, the center-right Social Democratic Center–Popular Party (*Centro Democrático Social–Partido Popular*—CDS-PP) trebled its representation, while the Communist-dominated Unitary Democratic Coalition (*Coligação Democrática Unitária*—CDU) lost ground. The Socialist leader, António GUTERRES, accordingly formed a minority government at the end of October that was expected to have CDU external support on most issues.

In a presidential election on January 14, 1996, the Socialist candidate and former mayor of Lisbon, Jorge SAMPAIO, scored a comfortable first-round victory, taking 53.8 percent of the vote against 46.2 percent for the PSD's Cavaco Silva. Sampaio was sworn in for a five-year term on March 9. The Socialists extended a string of electoral victories thereafter, unexpectedly adding 3 seats in the assembly election of October 10, 1999 (for a total of 115, exactly half the membership), and retaining the presidency in balloting on January 14, 2001. In the latter contest, President Sampaio won 55.8 percent of the vote, versus 34.5 percent for the PSD's candidate, Joaquim FERREIRA DO AMARAL.

The PS suffered significant losses in municipal elections on December 16, 2001, and the following day Prime Minister Guterres announced his resignation. On December 28 President Sampaio, following the unanimous advice of the Council of State, dissolved the assembly in preparation for national legislative balloting in March.

In assembly balloting on March 17, 2002, the PSD secured 40.2 percent of the vote and 105 seats, followed by the Socialists (37.9 percent of the vote and 96 seats). On March 28 President Sampaio named José Manuel Durão BARROSO of the PSD to form a new government, and the next day Barroso signed a coalition pact with the CDS-PP, which was given three ministerial posts in the new government appointed on April 6.

Strengthened by their victory in the June 2004 European Parliament elections, the PS and other opposition parties demanded early elections when Prime Minister Barroso resigned on July 5 to become president of the European Commission. Instead, President Sampaio opted to pursue "stability" by appointing Pedro SANTANA LOPES of the PSD to succeed Barroso. The selection of Santana Lopes, who, despite being the mayor of Lisbon, was not well known in the rest of the country and had little experience at the national level.

In light of the continued decline in popular support for the governing coalition, Sampaio dissolved the assembly on December 10, 2004, and directed that new elections be held on February 20, 2005, at which time the PS gained its first legislative majority (121 seats) since independence. Consequently, the new government installed on March 12 under the PS's José SÓCRATES included only PS members and a number of independents. Sócrates focused on improving Portugal's economy through public sector reforms. Decreased pension benefits, a reduction in the number of public sector workers, and spending cuts sparked widespread criticism.

After months of protests against Sócrates's austerity measures, voters on January 22, 2006, elected former prime minister Cavaco Silva to a five-year term as president. Cavaco Silva, who won 50.6 percent of the vote to defeat five left and center-left opponents, including PS member Manuel ALEGRE, who ran as an independent, and former president and official PS candidate Mário Soares, became the first center-right president to serve since the restoration of democracy in 1974. Although the Socialist Sócrates supported Soares for president, Cavaco Silva declared his intention to maintain a positive "dialogue" with the Socialist government and refrained from exercising his veto power to block government-supported bills, including a controversial law permitting abortion during the first 10 weeks of gestation.

Despite opposition, in November 2006 the governing PS pushed through its austerity budget for 2007, aimed at enabling Portugal to meet the EU deadline for reducing the budget deficit from 4.6 percent of GDP to 3 percent by 2008. The government exceeded its goal, shrinking the deficit to 2.6 percent of GDP, and broadened its reform efforts to include education, health care, and labor. In May 2008 the parliament approved a controversial measure standardizing the Portuguese language among the seven Portuguese-speaking countries by adopting Brazilian spelling. In July the government won a long-sought labor agreement with employer associations and one of the two main labor unions that critics claimed eroded job security.

The economy and government plans to reduce the deficit dominated political discussions in 2009. In an effort to win support before national elections scheduled on September 27, the PS in January issued an election platform that included a €200 subsidy for each child born in Portugal, mirroring similar measures introduced in other European countries with falling birth rates. However, widespread discontent with the government, especially its austerity measures amid a steep recession, led to a shift in the Portuguese delegation to the European Parliament in elections held on June 7, 2009. The opposition PSD won 8 of 22 seats, the PS won 7, and the Left Bloc won 3, marking a shift in the parties' fortunes. Preelection tensions mounted on July 2, when Finance Minister Manuel PINHO was forced to resign after insulting a Communist deputy during a parliamentary debate.

On election day, the PS won a leading 97 seats, but the loss of 24 seats from its 2005 total left it well short of a majority in the 230-seat legislature. Allegations that the prime minister's office had bugged the president's offices emerged in the midst of the September balloting, making it impossible for Sócrates to negotiate a coalition agreement with any other party. Instead, Sócrates formed a minority PS government that was sworn in on October 26. In December, the EU and IMF warned the government of the need to reduce a record deficit of more than 9 percent of GDP.

In March 2010, credit agencies downgraded Portugal's bond rating because of the deficit and national debt. In March the assembly enacted a four-year austerity program that included a wage freeze for government employees, cuts to the military and public services, and tax increases. Civil servants protested the cuts through a series of one-day strikes though the spring. Portugal's credit rating was further downgraded in December 2010.

In February 2011 the European Central Bank intervened to purchase Portuguese bonds as concerns mounted that the country would be forced to seek a bailout similar to those negotiated by Greece and Ireland with the IMF and EU (see the entries on Greece and Ireland). The Sócrates government developed a new austerity package in an effort to satisfy EU requirements for financial aid. However, the new economic program was defeated in the assembly in March. Sócrates resigned, and new elections were scheduled for June.

In balloting on January 23, 2011, incumbent president Silva was reelected with 52.9 percent of the vote in the first round of balloting, defeating Manuel Alegre (PS), who secured 19.8 percent, independent candidate Fernando NOBRE with 14.1 percent, and a number of minor candidates. Opposition parties voted against a new economic program on March 23 in a no-confidence measure. Sócrates subsequently resigned, and new elections were called for June 5. The PSD won a plurality of 108 seats in the legislature in the balloting, and party leader Pedro Passos COELHO formed a coalition government with the CDS-PP on June 21. The 12-member cabinet was considerably smaller than previous governments.

Constitution and government. The constitution of April 25, 1976, stemmed from a constitutional agreement concluded two months earlier by the leading parties and Costa Gomes in his capacity as chief of state and president of the SRC (subsequently the Council of the Revolution). Under the pact (which superseded an earlier agreement of April 1975), the council, while formally designated as the most important government organ after the presidency, became, in large part, a consultative body with powers of absolute veto only in regard to defense policy. The third most important organ, the Assembly of the Republic, was empowered to override the council (on nonmilitary matters) and the president by a two-thirds majority.

A series of constitutional reforms that came into effect in October 1982 abolished the Council of the Revolution and distributed its powers among a Supreme Council of National Defense, a 13-member Constitutional Tribunal, and an advisory Council of State of 16 members (plus national presidents elected since adoption of the existing basic law): five named by the president, five named by the assembly, and six ex officio (the prime minister; the national ombudsman; and the presidents of the assembly, the Supreme Court, and the regional governments of the Azores and the Madeira Islands).

The president, elected for a five-year term, serves as military chief of staff and as chair of the Council of State and appoints the prime minister, who is responsible to both the head of state and the assembly. Portugal's judicial system, based on European civil law and heavily influenced by the French model, includes, in addition to the Constitutional Tribunal, a Supreme Court, courts of appeal, and district courts as well as military courts and a Court of Audit.

Administratively, metropolitan Portugal is divided into 18 districts (each headed by a governor appointed by the minister of the interior), which are subdivided into 275 municipalities and more than 4,000 parochial authorities. The Azores and the Madeira Islands are governed separately as Autonomous Regions, each with an elected Regional Assembly and municipal subdivisions (a total of 30). In both regions the central government has been represented since March 2006 by a "representative of the republic" (previously called a minister of the republic), who is appointed by the president.

Portugal's constitution guarantees freedom of the press and free speech. All newspapers are privately owned. In 2013, Reporters Without Borders ranked Portugal 28th out of 179 countries in freedom of the press, an improvement from 33rd the previous year.

Foreign relations. Allied with England since 1373, Portugal nevertheless declared itself neutral in World War II. It currently participates in the North Atlantic Treaty Organization (NATO) and the OECD as well as in the UN and its specialized agencies. It became a member of the Council of Europe in September 1976 and, after years of negotiation, joined Spain in gaining admission to the EC on January 1, 1986.

The country's foreign policy efforts prior to the 1974 coup were directed primarily to retention of its overseas territories at a time when other European powers had largely divested themselves of colonial possessions. Subsequent to the 1974 coup, its African problems were significantly alleviated by the independence of Guinea-Bissau (formerly Portuguese Guinea) in 1974 and of Angola, Cape Verde, Mozambique, and São Tomé and Principe in 1975.

In late 1975 a dispute arose with Indonesia regarding the status of Portuguese Timor, the country's only remaining Asian possession except for Macao. On December 8 Indonesian Foreign Minister Adam Malik announced that pro-Indonesian parties in the Portuguese (eastern) sector of the island had set up a provisional government and that Indonesian military units had occupied Dili, the capital. Portugal promptly severed diplomatic relations with Indonesia, which had also announced the annexation of Ocussi Ambeno, a small Portuguese enclave on the northern coast of West Timor. On July 17, 1976, Jakarta proclaimed the formal incorporation of the remainder of Timor into Indonesia, although the UN continued to regard Portugal as the territory's legitimate administrative power.

Lisbon's objection to Indonesian control of East Timor was again manifested in the recall of its ambassador to Australia in August 1985, after Australian Prime Minister Bob Hawke had endorsed his predecessor's acceptance of the takeover. Relations with Canberra were further strained in 1989 when Australia concluded a treaty with Indonesia providing for the division of offshore oil resources in the Timor Gap. Claiming that Indonesia's illegal occupation of East Timor rendered the treaty invalid under international law, Portugal in 1991 took the matter to the International Court of Justice (ICJ). In June 1995, however, the ICJ ruled that it had no jurisdiction on the 1989 treaty, as it was precluded from giving a ruling on the legality of Indonesia's annexation of East Timor by Indonesia's nonrecognition of the court's jurisdiction in the matter and because Indonesia was not a party to the case brought by Portugal. UN-prompted "dialogue" between the Portuguese and Indonesian foreign ministers on the East Timor question made no substantive progress in 1995, with Portugal finding little merit in an Indonesian proposal that each side should establish "interest sections" in third-country embassies in Lisbon and Jakarta. Diplomatic relations were not restored with Indonesia until late 1999, following Jakarta's acceptance of an independence referendum in East Timor, which achieved independence as the Democratic Republic of Timor-Leste on May 20, 2002.

In early 1988 Portugal called for a "thorough overhaul" of a mutual defense treaty that permitted the United States to use Lajes air base in the Azores. Although the agreement was not due to expire until 1991, it included a provision for military aid, which the U.S. Congress had sharply reduced in approving the administration's foreign assistance budget for the year. The dispute was eventually settled in January 1989, with Washington pledging to increase levels of both military and economic compensation. An agreement granting a further extension on U.S. use of the Lajes base was signed in Lisbon on June 1, 1995.

In 1989, it was agreed that regular consultative meetings of the foreign ministers of Portugal and the five lusophone African countries would be convened to promote the latter's economic development. In 1991 the six countries plus Brazil agreed upon linguistic standardization, while plans were initiated for a common television satellite channel. Further meetings of the seven Portuguese-speaking states in the early 1990s led to the formal establishment in July 1996 of the Community of Portuguese Speaking Countries (CPLP), with a total population of some 200 million Portuguese speakers (80 percent of them in Brazil). Meanwhile, Portuguese diplomacy had scored a major success in brokering the 1991 Escuril Accord between the warring factions of postindependence Angola.

The 1991 Maastricht Treaty on the economic and political union of what became the EU was ratified by the Portuguese Assembly on December 10, 1992, by a large majority. Two days later the EU's Edinburgh summit agreed to set up a "cohesion fund" for its four poorest members, of which Portugal was one. Portugal was a founding member of the EU's Schengen zone in March 1995 and the Economic and Monetary Union (EMU) on January 1, 1999.

Portugal has been largely supportive of further European integration and supported Germany's 2007 successful rejection of an effort by Poland to allow a minority of EU states to delay EU legislation against the majority's wishes. Portugal traditionally has maintained close ties with its former colonies, and Sócrates scheduled an EU-African Union (AU) summit to be held in Lisbon in December 2007 with the aim of strengthening economic ties with the continent. But tensions heightened over the inclusion of Robert Mugabe, Zimbabwe's controversial president, and Britain boycotted the meeting.

The Barroso administration vigorously supported the U.S.-led campaign in Iraq in 2003, committing troops to the overthrow of Saddam Hussein and to subsequent security and reconstruction efforts. Responding to increasing public opposition to the war in Iraq and acting on a campaign promise, new Prime Minister Sócrates withdrew Portugal's 120 troops from Iraq in February 2005. Portugal also participated in NATO peacekeeping efforts in Afghanistan. In March 2009 Lisbon signed an agreement with the United States to install a climate observatory on the island of Graciosa in the Azores, and in June the government agreed to accept two to three detainees from the controversial U.S. prison camp at Guantánamo Bay, Cuba.

In September 2009, Barroso was reelected as head of the European Commission for a second five-year term by a vote of 382 to 219, with 117 deputies abstaining.

In February 2010, Portugal announced it would increase its troop deployment in Afghanistan to 250 soldiers. Meanwhile, in August Portugal and Indonesia signed an accord to increase bilateral cooperation. During a state visit in November, Chinese president Hu Jintao signed a range of bilateral cultural, economic, and educational agreements with Sócrates.

In April 2012, Portugal joined other EU states in opposing a French initiative to increase border controls in response to a wave of immigrants from the Middle East following the Arab Spring. High unemployment (see Current issues, below), prompted a 40 percent increase in the number of Portuguese immigrants to the former colonies of Angola and Brazil. By 2011, there were 100,000 Portuguese with work permits in Angola and 328,860 in Brazil.

In April 2012, the assembly approved the EU Treaty on Stability, Coordination, and Governance in the Economic and Monetary Union. As part of the continuing effort to reduce government spending (see Current issues, below), the cabinet reduced military spending by 3.9 percent for 2012.

Current issues. On April 6, 2011, Portugal formally requested a debt bailout from the EU after yields on Portuguese bonds soared to new records. In May, the EU and IMF agreed to provide Portugal with €78 billion over three years to service debt payments in exchange for additional austerity measures. Popular discontent with the government's management of the economy manifested itself in the June legislative balloting, in which the PS had its worst showing in more than 20 years. The PSD won a plurality in the parliament and formed a coalition government with the CDS-PP, with Pedro Passos Coelho of the PSD as prime minister. The new cabinet immediately began to implement the unpopular cuts to public sector salaries and social programs demanded by the EU and IMF.

In early 2012, the government announced that it had reached 60 percent of its EU-IMF mandated privatization goals and was on track to complete the requirement by 2014. Although Portugal consistently met its bailout goals, austerity measures were blamed for a high unemployment rate, which reached 14.9, the highest level ever recorded. Budget-squeezed citizens cut back on consumption, forcing the government to reduce revenue expectations. Tax revenue fell 3.5 percent in the first half of 2012, putting the target budget deficit of 4.5 percent of GDP out of reach. In an effort to increase competiveness, the government suspended 4 of the nation's 14 national holidays for a five-year period. These measures breached the patience and cooperation of the population.

Amid widespread protests in September, the government abandoned plans to raise employee social security contributions from 11 percent to 18 percent. That month international lenders relaxed the 2012 deficit goal to 5.0 percent and the 2013 goal from 3.0 to 4.5 percent. In November the government adopted another austerity-focused budget for 2013 that included tax hikes equivalent to a month's salary for the average citizen. Workers in Portugal and Spain staged an unprecedented joint general strike on November 14. Privatization of state assets, such as the national airline and airport operator, brought in €6.4 billion, easily meeting the €5.5 billion by 2013 target.

Exports of goods and services declined in the first quarter of 2013, as trading partners faced their own austerity measures.

Anti-austerity protests spread across the country on March 2, as unemployment neared 18 percent. Two days later, the Constitutional Court struck down four of the nine austerity measures in the 2013 budget. Justices ruled that cutting wages, benefits, and bonuses for civil servants constituted discrimination. The rejected measures left a €1.4 billion hole in the budget that had to be plugged to receive the next bailout payment. António José SEGURO MARTINS (PS) declared austerity had "failed on every level" and brought the country to the "brink of a social tragedy," but Portugal was granted a seven-year extension on repaying its emergency loans. Also, the budget deficit target for 2013 was raised to 5.5 percent of GDP.

A cabinet reshuffle occurred on April 13, following the resignation of Parliamentary Affairs Secretary Miguel RELVAS, who was discovered to have falsified his university degree. Luís Marques GUEDRES assumed a portfolio expanded to include gender, youth, and sport issues. On April 23 Economy Minister Alvaro Santos PEREIRA announced a far-reaching stimulus package to encourage business, including a reduction in the business tax.

The revised budget, issued in June, extended the workweek from 35 hours to 40 and increased employee contributions for health insurance. It also would streamline state-owned companies and think tanks. Public workers responded by shutting down transportation and other services.

Finance Minister Vitor GASPAR resigned on July 1, and Prime Minister Passos Coelho nominated Gaspar's deputy, Maria Luis ALBUQUERQUE, as his replacement, indicating an ongoing commitment to austerity. But this prompted the resignation of CDS-PP leader, Foreign Minister Paulo PORTAS, who insisted the government needed a new economic policy. Passos Coelho refused to accept Portas' resignation. To keep his coalition together and forestall new elections, he promoted Portas to deputy prime minister—a title not used for nearly 30 years. Passos Coelho completed this cabinet shuffle, his seventh, on July 23. Rui MACHETE (PSD) took the foreign affairs portfolio, while agriculture, marine affairs, environment and regional planning was split into two ministries.

President Cavaco Silva spoke to the nation on July 10, appealing to the PSD, CDS-PP, and PS to put politics aside and reach a national consensus. He also called for elections to be moved from 2015 to June 2014, when Portugal is scheduled to exit the bailout period. Unemployment fell from 17.6 percent in June to 16.5 percent in July, but the PSD still suffered heavy losses in the September 29 local elections, gaining only 26.5 percent of the overall popular vote and losing 34 mayoral seats and 137 councilors to the PS, the CDU, and other parties.

POLITICAL PARTIES

Government Parties:

Social Democratic Party (*Partido Social Democrata*—PSD). The PSD was founded in 1974 as the **Popular Democratic Party** (*Partido Popular Democrático*—PPD), under which name it won 26 percent of the vote for the Constituent Assembly on April 25, 1975, and 24 percent in the Assembly of the Republic election a year later. Although it initially advocated a number of left-of-center policies, including the nationalization of key sectors of the economy, a number of leftists withdrew in 1976, and the remainder of the party moved noticeably to the right.

An April 1979 disagreement over leadership opposition to the Socialist government's proposed budget led to a walkout of 40 PSD deputies prior to a final assembly vote. Shortly thereafter, 37 of the 73 PSD deputies withdrew and announced that they would sit in the assembly as the **Association of Independent Social Democrats** (*Associação dos Sociais Democratas Independentes*—ASDI). The party's losses were more than recouped in the December election, however, when the PSD-led alliance won a three-seat majority, as a result of which the party president, Francisco Sá Carneiro, was named prime minister. Francisco Pinto Balsemão was designated party leader in December 1980, following Sá Carneiro's death, and he became prime minister in January 1981.

In early 1983, following the formal designation of a three-member leadership at a party congress in late February, Balsemão was effectively succeeded by Carlos Mota PINTO. The party was runner-up to the PS at the April election, winning 75 assembly seats. In June 1985, Aníbal Cavaco Silva, who had succeeded Mota Pinto as PSD leader the previous month, withdrew from the ruling coalition and formed a minority government after the party had gained a slim plurality in legislative balloting in October. Defeated in a censure vote in April 1987, the PSD became the first party since 1974 to win an absolute majority of seats in the ensuing legislative poll in July. It retained control with a slightly reduced majority of 135 of 230 seats in 1991. A subsequent slide in the PSD's standing, including losses at the 1994 election for the European Parliament, compelled Cavaco Silva to vacate the party leadership in January 1995. At the same time, he hoped to position himself for a presidential challenge.

Under the new leadership of Joaquim Fernando NOGUEIRA, the party went down to an expected defeat in the October 1995 general election, retaining only 88 seats on a 34 percent vote share. In the January 1996 presidential balloting, moreover, Cavaco Silva was defeated by the socialist candidate in the first round. The party's response at the end of March was to elect as its new leader Marcelo REBELO DE SOUSA, a media personality on the party's liberal wing who had not held ministerial office during the period of PSD rule.

In early 1998, the PSD and CDS-PP (below) formed an electoral alliance, styled the AD, with the stated aim of presenting a single list for the upcoming European Parliament and national legislative elections. The AD Pact was formally ratified in February 1999; however, it collapsed the following month, and immediately thereafter Rebelo de Sousa resigned as leader of the PSD. His successor, José Manuel Durão Barroso, a former foreign affairs minister, led the party in the October 1999 election, but the PSD lost 7 of its 88 seats. In 2001 it failed to unseat President Sampaio, with its candidate, Joaquim Martins Ferreira do Amaral, finishing a distant second (34.5 percent of the vote).

Barroso was named prime minister following the March 2002 legislative balloting, at which the PSD won a plurality of 105 seats. He resigned as prime minister in July 2004 to become president of the European Commission. Pedro Santana Lopes succeeded Barroso as prime minister until the February 2005 legislative poll, in which the PSD fell to 75 seats. Santana Lopes resigned as PSD leader in April. In the 2006 presidential contest, Cavaco Silva won 50.6 percent of the vote, and avoided a runoff. In October 2007, the party chose member of parliament Luís Filipe MENEZES, a vocal critic of the government's austerity measures, to lead the PSD. Unable to mount a strong challenge to the government, Menezes resigned seven months later and was succeeded by former finance minister Manuela Ferreira LEITE on May 31, 2008.

The PSD gained one additional seat in the European Parliament in June 2009, bringing its total to eight. It also increased its representation in the assembly by six seats in the subsequent legislative balloting. Barroso was reelected president of the European Commission in September.

Cavaco was reelected president in January 2011. The PSD won 108 seats in legislative balloting in June and Pedro Passos Coelho formed a government with the CDS-PP.

Leaders: Aníbal CAVACO SILVA (President of the Republic), Pedro Passos COELHO (Prime Minister and Chair), Pedro SANTANA LOPES (Former Prime Minister), José Manuel Durão BARROSO (European Commission President and Former Prime Minister).

Social Democratic Center–Popular Party (*Centro Democrático Social–Partido Popular*—CDS-PP). This right-of-center Christian democratic party was founded in 1974 as the CDS. The name was changed to the CDS-PP in 1993. The party is strongest in the northern part of the country, and a number of its members were named to key government posts following the 1979 and 1980 legislative elections. Despite the party's having lost 8 of 30 assembly seats in the October 1985 election, its presidential candidate, Diogo Freitas do Amaral, won 46 percent of the vote in first-round presidential balloting in January 1986, but he lost to former prime minister Soares (PS) in the runoff. Freitas do Amaral resigned the CDS presidency after the 1991 election, in which the party won only five assembly seats. Standing on an anti-EU platform, the CDS-PP gained ground in the October 1995 national election, winning 15 seats on a vote share of 9.1 percent.

Despite having repulsed a leadership challenge by Paulo Portas, Manuel MONTEIRO resigned as CDS-PP president in September 1996 in protest against internal party feuding. He subsequently agreed to return as president, although he announced he would not run again in the party congress scheduled for March 1998. As promised, Monteiro left his party post in March, and in subsequent intraparty balloting Portas finally secured the presidency. A principal architect of the 1998 PSD/CDS-PP electoral alliance, Portas nevertheless quickly grew disenchanted with the PSD leadership, and just prior to the AD's dissolution, the PSD's Rebelo de Sousa accused Portas of publicizing confidential information. Despite a reduced vote share of 8.3 percent, the party retained its 15 assembly seats at the October 1999 election. In 2001 it endorsed President Sampaio for reelection.

Portas resigned as the CDS-PP leader in April 2005, two months after the party won only 12 assembly seats, but he regained the leadership in April 2007. The CDS-PP presence in the assembly dropped to 11 after a party member joined an unaffiliated group on December 17, 2008. The CDS-PP maintained its 2 seats in the EU Parliament balloting in 2009 but gained 9 seats in that year's legislative elections to bring its total to 21.

The CDS-PP supported Cavaco Silva of the PSD in presidential balloting in January 2011. The CDS-PP placed third in the June assembly balloting with 24 seats. It subsequently formed a coalition government with the PSD but grew uneasy at repeated tax increases. Portas was promoted from minister of state for foreign affairs to deputy prime minister in July 2013, to keep the governing coalition intact.

Leaders: Paulo PORTAS (President of Party, Deputy Prime Minister), Nuno MAGALHÃES (Parliamentary Leader), António Carlos MONTEIRO (General Secretary).

Other Legislative Parties:

Socialist Party (*Partido Socialista*—PS). Organized in 1973 as heir to the former Portuguese Socialist Action (*Acção Socialista Portuguesa*—ASP), the PS won a substantial plurality (38 percent) of the vote in the election of April 1975 and 35 percent a year later, remaining in power under Mário Soares until July 1978. In the December 1979 balloting the PS lost 33 of the 107 assembly seats it had won in 1976. It secured a plurality of 101 seats in 1983, with Soares being redesignated prime minister on June 9 and continuing in office until forced into caretaker status by the withdrawal of the Social Democrats (PSD) from the government coalition in July 1985. The party won only 57 seats in the October election, although Soares succeeded in winning the state presidency in February 1986, at which time he resigned as PS secretary general.

A party congress in June approved wide-ranging changes aimed at democratizing the party's structure and deleted all references to Marxism in its Declaration of Principles, committing the organization to an "open economy where private, public, and social institutions can coexist." The party's legislative strength gained only marginally (from 57 to 60 seats) in the balloting of July 16, 1987, but it secured 72 seats in the election of October 6, 1991.

Remaining in the opposition, the party elected António Guterres as its leader in February 1992 and registered its best ever national vote in the December 1993 local elections. In the general election of October 1995 the PS won 112 assembly seats, with Guterres forming a minority government. In 1996, the PS's Jorge Sampaio captured the national presidency with a majority in the first round. In the October 1999 legislative election the PS fell just short of a legislative majority, winning 115 seats in the 230-seat chamber. President Sampaio continued the party's string of successes in January 2001, easily winning reelection. However, the PS did poorly in the December 2001 municipal elections, setting the stage for Guterres's resignation as prime minister and the PS's fall from national power in 2002. Eduardo FERRO RODRIGUES, a former minister in Guterres's 1995 cabinet, was elected in January to succeed Guterres as PS secretary general and thereby the party's candidate for prime ministership. However, Rodrigues resigned the leadership in July 2004 to protest President Sampaio's decision not to call early elections following the resignation of Prime Minister Barroso. Former environment minister José Sócrates was elected as the new PS leader in late 2004, and having attempted to move the PS "to the center," he led the party to a resounding legislative victory in February 2005.

In September 2005, Manuel Alegre, a member of the assembly who had lost the race for party leader to Sócrates in 2004, announced that he would seek the presidency in 2006, even though the official socialist endorsement had gone to 81-year-old former president Soares. At the January 2006 polls Alegre finished second, with 20.7 percent of the vote, while Soares came in third, with 14.3 percent.

While in power, the PS focused on improving economic efficiency, especially through labor market reforms, spending cuts, and a reduction in public sector employment. The party's loss of 5 seats in the European Parliament in the June 2009 election suggested a narrowing of public support. Although the PS remained the largest party in the assembly after the September legislative balloting, the party lost 24 seats. Nonetheless, Sócrates formed a new minority government.

Alegre placed second in 2011 presidential election, with 19.7 percent of the vote. Sócrates lost a no-confidence vote in March and resigned as prime minister. In legislative balloting in June the PS fell to 74 seats. Maria de Belém Roseira was elected party president in September 2011, with 746 of 788 votes, but General Secretary António José Seguro Martins has gained a strong following in parliamentary debates over austerity.

Leaders: Maria de Belém ROSEIRA (President), António José SEGURO MARTINS (General Secretary), Jorge SAMPAIO (Former President of the Republic), António GUTERRES (UN High Commissioner for Refugees and Former Prime Minister), José SÓCRATES (Former Prime Minister).

Unified Democratic Coalition (*Coligação Democrática Unitária*—CDU). Prior to the 1979 election the Portuguese Communist Party (PCP, below) joined with the Popular Democratic Movement (*Movimento Democrático Popular*—MDP) in an electoral coalition known as the United People's Alliance (*Aliança Povo Unido*—APU). The APU won 47 legislative seats in 1979, 41 in 1980, and 38 in 1985, its constituent formations having campaigned separately in 1983. In the 1986 presidential race, the party formally endorsed independent Maria de Lourdes Pintasilgo, with some dissidents supporting Francisco Salgado ZENHA of the now-defunct Democratic Renewal Party (*Partido Renovador Democrático*—PRD); following the elimination of both from the runoff, a special Communist Party congress on February 2, 1986, urged Alliance supporters to "hold their nose, ignore the photograph," and vote for Soares.

Disturbed by allegations that it was merely a PCP front, the MDP withdrew from the Alliance in November 1986. The APU was thereupon dissolved in favor of the CDU, which embraced the PCP; a group of MDP dissidents calling themselves Democratic Intervention (*Intervenção Democrática*—ID), which effectively superseded the MDP; an environmentalist formation, The Greens (*Os Verdes*); and a number of independent leftists. The new group obtained 31 assembly seats in 1987, 7 fewer than the APU in 1985. In October 1991, having lauded the attempted hard-line coup in the Soviet Union two months earlier, the CDU's legislative representation was further reduced to 17. It slipped to 15 seats in the October 1995 legislative election but then added 2 more in 1999. The coalition received 14 seats in 2005 and 15 seats in 2009. During the 2011 election, the coalition took 16 seats: 14 for the PCP and 2 for PEV. CDU candidate Francisco LOPES placed fourth in the 2011 presidential election, with 7.1 percent of the vote.

Leader: Jerónimo Carvalho DE SOUSA.

Portuguese Communist Party (*Partido Comunista Português*—PCP). Founded in 1921 and historically one of the most Stalinist of the West European Communist parties, the PCP was the dominant force within both the military and the government in the year following the 1974 coup. Its influence waned during the latter half of 1975, particularly following the abortive rebellion of November 26, and its legislative strength dropped to fourth place in April 1976, prior to organization of the APU. The party made limited concessions to Soviet-style liberalization at its 12th congress in December 1988 by endorsing freedom of the press and multiparty politics. At a special congress called in May 1990, however, the PCP returned to a hard-line posture. It enjoys widespread support in rural and industrial areas.

In the 1999 assembly election, the PCP won 15 of the CDU's 17 seats. Its 2001 presidential candidate, António SIMÕES DE ABREU, finished third, with only 5 percent of the vote. In 2005 the party's assembly representation dropped to 12 (and later to 11 when a PCP delegate became unaffiliated in November 2007) but rose to 13 in 2009.

In 2006 presidential candidate Jerónimo Carvalho De Sousa finished fourth, with 8.6 percent of the vote. The party gained 14 seats in elections in June 2011. The party is a fierce critic of the international financial community.

Leaders: Jerónimo Carvalho DE SOUSA (General Secretary), Bernardino SOARES (Parliamentary Leader).

Ecologist Party "The Greens" (*Partido Ecologista "Os Verdes"*—PEV). The PEV began in 1982 as the Portuguese Ecologist Movement—"The Greens" Party (*Movimento Ecologista Português—Partido "Os Verdes"*). In the October 1999 election the party won two of the CDU's legislative seats. The PEV subsequently was described as having shifted its emphasis from purely Portuguese environmental issues to broader European concerns.

The Greens won two seats in each of the 2005, 2009, and 2011 legislative elections.

Leader: Heloísa APOLÓNIA (Parliamentary Leader).

Left Bloc (*Bloco de Esquerda*—BE). The BE held its first national convention in February 1999. The alliance included the socialist **Politics XXI** (*Politica XXI*), the Trotskyite **Revolutionary Left Front** (*Frente da Esquerda Revolucionária*—FER), the Marxist-Leninist **Popular Democratic Union** (*União Democrática Popular*—UDP), and the small Trotskyite **Revolutionary Socialist Party** (*Partido Socialista Revolucionário*—PSR). The BE won 2.4 percent of the vote and two seats in the general election of October 1999. Its 2001 presidential contender, Fernando ROSAS, won 3 percent. The BE, which presents itself as a mainstream, progressive alternative to the PCP, lost two of its constituent parties with the November 2005 dissolution of the UDP and FER.

BE leader Francisco LOUÇÃ finished fifth in the 2006 presidential election, with 5.3 percent of the vote. The BE tripled its presence in the Portuguese delegation to the European Parliament in the June 2009 election to that body, from 1 to 3 seats, a result that analysts attributed to public frustration over the government's austerity measures. The BE also benefited from voter dissatisfaction with the PS government in the 2009 legislative balloting when the party doubled its representation to 16 seats in the Assembly. The BE supported PS candidate Manuel Alegre in the 2011 presidential balloting. In legislative elections in June the BE lost half its seats, falling to 8, prompting Louçã to step down as leader. The BE led a series of strikes and protests against austerity measures in 2012.

Leaders: Catarina MARTINS (Leader of the Party), Luís FAZENDA (General Secretary), and Pedro Filipe SOARES (Parliamentary Leader).

Other Parties That Contested the 2011 Elections:

Parties that contested the June 2011 assembly balloting but failed to win a seat included the **Portuguese Workers' Communist Party/ Reorganizative Movement of the Party of the Proletariat** (*Partido Comunista dos Trabalhadores Portugueses/Movimento Reorganizativo do Partido do Proletariado*—PCTP/MRPP), a Maoist party led by Garcia PEREIRA; the **Party for Animals and Nature** (*Partido pelos Animais e pela Natureza*), which was founded in 2011; the **New Democracy Party** (*Partido da Nova Democracia*—PND), a conservative party founded in 2003 by its current leader, former CDS-PP president Manuel Monteiro; the center-left **Humanist Party** (*Partido Humanista*—PH), led by Luís Filipe GUERRA; the neo-fascist **National Renewal Party** (*Partido Nacional Renovador*—PNR), led by José PINTO-COELHO; the Trotskyite **United Socialist Workers' Party** (*Partido Operário de Unidade Socialista*—POUS), formed in 1976 and led by Aniceto BARBOSA; and the **Atlantic Democratic Party** (*Partido Democrático do Atlântico*—PDA), a grouping based in the Azores and the Madeira Islands and led by José VENTURA; the **Hope for Portugal Movement** (*Movimento Esperança Portugal*—MEP), a centrist party founded by businessman Rui MARQUES in 2008; the **People's Monarchist Party** (*Partido Popular Monárquico*—PPM), founded in 1974; the green, center-right **Earth Party** (*Partido da Terra*—MPT), founded in 1993; the **Labor Party** (*Partido Trabalhista*); and the small **Pro-Life Party**.

LEGISLATURE

The unicameral **Assembly of the Republic** (*Assembleia da República*) consists of 230 members elected for four-year terms (subject to dissolution) via proportional representation. (Four seats are elected by Portuguese living abroad.)

In the most recent balloting on June 5, 2011, the seat distribution was as follows: the Social Democratic Party, 108 seats; the Socialist

Party, 74; the Social Democratic Center-Popular Party, 24; the Unified Democratic Coalition, 16 (Portuguese Communist Party, 14; Ecologist Party "The Greens," 2), and the Left Bloc, 8.

President: Maria da ASSUNÇÃO ESTEVES.

CABINET

[as of September 5, 2013]

Prime Minister	Pedro Passos Coelho (PSD)
Deputy Prime Minister	Paulo Portas (CDS-PP)
Ministers of State	
Finance	Maria Luis Albuquerque (ind.) [f]
Foreign Affairs	Rui Machete (PSD)
Ministers	
Agriculture and Marine Affairs	Assunção Cristas (CDS-PP) [f]
Economy and Employment	Antonio Pires De Lima (CDS-PP)
Education, Higher Education, and Science	Nuno Crato (ind.)
Environment and Regional Planning	Jorge Moreira Da Silva (PSD)
Health	Paulo Macedo (ind.)
Internal Administration	Miguel Macedo (PSD)
Justice	Paula Teixeira da Cruz (PSD) [f]
National Defense	José Pedro Aguiar Branco (PSD)
Presidency and Parliamentary Affairs	Luís Marques Guedes (PSD)
Solidarity and Social Security	Pedro Mota Soares (CDS-PP)

[f] = female

INTERGOVERNMENTAL REPRESENTATION

Ambassador to the U.S.: Nuno Filipe Alves SALVADOR E BRITO.

U.S. Ambassador to Portugal: Allan J. KATZ.

Permanent Representative to the UN: José DE MENDONÇA E MOURA.

IGO Memberships (Non-UN): ADB, AfDB, CEUR, EBRD, EIB, EU, IADB, ICC, IEA, IOM, NATO, OECD, OSCE, WTO.

RELATED TERRITORIES

The Azores and the Madeira Islands have long been construed as insular components of metropolitan Portugal and, as such, were legally distinct from a group of Portuguese possessions whose status was changed in 1951 from that of "Colonies" to "Overseas Territories." Of the latter, the South Asian enclaves of Goa, Damão, and Diu were annexed by India in 1961; Portuguese Guinea became independent as Guinea-Bissau in 1974; and Angola, the Cape Verde Islands, Mozambique, and São Tomé and Principe became independent in 1975. Portuguese Timor (East Timor) was annexed by Indonesia on July 17, 1976, but the action was never recognized by Portugal, and diplomatic relations with Jakarta were not restored until late 1999, after the Indonesian government had accepted the results of the August 1999 independence referendum in East Timor (now Timor-Leste). Macao, which had been defined as a "collective entity" (*pessoa colectiva*) under a governing statute promulgated on February 17, 1976, reverted to Chinese sovereignty in 1999 (see entry on China). Under the 1976 constitution, the Azores and Madeira are defined as autonomous regions.

Azores (*Açores*). The Azores comprise three distinct groups of islands located in the Atlantic Ocean about 800 miles west of mainland Portugal. The most easterly of the islands are São Miguel and Santa Maria; the most westerly and least densely populated are Corvo and Flores; Fayal, Graciosa, Pico, São Jorge, and Terceira are in the center. There are three political districts, the capitals and chief seaports of which are Ponta Delgada (São Miguel), Horta (Fayal), and Angra do Heroísmo (Terceira). The islands' total area is 890 square miles (2,305 sq. km), and their resident population (2006E) is 244,100.

Following the 1974 coup, significant separatist sentiment emerged, particularly on Terceira, whose residents feared that the left-wing government at Lisbon might close the U.S. military base at Lajes. In August 1975 a recently organized **Azorean Liberation Front** (*Frente de Libertação dos Açores*—FLA) announced its opposition to continued rule from the mainland. Following the resignation of three appointed governors, the Portuguese government surrendered control of the islands' internal administration to local political leaders and in April 1976 provided for an elected Regional Assembly.

In March 1991, FLA leader José de ALMEIDA was acquitted of treason charges on the grounds that there was insufficient evidence of his having incited others to violence. In assembly balloting on October 11, 1992, the Social Democratic Party (PSD) regained its majority, winning 28 of 51 seats. The PSD and the Socialist Party (PS) each won 24 seats in the October 3, 1996, balloting, with the Popular Party (PP) gaining 2 seats and the Portuguese Communist Party (PCP), 1. In the election of October 15, 2000, the PS claimed a majority of 30 seats, while the PSD dropped to 18. The PP and the Unitary Democratic Coalition (the PCP and the Greens) each won 2 seats. The PS advanced to 44 of 52 seats in the assembly balloting of October 17, 2004. In October 2008 balloting the PS kept its majority in the assembly, winning 30 of 57 seats, followed by the PSD with 18; the CDS-PP, 5; the Left Bloc, 2; the PCP-PEV, 1; and the PPM, 1.

Two candidates from the PS, and one from the PSD, from the Azores won seats in the National Assembly in the June 2011 Portuguese election. The PS continued its dominance in the October 14, 2012, local election, winning 31 seats, followed by the PSD (20), and CDS-PP (3). President César retired after 16 years in office and was succeeded by Vasco Alves Cordeiro (PS).

President of the Regional Government: Vasco Alves CORDEIRO (PS).

Representative of the Republic: Pedro Manuel Alves dos Reis CATARINO.

Madeira Islands (*Ilhas da Madeira*). The Madeira Islands consist of Madeira and Porto Santo islands and the uninhabited islets of Desertas and Salvages. Lying west of Casablanca, Morocco, some 500 miles southwest of the Portuguese mainland, they have a total area of 308 square miles (797 sq. km) and a resident population (2006E) of 240,000. The capital is Funchal, on Madeira Island.

As in the case of the Azores, separatist sentiment exists, the **Madeira Archipelago Liberation Front** (*Frente de Libertação de Arquipélago da Madeira*—FLAM), which advocated independence from Portugal and possible federation with the Azores and the Spanish Canaries, claiming on August 29, 1975, to have established a provisional government. However, both the government that was installed on October 1, 1976, and the elected Regional Assembly that was convened on October 23 were pledged to maintain ties to the mainland.

In balloting on October 15, 2000, the Social Democratic Party (PSD) won its seventh regional election in a row, claiming 41 of the 61 seats in the assembly. The Socialist Party (PS) won only 13 seats and the Popular Party (PP), 3. Alberto João Jardim of the PSD has served as regional president for nearly a quarter of a century. The PSD won 44 of 68 assembly seats in balloting on October 17, 2004. In the February 2005 Portuguese election, three PS and three PS candidates from the Madeira Islands won seats in the National Assembly.

On February 19, 2007, President Jardim resigned to protest a new, government-supported law on regional financing that would reduce aid levels from the central government to Madeira. The resignation prompted early elections on May 6, which Jardim won easily. The government rejected his call to rescind the law, but a court ruling in September forced it to do so.

A February 2010 storm, described as the worst in a century, caused extensive flooding and landslides. More than 50 people were killed and there was extensive property damage. The Portuguese government initiated a program to repair homes and build replacement dwellings. Madeira's debt reached €6 billion in 2012, largely government loans matched by the EU. The island has become overdeveloped, with luxurious new tourist areas sitting empty. The PSD won 25 of 47 seats in balloting in October 2011, and Jardim was reelected.

President of the Regional Government: Alberto João JARDIM (PSD).

Representative of the Republic: Antero Alves MONTEIRO DINIZ.

QATAR

State of Qatar
Dawlat al-Qatar

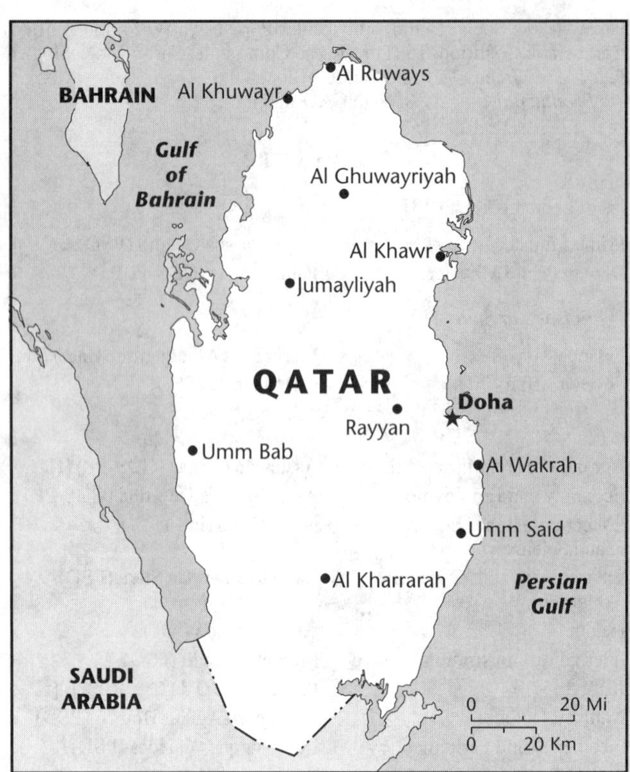

Political Status: Traditional sheikhdom; proclaimed fully independent September 1, 1971; first permanent constitution, approved in referendum of April 29, 2003, went into effect on June 8, 2004.

Area: 4,247 sq. mi. (11,000 sq. km).

Population: 1,940,773 (2012E—UN); 2,042,444 (2013E—U.S. Census), including nonnationals, who constitute more than two-thirds of the resident population.

Major Urban Centers (2010E): DOHA (796,947) (al-Dawhah, 353,000), Rayyan (455,623).

Official Language: Arabic.

Monetary Unit: Qatar Riyal (official rate November 1, 2013: 3.64 riyals = $1US).

Sovereign (Emir): Sheik Tamim ibn Hamad AL-THANI; assumed power on June 25, 2013, upon the abdication of his father Sheikh Hamad ibn Khalifa AL-THANI, who assumed leadership on June 27, 1995.

Heir to the Throne: [Vacant].

Prime Minister: Sheikh Abdullah ibn Nasser ibn Khalifa AL-THANI, appointed by the emir on June 27, 2013, succeeding Sheikh Hamad ibn Jasim ibn Jabir AL-THANI.

THE COUNTRY

A flat, barren, peninsular projection into the Persian Gulf from the Saudi Arabian mainland, Qatar consists largely of sand and rock. The climate is quite warm with very little rainfall, and the lack of fresh water has led to a reliance on desalination techniques. The population is almost entirely Arab, but indigenous Qataris (mainly Sunni Muslims of the conservative Wahhabi sect) comprise substantially less than a majority, as thousands have flocked from abroad to cash in on Qatar's booming economy; the nonindigenous groups include Pakistanis, Iranians, Indians, and Palestinians. The percentage of women in the workforce grew substantially in the 1990s, and religious and governmental strictures upon women are less severe than in most other Gulf states. In 2013 one female minister served in the cabinet: Hessa Sultan al-Jaber, Minister of Communications and Information Technology. However, most women continue to wear veils in public, accept arranged marriages, and generally defer to the wishes of the male members of their families. Qatari culture as a whole continues to reflect the long history of "feudal tribal autocracy" and the "puritanical" (in the eyes of many Western observers) nature of Wahhabism, which is also practiced in Saudi Arabia, Qatar's influential neighbor.

The economy remains largely dependent upon revenue from oil, which has been produced for export since 1949 and under local production and marketing control since 1977. During the oil boom years of the 1970s, Qatar became one of the world's wealthiest nations. The sheikhdom was therefore able to develop a modern infrastructure, emphasizing schools, hospitals, roads, communication facilities, and water and electric plants.

Qatar is also home to the world's third-largest reserves of liquid natural gas. As domestic supplies dwindle elsewhere, other industrialized countries are poised to invest in Qatar's developing natural gas sector, in which the government has invested extensively. Attention has also focused on the development of new small- and medium-scale industries under joint public-private ownership; the Qatar Exchange opened in 1997 to that end. In early 2005 Qatar was named the most competitive Arab economy by the World Economic Forum. Investments in new projects totaling more than $60 billion indicated growing confidence in the economy, with much of the revenue going to improve Qatar's infrastructure. Annual GDP growth averaged about 11 percent from 2004–2007, bolstered by the soaring price of crude oil.

The Qatari government continued to emphasize diversification, announcing plans in 2008 to transform Qatar's economy from one based on oil production to one "that has knowledge as its mainstay." It has invested heavily in education, including Doha's multibillion-dollar Education City, which incorporates branches of five U.S. universities, as well as in the tourism and health sectors. The financial forecast remained positive, despite high inflation. Annual GDP growth of 14.9 percent was recorded for 2008–2011, driven by a significant expansion in the production of liquefied natural gas, as well as growth in the non-hydrocarbon sector. The International Monetary Fund (IMF) commended Qatar for "successfully steering the economy through the global financial crisis." With a self-imposed moratorium on increased oil production, growth slowed to 6.5 percent in 2012, and slipped further to 5.2 percent in 2013. Inflation was 1.9 percent. Unemployment of Qataris dropped to 3.1 percent in 2012 from 3.9 percent the previous year, according to government statistics.

GOVERNMENT AND POLITICS

Political background. Qatar was dominated by Bahrain until 1868 and by the Ottoman Turks from 1878 through World War I, until it entered into treaty relations with Great Britain in 1916. Under the treaty, Qatar stipulated that it would not conclude agreements with other foreign governments without British consent; in return, Britain agreed to provide for the defense of the sheikhdom. When the British government announced in 1968 that it intended to withdraw from the Persian Gulf by 1971, Qatar attempted to associate itself with Bahrain and the Trucial Sheikhdoms in a Federation of Arab Emirates. Qatar declared independence when it became apparent that agreement on the structure of the proposed federation could not be obtained; its independence was realized in 1971.

The new state was governed initially by Sheikh Ahmad ibn Ali ibn Abdallah Al THANI, who proved to be an inattentive sovereign. In February 1972 his cousin, Prime Minister Sheikh Khalifa ibn Hamad Al THANI, deposed Sheikh Ahmad in a bloodless coup approved by the royal family. Although modernist elements subsequently emerged, the sheikhdom remained a virtually absolute monarch with close relatives of the emir occupying senior government posts.

In May 1989 Sheikh Hamad ibn Khalifa Al THANI, the emir's heir apparent, was named head of the newly formed Supreme Council for

Planning, which was commissioned to oversee Qatar's resource development projects. The government's economic efforts gained additional momentum on July 18 when the first cabinet reshuffling since 1978 resulted in the replacement of seven elderly ministers.

Like its Arab neighbors, Qatar faced international and domestic pressure for political reform following the 1990–1991 Gulf crisis, which drew Western attention on the dearth of democratic institutions in the region. The issue came to a head in early 1992 when 50 prominent Qataris expressed "concern and disappointment" over the ruling family's "abuse of power" and called for economic and educational reform, ultimately demanding the abolition of the Consultative Council in favor of a true legislative body. The government responded harshly to the criticism and briefly detained some of the petitioners, muting calls for democratization. However, reformists considered it a positive step when non-relatives of the royal family assumed several key ministerial positions in the cabinet reshuffle of September 1, 1992.

Though Qataris liked Sheikh Khalifa on a personal level, they reportedly believed he was allowing Qatar to slip behind other Gulf countries in economic and political progress. They expressed little dissent when Sheikh Hamad deposed his father on June 27, 1995, while the emir was on a private visit to Switzerland. Sheikh Hamad consolidated his authority and reorganized the cabinet on July 11, naming himself as prime minister and defense minister. (Sheikh Khalifa lived in Europe until he returned to Qatar for the first time since he was deposed on October 14, 2004, to attend his wife's funeral.)

In February 1996 the government announced that it had uncovered a coup plot, and those arrested reportedly included army and police officers. Although Sheikh Khalifa strongly denied any involvement in the alleged plot, he argued that it indicated popular support for his reinstatement. The government concluded an out-of-court financial settlement with Sheikh Khalifa in October 1996, which permitted Sheikh Hamad to establish a sense of permanence to his reign and facilitated an at least partial reconciliation between father and son. In November 1997 some 110 people, including many military officers, were tried for alleged participation in the February 1996 coup attempt. While 85 of the defendants were acquitted in February 2000, about 30 were convicted and received sentences of either life in prison or death. An appeals court upheld their sentences in May 2001. Meanwhile, Sheikh Hamad had gained broader support from the populace and continued to promote his liberalized administration as a potential model for other countries in the region where long-standing regimes have resisted political and economic reform.

On October 22, 1996, Sheikh Hamad appointed his third son, Sheikh Jassim ibn Hamad Al THANI, as crown prince and his heir apparent. Six days later the emir appointed his younger brother, Sheikh Abdallah ibn Khalifa AL THANI, as prime minister to the government named on October 20, which included a number of younger ministers.

On March 8, 1999, the nation's first elections were held for the transitional Consultative Central Municipal Council, which the government established to introduce representative popular elections in the country. In July a committee newly appointed by the emir held its first meeting to draft a constitution that would ultimately provide for a popularly elected legislature. In 2002 Qatar established a national human rights committee.

The crown prince relinquished his position on August 5, 2003, to his younger brother, Sheikh Tamim ibn Hamad Al THANI. In September the emir conferred the title of deputy prime minister upon two of his ministers, and the new crown prince also was named commander in chief of the armed forces. Sheikh Hamad also appointed the first woman to the Qatari cabinet, Sheikha Ahmad al-MAHMUD, in 2003 (see Cabinet, below).

Sheikh Abdallah ibn Khalifa Al Thani resigned as prime minister on April 3, 2007, and was replaced the same day by Sheikh Hamad ibn Jasim ibn Jabir Al Thani. The new prime minister was sworn in along with a reshuffled cabinet on April 3.

The cabinet was enlarged and reshuffled on July 2, 2008, with a second woman named to a ministerial post. Both women were replaced in a cabinet reshuffle on April 29, 2009. Three ministers were replaced in April and June 2010. The minister of energy and industry was replaced on January 18, 2011, by the minister of state for energy and industry, though the former retained his post as deputy prime minister.

On June 25, 2013, Sheikh Hamad abdicated the throne and Sheikh Tamim assumed power. The following day, he installed a new cabinet, naming Sheikh Abdullah ibn Nasser ibn Khalifa Al THANI as prime minister (see Current issues, below).

Constitution and government. Qatar employs traditional patterns of authority, onto which a limited number of modern governmental institutions have been grafted. The provisional constitution of 1970 provided for a Council of Ministers, headed by an appointed prime minister, and an Advisory Council (Consultative Council) of 20 (subsequently 35) members. Three of the Advisory Council members were to be appointed and the rest elected, although national elections were not held. The judicial system embraces five secular courts (two criminal as well as civil, labor, and appeal) and religious courts, which apply Islamic law (sharia).

In November 1998 Sheikh Hamad announced that a constitutional committee would draft a new permanent basic law, one that should provide for a directly elected National Assembly to replace the Consultative Council. The emir announced that all Qataris over 18, including women, would be permitted to vote, while those over 25, also including women, would be allowed to run for the new legislative body. The new constitution, promulgated on June 8, 2004, after gaining overwhelming approval by voters (96.6 percent) in a national referendum on April 29, 2003, identifies Islam as the state religion. However, officials say Islamic law only "inspires" the new charter and is not the only source for its content. Under the new charter, the emir retains executive powers, including control over general policy and the appointment of a prime minister and cabinet. The new constitution also states that 30 of 45 members of the Consultative Council will be elected, the remainder appointed by the emir. In 2011 the emir announced that elections would take place in 2013, but they were indefinitely postponed upon his abdication (see Current issues, below).

In 2013 Reporters Without Borders ranked Qatar as 110th out of 179 countries for press freedom. The country's newspapers are largely owned by members of the royal family, stifling journalistic criticism of the government.

Foreign relations. Until 1971 Qatar's foreign relations were administered by Britain. Since reaching independence it has pursued a policy of nonalignment in foreign affairs as a member of the United Nations (UN), the Arab League, and the Organization of Petroleum Exporting Countries (OPEC).

In 1981 Qatar joined with five other Gulf states (Bahrain, Kuwait, Oman, Saudi Arabia, and the United Arab Emirates) in establishing the Gulf Cooperation Council (GCC) and has since participated in joint military maneuvers and the formation of economic cooperation agreements, though territorial disputes sporadically threatened GCC unity. In April 1986 fighting nearly erupted between Qatari and Bahraini troops over a small, uninhabited island, Fasht al-Dibal, that Bahrain had reclaimed from an underlying coral reef. Although Qatar acquiesced to temporary Bahraini control of the island, sovereignty remained in question. In mid-1991, Qatar asked the International Court of Justice (ICJ) to rule on Fasht al-Dibal as well as several other contested Bahraini-controlled islands. In 1997 GCC mediation between Qatar and Bahrain resulted in an agreement to open embassies in each other's capitals and await the ICJ ruling. Ultimately, in 2001, the ICJ awarded the disputed islands to Bahrain while reaffirming Qatar's sovereignty over the town of Zubara and its surrounding territory (which Bahrain had claimed as part of the case). Relations between the two countries have warmed, and in 2006, they signed a deal to begin construction of a causeway connecting them.

Another long-simmering dispute erupted in violence in late September 1992 when two Qatari border guards were killed in a confrontation along the border with Saudi Arabia. Saudi leaders dismissed the incident as an inconsequential clash among Bedouin tribes, but Qatar reacted with hostility, boycotting several GCC ministerial sessions and reportedly threatening to quit the organization altogether. After years of negotiations, Qatar accepted Saudi Arabia's demands and a final agreement on land and sea border demarcation was signed in June 1999.

The sheikhdom denounced the August 1990 Iraqi invasion of Kuwait and responded further by offering its territory as a base for allied forces, expelling PLO representatives, and taking part in joint military exercises. At the GCC's December summit Qatar supported the "Doha Declaration," which called for a plan to prevent a repetition of Iraqi aggression, the departure of "friendly" forces upon the resolution of the crisis, and an Iranian role in security arrangements. In early 1991, Qatari forces (composed primarily of foreigners) participated in allied air and ground actions. Qatar remained closely aligned with the other GCC states on most security issues following the war and signed a defense agreement with the United States in June 1992 in the wake of similar U.S. pacts with Bahrain and Kuwait.

Meanwhile, Qatar, without GCC support, moved to improve relations with Iran for regional stability. In May 1992, Doha signed a number of agreements with Tehran (covering such matters as air traffic, customs procedure, and the possibility of supplying the sheikhdom with fresh water via a trans-Gulf pipeline), with Doha called for peaceful negotiations to resolve the Iranian nuclear issue.

Qatar has also adopted a more lenient posture than most of its GCC partners regarding Iraq, calling in early 1995 for UN sanctions against Iraq to be lifted for humanitarian reasons. However, in the wake of the brief crisis generated by the massing of Iraqi troops near the Kuwaiti border in October 1994, Doha agreed to let the U.S. permanently store its armor in Qatar.

In the early 21st century, Qatar has become an important American ally in the Middle East. In mid-2000, the United States financed and built a massive staging area for its ground troops in eastern Qatar, which later became the U.S. Central Command site in the 2003 invasion of Iraq.

On the second anniversary of the U.S.-Iraqi invasion in March 2005, a car bomb exploded in a Qatari theater frequented by Westerners. It was the first incident of its kind in Qatar; an Egyptian expatriate with alleged al-Qaida links was later blamed in the attack.

Qatar made efforts "to bring Israel into the Gulf" as a contribution to the Middle East peace process, despite contrary sentiments in the region. In May 2005, Israel agreed to Qatar's unprecedented request for support of Doha's candidacy for a rotating seat in the UN Security Council. The request marked the first time an Arab state had sought Israel's help in such a matter, and signaled the potential for increasingly positive relations between the two countries. In early 2006, however, Qatar was among 14 Arab nations attending a summit in Damascus to discuss tightening the boycott against Israel. Qatar allowed the governing Palestinian group, Hamas, to have an office in Doha in 2006 and pledged $50 million in aid to Hamas, despite pressure from the United States not to help the anti-Israel group financially. Qatar, for its part, has called for Israeli-Palestinian peace efforts.

Relations with Russia improved in 2007, evidenced by President Vladimir Putin's trip to Qatar, and in late 2008, the two countries announced that they were setting up an OPEC-style cartel, along with Iran, for natural gas. (The three countries were reported to control 60 percent of the world's gas reserves.)

Though Qatar has no diplomatic relationship with Israel, Israeli foreign minister Tzipi Livni visited Doha in April 2008, at the invitation of the emir, to lobby for Arab states' ties with Israel and for support against Iran's nuclear program. Her trip came in the wake of Qatar's offer in February to help broker a peace agreement between Israel and Hamas. Observers noted Qatar's recent engagement in regional mediation efforts, such as its March 2008 brokering of a peace accord between Yemen's government and an insurgent group. Following Israel's attacks on Gaza in response to Hamas's launching rockets into southern Israel in late 2008 and early 2009, Qatar closed Israel's trade office in Doha and cut off all economic and political ties with the state. However, in February Prime Minister Hamad ibn Jasim ibn Jabir Al Thani told French president Nicolas Sarkozy at a meeting in Paris that he would "intensively" engage Hamas in an effort to free a kidnapped Israel soldier upon learning that the soldier also held French citizenship.

In a move that reportedly surprised Qatari officials, Ethiopia in April 2008 suspended diplomatic relations with Qatar, claiming that media outlets in Qatar were supporting terrorism in Ethiopia and Somalia in the wake of Ethiopia's failed efforts to drive out Islamists who had gained control in Somalia.

In May 2010 Israel rejected Qatar's offer to reestablish trade relations between the two countries, provisioned on permission for Qatar to import materials into Gaza. The offer was regarded by Israel as "bolstering Hamas" and stirred concern from the United States and Egypt. Following Israel's attack on a flotilla bound for Gaza on May 31, Qatar backed a proposed UN Security Council resolution condemning Israel's action.

China and Qatar in 2011 pledged to expand energy cooperation.

During the so-called "Arab Spring" that same year, Qatar expressed its support to the Syrian president in the wake of mass antigovernment protests, though it later reversed its position to publicly oppose Bashar al Assad. In early 2011 Qatar tried to resolve a government crisis in Lebanon but was thwarted by Hezbollah and its supporters in Syria and Iran. Qatar adopted a more confrontational approach to relations with Assad. In August Qatar closed its Damascus embassy and threw support behind the opposition Syrian National Council, calling for a peaceful transfer of power. Qatar participated in the Arab League's peace initiative in Syria, with very limited success as of September 2012. Prime Minister Hamad ibn Jasim ibn Jabir Al Thani called for the Syrian opposition to be armed. Qatar's assertiveness in Syria has heightened tensions with Iran.

Qatar joined the NATO effort in Libya from March through October 2011 and was the first Arab country to recognize the authority of the Libyan rebels, winning the praise of Western leaders. However, Qatar supported Saudi Arabia in sending troops to defend Bahrain's minority Sunni king against the protesting Shiite majority, and, in May, deported a Libya woman who took refuge in Qatar after alleged sexual assault by Libyan government forces.

Despite the International Criminal Court's (ICC) appeal to Qatar to cooperate with an arrest warrant against Sudan's President Beshir for alleged war crimes, Qatari officials invited Beshir and did not detain him when he arrived on a 2009 visit. (Qatar is not a signatory to the agreement that dates to the establishment of the ICC.) Subsequently, Arab leaders in the summer rejected the ICC's arrest warrant, calling for it to be annulled. In 2012 Qatar pledged to make strategic investments in Sudan to help prop up Sudan's currency, and in April 2013, hosted a conference on reconstruction in Darfur.

In May 2011 Qatar withdrew from the GCC's initiative to secure the resignation of Yemeni president Ali Abdullah Saleh, saying that "the intensity of the conflict" and "a lack of wisdom" in Yemen made mediation by the GCC impossible. Saleh, who saw Qatar as a hostile party and Qatar-based television channel Al-Jazeera as a supporter of the Yemeni opposition, welcomed Qatar's withdrawal.

A visit by Pakistan President Asif Ali Zardari in November 2012 resulted in an effort to improve bilateral economic and trade relations between the two countries.

In January 2012 a spokesman for Afghanistan's Taliban movement announced that it had reached an agreement to open a representative office in Doha, a move meant to foster "negotiations with the international community." In June 2013 the Taliban opened their first official foreign office in Doha, expected to usher in talks with the United States, Pakistan, and the Afghan government led by Hamid Karzai. However, talks stalled almost immediately when Karzai and the United States objected to the display of the Taliban flag and a plaque reading the "Islamic Emirate of Afghanistan" (used when the Taliban rose to power in the 1990s). Upon their removal by Qatari officials, Taliban representatives, some 20 of whom are said to be in Qatar, refused to enter the office. Little progress has been made since.

Current issues. In November 2012 Qatari poet Mohammad AL-AJAMI was sentenced to life in prison for insulting the emir in a poem he recited before a small audience in Egypt in 2010 that was later posted online, though he is best known throughout the Middle East from a video of him reciting a poem lauding the Arab Spring. The ruling was internationally condemned, and, upon appeal in February 2013, the sentence was reduced to 15 years.

In a televised speech on June 25, 2013, Sheikh Hamad abdicated, transferring power to his 33-year-old son, Sheikh Tamim. The move was seen as a challenge to the region's monarchical traditions, where power is transferred only by death or palace coup. Sheikh Hamad handed the reins to his son, noting the shift represents "a new era where young leadership hoists the banner." No official explanation for the elder emir's abdication was given, but it was widely reported that he suffers from chronic medical problems. In contrast to his father, who left behind a legacy of foreign intervention and regional mediation, Sheihk Tamim is expected to focus on domestic affairs, assuming leadership of the Interior Ministry. On June 26, the new emir appointed his new cabinet, including former minister of state for internal affairs Sheikh Abdullah ibn Nasser ibn Khalifa al-Thani as prime minister. The cabinet includes the second woman to serve at the ministerial level in Qatar.

Meanwhile, the transfer of power further postponed Consultative Council elections. In May 2008, the council established direct elections for two-thirds of the 45-member body. No elections were scheduled at the time, and the emir extended the members' terms for two years in July, and then, in 2010, renewed the extension for three years. In November 2011 responding, in part, to the year's Arab Spring protests, the emir promised elections by the end of 2013, a promise complicated by the emir's abdication. As of mid-2013, no election date has yet been called.

POLITICAL PARTIES

The constitution promulgated on June 8, 2004 (see Constitution and government, above) does not provide for the formation of political parties.

LEGISLATURE

The **Consultative Council** (*Majlis al-Shura*), created in 1972, was increased from 20 members to 30 in 1975 and to 35 in 1988. The present council consists exclusively of the emir's appointees, most of them named in 1972 and subsequently reappointed. Arrangements for a partially elected National Assembly are included in the new constitution that was promulgated in June 2004 (see Constitution and government, above). On June 27, 2006, the emir appointed 35 members for a term of one-year to the Consultative Council. On July 2, 2007, the emir extended the term of Consultative Council members, though the length of the new term was unclear. On July 2, 2008, another decree of the emir extended the members' terms to June 30, 2010. The terms were renewed for three more years in 2010 and again in 2013.

Speaker: Muhammad ibn Mubarak AL-KHALIFI.

CABINET

[as of November 12, 2013]

Prime Minister	Sheikh Abdullah ibn Nasser ibn Khalifa al-Thani
Deputy Prime Minister	Ahmed ibn Abdullah ibn Zaid al-Mahmud
Ministers	
Administrative Development	Issa Saad al-Jafali al-Nuaimi
Awqaf and Islamic Affairs	Ghaith Mubarak Ali Imran Al Kuwari
Communications and Information Technology	Hessa Sultan al-Jaber [f]
Culture, Arts, and Heritage	Hamad ibn Abdul Azziz al-Kawari
Development Planning and Statistics	Saleh Mohamed Salem al-Nabit
Economy and Trade	Sheikh Ahmed ibn Jassim ibn Mohamed al-Thani
Education and Higher Education	Mohammed Abdul Wahed Ali al-Hammadi
Energy and Industry	Muhammad ibn Saleh al-Sada
Environment	Ahmed Amer Mohamed al-Humaidi
Finance	Ali Sherif al-Emadi
Foreign Affairs	Khalid ibn Mohammad al-Attiyah
Interior	Sheikh Abdullah ibn Nasser ibn Khalifa al-Thani
Justice	Hassan Lahdan Saqr al-Mohannadi
Labor and Social Affairs	Abdullah Saleh Mubarak al-Khulaifi
Municipalities and Urban Planning	Sheikh Abdul Raman bin Khalifa bin Abdul Azziz al-Thani
Public Health	Abdullah ibn Khalid al-Qahtani
Transport	Jassim Seif Ahmed al-Sulaiti
Youth and Sports	Saleh ibn Ghanem ibn Nasser al-Ali
Ministers of State	
Cabinet Affairs	Ahmed ibn Abdullah ibn Zaid al-Mahmud
Defense Affairs	Khalid ibn Ali al-Attiyah

[f] = female

INTERGOVERNMENTAL REPRESENTATION

Ambassador to the U.S.: Muhammad ibn Abdullah AL-RUMAIHI.

U.S. Ambassador to Qatar: Susan L. ZIADEH.

Permanent Representative to the UN: Alya Ahmed Saif AL-THANI.

IGO Memberships (Non-UN): GCC, NAM, OPEC, OIC, WTO.

ROMANIA

România

Political Status: Independence established 1878; People's Republic proclaimed December 30, 1947; designated a Socialist Republic by constitution adopted August 21, 1965; redesignated as Romania in December 1989; presidential multiparty constitution approved in referendum of December 8, 1991.

Area: 91,699 sq. mi. (237,500 sq. km).

Population: 22,101,441 (2012E—UN); 21,848,504 (2012E—U.S. Census).

Major Urban Centers (2011C): BUCHAREST (București, 1,883,000), Cluj-Napoca (325,000), Timișoara (319,000), Iași (290,000), Constanța (284,000), Craiova (270,000), Brașov (253,000), Galați (249,000).

Official Language: Romanian.

Monetary Unit: New Leu (market rate November 1, 2013: 3.30 new lei = $1US). The new leu was introduced on July 1, 2005, at the rate of 1 new leu = 10,000 old lei.

President: Traian BĂSESCU (formerly Democratic Party, currently independent [as constitutionally required]); elected (as the candidate of the Justice and Truth Alliance) in second-round balloting on December 12, 2004, and inaugurated for a five-year term on December 20 in succession to Ion ILIESCU (elected as a member of the Social Democratic Party); reelected (with the endorsement of the Democratic-Liberal Party) in second-round balloting on December 6, 2009, and inaugurated for a second five-year term on December 21.

Chair of the Council of Ministers (Prime Minister): Victor PONTA (Social Democratic Party); designated by the president on April 27, 2012, and sworn in on May 7, 2012, to succeed Mihai Razvan UNGUREANU (Democratic-Liberal Party), after his government lost a confidence motion in parliament; nominated for a second term on December 17, 2012 (following the legislative elections of December 9), and sworn in on December 21, 2012.

THE COUNTRY

Shaped by the geographic influence of the Carpathian Mountains and the Danube River, Romania occupies the northeastern quarter of the Balkan Peninsula. It served historically both as an outpost of Latin civilization and as a natural gateway for Russian expansion into southeastern Europe. Some 83 percent of the population is ethnically Romanian, claiming descent from the Romanized Dacians of ancient times. There are also some 1.2 million Magyars (Hungarians), situated mostly in Transylvanian lands acquired from the Austro-Hungarian Empire after World War I. A sizeable German community that totaled approximately one-half million after World War II has dwindled because of emigration. Traditionally, the Romanian (Eastern) Orthodox Church has been the largest religious community. Female participation in political affairs increased significantly under the former Communist regime, but the membership of Parliament in 2012 was only 11.5 percent women (7.4 percent in the Senate and 13.3 percent in the Chamber of Deputies).

Although one of the world's pioneer oil producers, Romania was long a predominantly agricultural country and continues to be largely self-sufficient in food production. After World War II most acreage was brought under the control of collective and state farms, while the agricultural component of the workforce dropped sharply from 65 percent in 1960 as the result of an emphasis on industrial development—particularly in metals, machinery, chemicals, and construction materials—under a series of five-year plans. Agriculture continues to account for about 8 percent of GDP and to employ about one-third of the labor force. Most farms have now been reprivatized. Leading crops include grains, potatoes, apples, and wine grapes. Industry contributes over one-third of GDP. Major exports include electrical machinery, clothing, light machinery, and chemicals. The leading trading partners are Germany, Italy, Hungary, and France.

Following the overthrow of the Ceaușescu regime in December 1989 and the new administration's espousal of a free-market orientation, Romania suffered serious economic reversals: a 33 percent contraction of GDP from 1990 to 1993, inflation averaging 140 percent per annum, currency depreciation of 97 percent, and an increase in official unemployment to over 10 percent of the labor force. Improvement from 1994 to 1996 was disrupted by GDP contraction and high inflation during economic crisis of 1997–1999, but this was followed by a high average annual GDP growth rate of 5.9 percent in 2001–2008, placing it among the fastest-growing economies in the region. The IMF reported significant privatization progress, liberalization of the electricity and gas markets, and modernization of the mining sector. Romania's accession to the European Union (EU) at the beginning of 2007 assisted continued growth.

Until recently, the main problems facing successive governments have been corruption and the large trade and budget deficits. However, those issues have been overshadowed since mid-2008 by domestic economic concerns, which played a significant role in that year's legislative campaign. The government estimated that GDP contracted by 7.2 percent in 2009 under the influence of the global economic downturn, while unemployment reached 7.6 percent by the end of the year. The IMF reported a further 1.2 percent decline in GDP in 2010, but GDP grew by 2.2 percent in 2011 and 0.3 percent in 2012. The IMF predicts 1.6 percent growth in 2013.

GOVERNMENT AND POLITICS

Political background. The twin principalities of Walachia and Moldavia were conquered by the Ottoman Turks in 1504. The principalities were unified in 1859 and became the core of the Romanian state. Recognized as independent at the Berlin Congress in 1878, Romania made large territorial gains as one of the victorious powers in World War I but lost substantial areas to Hungary (Northern Transylvania), to the Soviet Union (Bessarabia and Northern Bukovina), and to Bulgaria (Southern Dobruja) in 1940 under threats from its neighbors and pressure from Nazi Germany. The young King MIHAI (Michael), who took advantage of the entry of Soviet troops in 1944 to dismiss the pro-German regime and switch to the Allied side, was forced in 1945 to accept a Communist-led coalition government under Dr. Petru GROZA. Following rigged elections in 1946, the king abdicated in 1947. The Paris peace treaty in 1947 restored Northern Transylvania to Romania, but not the other territories lost in 1940. Thereafter, the Communists proceeded to eliminate the remnants of the traditional parties, and in 1952, after a series of internal purges, Gheorghe GHEORGHIU-DEJ emerged as the unchallenged party leader.

Following a decade of rigidity, Romania embarked in the early 1960s on a policy of increased independence from the Soviet Union in both military and economic affairs. This policy was continued and intensified under Nicolae CEAUŞESCU, who succeeded to leadership of the Romanian Communist Party (*Partidul Comunist Român*—PCR) on Gheorghiu-Dej's death in 1965 and became president of the Council of State in 1967. While maintaining relatively strict controls at home, the Ceauşescu regime consistently advocated maximum autonomy in international Communist affairs.

In November 1989 Romania appeared impervious to the winds of change sweeping over most other East European Communist regimes. Thus, the 14th PCR congress met without incident on November 20–24, and Ceauşescu made a state visit to Iran on December 19–20. During his absence, long-simmering unrest among ethnic Hungarians in the western city of Timişoara led to a bloody confrontation between police and antigovernment demonstrators. The protests quickly spread to other cities, and on December 21 an angry crowd jeered the president during what had been planned as a progovernment rally in Bucharest. By the following day army units had joined in a full-scale revolt, with a group known as the National Salvation Front (*Frontul Salvării Naţionale*—FSN) announcing that it had formed a provisional government. Unlike other East European revolutions, Romania's overthrow of Communist rule involved fierce fighting, in Bucharest and other cities, with many civilian casualties. On December 25 Ceauşescu and his wife Elena, who had been captured after fleeing the capital, were executed following a secret trial that had pronounced them guilty of genocide and the embezzlement of more than $1 billion. On December 26 Ion ILIESCU was sworn in as provisional head of state, with Petre ROMAN, a fellow member of the PCR *nomenklatura,* being named prime minister. The FSN quickly came under attack as a thinly disguised extension of the former regime, and on February 1, 1990, it agreed to share power with 29 other groups in a coalition styled the Provisional Council for National Unity (*Consiliul Provizoriu de Uniune Naţională*—CPUN).

In presidential and legislative elections (the latter involving 6,719 candidates) on May 20, 1990, Iliescu won 85.1 percent of the presidential vote, while the FSN secured 67.0 and 66.3 percent of the votes for the upper and lower houses of Parliament, respectively. The balloting went ahead despite demonstrations by opposition parties claiming that they had been accorded insufficient time to organize. The protesters were eventually evicted from Bucharest's University Square in mid-June by thousands of club-wielding coal miners summoned to the capital by the president. On June 20 Iliescu was formally invested for a two-year term as president, with Roman continuing as prime minister.

Following his reappointment, Roman declared that he would pursue a "historic transition from a supercentralized economy to a market economy" and asserted that only "shock therapy" could save the rapidly deteriorating economy from disaster. Thus, prices of essential goods doubled as the result of sharp cuts in state subsidies in April 1991, while a drastic revision of the foreign investment code, urged by the IMF, offered non-Romanian companies full ownership, capital protection, repatriation of profits, and multiyear tax concessions.

Despite rapidly eroding support for the government by mid-1991, the reforms continued unabated, including the enactment of legislation in August that authorized the privatization of all state enterprises except utilities. For their part, the miners responded to soaring inflation by returning to Bucharest in September for three days of violent demonstrations, and on October 1 it was announced that Theodor STOLOJAN, the nonparty finance minister, had been asked to form a new government. By December it was clear that President Iliescu and former prime minister Roman were engaged in a struggle for control of the FSN. Iliescu supporters, formally organized from April 1992 as the Democratic National Salvation Front (*Frontul Democrat al Salvării Naţionale*—FDSN), gained parliamentary support for simultaneous legislative and presidential elections in September, at which Roman's forces were decisively routed.

At his reinvestiture on October 30, President Iliescu endorsed further progress toward pluralism and a market economy, despite having long been accused by opponents of foot-dragging on both counts. Fourteen days later, a deeply divided Parliament ended a five-week impasse by agreeing to the formation of a government led by Nicolae VĂCĂROIU, a relatively unknown tax official then without party affiliation, who proceeded to combine liberal reform with "special care" for its social consequences. In July 1993 the FDSN absorbed three other progovernment parties and adopted a new name, the Social Democracy Party of Romania (*Partidul Democraţiei Sociale din România*—PDSR), which Văcăroiu later joined.

Despite deepening economic misery, the Văcăroiu government endured, with support from the (ex-Communist) Socialist Labor Party (*Partidul Socialist al Muncii*—PSM), the far-right Greater Romania Party (*Partidul România Mare*—PRM), and (after 1994) the rightist Romanian National Unity Party (*Partidul Unităţii Naţionale Române*—PUNR). In the course of 1995, however, the PDSR's relations with all three coalition partners deteriorated sharply, with the PRM and PSM leaving the government alliance in October, with the PUNR's exit confirmed in September 1996.

In the first round of presidential balloting held on November 3, 1996, incumbent Iliescu (PDSR) headed the poll against 15 other candidates, winning 32.3 percent of the vote. However, he was closely followed by the CDR candidate, Emil CONSTANTINESCU, with 28.2 percent, while Petre Roman, standing for the Social Democratic Union (*Uniunea Social Democrată*—USD), came in third with 20.5 percent. The USD and most other opposition parties then swung behind the CDR candidate for the runoff polling on November 17. As a result, Constantinescu won a decisive victory over Iliescu by 53.5 percent to 46.5 percent, the incumbent having been weighed down not only by Romania's economic and social deterioration, but also by evidence of abuse of power and pervasive corruption within ruling circles. In legislative balloting also held on November 3, the CDR won pluralities in both the Senate and the Chamber of Deputies, with the USD also polling strongly as the third grouping, after the PDSR.

Interparty talks following the elections yielded the signature of an agreement on December 6, 1996, providing for Victor CIORBEA, the youthful CDR mayor of Bucharest, to head a majority coalition government with the USD and the Hungarian Democratic Union of Romania (*Uniunea Democrată a Maghiarilor din România*—UDMR), the latter representing Romania's ethnic Hungarian minority. Accorded a 316–152 endorsement by a joint session of the two legislative houses on December 11, the new administration was sworn in the following day.

Ciorbea's government found it difficult to implement the reforms required to resolve Romania's economic problems. Coalition members, particularly the CDR's Christian and Democratic National Peasants' Party (*Partidul Naţional Ţărănesc Creştin şi Democrat*—PNŢCD) and the USD's Democratic Party (*Partidul Democrat*—PD, an FSN descendant), generally were unable to compromise. In the wake of persistent feuding and public discord, the cabinet was reshuffled in December, with a number of independents being appointed. On January 14, 1998, the PD withdrew its support from Ciorbea and threatened to quit the government if he did not resign and if no agreement was reached within the coalition on a reform program by March 31. On February 5 the PD's five cabinet ministers resigned, and a new coalition agreement was approved, the open ministerial posts going to the PNŢCD, the National Liberal Party (*Partidul Naţional Liberal*—PNL), and the Civic Alliance Party (*Partidul Alianţa Civică*—PAC). After three months of political instability, Ciorbea resigned on March 30.

On April 2, 1998, President Constantinescu named Radu VASILE, the general secretary of the PNŢCD, to replace Ciorbea; Vasile and his cabinet were sworn in on April 15. The new government included members from the PNŢCD, PD, UDMR, PNL, Romanian Social Democratic Party (*Partidul Social Democrat Român*—PSDR), and Romania's Alternative Party (*Partidul Alternativa României*—PAR). However, in October PAR quit the coalition government in protest over the slow pace of economic reform.

Himself an economist, Vasile promised to strengthen the market economy by accelerating privatization efforts, and in December 1998 he restructured the government, reducing the number of ministries to quicken the pace of reform. In early 1999, however, his plans were set back by a miners' strike in the Jiu Valley that escalated into Romania's worst civil disorder since 1991. In mid-January the government reached a compromise with the leader of the miners' union, Miron COZMA, agreeing to abandon immediate plans to close unprofitable coal mines. The agreement averted a potential armed conflict between security forces and 20,000 strikers, but in mid-February Cozma and several hundred others were arrested as he led 2,000 miners toward Bucharest in protest against his recent sentencing to 18 years in prison for his role in the September 1991 riots.

With inflation and unemployment at unacceptable levels, and with the leu having fallen by more than one-third of its value between January and mid-March 1999, general dissatisfaction with the state of the economy continued to grow. Squabbling within the governing coalition also persisted, hindering progress on reform measures, and by December Vasile had lost the support of his own PNŢCD, whose ministers, constituting the majority of the cabinet, resigned. On December 13 President Constantinescu dismissed Vasile, with Mugur ISĂRESCU, the governor of Romania's central bank, appointed on December 16 as the new prime minister. Isărescu and a largely unchanged Council of Ministers received the legislature's approbation on December 21.

The final years of the CDR-led government were marked by political infighting and a resultant inability to establish a course that would resolve Romania's economic difficulties. At the same time, the country continued to grapple with the legacy of the Ceauşescu era. The government decided to release files held by the former secret police, the *Securitate,* and supported measures covering restitution for personal property, farmland, and forests.

After mid-2000, with presidential and legislative elections approaching, the political alliance behind the governing coalition gradually dissolved. In August 2000 the PNŢCD and several allied parties reconstituted the CDR as the CDR 2000, but minus one of its previous principal components, the PNL. The PD, UDMR, and PNL prepared to contest the elections independently, while in September the PSDR left the government and formed an alliance with the PDSR. The legislative election of November 26 saw the PDSR capture a large plurality in both parliamentary houses, with the xenophobic PRM, in the election's most startling development, rising to second place with 20 percent of the vote and with the enfeebled CDR 2000 failing to meet the threshold for representation. In the presidential contest, former president Iliescu of the PDSR easily defeated the PRM's Corneliu VADIM TUDOR in a two-way runoff on December 10. (President Constantinescu had decided not to seek a second term, describing Romania's political parties as conducting "a blind struggle" for power.) Iliescu assumed office on December 21. His choice for prime minister, Adrian NĂSTASE, was confirmed by the Parliament and sworn in on December 28 at the head of a minority government dominated by the PDSR, with external backing from the PNL and the UDMR. On June 16, 2001, the PDSR and the PSDR completed their merger as the Social Democratic Party (*Partidul Social Democrat*—PSD).

At legislative balloting on November 28, 2004, the PSD, and its ally in the National Union coalition, the Humanist Party of Romania (*Partidul Umanist din România*—PUR), secured a plurality of 132 seats in the Chamber of Deputies. Following closely (with 112 seats) was the Justice and Truth Alliance (*Alianţa Dreptate şi Adevăr*—ADA), which had been formed in 2003 by the PNL and the PD. In concurrent first-round presidential balloting, Prime Minister Năstase led 12 candidates with 41 percent of the vote. The ADA's Traian BĂSESCU finished second with 34 percent of the vote, followed by the PRM's Vadim Tudor with 12.6 percent.

In the presidential runoff on December 12, 2004, Băsescu scored a surprising victory over Năstase, securing 51.2 percent of the vote. Observers were surprised by Năstase's loss since as prime minister he had successfully negotiated accession to NATO, overseen progress toward EU membership, and adopted policies that contributed to economic improvement. However, Băsescu was aided among voters still concerned about corruption by his reputation for rectitude as mayor of Bucharest. On December 28 the Parliament, by a vote of 265–200, approved a cabinet (led by Călin POPESCU-TĂRICEANU of the PNL) comprising the PNL, PD, UDMR, and PUR (which had split from the PSD).

In April 2005 Romania signed an accession treaty with the EU calling for Romania to become a member in January 2007, although analysts noted that significant reform was still required. Complicating matters at midyear was reported friction between the president and the prime minister on a number of issues.

The Conservative Party (*Partidul Conservator*—PC, as PUR had been renamed) left the government in December 2006 after a series of disagreements within the coalition over a number of issues. (Several PC leaders were also facing corruption investigations.) The government's legislative majority was also compromised by the defections of a number of PNL deputies to a new party (the Democratic Liberal Party [*Partidul Liberal Democrat*—PLD]) formed by former prime minister Stolojan and other PNL dissidents. Nevertheless, Prime Minister Popescu-Tăriceanu declined to call new elections, in part, apparently, in an effort to maintain stability in advance of the January 1, 2007, accession to the EU.

An even stronger threat to the government arose when the ADA was dissolved and the PD withdrew from the cabinet on April 1, 2007. However, on the following day Prime Minister Popescu-Tăriceanu named a new minority government comprising the PNL and UDMR, which was easily approved by the assembled Parliament on April 5, thanks primarily to support from the PSD. Turmoil nevertheless continued as the Parliament, at the prime minister's urging, on April 19 voted 322–108 to suspend President Băsescu and conduct a referendum on his possible permanent removal from office for alleged violation of the constitution in regard to the extent of presidential authority. Nicolae VĂCĂROIU, the chair of the Senate, served as acting president until the May 19 referendum, in which nearly 75 percent of the voters rejected the proposed removal of the president, who resumed his duties on May 23.

Another national referendum was held on November 25, 2007, concerning changes in the national electoral system supported by President Băsescu, who favored decentralizing the government and making Parliament more responsive to constituents by, among other things, introducing a majoritarian element to the legislative balloting. The proposal received an 80 percent endorsement in the referendum, although the results were ruled invalid due to insufficient turnout. Nevertheless, spurred by the debate, Parliament approved new electoral arrangements in March 2008. (See Legislature, below, for details.)

In the campaign for the November 2008 parliamentary elections, wage levels and domestic economic concerns emerged as significant factors. The PSD and PD-L, among others, sponsored legislation before the election promising wage hikes of up to 50 percent for civil servants, subsequently promising expenditures on infrastructure to stimulate the economy and to address regional disparities in regard to development. However, Prime Minister Popescu-Tăriceanu refused to implement the proposals, arguing that the budget lacked the necessary resources. In the November, 30, 2008, elections the Democratic-Liberal Party (*Partidul Democrat-Liberal*—PD-L), a recent merger of the PD and PLD, secured 115 seats in the Chamber of Deputies, compared to 114 for the alliance of the PSD and PC. The PNL won 65 seats and the UDMR 22, while the PRM failed to pass the threshold. The close results led to calls for a "Grand Coalition" between the PD-L and PSD. However, the first attempt at forming the new government was disrupted when prime minister designate Theodor Stolojan of the PD-L withdrew his name from consideration, citing the need for a "younger generation" to assume governmental responsibility. The PD-L's Emil BOC, the mayor of Cluj-Napoca, subsequently formed the coalition, which was approved by a vote of 324–115 in Parliament on December 22.

The June 7, 2009, European Parliament elections were conducted by nationwide proportional representation. The alliance of the PSD and PC won a plurality of 31.1 percent of the vote and 11 of the country's 33 seats. The PD-L finished second with 29.7 percent of the vote and 10 seats, followed by the PNL with 14.5 percent of the vote and 5 seats, and the UDMR with 8.9 percent of the vote and 3 seats. The PRM won 8.65 percent of the vote and 3 seats, and independent candidate Elena BĂSESCU (President Băsescu's daughter) won a seat with 4.2 percent of the vote.

The ministers from the Social Democratic Party (PSD) resigned from the cabinet on October 1, 2009, to protest the recent dismissal of Administration and Interior Minister Dan Nica, who had reportedly speculated about the possibility of fraud in the upcoming presidential poll. Without PSD support, the government of Prime Minister Emil Boc collapsed on October 13, when it lost a confidence motion by a vote of 254–176 in the Chamber of Deputies. Independent Lucian Croitoru and Liviu Negoiţă of the Democratic-Liberal Party (PD-L) successively failed to win legislative support for their proposed cabinets, and Boc on December 23 formed a new minority government comprising the PD-L, the Hungarian Democratic Union of Romania, independents, and rogue members of the PSD and National Liberal party who subsequently formed the National Union for the Progress of Romania (*Uniunea Naţională pentru Progresul României*—UNPR). The new government was approved by a 276–135 legislative vote. Meanwhile, President Traian Băsescu had been sworn in for another five-year term on December 21 after winning a runoff on December 6 with 50.3 percent of the vote against PSD chair Mircea GEOANĂ.

Protests in January 2012 (see Current issues, below) led to the resignation of Boc on February 6, 2012, and the announcement of a new government by Mihai Razvan UNGUREANU on February 9, again a coalition of the PD-L, UDMR, and UNPR. However, a vote of no confidence in the government on April 27 succeeded after a series of defections by PD-L legislators to the Social Liberal Union (*Uniunea Social Liberală*—USL), a coalition of the PSD, PC and PNL. Victor PONTA of the PSD was then asked to form a government. On May 7, Ponta formed a government of the PSD, PNL, and PC. Following a failed effort to impeach Băsescu in June through August 2012, however,

Ponta announced a significant reshuffle of the cabinet in August to "restore credibility" in the government.

In the December 9, 2012, elections the USL (now including the UNPR) secured 273 seats in the Chamber of Deputies, compared to 56 for the Right Romania Alliance (*Alianța România Dreaptă*—ARD), an electoral alliance of the PD-L, PNȚCD, Civic Force (*Forța Civică*—FC) and Romanian National Party (*Partidul Național Român*—PNR). Also in the opposition was the newly formed People's Party-Dan Diaconescu (*Partidul Poporului - Dan Diaconescu*—PP-DD), with 47 Chamber seats and the UDMR with 18.

Constitution and government. Upon assuming power in late 1989, the FSN suspended the constitution of 1974 and declared its support for a multiparty system and a market economy. The balloting of May 20, 1990, was for a president and a bicameral Parliament, the latter being empowered to draft a new constitution within 18 months, with new elections to follow within 12 months. A revised basic law providing for a strong presidency, political pluralism, human rights guarantees, and a commitment to market freedom was approved by Parliament (sitting as a Constituent Assembly) on November 21, 1991, and ratified by referendum on December 8.

A national referendum held October 18–19, 2003, approved (by a 90 percent "yes" vote in a 55.7 percent turnout) a number of constitutional amendments designed for the most part to facilitate Romania's planned accession to the EU. Among other things, the changes strengthened the protection of human rights (most notably for minority groups) and property rights. In addition, the presidential term was extended from four to five years.

Administratively, Romania is divided into 41 counties plus the city of Bucharest, in addition to a large number of towns and villages. A prefect represents the central government in each county, which elects its own council. Mayors and councils are elected at the lower level.

Reporters Without Borders ranked Romania as 42nd in the world in its 2013 Press Freedom Index.

Foreign relations. Romania during its first 15 years as a Communist state cooperated fully with the Soviet Union both in bilateral relations and as a member of the Council for Mutual Economic Assistance, the Warsaw Pact, and the United Nations. However, serious differences with Moscow arose in the early 1960s over the issue of East European economic integration, leading in 1964 to a formal rejection by Romania of all Soviet schemes of supranational planning and interference in the affairs of other Communist countries. Subsequently, Romania followed an independent line in many areas of foreign policy, refusing to participate in the 1968 Warsaw Pact intervention in Czechoslovakia, rejecting efforts to isolate Communist China, and remaining the only Soviet-bloc nation to continue diplomatic relations with both Egypt and Israel. Prior to the admission of Hungary in 1982, Romania was the only Eastern-bloc state to belong to the World Bank and the IMF.

A constant regional theme of Romania's external relations in the early 1990s was discord with Hungary over the status of Romania's substantial ethnic Hungarian minority population, concentrated in Transylvania. Tension mounted when the ultranationalist Gheorghe FUNAR, presidential candidate of the Romanian National Unity Party (*Partidul Unității Naționale Române*—PUNR), was elected mayor of Cluj-Napoca in Transylvania in February 1992, with subsequent restrictions on "anti-Romanian" public meetings. Collaterally, the central government named ethnic Romanians to replace ethnic Hungarian prefects in the two Hungarian-majority counties, the resultant outrage being only partially eased by the appointment of two prefects for each county, one Hungarian and one Romanian.

A second major preoccupation of post-Communist Romania has been the position of Moldova (the former Moldavian Soviet Socialist Republic), once the bulk of Romanian-ruled Bessarabia and inhabited predominantly by ethnic Romanians. On September 3, 1991, the Romanian Parliament adopted a resolution endorsing an August 27 declaration of independence by Moldova. On November 2, during a visit to Bucharest, Moldovan Prime Minister Valeriu Muravschi expressed the hope that intergovernmental exchanges could "speed up the process of [his country's] integration with Romania."

Advancing the concept of "two republics, one nation," the Romanian and Moldovan governments took a gradualist approach to unification and from May 1992 engaged in protracted diplomatic efforts with Russia and Ukraine to bring about a lasting cessation of hostilities between the warring ethnic groups in Moldova. (On the other hand, the Moldovan election of February 1994 yielding a legislative majority for proindependence parties represented a rebuff to the reunification effort.)

Romania was a founding member of the Black Sea Economic Cooperation (BSEC) grouping launched in June 1992, and on February 1, 1993, Romania signed an association agreement with the European Community (EC, subsequently the EU). However, its continuing problems in gaining international acceptance were highlighted by the refusal of the United States to extend most-favored-nation trade status until October 1993, although Washington had joined Western European governments in applauding the overthrow of the Ceaușescu regime.

In September 1993 the Parliamentary Assembly of the Council of Europe approved the admission of Romania to the organization. Subsequently, on January 26, 1994, Romania became the first former Communist state to join NATO's Partnership for Peace program, pursuant to its aim of eventual full NATO membership as well as accession to the EU. In the latter context, Romania in mid-1994 secured an EU pledge that it would be treated on a par with the four Visegrád states (Czech Republic, Hungary, Poland, Slovakia) also seeking membership. (On June 22, 1995, Romania became the third ex-Communist state [after Hungary and Poland] to submit a formal application for EU membership, although it was not invited to open accession negotiations until December 1999.)

The June 1994 advent of a Socialist government in Hungary led to an improvement in Bucharest-Budapest relations, including a visit to Hungary by the Romanian foreign minister in September. Nevertheless, difficulties continued, occasioned by such events as passage in the Romanian Parliament of legislation regulating Hungarian-language education and the display of the flag or the singing of the anthem of another state. In a new initiative in September 1995, the Romanian government submitted three draft documents to Hungary covering reconciliation between the two countries, bilateral cooperation, and a code of behavior on treatment of ethnic minorities. Although the response in Budapest was cool, Bucharest persisted, with the result that a 1996 bilateral treaty saw both sides make concessions on the minority question. Hungary renounced any claim to Romanian territory populated by ethnic Hungarians, and Romania undertook to guarantee ethnic minority rights within its borders. Although the treaty commanded majority support in both national legislatures, it attracted fierce criticism from nationalist parties in both Hungary and Romania.

Romanian-Hungarian relations continued to improve after the election of President Constantinescu in November 1996, and in February 1997 the defense ministers of the two countries met and agreed on the formation of a joint peacekeeping force, a move that was seen as enhancing both nations' prospects for gaining entry into NATO. In March, Prime Minister Ciorbea, in the first visit of a Romanian prime minister to Hungary since 1989, signed five agreements. The following month President Arpád Göncz became the first Hungarian head of state to visit Romania, while in June the two nations signed a friendship treaty, confirming existing borders.

Despite support from France, Italy, and Spain, Romania's request to be included in the first-round expansion of NATO was blocked in 1997 by the United States, with U.S. Defense Secretary William Cohen explaining that Washington had said "not yet" rather than simply "no." The rejection was seen as a desire by the United States to placate a nervous Russia and to delay admission until democracy and free-market reforms in Romania had become irreversible. In July U.S. President Clinton, in the first visit to Romania by an American president in more than 20 years, praised the Romanians and encouraged them to stay their course.

Romania became a member of the Central European Free Trade Agreement (CEFTA) on July 1, 1997, expecting to regain access to Eastern and Central European markets as well as to enhance its prospects for NATO membership (see Poland, Foreign relations, for more on CEFTA). A month earlier, the presidents of Ukraine and Romania had signed a friendship treaty, calling existing borders "inviolable" despite earlier friction over the status of Northern Bukovina and Southern Bessarabia, both of which Romania had been compelled to cede to the USSR in June 1940. Related issues of national identity delayed conclusion of a basic treaty with Russia until 2003, as had Romania's demand that Russia return the state treasury that has been held in Moscow since its delivery there for safekeeping during World War I.

A trip to Romania in May 1999 by John Paul II was the first visit by a Roman Catholic pope to a country with an Orthodox majority since the Great Schism of 1054. Although restricted to Bucharest, the pope was warmly greeted by the patriarch of the Romanian Orthodox Church, TEOCTIST.

A basic treaty between Romania and Moldova was initialed on April 28, 2000, but neither country's legislature ratified the agreement.

Subsequently, in November 2002, Romania and Hungary signed an agreement defining the future course of their bilateral partnership and guaranteeing each other support for EU membership.

In 2003 Romania was included in the "second wave" of candidates for membership in NATO, to which it formally acceded in March 2004 along with six other countries. Earlier, Romania had contributed a contingent of noncombat troops to the U.S.-UK–led operation in Iraq, withdrawing in 2009.

In October 2005 Romania and Hungary signed a number of potentially significant agreements providing for cooperation in environmental protection, law enforcement, border security, joint defense programs, and cultural and educational exchanges. The two countries also pledged to pursue common economic policies.

Romania acceded to the EU on January 1, 2007. However, Romania pledged to continue reforms, particularly judicial reforms and anticorruption measures, as specified by the European Commission Mechanism for Cooperation and Verification.

Tensions grew in 2007 concerning the large expatriate Romanian community in Italy. Among other things, widespread protests, including violent attacks on Romanian immigrants, broke out in Italy when an Italian woman was allegedly murdered by a Romanian citizen. The Italian government responded by using emergency measures to expel some Romanian citizens, drawing expressions of concern from the Romanian government. Many of those expelled were of Roma origin, highlighting problems of minority relations in both Italy and Romania.

The International Court of Justice in February 2009 resolved Romania's ongoing territorial dispute with Ukraine over the disposition of Serpents' Island (transferred at Soviet insistence in 1948) and related maritime borders. Some 9,700 square kilometers of maritime waters were slated to be transferred to Romanian sovereignty, an area that was believed to have significant oil and gas reserves.

In campaigning for the June 2009 European Parliament elections, the PD-L and PSD both proposed changes to Romanian citizenship laws to provide citizenship to ethnic Romanians living in the Republic of Moldova. EU officials subsequently criticized such rhetoric as offering blanket Romanian citizenship (and, consequently, EU citizenship) to Moldovans, leading the Romanian foreign ministry to repudiate such proposals. The PNL subsequently called for the relaxation of visa regimes and border controls with Moldova.

Ties between Romania and Moldova improved after the Moldovan elections of September 2009 led to the end of the Vladimir Voronin presidency. In November Romania relaxed its visa regime to allow Moldovan residents living in villages and towns within 30 kilometers of the border to enter without a visa, a category that extends to nearly half of the country's population. In January 2010 Băsescu offered Moldova €100 million in economic aid, further pledging to support Moldova's entry into the EU on a timeframe comparable to that of candidate countries in the western Balkans.

Relations with Russia saw considerable friction in 2011, chiefly due to Romania's offer to provide a site for U.S. SM-3 missile interceptors at Deveselu air base (formally signing an agreement in September). The use of anti-Russian rhetoric in domestic populist political appeals has also played a factor, such as Băsescu's statement on June 22, 2011, that he agreed with Romania's participation in the 1941 German-led invasion of the Soviet Union so far as it was driven by the desire to regain Moldova, ceded to the Soviets in 1940.

Current issues. EU criticism of government corruption in Romania has served to focus domestic political attention on the issue. European Commission President Jose Manuel Barroso in January 2009 called on Romania to show "concrete results" in fighting corruption. The PSD and PD-L, however, have issued frequent and mutual recriminations that anticorruption efforts are being used for political purposes.

The close results in the second round of the presidential elections of December 6, 2009, plus the fact that exit polls had indicated a lead for the PSD's Mircea Geoană led to accusations of fraud against Băsescu and the PD-L. Although the Constitutional Court certified Băsescu's reelection, the PSD did not withdraw its allegations.

In May 2010 the government embraced a series of austerity measures to gain access to an IMF loan, cutting salaries of state employees by 25 percent and raising the value-added tax on goods from 19 to 24 percent. A second series of initiatives in September 2010 raised the retirement age to 65 years (up from 63.5 years for men and 59.5 years for women) and lowered health care and social spending. The changes prompted widespread protests.

Although the European Commission in July 2011 praised Romania for its continued efforts to stem corruption, the report also underlined the need for further reform by 2012 to meet the guidelines laid out at Romania's accession to the EU. Issues of state corruption were underscored by the dismissal in February 2011 of Radu MĂRGINEAN, the head of the National Customs Authority, after his indictment on charges of taking bribes. Concern by other EU members over Romanian border controls and bribery of border guards was a significant factor in the decision in June 2011 to delay Romania's entry to the Schengen area, which waives border controls between members.

New austerity measures, particularly controversial measures to reform and privatize health care, sparked significant protests in several Romanian cities over January 12 through January 15, 2012. As many as 20,000 protested over the issue in Bucharest, joined by protesters concerned over a variety of issues, including shale gas fracking, the proposed Roşia Montană gold mine, and corruption. In response, Prime Minister Boc resigned on February 5.

In June 2012 tensions between Băsescu and Prime Minister Ponta erupted into an open clash over which figure had the legal right to represent Romania in the June 28, 2012, meeting of the European Council, with Parliament backing Ponta in a 249–30 vote. Subsequent developments heightened the political tensions. On June 19 Ponta was formally accused of plagiarizing his 2003 doctoral dissertation; then on June 20 former PSD leader Adrian Năstase attempted suicide when police attempted to arrest him to serve a two-year prison sentence for corruption. Ponta subsequently charged Băsescu with motivating the charges against himself and Năstase.

On June 27, the Constitutional Court ruled that Băsescu should attend the European Council, but the government delayed publishing the verdict and confirmed Ponta's attendance, leading Băsescu to publicly concede. The conflict, and particularly the Ponta government's use of emergency legislation during the crisis (for example, limiting the oversight of the Constitutional Court on parliamentary decisions), led to domestic and international criticism that Ponta was undermining the democratic process.

On July 6 Parliament voted 256–114 to suspend Băsescu, then voting 242–0 (the opposition boycotting the vote) to call for a public referendum to impeach Băsescu. The referendum on July 29 saw 88.7 percent of voters vote to impeach, but with only 46.2 percent of voters turning out, the Constitutional Court ruled on August 21, 2012, that the vote was invalid having failed to reach the specified 50 percent + 1 threshold. On August 27 Băsescu was reinstated.

In March 2013 the EU again postponed Romanian accession to the Schengen Zone, citing corruption issues. The decision raised concerns that the 2014 deadline to open the EU labor market to Romanians could be similarly postponed.

In April 2013 Ponta withdrew the government's target date of 2015 for joining the eurozone. No new target was offered, although Ponta states adoption of the Euro remains a "fundamental objective."

On May 20, 2013, the Romanian Supreme Court sentenced politician George BECALI and former Minister of Defense Victor BABIUC to prison terms for fraud related to the exchange of state land in the late 1990s.

The two-thirds parliamentary majority won by the USL in the December 2012 elections has opened the possibility for constitutional revision. In May 2013 a parliamentary constitution commission was created, which drafted a series of amendments. Many revisions provoked controversy, including proposals to limit the powers of the president; to redefine administrative boundaries, creating 7 or 8 economic regions that would encompass the present 41 counties; for the prime minister to represent Romania in EU bodies (overturning the 2012 Constitutional Court decision); to define marriage as solely between a man and a woman; and to restore the coat of arms to the national flag. The draft has been forwarded the parliament, for future debate and revision.

In July Băsescu threatened to call a new referendum on restructuring parliament if parliament did not take steps to fulfill the 2009 referendum.

On July 12, 2013, PNL member and Minister of Transport Relu FENECHIU was convicted of corruption and sentenced to five years in prison, the first minister to be convicted while in office.

POLITICAL PARTIES

Until late 1989 Romania's political system was based on the controlling position of the Romanian Communist Party (*Partidul Comunist Român*—PCR). Founded in 1921, the PCR changed its name to the Romanian Workers' Party (*Partidul Muncitoresc Român*—PMR) in 1948 after a merger with the left-wing Social Democrats, but the party reassumed its original name at the ninth party congress in 1965. Identified by the constitution as "the leading political force of the whole society," the PCR exercised its authority with the aid of the Front of Socialist Democracy and Unity (*Frontul Democrației și Unității Socialiste*—FDUS), which prepared the approved list of candidates for election to the Grand National Assembly and other bodies.

Following the rebellion of December 22, the new government of Ion Iliescu declared that the question of banning the PCR would be decided by a popular referendum on January 28, 1990. However, on January 19 the ruling National Salvation Front (*Frontul Salvării Naționale*—FSN) announced that the decision to schedule the referendum had been "a political mistake," with the result that the party quickly ceased to exist as an organized force.

Eleven parties and alliances and 31 independent candidates participated in the November 2008 elections, a significant decrease from the nearly 50 parties that registered in 2004.

Government Parties:

Social Liberal Union (*Uniunea Social Liberală*—USL). In April 2008 the PSD and the PC announced the formation of a common parliamentary group and a "permanent" electoral alliance, the **Social Democratic Party + Conservative Party Alliance** (*Alianța Politică Partidul Social Democrat + Partidul Conservator*—PSD+CP). In January 2011 the PC formed an additional alliance with the PNL, the **Center Right Alliance** (*Alianța de Centru Dreapta*—ACD). In February 2011 the three parties clarified the relationship: the ACD and the PSD comprised the **Social-Liberal Union** (*Uniunea Social Liberală*—USL). The fall of the Urgureanu government in April 2012 brought the USL coalition into government. The USL emerged as the winner in the June 2012 local elections, obtaining 42 percent of town hall seats and 50 percent of county councils. In July 2012 the PSD and the UNPR announced formation of the **Center Left Alliance** (*Alianța de Centru Strânga*—ACS), bringing the UNPR into the USL. In the December 2012 legislative elections, the USL secured 122 Senate with 60 percent of the vote, and 273 Chamber seats with 58.6 percent of the vote.

Center Left Alliance (*Alianța de Centru Strânga*—ACS). The PSD and UNPR announced an electoral alliance in July 2012, but before the December elections expanded this into a proposed merger between the two parties. Reportedly, tensions between the parties at the local level meant the merger has been indefinitely postponed.

Social Democratic Party (*Partidul Social Democrat*—PSD). The PSD was formally established on June 6, 2001, by merger of the Social Democracy Party of Romania (*Partidul Democrației Sociale din România*—PDSR) and the much smaller Romanian Social Democratic Party (*Partidul Social Democrat Român*—PSDR). The two had envisaged their eventual merger in a September 2000 electoral agreement establishing the three-party **Social Democratic Pole of Romania** (*Polul Democrat-Social din România*—PDSR) in partnership with the Humanist Party of Romania (now the PC, see below).

The PDSR had been formed as the "presidential" party on July 10, 1993, by the renaming of the Democratic National Salvation Front (FDSN) and its absorption of the Romanian Socialist Democratic Party (*Partidul Socialist Democrat Român*—PSDR), the Cooperative Party (*Partidul Cooperatist*—PC), and the Republican Party (*Partidul Republican*—PR). Less reform-oriented than their colleagues, a number of pro-Iliescu chamber deputies, had withdrawn from the FSN in March 1992 and registered as the FDSN in April. The new formation won a plurality of seats in both houses of Parliament in the September 1992 balloting and secured the reelection of Iliescu at the second-round presidential poll of October 11. The Socialist Democrats were a leftist formation that had once been closely allied with the FSN. A centrist party favoring free enterprise, the PR was formed in 1991 by merger of an existing Republican Party and the Social Liberal Party–20 May.

Having previously headed a minority government, the PDSR in August 1994 drew the right-wing PUNR (see Conservative Party, below) into a coalition that continued to attract external support from the Greater Romania Party (PRM) and the Socialist Labor Party (PSM). However, increasing strains resulted in all three withdrawing their support from the government between October 1995 and September 1996, after which the PDSR was technically reduced to minority status in the Chamber of Deputies. Hitherto identified as a nonparty technocrat, Prime Minister Nicolae Văcăroiu announced his adhesion to the PDSR in May 1996. In local elections the following month the PDSR saw its support decline, with former tennis champion Ilie NĂSTASE failing in a bid for the Bucharest mayoralty.

In the November 1996 balloting, Iliescu suffered a second-round defeat in his presidential reelection bid, while the PDSR fell to second place in the legislature (with 21.5 percent of the lower house vote) and went into opposition, whereupon Iliescu assumed the formal party leadership. As the party attempted to regroup in 1997, tensions emerged among the leadership. At the PDSR national conference in June reformers led by former foreign minister Teodor Meleșcanu criticized Iliescu for failing to dissociate the party from corrupt elements. After the conference Meleșcanu and others resigned from the PDSR and formed the Alliance for Romania (ApR; see PNL, below). In June 1999, however, the party agreed to absorb a PUNR splinter, the Alliance for Romanians' Unity Party (PAUR; see PUNR, below).

The left-of-center PSDR descended from the historic party founded in 1893 but was forced to merge with the Communist Party in 1948. Following its re-forming in late 1989, several competing groups claimed the inheritance, a court subsequently awarding the PSDR designation to the main faction, which had Socialist International recognition. Standing on the Democratic Convention of Romania (CDR) ticket in the 1992 balloting, the PSDR won 10 chamber seats and 1 in the Senate. While maintaining its links with some CDR parties for the November 1996 elections, the PSDR established a formal electoral alliance, the Social Democratic Union (*Uniunea Social Democrată*—USD), with the Democratic Party–National Salvation Front (see PD, above), winning 10 of the USD's 53 chamber seats and 1 of its 23 Senate seats. The USD subsequently agreed to join Victor Ciorbea's CDR-led coalition government.

In July 2000 the PSDR approved a merger with the Socialist Party (*Partidul Socialist*—PS), led by unsuccessful 1996 presidential candidate Tudor MOHORA, while on September 7 it not only agreed to an alliance with the opposition PDSR for the November elections, but to join the PDSR, after the elections, in forming the PSD. Accordingly, on September 8 it formally withdrew from the governing coalition. the agreement with the PDSR prompted longtime party leader Sergiu CUNESCU to resign, asserting that the PSDR had committed "self-enslavery" to an organization that was guilty of "confiscating the revolution" after 1990.

The Social Democratic Pole's 2000 presidential candidate, Ion Iliescu, finished first in the November 26 presidential contest, with 36.5 percent of the vote, and then defeated the Greater Romania Party's Vadim Tudor in the runoff on December 10, taking a 66.8 percent vote share. In the November legislative contests the alliance won 36.6 percent of the vote in the Chamber of Deputies, for a plurality of 155 seats, and 37.0 percent in the Senate, for a plurality of 65 seats. The minority government installed under Adrian Năstase on December 28 included one minister from the PSDR and one from PUR.

An extraordinary PDSR party conference held in January 2001 unanimously elected Prime Minister Năstase as chair, President Iliescu having resigned in accordance with a constitutional dictate. Upon formation of the PSD, Năstase remained chair.

In November 2001 the Party of Moldovans (*Partidul Moldovenilor*—PM) merged into the PSD. The PM had been organized by the mayor of Iași, Constantin SIMIRAD, as a vehicle for forging closer ties between Moldova and Romania. Despite discussions with the PNL in early 2000, the PM had chosen to join the CDR 2000 for the general election in November. In 2003 the PSD absorbed the Socialist Labor Party (*Partidul Socialist al Muncii*—PSM) and the National Revival Socialist Party (*Partidul Socialist al Renașterii Naționale*—PSRN).

The PSD participated in the 2004 UN alliance with PUR, securing a plurality of legislative seats. However, the PSD was forced into opposition when PUR and the UDMR agreed to join the ADA in a new coalition government. Adrian Năstase was narrowly defeated as the UN candidate in the 2004 presidential poll. He subsequently resigned from all party leadership posts in the wake of a corruption scandal.

Although still formally classified as an opposition party, the PSD agreed in April 2007 to support the new PNL/UDMR government in the legislature as necessary to ensure the coalition's continuation until the 2008 general elections. Although the PSD+PC won a plurality of votes in the November 2008 elections (33.1 percent in the Chamber of Deputies and 34.2 percent in the Senate), it received fewer seats (114 in the chamber, 49 in the Senate) than the PD-L. It therefore surrendered (albeit reluctantly) the lead in forming a new government to the PD-L. In December 2008 the PSD agreed to join a coalition government with the PD-L, stipulating that the new government not include the UDMR. On October 1, 2009, Interior Minister Dan Nica of the PSD was dismissed following his charge that fraud had been committed in the June European Parliamentary elections and that fraud was planned for the upcoming Romanian presidential elections. The PSD withdrew from the coalition in response to Nica's dismissal, leading to a lengthy cabinet crisis.

In the 2009 presidential elections the PSD nominated chair Mircea Geoană, who received 31.2 percent of the ballot (good for second place) in the first round and 49.7 percent in the second. (The results were challenged by the PSD as fraudulent.) In the wake of the defeat, a party congress in February 2010 replaced Geoană as chair with Victor Ponta.

As part of the USL in the December 2012 legislative elections, the PSD received 51 Senate seats and 149 Chamber seats.

Leaders: Victor PONTA (President of the Party; Prime Minister); Mircea GEOANĂ (Former President of the Party, 2009 presidential candidate); Ion ILIESCU (Honorary Party President and Former President of Romania); Ecaterina ANDRONESCU, Dan NICA (Vice Presidents); Adrian NASTASE (Former Prime Minister).

National Union for the Progress of Romania (*Uniunea Națională pentru Progresul României*—UNPR). Formed in March 2010 by members of parliament of the PSD and PNL that broke away to support President Băsescu, initially as independent deputies. The UNPR immediately joined the ruling coalition. In 2011 the UNPR absorbed the National Initiative Party (*Partidul Inițiativa Națională*—PIN), an offshoot of the PD. In 2012 the UNPR passed into the opposition, but following the June 2012 local elections, it formed an alliance with the PSD and shifted to support the government.

As part of the USL in the December 2012 legislative elections, the UNPR received 5 Senate seats and 10 Chamber seats.

Leader: Gabriel OPREA (President).

Center Right Alliance (*Alianța de Centru Dreapta*—ACD). Formed in January 2011 as an alliance between the PC and the PNL within the broader framework of the USL. In June 2013 PC Party President Daniel CONSTANTIN publically stated that the ACD was failing to function, leading to speculation the alliance might dissolve.

National Liberal Party (*Partidul Național Liberal*—PNL). Founded in the mid-19th century but banned by the Communists in 1947, the PNL was reconstituted in 1990 as a right-of-center party that, in addition to supporting a free-market economy, endorsed resumption of the throne by the exiled King Mihai. A founding member of the Democratic Convention (*Convenția Democrată Romāna*—CDR), the PNL withdrew from the alliance in April 1992. Two splinter groups, the party's Youth Wing and the PNL–Democratic Convention (*Partidul Național Liberal–Convenția Democrată*—PNL-CD), the latter led by Nicolae CERVENI, refused to endorse the action and remained affiliated with the CDR. Some of the youth wing members later helped form the Liberal Party 1993 (*Partidul Liberal 1993*—PL-93), although others, grouped as the New Liberal Party (*Noul Partid Liberal*—NPL), rejoined the PNL at a February 1993 PNL "unification" congress. Ironically, the 1993 congress ultimately led to formation of a third major splinter when the election of Mircea IONESCU-QUINTUS as chair was contested by his predecessor, Radu CÂMPEANU, who went on to form the **PNL-Câmpeanu** (PNL-C).

Having failed to win any seats in the Chamber of Deputies in September 1992, the PNL later reestablished a presence in that house through absorption in May 1995 of the PL-93's Political Liberal Group (*Grupul Politic Liberal*) and the Group for Liberal Unification (*Grupul pentru Unificarea Liberală*) of the Civic Alliance Party (*Partidul Alianța Civică*—PAC), although chamber rules to inhibit floor crossing meant that the dozen or so PNL representatives were technically classified as independents. (PAC was an outgrowth of the still active **Civic Alliance** [*Alianța Civică*—AC], which had been organized in November 1990 by a group of trade unionists and intellectuals to provide an extraparliamentary umbrella for post-Communist opposition groups, in partial emulation of East Germany's New Forum and Czechoslovakia's Civic Forum. At its second congress in July 1991 the AC had voted to establish PAC as its electoral affiliate under the leadership of literary critic Nicolae MANOLESCU. In the 1992 general election PAC had won 13 seats in the Chamber of Deputies and 7 in the Senate as a component of the CDR.)

The PNL rejoined the CDR in time for the November 1996 election and won 25 seats in the chamber and 17 in the Senate. The PNL-CD took 5 seats in the lower house and 4 in the upper, but the PL-93, having left the CDR in 1995, won no seats as part of the National Liberal Alliance (*Alianța Națională Liberală*—ANL), which it had formed with PAC.

In February 1997 PNL-CD dissidents, with unofficial support from the CDR, suspended Nicolae Cerveni as chair because of his efforts to join forces with liberals outside the CDR. In June Cerveni loyalists in the PNL-CD united with the PL-93 to form the Liberal Party (*Partidul Liberal*—PL), chaired by Cerveni. Subsequently, in February 1998 PAC merged with the PNL.

In March 1998 the PL and the PNL-Câmpeanu formed an umbrella group called the Liberal Federation (*Federația Liberală*—FL), but differences over the PL's relationship to the PNL and the CDR soon led to a bifurcation of the PL, with Cerveni heading one faction and Dinu PATRICIU, the former PL-93 chair, and his supporters constituting another. In May the Cerveni PL was renamed the Romanian Liberal Democratic Party (*Partidul Liberal Democrat Român*—PLDR), while in July 1999 the Patriciu PL was absorbed by the PNL. At the same time, the PNL-CD and PL-93 ceased to exist. In May 1999 Cerveni agreed to merge his party with the Romanian National Party (PNR; see PD), but differences soon emerged and Cerveni competed for the presidency in November 2000 as the candidate of the PLDR, finishing last among 12 contenders. Like the PLDR, the PNL-Câmpeanu, running independently, failed to win representation in either house in 2000.

As the 2000 general election approached, the PNL, increasingly dominated by Deputy Chair Valeriu STOICA, distanced itself from the CDR, and in June 2000 it offered its own candidates in local elections, placing fourth in terms of mayoral victories. When the party formally abandoned the CDR shortly thereafter, Stoica attempted to forge ties to the Alliance for Romania (*Alianța pentru România*—ApR), but many party members objected, Nicolae Manolescu being the most prominent member to resign as a consequence. In the 2000 presidential contest the PNL endorsed former prime minister Theodor Stolojan, but a group headed by Minister of Finance Decebal Traian REMEȘ, accusing the party of a leftward drift, denounced the selection and left to establish a new party that was registered in October as the National Liberal Party–Traditional (*Partidul Național Liberal–Tradițional*—PNL-T). At the November balloting Stolojan finished third, with 11.8 percent of the vote, while the party won 30 seats in the chamber and 13 in the Senate.

A party congress in February 2001 elected Stoica as PNL chair, the octogenarian Ionescu-Quintus having decided to step down. The following November, the ApR signed a merger agreement with the PNL, and the two united under the PNL rubric on January 19, 2002.

The ApR, a center-left party founded in August 1997, had been formed by reformers who had split off from the PDSR. Led by Teodor Meleșcanu, the ApR regarded itself as a "nonconfrontational" opposition party. It claimed 13 deputies in the chamber and 2 senators upon its formation, but in the November 2000 election it failed at the polls, taking only about 4 percent of the vote for each house. Meleșcanu finished seventh in the concurrent presidential balloting, with 1.9 percent of the vote. Prior to the election the ApR had discussed an alliance with the PNL, but the overtures fell through, in part because the PNL re-fused to accept the ApR leader as its presidential candidate. Because of the ApR's dismal electoral showing, the entire leadership stepped down in early December 2000. At a party conference in March 2001, however, Meleşcanu was returned to office, and the party redefined itself as "social-liberal" (center-right) in orientation. A social democratic (center-left) faction strongly opposed the redefinition, and subsequent efforts by Meleşcanu to negotiate an alliance with the Democratic Party (DP) failed to bear fruit. However, talks with the PNL proved more fruitful, and in 2002 the ApR merged with the PNL, Meleşcanu becoming vice president of the PNL.

With the goal of reuniting all the liberal factions under one banner, in April 2002 the PNL-C absorbed the PNL-T, led by Decebal Traian Remeş. In June the Cerveni wing of the liberal movement (the PLDR) also merged into the PNL-C. At that point, there were only two major liberal groupings—the PNL and the PNL-C. Final consolidation was achieved at the end of 2003 when the PNL-C merged into the PNL. Meanwhile, by that time the Union of Rightist Forces (*Uniunea Forţelor de Dreapta*—UFD) had also merged with the PNL. (See the 2000–2002 *Handbook* for additional information on the UFD.)

In November 2003 the PNL launched the Justice and Truth Alliance (*Alianţa Dreptate şi Adevăr*–ADA) with the PD (below), with the goal of presenting a strong opposition front to the PSD-led governing coalition. The ADA pledged to combat corruption, restore the independence of the judiciary, protect property rights, pursue EU membership, and adopt promarket economic reforms. PNL chair Theodor Stolojan resigned the party leadership and canceled plans to seek the ADA's presidential nomination due to health reasons, and the PNL supported the PD's Traian Băsescu, who was elected president in second-round balloting in December 2004. Subsequently, the ADA (which had finished second in the November legislative balloting to the PSD/PUR alliance) formed a coalition government with PUR and the UDMR, with new PNL leader Călin Popescu-Tăriceanu as prime minister.

The PNL and the PD presented separate candidate lists for the June 2004 local elections (except in Cluj and Bucharest, where joint lists were used). Analysts subsequently described the ADA as "walking a thin line" in representing the sometimes diverse aspirations of the PNL and PD while remaining sufficiently strong as an alliance. The PNL suffered severe factionalization in the second half of 2006 when a number of prominent members, including Stolojan, strongly criticized the policies and governing approach of Prime Minister Popescu-Tăriceanu. Stolojan and others were expelled from the PNL in October and subsequently formed the PLD, taking nearly 30 PNL legislators with them.

Although there had been talk of a formal merger of the PNL and the PD, the ADA collapsed in the spring of 2007 and the PD moved into opposition. In June 2007 the PNL announced the formation with the PNŢCD and the Popular Action (*Acţiunea Populară*—AP) of a new alliance called the Center-Right Pole (*Polul de Centru-Dreapta*), dedicated to representing the interests of the middle class and supporting liberal, Christian-democratic values. In 2008 the PNL formally absorbed the AP, which had been formed in mid-2003 by supporters of former president Emil Constantinescu, who was named chair of the new party even though he had announced his retirement from politics following his 2000 presidential defeat. Upon the AP's incorporation into the PNL, Constantinescu stated that the leadership and members of the AP would correct "false attitudes" within the PNL and strengthen the party's conservative wing.

Crin Antonescu assumed party leadership in March 2009 and was nominated for the 2009 presidential elections. He received 20 percent of the ballot in the first round and supported the PSD's Geoană in the second round.

On February 5, 2011, the PNL joined the PSD and the CP in a political alliance, the USL (above).

As part of the USL in the December 2012 legislative elections, the PNL received 51 Senate seats and 101 Chamber seats.

Leaders: Crin ANTONESCU (President of the Party; President of the Senate), Eduard HELLVIG (Secretary General).

Conservative Party (*Partidul Conservator*—PC). The PC is a successor to the Humanist Party of Romania (*Partidul Umanist din România*—PUR), which had been formed in the early 1990s and had subsequently called for adoption of a "third way" that rejected both doctrinaire socialism and "market fundamentalism." PUR allied with the PSD in 2000 as part of the Social Democratic Pole (see PSD, above, for details). As a result, it subsequently gained legislative seats and representation in the PSD-led cabinet.

For the 2004 legislative elections, PUR again presented joint lists with the PSD through the National Union (*Uniunea Naţională*—UN). However, following that balloting, PUR deserted the UN to join the new government led by the ADA.

In May 2005 PUR's national convention voted to adopt the PC rubric, although leaders stated that the change did not indicate a revision of what they now declared to be the party's long-standing devotion to conservative doctrine.

In February 2006 the PC merged with the **Romanian National Unity Party** (*Partidul Unităţii Naţionale Române*—PUNR). The PUNR was organized in 1990 as the political arm of the nationalist Romanian Hearth (*Vatra Românească*). It ran fifth in the 1992 parliamentary balloting on a hard-right ticket, securing 30 Chamber and 14 Senate seats on an 8 percent vote share, and was eventually co-opted into the government coalition in August 1994. Problems with coalition partners and internal dissent with party leader Gheorghe FUNAR (the mayor of Cluj-Napoca in Transylvania) weakened the PUNR. Funar was expelled as party leader in 1997, only to launch the rival **Alliance for Romanians' Unity Party** (*Partidul Alianţei pentru Unitatea Românilor*—PAUR), which subsequently joined the PDSR (Funar himself would join the PRM). (For additional information on the PUNR, see the 2008 *Handbook.*)

Gheorghe COPOS, a state minister (vice prime minister) in the ADA-led coalition government, resigned his cabinet post in June 2006 following his reported indictment on tax evasion charges. Although the PC, claiming ideological differences with the PNL, subsequently left the government, it continued to support the administration in the legislature on a case-by-case basis.

In April 2008 the PC announced a political alliance with the PSD, receiving four of the alliance's seats in the Chamber of Deputies and one in the Senate in the November elections. It did not, however, receive cabinet positions in the subsequent coalition government between the PD-L and PSD.

As part of the USL in the December 2012 legislative elections, the PC received eight Senate seats and 13 Chamber seats.

Leaders: Daniel CONSTANTIN (President), Dan VOICULESCU (Founding President).

Opposition Parties:

Right Romania Alliance (*Alianţa România Dreaptă*—ARD). An electoral alliance registered on September 15, 2013, that comprised the PD-L, PNŢCD, PNR, and the Center-Right Civic Initiative (*Iniţiativa Civică de Centru-Dreapta*—ICCD), founded in July 2012 by Former Prime Minister Mihai Ungureanu. It later expanded to include the **Civic Force** (*Forţa Civică*—FC). In the December 2012 elections, the alliance secured 24 Senate seats with 16.7 percent of the vote, and 56 Chamber seats with 16.5 percent of the vote.

Leader: Mihai Răzvan UNGUREANU.

Democratic-Liberal Party (*Partidul Democrat-Liberal*—PD-L). The PD-L was formed in January 2008 by the merger of the PD and the PLD. Although the PD and PLD had defined themselves as social-democratic parties, the PD-L has been described as a "populist" and centrist formation. The new party led the June 2008 local elections with 28 percent of the vote and took (barely) the leading role in parliament with 115 seats in the Chamber of Deputies and 51 in the Senate in the November national balloting. After the PD-L's initial discussions to form a coalition with the UDMR and PNL broke down over the latter's insistence on holding the position of prime minister, a collaboration protocol between the PD-L and PSD was signed instead in December 2008, despite significant tensions between the two parties and an anticipated clash in the upcoming presidential election between Băsescu and Mircea Geoană of the PSD. After the PSD withdrew from the cabinet in October 2009, the PD-L supported the reelection campaign of

Băsescu, who received 32.4 percent of the vote in the first round of balloting on November 22, finishing first among the 12 candidates. Băsescu was credited with 50.3 percent of the vote in the runoff against Geoană on December 6.

The PD-L's poor showing in the June 2012 local elections (winning 13 percent of the vote to 51 percent for the USL) led to an extraordinary congress that replaced the senior leadership of the party.

As part of the ARD in the December 2012 legislative elections, the PD-L received 22 Senate seats and 52 Chamber seats.

In March 2013 a party congress re-elected Blaga despite significant opposition within the party. In July 2013 a faction of the party led by Eugen TOMAC broke away to form the **Popular Movement** (*Partidul Miscarea Populara*—PMP).

Leaders: Vasile BLAGA (President), Anca BOAGIU, Dorin FLOREA, Liviu NEGOITA, Andreea PAUL (Senior Vice Presidents), Goerge FLUTUR (General Secretary), Emil BOC (Former President of the Party and Former Prime Minister).

Democratic Party (*Partidul Democrat*—PD). The PD was the direct descendant of the National Salvation Front (FSN), which was described as a "self-appointed" group that assumed governmental power following the overthrow of the Ceaușescu regime. Claiming initially to be a supraparty formation, the front reorganized as a party in February 1990 and, as such, swept the balloting of May 20. Ion Iliescu subsequently stepped down as FSN president to serve as head of state but later emerged as de facto leader of the Democratic National Salvation Front (FDSN), which opposed rapid economic reform.

At its first national convention held March 16–17, 1991, the FSN, despite criticism from the Iliescu faction, approved a free-market reform program entitled "A Future for Romania" that was presented by Prime Minister Petre Roman, who replaced Iliescu as party president its second convention in March 1992. With the FDSN faction having separated from the FSN, the FSN ran a distant fourth in the national presidential poll of September 1992, Roman having declined to stand as its candidate; in the legislative balloting the FSN was limited to third place behind the FDSN and CDR, winning 10 percent of the vote.

In May 1993 the FSN reconstituted itself as the Democratic Party–National Salvation Front (*Partidul Democrat–Frontul Salvării Naționale*—PD-FSN), and in October 1994 it absorbed the Democratic Party of Labor (*Partidul Democrat al Muncii*—PDM). In February 1996 Roman accepted nomination as the PD-FSN candidate in the November presidential election, proclaiming his intention to stand on a social-democratic platform. For the accompanying legislative balloting the PD-FSN not only entered into the Social Democratic Union (USD) with the PSDR, but also sought to rally other proreform groupings under its banner. These efforts yielded third place for Roman in the presidential contest, while the PD-FSN won 43 chamber and 22 Senate seats in the legislative balloting.

As part of the Ciorbea government the PD, which had dropped the FSN designation, frequently tussled with the PNȚCD (below), particularly over the forced resignation in early 1998 of PD minister of transport Traian Băsescu, who had called for more rapid economic reform. The PD was at the center of governmental turmoil until Ciorbea's resignation in March 1998. The PD subsequently supported both the Vasile and Isărescu administrations, with Petre Roman becoming foreign minister in the latter.

In the November 2000 election the PD finished third, declining to 31 seats in the Chamber of Deputies and 13 in the Senate, and then moved into the opposition when the new Parliament convened. Among the successful senatorial candidates on the PD list was former prime minister Radu Vasile, who, having been expelled from the PNȚCD in early 2000, accepted an invitation to bring his supporters into Cornel BRAHAS's Party of the Romanian Right (*Partidul Dreapta Româneasca*—PDR). After overcoming a court challenge from opponents within the PDR, the expanded party then reregistered under Vasile's chairship as the **Romanian People's Party** (*Partidul Popular din România*—PPDR), which espoused authoritarianism, opposed multiculturalism, and described suspicion of foreigners as "a natural instinct."

Roman, who had finished the 2000 presidential race in sixth place with 3.0 percent of the vote, subsequently proposed establishing a center-right "Alternative 2004" of the PD, the Alliance for Romania (ApR), and the National Alliance (PUNR-PRN). However, at an extraordinary national convention the following May, he was replaced as chair by Traian Băsescu, recently elected as mayor of Bucharest. In 2003 Roman left to form the **Democratic Front of Romania Party** (*Partidul Frontul Democrat din România*—PFDR).

Between June and September 2001 the PD absorbed the National Alliance, formation of which had been announced in late July 2000 by the Romanian National Unity Party (PUNR, below) and the Romanian National Party (*Partidul Național Român*—PNR). In the November 2000 election the grouping—formally on the ballot as the National Alliance Party (*Partidul Alianța Națională* [PUNR-PNR])—won only 1.4 percent of the vote in each house, and in February 2001 the former PUNR leadership indicated its intention to reregister their organization as a separate entity.

The PNR had been founded in March 1998 by the merger of the New Romania Party (*Partidul "Noua Românie"*—PNR) of Ovidiu TRAZNEA and the Agrarian Democratic Party of Romania (*Partidul Democrat Agrar din România*—PDAR) of Mihai BERCA, with the Christian Liberal Party (*Partidul Liberal Creștin*—PLC) joining soon after. The PDAR, an agricultural workers' party launched in 1990 on a nationalist platform, later served as a governing partner of the PDSR, but it withdrew from the alliance in April 1994 in protest over a bill introducing an IMF-mandated land tax. For the 1996 presidential election the PDAR initially nominated Ion COJA, a literature professor and prominent anti-Semite who had temporarily broken with the PUNR. However, the PDAR ultimately joined the Humanist Party (PUR) and the Ecologist Movement (MER) in the unsuccessful National Union of the Center (UNC) alliance, which backed Ion Pop de POPA as its presidential candidate.

In September 1999 Viorel CATARAMĂ resigned as PNR chair, ostensibly to distance the party from a failed company that he had led. His interim replacement, Virgil MÁGUREANU, a former director of the Romanian intelligence service, was elected chair in February 2000. Catarамă ultimately joined the ApR (which merged with the PNL in 2002), while Măgureanu led the PNR into the National Alliance, and then the alliance, minus the PUNR, into the PD.

Traian Băsescu, then mayor of Bucharest and chair of the PD, became the ADA's successful presidential candidate in 2004. He was succeeded as PD chair by Emil Boc, who in 2005 convinced the delegates at a PD national convention to adopt a platform favoring promarket economic policies, a shift to the center from its former left-leaning doctrine.

After the dissolution of the ADA coalition in the spring of 2007, the PD left the government and became an opposition party to the new PNL-led cabinet.

Democratic Liberal Party (*Partidul Liberal Democrat*—PLD). The PLD was formed by former prime minister Theodor Stolojan and other PNL dissenters in December 2006. It was reported that some 30 legislators had defected from the PNL to the PLD, along with approximately 11,500 PNL members. Stolojan, an aide to President Băsescu, attacked the PNL leaders as "oil tycoons," and pledged to cooperate with the PD in reviving the ADA's center-right principles.

Civic Force (*Forța Civică*—FC). Founded in 2004 as the **Christian Party** (*Partidul Creștin*), it took its present name in 2008. It contested the 2009 European Parliament elections but failed to pass the threshold. During negotiations to join the ARD in 2012, it became a "political wing" for the ICCD (see ARD, above) and elected Mihai Ungureanu as party present on September 7.

As part of the ARD in the December 2012 legislative elections, the FC received one Senate seat and three Chamber seats.

Leaders: Mihai Răzvan UNGUREANU (President), Adrian IURAȘCU (First Vice President).

Christian and Democratic National Peasants' Party (*Partidul Național Țărănesc Creștin și Democrat*—PNȚCD). Founded in the prewar period and banned by the Communists, the National Peasants' Party under its veteran leader, Ion PUIU, refused to cooperate with the FSN because of the large number of former

Communist officials within its ranks. Prior to the 1990 election members of the "historic" PNȚ agreed to merge with a younger group of Christian Democrats as the PNȚCD, with the leadership going to Corneliu COPOSU, another party veteran, who had spent 17 years in jail during the Communist era.

The PNȚCD was one of the core components of the Democratic Convention of Romania (*Conventia Democrata Romana*—CDR), an anti-FSN alliance launched prior to the local elections of February 1992 as a successor to the eight-party Democratic Union (*Uniunea Democrata*—UD) that had been formed in 1990. Embracing some 18 parties and organizations, the CDR ran second to the FDSN (see PDSR) in the 1992 parliamentary balloting (winning a 20 percent vote share), while its nominee, Emil Constantinescu, was runner-up to Ion Iliescu in the presidential poll. The ethnic Hungarian UDMR was also affiliated, although it presented a separate list in the 1992 election.

The PNȚCD's Coposu died in November 1995 and was succeeded in January 1996 by Ion DIACONESCU, who defeated Vice President Ion RAȚIU for the post. In the November legislative balloting the promarket PNȚCD was returned as substantially the largest CDR component party, therefore providing the prime minister in the resultant CDR-led coalition government.

Constantinescu again ran for the presidency in 1996, pledging to accelerate the privatization program and encourage domestic and foreign investment in Romania's economy. His candidacy, which had been proposed by the PNȚCD, provoked some opposition within the CDR. Nevertheless, Constantinescu was a strong second in the presidential balloting in November and comfortably defeated President Iliescu in the runoff. In simultaneous legislative elections, the CDR won pluralities in both the Senate (53 seats) and the chamber (122 seats), with vote shares of 30.7 and 30.2 percent, respectively.

At the time, the center-right CDR included the PNȚCD, the National Liberal Party (PNL), the PNL–Democratic Convention (PNL-CD), Romania's Alternative Party (PAR), the Romanian Ecologist Party (PER), and the Ecological Federation of Romania (FER). In conjunction with the UDMR and the two-party Social Democratic Union (USD), the CDR formed a majority coalition under the PNȚCD's Victor Ciorbea. The CDR remained the core of the government under his successors, Radu Vasile of the PNȚCD and then Mugur Isărescu (nonparty), but by mid-2000 the PNL was preparing to contest the upcoming presidential and legislative elections on its own. PAR had already withdrawn in October 1998.

In April 1998 Victor Ciorbea was succeeded as prime minister by the PNȚCD's Radu Vasile, who was in turn replaced in December 1999 by an independent, Mugur Isărescu. The party subsequently decided to support Isărescu's presidential candidacy in 2000, although several members left in August in support of the PNL candidate, former prime minister Theodor Stolojan. Now known as the CDR 2000, the alliance was formally reconstituted on August 31, 2000, under a protocol signed by the PNȚCD, the Union of Rightist Forces (UFD, successor to PAR), and FER. Subsequently joining were Ciorbea's new Christian Democratic National Alliance (ANCD; see below), the Traditional National Liberal Party (PNL-T), and the Party of Moldovans (PM). (The PM ultimately merged into the PSD in November 2001.)

In the November 2000 general elections the CDR 2000 was wiped out, winning barely 5 percent of the vote in each house and, as a consequence, no seats. Prime Minister Isărescu, who had received the alliance's endorsement for president, finished fourth in the contest, with 9.5 percent of the vote.

The disastrous showing of the CDR 2000 and the PNȚCD in the November 2000 election led the party's entire leadership to resign, with an interim governing board under Constantin Dudu IONESCU being elected on December 2, pending a party congress in early 2001. At the January session the party elected as chair Andrei MARGA, who defeated Ionescu on a third ballot.

In April 1999 Ciorbea had led a faction out of the PNȚCD and formed the Christian Democratic National Alliance (*Alianța Națională Creștin-Democrată*—ANCD). With neither party having won parliamentary seats in November 2000, the ANCD rejoined the parent organization in March 2001. The reunification rapidly led to yet another fissure, however, with Marga resigning as chair and being replaced by Ciorbea in early July. The opposing factions subsequently held competing extraordinary congresses, with Ciorbea being confirmed as chair by the first, on August 14. The forces loyal to Marga held their congress August 17–19 and then, on October 20, established the Popular Christian Party (PPC).

Following a poor showing by the PNȚCD in the mid-2004 local elections, Ciorbea relinquished the party leadership to Gheorghe CIUHANDU, who had just been elected mayor of Timișoara. After another dismal performance in the December 2004 legislative poll (1.85 percent of the vote in the balloting for the Chamber of Deputies), it was reported in 2005 that the party was soliciting consolidation with other centrist parties. In June 2007 the party entered the Center-Right Poll alliance with the PNL and AP, subsequently electing Marian Petre Miluț as chair. In view of the PNȚCD's poor standing in public opinion polls, the party supported the PNL's parliamentary list in the 2008 elections, but without a formal political alliance in which the PNȚCD would receive a proportion of the legislative seats. Instead, several party members (including Aurelian Pavelescu) ran as candidates on the PNL list. Party leadership defended this approach as providing time for reorganization of the party, but the agreement, as well as broader criticism of Miluț's leadership, led to a revolt in 2009 by the regional party leadership in Cluj and Bucharest counties, including Radu SÂRBU and Gheorghe CIUHANDU, who threatened legal action to gain control over the national leadership. In June 2009 the PNȚCD participated in Romania's European Parliament elections but failed to win any seats. Party congresses were held by the rival factions in July and September 2010, respectively, electing as chairs Aurelian Pavelescu and Radu Sârbu, both of whom claimed legitimacy as the rightful leader of the party as legal action continued. Each faction held separate extraordinary congresses in June 2011, at which the Pavelescu faction elected a new leader, Vasile Lupu; the Sârbu faction elected Victor Ciorbea, who was recognized by court officials in September 2011 as the leader of the registered PNȚCD.

As part of the ARD in the December 2012 legislative elections, the PNȚCD received one Senate seat and one Chamber seat.

Divisions within the party continued into 2013, as the Lupu faction condemned the April 2013 congress, which elected Aurelian Pavelescu as party president.

Leaders: Aurelian PAVELESCU (President, contested), Vasile LUPU (President, contested), Radu SÂRBU.

People's Party-Dan Diaconescu (*Partidul Poporului-Dan Diaconescu*—PP-DD). Founded in September 2011 by Dan DIACONESCU, owner of the OTV television station. The PP-DD offered a populist slate that included raising pension levels, restructuring taxation, eliminating salaries for members of parliament and top government officials, and offering cash grants both to Romanians who start businesses and to emigrants who return to Romania.

In the December 2012 legislative elections, the PP-DD won 21 Senate seats with 14.6 percent of the vote, and 47 Chamber seats with 14 percent of the vote. By June 2013, however, over a fifth of the PP-DD's members of parliament (two senators and 16 deputies) had left to sit as independents or to join other parties.

Leaders: Simona MAN (Chair), Diana VOICULESCU (First Vice President), Dan DIACONESCU (Honorary President).

Hungarian Democratic Union of Romania (*Uniunea Democrată a Maghiarilor din România*—UDMR/*Romániai Magyar Demokrata Szövetség*—RMDSz). Representing Romania's Hungarian minority, the newly organized UDMR placed second in the legislative poll of May 1990, winning 29 chamber and 12 Senate seats, despite a mere 7.2 percent vote share; it slipped to fifth in 1992 (with a slightly increased vote share), winning 27 chamber and 12 Senate seats.

Following the resignation of Géza DOMOKOS as UDMR president, the moderate Béla Marko was elected to the post in January 1993 after protestant bishop Lászlo TÖKÉS, a radical, had withdrawn his candidacy to accept appointment as honorary president. In mid-1995 the UDMR was rebuffed in efforts to establish political cooperation with other opposition parties, who claimed that it had become a party of extreme nationalism, favoring immediate local and regional autonomy for the Hungarian community. However, after the UDMR had won 25 chamber and 11 Senate seats in November 1996, it was accepted as a member of the CDR-led coalition government.

The UDMR's role in the coalition was frequently strained in subsequent years over Hungarian-language and minority education issues. The organization nevertheless remained part of the successor administrations of Radu Vasile and Mugur Isărescu. In the election of

November 2000 it won 27 seats in the chamber and 12 in the Senate, while its presidential candidate, György FRUNDA, finished fifth, with 6.2 percent of the national vote. In late December the party extended its external support to the PDSR-led minority government of Prime Minister Năstase, which had indicated it would quickly move forward on legislation designed to permit wider use of ethnic languages in localities and to resolve the status of property confiscated during the Communist era.

In 2003 the UDMR suffered a setback when several dissident groups announced their "independence" to protest what they considered the "betrayal" of party principles through continued association with the PSD. Bishop Tőkés resigned as the UDMR's honorary president at the 2003 party congress, and several splinter groups, the Reformist Bloc (*Blocul Reformist*—BR) and the Hungarian Civic Union (*Uniunea Civică Maghiară*—UCM), were formed at or subsequently to the congress.

The UDMR won 22 seats in the Chamber and 10 in the Senate in November 2004, and its decision to join the ADA-led coalition in December 2004 was considered crucial to the establishment of a legislative majority for the cabinet.

In the November 2007 European Parliament elections, Tőkés won a seat running as an independent candidate. UDMR leaders accused Tőkés of colluding with the PD-L to split the Hungarian vote.

The UDMR argued that the new electoral laws of 2008 would weaken the proportional voice of ethnic Hungarians in national elections. Despite these fears, the UDMR took 22 seats in the Chamber and 9 in the Senate in the November balloting. At the insistence of the PSD, the UDMR was excluded from the new ruling coalition, and the UDMR moved into the opposition for the first time since 1996. In the 2009 presidential elections the UDMR nominated Hunor Kelemen, who received 3.8 percent of the ballot in the first round. He supported the PSD's Geoană in the second round. Following the election, the UDMR successfully negotiated entry into a new PD-L–led government.

In May 2011 Tibor TORÓ led a faction of the party to form the **Hungarian People's Party in Transylvania** (*Partidul Popular Maghiar din Transilvania/Erdélyi Magyar Néppárt*—PPMT/EMN), campaigning for greater autonomy. It contested the December 2012 elections but failed to win any seats.

In the December 2012 legislative elections, the UDMR won nine Senate seats with 5.3 percent of the vote, and 18 Chamber seats with 5.2 percent of the vote.

Leaders: Hunor KELEMEN (Executive President and 2009 presidential candidate), Béla MARKO (Former President of the Party and 2004 presidential candidate), László BORBÉLY (Vice President), Péter KOVÁCS (Secretary General).

Ethnic Minority Legislative Parties:

Eighteen legislative seats are reserved for ethnic parties in Romania; following the 2012 legislative elections, the parties listed below secured representation.

Roma Party "Pro-Europe" (*Partida Romilor "Pro-Europa"*—PRPE). Representing Romania's substantial Roma (Gypsy) population, the Roma Party (*Partida Romilor*—PR) in March 1996 launched an electoral coalition with 11 other Roma groups with the aim of maximizing the impact of the Roma vote in the fall legislative elections. In 2000 the party won only 0.6 percent of the vote for the Chamber of Deputies but claimed one minority seat. The PR is frequently referred to under the rubric **Social Democratic Roma Party of Romania** (*Partida Romilor Social Democrată din România*—PRSDR).

Leaders: Nicolae PĂUN (President), Ivan GHEORGHE (Vice President).

Smaller parties include the **Association of Italians of Romania** (*Asociația Italienilor din România*—RO.AS.IT.), the **Association League of Albanians of Romania** (*Asociația Liga Albanezilor din România*—ALAR), the **Association of Macedonians of Romania** (*Asociația Macedonenilor din România*—AMR), the **Bulgarian Union of the Banat-Romania** (*Uniunea Bulgară din Banat-România*—UBBR), the **Cultural Union of Rusyns of Romania** (*Uniunea Culturală a Rutenilor din România*—UCRR), the **Democratic Forum of Germans in Romania** (*Forumul Democrat al Germanilor din România*—FDGR), the **Democratic Union of Slovaks and Czechs in Romania** (*Uniunea Democratică a Slovacilor și Cehilor din România*—UDSCR), the **Democratic Union of Turco-Islamic Tatars of Romania** (*Uniunea Democrată a Tătarilor Turco-Musulmani din România*—UDTTMR), the **Federation of Jewish Communities of Romania** (*Federația Comunităților Evreiești din România*—FCER), the **Greek Union of Romania** (*Uniunea Elenă din România*—UER), the **Lipovan Russian Community of Romania** (*Comunitatea Rușilor Lipoveni din România*—CRLR), the **Turkish Democratic Union of Romania** (*Uniunea Democrată Turcă din România*—UDTR), the **Union of Armenians of Romania** (*Uniunea Armenilor din România*—UAR), the **Union of Croatians of Romania** (*Uniunea Croaților din România*—UCR), the **Union of Poles of Romania "Polish Home"** (*Uniunea Polonezilor din România "Dom Polski"*—UPR), the **Union of Serbs of Romania** (*Uniunea Sârbilor din România*—USR), and the **Union of Ukrainians of Romania** (*Uniunea Ucrainenilor din România*—UUR).

Other Parties Contesting the 2012 Legislative Elections:

Greater Romania Party (*Partidul România Mare*—PRM). The political wing of the extreme nationalist Greater Romania movement, the PRM won a 4 percent vote share in the 1992 legislative balloting. In a March 1993 speech, Corneliu Vadim Tudor praised Nicolae Ceaușescu as a Romanian patriot and portrayed his 1989 overthrow as an "armed attack" by Hungary and the former Soviet Union. From mid-1994 the PRM gave external support to the incumbent government coalition but terminated the arrangement in October 1995 amid much acrimony. Tudor was subsequently named as the PRM's candidate in the November 1996 presidential election, although by vote of the Senate in April he lost his parliamentary immunity and faced possible legal proceedings on over a dozen assorted accusations. Also in April a PRM congress adopted a "blitz strategy" to be followed if the party came to power, including the banning of the ethnic Hungarian UDMR, strict control of foreign investment, and confiscation of "illegally acquired" property.

In early September 1996 the PRM absorbed the small Romanian Party for a New Society (*Partidul Român pentru Noua Societate*—PRNS), led by Gen. Victor VOICHIȚA. It nevertheless managed only 4.5 percent of the lower house vote in the November election, for 19 chamber and 8 Senate seats. Tudor finished fifth in the presidential race, winning 4.7 percent of the vote.

In September 1997 Tudor canceled plans for an alliance with the PDSR, saying PDSR leader Ion Iliescu's unification effort was designed to return him as head of state. In February 1998 the PRM signed a protocol with Gheorghe Funar's wing of the PUNR, which envisioned the establishment of a Great Alliance for the Resurrection of the Fatherland. The alliance's agenda included a new government and outlawing of the UDMR. Subsequently, however, Funar and his supporters were forced from the PUNR, and he eventually joined the PRM leadership.

In early 1999 Tudor publicly supported the Jiu Valley miners' strike, but he subsequently expelled the miners' leader, Miron Cozma, from the PRM for bringing the party into "disrepute." Meanwhile, the Senate suspended Tudor for his having supported the strikers.

The November 2000 elections constituted a major advance for the PRM, which saw its legislative representation jump to 84 seats in the lower house and 37 in the upper, second only to the PDSR; the party's vote share of 19.5 percent in the chamber and 21.0 percent in the Senate was more than a fourfold increase over its 1996 results. In the presidential race, Tudor won 28.3 percent of the first-round vote and advanced to a runoff against the PDSR's Iliescu, who, with support from all the other leading parties, prevailed two-to-one over the PRM leader. During the campaign and afterward, Tudor showed no inclination to tone down his ultranationalist, anti-Hungarian, anti-Roma, anti-Semitic, populist rhetoric, asserting, for example, that Ceaușescu had been "one of the world's great statesmen" and that the IMF and the World Bank were blackmailing Romania, demanding poisonous policy changes in return for vitally needed loans and credits. In the following two years the party lost more than a dozen chamber deputies as well as other defectors dissatisfied with Tudor's authoritarian leadership and the party's far-right rhetoric. Principal benefactors were the joint PSD-PUR parliamentary faction (which picked up about a dozen seats), the new Socialist Party of National Revival, and the Romanian Socialist Party.

Prior to the 2004 elections Tudor expressed remorse for his past actions and recanted previous attacks on various minority groups. He subsequently finished third in the first round of presidential balloting in December, while the PRM secured 48 seats in the Chamber of Deputies.

In March 2005 Tudor issued a surprise announcement that he was stepping down as PRM leader in favor of Corneliu CIONTU, hitherto deputy chair. It was subsequently reported that the PRM had changed its name to the Popular Greater Romania Party (*Partidul Popular România Mare*—PPRM) and had adopted a more moderate centrist platform. Tudor returned to the forefront in June and convinced the party's National Council to rescind the name change, return him to his leadership post, and force Ciontu from the party. The PRM subsequently lost roughly half of its members to the PC. Its rump agreed in April 2007 to support the new PNL/UDMR minority government as needed in the legislature to maintain government stability.

In the 2008 legislative elections the PRM did not pass the threshold for legislative representation and failed to take any seats in the Chamber of Deputies or Senate for the first time since 1996. The defeat led to an unprecedented agreement with the PNG-CD (below) to combine electoral lists for the June 2009 balloting for Romanian delegates to the European Parliament, with Tudor taking one of the three seats won by the alliance.

In the 2009 presidential elections the PRM nominated Tudor, who received 5.6 percent of the ballot in the first round and called upon PRM members to boycott the second round.

In the December 2012 parliamentary elections, the PRM received 1.5 percent of the ballot in the Senate elections and 1.2 percent in the Chamber, failing to win any seats. Tudor subsequently blamed the defeat on the rise of the PP-DD, which he argued was a surrogate created by other parties to weaken the PRM.

A party congress in July 2013 voted to eject Tudor from the party and elected Gheorghe FUNAR as chair. Tudor contested the move and filed legal appeals in August to overturn the decision.

Leaders: Gheorghe FUNAR (Chair, contested), Corneliu VADIM TUDOR (Former Chair), Lucian BOLCAS (Vice President).

Romanian Ecologist Party (*Partidul Ecologist Român*—PER). The PER is an ecological group founded in 1978 in opposition to Socialist-era economic development. In 1989 it was registered as a political party with a substantially smaller membership than the Ecologist Movement of Romania (*Mişcarea Ecologistă din România*) with which it cooperated in 1992. Standing in its own right as a CDR party in 1996, it won five chamber seats and one in the Senate.

For the November 2000 parliamentary elections PER spearheaded formation of an alliance called the **Romanian Ecologist Pole** (*Polul Ecologist din România*) that also included the smaller **Green Alternative Party–Ecologists** (*Partidul Alternativa Verde–Ecologiştii*—PAVE) and the **Romanian Ecologist Convention Party** (*Partidul Convenţia Ecologistă din România*—PCER). The alliance offered a joint candidate list that polled less than 1 percent of the vote in each house. In early 2003 it was reported that the PER, PAVE, and PCER had merged under the PER rubric. In 2008 the PER created an electoral alliance with the Green Party to form the electoral alliance **Green Ecologist Party** (*Partidul Verde Ecologist*), which failed to reach the electoral threshold.

In the 2009 presidential elections the PER nominated Ovidiu Cristian Iane, who was credited with 0.2 percent of the vote in the first round.

In the December 2012 parliamentary elections, the PER received 0.8 percent of the ballot in the Senate elections and 0.5 percent in the Chamber, failing to win any seats.

Leaders: Dănuţ POP (President), Mircea COSEA (Honorary President), Ovidiu-Cristian IANE (2009 presidential candidate).

Other parties participating in the 2012 legislative balloting included the **People's Party** (*Partidul Popular*—PP); the **Socialist Alliance Party** (*Partidul Alianţa Socialistă*—PAS); **The Popular Party for Social Protection** (*Partidul Popular şi al Protecţiei Sociale*—PPPS), formerly the **Romanian Party of Pensioners** (*Partidul Pensionarilor din România*—PPR); and the **Christian Democratic National Party** (*Partidul Naţional Democrat Creştin*—PNDC);

Other Parties Contesting the 2008 Legislative Elections:

New Generation Party-Christian Democrat (*Partidul Noua Generaţie-Creştin Democrat*—PNG-CD). The New Generation Party (PNG) was launched in 2000 under the leadership of Virel LIS, the former mayor of Bucharest. However, Lis subsequently left the party, and the leadership mantle eventually passed to George Becali, the owner of a prominent soccer club. Campaigning on a center-right platform, Becali secured 1.8 percent of the vote in the first round of the December 2004 presidential balloting. In April 2006 the party changed its name to the PNG-CD.

The PNG-CD won less than 3 percent of the vote in the 2008 balloting for the Senate and Chamber of Deputies, failing to reach the electoral thresholds. Consequently, merger talks were launched with the PD-L in early 2009, but Becali's subsequent arrest on charges of kidnapping (allegedly, thieves who had earlier stolen his car) led to a cessation of the talks. Cooperation with the PRM in the 2009 European Parliament elections, in which Becali won a seat, reignited speculation of a merger of the two significant far-right parties.

In the 2009 presidential elections the PNG-CD nominated Becali, who received 1.9 percent of the ballot in the first round and supported the PSD's Geoană in the second round.

The PNG-CD contested the 2012 local elections but did not nominate candidates for the 2012 legislative elections. Becali reportedly attempted to negotiate a merger of the PNG-CD with the PNL in 2012. Although this was declined by the PNL, he joined the latter party and won a parliamentary seat. On May 29, 2013, however, he was found guilty of fraud and sentenced to three years, losing his parliamentary seat.

Leader: George BECALI (President).

LEGISLATURE

The present Romanian legislature is a bicameral **Parliament** (*Parlament*) consisting of a Senate and a Chamber of Deputies, each with a four-year term. Elections from 1990 to 2004 were conducted via proportional representation on the basis of party lists. However, a complicated (and confusing to most analysts) system (combining majoritarian and proportional elements) was adopted by Parliament in March 2008, and then further modified in July 2012.

Voters now cast a single ballot for candidates within 311 single-member districts ("colleges") for the Chamber of Deputies and 135 for the Senate, these districts distributed across the 41 counties, Bucharest and a special district for nonresident Romanians. Candidates who receive more than 50 percent of the vote in a district are elected automatically. The remaining seats (including the supplemental seats) are distributed proportionately to parties that achieve the necessary threshold for representation (5 percent of the total national vote for single parties, 8 percent for two-party alliances, 9 percent for three-party alliances, and 10 percent for alliances of four or more parties), first within the 43 electoral counties and then at the national level. Additional seats can then be added to ensure the proportional representation of coalitions and parties; in December 2012 an additional 97 deputy and 39 Senate seats were thus created.

A national referendum on November 22, 2009, had endorsed a proposal from President Băsescu to combine the two houses of Parliament into a 300-seat unicameral legislature. However, further legislation has not been enacted to make the change.

Senate (*Senat*). The upper house currently comprises 176 members elected from 135 districts (two single-seat districts are reserved for nonresident Romanians), with 39 "supplementary" seats added to ensure proportional representation.

Following the elections of December 9, 2012, the alliance of the Social Liberal Union won 122 seats (58 for the Social Democratic Party, 51 for the National Liberal Party, 8 for the Conservative Party, and 5 for the National Union for the Progress of Romania); the Right Romania Alliance, 24 (22 for the Democratic Liberal Party, 1 for Civil Force, and 1 for the Christian-Democratic National Peasants' Party); the People's Party-Dan Diaconescu, 21; and the Hungarian Democratic Union of Romania, 9.

Chair: Crin ANTONESCU.

Chamber of Deputies (*Camera Deputaţilor*). The lower house currently comprises 412 members elected from 315 districts (4 single-seat districts are reserved for nonresident Romanians), with 79 seats added to ensure proportional representation. Organizations representing the following 18 ethnic communities are also given seats (assuming that no members of the ethnic community had otherwise been elected): Albanians, Armenians, Bulgarians, Croats, Czechs and Slovaks, Germans, Greeks, Italians, Jews, Lipovan Russians, Poles, Roma,

Ruthenians, Serbs, Slav Macedonians, Turko-Muslim Tatars, Turks, and Ukrainians. Voting for the minority seats is via nationwide balloting for each ethnic community, the party securing a plurality of votes for each community claiming that community's seat.

Following the elections of December 9, 2012, the alliance of the Social Liberal Union won 273 seats (149 for the Social Democratic Party, 101 for the National Liberal Party, 13 for the Conservative Party, and 10 for the National Union for the Progress of Romania); the Right Romania Alliance, 56 (52 for the Democratic Liberal Party, 3 for Civil Force, and 1 for the Christian-Democratic National Peasants' Party); the People's Party-Dan Diaconescu, 47; and the Hungarian Democratic Union of Romania, 18.

Chair: Valeriu ZGONEA.

CABINET

[as of August 1, 2013]

Prime Minister	Victor-Viorel Ponta (PSD)
Vice Prime Minister	Liviu Dragnea (PSD)
Vice Prime Minister	Daniel Chitoiu (PNL)
Vice Prime Minister	Gabriel Oprea (UNPR)
Ministers	
Agriculture and Rural Development	Daniel Constantin (PC)
Communications and Information Technology	Dan Nica (PSD)
Culture	Daniel Barbu (PNL)
Economy	Varujan Vosganian (PNL)
Education	Remus Pricopie (PSD)
Energy	Constantin Nita (PSD)
Environment and Climate Change	Rovana Plumb (PSD) [f]
European Funds	Eugen Teodorovici (PSD)
Finance	Daniel Chitoiu (PNL)
Foreign Affairs	Titus Corlățean (PSD)
Health	Eugen Nicolaescu (PNL)
Interior	Radu Stroe (PNL)
Justice	Robert-Marius Cazanciuc (ind.)
Labor, Family, and Social Protection for the Elderly	Mariana Câmpeanu (PNL) [f]
National Defense	Mircea Dușa (PSD)
Regional Development and Public Administration	Liviu Dragnea (PSD)
Small and Medium Enterprises, Tourism, and the Business Environment	Maria Grapini (PNL) [f]
Transport and Infrastructure	Victor-Viorel Ponta (PSD) (acting)
Water, Forests, and Fisheries	Lucia Varga (PNL) [f]
Youth and Sports	Nicolae Banicoiu (PSD)
Ministers Delegate	
Budget	Liviu Voinea (PSD)
Higher Education, Scientific Research, and Technological Development	Mihnea Costoiu (PSD)
Parliament Liaison	Mihai Voicu (PNL)
Romanians Abroad and Liaison with Moldova	Cristian David (PNL)
Social Dialogue	Doina Pana (PSD) [f]

[f] = female

INTERGOVERNMENTAL REPRESENTATION

Ambassador to the U.S.: Adrian Cosmin VIERITA.

U.S. Ambassador to Romania: (Vacant).

Permanent Representative to the UN: Simona-Mirela MICULESCU.

IGO Memberships (Non-UN): CEUR, EBRD, EIB, ICC, IOM, NATO, OSCE, WTO.

RUSSIA

Russian Federation/Russia
Rossiiskaya Federatsiya/Rossiya

Political Status: Formerly the Russian Soviet Federative Socialist Republic (RSFSR), a constituent republic of the Union of Soviet Socialist Republics (USSR); present official designations adopted on April 17, 1992; current constitution approved by referendum of December 12, 1993.

Area: 6,592,800 sq. mi. (17,075,400 sq. km).

Population: 146,946,522 (2012E—UN); 142,500,000 (2013E—U.S. Census).

Major Urban Centers (2010E): MOSCOW (11,514,000), St. Petersburg (formerly Leningrad, 4,849,000), Novosibirsk (1,474,000), Yekaterinburg (formerly Sverdlovsk, 1,350,000), Nizhny Novgorod (formerly Gorky, 1,251,000), Samara (formerly Kuibyshev, 1,165,000), Omsk (1,154,000), Rostov-na-Donu (1,090,000), Volgograd (1,021,000), Vladivostok (592,000).

Official Languages: Russian, in addition to languages recognized by the constituent republics and autonomous areas.

Monetary Unit: Ruble (official rate November 1, 2013: 32.39 rubles = $1US).

President: Vladimir PUTIN (United Russia); elected on March 4, 2012, and inaugurated for a four-year term on May 7, succeeding Dmitri MEDVEDEV (United Russia).

Chair of the Government (Prime Minister): Dmitri MEDVEDEV (United Russia); nominated by the president on May 7, 2012, and approved by the State Duma on May 8 to succeed Vladimir PUTIN.

THE COUNTRY

The world's largest country, with more than three-quarters of the former Soviet Union's land mass (though little more than half of its population), the Russian Federation stretches for more than 5,000 miles from the Baltic Sea in the west to the Pacific Ocean in the east. Its contiguous neighbors lie along an arc that encompasses Norway and Finland in the northwest; Estonia, Latvia, Lithuania, Poland, and Belarus in the west; Ukraine in the southwest; and Georgia, Azerbaijan, Kazakhstan, Mongolia, China, and North Korea in the south. Although there are upward of 100 nationalities, approximately 80 percent of the population is Russian. There are also many millions of ethnic Russians living in the "near abroad" of the other ex-Soviet republics. Women make up about 49 percent of the active labor force but remain underrepresented in government.

Russia possesses a highly diversified economy, including major manufacturing centers in the northwestern, central European, and Ural mountain regions; substantial hydroelectric capacity in the Volga River basin and Siberia; and widespread reserves of oil, natural gas, coal, gold, industrial diamonds, and other minerals.

Following the collapse of the Soviet Union in 1991, a commitment to radical economic reform became the centerpiece of Russian government policy, including price liberalization, currency convertibility, privatization, and encouragement of foreign investment. However, the rapid change to a free market system over nearly a decade led to economic collapse, forcing millions into poverty. Annual GDP contracted an average of nearly 14 percent between 1992 and 1995, and the inflation rate soared to 1,350 percent in 1992 before easing to 131 percent in 1995. Meanwhile, due to a currency crisis in October 1994, the ruble was valued at around 4,000 to the U.S. dollar (compared with an official one-to-one rate five years earlier), with further depreciation taking the rate above 5,500 by late 1996. Corruption was rampant, and billions in cash and other assets were reportedly taken out of the country.

The economy began to recover in 1997, as GDP increased by 0.4 percent, and currency reform at the end of the year led to a revaluation of the ruble (about 6 rubles to 1 U.S. dollar).

In August 1998 the economy was severely weakened due to low oil prices globally, a continuing East Asian financial crisis, and Russia's unmanageable debt. The ruble lost 70 percent of its value by the first quarter of 1999. In late April 1999 the International Monetary Fund (IMF), which had suspended loan disbursements to Russia the previous August, agreed to provide $4.5 billion to cover part of the country's massive debt servicing. Annual growth of 5.4 percent was recorded, owing in large part to progress in the country's conversion to a market economy.

From 2000 to 2007 annual average GDP growth was a robust 7.2 percent, due in large part to a boom in world oil prices and the increased competitiveness of the ruble. Inflation remained in double digits.

The 2008 global financial crisis, including a steep decline in oil prices, contributed significantly to the Russian economic crisis of 2008–2009. Other contributing factors included a decrease in exports, the republic's weak banking system, mortgage defaults and a credit crisis, and the flight of many foreign investors as a result of the fighting in Georgia (see earlier editions of the *Handbook*). Subsequently, in 2009 the Russian economy experienced its steepest decline in 15 years, with annual GDP contracting 7.8 percent from the 5.2 percent recorded in 2008. Double-digit declines were registered in the manufacturing, construction, and tourism sectors. To combat the contraction, the government initiated a large stimulus program and cut interest rates ten times. The approach was considered effective for the most part. However, the unemployment rate hovered around 9 percent, and the inflation rate was 8.8 percent.

Recovery was under way by 2010, when annual GDP of 4.5 percent was recorded, owing in large part to increased domestic spending and investment, and unemployment declined from a high for the year of 9.2 percent in January to 7.2 percent in December. The IMF noted a slowing of the economy in 2011 as a result of a severe drought, among other factors. Inflation began to "edge down," to about 8 percent, according to fund managers, and annual GDP growth was about 4.3 percent. Meanwhile, the IMF emphasized that the country's high commodity prices created "an opportunity to embark on bold and decisive reforms" and urged authorities to implement measures to create a more favorable climate for investment and economic diversification. GDP growth further slowed to 3.4 percent in 2012, while the IMF has forecast 3.4 percent growth for 2013.

GOVERNMENT AND POLITICS

Political background. Russia's early national history was that of a series of small medieval fiefs that gradually united under the leadership of the grand dukes of Moscow in the 15th and 16th centuries, expanding into a vast but unstable empire that collapsed midway through World War I. Military defeat and rising social unrest resulting from that conflict led directly to the "February" Revolution of 1917, which resulted in the abdication of Tsar NICHOLAS II (March 15, 1917, by the Western calendar), and the formation of a provisional government whose best-remembered leader was Aleksandr F. KERENSKY. Unable to cope with the country's mounting social, political, economic, and military problems, the provisional government was forcibly overthrown in the "October" Revolution of November 7, 1917, by the Bolshevik wing of the Russian Social Democratic Party under Vladimir Ilyich LENIN. The new Soviet regime—so called because it based its power on the support of newly formed workers,' peasants,' and soldiers' councils, or "soviets"—proceeded under Lenin's guidance to proclaim a dictatorship of the proletariat; to nationalize land, means of production, banks, and railroads; and to establish on July 10, 1918, a socialist state known as the Russian Soviet Federative Socialist Republic (RSFSR).

Draconian peace terms imposed by the Central Powers under the Brest-Litovsk Treaty of March 3, 1918, were invalidated by that alliance's eventual defeat in the west, but civil war between the Bolsheviks and the Whites, compounded by foreign intervention in Russia, lasted until 1922. Other Soviet Republics that had meanwhile been established in Ukraine, Byelorussia, and Transcaucasia joined with the RSFSR by treaty in 1922 to establish the Union of Soviet Socialist Republics (USSR), whose first constitution was adopted on July 6, 1923. The Central Asian territories of Turkmenistan and Uzbekistan became constituent republics in 1925, followed by Tajikistan in 1929 and Kazakhstan and Kyrgyzstan in 1936, at which time dissolution of the Transcaucasian SSR yielded separate union status for Armenia, Azerbaijan, and Georgia. The Estonian, Latvian, Lithuanian, and Moldavian SSRs were formally proclaimed in 1940.

Lenin's death in 1924 had been followed by struggles within the leadership of the ruling Communist Party before Joseph Vissarionovich STALIN emerged in the later 1920s as the unchallenged dictator of the party and country. There followed an era characterized by extremes: forced industrialization that began with the First Five-Year Plan in 1928; all-out collectivization in agriculture commencing 1929–1930; and far-reaching political and military purges from 1936 to 1938. The conclusion in August 1939, on the eve of World War II, of a ten-year nonaggression pact with Nazi Germany enabled Soviet military power to expand Soviet frontiers at the expense of Poland, Finland, Romania, and the Baltic states of Estonia, Latvia, and Lithuania. Nazi-Soviet collaboration came to an abrupt end when German forces attacked the USSR on June 22, 1941. The subsequent years of heavy fighting, which cost the USSR an estimated 20 million lives and left widespread devastation in European Russia, eliminated the military power of Germany and ultimately enabled the USSR to extend its influence into the heart of Europe.

Stalin's death in March 1953 initiated a new period of political maneuvering among his successors. The post of chair of the Council of Ministers, held successively by Georgy M. MALENKOV (1953–1955) and Nikolai A. BULGANIN (1955–1958), was assumed in March 1958 by Nikita S. KHRUSHCHEV, who had become first secretary of the Soviet Communist Party in September 1953. Khrushchev's denunciation of Stalin's despotism at the 20th Communist Party of the Soviet Union (CPSU) Congress in February 1956 gave impetus to a policy of "de-Stalinization" in the USSR and Eastern Europe, while emphasis in Soviet foreign policy shifted from military confrontation to "competitive coexistence," symbolized by a growing foreign aid program and by such achievements as the launching of the world's first artificial satellite, *Sputnik,* in 1957. Khrushchev's policies nevertheless contributed to a series of sharp crises within and beyond the Communist world. An incipient liberalization movement in Hungary was crushed by Soviet armed forces in 1956, relations with Communist China deteriorated, and recurrent challenges to the West culminated in a defeat for Soviet aims in the confrontation with the United States over Soviet missiles in Cuba in October 1962.

Khrushchev's erratic performance resulted in his dismissal in October 1964 and the substitution of collective rule, under which Leonid I. BREZHNEV became head of the CPSU and Aleksei N. KOSYGIN became chair of the Council of Ministers. In 1965 Nikolai V. PODGORNY succeeded Anastas I. MIKOYAN as chair of the Presidium of the Supreme Soviet and thereby as nominal head of state, while Brezhnev clearly emerged from the 24th party congress in 1971 as first among equals. His position as CPSU general secretary was reconfirmed at the 25th and 26th congresses in 1976 and 1981. In June

1977 the Supreme Soviet designated Secretary Brezhnev to succeed Podgorny as chair of the Presidium.

In October 1980 Kosygin asked to be relieved of his duties as chair of the Council of Ministers because of declining health, and he was replaced by First Deputy Chair Nikolai TIKHONOV. Of more far-reaching consequence was the death of Brezhnev in November 1982 and his replacement as party secretary by Yuri V. ANDROPOV, who had previously served as head of the KGB, the Soviet intelligence and internal security agency. Andropov was named chair of the Presidium in June 1983 but died in February 1984. He was succeeded as CPSU general secretary and, two months later, as head of state by Konstantin Y. CHERNENKO.

Long reputed to be in failing health and widely viewed as having been elevated to the top leadership on a "caretaker" basis, Chernenko died in March 1985. As evidence that the succession had already been agreed upon, the relatively young (54-year-old) Mikhail S. GORBACHEV was named general secretary on the following day. The Presidium chairship remained temporarily vacant.

During the ensuing four years, wide-ranging personnel changes occurred in both the party and the government. In July 1985 the long-time foreign minister, Andrei A. GROMYKO, was named Presidium chair, while Nikolai I. RYZHKOV replaced the aging Tikhonov as chair of the Council of Ministers in September. In October 1988 Secretary Gorbachev was elected to the additional post of Presidium chair, with Gromyko moving into retirement. Two months later extensive constitutional revisions introduced a new parliamentary system, competitive elections, heightened judicial independence, and other changes in keeping with Gorbachev's policies of openness (glasnost), restructuring (perestroika), and greater democracy.

In May 1989 a new, supra-legislative Congress of People's Deputies elected Gorbachev to a five-year term as chair of a restructured Supreme Soviet, with Anatoly I. LUKYANOV (vice chair of the Presidium since October) redesignated as Gorbachev's deputy. Following further constitutional amendments in December 1989 and March 1990 that sanctioned a multiparty system, increased the scope of direct elections, and broadened the rights of private property and enterprise, the Congress named Gorbachev in March 1990 to the new post of Union president. Concurrently, it elected Lukyanov chair of the Supreme Soviet.

In June 1990 the Russian Federation issued a declaration asserting the primacy of the RSFSR constitution within its territorial limits. The document also asserted a right to engage in foreign relations and "freely leave the USSR" in accordance with procedures set forth in Union law. Earlier, on the basis of constitutional reforms approved at the Union level in 1988, the Russian Federation had emulated the central USSR administration by establishing a two-tiered legislative system consisting of a Congress of People's Deputies and a bicameral Supreme Soviet elected by the Congress. On May 29, 1990, the 1,068 Congress deputies, who had been elected in competitive balloting on March 4, elected Boris YELTSIN as chair of the RSFSR Supreme Soviet, and hence, de facto president of the federation.

On July 20, 1990, Yeltsin announced a "500-day" drive toward a market economy within the federation, which subsequently became the core of an all-Union plan that secured approval in weakened form three months later. In mid-November, following a meeting with USSR President Gorbachev, Yeltsin called for a central "coalition government of national unity" as a prelude to further Union negotiations.

During the fall and winter of 1990–1991 conservative forces (principally elements of the administrative and Communist Party bureaucracies, the army, the interior police, and the KGB) ranged themselves against Gorbachev's pluralist measures. For a time, the Soviet leader appeared to offer little resistance to the backlash, but a six-month lapse into authoritarianism ended dramatically in April 1991 with a much-heralded "nine-plus-one" conference, at which the participating republics (with Armenia, Georgia, Moldova, and the Baltic states not attending) endorsed a new Union Treaty that called for extensive decentralization in social, political, and economic spheres. Under the plan, a new constitution would be drafted for a "Union of Soviet Sovereign Republics."

At a nonbinding referendum on the draft of the Union Treaty on March 17, 1991, RSFSR voters had registered 71.3 percent approval, with 69.9 percent also endorsing the creation of a directly elected RSFSR presidency. On April 5 the republican Congress voted to create the office, and on June 12 Yeltsin defeated five other candidates, including former Soviet ministerial chair Nikolai Ryzhkov, for the presidency, with Aleksandr RUTSKOI elected vice president.

During the week of August 19, 1991, a self-proclaimed State Committee for the State of Emergency (SCSE), led by Soviet Vice President Gennadi YANAYEV, responded to Gorbachev's reforms and the new Union proposal by launching an attempted coup. With RSFSR President Yeltsin in the forefront of the opposition, the coup quickly failed and USSR President Gorbachev resumed constitutional authority. By the end of the month, however, most of the republican parties had renounced the authority of the CPSU, Ukraine had declared its independence, and Yeltsin had called upon Gorbachev to recognize the independence of Estonia, Latvia, and Lithuania.

On September 6, 1991, Moscow accepted the withdrawal of the Baltic states. The remaining 12 republics, during a meeting at Alma-Ata (Almaty), Kazakhstan, held October 1–2, endorsed a plan for what Gorbachev characterized as a union of "confederal democratic states." However, in a referendum on December 1 Ukrainians overwhelmingly endorsed complete independence, and one week later in Brest, Belarus, both Russia and Belarus joined Ukraine in proclaiming the demise of the Soviet Union. On December 21 Russia and 10 of its sister republics (with Georgia not participating) proclaimed the formation of the Commonwealth of Independent States (CIS—see under Intergovernmental Organizations), and four days later Gorbachev, the last president of the USSR, resigned.

Meanwhile, in mid-July 1991 the RSFSR Congress of People's Deputies had encountered an impasse over the selection of Yeltsin's successor as chair of the Russian Supreme Soviet. When no candidate managed to muster a majority in six rounds of voting, the former deputy chair, Ruslan KHASBULATOV, who had been accused of an excessively authoritarian leadership style, was named acting chair. Two months later a dispute broke out in the Supreme Soviet over an attempt by the president to augment his executive powers, and on September 27 Ivan SILAYEV resigned as chair of the Council of Ministers. In late October Khasbulatov was confirmed as Supreme Soviet chair and Yeltsin personally took over Silayev's responsibilities, while continuing to press for enhanced capacity to move forward with his economic reforms. On November 1 the added powers were approved, as was authority to suspend the actions of the presidents of the autonomous republics within the RSFSR. On November 6 Yeltsin was formally invested as chair of the Council of Ministers. On the same day he issued a decree banning both the Union and the republican Communist parties and nationalizing their assets.

The abolition of most price controls and other "shock therapy" economic measures in 1992 intensified a clash between ministers and legislators, with Khasbulatov warning that the federation could encounter "a catastrophic decline in living standards, famine [and] social upheaval." The cabinet responded by submitting its resignation on April 12, with members withdrawing en masse from the Congress of People's Deputies. In the end, after defeating a proposal by Khasbulatov that would have stripped the president of most of his powers, the deputies adopted a declaration that permitted a resumption of governmental activity, with an architect of the Yeltsin reform program, Finance Minister Yegor GAIDAR, being named acting chair of the Council of Ministers on June 15. Yeltsin's victory was, however, less than total. He failed in a bid to further augment his executive powers and was precluded from effectively moving on land reform, most notably in regard to privatization.

During the final months of 1992 Yeltsin was forced into an increasingly defensive posture on domestic policy. In December, Yeltsin was obliged to abandon Gaidar, his leading reform advocate, and accept as prime minister Viktor S. CHERNOMYRDIN, previously in charge of the state fuel-energy complex.In early 1993 the contest between Yeltsin and Khasbulatov intensified, with the former campaigning for an April referendum on major provisions of a new constitution and the latter calling for early parliamentary and presidential elections in 1994. On March 28, 1993, during an emergency Ninth Congress, a motion to dismiss Yeltsin secured a substantial majority, but not the two-thirds required for implementation; a similar motion to dismiss Khasbulatov, which required only a simple majority, also failed. The Congress then proceeded to authorize an April 25 referendum at which the voters simultaneously voiced support for Yeltsin and his socioeconomic policies as well as for early legislative elections. (See the 2013 *Handbook* for details of this phase of the conflict between Yeltsin and Khasbulatov).

Two days before the referendum Yeltsin had unveiled his draft constitution, which called for a strong presidency, a bicameral legislature, and an independent judiciary. Not unexpectedly, the document was rejected on May 7, 1993, by the Supreme Soviet's Constitutional Commission, which preferred a parliament with expanded powers, including the capacity to reject government appointments. Undaunted, the president on June 5 convened a 700-member constitutional conference, which approved his draft on July 12.

Yeltsin's renewed ascendancy was demonstrated on September 16, 1993, by the reappointment of Gaidar as deputy prime minister and economics minister. Moreover, in actions that were immediately repudiated by the Constitutional Court, the president on September 21 issued a decree on constitutional reform, suspended both the Congress of People's Deputies and the Supreme Soviet, called for the election of a new bicameral legislature on December 11–12, and announced that presidential balloting would take place on June 12, 1994. The Congress, assembling in an emergency session, responded by voting to impeach the president and named the conservative Rutskoi, whom Yeltsin had suspended as vice president on September 1, as his successor.

Yeltsin thereupon mounted a series of measures against his legislative opponents that culminated in the House of Soviets ("White House") being sealed off by some 2,000 troops on September 27, 1993. A number of armed clashes followed, with the anti-Yeltsin leaders surrendering on the evening of October 4 after government forces had stormed the building. Overall, the fighting cost some 140 lives, while several hundred people were injured. As the power struggle drew to a close, Yeltsin announced that the December 12 elections would be augmented to include a referendum on the new constitution. However, the proposal for an early presidential election was abandoned.

In polling on December 12, 1993, for the State Duma, the lower house of the new Federal Assembly, the pro-reform Russia's Choice list won a plurality of seats but was strongly challenged by both right- and left-wing opponents. At the same time, 58.4 percent of participating voters approved the new constitution. The most startling success was that of the neofascist Liberal Democratic Party of Russia (*Liberalno-Demokraticheskaya Partiya Rossii*—LDPR), led by Vladimir ZHIRINOVSKY, which secured the largest share (22.8 percent) in the party preference poll and finished second overall in the State Duma race, with 64 of 450 seats.

Events in early 1994 illustrated Yeltsin's increased political vulnerability as a result of the 1993 election. In January both Gaidar and the reformist finance minister, Boris FEDOROV, resigned after failing to secure a number of objectives. A month later the State Duma voted to grant amnesty not only to the leaders of the October 1993 parliamentary maneuverings but also to those involved in the August 1991 coup attempt. Yeltsin responded on April 28 by concluding a two-year Treaty on Civil Accord with 245 political and social groups. The document specified, among other things, that controversial constitutional changes would be avoided, that there would be no early elections, that local self-government would be strengthened, and that the rights of ethnic minorities would be supported. Signatories of the document included not only arch-reformer Gaidar but also Zhirinovsky, whereas some rightists, notably former vice president Rutskoi, denounced it as unconstitutional.

The Treaty on Civil Accord yielded a measure of political stability for the Chernomyrdin government, while steps were taken to reduce the potential for presidential/ministerial tension. At the same time, the slowdown in the pace of economic reform attracted growing criticism from Gaidar, whose party was renamed Russia's Democratic Choice (*Demokraticheskii Vybor Rossii*—DVR) in June 1994. In October the government was jarred by a major currency crisis that halved the external value of the ruble and led, a month later, to a major reshuffle of economic portfolios.

The Russian government made some progress in 1994 in improving relations with its more fractious constituent republics, concluding accords with Tatarstan in February and with Bashkortostan in August that provided for substantial home rule. However, the self-declared "independent" Republic of Chechnya in the Caucasus proved to be obdurate. In the wake of mounting tensions Russian forces launched a full-scale invasion of the territory on December 11 with the aim of restoring central government authority. Despite fierce Chechen resistance, the Russians finally captured the capital, Grozny, on February 6, 1995, and thereafter extended their control to other population centers.

The invasion of Chechnya dominated Russian politics in the first half of 1995. The action was strongly supported by the nationalist right but opposed by important elements of the centrist/reformist parties that had usually backed the Yeltsin administration, notably Gaidar's DVR. Ministry of Defense figures in late February 1995 put the number of dead and missing Russian soldiers at about 1,500, but independent observers estimated that some 10,000 Russians might have been killed and that Chechen civilian deaths totaled 25,000 in Grozny alone. International criticism of the action was particularly strong in the Islamic world—the Chechens being predominantly Muslim—and was heightened by Red Cross reports that Russian soldiers had massacred at least 250 civilians during an April assault on the village of Samashki in western Chechnya. Moreover, it appeared that a protracted guerrilla war was a prospect, since the self-styled Chechen "president," Gen. Dzhokhar DUDAYEV, had gone underground with a considerable military entourage. In June 1995 a band of Chechen gunmen seized a hospital in the southern Russian town of Budennovsk, holding more than 1,000 people hostage for five days until securing safe passage back to Chechnya in return for the hostages' release. At least 120 people died in the crisis, including about 30 casualties when Russian forces tried unsuccessfully to storm the hospital.

The Chechen attack was perceived as humiliating for Russia and provoked a parliamentary motion of no confidence in the government, directed mainly at the three "power" ministers of defense, interior, and security—all Yeltsin supporters—rather than at Prime Minister Chernomyrdin, who had negotiated the hostages' release. On June 21 the motion was carried by 241 votes to 72, but the result was nonbinding under the constitution unless repeated within three months. With Yeltsin's announcement that several senior ministers and officials would be dismissed, a second motion at the beginning of July failed to obtain the requisite majority. Russian and Chechen negotiators eventually signed a cease-fire agreement on July 30, but general hostilities resumed in October amid continued wrangling over the future political status of Chechnya.

Party politics from mid-1995 focused on the forthcoming legislative and presidential elections, scheduled for December 1995 and June 1996, respectively. New parties, alliances, and realignments proliferated, including the launching in May of Our Home Is Russia (*Nash Dom–Rossiya*—NDR) by Prime Minister Chernomyrdin. Several prominent figures declared their presidential candidacies, including Zhirinovsky on the far right and Gennadi ZYUGANOV of the Communist Party of the Russian Federation (*Kommunisticheskaya Partiya Rossiiskoi Federatsii*—KPRF). Despite health problems, President Yeltsin subsequently confirmed his candidacy for election to a second term.

The outcome of the State Duma election on December 17, 1995, was a significant victory for the KPRF, which won a plurality of 157 of the 450 seats with 22.3 percent of the party list vote, more than double the tally of the second-place NDR, which managed only 55 seats. In third place came the LDPR with 51 seats, while the reformist Yavlinsky-Boldyrev-Lukin Bloc (*Yabloko*), with 45 seats, was the only other list to achieve the 5 percent threshold for the allocation of proportional seats. In the constituency section, however, a total of 19 other groupings won representation.

President Yeltsin responded to the Communist/conservative electoral advance by making major government changes in January 1996. Several prominent reformers were dropped, including privatization architect Anatoly CHUBAIS as first deputy premier. Andrei KOZYREV was replaced as foreign minister by Yevgeni PRIMAKOV, hitherto chief of foreign intelligence and known to be much less pro-Western than his predecessor. These changes and a collateral slowdown in the privatization program found favor with the dominant KPRF contingent in the State Duma.

Held on June 16, 1996, the first round of the presidential balloting found Yeltsin heading the field of ten candidates with 35.3 percent of the vote, but only narrowly ahead of Zyuganov, who obtained 32 percent. In third place, with 14.5 percent, was Gen. (Ret.) Aleksandr LEBED, the former Russian military commander in the separatist Moldovan region of Transnistria, standing as the candidate of the nationalist Congress of Russian Communities (*Kongress Russkikh Obshchin*—KRO), while Grigori YAVLINSKY (*Yabloko*) and Zhirinovsky (LDPR) trailed. Within two days of the polling Yeltsin had forged an alliance with Lebed, who was appointed secretary of the National Security Council. With Lebed's endorsement in the runoff ballot on July 3, Yeltsin won a decisive victory over Zyuganov by a margin of 53.7 to 40.3 percent. Reinaugurated on August 9, President Yeltsin immediately reappointed Chernomyrdin as prime minister, at the head of a reshaped government in which pro-reform elements regained some of the ground lost in the January reshuffle. In addition, Anatoly Chubais assumed the key post of presidential chief of staff at a time of mounting concern about the president's health.

In Chechnya, the collapse of the cease-fire in October 1995 was followed in January 1996 by major hostage seizures by Chechen rebels. Russian peace overtures were assisted by the death of Chechen leader Dudayev in a Russian rocket attack in April, following which his successor, Zelimkhan YANDARBIYEV, concluded a cease-fire agreement with President Yeltsin. The May cease-fire again broke down with

Yeltsin's reelection, but efforts by the new presidential security adviser, General Lebed, yielded a new agreement on August 31 that provided for the withdrawal of Russian and rebel forces from Grozny. Following Yeltsin's dismissal of Lebed in October, on grounds that he had proved to be a disruptive influence, the Russian president concluded yet another peace agreement with the Chechen leadership. The November accord provided for a complete Russian military withdrawal before the holding of presidential and parliamentary elections in Chechnya on January 27, 1997.

The winner in the presidential election was the most moderate of the candidates, Aslan MASKHADOV, who nevertheless continued to favor complete independence. In May Maskhadov and Yeltsin signed a peace treaty that rejected the use of force and postponed final resolution of Chechen-Russian relations to the year 2001. The situation nevertheless remained precarious as Chechen field commanders and extralegal groups continued to engage in abductions, politically motivated murders, and skirmishes with Russian troops along the Chechen frontier.

President Yeltsin underwent heart bypass surgery in November 1996 and spent most of the next several months in the hospital, prompting questions about his health that dominated the political scene into 1997. Attempts at impeachment by the opposition KPRF and LDPR over the health issue failed to pass constitutional muster, however, and in March Yeltsin significantly restructured the government, bringing in two noted reformers: Anatoly Chubais as a first deputy prime minister (the position from which he had been dismissed in January 1996) and the youthful governor of Nizhny Novgorod, Boris NEMTSOV. In November 1997 Chubais was dismissed as finance minister (but retained as deputy prime minister) following revelations that he had received money for his contribution to a book on privatization in Russia, a scandal widely linked to rivalry between financial conglomerates over the spoils of privatization.

Apparently determined to end infighting within the cabinet and to forge ahead with economic reform despite such adverse signs as a falling stock market and continuing wage arrears, on March 23, 1998, Yeltsin dismissed the government and named Sergei KIRIYENKO, a young reformer, as prime minister. Facing a threat of dissolution by the president after having rejected the nomination twice, the Duma finally approved Kiriyenko on April 24. His tenure proved to be short, however, as Russia's economic plight deepened, precipitated by falling oil prices on world markets and the impact of the recent East Asian financial turmoil. The crisis led on August 17 to a major devaluation of the ruble, the suspension of foreign debt payments, and the rescheduling of domestic short-term debt. Six days later, having dismissed Kiriyenko, Yeltsin nominated a former prime minister, Viktor Chernomyrdin, as his successor. However, the Duma twice rejected the nomination and Chernomyrdin withdrew his candidacy. On September 10 Yeltsin proposed in his stead a political veteran, Foreign Minister Primakov, who, with the support of the KPRF, won easy confirmation the following day.

Primakov's accomplishments included initiating an anticorruption campaign that targeted the "oligarchs," businessmen with powerful political connections who had made fortunes since the breakup of the Soviet Union, largely through the auction of state-owned enterprises in the mid-1990s. A principal target, Boris BEREZOVSKY, had close connections to Yeltsin's entourage ("the family"), and accusations surfaced that the president himself may have been involved, at least indirectly, in illegal business dealings.

On May 12, 1999, Yeltsin dismissed the government of Prime Minister Primakov, who, at the time, had been considered the frontrunner to succeed Yeltsin at the expiration of the presidential term in 2000. Primakov's replacement, First Deputy Prime Minister Sergei STEPASHIN, was confirmed by the State Duma on May 19 and thus became Russia's fourth prime minister in 14 months.

On August 9, 1999, Yeltsin once again dismissed his prime minister, designating as Stepashin's successor Vladimir PUTIN, theretofore head of the Federal Security Service (successor to the KGB) and secretary of the Security Council. Furthermore, Yeltsin identified Putin as his preferred presidential successor. The State Duma approved Putin's appointment as prime minister on August 16.

Speaking to the legislature before the confirmation vote, Putin not only outlined his government's economic goals, but also asserted that he would restore order to the North Caucasus and Chechnya. In early February 1999 Chechnya's President Maskhadov, under pressure from opposition field commanders, had issued a decree ordering an immediate transition to Islamic law (sharia), curtailed the legislature's powers, and created a commission to draft an Islamic constitution. On February 9 the field commanders set up a *Shura* (Islamic Council) and subsequently elected Shamil BASAYEV as its leader. On March 19 the instability of the entire North Caucasus region was exacerbated by a bombing in Vladikavkaz, the capital of North Ossetia, which killed at least 50 and wounded 100.

In early August 1999 Chechen rebels commanded by Basayev and Jordanian-born Omar ibn al-KHATTAB invaded Dagestan, capturing several border villages and declaring an independent Islamic state. Federal and Dagestani forces began a counteroffensive and within two weeks forced the insurgents to withdraw. On August 16 President Maskhadov declared a state of emergency in Chechnya, but the situation continued to deteriorate. When several massive bomb blasts in Moscow and elsewhere in August–September killed nearly 300 people, suspicion immediately fell on Chechen terrorists. Additional incursions into Dagestan prompted tighter security measures, and Russian forces renewed the push into Chechnya.

By late October 1999 nearly 200,000 civilians had fled the fighting, many into neighboring Ingushetia. Emphasizing air power and artillery in an effort to minimize Russian casualties, the strong military response served to strengthen Prime Minister Putin's standing in the polls. The government asserted that its intention was to convince the entire North Caucasus region—the Republics of Karachayevo-Cherkessia and North Ossetia as well as Chechnya, Dagestan, and Ingushetia—that Moscow would exert its full force to maintain central authority and defeat terrorism.

In the December 18, 1999, State Duma polling, the KPRF again won a plurality (113 seats on a 24 percent vote share), but, more significantly, the combined success of several recently formed, increasingly pro-Putin blocs secured a majority for the government. Two of the new electoral alliances, Unity (*Edinstvo*) and the Union of Right Forces (*Soyuz Pravyh Sil*—SPS), had been endorsed by Putin. A third, the Fatherland–All Russia bloc (*Otechestvo–Vsya Rossiya*—OVR), led by former prime minister Primakov and Moscow's mayor, Yuri LUZHKOV, found itself undercut by Putin's popularity. Most of the more than 100 representatives elected as independents soon joined progovernment parliamentary factions and deputies' groups.

With Putin's standing secured, President Yeltsin unexpectedly resigned on December 31, 1999, the prime minister thereby becoming acting president pending an election to be held within three months. Putin quickly decreed immunity from prosecution for Yeltsin, although not for "family" members. (Yeltsin died of heart failure on April 23, 2007.) In the presidential election on March 26, 2000, Putin secured 52.9 percent of the vote. Among the ten challengers, the KPRF's Zyuganov finished second, with 29.2 percent. Both former prime minister Primakov and Mayor Luzhkov of the Fatherland declined to run, given Putin's certain victory. Putin was inaugurated on May 7, and he nominated Mikhail KASYANOV as prime minister three days later. The State Duma approved the nomination on May 17 and over the next several days confirmed a revamped cabinet that featured, most notably, major changes in the structure and leadership of economic ministries.

Putin continued to take a hard line toward the Chechen rebels, Russian forces taking control of Grozny in February 2000, months after federal forces had advanced into the city with the support of pro-Russian Chechen contingents. The remaining Chechen rebels retreated, amid heavy casualties, to the southern mountains. At the same time charges of human rights abuses by Russian troops escalated, especially in "filtration camps" established to weed out belligerents. On April 25 the United Nations Commission on Human Rights voted to condemn a "disproportionate and indiscriminate use of Russian military forces." By then, pro-Russian Chechen officials were increasingly being targeted for assassination by the rebels, who also continued guerrilla assaults on Russian troops.

President Putin soon initiated steps to consolidate Moscow's authority, issuing a decree on May 13, 2000, establishing seven federal "superdistricts" to be funded by Moscow and headed by presidentially appointed envoys empowered to ensure regional compliance with federal law. The president also secured the authority to dismiss regional leaders for violating federal law (see Constitution and government, below).

On June 8, 2002, President Putin imposed direct rule on Chechnya and four days later named Mufti Akhmed KADYROV as acting head of administration.

In July 2001 Unity, All Russia, and Fatherland organized an alliance that was registered in December as Unity and Fatherland–United Russia (*Edinstvo i Otechestvo–Edinaya Rossiya*), and two months later the members of all three voted to dissolve as separate entities. On the right, many of the SPS participants had also merged into a single party, while on the left the continued domination of the KPRF was called into question by factional disputes as the 2003 State Duma election approached. At the December 7 poll the Putin-supportive United Russia won a majority of seats, while the KPRF lost support to a recently organized Motherland–People's Patriotic Union (*Rodina–Narodno-Patrioticheskii Soyuz*) electoral bloc. In a major setback, neither the SPS nor *Yabloko* met the 5 percent threshold for claiming proportional seats, while the LDPR doubled its representation to 36 seats. When the State Duma convened, the United Russia parliamentary faction surpassed the two-thirds majority needed to approve constitutional changes.

On February 24, 2004, three weeks before the presidential election, President Putin dismissed the Kasyanov government and on March 1 named Mikhail FRADKOV, Russia's ambassador to the European Union (EU) and considered an "outsider," as prime minister. Confirmed by the legislature on March 5, Fradkov completed his streamlined cabinet on March 9. Five days later Putin, running as an independent, easily won reelection, capturing 71.3 percent of the vote, defeating five challengers, the closest of whom, the KPRF's Nikolai KHARITONOV, won 13.7 percent. Required by the constitution to resign following the May 7 presidential inauguration, Fradkov was immediately reappointed by Putin and confirmed on May 12.

In 2002 the frequent suicide bombings and hostage taking in Chechnya continued to draw international attention. On October 23 separatists seized more than 800 hostages at a Moscow theater. An attack by Russian special forces on October 26 not only killed all the rebels but also resulted in the deaths of some 130 hostages. Two months later suicide bombers attacked the administrative headquarters in Grozny, killing 80 and wounding 150. In 2003, from May to August, suicide bombers, some of them women, included in their targets a music festival in Moscow, government buildings and a religious festival in Chechnya, and a military hospital in North Ossetia.

On March 23, 2003, a reported 96 percent of Chechen voters endorsed a draft constitution for a self-ruling republic with an elected legislature and president. Akhmed Kadyrov won the Chechen presidential election on October 3 with more than 80 percent of the vote, his principal rivals having withdrawn. He was assassinated by Chechen Islamists in Grozny in 2004. Prime Minister Sergei ABRAMOV, who had been in office less than two months, became acting president. On August 29 Maj. Gen. Alu ALKHANOV, theretofore the Chechen interior minister, was elected president with 74 percent of the vote. His principal rival, Chechen businessman Malik SAIDULLAYEV, was denied a place on the ballot due to a technicality. On September 1, 2004, some 30 rebels, reportedly including several operatives linked to the al-Qaida network, invaded a school at Beslan, North Ossetia, and took 1,200 teachers, parents, and children hostage. Two days later nearly 340 hostages died during a rescue mission.

President Putin continued to consolidate his authority, as in 2005 he tightened requirements for registration of political parties; eliminated single-mandate legislative districts beginning with the 2007 State Duma election; and raised to 7 percent the vote threshold needed for parties to claim lower house seats. Putin claimed that by switching to proportional representation for legislative elections, the party system would be strengthened since there would be fewer parties in the lower house. Putin's consolidation of power was interpreted by some observers as marking the ascendancy of the *siloviki* (roughly, the powerful), individuals with a background in the Soviet KGB or the Russian security and military services, at the expense of former president Yeltsin's "family"—particularly some of the oligarchs who had amassed fortunes through the sale of state assets in the 1990s. Early targets included Vladimir GUSINSKY, owner of Russia's largest independent media conglomerate, Media-MOST, which had angered the government with its unfavorable coverage of the war in Chechnya. Gusinsky, fleeing charges of tax evasion, relocated to Israel, while Media-MOST fell under the control of Gazprom, the state-owned natural gas company. Mikhail KHODORKOVSKY, the chief executive officer of a leading energy company, Yukos, was convicted of tax evasion and fraud in May 2005 and sentenced to nine years in prison. (Yukos was dismantled in 2007, furthering the government's aim of regaining a controlling share of the country's natural resources and other critical industries, such as pipelines, rail transport, shipping, and nuclear energy.)

The Chechen separatists suffered a significant blow on March 8, 2005, when Aslan Maskhadov died during an operation by the Federal Security Service. Two days later the separatist Chechen State Defense Committee announced that Abdul-Khalim SADULAYEV had succeeded Maskhadov as its chair. Moscow increased its control over the Chechen republic through the parliamentary elections called for November 27, 2005, which were widely criticized for irregularities and low turnout. The United Russia party was declared to have won 61 percent of the vote, giving it majorities in both upper and lower chambers.

In March 2006 pro-Moscow warlord Ramzan KADYROV, leader of a private army of thousands of irregular troops and son of slain president Akhmed Kadyrov, was approved as prime minister in a unanimous vote of the People's Assembly of Chechnya, succeeding Sergei Abramov, who had resigned in February. In mid-June Abdul-Khalim Sadulayev was killed in a Russian police operation. His deputy, Doku UMAROV, assumed the separatist leadership. On July 10 Shamil BASAYEV, the Chechen separatist leader who had claimed responsibility for attacks that killed hundreds of Russian civilians in the past decade, including the Beslan school massacre, died when a nearby truck carrying dynamite blew up.

In February 2007 Ramzan Kadyrov was appointed acting president of Chechnya, Alkhanov having been named federal deputy minister of justice in a cabinet reshuffle. On March 2 Kadyrov was elected president, and in April named a cousin, Odes BAYSULTANOV, as prime minister. By then, with the separatist leadership having been decimated, the pace and severity of separatist attacks had diminished.

On September 12, 2007, President Putin accepted the resignation of Prime Minister Fradkov, and according to law, the cabinet was dismissed. Fradkov remained as acting prime minister until Putin nominated Viktor ZUBKOV as his successor on September 14. Zubkov had been serving as first deputy finance minister and chair of the committee responsible for combating money laundering. On October 6 Putin appointed Fradkov as head of the Foreign Intelligence Service.

In the December 2, 2007, legislative elections, in which 11 parties participated, United Russia won 64.3 percent of the vote and 315 of the legislature's 450 seats. The KPRF, as expected, finished second, with 11.6 percent and 57 seats. Shortly after the election, President Putin, who was barred constitutionally from seeking a third consecutive term, announced his support for First Deputy Prime Minister Dmitri MEDVEDEV in the 2008 presidential election. Medvedev, in turn, indicated that if elected, he intended to nominate Putin as prime minister. All four pro-Kremlin parties—United Russia, Just Russia, Agrarian Party of Russia (*Agrarnaya Partiya Rossii*—APR), and Civil Force (*Grazhdanskaya Sila*—GS)—endorsed Medvedev as well. The Russian Ecological Party "The Greens" (*Rossiiskaya Ekologicheskaya Partiya "Zelenye"*—REP) also backed Medvedev.

In the election on March 2, 2008, Medvedev, who officially is an independent, received 70.3 percent of the vote, defeating Gennadi Zyuganov of the KPRF, with 19.96 percent of the vote; Vladimir Zhirinovsky of the LDPR, with 9.48 percent; and Andrei Bogdanov of the DPR, with 1.31 percent. As expected, Medvedev appointed Putin prime minister. Putin named a new cabinet on May 12. A minor reshuffle occurred in October.

One minister was replaced on March 12, 2009, and a ninth deputy chair of the Council of Ministers was appointed on January 19, 2010. Another deputy chair resigned on October 21 in order to contest the Moscow mayoral election.

In August 2011 the governor of St. Petersburg resigned in advance of filling the post of speaker of the Federation Council, which had been vacated by the resignation (under pressure by United Russia) of the previous speaker on May 18. Valentina MATVIYENKO, a senior member of United Russia, was installed as speaker on September 21.

The long-serving finance minister resigned on September 27, 2011, after refusing to withdraw the remarks he had made days earlier in the wake of Prime Minister Putin's announcement that he would seek reelection as president in 2012 and that Medvedev would stand on the United Russia ticket in the December parliamentary elections and would likely be prime minister. Aleksei KUDRIN, who was also a deputy prime minister, had said during a trip to Washington that he would refuse to serve under Medvedev.

The December 4, 2011, legislative elections included seven registered parties. United Russia won 49.32 percent of the vote and 238 of the legislature's 450 seats. The KPRF took second place, with 19.19 percent and 92 seats. United Russia secured a majority and the mandate to form a government, but it did lose the two-thirds constitutional majority it had previously enjoyed, while the three parliamentary opposition parties all gained seats. There were, subsequently, numerous protests against perceived flaws in the election (see Current issues, below).

In the presidential election on March 4, 2012, Putin received 63.64 percent of the vote, defeating Gennady Zyuganov of the KPRF, with 17.18 percent of the vote; Mikhail Prokhorov, an independent, with 7.94 percent; Vladimir Zhirinovsky of the LDPR, with 6.22 percent; and Sergey Mironov of A Just Russia with 3.85 percent. Putin appointed

Medvedev as prime minister, as he suggested in September 2011, and Medvedev named a new cabinet on May 15, 2012.

But Putin's new term of office saw the replacement of several key cabinet members. Oleg GOVORUN, minister for regional development and widely seen as an ally of Medvedev, was dismissed on October 17, 2012, after public criticism by Putin the preceding month. Putin dismissed defense minister and long-time ally Anatoly SERDYUKOV on November 6, 2012, after the police began a corruption investigation of how the defense ministry had privatized ministry land. Most notably, on May 8, 2013, Deputy Prime Minister Vladislav SURKOV resigned a day after Putin criticized his performance. The resignation was interpreted by the local media as a possible sign of a rift between Putin and Medvedev. Surkov, a former key political advisor of Putin, had distanced himself during the December 2011 elections.

Constitution and government. Under the 1993 constitution the Federation president "determine[s] guidelines for the domestic and foreign policy of the state." Directly elected for no more than two consecutive four-year terms, the president nominates the chair of government (the prime minister) as well as higher court judges; in addition, he serves as commander in chief of the armed forces, appoints and dismisses the top military commanders, and may issue decrees carrying the force of law. He may reject an initial vote of nonconfidence and upon the repassage of such a measure within three months may call for dissolution of the legislature and new elections. The current basic law makes no provision for a vice president. The president's main advisory body on security issues is the Security Council, whose powers were substantially strengthened by presidential decree in July 1996.

The bicameral Federal Assembly consists of the State Duma and, as an upper house, the Federation Council. The Duma votes on the president's nominee as government chair as well as his choices for other high positions. Legislation must first be approved by majority vote of the entire Duma; rejection by the upper house requires a two-thirds vote of the entire Duma to override. Measures vetoed by the president require approval by two-thirds of both houses. The Federation Council comprises two representatives from each of Russia's 85 territorial components (83 as of March 2008)—prior to 2002, the governing executive (governor or, in the case of republics, president) and the leader of the assembly. On August 7, 2000, however, President Putin signed into law a measure stripping regional officials of their ex officio seats and of their immunity from prosecution. With full effect from January 2002, the regional executives each appoint one member to the council (with legislative concurrence), and each territorial assembly elects a legislative representative. The Federation Council's powers include review of martial law and emergency decrees.

The judicial system includes a Constitutional Court, a Supreme Court, a Supreme Arbitration Court, and lesser federal entities as determined by law. Between 2001 and 2002 Russia introduced codes permitting the sale and private ownership of land, although the sale of agricultural land to foreigners and to companies with majority foreign ownership was prohibited. In July 2002 a new "Western-style" criminal code instituted a jury system nationwide for serious offenses, required police to obtain court warrants for arrests and searches, and set a 48-hour limit on detentions.

Local self-government is conducted through referenda, elections, and other means, with appropriate "consideration for historical and other local traditions." Mergers of territorial units have been encouraged by the central government as part of a larger plan to consolidate the federal structure, ostensibly to streamline public administration, but apparently also as a way to diminish the political authority of the often restless ethnic areas. As of 2008 the federation encompassed 21 republics (*respubliki*), nine territories (*kraia*), 46 regions (*oblasti*), the Jewish autonomous region (*avtonomnaya oblast*) of Birobijan, four autonomous areas (*avtonomnie okruga*), and two "cities of federal importance" (Moscow and St. Petersburg). (See the 2013 *Handbook* for recent changes to administrative divisions.)

By decree, on May 13, 2000, President Putin established seven federal districts—Central, Far Eastern, North Caucasus (renamed Southern by decree on June 23), Northwest, Siberian, Ural, and Volga—to oversee regional compliance with federal law. Later, in conjunction with the reform of the Federation Council, Putin signed into law measures intended to restructure the federal relationship, one giving the president authority to dismiss regional heads who violate federal law and the other permitting regional executives to remove local officials for similar cause. On September 1, again by decree, President Putin established a consultative State Council of the Russian Federation, to ensure that executives from all territorial subdivisions have an institutional voice in Moscow. Chaired by the president, the State Council has a seven-member Presidium consisting of a presidentially appointed representative from each of the "super-districts." Serving six-month terms, the appointees are chosen by rotation from among the leaders of Russia's constituent republics and regions. Legislation passed in 2004 brought an end to the election of regional governors and republican presidents, who are now appointed by the federation president with the concurrence of the legislature of the particular jurisdiction.

All mass media are licensed by the government, and most of the country's leading newspapers and broadcasting outlets are owned by companies close to the government or in which the government has majority ownership. Foreign ownership of broadcast media was prohibited by a 2011 law.

Reporters Without Borders listed Russia as 148th out of 179 countries in its 2013 Press Freedom Index, pointing to the failure to punish violence against journalists, "arbitrary" applications of anti-extremism legislation, and the continued repression of protests against the government. Freedom House in 2013 categorized the Russian press as "not free," noting the introduction of "vaguely worded" laws intended to stifle press freedoms and NGOs. Criminal defamation was reintroduced in July 2012.

Foreign relations. The Russian Federation was generally accepted as successor to the Soviet Union in respect to the latter's international commitments and affiliations, including membership in the United Nations and the Conference on (later Organization for) Security and Cooperation in Europe (CSCE/OSCE). It also assumed the Soviet Union's obligations under international and bilateral treaties, such as those on arms control with the United States.

Russian troops remained deployed in several areas of the "near abroad" following the disintegration of the Soviet Union. When Georgia declared its independence in 1991 after the collapse of the Soviet Union, two of its regions, South Ossetia and the Abkhaz Republic, now commonly known as Abkhazia, took up arms to gain autonomy. Hundreds were killed and hundreds of thousands displaced as independence fighters engaged Georgian troops. In the summer of 1992, Russian peacekeepers were deployed in South Ossetia, achieving an end to the violence but leaving the issue of sovereignty unresolved.

In June 1992 Russia was formally admitted to membership in the IMF and the World Bank.

In August 1992 tension between Russia and Ukraine eased in the wake of an agreement to place the former Soviet Black Sea fleet under joint command pending implementation of a June accord to divide the ships equally and jointly finance their bases. At a CIS meeting in 1994 the two countries agreed that 15 to 20 percent of the fleet's 800-plus ships would be retained by Ukraine, with Russia "purchasing" the remainder of Ukraine's share.

In the course of a highly productive summit in Washington in 1992, Presidents Yeltsin and George H. W. Bush concluded agreements on most-favored-nation trade status and a major extension of the 1991 Strategic Arms Reduction Treaty (START). Under the START II accord, each nation would be limited to 3,000–3,500 long-range weapons (down from 11,000–12,000 on the eve of START I), while all land-based multiple warhead missiles would be banned. In November 1992 the Supreme Soviet ratified the 1991 START I accord with the United States, although an exchange of ratification documents was deferred until Belarus, Kazakhstan, and Ukraine had signed the 1968 Nuclear Non-Proliferation Treaty (NPT) and agreement had been reached on the disposition of nuclear arms in their possession. (Under a protocol to START I signed in Lisbon in May 1992, the three ex-Soviet republics had agreed that Russia should be the sole nuclear power in the CIS.) By late 1993 Belarus and Kazakhstan had completed these procedures; Ukraine acceded to the NPT in December 1994.

With regard to areas of the "near abroad" populated by ethnic Russian minorities, the Yeltsin administration firmly opposed the demands of right-wing nationalists that they be brought under Russian sovereignty. At the same time, it insisted that the rights of Russian minorities must be fully respected by the governments concerned. Thus, in October 1992 Yeltsin suspended the withdrawal of Russian troops from the three Baltic states, citing "profound concern over the numerous infringements of rights of the Russian-speaking population" in Latvia and Estonia, in particular. However, Western pressure and assurances on ethnic Russian rights yielded the withdrawal of Russian forces from Lithuania by August 1993 and from Estonia and Latvia a year later, subject to Russian retention of certain defense facilities for a specified period.

Russian negotiators facilitated a cease-fire agreement between Georgia and the Abkhaz Republic in April 1994. Both South Ossetia and Abkhazia have operated as de facto independent states since then, and Russia has provided both regions with peacekeeping troops, financial support, and Russian passports.

The rapid transformation of Russia's external relations was highlighted in June 1994 when Russia acceded in principle to the North Atlantic Treaty Organization's (NATO's) Partnership for Peace (PfP) program for former Soviet-bloc and neutral European states, and also signed a new partnership and cooperation agreement with the EU.

In September 1994 President Jiang Zemin became the first senior Chinese leader to visit Moscow since 1957. Agreements signed on September 3 resolved most bilateral border demarcation disputes and committed each never to use force against the other.Further visits to Moscow by Chinese president Jiang in May 1995 and by Premier Li Peng in June continued the rapprochement, which was consolidated by President Yeltsin's April 1996 visit to Beijing. Troop reductions on the Sino-Russian border were agreed to as part of a new "strategic partnership."

Efforts at improving ties with Japan were long stalled due to a dispute over the four southern Kurile Islands seized by the Soviet Union at the end of World War II (see the Foreign relations section of the entry on Japan). In November 1997 President Yeltsin and Japanese Prime Minister Ryutaro Hashimoto pledged to sign a treaty by 2000 that would settle the dispute and normalize relations. The two leaders also concluded a fishing agreement covering the Kurile Islands and agreed to further economic cooperation. (The dispute remained unresolved in 2013, despite an April trip to Moscow by Japanese Prime Minister Shinzo Abe.)

The dominant foreign policy issue in 1997 was the proposed admission of former Warsaw Pact members Poland, the Czech Republic, and Hungary into an expanded NATO, despite Russian objections and its previous threat to withdraw from the 1990 Conventional Forces in Europe (CFE) treaty. Negotiations held in Moscow in May led to an accord, signed in Paris on May 27, known as the Founding Act. While Russia had sought a treaty, rather than a nonbinding accord, it accepted an agreement to strengthen the OSCE, acquiesced on the need for revisions to the CFE treaty, and received a pledge, but not a guarantee, from NATO that the Western alliance would not place nuclear weapons on the territory of any new member states. While the NATO Founding Act did not give Russia a veto over future NATO decisions, as Yeltsin had desired, a Russian-NATO joint council has afforded Russia a voice in NATO decisions. Russia also received a number of economic concessions, including enhanced status in the G-7. (In 1998 Russia became a full participant, and the G-7 officially became the G-8.) In addition, Washington pledged to support eventual Russian accession to the World Trade Organization (WTO).

On July 23, 1997, in Vienna 16 NATO and 14 former Warsaw Pact states agreed "in principle" on a new draft CFE accord that set national rather than bloc limitations on conventional armed forces, as Russia's objections to the 1990 CFE treaty had rested on a desire to limit NATO deployments in the former Warsaw Pact countries.

Agreements concluded in May 1997 permitted Russia to lease half of the Ukrainian naval base at Sevastopol for a period of 20 years and also signified Russian recognition of Crimea and Sevastopol as Ukrainian territory.

Related to the eastward expansion of NATO, Yeltsin advocated closer linkages with CIS member states, in particular regarding economic, political, and military ties between Russia and Belarus. In June 1997 the legislatures of both countries ratified a Charter of the Union, which set out a plan for greater integration (see entry on Belarus). On December 25, 1998, Yeltsin and Belarusan President Alyaksandr Lukashenka agreed to set up an integrated monetary system and customs policies and form a common leadership while retaining national sovereignty. Modeled on the EU, a formal Union Treaty was signed in Moscow on December 8, 1999, and unanimously ratified on December 22 by the upper houses of both countries.

Russian contingents have participated in several peacekeeping missions, including a UN-sponsored force in Bosnia and Herzegovina and a CIS contingent in Tajikistan. In the confrontation between Yugoslavia and NATO over the Kosovo question in 1998–1999, Moscow took a pro-Belgrade stance, owing in large part to the strong cultural ties between Russians and Yugoslavia's Serbs. Despite Russian anger over the bombing campaign against Yugoslavia in March 1999, in the aftermath Russian troops were successfully stationed alongside NATO-led peacekeepers in Kosovo.

In 2000 Russia announced its withdrawal from the 1992 Bishkek Treaty on visa-free travel among CIS members, citing threats posed by international terrorism, crime, and drug trafficking.

On April 14, 2000, the State Duma, at the urging of President-elect Vladimir Putin, ratified START II and on April 22 approved the 1996 Comprehensive Test Ban Treaty. At the same time, however, the legislature also endorsed a revised military doctrine authorizing use of nuclear weapons "if the very existence of the country" were in jeopardy.

A visit by U.S. president Bill Clinton to Russia in June 2000 produced a bilateral agreement on the disposal of weapons-grade plutonium and on setting up an early-warning center—the first permanent U.S.-Russian military operation—to reduce the risk of accidental nuclear war.

In July 2000 the government introduced a new foreign policy doctrine favoring pragmatism, cooperation with NATO, closer ties with China and India, and "active dialogue" with the United States. Moscow and Washington differed, however, over the contemplated U.S. limited missile defense plan, with Russian officials charging that the proposed warhead intercept system would violate the 1972 Anti-Ballistic Missile (ABM) Treaty. The United States formally withdrew from the ABM Treaty in 2002, straining relations with Russia.

In a meeting in Moscow on May 24, 2002, presidents Putin and George W. Bush signed the Treaty of Moscow (the Strategic Offensive Reductions Treaty—SORT), committing both countries to reducing nuclear stockpiles by two-thirds over the next decade. Other summit concerns included improved cooperation in counterterrorism and in trade relations, particularly with regard to the energy sector.

On May 28, 2002, in Rome, Italy, NATO and Russia signed Rome Declaration, establishing a NATO-Russia Council for the purpose of discussing nonproliferation, combating terrorism, and peacekeeping. On May 29, at a Russian-EU summit in Moscow, the EU recognized Russia as a market economy, as did the United States shortly thereafter, thereby advancing Russia's efforts to enter the WTO.

In September 2003 Kazakhstan and Ukraine joined Russia and Belarus in signing a treaty intended to create a Single Economic Space, which includes a free trade zone and greater coordination of economic policy.

In October 2004 the legislature ratified the Kyoto Protocol, aimed at combating global warming. Although President Putin had expressed reservations as to whether the protocol was in Russia's best interests, ratification became central to establishing closer relations with the EU.

In 2005 China and Russia held their first joint military exercises.

Following severe reductions in gas shipments to the Ukraine in 2006 over a debt dispute, the crisis was ultimately resolved peacefully, but tensions between the two countries remained, owing in part to Russia's opposition to Ukraine's goal of joining NATO and the EU.

Russia's relations with the United Kingdom in 2006 suffered in the wake of the murder of former security agent Aleksandr LITVINENKO, a vocal critic of President Putin, who had defected. Litvinenko died in London in November of poisoning by radioactive polonium-210. Russia refused to extradite Andrei LUGOVOI, an LDPR member of the State Duma and the principal target of the British investigation, and instead attempted to implicate the exiled Boris Berezovsky in Litvinenko's poisoning. Relations with the United Kingdom subsequently remained tense. (Russia has continued to reject requests to extradite Lugovoi.)

At a Russia-EU summit in May 2007, leaders addressed criticism of Russia's human rights record, especially in Chechnya, and the future status of Kosovo, among other issues. Russia continued to reject Kosovar independence without Serbian approval even after Kosovo declared independence in February 2008. Western recognition of Kosovo was viewed by some analysts as one of the provocations leading to Russia's recognition of South Ossetia and Abkhazia in Georgia, a staunch Western ally.

Russia continued to struggle against U.S. plans to deploy a defensive missile shield in Europe, which would include placing intercept missiles in Poland and a radar installation in the Czech Republic. Though the United States claimed that the shield would not target Russia and its purpose was to protect against "rogue" states such as Iran, Russia viewed the shield as a national security threat. Putin threatened to retarget Russian missiles on Europe if the missile defense system was deployed. Further, in July 2007 Putin announced that Russia intended to suspend its participation in the CFE Treaty, partly over the proposed missile shield and partly because some NATO members had never ratified the revised treaty.

Differences between Russia and the United States persisted over Iran's efforts to develop nuclear power, which would give it the capacity to enrich uranium for weapons. In 2007, when Iran reportedly violated requirements of the Non-Proliferation Treaty, the United States and other Western countries attempted to force Iran to dismantle its nuclear programs with threats of sanctions. Russia has consistently voted against sanctions against Iran in the UN Security Council, claiming that all states have a right to develop nuclear energy. Amid heightened tensions between the United States and Iran, Putin traveled to Tehran and met with President Mahmoud Ahmadinejad in October 2007, marking the first visit by a Russian or Soviet leader to Iran since 1943.

Following Russian occupation of South Ossetia and Abkhazia in August 2008, Russia recognized the provinces as independent.

U.S. president Barack Obama moved to "reset" relations with Russia in July 2009, when he met in Moscow with President Medvedev and Prime Minister Putin, both sides pledging cooperation. The two countries agreed to further reduce nuclear arsenals and resume military contacts that had been suspended during Russia's war with Georgia. Also, Russia agreed to open its airspace to allow U.S. troops and weapons to be transported to Afghanistan.

Relations with Belarus deteriorated in 2009, when a dispute was revived after President Lukashenka told his government the country must no longer rely on Russia. Putin subsequently pledged to continue to provide financial support to Belarus. The two countries ultimately reached an agreement on oil supplies in January 2010, but in June Russia dramatically cut gas supplies to Belarus. However, the matter was resolved in a few days when both sides agreed to repay the debts they owed to each other.

The election of Viktor Yanukovych as president of Ukraine in February 2010 brought an improvement in relations. In April agreements were reached on the cost of Russian gas supplies to the Ukraine, which will receive a rebate on prices until 2019. Collaterally, Ukraine granted permission to Russia to station its Black Sea Fleet at Sevastopol until 2042.

In March 2010 Russia and the United States agreed to the New START Treaty, which provides for both sides to ultimately reduce their deployments to no more than 1,550 strategic warheads and 700 launchers. The treaty was ratified by the U.S. Senate in December 2010. (It was signed by President Obama on February 2, 2011.)

Tensions with Poland heightened following a plane crash near Smolensk, Russia, in April 2010, which killed the Polish president, among other leading Polish political figures who were traveling to a ceremony honoring Polish soldiers killed by the Soviets in the Katyn Massacre during World War II. Russia and Poland subsequently sparred over how to assess blame for the crash. (See the 2013 *Handbook* for details.) Ultimately, however, the event resulted in warming relations between the two countries, as the Russian president and prime minister expressed their condolences and announced a national day of mourning. The gesture of President Putin laying flowers at the crash site and paying tribute alongside Polish prime minister Donald Tusk was reported to have contributed greatly to an enhanced opinion of the Russian leader by the Polish public and helped ease tensions. In November the State Duma passed a resolution stating that the Soviet leader Josef Stalin—not Nazi Germany as had previously been claimed—was responsible for the Katyn Massacre.

In June 2010 Russia was one of five countries that agreed to sanctions against Iran for its nuclear program. Russia's acquiescence was widely attributed to its better relations with the United States.

In 2011 relations between the United States and Russia remained cordial, and in the wake of the uprising against Libyan leader Muammar Qadhafi, Medvedev shifted his position after meeting with President Obama and agreed that the dictator must relinquish control. Also, Russia allowed the United States to transport military equipment over its territory to Afghanistan. After the outbreak of the Syrian civil war, however, Russia has blocked UN resolutions that would impose sanctions on the government of Bashar Al-Assad. a position that continued into 2013.

Trade with Germany increased significantly in 2011, and in June a German company agreed to develop a multimillion-dollar combat training center in Russia. During Medvedev's trip to Germany in July, the two countries signed a number of agreements on culture, politics, science, and economics.

The Eurasian Economic Space, consisting of Belarus, Kazakhstan, and Russia, went into effect on January 1, 2012, creating a single market between the three countries overseen by the Eurasian Commission. This builds on their 2010 customs union, and it is the foundation for the November 18, 2011, agreement to establish a Eurasian Union by 2015, roughly modeled on the European Union. Tajikistan and Kyrgyzstan have both expressed interest in joining.

In August 2012 Russia joined the WTO.

In July 2013 Russia disputed Western claims that the Syrian government had used chemical weapons against its own people. In August a foreign ministry spokesman suggested that rebels had used the weapons as a "provocation" to draw in international intervention, a position that Putin restated in a September 11 editorial in *The New York Times*. In September Russian leaders argued for a negotiated surrender of all Syrian chemical weapons as a way to avoid U.S. military intervention.

Relations with the United States were further complicated by the flight of Edward Snowden to Moscow on June 23. Snowden, a civilian contractor for the U.S. National Security Agency who exposed U.S. Internet and telephone surveillance programs, received temporary asylum in Russia on August 1.

Russia brought economic pressure to bear on several neighboring states in 2013. Energy prices for Armenia were raised in June 2013 and extensive customs checks were briefly declared for all Ukrainian goods entering Russia in August. Both policies were seen as linked to Armenia and Ukraine's efforts to negotiate Association Agreements with the European Union, including expanded trade links. In September Russia briefly imposed a ban on imports of Moldovan wine for the second time in seven years.

Current issues. Suicide bombers targeted major sites in Moscow and its suburbs in late 2009 and during 2010, raising questions about Russia's national security capacity. In January 2011 a suicide bomber killed 36 and wounded 168 at Moscow's Domodevovo airport. The bombing was reported to have caused extreme embarrassment to the Russian government ahead of President Medvedev's upcoming address before the World Economic Forum in Davos, Switzerland. As Medvedev sought international investment at the forum of some $15 billion to support tourism development, including ski resorts in the North Caucasus in advance of the 2014 Winter Olympics in Sochi, the bombings cast doubt on Russia's ability to provide the level of security required for the games. In February a Chechen terrorist group reportedly claimed responsibility for the attack.

Political uncertainty increasingly drew domestic attention, as speculation about the future leadership of the country centered on whether Prime Minister Putin would seek reelection or whether President Medvedev would stand for a second term. Analysts saw divisions between Putin and his supporters, who sought greater state control, and Medvedev and his backers, who favored more modernization and liberal political policies. Putin ended the speculation with an announcement on September 24 that he would contest the 2012 presidential election and that Medvedev, in turn, was likely to become prime minister. Some observers said that a Putin presidency raised concerns about further economic stagnation, as in 2011 alone, there had been some $70 billion leaving the country as investors shied away due to the political uncertainty.

The 2011 parliamentary elections were widely criticized as fraudulent by opposition parties and media, a charge partially supported by an OSCE report that stated that "there was no real competition" in the election. Protests in Moscow on December 5, 2011, grew by December 10 into the largest protests since the 1990s, spreading to St. Petersburg, Novosibirsk, Yekaterinburg, and almost 90 other towns and cities across Russia. Protesters demanded an annulment of the elections, official investigations into voting fraud, greater liberty to register parties, and new elections. Subsequent protests on December 24 and February 4, 2012, were even larger and marked by large counter-protests in support of the government. New rounds of protests broke out on March 5, in reaction to Putin's reelection, and May 6, the day before his inauguration. The May protest in Moscow was marred by clashes between police and protestors and the reported arrest of hundreds; prior to an additional round of protests on June 12, new laws on demonstrations went into effect that allow protestors engaging in unauthorized demonstrations to be fined or jailed.

A series of smaller terrorist attacks continued into 2012, chiefly in Chechnya and Dagestan. The most significant was a pair of bombings on May 3 in the capital of Dagestan that killed 13 and injured 130, but four other reported attacks (three in August 2012 alone) killed 25 people.

On August 17, 2012, three members of the Russian female punk band Pussy Riot were found guilty of "hooliganism" and sentenced to two years of labor in a penal colony for performing an anti-Putin protest song on February 21, 2012, in Moscow Cathedral of Christ the Savior. Their trial gathered international attention and helped spark a new major protest by opposition parties on September 12.

Opposition protests continued, with significant rallies on December 15, 2012, January 13, 2013 (in response to a recent law banning U.S. citizens from adopting Russian children), and May 6. The government has continued to take action against protest organizers. Opposition activist Sergei Udaltsov, who helped organize protests in 2011 and 2012, was charged with organizing "mass disorder" and placed under house arrest in February 2013. On July 18, 2013, opposition leader Aleksei NAVALNY was convicted of embezzlement and sentenced to five years' imprisonment. Despite the conviction, Navalny competed in the September 8, 2013, Moscow mayoral election, placing second with 27.2 percent of the vote (to 51.4 percent for Sergey Sobyanin, a member of United Russia).

In June 2013 the Duma adopted a law prohibiting the distribution to minors of "propaganda" that advocates "non-traditional sexual relations," and included provisions allowing the police to expel or detain "pro-gay" foreigners. In July a law was passed banning the adoption of Russian-born children by anyone from a country that allows same-sex marriage. The policies came under international scrutiny in the wake of the upcoming Olympic games in Sochi.

In August 2013 the Russian government began a popularly received roundup of illegal immigrants, mostly from Central Asia and Vietnam. The policy, triggered by the widely reported July 27 assault on a police officer in a Moscow open-air market by the family of an ethnic Dagestani detainee, had led to the arrest of nearly 5,000 illegal immigrants by mid-September.

POLITICAL PARTIES AND GROUPS

The advent of political pluralism in the Soviet Union in 1990 and the suspension of the CPSU in August 1991 stimulated the emergence of over 200 parties, most of which did not survive in the successor Russian Federation. Some three dozen formations were active in the run-up to the December 1993 legislative elections; ten ultimately gained representation in the State Duma. Thereafter, the party scene was characterized by frequent realignments and new formations, particularly among the pro-market and centrist groupings broadly supportive of the Yeltsin administration. The launching in May 1995 of the center-right Our Home Is Russia (NDR) formation as the "government" party and concurrent moves to form a center-left opposition bloc were seen as an attempt by the political establishment to create a two-party system that would exclude from power the ultranationalists on the far right and the revived Communists on the reactionary left. However, both camps retained sizeable popular constituencies in the complex party maneuverings preceding the legislative balloting of December 17, 1995, at which more than 40 parties, movements, and alliances offered candidates.

As of January 1, 1999, the Ministry of Justice reported 141 registered political organizations, more than 40 of which had sought official status during December 1998 to meet the eligibility deadline for the December 1999 legislative election. However, electoral laws permitted a political formation registered for less than a full year to contest the election if it constituted an alliance of at least two legally registered parties or movements. In the end, 26 organizations qualified for the election, including several alliances formed in 1999. Of the four most important groups active in September 2000, only the Communist Party of the Russian Federation (KPRF) predated 1998, the other three being the Putin-backed Unity, the left-centrist Fatherland, and the right- centrist Union of Right Forces (SPS).

At the beginning of 2001 there were 56 registered parties and 156 other political groups, but a law passed by both houses of the Federal Assembly in June and subsequently signed by President Putin rewrote registration requirements to the detriment of small parties. The law stipulated that to compete nationally parties must have at least 10,000 members, with no fewer than 100 members registered in each of 45 or more of the country's then 89 regions and republics.

The new parties law accelerated a process of political consolidation that had begun in anticipation of its passage. In May 2001, with most of its constituent groups having agreed to a formal merger, the SPS held a congress to authorize its restructuring as a unified party. A second congress in December confirmed the decision, and it was officially registered as such in March 2002. In July 2001 Unity, All Russia, and Fatherland had formed an alliance that was registered in December as the Unity and Fatherland–United Russia; its central component organizations voted to dissolve as separate entities in February 2002, by which time United Russia was already being referred to in some circles as the latest "party of power." Consolidations were also taking place among Russia's less significant parties.

For the State Duma election of December 2003 a total of 44 parties were eligible to present candidate lists for the proportional component. (Twenty public associations were also eligible, but only as members of electoral blocs.) In the end, 18 individual parties and 5 electoral blocs competed, with only 3 parties and 1 bloc meeting the 5 percent threshold for proportional seats: United Russia, the KPRF, the far-right Liberal Democratic Party of Russia (LDPR), and the Motherland–People's Patriotic Union bloc, elements of which subsequently united as the Motherland party. (For a complete discussion of parties and blocs that contested the 2003 election, see the 2005–2006 or 2007 *Handbook.*)

Shortly after the 2003 election, President Putin, backed by United Russia's overwhelming majority faction in the State Duma, began passing legislation intended to eliminate Russia's many medium-sized and small parties before the December 2007 election. For a party to register, it must now have at least 50,000 members, with at least 500 members in each of half the country's regions and 250 in each of the rest. Parties failing to meet the membership test must reregister as public organizations rather than parties or be disbanded by the courts. Single-mandate districts have been eliminated, and the threshold for winning proportional seats now stands at 7 percent of the total national vote. Parties and associations are no longer allowed to form electoral blocs, and members of one party are prohibited from appearing on the candidate list of another party, although individuals without a current party affiliation may be included. Except for those parties that won list seats in the preceding State Duma, parties must pay a deposit of $2.35 million (refundable for those winning at least 4 percent of the 2007 vote) or submit 200,000 supporting signatures; if more than 5 percent of a party's signatures are declared invalid, the party is disqualified. In addition, "none of the above" has been eliminated as a ballot option; it had frequently been used to cast a protest vote. Minimum turnout requirements for national elections have been eliminated, and lawmakers who switch parties after election are to be stripped of their seats.

In the run-up to the 2007 State Duma election, the Patriots of Russia (PR) formed a coalition with the Party of Russia's Rebirth (PVR). The Russian Ecological Party ("The Greens") was disqualified for allegedly faking signatures. While 11 registered parties were deemed eligible for the December election, only 4 reached the 7 percent threshold for election: United Russia, the KPRF, the LDPR, and Just Russia.

In May 2011 Prime Minister Putin established what he said was a new political movement, styled as the All Russian Popular Front, to bring together, with United Russia, "all people who are united by a common desire to strengthen our country," ahead of the December 2011 legislative and March 2012 presidential elections.

Governing Party:

United Russia (*Edinaya Rossiya*). In July 2001 Unity (*Edinstvo*), All Russia (*Vsya Rossiya*), and Fatherland (*Otechestvo*) organized an alliance that was registered in December as Unity and Fatherland–United Russia (*Edinstvo i Otechestvo–Edinaya Rossiya*). The members of all three then voted in February 2002 to dissolve as separate entities.

The Unity bloc, also known as the Inter-Regional Movement "Unity" (*Mezhregionalnoye Dvizhenie "Edinstvo"—Medved* [Bear]), had been announced in September 1999 by nearly three dozen leaders of regions and republics (some of whom later withdrew their support) to contest the State Duma elections in December. Backed by President Yeltsin and Prime Minister Putin as a counter to the Fatherland–All Russia bloc, Unity offered no ideological platform and was described by some commentators as a "virtual party."

Apparently benefiting from Putin's prosecution of the war in Chechnya and his accompanying rise in popularity, Unity finished second to the KPRF in the December 1999 federal election, winning 23 percent of the vote and 73 seats. In May 2000, with President Putin in attendance, Unity held its founding congress as a political party. On the same day former prime minister Viktor Chernomyrdin's Our Home Is Russia (*Nash Dom–Rossiya*—NDR), having won only 1.2 percent of the party list vote and 8 constituency seats at the most recent State Duma election, voted to disband in favor of Unity.

Little more than a year earlier, in April 1999, the organizing committee of All Russia had met in an effort to establish in the Federal Assembly a regionalist power bloc dominated by various regional governors and presidents. Two days later it allied with the Fatherland movement, which had been founded in late 1998 by Yuri Luzhkov, the mayor of Moscow. The resultant Fatherland–All Russia (*Otechestvo–Vsya Rossiya*—OVR) won 13 percent of the party list vote and 66 seats at the December State Duma election.

In April 2001 the Unity faction in the State Duma and the Fatherland–All Russia faction announced that they would work together with the goal of forming a unified party. Within days, two additional parliamentary factions, Russia's Regions and the People's Deputies, had agreed to cooperate with them on selected issues, thereby—at least on paper—creating a 234-seat majority bloc in the State Duma.

In the December 2003 parliamentary election, the unified party, now known as United Russia (sometimes translated as Unified Russia), with President Putin's backing, was the clear victor, winning 36.6 percent of the proportional vote and a slim majority of the filled seats. More important, it soon attracted additional support from independents and other parties, enabling its Duma faction to chair all committees and to surpass the two-thirds threshold for making constitutional changes.

United Russia has emerged as the vehicle for what Putin's supporters label "reform" (and his detractors, authoritarianism). It espouses "social conservatism"—a blend of market economics, promotion of the middle class, nationalism, and support for social order and stability. There has, however, been tension between the party's more rightist market forces and those committed to a more "social orientation," some of whom strongly objected to a Putin initiative that replaced guaranteed social service benefits with cash payments.

United Russia extended its political control in March 2006, winning 55 percent of the vote in eight regional and republican legislative elections. In March 2007 it took 46 percent in winning control in 13 out of 14 legislatures.

Prior to the December 2007 legislative election, United Russia continued to pick up adherents as smaller parties dissolved. Speaking at a party congress on October 1, 2007, President Putin announced that he had agreed to head the party's candidate list and would consider leading the party and serving as prime minister following the end of his presidential term in 2008. In the December election, United Russia won 64.3 percent of the vote. A month before the election, the Agrarian Party of Russia (*Agrarnaya Partiya Rossii*—APR), which had been aligned with the Communists, merged with United Russia. (See the 2009 *Handbook* for details on the APR.) Also in 2008 United Russia shortened its name by dropping the "All Russia" rubric.

Following the election of President Medvedev in 2008, whose candidacy was supported by United Russia, Putin, as had been expected, was named prime minister. In April Putin was elected to a four-year term in the newly created post of chair of the party. The party's strength was further consolidated by its victories in most of the March 2009 mayoral elections and in the regional elections of October. Following a series of televised political party debates in mid-2009, United Russia was reported to have achieved its highest-ever popularity rating of 58 percent. Earlier in the year the mayor of Smolensk was dismissed from the party allegedly because of the poor state of infrastructure in his district. However, observers said the party was backing another mayoral candidate, and when the incumbent defiantly added his name to the ballot, he was expelled.

United Russia was concerned about its relatively poor showing in the regional and municipal elections of March 2010. Consequently, the party began to hold mass meetings and to seek new candidates for leadership, particularly on the local level, while also looking for projects to help economic development, especially in Siberia.

United Russia held national party primaries in July 2011 to increase the number of candidates for the December election to the Duma and perhaps increase the party's appeal, which had been waning. The party was suffering from a reputation for corruption and authoritarianism; further, the Communist Party accused it of using state funds to finance the primaries.

In September 2011, at a party convention in Moscow, Medvedev announced that he would defer to Putin as the party's flagbearer in the 2012 presidential election. If Putin were to be elected, Medvedev would become prime minister.

In the December 4, 2011, parliamentary election, United Russia won 49.32 percent of the popular vote, securing 238 seats. In the presidential election on March 4, 2012, Putin received 63.64 percent of the vote, easily defeating Gennady Zyuganov of the KPRF, who placed second with 17.18 percent of the vote.

Following Putin's election, on May 26 Medvedev was announced as the new leader of the party.

Leaders: Dmitry MEDVEDEV (Chair and Prime Minister), Vladimir PUTIN (President), Boris GRYZLOV, Mintimer SHAIMIYEV, Sergei SHOIGU, Andrei VOROBYOV, Andrei ISAEV, Sergei NEVEROV (Secretary).

Other Parties in the State Duma:

Communist Party of the Russian Federation (*Kommunisticheskaya Partiya Rossiiskoi Federatsii*—KPRF). The KPRF is a late 1992 revival of the former Communist Party of the Soviet Union—CPSU (*Kommunisticheskaya Partiya Sovetskogo Soyuza*—KPSS), which was suspended in August 1991 and banned in November. The KPRF ran third in the legislative poll of December 1993 and thereafter generally opposed the Yeltsin administration, although in January 1995 a Communist was appointed justice minister. At the December State Duma election the KPRF won a plurality of 157 of the 450 seats, including 99 on a 22 percent share of the proportional vote.

KPRF leader Gennadi Zyuganov contested the mid-1996 presidential election on a platform deploring the erosion of Russia's industrial base by IMF-imposed policies and promising to restore economic sovereignty. He finished a close second to President Yeltsin in the first round on June 16, with 32 percent of the vote, but lost to the incumbent in the runoff on July 3, taking 40.3 percent of the vote. The KPRF then sought to consolidate the left-wing and conservative backing obtained by Zyuganov, initiating the formation in August of the opposition People's Patriotic Union of Russia (NPSR—see Patriots of Russia, below).

After having unsuccessfully attempted to forge a "For Victory" (*Za Pobedu*—ZP) electoral coalition of Communists, Agrarians, and others to contest the December 1999 State Duma balloting, the KPRF basically ran independently, with "For Victory" reduced to little more than a slogan. As in 1995, it won a plurality, taking 114 seats and a party list vote share of 24 percent. Three months later Zyuganov again finished second, with 29 percent of the vote, in the presidential contest.

In May 2002 the party's Central Committee expelled three leading members who refused to resign from leadership posts in the State Duma after the ascendant United Russia won committee chairs away from the KPRF. The most prominent dissenter was the chair of the Duma, Gennadi Seleznev, who subsequently built his patriotic Russia movement (*Rossiya*) into the Party of Russia's Rebirth (PVR, below).

At the December 2003 State Duma election the KPRF saw its support halved—to 12.6 percent of the proportional vote and a total of only 52 seats—in part because a significant fraction of the leftist vote was won by the new Motherland coalition. Sergei Glazyev, a former Communist who had sought an electoral alliance with the KPRF before forming the Motherland coalition, was one of several prominent leftists who had grown disenchanted with Zyuganov's continuing leadership, which led, in mid-2004, to further ruptures. In July supporters of Zyuganov and Vladimir TIKHONOV held competing congresses, with the Ministry of Justice ultimately ruling in Zyuganov's favor. Tikhonov went on to form the All-Russian Communist Party of the Future (*Vserossiiskaya Kommunisticheskaya Partiya Budushchego*—VKPB). Zyuganov also lost the support of Gennadi Semigin, chair of the NPSR, who was expelled from the KPRF and later formed the Patriots of Russia.

The KPRF's 2004 presidential candidate, Nikolai Kharitonov, finished second, with 13.7 percent of the vote.

The KPRF has subsequently led opposition to a number of President Putin's initiatives, including changes to social benefits policies. In March 2006 the KPRF came in second in six of eight regions holding legislative elections, improving its representation in five regions due in part to the fact that competing leftist party *Rodina* was excluded from the balloting in all but one of the regions. In March 2007 the KPRF received 16 percent of the vote in 14 regional and republican legislative elections.

In the December 2007 State Duma election the KPRF received 11.6 percent of the votes. Zyuganov stood as the party's presidential candidate for the third time on March 2, 2008, finishing second with 17.8 percent.

The KPRF fared poorly in the regional and municipal elections of October 2009, gaining only 5.3 percent of the vote nationwide. However, it was the only other party besides United Russia to win seats in the Moscow Duma (3 of 35 seats).

In the December 4, 2011, parliamentary election, the KPRF won 19.19 percent of the popular vote, securing 92 seats. In the March 4, 2012, presidential election, KPRF candidate Gennady Zyuganov won 17.18 percent of the popular vote, placing second.

Leaders: Gennadi ZYUGANOV (Chair and 2012 presidential candidate), Vladimir Stepanovich NIKITIN, Ivan MELNIKOV (Deputy Chair), Vladimir KASHIN (Deputy Chair), Nikolai AREFIEV.

A Just Russia–Motherland, Pensioners, Life (*Spravedlivaya Rossiya–Rodina/Persionery/Zhizn*—SR). (*Spravedlivaya Rossiya* is usually translated as A Just Russia, but at times the party is called Fair

Russia.) A Just Russia was established in October 2006 by the merger of three parties: Motherland, the Russian Party of Life, and the Russian Party of Pensioners. Also joining, in April 2007, was the People's Party of the Russian Federation (NPRF).

Motherland (*Rodina*) had originated as the Party of Russian Regions (*Partiya Rossiiskih Regionov*—PRR), which joined the Party of National Rebirth "People's Will" (see the People's Union, below), the Socialist United Party of Russia (Spiritual Heritage) (*Sotsialisticheskaya Edinaya Partiya Rossii [Dukhovnoe Nasledie]*—SEPR), and smaller groups in forming the Motherland–People's Patriotic Union (*Rodina–Narodno-Patrioticheskii Soyuz*) electoral bloc in September 2003. Appealing to the patriotic left, the Motherland bloc surprised most observers by drawing support from the Communists and winning 9 percent of the proportional vote and a total of 36 State Duma seats in December.

The bloc's principal organizers, Sergei GLAZYEV and Dmitri ROGOZIN, had been associated with a number of political formations since the breakup of the Soviet Union, including the Congress of Russian Communities (*Kongress Russkikh Obshchin*—KRO), a moderately nationalist movement that dated from 1995. Much of the KRO's membership had followed Rogozin into the NPRF after its formation in 2001. Glazyev later became the chair of the SEPR, founded in March 2002 by merger of the Socialist Party of Russia (*Sotsialisticheskaya Partiya Rossii*—SPR) and Alexei PODBEREZKIN's Spiritual Heritage (*Dukhovnoe Nasledie*), which dated from 1996 and 1995, respectively. For the 2003 elections Glazyev had approached the KPRF about an alliance but was turned down, leading to his involvement in forming the *Rodina* alliance with Rogozin.

Soon after the unexpected success of the Motherland–People's Patriotic Union in December 2003, their ideological differences and competing political ambitions caused a rupture between Glazyev and Rogozin. In February 2004 Rogozin engineered the renaming of the PRR as the *Rodina* party, after which Glazyev, who had decided to run against President Putin, was removed from the leadership. As an independent, Glazyev finished third, with 4.1 percent of the vote, in the March 2004 balloting. Three months later his new public-political organization, For a Decent Life (*Za Dostoinuyu Zhizn*—ZDZ), based on a loyal SEPR faction and various other elements of the Motherland coalition, was denied registration by the Ministry of Justice. In March 2006 Rogozin announced his resignation from all senior party posts but remained a member of *Rodina* until formation of A Just Russia. In 2007 he formed the Great Russia (VR, below) party. Glazyev, who initially supported formation of Just Russia, later announced his retirement from politics.

The Russian Party of Life (*Rossiiskaya Partiya Zhizni*—RPZh) was established in 2002 by Sergei Mironov, chair of the Federation Council. Centrist in nature, the RPZh focused on quality-of-life issues. For the 2003 State Duma election the RPZh forged an electoral bloc with the Party of Russia's Rebirth (PVR, below), but the bloc won only 1.9 percent of the proportional vote and 3 constituency seats. Mironov won less than 1 percent of the vote as a candidate for president in 2004.

The Russian Party of Pensioners (*Rossiiskaya Partiya Pensionerov*—RPP) dated from 1997. It contested the 2003 State Duma elections in a bloc with the Party of Social Justice (PSS, below), winning 3.1 percent of the vote but no seats, which contributed to the suspension of the party's chair, Sergei ATROSHENKO in January 2004. He was succeeded by Valery GARTUNG, initially in an acting capacity. In October the RPP joined in forming the Patriots of Russia coalition, but it remained separate from the subsequently organized Patriots of Russia party. In February 2005 Gartung broke with United Russia's parliamentary faction, primarily because of his opposition to President Putin's plan to replace guaranteed social service benefits with monetary payments (the so-called cash-for-benefits reform), which was widely viewed as adversely affecting pensioners. Seemingly as a direct result of this action, it was discovered that Gartung's election as party leader involved irregularities, which ultimately cost him the post that autumn.

The People's Party of the Russian Federation (*Narodnaya Partiya Rossiiskoi Federatsii*—NPRF), formed from Gennadi RAIKOV's preexisting People's Deputy group in the State Duma, was registered as a party in October 2001. At the December 2003 elections it won only 1.2 percent of the proportional vote but 17 district seats. Its deputies then elected to sit in the United Russia parliamentary faction. Citing his duties in the Duma, Raikov stepped down as party chair in April 2004 and has most recently served on the Central Electoral Commission.

At a January 2005 party congress the NPRF adopted a more social-democratic platform and criticized Putin's cash-for-benefits reform. The party leadership later threatened to pull its deputies from the United Russia deputy group, but in May the majority of the NPRF's 17 deputies instead opted to join United Russia to ensure their inclusion on the United Russia party list for the 2007 Duma election. Party chief Gennadi Gudkov later attempted to unite various leftist parties, but the effort failed and he joined A Just Russia in March 2007, a month before the NPRF was deregistered by the courts.

Since its formation, A Just Russia/Fair Russia has remained generally supportive of President Putin's policies while attempting to establish itself as the country's principal alternative to United Russia. Its candidate list for the 2007 State Duma election included various prominent figures whose parties had failed to meet the new stringent registration requirements, including Oleg SHEIN of the Russian Labor Party (*Rossiiskaya Partiya Truda*—RPT) and Ivan GRACHEV of the Development of Enterprise (*Razvitie Predprinimatelstva*—RP), a business-oriented party that was formed in 1998 and won 1 constituency seat in the 2003 State Duma election. A Just Russia received 7.8 percent of the vote in the December 2007 State Duma election.

In 2008 the Russian Ecological Party "The Greens" (*Rossiiskaya Ekologicheskaya Partiya "Zelenye"*—REP "The Greens") and the SEPR merged with A Just Russia, as did the Party of Social Justice (*Partiya Sotsialnoi Spravedlivosti*—PSS). (For details on these parties, see the 2009 *Handbook.*)

In February 2010 United Russia agreed to coordinate its actions with A Just Russia in support of Just Russia's Sergei Mironov in his role as chair of the Federation Council. However, prior to the March local elections, the LDPR, KPRF, and A Just Russia agreed to combine efforts against United Russia by refraining from campaigning against each other. Consequently, A Just Russia won several mayoral elections. In May 2011 Mironov was sacked as chair of the Federation Council, resulting in the party's losing much of its financial and administrative resources. In June, A Just Russia declared that it would not support the candidate (ultimately, Putin) from United Russia in the 2012 presidential elections.

In the December 4, 2011, parliamentary election, A Just Russia won 13.24 percent of the popular vote, securing 64 seats. REP "The Greens," however, had received no seats in the December 2011 election in the lists of A Just Russia and accordingly withdrew and reestablished itself as an independent party in February 2012.

In the March 4, 2012, presidential election, A Just Russia candidate Sergei Mironov won 3.85 percent of the popular vote, placing fifth.

On September 14 A Just Russia parliamentary deputy Gennady Gudkov was expelled from the Duma, leading to accusations by the party that United Russia was attempting to repress the opposition.

Leaders: Nikolai LEVICHEV (Chair), Sergei MIRONOV (Party Leader and 2012 presidential candidate), Aleksandr BABAKOV.

Political Party LDPR (*Politicheskaya partiya LDPR*). Founded as the **Liberal Democratic Party of Russia** (*Liberalno-Demokraticheskaya Partiya Rossii*), the LDPR took its current name, based on its former acronym, at its December 2012 congress. The far-right LDPR was launched in Moscow in March 1990 as an all-Union grouping. Its leader, the xenophobic Vladimir Zhirinovsky, drew over 6 million votes (7.8 percent) in the 1991 presidential poll. Zhirinovsky had made a number of extravagant promises, such as providing each Russian with cheap vodka and launching a campaign to reconquer Finland. The party was officially banned in August 1992 on grounds that it had falsified its membership lists; however, it was permitted to contest the 1993 legislative poll, at which it ran second to Russia's Choice overall, while heading the party list returns with 22.8 percent of the national vote.

Although Zhirinovsky signed the April 1994 Treaty on Civil Accord between President Yeltsin and more than 200 political groups, his increasingly controversial utterances caused him to be shunned by the political establishment, including his own natural allies. In the December 1995 legislative balloting the LDPR slipped to 11.4 percent of the proportional vote, coming in third with 51 seats. In the mid-1996 presidential contest, Zhirinovsky managed only fifth place in the first round, with 5.7 percent of the vote. The LDPR continued to fare poorly in regional elections in 1997.

In October 1999 the Central Electoral Commission disqualified the LDPR party list from the December State Duma election because two of its top three candidates—one of whom was being investigated for money laundering—had not fully declared their assets. Zhirinovsky cobbled together an alternative list, the Zhirinovsky Bloc (*Blok Zhirinovskogo*), based on the small affiliated Spiritual Revival of Russia Party (*Partiya Duhovnogo Vozrozhdeniya Rossii*—PDVR), led by his half-sister Lyubov ZHIRINOVSKAYA and Oleg FINKO, and the Russia Free

Youth Union (*Rossiiskii Soyuz Svobodnoi Molodezhi*—RSSM), led by Yegor SOLOMATIN. The bloc won a 6 percent party list vote share and 17 seats at the election. In the March 2000 presidential contest Zhirinovsky polled 2.7 percent of the vote, for fifth place.

At the December 2003 State Duma election the LDPR finished with an unexpected 11.5 percent of the proportional vote and a total of 36 seats. This momentum did not last, however. Zhirinovsky, acknowledging President Putin's insurmountable lead going into the 2004 presidential election, chose not to run. The party's candidate, Oleg MALYSHKIN, finished fifth with 2 percent of the vote. The LDPR did not reach the threshold for winning seats in two of eight regions holding legislative elections in March 2006, and lost significant ground in the other 6. In March 2007 it won only 9 percent of the total vote in the 14 regions and republics holding elections. In the December 2007 State Duma election, the LDPR won 8 percent of the vote. In the March 2008 presidential election, Zhirinovsky finished third with 9.5 percent.

In 2009 President Medvedev said that although the LDPR was an opposition party, he was certain compromise and cooperation were possible, the LDPR having often voted with United Russia in the past. The LDPR won 4.1 percent of the vote in the regional and municipal elections of October 2009, and it finished third behind United Russia and the Communists in local elections of March 2010.

In June 2011 Zhirinovsky called for repeal of anti-extremist legislation.

In the December 4, 2011, parliamentary election, the LDPR won 11.67 percent of the popular vote, securing 56 seats. In the March 4, 2012, presidential election, LDPR candidate Vladimir Zhirinovsky won 6.22 percent of the popular vote, placing fourth.

Leaders: Vladimir ZHIRINOVSKY (Chair and 2012 presidential candidate), Igor LEBEDEV, Vasily ZHURKO, Oleg LAVROV, Alexei OSTROVSKY, Maxim ROHMISTROV.

Other Parties That Contested the 2011 State Duma Election:

Yabloko—formally, the Russian Democratic Party *"Yabloko"* (*Rossiiskaya Demokraticheskaya Partiya "Yabloko"*)—descends from the Yavlinsky-Boldyrev-Lukin Bloc, an electoral grouping formed in October 1993 by economist Grigori Yavlinsky, scientist Yuri BOLDYREV, and former ambassador to the United States Vladimir LUKIN, who, while endorsing market reforms, opposed what they viewed as Yeltsin's "shock therapy." In December 1993 the grouping won 7.8 percent of the party list vote. Boldyrev left the party in 1994. (In 1999 he formed an electoral bloc with the KRO—see A Just Russia, above.) Yabloko's name (which translates as "Apple") comes from an acronym of the three figures' names (Ya-B-L-oko).

Yabloko finished fourth in the December 1995 legislative balloting, winning 45 seats. In the mid-1996 presidential contest Yavlinsky placed fourth in the first round, winning 7.3 percent of the vote and then giving qualified endorsement to Boris Yeltsin in the runoff balloting. Debates over the 1997 and 1998 budgets showed *Yabloko,* rather than the Communists or the nationalists, to be the most uncompromising opponent of the government's spending plans.

At the 1999 State Duma elections *Yabloko* won 21 seats. During the campaign it had been the only major party to criticize the government's conduct of the war in Chechnya, particularly the bombing of Grozny. Yavlinsky finished third, with 5.8 percent of the vote, in the March 2000 presidential election.

At the 2003 lower house election *Yabloko* won only 4.3 percent of the proportional vote and 4 seats. The poor showing of both *Yabloko* and the Union of Right Forces (SPS, below) rekindled discussions, first broached in 2000, of a merger, although Yavlinsky had significant differences with SPS leader Anatoly Chubais. In July 2004 Yavlinsky won reelection as party head over Yuri KUZNETSOV, who had advocated an alliance with the SPS. In the March 2006 regional elections *Yabloko* and the SPS, running as an electoral alliance, failed to win any legislative seats, and in June the *Yabloko* party congress voted not to pursue the merger. In the December 2007 State Duma election, Yabloko failed to reach the 7 percent threshold and lost its representation in the lower house. In a statement on election day, Yavlinsky claimed that the election had been rigged.

After 15 years as *Yabloko*'s leader, Yavlinsky stepped down on June 21, 2008, though he remained influential within the party. Sergei Mitrokhin, the leader of the party's Moscow branch, took over as party chair.

In January 2009 the party protested as illegal the arrests of its members who demonstrated in memory of slain journalists and liberal public figures. Another party activist was arrested at a demonstration in April.

Yabloko won only 4 seats of the more than 42,000 seats available nationally in the October 2009 regional and municipal elections and complained of fraud. (Mitrokhin stated that according to official returns *Yabloko* received no ballots in the precinct in which he and his family vote.) The March 2010 local elections were also dismal for the party, their candidates having been barred from competing in the Sverdlovsk and Kaluga regions because a large number of the signatures on the petitions for registration had been declared invalid.

In the December 4, 2011, parliamentary election, Yabloko won 3.43 percent of the popular vote, failing to pass the 7 percent threshold and gain representation.

Leaders: Sergei MITROKHIN (Chair), Alexei ARBATOV (Vice Chair), Mikhail AMOSOV, Elena DUBROVINA, Sergei V. IVANENKO (Treasurer).

Patriots of Russia (*Patrioty Rossii*—PR). Founder and former Communist Gennadi Semigin announced formation of the PR as a unified political party in April 2005. The previous October Semigin had spearheaded formation of a PR coalition encompassing ten predominantly leftist parties and movements, including his own People's Patriotic Union of Russia (*Narodno-Patrioticheskii Soyuz Rossii*—NPSR), which had been organized in 1996 by the KPRF's Gennadi Zyuganov as a means of consolidating left-wing, nationalist parties and movements. Zyuganov had lost control of the NPSR in mid-2004, however, during the dispute over leadership of the KPRF. Other initial participants in the PR coalition included the All-Russian Communist Party of the Future (VKPB; see under KPRF, above); the Eurasian Party–Union of Russian Patriots (EP-SPR; see under VR-ES, below); the National-Patriotic Forces of the Russian Federation (*Natsionalno-Patrioticheskii Sil Rossiiskoi Federatsii*—NPSRF), led by Shmidt DZOBLAEV; the Party of Russia's Rebirth (PVR, below); the Party of Workers' Self-Government (*Partiya Samoypravleniya Trudyashchikhsya*—PST), founded in 1995 by Svyatoslav FYODOROV, who finished sixth in the 1996 presidential election; the People's Patriotic Party of Russia (NPPR); the Russian Party of Pensioners (RPP; see under Just Russia, above), a wing of the Russian Labor Party (RPT) led by Sergei KHRAMOV; and the Union of People for Education and Science (*Soyuz Liudei za Obrazovanie i Nauku*—SLON), led by Vyacheslav IGRUNOV, one of the original *Yabloko* leaders. The PR also claimed the support of some 30 public organizations.

The PR took part in five of the eight races to regional legislatures in March 2006, passing the 5 percent threshold to win seats in the parliaments of the Kaliningrad and Orenburg regions. It had scant success in the March 2007 regional elections, and received less than 0.9 percent of the vote in the December 2007 State Duma election, failing to win any legislative seats.

The Party of Russia's Rebirth (*Partiya Vozrozhdeniya Rossii*—PVR), led by Gennadi SELEZNEV, and the Party of Peace and Unity (*Partiya Mira i Edinstva*—PME), led by Sazhi UMALATOVA, merged with the PR in 2008. (See the 2009 *Handbook* for details on the PVR and the PME.)

The PR won only 6 out of more than 42,000 seats contested in the October 2009 regional and municipal elections, and in February 2010 party spokesperson Nadezhda Korneeva complained of the elaborate and expensive process required to gather signatures in order to have candidates compete in an election.

In the December 4, 2011, parliamentary election, the PR won 0.97 percent of the popular vote, failing to pass the 7 percent threshold to gain representation.

Leaders: Gennadi SEMIGIN (Chair), Nadezhda KORNEEVA (Vice Chair).

Right Cause (*Pravoye Delo*—PD). The pro-business liberal Right Cause was formed in November 2008 by the merger of the Union of Right Forces (*Soyuz Pravyh Sil*—SPS), led by Leonid GOZMAN, Civil Force (*Grazhdanskaya Sila*—GS), led by Mikhail BARSHCHEVSKY, and Democratic Party of Russia (*Demokraticheskaya Partiya Rossii*—DPR), led by Andrei BOGDANOV. (See the 2009 *Handbook* for details on these three parties.) It was officially registered on February 18, 2009, becoming only the second new party to obtain registration in recent years (A Just Russia being the other). Right Cause promotes a civil society based on democratic principles and the rule of law, and it urges political and public freedom, along with free and fair elections. Its critics, however, have accused the party of being too closely aligned with President Medvedev and Prime Minister Putin and more or less controlled by the Kremlin.

Rifts in the party over the tripartite leadership and a campaign platform were reported in 2009, and it won only a few seats nationwide in the October regional and municipal elections. Following another self-acknowledged "dismal" performance in the March 2010 local polls, the party appeared to be in a state of disorganization and in danger of collapse

In June 2011 Mikhail PROKHOROV, described as the third richest man in Russia, was named party leader. However, rifts within the party had deepened by September, resulting in the ouster of Prokhorov as party chair because of his leadership style, followed by the resignations of several senior leaders. Some observers claimed the party was deliberately riven by Kremlin loyalists, who feared Prokhorov's potential as a political force. Prokhorov subsequently insisted that the party return $22.8 million in party investments that were intended for the parliamentary campaign. (Prokhorov subsequently stood in the March 4, 2012, presidential election as an independent, winning 7.94 percent of the vote and placing third.)

In the December 4, 2011, parliamentary election, Right Cause won 0.6 percent of the popular vote, failing to pass the 7 percent threshold to gain representation.

Leader: Maratkanov VYACHEVSLAV (Acting Chair).

(For information on parties that have been dissolved or denied registration, see earlier editions of the *Handbook.*)

Other Political Organizations:

Russian Opposition Coordination Council (*Koordinatsionnyi Sovet Rossiiskaya Oppositsii*—KSRO). In June 2012 activists involved in the ongoing protest movement triggered by the 2011 elections created a council to unify the aims and actions of the disparate opposition groups. Elections of 45 council members were held on October 20–22.

Leaders: Alexei NAVALNY, Gennady GUDKOV, Sergei UDALTSOV, Garry KASPAROV, Andrey PIONTKOVSKY, Yevgeniya CHIRIKOVA, Ilya YASHIN, Boris NEMTSOV, Oleg KASHIN.

The Other Russia (*Drugaya Rossiya*—DR). A forum organized in July 2006 by opponents of President Putin, the DR brought together a philosophically incongruous assortment of former government figures, human rights activists, communists, and nationalists. Organizers included former prime minister Mikhail Kasyanov of the **People's Democratic Union** (*Narodno-Demokraticheskii Soyuz*—NDS), a movement formed in March 2006 to unite left-wing and prodemocracy forces beneath a single banner; among the other NDS leaders were Irina Khakamada, SPS (above) founder and 2004 independent presidential candidate, and former SPS Policy Council secretary Ivan STARIKOV. Participants in the Other Russia also included former chess champion Garry Kasparov, founder in 2005 of the centrist **United Civic Front** (*Obyedinyonny Grazhdansky Front*—OGF); the writer Eduard Limonov, whose radical **National Bolshevik Party** (*Natsional-Bolshevistskaya Partiya*—NBP) had been banned as an extremist organization; and Vladimir Ryzhvov of the Republican Party of Russia (above). From December 2006 the principal DR tactic was to convene opposition rallies in major cities. The protests have often been dispersed by the police, with resultant arrests.

In September 2007 differences between Kasparov supporters and Kasyanov led Kasyanov to work outside the forum. He announced formation of **People for Democracy and Justice** (*Narod za demokratiyu i spravedlivost*—NDS) and was nominated as a candidate for the presidential election in December. He was then disqualified by the Central Election Commission, which claimed a large number of his 2 million supporting signatures were invalid. In October DR elements nominated Kasparov as their 2008 presidential candidate. Kasparov withdrew from the presidential election in December. In March 2010 Kasparov was a signatory to a petition circulated by "Putin Must Go," which calls for the resignation of Putin from the government in the interest of creating a free society.

An attempt by Kasyanov, Boris Nemtsov, and others to register a new party, the **People's Freedom Party**, was rejected by the justice ministry in June 2011, but organizers continued to hold rallies pushing their antityranny, anticorruption platform. They further declared that the December 2011 legislative elections would be illegitimate without the party's representation on the ballot.

Leaders: Garry KASPAROV, Eduard LIMONOV.

LEGISLATURE

The 1993 constitution provides for a **Federal Assembly** (*Federalnoe Sobranie*) consisting of a Federation Council and a State Duma. The normal term for each is four years.

Federation Council (*Sovet Federatsii*). The upper house comprises two representatives from each of Russia's constitutionally recognized territorial units (89 units in 2003, declining to 83 in March 2008—see under Constitution and government, above). Each jurisdiction returns two members, one selected by the unit's executive and one by the unit's legislature. (Prior to January 2002, the chief executive and legislative chair of each unit had served ex officio.) Most members are designated as independents, but a majority support United Russia.

Chair: Valentina MATVIYENKO.

State Duma (*Gosudarstvennaya Duma*). The lower house is a 450-member body. In the election of December 7, 2003, half of the seats were filled from single-member constituencies and half by proportional representation from party lists obtaining a minimum of 5 percent of the vote. Following repeat elections in several districts and significant realignments due to parliamentary factions, the 447 filled seats of the 2003–2007 Duma fell into bloc alignments as follows: United Russia, 306; Communist Party, 52; Motherland, 38; Liberal Democratic Party, 36; unaffiliated, 15.

In accordance with a law adopted in 2005, State Duma elections starting in 2007 were conducted on a party-list proportional representation basis. Following the December 4, 2011, election, the seat distribution was as follows: United Russia, 238 seats; Communist Party of the Russian Federation, 92; A Just Russia, 64; Liberal Democratic Party of Russia, 56.

Chair: Sergey NARYSHKIN.

CABINET

[as of September 15, 2013]

Prime Minister	Dmitry Medvedev
First Deputy Prime Ministers	Igor Shuvalov
Deputy Prime Ministers	Olga Golodets [f]
	Arkady Dvorkovich
	Dmitry Rogozin
	Aleksandr Khloponin
	Dmitry Kozak
Ministers	
Agriculture	Nikolai Fyodorov
Civil Defense, Emergencies, and Disaster Relief	Vladimir Puchkov
Communications and Mass Media	Nikolai Nikiforov
Culture	Vladimir Medinsky
Defense	Sergei Shoigu
Development of the Russian Far East	Viktor Ishayev
Economic Development	Alexei Ulyukayev
Education and Science	Dmitry Livanov
Energy	Alexander Novak
Finance	Anton Siluanov
Foreign Affairs	Sergei Lavrov
Health	Veronika Skvortsova [f]
Industry and Trade	Denis Manturov
Interior	Vladimir Kolokoltsev
Justice	Alexander Konovalov
Labor and Social Security	Maxim Topilin
Natural Resources and Environmental Protection	Sergei Donskoi
Regional Development	Igor Slyunyayev
Relations with the Open Government	Mikhail Abyzov
Sport, Youth, and Tourism	Vitaly Mutko
Transportation	Maxim Sokolov

[f] = female

INTERGOVERNMENTAL REPRESENTATION

Ambassador to the U.S.: Sergey Ivanovich KISLYAK.

U.S. Ambassador to Russia: Michael A. McFAUL.

Permanent Representative to the UN: Vitaly Ivanovich CHURKIN.

IGO Memberships (Non-UN): APEC, CEUR, CIS, EBRD, OSCE, WTO.

RWANDA

Republic of Rwanda
République Rwandaise (French)
Republika y'u Rwanda (Kinyarwanda)

Political Status: Republic proclaimed January 28, 1961; independent since July 1, 1962; multiparty constitution adopted June 10, 1991, but full implementation blocked by ethnic-based fighting; peace agreement signed August 4, 1993, in Arusha, Tanzania, providing for transitional government and multiparty elections by 1995; twenty-two-month transitional period announced January 5, 1994; new transitional government installed on July 19, 1994, by the Rwandan Patriotic Front (FPR) after taking military control in the wake of genocide of April 1994; new constitution (providing for a four-year, FPR-led transitional government but including provisions of the 1991 basic law and the 1993 Arusha peace agreement) adopted by the Transitional National Assembly on May 5, 1995; transitional period extended by the FPR for four years on June 8, 1999; new constitution providing for full transition to civilian rule adopted on June 4, 2003, following a national referendum on May 26.

Area: 10,169 sq. mi. (26,338 sq. km).

Population: 11,312,009 (2012E—UN); 12,012,589 (2013E—U.S. Census).

Major Urban Center (2012C): KIGALI (530,907).

Official Languages: English, French, Kinyarwanda.

Monetary Unit: Rwandan Franc (official rate November 1, 2013: 674.31 francs = $1US).

President: Maj. Gen. Paul KAGAME (Rwandan Patriotic Front); named interim president by the Supreme Court on March 24, 2000, following the resignation the previous day of Pasteur BIZIMUNGU (Rwandan Patriotic Front); elected in a permanent position by the combined Transitional National Assembly and cabinet on April 17, 2000, and inaugurated on April 22; reelected by popular vote on August 25, 2003, and inaugurated for a seven-year term on September 12; reelected for a second seven-year term on August 9, 2010.

Prime Minister: Pierre Damien HABUMUREMYI; appointed by the president on October 6, 2011, to replace Bernard MAKUSA (independent), who was appointed to the Senate after serving since March 2000.

THE COUNTRY

Situated in the heart of Africa (adjacent to Burundi, Tanzania, Uganda, and the Democratic Republic of the Congo), Rwanda consists mainly of grassy uplands and hills endowed with a temperate climate. The population comprises three main ethnic groups: the Hutu, or Bahutu (84 percent); the Tutsi, or Batutsi (15 percent); and the Twa, or pygmies (1 percent). Approximately 57 percent of the population is Roman Catholic, with Protestant (37 percent) and Muslim (5 percent) minorities. In addition to English, French, and Kinyarwanda (the three official languages), Kiswahili is widely spoken. Women account for about half of the labor force, primarily as unpaid agricultural workers on family plots; female representation in government and party posts is minimal, though the 2003 constitution called for increased participation by women in all levels of government, civil service, and policy-making. By 2008 the World Bank estimated that women owned 41 percent of Rwandan businesses, the highest percentage in Africa. Women also won a majority of seats in the 2013 legislative balloting with 51 of 80 posts. With women accounting for 63.8 percent of the seats, Rwanda is the only country in the world where women outnumber men in the legislature.

Economically poor, Rwanda has been hindered by high population growth (it is one of the most densely populated states in Africa), inadequate transportation facilities, distance from accessible ports, and the ravages of civil war. Services account for 43.6 percent of GDP, followed by agriculture, 42.1 percent, and industry, 14.3 percent. Approximately 80 percent of the population is employed in agriculture. Coffee is the leading cash crop and principal source of foreign exchange, although tea cultivation is expanding. Industry is concentrated in food processing and nondurable consumer goods, but the mining of cassiterite and wolframite ore is also important. International assistance has focused on economic diversification, while recent state budgets have concentrated on agricultural and infrastructural development.

Despite the subsequent problems associated with civil war and the massive displacement and return of perhaps 2 million Rwandans, as of mid-2002 Rwanda was continuing to make considerable progress in rebuilding its economy (for information on the economy prior to 2002, see the 2010 *Handbook*). Reinforcing the country's economic infrastructure subsequently became the primary focus of governmental policy, which attracted substantial donor assistance. The IMF and World Bank, noting the progress in structural reform, offered debt relief, while at the same time encouraging the government to improve its revenue collection system and intensify the privatization of state-run enterprises.

Rwanda's GDP growth averaged 8.1 percent from 2002 through 2008, and the government was credited with continued liberalization of the economy and retrenchment in public spending. In 2005 the IMF and World Bank announced that Rwanda had met the requirements for large-scale debt reduction through the Heavily Indebted Poor Countries (HIPC) initiative which allowed the country to write off $1 billion of its $1.4 billion in foreign debt. For its part, the government launched programs designed to attract foreign investment, particularly in regard to an ambitious plan to make Rwanda a "high-tech hub" for central Africa by extending phone and Internet service into rural areas. Subsequently, Rwanda's entry into the East African Community (EAC) in July 2007 was expected to further accelerate development by, among other things, opening neighboring markets to Rwandan goods.

In 2008 the government consolidated seven development agencies into a single body, the Rwanda Development Board, to better facilitate the disbursement of international assistance. The reform was part of a larger program designed to increase annual per capita income in Rwanda from $371 in 2008 to $900 by 2020. In addition, the country passed a milestone when its domestic government revenues exceeded foreign aid for the first time since the 1994 genocide. The global economic crisis caused a decline in agricultural exports in 2009 and GDP growth slowed to 4.14 percent. In 2010 the UN ranked Rwanda 152nd out of 169 countries in its Human Development Index. That year GDP grew by 6.5 percent, while inflation was 2.3 percent. In 2011 GDP grew by 8.6 percent, owing to increased agricultural output, strong exports, and domestic demand. High food and fuel prices, as well as an accommodative monetary policy, drove inflation to its peak of 8.3 percent by the end of 2011. A household expenditure survey released in February 2012 showed substantial progress in poverty reduction over the previous five years across all provinces, particularly outside the capital. The IMF reported that GDP grew by 8 percent in 2012, while inflation was 6.3 percent, and GDP per capita was $681. In its 2013 Doing Business survey, the World Bank ranked Rwanda 52nd out of 185 countries, behind only South Africa among sub-Saharan African countries.

GOVERNMENT AND POLITICS

Political background. Like Burundi, Rwanda was long a feudal monarchy ruled by nobles of the Tutsi tribe. A German protectorate from 1899 to 1916, it constituted the northern half of the Belgian mandate of Ruanda-Urundi after World War I and of the Belgian-administered trust territory of the same name after World War II.

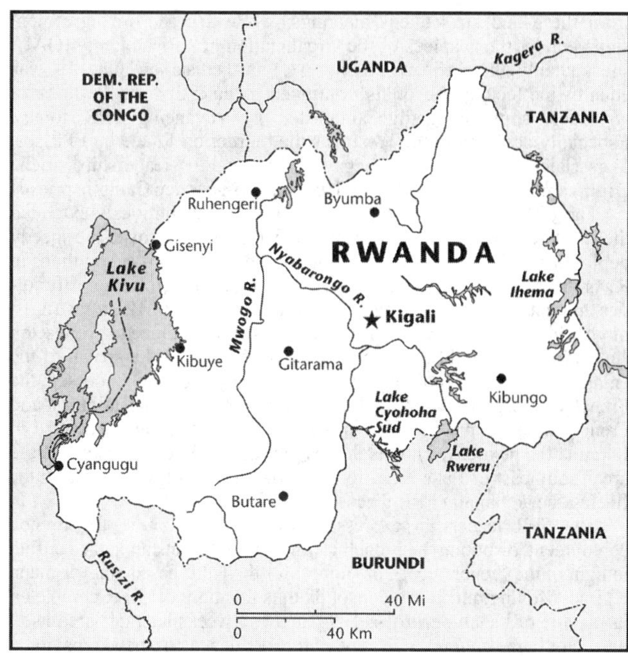

Resistance to the Tutsi monarchy by the more numerous Hutus intensified in the 1950s and culminated in November 1959 in a bloody revolt that overthrew the monarchy and led to the emigration of thousands of Tutsis. The Party of the Movement for Hutu Emancipation (*Parti du Mouvement de l'Émancipation Hutu*—Parmehutu), founded by Grégoire KAYIBANDA, won an overwhelming electoral victory in 1960, and Rwanda proclaimed itself a republic on January 28, 1961, under the leadership of Dominique MBONYUMUTWA. Since the United Nations did not recognize the action, new elections were held under UN auspices in September 1961, with the Hutu party repeating its victory. Kayibanda was accordingly designated president on October 26, 1961, and trusteeship status was formally terminated on July 1, 1962. Subsequently, Tutsi émigrés invaded the country in an attempt to restore the monarchy; their defeat in December 1963 set off mass reprisals against the remaining Tutsis, resulting in 10,000–15,000 deaths and the flight of 150,000–200,000 Tutsis to neighboring countries.

The Hutu-dominated government consolidated its position in the elections of 1965 and 1969. Moreover, with President Kayibanda legally barred from seeking another term in the approaching 1973 election, the constitution was altered to assure continuance of the existing regime. The change fanned hostility between political elements from the northern region and those from the southern and central regions, the latter having dominated the government since independence. Beginning in February 1973 at the National University in Butare, renewed Hutu moves against the Tutsis spread quickly to other areas. The government did not attempt to quell the actions of the extremists, and continued instability raised the prospect of another tribal bloodbath or even war with Tutsi-ruled Burundi. In this context, a bloodless coup took place on July 5, 1973.

The new government, under Maj. Gen. Juvénal HABYARIMANA, moved quickly to dissolve the legislature, ban political organizations, and suspend portions of the constitution. A civilian-military government, composed largely of young technocrats, was subsequently installed, and it established a more centralized administrative system. A regime-supportive National Revolutionary Movement for Development (*Mouvement Républicain National pour le Développement*—MRND) was organized in mid-1976 and was accorded formal status as the sole legal party under a new constitution adopted by referendum on December 17, 1978. Subsequently, it was announced that the same poll had confirmed Habyarimana for an additional five-year term as president.

In 1980 the administration declared that it had foiled a coup attempt allegedly involving current and former government officials, including Maj. Théonaste LIZINDE, who had recently been removed as security chief after being charged with corruption. Lizinde received a death sentence, which was subsequently commuted to life imprisonment.

Single-party legislative balloting was conducted in 1981, 1983, and on December 26, 1988. Habyarimana, the sole candidate, was accorded additional five-year terms as president by means of referendums in 1983 and on December 19, 1988. In July 1990 Habyarimana called for the drafting by 1992 of a new national charter, which would separate governmental and MRND powers, reduce the size of the bureaucracy, and establish guidelines for the creation of a multiparty system. However, political reform was delayed by an October 1990 invasion from bases in Uganda of the Tutsi-dominated Rwandan Patriotic Front (*Front Patriotique Rwandais*—FPR), obliging the government to call in French, Belgian, and Zairean troops to help repel an FPR advance on Kigali. In March 1991 a cease-fire was negotiated, although fighting continued intermittently thereafter.

On April 6, 1991, a National Synthesis Commission was charged with revising the constitution, and a draft charter was completed on April 30. On June 2 the president announced the legalization of multiparty politics, and the revised constitution was adopted on June 10, one year ahead of schedule. (Earlier, plans for a national referendum were reportedly abandoned for economic reasons.) On October 12 Justice Minister Sylvestre NSANZIMANA was named to the newly created post of prime minister, and on December 30 he announced the installation of a bipartisan administration drawn from what was now termed the National Republican Movement for Democracy and Development (*Mouvement Républicain National pour la Démocratie et le Développement*—MRNDD) and the Christian Democratic Party (*Parti Démocratique Chrétien*—PDC), one of a number of newly registered formations.

In April 1992 the Social Democratic Party (*Parti Social Démocrate*—PSD), Liberal Party (*Parti Liberal*—PL), and Republican Democratic Party (*Parti Démocratique Républicain*—MDR), which had refused to enter the government unless an opposition leader was named prime minister, agreed to join an expanded five-party administration headed by the MDR's Dismas NSENGIYAREMYE pending legislative balloting within a year. In early June the new administration's plan to expedite a debate on a national conference and then hold general elections was foiled when the FPR ejected government forces from a large area of northern Rwanda and threatened to continue its advance unless granted a role in the administration. During preliminary talks held June 5–7 in Paris, the FPR and the government agreed to revive the March 1991 cease-fire and hold a full-scale peace conference.

The first round of talks held July 10–14, 1992, in Arusha, Tanzania, with Western and regional observers in attendance, yielded a truce and a new cease-fire to take effect July 19 and 31, respectively. Thereafter, despite reports of continued fighting, negotiations continued, and on October 31 a power-sharing protocol was announced. On January 10, 1993, following two months of debate on the composition of a transitional government, a formal peace agreement was signed that would give the FPR, MDR, PDC, PL, and PSD a majority of seats in the cabinet and National Assembly. The MRNDD, which was assigned six cabinet seats, and a weakened presidency, denounced the agreement, saying that it categorically refused to participate in the future broad-based transitional government. By early February more than 300 people, predominantly Tutsis, had reportedly been killed in violent anti-accord demonstrations allegedly orchestrated by the MRNDD and the Coalition for the Defense of the Republic (*Coalition pour la Défense de la République*—CDR), an openly anti-Tutsi group, which had been excluded from the government. In response to continuing violence, the FPR announced that it was withdrawing from peace negotiations, and on February 8 it launched an attack on government forces in northern Rwanda near the site of a recent Tutsi massacre. However, the deployment of additional French troops (bringing their number to 600), officially to protect foreign nationals, enabled the regime to survive.

Following further negotiations with the FPR in Arusha in March 1993, Habyarimana was able in July to appoint a new coalition government of the same five internal parties, although this time with a more accommodating faction of the MDR, headed by Agathe UWILINGIYIMANA as prime minister. Renewed Arusha talks subsequently yielded a new 300-page treaty that was signed by President Habyarimana and FPR chair Alexis KANYERENGWE on August 4. Under the new accord, a Hutu prime minister acceptable to both sides would be named and the FPR would be allocated 5 of 21 cabinet posts in a government to be installed by September 10, with multiparty presidential and legislative elections to be held by mid-1995. In addition, a united military force would be formed, 40 percent of which would be Tutsi and 60 percent Hutu. Earlier, on June 22, the UN Security Council had voted to establish a UN Observer Mission Uganda–Rwanda (UNOMUR) to verify that no external military assistance was reaching the FPR. In accordance with the August agreement, the Security Council voted on October 4 to establish a UN Assistance Mission in Rwanda (UNAMIR), which was mandated to monitor the cease-fire and to contribute to security and national rehabilitation in the run-up to the planned elections.

Bickering among the Rwandan parties and delays in UNAMIR deployment made it impossible to meet a September 1993 deadline for the start of the transitional period or a revised target date of December 31. Thus, a new timetable was announced by Habyarimana when, on January 5, 1994, he assumed the presidency for a 22-month transitional period preparatory to multiparty elections in October 1995. However, intense criticism from both the FPR and the internal prodemocracy parties forced the president to postpone the designation of a transitional government and interim legislature. The assassination by unknown assailants on February 21 of PSD leader and government minister Félicien GATABAZI, a Hutu who had promoted rapprochement with the FPR, provoked a new crisis. On February 22 Habyarimana declared an indefinite extension of the transitional phase amid street clashes in which the chair of the Hutu CDR, Martin BUCYANA, was slain by a mob of PSD supporters.

Previous violence in Rwanda paled in significance compared with the wholesale slaughter that followed the death of Habyarimana on April 6, 1994. Both he and President Ntaryamira of Burundi died when their plane was shot down on approach to Kigali airport. The reaction of Hutu militants in Rwanda, led by the Presidential Guard and CDR militia, was to embark on an orgy of killing, not only of Tutsis but also of Hutus believed to favor accommodation with the FPR. Among those murdered within hours of the president's death were Prime Minister Uwilingiyimana and members of her family, at least one minister, Constitutional Court chair Joseph KAVAUNGANDA, and ten Belgian soldiers of the UNAMIR force.

As prescribed by the constitution, the president of the National Development Council, Theodore SINDIKUBWABO, assumed the presidency on April 9, 1994, appointing an interim government headed by Jean KAMBANDA as prime minister and including the five parties represented in the previous coalition. Although a broader-based transitional administration was promised within six weeks, the FPR rejected the legitimacy of the new government (claiming that the presidency should have passed to the president of the yet-to-be-inaugurated transitional legislature) and declared a new military offensive. On April 12, as FPR forces closed in on Kigali, the new government fled to Gitarama, some 30 miles to the south. Meanwhile, French, Belgian, and U.S. troops had been deployed in Rwanda to evacuate foreign nationals. On April 14, upon completion of the transfer of the foreign nationals, Belgium withdrew its 420-strong contingent from UNAMIR. That action, coupled with the failure of UN mediators to arrange a lasting cease-fire, prompted the UN Security Council, in a controversial decision on April 22, to vote unanimously for a reduction of UNAMIR from 2,500 to 270 personnel.

The FPR offensive and the effective absence of an international military presence served to incite the Hutu militants in Rwanda to even greater savagery against the Tutsi minority and presumed Hutu opponents. Gangs of machete-wielding soldiers and militia members reportedly roamed the countryside, engaging in systematic and indiscriminate slaughter of men, women, and children. Although numbers were impossible to verify, the death toll was estimated to be at least 200,000 by late April and perhaps as high as 800,000—a scale of killing officially described by the UN as genocidal. The carnage caused a mass exodus from the country, both of surviving Tutsis and of Hutus fearing FPR vengeance. By early May some 1.5 million refugees had crossed into neighboring countries, creating one of the most severe humanitarian crises ever to afflict independent Africa.

Following widespread criticism of its April 22 decision, the UN Security Council on May 17, 1994, reversed itself by approving the creation of a UNAMIR II force of 5,500 troops, while embargoing arms supplies to the Rwandan combatants. Mainly at U.S. insistence, however, only 150 unarmed observers were initially dispatched, followed by an 800-strong Ghanaian contingent charged with securing Kigali airport. Deployment of the bulk of the force was contingent on a further report from the UN secretary general on its duration, mandate, and composition, and on the attitude of the warring factions to a heightened UN presence. The immediate reaction of the FPR to the UN decision was one of suspicion that UNAMIR II would forestall its imminent military victory. On May 30, with FPR forces controlling portions of Kigali, UN mediators succeeded in bringing about talks between government and rebel representatives. However, little of substance resulted from these and subsequent meetings, while a cease-fire agreement signed under the auspices of the Organization of African Unity (OAU, subsequently the African Union—AU) in Tunisia on June 14 was equally ineffectual. Accounts continued to emerge from Rwanda of atrocities, some allegedly committed by advancing FPR forces. Especially deplored in the West was the murder on June 9 by FPR soldiers (later described as "renegades" by the FPR leadership) of the (Hutu) archbishop of Kigali, two Hutu bishops, and ten Catholic priests.

The UN Security Council on June 9, 1994, unanimously extended the UNAMIR mandate for a six-month period and approved the speedy deployment of two further battalions, which were to protect civilians in Rwanda and facilitate the international relief effort. However, difficulties and delays in assembling and equipping the UNAMIR force (most of which was to be provided by African states) led France to propose on June 15 that it should dispatch 2,500 troops pending the arrival of the enlarged UNAMIR contingent. The Security Council endorsed the French proposal on June 22 (albeit with five members abstaining), and French troops (supported by a small Senegalese contingent) arrived in Rwanda the next day. The result was the establishment of a large "safe area" southeast of Lake Kivu for surviving Tutsis as well as for Hutus fleeing the advancing FPR forces.

The FPR leadership expressed strong opposition to the French deployment, disputing the French claim to nonpartisanship in the conflict in light of the French record of support for the Hutu-based Habyarimana regime. Moving quickly to consolidate its position, the FPR completed its capture of Kigali on July 4, 1994, and two weeks later declared itself the victor in the civil war. On July 19 the FPR installed a new transitional government, with a moderate Hutu, Pasteur BIZIMUNGU, as president, and another Hutu, Faustin TWAGIRAMUNGU (the opposition's nominee for the post following the August 1993 agreement) as prime minister. The FPR military commander, Maj. Gen. Paul KAGAME, became vice president and defense minister, while Tutsis took most of the remaining portfolios. In addition to the FPR and MDR, the PDC, PL, and PSD were represented in the new administration, while the MRNDD and CDR were excluded.

Because of widespread reports of mass killings, the Office of the UN High Commissioner for Refugees (UNHCR) in September 1994 suspended its policy of encouraging Rwandan refugees in Zaire to return home, and on November 8 the Security Council established an International Criminal Tribunal for Rwanda (ICTR) to prosecute those responsible for genocide "and other serious violations of international humanitarian law." Subsequently, the 70-member Transitional National Assembly provided for under the 1993 Arusha agreement convened in Kigali on December 12 (see Legislature, below).

On April 22, 1995, the image of the FPR-controlled government was severely tarnished by the Tutsi-dominated army's massacre of some 2,000 Hutus in the Kibeho refugee camp near Gikongoro. The universally condemned action slowed the voluntary return of Rwandans from Zaire, in addition to setting back efforts to secure badly needed international aid. This and other atrocities by the victorious Tutsis were reportedly the reason for the resignation of Prime Minister Twagiramungu on August 28, with Pierre-Célestin RWIGEMA, the relatively obscure primary and secondary education minister, being named three days later as Twagiramungu's successor and the head of a government which included a number of new Tutsi members in posts formerly assigned to Hutus.

By the end of 1997 an estimated 1.5 million refugees had returned, but the FPR regime still fell short of fulfilling what it had delineated as one of the top prerequisites for national reconciliation—resolution of the judicial process for the tens of thousands of predominantly Hutu prisoners imprisoned (in reportedly subhuman conditions) for their alleged roles in the 1994 genocide. In fact, the FPR continued to be plagued by charges, largely unsubstantiated, that the Tutsi-controlled military was engaging in its own campaign of revenge killings. Meanwhile, the ICTR—26 justices assigned to more than 100,000 cases—proceeded at a glacial pace, hampered, according to a January 1998 UN internal investigation, by a mismanaged judicial system. By the end of 1997, three years after the massacres, the ICTR had not convicted a single defendant. Kigali's judicial efforts, which disposed of fewer than 300 cases in 1997, also foundered when a plea-bargaining program failed to break the logjam, causing observers to note that, barring new developments, most prisoners would die in prison long before their cases could come to trial.

Meanwhile, the toll from ethnic conflict increased in the second half of 1997 (with at least 6,000 more murders during the year, according to UN monitors) as Hutu guerrillas grew in strength and began making daylight raids, particularly in the northwest, where they had wide popular support. Although the guerrillas appeared to have no hope of a military victory, their attacks seemed aimed at making Rwanda ungovernable.

During ICTR testimony in February 1998 the former UNAMIR commander in Rwanda said he had advised the UN leadership of the impending genocide and asked for authorization (never granted) to prevent it. Similarly, a report by the Belgian parliament released in February 1998 claimed the Belgian, French, and U.S. governments also had credible advance warning of the genocide. U.S. president Bill Clinton visited Rwanda in March as part of an African tour, and he acknowledged that the United States and other Western nations had been slow to react to the developments of 1994. (In July 2000 an OAU panel strongly criticized the United States, France, Belgium, the UN, and others—including church groups—for failing to prevent or stop the genocide and called for a "significant level of reparations.")

In April 1998 Rwanda publicly executed 22 persons convicted of murders committed during 1994, and by June thousands of other prisoners had pleaded guilty, apparently to avoid death sentences. In early September the ICTR (recently expanded by the UN in response to widespread criticism) issued its first guilty verdict. Shortly thereafter, the tribunal sentenced former interim prime minister Jean Kambanda to life in prison following his conviction on genocide charges. (Kambanda had admitted his guilt earlier and had reportedly provided evidence against other officials.)

Despite the ongoing judicial quagmire, a degree of normalcy had returned to Rwanda by early 1999, as evidenced by the successful completion of nonparty local elections in March, the first balloting since 1988. At the same time, however, instability persisted near the DRC border, hundreds of thousands of civilians having moved into camps protected by government troops. International attention also remained focused on the Rwandan government's significant role in the DRC civil war (see article on the DRC). Under those circumstances, it was not surprising that the transitional government in July extended its mandate for four more years, with FPR leaders concluding that security conditions did not permit the organization of multiparty elections.

Major General Kagame remained the most powerful figure in the administration, and on March 24, 2000, he moved into the presidency following the resignation of President Bizimungu. Earlier, on March 8, Bernard MAKUSA, a relatively unknown former ambassador to Burundi and Germany, was appointed to succeed Rwigema as prime minister.

Prime Minister Rwigema's resignation in late February 2000 was attributed to his deteriorating relationship with the Transitional National Assembly (which was investigating alleged financial improprieties on the part of government officials) as well as conflict with other MDR leaders. Likewise, an intraparty power struggle in the FPR apparently contributed to the resignation of President Bizimungu in March. The installation of Major General Kagame as president merely formalized his already de facto authority. Kagame called upon all Rwandan refugees to return home and pledged to pursue national reconciliation, although his status as the nation's first Tutsi president since independence created additional unease for those already concerned over the lack of Hutu representation in government. That worry was not alleviated by the March 2001 district elections, in which party activity was again barred and most of the successful candidates appeared to be aligned with the FPR.

The return to normality continued with the government in December 2001 adopting a new flag, national anthem, and national seal. However, Hutu groups continued to assert periodic discrimination and retaliation by the FPR-dominated government. Domestically, hopes for Tutsi-Hutu reconciliation rested, in part, on the reestablishment in early 2002 of the traditional *gacaca* system, in which elected village judges were to adjudicate the cases of some 90,000 detainees still facing charges relating to the events of 1994. (Most of the other cases, involving those accused of ordering mass killings or participating in rapes, were to be handled by the normal court system. Meanwhile, the "masterminds" of the genocide still faced trial at the ICTR, which as of April 2002 had arrested 60 of the 75 people who had been indicted so far. Only eight convictions had been achieved by that time, although a number of high-profile cases were on the docket for the remainder of the year.)

In January 2003 the government ordered the release of 40,000 detainees but reserved the right to arrest the released people if new evidence emerged. By the end of the year some 25,000 had been released. Survivor groups severely criticized the measure, claiming that many involved in the genocide were being released. Meanwhile, the *gacaca* courts began to adjudicate an increasing number of cases. In August 2003 one *gacaca* court convicted 105 people in a mass two-day trial.

In April 2003 the Transitional National Assembly approved a new draft constitution that was put before voters in a national referendum on May 26, 2003. The new basic law was approved by a 93.4 percent vote and became effective June 4. Among other provisions, the constitution created a bicameral legislature and provided for direct election of the president. In an effort to prevent further ethnic conflict, the constitution also prohibited any parties based solely on race, gender, or religion. However, some opposition parties and international human rights groups charged that this provision was enacted to reinforce the political domination of the FPR.

Prior to the presidential elections, the constitutional court ruled that the MDR and the PDC were illegal parties because of their role in the events of 1994. Consequently, the MDR candidate—former prime minister Twagiramungu—and the PDC candidate—Jean-Népomuscéne NAYINZIRA—were forced to run as independents. In the balloting on August 25, 2003, Kagame was elected with 95.1 percent of the vote, followed by Twagiramungu with 3.6 percent and Nayinzira with 1.3 percent.

Legislative balloting took place September 29–30 and October 2, 2003. Of the 53 directly contested seats, a coalition led by the FPR secured 40 seats; the PSD, 7; and the PL, 6. Makusa was reappointed prime minister and formed a new unity government on October 19. The government included representatives of all 7 parties that secured representation in the Chamber of Deputies. Kagame carried out several cabinet reorganizations, including a major reshuffle on March 7, 2008, in which 5 new ministers were appointed, and 11 had their portfolios changed.

By March 2005 the ICTR had convicted 22 defendants and acquitted 3. In addition to complaints about the continued slow pace of case resolution, criticism emanated from Rwandan Hutus over the fact that no Tutsis had been indicted by the ICTR, despite Hutu assertions that revenge killings and other atrocities had been committed by Tutsis from the FPR in 1994. Meanwhile, the *gacaca* courts faced a backlog of some 95,000 cases by the end of the year. Tension also arose from the release of documents from the Kambanda trial that appeared to support Tutsi arguments that the Hutu attacks in 1994 had been well coordinated and discussed in advance at high levels of government.

In an effort to promote national reconciliation, more than 9,000 prisoners who had been accused of participation in the 1994 genocide were released in February 2007. Although none of those released had faced charges of so-called "major crimes," genocide victims groups still criticized the action. In April former president Bizimungu was also pardoned. Meanwhile, former Maj. Gen. Laurent MUNYAKAZI became the most senior military figure to be convicted when he was found guilty of 13 counts of genocide by a Rwandan court. He was sentenced to life in prison.

A 2007 controversial family planning law met with widespread opposition in the Catholic community. It limited couples to three children in an effort to slow population growth. Meanwhile, the death penalty was abolished in June and replaced by life imprisonment.

In the 2008 legislative elections, the FPR again formed an electoral coalition. The grouping won 42 seats in the direct elections, while the Social Democratic Party secured 7, and the Liberal Party, 4. The main opposition groups boycotted the elections, but international observers declared the elections free and fair and noted that the National Election Commission had implemented all of the reforms recommended after the 2003 polling. In balloting for the Chamber of Deputies in October 2008, women secured 45 posts, or more than 56 percent of the seats, making Rwanda the first country to have a majority female legislative chamber. Rwanda was also the first country to meet the AU's Protocol to the African Charter on the Rights of Women in Africa, which called for countries to have 50 percent of their legislature made up of women deputies. The FPR-led coalition led won the legislative balloting and Kagame subsequently reappointed Makusa as prime minister of a coalition government that included only minor alterations from the previous cabinet.

Kagame carried out a major cabinet reshuffle on November 29, 2009. The 2010 presidential election was marred by violence against opposition candidates (see Current issues, below). Kagame won the balloting on August 9, with more than 90 percent of the vote against three candidates from progovernment parties. Leading opposition leaders were barred from entering the race. On September 14 Kagame reappointed Makusa as prime minister and renewed the existing cabinet.

Local balloting was held on February 4 and 21, 2011. Candidates ran as independents, but reports indicated that the majority were supportive of Kagame and the FPR. On May 7 Kagame conducted a cabinet reshuffle and reduced the number of portfolios in the government. Pierre Damien HABUMUREMYI was appointed by the president on October 6, to succeed Makusa as prime minister.

Kagame undertook a cabinet reshuffle on February 25, 2013, which included the appointment of three additional ministers of state. In the September 16–18, Chamber of Deputies balloting, the FPR and its allies again won a majority, with 41 votes (see Political parties, below); followed by the PSD, 7; and the PL, 5 (see Current issues, below).

Constitution and government. Under the 1978 constitution, executive power was vested in a president elected by universal suffrage for a five-year term, the president of the MRND being the only candidate. He presided over a Council of Ministers, which he appointed, with the secretary general of the MRND being empowered to serve as interim president should the incumbent be incapacitated. A unicameral National Development Council, also elected for a five-year term, was to share legislative authority with the president and, by four-fifths vote, could censure (but not dismiss) him.

On June 10, 1991, President Habyarimana signed into law a new charter distinguished by the introduction of a multiparty system and the separation of executive, legislative, and judiciary powers. Under the 1991 constitution, executive powers were shared by the president and a presidentially appointed prime minister, who named his own cabinet. In addition, the legislature's presiding officer was empowered to serve as interim president if the incumbent left the country or became incapacitated. The constitution also stated that while political party formations could organize along ethnic and tribal lines, they had to be open to all.

On May 5, 1995, the Transitional National Assembly that had convened five months earlier adopted a new constitution incorporating the essentials of the 1991 document as well as elements of the 1993 power-sharing peace agreement. On June 8, 1999, the transition period, initially scheduled to expire in 1999, was extended to 2003.

The new constitution adopted on June 4, 2003, created a bicameral legislature and provided for a directly elected president, limited to two seven-year terms. Amendments to the constitution in October 2005 reduced the number of provinces from 12 to 5, the number of districts from 106 to 30, and the number of "sectors" (local administrative units) from 1,545 to 416. The consolidation was seen as a way to save money and streamline government. In February 2006 the language in the constitution regarding property rights was strengthened to assist returning refugees in recovering their property. In July 2008 the constitution was amended to ensure that the country's budgetary process was in accordance with requirements of the EAC. Amendments also clarified the duties of some cabinet ministers, changed the title of the country's senior military officer to chief of the defense staff, and granted perpetual immunity to former presidents of the republic.

The judiciary, headed by a Supreme Court, includes magistrates,' prefectural, and appeals courts; a Court of Accounts; a Court of Cassation; and a Constitutional Court composed of the Court of Cassation and a Council of State. The president and vice president of the Supreme Court are elected by the Senate. In 2008 the tenure of judges was reduced from lifetime appointments to four-year periods, followed by a legislative review and potential reappointment.

On August 14, 1991, the legislature adopted a press law guaranteeing, with certain restrictions, a free press. Most papers stopped publishing as the result of the 1994 genocide, although the situation has since returned to normal. The press is generally considered to be supportive of the government and exercises a degree of self-censorship in that regard. In its annual index on press freedom in 2013, the journalism watchdog group Reporters Without Borders ranked Rwanda 161st out of 179 countries. In March 2013 a new law eliminated restrictions on print media, although some constraints remained on broadcast journalism.

Foreign relations. Under President Kayibanda, Rwandan foreign policy exhibited a generally pro-Western bias but did not exclude relations with a number of communist countries, including the Soviet Union and the People's Republic of China. Following the 1973 coup, however, the country took a pronounced "anti-imperialist" turn; Rwanda became the first African nation to break relations with Israel as a result of the October 1973 Arab-Israeli war, and it also contributed to the support of liberation movements in southern Africa. At the same time, President Habyarimana initiated a policy of "opening" (*l'ouverture*) with adjacent countries. Despite a tradition of ethnic conflict between Burundi's ruling Tutsis and Rwanda's ruling Hutus, a number of commercial, cultural, and economic agreements were concluded during a visit by Burundian president Michel Micombero in June 1976, while similar agreements were subsequently negotiated with Tanzania and Côte d'Ivoire. Burundi, Rwanda, and Zaire established the Economic Community of the Great Lakes Countries in 1976.

Relations with Uganda were strained for several decades following independence by large numbers of refugees crossing the border in both directions to escape tribal-based hostilities (for more on relations between the countries from 1985 to 1995, see the 2012 *Handbook*).

In 1995 and 1996 Rwanda's foreign relations continued to be defined by the encampment of an estimated 2 million Rwandans outside its borders. In August 1995 the UN lifted its embargo on the sale of weapons to Rwanda after months of lobbying by Rwanda, which claimed that members of the former Hutu government now exiled in Zaire were engaging in cross-border guerrilla attacks. In response to the end of the embargo, Kinshasa launched a violent and unsuccessful repatriation program, claiming that Kigali was preparing to attack the refugee camps. A subsequent repatriation attempt in February 1996 strained relations even further, and throughout the first half of 1996 the two capitals accused each other of employing "destabilization" tactics. Meanwhile, in mid-April the FPR cheered the withdrawal of the last UN peacekeepers from Rwanda. (The Tutsi regime held the UN forces responsible for both allegedly collaborating in the 1994 genocide and undermining the regime's attempts to govern.) During the second half of 1996 a stunning sequence of events in Burundi, Zaire, and Tanzania, respectively, resulted in the repatriation of approximately 650,000 refugees to Rwanda. In Burundi the military coup by Tutsi officers in late July reportedly sparked fear of reprisal attacks among the refugees, and, following the departure of 130,000 people, Bujumbura on August 27 announced the closing of the last of Burundi's camps. Thereafter, in mid-November, several hundred thousand refugees were reported to have fled back across the border from their encampments in eastern Zaire after an allegedly Kigali-funded rebellion on behalf of Zairean Tutsis, the Banyamulenge, resulted in the rout of Zairean troops and Rwandan Hutu militiamen who had been seeking to establish a "Hutuland" in the region. In December Tanzanian government forces, with the tacit and unprecedented approval of the UNHCR, forcibly repatriated over 200,000 refugees to Rwanda.

In 1997 Rwanda, along with five other nations, supported the forces of Laurent Kabila in Zaire, hoping a rebel victory there would enable Rwanda to close the rear bases of the Hutu guerrillas as well as the camps where they sought refuge. After the Kabila victory, the refugee camps along the border were closed, but guerrillas drifted across into Rwanda with returning refugees and regrouped in Rwanda. Meanwhile, Rwandan government forces who had crossed the border into the former Zaire (now known as the Democratic Republic of the Congo or DRC) remained in two provinces, North and South Kivu, in a de facto occupation apparently with Kabila's tacit approval. Relations between Kinshasa and Kigali subsequently deteriorated, as Kabila distanced himself from Tutsi influence, prompting hostility among the Banyamulenge Tutsis in the eastern portion of the DRC, as Zaire had been renamed. In July 1998 Kabila announced an end to military cooperation with Rwanda, and in August a full-fledged rebellion broke out against his administration (see article on the DRC). By November Rwanda acknowledged that its troops were allied with the anti-Kabila rebels, claiming that the DRC government was rearming the Hutus responsible for the 1994 genocide.

In an unexpected turn of events, forces from Rwanda and Uganda, previously allied in support of anti-Kabila rebels in the DRC, clashed in northeast DRC in August 1999, with underlying factors apparently including support for different anti-Kabila factions in the DRC and perhaps most importantly, rivalry regarding eventual preeminence in the region. Fighting between the Rwandan and Ugandan troops erupted again in the spring of 2000.

In November 2001, Kagame began a series of meetings with the leader of Uganda, president Museveni. Following mediation efforts by South Africa and the United Kingdom, in 2003, the two governments agreed to take stronger action to prevent rebels and dissident groups from crossing each other's borders and initiating conflicts. In addition, the two heads of state agreed on the voluntary repatriation of 26,000 Rwandans remaining in refugee camps in Uganda. In July 2002 a separate peace accord was signed in Pretoria, South Africa, between Rwanda and the DRC. By October, all 23,400 Rwandan troops had withdrawn from the DRC, and in September 2003 the two countries reestablished diplomatic relations.

In 2005 the government deployed 2,000 troops to the UN peacekeeping mission in Darfur, Sudan.

Burundi and Rwanda established a joint committee to resolve border issues in August 2006. Subsequently, Rwanda and Uganda agreed to increase security cooperation to suppress Hutu militias operating in the border regions of the two countries.

In November 2006, a French judge issued an international arrest warrant for nine senior Rwandan officials on charges that they had been involved in the downing of President Habyarimana's plane in 1994. All nine were close allies of Kagame. The Rwandan government adamantly rejected the charges and broke off diplomatic relations with France. Rwanda also closed its embassy in Paris and opened a new one in Sweden. Meanwhile, there were large demonstrations against France in Rwanda, including one in Kigali involving more than 25,000 people. During local trials in Rwanda, new allegations emerged that French military officers had ignored calls to help victims of the genocide. A memorandum of understanding between Rwanda and the UK led to the arrest of four genocide suspects in London in December 2006. Rwanda subsequently applied for membership in the Commonwealth as a manifestation of the country's growing ties with the UK.

In April 2007 the UN lifted the arms embargo that had been in place against Rwanda since 1994, and in July Rwanda became a member of the EAC. As part of the accession agreement, other EAC members reduced tariffs on Rwandan agricultural exports. The Rwandan government also initiated a program to change the language of instruction from French to English. Officially this was part of a broader effort to integrate into the EAC, but it also indicated the continuing tense relations between Rwanda and France. French president Nicholas Sarkozy visited Rwanda in October in an effort to improve relations between the two countries. In November, an agreement was reached between Rwanda and the DRC to disarm the Hutu resistance group, the Democratic Forces for the Liberation of Rwanda (*Forces Démocratiques pour la Libération du Rwanda*—FDLR), and to suppress other armed groups in both countries. The agreement was followed by a DRC offensive against the FDLR. Kagame attended the meeting of heads of state of the Commonwealth in November, and the country began negotiations to join the organization.

During the crisis in Zimbabwe (see article on Zimbabwe), Kagame emerged as one of the foremost critics of President Robert Mugabe and a proponent for new elections in that country. In March Rwanda and the UN finalized an agreement whereby those convicted by the ITCR would be allowed to serve their sentences in Rwanda. In August a commission created by the Rwandan government charged various French officials, including former president Francois Mitterrand, with complicity in the 1994 genocide. The French government rejected the accusations.

Joint Rwanda-DRC military operations against the FDLR in 2008 and 2009, resulted in a number of the rebel group's top leaders being killed or captured and allowed for the return of more than 2,000 Hutu refugees. In January 2009 it was reported that Rwanda arrested the leader of the DRC Tutsi rebel group, the National Congress for the Defense of the People (*Congrès National pour la Dèfense du Peuple*—CNDP) that had been supported by Rwanda. The CNDP had split into rival factions with one group, led by Bosco NTAGANDA, signing a cease-fire with the DRC in January. Rwanda reportedly backed the Ntaganda faction. In April Rwanda and Uganda signed an agreement to return more than 20,000 Rwandan refugees. The UNHCR pledged aid and material support to facilitate the resettlement. At the November 2009 meeting of the Commonwealth, Rwanda was formally admitted to the organization as its 54th member.

In January 2010 publication of a government report absolved France of any role in the 1994 assassination of Habyarimana (see Current issues, below). Relations between Rwanda and France subsequently improved significantly. French president Sarkozy, during a trip to Rwanda, in February acknowledged that actions by his country contributed to the genocide. Following a meeting between high-ranking military officials, Rwanda and China announced closer security ties. In June 2010 Rwanda and South Africa recalled their respective ambassadors after an aborted assassination attempt against the Rwandan opposition figure Kayumba NYAMWASA. In August Ugandan authorities arrested fugitive Hutu leader Augustin NKUNDABAZUNGU and extradited him to Rwanda to stand trial for genocide related to the 1994 civil war.

In October a report by the UN accused Rwandan troops of committing crimes against humanity, including rape and extrajudicial killings, during the 1990s. The Rwandan government rejected the report and threatened to withdraw its peacekeeping forces from Sudan. Intervention by UN secretary general, Ban Ki Moon, defused the crisis. Also in October the French authorities arrested Callixte MBARUSHIMANA, a leader of the FDLR. He was subsequently turned over to the International Criminal Court on charges of war crimes (in December 2011 the ICC freed Mbarushimana for lack of evidence).

In late May 2012, a leaked UN report claimed Rwandan authorities were complicit in the recruitment of Rwandans to fight with rebels who broke away from the control of Congo's national army in April. In late June the United Nations published its full investigation into Rwanda's involvement with the M23 rebel group in eastern Congo, documenting numerous violations of international law and UN resolutions (see entry on the DRC). In addition to sending troops and arms to the fight, the report claimed that Rwandan officials had encouraged the secession of North and South Kivu and may have tried to sponsor a rebellion in South Kivu. In response, the United States announced on July 21 that it would cut $200,000 in military aid to Rwanda, a symbolic move that, according to analysts, reflects a dramatic change in perception from one of Rwanda's staunchest allies. Similar aid cuts or delays soon followed from Germany ($26 million), the Netherlands ($6.1 million), and the United Kingdom ($25 million). Despite the controversy, on October 18, Rwanda was elected to a non-permanent seat on the UN Security Council. Meanwhile, Rwanda announced it would withdraw its remaining forces in the DRC.

On February 1, 2013, Germany restored aid to Rwanda. Also in February, Rwanda and the Netherlands pledged to further increase collaboration following the signing of an aviation treaty. That month Rwanda, the DRC, and Uganda, signed a conservation treaty to encourage wildlife preservation. In June Rwanda signed an agricultural cooperation agreement with Ethiopia, followed by a broader trade accord in August.

Current issues. In January 2009, Agnes NTAMABYALIRO, became the first former government minister of the 1994 Hutu cabinet to be tried and sentenced in Rwanda for her part in the 1994 genocide. In June a *gacaca* court sentenced senator Stanley SAFARI, the leader of the Prosperity and Solidarity Party (PSP), to life in prison for his role in the genocide and the PSP leader subsequently fled to Uganda to avoid detention. The Senate subsequently expelled Safari from the chamber. In December 2009 the UN extended the mandate of the ICTR through 2012 and approved the appointment of additional judges to address the backlog of cases. Meanwhile Ephrem NKEZABERA was convicted and sentenced to 30 years of imprisonment for involvement in the genocide.

On January 11, 2010, an independent commission led by Jean MUTSINZI issued a comprehensive report on the 1994 genocide. The report blamed the 1994 assassinations of the Rwandan and Burundian presidents on a small group of Hutu officials. In March Agathe HABYARIMANA, the widow of the assassinated former president, was arrested outside Paris on a warrant issued by Rwanda on charges of involvement in genocide. The arrest was reportedly a manifestation of closer ties between the two countries. In April Victoire INGABIRE, leader of the United Democratic Forces (FDU-Inkingi) and her party's presidential candidate, was arrested on charges of genocide denial and that she was illegally working with the FDLR (in October 2012, she was sentenced to eight years in prison).

Former army chief of staff and opposition leader Kayumba Nyamwasa was wounded in an assassination attempt in Johannesburg on June 19, 2010. Reports initially blamed Rwandan intelligence agents, but six people were subsequently arrested in the attack. Meanwhile, opposition newspaper editor Jean-Léonard RUGAMBAGE was killed on June 24. On July 13 André Kagwa RWISEREKA, the vice president of the **Democratic Green Party of Rwanda** (*Parti Democratique Vert du Rwanda*), was murdered and beheaded. Kagame was reelected on August 9 in balloting described by international observers as free and fair. However, opposition parties rejected the balloting. After the results were announced, a grenade attack injured more than 20 in Kigali. In June 2011 Pauline NYIRAMASUHUKO became the first woman to be convicted of genocide and incitement to rape by the ICTR. She was sentenced to life in prison.

On January 11, 2012, two French judges cleared the FPR of shooting down the plane carrying Habyarimana, and they agreed with a team of British experts that the missiles were fired from a camp under the control of the Rwandan army. The decision angered Kagame's critics in France and Rwanda. In December 2012 Augustin NGIRABATWARE, former minister of planning and cooperation, was convicted by the ICTR of genocide. He was the last person to be tried by the ICTR, which did continue to hear appeals.

On September 16–18, 2013, elections for the Chambers of Deputies were held. There was minor violence prior to the balloting, including two grenade attacks in Kigali that killed two and injured 14, and was blamed on the FDLR. The FPR-led alliance won an absolute majority of 41 seats in the 80 member chamber, in balloting that was criticized by opposition groups who claimed that their supporters faced harassment and intimidation at polling centers.

POLITICAL PARTIES

A one-party state after the 1973 coup, Rwanda adopted a multiparty constitution on June 10, 1991. Under the terms of the 2003 constitution, the government has the power to ban political parties that might advocate civic unrest or exacerbate ethnic differences. Using this provision, the government banned the MDR, PDC, and several smaller parties prior to the 2003 elections (see below). Prior to the 2008 legislative elections, it was announced that the same parties that formed an FPR-led grouping in the 2003 balloting would campaign as an electoral coalition. The parties included the FPR, the PDC, the **Islamic Democratic Party** (*Parti Démocratique Islamique*—PDI), the **Rwandan Socialist Party** (*Parti Socialiste Rwandais*—PSR), and the **Rwandan People's Democratic Union** (*Union Démocratique du Peuple Rwandais*—UDPR). The **Party for Progress and Concord** (*Parti pour le Progrès et la Concorde*—PPC) and the **Prosperity and Solidarity Party** (*Parti de la Solidarité et du Progrès*—PSP) also joined the FPR-led coalition. Reports in 2010 indicated that three small parties, the **United Democratic Forces** (FDU-Inkingi), the **Democratic Green Party of Rwanda** (*Parti Democratique Vert du Rwanda*), and **Social Party Imberakuri** (*Parti Social Imberakuri*—PS Imberakuri), formed an opposition coalition, the Permanent Consultative Council of Opposition Parties.

Government and Progovernment Parties:

Rwandan Patriotic Front (*Front Patriotique Rwandais*—FPR). Currently the dominant political force in Rwanda, the FPR is a largely Tutsi formation that invaded Rwanda in October 1990 from Uganda under the command of Rwandan refugees who were formerly officers in the Ugandan armed forces. However, most of the original leadership, including FPR founder Fred RWIGYEMA, were killed in fighting with government troops in late 1990 and early 1991.

Buoyed by a series of stunning victories in early June 1992, which yielded control of much of northern Rwanda, the FPR called on the Rwandan government to integrate FPR members into both the military and the government, reduce the president's power, allow all refugees to return, and hold multiparty elections. The FPR signed the Arusha peace agreement on August 4, 1993, but implementation was subject to repeated delays. The massacres of Tutsis and moderate Hutus, which followed the death of President Habyarimana in April 1994, impelled the FPR to launch a new offensive, which brought it to power three months later. The victory was attributed largely to the military leadership of Maj. Gen. Paul Kagame, who, although designated as vice president in the new regime, was widely regarded as its preeminent figure. Kagame consolidated his power when he was elected FPR president in February 1998 and president of the republic in March 2000. Kagame was subsequently reelected president for a seven-year term in 2003. During legislative elections, the FPR led an electoral coalition that received 73.78 percent of the vote and 40 seats. (The FPR gained 33 seats alone.) The FPR conducted elections in July 2007 for local and regional party organizations. Allies of Kagame won the majority of posts.

In 2008 the party vehemently rejected the 40 arrest warrants issued by a Spanish judge for FPR members who were currently military or government officials (see Current issues, above). In elections for the Chamber of Deputies, the FPR again led a coalition of progovernment parties. The coalition won 78.8 percent of the vote and 42 of the directly elected seats. The FPR had to replace one of its deputies in the assembly, Beatrice NIRIERE, after she was convicted of genocide in June 2009.

Kagame was reelected president with 93.1 percent of the vote in balloting on August 9, 2010. In October Kagame publicly rejected speculation that he would attempt to change the constitution in order to seek a third term. In legislative balloting in September 2013, the FPR-led coalition won 76.2 percent of the vote and renewed its majority in the Chamber.

Leaders: Maj. Gen. Paul KAGAME (President of the Republic and Chair of the Party), Christophe BAZIVAMO (Vice Chair), Col. Alexis KANYARENGWE (Former President of the Front), Francois NGARAMBE (Secretary General).

Christian Democratic Party/Centrist Democratic Party (*Parti Démocratique Chrétien*—PDC). The PDC accepted one cabinet post in the governments of December 1991 and April 1992. A PDC member also served in the Makusa government until March 2001. Prior to the 2003 presidential elections, the PDC was banned since the Constitution forbade religious parties. It reconstituted itself as the **Centrist Democratic Party** (*Parti Démocrate Centriste*—PDC) before legislative elections, and the reconstituted PDC joined the FPR-led coalition. It won three seats. Former PDC president Jean-Népomuscéne Nayinzira placed third in the national presidential polling in 2003. Party leader Alfred Mukezamfura was elected speaker of the Chamber of Deputies in 2003, but he fell ill in September 2007 and was temporarily replaced, before resuming his duties. Mukezamfura announced in August 2008 that he would not seek reelection to the Chamber of Deputies, but that the PDC would join the FPR-led electoral coalition. In June 2009 Agnes MUKABARABGA was elected chair of the PDC at a party congress. The PDC supported Kagame in the 2010 presidential elections and was part of the FPR-led electoral coalition in the 2013 legislative balloting (the PDC won one seat in the polling).

Leaders: Agnes MUKABARABGA (Chair), Alfred MUKEZAMFURA (Former Speaker of the Chamber of Deputies).

Party for Progress and Concord (*Parti pour le Progrès et la Concorde*—PPC). The PPC was formed in 2003 after the MDR was outlawed. It is comprised mainly of Hutus. In the 2003 legislative elections, the PPC received 2.2 percent of the vote, below the 5 percent threshold needed for representation. Party leader Alivera MUKABARAMBA was the PPC's 2003 presidential candidate. She was appointed to the Senate in 2003. In February 2008 an internal split emerged in the PPC. Christian MARARA claimed to be president of the PPC after the group's leadership dismissed him and affirmed Mukabarama as party president. The PPC joined the FPR-led coalition for the 2008 assembly balloting. Mukabaramba was the PPC candidate in the 2010 presidential elections but received less than 1 percent of the vote. She was appointed minister of state for community development and social affairs in 2011. The PPC remained part of the FPR-led alliance in the 2013 legislative balloting and won one seat.

Leaders: Alivera MUKABARAMBA (Party President and 2003 and 2010 presidential candidate), Etienne NIYONZIMA (Vice President).

Ideal Democratic Party (*Parti Démocratique Idéal*—PDI). Originally formed in 1992 as the **Islamic Democratic Party** (*Parti Démocratique Islamique*—PDI), the PDI changed its title in 2003 in response to a constitutional ban on religious parties and as part of a broader effort to attract voters. The PDI joined the FPR-led coalition in the 2003 and 2008 legislative elections. PDI party leader Sheikh Mussa Harerimana was appointed interior minister after the 2003 balloting. The PDI backed Kagame in the 2010 presidential polling, and Harerimana was reappointed interior minister. The PDI won one seat as part of the FPR coalition in the 2013 elections.

Leader: Sheikh Mussa HARERIMANA (Chair).

Other members of either the 2008 or 2103 FPR-led electoral coalition, which all supported Kagame in the 2010 presidential elections, included the the **Rwandan Socialist Party** (*Parti Socialiste Rwandais*—PSR), a workers' rights party launched in 1991, which was led by Medard RUTIJANWA and which won one seat in 2013; **Rwandan People's Democratic Union** (*Union Démocratique du Peuple Rwandais*—UDPR), formed in 1992 and led by Gonzague RWIGEMA; and the **Prosperity and Solidarity Party** (*Parti de la Solidarité et du Progrès*—PSP), led by Stanley SAFARI (see Current issues, above).

Social Democratic Party (*Parti Social-Démocrate*—PSD). One of the first three opposition parties to be recognized under the 1991 constitution, the PSD was one of several prodemocracy parties that accepted cabinet posts from April 1992, and in August 1993 it was a signatory of the Arusha peace agreement. The assassination of its leader, Félicien GATABAZI, in February 1994 sparked the violence in Rwanda, which escalated to genocidal proportions from April onward. Following the death of President Habyarimana two months later, PSD president Frederic NZAMURAMBAHO and vice president Felicien NGANGO also died. The PSD's Juvénal Nksui, then Speaker of the assembly, was sacked by the legislature in March 1997 and accused of incompetence after failing to sign into law a bill passed by the assembly that would make the president accountable to it. The PSD won 6 seats in the 2003 legislative elections. Party leader Vincent Biruta was elected to the Senate and was subsequently elected Speaker of that body. The PSD participated in the subsequent Kagame unity government. Prior to the September 2008 legislative elections, the PSD announced an electoral list that included 64 candidates. It declined an invitation to join the FPR-led coalition. In the balloting, the PSD won 13.1 percent of the vote and 7 seats in the assembly. Jean Damascene NTAWUKURIRYAYO was the PSD presidential candidate in 2010. He placed second to Kagame with 5.15 percent of the vote but was subsequently elected president of the Senate. Biruta was appointed minister of education in the FPR-led cabinet. In January 2011 the PSD member of Parliament Jacqueline MUKAKANYAMUGENGE was elected to chair the National Consultative Forum for Political Organizations, an umbrella group of Rwandan political parties.

In the 2013 legislative balloting, the PSD secured 13 percent of the vote and seven seats.

Leaders: Vincent BIRUTA (Chair and Minister of Education), Juvénal NKSUI (Former Speaker of the Assembly), Jean Damascene NTAWUKURIRYAYO (President of the Senate and 2010 presidential candidate).

Liberal Party (*Parti Liberal*—PL). Joining the MDR and PSD in refusing to enter the Nsanzimana government of December 1991, the PL accepted three cabinet posts under the MDR's Dismas Nsengiyaremye in April 1992 and also participated in subsequent coalitions, becoming as a consequence split into progovernment and antigovernment factions. The latter joined the government installed by the FPR following its military victory in July 1994. The PL's Joseph SEBARENZI became Speaker of the assembly when that body sacked Juvénal Nksui (see PSD, above); however, Sebarenzi resigned his speaker's position in January 2000 amid a power struggle within the party and in the face of parliamentary criticism. He was subsequently reported to have assumed self-imposed exile in the United States. Prosper Higiro became party chair in 2001. In the 2003 elections, the PL secured seven seats. The PL was given a cabinet post in the subsequent Kagame unity government.

Following elections for regional party officials in August 2007, the PL was divided by a power struggle. The party leadership expelled two of its parliamentarians and five other party officials after they accused senior PL officials of corruption in the party's September 2007 leadership election, which was won by Protais MITALI. The members appealed their expulsion, but on November 9 the high court rejected their appeal, and the party replaced the parliamentarians. The PL ran 62 candidates in the 2008 legislative elections. Most of the candidates were reported to be members of the Mitali-led faction of the party. The PL secured 7.5 percent of the vote and four seats in the assembly. Mitali was reappointed minister of youth in the subsequent FPR-led government and appointed minister of sports and culture following subsequent cabinet reshuffles. Higiro was the PL candidate in the 2010 presidential balloting. He received 1.37 percent of the vote.

The PL received 9 percent of the vote in the 2013 legislative elections and five seats. Party member Donatille MUKABALISA was elected speaker of the assembly in October 2013.

Leaders: Protais MITALI (President of the Party and Minister of Sports and Culture), Leopold NDORUHIRWE (General Secretary), Donatille MUKABALISA (Speaker of the Chamber of Deputies), Prosper HIGIRO (Vice President of the Senate).

Other Parties and Groups:

Social Party Imberakuri (*Parti Social Imberakuri*—PS Imberakuri). Formed in 2008 by Bernard NTAGANDA, the party emerged as one of the main opposition groupings. In 2009 reports indicated that the party split between Ntaganda and former party vice president Christine MUKABUNANI. Ntaganda sought to campaign against Kagame in the 2010 presidential elections. However, he was arrested in June for his role in what the government described as illegal demonstrations. In 2011 reports indicated that dissidents loyal to Ntaganda had created a new grouping. The party participated in the 2013 assembly elections but failed to secure any seats with only 0.6 percent of the vote.

Leaders: Bernard NTAGANDA, Christine MUKABUNANI.

Republican Democratic Movement (*Mouvement Démocratique Républicain*—MDR). A predominantly Hutu party, the MDR drew its support from the central Rwandan capital region. Prior to the 2003 legislative elections the National Assembly voted to dissolve the MDR under the terms of the 2003 constitution. Former MDR member Twagiramungu ran for the presidency in 2003 and placed third. Subsequently, many members of the MDR joined the new Hutu-based party, the Party for Progress and Concord (*Parti pour le Progrès et la Concorde*—PPC). For more information on the MDR, see the 2009 *Handbook.*

Resistance Forces for Democracy (*Forces de Résistance pour la Démocratie*—FRD). The FRD was launched by former Hutu prime minister Faustin Twagiramungu and former interior minister Seth SENDASHONGHA in Brussels on March 26, 1996, following their breaks from the MDR and FPR, respectively. The new party's platform called for the ouster of the Tutsi regime (which the FRD cited as an unbreachable impediment to the return of Rwanda's primarily Hutu refugees) and the drafting of a new power-sharing constitution based on the 1993 Arusha peace agreement. Furthermore, the FRD accused the FPR regime of engaging in genocide against the Hutu population. Party leader Sendashongha was in exile in Nairobi when he was assassinated in May 1998. Moderates had wanted Sendashongha to return to Kigali to lead reconciliation efforts. Twagiramungu strongly criticized President Kagame's call in April 2000 for exiles to return to Rwanda, charging that Kagame was attempting to cover up his "crimes against humanity." Nonetheless, Twagiramungu returned to Rwanda in June 2003 and launched a bid for the presidency as an independent. He placed second in the balloting but challenged the results. His challenge was overturned by the Supreme Court. Reports indicated in 2013 that Twagiramungu had formed a new political grouping, the Rwandan Dream Initiative—Rwanda Rwiza.

Leader: Faustin TWAGIRAMUNGU (Former Prime Minister).

Democratic Forces for the Liberation of Rwanda (*Forces Démocratiques pour la Libération du Rwanda*—FDLR). Described in 2004 and early 2005 as one of the last major organized resistance groups outside Rwanda, the Hutu FDLR was accused by some Western leaders of involvement in the killing of civilians in the DRC. In March 2005 the FDLR formally apologized for its role in the 1994 killings in Rwanda. In April 2005 the FDLR declared it was disarming, and the leadership announced the group's intention to return to Rwanda from the DRC and to try to establish a legal political movement.

FDLR leader Ignace MURWANASHYAKA was arrested in Germany in April 2006 on alleged immigration violations. The Rwandan government asked for his extradition, but the German government refused the request. In November 2007 the DRC and Rwanda signed an agreement to disarm the FDLR (see Foreign relations, above). In December the United States announced an effort to initiate sanctions against the FDLR through the UN. In 2008 the UN estimated that approximately 6,000 FDLR fighters remained, but more than 1,000 surrendered or were killed during a joint DRC-Rwandan offensive in December 2008 and January 2009. In 2010 an amnesty program was credited with encouraging the repatriation of more than 200 FDLR fighters and their families. The FDLR was blamed for a number of terrorist attacks from 2010 through 2013 (see Current issues, above). In September 2011 DRC security forces killed 40 FDLR fighters in the Talama region. Reports in 2013 from former FDLR fighters accused the DRC of supporting some FDLR militias. An October 2013 UN report praised Rwanda for its efforts to reintegrate FDLR militias into society, noting that since 2004 more than 10,000 FDLR fighters had been demobilized and rehabilitated.

Leader: Ignace MURWANASHYAKA.

The Dutch-based **United Democratic Forces** (*Forces Democratiques Unifiées*--FDU-Inkingi), led by Victoire INGABIRE, absorbed the **Rally for Return and Democracy** (*Rassemblement pour la Démocratie et le Retour*—RDR) in 2006 (see the 2013 *Handbook* for more information on the RDR). The FDU-Inkingi attempted to compete in the 2010 presidential balloting, but Ingabire was arrested (see Current issues, above). The **Democratic Green Party of Rwanda** (*Parti Democratique Vert du Rwanda*) was formed in 2009 and led by Frank HABBINEZA. The party was denied official registration prior to the 2010 presidential balloting but was registered in August 2013, too late for that year's legislative election.

For more information on the **Party for Democracy and Renewal** (*Parti pour la Démocratie et le Renouveau*—PDR), please see the 2013 *Handbook.*

LEGISLATURE

Prior to the resumption of hostilities between the Rwandan armed forces and the Rwandan Patriotic Front in April 1994, the legislature consisted of a unicameral National Development Council (*Conseil pour le Développement National*) of 70 members elected on December 26, 1988, from 140 candidates nominated by the MRND. Under the terms of the power-sharing agreement reached by the government and FPR on January 10, 1993, and confirmed by the Arusha peace agreement of August 4, 1993, a transitional legislative body was formally launched on December 12, 1994.

Under the terms of the 2003 constitution, a bicameral **Parliament** (*Inteko Ishinga Amategeko*) was created.

Senate. The Senate (*Umutwe wa Sena*) consists of 26 indirectly elected members who serve eight-year terms. Twelve senators are elected by regional councils; 8 are appointed by the president; 4 are elected by a regulatory forum of the country's political parties; and the remaining 2 are elected by university staffs and faculty. In addition, former presidents of the republic can request to be members of the Senate. The first senators were sworn in on October 10, 2003.

President: Jean Damascene NTAWUKULIRYAYO.

Chamber of Deputies. The lower house (*Umutwe w'Abadepite*) consists of 80 members who serve five-year terms. Fifty-three are directly elected by a system of proportional representation in which parties must achieve a 5 percent threshold to gain representation. Two deputies are elected by the National Youth Council and 1 by the Federation of the Associations of the Disabled. The remaining 24 deputies are elected by a joint council, which includes representatives from provincial, district, and city governments, as well as members of the executive committees of women's groups at various regional levels. In balloting for the 53 directly elected members of the Chamber of Deputies from September 16–18, 2013, the Rwandan Patriotic Front–led coalition won 41 seats; the Social Democratic Party, 7; and the Liberal Party, 5.

Speaker: Donatille MUKABALISA.

CABINET

[as of October 15, 2013]

Prime Minister	Pierre Damien Habumuremyi
Ministers	
Agriculture and Animal Resources	Agnes Kalibata [f]
Cabinet Affairs	Stella Ford Mugabo [f]
Defense	Gen. James Kabarebe
Disaster Management and Refugee Affairs	Serafine Mukantabana (ind.) [f]
East African Community	Jacqueline Muhongayire [f]
Education	Vicent Biruta (PSD)
Finance and Economic Planning	Claver Gatete
Foreign Affairs and Cooperation	Louise Mushikiwabo [f]
Health	Agnes Binagwaho [f]
Infrastructure	Silas Lwakabamba
Internal Security	Sheikh Mussa Harerimana (PDI)
Justice; Attorney General	Johnston Busingye
Local Government	James Musoni
Natural Resources, Lands, Forestry, Environment and Mines	Stanislas Kamanzi
Office of the President	Venantia Tugireyezu
Office of the Prime Minister, in Charge of Gender and Family Promotion	Oda Gasinzigwa [f]
Public Service and Labor	Anastase Murekezi
Sports and Culture	Protais Mitali (PL)
Trade and Industry	Françoise Kanimba
Youth and Information Communication Technology	Jean Philbert Nsengimana
Ministers of State	
Cooperation	Eugène-Richard Gasana
Energy and Water	Emma Francoise Isumbingabo [f]
Mining	Evode Imena
Primary and Secondary Education	Anita Aslimwe [f]
Public Health and Primary Healthcare	Mathias Harebamungu
Social Affairs	Alvera Mukabaramba (PPC) [f]
Technical and Vocational Education	Albert Nsenglyumva
Transport	Alexis Nzahabwanimana

[f] = female

Note: Unless indicated, cabinet officials belong to the FPR.

INTERGOVERNMENTAL REPRESENTATION

Ambassador to the U.S.: Mathilde MUKANTABANA.

U.S. Ambassador to Rwanda: Donald KORAN.

Permanent Representative to the UN: Eugène-Richard GASANA.

IGO Memberships (Non-UN): AfDB, AU, Comesa, CWTH, IOM, NAM, WTO.

ST. KITTS AND NEVIS

Federation of Saint Kitts and Nevis
Federation of Saint Christopher and Nevis

Note: Both versions of the name are official, although "Federation of Saint Kitts and Nevis" is preferred.

Political Status: Former British dependency; joined West Indies Associated States in 1967; independent member of the Commonwealth since September 19, 1983.

Area: 101 sq. mi. (262 sq. km), encompassing Saint Christopher (65 sq. mi.) and Nevis (36 sq. mi.).

Population: 53,000 (2011E—UN); 51,134 (2013E—U.S. Census).

Major Urban Center (2011E): BASSETERRE (13,000).

Official Language: English.

Monetary Unit: East Caribbean Dollar (market rate November 1, 2013: 2.70 dollars = $1US).

Sovereign: Queen ELIZABETH II.

Governor General: Sir Edmund Wickham LAWRENCE; sworn in on January 2, 2013, succeeding Sir Cuthbert Montroville SEBASTIAN.

Prime Minister: Dr. Denzil Llewellyn DOUGLAS (St. Kitts-Nevis Labour Party); sworn in on July 7, 1995, succeeding Dr. Kennedy Alphonse SIMMONDS (People's Action Movement) following election of July 3; retained office following elections of March 6, 2000, October 25, 2004, and January 25, 2010.

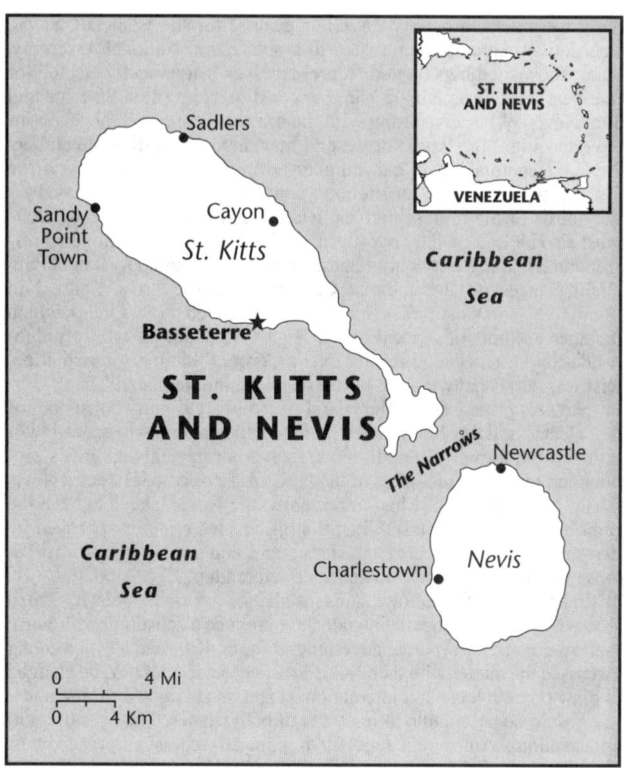

THE COUNTRY

Conventionally styled St. Kitts-Nevis, Saint Christopher and Nevis form part of the northern Leeward Islands group of the Eastern Caribbean. The population is largely of African descent and the religion primarily Anglican. The economy is dependent on tourism, with several hotels currently under construction; agriculture on the large island is devoted primarily to sugarcane and its derivatives, and on Nevis to coconuts and vegetables. Recent economic planning has focused on the promotion of small-scale local industry and agricultural diversification to reduce the islands' dependence on food imports and fluctuating sugar prices.

In October 1993, St. Kitts-Nevis graduated from concessionary loan financing by the World Bank, with future loans to be at commercial rates; however, the islands were dealt serious blows by two major hurricanes in the 1990s causing more than $500 million in damage. The terrorist attacks in the United States in September 2001 significantly depressed the tourism sector in St. Kitts-Nevis. After several years of steady growth, GDP contracted by 4.2 percent in 2009 as the global recession took a dramatic toll on the island. The island nation's economy remained stagnant through 2012, before experiencing slight growth of 1.9 percent. Inflation in 2013 was 2.9 percent.

GOVERNMENT AND POLITICS

Political background. Although one of the smallest territories of the West Indies, St. Kitts was Britain's first colony in the region, settled in 1623. Ownership was disputed with France until 1783, when Britain acquired undisputed title in the Treaty of Versailles. The tripartite entity encompassing St. Kitts, Nevis, and the northern island of Anguilla entered the West Indies Federation in 1952 and was granted internal autonomy as a member of the West Indies Associated States in February 1967. Three months later Anguilla repudiated government from Basseterre and in 1976 was accorded a separate constitution that reconfirmed its status as a dependency of the United Kingdom (see United Kingdom: Related Territories).

The parliamentary election of February 18, 1980, yielded the first defeat of the St. Kitts Labour Party (SKLP) in nearly three decades and the formation of a government under Dr. Kennedy A. SIMMONDS of the People's Action Movement (PAM), with the support of the Nevis Reformation Party (NRP). Despite protests by the SKLP, which insisted that the coalition did not have an independence mandate, the Simmonds government issued a white paper on a proposed federal constitution in July 1982. A revised version of the document, which formed the basis of discussions in London the following December, was endorsed by the St. Kitts-Nevis House of Assembly in March 1983 and secured the approval of the British Parliament in early May. Formal independence followed on September 19.

The PAM/NRP coalition maintained its majority until 1993. The election of November 29, 1993, yielded four seats each for the PAM and SKNLP (Nevis having been added to the opposition party's name), with the NRP losing one of its remaining seats to its Nevis-based opponent, the Concerned Citizens' Movement (CCM). After the CCM had refused to form a majority coalition with either the PAM or the SKNLP, the governor general on December 1 asked Simmonds to continue as head of a PAM-NRP minority government.

Following an outbreak of what appeared to be drug-related crime in October 1994, political, religious, business, and labor leaders agreed at a "forum for national unity" on November 12 that all parties represented in the National Assembly would be permitted to participate in key government decisions and that the next general election would be held by November 1995, three years ahead of schedule. However, Prime Minister Simmonds scheduled the poll even earlier, on July 3. He lost his own seat in a seven-to-one SKNLP victory on St. Kitts; consequently, Denzil DOUGLAS was installed as head of a new government on July 7. Douglas retained office in an early election on March 6, 2000, the SKNLP gaining an additional legislative seat for a majority of eight.

In early elections in October 2004, the SKNLP majority declined to seven seats. A further SKNLP decline to six seats on January 25, 2010, did not preclude the formation of a fourth Douglas administration. Divisions within the SKNLP government led to the resignation of Deputy Prime Minister Sam CONDOR in January 2013, prompting Douglas to reorganize the cabinet (see Current issues, below).

Constitution and government. The 1983 constitution describes St. Kitts-Nevis as a "sovereign democratic federal state" whose ceremonial head, the British monarch, is represented by a governor general of local citizenship. The governor general appoints as prime minister an individual commanding a parliamentary majority and, on the latter's advice, other ministers, all of whom, except for the attorney general, must be members of the legislature. He also appoints, on the advice of the government, a deputy governor general for the island of Nevis. Legislative matters are entrusted to a unicameral National Assembly, 11 of whose members (styled "representatives") are directly elected for five-year terms from single-member constituencies (8 on St. Kitts and 3 on Nevis). After consulting with the prime minister and the leader of the opposition, the governor general may appoint additional members (styled "senators") who can number no more than two-thirds of the elected membership. Constitutional amendments require approval by two-thirds of the representatives, while certain entrenched provisions must also be endorsed by two-thirds of the valid votes in a national referendum. The highest court—apart from the right of appeal, in certain circumstances, to the Judicial Committee of the Privy Council in London—is the West Indies Supreme Court (based on St. Lucia), which includes a Court of Appeal and a High Court, one of whose judges resides on St. Kitts and presides over a Court of Summary Jurisdiction. District courts deal with petty offenses and minor civil actions.

Nevis is provided with an island Assembly, currently consisting of five elected and three nominated members (the latter not to exceed two-thirds of the former); in addition, the governor general appoints a premier and two other members of the Nevis Assembly to serve as a Nevis Island Administration. Most importantly, the Nevis Islanders have the right of secession from St. Kitts, if a bill to such effect is approved by two-thirds of their elected legislators and endorsed by two-thirds of those voting on the matter in an island referendum.

In late July 1995, following his installation as prime minister, Denzil Douglas announced that he intended to introduce a constitutional reform that would provide separate governments for St. Kitts and Nevis. Having discussed the matter with then Nevis premier Vance AMORY, he pledged to draw on both local and international expertise to draw up a document that would be acceptable to residents of both islands. The overture notwithstanding, Amory in June 1996 initiated secession proceedings, Douglas characterizing the action as indicating that the Nevis leader had "no other issue of note to bring to the people." Nonetheless, the inhabitants of the smaller island had long chafed at alleged policy discrimination by the federal government at Basseterre. Involved were a variety of complaints ranging from slow response to a proposed upgrading of public services and fears of exclusion from offshore banking opportunities.

Efforts by regional representatives to mediate the dispute having failed, the Nevis Assembly voted unanimously on October 13, 1997, for secession, opposition members indicating their support "on principle." In August 1998, however, only 61.8 percent of Nevis voters in an island referendum backed secession, thus defeating the measure because it failed to gain the constitutionally required two-thirds majority.

The St. Kitts-Nevis constitution provides for freedom of speech, and freedom of the press is generally respected in privately owned media, though opposition parties claimed the government-run TV and radio stations unfairly favored the SKNLP in the 2010 election.

Foreign relations. At independence, St. Kitts-Nevis became an independent member of the Commonwealth and shortly thereafter was admitted to the United Nations. It joined the Organization of American States (OAS) in March 1984. Regionally, it is a member of the Association of Caribbean States (ACS), the Caribbean Community and Common Market (Caricom), and the Organization of Eastern Caribbean States (OECS). Most of its bilateral aid has come from Britain, which, at independence, provided a special grant-loan package of £10 million for capital projects and technical cooperation. The Simmonds government endorsed the U.S. intervention in Grenada in October 1983, subsequently receiving modest military assistance from the United States in support of its small voluntary defense force.

In June 2010, St. Kitts became the 17th signatory of the Tax Information Exchange Agreement (TIEA) with Canada. As a result, the country was moved from the Organization for Economic Cooperation and Development's "gray list" of tax havens to its "white list" of compliant regimes. In February 2011 St. Kitts-Nevis approved an agreement with India. In addition to the 18 existing TIEAs, the government has concluded its discussions and negotiations with three other countries and is currently in discussions with an additional three countries, including the United States.

Despite major revenue from Nevis's status as an offshore financial services center, the government, in response to mounting criticism by the U.S. Congress, approved legislation for the registration of international funds as of January 1, 2008.

St. Kitts signed a treaty in January 2011 with the other countries of the OECS to form an economic union to allow easier movement of people and goods between member states. In 2012, the Douglas government renewed commitment to fully embrace the Caribbean Court of Justice (CCJ) as the highest appellate court, replacing the London-based privy court, along with the other members of the OECS. No action had been taken as of mid-2013.

Current issues. In the July 2011 Nevis Island Administration general election, the Nevis Reformation Party (NRP) retained its slender majority over the Concerned Citizens' Movement (CCM). Two seats, including that of Deputy Premier Hensley DANIEL, were won by a narrow margin of fewer than 35 votes. The CCM filed an election petition, and the High Court voided the results for Daniel's district on March 21, 2012. The Eastern Caribbean Supreme Court upheld the decision, leading Daniel to tender his resignation on August 27. Constitutionally required to call a by-election within 90 days, Parry instead called general elections and dissolved the Nevis parliament on November 8. In January 22, 2013, balloting, the CCM won three seats defeating the NRP, which took two.

Sir Edmund Wickham LAWRENCE was sworn in as governor general on January 2, 2013, following Sir Cuthbert SEBASTIAN's retirement.

In December 2012, opposition leader Mark BRANTLEY filed a no-confidence motion against the SKNLP government, which was tabled. Prime Minister Douglas dismissed Agriculture Minister Timothy HARRIS in January for opposing a bill to increase the number of senators in the Assembly; Deputy Prime Minister Sam Condor resigned over the matter days later. In February, Douglas named Housing Minister Earl Asim MARTIN as his deputy, and reassigned vacant portfolios. In March, Harris and Condor joined the PAM/CCM bloc in voicing support for the still-tabled no confidence motion (giving it majority support). In April, the opposition appealed to the High Court to force a vote on the no-confidence motion, which was withdrawn in July after the Douglas administration noted that a vote would not occur until legal proceedings concluded. Condor and Harris launched the People's Labour Party (PLP) in June. In July, the opposition filed a new no-confidence motion.

In August 2013, Brantley announced that the PAM, CCM, and PLP would form a unity platform.

POLITICAL PARTIES

Government Parties:

St. Kitts-Nevis Labour Party (SKNLP). What was then styled the St. Kitts Labour Party (SKLP) was organized as a socialist party in 1932. Long the dominant grouping on St. Kitts, it won seven of nine Assembly seats in 1971 and retained a plurality of four in 1980 but was forced from office by the PAM/NRP coalition. The party initially opposed federal status for Nevis, claiming that it made Nevis "more equal" than St. Kitts; however, this position was reversed following the SKLP's crushing defeat in the 1984 election, in which it lost all but two of its legislative seats, including that of opposition leader Lee L. MOORE. Youth leader Henry BROWNE succeeded Moore. Though it increased its Assembly representation from two to four in 1993, it was unable to persuade the CCM (below) to join a government coalition. The party swept to victory on July 3, 1995, winning seven of eight seats on St. Kitts. It added the eighth seat in the election of March 6, 2000, but returned to seven in 2004. An additional seat was lost in January 2010, leaving the SKNLP with a bare majority. Prime Minister Douglas was reelected for a 22nd consecutive year as Labour Party leader.

Cracks within the SKNLP emerged in January 2013 leading Sam Condor and Timothy Harris to leave the government and party, and in June, launch the PLP (see Current issues, above, and the PLP entry, below). The SKNLP elected their replacements at a party conference in May.

Leaders: Dr. Denzil Llewellyn DOUGLAS (Prime Minister and Political Leader), Nigel CARTY (Deputy Political Leader), Marcella LIBURD (Chair).

Nevis Reformation Party (NRP). Organized in 1970, the NRP had, before 1980, campaigned for Nevis's secession from St. Kitts. It won two National Assembly seats in 1980 and participated in the independence discussions that led to the formation of the federal state. It captured all three seats from Nevis in 1984, after having won all five seats to the Nevis Island assembly in August 1983; it lost one of the latter in December 1987 and one of the former in March 1989, both to the CCM. In the Nevis election of June 1, 1992, it retained only two assembly seats. It lost one of two National Assembly seats in November 1993, with no change in 1995, 2000, 2004, and 2010.

Following the 1997 Nevis poll, in which the NRP retained two seats, former premier Simeon DANIEL stated that he would not contest future elections, since speculation that his party favored the central government's position may have weakened its position with voters. The NRP lost one of its two seats in balloting for the Nevis assembly in September 2001 but secured three seats (a majority) in July 2006. In 2010, NRP parliamentary representative Patrice NISBETT was named Attorney General of the Federated States of St. Kitts and Nevis, becoming the first NRP member of the federal cabinet. In the 2011 balloting for the Nevis assembly, the NRP retained its three seats in one of the closest elections in Nevis's history. In August 2012 the court nullified Hensley Daniel's 14-vote victory. Joseph Parry called for general elections (rather than by-elections). In January 2013 balloting, the NRP lost its majority, winning two seats.

Leader: Joseph W. PARRY (Former Premier of Nevis and President of the Party).

Opposition Parties:

Concerned Citizens' Movement (CCM). The CCM is a Nevis-based party that in 1987 captured one local assembly seat and in 1989 one National Assembly seat from the NRP. It won control of Nevis on June 1, 1992, by securing three of five assembly seats, retaining them on February 24, 1997. It increased its National Assembly representation from one to two in 1993, retaining both in 1995, 2000, 2004, and 2010. In the balloting for the Nevis Assembly in September 2001, the CCM secured four of the five elected seats, two of which were lost in July 2006. In the July 2011 Nevis Assembly elections, the CCM retained its two seats in what was one of the closest elections in the island's history, with two of five seats decided by fewer than 35 votes. In the early election in January 2013, the CCM won three seats and Vance Amory assumed premiership.

Leaders: Vance W. AMORY (Party Leader), Mark BRANTLEY (Deputy Leader), Stedmond TROSS (Chair).

People's Action Movement (PAM). The PAM is a moderately left-of-center party formed in 1965. It won only 3 of 9 elective seats in the 1980 preindependence balloting, but with the support of 2 members from Nevis was able to force resignation of the existing Labour government. It captured 6 of the 8 seats from St. Kitts in June 1984, thus securing an absolute majority in a new house that had been expanded to 11 elected members; it retained all 6 seats in 1989 but slipped to 4 in 1993. Although finishing second in the popular vote, the PAM, despite SKNLP objections, retained office in coalition with the NRP. It won only 1 legislative seat in the July 1995 election, which was lost in the March 2000 poll but regained in 2004. The PAM secured 2 seats in January 2010. In internal elections in September 2012, Shawn Richards became party leader. A PAM faction reportedly expelled for speaking out about party corruption formed the National Integrity Party in April 2013.

Leaders: Shawn K. RICHARDS (Party Leader), Selwyn "Rusty" LIBURD (Chair).

People's Labour Party (PLP). Former SKNLP members Timothy Harris and Sam Condor launched the PLP in June 2013 as an alternative to the leading party.

Leaders: Timothy HARRIS (Party Leader), Sam CONDOR (Chair).

Other Parties:

National Integrity Party (NIP). The NIP was formed in April 2013 by five former PAM members. The party aims to eliminate corruption in government.

Leader: Glenroy BLANCHETTE (Party Leader).

United National Empowerment Party (UNEP). The UNEP was launched in May 2004 on a platform of constitutional reform and opposition to independence for Nevis. They unsuccessfully contested the 2004 election, gaining only 1.2 percent of the popular vote.

Leader: Henry L. O. BROWNE.

LEGISLATURE

The unicameral **National Assembly** presently consists of 11 elected members, plus three appointed senators (two-thirds by the government, one-third by the opposition) and the attorney general, if he or she is not already a member of parliament. The legislative mandate is five years, subject to dissolution. In the most recent balloting of January 25, 2010, the St. Kitts-Nevis Labour Party elected 6 members; the People's Action Movement, 2; the Concerned Citizens' Movement, 2; and the Nevis Reformation Party, 1. Two SKNLP members defected in 2013 and subsequently established the People's Labour Party, reducing SKNLP membership to 4.

Speaker: Curtis MARTIN.

CABINET

[as of August 1, 2013]

Prime Minister	Dr. Denzil Llewellyn Douglas (SKNLP)
Deputy Prime Minister	Dr. Earl Asim Martin (SKNLP)
Ministers	
Education, Information, Agriculture, Marine Resources, and Co-operatives	Nigel Carty (SKNLP)
Finance, Sustainable Development, Human Resource Development, Constituency Empowerment, and Social Security	Dr. Denzil Llewellyn Douglas (SKNLP)
Health, Social Services, Community Development, Culture, and Gender Affairs	Marcella Liburd (SKNLP) [f]
Housing, Energy, Public Works, and Utilities	Dr. Earl Asim Martin (SKNLP)
International Trade, Industry, Commerce, Consumer Affairs, Tourism, and International Transport	Richard Skerritt (SKNLP)
Justice, Legal Affairs, Homeland Security, Labor, and Foreign Affairs	Patrice Nisbett (NRP)
Youth Empowerment, Sports, Information Technology, and Telecommunications and Posts	Glen Phillip (SKNLP)

[f] = female

INTERGOVERNMENTAL REPRESENTATION

Ambassador to the U.S.: Jacinth Lorna HENRY-MARTIN.

U.S. Ambassador to St. Kitts-Nevis: Larry L. PALMER.

Permanent Representative to the UN: Delano Frank BART.

IGO Memberships (Non-UN): Caricom, CWTH, ICC, NAM, OAS, WTO.

ST. LUCIA

Saint Lucia

Political Status: Former British dependency; joined West Indies Associated States in 1967; independent member of the Commonwealth since February 22, 1979.

Area: 238 sq. mi. (616 sq. km).

Population: 180,747 (2012E—UN); 162,781 (2013E—U.S. Census).

Major Urban Center (2005E): CASTRIES (14,600).

Official Language: English.

Monetary Unit: East Caribbean Dollar (official rate November 1, 2013: 2.70 dollars = $1US).

Sovereign: Queen ELIZABETH II.

Governor General: Dame Pearlette LOUISY; sworn in September 17, 1997, succeeding Sir W. George MALLET.

Prime Minister: Kenny ANTHONY (St Lucia Labour Party); sworn in on December 6, 2011, succeeding Stevenson KING (United Workers' Party) following the election of November 28.

THE COUNTRY

The second largest of the former West Indies Associated States, St. Lucia lies between Martinique and St. Vincent in the Windward Islands chain of the eastern Caribbean. As in the case of adjacent territories, most of the inhabitants are descendants of West African slaves who were brought as plantation laborers in the 17th and 18th centuries. Following the conclusion of a treaty with the indigenous Carib Indians in 1660, France settled the island and significant traces of French culture remain despite undisputed British control after 1803. At least 80 percent of the population is Roman Catholic.

The principal economic sectors are agriculture, with bananas and coconuts as the leading export items; tourism, which has been growing rapidly in recent years; and manufacturing, which currently embraces more than 40 relatively diversified enterprises. Despite satisfactory infrastructural development and significant geothermal energy potential, the economy has been hampered by rapid population growth, which has yielded widespread unemployment. (For more on the economy of the 1980s and 1990s, see the 2012 *Handbook.*)

Though the economy was hit hard in 2001, shrinking by 4.8 percent due to a combination of drought and the reduction in tourism following the terrorist attacks of September 11, St. Lucia saw growth through the decade. In 2008, GDP increased by 5.8 percent, but slowed to 0.4 percent the following year with the impact of the global economic crisis. The economy recovered somewhat in 2010, with 3.5 percent growth. Hurricane Tomas devastated the country in October 2010, causing an estimated $336 million in damage. Subsequently, unemployment rose to 24.5 percent, up from 14 percent in 2006. Economic growth has floundered in recent years, averaging 0.4 percent between 2010 and 2012, reflecting low tourism rates, an outbreak of banana leaf disease, and the introduction of a value-added tax (VAT) in October 2012. The IMF projected 1.1 percent GDP growth in 2013, with inflation at 4.8 percent.

GOVERNMENT AND POLITICS

Political background. Administered after 1833 as part of the British Leeward Islands, St. Lucia was incorporated in 1940 into the Windward Islands group, which also included Dominica, Grenada, and St. Vincent. It participated in the Federation of the West Indies from 1958 to 1962 and became one of the six internally self-governing West Indies Associated States in March 1967. St. Lucia, under Premier John G. M. COMPTON of the long-dominant United Workers' Party (UWP), applied for independence under a provision of the West Indies Act of 1966 requiring only that an Order in Council be laid before the British Parliament. After initially calling for a referendum, the opposition St. Lucia Labour Party (SLP), led by Allan LOUISY, participated in a constitutional conference held in London in July 1978. Following approval of the proposed constitution by the St. Lucia House of Assembly on October 24 and a draft termination order by both houses of Parliament in December, independence within the Commonwealth was proclaimed on February 22, 1979, with Premier Compton assuming the office of prime minister. Compton was succeeded by Louisy following a landslide victory by the leftist-oriented SLP on July 2, 1979.

In the wake of mounting conflict between the prime minister and a radical SLP faction led by Foreign Minister George ODLUM, Louisy resigned on April 30, 1981, paving way for centrist Winston CENAC. After Cenac was forced to step down on January 16, 1982, the governor general named Michael PILGRIM to head an all-party administration pending a general election on May 3 in which Compton's UWP secured a decisive victory, sweeping all but three parliamentary seats. Retaining control by one seat in the balloting of April 6, 1987, Compton called for a second election only three weeks later, which yielded the same outcome.

Buoyed by a resilient economy and campaigning on the slogan "Keep St. Lucia in good hands," Compton led the UWP to an 11–6 victory over the SLP in parliamentary balloting on April 27, 1992. He retired on March 31, 1996, and was succeeded by his recently designated party successor, Dr. Vaughan A. LEWIS, on April 2. Compton, however, returned as party leader in mid-1998.

In the election of May 23, 1997, the SLP crushed the UWP, 16–1, winning 61.3 percent of the valid votes under its new leader, Kenny D. ANTHONY. Anthony called early assembly elections for December 3, 2001, the SLP securing 14 seats compared to 3 for the UWP.

In another reversal, on December 11, 2006, the UWP regained power with 11 seats to the SLP's 6. The 82-year-old Compton was invested for the fifth time as prime minister. Following Compton's death less than a year later on September 7, 2007, Stevenson KING, who had served as acting prime minister since May 1, 2007, was named prime minister. (For more on King's cabinet, see the 2012 *Handbook.*)

Ahead of the November 2011 elections, two UWP parliamentarians resigned in protest of government policies. Meanwhile, controversy brewed over a revelation published in a Trinidadian newspaper in July 2011 alleging that Taiwan spent $3.8 million in an effort to keep the UWP in power (see Current Affairs, below). Against a backdrop of economic stagnation and an unemployment rate over 20 percent, both the UWP and SLP platforms touted job creation. The SLP returned to power with 11 seats, claiming victory over the UWP's 6. Kenny Anthony was sworn in on December 6 to serve his third term as prime minister.

Constitution and government. Under the 1979 constitution, the St. Lucia Parliament consists of "Her Majesty, a Senate and a House of Assembly." The queen, as titular head of state, is represented locally by a governor general whose emergency powers are subject to legislative review. Senators are appointed, serve only for the duration of a given Parliament, may not introduce money bills, and can only delay other legislation. The size of the Assembly is not fixed, although the present house has not been expanded beyond the preindependence membership of 17. The prime minister must be a member of the Assembly and command a majority therein; other ministers are appointed on the prime minister's advice from either of the two houses. Appointments to various public commissions, as well as the designation of a parliamentary ombudsman, require consultation with the leader of the opposition. The judicial system includes membership in the Eastern Caribbean Supreme Court, with appeals from its Court of Appeal transferred from the Judicial Committee of the Privy Council in London to the Caribbean Court of Justice upon the latter's launching in April 2005.

In 1985, the Compton government announced a plan to divide the island into eight regions, each with its own council and administrative services; implementation of the decentralization plan began in December 1985 and was completed the following year.

Calls for a number of constitutional changes, including abandonment of the link to the British Crown, were made to a Constitutional Reform Commission in early 2009. In March 2009, the Constitutional Reform Commission received submissions from individuals and organizations seeking changes in the island's basic law, including calls for the adoption of a republican form of government, a fixed date for general elections, changes in the appointment and function of the Senate, and expansion of the Bill of Rights to encompass education, health, and protection of the environment. The commission submitted its report to parliament in September 2012 and was tabled by Prime Minister Anthony in April 2013. Debate was expected during the next parliamentary session.

Freedom of speech is constitutionally guaranteed, and libel was removed from the criminal code in 2006.

Foreign relations. In May 1982, Prime Minister Compton reaffirmed his earlier wariness of Havana while indicating that his administration would cooperate with all regional governments participating in the Organization of Eastern Caribbean States (OECS), established in June 1981. In May 1987 Compton joined with James Mitchell of St. Vincent in urging that the seven OECS members work toward the formation of a single unitary state. Prime Minister Vere C. Bird Sr. of Antigua criticized the proposal as neocolonial, while other regional leaders showed only modest support.

Given the apparent failure of the OECS unification scheme, St. Lucia joined with its Windward Island neighbors (Dominica, Grenada, and St. Vincent and the Grenadines) in an effort to launch a less inclusive grouping. In September 1991, agreement was reached on a federal system with a common legislature and executive; however, there was opposition to the recent proposal. Prime Minister Compton subsequently sought a structure of association that would not require modification of the participants' constitutions.

St. Lucia joined with the five other OECS member states to officially create the OECS Economic Union on January 21, 2011. The accord provided a framework for an OECS Commission, an executive body with decision-making capability. A multilateral decision was finalized concerning the allowance of free movement of people and goods amongst OECS states, and the measure took effect on August 1 of that year. In January 2012, St. Lucia joined the OECS states in affirming commitment to fully embrace the jurisdiction of the Caribbean Court of Justice (CCJ), replacing the London-based Privy Court as the highest appeals court in the region. In May 2013, the Eastern Caribbean Supreme Court of Appeals ruled St. Lucia could adopt the CCJ without a referendum. In July Prime Minister Anthony began the process of negotiating the terms of adoption with the opposition UWP.

On September 1, 1997, diplomatic relations were established with the People's Republic of China, three days after a severance of ties with Taiwan, notwithstanding offers from Prime Minister Anthony to maintain economic and trade relations. Prime Minister Compton's denied after the December 2006 election that his administration sought refreshed ties with Taiwan. However, early the next year, the government invited a Taiwanese delegation to examine how "the interests of both parties could be advanced." Four months later, the Taiwanese flag was again raised in Castries, casting the diplomatic relationship with China into turmoil and stirring domestic controversy over the way the matter was handled. The relationship between Taiwan and St. Lucia is further complicated by the so-called Red Envelope Affair, in which the Taiwanese ambassador allegedly distributed $37,000 to each UWP candidate before the 2011 election. Nonetheless, Prime Minister Anthony surprised observers in September 2012 when he announced St. Lucia would maintain diplomatic ties with Taiwan while also seeking to maintain economic and other ties with China.

Following the conclusion of a number of Tax Information Exchange Agreements (TIEAs) that brought the total to more than the benchmark number of 12, the OECD elevated St. Lucia from its "gray list" of tax havens to its "white list" of compliant regimes, thus averting the possibility of sanctions by either the G-20 or the OECD.

In February 2012, St. Lucia was made a "special guest member" state of the Venezuelan-led regional organization, the Bolivarian Alliance for the Americas (ALBA). Despite claims from the UWP that the move would damage relations with the United States, St. Lucia fully acceded in August 2013.

Canada revoked visa-free entry for St. Lucian citizens in September 2012, citing concerns over the reliable authenticity of St. Lucian passports.

During a state visit to Cuba in May 2013, Prime Minister Anthony reinforced the strength of the relationship between the countries.

Current issues. Stephenson King's administration appeared reluctant to press for implementation of a VAT, to which it had long been committed, apparently reflective of concerns within the business community as to which lesser levies (ranging from personal taxes to import duties) the VAT would supersede. Nonetheless, Prime Minister Anthony embraced King's VAT proposal, and the VAT was implemented on October 1, 2013, delayed one month to address details pertaining to the service sector and other particularities. Though initially met with disgruntlement, the VAT is expected to improve long-term economic development.

Meanwhile, St. Lucian officials are cautious of deepening foreign direct investment and foreign aid ties. Prime Minister Anthony has ruled out pursuing a stronger relationship with the International Monetary Fund (IMF) after the organization provided $8 million in emergency financing for reconstruction after Hurricane Tomas and hopes to build an economy that will not require outside assistance.

Public sector workers went on strike in March 2013 as the government refused to meet union demands of a salary increase of at least 6 percent, citing the country's "unsustainable" debt. While some unions within the umbrella organization agreed to the 4 percent raise, other groups maintained the strike for three weeks at an estimated cost of $1.1 million.

POLITICAL PARTIES

Government Party:

St. Lucia Labour Party (SLP). The SLP is a left-of-center party formed in 1946. After boycotting the independence ceremonies because they were not immediately preceded by balloting for a new assembly, it won a landslide victory in the election of July 2, 1979. Party leader Allan Louisy resigned as prime minister in April 1981 because of intraparty conflict with "new Left" advocate George Odlum, who subsequently withdrew to form the **Progressive Labour Party** (PLP) in opposition to the government of Louisy's successor, Winston Cenac. At its 1984 annual convention, the SLP voted to assign the roles of party leader and leader of the opposition to different individuals, and in a move interpreted as a swing to the right, named Castries businessman Julian HUNTE to the former post. The party was unable to secure a majority in either of the 1987 elections and secured only 6 of 17 seats in 1992. Hunte resigned his leadership post in February 1996 because of the party's poor showing in a Castries by-election and was succeeded in March by Dr. Kenny Anthony.

Dr. Anthony led the SLP to a near sweep (16 of 17 assembly seats) in the election of May 23, 1997, resulting in his appointment as prime minister. George Odlum joined the subsequent cabinet as minister of foreign affairs and international trade. However, he left the government in March 2001 after announcing that he would not stand as an SLP candidate in the 2001 balloting. (See National Alliance, below, for information on Odlum's subsequent activities.) The SLP maintained a strong showing in the 2001 election, capturing 14 seats. After losing control of the government 6 seats to the UWP's 11 in 2006, Anthony led the party to victory in the 2011 elections, unseating the UWP by winning a 5-seat majority.

Leaders: Dr. Kenny Davis ANTHONY (Party Leader and Prime Minister), Phillip J. PIERRE (Deputy Political Leader), Alva BAPTISTE (Second Deputy Political Leader).

Opposition Party:

United Workers' Party (UWP). The UWP was organized in 1964 by members of the former National Labour Movement and the People's Progressive Party. The party's basically moderate leader, Sir John G. M. Compton, served as chief minister from 1964 to 1967 and as premier from 1967 to 1979, becoming prime minister upon independence. Decisively defeated in July 1979, the UWP returned to power on May 3, 1982. It obtained a bare majority of one assembly seat in the election of April 6, 1987, and failed to improve its standing in a second election on April 30. By contrast, the party won a healthy margin of five seats in April 1992. In January 1996, Compton retired as party leader in favor of Dr. Vaughan Lewis, who succeeded as prime minister on April 2 before the election of May 23, 1997, in which the party secured only one seat.

Morella Joseph, a retired school principal, was elected unopposed as the UWP party leader at the October 2000 annual convention. Despite an increase in UWP representation to three seats with a vote share of 36.6 percent in the 2001 election, Joseph subsequently resigned and was replaced on an interim basis by Marius Wilson. In mid-2004 the parliamentary leader of the opposition, Marcus NICHOLS, was sacked after calling for UWP leader Lewis to resign. In March 2005 former prime minister Compton came out of political retirement to defeat Lewis for the UWP leadership. In May 2007 Stevenson King was appointed acting prime minister when Prime Minister Crompton was incapacitated because of illness. Upon Crompton's death on September 7, 2007, King was named prime minister and was elected party leader at the 2007 UWP annual convention.

In January 2011, Member of Parliament Jeannine COMPTON-ANTOINE, daughter of party founder and former prime minister John G. M. Compton, resigned from the UWP, claiming that the ministers often ignored her when discussing issues pertaining to her constituency and noting that for some time many within the party had made it clear that she was not wanted as a party member.

In internal elections of July 2013, former tourism minister Allen Chastanet won a decisive victory for party leadership, defeating King, 264 to 99.

Leaders: Allen CHASTANET (Party Leader), Mary POLIUS (Deputy Party Leader), Andy DANIEL (Deputy Political Leader).

Other Parties:

Lucian People's Movement (LPM). Created in 2010 as a third party alternative to the SLP and the UWP, the LPM is devoted to promoting equity, social equality, and increased standards of living for all of St. Lucia's citizens. It appeals to democratic tools, such as referendum, to accurately gage the will of the people in their governance. The LPM places a heavy influence on youth as the future of the nation and accordingly desires to incorporate youth into the decision making of the government. Six candidates ran without success in 2011. In July 2013, the LPM urged the government to hold a referendum on the CCJ (see Foreign relations, above).

Leader: Therold PRUDENT (Party Leader).

National Democratic Movement (NDM). The NDM was created in 2004. Five candidates ran unsuccessfully in the 2011 election.

Leader: Ausbert D'AUVERGNE (Party Leader).

An additional party, the **Lucian Greens** headed by Andre DeCaires, unsuccessfully contested the 2011 election in three districts.

LEGISLATURE

The **Parliament** of St. Lucia consists of an appointed Senate and an elected House of Assembly, each with a normal term of five years, subject to dissolution.

Senate. The upper house encompasses 11 members, of whom 6 are appointed on the advice of the prime minister, 3 on the advice of the leader of the opposition, and 2 after consultation with religious, economic, and social groups.

President: Claudius FRANCIS.

House of Assembly. The lower house presently consists of 17 directly elected members plus an appointed speaker. In the election of November 28, 2011, the St. Lucia Labour Party won 11 seats and the United Workers' Party, 6.

Speaker: Peter FOSTER.

CABINET

[as of September 15, 2013]

Prime Minister	Kenny Davis Anthony
Ministers	
Agriculture, Land, Forestry, and Fisheries	Moses Jean Baptiste
Commerce, Business Development, and Consumer Affairs	Emma Hippolyte [f]
Education, Human Resource Development, and Labor	Robert Lewis
Finance and Economic Affairs	Kenny Davis Anthony
Foreign Affairs, International Trade, and Civil Aviation	Alva Baptiste
Health, Wellness, Human Services, and Gender Development	Alvina Reynolds [f]
Infrastructure, Ports, and Transport	Philip Pierre
Legal Affairs, Home Affairs, and National Security	Sen. Victor Phillip LaCorbiniere
Physical Development, Housing, and Urban Renewal	Sen. Stanley Felix
Public Service, Sustainable Development, Energy, Science, and Technology	Sen. James Fletcher
Social Transformation, Local Government, and Community Empowerment	Harold Dalson
Tourism, Heritage, and the Creative Industries	Lorne Theophilus
Youth Development and Sports	Shawn Edward

[f] = female

Note: All Members belong to SLP.

INTERGOVERNMENTAL REPRESENTATION

Ambassador to the U.S.: Sonia Merlyn JOHNNY.

U.S. Ambassador to St. Lucia: Larry Leon PALMER.

Permanent Representative to the UN: Menissa RAMBALLY.

IGO Memberships (Non-UN): ALBA, Caricom, CWTH, ICC, NAM, OAS, WTO.

ST. VINCENT AND THE GRENADINES

Political Status: Former British dependency; joined West Indies Associated States in 1967; independent member of the Commonwealth since October 27, 1979.

Area: 150 sq. mi. (389 sq. km), including the Grenadine dependencies, which encompass 17 sq. mi. (44 sq. km).

Population: 110,866 (2012E—UN; 103,537 (2012E—U.S. Census)

Major Urban Center (2005E): KINGSTOWN (30,400, including suburbs).

Official Language: English.

Monetary Unit: East Caribbean Dollar (market rate November 1, 2013: 2.70 EC dollars = $1US).

Sovereign: Queen ELIZABETH II.

Governor General: Sir Frederick Nathaniel BALLANTYNE; sworn in on September 2, 2002, after being appointed by the Queen following the death of Sir Charles James ANTROBUS on June 3. (Deputy Governor General Monica DACON had served in an acting capacity during the interim period.)

Prime Minister: Dr. Ralph E. GONSALVES (Unity Labour Party); sworn in March 29, 2001, following the election of March 28 in succession to Arnhim EUSTACE (New Democratic Party); remained in office following elections of December 7, 2005, and December 13, 2010.

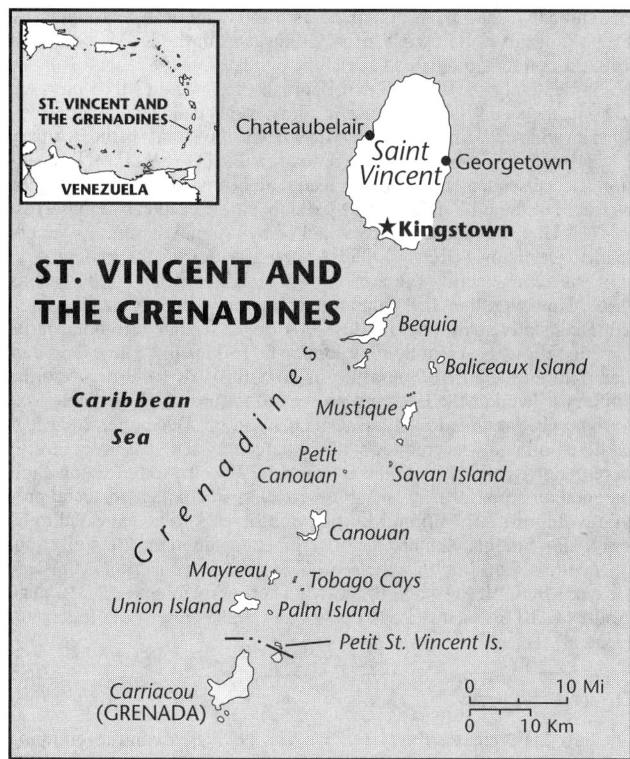

THE COUNTRY

St. Vincent and the Grenadines (comprising some 32 islands and keys) is located in the Windward group of the eastern Caribbean, south of St. Lucia and west of Barbados. Its jurisdiction encompasses the northern Grenadine islets of Beguia, Canouan, Mayreau, Mustique, Prune Island, Petit St. Vincent, and Union Island, the southern portion of the chain being part of Grenada. The population is mainly of African and mixed origin, with small numbers of Asians, Caribs, and Europeans. The economy is based almost entirely on tourism (the leading earner of foreign exchange) and agriculture, with bananas, arrowroot, and coconuts being the principal export commodities. An extended series of volcanic eruptions in April 1979 caused massive devastation and necessitated temporary evacuation of the northern two-thirds of the main island, although substantial recovery was registered by early 1984.

Real GDP growth fell to 2 percent in 2000 and was close to zero in the ensuing two years because of declining banana exports and the negative impact on tourism of the September 2001 terrorist attacks on the United States. It then rose steadily to a vigorous 8.0 percent in 2007 before plummeting to –1.0 percent in 2009 and –2.0 percent in 2010 because of the global recession, which, among other things, depressed tourism and foreign investment. Recovery was subsequently compromised by natural disasters, prompting assistance from the International Monetary Fund (IMF), which called for structural reforms such as improved tax compliance, reduced government spending, and promotion of the private sector. Growth of just under 1 percent was reported for 2012.

GOVERNMENT AND POLITICS

Political background. Claimed by both Great Britain and France during the 17th and 18th centuries, St. Vincent was definitively assigned to the former by the Treaty of Versailles in 1783. The islands, 50 years later, became part of the general government of Barbados and the Windward Islands and, after the separation of the two in 1885, were administered from Grenada. A founding member in 1958 of the Federation of the West Indies (which dissolved in 1962), St. Vincent and the Grenadines joined the West Indies Associated States in 1969 as an internally self-governing territory with a right of unilateral termination, which was exercised on October 27, 1979. After the state's admission to the Commonwealth as a special member in 1979, Sir Sydney GUN-MUNRO, the former governor, assumed the titular role of governor general, while Premier Robert Milton CATO became prime minister and continued in office after balloting on December 5, in which his St. Vincent Labour Party (SVLP) captured 11 of 13 elective parliamentary seats.

In the election of July 25, 1984, the SVLP was defeated by the New Democratic Party (NDP), whose nine-member majority forced the resignation of Prime Minister Cato in favor of former premier James F. MITCHELL. The NDP swept the balloting of May 20, 1989, the country being bereft of an elected opposition. The NDP continued in office by winning 12 of 15 elective seats on February 21, 1994, before being reduced to a bare majority of 8 seats on June 18, 1998. Arnhim EUSTACE, theretofore finance minister, succeeded Mitchell as prime minister upon the latter's retirement on October 27, 2000.

In accordance with an agreement reached the previous year, early elections were held on March 28, 2001. The center-left Unity Labour Party (ULP, a successor, in part, to the SVLP) captured 12 elective seats to the NDP's 3. ULP leader Ralph GONSALVES was appointed prime minister on March 29 and announced a ULP cabinet on April 2, thus ending 16 years of uninterrupted NDP control. Gonsalves remained in office after the election of December 7, 2005, which yielded no change in the legislative distribution. Gonsalves also retained his post as head of a new cabinet formed on December 19, 2010, although the ULP's majority over the NDP had fallen to a single seat in the legislative balloting of December 13, in part as a result of recent economic shocks.

Constitution and government. An amended version of the 1969 document defining St. Vincent's status as an Associated State, the present constitution, adopted at independence in 1979, provides for a governor general who acts on behalf of the British Crown and who appoints as prime minister the individual best able to command a majority within the legislature. Other cabinet members are appointed on the advice of the prime minister. Legislative authority is exercised by a unicameral House of Assembly. The highest court—apart from a right of appeal in certain circumstances to the Judicial Committee of the Privy Council in London—is the West Indies Supreme Court (based in St. Lucia), which includes a Court of Appeal and a High Court, one of whose judges is resident in St. Vincent and the Grenadines and presides over a Court of Summary Jurisdiction. District Courts deal with petty offenses and minor civil actions. The main island of St. Vincent is divided into five local parishes (Charlotte, St. George, St. Andrew, St. David, and St. Patrick); a sixth parish covers all of the Grenadine islands.

In what was considered a major setback to the ULP government, 55 percent of the voters in a national referendum on November 25, 2009, rejected a proposed new constitution that, among other things, would have replaced Queen Elizabeth II as head of state with a president chosen by the legislature and would have replaced the UK's Privy Council with the Caribbean Court of Justice as the country's final appellate court.

Freedom of the press is constitutionally guaranteed, and the country's several private newspapers and radio stations operate without government interference.

Foreign relations. Admitted to the United Nations in September 1980, St. Vincent obtained full membership in the Commonwealth in June 1985.

One of the more moderate Caribbean leaders, Prime Minister Cato declared during independence ceremonies in 1979 that his government would "not succumb to pressure from any power bloc" and would not seek admission to the Nonaligned Movement because such participation "is to be aligned." Although Cato assisted in establishing the U.S.-backed Regional Security System (RSS), his successor, James Mitchell, strongly opposed "militarization" of the region and in 1986 helped block the U.S. effort to upgrade the RSS to a stronger alignment that would have established a centralized military force to fight "subversion" in the Eastern Caribbean. Mitchell also canceled St. Vincent and the Grenadines' participation in U.S.–Eastern Caribbean joint military maneuvers late in the year. In July 1996, on the other hand, he agreed to the conclusion of an extradition treaty with Washington that was aimed primarily at drug traffickers.

While opposing military enhancement, Mitchell was long viewed as the "father" of regional political integration. Following failure by the seven-member Organization of Eastern Caribbean States (OECS) to move toward a single unitary state, he advocated unification of St. Vincent and the Grenadines with the neighboring Windward Island states of Dominica, Grenada, and St. Lucia. However, the third session of a Regional Constituent Assembly that convened in Roseau, Dominica, in September 1991 could reach agreement only on a federal system, preliminary approval for which was to be sought by referendums (never held) in the four nations.

In December 1991 a four-member government delegation headed by St. Vincent and the Grenadines' ambassador to the United States,

Kingsley LAYNE, was the first such group to visit Cuba. Five months later formal diplomatic relations were established with Havana.

St. Vincent and the Grenadines is one of about two dozen (mainly small) countries maintaining relations with Taiwan, whose foreign minister, in a discussion of financing for a variety of projects, declared in September 2006 that even a small country could speak in support of his government's bid to join international organizations. Apart from Taiwan, the principal sources of external aid for St. Vincent and the Grenadines are the United Kingdom, Canada, and the United States, which contribute both bilaterally and through donations to the World Bank, the United Nations Development Programme, and the Caribbean Development Bank. However, a $7 million aid package was negotiated with Iran in 2008.

St. Vincent and the Grenadines distanced itself from the United States somewhat with a declaration by Prime Minister Gonsalves in early 2009 that it would join the Bolivarian Alternative for the Americas (ALBA), launched by Venezuelan President Huge Chávez as a counter to the U.S.-backed Free Trade Area of the Americas. In addition, unlike several of its Caribbean neighbors, St. Vincent and the Grenadines initially did little to assist the campaign by the Organization for Economic Cooperation and Development (OECD) to eliminate tax havens.

Prime Minister Gonsalves warmly welcomed integrationist initiatives in 2011–2012 within the OECS, including the implementation of the free movement of nationals among the member countries and progress toward economic union. He also strongly criticized the lack of similar progress within the Caribbean Community and the Common Market (Caricom), while continuing to promote ALBA as an important regional grouping. Earlier, Iranian President Mahmoud Ahmadinejad had praised St. Vincent and the Grenadines for having resisted the "bullying" of Western states.

On the other hand, the government's stance in regard to OECD demands about tax havens has softened recently, and in April 2012, Gonsalves announced the completion of the first phase of efforts to improve the regulatory framework of the nation's financial sector in consonance with OECD guidelines. In addition, bilateral agreements have been concluded regarding the exchange of tax information with many countries, including France, which in 2012, removed St. Vincent and the Grenadines from its blacklist in that regard.

In March 2013 Gonsalves urged the creation of a Caribbean-wide initiative to seek reparations from the United Kingdom for Britain's role in the slave trade in the region and for the "theft" of land during colonial rule.

Current issues. The government announced in the first half of 2012 that economic recovery had begun while predicting that construction of the nation's new international airport would boost the tourism sector significantly. However, the opening of the $280 million facility was subsequently postponed until at least the end of 2014. Also on the economic front, the government's proposed bond issue ($14.7 million over ten years for various projects) was reportedly significantly undersubscribed in March 2013 due to investor concern over domestic and regional economic doldrums.

POLITICAL PARTIES

Government Party:

Unity Labour Party (ULP). The ULP was formed in October 1994 by the merger of two opposition groups, the St. Vincent and Grenadines Labour Party (SVGLP) and the Movement for National Unity (MNU).

The SVGLP was launched in 1955 as the St. Vincent Labour Party (SVLP), a moderate socialist formation that obtained 10 of 13 elective legislative seats in the preindependence balloting of 1974 and 11 seats in the first postindependence poll in December 1979. The party was forced into opposition after winning only 4 seats in 1984. Soon afterward, former prime minister Robert Cato, whose relatively advanced age of 69 and recent ill health were viewed as contributing factors in the election reversal, announced his retirement from politics. Hudson TANNIS was elected party leader at a special congress in January 1985. His rival for the party leadership, Sir Vincent Ian BEACHE, was later elected parliamentary opposition leader, indicating continued competition for control of the SVLP before Tannis's death in a plane crash in August 1986. Beache retired in September 1992, Stanley JOHN being elected his successor.

The MNU had been organized as a moderate leftist grouping by Ralph Gonsalves following his withdrawal from the UPM (below) in 1982; it nominated two unsuccessful candidates in 1989.

In September 1993 the SVGLP initially rejected an MNU proposal to conclude an anti-NDP alliance for the next general election; however, such an alliance, formed in January 1994, won three seats in the February 21 poll. After the election Beache returned to lead the SVLP/MNU coalition and subsequently the ULP (as leader of the opposition). He resigned as leader of the ULP in December 1998, being succeeded by Gonsalves.

The ULP was subsequently wracked by internal dissent, its deputy leader, Ormiston ("Ken") BOYEA, being criticized for joining government representatives in a meeting with EC officials on the banana issue. However, the ULP won an overwhelming victory in the March 2001 legislative balloting. In May 2004 Boyea resigned from the party, joining fellow dissident Stanley John, who had resigned nine days earlier. The two accused Gonsalves of activities that were dividing the country as well as the ULP and proceeded to form the PPM (below).

The ULP retained its 12-seat majority in the December 2005 legislative poll and was credited with 51 percent of the vote in securing a bare majority of 8 seats in the December 2010 elections, having campaigned on a platform stressing job creation and expanded social programs. In mid-2012 Prime Minister Gonsalves said he expected to be the ULP's candidate to lead the government again in the 2015 election.

Leaders: Dr. Ralph E. GONSALVES (Leader and Prime Minister), Girlyn MIGUEL (Deputy Prime Minister), Edwin SNAGG (Chair), Audrey GITTENS-GILKES (Deputy Chair), Julian FRANCIS (Secretary General).

Opposition Party:

New Democratic Party (NDP). The NDP is a centrist grouping formed in 1975. It became the formal opposition party after the 1979 election, although it had captured only 2 legislative seats and NDP leader James Mitchell had lost his bid for reelection after abandoning his traditional seat from Beguia for a main-island constituency. Subsequently, Mitchell's successor from the Grenadines resigned, permitting Mitchell to regain the seat in a by-election in June 1980. Following a thorough reorganization, the NDP, campaigning in July 1984 under the slogan "Time for a Change," won 9 of the (then) 13 elective assembly seats; it captured all 15 such seats in May 1989, with a vote share of 66.2 percent. In February 1994 it dropped to 12 seats on a vote share of 54.5 percent.

Mitchell resigned as prime minister in October 2000 and was succeeded by Finance Minister Arnhim Eustace, who led the party to defeat in March 2001 and December 2005. The NDP closed significantly on the ULP by securing 49 percent of the vote (good for 7 of the assembly's 15 elected seats) in the December 2010 elections. The NDP campaign manifesto emphasized the pursuit of foreign investment and characterized the ULP government as corrupt and too closely aligned with leftist governments in the region. Several prominent NDP members have reportedly criticized Eustace's leadership style recently.

Leaders: Arnhim Ulric EUSTACE (Former Prime Minister, President of the Party, and Leader of the Opposition); Linton LEWIS (Chair); St. Clair LEACOCK and Goodwin FRIDAY (Vice Presidents); Sir James F. MITCHELL (Former Prime Minister and Former President of the Party); Allan CRUICKSHANK (Secretary General).

Other Party Contesting the 2010 Election:

St. Vincent and the Grenadines Green Party (SVGGP). Launched in January 2005, the Green Party won no seats in the 2005 balloting or in the 2010 poll, in which it was credited with 0.2 percent of the vote.

Leaders: Ivan O'NEAL (Leader), Don O'NEAL, Ordan O. GRAHAM (Secretary).

Other Parties:

People's Progressive Movement (PPM). The PPM was launched on August 13, 2000, by former members of the ULP, including Ormiston "Ken" BOYEA. It presented 11 candidates in the March 2001 balloting but won no seats, securing only 2.6 percent of the vote.

Leaders: Ormiston ("Ken") BOYEA, Stanley ("Stalley") JOHN.

United People's Movement (UPM). The UPM was organized, under the leadership of Ralph Gonsalves, as a coalition of left-wing groups before the 1979 election, in which it obtained no parliamentary representation. Gonsalves, once described as "the leading Marxist theoretician in the Caribbean," left the party in 1982 to form the MNU (see ULP, above), his role as radical leftist advocate being assumed by Oscar ALLEN. The party never secured legislative representation, having last competed in 1989.

People's Movement For Change (PMC). The PMC was launched in July 2008 as a "social-political movement" designed to "raise the consciousness of the people" by focusing on crucial national issues.
Leaders: Oscar ALLEN (Chair), Jomo THOMAS (General Secretary).

Canovan People's Movement (CPM). The CPM represents inhabitants of the Grenadine islet of Canovan.
Leader: Terry BYNOE.

LEGISLATURE

The unicameral **House of Assembly** currently consists of 6 appointed senators (4 appointed by the government party and 2 by the opposition) and 15 representatives elected from single-member constituencies for five-year terms, subject to dissolution. The speaker of the assembly and the attorney general serve as ex officio members, with the right to vote except on financial or constitutional matters. In the most recent balloting of December 13, 2010, the Unity Labour Party won 8 of the elective seats and the New Democratic Party, 7.
Speaker: Hendrick ALEXANDER.

CABINET

[as of July 1, 2013]

Prime Minister	Ralph E. Gonsalves
Deputy Prime Minister	Girlyn Miguel [f]
Ministers	
Agriculture, Industry, Forestry, Fisheries, and Rural Transformation	Saboto Caesar
Education	Girlyn Miguel [f]
Finance and Economic Planning	Ralph E. Gonsalves
Foreign Affairs, Foreign Trade, and Consumer Affairs	Sen. Dr. Douglas Slater
Grenadine Affairs	Ralph E. Gonsalves
Health, Wellness, and the Environment	Clayton Burgin
Housing, Informal Human Settlements, Physical Planning, and Lands and Surveys	Montgomery Daniel
Legal Affairs	Ralph E. Gonsalves
National Mobilization, Social Development, Family, Gender Affairs, Persons with Disabilities, and Youth	Frederick A. Stephenson
National Reconciliation, Public Service, Labor, Information, and Ecclesiastical Affairs	Maxwell Charles
National Security and Air and Sea Port Development	Ralph E. Gonsalves
Tourism, Sports, and Culture	Cecil McKie
Transport, Works, Urban Development, and Local Government	Sen. Julian Francis
Attorney General	Judith S. Jones-Morgan [f]

[f] = female

INTERGOVERNMENTAL REPRESENTATION

Ambassador to the U.S.: La Celia Aritha PRINCE.

U.S. Ambassador to St. Vincent: Larry Leon PALMER (resident in Barbados).

Permanent Representative to the UN: Camillo GONSALVES.

IGO Memberships (Non-UN): Caricom, CWTH, ICC, NAM, WTO.

SAMOA

Independent State of Samoa
Sa 'oloto Tuto 'atasi o Samoa

Note: There is considerable confusion regarding Samoan proper names, the initial component being generally accorded benchmark status and, with some exceptions, utilized herein as such.

Political Status: Gained independence (as Western Samoa) on January 1, 1962; member of the Commonwealth since 1970; current name adopted in 1977; under mixed political system approximating a constitutional monarchy.

Area: 1,097 sq. mi. (2,842 sq. km).

Population: 188,097 (2013E—UN); 195,476 (2013E—U.S. Census).

Major Urban Center (2005E): APIA (40,700).

Official Languages: English, Samoan.

Monetary Unit: Tala (market rate November 1, 2013: 2.33 tala = $1US).

Head of State: Tui Atua TUPUA Tamasese Taisi Efi; elected by the Legislative Assembly and installed for a five-year term on June 20, 2007, succeeding Susuga MALIETOA Tanumafili II, who had died on May 12; reelected July 20, 2012, and sworn in for a second five-year term on July 25.

Prime Minister: TUILAEPA Lupesoliai Neioti Aiono Sailele Malielegaoi (Human Rights Protection Party); confirmed by the Legislative Assembly on November 23, 1998, following the resignation of TOFILAU Eti Alesana (Human Rights Protection Party); continued in office following the elections of March 2, 2001, March 31, 2006, and March 4, 2011.

THE COUNTRY

What was formerly called Western Samoa consists of two volcanic islands (Savai'i and Upolu) and several minor islets located east of Fiji and west of American Samoa in the south-central Pacific. The country enjoys a tropical climate and good volcanic soils, but rugged topography limits the cultivated and populated areas to the lowlands and coastal fringes. The Christian, highly literate Samoans are representatives of the second-largest ethnic group of Polynesia. They have had lengthy contact with the West but retain their traditional social structure, which is based on an extended family grouping known as the *aiga,* whose chief, or *matai,* also serves as the *aiga's* political representative.

The economy is largely based on subsistence agriculture (which involves two-thirds of the labor force) and fishing (which accounts for 60 percent of exports), supplemented by the production of coconut oil, coffee, and bananas for export. (Cocoa was an increasingly important cash crop in the 1980s but is currently limited primarily to domestic consumption.) Basic raw materials are lacking, and the country suffers from a chronic trade deficit, part of which is offset by tourism (20 percent of GDP), remittances (25 percent of GDP) from Samoans living in New Zealand and the United States, and foreign aid.

Listed by the United Nations as a least developed country, Samoa in 1990–1991 was ravaged by cyclones that decimated crucial banana, cocoa, and coconut plantations, leaving the economy in tatters. Economic improvement over the next decade was attributed, in part, to government initiatives to support the private sector, which included tax breaks for foreign investors, modernization of customs procedures, and reduction of import tariffs. The government also privatized some state-run enterprises while promoting the fledgling offshore banking sector. Efforts to improve oversight of offshore facilities followed criticism in June 2001 by the Organization for Economic Cooperation and Development, which included Samoa on a list of jurisdictions with questionable tax policies. Although formally deleted from the list a year later, Samoa continued to attract attention as a tax haven.

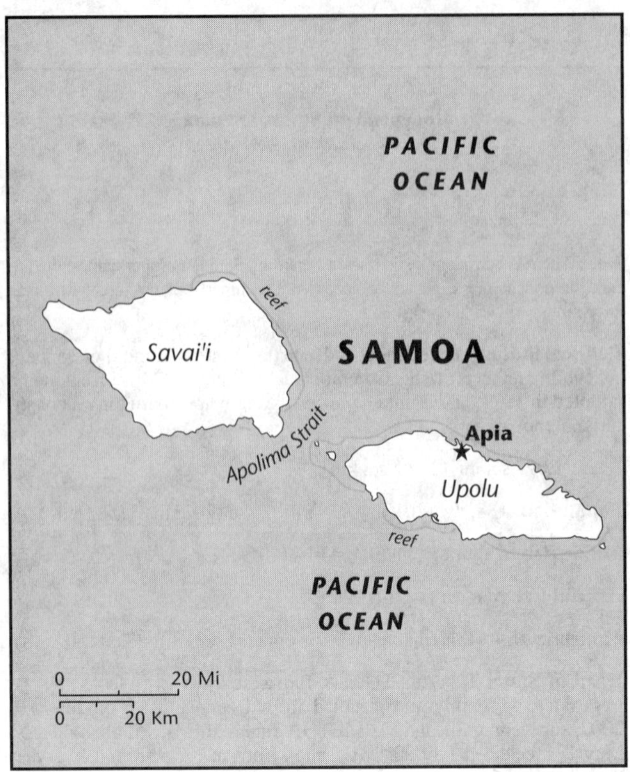

After a decade of steady growth, GDP plummeted by more than 5 percent in 2009 as a result of the global economic crisis and a massive tsunami in September that inflicted unprecedented damage to both physical infrastructure and tourism and killed more than 180 people. In part due to post-tsunami reconstruction and a government stimulus program, GDP rose by more than 2 percent in 2011 and 2012.

In March 2012, the World Bank announced it would provide $100 million in grants and concessionary lending over the next five years. An economic boost was also anticipated from Samoa's accession to the World Trade Organization (WTO) the following May. However, the economy suffered another severe shock when Cyclone Evan hit in December (see Current issues, below).

GOVERNMENT AND POLITICS

Political background. An object of missionary interest since the 1830s, the Samoan Islands came under joint British, German, and American supervision in 1889 but were politically divided as a consequence of an 1899 treaty whereby the United States annexed Eastern (American) Samoa, while Western Samoa became a German protectorate. New Zealand occupied Western Samoa during World War I and acquired subsequent control of the territory under a League of Nations mandate. Opposition to the New Zealand administration resulted in the formation of a nationalist organization known as the "Mau," which was active between 1927 and 1936.

Following World War II a Samoan request for independence was rejected, and Western Samoa continued under New Zealand administration as a United Nations Trust Territory. However, political evolution subsequently gained momentum. Cabinet government was introduced in 1959; a new constitution, adopted in 1960, was approved by plebiscite in 1961; and the country became fully independent by agreement with New Zealand and the United Nations on January 1, 1962. The largely ceremonial position of head of state was at first held jointly by the representatives of two of the four royal lines (the Tuiaana/Tuiatua and the Malietoa), but one of the incumbents died in 1963.

Political life since independence has seen a number of changes as well as a series of recent challenges to certain aspects of the country's constitutional structure. The first government after independence, headed by Prime Minister FIAME Mata'afa, lasted through 1970, when it was replaced by an administration headed by Tupua TAMASESE Lealofi IV. The Tamasese regime was succeeded in 1973 by another Fiame government, although Tamasese returned as acting prime minister to serve the remainder of Fiame's term upon the latter's death in May 1975. In March 1976, following a legislative election in which more than half of the incumbents lost their seats, TUPUOLA Taisi Efi became the first prime minister not a *Tama Aiga* ("Royal Son") from one of the four leading families. After balloting on February 24, 1979, that again saw more than half of the incumbents defeated, Tupuola was redesignated prime minister following legislative endorsement by a vote of 24–23.

In the election of February 27, 1982, the islands' first formally constituted political group, the Human Rights Protection Party (HRPP), won a plurality of 22 parliamentary seats, and, after a lengthy period of consultation with independent members, it organized a government under VA'AI Kolone on April 13. However, the party lost its 1-seat majority in late June upon the ouster of a member found guilty of electoral malpractice, and on September 18 Va'ai's seat was vacated by the Supreme Court on similar grounds. Former prime minister Tupuola was thereupon returned to office, although his attempt to form a coalition government was rebuffed by the HRPP, which argued that the court had exceeded its authority in its expulsion orders. Upon rejection of a budget bill, Tupuola was again forced to resign, and the new HRPP leader, TOFILAU Eti Alesana, succeeded him on December 30, the party having regained its majority in special elections to refill the vacated seats. In mid-1984 opposition leader Tupuola was designated a *Tama Aiga* in succession to his cousin, former prime minister Tamasese Lealofi IV; thenceforth Tupuola was addressed as Tui Atua TUPUA Tamasese Efi.

The HRPP captured 31 of 47 assembly seats in the election of February 22, 1985, Tofilau Eti being redesignated prime minister after former prime minister Va'ai Kolone had withdrawn a bid to recover the party leadership. Despite his party's technical majority, Tofilau was forced to resign on December 27, 1985, after members of the HRPP joined with the opposition (now including Va'ai) to defeat the 1986 budget bill on a 27–19 vote. During the following week a new coalition government headed by Va'ai was formed, the head of state having rejected a request to dissolve the assembly.

The results of the extremely close election of February 26, 1988, were not announced until the new assembly convened on April 7, at which time the HRPP was declared to have obtained a bare majority of 24 seats, with Tofilau Eti returning as prime minister. By late summer, following a number of Supreme Court rulings on electoral challenges and a series of special elections, the HRPP's representation had increased to 27.

In a popular referendum on October 29, 1990, voters by a narrow margin indicated that they favored the adoption of universal suffrage for all persons age 21 and above (albeit with only chiefs eligible as candidates), while rejecting by a 3–2 margin the proposed establishment of an upper chamber reserved for *matai.* Under the new procedure the HRPP won an increased majority of 30 seats (1 of which was subsequently vacated) in the election of April 5, 1991, with Tofilau Eti forming a new government on May 14.

In early 1994 the introduction of a value-added tax on goods and services generated a series of demonstrations and protest marches. The HRPP responded by expelling 3 antitax members, thereby reducing its position (in the wake of several 1993 defections) to a legislative plurality of 23 seats. However, by March 1995, after special elections and other realignments, the HRPP had regained a majority of 33.

In the election of April 26, 1996, HRPP government representation declined to 22 seats, with a loss of 3 cabinet members and the assembly speaker. However, Tofilau Eti retained office by a 34–14 vote on May 17, with a number of independents entering the HRPP to establish its majority once more.

In early 1997, Prime Minister Tofilau Eti introduced a constitutional amendment, which was subsequently approved, to change the country's name from Western Samoa to Samoa. The change was bitterly opposed by American Samoans, who were, however, unable to secure a reversal.

Tofilau Eti, who had long been in ill health, resigned as prime minister in favor of his deputy, TUILAEPA Sailele Malielegaoi, on November 23, 1998, and died four months later. Prime Minister Tuilaepa was returned to office following the legislative election of March 2, 2001, although the HRPP required the adherence of independents to secure his confirmation and establish a working majority in the Legislative Assembly. Tuilaepa was returned with a far more commanding majority of 33 after the election of March 31, 2006.

Prior to his death at age 95 on May 12, 2007, MALIETOA Tanumafili II had been recognized as the world's oldest surviving head of state, having served since Samoa's independence in 1962. He was succeeded on May 12 by former prime minister Tui Atua Tupua Tamasese Efi, the first head of state to be elected for a five-year term rather than for life.

Although it faced a significant challenge from the recently formed Tautua Samoa Party (TSP), the HRPP retained a clear majority in the March 4, 2011, legislative poll. Prime Minister Tuilaepa named nine new ministers to the cabinet appointed on March 19.

Head of State Tupua was reelected unopposed for a second five-year term on July 20, 2012.

Constitution and government. As defined by the constitution of October 28, 1960, Samoa's political institutions combine the forms of British-style parliamentary democracy with elements of the traditional Samoan social structure. The head of state (*O le Ao o le Malo*) performs the duties of a constitutional sovereign. Formerly designated for life, heads of state are now elected by the Legislative Assembly (*Fono Aoao Faitulafono*) for five-year terms. The head of state appoints the prime minister upon the recommendation of the assembly; the prime minister appoints the members of the cabinet, who are drawn from the assembly and are responsible to that body. Traditionally, most members of the legislature were indirectly elected by *matai,* or family heads, whose number was increased by one-third to 16,000 in a series of controversial appointments before the 1985 balloting; direct election was limited to two special representatives chosen by universal adult suffrage of persons outside the *matai* system.

A measure calling for universal suffrage (without a universal right of candidacy) was rejected by the assembly in 1981. However, with chiefly titles being created at a rate exceeding that of population growth and with some individuals holding multiple titles (each carrying an electoral vote), the *matai* system had come under mounting criticism. Given the increasingly prevalent practice of bestowing titles for political purposes, universal suffrage (endorsed in the October 1990 referendum), ironically, came to be viewed as a means of maintaining historic Samoan values.

The judicial system is headed by a Supreme Court and includes a Court of Appeal, magistrates' courts, and a special Land and Titles Court for dealing with disputes over customary land and Samoan titles.

For the most part, local government is carried out through the *matai* system and includes the institution of the village *fono,* or council. There are some part-time government officials who operate in rural areas.

Freedom of the press is constitutionally guaranteed, although instances of implicit censorship or of contempt citations against journalists have occurred in the past. Calling the media "weak" in regard to professional standards, Prime Minister Tuilaepa in 2012 proposed the establishment of a media regulatory body. However, some Samoan journalists in 2013 described the proposed council as an inappropriate attempt by the government to further control an already constrained media.

Foreign relations. Samoa has established diplomatic relations with more than two dozen other countries (including the People's Republic of China), most of which conduct relations with Apia through diplomats accredited to New Zealand. Although not choosing to apply for UN membership until 1976, Western Samoa had previously joined a number of UN subsidiary agencies and other international organizations, including the World Health Organization, the International Monetary Fund, and the World Bank, in addition to such regional organizations as the South Pacific Commission (subsequently the Pacific Community).

Relations with the country's principal trading partner, New Zealand, which had been cordial since independence, cooled in 1978 and 1979 as a result of Wellington's attempt to expel some 200 Samoan "overstayers" who had expected to be granted New Zealand citizenship. Subsequently, the Judicial Committee of the Privy Council in London ruled that all Western Samoans born between 1928 and 1949 (when New Zealand passed legislation separating its citizenship from that of Britain), as well as their children, were entitled to New Zealand citizenship. However, the decision was effectively invalidated by an agreement concluded in mid-1982 by Prime Minister Va'ai Kolone and New Zealand prime minister Robert Muldoon whereby only the estimated 50,000 Samoans resident in New Zealand could claim such citizenship. The accord was widely criticized within Western Samoa, then opposition leader Tupuola Efi chastising the Samoan government for abrogating "a basic tenet of the Anglo-Saxon legal heritage that the right to legal citizenship can only be surrendered by personal choice." A related issue arose in early 1989, when Wellington announced that it might terminate a special immigration quota for Samoans on the ground that the immigrants were contributing to New Zealand's high rate of unemployment. The dispute was partially resolved at midyear with a statement from Prime Minister David Lange that the quota would remain, with a stricter application of its rules. Subsequently, in September 1991, the Western Samoan government indicated that it would not seek amnesty from Wellington for 7,500 overstayers, following assurances by New Zealand authorities that their appeal rights would be protected. There have also been many visa overstayers in American Samoa, where it is estimated that some two-thirds of the territory's inhabitants are nonnative. The problem is not viewed as seriously as elsewhere because of the shared cultural identity of the two island peoples; their shared identity was, however, central to American Samoa's strong objection to adoption of the unqualified name "Samoa" by its western neighbor in 1997.

As with a number of other financially strapped countries, accusations have been made of the illegal sale of Samoan passports to Chinese nationals. Former prime minister Tofilau Eti denied any knowledge of such a practice, although a number of individuals were formally indicted in the matter. Major Chinese officials have recently made well-publicized visits to Samoa, often in connection with the announcement of development assistance. In 2012 Prime Minister Tuilaepa praised China for providing aid with "no strings attached," unlike Western donors.

Current issues. The Supreme Court stirred up controversy in February 2011 when it disqualified three potential TSP candidates from the March *Fono* poll. Among other things, the disqualifications meant that Prime Minister Tuilaepa ran unopposed in the elections, in which the HRPP saw its majority decline, the TSP having accused the administration of mismanaging aid money allocated for recovery from the 2009 tsunami. The TSP also called for less emphasis on large infrastructure projects and more attention to the "needs of the people."

At the end of 2011 Samoa "moved" west of the international dateline so that it would be more closely aligned in regard to time with its trading partners in Asia and Australasia. The government acknowledged that the dateline decision was only the latest in a series of measures underscoring the decline of U.S. influence in the region recently. Among other things, Prime Minister Tuilaepa argued that the peaceful conditions of the South Pacific had resulted in reduced U.S. attention. However, in marking the nation's 50th independence anniversary in May 2012, he expressed confidence that Samoa's accession to the WTO would promote increased trade with American Samoa.

Cyclone Evan struck the island of Upolu (home to 70 percent of the population) on December 13, 2012, causing flash floods, crop destruction, and widespread dislocation. Observers described the damage from the storm as at least as bad as that from the 2009 tsunami, with many schools and other buildings being destroyed. International donors (including Australia and New Zealand) subsequently provided emergency aid, and the Samoan government in 2013 approved another stimulus package to help the tourism and housing sectors recover. The 2013/2014 budget focused on capital expenditures for infrastructure, in part to prepare for the UN's Third International Conference of Small Island Developing States, which was scheduled to be held in Samoa in the fall of 2014.

POLITICAL PARTIES

Although there traditionally had been no political parties in Western Samoa, the Human Rights Protection Party was formed following the 1979 election. Other parties followed, including several short-lived groups formed during the 1990s (see the 2012 *Handbook* for details).

Governing Party:

Human Rights Protection Party (HRPP). The HRPP was organized by Va'ai Kolone following the 1979 election to oppose the reconfirmation of Tupuola Efi as prime minister. The new party subsequently claimed the support of a near majority of legislators. It won 22 of 47 seats in the February 1982 balloting and, after protracted negotiation with independent members, secured a 1-seat majority that permitted the installation of a Va'ai Kolone government on April 13. As a result of legal actions in late June and mid-September, 2 seats, including the prime minister's, were lost, Va'ai temporarily turning the party leadership over to Tofilau Eti Alesana, who was able to form a new HRPP government at the end of the year. Va'ai, who had regained his legislative seat in a by-election, failed in his effort to regain the HRPP leadership prior to the February 1985 election. He consequently resigned from the HRPP, moving into opposition (formally as an independent).

Tofilau Eti led the HRPP to a landslide 31–16 victory in the election of February 22, 1985, but the HRPP lost control of the government in

December by defection of its members to the opposition. (Va'ai Kolone returned to the premiership with the support of Tupuola's Christian Democratic Party [see SDUP, below].) Gaining a new term as prime minister by the barest possible legislative majority in April 1988, Tofilau Eti described the HRPP's program as emphasizing "electrification, sealed roads, and water supplies for the whole country." Declaring that it would be his last, the HRPP leader formed a drastically restructured government following the election of April 5, 1991. Despite a serious heart condition, he reversed himself in 1996 and won easy reelection. His party was less successful, declining to a plurality of 22 seats before regaining a majority with the conversion of independents.

Tofilau Eti's successor as prime minister, Tuilaepa Malielegaoi, carried the party to a plurality in the March 2001 election, after which the HRPP attracted enough independents to claim a majority of 28 seats when the new Legislative Assembly convened. It gained 2 additional seats as a result of subsequent special elections.

The HRPP led the balloting of March 31, 2006, securing 33 seats and, with the support of five members who had campaigned as independents, holding a commanding legislative majority. Defections reduced the HRPP's majority to 30 seats (plus the continued support of five independents) prior to the March 2011 assembly poll, in which the HRPP secured 28 seats (augmented by 1 following by-elections in August [see Legislature, below]).

Leaders: TUILAEPA Sailele Malielegaoi (Prime Minister), FONOTOE Nuafesili Pierre Lauofo (Deputy Prime Minister), Laulu Dan STANLEY (General Secretary).

Parliamentary Opposition:

Tautua Samoa Party (TSP). Formation of the TSP was announced in December 2008 by nine members of the Legislative Assembly (including two members who had resigned from the HRPP in April and a number of members formerly from the SNDP [see SDUP, below]). The seats of the 9 legislators were promptly declared vacant by the speaker because the legislators had violated Statutory Orders by establishing a new party prior to parliamentary dissolution. Samoa's Supreme Court subsequently ruled that the expulsion of the 9 was invalid, but the *Fono* passed new legislation requiring that any legislator who switched allegiance to a different party (regardless of whether it was officially registered or not) lose his or her seat. The TSP (registered in November 2009) subsequently claimed the allegiance of 11 legislators, who formally continued to sit as independents.

The TSP, criticizing the government's handling of the 2009 tsunami, won 13 seats in the March 2011 legislative poll, including a seat for TSP leader VA'AI Papu Vailupe. However, Va'ai was subsequently charged with bribery and lost his seat, which was secured by the HRPP in the August by-election. (Va'ai was convicted in May 2012.)

TSP president VA'AELUA Eti Alesana died in October 2011. He was succeeded by Leatinu'u Salote Lesa, one of the few women in Samoa to hold a position of significant political influence.

Leaders: LEATINU'U Salote Lesa (President), Paul SALELE (Treasurer), PALUSALUE Faapo II (Leader of the Opposition and Former President of the Party), A'EAU Peniamina Leavi (Deputy Leader of the Opposition), LEALAILEPULE Rimoni Aiafi (Founder and Former Chair), VA'AI Papu Vailupe (Former President), LEFAU Harry Schuster.

Other Parties:

Samoa Democratic United Party (SDUP). The SDUP was formed in 2003 by the merger of the Samoan National Development Party (SNDP) and the Samoan United Independent Party (SUIP) following disqualification of the SNDP for allegedly providing the Interparliamentary Union with false information about the government.

The SDNP was an outgrowth, at least in part, of the Christian Democratic Party (CDP), which supported Tupuola Taisi Tufuga Efi, who served as prime minister for two consecutive terms in 1976–1982. Tupuola became leader of the opposition following the 1982 election, and the CDP secured 16 seats in the 1985 balloting. Late in the year, the CDP joined with 11 HRPP defectors to defeat the budget proposed by Prime Minister Tofilau and to support the return of former HRPP prime minister Va'ai Kolone to the premiership, despite Va'ai's earlier opposition to Tupuola. The coalition of the CDP and the HRPP defectors was formalized by the launching of the SDNP after the 1988 election, in which the HRPP returned to power. The small Samoa National Party also participated in the formation of the SNDP, which was led by Tupuola (by then referenced as Tui Atua Tupua Tamasese Efi following his designation as a *Tama Aiga* in 1984). The SNDP slipped to 14 seats in 1991 and 13 in 1996.

The SUIP was registered as a party before the March 2001 election, in which it initially claimed 13 seats after the balloting; however, the number fell to 7 following recounts and defections to the HRPP. Meanwhile, the SNDP was credited with winning 13 seats in that poll and proceeded to fashion a coalition with the SUIP. Before the opening of the new legislative session the coalition claimed to have sufficient support to form a new government, but it ended up 4 seats short of a majority, with 21. Asiata Saleimoa Va'ai, a son of former prime minister Va'ai Kolone (who had died shortly after the election), was initially selected as leader of the opposition in the *Fono,* but he voluntarily surrendered the post to Le MAMEA Ropati Mualia, who had replaced Tupua as leader of the larger SNDP. (Tupua was elected head of state in 2007.) However, in September 2006, Mamea left the SDUP to sit as an independent, with Asiata resuming the role of opposition leader (until his death in 2010).

The SDUP secured 13 seats in the 2007 legislative poll but subsequently disintegrated under the influence of ongoing leadership battles. A number of SNDP legislators joined the TSP (above), while Mamea secured a *Fono* seat in 2011 on the HRPP ticket and was named minister of agriculture and fisheries in the new cabinet.

People's Party (PP). The PP, a successor to a civic group called People Against Switching Sides (PASS), was launched in July 2008 and held its first convention two months later. Its immediate objective was revocation of the controversial Road Transport Reform Bill that in September 2009, amid much acrimony, changed road driving from right to left, in accordance with the procedure in Australia and New Zealand. The PP insisted the change would generate an increase in highway accidents.

Leader: MAPOSUA Teleafoa Punafelutu Solomona Toailoa (President).

Samoan Christian Party (SCP). Also referenced simply as the Christian Party (CP), the SCP is primarily a women's party.

Leader: Tuala TIRESA Malietoa.

The **Samoan Progressive Political Party** (SPPP), led by TOEOLESULUSULU Siueva, unsuccessfully contested the 2001 and 2006 elections but has not been referenced regularly in recent years. In addition, a number of parties that presented candidates in 2001, including the *Faamatai* Party (FP), the *Pati Samoa Aoao* (PSA), and the Samoa United People's Party (SUPP), are now considered defunct. A Samoan Party (SP), launched in September 2005, won no seats in the March 2006 balloting, and in September its founder, SU'A Rimoni Ah Chong, was convicted of bribery during the electoral campaign. The party was dissolved in September 2010, after declaring its support for Tautua Samoa in the 2011 poll. A **United Samoa People's Party** (possibly related to the PP, above) also aligned with the TSP for that balloting.

LEGISLATURE

In November 1991 the term of the unicameral **Legislative Assembly** (*Fono Aoao Faitulafono*) was changed from three to five years (subject to dissolution), with 2 seats being added to the existing 47. Currently, 47 *matai* are elected from territorial constituencies (6 multimember, 35 single-member) by universal suffrage of all persons age 21 and above, with an additional 2 members elected (in 1 multimember constituency) by and from those ("part-Samoans" and non-Samoans) outside the *matai* system. The initial results of the most recent balloting on March 4, 2011, were as follows: the Human Rights Protection Party (HRPP), 28; the Tautua Samoa Party (TSP), 13; and independents, 8 (all of the independents were reportedly aligned with the HRPP). However, 4 of the successful candidates (3 from the HRPP and 1 from the TSP) subsequently lost their seats after being convicted of bribery or other charges in regard to the recent campaign. In the by-elections held in early August, the HRPP won all 4 vacant seats, giving it 29 seats of its own plus the continued support of the 8 independents.

In 2013 the assembly approved a bill mandating that at least 10 percent of the membership of subsequent assemblies be female (there are currently two female legislators). If fewer than five women are elected outright in future polls, additional women (up to five) will be accorded seats based on the number of votes they received in the general election. Consequently, subsequent assemblies could comprise as many as 54 members.

Speaker: LAAULI Leuatea Polataivao Fosi.

CABINET

[as of August 1, 2013]

Prime Minister	Tuilaepa Lupesoliai Sailele Malielegaoi
Deputy Prime Minister	Fonotoe Nuafesili Pierre Lauofo
Ministers	
Agriculture and Fisheries	Le Mamea Ropati
Commerce, Industry, Trade and Labor	Fonotoe Nuafesili Pierre Lauofo
Communication and Information Technology	Tuisugaletaura Sofara Aveau
Education, Sports, and Culture	Magele Mauiliu
Finance	Faumuina Liuga
Foreign Affairs and Trade	Tuilaepa Lupesoliai Sailele Malielegaoi
Health	Dr. Tuitama Talalelei Tuitama
Justice and Courts Administration	Fiame Naomi Mataafa [f]
Natural Resources and Environment	Faamoetauloa Ulaitino Faale Tumaalii
Police, Prisons, and Fire Service	Sala Fata Pinati
Revenue	Tuiloma Pule Lameko
Samoa Land Corporation	Tuilaepa Lupesoliai Sailele Malielegaoi
Women's Affairs and Community and Social Development	Tolofuaivalelei Falemoe Leiataua
Works, Transport, and Infrastructure	Manualesegalala Enokati Posala

[f] = female

INTERGOVERNMENTAL REPRESENTATION

Ambassador to the U.S. and Permanent Representative to the UN: Ali'ioaiga Feturi ELISAIA.

U.S. Ambassador to Samoa: David HUEBNER (resident in New Zealand).

IGO Memberships (Non-UN): ADB, CWTH, ICC, PIF.

SAN MARINO

Republic of San Marino
Repubblica di San Marino

Political Status: Independent republic dating from the early Middle Ages; under multiparty parliamentary regime.

Area: 23.6 sq. mi. (61 sq. km).

Population: 33,629 (2013E—UN); 32,448 (2013E—U.S. Census).

Major Urban Center (2005E): SAN MARINO (4,800).

Official Language: Italian.

Monetary Unit: Euro (market rate November 1, 2013: 0.74 euro = $1 US). (Although San Marino is not a member of the European Union [EU], it has negotiated a monetary agreement with the EU to permit usage of the euro as the national currency.)

Captains Regent: Gian Carlo CAPICCHIONI (Party of Socialists and Democrats) and Anna Maria MUCCIOLI (San Marino Christian Democratic Party); inaugurated for a six-month term on October 1, 2013, to succeed Denis AMICI (San Marino Christian Democratic Party) and Antonella MULARONI (Popular Alliance). (Captains regent are elected every six months, and the next election was scheduled for March 2014.)

THE COUNTRY

An enclave within the Italian province of Emilia-Romagna, San Marino is the world's oldest and second-smallest republic (after Nauru). Its terrain is mountainous, the highest point being Mount Titano, on the western slope of which is located the city of San Marino. The Sammarinese are ethnically and culturally Italian, but their long history has created a strong sense of separate identity and independence. The population enjoys one of the highest rates of life expectancy in the world, supported by extensive social benefits provided by the government. The principal economic activities are tourism (some 2 million tourists visit annually), light manufacturing, and service-related industries, especially nonresident banking and financial services (known, until recently, for strict secrecy laws that have attracted many foreign depositors, especially from Italy). Agriculture employs fewer than 2 percent of the workforce; olives and wine grapes rank with various grains as important crops. Wine, textiles, varnishes, ceramics, woolen goods, furniture, and building stone are chief exports. Traditional sources of income include the sale of coins and postage stamps and an annual budget subsidy from the Italian government.

By virtue of its economic union with Italy, San Marino became part of the European Economic Community (EEC) in the 1950s. It now has a separate customs union and cooperation agreement with the European Union (EU). Annual GDP grew steadily throughout the 1990s, averaging 7 percent annually, while the growth of the tourism industry contributed to an influx of cross-border workers (nearly one-fourth of the labor force). After stagnating early in the 2000s in the wake of a decline in the manufacturing sector, growth was robust in 2006 and 2007, thanks largely to a series of regulatory reforms, spending cuts, and initiatives to boost competitiveness in services. However, the global recession began to take a severe toll on San Marino in 2008, as focus intensified on San Marino's status as a tax haven. Italian measures (see Current issues, below) in particular contributed to a major outflow of nonresident deposits from Sammarinese banks while also compromising exports from San Marino. GDP had declined by more than 30 percent cumulatively by 2013, while unemployment had risen to 7 percent (up from 3 percent in 2007).

GOVERNMENT AND POLITICS

Political background. Reputedly founded in 301 A.D., San Marino is the sole survivor of the numerous independent states that existed in Italy prior to unification in the 19th century. A treaty of friendship and cooperation concluded with the Kingdom of Italy in 1862 has subsequently been renewed and amended at varying intervals.

A coalition of Communists (*Partito Comunista Sammarinese*—PCS) and Socialists (*Partito Socialista Sammarinese*—PSS) controlled the government from 1945 until 1957, when, because of defections from its ranks, the coalition lost its majority to the opposition Popular Alliance (composed mainly of Christian Democrats and Social Democrats). The San Marino Christian Democratic Party (*Partito Democratico Cristiano Sammarinese*—PDCS) was the plurality party in the elections of 1959, 1964, and 1969, but it required the continuing support of the San Marino Independent Social Democratic Party (*Partito Socialista Democratico Indipendente Sammarinese*—PSDIS) to ensure a governing majority. The coalition split over economic policy in January 1973, enabling the Socialists to return to power in alliance with the Christian Democrats. In the September 1974 election (the first in which women were allowed to present themselves as candidates for the country's legislative body—the Grand and General Council), the Christian Democrats and the Social Democrats each lost two seats, while the Communists and the Socialists experienced small gains.

In November 1977 the Socialists withdrew from the government, accusing the Christian Democrats of being bereft of ideas for resolving the country's economic difficulties. Following a lengthy impasse marked by successive failures of the Christian Democrats, Communists, and Socialists to form a new government, a premature general

election was held in May 1978, but the balance of legislative power remained virtually unchanged. Subsequently, the Christian Democrats again failed to secure a governing mandate, and in July a "Government of Democratic Collaboration" involving the Communists, Socialists, and the Socialist Unity Party (*Partito Socialista Unitario*—PSU, principal successor to the PSDIS) was approved by a bare parliamentary majority of 31 votes. The other PSDIS successor, the San Marino Social Democratic Party (*Partito Socialista Democratico Sammarinese*—PSDS), joined the governing coalition in 1982 but returned to opposition after the May 1983 election, in which the ruling parties gained an additional council seat. The leftist government fell in June 1986, when the Communist and Socialist Unity parties withdrew over foreign policy and other issues. In late July the council, by a 39–13 vote, approved a new program advanced by the Christian Democratic and Communist parties, the first such coalition in the country's history. The coalition was renewed in June 1988, following a general election in May in which the governing parties gained four seats at the expense of a divided Socialist opposition. In 1990 the PCS, responding to recent events in Eastern Europe, recast itself as the San Marino Progressive Democratic Party (*Partito Progressista Democratico Sammarinese*—PPDS).

On February 24, 1992, the Christian Democrats withdrew from their coalition with the PPDS and forged a new ruling alliance with the recently reunified Socialists. The outcome of the May 30, 1993, election was notable for the emergence of three smaller parties, although the ruling center-left coalition of the PDCS and the PSS retained a comfortable majority in the Grand and General Council. The coalition was renewed following the May 1998 legislative elections.

In February 2000 the Socialists withdrew from the government because of policy differences. The Christian Democrats then turned to the PPDS to ensure a new legislative majority, and on March 28 a government of the Christian Democrats, the Progressive Democrats, and the Socialists for Reform (*Socialisti per le Riforme*—SpR) assumed office. In February 2001, after the Christian Democrats rebuffed efforts to introduce measures aimed at tightening the country's financial and tax regulations, another crisis ensued, leading to premature dissolution of the legislature on March 11.

As in 1998, the 2001 preelection debate raised questions about the republic's relationship with the EU, which centered on San Marino's status as a tax haven. The EU, which in November 2000 had proposed an open exchange of information on nonresident investment accounts, maintained that financial secrecy in San Marino created an uneven playing field in the markets, eroded the tax bases of EU members, and facilitated fraud. Indeed, Italian tax officials had launched raids throughout San Marino in July 1998 to snare tax evaders, estimated to have been costing Rome $600 million annually.

The legislative election held on June 10, 2001, resulted in only minor changes in the makeup of the Grand and General Council. The PDCS remained in the plurality, claiming 25 seats on a vote share of 41.5 percent, while the PSS took 15 seats on 24.2 percent of the vote. Third place (20.8 percent of the vote and 12 seats) went to the newly organized Party of Democrats (*Partito dei Democratici*—PdD), successor to the PPDS, the SpR, and Ideas in Motion (*Idee in Movimento*—IM). Following the election, the PDCS and PSS established a new coalition, but the PSS withdrew on June 5, 2002. Subsequently, the PSS, the PdD, and the small San Marino Popular Democratic Alliance (*Alleanza Popolare dei Democratici Sammarinesi*—APDS) formed a new government that excluded the Christian Democrats. However, that government collapsed in December and was replaced with a PSS/PDCS coalition; the PdD rejoined the government in December 2003.

Following the election of June 4, 2006, a center-left coalition government was formed by the recently established Party of Socialists and Democrats (*Partito dei Socialisti e dei Democratici*—PSD), which resulted from the merger of the PSS and PdD; the Popular Alliance (*Alleanza Popolare*—AP, as the APDS had been renamed); and the small United Left (*Sinistra Unita*—SU) alliance. On July 17 the new government presented its program, which called for broad-based political and economic reforms to overcome economic stagnation and political corruption.

Under heavy criticism from the PDCS, which had been excluded from the center-left coalition despite winning a plurality of seats in the council in the June 2006 election, the government lost a confidence vote and resigned on October 29, 2007. It was replaced on November 28 by a coalition that included the previous government parties (PSD, AP, and SU) and the Center Democrats (*Democratici di Centro*—DdC), a new party founded by former Christian Democrats who had quit over the PDCS's inability to exert influence in the council. Also in 2007, another group of PDCS defectors, critical of the party's inability to attract moderates, founded yet another new party, Euro-Populars for San Marino (*Europopolari per San Marino*—EpS).

The center-left coalition subsequently was unable to garner enough consensus to surmount legislative gridlock, and the government collapsed on July 9, 2008. After another proposed coalition fell apart before it could be approved by the council, the captains regent on August 5 called for early elections.

The center-right returned to power following the election on November 9, 2008, winning 35 seats on the council as the Pact for San Marino (*Patto per San Marino*) coalition, compared with 25 for the center-left opposition coalition, Reforms and Liberty (*Riforme e Libertà*). However, the government's legislative support had fallen by mid-2011, in part due to severe economic decline, and early elections were held on November 11, 2012, with a ticket comprising the PDCS, AP, and PSD securing 35 seats and subsequently forming a government on December 5.

Constitution and government. Although a document dating from 1600 is sometimes referenced as San Marino's constitution, it is perhaps more accurate to say the republic has no codified, formal constitution but rather a constitutional tradition that is hundreds of years old. Legislative power is vested in the Grand and General Council (*Consiglio Grande e Generale*) of 60 members directly elected for five-year terms, subject to dissolution. A 10-member Congress of State (*Congresso di Stato*), or cabinet, is elected by the Grand and General Council for the duration of its term. Two members of the council are designated for six-month terms as captains regent (*capitani reggenti*), who serve as the heads of state but under normal circumstances do not set policy; both have equal power. Each is eligible for reelection three years after the expiration of his or her term. The judicial system encompasses justices of the peace (the only level not entrusted to Italian personnel); a law commissioner and assistant law commissioner, who deal with both civil and criminal cases; a criminal judge of the Primary Court of Claims (involving penalties greater than three years); two Appeals Court judges; and a Council of Twelve (*Consiglio dei XII*), which serves as a final court of appeals in civil cases only.

Administratively, San Marino is divided into nine districts called castles (*castelli*), each of which is directed by an elected Castle Board led by the captain of the castle, both serving five-year terms (increased from two years in 1994).

Although San Marino has no formal constitution, freedom of expression is protected by legal precedent and, more explicitly, by the Declaration of the Rights of Citizens and the Fundamental Principles of the Juridical Order of San Marino, issued by the council on July 12,

1974. Newspapers and periodicals are published primarily by the government, political parties, or trade unions.

Foreign relations. On March 2, 1992, San Marino was admitted to full United Nations membership, having previously been accorded observer status with the world body, and on September 23 it became a member of the International Monetary Fund. The republic is also a member of other international organizations, including the Conference on (later Organization for) Security and Cooperation in Europe, in whose review sessions it has been an active participant.

San Marino's relations with Italy (raised to the ambassadorial level in 1979) are governed by a series of treaties and conventions establishing a customs union, regulating public-service facilities, and defining general principles of good neighborly relations. Despite San Marino's staunchly reiterated independence, its reliance on Italy for a variety of necessities, ranging from daily newspapers to currency, provides little evidence that it will break with a tradition of alignment with Italian social and political processes.

Bilateral talks aimed at forging closer financial ties with Italy continued in 2009, prompting concern that the central Bank of Italy might gain undue influence over San Marino's domestic economic policy. At the same time, multilateral talks were held among the EU, San Marino, and four other small non-EU countries aimed at including them in the EU's tax information-sharing system.

Current issues. The most vexing problem faced by the new center-right government installed in late 2008 was the status of San Marino's banks in light of growing international pressure on so-called tax havens to become significantly more transparent in regard to foreign deposits. Although the Organization for Economic Cooperation and Development (OECD) in 2009 removed San Marino from its list of uncooperative states in regard to the exchange of financial information among nations, Italy continued to accuse San Marino of providing Italians with broad opportunities to avoid paying Italian taxes. When Italy offered its citizens an amnesty in 2010 regarding back taxes if foreign deposits were "repatriated" to Italian banks, it was estimated that some 5 billion euros in deposits were switched from San Marino to Italy. Italy also decreed in mid-2010 that any transactions conducted in San Marino totaling more than 5,000 euros would have to be reported to Italian tax authorities, which the government of San Marino characterized as an attempted "trade embargo" by Italy (the recipient of 95 percent of San Marino's exports) against San Marino.

In March 2012 San Marino pledged to adopt EU guidelines on certain bank regulations designed, among other things, to combat money laundering. Upon concluding a treaty with Italy in June providing for "data-sharing" regarding bank accounts, San Marino emphasized its hope that the financial sector would soon experience a resurgence following adoption of all international standards.

In part in an effort to achieve "national unity" to deal with, among other things, the ongoing deep recession, the PDCS (the majority partner in the incumbent government) agreed to participate in the San Marino Common Good coalition in the early elections of November 2012 along with the PSD (until then the major opposition party). Some observers anticipated strains within the new government in regard to a number of issues, including the country's unfolding relationship with the EU. Although the EU had already indicated reluctance to offer full accession to microstates such as San Marino, a referendum was held on October 20, 2013, in San Marino to determine the electorate's sentiment in regard to applying for EU membership. A yes vote of 50.3 percent was reported, but the proposal failed due to inadequate turnout (30 percent turnout was required, but only 22 percent of the voters participated).

POLITICAL PARTIES

San Marino's older political parties traditionally had close ties with and resembled corresponding parties in Italy, although recent mergers and name changes have led to more distinct identities for the parties in San Marino. Electoral law revision was proposed following the 2006 legislative balloting to permit parties to form coalitions for subsequent polls, with the hope that "fragmentation" in the Grand and General Council would give way to something similar to a two-party (or at least a two-coalition) system. The change was approved in 2007, with subsequent changes in 2008 establishing a complicated threshold structure (see Legislature, below, for details) and requiring coalitions to present their proposed governments and policy plans prior to the balloting, with no significant changes being permitted through a coalition's term in office.

Two coalitions were formed prior to the November 2008 legislative poll, the first to be conducted under the new electoral law. They were the Pact for San Marino (*Patto per San Marino*), which included the PDCS (and its affiliated parties [the EpS and the AeL]), AP, LdL (comprising the NPS and NS), and USDM (comprising the San Marino Populars and the ANS); and Reforms and Freedom (*Riforme e Libertà*), which included the PSD list (comprising the PSD and the SpL), SU (comprising the RCS and ZF), and DdC. The center-left Reforms and Freedom campaigned on a platform calling for increased social benefits and additional cooperation with Italy in regard to banking and tax issues. The center-right Pact for San Marino promised to promote domestic political stability and stronger ties with the EU. The Pact for San Marino parties secured 35 seats (on a vote share of 54 percent), with the remaining 25 seats going to Reforms and Freedom (46 percent). The primary reason for the Pact for San Marino's victory appeared to be its inclusion of the AP, which had previously been aligned in the center-left government with the PSD and SU.

Three individual parties and three coalitions (significantly altered from 2008) contested the November 2012 legislative balloting. The coalitions were the San Marino Common Good (*San Marino Bene Commune*), comprising the PDCS-NS joint list, the PSD, and the AP; the Agreement for the Country (*Intera Per Il Paese*), comprising the PS, UPR, and Moderate Sammarinese; and Active Citizenship (*Cittadinanza Attiva*), comprising the SU and Civic Movement 10.

Government Parties:

San Marino Christian Democratic Party (*Partito Democratico Cristiano Sammarinese*—PDCS). Catholic and conservative in outlook, the PDCS was established on April 9, 1948, and first came to power in 1957. In recent years it has been the strongest party in the Grand and General Council, winning at least 21 seats in every election since 1974. It ruled as the senior partner in coalitions with the San Marino Socialist Party (*Partito Socialista Sammarinese*—PSS) from 1973 until the latter's withdrawal in December 1977, at which time the PDCS was unable to organize a new government majority and went into opposition. It returned to power in an unprecedented coalition with the Communist Party (subsequently the San Marino Progressive Democratic Party [*Partito Progressista Democratico Sammarinese*—PPDS]) in July 1986, from which it withdrew in February 1992 to revive the alliance with the PSS. The PDCS again won a plurality in the 1993 balloting, following which its coalition with the PSS was continued.

The PDCS lost 1 of its 26 seats in the legislative election of May 1998. The subsequent collapse in 2000 of the PDCS-PSS coalition led the PDCS to reunite with the PPDS in a tripartite coalition that also included the SpR (see PSD, below). Although the PDCS retained its 25 seats in the June 2001 election, a revived PDCS-PSS coalition lasted only one year, and the PDCS was forced into opposition. In the June 2006 election the PDCS won 21 seats, more than any other party, but not enough to outweigh the combined strength of 32 seats won by the center-left governing coalition. The PDCS subsequently lost 9 council seats due to resignations from the party (5 to the EpS and 4 to the DdC [see UPR, below, for both]). The PDCS list, which included the candidates from the EpS and the new AeL (below), secured 22 of the seats won by the Pact for San Marino in the November 2008 election. However, three legislators left the PDCS/EpS/AeL parliamentary group in September 2010 to form an autonomous legislative faction. The new grouping was initially viewed as a de facto component of the majority, but one of the three defectors subsequently became an official independent, while the other two aligned with the opposition DdC.

Leaders: Teodora LONFERNINI (Leader), Marco GATTI (Political Secretary), Luigi MAZZA (Parliamentary Leader).

We Sammarinese (*Noi Sammarinesi*—NS). Founded in 2006, the NS defined itself as defending the republic's traditional values. It won 2.5 percent of the vote and one seat on the council in 2006 and presented its candidates on the Freedom List with the NPS (see PS, below) in 2008 as part of the Pact for San Marino. The Freedom List secured 4 of the Pact's 35 seats in that poll. For the 2012 poll the NS participated in a joint list with the PDCS within the San Marino Common Good coalition.

Leaders: Marco ARZILLI, Gabrielle BUCCI.

Party of Socialists and Democrats (*Partito dei Socialisti e dei Democratici*—PSD). The PSD was founded on February 25, 2005, as a merger of the leftist Socialist Party of San Marino (*Partito Socialista Sammarinese*—PSS) and the Party of Democrats (*Partito* *dei Democratici*—PdD), both of which were participating in a governing coalition that also included the PDCS. (The PSD's Italian counterpart is the Democratic Party.)

The PSS and the San Marino Communist Party (*Partito Comunista Sammarinese*—PCS) ruled jointly during 1945–1957. In 1973 the PSS returned to power upon forming a coalition government with the Christian Democrats that was continued after the 1974 election, in which the PSS won eight council seats. (The coalition gained an additional representative when the San Marino Independent Social Democratic Party [*Partito Socialista Democratico Indipendente Sammarinese*—PSDIS], originally a right-wing splinter from the PSS, split in 1975.) In November 1977, however, the PSS withdrew from the coalition, precipitating the fall of the PDCS-led administration. The PSS went on to win eight council seats in 1978 and nine in 1983, entering the government on both occasions. However, the unprecedented PDCS-PCS coalition formed in July 1986 excluded the PSS.

In 1990 the Socialist Unity Party (*Partito Socialista Unitario*—PSU), the more extreme remnant of the PSDIS, reunited with the PSS, which revived its coalition with the Christian Democrats in February 1992. In the May 1998 balloting the PSS retained its 14 legislative seats, continuing as the junior coalition partner until withdrawing from the government in February 2000. After winning 15 seats in June 2001, the PSS reentered a PDCS-led coalition. A year later it joined the PdD and APDS in a left-leaning government.

The PdD was established in March 2001 by merger of three groups: the San Marino Progressive Democratic Party (*Partito Progressista Democratico Sammarinese*—PPDS); Ideas in Motion (*Idee in Movimento*—IM); and the Reformist Democrats and Socialists (*Riformisti Democratici e Socialisti*), led by Emma ROSSI. In the context of the political upheaval of late 1989 in Eastern Europe, the PPDS had been formally launched on April 15, 1990, as heir to the San Marino Communist Party (*Partito Comunista Sammarinese*—PCS), which had won 18 legislative seats in 1988. The PCS, a nominally independent offshoot of the Italian Communist Party, had generally followed the line of its Italian counterpart.

The PPDS was forced into opposition following the breakup of its coalition with the Christian Democrats in early 1992, and it fell back to 11 legislative seats in 1993. For the May 1998 election it formed a joint list with the IM and others that retained 11 seats on 18.6 percent of the vote. The February 2000 departure of the PSS from the government enabled the PPDS to reestablish a coalition with the Christian Democrats in March, but the resultant government collapsed a year later.

Meanwhile, the leftist IM had been established in 1998 by Alessandro ROSSI as principal successor to the Democratic Movement (*Movimento Democratico*—MD); following the 1998 election, the nascent IM extended its support to the newly formed PDCS-PPDS government. The MD had been formed in 1990 by members of the San Marino Social Democratic Party (*Partito Socialista Democratico Sammarinese*—PSDS), the most moderate of San Marino's several socialist parties and itself a partial successor to the PSDIS, which had bifurcated in 1975. In the 1993 general election the MD had won three seats. Emma Rossi's reformist group was largely a continuation of the Socialists for Reform (*Socialisti per le Riforme*—SpR), which she had formed in 1998 after quitting the PSS on the ground that it had become too closely aligned with the PDCS. The SpR won two seats in the 1998 poll. In March 2000 Rossi entered the newly formed government coalition.

Formation of the PdD was announced in preparation for the premature election of June 2001. Having won 12 seats in that poll, the PdD joined the PSS and the APDS in a new coalition government in mid-2002.

Following its formation in 2005, the PSD won 31.8 percent of the vote and 20 seats in the 2006 legislative poll. (The PSD total was 7 fewer than the total won in the previous election by its constituent parties [the PSS and PdD].) On July 12 the PSD formed a center-left governing coalition with the AP and SU that controlled 32 seats in the legislature until it fell on October 29, 2007. The PSD led a successor coalition government with the AP, the SU, and the DdC from November 28, 2007, to July 9, 2008.

The PSD list (which included candidates from the SpL [below]) secured 32 percent of the vote and 18 of the 25 seats won by the Reforms and Freedom coalition in the November 2008 legislative poll. However, citing the need for a new group in the Grand and General Council to promote traditional socialist values, PSD secretary Paride Andreoli and seven other PSD council members left the party and the Reforms and Liberty coalition on July 1, 2009, to form the PSRS (see PS, below). The move reduced the number of Reforms and Freedom seats in the council to 17 and PSD seats to 10, threw the opposition coalition into disarray, and prompted a number of other PSD members to resign.

Despite having previously been highly critical of the PDCS-led government (particularly in regard to slow progress in the reform of bank secrecy laws), the PSD opted to join the PDCS, NS, and AP in the "national unity" ticket presented under the San Marino Common Good electoral umbrella for the 2012 legislative poll.

Leaders: Denise BRONZETTI (Party Leader and Parliamentary Leader), Claudio FELICI (Council Leader).

Popular Alliance (*Alleanza Popolare*—AP). This centrist, liberal party, formerly known as the San Marino Popular Democratic Alliance for the Republic (*Alleanza Popolare dei Democratici Sammarinesi per la Repubblica*—APDS), was formed prior to the 1993 election under the leadership of former Christian Democrats. The APDS won four Grand and General Council seats in 1993 and six seats in 1998. In 2001 it slipped to five seats. In 2006 the party, by that time known as the AP, won 12.1 percent of the vote and seven seats, making it the third-largest party in the council.

Amid mounting discord with the United Left (*Sinistra Unita*—SU), one of the AP's partners in the governing center-left coalition that collapsed in 2008, the AP joined the center-right Pact for San Marino for the November 2008 election. It won 11.5 percent of the vote and 7 of that Pact's 35 seats and 4 of the 35 seats secured by the San Marino Common Good coalition in 2012.

Leaders: Mario VENTURINI (President and Parliamentary Leader), Stefano PALMIERI (Coordinator), Roberto GIORGETTI.

Opposition Parties:

Socialist Party (*Partito Socialista*—PS). Formed in March 2012 by the New Socialist Party (*Nuovo Partito Socialista*—NPS) and the San Marino Socialist Reformist Party (*Partito Socialista Riformista Sammarinese*—PSRS), the PS secured 7 of the 12 seats won by the Agreement for the Country coalition in the November legislative balloting.

The social-democratic NPS had been founded in November 2005 by defectors from the PSD to protest what they perceived as corruption in the PSD-led government and to restore to what the leaders of the new party described as traditional socialist values. The NPS won 5.4 percent of the vote and 3 seats in the 2006 election and was part of the opposition to the PSD-SU-AP governing coalition that collapsed in 2008. In advance of the 2008 election, the NPS formed an electoral list called the Freedom List (*Listadella Libertà*—LdL) with the NS.

Founded on July 1, 2009, by eight defectors from the PSD as a new opposition group in the Grand and General Council, the PSRS was formally launched as a new political party shortly thereafter.

Leader: Paolo CRESCENTINI (Parliamentary Leader).

Union for the Republic (*Unione per la Republica*—UPR). The UPR is an outgrowth, at least in part, of the Center Democrats (*Democratici di Centro*—DdC), a Catholic, populist movement founded in March 2007 by four defectors from the PDCS who were frustrated by the PDCS's poor showing in the 2006 elections. The defectors, including sitting Captain Regent Rosa Zafferani, resigned from the PDCS, but not from the legislature, in an effort to promote the DdC as a more viable centrist party. In November the DdC joined the center-left governing coalition.

In November 2008 the DdC won 4.9 percent of the vote and two council seats as a component of the Reform and Freedom coalition. In March 2011 the two DdC parliamentarians joined with the three defectors from the government to form the UPR faction in the council. The UPR subsequently became a formal party with the inclusion of the Euro-Populars for San Marino (*Europopolari per San Marino*—EpS).

The centrist EpS had been formed in July 2007 by former PDCS political secretary Marino Menicucci and several other prominent PDCS members who had resigned from the PDCS in 2006, citing the party's inability to adapt to the changing political climate and the need to widen its base of support to include moderates. However, the EpS realigned with the PDCS for the 2008 elections as the EpS candidates ran on the PDCS list.

Legislator Gian Marco Marcucci, the leader of the EpS, resigned from his position as minister for labor, cooperation, and postal service relations in March 2011 and subsequently joined the new opposition parliamentary faction formed with the DdC.

The UPR secured 5 of the 12 seats won by the Agreement for the Country coalition in the November 2012 legislative balloting.

Leaders: Marino MENICUCCI, Gian Marco MARCUCCI, Giovanni LONFERNINI (Parliamentary Leader), Lorenzo LONFERNINI (Coordinator).

Moderate Sammarinese (*Moderati Sammarinese*). This party is an outgrowth of the San Marino Populars (*Popolari Sammarinese*), a centrist, Catholic party that was founded in 2003 and that won 2.4 percent of the vote and one seat on the Grand and General Council in 2006. The San Marino Populars formed an electoral list called the San Marino Union of Moderates (*Unione Sammarinese dei Moderati*—USDM) with the ANS (below) prior to the November 2008 legislative poll, at which the USDM won 4.2 percent of the vote and 2 of the 35 seats secured by the Pact for San Marino. However, legislative cooperation between the San Marino Populars and the ANS declined in 2011, and members of the San Marino Populars formed Moderate Sammarinese to participate in the Agreement for the Country Coalition for the November 2012 legislative elections. Candidates from Moderate Sammarinese did not secure any of the coalition's 12 seats.

Leader: Angela VENTURINI.

United Left (*Sinistra Unita*—SU). The leftist SU political alliance was formed in 2005 by the **San Marino Communist Refoundation** (*Rifondazione Comunista Sammarinese*—RCS) and the **Left Party–Free Port** (*Partito della Sinistra–Zona Franca*—ZF). In the 2006 legislative poll the SU won 8.7 percent of the vote and five seats. It retained its five seats in 2008 as a component of the Reforms and Freedom coalition and in 2012 as a component of the Active Citizenship coalition. The other 2012 coalition member, **Civic Movement 10** (*Movimento Civico 10*—Civico 10) led by Andrea ZAFFERNINI (Parliamentary Leader) and Marco Rossi, won four seats.

Leaders: Gastone PASOLINI (President), Alessandro ROSSI (Coordinator), Francesca MICHELOTTI (Parliamentary Leader), Ivan FOSCHI, Roberto TAMAGNINI (ZF Coordinator), Angelo DELLA VALLE (RCS Secretary).

Renewal, Equity, Transparency, and Eco-sustainability Civic Movement (*Rinnovamento, Equità, Transparenza, Ecosostenibilità Movimento Civico*—RETA Movement). Recently formed by activist groups concerned with, among other things, the environment, civil rights, and the arts, the RETE Movement, competing on its own, won four seats on a vote share of 6.3 percent in the November 2012 legislative poll.

Leaders: Grazia ZEFFERANI (President), Roberto CIAVATTA (Parliamentary Leader).

Other Parties:

Arengo and Freedom (*Arengo e Libertà*—AeL). The center-left AeL was founded in September 2008 by council members Fabio Berardi and Nadia Ottaviani, who left the PSD because they thought the party had moved too far to the left. The AeL was named for the assembly (*Arengo*) that ruled San Marino during the Middle Ages. The new party presented its candidates for the 2008 elections on the PDCS list. There was no reference to the AeL in regard to the 2012 balloting.

Leaders: Fabio BERARDI, Nadia OTTAVIANA.

San Marino National Alliance (*Alleanza Nazionale Sammarinese*—ANS). The right-wing ANS, founded in 2001 and linked to the Italian post-fascist National Alliance (*Alleanza Nazionale*), won one seat in the June 2001 council election. In 2006 it won 2.3 percent of the vote and retained its seat on the council. In 2008 the ANS presented its candidates with the San Marino Populars on the USDM list (a component of the Pact for San Marino). There was no reference to the ANS in regard to the 2012 elections.

Leaders: Glauco SANSOVINI (Political Secretary), Ennio Vittorio PELLANDRA (President).

Sammarinese for Freedom (*Sammarinesi per la Libertà*—SpL). Founded in 2002, the center-left SpL won 1.8 percent of the vote and one council seat in 2006. It participated in the PSD electoral list for the 2008 poll as a member of the Reforms and Freedom coalition. A report in 2012 indicated that the SpL had expressed interest in the formation of the Socialist Party.

Leaders: Giuseppe ROSSI (President), Monica BOLLINI.

New parties that ran unsuccessfully on their own in the 2012 legislative elections were: **San Marino 3.0** (led by Simone DELLA VALLE and Mickael BORKHOLZ), which received 1.8 percent of the vote; and **For San Marino** (*Per San Marino*), which received 2.8 percent of the vote under the leadership of Emilio DELLA BALDE and Alvara SELVA.

LEGISLATURE

The **Grand and General Council** (*Consiglio Grande e Generale*) is a unicameral body consisting of 60 members elected on a proportional basis for five-year terms (subject to dissolution) by direct popular vote in a single nationwide constituency. The captains regent serve as presiding officers.

Electoral law revisions following the 2006 poll permitted parties to form coalitions for subsequent elections (see Political Parties, above). In addition, a minimum threshold of 3.5 percent was established for a party or coalition to secure representation in most cases. (Lower thresholds are possible depending on how many lists are presented in any given election and how many parties participate in a list.) Finally, "bonus seats" were authorized to ensure that the leading coalition secures at least 35 seats.

Following the most recent election on November 11, 2013, the seat distribution was as follows: the San Marino Common Good coalition, 35 (the joint list of the San Marino Christian Democratic Party [PDCS] and We Sammarinese [NS], 21 [PDCS, 18; NS, 3]; the Party of Socialists and Democrats, 10; the Popular Alliance, 4); the Agreement for the Country coalition, 12 (the Socialist Party, 7; the Union for the Republic, 5); the Active Citizenship coalition, 9 (the United Left, 5; the Civic Movement 10, 4); and the Renewal, Equity, Transparency, and Eco-sustainability Civic Movement, 4.

Speakers (Captains Regent of the Republic): Gian Carlo CAPICCHIONI and Anna Maria MUCCIOLI (until April 1, 2014).

CABINET

[as of October 1, 2013]

Captains Regent	Gian Carlo Capicchioni (PSD) Anna Maria Muccioli (PDCS) [f]
Secretaries of State	
Education, Culture, the University, Scientific Research, Social Affairs, and Gender Equality	Giuseppe M. Morganti (PSD)
Finance and Budget, Posts, and Relations with the Philatelic and Numismatic State Corporation	Claudio Felici (PSD)
Foreign and Political Affairs	Pasquale Valentini (PDCS)
Health and Social Security, National Insurance, Family, and Economic Planning	Francesco Mussoni (PDCS)
Industry, Crafts, Trade, Transportation, and Research	Marco Arzilli (NS)
Internal Affairs, Civil Service, Justice, and Relations with Township Councils	Gian Carlo Venturini (PDCS)
Labor, Cooperation, and Information	Iro Belluzi (PSD)
Territory and Environment, Agriculture, Telecommunications, Youth, Sports, Civil Protection, and Relations with the Public Works State Corporation	Matteo Fiorini (AP)
Tourism and Relations with the Public Utilities State Corporation	Teodoro Lonfernini (PDCS)

[f] = female

INTERGOVERNMENTAL REPRESENTATION

Ambassador to the U.S.: Paolo RONDELLI.

U.S. Ambassador to San Marino: David H. THORNE (resident in Italy).

Permanent Representative to the UN: Daniele D. BODINI.

IGO Memberships (Non-UN): CEUR, ICC, OSCE.

SÃO TOMÉ AND PRÍNCIPE

Democratic Republic of São Tomé and Príncipe
República Democrática de São Tomé e Príncipe

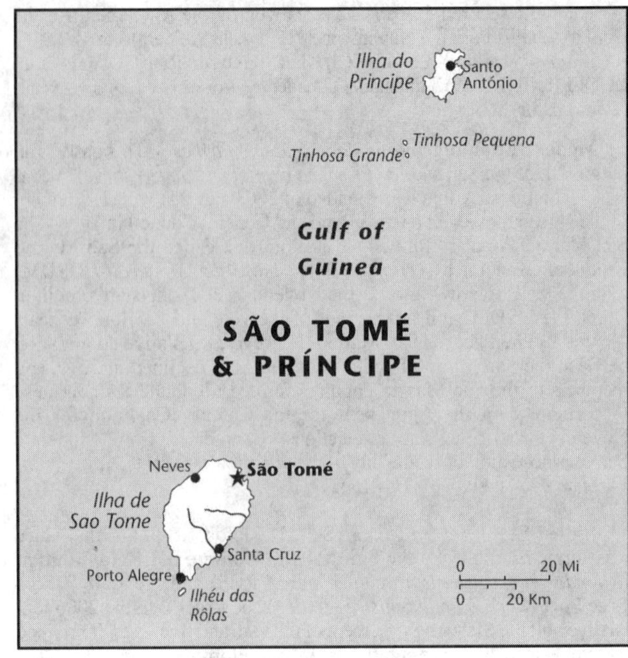

Political Status: Achieved independence from Portugal on July 12, 1975; constitution of November 5, 1975, revised in December 1982, October 1987, August 1990, and March 2003.

Area: 387 sq. mi. (1,001 sq. km).

Population: 187,303 (2013E—UN); 186,817 (2013E—U.S. Census).

Major Urban Center (2008E): SÃO TOMÉ (62,500).

Official Language: Portuguese.

Monetary Unit: Dobra (market rate November 1, 2013: 17,905.10 dobras = $1US).

President: Manuel PINTO DA COSTA (independent); directly elected in runoff balloting on August 7, 2011, and sworn in for a five-year term on September 3, succeeding Fradique de MENEZES (Democratic Movement of Forces for Change–Liberal Party). (Pinto Da Costa had previously served as president from independence in 1975 until 1991.)

Prime Minister: Gabriel Arcanjo Ferreira da COSTA (Union of Democrats for Citizenship and Development); appointed by the president on December 10, 2012, and inaugurated (along with his new cabinet) on December 12 in succession to Patrice Emery TROVOADO (Independent Democratic Action), whose government had been dismissed by the president on December 4 after losing a confidence motion in the National Assembly on November 28.

THE COUNTRY

Located in the Gulf of Guinea some 125 miles off the coast of Gabon, São Tomé and Príncipe consists of a small archipelago of two main islands (after which the country is named) and four islets: Cabras, Gago Coutinho, Pedras Tinhosas, and Rôlas. Volcanic in origin, the islands exhibit numerous craters and lava flows; the climate is warm and humid most of the year. The indigenous inhabitants are primarily descended from plantation laborers imported from the African mainland. The Portuguese population, estimated at more than 3,000 before independence, has declined substantially. Roman Catholicism is the principal religion. Women constitute about one-third of the economically active population and hold a limited number of leadership positions in politics and government. Ten women were elected to the National Assembly in 2010.

São Tomé and Príncipe was once the world's leading producer of cocoa, although production has declined. Tourism and construction have contributed significantly to growth, and the government hopes that oil revenues from the Gulf of Guinea will boost the nation's economic status. (São Tomé and Príncipe shares with Nigeria an economic development zone believed to hold more than 11 billion barrels of crude oil. Chevron began exploration in early 2006, and many other oil companies have shown interest in developing the region.) Most food is imported, often in the form of donations, with copra, coffee, palm kernels, sugar, and bananas being produced domestically. Consumables dominate the small industrial sector, and the country relies heavily on foreign aid, which provides approximately 80 percent of the government's budget.

The flight of Portuguese managers and skilled labor at independence took a toll on the economy, as did cyclical droughts and, beginning in 1980, low world cocoa prices. The government began moving away from a Marxist orientation in the mid-1980s and subsequently began to emphasize economic denationalization (most importantly in the cocoa industry), foreign investment, reduction of subsidies, currency devaluation, and other liberalization measures that won the support of the International Monetary Fund (IMF) and World Bank. In addition, the administration tried to diversify the economy by developing fishing and tourism.

In 2009 the IMF approved $3.8 million in assistance for the following three years to support the government's economic reforms (including improvements in the banking sector) and efforts to reduce poverty, which reportedly affects more than one-half of the population. The IMF in 2012 continued to praise the government for its "fiscal prudence" and probusiness regulatory reforms and approved another three-year, $3.9 million program. GDP growth of 4 percent was reported for 2012, with annual inflation registering 10 percent.

The World Bank announced grants of $5.5 million in mid-2013 to support the government's efforts to, among other things, improve the investment climate. As of that time, analysts predicted that oil would start to flow no earlier than 2015 in view of disappointing exploratory results to date. Business leaders also described progress on the proposed deepwater port in Fernão Dias on São Tomé as sluggish.

GOVERNMENT AND POLITICS

Political background. Discovered by Portuguese explorers in 1471, São Tomé and Príncipe became Portuguese territories in 1552–1523 and, collectively, an Overseas Province of Portugal in 1951. Nationalistic sentiment became apparent in 1960 with the formation of the Committee for the Liberation of São Tomé and Príncipe (*Comité de Libertaçã de São Tomé e Príncipe*—CLSTP). In 1972 the CLSTP became the Movement for the Liberation of São Tomé and Príncipe (*Movimento de Libertaçã de São Tomé e Príncipe*—MLSTP), which quickly became the leading advocate of independence from Portugal. Based in Gabon under the leadership of Manuel PINTO DA COSTA, the MLSTP carried out a variety of underground activities, particularly in support of protests by African workers against low wages.

In 1973 the Organization of African Unity (OAU, subsequently the African Union—AU) recognized the MLSTP, and Portugal granted the country local autonomy. After the 1974 military coup in Lisbon, the Portuguese government began negotiations with the MLSTP, which it recognized as the sole official representative for the islands. The two agreed in November 1974 that independence would be proclaimed on July 12, 1975, and that a transitional government would be formed under MLSTP leadership until that time. Installed on December 21, 1974, the transitional government council comprised four members appointed by the MLSTP and one by Portugal. Upon independence, Pinto da Costa assumed the presidency and promptly designated his MLSTP associate, Miguel Anjos da Cunha Lisboa TROVOADA, as prime minister. In December 1978, however, Trovoada was relieved of his duties, and in October 1979 he was arrested on charges that he had been involved in a projected coup, one of a series that Pinto da Costa claimed to have foiled with the aid of Angolan troops. The president subsequently served as both head of state and chief executive without serious domestic challenge, despite Trovoada's release in 1981. In late 1987 the government, which had already introduced many economic liberalization measures, launched a political liberalization campaign as well (see Constitution and government, below). One of the first official changes was the revival of the office of prime minister; Celestino ROCHA DA COSTA was appointed to the post in January 1988.

The reform process culminated in an August 1990 referendum that endorsed abandonment of the country's single-party system, and on January 20, 1991, the recently legalized Party of Democratic Convergence (*Partido da Convergência Democrática*—PCD) outdistanced the restyled MLSTP–Social Democratic Party (MLSTP–*Partido Social Democrata*—MLSPT-PSD) by winning 33 of 55 seats in the new National Assembly. On February 8 PCD general secretary Daniel Lima dos Santos DAIO was named to head a new government, and on March 3 former prime minister Trovoada secured election as head of state. (Incumbent president Pinto da Costa had earlier announced his retirement from public life, although he subsequently returned to politics [see below].)

Prime Minister Daio was dismissed on April 22, 1992, in favor of his finance minister, Norberto José d'Alva COSTA ALEGRE. Despite an MLSTP-PSD call for a unity government, the cabinet announced by Costa Alegre on May 16 was composed solely of PCD members.

On July 2, 1994, President Trovoada sacked Prime Minister Costa Alegre in favor of Evaristo de CARVALHO, who, although a PCD member, had long been close to the president. Four days later Carvalho was expelled from the PCD, which called for a new presidential election. Trovoada responded by appointing a Carvalho-recommended government of "presidential friends." On July 10, after the PCD had announced that it intended to introduce a motion declaring the new administration unconstitutional, Trovoada dissolved the National Assembly and called for the election of its successor.

In legislative balloting on October 2, 1994, the MLSTP-PSD returned to power with the capture of a near-majoritarian 27 seats, while the PCD and President Trovoada's recently legalized Independent Democratic Action (Acção Democrática Independente—ADI) each secured 14. On October 25 Trovoada appointed MLSTP-PSD secretary general Carlos Alberto Dias Monteiro da GRAÇA as prime minister. Although da Graça had pledged to form a government of "national union," he named a cabinet dominated by MLSTP-PSD members on October 28.

On August 16, 1995, a group of Cuban-trained rebel soldiers led by Lt. Orlando das NEVES stormed the presidential palace, taking President Trovoada prisoner. However, Trovoada resumed his duties a week later after issuing a pardon to the officers who had seized him. Among the concessions reportedly made to secure Trovoada's release were pledges to name the long-anticipated unity government and restructure the military.

After the MLSTP-PSD, ADI, and the Opposition Democratic Coalition (*Coligação Democrática da Oposição*—Codo) had signed a cooperation pact on December 29, 1995, MLSTP-PSD deputy secretary general Armindo Vaz de ALMEIDA on January 5, 1996, formed a cabinet that included seven members from the MLSTP-PSD, four from the ADI, and one from Codo, despite Codo's lack of legislative representation.

In delayed first-round presidential balloting on June 30, 1996, incumbent president Trovoada led a five-man field with 40.9 percent of the vote, followed by former president Pinto da Costa (39.1 percent), the PCD's Alda BANDEIRA (14.6 percent), former prime minister da Graça, and Armindo TOMBA, an anticorruption journalist. In the runoff on July 21, Trovoada defeated Pinto da Costa by 52–48 percent.

On September 20, 1996, an assembly nonconfidence motion reportedly orchestrated by the assembly president, Fortunato PIRES, forced the resignation of the Almeida government. Subsequent MLSTP-PSD efforts to have Pires appointed to the vacant post were blocked by Trovoada and the ADI, however, and on November 13 Trovoada appointed MLSTP-PSD deputy secretary general Raúl Bragança NETO as prime minister. On November 28 Neto named a government that included six MLSTP-PSD ministers, three from the PCD, and one independent.

The MLSTP-PSD won 31 legislative seats in polling on November 8, 1998, with the ADI improving to 16 seats and the PCD falling to 8. The MLSTP-PSD subsequently nominated Guilherme POSSER DA COSTA, a former foreign minister and ambassador, to be the next prime minister, and Posser da Costa and his MLSTP-PSD government were sworn in on January 5, 1999.

In first-round presidential balloting on July 29, 2001, ADI candidate Fradique de MENEZES (56.3 percent of the vote) defeated former president Manuel Pinto da Costa (38.4 percent) and three minor candidates. Several attempts to form a "cohabitation" government failed, in part because President Menezes rejected cabinet recommendations from the MLSTD-PSD. Menezes, who was inaugurated in September, dismissed Prime Minister Posser da Costa and his cabinet and named former prime minister Carvalho to head a "presidential initiative" government including members from the ADI and the PCD. Calling the minority government "unconstitutional," the MLSTP-PSD walked out of the assembly, initiating a political crisis that prompted President Menezes to dissolve the assembly on December 7 and call for early elections. Concurrently, it was reported that the leading political parties had agreed to allocate cabinet posts according to the seats won by each party in the new legislative balloting.

In the assembly poll on March 3, 2002, the MLSTP-PSD secured a 1-seat plurality of 24 seats over the new electoral coalition formed by the PCD and the recently launched, pro-Menezes Democratic Movement of Forces for Change–Liberal Party (*Movimento Democrático das Forças para da Mudunça–Partido Liberal*—MDFM-PL). On March 26, the president appointed Gabriel COSTA (a former leader of the MLSTP-PSD but now an independent described as "close" to the MDFM–PL) as the new prime minister. The cabinet that took office in April contained, according to the previously determined proportion, members of the MLSTP-PSD, the coalition of the MDFM-PL and the PCD, and the new Uê Kédadji alliance that had been formed by the ADI, Codo, and others prior to the assembly poll, at which the alliance had captured third place with 8 seats.

Following a dispute between Prime Minister Costa and Defense Minister Victor MONTEIRO, President Menezes dismissed Costa and the rest of the cabinet on September 27, 2002. On October 3 the president appointed Maria das NEVES de Souza (MLSTP-PSD) as the new prime minister. On October 6 das Neves announced her new cabinet, which again included members of her own party, the coalition of the MDFM-PL and PCD, and the Uê Kédadji alliance.

In 2003 the potential windfall from oil exploration raised concerns regarding government accountability and corruption. In June a military group briefly deposed President Menezes while he was in Nigeria, but he returned to office on July 23 after successful negotiations with the rebels. Among other things, the assembly agreed to a deal arranged by international negotiators to grant amnesty to the junta and to the political group linked to it, the Christian Democratic Front (*Frente Democrática Cristã*—FDC). However, the fractious debate over energy resources, which inspired the coup, continued over the terms of a contract with the Environmental Remediation Holding Company (ERHC), a Nigerian company involved in the Joint Development Zone (JDZ).

President Menezes appointed Damiao ALMEIDA as prime minister on September 17, 2003, and a reshuffled cabinet made up of the MLSTP-PSD and ADI was sworn in the next day. The award of five blocs of the JDZ to international oil companies in May 2005 caused disagreement in the government's inner circles, and Patrice TROVOADA, an oil broker and the son of the former president, was dismissed as oil adviser to the president. Menezes then flew to Nigeria, where he signed off on the bloc awards, prompting the resignation of Prime Minister Almeida and the entire cabinet on June 3. Maria do Carmo SILVEIRA was named prime minister on June 7, and a new cabinet, dominated by the MLSTP-PSD, was appointed on June 8.

In legislative elections on March 26, 2006, MDFM-PL supporters of President Menezes won 23 seats, surprising many by finishing ahead of the MLSTP-PSD, whose seat count fell to 20. The ADI secured the other 11 seats. Menezes subsequently named Tomé Soares da VERA

CRUZ—an engineer who had previously held the position of minister of natural resources—as head of a new minority MDFM-PL/PCD government.

On July 30, 2006, with the backing of the MDFM-PL and PCD, President Menezes was reelected with 60.6 percent of the vote in the first round of balloting. Menezes's main opponent was Patrice Trovoada, who was backed by the ADI and the MLSTP-PSD and received 38.8 percent of the vote. In August, in the first regional balloting since 1992, the coalition of the MDFM-PL and PCD won majorities in six of seven districts that held elections, with the MLSTP-PSD winning the other. Meanwhile, the Union for Change and Progress in Príncipe (*União para Mudança e Progresso do Príncipe*—UMPP), supported by the MDFM-PL and PCD, won all seven seats in the regional assembly of Príncipe in concurrent balloting. José CASSANDRA, the UMPP leader, subsequently became president of the regional assembly on October 5.

When the assembly rejected his proposed budget, Prime Minister Vera Cruz resigned in February 2008, and President Menezes subsequently appointed Patrice Trovoada of the ADI to head a new coalition government of the MDFM-PL, PCD, and ADI. However, on May 30, the government lost a vote of no confidence when the PCD voted with the opposition. Consequently, on June 10 Menezes appointed Joachim Rafael BRANCO of the MLSTP-PSD as prime minister. The new government sworn in on June 21 included the MDFM-PL, PCD, and MLSTP-PSD.

In December 2009, President Menenzes was elected president of the MDFM-PL, but the MLSTP-PSD and PCD criticized his elevation in the party as illegal and asked the Constitutional Court for a ruling. (The constitution forbids a sitting president from engaging in "other political activities.") As a result, the MDFM-PL announced it was leaving the government, although several MDFM-PL ministers reportedly indicated a desire to resist the decision. On January 12, 2010, Branco announced a new minority cabinet comprising the MLSTP-PSD and the PCD. Menezes subsequently withdrew from his party responsibilities (see section on the MDFM-PL, below).

The ADI won a plurality of 26 seats in the August 1, 2010, assembly balloting, while the MDFM-PL, running on its own, plummeted to only 1 seat. ADI leader Trovoada formed a minority government (comprising only ADI members and independents) on August 14.

Ten candidates—seven running as independents—contested the first round of presidential elections on July 17, 2011. Former president Manuel Pinta da Costa, running as an independent, finished first with 35.8 percent of the vote, followed by the ADI's Evaristo CARVALHO (the speaker of the National Assembly) with 21.8 percent. Pinto da Costa won a narrow victory with 52.9 percent of the vote in the second round on August 7. He was sworn in on September 3, 20 years since he had last held the office.

Having faced sustained criticism ever since its 2010 installation, the ADI-led administration lost a confidence motion in the assembly on November 28, 2012, when all the non-ADI legislators supported the government's ouster. President Pinto da Costa dismissed Prime Minister Trovoada and his cabinet on December 4, and former prime minister Gabriel Costa subsequently formed a new government that included the MSLPT-PSD, PCD, and the MDFM-PL, but not the disgruntled ADI.

Constitution and government. The constitution, as revised in 1982, identified the MLSTP as the "directing political force" for the country, provided for an indirectly elected National Popular Assembly as the supreme organ of state, and conferred broad powers on a president, who was named by the assembly for a five-year term. In October 1987 the MLSTP Central Committee proposed a number of constitutional changes as part of a broad democratization program. Theretofore elected by the People's District Assemblies from candidates nominated by an MLSTP-dominated Candidature Commission, legislators would now be chosen by direct and universal suffrage. Independent candidates would be permitted in addition to candidates presented by the party and "recognized organizations," such as trade unions or youth groups. The president would be elected by popular vote rather than being designated by the assembly; however, only the MLSTP president (elected by secret ballot at a party congress) could stand as a candidate. In the course of approving the reform program, the assembly provided for the restoration of a presidentially appointed prime minister.

As a consequence of the August 1990 referendum, a multiparty system was introduced, together with multicandidature and popular balloting for legislators and the president. In addition, the president was limited to two five-year terms. The National Assembly conferred local autonomy upon Príncipe in 1994, and elections were held there in March 1995 for a seven-member regional assembly and a five-member regional government (headed by a president). The new bodies were installed April 29, 1995.

In November 2002, the assembly endorsed constitutional revision designed to diminish presidential power. Despite the objections of President Menezes, the changes took effect in March 2003. Among other things, the new basic law eliminated the president's right to veto constitutional amendments and provided for the establishment of two new bodies—an advisory Council of State and a Constitutional Tribunal.

The judiciary is headed by a Supreme Court, whose members are designated by and are responsible to the assembly. Administratively, the country is divided into two provinces (coterminous with each of the main islands) and 12 counties (11 of which are located on São Tomé).

São Tomé and Príncipe's constitution protects free speech and freedom of the press. Among other things, opposition groups and parties are guaranteed access to state-controlled radio and television.

Foreign relations. Despite the exodus of much of the country's Portuguese population from 1974 to 1975, São Tomé and Príncipe continued to maintain an active commercial trade with the former colonial power. Following independence, diplomatic relations were established with the Soviet Union and the Eastern-bloc countries as well as the major Western states and other former Portuguese dependencies in Africa, most notably Angola. In 1978 some 1,000 troops from Angola, augmented by a small contingent from Guinea-Bissau, were dispatched to São Tomé to guard against what President Pinto da Costa claimed to be a series of coup plots by expatriates in Angola, Gabon, and Portugal. However, most of the troops were withdrawn by the mid-1980s as part of a rapprochement with the west.

Ties with nearby Francophone nations subsequently grew, and France became São Tomé and Príncipe's leading trade partner. The county has also enjoyed significant aid from Taiwan, which São Tomé and Príncipe recognized in 1997.

In November 1999, São Tomé and Príncipe joined six of its Gulf of Guinea neighbors in agreeing to establish the Gulf of Guinea Commission (GGC) to coordinate "cooperation and development" in the oil- and fish-rich region. In early 2001 São Tomé and Príncipe reached an accord with Nigeria to establish the JDZ in disputed waters in the Gulf of Guinea; however, in May 2005, tensions arose between the countries over operating rights in the zone. Cooperation subsequently appeared back on track, and in 2007 São Tomé and Príncipe and Nigeria created a joint military commission to enhance bilateral security cooperation. Nigeria also supported São Tomé and Príncipe by selling it subsidized oil and providing a $30 million credit line. (In May 2009, the Nigerian legislature approved a $10 million interest-free loan for São Tomé and Príncipe to be paid back over six years with revenue from the JDZ.)

The United States has provided training to local security forces and has assisted in numerous infrastructure projects in the islands. The two countries conducted a joint military training exercise in March 2007, and in May 2007 the United States announced that it would assist São Tomé and Príncipe in coastal security to protect oil shipments passing through the Gulf of Guinea.

In 2013 government officials from São Tomé and Príncipe emphasized the country's continued good relationships with Angola and Cuba.

Current issues. Former prime minister Patrice Trovoada's ADI was particularly critical of the government in the run-up to the 2010 elections in regard to perceived corruption, a stance that apparently resonated with the electorate. The ADI dominated the balloting in the major districts in the local elections that were finally held on July 25, having been postponed from August 2009 due to funding constraints. The ADI also secured a plurality of 23 seats in the August 1 balloting for the National Assembly. Although he formed a minority government (comprising "new faces" from the ADI and independents), Trovoada pledged to consult with the opposition parties on policy initiatives. Nevertheless, subsequent legislative action remained constrained by interparty friction, particularly between the ADI and the MLSTP-PSD, that had contributed to decades of political instability (18 prime ministers since 1991).

After failing to secure the nomination from the MLSTP-PSD, former president Manuel Pinto da Costa ran as an independent in the 2011 presidential campaign. By that time, popular support for the ADI had apparently waned, and Pinto da Costa's second-round victory was considered a personal setback for Prime Minister Trovada. Pinto da Costa, 74, pledged to fight poverty and corruption in response to growing popular frustration over those issues. Although much presidential authority had been shifted to the prime minister since Pinto da Costa had last held office two decades earlier, some observers worried about a possible return to the authoritarian approach that had marked Pinto da Costa's previous presidency.

All the non-ADI legislative parties participated in a mass "Save Democracy" demonstration in October 2012, as Prime Minister Trovoada's critics accused him of hard-line tactics against the opposition, manipulation of the media, and a lack of transparency in regard to various financial dealings. Consequently, the November nonconfidence vote, which focused on the proposed 2013 budget, was not surprising. Trovoada, who reportedly retained substantial popular support, decried his dismissal by the president in early December as "illegitimate," and the ADI refused to nominate another candidate for the premiership, calling instead for new elections. Meanwhile, new prime minister Gabriel Costa was viewed as a "consensus builder" whose government would at least enjoy a relatively collegial relationship with the president.

POLITICAL PARTIES

Government Parties:

Movement for the Liberation of São Tomé and Príncipe–Social Democratic Party (*Movimento de Libertaçã de São Tomé e Príncipe–Partido Social Democrata*—MLSTP-PSD). An outgrowth of an earlier Committee for the Liberation of São Tomé and Príncipe (*Comité de Libertação de São Tomé e Príncipe*—CLSTP), the MLSTP was founded in 1972 and became the leading force in the campaign for independence from Portugal. At its first congress in 1978, the movement defined itself as a "revolutionary front of democratic, anti-neocolonialist, and anti-imperialist forces"; however, it did not formally adopt Marxism-Leninism despite that ideology's influence on its leaders and their economic policies. The MLSTP was the country's only authorized political group until the adoption of a multiparty system in August 1990. Two months later, President Manuel Pinto da Costa retired from leadership of what had been redesignated the MLSTP-PSD.

Pinto da Costa returned to political activity in 1996 and was elected to the party presidency in May 1998, prompting the resignation of Francisco Pires, a senior MLSTP-PSD leader who decried Pinto da Costa's "authoritarianism." Promising to reverse the country's declining economic conditions, the MLSTP-PSD secured a majority of assembly seats in the November election. However, Pinto da Costa was defeated in his bid for the presidency in 2001, and the MLSTP-PSD was excluded from the new government. In February 2005 former prime minister and party vice president Guilherme Posser da Costa replaced Pinto da Costa as the party's president. In June 2005 the MLSTP-PSD threatened to resign from the government, but the party subsequently agreed to form a new government to avoid early elections. Party member Maria do Carmo Silveira became the new prime minister and finance minister.

In the March 2006 legislative elections, the MLSTP-PSD won 20 seats, finishing second behind the coalition of the MDFM-PL and PCD. In the July presidential election, the MLSTP-PSD chose not to field its own candidate, instead supporting the ADI's Patrice Trovoada. In regional balloting in August 2006, the MLSTP-PSD won a majority in only one of seven districts. In light of the poor showing, party president Posser da Costa resigned the leadership post; he was replaced in February 2007 by Joaquim Rafael Branco, a party veteran who promised to rebuild the base before the next legislative elections in 2010. Following the collapse of the short-lived Trovoada government in May 2008, Branco was named to head a new coalition government. He lost the premiership following the August 2010 assembly balloting, in which the MLSTP-PSD won 21 seats (on a vote share of 33 percent) to finish second to the surging ADI.

In January 2011 businessman Aurelio Martins was elected party president over rival Jorge Amado. Martins subsequently became the party's flagbearer for the July presidential elections, while former party leader Pinto da Costa, as well as party stalwarts Maria das Neves and Elsa PINTO, ran as independents. Eventual winner Pinto da Costa received 35.8 percent of the first-round vote, while das Neves secured 13.9 percent, Pinto 4.6 percent, and Martins 4.1 percent. Jorge Amado was elected as the new party president at the MLSTP-PSD congress in June 2012. He was a prominent leader in the demonstrations in October that contributed to the downfall of the Trovoada government.

Leaders: Jorge AMADO (President), Américo BARROS (Vice President), Aurelio MARTINS (Former President and 2011 presidential candidate), Joaquim Rafael BRANCO (Former President of the Party and Former Prime Minister), Guilherme POSSER DA COSTA (Former Prime Minister), Armindo Vaz de ALMEIDA (Former Prime Minister), Alcino Martinho de Barros PINTO (President of the National Assembly), Fernando MAQUENGO (Secretary General).

Democratic Movement of Forces for Change–Liberal Party (*Movimento Democrático das Forças para da Mudança–Partido Liberal*—MDFM-PL). The MDFM-PL was formed in late 2001 by former members of the ADI (below) close to President Menezes and later established an electoral alliance with the PCD (below) for legislative balloting in 2002. That alliance won the largest number of seats (23) in the March 2006 election and went on to win majorities in six of seven districts in regional voting in August. In July President Menezes easily won reelection with more than 60 percent of the vote in the first round.

The MDFM-PL participated in the brief Trovoada government of February–May 2008 and in the subsequent Branco cabinet. However, apparently at Menezes's direction, the MDFM-PL officially withdrew from the government in late 2009. Menezes had been elected president of the MDFM-PL at an extraordinary congress in December 2009 and had indicated he would become prime minister if the party won the upcoming assembly poll. However, the leaders of other parties charged that Menezes's elevation to the MDFM-PL presidency was a violation of the constitutional provision that the president of the republic may not engage in "other public activity." When the legal community appeared to side with his critics, Menezes in January 2010 announced he was relinquishing the party's leadership responsibilities to MDFM-PL vice president Joao Costa Alegre. Running on its own in the August assembly poll, the MDFM-PL secured only one seat on a vote share of 7.3 percent and, after Menezes left office in 2011, was described by one analyst as "in the political graveyard." The MDFM-PL supported Delfim Neves of the PCD in the 2011 presidential race.

Leaders: Fradique de MENEZES (Former President of the Republic), João COSTA ALEGRE (Acting President of the Party), Tomé Soares da VERA CRUZ (Secretary General).

Party of Democratic Convergence (*Partido da Convergência Democrática*—PCD). The PCD was launched in 1987, initially as an underground movement styled after the Reflection Group (*Grupo de Reflexão*—GR), which surfaced as an open opposition formation following the introduction of multiparty politics in August 1990.

In early 1996 the PCD refused to participate in the new government. Subsequently, it named party president Alda Bandeira de Conceicão as its presidential candidate; following his third-place finish in the first round of presidential polling in June, the PCD supported Miguel Trovoada in the second round.

In the November 1998 legislative polling, the PCD's representation fell from 14 to 8 seats. The PCD supported the ADI's candidate in the 2001 presidential election, and the PCD was given posts in the new cabinet in September 2001. In 2002 and again in 2006, the PCD entered into an electoral alliance with the MDFM-PL. Running on its own in the 2010 assembly poll, the PCD finished third, securing 7 seats on a vote share of 13.9 percent.

In the 2011 presidential election, Delfim Neves, party secretary general, received 13.9 percent of the vote in the first round, finishing fourth. In 2012, the PCD criticized President Pinto da Costa for a perceived failure to pursue political dialogue with the assembly.

Leaders: Daniel Lima dos Santos DAIO (Former Prime Minister), Carlos Alberto Pires GOMES (Vice President), Alda BANDEIRA de Conceicão (1996 presidential candidate), Delfim NEVES (2011 presidential candidate and Secretary General).

Union of Democrats for Citizenship and Development (*União dos Democrates para e Cidadania e Denvolvimento*—UDD). Launched by ADI dissidents, including ADI cofounder Gabriel Costa, the UDD secured 2.4 percent of the vote in the March 2006 legislative poll and 1.2 percent (and again no seats) in 2010.

Leader: Gabriel COSTA (Prime Minister).

Opposition Party:

Independent Democratic Action (*Acção Democrática Independente*—ADI). Formed in 1992 under the leadership of President Miguel Trovoada's political advisor, Gabriel Costa, the ADI participated in municipal elections that year as an "independent group." It was legally registered in early 1994 and won 14 seats in the 1994 assembly balloting and 16 in 1998, claiming irregularities in the latter poll. In 2000 the ADI formed an electoral alliance with the PCD, Codo, UNDP, and PPP called the "Democratic Platform," which backed

ADI candidate Fradique de Menezes in the 2001 presidential election. The ADI subsequently formed a coalition government with the PCD. However, Menezes later fell into disagreement with pro-Trovoada factions within the ADI, and his allies formed the MDFM-PL (below). Meanwhile, Costa objected to the elevation of Patrice Trovoada, son of the former president, to ADI leader and left the party, eventually founding the UDD (above).

The ADI participated in the UK coalition (below) from late 2001 until early 2006 but won 11 seats on its own in the March 2006 legislative election. Party Secretary Patrice Trovoada, the son of the former president, became prime minister for a short time in the first half of 2008 but was unable to hold the fledgling coalition together. Calling for fresh legislative elections, the ADI rejected the negotiations that brought about Prime Minister Branco's coalition government in June 2008. The ADI subsequently maintained the position that Branco's government was unconstitutional. Trovoada was named prime minister again after the ADI secured a plurality of 26 seats (on a vote share of 42 percent) in the 2010 assembly balloting.

Party secretary general Evaristo Carvalho lost in the 2011 runoff presidential balloting to Manuel Pinta da Costa with 47.1 percent of the vote.

Leaders: Patrice TROVOADA (Chair and Former Prime Minister), Evaristo CARVALHO (2011 presidential candidate and Secretary General).

Other Parties and Groups:

New Way Movement (*Movimento Novo Rumo*—NR). The NR won one seat (from Príncipe) in the March 2006 assembly elections but did not join the new coalition government.

Leader: João GOMES.

Uê Kédadji (UK). The UK was established in late 2001 as an alliance of the ADI (above); Codo; the **National Union for Democracy and Progress** (*União Nacional para a Democracia e Progresso*—UNDP), led by Manuel Paixao LIMA; the **People's Progress Party** (*Partida Progresso do Povo*—PPP), led by Francisco SILVA; and the **Democratic Renovation Party** (*Partido da Renovação Democrática*—PRD), led by Armindo GRAÇA. The UNDP and the PPP had been recognized in September 1998 and were part of the Democratic Platform that supported the ADI candidate in the 2001 presidential balloting. After the 2002 balloting, the UK held eight seats in the legislature, but the ADI left the alliance in early 2006. In February 2006 the **Social Renovation Party** (*Partido Social Renovado*—PSR), led by Hamilton VAZ, joined the UK, which failed to win any seats in the 2006 legislative elections. The UNDP ran on its own in 2010.

Opposition Democratic Coalition (*Coligação Democrática da Oposição*—Codo). Codo was launched in March 1986 as an alliance of two Lisbon-based opposition groups—the **Independent Democratic Union of São Tomé and Príncipe** (*União Democrática Independente de São Tomé e Príncipe*—UDISTP) and the **São Tomé and Príncipe National Resistance Front** (*Frente da Resistência Nacional de São Tomé e Príncipe*—FRNSTP)—to combat what they called the "totalitarianism" of the da Costa government. Although the UDISTP previously had stated that it would reach its goals through "peaceful means," its association with the FRNSTP, generally considered a more radical group, led to a Codo posture that did not rule out "recourse to armed struggle."

Leader: Manuel Neves e SILVA.

Union for Change and Progress in Príncipe (*União para Mudança e Progresso do Príncipe*—UMPP). The UMPP was founded by José Cassandra, an ally of former prime minister Vera Cruz. The party won control of the regional assembly in Príncipe in the 2006 balloting, and Cassandra was subsequently elected president of that assembly, promising to increase development of the island and to decrease its dependence on the island of São Tomé. Cassandra and other party leaders subsequently threatened to resign from the regional assembly if the central government on São Tomé did not reverse its decision to delay municipal and regional elections originally scheduled for August 2009. Cassandra was reelected regional president in the July 25, 2010, municipal and regional elections, which were dominated by the MLSTP-PSD. Cassandra had the support of the ADI, the PCD, and the MDFM-PL.

In early 2012, the UMPP urged the residents of Príncipe to participate in protest demonstrations against the national government's decision not to ratify an investment agreement recently negotiated between the regional government and a prominent South African financier. The UMPP and others argued that political and business leaders on São Tomé were envious of the investment accord, which called for development of a "luxury eco-tourism" project on Príncipe.

Leader: José CASSANDRA.

Christian Democratic Front (Frente Democrática Cristã—FDC). The FDC leader, Arlécio Costa, first became known for his role in fighting for the apartheid government in South Africa in the 1980s as commander of the South African military's Buffalo Battalion. FDC members were also implicated in a coup attempt in São Tomé and Príncipe in 2003 and subsequently maintained an uneasy relationship with the government.

Costa and some 30 others were arrested in February 2009 for allegedly plotting a coup. About half of the detainees were released in August, but Costa and others were convicted later in the year for illegal arms possession and "acts amounting to rebellion." Costa was released in January 2010 as part of President Menezes's yearly amnesty.

Leader: Arlécio COSTA.

Other recently active groups include the **São Tomé Workers' Party** (*Partido Trabalhista São Tomense*—PTS), led by Anacleto ROLIM; the **Democratic Alliance for the Development of Príncipe** (*Aliança Democrática para Desenvolvimento do Príncipe*—ADDP), a regional party in Príncipe supported by the MLSTP-PSD; and the **Renaissance Movement of Agua Grande,** which won two seats in regional elections in Príncipe in August 2006.

LEGISLATURE

Formerly an indirectly elected National Popular Assembly (*Assembleia Popular Nacional*) of 40 members, the current **National Assembly** (*Assembleia Nacional*) is a unicameral body of 55 members directly elected via proportional representation (primarily from party lists, although independent candidates are permitted) for four-year terms from seven multimember constituencies.

Following the most recent balloting of August 1, 2010, the seat distribution was as follows: Independent Democratic Action, 26; the Movement for the Liberation of São Tomé and Príncipe–Social Democratic Party, 21; the Party of Democratic Convergence, 7; and the Democratic Movement of Forces for Change–Liberal Party, 1.

President: Alcino Martinho de Barros PINTO.

CABINET

[as of November 12, 2013]

Prime Minister	Gabriel Arcanjo Ferreira da Costa (UDD)
Ministers	
Agriculture, Fishing, and Rural Development	Antonio Alvaro da Graça Dias (PCD)
Commerce, Industry, and Tourism	Demóstenes Vasconcelos Pires dos Santos (PCD)
Defense and Internal Security	Lt. Col. Oscar Aguiar Sacramento e Sousa (MDFM-PL)
Education, Culture, and Training	Jorge Lopes Bom Jesus (MLSTP-PSD)
Foreign Affairs, Cooperation, and Communities	Natália Pedro da Costa Umbelina Neto (ind.) [f]
Health and Social Affairs	Leonel Pinto d'Assunção Pontes (MDFM-PL)
Justice, Public Administration, and Parliamentary Affairs	Edite Ramos da Costa Tem Jua (MLSTP-PSD)
Planning and Finance	Hélio Silva Vaz de Almeida (MLSTP-PSD)
Public Works, Infrastructure, and Natural Resources	Osvaldo Cravid Viegas d'Abreu (MLSTP-PSD)
Youth and Sports	Albertino Francisco Boa Morte (PCD)

[f] = female

INTERGOVERNMENTAL REPRESENTATION

Ambassador to the U.S.: (Vacant).

U.S. Ambassador to São Tomé and Príncipe: Eric BENJAMINSON (resident in Gabon).

Permanent Representative to the UN: Carlos Filomeno Agostinho DAS NEVES.

IGO Memberships (Non-UN): AfDB, AU, NAM.

SAUDI ARABIA

Kingdom of Saudi Arabia
al-Mamlakah al-Arabiyah al-Saudiyah

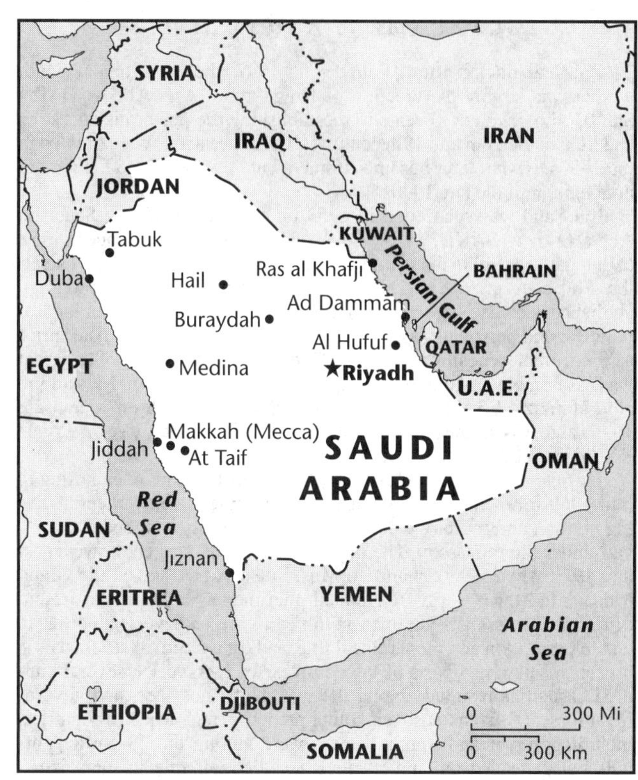

Political Status: Unified kingdom established September 23, 1932; under absolute monarchical system; Basic Law of Government based on Islamic law promulgated by royal decree on March 1, 1992.

Area: 829,995 sq. mi. (2,149,690 sq. km).

Population: 28,877,141 (2012E—UN); 26,939,583 (2013E—U.S. Census). Foreign nationals constitute approximately one quarter of both figures.

Major Urban Centers (2005E): RIYADH (royal capital, 5,126,000), Jiddah (administrative capital, 3,557,000), Makkah (Mecca, 1,446,000).

Official Language: Arabic.

Monetary Unit: Riyal (market rate November 1, 2013: 3.75 riyals = $1US).

Ruler and Prime Minister: King Abdallah ibn Abd al-Aziz Al SAUD; confirmed on August 1, 2005, by the royal court upon the death of King Fahd ibn Abd al-Aziz Al SAUD.

Heir Apparent: Crown Prince Salman ibn Abd al-Aziz Al SAUD; appointed crown prince and heir to the throne on June 18, 2012, upon the death of former Crown Prince Nayef ibn Abd al-Aziz.

THE COUNTRY

A vast, largely desert country occupying the greater part of the Arabian Peninsula, the Kingdom of Saudi Arabia exhibits both traditional and contemporary lifestyles. Frontiers were poorly defined for many years, and no census was undertaken prior to 1974. Some 85 percent of the indigenous inhabitants, who have traditionally adhered to patriarchal forms of social organization, are Sunni Muslim of the conservative Wahhabi sect. The Shiite population (15 percent) is located primarily in the east. Despite a strict interpretation of Islam, female participation in the paid labor force has tripled to 15 percent over the last two decades. Mecca and Medina, the two holiest cities of Islam and the goals of an annual pilgrimage by Muslims from all over the world, lie within the western region known as the Hijaz, where the commercial and administrative center of Jiddah is also located.

Saudi Arabia is the leading exporter of oil and possesses the world's largest known petroleum reserves (estimated at upward of 200 billion barrels), which have made it one of the world's richest nations. The government acquired full interest in the Arabian-American Oil Company (Aramco) in 1980. Dramatic surges in oil revenue permitted heightened expenditures after 1973 that focused on the development of airports, seaports, and roads, as well as the modernization of medical, educational, and telecommunications systems. In addition, large-scale irrigation projects and heavy price subsidies yielded agricultural self-sufficiency in a country that once produced only 10 percent of its food needs. Vast sums were also committed to armaments, particularly modern fighter planes, missiles, and air defense systems.

Because of a reversal in oil prices and substantial support to Iraq in its eight-year war with Iran, the Saudis experienced a major recession in the early 1980s. An economic revival was sparked in the early 1990s, however, by increased oil production as an offshoot of Iraq's invasion of Kuwait in 1991. Subsequently, concern over falling cash reserves and growing external debt prompted substantial budgetary retrenchment, including reductions in the traditionally high subsidies upon which Saudis had come to rely. The government also introduced programs designed to help move Saudis into private-sector jobs, which are held primarily by foreign workers.

Generally higher oil prices in 1996 and 1997 permitted a return to moderately expansive budgets, with emphasis being placed on infrastructure designed to promote private-sector development. However, financial difficulties returned in 1998 as the result of a sharp drop in oil prices and the effects of the Asian economic crisis. In July 2003 the government bolstered its "Saudization" effort to help reduce unemployment, most significantly by replacing 17,800 foreign white-collar workers with Saudis. Unemployment, widely estimated at nearly 30 percent (though the government says it is in the single digits), has been a particular problem among those under age 20, a group that constitutes more than half the population.

As a result of the U.S. war in Iraq since 2003, Saudi oil prices and production increased significantly. In September 2003, Russia and Saudi Arabia agreed to a landmark deal paving the way for a multi-billion-dollar Saudi investment in the Russian oil industry, thus ensuring long-term capacity for both. As a result of surging economic growth, the kingdom has improved roads, schools, and hospitals. It has also continued to move ahead with privatization efforts and in 2006 opened its stock market to foreign investors. Annual GDP growth averaged 5.2 percent in 2006–2008 but contracted to less than 1 percent in 2009 due to a dramatic decline in the price of oil during the global economic crisis. Meanwhile, authorities drew from the country's $400 billion reserves to fund key projects and maintain growth in the wake of the worldwide financial turmoil, and the International Monetary Fund (IMF) praised the government's efforts to diversify. Annual growth accelerated to an average 7.6 percent in 2010–2012, owing in large part to a rebound in the private sector, boosted by government spending, and growth in the non-oil sector. The IMF expected growth of 4.4 percent in 2013, with inflation at 3.7 percent.

GOVERNMENT AND POLITICS

Political background. Founded in 1932, the Kingdom of Saudi Arabia was largely the creation of King Abd al-Aziz Al SAUD (Ibn Saud), who devoted 30 years to reestablishing the power his ancestors had held in the 18th and 19th centuries. Oil concessions were granted in the 1930s to what later became Aramco, but large-scale production did not begin until the late 1940s.

Ibn Saud was succeeded in 1953 by an ineffectual son, Saud ibn Abd al-Aziz Al SAUD, who was persuaded by family influence in 1958 to delegate control to his younger brother, Crown Prince Faysal (Faisal) ibn Abd al-Aziz Al SAUD. Faysal began a modernization program, abolished slavery, curbed royal extravagance, adopted sound fiscal policies, and personally assumed the functions of prime minister prior to the formal deposition of King Saud on November 2, 1964. Faysal was assassinated by one of his nephews, Prince Faysal ibn Musaid ibn Abd al-Aziz Al SAUD, while holding court in Riyadh on March 25, 1975, and was immediately succeeded by his brother, Crown Prince Khalid ibn Abd al-Aziz Al SAUD.

Despite a number of coup attempts, the most important occurring in mid-1969 following the discovery of a widespread conspiracy involving civilian and military elements, internal stability has tended to prevail under the monarchy. The regime was visibly shaken, however, in late 1979 when several hundred Muslim extremists seized the Grand Mosque in Mecca during the annual pilgrimage. Under the leadership of a *mahdi* (messiah), the men involved in the takeover called for an end to corruption and monarchical rule, and for a return to strict Islamic precepts. They held parts of the complex for two weeks; several hundred casualties resulted among the insurgents, hostages, and government forces. Citizens of several other predominantly Muslim countries, including Egypt and South Yemen, were among the 63 participants publicly beheaded on January 9, 1980, for their role in the seizure. Collaterally, the Shiite minority initiated antigovernment demonstrations in eastern areas of the kingdom.

King Khalid died on June 13, 1982, and was immediately succeeded as monarch and prime minister by his half-brother and heir, Crown Prince Fahd ibn Abd al-Aziz Al SAUD. On the same day, Prince Abdallah ibn Abd al-Aziz Al SAUD was designated heir to the throne and first deputy prime minister. King Fahd's rule subsequently encountered potential instability, with declining oil revenues threatening social programs, and a radical Islamic movement, supported by Iran, attempting to undermine the regime diplomatically and militarily.

King Fahd's decision in August 1990 to request Western and regional assistance in defending Saudi Arabia's border against the possibility of an Iraqi invasion was widely supported within the kingdom. However, the presence of Western forces and media resulted in intense scrutiny of Saudi government and society, raising questions about the nation's inability to defend itself despite massive defense expenditures; generating calls for modernization of the political system, which the king answered by promising reforms; and eliciting signs of dissent, including a quickly suppressed, but highly publicized protest by Saudi women for greater personal liberties. The government also faced growing pressure from Islamists, even though the regime was already considered one of the most conservative in the Arab world because of its active enforcement of Islamic interdictions. In May 1991 Islamist leaders sent a highly publicized letter to King Fahd demanding 12 reforms, including extended implementation of sharia and creation of an independent consultative council that would be responsible for domestic and foreign policy. King Fahd issued royal decrees on March 1, 1992, creating Saudi Arabia's first written rules of governance and providing for the formation of a national Consultative Council. But, he rejected the notion that "the prevailing democratic system in the world" was suitable for Saudi Arabia and insisted that no elections would be in the offing.

In September 1992, Islamist leaders again formally challenged government policy, this time in a "memorandum" to religious leaders that was viewed as "more defiant and bolder" than the 1991 document. The action was followed in May 1993 by the establishment of a Committee for the Defense of Legitimate Rights (CDLR; see Political Groups, below). However, the government quickly declared the organization illegal, with King Fahd warning the Islamists to cease distributing antigovernment material and using mosques as "political pulpits."

The most conspicuous result of a July 1993 cabinet reshuffle was the creation of a new Ministry of Islamic Guidance, which was seen as an attempt to buttress the kingdom's "religious establishment" against Islamist pressure within the Shiite and Sunni populations. The following month the king appointed the members of the national Consultative Council. The council consisted entirely of men, none drawn from the royal family, representing a broad social spectrum. Although the government heralded the inauguration of the council in December 1993 as a major advance, some observers derided it as a "public relations exercise," noting that council sessions would not be open to the public and that topics for debate required advance approval by the king.

Questions also surrounded the king's October 1994 appointment of the new Supreme Council on Islamic Affairs, which was dominated by members of the royal family and technocrats owing their livelihood to the government. The new body was viewed as a further effort by the monarchy to undercut the appeal of the Islamists, who had been pressing for further Islamization of government policy and a curtailment of Western ties since the 1990–1991 Gulf crisis and war.

On August 2, 1995, in the most sweeping ministerial shakeup in two decades, no less than 13 portfolios, including those of finance, industry, and petroleum, changed hands, with many political veterans being succeeded by younger, Western-educated technocrats. While members of the royal family were left in charge of several key ministries (notably defense, interior, and foreign affairs), the obvious intent was to improve efficiency by bringing in a new generation of officials.

King Fahd was hospitalized in early November 1995, suffering from what was widely reported but never officially confirmed to be a stroke. On January 1, 1996, he formally transferred responsibility for "affairs of state" to Crown Prince Abdallah, interpreted by many observers to be a step toward permanent succession, but King Fahd formally reassumed full authority on February 22.

An explosion near a U.S. Air Force building, the Khobar Towers, in Dhahran in June 1996 killed 19 U.S. servicemen and wounded 350, prompting the transfer of American forces to more secure desert bases. Meanwhile, in what was seen as a related development, the Saudi government launched a crackdown on Shiite dissidents in the east, where antimonarchical and anti-Western sentiment appeared to be the strongest. Members of a pro-Iran Shiite group were later accused by the United States of being responsible for the attack (see Political Groups, below).

A cabinet reshuffle was announced on June 6, 1999, with members of the ruling family retaining six key posts. A Supreme Economic Council was established in August to oversee proposed reform in non-oil sectors, and a Supreme Council for Petroleum and Mineral Affairs was created in January 2000. By 2003 major reforms had begun to take shape. In an unprecedented move in January of that year, Crown Prince Abdallah met with reformists, some of whom the government had jailed in the 1990s for advocating reforms. Government representatives also met for the first time on Saudi soil with a UN human rights group, and in October, for the first time a woman was named dean at a major university. The most stunning news, however, came on October 13, 2003, when the government announced that it would hold nationwide elections for municipal councils in 2004 (postponed to 2005), to be followed by elections for city councilors and, ultimately, members of the Consultative Council. The announcement coincided with the country's first human rights conference, held in Riyadh, October 13–15.

Further, King Fahd granted greater legislative powers to the Consultative Council in November 2003, effectively shifting some influence from the cabinet to the legislative body. The reforms followed in the wake of increasing pressure from "liberals," but more significantly after an attack in May 2003 on a luxury residential compound that killed 35 and wounded hundreds (see Foreign relations, below). The government, which came under increasing pressure from the United States since the September 11, 2001, attacks to undertake social and political reforms, in 2003 approved direct elections for half of the seats of the 178 municipal councils, though women were not allowed to vote. The first municipal elections in more than 30 years were held February 10–April 21, 2005. Islamists won the vast majority of seats.

King Fahd died on August 1, 2005, at age 82 after an extended illness and a 23-year reign. He was immediately succeeded by 82-year-old Crown Prince Abdallah, his half-brother. Sultan ibn Abd al-Aziz Al SAUD, the longtime defense minister, replaced Abdallah as crown prince (while continuing to hold the defense portfolio and several other positions).

In his first major cabinet reshuffle, King Abdallah appointed several reformers and dismissed "reactionaries," according to news reports, in new appointments announced February 14, 2009. The king also appointed the first female cabinet member, naming her to the post of deputy minister for girls' education. In March the king postponed the country's second local elections for at least two years, stating that more time was needed to change the laws in order to "expand the participation of citizens in the management of local affairs." On March 28 Prince Nayif ibn Abd al-Aziz AL SAUD was sworn in as second deputy prime minister, placing him third in line for the throne behind the king and the crown prince. Prince Nayif became deputy prime minister and crown prince upon the death of Crown Prince Sultan on September 22, 2011. Nayif died on June 16, 2012, and Salman ibn Abd al-Aziz Al SAUD became the next in line to the throne.

On March 26, 2011, King Abdallah established a new ministry of housing. On September 25, he granted women the right to vote and to run in future municipal elections. He appointed 30 women to the Consultative council in January 2013 (see Current issues, below).

Constitution and government. Saudi Arabia is a traditional monarchy with all power ultimately vested in the king, who is also the country's supreme religious leader. The kingdom held its first national municipal elections in some 30 years in 2005, though women continued to be disenfranchised. There are no political parties in Saudi Arabia, and legislation is by royal decree, though in 2004 King Fahd granted a greater legislative role to the Consultative Council, shifting some influence from the cabinet. In recent years an attempt was made to modernize the machinery of government by creating ministries to manage affairs of state. However, the king serves additionally as prime minister, and many sensitive cabinet posts are held by members of the royal family, often for long periods of time. The judicial system, encompassing summary and general courts, a Court of Cassation, and a Supreme Council of Justice, is largely based on Islamic religious law (sharia), but tribal and customary law are also applied. Sweeping judicial reforms were announced on April 3, 2005, including establishment of a supreme court and appeals courts in the 13 provinces.

For administrative purposes Saudi Arabia is divided into 13 provinces or regions, each headed by a governor appointed by the king. In April 1994 the provinces were subdivided into 103 governorates. The principal urban areas have half-elected, half-appointed municipal councils, while villages and tribes are governed by sheikhs in conjunction with legal advisers and other community leaders.

On March 1, 1992, King Fahd authorized the creation of a 60-member national Consultative Council (*Majlis al-Shura*) headed by a chair (speaker) appointed by the king to a four-year term. The *Majlis* (inaugurated on December 29, 1993) was empowered to initiate laws, review domestic and foreign policies, and scrutinize budgets "in the tradition of Islamic consultation." Council membership was raised to 90 in 1997 and to 120 in 2001. In late 1993 the king also issued a decree authorizing the formation of consultative councils in each province, encompassing the provincial governor and at least ten appointed individuals. Another decree codified a "basic system of government" based on Islamic law. The 83-article document is widely described as the country's first written constitution, which went beyond previous unwritten conventions by guaranteeing individual rights. It also formally delineated the rules of succession, institutionalizing the king's unilateral authority to designate (and dismiss) his heir, a son or grandson of King Abd al-Aziz Al Saud, who died in 1953.

In October 1994, King Fahd appointed the Supreme Council on Islamic Affairs to review educational, economic, and foreign policies to ensure that they were conducted in concert with Islamic precepts.

On October 20, 2006, the king issued a new law establishing a committee made up of the sons and grandsons of King Fahd to choose future kings and crown princes. The changes do not go into effect until the current crown prince becomes king. (See Current issues, below.) On October 1, 2007, King Abdallah issued a decree approving the formation of a supreme court, special tribunals for labor and commercial disputes, and appeals courts—all in accordance with Islamic law.

The king renewed the Consultative Council on February 28, 2009, appointing 150 members to four-year terms.

In the wake of Arab Spring movements, Saudi Arabian authorities further tightened laws prohibiting criticism of the government. The Ministry of Culture and Information heavily censors print and broadcast media. Reporters Without Borders ranked Saudi Arabia 163rd of 179 countries for press freedom in 2013.

Foreign relations. Since the late 1950s, Saudi Arabia has stood as the leading conservative power in the Arab world. The early 1960s were marked by hostility toward Egypt over North Yemen, with Riyadh supporting the royalists and Cairo backing the ultimately victorious republicans during the civil war that broke out in 1962. By 1969, however, Saudi Arabia had become a prime mover behind the pan-Islamic movement and subsequently sought to mediate such disputes as the Lebanese conflict in 1976 and the Iran-Iraq war. An influential member of the Organization of the Petroleum Exporting Countries (OPEC), the kingdom was long a restraining influence on oil price increases. Since the U.S.-led invasion of Iraq in 2003, Saudi Arabia, a swing producer, has been authorized by OPEC to continue to boost production to meet global demand.

The Saudis provided financial support for other Arab countries involved in the 1967 and 1973 Arab-Israeli conflicts and broke diplomatic relations with Cairo in April 1979 to oppose the Egyptian-Israeli peace treaty. Otherwise, the kingdom has been generally allied with the United States. The outbreak of war between Iraq and Iran in September 1980 prompted the Carter administration, which earlier in the year had rejected a Saudi request for assistance in upgrading its military capability, to announce the "temporary deployment" of four Airborne Warning and Control Systems (AWAC aircraft), a decision influenced by Riyadh's support of Washington's plan to increase U.S. military presence in the Gulf region upon the 1979 Soviet intervention in Afghanistan. Despite Israel's objections, the Reagan administration secured Senate approval in October 1981 of a major package of arms sales to Saudi Arabia that included five surveillance aircraft, although delivery did not commence until mid-1986 because of controversy over U.S. supervisory rights. Earlier, in an effort to win congressional support for their arms purchases, the Saudis had indicated a willingness to allow American use of bases in the kingdom in the event of Soviet military action in the Gulf. As the U.S. Iran-contra scandal unfolded in late 1986 and 1987, it was alleged that the Saudis had agreed to aid anti-communist resistance groups around the world as part of the AWAC purchase deal, ultimately making some $32 million available to the Nicaraguan rebels between July 1984 and March 1985. In July 1988, relations were further strained when Riyadh, citing congressional delays and other "embarrassments" caused by Washington's criticism of Chinese missile imports, purchased $25 billion of British armaments, thus undercutting reliance on the United States as its leading military supplier.

During 1987 and 1988, the Iran–Iraq war yielded continued political tension between revolutionary Tehran and pro-Western Riyadh. In July 1987 the seizure of Mecca's Grand Mosque by Muslim extremists resulted in the death of an estimated 400 Iranian pilgrims; subsequently, Iranian officials called for the immediate "uprooting" of the Saudi royal family, while King Fahd, supported by most of the Arab states, vowed to continue as "custodian" of Islam's holy shrines. In April 1988, citing the Mecca riot and increasing Iranian attacks on its shipping vessels, Saudi Arabia became the first member of the Gulf Cooperation Council (GCC) to sever diplomatic relations with Tehran. The Khomeini regime's subsequent decision to forbid its citizens from participating in the 1988 pilgrimage was seen as an attempt to discredit Saudi administration of the holy cities. Diplomatic relations were restored in March 1991 upon the rise of more moderate Irani leadership.

Relations with the Soviet Union, which were suspended in 1938, briefly saw potential for improvement when Foreign Minister Saud al-Faisal visited Moscow in 1982. After Moscow's 1988 announcement that it would withdraw from Afghanistan (Riyadh long having been a highly vocal supporter of the rebel president-in-exile, Sibgahatullah Mojaddidi) resolution of the impasse became possible. Diplomatic relations were restored in 1990, the same year ties were established with China. In 1992, the kingdom moved quickly to establish ties with the Commonwealth of Independent States (CIS), offering economic aid and pursuing private-sector ties. Particular attention was given to the Central Asian republics, where the Saudis were expected to vie with Turkey and Iran for influence.

In March 1989, Iraqi and Saudi officials signed a mutual noninterference pact. However, in the wake of Iraq's invasion of Kuwait on August 2, 1990, and amid reports that Iraqi troops were massing on the Saudi border, the Saudi government shed its traditional role as regional consensus builder, criticized the invasion as "vile aggression," and called for international assistance to prevent further Iraqi gains. The ensuing buildup of Western and regional forces along the Saudi border with Kuwait caused a rupture in relations with pro-Iraqi leaders of Yemen, Jordan, and the Palestine Liberation Organization (PLO). On September 19, Riyadh rescinded special privileges for Yemeni and PLO workers, prompting repatriation of more than half of the 1.5 million Yemeni citizens in the kingdom. Shortly thereafter oil deliveries to Jordan were suspended, Jordanian diplomats were expelled, and the Saudi ambassador to Amman was recalled. Meanwhile, the Saudi government moved to reimburse and reward its allies, particularly Egypt and Syria. The kingdom's most dramatic Gulf crisis decision, however, was to acknowledge its effective alliance with the United States, which responded by promising to sell the Saudis $20 billion in armaments.

Saudi Arabia's pivotal role in the U.S.-led coalition against Iraq during the 1991 war included participation in 6,500 air sorties, the eviction of Iraqi forces from Khafji, and the liberation of Kuwait City.

After the Gulf war, the Saudi government allowed U.S. troops to remain in the kingdom—the birthplace of Islam and home to its most sacred places—angering many, including Osama bin Laden and his supporters. During the buildup to the 2003 U.S. invasion of Iraq, King Fahd announced that the kingdom would not participate in a war against Iraq, and he proposed that Iraqi leader Saddam Hussein go into exile to avert a war. However, U.S. forces were eventually allowed to deploy to Saudi Arabia prior to the war. After the May 12, 2003, suicide bombings of a compound in Riyadh that killed 35 and wounded hundreds, Riyadh became more attuned to the U.S. war on terror, with the government declaring its own such war in August 2003.

In 2004 the relationship between the two countries further strengthened when they jointly asked the United Nations to crack down on one of the kingdom's largest charities, which reportedly funded al-Qaida. In June 2005 some 57 Islamic nations—Saudi Arabia among them—met in Yemen and agreed to fight terrorism, now a defining issue in the Middle East. Analysts said that Riyadh was concerned that sectarian violence between Sunnis and Shiites in Iraq might make its way into Saudi Arabia if armed militants gained support from Shiite hardliners in the kingdom.

Saudi Arabia's relations with North Yemen and South Yemen and, since 1990, the unified Republic of Yemen have often been strained, particularly regarding border demarcations. In March 2005 the two countries signed a border agreement, influenced by their desire to halt the flow of weapons and drug smuggling and an increasing number of terrorist suspects. In April Yemen and Saudi Arabia held their first joint military exercise.

Saudi Arabia has played a role in supporting a negotiated settlement between Israel and the Palestinians, at times acceding to foreign pressure. In early 1993 the Saudis responded favorably to a U.S. request for resumption of aid to the PLO as an inducement to the Palestinians to rejoin stalled peace talks with Israel. Riyadh also underscored its backing for the regional peace process the following September, when it convinced the GCC countries to end their long-standing boycott of companies doing business with Israel (see Arab League entry for details). In 2003 Crown Prince Abdallah presented the Arab League with an initiative for peace with Israel in return for its withdrawal from occupied territories. (The following day, however, Israel launched a massive invasion to reoccupy the West Bank.) When Saudi Arabia was granted membership in the World Trade Organization (WTO) in December 2005, the kingdom granted assurances that it had ended its trade boycott against Israel, though later acknowledged that it had lifted only "certain aspects" of the boycott. In February 2006 Riyadh joined other Arab countries in rejecting a U.S. request that they cut off aid to Hamas (which won election to the new Palestinian government a month earlier). The kingdom has continued to support what it has described as the legitimate rights of Palestinians.

In February 2007, Saudi Arabia invited the leaders of Hamas and Fatah to a summit in Mecca, where the warring Palestinian factions agreed to form a unity government (which subsequently failed). Shortly after the Mecca meeting, Riyadh hosted an Arab League summit that renewed the peace initiative, offering Israel normalized ties with Arab states if it would agree to return to its pre-1967 borders. Following the collapse of the peace deal and a visit in August by U.S. Secretary of State Condoleezza Rice and U.S. Defense Secretary Robert Gates, Saudi Arabia agreed to send its foreign minister to the U.S.-sponsored Middle East peace conference in Annapolis, Maryland, in November—its participation seen as bolstering President George W. Bush's initiative at a time when U.S. standing in the region was at a low point.

Relations with Syria deteriorated in 2008, with Saudi Arabia ultimately joining Egypt, Jordan, and Lebanon in boycotting an Arab summit in Damascus following Syria's failure to help facilitate the election of a new government in Lebanon. Riyadh grew increasingly concerned over the tumultuous events in Beirut (see entry on Lebanon), calling on "all regional sides to respect the sovereignty and independence of Lebanon," with particular references to Syria and Iran. Tensions with Iran heightened following Saudi Arabia's describing Hezbollah's military attacks in Lebanon as a "coup" backed by Iran, highlighting Saudi Arabia's efforts to counter Iran's growing Shiite influence in the region. Meanwhile, the kingdom strengthened ties with the United States, signing agreements in May to broaden counterterrorism efforts and bolster peaceful nuclear cooperation, among other things. In addition, President Bush pledged to push for a $20 billion arms deal for Saudi Arabia, despite the objections of Israel and some members of the U.S. Congress. Meanwhile, relations with Syria warmed somewhat following a visit by President Bashar al-Assad to Saudi Arabia in March. Seven months later, King Abdallah, made a "highly symbolic" visit to Syria to ease tensions. The king and President Assad agreed to work toward closer ties between their countries. (For more on Saudi Arabia's counterterrorism efforts and oil policies in 2007–2008, see the 2013 *Handbook*.)

Agreements on security issues strengthened with Yemen in 2009 as a result of that country's crackdown in particular on al-Qaida terrorists, who were reported to be using Yemen as a staging ground for radical Islamist activities. In November Yemen's war against Huthi rebels spilled over into Saudi Arabia when the rebels killed a Saudi border official. The rebels accused Saudi Arabia of allowing Yemeni government forces to attack them from a Saudi military base.

In January 2010 Saudi authorities held talks with Iran in an effort to repatriate the 17-year-old daughter of Osama bin Laden. She had reportedly fled to the Saudi embassy in Tehran from a compound outside the city where the family had been under house arrest for years.

A long-simmering dispute with the United Arab Emirates (UAE) over maritime and land borders erupted in April 2010, when vessels from both countries exchanged gunfire. Subsequently, two Saudi border guards arrested by the UAE were released. Despite an accord signed by the two countries in 1974 that supposedly resolved the matter, Abu Dhabi has resented that the pact put a huge oilfield in Saudi territory.

In July 2010, King Abdallah visited Jordan, Syria, and Egypt in an effort to bolster Arab unity in the region. In September reports revealed details of what was said to be the largest single arms sale ever by the United States to Saudi Arabia, totaling some $67 billion over 10 years.

In 2011, Saudi Arabia and Pakistan agreed to enhance ties, and Saudi Arabia established a diplomatic mission in Cuba. Relations with Iran, a predominantly Shiite country, were strained after Saudi Arabia sent troops into Bahrain to back the Sunni king against antigovernment demonstrators (see Current issues, below).

Relations with Iran became tense in June 2012 after Saudi Arabia executed four Iranians for drug trafficking. The matter was resolved with a treaty in July addressing the repatriation of criminals between the two countries. In January 2013 Sri Lanka withdrew its envoy in Saudi Arabia in protest after a Sri Lankan nanny was executed because of the death of an infant in her care.

In 2013 Saudi Arabia established itself as the main outside support for antigovernment fighters in Syria. The kingdom financed a major purchase of weaponry from Croatia to arm Syrian rebels in February. In June Saudi authorities called for a ban on supplying arms to the Syrian government and condemned the role of Iran and Hezbollah in the civil war.

In late March 2013, in an effort to lower unemployment rates, Saudi Arabia began deporting thousands of Yemenis and other foreign workers. After two weeks, in which time Yemen reported some 20,000 had returned, the policy was revised to give a three-month grace period.

Current issues. In other moves toward reform, the government took steps toward the establishment of the first coed, public university in the kingdom, and Saudi authorities reportedly held secret talks with the Vatican regarding the opening of the first Roman Catholic church in the kingdom, which historically has banned all Christian denominations. The talks followed an unprecedented visit to the Vatican by King Abdallah in November 2007.

In 2009, attention turned to what was described by observers as "a sweeping shake-up" by the king, who replaced four key cabinet ministers, most notably those in education and justice, and appointed new leaders to almost all justice-related bodies. All of these changes, including the king's appointment of a woman as deputy education minister—making her the kingdom's highest-ranking female political figure ever—were seen as significant moves toward reform. The deputy minister's appointments were seen as particularly important in the religious-based education system, which had been viewed as fostering extremism, and in the effort to codify sharia law. Some analysts said the king's most far-reaching change was his reconfiguration of the Grand Ulema Council, the country's premier religious body, to include more moderates. Further, the king appointed as head of the Supreme Judicial Council the former chair of the Consultative Council, Salih ibn HUMAYD, who was seen as more likely to advance the king's reforms than his predecessor. In addition, the king replaced the head of the "notoriously strict" religious police with a more moderate figure, according to published reports. Meanwhile, the king delayed the next municipal elections for at least two years in an effort to grant more power to the local councils and to expand the electoral process. The government explained the postponement as having "extended the mandate" of the sitting councils by two years while necessary changes to the law were prepared.

In April 2010, the government announced plans to establish a civil nuclear and renewable energy center in Riyadh to meet the country's increasing demand for power. Regarding other domestic issues, observers have said in recent years public debate on a range of issues has increased significantly, owing in large part to expanded media coverage of women's rights, government accountability, and freedom of speech, among other things. In what observers said was an attempt to bring order to the religious sector, the king in August issued a decree stating that only officially appointed Islamic scholars could issue fatwas (religious rulings).

Issues related to terrorism and security dominated 2010, as in December the intelligence director announced a special security unit to combat terrorism. He pointedly rejected any attempts to link terrorism with Islam. The launch of the new security team was preceded in November by announcements of the arrests of some 146 al-Qaida militants over the past eight months.

As the so-called Arab Spring of political unrest unfolded in early 2011, Saudi Arabia found itself caught up in the tumultuous events in the neighboring countries. When antigovernment protests in Tunisia escalated in January and spread across the country, President Zine Ben Ali deployed troops to curb the demonstrations and on January 14 fled to Saudi Arabia, where he was granted refuge. In February, as protests spread across the region, majority Shiites rebelled against minority Sunni rule in Bahrain, where the royal family was supported by Saudi Arabia. The repressive tactics of Yemen's president Ali Abdullah Saleh continued against the protesters, and in April Saudi Arabia and the UAE sent some 1,500 troops to back up the Bahraini forces. On April 18 opposition activists in Bahrain claimed that the Saudi-backed Bahraini troops had demolished or desecrated seven Shiite mosques and many prayer centers and shrines. On April 23 President Saleh, under intense domestic and international pressure, agreed to accept a plan for his departure brokered by Saudi Arabia and the other GCC member countries. Meanwhile, that same month, Tunisia sought to extradite President Ben Ali from Saudi Arabia. (He was sentenced in absentia in July to 15 years' imprisonment.)

While political turmoil churned the region, the Saudi monarchy focused mainly on domestic issues, though it wasn't fully spared its own homegrown protests. The king had poured $130 billion into the economy in June 2010 to boost the salaries of civil servants, build houses, and finance religious organizations, among other things, effectively quelling most of the opposition. In July 2011, the council passed legislation asserting the government's determination to prevent the Arab Spring from spilling over into Saudi Arabia. Saudi authorities were granted sweeping new powers to combat sedition, allowing for one-year detention without trial, secret trials, the tapping of phones, and extrajudicial searching of homes.

In the summer of 2011, a small group of women demanded that the law be changed to allow them to drive, a cause that was publicly endorsed by U.S. secretary of state Hillary Clinton. The woman who had started the "movement" on Facebook was arrested after she posted a video of herself. Her sentence of nine days in jail was seen as surprisingly harsh and taken as a warning that the monarchy was sending a message against any type of movement organized via social media. On February 5, 2012, a group of women filed a lawsuit against the traffic department for refusing to issue drivers licenses to women. Meanwhile, the Consultative Council recommended that women be allowed to vote and be candidates in municipal elections, and King Abdallah decreed on September 25, 2011, that women would be given the vote and the right to run for election to local councils in the 2015 elections. He also announced that they would be eligible to be appointed to the Consultative Council. On September 29, the long-delayed municipal council elections were held. Turnout among the still-all-male electorate was low, possibly because of the presumed powerlessness of the councils. Half of the council's membership was filled, with the other half to be appointed. In January 2013 King Abdallah appointed 30 women to the Consultative Council and decreed that henceforth 20 percent of council members must be women. Though in many ways an unprecedented move, female councilors will be segregated with their own door and seating area.

In February 2012 two men were killed and several were wounded when police opened fire on Shiite demonstrators in Al-Qatif, a coastal town in the Eastern Province. (Public gatherings are illegal, though social media have gained significant momentum.) Small-scale, protests cropped up sporadically throughout the year: in July a government crackdown on Shiite protesters in Eastern Province reportedly left 14 injured; relatives of political prisoners demonstrated in September in Riyadh, with dozens detained; a similar protest of about 40 people took place outside the Saudi Human Rights Commission in November.

A recent change of faces in the Cabinet indicates the passing of the torch to the younger generation of Saudi leaders. In November 2012 Prince Mohammad ibn Nayef ibn Abd al-Aziz Al Saud was appointed minister of the interior, succeeding his uncle, who resigned after just five months in office. Prince Muqrin, the former head of Saudi intelligence, was named second deputy prime minister in February 2013, making the 67-year-old third in line for the throne. In May King Abdallah elevated the department of the National Guard to the cabinet and named his son Prince Miteb to the post. Governorships of Riyadh and Eastern Province were also passed down to younger members.

POLITICAL GROUPS

There are no political parties, as such, in Saudi Arabia.

Committee for the Defense of Legitimate Rights—CDLR. The CDLR was formed in May 1993 by several prominent Islamists who described the grouping as the kingdom's first human rights organization. However, the government charged that the CDLR was in reality a vehicle for extending fundamentalist criticism of the monarchy, which had been on the rise since the Gulf crisis. Consequently, the CDLR was ordered to disband only two weeks after its creation; in addition, CDLR leader Muhammad al-MASARI and some 1,000 followers were arrested, and a number of CDLR supporters were fired from their government positions. After his release the following November, al-Masari moved to London, where the CDLR was reestablished in April 1994 as an exile organization. The committee subsequently issued numerous communiqués criticizing the Saudi regime's human rights and economic policies. Although accused by Riyadh of attempting to promote "destabilization" so as to facilitate elimination of the monarchy in favor of a fundamentalist regime, CDLR leaders took no official antimonarchical stance and steadfastly avowed a policy of nonviolence. However, the CDLR remained critical of what it alleged to be widespread corruption within the ruling family and direct in its call for imposition of strict Islamic rule in the kingdom. (In 1998 the Saudi government released Sheikh Sulaymah al-RUSHUDI, reportedly one of the founders of the CDLR.)

In 1996 a conflict was reported between CDLR leaders Muhammad al-Masari and Saad al-FAQIH, with the latter forming a breakaway grouping called the **Movement for Islamic Reform in Arabia** (MIRA). Subsequent activity has been minimal on the part of both groups, although in 2003 MIRA led an unprecedented demonstration in Riyadh, coinciding with the opening of the kingdom's first human rights conference. MIRA's antigovernment Web site in March 2005 posted an audiotape purporting to represent the new al-Qaida leader in Saudi Arabia. According to MIRA, he was killed in April 2005. A year later, Abd al Aziz al SHANBARI, a former Saudi dissident who had been affiliated with MIRA, denounced the group during a meeting with King Abdallah. Al Shanbari returned to Saudi Arabia after two years in exile in London, reportedly having made some sort of private arrangement with the king. MIRA reportedly operates out of London.

MIRA's Web site in 2006 addressed the new succession law issued by the king, claiming that the real aim of the law was to exclude Prince Nayif ibn Abd al-Aziz Al SAUD, the interior minister and a brother of King Fahd, from ascending the throne. The reported reasons for excluding Nayif were his alleged defiance of many of the king's orders and pressure from U.S. officials who were said to be dissatisfied with the level of cooperation from Nayif. In 2007 MIRA started television broadcasts via satellite from London.

In 2010, Muhammad al-MASARI, formerly described as leader of the CDLR, was reported to be the head of a group called the **Party for Islamic Renewal**, based in London.

Reform Movement. A loosely organized Shiite grouping, the Reform Movement (also referenced as the Islamic Revolutionary Organization in the Arabian Peninsula) originally operated out of London and Damascus, its activities including publication of the *Arabian Peninsula,* a newsletter critical of, among other things, the Saudi government's human rights record. In late 1993, the movement's leaders agreed to discontinue its attacks on the government in return for the release of Shiite dissidents from prison and permission for Shiite expatriates to return to Saudi Arabia. However, some members reportedly remained in "revolutionary" mode and opposed to the proposed reconciliation pact. A number of Shiites were arrested in the government crackdown that followed the 1996 bombing in Dhahran, prompting observers to suggest that the agreement with the Reform Movement had collapsed. However, little formal activity was subsequently reported on behalf of the movement, though it continues to press for change and its members are routinely arrested, convicted, and jailed. The leader, Sheikh Hassan al-Safar, was reportedly living in exile in Damascus in 1993. At some point al-Safar, a cleric, returned to the Shiite-dominated area of eastern Saudi Arabia. In 2003 al-Safar was among those invited to participate in the king's "national dialogue" in Mecca, where measures to counter extremism were among the topics. It was reported to be the first such gathering in the country to include Shiites and Sunnis, and observers made note of the fact that leaders from the two main religious branches were seen together on television.

Leader: Sheikh Hassan al-SAFAR.

LEGISLATURE

On March 1, 1992, King Fahd decreed that a **Consultative Council** (*Majlis al-Shura*) of 60 members (plus a speaker) would be appointed within six months. In accordance with the decree, a speaker was named the following September. Other members were not appointed until August 20, 1993, and the council convened on December 29. Upon the expiration of the first term of the council in July 1997, King Fahd increased its membership to 90 for the subsequent four-year term. Membership increased to 120 for the new council appointed on May 24, 2001, and the council was renewed on April 11, 2005. The king appointed an expanded 150-member council on February 28, 2009. In January 2013 King Abdallah decreed that 20 percent of the council members must be women and appointed 30 women to the council (see Current issues, above).

Chair: Abdullah Al ASHAIKH.

CABINET

[as of November 22, 2013]

Prime Minister	King Abdallah ibn Abd al-Aziz Al Saud
Deputy Prime Minister	Prince Salman ibn Abd al-Aziz Al Saud
Second Deputy Prime Minister	Prince Muqrin ibn Abd al-Aziz Al Saud
Ministers	
Agriculture	Fahd ibn Abd al-Rahman ibn Sulayman Balqhanaim
Civil Service	Abd al-Rahman ibn Abdullah ibn Abdul Aziz Al Barak
Commerce and Industry	Tawfeeq ibn Faozan ibn Muhammad al-Rabiah
Communications and Information Technology	Muhammad ibn Jamil ibn Ahmad Mulla
Culture and Information	Abd al-Aziz ibn Mohieddin Khoja
Defense and Aviation	Prince Salman ibn Abd al-Aziz Al Saud
Economy and Planning	Muhammad ibn Sulaiman ibn Muhammad Al Jasser
Education	Prince Faisal ibn Abdullah Muhammad Al Saud
Finance	Ibrahim ibn Abd al-Aziz al-Assaf
Foreign Affairs	Prince Saud al-Faisal ibn Abd al-Aziz Al Saud
Health	Abdullah ibn Abd al-Aziz al-Rabiah
Higher Education	Khalid ibn Muhammad al-Anqari
Interior	Prince Mohammad ibn Nayef ibn Abd al-Aziz Al Saud
Housing	Shuwaish ibn Saudi bin Duwaihi al-Duwaihi
Islamic Affairs, Endowments, Call, and Guidance	Salih ibn Abd al-Aziz al-Ashaikh
Justice	Mohammad ibn Abdulkarim ibn Abd al-Aziz al-Issa
Labor	Adel ibn Muhammad ibn Abd al-Gader al-Faqih
Municipal and Rural Affairs	Prince Mansur ibn Mitib Abd al-Aziz Al Saud
National Guard	Prince Miteb ibn Abdullah
Petroleum and Mineral Resources	Ali ibn Ibrahim al-Naimi
Pilgrimage	Bandar ibn Muhammad ibn Hamza Asaad Hajjar
Social Affairs	Yusuf ibn Ahmed al-Othaimeen
Transport	Jubarah ibn Ayd al-Suraysiri
Water and Electricity	Abdallah ibn Abd al-Rahman al-Husayn
Ministers of State	
Foreign Affairs	Nizar ibn Ubayd Madani
Shura Affairs	Saud bin Said al-Methami
Without Portfolio	Musaid ibn Muhammad al-Ayban
	Abd al-Aziz ibn Abdallah al-Khuwaytir
	Mutlaab ibn Abdallah al-Nafissa
	Prince Abd al-Aziz ibn Fahd ibn Abd al-Aziz
	Prince Abd al-Aziz ibn Abdullah bin Abd al-Aziz

INTERGOVERNMENTAL REPRESENTATION

Ambassador to the U.S.: Adel bin Ahmed al-JUBEIR.

U.S. Ambassador to Saudi Arabia: James B. SMITH.

Permanent Representative to the UN: Abdallah Yahya A. al-MOUALLIMI.

IGO Memberships (Non-UN): AfDB, GCC, LAS, NAM, OIC, OPEC, WTO.

SENEGAL

Republic of Senegal
République du Sénégal

Political Status: Former French dependency, independent since August 20, 1960; presidential system established under constitution promulgated March 7, 1963; Senegalese-Gambian Confederation of Senegambia, formed with effect from February 1, 1982, dissolved as of September 30, 1989.

Area: 75,750 sq. mi. (196,192 sq. km).

Population: 13,125,027 (2012E—UN); 13,300,410 (2013—U.S. Census).

Major Urban Center (2011E—UN): DAKAR (1,056,009).

Official Language: French.

Monetary Unit: CFA Franc (official rate November 1, 2013: 486.52 francs = $1US). The CFA franc, previously pegged to the French franc, is now permanently pegged to the euro at 655.957 francs = 1 euro.

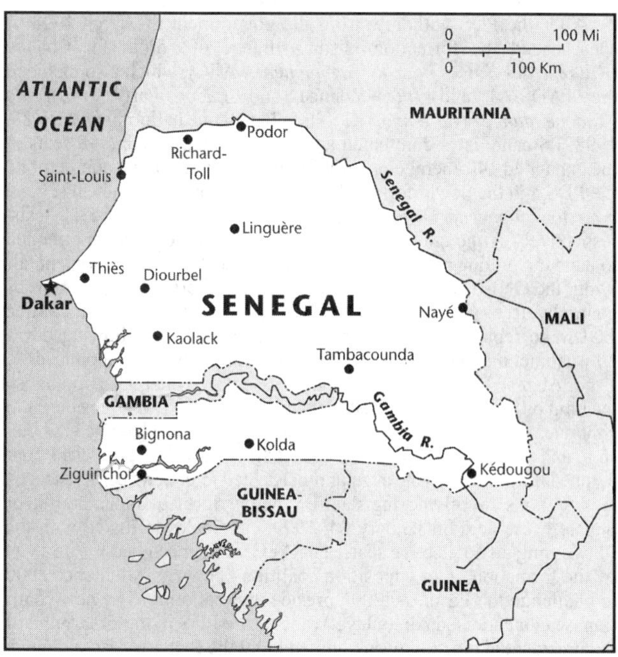

President: Macky SALL (APR-*Yakaar*); elected in second-round balloting on March 18, 2012, and inaugurated for a seven-year term on April 2 in succession to Abdoulaye WADE (Senegalese Democratic Party).

Prime Minister: Abdoul MBAYE (Independent); appointed by the president on April 5, 2012, to succeed Souleymane Ndéné NDIAYE (Senegalese Democratic Party).

THE COUNTRY

Senegal is situated on the bulge of West Africa between Mauritania on the north, Mali on the east, and Guinea and Guinea-Bissau on the south. Gambia forms an enclave extending into Senegal's territory for 200 miles along one of the area's four major rivers. The predominantly flat or rolling savanna country in Senegal has a population of varied ethnic backgrounds, with the Wolof, whose language is widely used commercially, being the largest group. French, the official language, is spoken only by a literate minority. More than 94 percent of the population is Muslim, the remainder being animist or Christian. Islamic "brotherhoods" exercise significant economic and political influence throughout the country, most of them espousing what Western observers would describe as a moderate version of Islam. The illiteracy rate remains above 50 percent. In addition, it is estimated that about 57 percent of the population lives in poverty. In 2013, the UN Human Development Index ranked Senegal 154th out of 186 nations. Women have made significant political strides in recent years. In the 2012 elections, women secured 64 of 150 seats in the assembly or 42.7 percent, the seventh highest percentage in the world. Women also held 40 seats in the Senate (40 percent).

GDP grew by an average of more than 5 percent annually from 1996 to 2008, earning praise from the International Monetary Fund (IMF) and World Bank, while inflation averaged less than 4 percent (for an overview of the economy prior to 2000, see the 2011 *Handbook*). At the same time, Senegal entered the new millennium with an economy that remained peasant-based and stressed by unequal distribution of wealth, high unemployment, an external debt of $3.5 billion, and deteriorating social services. Nonetheless, Senegal subsequently experienced steady, if modest, economic growth, which was accompanied by low inflation. As a result of sound fiscal policy, the government was also able to lower deficits and increase tax revenue.

In 2003 the IMF declared that Senegal had completed the necessary steps under the Heavily Indebted Poor Countries (HIPC) initiative and was accorded nearly $500 million in debt relief.

In 2006, the World Bank announced that Senegal had qualified for additional debt relief under the Multilateral Debt Relief Initiative. Spain announced in February 2008 that it would cancel Senegal's $75 million debt. In December the IMF granted Senegal $75.6 million in emergency assistance to help offset the impact of rising energy and food costs, however, it also criticized the government for delays in implementing economic reforms. In addition, China extended a $57 million loan to Senegal to improve public transportation and information technology. France also announced a $174.7 million emergency loan to pay-off the country's domestic debt after ending a boycott of aid to the country (see Foreign relations, below).

The global economic crisis slowed Senegal's economy in 2009 because of declines in commodity exports and decreases in remittances. GDP growth was 2.1 percent for the year, while inflation was –1.7 percent. In September 2009, Senegal concluded an agreement with the Millennium Challenge Corporation to provide $540 million in funding for road construction and irrigation projects. GDP grew 4.1 percent in 2010 and 2.6 percent the next year. Inflation was 3.4 percent in 2011, GDP grew by 3.5 percent in 2012, while inflation expanded by 1.1 percent, and GDP per capita was $1,119. That year, in its annual Doing Business survey, the World Bank ranked Senegal 166th out of 185 countries.

GOVERNMENT AND POLITICS

Political background. Under French influence since the 17th century, Senegal became a French colony in 1920 and a self-governing member of the French Community in November 1958. In January 1959 it joined with the adjacent French Soudan (now Mali) to form the Federation of Mali, which became fully independent within the Community on June 20, 1960. Two months later Senegal seceded from the federation, and the separate Republic of Senegal was proclaimed on September 5. President Léopold Sédar SENGHOR, a well-known poet and the leader of Senegal's strongest political party, the Senegalese Progressive Union (*Union Progressiste Sénégalaise*—UPS), governed initially under a parliamentary system in which political rival Mamadou DIA was prime minister. An unsuccessful coup in December 1962 resulted in Dia's arrest and imprisonment (until his release in 1974) and the establishment by Senghor of a presidential form of government under his exclusive direction. In an election held under violent conditions on December 1, 1963, Senghor retained the presidency, and his party won all of the seats in the National Assembly, as it also did in the elections of 1968 and 1973.

In response to demands for political and constitutional reform, Senghor in early 1970 reinstituted the post of prime minister, while a constitutional amendment adopted in 1976 sanctioned three political parties, the ideology of each being prescribed by law. In early 1979 a fourth, essentially conservative, party was also accorded recognition. Additional parties were legalized under legislation enacted in April 1981.

Although he had been overwhelmingly reelected to a fourth five-year term on February 26, 1978, President Senghor resigned on December 31, 1980, and, as prescribed by the constitution, he was succeeded by Prime Minister Abdou DIOUF. Coalitions remained prohibited in national balloting on February 27, 1983. Diouf was reelected with 83 percent of the vote, and the ruling Socialist Party (*Parti Socialiste*—PS) captured 111 of 120 assembly seats. In the subsequent poll of February 28, 1988, Diouf was reelected by a reported 73 percent of the vote, with the PS being awarded 103 assembly seats. However, controversy surrounding this election, and its aftermath tarnished Senegal's long-standing democratic reputation.

While the major opposition parties boycotted local elections in November 1990, a number of their leaders, including Abdoulaye WADE, Diouf's principal opponent in the 1982 and 1988 presidential campaigns, were named to a government headed by Habib THIAM on April 7, 1991. However, in October 1992 Wade and three other cabinet members from Wade's Senegalese Democratic Party (*Parti Démocratique Sénégalais*—PDS) resigned from the government, claiming they had been marginalized by their PS colleagues and included in only "trivial" decision making.

In first-round balloting on February 21, 1993, President Diouf was credited with winning 58 percent of the valid vote, thus eliminating the need for a second round. Wade was runner-up with a vote share of 32 percent. In the legislative poll of May 9, the PS won a reduced majority of 84 assembly seats, with the PDS securing 27 seats.

On May 15, 1993, the Constitutional Council's vice president, Babacar SEYE, was assassinated by a group identifying themselves as the People's Army. On May 16 Wade and a number of his PDS colleagues were detained after one of the alleged conspirators, Cledor SENE, claimed to be acting on their orders. On June 7, Sene recanted his story and publicly apologized to Wade for attempting to "decapitate" the PDS. Thereafter, relations between the government and the opposition grew increasingly acrimonious, as two PDS deputies, Mody SY and Samuel SARR, remained imprisoned for alleged involvement in the assassination, and the PDS mounted a demonstration in late July on behalf of their release. On August 24, the National Assembly further aggravated the situation by approving an emergency economic austerity plan that called for cuts in civil service salaries. Implementation of the measure was subsequently temporarily suspended following a general strike on September 2. In early October, Wade and his wife, Viviane WADE, who had previously been released, were rearrested for their alleged involvement in Seye's assassination, and on November 5 more than 130 opposition activists were arrested for participating in an antigovernment rally organized by the PDS and the African Party for Democracy and Socialism/And Jëf (*Parti Africain pour la Démocratie et le Socialisme/And Jëf*—PADS/AJ). Violent clashes erupted during a demonstration against the effects of the mid-January 1994 CFA devaluation, and the government moved quickly to indict Abdoulaye Wade and Landing SAVANE, leader of the PADS/AJ, for "breach against the state security," a charge for which 73 others were also being detained. However, on May 26, the Wades and their fellow PDS members were cleared of involvement in the Seye assassination, and at midyear Sy and Sarr were released after launching hunger strikes. In August Wade and Savane were acquitted of the February charges. In October three people were sentenced for their roles in Seye's assassination, although no motive was revealed.

In March 1995, the Diouf administration scored what appeared to be a major political victory when Wade accepted a cabinet-level post. As a result, the government contained three of the four leading groups previously aligned as regime opponents. In addition, although Wade had previously refused to enter the government unless the PDS was given half the posts in a 20-member cabinet, he now agreed to accept only 5 portfolios in a 33-member cabinet. A number of opposition parties, including the PDS, the PADS/AJ, and the Movement for Socialism and Unity (*Mouvement pour le Socialisme et l'Unité*—MSU), operated in a loose coalition called Uniting to Change Senegal until that grouping's demise following the PDS's decision to join the government in 1995.

Amid reports of increasing violations of a two-year-old cease-fire between the government and secessionist Casamance rebels in southern Senegal, security forces in May 1995 arrested Fr. Augustin DIAMACOUNE Senghor, leader of the Movement of Democratic Forces of Casamance (*Mouvement des Forces Démocratiques de la Casamance*—MFDC). Full-scale fighting erupted following Diamacoune's detention, and in mid-June the cease-fire was formally abandoned. In September the government attempted to start peace talks in Ziguinchor, but fighting continued as MFDC militants refused to negotiate until Diamacoune, who had been placed under house arrest, was freed. In response to the release of a number of his associates in early December, Diamacoune called for an end to the uprising, and on December 30 charges against him were dropped. The following day Diouf announced the creation of a parliamentary upper house, a Senate, which he described as the first step in an effort to decentralize power through a process of "regionalization."

In early 1996, the Diouf administration announced that independent candidates would be prohibited from participating in the rural, regional, and municipal elections scheduled for November. Grassroots groups and small opposition parties then accused Diouf of retreating from his pledge to decentralize power. Meanwhile, electoral preparations were threatened by the renewal of Casamance rebel activity, and in May the president's party rebuffed proposals to form an independent electoral commission. In balloting on November 24 the PS won what was described as a landslide victory, although voter turnout was reported at only about 50 percent and opposition parties criticized some aspects of the way the elections were conducted.

In March 1997, President Diouf convened a conference to review the 1996 elections with the purported aim of improving polling procedures. However, 19 opposition parties accused the PS of attempting to dominate the proceedings and withdrew from the conference in May. In August the Diouf administration, in an abrupt about-face, announced that it would establish an independent electoral commission, the National Elections Observatory (*Observatoire National des Elections*—ONEL) and published a draft electoral reform document that opposition leaders described as meeting "80 percent" of their demands.

After the PDS withdrew from the government in March 1998, it spearheaded the formation of an Alliance of Forces for Change (*Alliance des Forces pour le Changement*—AFC), which also included the PADS/AJ and Independence and Labor Party (*Parti de l'Indépendance et du Travail*—PIT). In legislative balloting on May 25, 1998, PS candidates dominated an 18-party field, winning 93 seats in the expanded 140-member assembly; the PS's nearest two competitors, the PDS and the newly formed Union for Democratic Renewal (*Union pour le Renouveau Démocratique*—URD), secured 23 and 11 seats, respectively. Although the PDS, URD, and four other parties petitioned to have the polling results overturned because of alleged fraudulent tallying, the ONEL and international observers described the elections as generally free and fair. On July 3 Diouf named Mamadou Lamine LOUM to replace Thiam as prime minister, and the following day a new cabinet that included only one non-PS member was announced.

In August 1998, the PS-dominated assembly voted 93–1 to abolish the limit on presidential terms, thereby permitting the Diouf presidency to continue past 2000. All but two opposition legislators boycotted the session, and the following day all of the leading opposition politicians condemned the assembly vote at an unprecedented joint news conference.

Elections to fill the legislature's newly formed upper house, or Senate, were held on January 24, 1999, candidates affiliated with the PS winning all 45 elective seats. The AFC was superseded in late 1999 by the formation of an opposition coalition known as Alternance 2000 to challenge the PS in the 2000 presidential balloting. The new coalition, which endorsed Abdoulaye Wade of the PDS in the first round of the presidential election, was dominated by the PDS but also included, among other groupings, the PADS/AJ, MSU, PIT, Democratic League–Labor Party Movement (*Ligue Démocratique–Mouvement pour le Parti du Travail*—LD-MPT), and the Action Front for Renewal/The Way (*Front d'Action pour le Renouveav/Yoon Wi*—FAR/Yoon Wi). In early 2000 Alternance 2000 joined with a number of other opposition groupings to form the Front for Fair and Transparent Elections (*Front pour la Régularité et la Transparence des Elections*—FRTE) to combat what the members perceived to be efforts by the PS to sabotage the election. The FRTE was not an electoral coalition; several members, including Alternance 2000, the Alliance of Forces for Progress (*Alliance des Forces pour le Progrès*—AFP), and the URD, presented their own presidential candidates in the first round.

Eight candidates contested the first round of presidential balloting on February 27, 2000, with Diouf securing 43 percent of the vote and Wade 30 percent. Following the first round of presidential balloting, a number of groups previously aligned in the FRTE (including Alternance 2000, the AFP and the CDP) formed the Front for Change (*Front pour l'Alternance*—FAL) to support Wade in the second round after the PDS/Alternance 2000 leader promised that his victory would be followed by installation of a coalition government. Meanwhile President Diouf of the PS was also endorsed in his reelection bid by a coalition called the Patriotic Convergence (*Convergence Patriotique*—CP). Wade won the second round, 58.7 to 41.3 percent. Following his inauguration on April 1, Wade appointed Moustapha NIASSE of the AFP as prime minister to head a coalition cabinet that also included the PADS/AJ, the PIT, and the LD-MPT.

As promised during the 2000 presidential campaign, the PDS and its allies presented a number of constitutional amendments for a national referendum on January 7, 2001. The measures, which abolished the presidentially appointed Senate and otherwise reduced the president's authority, were approved by 94 percent of the voters in a reported 66 percent turnout.

Invoking a provision in the new basic law that authorized the president to call for new legislative elections after the most recently elected assembly had served for at least two years, Wade dissolved the assembly on February 15, 2001, and ordered new elections for April 29. Meanwhile, friction grew between Wade and Niasse, and the prime minister left his post (having either resigned or been dismissed, depending on whose account was accurate) on March 3. He was succeeded by Mame Madiou BOYE, an independent who had been serving as justice minister; Boye thereby became Senegal's first female prime minister.

The FAL essentially collapsed when Niasse resigned as prime minister and the AFP cabinet members also left the government. Consequently, the PDS organized the *Sopi* (Wolof for "Change") Coalition, which ultimately included upward of 40 smaller groups, to contest the April 29, 2001, assembly balloting. Meanwhile, the AFP, PIT, and a number of other opposition parties formed a loose preelection coalition called the Front for Defense of Democracy (*Front pour la Défence de la Démocratie*—FDD), under the leadership of the PIT's

Amath DANSOKHO. The *Sopi* Coalition was credited with winning 89 of the legislative seats. The new government named by Boye on May 12 was again led by the PDS and several of its smaller electoral partners.

Subsequently, opposition parties (including the PS, AFP, URD, and PIT) organized a Permanent Framework for Consultation (*Cadre Permanent de Concertation*—CPC) to work against the policies of the PDS-led government. In response, the PDS organized a grouping known as the Convergence of Actions around the President for the 21st Century (*Convergence des Actions autour du Président en Perspective du 21ème Siècle*—CAP-21). The CAP-21, which included the PADS/AJ, the LD-MPT, and some 20 other smaller groups, contested the May 2002 municipal balloting as an electoral coalition, as did the CPC.

On November 4, 2002, President Wade dismissed Prime Minister Boye in the wake of a ferry disaster that claimed 1,200 lives and attracted intense international scrutiny. Wade appointed Idrissa SECK, his chief of cabinet, to form a new government. However, in August 2003 the Seck government resigned in response to growing public discontent with the inquiry into the ferry's sinking and negative reaction to the government's response to recent severe flooding. Seck was reappointed prime minister and was asked to develop a government of national unity, but most opposition parties declined to join the government, which remained largely dominated by propresidential parties. Tensions between Wade and Seck resulted in the latter's dismissal as prime minister on April 21, 2004. Former interior minister Macky SALL was named the next day to lead a reshuffled cabinet, while Seck was subsequently charged with subversion and embezzlement and kicked out of the PDS.

On July 15, 2005, former prime minister Seck was arrested and charged with embezzlement and later with endangering national security. In August the assembly voted to strip Seck of immunity and forced him to appear before a special anticorruption court. The court dismissed the embezzlement and subversion charges, and the former prime minister was released from prison in February 2006. Seck continued to face a minor charge of overspending government funds; however, his release allowed him to launch his 2007 presidential campaign.

In late 2005, legislative elections scheduled for May 2006 were postponed until June 2007, ostensibly to save money by combining the polling with presidential elections. Wade redirected the $13 million allocated for the 2006 balloting to help relocate Senegalese displaced by flooding. Opposition leaders met in Dakar in December 2005 and issued a joint statement condemning the postponement. Meanwhile, in spite of his age, Wade announced his intention to campaign for reelection.

Seck ran against Wade in the 2007 presidential elections, which were marked by violent clashes between the supporters of the two candidates. Wade received 55.9 percent of the vote in the first round of voting on February 25, followed by Seck (running as the candidate of a new party called The Nation) with 14.9 percent and Ousmane Tanor DIENG of the PS with 13.6 percent. None of the other 12 candidates received more than 6 percent of the vote. After Wade was sworn in on April 3, the Sall government resigned, but it was immediately reappointed by the president.

Citing irregularities in the presidential balloting, many opposition parties boycotted the June 2007 legislative elections, in which the propresidential *Sopi* 2007 Coalition won 131 seats and no other party secured more than 3 seats. Wade subsequently appointed independent Cheikh Hadjibou SOUMARÉ as prime minister of a cabinet dominated by the PDS, while Sall was elected speaker of the National Assembly. In balloting for the Senate in August the PDS won 34 of the elected seats, while the African Party for Democracy and Socialism/And Jëf won 1. Wade appointed the remaining 65 seats in September. Wade ally and mayor of Dakar, Pape DIOP was subsequently elected speaker of the Senate. A major cabinet reshuffle in December reduced the number of members from 38 to 28 in an effort to streamline the government. Wade faced significant criticism as 8 of the dismissed ministers were women.

The PS and other opposition groups announced that they would participate in local and regional elections scheduled for May 18, 2008. However, the assembly postponed the balloting until March 2009. The action led to protests by the opposition, especially after the assembly enacted legislation in May 2008 to consolidate the number of local and regional offices. In October the terms of office of speaker in both the Senate and Assembly were reduced from five years to one year.

There were a series of cabinet reshuffles in late 2008 and early 2009 as part of an effort to enhance the popularity of the government. Nonetheless, in balloting for local and municipal offices on March 22, opposition parties won the majority of posts (see Current issues, below), including a number of seats in areas that were strongholds for the ruling *Sopi* Coalition. The defeat was the first broad electoral loss for Wade's coalition since 2000. Following the losses, Wade replaced Soumaré as prime minister on April 30 with a close political ally, Souleymane Ndéné NDIAYE. Ndiaye reshuffled the cabinet and formed a new government on May 1. Wade's son Karim WADE was subsequently appointed to a cabinet post, leading to speculation that he was being groomed to succeed his father.

President Wade conducted more cabinet reshuffles through 2009 and 2010. On October 5, 2010, after a series of widespread power outages, Wade appointed his son Karim, already a minister of state for international cooperation, as minister of energy (see Current issues, below). Wade reshuffled the cabinet again on January 25, 2011, and on May 7.

Former prime minister Sall won the presidential election in run-off balloting on March 18, 2012 (see Current issues, below). Sall was the candidate of the Alliance for the Republic—Hope (*Allaince pour le Republique—Yaakar*—APR-*Yakaar*). Sall appointed independent Abdoul MBAYE prime minister of a coalition cabinet that was significantly smaller than its predecessor. The APR-*Yakaar* subsequently formed an electoral coalition, United in Hope (*Benno Bokk Yakaar*), which won 119 seats out of 150 in balloting for the National Assembly on July 1. On October 29, the cabinet underwent a major reshuffle, including the addition of five ministries (see Current issues, below).

Constitution and government. Senegal is administratively divided into eleven regions, each headed by a presidentially appointed governor who is assisted by an elected Regional Assembly; the regions are divided into departments. The constitution provides for a president elected by direct universal suffrage, with runoff balloting for the two top contenders if none secures an absolute majority. Under amendments approved in 1991, presidents were limited to two terms, although the incumbent (Abdou Diouf), already elected twice, was permitted to stand one more time. An amendment in 1993 extended presidential terms to seven years. The two-term restriction was formally abandoned in 1998, thereby permitting Diouf to contest the 2000 balloting as well. Amendments in 2001 reimposed the two-term limit and returned the length of the term to five years. In 2008, the presidential term was again extended to seven years, to take effect after the 2012 balloting. The president appoints the prime minister (the office having been abolished in 1983 and revived in 1991), who in turn appoints the Council of Ministers in consultation with the president.

Legislative power was vested in a unicameral National Assembly until December 31, 1995, when President Diouf announced the creation of a Senate to act as an upper house. The first Senate was elected in January 1999, but that body was abolished in the 2001 constitutional amendments. Under initial procedures, half of the assembly members were elected from Senegal's departments on a "first past the post" basis, the other half by proportional representation from a national list. However, electoral changes adopted in 1989 provided that national lists would be dropped from future elections, with all members being chosen on a departmental basis. Only parties registered at least four months before an election were allowed to participate; neither independent candidacies nor opposition coalitions were permitted. However, the combination of departmental and national lists was reestablished for the April 2001 assembly election in accordance with the January constitutional revisions. Party restrictions were also lifted as were barriers to electoral coalitions. The principal judicial organs, under a system revised in 1992, include a Constitutional Council, one of whose functions is to rule on electoral issues; a Council of State; a Court of Cassation; and a Court of Appeal; with magistrate courts at the local level. In addition, a High Court of Justice, chosen by the assembly from among its own membership, is responsible for impeachment proceedings. Elections for municipal and rural community councilors were held in May 2002.

In January 2007, the National Assembly voted to reinstate the Senate, and elections for the chamber were held in August. In 2008 the presidential term of office was extended from five to seven years (see Current issues, below).

Newspapers are subject to government censorship and regulation, although a number of opposition papers appeared in the 1990s, some evading official registration by means of irregular publication, and restrictions have eased significantly in recent years. Prior to the 2007 elections, the government reportedly forced the closure of some private radio stations, seized editions of newspapers, and detained journalists who were critical of the regime. In its 2013 press freedom index, the media organization Reporters Without Borders ranked Senegal 59th out of 179 countries, a significant improvement from 2010, when Senegal was ranked 93rd.

Foreign relations. Formally nonaligned, Senegal has retained especially close political, cultural, and economic ties with France. An active advocate of West African cooperation, it has participated in such regional groupings as the Economic Community of West African States, the Permanent Inter-State Committee on Drought Control in the Sahel, and the Organization for the Development of the Senegal River. (The members of the latter are Mali and Mauritania.) Regional relations improved substantially as the result of a "reconciliation" pact signed in Monrovia, Liberia, in March 1978, ending five years of friction with Guinea and Côte d'Ivoire.

Under President Senghor, Senegal maintained a generally conservative posture in African affairs, refusing to recognize Angola because of the presence of Cuban troops there, supporting Morocco against the claims of the insurgent Polisario Front in the Western Sahara, and breaking relations with Libya in mid-1980 because of that country's alleged efforts to destabilize the governments of Chad, Mali, and Niger, as well as Senegal. Reflecting the "spirit of our new diplomacy"—essentially an effort to introduce greater flexibility in its relations with other African governments—Dakar announced in February 1982 that it would reverse its long-standing support of the Angolan resistance movement and recognize the Mouvement Populaire de Libération de l'Azawad (MPLA) government in Luanda. Ties with Algeria were strengthened in the course of reciprocal visits by the respective heads of state in 1984 and 1985; relations with Libya eased as the result of a visit by Colonel Muammar Qadhafi in December 1985 and were formally restored in November 1988.

In light of the unusual geographic relationship between the two countries, one of Senegal's most prominent regional concerns has been its association with Gambia. A 1967 treaty provided for cooperation in foreign affairs, development of the Gambia River basin, and, most important, defense. Consequently, Senegalese troops were dispatched to Banjul, Gambia, in October 1980 amid rumors of Libyan involvement in a projected coup and again in July 1981 when an uprising threatened to topple the Jawara administration (see article on Gambia). The latter incident was followed by an agreement to establish a Confederation of Senegambia, completed on February 1, 1982. Although the component states remained politically independent entities, the Confederation agreement called for the integration of security forces, the establishment of an economic and monetary union, and the coordination of policies in foreign affairs, internal communications, and other areas. A joint Council of Ministers and an appointed Confederal Assembly were established, and it was agreed that the presidents of Senegal and Gambia would serve as president and vice president, respectively, of the confederation. In practical terms, however, little progress was made in actualizing the confederation. Many Gambians criticized what was perceived as an unequal relationship, while Gambian government and business leaders questioned the wisdom of their country's proposed entrance into the franc zone. Economic union was also hindered by the fact that Gambia had long favored liberal trade policies in contrast to Senegal's imposition of high protective tariffs. In August 1989, Senegal unilaterally withdrew some of its troops from Gambia, and President Diouf declared that the confederation, having "failed in its purpose," should be "frozen." Gambian President Jawara responded by suggesting it be terminated completely, and a protocol was quickly negotiated formally dissolving the grouping as of September 30. Despite a presidential summit in December 1989, relations remained cool through 1990 as Senegal enacted trade sanctions aimed at stemming the importation of foreign goods via its relatively duty-free neighbor. In January 1991 the two countries moved to reestablish bilateral links by the conclusion of a treaty of friendship and cooperation. As finalized in June, the treaty provided for annual summits and the establishment of joint commissions to ensure implementation of summit agreements.

In May 1989, the third conference of francophone heads of state met in Dakar amid deepening hostility between Senegal and Mauritania that had been triggered by a dispute on April 9 over farming rights along their border. Rioting in both Dakar and Nouakchott ensued, causing death or injury to several hundred people and the cross-repatriation of an estimated 150,000–300,000, including a substantial number of Moors, who had dominated the crucial small-business retail sector in the Senegalese capital. The situation continued in crisis for the balance of the year. Relations remained broken, with a continuing exodus (forced, according to Senegalese charges) of blacks from Mauritania to Senegal; Nouakchott announced preparations for a possible war. In January 1990 border forces exchanged artillery fire across the Senegal River, but diplomatic efforts, led by Organization of African Unity (OAU, subsequently the African Union—AU) president Hosni Mubarak, helped avert additional violence. By early 1991 relations had again deteriorated, as Nouackchott accused Senegal of aiding antigovernment rebels and Dakar charged Mauritania with arming Casamance separatists with Iraqi weapons. Meanwhile, relations with Guinea-Bissau, already strained by Bissau's refusal to recognize a July 1989 international court decision favoring Senegal in their maritime border dispute, were exacerbated by a clash in May 1991 that left 17 dead and by reports that Bissau was also supporting the Casamance rebels.

A May 1991 rapprochement between Dakar and the Casamance insurgents had a positive effect on relations with both Guinea-Bissau and Mauritania. The choice of the former as the site for the signing of a cease-fire agreement signaled a further lessening of tensions, and on July 18 an agreement to reopen the Senegalese-Mauritanian border paved the way for restoration of diplomatic relations on April 23, 1992. However, on December 12 tension again flared with the bombing by Senegalese forces of alleged Casamance bases in northern Guinea-Bissau. Four days later the Senegalese government offered its apologies after Bissau had protested the violation of its border, and on December 22 it was reported that Casamance leader Diamacoune had been expelled from Guinea-Bissau.

In May 1994, Dakar demanded the withdrawal of Iran's ambassador, accusing Tehran of supporting the activities of the Islamic fundamentalist movement in Senegal. Fear of the spread of Islamic fundamentalism also dominated a meeting among Senegal, Mali, and Mauritania in January 1995, with the three agreeing to "combat fanaticism in all its forms." On February 10 Senegalese aircraft bombed a suspected Casamance rebel base in Guinea-Bissau, Dakar ignoring Bissau's subsequent demand for an explanation of the attack. However, in September, Dakar and Bissau signed a security cooperation pact, and in December the prospect of closer relations improved markedly when Bissau agreed to withdraw its earlier objections to the 1989 court ruling on their shared maritime border. In 1996, Senegal continued to enjoy improved relations with its neighbors, signing cooperation agreements with Guinea, Guinea-Bissau, Mali, and Mauritania. On a less positive note, efforts to repatriate the Mauritanian refugees residing in Senegal since 1989 were only haltingly successful.

In June 1998, President Diouf deployed troops to Guinea-Bissau to shore up the embattled government there, underlining Dakar's concern that the Casamance region in Senegal would erupt in violence if the pro-Casamance Bissaun rebels secured power in Guinea-Bissau (see article on Guinea-Bissau). The administration's military strategy initially drew widespread support; however, by August opposition leaders had begun to question the effort. In March 1999, the last of the Senegalese troops were withdrawn. In 2001 armed forces from Guinea-Bissau destroyed the main Casamance rebel bases in that country. In 2002, separatist groups launched a new round of negotiations with the Senegalese government following the appointment of a new government peace commission. The government committed to a number of infrastructure programs in the province and released some government-held rebels on bail. In response the rebels adopted a cease-fire, although rebels opposed to the negotiations continued to launch minor attacks.

Wade maintained close ties with France but also reached out to other major powers. In February 2002 he hosted Tony Blair, the first British prime minister to visit Senegal. During the meeting Blair pledged support for the New Partnership for Africa's Development (NEPAD), an organization launched through the OAU in October 2001 to promote socioeconomic recovery in Africa. In April 2002, Wade hosted the first major NEPAD conference. Wade also worked to improve relations with the United States and met with U.S. president George W. Bush in Senegal in July 2003. In addition, Senegal pledged to cooperate with the United States in the global war on terrorism. In 2003 Wade angered France by his refusal to condemn the U.S.-led war in Iraq.

On December 30, 2004, the government and the main rebel group in Casamance, the MFDC, signed a comprehensive peace settlement, although some minor rebel factions continued to fight the central government. (In March 2006, fighting between competing factions of the MFDC displaced 5,000 civilians along the border between Senegal and Guinea-Bissau.)

Tensions emerged in 2005 over a Gambian decision to double the tariff on ferry traffic on the Gambia River, which prompted Wade to close border crossings. The dispute was later resolved with a 15 percent reduction in the tariffs.

In October 2005, Senegal reestablished diplomatic relations with the People's Republic of China, ending Senegal's long-standing recognition of Taiwan. Economic relations between Dakar and Beijing were the main reason for the action, as trade between the two countries had increased by 25 percent per year since 2003.

Renewed fighting in Casamance between rival wings of the MFDC in September 2006 created 15,000 refugees, and at least 5,000 people fled across the border into Gambia. In December, Senegal and Gambia launched new talks to resolve tensions over the presence of Senegalese rebel bases in Gambia. In July 2007 the government announced that it would try former Chadian President Hisséne Habré (see article on Chad), in custody in Senegal, on charges of murder and torture following a request for such a trial from the AU. In April 2008 the National Assembly amended the constitution to allow Habré's trial on retroactive charges of crimes against humanity.

In 2006, Senegal and Spain agreed to joint patrols of Senegalese waters to deter illegal immigration to the Canary Islands. Senegal also reached an immigration agreement with France that eased restrictions on Senegalese immigrating to France but also simplified repatriation for illegal immigrants.

France announced in October 2007 that it would resume development loans to Senegal for the first time in 17 years. Senegal agreed in November to a governance program sponsored by the IMF. Under the terms of the initiative, the IMF provided technical advice and assistance on monetary and fiscal policy. In December Morocco recalled its ambassador to Senegal over remarks made by a member of the assembly that supported independence for the Western Sahara. Diplomatic ties were restored the following month.

In March 2008, Wade helped negotiate a nonaggression pact between Sudan and Chad. Also in March Senegal hosted the meeting of the Organization of Islamic States (OIC) in Dakar. South Africa and Senegal signed a bilateral trade agreement in April in what was reported to be a sign of growing ties between the two nations. In November Senegal deployed troops along its border with Guinea Bissau in response to an attempted coup.

In February 2009, Belgium filed a motion before the International Court of Justice in an effort to force Senegal to try former Chadian president Habré. Senegal had reportedly delayed prosecution because of the costs associated with a trial. During a visit to Senegal by Chinese president Hu Jintao, a number of new bilateral economic agreements were signed. In May, Wade helped negotiate an agreement to allow elections in Mauritania in July 2009, following a 2008 coup.

Following the January 2010 Haiti earthquake, Wade offered to allow survivors of the disaster to resettle in Senegal and provided $1 million in aid for the country. In June, France withdrew 900 of its 1,200 troops from Senegal and turned three military facilities over to the Senegalese. The remaining French soldiers continued the long-standing training mission in the country. Meanwhile, in September Senegal joined five other West African nations in a multilateral agreement, sponsored by Norway, to delineate the maritime borders of the nations. In 2010, China and Senegal signed two economic agreements whereby Chinese firms were awarded contracts to modernize Senegal's aging power system (see Current issues, below). In addition, in December China provided 50 vehicles to the Senegalese government. By the end of 2010 trade between the two countries had reached $459 million annually, and there was more than $1.5 billion in infrastructure agreements in place. In September 2011, Sierra Leone opened an embassy in Dakar, three years after the restoration of ties with Senegal.

In August 2012, the United States announced that it would expand military cooperation with Senegal, including an increase in joint training exercises. Also in August, Senegal signed an accord with the AU to create a special court to try Habré, following a ruling from the ICJ that Senegal either extradite the former Chadian leader or prosecute him. In September, a Gambian opposition group, the National Transitional Council of the Gambia, was launched in Dakar. Also that month, Senegal banned certain classes of supertrawlers from fishing in Senegalese waters following reports of overfishing.

In January 2013, Senegal agreed to contribute 500 troops to the ECOWAS-led peacekeeping force in Mali, the African International Support Mission to Mali (AFISMA). As the fighting in Mali escalated (see entry on Mali), Senegal increased security throughout the country and deployed additional forces along the border with Mali. In August, Senegal and Chad finalized an agreement to finally allow the trial of Habré to begin.

Current issues. In January 2009, Diadji DIOUF, a well-known gay rights activist, and eight others were tried and convicted of homosexuality. They were each sentenced to eight years in prison. International and domestic human rights groups condemned the trial and sentence. The deteriorating economy and rising costs were reportedly responsible for electoral losses by the *Sopi* Coalition in the March local elections. *Sopi* faced a coalition of opposition groups, United to Boost Senegal (see Political Parties, below). Wade's coalition even lost control of the governing council of Dakar, and opposition leader Khalifa SALL was elected mayor of the capital city. Following the loss, Wade replaced the prime minister. In June, the assembly approved the creation of the post of vice president, a post that remained vacant through 2009.

A massive 160-foot statue was unveiled at independence celebrations in April 2010. The $27 million cost of the monument drew criticism from opposition groups and public protests. In October the president dismissed Samuel SARR, the minister of energy, following widespread power outages and concurrent public protests and demonstrations. Wade appointed his son Karim to replace Sarr and ordered audits of the national electric company and changes in personnel. Reports indicated that the appointment was a further signal that the younger Wade was being groomed to take over the presidency in the future.

Riots and protests swept the capital and other major cities on June 22 and 23, 2011, after Wade introduced a constitutional amendment that would have lowered the threshold to win a presidential election, without a runoff, from 50 percent to 25 percent. The measure was perceived as a ploy by the president to ease his reelection bid. The demonstrations left more than 100 injured and led the government to deploy military forces. A second measure to create an elected vice president also met with widespread opposition as most assumed that Wade would name his son Karim as his vice-presidential running mate. The violence prompted Wade to withdraw the measures. On June 28, new rioting commenced following widespread power outages that left some areas of Dakar without electricity for more than 30 hours. Power availability improved after the government tapped an emergency fund to buy additional diesel fuel for power plants. A new, loose coalition of opposition parties and civil society groups, known as the June 23 Movement, emerged following the riots. The group sought to prevent Wade from seeking a third term as president and later rallied behind opposition figures in the 2012 balloting.

On January 27, 2012, a court ruled that Wade's first term did not count toward the two-term limit because the constitution was amended in 2001, after he had initially been elected. The decision allowed Wade to run in the February balloting but was met with widespread protests and violence. Wade placed first among 14 candidates with 34.8 percent of the vote, followed by former prime minister Sall, with 26.6 percent. The two advanced to run-off balloting that was won by Sall, with 65.8 percent of the vote, after opposition leaders rallied behind the challenger. Sall's APR-*Yakaar*-led coalition, United in Hope, went on to win legislative balloting in July. In September, the assembly voted to abolish the Senate rather than hold new elections, but the measure stalled in the upper chamber.

In April 2012, riots swept through Dakar following the arrest of Cheikh Bethio THIOUNE, a leader of the Islamist Mouride Sufi Brotherhood on murder charges after his followers beat and killed two youths. In October, Sall replaced Minister of the Interior Mbaye NDIAYE over his management of the protests.

Sall was praised by international observers for his anticorruption efforts, including the creation in January 2013 of a new office to investigate and prosecute malfeasance in office. Sall signed a series of emergency decrees that allowed the government to spend more than $200 million on a range of security and infrastructure projects without parliamentary approval. Opposition groups decried the spending as an effort to bolster the president's popularity and argued that the funds were being used for nonemergencies. The dispute led to the passage of a revised finance law in July 2013.

POLITICAL PARTIES

In March 1976, the National Assembly approved a constitutional amendment authorizing three political parties (for more on the development of the three parties, see the 2013 *Handbook*). In early 1979 the amendment was altered to permit the legal establishment of a fourth, essentially right-wing, party—the Senegalese Republican Movement. In April 1981, the assembly removed the remaining restrictions on party activity.

For the 2007 presidential and legislative elections, propresidential parties ran as the *Sopi* 2007 Coalition. Leading opposition parties boycotted the legislative balloting under the *Siggil Sénégal Front,* while a number of other parties formed coalitions for the polling. For the 2009 local elections, 79 parties were registered. A new opposition coalition, United to Boost Senegal (*Benno Siggil Senegaal*—BSS), brought together 35 opposition parties prior to the municipal balloting. The BSS was led by former PS parliamentarian, Khalifa Sall, and it included a number of parties that had boycotted the 2007 legislative elections, including the PS, the PIT, and the PPS. The BSS won a number of key constituencies in the elections. Ahead of the 2012 balloting, a number of parties in the BSS broke away to form the United in Hope Coalition (*Benno Bokk Yakaar*) coalition in 2012.

In the 2012 balloting, 24 parties or groupings fielded candidates. New electoral laws required that women comprise at least 50 percent of party lists.

Government and Government-Supportive Parties:

United in Hope Coalition (*Benno Bokk Yakaar*). The pro-Mackey Sall coalition was formed in 2012 by opposition parties in an effort to end the political dominance of the PDS. United in Hope won 119 seats in the 2012 assembly balloting. Tensions within the coalition were reported ahead of planned local balloting in 2014, casting doubts on the ability of Sall to maintain all parties in the grouping.

Leaders: Mackey SALL (President of the Republic), Moustapha NIASSE (Speaker of the Assembly).

Alliance for the Republic—Hope (*Allaince pour le Republique–Yaakar*—APR-*Yakaar*). The APR-*Yakaar* was formed in 2008 by former prime minister Mackey SALL to oppose Wade and the PDS. Sall won the 2012 presidential balloting and the APR-*Yakaar* formed the United in Hope coalition to contest legislative balloting that year.

Leader: Mackey SALL (President of the Republic).

Alliance of Forces for Progress (*Alliance des Forces pour le Progrès*—AFP). Formed by Moustapha Niasse in the fall of 1999 after he had left the PS, the AFP supported Abdoulaye Wade in the second round of the 2000 presidential election, after Niasse had finished third in the first round with 16.7 percent. Under an apparent electoral agreement with Wade, Niasse was named prime minister in Wade's first cabinet, but he subsequently quit that post in early 2001. The AFP, some of whose support comes from the Tidjane Islamic Brotherhood, competed alone in the 2001 legislative elections, finishing second to the *Sopi* Coalition.

Niasse was the AFP's 2007 presidential candidate and placed fourth in the balloting. The AFP joined the opposition boycott of that year's legislative polling. In 2008, Niasse led a failed effort by opposition parties to replace the national election commission, seen as being dominated by the PDS, with an independent agency. The AFP joined the BSS coalition for the 2009 local elections. Niasse placed third in the first round of presidential balloting in 2012 and then supported Sall in the second round. Niasse was elected speaker of the assembly in July 2012. The AFP was given two posts in the October 2012 cabinet.

Leader: Moustapha NIASSE (Speaker of the Assembly and Former Prime Minister).

Socialist Party (*Parti Socialiste*—PS). Known until December 1976 as the Senegalese Progressive Union (*Union Progressiste Sénégalaise*—UPS), the PS consistently held a preponderance of seats in the National Assembly until 2001. A moderate Francophile party long identified with the cause of Senegalese independence, the UPS, was founded by Léopold Senghor in 1949 in a secession from the dominant local branch of the French Socialist Party. From 1963 to 1974, it was the only legal party in Senegal; it absorbed the only significant opposition grouping, the leftist *Parti de Regroupement Africain-Sénégal* (PRA) in 1966 in furtherance of Senghor's "national reconciliation" policy. In early 1981, following his resignation of the presidency, Senghor withdrew as party secretary general. During an extraordinary conference in March 1989, the PS voted to assign internal authority to a ten-member Executive Committee that was directed to recruit new members and assist in "rejuvenation" of the party. At the PS congress in 1990, Abdou Diouf was reappointed secretary general and given unchecked control of a restructured, "nonhierarchical," 30-member Politburo.

The PS experienced unprecedented levels of intraparty violence prior to its 1996 congress, spurring a call from Diouf for "reconciliation." Meanwhile, Diouf and Ousmane Tanor Dieng were elected to the newly created party presidency and executive secretaryship, respectively, with the latter assuming administrative responsibilities previously assigned to the secretary general.

In March 1998, a PS faction, led by Djibo KA, broke off from the party and formed the URD (see above). Among the reasons cited for Ka's decision was Diouf's reported elevation of Dieng to the status of heir apparent.

Another prominent PS member, Moustapha Niasse, left the PS after 40 years to form the AFP (see below), the recent departures contributing to Diouf's failure in his 2000 reelection bid. Although Diouf was reconfirmed as the PS leader at an October 2000 congress, he subsequently announced plans to retire from politics.

The PS led the opposition to the 2006 postponement of legislative elections and tried to rally opposition parties. It was also reportedly active in unsuccessful efforts to form an opposition electoral coalition ahead of the 2007 balloting. Dieng was the party's candidate in the presidential polling, placing third. The PS boycotted the 2007 legislative balloting. Dieng was formally elected party leader in October. The PS agreed to participate in local and regional elections in 2008, in which it gained mayoral posts and majorities on councils in a number of areas. The PS was instrumental in the creation of the opposition BSS coalition and sought to use the grouping as a potential base for an alliance ahead of future legislative balloting. Dieng placed fourth in the first round of presidential balloting in 2012 and then supported Sall in the second round. Reports in 2013 indicated that Sall might replace Prime Minister Mbaye with former prime minister Mamadou Lamine Loum of the PS.

Leaders: Ousmane Tanor DIENG (Chair and 2012 Presidential Candidate), Abdou DIOUF (Former President of the Republic), Mamadou Lamine LOUM (Former Prime Minister), Cheikh Abdoul Khadre CISSOKHO (Former National Assembly President).

Democratic League–Labor Party Movement (*Ligue Démocratique–Mouvement pour le Parti du Travail*—LD-MPT). A self-proclaimed independent Marxist group with links to Senegal's leading teachers' union, the LD-MPT contested both the 1983 and 1984 elections. At its second congress in December 1986, the League's Secretary General Abdoulaye Bathily called for "disorganized alliances" among opposition parties and advanced an economic "alternative to the recipes of the International Monetary Fund and the World Bank" as a means of establishing a socialist society. The party supported PDS candidate Abdoulaye Wade in the 1988 presidential poll but presented its own legislative candidates, securing no seats on a 1.4 percent vote share.

In April 1988, LD-MPT's Bathily was given a suspended sentence for having organized an illegal antigovernment demonstration, while five other party activists were indicted on similar charges late in the year. In 1990, Bathily intensified his criticism of the Diouf administration's policies and called for a non-Diouf "unity" government. Thereafter, despite the co-option of a number of opposition colleagues, Bathily initially refused Diouf's offer of a cabinet portfolio, citing Dakar's repressive policies in Casamance. However, Bathily ultimately agreed to become environment minister in June 1993, with the party being awarded a second portfolio in August 1995. Following the May 1998 legislative poll (in which it won three seats), the LD-MPT declined to participate in the next government. Instead, it proposed the formation of a unified opposition front against the PS and President Diouf. In the 2001 legislative balloting, 6 of the 89 successful candidates from the *Sopi* Coalition were identified as LD-MPT members. Two LD-MPT deputies briefly served in the government in 2005 before disputes with Wade led to their dismissal during a cabinet reshuffle.

Bathily was the LD-MPT's presidential candidate in 2007 (he received 2.2 percent of the vote). The LD-MPT boycotted the 2007 legislative election. The LD-MPT participated in the postponed 2009 local and regional elections as a member of the PS-led opposition BSS grouping. Bathily supported Sall in the 2012 balloting. He was appointed as the UN Deputy Special Representative for the world body's peacekeeping mission in Mali in July 2013.

Leader: Dr. Abdoulaye BATHILY (1993 and 2007 presidential candidate and Secretary General).

Independence and Labor Party (*Parti de l'Indépendance et du Travail*—PIT). Organized by a group of PAI dissidents and permitted to register in 1981, the PIT was recognized by Moscow as Senegal's "official" Communist Party. It contested both the 1983 and 1984 elections but won no assembly or town council seats. The party joined the LD-MPT in supporting PDS presidential candidate Wade in 1988, while its legislative candidates won only 0.8 percent of the vote and no seats. The PIT secretary general was among those arrested after the elections, but the charges were later dismissed. In mid-1989, the PIT entered into negotiations with the ruling Socialist Party, and the party was awarded two portfolios in the cabinet reshuffle of August 1995. However, both ministers were ousted a month later in the wake of a PIT Central Committee statement critical of the Diouf administration.

The PIT was a member of Alternance 2000 in support of the 2000 presidential bid of Abdoulaye Wade, and the party's secretary general, Amath Dansokho, served in the first Wade cabinet. However, the two leaders subsequently quarreled, and Dansokho resigned from the government in early 2001. Dansokho was briefly arrested in July 2005 for making antigovernment statements. The PIT participated in the 2007 boycott of legislative elections but took part in the local elections that were postponed until 2009. The PIT was a member of the BSS coalition during the balloting; however, a dispute within the PIT led Dansokho to withdraw his mayoral candidacy for Kedougou. The PIT supported Sall in the 2012 presidential balloting and subsequently joined the United in Hope Coalition. Dansokho has been named as the leader of the opposition grouping, M23.

Leader: Amath DANSOKHO (Secretary General).

Opposition Parties:

Senegalese Democratic Party (*Parti Démocratique Sénégalais*—PDS). The PDS was launched in October 1974 as a youth-oriented opposition group to implement the pluralistic democracy guaranteed by the Senegalese constitution. Although standing to the left of President Senghor on certain issues, it was required by the constitutional amendment of March 1976 to adopt a formal position to the right of the government party. Having charged fraud in both the 1980 and 1983 legislative elections (although the PDS was one of two opposition parties to gain representation on the latter occasion), PDS leaders participated in the 1984 municipal boycott and asserted their regret at having campaigned in 1983. Following the return from abroad of party leader Abdoulaye Wade in early 1985, the PDS led a number of mass prayer demonstrations for radical change, with Wade calling for "a transitional government of national unity."

As the major force in Senegal's growing opposition movement, the PDS appeared to pose a genuine threat to the PS in the 1988 legislative and presidential campaigns, partly as a result of its alliance with the LD-MPT and the PIT (below). Although presidential candidate Wade was officially credited with 26 percent of the vote, widespread indications of electoral abuse suggested that his actual total may have been higher.

In 1991, Wade attributed his acceptance of a cabinet post to fears that continued opposition activity would destabilize the country. However, Wade resigned from the government in October 1992 in what was viewed as an attempt to recapture the allegiance of PDS members estranged by his alliance with Diouf. Shortly thereafter Wade announced that the party would present candidates at the forthcoming legislative poll and entered the presidential contest in which he ran second to the incumbent, with a 32 percent share of the vote.

In July 1993 the PDS, ignoring a government ban, organized a demonstration for the release of jailed party deputies Mody Sy and Samuel Sarr, both of whom had been held since mid-May for their alleged involvement in the assassination of the Constitutional Council's vice president. On October 1 Wade, who had himself been detained for two days after the assassination, was arrested along with his wife for their alleged roles in the killing. Within days a number of other prominent PDS leaders, including Abdoulaye FAYE and Ousmane NGOM, were also implicated in the assassination.

On November 5, 1993, a number of party members were arrested for leading antigovernment demonstrations, and on February 18, 1994, Wade was reimprisoned for his participation in rioting, which erupted following the devaluation of the CFA franc. At a perfunctory military trial on February 24 Wade was convicted of a "breach against state security." However, on May 26, charges against him and his associates in connection with the 1993 assassination were dropped. Wade was one of five PDS leaders to accept cabinet portfolios in August 1995.

In March 1998, the PDS withdrew from the government and legislature after the PS legislators increased the size of the latter. At the same time Wade reportedly predicted that the PDS would win as many as 80 seats in the May polling. However, the party fell far short of such expectations, securing just 23 seats. In July Wade resigned his assembly post, saying that he would focus his efforts on resolving the PDS's intraparty disputes.

Wade finished second with 31 percent of the vote in the first round of presidential balloting in February 2000. However, after securing the support of most of the other first-round runners-up, Wade went on to defeat President Diouf in the second round in March with 58.7 percent of the vote, setting the stage, in conjunction with the PDS legislative victory in April 2001, for one of the continent's most remarkably peaceful shifts in political power.

In April 2002, the **Party for Progress and Citizenship** (*Parti pour le Progrès et la Citoyenneté*—PPC) agreed to merge with the PDS. The PPC, formed in 2001 by Mbaye Jacques DIOP after he quit the PS, had secured one seat in the 2001 legislative balloting. The **Senegalese Democratic Party–Renewal** (*Parti Démocratique Sénégalais–Rénovation*—PDS-R) also merged with the PDS. The PDS-R was originally organized in June 1987 by an anti-Wade faction within the PDS that announced as its goal the establishment of a "truly secular and pluralist democracy." PDS-R candidates secured minuscule legislative vote shares in the 1988 and 1993 elections, while supporting Diouf for president on both occasions. Serigne Lamine DIOP, the PDS-R secretary general, was named minister of justice and keeper of the seals in the Loum government formed in July 1998, the party having secured one seat in the May legislative balloting. In 2003, the **Senegalese Liberal Party** (*Parti Libéral Sénégalais*—PLS) merged with the PDS. The PLS had been formed in June 1998 by Ousmane Ngom and a number of other party leaders who left the PDS after they failed to gain central committee posts in their former party. At the group's founding meeting, Ngom described the PLS as a vehicle of "liberalism" and denounced Wade's rule of the PDS as monarchical.

In April 2005, 14 PDS members of parliament announced their intention to leave the party and form a new group, the Forces of Change. After it was ruled that the 14 would have to resign their seats and campaign in special elections, they returned to the PDS. In May the Convention of Democrats and Patriots (*Convention des Démocrates et des Patriotes*—CDP) merged with the PDS. Also known as *Garab-Gi* ("The Cure"), the CDP was founded in May 1992 by Iba Der THIAM, a former education minister and UNESCO Executive Council member. In December 1994 the CDP and the RND (below) issued a joint statement rejecting the Uniting to Change coalition's call for the drafting of a national consensus program, describing it as a self-serving PDS maneuver. However, after Thiam secured 1.2 percent of the vote in the first round of the 2000 presidential poll, he threw his support behind Wade in the second round, becoming the coordinator of the FAL. The CDP, noted for its antipoverty platform and, more recently, an increasingly Islamic orientation, secured one seat as a member of the *Sopi* Coalition in the 2001 legislative balloting before joining the PDS.

Wade's main political rival within the PDS, Idrissa Seck, was dismissed as prime minister in April 2004. In August, Seck was also dismissed from his post as PDS executive secretary, and he and several of his supporters were expelled from the party. In November 2007 former prime minister Macky SALL, and then speaker of the assembly, was dismissed from his post as a deputy secretary general of the party, reportedly because he was perceived to be a threat to plans for Wade's son to be the future leader of the party. In November 2008, Sall was voted out of the speakership by the PDS. Sall subsequently formed a new political party, **Alliance for the Republic—Hope** (*Allaince pour le Republique—Yaakar*—APR-*Yakaar*), which joined the BSS opposition coalition in the 2009 local elections. Reports indicated that three factions had emerged within the party: the first led by Karim WADE, the second supportive of Pape Dion, and the third under former presidential advisor Moustapha DIAKHATE.

Wade reconciled with Seck in an effort to consolidate the party ahead of municipal elections in 2009, but the party suffered significant losses, including the defeat of Senate Speaker Pape Diop in his reelection bid as mayor of Dakar.

Wade announced in July 2010 that he intended to run for the presidency again in 2012. This set off a constitutional debate and disagreements within the party since presidents were limited to two terms. However, Wade's supporters within the PDS argued that since the term of office had been changed from five years to seven years, the incumbent had not served two full terms. In April 2011 Seck was expelled from the party after he announced his public opposition to Wade's 2012 presidential candidacy. Seck subsequently launched an independent presidential campaign.

Wade lost the 2012 presidential election, and the PDS only secured 12 seats in the subsequent assembly balloting after a group of dissidents broke from the party to form the United for a Common Vision Coalition (*Bokk Gis Gis*).

In April 2013, Karim Wade was arrested on corruption charges that much of his estimated personal fortune of $1.4 billion was illicitly gained through misuse of office. The arrest prompted protests and demonstrations in Dakar by the PDS.

Leaders: Abdoulaye WADE (Secretary General of the Party and Former President of the Republic), Pape DIOP (Speaker of the Senate).

African Party for Democracy and Socialism/And Jëf (*Parti Africain pour la Démocratie et le Socialisme/And Jëf*—PADS/AJ). The PADS/AJ was formed in 1991 by merger of the Revolutionary Movement for the New Democracy (*Mouvement Révolutionnaire pour la Démocratie Nouvelle*—MRDN) and two other left-wing groups, the People's Democratic Union (*Union pour la Démocratie Populaire*—UDP) and the Socialist Workers' Organization (*Organisation Socialist des Travailleurs*—OST).

Also known as *And Jë,* a Wolof expression meaning "to unite for a purpose," the MRDN was a populist southern party of the extreme left that included former socialists and Maoists. It was permitted to register in June 1981 but joined the 1983 and 1984 election boycotts. The UDP was organized in 1981 by a pro-Albanian MRDN splinter group, while the OST was a small Marxist–Leninist formation launched in 1982.

Landing Savane ran a distant third as the 1993 presidential nominee of the PADS/AJ. For the May legislative balloting, the party participated with the RND (see below) in a **Let Us Unite** (*Jappoo Liggeeyal*) **Senegal** coalition that won three assembly seats. In November, Savane was arrested for organizing a demonstration against the Diouf administration's economic austerity program. Given a suspended sentence for the incident, the PADS leader was rearrested in February 1994 and, along with Wade, he was subsequently convicted of provoking anti-government riots.

The PADS/AJ captured four seats in the 1998 legislative balloting; subsequently, it cooperated with the PIT and PLS to run a joint slate of candidates in the January 1999 Senate elections under the banner of "*And Fippu.*" After supporting Abdoulaye Wade of the PDS in the 2000 presidential campaign, the PADS/AJ secured two seats in the 2001 legislative poll and joined the PDS-led parliamentary faction. Savane and Mamadou DIOP were given posts in subsequent PDS-led governments.

Savane was the PADS/AJ candidate in the 2007 presidential election, in which he secured a little more than 2 percent of the vote. The PADS/AJ was the main component of the **Build Senegal Together** (*And Defar Sénégal*) coalition that secured three seats in the assembly in 2007. In 2007, divisions within the party emerged between the supporters of Savané and a group led by Madièye MBODJ that criticized the leadership for abandoning the core principles of the party. PADS/AJ won one senate seat in the 2007 balloting. In 2008, Savané was appointed a minister of state and party official Mamadou Diop DECROIX was appointed commerce minister. Following the 2009 municipal elections, both Savané and Diop lost their positions during a cabinet reshuffle. Savané subsequently moved the PADS/AJ into the opposition. Decroix was expelled from the party in 2009 during an internal feud with Savané.

The PADS/AJ supported Wade in the 2012 presidential balloting and won one seat in the July legislative polling.

Leader: Landing SAVANÉ (Secretary General and 1993 and 2007 presidential candidate).

Union for Democratic Renewal (*Union pour le Renouveau Démocratique*—URD). The URD, originally styled the Democratic Renewal (*Renouveau Démocratique*—RD), was formed by former interior minister Djibo Ka in November 1997 to act as a reform group within the PS; however, in December, Ka and ten of his dissident colleagues were suspended from the PS for three months. Subsequently, Ka declared his intention to forward an independent list of candidates for legislative balloting in May 1998. In March 1998, the PS rejected Ka's list, and on April 1, he resigned from the group and formally launched the URD. Having emerged from the 1998 legislative polling with 11 seats, the URD presented Ka as its candidate in the first round of the 2000 presidential election. He finished fourth and surprisingly threw his support to Abdou Diouf in the second round. A split in the URD regarding that decision (one faction joined the *Sopi* Coalition) apparently contributed to the URD's decline to three seats following the 2001 legislative poll.

Ka was appointed minister of state for fisheries in the Sall government and reappointed to a post in the Soumaré cabinet. Following a 2007 cabinet reshuffle, Ka became minister of state for the environment and protection of nature, reservoirs, and artificial lakes. He retained that post in the new government formed after the 2009 municipal elections and in subsequent cabinet reshuffles through the summer of 2011. Ka won the URD's sole seat in the 2012 legislative balloting. Once in the assembly, he declined to join the formal opposition grouping.

Leader: Djibo KA (Secretary General and 2000 presidential candidate).

Other parties that won seats in the 2012 Assembly elections included: **United for a Common Vision Coalition** (*Bokk Gis Gis*); the **Citizen Movement for Reform** (*Mouvement Citoyen pour la Réforme Nationale*—MCRN); the **Republican Movement for Socialism and Democracy** (*Mouvement Républicain pour le Socialisme et la Démocratie*—MRSD); the **Party for Truth and Development** (*Parti pour la Vérité et le Développement*—PVD); the **Senegalese Patriotic Movement** (*Sénégalais Mouvement Patriotique*—SMP); **Patriotic Convergence for Justice and Equity** (*Convergence Patriotique pour la Justice et l'Équité*—CPJE-Nay Leer); the **Party for the Emergence of Citizens** (*Parti pour l'Émergence de Citoyens*—Tekki 2012); ***Deggo Souxali Transport ak Commerce***; the **Enlighten the People** (*Leeral Askanwi*).

Other Parties Contesting the 2012 Legislative Elections:

Other parties that contested the 2012 Assembly elections (none received more than 1 percent of the vote), included: the **Rally of Ecologists of Senegal** (*Rassemblement des Écologists du Sénégal*—RES), led by Ousmane Sow HUCHARD; the **Democratic Alliance** (*Alliance Démocratique*); the **Authentic Socialist Party** (*Parti Socialiste–Authentique*—PS-A), led by Souty TOURÉ; the **Allied Coalition of the People** (*Coalition Alliée du Peuple*—CAP 21); the **Taxawal Askan Wi Coalition;** the **Lii Dal Na Xel Coalition;** and the **Taxawu Askan Wi Party.**

Other Parties and Groups:

Smaller pro-Wade formations include the **Senegalese Democratic Rally** (*Rassemblement Démocratique Sénegalais*—RDS); the **Union of Senegalese Patriots**; the **Popular Democratic Rally** (*Rassemblement Démocratique Populaire*—RDP); the **Democratic Union for Federalism/Mboloomi** (*Union Démocratique pour le Fédéralisme/ Mboloomi*—UDF/Mboloomi); and the **Union for Democratic Renewal/Front for Change** (*Union pour le Renouveau Démocratique/ Front pour l'Alternance*—URD/FAL).

Front for Socialism and Democracy–Unite and Correct (*Front pour le Socialisme et la Démocratie–Benno Jubël*—FSD-JB). Launched under the direction of a prominent Muslim leader, Cheikh Abdoulaye Dieye, the FSD-JB captured one seat in the 1998 legislative balloting on a platform emphasizing care for the elderly and women. Dieye captured 1 percent of the first-round vote in the 2000 presidential election, and the FSD-JB subsequently joined the FAL. Cheikh Bamba DIEYE succeeded his father as party leader following the former's death in 2002.

The younger Dieye received less than 1 percent of the vote in the 2007 presidential balloting, while the party gained one seat in the assembly in 2007. The FSD-JB participated in the opposition BSS coalition in the 2009 municipal elections, in which party leader Dieye was elected mayor of Saint-Louis. Dieye publicly opposed the proposed constitutional amendment to create an elected vice president. Dieye placed sixth in presidential balloting in 2012. Dieye was appointed minister of communication and information technology in October 2012.

Leader: Cheikh Bamba DIEYE (2007 and 2012 presidential candidate).

Alliance Jëf Jël. Formerly known as the Alliance for Progress and Justice/Jëf Jël, this grouping adopted its current name at a party congress in June 2000. Party leader Talla Sylla placed eighth in the 2007 presidential balloting, but was the sole party member elected to the National Assembly. He subsequently announced his intention to retire as party president in June for health reasons but has remained at the helm of the party after he emerged as one of the most visible leaders of the opposition. The party joined the BSS coalition for the 2009 local elections. The party joined the small Benno Alliance 2012 and supported Abdou Latif COULIBALY for the 2012 presidential election, but the candidate withdrew a month before the balloting.

Leaders: Talla SYLLA (President), Moussa TINE.

Movement for Socialism and Unity (*Mouvement pour le Socialisme et l'Unité*—MSU). The MSU was registered in 1981 as the People's Democratic Movement (*Mouvement Démocratique Populaire*—MDP), which, led by longtime Senghor opponent Mamadou Dia, called for a program of socialist self-management of the economy. Dia was one of the few prominent Senegalese political figures to oppose establishment of the Senegambian Confederation. The MDP contested the 1983 general election but boycotted subsequent balloting.

The MSU was listed as a member of Alternance 2000, and official government sources indicated that one MSU member was elected in the

2001 legislative balloting as a member of the *Sopi* Coalition. However, perhaps indicating a split within the party, news reports described the MSU, under the leadership of Sheikh Tidiane BA, as aligning with the PIT for the assembly elections. As of 2002 Ba was still being described as an opponent of the Wade government. In 2008 the MSU executive council was reported to be based in France. The MSU was part of the BSS coalition in the 2009 municipal balloting. Longtime party figure Dia died at age 98 in 2009. Former MSU member Aminata TOURÉ was appointed minister of justice by Sall in 2012.

Leader: Mouhamadou N'DIAYE (National Coordinator).

National Democratic Rally (*Rassemblement National Démocratique*—RND). Established in February 1976, the RND described itself as a "party of the masses." It applied, without success, for recognition in September 1977, and two years later its founder, Cheikh Anta DIOP (who died in 1986), was ordered to stand trial for engaging in unauthorized party activity. The RND was legalized in June 1981; it subsequently repeatedly criticized the government for its position on Chad and for its "systematic alignment with the positions of France and the United States." Evincing an anti-Wade orientation, the RND retained its single legislative seat in 2001, although it garnered only 0.7 percent of the vote. In June 2006 the party's sole deputy in the assembly resigned in protest over the postponement of legislative elections. The party boycotted the 2007 elections. After the boycott, Diouf was reported to have announced his retirement from politics. The RND was a member of the BSS coalition in the 2009 balloting.

Leader: Dialo DIOP (Secretary General).

African Independence Party (*Parti Africain de l'Indépendance*—PAI). Founded in 1957 and composed mainly of intellectuals in southern Senegal, the PAI was legally dissolved in 1960 but was subsequently recognized as the "Marxist-Leninist" party called for by the 1976 constitutional amendment. Claiming to be the "real PAI," a clandestine wing of the party denounced recognition as a self-serving maneuver by the Senghor government. In March 1980 two leaders of the splinter faction, Amath Dansokho and Maguette THIAM, were charged with inciting workers to strike, but in 1981 they were permitted to register the group as a distinct party (see PIT, above). Having unsuccessfully contested the 1983 election, the PAI joined the November 1984 boycott. In early 1987 the formation of a front uniting the PAI with the MDP (see under MSU, above) and the former Communist Workers' League (*Ligue Communiste des Travailleurs*—LCT) was announced, although no legislative candidates were presented by any of the three in 1988.

The PAI supported Abdou Diouf in the 2000 presidential campaign and presented its own candidates (unsuccessfully) in the 2001 legislative poll. The PAI boycotted the 2007 legislative elections and failed to gain any seats in the 2012 balloting.

Leaders: Majhemouth DIOP (President), Balla N'DIAYE (Vice President), Siaka SANE (Secretary General).

Other parties that gained seats in the 2007 election include the **Rally for the People** (*Rassemblement pour le Peuple*—RP); the **Reform Movement for Social Development** (*Mouvement de la Réforme pour le Développement Social*—MRDS), led by Mbaye NIANG, which initially joined the BSS in the 2009 municipal balloting but withdrew from the coalition prior to the elections because of differences with the PS; **Convergence for Renewal and Citizenship** (*La Convergence pour le Renouveau et la Citoyenneté*—CRC), led by Aliou DIA; the **National Patriotic Union** (*Union Nationale Patriotique*—UNP), led by Me Ndèye FATOU TOURÉ; and the **Social Democrat Party–The Sun** (*Parti Social-Démocrate–Jant Bi*—PSD-JB), led by Mamour CISSE.

Other parties include the **Party of Renewal and Citizenship** (*Partide la Renaissance et de la Citoyenneté*—PRC); the **Assembly of African Workers–Senegal** (*Rassemblement des Travailleurs Africains–Sénégal*—RTA-S), a social-democratic party recognized in March 1997 and a member of the BSS coalition in 2009; the **Movement for Democracy and Socialism/Naxx Jarinu** (*Mouvement pour la Démocratie et le Socialisme/Naxx Jarinu*—MDS/NJ); the **Union for the Republic** (*Union pour la République*—UPR); the **Social Democratic Party/Jant-Bi**; the **Democratic Union of Progressive Patriotic Forces** (*Union Démocratique des Forces Progressistes Patriotiques*—UDFP); the **Citizens' Movement for a Democracy of Development** (*Mouvement des Citoyens pour une Démocratie de Développement*); the **Action Front for Renewal/The Way** (*Front d'Action pour le Renouveav/Yoon Wi*—FAR/Yoon Wi), led by Bathie SECK; the **Gainde Centrist Bloc** (*Bloc des Gainde Centristes*—BGC); the **Reform Party** (*Parti de la Réforme*—PR); the **Rally for Unity and Peace** (*Rassemblement pour l'Unité et la Paix*—RUP); **The Nation** (*Rewmi*), formed by former Prime Minister Idrissa SECK, who placed second in national polling as the party's 2007 presidential candidate (*Rewmi* boycotted the 2007 legislative elections) and fifth in the 2012 presidential balloting; and the **Senegalese People's Party** (*Parti Populaire Sénégalais*—PPS), which was legalized in 1981 and was part of the BSS coalition in the 2009 local elections.

For information on the **Senegalese Democratic Union–Renewal** (*Union Démocratique Sénégalais–Rénovation*—UDS-R), the **Senegalese Republican Movement** (*Mouvement Républicain Sénégalais*—MRS), and the **Party for the African Renaissance** (*Parti pour la Renaissance Africaine*—PARENA), see the 2009 *Handbook*. For more on the **Action for National Development** (*Action pour le Développement National*—ADN), **Senegalese Republican Party** (*Parti Sénégalais Républicain*—PSR), the **Engagement and Reconstruction of Senegal Coalition** (*Takku Defaraat Sénégal*), **The Field** (*Waar Wi*), and the **Senegalese Patriotic Rally** (*Rassemblement Patriotique Sénégalais–Jammi Rewmi*—RPS-JR), please see the 2012 *Handbook*.

Illegal Groups:

Movement of Democratic Forces of Casamance (*Mouvement des Forces Démocratiques de la Casamance*—MFDC). The MFDC was launched as a clandestine grouping advocating the secession of the Casamance region of southern Senegal. Many supporters, including MFDC leader Fr. Augustin Diamacoune Senghor, were jailed following demonstrations in the provincial capital of Ziguinchor in the early 1980s, and another 152 people were arrested in 1986 for allegedly attending a secret MFDC meeting. Diamacoune and most of the other detainees were subsequently released. However, new MFDC-army clashes were reported in late 1988.

In mid-1990, Diamacoune and most other MFDC civilian leaders were arrested or forced into exile following a resurgence of separatist violence spearheaded by *Attika* ("Fighter"), the MFDC's military wing. The uprising, which the separatists claimed was the result of their being economically and socially marginalized, continued through late 1990. However, in May 1991, following a series of secret meetings with ethnic Diola parliamentarians negotiating on Diouf's behalf, MFDC leaders agreed to a cease-fire and disarmament. Reports of the negotiations supported observers' suspicions that the separatists encompassed a limited number (300–500) of ethnic Diolas.

In April and May 1992, renewed separatist activity was attributed to a militant MFDC splinter and despite an escalating verbal confrontation between Dakar and the MFDC leadership over the military's allegedly heavy-handed response to the violence, the Diouf administration, as late as September, absolved the MFDC leadership of blame for the cease-fire breakdown.

On July 8, 1993, the MFDC signed a cease-fire agreement with the government that included provisions for further negotiations, a bilateral prisoner release, the deployment of French military observers, and the establishment of a refugee repatriation program. However, renewed clashes were reported three days later, and open fighting resumed following the government's killing of an MFDC activist in September. Thereafter, no serious cease-fire violations were reported until January 1995, when a pro-independence faction led by Léopold SANIA rejected the peace accord and resumed guerrilla activities.

In April 1995, the government deployed an additional 1,000 troops in the Casamance region in response to persistent breaches of the cease-fire, including the disappearance of 4 French tourists who were assumed to have been kidnapped by the MFDC. In late April the government announced the arrest of some 50 suspected activists, including Father Diamacoune, and in mid-July the separatists formally abandoned the cease-fire. While Diamacoune's imprisonment served as a rallying point for MFDC faithful during the 1995 crisis, his influence with party militants reportedly had already begun to wane. Subsequently, despite his declaration of a unilateral cease-fire in January 1996, rebel attacks continued throughout the first half of the year.

Fierce fighting broke out in August 1997 as the government responded to renewed rebel activity with a massive offensive, and by late September more than 100 people were reported dead. Meanwhile, the fighting widened the split in the MFDC between the hard-line northern wing, led by Mamadou SANE, and Diamacoune's predominantly southern followers, who were described as prepared to abandon their demand for independence in return for a government promise to speed development of the region. In early 1998 the two factions were reported to be in open conflict. Furthermore, troops from Guinea-Bissau were reportedly laying siege to Sane's longtime safe havens within Bissau's border.

In March 1998, the government claimed to have killed 50 MFDC fighters preparing to attack a village near Ziguinchor. Thereafter, fighting was reported throughout the region during the run-up to legislative polling; however, the government deployed a large number of forces to the area for the balloting period, and few incidents were reported.

Amid reports that the MFDC was preparing to enter into negotiations with the Diouf administration, the group's military and political leaders met in Banjul, Gambia, in April 1999. However, on April 30, 17 people were reported killed in a clash between the rebels and government forces, thus underscoring continued reports that the movement was splintered.

Some MFDC fighters were reported to have disarmed in mid-1999, and another questionable cease-fire was announced late in the year. However, the leadership dispute within the MFDC continued, as did the low-level war between rebels and government troops. Additional negotiations were launched in December 2000, new Senegalese President Abdoulaye Wade having declared resolution of the conflict a top priority for his government. A peace pact was again announced in March 2001. It also appeared that Diamacoune and his supporters had renounced their secessionist stance and instead had agreed to pursue greater autonomy for the region while remaining a part of Senegal. The accord was greeted hopefully by many observers, especially following a face-to-face meeting between Wade and Diamacoune and the MFDC's call for fighters to lay down their guns for the April national legislative balloting. Banditry and sporadic killings continued, however, precluding finalization of a permanent settlement.

At a mid-2001 MFDC congress, Diamacoune became the group's president, a role considered more ceremonial in nature than his previous post. Meanwhile, Sidi Badji, a hard-liner rival to Diamacoune, was reportedly named head of military affairs. Badji subsequently claimed the secretary general's position, and the power struggle between his "radical" faction (which also included military commander Salif SADIO) and Diamacoune's "peacemaking" faction continued into mid-2002. On September 19, 2004, Diamacoune became honorary president, while Biagui became the effective leader of the MFDC.

The MFDC signed a peace agreement with the government on December 30, 2004, and it announced plans to reestablish itself as a legitimate political party and contest legislative elections in 2007. However, in March 2006 the Sadio-led faction of the MFDC initiated attacks against other MFDC groupings. In response, security forces from Guinea-Bissau launched an offensive against MFDC positions in an attempt to end the factional fighting.

On January 14, 2007, Diamacoune died of natural causes in a Paris hospital, creating an unresolved internal struggle over the leadership of the MFDC. In December a faction of the MFDC assassinated a presidential envoy during negotiations over Casamance. The attack was condemned by most of the leadership of the MFDC. There was sporadic fighting between the MFDC and government forces in May 2008. During the summer of 2009 there was a significant increase in violence in the region, which reports attributed to younger members of the MFDC who opposed a settlement with the government. In response, in March 2010, the Senegalese military launched a new campaign in the region. That month, Cesar Atoute BADIATE, the leader of one MFDC faction agreed to talks with the government as long as they were hosted by a neutral country. However, other MFDC leaders rejected negotiations. In August Wade formally requested that Gambia assume a formal role in a negotiated settlement with the MFDC. Meanwhile, new fighting erupted in August in Diango between the MFDC and government security forces.

After the election of Sall in 2012, the MFDC announced it was willing to reenter negotiations with the government; however, new fighting broke out in July along the Gambian border. In July, the MFDC freed nine hostages who were working as part of a demining operation. They had been captured in May. Following negotiations with Senegal in August, Gambia announced it would pardon two suspected Senegalese MFDC members who had been sentenced to death.

Leaders: Mamadou SANE, Sidi BADJI, Jean-Marie BIAGUI (Secretary General).

LEGISLATURE

The **Parliament** consists of a National Assembly, which was established in 1963, and a Senate, which was established in 1999, abolished in 2001, and reestablished in 2007.

Senate. Legislation adopted by the assembly in January 2007 mandated the reestablishment of the upper house, the Senate, with 100 members serving five-year terms. Of these 100 senators, 35 (one from each district) are indirectly elected for five-year terms by members of regional, rural, and municipal councils. The remaining 65 senators are appointed by the president.

In balloting (boycotted by most of the main opposition parties) for the 35 elected senators on August 19, 2007, the Senegalese Democratic Party (PDS) won 34 seats, and the African Party for Democracy and Socialism/And Jëf won 1. President Wade appointed the remaining 65 members on September 21; most were members of the PDS, although the appointees reportedly included members of opposition parties and a number of independents.

President: Pape DIOP.

National Assembly. The assembly currently consists of 150 members, 90 elected on a majoritarian basis at the department level and 60 elected on a proportional basis from national party lists. (The assembly voted in November 2006 to increase its size from 120 to 150 members.) Members serve five-year terms, although the assembly is subject to presidential dissolution after two years.

In the most recent balloting of July 1, 2012, the United in Hope Coalition won 119 seats; the Senegalese Democratic Party, 12; United for a Common Vision Coalition, 4; Citizen Movement for National Reform, 4; Republican Movement for Socialism and Democracy, 2; Party for Truth and Development, 2; Union for Democratic Renewal, 1; Senegalese Patriotic Movement, 1; Patriotic Convergence for Justice and Equity, 1; Party for the Emergence of Citizens, 1; Deggo Souxali Transport ak Commerce, 1; Enlighten the People, 1; and the African Party for Democracy and Socialism/And Jëf, 1.

President: Moustapha NIASSE.

CABINET

[as of August 15, 2013]

Prime Minister	Abdoul Mbaye
Ministers	
Agriculture and Rural Equipment	Abdoulaye Baldé
Armed Forces	Augustine Tine
Commerce, Industry, and Handicrafts	El Hadji Malick Gackou
Communication and Information Technology	Bamba Diéye
Culture and Tourism	Abdoul Aziz Mbaye
Ecology and Nature Protection	Haidar Ali
Education	Serigne Mbaye Thiam
Energy and Mines	Ngouille Aly Ndiaye
Finance and Economy	Amadou Kane
Fisheries and Maritime Affairs	Pape Diouf
Foreign Affairs	Mankeur Ndiaye
Good Governance	Abdoul Latif Coulibaly
Health and Social Action	Eva Marie Coll Seck [f]
Higher Education and Research	Marie-Tew Niane
Infrastructure and Transport	Theirno Alassane Sall
Interior	Gen. (ret.) Pathe Seck
Justice	Aminata Touré
Livestock	Aminata Mbengue Ndiaye
Planning and Local Government	Arame Ndoye [f]
Professional Training, Apprenticeships, and Handicrafts	Mamadou Talla
Public Service, Labor, and Relations with Institutions	Mansour Sy
Restructuring and Planning of Flood Zones	Khadim Diop
Sport	Mbagnick Ndiaye

Tourism and Leisure	Youssou Ndour
Urban Development and Housing	Khoudia Mbaye
Water and Sanitation	Oumar Gueye
Women, Children, and Women Entrepreneurs	Mariama Sarr [f]
Youth, Training, and Employment	Benedict Sambou
Ministers Delegate	
Economy and Finance, in Charge of Budget	Abdoulaye Diallo Daouda
Foreign Affairs, in Charge of Senegalese Abroad	Seynabou Gaye Touré [f]

[f] = female

INTERGOVERNMENTAL REPRESENTATION

Ambassador to the U.S.: Cheikh NIANG.

U.S. Ambassador to Senegal: Lewis LUKENS.

Permanent Representative to the UN: Andou Salam DIALLO.

IGO Memberships (Non-UN): AfDB, AU, ECOWAS, ICC, IOM, NAM, OIC, WTO.

SERBIA

Republic of Serbia
Republika Srbija

Political Status: Incorporated in the Kingdom of the Serbs, Croats, and Slovenes, which was constituted as an independent monarchy on December 1, 1918, and formally renamed Yugoslavia on October 3, 1929; became constituent republic of the communist Federal People's Republic of Yugoslavia, instituted November 29, 1945, and then of the Socialist Federal Republic of Yugoslavia, proclaimed April 7, 1963; continued as constituent republic, along with Montenegro, of the Federal Republic of Yugoslavia (FRY), proclaimed April 27, 1992; included in the "state union" of Serbia and Montenegro, established February 4, 2003, under new Constitutional Charter; proclaimed as the independent Republic of Serbia on June 5, 2006, following Montenegro's declaration of independence on June 3; currently governed under new constitution approved by referendum on October 28–29, 2006, and formally adopted by the National Assembly on November 8. (Serbia's Autonomous Province of Kosovo and Metohija was placed under administration of the United Nations Interim Administrative Mission in Kosovo with effect from June 14, 1999, by authorization of United Nations Security Council Resolution 1244. The autonomous province declared independence as the Republic of Kosovo on February 17, 2008, an action unrecognized by Serbia, which labeled it as illegal and in violation of international principles of sovereignty and territorial integrity.)

Area: 34,116 sq. mi. (88,361 sq. km). Included are the autonomous provinces of Kosovo and Metohija, 4,211 sq. mi. (10,908 sq. km), and Vojvodina, 8,304 sq. mi. (21,506 sq. km).

Population: 7,186,862 (2011C; excludes Kosovo and Metohija); 8,342,613 (2012E—UN); 7,276,604 (2012E—U.S. Census).

Major Urban Centers (2011C): BELGRADE (1,233,000), Novi Sad (Vojvodina, 222,000), Niš (183,164).

Official Languages: Serbian. National minorities may officially use their languages in localities where they comprise at least 15 percent of the population.

Monetary Unit: Dinar (market rate November 1, 2013: 84.58 dinars = $1US).

President: Tomislav NIKOLIĆ (elected as the candidate of the Serbian Progressive Party [SNS], from which he resigned following his election); elected in second-round voting on May 20, 2012, and inaugurated for a five-year term on May 31, succeeding Boris TADIĆ (Democratic Party), who resigned on April 5, 2012. Slavica DJUKIĆ-DEJANOVIĆ (Socialist Party of Serbia) served as acting president between April 5 and May 31.

Prime Minister: Ivica DAČIĆ (Serbian Socialist Party); nominated by the president June 28, 2012, following the National Assembly election of May 6; confirmed by the National Assembly on July 27, succeeding Mirko CVETKOVIĆ (Democratic Party).

THE COUNTRY

The Republic of Serbia, encompassing approximately 35 percent of pre-1992 Yugoslavia's area, is a landlocked Balkan state. While it has a Serb ethnic majority of 83 percent, Serbs are unevenly distributed. There have been particularly destabilizing effects in Serbia's Kosovo and Metohija Province, more than 90 percent of whose 2.2 million inhabitants are ethnic Albanians, and in the Sandžak region of western Serbia, where half the population are Bosniak Muslims. Serbia's Vojvodina Province, in the north, has a notable ethnic Hungarian minority (some 4 percent of the country's total population). Eastern Orthodox Christianity predominates, with regional Muslim and Roman Catholic Vojvodina minorities.

Mostly underdeveloped before World War II, Yugoslavia, comprising six constituent republics (Bosnia and Herzegovina, Croatia, Macedonia, Montenegro, Serbia, and Slovenia), made rapid advances after 1945 under a Communist regime that applied pragmatic and flexible methods of economic management.

Political transition and the outbreak of regional conflict in mid-1991 caused the economy to deteriorate rapidly, the decline being aggravated by the imposition of economic sanctions against the new Federal Republic of Yugoslavia (FRY, encompassing the constituent republics of Serbia and Montenegro) by the United Nations from May 1992 until November 1995. Substantial currency devaluations were undertaken in early 1992, with inflation soaring to a historically unprecedented rate of 1 million percent a month by December 1993. The "super dinar," introduced in January 1994, was valued at 13 million old dinars and had the effect of ending hyperinflation. The GDP of Serbia and Montenegro declined by more than 40 percent in the period

1990–1995. For the rest of the decade, growth averaged only about 2 percent annually.

Beginning in early 1998, escalating violence in Kosovo led to a renewal of international sanctions and then to a bombing campaign conducted by the North Atlantic Treaty Organization (NATO) in March–June 1999, severely damaging Serbia's economic infrastructure. In late September the government claimed that the NATO air war had caused $100 billion in damage, compared to the $30–50 billion estimated by international sources. According to FRY government figures, GDP declined by 16 percent in 1999 because of the Kosovo conflict but increased by 5 percent in 2000. (Beginning in 2000 basic economic statistics have excluded Kosovo.) Output nevertheless stood at only half of its 1989 level, and 30 percent of the labor force was unemployed. From 2006–2008, GDP grew at an average of 5.8 percent. In 2009, GDP fell by 4 percent due to reductions in trade, consumer demand, output, and fiscal revenues during the global economic downturn, but annual average growth of 1.3 percent returned in 2010–2011.

In 2011, Serbia's agricultural sector accounted for about 11 percent of GDP and employed about 22 percent of the active labor force. Leading crops include maize, wheat, and sugar beets. Industry contributed about 19 percent of GDP and engaged 20 percent of workers. Coal, lead, and zinc were mined in significant quantities, particularly in Kosovo. Major exports have included iron and steel, textiles, machinery and transport equipment, and agricultural products.

Inflation has averaged more than 10 percent annually from 2006 through 2011. Unemployment has eased from 1999 levels, but in April 2013 had risen to over 27 percent. GDP contracted in 2012 by 1.8 percent, with the International Monetary Fund (IMF) predicting 2 percent growth in 2013.

GOVERNMENT AND POLITICS

Political background. The Kingdom of the Serbs, Croats, and Slovenes, was formed on December 1, 1918, under the Serbian House of Karadjordjević. Uniting the independent kingdoms of Serbia and Montenegro with the Croatian, Dalmatian, and Bosnian and Herzegovinian territories previously ruled by Austria-Hungary, the new entity (formally renamed Yugoslavia on October 3, 1929) was ruled between World Wars I and II as a highly centralized, Serb-dominated state in which the Croats became an increasingly disaffected minority. The Serb-Croat antagonism, which caused many Croats to sympathize with Nazi Germany and Fascist Italy, continued even after the two Axis powers attacked and occupied the country in April 1941 and set up a pro-Axis puppet state of Croatia that included most of Bosnia and Herzegovina.

Wartime resistance to the Axis was led by two rival groups, the proroyalist Chetniks, under Gen. Draža MIHAILOVIĆ, and the Communist-inspired Partisans, led by Marshal Josip Broz TITO, a Croat who sought to enlist all the country's national groups in the liberation struggle. The Partisans' greater effectiveness in opposing the occupation forces and securing Allied aid paved the way for their assumption of power at the end of the war. In March 1945, Tito became prime minister in a government of national unity; eight months later, on November 29, the monarchy was abolished and a Federal People's Republic of Yugoslavia, based on the equality of the country's principal national groups, was proclaimed. On January 14, 1953, under a new constitution, Tito was elected president of the republic.

Yugoslavia developed along orthodox Communist lines until 1948, when its refusal to submit to Soviet directives led to its expulsion from the Communist bloc and the imposition of a political and economic blockade by the Soviet Union and its East European allies. Aided by Western arms and economic support, Yugoslavia maintained its autonomy throughout the Stalin era and by the late 1950s had achieved a partial reconciliation with the Soviet-led Warsaw Pact states, although it still insisted on complete independence and the right to find its own "road to socialism." A federal constitution promulgated in 1963 consolidated the system of "social self-management" by attempting to draw the people into economic and administrative decision-making at all levels; it also expanded the independence of the judiciary, increased the responsibilities of the federal legislature and those of the country's six constituent republics and two autonomous provinces (Kosovo and Metohija, and Vojvodina), and widened freedom of choice in elections.

In May 1980, Marshal Tito, president for life of the republic and of the League of Communists of Yugoslavia (*Savez Komunista Jugoslavija*—SKJ), died at age 87. The leadership of state and party thereupon passed to collegial executives—the eight-member State Presidency and the eight-member Presidium of the SKJ Central Committee. Yugoslavia's six republics and two autonomous provinces were equally represented in both. Through the 1980s the president of the State Presidency and the president of the Presidium rotated on an annual basis.

During 1990, both the federal government and the SKJ experienced acute crises as economic ills exacerbated long-standing political animosities. An SKJ congress that convened in January 1990 was forced to adjourn because of a split over introduction of a multiparty system. Croatia and Slovenia both subsequently conducted open legislative elections in which the SKJ's republic-level affiliates were defeated. The situation was further aggravated in May when the hard-line Borisav JOVIĆ of Serbia became president of the State Presidency.

In July 1990, Slovenia and Macedonia declared their "full sovereignty" within Yugoslavia, while Croatia approved constitutional changes having much the same effect. In Serbia, a majority of voters endorsed a new Serbian constitution that, contrary to the federal document, effectively stripped the provinces of Kosovo and Vojvodina of autonomous status. Concurrently, ethnic Albanian delegates to the Kosovo Assembly declared their province independent of Serbia and a constituent republic of the Yugoslav federation. Serbia responded three days later by dissolving the Kosovo legislature. In a series of multiparty elections during November and December, former Communists won overwhelmingly in Serbia and Montenegro but were decisively defeated in Bosnia and Herzegovina.

The elections occurred at a time of mounting confrontation between the government of Croatia and the Serb-dominated Yugoslav National Army (*Jugoslovenske Narodne Armije*—JNA). In January 1991 Croatia and Slovenia concluded a mutual defense pact. In February the Slovene Assembly voted for phased secession from the federation. Shortly thereafter, the Serb-populated regions of Croatia opted for effective secession from that republic, prior to proclaiming at year's end a self-styled "Republic of Serbian Krajina."

In June 1991, the presidents of the six constituent republics were reported to have agreed to a plan whereby the republics would retain sovereignty within Yugoslavia but would not seek international recognition as independent states. However, the relatively prosperous Slovenes subsequently indicated their unwillingness to continue financial support for the less-developed republics, while Croatia feared that its sizable Serbian minority would force geographic dismemberment if it remained in the federation. As a result, the two western republics declared their independence on June 25.

That the federation had in fact expired was quickly apparent in the failure of the JNA to mount real opposition to Slovenia's secession, while JNA engagement in Croatia was mainly directed to backing local Serbs against Croatian government forces. By late August 1991 the conflict had cost Croatia nearly one-third of its territory, although some was later retaken. On September 8, Macedonians voted overwhelmingly in favor of establishing a sovereign and independent Macedonia. Bosnia and Herzegovina followed suit, issuing a declaration of sovereignty on October 15. On December 5 Croatia's Stjepan MESIĆ resigned as president of the State Presidency, stating, "Yugoslavia no longer exists." The Croatian Assembly backdated the action to October 8, when its declaration of independence formally came into effect.

On January 15, 1992, one day after the advance contingent of a UN peacekeeping force had arrived in Yugoslavia, the European Community (EC, subsequently the European Union—EU) recognized the independence of Croatia and Slovenia. In contrast, on February 12 Serbia and Montenegro agreed to join in upholding "the principles of a common state which would be a continuation of Yugoslavia." In a referendum held February 29–March 1, Bosnia and Herzegovina opted for independence, and on March 26 Macedonia moved in the same direction by securing the withdrawal of JNA forces from its territory.

On April 27, 1992, a rump Federal Assembly adopted the constitution of a new Federal Republic of Yugoslavia (FRY), under which elections for a successor assembly were held in Serbia and Montenegro in May. The Socialist Party of Serbia (*Socijalistička Partija Srbije*—SPS), led by the president of Serbia, Slobodan MILOŠEVIĆ, won a slim majority in the new lower house, the Chamber of Citizens, in part because opposition elements, including the new Democratic Movement of Serbia coalition (*Demokratska Pokret Srbije*—Depos) boycotted the balloting. On June 15 the assembly elected Dobrica ĆOSIĆ, a well-known writer and political independent, as federal president. Under the new basic law, Ćosić, a Serb, was obligated to name a Montenegrin to the post of prime minister; however, in an unusual move apparently instigated by Milošević in the hope of currying favor in Washington, Ćosić nominated Milan PANIĆ, a wealthy U.S. citizen born in Serbia, who was formally confirmed by the assembly in July.

Milošević soon became increasingly critical of Panić, who, despite his questionable residential qualifications, then ran against Milošević in the Serbian presidential election in December 1992 but was soundly defeated. In the simultaneous legislative election Milošević's SPS maintained its dominance of the Serbian National Assembly. Although the SPS lost ground in the FRY's Federal Assembly, the hard-liners and anti-Panić forces were sufficiently strong to secure the overwhelming passage of a nonconfidence motion against the prime minister.

Amid uncertainty stemming from Panić's refusal to resign, his deputy, Radoje KONTIĆ of Montenegro, was named prime minister in February 1993. Thereafter, as the FRY's international isolation increased because of its involvement in the worsening ethnic conflict in Bosnia and Herzegovina, the ire of the Serbian hard-liners focused on the nonparty federal president, Ćosić, replacing him in June with the chair of the Serbian legislature, Zoran LILIĆ (see the 2012 *Handbook* for details).

Thereafter, Milošević was increasingly aligned with the "greater Serbia" school, although international pressure had obliged him in early May 1993 to accept the Vance-Owen plan for the cantonization of Bosnia and Herzegovina. Milošević was bitterly denounced for his action by the leader of the ultranationalist Serbian Radical Party (*Srpska Radikalna Stranka*—SRS), Vojislav ŠEŠELJ, whose call for a nonconfidence vote forced dissolution of the Serbian National Assembly in October. In the resultant December election, the SPS increased its strength in the 250-member body from 101 to 123 seats, while SRS representation declined from 73 to 39 in a contest that nevertheless saw a marked shift to right-wing nationalist attitudes among the opposition parties. Postelection negotiations led to the formation in March 1994 of a Serbian "cabinet of economists" that was headed by Mirko MARJANOVIĆ (SPS) and also included representation for the New Democracy (*Nova Demokratija*—ND) party.

In 1995, a major offensive by Croatian government forces had recovered most of the "Republic of Serbian Krajina" by early August (see the entry on Croatia). In Yugoslavia, this provoked a storm of criticism directed against Milošević by hard-line Serb leaders. Political difficulties were compounded by the flight of an estimated 200,000 Serbian refugees from Krajina, most of them into Yugoslavia, where many supported opposition demands for the government's ouster. Milošević's muted response to the Croat successes (and to subsequent advances by allied Muslim and Croat forces in Bosnia) was widely seen as in line with his recent policy of distancing the Belgrade government from the Croatian and Bosnian Serbs, in part to secure a settlement that would fully lift UN sanctions on Yugoslavia (see Foreign relations, below).

Serbian relations with the province of Kosovo remained in a state of crisis in 1995 and 1996 as ethnic Albanians, resisting Serbian attempts to impose political, social, and educational control, established an underground administration. Elections to the Kosovo Assembly in May 1992, won by the pro-independence Democratic League of Kosovo (*Lidhja Demokratike e Kosovës*—LDK), had been condemned as illegal by Belgrade, which had officially dissolved the body in 1990. Nevertheless, the LDK leader, Ibrahim RUGOVA, was proclaimed president of a self-declared "Republic of Kosovo," which secured international recognition only from Albania. The local situation deteriorated in December 1994, when Serbian security forces carried out the most sweeping wave of arrests since 1990 in an effort to eliminate the unauthorized police force created by the ethnic Albanians. Tension intensified further in mid-1995 when the Belgrade government announced that Serb refugees from Krajina would be resettled in Kosovo with the aim of redressing the province's ethnic imbalance.

Elections in November 1996 took place amid increasing voter dissatisfaction with government mismanagement, crime, and corruption, as well as with the lack of economic improvement following the suspension a year earlier of UN sanctions. In the election for the federal Chamber of Citizens an SPS-led alliance won 64 of the 138 seats, with the government-aligned Democratic Party of Socialists of Montenegro (*Demokratska Partija Socijalista Crne Gore*—DPSCG) adding another 20 seats. SRS representation fell to 16, while the Together (*Zajedno*) coalition of moderate opposition parties obtained a disappointing 22 seats in the federal contest. In contrast, in mid-November, following a second-round election for local assemblies, the opposition parties claimed victory in most of Serbia's cities, including Belgrade. The SPS-controlled courts and electoral commissions quickly annulled the municipal results, alleging irregularities. In response, the opposition parties, joined by students and later the Serbian Orthodox Church and teachers, staged mass demonstrations of up to 250,000 people in the streets of Belgrade. After 88 days of marches, Milošević, in February 1997, finally felt compelled to have the Serbian National Assembly confirm the opposition victories.

Once in office, however, the opposition found its hands tied, the pro-Milošević bureaucracy having collaborated with departing SPS politicians in the mass transfer of government property from localities to the SPS-dominated Serbian republic. Moreover, by summer the *Zajedno* coalition had collapsed, its constituent parties having failed to agree on a common candidate to oppose Milošević for the presidency of Yugoslavia. (He was constitutionally barred from running for a third term as president of Serbia.) Thus, in July 1997 the federal legislature elected an unopposed Milošević as federal president. Two months later, in Serbia's parliamentary elections, Milošević's SPS and allies won a plurality of seats but were faced with having to rely on either the second-place SRS or the third-place opposition Serbian Renewal Movement (*Srpski Pokret Obnove*—SPO) for a parliamentary majority. After months of negotiations, in March 1998 the SPS and an ally, the Yugoslav Left (*Jugoslovenska Levica*—JUL), formed a government with the SRS under the continued leadership of Prime Minister Marjanović.

In the first round of the Serbian presidential election (held in tandem with the September 1997 parliamentary election), no candidate had won an absolute majority, forcing a runoff between Milošević's hand-picked SPS candidate, Zoran Lilić, and SRS leader Vojislav Šešelj. The results of the October 1997 second round favored Šešelj but were annulled by law as turnout had fallen below 50 percent. New first-round elections were held in early December, with Šešelj facing six candidates, including the SPS's Milan MILUTINOVIĆ. In the runoff two weeks later, Milutinović handily defeated Šešelj with 59 percent of the vote. The election was subsequently characterized as "fundamentally flawed" by the Conference on (later Organization for) Security and Cooperation in Europe (CSCE/OSCE).

Having fallen out of favor with President Milošević, in May 1998 the federal prime minister, Radoje Kontić, after more than five years in office, lost a confidence vote in the upper chamber of the Federal Assembly and was succeeded by Milošević ally and former Montenegrin president Momir BULATOVIĆ of the recently organized Socialist People's Party of Montenegro (*Socijalistička Narodna Partija Crne Gore*—SNPCG). In October 1997 Bulatović had lost a close bid for reelection as Montenegro's president, largely because of a split between pro- and anti-Milošević forces in his previous party, the DPSCG.

By this point, tensions had worsened in Kosovo. Following the murder of four Serbian policemen in February 1998 by members of the separatist Kosovo Liberation Army (KLA), a retaliatory security operation killed 24 ethnic Albanian villagers, many apparently by summary execution. Later in March, ethnic Albanians, in addition to casting ballots for the shadow "Republic of Kosovo" legislature, reelected the LDK's Ibrahim Rugova as shadow president (see the entry on Kosovo).

With daily demonstrations continuing in the province, U.S. diplomats succeeded in convincing Milošević and Rugova to meet for the first time in May 1998. Although both sides agreed to initiate weekly talks in Priština, the violence in Kosovo continued to escalate over October to January 1999, despite a cease-fire in December and Milošević's agreement to withdraw in the face of imminent NATO air strikes. In February 1999, peace talks between Serbian officials and ethnic Albanians—including KLA representatives—opened in Rambouillet, France. Cosponsored by France and the United States, the negotiations were aimed at almost complete administrative autonomy for the province with the end of hostilities to be overseen by NATO troops. In March, the Kosovar delegation signed the pact, but the Serbian delegation continued to reject the presence of NATO peacekeepers (see the entry on Kosovo).

On March 24, 1999, NATO forces from eight countries initiated Operation Allied Force, the most extensive air campaign in Europe since the close of World War II. Serbian forces stepped up a widespread campaign of "ethnic cleansing" that saw the entire Albanian population forced from some cities and villages, creating an immediate refugee crisis at the borders of Albania and Macedonia. By the end of April the refugee exodus was swelling toward 750,000, with additional hundreds of thousands displaced within the province itself.

The main Serbian opposition parties, a number of which had earlier joined various nongovernmental organizations in an umbrella grouping, the Alliance for Change (*Savez za Promene*—SZP), were largely silenced by the country's war footing. The loudest dissenting voice was that of Deputy Prime Minister Vuk DRAŠKOVIĆ of the SPO. Having joined the government in January in a show of national solidarity, he was dismissed in late April for having stated that the populace should be told, contrary to government contentions, "that NATO is not facing a breakdown, that Russia will not help Yugoslavia militarily, and that world public opinion is against us." In Montenegro, President Milo DJUKANOVIĆ (Bulatović's successor) continued his efforts to distance his administration from federal policies. Even though Montenegro was not exempt from the NATO air campaign, and despite rumors that the Serbian military was preparing to depose him, Djukanović rejected orders that the Montenegrin police be placed under the command of the army. Djukanović accused Milošević of using "the pretext of the defense of the country" to displace the civil government.

On May 6, 1999, the Group of Seven countries plus Russia (G-8) proposed a peace plan providing for "deployment in Kosovo of effective international civil and security presences" and formation of an interim provincial administration under the UN Security Council. On June 3 President Milošević accepted the terms of an amended peace agreement offered by President Martii Ahtisaari of Finland and Russia's Viktor Chernomyrdin, including the deployment in Kosovo—but not in the rest of Serbia—of a UN-sponsored, NATO-dominated peacekeeping contingent (Kosovo Force, or KFOR) expected to number some 50,000 troops. The agreement also called for the complete withdrawal of the Serb army, police, and paramilitary forces from Kosovo.

On June 10, 1999, NATO suspended its bombing campaign and the UN Security Council adopted Resolution 1244, authorizing international troop deployment and the establishment of an interim civilian administration in Kosovo. The resolution also reaffirmed Yugoslavia's "sovereignty and territorial integrity" but echoed previous calls for "substantial autonomy and meaningful self-administration in Kosovo." The agreement was widely, though often reluctantly, accepted by most of the opposition, including Serbian nationalists, the principal exception being the SRS, which protested by announcing its withdrawal from the coalition government in Serbia. (The withdrawal was technically prohibited by Serbian president Milutinović because of the state of war.) Meanwhile, on May 27 the International Criminal Tribunal for the former Yugoslavia (ICTY) had indicted Milošević and four others, including the interior minister and army chief of staff, for crimes against humanity related to events in Kosovo.

On June 14, 1999, the UN Security Council received a plan for the civil Kosovo administration that included a new UN Interim Administration in Kosovo (UNMIK). On June 20, with the Yugoslav army having completely withdrawn from Kosovo, NATO formally concluded its bombing campaign. On the same day NATO and the KLA signed an agreement providing for KLA demilitarization. Most of the 1 million or more Kosovo Albanian refugees and displaced persons were already returning to their homes, contributing to the collateral flight from the province of ethnic Serbs, many of whom feared reprisals.

In December 1999, UNMIK announced formation of an Interim Administrative Council (IAC) of Rugova, the KLA's Hashim THAÇI, and Rexhep QOSJA of the United Democratic Movement (*Lëvizja Bashimit Demokratike*—LBD); a fourth seat on the IAC was reserved for a representative of the Serb community, which refused to participate. By then, forensic specialists from the international war crimes tribunal had already exhumed thousands of Albanian bodies from mass graves in Kosovo. (Late in the year, the Albanian death toll was estimated at 4,000–5,000, considerably less than originally projected.)

A federal cabinet reshuffle in August 1999 saw the addition of SRS ministers to the Bulatović administration in an effort to shore up support for Milošević. Political opposition to Milošević nevertheless continued to mount. In January 2000 the SPO's Drašković joined his principal opposition rival, Zoran DJINDJIĆ of the Democratic Party (*Demokratska Stranka*—DS), in forging a unified strategy that was signed by 16 opposition parties.

On April 18, 2000, the Eurocorps, with troop contingents from Germany, Spain, France, Belgium, and Luxembourg, took over control of the Kosovo peacekeeping effort from NATO, but KFOR was encountering increasing difficulty in preventing violent clashes between Albanian and Serb communities. The climate of violence was not, however, limited to Kosovo: in February the Yugoslav defense minister, Pavle BULATOVIĆ, had been assassinated in Belgrade, and in June the SPO's Drašković was wounded in Montenegro.

In a gambit designed to maintain Milošević's hold on power, on July 6, 2000, the SPS pushed through the Federal Assembly constitutional changes authorizing direct election of the president and of the upper legislative house. With most of the opposition continuing a boycott of parliament, the proposals easily received the necessary two-thirds support. The changes, in addition to permitting the incumbent to serve two additional four-year terms, put organization of elections under the FRY instead of the individual republics. On July 8, the Montenegrin assembly described the changes as illegal and "a gross violation of the constitutional rights of the Republic of Montenegro."

On July 27, 2000, Milošević called elections for September, even though his presidential term would not expire until July 2001. The governing coalition in Montenegro quickly announced that it would boycott the balloting. On August 7 the Democratic Opposition of Serbia (*Demokratske Opozicije Srbije*—DOS), ultimately encompassing some 18 parties and a trade union association, nominated Vojislav KOŠTUNICA, leader of the Democratic Party of Serbia (*Demokratska Stranka Srbije*—DSS), as their joint presidential candidate. The SPO, running independently, nominated the mayor of Belgrade, Vojislav MIHAJLOVIĆ, raising the prospect of a split in the opposition vote.

Despite allegations of vote rigging and other irregularities committed by Milošević's supporters, Koštunica emerged from the September 24, 2000, presidential election as the likely leader, although the SPS initially claimed otherwise. In the legislative contests, the DOS won a plurality in the lower house, but the electoral boycott by Montenegro's governing parties left the balance of power in the hands of the pro-Milošević SNPCG. On September 26 the government-controlled election commission admitted that Koštunica held the lead in the presidential tally, but with less than the 50 percent needed to avoid a runoff with Milošević. Rejecting the commission's count, Koštunica refused to participate in a second round of voting scheduled for October 8.

In the following days massive street demonstrations called for Milošević to step down, the Serb Orthodox Church began referring to Koštunica as the president, the Yugoslav army made it clear that it would not intervene, and ultranationalist SRS leader Vojislav Šešelj announced that he, too, would support Koštunica's claim to the presidency. On October 4, 2000, the Constitutional Court annulled the presidential poll, but two days later, with the country in the grip of a general strike and with pro-DOS demonstrators in Belgrade having burned the Federal Assembly and other buildings, the court reversed itself and declared that Koštunica had won 50.2 percent of the vote (some sources put the total at 55–56 percent). On the same day Milošević conceded, and the new president took office on October 7.

Faced with mounting opposition, the SPS-led government of Serbia resigned on October 21, 2000. The SPS's Milomir MINIĆ assumed office as prime minister on October 24 at the head of a transitional cabinet of the SPS, DOS, and SPO, pending a Serbian National Assembly election set for December 23. On November 4 the Federal Assembly confirmed the nomination of Zoran ŽIŽIĆ of the SNPCG as federal prime minister, Momir Bulatović having resigned on October 9. The Žižić cabinet included an equal number of ministers from the SNPCG and the DOS, plus two reform-oriented, nominally unaffiliated economists with strong ties to the DOS.

At the Serbian republican election in December 2000, the DOS handily defeated Milošević's SPS, winning 176 of the National Assembly's 250 seats, with 64 percent of the vote. On January 25, 2001, Zoran Djindjić of the DS took office as prime minister of Serbia, heading a new DOS-dominated Serbian cabinet that also included independents and members of the DOS-supportive G17 Plus economic think tank.

On April 1, 2001, after a violent standoff outside the former president's villa, Serbian police arrested Milošević on charges of corruption and abuse of power. A debate continued over where he should be tried. Some members of the federal administration called for surrendering him to the ICTY, even though President Koštunica opposed any such action in the absence of legislation or a constitutional change authorizing extradition. In the Federal Assembly, efforts to pass extradition legislation were repeatedly stymied by the SNPCG. As a consequence, on June 23 the majority of the federal cabinet—minus the absent Prime Minister Žižić and all but one SNPCG minister—issued a decree on cooperation with the war crimes tribunal. On June 28, the FRY Constitutional Court stayed the decree pending determination of its constitutionality, but Serbian Prime Minister Djindjić and his cabinet, meeting in an emergency session and in near unanimity, discredited the court and refused to accept the stay. Justifying their action under a provision of the Serbian constitution that allowed the Serbian government to act unilaterally and temporarily on behalf of the whole country if federal authorities were unable to do so, the Serbian authorities immediately surrendered Milošević to UN representatives, who flew him to the Netherlands. (On March 11, 2006, 444 days into his trial before the

ICTY, Milošević would be found dead of a heart attack in his cell.) In reaction, FRY Prime Minister Žižić resigned on June 29, although he remained in a caretaker capacity until the confirmation on July 17 of Dragiša PEŠIĆ, also of the SNPCG.

In the context of a growing rivalry between Federal president Koštunica and Serbian prime minister Djindjić, Koštunica's DSS withdrew from the Serbian coalition government on August 17, 2001, ostensibly over the government's inaction in fighting organized crime. The increasing distance between the DSS and the DOS culminated on June 12, 2002, when the DSS withdrew from the Serbian legislature in protest of a government effort to replace 21 DSS deputies for absenteeism and to distribute some of their seats to other parties.

On March 14, 2002, the governments of Serbia, Montenegro, and the FRY announced an "agreement in principle" that would replace Yugoslavia with a "state union" to be called Serbia and Montenegro. Over the objections of parties that wanted a separate and independent Serbia, the Serbian legislature ratified the accord 149–79 on April 9. The same day, the Montenegrin legislature voted in favor of the agreement 58–11, but dissatisfaction on the part of proindependence parties soon cost the Montenegrin government its majority. On May 31, both chambers of the Federal Assembly approved the state union agreement by wide margins.

In August 2002, with the federal presidency certain to be replaced by a much weaker union presidency, federal president Koštunica entered the race for the Serbian presidency. In the September 29 election he won a leading 31 percent of the vote. Second place, with 27 percent, went to Miroljub LABUS, the federal deputy prime minister and the hand-picked candidate of Serbian prime minister Djindjić. In a runoff election on October 13 Koštunica took about 67 percent of the vote, but the turnout fell under 50 percent, invalidating the results. A repeat election on December 8, which pitted Koštunica against the SRS's Vojislav Šešelj and one other candidate, met the same fate, leaving Serbia without an elected president when Milutinović's term expired near the end of the month.

On January 27 and 29, 2003, the Serbian and then the Montenegrin assemblies approved a Constitutional Charter for the state union of Serbia and Montenegro. The Federal Assembly concurred on February 4 (by votes of 26–7 in the upper chamber and 84–31 in the lower), thereby excising Yugoslavia from the political map. Under the charter a new state union Assembly of Serbia and Montenegro was elected by and from among the members of the FRY, Serbian, and Montenegrin legislatures, and on March 7 the new assembly in turn elected the DPSCG's Svetozar MAROVIĆ, the only candidate, as state union president and chair of the Council of Ministers.

Five days later Serbian prime minister Zoran Djindjić was assassinated by an organized Belgrade criminal gang, the Zemun Clan, many of whose members had served in Milošević's Special Operations Unit, the so-called Red Berets. (In May 2007 a dozen defendants were convicted in connection with the assassination and sentenced to prison terms of between 8 and 37 years.) Djindjić was succeeded in an acting capacity by Deputy Prime Minister Nebojša ČOVIĆ of the DOS-affiliated Democratic Alternative (*Demokratska Alternativa*—DA), with the Serbian legislature then confirming the DS's Zoran ŽIVKOVIĆ as the new prime minister on March 18, 2003.

Later in 2003, the DOS-led government of the Serbian Republic lost its legislative majority, precipitating an early National Assembly election on December 28. With the DOS alliance having dissolved, the ultranationalist SRS won a plurality of 82 seats but was unable to form a government. Thus, Vojislav Koštunica, who had stepped down as the last president of the FRY on March 3, 2003, was named Serbian prime minister-designate on February 20, 2004, by Dragan MARŠIĆANIN—the second of three acting Serbian presidents following the expiration of Milutinović's term in 2002. On March 3, 2004, the newly elected Serbian legislature confirmed Koštunica as the head of a minority government that included his DSS, the allied SPO and New Serbia (*Nova Srbija*—NS), and the G17 Plus. Because of its minority status, the new government depended on parliamentary support from the SPS.

In February 2004, three months after another invalidated Serbian presidential election, the Serbian Assembly eliminated the 50 percent turnout requirement. In a fresh election on June 13 Tomislav NIKOLIĆ of the ultranationalist SRS finished first, with 31 percent of the vote, against a dozen other candidates, including the DS's Boris TADIĆ (28 percent) and independent businessman Bogoljub KARIĆ (18 percent). In runoff balloting on June 27, however, Tadić, having gained the support of most mainstream parties, won 54 percent to Nikolić's 46 percent, and he was inaugurated as Serbian president on July 11.

Under their 2003 EU-backed state union agreement, both Serbia and Montenegro had the right to vote on the question of independence in three years. On May 21, 2006, by a half a percentage point above the EU-set threshold of 55 percent for approval, Montenegro's voters chose separation from Serbia, and on June 3 the Montenegrin assembly passed a declaration of independence. Although many Serbians were unhappy with what they viewed as an abrupt divorce, on June 5 the Serbian National Assembly declared Serbia to be the independent successor state to the state union, as had been agreed upon under the charter, and thereby extinguished the last remnants of the former Yugoslavia. The two new countries then began the process of disentangling their institutions.

Independent Serbia's adoption of a new constitution, which was approved by 96.6 percent of those voting in a referendum on October 28–29, 2006, prepared the way for election of a new National Assembly on January 21, 2007. The SRS again won a plurality, 81 of 250 seats, but protracted negotiations among the other leading parties led to formation of a coalition by the DS, DSS, NS (now allied with the DSS), and the G17 Plus, which together commanded 130 seats. The new government, once again headed by Prime Minister Koštunica, took office on May 15.

Meanwhile, Kosovo, still under UNMIK administration, continued to press for independence from Serbia. Under a May 2001 Constitutional Framework for Provisional Self-Government, UNMIK had created "provisional institutions of self-government," lending legitimacy to Kosovo's presidency, government, and assembly. Following President Rugova's death from cancer on February 10, 2006, the Kosovar legislature elected the LDK's Fatmir SEJDIU as president, with Agim ÇEKU then being named prime minister in an effort to provide stronger leadership during UN-mediated negotiations over Kosovo's future political status.

On March 26, 2007, having abandoned futile efforts to achieve a compromise between the Serbian and Kosovar governments, UN Special Envoy Martii Ahtisaari submitted to the UN Security Council his plan for Kosovo's "supervised independence." The Ahtisaari plan gave considerable attention to the status of the minority Serb population. (Only a fraction of the estimated 200,000 Serbs who had fled Kosovo since 1999 had returned.) Serbs would be granted broad governmental powers in six municipalities, each of which could receive direct aid from Serbia. In addition, Serbs and other minorities would be guaranteed seats in the legislature. Although the Kosovo assembly voted its approval of the Ahtisaari plan in early April 2007, Serbia rejected it.

Given a December 2007 deadline for reaching a final decision on Kosovo's future, representatives of Serbia and Kosovo, including both presidents and both prime ministers, met in New York on September 28 for face-to-face discussions. Between then and November 26 five additional negotiating rounds were held. Serbia's final offer of self-government except in foreign relations, defense, and border control was rejected by Kosovo, the only significant point of agreement being that both would avoid threats and violence.

On November 17, 2007, the PDK won a plurality in an election for the Assembly of Kosovo. On January 9, 2008, the new legislature reelected Fatmir Sejdiu as president and then endorsed Hashim Thaçi as prime minister of a coalition cabinet comprising ministers from the PDK and the LDK, as well as two Serbs and a Turk.

In the presidential election on January 20, 2008, the SRS's Tomislav Nikolić led in the first round of voting, winning 40.0 percent in a nine-way contest. The incumbent, Boris Tadić, finished second, with 35.4 percent, but went on to win reelection in the February 3 runoff, with 50.3 percent versus Nikolić's 48.0 percent. Prime Minister Koštunica, taking a harder line than the president on Kosovar independence and EU integration, had refused to support Tadić.

On February 17, 2008, Prime Minister Thaçi declared Kosovo to be "proud, independent, and free." The unilateral declaration was immediately condemned as illegal by Serbia. Addressing the UN Security Council on February 18, President Tadić asserted that Kosovo's action violated guarantees of sovereignty and territorial integrity contained in the UN charter. Protests by ethnic Serbs on both sides of the Kosovo border erupted, and in Belgrade tens of thousands of sometimes-violent demonstrators took to the streets on February 21.

On March 8, 2008, having vowed that he would not support further negotiations with the EU until it accepted that Kosovo remained part of Serbia, Prime Minister Koštunica announced that the government coalition had collapsed, and five days later President Tadić dissolved the National Assembly. The resultant May 11 election saw Tadić's For a European Serbia (*Za Evropsku Srbiju*—ZES) coalition, led by the DS and G17 Plus, win 102 seats, to 78 for the SRS and 30 for Koštunica's coalition of the DSS and NS. Negotiations on forming a new coalition government concluded on June 26 with the announcement that the ZES would be joined by the SPS and several smaller parties. On July 7 the National Assembly confirmed a new cabinet headed by the DS's Mirko CVETKOVIĆ, theretofore the minister of finance.

President Tadić resigned on April 5, 2012, ten months before his term was slated to expire, allowing the presidential and parliamentary elections to be run concurrently, in hopes of boosting the fortunes of the DS.

The May 6, 2012, parliamentary election saw the Nikolić's Let's Get Serbia Moving (*Pokrenimo Serbiju*—PS) coalition, led by the SNS, win 73 seats with 24 percent of the vote, and Tadić's Choice For a Better Life (*Izbor za Bolji Život*—IzBZ) won 67 seats with 22 percent of the vote. In the subsequent negotiations to form a government, the SPS emerged as a key player, their own coalition having secured 44 seats with 14.5 percent of the vote. The SPS agreed on May 9 that they would support the DS in forming a government, pending the results of the second round of the presidential elections.

Meanwhile, the incumbent, Boris Tadić, won 25.3 percent of the vote in a 12-way contest. The SNS's Tomislav Nikolić finished second, winning 25.0 percent but went on to win in the second round with 49.5 percent to Tadić's 47.3 percent.

Following Nikolić's election, the SPS shifted to negotiate with the SNS; the government subsequently announced on July 23 included the SPS, SNS, URS (a coalition group led by G17 Plus), PUPS, SDPS, DS, and NS.

Conflicts within the ruling coalition had emerged by January 2013. In July, Prime Minister Ivica DAČIĆ (SPS) demanded the ouster of the URS from the government; the resulting conflict between the SPS and SNS threatened to shatter the government and trigger early elections. In August a compromise created a new cabinet joined by a slate of nonparty experts. The URS moved to the opposition, but the SPO and DHSS supported the cabinet reshuffle, which was approved on September 3.

Constitution and government. Yugoslavia under successive postwar constitutions remained a Communist one-party state until the emergence of a variety of opposition groups at the republican level in early 1990. The constitution of the Federal Republic of Yugoslavia, adopted in 1992, provided for a bicameral Federal Assembly, encompassing a Chamber of Republics (with equal representation for Serbia and Montenegro) and a Chamber of Citizens apportioned on the basis of population. The federal president was elected to a four-year term by the assembly until July 2000, when constitutional changes instituted direct elections for the presidency as well as for the Chamber of Republics. The president was expected to nominate a prime minister from the other constituent republic.

The Constitutional Charter of the state union of Serbia and Montenegro (including Serbia's Autonomous Province of Vojvodina and Autonomous Province of Kosovo and Metohija) was formally adopted in February 2003 and lasted until both countries chose independence in 2006. It established a presidency with circumscribed powers, although the head of state also served as chair of the Council of Ministers. The president was elected for a single four-year term by the unicameral legislature, the Assembly of Serbia and Montenegro, comprising 91 Serbian and 35 Montenegrin deputies. Each of the constituent republics had a popularly elected president and unicameral assembly, with a prime minister nominated by the former and confirmed by the latter.

Serbia's 2006 constitution retains a mixed presidential-parliamentary system. The president, elected by majority vote, serves a five-year, once-renewable term. The National Assembly, elected by proportional representation, also serves a five-year term, subject to dissolution. The president proposes a prime minister, who is approved by the legislature along with a cabinet. The president may return legislation to the National Assembly for reconsideration but, following repeat passage by a majority of the whole legislature, must then promulgate the resultant law. The president may also dissolve the National Assembly "upon the elaborated proposal of the Government."

A Supreme Court of Cassation sits at the apex of the judicial system. The National Assembly elects the president of the Supreme Court (for a nonrenewable five-year term) and first-time judges (for terms of three years). The latter may then be given permanent tenure by a High Judicial Council, an autonomous body elected by the National Assembly. There is also an autonomous Constitutional Court, whose authority extends to such matters as the constitutionality of laws, intergovernmental disputes, and compatibility of ratified treaties with the constitution. Local jurisdictions include 29 districts (5 in Kosovo), municipalities, towns, and the capital of Belgrade. A law passed in 2009 and amended in 2010 created five statistical development regions: Belgrade; Kosovo and Metohija; Southern and Eastern Serbia; Šumadija and Western Serbia; and Vojvodina.

The constitution begins by affirming the "equality of all citizens and ethnic communities in Serbia" and adds that Kosovo and Metohija is "an integral part of the territory of Serbia," albeit with "substantial autonomy." Vojvodina is also recognized as an autonomous province. Despite Kosovo's February 2008 unilateral declaration of independence, Serb representatives from 26 municipalities from the mainly northern, Serb-dominated areas of Kosovo convened in May in Mitrovica as a 45-member Assembly of the Community of the Municipalities of the Autonomous Province of Kosovo and Metohija (see the 2012 *Handbook* for details).

In 2013 Freedom House described the press in Serbia as only "partially free" due to widespread corruption, laws which restrict media freedom, and economic and political pressure. In 2013 Reporters Without Borders ranked Serbia 62nd out of 179 countries in its press freedom index.

Foreign relations. Following the 1948 break with Moscow, Yugoslav foreign policy concentrated on maintaining the country's independence from both major power blocs. The Tito regime consistently advocated peace, disarmament, détente, and aid to anticolonial and developmental struggles of third world countries. Along with Egypt's Nasser and India's Nehru, Tito was considered a founder of the Nonaligned Movement.

Federal Yugoslavia was ostracized by much of the international community because of military action in support of Serbs in Croatia and in Bosnia and Herzegovina. The Bosnian conflict led to UN Security Council sanctions on May 30, 1992, as well as an EC trade embargo and the dispatch of NATO and Western European Union military units to enforce these sanctions. By the end of 1992, Yugoslavia was suspended from the IMF, the OSCE, and the Central European Initiative (see the entry on Yugoslavia in the 2011 *Handbook* for details).

Intensified UN sanctions on the FRY compelled the Belgrade government to take an overtly stronger line with the Bosnian Serbs following the tabling of new peace proposals—the so-called Stoltenberg-Owen plan—in July 1994 by the Contact Group (of the UK, France, Germany, Russia, and the United States, together with the UN and EU). When the Bosnian Serbs rejected the plan, Belgrade's response was to announce the severance of all political and economic ties with the Bosnian Serbs and to agree to the deployment of international observers on the Yugoslav-Bosnian border to monitor compliance with the official blockade.

Belgrade's reward was UN Security Council approval on September 24, 1994, of a selective suspension of sanctions. Following the intensification of NATO aerial attacks in late August 1995, the Bosnian and Croatian Serb leaders were pressured into accepting the primary role of the Serbian president Milošević in peace negotiations. As a result, after three weeks of intense negotiations between the protagonists conducted under U.S. sponsorship in Dayton, Ohio, a peace agreement was concluded on November 21, 1995 (see the entry on Bosnia and Herzegovina), and initialed on behalf of Yugoslavia and the Bosnian Serbs by Milošević. Suspended the following day, UN sanctions against Belgrade were formally lifted by a unanimous Security Council vote on October 1, 1996 (although FRY assets remained frozen because of disputes and claims from other Yugoslav successor states).

Beginning in February 1998, however, Serbian police and military actions in Kosovo again put Yugoslavia at odds with much of the rest of the world, and on March 31 the UN Security Council imposed an arms embargo on Yugoslavia. From April to June the Contact Group, which now included Italy, met several times, with only Russia dissenting from the imposition of various economic sanctions. A September UN Security Council called for a cease-fire and condemned the "excessive and indiscriminate use of force" by the Serb military and security units. In November Belgrade barred members of the UN war crimes tribunal from entering Kosovo to investigate allegations of extrajudicial killings, prompting the U.S. president of the tribunal to brand Yugoslavia as a "rogue state, one that holds the international rule of law in contempt."

Although Yugoslavia stated during the February 1999 peace talks in Rambouillet, France, that it was prepared to consider regional autonomy for Kosovo, it continued to reject a NATO presence on its soil. Immediately following the start of the NATO bombing campaign on

March 24, 1999, Belgrade declared a state of war and broke diplomatic relations with France, Germany, the UK, and the United States. Relations with all four were restored in November 2000 as Yugoslavia, now headed by Vojislav Koštunica, moved broadly to reestablish its international linkages. The FRY was formally reintegrated into the UN on November 1 and into the OSCE on November 27. On May 25, 2001, meeting in Vienna, the FRY and the other four Yugoslav successor states reached agreement on the division of assets from the former Yugoslavia. In April 2003 the FRY joined the Council of Europe.

A 2004 report by the government acknowledged Serbian involvement in the 1995 massacre of some 8,000 Muslim men and boys outside Srebrenica, Bosnia and Herzegovina. During a visit to Bosnia and Herzegovina in December 2004, President Tadić drew considerable international attention by apologizing "to all against whom a crime was committed in the name of the Serbian people."

On February 26, 2007, the International Court of Justice (ICJ), ruling in a case brought against the Federal Republic of Yugoslavia in 1993, concluded that Serbia was not responsible for genocide committed in Bosnia and Herzegovina during that country's conflict and did not owe reparations. The court severely criticized Serbia, however, for neglecting its obligations under the Convention on the Prevention and Punishment of the Crime of Genocide, both by failing to prevent the 1995 Srebrenica massacre in Bosnia and by failing to cooperate fully with the ICTY.

Prior to Montenegro's declaration of independence, the state union's ambitions to join the EU were complicated by the differences between the Serbian and Montenegrin currency, customs, and market regimes. Negotiations with the EU on a Stabilization and Association Agreement (SAA) as a precursor to EU membership primarily stalled, however, because of Serbia's testy relationship with the ICTY and the unresolved status of Kosovo. At the ICTY, the trial of former Serbian president Milan Milutinović began in July 2006, while that of SRS ultranationalist leader Vojislav Šešelj began in November 2007. Milutinović and Šešelj had surrendered to the ICTY in January and February 2003, respectively, to defend themselves against charges that included crimes against humanity and violations of the conventions of war. Although a number of once-prominent Serbian military leaders had also voluntarily surrendered to the ICTY in 2004 and 2005, the prosecutors in The Hague, Netherlands, continued to insist that Belgrade had not rigorously pursued Radovan KARADŽIĆ and Ratko MLADIĆ, the most notorious Bosnian Serb commanders. Some human rights advocates charged that Serbia was actively protecting the two, who were under indictment for genocide, crimes against humanity, and war crimes. The Serbian government denied the accusations, even though Prime Minister Koštunica consistently argued that Serbians suspected of criminal acts during the Croatian, Bosnian, and Kosovar conflicts should be tried by a Serbian war crimes court.

The matter of cooperation with the ICTY had also delayed consideration by NATO of Serbia's participation in its Partnership for Peace (PfP) program. PfP membership was eventually offered by NATO in November 2006.

In December 2007, despite negotiations led by a troika of mediators representing the EU, Russia, and the United States, the deadline passed for Serbia and Kosovo to reach an accommodation on Kosovo's future status. Kosovo's February 2008 unilateral declaration of independence was quickly recognized by France, Germany, the UK, and the United States, among other countries, prompting some Serb nationalists to call for breaking off diplomatic relations with those states and to withdraw from an SAA with the EU that had been initialed on November 7, 2007. Nevertheless, the SAA was signed on April 29, 2008, two weeks before the legislative election that President Tadić described as setting out a "clear European path for Serbia." As of July 2013, 103 countries and Taiwan had recognized the Republic of Kosovo.

On March 30, 2010, the Serbian parliament passed a resolution condemning and apologizing for the massacre of 8,000 Muslims at Srebrenica in 1995. President Tadić on July 11 attended the commemoration of the 15th anniversary of the Srebrenica massacre. Taken together, the two events constituted an unprecedented recognition by the Serbian state of the crimes committed during the conflict in Bosnia.

The May 26, 2011, arrest of Ratko Mladić and July 20, 2011, detainment of Goran HADŽIĆ, a Croatian Serb who acted as president of the "Republic of Serbian Krajina," meant that the Serbian authorities had captured the last two ethnic Serbian fugitives from ICTY indictments. The step was praised by the European Commission and by EU officials as demonstrating the "determination and commitment" of Serbia to pursue the rule of law and as an important step in Serbia's goal of joining the EU. On March 1, 2012, Serbia moved to full candidate status for accession to the EU.

On April 17, 2013, Serbia and Kosovo accepted a 15-point draft document to normalize their relations. Much of the document addressed the status of the Mitrovica region, including provisions that local Serbian communities would retain significant autonomy. The EU had helped broker the negotiations and hailed Serbia's participation as a key step in moving toward accession. On April 22, 2013, the European Commission recommended the start of EU entry talks with Serbia. The European Council announced on June 28 that negotiations would begin by January 2014.

Current issues. The two principal issues that continue to face Serbia are the status of Kosovo and the country's relationship with the EU. None of the major Serbian parties, let alone the government, has dared characterize Kosovo's independence as a fait accompli, but entry into the EU undoubtedly depends on how the Kosovo question is resolved.

As a step toward preparing for EU membership, in 2009 the National Assembly passed a regionalization bill to consolidate the country's 29 districts into development regions based on EU standards. Concerns about further ethnic partition and strife contributed to opposition from the SRS and other nationalist parties. The government reassured critics that regional boundaries would be determined on a statistical basis and would avoid ethnic homogeneity.

On July 21, 2008, a Serbian security team arrested Radovan Karadžić in a Belgrade suburb, and on the following day a judge ordered his transfer to The Hague to stand trial. Meanwhile, the ICTY has continued its activities. The trial of former Yugoslav army chief of staff Momčilo PERIŠIĆ, who had surrendered to the ICTY in 2005, opened in October 2008 and entered the defense phase in February 2010. Perišić faced 13 charges related to war crimes and crimes against humanity committed in 1993–1995 in Bosnia and Croatia. He was found guilty on September 6, 2011, and sentenced to 27 years, but on February 28, 2013, the Appeals Chamber overturned the verdict and acquitted him. On February 26, 2009, former Serbian president Milan Milutinović was acquitted of similar charges against him, although five codefendants were found guilty and sentenced to between 15 and 22 years in prison. The trial of SRS leader Vojislav Šešelj was interrupted in February 2009 when prosecutors alleged intimidation of witnesses. In July Šešelj was found guilty of contempt of court and sentenced to 15 months in prison for having revealed the names of three protected witnesses. The original trial was again interrupted in 2010 by further alleged intimidation of witnesses and another trial for contempt in February 2011 and a third trial in June 2012. The trial entered its closing arguments in March 2013, with a verdict expected in October. War crimes trials conducted by Serbia itself also continued. As of November 2010, 49 people had been convicted and more than 50 others were on trial.

In August 2009, the National Assembly adopted controversial amendments to the Public Information Law that established heavy fines on journalists and media outlets for publishing false or libelous information. Media associations and watchdogs criticized the changes as likely to result in self-censorship and the closure of electronic and print outlets that are found to violate the law.

On June 22, 2010, the ICJ issued an advisory opinion that found that Kosovo's 2008 declaration of independence did not violate international law. The Serbian government in response noted that the ICJ opinion did not recognize Kosovo's right to independence but merely that the "technical content" of the declaration did not violate international law. On September 9 Serbia dropped its formal complaint to the UN regarding the unilateral nature of the declaration and called for EU-facilitated direct dialogue with Kosovo. However, Tadić reaffirmed in 2010 that Serbia will not recognize the independence of Kosovo.

In November 2010, the EC praised Serbia's commitment to regional reconciliation and combating organized crime but stressed that EU candidate status would first require the country to be "more co-operative towards independent Kosovo" and undertake judicial reform. Underscoring the problem were clashes between Kosovo border police and Serb protestors in June 2011, when the former attempted to establish Prishtina's control over parts of the northern border between Serb-inhabited Kosovo and Serbia. On August 23, 2011, the German chancellor, Angela Merkel, stated that Serbia must shut down the "parallel structures" of administration it operates in northern Kosovo before it could gain EU candidate status. Protests against the extension of Pristina's control into the Mitrovica region continued through August and September, leading to clashes between the protestors and KFOR personnel.

On August 25, President Tadić stated that Serbia's commitment to joining the EU does not come at the price of abandoning Kosovo and Metohija, leading to criticism from within his party and from allied parties that he risked the loss of EU candidacy status.

Corruption emerged as a prominent theme in the May 2012 legislative elections, with Deputy Prime Minister Aleksandar VUČIĆ leading the government's anticorruption efforts. A series of high-profile arrests were subsequently made, including the November 26, 2012, arrest of former minister of agriculture Saša DRAGIN and the December 12, 2012, arrest of Miroslav MIŠKOVIĆ, the richest businessman in Serbia. Both arrests were related to accusations of fraud in the privatization of state-owned companies.

POLITICAL PARTIES

For four-and-a-half decades after World War II, Yugoslavia's only authorized political party was the Communist Party, which was redesignated as the League of Communists of Yugoslavia (*Savez Komunista Jugoslavija*—SKJ) in 1952. Political control was also exercised by its "front" organization, the Socialist Alliance of the Working People of Yugoslavia (*Socijalistički Savez Radnog Naroda Jugoslavije*—SSRNJ). The collapse of Communist rule in 1989–1990 led to the formation of a large number of successor and other parties, including several "federal" groupings that sought, without success, to preserve the Yugoslav federation (see the 1994–1995 edition of the *Handbook,* p. 991).

Until late 2000, the dominant party in Serbia and at the federal level was Slobodan Milošević's Socialist Party of Serbia (SPS). Beginning in 1992 a number of opposition coalitions attempted to dislodge the SPS and its allies. The Democratic Movement of Serbia (*Demokratska Pokret Srbije*—Depos) was formed in May 1992 as an alliance whose principal members were the Serbian Renewal Movement (SPO), New Democracy (ND, subsequently the Serbian Liberals), and, following its separation from the Democratic Party (DS), Vojislav Koštunica's Democratic Party of Serbia (DSS). Depos quickly fractured, however, although the SPO and the ND, joined by the Civic Alliance of Serbia (GSS; see the Liberal Democratic Party, below), attempted to rejuvenate the alliance (dubbed Depos II) prior to the December 1993 Serbian Assembly election, in which it won 45 seats. In February 1994 the ND decided to support the Serbian government, and that, coupled with a move to the right by the SPO, brought an end to Depos.

In early 1996, the Together (*Zajedno*) coalition was established by the SPO, DS, and GSS, which were later joined by the Democratic Center (DC; see the DS, below) and, at the federal level, the DSS. The alliance captured a disappointing 22 seats in the federal poll of November 1996 but was far more successful in municipal elections later in the month, although the federal government did not acknowledge the victories for several months. Thereafter, with Serbian legislative elections approaching, relations between the SPO and its partners turned acrimonious, and in mid-1997 *Zajedno* collapsed.

A more inclusive Alliance for Change (*Savez za Promene*—SZP) originated in a June 1998 agreement by half a dozen parties to adopt a uniform opposition strategy. Among the initial participants were the DS, the GSS, and the Christian Democratic Party of Serbia (DHSS). Organizations joining later included the DC, the Democratic Party of Vojvodina Hungarians (DSVM), the New Serbia (NS), the Association of Free and Independent Trade Unions (*Asocijacija Slobodnih i Nezavisnih Sindikata*—ASNS), some 20 smaller parties, and various civic groups.

A smaller opposition grouping, the Alliance of Democratic Parties (*Savez Demokratskih Partija*—SDP), had been organized in October 1997 by the Alliance of Vojvodina Hungarians (SVM), the League of Vojvodina Social Democrats (LSV), the Reformist Democratic Party of Vojvodina (RDSV, subsequently the RVSP—see the Vojvodina Party, below), the Sandžak Coalition (KS), the Social Democratic Union (SDU), and the Šumadija Coalition (*Koalicija Šumadija*—KŠ).

The SZP and SDP, often in conjunction with the SPO, organized or participated in a number of anti-Milošević demonstrations and, beginning in September 1999, a series of opposition roundtables. These led to a January 10, 2000, meeting at which 16 opposition party leaders, spearheaded by the SPO's Vuk Drašković and the DS's Zoran Djindjić, committed their organizations to a joint strategy for forcing early elections. Following the July adoption by the Milošević-controlled Federal Assembly of constitutional changes permitting direct election of the president and the upper house, the opposition prepared for the September 24 federal elections by attempting to forge a comprehensive electoral alliance. Although the SPO and many less-influential parties ultimately chose to remain independent, the unification effort culminated in formation of the Democratic Opposition of Serbia (*Demokratske Opozicije Srbije*—DOS), which nominated the DSS's Koštunica for the presidency. By the time of the September balloting the DOS encompassed 18 parties (plus the ASNS), among them the DS, DSS, GSS, NS, and the 6 SDP parties. The DOS followed up its federal victories in September by winning 176 of the 250 seats in the December Serbian National Assembly election. By the time of the December 2003 Serbian election, however, the cumbersome DOS had dissolved.

For the May 2012 Serbian national election, 18 parties and coalitions offered party lists, down from 22 in May 2008. The leading coalition, **Let's Get Serbia Moving** (*Pokrenimo Serbiju*—PS), included as the principal participant Tomislav Nikolić's SNS. Other significant coalitions were formed by the SNS, United Pensioners of Serbia (PUPS), and United Serbia (JS); by G17 Plus and a group of regional parties; by the DS, Social Democratic Party of Serbia (SDPS), and LSV; and by the LDP and SPO. A 5 percent threshold for seats continued in effect except for ethnic minority parties, which needed only 0.4 percent of the vote to obtain a seat. Five such parties or coalitions won a total of 10 seats. A plethora of other minor organizations exist, many with a predominantly regional or ethnic character.

Government Parties:

Let's Get Serbia Moving (*Pokrenimo Serbiju*—PS). Formed in preparation for the 2012 legislative elections as a coalition among the SNS, NS, and a group of smaller parties that included Bogoljub KARIĆ's **Strength of Serbia Movement** (*Pokret "Snaga Serbije"*—PSS), the **Socialist Movement** (*Pokret Socijalista*—PS), **the Serbian Association of Small and Medium Companies and Entrepreneurs** (*Asocijacija Malih i Srednjih Preduzeća i Preduzetnika Srbije*—AMSPPS), **the Association of Refugees in Serbia** (*Stvaranje Udruženje Izbeglica u Srbiji*—SUIS), the **People's Peasant Party** (*Narodna Seljačka Stranka*—NSS), the **Bosniak People's Party** (*Bošnjačka Narodna Stranka*—BNS), the **Democratic Party of Macedonians** (*Demokratska Partija Makedonaca*—DPM), **the Roma Party** (*Romska Partija*—RP), the **Movement for the Economic Renewal of Serbia** (*Pokret Privredni Preporod Srbije*—PPPS), and the *Vlach Unity Movement* (*Uzdruženje Izbeglica u Srbiji*—UIS). The PS won 73 seats with 24 percent of the vote in the May 6, 2012, elections; in the subsequent distribution of seats, the PSS received 2 seats, and each smaller party (except the Vlach Unity Movement) received 1 seat. After the elections, the coalition was retained as a parliamentary group, with the exception of the NS, which formed its own group.

Serbian Progressive Party (*Srpska Napredna Stranka*—SNS). The SNS was formed in September 2008 by a group of SRS members, including about 20 members of the National Assembly, who broke with party policy because they supported greater European integration, including EU membership. The dissenters, led by former SRS presidential candidate Tomislav Nikolić, were expelled by the SRS leadership, prompting formation of a separate faction in the National Assembly, the Go, Serbia! (*Napred Srbijo*) floor group, and confirmation of their intention to establish a new "radical" party. Apart from the issue of closer ties to Western Europe, the SNS remains ideologically nationalistic, supporting the integrity of the state and rejecting independence for Kosovo. It also advocates military neutrality and support for ethnic Serbs throughout the former Yugoslavia.

In the coalition of PS's distribution of seats following the May 2012 legislative elections, the SNS received 55 seats in parliament. The SNS nominated Tomislav Nikolić as its candidate for the 2012 presidential elections. Nikolić won 25.1 percent of the vote in the first round on May 6 and won the second round on May 20 with 49.5 percent of the vote. Nikolić stood down as party leader on May 24.

Leaders: Tomislav NIKOLIĆ (President of the Republic; Former President of the Party), Aleksandar VUČIĆ (President of the Party), Jorgovanka TABAKOVIĆ (Vice-President); Nebojša SEFANOVIĆ (President of Parliament).

New Serbia (*Nova Srbija*—NS). The NS was organized following the expulsion of Čačak's controversial mayor, Velimir Ilić, from the SPO in 1998 and his subsequent departure from Serbia-Together (*Srbija-Zajedno*), an SPO offshoot.

The NS joined the Alliance for Change and then the DOS. In November 2003 Ilić ran third in the invalidated Serbian presidential election. A month later the NS and the SPO ran as a coalition in balloting for the Serbian legislature, with the NS being awarded nine seats.

In November 2006, the NS allied with the DSS in preparation for the 2007 National Assembly election, in which the NS won 10 seats. Ilić finished third, with 7.4 percent of the vote, in the first round of the 2008 presidential contest. In May it won 9 National Assembly seats and then formed its own floor group. Following the May 2012 election, it received 8 seats as part of the PS coalition and again formed its own floor group.

Leader: Velimir ILIĆ (President).

Socialist Party of Serbia (*Socijalistička Partija Srbije*—SPS). The SPS was formed in July 1990 by consolidation of the former League of Communists of Serbia and its associated Socialist Alliance. The party won 194 of 250 seats in the Serbian Assembly in December 1990, while its leader, Slobodan Milošević, defeated 30 other candidates in retaining the Serbian presidency with a 65 percent vote share. The SPS won a narrow majority (73 of 138 seats) in the federal Chamber of Citizens in May 1992. Following the imposition of UN sanctions on May 30, anti-Milošević social democrats within the party formed several splinter groups; however, Milošević remained firmly in charge and was reelected in December, when the party also retained its pluralities in both the federal and the republican assemblies.

Thereafter, the SPS moved closer to the ultranationalist SRS (below), with which it cooperated to oust President Ćosić from the FRY presidency in June 1993. Four months later the SRS terminated the relationship, prior to the Serbian legislative poll in December, in which the SPS won 123 seats. In late 1995, Milošević dismissed several hard-line nationalists in the SPS leadership who were critical of the Dayton peace accord. Subsequently, an SPS-led electoral alliance, the Joint List, dominated federal parliamentary elections in November 1996 as well as the September 1997 presidential and legislative elections in Serbia. The Joint List also included the ND and the Yugoslav Left (*Jugoslovenska Levica*—JUL), an umbrella grouping of some two dozen communist and other leftist organizations led by Mirjana MARKOVIĆ, Milošević's wife.

At the federal presidential election of September 2000 President Milošević finished second, with some 35–37 percent of the vote, although he refused to acknowledge his loss to the DOS's Koštunica until early October. In simultaneous parliamentary elections, the SPS-JUL alliance saw its seat total in the lower house drop to 44, while it won only 7 of Serbia's 20 seats in the newly elective upper house. Although the SPS continued to control the republican government and legislature in Serbia, the success of the DOS precipitated a premature dissolution of the Serbian National Assembly in late October and the swearing in of an interim coalition government of the SPS, DOS, and SPO, pending an election in late December. In the meantime, a defiant Milošević was reelected party chair at a party congress in November.

The erosion of public support for the SPS continued in the December 2000 Serbian Assembly balloting. The SPS won only 37 seats, in contrast to the 86 won in 1997 as part of the Joint List with the JUL and ND. In the December 2003 election, it won only 7.7 percent of the votes, good for 22 seats. Milošević, despite being on trial in The Hague, remained the SPS chair until his death in 2006.

Struggles over leadership of the SPS began after Milošević's death. The infighting undermined party unity in the assembly; this threatened the government, which depended on SPS support. In December 2006 the party elected Ivica Dačić over Milorad VUČELIĆ as successor to the late president. In the January 2007 election the SPS won just 5.6 percent of the vote and 16 seats. A year later, its presidential candidate, Milutin Mrkonjić, finished fourth, with 6.0 percent of the vote in the first round.

In the May 2008 legislative election the SPS ran in coalition with the **Party of United Pensioners of Serbia** (*Partija Ujedinjenih Penzionera Srbije*—PUPS) and the **United Serbia** (*Jedinstvena Srbija*—JS), winning 12 of the alliance's 20 seats. The PUPS won 5 seats and then established its own deputy group, led by Momo ČOLAKOVIĆ, in the National Assembly. The JS won 3 seats, while 1 seat went to an SPS electoral partner, the **Movement of Veterans of Serbia** (*Pokret Veterana Srbije*—PVS).

In the May 2012 legislative election, the SPS again ran in coalition with the PUPS and the JS; the coalition won 44 seats with 14.5 percent of the vote. The SPS won 24 seats, with 1 additional seat being allocated to the PVS, led by Saša DUJOVIĆ. The PUPS, led by Jovan KRKOBABIĆ, won 12 seats. The JS, led by Dragan MARKOVIĆ, won 7 seats. Both the PUPS and JS established their own deputy groups in parliament. In the 2012 presidential election, the coalition supported Dačić, who secured 14.2 percent of the vote in the first round, taking third place and failing to advance to the second round.

Leaders: Ivica DAČIĆ (Prime Minister and President of the Party), Slavica DJUKIĆ-DEJANOVIĆ (Minister of Health and Vice President of the Party), Milutin MRKONJIĆ (Minister of Transport and Vice President of the Party), Dijana BUKOMANOVIĆ (Vice President), Žarko OBRADOVIĆ (Minister of Education and Vice President of the Party), Branko RUŽIĆ (Chair, Executive Committee).

Social Democratic Party of Serbia (*Socijaldemokratska Partija Srbije*—SDPS). Formation of the SDPS was announced in August 2009 by Rasim Ljajić, minister of labor and social policy. Ljajić stated that the SDPS was an effort to unite various social democratic parties, including his own Sandžak Democratic Party, the Social Democratic Party (SDP) of Nebojša Čović, and the Independent Social Democrats (*Nezavisni Socijaldemokrata*—NSD), led by Zoran DRAGIŠIĆ. The SDPS was registered in October.

The SDP had been established in April 2002 by merger of one wing of Social Democracy (*Socijaldemokratija*—SD), led by Slobodan ORLIĆ, and the Social Democratic Union (SDU, below), led by Žarko KORAĆ. The SD-SDU merger proved short-lived: In March 2003 the SDU was reestablished as a separate party, with the rump group retaining the SDP name. (In June 2002 the SD wing loyal to party founder Vuk OBRADOVIĆ had won title to the SD name in the courts.)

In October 2003 the SDP withdrew its support for the DOS-led Serbian government, which contributed to the collapse of the government and accelerated the alliance's disintegration. In the December 2003 parliamentary election the SDP candidates joined the G17 Plus electoral list, winning three seats.

In September 2004, Nebojša Čović's Democratic Alternative (*Demokratska Alternativa*—DA) merged into the SDP. The DA, dating from 1997, had participated in the Alliance for Change but departed and formed the DAN Coalition with the New Democracy and the Democratic Center (see DS, above) in late 1999 before joining the DOS in 2000. In the December 2003 Serbian legislative election, the DA won only 2.2 percent of the vote and no seats.

In August 2005, Prime Minister Koštunica asked the SDP to leave the government after two of its three assembly members voted against privatization of the state oil and gas company. Party chair Čović, who had been serving as head of the Serbia and Montenegro Coordination Center for Kosovo, was then dismissed, and the party formally entered the opposition. Minister of Labor Slobodan LALOVIĆ sided with the government and left the party. In 2007 the SDP joined forces with the PUPS (see under SPS, above), but the coalition won only 3.1 percent of the vote and therefore failed to meet the threshold for representation.

The NSD was established by Zoran Dragišić, a security analyst, in January 2008. The new party drew most of its members from what remained of the SD, then led by Nanad VUKASOVIĆ.

In 2009, the SDPS fully merged with the **Sandžak Democratic Party** (*Sandžačka Demokratska Partija*—SDP). The SDP was founded as a result of factional strife within the Sandžak SDA (see Leading Sandžak Parties, below) and was founded in October 2000. It participated unsuccessfully in the 2003 Serbian legislative election, although Ljajić as leader of the SDP received a cabinet position in 2006 (see the 2012 *Handbook* for details). In 2007, running on the DS list, the SDP was awarded three National Assembly seats. It received four in 2008 as part of the ZES.

In 2012, the SDPS joined the Choice for a Better Life coalition (see IzBZ, below). The coalition won 67 seats with 22.1 percent of the vote, the SDPS subsequently receiving 9 of those seats. The SDPS subsequently left the coalition and joined the SNS-led government in July 2012, forming its own progovernment deputy group.

Leaders: Rasim LJAJIĆ (Deputy Prime Minister, Minister of Foreign and Domestic Trade, Telecommunications and Information Society, and President of the Party), Miodrag MIJATOVIĆ (Leader of Deputy Group).

Government-Supportive Parties:

Serbian Renewal Movement (*Srpski Pokret Obnove*—SPO). The SPO was founded in March 1990 as a merger of four parties, most notably those led by Vojislav Šešelj and Vuk Drašković. In less than three months, however, internal squabbling led to the departure of Šešelj to found a new party, the SRS (below). Without Šešelj the SPO moderated its extreme nationalism and participated in the Depos coalitions in 1992 and 1993. During this time, Drašković spoke out against war crimes, and as a result, he and his wife Danica were arrested and allegedly beaten by Serbian police. Following the disappointing showing of *Zajedno* in the 1996 federal election, the SPO was the sole opposition party to contest the 1997 Serbian elections for both parliament and the presidency, finishing third in both contests.

In January 1999 Drašković joined Prime Minister Bulatović's government as a deputy prime minister, but his show of national solidarity ended three months later when comments made contrary to policy led to his dismissal. The other three SPO ministers immediately resigned.

In 2000 the SPO remained aloof from the DOS alliance—a move that Drašković subsequently acknowledged as a mistake. In the September elections the SPO won only one upper house seat, while its presidential candidate, Vojislav Mihajlović, the mayor of Belgrade, took only 3 percent of the vote. In the December election for the Serbian assembly, the SPO won less than 4 percent of the vote and no seats. Drašković subsequently voiced support for reestablishing Serbia as a constitutional parliamentary monarchy.

For the 2003 Serbian legislative election, the SPO joined forces with New Serbia, winning 13 of the coalition's 22 seats (based on a 7.7 percent vote share). Intraparty differences led in 2005 to formation of the Serbian Democratic Renewal Movement (SDPO, below) by 9 of the SPO's deputies. In 2007 the SPO list, which included members of the Serbian Liberals and the People's Peasant Party (below), won only 3.3 percent of the vote and thus no National Assembly seats. In the May 2008 election, the SPO ran as part of the ZES and was awarded 4 seats.

The SPO joined the Turn Around electoral coalition (below) for the May 2012 legislative elections, winning four seats. Following the election, it left the alliance and formed a deputy group with the DHSS. In September 2013 the SPO-DHSS supported the new cabinet proposed by Ivica Dačić, although the parties did not join the government.

Leader: Vuk DRAŠKOVIĆ (President).

Christian Democratic Party of Serbia (*Demohrišćanska Stranka Srbije*—DHSS). The DHSS dates from 1997, when a dispute with Vojislav Koštunica led a number of DSS members to leave the party under the former DSS vice president, Vladan BATIĆ. He subsequently served as coordinator of the Alliance for Change and as a principal leader of the DOS.

At the December 2003 Serbian legislative election, the DHSS headed the Independent Serbia *(Samostalna Srbija)* list, which won 1.1 percent of the vote. In 2007 DHSS candidates were included on the coalition list headed by the LDP and GSS; the DHSS was awarded one seat.

In February 2008 the DHSS blamed the Koštunica government for instigating the Belgrade riots ("an act of state terrorism") that followed Kosovo's unilateral declaration of independence. In May the party again ran on the LDP list, with Batić claiming the party's sole seat.

In May 2010 the My Serbia Movement (*Pokret Moja Srbija*) merged with the DHSS. The My Serbia Movement had participated in the 2008 elections but failed to gain seats.

The DHSS joined the Choice for a Better Life electoral coalition (see below) in the 2012 legislative election, securing one seat. Following the elections, however, it formed a deputy group with the SPO (above).

Leader: Olgica BATIĆ (President).

Opposition Parties:

Choice for a Better Life (*Izbor za Bolji Život*—IzBZ). Announced on March 16, 2012, this coalition formed around the Democratic Party, the Social Democratic Party of Serbia (see SDPS, above), the Christian Democratic Party of Serbia, the League of Social Democrats of Vojvodina (LSV; see Leading Vojvodina Parties, below), The Greens of Serbia (*Zeleni Srbije*—ZS), the Democratic Alliance of Croats in Vojvodina (DSHV; see Leading Vojvodina Parties, below), and the Original Serbian Renewal Movement (*Izvorni Srpski Pokret Obnove*—ISPO). The ISPO, led by Srdjan SREĆKOVIĆ, was formed in February 2012 by a faction of the SPO (see below). The IzBZ won 67 seats with 22.1 percent of the vote in the May 6, 2012, parliamentary election. In the subsequent allocation of seats, the DS received 49 seats, the SDPS 9, the LSV 5, and the ZS, DHSS, DSHV, and ISPO 1 seat each. The SDPS subsequently broke with the coalition in the negotiations over the new government, while the DHSS formed a deputy group with the SPO (see above).

Democratic Party (*Demokratska Stranka*—DS). The descendant of a post–World War I governing democratic party, the DS was revived in December 1989 and held a constituent convention in February 1990. A centrist party committed to a democratic multiparty system, human rights, and a free press, the DS boycotted the May 1992 Federal Assembly election. Its reluctance to join the opposition coalition Depos in 1992 resulted in a party split, with the departing faction, the DSS, joining the alliance. Building on its modest success in the December 1992 balloting, the DS won 29 Serbian Assembly seats a year later as the party's turn toward nationalism won it surreptitious support from the Milošević-run media. At the head of the nationalist faction was Zoran Djindjić, who led the electoral campaign and in 1994 was elected party president.

The party returned to active opposition in 1996 by joining *Zajedno.* The SPO's withdrawal in mid-1977 meant the demise of *Zajedno,* and the DS boycotted the 1997 Serbian elections. In 1998 Djindjić joined a number of other opposition politicians in announcing formation of the Alliance for Change (SZP). In 2000 Djindjić was a leading participant in the formation of the DOS as well as coordinator of the SZP. As prime minister of Serbia, he led the more reform-minded majority within the DOS, often in opposition to his chief rival, Vojislav Koštunica of the DSS. Djindjić was assassinated on March 12, 2003. A week later Zoran Živković was confirmed as prime minister.

Following the breakup of the DOS, the DS ran independently in the Serbian legislative election of December 2003, although various candidates from other parties, including the Civic Alliance of Serbia (GSS, below) and the DC, were included on the DS electoral list. The DS's Boris Tadić was elected president of Serbia in June 2004.

In January 2005, the DC merged into the DS. Following its formation in 1995, the DC had participated in both the Depos and the *Zajedno* opposition alliances before forming the DAN Coalition (*Koalicija DAN*) in late 1999 with New Democracy (*Nova Demokratija*—ND; renamed the Serbian Liberals [*Liberali Srbije*—LS] in 2003) and the Democratic Alternative (DA; see the SDP, below). All three DAN parties then joined the DOS in 2000. The DC's Mićunović ran as the DOS candidate in the invalidated Serbian presidential election of November 2003, finishing second. In the 2003 Serbian National Assembly election, five DC candidates on the DS electoral list were awarded seats.

Following the separation of Serbia and Montenegro, and with an eye toward the growing popularity of the SRS, Tadić backed a call for early elections. In the January 2007 election the DS list won 64 seats, including 3 awarded to the Sandžak Democratic Party and 1 to the Democratic Alliance of Croats in Vojvodina (both below). It then formed a coalition government with the DSS, the NS, and G17 Plus. Tadić later confirmed his intention to seek reelection as president in January 2008. Although he finished second to the SRS candidate in the first round, with 35.4 percent of the vote, he won the February runoff, with 50.3 percent.

Following the withdrawal of the DSS from the government in March 2008 and the consequent dissolution of the National Assembly, the DS formed the ZES coalition to contest the May legislative election, in which its list won 64 of the alliance's 102 seats.

Following the May 6, 2012, parliamentary elections, the DS received 49 seats from the 67 won by the IzBZ coalition. As presidential candidate, Tadić took first place in the first round of the presidential election with 25.3 percent but lost the second round with 47.3 percent to 49.5 percent for Tomislav Nikolić. In August, dissatisfaction with election results led elements of the party, including Deputy President Dragan Djilas, to call for significant reforms by the leadership or risk a split. Tadić stepped down as party leader in November, and a party congress the same month elected Djilas as party leader.

Leaders: Dragan DJILAS (President; Mayor of Belgrade), Boris TADIĆ (Former President of the Republic; Honorary President of the Party), Mirko CVETKOVIĆ (Former Prime Minister), Bojan PAJTIĆ (Vice President), Balsa BOZOVIĆ (Secretary General).

Democratic Party of Serbia (*Demokratska Stranka Srbije*—DSS). The DSS was established shortly before the December 1992 election by a dissident faction of the Democratic Party that wished to join the Depos opposition bloc in that contest. Under Vojislav Koštunica it later swung further to the right than its parent.

Standing on its own in the December 1993 Serbian Assembly election, the DSS won seven seats. Although a constituent of the *Zajedno* alliance in the November 1996 election, in which it won four seats, the DSS ran separately in some municipalities in the subsequent local balloting. Like the DS, it boycotted the 1997 Serbian elections.

In August 2000, Koštunica emerged as the consensus DOS presidential candidate to oppose Slobodan Milošević, and he was declared the winner of the September election in early October. Subsequently, the conservative Koštunica had differences with the DOS majority, not least over the handling of Milošević.

In August 2001, the DSS withdrew from the Serbian government, which it accused of failing to address the problem of organized crime. Relations with the DOS and, more specifically, the DS continued to worsen thereafter, and in December the DSS's Dragan Maršićanin was forced out as speaker of the Serbian National Assembly after being accused of vote rigging. With the rivalry between DS leader Djindjić and Koštunica heating up, the DSS in effect withdrew from the DOS.

Koštunica was denied the Serbian presidency in 2002 when a low voter turnout invalidated elections in October and December. Having led the DSS to a second-place finish, with 17.7 percent of the vote and 53 seats, in the Serbian legislative election of December 2003, he was confirmed as the head of a minority government in March 2004. For the December election the DSS had included on its electoral list a handful of candidates from several small parties, including the People's Democratic Party (*Narodna Demokratska Stranka*—NDS), led by Slobodan VUKSANOVIĆ, which then merged into the DSS in October 2004.

In November 2006, looking toward the January 2007 general election, the DSS formed an alliance with New Serbia (below). The coalition won 47 seats, including the DSS's 33 and the NS's 10. Also awarded 2 seats each on the DSS-NS list were the Serbian Democratic Renewal Movement (SDPO, below) and the United Serbia (see SPS, above). For the January 2008 presidential contest the DSS supported Velimir Ilić of the NS. In May 2008 a coalition of the DSS and the NS won 30 seats (21 for the DSS) on an 11.6 percent vote share. The DSS, adamantly opposed to Kosovo's independence and its recognition by the majority of EU members, joined the opposition.

In the May 6, 2012, election, the DSS won 21 seats with 7.0 percent of the vote. Koštunica secured 7.4 percent of the vote in the first round of the presidential election, taking fourth place and failing to advance to the second round.

Leaders: Vojislav KOŠTUNICA (Former Prime Minister of Serbia and President of the Party), Dragan JOČIĆ (Vice President).

United Regions of Serbia (*Ujedinjeni Regioni Srbije*—URS). This political coalition was founded on May 16, 2010 by G17 Plus, Together for Šumadija, and six smaller parties: the **People's Party** (*Narodna Partija*—NP), the **Coalition for Pirot** (*Koalicija za Pirot*—KZP), **I Live for Krajina** (*Živim za Krajinu*—ZZK), the **Bunjevac Party** (*Bunjevačka Partija*—BP), the **Sandžak People's Party** (*Sandžačka Narodna Partija*—SNP), and the **Vlach People's Party** (*Vlaška Demokratska Stranka*—VDS). In the May 6, 2012, parliamentary election, the URS won 16 seats with 5.5 percent of the vote; in the subsequent distribution of seats, G17 Plus received 10, the ZZS 2, the NP 2, and the ZZK and KZP each won 1 seat. In June 2012, the NP was expelled from the coalition after it was revealed they were negotiating a coalition agreement with the Democratic Party.

The NP subsequently, however, has formed a progovernment deputy group along with the Party of Democratic Action Sandžak (see Leading Sandžak Parties, below) and the **Rich in Serbia** (*Bogata Serbija*—BS).

In the 2012 presidential election, the URS supported Zoran STANKOVIĆ of the G17 Plus. In the first round, he secured 6.6 percent of the vote, placing fifth and failing to advance to the second round.

G17 Plus. The G17 Plus originated in a think tank of reform-minded, nonparty economists that participated in the FRY and Serbian cabinets following the ouster of Slobodan Milošević. It was established as a political party in December 2002 under the leadership of Miroljub Labus, former FRY deputy prime minister and presidential candidate of the DS. In the December 2003 election for the Serbian National Assembly the G17 Plus electoral list finished fourth, with 11.5 percent of the vote and 34 seats, including 3 that went to members of the Social Democratic Party (SDP, below). The G17 Plus then joined the minority Koštunica government.

After the EU, dissatisfied with Belgrade's failure to capture war crimes suspects, suspended negotiations on a preaccession agreement, G17 Plus leader and Deputy Prime Minister Mladjan Dinkić protested the government's inaction by withdrawing his party from the government on October 1, 2006, although the G17 Plus ministers remained in place pending a new election. In the January 2007 voting the party saw a steep decline in its support, winning only 6.8 percent of the vote and 19 seats. In May 2008, as part of the ZES, it took 21 seats.

The G17 floor group in the National Assembly includes three additional deputies who were elected on the ZES list: one nonparty member and two members of the **Together for Šumadija** (*Zajedno za Šumadiju*—ZZS), a regional party led by Veroljub STEVANOVIĆ, the mayor of Kragujevac and a former copresident of the Serbian Democratic Renewal Movement (SDPO). The ZZS members had been associated with the Together for Kragujevac (*Zajedno za Kragujevac*—ZZK) civic movement until formation of the ZZS in May 2009.

Leaders: Mladjan DINKIĆ (President), Suzana GRUBJEŠIĆ (Leader of Deputy Group and Vice President of the Party), Verica KALANOVIĆ, Snežana Samardzić MARKOVIĆ (Vice Presidents).

Together for Šumadija (*Zajedno za Šumadiju*—ZZS). Originally formed as part of the *Zajedno* coalition, this group won the 1996 local elections in Kagujevac, the fourth-largest city in Serbia. By 2002, it had evolved into a regional party, **Together for Kragujevac** (*Zajedno za Kragujevac*—ZZK). The party platform stresses economic revival, membership in the EU, and decentralization of government power—decrying what it terms the "Belgradization" of Serbia and subordination of regional interests to those of the capital. In 2008, the party received two parliamentary seats as part of a coalition with G17 Plus and subsequently was refounded as the ZZS on June 10, 2008. In 2012, it again received two seats as part of the URS.

Leader: Veroljub STEVANOVIĆ.

Turn Around (*Preokret*). The origins of the coalition Turn Around (also often translated as "Turnover") lie in a joint statement by the LDP, SPO, and SDU on November 5, 2011. The text argued that the government will have to adopt new policies (e.g., "turn around" policy) given the reality of Kosovo's secession if Serbia is to obtain EU membership and criticized the government as indulging in anti-European hysteria. On March 11, 2012, a formal coalition between the three parties was announced, which further included **Rich Serbia** (*Bogata Srbija*—BS), led by Zaharije TRNAVCEVIĆ**; the Association of Free and Independent Trade Unions** (*Asocijacija Samostalnih i Nezavisnih Sindikata*—ASNS), led by Ranka SAVIĆ; the **Vojvodina Party** (see Leading Vojvodina Parties, below); the Democratic Party of Sandžak (SDA Sandžak; see Leading Sandžak Parties, below) **the Green Ecological Party-Green** (*Zelena Ekološka Partija-Zeleni*—ZEPZ); and **the Party of Bulgarians from Serbia** (*Partija Bugara Srbije*—PBS). In the May 6, 2012, parliamentary election, Turn Around won 19 seats with 6.5 percent of the vote; in the subsequent distribution of seats, the LDP received 11 seats, the SPO 4, the SDU 1, the BS 1, the ASNS 1, with 1 seat allocated to a nonparty candidate. The SPO subsequently formed a deputy group with the DHSS, and the BS formed a group with the NP, with the remaining deputies in an LDP-led group.

Liberal Democratic Party (*Liberalno Demokratska Partija*—LDP). The LDP was formed in 2005 by a dissenting faction of the DS following the ouster from the leadership of the LDP's founder, Čedomir Jovanović. It ran in the 2007 legislative election in coalition with the Civic Alliance of Serbia (*Gradjanski Savez Srbije*—GSS), the Social Democratic Union (SDU, below), and the League of Social Democrats of Vojvodina (LSV, below). The coalition won 15 seats, 5 of which were assigned to the LDP. In April 2007 the GSS merged into the LDP.

The GSS, founded in 1992 by antiwar activist Dr. Vesna PEŠIĆ, never achieved notable success in the polls despite participating in Depos, *Zajedno,* the Alliance for Change, and the DOS. In December 2003 GSS candidates for the Serbian legislature ran on the DS electoral list, ending up with five seats. In the following year a number of GSS leaders, including the party's president, Goran SVILANOVIĆ, resigned and joined the DS.

In the 2008 presidential election, Jovanović finished with 5.3 percent of the vote. In May the LDP list won 5.2 percent of the National Assembly vote, for 13 seats, including 1 for the SDU and 1 for the Christian Democratic Party of Serbia (below).

The LDP received 11 seats in the distribution by the Turn Around coalition following the May 6, 2012, parliamentary election. Jovanović was again nominated for the 2012 presidential election, receiving 5.0 percent of the vote in the first round, placing sixth.

Leaders: Čedomir JOVANOVIĆ (President); Nenad MILIĆ (Deputy President); Nastaša MIĆIĆ, Ivan ANDRIĆ, Dusan MIJIĆ, Dušica ANDJELKOVIĆ (Vice Presidents).

Social Democratic Union (*Socijaldemokratska Unija*—SDU). The SDU was formed by a former associate of the Civic Alliance, Žarko Korać. He was also linked to the student-led Resistance (*Otpor*), which repeatedly took to the streets in opposition to the Milošević regime. The SDU participated in the DOS alliance in 2000.

Following an abortive merger with a wing of Social Democracy in 2002, the SDU reemerged as a separate party in March 2003. In the December 2003 Serbian National Assembly election its candidates ran on the DS electoral list, ending up with one seat. In 2007 it competed in coalition with the LDP, GSS, and LSV and was awarded one seat. In 2008, once again allied with the LDP, it again received one seat.

Leader: Žarko KORAĆ (President).

In addition to those already mentioned above, three ethnic minority parties and an ethnic minority coalition won seats in the May 2012 legislative election. The **Alliance of Vojvodina Hungarians** (SVM; see below, under Vojvodina Parties) won 5 seats. **None of the Above** (*Nijedan od Ponudjenih Odgovora*—NOPO), a party representing the Vlach minority, won 1 seat. The **Coalition of Albanians from the Preševo Valley** (*Koalicija Albanaca Preševske Doline*—KAPD) won 1 seat. The KAPD had been formed by two ethnic parties based in the southern localities of Preševo, Bujanovac, and Medvedja: the **Democratic Action Party** (*Partija za Demokratskoe Delovanje/Partia për Veprim Demokratik*—PDD/PVD), led by Riza HALIMI, and the **Democratic Union of the Valley** (*Demokratske Unije Doline*—DUD), led by Skender DESTANI. In 2007, the two were the first ethnic Albanian parties to contest a national election since 1993. The coalition **All Together** (*Sve Zajedno*—SZ) was formed by the **Bosniak Democratic Union**, **Civil Alliance of Hungarians**, **Democratic Union of Croats**, **Democratic Fellowship of Vojvodina Hungarians**, and **Slovak Party** and won 1 seat.

Other Parties That Contested the 2012 Election:

Serbian Radical Party (*Srpska Radikalna Stranka*—SRS). Founded in 1991 and runner-up to the SPS in the federal lower house elections of May and December 1992, the SRS advocates a "Greater Serbia." It withdrew its support of the SPS at both the republican and federal levels in September 1993 and mounted a campaign to undercut the ruling party in the run-up to the 1993 legislative election, in which, however, its representation dropped from 73 to 39 seats.

In 1994 the SRS abolished its paramilitary wing, the Serbian Chetnik Movement, following charges that it was guilty of war crimes in Croatia during 1991 and 1992. It was also implicated in the Bosnia and Herzegovina conflict. Party leader Vojislav Šešelj was given a four-month prison sentence in September 1994 for repeated acts of violence in the assembly. In opposition to his continuing leadership, party dissidents left to form a new party, the Radical Party of the Left Nikola Pašić (*Radikolna Stranka Levice Nikola Pašić*—RSLNP), but had no success in the polls.

In the November 1996 federal election SRS lower house representation slipped further, to 16 seats. In the first runoff of the 1997 Serbian presidential election, Šešelj appeared to have beaten SPS candidate Zoran Lilić, but due to a low turnout the election was invalidated. Šešelj ultimately lost to new SPS candidate Milan Milutinović in December, though the official count and turnout levels were questionable. In the parliamentary election, the SRS, attacking Milošević as the cause of Serbia's woes, finished a strong second with 82 seats. As a result, the SPS approached the SRS about joining the Serbian government, with Šešelj being named a deputy prime minister in March 1998. The SRS was the only prominent Serb party to reject the June 1999 Kosovo peace plan.

At the federal level, the SRS 2000 presidential candidate, Tomislav Nikolić, finished third, with 6 percent of the vote, while the party captured only 5 seats in the lower house and 2 in the upper. In the December 2000 Serbian National Assembly election the SRS finished third, with 23 seats, a loss of 59.

In February 2003, Vojislav Šešelj surrendered to ICTY authorities to face charges that included crimes against humanity from 1991 to 1995. In December, with the DOS having dissolved, the SRS won a leading 27.6 percent of the vote and 82 seats in the National Assembly, far outdistancing the second-place DSS. Although the victory also gave the SRS a plurality of 30 indirectly elected seats in the new state union assembly, the party was unable to muster enough additional support to form a government in Serbia. Nikolić finished first in the June 2004 first-round voting for president of Serbia but was defeated in the second round, winning 46 percent of the vote.

In November 2006, in the midst of a four-week hunger strike, Vojislav Šešelj refused to appear at the opening of his trial in The Hague. A month earlier, the SRS had reelected him as leader. In January 2007 the SRS again emerged from the legislative election with a plurality, 81 seats based on a 28.6 percent vote share.

In late December 2007, the SRS absorbed the Serbian Unity Party (*Stranka Srpskog Jedinstva*—SSJ), an ultranationalist group launched prior to the December 1992 election, with the reported support of President Milošević, as a counter to the SRS. Its leader, Željko RAŽNJATOVIĆ ("Arkan"), a commander of the paramilitary Tigers group, had been linked in press reports to a variety of atrocities in Bosnia and Croatia. In March 1999 the ICTY announced that it had sent Belgrade a warrant for Arkan, who was killed by masked gunmen in January 2000. The hard-line stance of the SSJ won it 14 seats in the December 2000 Serbian Assembly election. In 2003 it ran under the banner of the unsuccessful ZNJ electoral list (see People's Peasant Party, above). Its chair, Borislav PELEVIĆ, ran for president in 2004.

In the January 2008 presidential race, Nikolić again led after the first round but lost in the runoff, with 48 percent of the vote. In the May National Assembly election, the SRS increased its vote share to 29.5 percent but won 3 fewer seats, finishing second to the ZES coalition. Four months later the party split over the issue of EU integration. Nikolić and others who supported eventual EU membership were expelled from the SRS, having been branded by Šešelj as traitors and "Western puppets." The departure of Nikolić and his supporters, including the SRS's general secretary, Aleksandar Vučić, reduced the SRS contingent in the National Assembly to 57 seats. In late September Nikolić formed the Serbian Progressive Party (SNS, above).

In July 2009, the ICTY sentenced Vojislav Šešelj to 15 months in jail for contempt of court after he revealed the identities of three protected witnesses. He was charged with contempt a second time in February 2010 and a third time in July 2011. As of October 2011 his trial for crimes against humanity had not concluded, delayed in part due to Šešelj's apparent poor health and to repeated accusations that Šešelj has publicly revealed the names of prosecution witnesses.

In the May 2012 parliamentary election, the SRS won 4.63 percent of the vote, failing to clear the threshold and winning no seats in parliament. Jadranka ŠEŠELJ, wife of the party leader, was the SRS's presidential candidate in the May 2012 presidential election, winning 3.78 percent of the vote and failing to advance to the second round.

Leaders: Vojislav ŠEŠELJ, Dragan TODOROVIĆ (Acting Chair), Gordana POP-LAZIĆ.

Other unsuccessful parties/electoral lists contesting the May 2012 election included Branimir NEŠIĆ's **Doors** (*Pokret Dveri*—PD), Zoranom DRAGIŠIĆEM's **Movement of Workers and Peasants** (*Pokret Radnika i Seljaka*—PRS), the **Communist Party** (*Komunistička Partija*—KP), and Milan VIŠNJIĆ's **Reformist Party** (*Reformistička Stranka*—RS).

Leading Sandžak Parties:

Party of Democratic Action Sandžak (*Stranka Demokratske Akcije Sandžaka*—SDA Sandžak). Linked to the Party of Democratic Action in Bosnia and Herzegovina, the ethnically Bosniac SDA has distinct organizations based in the Albanian/Muslim communities of the Sandžak region (in southwestern Serbia, adjacent to Montenegro), Montenegro, Preševo, and Kosovo.

In 1995 conflicts between factions led by the chair of the SDA Sandžak, Sulejman Ugljanin, and by the party's secretary general, Rasim Ljajić, fragmented the group into five similarly named Sandžak parties. Ugljanin would continue at the head of what he deemed the "true" SDA Sandžak and organized a three-party coalition, the Sandžak List Dr. Sulejman Ugljanin (*Koalicija "Lista za Sandžak Dr. Sulejman Ugljanin"*—LZS), which won a seat in the November election for the federal legislature and three seats in the Serbian Assembly in 1997. In 2000 Ljajić's SDA Sandžak adopted the name Sandžak Democratic Party (SDP; see SDPS, above), which remains the principal regional rival of Ugljanin's SDA.

For the 2003 Serbian election various participants in the Sandžak List, including the **Bosniac Democratic Party of Sandžak** (*Bošnjačke Demokratske Stranke Sandžaka*—BDSS), led by Esad DŽUDŽEVIĆ, and Bajram OMERAGIĆ's **Social Liberal Party of Sandžak** (*Socijalno-Liberalna Stranka Sandžaka*—SLSS), were included on the DS party list. In 2007 the Sandžak List, which won two National Assembly seats, also included the **Sandžak Reformists** (*Reformisti Sandžaka*—RS). In 2008, the LZS was renamed the **Bosniac List for a European Sandžak** (*Bošnjačka Lista za Evropski Sandžak*), which again won two seats, one for the BDSS and one for the SLSS.

Ugljanin, who accepted appointment to the Cvetković cabinet after the 2008 election, has also chaired the Bosniac National Council of Sandžak (*Bošnjačko Nacionalno Vijeće Sandžaka*—BNVS), which claims to be the highest representative body of Bosniacs in the region.

In the May 6, 2012, election, the SDA Sandžak won two seats in parliament as a minority list.

Leader: Sulejman UGLJANIN (President).

Leading Vojvodina Parties:

League of Vojvodina Social Democrats (*Liga Socijaldemokrata Vojvodine*—LSV). The moderate left-wing LSV was a founding member of the Vojvodina Coalition (see the Vojvodina Party, below) and continues to support autonomy for the region. The party competed in the September election as part of the DOS alliance.

In 2004 the LSV led formation of the **Coalition "Together for Vojvodina"** (*Koalicija "Zajedno za Vojvodinu"*), which won seven seats in that year's Vojvodina Assembly election. After the election the LSV joined the DS-led provincial government. For the 2007 National Assembly election the LSV ran in coalition with the LDP, GSS, and SDU and claimed four seats.

For the May 2008 National Assembly election, the LSV ran as part of the ZES, winning five seats. For the provincial election, however, it again led a Together for Vojvodina Coalition, which won six seats.

The LSV was part of the IzBZ coalition (see above) in the May 2012 election, receiving five seats in the subsequent distribution.

Leaders: Nenad ČANAK (Chair), Bojan KOSTREŠ (Deputy Chair).

Alliance of Vojvodina Hungarians (*Savez Vojvodjanskih Madjara/Vajdasági Magyar Szövetség*—SVM/VMSZ). Founded in 1994 as an offshoot of the DZVM (below), this minority party won 3 seats in the 1996 federal election and 4 in the 1997 Serbian election. It joined the DOS in 2000 but nevertheless offered a separate candidate list in several constituencies, winning 1 lower house seat in the September federal election and, in conjunction with the DOS, an overwhelming majority of seats in the Vojvodina Assembly election of September–October. In the 2004 provincial election the SVM finished third, with 11 seats, far behind the DS's 38 and the SRS's 35. It suffered similar losses in local council elections but joined in forming a DS-led provincial government.

In the 2007 national election, the SVM won 3 seats. In May 2008, the party ran at the national and provincial levels as part of the **Hungarian Coalition** (*Madjarska Koalicija*—MK) along with the DZVM and the DSVM (below). The MK won 4 National Assembly seats and 9 in the 120-member Vojvodina Assembly, where the ZES won a majority. In January the SVM's chair, István Pásztor, had won 2.3 percent of the first-round vote for president.

In the May 6, 2012, parliamentary election, the SVM won 5 seats from the minority list (with 1.8 percent of the national vote).

Leaders: Jósef KASZA (Honorary President), István PÁSZTOR (President), Károly PÁL (Executive Vice President).

Democratic Community of Vojvodina Hungarians (*Demokratska Zajednica Vojvodjanskih* Madjara/*Vajdasági Magyarok Demokratikus Közössége*—DZVM/VMDK). The DZVM was formed in 1990 to represent the interests of the ethnic Hungarian population of Vojvodina. In the December 1993 regional elections the DZVM leader, Andraš Agošton, disclosed that proautonomy Hungarian organizations in Vojvodina had been financed from Hungary. Agošton was replaced as chair in 1996 and organized the DSVM (below) in 1997. Remaining aloof from the DOS, the party failed to win any seats in the Vojvodina Assembly election in September–October 2000.

For the 2007 national election, the DZVM joined forces with the DSVM in the Coalition of Hungarian Unity (*Koalicija Madjarska Sloga*—KMS), which won less than the 0.4 percent threshold for minority parties. In May 2008 it competed as part of the MK. The party's longtime leader, Sándor PÁL, died in July 2010.

Leader: Aron ČONKA (Chair).

Democratic Party of Vojvodina Hungarians (*Demokratska Stranka Vojvodjanskih Madjara/Vajdasági Magyar Demokrata Párt*—DSVM/VMDP). The DSVM was formed in 1997 by András Ágoston, former chair of the DZVM. The party did not join the DOS in 2000. It won one Vojvodina Assembly seat in 2004. It joined the DZVM in 2007's KMS alliance and in 2008 participated in the MK.

Leader: András ÁGOSTON.

Democratic Alliance of Croats in Vojvodina (*Demokratski Savez Hrvata u Vojvodini*—DSHV). Founded in 1990, the DSHV represents the small ethnic Croat minority in Vojvodina. For the 2004 Vojvodina election it cooperated with the SVM. In the January 2007 National Assembly election its candidates ran on the DS list and received one seat. In 2008, running with the ZES, it again claimed 1 seat. In 2012, it again claimed one seat, running with the IzBZ.

Leader: Petar KUNTIĆ (Chair).

Vojvodina Party (*Vojvodjanska Partija*—VP). Formation of the Vojvodina Party was accomplished in June 2005 by the merger of half a dozen small parties, including the Reformists of Vojvodina–Social Democratic Party (*Reformisti Vojvodine–Socijaldemokratska Partija*—RVSP), the Vojvodina Civic Movement (Vojvodjanski *Gradjanski Pokret*—VGP), and the Vojvodina Coalition (*Koalicija Vojvodina*—KV). A principal goal of the new formation was full autonomy for the province.

At the 2007 National Assembly election, the VP headed a Coalition "Vojvodina Parties" (*Koalicija "Vojvodjanske Partije"*) that failed to win representation. In 2008, running independently, it took only 0.1 percent of the vote. In 2012, it ran as part of the Turn Around coalition but received no seats.

Leader: Igor KURJAČKI.

Kosovo Parties:

Ethnic Albanian parties in Kosovo uniformly refused to participate in national elections, and most ethnic Serb parties in Kosovo have boycotted Kosovar elections. The Kosovo parliamentary and local elections held on December 12, 2010, saw 28 parties and "citizens initiatives" and 1 coalition competing, including an assortment of Serb and other minority parties vying for reserved minority seats. The **Democratic Party of Kosovo**, led by former Kosovo Liberation Army head Hashim THAÇI, won a plurality of 34 seats in the Assembly of Kosovo. The **Democratic League of Kosovo,** led by President Fatmir SEJDIU, finished second, with 27 seats. Other parties passing the 5 percent minimum threshold for proportional seats were *Vetëndosje,* taking 14; the **AAK,** which claimed 8; the **New Kosovo Coalition,** with 8, and the **SLS,** winning 8. Eleven minority parties split the remaining 17 seats. The election saw a considerably larger number of Kosovo Serbs participating than in the past.

For a full discussion of these and other parties, see the entry on Kosovo.

Other Ethnic or Regional Parties:

In the 2007 National Assembly election, the **Roma Party** (*Romska Partija*—RP), led by Šajn SRDJAN, and the **Union of Roma in Serbia** (*Unija Roma Srbije*—URS), led by Rajko DJURIĆ, each received one seat. Neither was successful in May 2008. The URS did not compete in the 2012 elections, but the RP received one seat in 2012 as part of the PS coalition (see above). The ethnically based **Montenegrin Party** (*Crnogorska Partija*—CP), led by Nenad SATEVOVIĆ, also competed in the 2012 elections.

LEGISLATURE

The **Serbian National Assembly** (*Narodna Skupština Srbije*) comprises 250 members elected to four-year terms by proportional representation. In general, party lists must meet a 5 percent threshold to qualify for seats, except that minority parties are awarded a seat for each 0.4 percent of the vote they receive. In the most recent election, held May 6, 2012, the Let's Get Serbia Moving coalition won 73 seats (Serbian Progressive Party, 55; New Serbia, 8; Strength of Serbia

Movement, 2; Socialist movement, 1; Serbian Association of Small and Medium Companies and Entrepreneurs, 1; Association of Refugees in Serbia, 1; People's Peasant Party, 1; Bosniak People's Party, 1; Democratic Party of Macedonians, 1; Roma Party, 1; Economic Renewal of Serbia, 1; the Choice for a Better Life coalition won 67 seats (Democratic Party, 49; Social Democratic Party of Serbia, 9; League of Social Democrats of Vojvodina, 5; Greens of Serbia, 1; Democratic Alliance of Croats in Vojvodina, 1; Christian Democratic Party of Serbia, 1; Original Serbian Renewal Movement, 1); the coalition Socialist Party of Serbia (SPS), Party of United Pensioners of Serbia (PUPS), United Serbia (JS), 44 (SPS, 25 [including 1 assigned to the Movement of Veterans of Serbia]; PUPS, 12; JS, 7); the Democratic Party of Serbia, 21; the coalition Turnover, 19 (the Liberal Democratic party, 11; the Serbian Renewal Movement, 4; the Social Democratic Union, 1; Rich Serbia, 1; the Association of Free and Independent Trade Unions 1; nonparty, 1); the coalition United Regions of Serbia, 16 (G17 Plus, 10; Together for Šumadija, 2; the People's Party, 2; the Coalition for Pirot, 1; I Live for Krajina, 1); the Alliance for Vojvodina Hungarians, 5; the Party of Democratic Action of Sandžak, 2; the coalition All Together, 1; None of the Above, 1; the Coalition of Albanians from the Preševo Valley, 1.

President: Nebojša SEFANOVIĆ.

CABINET

[as of September 15, 2013]

Prime Minister	Ivica Dačić (SPS)
First Deputy Prime Minister for Defense, Security, the Fight against Corruption and Crime	Aleksandar Vučić (SNS)
Deputy Prime Ministers	Jovan Krkobabić (PUPS) Rasim Ljajić (SDPS)
Ministers	
Agriculture, Forestry, and Water Management	Dragan Glamočić (Ind.)
Culture and Media	Ivan Tasovac (Ind.)
Defense	Nebojsa Rodić (SNS)
Education, Science and Technological Development	Tomislav Jovanović (Ind.)
Energy, Development and Environmental Protection	Zorana Mihajlović (SNS) [f]
Engineering and Urbanism	Velimir Ilić (NS)
Finance	Lazar Krstić (Ind.)
Foreign Affairs	Ivan Mrkić (Ind.)
Foreign and Domestic Trade and Telecommunications	Rasim Ljajić (SDPS)
Health	Slavica Dukić-Dejanović (SPS) [f]
Interior Affairs	Ivica Dačić (SPS)
Justice and Public Administration	Nikola Selaković (SNS)
Labor and Social Policy	Jovan Krkobabić (PUPS)
Natural Resources, Mining, and Spatial Planning	Mila Bacević (SNS)
Regional Development and Local Self-Government	Igor Mirović (SNS)
Sport and Youth	Vanja Udovičić (Ind.)
Transport	Aleksandar Antić (SPS)
Without Portfolio	Sulejman Ugljanin (SDA) Aleksandar Vulin (SNS) Branko Ružić

[f] = female

INTERGOVERNMENTAL REPRESENTATION

Ambassador to the U.S.: Vladimir PETROVIĆ.

U.S. Ambassador to Serbia: Michael D. KIRBY.

Ambassador to the UN: Feodor STARČEVIĆ.

IGO Memberships (Non-UN): CEUR, EBRD, ICC, IOM, OSCE.

SEYCHELLES

Republic of Seychelles
Repiblik Sesel
République des Seychelles

Political Status: Independent member of the Commonwealth since June 29, 1976; present constitution approved by referendum of June 18, 1993.

Area: 171 sq. mi. (429 sq. km).

Resident Population: 90,024 (2012E—U.S. Census); some 30,000 Seychellois live abroad, mainly in Australia and the United Kingdom.

Major Urban Center (2011E): VICTORIA (27,000).

National Languages: Creole, English, French.

Monetary Unit: Seychellois Rupee (market rate November 1, 2013: 12.02 rupees = $1US).

President: James Alix MICHEL (Seychelles People's Progressive Front); elevated (from vice president) to the presidency on April 14, 2004, following the retirement of France Albert RENÉ (Seychelles People's Progressive Front); directly elected in balloting of July 28–30, 2006, and sworn in for a five-year term on August 1; formed new government on July 1, 2010; reelected in multiparty balloting on May 19–21, 2011, and sworn in for a second five-year term on May 23.

Vice President: Daniel FAURE (Seychelles People's Progressive Front), appointed by the president on June 8, 2010, and sworn in on July 1 to succeed Joseph BELMONT (Seychelles People's Progressive Front), who retired on June 30; reelected with the president on May 19–21, 2011, and sworn in on May 23, for a term concurrent with that of the president.

THE COUNTRY

The Seychelles archipelago consists of some 115 islands in the Indian Ocean about 600 miles northeast of Madagascar. More than 85 percent of the population is concentrated on the largest island, Mahé, which has an area of approximately 55 square miles (142 sq. km); most of the remainder is distributed between the two northern islands of Praslin and La Digue. Most Seychellois are of mixed French-African descent and adhere to Roman Catholicism. There are small minority groups of Indians and Chinese. Nearly 98 percent of adult women are classified as "economically active," largely in subsistence agriculture; women are more likely than men to be literate.

Tourism is a significant source of national income and employs about 30 percent of the labor force. Small-scale industries provide about one-quarter of GDP, while the fishing sector produces about 30 percent of export earnings. The economy is also underpinned by a growing offshore banking sector. There has been cautious hope of finding oil, with a U.S. firm awarded a bid to drill south of the islands in 2005.

In 2001 the Seychelles agreed to make changes and was added to the list of Organization for Economic Cooperation and Development (OECD) countries committing to eliminating harmful tax practices.

Following the Indian Ocean tsunami in December 2004, the Paris Club canceled Seychelles's debt. The government began soliciting foreign investment for the tourism sector and promoted the Seychelles as a provider of offshore financial services, but the International Monetary Fund (IMF) reported there was little activity in that area due to the lack of financial supervision. The IMF cited an "urgent" need for banking reforms and legislation to criminalize the financing of terrorism.

Post-tsunami recovery, slow at first, peaked in 2007 with GDP growth of 10 percent, thanks to foreign investment in tourism. However, in 2008–2009, GDP contracted by an annual average of 1 percent due to increasing international oil prices and, subsequently, as the result of the global financial crisis and a related decline in tourism. In December 2009, the IMF approved $31 million under a stand-by arrangement to

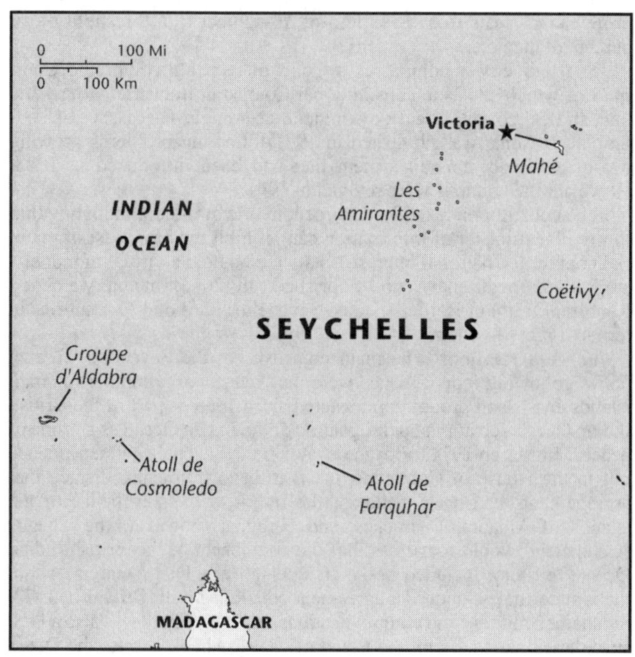

support Seychelles's economic program in 2010–2012. Annual growth for 2010 was 5.6 percent, reflecting a rebound in tourism. In 2011 Seychelles was set to receive a $5.5 million installment as part of a three-year economic program. The IMF commended authorities for modernizing the tax system, including progress toward initiating a value-added tax in 2012. The IMF completed its fourth review of the finance program in January 2012, allowing for the disbursement of an additional $4.7 million.

In 2012, the IMF revised down its GDP growth forecast for the Seychelles's economy to 2.8 percent from the 4.9 percent forecast in 2011, citing a slowdown in tourism due to the 2010 European debt crisis. Tensions in the oil markets and depreciation of the Euro against the dollar also contributed to negative growth, the IMF said. In April 2012, the World Bank announced a $21 million Country Partnership Strategy with the Seychelles, designed to reduce the country's vulnerability to economic shocks, and in October, the IMF extended the support program until December 2013. Slight recovery in 2013 brought GDP growth of 3.2 percent, with inflation of 4.6 percent. Unemployment was 3.3 percent.

GOVERNMENT AND POLITICS

Political background. Following a half-century of French rule, the Seychelles became a British possession under the Treaty of Paris in 1814. Originally administered from Mauritius, it became a Crown Colony in 1903. A partially elected governing council was established in 1967, and limited self-government under a chief minister was introduced in 1970. Following a constitutional conference in London in March 1975, the legislative assembly established in 1970 was increased from 15 to 25 members, the 10 new members being nominated by the two parties in the government coalition. Concurrent with the achievement of independence on June 29, 1976, the former chief minister, James R. MANCHAM, was designated president, and the former leader of the opposition, France Albert RENÉ, became prime minister.

On June 5, 1977, while the president was attending a Commonwealth conference in London, the government was overthrown in a near-bloodless coup that installed René as the new head of state. In balloting on June 23–26, 1979, conducted under a single-party socialist constitution adopted on March 26, René was confirmed in office for a five-year term. After assuming power, President René encountered a series of external and internal challenges to his authority.

In November 1979, he announced the discovery of an antigovernment plot "sponsored from abroad" that allegedly involved ousted president Mancham and a force of mercenaries based in Durban, South Africa. About 85–100 people were arrested in the wake of the allegations including the head of the country's immigration service. A potentially more serious threat was averted in November 1981 with the detection at Mahé's Pointe Larue airport of a group of mercenaries led by the celebrated Col. Michael ("Mad Mike") Hoare, an Irishman who had been involved in a number of African destabilization efforts during the previous two decades. In the course of a pitched battle with units of the Seychelles People's Defence Force (SPDF), some 45 of the invaders commandeered an Air India Boeing 707 and ordered the pilot to fly them to Durban, where they eventually surrendered to South African police. Released on bail in early December, the mercenaries were rearrested on January 5, 1982, in the wake of mounting international criticism. Most were given modest jail sentences under the South African Civil Aviation Offenses Act, Colonel Hoare ultimately being released in May 1985.

In August 1982, some 150 lower-ranked members of the SPDF seized key installations on Mahé in an abortive protest against alleged ill-treatment by senior military officials, while in September 1986 a number of army officers loyal to the minister of defense, Col. Ogilvy BERLOUIS, were charged with plotting to assassinate the president. In London, the exiled Seychelles National Movement (*Mouvement National Seychellois*—MNS) claimed knowledge of the 1986 plot, saying that the principals had been divided as to its implementation; subsequently, Colonel Berlouis resigned his post and left the country for Britain.

Despite exile opposition calls for a boycott, President René was reelected by a reported 92.6 percent of the vote on June 17, 1984, after having announced that those failing to participate would lose their right to public assistance. The National Assembly was subsequently replenished in single-party balloting on December 5, 1987, while the president was accorded a third term on June 9–11, 1989. Over the next two years, President René made tentative steps toward political change.

In November 1990, President René commented favorably on the possibility of a reform referendum, although with reference only to the conduct of intraparty affairs. In March 1991 he was further reported to favor limited administrative decentralization through the reestablishment of district councils, whose members would, however, have to be supporters of the ruling Seychelles People's Progressive Front (SPPF).

On September 12, 1991, the assembly approved a Local Government Bill that provided for the multiple candidature, one-party election of local councils, whose heads were to meet with the Central Committee of the SPPF to rule on the desirability of a referendum on constitutional revision. However, in a remarkable turnabout on December 3, an extraordinary SPPF congress (meeting with the council heads elected two days earlier and identified as constituting a new assembly) voted unanimously to endorse an unexpected proposal by René to introduce a pluralist system. Under the plan, opposition parties would be permitted to register by January 1992 and a Constituent Committee would be elected by proportional representation in July to draft a new constitution. The president had also called on political exiles to return to the Seychelles, provided they retract their "accusations" against his regime.

In the Constituent Committee balloting on July 26, 1992, the SPPF won 14 seats on the basis of a 58.4 percent vote share, while the Democratic Party (DP) of former president Mancham was awarded 8 seats on the basis of a 33.7 percent share; no other groups secured representation.

The DP eventually boycotted the following constitutional proceedings after accusing the SPPF of "bulldozer tactics," and the SPPF delegation (which constituted a quorum) continued alone. On October 6, the opposition set out specific objectives, which included the termination of links between the SPPF and the armed forces and a halt to state funding for the SPPF.

In the face of opposition criticism, the draft constitution secured the approval of only 53.7 percent of the votes cast (60 percent being needed for acceptance) at the referendum of November 15, 1992. The DP thereupon returned to the Constituent Committee and participated in the approval on May 7, 1993, of a revised draft that received popular endorsement by 73.6 percent of participating voters on June 18 (For more on the 1992 constitution, see the 2012 *Handbook*.)

New presidential and assembly elections were held on March 20–22, 1998, with President René and the SPPF again winning by convincing margins. René was reelected with 67 percent of the vote, 7 points higher than he had scored in the 1993 election; in addition, James MICHEL, whom René had appointed as vice president the previous year, was elected as René's running mate. René's nearest competitor was Rev. Wavel RAMKALAWAN, leader of the United

Opposition (UO), who secured 20 percent of the vote, while former president Mancham of the DP finished with 14 percent. The DP also fared poorly in the assembly balloting, winning only one seat (down from the five they had held previously). Meanwhile, the SPPF, with 30 legislative seats, improved its total by 3 from 1993; the UO became the main opposition party, such as it was, with 3 assembly seats.

Following the approval by the National Assembly in 2000 of a constitutional amendment allowing the president to call presidential elections separately from legislative elections, René called for an early presidential poll on August 31–September 2, 2001. Once again facing Ramkalawan (representing the Seychelles National Party [SNP], as the UO had been renamed), René was reelected with 54.19 percent of the vote. Ramkalawan, however, significantly improved his vote share to 44.95 percent, partly because of Mancham's decision not to run. The cabinet announced by René on September 5 included reshuffled assignments but no new members.

In October 2002, the assembly voted to dissolve and hold new legislative balloting on December 4–6. Although the SPPF retained its majority (23 of 34 seats on a 54 percent vote share), the SNP improved from 3 to 11 seats (on a 40 percent vote share).

President René, citing the fact that he was "getting older," resigned the presidency on March 31, 2004, and Michel was inaugurated as his successor on April 14. Joseph BELMONT, a cabinet member since 1982, was confirmed as vice president by the assembly on April 16. Initial objection to Michel's appointment on behalf of the SNP subsided and his leadership was accepted. An opposition (SNP) motion to dissolve the assembly to allow for parliamentary elections at the same time as presidential balloting in 2006—a year ahead of schedule—was rejected by the full body in May 2006. Presidential elections subsequently were held July 28–30, 2006, in which the incumbent Michel and running mate Vice President Belmont garnered 53.7 percent of the votes, defeating the SNP's Ramkalawan and running mate Annette GEORGES (45.7 percent of the vote), and independent Philippe BOULLÉ (0.6 percent). A reshuffled cabinet was sworn in on August 9, 2006.

Following a violent confrontation with police in October 2006 over a law banning political parties and religious groups from owning radio stations, the 11 opposition legislators boycotted parliament, and their five-month absence prompted President Michel to dissolve the National Assembly in March 2007, setting the stage for early legislative elections on May 10–12. The SNP on March 27 formed an electoral alliance with the DP. The ruling SPPF retained its 23-seat majority with a 57 percent vote share; the DP-SNP coalition won 11 seats on a vote share of 43 percent. The president reshuffled the cabinet on July 3.

On June 8, 2010, the president announced a major reshuffle of the cabinet and named a new vice president, Daniel FAURE, in light of the retirement of Vice President Belmont at the end of June after more than 40 years of public service. The new, restructured government and the new vice president took office on July 1, following approval by the National Assembly.

President Michel was reelected in balloting on May 19–21, 2011, (several days were set to accommodate the distances across the archipelago) with 55.4 percent of the vote, defeating perennial candidate Wavel Ramkalawan, who secured 41.4 percent. Philippe Boullé was a distant third with 1.7 percent, followed by the DP's Ralph VOLCERE with 1.5 percent. The president and Vice President Faure were sworn in on May 23, 2011.

President Michel dissolved the National Assembly in July 2011 after the SNP boycotted most the assembly's sessions. The SNP, the NDP, and the Seychelles Freedom Party also boycotted the resulting legislative elections to protest the systematic use of state resources by the ruling party. Consequently, the SPPF won all 31 directly elected seats and 6 of the 7 proportional seats. The newly formed Popular Democratic Movement (PDM) gained the remaining proportional seat (see Current issues, below).

President Michel announced a restructuring of ministries on February 29, 2012, and named a reshuffled cabinet on March 7, appointing several new ministers and creating the Ministry of Tourism and Culture. Former Indian archipelago central bank governor, Pierre LAPORTE, was appointed Minister of Finance.

Constitution and government. The 1993 constitution provides for a multiparty presidential system, under which the chief executive is elected for a thrice-renewable five-year term. Legislative authority is vested in a unicameral National Assembly. Constitutional amendments introduced in July 1996, following their adoption by an SPPF congress in late May, created the post of vice president and also increased the number of directly elective seats in the assembly from 22 to 25, while reducing the proportional seats to a maximum of 10 subject to a threshold of 10 percent of the vote.

The judiciary encompasses a Court of Appeal, a Supreme Court (part of which sits as a Constitutional Court), an Industrial Court, and magistrates' courts. Local government, seemingly necessary for geographic reasons, was abolished in 1971 following problems growing out of a district council system that had been introduced in 1948. However, the councils were revived in 1991.

The constitution provides for freedom of expression, though within limits. The minister of information can prohibit the broadcast of material counter to "national interest." State media hold a virtual monopoly, as private media have not flourished. In 2013, media watchdog Reporters Without Borders ranked Seychelles 93rd of 179 countries in terms of press freedom.

Foreign relations. The main objectives of the Seychelles foreign policy following independence were the "return" of a number of small islands and island groups administered since 1965 as part of the British Indian Ocean Territory and designation of the Indian Ocean as a "zone of peace." In March 1976, prior to debate on the Seychelles independence bill in the House of Commons, the British government indicated that arrangements had been made for the return to the Seychelles of the islands of Aldabra, Desroches, and Farquhar; however, the Chagos Archipelago would remain as the sole component of the British Indian Ocean Territory. Included in the archipelago was Diego Garcia, where the United States, under an agreement concluded with Britain in 1972, maintained military and communications facilities. There was also a U.S. space-tracking station on the island of Mahé, where, despite the Diego Garcia issue, relations between American personnel and the Seychellois were relatively cordial. In July 1989, while visiting Washington, President René agreed to a five-year extension of the station's lease, which in 1984 provided 5 percent of the state's revenue. In 1995 Washington announced it was closing the Mahé station in a cost-cutting move and transferring its activity to a new facility on Diego Garcia.

Relations between the Seychelles and South Africa were by no means enhanced as a result of the 1981 coup attempt on Mahé. Colonel Hoare and the other defendants, tried under air piracy charges, argued that South Africa's National Intelligence Service (NIS) had full knowledge of the plot, and the trial judge conceded that it would be naïve to assume otherwise as one of the mercenaries was a former NIS agent. South African Prime Minister P. W. Botha did not dispute this finding but argued that "neither the South African Government, the Cabinet, nor the State Security Council" had been informed and that, therefore, no authorization had been given. Significantly, 34 of the mercenaries convicted on the air piracy charges were given time off for good behavior and released on November 27, 1982, after spending only four months in prison. But, by early 1992, relations between the two countries had warmed, permitting the establishment of consular and trade (though not ambassadorial) relations.

In mid-1988, the Seychelles established diplomatic relations with Mauritius and the Comoros. The three, along with Madagascar and France (representing Réunion), are members of the Indian Ocean Commission (IOC) set up in 1982 to promote regional cooperation and economic development.

Relations with the United States cooled in 1996 following the closure of the U.S. embassy in Victoria (responsibility for the Seychelles transferring to the U.S. ambassador to Mauritius). In addition, a U.S. State Department report in March criticized the Seychelles's human rights record, referring to the ruling party's "pervasive system of political patronage and control over government jobs, contracts, and resources." In the wake of increasing global terrorist attacks, the United States in 2005 pledged continued support to the Seychelles military. Washington reportedly valued the Seychelles geographical location for transit for U.S. shops, though also viewed the islands as a potential transfer point by terrorists seeking access to Africa.

Although the Seychelles agreed to a regional free trade pact with the European Union (EU) in 2007, it was one of several African countries that in 2008 rejected participation in a free trade zone and a customs union as proposed by the Common Market for Eastern and Southern Africa (Comesa).

In 2009 the Seychelles allowed EU troops on the islands and expanded its military cooperation with the United States, China, France, and the United Arab Emirates in intensified efforts to combat piracy (see Current issues, below). Strengthened relations with China, which the Seychelles had been fostering for several years, led to China's pledging $6 million for development projects in the islands in May 2010.

China announced in December 2011 that it would accept the Seychelles's offer of establishing a naval refueling port on Mahé (China's first overseas military base) to support its antipiracy operations. In 2011, China and Seychelles also renewed a defense agreement signed in 2004, under which China provides training and equipment to Seychellois military personnel.

In 2011, Seychelles signed an agreement with Denmark to fight piracy in the Indian Ocean, and with international support, the country remained a hub for combating piracy (see Current issues, below).

In February 2012, India and Seychelles signed a pact to install a surveillance system in the Seychelles's exclusive economic zone to combat piracy and terrorism. India has since deployed several ships to the Seychelles, and the two nations are discussing further bilateral cooperation in defense, including the training of experts and police. In April, India signed a $75 million credit line and grant agreement with the Seychelles.

Seychelles joined the Combined Maritime Forces, an antipiracy alliance of 26 countries. Seychelles and Qatar in November 2012 iterated an interest in strengthening ties between the two countries.

In April 2013, Seychelles granted asylum to Sakhr el-Materi, son-in-law of deposed Tunisian leader Zine al-Abidine Ben Ali, who was convicted of corruption in absentia in Tunisian court. Seychelles did not comply with Tunisian extradition requests, claiming that there were no conditions for a free and fair trial.

Current issues. Vice President Belmont chaired a constitutional review committee in 2008. Though officials sought public comments for the review, they indicated that any amendments would be approved by the National Assembly rather than made subject to a popular referendum.

Attention turned in 2009 to the growing problem of piracy, the Seychelles having arrested more than a dozen suspected pirates early in the year. Indian and European naval forces joined the Seychelles's coast guard in antipiracy efforts in the Indian Ocean. Reports late in the year indicated that hijackings had increased, despite the deployment of what had now become an international armada in coastal waters. By 2010, the Seychelles had become a hub for antipiracy action as it boosted surveillance with the help of the U.S. government in providing an unarmed aerial vehicle.

The constitution review panel, chaired by Francis CHANG-SAM, turned its recommendations in to President Michel in April 2010, and the president subsequently asked the attorney general to begin the process to update the charter. The government posted the review on its Web site and invited the public to submit comments. The authorities said a national consultation exercise would be conducted in 2011.

In July 2010—in the first such ruling in the islands—the government sentenced 11 Somali pirates to 10 years in jail for attacking a coast guard vessel inside territorial waters. Piracy continued to be a high-priority issue in 2011, when the Seychelles changed its laws to allow pirates captured anywhere beyond its territorial waters to be prosecuted. In February, 10 Somalis who had seized a fishing boat with seven Seychellois on board in November 2010 were sentenced to 20 years in jail on two counts of piracy. The Somalis were sent back to Somalia in accordance with an agreement between the two countries.

Following his reelection to a second term in May 2011, President Michel called for a bipartisan effort toward a "new Seychelles." Though some opposition members claimed there were electoral violations, the polling was declared free and fair by observers, who recommended equal access to the state media by all candidates.

Due to a boycott of the legislative elections, the SPPF initially won all the seats in the National Assembly, prompting concern from other parties and observers about the country returning to one-party rule. The newly formed People's Democratic Movement, founded by former SNP member Daniel Pierre in August 2011, won 9.6 percent of votes nationwide, but the Electoral Commission declared this was not enough to claim a proportionally allocated seat. The MDP contested the outcome and was eventually awarded the seat by the Court of Appeals, a decision that was criticized by the SPPF. The SNP and the other political parties called for electoral reform as proposed by the Electoral Commission. In May 2012, the first piece of legislation for the Electoral Reform Process was sent to the Cabinet. The proposed Public Assembly Act would eliminate the current requirement that political parties request permission from the Commissioner of Police before holding a meeting; parties still, however, would be required to notify the Commissioner five days in advance.

The island nation continued to be a venue for prosecuting piracy in 2012. In January, 15 Somali pirates who had hijacked an Iranian ship were captured by the U.S. Navy and, in March, were transferred from Djibouti to the Seychelles to stand trial.

Meanwhile, in two separate incidents, in December 2011 and April 2012, U.S.-operated unarmed aerial vehicles (or "drones") crashed near or on the Seychelles. U.S. officials said unmanned aerial vehicles are being operated from the island to track pirates in the Indian Ocean.

In January 2013, Seychelles won an award recognizing its efforts toward protection of the ozone layer. The Seychelles was among the first countries to ratify the Montreal Protocol.

Following a two-year moratorium, the Seychelles reopened bidding for oil and gas exploration rights in its exclusive economic zone in June 2013. Meanwhile, antipiracy efforts have continued through 2013, with a conviction of 11 pirates, likely of Somali origin, in October.

POLITICAL PARTIES

Prior to the 1977 coup, government was shared by the centrist Seychelles Democratic Party (SDP), led by President James R. Mancham, and the left-of-center Seychelles People's United Party (SPUP), headed by Prime Minister France René. Following the coup, René stated that the SDP "has not been banned, it has simply disappeared." The government-supportive Seychelles People's Progressive Front (SPPF) was the sole legal party from June 1978 until January 1991, following which other parties, including Mancham's Democratic Party, were recognized. Provision was also made for the financial support of parties from public funds.

Government Party:

Seychelles People's Progressive Front—SPPF (*Front Populaire Progressiste des Seychelles*—FPPS). The SPPF was organized in early 1978 as successor to the SPUP. (It is also referred to as *Parti Lepep* after it changed its name to People's Party in 2009.) Like its predecessor, it advocated a broad spectrum of "progressive" policies while attempting to cultivate relations with Catholic clergy sympathetic to its approach to social issues. Upon the retirement of Secretary General Guy SINON in May 1984, President René was named to succeed him as head of an expanded secretariat of 13 members, René's former position as party president being abolished.

Delegates to the party's congress in 1991 approved a Central Committee declaration that "the SPPF believes in the one-party system and in the socialist option" but left open the possibility of a future referendum on multipartyism. It also endorsed revival of an earlier system of party-controlled elective district councils, prior to approving a return to political pluralism at an extraordinary congress in December (see Political background, above). René was reelected as party chair during the annual SPPF conference on April 3, 2005, even though many observers had expected him to vacate the post following his resignation as president of the republic in 2004.

In June 2009, upon the 45th anniversary of the party's founding, René relinquished party leadership to President Michel. Finance minister Daniel Faure, who later became vice president, was elected secretary general.

Leaders: James Alix MICHEL (President of the Republic and President of the Party), Daniel FAURE (Vice President of the Republic, Secretary General of the Party), Joseph BELMONT (Former Vice President of the Republic), France Albert RENÉ (Former President of the Republic and Chair of the Party).

Opposition Parties:

Seychelles National Party (SNP). The SNP is the successor to the United Opposition (UO), which changed its name at a July 1998 congress. The UO had been formed by the three parties immediately below to oppose the 1993 constitution in both its original and final forms. Its candidate, Philip BOULLÉ, ran a distant third in the presidential balloting of July 23, and the party won only one proportionally allocated seat. Boullé retired from politics in 1995 (see National Alliance Party, below), during the party's first convention in September 1995 at which its member of parliament, Rev. Wavel Ramkalawan, defeated Gabriel Hoareau of the MNS for the party presidency. Ramkalawan finished second in the 1998 presidential election with 20 percent of the vote. The UO won three seats in parliament, making it the leading opposition group, and Ramkawalan was reelected as party leader during the July 1998 congress, when the party adopted the SNP rubric.

In the 2001 presidential election, Ramkalawan received 45 percent of the vote in his loss to René.

While relations between Ramkalawan and René appeared to improve during the 2002 parliamentary elections, government forces launched a crackdown on an SNP demonstration in July 2003. The SNP subsequently won 11 seats in the December 2002 legislative elections.

Ramkalawan, with a 45.7 percent vote share and an endorsement by the DP, failed to defeat James Michel in the July 2006 presidential election. In October 2006 Ramkalawan reportedly was among those arrested during a demonstration protesting a law banning political parties and religious groups from owning radio stations. In March 2007 the SNP and the DP formed an electoral alliance with the DP for the May legislative elections, the coalition retaining 11 opposition seats.

Following published attacks on SNP leaders, the party's secretary general Roger Mancienne, who owned a printing company, stopped printing the DP's newspaper, *Le Nouveau Seychelles Weekly*, which he said his company had agreed to publish "in support of freedom of expression and the work of the opposition." The newspaper's editor responded that those involved in politics should be ready to accept criticism.

Ramkalawan again failed in his bid for the presidency in 2011, when Michel was reelected. Following Michel's reelection, Ramkalawan called for a boycott of the 2011 National Assembly elections over "deficiencies in political and electoral conditions," and some former members of the party broke away to form the Popular Democratic Movement (PDM) in order to field an opposition to the ruling SPPF (see below).

Leaders: Rev. Wavel RAMKALAWAN (President of the Party and 1998, 2001, 2006, and 2011 presidential candidate), Bryan JULIE (Treasurer), Nicolas PREA (Secretary General).

Seychelles Party (*Parti Seselwa*—PS). Led by Jean-François Ferrari, son of Maxime FERRARI (former foreign minister and leader of the RPSD, see below), and formerly referenced most frequently by its French rubric, *Parti Seychellois,* the free enterprise-oriented PS was, prior to its legalization, the domestic clandestine affiliate of the RPSD/UDF (see below). Jean-François Ferrari, publisher of the opposition weekly *Regar,* was among those arrested in the July 2003 crackdown.

Leaders: Rev. Wavel RAMKALAWAN, Jean-François FERRARI (Secretary).

Seychelles National Movement (*Mouvement National Seychellois*—MNS). The MNS was originally formed in Brussels in 1984 as an affiliate of the MPR (below).

Leaders: Gabriel (Gaby) HOAREAU (President), Robert FRICHOT (Vice President), Terry SANDAPIN (Secretary).

National Alliance Party—NAP. The NAP was organized in early 1992 by Philippe Boullé and Kathleen Pillay, a former UDF (see below) leader. Boulle later ran as the UO's presidential candidate in balloting in 1993 and announced his retirement in 1995 from active politics. However, he ran as an independent candidate in presidential balloting in 2001, securing only 0.86 percent of the vote, and again in 2006, winning a mere 0.56 percent. In 2011 he secured 1.7 percent of the vote, again as an independent candidate.

Leader: Kathleen PILLAY (Secretary).

Democratic Party—DP. The DP was legalized in March 1992 as a revival of the former SDP. Its leader, Sir James Mancham, returned from exile on April 12, 1992. Subsequently, the DP and the SPPF were viewed as the country's two principal political "currents."

Mancham was reelected party leader at an extraordinary party congress on March 18, 1995, from which his intraparty opponents were excluded. DP dissident Christopher Gill, expelled for complaining about Mancham's "tightfisted" control, founded the short-lived New Democratic Party in 1995 before joining the SPPF in 1997, despite his previous criticism of the René government. The DP secured only one seat in the 1998 elections, while Mancham won only 14 percent of the vote in the Presidential election. The DP lost its seat in the National Assembly in the 2002 election, polling only 3.1 percent. Mancham retired as party leader in January 2005, although he subsequently was reportedly involved in planning a conference of opposition leaders designed to promote "reconciliation."

In 2006 the DP supported the SNP's Ramkalawan in the presidential election (DP members being assured of several ministerial posts if Ramkalawan were elected). In 2007 the DP contested the National Assembly elections in a coalition with the SNP, winning 11 seats.

In March 2009 it was reported that Ralph Volcere was elected party president following the resignation of Paul CHOW. The Party changed its name to New Democratic Party in June 2009 but is distinct from Gill's New Democratic Party. Following the 2011 presidential election, in which Volcere finished a distant fourth with just 1.5 percent of the vote, he offered to resign as party president, but the party's executive committee rejected the offer, and Volcere remained party leader. The DP boycotted the 2011 National Assembly elections.

Leaders: Ralph VOLCERE (Party President), Sir James R. MANCHAM (Former President of the Republic), Nichol GABRIEL (Secretary).

Popular Democratic Movement—PDM. Registered with the Electoral Commission in August 2011, the PDM (initially named the Popular Democratic Party) was hurriedly formed by breakaway members of the SNP following the party's boycott of the 2011 National Assembly elections. The PDM was the only opposition party that fielded candidates and was awarded one proportionally elected seat.

Leaders: David PIERRE (Party Leader and Former Deputy Secretary General of the SNP), Francheseca MONNAIE (Secretary General).

Seychelles Freedom Party—SFP. The SFP was registered in August 2011. It was founded by Christopher GILL, formerly of the Democratic Party (see also DP, above). In the mid-1990s, Gill formed a breakaway New Democratic Party but then later joined the SPPF in 1997. Gill tried to register the party under the name Mouvman Seselwa Rasin (Seychelles Roots Movement), but the name was deemed too xenophobic by authorities. The SFP campaigns against what it perceives as unfair rights and privileges, like tax breaks and land ownership enjoyed by wealthy foreigners. The party has been accused of inciting racism. Gill's SFP, along with the SNP and DP, boycotted the 2011 National Assembly elections and, like the SNP, pushes for electoral reform and the de-linking of the state and the ruling party.

Leader: Christopher GILL (Party Leader).

Other Parties and Groups:

The only other party to present candidates in the 2002 assembly balloting was the **Social Democratic Alliance**, which fielded one candidate. However, several independent candidates contested the elections.

A British-based organization known simply as the **Resistance Movement** (*Mouvement pour la Résistance*—MPR) appeared to have been implicated in the November 1981 coup attempt, while a South African-based **Seychelles Popular Anti-Marxist Front** (SPAMF) announced late in the year that it had known of the mercenary effort but had declined to participate on the ground that it was unworkable. A third group, the **Seychelles Liberation Committee** (*Comité de la Libération Seychelles*—CLS) was launched in Paris in 1979. In November 1985 MPR leader Gérard HOAREAU was assassinated outside his London residence by an unknown assailant. Former president Mancham charged the René government with the killing, which was vehemently denied by a spokesperson for the Seychelles embassy.

During a speech before a House of Commons committee in February 1990 Mancham invited all of the exile groups to join him in a **Crusade for Democracy in Seychelles** (CDS) and subsequently called for the formation of an opposition **United Democratic Front** (UDF). A less conservative London exile, former foreign minister Maxime Ferrari, displayed ambivalence toward the Mancham overture and in December 1990 launched a **Rally of the Seychelles People for Democracy** (*Rassemblement du Peuähple Seychellois pour la Démocratie*—RPSD) that, somewhat unrealistically, appeared to seek common ground between Mancham and René. Ferrari returned to the Seychelles in 1991.

LEGISLATURE

The unicameral **National Assembly** (*Assemblée Nationale*) has 25 directly contested seats from 25 single-member constituencies, plus up to 10 seats allocated on a proportional basis to parties winning at least 10 percent of the vote. (A party gets one proportional seat for each 10 percent of the vote it receives in the balloting for the directly contested seats.) The term of office is five years. The results of the most recent elections on September 29–October 1, 2011, were as follows: Seychelles People's Progressive Front, 31 (25 directly contested, 6 proportional); Popular Democratic Movement, 1 proportional seat.

Speaker: Patrick HERMINIE.

CABINET

[as of October 1, 2013]

President	James Alix Michel
Vice President	Daniel Faure
Ministers	
Community Development, Social Affairs, Youth, and Sport	Vincent Meriton
Defense	James Alix Michel
Education	MacSuzy Mondon [f]
Employment and Human Resources Development	Iudith Alexander [f]
Environment and Energy	Rolph Payet
Finance, Trade and Investment	Pierre La Porte
Foreign Affairs	Jean-Paul Adam
Health	Mitsy Larue [f]
Home Affairs, in Charge of Immigration, Prisons, and Police (Internal Affairs and Transport)	Joel Morgan
Information Communication Technology	Daniel Faure
Investment, Natural Resources, and Industry	Peter Sinon
Land Use and Housing	Christian Lionnet
Legal Affairs	James Alix Michel
Tourism and Culture	Alain St. Ange

[f] = female

INTERGOVERNMENTAL REPRESENTATION

Ambassador to the U.S. and Permanent Representative to the UN: Marie-Louis Cecile POTTER.

U.S. Ambassador to the Seychelles and Mauritius: Shari VILLAROSA.

IGO Memberships (Non-UN): AfDB, AU, Comesa, CWTH, NAM, WTO.

SIERRA LEONE

Republic of Sierra Leone

Political Status: Independent member of the Commonwealth since April 27, 1961; republic proclaimed April 19, 1971; one-party constitution adopted June 1978; multiparty constitution approved by popular referendum on August 23–30, 1991, with effect from September 24; government overthrown in military coup of April 29, 1992; ruling military council overthrown and replaced by "reconstituted" military council on January 16, 1996; democratically elected president inaugurated on March 29, 1996; government overthrown in military coup of May 25, 1997; ruling military council forcibly removed by regional forces on February 13, 1998; previously elected government reinstalled on March 10, 1998; July 1999 Lomé peace accord and UN peacekeepers unable to halt ongoing violence; cease-fire agreed between government and insurgents on May 16, 2001; previously elected president and majority party won elections of May 14, 2002.

Area: 27,699 sq. mi. (71,740 sq. km).

Population: 6,245,640 (2013—UN); 5,612,685 (2013E—U.S. Census).

Major Urban Center (2005E): FREETOWN (824,000, including suburbs).

Official Language: English.

Monetary Unit: Leone (market rate November 1, 2013: 4,347.83 leones = $1US).

President: Ernest Bai KOROMA (All People's Congress), elected in second-round balloting on September 8, 2007, and sworn in for a five-year term on September 17 to succeed Ahmad Tejan KABBAH (Sierra Leone People's Party); reelected on November 17, 2012, and sworn in on November 23.

Vice President: Sahr SAM-SUMANA (All People's Congress), elected on September 8, 2007, and sworn in on September 17 for a term concurrent with the president's in succession to Solomon BEREWA (Sierra Leone People's Party); reelected on November 17, 2012, and sworn in for a term concurrent with the president on November 23.

THE COUNTRY

The West African nation of Sierra Leone ("lion mountain"), facing the South Atlantic and nearly surrounded by the Republic of Guinea on the northwest, north, and east, encompasses three geographic regions: a peninsula in the west; a western coastal region, which consists of mangrove swamps and a coastal plain; and a plateau in the east and northeast. The indigenous inhabitants range over 12 principal tribal groups, the most important being the Mende in the south and the Temne in the north. There are also numerous Creole descendants of freed slaves. A variety of tribal languages are spoken, with Krio, a form of pidgin English, serving as a lingua franca. Traditional religions predominate, but there are many Muslims in the north and Christians in the west.

The agricultural sector of the economy employs about two-thirds of the workforce. Rice is the main subsistence crop, while cocoa, coffee, and palm kernels are the leading agricultural exports. Gold, bauxite, and rutile are among the minerals extracted, with a diamond reserve providing approximately 55 percent of export earnings in 2013. The International Monetary Fund (IMF), the World Bank group, and the European Community/Union (EC/EU) have been among the international agencies extending recent aid in support of efforts to revive an economy that has deteriorated markedly since the mid-1970s (for more on the economy between the 1970s and 1990s, please see the 2012 *Handbook*). Economic activity reportedly ground to a virtual standstill during the military's control of power from May 1997 to February 1998. A blockade of the Freetown harbor was lifted in late February 1998, thus allowing commercial activity to resume.

In late 1998, observers reported that mining and agriculture sectors in the north and east had been decimated by fighting. Furthermore, the subsequent return to full-scale civil war effectively dashed hopes for economic growth in 1998 and 1999. In December 1999 the IMF approved emergency assistance for the country, and a cease-fire in 2001 fostered the resumption of normal activity.

Diamond mining, the country's third-largest employer, has been a prime beneficiary of the cessation of hostilities. The smuggling of "blood diamonds," a key feature of the civil war, was curbed somewhat by a United Nations diamond embargo on Sierra Leone in 2000 and a subsequent diamond-certification scheme known as the Kimberley process. Since then, the government has regained partial control over the diamond trade; however, smuggling continued to be a problem.

Economic growth improved in 2005–2006, with a decline in inflation (to 9.5 percent) and increased foreign investment in oil and mining. The IMF approved a new three-year poverty reduction program for Sierra Leone, citing the government's "considerable progress" toward economic stability and addressing widespread poverty. (The IMF noted that 80 percent of the population lives on less than $1US per day.) The fund urged the government to enforce tax regulations, accelerate privatization efforts, and diversify and expand exports to bolster revenue. In 2006, the country qualified for $994 million in debt relief under the Heavily Indebted Poor Countries (HIPC) initiative.

The return of "peace and stability" to Sierra Leone contributed to robust economic growth of about 5.5 annually in 2008, according to the IMF, which continued to press for increased spending to help relieve pervasive poverty and for the acceleration of structural reforms. Annual growth was 5.3 percent in 2010, while inflation soared to 17.8 percent "reflecting largely the challenges associated with the new goods and services tax," according to the IMF. GDP grew by 6 percent in 2011, while inflation rose to 18.5 percent, owing in large part to foreign investment in the mining sector and expansion in construction. GDP soared by 15.2 percent in 2012 and 13 percent the following year, mainly on increased foreign investment in the mineral sector and economic assistance. Inflation slowed to 13.8 percent in 2012, and 8.7 percent in 2013. Poverty remained prevalent, and the UN ranked Sierra Leone 177th out of 186 countries in its 2013 Human Development Index.

GOVERNMENT AND POLITICS

Political background. Growing out of a coastal settlement established by English interests in the 18th century as a haven for freed slaves, Sierra Leone became independent within the Commonwealth in 1961. Political leadership from 1961 to 1967 was exercised exclusively through the Sierra Leone People's Party (SLPP), a predominantly Mende grouping led successively by Sir Milton MARGAI and his half-brother, Sir Albert M. MARGAI. Attempts to establish a one-party system under the SLPP were successfully resisted by the opposition All People's Congress (APC), a predominantly Temne formation headed by Dr. Siaka P. STEVENS, a militant trade-union leader belonging to the smaller Limba tribe.

Following an unexpectedly strong showing by the APC in the election of 1967, Stevens was appointed prime minister, but he was prevented from taking office by Brig. David LANSANA's declaration of martial law on March 21. Two days later, Lt. Col. Andrew JUXON-SMITH assumed the leadership of a National Reformation Council (NRC) that suspended the constitution, dissolved the parties, and ruled for the ensuing 13 months. The NRC was itself overthrown in April 1968 by a group of noncommissioned officers, the Anti-Corruption Revolutionary Movement, which restored civilian government with Stevens as prime minister.

The ensuing decade was marked by a series of coup attempts and government harassment of political opponents. In 1973 official intimidation contributed to an SLPP boycott of the general election, with the APC winning all but one of the seats in the House of Representatives. In 1975 six civilians and two soldiers were executed in Freetown after being convicted of an attempt to assassinate (then) Finance Minister Christian KAMARA-TAYLOR and take over the government. Under a new constitution adopted by referendum in June 1978, Sierra Leone became a one-party state; President Stevens was reinvested for a seven-year term on June 14.

In early 1985, the president announced his intention to retire, naming army commander Maj. Gen. Joseph Saidu MOMOH as his successor. The new president was confirmed in single-party balloting on October 1; Stevens transferred power to him on November 28, although formal swearing-in ceremonies were not held until January 26, 1986. The House of Representatives was renewed in a multicandidate, one-party poll held on May 29–30, a year prior to expiry of its normal term.

Enthusiasm over Momoh's accession subsided when a campaign to "instill military discipline" in fighting corruption and managing the economy failed to yield tangible results. By mid-1990, the Momoh regime's inability to check inflation, generate the funds for civil service salary payments, or maintain basic services had provoked widespread civil unrest and calls for the adoption of a new, multiparty constitution. Consequently, at an extraordinary APC meeting in August, President Momoh named economist Peter TUCKER to head a National Constitution Review Commission to explore government reorganization along "democratic lines." (At the same time, Momoh described multiparty activity as incompatible with Sierra Leone's tribal structures and widespread illiteracy.)

In late March 1991, less than a week after having reiterated his opposition to the idea, Momoh announced that he welcomed the introduction of a multiparty system. Two months later, the Tucker Commission submitted its report, and in early June the life of the existing House of Representatives was extended to enable it to approve a pluralistic basic law. On July 2, following intense debate both within and outside the government, the House of Representatives ratified the new constitution, and on August 23–30 the document was approved by popular referendum; more than 60 percent of the 2.5 million participants reportedly favored its enactment. On September 23, President Momoh named a transitional government to rule until multiparty elections, tentatively scheduled for late 1992. One day later, the constitution was promulgated, and on September 30 the ban on political parties was officially lifted.

On April 29, 1992, army units, angered at a lack of pay and the failure of the government to provide them equipment to end a 13-week rebellion in eastern Sierra Leone, ousted President Momoh, who flew to exile in Guinea. On May 1 Capt. Valentine Strasser and (then) Lt. Solomon Anthony James MUSA were named chair and vice chair, respectively, of a National Provisional Ruling Council (NPRC), which suspended the constitution and ruled by decree. On May 2, the NPRC appointed a 19-member government, which included several members of the NPRC and six civilians. Two days later the NPRC dissolved the legislature and suspended political activity. On July 14 Captain Strasser announced that the NPRC would thenceforth be known as the Supreme Council of State (SCS) and would no longer be involved in day-to-day administration. Concurrently, ministers were redesignated as secretaries of state, with Musa serving in the quasi-prime ministerial post of chief secretary. In October, a 15-member advisory council was established with a mandate to work out a return to multipartyism, with an emphasis on involving citizens in the democratization process.

In mid-December 1992, the regime established a special military tribunal "in the interest of maintaining peace, security, and public order." On December 28 government troops violently repulsed an alleged coup attempt by the so-called Anti-Corruption Revolutionary Movement (ACRM), a grouping of pro-Momoh civilians and military personnel (some of whom were already incarcerated). On December 30, following a summary military trial, 26 people (9 ACRM members and 17 others who had been convicted of high treason for their involvement in an earlier incident) were executed. The executions drew international condemnation; several Western donors announced suspension of aid payments.

On April 29, 1993, Strasser announced the commencement of a three-year transition period to culminate in multiparty elections. In addition, the chair promised to launch an inquiry into the special military tribunal's activities and to ease some security measures.

In a government reshuffle on July 5, 1993, Capt. Julius Maada BIO replaced Musa as SCS vice chair and chief secretary. Musa's dismissal came amid reports that he had clashed with Strasser about the return to multipartyism and that he harbored his own presidential ambitions. In December Dr. James JONAH was appointed chair of the newly established Interim National Electoral Commission (INEC), which had been charged with preparing for presidential and legislative elections tentatively scheduled for 1995.

In 1994, the Strasser regime's credibility was impaired by its inability to suppress the Revolutionary United Front (RUF, below), a Sierra Leonean offshoot of Charles Taylor's National Patriotic Front of Liberia (NPFL, see Liberia entry) led by Foday Savannah SANKOH; the Strasser regime claimed the RUF had been organized to punish Sierra Leone for its peacekeeping role in Liberia. By midyear, RUF-related violence was reportedly responsible for the deaths of hundreds of individuals and the dislocation of thousands. Consequently, in July the State Advisory Council, noting that "local people must be collaborating" with the insurgents, announced the creation of a National Security Council charged with ending the hostilities. Thereafter, despite reports that most of the country was "lawless," the government released a draft constitution in October, which included provisions for a return to civilian rule by 1996.

On November 12, 1994, the junta executed 12 soldiers in an apparent attempt to intimidate the so-called "sobels" (soldiers during the day, rebels at night) whom observers described as increasingly beyond Freetown's control. On November 25, bolstered by reports that an offensive had severely weakened the rebels, the Strasser government called on the RUF to begin negotiations on a peace accord and cease-fire, pledging that they would be allowed to form a political party in preparation for multiparty elections. The RUF, which had gained international attention two weeks earlier when it kidnapped two British citizens, initially rejected the offer but on December 4 met with government negotiators for discussions, which were described as "frank." However, the rebels' kidnapping campaign continued into 1995; they reportedly seized an additional 15 foreigners by February. (All of the hostages were eventually handed over to International Red Cross representatives on April 20.)

On March 31, 1995, Captain Strasser announced a major government restructuring, under which Health and Social Services Secretary Lt. Col. Akim GIBRIL would become chief secretary in place of Bio, who remained SCS vice chair while assuming the position of chief of the defense staff "to provide additional mettle" to the armed forces in their campaign against the RUF. On April 27, Strasser promised to lift the ban on political parties and relinquish power to a democratically elected president in January 1996. He also offered the RUF a truce to negotiate an end to the conflict that had claimed some 5,000 lives since 1991. On May 18, he asked the Economic Community of West African States (ECOWAS) to broker negotiations with the rebels; however, the RUF rejected the initiative, calling instead for Strasser to convene a sovereign national conference to decide the future of the country.

On June 21, 1995, the regime lifted the ban on political parties, but two days later it issued a list of 57 people, headed by former president Momoh, who were ineligible to compete in the upcoming balloting. On August 18, the government convened a National Consultative Conference; however, despite its earlier entreaties, the RUF refused to attend. Among the rulings adopted by the conference were the postponement of balloting until February 1996 and the organization of simultaneous presidential and legislative polling.

On October 3, 1995, a coup attempt led by at least eight senior military officers was quashed by troops loyal to Strasser, who was out of the country. The failed uprising highlighted the growing chasm in the SCS between those who opposed the return to a civilian government and its advocates, purportedly led by Strasser.

On January 16, 1996, Strasser was overthrown by his second-in-command, Brigadier General Bio, who announced that he would lead a "Reconstituted" Supreme Council of the State (RSCS). At his inauguration the following day, Bio promised to continue preparations for "transparent, free, and fair" elections and urged the RUF to begin peace talks. In response, the RUF announced a one-week, unconditional cease-fire and called for postponement of the elections, saying it would not negotiate with a civilian government.

In the first round of legislative and presidential balloting on February 26–27, 1996, held under provisions of the 1991 constitution, the SLPP captured 36.1 percent of the vote, easily outpacing the United People's Party (UNPP, below), which finished second with 21.6 percent, and 11 other parties. Meanwhile, SLPP presidential candidate Ahmad Tejan KABBAH and UNPP leader John KARIFA-SMART finished first and second, respectively, in their 12-candidate race. However, because neither captured a majority, a second round of balloting was held on March 15, with Kabbah winning with 59.5 percent of the vote.

The Kabbah administration moved quickly to build on the peace initiative its predecessor had begun with the RUF, and on April 23, 1996, agreement was reached between Kabbah and Sankoh on a "definitive" cease-fire and the establishment of committees to draft disarmament and peace accords. On May 30, Freetown announced that it had reached agreement with the RUF on 26 of 28 articles in a proposed peace plan, leaving unresolved only the timetable for the withdrawal of foreign troops and the establishment of a national debt commission. However, the rebels continued to refuse to recognize the Kabbah government publicly and insisted that the cease-fire was only provisional. At the same time, the administration's announced intention to reduce the military ranks from 18,000 to approximately 4,000 added the threat of yet another military coup to a domestic security landscape already populated by RUF dissidents, "sobels," and escaped prisoners.

On September 8, 1996, at least six soldiers were arrested after senior military officials were alerted to their alleged plans to overthrow the government, and within a week 150 more soldiers were purged in response to an executive order demanding the dismissal of suspected dissidents. Meanwhile, a series of clashes between government forces and rebels in the east threatened the six-month-old cease-fire. However, when government troops reportedly gained the upper hand on the battlefield, President Kabbah and RUF leader Sankoh signed a peace treaty in Abidjan, Côte d'Ivoire, on November 30. Highlighting the accord were provisions for the immediate end to hostilities, the demobilization and disarmament of the RUF, and the integration of rebel soldiers into the national army. Furthermore, the agreement entitled the RUF to transform itself into a legal political party.

Sporadic fighting was reported throughout late 1996 and early 1997; the RUF and government accused each other of violating the peace accord. In addition, clashes were reported between alleged "sobels" and ethnic Kamajor militiamen allied with the president. On March 12, the RUF's Sankoh was detained in Nigeria, and on March 15 he was dismissed from the RUF by senior party officials who accused him of blocking implementation of the peace accord. Subsequently, Sankoh's supporters threatened to attack Freetown unless he was returned from Lagos.

On May 25, 1997, junior army officers fighting alongside RUF militants overran the prison where the defendants in the September 1996 coup plot were being held. Subsequently, under the leadership of one of the freed prisoners, Maj. Johnny Paul KOROMA, the combined forces took control of Freetown and overthrew the government (with Kabbah fleeing to Guinea). On May 28, the military junta abolished the constitution and banned political parties. Meanwhile, 300,000 people reportedly fled the country amid heavy fighting between the junta's forces and Nigerian-led ECOWAS troops, who had launched a countercoup offensive. On June 1 the junta established a 20-member Armed Forces Revolutionary Council (AFRC) and named Koroma its chair. Unable to dislodge the rebel soldiers, the Economic Community of West African States Monitoring Group (Ecomog) announced a cease-fire on June 2. Nevertheless, regional and international observers vowed not to let the coup stand and refused to recognize the Koroma regime.

On June 17, 1997, Major Koroma was sworn in as the leader of the AFRC, and he subsequently agreed to participate in internationally mediated negotiations. However, the talks were promptly abandoned after the junta leader demanded a four-year term. Frustrated with Koroma's intransigence, ECOWAS officials tightened sanctions against the AFRC in late August, and on September 2, Ecomog forces bombed Freetown in an effort to enforce an embargo on imported goods. Furthermore, on October 8 the UN Security Council adopted a resolution empowering Ecomog forces to enforce oil and arms sanctions against the regime. On October 24, under pressure of heavy shelling, AFRC negotiators agreed to a peace plan that included provisions for a disarmament process (beginning December 1), Kabbah's reinstallment on April 22, 1998, immunity for the junta's forces, and a future government role for RUF leader Sankoh. Despite the accord, clashes continued between the AFRC and Ecomog forces, and in mid-December 1997 Koroma asserted that the timetable for implementing the pact would be delayed.

Following a week of particularly intense fighting, Ecomog forces captured Freetown on February 13, 1998. On February 17 ECOWAS announced the formation of an interim "special supervision committee," headed by Vice President Albert DEMBY and the Nigerian leader of the Ecomog forces, Col. Maxwell Khobe. On February 20, 25 of the AFRC leaders were captured as they attempted to escape into Liberia (Johnny Paul Koroma is widely believed to be dead). President Kabbah was officially reinstated on March 10 and promptly named a 15-member cabinet.

As of March 1998, Ecomog-directed, propresidential forces reportedly controlled 90 percent of Sierra Leone. In addition to attempting to wrest control of the remainder of the country from the remnants of the combined AFRC-RUF forces, the reinstalled Kabbah government faced a myriad of other challenges, including resurrecting a devastated economy; reintegrating tens of thousands of dislocated and homeless citizens; and reestablishing relations with Sankoh and the RUF, many of whose fighters reportedly had hidden their weapons when confronted by the Ecomog offensive. Meanwhile, the Kabbah administration pressed ahead with legal actions against former Koroma coup members and their alleged collaborators. In October, Freetown ignored observers' calls for leniency and executed 24 people for treasonous acts, including Koroma's brother, Brig. Gen. Samuel KOROMA. On October 23 Sankoh, who had been returned for trial from Nigeria in July, was sentenced to death for similar offenses. (Collaterally, on November 5 former president Momoh received a ten-year jail term for his ties to Koroma, who remained a fugitive.) Following Sankoh's sentencing, a dramatic upsurge in rebel attacks against civilians was reported; thousands subsequently fled to the capital to escape a campaign marked by atrocities. Despite initial depictions of the violence as being the rebels' last gasp, the RUF and its AFRC military allies advanced to within striking distance of Freetown by December.

In late December 1998, RUF commander Sam BOCKARIE rejected calls for a cease-fire, and on January 6, 1999, the rebels invaded the capital. Approximately 5,000 people were killed before Ecomog troops regained control of the city in mid-month. Thereafter, President Kabbah agreed to let Sankoh participate in cease-fire negotiations; however, apparently emboldened by reports of Ecomog gains elsewhere in the country, Kabbah insisted that the rebels respect the dictates of the 1996 peace accord. Consequently, negotiations proceeded fitfully through February and early March. On March 16 Bockarie broke off talks, reportedly suspecting the government of employing delaying tactics while it won back territory. Subsequently, the Kabbah administration came under pressure from its two largest military backers, the United Kingdom and Nigeria, to seek a negotiated end to its "unwinnable" war.

On May 18, 1999, President Kabbah and rebel leader Sankoh signed an agreement in Togo calling for a cease-fire effective May 25, and a formal peace accord was signed in July. The agreement promised to give the RUF and the AFRC four key government posts and extended total amnesty to RUF and AFRC leaders, including Sankoh, as well as former head of state Momoh, who had been charged with collaborating with the AFRC junta. Amid reports of internal divisions, the RUF and the AFRC agreed to demobilize and disarm and also dropped their demands for an immediate withdrawal of Ecomog troops. The AFRC wing that accepted Koroma's call to stop violence immediately was then reincorporated into the political arena. In October the UN Security Council authorized the United Nations Mission in Sierra Leone (UNAMSIL) to replace the Ecomog troops gradually. In November Sankoh was given powers equivalent to those of vice president, and the RUF and the AFRC were allocated nonsenior cabinet posts. Concurrently, the RUF decided to transform itself into a registered political party, adopting the rubric Revolutionary United Front Party (RUFP). However, the issues of demobilization and disarmament created problems during much of early 2000, and in May the peace agreement broke down as UNAMSIL was moving to replace the Ecomog troops. RUF fighters and some renegade AFRC militia (linked with Eddie KANNEH's wing, which was uneasy with Koroma's call to stop the violence) attacked UNAMSIL detachments, and 19 civilians were killed by Sankoh's bodyguards during a demonstration in front of his residence. Although Sankoh fled the country following the incident, he was apprehended in Nigeria on May 17. Due to advances by UNAMSIL, the progovernment Kamajor militia (styled as the Civil Defense Force [CDF]), Guinean forces opposed to the RUF, and renegade AFRC forces, the rebels were on the defensive for much of the year. In November, the RUF agreed once again to commit itself to the peace process and to disarm its troops and relinquish most of its territory to government and UNAMSIL control. In February 2001, Kabbah asked the National Assembly to postpone the presidential and legislative elections due to be held in February and March because of the "uncertain security situation." He also reshuffled his cabinet to include some opposition figures.

As Liberian president Charles Taylor tried to distance himself from the RUF in an effort to clean up his country's image as a protector of the rebels, the RUF signed a peace agreement in May 2001 and another cease-fire was implemented. In August it was announced that elections were expected to be held in June 2002 under a "constituency electoral system," although in September the National Electoral Commission advised the assembly to adopt a proportional representation system instead. Despite criticism from the opposition that Kabbah was trying to eliminate his potential rivals in the coming elections, as well as fears that some RUF forces might resume fighting, the country appeared to be moving toward normalization.

At a dramatic weapons-burning ceremony on January 18, 2002, which marked the completion of the disarmament process, President Kabbah declared the "war is over," and the four-year state of emergency was formally lifted on March 1. (An estimated 50,000 people died as a result of the conflict.) In presidential balloting on May 14, President Kabbah was elected to another four-year term by securing more than 70 percent of the vote against eight opponents. (Kabbah's running mate, Solomon BEREWA, the sitting minister of justice and attorney general and also from the SLPP, was elected to the vice presidency in succession to Albert Joe Demby, who had been dropped from the ticket at the SLPP congress in March.) In concurrent voting for the National Assembly, which had been expanded to 112 members elected on a proportional basis, the SLPP secured the majority of seats, followed by the All People's Congress (APC). A small number of seats were won by the Peace and Liberation Party (PLP); the RUF failed to win any seats. A new cabinet of the SLPP and two independents was sworn in on July 9, the independents subsequently joining the SLPP.

After the elections, international troops who had overseen the cease-fire ending Sierra Leone's civil war began to withdraw. In 2005, UNAMSIL forces were replaced by a small contingent of military advisers—the United Nations Integrated Office in Sierra Leone (UNIOSL)—charged with monitoring the security situation and guarding the war crimes tribunal (see Current issues, below).

The cabinet was reshuffled on September 6, 2005, all ministers representing the SLPP.

The APC was victorious in the parliamentary and presidential elections of 2007, unseating the governing SLPP, as the APC secured 40.7 percent of the seats in first-past-the-post legislative elections on August 11, followed by the SLPP with 39.5 percent and the newly formed People's Movement for Democratic Change (PMDC), an SLPP breakaway party, with 15.4 percent. Among the 572 candidates vying for 112 parliamentary seats, none was chosen from four other parties contesting the elections, nor were any independent candidates successful. In the first round of presidential balloting on August 11, APC chair Ernest Bai Koroma's vote share of 44.3 percent and Solomon Berewa's 38.3 percent as the SLPP candidate led five other contenders (from the PMDC, the Convention People's Party—CPP, the NDA, PLP, and UNPP). Since neither Koroma nor Berewa secured the 55 percent required for election, a runoff was held on September 8, in which Koroma won 54.6 percent to Berewa's 45.4 percent. President Koroma and his running mate, Sahr SAM-SUMANA, were sworn in on September 17. The president named a new APC-dominated cabinet, which included four members of the PMDC but none from the SLPP, on October 8 and October 16.

Among Koroma's first acts as president was the invocation of a "certificate of emergency," granting him the authority to push laws through the National Assembly, most notably one giving prosecutorial powers to the Anti-Corruption Commission (ACC). In addition to his pronounced "zero tolerance" for corruption, he also pledged to restore electricity, available in short, sporadic supply only through private generators, in Freetown and the provincial capitals. To this end, he replaced the top tier at the National Power Authority, which had been accused of selling diesel fuel on the black market. Western leaders were also buoyed by President Koroma's decision to break with tradition and relinquish control of the defense ministry.

In 2007, legislation was approved granting unprecedented rights to women. New laws made domestic violence a crime, allowed women to inherit property, and protected young women against forced marriage. Other new laws prohibited exploitative labor practices and set up national agencies to protect the rights of children.

On July 5, 2008, local elections were held without incident, the first such balloting since the country's civil war ended. In a further sign of peace and stability, the UN's Integrated Office in Sierra Leone (Uniosil), was established as a follow-up to UN peacekeepers and began working on good governance and human rights issues.

The cabinet was reshuffled on February 27, 2009, with the replacement of 9 of 20 ministers, including, most notably, the appointment of the former central bank governor as finance minister. Observers said the appointment was significant as the government struggled to deal with the slumping economy. Furthermore, analysts said, the reshuffle was necessary in the wake of corruption scandals in the ministries of mines, energy, and transport. The minister for health and sanitation was suspended in November after being indicted on corruption charges (he was subsequently convicted). That portfolio fell under the supervision of Vice President Sam-Sumana. The minister of state in the office of the vice president was replaced the same day.

Attention in early 2009 quickly turned to what was reported as the worst political violence in the country since 2007, when supporters of the APC and the SLPP attacked each other over a period of five days in March. Thousands of youthful fighters took to the streets; the SLPP's headquarters were ransacked, and women were reported to have been sexually assaulted inside the headquarters building. Two radio stations accused of inflaming tensions were indefinitely suspended by the government. Meanwhile, the APC was angered by the reappearance in the SLPP leadership of former NPRC members, including its secretary general, John BENJAMIN, and both the SLPP and the APC reportedly used "youth protection squads" that included former fighters. The fragility of the political situation prompted intercession by the UN, which mediated a peace agreement between the two parties in April.

A long-standing trial of war criminals concluded in April 2009 when the special court in Sierra Leone convicted three RUF leaders (see Political Parties, below) and imposed lengthy sentences. Of added significance, the court also determined that it was the AFRC that was responsible for a February 1999 invasion of Freetown in which 6,000 people died. In that case, the court determined that the RUF was not involved in the atrocities. The court made a point of highlighting that the AFRC and army dissidents had a major role in war crimes, not just the RUF as many believed. Further, the court set forth five new violations of international humanitarian law: forced marriage, sexual slavery, enlisting child soldiers under the age of 15, attacks on peacekeepers, and acts of terrorism against civilians.

Drug trafficking, in conjunction with corruption and a high unemployment rate among youth, was described in 2009 as the "main destabilizing force" in the country, as well as in neighboring West African nations, as they became transit points for the smuggling of cocaine from South America to Europe. On a positive note, the government's Anti-Corruption Act, adopted in 2008, granted more powers to the Anti-Corruption Commission (ACC) to review ministries, among other things. Despite efforts to fight corruption, however, the Koroma administration continued to lose support, as the opposition rallied against the replacement of some 200 government workers from the southeast region with appointees from Koroma's home region in the northwest, and as the economic recovery was deemed to be too slow. A positive development was the restoration of electric power to much of the capital in November, when the Bumbuna dam came online after nearly 40 years of construction. At the end of October the Special Court for Sierra Leone, which was hearing war crimes cases, upheld the sentences of former RUF interim leader Issa SESAY and two other high-ranking members (see Political Parties, below). In December, eight men who had been found guilty in the UN-backed war crimes court were transferred to prisons in Rwanda because no facilities in Sierra Leone met the required international standards.

On March 15, 2010, the marine resources minister was removed as a result of corruption charges and replaced by the minister of presidential and parliamentary affairs. The cabinet was extensively reshuffled on December 4, dominated by members of the APC and a few from the PMDC. The foreign affairs minister was a member of the SLPP, but he was immediately suspended by the party and officially resigned from the SLPP on February 9, 2011. The president replaced the minister for energy and water resources in January 2012.

In elections held on November 17, 2012, Koroma won a second term as president, defeating opponent Julius Maada Bio (Sierra Leone People's Party) and seven other candidates. The APC also strengthened its parliamentary majority, winning 67 seats to the SLPP's 42. No other parties secured seats in the parliament. Koroma named a reshuffled cabinet over the next three months.

Constitution and government. The 1991 constitution provided for a popularly elected executive president who could serve for no more than two five-year terms; a parliament whose members could not serve simultaneously as ministers; and a State Advisory Council composed of 12 paramount chiefs (one from each local district) and ten "emergent citizens" nominated by the president. There was no limit on the number of political parties, provided they met basic requirements. The judicial system included a Supreme Court and a Court of Appeal, as well as a lower tier of high, magistrates', and native courts.

Following the establishment of the NPRC in 1992, the constitution was suspended, and on July 14 the Supreme Council of State (as the NPRC was subsequently named) called for the designation of three SCS members as "principal liaison officers," each of whom would oversee a number of government departments (successors to the former ministries). The department heads were to be styled secretaries of state under a chief who would report to the SCS. Meanwhile, the SCS had assumed a quasi-legislative function by the issuance of decrees. In 1993, the Strasser regime named a national advisory council to prepare a draft document as the basis for a new constitution (with the aim of holding a referendum in 1995). The draft, published in September 1994, included stipulations that future presidents be at least 40 years old and native-born Sierra Leoneans. It also included provisions for restoring basic human rights, guaranteeing freedom of expression, establishing a unicameral legislature, and empowering parliament to remove a president who became mentally or physically incapacitated, or who was dishonest.

On February 7, 2002, the constitution was amended in accordance with the Electoral Laws Act of 2002 adopted by parliament to provide for a party-list proportional voting system for the National Assembly. In October 2006, the government established the Constitutional Review Committee to consider changes to the charter (see Current issues, below). The constitution was amended in 2007 in accordance with the Electoral Laws Act of 2002 to provide for a first-past-the-post voting system for the National Assembly.

Freedom of the press is guaranteed and Reporters Without Borders ranked Sierra Leone 61st out of 179 countries in media freedom in 2013, one of the higher rankings in the region.

Sierra Leone is administratively divided into three provinces (Northern, Eastern, Southern), in addition to a Western Area that includes Freetown. The provinces are subdivided into 12 districts and 147 chiefdoms.

Foreign relations. Sierra Leone has long subscribed to a generally pro-Western foreign policy, while maintaining diplomatic relations with the former Soviet Union, several East European countries, the People's Republic of China, and North Korea. Regionally, it has been an active participant in the Organization of African Unity (OAU, subsequently the African Union—AU) and a long-standing member of OAU committees established to resolve the disputes in Chad and the Western Sahara. Traditionally cordial relations with bordering states were strained by the overthrow of civilian governments in Liberia and Guinea; however, the three countries signed a security agreement in September 1986 and revived the Mano River Union plan for economic cooperation. In early 1989 continuing efforts by Freetown to "intensify existing friendly relations" with regional neighbors led to the establishment of joint economic and social commissions with Nigeria and Togo.

Civil war in neighboring Liberia topped Freetown's foreign policy agenda in 1990 as ECOWAS's peacekeeping forces, including Sierra Leonean troops, were dispatched from Freetown. In November Momoh described the influx of Liberian refugees as "stretching thin" his government's resources and characterized Liberian rebel leader Charles Taylor, who had threatened retaliation for Sierra Leone's involvement, as "ungrateful." In March 1991, Taylor, angered by Freetown's participation in the ECOWAS operation, began launching raids into Sierra Leone, and Nigeria and Guinea were reported in mid-April to have dispatched troops to aid in repulsing the intruders. Meanwhile, Freetown also accused Libya, Burkina Faso, and Côte d'Ivoire of aiding the rebels.

By early November 1991, the government and its allies claimed to have routed the guerrillas, and Guinean forces began their withdrawal. However, a cease-fire signed earlier in Côte d'Ivoire proved short-lived; in December Taylor charged Freetown with backing incursions by the Liberian United Movement for Freedom and Democracy (ULIMO), a group linked to the deposed Doe regime. ULIMO admitted to having engaged Taylor's forces but denied being based in Sierra Leone.

During the second half of 1992, Captain Strasser reportedly developed close ties with Nigerian military leader General Babangida, who in early 1993 agreed to provide Sierra Leone with military advisers. Subsequently, Sierra Leone and ULIMO forces were reported to have participated in joint operations against RUF rebels.

In March 1994, the Strasser government pressed Ecomog commanders to establish a buffer zone along its shared border with Liberia, citing increased rebel activity as well as the volatility of Liberia's disarmament process. One month later, the Strasser government expelled Germany's ambassador to Freetown, claiming that his "undiplomatic" behavior, including meetings with Liberia's Taylor, were undermining Sierra Leone's interests and threatening relations between the two countries. However, other reports linked the German's ouster to his defense of a Sierra Leonean journalist who had been arrested for criticizing Strasser. In September 1995, seven Guinean soldiers, stationed in Sierra Leone to fulfill a defense pact between the two nations, were killed during a clash with the RUF.

In mid-1998, the UN Security Council announced the establishment of a United Nations Observer Mission in Sierra Leone (UNOMSIL) which it charged with overseeing peacekeeping efforts. In February 1999 UNOMSIL personnel accused Nigerian members of Ecomog of executing civilians suspected of aiding the antigovernment insurgents. Subsequently, observers in Lagos reported that support for continued involvement in Sierra Leone had reached a new low. Meanwhile, Liberia, Libya, and Burkina Faso were alleged to be supplying the rebels with armaments and refuge. Following the May 1999 agreement between Sierra Leone and the RUF, the Liberian border was reopened in May, and in December, Sierra Leone and Liberia established a joint security committee.

However, with the breakdown of the agreement and the resumption of violence in May 2000, Sierra Leone's relations with all three countries suspected of helping the RUF deteriorated once again. Although the Mano River Union summit held in May and attended by Sierra Leone, Liberia, Guinea, and Mali "deplored the attacks by the RUF," Kabbah's government and much of the international community continued to charge Liberia with assisting the rebels. With the RUF rebels crossing into the Guinean territory, and the Guinean President Lasana Conté accusing Sierra Leonean and Liberian refugees in his country of assisting the rebels, the Mano River region became a crisis zone and the scene of a severe refugee tragedy.

After the fighting in Liberia's Lofa county intensified in early 2001, Liberian president Taylor renewed his claim that the Sierra Leonean and Guinean authorities were assisting the Liberian rebels. In March the ambassadors of Sierra Leone and Guinea were expelled from Liberia. Relations improved following a new peace agreement between Sierra Leone and the RUF in May 2001.

In 2006, Sierra Leone became a full member of the Community of Sahel and Saharan States (CEN-SAD). On June 4, 2007, Sierra Leone and Liberia reached a border agreement, culminating in the reopening on June 7 of the Mano River bridge connecting the two countries. Peace talks continued at another Mano River Union summit in July.

In May 2008, during a summit in Monrovia, Sierra Leone and Guinea joined with their Liberian host in pledging that the Mano River Union, soon to include Côte d'Ivoire, would sustain peace and security in the region. In August, the UN Security Council approved the transition of UNOMSIL to a smaller mission, the UN Integrated Peacebuilding Office in Sierra Leone (UNIPSIL). Also in 2008 relations with China were strengthened as the two countries signed a cooperation agreement following China's granting of interest-free loans to Sierra Leone to help rebuild its war-torn economy. The leaders of China and Sierra Leone agreed in 2009 to enhance bilateral relations.

In April 2009, former British prime minister Tony Blair visited Sierra Leone on a trip designed to promote tourism in the country, and the United Kingdom promised aid of nearly $71 million in 2010. In September the UN extended the mandate of the peace-building operation in Sierra Leone through September 2010.

In October 2009, Sierra Leone prepared to send its first troops to join a UN peacekeeping mission in Sudan. Britain provided financial assistance for the restructuring of Sierra Leone's significantly reduced army.

The first group of U.S. Peace Corps volunteers since 1994 arrived in Sierra Leone in June 2010.

In the midst of the Arab Spring of civil unrest in the Middle East and North Africa, Sierra Leone said its diplomatic relations with the embattled country would not change, while at the same time the government said it had "nothing against regime change."

In February 2012, the UN recalled its representative in Sierra Leone, Michael von der SCHULENBURG, after Koroma complained that the diplomat inappropriately supported the SLPP in upcoming elections. Schulenburg denied the charge.

In April 2012, former Liberian leader Taylor was convicted of war crimes (see entry on Liberia) and sentenced to 50 years in prison. Also in April, Sierra Leone announced it would deploy 850 troops as part of the African Union (AU) peacekeeping force in Somalia. Sierra Leone and Sri Lanka established full diplomatic relations with each other in 2012, while Sierra Leone and the United States finalized an open skies agreement that year in an effort to increase air traffic between the two countries. In September, under pressure from the United States, the Koroma government de-registered ten Iranian ships that had been using Sierra Leonean registration to evade international sanctions on oil sales from the Islamic republic.

In March 2013, the UN Security Council approved an extension of UNIPSIL until March 2014 and announced that the mission would cease on that date.

Current issues. In January 2010, the Koroma government took control of the logging industry, reportedly to help restore depleted forests, and banned the transport and export of lumber. Observers said many logging companies were operating illegally. In March a minister was dismissed as a result of corruption charges, and the anticorruption chief quit in May, "signaling a growing malaise in the government," according to *Africa Confidential*. The ACC chair, who had spearheaded what was recognized as among the best anticorruption effort in Africa, resigned in the wake of rioting by APC members, who stormed the courts in Freetown following the trial of the marine resources minister on 17 counts of corruption. On a positive note, the UN Security Council on September 29 lifted all sanctions it had imposed on Sierra Leone in 1997 as a result of the civil war and related atrocities. The move, which allowed for the free flow of goods and services, was hailed as opening the way for economic recovery and stimulating trade, investment, and tourism. At year's end, however, observers said international drug cartels selling cocaine within the country continued to be a major problem, along with alleged misappropriation of mining revenues.

In January 2011, the government addressed a long-standing issue by paying out $1.4 million to families of soldiers said to be missing in action during the conflict that ended in 2002. Meanwhile, a British team began helping to train Sierra Leone's reorganized armed forces, pared down from 13,500 in 2007 to 8,500. Tensions increased in May when the government slashed the gas subsidy by half, reportedly resulting in a 30 percent increase in price at the pump. Analysts said the cut was meant to provide revenue to help pay off the government's external debt, but it was alleged that a large portion of the money was used by the APC for the country's Golden Jubilee anniversary celebration of independence. On a positive note, the government stepped up efforts to involve more women in governance, an initiative also backed by the SLPP, and established the All Political Parties Women's Association–Sierra Leone (APPWA-SL) to encourage active participation by women. Subsequently, the government said it would implement measures to ensure that women represented 30 percent of public and private sector jobs.

In August 2012, allegations emerged that Vice President Sam-Sumana had used foreign commercial funds to support the APC in the 2007 election. Also in August, a cholera outbreak prompted Koroma to declare a nationwide state of emergency. By the end of the month, reports indicated that more than 230 had died from the disease, which had sickened more than 14,000.

Reports indicated that the president was considering a new running mate for the 2012 balloting but announced he would maintain Sam-Sumana on October 1. He was easily reelected in the November balloting, defeating eight other candidates. Meanwhile the APC expanded its parliamentary majority. International observers reported the balloting was generally free and credible, but they noted some irregularities and delays in vote counting.

In January 2013, protests and demonstrations against widespread fuel shortages occurred in Freetown following the disruption of petroleum from Benin and Côte d'Ivoire. In March, the ACC charged 29 government officials with corruption in a scandal over the misappropriation of vaccines.

POLITICAL PARTIES

During Sierra Leone's first 17 years of independence, the principal political groupings were the Sierra Leone People's Party (SLPP), strongest in the Mende area of the south, and the All People's Congress (APC), based in the Temne region of the north. The SLPP dominated from 1961 to 1967 and the APC from 1967 to 1978, when it was accorded monopoly status. Following adoption of the 1991 constitution, a number of new parties emerged, most of which were accorded legal recognition prior to the suspension of political activity in May 1992.

By late 1992 the regime had released the majority of the political figures detained in the aftermath of the coup, the most prominent of whom included SLPP leader Salia JUSU-SHERRIFF and National Action Party (NAP) co-founder Dr. Sheka KANU.

The ban on political party activity was rescinded on June 21, 1995, in preparation for elections promised by early 1996. In August the Interim National Electoral Commission granted provisional registration certificates to approximately 15 groups, 11 of which were granted permission in November to participate in the upcoming elections.

Political parties were banned by the Koroma military junta upon its seizure of power in May 1997. Following his reinstallation in March 1998, President Kabbah authorized parties to resume their activities. His decision to include representatives from only four groups in his reshuffled government was criticized by his opponents, who had expected a more inclusive cabinet.

Following the July 1999 peace and power-sharing agreement, Kabbah reshuffled his cabinet in November, and the rebels (the RUF and AFRC) were given four nonsenior posts. After the resumption of fighting in May 2000, however, three rebel ministers were jailed. In March 2001 Kabbah reshuffled his cabinet to replace retiring and jailed rebel ministers. In an effort described as "forming a more inclusive national unity government" but criticized by opponents as "trying to silence and co-opt" his rivals, Kabbah appointed four new ministers. Three came from the opposition National Unity Party (NUP), People's Democratic Party (PDP), and UNPP to supplement Kabbah's SLPP-dominated government (which had also included civilians); one minister came from the Democratic Center Party (DCP). The latter party, chaired by Aiah Abu KOROMA, reportedly dissolved in 2002 after pledging its support to Kabbah. However, the UNPP, NUP, and PDP announced they were not supporting Kabbah's rule by joining the government but were merely trying to help the country in difficult times. (In 2003, however, NUP leader John BENJAMIN joined the SLPP, following the party's former chair, Dr. John KARIMU, who had defected in 2001.) Indeed, the APC, People's Democratic Alliance (PDA), People's National Convention (PNC), People's Progressive Party (PPP), PDP, and UNPP had formed an opposition alliance styled as the Grand Alliance (GA) in August 2000. A number of smaller parties reportedly joined the GA later. Although the GA members announced they would "unite under a single political party in due course," by mid-2001 various internal rifts seemed to have rendered that aim difficult to achieve. The APC and UNPP subsequently left the alliance.

In the May 14, 2002, balloting, 11 parties presented candidates for the presidency, and 12 parties were represented in the legislative contest. Seven political parties participated in the 2007 parliamentary and presidential elections, while ten took part in the 2012 balloting.

Government Parties:

All People's Congress—APC. Leftist and republican in outlook, the APC was formed in 1960 by Dr. Siaka Probyn Stevens in a split with a dissident group headed at that time by Albert M. Margai. Although strongest in Temne territory, the party was not exclusively tribal in character, drawing its support from wage-earning and lower-middle-class elements in both Temne and non-Temne areas. The APC won all but one of the legislative seats in the 1973 election, which was boycotted by the opposition SLPP; it won all but 15 seats in 1977 and was constitutionally unopposed in 1982 and 1986. At the conclusion of an APC conference in August 1985, despite strong support for (then) first vice president Sorie KOROMA, Maj. Gen. Joseph Momoh was nominated as the sole candidate to succeed Stevens as president of the republic. While yielding the post of secretary general to Momoh, Stevens retained the title of chair, as well as the primary loyalty of much of the party's membership, until his death in June 1988. Momoh was reelected unopposed to the party's top post at the tenth APC conference in January 1989, which also yielded abandonment of the positions of chair and vice chair and adoption of a demanding "Code of Conduct" for political leaders and public servants.

At an APC Central Committee and Governing Council joint session on August 17–20, 1990, President Momoh, pressured by calls for political reform, proposed an "overhauling" of Sierra Leone's political system. However, his support in March 1991 for the adoption of a multiparty constitution generated deep fissures within the party. In mid-July two of its leaders resigned their posts, and ten others were suspended for criticizing the document that was approved in late August. In early 1992 the party further redefined its policies and principles, and, by providing for rank-and-file balloting, underwent sweeping personnel changes.

APC presidential candidate Edward Mohammed Turay captured just 5.1 percent of the vote in 1996 balloting, while the party finished fourth in the legislative contest. In March 2002 Ernest Bai Koroma was elected party president and chosen as the party's candidate for president in the 2002 elections. Koroma won 22.3 percent of the vote, and the party finished second in the legislative election, winning 27 seats, including a seat won by Koroma. Rifts in the party resulted in Koroma's losing the top party post in June 2005, but he was reinstated in September and subsequently ran unopposed for the party leadership. Tensions within the party eased as Koroma was tapped to represent the APC in the 2007 presidential election, securing his victory in two rounds of voting. His win came as a surprise to observers, who had forecast victory by Koroma's main challenger, Vice President Berewa of the long-governing SLPP. But Koroma's leadership in the party reportedly helped it to regain support in the north, its traditional stronghold, and the APC also benefited from newfound support in the south in the runoff, with backing from the PMDC (below), which split the SLPP's support in that region. Also adding to Koroma's popularity, according to *Africa Confidential*, was the fact that "voters seem to think that since he already made so much money (in insurance), he would be less corrupt in power."

In May 2008, the party was said to have lost favor with some members in the wake of reports that the government had shut down the radio station of the SLPP. Soon thereafter, the station was cleared of four charges of misconduct.

Following the peace agreement between the APC and the SLPP in April 2009, SLPP leader John Benjamin, in a show of support for stability, spoke at the APC congress shortly thereafter. President Koroma was reelected party leader, as well as its presidential candidate at a congress in April 2012. Koroma won the November presidential election with 58.7 percent of the vote, while the APC expanded its majority in parliament, securing 67 seats with 53.7 percent of the vote.

Leaders: Ernest Bai KOROMA (President of the Republic and Party Leader and 2002, 2007, and 2012 presidential candidate), Victor CHUKUMA-JOHNSON (Chair), Edward Mohammed TURAY (1996 presidential candidate), Alpha KANU (Spokesperson), Victor FOH (Secretary General).

Opposition Party:

Sierra Leone People's Party—SLPP. Led by former second vice president Salia JUSU-SHERIFF, whose identification with the Momoh regime was viewed as a political liability, the SLPP was launched as a revival of the party outlawed in 1978.

Ahmad Tejan Kabbah, a 64-year-old veteran politician and former UN development worker, emerged as the SLPP's presidential candidate after an intraparty contest with Charles Margai in early 1996. Subsequently, in the February 1996 parliamentary balloting, the SLPP secured 10 more seats than its nearest competitor while its allies (the PDP, APC, NUP, and DCP) gained an additional 24 seats.

In mid-1998, Kabbah reportedly signaled that he would not seek another term in office. Among those cited by observers as potential successors were Margai, cabinet member Harry WILL, and Sam Hinga Norman, whose command of Kamajor militias had won him wide acclaim. Kabbah reversed his previous announcement, however, during a period of peace, which was followed by a resumption of violence and another time of peace from 1999 to 2001, when he won enough support to ensure another election victory for himself and his party in 2002. Former military leader Julius Bio returned to Sierra Leone in 2004 after ten years in exile and reportedly stated his interest in party leadership while condemning the current regime for its alleged corruption and incompetence. Margai left the party in 2005 after losing the leadership post—and, thus, the opportunity to be the party's presidential candidate—to Solomon Berewa, who *Africa Confidential* said was "generally referred to as President Number Two" because Kabbah delegated many official duties to him. Margai then formed the PMDC (above) with other SLPP defectors. Bio, for his part, announced he would not follow Margai and reiterated his support for the SLPP.

Kabbah, who observers said was increasingly unpopular at home and abroad, was barred by the constitution from seeking a third term as president, paving the way for the nomination of Vice President Berewa as the party's standard-bearer in the 2007 election. Berewa chose as his running mate Momodu KOROMA, the minister of foreign affairs, widely known as a Kabbah loyalist. Observers explained Berewa's selection as one of demographics: since Berewa is from the southeast, it was important for him to choose a running mate from the north, where the APC's Ernest Koroma had a stronghold. Though Momodu Koroma was born in the south, his father is a northerner like Kabbah. Party stalwarts reportedly opposed the selection of Koroma, based on his ties to Kabbah and on speculation that Berewa, 67 and in ill health, might not survive a first term.

Though Berewa, described as a shrewd politician, was seen by many as the near-certain successor to Kabbah, the 2007 presidential election proved to be an upset victory for the APC's candidate, bolstered in large part by support from Margai's SLPP-breakaway PMDC, which split the vote in the south. Berewa, who observers said symbolized continuity (versus the change promised by the APC's Koroma), lost in the runoff with 45.4 percent versus Koroma's 54.6 percent. Berewa subsequently resigned as party leader, the post being assumed by U. N. S. JAH.

In 2008 tensions heightened between the SLPP and the APC in advance of local elections in July, with the SLPP threatening to boycott the balloting unless ECOWAS replaced the elections commission as organizer of the poll. (The SLPP had accused the commission of improper conduct during the 2007 elections.) The SLPP ultimately participated, but it faired poorly, leading to discord within the ranks. In early 2009 party veteran John Benjamin was elected chair, and the party began to formulate its strategy ahead of the 2012 general elections. In April the party signed a peace agreement with the APC in the wake of violent confrontations involving both parties in March (see Current issues, above).

Party members began vying for position in early 2010 to become the SLPP's candidate in the 2012 presidential election, as in March 23 members made their intentions known. However, in May Alpha Osman TIMBO, a former labor minister, declared himself the flagbearer, purportedly to mend divisions within the party. In June another long-time party member, Umaru DUMBUYA, who had worked as a prison guard in the United States for many years, said he intended to be the flag bearer. Ultimately, 19 challengers stepped forward but their bids were halted in May 2011 when one of the candidates, Bu-buaker JABBI, took the party to court, claiming the leadership could not hold an election because its tenure had expired. The Supreme Court ruled in his favor. The court also granted the party the right to appeal a Court of Appeal ruling regarding the voiding of several hundred votes in the 2007 presidential runoff election.

Rifts continued to develop in mid-2011, as Brigadier General Bio, a rival of Benjamin's dating to the 1990s, put himself forth as the main presidential candidate of the SLPP. On July 20 the Supreme Court lifted the injunction against the party holding a congress, and when the SLPP convened on July 29–31, Bio secured the presidential nomination with 238 of 602 votes. His closest rival was Usman Boie KAMARA with 186 votes. Timbo received 44 votes and Dumbuya, 2, while Jabbi received just 1 vote. Bio was allied with Abass BUNDU, who lost his bid at the helm to Benjamin, who did not contest the presidential bid. In November 2011, Bio chose Kadi SESAY, a well-known feminist and human rights advocate, as his running mate for the 2012 balloting. Bio lost that election to incumbent president Koroma of the APC, securing 37.4 percent of the vote. Meanwhile Kamara defected to the APC and was appointed to a cabinet post following the November balloting.

Leaders: John BENJAMIN (Chair), Kadi SESAY (Deputy Chair), Solomon BEREWA (Former Vice President of the Republic, and 2007 presidential candidate), Ahmad Tejan KABBAH (Former President of the Republic), Ibrahim SESAY (Deputy Secretary General), Sulaiman Banja TEJANSIE (Secretary General).

Other Parties That Contested the 2012 Elections:

People's Movement for Democratic Change—PMDC. Registered by the government in April 2006, the PMDC was founded by Charles Margai, who left the SLPP after he lost his bid for the chairship, to promote a civilian, democratic government. Margai was arrested in 2006 on a variety of charges related to disorderly behavior against the government and was later released on bail. Several student members reportedly defected to the SLPP in mid-2007, and in midyear Margai was slated as the PMDC's presidential candidate. His defection from the SLPP caused the former governing party to lose a significant number of votes in 2007 in the south and southeast regions of the country, particularly among younger voters, who make up 56 percent of the electorate.

Following the first-round balloting in the 2007 presidential election, in which Margai secured just 13.9 percent of the vote, he backed Ernest Bai Koroma in the runoff. The new president subsequently named four PMDC members to his cabinet, including party co-founder Moses Moisa-Kapu. In the concurrent parliamentary elections, the PMDC secured a small number of seats, trailing the APC and the SLPP.

Rifts reportedly began developing between the PMDC and the APC in early 2008 when Margai accused the new APC government of "chronic tribalism." Merger talks with the SLPP later in the year did not come to fruition at a time when the PMDC was widely reported to be in disarray. Subsequently, in 2009 the national women's leader of the party blamed Margai for bringing about the "disintegration" of the PMDC. However, in February President Koroma included PMDC members in his reshuffled cabinet. Meanwhile, rifts within the party deepened, and in January 2010 more than 600 members reportedly defected to the APC. More defections, this time to the SLPP, were reported in September. Margai again publicly lashed out at the APC in October, claiming that President Koroma gave former party chair Mohamed Bangura $300,000 to form a new political party. Bangura, who was suspended in July for three years for allegedly offending the values of the party, denied that he had been given any money. Bangura and others in the party who had protested his suspension called for Margai to step down from the helm, but a court ruling upheld Bangura's suspension, and Margai retained his post. Bangura subsequently formed a new party, the **United Democratic Movement** (UDM), in 2011 (see below).

In July 2011, Margai shocked party members with the remarks he made at the SLPP party congress indicating that the PMDC would align with the SLPP during presidential and parliamentary elections in 2012 and that he aimed to remove the APC from power. The PMDC immediately issued a statement condemning Margai for his comments and vowing that the party would remain united and "focused on its political objectives for the 2012 elections." In September 2012, Margai was reelected party leader. Margai placed third the November presidential election, securing just 1.3 percent of the vote. The PMDC received just 3.2 percent of the vote in concurrent legislative balloting and failed to gain any seats in the parliament.

Leaders: Charles MARGAI (President of the Party and 2007 presidential candidate), Moses MOISA-KAPU, Ansu LANSANA, William A. B. TUCKER (Secretary General).

National Democratic Alliance—NDA. The NDA fielded candidates for the legislature but not the presidency in 2002. The party reconvened in 2005 after having been inactive for several years.

In 2007, the NDA formed an alliance with the PLP to back Vice President Solomon Berewa of the SLPP in the presidential runoff election. The NDA's candidate, Amadu Jalloh, finished fifth, with about 1 percent of the vote, in the first round of balloting. The NDA did not field a candidate in the 2012 presidential balloting. It received 1.29 percent of the vote in the assembly elections and no seats.

Leaders: Ansu MASSAQUOI (Chair), Amadu JALLOH (2007 presidential candidate), Abdul BAH, Margaret SEDIKIE, Francis BAWOH (Secretary General).

Peace and Liberation Party—PLP. Established in 2001, the PLP was led by the former AFRC leader Johnny Paul Koroma. It was linked with the Grassroots Awareness movement, one of many peace promotion organizations. In the May 2002 elections, Koroma came in third in the presidential race, while the party won 3.6 percent of the vote—and two seats—in the legislative contest. Though Koroma was indicted in 2003, he remained the party's leader, the party spokesperson said in 2007. However, it was later reported that Koroma was dead.

In the 2007 presidential election, Kandeh Baba Conteh came in sixth in the first round, with 0.6 percent of the vote.

The PLP was ruled ineligible to participate in the 2008 local elections. Conteh was the party's presidential candidate in the 2012 elections. He placed seventh with 0.3 percent of the vote. The PLP secured just 0.1 percent of the vote in the legislative elections.

Leaders: Kandeh Baba CONTEH (2007 and 2012 presidential candidate), Darlington MORRISON (Chair), Bai MORROW, Amadu BAH (Spokesperson).

United National People's Party—UNPP. The UNPP secured 17 seats behind a 21 percent vote tally in the February 1996 balloting. Meanwhile, its leader, banker John KARIFA-SMART, placed second in concurrent presidential balloting. In March 1997 Karifa-Smart was charged with contempt and suspended from the assembly. He also unsuccessfully attempted in April 2001 to expel some legislators from the party due to differences on certain policies. Karifa-Smart came in last, with 1 percent of the vote, in the May 2002 presidential election, and the UNPP failed to win any seats in the legislative contest, with 1.3 percent of the vote. Following the election, a cabinet minister who had been a member of the UNPP joined the SLPP. In May 2005 the UNPP joined in coalition with the National Unity Movement (NUM, below) in advance of the next presidential elections. It backed out of a so-called merger with the RUF after some of the latter's leaders were charged with war crimes.

Karifa-Smart retired from politics in 2006, and Abdul Kadi Karim was elected as party leader and 2007 presidential candidate. He came in last with 0.4 percent of votes. In 2008 the party was one of three ruled ineligible to take part in local elections in March.

James Obai Fullah emerged as the UNPP's presidential candidate in the 2012 elections. He came in ninth (last) with 0.2 percent of the vote. The UNPP secured just 0.2 percent of the vote in assembly balloting.

Leaders: James Obai FULLAH (Party Leader and 2012 presidential candidate), Abdul Kadi KARIM (2007 presidential candidate), Mohamed

Husman FORNAH (Chair), Osman CONTEH (Secretary General).

People's Democratic Party—PDP. The PDP was characterized by *West Africa* as the "loudest" of the new parties, whose "main handicap is the uncharismatic quality" of its leader, former information minister Thaimu BANGURA. In September 1991 Bangura had been named chair of a United Front of Political Movements (UNIFORM), a six-party opposition formation that was subsequently dissolved.

In the February 1996 balloting, Bangura placed third in the presidential contest, with 16.1 percent of the vote, and the party won 12 seats. Subsequently, as an apparent reward for supporting Kabbah in the second round of presidential balloting, the PDP secured three cabinet portfolios.

Bangura died in March 1999. Following infighting between Osman Kamara and former NPRC member Abdul Rahman KAMARA to replace Bangura, Osman Kamara was elected chair. Abdul Rahman Kamara quit the party to form his own organization, the **People's Democratic Alliance** (PDA) in November. In a cabinet reshuffle in March 2001, Osman Kamara was given the post of the trade and industry minister, although he claimed that the PDP was still an opposition party. He was subsequently replaced. The PDP, with 1 percent of the vote, failed to win a seat in the legislative election of May 2002. Following the election, one cabinet member affiliated with the PDP subsequently joined the SLPP. The party did not present a presidential candidate but came out in support of Kabbah. Several party officials were expelled in 2006 for alleged financial malfeasance. The party did not participate in the 2007 elections.

In May 2009, there was speculation that former APC minister of transport and aviation, Kemoh SESAY, was planning to revive and lead the PDP. Sesay was dismissed in the cabinet reshuffle of February 2009 because of suspicions related to a cocaine deal.

In September, the party elected Gibrilla KAMARA as its 2012 presidential candidate and the PDP leader. He placed sixth in the November polling with 0.4 percent of the vote. The PDP received 0.4 percent of the vote in the concurrent legislative balloting.

Leader: Gibrillia KAMARA (Secretary General and 2012 presidential candidate).

Revolutionary United Front—RUF. The Revolutionary United Front (RUF) surfaced in early 1991 as a group of Sierra Leone dissidents who had joined forces with Liberian guerrillas loyal to Charles Taylor along the Sierra Leone–Liberia border, where diamond smuggling had been estimated to yield some $100 million annually. In July 1992 the rebels rejected an appeal by the Strasser regime to surrender and negotiate a resolution of their estrangement from Freetown, demanding instead a national interim government and free democratic elections.

In August 1993, the RUF was described as "unorganized" amid indications that attempts had been made to oust its leader, Foday Sankannah Sankoh (who earlier was rumored to have died). On December 30 Sankoh's personal bodyguards surrendered when government troops overran Pujehin, and in early 1994 the RUF leader was reported to have barely escaped arrest during fighting at Kailahun, which resulted in the further capture of elite rebel troops.

Thereafter, although estimates of the actual number of RUF members fluctuated between 100 and 1,000, the group, which had reportedly broken into four units, was credited with orchestrating military activities in over two-thirds of the country. By October 1994 some observers suggested that the government's war with the rebels was nearly concluded. However, in early November the RUF appeared to be invigorated when its seizure of two British nationals drew international attention, and on November 28 the rebels rejected Freetown's cease-fire entreaties, saying it would only negotiate with the British government.

On January 18–20, 1995, the RUF captured two of the country's most important mines; however, the rebels suffered numerous casualties in a government counter-offensive that dislodged the insurgents. Subsequently, the RUF requested that the International Committee of the Red Cross act as a mediator in the conflict.

Confronted with a reorganized Sierra Leonean Army and near starvation conditions in areas under their control, RUF political leaders in September 1995 reportedly sought a dialogue with Freetown. However, rebel military activities continued unabated, underscoring the reported split between RUF moderates and militants.

Following the overthrow of the Strasser regime in mid-January 1996, the RUF announced a one-week unconditional cease-fire, and on February 25 the rebels held their first direct talks with the new government in Côte d'Ivoire, where they unsuccessfully sought a delay in nationwide elections. Subsequently, the rebels were blamed for disrupting polling in a number of regions. At a meeting with Brigadier General Bio on March 24, Sankoh agreed to a cease-fire but refused to recognize the civilian government-elect. Thereafter, the Kabbah government expressed "cautious optimism" following a meeting between Sankoh and the new president on April 22–23, which yielded a "definitive" cease-fire. The final accord signed on November 30 permitted the RUF to begin functioning as a political movement immediately, with the understanding that it would apply for formal party recognition within 30 days.

Subsequently, implementation of the peace pact stalled because Sankoh refused to meet with officials seeking to finalize the scheduling of the RUF's disarmament and reintegration, and in early 1997 the government accused Sankoh of failing to meet his responsibilities as dictated by the accord. Following a meeting with Nigerian officials, Sankoh was arrested in Lagos on March 12. Three days later, a senior RUF official, Philip Sylvester PALMER, announced that Sankoh had been dismissed from the RUF for "thwarting the peace process." The arrest and ouster of Sankoh (an "international conspiracy" according to his followers) sparked fierce internecine fighting between his loyalists and opponents.

RUF militants played a major role in the fighting, which led to President Kabbah's overthrow in May 1997, and in June at least three RUF representatives were included in the AFRC. Moreover, the AFRC's exhaustive diplomatic efforts to win Sankoh's freedom from detention in Nigeria fueled reports that the RUF was steering the junta's activities. During negotiations with the AFRC in late 1997, representatives of the Kabbah administration agreed to find a role for Sankoh upon their proposed reinstallation in Freetown. Meanwhile, RUF fighters who had aligned with rebel soldiers were being targeted by Ecomog troops.

Following the peace agreement with the government in July 1999, the RUF was promised cabinet posts, and Sankoh was given powers equivalent to those of vice president. In the meantime, the RUF decided to transform itself into a registered political party (the RUFP). However, after the breakdown of the agreement and the resumption of fighting in May 2000, Sankoh was jailed, and Issa Sesay replaced him as the interim leader. In June the government asked the UN to set up a special court to try Sankoh and other RUF officials for "war crimes."

Before and after the RUF's announcement of commitment to the peace process once again in May 2001, there were signs of a split within the organization. Reportedly, the faction for continuing the war, represented by an uneasy coalition of Sam Bockarie and Dennis Superman Mingo, was in conflict with the official leadership of Sesay and the faction committed to the peace process.

The RUFP's presidential candidate, Alimamy Pallo BANGURA, came in fourth, with 1.7 percent of the vote, in May 2002, while the party won 2.2 percent of the vote—and no seats—in the legislative contest.

Sesay, who had been indicted on war crimes charges by the special court, was replaced as interim leader in January 2005 by Peter VANDY. The following month, however, Vandy resigned from the party and joined the SLPP, declaring his belief in the SLPP as the party of reconciliation and multiparty democracy. In early 2006 Sesay was in detention on war crimes charges. Meanwhile, party official Omrie Golley was charged in 2006 with plotting to overthrow the government. Former presidential candidate Bangura resigned from the party in 2006.

In 2007, Secretary General Jonathan Kposova said the party would not contest the upcoming presidential and parliamentary elections because of a lack of financial support.

The war crimes trial of Sesay and other RUF leaders, which began in mid-2008, concluded in March 2009 with the convictions of Sesay, Morris KALLON, and Augustine GBAO on 14–16 charges of war crimes and crimes against humanity. Sesay was sentenced in April to 52 years in prison, Kallon received a 40-year sentence, and Gbao received 25 years. (The court did not have the authority to impose life sentences.) In October the court upheld the sentences for Sesay, Kallon, and Gbao.

In August 2010, at the trial of former Liberian president Charles Taylor, Sesay (a defense witness for Taylor) apologized to the people of Sierra Leone for his role in the war. In September 2012, Eldred Collins was elected the leader of the RUFP and became the party's 2012 presidential candidate. Collins secured 0.6 percent of the vote while the RUF received 0.6 percent in the legislative polling.

Leaders: Eldred COLLINS (Party Leader and 2012 presidential candidate), Issa SESAY (in detention), Gibril MASSAQUOI (Spokesperson), Dennis Superman MINGO, Omrie GOLLEY (Peace and Political Council Chair; in detention), Jonathan KPOSOVA (Secretary General).

United Democratic Movement—UDM. With the goal of contesting the 2012 elections, the UDM was established by former PMDC chair Mohamed Bangura in early 2011. The party received its official legal approval on May 31. Bangura was the UDM presidential candidate in 2012. He received 0.2 percent of the vote, while the UDM received 0.6 percent in the concurrent assembly elections.

Leader: Martin BANGURA (Party Chair and 2012 presidential candidate).

Citizens Democratic Party—CDP. Led by Joshua Albert Carew, the party's 2012 presidential candidate, the CDP secured 0.4 percent of the vote in the 2012 legislative elections.

Leader: Joshua Albert CAREW (Chair and 2012 presidential candidate).

Other Parties and Groups:

Other groups include the **People's Progressive Party** (PPP), led by former ECOWAS executive secretary Dr. Abass Bundu who was a 1996 presidential candidate but in 2007 was said to be in the SLPP camp; the **People's National Convention** (PNC), led by 1996 presidential candidate Edward KARGBO, reported in 2002 to be retired; the **National Unity Movement** (NUM), led by Sam LEIGH, which formed a political alliance with the UNPP in 2005; the **National Alliance Democratic Party** (NADP), an opposition party based in the United States and led by Mohamed Yahya SILLAH; the **Sierra Leoneans Advocate for Progress** (SLAP), led by Christian JOHNSON and Jon KANU; and the **Liberal Democratic Party** (LDP) and the **Sierra Leone Socialist Party** (SLSP), both organized in 2000.

For more on the **Convention People's Party**—CPP, and the **Citizens United for Peace and Progress**—CUPP, see the 2012 *Handbook.* For information on the **Movement for Progress**—MOP, see the 2013 *Handbook.*

LEGISLATURE

The Sierra Leone **National Assembly** is a 124-member unicameral body. In accordance with the Electoral Laws Act of 2002, a constitutional amendment was enacted on February 7, 2002, providing for 112 assembly members to be elected on a party-list proportional basis (5 percent threshold required) from 12 multimember constituencies for five-year terms. In addition, 12 seats are filled by paramount chiefs, representing the 12 provincial districts.

In the most recent election of November 17, 2012, the All People's Congress won 67 seats, and the Sierra Leone People's Party, 42 (three seats remained undecided as of June 20, 2013). The 12 seats for paramount chiefs were filled on December 7, 2012.

Speaker: Abel N. STRONG.

CABINET

[as of November 15, 2013]

President	Ernest Bai Koroma
Vice President	Sahr Sam-Sumana
Ministers	
Agriculture, Food Security, and Forestry	Sam Sesay (APC)
Defense	Maj. (Ret.) Paolo Conteh
Education, Science, and Technology	Minkailu Bah
Energy	Oluniyi Robbin-Coker
Finance and Development	Kaifala Marrah (APC)
Foreign Affairs	Samura Kamara
Health and Sanitation	Miatta Kargbo [f]
Information and Communications	Alpha Kanu (APC)
Internal Affairs	Joseph B. Dauda (APC)
Justice and Attorney General	Frank Kargbo
Labor and Social Security	Matthew Teambo
Lands, Country Planning, and Environment	Musa Tarawally
Local Government and Rural Development	Finda Diana Konomanyi [f]
Marine Resources and Fisheries	Capt. Allieu Pat-Sowe
Mineral Resources	Minkailu Mansaray (APC)
Political and Public Affairs	Ibrahim Kemoh Sesay
Resident Minister, East	William Juana Smith (APC)
Resident Minister, North	Alie Kamara
Resident Minister, South	Muctarr Conteh
Social Welfare, Gender, and Children's Affairs	Emmanuel Moijueh Kaikai
Sports	Paul Kamara
Tourism and Cultural Affairs	Peter Bayuku Konteh
Trade and Industry	Osman Boie Kamara (APC)
Transport and Aviation	Leonard Balogun Koroma
Youth	Alimamy Kamara
Water Resources	Momodu Maligie
Works and Housing and Infrastructural Development	Alimamy P. Koroma (APC)

[f] = female

INTERGOVERNMENTAL REPRESENTATION

Ambassador to the U.S.: Bockari K. STEVENS.

U.S. Ambassador to Sierra Leone: Michael S. OWEN.

Permanent Representative to the UN: Shekou M. TOURAY.

IGO Memberships (Non-UN): AfDB, AU, CWTH, ECOWAS, IOM, NAM, OIC, WTO.

SINGAPORE

Republic of Singapore
Xinjiapo Gongheguo (Chinese)
Republik Singapura (Malay)
Singapur Kutiyarasu (Tamil)

Political Status: Attained self-rule within the British Commonwealth June 3, 1959; joined in formation of Malaysia on September 16, 1963; independent republic since August 9, 1965.

Area: 246 sq. mi. (636 sq. km), including adjacent islets that encompass some 15 sq. mi. (39 sq. km).

Population: 5,259,252 (2012E—UN); 5,460,302 (2013E—U.S. Census).

Major Urban Center (2011E): SINGAPORE (5,183,700).

Official Languages: Chinese (Mandarin is the preferred form), English, Malay, Tamil.

Monetary Unit: Singapore Dollar (market rate November 1, 2013: 1.24 dollars = $1US).

President: Tony TAN Keng Yam (nonparty); declared president-elect on August 27, 2011; inaugurated on September 1 for a six-year term, following presidential elections on August 27, 2011, succeeding Sellapan Ramanathan NATHAN (nonparty).

Prime Minister: LEE Hsien Loong (People's Action Party); sworn in on August 12, 2004, upon the resignation of GOH Chok Tong (People's Action Party); continued in office following the election of May 7, 2011.

THE COUNTRY

Joined to the southern tip of the Malay Peninsula by a three-quarter-mile-long causeway, Singapore consists of a single large island, on which

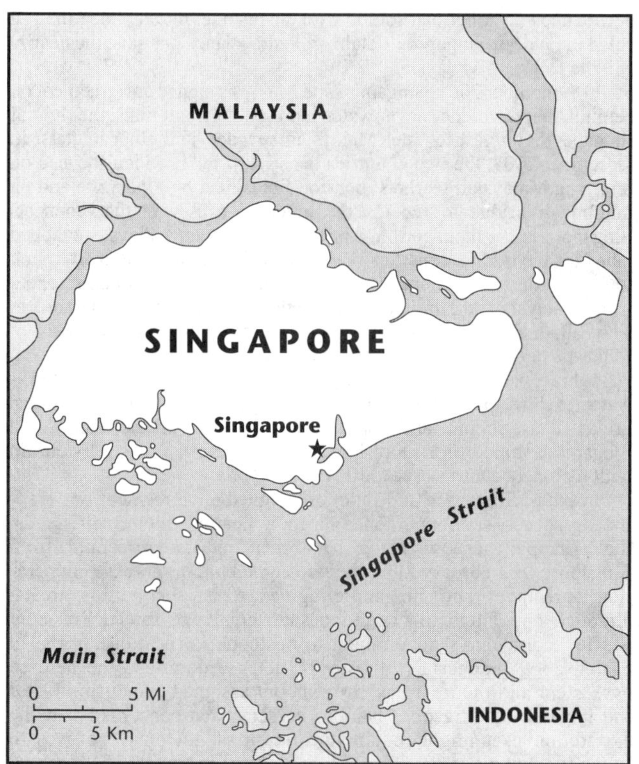

the city of Singapore is located, and about 50 adjacent islets. Situated at the crossroads of Southeast Asian trade routes, the country is one of the world's most densely populated, with two-thirds of the population—about 74 percent ethnic Chinese, 13 percent Malay, and 9 percent Indian and Pakistani—residing in Singapore City. Religious divisions follow ethnic divisions: the Malays and Pakistanis are overwhelmingly Muslim, the Indians are Hindu, and the Chinese include Buddhists, Christians, Taoists, and Confucianists. Women constitute 43 percent of the active labor force and 23.5 percent of the members of parliament.

Singapore's economy has traditionally been geared to the entrepôt trade, with a heavy emphasis on the processing and transshipment of petroleum, rubber, timber, and other regional products, and on related banking, shipping, insurance, and storage services. In addition, tourism has become a significant source of earnings. In all, services account for 74 percent of GDP and employ 76 percent of the labor force. Singapore is a leading oil-refining hub and a "global operations center" for more than 3,500 multinational firms. (For more information on Singapore's economy, see the 2010 *Handbook*.) Singapore is now a major producer of computer-related electronics as well as pharmaceuticals. Manufacturing as a whole contributes 26 percent of GDP and employs 17 percent of the active labor force.

For 2005–2008 average annual GDP growth was 7.5 percent. Following a record downturn in the first half of 2009, the economy quickly recovered and GDP growth rebounded to 14.7 percent in 2010 as a result of renewed exports. Government gross debt has steadily decreased since 2009, when it totaled 105 percent of GDP, falling to 96.2 percent in 2010 and 93.4 percent in 2011. In 2012, GDP grew by 1.3 percent, while inflation was 4 percent, and unemployment 2 percent. GDP per capita that year was $51,162, while the government again posted a surplus, $3.9 billion or 1.1 percent of GDP. In 2013, once again, the World Bank ranked Singapore first in its annual Doing Business index.

GOVERNMENT AND POLITICS

Political background. Established as a trading station by Sir Stamford RAFFLES in 1819, purchased by Great Britain in 1824, and subsequently organized as part of the Straits Settlements (with Penang and Malacca), Singapore became a crown colony in 1867. It was occupied by the Japanese in World War II but achieved internal self-rule within the Commonwealth on June 3, 1959. Led by LEE Kuan Yew of the People's Action Party (PAP), it joined in 1963 with the Federation of Malaya, Sarawak, and Sabah to form Malaysia. Malay opinion subsequently became alarmed by the efforts of Lee and his largely Chinese party to extend their influence into other parts of Malaysia, and Singapore was consequently excluded on August 9, 1965.

As a fully independent state, Singapore adopted a republican form of government. The PAP, which had been seriously challenged in the early 1960s by the more radical Socialist Front (*Barisan Sosialis*), subsequently consolidated its position, obtaining a monopoly of all legislative seats in the four elections from 1968 through 1980 and then losing no more than two seats through 1988. By then, Prime Minister Lee had made a strong effort to bring "second-liners" (second-generation leaders) into government and the PAP hierarchy.

In October 1989, Lee, having become the world's longest-serving prime minister, confirmed reports that he planned to step down as prime minister. In November 1990 GOH Chok Tong formally succeeded Lee, who nevertheless retained backstage power in the post of senior minister and, until 1992, as PAP secretary general.

Although retaining its political dominance, the PAP was jolted by the outcome of an early election called by Goh for August 1991: The opposition captured four seats while the ruling party's popular support fell to a 23-year low of 61 percent. In response, the prime minister undertook a September cabinet shakeup that dispensed with most of his second-generation colleagues in favor of a third-generation cohort, including his predecessor's son, LEE Hsien Loong. Conscious that the anti-PAP vote had secured inadequate representation, and in an apparent effort to undermine by-election campaigns by the opposition, the government approved a 1992 parliamentary recommendation that six nonelected persons should become MPs, as allowed under a 1990 constitutional amendment.

In the legislative election of January 1997, the PAP won 81 of 83 seats with about 65 percent of the popular vote. The following May J. B. JEYARETNAM, secretary general of the Workers' Party (WP) and a longtime opponent of Lee Kuan Yew and the PAP, was awarded a nonconstituency seat to bring the opposition total up to the constitutionally mandated minimum of three.

In July 1999, ONG Teng Cheong, who had been installed in 1993 as Singapore's first popularly elected president, announced that he would not seek reelection. S. R. NATHAN, a former military intelligence official and ambassador to the United States, was designated president-elect on August 18 by the Presidential Elections Commission, which had declared that the two other potential nominees did not meet the standards for office. On September 1 Nathan took the oath of office.

Hoping to forestall negative political consequences of an economic downturn, in October 2001, Prime Minister Goh announced an early legislative election for November 3. Earlier, four opposition parties had organized a Singapore Democratic Alliance (SDA), but the PAP nevertheless retained its stranglehold on Parliament, winning 82 elective seats, compared to 1 for the SDA and 1 for the WP.

On August 17, 2003, Prime Minister Goh confirmed what had long been anticipated in announcing the appointment of Deputy Prime Minister Lee Hsien Loong, officially taking over on August 12, 2004.

On April 20, 2006, Parliament was dissolved and an early election called on May 6. Although the PAP experienced a drop to 67 percent in overall support compared with 75 percent in 2001, it again won 82 seats. On May 7, 2011, the PAP received its lowest level of popular support since 1965, taking 60.1 percent of the vote in the general election, which cost the party one seat. Loong continued to occupy the office of prime minister after the general election in May (see Current issues, below), which was followed by the election of Tony TAN Keng Yam (IND) as president on August 27, 2011.

On August 1, 2012, Loong announced a cabinet reform whereby the ministry of community development, youth, and sport and the ministry of information, communication, and the arts would be reconfigured to create three new portfolios beginning in November.

On January 14, 2013, Halimah YACOB (PAP) became the first woman elected speaker of Singapore's parliament.

Constitution and government. Singapore's current basic law has evolved since 1959, with amendments necessitated by its temporary Malaysian affiliation and the subsequent adoption of republican status. The executive branch is headed by a president with limited powers—the chief executive's principal role is to safeguard the country's financial reserves—and a presidentially designated prime minister, who must command a parliamentary majority and who selects a cabinet that is collectively responsible to the Parliament. A Presidential Elections Commission is responsible for vetting presidential nominees, who must have sufficient governmental or corporate experience and be able to demonstrate "good integrity, character, and reputation." A Presidential Council for Minority Rights reviews legislation (except money bills or security-related legislation) to ensure racial and religious nondiscrimination.

The unicameral legislature is elected by universal suffrage and compulsory voting for a maximum term of five years. Under 1984 and 2010 constitutional amendments, up to nine nonconstituency seats (originally six) may be awarded to ensure opposition representation in Parliament, with the precise minimum number of opposition seats (currently three) determined by electoral law. Should fewer than three members of the opposition win election, the requisite number of nonconstituency seats are awarded to the opposition candidate(s) who came closest to winning. In addition, 1990 and 1997 constitutional amendments authorize the president, based on recommendations from a Special Select Committee of Parliament, to name up to nine (originally six) similarly constrained "nonpolitical Singaporeans." A 2010 amendment made the nonpolitical appointee system permanent. Nonelected members are not permitted, however, to vote on key measures, such as money bills, nonconfidence motions, and constitutional amendments.

Singapore's Supreme Court encompasses a High Court and a Court of Appeal. Since 1994 the Court of Appeal has served as the highest appellate court, replacing in that capacity the Judicial Committee of the UK Privy Council. Subordinate courts include district and magistrate's courts.

Even before independence, Singapore was administered as a unified city-state, local government bodies having been absorbed by departments of the central government in 1959. In 1960 Parliament created a People's Association (PA), a statutory board chaired by the prime minister and led by a chief executive director. Its goals have included achieving multiracial harmony, advancing social cohesion, and organizing community work. As such, it has sponsored residential committees, a Social Development Service, volunteer and grassroots organizations, community clubs, and youth programs, among other bodies and activities. The PA is also responsible for appointing members of Community Development Councils (CDCs). In 2000 Prime Minister Goh stated that the government planned to give the CDCs greater authority, responsibilities, and funding, in order to decentralize delivery of various services and other government functions. At present, the country's 23 electoral constituencies are grouped into five regions, each of which has an appointed mayor (a member of Parliament) and a CDC of roughly 12–80 councilors drawn from among community leaders, administrators, and professionals.

The domestic press has long been free in principle although restrained in practice by government ownership or control of major outlets, continuous monitoring, and periodic crackdowns for exceeding official perceptions of acceptable criticism. The government has also taken action against a number of foreign publications, several of which have been forced to apologize for articles and to make civil payments to government officials for critical stories. Internet sites posting political or religious content must register. In 2013, Reporters Without Borders ranked Singapore 149th out of 179 countries in press freedom, a decline from 135th the previous year. In April 2013, cartoonist Leslie Chew was arrested for sedition following the publication of a cartoon that implied the government was racist toward ethnic Malays.

Foreign relations. Singapore joined the United Nations in 1965 and in 1967 helped found the Association of Southeast Asian Nations (ASEAN). Upon the departure of most British defense forces in 1971, Singapore became a member of the Five Power Defense Arrangement (along with Britain, Australia, New Zealand, and Malaysia), a regional security system that calls for the maintenance of Commonwealth forces in Singapore.

Following independence, Singapore's relations with its immediate neighbors were initially tense. However, in 1989 Malaysia and Singapore held their first joint military exercises since 1965, and the Lee government signed defense agreements with both Malaysia and Indonesia. In early 1992, however, Singapore-Malaysia relations were strained when a visit to Singapore by U.S. President George H. W. Bush produced an agreement on relocating a U.S. naval logistical command headquarters from Subic Bay, Philippines, to Singapore.

In 1998 Singapore and Malaysia agreed to submit to the International Court of Justice (ICJ) competing claims to the islet of Pedra Blanca (Pulau Batu Putih), although a formal agreement to that effect was not signed until February 2003. Eight months later the International Tribunal for the Law of the Sea ruled against Malaysia and in favor of Singapore's right to conduct land reclamation on Pulau Tekong island. In January 2005 the neighbors reached a "mutually acceptable and beneficial solution" to the dispute. In May 2008 the ICJ ruled in favor of Singapore's claim to Pedra Blanca but gave the nearby Middle Rocks to Malaysia.

In September 2001, Singapore and Malaysia signed an agreement on settling their differences over water supplies, transport links, the right of Singapore's aircraft to enter Malaysian airspace, and other matters. In December 2004, the two countries began new talks, which focused on releasing Malaysian workers' pension funds held by Singapore and on building a bridge to replace the outdated causeway that connects Singapore to the mainland. In April 2006, however, Malaysia scrapped plans for the bridge, construction of which Singapore continued to link to restoration of full airspace rights as well as to a 20-year commitment from Malaysia for 1 billion cubic meters of sand for reclamation. In May 2010, Prime Minister Lee and Prime Minister Najib Razak of Malaysia agreed to resolve differences over rail stations and transit. In 2011, however, disputes persisted with Malaysia over delivering freshwater to Singapore, Singapore's extensive land reclamation works, bridge construction, and maritime boundaries in the Johor and Singapore Straits. (For more information on Singapore's relationship with regional countries, see the 2010 *Handbook.*)

In 2006, Singapore and Indonesia signed an agreement on establishing special economic zones on three nearby Indonesian islands, the principal purpose being to attract investment capital from Singapore. In February 2007 the two signed a joint defense cooperation agreement and Singapore agreed to an extradition treaty, although opposition in the Indonesian legislature forced President Susilo Yudhoyono's government to postpone ratification efforts. In March 2009 Indonesia's minister of defense described the defense agreement and the treaty as "frozen" but assigned responsibility for the impasse to Singapore, which, he said, was concerned that the extradition pact might require the return of not only fugitives to Indonesia, but also their funds. More recently, in August 2010 the two countries' foreign ministers concluded an agreement defining the maritime border in the western Singapore Strait. (For more information on Singapore's relationship with Indonesia prior to 2006, please see the 2010 *Handbook.*)

The government supported the U.S.-led invasion of Iraq in March 2003 and committed a landing ship (LST) and a handful of support aircraft, but no combat troops, to the multinational operation.

Effective January 2010, Singapore and five other ASEAN states (Brunei, Indonesia, Malaysia, Philippines, and Thailand) inaugurated a trade agreement with China under which 90 percent of mutual trade was tariff-free. The resultant trade zone is the largest in the world in terms of overall population and third, behind the European Union and the North American Free Trade Association, in terms of potential value. Territorial disputes in the South China Sea between China and several ASEAN countries surfaced in 2010 and 2011. Foreign ministers from Singapore and Cambodia jointly urged a peaceful solution in October 2011. Also in October, Singapore donated 45 military patrol boats to Thailand.

The United States announced the deployment of three additional naval vessels to Singapore. The two countries also promised to increase bilateral military exercises. The increased cooperation was reported to be a reaction to the rising Chinese military presence in the region. In April 2012, Singapore agreed to contribute $4 billion to the $430 billion International Monetary Fund (IMF) emergency fund used to support Eurozone bailout programs. The pledge was challenged in court by opposition lawmakers but approved by the high court in October. In June, Singapore and Thailand announced a series of initiatives to ease restrictions on private financial transactions between the two countries. In December, Singapore finalized negotiations with the EU over a free trade agreement.

In March 2013, Singapore requested the assistance of the Federal Bureau of Investigation of the United States in the investigation of the death of U.S. citizen Shane Todd. The death was initially ruled a suicide, but Todd's family and U.S. officials sought a more thorough investigation.

In June 2013, Singapore and Australia signed an agreement to expand sports cooperation in areas such as training, illegal sports betting, and antidoping efforts. The following month, Singapore and Thailand agreed to revise their 35-year-old tax and investment treaty. Meanwhile, Singapore and Japan pledged greater cooperation on antipiracy efforts in the Pacific.

Current issues. Criticism of the government remains circumscribed by legal impediments, including the country's severe slander laws and the Internal Security Act (ISA). Moreover, the PAP continues to use lawsuits and the threat of consequent bankruptcy against opponents. The ISA has also been used to detain suspected terrorists, including members of the *Jemaah Islamiah* (JI), the Indonesian-based terrorist network that has called for creation of a regional Muslim state. In September 2009 Singapore released three suspected terrorists, two from the JI and one from the Philippine-based Moro Islamic Liberation Front, because they had cooperated with the government and had made "significant progress" toward rehabilitation. Two of them had been held since 2002 and the third, since 2005. In September 2010 Indonesia extradited Mas Salamat KASTARI to Singapore to face charges involving a plot to hijack an aircraft and crash it at Singapore's international airport. Kastari has been described as the former leader of Singapore's JI branch.

The 2010 census revealed that the national population has surpassed 5 million, including 540,000 permanent residents and 1.3 million nonresidents. The number of nonresidents grew from 750,000 in 2000.

In the May 7, 2011, parliamentary elections, the overwhelmingly dominant PAP received its lowest level of support in 46 years, reflecting voter concerns over the economy. Nonetheless, the party secured 81 of the 87 elected seats.

In January 2012, the government approved recommendations to cut the pay of ministers by an average of 36 percent (Singapore's cabinet members are among the highest-paid government officials in the world). The president's salary would also be cut by 51 percent, while members of parliament would see 3 percent reductions. In July, the government reduced the number of criminal offences that were eligible for capital punishment. In August, two new universities, the Singapore Institute of Technology and SIM University, opened. They were Singapore's fifth and sixth universities and part of an effort to expand the number of graduating high-school Singaporeans able to enter university in the city state from 27 percent to 40 percent.

In response to growing international criticism, a new law in March 2013 mandated that domestic workers such as maids and housekeepers be given at least one day off per week; at the time, estimates were that fewer than 10 percent of household workers were given one day off per week.

In late June 2013, activist and former SDP treasurer Vincent WIJEYSINGHA became Singapore's first openly homosexual politician. By August, Wijeysingha had resigned from the SDP to focus full-time on activism related to civil liberties and human rights.

POLITICAL PARTIES

Since Singapore achieved self-rule in 1959, the People's Action Party (PAP) has never been out of power. Newly registered parties continue to show low membership.

Governing Party:

People's Action Party (PAP). Organized as a radical socialist party in 1954, the PAP has been Singapore's ruling party since 1959. Some of its more militant leaders were arrested by the British in 1957, and other radicals split off in 1961 to form the Socialist Front (see under WP, below). What remained was the more moderate, anti-Communist wing of the original party, which has supported a pragmatic program emphasizing social welfare and economic development.

Despite its legislative dominance, the party's share of the total vote declined steadily from 78 percent in 1980 to 61 percent in 1991. It rebounded to a 65 percent share in January 1997, when the PAP won 81 of 83 parliamentary seats, and to nearly 75 percent in 2001, when it won 82 of 84 seats. Prime Minister Goh soon announced that a "People's Action Forum" of 20 MPs would be set up as an internal opposition to encourage debate within the PAP.

Under the leadership of Goh's successor, Lee Hsien Loong, the PAP's support declined to 67 percent of the vote and 82 elective seats in the May 2006 election and again in May 2011, with 60.1 percent of the vote and 81 of 87 seats. Loong was appointed chair of the Government of Singapore Investment Corporation (GIC) in June 2011.

In January 2013, the PAP suffered its second by-election defeat since the 2011 polling, reducing its majority to 80 seats.

Leaders: LEE Hsien Loong (Prime Minister and Secretary General of the Party), TEO Chee Hean (Assistant Secretary General and Deputy Prime Minister), KHAW Boon Wan (Chair and Minister for National Development), YAACOB Ibrahim (Vice Chair and Minister for Communications and Information), LIM Swee Say (Treasurer and Minister in the Prime Minister's Office).

Parliamentary Opposition:

Workers' Party—WP (*Parti Pekerja*). Founded in 1957 and reorganized in 1971, the WP long advocated a more democratic constitution and closer relations with Malaysia. In its early years a number of WP leaders were arrested for alleged pro-Communist activities, and in 1978 its secretary general, Joshua Benjamin Jeyaretnam, was convicted of having committed "a very grave slander" against Prime Minister Lee. In a by-election in October 1981, the Sri Lankan–born Jeyaretnam became the first opposition member of Parliament since 1968. Despite having previously been acquitted of making a false declaration about party finances, Jeyaretnam and the party chair, WONG Hong Toy, were retried in September 1985. Jeyaretnam was fined and imprisoned for one month in late 1986, which cost him his legislative seat.

Prior to the 1988 election, the Socialist Front (Barisan Sosialis) and the Singapore United Front—SUF (Barisan Bersatu Singapura) merged with the WP. Formed in 1961 by a group of pro-Beijing PAP militants under the leadership of trade unionist LIM Chin Siong, the Barisan Sosialis was the leading opposition party until 1966, when 11 members resigned their seats and 2 went underground. The SUF, organized in 1973, ran third in 1984 but won no legislative seats. In 1989 Singapore's most celebrated political prisoner, former Barisan Sosialis leader CHIA Thye Poh, was released after 23 years' detention. Remaining restrictions imposed on Chia's political activity were finally lifted in 1998.

The WP elected one MP in 1991 and again in January 1997. In May 1997 Secretary General Jeyaretnam was awarded a nonconstituency seat, even though he and fellow WP candidate TANG Liang Hong had been sued by Prime Minister Goh and other PAP members for defaming them during the election campaign. Claiming his life had been threatened, Tang fled abroad, and in March he was found guilty in absentia and ordered to pay heavy damages. Late in 1997 the government issued a warrant for his arrest on tax evasion charges. Jeyaretnam also lost his case, and in July 1998 a court not only dismissed his appeal but also raised the damage award. A subsequent report indicated that Jeyaretnam had agreed to pay some $61,500 in installments to avoid bankruptcy and forfeiture of his seat in Parliament.

In May 1999, the Court of Appeal dismissed a request by the WP to throw out a defamation award of more than $150,000 won by a group called the Tamil Language Committee, which had sued over an article in the party newsletter. The septuagenarian Jeyaretnam himself lost an appeal of a bankruptcy order in July 2001 and was thereby forced to vacate his parliamentary seat. Citing lack of support for his case, he resigned from the WP before the November 2001 election, at which the party again won one seat. In April 2002 Jeyaretnam publicly apologized for his 1997 remarks, in return for which the government dropped seven other lawsuits against him.

In 2003, Sylvia Lim was elected to chair the party, thereby becoming the first woman to assume that role. In the 2006 election the WP won one seat. Lim claimed a second, nonconstituency seat. In June 2008 she was reelected chair. In May 2011 the WP secured six seats. In February 2012, WP MP Yaw SHIN Leong resigned. In the subsequent by-election, the WP retained the seat and won a second by-election in January 2013.

Leaders: Sylvia LIM Swee Lian (Chair), Mohammed RAHIZAN Yaacob (Vice Chair), LOW Thia Khiang (Leader of the Opposition and Secretary General of the Party).

Singapore Democratic Alliance (SDA). Formation of the four-party SDA was announced on July 28, 2001. In the November 2001 election it won only one seat but was later awarded an additional nonconstituency seat. In May 2006 it retained only its electoral seat. Afterward, the SDA's lack of success led to calls from some quarters for a change of leadership and the merger of the participating parties.

In January 2007, the National Solidarity Party (NSP, below) withdrew from the SDA, which consisted of the Singapore People's Party (SPP), the Singapore Malay National Organization (PKMS), and the Singapore Justice Party (SJP). The SDA's Executive Council was most recently elected in January 2009. In February 2011 the SDA's council voted to relieve Chiam See Tong of the SPP of his role as chair, following which Chiam announced that his party was withdrawing from the SDA.

In March 2013, the dormant Democratic Progressive Party was revived and agreed to join the SDA.

Leader: Desmond LIM Bak Chuan (Secretary General).

Singapore Malay National Organization (*Pertubuhan Kebangsaan Melayu Singapura*—PKMS). Originally an affiliate of the United Malays National Organization in Malaysia, the PKMS assumed its present name in 1967. It supports Malay interests, racial harmony, national unity, and "the advancement of Islam without interfering in the affairs of other religions." In 1999 it called for government creation of a "supervisory council" charged with eliminating racial discrimination.

In recent years, the party has suffered from a number of intraparty disputes. In September 2006 the party's sitting president and vice president, Borhan Ariffin and MUHAMMAD Ali Aman, were ousted in a party election but then challenged the results. In January 2007 the courts ruled that a new election should be held by the following September. That election concluded with the apparent reelection of the unopposed sitting president, Osman Hassan, and other officers. Borhan's supporters again challenged the results, however, with the Registrar of Societies refusing to recognize the outcome of the election until its validity was examined by the courts.

The factional dispute continued into 2008, when an extraordinary general meeting in November elected a new slate of officers, led by Borhan. The Osman faction refused, however, to acknowledge the legitimacy of the election, and in September 2009, when a group of Borhan supporters attempted to enter the party headquarters, a riot ensued. The police arrested 21 individuals. Each side accused the other of misusing party funds and violating the party constitution.

Following an August 7, 2010, general meeting, the Borhan faction asked the Registrar of Societies to resolve the dispute with the Osman faction. Meeting a day later, the Osman faction elected Ali Asjadi to assume the presidency, with Osman taking on the role of chief adviser. On August 10 the High Court ordered the Borhan faction to turn over the keys to party headquarters to its rival, but Borhan announced his intention to appeal the decision. Still a member party of SDA, PKMS also maintains ties with UMNO Malaysia. The party continues to weaken due to unresolved infighting. In October 2011, Asjadi was convicted of selling contraband cigarettes and sentenced to 30 months in prison. He was subsequently expelled from the party and Deputy President ABU Mohmed was made acting leader of the PKMS. In 2013, a former member of the PKMS executive committee, Sulaiman GANI, was convicted of stealing jewelry from Asjadi and sentenced to seven months in prison.

Osman Faction Leaders: ABU Mohmed (Acting President), MOHD Nazem Suki (Secretary General).

Borhan Faction Leaders: BORHAN Ariffin (President), ALI Aman, ATAR Rafiee, KAMSON Moyong.

Singapore Justice Party (SJP). The SJP is a small group organized in 1972. It has contested only a handful of parliamentary seats, none since 1991. Internal disputes weakened the party, but when the SDP's Chiam See Tong became SPP's leader in 1997, several SJP members joined SPP. In 2001 SJP and others became an inaugural component of SDA. After the SPP pulled out of SDA in 2011, ex-SJP member Desmond LIM resigned from SPP in order to stay within SDA.

Leaders: Habibi binte JOHARI (Chair), AMINUDDIN Ami (Secretary General).

Singapore People's Party (SPP). A moderate breakaway faction of the SDP (below), the SPP was registered in November 1994. In January 1997 the party won one seat, tying the WP for opposition representation in the Parliament. The SPP's sole seat was held by Chiam See Tong, a longtime legislator who joined the party in 1996 after losing a power struggle in the SDP (below).

In 2010, Chiam indicated that he favored his wife, Lina Chiam, as his successor rather than his longtime assistant, Desmond Lim. At the same time, Chiam supported, but Lim opposed, accepting the Reform Party (below) into the SDA. Lina Chiam is now the SPP's sole representative and serves as a Non-Constituency MP (NCMP), often emphasizing her role as "a voice for other opposition parties."

In January 2012, after six SPP central executive committee members resigned, a new central body was elected. In January 2013, SPP member Benjamin PWEE left the party to relaunch the Democratic Progressive Party.

Leaders: CHIAM See Tong (Secretary General), SIN Kek Tong (Chair), YONG Seng Fatt (First Vice Chair), Lina CHIAM (Second Vice Chair and Member of Parliament), YEN Kim Khooi (Treasurer).

Other Opposition Parties:

National Solidarity Party (NSP). Conceived in April 1986 by a group of former SDP and SUF leaders, the NSP gained its first legislative representative when Steve Chia Kiah Hong was named a nonconstituency member after the 2001 election. In December 2003 Chia resigned as NSP secretary general because of admitted sexual peccadilloes, but he was reelected to the vacant post in July 2005 and continues to serve on the party's governing council.

A founding member of the SDA, the NSP left the alliance in January 2007. The "amicable parting" was intended to afford the party room to "maneuver, reengineer, and rebuild." In the May 7, 2011, elections it fielded the largest number of candidates. A new central executive committee was elected in April 2013, with party president Sebastian Teo reelected.

Leaders: Sebastian TEO (President), Jeannette CHONG Aruldoss (Acting Vice President), Christopher NEO (Treasurer), HAZEL Poa (Secretary General).

Reform Party (RP). The RP was launched in early 2008 by Ng Teck Siong and longtime Workers' Party stalwart J. B. Jeyaretnam, who had recently emerged from bankruptcy, on a platform that included abolition of the death penalty and of the ISA. One of the government's staunchest critics as well as an advocate for multiparty democracy, Jeyaretnam, 82, died in September 2008. In April 2009 a son, Kenneth, stepped into the leadership, and, Ng Teck Siong, following a vote of no confidence by the Central Executive Committee, resigned as chair. (In 2010, Ng formed the Socialist Front—see below.)

At its May 2010 annual meeting the RP conditionally approved joining the SDA, but some members of the alliance's leadership objected to what it perceived not as negotiating points but as unreasonable demands by the RP. Discussions on the potential affiliation subsequently resumed. In the 2011 general election many RP members defected to the NSP. Discussions on a possible alliance with SDA and SPP also broke down. The RP candidate received less than 1 percent of the vote in the January 2013 Punggoi East by-election.

Leaders: Andy ZHU (Chair), Kenneth JEYARETNAM (Secretary General).

Singapore Democratic Party (SDP). Organized in 1980 by Chiam See Tong, the SDP attracted liberal-minded Singaporeans seeking a degree of formal opposition to the PAP. Chiam won one of the two seats lost by the PAP in 1984; the seat was retained in 1988. The party won three parliamentary seats in 1991, but in June 1993 Chiam resigned as the SDP secretary general and later joined the SPP.

Having been targeted by the PAP, the SDP lost all its seats in the 1997 parliamentary elections. Four years later, despite attracting about 8 percent of the vote, the SDP failed to win any seats. It had campaigned on a "Singaporeans First" platform that blamed foreign workers for rising unemployment.

Since 1999, party leader Chee Soon Juan has been repeatedly fined and jailed for offenses that have included making unlicensed public policy speeches, illegally selling a book he had written, and defaming government officials, including the current prime minister and his two predecessors. Forced into bankruptcy in 2006, Chee was thereby disqualified to run for Parliament in May. In November he was jailed for five weeks for refusing to pay a fine of S$5,000 imposed for speaking in public without a permit during the parliamentary election campaign. Also sentenced to jail were party leaders Ghandi Ambalam and YAP Keng Ho. Earlier in the year, longtime party leader Wong Hong Toy (previously a leader of the WP) resigned as assistant secretary general because of policy differences with Chee.

Chee has since been charged with additional offenses, including leading an illegal march in September 2007, attempting in October 2007 to deliver to the prime minister's office a petition regarding Singapore's relationship with Myanmar's ruling junta, and holding an illegal assembly outside Parliament in March 2008 to protest rising prices. In June 2008 he and his sister, CHEE Siok Chin, served 12- and 10-day sentences, respectively, for contempt of court during a defamation proceeding. In December 2009 they and party chair Gandhi Ambalam served a week in jail rather than pay a fine for having distributed fliers without a permit in 2006. As of October 2010 several court cases and appeals involving the party leaders were pending, and ultimately Chee went bankrupt, foreshadowing an unstable future for the party. Negotiations between the SDP and the WP on fielding joint candidates in by-elections failed in 2013.

Leaders: Jufrie MAHMOOD (Chair), Vincent CHENG (Vice Chair), CHEE Soon Juan (Secretary General), John L. TAN (Assistant Secretary General).

Socialist Front—SF (*Angkatan Sosialis*). The SF was established and registered in September 2010 at the instigation of Ng Teck Siong, who had previously belonged to the SDP, the WP, and the RP. He left the RP in April 2009 after a vote of no confidence in his leadership. During the May 7, 2011, elections party leaders were divided over whether to contest the balloting, further dividing what many viewed as a short-lived party.

Leaders: NG Teck Siong (Chair), CHIA Ti Lik (Secretary General).

For information on the **United Singapore Democrats** (USD), please see the 2012 *Handbook*.

LEGISLATURE

The unicameral **Parliament** currently includes 87 members directly elected (from a mix of group representation and single-member constituencies) for five-year terms, subject to dissolution. In the general election of May 7, 2011, the PAP took 81 seats, while the WP won 6. As of the May 2011 election, the Parliament comprises 87 members of Parliament (MPs), 3 nonconstituency members of Parliament (NCMPs), and 9 nominated members of Parliament (NMPs), who are appointed once Parliament convenes.

Speaker: Halimah YACOB.

CABINET

[as of August 1, 2013]

Prime Minister	Lee Hsien Loong
Deputy Prime Ministers	Rear Adm. (ret.) Teo Chee Hean
	Tharman Shanmugaratnam
Ministers	
Communications and Information	Yaacob Ibrahim
Culture, Community, and Youth (Acting)	Lawrence Wong
Defense	Ng Eng Heng
Education	Heng Swee Keat
Environment and Water Resources	Vivian Balakrishnan [f]
Finance	Tharman Shanmugaratnam
Foreign Affairs	Kasiviswanathan Shanmugam
Health	Gan Kim Yong
Home Affairs	Rear Adm. (ret.) Teo Chee Hean
Law	Kasiviswanathan Shanmugam
Manpower (Acting)	Tan Chuan-Jin
National Development	Khaw Boon Wan
National Security, Coordinating Minister	Rear Adm. (ret.) Teo Chee Hean
Prime Minister's Office	Lim Swee Say
	Grace Fu Hai Yien [f]
Social and Family Development (Acting)	Maj. Gen. (ret.) Chan Chun Sing
Trade and Industry	Lim Hng Kiang
Transport	Lui Tuck Yew
Senior Ministers of State	
Defense	Maj. Gen. (ret.) Chan Chun Sing
National Development	Tan Chuan-Jin
Communications and Information	Lawrence Wong

[f] = female

INTERGOVERNMENTAL REPRESENTATION

Ambassador to the U.S.: Ashok Kumar MIRPURI.

U.S. Ambassador to Singapore: Kirk WAGAR.

Permanent Representative to the UN: Albert CHUA.

IGO Memberships (Non-UN): ADB, APEC, ASEAN, CWTH, NAM, WTO.

SLOVAKIA

Slovak Republic
Slovenská Republika

Political Status: Slovak Republic proclaimed upon separation of the constituent components of the Czech and Slovak Federative Republic (see article on Czech Republic) on January 1, 1993.

Area: 18,933 sq. mi. (49,035 sq. km).

Population: 5,408,000 (2013E—UN); 5,488,339 (2013E—U.S. Census).

Major Urban Centers (2013E): BRATISLAVA (415,589), Košice (240,164), Prešov (91,352).

Official Language: Slovak.

Monetary Unit: Euro (market rate November 1, 2013: 0.74 euro = $1US). The monetary unit was the koruna until Slovakia adopted the euro on January 1, 2009, at an exchange rate of 30.1260 koruny = 1 euro. (The official rate of the koruna on December 31, 2008, was 21.45 koruny = $1US.)

President: Ivan GAŠPAROVIČ; popularly elected (as the candidate of the People's Union–Movement for Democracy) in runoff balloting on April 17, 2004, and inaugurated on June 15 for a five-year term, succeeding Rudolf SCHUSTER (Party of Civic Understanding); reelected (officially as an independent candidate but with the support of Direction–Social Democracy and other parties) in runoff balloting on April 4, 2009, and inaugurated on June 15 for a second five-year term.

Prime Minister: Robert FICO (Direction-Social Democracy) designated by the president on March 15, 2012, to form a new government following the legislative elections of March 10 and formally appointed by the president on April 4 to head a new government in succession to Iveta RADIČOVÁ (Slovak Democratic and Christian Union).

THE COUNTRY

Situated in the geographical center of Europe, Slovakia consists of some 40 percent of the area of the former Czechoslovak federation. It is bounded by the Czech Republic to the west, Poland to the north, Ukraine to the east, Hungary to the south, and Austria to the southwest. A former province of the Hungarian-ruled part of the Austro-Hungarian Empire, the country's population is 86 percent Slovak and 10 percent Hungarian (Magyar), with small minorities of Czechs, Roma (Gypsies), Ruthenes, and Ukrainians. Approximately 69 percent of the population is Roman Catholic, the other Christian denominations include Protestant (11 percent) and Greek–Catholic (Orthodox-rite Christians who acknowledge the hierarchy of the Catholic Church; 4 percent).

A substantial proportion of former Czechoslovakia's heavy industry is located in Slovakia. Industry as a whole accounted for 35.5 percent of GDP in 2011. The principal manufactures include machinery, chemicals, plastics, and processed foods; Slovakia is also the world's biggest per capita car producer. The agricultural sector contributes less than 4 percent of GDP; its leading crops are wheat, other grains, and sugar beets. Leading trade partners include Germany, the Czech Republic, Russia, Italy, and Poland.

Long less affluent than Bohemia and Moravia, reform efforts in the immediate post-Communist period in Slovakia accentuated economic differences with the Czech Republic, fueling pressure for political separation on January 1, 1993. State control and central planning were much more entrenched in the Slovak bureaucracy, which continued to be dominated by officials who had prospered under the previous regime. In 1993 Slovakia's estimated per capita GNP was only $1,500, as contrasted with $2,500 in the Czech lands, with Slovak GDP falling by an estimated 5 percent during the year; at the same time, unemployment and inflation in Slovakia rose well above Czech levels, to 15 percent and around 25 percent, respectively.

The lackluster economic performance was widely attributed to the authoritarian policies of the postseparation government, which favored

a slow transfer to the free market and retained significant elements of the bloated Communist bureaucracy. However, the situation improved in the wake of the installation in 1998 of a center-right administration that implemented numerous belt-tightening measures, including the privatization of state-owned banks and other enterprises. Reform (lower corporate taxes, paring of welfare and pension benefits, and more privatization) intensified even further when the government retained control in the 2002 general election. Slovakia was described as one of Central Europe's brightest economic performers upon its accession to the EU in 2004. Slovakia joined the European Exchange Rate Mechanism II agreement on November 28, 2005, a key step toward entry into the Eurozone.

The country achieved a long-standing objective by adopting the euro in January 2009. However, that success was partially overshadowed by the impact of the global financial crisis, with unemployment surpassing 12 percent in 2009. GDP fell by 4.7 percent. In 2010 strong exports helped lift the country out of recession. GDP growth was 3.5 in 2011 and 2.0 for 2012. Inflation dipped from 4 percent in 2011 to 3.7 percent, while unemployment rose from 13.4 percent in 2011 to 14.0 percent in 2012. In its 2012 annual survey, Doing Business, the World Bank ranked Slovakia 46th out of 183 countries. GDP per capita that year was $16,899,025.

GOVERNMENT AND POLITICS

Political background. Founded in 1918, Czechoslovakia was considered to be the most politically mature and democratically governed of the new states of Eastern Europe, but it was dismembered following the 1938 Munich agreement. The preponderant role of Soviet military forces in liberating the country at the close of World War II enabled the Communists to gain a leading position in the postwar cabinet headed by strongly pro-Soviet Premier Zdeněk FIERLINGER, although President Eduard BENEŠ was perceived as nonaligned. Communist control was consolidated in February 1948, and, under Marxist-Leninist precepts, Czech-Slovak differences officially ceased to exist, the two ethnic groups being charged with building socialism in amity and cooperation. (For subsequent political developments during the Communist era, see the article on the Czech Republic.)

Communist power in Czechoslovakia crumbled in late 1989. On November 20, one day after formation of the opposition Civic Forum (*Občanské Fórum*—OF), 250,000 antiregime demonstrators marched in Prague, and 24 hours later government leaders held initial discussions with Forum representatives. On November 22 the widely admired Alexander DUBČEK (who had attempted to introduce "socialism with a human face" while serving as leader of the Czechoslovakian Communist Party in the "Prague Spring" of 1968) returned to the limelight with an address before an enthusiastic rally in Bratislava. Following a nationwide strike on November 28 (preceded by a three-day rally of 500,000 in Prague), the regime accepted loss of its monopoly status, and on December 7 Prime Minister Ladislav ADAMEC quit in favor of the little-known Marián ČALFA. On December 10 President Gustáv HUSÁK resigned after swearing in the first non–Communist-dominated government in 41 years, with the Federal Assembly naming Václav HAVEL as his successor on December 29. The Civic Forum and its Slovak counterpart, Public Against Violence (*Verejnost Proti Násili*—VPN), won a majority of federal legislative seats in nationwide balloting on June 8 and 9, 1990, with Čalfa (who had resigned from the Communist Party on January 18) forming a new government on June 27 and Havel being elected to a regular two-year term as president on July 5.

During 1991, the anti-Communist coalition, its major objective achieved, crumbled into less-inclusive party formations. The Civic Forum gave rise to two Czech groups in February, while in Slovakia the VPN assumed a new identity, the Civic Democratic Union–Public Against Violence (*Občanská Demokratická Únie–Verejnost Proti Násili*—ODU-VPN), in October after having been substantially weakened by the defection of a Slovak separatist faction, the Movement for a Democratic Slovakia (*Hnutie za Demokratické Slovensko*—HZDS). In November, negotiations between federal and republican leaders over the country's future political status collapsed, with the Federal Assembly becoming deadlocked over the issue of a referendum on separate Czech and Slovak states.

On March 3, 1992, the Federal Assembly presidium scheduled a general election (coinciding with elections to the Czech and Slovak National Councils) for June 5–6, and on April 14, Havel announced that he would seek a further term as president. By then, however, a contest between Czech Finance Minister Václav KLAUS and former Slovak prime minister Vladimír MEČIAR had emerged as the major determinant of federal politics, Klaus favoring a right-of-center liberal economic policy with rapid privatization and Mečiar preferring a slower transition to capitalism. The two remained in firm control of their respective regions in the election of June 5–6, after which Mečiar returned to the post of Slovak prime minister, from which he had been dismissed in April 1991. Paralleling their differing economic outlooks, the Czech and Slovak leaders entertained divergent views as to the federation's political future. Klaus insisted that Czechoslovakia should remain a state with strong central authority or divide into separate entities, while Mečiar favored a weakened central government with most powers assigned to the individual republics. In the end, the death knell of the combined state was sounded by successful Slovak opposition in the assembly to the reelection of Havel as federal president on July 3. Thereafter, events moved quickly toward formal dissolution, with agreement being reached between the two governments by the end of August and the Slovak National Council adopting an independent constitution on September 1. Ironically, public opinion in both regions opposed separation. Thus, Klaus and Mečiar were obliged to act through the Federal Assembly, 183 of whose deputies (3 more than the required minimum) on November 25 endorsed the breakup with effect from January 1, 1993.

The Mečiar government of independent Slovakia quickly came under criticism for its alleged dictatorial tendencies and its reluctance to tackle the entrenched position of former Communists in the state bureaucracy. The election of Michal KOVÁČ as president on February 15, 1993, added to the divisions in the ruling HZDS. Although Kováč, a former reform Communist, was then backed by Mečiar, his postelection offer to resign from the HZDS highlighted an internal rift between the prime minister and leading cabinet colleagues. In a cabinet reshuffle in March, Mečiar ejected his main HZDS opponent, Foreign Minister and Deputy Prime Minister Milan KŇAŽKO, who promptly defected from the party to found a new group, the Alliance of Democrats of the Slovak Republic (*Aliancia Demokratov Slovenskej Republiky*—ADSR). Mečiar also insisted on appointing a former Communist military officer, Imrich ANDREJČÁK, as defense minister. The one ministerial representative of the Slovak National Party (*Slovenská Národná Strana*—SNS) thereupon resigned in protest, although the SNS, a strongly nationalistic formation with an anti-Hungarian orientation, announced that it would continue to support the government.

Mečiar governed the country for the next seven months as head of a minority government, failing during this period to entice the (ex-Communist) Party of the Democratic Left (*Strana Demokratickej*

L'avice—SDL'; see *Smer,* below) to join his administration. In October 1993, the HZDS-SNS coalition was formally revived, this time with the junior partner holding several key portfolios. However, divisions within both ruling parties became irresolvable in early 1994, and defections led to Mečiar's defeat in a parliamentary nonconfidence vote on March 11. Mečiar resigned three days later and was replaced as prime minister on March 16 by Jozef MORAVČÍK, who had resigned as foreign minister the previous month and had set up a new party opposed to the HZDS. He formed a center-left coalition, headed by his Democratic Union of Slovakia (*Demokratická Únia Slovenska*—DÚS) and including the SDL'.

The ouster of the Mečiar government, described as a "parliamentary putsch" by the former prime minister, served to enflame political antagonisms in the run-up to the election. Particularly venomous were relations between Mečiar and President Kováč, whose open criticism of the HZDS leader had been a major cause of the government's collapse. Nevertheless, in legislative balloting on September 30–October 1, 1994, Mečiar and the HZDS won a plurality, campaigning on a populist platform that appealed to the large rural population. Despite an economic upturn under the Moravčík government, the new DÚS could manage only fifth place, being outpolled by the center-left Common Choice bloc (headed by the SDL'), the Hungarian Coalition (*Mad'arská Koalícia*—MK), and the Christian Democratic Movement (*Křest'ansko-demokratické Hnutie*—KDH). Six weeks later, on December 13, Mečiar embarked upon his third term as prime minister, heading a "red-brown" coalition of the HZDS, the far-right SNS, and the now-defunct leftist Association of Workers of Slovakia (*Združenie Robotníkov Slovenska*—ZRS) that commanded 83 of the 150 legislative seats (for more background on the ZRS, see the 2007 *Handbook*).

In March 1995, tensions between Mečiar and President Kováč flared when the latter delayed a bill transferring overall control of the national intelligence agency, the Slovak Information Service (*Slovenská Informačna Služba*—SIS), from the presidency to the government. Although the president signed the bill on April 8, following its readoption by the legislature, the National Council on May 5 passed a motion censuring him for mismanagement of the SIS. The 80-vote tally in favor was below the two-thirds majority required to remove the president; nevertheless, Mečiar backed an HZDS executive call for Kováč's resignation and urged his expulsion from the party. The following month the prime minister called for a national referendum to decide whether Kováč should continue in office, while on June 23 the National Council voted to strip the president of his duties as commander in chief and to transfer them to the government.

Early in 1997, the opposition completed a petition drive to hold a referendum on instituting direct presidential elections, but the government suspended the referendum on April 22, claiming that the constitution could only be changed by the parliament. On May 22 the Constitutional Court ruled that the referendum would be legal, but the government asserted that the result would not be binding and, therefore, should not appear on the same ballot as a separate referendum on whether the Slovak Republic should join NATO. On the eve of the referendum the interior minister, Gustáv KRAJČÍ, ordered new ballots to be printed without the presidential question, creating voter confusion and provoking a boycott. As a result, the turnout was less than 10 percent, invalidating the results.

As was widely expected, in early 1998 the legislature failed to elect a new president, no candidate being able to command the required three-fifths majority. When President Kováč's term expired on March 2, the constitution authorized Prime Minister Mečiar to assume various presidential powers. He quickly dismissed nearly half of the government's overseas ambassadors and canceled further referendums on NATO membership and direct presidential elections. By then, Mečiar had already been attacked for alleged intimidation of the media, abuse of police powers, and the apparent enrichment of cronies through the sale of state-run enterprises. Popular support for his administration continued to decline as the HZDS repeatedly blocked the National Council from selecting a new president and also, in May, changed the electoral law to make it more difficult for small parties to win seats in the legislature (see Constitution and government, below).

In the National Council election of September 25–26, 1998, the HZDS secured only 27 percent of the vote. Although it retained a slim plurality of seats (43, down from 61 in 1994), its only potential coalition partner was the SNS, with 15 seats, the ZRS having failed to achieve representation. Consequently, the newly formed Slovak Democratic Coalition (*Slovenská Demokratická Koalícia*—SDK) allied with the SDL,' the Party of the Hungarian Coalition (*Strana Mad'arskej Koalície*—SMK), and the Party of Civic Understanding (*Strana Občianskeho Porozumenia*—SOP) to form a new government on October 30 under the leadership of the SDK's Mikuláš Dzurinda. Dzurinda quickly pledged to repair the nation's international image in order to attract foreign investment and enhance chances for EU and NATO accession. Domestic reform included curtailment of strictures on the media and unions as well as the appointment of an ethnic Hungarian to the newly created post of deputy prime minister for human and minority rights.

In January 1999, the new legislature resolved the presidential impasse by approving the long-delayed constitutional amendment to provide for the direct election of the president. The governing coalition nominated SOP leader Rudolf SCHUSTER, the mayor of Košice (and a former prominent member of the Czechoslovakian Communist Party), as its candidate for the May 15 presidential election. Schuster was initially expected to face the strongest opposition from former president Kováč and actress and former ambassador Magda VÁŠÁRYOVÁ, both of whom ran as nonparty, or "civic," candidates. However, in early April former prime minister Mečiar, who had left the public arena following his regime's 1998 loss, reappeared to announce that he had accepted the nomination of the HZDS for the post, immediately positioning himself as Schuster's primary opponent. On May 15 Schuster garnered 47.4 percent of the vote, shy of the 50 percent needed for an outright victory despite Kováč's late withdrawal in his favor. In runoff balloting on May 29 against Mečiar, who had claimed second place with 37.2 percent support, Schuster won 57.2 percent and was therefore inaugurated on June 15.

The apparent stability of the multiparty Dzurinda government during its first two years in office belied the tensions in the underlying political party structure. In January 2000, acknowledging that the SDK would not outlive the current legislative term, Dzurinda announced that he planned to organize a new party, the Slovak Democratic and Christian Union (*Slovenská Demokratická Krest'anská Únia*—SDKÚ), in preparation for the 2002 election. By the end of the year the Christian Democrats and others had formally withdrawn from the SDK (see Political Parties and Groups, below), although not from the government.

The HZDS led all parties with a plurality of 36 seats in the September 20–21, 2002, legislative balloting followed by the SDKÚ with 28 and the recently formed Direction (*Smer*). Despite the HZDS's plurality, Dzurinda was subsequently able to form a new government comprised of the SDKÚ, SMK, KDH, and the recently formed New Citizen's Alliance (*Alliancia Nového Občana*—ANO). The coalition fell to minority status in September 2003, when seven SDKÚ legislators left the party.

The first round of new presidential balloting was held on April 3, 2004, with Mečiar leading all candidates with 32.7 percent of the vote, followed by Ivan GAŠPAROVIČ of the new People's Union–Movement for Democracy (*L'udová Únia–Hnutie za Demokraciu*—L'U-HZD) with 22.3 percent and the SDKÚ's Eduard KUKAN with 22.1 percent. In the runoff election on April 17, Gašparovič defeated Mečiar with a 59.1 to 40.1 percent vote share.

Dzurinda's minority coalition government collapsed in February 2006 upon the KDH's decision to quit the cabinet in a dispute over abortion policy. (The KDH had unsuccessfully promoted legislation that would have allowed hospital workers to decline to assist in abortions because of their religious beliefs.)

Early legislative elections were held on June 17, 2006, with Direction–Social Democracy *(Smer–Sociálna Demokracia,* formed in 2005 via the merger of *Smer,* the SDL,' and several other parties) leading all parties with 50 seats after campaigning on a populist platform of reduced taxes, increased social spending, ending privatization of state-run enterprises, and withdrawal from Iraq. *Smer* leader Robert FICO on July 4 formed a coalition government comprised of *Smer,* the far-right SNS, and the renamed People's Party–HZDS (*L'udová Strana–HZDS*—L'S-HZDS). The coalition government maintained a comfortable majority in the National Council, with 85 of the 150 seats. A strong economy allowed Fico to maintain high approval ratings, mixing populist slogans with modest reform, such as eliminating a nominal but unpopular fee for accessing the healthcare system, while generally not reversing the Dzurinda reforms.

Following the 2006 elections, Prime Minister Fico criticized the country's media for a lack of professionalism in reporting, claiming it showed bias in favor of opposition parties and special interests. A new "Right of Reply" media law proposed in April 2007 required media to allow interested parties to respond to published material (whether true or not) and promised the Ministry of Culture powers to sanction publishers. The proposal drew domestic and international allegations that the government sought merely to limit media criticism and that the law fell out of line with Western European practices. To prevent the law from passing, opposition parties—the SDKU, KDS, and KDH—tied their support of the EU Lisbon treaty to revisions to the new law, invoking criticisms of the law supplied by the OSCE. In April 2008, however, Fico broke the opposition alliance against the media bill, pushing through the controversial proposal by drawing KDH support for the governing coalition's position on the Lisbon treaty. This KDH "betrayal" was symptomatic of a general fragmentation of Slovak center-right politics in 2008, a consequence of which was the formation in July of a new political party, the Conservative Democrats of Slovakia (*Konzervatívni Demokrati Slovenska*—KDS), by four former KDH deputies (see Political Parties and Groups, below).

Meanwhile, in November 2007, it had emerged that Branislav BRIZA, deputy director of a Ministry of Agriculture agency—the Slovak Land Fund (SPF)—and an HZDS appointee, had authorized a cut-price land sale to a company alleged to be close to Vladimír Mečiar. Fico responded by calling for the resignations of Briza and Miroslav JURENA, agriculture minister and deputy leader of the HZDS. Meanwhile, Mečiar not only backed Jurena, but also called for the director of the SPF, a *Smer* appointee, to resign. The situation finally deescalated when Mečiar consented to Jurena's replacement by another deputy from his party. While his statements at the time suggested that Mečiar was considering suspending the coalition upon the EU's approval of Slovakia's euro bid, the coalition remained steady even following the euro assessment. The coalition weathered several other major cabinet resignations and reshuffles in 2008.

Presidential elections were held on March 21, 2009, with Gašparovič (supported by *Smer,* the SNS, and the Movement for Democracy [*Hnutie za Demokarciu*—HZD]) leading all candidates with 46.7 percent of the vote. He was followed by Iveta RADIČOVÁ of the SDKÚ–Democratic Party (SDKÚ–*Demokratická Strana*—SDKÚ-DS, formed in 2006 when the SDKÚ merged with the DS) with 38.1 percent. (Radičová was also supported by the SMK, KDH, and the small Civic Conservative Party [*Občianska Konzervativna Strana*—OKS].) Five other candidates received support in the single digits. In the runoff balloting on April 4, Gašparovič defeated Radičová with a 55.5 to 44.5 percent vote share.

Slovakia's European Parliament election on June 6, 2009, demonstrated *Smer*'s continued popularity and roughly paralleled the 2006 parliamentary elections. The 13 seats were distributed as follows: *Smer,* 5; SDKÚ-DS, 2; SMK, 2; KDH, 2; L'S-HZDS, 1; and SNS, 1.

In legislative elections on June 12, 2010, *Smer* placed first and increased its seats in the parliament from 50 to 62, still short of a majority. In the balloting, women secured 24 seats, or 16 percent of the total. One of parties in the Fico government, the L'S-HZDS, failed to secure any seats in the National Council, while another partner, the SNS, lost more than half its seats. Consequently, although *Smer* increased its representation in the parliament, Fico was unable to negotiate a new coalition. Iveta RADIČOVÁ, of the SDKÚ-DS, was subsequently named to organize a government and she concluded a coalition agreement on June 28 between her party, and three other center-right parties, the KDH, the Freedom and Solidarity (*Sloboda a Solidarita*—SaS), and the Bridge (*Most–Híd*—MH). The resultant government had the support of 79 deputies and was sworn in on July 9. It survived a no-confidence vote on August 10. The ministry of the environment, which had been consolidated into another ministry, was reestablished in November. The budget deficit rose to 7.9 percent of GDP in 2010 as the Radičová government endeavored to stimulate the economy and was forced to expand unemployment benefits.

A September 19, 2010, national referendum on reducing the number of deputies in parliament from 150 to 100, failed because only 22.8 percent of voters participated, less than the 50 percent required.

Rising unemployment was one of the main reasons for the defeat of the SDKÚ-DS in local elections on November 27. In the balloting, among formal parties, the SDKÚ-DS was placed third with 159 mayoral posts, behind *Smer*, with 599 posts, and the KDH, with 161. However, independent candidates won 979 mayorships in what was reported to be a broad rejection of established parties.

In October 2011, the ruling coalition fell apart after the SaS refused to support Slovakian approval for the European financial stability accord. In early elections on March 10, 2012, *Smer* won an absolute majority with 83 seats (see Current issues, below). Fico subsequently formed a new government composed of *Smer* members and three independents.

Constitution and government. The constitution of the Slovak Republic came into effect on January 1, 1993, on dissolution of the Czechoslovak federation. It defines Slovakia as a unitary state with a unicameral legislature, the 150-member National Council of the Slovak Republic, which sits for a maximum term of four years. Elections are by proportional representation. Prior to passage of a May 1998 electoral reform, individual parties were required to obtain at least 5 percent of the national vote to claim council seats, while alliances of two or three parties needed at least 7 percent, and alliances of four or more parties, at least 10 percent. Under the amended law, however, all parties, regardless of their participation in coalitions, are required to meet a 5 percent threshold, as a result of which numerous previously allied organizations merged before the September 1998 election (see Political Parties and Groups, below).

In another major change, a January 1999 constitutional amendment introduced direct presidential elections. Previously, the National Council chose the president by secret ballot, a three-fifths majority being required for election. The president serves a five-year term and performs a largely ceremonial role, although legislation and treaties require presidential approval and the president may dissolve the National Council and declare a state of emergency. In addition, the president appoints the prime minister and, on the latter's recommendation, other government ministers, who are collectively responsible to the legislature. A set of amendments were passed in 2001 to address prerequisites required for membership in NATO and the EU (see Current issues, below).

Under legislation enacted in 1996, Slovakia is divided into eight regions (Bratislava, Trnava, Nitra, Trenčín, Žilina, Banská Bystrica, Prešov, and Košice), which are themselves divided into 79 districts. Regional officials were nominated at the federal level until 2002 (see Current issues, below); district officials are elected.

A feature of the Slovak constitution is its guarantee of the rights of ethnic minorities, including freedom to choose national identity and prohibition of enforced assimilation and discrimination. Under associated legislation, use of minority languages in dealings with public authorities is guaranteed in administrative areas where a minority forms 20 percent or more of the total population.

Earlier, the National Council had decreed that Czechoslovak federal law would continue to apply in Slovakia but that, in cases of conflict between Slovak and federal law, the former would prevail. In addition, following the deletion from the Czechoslovak constitution in December 1989 of the guarantee of Communist power, a systematic revision of legal codes had been initiated to reestablish "fundamental legal norms." A revision of the criminal law included abolition of the death penalty and provision of a full guarantee of judicial review, while a law on judicial rehabilitation facilitated the quashing of nearly all of the political trials of the Communist era. Commercial and civil law revisions established the supremacy of the courts in making decisions relating to rights, and property rights were reinstituted.

Freedom of the press is constitutionally guaranteed. In 2013 Reporters Without Borders ranked Slovakia 23th out of 179 countries in its annual index of press freedom.

Foreign relations. On December 21, 1992, the "Visegrád" countries (Poland, Hungary, and Czechoslovakia) concluded a Central European Free Trade Agreement (CEFTA), to which the Czech and Slovak republics were deemed to have acceded at their attainment of separate sovereignty on January 1, 1993. (For additional information on CEFTA, see Foreign relations in the Poland entry.) On December 30 the International Monetary Fund (IMF) decided to admit both the Czech and Slovak republics as full members, effective January 1. On January 19, 1993, the UN General Assembly admitted the two republics to membership, dividing between them their seats on various subsidiary organs held by the former Czechoslovakia. The two states also became separate members of the Council of Europe, the Conference on (later Organization for) Security and Cooperation in Europe (CSCE/OSCE), and the European Bank for Reconstruction and Development (EBRD), sovereign Slovakia having declared its intention to honor and fulfill all the international treaties and obligations entered into by the Czechoslovak federation. In October 1993 agreements were signed with the EU transferring the latter's 1991 association agreement with Czechoslovakia to the two successor states in renegotiated form. (For foreign relations of the former federative republic prior to December 31, 1992, see entry under the Czech Republic article.)

As part of its orientation toward the West, Slovakia in February 1994 joined NATO's Partnership for Peace program for former

Communist and neutral states, becoming in addition an associate partner of the Western European Union (WEU) in May. Shortly thereafter, it signed military cooperation agreements with Germany and France, receiving from both countries assurances of support for eventual Slovakian membership in NATO and the EU.

Following the breakup of Czechoslovakia, the Slovak government applied itself to the implementation of some 30 treaties and agreements designed to regulate relations with the Czech Republic, but some aspects of the separation (including the division of federal property, debt settlement, and border arrangements) proved difficult to finalize. A temporary currency union between the two states was terminated on February 8, 1993, accompanied by a dramatic slump in bilateral trade despite the commitment of both sides to a customs union. In 1994, Slovak-Czech trade began to recover, while the Moravčík government upon assuming office in March sought improved relations by moving quickly to conclude an agreement with Prague on police and customs arrangements.

The Czech government's unilateral decision in June 1995 to terminate the payments clearance system operating with Slovakia drew strong condemnation from Bratislava, where Czech charges of Slovak noncompliance with its rules were rejected. The premiers of the two countries met at a CEFTA summit in Brno, Czech Republic, on September 11, when a mutual desire to preserve the Czech-Slovak customs union was expressed. In January 1996 Bratislava and Prague signed a treaty defining the 155-mile Slovak-Czech border and involving land exchanges totaling some 6,000 acres in resolution of outstanding claims. Remaining property and debt disputes were resolved at prime ministerial meetings in November 1999 and May 2000.

Slovakia's relations with neighboring Hungary have long been colored by the presence of a 600,000-strong ethnic Hungarian minority: allegations of official discrimination against it inevitably draw the attention of the Budapest government, which regards itself as the protector of Magyars beyond its borders. Under the 1992–1994 Mečiar government, the influence of the nationalist SNS contributed to a worsening of relations with the ethnic Hungarian community. The Moravčík government took a more conciliatory line and also sought to improve relations with Budapest later in 1994. On Mečiar's return to office in December, rapprochement with Hungary continued to be a government aim.

A long-negotiated treaty of friendship and cooperation was signed in Paris on March 19, 1995, by the Slovak and Hungarian prime ministers that recognized the rights of national minorities and enjoined their protection, while declaring the Slovakian-Hungarian border to be "inviolable." The treaty was ratified by the Slovak legislature on March 27, 1996. A remaining disagreement involves the controversial Gabčíkovo-Nagymaros dam being built by Slovakia on the Danube. In early 1999 tentative agreement was reportedly reached for joint operation of the dam and the discontinuation of plans to build another on the Danube, but no final resolution followed. In September 2000 UN Secretary General Kofi Annan apparently offered to mediate the dispute, but Prime Minister Dzurinda rejected the offer as unnecessary.

On June 27, 1995, Slovakia formally submitted an application for full EU membership, and it subsequently expressed its desire to join NATO. However, in July 1997 the Madrid summit of NATO leaders did not include Slovakia among the three former Warsaw Pact nations, including the Czech Republic, invited to join the alliance. Neither was Slovakia numbered in December among the six nations invited to begin formal membership discussions with the EU, though it remained one of five East European countries expected to participate in a "second wave" of expansion. The decisions were reportedly based on political grounds, including the perceived lack of democratic reforms in Slovakia and its treatment of ethnic Hungarians. The change of government in the fall of 1998 improved Slovakia's prospects for EU and NATO accession, as new Prime Minister Dzurinda indicated his desire to redirect the nation's focus away from Russia and Ukraine (his predecessor's favored direction) and toward the West. Slovakia's standing with regard to NATO admission was also improved by the government's support for the 1999 air campaign against Yugoslavia.

Despite initial objections from the United States, Slovakia was invited on July 28, 2000, to join the Organization for Economic Cooperation and Development (OECD), which the Dzurinda government viewed as further recognition of the country's readiness for full integration with Western institutions. A favorable progress report in November from the European Commission offered additional encouragement that the goal of EU accession might be achieved by 2004, although the status of Slovakia's large Roma (Gypsy) minority remained a concern.

Slovakia was formally invited in November 2002 to begin membership negotiations with NATO. In what was seen as a related development, Slovakia and a group of other Eastern European countries publicly endorsed the stance of U.S. president George W. Bush regarding Iraq in early 2003. On April 10 the National Council approved NATO accession by a vote of 124–11, and in June Slovakia sent some 100 military engineers to support the U.S.-led coalition in Iraq (despite the fact that polls indicated that 75 percent of Slovakia's population opposed the war). Slovakia officially joined NATO with six other new members on March 29, 2004. EU accession followed on May 1, a national referendum on May 16–17, 2003, having approved EU membership by a 94 percent "yes" vote, albeit with a modest turnout of only 52 percent.

Prime Minister Dzurinda's defeat in the legislative balloting of June 2006 was initially seen as a possible setback in the country's goal of adopting the euro on January 1, 2009. However, in July new Prime Minister Robert Fico announced that he would support the 2009 schedule. Twelve months later the EU ratified Slovakia's entry into the euro area on the existing schedule, despite the European Central Bank's "considerable concerns" voiced in May 2008 that Slovak inflation could rise more than the euro average. On December 21, 2007, Slovakia was one of nine new countries incorporated into the Schengen Agreement, Europe's free movement zone.

Following his alliance with the HZDS (led by the former authoritarian Vladimír Mečiar) and the SNS (led by Ján SLOTA, a politician known for his xenophobic rhetoric), Fico's *Smer* party found itself excluded from the Party of European Socialists (PES), the social democratic grouping in the European Parliament. In November 2007 PES head Hannes Swoboda visited Slovakia to monitor minority issues and concluded that Slota's inflammatory statements against ethnic Hungarians caused real damage to Slovakia's international standing. *Smer* was reinstated by the PES in early 2008 after Fico and Slota reaffirmed their commitment to human rights. But in April the Slovak government further tarnished its image in Europe by approving a controversial media law (see Current issues), despite objections from the Organization for Security and Cooperation in Europe (OSCE).

Tensions with Hungary increased in September 2007, when the Slovak parliament approved a declaration on the inviolability of the Beneš decrees. Enacted in the 1940s by the Czechoslovak government-in-exile, this series of laws forced thousands of ethnic Hungarians out of the country following World War II. In September 2008 Hungarian Prime Minister Ferenc Gyurcsány agreed to an official visit to Slovakia to help ease bilateral tensions, having refused a similar invitation in October 2007. However, Fico's coalition arrangement with the nationalist SNS continued to strain relations, while anxiety about Hungarian irredentism has prevented the Slovak government from recognizing the unilateral declaration of independence by Kosovo.

During Fico's first stint as prime minister, Slovakia recast its bilateral relationships with both the United States and Russia. In a break with the pro-American stance of his predecessor, the prime minister withdrew the majority of Slovakia's small contingent in Iraq in early 2007 and made visits to Libya, Venezuela, and the Cuban embassy in Bratislava. Meanwhile, in anticipation of the renegotiation of its gas supply contract with Russian gas monopoly Gazprom at the end of 2008, Slovakia signaled that its support of Russia was on the upswing. "We consider [Russia] a reliable partner," said Slovak Foreign Minister Ján Kubiš. In an apparent contradiction of the official Slovak line on Kosovar independence, the official reaction to the August 2008 conflict between Russia and Georgia over South Ossetia set Slovakia apart from the pro-Georgian stances taken by its neighbors Poland and the Czech Republic, with Deputy Prime Minister Dušan Čaplovič declaring that South Ossetia should be allowed a chance at independence.

Tension between Slovakia and Hungary continued to worsen, and the European Commission in November 2008 expressed concern over the nature of political discourse in both countries. The Slovak State Language Act of June 2009 was criticized by Hungarian government officials. In turn, Hungarian president László Sólyom was denied permission to enter Slovakia in August to participate in a celebration of St. Stephen's Day, the Hungarian national holiday.

Slovakia and Russia signed a series of accords on economic cooperation in energy and transport on April 7, 2010. In May Slovakia and Moldova signed an agreement to increase bilateral diplomatic cooperation and ease travel barriers between the two nations. In July Slovakia agreed to provide €4.3 billion to the €750 billion EU stabilization fund, but rejected participation in the separate €110 billion EU-led bailout program for Greece. Slovakia strongly condemned the expulsion of the

Roma from France in September 2010 (see entry on France) and called for intervention by the European Commission.

When Hungary extended citizenship to Hungarians living abroad in spring 2010, the Fico government passed a controversial law banning dual citizenship, effective July 17, 2010.

In November 2011, Estonia opened its first consul in Slovakia. In June 2012, Slovakia announced that it could not continue with decommissioning two nuclear power plants without additional funding from the EU, which had already provided €115 million.

Fico has not resumed the open confrontations with Hungary and policy tilt toward Russia that characterized his first time as prime minister, although he has promoted Russia's membership in the OECD. Slovakia opened an embassy in Tunisia in late 2012 and is advising the Tunisian government on the democratic transition process.

President Gašparovič met with his Hungarian counterpart in Budapest on February 19, 2013, the first presidential summit in nine years.

Fico upset minorities, including Roma and homosexuals, by declaring in a March 2013 speech that Slovakia had been "established for Slovaks, not minorities." He backtracked on the statement, and Foreign Minister Miroslav Lajčák signaled a willingness to reexamine the Benes Decrees.

Current issues. Slovakia's politicians face ongoing challenges related to minority rights, corruption scandals, and a slowing economy.

In late June 2009, amendments to Slovakia's State Language Act were passed to formalize the use of Slovak in official communication. The SMK criticized the law as restricting the use of the Hungarian language and discriminating against the ethnic Hungarian minority. Analysts noted that although the practical implication of the law may be minor, it served to create populist platforms for its sponsors in government ahead of the 2010 parliamentary campaigns. In September more than 10,000 ethnic Hungarians protested the measure in the town of Dunajska Streda.

In June 2011, the assembly overrode a veto by President Gašparovič on a Hungarian language bill. The measure reduced from 20 to 15 percent the minimum ethnic population required in a municipality for the official use of a minority language, including Hungarian, German, Roma, and Ruthenian.

On October 11, 2011, the governing coalition lost its majority in parliament when the SaS withdrew over opposition to the government-backed EU fiscal and stability pact. Radičová gained approval of the measure by agreeing to a *Smer* demand for early elections in March 2012. Meanwhile, on November 23, Defense Minister Lubomir GALKO resigned following revelations that military intelligence had wiretapped three journalists. On November 28, a state of emergency was declared throughout the country after more than 2,400 doctors resigned in a dispute over pay.

In December 2011, revelations emerged that the financial firm Penta had bribed members of the SDKÚ-DS-led coalition government in the early 2000s in exchange for privatization contracts. The so-called Gorilla scandal was followed by the "Sea Flower" affair in January 2013, in which MPs were allegedly paid to vote for Jozef ČENTÉŠ, the government coalition's candidate for prosecutor-general in 2011. Together, the scandals seriously undermined the Radičová government ahead of the early elections. The newly formed conservative **Ordinary People and Independent Personalities** (*Obyčajní Ľudia a Nezávislé Osobnosti*—OĽaNO) was one of several parties to campaign on anti-corruption platforms.

In January and February 2012, international credit agencies downgraded Slovakia's bond ratings in light of rising debt.

In early elections on March 10, 2012, *Smer* won 44 percent of the vote, enough for a majority 83 seats. *Smer* thus became the first party in Slovakia's history to rule without a coalition. All other parties took less than 9 percent of the vote, with seats allocated as follows: KDH, 16; OL'aNO, 16; MH, 13; SDKU-DS, 11; and SaS, 11. Former prime minister and Smer leader Robert Fico formed a center-left majority government with three independent members. Fico pledged to create a social dialog to find less painful ways to bring the deficit below 3 percent of GDP in 2013, raised the corporate tax rate, and canceled the previous government's 19 percent flat tax. He also announced that Slovakia would no longer be the euro zone's troublemaker and immediately approved the EU's expanded stability facilty. The SDKU-DS, KDH, and MH subsequently allied in parliament as the People's Platform.

In July 2012, Archbishop Róbert BEZÁK of Trnava was fired by Pope Benedict XVI. No explanation was given by the Vatican, but in December 2012 a fraud investigation was launched against Bezák's predecessor, Archbishop Jan SOKOL. Critics suggested that Sokol's allies were behind Bezák's sacking. Sokol is no stranger to controversy, after it was revealed in January 2007 that he had worked for the Secret Service (*Štátna Bezpečnosú*—ŠtB). Earlier that month, he had praised the wartime pro-German government of Archbishop Jozef Tiso, drawing protests from Slovakia's Jewish community. (For more on allegations of ŠtB collaboration, see the 2013 *Handbook*.)

In January 2013 the opposition introduced a motion to impeach President Gašparovič. At issue was the president's refusal to appoint Čentéš as attorney general. Although parliament nominated Čentéš in 2011, Gašparovič refused the appointment, due to rumors of vote buying (the "Sea Flower" affair). Only 45 MPs voted for the impeachment motion, half of the 90 needed to move the issue to the Constitutional Court. Public confidence in the judiciary is very low; 67 percent of respondents in a June 2012 poll said they did not trust the court system.

A government proposal to create boarding schools for Roma children prompted public demonstrations in March, while opposition parties offered ever-harsher proposals, ranging from razing Roma communities to capping welfare payments to a maximum of four children per family.

In June, parliament nominated Jaromir CIZNAR as prosecutor general, although many opposition parties denounced the vote as anticonstitutional. Gašparovič subsequently appointed Ciznar in July.

Fico eased some minority concerns when he signed a Memorandum of Mutual Cooperation with his Hungarian counterpart on July 2, 2013. The two leaders agreed to upgrade roads and increase border crossings.

By mid-2013, unemployment had risen to 15 percent with youth unemployment a staggering 35 percent. Fico lashed out against austerity programs, calling them "completely counter-productive," and offered economic and environmental concessions to keep open a U.S. Steel plant that provides 11,000 jobs. The prime minister insisted that austerity programs in Germany and other EU countries had slashed sales of Slovak exports.

POLITICAL PARTIES AND GROUPS

From 1948 to 1989 Czechoslovakia displayed the façade of a multiparty system through the National Front of the Czechoslovak Socialist Republic (*Národní Fronta*—ČSR), which was controlled by the Communist Party. The Front became moribund in late 1989, as most popular sentiment coalesced behind the recently organized coalition of the Civic Forum (*Občanské Fórum*—OF) in the Czech lands and its Slovak counterpart, the Public Against Violence (*Verejnost Proti Násilí*—VPN), which swept the legislative balloting of June 8–9, 1990. The Movement for a Democratic Slovakia (HZDS) emerged as a new party under the Slovak prime minister, Vladimír Mečiar, on June 22, 1991.

A controversial May 1998 electoral law revision mandated that individual parties, even those in coalitions, would claim National Council seats only if they obtained 5 percent of the national vote. As a direct result, a number of small parties merged with larger formations—principally the HZDS and the Slovak National Party (SNS)—while the principal opposition alliances, the Slovak Democratic Coalition (SDK) and the Hungarian Coalition (MK), technically transformed themselves into unified parties in preparation for the September 1998 election. Both participated in the formation of the multiparty Dzurinda government that took office a month later. In less than a year the diverse SDK began to fracture, leading Prime Minister Dzurinda to announce on January 17, 2000, his intention to organize a Slovak Democratic and Christian Union (SDKÚ), which held a founding congress the following November. By then, it had become apparent that the SDK would survive only until the 2002 election campaign, Dzurinda having announced that he would remain its chair while advancing the SDKÚ as a leading contender for 2002. The SDKÚ congress was soon followed by the withdrawal of the Christian Democratic Movement (KDH) and much of the Democratic Party (DS) from the SDK's parliamentary organization, although both pledged continued support for the government.

Government Parties:

Direction–Social Democracy (*Smer–Sociálna Demokracia*—*Smer*). Following the Communist defeat in late 1989, elements of the Communist Party of Slovakia (*Komunistická Strana Slovenska*—KSS) reestablished themselves as the Party of the Democratic Left (*Strana* Demokratickej *L'avice*—SDL') in 1990. By 1994, the party had emerged as the strongest component of a new center-left coalition but was unable to transform this into electoral success. Disputes over whether or not to join the HZDS in a coalition divided the party resulted in the emergence of Jozeph MIGAŠ as the party's chair, with several factions breaking away to form new parties.

Smer was formally established on December 11, 1999, by former members of the SDL,' and quickly emerged as a potentially significant force for the 2002 election due to the strength of its leader's popularity. Robert Fico, previously an SDL' deputy chair, organized *Smer* as a center-left, third-way party supporting EU accession, political reform, and caution with regard to majority foreign ownership of key industries. In late 2000, opinion polls ranked Fico as the country's most trustworthy and popular politician.

Smer won 13.5 percent of the vote and 25 seats in the September 2002 general election and subsequently served as one of the strongest left-leaning opponents of the Dzurinda government. *Smer* supported Ivan Gašparovič of the HZDS in his successful run for president in 2004.

In early 2005, *Smer* merged with the SDL', the Social Democratic Party of Slovakia (*Sociálnodemokratická Strana Slovenska*—SDSS), and the Social Democratic Alternative (*Sociálnodemokratická Alternatíva*—SDA), a small party formed by former SDL' ministers that had competed unsuccessfully in the 2002 legislative poll. (For information on the historically significant SDSS, see the 2006 *Handbook.*) The SDL' had been heir to the Communist Party of Slovakia (*Komunistická Strana Slovenska*—KSS), originally formed in 1939 but subsequently absorbed by the Communist Party of Czechoslovakia. The SDL' was reestablished in 1989, and in October 1990, its majority wing renamed itself the Communist Party of Slovakia–Party of the Democratic Left, which became simply Party of the Democratic Left later in the year.

The SDL' ran third in Slovakian local elections in November 1990 and second in the June 1992 general election. In 1993, it resisted overtures from the then-ruling HZDS to join the government, and in March 1994, it became the strongest component of a new center-left coalition. For the general election in fall 1994, it headed the Common Choice (SV) alliance, which won 18 seats (13 filled by members of the SDL', which had won 29 seats in 1992). The failure of the SDL' to emulate the recent electoral success of other East European ex-Communist parties was attributed in part to the preference of the old Slovak *nomenklatura* for Mečiar's HZDS.

From 1995, the SDL' experienced internal strife over whether to join the coalition government, as proposed by the HZDS. The election of compromise candidate Jozef Migaš as party leader in April 1996 (in succession to Peter WEISS) failed to end the dissension, which intensified when the SDL' leadership gave qualified external support to the government during a midyear cabinet crisis. Having finished third in the 1998 legislative election with 23 seats, the SDL' signed a coalition agreement under which it accepted six ministerial portfolios, compared with nine for the SDK, three for the SMK, and two for the SOP. Migaš was reelected chair at a July 2000 party conference despite considerable dissension over antigovernment statements, including his support for a no-confidence motion in April. On December 16, 2000, the SDL' minister of defense, Pavol KANIS, announced that he would shortly leave the cabinet, primarily over allegations concerning the financing of a luxury villa he had built.

The new 2005 grouping, which also reportedly attracted former members of the SOP, adopted the Direction–Social Democracy rubric, although it continued to be routinely referenced as simply *Smer.* The party secured a plurality of 29.1 percent of the legislative vote in 2006 and formed a government in coalition with two junior parties, the SNS and the HZDS. Since his election in 2006, Fico has consolidated his position within *Smer,* displacing rivals such as Monika FLAŠIKOVÁ-BEŇOVÁ (who was demoted from a deputy chair position in August 2006 after criticizing the coalition agreement with the SNS). The small Left Bloc (*L'avicový Blok*—L'B) merged with *Smer* in 2008.

Smer backed Ivan Gašparovič in his 2009 reelection bid, with the president going so far at some rallies as to identify his campaign with *Smer*'s political future. Although *Smer* won a plurality in the June 2010 legislative balloting, it could not negotiate a coalition government. In the March 2012 parliamentary elections, *Smer* secured 34.8 percent of the vote and 83 seats. Fico subsequently formed a new government.

Fico may run for the presidency in 2014, although mid-2013 polls suggest he would not secure victory in the first round of voting. His plans may affect the economy, as his entire cabinet would have to resign if he stepped down as prime minister.

Leaders: Robert FICO (Chair and Prime Minister), Robert KALIŇÁK and Peter KAŽIMÍR (Deputy Prime Ministers).

Opposition Parties:

Christian Democratic Movement (*Křesťansko-demokratické Hnutie*—KDH). Previously a partner of the Czech Christian Democrats, the KDH presented its own list in Slovakia for the 1990 poll. Its chair, Ján Čarnogurský, served as Slovakian prime minister following Mečiar's dismissal in April 1991. The party went into opposition after the June 1992 election but returned to government in the center-left coalition formed in March 1994. Polling a creditable 10.1 percent and winning 17 seats in the fall election, the KDH again went into opposition and subsequently rejected cooperation overtures from the ruling HZDS. In late 1996, the KDH joined with the DÚS and DS to form the Blue opposition alliance, named after the color of the EU flag to demonstrate the participants' pro-Europeanism.

Following the 1998 election, the KDH strongly argued for maintaining its separate identity within the SDK. In response to the formation of the SDKÚ (an obvious rival for Christian Democratic support), the KDH withdrew from the SDK in November 2000, taking with it nine members of the National Council. Late in the month, however, it officially joined the governing coalition. A month earlier, Čarnogurský had resigned the party chairship after ten years in office.

The KDH secured 8.3 percent of the votes in the 2002 legislative poll, while its presidential candidate, legislator František MIKLOŠKO, won 6.5 percent of the votes in the first round of balloting in April 2004. In February 2006, the party left the government coalition due to objections to an international treaty signed between Slovakia and the Holy See. The KDH won 8.3 percent of the vote in the 2006 legislative poll.

On February 21, 2008, four prominent members of the KDH left the party, citing dissatisfaction with its deviation from Christian Democratic ideals. On July 15, the four members submitted a successful petition to the Interior Ministry to form a new party, the Conservative Democrats of Slovakia (see below).

In the 2009 presidential elections, the KDH supported SDKÚ-DS candidate Iveta Radičová as part of a broader strategy of cooperation with other opposition parties. In September 2009, the party elected a new leader, Ján Figel', who pledged to reverse the party's declining fortunes. The party secured 16 seats in the June 2010 legislative balloting and subsequently joined the Radičová coalition government. Figel' was appointed a deputy prime minister. The KDH placed second in assembly balloting in March 2012 with 8.82 percent of the vote and 16 seats. Former interior minister Daniel LIPSIC and Jana ZITNANSKA left the KDH in 2013 to form the New Majority (*Nová väčšina*) party. Radoslav PROCHAZKA established a separate Alfa platform, then quit the party in February.

Leaders: Ján FIGEL' (Chair and Former EU Commissioner); Pavol ABRHAN, Peter BELINSKY, Julius BROCK, John HUDACKY, Milos MORAVCIK, Miroslava SZITOVÁ (Deputy Chairs); Ján ČARNOGURSKÝ (Former Prime Minister and Member of the Presidency of the Party); Pavol HRUŠOVSKÝ (Former Chair and Former Speaker of the National Council).

Ordinary People and Independent Personalities (*Obyčajní Ľudia a Nezávislé Osobnosti*—OĽaNO). The OL'aNO, a conservative grouping, was founded in October 2011 by Igor Matovič and former members of the SaS. The party placed third in the March 2012 elections with 8.55 percent of the vote and 16 seats. Peter POLLAK become the country's only Roma MP and the government's commissioner for the Roma community.

Leader: Igor MATOVIČ.

Bridge (*Most–Híd*—MH). This party was founded in June 2009 by Béla Bugár, the former president of the SMK. The party's name, which translates as "bridge" in both Hungarian and Slovak, is symbolic of its platform. Bugár described the MH as a moderate formation representing the interests of the ethnic Hungarian minority in cooperation with Slovak parties. The small Civic Conservative Party (*Občianska Konzervatívna Strana*—OKS) joined in an electoral alliance with the MH for the 2010 Council elections. The grouping placed fifth in the balloting with 8.1 percent of the vote and 14 seats in the parliament. The MH joined the SDKÚ-DS-led government and party Vice President Rudolf Chmel was appointed a deputy prime minister. In the March 2012 polling, the MH won 6.89 percent of the vote and 13 seats.

Leaders: Béla BUGÁR (President), Rudolf CHMEL (Vice President).

Slovak Democratic and Christian Union–Democratic Party (*Slovenská Demokratická Kresťanská Únia–Demokratická

Strana—SDKÚ-DS). Officially registered as a party on February 14, 2000, by Prime Minister Dzurinda (formerly of the KDH), the SDKÚ held its initial congress on November 18–19, 2000. Some 19 deputies and numerous government ministers affiliated with the Slovak Democratic Coalition (*Slovenská Demokratická Koalicia*—SDK) had pledged allegiance to it by the end of the year. The SDK had emerged in 1997 as a loose, philosophically diverse coalition of opposition parties—including the SDSS; the SZS; the DÚ, which dissolved in favor of the SDKÚ; the KDH; and DS, both of which withdrew in late 2000. In February 1998, the SDK evolved into an electoral alliance, and four months later, it officially registered as a unified party to ensure that none of its constituent organizations would fail to meet the new 5 percent threshold for claiming National Council seats. As a result, the SDK secured 42 seats in the September 1998 legislative balloting (on 26 percent of the votes) and led the subsequent coalition government. Following the withdrawal of the KDH and DS in late 2000, the SDK deputies numbered 27, including those who had announced support for the new SDKÚ and 2 (including former DÚ deputy chair and Velvet Revolution leader Ján BUDAJ) who had recently formed the Liberal Democratic Union (*Liberálnodemokratická Únia*—LDÚ).

On August 26, 2000, the Democratic Union (*Demokratická Únia*—DÚ, one of the founding members of the SDK, officially dissolved to join the SDKÚ, as did the minor Slovak Union of Small Tradesmen, Entrepreneurs, and Farmers (*Únie Živnostníkov, Podnikatel'ov a Rolníkov*—ÚŽPR) on June 30. (The ÚŽPR, led by Pavol PROKOPOVIĆ, had cooperated with the SDK in the 1998 election, contributing one seat to the alliance.) The DÚ had been founded at a Bratislava congress on April 23, 1994, as a merger of two components of the coalition government that came to power the previous month: the Democratic Union of Slovakia (DÚS), led by Prime Minister Jozef Moravčík, which had originated in February as a breakaway group of the then-ruling HZDS called the Alternative of Political Realism, and the Alliance of Democrats of the Slovak Republic (*Aliancia Demokratov Slovenské Republiky*—ADSR), another HZDS splinter group formed in June 1993 by Milan Kňažko, who had been ousted as foreign minister three months earlier. Commanding the support of 18 members of the National Council at the time of the merger, the DÚS adopted a centrist orientation and sought to build an alliance of similar formations for the fall 1994 general election. It largely failed to do so, attracting only the National Democratic Party–New Alternative (*Národná Demokratická Strana–Nová Alternatíva*—NDS-NA) onto its list, which polled an 8.6 percent vote share and won 15 seats. Founded in March 1994 by a moderate faction of the SNS and led by L'udovit ČERNÁK, the NDS-NA was formally absorbed by the DÚS in early 1995. In 1998, the DÚS won 12 of the SDK's 42 National Council seats.

The SDK officially dissolved in 2001; some core components formally transferred their allegiance to the SKDÚ, while the DS, SDSS, SZS, and KDH continued as independent parties. Following the 2002 legislative balloting (in which the SDKÚ finished second to the HZDS with 28 seats and a 19 percent vote share), Prime Minister Dzurinda was again asked to head a coalition government.

Following his dismissal as defense minister in September 2003, SDKÚ legislator Ivan ŠIMKO launched the Free Forum (below), the defections throwing the SDKÚ coalition into the status of a minority government. Continuing the SDKÚ slide, Eduard Kukan finished third (with 22.1 percent of the vote) as the party's candidate in the first round of presidential balloting in April 2004.

In January 2006, the SDKÚ merged with the Democratic Party (*Demokraticka Strana*—DS), the new grouping adopting the SDKÚ-DS rubric. (For information on the DS, see the 2006 *Handbook.*) In the legislative election of June 2006, Prime Minister Dzurinda and the SDKÚ-DS lost to Robert Fico's *Smer,* 29.1 percent to 18.4 percent. Dzurinda said that his reforms "should continue," a rather unlikely prospect as they were one of the main causes of the voters' desire for a change in government. Opinion polls in August 2007 continued to list Dzurinda as one of the least popular political figures in the country, while Deputy Chair Iveta Radičová polled as the third "most trusted" politician.

The SDKÚ-DS declined by 1,300 members in 2007, a 15 percent loss, and in March 2008, the party ejected 14 members for challenging the leadership of Dzurinda. In July 2008, Radičová called for a "restructuring" of the party and its communications strategy.

Despite divisions on several issues, in May 2008, the SDKÚ and KDH announced a common strategy for the 2010 parliamentary election, an agreement that initially excluded the SMK following its disloyalty in supporting the ratification of the EU treaty in April (see Current issues). Dzurinda, however, suggested that the SMK partnership would eventually resume, specifically in the three parties' backing (along with the OKS, below) of a single candidate, Radičová, to challenge popular incumbent Ivan Gašparovič in the 2009 presidential election. Radičová won 38.1 percent of the vote in the first round of balloting on March 21 and 44.5 percent in the second round on April 4. Despite her loss, analysts characterized her performance as a substantial personal victory, and there was widespread speculation she might emerge as leader of the party, although she chose not to challenge Dzurinda for leadership in party primaries in May. Although, the SDKÚ-DS placed second in legislative balloting in June 2010, Radičová formed a center-right coalition government.

Following legislative elections in March 2012, Radičová resigned from the party. In that balloting, the party placed fifth with 6.1 percent of the vote and 11 seats. The huge defeat led to the election of a new leadership team at the May 2012 party congress, where Pavol Frešo, president of the Bratislava Self-Governing Region, narrowly defeated former justice minister Lucia ALITNANSKA. Miroslav BEBLAVY and Alitnanska established their own platform, "We Are Creating Slovakia."

Leaders: Pavol FREŠO, (Chair); Viliam NOVOTNY, Ivan STEFANEC, Jozef MIKUS, Martin FEDOR (Deputy Chairs); Štefan KUZMA (Secretary).

Freedom and Solidarity (*Sloboda a Solidarita*—SaS). Founded in February 2009 by economist Richard Sulík, the SaS called for economic and social liberalism. It won 4.7 percent of the vote in the June European Parliament elections. The SaS placed third in the June 2010 legislative balloting with 12.1 percent of the vote, and it secured 22 seats. Sulík was elected speaker of the National Council on July 8, and the SaS joined the SDKÚ-DS–led coalition government. The SaS split with its coalition partners and opposed a second EU bailout package for Greece in 2011. In the 2012 parliamentary balloting, the SaS was sixth with 5.88 percent of the vote and 11 seats. The party split in March 2013 when Jozef KOLLAR failed to unseat Richard Sulik as chair and left to form a civic association, Liberal Agreement, that later joined the New Majority party. Four MPs also quit the party.

Leader: Richard SULIK (Chair and Former Speaker of the National Assembly).

Other Parties Contesting the 2012 Elections:

Slovak National Party (*Slovenská Národná Strana*—SNS). Founded in December 1989, the SNS is an intensely nationalist and anti-Hungarian formation defining itself as Christian, national, and social. In the 1990 National Council balloting it received 13.9 percent of the vote but took only 7.9 percent in June 1992, after which it entered into a coalition with the HZDS. It continued to support the government after the resignation of its sole minister in March 1993 and in October resumed formal coalition status, obtaining several key ministries. Its moderate wing, led by Chair L'udovit Černák, broke away in February 1994 (see NDS-NA, under SDKÚ, below), and the SNS went into opposition after the fall of the Mečiar government in March. In May the SNS Central Council decided that only ethnic Slovaks could be members of the party, which was awarded two portfolios in the coalition formed in December 1994 after winning 9 seats in the preceding election. The party advocated a "no" vote on the NATO referendum of May 1997 and joined the ZRS in backing President Mečiar's proposal for a "voluntary exchange of minorities" between Slovakia and Hungary. Its legislative representation rose to 14 in 1998 after securing 9 percent of votes.

On June 27, 1998, the Slovak Green Alternative (*Slovenská Zelených Alternatíva*—SZA), led by Zora LAZAROVÁ, merged into the SNS. (For the 1994 election the SZA had participated in a joint list with the HZDS, drawing some environmental support away from the SZS.) On the same day the Christian Social Union (*Křest'anská Socialná Únia*—KSÚ) ratified a merger agreement signed in May by the SNS's Ján Slota and the KSÚ Chair Viliam OBERHAUSER.

In the 1999 presidential election, Slota drew only 2.5 percent of the popular vote, in fifth place, and at a party congress in September he lost his chairship. In March 2000 the SNS renewed its alliance with the HZDS, the two parties agreeing to work together in parliament and in an effort to force an early election. Unlike the HZDS, the SNS opposed NATO membership.

In September 2000, the National Council stripped an SNS MP, Vít'azoslav MORIC, of parliamentary immunity, and in early October he was charged with inciting ethnic and racial hatred for having proposed that "unadaptable Gypsies" be sent to "reservations." The charges were subsequently dropped.

Slota and a number of his supporters were expelled from the SNS in late 2001. They subsequently announced the establishment of a "Real SNS," although the selection of that name was challenged by the SNS proper. The Real SNS was credited with 3.7 percent of the legislative vote in 2002, while the SNS was credited with 3.3 percent. The two factions reunited in April 2005, restoring Slota as leader. The SNS was surprisingly successful in the 2006 legislative poll, securing 20 seats on a vote share of 11.7 percent. However, in a political upset on December 2, 2006, Slota's reelection as mayor of Žilina failed, despite its status as a political stronghold of the SNS. Subsequent polls revealed public frustration with Slota for his perceived failure to establish transparency in decision making.

In 2006, SNS joined *Smer* and the L'S-HZDS in Fico's center-left governing coalition, a move that increased tensions with Hungary and contributed to a rift between the Slovak government and the social democratic faction of the European Parliament (see Foreign relations). The SNS demonstrated its role as a generally pliant coalition partner by accepting three successive requests from Fico in 2008 and 2009 that SNS environment ministers resign after criticism was raised regarding the disbursement of environmental-related government contracts. Fico subsequently withdrew the ministry of the environment from the purview of the SNS. The SNS joined *Smer* in supporting President Gašparovič's 2009 reelection bid. The earlier scandals undermined support for the SNS in the 2010 Council balloting and the party only secured 5.1 percent of the vote, reducing its seats in the parliament from 20 to 9. In July 2011 the SNS signed a memorandum of understanding with the far-right Austrian Freedom Party to oppose Turkey's bid for EU membership.

Following the party's disastrous showing in the March 2012 balloting, 4.55 percent of the vote and no seats, Slota was replaced as party chair by his deputy, Andrej Danko.

Leaders: Andrej DANKO (Chair); Rafael RAFAJ (First Deputy Chair), Milan FRIC, Roman STEM (Deputy Chairs).

Party of the Hungarian Coalition (*Strana Mad'arskej Koalície*—SMK/*Magyar Koalíció Partja*—MKP). The SMK was established in June 1998 as an outgrowth of the Hungarian Coalition (*Mad'arská Koalícia*—MK). Based in Slovakia's 600,000-strong ethnic Hungarian population, the MK had been formed for the 1994 national election by three parties, of which the first two had presented a joint list in the 1990 and 1992 elections, winning 7.4 percent of the vote on the latter occasion. In the 1994 balloting the three-party alliance came in third place with 17 seats on a 10.2 percent vote share. The ethnic Hungarian parties were the only groups in favor of across-the-board support of NATO in the 1997 referendum, endorsing membership as well as the deployment of nuclear weapons and placement of foreign military bases in Slovakia. In September they called upon Prime Minister Mečiar to resign over his suggestion that Hungary and Slovakia "exchange" minorities, which had reminded them of the postwar deportations 50 years ago. The SMK captured 15 National Council seats in the September 1998 election, in which it won 9.1 percent of the vote.

In August 2000, the party called for establishment of a self-governing region in the south, threatening to withdraw its support for the Dzurinda government. The call came in the context of national plans to establish new local administrative boundaries, creating 12 regions from the current 8. Ethnic Hungarians objected, in particular, to division of the Komárno region, fearing a dilution of their political power.

The SMK secured 11.7 percent of the vote in the 2006 legislative balloting. New party elections in March 31, 2007, ousted Béla Bugár from the chair in favor of former deputy prime minister Pál Csáky.

In the 2009 presidential election, the SMK supported SDKÚ candidate Iveta Radičová. In the 2010 legislative elections, the SMK lost support to another Hungarian party, the Bridge. In the balloting, the SMK received 4.3 percent of the vote and no representation in the Council. Because of the poor electoral showing, the senior party leadership resigned on June 13. The SMK secured 4.4 percent in local balloting in November. In Council elections in March 2012, the SMK failed to gain any seats.

Leaders: József BERÉNYI (Chair), László SZIGETI (Vice Chair).

People's Party–Movement for a Democratic Slovakia (*L'udová Strana–Hnutie za Demokratické Slovensko*—L'S-HZDS). The L'S-HZDS and its original version, HZDS, dominated Slovak politics in the 1990s and served in the Fico government of 2006–2010. Party leader Vladimir Mečiar served three terms as prime minister. However, its popularity plummeted and membership fragmented after 2006, and the party was shut out of parliament in the 2010 and 2012 elections, taking barely 1 percent of the vote in 2012. Mečiar resigned as party chair in May 2012. Although the party has one MEP, Sergej KOZLÍK, it has effectively dissolved. (For more on L'S-HZDS, see the 2013 *Handbook.*)

Communist Party of Slovakia (*Komunistická Strana Slovenska*—KSS). Descended from the original Slovak Communist Party founded in 1939, the present KSS consists of the Marxist-Leninist minority that rejected transitioning to the democratic socialist SDL' in 1990. The party won a 2.7 percent vote share in the 1994 legislative balloting and 2.8 percent in 1998. In 1999 its candidate for president attracted only 0.5 percent of the vote. The KSS improved to 6.3 percent of the vote (and 11 seats) in the 2002 legislative poll. However, it failed to secure representation in 2006 on a vote share of 3.9 percent.

On August 12, 2008, an unaffiliated candidate, Milan SIDOR began collecting signatures in preparation for a presidential bid with the support of the KSS. Earlier, in April, KSS member and former MP Dagmara BOLLOVÁ left the party in order to launch an independent run for the presidency. Bollová took 1.13 percent and Sidor 1.11 percent of the vote in the first round of balloting in March 2009. In the 2010 and 2012 legislative balloting, the KSS received less than 1 percent of the vote.

Leader: Jozef HRDLIČKA (Chair).

Green Party (*Strana Zelených*—SZ). Founded in December 1989 as the Green Party in Slovakia (*Strana Zelených na Slovensku*—SZS), the SZ failed to secure federal parliamentary representation in 1990 but obtained six seats in the Slovak National Council. Having lost all six in the 1992 balloting, the party regained two seats in 1994 as part of the Common Choice coalition. In 1998, the Greens won three SDK seats, agreeing in late 2000 to work with the newly formed LDÚ on leftist concerns. The SZ adopted its current designation in January 2006.

In a move that was widely seen as a means for *Smer* to improve its environmental credentials, in March 2008, the SZ signed an agreement with *Smer,* pledging to cooperate on drawing up environmental legislation. However, Fico and (then) SZ Chair Pavel PETRIK denied that the agreement was a step on the road to a merger. The SZ won 2.1 percent of the vote in the 2009 European Parliament elections but only 0.4 percent in the 2012 Council elections.

Leaders: Peter PILINSKÝ (Chair), Ivan HIRLÄNDER (Deputy Chair), Martin JÓNA (Secretary).

Among the small parties that unsuccessfully contested the 2012 legislative poll were the **Party of the Democratic Left** (*Strana Demokratickej Lavice*—SDL) led by Mark BLAHA; the **Party of the Slovak Roma Union** (*Strana Romské Unie na Slovensku*—SRÚS), led by František TANKO; the **99 Percent—Civic Voice** (*99%–Občiansky Hlas*); the **Free Forum** (*Slobodné Fórum*—SF), formed in November 2003 and whose leader, Zuzana MARTINÁKOV, secured approximately 5 percent of the vote in the 2009; and the **Free Word Party of Nora Mojsejová** (*Strana Slobodné Slovo–Nory Mojsejovej*, SSS).

Other Parties:

Movement for Democracy (*Hnutie za Demokraciu*—HZD). The HZD was launched in 2002 by Ivan Gašparovič, a former supporter of HZDS leader and former prime minister Vladimír Mečiar. The defection was attributed to Gašparovič's anger at being left off the HZDS candidate list for the September 2002 National Council balloting. The HZD secured 3.3 percent of the vote in the legislative poll. In January 2004 the HZD merged its candidate lists with the People's Union (*L'udová únia*—L'U; see Liberal Party, below). In the presidential elections the group nominated Ivan Gašparovič, a former speaker of the National Council, as the presidential candidate of an L'U-HZD-led Confederation of the National Forces of Slovakia that also included the SNS (above) and another small grouping called **Slovak National Unity** (*Slovenská Národná Jednota*—SNJ). Gašparovič surprised most observers by finishing second in the first round of balloting with 22.3 percent of the vote and then handily defeating his former mentor Mečiar in the runoff. Following the election, Gašparovič resigned his post as chair of the HZD so as not to appear beholden to any single party, although honorary ties to the party are often ascribed to him. In the 2009 presidential elections the HZD supported Gašparovič's reelection bid, although he ran as an independent candidate.

Polls in early 2009 suggested that only 1 percent of the electorate would support the HZD in a parliamentary election. Party leader Joseph Grapa subsequently declared that the party would not compete in the 2010 legislative balloting, but would instead support *Smer.* The HZD also supported *Smer* in municipal balloting in November and the March 2012 elections.

Leaders: Josef GRAPA (Chair), Ivan GAŠPAROVIČ (President of the Republic and Honorary Chair of the Party).

For more information on the **New Citizens' Alliance** (*Alliancia Nového Občana*—ANO), the **Liberal Party** (*Liberálna Strana*—LS), and the **Party of Civic Understanding** (*Strana Občianskeho Porozumenia*—SOP), see the 2009 *Handbook.* For information on the the **Conservative Democrats of Slovakia** (*Konzervatívni Demokrati Slovenska*—KDS); the **Free Forum** (*Slobodné Fórum*—SF); the **Romany Civic Initiative** (*Rómska Občanská Iniciatíva*—ROI); and the **Romany Initiative of Slovakia** (*Rómska Iniciatíva Slovenska*—RIS), please see the 2012 *Handbook.*

LEGISLATURE

The unicameral **National Council of the Slovak Republic** (*Národná Rada Slovenské Republiky*) consists of 150 members directly elected via proportional representation in one countrywide constituency for four-year terms. Parties must secure at least 5 percent of the vote to achieve representation. Following the most recent balloting of March 10, 2012, the seats were distributed as follows: Direction–Social Democracy, 83; the Christian Democratic Movement, 16; Ordinary People, 16; the Bridge 13; the Slovak Democratic and Christian Union–Democratic Party, 11; and Freedom and Solidarity, 11.

Speaker: Pavol PAŠKA.

CABINET

[as of August 8, 2013]

Prime Minister	Robert Fico
Deputy Prime Ministers	Robert Kaliňák
	Peter Kažimír
	Miroslav Lajčák (ind.)
Ministers	
Agriculture and Regional Development	L'ubomir Jahnátek
Culture and Tourism	Marek Mad'arič
Defense	Martin Glváč
Economy and Construction	Tomáš Malatinský (ind.)
Education, Science, Research, and Sport	Dušan Čaplovič
Environment	Peter Žiga
Finance	Peter Kažimír
Foreign Affairs	Miroslav Lajčák (ind.)
Health	Zuzana Zvolenská [f]
Interior	Robert Kaliňák
Justice	Tomáš Borec (ind.)
Labor, Social Affairs, and Family	Ján Richter
Transport, Posts, and Telecommunications	Ján Počiatek

[f] = female

Note: Unless indicted, all ministers belong to *Smer.*

INTERGOVERNMENTAL REPRESENTATION

Ambassador to the U.S.: Peter KMEC.

U.S. Ambassador to the Slovak Republic: Theodore SEDGWICK.

Permanent Representative to the UN: František RUŽIČKA.

IGO Memberships (Non-UN): CEUR, EBRD, EIB, EU, ICC, IOM, NATO, OECD, OSCE, WTO.

SLOVENIA

Republic of Slovenia
Republika Slovenija

Political Status: Former constituent republic of the Socialist Federal Republic of Yugoslavia; independence declared June 25, 1991, on the basis of a referendum held December 23, 1990; present constitution adopted December 23, 1991.

Area: 7,818 sq. mi. (20,251 sq. km).

Population: 2,056, 262 (2013E—UN); 1,992,690 (2013E—U.S. Census).

Major Urban Centers (2011E): LJUBLJANA (272,220), Maribor (95,171).

Official Language: Slovene.

Monetary Unit: Euro (market rate November 1, 2013: 0.74 euro = $1US). Slovenia adopted the euro as its official currency on January 1, 2007. Its former currency was the tolar.

President: On December 2, 2012, Borut PAHOR (Social Democrats) defeated incumbent Danilo TÜRK (nonparty) in the second round of presidential balloting, 67.4 percent to 32.6 percent. Inaugurated on December 22, Pahor was born in 1963, making him the youngest president in the country's history.

President of the Executive Council (Prime Minister): Alenka BRATUŠEK (Positive Slovenia); nominated by the National Assembly on February 27, following a vote of no confidence in Janez JANŠA (Slovenian Democratic Party); nominated by the president on January 25, 2012, following the legislative election of December 4, 2011. Bratušek's government was approved by the National Assembly on March 20, making her Slovenia's first female prime minister and the first from the PS.

THE COUNTRY

Located in the extreme northwest of post–World War II Yugoslavia, with a short Adriatic coastline south of Trieste, Slovenia is bordered on the west by Italy, on the south and east by Croatia, on the northeast by Hungary, and on the north by Austria. The population is predominantly Slovene (83.1 percent), with small Croat, Serb, Magyar (Hungarian), and Italian minorities. About 58 percent of the population is Roman Catholic. Women and men are equal participants in the labor force. Following the elections in 2007 and 2011, women made up 2.5 percent (1 member) of the National Council and 32.2 percent (29 members) of the National Assembly.

Leading manufactures include transport equipment, textiles, and chemicals and pharmaceuticals. Tourism is another significant contributor to the economy. The European Union (EU) now accounts for about two-thirds of trade, with Germany and Italy in the lead.

Slovenia's industrial production declined by 21 percent in 1991 (to its 1975 level), while GDP fell by 9 percent and inflation soared to more than 200 percent (for information on Slovenia's economy prior to 1991, please see the 2012 *Handbook*). However, its economy recovered quickly, and Slovenia is the most prosperous country to emerge from the former Yugoslavia. GDP growth was steady throughout most of the 1990s, reaching 4.9 percent in 1999.

In March 2003 Slovenian voters approved a referendum on EU membership, and the country formally joined the organization on May 1, 2004. Between 2000 and 2008, GDP growth averaged 4.3 percent, while inflation averaged 5.3 percent and unemployment 6 percent. In January 2007 Slovenia became the first Eastern or Central European state to adopt the euro as its currency. The economy went into recession in the last quarter of 2008, and GDP declined by 7.8 percent in 2009 because of the global economic slowdown. That year inflation fell to less than 1 percent but unemployment rose from 4.4 percent to 9.2 percent. Meanwhile, the deficit expanded in 2009 because of lower tax revenues and increased public spending. In 2010, GDP grew 1.4 percent, while the following year, the country fell in to recession as GDP

fell by 0.2 percent, followed by –2.3 percent in 2012. Inflation was 1.8 percent in 2011 and 2.6 in 2012, while unemployment rose from 8.1 percent in 2011 to 11 percent in 2012.

GOVERNMENT AND POLITICS

Political background. Previously consisting of a number of Austrian crown lands, modern Slovenia was included in the Kingdom of the Serbs, Croats, and Slovenes, which was officially renamed Yugoslavia in October 1929. During World War II it was divided between Germany, Hungary, and Italy, and in 1945 it became a constituent republic of the Yugoslavian federation.

After 45 years of Communist one-party rule, a six-party Democratic Opposition of Slovenia (*Demokratične Opozicije Slovenije*—Demos) obtained a majority of legislative seats in the tricameral Slovenian Assembly in balloting on April 8 and 22, 1990, with Demos leader Lojze PETERLE being named president of the Executive Council (prime minister) on May 16. However, in the contest for president of the republic the former Communist leader, Milan KUČAN, outpolled three competitors by winning 44.5 percent of the vote in the first round and defeated the runner-up, Demos candidate Jože PUČNIK, with a 58.7 percent vote share in the second. On July 2 the assembly issued a declaration of full sovereignty for the Slovene Republic, and in a referendum on December 23 an overwhelming majority of voters opted for independence.

On February 20, 1991, the assembly approved a resolution announcing the phased "dissociation of Slovenia from Yugoslavia," and on June 25 Slovenia joined neighboring Croatia in issuing a formal declaration of independence. A brief war ensued with federal Yugoslav forces, resulting in the withdrawal of the latter after ten days of relatively minor skirmishing. Having achieved its primary objective, the Demos coalition proved unstable and was formally dissolved in December 1991. This left what became the Party of Democratic Reform (*Stranka Demokratične Prenove*—SDP) and the Liberal Democratic Party (*Liberalna Demokratična Slovenije*—LDS)—with the former having descended from the League of Communists and the latter from the former Communist youth organization—more strongly represented than any other grouping. Even so, Peterle, leader of the conservative Slovenian Christian Democrats (*Slovenski Krščanski Demokrati*—SKD), remained premier.

In early 1992, the government encountered criticism for the slow pace of economic reform, and on April 22 Peterle was obliged to resign upon passage of a parliamentary vote of no confidence. The assembly thereupon named Janez DRNOVŠEK of the LDS to form a new government, which, after being installed on May 14, announced a program that included reducing inflation and unemployment, privatizing the economy, and establishing linkages with international financial institutions.

The LDS became the strongest parliamentary party in the first postindependence general election, held on December 6, 1992, with the SKD taking second place. In simultaneous presidential balloting, Kučan, abandoning his party affiliation, was returned for a five-year term by 63.8 percent of the vote against seven other candidates. The governmental outcome was the formation of a new center-left coalition under the continued incumbency of Drnovšek, with Peterle as deputy premier and foreign minister.

The new Drnovšek government reaffirmed its commitment to the "Economic Policy Program" aimed at galvanizing the private sector, reforming fiscal legislation, restructuring the banking system, and rehabilitating state-owned enterprises. However, it took a cautious line in its economic reform, preferring to adapt existing structures rather than abolish them. Observers noted that the center-left cabinet included former Communists in all the key economic portfolios. Moreover, President Kučan, once Slovenia's Communist leader, retained considerable personal influence (and public popularity), even though the 1991 constitution reduced the presidency to a largely symbolic role.

In June 1993, the president and various ministers became involved in a major arms-trading scandal when some 120 tons of weaponry were discovered at Ljubljana's Maribor airport, apparently en route from Saudi Arabia to the Bosnian Muslims in contravention of a United Nations (UN) embargo. Amid conflicting allegations as to who had instigated the shipment, the affair became a power struggle between Defense Minister Janez JANŠA of the Social Democratic Party of Slovenia (*Socialdemokratična Stranka Slovenije*—SDS) and President Kučan, with the former depicting the episode as characteristic of the corrupt practices surrounding the ex-Communist ruling clique. The confrontation persisted until March 1994, when reported misconduct by military police under the defense minister's authority prompted the prime minister to dismiss Janša from the government, whereupon the SDS joined the opposition.

The transfer to opposition of the SDS was not seen as affecting survival of the Drnovšek government, which continued to command a parliamentary majority. Indeed, prior to the ouster Drnovšek had consolidated his assembly support by restructuring the LDS, now called the Liberal Democracy of Slovenia (*Liberalna Demokracija Slovenije*—LDS), to include elements of three smaller parties, two with parliamentary representation.

The SKD's participation in the ruling coalition became strained in 1994, culminating in the resignation of Peterle from his government posts in September to protest the selection of an LDS deputy to be the new president of the National Assembly. Other Christian Democrats continued to hold important portfolios, however, and the government remained secure in the National Assembly. More ominous for the LDS was the withdrawal of the United List of Social Democrats (*Združena Lista Socialnih Demokratov*—ZLSD) from the coalition in January 1996 (in protest against the prime minister's move to dismiss a ZLSD minister), while in May a parliamentary nonconfidence vote against the foreign minister, Zoran THALER, obliged Drnovšek to make a new appointment to the post.

In assembly balloting on November 10, 1996, the LDS remained the largest single party but fell back to 25 seats out of 90, while a center-right Slovenian Spring (*Slovenije Pomladi*—SP) alliance of the Slovenian People's Party (*Slovenska Ljudska Stranka*—SLS), the SDS, and the SKD won a combined total of 45 seats. Drnovšek was asked to remain as head of a caretaker government, and he immediately announced his intention to form a new government comprised of the LDS and the other non-SP parties. However, the 45–45 parliamentary split between the SP and the LDS-allied parties delayed not only the quick formation of a new government, but also the election of a permanent prime minister. The latter stalemate was finally broken in early January 1997 when an SKD deputy announced support for Drnovšek, who was reelected on January 9 by a vote of 46–44. Nevertheless, wrangling over the formation of a new cabinet continued for some seven weeks until the SLS broke with the SP to participate with the LDS and the small Slovenian Democratic Party of Pensioners (*Demokratična Stranka Upokojencev Slovenije*—DeSUS) in a government approved on February 27. President Kučan won reelection on November 23, 1997, taking 55 percent of the vote in a field of eight candidates in the first-round balloting, thereby avoiding a runoff.

Drnovšek survived two nonconfidence votes in May and December 1998, both relating to claims by opposition leader Janša that the prime minister knew about a secret 1995 security agreement with Israel and failed in his constitutional duty to make it public. In the December election the opposition could muster only 24 votes in the 90-seat National Assembly.

On March 15, 2000, nine SLS ministers announced that they would leave the government on April 15, at which time the SLS and the SKD would merge in preparation for an autumn general election. With the SLS controlling 19 of the government's 49 seats in the National Assembly, Prime Minister Drnovšek faced the imminent demise of his government. On April 3 he proposed adding eight nonparty experts to the cabinet, but lack of support forced his resignation on April 8. The unified center-right SLS+SKD Slovenian People's Party (*SLS+SKD Slovenska Ljudska Stranka*—SLS+SKD) put forward Andrej BAJUK as his successor, but Bajuk, an economist with the Inter-American Development Bank who had spent all but a fraction of his life abroad, twice failed to win majority support in the legislature, obtaining 44 votes on April 20—2 shy of the required 46—and then 43 on April 26. Following negotiation of a coalition agreement with the SDS, Bajuk won confirmation, 46–44, on May 3, although on May 23 the legislature split evenly on his proposed cabinet, which did not win approval until June 7, also by a 46–44 vote. The new government included eight SLS+SKD ministers, five SDS ministers, and five independents.

The government suffered a serious rupture in late July 2000 when the majority of the SLS+SKD, but not Prime Minister Bajuk, reversed course and joined the LDS in backing retention of proportional representation in the National Assembly. (In a 1996 binding referendum the public had endorsed a majoritarian system, but the legislature had failed to enact the change because of opposition from the left.) As a result, the SDS ended its agreement with the SLS+SKD, and on July 27 President Kučan called an election for October. In the interim, Prime Minister Bajuk left the SLS+SKD and formed the New Slovenia–Christian People's Party (*Nova Slovenija–Krščanska Ljudska Stranka*—NSi), which quickly formed an electoral coalition with the SDS.

In the October 15, 2000, balloting the LDS won a plurality of 34 seats. Prime Minister Drnovšek returned to power in November as the head of a four-party coalition that also included the ZLSD, the SLS+SKD, and the DeSUS. Easily confirmed by the National Assembly on November 17, Drnovšek fashioned a restructured cabinet comprised of nine LDS ministers and three each from the ZLSD and the SLS+SKD. In addition, the ZLSD chair, Borut PAHOR, took over as president of the legislature.

In runoff balloting on December 1, 2002, Prime Minister Drnovšek won the presidency of Slovenia, capturing about 56.5 percent of the vote against Barbara BREZIGAR, a state prosecutor. Drnovšek resigned as prime minister the next day, and on December 6 President Kučan (who had been barred from seeking a third term) nominated Finance Minister Anton ROP (LDS) as the new prime minister. Confirmed by the National Assembly on December 19, Rop and his cabinet took office on December 20. President Drnovšek was sworn in on December 22 and assumed his duties the following day.

In November 2002, Slovenia was invited to join the North Atlantic Treaty Organization (NATO) along with six other countries, and in December 2002 Slovenia was one of ten countries that were offered EU membership. At a national referendum on March 23, 2003, voters approved entry into both organizations. EU membership was approved by 89.6 percent of the voters, while NATO membership was supported by 66.1 percent. On March 29, 2004, Slovenia joined NATO, and on May 1, it became a member of the EU.

In 2004, the assembly enacted controversial legislation to grant Slovenian citizenship to refugees from the former Yugoslavia. Opposition groups argued against the measure, which undermined public support for the LDS-led government and prompted the SLS (the SLS+SKD having returned to the SLS rubric) to withdraw from the government on April 7, 2004. The issue was also prominent in European parliamentary elections on June 13, 2004, in which the opposition NSi received 23.5 percent of the vote and two seats, while an alliance of the LDS and the DeSUS secured 21.9 percent and two seats; the SDS, 17.7 percent and two seats; and the ZLSD, 14.2 percent and one seat. Previously, on February 26, 2004, the National Assembly had approved legislation that required 40 percent of party candidates for the EU seats to be female.

In addition to the unpopular citizenship policy, the ruling coalition faced problems over internal strife surrounding the 2004 legislative elections. On June 24 Rop requested that the assembly approve a no-confidence vote for Foreign Minister Dimitrij RUPEL, whom the prime minister accused of cooperating with the opposition. The assembly removed Rupel through such a vote on July 5 (Rupel subsequently joined the SDS).

In the legislative elections on October 3, 2004, the SDS became the largest party in the legislature when it received 29.1 percent of the vote and 29 seats in the assembly, while the LDS only secured 22.8 percent and 23 seats. SDS leader Janša was subsequently nominated by the president to form a government, and his new cabinet, which included the SDS, NSi, DeSUS, and SLS, was approved by the assembly on December 3. His government initiated a range of economic reforms, including tax reductions. However, its privatization program subsequently stalled, and the government faced calls from the EU and the IMF to reduce state involvement in the banking and financial sectors. Nevertheless, Slovenia was praised by the EU for its management of the adoption of the euro in 2007.

President Drnovšek announced that he would not seek reelection due to ill health in February 2007. (Drnovšek died on February 23, 2008, of cancer.) Seven candidates contested the first round of presidential balloting on October 21. Former prime minister Lojze Peterle, an independent supported by the SDS, the SLS, and the NSi, placed first with 28.7 percent of the vote. Independent Danilo TÜRK came in second with 24.5 percent of the vote. Türk was endorsed by the SD, DeSUS, Active Slovenia (*Aktivna Slovenia*—AS), and For Real (*Zares*). In the second round of polling on November 11, Türk won with 68.0 percent of the vote to Peterle's 32.0 percent. He assumed office on December 22. Meanwhile, the endorsement of Türk by the DeSUS, a member of the SDS-led government, led Janša to call for a confidence vote after the election. On November 19 the Janša government won the confidence vote by a margin of 51 to 33 votes as the DeSUS continued to support the government. The prime minister and new president subsequently pledged to work together as Slovenia assumed the rotating presidency of the EU.

In summer 2008, Janša was accused by Finnish reporters of accepting cash payments to approve a 2006 procurement deal whereby Slovenia bought 135 armored vehicles from the Finnish company Patria Ojy for $402 million, the largest defense contract in Slovenian history. Janša strongly denied the charges. In September the National Assembly debated the allegations and conducted a confidence vote, which the government won with 41 votes in favor and 11 opposed. The charges emerged as a significant factor in the campaign for the assembly election on September 21. The SD received 30.5 percent of the vote and 29 seats, followed by the ruling SDS with 29.3 percent and 28 seats. Thus, the SD won one more seat in the balloting than the ruling SDS; however, the SD did not secure a majority and negotiations continued until November 3, when SD Borut Pahor was nominated as prime minister of an SD-led coalition government supported by 50 deputies in the assembly. Meanwhile, on October 15, Pavel GANTAR of *Zares* was elected president of the National Assembly with support from the SD.

In April 2009, the Pahor government announced deep cuts in defense spending to shift resources to social programs as a recession cut government revenues. In elections for the European Parliament on June 7, the SDS retained its two seats, while the SD gained one to bring its total to two. The NSi, the LDS, and *Zares* each secured one seat in the balloting, which saw a voter turnout rate of 28.3 percent and reflected the continuing division of public sentiment between parties of the left and right. In November the new government announced that Slovenia would construct a second nuclear power plant that would become operational between 2020 and 2025.

On January 26, 2010, Karl ERJAVEC, the chair of DeSUS and the minister of the environment and physical planning, resigned after losing a confidence vote requested by Pahor. The prime minister requested the motion after he accused the minister of inefficiency and poor management. Three other ministers resigned in 2010.

In April 2011, DeSUS withdrew from Pahor's coalition government, and the following month, *Zares* pulled out. The loss of the two partners left the government with only 33 votes in the assembly. Following the loss of a confidence vote in September, Pahor announced that he would remain at the head of a minority government until early elections on December 4, 2011. In the balloting, the newly formed center-left Positive Slovenia (*Pozitivna Slovenija*—PS) placed first with 28 seats but was unable to form a government (see Current issues, below). Instead, Janša negotiated a center-right coalition government that included the SDS, SLS, NSi, DeSUS, and the new Civic List (*Državljanska Lista*—DL). The new government was approved on February 10, 2012.

Constitution and government. The Slovenian elections of April 1990 were the first to be freely contested in former Yugoslavia in 51 years. The current constitution was adopted on December 23, 1991, and was amended by the Constitutional Act of July 14, 1997, and the Constitutional Act of July 25, 2000.

The head of state is the president, who is directly elected for a five-year term but has a largely ceremonial role. The principal executive officer is the prime minister, who is designated (and may be removed) by the National Assembly.

The 1991 document endorses basic human rights on the European model, one of the aims of the drafters having been to demonstrate Slovenia's suitability for admittance into European democratic organizations. The judiciary includes district and regional courts, with a Supreme Court at the apex. Administratively, Slovenia encompasses 210 municipalities, each consisting of 1 or more of the country's approximately 2,700 cadastral communities. Municipalities may choose to form larger districts (*upravne enote*), of which there are currently 58. Eleven large municipalities have been granted "urban status," which allows them greater autonomy. On June 22, 2008, Slovenians voted in favor of the creation of 13 regions in a nonbinding referendum that was marred by low voter turnout of 10.9 percent.

In 2004, the assembly passed legislation, requested by the Supreme Court, which granted citizenship to residents of Slovenia who had immigrated from other areas of the former Yugoslavia and who had lost their legal status because they failed to apply for citizenship within a six-month grace period following Slovenian independence. (This group became known as the "erased" since they were struck from the census records and therefore were ineligible for government benefits and services.) Conservative and opposition parties forced a national referendum on the issue, and on April 4, 2004, voters overwhelmingly rejected the citizenship law with 94 percent voting against amnesty. The government and LDS had urged citizens to boycott the referendum and turnout was low at 31 percent. Then interior minister Rado BOHINC vowed to continue registering the erased, and the Supreme Court subsequently ruled that the referendum was illegal.

Slovenia has a comparatively free and open press. In its 2012 annual index, the media watchdog group Reporters Without Borders ranked Slovenia at 35th out of 179 countries in terms of freedom of the press.

Foreign relations. The European Community (EC, later the EU) recognized the independence of both Croatia and Slovenia on January 15, 1992, with the two countries establishing diplomatic relations on February 17. (Relations with Yugoslavia were not normalized until December 8, 2000.) In February 1992, Slovenia joined the Conference on (later Organization for) Security and Cooperation in Europe (CSCE/OSCE). On May 23, Slovenia, Croatia, and Bosnia and Herzegovina were admitted to the UN.

In March 1992 Slovenia was admitted to membership of the Central European Initiative (CEI), becoming active in efforts to revive the Slovenian and Italian Adriatic ports as entrepôts for the CEI countries. Slovenian officials recalled that the Trieste-Vienna railway, running through Slovenia, had been one of the first built in continental Europe and saw the CEI as a framework for recreating the economic links of the imperial era. In the longer term, Slovenia aspired to membership in the EC/EU, as did the other non-EU CEI states. On January 15, 1993, it became a member of the International Monetary Fund (IMF), and in May it was admitted to membership of the Council of Europe. In February 1994 Slovenia joined the Partnership for Peace program launched by NATO the previous month for former Communist and neutral states.

Slovenia contributed troops to the international peacekeeping mission in Bosnia. In addition, Slovenia was instrumental in creating the International Fund for Demining and Mine Victims' Assistance to support demining operations in Bosnia. In March 2004, Slovenia deployed troops and equipment to Afghanistan as part of the UN-led peacekeeping operation. In August, firefighting units were also sent to Kabul, Afghanistan, to train locals.

Unresolved border disputes have strained Slovenia's postindependence relations with Croatia. The issue flared up in October 1994 when the Slovenian Assembly adopted local boundary changes that assigned territory claimed by Croatia to the Slovenian municipality of Piran. Although the Slovenian government quickly called for revision of the measure, Croatia lodged an official protest. Talks at the prime ministerial level in June 1995 were reported to have yielded agreement on "98 percent" of land and maritime border issues. However, relations cooled in December 1997 when Croatia amended its constitution, dropping Slovenes from a list of recognized ethnic minorities and raising suspicions about Zagreb's intentions.

Notwithstanding their bilateral territorial dispute, Slovenia and Croatia remained in agreement on the need to resist any revival of irredentism on the part of Italy, which had long pressed the issue of compensation for Italians whose property in Istria had been appropriated following post–World War II border changes that favored Yugoslavia. The pressure on Slovenia intensified in May 1994 with the advent of the right-wing government of Italian prime minister Silvio Berlusconi, with Rome making it clear that it would block Slovenia's EU membership aspirations until it obtained satisfaction. However, following the fall of Berlusconi in December, the new nonparty Italian government lifted the veto on March 4, 1995, enabling Slovenia to commence associate membership talks with the EU, which were assisted by Spanish mediation on the dispute with Italy. Following the resolution of most outstanding issues, Slovenia signed an association agreement with the EU in June 1996, also lodging an application for full EU membership. In the same month Slovenia became an "associate partner" of the Western European Union (WEU), seeing such status as a necessary precursor to the goal of NATO membership. Subsequently, in February 1998, Slovenia agreed to compensate 21,000 ethnic Italians for property they left behind when they fled to Italy at the end of World War II.

Relations with Croatia took a step forward after the death of Croatian president Franjo Tudjman in December 1999 and the election of a new president, Stipe Mesič, two months later. Following talks with President Kučan during a March visit to Ljubljana, Mesič described bilateral issues as "solvable with just a little stronger will on both sides." Border concerns, including Slovenian access to Piran Bay, were largely resolved in July 2001, as was a disagreement over management of the jointly owned nuclear power plant in Krško, Slovenia. Austria also expressed concern about the safety of the nuclear facility, but a more contentious issue involved Austrian calls, particularly from the right, for Slovenia to renounce the World War II–era decrees under which the partisan-led Antifascist Council for the National Liberation of Yugoslavia (*Antifašističko Vee Narodnog Oslobodjenja Jugoslavije*—AVNOJ) expelled the German minority from Yugoslavia and confiscated German property.

At the NATO Summit Meeting in Prague, on November 21–22, 2002, Slovenia was invited to begin accession talks for NATO membership along with six other countries: Bulgaria, Estonia, Latvia, Lithuania, Romania, and Slovakia. On March 29, 2004, Slovenia became a member of NATO, and on May 1 it joined the EU. The assembly approved the proposed EU Constitution on February 2, 2005.

Once in office in December 2004, the Janša government announced its intention to maintain close ties with the United States. (Tension between the two countries over the International Criminal Court had strained what had previously been very good relations.) The administration also pursued deeper ties with Romania, actively working to aid Romania's successful quest to join the EU.

Ongoing disputes with Croatia over the border continued in 2005–2006, including the demarcation of fishing areas in the Adriatic Sea (the talks over that issue also included Italy). Additionally, the two countries maintained overlapping claims in the Bay of Piran, Slovenia's only deepwater access to the Adriatic.

In response to complaints from Slovenia and other new EU members, the European Central Bank called in February 2007 for countries such as Germany and France to remove restrictions on the migration of workers from the Central and Eastern European states. Subsequently, in April, Slovenia and Greece signed three bilateral agreements on maritime transport, coordination of oceanographic services, and tourism.

On January 1, 2008, Slovenia assumed the rotating presidency of the EU. The country's priorities during its presidency were ratification of the Lisbon Treaty by the EU member states, increased economic integration, and addressing climate change. Slovenia ratified the Lisbon Treaty on January 29. Slovenia also championed EU membership for Macedonia but was unable to secure an agreement to open accession discussions because of opposition from Greece (see the entry on Greece). In December the new government announced its opposition to EU membership for Croatia because of the continuing border dispute between the two countries. However, the assembly approved NATO membership for Croatia in February 2009. Slovenia subsequently withdrew its veto of EU membership for Croatia in September. In November the two countries signed an accord pledging to accept international arbitration to settle the boundary controversy.

In November 2009, Slovenia signed an agreement with Russia to allow the construction of a gas pipeline into Western Europe, known as the South Stream pipeline. The agreement was the culmination of several years of negotiations and resulted in concessions for Slovenia, including a 50 percent stake in the construction of the pipeline.

By 2009, Slovenia had become the largest foreign investor in Kosovo. In February Slovenia extended its participation in the NATO-led peacekeeping mission in Kosovo for an additional year, and in July Slovenia announced the donation of $794,000 to Kosovo for infrastructure programs as part of an ongoing aid initiative. In April, the Pahor government approved the continuation of the nation's participation in the NATO mission in Afghanistan. In October 2010, the government announced that it would expand the mission to include civilian instructors as part of an effort to train Afghan security forces. Also in October Iran opened its first embassy in Slovenia. Also in October two Islamic extremists, wanted in Germany, were arrested in northwestern Slovenia and extradited.

In March 2010, Pahor accepted an opposition plan to hold a referendum on the country's agreement to allow the EU to arbitrate Slovenia's border dispute with Croatia. In voting on June 6, the accord was approved by 52 percent of voters. Negotiations on Croatia's EU bid were subsequently restarted.

On February 24, 2011, the legislature enacted measures to allow the United States to send prisoners from Guantanamo Bay to Slovenia. In March, Russian President Vladimir Putin travelled to Slovenia to finalize agreement on Slovenia's participation in the South Stream pipeline. An additional 31 economic cooperation agreements were signed between Russia and Slovenia. The following month Pahor met with the leaders of Croatia and Serbia and pledged Slovenian support for EU membership for both countries. In July Slovenia recognized South Sudan as an independent nation. In December, the EU parliament was increased in size from 736 to 752 members. Slovenia's delegation would rise from seven to eight in the 2014 elections.

Slovenia was nominated for a rotating seat on the UN Security Council in October 2011; however, it withdrew its candidacy after 16 rounds of voting failed to produce the two-thirds majority needed to secure the seat (Azerbaijan eventually won).

Slovenia closed its embassies in Iran, Ireland, Finland, Portugal, and Sweden, as well as its consulate in New York City, in 2012–2013, as part of the government austerity program.

Current issues. In July 2010, Matej LAHOVNIK, one of the founders of *Zares* and the economy minister, resigned following a dispute with his party leader, Gregor GOLOBIČ (see Political Parties, below). Lahovnik alleged corruption on the part of the *Zares* leader in a public dispute that undermined confidence in the government. In local elections in October, the SDS defeated the SD, gaining more seats and securing 18.9 percent of the total vote to 12 percent for the SD.

On April 18, 2011, the minister without portfolio, in charge of local government and regional development, Dusa Trobec BUSAN of DeSUS, resigned, citing increasing tensions within the coalition government over economic policy. On May 9 the remaining DeSUS ministers also resigned, and the party withdrew from the government. On June 5 a three-part, government-sponsored referendum was defeated. Voters rejected a pension reform measure to raise the retirement age to 65 years by a vote of 72.1 against to 27.9 percent in favor. Separate initiatives to increase penalties for unregistered or informal work and to restrict access to communist era archives were rejected by similar margins. *Zares* withdrew from the coalition government following the rejection of the measures. Pahor remained in office at the head of a minority government. President Türk and opposition parties called for early elections. On August 11 Katarina KRESAL, the minister of the interior and leader of the LDS, resigned in the wake of allegations of corruption involving a conflict of interest over the lease of a building to Slovenian law enforcement.

In early elections on December 4, 2011, the newly formed **Positive Slovenia** (*Pozitivna Slovenija*—PS), led by Zoran JANKOVIĆ, the popular mayor of Ljubljana, secured the most votes. When coalition talks between Janković, Pahor, and other parties failed, the president nominated Janša to form a government, despite his ongoing trial for corruption. The former prime minister crafted a coalition government that took power in February 2012. That month, international credit agencies downgraded Slovenia's debt in light of rising debt.

Janša faced mounting economic crises in 2012, while his corruption trial proceeded in the background. He introduced an austerity package that included a 7.5 percent pay cut for civil servants and raised the retirement age to 65.

The government was forced to bail out Nova Ljubljanska Banka, the country's largest bank, for €380 million in July. Slovenia's state-owned banks were saddled with bad debt incurred when the bankers lent money to a small circle of friends who wanted to buy the state-owned companies they had managed. The buyers were offered cut-rate prices to keep the businesses in Slovene hands, and they used the firms as collateral. When the businesses collapsed in the global slump of 2008, their loss wiped out the equity of many banks. In total, Slovenia's banks held some €6.8 billion in bad debt, an amount equal to one-fifth of the national economy.

Popular protests against governing elites and high-level corruption began in Maribor in November 2012 and soon moved to Ljubljana. Participants stressed they were not complaining about the economy, but rather that the composition of the social elites had changed little since 1945. A protest in Ljubljana on January 11, 2013, brought out 10,000 protestors—0.5 percent of the country's entire population.

Presidential elections on November 11, 2012, were expected to give President Türk a second term, but he unexpectedly placed second, with 36 percent of the vote, behind former prime minister Borut Pahor (SD), with 40 percent. Pahor soundly defeated Türk 67.4 percent to 32.6 percent in the December 2 runoff, results widely interpreted as criticism of Janša's austerity program. Also in December, the National Assembly adopted the budget for 2013, which aimed to reduce the budget deficit from 4.2 percent of GDP in 2012, to 2.8 percent in 2013 and 2.5 percent in 2014.

On January 8, the Corruption Prevention Commission ruled that Prime Minister Janša had "systematically and repeatedly violated the law" by failing to report more than €200,000 in assets of "unknown origin." The charges enraged public sector workers whose wages had been slashed 5 percent for 2013 while Janša's income mysteriously grew. Teachers, doctors, and other civil servants staged a one-day strike on January 23. The commission also suggested that PS leader and Ljubljana mayor Zoran JANKOVIĆ had benefitted from lucrative contracts given to firms owned by his sons. Janković resigned from PS and was replaced by Alenka BRATUŠEK, a PS legislator and former state budget director.

On January 24, the DL pulled out of the government coalition when Janša refused to resign over the corruption charges, leaving the government 42 out of 90 seats. The ministers of justice and finance, both from DL, also submitted their resignations. The SLS and DeSUS also called for Janša's exit, but remained in the now-minority government.

The National Assembly passed a vote of no confidence in Janša on February 27 and selected Alenka Bratušek (Positive Slovenia) as interim prime minister. Bratušek formed a government comprised of the PS, DeSUS, DL, and SD on March 14, becoming Slovenia's first female prime minister. Departing from Janša's austerity program, Bratušek pledged to promote growth and fiscal stability and repeatedly insisted that Slovenia would not need an EU or IMF bailout. She authorized the creation of a "bad bank" for unrecoverable loans that would stabilize the banking system.

Croatia and Slovenia reached a deal on March 20 that resolved the last obstacle to Croatia's July 1 accession to the EU. The two countries agreed to have the Bank for International Settlements resolve Croatia's demand for €270 million paid to 430,000 Croats whose Nova Ljubljanska Banka accounts were frozen when Yugoslavia began to collapse in 1990.

The government successfully raised $1.3 billion in a bond sale in April and another $15 billion in May, even though Moody's had downgraded it to junk status. Bratušek announced on May 9 plans to raise the value-added tax from 20 percent to 22 percent and to sell 15 state-owned companies, including Telekom Slovenje, Adria Airways, and Nova Kreditna Banka Maribor.

In May the EU granted Slovenia an additional two years to reach the 3 percent deficit ceiling. Bratušek responded with a supplemental budget bill in July that set a 4.4 percent deficit, using the additional funds for pensions, public sector wages, bank recapitalization, and other growth measures. Two constitutional amendments took effect in May, one requiring a balanced budget as of 2015 and the second amending the referendum law so that referendum requests must come from voters, not legislators.

Janša and two other defendants in the Patria case were sentenced to two years in jail on June 5. Janša denounced his conviction as politically motivated.

POLITICAL PARTIES

For four-and-a-half decades after World War II the only authorized political party in Yugoslavia was the Communist Party, which was redesignated in 1952 as the League of Communists of Yugoslavia (*Savez Komunista Jugoslavija*—SKJ). In 1989 noncommunist groups began to emerge in the republics, and in early 1990 the SKJ approved the introduction of a multiparty system, thereby effectively triggering its own demise. The most important initial outgrowth of liberalization was the creation of the broad electoral alliance the Democratic Opposition of Slovenia (*Demokratične Opozicije Slovenije*—Demos). For more information on political parties and coalitions between 1990 and 2008, see the 2011 *Handbook.*

Government Parties:

Postive Slovenia (*Pozitivna Slovenija*—PS). Originally established as **Zoran Janković's List–Positive Slovenia** (*Lista Zorana Jankovića–Pozitivna Slovenija*—LZJ-PS) by Ljubljana mayor Zoran Janković in October 2011, the PS is a center-left grouping. When the PS placed first in the 2011 assembly elections, with 28 seats, Janković resigned as mayor with plans to become prime minister. When he was unable to form a coalition government, he entered and won the by-election to replace himself as mayor of Ljubljana. In January 2013 the Corruption Prevention Commission ruled that Janković had benefitted from lucrative contracts given to firms owned by his sons. Janković suspended his PS chairmanship. The party replaced him with Alenka Bratušek. When Prime Minister Janša (SDS) lost a vote of confidence in February, Bratušek created a governing coalition consisting of the PS, DeSUS, DL, and SD on March 14, becoming Slovenia's first female prime minister.

Leaders: Alenka BRATUŠEK (Prime Minister and Party President); Zoran JANKOVIĆ (Founder); Maša KOCIPER, Melita ZUPEVIC, Robert GOLOB (Vice Presidents).

Slovenian Democratic Party of Pensioners (*Demokratična Stranka Upokojencev Slovenije*—DeSUS). Also known as the Grey Panthers, the DeSUS was a component of the leftist ZLSD until it opted to contest the November 1996 election in its own right, winning five seats and 4.3 percent of the vote. The party's decision to join the government in February 1997 was crucial in providing the coalition with a slim majority in the assembly. The DeSUS saw its vote share rise to 5.2 percent in 2000, but it won only four seats. It agreed to accept junior status in the subsequent LDS-led government. The DeSUS gained four seats in the 2004 elections. It joined the SDS-led coalition government. The DeSUS split with its government coalition partners and backed Danilo Türk in the 2007 presidential polling. However, the party continued to support the SDS-led coalition government. It secured seven seats in the 2008 assembly balloting and joined the SD-led coalition government. Party leader Karl Erjavec was appointed minister of the environment and physical planning. In 2010, Erjavec was forced to resign by Pahor, but DeSUS agreed to continue to support the government; however, it withdrew in May 2011. Minister of the Environment and Physical Planning Roko ŽARNIĆ resigned from DeSUS at that time and became an independent in order to remain in office. DeSUS secured six seats in the 2011 elections, and the party joined the SDS-led government in 2012. Erjavec was appointed a deputy prime minister and foreign minister.

Leaders: Karl ERJAVEC (Deputy Prime Minister and President of the Party), Franc JURŠA (Parliamentary Leader), Branko SIMONOVIČ (General Secretary).

Civic List (*Državljanska Lista*—DL). Formed by Gregor Virant in October 2011, the centrist DL was intially known as **Gregor Virant's Civic List** (*Državljanska lista Gregorja Viranta*—LGV). It sought to offer an alternative to existing center-right parties. In the 2011 balloting, the then LGV placed fourth with eight seats. It joined the SDS coalition government in 2012. At an April 2012 party congress, the DL adopted its current name. Virant and the DL have pushed for greater transparency in party funding.

Leaders: Gregor VIRANT (President); Aleksandra MARKOVIČ, Alois SELIŠNIK (Vice Presidents).

Social Democrats (*Socialni Demokrati*—SD). The SD was known as the **United List of Social Democrats** (*Združena Lista Socialnih Demokratov*—ZLSD) until 2005. The ZLSD was originally formed prior to the December 1992 election as a United List (ZL) of groups deriving from the Communist era, winning 14 seats and joining a coalition headed by the LDS. The original components were the SDP, the Social Democratic Union (*Socialdemokratska Unija*—SDU), the Workers' Party of Slovenia (*Delavska Stranka Slovenije*—DSS), and the DeSUS. Of these, the SDR declined to join a formal merger creating the ZLSD in 1993, while the DeSUS reverted to independent status after the ZLSD left the government in January 1996. Advocating neutrality as an alternative to NATO membership (but favoring EU accession), the ZLSD won 9 lower house seats on a 9 percent vote share in the November balloting. In the October 2000 election, it won 12 percent of the vote and 11 seats, after which it agreed to join Prime Minister Drnovšek's new government. The ZLSD secured 14.2 percent of the vote and 1 seat in the June 2004 European parliamentary elections. In the October 2004 legislative elections, the ZLSD received 10.2 percent of the vote and 10 seats. Former prime minister Anton Rop and three other LDS members of parliament left the LDS to join the SD in March 2007, making the SD the largest opposition group. Party leader Borut Pahor was expected to be the SD presidential candidate in 2007, but the party instead endorsed the independent candidate Danilo Türk, who eventually won the balloting.

The SD won the legislative balloting in 2008, and party leader Pahor was named prime minister of an SD-led coalition government. Pahor was reelected party leader at a Congress in March 2009. In protest of the party opposition to Croatian entry into the EU, SD member of the EU Parliament Aurelio JURI resigned from the party in June 2009. Following a disappointing showing in local balloting in 2010, Pahor pledged to redouble the government's efforts to revive the economy. Nonetheless, in the local balloting Peter BOSSMAN of the SD, who was born in Ghana, became the first African-born Slovene mayor when he was elected chief executive of Piran. Pahor refused calls to resign after DeSUS and *Zares* withdrew from the governing coalition. The SD secured only 10 seats in the 2011 balloting. At a 2012 party congress, Igor Lukšič was elected president of the SD.

Leaders: Igor LUKŠIČ (President); Tanja FAJON, Mojca KLEVA, Bojan KONTIČ, and Dejan ŽIDAN (Vice Presidents).

Other Parliamentary Parties:

Slovenian Democratic Party (*Slovenska Demokratska Stranka*—SDS). Founded in 1989 as the Social Democratic League of Slovenia (*Socialdemokratska Zevza Slovenije*—SDZS), one of the Demos participants, the SDS has described itself as a "social-democratic party in the traditions of European democracy and the social state." However, the party has adopted center-right policies and aligned itself with Christian Democrat parties and the European People's Party (EPP) in the European Parliament.

Although its presidential candidate in 1992 registered only 0.6 percent of the vote, the party won 3.3 percent and four seats in the legislative election, subsequently participating in the LDS-led coalition government. On the dismissal of party leader Janez Janša as defense minister in March 1994, the SDS joined the parliamentary opposition. In May 1995, it absorbed the National Democrats (*Narodnimi Demokrati*—ND), which had separated from the Slovenian Democratic League (SDZ) in 1991.

As part of the SP in the November 1996 balloting, the party took third place with 16 seats on a 16.1 percent vote share. It remained in opposition until formation of the SLS+SKD-led government of Andrej Bajuk in April 2000. Holding five ministerial portfolios, the SDS remained in the cabinet despite termination of the coalition agreement in July. For the October 2000 election, the party concluded a cooperation pact, Coalition Slovenia (*Koalicija Slovenija*), with the new NSi (below) and went on to win 14 National Assembly seats.

In September 2003, the party changed its name from the Social Democratic Party of Slovenia (*Socialdemokratična Stranka Slovenije*) to the Slovenian Democratic Party (*Slovenska Demokratska Stranka*) but kept the initials SDS. The change was designed to align the party with center-right groups in the European Parliament, including the EPP. In the European parliamentary elections of June 2004, the SDS secured 2 seats. In the October legislative elections, the SDS became the largest parliamentary group after it won the elections with 29 seats. Party leader Janez Janša was subsequently nominated as prime minister and formed a coalition government on December 3. On May 15, 2005, Janša was reelected as party president at the Eighth SDS Congress.

In June 2007, the SDS endorsed Lojze Peterle for the 2007 presidential balloting. Despite bribery allegations (see Current issues, above), Janša continued to enjoy strong backing from the SDS ahead of the 2008 legislative elections. The SDS placed second in the assembly balloting with 28 seats and became the largest opposition party. In 2009, SDS member of parliament Franc PUKŠIČ defected from the party to join the SLS.

The SDS placed second in balloting in the 2011 elections, and Janša became prime minister of a coalition government in February 2012. He lost a parliamentary vote of no confidence in March 2013, and was removed as prime minister, but was confirmed as party president at the May 2013 SDS party congress.

Leaders: Janez JANŠA (Party President), Jože TANKO (Parliamentary Leader), Anja Bah ZIBERT (Secretary General).

Slovenian People's Party (*Slovenska Ljudska Stranka*—SLS). The SLS is the current rubric of the party that had been named the SLS+SKD Slovenian People's Party (SLS+SKD) in April 2000 upon the merger of the longstanding SLS and the Slovenian Christian Democrats (*Slovenski Krščanski Demokrati*—SKD). The 2000 merger had occurred following the decision by nine SLS ministers to leave the government. (For party history prior to 2000, see the 2013 *Handbook.*)

At the congress that formally approved the merger into the SLS+SKD in 2000, Franc ZAGOŽEN, the SLS parliamentary leader, was elected party president; his deputies included Lojze Peterle and Andrej Bajuk. The new party immediately claimed a plurality of 28 seats in the 90-seat National Assembly, and on April 28, it renewed its coalition with its former SP partner, the SDS. That agreement produced assembly approval of Bajuk as prime minister on May 3, although it took until June 7 for the legislature to approve an SLS+SKD-led cabinet. The coalition soon began unraveling, however, over the issue of whether to adopt a majoritarian electoral system. On July 25, most of the SLS—but not Bajuk and Peterle—sided with the LDS and other opposition parties in supporting retention of proportional representation. A day later, the SLS+SKD and SDS announced the end of their coalition agreement, although they agreed to remain in a caretaker government pending legislative elections in October. On August 4, Bajuk and Peterle established the New Slovenia–Christian People's Party (see NSi).

In the October 2000 election, the SLS+SKD won only nine seats, on a 9.5 percent vote share. It subsequently agreed to accept three ministries in a reconstituted LDS-led government. In 2002, the SLS+SKD decided to readopt the SLS rubric. At a party congress in November 2003, Janez PODOBNIK was elected party president. The SLS withdrew from the LDS-led government in April 2004 over the unpopular citizenship law (see Political background, above). In the October 2004 legislative elections, the SLS secured seven seats in the assembly. It subsequently joined the SDS-led coalition government. The party announced in June 2007 that it would support Lojze Peterle in the upcoming presidential election. Bojan ŠROT was elected party president in November 2007. In August 2008, Šrot received the endorsement of the SLS executive committee and party members as president of the party following a challenge by Ales PRIMC, who accused Šrot of corruption. The SLS campaigned in a coalition with the SMS in the 2008 assembly balloting, and the grouping won five seats (all were SLS candidates). Šrot resigned as SLS leader in March. At a May 2009 party congress, Radovan ŽERJAV was elected party president. The SLS placed third in the 2010 local balloting with 9.8 percent of the vote. It also secured 32 mayoral posts, more than any other party in the elections. In the 2011 elections, the SLS gained six seats. It joined the SDS-led governing coalition in 2012, but not the PS-led coalition formed in 2013. Franc Bogovič was unanimously elected party president on March 2, 2013.

Leaders: Franc BOGOVIČ (President); Olga FRANCA, Janez TOMŠIČ, Jasmina OPEC (Vice Presidents); Jakob PRESEČNIK (Parliamentary Leader).

New Slovenia–Christian People's Party (*Nova Slovenija–Krščanska Ljudska Stranka*—NSi). The NSi was established on August 4, 2000, following a split within the SLS+SKD over the issue of adopting a majoritarian electoral system for the National Assembly, as favored by then Prime Minister Bajuk. Like its predecessor, the SKD, the NSi is a conservative, Christian democratic formation supporting deregulation, privatization, a market economy, and membership in both the EU and NATO. For the October 2000 election, it concluded a cooperation agreement with the SDS and won eight seats on an 8.8 percent vote share. The NSi received the highest number of votes in the June 2004 European parliamentary elections, with 23.5 percent and two seats. The NSi won 9.0 percent of the vote and nine seats in the 2004 National Assembly elections. The party subsequently joined the SDS-led coalition government, and Bajuk was appointed finance minister.

Lojze Peterle, a member of the European Parliament from the NSi, was chosen as the party's presidential candidate for the 2007 balloting. He ran as an independent and was subsequently endorsed by all of the members of the governing coalition. Peterle placed second in the presidential polling. A group of conservative members of the party, led by Janez DROBNIC, defected to form the Christian Democratic Party (KDS) in August 2008. The NSi received no seats in the 2008 assembly elections. Following the balloting, Bajuk resigned. Ljudmila Novak became party president. The NSi did gain one seat in the EU parliamentary elections in June 2009. Reports in 2011 indicated that Peterle had revived the defunct **Slovenian Christian Democrats** (*Slovenski Krščanski Demokrati*—SKD). In the 2011 elections, the NSi secured four seats and subsequently became part of the SDS-led governing coalition. New party vice presidents were elected at the December 2012 party congress.

Leaders: Ljudmila NOVAK (President of the Party); Alojz PETERLE (2007 presidential candidate); Aleš HOJS, Iva DIMIC (Vice Presidents).

Other Parties:

Liberal Democracy of Slovenia (*Liberalna Demokracija Slovenije*—LDS). The LDS was formed in March 1994 as a merger of the main government formation, the Liberal Democratic Party (*Liberalna Demokratična Stranka*—LDS), led by Prime Minister Drnovšek, and three small groupings. (For the early history of the LDS, please see the 2013 *Handbook.*)

Prime Minister Janez Drnovšek was narrowly reelected in January 1997 and subsequently established a coalition government with the SLS and the DeSUS. The April 2000 departure of the SLS led to Drnovšek's resignation, although he returned to office following the October 2000 election, the LDS having won a plurality of 34 seats. Drnovšek was elected president of the republic in 2002 and successfully nominated Anton Rop as prime minister.

The LDS participated in the 2004 EU elections in an alliance with the DeSUS, but the alliance performed poorly, securing 2 seats. The LDS subsequently fell to second place in the October legislative elections with 23 seats and then began to fragment.

In January 2007, Drnovšek left the LDS and did not seek reelection as president of the republic. When Rop and a number of other LDS members left in March 2007 to join the ZLSD the party's parliamentary grouping dropped from 23 to 11. Six former ZLSD parliamentary members formed the grouping **For Real** (*Zares*), while others became independents. On June 30, Katerina Kresal was elected as the LDS president, becoming the first woman to lead a Slovenian political party. In the 2007 presidential balloting, the LDS supported Mitja GASPARI, who placed third in the first round of balloting.

The LDS secured five seats in the assembly in 2008 and joined the SD-led coalition government. Kresal was appointed interior minister. The LDS campaigned strongly in support of the June 2010 referendum on the border agreement with Croatia. Following charges of corruption, Kresal resigned her cabinet post on August 10, 2011, and vowed to allow the party to conduct a confidence vote on her leadership. Despite her resignation, the LDS remained part of the SD-led coalition government. The LDS secured no seats in the 2011 parliamentary elections. Iztok PODBREGAR was elected president in March 2012, but resigned three months later, citing personal reasons.

Leaders: Anton ANDERLIĆ (President); Anton PRESKAR, Milan RAZDEVŠEK, Debora BURIĆ, Tadeja DRENOVEC (Vice Presidents).

For Real (*Zares*). *Zares* was formed in 2007 by dissidents from the ZLSD, led by Minister of the Economy Matej Lahovnik. **Active Slovenia** (*Aktivna Slovenia*—AS), led by Franci KEK, which won 3 percent of the vote in the 2004 balloting, merged with *Zares* in 2007. *Zares* supported Danilo Türk in the 2007 presidential balloting. *Zares* placed third in the assembly elections in September 2008 and secured nine seats. It subsequently joined the SD-led coalition government. Party founder Lahovnik resigned from the government and from the party after accusing *Zares* chair Gregor Golobič of corruption. *Zares* withdrew from the governing coalition in June 2011, and party member Pavel Gantar announced he would resign as speaker of the assembly on September 1 as *Zares* had joined the opposition. *Zares* secured no seats in the assembly in the 2011 balloting. Gantar was elected party chair in February 2012.

Leaders: Pavel GANTAR (Chair); Cveta RIBARIČ LASNIK, Vito ROZEJ (Vice Presidents).

Slovenian National Party (*Slovenska Narodna Stranka*—SNS). The SNS is an extreme right-wing grouping that stands for a militarily strong and sovereign Slovenia, the family as the basic unit of society, and preservation and restoration of the country's cultural heritage. It won 9.9 percent of the vote and 12 lower house seats in December 1992 but entered a divisive phase in 1993 after party leader Zmago Jelinčič was named as a federal Yugoslav agent. Also contributing to party disunity were disclosures that prominent members were listed in police files as informers in the communist era. As a result, five of its assembly members formed an Independent SNS Deputy Group, three others launched a breakaway Slovenian National Right (*Slovenska Nacionala Desnica*—SND), and one withdrew to sit as an independent.

In the 1996 election, the SNS won four seats. It again won four seats in October 2000. In the 2004 assembly elections, the SNS increased its representation to six seats. Jelinčič announced his presidential candidacy in May 2007. He placed fourth in the first round of polling. In 2008, SNS Vice President Sašo PEČE led a number of members out of the SNS to form a new party, Lipa (see below). The SNS secured five seats in the 2008 assembly balloting. The SNS led the unsuccessful campaign against ratification of the border agreement with Croatia during the national referendum in June 2010. It also continued to oppose Croatian EU membership after Slovenia officially endorsed the neighboring country's bid in 2011. The SNS failed to secure any seats in the 2011 legislative balloting.

Leader: Zmago JELINČIČ (President).

Youth Party of Slovenia—European Greens (*Stranka Mladih Slovenije—Zeleni Evrope*—SMS—Zeleni). The SMS was organized in July 2000 by former members of youth groups at the universities of Maribor and Ljubljana. Claiming no firm ideology, but emphasizing youth-oriented issues, the party won a surprising four seats in the October 2000 National Assembly election on a vote share of 4.3 percent. It subsequently agreed to support the return of Janez Drnovšek as prime minister. The SMS did not gain any seats in the 2004 legislative election. In April 2007, party leader Darko Krajnc was chosen as the SMS candidate for the upcoming presidential elections. He placed fifth in the first round of balloting with 2.2 percent of the vote and failed to qualify to advance to the second round. The SMS joined the SLS in an electoral coalition in the 2008 balloting, but none of its candidates were elected to office. Krajnc was reelected as party leader in June 2009. Later that year the party adopted its new name, the Youth Party of Slovenia—European Greens. It secured 0.9 percent of the vote in the 2011 assembly and no seats.

Leaders: Darko KRAJNC (President), Uroš BREŽAN (Vice President), Jože VOZELJ (Secretary General).

Other parties that contested the 2011 assembly elections included (the parties received less than 1 percent of the vote): the **Party of the Slovenian Nation** (*Stranka Slovenskega Naroda*—SSN); the **Greens of Slovenia** (*Zeleni Slovenije*—ZS); **Acacias** (*Akacije*); the **Party for Sustainable Development of Slovenia** (*Stranka za Trajnostni Razvoj Slovenije*—TRS); the **Youth Party—European Greens** (*Stranka Mladih-Zeleni Evrope*—SMS-*Zeleni*); the **Democratic Labour Party** (*Demokratična Stranka Dela*—DSD); the **Movement for Slovenia** (*Gibanje za Slovenijo*); the **Slovenian Party of Equal Opportunities** (*Stranka Enakih Možnosti Slovenije*—SEM-Si); **Forward Slovenia** (*Naprej Slovenija*—NPS); the **Party of the Slovenian Nation** (*Stranka Slovenskega Naroda*—SSN); and the **Humana Party** (*Stranka Humana*).

For more information on **Lipa** (Linden Tree), the **List for Justice and Development** (*Lista za Pravičnost in Razvoj*—LPR), **Go, Slovenia!** (*Naprez Slovenija*—NPS), and the **Christian Democratic Party** (*Krščanski Demokrati Stranka*—KDS), please see the 2012 *Handbook.*

LEGISLATURE

Prior to implementation of the 1991 constitution, the Slovene Assembly (*Zbòr*) was a directly elected tricameral body consisting of a Socio-Political Chamber, a Chamber of Associated Labor, and a Chamber of Communes. On December 6, 1992, the first elections were held for a National Assembly and a portion of a National Council.

National Council (*Državni Svet*). The 40 members of the council, who serve five-year terms, are chosen by electoral colleges of local (22 seats) and functional (18 seats) interest groups. The breakdown is as follows: 4 seats for employer groups; 4 for employee groups; 4 for farmers, tradespeople, and professions; 6 for noncommercial activities; and 22 for local interests. The council is able to propose new laws, require the holding of referendums relating to legislation, call for a parliamentary inquiry, request the Constitutional Court to review the constitutionality and legality of legislative acts, and direct the National Assembly to reconsider newly passed legislation. The last election for the National Council was conducted on November 20–21, 2012.

President: Mitja BERVAR.

National Assembly (*Državni Zbor*). The 90 members of the assembly are elected for four-year terms, with 88 of the members elected in eight electoral districts by proportional representation. Lists must receive a minimum of 4 percent of the national vote to achieve representation. The remaining 2 seats are reserved for Hungarian and Italian ethnic minorities, with 1 seat going to each group and with each elected in a special nationwide electoral district. The balloting on December 4, 2011, resulted in the following seat distribution: Positive Slovenia, 28; Slovenian Democratic Party, 26; Social Democrats, 10; Civic List, 8; Slovenian Democratic Party of Pensioners, 6; Slovenian People's Party, 6; New Slovenia, 4; minority representatives, 2.

President: Janko VEBER.

CABINET

[as of August 10, 2013]

Prime Minister	Alenka Bratušek (PS) [f]
Deputy Prime Ministers	Dejan Židan (SD)
	Karl Erjavec (DeSUS)
	Gregor Virant (DL)
Ministers	
Agriculture and Environment	Dejan Židan (SD)
Culture	Uroš Grilc (PS)
Defense	Roman Jakič (PS)
Economic Development and Technology	Stanko Stepišnik (PS)
Education, Science, and Sports	Jernej Pikalo (SD)
Finance	Uroš Čufer (PS)
Foreign Affairs	Karl Erjavec (DeSUS)
Health	Tomaž Gantar (DeSUS)
Infrastructure and Urban Planning	Samo Omerzel (DL)
Interior and Public Administration	Gregor Virant (DL)
Justice	Senko Pličanič (DL)
Labor, Family, and Social Affairs	Anja Kopač Mrak (SD) [f]
Without Portfolio, Responsible for Relations with Slovenes Abroad	Tina Komel (PS) [f]

[f] = female

INTERGOVERNMENTAL REPRESENTATION

Ambassador to the U.S.: Roman KIRN.

U.S. Ambassador to Slovenia: Joseph MUSSOMELI.

Permanent Representative to the UN: Andrej LOGAR.

IGO Memberships (Non-UN): CEUR, EBRD, EIB, EU, IADB, ICC, IOM, NATO, OSCE, WTO.

SOLOMON ISLANDS

Political Status: Former British-administered territory; achieved internal self-government on January 2, 1976, and full independence within the Commonwealth on July 7, 1978.

Area: 10,639 sq. mi. (27,556 sq. km).

Population: 568,501 (2012E—UN); 585,578 (2012E—U.S. Census).

Major Urban Center (2011E): HONIARA (68,000).

Official Language: English (Solomons Pidgin is the effective lingua franca).

Monetary Unit: Solomon Islander Dollar (market rate November 1, 2013: 7.16 dollars = $1US).

Sovereign: Queen ELIZABETH II.

Governor General: Sir Frank Ofagioro KABUI; elected by the National Parliament on June 15, 2009, and sworn in on July 7 for a five-year term, succeeding Sir Nathaniel WAENA.

Prime Minister: Gordon Darcy LILO (National Coalition for Reform and Advancement); elected by the National Parliament on November 16, 2011, succeeding Danny PHILIP (Solomon Islands Reform and Democratic Party).

THE COUNTRY

The Solomons comprise a twin chain of 922 Pacific islands stretching nearly 900 miles in a southeasterly direction from the Papua New Guinean territory of Bougainville to the northern New Hebrides. The 6 largest islands are Guadalcanal (on which the capital, Honiara, is located), Choiseul, Malaita, New Georgia, San Cristobal, and Santa Isabel. Approximately 94 percent of the inhabitants are Melanesian, with smaller groups of Polynesians (3 percent), Micronesians (1.5 percent), Europeans (0.7 percent), and Chinese (0.3 percent). Anglicans are the most numerous among the largely Christian population, followed by Roman Catholics and adherents of a variety of evangelical sects. An estimated 85 percent of the population is rural, with women bearing much of the responsibility for subsistence agriculture. One woman serves in the current legislature; meanwhile, the present government has pledged action to improve their status and a women's party was launched in June 2010 (see Political Parties, below).

More than 90 percent of the land is governed by customary landownership practices, creating, in combination with the strong influence of tribal nationalism, some barriers to recent development efforts. The principal export commodities are copra, gold, timber, fish, and palm oil. Untapped resources include lead, zinc, and bauxite.

The economy has encountered severe difficulty in past years, with timber resources (the second most important source of foreign earnings) rapidly dwindling. Civil unrest in 1999–2000, coupled with major shortfalls in export earnings from copra, palm oil, and fish, brought the economy to the verge of collapse. GDP collapsed in 2000, but recovery thereafter yielded a rise in GDP to an annual average in 2006–2008 of 8.2 percent. Growth plunged to 0.4 percent in 2009 because of the global recession, coupled with declining copra and lumber sales. Conditions improved in 2010, with GDP growth of 6.5 percent for the year and inflation at a low of 1 percent. GDP per capita was $1,261. In October 2010 the World Bank agreed to provide $3 million in aid for rural development. In May 2012, the government signed a $2 million grant agreement with the World Bank to help the Solomons identify areas of growth economic reform and protect it from the effects of climate change, and in December, the International Monetary Fund initiated a three-year extended credit facility arrangement. In 2013, GDP growth was 4 percent, with inflation of 5.4 percent.

GOVERNMENT AND POLITICS

Political background. Originally named on the basis of rumors that the 16th-century Spanish explorer Alvaro de Mendana had discovered the source of the riches of King Solomon, the islands became the object of European labor "blackbirding" in the 1870s. The excesses of the indenture trade prompted Britain to declare a protectorate over the southern islands in 1893, the remaining territory being added between 1898 and 1900. Occupied by the Japanese in 1941, some of the most bitter fighting of the Pacific war occurred near Guadalcanal and in the adjacent Coral Sea during 1942–1943. After the war, a number of changes in British administration were introduced in response to a series of indigenous political and evangelical movements. The territory became internally self-governing in January 1976, and the country was administered by an elected Legislative Council, led by a chief minister who appointed his own cabinet. After lengthy constitutional discussions in London in 1977, full independence was achieved on July 7, 1978. Former chief minister Peter KENILOREA was designated prime minister.

Kenilorea was redesignated following a legislative election on August 6, 1980, but was defeated 20–17 in intraparliamentary balloting on August 31, 1981, and obliged to yield office to Solomon MAMALONI, who had served briefly as chief minister during the transition period immediately preceding independence.

Neither of the leading parties gained an absolute majority in the election of October 24, 1984. Following a 21–17 legislative vote on November 19, Kenilorea formed a coalition government that included members of his United Party and the recently organized *Solomone Agu Sogufenua,* in addition to a number of independents.

Although the opposition charged the ruling coalition with inefficiency and "inexplicable delays" in presenting a national development plan, Kenilorea survived a nonconfidence vote on September 6, 1985. However, he was obliged to resign on November 14, 1986, because of controversy surrounding the allocation of aid in the wake of a severe cyclone. The National Parliament approved Deputy Prime Minister Ezekiel ALEBUA as Kenilorea's successor on December 1.

While the opposition People's Alliance Party (PAP) obtained a plurality of only 11 legislative seats in the election of February 22, 1989, its leader, former prime minister Mamaloni, benefiting from crossover and independent support, was returned to office with 21 of 38 MP votes on March 28. In May the High Court ruled the 1988 appointment of Sir George LEPPING as governor general unconstitutional on the ground that he had not taken a leave of absence from a civil service position.

In a startling move on October 9, 1990, shortly before he was to face a leadership challenge at the ruling party's annual convention, Mamaloni resigned from the PAP to form a government of "national unity" that included a number of theretofore opposition parliamentarians and was designed to be broadly representative of the country's principal islands in terms of both geography and population. The action was later formalized by the launching of a Group for National Unity and Reconciliation (GNUR), which won 21 of 47 parliamentary seats in legislative balloting on May 26, 1993. However, the GNUR was unable to attract sufficient additional support to ensure the incumbent's retention of office on June 18. By a one-vote margin, the National Coalition Partners (NCP), an alliance of six anti-Mamaloni groups, elected Francis Billy HILLY, an independent who had not participated in national politics for eight years, as the new prime minister. Mamaloni immediately charged that Hilly's 24–23 victory did not meet the constitution's definition of an absolute majority as "at least one half of all the members plus one." Eventually both the governor general and the Court of Appeal ruled against the contention, although the issue was rendered moot in November, when three government ministers joined the opposition and one opposition MP joined the government, presumably giving Mamaloni the capacity to defeat Hilly on a 25–22 vote. However, a further shift in the fragile balance yielded approval of the government's budget on a 25–21 vote late in the year.

The defection of two ministers during a legislative adjournment in early October 1994 again reduced the Hilly coalition to a minority, and on October 13, Governor General Moses PITAKAKA dismissed the prime minister. A government crisis ensued, with Hilly refusing to stand down and the Court of Appeal upholding the action of the governor general, who proceeded to swear in Mamaloni on a caretaker basis on October 24. Two days later the judiciary reversed itself by agreeing with Hilly that dismissal required a legislative vote of nonconfidence, but added that the governor general was not obligated to take advice from a minority administration. As a result, Hilly resigned on October 31 and Mamaloni, buttressed by additional NCP defections, was formally confirmed as his successor by a 29–18 vote on November 7.

In the face of a growing financial crisis, Mamaloni called for an election on August 6, 1997. While it appeared after the vote that his National Unity group had won a plurality, Mamaloni was unable to command a legislative majority, and on August 27 Bartholomew ULUFA'ALU of the Solomon Islands Liberal Party (SILP) was elected as his successor.

Soon after assuming office, Ulufa'alu became embroiled in a longstanding ethnic dispute between the indigenous (Isatambu) inhabitants of Guadalcanal and those of the adjacent island of Malaita, many of whom had migrated to Honiara, an urban area that had emerged from the World War II American base at Henderson Field as the nation's capital. In early 1999 leaders of the Guadalcanal Revolutionary Army (GRA) demanded $4 million annual rent for accommodating the capital, eventually accepting $103,000 as a "temporary goodwill gesture." Hostilities continued, however, between the GRA, restyled as the Isatambu Freedom Movement (IFM), and the so-called Malaita Eagles Force (MEF), despite the formal signing of a peace accord on June 28. A second accord was concluded on August 12, while a third, cosigned by Fiji, Papua New Guinea, and Vanuatu on October 23, paved the way for a multinational peace-monitoring group that began arriving two days later.

On April 10, 2000, following a series of riots in Honiara, further peace talks were postponed, and on June 5 the MEF mounted a coup that included the kidnapping of Prime Minister Ulufa'alu, who, although himself a Malaitan, was charged with failure to resolve the conflict. Ulufa'alu was released on June 9 and resigned under pressure four days later, former finance minister Manasseh SOGAVARE succeeded him on June 30.

Another cease-fire agreement between the IFM and MEF was concluded under Australian auspices on August 3, 2000, while additional peace talks were conducted on September 7–13 on a New Zealand frigate before the conclusion on October 15 in Townsville, Queensland, of a peace agreement that included provision for Australia and New Zealand to provide peace monitors. Forces on both sides nevertheless remained reluctant to turn in their weapons, as called for in the Townsville Peace Agreement, and by the initial deadline of December 15 only about half of the anticipated weapons—and virtually none of the more modern ones—had been surrendered. Four days later parliament passed a bill granting amnesty to the militias for crimes committed during the civil uprising. On February 7, 2001, the IFM and another group, the Marau Eagles Force from east Guadalcanal, completed a peace agreement.

In August 2001, parliament was dissolved ahead of the general election. In the balloting of December 5 the PAP captured a plurality of 20 seats, and on December 17 the PAP's Sir Allan KEMAKEZA was named prime minister by the National Parliament.

In May 2005 a new rebel group, the Malaita Separatist Movement (MSM), was reported to have been launched by former members of the MEF to oppose what were perceived as injustices perpetrated by the Kemakeza government and what had become known as the Regional Assistance Mission to the Solomon Islands (RAMSI).

The turmoil intensified after the April 2006 election, with rioting erupting in Honiara upon the appointment as prime minister of Snyder RINI, who was accused of being influenced by local Chinese on behalf of Taiwan, which the Solomon Islands recognized rather than the People's Republic of China (PRC). In the wake of widespread looting of Chinese businesses, Rini resigned and was replaced on May 4 by former prime minister Sogavare. Sogavare was again obliged to step down in the wake of an adverse nonconfidence vote on December 13, 2007, and was succeeded on December 30 by Dr. Derek SIKUA. Sikua was succeeded by Danny PHILIP of the newly formed Solomon Islands Reform and Democratic Party (see Political Parties, below) on August 25, 2010, following parliamentary elections on August 4. Philip appointed a new cabinet on August 28 and conducted a cabinet reshuffle on April 18, 2011. Meanwhile, a number of opposition legislators joined the governing coalition, raising its parliamentary majority to 32.

Gordon Darcy LILO, Philip's finance minister, was elected prime minister on November 17, 2011, after Philip's resignation. The administration several ministerial posts turned over before a no-confidence motion came up for vote in October 2012 (see Current issues, below).

Constitution and government. The independence agreement negotiated in September 1977 provided for a constitutional monarchy with the queen represented by a governor general of local nationality, who is appointed for a five-year term on the advice of parliament. Upon independence, the unicameral Legislative Assembly, which had been increased to 38 members in April 1976, became the National Parliament, with the authority to elect a prime minister from among its membership (subsequently increased to 47 and then to 50 legislators). The cabinet, which is appointed by the governor general on advice of the prime minister, is responsible to the parliament. In addition, the independence agreement called for devolution of authority to local government units, within which the traditional chiefs retain formal status. The most seriously contested issue yielded a provision that nonindigenous Solomon Islanders (mainly Gilbertese, Chinese, and European expatriates) would be granted automatic citizenship upon application within two years of independence. The judicial system includes a Court of Appeal, a High Court, magistrates' courts, and local courts whose jurisdiction encompasses cases dealing with customary land titles. Ultimate appeal, as in certain other nonrepublican Commonwealth nations, is to the Judicial Committee of the Privy Council in London.

For administrative purposes the islands are currently divided into nine provinces, each headed by a premier.

Prime Minister Hilly informed the provincial premiers in mid-1994 that he was committed to a responsible partnership between the national and provincial administrations. By contrast, three provincial premiers threatened secession in mid-1996 after the Mamaloni administration secured legislation transferring powers of the provincial assemblies to 75 local assemblies and councils. In 2001 adoption of a state-based federal system was again being considered.

The first draft of a document detailing a proposed federal system became available in mid-2009, but the review process was placed on hold in January 2010 for lack of funding, with no report of its resumption following the August election. Earlier, parliament rejected a proposal advanced by a 2009 Constituency Boundaries Commission report that 17 new constituencies be created.

The constitutional provision for freedom of expression is generally well respected. However, media outlets are restricted by criminal defamation laws.

Foreign relations. The nation retains close links with Britain, which agreed in 1977 to provide some $43 million in nonrepayable financial assistance during 1978–1982. Additional aid has been obtained from Australia, New Zealand, Japan, and such multilateral sources as the Asian Development Bank. Regionally, Honiara has been a strong supporter of the South Pacific Nuclear Free Zone movement and an opponent of what former prime minister Kenilorea called French "imperialism," although he stopped short of offering material aid to independence activists on New Caledonia. Despite its antinuclear posture, the Solomons was one of the few Pacific island states to express concern about the future of the Australia, New Zealand, United States Security Treaty (ANZUS), given its own lack of defense forces.

Relations between PNG and the Solomon Islands were strained from the mid-1980s over an insurrection in PNG's province of Bougainville. In late 1990, then Foreign Minister Kenilorea flew to Port Moresby to discuss the provision of humanitarian aid for the rebellious province, which is geographically and ethnically closer to the Solomons than to the PNG mainland. In March 1991, the Solomons reiterated that the rebellion was an internal PNG matter—but the Namaliu government charged that the Bougainville rebels were using the Solomons as both a safe haven and a conduit for arms.

The strain between the two Melanesian governments was exacerbated in April 1992, when PNG military units on two occasions crossed into Solomons territory on search-and-destroy missions. A third incursion in mid-September, during which two Solomon Islanders were killed and a third abducted, further strained relations, despite PNG acceptance of full responsibility for what its prime minister termed an "atrocious act." Subsequently, Prime Minister Mamaloni was accused of meddling in PNG internal affairs upon publication of a confidential letter to a Papuan provincial premier that seemed to support secession if PNG Prime Minister Wingti abolished the regional government system. Tension between the two governments eased somewhat, with a series of ministerial-level meetings in early 1993 yielding tentative agreement on rules for "hot pursuit" in border areas affected by the insurrection. Comprehensive border talks in 1996 yielded the Basic Border Agreement, signed in July 1997, which recognized Bougainville as part of PNG, endorsed cooperation in security matters, and acknowledged the rights of indigenous peoples in the border area. (A revised treaty was concluded in July 2009.)

In July 2006, Prime Minister Sogavare announced a one-year extension of the Australian-led RAMSI, which had been augmented to include personnel from 14 countries, indicating that after three years it was still needed to suppress ethnic violence and secure law and order. In mid-September, however, Australia's high commissioner, Patrick Cole, was declared persona non grata in the Solomons, apparently because he had criticized Sogavare's handling of an inquiry into the riots that followed the April election. In late September relations deteriorated further because of Sogavare's refusal to permit the extradition to Australia of his recently appointed attorney general, Julian MOTI, who had been charged with an underage sex offense in Vanuatu. Thereafter, the deportation of an Australian national accused of complicity in a plot to assassinate Sogavare contributed to a thaw, and in March 2007 the prime minister agreed to accept the credentials of a new high commissioner.

On September 5, 2007, Sogavare's police minister reiterated the government's refusal to turn Moti over to Australian authorities. Two weeks later, Sogavare called for a review of RAMSI operations. His successor, Derek Sikua, promised renewed support for RAMSI and on December 27 ordered Moti's deportation. In mid-2010 the Queensland Court of Appeals overruled a stay on charges against the former attorney general, thus clearing the way for his trial.

In September 2011, Australia announced that it would allow guest workers from the Solomon Islands, Nauru, Tuvalu, and Samoa. In order to support greater participation by women in politics, Australia granted the Solomon Islands $1 million in October. Meanwhile total aid from Australia increased to $68 million per year. The Solomons government supports Australia's UN Security Council seat bid, and in July 2012, Australia reaffirmed its commitment to bilateral relations, pledging $239.4 million in development assistance for 2012–2013. New Zealand also signed a Joint Commitment for Development in September 2011.

In April 2012, Australia and the Solomon Islands began preliminary talks on a timetable for withdrawing RAMSI troops. Shortly after the tenth anniversary of the start of the mission, the final rotation of Australian troops withdrew in August 2013.

In January 2013, concerns arose over transborder crime between the Solomon Islands and PNG after there was a raid on a Solomon logging settlement.

Current issues. In October 2010 new prime minister Philip reaffirmed the Solomons' commitment to RAMSI. However, in January 2011 the government accused RAMSI of working with the opposition to undermine Philip's cabinet by bribing members of parliament to switch parties. Australia rejected the accusations. In May 2011, the governor general, Sir Frank Ofagioro KABUI, refused to swear in newly reappointed fisheries minister Jimmy LUSIBAEA, who had been convicted of assault, and following a case brought by the opposition on October 17, 2011, the country's High Court ruled that Lusibaea was officially barred from serving in Parliament. (For more on Lusibaea, see the 2011 *Handbook.*) In a by-election on August 1, 2012, his wife, Vika Lusibaea, became the second woman to be elected to National Parliament.

On November 11, 2011, Prime Minister Danny Philip resigned rather than face a vote of no confidence over allegations regarding the misuse of development aid from Taiwan. His former finance minister, Gordon Darcy Lilo, was elected five days later amid controversy. Opposition leader Derek Sikua filed a motion of no confidence against Lilo's government one a day after his election drew protests in the capital due to his close links with the former government.

In February 2012, Lilo dismissed Foreign Minister Peter SHANEL two days after Shanel announced that the country would establish diplomatic ties with Russia, which Lilo allegedly found to be an overreach of Shanel's mandate. Shanel claimed that his removal had been planned beforehand.

A motion of no confidence filed by Sikua triggered a reshuffle of the cabinet in October 2012 before the parliament vote. Reportedly, nine government legislators were expected to support the motion. However, most opposition members, including Sikua, did not turn up to the scheduled vote on October 26. The motion was opposed by 28 votes, with three abstentions and no supporters.

An underwater earthquake off the Solomon Islands triggered a tsunami on February 6, 2013, killing at least six people and causing significant damage to coastal villages and a provincial capital.

POLITICAL PARTIES

As in neighboring Papua New Guinea, party affiliations tend to be transient and based more on personality than ideology. The People's Alliance Party (PAP) government formed by Prime Minister Mamaloni in 1989 was the first single-party administration since independence; in 1990, by contrast, Mamaloni withdrew from the PAP to form a "national unity" government that included a number of theretofore opposition figures and became the basis of the Group for National Unity and Reconciliation (GNUR). In June 1993 the five anti-Mamaloni parliamentary parties, led by Francis Billy Hilly, joined with Christian Fellowship and independent members to form a government alliance called the National Coalition Partners (NCP), which lost its slim legislative majority and became effectively moribund in October 1994. The GNUR, having regrouped after the 1997 election, had faded from the political scene by the 2001 balloting.

The government grouping during the Sogavare administration was styled the Grand Coalition for Change, while the opposition, in early December 2007, announced formation of a Coalition for National Unity and Rural Advancement (CNURA), led by theretofore independent Derek Sikua, that was victorious in the December 20 balloting.

In 2001, a Solomon Islands Alliance for Change Coalition (SIACC) evolved from the Solomon Islands Alliance for Change (SIAC), which had contested the 1997 election and saw its leader, Bartholomew Ulufa'alu, form a government on August 30. (As a consequence of its origins and name, the group was frequently referenced simply as the SIAC.) Ulufa'alu was forced to resign in June 2000 but a year later filed a constitutional challenge to the action and the election of Prime Minister Sogavare of the People's Progressive Party (PPP). In November 2001 the High Court dismissed Ulufa'alu's case.

An effort by the Sikua administration to require the registration of political parties and control their activity, particularly during election campaigns, was defeated by parliament in April 2010. As a result, numerous new parties were launched prior to the August poll.

Legislative Parties:

Solomon Islands Reform and Democratic Party (SIRDP). Also styled the Solomon Islands Reform Democratic Party, the SIRDP was launched in April 2010 by a group pledged to restructuring the building blocks of Solomons' society. Party founder Danny Philip was elected prime minister in August 2011 but resigned in November.

Leader: Danny PHILIP.

Solomon Islands Democratic Party (SIDP). The SIDP was formed in October 2005 to offer the country an "alternative leadership." It won three legislative seats in April 2006 and 15 in August 2010. Party leader Steve Abana became leader of the parliamentary opposition after the balloting. However, three members of the party, including deputy prime minister Manasseh MAELANGA, joined the government. Reports in 2011 indicated that Abana resigned as opposition leader and agreed to support the Philip government. That year, Alice Pollard assumed party leadership.

Leaders: Alice POLLARD (President), Gabriel SURI (Vice President).

Ownership, Unity, and Responsibility (OUR). OUR was cofounded by former prime minister and Social Credit Party Leader Manasseh Damukana Sogavare and seven other MPs prior to the election of August 2010, at which it won four legislative seats.

Leader: Manasseh SOGAVARE (Former Prime Minister).

Direct Development Party (DDP). The DDP was launched in the lead-up to the 2010 election, at which it won two legislative seats.

Leaders: Dick HA'AMORI, Alfred SASAKO.

People's Alliance Party (PAP). Also called the Solomon Islands People Alliance (SIPA), the PAP was formed in late 1979 by merger of the People's Progressive Party (PPP), led by former chief minister Solomon Mamaloni, and the Rural Alliance Party (RAP), led by David KAUSIMAE. Chosen to succeed Peter Kenilorea as prime minister in August 1981, Mamaloni was forced into opposition after the election of October 1984 but returned to the office on March 28, 1989. He resigned from the PAP in October 1990 to head a coalition administration that included a revived PPP, thus effectively splitting the alliance. In January 1992 PAP leader Kausimae announced the expulsion from the party of ten MPs who were serving in the second Mamaloni government.

Despite participating in the first Sogavare government, the PAP strongly opposed extension of the 1997–2001 legislative term by a year. Party leader Allan Kemakeza served as deputy prime minister under Sogavare until his dismissal in August 2001 for alleged mishandling of compensation funds related to the recent civil disruptions. With the PAP having achieved a plurality of 20 seats in the December parliamentary election, Kemakeza, with independent support, was elected prime minister, continuing in office until after the April 2006 election. The PAP has called for adoption of a federal republic headed by a president.

Leaders: Clement KENGAZA (President), Edward KINGMELE (General Secretary).

Independent Democratic Party (IDP). The IDP was formed after the 2010 election by Snyder Rini, a former prime minister, who previously led the Association of Independent Members of Parliament (AIMP).

The AIMP had not been a party in the strict sense of the word, since it was composed of independents (some of whom were party aligned). The AIMP secured 13 seats in 2001 30 in 2006 and 2 in 2010.

Leader: Snyder RINI (Former Prime Minister).

Solomon Islands Liberal Party (SILP). The SILP was originally founded in 1976 by Bartholomew Ulufa'alu as the National Democratic Party (Nadepa). The only formal party to contest the 1976 election, Nadepa won five legislative seats. Having won four seats in 1989 (three years after redefining itself as the SILP), the party joined a number of smaller groups and independents in a parliamentary formation called the Coalition for National Unity. In the course of the 1990 realignment, Mamaloni persuaded SILP leader Ulufa'alu to resign from parliament and accept appointment as a government consultant.

Joining Ulufa'alu in the formation of the SIACC grouping in 2001 was former prime minister Francis Billy Hilly, Fred FONO, and Patteson Oti. In the December parliamentary election the SILP won 12 seats. Shortly thereafter Ulufa'alu decided to seek the prime ministership despite the party's endorsement of Oti. Oti ultimately finished second to the PAP's Kemakeza, with 13 votes, while Ulufa'alu won only 3. Although a member of the SIACC, Fono served in the Kemakeza cabinet. Ulufa'alu died on May 25, 2007. The SILP won 1 seat in the 2010 balloting. As opposition leader, Derek Sikua initiated two unsuccessful no-confidence motions against the Lilo administration in 2011 and 2012.

Leader: Derek SIKUA (Former Prime Minister).

Solomon Islands National Party (NP). The NP was established in 1997 by former prime minister Francis Billy Hilly. In 2001 the NP joined the Solomon Islands Alliance for Change Coalition (SIACC). Hilly was replaced as party president by Warren Paia in August 2006. Ezekiel Alebu, former prime minister and former head of the Solomon Islands United Party (Siupa), subsequently joined the NP.

Leaders: Warren PAIA (President), Ezekiel ALEBUA (Former Prime Minister).

Solomon Islands Party for Rural Advancement (SIPRA). SIPRA was launched in July 2005 by former prime minister Manasseh Damukana Sogavare. Sogavare had previously headed the now defunct PPP, which had been founded and led, through a number of changes, by former prime minister Mamaloni before his death in January 2000. SIPRA secured one seat in the 2010 legislative balloting.

Leaders: Job Dudley TAUSINGA (Parliamentary Leader), Gordon Darcy LILO (Prime Minister).

Other minor parties that secured one seat in the 2010 balloting include the **Solomon Islands People's Congress Party** (SIPCP), founded in 2010; the **Rural and Urban Political Party** (RUPP), launched prior to the 2010 poll and led by Samuel MANETOALI (President) and Trevor OLAVAE; and the **People's Federation Party** (PFP), founded by Rudolf Henry DORAH and led by Clay Forau SOALAOI.

Other Parties:

Solomon Islands United Democratic Party (SIUDP). The SIUDP adopted its current name before the 2001 election. It traced its origins to the Siupa, an outgrowth of the Civil Servants' Association, Its president, Peter Kenilorea, entered the assembly in 1976 and served as prime minister from independence until supplanted by Solomon Mamaloni in 1981. He returned to office in 1984–1986 and continued thereafter to play a central role in Solomon politics, serving as chair of the Peace Monitoring Council and, after the December 2001 election, as speaker of parliament, a post to which he was reelected in 2006. Prior to the 2010 balloting, Joel Moffat Konofilia was elected president of the party. The SIUDP did not secure any seats in the 2010 balloting.

Leaders: Sir Peter KENILOREA (Former Speaker of Parliament and Former Prime Minister), Joel Moffat KONOFILIA (President).

Solomon Islands New Generation Party. The youth-focused party was founded in February 2012 to represent young people's interests, particularly in the area of education. Party membership is restricted to those between the ages of 18–40.

Leader: Ishmael NORI (President).

Other minor parties include the **Autonomous Solomon Islanders Party** (ASIP), founded in January 2010; the **Direct Development Party**, founded by Dick Ha'amori and Alfred SASAKOAND; the **Twelve Pillars to Peace and Prosperity Party** (TP4), which was launched in June 2010 as the Solomons' first women's party; the **Solomon United Nationalist Party** (SUN), founded in January 2010 and led by Ramon QUITALES; and the **New Nations Solomon Islands Party**, established by Belani TEKULU.

LEGISLATURE

The unicameral **National Parliament** currently consists of 50 members elected for four-year terms. The last legislative election on August 4, 2010, and a by-election on August 1, 2012, gave the Solomon Islands Democratic Party, 14 seats; Ownership, Unity, and Responsibility, 4; the Solomon Islands Party for Rural Advancement, 3; the People's Alliance Party, 2; the Solomon Islands Reform and Democratic Party, 3; the Direct Development Party, 2; the Independent Democratic Party, 2, the People's Federation Party, the Rural and Urban Political Party, the Solomon Islands Liberal Party, and the Solomon Islands National Party, 1 each; independents, 16.

Speaker: Sir Allan KEMAKEZA.

CABINET

[as of October 7, 2013]

Prime Minister	Gordon Darcy Lilo (SIRDP)
Deputy Prime Minister	Manasseh Maelanga (SIDP)
Ministers	
Agriculture and Livestock	David Tome
Aid Coordination and Planning	Connelly Sandakabatu
Aviation and Communication	Walter Folotalu (SIDP)
Commerce, Industry, and Employment	Elijah Dore Muala (NP)
Education and Human Resources	Dickson Ha'amori (SIPRA)
Environment and Conservation	Bradley Tovosia (ind.)
Finance and Development Planning	Rick Houenipwela (SIDP)
Fisheries and Marine Resources	Alfred Ghiro (SIDP)
Foreign Affairs and Trade Relations	Clay Forau Soalaoi (ind.)
Forestry	Dickson Mua (OUR)
Health and Medical Services	Charles Sigoto (SIRDP)
Home Affairs	Manasseh Maelanga (SIDP)
Infrastructure and Development	Seth Gukuna (SIPCP)
Justice and Legal Affairs	Commins Aston Mewa (ind.)
Lands and Housing	Joseph Onika (ind.)
Mines and Energy	Moses Garu (SIDP)
Peace and Reconciliation	Hypolite Taremae (ind.)
Police and National Security	Christopher Laore (ind.)
Provincial Government	Silas Tausinga (SIPRA)

Public Service	Stanley Sofu (SIDP)
Rural Development and Indigenous Affairs	Lionel Alex (Ind.)
Tourism and Culture	Samuel Manetoali (RUPP)
Women, Youth, and Sports	Peter Tom (SIDP)
Attorney General	Billy Titiulu

INTERGOVERNMENTAL REPRESENTATION

Ambassador to the U.S. and Permanent Representative to the UN: Collin David BECK.

U.S. Ambassador to the Solomon Islands: Walter NORTH.

IGO Memberships (Non-UN): ADB, CWTH, PIF, WTO.

SOMALIA

Somali Republic
Jamhuuriyada Soomaaliyeed

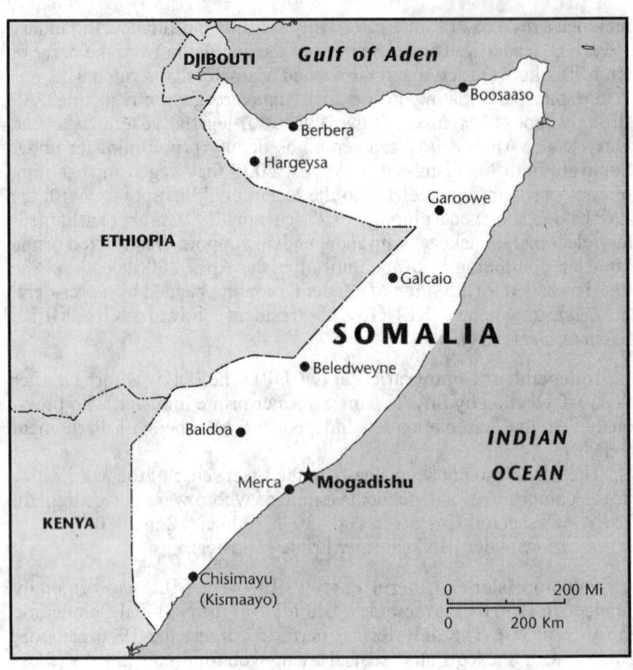

Political Status: Independent republic established July 1, 1960; revolutionary military regime installed October 21, 1969; one-party state proclaimed July 1, 1976; multiparty system authorized on December 25, 1990, but unimplemented prior to the assumption of power by rebel forces on January 27, 1991; national charter providing for three-year transitional national government adopted by Somali National Peace Conference July 16, 2000, in Arta, Djibouti; Transitional Federal Charter approved January 29, 2004, providing for a four-year transitional government; provisional constitution approved on August 1, 2012.

Area: 246,199 sq. mi. (637,657 sq. km), including Somaliland (68,000 sq. mi.; 176,120 sq. km).

Population: 9,826,616 (2012E—UN); 10,251,568 (2013E—U.S. Census).

Major Urban Center (2005E): MOGADISHU (1,257,000, preliminary, including suburbs).

Principal Language: Somali.

Monetary Unit: Somali Shilling. Conditions in Somalia in recent years have rendered attempts to determine a genuine national currency rate essentially futile; approximate market rate in November 2013 was 1,227.97 shillings = $1US.

President: Hassan Sheikh MOHAMUD (Peace and Development Party); elected by the Federal Parliament on September 10, 2012, and inaugurated on September 16 for a four-year term to succeed acting President Mohamed Osman JAWARI (nonparty).

Prime Minister: Abdi Farah SHIRDON (nonparty); appointed prime minister by the president on October 6, 2012, and approved by the parliament on October 17, succeeding Abdiweli Mohamed ALI (nonparty).

THE COUNTRY

The easternmost country in Africa, Somalia (including Somaliland) encompasses a broad band of desert and semidesert territory extending eastward along the Gulf of Aden and continuing southwestward to a point just south of the equator. The Somalis, who constitute 85 percent of the population, are a people of nomadic and pastoral traditions who share a common religion (Islam) and a common language (Somali). However, interclan rivalry has generated numerous economic and political cleavages, particularly between northern and southern groups. Nonindigenous inhabitants include Arabs, Ethiopians, Italians, Indians, and Pakistanis.

The economy is largely undeveloped, and the country remains one of the world's poorest. Agriculture accounts for more than 60 percent of economic activity, although it is compromised by irregular rainfall. The country possesses some mineral deposits that have not been commercially exploited. Although fishing, textile, and food processing industries have been established, much of the country's foreign exchange is derived from livestock and livestock-related products. In addition, Somalia has long been the world's largest producer of myrrh, an incense that is widely used in the Gulf region. Inflation, drought, inefficiency in state enterprises, bureaucratic corruption, and disruptions occasioned by civil war and interclan hostilities contributed to economic stagnation.

As momentum developed toward the resolution of the long-standing hostilities, the World Bank, European Union (EU), and United Nations (UN) relaunched some of its aid programs to Somalia in 2003. However, the resumption of conflict in the spring of 2006 prompted many aid groups to withdraw personnel and suspend assistance (see Current issues, below). GDP grew by an average of 2 percent from 2008 to 2011, partly as the result of ransoms paid by international shippers for hijacked vessels during that period (see Foreign relations, below). Annual GDP per capita in 2013 was approximately $650. That year GDP grew by about 2.4 percent. Most economic activity continued to be in the informal sectors of the economy or based on remittances, estimated to be $1.6 billion in 2013. However counterterrorism laws in the United States led a succession of banks to cease money transfers to Somalia in 2012–2013, severely constraining remittances.

GOVERNMENT AND POLITICS

Political background. Divided into British, French, and Italian sectors at the end of the 19th century, Somalia was partially reunited in 1960 when British Somaliland in the north and the Italian-administered Trust Territory in the south achieved their independence and promptly merged to form the United Republic of Somalia. Large numbers of Somalis remained in Ethiopia, Kenya, and the French Territory of the Afars and the Issas (subsequently Djibouti), and the new Somali regime announced that their inclusion in a "Greater Somalia" was a leading political objective.

The Somali Youth league (SYL) was the country's principal political party at independence and formed the republic's initial governments. During the late 1950s and early 1960s Somalia pursued a strongly irredentist policy toward Ethiopia and Kenya, relying increasingly on aid from the Soviet Union and other communist states. A change of policy occurred in 1967 with the presidential election of Abdirashid Ali SHERMARKE and his appointment of Mohamed Haji Ibrahim EGAL as prime minister.

The Egal regime was ousted by military units under the command of Maj. Gen. Mohamed SIAD BARRE on October 21, 1969, in an action that included the assassination of President Shermarke. Pledging to reduce tribalism and corruption, the new military government launched a restructuring along socialist lines of what was now termed the Somali Democratic Republic. Although briefly interrupted by anti-government plots in 1970 and 1971, the program moved forward at a deliberate pace. In 1970 foreign banks and other foreign-controlled enterprises were nationalized, and in October 1972 local government reorganization was begun. On July 1, 1976, the Supreme Revolutionary Council (SRC) that had been established in the wake of the 1969 coup was abolished, and its powers were transferred to a newly created Somali Revolutionary Socialist Party (SRSP) of which Siad Barre was named secretary general. Civilian government was nominally reinstituted following popular approval of a new constitution on August 25, 1979, the one-party election of a People's Assembly on December 30, and the assembly's election of General Siad Barre as president on January 26, 1980.

A state of emergency was declared on October 21, 1980, following a resurgence of conflict with Ethiopia (for a discussion of earlier hostilities, see Foreign relations, below). Radio Mogadishu announced two days later that the SRC had been reconstituted. The emergency decree was rescinded on March 1, 1982, despite reports of a northern army mutiny in mid-February and sporadic border incidents that persisted thereafter. In the legislative election of December 31, 1984, 99.8 percent of the voters were reported to have cast ballots, with less than 1 percent opposing the SRSP's nominees.

In May 1986, Siad Barre suffered severe injuries in an automobile accident, and First Vice President Lt. Gen. Mohamed Ali SAMATAR served as de facto chief executive for several months. Although Siad Barre recovered sufficiently to be the sole candidate for reelection to a seven-year presidential term on December 23, 1986 (in the country's first direct balloting for the position), his poor health and advanced age generated intense speculation as to a successor. Samatar appeared to be a leading candidate, particularly after being additionally named to the new post of prime minister in January 1987. However, in the wake of a government reshuffle in December, all references to his vice presidential role ceased. Given the constitutional significance of the office in regard to succession, the change was interpreted as reflecting Siad Barre's desire to be succeeded either by a family member or an individual from his Marehan clan, to which Samatar did not belong.

During 1988 the Somali National Movement (SNM), a northwestern rebel group that had joined Ethiopian units in a cross-border assault the year before, mounted a broad offensive that eventually succeeded in driving government forces from most of the region's rural areas by mid-1989. President Siad Barre thereupon announced the appointment of a constitutional review committee charged with laying the groundwork for a multiparty system that would permit the SNM to engage in electoral activity, provided it did "not solely seek to satisfy tribal interests." Meanwhile, other clan-based groups had taken up arms, including the United Somali Congress (USC) in the center and the Somali Patriotic Movement (SPM) in the south.

On September 3, 1990, in the wake of heightened rebel activity, Prime Minister Samatar was dismissed in favor of Mohamed HAWADIE MADAR. On January 20, 1991, as USC forces converged on the capital, Umar ARTEH GHALIB, a former foreign minister who had only recently been released from house arrest, was asked to form an essentially transitional government, and six days later Siad Barre departed for exile in Kenya. (He died in Nigeria on January 2, 1995.) On January 28, one day after assuming control in Mogadishu, the USC appointed its principal financial backer, Ali MAHDI MOHAMED, to the post of interim president. Mahdi, in turn, named Arteh Ghalib to head a reconstituted administration on January 29. However, neither appointment proved acceptable to the SNM, which, after rejecting two invitations to attend "national reconciliation" meetings with its erstwhile allies, announced the secession of the former British Somaliland on May 18 (see entry Somaliland). Subsequently, Gen. Mohamed Farah AIDID was elected USC chair at the party's third congress held July 4–5, provoking a bitter dispute with President Mahdi because the two came from different Hawiye subclans. In early September, at least 300 people were killed in a clash between the two factions in Mogadishu, while more intense fighting, which erupted in mid-November, resulted in the slaughter of at least 4,000 civilians by the end of the year, with some 100,000 having fled the city.

In early February 1992, General Aidid was dismissed as USC chair, formalizing the cleavage between the group's pro- and anti-Mahdi factions. The action came after the announcement by UN Secretary General Boutros Boutros-Ghali of the first of a number of cease-fires, none of which proved effective. On April 24, in response to the team's recommendations, the Security Council authorized the creation of a United Nations Operation in Somalia (UNOSOM). Meanwhile, General Aidid launched a new opposition grouping called the Somali National Alliance (SNA).

On June 6, 1992, representatives of 11 Somali factions, meeting in Bahr Dar in northwest Ethiopia, agreed to support a UN-implemented cease-fire and convene a "comprehensive and joint conference" to "smooth the way" for the establishment of a provisional government in Somalia within three months. However, by late August, with reports that some 2,000 people were perishing daily from starvation, arrangements were made for the deployment of a 500-member UN peacekeeping force to guard relief supplies. In mid-September, responding to heightened evidence of famine, U.S. president George H. W. Bush ordered four warships with 2,400 marines to the Somali coast. On October 1, the UN announced that it was increasing its peacekeeping body to 1,200, despite protests from General Aidid, whose forces claimed control of two-thirds of the capital and most of southern Somalia. On November 27, Washington offered to provide 30,000 troops as part of a UN military intervention effort to thwart the theft of food aid. General Aidid thereupon reversed himself and hailed the U.S. overture as a way to "solve our political, economic, and social problems." On December 4, President Bush ordered the U.S. forces to Somalia as part of a projected multinational United Task Force (UNITAF) of some 35,000 soldiers.

Despite the breakdown of peace talks among 14 warring Somali factions in early January 1993, agreement was subsequently reached on a cease-fire and the appointment of a 7-member committee to lay the groundwork for a national reconciliation conference in mid-March. Meanwhile, the U.S. forces committed to "Operation Restore Hope" commenced a withdrawal, preparatory to handing peacekeeping operations over to a new 28,000-member UN Operation in Somalia (UNOSOM II) in early May.

Intense fighting erupted in the southern port city of Kismayu in mid-March 1993 between forces commanded by Siad Barre's son-in-law, Gen. Mohamed SAID HERSI, and Col. Ahmed UMAR JESS, an ally of General Aidid. However, at the conclusion of the conference in Addis Ababa, Ethiopia, on March 27, 1993, it was announced that agreement had been reached on a Transitional National Council for Somalia, which was given a mandate to lead the country to elections within two years.

On May 4, 1993, the UN formally assumed control of the multinational relief effort led since December by a U.S. commander. Unlike previous peacekeeping missions, however, the UN troops were provided with rules of engagement that permitted them to use offensive force to disarm Somali clans. This mandate was invoked on June 11 in retaliation against General Aidid, whose faction was accused of ambushing and killing 23 Pakistani peacekeepers on June 5. The action, which commenced with an attack by U.S. helicopter gunships on Aidid's Mogadishu compound, concluded on June 17 with a ground assault that failed to curb the general's military capability, Aidid himself evading capture. On November 16, the UN Security Council revoked its warrant for the arrest of Aidid, who nonetheless boycotted a further UN-sponsored peace conference in Addis Ababa in November.

A more positive note was sounded at a January 1994 meeting in Mogadishu of elders of Mahdi's Abgal and Aidid's Habr Gedir subclans. Two months later, the two leaders met for the first time in over a year in Nairobi, and on March 24 they signed a somewhat vaguely worded peace accord that called for the formation of a coalition government during a "national reconciliation" meeting on May 15. However, no action was taken on the date specified, and in late June heavy factional fighting again broke out in Mogadishu.

Frustrated in its efforts to reconcile Somalia's rival factions, the UN Security Council voted on November 4, 1994, to withdraw the UNOSOM II force by March 31, 1995. In fact, the UN completed its withdrawal on March 1. Eleven days later Aidid and Mahdi concluded an agreement for joint control of the port and airport, both of which reopened on March 14. However, by mid-May the agreement appeared to be fading, each side charging the other with violating its terms, and on May 25 Aidid's sector of Mogadishu came under shelling from the north. On June 12, Aidid was formally ousted as SNA leader by a joint SNA-USC conference called by his longtime ally and fellow Habr Gedir subclansman, Osman HASAN ALI ("Osman Ato"), who was named the general's successor. Aidid, who refused to accept the conference action, responded by convening a meeting of representatives from a number of groups of supporters who unanimously elected him Somali "president" for a three-year term. On June 16 Interim President Mahdi joined Osman Ato in condemning Aidid's "self-appointment."

In late August 1995, fighting broke out along a Green Line demarcating sectors of Mogadishu controlled by Aidid and Mahdi. The clash was apparently triggered by Aidid's efforts to confiscate weapons from civilians as part of a "rehabilitation and disarmament" drive, which followed the failure of a "reconciliation" conference launched by Osman Ato in Nairobi with the support of the Organization of the Islamic Conference (OIC). In September Aidid's forces captured the important town of Baidoa, some 90 miles northwest of the capital.

Aidid and his militiamen continued their offensive through early 1996, scoring a number of victories outside of the capital, including the capture of at least two more towns, before being slowed by the Mahdi-allied Rahanweyn Resistance Army (RRA). Subsequently, theretofore low-level hostilities erupted into widespread fighting following the collapse of peace talks in April. Particularly intense clashes were reported in Mogadishu, where, in July, the warring factions were reported to be preparing for an all-out battle for control of the capital. However, on August 1, 1996, General Aidid died from wounds reportedly suffered one week earlier in a battle against Ato's forces in the Medina neighborhood of Mogadishu. Calling Aidid's death an opportunity to launch fresh peace negotiations, Mahdi and Ato immediately announced a cease-fire.

Optimism was quickly dampened, however, by the SNA's election of Aidid's son, Hussein Mohamed Farah AIDID, as "interim president of Somalia." At his "inauguration" on August 4, 1996, Aidid, a U.S.-educated former Marine who had returned to Somalia a year earlier, pledged to gain revenge on his father's killers and renewed fighting was subsequently reported in Mogadishu. Meanwhile, international observers had persuaded Aidid, Mahdi, and Ato to accept the establishment of a commission to prepare for reconciliation negotiations, and in Nairobi on October 15 the three agreed to begin a cease-fire, remove roadblocks between the areas under their control, and facilitate the distribution of humanitarian aid. The cease-fire proved short-lived, however, with fighting beginning anew in late October.

In mid-November 1996 representatives of 26 groups, including nearly all of the major factions (with the notable exception of Aidid's), convened in Sodere, Ethiopia, for peace talks sponsored by the Organization of African Unity (OAU, subsequently the African Union—AU). On January 3, 1997, the participants announced the creation of a 41-member National Salvation Council (NSC) under the leadership of five faction leaders (including Mahdi and Ato), as well as an 11-member National Executive Committee (NEC). The NSC was charged with organizing a national reconciliation conference (then scheduled for June 1997) at which a transitional government would be formed. For his part, Aidid rejected the NSC's entreaties to participate, reasserting that he was already the "legitimate leader of all Somalia."

Aidid actively sought to resuscitate the October 1996 accord, meeting and signing new pacts with Ato and Mahdi in Cairo, Egypt, in early and late May, respectively. In June the NSC rescheduled the proposed reconciliation conference to November; however, in October the conference was postponed indefinitely, ostensibly because of a lack of international funding. On the other hand, Egypt continued its efforts to provide an alternative to the now-stalemated Sodere plan, and in early December Aidid and leaders of other factions signed an accord in Cairo that included provisions for a "government of national union." The NSC ratified the accord in early January 1998 and scheduled a national reconciliation conference for February 15 to select a transitional president, government, and Council of Deputies. However, the conference was postponed, and, despite subsequent efforts to resuscitate the pact, Somalia remained without a national governing authority. (On March 20 Aidid had reportedly renounced his claim to the presidency and, restyling himself "co-president," had pledged to cooperate with nominal president Mahdi.)

On July 23, 1998, a conference of some 300 leaders from the northeast region of Puntland declared the establishment of an autonomous government under the presidency of Col. Abdullahi YUSUF AHMED, a longtime military and political leader (see Somali Salvation Democratic Front under Political Parties and Groups, below). Although the conference also established a 66-member House of Representatives (appointed by local leaders, essentially on a subclan basis), a charter endorsed by the house (as well as an informal council of traditional leaders) in September rejected secession for the region, calling instead for eventual establishment of a federal system in which regional governments would enjoy extensive autonomy. A transitional government of three years' duration was initially envisioned for Puntland.

On May 2, 2000, in Arta, Djibouti, Ismail Omar Guelleh, the new president of Djibouti, convened a Somali National Peace Conference (SNPC) of prominent Somali figures representing a wide range of constituencies, including religious groups, the business community, traditional elders, intellectuals, women's organizations, and clans. (The conference was endorsed by the UN, OAU, and the Inter-Governmental Authority on Development [IGAD].) On July 16 the SNPC approved a national charter providing for a three-year Transitional National Government (TNG) to be led by a Transitional National Assembly (TNA, appointed on a clan basis) and a president (elected by the TNA). The TNA convened for the first time in Arta on August 13, and on August 27 it elected Abdiqassim SALAD HASSAN, a former deputy prime minister and interior minister in the Siad Barre regime, as president. On October 2 Salad Hassan appointed Ali Khalif GALAYDH, a professor and prominent businessman, as prime minister. Galaydh announced his first ministerial appointments, carefully balanced among clans, on October 20. Although the fledgling interim central government subsequently moved to Mogadishu, its potential effectiveness remained in serious question because it had not received the endorsement of Somaliland, the regional administration established in Puntland, or most factional militia leaders. Of the prominent Somali "warlords," only Mahdi had attended the SNPC. He was subsequently appointed to the new assembly and pledged his support to the TNG.

In February 2001, Prime Minister Galaydh announced a cabinet reshuffle, with the pro-Mahdi faction of the USC formally joining the government. However, Galaydh's government, apparently being blamed by the public for the lack of progress in negotiations with the recalcitrant warlords, lost a confidence motion in the assembly by a reported vote of 141–29 on October 28. President Salad Hassan on November 12 named Hasan Abshir FARAH, a former cabinet member, to replace Galaydh. Following the successful negotiation of a power-sharing agreement with several minor warlords in late December, Farah announced a new cabinet on February 16, 2002.

In Puntland, as the conclusion neared of the three-year mandate accorded the transitional government of Yusuf Ahmed in 1998, in late June 2001, the House of Representatives and clan elders extended the government's authority for another three years. However, Puntland Chief Justice Yusuf Haji NUR in early July declared the extension "unconstitutional" and announced he had assumed authority as "acting president" pending new regional elections. Yusuf Ahmed rejected Nur's dictate, and fighting was reported in August between Yusuf Ahmed's forces (reportedly supported by Ethiopia) and those of Nur's (believed to have the support of the TNG and, according to charges from Yusuf Ahmed, the Islamic Union [see Political Parties and Groups, below].) With Yusuf Ahmed now "ruling" from the city of Galkacyo and Nur controlling the regional capital of Garowe, a controversial congress of clan elders opened in Garowe in late August. On November 14 the congress, deemed "illegal and destabilizing" by Yusuf Ahmed, elected Jama Ali JAMA, a former army colonel who had been imprisoned during the Siad Barre regime's tenure, as the new president of Puntland from among 12 candidates. Although Jama was inaugurated on November 19, Yusuf Ahmed's forces by May 2002 had effectively regained control of the region. The TNG subsequently continued to reference Jama as the "legitimate" president, but Yusuf Ahmed was still exercising full authority as the year ended.

On April 1, 2002, the self-described State of Southwestern Somalia, the third such breakaway administration (the others being Somaliland and Puntland) was formed. Although internal dissension was reported on the matter, the new regional government was launched under the umbrella of the Somali Reconciliation and Reconstruction Council (SRRC), a loose coalition of southern factions that had been launched in 2001 in opposition to the TNG (see Somali National Alliance under Political Parties and Groups, below, for additional information on the SRRC). Col. Hassan Mohammed NUR ("Shatigadud") of the RRA was named president of the new administration.

The warring factions resumed negotiations in October 2002 in Kenya, although Somaliland declined to attend. On July 5, 2003, the parties appeared to agree on a transitional peace plan, but Salad Hassan rejected the proposal, claiming that Prime Minister Farah had exceeded his authority by agreeing to allow too much power to remain at the regional level under the tentative agreement. On August 9 Salad Hassan dismissed Farah as prime minister, naming Osman JAMA ALI (former deputy prime minister) to the post. However, Jama Ali resigned on November 28, reportedly due to conflict with the president. He was succeeded on December 8 by Mohamed Abdi YUSUF, the deputy speaker of the TNA, which subsequently endorsed a new 37-member cabinet. Meanwhile, in Puntland, Yusuf Ahmed had initiated peace talks with rival groups in May 2003 that had yielded an agreement under which he was fully recognized as president while former opponents were named to the new Puntland cabinet.

In January 2004, several hitherto reluctant rebel and opposition groups (including the RRA) joined the peace negotiations in Kenya, and on January 29 some 42 factions and warlords signed a potentially historic comprehensive accord based on a Transitional Federal Charter (TFC) that provided for a transitional legislature that would elect a president and confirm a new transitional government. The TNA approved the settlement on February 9, and the new legislature (the Transitional Federal Parliament—TFP) was filled by clan and subclan appointees by early August.

In the third round of balloting for a national president in the TFP on October 10, 2004, Yusuf Ahmed was elected by a vote of 189–79. (Eleven candidates had contended the first round.) On November 3, the new president appointed Ali Mohammed GHEDI as prime minister, but the TFP on December 11 voted down his first proposed cabinet, apparently because a number of clans were not happy with their representation. However, an expanded and revised Transitional Federal Government (TFG) won TFP approval on January 7, 2005, all activity occurring in Kenya due to continued unsettled conditions in Somalia. Somaliland remained divorced from the new institutions, although the breakaway status of the State of Southwestern Somalia appeared resolved by Colonel Shatigadud's inclusion in the new national government.

Tensions over where the government should locate subsequently constrained the TFG's effectiveness, as did reported clan rivalries within the cabinet. Consequently, plans for the demobilization of clan militias in favor of a unified national army failed to produce significant results. Ghedi, the cabinet, and some legislators settled in Jowhar, while other legislators attempted to operate out of Mogadishu. Ghedi survived another assassination attempt during a trip to Mogadishu in November, an event that triggered a new round of fighting in the capital. At the same time it was reported that Islamic fighters were filtering into Mogadishu to support the Islamic Courts Union (ICU). Formed in 2004, the ICU was a fundamentalist movement devoted to the creation of an Islamic state in Somalia governed by sharia (Islamic religious law). Dominated by the Hawiye clan, the ICU created its own militia to protect the courts and help to enforce the courts' decisions (for more on the ICU, see the 2013 *Handbook*). The Ifka Halam court, led by Sheikh Hassan Dahir AWEYS, took control of Mogadishu along with other ICU fighters in June 2006 and held the city until December, when they were ousted by TNG-allied militias with the support of Ethiopian troops.

The TNG faced numerous internal challenges in addition to its struggle with the ICU. While Ghedi retained his post during a reorganization of the cabinet in February 2007, he resigned under intense pressure on October 29, 2007, for his inability to pacify the capital and for his support for Ethiopian troops stationed in Somalia. He was replaced by an interim prime minister, Salim Aliyow IBROW, on October 30. Tensions between Ibrow and the president led Yusuf Ahmed to name a new prime minister, Nur Hassan HUSSEIN ("Nur Adde"), on November 22. Nur Adde was confirmed by the TFP two days later. On December 2 Nur Adde named a new cabinet, but that government was dismissed and a new one formed on January 5, 2008. It was confirmed by the TFP on January 10. On June 9 a peace agreement was signed by the TNG and the main opposition (see Current issues, below). Ten ministers resigned on August 2 in protest over an effort by Nur Adde to dismiss the mayor of Mogadishu, an ally of Yusuf Ahmed. A new, smaller cabinet, with six vacancies, was named on August 3. Tensions between Nur Adde and the president led Yusuf Ahmed to attempt to dismiss the prime minister on December 14. However, the legislature voted to block the president's action, even as Ahmed tried to appoint former minister of internal affairs Mohammed Mahmud GULED as prime minister. Unable to remove Nur Adde, the president resigned on December 29 and was replaced on an interim basis by the speaker of the legislature, Sheikh Adan MADOBE.

On January 8, 2009, Abdirahman Mohamed MOHAMUD ("Farole") was elected president of Puntland. Mohamud campaigned as a reformer and promised to improve security and economic development. Once in office, the new president undertook steps to improve cooperation with other powers to repress pirates in the region. The Puntland parliament ratified a new constitution on June 30 that introduced a multiparty political system.

Meanwhile, on January 30 Sheikh Sharif AHMED of the Islamist group the Alliance for the Liberation and Reconstruction of Somalia (ALRS) was elected president of the Somali TNG by the transitional assembly. During the second round of run-off balloting, Ahmed received 293 votes to 126 for Gen. Maslah Mohammed SIYAD, a son of the former dictator. Ahmed was a leader of the moderate faction of the ALRS (known as the "Djibouti wing"), so members of the TNG and the international community hoped his election would ease the Islamic insurgency in Somalia. The new president appointed as prime minister Omar Abdirashid Ali SHERMARKE, the son of former president Shermarke and a Western-educated diplomat. His appointment was seen as an effort to gain the backing of both the Darod clan and the Somali expatriate community for the new government. Shermanke formed a government of national unity that was approved by the TFP on February 22. The new cabinet initially met in Djibouti, then transitioned to Mogadishu before being forced to withdraw (see Current issues, below).

Following an agreement with the moderate Islamic group *Ahlu Sunnah Wal-Jamaa* (ASWJ) in March 2010, Shermarke carried out a cabinet reshuffle in order to provide the ASWJ with cabinet positions. In addition, Adan Muhammad Nur MADOBE, former speaker of the transitional parliament, was appointed a deputy prime minister, and deputy prime minister Sharif Hassan Sheikh ADEN was elected speaker of the assembly. On September 21 Shermarke resigned as prime minister, and Ahmed named Mohamed Abdullahi MOHAMED to replace him (see Current issues, below). Mohamed named a new cabinet on November 12, including members of the ASWJ.

The UN brokered a new political agreement in the spring of 2011 in which the terms of the president and parliament were extended and a new prime minister appointed (see Current issues, below). Consequently, on June 19, 2011, Mohamed resigned. Abdiweli Mohamed ALI was named prime minister and confirmed on June 23. He named a smaller, inclusive cabinet on July 23.

On March 28, 2012 Ahmed dismissed Deputy Prime Minister and Minister of Agriculture and Livestock, Mohamed Mohamud IBRAHIM, accusing him of corruption. He was replaced by Hussein Sheikh Mohamed HUSSEIN on May 3. With the TNG's mandate set to expire in August, a constituent assembly was created to draft a new constitution. The new basic law was approved on August 1.

A new federal parliament was established on August 20, 2012, under the guidelines of the new constitution. Members of the parliament were chosen by tribal and clan leaders and approved by a federal transition committee (see Legislature, below). Also on August 20, Ahmed left office and was succeeded on an interim basis by the speaker of the parliament, Muse Hassan ABDULLE (nonparty), who served for eight days until another interim president, Mohamed Osman JAWARI (nonparty), took over. Hassan Sheikh MOHAMUD (Peace and Development Party) subsequently won the second round of indirect presidential balloting by the parliament on September 10 (see Current issues). He appointed Abdi Farah SHIRDON (nonparty) prime minister. Shirdon named a new cabinet that was approved by the parliament on November 13. Fowsiyo Yusseuf Haji AADAN was appointed deputy prime minister and foreign minister, the first woman in Somalia to hold these positions.

Constitution and government. For the decade after the October 1969 coup, supreme power was vested in the Central Committee of the SRSP, whose secretary general served as head of state and chief executive. For all practical purposes these arrangements were continued under a constitution approved in 1979, which provided additionally for a People's Assembly of 177 members, 171 of whom were nominated by the party and 6 by the president. The president was popularly elected for a seven-year term after having been nominated by the SRSP as the sole candidate. These and other provisions of the 1979 basic law were effectively suspended with the collapse of the Siad Barre regime in January 1991, following which the independent republic of Somaliland was declared in May in the northwest (see separate entry for details on the administration in Somaliland).

In part with the goal of encouraging eventual participation by the administrations already established in Somaliland and Puntland, the national charter adopted by the SNPC in July 2000 called for a federal system with strong regional governments. Pending formal establishment of such a system under a new constitution, the SNPC authorized a three-year TNG, with legislative responsibility delegated to an appointed House of Representatives. The charter also promised an independent judiciary, protection of the freedom of expression and other human rights, and support for multiparty activity. (For details of transitional institutions established through the Transitional Federal Charter of January 2004, see Political background, above.) In March 2009 the cabinet voted to impose sharia law throughout Somalia.

A constituent assembly approved a new constitution on August 1, 2012. The new basic law created a bicameral legislature with members directly elected for four-year terms. The head of state is the president who is elected by both chambers of the legislature for a four-year term. The president is commander-in-chief of the military. The head of government is a prime minister appointed by the president and confirmed by the parliament. The judiciary consists of national and regional courts, with a constitutional court as the nation's supreme judicial body.

Administratively, the country is divided into 18 regions (including the autonomous areas of Somaliland and Puntland), which are subdivided into 70 districts, plus the city of Mogadishu.

The press is undeveloped. Few people are literate enough to read newspapers or wealthy enough to buy them. Both the ICU and the interim government have reportedly repressed independent media and have harassed and assassinated journalists. In 2011 the government launched a state-run television service, the first since 1991. In 2012 more than 20 journalists or media figures were killed in Somalia. In its 2013 ranking of press freedom, Reporters Without Borders ranked Somalia 175th out of 179 countries.

Foreign relations. Although a member of the United Nations, the AU, and the Arab League, Somalia has been chiefly concerned with the problems of its own immediate area, where seasonal migrations by Somali herdsmen have long strained relations with neighboring states (for information on Somalia's foreign relations prior to 1979, please see the 2012 *Handbook*). Although the 1979 constitution called for "the liberation of Somali territories under colonial occupation"—implicitly referencing Somali-populated areas of Kenya as well as of Ethiopia—the Somalis promised that they would not intervene militarily in support of external dissidents. Tense relations and occasional border hostilities continued, however, with Ethiopia supporting the major Somali opposition groups in guerrilla operations. In January 1986 President Siad Barre and Ethiopian leader Mengistu Haile Mariam established a joint ministerial commission to resolve the Ogaden question, but no results were achieved during the ensuing year, with Somalia condemning Ethiopia for a cross-border attack in February 1987. Following major Ethiopian reverses at the hands of Eritrean secessionists in the north, Siad Barre and Mengistu conferred during a drought conference in Djibouti in March 1988 and agreed to peace talks in Mogadishu in early April. The discussions yielded a communiqué that pledged a military "disengagement and separation," an exchange of prisoners, the reestablishment of diplomatic relations, and the joint cessation of support for opposition groups.

In early August 1996, Ethiopian forces attacked three towns in Somalia's Gedo region in an apparent attempt to squash the activities of the Islamic Union (see Political Parties and Groups, below), which had claimed credit for bombings and assassination attempts in Ethiopia as part of its campaign for the Ogaden region's independence. The offensive continued into 1997, and by early February Ethiopian troops had reportedly overrun the Islamic fighters' last base in the region. Ethiopia's military advances proved costly on the diplomatic front, however, as a number of Somalian faction leaders, most important the SNA's Aidid, condemned the "occupation" and refused to participate in the peace process launched in November 1996 in Sodere, Ethiopia. Thereafter, Aidid's efforts to revive the short-lived Nairobi accord of October 1996 were actively supported by Kenya and Egypt. The latter championed the establishment of a unified and centrally governed Somalia as opposed to an Ethiopian diplomatic advance, which one analyst labeled "divisive." Much of southern Somalia subsequently came under Ethiopian influence as the result of Ethiopian initiatives relating to its war with Eritrea in 1998–2000. The TNG in Somalia subsequently accused Ethiopia of supplying weapons to anti-TNG warlords in Somalia. Meanwhile, the activities of the Islamic Union also attracted the interest of the United States because of the latter's "war on terrorism" following the terrorist attacks in September 2001.

Many African states recognized the TFG established in late 2004 and early 2005 to govern Somalia, and the AU authorized a contingency peacekeeping force for possible deployment in Somalia. Meanwhile, the EU pledged financial and technical aid for the new administration, but the United States had developed only "informal ties" with the TFG as of mid-2005. However, responding to the risk of potential Islamic terrorist activity in the region, the U.S. government has tacitly supported the TFG in its battles against Islamist militias and was directly involved in at least one air-strike against al-Qaida targets near the Somali-Kenyan border in January 2007 (see Current issues, below). Negotiations over the proposed AU peacekeeping force continued through 2006. The UN authorized the deployment of the AU force, the African Union Mission in Somalia (AMISOM), in February 2007. Although AMISOM was designated to have up to 8,000 troops, only 2,600 peacekeepers were dispatched, mainly from Uganda and Burundi. AMISOM was initially deployed only in Mogadishu.

In April 2006, Prime Minister Ghedi gave the United States permission to patrol the waters off the coast of Somalia to suppress piracy. Reports had also previously surfaced that U.S. marines and special forces had undertaken several covert antiterrorist operations in Somalia, prompting minor rioting and protests in some cities. During 2007, the United States launched at least four airstrikes against suspected terrorist targets. More than 40 pirate attacks occurred in Somali waters during 2007 and early 2008, including an attack on a Spanish fishing boat with a crew of 26 that was captured in April 2008 and released only after a ransom of $1.2 million was paid. In response to these attacks, the UN Security Council on June 2 authorized countries that had prior agreements with the TNG to enter Somali waters to interdict or apprehend pirates, based on the existing model between the United States and Somalia. After a Ukrainian vessel carrying 33 tanks en route to Kenya was hijacked in September, Russia deployed naval forces to the region. In April Somali pirates captured a U.S. vessel, the *Maersk Alabama.* U.S. naval forces killed three pirates while rescuing the ship's captain on April 12. Meanwhile, a hostage was killed when French forces recaptured the *Tanit.* In December the EU initiated a joint naval deployment to suppress pirates in Somali waters. The mission was undertaken following a UN Security Council Resolution that granted member states expanded authority to take steps to counter piracy in the region, including pursuing pirates on land.

In November 2008, Ethiopia announced the withdrawal of all its forces from Somalia. The last Ethiopian troops departed in January 2009, but reports in June indicated that Ethiopian forces had again crossed the border. Meanwhile, on January 16 the UN Security Council authorized the deployment of a UN peacekeeping force to replace AMISOM, but no formal steps had been taken to deploy a force by the summer of 2011. By January 2009 pirates had possession of at least 14 vessels captured in Somali waters. In April international donors pledged more than $250 million in economic and security aid for the TNG.

Through 2009, piracy continued in Somali waters despite increased international naval patrols and deaths of pirates in 214 attacks and 47 hijackings. By year's end more than 100 suspected Somali pirates were in custody awaiting trial in various locations outside of Somalia.

Ethiopian forces crossed into Somalia in May 2010, during fighting that left 13 dead and dozens wounded. Reports through the year indicated that Ethiopian incursions into Somalia continued. In July *al-Shabab* terrorists launched a series of bomb attacks in Kampala, Uganda, that killed 76 people. The strikes were reportedly in retaliation for Uganda's participation in AMISOM. Also in July, AU leaders rejected a UN call to expand AMISOM's mandate but pledged to contribute more troops to the peacekeeping mission. AMISOM troops were subsequently increased from 5,000 to 6,300. A covert U.S. military mission on September 14 killed a leading Somali al-Qaida figure, Saleh Ali Saleh NABHAN. In response *al-Shabab* conducted a suicide bombing against the main AMISOM headquarters in Mogadishu.

In January 2011, the International Maritime Bureau reported that 49 ships had been hijacked by Somali pirates in 2010 and more than 1,000 foreign sailors had been taken hostage. By the end of that year, pirates held 31 vessels and more than 700 crewmen hostage.

AMISOM and progovernment forces launched a major campaign against *al-Shabab* in February 2011 in the southern areas of the country. More than 50 coalition troops and more than 100 insurgents were killed. In order to bolster AMISOM, Uganda deployed an additional 750 troops in 2011, and the EU provided a further €47 million to support the mission. Increased antipiracy patrols led to a series of setbacks for would-be pirates. For instance, on March 13 two Indian naval vessels captured 61 pirates from a mother ship that was used to launch raids against commercial vessels. On June 23 a U.S. pilotless drone attack killed two *al-Shabab* leaders in the first such strike in Somalia. Two days later, the United States pledged $45 million to Burundi and Uganda to fight *al-Shabab*.

On October 16, 2011, 1,600 Kenyan troops invaded Somalia as part of a coordinated effort, with Ethiopia, to suppress *al-Shabab* (see entry on Kenya). Also in October, African Union Mission in Somalia

(ANISOM) troops recaptured the last areas of Mogadishu held by *al-Shabab*. Twelve ANISOM troops were killed in the fighting. ANISOM subsequently expanded its operations into other regions of Somalia. On October 24, the UN Security Council adopted a resolution that called for member states to cooperate in efforts to suppress piracy and hostage taking in the region. Meanwhile, U.S., British, and Kenyan naval and security forces conducted a series of operations and rescue missions to free hijacked vessels off of Somalia.

On February 23, 2012, the London Summit brought together representatives from 55 countries and international groups for talks on Somalia. Participants called for greater international cooperation to suppress piracy and terrorism and for the creation of a permanent government to replace the TFG. On February 25, the UN Security Council approved the expansion of ANISOM to 17,700 troops and the integration of Kenyan forces in Somalia as part of the mission. In March, South Africa established diplomatic relations with Somalia.

Kenyan and progovernment forces conducted an amphibious landing on Kismaayo on September 28, 2012. The city was the last major stronghold of *al-Shabab*. Allied forces quickly captured the town. In October, security officials in Puntland captured a Yemeni vessel loaded with weapons for *al-Shabab*. The incident led international security officials to express concerns over expanding cooperation between *al-Shabab* and al-Qaida in the Arabian Peninsula (AQAP). Puntland forces also freed the crew of a Panamanian vessel on December 23. The hostages had been held since 2010, the longest of any hijacked crew. Meanwhile, by the end of 2012, pirate attacks in Somali waters had fallen to a three-year low.

A failed attempt by French security forces to rescue French intelligence agent Denis ALLEX on January 11, 2013, left the hostage, two soldiers, and 17 *al-Shabab* fighters dead. Allex had been captured by *al-Shabab* in July 2009.

On January 17, 2013, the United States recognized the government of Somalia for the first time since 1991 as part of a broader international effort to bolster the legitimacy of the new government. International donors, including the United States, the UK, China, and the World Bank, pledged more than $300 million in aid for Somalia at a conference in London that ended on May 7.

In March 2013, the UN Security Council curtailed its arms embargo on Somalia, in place since 1992, to allow the government to purchase weapons and munitions. In May the UN Security Council voted to end the world body's existing political mission in Somalia, the UN Political Office for Somalia (UNPOS), and replace it with the UN Assistance Mission in Somalia (UNSOM). Whereas UNPOS focused on political reconciliation, UNSOM was tasked to aid in reconstruction. UNSOM began operations in June.

Current issues. The full TNA met for the first time in Baidoa in February 2006. However, it remained clear that the TFG lacked the military means to confront the warlords who had controlled Mogadishu. Following severe rioting in February, prompted by the publication of cartoons in Denmark deemed offensive to Muslims, fighting intensified in Mogadishu between the ICU militias and the warlords, who had formed the Alliance for the Restoration of Peace and Counter-Terrorism (ARPCT), supported by the United States. These battles culminated in the Islamists taking control of Mogadishu and surrounding areas in June. The ICU subsequently established a Council of the Islamic Courts to govern the capital.

Much of the population in Mogadishu reportedly welcomed the ICU victory as representing relief from the violence and anarchy that had marked the reign of the warlords. Concern was voiced over the imposition of extreme religious strictures. Meanwhile, hard-liners in the group reportedly called for an Islamic state that would also include parts of Ethiopia, Kenya, and Djibouti. The international community urged negotiations between the TFG (located in Baidoa) and the Islamists toward creation of a government of national unity. However, talks stalled. The ICU was then ousted after an assault on Mogadishu by an interim government militia backed by Ethiopian troops in December 2006 and January 2007, with the interim government subsequently imposing a three-month state of emergency. An AU peacekeeping force started to deploy in March in Baidoa amid signs of a guerilla-style insurgency by Islamists in the capital. Earlier in the year, the AU had promised to send 8,000 troops to replace the Ethiopian contingent and then hand authority over to a UN mission later in 2007. However, the Ethiopian troops remain in the country despite widespread anger at their presence, which fueled additional violence. As a result, the government of Uganda was the only AU country to fulfill its commitment to the mission, sending 1,600 troops that protect installations in Mogadishu. The interim government, as well as Ethiopian and Ugandan troops, continue to be targeted by the ICU insurgency's bomb, grenade, and sniper attacks.

On the heels of the crisis, the cabinet was reconstituted in February 2007 in response TFP dissatisfaction with cabinet members' attendance and work ethic. In September 2007, at a congress of opposition groups in Eritrea, a new coalition, the Alliance for the Liberation and Reconstruction of Somalia (ALRS), alternatively known as the Alliance for the Reliberation of Somalia (ARS), was created. The ALRS hoped to coordinate political and military efforts against the TNG (see Political Parties and Groups, below). Meanwhile, the TFG was hampered by infighting between President Ahmed and Prime Minister Ghedi, who were at odds over the handling of the Islamist insurgency. Ghedi resigned on October 29, 2007, following immense pressure from Ahmed and the transitional parliament. President Ahmed designated Deputy Prime Minister Salim Aliyow Ibrow as interim prime minister on October 30. (The president is required to appoint a permanent replacement within 30 days.) Nur Hassan Hussein ("Nur Adde") was appointed prime minister on November 22. However, conflicts quickly emerged between Yusuf Ahmed and Nur Adde over the insurgency.

Ongoing territorial disagreements between Puntland and neighboring Somaliland continued to complicate relations in the Horn of Africa in 2007. Fighting subsequently broke out between the neighbors in early October 2007 in one of the contested cities, Sool, which itself is split between sub-clans calling for Sool's independence, or backing either Somaliland or Puntland in the dispute (see Somaliland entry).

In March 2008, renewed violence in the capital killed scores of people and prompted an estimated 20,000 to flee Mogadishu. Then in May massive food riots in Mogadishu over rising prices led to a new wave of refugees. On June 9 an 11-point peace agreement was signed between the TNG and the ALRS following negotiations sponsored by the UN. However, hard-line factions within the ALRS rejected the agreement and vowed to continue fighting until Ethiopian troops were withdrawn. The factions rejected a new round of negotiations between the TNG and the ALRS in August in Djibouti. Osman Ali Ahmed, the head of the UN's development program in Somalia, was killed by gunmen on July 6. Renewed fighting in Mogadishu in September left at least 100 dead and prompted a new wave of refugees. In addition, 30 trucks of the World Food Program were looted by hungry crowds on September 25.

Islamic fighters formed a new group, *al-Shabab*, in late 2008. *Al-Shabab* opposed both the TNG and the ICU and as Ethiopian troops withdrew in 2009 was able to capture large areas of Somalia, including Baidoa, the interim site of the nominal government. In February 2009 *al-Shabab* forces killed 11 AMISOM troops in a battle in Mogadishu and subsequently launched a series of targeted assassinations and suicide bombings. The group claimed responsibility for a suicide bombing that killed Security Minister Omar HASHI on June 18 and a subsequent failed assassination attempt on the interior minister. Fighting forced the TNG to again withdraw from Mogadishu. By the end of July renewed fighting in and around Mogadishu was estimated to have killed 200 civilians and displaced more than 100,000. In October fighting broke out between *al-Shabab* and the **Party of Islam** (*Hizb al-Islam*). An *al-Shabab* suicide attack on December 3 killed 22, including 3 government ministers, at a university graduation ceremony in Mogadishu.

On January 5, 2010, the World Food Program suspended operations in southern Somalia due to violence and demands from *al-Shabab* that the program pay the Islamic group for security and dismiss its female staff members. From March through June, heavy fighting in Mogadishu between *al-Shabab* and government forces, supported by AMISOM and ASWJ fighters, left more than 100 dead and at least 1,000 wounded. Meanwhile, in combat in Kismaayo between Islamic militants and AMISOM, Sheikh Daud Ali HASAN, an *al-Shabab* leader, was killed. An *al-Shabab* attack on a hotel in Mogadishu killed 33, including 6 members of the interim assembly on August 24. Also in August Mohamed Abdi GAG declared a new autonomous republic in Hiiraan region of central Somalia.

In May 2010, President Ahmed attempted unsuccessfully to dismiss Prime Minister Shermarke. Shermarke subsequently resigned on September 21, citing disputes with Ahmed over a new draft constitution. Deputy Prime Minister Abdiwahid Ilmi GONJEH was appointed interim prime minister. The president appointed Mohamed Abdullahi MOHAMED on October 14, but his confirmation was stalled in the legislature due to a dispute over the manner in which his confirmation vote would be held. Mohamed was sworn in on November 1 and appointed a new cabinet the following day. Meanwhile, government troops and allied militia forces were able to recapture large portions of Mogadishu and areas near the Kenyan border in an offensive in October. The fighting created more than 60,000 new refugees.

International efforts to resolve tensions between President Ahmed and the powerful speaker of the legislature, Sharif Hassan Sheikh Aden, led to the June 9, 2011, Kampala accord. Brokered by the UN and Uganda, the deal allowed Ahmed and TFP to remain in office for an additional year in exchange for a pledge to conduct elections before August 2012. Mohamed was forced to resign, and Abdiweli Mohamed Ali was appointed prime minister on June 23. Reports indicated that Mohamed's resignation was a precondition for Aden's acceptance of the accord. Mohamed was widely perceived as the most proficient prime minister in recent history, and news of his resignation prompted demonstrations and riots in Mogadishu. Meanwhile, on June 10 the Interior and National Security Minister, Abdishakur Sheikh Hasan Farah, was assassinated by a suicide bomber.

Throughout the summer of 2011, a severe drought put an estimated 2 million people at risk of starvation. The famine was exacerbated by continued fighting, which prevented international aid groups from conducting humanitarian operations. On October 4, an *al-Shabab* suicide bomber killed more than 100 in Mogadishu.

By February 2012, the famine and drought had ended as the country experienced a record harvest. Following the adoption of a new constitution on August 1 and the inauguration of the new lower chamber of parliament on August 20, 22 candidates contested the indirect balloting for president. Former president Ahmed received a plurality in the first round, prompting a run-off election. He was defeated in the second round on September 10 by Hassan Sheikh Mohamud who was sworn in six days later. Meanwhile, Mohamud survived an assassination attempt on September 12.

On March 18, 2013, ten people were killed and dozens injured in a car bomb attack in Mogadishu that was described as the worst terrorist attack in the capital in more than a year. In response, General Ahmed Moallim FIQI, the director of Somalia's intelligence and security agency, resigned. In April Puntland postponed local elections scheduled for May 15. Reports indicated that presidential balloting scheduled for January 2014 would also likely be delayed in an apparent effort to extend the term of President Farole.

Ahmed Mohamed ISLAAN ("Madobe"), the leader of the pro-Kenyan Oagden Ras Kambori Brigade, was declared president of Jubaland in May 2013, following a conference of tribal elders. The Mohamud government refused to recognize Madobe. Meanwhile, rival claimants launched a series of attacks on the areas under control of Madobe's militia.

POLITICAL PARTIES AND GROUPS

From the time of its inaugural congress in June 1976 to the nominal authorization of a multiparty system in December 1990, the Somali Revolutionary Socialist Party (SRSP) was the country's only authorized political formation. The SRSP virtually ceased to exist with the collapse of the Siad Barre regime in January 1991, at which time a large number of additional groups, almost all of them clan-based, emerged from clandestine or insurrectionary activity. The most important of the new formations was the United Somali Congress (USC), organized in January 1989. Subsequently, in November 1993, several components of the USC helped to launch the **Somali Salvation Alliance** (SSA), a loose coalition that also included components of the SDM, SAMO, SPM, SSDF, SNA, and SSNM, as well as the **Somali Democratic Front,** led by Ali MOHAMED HAMED; the **Somali National Democratic Union** (SNDU); and the **Somali National Union** (SNU), led by Mohamed RAJIS MOHAMED. The SSA was supportive of Ali MAHDI MOHAMED (who had become the nominal president of Somalia in 1991 following the ouster of Gen. Siad Barre) in his leadership fight with Gen. Mohamed Farah Aidid and, after 1996, General Aidid's son, Hussein Mohamed Farah Aidid. Both Aidids were supported by the Somali National Alliance (SNA, see below).

Peace and Development Party (*Xisbiga Nabadda Iyo Horumarka*—PDP). The PDP was a social democratic grouping launched in April 2011 at a congress that also elected Hassan Sheikh MOHAMUD as party chairman. The PDP is comprised mainly of members of the New Blood (*Damul Jadiid*) faction of the **Muslim Brotherhood** (*al-Islah*). In September 2012 Mohamud was elected president of Somalia by the country's new parliament.

Leaders: Hassan Sheikh MOHAMUD (President of the Republic and Party Chair). Hamza Abdi AAR (Secretary General).

Alliance for the Liberation and Restoration of Somalia (ALRS). The ALRS was a loose coalition of opposition groups formed following a congress in Asmara, Eritrea, in September 2007. The coalition was an effort by Islamic resistance groups, such as the ICU, to reach out to secular and other opposition parties. Sheikh Sharif Ahmed of the ICU was named chair of the group, while Sheikh Hassan Dahir Aweys of the ICU emerged as the main leader of the ALRS's central committee. By late 2008 the ALRS was divided into two broad camps, the moderate Djibouti faction, which sought reconciliation with the TNG, and the hard-line Asmara wing, led by Aweys, which refused to negotiate with the interim government and eventually formed the **Party of Islam** (*Hizb al-Islam*) and then merged with *al-Shabab* (see below). The ALRS signed a new peace accord with the TNG in October 2008. Although the agreement was rejected by the Asmara faction, the accord paved the way for the expansion of the TFP to include ALRS deputies and the election of Ahmed as the president of the TNG. The new cabinet included a number of ALRS ministers. In July 2010 Mohammad Ahmed TARZAN of the ALRS was appointed mayor of Mogadishu. President Ahmed rejected a UN plan for elections in April 2011 and instead agreed to an extension of his term until August 2012. Ahmed faced criticism within the ALRS for cooperating with Kenya and Ethiopia, two mainly Christian nations, in the campaign against *al-Shabab.* Ahmed was defeated in the second round of indirect balloting for the Somali presidency in September 2012.

Leaders: Sheikh Sharif AHMED (Former President of the Transitional National Government and Leader of the Djibouti Faction), Sheikh Yusuf Mohammad SIYAD ("Indha Adde").

United Somali Congress (USC). Organized in January 1989 by members of the Hawiye clan of central Somalia, the USC was instrumental in the ouster of President Siad Barre in 1991, and the grouping's principal financial backer, Ali Mahdi Mohamed, was shortly thereafter named interim president of the republic. However, at the party's third congress held July 4–5, Gen. Mohamed Farah Aidid was elected USC chair, provoking a bitter dispute with Mahdi and clashes between their respective factions in the autumn that produced widespread death and dislocation in Mogadishu. The USC subsequently remained split between pro-Mahdi and pro-Aidid factions referenced as the USC-SSA and USC-SNA, respectively. Further splintering occurred in June 1995 when Osman Hasan Ali ("Osman Ato"), a longtime ally of Aidid's, turned against the general and was named chair of a dissident USC-SNA. The USC-SNA later became the core of the Somali Reconciliation and Reconstruction Council (SRRC).

In February 2001, Muhammad Qanyarsh AFRAH, a USC leader, was named to the cabinet. However, a major USC-SSA faction, under the leadership of Musa Sudi YALLAHOW (who had challenged Mahdi for the SSA leadership in 1999) and Umar Muhammad MAHMUD ("Umar Finish"), continued to reject participation in the government. Further splintering occurred in December when Umar Finish and his supporters signed the proposed expanded power-sharing agreement, while Yallahow opposed the pact. Fighters loyal to Yallahow engaged TNG troops routinely throughout 2002, and his faction remained an integral part of the SRRC and joined in the launching of the breakaway autonomous administration in the southwest (see Political background, above). Some factions joined in the negotiations, which resulted in the 2004 TFC, and Osman Ato and Yallahow joined the 2004 transitional government. No longer a united front, factions of the party support different warlords, such as Ato and Yallahow, and continue to support the TNG. However, other faction leaders opposed the presidency of Yusuf Ahmed. Most of the former USC factions are united in their opposition to *al-Shabab* and other fundamentalist Islamic groups.

Somali National Alliance (SNA). The SNA was launched by Gen. Mohamed Farah Aidid following the leadership conflict in 1992 in the USC (see above). The SNA claimed the support of some two dozen affiliates, including factions of the USC, SDM, SPM, SSDF, and SSNM.

In October 1994 General Aidid, responding to the announcement by his adversary, Ali Mahdi Mohamed, of a Group of Twelve alliance, announced a G-12 of his own that encompassed Aidid supporters from the previous five formations; a number of SSA dissidents; the **National Democratic Union** (NDU); an SNU faction led by Umar MUNGANI AWEYS; a SAMO faction led by Sheikh JAMA HUSSEIN; a faction of the **Somali National Democratic Union** (SNDU) led by Ali ISMAIL ABDI and Ahmad MAHMUD ATO; and a United Somalia

Party (USP) faction led by Hasan Haji UMAR AMI. The other two places on Aidid's G-12 list were assigned to a northwestern clan grouping, the Somali Democratic Alliance (SDA), and Somaliland's Somali National Movement (SNM), which Abdurahmane Ahmed Ali insisted that he still led (see the Somaliland entry for both groups).

In May 1995, Osman Hasan Ali ("Osman Ato"), a longtime adviser to General Aidid, broke with Aidid and announced he had assumed the leadership of the SNA. Osman Ato and his supporters were subsequently referenced as representing a dissident branch of the USC-SNA.

Several additional groups reportedly supported General Aidid at the time of his presidential self-proclamation in June 1995, including the **Somali Democratic Movement–Original** (SDM–*Asalow*), led by Dr. Yusuf ALI YUSUF, and an SPM faction led by Barreh UGAS GEDI.

Following the death of General Aidid in August 1996, his son, Hussein Mohamed Farah Aidid, an American-educated former U.S. Marine, was elected "president" and SNA leader in a three-day, two-part electoral process that reportedly split the clan along generational lines. Subsequently, although there was widespread speculation that the younger Aidid would only serve as a figurehead for the SNA's militia, he immediately pursued reconciliation pacts with a number of SNA clan leaders whom his father had alienated.

In April 1997, approximately 800 SNA militants broke off from the grouping, accusing the Farah Aidid "government" of corruption and complaining that they had not been given the respect due a national army. SNA militiamen subsequently battled with forces from the RRA (below) for control of Baidoa.

Aidid, whose militia continued to control portions of Mogadishu and surrounding areas, declined to participate in the SNPC, held in Arta, Djibouti, in 2000, and rejected the resultant transitional government. In early 2001 Aidid, still referring to himself as chair of the SNA, was announced as chair of the Somali Reconciliation and Reconstruction Council (SRRC), a new grouping of some 21 southern faction leaders committed to establishing their own interim central government as an alternative to the "Arta" plan.

Other prominent SRRC members included the RRA, SSNM, and a main faction of the SPM. Aidid was elected as the first SRRC chair, while Mawlid MA'ANE MAGMUD was named as the group's general secretary. However, Ma'ane Magmud, described as the leader of the Bantu community in Somalia, broke from the SRRC and endorsed the December 2001 power-sharing agreement between the TNG and several warlords and faction leaders. The SRRC subsequently continued to serve as the primary challenge to the TNG's authority, and in April 2002 it announced the formation of a breakaway state in southern Somalia. Farah Aidid supported the 2004 TFC and was appointed a deputy prime minister and the internal affairs minister in the December transitional government. Aidid's portfolio was then shifted to minister of public works and housing during the cabinet reshuffle of February 2007. In May 2007, PM Ghedi sacked him from the cabinet completely, though he maintained a parliamentary seat in the TFP and was a vocal opponent of the Ethiopian troop presence in the country. Reports in 2008 indicated that Aidid and his followers had joined the ALRS and had established a base of operations in Asmara, Eritrea. In February 2012, Aidid ally Abdi Hasan Awale QEYBDID survived a suicide bombing in Puntland.

Leader: Hussein Mohamed FARAH AIDID (Chair).

Rahanweyn Resistance Army (RRA). Assisted by troops from Ethiopia, the RRA in 1999 seized control of much of south-central Somalia (home to the Digil and Mirifle clans) and expelled Ethiopian rebel groups from the region. The RRA was a core component of the Somali Peace Alliance (SPA), established in August 1999 to promote the "rebuilding" of a central government through the initial establishment of a number of autonomous regional governments. (The SPA was led by Col. Abdullahi Yusuf Ahmed of Puntland and also included the pro-Ethiopian wing of the SNF.) In December 2000, the leader of the RRA, Col. Hassan Mohammed Nur ("Shatigadud"), rejected the authority of the TNG, and the RRA subsequently indicated plans to set up its own regional administration. In January 2001 the SPA appeared to have been superseded by a National Restoration Council (NRC), itself a precursor, in part at least, to the SRRC (see SNA, above). Colonel Shatigadud was elected president of the Southwestern Regional Government announced in April 2002, although some RRA members, led by Muhammad Ibrahim HABSADE and Adan Muhammad Nur MADOBE, opposed that initiative. Fierce fighting was subsequently reported between the two RRA factions. Shatigadud was appointed agriculture minister in December 2004 and changed his portfolio to finance minister in 2005, but resigned from the government in December 2007 after being appointed minister of national security. Madobe was appointed minister of justice in the transitional government and became speaker of parliament in January 2007. He briefly served as interim president of the TNG following the resignation of Ahmed in 2008 and was instrumental in the negotiations that led to the reconciliation between the government and the ALRS in January 2009. He was appointed a deputy prime minister in 2009 but lost his position in a subsequent cabinet reshuffle. The RRA was reported to be in talks with other groups for an alliance ahead of the selection of a new president in August 2012. On April 8, 2013, Shatigadud died of a heart attack.

Leaders: Adan Muhammad Nur MADOBE, Mohamed Ali Adeh QALINLEH.

Southern Somali National Movement (SSNM). A south coastal formation, the SSNM was led by Abdi Warsame ISSAQ, who withdrew from the SNA in August 1993 to enter the pro-Mahdi G-12. In August 1997 one faction of the SSNM rejoined the pro-Aidid wing of the SNA. The SSNM-SNA, now under the leadership of Abdullahi Sheikh ISMAIL, participated in the formation of the SRRC in 2001 and the subsequent negotiations over the TFC. Ismail was appointed foreign minister in the transitional government installed in late 2004. He served as deputy prime minister but left the government in 2007. In 2011, party leader Abdullahi Sheikh ISMAIL was reported to have formed a new grouping, the **Peace Alliance.**

Leader: Abdullahi Sheikh ISMAIL.

Ahl al-Sunnah wal-Jamaa (ASWJ). The ASWJ is a moderate, Sufi Islamic group founded in 1991 in an effort to counter the growing militancy of some sects in Somalia. Over the next decade it slowly increased its authority in Galguduud Province in central Somalia with military and financial support from Ethiopia. In 2009, the ASWJ created a semi-autonomous government for the region. However, in March 2010, the ASWJ agreed to support the TFG and several group leaders were appointed to the government. In September 2010 reports indicated a division within the group, with one faction advocating withdrawal from the TFG and the other pledging to continue to work with the interim government. ASWJ militias were instrumental in the campaign against *al-Shabab* from 2010 through 2012.

Leaders: Sheikh Muhammad Sheikh HASSAN, Sheikh Omar Sheikh Muhammad FARAH.

Mujahideen Youth Movement (*Harakat al-Shabab al-Mujahidin,* or more commonly *"al-Shabab"*). *Al-Shabab* is a fundamentalist Islamic movement led by Sheikh Muktar Abdirahman GODANE, which captured large areas of Somalia in 2009 in an alliance with *Hizb al-Islam.* It also launched an increasing number of terrorist attacks in 2009 and 2010, including suicide bombings. *Al-Shabab* was reported to have received substantial financial and military support from Saudi Arabia and has drawn a significant number of foreign fighters to Somalia. Aden Hashi AYRO, the leader of *al-Shabab* and the head of al-Qaida in Somalia, was killed in U.S. air strikes on May 1, 2008. In 2010, the **Party of Islam** (*Hizb al-Islam*), formed in 2008 as an Islamic party, was absorbed into *al-Shabab* (for more information on *Hizb al-Islam*, please see the 2012 *Handbook*). Former ICU and *Hizb al-Islam* leader Sheikh Hassan Dahir AWEYS became a leader in *al-Shabab* in 2011. Through 2013, the group suffered a number of military defeats by AMISOM and progovernment forces. In 2013, *al-Shabab* was estimated to have approximately 10,000 fighters and allied militiamen.

Leaders: Sheikh Muktar Abdirahman GODANE, Sheikh Hassan Dahir AWEYS.

Horseed. Formed in November 2012 in anticipation of presidential elections in 2014, *Horseed* is a regional grouping in Puntland. *Horseed* is the political base of incumbent Puntland president Abdirahman Mohamed Mohamud ("Farole").

Leaders: Abdirahman Mohamed MOHAMUD ("Farole") (President of Puntland), Abdisamad Ali SHIRE (Vice President of Puntland).

Other groupings include the **United Somali Parliamentarians,** formed in 2007 to support then prime minister Ali Mohammad Ghedi; Islamist **Unity Party** (*Midnimo*), formed in 2012 by Sheikh Umar Dahir Abdurahman MUHAMMAD; **Quality** (*Tayo)*, formed in 2012 by former prime minister Mohamed Abdullahi Mohamed; the **Democratic Party of Somalia,** formed in 2010 and led by Maslah MUHAMMAD, the son of former president Siad Barre; the **Hiil Qaran Party,** founded in 2011 and led by 2012 presidential candidate Ahmad Ismail SAMATAR; and the **Daljir Party,** led by Sheikh Dahir Muhammad GELLE.

For more information on the **Juba Valley Alliance** (JVA), the **Muslim Youth Party,** the **Somali African Muki Organization** (SAMO), the **Somali Islamic Party** (SIP), the **Unity for the Somali Republic Party** (USRP), and the **National Democratic League**, please see the 2012 *Handbook*.

For more information on the **Somali National Front** (SNF), the **Somali Salvation Democratic Front** (SSDF), the **Islamic Union** (*al-Ittihad al-Islami*), the **Somali Democratic Party,** the **Somali Peace Loving Party,** the **Somali Solidarity Party** (SSP), the **Somali Unification Party,** and the **Somali Patriotic Movement** (SPM), see the 2009 *Handbook*.

LEGISLATURE

The former People's Assembly was dissolved after the overthrow of the SRSP government in January 1991. On August 13, 2000, a Transitional National Assembly (TNA) was inaugurated in accordance with the national charter adopted by the Somali National Peace Conference meeting in Arta, Djibouti (for more information on the TNA, see the 2013 *Handbook*).

In January 2004 most of the parties involved in the political and military conflict in Somalia agreed to a comprehensive agreement that included provision for the creation of an appointed Transitional Federal Parliament (TFP) to serve for four years, after which direct elections were to be held for a permanent legislature. The TFP, sworn in on August 29, 2004, comprised 275 deputies; each of the four major clans (Hawiye, Rahanweyn, Dir, and Darod) appointed 61 members, while 31 seats were allocated to smaller clans and subclans. On January 26, 2009, the TFP voted to expand to 550 members, including 200 deputies from the ALRS and an additional 75 members from civil society groups.

Under the terms of the constitution approved in August 2012, a new bicameral legislature, the **Federal Parliament** (*Golaha Shacabka Soomaaliya*) was created. Owing to the difficulty of conducting elections, it was agreed that the initial members of the new parliament would be selected by the clans, using the same formula that was utilized for the TFP in 2004. The constitution mandated that 30 percent of the seats in parliament were reserved for women, but only 38 women were appointed (13.8 percent) during the clan selection process.

Senate. The upper chamber has 54 members, directly elected to represent the 18 regions of the country. Selections for the Upper House were ongoing in 2013.

Speaker: Vacant.

House of the People. The lower house has a maximum of 275 members, directly elected for four-year terms. Initially 215 members were appointed and sworn-in on August 21, 2012, with the remaining members taking office on September 10.

Speaker: Mohamed Osman JAWARI.

CABINET

[as of November 1, 2013]

Prime Minister	Abdi Farah Shirdon
Deputy Prime Minister	Fowsiyo Yusseuf Haji Aadan [f]
Ministers	
Defense	Abdihakim Mohamoud Fiqi
Finance and Treasury	Mohamud Hassan Suleiman
Foreign Affairs and International Cooperation	Fowsiyo Yusseuf Haji Aadan [f]
Information, Communication, and Transport	Abdullahi Alimoge Hirsi
Industry and Trade	Mohamud Ahmed Hassan
Interior and National Security	Abdikarim Hussein Guled
Justice, Religious Affairs, and Endowment	Abdullahi Abyan Nur
Natural Resources	Abdirisak Omar Mohamed
Public Works, Ports, and Water Transportation	Muhayadin Mohamed Kalmoi
Social Development	Maryam Kassim [f]

[f] = female

INTERGOVERNMENTAL REPRESENTATION

Ambassador to the U.S.: (The Washington embassy closed on May 8, 1991).

U.S. Ambassador to Somalia: (Vacant).

Permanent Representative to the UN: Elmi Ahmed DUALE.

IGO Memberships (Non-UN): AfDB, AU, IOM, LAS, NAM, OIC.

SOMALILAND

Republic of Somaliland
Jamhuuriyada Soomaaliland

Political Status: Former British Somaliland Protectorate; joined with (Italian) Trust Territory of Somalia on July 1, 1960, to form Somali Republic; announced secession as independent state on May 18, 1991; constitution endorsing independence and providing for multiparty activity approved by national referendum on May 31, 2001.

Area: 68,000 sq. mi. (176,120 sq. km).

Population: 3,835,694 (2012E).

Major Urban Centers (2004E): HARGEISA (500,000), Berbera (35,000).

Principal Language: Somali.

Monetary Unit: Somaliland shilling, which became Somaliland's sole legal tender on January 31, 1995, with an initial value of 100 Somali shillings = $1US. Due to the lack of international recognition of Somaliland's self-declared independent status, the exchange value of the shilling is not reported in regular currency listings. However, it reportedly has averaged 6,500–7,000 Somaliland shillings = $1US.

President: Ahmed Mohamed MOHAMOUD ("Silanyo") (Solidarity Party); popularly elected on June 26, 2010, and sworn in for a five-year term on July 27 to succeed Dahir Riyale KAHIN (United and Democratic People's Alliance).

Vice President: Abdirahman Abdallahi ISMAIL ("Saylici") (Solidarity Party); popularly elected along with the president on June 26, 2010, and sworn in for a five-term term, concurrent with that of the president, on July 27 to succeed Ahmad Yusuf YASIN (United and Democratic People's Alliance).

THE COUNTRY

The northwest portion of the Somali Republic as constituted in 1960, Somaliland extends some 400 miles eastward from Djibouti along the Gulf of Aden (see map). Most of the terrain is desert or semidesert, and it is estimated that nomadic animal-herders still constitute about one-half of the population. While sharing, as throughout Somalia, a common religion (Islam) and a common language (Somali), the people are divided into numerous clans and subclans, which contributed to the 1991 break with the south as well as subsequent difficulty in forging a wholly unified regime in the north.

Largely stable and peaceful since 1997, Somaliland has nevertheless failed to achieve international recognition for its independence as the result of concern, particularly among African leaders, that the "Balkanization" of Somalia would embolden secessionists throughout the continent. Consequently, international aid has been constrained, and the economy has depended primarily on remittances from workers abroad (an estimated $350 million in 2012). About 60 percent of the population reportedly relies on agriculture, including livestock, for a living, and annual GDP per capita is currently estimated at only $420. To attract the interest of the international private sector, the government

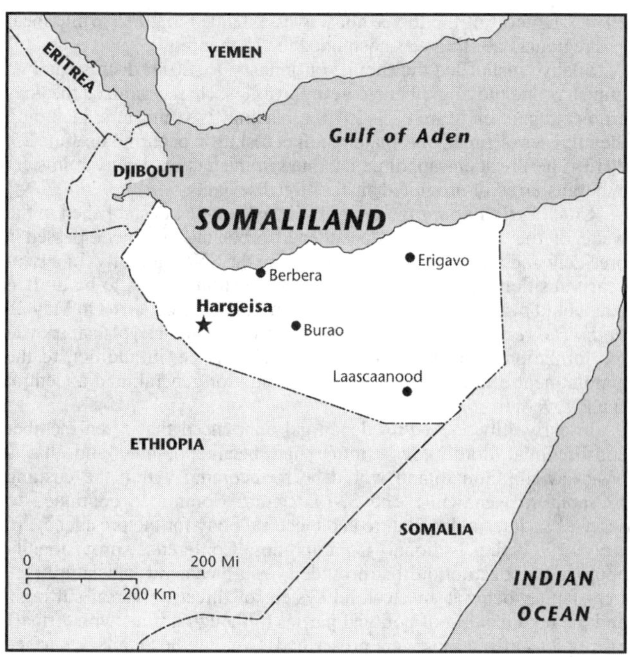

has adopted a free-market orientation, including liberal investment policies. Development plans focus on expanding the production of frankincense and myrrh, exploiting rich coastal fishing grounds, and exploring the potentially lucrative gem sector. A degree of economic progress (particularly around Hargeisa and the port of Berbera) has occurred in recent years, lending support to the contention of the government that Somaliland would best be served by remaining outside the political and economic "maelstrom" of Somalia proper. Oil companies from South Africa, Malaysia, India, and the United Kingdom were authorized by the Somaliland administration to pursue offshore oil exploration. However, the people of Somaliland continue to rely overwhelmingly on livestock and export more than 2 million head of cattle, camels, and goats per year. The United States announced that it would increase its aid to Somaliland from $7 million to $25 million per year in 2010 following successful presidential elections (see Current issues, below). According to the UN, Somaliland received approximately $100 million in international aid and assistance in 2011. Somaliland's GDP was estimated to be approximately $3 billion in 2012, although the majority of economic activity remained in the unregulated informal sector. The Somaliland government budget for 2013 was $185 million.

GOVERNMENT AND POLITICS

Political background. A British protectorate since 1887, Somaliland was overrun by Italian forces at the outbreak of World War II but was recaptured by Britain in 1941. The protectorate was terminated on June 26, 1960, and on July 1 Somaliland joined its theretofore Italian-administered counterpart in the south to form what was styled the United Republic of Somalia, prior to its redesignation as the Somali Democratic Republic in 1969.

In 1988, the Somali National Movement (SNM), a rebel group that had joined with Ethiopian units in a cross-border assault the year before, mounted a broad-gauged offensive that succeeded in driving government forces from most of the northern region's rural areas by mid-1989. However, the government continued its heavy bombing campaign against Hargeisa and other towns, much of the northern population reportedly fleeing to Ethiopia to escape the "genocidal campaign" of the Siad Barre regime. Meanwhile, elsewhere in Somalia, other clan-based groups had taken up arms, most important among them the United Somali Congress (USC) in central regions and the Somali Patriotic Movement (SPM) in the south (see Political Parties and Groups in entry on Somalia for details).

On January 27, 1991, USC forces assumed control in Mogadishu, the Somalia capital, and appointed their principal backer, Ali Mahdi Mohamed, to the post of interim president. Ali Mahdi attempted to convene a "conference of national reconciliation" on February 28 but was rebuked by the SNM for having taken the initiative without prior consultation. A second such effort on March 14 also failed, and on May 18 the north proclaimed its independence as the Republic of Somaliland under the presidency of Abdurahman AHMED ALI ("Taur"). Many refugees subsequently returned to Somaliland from Ethiopia, discovering that the recent fighting, which had reportedly left 40,000 dead, had also devastated the region's infrastructure.

Ahmed Ali's control proved to be somewhat tenuous, and he did not attend a grand *shir* (gathering) of leading tribal, political, and military figures in Somaliland that met for most of February 1993 to discuss clan relations and the formalization of independence. Subsequently, a "parliamentary" meeting of the SNM Central Committee was convened to implement the *shir*'s conclusions. On May 5, the same body named Mohamed Ibrahim EGAL, a former prime minister of Somalia who had been imprisoned by the Siad Barre regime for many years, to succeed Ahmed Ali as president, with Col. Abdurahman ALI, who had been sacked as education minister in February, as vice president.

During a meeting with Gen. Mohamed Farah Aidid of the Somali National Alliance (SNA) in Ethiopia in April 1994, Ahmed Ali unexpectedly called for Somaliland to rejoin Somalia. The appeal was immediately rejected by President Egal, who branded his predecessor as a traitor and termed Somaliland's independence as "irrevocable." Egal reiterated the position in late May by rejecting inclusion in a federal state. On October 15, 1994, fighting erupted in Hargeisa airport between government forces and defecting militiamen of the Issaq subclan of Eidegalla. By late November the rebels appeared to control most of the capital, despite claims by President Egal to the contrary, and by early December about three-quarters of the city's population had reportedly fled.

In January 1995, having embarked on a build-up of arms (reportedly supplied by Albania) and with an army increased to more than 3,000 men, Egal mounted an offensive that succeeded in driving the rebels from Hargeisa. Further clashes occurred in Hargeisa airport in August 1995 and along the frontier with Djibouti three months later. On the latter occasion the government blamed the Djibouti regime for providing support to dissident Issa militiamen belonging to the United Somali Front (see Political Parties and Groups, below).

In May 1995, the SNM Central Committee, acting as an interim parliament, reelected Egal president. In July Egal appointed a ten-member constitutional drafting committee that he charged with writing a new basic charter within 12 months. However, immediately thereafter, the president employed a Sudanese constitutional consultant who, along with the president and a reportedly shrinking circle of presidential advisors, drew up a draft document that included provisions for a U.S.-style presidency. In response to Egal's proposed constitution, the Central Committee, many of whose members were described as "infuriated" by the president's actions, presented a rival draft highlighted by a parliamentary democracy. The constitutional deadlock continued through mid-1996, thus "forcing" Egal to continue governing by decree.

Concurrent with the expiration of its own charter, the advisory Council of Elders in October 1996 convened a 315-member National Communities Conference to which President Egal presented the two draft documents. In early 1997 the conference provisionally approved a new constitution (see Constitution and government, below), and on February 23 the delegates reelected Egal to a five-year term (the incumbent secured 223 votes in what observers described as remarkably "amicable" polling). In May Egal appointed a new government.

In December 1997, President Egal submitted his resignation to the legislature. He complained of a "lack of collaboration" from his government and other senior officials, but the legislators voted overwhelmingly to reject his request. A number of analysts attributed Egal's actions to his desire to fortify his position amid accusations of rampant corruption as well as to underline Somaliland's independence claims at the same time that Somalian faction leaders held unity talks in Cairo, Egypt.

Constitutional amendments were proposed by the government in mid-1999 with the goals of strengthening the role of the president and responding to opposition demands for greater judicial independence. Following a number of further revisions, the new constitution received a reported 97 percent endorsement from those voting in a national referendum on May 31, 2001. Among other things, the new basic law contained an entry affirming Somaliland's status as an independent republic. The first multiparty elections under the new constitution were initially scheduled at the local level for December 2001. However, they were subsequently postponed, and in early 2002 the legislature reportedly extended Egal's term of office (as well as that of Vice President Dahir Riyale KAHIN) until February 2003, although opponents of the administration criticized that decision and demanded that another all-inclusive conference of clan elders be held to determine the presidential status.

President Egal died on May 3, 2002, and he was succeeded on the same day by Kahin. Local elections were conducted in December 2002, with Kahin's United and Democratic People's Alliance (*Ururka Dimuqraadiga Ummadda Bahawday*—UDUB) securing a reported 41 percent of the vote, followed by the Solidarity Party (*Hisbiga Kulmiye*) with 19 percent and the Justice and Welfare Party (*Uruka Caddaalada Iyo Daryeelka*—UCID) with 11.2 percent. Those three parties consequently qualified for legal status under new constitutional provisions (see Political Parties and Groups, below, for details).

In presidential balloting on April 14, 2003, Kahin was reelected by a razor-thin margin (42.08 percent to 42.06 percent or 80 votes out of 490,000 cast) over Ahmed Mohamed MOHAMOUD ("Silanyo") of *Kulmiye.* A new "propresidential" government was announced on July 3. Silanyo initially protested the results, but following a ruling from the Constitutional Court that validated the outcome, he urged his supporters to accept the verdict. In October 2003 the government initiated a series of "antiterrorism" measures following an attack on Westerners, which Kahin blamed on illegal immigrants with connections to militant Islamic organizations. Foreigners without legal permits were expelled from the country.

In Somaliland's first national legislative balloting since its declaration of independence, the UDUB secured a plurality of 33 seats in the elections to the House of Representatives on September 25, 2005. However, following the elections, the UCID and *Kulmiye* announced a cooperation agreement that produced immediate results—the election of a member of the UCID as speaker. In the poll, there was reportedly severe tension over Somaliland's inclusion of the disputed territory of Sool along the border with Puntland. (Fighting broke out in 2004 between forces from Somaliland and Puntland.) However, the balloting was completed in Sool without violence.

Foreign observers described the 2005 elections as generally fair and free, further bolstering Somaliland's argument that it represented an oasis of developing democracy in an otherwise turbulent region and should be rewarded with international recognition. However, conflict over the election of the speaker of the House of Representatives prompted a walkout by UDUB legislators and riots outside the parliament buildings. After securing the speaker's post, the UCID/*Kulmiye* coalition presented a legislative agenda calling for, among other things, sweeping anticorruption measures and a reduction in the president's national security powers. Meanwhile, the government announced that security forces had arrested a group of heavily armed men accused of plotting assassinations and other terrorist acts. The government characterized the detainees as members of al-Qaida who had been trained in Afghanistan.

In May 2006, the House of Elders announced that it had extended its term of office until October 2010 even though elections had been scheduled for October 2006. President Kahin supported the extension, and he and the House of Elders were strongly criticized by UCID and *Kulmiye* leaders for seemingly trying to hold on to a degree of legislative authority through extraconstitutional means. In response to the rise of the Union of Islamic Courts in Somalia, a debate over the role of Islam in Somaliland's public life gained prominence in late 2006, with President Kahin announcing in October that the country would be run by Islamic law (sharia). However, specifics regarding the timing and implementation of sharia remained unknown.

Kahin's term was extended by the House of Elders in 2008 and 2009, a decision that was roundly criticized by the UCID and *Kulmiye.* Meanwhile, presidential balloting was postponed until September 2009 (see Current issues, below). Kahin rejected opposition calls to step down and appoint an interim government until the presidential balloting. In April 2009 the new Somali government (see Somalia entry) initiated negotiations with Somaliland on mutual recognition. In September the House of Elders voted to extend Kahin's term if a date was set for presidential balloting.

After repeated delays, presidential elections were held on June 26, 2010. Silanyo defeated Kahin in the balloting with 49.6 percent of the vote, compared with 33.2 percent for the incumbent. Faisal Farah ALI ("Warabe") of the UCID placed third with 17.2 percent. After his inauguration, Silanyo named a new cabinet on July 28. Silanyo also appointed new governors in seven of the country's provinces. On September 11, elections for the House of Elders were postponed until 2014. The term of the lower house was extended to 2012, while local and regional balloting was postponed for 18 months.

Silanyo reshuffled the cabinet on January 15, 2011, dismissing two ministers and moving others to new portfolios. He reorganized the government again on March 15, 2012, replacing five ministers, including the minister of finance. A major cabinet reshuffle occurred on June 25, 2013. The president appointed 19 new ministers or deputy ministers and transferred or promoted an additional seven.

Constitution and government. The government established in the wake of the May 1991 independence proclamation encompassed a president and vice president, appointed by the SNM, initially for a two-year transitional period during which a constitution was to be drafted that would permit the holding of open, multiparty elections. On May 28 *Radio Hargeisa* announced that the SNM leadership had also approved the formation of a high court and a civil service, in addition to the appointment of an attorney general, an auditor general, and a Central Bank governor.

In early July 1995 President Egal announced that a ten-member constitutional drafting committee had been appointed and that a basic law for Somaliland would be forthcoming within the ensuing 12 months. Meanwhile, the SNM Central Committee continued to serve as an interim legislature and electoral body for the presidency. In early 1997 the National Communities Conference provisionally approved a constitution that provided for a bicameral legislature (see Legislature, below), an electoral system of direct universal suffrage, and the organization of political parties (although groups with "tribal" or religious affiliations were proscribed). Among the details to surface subsequently about the document were stipulations that future presidents and their spouses be both native Somalians and Muslims. In late 1998 the legislature reportedly approved the implementation of measures based on Islamic religious law.

The 1997 constitution was approved with the provision that it be presented to a national referendum within three years. A one-year extension was granted in February 2000 and a three-month extension in February 2001, with the referendum finally being held on May 31, 2001. The new basic law confirmed Somaliland's independence, strengthened the executive branch, confirmed Islam as the "national faith," provided for a free press, and endorsed multiparty elections at all levels of government through universal suffrage. In March 2008, legislation reconfigured Somaliland into 12 regions and 57 districts.

Freedom of the press was codified in the constitution approved by national referendum in 2001. However, the government still controls the media, and a number of journalists have been imprisoned for criticizing the regime. In December 2007, 24 exiled Somali reporters were ordered to leave Somaliland. From March through July 2009, more than 20 journalists were arrested and imprisoned for varying lengths of time. In January 2011 the editor of a private newspaper was sentenced for three years on criminal defamation charges. In January 2012, more than 21 journalists were arrested for disseminating "propaganda" against the government. On April 24 masked assailants attacked a Hargeisa newspaper office. It was later discovered that one of the attackers was a police officer.

Foreign relations. Refusals to attend "reconciliation" conferences in Djibouti in 1991 were defended by SNM leaders on the ground that the meetings were called to address matters of domestic concern to "Southern Somalia." However, relations between Djibouti and Somaliland had been less than cordial because of conflict between the Issa community common to both countries and the Issaq grouping in Somaliland.

Despite what was described as a "flurry of meetings" designed to promote international recognition, by mid-1995 no foreign government had complied, partly because of long-standing opposition by the Organization of African Unity (OAU, subsequently the African Union—AU) to secessionist regimes and partly because of uncertainties surrounding continued anarchic conditions in the south. Significantly, while Somaliland had agreed in 1993 to the introduction of 500 UN peacekeepers to supervise the distribution of relief supplies, it rejected any deployment of U.S. troops on the ground that its claim to autonomy would thereby be jeopardized. In May 1994 President Egal threatened to expel any UN personnel advocating reintegration into Somalia.

In mid-1995, President Egal was reported to have sent a fax message to Israeli Prime Minister Yitzhak Rabin proposing the establishment of "strategic links" between their two countries. Egal spoke of the need to counter Islamic fundamentalism in the Horn of Africa, attributed with some degree of imprecision to "the growing influence of Saudi Arabia and the pro-Islamic Yemen."

Egal's efforts to gain international support bore fruit in late 1997 as Djibouti announced that it would exchange diplomatic credentials with Somalia. Italy subsequently told Egal in early 1998 that it would support an EU proposal to grant Somaliland "semi-diplomatic" recognition. For his part, Egal agreed to accept the offer of limited recognition for an interim period. Such concerns dominated Somaliland's foreign policy agenda through early 1999, with reports of Somaliland's enhanced international standing being balanced by continued calls from regional leaders for it to be included in a unified Somalia.

Relations with Djibouti deteriorated in 2000 when that country's leadership played a major role in the establishment of the transitional government in Somalia. However, Somaliland and Djibouti agreed to "normalize" their ties again in 2001. By that time it was clear that, in addition to opposing the notion of reunification with Somalia, Somaliland was in the midst of an ongoing territorial dispute with the Puntland autonomous region in Somalia.

Relations with Ethiopia improved in January 2002, when Ethiopia appointed an ambassador to Somaliland, and the Ethiopian government has since indicated that it may recognize Somaliland unilaterally if the AU refuses its membership bid. Reports indicated in 2008 that Somaliland and Ethiopia had increased military ties.

Intense lobbying efforts by officials from Somaliland to convince the UK government to recognize Somaliland's status as a fully independent nation continue to the present day. UK lawmakers visited Somaliland, and London agreed to help pay costs involved in the 2003 presidential poll. In addition, British companies reportedly began negotiations with Somaliland regarding offshore oil exploration. However, no official recognition was forthcoming, as most of the international community pressed (unsuccessfully) the Kahin administration to participate in the comprehensive Somalia peace talks. The Arab League in 2005 declined a request for membership from Somaliland, and the country's application for AU membership is still pending.

In January and July 2007 the EU sent foreign affairs delegations to discuss future cooperation between the EU and Somaliland. The EU has also pledged to support the upcoming elections in the country. Additionally, Somaliland interacts directly with the Swedish government in aid negotiations, despite the fact that Sweden has not yet granted formal recognition to the country.

In February 2008, France announced an initiative to improve ties with Somaliland by funding French language and cultural programs. In June the United Nations provided Somaliland with vehicles for its security forces and judiciary. The UN Development Program concurrently announced that it was doubling its aid to Somaliland to $7 million per year. Beginning in September 2008, Somaliland security forces launched an aggressive antipiracy campaign that resulted in the arrest of more than 100 alleged pirates by May 2009. The effort was reportedly part of the larger campaign to gain support from the West. In May 2009, following negotiations with Puntland officials, Ethiopia offered to host discussions in an effort to mediate the dispute over the Sool region. Renewed fighting in Somalia led an estimated 26,000 Somalis to flee to Somaliland by the summer of 2009.

In October 2010, Somaliland and Ethiopia agreed to increase security cooperation to suppress terrorism and piracy. Somali-backed antigovernment groups were reportedly responsible for terrorist attacks in early 2010 in Laas Anood, the capital of the Sool region.

In August 2011, the government announced that a Chinese firm would refurbish the port of Berbera and construct a refinery. In December, Somaliland granted additional licenses to British and Italian and energy companies to explore for oil.

In May 2012, reports indicated that the project to rebuild Berbera was placed on hiatus after Chinese officials refused to grant Somaliland diplomatic recognition as a condition for the deal. In June, the United States announced a $1 million program to promote economic development in Somaliland. This was followed by an additional $17 million economic development aid package in December.

In June 2013, Somaliland's foreign minister announced that the UN Assistance Mission in Somalia (UNSOM) would not be allowed to operate in the country. Reports indicated that the decision was based on apprehension that UNSOM would promote reunification of Somalia.

Current issues. Controversy erupted in the capital after the formation in April 2007 of the Qaran Party, whose leaders challenged administration claims that the constitution requires politicians to join one of the existing three political parties to enter government. The QP leaders were arrested in July (see Political Parties and Groups, below). On October 8, 2007, the National Electoral Commission announced it was delaying upcoming presidential and local government polls, scheduled for December 2007 and April 2008. An agreement was reached on June 9, 2008, between the three official political parties for presidential balloting to be held on April 6, 2009, followed by legislative polling on an unspecified date.

Long-standing territorial disputes between Somaliland and neighboring Puntland deepened in 2007. Puntland claimed the Bari, Nugaal, and Mudug regions as well as the Sanaag and Sool regions, which Somaliland also claimed. Sanaag declared independence from both in July 2007, renaming itself Makhir and choosing Badhan as a capital. Somaliland Defense Minister Adan Mire Mohamed was dismissed by Kahin for failing to prevent the fighting in Sanaag in April. Fighting then broke out between the neighbors in early October 2007, as Sool was rent by conflict between sub-clans calling for Sool's independence or backing the claims of either Somaliland, which claimed Sool due to the regions' shared history under British rule, or Puntland, which asserted its rights to the region based on common Darod clan ethnicity. By the end of October, Somaliland forces had captured Las Anod, the regional capital of Sool. The strife created an estimated 20,000 refugees. Later in the month, Somaliland levied an additional tax of 2 percent on its inhabitants, reportedly for the purpose of providing relief to displaced residents of Sool. There was renewed fighting in the region in January 2008 and again in July. Also in January pro-independence Somaliland demonstrators in northwestern Somalia were fired upon by Somali security forces. The minister for rural development, Fuad Adan Adde, was dismissed in April after criticizing the president.

On September 29, 2008, suicide bombers attacked the presidential palace and Ethiopian embassy in Hargeisa. The attacks killed 19, including the president's secretary, and wounded more than 100. The strikes were believed to have been carried out by Islamic extremists.

Somali member of the Transitional Federal Parliament Mohamed Mohamud ("Indhohur") was arrested in Somaliland on February 27 and held for 11 days before being expelled. Indhohur had been Somaliland's deputy regional governor for Sool before defecting to join the Somali national government. On March 28, the president's term was extended through September by the House of Elders, and Kahin issued a decree setting September 27 as the date for presidential elections. Officially, continued fighting in Sool, caused the delay, but opposition parties and groups decried it and threatened to withdraw recognition of the government. Meanwhile, a new dispute arose over voter registration when the president ordered the head of an international rights group, which was overseeing a new registration drive, to leave the country. On April 6 police used force to disperse opposition-led demonstrations in Hargeisa. The government subsequently banned demonstrations in the capital until the September balloting. On July 11, 2009, negotiations resulted in an agreement between the three major parties to support presidential elections in September. The balloting was subsequently postponed until June 2010.

In the long-delayed presidential elections on June 26, 2010, Silanyo won comfortably over Kahin and Warabe in balloting that international observers described as mostly free and fair. Despite threats from extremist groups, the polling was also peaceful. After his inauguration on July 27, the new president appointed a cabinet that was smaller than any since independence. The government included a number of Western-educated technocrats. In one of its first acts, it imposed a hiring freeze to reduce the deficit. Silanyo also released a number of political prisoners and pledged not to issue emergency decrees, as his predecessor had.

A drought and a devastating famine reduced crop production in 2011. In February 2011 a new prison, built with Norwegian funds, was opened to house suspected pirates. On March 23, for the first time, Somaliland naval forces captured Somali pirates. Meanwhile, the government announced on September 5 that it would expel all illegal immigrants and refugees. The announcement was criticized by human rights groups. In September the government launched a program to expand the use of the Somaliland shilling by replacing the widely used Somali shilling with the currency. The initiative was part of a larger program to increase tax revenues by reducing the informal economy. On October 8, a Somaliland court convicted seven of piracy and sentenced them to five years in prison.

In May 2012, ten opposition leaders were arrested and political demonstrations banned following the disqualification of several new political parties. In June, Silyano met with the president of Somalia's interim government for discussions in Dubai. The two leaders signed a general accord that called for greater cooperation between the two governments.

There were large demonstrations in support of the talks in the Mogadishu, but the meeting was criticized by officials from Puntland. Meanwhile, Turkey sponsored further negotiations in April and July 2013.

Seven political parties or groupings competed in local elections in November 2012. *Kulmiye* won the majority of the vote with 30.2 percent, followed by the newly formed **Somaliland National Party** (*Wadani*), 20.2 percent, and the UCID, 13 percent. Three people were killed and dozens injured in postelection violence as opposition parties protested the results. Security forces imposed a curfew in Hargeisa to contain the violence.

POLITICAL PARTIES AND GROUPS

The constitution endorsed by national referendum in May 2001 provided for multiparty activity, with the restriction that parties could not be based on tribal/clan or religious affiliations. The parties were provisionally recognized but had to secure 20 percent of the vote in four of the country's six provinces in local balloting in December 2002 in order to be registered for national elections. In local balloting in 2012, *Kulmiye,* the UCID, and *Wadani*, secured the right to compete in the next round of presidential and legislative elections.

Official Parties:

Solidarity Party (*Hisbiga Kulmiye*). Established in early 2002, *Kulmiye* is led by Ahmed Mohamed Mohamoud ("Silanyo"), who was chair of the SNM from 1984–1990. Silanyo had resigned from the Egal government in 2001, indicating his desire to campaign for the presidency. *Kulmiye* finished second to the UDUB in the December 2002 municipal balloting, securing, according to the government, about 83,000 votes to UDUB's 198,000. Silanyo finished second in the very close vote for president in April 2003. Subsequently, when the Kahin government was criticized by world leaders for refusing to participate in the Somali peace negotiations, Silanyo announced that he supported Kahin in the matter.

Kulmiye finished second in the 2005 legislative balloting with 30.3 percent of the vote. Following the election, *Kulmiye* announced a cooperative agreement with the other "opposition" party—the UCID (below). The party has supported the efforts of the Qaran party to become a registered political party. Silanyo was chosen as the *Kulmiye* presidential candidate in the 2009 elections at a September 2008 party convention. A division in the party emerged over the selection of the vice presidential candidate, Mudane SAYLICI. The choice was deeply opposed by a faction led by Ahmed Ali ADAMI. Through the spring and summer of 2009, *Kulmiye* members and supporters held a series of demonstrations against the extension of President Kahin's term. Silanyo won in the presidential balloting of June 2010. Deputy party chair Abdirahman ABDIQADIR was removed from office at a party conference in April 2012 for criticizing Silyano. At the same conference, Muse BIHI was elected party chair.

Leaders: Ahmed Mohamed MOHAMOUD ("Silanyo") (President of the Republic), Muse BIHI (Chair).

Justice and Welfare Party (*Ururka Caddaalada Iyo Daryeelka*—UCID). Established as a "modern" party devoted to "good governance," the staunchly nationalist UCID was described as an outgrowth of a Social Democratic Party that had been previously organized within the diaspora. UCID leader Faisal Farah Ali ("Warabe") was one of the founders of the SNM. In December 2002 the UCID secured the third place out of six contesting parties in the municipal elections. Warabe placed third in the 2003 presidential election with 16 percent of the vote. The UCID secured 29 percent of the vote in the 2005 legislative elections, and after announcement of a UCID/*Kulmiye* cooperation agreement, the UCID's Abdirahman Muhammad Abdullahi IRRO was elected speaker of the House of Representatives. The UCID choose Warabe as its presidential candidate at a party congress in 2009. He placed third in the June 2010 presidential polling. In June 2012, Warabe was appointed to a reconciliation commission charged to open new discussions with Somalia.

Leaders: Faisal Farah ALI ("Warabe") (Chair), Mohamed Osman FADAL (Vice Chair), Abdirahman Muhammad Abdullahi IRRO (Speaker of the House of Representatives).

Somaliland National Party (*Wadani*). Formed in 2012, by the speaker of the House of Representatives, Abdirahman Muhammad Abdullahi Irro, *Wadani* drew supporters from the UDUB and other opposition parties. *Wadani* placed second in the local elections in November 2012.

Leader: Abdirahman Muhammad Abdullahi IRRO.

Other Parties and Groups:

United and Democratic People's Alliance (*Ururka Dimuqraadiga Ummadda Bahawday*—UDUB). Launched in June 2001 by President Egal, the UDUB was subsequently routinely referenced as the "ruling" party in Somaliland. Although some observers viewed the UDUB as primarily a personal vehicle for Egal, the party was reportedly "resuscitated" by President Kahin following Egal's death in May 2002. The party went on to dominate the December 2002 municipal elections and to achieve a plurality in the 2005 legislative balloting on a vote share of 40.7 percent. In February 2009 a party congress elected Kahin as the UDUB candidate for the upcoming presidential balloting. However, UDUB opponents of Kahin, led by Abdullahi DARAWEL, left the meeting and held a rival congress. Kahin placed second in the presidential election in 2010. The UDUB failed to qualify as one of the three official parties following the November 2012 local elections.

Leaders: Dahir Riyale KAHIN (Chair and Former President of the Republic), Ahmad Yusuf YASIN (Former Vice President of the Republic), Usman GARAD (Secretary).

Somali National Movement (SNM). The SNM was organized in London in April 1981 by an exile group that declared its commitment to the overthrow of the Mogadishu regime but did not wish to ally itself with either the United States or the Soviet Union. Deriving most of its support from Somaliland's Issaq clan, the SNM long supported greater autonomy for the area. Ideologically, however, the movement suffered from a lack of cohesion, apparently counting Marxist, pro-Western, and Islamic fundamentalist groups within its ranks.

Following the Ethiopian-Somali agreement in April 1988, the SNM was left with no external source of support as its fighters were forced to leave Ethiopia. Subsequently, the SNM initiated wide-scale military activity against the government in the north and announced the capture of Hargeisa, the country's second city, in December 1989. The SNM formed an operational alliance with Somalia's other leading rebel groups in mid-1990. Reportedly, the SNM leadership was initially willing to participate in a federal system after the fall of the Siad Barre regime in January 1991, but it bowed to rank-and-file sentiment in opting for independence in May.

After being ousted from the Somaliland presidency in favor of Ibrahim Egal in May 1993, Abdurahman Ahmed Ali took up residence in London before surfacing in Mogadishu in August 1994 as a pro-Aidid opponent of secession. In September President Egal denounced a claim from Ahmed Ali that Ahmed Ali remained SNM chair. Thereafter, in early 1996 it was reported that Ahmed Ali was advising an anti-Egal rebel group in the Burao region.

Anti-Egal forces within the SNM accused the president of corruption in 1997 and threatened to launch a legal challenge against the composition of the National Communities Conference. However, such opposition reportedly failed to materialize. The SNM subsequently remained fractionalized concerning Egal's role and other issues, the president's critics also questioning his commitment to independence. Egal in 2001 formed his own political party (see the UDUB, above), with several other former SNM leaders following suit. The SNM ceased to function as a political entity after the 2001 referendum.

Qaran Party (QP). Founded in 2007, the party has met fierce resistance from the national government, which argues that the constitution requires that only three parties can exist in Somaliland. Despite this, the leaders of the Qaran Party announced its founding in April 2007. The three top officials in the party were then arrested by the Somaliland government on July 28, 2007, for engaging in unauthorized political activity. They were released in December 2007 and the charges against them dismissed. Efforts to gain official recognition of Qaran prior to the September 2009 presidential elections were unsuccessful. Party leader Mohammad Gabose was appointed interior minister in the 2010 government, but he resigned in March 2011, to form a new political grouping, **Ummada**.

Other minor groupings include the **Party of God** (*Hizbullah*), formed in 2012; **Rays**, led by Hasan Muhammad Ali ("GAAFAADHI"); and **Haqsoor**, led by Hassan ISSE.

For information on the **United Somali Front** (USF), see the 2009 *Handbook.*

LEGISLATURE

Following Somaliland's declaration of independence in 1991, the Central Committee of the Somali National Movement (SNM) served as a nominal "provisional" legislature for several years, although its actual authority was limited due to the subclan conflict that left substantial territory outside SNM control. In May 1993 the SNM "parliament" endorsed the recommendation of a recently concluded grand *shir* (gathering) for the formal establishment of a two-chamber legislature, comprised of a House of Elders and a House of Representatives (initially to be appointed on a clan basis but ultimately to be filled by elections). The two chambers began to operate shortly thereafter, although some clan seats in the House of Representatives remained vacant until August 1994. The new constitution approved by national referendum in 2001 provided for a bicameral **Parliament.**

House of Elders (*Golaha Guurtida*). The upper house is authorized to review legislation passed by the House of Representatives and to approve legislation on its own in regard to religion, culture, and security. It comprises 82 members and a number of nonvoting honorary members. The first elections to the House of Elders were scheduled for October 2006, but in a controversial decision the current appointed membership decided in May 2006 to extend its mandate until October 2010, and then again until 2014.

Speaker: Saleban Muhammad ADAN.

House of Representatives (*Golaha Wakiilada*). The lower house comprises 82 members directly elected via proportional representation (in six regions) for five-year terms. In the first elections for the house on September 29, 2005, the United and Democratic People's Alliance reportedly secured 33 seats; the Solidarity Party, 28; and the Justice and Welfare Party, 21.

Speaker: Abdirahman Muhammad Abdullahi IRRO.

CABINET

[as of November 15, 2013]

President	Ahmed Mohamed Mohamoud ("Silanyo")
Vice President	Abdirahman Abdallahi Ismail ("Saylici")
Ministers	
Agriculture	Farah Elmi Mohamed
Civil Aviation	Mohamoud Hashi Abdi
Commerce	Mohamed Abdilahi Omer
Defense	Ahmed Haji Ali Adam
Development of Rural Areas and Environment	Shukri Ismael Bandare [f]
Education	Samsam Abdi Adan [f]
Fisheries and Marine Resources	Ali Jama Farah ("Bureed")
Foreign Affairs	Mohamed Bihi Younis
Health	Saleiban Esa Ahmed
Industry	Abdirisaq Ali Osman
Interior	Ali Mohamed Waran'ade
Information	Abdilahi Mohamed Dahir
Justice and Attorney General	Hussein Ahmed Aided
Labor and Social Welfare	Mohamud Ahmed Barre ("Garaad")
Livestock	Abdi Aw Dahir
Mineral and Water Resources	Hussein Abdi Duale
Parliament	Aden Ahmed Warsame
Planning and Development	Saad ali Shire
Post and Telecommunication	Ali Elmi Abgal
Presidency	Hersi Ali Haji Hassan
Public Works and Housing	Ahmed Abdi Mohamud
Religion	Sheikh Khalil Abdullahi Ahmed
Resettlement and Rehabilitation	Ahmed Abdi Kahin
Sports, Youth, and Culture	Ali Said Raygal

[f] = female

INTERGOVERNMENTAL REPRESENTATION

As of July 2013, Somaliland was not a member of the UN.

IGO Memberships (Non-UN): None.

SOUTH AFRICA

Republic of South Africa
Republiek van Suid-Afrika

Political Status: Fully independent state since 1934; republic established May 31, 1961; Interim Constitution ratified on December 22, 1993, with effect from April 27, 1994, for a five-year term; new text signed into law on December 10, 1996, effective February 4, 1997, with certain provisions implemented gradually through 1999.

Area: 470,882 sq. mi. (1,221,037 sq. km).

Population: 51,447,705 (2013E—UN); 48,601,098 (2013E—U.S. Census).

Major Urban Centers (urban areas, 2005E): PRETORIA (administrative capital, 2,534,000), Cape Town (legislative capital, 3,143,000), Bloemfontein (judicial capital, 793,000), Durban (4,610,000), Johannesburg (3,974,000). Pretoria is part of the City of Tshwane Metropolitan Municipality.

Official Languages: There are 11 official languages, of which English and Afrikaans are the languages of record.

Monetary Unit: Rand (market rate November 1, 2013: 10.17 rand = $1US).

President: Jacob Gedleyihlekisa ZUMA (African National Congress); elected by the National Assembly on May 6, 2009, and inaugurated for a five-year term on May 9, succeeding Kgalema Petrus MOTLANTHE (African National Congress); named new government on May 10, 2009.

Deputy President: Kgalema Petrus MOTLANTHE (African National Congress); appointed by President Zuma on May 9, 2009, and sworn in on May 10, succeeding Baleka MBETE (African National Congress).

THE COUNTRY

Industrially the most developed country in Africa, the Republic of South Africa is a land of rolling plateaus within a mountainous escarpment that rims its territory on the seaward side and separates the coastal cities of Cape Town and Durban from the inland centers of Johannesburg and Pretoria. The country is peopled by four separate ethnic elements as unequal in numbers as they used to be in political status. The largest and historically least favored group, comprising approximately 79 percent of the population, consists of the Xhosa, Zulu, and Sotho, who are collectively known as the Bantu. Whites comprise 9.6 percent of the population; mixed-race people, 8.9 percent; and Asians, mainly Indians living in KwaZulu-Natal Province, 2.5 percent.

Some three-fifths of the whites are "Afrikaners," who descend from the Dutch, German, and French Huguenot settlers who colonized the country beginning in the 17th century. Traditionally agrarian in their social traditions and outlook, their native language is Afrikaans, a language closely related to Dutch (although many Afrikaners also speak English). Afrikaners, predominantly affiliated with the Dutch Reformed Church, were the most resolute supporters of the policy of separation of the races (apartheid). Most other whites speak English as their first language, identify with the British tradition, and are more involved in business and industry than Afrikaners, although this pattern has changed as Afrikaners have moved to urban areas.

South Africa has become a highly urbanized country, with half of the white population, a third of the blacks, and most Asians and mixed-race

people (known in South Africa as "Cape Coloureds" or simply "Coloureds") residing in and around the dozen large cities and towns. The Coloureds form a distinct group. They are frequently of mixed non-white and Afrikaner descent, with Afrikaner-sounding last names and Afrikaans often their first language. They are concentrated in Western Cape Province. The term "Coloured," while still in general and official use, is coming under increasing criticism.

In predominantly white areas, black women are employed mainly as domestic servants and casual agricultural laborers. Men's migration to white-controlled employment sites has left women largely in charge of subsistence agriculture. Women's participation in government was long limited to minor representation by white women in national and provincial legislatures; however, women of all races were prominent in the anti-apartheid movement. The award of cabinet portfolios to women in the current administration has fulfilled a pledge by former president Nelson Mandela to give women one-third of all posts at all levels. Following the 2009 legislative elections, women held 169 seats in the lower house (42.3 percent), and 17 in the upper chamber (32.1 percent).

The first African country to experience the full force of the industrial revolution, South Africa now has an advanced economy and plays an important role in international economic affairs. The world's leading gold producer, the country's mines yield nearly one-third of global output. South Africa also mines diamonds, copper, asbestos, chrome, platinum, and vanadium, and is tapping recently discovered ocean reserves of oil. The country has abundant coal, which provides a large share of energy. Agriculturally, South Africa is self-sufficient (except in coffee, rice, and tea) and exports wool, maize, sugar, and fruit. Although agriculture now contributes only about 3 percent of GDP, it continues to employ almost 10 percent of the labor force. The manufacturing sector, spurred by the government during the apartheid era to promote industrial self-sufficiency, presently accounts for approximately 25 percent of GDP; mining adds another 6 percent. Industry employs approximately 25 percent of workers. South Africa's leading trade partner is China.

In 2000, South Africa concluded with the European Union (EU) a free-trade agreement, which covered some 90 percent of transactions by 2012 (for more on the economy prior to 2000, please see the 2013 *Handbook*).

In recent years, South Africa has seemed to prefer public–private partnerships to large-scale privatization. All economic sectors are required to draw up charters that commit them to black economic empowerment.

Annual GDP growth averaged 4.7 percent in 2006–2008, and inflation soared to 11.3 percent in 2008 in response to high commodity prices. The unemployment rate decreased to approximately 23 percent by mid-2008. The economy went into recession in 2009, owing in large part to the global economic downturn. GDP fell that year by –1.5 percent. International Monetary Fund (IMF) managers said South Africa weathered the global crisis without major problems or need for public stimulus. GDP growth of 3.1 percent was recorded for 2010, and the IMF commended South Africa for its "impressive economic performance in recent years" and its efforts toward improving infrastructure and educational and health services. Meanwhile, the World Bank approved a $3.75-billion loan in 2010 to develop renewable energy and help pay for work on a coal-fired plant, described as one of the largest of its kind in the world.

Another recent focus of attention has been HIV/AIDS. In 2010, South Africa was reported to have the world's largest number of HIV-positive citizens, an estimated 10 percent of the population. The government estimated that $88 billion would be required over the next two decades to pay for the cost of caring for AIDS patients and for prevention efforts.

In 2012, the economy struggled under flagging demand for South African exports as a result of the European debt crisis. On July 19, 2012, the South African Reserve Bank cut interest rates by half a percentage point to 5 percent to bolster growth. GDP grew by 2.6 percent in 2012, while inflation rose by 5.7 percent and the unemployment rate remained high at 25.2 percent. A 2012 World Bank report highlighted that uneven distribution of growth in South Africa has perpetuated inequality: The top decile of the population accounted for 58 percent of the country's income, while the bottom decile accounted for just 0.5 percent.

GOVERNMENT AND POLITICS

Political background. The Republic of South Africa as it exists today is the result of a long and complicated process of interaction between indigenous peoples and the Dutch and British colonists who came to exploit the territory. The original Cape Colony was settled by the Dutch in the 17th century but fell into British hands as a result of the Napoleonic wars. Discontented Afrikaners, known as "Boers," the Afrikaans word for farmers, trekked northward in 1835–1837, commencing a half-century subjugation of the Zulu and other native peoples and establishing the independent republics of Transvaal and Orange Free State. Following the discovery of diamonds and gold in the late 19th century, the two Boer republics were conquered by Britain in the Anglo-Boer War of 1899–1902. In 1910 they were joined with the British colonies of the Cape and Natal (annexed in 1843) to form the Union of South Africa, which obtained full independence within the Commonwealth in 1931.

Although South Africa joined with Britain in both world wars, its British and Commonwealth attachments progressively weakened as the result of widespread anti-British sentiment and racial preoccupations. The National Party (*Nasionale Party*—NP), led by Daniel F. MALAN, came to power in 1948 with a program strongly reinforcing racial separation under white "guardianship." It proceeded to enact a body of openly discriminatory legislation that was further amplified under Hendrik F. VERWOERD (1958–1966). Segregation was strictly enforced, the already token political representation of nonwhites was progressively reduced, and overt opposition was severely repressed. Similar policies were applied in South West Africa, a former German territory occupied by South Africa in World War I and subsequently administered under a mandate from the League of Nations (see entry under Namibia).

With apartheid, the African National Congress (ANC), the largest party advocating racial partnership, went underground and began a three-decade-long "armed struggle" against the NP government. Much of its leadership either was imprisoned or went abroad. Many received military training in the USSR or other communist countries.

Increasing institutionalization of segregation under the Verwoerd regime led to international condemnation. External opposition was intensified by the "Sharpeville incident" of March 21, 1960, during which South African police fired on black demonstrators, killing 69 of them. In view of the increasingly critical stand of other Commonwealth members, South Africa formally withdrew from the grouping and declared itself a republic on May 31, 1961.

Prime Minister Verwoerd was assassinated by a deranged white man in September 1966, but his successor, Balthazar J. VORSTER, continued Verwoerd's policies, bringing to fruition the idea of dividing the blacks into separate tribal homelands, or "Bantustans." These areas, encompassing approximately 13 percent of the country's land, were ultimately intended to house upward of three-quarters of the population. However, a series of minor concessions to the blacks brought about a challenge from the right-wing, or *verkrampte* ("unenlightened" or "ultra-Conservative"), faction of the NP under the leadership of Dr. Albert HERTZOG, who formed the Refounded National Party (*Herstigte Nasionale Party*—HNP) to compete, with little success, in the 1970 election.

The 1974 Portuguese revolution and subsequent changes in Angola and Mozambique further isolated the South African regime. Early in 1975 the government announced a policy of "ending discrimination" within South Africa and of working for détente in external affairs. During the following year, however, the country experienced its worst outbreak of racial violence since the Sharpeville episode in 1960. The rioting, which began in Soweto, the huge black township next to Johannesburg, in mid-June, grew out of black student protests against the compulsory use of Afrikaans as a medium of instruction. Although the government announced in early July that it would begin phasing out Afrikaans at the primary and secondary school levels, the disturbances spread to townships around Pretoria and, in late August and early September, to the heart of Cape Town. Despite the unrest, the Vorster government gave no indication of abandoning its commitment to "separate development" of the races, with the official position being that the policy was not based on race but on the conviction that, within South Africa, blacks made up distinct "nations" to which special political and constitutional arrangements should apply. It was in accordance with this philosophy that nominal independence was granted to the territories that would become known as the black homelands: Transkei in October 1976, Bophuthatswana in December 1977, Venda in September 1979, and Ciskei in December 1981.

Rioting intensified during 1977 amid growing signs that the Vorster government felt itself under siege. Drastic new security legislation was approved, and the government instituted its most drastic crackdown in two decades, closing the leading black newspaper, arresting its editor, and banning a number of protest groups. Apparent white endorsement of these moves was revealed in a parliamentary election on November 30, in which the NP captured 134 of 165 lower house seats.

On September 20, 1978, Prime Minister Vorster announced his intention to resign for reasons of health. Nine days later he was elected by a joint session of Parliament to the essentially titular post of president, succeeding Nicolaas J. DIEDERICHS, who had died on August 21. One day earlier the NP elected Defense Minister Pieter W. BOTHA as its new leader (hence prime minister). On June 4, 1979, President Vorster also resigned after being charged with participation in a variety of clandestine propaganda activities and of giving false evidence in an effort to conceal gross irregularities in the affair. He was immediately succeeded, on an interim basis, by Senate president Marais VILJOEN, who was elected to a full term as head of state by Parliament on June 19. Despite the scandal and increasingly vocal opposition from both the HNP and remaining *verkrampte* elements within the NP, the Botha government remained in power with a marginally reduced parliamentary majority after the election of April 29, 1981, having campaigned on a 12-point platform, first advanced in 1979, that called for constitutional power-sharing among whites, Coloureds, and Asians, with "full independence" for the black homelands.

In a referendum conducted November 2, 1982, a Constitution Bill, providing for an executive state president and a tricameral parliament excluding blacks, was endorsed by 66 percent of white voters and was approved by the House of Assembly on September 9, 1983. After balloting for delegates to the Coloured and Indian chambers in August 1984, Prime Minister Botha was unanimously elected president by an electoral college of the majority parties in each house on September 5, and he was inaugurated in Cape Town on September 14.

Faced with mounting internal unrest and near-universal foreign condemnation, the government in April 1985 abandoned legislation outlawing sex between the races and the prohibition of multiracial political movements. These moves, while provoking an immediate backlash from right-wing extremists, were received by black and moderate white leaders as "too little, too late." Clashes between police and demonstrators increased, prompting a state of emergency in 36 black townships, the first in a quarter-century. On August 15, in a speech in Durban, President Botha rejected demands for further racial concessions, insisting that they would constitute "a road to abdication and suicide" by white South Africans.

In an address at the opening of Parliament on January 31, 1986, President Botha shocked the extreme right by declaring that "We have outgrown the outdated colonial system of paternalism, as well as the outdated concept of apartheid." In late April, he announced that a bill would be introduced terminating the hated pass laws, which required black South Africans to carry a document showing any white areas they were allowed to enter, though the legislation would not affect segregation in schools, hospitals, and residential areas. Earlier, on March 7, the partial state of emergency imposed eight months before was rescinded; however, a nationwide state of emergency was declared on June 12 to quell anticipated violence on June 16, the anniversary of the Soweto uprising.

Although the term of the House of Assembly had been extended from 1986 to 1989 to coincide with the five-year mandates of the Coloured and Indian chambers, President Botha announced in January 1987 that an early election for a new white chamber would be held on May 6. The results of the poll reflected a distinctly rightward swing by the white voters.

During the ensuing months the government continued grudgingly yielding on the substance of apartheid while severely limiting the freedom of its opponents. A variety of new press restrictions were announced in August, while the government banned the activities of numerous groups. Banned groups included labor unions; civic, educational, and youth associations; the umbrella United Democratic Front (UDF), which linked some 650 anti-apartheid organizations; and a new Committee for the Defence of Democracy (CDD), organized in Cape Town in March 1988. In September a major constitutional crisis was averted by the government's withdrawal of five bills designed to tighten residential segregation laws, upon which the two nonwhite parliamentary chambers had refused to act. Throughout the period numerous long-incarcerated regime opponents were released, while others, primarily from the "new generation" of UDF and other leaders, were arrested and convicted of treason.

On January 18, 1989, President Botha suffered a stroke, and Constitutional Development Minister J. Christiaan HEUNIS was sworn in as acting chief executive the following day. On February 2 Botha resigned as NP leader, with Education Minister Frederik W. DE KLERK being named his successor. On March 13 the party's parliamentary caucus voted unanimously that de Klerk should also become state president; Botha, however, refused to step down and on March 15 resumed the presidency, vowing to stay in office for the remainder of his term. Less than five months later Botha complained of not being advised of a proposed meeting that de Klerk and Foreign Minister "Pik" Botha had scheduled with Zambian president Kenneth Kaunda. Terming the proposed meeting "inopportune," President Botha resigned on August 14, with de Klerk succeeding him on an acting basis the following day.

At balloting for all three legislative chambers on September 6, 1989, the NP retained its overall majority in the House of Assembly, although its share of the vote fell to less than half (48.6 percent). On September 14 de Klerk was named by the parliamentary electoral college to a regular five-year term as president. In October his administration released seven prominent ANC leaders from prison, including Walter SISULU, who had been incarcerated for 26 years.

On February 2, 1990, de Klerk lifted the bans against the main anti-apartheid organization, the African National Congress (ANC), the Pan-Africanist Congress (PAC), and the South African Communist Party (SACP), and on February 11 he freed the long-incarcerated ANC leader, Nelson Rolihlahla MANDELA. However, on April 17, two weeks before the start of talks with ANC leaders, the president flatly rejected majority rule on the ground that it would "lead to the domination and even the suppression of minorities." He also rejected a demand by right-wing whites for racially based partition of the country and proposed a system under which power would be shared by all groups and minority rights would be constitutionally guaranteed. For its part, the ANC indicated that it would not engage in full negotiations until the nearly four-year state of emergency had been rescinded and all political prisoners and exiles had been amnestied.

On June 1, 1990, the government introduced legislation to rescind the Reservation of Separate Amenities Act that had sanctioned "petty apartheid" at public locations, such as beaches, libraries, and places of entertainment.

On June 27, 1990, de Klerk stated that he was prepared to negotiate a new constitution that would eliminate all aspects of apartheid, and on August 7, one day after his second meeting with the president, Mandela announced that the ANC was suspending its 30-year armed struggle. In early October de Klerk and the leaders of the six "self-governing" homelands agreed to scrap the Lands Acts, and on October 15 the Separate Amenities Act was formally repealed. Subsequently, in a historic move, de Klerk asked the National Party to open its rolls to all races. On December 13 ANC President Oliver TAMBO was permitted to return from more than three decades' exile.

In January 1991, the government and the ANC agreed to convene an all-party conference on the constitutional drafting process, although Chief Mangosuthu BUTHELEZI, leader of the Zulu-based *Inkatha* Freedom Party (IFP), responded coolly, while the CPSA, the PAC, and the Azanian People's Organization (Azapo) indicated that they would not participate. Meanwhile, on January 29, the ANC's Mandela and *Inkatha*'s Buthelezi met for the first time in 30 years to defuse the bitter rivalry that had caused the death of more than 4,000 people and had split the anti-apartheid movement. However, within two days of the leaders' reconciliation renewed fighting had broken out between their followers.

The Lands Acts of 1913 and 1936, which reserved 87 percent of the country's land for the white minority, and the Group Areas Act, which provided for racially segregated residential areas, were abolished on June 5, 1991. Five days later, the Population Registration Act, which mandated the classification of South Africans by race from birth, was repealed. Revocation of the Population Act left the capacity to vote (promised by the government under the new constitution) as the major remaining obstacle to black emancipation.

The first session of the Convention for a Democratic South Africa (Codesa), held December 20–21, 1991, featured a "declaration of intent" whereby constitutional proposals would require the approval of both the ANC and the government, with the latter pledging to employ its parliamentary majority to translate Codesa's decisions into law. Meanwhile, the de Klerk administration had become embroiled in an "Inkathagate" scandal stemming from evidence that the South Africa Defence Force (SADF) had been engaged over a three-year period in providing IFP members with anti-ANC military training.

On February 20, 1992, President de Klerk announced that a "whites-only" referendum would be held March 17 to renew his mandate for negotiating with anti-apartheid organizations. The projected poll was immediately denounced by white extremist groups as well as by the leftist PAC and Azapo, which had long demanded that a new basic law be approved by a broadly based constituent assembly rather than by the existing nonblack Parliament. The result of the referendum was a triumph for the president, with 68.7 percent of the participants endorsing continuation of the reform process.

The Codesa II session held May 15–16, 1992, proved unproductive, largely because the parties were unable to resolve an impasse over the size of the majority required for interim legislative approval of key constitutional provisions. On May 27 a commission headed by Richard GOLDSTONE, a respected South African jurist, issued a six-month study on the sources of internal violence. While not completely exonerating the government, the commission found no evidence of "a sinister and secret organization orchestrating political violence on a wide front." Rather, it attributed the disturbances in the townships to "the political battle between supporters of the ANC and the *Inkatha* Freedom Party." The conclusions of the commission were sorely tested on June 17, when South African police were accused of transporting a group of Zulu speakers to Boipatong township, south of Johannesburg, where a bloody massacre ensued that claimed 45 lives. After touring Boipatong, ANC Secretary General Cyril RAMAPHOSA insisted that the slaughter was a government response to the launching of an ANC mass action campaign designed to force majority rule. While the government vehemently denied the charge, Nelson Mandela declared on June 21 that negotiations were "in tatters," and the ANC Executive Committee voted two days later to withdraw from Codesa.

ANC suspicions that the Goldstone Commission had not uncovered the whole truth about township violence were confirmed when a raid on a covert operations center of military intelligence in Pretoria yielded information that impelled President de Klerk to announce on December 19, 1992, that illegal activities by senior SADF officers were under investigation. In further reports, the commission in October 1993 found strong circumstantial evidence of security force involvement in the violence. In March 1994 it cited allegations of a conspiracy among senior police officers involving a "third force" of *agents provocateurs* tasked with anti-ANC destabilization in collaboration with the IFP.

Meanwhile, a "record of understanding" drawn up in September 1992 between the ANC and the NP had given renewed impetus to constitutional talks, which were resumed in March 1993 within what was later designated the Multi-Party Negotiating Process (MPNP). The 26 parties involved included several that had boycotted Codesa, notably the PAC and the SACP, the latter being a leading component of the Concerned South Africans Group (COSAG) of apartheid-era formations, including the IFP. The MPNP came under immediate strain as a result of the assassination on April 10 of Chris HANI, SACP general secretary and an ANC executive member. However, counsels of restraint from Mandela and others prevented the violent reaction in the black townships from getting out of control.

Negotiating breakthroughs came in May and June 1993, when most of the MPNP parties agreed that nonracial elections for a five-year transitional government of national unity would take place on April 27, 1994. Also crucial was the ANC's shift from insistence on a centralized state to acceptance of a federal structure with entrenched powers for provincial governments. The concession did not prevent the IFP and the CPSA from withdrawing from the MPNP shortly before the publication on July 26 of a draft interim constitution providing for equal citizenship rights for all races and a nine-province federal structure integrating the black homelands into the new South Africa. In September the remaining MPNP parties also reached agreement on the creation of a multiracial Transitional Executive Council (TEC), which as approved by Parliament on September 23, was to operate alongside the government in the election run-up to ensure fair play and to monitor the operations of the security forces. After the package of texts had been formally adopted by the MPNP on November 18, the TEC was installed on December 7. Finally, on December 22 Parliament ratified the Constitution of the Republic of South Africa Bill by 237 votes to 45, most of those against being CPSA members.

The problem of reconciling opponents, both white and black, to the settlement remained. In May 1993 the CPSA had joined with various right-wing Afrikaner groups to form the Afrikaner People's Front (*Afrikaner Volksfront*—AVF) under the leadership of Gen. (Ret.) Constand VILJOEN, a former head of the SADF, with the aim of achieving self-determination for Afrikaners in a separate homeland. In June tensions mounted when armed members of the Afrikaner Resistance Movement (*Afrikaner Weerstandsbeweging*—AWB), a paramilitary group led by Eugene TERRE'BLANCHE, forcibly occupied the building where MPNP talks were in progress, with no resistance from the police. In October the AVF, together with the IFP and other conservative black elements, launched the Freedom Alliance as successor to COSAG. Its constituent elements at first presented a united front against the constitutional settlement, although a January 1994 decision in favor of electoral participation by the Ciskei government (originally a Freedom Alliance member) was a serious setback.

The situation was transformed in March 1994 when the AWB and other Afrikaner paramilitaries, apparently sanctioned by the AVF, tried to protect the Bophuthatswana government of Chief Lucas MANGOPE (a Freedom Alliance member) from ANC-led protests against his decision to boycott the elections. Order was restored by speedy deployment of SADF troops, the Afrikaners being routed with 3 fatalities among at least 60 deaths overall and Mangope being removed from office by decision of the TEC on March 12. In light of this debacle and earlier divisions in the Freedom Alliance, Viljoen broke ranks with the AVF by forming the Freedom Front (*Vryheidsfront*—VF), which registered for the elections, whereas the CPSA and the other AVF formations maintained their nonparticipatory stance. The split marked the effective collapse of the Freedom Alliance, as confirmed by the eleventh-hour decision of the IFP on April 19 that it too would contest the forthcoming elections, despite bloody ANC-IFP clashes near the ANC's Shell House headquarters in Johannesburg on March 28 in which over 50 IFP demonstrators had been killed.

The IFP's participation ensured that South Africa's first multiracial balloting, to be held April 26–29, 1994, would be relatively free of violence. According to the Independent Electoral Commission and numerous foreign observers, the election was in the main conducted fairly. As expected, the ANC registered an overwhelming victory in the national contest, winning 252 of 400 seats in the new National Assembly, against 82 for the NP, 43 for the IFP, 9 for the VF, and 14 for three smaller parties. In simultaneous polls for new provincial assemblies, the ANC won majorities in seven provinces, losing only Western Cape (to the NP) and KwaZulu-Natal (to the IFP).

Elected president by unanimous vote of the new assembly on May 9, 1994, Nelson Mandela was sworn in the following day. Under the terms of the constitutional settlement, the ANC's Thabo MBEKI became first deputy president and de Klerk second deputy president. The new cabinet installed on May 11 contained 19 ANC representatives, 5 from the NP, and 3 from the IFP (including Chief Buthelezi as home affairs minister). The new Senate, its members designated by the newly elected provincial assemblies, convened on May 20, with the ANC holding 60 of 90 seats.

Nelson Mandela was inaugurated as South African president on May 10, 1994. Far-right Afrikaners continued to press for political autonomy, although talks between Mandela and CPSA leader Ferdi HARTZENBERG in Pretoria on August 12 suggested that the AVF did not intend to resort to force. As for the IFP, while Chief Buthelezi had accepted cabinet membership, relations between his Zulu-based formation and Mandela's ANC remained tense. Intensifying post-election controversy was the disclosure on May 19 that on the eve of the election some 7.4 million acres of state land in KwaZulu, about a third of the ex-homeland's area, had been transferred to the control of the Zulu King Goodwill ZWELITHINI under legislation adopted by the outgoing KwaZulu Assembly and approved by President de Klerk, without the knowledge of the ANC. Although the new minister of land affairs, Derek HANEKOM (ANC), announced on June 15 that the transfer would stand, the affair angered many ANC members, who suspected that its purpose had been to entice the IFP into the electoral process.

A year after the advent of majority rule, the most serious political problem facing the government was the disaffection of the IFP and its Zulu supporters, centering on their demand for a degree of autonomy for KwaZulu-Natal. Accompanied by periodic clashes between ANC and IFP supporters, the confrontation worsened in April 1995 when IFP members withdrew from the Constituent Assembly charged with drafting a permanent constitution. Although Chief Buthelezi remained a member of the government, he asserted that his party would not accept any constitution drawn up in its absence and repeated his demand for international mediation of KwaZulu-Natal's dispute with the central authorities. ANC ministers and officials responded that a formal international role in the dispute would imply acceptance of KwaZulu-Natal's claim to separate status; they also insisted that drafting of the new constitution would proceed according to schedule, if necessary without IFP participation.

ANC-IFP relations were further aggravated by President Mandela's admission on June 1, 1995, that he had personally authorized ANC members "to shoot to kill if necessary" during bloody clashes between the ANC and IFP on March 28, 1994, near the ANC's headquarters in Johannesburg, in which over 50 IFP demonstrators had died. Amid IFP calls for his impeachment over this admission, the president sought to regain the initiative by proposing on June 14 that responsibility for the pay and perquisites of tribal chiefs should be transferred from the provincial authorities to the central government. Such a change would pose a special threat to Chief Buthelezi's power base in the KwaZulu-Natal countryside, where control of the purse strings sustained the IFP's network of support among tribal chiefs. Serious IFP-ANC clashes in August 1995 were followed on December 25 by an attack by IFP supporters on the village of Shobashobane (an ANC enclave in KwaZulu-Natal) in which at least 19 people were killed, with the security forces failing to intervene.

In sharp contrast, relations between the ANC and the white minority continued to be accommodating, with occasional rifts within the transitional government being quickly resolved. The discovery by the ANC justice minister in January 1995 that the outgoing NP government had secretly granted indemnities from prosecution to over 3,500 policemen and security officials provoked a cabinet crisis in which de Klerk claimed that he and the NP had been subjected to "insulting attack." However, the possibility of an NP withdrawal receded when de Klerk and Mandela met on January 20 and agreed that a "fresh start" should be made. The president also established working relations with several Afrikaner groups that had vigorously opposed black majority rule, with a disavowal of violence by General Viljoen and the VF seen as particularly helpful.

Two days after the endorsement of the new constitution in Parliament, de Klerk announced on May 10, 1996, that the NP was withdrawing from the government of national unity with effect from June 30. He cited the diminishing influence of the NP on government policy, the refusal of the ANC to include power-sharing arrangements in the new constitution, and the need for an effective opposition. Commentators considered that the decision was motivated by a desire to assert the NP's independence well in advance of legislative elections in 1999. The party subsequently also withdrew from all provincial governments except that of Western Cape, where it was in the majority. President Mandela appointed ANC members to replace the outgoing NP ministers and abolished the post of second deputy president vacated by de Klerk.

Much domestic attention subsequently focused on the initial proceedings of the Truth and Reconciliation Commission (TRC), which had been created in July 1995 to investigate human rights abuses and political crimes of the apartheid era with the aim of consigning their legacy to history. Chaired by Archbishop Desmond TUTU (head of the Anglican Church in South Africa until his retirement in June 1996), the TRC was empowered to grant judicial amnesties to people confessing to apartheid-era crimes (depending on their gravity) if it was satisfied that full disclosure had been made and that the crime in question had been politically motivated. The TRC began a scheduled two years of hearings in April 1996, its authority to grant amnesties being upheld by the Constitutional Court in July after Azapo and the families of several murdered political activists had argued that the commission's power to protect human rights violators from prosecution and civil damages denied them the opportunity to obtain justice through the courts.

Former state president de Klerk gave evidence to the TRC on August 21, 1996. He stated that the security forces had not, to his knowledge, been authorized during the period of NP government to commit human rights abuses, although he apologized for suffering caused by the apartheid system. However, Eugene DE KOCK, a former colonel in the South African police who was convicted in the same month for murder and other crimes during the apartheid era, subsequently claimed in court that members of the former NP government had had full knowledge of a systematic campaign by the police, armed forces, and covert security units against apartheid opponents. Furthermore, in testimony to the TRC in October, several former members of the police claimed that former president P. W. Botha and two former ministers, Louis LE GRANGE and Adriaan VLOK, had ordered state violence against anti-apartheid organizations in the 1980s. In May 1997 de Klerk, in a second appearance, again denied knowledge of human rights violations. He retired from politics in August, and the NP inaugurated a new leadership under Marthinus van SCHALKWYK, by which time the party had ended its cooperation with the TRC on the grounds of political bias.

In September 1997, the deadline for submitting petitions to the TRC passed. Among those who did not file and attempted to stave off the TRC's calls to testify were former president Botha and a number of apartheid-era judicial officials. (Botha was convicted in August 1998 for refusing to appear before the TRC, although in June 1999 his appeal was upheld on technical grounds.) The ANC was the most prominent of the organizations to apply and in its petition admitted to torture, abuse, and even executions; however, the party attempted to justify such actions as being in the name of the "dirty war" fought against apartheid.

The dominant event of 1998 was the October release of a comprehensive report from the TRC. Having reviewed evidence from some 20,000 people, the TRC described apartheid as a "crime against humanity." It also declared the government responsible for a large majority of the abuses committed between 1960 and 1994, condemning the NP regime for a broad range of atrocities that included kidnappings, torture, killings, and bombings. However, the ANC and other liberation groups as well as extreme right organizations were also held accountable for violent acts. The report caused controversy, and every major party rejected its conclusions to some degree. It cited prominent individuals from across the entire political spectrum for human rights abuses. They included P. W. Botha, Chief Buthelezi, General Viljoen, Eugene Terre'Blanche, and President Mandela's ex-wife, Winnie MADIKIZELA-MANDELA, one of the country's most popular female politicians and an ANC leader, who was implicated in a dozen violent acts, including murder. Although the activities of two of the TRC's three committees—the Reparation and Rehabilitation Committee and the Human Rights Violations Committee—drew to a close with the release of the report, the mandate of the Amnesty Committee, with over 1,000 cases yet to review, was extended by act of Parliament "until a date determined by the President."

In December 1997, President Mandela had resigned as ANC president and was succeeded, as expected, by Thabo Mbeki, who led the ANC into the June 2, 1999, national elections. The ANC emerged from the balloting with 266 National Assembly seats, one short of the two-thirds majority needed to amend the constitution, prompting party leaders to quickly negotiate a coalition with the Minority Front (MF), an Indian party that had won a single seat. On June 14 the National Assembly unanimously elected Mbeki as president, and he took the oath of office two days later. On June 17 the new president named ANC deputy leader Jacob ZUMA as deputy president and appointed a cabinet in which Chief Buthelezi retained his position as home affairs minister.

In the June 1999 balloting, the dominance of the ANC was evident not only at the national level but also in the provinces, where it retained outright majorities in seven, formed a coalition government with the IFP in KwaZulu-Natal, and won a plurality in Western Cape. In the national balloting, the Democratic Party (DP), led by Tony LEON, displaced the NP (subsequently reconstituted as the New National Party [NNP]) as the leading opposition formation, winning 38 seats (up from 7 in 1994), while the NNP managed only 28, a net loss of 54. Facing diminished prospects, in June 2000 the NNP joined the DP in forming a Democratic Alliance (DA), the expectation being that a full merger of the parties would eventually occur. The DA surprised many observers by winning 23 percent of the national vote in the December municipal elections, but policy and leadership clashes ultimately led the NNP to part ways with the DP in October 2001. In abandoning the DA for a closer relationship with the ANC, the NNP's van Schalkwyk noted that the two erstwhile antagonists no longer had significant ideological differences. Thus, at the end of 2001 the only opposition formations with more than a handful of National Assembly members were the rump DA (the DP plus the small Federal Alliance) and the United Democratic Movement.

In June 2001, public hearings opened into a December 1999 arms deal involving the purchase of surface ships, submarines, helicopters, and jet aircraft from a number of EU countries, at a cost of $5.4 billion. Despite accusations that officials had received kickbacks and engaged in other illegalities, in November the resultant report concluded that the procurement procedure had been flawed but not corrupt, although individuals who had derived "some form of benefit from the acquisition process" could be held criminally liable. The National Assembly opposition condemned the report as a whitewash. Throughout much of the following decade, the affair led to legal troubles for Jacob Zuma.

The Truth and Reconciliation Commission intended to release the final volumes of its report in 2002, but publication was delayed when the IFP went to court in opposition to conclusions that it had been responsible for major human rights violations. The final report was presented to the president in 2003. The commission granted amnesty to 1,200 people but rejected more than 5,000 other applications. After rejecting a suggestion that a special tax be imposed on companies that had profited from apartheid, Mbeki announced that those designated as victims by the TRC would each receive a single payment worth $3,800.

In 2000–2002 the Mbeki administration drew severe criticism for its failure to present a cohesive plan for fighting the HIV/AIDS crisis. Late in 2002 the government announced that it would look into making crucial antiretroviral drugs available through the public health system.

In February 2004 Mbeki signed into law the controversial Restitution of Land Rights Amendment Act, which gave the state the right to expropriate land for restitution purposes without a court order or the seller's agreement. The act applied only to land from which blacks were forcibly removed under the colonial and apartheid regimes. "Just and equitable" compensation was guaranteed to farmers whose land was expropriated. The legislation was an attempt to overcome logjams under the "willing buyer, willing seller" policy, which had been marked by disputes over fair market value of land.

In the elections to the National Assembly and the provincial councils on April 14, 2004, the ANC emerged as the dominant party, winning 279 of the 400 National Assembly seats with 69.7 percent of the vote. The ANC also took control of seven of the nine provincial assemblies and nominated premiers to head all nine provincial governments. On April 23, President Mbeki was reelected by the National Assembly for a second term. Members of the NNP and Azapo were included in the subsequent cabinet, as were six members of the SACP. On August 7 Marthinus VAN SCHALKWYK announced the dissolution of the NNP, asked its members to join the ANC (as van Schalkwyk and some of his colleagues had, former president de Klerk being a notable exception), and agreed to contest all future elections under the ANC banner. In June former president Nelson Mandela officially retired from public life.

In June 2005, Schabir SHAIK, financial adviser to deputy president Jacob Zuma, was found guilty of two counts of corruption and one count of fraud in one of the most closely watched criminal trials since the end of apartheid. On June 15 Zuma, who the judge said was "compliant" in the malfeasance, was dismissed as deputy president. Two weeks later he was charged with two counts of bribery. However, a groundswell of popular support developed for Zuma, a key figure in the fight against apartheid, COSATU describing the pending legal action as a "political trial" and calling on President Mbeki to reinstate Zuma. At year's end, matters became further complicated when Zuma was charged with raping the 31-year-old daughter of a friend. In May 2006 a judge acquitted Zuma of the rape charge, and within days Zuma was reinstated as ANC deputy president.

In local elections on March 1, 2006, the ANC was unseated in Cape Town where Helen ZILLE of the DA became mayor of the only opposition-controlled city in the country. The DA cited subsequent ANC maneuvers to abolish Zille's position as further evidence of the ANC's drive for power and inability to accept electoral defeat.

In the midst of the ANC's June 2007 national policy conference and a huge public service strike, COSATU's general secretary, Zwelinzima VAVI, claimed Mbeki's government had marginalized not only COSATU and the SACP, but also the ANC. COSATU and the SACP became increasingly vocal critics of President Mbeki, denouncing what they said were his autocratic tendencies, conservative and probusiness economic policies, and alleged failure to address unemployment, poverty, and inequality effectively.

Mbeki's status declined after he lost the ANC chair at the party's 2008 convention (see Political Parties, below). Further, Zuma appeared to be encroaching on his position. In March Zuma declared that the ANC, rather than the government, was the main source of political power in South Africa, and in April he visited the United Kingdom, where he met with Prime Minister Gordon Brown in a manner more suggestive of a head of government than a party leader. Together, they called for a break in the Zimbabwean electoral stalemate (see article on Zimbabwe), demanding that Zimbabwean president Robert Mugabe release the election results.

The criminal case against Zuma proceeded slowly through much of 2008. Some of Zuma's ANC supporters, particularly in the party's youth wing, threatened bloodshed if he were convicted. Zuma, in turn, promised to name names if he were ever made to give evidence. Some news reports had linked President Mbeki to the arms scandal, and it was assumed that Zuma would accuse Mbeki if necessary. After numerous postponements, the case appeared to have finally collapsed on September 12, 2008, when a High Court judge ruled that the case against Zuma could not continue. The judge said that Zuma's constitutional rights had been denied because he had not been questioned before charges were brought. In a blow to Mbeki's reputation, the judge expressed suspicion that the prosecution had been politically motivated, noting that the latest round of charges against Zuma came shortly after he defeated Mbeki for the ANC presidency. The judge criticized all parties in the case and emphasized that they were eroding South Africa's reputation for electoral freedom and an independent judiciary. (Charges against Zuma were reinstated but were thrown out of court shortly before the April 2009 elections.)

After the High Court ruling, the ANC voted on September 24, 2008, to ask Mbeki to step down as president. Mbeki agreed to honor the motion when parliament named his replacement. The ANC nominated Kgalema MOTLANTHE, its deputy leader and an ally of Zuma, as caretaker president until the 2009 presidential election. Parliament ratified the choice on September 25, and Motlanthe was sworn in. Mbeki's departure prompted 11 cabinet resignations. Some resignations were a courtesy to the new president, as in the case of Trevor Manuel, the well-respected finance minister who resigned but was reappointed. Other ministers were unwilling to serve in the new administration. The replacement of health minister Mantombazana TSHABALALA-MSIMANG, who had advocated garlic and beetroot to combat HIV, was widely praised.

President Mbeki's forced resignation angered many within the ANC. Among the ministers resigning in protest was Defense Minister Mosiuoa LEKOTA, who led a dissident group in forming a new political party to contest the spring 2009 elections. Many observers believed the new party might deny the ANC the two-thirds majority necessary to change the constitution. The ANC successfully challenged two names proposed for the new party by claiming ownership rights over each. Ultimately, the new party was granted the name Congress of the People (COPE) over the ANC's objections. In January 2011, a document from WikiLeaks suggested that Mbeki had been involved in writing a policy statement for COPE. Mbeki denied this, and the ANC declared that he was still a member in good standing.

In the run-up to the 2009 elections, the Constitutional Court confirmed an earlier High Court decision allowing South African citizens living outside the country to vote. The campaign was marked by intermittent violence, and several unions vowed to boycott the elections. Desmond Tutu initially said he would not vote but later changed his mind. Critics also objected to Zuma's appeal for support from members of his tribe, the Zulus, and his apparent willingness to distribute key positions to loyalists. They argued that tribalism and related practices were incompatible with South Africa's modern social aspirations and norms. Despite increasing poverty and persistent inequality during the period of ANC rule, Zuma remained popular with poor black voters. He also made significant efforts to court Afrikaners, addressing them as a "white tribe" implicitly superior to English-speaking (and presumably nontribal) whites. Middle-class blacks and ANC dissidents, however, increasingly gravitated toward COPE, while the DA remained the party of choice for many whites and made inroads with the Coloureds.

The ANC won the poll on April 22, 2009, with a vote share of 65.9 percent, just short of the two-thirds majority required to amend the constitution, something observers attributed to the rising profile of COPE. The ANC won 294 Assembly seats, followed by the Democratic Alliance with 67. On May 6, the National Assembly elected Zuma president. Days later, he named Kgalema Petrus MOTLANTHE as deputy president and formed a new government.

Facing an economic recession and high unemployment, the government announced in June that it would not expropriate white-owned farms, a move deemed harmful to the economy. Zuma's first two years in office were met with praise for programs to providing AIDS treatment drugs for pregnant women. But the country was plagued by intermittent strikes, including tens of thousands of government workers demanding an 8.6 percent pay raise in hospitals and schools. Zuma's administration took some measures to fight corruption, but observers noted troublesome issues remain, including a lack of transparency in government and the militarization of police.

A major cabinet reshuffle occurred on October 31, 2010; 7 ministers were dismissed, and 14 new deputy ministers were appointed, among other changes. The move was widely seen as an attempt by Zuma to cater to allies in the ANC rather than enhance the effectiveness of government. Another, albeit minor, cabinet reshuffle occurred in June 2012.

Constitution and government. Under the Interim Constitution adopted by the outgoing Parliament on December 22, 1993, a president, named for a five-year term by the National Assembly, exercised executive power. Legislative authority was vested in a bicameral Parliament consisting of a Senate, 10 of whose 90 members were elected from each of nine regional legislatures, and a National Assembly, half of whose 400 members were elected from national and half from regional party lists. The two houses sat jointly as a Constituent Assembly, which debated and approved a permanent constitution (see below). The Interim Constitution detailed rights of citizenship, which for the first time constituted a universal bill of rights applying equally to all races, to be safeguarded by a Constitutional Court as the supreme judicial authority. In its first major ruling on June 6, 1995, the Court decided unanimously to abolish the death penalty in South Africa.

The four historic provinces (Cape, Natal, Orange Free State, and Transvaal) were replaced by nine new provinces: Eastern Cape, Eastern Transvaal (now Mpumalanga), KwaZulu-Natal, Northern Cape, Northern Transvaal (now Limpopo), North-West, Orange Free State (now Free State), Pretoria-Witwatersrand-Vereeniging (PWV, now Gauteng), and Western Cape, each with an elected legislature. Under the new provincial structure, the four "independent" and six "self- governing" black homelands created by the apartheid government were effectively abolished. (For details regarding the "independent" homelands, see the 1993 edition of the *Handbook,* pp. 762–772.) Town and city councils were established as multiracial, with white and black voters each electing 30 percent of the councilors and the remainder being selected on a nonracial basis.

In November 1995, following 18 months of work by the Constituent Assembly, the first draft of the new permanent constitution was published, with the main political parties reaching agreement on a final version on May 7, 1996, shortly before the expiry of the deadline set during the transitional period. The following day the text was approved overwhelmingly by Parliament. The NP voted in favor, despite its reservations over provisions relating to labor relations, property rights, language, and education, in order to safeguard concessions already secured from the ANC. The IFP was absent for the vote, maintaining its boycott of the Constituent Assembly, from which it had withdrawn in April 1995. Ratified in its final version on December 4 by the Constitutional Court, which had previously rejected certain draft clauses, particularly in relation to the reduction of provincial powers, the new constitution was finally signed into law on December 10 by President Mandela in a ceremony in Sharpeville. The IFP, which had briefly returned to the Constituent Assembly on October 1 before withdrawing again on October 7, accepted the legitimacy of the new document.

The new constitution took effect February 4, 1997. The new basic law incorporated many essentials of the 1993 text, although it abandoned the principle that all parties with 5 percent of the vote should be represented in the cabinet. It also provided for a National Council of Provinces (NCOP) to replace the existing Senate, with the aim of enhancing the influence of the provinces on the policy of the central government—although it fell short of guaranteeing the provincial powers that the IFP had demanded. In addition, it enshrined an extensive bill of rights, one of the most liberal in the world. In the future, changes to the constitution would require the approval of at least two-thirds of the members of the National Assembly and at least six of the nine provinces represented in the National Council.

With regard to ordinary legislation, the powers exercised by the two houses vary. Bills affecting the republic as a whole are introduced in the National Assembly and, if passed, proceed to the NCOP, where the members, voting individually, may concur or may propose changes for consideration by the assembly. Bills affecting the provinces may be introduced in either house, but in the NCOP each of the nine provincial delegations has one vote. If the two chambers disagree on a provincial bill, an 18-member mediation committee (9 members from each chamber) attempts to reconcile the differences and return compromise legislation for a new vote in both houses. Failing that, the National Assembly may pass the bill with a two-thirds vote and send it on for presidential signature.

In early 1997, the legislature approved the creation of a National House of Traditional Leaders, aiming to provide a forum for the leaders of tribal groups and increasing communication between the legislature and the provinces. The new body was inaugurated on April 17. Members are named by provincial-level Houses of Traditional Leaders. In 2001 the Department of Justice and Constitutional Development, responding largely to requests from rural areas, announced that traditional leaders would be permitted to function as Commissioners of Oaths (with a function similar to that of a notary public). At the same time, the Department of Provincial and Local Government has begun the process of more clearly delineating the powers and functions of the traditional leadership.

Provincial governments are led by elected legislatures of 30 to 80 members. Each legislature elects a provincial premier, who heads an Executive Council. Beneath the provincial level are 284 municipalities, including 6 metropolitan municipalities ("megacities," incorporating surrounding townships): Cape Town, Durban Unicity, Ekurhuleni (East Rand), Johannesburg, Nelson Mandela (Port Elizabeth), and Tshwane (Pretoria). Legislatures are elected at each municipal level. In 2000 the proportion of traditional representatives on councils was raised from 10 to 20 percent. The smaller jurisdictions are represented throughout the governmental system by the South African Local Government Association (SALGA).

The 1996 constitution had an antidefection clause prohibiting floor-crossing because it was felt that permitting representatives to change parties would interfere with the proportional electoral system. In June 2002 legislation regulated floor-crossing in national, provincial, and local government elections. Legislators wishing to change parties were required to do so within the first 15 days of the second year of a legislative term; they could form another party or merge with a party without losing their seats. The UDM and others submitted an urgent application to the Constitutional Court challenging the constitutionality of the new legislation. In October the court ruled that floor-crossing at the municipal level could proceed but indicated that the legislation for the national and provincial levels had technical deficiencies and would require redrafting. In February 2003 the constitution was amended to permit members of the National Assembly and the nine provincial legislatures to switch allegiances from one party to another, thus bringing uniformity to the three levels of government regarding defections. In January 2009, floor crossing was again abolished by the parliament.

Freedom of the press is guaranteed, and Reporters Without Borders ranked South Africa 52nd out of 179 countries in media freedom in 2013, the sixth highest rating for an African state.

Foreign relations. Although South Africa was a founding member of the United Nations, its international standing was greatly impaired as a result of the racial restrictions maintained in its own territory and, until late 1988, that of Namibia (South West Africa). In the post–World War II period its rejection of external advice and pressure resulted in an atrophy of international contacts, notably through its departure from the Commonwealth in 1961, its suspension from membership in the Economic Commission for Africa in 1963, and its withdrawal or expulsion from a number of UN Specialized Agencies. It was also denied participation in the UN General Assembly, which repeatedly condemned the policy and practice of apartheid and advocated "universally applied economic sanctions" as the only means of achieving a peaceful solution to the problem. The UN Security Council, while stopping short of economic measures, called as early as 1963 for an embargo on the sale and shipment to South Africa of military equipment and materials.

Relations with the United Nations were further aggravated by South Africa's refusal to apply economic sanctions against Rhodesia, as ordered by the Security Council in 1966, and its long-standing refusal to relinquish control over Namibia, as ordered by both the General Assembly and the Security Council. Despite its political isolation on these key issues, Pretoria refrained from quitting the world body and attempted to maintain friendly political relations and close economic ties with most Western countries. Regionally, it belonged to the Southern African Customs Union (SACU), along with Botswana, Lesotho, Swaziland, and, later, Namibia. It also cooperated closely with the Ian Smith regime in Rhodesia over economic and defense matters, assisting its neighbor in circumventing UN sanctions. However, in accordance with its policy of seeking détente with neighboring black regimes, it publicly called for a "resolution of the Rhodesian question," endorsing in 1976 the principle of black majority rule if appropriate guarantees were extended to the white minority of what became in 1980 the Republic of Zimbabwe.

For more than a decade the government mounted repeated forays into Angola in its protracted conflict with Namibian insurgents, while relations with Swaziland and Mozambique were aggravated by the presence of ANC guerrilla bases in both countries, despite the conclusion of a nonaggression pact with the former in 1982 and with the latter in May 1984.

During 1985, Western states came under increased pressure to impose sanctions on the Botha government. U.S. president Ronald Reagan had long opposed any action that would disrupt the South African economy, but faced in mid-September with a congressional threat to act on its own, he ordered a number of modest punitive actions, with the countries of the European Community (EC, subsequently the EU) following in an equally restrained manner. The principal American prohibitions focused on bank loans and the export of nuclear technology and computers, while the Europeans imposed an oil embargo, halted most arms sales, and withdrew their military attachés. In addition, substantial corporate divestment occurred, particularly by U.S. firms. None of these sanctions presented a serious challenge to South Africa, which was, however, sufficiently aggrieved to threaten an embargo on the export of strategic metals to the United States.

Pretoria's capacity to act with impunity in regard to neighboring states was amply demonstrated during 1986. On January 1 Lesotho was effectively blockaded, and three weeks later its government was overthrown by forces supportive of South African efforts to contain cross-border attacks by ANC guerrillas. Subsequently, on May 19, ANC targets in Botswana, Zambia, and Zimbabwe were subjected to bombing attacks by the South African Air Force, in addition to ground raids by units of the SADF. Additional forays were conducted against alleged ANC bases in Swaziland late in the year and in Zambia in early 1987.

During 1988, South Africa's regional posture softened dramatically. In September, President Botha traveled to Mozambique for his first state visit to a black African country. "Fruitful and cordial" discussions were held with President Chissano on a variety of topics, including the supply of power from Mozambique's Cahora Bassa hydroelectric facility, the status of Mozambican workers in South Africa, and "reactivation and reinforcement" of the Nkomati agreement of March 1984, which promised mutual nonaggression between South Africa and Mozambique. Subsequently, Botha visited Zaire and Côte d'Ivoire for talks with presidents Mobuto and Houphouët-Boigny, respectively. The most important development, however, concerned the Angola-Namibia conflict. During a November meeting in Geneva, Switzerland, Pretoria accepted a U.S.-mediated agreement, previously endorsed by Angola and Cuba, for the phased withdrawal of Cuban troops from Angola, accompanied by a withdrawal of all but 1,000 South African troops from Namibia and a UN-supervised election seven months thereafter in implementation of UN Security Council Resolution 435 of 1978. A protocol finalizing the agreement was signed in Brazzaville, Congo, on December 13, followed by the formal conclusion of a tripartite peace accord at UN headquarters in New York on December 22 (for details, see articles on Angola and Namibia). Not addressed by the Namibia settlement was the status of the port enclave of Walvis Bay, which, although historically South African territory, had been administered since 1977 as part of South West Africa. Discussions on the issue began in March 1991, but it was not until August 16, 1993, in a major decision of the multiparty forum convened to decide the future of South Africa, that the South African government delegation agreed under pressure from the ANC and other participants to transfer the Walvis Bay enclave to Namibia. Formal conveyance occurred at midnight on February 28, 1994.

In a setback for ANC efforts to increase Pretoria's diplomatic isolation, in September 1990 President de Klerk was received at the White House by U.S. president George H. W. Bush. A few days earlier Foreign Minister Botha had announced that South Africa was prepared to accede to the UN Nuclear Non-Proliferation Treaty (see International Atomic Energy Agency, under UN: Related Organizations) in furtherance of an effort to make the African continent a nuclear weapons–free zone.

The progress made in dismantling apartheid during 1991 yielded significant diplomatic gains for Pretoria globally and on the African continent. Most economic sanctions imposed by Western nations (save in regard to military items) were relaxed, and in April 1992, after a number of political exchanges with neighboring regimes, President de Klerk made a highly symbolic state visit to Nigeria for talks with the incumbent chair of the Organization of African Unity (OAU, subsequently the AU, Ibrahim Babangida. No less symbolic was South Africa's return to international sport.

On July 1, 1993, President de Klerk and ANC President Mandela held separate meetings in Washington with U.S. president Bill Clinton and three days later were joint recipients of Liberty Medals in Philadelphia, with President Clinton in attendance. The end of apartheid was further celebrated on October 15, when de Klerk and Mandela were jointly awarded the 1993 Nobel Peace Prize. At the same time, most UN economic sanctions against South Africa were terminated.

During 1994, South Africa gradually reentered the international community. On June 1 it rejoined the Commonwealth after a break of 33 years; two weeks later it became the 53rd member of the OAU. On June 23, following the Security Council's lifting of its long-standing arms embargo on South Africa, the suspension of Pretoria's participation in the UN General Assembly was rescinded, thus facilitating full reintegration into the world body. Two months later, South Africa joined the Southern African Development Community (SADC), and in October it signed an economic cooperation agreement with the EU.

In November 1996, the South African government announced that it was canceling its diplomatic relations with Taiwan, one of its foremost trading partners, and establishing formal relations with the People's Republic of China.

In the fall of 1998, South Africa deployed troops to help restore order in Lesotho in the fall (see article on Lesotho for details). President Mandela also continued to pursue a role as Africa's most prominent peacemaker, becoming heavily involved, for example, in efforts to resolve the conflict in the Democratic Republic of the Congo. In addition, the government further exhibited the independent nature of its foreign policy by extending ties with Iraq and North Korea, despite strong objections from Washington and several EU capitals.

South Africa has emerged in recent years as an ambitious diplomatic power. Mbeki was the leading figure behind the New Partnership for Africa's Development (NEPAD) and was instrumental in brokering peace in Burundi and the Democratic Republic of the Congo, providing 3,000 troops in the two countries as part of UN peacekeeping operations and also shouldering most of the financial burden. South African companies have struck out north with strong investment strategies. With 40 percent of sub-Saharan Africa's GDP, South Africa is the only country capable of projecting both military power and economic clout.

South Africa consistently opposed the U.S.-led war in Iraq and has promoted relations with many countries with whom the United States is at odds. Nevertheless, the United States considers South Africa as an ally in its efforts to promote democracy in the continent.

Mbeki was deeply involved in efforts to resolve the 2008 political crisis in neighboring Zimbabwe (see entry on Zimbabwe).

The Zuma administration has made a strong push to enhance South Africa's international stance. U.S. Secretary of State Hillary Rodham Clinton visited South Africa in August 2009 in an effort to improve bilateral relations. She also suggested that South Africa take a leading role in helping poorer African countries and work for political stability in Zimbabwe. In the same month, South Africa and India pledged stronger economic ties.

In August 2010, Zuma made a state visit to China, where he signed numerous business deals and announced that talks were in progress for South Africa to join BRIC, an economic coalition of Brazil, Russia, India, and China. South Africa formally joined the group, hereafter known as BRICS, in January 2011.

In September 2010, at the South African–European Union summit, Brussels reaffirmed the EU's commitment to a strategic partnership with South Africa, the EU's leading trade partner in Africa.

Prior to the 2011 Libyan civil war, Zuma's relations with strongman Muammar Qadhafi had been quite friendly, and his attitude to the conflict was somewhat inconsistent. In early March South Africa, a nonpermanent member of the UN Security Council, voted to impose a no-fly zone over Libya, authorizing military action, if necessary, to enforce it and to protect civilians. And Zuma telephoned Qadhafi, demanding that he stop killing civilians. On March 10 he introduced a resolution in the AU to suspend Libya's membership in that body and instructed the South African Treasury to freeze any asset transactions involving the Libyan leader. But Zuma spoke out against regime change in Libya, and called on the NATO (North Atlantic Treaty Organization) countries to use restraint. On May 30 he visited Tripoli as an AU representative in an attempt to find a diplomatic solution to the conflict.

On October 4, 2012, four months after several months of waiting for a visa to visit South Africa for the 80th birthday of Archbishop Desmond Tutu, the Dalai Lama withdrew his application. In response, Tutu surprised journalists with an angry tirade alleging that the South African government had caved to pressure from China and comparing the ANC's rule to that of the apartheid regime and the governments of Hosni Mubarak and Qadhafi.

In November 2011, *Africa Confidential* reported that two teams of South African mercenaries—ex-soldiers and police recruited in Cape Town—had been working in Libya, presumably with some level of support from South African officials; one team was helping members of the Qadhafi family escape, and another was escorting Muammar Qadhafi when his convoy was bombed. South African officials had also reportedly asked Zimbabwe to take in Qadhafi's son, Seif al Islam, but were rebuffed.

In June 2012, South Africa was one of seven states granted waivers by the United States on oil imports from Iran. The waiver allowed South Africa to avoid U.S. sanctions targeted at countries that imported Iranian oil.

In April 2013, the Central African Republic (CAR) requested that South African peacekeeping forces be withdrawn from the country. Meanwhile, the mission, which had suffered 13 dead and 27 wounded by April, grew increasingly unpopular among the South African public. Opposition figures asserted that the mission was undertaken solely at the behest of mining interests seeking access to the CAR's mineral resources. In May, South Africa announced it would consider rebuilding a border fence in an effort to stop poaching in Kruger National Park. The original fence had been demolished in an effort to create a supranational park, the Great Limpopo Transfrontier Park, with Mozambique. However, by 2013, more than 240 rhinos were being killed annually, mainly by poachers from Mozambique (see entry on Mozambique).

Current issues. Throughout 2011 and 2012, corruption allegations provided ammunition for Zuma's critics in a deepening rift within the ANC over his bid for a second term as president (see Political Parties, below). In October 2011, under mounting pressure from the opposition to tackle corruption, Zuma fired two government ministers and suspended a police chief: Cooperative Governance Minister Sicelo SHICEKA stood accused of spending more than $68,000 of government money on unauthorized travel and hotel bills, including a visit to a girlfriend jailed in Switzerland for drug smuggling; Public Works Minister Gwendeline MAHLANGU-NKABINDE and police chief Bheki CELE, a close Zuma ally, were accused of authorizing deals to lease property for police headquarters at inflated prices from a well-connected businessman.

In his state-of-the-nation speech on February 9, 2012, Zuma announced a massive public spending program: $112 billion in power generation, transport, and telecom investments and more than $50 billion to build six new power stations by 2030. While the government's stated goals included doubling the current average growth rate of 3.5 percent and creating 5 million new jobs by 2020, critics allege that wealthy ANC supporters will receive state contracts for the program in exchange for political and financial backing of Zuma.

On July 15, Nkosazana DLAMINI-ZUMA, South Africa's home affairs minister and the ex-wife of President Zuma, won the chairmanship of the AU over Gabon's incumbent Jean Ping. The vote ended months of gridlock after neither secured the required two-thirds majority at an AU summit in January. *Africa Confidential* reported that some believe Zuma supported his ex-wife's AU candidacy to keep her out of the impending contest for the ANC presidency.

On August 16, police opened fire on a crowd of 3,000 striking miners at the Marikana platinum mine in Lonmin, killing 34 and wounding 78 others. The police claimed they were defending themselves from a crowd armed with machetes and spears. But, the Marikana Massacre touched a political nerve as the mining sector is considered by some in the ANC to be a bastion of white control. In the week before the shooting, 10 people, including 2 police officers, had been killed at the mine in a conflict between rival unions: The long-dominant National Union of Mineworkers (NUM), a key supporter of the ANC, was challenged by the Association of Mineworkers and Construction Union (AMCU). Zuma cut short a trip to a regional summit in Mozambique to visit the mine and announce an inquiry; critics attacked Zuma for spending more time talking to Lonmin executives than to the miners. Analysts suggested that, because Zuma could order police to bring strikers under control, he was vulnerable to charges of complicity, complicating his reelection bid. In the weeks that followed, the mine's operations came to a halt, and global platinum prices jumped.

A new round of labor unrest peaked in October 2012 when wildcat mine strikes spread to other sectors, eventually involving an estimated 100,000 workers and including employers such as Toyota. Most of the strikes were settled by late October following a negotiated settlement with mine companies that included series of concessions and minor wage increases. The labor strife cost South Africa an estimated $5 billion and reportedly prompted foreign firms to reconsider locating new plants in the country. Continuing labor unrest led Fitch to downgrade South Africa's credit rating in January 2013.

On February 14, 2013, South African Olympian Oscar PISTORIUS was arrested for the murder of his girlfriend. The high-profile case, combined with the brutal murder of 17-year-old Anene BOOYSEN, prompted renewed public attention on the problem of violence toward women and gun ownership (South Africa has one of the highest rates of gun ownership in Africa). Meanwhile, also in February, Zuma announced the National Development Plan, a $33 billion stimulus program designed to improve infrastructure and create 11 million jobs.

In May 2013, the AMCU refused to sign a new mining pact, and violence again flared in Lonmin. Security forces used rubber bullets to disperse protesting miners. Meanwhile, the NUM renewed a call for the nationalization of the mining sector following an announcement that the Anglo-American Platinum Corporation would lay-off some 14,000 workers. The unrest spread to farms and an estimated 1,500 agricultural workers went on strike.

Nelson Mandela was hospitalized on June 8, 2013, for a lung infection and remained in critical care for his 95th birthday on July 18. He passed away at his home on December 5.

In late summer, Zuma signed the controversial Protection of Personal Information Bill (POPI). The measure allowed the government to classify almost any information about government activities as secret. A companion measure established an independent commission to sanction elements of the press that did not sufficiently censor themselves. Both measures were vigorously opposed as attacking the roots of South African democracy and a serious turn away from postapartheid South Africa's tradition of openness and toleration of free speech.

POLITICAL PARTIES

During most of the apartheid era South Africa's leading political party was the predominantly Afrikaner National Party (NP), which came to power in 1948 and steadily increased its parliamentary strength to a high of 134 (64.8 percent) of lower house seats in the November 1977 election, before falling to 94 seats (48.1 percent) in 1989.

In 2003, five new parties were represented in the assembly: the **African Independent Movement** (AIM), the ADP, the ID, **National Action** (NA), and the **Peace and Justice Congress** (PJC), as the result of floor crossing.

By 2007 the Democratic Alliance (DA) was the chief opposition party, holding 50 seats while the ANC had 279 seats. By this time AIM, the ADP, the NA, and the PJC had disappeared from the National Assembly. The 2009 elections granted Congress of the People (COPE), an ANC splinter group, the third largest number of seats in Parliament.

Government Parties:

African National Congress (ANC). Organized in 1912 as the South African Native National Congress and long recognized as South Africa's leading black formation, the ANC (as it became known in 1923) was banned from 1960 to February 1990. The organization's most charismatic figure, Nelson Mandela, was released from prison in February 1990, while its president, Oliver Tambo, was permitted to return from more than three decades' exile the following December. (Tambo died in 1993.)

On May 28–31, 1992, the ANC held a policy conference in Johannesburg, during which it celebrated its evolution from a liberation movement to a political party and replaced a 1955 commitment to comprehensive nationalization with an emphasis on a mixed economy. In January 1994, prior to its assumption of power, it did, however, announce an ambitious program to end economic apartheid by redistributing land, building more than a million low-income dwellings, assuming state control of the mining industry, and breaking up white-owned conglomerates. The draft plan, known as the Reconstruction and Development Program, drew immediate criticism from the country's business leaders and yielded a caveat from Mandela that it required "a substantial amount of additional work to be anywhere near what we want it to be."

Since April 1994, the ANC has governed in a tripartite alliance with COSATU and the SACP, whose leaders appear on ANC party lists. Among those elected on the ANC ticket in the party's landslide election victory in April 1994 was Winnie Mandela, the controversial estranged wife of the new president, whose 1991 conviction for kidnapping and being an accessory to assault did not prevent her appointment as a deputy minister in the new government. In a strengthening of radical elements in the party leadership, Winnie Mandela regained her position on the ANC executive at the 49th congress in December, when First Deputy President Thabo Mbeki succeeded the ailing Sisulu as ANC vice president, thus becoming President Mandela's heir apparent. Mrs. Mandela's dismissal from the government in March 1995, following her public assertions that it lacked radicalism, drew official endorsement from ANC bodies, although she retained strong rank-and-file support. The Mandelas' 38-year marriage ended in divorce in March 1996.

In November 1995, the ANC won 66.4 percent of the votes cast in South Africa's first democratic local elections. In August 1996 President Mandela formally notified the ANC executive committee that he would not seek a second presidential term in the elections due in 1999 and that he would relinquish the ANC presidency at the party's next national conference in 1997.

As expected, at the ANC's congress held December 16–20, 1997, Nelson Mandela announced his retirement from the party's top post and his chosen successor, Thabo Mbeki, was unopposed in the subsequent election for party president. Also unopposed in their runs for party posts were Zuma, Kgalema Motlanthe (secretary general), and Mendi MSIMANG (treasurer general). Winnie Mandela secured a seat on the National Executive Committee.

The ANC unsuccessfully tried to block release of the comprehensive TRC report in the fall of 1998, objecting to conclusions that the ANC had been responsible for human rights abuses and acts of terrorism against its opponents during the anti-apartheid campaign and prior to the 1994 balloting. Party officials, led by Mbeki, condemned the report as "scurrilous," but President Mandela, in a pointed departure from the views of his successor, acknowledged that some of the abuses reported by the TRC had occurred and chastised the other ANC leaders for their angry response. Winnie Mandela was singled out in the TRC report for her alleged role in violent acts committed by the Mandela United Football Club, described as her "private army."

In the June 1999 elections, the ANC widened its parliamentary majority to 266 seats (with a 66.4 percent vote share) and retained control of seven provincial legislatures. It joined the IFP in a coalition government in KwaZulu-Natal and then in November 2001, having negotiated a cooperation agreement with the NNP, joined in forming a new administration in the ninth province, Western Cape, where it held a plurality of council seats.

The ANC's entrenchment as the dominant party in South African politics was helped by the splintering of opposition parties and by its ability to woo opposition legislators and career politicians with jobs and favors. The ANC has made heavy inroads among Zulus, other working-class blacks, Indians, and Coloureds. It still has not won over many white voters, who generally vote for the DA or other white liberal or right-wing parties.

At the ANC's five-yearly national policy conference, June 27–30, 2007, Mbeki warned the SACP and COSATU not to try to dictate ANC policy. The conference adopted a compromise on the succession issue. It was agreed that it was party "preference" but not a "principle" that the party leader and the president be the same person.

ANC custom makes it inappropriate for candidates to declare their interest in the party's presidential post, as one is supposed to be asked to serve. Mbeki said he would be willing to continue to serve as ANC president if asked to do so. At the same time, the COSATU and SACP leadership announced their support for Zuma, in part due to his pledge to pursue a more left-wing agenda than Mbeki should he come to power.

In 2007, many Mbeki loyalists were also ousted from ANC leadership positions, and some of them eventually left the ANC to form the COPE. Jacob Zuma was elected president of the ANC at the party's leadership convention on December 18, easily defeating Mbeki. Zuma, a populist who enjoyed the support of trade unions, the Communist Party of South Africa, and other left-wing elements of the ANC, consequently became the presumptive ANC candidate for the 2009 presidential election. His status remained compromised by corruption charges that were reinstated shortly after the convention but were dropped just before his April 2009 election as president of the republic. The party dominated the April 2009 national elections, but while retaining a large overall majority among voters, it suffered a noticeable decline in the May 2011 local elections, with its share reduced to 63.7 percent.

Throughout much of 2011 and 2012, a growing power struggle pitted Zuma against ANC Youth League President Julius MALEMA, who was quietly pushing Deputy President Kgalema Motlanthe to replace him, and others disappointed by Zuma's leadership and the abandonment of his initial promise to serve for only one term. Some party members reportedly claim that Zuma's primary motivation for seeking a second term is the fear that Mbeki's allies, angry at his ouster, may pursue criminal charges against Zuma after he leaves office (possibly over his role in the 1999 arms deal scandal). Consequently, Zuma was said to be taking greater control of the security services and using investigators to keep his political opponents off balance, including an investigation into Malema's financial affairs. In September, Zuma reportedly told the party's national executive committee he had appointed a commission of inquiry into the arms deal in order to head off a Constitutional Court inquiry into the matter. Meanwhile, General Secretary Gwede Mantashe's candid report on the state of the party, as described by *Africa Confidential,* said the ANC was in "shambles," divided into factions supporting or opposing Zuma's reelection and by groups trying to profit from access to state resources.

By November 2012, fierce purges were underway among opponents and supporters of Zuma's reelection bid. Citing "political risk issues," Moody's Investors Services downgraded the state-owned electrical utility Eskom's rating to "negative" on November 11. Within a week, the ANC disciplinary committee had suspended Malema for five years for undermining the presidency and bringing the party into disrepute, a decision Malema tried to appeal. By the February State of Union address, Zuma was seen to have strengthened his position. However, when he gathered the party's top leaders in April to endorse Molina's suspension, three refused: Deputy President Motlanthe, Deputy General Secretary Thandi MODISE, and Treasurer Mathews Phosa. By May, the power struggle encompassed not only the ranks of the party's leadership but also the security services, courts, and the state broadcasting service, where journalists were reportedly under pressure to uncover evidence of wrongdoing by Zuma's opponents. Still, other serious contenders for the presidency had emerged, including Human Settlements Minister Tokyo SEXWALE and businessman Cyril Ramaphosa (Ramaphosa, however, was subsequently tainted by his post on the board of the mine at Lonmin, where police killed workers. See Current issues, above). Julius Malema continued working to shore up support for Zuma's opponents in ANC Youth League structures across the provinces.

Rather than a substantive debate on issues, the June 25–29 ANC National Policy Conference was reportedly dominated by the clash of personalities and their supporters, who reportedly threw plastic water bottles at each other. Malema's office at the ANC headquarters was also burgled and computer hard drives stolen, and on June 30, a prominent ANC leader from KwaZulu-Natal was shot outside his home, a murder allegedly tied to the election controversy. Supporters of both Motlanthe and Sexwale looked to influence the choice of delegates, who would in turn elect the party leaders in the country's nine provinces. In the three largest provinces, Zuma was said to have near-total support in KwaZulu-Natal, Guateng was mostly split between Motlanthe and Sexwale, and Eastern Cape split between Zuma and Sexwale. Late in the year, Zuma was also challenged by Motlanthe for party leadership. Nevertheless, on December 19, 2012, Zuma was overwhelmingly reelected as the head of the ANC. Meanwhile, former pro-Zuma official, Malema, was expelled from the party after campaigning against the president. In January 2013, pro-Motlanthe members of the ANC executive committee were purged.

Reports in 2013 indicated a division within the party between General Secretary Gwede Manthase and deputy party president Cyril Ramaphose. In July, Limpopo premier Cassel MATHALE was recalled by the party, ostensibly for "poor performance." Reports indicated that Mathale's resignation was part of Zuma's continuing purge of potential rivals within the ANC. In July 2013, a new political grouping, the **Economic Freedom Fighters**—EFF, was formed by Malema.

Leaders: Jacob ZUMA (President of the Republic), Kgalema MOTLANTHE (Deputy President of the Republic), Baleka MBETE (National Chair), Cyril RAMAPHOSE (Deputy ANC President), Gwede MANTASHE (Secretary General), Mathews PHOSA (Treasurer General).

South African Communist Party (SACP). The SACP was formed in 1953, following the dissolution in 1950 of the original Communist Party of South Africa (CPSA), which had been organized in 1921 but had been banned by the Suppression of Communism Bill in 1950. The SACP has long cooperated closely with the ANC, to which a number of senior SACP members have been appointed. The party's former chair, Dr. Yusef DADOO, died in 1983, while its former general secretary, Moses MABHIDA, died in Maputo, Mozambique, in March 1986. A year later, following his appointment as Mabhida's successor, Joe SLOVO resigned as chief of staff of the ANC's military wing, *Umkhonto we Sizwe* (Spear of the Nation). He returned to South Africa in April 1990. The party gathered for a "relaunching"—its first public rally within South Africa in 40 years—on July 29, 1990. In a stinging opening address to the SACP's first legal congress on December 8, 1991, Slovo insisted that former Soviet President Mikhail Gorbachev had "completely lost his way" and that what was being buried in Eastern Europe was not true socialism. Subsequently, Slovo was elected party chair, with the longtime chief of *Umkhonto we Sizwe,* Chris Hani, being named his successor as general secretary. Hani was assassinated on April 10, 1993.

As members of the governing coalition, SACP members sit as ANC members in parliament, though they are identified as SACP in their cabinet biographies. Slovo was awarded the housing portfolio in the Mandela administration, but he died in January 1995. About 80 of the ANC's National Assembly representatives have SACP membership, as do a number of cabinet ministers.

At the SACP's national conference held in Port Elizabeth in July 2007, most of those elected to the Central Committee supported Jacob Zuma in his bid to become the next ANC president, while a number of pro-Mbeki cabinet members lost their committee posts. Several of the latter subsequently resigned from the party to protest the militant anti-Mbeki stance. Meanwhile, COSATU's president, Willie Madisha, was voted off the Central Committee for being perceived as pro-Mbeki. SACP General Secretary Blade Nzimande warned that the party would hold an extraordinary congress to consider a break with the ANC if Zuma was not elected as the next ANC president.

The SACP's membership has grown to over 50,000, 70 percent of whom are under 35 years old. The Young Communist League (YCL), the youth wing of the SACP, has thus become an important power broker in the SACP.

In July 2013, the SACP endorsed new restrictions on the media, including legislation that would criminalize criticism of the president and senior political leaders.

Leaders: Blade NZIMANDE (General Secretary), Jeremy CRONIN (Deputy General Secretary), Senzeni ZOKWANA (National Chair), Joyce MOLOI-MOROPA (National Treasurer).

Freedom Front Plus (*Vryheidsfront Plus*—VF Plus). This group was founded in 2004 by the Freedom Front (*Vryheidsfront*—VF), the CPSA, and the *Afrikaner Eenheids Beweging* to contest the upcoming national election as a single party.

The VF was launched by Gen. (Ret.) Constand Viljoen in March 1994 following a split in the Afrikaner People's Front (AVF; see discussion under CPSA, below) over the issue of participation in the April election, with the VF opting to register to present the case for a "white homeland." Several prominent members of the Conservative Party also defected to the new grouping. In late March the VF stated that its objective was a confederal South Africa based on the "inalienable and non-negotiable" right of self-determination for Afrikaners and all other groups. Subsequent to the April poll, in which it placed fourth with 2.2 percent of the vote, the Front insisted that blatant irregularities had occurred at 80 percent of the voting stations. Having achieved a measure of accommodation with the government under black majority rule, the VF welcomed President Mandela's proposal of June 1995 that a consultative referendum should be held to ascertain Afrikaners' views on the concept of a separate Afrikaner state.

In the TRC report issued in October 1998, General Viljoen was held accountable for certain acts of violence committed by right-wingers during the run-up to the 1994 balloting. Meanwhile, the VF was described as hoping to cooperate with the DP for the 1999 election, in which it won only 0.8 percent of the vote and three National Assembly seats (a loss of six). In August Viljoen was reelected party leader by one vote over Pieter Mulder, but in March 2001 he announced his retirement from active politics. On March 31 Mulder was unanimously elected as his successor.

Following the VF's legacy, the VF Plus seeks to protect and enhance Afrikaner rights and interests through the creation of an autonomous region. The proposed region lies between Northern Cape and Western Cape provinces. The VF Plus currently holds four assembly seats. In May 2008 Mulder announced that the VF Plus had established Afrikaners as a member group in the Unrepresented Nations and Peoples Organization (UNPO), an international organization, based in the Netherlands, that campaigns for the rights of minority and indigenous populations. The party has actively, and thus far successfully, opposed changing the name of South Africa's capital from Pretoria to Tshwane.

In the 2009 elections, the party retained its four seats in the National Assembly. Following the spring 2009 elections, the VF Plus offered its support to the incoming Zuma administration, and Mulder was named deputy minister of agriculture, forestry, and fisheries. Reports in 2013 indicated that the VF Plus was in negotiations to form an opposition coalition ahead of the 2014 balloting.

Leaders: Pieter MULDER (Party Leader), Abrie OOSTHUIZEN (Chair and Provincial Leader).

Other Parliamentary Parties:

Democratic Alliance (DA). The DA was established in late June 2000 by the Democratic Party (DP); the New National Party (NNP); and the small Federal Alliance (FA), which earlier in the month had agreed to present its candidates for upcoming local elections on the DP list. Formal merger of the three was delayed, however, pending passage of legislation permitting party consolidations. Initially seen as an attempt by the principal white formations to form a united front, the DA registered considerable success in the December municipal elections, taking 23 percent of the national vote and capturing Cape Town from the ANC. However, differences within the leadership resulted in the departure of the NNP from the DA in November 2001, and local defections in October 2002 delivered control of Cape Town to an ANC-NNP coalition.

Since it had been formed especially to contest the 2000 municipal elections, the DA's legal status was initially limited to the local level. Therefore, in order to constitute itself as a party at the provincial and national levels, the DA in 2001 launched an initiative in support of floor-crossing legislation, which, with the crucial support of the ANC, was passed by parliament in 2002. In the 2004 assembly balloting the DA emerged as the principal opposition party in the national parliament with 50 seats.

Tony Leon, leader of the DP/DA since 1994, said in November 2006 that he would not seek reelection at the 2007 party congress. At the DA's congress in March 2007, Helen Zille won 70 percent of the delegates' votes to replace Leon. Joe Seremane, the only black rival, won 6 percent of votes. In her acceptance speech, Zille criticized the ANC's "race-based politics," indicating that, like Leon, she would oppose affirmative action.

In the 2009 parliamentary elections, the DA won 67 seats in the National Assembly and 10 in the National Council of Provinces.

Throughout 2009 and 2010, the DA campaigned to have the corruption charges against President Zuma reinstated. In the July 2010 DA federal congress election, no black candidates were elected to senior positions in the party. The outcome embarrassed Zille, who vowed that in future the party would use democratic persuasion to ensure a more racially balanced ticket. The DA did well in the May 18, 2011, local elections. While failing to gain control of any major city in addition to its base in Cape Town, the party increased its share of the popular vote to 24.2 percent, as against 16.6 percent in the 2009 national election.

On October 27, 2011, the DA elected Lindiwe Mazibuko as its first black female parliamentary leader, a strategy to reach out to young black voters outside its traditional support base. Critics alleged she lacks support in black communities. In December 2012, Zille was reelected president of the DA, while Wilmot James was reelected chair.

Leaders: Helen ZILLE (President), Wilmot JAMES (Chair), Lindiwe MAZIBUKO (Parliamentary Leader), Mmusi MAIMANE (National Spokesperson).

Congress of the People (COPE). Congress of the People was the name finally given to the group that broke away from the ANC after Thabo Mbeki's forced resignation from the presidency in September 2008. Led by former defense minister Mosiuoa LEKOTA, COPE was formed to contest the April 2009 elections. Its aim was to deny the ANC the two-thirds majority needed to change the constitution. In this, COPE was successful, returning 30 members and becoming the third-largest parliamentary party behind the ANC and the DA. COPE's manifesto presents an alternative to a race-based, one-party state under the ANC to "depoliticize the institutions of state" and expedite economic growth for "large-scale labor absorption." COPE's December 2010 conference ended in a bitter, actually physical, struggle between President Mosiuoa LEKOTA and Deputy President Mbhazima SHILOWA for leadership of the party. Since that time the party has had two rival leaderships, with the dispute still in court in July 2013. COPE's credibility has declined greatly, and some of its parliamentarians returned to the ANC. In July 2013, there were calls to disband the Lekota-affiliated youth wing after the group's leader, Nqaba BHANGA, began negotiations with the Shilowa youth faction.

Leader: Mosiuoa LEKOTA (President and Parliamentary Leader).

Inkatha Freedom Party (IFP). In response to charges of tribalism, the *Inkatha,* a predominantly Zulu organization, voted at a general conference in 1990 to transform itself into a political party that would be open to all races; however, most observers felt that the organization remained primarily a vehicle for the expression of Zulu interests in KwaZulu. Dr. Mangosuthu Buthelezi, the KwaZulu homeland leader from 1978 to 1994, was unanimously elected president of the IFP. The party shares many ANC positions, except what it considers are the rights and prerogatives of "traditional leaders," as well as its emphasis on individual responsibility.

Bitterly opposed to the ANC and frequently engaged in violence with its larger rival, *Inkatha* declared in mid-1993 that it would not participate in the 1994 election and joined in an improbable alliance with the leading right-extremist parties and representatives of nominally independent Bophuthatswana and Ciskei in a Concerned South Africans Group (COSAG) that was subsequently styled the Freedom Alliance. Following the ouster of Bophuthatswana's Lucas Mangope in March 1994, however, the Alliance disintegrated, and the IFP agreed on April 19 to abandon its boycott of the election. It placed third. The group was awarded three portfolios in the ensuing Mandela administration, including the designation of IFP leader Buthelezi as home affairs minister. It nevertheless continued its deep disagreement with the ANC over constitutional and other issues, boycotting the Constituent Assembly charged with drafting a new constitution.

The intraparty schism between those members favoring continued participation in the national government (so-called moderates) and the Buthelezi-led, anti-ANC faction widened in early 1997. At a meeting of the National Council in January, the IFP's national chair, Frank MDLALOSE, and Secretary General Ziba Jiyane resigned and were replaced by Buthelezi supporters Ben NGUBANE and Zakhele KHUMALO, respectively. Subsequently, in March, 13 IFP activists were convicted for their roles in the slaying of 19 ANC members in 1995.

The TRC accused the IFP of having caused the death of nearly 4,000 opponents in KwaZulu in 1982–1994, attributing ultimate responsibility for the violence in large part to Chief Buthelezi, who did not testify before the commission or request amnesty. Subsequently, the IFP election campaign in 1999 focused on economic issues. In the June balloting the party won 34 seats in the National Assembly on an 8.6 percent vote share. It continued as national government partner of the ANC, with which it also formed a coalition in KwaZulu-Natal.

Relations between the IFP and ANC in 2002 fell to their lowest ebb since 1994. The main arena of the quarrel between the two parties was KwaZulu-Natal, where, in late 2002, the ruling IFP ejected two ANC ministers from the provincial government and formed a partnership with the opposition Democratic Alliance. After floor-crossing in 2003, the IFP held 31 assembly seats.

The IFP suffered considerable erosion of support in the 2004 general election, in which it secured 28 seats. For the first time since 1994, the IFP subsequently had no representation in the cabinet.

At the IFP's annual conference in July 2004, Ziba Jiyane was nominated from the floor, against the leadership's wishes, to run against the incumbent national chair and former provincial premier, Lionel MTSHALI, whom he defeated in a landslide victory. Rev. Musa Zondi was nominated for the revived position of secretary general. In the 2004 elections, the party won 28 seats in the National Assembly, making it the fourth largest party.

After floor-crossing in 2005, the IFP lost an additional five assembly seats, ceding four to the newly formed Nadeco and one to the DA. (In April 2006, three IFP defectors to Nadeco returned to the IFP, whose Operation *Buyela eKhaya* [Come Back Home] encouraged defectors to return to the party.) At the IFP's annual national conference in September 2005, Zondi was elected secretary general and Zanele Magwaza was unanimously elected national chair, replacing Ziba Jiyane, who had defected earlier to help form Nadeco.

Ideologically, the IFP views itself as right of the ANC. It opposed the passage of legislation in 2005 to expropriate white-owned land because of its opposition to state intervention in the market. In 2007 the IFP submitted a private member's bill calling for an end to floor-crossing, which it considers a betrayal of the electorate. The party's main support base is among Zulus in rural KwaZulu-Natal. However, the party seeks to project itself as a national party, and IFP parliamentarians have included non-Zulus.

The IFP, a regional party, estimates its membership was 1–2 million in the 1980s and 1990s, though officials concede there has been a decline since then. If the numbers are accurate, the IFP has the largest party membership in the country.

In the 2009 national elections, the IFP posted its worst results in recent years, securing just 4.5 percent of the vote and 18 seats in the National Assembly, down from 28 seats in 2004.

The party's secretary general Musa Zondi, who was considered by some to be next in line for the IFP presidency, resigned his seat in the National Assembly in a letter dated January 24, 2012, a month after alleging that IFP members were maliciously trying to discredit him with sex scandal rumors. After two former members of parliament defected to the ANC in June 2013, the IFP charged that the rival party had launched a concerted campaign to lure defectors through illicit incentives.

Leaders: Chief Mangosuthu (Gatsha) BUTHELEZI (President), Rev. Musa ZONDI (Secretary General), Themba C. MSIMANG (Deputy Secretary General).

African Christian Democratic Party (ACDP). The ACDP, a conservative Christian group, was organized in 1993 with the aim of representing Christians in parliament. Sixty percent of its members are black. Prior to the 1994 balloting, in which it won two seats on a 0.5 percent vote share, the ACDP also secured representation in three provincial assemblies. The party won six assembly seats and its first NCOP seat in the 1999 general election, securing an additional assembly seat during the floor-crossing window in 2003. The ACDP also contested the 2004 elections, in which it won 1.4 percent of the vote and six assembly seats. This seat share was reduced to three after the 2005 floor-crossing, as the party lost two to the ANC and one to the Federation of Democrats.

The ACDP was the only party in the National Assembly that voted against adoption of the 1996 constitution because of moral and "biblical" objections to clauses, including the prohibition of government discrimination on the basis of sexual orientation. In 1997 the ACDP also expressed outrage at the government's decision to legalize abortion, and in 2000 its manifesto opposed the promotion of condoms and safe sex as preventive measures against HIV transmission. The party opposed (as did the IFP) the 2006 Civil Union Bill, which legalized same-sex marriages.

In the 2009 National Assembly elections, the party won three seats, down from seven in 2004. In June 2013, party leader Kenneth Meshoe resigned from parliament in order lead a fundraising campaign for the party.

Leaders: Rev. Kenneth MESHOE (President), Wayne M. THRING (Deputy President), Raymond TLAELI (Secretary General), Jo-Ann DOWNS (NEC Chair).

Independent Democrats (ID). The ID was formed during the floor-crossing window in March–April 2003 under the leadership of Patricia de Lille, a former trade unionist and a long-time member of the Pan Africanist Congress, which she left to form the ID. The party's main support area is the Cape metro area, but it is expanding. With the motto "Back to Basics," the ID's policies are generally centrist.

The ID won seven seats in the 2004 assembly elections. To forestall defections in the 2005 floor-crossing window, the ID sacked its deputy leader and Gauteng provincial legislature member, Themba SONO. Sono obtained a temporary court order preventing the Gauteng speaker from swearing in anyone in his place until the matter was heard in court. A temporary court order was also issued to prevent the ID from filling the Western Cape legislature seat of Lennit MAX until the party heard his internal appeal against his expulsion. Despite the party's efforts to prevent defections, the ID lost two assembly seats to the ANC during the 2005 floor-crossing window.

In June 2007, the ID held its first national policy conference, followed by its inaugural national congress in July. De Lille positioned the ID as a "people-oriented" party, favoring a role for both the state and the market. She criticized the government's black economic empowerment policy for benefiting only a small elite and identified other perceived policy failures regarding crime control, HIV/AIDS prevention, and the delivery of essential services. She also called for draft legislation to regulate party funding and for the government to institute immediate temporary relief measures and an economic recovery plan for fishing communities.

In the 2009 national elections, the party won four seats in the National Assembly, down from seven in 2004.

In August 2010 the ID entered into an electoral pact with the DA, with the aim of completely merging before the 2014 general election. De Lille left the national parliament to become a member of Helen Zille's administration in the Eastern Cape. In preparation for the 2014 merger, members of the ID were appointed to the DA's shadow cabinet.

Leaders: Patricia de LILLE (President), Agnes TSAMAI (Deputy President), Mervyn CIROTA (National Chair), Schalk LUBBE (National Treasurer), Joe MCGLUWA (National Organizer), Haniff HOOSEN (Secretary General).

Pan Africanist Congress of Azania (PAC). A militant ANC offshoot that was banned in 1960, the PAC long sought to unite all black South Africans in a single national front. Based in Lusaka, Zambia, the PAC announced in May 1979 the establishment in the Sudan of a "June 16 Azania Institute" (named after the June 1976 Soweto uprising) to instruct displaced South African students in a variety of academic and artisan skills. Its underground affiliate, the Azanian People's Liberation Army (APLA), was relatively small, compared to the military wing of the rival ANC. The PAC's longtime leader, John Nyati POKELA, died in June 1985; its president, Zephania MOTHOPENG, was released from nine years' imprisonment in November 1988, while another leader, Jafta MASEMOLA, was released in October 1989. In September 1990 the PAC rejected a government invitation to participate in constitutional talks, branding the overture as "not serious or honest." In October, the PAC joined the ANC and some 60 other groups (*Inkatha* being the most notable exception) in the attempted formation of a united Patriotic Front. However, the PAC subsequently broke with the Mandela-led formation in opposing Codesa, insisting that it would settle for nothing less than "a democratically elected constituent assembly." The PAC has abandoned its more radical programs and now concentrates on the plight of the poor and related issues.

The PAC announced in the early 1990s that it was abandoning armed struggle, thus permitting it to register for elections. The party won 1.2 percent of the vote and five assembly seats in the 1994 balloting. Following a protracted leadership struggle, Clarence MAKWETU stepped down as PAC president in December 1996 and was replaced by Rev. Mmutlanyane Stanley MOGOBA. Makwetu was expelled from the party in 1997.

Under Mogoba's leadership the PAC in 1997 evinced a conciliatory attitude toward whites, while party leaders also expressed an interest in opening a dialogue with the ANC, the PAC's longtime rival. Subsequently, in January 1999, it was announced that the APLA had been officially disbanded, and the PAC was registered to contest the June national elections, in which it won three seats on a 0.7 percent vote share. In July 2001 the PAC, responding to delays in land distribution and government housing construction, began helping thousands of homeless people occupy a wasteland near Johannesburg. The government quickly evicted them.

In the 2003 floor-crossing, Patricia de Lille left the PAC to form the ID, thus leaving the PAC with only two assembly seats. The PAC deputy president, Dr. Motsoko PHEKO, was elected president on June 15, replacing Mogoba, who had continued as president after the dispute over 2002 party congress results. In February 2004, Mogoba resigned from parliament to give his seat to the deputy president of the party, Themba Godi. After the April 2004 national election, the PAC again had three assembly seats. In 2006 the PAC congress elected a new president, Letlapa Mphahlele. At the September 2007 floor-crossing, two members left to form the **African People's Convention.** The party has since experienced severe factional infighting, with supporters of Pheko and MPHAHLELE each claiming to be the "real PAC." Mphahlele was elected to parliament in place of Pheko in April 2009, when the party won one seat in the assembly.

In May 2013, PAC's executive committee suspended Secretary General Narius Moloto and two other senior party officials. In response, Moloto and a group of supporters voted to expel Mphahlele, creating a new rift within PAC.

Leaders: Letlapa MPHAHLELE (President), Narius MOLOTO (Secretary General), Andiswa MJALI (Deputy Secretary General).

African People's Convention (APC). The APC was founded at the September 2007 floor-crossing with the withdrawal of Themba Godi and Mofihli Dikotsi from the Pan Africanist Congress.

After the April 2009 election, Godi was the only APC member in the National Assembly.

Leaders: Themba GODI (President), Hlabirwa MATHUME (Secretary General).

United Christian Democratic Party (UCDP). The UCDP was founded by Chief Lucas Mangope, former president of the Bophuthatswana homeland. The conservative formation includes in its platform support for the authority of traditional leaders. Despite reports that Mangope considered merging the UCDP with the newly formed UDM in 1997, it contested the 1999 elections independently, winning three seats in the National Assembly on a 0.8 percent vote share. In 2004 it retained its three seats but in 2009 was reduced to two. The main UCDP power base is in the North West province.

Leaders: Isaac Sipho MFUNDISI (President), Tediye Phillip MOERANE (Deputy President), Ipuseng Celia DITSHETELO (National Chair).

United Democratic Movement (UDM). The UDM was launched on September 27, 1997, by former NP secretary general Roelf MEYER and former ANC deputy minister Bantu Holomisa, also a former Transkei homeland leader. The new grouping, which promoted a moderate and nonracial platform, was reportedly immediately bolstered by the enrollment of a number of young, liberal NP defectors. Its first secretary general, Sifiso NKABINDE, was murdered in January 1999. Like Holomisa, Nkabinde had been expelled from the ANC.

The UDM subsequently was reported to be gaining popular support, and it competed in the 1999 assembly campaign on a pledge to narrow the gap between rich and poor without imperiling the wealth of the financial elite. The party won 14 seats on a 3.4 percent vote share. In January 2000 Meyer announced his retirement from politics, and on August 31, 2007, he joined the ANC. The second National Congress in December 2001 confirmed Holomisa as president.

The UDM is identified with Xhosa interests in Eastern Cape province. It supported the ANC during the latter's bitter struggle with the IFP for control of the KwaZulu-Natal legislature (for more on the defections and expulsions form the party during the 2003 floor-crossing window, see the 2011 *Handbook*).

In 2009 the party won four seats in the National Assembly, down from nine in 2004. In 2013, the UDM began negotiations to create a broad opposition coalition ahead of the 2014 balloting.

Leaders: Bantu HOLOMISA (President), Bongani MSOMI (General Secretary), Zolisa LAVISA (National Chair).

Azanian People's Organization (Azapo). Azapo was founded in April 1978 to carry on the work of the black consciousness movement that was banned in October 1977; however, its founders were immediately detained, and it did not hold its first congress until September 1979. Although never a mass party, it enjoyed the support of black intellectuals. Avowedly nonviolent, it adopted a hard line on the possibility of negotiating with the white government and was strongly anti-Codesa. In early 1994 Azapo declared its opposition to the forthcoming all-party election and announced that it would intensify its struggle until land had been returned to the country's blacks. Although Azapo had boycotted the 1994 balloting, it was registered for the 1999 elections, in which it won 0.2 percent of the vote and one National

Assembly seat. Some Azapo members had defected to join the **Socialist Party of Azania** (SOPA), which was formed on March 21, 1998, allegedly because Azapo had abandoned its socialist principles and its leadership was undemocratic. In January 2001, the Azapo leader, Mosibudi Mangena, was named deputy minister of education, prompting mass resignations by Azapo members who accused him of betrayal for participating in the ANC's nonsocialist and multiracial government.

In the cabinet announced after the 2004 election, Azapo leader Mangena was appointed minister of science and technology, again generating criticism that Azapo should not be in the ANC government. In the 2009 elections, the party won one seat. No members were named in President Zuma's new government appointed in May. Mangena retired in March 2010.

In 2013, AZAPO and SOPA announced they would merge.

Leaders: Jacob DIKOBO (President), Strike THOKOANE (Deputy President), Zithulele N. A. CINDI (National Chair), Mpotseng KGOKONG (Secretary General).

Minority Front (MF). The MF represents the rights of Indians in South Africa; it participated without success in the 1994 balloting but won one National Assembly seat in 1999 on a vote share of 0.3 percent. It then formed an alliance with the ANC, giving the latter the 267 votes needed to amend the constitution. In 2004 the MF won two assembly seats. The MF manifesto supports increased subsidies for education and housing, job creation, improving social grants and pensions, fighting unfair implementation of affirmative action, and protecting minority rights.

In the 2009 elections, the party won one assembly seat.

Leader: Amichand RAJBANSI.

Other Parties and Groups:

Afrikaner Resistance Movement (*Afrikaner Weerstands beweging*—AWB). Founded in 1973, the extreme right-wing AWB became the most visible of the Afrikaner paramilitary formations opposed to majority rule. In June 1993 armed AWB members invaded the Johannesburg building where constitutional talks were in progress, meeting no resistance from the police on duty. Having been convicted and fined in October for electoral violence in 1991, controversial AWB leader Eugene Terre'Blanche in November urged whites to arm themselves for "inevitable" civil war. In March 1994, however, the failure of AWB and other Afrikaner paramilitaries to preserve the Bophuthatswana regime contributed to the collapse of the broad Freedom Alliance of conservative forces. In April 1996 ten AWB members were imprisoned for their part in a bombing campaign aimed at disrupting the 1994 election.

Further arrests of AWB activists were reported in early 1997. Moreover, in June Terre'Blanche was sentenced to prison for six years for allegedly attempting to murder a black laborer. (In March 2001, he lost his final appeal and began serving his sentence.) He was released in 2004. He was also condemned by the TRC for his role in the 1993–1994 violence. In March 2008 Terre'Blanche announced that he was re-founding the movement, which had become defunct. In April 2010, Terre'Blanche was killed by Chris Mahlangu, a young black man who worked on his farm, in a dispute over unpaid wages. Steyn Van Ronge succeeded him as party leader. The AWB has continued to recruit members and hold rallies. On August 22, 2012, Mahlangu was sentenced to life in prison. In December, seven members of the AWB were arrested with weapons outside of a white-owned farm in the midst of a strike.

Leader: Steyn van RONGE.

Refounded National Party (*Herstigte Nasionale Party*—HNP). The HNP is a right-wing Calvinist party organized by Dr. Albert Hertzog following his dismissal from the government in 1968. The party, which adopted the racist doctrine that blacks are genetically inferior to whites, competed in four subsequent elections without securing parliamentary representation. Dr. Hertzog (son of original National Party founder J. B. M. Hertzog) relinquished the HNP leadership in May 1977. In March 1979, the NP-dominated Parliament, by amendment to a 1978 electoral act, refused to register the HNP as a political party, although it was permitted to contest most constituencies (none successfully) in 1981 by producing 300 signatures in support of each nomination. It secured its first parliamentary seat, previously held by the NP, in a by-election in October 1985 but was unable to retain it in 1987. Although the HNP withdrew from the AVF shortly after its formation in May 1993, it nevertheless joined the AVF in boycotting the April 1994 election.

The HNP's attempts to reach a broader constituency were reportedly hindered in 1997 by its well-publicized conflicts with other Afrikaner groups, most notably the VF. It was reported in 1998 that the HNP was hoping to contest the 1999 balloting, but it did not appear on the final list of approved parties. Longtime leader Jaap MARAIS died in August 2000 and was officially succeeded by Willem Marais at a March 2001 party congress. Marais died in 2007 and was replaced as leader by Japie Theart, who was subsequently replaced by Andries Breytenbach in 2011.

Leaders: Andries BREYTENBACH (Chair), Simon DUVENAGE (Deputy Chair).

Other recently formed parties include **To Build** (*Agang*), formed in 2013 and led by Mamphela RAMPHELE; and **Democracy From Below**—DFB, established in 2013 and led by Ronnie KASRILS.

For more information on the **United Independent Front** (UIF), and the **New National Party** (NNP), the name adopted by the now defunct **National Party** (*Nasionale Party*—NP) at a December 1998 congress, please see the 2013 *Handbook.*

LEGISLATURE

Prior to 1981 the South African **Parliament** was a bicameral body consisting of a Senate and a House of Assembly, from which blacks and Coloureds lost their previous limited indirect representation in 1959 and 1968, respectively. The Senate (consisting largely of members designated by the provincial assemblies) was abolished, effective January 1, 1981, some of its duties being assumed by a newly created President's Council of nominated members.

The 1983 document provided for a tricameral body encompassing a House of Assembly, a continuation of the former lower house; a House of Representatives, representing Coloured voters; and a House of Delegates, representing Indian voters. Each was empowered to legislate in regard to "its own" affairs, while the assent of all was required in regard to collective issues.

The interim constitution, which was in effect from April 27, 1994, to February 4, 1997, was the first to be based on the one-person–one-vote principle. It provided for a Senate of indirectly elected members and a directly elected National Assembly, both with five-year mandates. The two bodies sat jointly as the Constituent Assembly that drafted the permanent basic law, which entered into effect on February 4, 1997, and, among other things, replaced the Senate with a National Council of Provinces.

National Council of Provinces. The National Council replaced the Senate on February 6, 1997, at which time 54 permanent elected members (6 from each of the nine provinces) and 36 special delegates (4 from each province) were inaugurated. Members are elected by each provincial legislature from among its own ranks. Each delegation is headed by the provincial premier who is one of the special delegates.

Delegations are required to reflect the party makeup of the provincial legislatures. Following elections on August 22, 2009, the seat distribution was as follows: the African National Congress, 35; Democratic Alliance, 10; Congress of the People, 7; *Inkatha* Freedom Party, 1; and Independent Democrats, 1.

Chair: Mninwa MAHLANGU.

National Assembly. The lower house contains 400 members, 200 of whom are elected by proportional representation from national party lists and 200 from regional lists. All serve a five-year term.

Following the election of April 22, 2009, the seat distribution was as follows: the African National Congress, 264 seats; Democratic Alliance, 67; Congress of the People, 30; *Inkatha* Freedom Party, 18; Independent Democrats, 4; the Freedom Front Plus, 4; United Democratic Movement, 4; African Christian Democratic Party, 3; United Christian Democratic Party, 2; Minority Front, 1; Pan Africanist Congress of Azania, 1; Azanian People's Organization, 1, and African People's Convention, 1.

Speaker: M. V. SISULU.

CABINET

[as of November 12, 2013]

President	Jacob Gedleyihlekisa Zuma
Deputy President	Kgalema Petrus Motlanthe
Ministers	
Agriculture, Forestry, and Fisheries	Tina Joemat-Pettersson [f]
Arts and Culture	Paul Mashatile (SACP)
Basic Education	Matsie Angelina Motshekga [f]
Communications	Yunus Carrim
Cooperative Governance and Traditional Affairs	Lechesa Tsenoli
Correctional Services	Joel Sibusiso Ndebele
Defense and Military Veterans	Nosiviwe Noluthando Mapisa-Nqakula [f]
Economic Development	Ebrahim Patel
Energy	Dikobe Ben Martins (SACP)
Finance	Pravin Jamnadas Gordhan
Health	Pakishe Aaron Motsoaledi
Higher Education and Training	Bonginkosi Emmanuel (Blade) Nzimande (SACP)
Home Affairs	Grace Naledi Mandisa Pandor [f]
Human Settlements	Connie September [f]
International Relations and Cooperation	Maite Nkoana-Mashabane [f]
Justice and Constitutional Development	Jeffrey Thamsanqa Radebe (SACP)
Labor	Nelisiwe Mildred Oliphant [f]
Mineral Resources	Susan Shabangu [f]
National Planning Commission	Trevor Andrew Manuel
Performance Monitoring and Evaluation and Administration in the Presidency	Ohm Collins Chabane
Police	Nathi Mthethwa
Public Enterprises	Malusi Nkanyezi Gigaba
Public Service and Administration	Lindiwe Nonceba Sisulu [f]
Public Works	Thembelani Thulas Nxesi
Rural Development and Land Reform	Gugile Nkwinti
Science and Technology	Derek Andre Hanekom
Social Development	Bathaqbile Olive Dlamini [f]
Sport and Recreation	Fikile April Mbalula
State Security	Siyabonga Cyprian Cwele
Tourism	Marthinus van Schalkwyk
Trade and Industry	Rob Davies (SACP)
Transport	Elizabeth Dipuo Peters [f]
Water and Environmental Affairs	Edna Molewa [f]
Women, Children and People with Disabilities	Lulama Xingwana [f]

[f] = female

Note: Except as otherwise stated, all ministers are members of the ANC. Ministers designated as SACP are also members of the ANC.

INTERGOVERNMENTAL REPRESENTATION

Ambassador to the U.S.: Ebrahim RASOOL.

U.S. Ambassador to South Africa: Patrick GASPARD.

Permanent Representative to the UN: Kingsley MAMABOLO.

IGO Memberships (non-UN): AU, CWTH, G-20, ICC, IOM, NAM, SADC, WTO.

SOUTH SUDAN

Republic of South Sudan
Junhuriyat Janub Al-Sudan

Political Status: Independent republic established in 2011; transitional constitution approved on July 7, 2011.

Area: 967,494 sq. mi. (2,505,813 sq. km).

Population: 11,090,104 (2011E—U.S. Census).

Major Urban Centers (2008E): Juba (300,000).

Official Language: English.

Monetary Unit: South Sudanese Pound (market rate November 1, 2013: 3.11 pounds = $1US). The South Sudanese pound was introduced after independence in 2011.

President and Prime Minister: Salva KIIR Mayardit (Sudan People's Liberation Movement); sworn in on July 9, 2011, following independence; previously appointed as president of the autonomous regional government of South Sudan (GOSS) on August 11, 2005, to succeed John GARANG (Sudan People's Liberation Movement), who died in a helicopter crash on July 30, 2005; reappointed on May 28, 2010, following presidential elections during April 11–15.

Vice President: (Vacant); following the dismissal on July 23, 2013, of Riek MACHAR Teny Dhurgon (Sudan People's Liberation Movement) who had been sworn in on July 9, 2011, following independence; previously appointed as vice president of the autonomous regional GOSS on August 11, 2005, to succeed Kiir Mayardit; reappointed on May 28, 2010, following presidential elections on April 11–15.

THE COUNTRY

Formerly the southern ten provinces of Sudan, South Sudan gained independence in 2011. It borders the Central African Republic, the Democratic Republic of the Congo, Ethiopia, Kenya, Sudan, and Uganda. The area traditionally marked the beginning of Africa's subtropical zone, and the White Nile flows through the country that is home to the Sudd—a wetlands area that constitutes about 15 percent of the total area of South Sudan. More than 90 percent of the population practices Christianity or traditional beliefs. The majority of the population is African, with a small Arab minority. Following elections in 2011, women secured 88 of 332 seats in the assembly (26.5 percent), and 5 of 50 seats in the upper chamber (10 percent). Women also held 5 of 21 cabinet positions in 2013.

South Sudan possesses significant mineral resources and produces about 600,000 barrels of oil per day. Petroleum accounts for 98 percent of government revenues; however, oil is currently exported through two pipelines that run through Sudan, forcing the GOSS to share revenues. In addition to fossil fuels, there are deposits of iron, copper, tungsten, silver, and zinc. South Sudan has extensive agricultural capabilities, producing bananas, cotton, mangos, papayas, peanuts, rice, sesame, sorghum, sugarcane, and wheat. The country is also home to 10–20 million head of cattle.

South Sudan faced decades of repeated droughts and civil war. The World Bank and International Monetary Fund (IMF) called for substantial new investments to overcome the damage to infrastructure caused by the civil war.

GDP growth was 6 percent in 2011, while inflation was 8.6 percent. A dispute with Sudan over export fees led South Sudan to suspend oil exports in January 2012 (see Current issues, below). The result was a significant reduction in GDP in 2012. The IMF and World Bank estimated GDP fell by more than 50 percent, while inflation rose grew by more than 45 percent. Observers complemented the government for its ability to function, with the aid of loans and grants, during this crisis. GDP was expected to grow by 32.1 percent in 2013 with the resumption of oil shipments (see Foreign relations, below). In 2012, GDP per capita was $1,174.

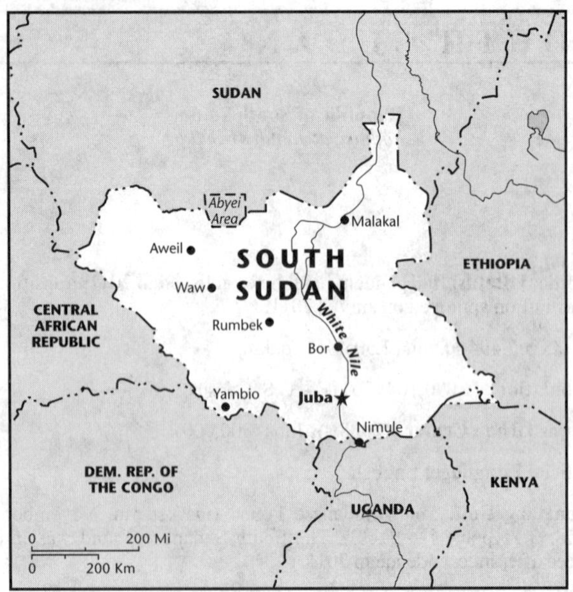

GOVERNMENT AND POLITICS

Political background. After a period of informal rule by Egypt, the territory that is now South Sudan was united as the Egyptian province of Equatoria in 1869. The region became part of the area controlled by Muhammad Ahmad, the MAHDI ("awaited religious leader"), following a rebellion (1881–1885) against Egyptian rule. By 1898 Anglo-Egyptian forces had reestablished control over the area. North and South Sudan were ruled as two relatively distinct colonies until after World War II. In 1946 the British endeavored unsuccessfully to merge South Sudan with Uganda. However, at the 1947 Juba Conference, North and South Sudan were combined into a single unitary state that became self-governing in 1954 and independent two years later.

Two bloody civil wars (1955–1972 and 1983–2005) were fought between the mainly African, Christian south and the Arab, Muslim north (for more details on the history of South Sudan prior to independence in 2011, see the entry on Sudan). More than 2.5 million were killed during the conflicts and the concurrent droughts and famines. The conflicts also produced more than 4 million refugees. The Sudanese People's Liberation Army (SPLA), led by Col. John GARANG, emerged as the main rebel group in the South. A peace accord, the Comprehensive Peace Agreement (CPA), was finalized in January 2005. The agreement created a system of power sharing between the national government of Sudan, led by General and President Umar Hassan Ahmad al-BASHIR of the National Congress (NC), and groups in the South, including the political arm of the SPLA, the Sudanese People's Liberation Movement (SLPM). In addition, the ten southern provinces were granted autonomy, and on October 21, 2005, the GOSS was established. Garang, the SPLA's leader, was appointed the first president of South Sudan, but he died in a helicopter crash on July 30 and was succeeded by Vice President Salva KIIR Mayardit of the SPLM. Riek MACHAR Teny Dhurgon of the SPLM was appointed vice president to replace Kiir. National elections were scheduled for 2009 (these were delayed until 2010), with a referendum on independence for South Sudan planned for 2011.

In suspect elections held during April 11–15, 2010, Bashir was reelected president after the SPLM candidate Yasir ARMAN withdrew from the balloting. Meanwhile, Kiir was reelected president of the GOSS. The SPLM subsequently joined a unity government led by Bashir.

The South Sudan referendum on independence was conducted January 9–15, 2011. More than 98 percent of the voters cast ballots in favor of forming a new nation. A new, transitional constitution was subsequently drafted (see Constitution and government, below). South Sudan became independent on July 9. Kiir resigned that day as vice president to become the president of South Sudan. He named a new cabinet on August 26, which included the SPLM, the NC, the United Sudan African Party (USAP), the South Sudan Democratic Front (SSDF), and the United Democratic Salvation Front—Mainstream (UDSF-M). The government was formally approved on September 1. Also in September, the government announced plans to relocate the capital from Juba to Ramciel.

On July 23, 2013, Kiir unexpectedly dismissed the vice president and cabinet. A new cabinet was appointed July 27–31, but not a new vice president (see Current issues, below). Another reshuffle occurred on August 4 that expanded the cabinet.

Constitution and government. A transitional constitution was approved by the parliament on July 7, 2011. The new basic law was scheduled to remain in place for four years, during which time a permanent constitution was to be developed. The interim basic law provided for a bicameral legislature, consisting of both previously elected legislators and appointees. Presidential and legislative elections were scheduled for 2015. The constitution also created an independent judiciary with a Supreme Court. Opposition groups criticized the interim constitution for concentrating too much power in the hands of the president, including the authority to dismiss elected governors and to declare war without parliamentary consent.

South Sudan is divided into ten states, with 86 counties. The Kiir government sought to include the disputed Abyei region in the 2011 referendum. However, in May an estimated 5,000 Sudanese troops invaded the region (see Foreign relations, below), and the status of the area remains unresolved as of July 2012.

The transitional constitution established English as the official language but also recognized indigenous languages. The interim government pledged to maintain freedom of the press. There are a number of newspapers, including the *Juba Post* and the *Akhbar al-Yaum*. In 2013, the media watchdog group Reporters Without Borders, ranked South Sudan 124th out of 179 countries in freedom of the press.

Foreign relations. In September 1993, Eritrea, Ethiopia, Kenya, and Uganda created the Intergovernmental Authority on Drought and Development (IGADD), which became the Intergovernmental Authority on Development (IGAD). IGAD endeavored to mediate the Sudanese conflict. IGAD and regional powers, including Egypt and Ethiopia, played an important role in fostering the 2005 CPA (for more information on the civil wars and international efforts to mediate the crises prior to 2011, see the entry on Sudan).

After South Sudan became independent in July 2011, it joined the UN and African Union (AU). Concurrently, the United States and other countries ended sanctions against South Sudan, while maintaining them against Sudan. In 2011, there were an estimated 81,000 refugees in South Sudan, mainly from Ethiopia and the Democratic Republic of the Congo.

The AU sponsored negotiations over the status of the disputed region of Abyei in Addis Ababa, Ethiopia, in June 2011. On June 20, South Sudan and Sudan signed an accord to demilitarize the area and allow a 7,000-member UN peacekeeping force (the UN Mission in the Republic of South Sudan, or UNMISS) to be deployed. Despite the presence of UNMISS and ongoing peace negotiations between Sudan and South Sudan, renewed fighting broke out in December 2011 and continued into 2012.

In February 2012, South Sudan and Sudan agreed on a plan to repatriate more than 300,000 South Sudanese from the north and to finalize the demarcation of the remaining disputed border areas. However, in March, renewed fighting commenced along the border, and SPLA troops captured the oil town of Heglig. However, the South Sudanese forces withdrew under international pressure. Sudan then undertook an irregular aerial bombing campaign of South Sudan despite repeated calls from the UN and international actors to end the strikes.

On January 20, 2012, Kiir announced that South Sudan would cease oil exports through Sudan because of a dispute over transit fees. South Sudanese officials claimed that the Sudanese had illegally diverted more than $815 million of oil. The suspension of production cut government revenues by 90 percent, leading to increased inflation. Meanwhile, South Sudan finalized an agreement to build a pipeline through Kenya for its energy exports. In April, South Sudan became the 188th member of the IMF.

On September 27, 2012, South Sudan and Sudan signed a series of agreements to resolve issues remaining from succession (see entry on

Sudan). The accords paved the wave for the resumption of oil shipments in April 2013.

On December 26, 2012, South Sudan filed a complaint with the UN Security Council after Sudan conducted aerial attacks on Kiir Adem. On December 4, the East African Community rejected South Sudan's membership bid.

In January 2013, South Sudan agreed to sell oil to Israel. In March the United Kingdom announced it would expand economic and cultural cooperation with South Sudan.

Current issues. After 21 years of civil war, the people of the southern provinces of Sudan voted in a referendum during January 9–15, 2011, to form the new nation of South Sudan. Formal independence came on July 9. After independence, there remained an estimated 100,000 internally displaced persons in South Sudan.

A renegade SPLA force led by George ATHOR signed a cease-fire agreement with the GOSS on January 5, 2011. However, new fighting broke out, and the militia group captured Fangak in Jonglei state on February 15, 2011. SPLA forces quickly recaptured the town, but more than 210 people were killed, mainly civilians. In April militias under the command of Maj. Gen. Gabriel "TANGINYE" CHAN and loyal to Khartoum, launched a series of attacks in the Upper Nile state. After a counteroffensive, Tanginye surrendered on April 25, and was placed under house arrest. By November 2011, the UN estimated that more than 1,500 people had been killed in fighting in South Sudan between the government and rebel militias since independence. On December 19, Athor was killed while fighting government forces.

Ethnic clashes in Jonglei killed an estimated 3,000 civilians in January 2012. The government declared martial law and dispatched troops to end the fighting. On March 19, the SPLA and the UN launched a program to demobilize an estimated 4,000 child soldiers.

In April 2013, the government and rebel groups, including the South Sudan Liberation Army, the South Sudan Democratic Army, and South Sudan Defense Force, signed a comprehensive peace agreement. However, renewed fighting in Jonglei with other groups created an additional 23,000 refugees. In June, Kiir dismissed the Minister of Cabinet Affairs Deng Alor KUOL and Finance Minister Kosti Manibe NGAL, following allegations of corruption. The next month, the president dismissed the vice president and cabinet in a reported effort to consolidate power. The firing of the vice president came amid rising tension between the two.

POLITICAL PARTIES AND GROUPS

The SPLM led the effort to gain independence and was the dominant political force in the postindependence government. The transitional Constitution guaranteed the right to develop new political parties.

Parties and Groupings:

Sudanese People's Liberation Movement/Army (SPLM/A). Originally formed in 1983 as a Marxist-Leninist grouping, the SPLM and its military wing, the SPLA, were led by Col. John Garang until his death in 2005. Salva Kiir Mayardit succeeded Garang and was reelected president of South Sudan in 2010. (For more information on the SPLM/A prior to South Sudanese independence in 2011, see the entry on Sudan.) Yasir ARMAN became the SPLM leader in the north (SPLM-N) after independence, although the party was banned in Sudan. After independence in July 2011, Kiir was automatically appointed interim president for a four-year term. Kiir appointed an SPLM-dominated cabinet in August. Following his dismissal as vice president, Riak MACHAR pledged to challenge Kiir for the presidency of South Sudan.

Leaders: Salva KIIR Mayardit (President of South Sudan, and Party Chair), Riak MACHAR (Former Vice President of South Sudan), Yasir ARMAN (2010 presidential candidate and SPLM-N).

Sudanese People's Liberation Army—United (SPLA-United). The SPLA-United was formed in 1993 in Nairobi, Kenya, by an anti-Garang faction of the SPLA. The SPLA-United was led by Lam Akol, who established the **Sudan Peoples' Liberation Movement—Democratic Change** (SPLM-DC) ahead of the 2010 legislative and presidential elections. Akol was the SPLM-DC candidate in the GOSS presidential balloting but was defeated by Kiir. (For more on the SPLA-United prior to South Sudanese independence, see the Sudan entry.)

The SPLM-DC emerged as the main opposition party after independence and did not join the SPLM-led coalition cabinet. Nonetheless, it was estimated that more than 500 members of the party defected to the SPLM during the transition to independence. In September 2011 Sisto Olur was appointed interim secretary general of the party. Following a meeting between Akol and Kiir in Nairobi, Kenya, in October, the SPLM-DC leader pledged to cooperate with the new government.

Leaders: Lam AKOL (Commander in Chief and 2010 presidential candidate), Sisto OLUR (Secretary General).

National Congress (NC). The NC was originally founded in 1986 as the National Islamic Front (NIF) (*al-Jabhah al-Watani al-Islami*). The NC emerged as the dominant northern Sudanese party. (For more information on the NC, see the entry on Sudan.) The southern faction of the NC agreed to participate in the SPLM-led coalition government. NC member Gen. Alison Manani MAGAYA was appointed minister of internal affairs and Agnes Kwaje LASUBA, minister of Gender, Children, and Social Welfare (Lasuba resigned in October 2011). Party chair Agnes Poni LUKUDU reportedly defected to the SPLM in July 2012. Subsequent reports indicated that the NC was largely defunct in South Sudan.

Leader: Agnes Poni LUKUDU.

United Democratic Salvation Front (UDSF). The USDF was formed by dissident members of SPLA as a moderate faction that initially promoted reconciliation between the north and south. The original leader, Riak MACHAR, left the party in 2002 and joined the SPLA. Following South Sudanese independence in July 2011, the UDSF retained a cabinet post in the Sudanese government. The southern branch of the USDF became known as the United Democratic Salvation Front—Mainstream (UDSF-M). The UDSF-M was given two cabinet posts in the government appointed by President Kiir in August 2011. In September the UDSF executive council dismissed party leader Joseph Malual DOUNG. Martin Tako Moyi was appointed as interim UDSF chair. Following the cabinet reshuffle in July 2013, the UDSF called for Kiir to step down.

Leaders: Martin Tako MOYI (Chair), Maj. Gen. (Ret.) Albino Akol AKOL (General Secretary).

United Sudan African Parties (USAP). The USAP was formed in 1987 as a coalition of seven minor parties. Initially led by Hilary LOGALI, the USAP joined the opposition National Democratic Alliance in 1994. After Logali died in 1998, he was succeeded by the current chair, Joseph Ukel Abango. Ukel was appointed minister of education in the South Sudanese postindependence government but lost his post in the July 2013 cabinet reshuffle.

Leader: Joseph UKEL Abango.

South Sudan Democratic Front (SSDF). The SSDF was formed in 2007 through the merger of the South Sudan Democratic Forum and the South Sudan United Democratic Alliance. The SSDF was a centrist organization that supported a negotiated settlement between the north and the south. Following independence, a member of the SSDF was appointed to the SPLM-led government, although reports indicated that the party portrayed itself as an opposition grouping. In July 2012, SSDF Maj. Gen. James Duit YIETCH and a number of party members defected to the SPLM/A. In July 2013, Martin Elia LOMORO was appointed minister of cabinet affairs.

Leader: Gordon BUAY.

United Democratic Front (UDF). Formed in 2003 and led by Peter Abdrhaman Sule, the UDF was a pro-independence South Sudanese party. In 2003 Sule became the only representative from South Sudan in the Sudanese national parliament. The UDF supported the 2005 CPA and sought to unite South Sudanese parties into a single, unified opposition coalition. In November 2011, Philip Yona JAMBI was elected party chair. Former UDF member David YAUYAU launched a rebellion against the kIir government in June 2012.

Leader: Philip Yona JAMBI.

Other parties include the small **African National Congress**, led by George Kongor AROP, a former vice president of the national Sudanese government.

LEGISLATURE

The **National Legislature** currently comprises the Council of States and the National Assembly. After independence, South Sudanese members of the Sudanese national legislature were automatically appointed to the parliament of the new nation.

The **Council of States** comprises 50 members, including the 20 South Sudanese former members of the Sudanese Council of States, 2 from each state, and 30 additional members appointed by the presidents.

Speaker: Joseph Bul CHAN.

The **National Assembly** is composed of 332 members, including 170 members elected in balloting for the South Sudan regional assembly during April 11–15, 2010; 96 South Sudanese members of the Sudanese assembly who were elected in concurrent balloting but who resigned after the January 2011 independence referendum; and 66 members appointed by the president.

President: James Wani IGGA.

CABINET

[as of August 15, 2013]

President	Salva Kiir Mayardit (SPLM)
Vice President	(Vacant)
Ministers	
Agriculture, Forestry, Tourism, Animal Resources, Fisheries	Beda Machar Deng
Cabinet Affairs	Martin Elia Lomuro (SSDF)
Culture, Youth, and Sports	Nadia Arop Dudi [f]
Defense and Veterans Affairs	Koul Manyang Juuk
Education, Science, and Technology	John Gai Yoh
Electricity, Dams, Irrigation, and Water Resources	Jemma Nunu Kumba (SPLM) [f]
Environment	Abdalla Deng Nhial
Finance, Commerce, and Economic Planning	Aggrey Tisa Sabuni
Foreign Affairs	Barnaba Marial Benjamin (SPLM)
Gender and Social Development	Awut Deng Acuil [f]
Health	Riek Gai Kok
Information and Broadcasting	Michael Makuei Lueth (SPLM)
Interior and Wildlife Conservation	Aleu Ayieny Aleu
Justice	Telar Ring Deng
Labor, Public Service, and Human Resource Development	Ngor Kolong Ngor
Lands, Housing, and Physical Planning	Catherine Juan Bennia [f]
National Security	Obuto Mamur Mete
Office of the Presidency	(Vacant)
Petroleum and Mining	Stephen Dhieu Dau (SPLM)
Telecommunications and Postal Services	Rebecca Joshua Okwachi [f]
Transport, Roads, and Bridges	Kuong Danhier Gatluak

[f] = female

INTERGOVERNMENTAL REPRESENTATION

Ambassador to the U.S.: Akec Khoc ACIEW.

U.S. Ambassador to South Sudan: Susan Denise PAGE.

Permanent Representative to the UN: Francis Mading DENG.

IGO Memberships (Non-UN): AU, Comesa, IMF.

SPAIN

Kingdom of Spain
Reino de España

Political Status: Formerly under a system of personal rule instituted in 1936; monarchy reestablished November 22, 1975, in accordance with the Law of Succession of July 26, 1947, as amended in 1969 and 1971; parliamentary monarchy confirmed by constitution effective December 29, 1978.

Area: 194,896 sq. mi. (504,782 sq. km).

Population: 46,163,114 (2013E—UN); 47,370,542 (2013E—U.S. Census).

Major Urban Areas (2013E): MADRID (3,198,000), Barcelona (1,611,000), Valencia (792,000), Seville (698,000), Zaragoza (678,000), Málaga (561,000), Murcia (438,000).

Official Languages: Spanish and regional languages (principally Basque, Catalan, Galician, and Valencian).

Monetary Unit: Euro (market rate November 1, 2013: 0.74 euro = $1US).

Monarch: JUAN CARLOS I de Borbón y Borbón; invested before the Spanish Legislative Assembly in 1969; sworn in as king on November 22, 1975, following the death of the former chief of state and president of government, Gen. Francisco FRANCO Bahamonde, on November 20.

Heir to the Throne: Prince FELIPE; sworn in as heir apparent on January 30, 1986.

President of Government (Prime Minister): Mariano RAJOY Brey (Popular Party); nominated by the king on December 16, 2011, following the parliamentary election of November 20, elected by the Congress of Deputies on December 20, sworn in on December 21 for a four-year term, succeeding José Luis Rodríguez ZAPATERO (Spanish Socialist Workers' Party).

THE COUNTRY

Occupying more than four-fifths of the Iberian peninsula (which it shares with Portugal), Spain is separated by the Pyrenees from France and the rest of Europe and includes within its national territory the Balearic Islands in the Mediterranean, the Canary Islands in the Atlantic, and small North African enclaves, including the *presidios* of Ceuta and Melilla. Continental Spain, a region of varied topography and climate, has been noted more for its beautiful landscape than for wealth of resources, but possesses valuable deposits of slate, iron, coal, and other minerals, as well as petroleum. The Spanish are a mixture of the original mainly Iberian population with later invading peoples. The population includes several cultural/linguistic groups: Castilians, Galicians, Andalusians, Catalans, and Basques (who claim distinct ethnicity). Regional feelings remain strong, particularly in the Basque and Catalan areas in the north and east, and various local languages and dialects are used in addition to the long-dominant Castilian Spanish and are increasingly taught in schools. About 94 percent of the population is Roman Catholic, although religious liberty is formally guaranteed. Women's participation in government is increasing, and several parties have adopted quota systems to ensure women have access to senior party posts. Following the 2008 elections, the national cabinet contained more women than men for the first time in the country's history. Women make up 34.8 percent of the legislature.

Spain's economy is largely driven by production of processed foods, textiles, footwear, petrochemicals, steel, automobiles, consumer goods, and electronics. Tourism contributes 10 percent of gross domestic product (GDP), and agriculture and fisheries yield less than 3 percent, though grain, vegetables, fruit, wine, olives and olive oil, sunflowers, and livestock remain important exports. Roughly 70 percent

of Spain's exports go to European Union (EU) member states, and Morocco is an important trading partner. Spain's entrance into the European Community (EC, subsequently the EU) in 1986 stimulated the economy, although the country experienced recessions in the early 1990s. Spain participated in the launch of the EU's Economic Monetary Union in 1999.

Between 1999 and 2008, economic growth transformed Spain from an economy with high unemployment, public deficits, and high inflation to a modern, dynamic economy with fiscal surpluses, low inflation, a strong currency, and low interest rates. However, the construction boom and housing bubble burst, plunging Spain into one of the worst recessions in Europe. Home values dropped 31 percent between 2008 and 2012. The federal bureaucracy and the legal system discourage foreign investment, and the recent devolution of powers to the regional level has increased bureaucracy. Basque terrorism also remains a concern to potential foreign investors. In its 2012 report on the ease of conducting business, the World Bank ranked Spain 44th out of 185 countries.

Economic conditions deteriorated significantly beginning in 2008. The combination of falling tax revenue and increased spending on fiscal stimulus measures widened Spain's budget deficit from 3.8 percent in 2008 to 9.3 percent of GDP in 2010. That year GDP fell by 0.2 percent, marking the second year of GDP contraction. In 2011, GDP declined by 0.7 percent, while inflation was 2 percent, and unemployment was a crippling 21.6 percent. GDP declined again in 2012, by 1.8 percent, inflation rose 1.9 percent, and unemployment grew to 26.6 percent. Unemployment for persons under age 25 exceeded 60 percent. Debt pressures led Spain to negotiate a financial rescue package from the EU and International Monetary Fund (IMF) in June 2012 (see Current issues, below).

GOVERNMENT AND POLITICS

Political background. Conquered in the 8th century by North African Moors (Arabs and Berbers), who established a flourishing Islamic civilization in the south of the peninsula, Christian Spain completed its self-liberation in 1492 and went on to found a world empire that reached its apogee in the 16th century and then gradually disintegrated. Monarchical rule under the House of Bourbon continued into the 20th century, surviving the dictatorship of Miguel PRIMO de Rivera in 1923–1930 but giving way in 1931 to a multiparty republic that became increasingly subject to leftist influences. The electoral victory of a leftist Popular Front coalition in 1936 provoked a military uprising led by Gen. Francisco FRANCO Bahamonde, precipitating the three-year civil war in which the republican forces, although assisted by Soviet and other foreign volunteers, were ultimately defeated with aid from Fascist Italy and Nazi Germany. A fascist regime was then established, Franco ruling as leader (*caudillo*) and chief of state with the support of the armed forces; the Catholic Church; and commercial, financial, and landed interests.

Having preserved its neutrality throughout World War II and suffered a period of ostracism thereafter by the United Nations (UN), Spain was gradually readmitted to international society. The political structure was modified in 1947 with the adoption of a Law of Succession, which declared Spain to be a monarchy (although without a monarch), and again in 1967 by an Organic Law confirming Franco's position as chief of state, defining the structure of other government bodies, and providing for strictly limited public participation in elections to the legislature (*Cortes*). Political and administrative controls in effect since the Civil War were considerably relaxed during the early 1960s, but subsequent demands for change generated increasing instability. In December 1973 Prime Minister Luis CARRERO Blanco was assassinated by Basque separatists and was succeeded by Carlos ARIAS Navarro.

Franco became terminally ill on October 17, 1975, and on October 30 Prince JUAN CARLOS I de Borbón y Borbón, who had been designated heir to the Spanish throne, assumed the powers of provisional chief of state and head of government. Franco died on November 20, and two days later Juan Carlos was sworn in as king, in accordance with the 1947 Law of Succession.

On July 1, 1976, Arias Navarro resigned as prime minister—reportedly at the king's request—following criticism of his somewhat cautious approach to promised reform of the political system. His successor, Adolfo SUÁREZ González, moved energetically to advance the reform program, securing its approval by the National Council of the National (Francoist) Movement on October 8, by the *Cortes* on November 10, and by the public in a referendum conducted on December 15. The National Movement was abolished by cabinet decree on April 1, 1977, and on June 15 balloting took place for a new, bicameral *Cortes,* with Prime Minister Suárez's Union of the Democratic Center (*Unión de Centro Democrático*—UCD) obtaining a substantial plurality in both houses. A new constitution went into force on December 29, 1978, following overwhelming approval by the *Cortes* on October 31, endorsement in a referendum on December 6, and ratification by King Juan Carlos on December 27. Suárez was formally reappointed on April 2, 1979, a general election on March 1 having yielded no substantial party realignment within the legislature.

During 1979–1980, an increase in terrorist activity, particularly in the Basque region, gave rise to manifest uneasiness within military circles, while the Union of the Democratic Center (*Unión de Centro Democrático*; please see the 2013 *Handbook* for more on the party) experienced internal dissension following the introduction of a liberal divorce bill that the Catholic Church and most right-wing elements bitterly opposed. On January 29, 1981, Suárez unexpectedly resigned. Before his designated successor had been confirmed, a group of Civil Guards, led by Lt. Col. Antonio TEJERO Molina, seized control of the Congress of Deputies chamber in an attempted coup on February 23. Due largely to the prompt intervention of King Juan Carlos, the rebellion failed, with Leopoldo CALVO Sotelo i Bustelo, the UCD secretary general, being sworn in as prime minister on February 26. However, the fissures between moderate and rightist elements within the UCD continued to deepen, with a number of new parties being spawned during late 1981 and the first half of 1982. As a result, lower house UCD representation plummeted to a mere dozen deputies at an election held October 12, when the Spanish Socialist Workers' Party (*Partido Socialista Obrero Español*—PSOE) obtained a comfortable majority (202 to 106 seats) over the Popular Alliance (*Alianza Popular*—AP), an emergent right-wing group that had previously held only a handful of seats. On December 2, PSOE leader Felipe GONZÁLEZ Márquez was inaugurated as the first left-wing head of government since the 1930s. González was sworn in for a second term on July 24, 1986, following an early election on June 22 at which the PSOE, despite marginally declining strength, retained majority control of both houses of the *Cortes.*

Throughout the 1980s, the Socialists continued to dominate as the conservative Popular Party (*Partido Popular*—PP, successor to the AP) engaged in a process of ideological self-examination and as the Communist Party reeled from events in Eastern Europe. The PSOE was rocked by a financial corruption scandal in 1992 and combined with economic problems narrowly avoided defeat in June 6, 1993 balloting due to support from the main Catalan (*Convergéncia i Unió*—CiU) and Basque nationalist (*Partido Nacionalista Vasco*—PNV) parties, which gave the minority PSOE government a 181-seat majority. The immediate price of CiU support was a government commitment to transfer 15 percent of taxes raised in Catalonia to the regional Catalan government and CiU demands for "real" autonomy for Catalonia.

To add to the government's problems, the Basque *Euzkadi ta Azkatasuna* (ETA), which had been engaged in a violent separatist campaign since the 1960s, launched a new wave of terrorist attacks in 1995, including an attempt to assassinate PP leader José María AZNAR López in a Madrid car bomb attack on April 19.

Parliamentary balloting on March 3, 1996, brought the PP to power, and its leader, Aznar, formed a minority government with external support from Basque (PNV), Catalan (CiU), and Canarian (*Coalición Canaria*—CC) regionalist parties, which won concessions that included a doubling (to 30 percent) of the proportion of income tax revenues accruing to the autonomous regions.

An increase in civilian deaths due to ETA terrorism led to a government crackdown in which the entire national committee of the political wing of the organization, the *Herri Batasuna* (HB), was placed on trial and sentenced to a minimum of seven years, although the Constitutional Court ultimately ordered their release in July 1999.

In September 1998, ETA announced a unilateral cease-fire and, having finished third in the regional elections, participated in the formation of a Basque regional government—a first for an ETA-linked group—with the PNV and the Basque Solidarity (*Eusko Alkartasuna*—EA).

In direct talks between the Aznar administration and ETA representatives, ETA continued to insist on the withdrawal of security forces from the Basque region, the release of some 450 jailed comrades (or, at the very least, their transfer to prisons in Basque Country), and an independence referendum. Citing the lack of progress toward any of its goals, ETA announced that it would end its cease-fire as of December 3 and was forced to withdraw from the Basque regional government.

At the general election of March 12, 2000, Prime Minister Aznar's PP surpassed expectations, winning an outright majority in both houses of the *Cortes,* including 183 seats in the Congress of Deputies. Reelected prime minister by the lower house on April 26, with external support from the CiU and the CC, Aznar was sworn in for a second term on April 27 at the head of a revamped and expanded cabinet. A ministerial reshuffle announced on July 9, 2002, was highlighted by the selection of Spain's first woman foreign minister, Ana PALACIO Vallelersundi, who was sworn in the following day.

On March 11, 2004, in the worst peacetime attack on Spanish civilians since the Civil War of the 1930s, a series of bombs exploded on four Madrid commuter trains, killing 191 and injuring another 1,400. The bombings had clearly been timed to affect the general election scheduled for March 14. Although the Aznar government immediately focused blame on ETA, it soon emerged that the coordinated assault had been perpetrated by militants associated with the al-Qaida terrorist network.

Prior to the March 2004 terrorist bombings in Madrid, the PP appeared on its way to a comfortable victory in the March 14 election. The Aznar government had weathered a number of difficulties, including a mishandling of the environmental crisis caused by the sinking of the Greek oil tanker *Prestige* off the coast of Galicia in November 2002. It had also overcome an 80 percent public disapproval rating of Spain's military involvement in Iraq.

Fearing adverse repercussions from the Madrid bombings, the government argued that a defeat at the polls would constitute a victory for the bombers, but by election day many Spaniards believed that the government had tried to manipulate the flow of information for political reasons, and voters displayed their anger through the ballot. On March 14 the voters gave the PSOE 42.6 percent of the vote, good for 164 seats, versus 37.6 percent and 148 seats for the PP. The rapid reversal of the PP's fortunes was generally attributed to the bombings, the government's misplaced blame, and underlying public opposition to Spain's military involvement in Iraq. With support from the IU and a handful of regional parties, the PSOE's José Luis Rodríguez ZAPATERO was confirmed as prime minister on April 16.

Some dozen seats short of a majority in the Chamber of Deputies, the Zapatero government came into office in 2004 through the support of a number of small regional parties, including the Catalan Republican Left (*Esquerra Republicana de Catalunya*—ERC), the Canarian Coalition, and the Galician Nationalist Bloc (*Bloque Nacionalista Galego*—BNG). In addition to quickly fulfilling a campaign pledge to withdraw from Iraq, Prime Minister Zapatero advanced a social agenda that included recognition of gay marriage (approved by both houses of the *Cortes* in 2005), streamlined divorce proceedings, allowed scientific research on embryonic stem cells, and reduced the role of religion in state schools. However, the policy changes provoked a backlash by conservatives, led by the Roman Catholic Church. The government maintained that advancing secular values was key to the modernization of Spain.

On December 20, 2007, Zapatero called a general election for March 9. Analysts predicted a tight race against the PP, stemming from public discontent over the ruling party's perceived leniency toward ETA and uneasiness over Spain's economic slowdown after more than a decade of expansion. High turnout, prompted in part by the March 7 assassination of PSOE councilor Isaias CARRASCO by a suspected ETA gunman, helped the PSOE secure 169 seats in the balloting with 43.6 percent of the vote, 7 short of an absolute majority, while the PP won 153 seats with 40.1 percent of the vote. Both leading parties expanded at the expense of smaller, regional parties such as the United Left and the Catalan Republican Left, which suffered a steep drop in support.

Although the PSOE was 7 short of an absolute majority, Zapatero said he had a "sufficient majority" to carry out his agenda. The PSOE shunned a formal coalition government, opting instead to negotiate with opposition parties on a case-by-case basis. His newly created cabinet, Spain's first with a female majority, included two new ministries: science and innovation as well as equality. The latter was headed by Bibiana AÍDO, who at 31 became Spain's youngest-ever cabinet minister.

Zapatero immediately turned his attention to the deteriorating economy. On April 18, 2008, the government announced a two-year, US$28.5 billion stimulus plan to support the real estate sector and small- to medium-sized businesses. In October the government raised guarantees on bank deposits and new debt and announced an $87 billion fund to buy state shares of healthy financial institutions to inject liquidity into the market. A stimulus package was directed toward job creation in the public works and automobile industries.

To cobble together enough support for the 2009 budget, Zapatero won key votes from nationalist parties in the Basque Country and Galicia with an agreement to provide the two regions with $283 million in infrastructure and research funds. However, in order to make the budget numbers work, Zapatero inserted a 1 percent growth forecast for 2009, an amount the PP called "legal fraud." Even the Economy Minister Pedro SOLBES deemed the growth forecast unrealistic.

In February 2009, Justice Minister Mariano Fernández BERMEJO resigned following a judges' strike and a scandal involving a hunting trip he took with a prominent judge. He was replaced by Francisco CAAMAÑO Domínguez.

In early April, only a year after the start of his second term, Zapatero announced a major cabinet reshuffle to boost public confidence in the PSOE, which had declined as the economic recession deepened. The PSOE was defeated in the June 7 European Parliament election, in which the PP won 42 percent of the vote compared to the PSOE's 39 percent. Analysts saw the PSEO's loss of 5 percentage points from the previous election as a reflection of the poor economy and not necessarily a lengthy move away from the party.

Zapatero reshuffled seven cabinet posts on October 20 after the introduction of unpopular austerity measures. A new minister of labor was appointed in an attempt to restart talks with trade unions following major changes to the country's labor laws in June. Zapatero put more power in the hands of popular interior minister Alfredo Perez RUBALCABA who, renowned for his success in suppressing the ETA, gained two extra portfolios in the arrangement—deputy prime minister and official government spokesperson. In cost-cutting moves, Zapatero incorporated the ministries of equality and housing into other portfolios.

In May 2010, under pressure from the EU to drive down Spain's budget deficit to the mandatory 3 percent by 2013, Zapatero pushed through the Congress of Deputies a highly unpopular austerity package (the measures passed by one vote). They included cuts to civil service salaries, a freeze on state pensions, and the abolition of the "baby bonus" for families. Civil servants held strikes in June, which disrupted schools, transit, and the postal service. In June Zapatero's labor reform legislation, designed to lower the country's 20 percent unemployment by reducing the cost of hiring and dismissing permanent employees, was passed by the Congress of Deputies solely by the PSOE as most deputies abstained from the vote.

Zapatero's 2011 austerity budget, presented in September 2010, proposed new income taxes for the wealthy and an 8 percent cut in federal spending. To gain minimal support for passage, the PSOE secured backing from the Basque National Party and the Canarian Coalition by agreeing to transfer funds and power to the Basque region and the Canary Islands.

The retirement age was raised from 65 to 67 in January 2011 as part of a broader effort to reform the pension system. On January 2 Spain introduced a nationwide smoking ban in public areas, including restaurants. In June the government enacted a 3.8 percent cut in the national budget in response to increased concern by the EU and IMF that Spain could need an economic bailout similar to those granted to Ireland, Greece, and Portugal. The IMF warned that the €150 billion debt accumulated by regional governments threatened Spain's future borrowing ability. On June 19 massive protests erupted across the country over the government's management of the economy.

In April 2011, Zapatero announced that he would not seek reelection. The following month the PSOE suffered its worst electoral defeat in decades in local and regional balloting as the PP won 11 of the 13 regions that held elections. The PSOE also lost the mayorship of Barcelona for the first time since 1979. In response, Zapatero announced snap elections scheduled for November 20, and Rubalcaba resigned in July 2011 to lead the PSOE in the November balloting, but to no avail. The PP retained its majority in the Senate and gained a majority in the Congress of Deputies. PP leader Mariano RAJOY Brey was sworn in as prime minister of a PP government on December 21.

Constitution and government. The 169-article Spanish constitution of 1978, the seventh since 1812, abrogated the "fundamental principles" and organic legislation under which General Franco had ruled as chief of state (*jefe del estado*) until his death in 1975. The document defines the Spanish state as a parliamentary monarchy and guarantees a variety of basic rights, including those of speech and press, association, and collective bargaining. "Bordering provinces" and "island territories and provinces" with common characteristics and/or historic regional status may, under prescribed circumstances, form "autonomous communities," but no federation of such communities is to be permitted. Roman Catholicism was disestablished as the state religion, although authorities were directed to "keep in mind the religious beliefs of Spanish society." Torture was outlawed, the death penalty abolished, and "a more equitable distribution of regional and personal incomes" enjoined. Freedom of the press is guaranteed, and in 2013, the media watchdog group Reporters Without Borders ranked Spain 36th out of 179 countries.

The powers of the king include nominating a candidate for the post of prime minister, after consulting the parties in the *Cortes;* dissolving the house and calling fresh elections if such approval is not forthcoming; serving as commander in chief of the armed forces, which are specifically recognized as guardians of the constitutional order; and calling referenda. The prime minister, who is empowered to dissolve the *Cortes* and call an election at any time, is assisted by a cabinet that is collectively responsible to the lower house.

Legislative authority is exercised by the bicameral *Cortes,* consisting of a 264-member Senate (208 directly elected territorial representatives plus 56 indirectly chosen by the assemblies of the autonomous regions and representing one senator for every million inhabitants) and a Congress of Deputies of 300–400 (currently 350) members elected on the basis of universal adult suffrage and proportional representation. Both houses serve four-year terms, barring dissolution; each can initiate legislation, although the upper house can only delay measures approved by the lower.

The judicial system is headed by a Supreme Tribunal (*Tribunal Supremo*) and includes territorial courts, provincial courts, regional courts, courts of the first instance, and municipal courts. An independent General Council of Judicial Power (*Consejo General del Poder Judicial*) oversees the judiciary.

The country is divided into 19 regions containing 50 administrative provinces, including the island provinces of Baleares, Las Palmas, and Santa Cruz de Tenerife. Although it was envisaged in 1978 that devolution to the regions would involve only a limited range of powers, such as alteration of municipal boundaries, control of health and tourism, instruction in regional languages, and the establishment of local police agencies, the tendency has been to delegate ever more functions to regional governments.

In October 1979, devolution statutes presented for the Basque and Catalan regions were overwhelmingly approved in regional referenda. In March 1980 elections for regional Legislative Assemblies were held in the Basque provinces of Alava, Guipúzcoa, and Vizcaya, and in the Catalan provinces of Barcelona, Gerona, Lérida, and Tarragona. Similar elections were held in Galicia in October 1981 and in Andalucía in May 1982. By February 1983 autonomy statutes had been approved for the (then) remaining 13 regions, with balloting in each being conducted in May. In 1994 the African enclaves of Ceuta and Melilla were also accorded the status of autonomous regions, bringing the total to 19. A referendum in Catalonia in 2006 on a proposal already approved by the Spanish parliament endorsed even greater autonomy for Catalonia, giving the regional parliament more powers on taxation and judicial affairs.

Known as one of the most decentralized countries in Europe, Spain has struggled to respect regional allegiances while fulfilling the essential obligations of the central government. Spain's electoral system of proportional representation is structured around provincial constituencies and is partly responsible for regional parties gaining more seats in parliament than parties that compete nationwide.

The presidents of government of the autonomous regions are elected by the regional legislatures.

Autonomous Region	*President of Government [as of September 1, 2013]*
Andalucía	(PSOE)
Aragón	Luisa Fernanda Rudi (PP) [f]
Asturias	Javier Fernández Fernández (PSOE)
Baleares (Balearic Islands)	José Ramón Bauzá (PP)
Canarias (Canary Islands)	Paulino Rivero Baute (CC)
Cantábria	Ignacio Diego (PP)
Castilla y León	Juan Vicente Herrera Campo (PP)
Castilla–La Mancha	Mariá Dolores de Cospedal Garcia (PP) [f]
Catalunya (Catalonia)	Artur Mas I Gavarro (CiU)
Ceuta	Juan Jesús Vivas Lara (PP)
Euzkadi/País Vasco (Basque Country)	Iñigo Urkullu (PNV)
Extremadura	José Antonio Monago Terraza (PP)
Galicia	Alberto Núñez Feijóo (PP)
Madrid	Jamie Ignacio González González (PP)
Melilla	Juan José Imbroda Ortiz (PP)
Murcia	Ramón Luis Valcarel Siso (PP)
Navarra	Yolanda Barcina (UPN) [f]
La Rioja	Pedro María Sánz Alonso (PP)
Valencia	Alberto Fabra (PP)

[f] = female

Foreign relations. Neutral in both world wars, Spain sided with the anti-communist powers after World War II but under Franco was prevented by certain democratic governments from becoming a member of the North Atlantic Treaty Organization (NATO), the EC (subsequently the EU), and other Western organizations. It was, however, admitted to the UN in 1955 and, in due course, to all of the latter's specialized agencies. The 1970s and early 1980s saw a strengthening of relations with Portugal, France, and West Germany. There also was a reduction of tension with Britain over Gibraltar (see entry on United Kingdom: Related Territories), which resulted in reopening of the border in early 1985 and a British commitment to talks from which the sovereignty question was not excluded. Relations with the United States remained cordial following the conclusion in 1970 of an Agreement of Friendship and Cooperation to replace the original U.S.-Spanish defense agreement of 1953. Following the restoration of democracy in 1975–1976, Spain was admitted to the Council of Europe in 1977 and to NATO in 1982, with membership in the EC following on January 1, 1986.

In February 1976, Spain yielded control of its North African territory of Spanish (Western) Sahara to Morocco and Mauritania. The action was taken despite strong protests by Algeria and the passage of a resolution by the UN General Assembly's Committee on Trust and Non-Self-Governing Territories in December 1975 that called for a UN-sponsored plebiscite to permit the Saharans to exercise their right to self-determination. Formerly cordial relations with the Saharan representative group Polisario (see entry on Morocco) were broken and its envoys expelled following a late 1985 Polisario attack on two Spanish vessels off the coast near Mauritania.

In May 1986 voters endorsed NATO membership, but on condition that Spain remain outside the alliance's command structure, ban nuclear weapons from Spanish territory, and reduce the number of U.S. forces in Spain. Subsequent negotiations yielded an agreement in principle on January 15, 1988, whereby the United States would, within three years, withdraw from the Torrejón facility outside Madrid and transfer its 72 F-16 jet fighters to a new base in Italy. The accord, as finalized at UN headquarters in September, contained no provision for continued military or economic assistance to Spain, while permitting U.S. military activity at a number of bases, including naval operations at Rota (near Cadiz). Most importantly, it allowed both sides to maintain their positions on nuclear arms, Spain reaffirming its opposition to the presence of such weapons but agreeing not to ask for compliance by inspection of U.S. vessels. In September 1990 González defied Spanish public opinion by contributing three warships to the buildup of allied forces in response to Iraq's August invasion of Kuwait. In the early 1990s, Spain signed a series of agreements that placed some of its forces under NATO's operational control.

A perennial obstacle to Spain's participation in NATO exercises was its refusal to join in any military activity that appeared to endorse British rule in Gibraltar. Full participation in NATO came on the heels of the installation of a conservative government in May 1996. A number of administrative accommodations regarding control of Gibraltar were achieved in 2000.

The Spanish Parliament overwhelmingly approved the EC's Maastricht Treaty in October–November 1992. Subsequently, Spain, together with Portugal, secured agreement on the creation of a "cohesion fund" for the four poorer members, including itself. Spain was also due to benefit from a similar fund established under the European Economic Area (EEA) agreement signed between the EC and five countries of the European Free Trade Association in March 1993.

In 2003, Zapatero won continued EU structural and cohesion funds for Spain in the EU's 2007–2013 budget, following concerns that it would lose EU funds as a result of the increase in membership in the EU. In February 2005 Spanish voters overwhelmingly endorsed the proposed EU constitution, which had the support of both the PSOE and the PP.

A frequent source of tension in Spain's external relations has been the activities of its 18,000-vessel fishing fleet (the EU's largest), whose crews combined a determination to protect home waters with a desire to exploit distant fishing grounds, often in alleged contravention of conservation and other international agreements (See the 2013 *Handbook* and the entry on Canada for details.) In December Spain's endorsement of the admission of three new EU members was only granted after it had secured additional fishing access to Irish and UK waters.

In early 2003, despite wide public opposition, the Aznar government dispatched Spanish forces to aid in peacekeeping and humanitarian efforts in Iraq following the U.S.-led ouster of Saddam Hussein's regime. A pledge by PSOE candidate Zapatero to withdraw Spanish troops from Iraq contributed to the March 2004 Socialist victory at the polls. By late May all 1,300 troops had returned home, beginning three years of frosty relations between Spain and the United States.

More tension with the United States arose in November 2005, when EADS-CASA, the Spanish subsidiary of the European aerospace consortium, began negotiating the sale of military aircraft to the Venezuelan government of Hugo Chávez. In June 2006 the United States officially blocked the sale because the planes in question contained U.S. technology.

In June 2006, the United Kingdom, Gibraltar, and Spain concluded talks in Cordoba, Spain, concerning several issues affecting the Rock and the Campo de Gibraltar, removing many of the restrictions imposed by Spain. The agreement allowed improved traffic flow at the frontier, direct flights between Gibraltar Airport and Madrid-Baraja, and recognition of the "350" telephone code. In March 2007 talks resumed in Cordoba with an agenda that included work on cooperation on environmental issues, financial services and tax issues, judicial and law enforcement cooperation, education, maritime communications, and Schengen visa issues.

In June 2007, U.S. secretary of state Condoleezza Rice visited Spain. While the trip was billed as an opportunity to improve bilateral relations, Rice expressed displeasure that Spanish foreign minister Miguel Angel MORANTIS would not visit with Cuban dissident groups during his April 2007 visit to Cuba, arguing that Spain's willingness to engage Castro would not aid democratization in Cuba. Spain has a policy of "constructive engagement" with Cuba, following a 2007 agreement that improved relations by aiding Cuban businesses and social programs in exchange for human rights reforms and the release of political prisoners. Spain supported Castro's decision to hand over power to his brother, Raúl, saying the move would advance political reforms. In June 2008 Spain urged an easing of international sanctions against Cuba because of progress made in reforms.

In July 2008 Spain's Senate approved the EU's Lisbon Treaty after Irish voters rejected it.

Faced with its own troubles with separatist movements, Spain in February 2008 became one of the few European countries not to recognize Kosovo's declaration of independence from Serbia. The government faced considerable domestic criticism over its deployment of nearly 600 troops in the NATO peacekeeping operation in Kosovo.

Upon winning a second term, Zapatero said he would seek a "new chapter" in relations with the United States based on "mutual respect." The election of Barack Obama to the U.S. presidency in November 2008 brought renewed commitments in Spanish support for U.S. military operations. In December Spain lifted a 3,000-troop ceiling on the number of soldiers that may be deployed overseas, thereby clearing the way for a troop increase in Afghanistan, and in February 2009 expressed a willingness to accept detainees from the U.S. military camp at Guantanamo on a case-by-case basis.

Angered at not being invited to a European meeting on the global financial crisis in October 2008, Zapatero lobbied heavily to attend a Group of 20 summit in Washington in November on the grounds that, as the world's eighth largest economy, Spain deserved a seat at the table. Spain eventually prevailed when France ceded one of its two seats. Subsequently, Zapatero called for a permanent seat at the Group of 20, while analysts saw the incident as an effort to enlarge Spain's international standing. In further such efforts, Zapatero interjected in a violent flare-up in the Gaza Strip in late 2008 by approving $1.5 million in medical aid to the Palestinians and offering his services in brokering peace. Opposition politicians accused Zapatero of trying to revive the antiwar sentiment that helped bring him to power.

In December 2008 Spain and Morocco sought to patch up lingering resentments over the 2007 visit of Spanish King Juan Carlos and Queen Sofia to Ceuta and Melilla by hosting a bilateral summit in Madrid during which Spain pledged $730 million to finance "projects of common interest" in Morocco with the aim of strengthening the two countries' economic ties (see Related territories, below). Zapatero and Moroccan Prime Minister Abbas El Fassi reportedly also discussed construction of a tunnel under the Straits of Gibraltar.

To advance Spanish business prospects, Spanish King Juan Carlos visited Libyan President Muammar Gadhafi in early 2009 to finalize an investment pact that would boost Spanish oil and construction interests there. In March Spain hosted Russian President Dmitry Medvedev and signed an energy agreement that allows Spanish oil companies to help develop Russia's vast Shtokman gas field and to partake in joint energy sector projects with Russia around the globe. The agreement came following a controversial debate in Spain over the possibility of a Russian oil firm purchasing a large stake in Spain's major energy supplier, Repsol SA.

Revelations in January 2009 that Gibraltan authorities were extending into Spanish territorial waters by reclaiming land for building projects aroused the PP, which threatened to seek a European Commission investigation into the matter and demanded Zapatero oppose an official visit to Gibraltar in March by Britain's Princess Anne. In July foreign minister Miguel Moratinos went to Gibraltar to sign agreements on judicial, environmental, security, and customs measures, while the PP argued that the visit validated the territory as a sovereign state.

Spain angered NATO allies with an unexpected decision to withdraw all peacekeeping forces from Kosovo by the autumn of 2009, saying that postwar operations there no longer needed outside support. U.S. officials complained that Spain made its decision without coordinating with other NATO members. Analysts believe that Spain withdrew to avoid appearing to endorse the precedent of Kosovar independence.

In response to growing tensions with foreign governments, the Congress of Deputies in June 2009 voted to restrict the ability of Spanish judges to investigate crimes against humanity around the world to cases only involving Spanish citizens. Spain had first used the principle of "universal jurisdiction" in an unsuccessful attempt to extradite Chilean dictator Augustus Pinochet in 1998. The Spanish judge in that case, Baltasar GARZÓN Real, also invoked the principle in May 2009 against six former White House officials who he alleged provided the legal cover for torture at the U.S. prison at Guantanamo, and to investigate a deadly Israeli incursion into Gaza in 2002. At the time of the lower house vote, the Spanish High Court was investigating 13 crimes against humanity around the world involving both Spanish and non-Spanish victims.

In January 2010, Spain assumed the six-month rotating EU presidency, a tenure that was marred by the European debt crisis and the Greek financial bailout. Zapatero led a successful effort to require public disclosure of stress tests on banks, and he concluded the signing of a free trade agreement between the EU and Central America. Efforts to normalize relations between the EU and Cuba were resisted by a number of EU nations, including France, Sweden, and the Czech Republic, which argued that the 1996 EU "common position" on the Caribbean island be preceded by democratic reforms.

In July 2010, Spain's foreign minister, Miguel Moratinos, supported by the Catholic Church, negotiated the release of 52 Cuban political prisoners and arranged their asylum in Spain. In October Spain called on Venezuela to examine evidence that several suspected ETA members, who had been arrested in Spain, had received weapons training in the South American country. Spain requested "concrete action" against ETA member Arturo Cubillas Fontan, who had been given a senior post in the administration of Venezuelan president Hugo Chavez in 2005. The Venezuelan government insisted it had no ties with ETA.

Also in 2010, tensions flared between Spain and Great Britain over Gibraltar. In June Spain refused to allow the British air force to use airspace over Gibraltar for military exercises, and in October Gibraltar asked the British Royal Navy to intercede because of a growing number of face-offs with Spanish naval and police boats in Gibraltar's waters. In October Spain agreed to resume talks with the UK over the future of the British enclave.

In October 2010, Argentine judge Mariá Servini announced that her court would begin investigating the atrocities committed during the Franco era since the 1977 amnesty law in Spain prevented prosecution for crimes during the period. On December 10 Spain expelled two Russian diplomats following charges of espionage. Russia retaliated by expelling two Spanish diplomats on December 24. In October 2011, Spain announced that it would participate in the NATO missile defense shield, despite opposition from Russia.

After Argentina took control of 51 percent of the Spanish oil company Repsol's South American operations in April 2012, Spain imposed restrictions on the import of biodiesel from Argentina. (Repsol later filed suit against Argentina for a loss of $10.5 billion.) The legislature approved a treaty with the Philippines in May 2012, whereby Filipinos working in Spain would be eligible for social security benefits. As a result of Spain's growing budget deficit, the government canceled development aid for Central and South America in May, and in November appealed to its former colonies to expand trade. Spain agreed to host four U.S. missile-interceptors in October. Two guided-missile-equipped ships will arrive in 2014 and two more in 2015.

Gibraltar dropped 70 concrete blocks into the sea to create an artificial reef in August 2013, but failed to alert Spain. Madrid protested the development, saying it impeded Spanish fishing rights, and increased border checks. The United Kingdom filed a protest with the European Commission, saying the Spanish move impeded the flow of goods and people.

Current issues. Following the 2004 Madrid train bombings, the government initiated proactive measures to reduce the threat of terrorism. In September 2005, in Europe's largest trial of Islamic militants, a Spanish court convicted 18 of 24 defendants of belonging to al-Qaida, including the alleged leader of al-Qaida in Spain. In October 2007, following a trial against 28 defendants in the Madrid bombings, many of them from Morocco or elsewhere in North Africa, 21 were convicted of charges ranging from forgery to murder. Further arrests in 2008 and 2009 were aimed at stopping a suspected attack against Barcelona's transport system and disrupting terrorism financing networks.

By 2008, Spain's immigrant population, largely from South America, Eastern Europe, and North Africa, had swelled to nearly 5 million people, or 10 percent of the population. At the height of the economic boom in 2005 Zapatero approved an amnesty that legalized some 600,000 illegal immigrants, to the dismay of EU leaders seeking greater immigration controls in the border-free block. The Zapatero administration announced plans to allow immigrants to vote in local elections. When the economy entered a severe downturn in 2009, the Zapatero government offered financial incentives for unemployed immigrants to return to their home countries, halted a program to recruit immigrants from abroad, and enacted harsher penalties on illegal immigration. As a result, the number of immigrants arriving on Spanish shores dropped by 40 percent between 2008 and 2010. The Spanish government reported that the number of immigrants in 2009 dropped to less than one-tenth of that of the previous year, and that the number of illegal immigrants dropped by half.

Spain's Muslim population of approximately 1 million has met public resistance in its efforts to build new mosques. The Popular Party unveiled proposals during the 2008 elections to require immigrants to renew residency permits, sign a pledge to learn Spanish, and respect Spanish customs. It also supported a ban on Muslim headscarves in public schools.

To counter threats emanating from North Africa in February 2009, Spain signed a comprehensive security agreement with Algeria on anti-terrorism intelligence, training, and technology cooperation. In June, a similar accord was struck with Morocco, although Spain continued to deny extradition to Morocco for anyone who would face the death penalty or life imprisonment.

Since the rise of Islamic terrorism, public tolerance for violent Basque separatists has waned considerably, although the issue of nationhood for the Basque County remains unresolved. Under Prime Minister Aznar, Spain had clamped down on groups associated with ETA, banning the Unity (*Batasuna*) party in 2003 (see Political parties, below). The Zapatero administration sought a more conciliatory approach with ETA, brokering a peace deal in March 2006, which collapsed 15 months later when a faction of ETA detonated a bomb at the Madrid airport. In response, the government arrested ETA leaders and initiated efforts to ban political parties that are suspected fronts (see Illegal Groups, below).

In June 2006 voters in Catalonia overwhelmingly approved a referendum giving their region greater autonomy, including retention of a higher percentage of tax collections and greater authority over judicial appointments, immigration, licensing, and mass transportation. It also recognized Catâlan as the "preferential" language over Castilian Spanish and acknowledged that Catalonia considers itself a distinct nation. Prime Minister Zapatero supported the Catalan referendum and said other regions were free to propose their own such referenda.

Voters in Andalusia acted on Zapatero's comment and in February 2007 overwhelmingly approved a referendum that expanded that region's autonomy, especially in the area of fiscal management. However, an effort by the **Basque Nationalist Party** (*Partido Nacionalista Vasco*—PNV/*Euzko Alderdi Jeltzalea*—EAJ) to hold a referendum on self-determination was blocked by the central government in October 2007 on grounds that it was unconstitutional. The referendum also sought approval for a negotiated peace accord with ETA.

In October 2007, the government passed the controversial Law of Historical Memory to wipe out remaining monuments to Franco's dictatorship and compensate the families of victims of the regime and the Spanish Civil War. Conservative parties, which in some cases had not explicitly renounced the fascist era, argued that the law was socially divisive and did not address the suffering inflicted by leftist Republican forces on Catholics and other groups. The Catholic Church, which opposed the law, won a concession to keep memorials of fascist-era symbols on church property so long as there were "artistic–religious" reasons to keep them. In November right-wing supporters honored Franco for the last time at his tomb at the Valle de los Caidos monument outside Madrid before the new law, which banned such public homage to fascist icons, took effect. The Spanish parliament in 2008 approved decrees under the historical memory law that compensated victims' families, cleared victims' names, and extended Spanish citizenship to the children and grandchildren of Spaniards who fled the country during the civil war. Approximately 150,000 Mexicans were expected to qualify for citizenship under the new provision.

Basque regional elections on March 1, 2009, terminated the three-decades-old reign of the Basque Nationalist Party, which failed to gain an absolute majority and was thereby defeated in a governing agreement led by the PSE-EE, a PSOE affiliate. Analysts saw the results as a blow to the radical left and a sign that voters valued Zapatero's efforts, however unsuccessful, toward a negotiated peace. However, the PSOE's success was tempered by an upset in Galicia, where the PP ousted the PSOE-led coalition in a vote of 39 for the PP and 24 for the PSOE in the 75-seat regional assembly. Analysts blamed voter discontent with the coalition on the PSOE's response to the severe economic recession, although clashes over requirements that the regional language, Galician, be taught in schools also featured prominently in the election.

In July 2009, the Zapatero administration approved a new financing mechanism for the regions, following two years of tense negotiations that were heavily promoted by the autonomous government of

Catalonia. The agreement allows regional governments to keep more tax revenue without reducing net transfers to poorer regions in Spain. Critics complained that the result significantly increased the central government's contribution to the system by about 1 percent of GDP.

In a major blow to regional demands for autonomy, the Constitutional Court in June 2010 struck down or changed more than a dozen articles in Catalonia's autonomy statute, including preferential use of Catalan over Spanish. Significantly, the court declared that use of the word "nation" to describe the region had "no legal value." The ruling was instigated by a challenge brought by the PP, but it provoked a backlash against Zapatero from Catalonian political leaders, who urged him to take a stronger stance against the ruling. It also resulted in calls for constitutional recognition of pluralism.

The national elections on November 20, swept the PSOE out of power. The PP increased its majority in the Senate and won an absolute majority in the lower chamber. Party leader Rajoy was sworn in as prime minister of a PP government in December.

In February 2012, the finance minister announced that Spain's budget deficit for 2011 was 8.5 percent of GDP, far above estimations by the former PSOE government. Credit firms again downgraded Spain's debt. The government instituted a new round of austerity measures, including the elimination of public-sector jobs, reducing severance packages, providing benefits to part-time workers, and incentives for firms hiring people under age 30. The measures were met with widespread protests and strikes. In regional elections in March 2012, the PP increased its seats in Andalusia but failed to gain a majority. The PSOE was able to form a coalition government for the region. Meanwhile, the PSOE won balloting in Asturias.

In June, following contentious negotiations, the EU and IMF agreed to provide Spain up to €100 billion to shore up its financial sector and to create an independent agency to monitor government finances. Unlike the bailout packages given to Greece or Ireland, these funds would go straight to the banks, not the government. In July, the EU-IMF released the first €30 billion of the deal after Spain agreed to limit its deficit in 2012 to 6.3 percent of GDP. However, depositors transferred €74.2 billion from Spanish banks to foreign banks that month—4.7 percent of holdings—amid fears that Spain would withdraw from the eurozone. Spain also agreed to establish a bad bank, the Fund for Orderly Bank Restructuring, to absorb €50 billion in toxic assets from the financial sector.

The government unveiled its 2013 budget in September, which included €40 billion in government spending cuts and a value-added tax rate increase from 18 to 21 percent. The government also acknowledged an unexpected 5 percent increase in benefit costs due to the high unemployment rate. The budget included a deficit of 4.5 percent of GDP. Proposed €1 billion cuts to education led parents to pull their children out of school in protest on October 18. Nearly 80 percent of the national student body was absent.

Regional leaders used the dire financial situation to press for independence. When Prime Minister Rajoy rejected his request for increased tax authority, the president of Catalonia, Artur MAS (CiU) called snap regional elections for November 25. Some 1.5 million Catalans had staged a rally for independence in Barcelona on September 11, angry that they paid more taxes to Madrid than they received in benefits. Meanwhile Andalusia, Castilla-La Mancha, Catalonia, Murcia, and Valencia regions requested a total of €14.5 billion from the central government's €18 billion regional rescue fund.

Pro-independence parties won regional elections in Basque country on October 21. The moderate Basque Nationalist Party (PNV) took 27 seats, followed by the new coalition Basque Country Assembly (*Euskal Herria Bildu*) with 21. The PSOE placed third, with 16 seats. Also on October 21, the ruling PP won a majority (41 of 75 seats) in Galicia, while a new nationalist group, the Galician Left Alternative, won 9 seats.

In November the European Commission released €37 billion to four Spanish banks, conditioned on their closing offices and laying off thousands of employees to cut costs. Industry analysts warned that the banks might need up to €60 billion to recapitalize. Meanwhile, separatist parties won 71 of the 135 seats in elections to Catalonia's regional parliament on November 25. On January 23 Catalonia's parliament passed a motion stating that Catalonia is a sovereign entity. Yet six days later, Catalonia's leaders asked Madrid for €9.1 billion in regional development funds.

Also in January, Prime Minister Rajoy and the ruling PP became embroiled in a corruption scandal that undermined public confidence in the government. Luis BÁRCENAS, who had resigned as PP treasurer in 2009 amid bribery charges, was discovered to have €22 million in Swiss bank accounts. Facing jail time, Bárcenas disclosed that he had presided over an elaborate kickback scheme whereby PP leaders, including Rajoy, had received regular cash payments from Spanish businessmen for more than 20 years. The news left voters disgusted and disillusioned and prompted calls for improved oversight of political contributions. A February poll showed that 96 percent of Spaniards believed most politicians are corrupt.

Corruption also sapped public support for the monarchy. King Juan Carlos continued to suffer the fallout from his lavish April 2012 African safari, which became public knowledge when he broke his hip and had to be flown home. Cash-strapped Spaniards had little sympathy for the king, and his staff staged an unprecedented strike in March 2013. Inaki Urdangarin, the king's son-in-law, stood accused of taking €6 million from regional governments in return for organizing sports and tourism events. In April, the PSOE introduced a motion requesting information on the king's finances, especially how public funds were spent. Many Spaniards called for Juan Carlos to abdicate in favor of his son.

The government announced plans in March to help residents fight evictions when they fall behind on their mortgage payments. To raise additional cash, the government decided on March 28 to sell part of its stake in the European Aeronautic Defense and Space Company for €400 million. Meanwhile, employees of Iberia airways called off their strike when the company agreed to lay off 3,141 workers instead of 4,500 and to reduce planned pay cuts.

By mid-2013, the Spanish economy was at a standstill. With slashed wages, meager benefits, and unemployment near 28 percent—almost 60 percent for youth—Spaniards limited consumption. Nearly 2 million unemployed individuals were no longer receiving benefits. Domestic demand was flat, and exports struggled as most went to other eurozone countries in similarly dire circumstances. High interest rates discouraged job creation. The government revised growth predictions, seeing little chance of growth before 2014. In April Finance and Public Administration Minister Cristóbal Montoro ROMERO admitted that the budget deficit would likely be 6.3 percent of GDP for 2013 and that it would not dip below 3 percent before 2016.

In May Rajoy proposed overturning the country's liberal abortion policy, a move seen as a ploy to shore up support among conservative members of the PP. He also moved to rein-in excessive spending of regional governments by lowering their deficit targets from 1.7 percent of GDP to 1.2 percent. However, compliance with the 2012 target varied widely. PP-run regions, such as Castille-La Mancha went from 7.9 percent in 2011 to 1.5 percent in 2012, while CiU-dominant Catalonia registered 2 percent and PSOE-run Andalusia at 1.72 for 2012. Regional leaders complained, resulting in individual targets for each region.

In late May, the EU granted Spain two additional years to meet the 3 percent deficit target.

In July 28, a commuter train derailed in Galicia, injuring nearly 200 passengers and killing 79. It was the worst train accident in over 40 years. The driver was arrested as records indicated he was traveling at more than twice the posted speed limit and talking on the phone as he approached a sharp curve.

While the October 2011 ceasefire with the ETA has held, the PP government has insisted that the organization most concede defeat and give up any remaining weapons, which leaders have refused to do. Rajoy pressured Norway to expel three ETA leaders, David Pla, Iratxe Sorzabel, and Josu Ternera, in March over their noncompliance. Following the strong showing of EH Bildu in the Basque elections in 2012, Sortu (see Political Parties, below) has been pressuring the remaining ETA leaders to consider turning in weapons in return for transferring Basque prisoners to facilities in the Basque territory.

POLITICAL PARTIES

The only authorized political formation during most of the Franco era was the Spanish Falange (*Falange Española Tradicionalista y de las Juntas de Ofensiva Nacional-Sindicalista*—FET y JONS), subsequently referred to as "The National Movement." In January 1975, prior to Franco's death, a law permitting the establishment of noncommunist and nonseparatist "political associations" went into effect, and during the next two years a large number of parties, both legal and illegal, proceeded to organize. In March 1976 the Democratic Coordination (*Coordinación Democrática*—CD) was launched as a unified front embracing all strands of the opposition, from communists to liberal monarchists.

Following a December 1976 referendum on political reform and the subsequent enactment of legislation simplifying the registration of political parties, the CD broke up. Most of its moderate members joined with a number of non-CD parties in establishing the Union of the Democratic Center (UCD), which won the June 1977 election and controlled the government for the ensuing five years. Following a disastrous showing against the PSOE in the October 1982 election, the UCD leadership voted in February 1983 to dissolve the party. By then what was to become the Popular Party had emerged as the main conservative alternative to the PSOE. Although 92.8 percent of the 1996 congressional vote was shared by just five parties (with no other party securing even 1 percent), the development of a straight two-party system was qualified by a diversity of regional parties and continuing support for left-wing groups. There are presently more than 2,000 registered national, regional, and local parties.

Government Party:

Popular Party (*Partido Popular*—PP). The PP was known until January 1989 as the Popular Alliance (*Alianza Popular*—AP), which emerged in 1976 as a right-wing challenger to the Union of the Democratic Center (UCD). Following the UCD victory in 1977, most AP deputies in late 1978 joined with representatives of a number of other rightist parties in an alliance that contested the 1979 election as the Democratic Coalition (*Coalición Democrática*—CD), winning nine lower house seats. Despite its Francoist image, the AP opposed the 1981 coup attempt. Prior to the 1982 poll, the UCD national executive, by a narrow margin, rejected a proposal to form an alliance with the AP, although a constituent group, the Popular Democratic Party (*Partido Demócrata Popular*—PDP), formerly the Christian Democracy (*Democracia Cristiana*—DC), elected to do so. In the October voting the AP/PDP coalition, benefiting from the effective demise of the UCD, garnered 106 congressional seats, thus becoming the second-ranked group in the lower house. Although pro-NATO, the AP urged a boycott of the March 1986 referendum on the NATO membership issue in an effort to undermine the González government.

The AP contested the June 1986 election as part of the Popular Coalition (*Coalición Popular*—CP), which included the PDP and secured 105 congressional seats. Describing the outcome as "unsatisfactory," the PDP (with 21 deputies and 11 senators) broke with the Coalition upon convening of the new *Cortes* on July 15, while four members of the AP also defected in opposition to Manuel FRAGA Iribarne's CP/AP leadership. Further disintegration of the CP at the regional level prompted Fraga's resignation as AP president on December 2, 1986. Antonio HERNÁNDEZ Mancha was named AP president (and leader of what remained of the CP) in February 1987.

At a party congress held January 20–22, 1989, the formation undertook a number of moves, including the change of name, to reorient itself toward the center as a moderate conservative alternative to the PSOE. In the same year, it absorbed the Liberal Party (*Partido Liberal*—PL), which nevertheless elected to retain its legal identity. The PP also has, from time to time, had local and regional pacts with a variety of other parties.

The PP retained its second-ranked standing in the October 1989 poll (albeit with a gain of only 1 lower house seat, for a total of 106) and, on December 17, won an absolute majority in the Galician Parliament. Recently reinstated party chief Fraga was thereupon installed as regional president, being succeeded as PP leader by José María Aznar.

The party was able to mount an impressive opposition threat in the run-up to the June 1993 parliamentary balloting, in which it won 141 congressional and 107 senatorial seats on a vote share of 34.8 percent, less than four points behind the PSOE. Having overtaken the PSOE in the June 1994 European Parliament balloting, the PP solidified its standing as the largest party in the March 1996 national balloting, winning 156 seats and 38.9 percent of the vote, enabling Aznar to form a minority government supported by three regionalist groupings: Catalonia's Convergence and Union (CiU), the Canarian Coalition (CC), and the Basque Nationalist Party (PNV).

At a party congress in January 1999, Aznar's handpicked candidate, Javier ARENAS Bocanegra, was chosen to succeed Francisco ÁLVAREZ-CASCOS as secretary general. Bocanegra's ascendancy reportedly underlined the prime minister's professed desire to foster the image of a more centrist PP as well as his increasing control over the party.

In March 2000, the PP won 183 seats on an unexpectedly high vote share of 46.6 percent, but the PP's quest for a third term in office failed in March 2004, when its results fell to 37.6 percent and 148 seats. In September 2003, Aznar announced that Deputy Prime Minister Mariano Rajoy would lead the PP in the next election.

After the PP's surprise loss in the 2004 elections following terrorist attacks in March, the PP became the lead opposition party, shifting further to the right. In the 2008 elections, Rajoy led a campaign against Zapatero that centered on tax cuts, a tough stance on terrorism with no engagement with ETA, tough immigration laws, and the promotion of "family values" as a counterweight to the PSOE's radical social policies.

In June 2008, Maria Dolores de Cospedal became the first woman general secretary of the party, replacing Ángel ACEBES Paniagua. The move was seen as a way to renew leadership. Rajoy was reelected with 84 percent of the vote at a party congress in November, which did little to mask emerging fractures within the party and with PP allies. A long-standing partner in Navarre, the UPN, split from the PP in October.

The PP was beset by a series of corruption scandals and political infighting in 2009. Several top Madrid officials accused PP rivals of using a regional government agency to spy on them during an internal battle for power within the party. A judge in the Gürtel case subsequently charged 37 members of the PP with corruption related to a network that allegedly ran building permits and lucrative contracts in Madrid. The highest-ranking officials implicated were the PP's national treasurer, Luis Bárcenas, and the president of Valencia's regional government, Francisco CAMPS. Rajoy reacted by accusing state prosecutors of acting in concert with the PSOE to smear the party's name and influence regional elections. Despite the scandal, regional elections on March 1 in Rajoy's home region of Galicia handed the PP a victory, while the June 7 European parliamentary elections resulted in the party's first victory in European elections.

In July 2009, Bárcenas quit his post as Valencia's president as his case came before the Supreme Court. In August, the Supreme Court dropped bribery charges against Camps and two other Valancian party members. Meanwhile, the PP secretary general Maria Dolores De Cospedal accused the government of using law enforcement to spy on PP members. In November, Rajoy announced he would strengthen his party's ethics code in reaction to the corruption scandal and called for those found guilty to feel the "full weight of the law." In April, Bárcenas resigned as treasurer of the party following the public release of a large dossier on him in the corruption investigation. In spite of the PP's corruption problems, polls consistently showed it to be more popular than the PSOE.

The PP swept regional and municipal balloting in May 2011, securing 37 percent of the vote and winning 11 of 13 regional presidencies while securing majorities in 3,317 of 8,078 councils. Prior to balloting, in January, former general secretary and deputy prime minister Francisco Álvarez-Cascos left the PP to form the **Forum Asturias** (*Foro Asturias*—FAC, below). In November, the PP swept national elections, and Rajoy became prime minister.

Leaders: Mariano RAJOY Brey (Prime Minister and President of the Party), José María AZNAR López (Honorary President), Maria Dolores DE COSPEDAL (Secretary General), Soraya Sáenz DE SANTAMARÍA (Deputy Prime Minister).

Other National Parties:

Spanish Socialist Workers' Party (*Partido Socialista Obrero Español*—PSOE). Founded in 1879 and a member of the Socialist International, the PSOE, under the young and dynamic Felipe González Márquez, held its first legal congress in 44 years in December 1976, and in 1979, the PSOE became the second-strongest party in the *Cortes,* winning 121 seats in the Congress of Deputies and 68 seats in the Senate at the election of March 1 in conjunction with a regional ally, the Party of Socialists of Catalonia (see PSC, below). In April 1978, the Popular Socialist Party (*Partido Socialista Popular*—PSP), which had contested the 1977 election as part of the Socialist Union (*Unidad Socialista*—US), formally merged with the PSOE.

At a centennial congress in May 1979, González unexpectedly stepped down as party leader after a majority of delegates refused to abandon a doctrinal commitment to Marxism. His control was reestablished during a special congress in late September, the hard-liners being defeated by a vote of more than ten to one. In the 1982 election, the PSOE/PSC won an absolute majority in both the Congress and Senate, González being invested as prime minister on December 2. In the following year, the PSOE absorbed the centrist Democratic Action Party (*Partido de Acción Democrática*—PAD). Subsequently, the PSOE experienced internal strain as a result of the government's pro-NATO posture, which ran counter to the party's long-standing rejection of participation in any military alliance. The issue was resolved in favor of qualified NATO membership by the March 1986 referendum, held shortly after the PSOE government had taken Spain into the EC.

The PSOE held power with a reduced majority in 1986. Its retention of only 175 lower house seats in the 1989 balloting was blamed, in part, on the emergence in September of a dissident internal faction, Socialist Democracy (*Democracia Socialista*—DS), and the subsequent defection of party members to the IU (see below). Thereafter, the PSOE's standing was adversely affected by a series of financial scandals involving prominent party figures, although at an early election in June 1993, the party retained a narrow plurality of 159 seats, sufficient for González to form a minority government with regional party support.

Continuing financial and security scandals led to the defeat of the PSOE in the election of March 1996, which left it with 141 seats in the lower house on a vote share of 35.5 percent. González declined to run for reelection as PSOE general secretary in 1997 and was succeeded by Joaquín ALMUNIA Amann.

In 1999–2000, the PSOE suffered a series of setbacks. On May 14, 1999, Josep BORRELL Fontelles, the party's candidate for prime minister in the next election, withdrew because of a financial scandal involving two former associates. Ten days later, the man who had served as the PSOE's president for more than 20 years, Ramón RUBIAL Cavia, died. On June 13, at local and regional elections, the PSOE saw its vote share increase, largely at the expense of the IU, but succeeded in gaining control of only one regional government, in Asturias. In the May 2000 national balloting, the party and its affiliates lost ground to the PP, losing 16 of their 141 seats in the lower house and prompting its prime ministerial candidate, Almunia, to immediately resign from the leadership.

Almunia's successor as secretary general, José Luis Rodríguez Zapatero, was elected by a party conference on July 23, 2000, narrowly defeating José BONO Martínez, the heavily favored president of Castilla–La Mancha. Rodríguez Zapatero, whose supporters compared him to the UK's Tony Blair, soon made wholesale changes in the party's hierarchy in the interest of "modernization" and a "New Way" (*Nueva Via*).

In July 2001, the Democratic Party of the New Left (*Partido Democrático de la Nueva Izquierda*—PDNI), which had been organized in 1996 by former members of the United Left, principally Cristina ALMEIDA and Diego LÓPEZ Garrido, merged with the PSOE. The PDNI had been allied with the PSOE in recent elections.

In the general election of March 2004, the PSOE won an unexpected victory, taking 42.6 percent of the vote and 164 seats (including those won by regional affiliates). With the support of the IU and several small regional parties allowing the party a majority, Zapatero was confirmed as prime minister in April. The PSOE then reversed some of the reforms implemented by the Anzar government, countering a strengthened role for private education and focusing primarily on social, as opposed to economic, concerns.

Since forming the government in 2004, the PSOE has decreased in popularity, due in part to its response to the Basque problem. The PSOE publicly condemned the arrest of the Batasuna party members in October 2007 (see Current issues, above) and endorsed engagement with ETA, in contrast to the opposition PP position. The PSOE also supports increased autonomy for Spain's regions.

At a congress on October 21, 2007, Juan Fernando López Aguilar was named the new PSOE general secretary, succeeding Prime Minister Zapatero with 92.97 percent of delegates' votes.

The PSOE performed better than expected in the March 9, 2008, election, winning the largest majority in both legislative houses and slightly boosting its membership. In the Congress of Deputies, the number of seats increased from 164 to 169 and in the Senate increased from 100 to 101. However, the PSOE's minority status meant the small regional parties would continue to hold the balance of power. At the July party convention, Zapatero won the position of secretary general a second time with 98.5 percent of the vote.

The 2008 elections led to significant policy shifts in the party. Among them was a renunciation of negotiations with ETA following the murder of a PSOE local politician two days prior to the poll as well as muted support for further concessions on regional autonomy, particularly concerning the Basque Country.

However, the PSOE refused to back down on its liberal social policies after drawing ire from leaders of the Catholic Church, which joined hands with the PP to condemn the PSOE for policies that legalized same-sex marriage, instituted fast-track divorce, and introduced a new civics course for students as an alternative to religious studies. The party's policies stoked deep divisions within Spain. Particularly controversial was a plan to ease restrictions on abortions that the PSOE introduced in early 2009, which the Vatican denounced on a state visit to Spain in February.

Opposition to the PSOE's sweeping social policies was compounded by the onset of the severe economic recession, which battered the party's popularity in public polls and in the June 7, 2009, European Parliament election.

Ironically, the PSOE's victory in regional elections in the Basque Country on March 1 served to further isolate the party in parliament. The Basque Nationalist Party, a crucial legislative ally, said it would no longer support Zapatero's government after it lost governing power in the Basque parliament. However, a regional financing agreement passed in July helped shore up support among Catalan nationalist parties for an autumn debate over the 2010 budget, which was expected to be especially contentious. An unexpected agreement was reached in November when the Basque National Party and Canarian Coalition lent the PSOE enough support to ensure passage of the 2010 budget. However, in 2010, the Zapatero government faced close votes on a series of economic reforms that, had they failed, would have precipitated a vote of no confidence and potentially an early election. As a result of the reforms, PSOE popularity plunged among an electorate largely unwilling to accept deep cuts to social services.

The PSOE secured only 28 percent of the vote in regional and local balloting in May 2011, winning majorities in 1,860 of 8,078 municipal councils. Deputy Prime Minister and Interior Minister Alfredo Pérez Rubalcaba subsequently resigned his government posts after he was chosen at a party primary to lead the PSOE in the November national elections, which the party lost to the PP.

In addition to the PSC, regional parties affiliated with the PSOE include the Basque Socialist Party–Basque Left (see PSE-EE, below), the Party of Galician Socialists (see PSdeG, below), the **Madrid Socialist Federation** (*Federación Socialista Madrileña*—FSM), the **Socialist Party of Navarra** (*Partido Socialista de Navarra*—PSN), and the **Socialist Party of the Valencian Country** (*Partido Socialista del País Valenciano*—PSPV).

Leaders: José Antonio GRIÑÁN Martíne (President), Alfredo Pérez RUBALCABA (General Secretary), Elena VALENCIANO (Vice General Secretary), María del Carmen SILVA REGO (Parliamentary Spokesperson).

United Left (*Izquierda Unida*—IU). The IU was formed in April 1986 as an anti-NATO electoral coalition that principally included the Spanish Communist Party (PCE, below), the **Republican Left** *(Izquierda Republicana*—IR), the **Socialist Action Party** (*Partido de Acción Socialista*—Pasoc), the **Progressive Federation** (*Federación Progresista*—FP), the left-wing liberal **Carlist Party** (*Partido Carlista*—PC), and the libertarian **Humanist Party** (*Partido Humanista*—PH). It won a total of seven congressional seats at the June 1986 election.

The PCE's Julio ANGUITA González resigned as IU general coordinator in November 1991, after opposing suggestions by members of several groups, including the PCE, that the coalition members dissolve as separate entities to form a single party; subsequently, however, he resumed the position. The IU made only marginal headway in the June 1993 election, winning 18 lower house seats with 9.6 percent of the vote. It retained third place in the 1996 national election, winning 21 lower house seats on a 10.6 percent vote share, but thereafter experienced a marked decline. In the June 1999 local elections its vote share fell from 11.7 to 6.5 percent, and in the March 2000 national election it won only 8 congressional seats. In March 2004 the IU won 5.0 percent of the vote and 5 lower house seats.

In 2007, the communist-led IU supported the PSOE-sponsored Law of Historical Memory, condemning the Franco regime, which had executed many of its political forebears. The IU was also the only parliamentary party to vote against the deployment of an additional 52 Spanish troops to Afghanistan in September. In November, IU leader Gaspar LLAMAZARES Trigo won reelection with 62 percent of the vote under a pledge to form a coalition of all "forces of the left," including the **Green Confederation** (*Confederación de Los Verdes*) and nationalist groups. His rival, Marga SANZ, was backed by a PCE faction whose criticism of Llamazares led Llamazares supporters to oust three PCE members from the executive board in December. The ousting included PCE leader Francisco Frutose and was meant to unify the party going into the 2008 election. However, continued infighting was partially to blame for the IU's dismal performance in the March 9, 2008, election, in which the IU lost one-quarter of its voters to the PSOE and two of the party's five seats in Congress.

Afterward, Llamazares announced he would not be standing for reelection in November, complaining of a "bipartisan tsunami" that was limiting political diversity. The IU's ninth party convention met in November and elected a new national committee but failed to agree on a new leader. Still stinging from losses in the March election, it approved a document stating that the IU must change because "it has reached the end of a political era" and "needs to return a sense of credibility and urgency to its leftist, anti-capitalist, alternative and transformational agenda." In December the party settled on a PCE leader, Cayo Lara Moyo, as general coordinator of the IU in a vote of 55 percent. Lara threatened to call a general strike if the PSOE did not change its response to the economic crisis by doing more to support workers.

In April 2009, the IU's only remaining city mayor left her post to become part of the PSOE government in Andalusia. However, the IU kept its two seats in the European Parliament following the June 7 election.

Other closely linked organizations include the **Ezker Batua** (EB—also translated as **United Left**) in Basque Country and Navarre, the **United Left of the Balearic Islands** (*Esquerra Unida de los Illes Balears*—EU), the **United Left of Valencia** (*Esquerra Unida del País Valenciá*—EUPV), and the Catalan **United and Alternative Left** (*Esquerra Unida i Alternativa*—EUiA). The IU has frequently formed coalitions with other small parties to contest regional elections. In the May 2011 regional and local polling the IU secured 6.31 percent of the vote and majorities on 58 municipal councils. The IU placed fourth and secured 11 seats in the 2011 Congress of Deputies balloting.

Leaders: Cayo LARA Moyo (General Coordinator), Ramón LUQUE (Parliamentary Group Coordinator), Montserrat MUÑOZ DE DIEGO (Institutional Relations).

Spanish Communist Party (*Partido Comunista de España*—PCE). Founded in 1920 but soon banned, the PCE was legalized in April 1977, following the release from detention in December 1976 of its secretary general, Santiago CARRILLO Solares. On April 19–23, 1977, in Madrid, it held its first legal congress in 45 years, while on May 13 the PCE's most celebrated figure, Dolores IBÁRRURI Gómez ("La Pasionaria"), returned to Spain after 38 years in exile. The PCE and its regional ally, the **Unified Socialist Party of Catalonia** (*Partit Socialista Unificat de Catalunya*—PSUC), secured 20 seats in the Congress of Deputies and 12 seats in the Senate in the June 1977 election. In March 1979, with Ibarruri having declined to seek legislative reelection for reasons of health and age, it placed three additional deputies in the lower house but lost all of its upper house seats. In the context of sharp differences between pro-Soviet and "Eurocommunist" factions, its congressional representation declined sharply in 1982 to only four members, with the result that Carrillo, the only survivor of the Civil War still to lead a major party, was forced to step down in November. Carrillo's influence was eroded still further by the decision of new party leaders, who favored nonalignment, to adopt internal reforms and work for a "convergence of progressive forces" with other leftist groups, both elective and nonelective; in April 1985, Carrillo and 18 supporters were expelled following an emergency national congress in March, subsequently forming the Spanish Workers' Party–Communist Unity (*Partido de los Trabajadores de España–Unidad Comunista*—PTE-UC), which joined the PSOE in February 1991.

Immediately prior to the 1986 election a pro-Soviet splinter group, the Spanish Communist Workers' Party (*Partido Comunista Obrero Español*—PCOE), led by Enrique LISTER, voted to disband and rejoin the PCE. Subsequently, in February 1987, a PCE delegation visited Moscow, pledging a strengthening of relations with the Soviet Communists. A second pro-Soviet splinter, the Communist Party of the Peoples of Spain (*Partido Comunista de los Pueblos de España*—PCPE), rejoined the party at a congress of unity in January 1989. The PCPE, led by Ignacio GALLEGO, had broken from the party in 1984 because of the "politico-ideological degeneration . . . which introduced Eurocommunism."

At a party congress in December 1998, the PCE elected Francisco FRUTOS as its new secretary general. In 2007 the PCE sought to build collaboration between European leftists to counter the influence of new center-right formations such as the Sarkozy government in France (see entry on France). The PCE is the largest member organization of the IU.

In April 2009, the PCE brought a suit to the Supreme Court against former prime minister José Maria Aznar and his former ministers of defense and foreign affairs, alleging that the March 2004 train bombings were a result of Spain's involvement in the U.S.-led invasion of Iraq. In November José Luis CENTELLA became the new leader of the PCE, and he struck a more moderate tone than his predecessor.

In May 2010, Centella met with Cuban president Raul Castro in Havana to boost ties between the countries' communist parties. Through 2012, the PCE was a leading force in organizing protests against the government's austerity measures.

Leader: José Luis CENTELLA Gómez (Secretary General).

The Greens (*Los Verdes*). Long a somewhat disparate movement of pacifists, feminists, and ecologists, the Spanish Green Party (*Partido Verde Español*—PVE) was established in June 1984. In the 1986 election the Green Alternative (*Alternativa Verde*) list fared poorly, and the Greens made little headway thereafter until a congress held at Grenada in 1993 resulted in formation of a **Green Confederation** (*Confederación de Los Verdes*) was established in 1993, following the collapse of the Spanish Green Party (*Partido Verde Español*—PVE). At its peak, the Confederation consisted of 16 national and regional parties, including the **Initiative for Catalonia–Greens** (below). It was part of the United Left coalition in the 2011 parliamentary elections. In May 2012, 13 of the 16 parties joined the new EQUO movement, and the European Greens Council canceled the Confederation's membership.

EQUO (*Partido Equo*) is comprised of 35 green parties and individuals, including 13 parties from the Green Confederation. EQUO was established as a political movement in 2011 and as a party in 2012. Members include Green organizations from all parts of Spain that seek sustainable solutions to global problems. It offers alternative values to consumerism and the accumulation of property and debt.

Cospokespersons: Juan López DE URALDE, Reyes MONTIEL

Union, Progress and Democracy (*Unión Progreso y Democracia*—UPyD). Founded in 2007, the UPyD is a liberal, progressive party that advocates expanded federalism, including restoring central control over education and health care. It tried to garner support as a centrist alternative to both the PP and PSOE. The UPyD secured five seats in the 2011 lower chamber balloting. As corruption allegations damaged PP and PSOE in 2013, UPyD emerged as the third national party.

Leader: Rosa DÍEZ.

Spain has a long history of right-wing formations, many of them descendants of the Franco-era **Spanish Falange**. Reduced to little more than a shadow of its former significance, the Falange joined with a number of other neo-fascist groups in forming a National Union (*Unión Nacional*) that secured one legislative seat in 1979. It did not contest the 1982 election to avoid divisiveness within "the forces opposing Marxism." Subsequently, it appeared to have been largely superseded by the formation in October 1984 of a new right-wing grouping, the Spanish Integration Committees (*Juntas Españolas de Integración*), which in 1993 was absorbed by the **National Front** (*Frente Nacional*—FN). Formation of the far-right FN was announced in October 1986 by Blas PIÑAR López, former secretary general of the New Force (*Fuerza Nueva*), which had been dissolved in 1982. The FN has not contested recent elections, but some of its supporters participated in the **Alliance for National Unity** (*Alianza por la Unidad Nacional*—AUN), with little impact in the 1996 election. With its leader, Ricardo SAENZ de Ynestrillas, in prison for attempted murder, the AUN did not contest the 2000 national election. In the 1996 national election the rump Falange, which had split into "Authentic" and "Independent" wings, secured less than 0.1 percent of the vote. In 2000 a new four-party far-right electoral alliance, **Spain 2000** (*España 2000*), suffered a similar fate. The four constituent groups in the alliance were the **National Democracy** (*Democracia Nacional*—DN) of Francisco PEREZ Corrales, the **National Workers' Party** (*Partido Nacional de los Trabajadores*—PNT), the **Republican Social Movement** (*Movimiento Social Republicano*—MSR), and the **Spanish Social Apex** (*Vértice Social Español*—VSE). In late 2005 National Democracy, the Falange, and **Spanish Alternative** (*Alternativa Española*) began negotiations to form a new electoral coalition in anticipation of municipal elections in 2007 and general elections in 2008. The Spanish Alternative won 0.12 percent of the vote in the June 7, 2009, European Parliament election.

In November 2007, the Falange won a controversial court case to hold a rally to commemorate the killing of Falange founder Jose Antonio PRIMO de Rivera in 1936 by leftist forces during the Spanish Civil War. Madrid's regional government had initially banned the rally out of fear it would provoke clashes with leftist groups, a problem that had occurred earlier and continued at a number of right-wing rallies in 2008. Falange's symbol, the arrow and yoke, was banned in Spain under the Law of Historical Memory (see Current issues, above). Falange ran candidates but failed to win any seats in the March 9, 2008, election.

Regional Parties:

There are hundreds of regional parties in addition to the local affiliates of the PP, PSOE, and IU/PCE. Grouped by alphabetical order of region, the parties discussed below are represented in the *Cortes* or regional assemblies.

Andalusian Party (*Partido Andalucista*—PA). Known until 1984 as the Andalusian Socialist Party (*Partido Socialista de Andalucía*—PSA), the PA won 1 seat in the Congress of Deputies in 2000 and none in 2004. At the regional level, the PA won 5 of 109 seats in the Andalusian elections in 2000 and 2004. The PA collaborated with a previously unknown grouping, Andalusian Platform (*Plataforma Andaluces*) to push for separate elections for Andalusia, emphasizing its distinct sense of nationhood.

PA returns for regional elections held May 27, 2007, were as follows: Almería, 4.3 percent; Cádiz, 9.05 percent; Córdoba, 6.5 percent; Granada, 3.12 percent; Huelva, 7.27 percent; Jaén, 4.55 percent; Málaga, 4.76 percent; Sevilla, 7.98 percent.

After its loss of 5 seats in the March 9, 2008, regional election, the party failed to enter the regional parliament for the first time in its history. In the May 2011 regional and local balloting, the party secured 470 seats and majorities on 11 councils. A leadership shuffle at the 2012 party congress installed Antonio Jesús Ruiz to reorient the PA.

Leader: Antonio Jesús RUIZ (Secretary General).

Aragonese Party (*Partido Aragonés*—PAR). Called the Aragonese Regionalist Party (*Partido Aragonés Regionalista*—PAR) until February 1990, the PAR is a center-right grouping that retains its predecessor's initials. Although the party did not contest the 1996 national congressional election in its own right, it won three Senate seats on the strength of an alliance with the PP. In the May 2003 regional election it won eight seats and then joined a governing coalition as junior partner to the PSOE, as it had in 1999. In the 2004 national election it failed to win any seats but continued to hold one designated Senate seat.

PAR returns for regional elections held in May 2007 were as follows: Huesca, 15 percent; Teruel, 22 percent; Zaragoza, 12.24 percent.

On September 19, 2007, the PAR National Committee elected Alfredo Boné Pueyo as secretary general, succeeding Juan Carlos TRILLO Baigorri. An Executive Commission meeting on November 30 finalized candidate lists for the 2008 general elections.

In the March 9, 2008, election the PAR failed to win any seats, registering 0.16 percent of the vote for Congress. In 2009 PAR president José Ángel Biel was reportedly behind a controversial project to build a casino resort complex in Aragon. PAR won 992 seats and majorities on 147 councils in local balloting in May 2011.

Leaders: José Ángel BIEL Rivera (President), Arturo López ALIAGA (Secretary General).

Aragonese Junta (*Chunta Aragonesista*—ChA). The ChA won five seats in the regional *Cortes* in 1999 and nine in the 2003 election, after which it joined the PSOE in forming a government. Nationally, it won one seat in the 2000 and 2004 congressional polls.

ChA regional vote shares on May 27, 2007, were as follows: Huesca, 8.24 percent; Teruel, 5.64 percent; Zaragoza, 9.35 percent. In the March 9, 2008, national election, the party won no seats, registering 0.15 percent of the vote for Congress. The ChA secured 184 seats on councils in the 2011 local elections.

Leaders: José Luis SORO (President), Juan MARTIN (General Secretary).

PSM–Nationalist Union of Majorca (PSM–*Entesa Nacionalista de Mallorca*—PSM-EN). The PSM-EN traces its origins to 1976, when the Socialist Party of the Islands (*Partit Socialist de les Illes*—PSI) was established. In December 1977 the party changed its name to the Socialist Party of Majorca (*Partit Socialista de Mallorca*—PSM), to which the Nationalist Left (*Esquerra Nacionalista*—EN) was added in 1984. Between then and 1990, when the PSM-EN restyled itself as the PSM–Majorca Nationalists (*PSM–Nacionalistes de Mallorca*), the party contested regional, national, and European elections in a number of alliances with other left-oriented formations. In November 1998 the organization assumed its current name.

Following the June 1999 regional election the PSOE negotiated an anti-PP governing alliance that was joined by the PSM-EN, which had won 5 of the 59 legislative seats. In May 2003 the PSM-EN retained 4 seats, but the PP returned to power. Nationally, the party contested the March 2004 lower house elections as part of a coalition, the **Balearic Islands Progressives** (*Progressistes per les Illes Balears*—PIB), that also included the IU-affiliated United Left of the Balearic Islands (EU), the regional Greens, and the Catalan Republican Left (ERC, below).

Initiatives in 2007 included motions to protect Mediterranean coral and ensure protections for minority languages under the European Charter for Regional and Minority Languages, first passed in 1992. The PSM-EN received 6.76 percent of votes in Illes Balears during the May 2007 regional elections.

Leaders: Joana Llüisa MASCARÓ Melià (President), Gabriel BARCELÓ Milta (General Secretary).

Amaiur. A leftist Basque separatist grouping that was formed in September 2011, Amaiur brought together a range of smaller Basque parties and supporters who were dissatisfied with the Basque Nationalist Party. In the 2011 national elections, Amaiur outpolled the Basque Nationalist Party and secured three seats in the Senate and seven in the Congress of Deputies.

Leader: Iñaki ANTIGÜEDAD.

Aralar. Named for a Basque mountain range, *Aralar* is a recent leftist-nationalist splinter from the now-outlawed *Batasuna* (below). Advocating nonviolence, the party won four seats in the Navarre legislature in May 2003 and one in the Basque regional election in April 2005. For the 2004 national election *Aralar* joined with the Basque Nationalist Party (PNV), the Basque Solidarity (EA), and another nationalist Basque party, **Batzarro,** in the **Navarre Yes** (*Naffaroa Bai*—Na-Bai) coalition, which won one seat in the Chamber of Deputies.

Aralar received 6.22 percent of votes in Vizvaya in the 2007 regional elections. In May 2008 party members and Basque separatist lawmakers helped pass a motion in the regional parliament accusing the Spanish government of complicity in police torture of a suspected ETA member. The group also voiced support for Kosovo's declaration of independence in February 2008. In September 2008, Aralar joined the Basque Nationalist Party to continue pressing for a referendum on Basque self-determination, despite a block by the Constitutional Court.

During the Basque regional elections on March 1, 2009, Aralar boosted its seats in the regional parliament from one to four, winning 6 percent of the vote. Its success was taken as a sign that voters had rejected more extremist parties. Following the election, Aralar asserted that it would only consider working with *Batasuna* if it used "exclusively political means" to try to achieve its goals. Because their activities allegedly occurred prior to the 1999 ban on *Batasuna,* in September 2010 Aralar publicly supported 20 of its members who were on trial for having links to ETA. In October Aralar called on ETA to impose a "permanent, unilateral, and verifiable" cease-fire in exchange for the government's transfer of ETA prisoners to jails in the Basque Country. Aralar secured 42 seats on local councils in the 2011 municipal balloting.

Leader: Patxi ZABALETA (General Coordinator).

Basque Country Assembly (*Euskal Herria Bildu—EH Bildu*), a coalition of pro-independence, left-wing forces, placed second in the October 21, 2012, regional parliamentary election, winning 21 seats. Founded in June 2012, *EH Bildu* unites Aralar, Basque Solidarity, Alternatiba, and *Batasuna*, the political wing of the ETA. The new coalition grew out of ETA's decision to end violence. Laura Mintegi, a University of Basque Country professor and *EH Bildu*'s candidate for the regional presidency, won praise for publically insisting on the need to acknowledge all victims of separatist violence in the region.

Leader: Laura MINTEGI (Candidate for Basque President).

Basque Nationalist Party (*Partido Nacionalista Vasco*—PNV/*Euzko Alderdi Jeltzalea*—EAJ). A moderate party that has campaigned for Basque autonomy since 1895, the PNV obtained a plurality in the 1980 Basque election and formed a regional government headed by Carlos GARAICOETXEA Urizza. After the 1984 regional election a dispute regarding devolution of power to individual Basque provinces led to Garaicoetxea's replacement as premier and party leader by José Antonio ARDANZA in January 1985, with the PNV eventually concluding a legislative pact with the PSOE's local affiliate, the Basque Socialist Party (see PSE-EE, below), while Garaicoetxea joined Basque Solidarity (EA, below).

In 1989, the PNV organized mass demonstrations in Bilbao to pressure separatist militants to end their armed struggle. However, subsequent efforts to form an electoral coalition with the EA and the Basque Left (see PSE-EE, below) failed, and in October 1989 the PNV's representation in the Spanish Congress and Senate fell to five and six seats, respectively. One of the latter was lost in the 1993 balloting, after which the PNV gave intermittent support to the PSOE minority government. In the March 1996 national balloting it retained five lower house seats, whereupon it agreed to support a minority PP government in return for more devolution. However, it later withdrew that support.

In balloting for the Basque regional legislature in October 1998, the PNV led all the parties, but its lack of a majority led it to form a coalition government with "We the Basque Citizens" (EH, the restyled political arm of the ETA) and the EA. In January–February 2000, following a renewal of ETA violence, the PNV ended its alliance with the EH. In the national election of March 2000 the PNV picked up 2 seats in the Congress of Deputies, for a total of 7, while at an early regional election on May 13, 2001, it registered its biggest success in a quarter-century, winning 33 seats (a gain of 6) on a 43 percent vote share.

Having retained seven seats in the March 2004 election, the PNV entered the April 2005 regional election seeking support for the "Plan Ibarretxe," a proposal for increased autonomy that had been put forward by PNV leader and Euzkadi President Juan José Ibarretxe. The plan, which included establishment of a union with French Basque areas as well as Basque representation in the EU, had been described by Prime Minister Zapatero as secessionist and unconstitutional and then rejected by the *Cortes* earlier in the year. At the polls, the PNV lost four seats, and Ibarretxe managed to retain the presidency by only one vote when the regional legislature met in June.

The PNV received 38.76 percent of votes in the province of Vizcaya during the 2007 regional elections. The PNV's moderate president, Josu Jon IMAZ, later resigned, citing the growing influence of separatists. He was replaced in November 2007 by Iñigo Uukullu, who condemned ETA violence but nonetheless announced he would meet with all the political forces in the Basque region, including the banned *Batasuna.* The power shift prompted the party to call for a referendum on self-determination, a move swiftly rejected by Prime Minister Zapatero, to preempt further PP criticism of his line on the Basque question.

In July 2008 the party's efforts to conduct the referendum in October 2008 were suspended by a Spanish court pending a review of its legality. The referendum was to be part of a "new model," announced by the PNV earlier in the year, for political relations between Basque Country and the federal government based on the "free accession of its nations."

In the March 9, 2008, election the PNV won 27 percent of the vote in the Basque region, granting the party six seats in the Congress. However, voter turnout was a low 35 percent in the region, owing to a call by separatists to boycott the election to protest "oppression" by the Spanish state. In October the PNV secured $114 million from the PSOE for research and development projects in the region in exchange for supporting the 2009 budget.

On March 1, 2009, the PNV captured 38 percent of the vote in regional elections, winning 30 seats, but was 8 short of an absolute majority. In the following days party leader and Euzkadi President Juan José Ibarretxe scrambled to maintain control by attempting to cobble together support from minority parties and offering a "stability agreement" with the PSE-EE. The PSE-EE instead formed a governing agreement with the PP, forcing the PNV to enter opposition status for the first time since 1980. In May Ibarretxe announced he would be retiring from politics.

In November 2009, in an unexpected accord following the tense March regional elections, the Zapatero government passed its 2010 budget with support from the PNV and in return agreed to strengthen the Basque region's fiscal autonomy.

In September 2010, the PNV struck a deal to support the 2011 budget in exchange for $700 million to generate employment in the region. In October the PNV traded support of upcoming measures to alleviate the economic crisis for 32 concessions for the Basque region. The concessions had been outlined in the 1979 Basque autonomy ruling, the Gernika Statute, but had been stalled by successive governments. Additionally, the PSOE agreed to send $157 million in investment money to the region as part of the coalition arrangement. The party won 882 seats and majorities on 59 municipal councils in local balloting in 2011, and 5 Congress seats. PVN prevailed in the October 21, 2012, regional parliamentary election, winning 27 seats. Party leader Iñigo Urkullu Renteria was elected regional president on December 13, 2012.

Leaders: Iñigo URKULLU Renteria (Party President, Basque President), Juan José IBARRETXE Markuartu (Former Basque President), Belén GREAVES (Secretary), Josu ERKOREKA (Parliamentary Spokesperson).

Basque Socialist Party–Basque Left (*Partido Socialista de Euzkadi–Euzkadiko Ezkerra*—PSE-EE). The PSE-EE was formed in March 1993 by merger of the PSOE-affiliated Basque Socialist Party, led by Ramón JÁUREGUI, and the smaller, more radical Basque Left, led by Juan María BANDRÉS and Jon LARRINAGA. In the May 2001 regional election the PSE-EE finished third, winning 13 of 75 seats, a relatively weak performance that contributed to the resignation of the party's secretary general, Nicolás REDONDO Terreros, in December. In the balloting of April 2005 the party finished second, with 18 seats. Despite the support of the PP, the new PSE-EE leader, Paxti López, lost the contest for regional president to the incumbent, the PNV's Ibarretxe, by one vote. The PSE-EE took a 23 percent vote share during the 2007 regional poll in the Vizcaya province.

The PSE-EE performed well in the March 9, 2008, election, capturing 38 percent of the vote in the Basque region. In April 2008 ETA set off a bomb in front of the group's offices in Bilbao, injuring seven police officers and causing extensive property damage.

In October 2007, a Spanish High Court opened proceedings against PSE-EE leaders Patxi López and Rodolfo ARES, as well as Ibarretxe of the Basque Nationalist Party, under charges that they conducted meetings with *Batasuna* after the group's cease-fire was announced to discuss the political future of the Basque Country.

Basque regional elections on March 1, 2009, handed the PSE-EE/PSOE 25 seats, an increase of 18. The PSE's success catapulted López to the premiership after nearly a month of tense negotiations with non-nationalist parties. On March 30 the PSE-EE and the PP, which held 13 seats, announced a coalition agreement. On May 5 López was elected as the first nonnationalist president of the Basque parliament with the support of the PP and the sole representative of the UPyD party. Upon taking office, López announced his "priority task" was to fight ETA. He said he would also halt a program that made Basque the main language in schools. ETA responded by announcing that the López government would be its "priority target" (see ETA, below).

In January 2010, the Supreme Court dismissed the case against López and other officials, writing that "meeting contacts in not a crime." In November it was reported that the PSE-EE held talks with *Batasuna* to discuss the nationalist party's strategy of pursuing its goals by exclusively political means. The meeting was noteworthy because the PSE-EE had repeatedly denied it had contacts with the outlawed group. The party tumbled to third place in the October 21, 2012, regional elections with 16 seats, down from 25. Lopez lost the regional presidency as well.

Leaders: Jesus EGUIGUREN (President), Patxi LÓPEZ (Secretary General).

Basque Solidarity (*Eusko Alkartasuna*—EA). The EA was formed in September 1986 as the Basque Patriots (*Eusko Abertzaleak*) by a group of PNV dissidents, subsequently joined by former Basque premier Carlos Garaicoetxea Urriza. A left-wing nationalist group opposed to political violence, it currently holds one seat in the national Chamber of Deputies. It contested the 1996 election in alliance with the now-defunct Basque Left (*Euskal Ezkerra*—EuE), which had separated from the *Euskadiko Ezkerra* (also translated as Basque Left) in 1993.

In late 1998, the EA agreed to participate in the formation of a Basque regional coalition government with the PNV and EH, and in the May 2001 and April 2005 elections it remained allied with the PNV. The party received 5.4 percent of votes during Basque local elections in 2007. In the March 1, 2009, regional election, the EA won 3.6 percent of the vote, taking one seat. In September 2010 the EA and *Batasuna* presented a roadmap for peace that called on ETA to declare a "permanent cease-fire under international verification," among other measures. The EA joined with the small grouping, *Alternatiba,* to form the electoral alliance **Join Together** (*Bildu*) for the 2011 regional and local balloting. *Bildu* secured 1,138 seats on local councils.

Leader: Pello URIZAR Karetxe (President).

Create (*Sortu*). In February 2011 *Batasuna* attempted to launch a new political grouping, **Create** (*Sortu*), to compete in regional and local balloting in May. However, in March the Supreme Court ruled that *Sortu* could not be registered as a party. Instead, *Batasuna* leaders established **Basque Country Assembly** (see above). Following the electoral success of EH Bildu, *Batasuna* announced its dissolution on

January 3, 2013. Meanwhile, the Constitutional Court ruled on June 20, 2012, that Sortu was separate from the ETA and thus legal. Sortu held its founding congress in February 2013. Members elected Hasier Arraiz as president, and Arnaldo Otegi as general secretary. Since 2009 Otegi has been serving a 10-year jail sentence for trying to re-establish *Batasuna* in 2009.

Leaders: Hasier ARRAIZ (President), Arnaldo OTEGI (General Secretary).

Unity (*Batasuna*). *Batasuna* descends from the United People (*Herri Batasuna*—HB), which was founded in 1978. Linked with the political wing of the terrorist ETA, the Marxist HB coalition had limited success in regional elections throughout the 1980s and in the 1993 national election won two congressional seats and one senatorial seat. However, the party has persistently faced government censure (see the entry in the 2010 *Handbook* for details). On December 1, 1997, the entire 23-member National Committee was convicted of supporting terrorism, and members were sentenced to at least seven years in prison. In 1999 the Constitutional Court threw out the convictions.

In the 1998 regional elections, the HB joined a leftist coalition, or "platform," styled We the Basque Citizens (*Euskal Herritarrok*—EH) and finished third with 14 seats. It participated in a regional coalition government with the PNV and EA, although an ETA decision to end its 14-month cease-fire led directly to EH's ouster from the coalition. On June 23, 2001, the EH joined in forming the unified *Batasuna* party.

Amid an upsurge in ETA attacks, on April 30, 2002, police detained 11 *Batasuna* members suspected of channeling funds to ETA or laundering "taxes" collected by ETA. In August a judge suspended the organization's activities for three years and ordered its offices closed, citing its relationship with ETA. In the same month the national legislature supported a government request that the Supreme Court ban *Batasuna* altogether, and on March 17, 2003, the court concurred. The ban, which extended to the HB and EH designations, was the first of its kind since the Franco era. Subsequent efforts by *Batasuna* members to register other organizations, most prominently an *Autodeterminaziorako Bilgunea* (AuB) coalition, were rejected.

In May 2003, the United States added *Batasuna* to its list of terrorist organizations, and the United Kingdom followed suit in June. In November 2004 *Batasuna* called for peaceful dialogue among all sides to end the decades of violence, but a Spanish court extended the ban on party activity for two more years in January 2006. On March 22, 2006, ETA announced a permanent cease-fire, and the Zapatero government began direct negotiations with ETA. However, in December 2006 the truce was broken by an ETA attack at Barajas, the Madrid airport, revealing splinters within ETA that undermined *Batasuna*'s leverage.

In October 2007, Spanish police arrested 22 senior *Batasuna* members, nearly the entire leadership, in a raid on an important meeting that government officials believed was held to transfer power to a new cadre of leaders.

In late August 2008, *Batasuna* leader Arnaldo Otegi, who was reportedly instrumental in brokering the 2006 peace negotiation with ETA, was released from jail after serving a 15-month sentence for glorifying terrorism. After his release Otegi served as the group's de facto spokesperson and called for renewed peace talks. A series of bomb attacks that month by ETA prompted *Batasuna* to call the violence an "obstacle" to the Basque independence movement and to begin promoting a clean list of candidates with no criminal records for the regional elections in March 2009.

In January 2009, Spanish authorities carried out raids on two new entities, Askatasuna and 3DM (Democracy 3,000,000) for suspected links to *Batasuna* and later banned the groups from participating in the March regional election.

The Supreme Court in mid-May banned the *Iniciativa Internacionalista II* from taking part in the June 7 European Parliament election on the grounds that it was a front for *Batasuna*. However, weeks later the Constitutional Court reversed the decision because of insufficient evidence. Otegi then endorsed the group, and *Iniciativa* won 1.12 percent of the vote but failed to take a seat.

In June the European Court of Human Rights upheld the Spanish court's ban on *Batasuna* on the grounds that it was a front for ETA. In November it rejected an appeal, effectively closing all avenues for the party to resume its political presence. In March 2010 Spain's High Court sentenced Otegi to two years for "glorifying terrorism" for comments he made at a 2005 rally. In 2010 *Batasuna* sought to salvage its political standing in advance of the 2011 regional elections by signing an agreement in June with the small left-leaning nationalist party Eusko Alkartasuna to use peaceful and democratic means to achieve Basque independence. Interior Minister Alfredo PÉREZ Rubalcaba rejected the move, saying the agreement would have little effect on ETA's renouncing violence. Subsequently, *Batasuna* toughened its stance by calling for ETA to unconditionally abandon its armed struggle.

Canarian Coalition (*Coalición Canaria*—CC). The CC was formed prior to the 1993 general election as a regional alliance that included the **Canarian Independent Groupings** (*Agrupaciones Independientes de Canarias*—AIC); the socialist **Canarian Initiative** (*Iniciativa Canaria*—ICAN); and the left-wing **Mazorca Assembly** (*Asamblea Majorera*—AM). Also initially part of the alliance were the **Canarian Nationalist Party** (*Partido Nacionalista Canario*—PNC) and the **Canarian Independent Center** (*Centro Canario Independiente*—CCI), predecessor of the current **Canarian Nationalist Center** (*Centro Canario Nacionalista*—CCN). More recently, the CC was joined by the **Lanzarote Nationalist Party** (*Partido Nacionalista de Lanzarote*—PNL).

The AIC, consisting principally of the **Tenerife Independents Group** (*Agrupación Tinerfeña de Independientes*—ATI) and the **Las Palmas Independent Group** (*Agrupación Palmera de Independientes*—API), had captured one congressional seat in the 1989 general election and was subsequently the only non-PSOE party to support Prime Minister González's reelection; in the 1991 regional balloting it took second place behind the PSOE in the Canaries, and the AIC nominee, ATI leader Manuel HERMOSO Rojas, secured the island presidency.

In the 1993 general election, the CC returned four deputies and six senators, proceeding thereafter to give qualified support to the minority PSOE government. In September 1994 the CC-led regional government lost its narrow majority when the PNC withdrew from the coalition. The coalition won a plurality of 21 regional assembly seats in 1995, so Hermoso remained in office. Its four national deputies, reelected in 1996, backed the formation of a PP government in exchange for various concessions. The CC won 25 seats in the June 1999 Canarian election and continued to rule, with PP support. In the May 2000 national balloting, the coalition won four Chamber and five Senate seats.

Following the May 2003 regional election, in which the CC won a plurality of 22 seats, the CC and the PP formed a coalition government. Nationally, the CC won 3 lower house seats in 2004 and then voted to approve the PSOE's Zapatero as prime minister. During the 2007 regional elections, the CC ran a joint ballot with a former ally, the previously unknown Canarian Nationalist Party (*Partido Nacionalista Canario*—PNC), with whom it championed Canarian identity, taking 9.54 percent of votes in Las Palmas and 37.7 percent in Santa Cruz de Tenerife.

In the March 9, 2008, election the CC-PNC won 17.5 percent of the vote for the Congress in the region, taking two seats in the lower house and one in the Senate. In January 2009 the CC was reportedly debating whether to give the federal government control over underage migrants, hundreds of whom have arrived on the island in recent years on boats from sub-Saharan Africa. The debate was significant because it represented an unusual decision to cede regional authority to the central government. In November 2009 the Zapatero administration passed its 2010 budget with support from the CC and agreed to earmark additional budget commitments to the Canary Islands. Again in October 2010, Zapatero won the much-needed support of the CC to pass its 2011 budget. In local balloting in 2011 the CC secured 391 seats on local councils. The CC secured 2 seats in the 2011 lower house elections. The coalition condemned the 1.2 percent of GDP deficit limit for 2013 set by Prime Minister Rajoy, asking for 2 percent instead. In June 2012 the CC elected Paulino Riveror to a fourth term as president.

Leaders: Paulino RIVERO (President), José Miguel BARRAGÁN (Secretary General).

Party of Independents from Lanzarote (*Partido de Independientes de Lanzarote*—PIL). Based on the Canarian island of Lanzarote, the PIL held one seat in the previous Spanish Senate. In March 2001, having been sentenced to a three-year prison term for bribery, Dimas MARTÍN Martín, the PIL president and senator, announced his resignation from both posts. In 2003 the PIL won three seats in the regional legislature as part of the **Canarian Nationalist Federation** (*Federación Nacionalista Canaria*—FNC). The PIL received a 1.82 percent vote share during the 2007 local elections in Las Palmas.

In May 2009, police arrested Dimas Martín and several members of the PIL on charges of operating a corruption ring in Lanzarote. Martín was sentenced to eight years in prison for embezzlement and social security fraud. Martín's son Fabian Martín Martín was elected party president in 2010. Infighting led to the expulsion of popular Arrecife

In 2011, the newly formed Basque grouping, **Yes to the Future** (*Geroa Bai*), and the Valencian leftist **Compromise Coalition** (*Coalició Compromís*) each won one seat in the lower chamber in national elections.

For information on the **The Rebirth and Union of Spain** (*Partido Renacimiento y Unión de España—PRUNE*), and the **Convergence of Navarran Democrats** (*Convergencia de Demócratas Navarros*—CDN), please see the 2012 *Handbook.* For more information on the **Majorcan Union** (*Unió Mallorquina*—UM), and the **Valencia Entesa** (*Entesa pel País Valenciá*), see the 2010 *Handbook.*

Illegal Groups:

Basque Homeland and Liberty (*Euzkadi ta Azkatasuna*—ETA). Founded in 1959, ETA has long engaged in a violent separatist campaign directed primarily at police and government targets, although in recent years journalists and anti-ETA civilians have increasingly been targeted as well. By 2001 the number of deaths attributed to ETA attacks approached 800.

In 1978, ETA's political wing was indirectly involved in formation of the United People (HB; see Unity, below). More recently, the HB was the driving force behind the "We the Basque Citizens" (*Euskal Herritarrok*—EH) coalition, which contested the 1998 regional election. The EH participated in the resultant governing alliance until the end of a unilateral ETA cease-fire (September 1998–December 1999) that led to the EH's expulsion. In June 2001 elements of the EH established a unified party, Unity. In its more than three decades of operations ETA has demonstrated considerable resiliency despite the arrests or deaths of numerous leaders. In September 2000 French authorities captured the reputed ETA chief, Ignacio GRACIA Arregui (also known as Iñaki de RENTERÍA), for whom a French arrest warrant had been issued in 1987. The French also arrested the suspected ETA military commander, Francisco Xabier GARCÍA Gaztelu, in February 2001 and the alleged head of logistics, Asier OIARZABAL Txapartogi, in September 2001. In September 2002, senior leaders Juan Antonio OLARRA Guridi and Ainhoa MUGIKA Goni were arrested in Bordeaux, France, while in December Ibón FERNÁNDEZ Iradi and half a dozen other ETA leaders were arrested near Bayonne. Fernández Iradi escaped from custody two days later but was recaptured by the French in December 2003. By then, increased French-Spanish cooperation against ETA was severely hampering the organization's activities, with nearly four dozen suspected operatives having been arrested in October–November 2003 alone. Key suspects arrested in April 2004 included Félix Alberto LÓPEZ de la Calle, a military commander, and Félix Ignacio ESPARZA Luri, a logistics chief; in December alleged political leader Mikel ALBIZU Iriarte and Soledad IPARRAGUIRRE Genetxea, a suspected military commander, were also captured. In response to overtures from the Zapatero government for peace talks, ETA offered a partial truce in June 2005, involving a commitment not to attack elected officials, an offer that was deemed as insufficient by the government to begin talks. On March 22, 2006, the group announced a permanent cease-fire. The Zapatero government began to directly negotiate with the group. Unfortunately, the group itself was splintered and a part of it took responsibility for the bombing of a parking structure in the Madrid airport in December 2006. The cease-fire was officially called off by ETA in June 2007, following the attack of the previous year. In September the ETA released a statement blaming the breakup of the peace accord on the government's failure to set the "minimum conditions" for a negotiated solution and vowed to "open all its fronts" to further the creation of a Basque state.

In the aftermath of the failed peace process, ETA announced its intentions to replace would-be moderates who had been open to negotiations, implementing a stricter hierarchy of control over related groups to ensure sufficient militancy. This was confirmed by the dismissal of Rafael DÍEZ Usabiaga, who in October 2007 was replaced as secretary general of the ETA-affiliated Union of Patriotic Workers (*Langile Abertzale Sozialista*—LAB) by Ainhoa ETXAIDE Amorrortu, who represents ETA's radical wing.

In 2008, Spanish authorities made a series of arrests of prominent ETA suspects and shut down several active cells. Nevetheless, the group's violent campaign continued into the summer tourist season with a series of bomb attacks on seaside resorts.

In late July Spanish authorities reportedly stepped up security measures in the Basque region after issuing an unusual warning that a huge attack by ETA would take place. In an effort to enhance secrecy and prevent more arrests, ETA leaders reportedly removed members in prison from the group's national committee and appointed a new set of leaders and sent them underground.

In August 2008, the release of ETA member De Juana CHAOS, who served 20 years of a 3,000-year sentence for a bomb blast that killed 25 people, provoked considerable public outrage. Further attacks in northern Spain later in the month were found to be staged from France, where ETA members had apparently reorganized their logistical base. Prosecutors launched more arrests and indictments on ETA supporters into the fall, including 24 people who were charged in October with extorting money from businesses in the Basque region in the form of a "revolutionary tax." The suspected military chief of ETA was arrested in southwestern France in November, delivering what Zapatero described as a "decisive blow" against the organization.

ETA was reportedly responsible for the December killing of a businessman whose construction company had been working on a high-speed rail project in the Basque Country. In January 2009 ETA marked its 50th anniversary by vowing to continue fighting for Basque independence and warning that it would target Spanish media outlets and those involved in the construction of the rail line.

In advance of the March 1, 2009, regional elections in Basque Country, ETA issued a statement calling the elections "anti-democratic" because of bans of two far-left independence parties and urged voters to support those parties. ETA reportedly set off a bomb in front of the PSOE headquarters in the Basque Country in late February, causing extensive damage but no injuries. Nevertheless, election results demonstrated ETA's waning support in the region, according to analysts. The number of spoilt ballot papers, a common sign of ETA's support within the population, dropped by a third from previous polls to about 10 percent of the vote. Furthermore, Aralar, a new leftist independence party that is against violence, boosted its number of seats in the regional parliament from one to four. At the end of March police arrested eight members of an ETA-affiliated youth group, following the group's alleged planned attacks on the high-speed rail line project.

The election of the new Basque Country premier, Paxi López of the PSE-EE, in May ushered in a tougher stance against ETA activity. Efforts were directed at minimizing the legitimacy of a separate Basque state, including removal of pro-independence posters and other material from public buildings and the refusal to give permits to pro-ETA demonstrators. ETA stepped up attacks over the summer, which resulted in the death of a police investigator of ETA, nearly three dozen injuries in a Civil Guard barracks attack in the northern city of Burgos, and the deaths of two police officers on the resort island of Mallorca. A second explosion on Mallorca in August at a restaurant, in which no one was harmed, called into question government claims that ETA had been seriously weakened by the surge in arrests.

As of July 2009, there were nearly 1,000 ETA members jailed in Spain and France. ETA has been blamed for 828 deaths in its campaign for independence.

In 2010, the government refused to resume peace talks unless ETA agreed to an unconditional and permanent end to its armed struggle. In March the interior ministry sought legislative measures that would give it the ability to ban any separatist party that had not purposefully condemned ETA violence. An ETA-declared cease-fire in September was roundly rejected by government officials and opposition parties because it did not explicitly call for ETA to surrender weapons, renounce violence permanently, and halt other illegal activities such as extortion.

In October 2011, the ETA renounced the use of force and called for negotiations with the Spanish and French governments.

Communist Party of the Basque Lands (*Partido Comunista de las Tierras Vascas*—PCTV/*Euskal Herrialdeetako Alderi Komunista*—EHAK). The PCTV/EHAK was established by former members of *Batasuna* after that party was banned in March 2003. In late 2008 the court ordered the liquidation of all PCTV assets and froze its bank accounts, and the PCTV was not allowed to enter the 2009. (For more information, see the 2013 *Handbook.*)

LEGISLATURE

Traditionally designated as the *Cortes* (Courts), the Spanish legislature was revived by General Franco in 1942 as a unicameral body with strictly limited powers and officially named *Las Cortes Españolas.* Initially, it had no directly elected members, but provision was made in 1967 for the election of 198 "family representatives." The essentially corporative character of the body was retained in 1971, when several new categories of indirectly elected and appointed members were added.

In November 1976, the *Cortes* approved a long-debated Political Reform Bill, which, calling for a largely elected bicameral assembly, secured overwhelming public endorsement in a referendum held on December 15. The new **Cortes Generales,** consisting of a Senate and a Congress of Deputies, held its inaugural session in July 1977. Both houses serve four-year terms, subject to dissolution.

Senate (*Senado*). The upper house currently has 266 members, of whom 208 were directly elected in 2011: 4 from each of the 47 mainland provinces; 6 from Santa Cruz de Tenerife (3 from Tenerife and 1 each from La Gomera, La Palma, and Hierro); 5 from the Balearic Islands (3 from Mallorca and 1 each from Menorca and Ibiza-Formentera); 5 from Las Palmas (3 from Gran Canaria and 1 each from Fuerteventura and Lanzarote); and 2 each from the North African enclaves of Ceuta and Melilla. The remaining 56 members are designated at varying times (depending on regional elections) by 17 autonomous regional legislatures (Ceuta and Melilla being excluded). Each designates at least 1 senator, with the more populous regions entitled to an additional senator for each million inhabitants. The current distribution is Andalucía, 9; Aragón, 2; Asturias, 2; Balearic Islands, 2; Basque Country, 3; Canary Islands, 3; Cantábria, 1; Castilla y León, 3; Castilla–La Mancha, 2; Catalonia, 8; Extremadura, 2; Galicia, 3; Madrid, 7; Murcia, 2; Navarra, 1; La Rioja, 1; and Valencia, 5.

The overall party distribution after the elections of November 20, 2011, was as follows (directly elected members in parentheses): Popular Party, 162 (133); Spanish Socialist Workers' Party, 64 (48); Convergence and Union, 13 (9); Catalan Accord for Progress (including the Catalan Republican Left, the Socialist Party of Catalonia, the Initiative for Catalonia Greens, and the United and Alternative Left), 10 (7); Basque Nationalist Party, 5 (4); Amaiur, 3 (3); Navarrese People's Union, 3 (2); Canary Islands Coalition, 2 (1); United Left, 2 (1); Asturian Forum, 1 (0); Independen,t 1 (0).

Speaker: Pío GARCÍA-ESCUDERO Márquez.

Congress of Deputies (*Congreso de los Diputados*). The lower house currently consists of 350 deputies elected on block lists by proportional representation. Each province is entitled to a minimum of 3 deputies, with 1 deputy each from the African enclaves of Ceuta and Melilla.

The balloting on November 20, 2011, produced the following seat distribution: Popular Party, 186; Spanish Socialist Workers' Party, 110; Convergence and Union, 16; United Left, 11; Amaiur, 7; Union, Progress and Democracy, 5; Basque Nationalist Party, 5; Catalan Republican Left, 3; Galacian Nationalist Bloc, 2; Canary Islands Coalition, 2; Compromise Coalition, 1; Asturian Forum, 1; Navarre Yes, 1.

President: Jesús POSADO Moreno.

CABINET

[as of August 31, 2013]

Prime Minister	Mariano Rajoy
Deputy Prime Minister	Soraya Sáenz de Santamaría [f]
Ministers	
Agriculture, Food and Environmental Affairs	Miguel Arias Cañete
Defense	Pedro Morenés Eulate
Development	Ana María Pastor Juliás [f]
Economy and Competitiveness	Luis de Guindos Jurado
Education, Culture and Sport	José Ignacio Wert Ortega
Employment and Social Security	María Fátima Báñez García [f]
Finance and Public Administration	Cristóbal Montoro Romero
Health, Equality, and Social Policy	Ana Mato Adrover [f]
Interior	Jorge Fernández Díaz
Foreign Affairs and Cooperation	José Manuel García-Margallo y Marfil
Government Spokesperson	Soraya Sáenz de Santamaría [f]
Industry, Energy and Tourism	José Manuel Soria López
Justice	Alberto Ruiz-Gallardón
Presidency	Soraya Sáenz de Santamaría [f]

[f] = female

INTERGOVERNMENTAL REPRESENTATION

Ambassador to the U.S.: Ramón Gil-Casares SATRÚSTEGU.

U.S. Ambassador to Spain: James COSTOS.

Permanent Representative to the UN: Fernando GONZÁLEZ Arias.

IGO Memberships (Non-UN): ADB, AfDB, CEUR, EBRD, EIB, EU, ICC, IEA, IOM, NATO, OECD, OSCE, WTO.

RELATED TERRITORIES

Virtually nothing remains of Spain's former colonial empire, the bulk of which was lost with the independence of the American colonies in the early 19th century. Cuba, Puerto Rico, and the Philippines were acquired by the United States in 1898. More recently, the West African territories of Río Muni and Fernando Pó became independent in 1968 as the state of Equatorial Guinea; Ifní was ceded to Morocco in 1969; and the Western (Spanish) Sahara was divided between Morocco and Mauritania in February 1976 (the latter subsequently renouncing its claim on August 5, 1979). Thereafter, the only remaining European possessions in the African continent were the small Spanish enclaves discussed below.

Places of Sovereignty in North Africa (*Plazas de Soberanía del Norte de Africa*). These Spanish outposts on the Mediterranean coast of Morocco, dating from the 15th century, encompass the two enclaves of Ceuta and Melilla, officially referred to as *presidios,* or garrison towns, and three "Minor Places" (*Plazas Menores*): the tiny, volcanic Chafarinas and Alhucemas islands, and Peñón de Vélez de la Gomera, an arid garrison spot on the north Moroccan coast. Ceuta, with an area of 7.6 square miles (19.7 sq. km) and a population of 70,400 (2007E), and Melilla, with an area of 4.8 square miles (12.5 sq. km) and a population of 67,700 (2007E), are considered parts of metropolitan Spain, and before being accorded the status of autonomous regions in September 1994, they were organized as municipalities of the provinces of Cádiz and Málaga, respectively. The Minor Places, with military garrisons of about one hundred each, are under the jurisdiction of Málaga (for information on areas prior to 1991, please see the 2012 *Handbook*).

During a state visit to Morocco in July 1991 by King Juan Carlos, the Spanish and Moroccan prime ministers signed a friendship treaty (the first between Spain and an Arab country) providing in particular for the peaceful settlement of disputes between the two countries. Madrid had long felt that any attempt to alter the status of the enclaves would be interpreted by Rabat as an "annexation" of "occupied territory." Thus, it had branded as "unconstitutional" a unilateral pronouncement by Melilla's mayor in early 1993 that the city was an "autonomous community" within Spain. On September 2, 1994, however, the Spanish government approved statutes of autonomy, effective from March 13, 1995, that upgraded the status of the enclaves by authorizing the replacement of their local councils by 25-member assemblies, to which an executive and president would be responsible. The Moroccan government responded by launching a major diplomatic offensive against Spanish possession of the enclaves, contending that the forthcoming reversion of Hong Kong and Macao to China provided an example that Spain should follow. Madrid rejected such arguments, and in 1998 Spanish officials refused a Moroccan invitation to take part in a panel discussion on granting residents of the enclaves dual citizenship.

In the elections of June 13, 1999, the recently formed Independent Liberal Group (*Grupo Independiente Liberal*—GIL), led by a mainland mayor, Jesús GIL, won pluralities in the 25-seat assemblies of both Ceuta and Melilla, but in both jurisdictions anti-GIL coalitions prevailed in forming governments. (See the entry in the 2010 *Handbook* for details.)

Tensions with Morocco flared again in July 2002 when Moroccan police set up camp on the offshore islet of Perejil (also known as Tourah or Leila), five miles west of Ceuta, ostensibly to combat smuggling and drug trafficking. In response, Spain dispatched members of its armed forces to Perejil. In an effort to mediate the dispute, then U.S. Secretary of State Colin Powell proposed that the islet be returned to its pre-July status. Both Spain and Morocco agreed, although Morocco subsequently voiced objection to the presence of a Spanish naval vessel near another islet, Nekor. On July 30 Morocco's King Mohamed VI reasserted his country's claims to Ceuta, Melilla, and the offshore islands and stated that Spain should end its "occupation."

The balloting on May 25, 2003, was more definitive. In Ceuta the PP won an overwhelming majority, taking 19 seats; the second-place **Ceuta Democratic Union** (*Unión Demócrata Ceuti*—UDCE), a Muslim formation led by Muhammad MUHAMMAD Ali, won 3, while the PSOE and PDSC each won 1. In Melilla, Imbroda Ortiz's UPM took 15 seats, followed by the CpM with 7 and the PSOE with 3. In 2004, as in 2000, all six representatives elected to the *Cortes Generales* from the enclaves ran as PP candidates or chose to sit with the PP parliamentary group.

On September 29, 2005, five Africans were shot to death and dozens of others were injured when hundreds of individuals tried to scale the fence separating Morocco from Ceuta. The fatal shots reportedly came from the Moroccan side of the border. On the same day Madrid announced that it would deploy some 500 troops to Melilla and Ceuta in an effort to prevent such attempts, which had claimed nine lives in the preceding two months. The incidents led directly to a decision by 60 African and European countries to meet in Rabat, Morocco, in July 2006, in an effort to formulate a strategy that would stem the flow of illegal immigrants into EU countries.

In regional elections in May 2007, the PP retained its absolute majorities in Ceuta and Melilla.

In August a series of protests in Melilla concerning alleged mistreatment of Moroccans by Spanish police shut down the border for days and triggered supply problems. The protestors claimed that police were preventing Moroccans, particularly pregnant women, from crossing the border to prevent births that would lead to Spanish citizenship. Morocco temporarily recalled its ambassador to Spain in protest of the first official visit to Ceuta and Melilla in November 2007 by Spain's King Juan Carlos and Queen Sofia.

In the March 9, 2008, national election the PP won the seats representing Ceuta and Melilla in the congress and senate. In a July visit to Morocco, Zapatero was reportedly pressed by his Moroccan counterpart, Abbas El Fassi, about the return of Ceuta and Melilla to Moroccan sovereignty.

After the storming of a border fence by a large group of African migrants in June 2008, Spain's Defense Minister Carme Chacón announced she would station 100 extra troops in Ceuta and 250 extra in Melilla. However, the additional troops failed to quell violence in subsequent incidents. In November about 200 African migrants in Melilla stormed the border in a series of clashes with security forces. In January 2009 troops in Melilla opened fire on a group of about 80 migrants, killing one man, who were attempting to cross illegally, prompting calls by human rights groups for an investigation. Meanwhile, a stampede at a border crossing near Ceuta in May resulted in the deaths of two women and brought attention to the high amount of trade, including contraband business, between the two sides.

In May 2010, Spain reaffirmed the "absolute Spanishness" of Ceuta and Melilla following Moroccan demands for new talks over the status of the territory. In August mounting tension over a number of incidents involving harsh treatment of Moroccan nationals by Spanish police led to a flurry of diplomatic contacts between both countries' high officials, including their kings. When PP leader Mariano Rajoy attended anniversary festivities in Melilla to mark the city's incorporation into Spain, Moroccan politicians became enraged. Moroccan prime minister Abbas el Fassi sent a letter of protest to Rajoy, calling his visit "an attack on the dignity and national feelings of Moroccans."

Regional elections in May 2011 gave the PP 18 of 25 seats in Ceuta and 15 of 25 in Melilla.

In May 2012, joint Spanish–Moroccan police posts were established in Tangiers and Algeciras to improve cooperation between the two states in counternarcotics efforts and human trafficking.

Spain's foreign minister José Manuel García-Margallo warned Morocco in April 2013 not to raise the issue of Ceuta and Melilla, while Moroccan deputy foreign minister Youssef Amrani complained of illegal immigrants trying to scale the fence around Melilla. "If we let them climb the border fence and enter Spain, we fail to honor our commitments to the European Union," he said. "But if we prevent them from doing so, we will be accused of committing human rights violations."

SRI LANKA

Democratic Socialist Republic of Sri Lanka
Sri Lanka Prajatantrika Samajawadi Janarajaya (Sinhala)
Llankais Sananayaka Socialisak Kutiyarasa (Tamil)

Political Status: Independent since February 4, 1948; present constitution adopted on August 6, 1978, effective September 7.

Area: 25,332 sq. mi. (65,610 sq. km).

Population: 21,553,031 (2012E—UN); 21,675,648 (2013E—U.S. Census).

Major Urban Centers (2005E): SRI JAYEWARDENEPURA (Kotte, administrative capital, 119,000), Colombo (Kolamba, commercial capital, 650,000), Dehiwala–Mount Lavinia (219,000), Jaffna (154,000), Kandy (Maha Nuwara, 111,000).

Official Languages: Sinhala, Tamil. English is recognized as a link language.

Monetary Unit: Sri Lankan Rupee (market rate November 1, 2013: 131.02 rupees = $1US).

President: Mahinda RAJAPAKSE (United People's Freedom Alliance); elected president on November 17, 2005, and sworn in November 19 for a six-year term, succeeding Chandrika Bandaranaike KUMARATUNGA (United People's Freedom Alliance); reelected on January 26, 2010.

Prime Minister: Disanayaka Mudiyanselage JAYARATNE (United People's Freedom Alliance); designated by the president and sworn in on April 21, 2010, succeeding Ratnasiri WICKREMANAYAKE (United People's Freedom Alliance).

THE COUNTRY

The insular location of Sri Lanka (formerly Ceylon) off the coast of southeast India has not prevented the development of an ethnic and religious diversity comparable to that of other parts of southern Asia. Approximately 74 percent of the people are of Sinhalese extraction, descended from Aryan stock of northern India, while 18 percent are Tamil, akin to the Dravidian population of southern India, and 7 percent are Moors; small minority groups include Europeans, Burghers (Eurasians), and Veddah aborigines. Roughly 70 percent of the inhabitants are Buddhist, while about 8 percent are Hindu, 7 percent Christian, and 7 percent Muslim.

The country's major ethnic problem has long centered on the Tamil population, which is divided into two groups: "Ceylon Tamils," whose ancestors have lived in Sri Lanka for many generations, and "Indian Tamils," whose forebears were brought to the island late in the 19th century as plantation laborers. The former, numbering nearly 2 million, predominate in the north and constitute about 40 percent of the population in the east. The latter, numbering about 900,000, are concentrated on the central tea plantations and were not been prominently involved in the Tamil *eelam* (homeland) movement.

Women constitute 33 percent of the active labor force. Even though they have occupied both the presidency and the prime ministership, they make up only 5.8 percent of the parliament (13 of 225 seats) following the 2010 elections.

Sri Lanka ranks with Kenya as the world's leading exporter of tea; other traditional exports include rubber, coconuts, and coconut products, with cinnamon being a leader among the specialized export crops promoted by a government-sponsored diversification program. Small-scale manufacturing has advanced significantly, with garments and textiles now accounting for over 40 percent of export earnings.

In the early 1980s Sri Lanka possessed one of Asia's most promising economies. However, falling commodity prices, drought, Sinhalese militancy in the south (1987–1989), and widespread Tamil unrest in the north and east (since 1983) have held back growth. The complex, at

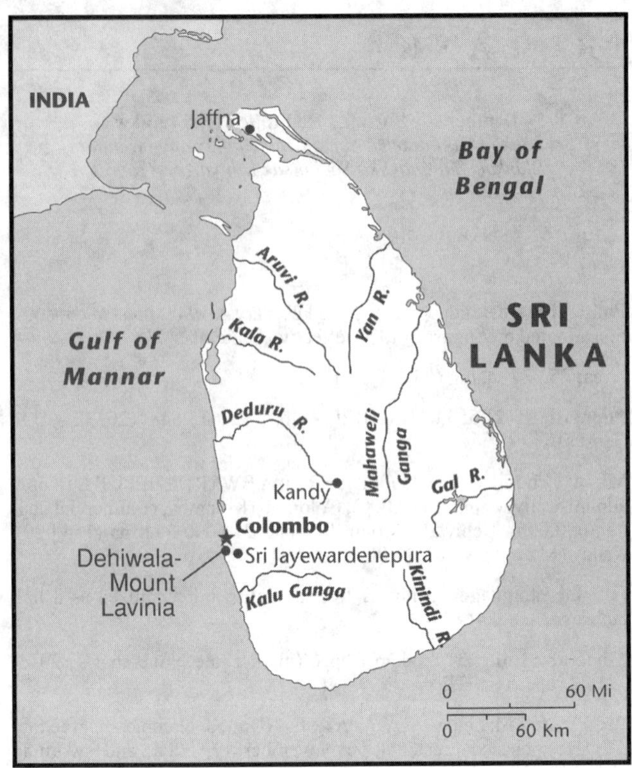

times fratricidal, maelstrom of violence left more than 100,000 dead, with some 1 million displaced during the Tamil conflict. It also has contributed to infrastructure decay (particularly in the Tamil areas). GDP growth averaged 5.2 percent between 2000 and 2008. Inflation averaged 11.9 percent, and unemployment was 7.5 percent.

In late December 2004 the Indian Ocean tsunami disaster, killed more than 35,000 Sri Lankans, displaced hundreds of thousands, and caused an estimated $1 billion in damage.

High inflation led the government to impose price controls on rice in April 2008; however, inflation continued to spike, rising to 28.2 percent in June, before moderating. Despite the global economic slowdown, Sri Lanka recorded more than $850 million in foreign investment in 2009, a record for the country. In 2010, the International Monetary Fund (IMF) extended a $2.6 billion loan to the country. GDP grew by an average of 8.1 percent in 2010 and 2011. In 2012, GDP grew by 6.4 percent, inflation was 7.4 percent, and unemployment 4.9 percent. GDP per capita was $2,956. In its annual Doing Business survey, the World Bank ranked Sri Lanka, 81st out of 185 countries.

GOVERNMENT AND POLITICS

Political background. After nearly four and a half centuries of foreign domination, beginning with the arrival of the Portuguese in 1505, followed by the Dutch (1658–1815) and the British (1815–1948), Sri Lanka (then Ceylon) became an independent state within the Commonwealth on February 4, 1948. Since the country's first parliamentary election in 1947, political power has oscillated between the moderate and generally pro-Western United National Party (UNP) and the Sri Lanka Freedom Party (SLFP), which has emphasized Buddhism, nationalism, "democratic socialism," and nonalignment in international affairs. Until 1956 the country was governed by the UNP, led successively by D. S. SENANAYAKE, his son Dudley SENANAYAKE, and Sir John KOTELAWALA. The SLFP, led by S. W. R. D. BANDARANAIKE, came to power in the 1956 election with an aggressively Sinhalese program reflecting the emergence of a nationalist, Sinhala-educated professional class, but a series of disorders culminated in the prime minister's assassination in 1959. The UNP formed a shaky minority government following the March 1960 general election but was unable to withstand a no-confidence vote shortly thereafter.

In July 1960, the SLFP, under the leadership of Sirimavo R. D. BANDARANAIKE, wife of the former prime minister, won a near-majority in the legislature and organized an all-SLFP government. Ceylonese policy under her leadership acquired an increasingly anti-Western character, accompanied by allegations of rightist plots and attempted coups. The UNP, however, regained a leading position in the 1965 election and organized a coalition government under the premiership of Dudley Senanayake. Subsequently, political power shifted back to the SLFP under Mrs. Bandaranaike, the UNP winning a bare 17 seats in a house of 157 members in 1970.

Sri Lanka's democratic tradition received a serious setback in 1971 when a radical Sinhalese group with Maoist underpinnings, the People's Liberation Front (*Janatha Vimukthi Peramuna*—JVP), attempted unsuccessfully to overthrow the government at the cost of an estimated 20,000 deaths.

An extremely bitter election campaign culminated in July 1977 in an unprecedented victory for the UNP, which, led by J. R. JAYEWARDENE, obtained 142 of the 168 legislative seats. SLFP representation plummeted from 91 to 8. Following adoption by the National State Assembly of a constitutional amendment providing for a French-style executive system, Jayewardene assumed the presidency in February 1978 and named Ranasinghe PREMADASA prime minister.

Having secured passage of a constitutional revision permitting the president to call an election after a minimum of four years in office, Jayewardene was reelected for a second six-year term in October 1982 (effective from February 1983). In November, by a near-unanimous vote, the Parliament endorsed a government proposal that its own term be extended by six years to August 1989, subject to approval in a popular referendum. In December, the measure was approved with 54.7 percent of the vote.

In July 1983, the killing of 13 soldiers near the northern city of Jaffna set off a wave of anti-Tamil rioting. Over 400 people, mainly Tamils, died in the disturbances. In addition to proscribing three leftist parties, President Jayewardene secured passage of a constitutional amendment banning all separatist activity and requiring MPs to take loyalty oaths. The 16 MPs of the Tamil United Liberation Front (TULF) responded by withdrawing from Parliament and were subsequently declared to have forfeited their seats.

Indian Prime Minister Indira Gandhi sent an envoy to mediate between the Jayewardene government and the Tamil militants; however, most opposition leaders boycotted projected multiparty talks in October 1983. It was not until late December that the president agreed to invite the TULF to attend, without preconditions, a roundtable conference scheduled for January 1984. A series of "amity talks" ensued, with Tamil representatives advancing, as a minimal demand, the creation of an autonomous regional council encompassing the northern and eastern regions of the country. At midyear Jayewardene countered with a proposal for a second legislative chamber consisting of district representatives plus spokespersons for special interests. The overture was quickly rejected by the TULF.

During 1985, the level of violence intensified. Four of five exile groups based in Madras (now Chennai), India, announced in mid-April that they had formed a coalition to facilitate "armed revolutionary struggle for national independence." Meanwhile, the new Indian prime minister, Rajiv Gandhi, retreated somewhat from the overtly pro-Tamil posture of his recently assassinated mother. He declared his opposition to any attempt by the Tamils to establish an autonomous regime in Sri Lanka but sponsored a series of ultimately inconclusive talks between the rebels and Sri Lankan officials in Thimphu, Bhutan.

In December 1986, the government cut off essential northern services. Two months later, it mounted a major offensive against the rebels that recaptured most of the Jaffna peninsula by late May. The Indian government, under strong domestic pressure to take action on the insurgents' behalf, responded by airlifting humanitarian supplies to the north in early June, which drew a sharp diplomatic protest from Colombo. Subsequently, high-level discussions between the two governments produced an India–Sri Lanka Accord (ISLA) that brought Indian troops to Sri Lanka in support of a cease-fire and the establishment by an elected provincial council of an integrated northeastern government. On July 30, the day after conclusion of the ISLA, a 3,000-man Indian Peacekeeping Force (IPKF) arrived in Jaffna to assist in disarming the Tamils. However, the IPKF found itself in a major confrontation with the Liberation Tigers of Tamil Eelam (LTTE), the largest of the guerrilla groups. While the IPKF, augmented to a force of some 30,000, eventually gained control of much of the contested area, heavy fighting resumed in October. The LTTE rebuffed an Indian call to surrender during a unilateral cease-fire in late November, and by early 1988, IPKF troop strength had risen to 70,000.

In the south, the extremist JVP experienced a resurgence because of its insistence that the ISLA conceded too much ultimate power to the Tamil minority. From mid-1987 the JVP engaged in a widespread assassination campaign against political figures and on August 18 almost succeeded in killing President Jayawardene in a grenade attack in the Parliament building. The government nonetheless proceeded to enact legislation that provided for elected provincial councils patterned after the Indian state legislatures.

The UNP swept a series of provincial council elections in non-Tamil areas during April and June 1988. With the SLFP refusing to participate because of alleged UNP concessions to the northern rebels, most of the remaining seats were won by the recently organized United Socialist Alliance (USA) which, although a leftist formation, had supported the mid-1987 pact with India. On September 8 Jayawardene signed a proclamation merging the Northern and Eastern Provinces. However, both the LTTE and the TULF declared a boycott of the subsequent provincial council election. Consequently, the Eelam People's Revolutionary Liberation Front (EPRLF) and the Eelam National Democratic Liberation Front (ENDLF) filled the council seats from the north without an election, while in the east the EPRLF and the Sri Lanka Muslim Congress (SLMC) each won 17 seats, compared to 1 for the UNP, in November.

In December 1988 Prime Minister Premadasa was elected to succeed the aging President Jayawardene, barely avoiding the necessity of a runoff by capturing 50.4 percent of the vote; Mrs. Bandaranaike received 44.9 percent, while USA candidate Ossie ABEYGUNASEKERA ran a distant third, with 4.6 percent. Parliament was immediately dissolved, and in the resultant legislative election in February 1989 the UNP won 125 of 225 seats. The SLFP, benefiting from the introduction of proportional representation, won 67 seats.

In March 1989, Premadasa selected former finance minister Dingiri Banda WIJETUNGE as prime minister. A month later he offered amnesty to Tamil guerrillas in the north and JVP militants in the south if they would renounce violence and join the political process. As an inducement he offered them 29 of the UNP's legislative seats. Although the LTTE agreed to negotiations, the JVP responded with a fresh wave of bombings and killings. The subsequent average daily death toll of 35–40 led to the June reimposition of a nationwide state of emergency.

In an apparent effort to neutralize one of the JVP's most popular positions, Premadasa, never a supporter of the 1987 accord with New Delhi, requested in mid-1989 that the Indian troops in Sri Lanka (then estimated at 50,000) leave immediately. An international crisis loomed over the issue until an agreement was reached in September for complete withdrawal by the end of the year. Fighting among Tamil groups broke out again, however, and the new Indian government announced in December that the deadline would be extended into 1990.

Meanwhile, bombings and assassinations continued in the south despite the killing of all known JVP leaders during an intensified anti-insurgency campaign that apparently included the use of shadowy "death squads."

India completed its withdrawal from Sri Lanka on March 24, 1990, leaving the LTTE in virtual control of the northern region. Three weeks earlier, the North-East Provincial Council had approved a resolution proclaiming the area to be an independent state of Eelam. The action was repudiated by New Delhi and seen as a "last gesture" by the council's chief minister, Annamalai Varatharaja PERUMAL, who, with numerous EPRLF associates, subsequently sought refuge in South India from the advancing LTTE.

In June 1990, President Premadasa agreed to dissolve the North-East Provincial Council and hold fresh elections, but the LTTE launched a new wave of insurgent activity and the elections were indefinitely postponed. In mid-1992 the government mounted a new offensive in the north that produced widely divergent casualty estimates. The LTTE responded in August–November with a series of assassinations and terrorist attacks on both military and civilian targets. In April 1993 opposition leader Lalith ATHULATHMUDALI of the Democratic United National Front (DUNF, subsequently the United Lalith Front) was killed by an LTTE suicide attack, as was President Premadasa on May 1. Prime Minister Wijetunge, who immediately succeeded Premadasa on an acting basis, was elected by parliament on May 7 to serve the balance of his predecessor's term, with Ranil WICKREMESINGHE filling the prime ministerial vacancy.

In the parliamentary election of August 1994, an SLFP-led People's Alliance (PA), in coalition with the SLMC, won 112 of 225 seats and obtained sufficient support from minor groups to provide a solid majority for PA leader Chandrika Bandaranaike KUMARATUNGA, who became the third member of her family to serve as prime minister. Concurrently, most mainstream Tamil parliamentarians extended their support to the new administration.

In October 1994, the UNP presidential candidate, Gamini DISSANAYAKE, and a number of his associates were assassinated in a suicide bomb attack at an election rally in Colombo. The UNP named as Gamini's replacement his widow, Srima DISSANAYAKE, who failed to prevent Kumaratunga from winning with a record-setting 62.2 percent of the vote. Following her inauguration in November, the new president not only reappointed her mother, Sirimavo Bandaranaike, to her former post as prime minister but also pledged to abolish the executive presidency by July 1995—a pledge she proved unable to keep.

In December 1994, President Kumaratunga announced that a government proposal for a cease-fire had been accepted by the LTTE, and talks aimed at ending the conflict opened in Jaffna in January 1995. The talks collapsed in April with a resumption of attacks by the rebels. Tiring of the search for a negotiated solution, in October the government launched a major military offensive, code-named *Rivirasa* (Sunshine), aimed at capturing the rebel stronghold of Jaffna. Government forces encountered fierce LTTE resistance and terrorist counteractions. Nevertheless, in December the city of Jaffna finally came under government control.

In January 1996, the financial center of Colombo was devastated by a huge LTTE truck bomb, killing over 90 people and injuring more than 1,400. With heavy fighting continuing, the government declared an extended nationwide emergency that secured parliamentary approval in April despite opposition objections, and a week later the military launched operation *Rivirasa* II to capture the areas around the city of Jaffna. On May 17 the government claimed that its forces were in control of the whole of the Jaffna peninsula, but its assertions that the LTTE had been effectively destroyed as a fighting force were disproved in mid-July when Tamil guerrillas overran the army garrison in Mullaittivu, southeast of Jaffna, inflicting the heaviest defeat on government forces since 1993. The military responded by launching another offensive in the north, during which an estimated 200,000 refugees fled.

In April 1997, Sri Lanka's two leading political parties agreed to a pact, brokered by the United Kingdom, to end the civil war. In May the military launched operation *Jaya Sikuru* (Victory Assured) in an effort to establish a stable overland supply route to Jaffna (for more on the operation, see the 2013 *Handbook*). Efforts by the government to restore normalcy to the Jaffna region included holding local elections in January 1998. Most of the leading Tamil parties participated despite threats from the LTTE, which the government had formally outlawed in response to the bombing of the country's most sacred Buddhist site, the Temple of Tooth in Kandy. Thereafter the LTTE undertook a bombing and assassination campaign to eliminate key leaders of the TULF and other government-supportive parties. In August the government again declared a nationwide state of emergency, thereby permitting it, under the constitution, to cancel elections scheduled for late August in five provinces.

In January 1999, the PA won a majority in the North-Western Provincial Council election, wresting control from the UNP. Two days later the Supreme Court censured President Kumaratunga for having illegally postponed the August 1998 elections; polling in the five provinces, held in April, saw the PA uniformly finish ahead of the UNP, which had previously controlled four of the five councils. In June the voters in Southern Province also went to the polls, with the PA again besting the UNP. The 1999 local elections had, however, collectively confirmed the JVP as the country's third most influential party.

In October 1999, President Kumaratunga called an early presidential election with a year left in her term. A suicide bombing three days before the balloting killed 26 individuals and wounded many others, including the president, who won reelection with 51.1 percent of the vote and was sworn in for a second term. She again named her mother as prime minister.

In early November 1999, the LTTE had initiated its latest military campaign, "Unceasing Waves III," which within five days had cost the government ten towns, including, once again, Mankulam. The offensive constituted the most sustained operation ever by the insurgents. In April 2000 the LTTE forced some 17,000 government troops to retreat northward from the strategic causeway at Elephant Pass, severing the army's land connection to the south. On May 3 President Kumaratunga invoked, for the first time in the country's history, the Public Security

Ordinance, which placed the country on a war footing. She also banned strikes and political demonstrations and imposed strict media censorship. Although the LTTE moved to within several kilometers of Jaffna city and also launched an assault in the east, around Batticaloa, the offensive stalled in June.

In February 2000, the government had confirmed that Norway was prepared to act as a mediator in direct talks with the LTTE. The Tamil Tigers insisted, however, on several preconditions, principally that government forces be withdrawn from the north and east and restricted to barracks during the discussions. The government refused. Meanwhile, the resurgent JVP questioned Norway's neutrality and demonstrated against its involvement in the peace process. Staunch Sinhalese Buddhists, including hundreds of monks, also were taking to the streets, demanding that the government achieve a military victory over the separatists and accusing Norway of giving LTTE leaders a safe haven.

In August 2000, the government introduced a long-delayed, controversial constitutional reform bill in Parliament that had already been rejected by the UNP and all the main Tamil parties. The bill's provisions included devolving powers to seven elected provincial councils and establishing an interim appointed council for a North-East region, with the final status of the latter jurisdiction dependent on whether the multiethnic population in the east approved a future referendum on union with the north. The government quickly acknowledged, however, that it could not marshal the needed two-thirds parliamentary majority to pass the 31-chapter bill and therefore withdrew it. Ten days later President Kumaratunga dissolved Parliament in preparation for a general election.

Octogenarian Prime Minister Bandaranaike resigned for health reasons on August 10, 2000, and was replaced by the minister for public administration and home affairs, Ratnasiri WICKREMANAYAKE. The retired prime minister died shortly after casting her ballot in the general election of October 10, which saw the PA capture 107 seats in the 225-member Parliament. Six seats short of a majority, the PA quickly negotiated a coalition with the National Unity Alliance (an affiliate of the PA-supportive SLMC), the Tamil-based Eelam People's Democratic Party (EPDP), and an independent deputy, which permitted Prime Minister Wickremanayake to remain in office.

On November 27, 2000, the LTTE leader, Velupillai PRABHAKARAN, reversed his stance and called for unconditional peace talks. In December the LTTE initiated a month-long unilateral cease-fire but the government rejected the overture. Despite cease-fire extensions into April 2001, as well as the efforts of Norwegian negotiator Erik Solheim, at midyear the two sides appeared no closer to peace negotiations.

On June 20, 2001, President Kumaratunga dismissed SLMC leader Rauff HAKEEM from the cabinet, leading Hakeem and 6 other MPs from the SLMC to defect to the opposition. The loss cost the PA-led coalition its parliamentary majority and left the president's administration subject to a vote of no confidence. On July 10 the president suspended Parliament until September to avoid that consequence, and then on September 5 the PA announced a formal agreement with the JVP that restored the government majority's to 119 parliamentary seats. Although the JVP remained outside the reshuffled cabinet, it won a number of policy concessions, including an end to further moves toward Tamil autonomy, a halt to privatizations, a major reduction in the size of the cabinet, and loan relief for farmers. The pact was severely criticized by the TULF and other Tamil parties and ultimately served only to postpone the government's collapse.

On October 10, 2001, 13 PA legislators, including S. B. DISSANAYAKE, secretary general of the president's own SLFP, defected to the opposition. With a no-confidence motion looming, Kumaratunga dissolved Parliament and called a general election for December 5, only 14 months after the previous election. This latest setback also brought to an end the president's effort to hold a referendum on a new constitution, which had been scheduled for mid-October. Meanwhile, in a daring raid on July 24 an LTTE assault team had attacked the country's principal international airport and an adjoining military air base, causing an estimated $400 million in damages. Although all 13 LTTE assailants were killed, the attack constituted a major blow to the administration and also harmed an ailing economy.

With much of the public having turned against President Kumaratunga's increasingly hard-line stance toward the LTTE, the UNP surged ahead during a violence-plagued campaign, and in the December 2001 parliamentary election it captured a plurality of 109 seats, compared to the PA's 77. As a consequence, Prime Minister Wickremanayake handed in his resignation, and Kumaratunga was forced to turn to her longtime foe, the UNP's Wickremesinghe, to form a new cabinet. The UNP leader quickly established a majority coalition, dubbed the United National Front (UNF), with the SLMC, which had won 5 seats, and also secured the external support of the TULF-led Tamil National Alliance (TNA). The bulk of the new cabinet was sworn in on December 12, with most remaining appointments then being made in February 2002. The president was forced to surrender the defense and finance portfolios she had held in the preceding cabinet.

Although the LTTE had launched a series of attacks to coincide with induction of the Wickremesinghe cabinet, it declared a unilateral cease-fire from December 24. The government reciprocated, reiterating, over the president's objections, its intention to open negotiations with the LTTE. Wide public relief, if not unanimous acclaim, greeted the announcement on February 22, 2002, of an indefinite cease-fire. The first direct government-LTTE talks in seven years were launched on September 16–18 in Thailand under Norwegian sponsorship, with the principals quickly reaching agreement on formation of a joint committee on security and a joint task force on reconstruction. An estimated 65,000 people had been killed since the beginning of the Tamil conflict.

Through early February 2003, four additional negotiating sessions were held at various locations, but on April 21 the LTTE announced its withdrawal from further talks, citing the government's unwillingness to put establishment of an interim administration for Tamil areas at the top of the agenda. It also complained of too little progress on reconstruction and rehabilitation. Meanwhile, President Kumaratunga continued to assert that Prime Minister Wickremesinghe was conceding too much to the LTTE; she insisted that a political settlement should be concluded only after the LTTE disarmed—a proposition that the LTTE labeled as "suicidal." She further insisted that the LTTE disband the Black Tigers squad of suicide bombers and fulfill its pledge to end the induction of child soldiers.

On November 4, 2003, during a visit by Prime Minister Wickremesinghe to Washington, President Kumaratunga suspended Parliament for two weeks and dismissed three key ministers, taking over the defense, interior, and mass communications portfolios herself. In response to the resultant governmental crisis, on November 14 Norway withdrew from its role as mediator of the peace process, although it left its Sri Lanka Monitoring Mission in place to continue supervising the cease-fire.

In January 2004, the SLFP and the JVP concluded an alliance, and on February 7 Kumaratunga dissolved Parliament and called an election for April 2. The multiparty United People's Freedom Alliance (UPFA, successor to the PA) won 105 seats to 82 for the UNP, and on April 6 the popular SLFP parliamentary leader, Mahinda RAJAPAKSE, was sworn in as prime minister. Although the UPFA remained 8 seats short of a parliamentary majority, Rajapakse won the external support of the newly organized Buddhist National Heritage Party (*Jathika Hela Urumaya*—JHU), which had won an unexpected 9 seats. It took the UPFA government until September 10, 2004, to cement a legislative majority, by bringing in an erstwhile UNP ally, the Ceylon Workers' Congress (CWC). Earlier, an MP from the SLMC had defected to the government, and in late October three additional members of the SLMC joined the government as noncabinet ministers.

The coalition government lost its legislative majority on June 15, 2005, when the JVP withdrew in opposition to the inclusion of Tamil separatist organizations in the distribution of international aid following the 2004 Indian Ocean tsunami. In a further blow to the UPFA, Foreign Minister Lakshman KADIRGAMAR, the government's senior ethnic Tamil, was assassinated by an unidentified gunman on August 12, 2005. The Supreme Court ruled on August 26, 2005, that President Kumaratunga's second term would expire in December 2005—not a year later to compensate for the year lost by the early election of December 1999. With the incumbent prohibited from seeking a third term, the presidential election was contested by Prime Minister Rajapakse, the UNP's Ranil Wickremesinghe, and 11 other minor candidates, several of whom withdrew at the last minute. Rajapakse had won the endorsement of the JVP and JHU by agreeing to support a unitary state rather than broad provincial or regional autonomy, to end privatization of state-run companies, and to renegotiate the terms of the cease-fire with the LTTE. On November 17 Rajapakse won 50.3 percent of the vote versus 48.4 percent for Wickremesinghe, who almost certainly lost because of a low voter turnout among Tamils following an expression of "disinterest" in the outcome by the LTTE and its political partner, the TNA. Sworn in as president on November 19, Rajapakse named Ratnasiri Wickremanayake as prime minister.

The JVP's external support remained vital to the Rajapakse administration until late January 2007, when 18 UNP legislators crossed the aisle. In the interim, the CWC and the Up-Country People's Front (UCPF) had joined the government. On January 28 President Rajapakse announced a greatly expanded cabinet, which included 10 new UNP ministers as well as the leader of the SLMC. Two days later, the JHU agreed to accept its first cabinet post. In December, however, the SLMC withdrew because of what it considered lack of progress on Muslim issues.

In balloting for the Eastern Province regional council in May 2008, the Tamil People's Liberation Party (*Tamileela Makkal Viduthalai Pulikal*—TMVP), a progovernment Tamil group that is part of the UPFA, won 20 of the council's 37 seats. The government claimed the victory was a rejection of the LTTE and a mandate for its policies.

In January 2009, government forces captured most of the remaining LTTE strongholds and forced the rebels into a remote region of the northeast. In February 2009, the UPFA swept provincial elections in the North-Western and Central provinces. The UPFA continued its electoral success in April when it won elections for the Western Province. Government forces defeated the last significant LTTE units in May 2009 and killed Prabhakaran, effectively ending the organized Tamil insurgency (see Current issues, below).

Ahead of parliamentary balloting scheduled for 2010, the UNP relaunched its electoral alliance, the United National Front (UNF), including the SLMC and a dozen smaller parties. In November General Sarath FONSEKA, the military commander who had led the forces that defeated the LTTE, announced his resignation. Fonseka subsequently launched a campaign ahead of presidential elections, which had been called for 22 months early (see Current issues, below). In the balloting on January 26, 2010, Rajapakse was reelected with 57.9 percent of the vote, and Fonseka placed second with 40.2 percent. There were 20 other candidates, none of whom received more than 1 percent of the vote. After the election Fonseka emerged as the leader of the new opposition grouping, the Democratic National Alliance (DNA).

In legislative elections on April 8, the UPFA won a significant victory, increasing its number of seats in the 225-member parliament to 144, six votes short of the two-thirds majority necessary to amend the constitution. The UNF secured 60 seats; the TNA, 14, and the DNA, 7. Disanayaka Mudiyanselage JAYARATNE was appointed prime minister of a new UPFA government on April 22. On November 22, Rajapakse appointed a reshuffled and enlarged 58-member cabinet.

On March 17, 2011, the ruling coalition won local balloting, securing a majority of 205 of the 234 municipal councils. In local elections, from October 8–23, the UPFA won 21 of 23 councils. In September 2012, the UPFA won majorities in provincial three councils where elections were held, securing 63 of 114 contested seats. In January 2013, Rajapakse reshuffled and expanded the cabinet.

Constitution and government. In May 1972, under the country's second constitution since independence, Ceylon was redesignated the Republic of Sri Lanka. Under the present constitution (adopted August 16, 1978, as a codification and enlargement of a series of constitutional amendments approved October 20, 1977), the name was further changed to Democratic Socialist Republic of Sri Lanka, and a British-style parliamentary structure was abandoned in favor of a "Gaullist" presidential-parliamentary system. The most visible feature of the present system is the concentration of powers in a "strong" president who serves a renewable six-year term (a September 2010 constitutional amendment removed a two-term limit on the presidency). The president appoints a prime minister and, in consultation with the latter, other senior administrative officials, the only restriction being that all ministers and deputy ministers must hold legislative seats. Should Parliament reject an appropriations bill or approve a no-confidence motion, the president may appoint a new government.

The legislative term is six years, subject to presidential dissolution. A constitutional amendment passed in August 1983 requires all members of parliament to take an oath of loyalty to the unified state of Sri Lanka and bans all activity advocating "the division of the state."

Judges of the Supreme Court and the Court of Appeal are appointed by the president. Courts of first instance include a High Court, which tries criminal cases, and district courts. A presidentially appointed parliamentary commissioner for administration (ombudsman) investigates complaints of wrongdoing by public officials.

In September 2001, parliament passed legislation authorizing creation of a Constitutional Council that has as part of its mandate naming independent commissions with responsibilities over police, the judiciary, public servants, and elections.

Prior to 1988 the country was divided into nine provinces, each with an appointed governor and elected Development Council. In November 1987 a constitutional amendment provided for the election of substantially more autonomous provincial councils, each headed by a chief minister. The amendment also authorized the president to merge the Northern and Eastern Provinces, a long-sought objective of their Tamil inhabitants. President Jayawardene implemented the change in September 1988. A North-East provincial government was temporarily installed, but the continuing civil strife rendered the merger moot by the early 1990s. (In October 2006 the Supreme Court ruled the merger unconstitutional.) Further devolutionary measures, approved in January 1988, called for a network of district councils (*pradeshiya sabhas*) throughout the country. Municipalities have urban or town councils, while rural areas are administered by elected village councils.

The 1978 constitution guarantees free speech and publication, but these and other rights are "subject to such restrictions as may be presented by law." "Restrictions" have been enforced to maintain racial and religious harmony, national security, and public order and welfare. As a consequence, varying degrees of censorship and other forms of media control prevail. In particular, the government periodically banned news coverage of military operations against the Tamil Tigers. In February 2009, the British Broadcasting Service stopped providing news stories to the Sri Lankan national broadcasting service because of continuing censorship. In 2011 Sri Lanka refused entry to Frank La Rue, a UN envoy tasked to promote freedom of expression. In 2013, the media watchdog group Reporters Without Borders ranked Sri Lanka 162nd out of 179 countries in press freedom (see Current issues, below).

Foreign relations. Sri Lanka has long maintained a nonaligned position in world politics despite its membership in the Commonwealth and a mutual defense agreement that grants the United Kingdom the right to maintain naval and air bases, as well as land forces, on its territory. While the Jayawardene government stressed Sri Lanka's economic similarity and cultural affinity with Southeast Asia, the country's application for admission to the Association of Southeast Asian Nations (ASEAN) was rejected in 1982 on geographical grounds. The action helped to precipitate the 1985 launching of the South Asian Association for Regional Cooperation (SAARC), of which Sri Lanka was a founding member.

The island state's major foreign policy problems since independence have involved relations with India. Conflicting claims to Kachchativu Island in the Palk Strait, which separates the two countries, were resolved in 1974; India yielded its claim, and Sri Lanka agreed to permit Indian fishermen and pilgrims easy access to the island. The Palk Strait accord was supplemented in 1976 by a general agreement on maritime economic zones. At the end of 1998 New Delhi and Colombo signed a trade agreement designed to phase out most tariffs and to facilitate trade, investment, and development.

Much more explosive has been the situation involving Sri Lanka's Tamil dissidents, who have strong ties to some 50 million Tamils in southern India. As ethnic violence on the island escalated, relations between Colombo and New Delhi became strained, largely because of the use of Indian territory as a refuge and staging area by Tamil guerrilla groups. By 1986, local authorities in the Indian state of Tamil Nadu were becoming increasingly disenchanted with the LTTE presence, and the rebels transferred most of their operations to Sri Lanka's Jaffna area. In addition, New Delhi and Colombo concluded a treaty in mid-1987 under which Indian troops attempted a peacekeeping role in Sri Lanka, although the accord ultimately became a political liability for both governments, and the troops were withdrawn in March 1990 (see Political background). In 1995, the Indian government again attempted to come to its neighbor's aid by setting up the equivalent of a naval quarantine around Sri Lanka's northern coast, thereby depriving the rebels of easy access to supply bases in Tamil Nadu. Since then, Indian support has been less direct. The breakdown of the cease-fire in 2006–2007 generated renewed interest on the part of many Sri Lankans, including many Tamils, for Indian mediation.

In 1997, the United States announced that it had added the LTTE to its list of terrorist organizations. The European Union (EU) did likewise in May 2006, which prompted the LTTE to demand the removal of the European members of the five-country, 57-person Sri Lanka Monitoring Mission (SLMM), which had been established in 2002 to assist with the cease-fire.

In 2007, Brazil announced that it was reopening its mission to Sri Lanka after a 40-year absence. The move was a reflection of increasing commercial ties between the two countries.

In April 2008, Sri Lanka signed six new commercial agreements with Iran, including an arrangement whereby Iran pledged $1.9 billion in loans and grants to increase Sri Lanka's energy output. Through the year, the government continued to reject calls for the establishment of a UN human rights office in the country.

A continuing government offensive in 2009 was condemned by a number of foreign governments, including the United States, members of the EU, and India. International offers to mediate the conflict were rebuffed by both the government and the LTTE, which refused to lay down its weapons as a precondition to negotiations. International actors also criticized the government's policy of detaining an estimated 300,000 ethnic Tamil refugees in 15 camps and the conditions at the facilities. The United States and other governments subsequently suspended military aid and sales to Sri Lanka.

The government expelled UNICEF official James Elder on September 6, 2009, after he criticized the government's management of Tamil internment camps. In October India offered Sri Lanka $100 million to resettle displaced Tamils. The next month, 21 Tamils, including French LTTE leader Nadaraja MATINTHIRAN, were convicted in Paris of illegally providing funds to the LTTE. In addition, the Tamil Coordinating Committee in France (CCTF) was designated a terrorist group and ordered dissolved.

In February 2010, the EU suspended Sri Lanka's participation in a preferential economic program because of what the body described as the government's "failure" to abide by basic human rights standards during the final months of fighting with the LTTE. On a state visit to India in June, Rajapakse signed new agreements with his Indian counterpart, including accords on energy and defense cooperation.

In February 2011, 25 Indian vessels and 136 crewmen were arrested by Sri Lankan naval forces for illegally fishing in Sri Lankan waters. The ships and crewmembers were released two days later following the intervention of the Indian government. Reports that the Sri Lankan navy killed two Indian fishermen prompted an accord between the two countries that pledged no force would be used against fishing vessels.

In January 2012, India's foreign minister visited Sri Lanka for the first time since November 2010. Bilateral agreements on transportation, communications, and education were signed during the visit. In August, Sri Lanka and Swaziland signed a series of economic cooperation accords. Meanwhile, as part of a broader effort to expand its diplomatic influence, Sri Lanka announced that it would open diplomatic relations with 13 nations in the Caribbean and Latin America (the country had formal ties with 20 of the region's 33 countries).

On September 3–4, 2012, 150 Sri Lankan Christian pilgrims were attacked in Tamil Nadu state in India by pro-Tamil activists. Sri Lanka evacuated the pilgrims amidst rising tensions with India. China, Japan, and India increased foreign aid to an estimated $1.4 billion for 2012, with $920 million from China alone. However, China refused a $500 million loan request from Sri Lanka. The government sought the funds to purchase oil to reduce energy costs.

India cancelled annual security talks with Sri Lanka in March 2013. Also in March, the government negotiated a $510 million, 40-year, infrastructure loan from Japan. The following month, Sri Lanka and Pakistan signed a new agreement designed to enhance economic and cultural cooperation. In July, the United States threatened to reduce development aid to Sri Lanka by 20 percent over concerns about human rights. Sri Lanka launched negotiations with China and Japan on free trade agreements in 2013.

Current issues. In May 2006, Swedish negotiator Ulf Henricsson asserted that the four-year-old cease-fire between the government and the LTTE had become a "low-intensity war," and by August 21, when the SLMM withdrew from Jaffna and Trincomalee to Colombo, no objective observer could characterize what was happening—ground assaults, sea battles, air strikes, suicide bombings—as anything remotely resembling a cease-fire. LTTE and government representatives met in Geneva, Switzerland, on February 22–23, 2006, to discuss the escalation in cease-fire violations, but a second round of talks scheduled for April 24–25 was canceled because the Sri Lankan navy had denied sea access to eastern LTTE leaders. In early August both sides accused the other of responsibility for the latest atrocity in the conflict: the execution in Muttur of 17 Tamils who were working for the French aid agency Action Against Hunger (*Action Contre le Faim*). Later in the month, an air strike by government forces killed some 60 Tamil schoolgirls, while in mid-October an LTTE suicide bomber attacked a military convoy and killed nearly 100 people. A further effort on October 28–29 to restart peace talks concluded without an agreement. Also in October, President Rajapakse and the UNP's Wickremesinghe signed a memorandum of understanding that called for cooperation on a range of issues, including the LTTE, electoral reform, and good governance. The agreement proved to be short-lived after 18 UNP legislators defected to the government in January 2007.

The Tamil conflict continued unabated into 2007. In March the LTTE used at least one light aircraft to launch its first-ever bombing run (against an airport), but the Sri Lankan Army was gradually gaining ground. In July the army claimed to have full control of the east and was pressing ahead in the north. At the same time, reports continued to surface about what Human Rights Watch termed "shocking abuses" of human rights by the military.

The government ended a 2002 ceasefire and launched a major offensive against the LTTE in January 2008. By November, 172 security forces had been killed and 1,122 wounded, and losses among the LTTE were reported to be close to 2,000 killed or wounded. Meanwhile, on April 6 the minister for highway and road development was killed by a suicide bomber affiliated with LTTE near Colombo. The attack also killed 12 others and wounded more than 100. Three weeks later, another suicide bomber killed 24 and injured 40 on a bus in Colombo; subsequent attacks continued through the spring and summer. In June security forces began the forced mass relocation of Tamils living in Colombo. At least 370 ethnic Tamils were removed by security forces before a court order halted the deportations. The renewed fighting left an estimated 300,000 civilians displaced and at least 250,000 trapped in the combat zone. Meanwhile, the UN reported that at least 6,000 civilians had been killed and 14,000 wounded since the offensive began. Also in June, heavy monsoons killed at least 20 and displaced more than 350,000.

In May 2009, government forces captured the last remaining LTTE stronghold in the Mullaitavu district. On May 19 government forces announced that Prabhakaran; his son and heir, Charles Anthony; and other senior LTTE leaders were killed in the final fighting. Even after the formal defeat of the LTTE, sporadic attacks continued against government figures and facilities by Tamil separatist groups. Also in May, the government revealed a plan to resettle up to 80 percent of the 260,000 Tamils held in refugee camps by the end of the year and announced that it would fully implement the Thirteenth Amendment to the country's constitution, which devolves political power to local and regional governments.

In October 2009, the government reported that it had resettled more than 130,000 of the estimated 260,000 displaced Tamils. Meanwhile, the EU and the U.S. State Department accused the Sri Lankan government of numerous human rights violations against civilians during the final campaign against the LTTE. The government rejected the accusations. After the defeat of the LTTE, Rajapakse called for early presidential elections to capitalize on his popularity.

Rajapakse easily won reelection as president in January 2010, defeating opposition candidate and former general Sarath Fonseka, who placed second in the polling. Fonseka was supported by the major opposition parties, including the TNA, the UNP, and the People's Liberation Front (JVP). Fonseka was subsequently arrested on February 8 as part of a sweep that included the arrests of more than 40 people on charges of conspiracy and treason. Most of those detained were members of the military. The arrests prompted widespread protests. Although still in detention and awaiting trial, Fonseka was elected a member of parliament in April. The president's brother Chamal RAJAPAKSE, was subsequently elected speaker of the parliament, while another brother, Basil RAJAPAKSE, was appointed minister of economic development.

In May the government lifted about half of the state of emergency restrictions that had been in place for 27 years because of the LTTE insurgency. Demonstrations against the UN prompted the world body to close its main office in Sri Lanka in July. Protestors objected to the creation of a UN panel to investigate abuses against Tamil civilians in 2009. Also in July additional charges of embezzlement and illegal arms trafficking were filed against Fonseka. He was convicted in September of engaging in political activities while still a member of the military and sentenced to three years in prison (in January 2011 the Supreme Court rejected an appeal by Fonseka).

The UN issued a report on April 25, 2011, that criticized both sides for civilian deaths during the civil war, but the Sri Lankan Army was blamed for the majority of casualties. The report recommended an investigation of war crimes. The Sri Lankan government rejected the findings. On May 30, the police fired on striking workers in Colombo, wounding more than 250. The incident prompted the resignation of the head of the national police, Gen. Mahinda Balasuriya. On August 25, Rajapakse ended the state of emergency that had been in place off and on since the start of the civil war. The measures gave security forces wide powers of arrest and detention.

On January 22, 2012, the government expelled 161 foreign Muslim clerics who were accused of promoting radical Islam. In March, the UN Human Rights Council (UNHRC) passed a resolution calling for Sri Lanka to launch an independent investigation of human rights violations during the civil war. On May 21, Fonseka was released after pledging not to seek political office for seven years. In September, the main camp for displaced Tamils was closed, following the release of the remaining 1,160 persons.

In March 2013, the UNHRC passed a second resolution that criticized Sri Lanka's human rights record and called for investigations into atrocities during the civil war. Also in March reports indicated that a new Sinhalese grouping, the Buddhist Strength Force (*Bodu Bala Sena*—BBS), had carried out a number of attacks on Christians and Muslims.

In June 2013, police closed the offices of two internet news sites and arrested nine journalists after charging that the media outlets presented "false and malicious reports." The government subsequently dismissed concerns expressed by the United States and the European Union over intimidation of the media. Concerns over media freedom and human rights led to considerable controversy over the decision of the Commonwealth heads of state to meet in Sri Lanka in November and prompted the government to issue a series of assurances that journalists would have complete freedom to cover the sessions. Local elections were scheduled for the war-torn Northern Province for September 2013 for the first time in 25 years.

POLITICAL PARTIES AND GROUPS

Government Parties:

United People's Freedom Alliance (UPFA). The UPFA coalition was formed for the April 2004 parliamentary election primarily by the Sri Lanka Freedom Party (SLFP) and the People's Liberation Front (JVP). The UPFA was an expansion of the **People's Alliance** (PA; *Bahejana Nidasa Pakshaya*), formed as an SLFP-dominated coalition prior to the 1993 provincial elections. A number of the PA parties, but not the SLFP, had theretofore operated under the banner of the opposition United Socialist Alliance (USA), formed by Chandrika Kumaratunga in 1988 on the basis of her Sri Lanka People's Party (SLMP). In the 1993 elections the PA defeated the United National Party (UNP) in Western Province (including Colombo) while limiting the ruling party's majorities elsewhere. In August 1994, a broader coalition formed with the SLMC produced, with the support of minor parties, a parliamentary majority of one seat.

In the first half of 1999, the PA claimed victories in all seven provincial council elections, winning clear majorities in two, exactly half the seats in two others, and pluralities in three. In the October 10, 2000, parliamentary election the PA won 45 percent of the vote and 107 seats, 6 short of a majority, although President Kumaratunga quickly picked up sufficient support from the National Unity Alliance (NUA), the Tamil Eelam People's Democratic Party (EPDP), and an independent to form a governing coalition. In the December 2001 election the PA won only 37 percent of the national vote and 77 parliamentary seats.

Formation of the UPFA was announced in January 2004 by the SLFP and the JVP. On February 3 the National Liberation People's Party (DVJP), the NUA, the People's United Front (MEP), and the Sri Lanka People's Party (SLMP) announced their participation, as did the Lanka Equal Society Party (LSSP) and the Sri Lanka Communist Party (SLCP) two weeks later.

The participation of the JVP, which won 39 of the alliance's 105 seats, propelled the UPFA to 45.6 percent of the vote and a near-majority in the April 2004 parliamentary election. In July the UPFA also won victories in all six provinces that held elections. Sharp differences between the staunchly leftist JVP and other alliance parties persisted, however, especially over the terms of peace negotiations with the LTTE. In August President Kumaratunga resigned as alliance leader, reportedly because of differences with the JVP.

In June 2005, the JVP withdrew from the government, although it continued to provide external support. By late January 2007, however, President Rajapakse had brought several additional parties, including the Ceylon Workers' Congress (CWC) and the SLMC, plus defectors from the UNP, into the governing coalition and was therefore no longer dependent on JVP support. (For information on the defunct Socialist People's Alliance [SPA], please see the 2012 *Handbook*.)

In July 2013, a UNP member of parliament and six other party officials defected to the UPFA. Also in July, Wasantha KUMARA, the UPFA member and chair of the Yatiyantota provincial council, was arrested on bribery charges.

Leaders: Mahinda RAJAPAKSE (President of the Republic), Susil PREMAJAYANTHA (Secretary General).

Sri Lanka Freedom Party—SLFP (*Sri Lanka Nidahas Pakshaya*). Founded in 1951 and a leading advocate of republican status prior to adoption of the 1972 constitution, the SLFP initially advocated a neutralist foreign policy and the progressive nationalization of industry. Although winning a clear majority of seats in the House of Representatives in the election of 1970, it governed in coalition with the *Lanka Sama Samaja* and communist parties until September 1975. Its legislative representation plummeted from 90 seats to 8 in the election of July 1977.

In October 1980, former prime minister Sirimavo Bandaranaike was deprived of her civil rights for a seven-year period for alleged corruption while in office. She nevertheless remained active in party affairs, causing a split between her supporters and those of the nominal president, Maithripala SENANAYAKE. Mrs. Bandaranaike's rights were restored by means of a presidential "free pardon" issued on January 1, 1986, and she immediately launched a campaign for early general elections. In August, the SLFP joined with some 20 groups, as well as prominent Buddhist leaders, in establishing the Movement for the Defense of the Nation (MDN) to oppose government policy that "conceded too much" on the Tamil question.

The party boycotted the 1988 provincial council elections but provided the main challenge to the United National Party (UNP) in subsequent presidential and legislative balloting. Mrs. Bandaranaike won nearly 45 percent of the December presidential vote, while the SLFP secured 67 parliamentary seats in February 1989.

In October 1993, Anura Bandaranaike, the former prime minister's son and theretofore leader of the opposition, withdrew from the party amid reports of a family power struggle, and subsequently joined the first Wickremesinghe administration. His departure opened the way for Mrs. Bandaranaike's younger daughter, Chandrika Kumaratunga, to assume a leading role in the SLFP-led PA and to become prime minister after the PA's electoral victory in August 1994. (Anura rejoined the SLFP prior to the December 2001 election.)

In October 2001, the SLFP general secretary, S. B. Dissanayake, was among the 13 PA defectors to the opposition, which precipitated the dissolution of Parliament. Following the PA's election loss in December, former prime minister Ratnasiri Wickremanayake, under pressure, resigned as leader of the opposition. In December 2004, Dissanayake was sentenced to two years in prison for defaming Supreme Court judges while he was SLFP general secretary.

In June 2006 President Rajapakse was elected party president, replacing former president Kumaratunga, who was resident in the United Kingdom. A year later, former foreign minister Mangala SAMARAWEERA, who had been removed from the cabinet in January 2007 after voicing policy differences with the president, announced formation of a breakaway **Sri Lanka Freedom Party–Mahagana** (SLFP-M), which quickly formed an alliance with the UNP.

In June 2008, it was reported that as many as 1,000 former members of the UNP and the JVP had defected and joined the SLFP. The SLFP led the UPFA coalition to 15 consecutive local and regional electoral victories from 2007 to 2009, through campaigns that emphasized the government's success in suppressing the LTTE. Two JVA leaders, Johnston FERNANDO and Indika BANDARANAYAKE, defected to the UPFA and were appointed to government posts in December 2009. In 2010, the **National Unity Alliance** (NUA) merged with the SLFP (for more on the grouping, please see the 2012 *Handbook*).

Rajapakse was reelected president in January 2010, and the UPFA received 60.3 percent of the vote in the April parliamentary balloting. The UPFA placed first in local balloting on March 17, 2011, securing 1,839 out of 3,036 seats in the local councils. It also won the second round of local elections in October with 51.9 percent of the vote.

In June 2013, the SLFP announced it supported amendments to the Thirteenth Amendment that critics argued would dilute the power of provincial councils.

Leaders: Mahinda RAJAPAKSE (President of the Republic and of the Party), Chandrika Bandaranaike KUMARATUNGA (Patron), Disanayaka Mudiyanselage JAYARATNE (Prime Minister), Ratnasiri WICKREMANAYAKE (Senior Minister of

Good Governance and Infrastructure and Former Prime Minister), Maithiripala SIRISENA (General Secretary).

Ceylon Workers' Congress (CWC). Formed as part of the labor union movement in 1939, the CWC is a Tamil group that participated in formation of the Tamil United Liberation Front (TULF, below) in 1976. It regards itself as the main spokesperson for the Indian Tamils who work primarily as laborers on centrally located tea plantations. It has attempted to prevent their forging links with the Tamil insurgents in the north and east.

In 1994, the CWC elected seven members of parliament on the UNP list, but they subsequently withdrew to sit as a group of progovernment independents. In the April 1999 provincial elections, the party campaigned under the banner of the National Union of Workers (NUW) because of a legal dispute over use of the party symbol. In three provinces the NUW's support was sufficient to give the PA a working legislative majority.

The CWC's longtime president, Sauvmiamoothy THONDAMAN, died in 1999. He was succeeded as minister of livestock development and estate infrastructure by his grandson Arumugam.

In late August 2000, five MPs broke from the CWC over a leadership dispute and announced their support for the UNP. In September 2001 the party severed its ties to the PA and then negotiated an electoral pact with the UNP, but not before the original dissidents rejoined the PA as the Ceylon Workers' Alliance. Following the December 2001 election, Thondaman joined the new UNP-led cabinet.

In 2004, the CWC ran as the UNP's partner in the United National Front (UNF), winning eight parliamentary seats. Following the election, the CWC was courted by the UPFA, which needed eight seats to claim a majority. In early June the CWC leadership rejected joining the minority government, but in early September it offered its "unconditional full support," thereby giving the UPFA a parliamentary majority and earning a cabinet post. Less than a year later, however, in February 2005, the CWC threatened to resign from the government, which it accused of neglecting the needs of its Tamil constituency. Differences were patched up late in the month and the CWC remained in the government, but in October the party announced that it would support the UNP's Wickremesinghe for the presidency.

In August 2006, the CWC rejoined the government, which it had supported in the March 2006 local elections. It left again in August 2007 but returned in October. In regional balloting through the summer of 2008, the CWC did poorly and failed to win seats in previously secure districts. In April 2009 public officials in the CWC agreed to donate one month's salary to relief efforts among Tamils displaced by fighting between the government and the LTTE. The CWC remained part of the UPFA-led government after the 2010 legislative elections. Meanwhile, CWC member of parliament V. S. RADHAKRISHNAN left the party to join the **Up-Country Peoples Front** (UCPF), which was also a member of the UPFA. The CWC ran as part of the UPFA coalition in local balloting in March 2011 but joined a coalition with the UCPF and the small **Democratic People's Front** (DPF) for provincial balloting in July 2012.

Reports in February 2013 indicated that the Plantation Trade Union Federation had begun to attract members of the CWC.

Leaders: Arumugam THONDAMAN (General Secretary of the Party and Minister of Livestock and Rural Community Development).

Eelam People's Democratic Party (EPDP). The EPDP was formed in the late 1980s by Douglas Devananda, a founding member of the EROS (see EDF, below) in the 1970s and of the EPRLF (below) in the 1980s. Having abandoned armed conflict, Devananda joined the political mainstream following the India–Sri Lanka Accord.

In the 1994 legislative election, EPDP members won nine "independent" seats from Jaffna, while in January 1998, defying LTTE threats and the deaths of at least two of its candidates, the party claimed victories in a majority of the 17 local council elections in the region. Nadarajah ATAPUTHARAJAH, an influential EPDP MP and editor of a widely read Tamil weekly, was assassinated in 1999.

The party backed President Kumaratunga's reelection in December 1999. Following the October 2000 general election, in which the party won four seats, it agreed to support the PA government. Its leader was awarded a cabinet post. In December 2001 the EPDP won two parliamentary seats on a vote share of 0.8 percent. In April 2004, it won only 0.3 percent and one seat. Devananda was then named to the Rajapakse cabinet, and he continues to serve under Prime Minister Wikremanayake. A close aide, Maha KANAPATHIPILLAI, was assassinated in July 2006. In 2008 Tharmalingam ELANGAKUMARAN, a regional EPDP leader, was arrested on criminal charges, including kidnapping and murder, and the party's office in Chenkaladi was reportedly closed by authorities. In 2009 the EPDP campaigned against the UPFA in local balloting in Jaffna and Vavuniya. But the EPDP campaigned as part of the UPFA in the 2010 parliamentary elections, winning three seats, and joined the subsequent UPFA government. The EPDP campaigned as part of the UPFA coalition in the March 2011 municipal balloting and the 2012 provincial elections. The EPDP also announced in July 2013 it would participate within the UPFA in polling in September in the Northern Province.

Leader: Douglas DEVANANDA (General Secretary of the Party and Minister of Traditional Industries and Small Enterprise Development).

Lanka Equal Society Party (*Lanka Sama Samaja Pakshaya*—LSSP). Established in 1935 as a Trotskyite formation named the Ceylon Equal Society Party, the LSSP first entered into a coalition with Mrs. Bandaranaike's SLFP in 1964. The party, which went into opposition in September 1975, lost all 19 of its legislative seats as a component of the ULF in the election of July 1977. Subsequently, it joined the SLMP and the SLCP in supporting measures to negotiate a settlement with Tamil activists.

In 1994, Vasudeva Nanayakkara rejoined the party. A presidential candidate in 1982, the outspoken Nanayakkara formed a new group during his hiatus from the LSSP. In 1999 he was expelled from party membership for crossing to the parliamentary opposition, thereby technically depriving the PA of its one-vote majority. Nanayakkara ran as the candidate of the Left and Democratic Alliance in the presidential balloting of December 1999.

The party's Wimalasiri de Mel was minister of science and technology under Prime Minister Wickremanayake, having joined the cabinet in January 1998 as a replacement for recently deceased party leader Bernard SOYSA. A year later the party leadership openly criticized the government for its failure to contain the violence that preceded the January 25, 1999, North-Western Provincial Council election. It subsequently threatened to leave the PA unless the government moved forward with abolition of the executive presidency and a return to the Westminster model.

In February 2004, despite some initial objections to the SLFP-JVP alliance, the LSSP decided to join the UPFA for the April parliamentary election and party leader de Mel won the LSSP's lone seat in Parliament. Shortly after the election, longtime LSSP Secretary Batty WEERAKOON resigned. LSSP member and constitutional advisor to the government, Jayampathy WICKRAMARATNE, resigned in protest over what he described as a lack of commitment on the part of the SLFP-led government on Tamil issues. The LSSP participated in regional elections in 2008 as a member of the SPA. It was part of the UPFA in the 2010 legislative elections, the 2011 local balloting, and the 2012 provincial polling. In May 2013, the LSSP joined the opposition in opposing a UPFA-sponsored increased in electricity process.

Leaders: Wimalasiri de MEL (Secretary to the Central Committee), Tissa VITHARANA (Senior Minister of Scientific Affairs).

National Congress (NC). The NC, initially called the National Muslim Congress, was formed in 2004 by A. L. M. Athaullah, who had previously been a leader in the SLMC and a noncabinet minister under Prime Minister Wickremesinghe. In 2003, having criticized the government for favoring the LTTE and not addressing the needs of the eastern Muslim community, Athaullah and S. SUBAIRDEEN broke away from the SLMC and established the Ashraff Congress. In February 2004 Athaullah left the Ashraff Congress and allied himself with the UPFA, joining the cabinet under Prime Minister Rajapakse. The party adopted its present name in September 2005. Shortly thereafter, some of its original members, dissatisfied with the UPFA government, returned to the SLMC. However, reports in 2009 indicated that a number of SLMC members continued to defect to the NC. The NC was part of the UPFA in the 2010 legislative elections and party leader Athaullah was given a cabinet post in the subsequent UPFA government.

Leader: Ahamed Lebbe Marikkan ATHAULLAH (Minister of Local Government and Provincial Councils).

National Heritage Party (*Jathika Hela Urumaya*—JHU). Launched in March 2004 with a platform that called for protecting Buddhism as the state religion, rooting out government corruption, and rejecting concessions to the Tamil Tigers, the JHU grew out of the strongly nationalist **Sinhalese Heritage** (*Sihala Urumaya*—SU). The SU was established in April 2000 on a similar platform that opposed concessions to Tamil militants, including any movement toward a federal state. In the October 2000 election the party won only one national list seat. An intraparty dispute over who should occupy the parliamentary seat led the SU president, S. L. GUNESEKARA, to resign and form the **Sinhala National Front** (*Sinhala Jathika Sangamaya*—SJS). In December 2001 the SU won under 0.6 percent of the vote and no seats in Parliament.

In the April 2004 election, the Buddhist JHU won an unexpected nine seats with 6.0 percent of the vote, after which it gave its external support to Prime Minister Rajapakse. Differences subsequently surfaced over whether the organization should abandon any future electoral role. The JHU supported Rajapakse in the 2005 presidential election. The JHU agreed to accept its first-ever cabinet post in January 2007.

In June 2008, the JHU announced a boycott of the All Party Representative Committee (APRC), a group formed to promote dialogue among the country's political parties. The JHU returned to the talks in August. The JHU was highly critical of international efforts to mediate the Tamil insurgency, and the party organized a series of protests outside of Western embassies in 2009 and petitioned for the UN to investigate human rights violations by the United States. The JHU campaigned with as part of the UPFA in the 2010 legislative elections and joined the subsequent government. At a 2011 party congress the JHU called for the government to undertake sterner measures to combat terrorism. In May 2013, a former JHU official committed suicide through self-immolation following his expulsion from the party.

Leaders: Katapola AMARAKITHTHI Thera (Chair), Patali Champika RANAWAKA (Minister of Power and Energy), Omalpe SOBHITHA (Secretary General).

National Liberation People's Party (*Desha Vimukthi Janatha Pakshaya*—DVJP). Active nationally since 1988, the DVJP is a leftist group often linked to the SLCP, SLMP, and LSSP. The DVJP was one of the founding members of the SPA.

Leader: Ven Galagama DHAMMARANSI (Chair).

People's United Front (*Mahajana Eksath Peramuna*—MEP). The MEP, a left-wing party formed in 1956, was formerly allied with the JVP. Strongly Sinhalese and Buddhist, it long advocated the nationalization of foreign estates. In April 1999 it captured three legislative seats in Western Province and subsequently backed President Kumaratunga's reelection. Although it later protested against the government's proposed constitutional changes, the MEP joined the PA for the October 2000 general election. Its president was named transport minister in the reshuffled Wickremanayake cabinet.

In 2004, the MEP won two seats in the legislative balloting, and Dinesh Gunawardena was appointed to the Rajapakse cabinet, a status he retained under Prime Minister Wickremanayake. The MEP campaigned for the UPFA during regional balloting in 2008. However, it joined the JHU in boycotting all-party talks during the summer of 2008. The MEP was part of the UPFA in the 2010 parliamentary elections, and Gunawardena was given a cabinet post in the subsequent government. The MEP participated with the UPFA in provincial elections in 2012.

Leaders: Dinesh GUNAWARDENA (President of the Party and Minister of Water Supply and Drainage), Piyasena DISSANAYAKE (General Secretary).

Sri Lanka Communist Party (SLCP). Founded in 1943, Sri Lanka's official Communist party consistently urged the nationalization of all banks, estates, and factories and the use of national languages rather than English. Initially, differences within the party membership prevented it from taking a clear position on Sino-Soviet relations, but subsequent trends yielded a strongly pro-Soviet posture. During 1976 the SLCP proposed a United Socialist Front with what it called the "centralized Left" in the SLFP. The initiative resulted in the formation in April 1977 of the United Left Front (ULF), comprising the SLCP, the LSSP, and the now-defunct People's Democratic Party (PDP); however, the ULF obtained no national state assembly seats in the July election. Briefly banned in 1983, the SLCP joined the SLFP in forming the USA in 1988 and then the PA in 1993. Longtime party leader Pieter KEUNEMAN died in 1997.

In May 2004, following the UPFA's victory at the polls, the SLCP secretary general, D. E. W. Gunasekera, was named minister for constitutional reforms. The SLCP helped create the SPA in 2006 and ran with the coalition in regional polling that year. It campaigned as part of the UPFA in 2010, and won two seats. Gunasekera was appointed to a cabinet post in the UPFA-led government and given another portfolio after the cabinet was reshuffled in 2010. Through 2013, the SLCP attempted to block efforts by the JVP to join the Communist International.

Leaders: D. E. W. GUNASEKERA (Secretary General of the Party and Minister of Human Resources), Raja COLLURE.

Sri Lanka People's Party (*Sri Lanka Mahajana Pakshaya*—SLMP). The socialist SLMP was formed in 1984 by Vijaya KUMARATUNGA, a popular film star, and his wife, Chandrika Kumaratunga, who had left the SLMP because of policy differences and the leadership style of her brother, Anura Bandaranaike. Vijaya was assassinated in February 1988, apparently as part of a campaign by the JVP (below) to suppress support of the 1987 India–Sri Lanka Accord. After several years abroad, Chandrika returned to Sri Lanka, organized the USA, and ultimately assumed leadership of the SLFP.

The party's general secretary and USA presidential candidate in 1988, Ossie Abeygunasekera, was among those killed in the October 1994 bomb attack that also took the life of UNP presidential nominee Gamini Dissanayake. The SLMP participated in regional balloting in 2008 as part of the SPA. The SLMP was part of the UPFA in the 2010 parliamentary balloting, the 2011 local polling, and the 2012 provincial elections.

Leader: Ranjith NAWARATNE (General Secretary).

Up-Country People's Front (UCPF). Representing Indian Tamil plantation workers, the UCPF was organized as an alternative to the CWC by former CWC member P. Chandrasekaran, who was elected to parliament as an independent in 1994 but aligned with the PA. The party won two seats on the Central Provincial Council in April 1999, but on December 7 Chandrasekaran resigned as President Kumaratunga's deputy minister for estate housing and threw his support to the opposition UNP, which he described as "offering more benefits to the estate Tamils." In December 2001 he was named to the incoming UNP-led cabinet.

In 2004, the UCPF won one parliamentary seat. It backed the UNP's Wickremesinghe for president in 2005 but shifted its support to the Rajapakse government in 2006. The party's leader has proposed the direct participation of India in settling the Tamil question, a call that Chandrasekaran repeated in 2008. The UCPF backed the UPFA in the 2010 legislative elections. It campaigned independently in the 2011 local balloting but participated in subsequent governing coalitions with the UPFA.

Leaders: Periyasamy CHANDRASEKARAN (President), P. RADHAKRISHNAN.

Tamil People's Liberation Party (*Tamileela Makkal Viduthalai Pulikal*—TMVP). Formation of the TMVP was announced in October 2004 by Colonel Karuna, the former LTTE eastern commander who broke with the LTTE in March 2004 and quickly saw his forces, numbering some 6,000, bear the brunt of an LTTE offensive. Later in October, Karuna and the leaders of the long-dormant ENDLF announced formation of the TIVM front "to achieve the cherished rights and the reasonable aspirations" of Sri Lanka's Tamils. Since then, the Karuna breakaway group has continued to engage in open hostilities with the LTTE, amid indications that it was cooperating with the Sri Lankan military. In 2007 Karuna announced that the TMVP was prepared to enter parliamentary politics. The TMVP campaigned as part of the UPFA in provincial balloting in 2008 and won 20 of 37 seats in the Eastern regional council elections. Karuna was appointed minister of national reconciliation and integration in March 2009. In 2009 it was reported that many TMVP members had defected to join the SLFP. The TMVP contested local balloting in 2011 and 2012 with the UPFA. In September 2012, TMVP leader Sivanesathurai Chandrakanthan was appointed as a presidential advisor.

Leader: Sivanesathurai CHANDRAKANTHAN.

National Freedom Front (NFF). The NFF was formed in June 2008 and subsequently expanded by attracting officials and members of other political parties, including the JVP. The NFF signed a memorandum of understanding with the UPFA in December 2008. In the 2010 coalition government, party leader Wimal Weerawansa was appointed minister of housing and construction. In the September 2012 provincial balloting, the NFF won its first council seat.

Leaders: Wimal WEERAWANSA (President of the Party and Minister of Housing and Construction), Nandana GUNATHILAKE (General Secretary).

Other Parliamentary Parties:

United National Front (UNF). Formed in October 2009, the UNF was a revival of an electoral alliance launched in 2001. Led by the UNP, the UNF included the SLMC, the mainly Tamil Democratic People's Front (DPF) and a dozen smaller parties. The UNF backed opposition candidate Fonseka in the January 2010 presidential balloting. In the April 2010 parliamentary balloting, the UNF placed second with 29.3 percent of the vote and 60 seats in the 225-member parliament. The constituent parties did not campaign as a coalition in the 2011 or 2012 local and regional balloting.

Leaders: Ranil WICKREMESINGHE, Mangala SAMARAWEERA (Cochairs).

United National Party—UNP (*Ekshat Jathika Pakshaya*). A democratic-socialist party founded in 1946, the UNP advocates a moderate line and the avoidance of a narrowly "communal" posture. Having survived virtual annihilation as a legislative force in 1970, the party swept 142 of 168 assembly seats in 1977 and remained in power by subsequent extension of the parliamentary term to 1989. It won 125 of 225 seats in the 1989 election. From 1978 until 1989 the UNP's Junius R. Jayewardene served as executive president of Sri Lanka.

The UNP finished second in 1994 with 94 of 225 seats, including 7 won by members of the CWC, who ran on the UNP ticket but subsequently announced that they would sit as progovernment independents. The party's initial choice as 1994 presidential candidate, Gamini Dissanayake, was assassinated less than three weeks before the November election, in which his widow, Srima, won 35.9 percent of the vote as his replacement. In the first half of 1999 the UNP uniformly finished second to the PA in elections for seven provincial councils, despite having won majorities in five of them in the previous provincial elections.

In November 1999, five members of parliament and two dozen or so other elected officials announced their break from the UNP leadership over the party's lack of support for constitutional reform. The MPs indicated that they would remain within the party but function independently. They also threatened a judicial challenge if the leadership formally expelled them, which it did. Two of the five were named to President Kumaratunga's cabinet as "special assignment" ministers.

UNP presidential candidate Ranil Wickremesinghe finished second in December 1999, with 42.6 percent of the vote. In the October 2000 parliamentary election the UNP won 89 seats on a 40 percent vote share. Three UNP dissidents received cabinet portfolios in the subsequent Wickremanayake government.

In the run-up to the December 2001 election, Wickremesinghe negotiated electoral alliances with the Sri Lanka Muslim Congress (SLMC), the recently formed four-party Tamil National Alliance (TNA, below), and the CWC. With the UNP having won 109 seats and 46 percent of the vote, Wickremesinghe formed a governing coalition with the SLMC, also brought the CWC leader into the cabinet, and obtained external support from the TNA.

In April 2004, the UNP and the CWC, running together as the **United National Front** (UNF), won 37.8 percent of the vote and 82 seats (74 claimed by the UNP). In November 2005 former prime minister Wickremesinghe once again lost the presidency, this time by only 2 percent of the vote.

In 2006 several MPs defect to the UPFA. At the same time, some party members voiced dissatisfaction with Wickremesinghe's continuing leadership. In January 2007 the UNP saw another 18 MPs, led by former deputy leader Karu JAYASURIYA, cross the aisle, with 10 being named to the cabinet and the others assuming lesser ministerial posts. Jayisuriya subsequently indicated that he intended to form a **Democratic Group** party. In 2008 the leader of the UNP's women's wing, Chandra WANNIARACHCHI, led an estimated 500 members of the UNP in a mass defection to the SLFP. Regional UNP leaders increasingly criticized party leaders and called for a reorganization to make the grouping more competitive. In July 2009, a court issued an order preventing the UNP from expelling party members that joined the UPFA government. Wickremesinghe declined to run for the presidency in 2010. He instead called on the party to support Fonseka. In September 2010, the UNP expelled six senior members for supporting an amendment to abolish the presidential term limit. In the March 2011 local elections, the UNP secured majorities in only nine councils, and it won one council in the October balloting.

Reports in July 2013 indicated a rift within the party between stalwarts and a faction led by Sajith PREMADASA.

Leaders: Ranil WICKREMESINGHE (Former Prime Minister), Rukman SENANAYAKE (Chair), Tissa ATTANAYAKE (General Secretary).

Sri Lanka Muslim Congress (SLMC). Formed in 1980, the SLMC declared itself a political party at a conference convened in 1986 to represent Muslim interests in the negotiations for a political settlement of the Tamil question. The party won 17 seats in the North-East Provincial Council balloting in November 1988 and supported Mrs. Bandaranaike's bid for the presidency in December 1988. It obtained 3 legislative seats in 1989, adding 4 more as a coalition partner of the PA in 1994.

In August 2000, comments by SLFP minister A. H. M. FOWZIE belittling the SLMC's importance to the PA led President Mohamed H. M. ASHRAFF to submit his resignation as ports minister, but the rift was patched at the end of the month. At the same time, the SLMC agreed to remain partnered with the PA for the October general election, although it decided to contest four districts separately. To broaden its appeal beyond its Muslim constituency, the party also decided to campaign as the National Unity Alliance (see SLFP, above). In the balloting the NUA won four seats in addition to those won under the PA banner.

Party founder Ashraff died in September 2000 in a helicopter crash. His widow, Ferial, was named to the cabinet announced after the October election, as was her party coleader, Rauff Hakeem. Hakeem soon supplanted Mrs. Ashraff within the SLMC, although she became the NUA leader.

In June 2001, President Kumaratunga removed Hakeem from the cabinet, at which time he and six other SLMC members of parliament abandoned the government, thereby costing it its legislative majority. Ashraff initially resigned her cabinet post but continued her support for the government. She resumed her ministerial position in early July, leaving the SLMC/NUA asunder. Following the December 2001 election, in which the SLMC won five seats, Hakeem negotiated a coalition agreement with the UNP and joined the new cabinet. Mrs. Ashraff's NUA had remained with the PA. Subsequent efforts to resolve their differences did not succeed. In 2002–2003 the party splintered further, largely over the perception of a faction led by A. L. M. Athaullah that the UNP government was favoring the LTTE at the expense of eastern Muslims (see NC, above).

For the April 2004 general election, the SLMC ran independently, capturing five parliamentary seats. In May one SLMC MP defected to the UPFA, and three others did likewise in October, for which the three were named noncabinet ministers responsible for rehabilitation and district development in three Tamil districts. The SLMC leadership attempted to expel the three but was overruled by the Supreme Court.

The SLMC supported the UNP's Ranil Wickremesinghe in the 2005 presidential contest. In 2006, however, it announced that it would extend issue-based support to the government, and in January 2007, Hakeem brought the SLMC back into the government, only to withdraw on December 12 because of insufficient progress on Muslim-related issues. In 2008, a faction of the party, led by M. Lalith GUNARATNE, announced that they would support the government at the local and regional level and rejected Hakeem's call for noncooperation. In 2009 several leading SLMC figures were reported to have left the party and joined the NC. The SLMC broke with other parties in the UNF and supported the constitutional amendment that abolished presidential term limits. In local balloting in March 2011 the SLMC gained majorities in just 4 out of 234 councils. It won a majority in one additional council in October.

In September 2012, the SLMC agreed to join with the UFPA to establish a coalition government for the Eastern Province.

Leaders: Rauff HAKEEM (Former Minister of Posts and Telecommunications), Basheer Cego DAWOOD (Chair), Hasan ALI (General Secretary).

Other parties in the UNF include the **Democratic People's Front** (DPF), a Tamil grouping, and the **Sri Lanka Freedom Party** (Mahajana Wing).

Democratic National Alliance (DNA). Formed in February 2010, the DNA was created by the JVP in an effort to bring together opposition parties to defeat the UPFA legislative balloting in April 2010. The DNA also served as a political vehicle for former general and opposition leader Fonseka, who was elected as a member of parliament. The JVP placed fourth in the balloting with 5.49 percent of the vote and 7 seats in the parliament. Reports in 2013 indicated that Fonseka had registered to form a new political party.

Leaders: Sarath FONSEKA; Vijitha HERATH (General Secretary).

People's Liberation Front (*Janatha Vimukthi Peramuna*—JVP). The Sinhalese JVP (not to be confused with the Tamil National Liberation Front—JVP, under TULF, below) was formed as a legal Maoist party in the mid-1960s. It led an attempt to overthrow the government in 1971. The front regained legal status in 1977 and emerged as the third-ranked party in Colombo as the result of local elections in 1979. It was again proscribed after the July 1983 riots, reemerging in 1987 as a major threat to the government through a campaign of killing and terror in the south directed at government targets and Sinhalese supporters of the India–Sri Lanka Accord. In an attempt to win the JVP over to conventional politics, the government again legalized the party in 1988, but JVP leaders renounced the offer and remained underground.

The JVP subsequently expanded its guerrilla campaign in the south, apparently operating through a military wing called the Patriotic People's Movement (*Deshapriya Janatha Viyaparaya*—DJV). Having disrupted provincial, presidential, and legislative elections in 1988 and early 1989, the front again rejected government overtures in September 1989. Subsequently, JVP founder and leader Rohana WIJEWEERA, General Secretary Upatissa GAANAYAKE, and other senior JVP members were killed by security forces under questionable circumstances. In all, the armed struggle in the south may have cost 50,000 lives or more.

Having disavowed violence in the mid-1990s, the JVP gathered strength late in the decade as a "third force" in opposition to the PA and the UNP, sometimes releasing joint statements with other leftist formations. In 1999 it presented candidates for all seven provincial council elections, capturing at least one seat at each. In Western and Southern Provinces, where neither the PA nor the UNP secured a majority, the JVP held the balance of power, although JVP leaders stated that they had no intention of entering either provincial government. Its December 1999 presidential candidate, Nandana GUNATHILAKE, finished third, with 4.1 percent of the vote, having campaigned on a platform that included abolition of the executive presidency and rejection of World Bank and IMF prescriptions for economic reform. In October 2000, the party won 6 percent of the vote and ten seats in parliament.

In September 2001, the JVP's Gunathilake and President Kumaratunga signed a 28-point agreement that guaranteed the JVP's support to the PA government, in return for which the JVP obtained key policy concessions. Parliament was nevertheless dissolved in October, and in the December election the JVP picked up an additional 6 seats on a 9 percent vote share. In 2004 the JVP was credited with 39 of the UPFA's seats. Despite participating in the Rajapakse cabinet, the JVP continued to press its own agenda, including an end to privatization, noncooperation with World Bank and IMF economic prescriptions, and opposition to broad autonomy for Tamil areas.

Despite having left the Rajapakse government in June 2005, the JVP lent its support to Rajapakse's presidential candidacy later in the year in return for his commitment to key elements of the JVP's agenda, including renegotiation of the cease-fire agreement with the LTTE. The JVP nevertheless remained outside the subsequent Wickremanayake government and reconfirmed its decision in July 2006, when it rebuffed overtures from the UPFA and demanded the expulsion of the Sri Lanka Monitoring Mission.

In 2008, the JVP called for a boycott of Indian goods and declared that reducing Indian influence in Sri Lanka would henceforth be one of the planks in its party platform. It was reported that a large number of JVP stalwarts defected from the party to the SLFP. In April 2009, the JVP experienced its worst electoral defeat, losing regional balloting in its political base in the Western Provincial Council elections. Its representation dropped from 23 to 3 seats. Several senior party members defected to the UPFA to protest the JVA's endorsement of Fonseka as a presidential candidate in January 2010 (see UPFA, above). Reports in 2011 indicated a continuing split within the party. Reports in 2013 indicated continuing defections to the UPFA.

Leaders: Somawansa AMARASINGHE (Chair), M. Tilvin SILVA (General Secretary).

Tamil National Alliance (TNA). The TNA was established on October 18, 2001, by Tamil parties in preparation for the December general election, in which it ran under the symbol of the TULF, the "rising sun." The TNA, strongly supportive of a negotiated settlement with the Tamil Tigers (LTTE, below), soon concluded an electoral pact with the opposition UNP and went on to win 15 parliamentary seats on a vote share of 3.9 percent. Following the election, it extended its external support to the United National Front government.

In the April 2004 election, the TNA appeared on the ballot under the house symbol of the **Sri Lanka Tamil Government Party** (*Ilankai Tamil Arasu Kachchi*—ITAK), an original component of the TULF that had been revived because of a split in the TULF. For the first time the TNA explicitly served as the proxy of the LTTE, winning 22 seats in the north and east.

In November 2005, the LTTE and TNA indicated their "disinterest" in the outcome of the presidential election, which probably contributed to a low voter turnout in Tamil areas and a resultant loss for UNP candidate Wickremesinghe. The TNA officially boycotted regional balloting in 2008 to protest the manner in which district lines were drawn. Between 2005 and 2008, three TNA legislators were killed in attacks. In February 2009 the TNA was invited to rejoin all-party negotiations. After the defeat of the LTTE in 2009, the TNA launched an initiative to develop closer ties with India and seek that country's assistance in protecting the Tamil minority. In March 2010, the TNA renounced its longtime goal of an independent Tamil homeland. In the April parliamentary balloting, the TNA placed third with 14 seats in the legislature.

In 2013 reports indicted a division within the TNA over the selection of candidates for provincial balloting scheduled for September.

Leaders: Rajavarothiyam SAMPANTHAN (Parliamentary Leader), Mavai S. SENATHIRAJAH (ITAK).

Tamil United Liberation Front—TULF (*Tamil Vimuktasi Peramuna*). The TULF was initially organized as the Tamil Liberation Front (*Tamil Vimukthi Peramuna*—TVP) in 1976 by a number of Tamil groups, including the CWC, the All Ceylon Tamil Congress (ACTC), the ITAK, the National Liberation Front (*Jatika Vimukthi Peramuna*—JVP), and the Muslim United Front.

The TULF stated in its 1977 election manifesto that its successful candidates would serve as the constituent assembly of a proposed Tamil state (Tamil Eelam). In the July election the front obtained 16 seats in the Northern and Eastern Provinces, becoming the largest opposition group in the National Assembly. Having previously declared their intention to resign from Parliament to protest the extension of the existing body beyond its normal term, the TULF MPs failed to appear for an oath renouncing separatism in August 1983, and their seats were thereupon declared constitutionally vacant.

Despite pressure from militants, the TULF maintained an essentially moderate posture, engaging in talks with the government and supporting the 1987 India–Sri Lanka Accord. Under pressure from the LTTE, the TULF boycotted the North-East Provincial Council balloting of November 1988; however, it won ten seats in the February 1989 parliamentary poll, its candidates reportedly having been supported by other proaccord Tamil groups. The TULF secretary general, Appapillai AMIRTHALINGAM, was killed and the party president seriously wounded in a July 1989 attack attributed by some reports to a "rogue cell" of the LTTE.

The TULF won five seats in Parliament in the 1994 election, after which it agreed to support the PA. In January 1998 the TULF won a majority of seats on the Jaffna Municipal Council, but in March the party president was quoted as saying that his organization would step aside in favor of the LTTE if the PA and the UNP would reopen talks with the group and accept it as the legitimate representative of the Tamils. In May the newly elected TULF mayor of Jaffna, Sarojini YOGESWARAN, was assassinated by a group claiming allegiance to the LTTE. Four months later her successor, Ponnuthurai SIVAPALAN, was also killed, and in December a party secretary, Ponnathurai MATHIMUGARAJAH, was assassinated at a public rally. The well-respected party vice president, Neelan TIRUCHELVAM, was killed by an LTTE suicide bomber in July 1999.

Because of intraparty differences, the TULF did not officially endorse a presidential candidate in December 1999. In October 2000 it won five seats in Parliament. In 2001 it was a prime mover in forming the TNA.

Technically, the TULF did not contest the April 2004 parliamentary election because of a leadership dispute that remained in the courts. The TNA-supportive wing of the party, led by R. Sampanthan, backed the LTTE as the sole representative of the Tamil people, while the other wing refused to accept the LTTE's contention. The latter wing, led by V. Anandasangaree, offered a slate of independent candidates but won no seats.

In December 2005, party leader and TNA legislator Joseph PARARAJASINGHAM was assassinated. The government blamed the LTTE; the LTTE blamed government-backed paramilitaries. In January 2006 the Anandasangaree wing, the anti-LTTE faction of the Eelam People's Revolutionary Liberation Front (EPRLF, below), and the People's Liberation Organization of Tamil Eelam (PLOTE, below) formed a new Tamil electoral alliance, the Tamil Democratic National Alliance, to compete in regional elections. However, reports in 2009 indicated that Anandasangaree had reconciled with the mainline TULF leaders. In 2012, TULF reaffirmed its call for Tamil autonomy.

Leaders: Veerasingham ANANDASANGAREE, Rajavarothiyam SAMPANTHAN.

All Ceylon Tamil Congress—ACTC (*Akila Ilankai* Tamil Congress). Organized in 1944 and generally regarded as the founder of the movement for Tamil statehood, the ACTC participated in formation of the TULF in 1976 but subsequently reregistered as a separate party.

On January 5, 2000, its leader, Kumar PONNAMBALAM, was assassinated. An anti-LTTE group calling itself the National Front Against Tigers later claimed responsibility. The party won one seat in the 2000 and 2004 parliament elections but failed to gain any seats in the 2010 balloting. Reports in 2013 indicated that the ACTC would not participate with the TNA in future balloting.

Leaders: Gajendrakumar PONNAMBALAM (General Secretary), Kumar PONNAMBALAM.

Eelam People's Revolutionary Liberation Front (EPRLF). Founded in 1980, the EPRLF conducted guerrilla activity in Tamil areas in the first half of the 1980s before being decimated by a full-scale LTTE offensive in late 1986. In the wake of the 1987 accord that brought Indian troops to the region, the EPRLF was rebuilt, with New Delhi's support, to serve as a vehicle for the assumption by moderate Tamils of local political autonomy. In November 1988 the EPRLF gained 40 of 71 seats in the newly created North-East Provincial Council: It won 17 of 35 seats in the east and, under an agreement with the Eelam National Democratic Liberation Front (ENDLF, below), filled 23 seats in the uncontested north. In addition, an EPRLF leader was appointed chief minister of the province, and an EPRLF-dominated militia, the Tamil National Army, was formed. Upon completion of the Indian withdrawal in March 1990, however, the Tamil army proved to be no match for the LTTE, and many of its members joined most of the EPRLF leadership in fleeing to India. Party leader K. PATHMANABA was assassinated in 1990.

The party failed to win control of any of the local bodies in the January 1998 Jaffna balloting. A year later former party chief and North-East chief minister Annamalai Varatharaja Perumal returned from exile, reportedly to rebuild the EPRLF, but in January 2000 he was expelled by the party's central committee for "antiparty" activities. Two months earlier he had stated that he no longer considered Tamil independence realistic. Perumal and his dissident supporters contested the October 2000 elections on independent district lists while voicing support for the PA at the national level.

In June 2003, the leader of Perumal's faction, Thambirajah SUBATHIRAN, was assassinated, apparently by the LTTE. The party remained divided through 2004, with the wing loyal to Suresh Premachandran (Suresh Faction) and continuing its participation with the TNA. The Perumal faction, led by T. Sritharan, backed the presidential candidacy of Prime Minister Rajapakse in 2005. In 2008, a faction of the EPRLF joined with the TULF in the Tamil Democratic National Alliance. The grouping, led by G. SRITHARAN, declared its intention to elect a Tamil as the chief minister of the regional council. In June 2009 EPRLF fighters engaged in a series of gun battles in Jaffna with LTTE guerillas, which left an estimated 75 dead and scores wounded. Reports indicated that a large number of EPRLF members surrendered and subsequently joined the LTTE. The EPRLF won 2 of the TNA's 14 seats in the 2010 parliamentary elections. In 2011, the party opposed the inclusion of the EPRLF—Pathmanabha faction as part of the TNA for future balloting.

Faction Leaders: Suresh K. PREMACHANDRAN (Suresh Faction), Thirunavakkarasu SRITHARAN (Pathmanabha Faction).

Tamil Eelam Liberation Organization (TELO). The TELO resulted from the merger, in Madras, India, in 1984, of a preexisting group of the same name with the Eelam Revolutionary Organization (EROS; see under EDF, below) and the Eelam People's Revolutionary Front (EPRF). The organization was reported to have been "virtually eliminated" in battles with the LTTE in 1986, with its principal leader, Mohan Sri SABARATNAM, among the estimated 300 casualties.

In the January 1998 balloting, the TELO won control of only one village council. In the 2000 and 2004 national elections the party won three seats in parliament. In 2007 and 2008 a number of TELO regional officials were attacked or killed by the LTTE, which rejected TELO's political accommodation with establishment parties. In some local elections in 2009, TELO candidates campaigned jointly with the UPFA. TELO campaigned as part of the TNA in the 2010 legislative balloting and secured 2 of the alliance's 14 seats. A breakaway faction of the TELO registered as the **Tamil National Liberation Alliance** (TNLA) in 2010.

Leaders: Selvam ADAIKALANATHAN (President), Indrakumar PRASANNA (General Secretary).

Sri Lanka Tamil Government Party (*Ilankai Tamil Arasu Kachchi*—ITAK) Organized in the 1940s, the ITAK, also known as the Federal Party, was revived in 2004. It had not directly competed in a national election since 1970. In the 2004 balloting it secured five seats as part of the TNA. In the 2010 elections, it won 8 of the TNA's 14 seats. In local balloting in 2011, ITAK won 17 seats on municipal councils. In 2013, ITAK threatened to withdraw from the TNA over the division of responsibilities within the grouping.

Leaders: R. SAMPANTHAN (Chair), Mawai SENATHIRAJAH (Secretary General).

Other National or Sinhalese Parties:

Liberal Party (LP). The LP began as the Council for Liberal Democracy, founded in 1981 by UNP member Chanaka AMARATUNGA, who ultimately formed the LP in 1987. It won two Western Province council seats in 1988 and ran on the SLFP ticket in 1989. In August 1996 Amaratunga, who had helped draft the revolutionary constitutional amendments favored by the Kumaratunga administration, died in an automobile accident.

The LP won no provincial council seats in 1999 despite offering candidates in six provinces. Its current leader ran for president in December 1999 but attracted little support, and in December 2001 and April 2004 the LP won only a handful of votes. Party leader Rajiva Wijesinha was appointed secretary general of the peace group, the Secretariat for Coordinating the Peace Process (SCOPP) in 2007. He was replaced by Kamal Nissanka, who was elected general secretary at a party congress. The LP received less than 1 percent of the vote in the 2010 legislative elections.

Leaders: Kamal NISSANKA (General Secretary), Swarma AMARATUNGA (Honorary President).

Muslim National Alliance (MNA). The MNA was established in May 2005 by three parties: the **Democratic Unity Alliance** (DUA); **the Sri Lanka Muslim Kachchi** (SLMK), led by Abdul RASOOL; and the **United Muslim People's Alliance** (UMPA), led by Nizar MOULANA. The alliance backed the UNP's Wickremesinghe. In October 2005, however, it switched its allegiance to Prime Minister Rajapakse of the UPFA. Other organizations joining the MNA included the Ashraff Congress (see NC, above) and the **Muslim United Liberation Front** (MULF). The MNA received less than 0.01 percent of the vote in the 2010 parliamentary elections.

Leader: Hafiz Nazeer AHAMED.

Sri Lanka Progressive Front (SLPF). The SLPF, which was formed in the late 1980s by former SLFP leader Ariya BULEGODA, won one seat in the 1994 balloting for Parliament. Its 1994 presidential candidate, Nihal Galappathy, won only 0.3 percent of the vote; Galappathy later joined the JVP. The SLPF failed to secure provincial council representation in balloting in 1999. Bulegoda died in April

2004. The party's 2005 presidential candidate, Nelson PERERA, withdrew in favor of Prime Minister Rajapakse. In the 2000, 2001, 2004, and 2010 general elections, it failed to gain any seats.

Leader: Rohan JAYATUNGA (Secretary).

Among other parties that contested the 2010 election (none obtained more than 0.2 percent of the vote) were the **Ceylon Democratic Unity Alliance** (CDUA), led by S. SATHASIVAM; the **Jathika Sangwardhena Peramuna** (JSP), led by 2005 presidential candidate Achala Ashoka SURAWEERA; the **National People's Party** (NPP), led by Mudhitha KARUNAMANI; the **Ruhuna Janatha Party** (RJP), led by Aruna SOYZA; the **Socialist Equality Party** (SEP), led by 2005 presidential candidate Wije DIAS; the **Sri Lanka National Front** (SLNF), led by Piyasena DISSANAYAKE; and the **United Socialist Party** (USP), led by 2005 presidential candidate, Siritunga JAYASURIYA.

For more information on the **New Equal Society Party** (*Nawa Sama Samaja Pakshaya*—NSSP) and the **Sons of the Soil Party** (*Sinhalaye Mahasammatha Bhoomiputra Pakshaya*—SMBP), see the 2011 *Handbook.*

Other Tamil Parties and Groups:

Liberation Tigers of Tamil Eelam (LTTE). Founded in 1972 as the Tamil New Tigers, the LTTE is the largest and most hard-line of the militant Tamil groups. It has proposed a socialist Tamil homeland, although ideology has recently been overshadowed by military considerations. In 1985 the Tigers joined the EPRLF, EROS (see under EDF, below), and TELO in an antigovernment coalition, the Eelam National Liberation Front (ENLF), to fight for a separate Tamil state. However, the LTTE was soon engaged in a bloody campaign against some of its former allies, assuming effective control of much of northern Sri Lanka, especially the Jaffna peninsula. The Tigers also conducted extensive guerrilla activity against the Indian troops brought into the region as peacekeepers under the 1987 accord between Colombo and New Delhi. The LTTE boycotted and partially sabotaged the provincial elections in November 1988 and the presidential elections in December.

In 1989, the LTTE agreed to peace negotiations with the government, announced a temporary cease-fire, and vowed to renounce violence if the other militant Tamil groups did likewise. It also launched the People's Front of Liberation Tigers (PFLT) as a "democratic socialist" political party. However, fighting was reported at year's end between the LTTE and the EPRLF, the Tigers' primary opposition in the struggle for Tamil dominance. Completion of the Indian withdrawal in March 1990 left the LTTE in virtual control in the north. Amid periodic hostilities and an ongoing LTTE terrorist campaign against civilian targets, various peace initiatives in the 1990s failed to yield a durable settlement. The government consistently rejected LTTE demands for third-party mediation of the conflict.

In January 1998, in response to the bombing of the country's holiest Buddhist shrine in Kandy, the government officially banned the LTTE. In November the High Court ruled that party members could be tried in absentia on charges related to the January 1996 Colombo financial center bombing that killed nearly 100 and injured another 1,400. Near the end of the year, for the second time since 1995, the LTTE reportedly responded to a revolt in its ranks with a crackdown against dissident troops.

A major LTTE offensive begun in November 1999 continued into 2000, reversing many of the losses suffered in the preceding 18 months and threatening government control of Jaffna. Meanwhile, a series of LTTE-sponsored assassinations and suicide bombings continued unabated. The targets included leaders of the government-supportive Tamil parties as well as President Kumaratunga, who narrowly escaped assassination in December 1999. In the two years following the January 1998 local elections in the north, the LTTE killed at least 25 councilors.

In March–April 2000, the LTTE appeared to be inching closer to talks with the government, with Norway to serve as mediator, although the Kumaratunga administration steadfastly rejected an LTTE demand that government forces be confined to barracks during any such negotiations. A breakthrough finally occurred in the wake of the December 2001 parliamentary election, and in February 2002 the LTTE and the new UNP-led government concluded an indefinite cease-fire agreement, with formal negotiations then opening in September. In April 2003, after four additional rounds of negotiations, the LTTE called a halt to the peace process, citing lack of progress with regard to autonomy, rehabilitation, and reconstruction.

On October 31, 2003, the LTTE published its proposal for an Interim Self-Governing Authority (ISGA) for the northeast. The plan called for Tamils to exert complete control over the region for five years, after which an election would be held.

The most significant challenge to the LTTE leadership of Velupillai Prabhakaran was launched in March 2004 by the commander of forces in the east, Colonel Karuna, who led an estimated 6,000 troops (out of the LTTE's total of 15,000) in a revolt against northern domination. The rebellion was largely suppressed in April, however, and Karuna went underground. In October he announced formation of the Tamil People's Liberation Party (TMVP, below). By early 2005, his forces were again challenging the LTTE, which accused the Sri Lanka Army and Karuna of cooperating in a "secret war" against the LTTE.

The LTTE and the Rajapakse government met in February 2006 in Switzerland to discuss increasingly frequent cease-fire violations, but the severity of the clashes continued to escalate. Talks scheduled for April were canceled, and in May the EU labeled the LTTE a terrorist organization, threatening its main fund-raising activities. (In 2007 the United States, France, and the United Kingdom all arrested LTTE representatives for criminal fund-raising.) An attempt to renew peace talks in October 2006 proved unsuccessful. In December the LTTE's chief negotiator, Anton BALASINGHAM, died in London of cancer.

On March 26, 2007, the LTTE, using one or two light aircraft, conducted its first air attack, but the additional capability did nothing to halt the Sri Lankan army's progress. By mid-July the army had claimed control in the east and continued on the offensive in the north. On November 2, the LTTE's political leader, S. P. THAMISELVAN, was killed in an air attack.

A new government offensive begun in January 2008 reduced the amount of territory under the control of LTTE from about 15,000 square kilometers to 4,000 square kilometers. However, Prabhakaran pledged not to negotiate with the government but to continue LTTE's armed struggle. Into 2009, government forces continued to advance, and Prabhakaran and other senior LTTE leaders were killed in fighting in May as the last rebel stronghold was captured by security forces. Although organized military resistance ceased, an estimated 5,000–7,000 fighters continued to wage a guerilla campaign against the government and progovernment Tamil groups. Selvarasa Pathmanathan was named as Prabhakaran's replacement in July by the LTTE's central committee, but the new leader was captured by authorities on August 5. In 2011 joint efforts were launched by Germany, the Netherlands, and Switzerland to suppress illegal fund-raising for the LTTE. A 2012 investigation by the United States reported that the LTTE used charitable organizations and humanitarian groups to illegally raise funds. The United States subsequently kept the LTTE on its list of international terrorist groups. Reports in 2013 indicated that the LTTE had trained terrorist groups in India.

Leader: Selvarasa PATHMANATHAN.

Eelam National Democratic Liberation Front (ENDLF). Initially a strong ally of the EPRLF and a supporter of the India–Sri Lanka Accord of 1987, the ENDLF filled 13 uncontested seats from the north in the creation of the North-East Provincial Council in November 1988. Since the withdrawal of Indian troops from Sri Lanka, the ENDLF has operated primarily in India. In October 2004, however, it announced formation of the **Tamil Eelam United Liberation Front** (*Tamileela Iykkiya Viduthalai Munnani*—TIVM) with the TMVP, the new party of ex-LTTE commander Karuna. In 2008 ENDLF leader G. Gnanasekaran called for military intervention by India to end the conflict between the government and the LTTE and to protect the Tamil minority. In August 2011 the Sri Lankan government deregistered the ENDLF as a political party.

Leaders: G. GNANASEKARAN, Parathan RAJAN (TIVM Coleader), R. RAJARATTINAM (General Secretary).

Eelavar Democratic Front (EDF). The EDF emerged in 1988 from reorganization of the Eelam Revolutionary Organization of Students (EROS, but also known as the Eelam Revolutionary Organization), which had been organized in London in the mid-1970s. Although not legally registered, the EDF presented a slate of independent candidates (with the reported tacit approval of the LTTE) in the February 1989 parliamentary balloting, securing 13 seats and becoming the third largest legislative block. EDF representatives boycotted subsequent parliamentary sessions, calling for repudiation of the 1987 India–Sri Lanka Accord, immediate withdrawal of Indian troops, and the release of all Tamil prisoners. Two of its parliamentary members resigned their seats in early 1990, while the remaining 11 followed suit in July, saying they did "not want to be dormant spectators who witness the torment of our people." The EDF did not present a slate of candidates for the 2004 general election.

In mid-2007, the EROS reemerged as the **Eelam Revolutionary Organization** under the leadership of Nesan Shankar Raji (son of an original EROS founder), who described the revived EROS as a democratic Tamil front committed to a federal secular state. The EDF participated in regional and local balloting in 2008, but its candidates faced attacks and intimidation from other Tamil groups, and two were killed. The EDF failed to gain any seats in local and regional balloting in 2012.

Leaders: Nesan Shankar RAJI (Nesan THIRUNESAN), Rajanathan PRABAHARAN (Secretary General).

People's Liberation Organization of Tamil Eelam (PLOTE). The PLOTE was the most important of the separatist groups not involved in the May 1985 coalition (see LTTE, above). Attempts were made on the lives of a number of its leaders in Madras in March 1985, apparently by the LTTE, which severely curtailed PLOTE rebel activity in 1986. PLOTE General Secretary Uma WAHESWARAN, who along with other PLOTE members had been implicated in an attempted coup in the Maldives in late 1988, was reportedly assassinated in Colombo in July 1989.

Since 1988, the PLOTE's political wing has been the **Democratic People's Liberation Front** (DPLF), which won three parliamentary seats in 1994 and extended its support to the PA (even though the leader of a progovernment faction, N. S. K. Uma PRAKASH, had been assassinated early in the year). The DPLF's vice president, Karavai KANDASAMY, was assassinated in December 1994.

The DPLF contested the January 1998 local elections in Jaffna, but it won control only of two urban and two village councils. The PLOTE, running under its own banner, had even less success, achieving no majorities. In September 1999 the PLOTE military commander, Thasan MANIKKADASAN, and a deputy were killed by a suspected LTTE suicide bomber. The party backed President Kumaratunga's reelection two months later.

In the December 2001 general election, the DPLF won under 0.2 percent of the vote but one seat in parliament. It failed to hold the seat in 2004. In 2008 it joined with other Tamil parties to form the Tamil Democratic National Alliance in regional balloting. In June 2009 the PLOTE joined discussions with the TNA in developing a common platform on Tamil issues. In the April 2010 parliamentary elections, the DPLF received 0.08 percent of the vote. In 2011 the DPLF requested that the government implement programs to reintegrate former youth fighters into civil society. In 2012, the DPLF rejected a TNA coalition offer. Reports in 2013 indicated that PLOTE would join the TNA.

Leaders: Dharmalingam SIDDHARTHAN (President), S. SATHANANTHAN (DPLF).

LEGISLATURE

Under the 1978 constitution the National State Assembly was redesignated as the **Parliament.** In December 1982 the life of the existing parliament was extended by referendum for an additional six years to August 1989 (although dissolution was decreed on December 20, 1988). The current 225-member body serves a six-year term, subject to dissolution.

In the early election of April 8, 2010, 196 members were chosen by proportional representation at the district level, while 29 members were elected on the basis of nationwide vote totals. Following the balloting, the United People's Freedom Alliance held 144 seats (127 district, 17 national); the United National Front, 60 (51, 9); the Tamil National Alliance, 14 (13, 1); Democratic National Alliance, 7 (5, 2).

Speaker: Chamal RAJAPAKSE.

CABINET

[as of July 20, 2013]

Prime Minister	Disanayaka Mudiyanselage Jayaratne
Senior Ministers	
Consumer Welfare	Seneviratne Bandara Navinne
Food and Nutrition	P. Dayaratne
Good Governance and Infrastructure	Ratnasiri Wickeremanayake
Human Resources	Don Edwin Weerasinghe Gunasekera
International Monetary Cooperation	Sarath Amunugama
National Resources	Piyasena Gamage
Rural Affairs	Athauda Seneviratne
Scientific Affairs	Tissa Vitarana
Social Welfare	Milroy Fernando
Urban Affairs	A. H. M Fowzie
Ministers	
Agriculture	Mahinda Yapa Abeywardena
Child Development and Women's Empowerment	Tissa Karaliyadde
Civil Aviation	Prijankara Jayaratna
Coconut Development and State Plantations	Jagath Pushpakumara
Cooperatives and Internal Trade	Johnston Fernando
Construction and Engineering	Wimal Weerawansa
Culture and Aesthetics	T. B. Ekanayake
Defense, Public Security, and Law and Order	Mahinda Rajapakse
Disaster Management	Mahinda Amaraweera
Economic Development	Basil Rajapaksa
Education	Bandula Gunawardena
Educational Services	Duaminda Dissanayake
Environment and Natural Resources	Susil Premajayantha
Finance and Planning	Mahinda Rajapakse
Fisheries and Aquatic Resources	Rajitha Senaratne
Foreign Affairs	Gamini Lakshman Peiris
Foreign Employment Promotion and Welfare	Dilan Perera
Health	Maithripala Sirisena
Higher Education	Sumanaweera Banda Dissanayake
Highways and Road Development	Mahinda Rajapakse
Indigenous Medicine	Salinda Dissanayake
Industry and Commerce	Rishad Bathiyutheen
Investment Promotion	Lakshman Yapa Abeywardena
Irrigation and Water Management	Nimal Siripala de Silva
Justice and Law Reforms	Rauf Hakeem
Labor Relations and Manpower	Gamini Lokuge
Land and Land Development	Janaka Bandara Tennekoon
Livestock and Rural Community Development	Arumugam Thondaman
Local Government and Provincial Councils	Ahamed Lebbe Marikkan Athaullah
Mass Media and Information	Keheliya Rambukwella
National Heritage and Cultural Affairs	Jagath Balasuriya
National Languages and Social Integration	Vasudeva Nanayakkara
Parliamentary Affairs	Sumedha Jayasena [f]
Petroleum and Petroleum Resource Development	Anura Priyadarshana Yapa
Plantation Industries	Mahinda Samarasinghe
Ports and Aviation	Mahinda Rajapaksa
Posts and Telecommunication	Jeewan Kumaranatunga
Power and Energy	Pavithra Wanniararchichi [f]
Private Transport Services	C. B. Rathnayake
Productivity	Basir Segudaud
Public Administration and Home Affairs	John Seneviratne
Public Coordination and Public Affairs	Mervin Silva
Public Management Reforms	Navin Dissanayake
Public Recreation and Botanical Gardens	Jayaratna Herath
Rehabilitation and Prison Reforms	Chandrasiri Gajadeera
Religious Affairs	Disanayaka Mudiyanselage Jayaratne
Resettlement and Disaster Relief Services	Gunaratne Weerakoon
Small Export Crops	Reginold Cooray
Social Services and Social Welfare	Felix Perera

Sports and Public Recreation	Mahindananda Aluthgamage
State Resources and Enterprise Development	Dayasritha Tissera
Sugar Industry Development	Lakshman Senevirathne
Technology and Research	Patali Champika Ranawaka
Telecommunications and Information Technology	Ranjith Siyambalapitiya
Traditional Industries and Small Enterprise Development	Douglas Devananda
Transport	Kumara Welgama
Water Supply and Drainage	Dinesh Gunawardena
Wildlife Resources Conservation	Gamini Vijith Wilayamuni
Youth Affairs	Dullas Alahaperuma

[f] = female

Note: All ministers are affiliated with the UPFA.

INTERGOVERNMENTAL REPRESENTATION

Ambassador to the U.S.: Jaliya WICKRAMASURIYA.

U.S. Ambassador to Sri Lanka: Michele J. SISON.

Permanent Representative to the UN: Palitha T. B. KOHONA.

IGO Memberships (Non-UN): ADB, CWTH, IOM, NAM, SAARC, WTO.

SUDAN

Republic of the Sudan
Jumhuriyat al-Sudan

Political Status: Independent republic established in 1956; revolutionary military regime instituted in 1969; one-party system established in 1971; constitution of May 8, 1973, suspended following military coup of April 6, 1985; military regime reinstituted on June 30, 1989; ruling military council dissolved and nominal civilian government reinstated on October 16, 1993; nonparty presidential and legislative elections held on March 6–17, 1996; new constitution providing for limited multiparty system ratified on June 30, 1998; peace agreement signed between the government of Sudan and the Sudanese People's Liberation Movement on January 9, 2005, effectively ending a civil war between the north and the south; six-year power-sharing period initiated on July 9, 2005, with the signing of an interim constitution; peace agreement signed on October 14, 2006, between the government of Sudan and the Eastern Front, effectively ending the rebellion by eastern rebel groups; succession of South Sudan, following referendum, on July 9, 2011.

Area: 718,722 sq. mi. (1,861,484 sq. km).

Population: 37,956,724 (2013E—UN); 34,847,910 (2013E—U.S. Census).

Major Urban Centers (2008C): KHARTOUM (639,598), Omdurman (2,395,159), Wad Medani (423,863), El Obeid (380,552), Kassala (298,529), Port Sudan (283,953), Gedaref (269,395).

Official Language: Arabic.

Monetary Unit: Sudanese Pound (market rate November 1, 2013: 4.40 pounds = $1US). The Sudanese pound was introduced in 2007 to replace the dinar, the official currency since 1992, at a rate of 1 pound = 100 dinars.

President and Prime Minister: Umar Hassan Ahmad al-BASHIR (National Congress); installed as chair of the Revolutionary Command Council for National Salvation (RCC) following overthrow of the government of Prime Minister Sadiq al-MAHDI (Umma Party) on June 30, 1989, succeeding the former chair of the Supreme Council, Ahmad al-MIRGHANI (Democratic Unionist Party); assumed title of prime minister upon formation of government of July 9, 1989; named president by the RCC on October 16, 1993; elected to a five-year term as president in nonparty multicandidate balloting on March 6–17, 1996, and inaugurated on April 1; formed new government on April 21, 1996; reelected on December 13–20, 2000, and inaugurated for a second five-year presidential term on February 13, 2001; formed new government on February 23, 2001; reelected April 11–15, 2010, and inaugurated for a third five-year term on May 27; formed new government on June 15.

First Vice President: Ali Uthman Muhammad TAHA (National Congress); appointed on February 17, 1998, to succeed Maj. Gen. al-Zubayr Muhammad SALIH, who died in a plane crash on February 12, 1998; reappointed on May 28, 2010, following presidential elections during April 11–15.

Second Vice President: Al-Hadj Adam YOUSSEF (National Congress); appointed on September 13, 2011, to replace Salva KIIR Mayardit (Sudan People's Liberation Movement), who resigned on July 9.

THE COUNTRY

One of the largest countries in Africa, Sudan shares its borders with seven neighboring states as well as the Red Sea and forms part of the transitional zone between the continent's largely desert north and its densely forested, subtropical south. The White Nile flows north for almost 2,500 miles, from the Ugandan border, past the river's union with the Blue Nile near Khartoum, to Egypt above Aswan. Approximately 90 percent of the population is Arab and/or Muslim. The geographic, ethnic, and religious cleavages have yielded political discord marked by prolonged periods of southern rebellion.

Women continue to be underrepresented in the economic and political spheres. However, women are allocated a minimum of 88 seats in the assembly through a separate electoral list. Following the 2011 reduction of seats after the independence of South Sudan (see Legislature, below), women held 87 of 354 seats in the assembly (24.6 percent) and 5 of 28 seats in the council (17.9 percent).

The economy is predominantly agricultural, although only a small part of the arable land is cultivated. Cotton is the most important cash crop, followed by gum arabic, of which Sudan produces four-fifths of the world supply. Other crops include sesame seeds, peanuts, castor beans, sorghum, wheat, and sugarcane. The country has major livestock-producing potential, and large numbers of camels and sheep are raised for export. Industry is largely limited to the processing of agricultural products and the manufacture of light consumer goods.

Sudan was plagued in the 1980s and 1990s by persistent drought, starvation, and civil war. By 1999, it was estimated that as many as 1.5 million Sudanese had died in the previous 16 years as the result of famine and war, while more than 2 million were in danger of starving as a result of drought (for more information, please see the 2012 *Handbook*).

Economic distress resulted in more than $15 billion of external debt. Foreign aid decreased sharply in the 1990s due to Khartoum's human rights abuses and its failure to democratize (for information on relations with the International Monetary Fund [IMF] in the 1990s, see the 2013 *Handbook*).

The fighting in Darfur compounded the instability, starting in early 2003, with an estimated 113,000 villagers fleeing to Chad by January 2004 and a death toll leading U.S. officials to declare the killing a genocide (see Current issues, below). By 2005 the economic outlook for Sudan had become more positive, owing primarily to higher revenues from oil and other sectors. In 2007 Sudan repaid $50.6 million to the IMF and made payments of $50 million annually thereafter.

On January 8, 2007, as part of the Comprehensive Peace Agreement (CPA) mandate, the Central Bank of Sudan (CBS) introduced its new currency, the Sudanese pound, valued at US$2 = S£1. The pound replaced the dinar, which was seen, especially in the south, as a symbol of Islamization and Arabization. In 2010, GDP growth was 5.1 percent as international fuel prices declined. Rising food costs kept inflation high at 12.9 percent. The economy continued to be hampered by ongoing conflict, with 14.9 percent of the population unemployed and 40 percent below the poverty line in 2010. In its 2013 Human Development Index, the UN ranked Sudan 171st out of 186 countries. After the independence of South Sudan, the new country secured control over approximately 75 percent of the nation's oil production but agreed to pay fees to Sudan for the transshipment of oil through pipelines to the Red Sea. In 2011, the country plunged into recession. GDP declined 1.9 percent that year and fell by 4.4 percent the next as South Sudan stopped oil transshipments (see Foreign relations, below). Inflation rose by 18.1 percent in 2011 (see Current issues, below), and then doubled to 35.6 percent in 2012. Unemployment was 12 percent in 2011 and 10.8 percent in 2012. In February 2012, the government announced that new oil discoveries would allow Sudan to increase production from 115,000 barrels per day to 180,000.

GOVERNMENT AND POLITICS

Political background. Historically known as the land of Kush, Sudan was conquered and unified by Egypt in 1820–1821. Under the leadership of Muhammad Ahmad, the MAHDI ("awaited religious leader"), opposition to Egyptian administration broke into open revolt in 1881; the insurrection had succeeded by 1885, and the Mahdist state controlled the region until its reconquest by an Anglo-Egyptian force in 1896–1898. Thereafter, Sudan was governed by an Anglo-Egyptian condominium, becoming self-governing in 1954 and fully independent on January 1, 1956, under a transitional constitution that provided for a democratic parliamentary regime. A civilian government, led successively by Ismail al-AZHARI and Abdallah KHALIL, was overthrown in November 1958 by Lt. Gen. Ibrahim ABBUD, whose military regime was itself dislodged following protest demonstrations in October and November 1964. The restored constitutional regime, headed in turn by Sir al-Khatim KHALIFA, Muhammad Ahmad MAHGUB, and Dr. Sadiq al-MAHDI (a descendant of the 19th century religious leader), was weakened both by political party instability and by revolt in the southern provinces.

Beginning in 1955 as a protest against Arab-Muslim domination, the southern insurgency rapidly assumed the proportions of a civil war. Led by the *Anyanya* (scorpion) movement under the command of Joseph LAGU, the revolt prompted military reprisals and the flight of thousands of refugees to neighboring countries. While moderate southern parties continued to seek regional autonomy within the framework of a united Sudan, exile groups worked for complete independence, and a so-called Provisional Government of Southern Sudan was established in January 1967 under the leadership of Agrev JADEN, a prominent exile leader.

The stability of the new Mahgub government was interrupted in May 1969 by a military coup organized by a group of nationalist, left-wing officers led by Col. Jafar Muhammad NUMAYRI. In response to Numayri's ten-man Revolutionary Council, a former chief justice, Abu-Bakr AWADALLA, formed a civilian administration of communists and extreme leftists. Revolutionary activity continued, however, including successive communist attempts in 1969 and 1971 to overthrow the Numayri regime. The latter effort succeeded for three days, after which Numayri regained power with Egyptian and Libyan help and instituted reprisals that included the execution of Abd al-Khaliq MAHGUB, the Communist Party's secretary general.

Subsequent to a temporary constitution in August 1971, Numayri was elected to the presidency in September. A month later, in an effort to consolidate his position, Numayri dissolved the Revolutionary Council and established the Sudanese Socialist Union (SSU) as the only recognized political party. Of equal significance was the ratification in April 1973 of a negotiated settlement that temporarily brought the southern rebellion to an end. The terms of the agreement, which provided for an autonomous Southern Sudan, were included in a new national constitution that became effective May 8, 1973. In November, the Southern Region voted for a Regional People's Assembly, while the first national election under the new basic law took place in May 1974 for a 250-member National People's Assembly.

In September 1975, rebel army personnel led by a paratroop officer, Lt. Col. Hassan Husayn USMAN, seized the government radio station in Omdurman in an attempted coup. President Numayri subsequently blamed Libya for instigating the uprising, which was quickly suppressed. The attack had been preceded by an army mutiny in Akobo on the Ethiopian border in March and was followed by an uprising in Khartoum in July 1976 that reportedly claimed 300 lives. At a news conference in London on August 4, former prime minister Mahdi, on behalf of the outlawed Sudanese National Front (SNF), a coalition of former centrist and rightist parties that had been organized in late 1969, accepted responsibility for having organized the July rebellion but denied that it had involved foreign mercenaries. President Numayri attempted to accommodate the dissidents. In July 1977 a number of SNF leaders, including Dr. Mahdi, returned from abroad and were immediately appointed to the Central Committee of the SSU. A year later the Rev. Philip Abbas GHABUSH, titular president of the SNF, expressed his conviction that the government was committed to the building of "a genuine democracy in Sudan" and ordered the dissolution of both the internal and external wings of the Front.

In early 1980, the north was divided into five new regions to provide for more effective local self-government, and in October 1981 the president dissolved the National Assembly and the Southern Regional Assembly to decentralize legislative power to new regional bodies. He appointed Gen. Gasmallah Abdallah RASSA, a southern Muslim, as interim president of the Southern Region's High Executive Council (HEC) in place of Abel ALIER, who continued as second vice president of the republic. Immediately thereafter a plan was advanced to divide the south into three regions based on the historic provinces of Bahr al-Ghazal, Equatoria, and Upper Nile.

The projected redivision of the south yielded three regional blocs: a "unity" group led by Vice President Alier of the numerically dominant Dinka tribe, who branded the scheme a repudiation of the 1973 agreement; a "divisionist" group led by former rebel commander Joseph Lagu of the Wahdi tribe of eastern Equatoria; and a "compromise" group, led by Clement MBORO and Samuel ARU Bol, which styled itself "Change Two" (C2) after an earlier "Wind for Change Alliance" that had opposed Alier's election to the HEC presidency. None of the three obtained a majority in an April 1982 election to the Southern Regional Assembly, and on June 23 a divisionist, Joseph James TOMBURA, was designated by the assembly as regional president with C2 backing (the alliance being styled "C3"). Six days later President Numayri named General Lagu to succeed Alier as second vice president of the republic. Earlier, on April 11, Maj. Gen. Umar Muhammad al-TAYYIB (who had been designated third vice president in October 1981) was named to the first vice presidency in succession to Lt. Gen. Abd al-Majid Hamid KHALIL, who had been dismissed on January 25.

As expected, President Numayri was nominated for a third term by an SSU congress in February 1983 and reelected by a national plebiscite held April 15–26. In June 1983 the tripartite division of the south was formally implemented, with both the HEC and the southern assembly being abolished.

In the face of renewed rebellion in the south and rapidly deteriorating economic conditions, which prompted food riots and the launching of a general strike in Khartoum, a group of army officers, led by Gen. Abd al-Rahman SIWAR al-DAHAB, seized power on April 6, 1985, while the president was returning from the United States. Numayri's ouster was attributed in part to opposition by southerners and some urban northerners and to the adoption of Islamic religious law (sharia) in September 1983.

On April 9, 1985, after inconclusive discussions between a civilian National Alliance for the Salvation of the Country (NASC), General Siwar al-Dahab formed a 14-member Transitional Military Council (TMC), with himself as chair and Gen. Taq al-Din Abdallah FADUL as his deputy. After further consultation with NASC leaders, Dr. al-Gizouli DAFALLAH, who had played a prominent role in organizing the pre-coup demonstrations, was named head of an interim Council of Ministers on April 22. On May 25 a seven-member southern cabinet that included representatives of the three historic areas (henceforth to be known as "administrative regions") was appointed. Concurrently, the Sudanese People's Liberation Army (SPLA), which had become the primary rebel force in the south under the leadership of Col. John GARANG, resumed antigovernment military activity.

Under Numayri, the size and composition of the unicameral National People's Assembly changed several times; the assembly elected in 1974 was the only one to complete its full constitutional term of four years. All existing legislative bodies were dissolved by the TMC in April 1985. Adhering to its promise to hold a national election within a year, the TMC sponsored legislative balloting April 1–12, 1986, despite continued insurgent activity that precluded polling in 41 southern districts. The new body, serving as both a Constituent and Legislative Assembly, convened on April 26 but disagreed on the composition of a Supreme (Presidential) Council and the designation of a prime minister until May 6, with a coalition government being formed under former prime minister Mahdi of the Umma Party (UP) on May 15. The UP's principal partner was the Democratic Unionist Party (DUP), which had finished second in the assembly balloting. Although several southern parties were awarded cabinet posts, most "African bloc" deputies boycotted assembly activity because of alleged lack of representation and unsatisfactory progress towards repealing sharia.

The Council of Ministers was dissolved on May 13, 1987, primarily because of a split within the DUP that weakened the government's capacity to implement policy. A new government was formed on June 3 with little change in personnel. On August 22, while cooperating with the UP, the DUP formally withdrew from the coalition because of a dispute over an appointment to the Supreme Council. Eight months later the DUP rejected a proposal by Mahdi to form a more broadly based administration that would include the opposition National Islamic Front (NIF). Undaunted, the prime minister resigned on April 16, 1988, to make way for a government of "national reconciliation." Reappointed on April 27, he issued an appeal for all of the parties to join in a proposed national constitutional conference to decide the role of Islam in a future state structure. Mahdi formed a new administration that included the DUP and NIF on May 14. In July 1988 the DUP joined the fundamentalists in calling for a legislative vote on the introduction of sharia prior to the constitutional conference. On September 19, following the government's introduction of a sharia-based penal code, the southern deputies withdrew from the assembly. In mid-November, purportedly with the prime minister's approval, DUP representatives met with SPLA leader Garang in the Ethiopian capital of Addis Ababa to negotiate a peace treaty that entailed abandoning sharia legislation, lifting the state of emergency, and convening of a national constitutional conference. However, rioting subsequently broke out in Khartoum, and on December 20, in the wake of a reported coup attempt and suspension of parliamentary debate on policy toward the south, Prime Minister Mahdi declared another state of emergency. On December 28, the DUP withdrew from the government in response to Mahdi's failure to recognize the agreement with the SPLA, the DUP ministerial posts being refilled by NIF representatives. On February 27, 1989, after another cabinet reshuffle in which the DUP did not participate, Mahdi threatened to resign if the army refused him the latitude to negotiate peace with the rebels. On March 5 some 48 parties and trade unions indicated their general acceptance of the November peace accord, and on March 22 a new governing coalition was announced composed of the UP, the DUP, and representatives of the unions and southern parties, with the NIF in opposition.

In May 1989, complaining that Khartoum had "done absolutely nothing" to advance peace, Colonel Garang announced a cease-fire in the south. A month later he met with northern representatives in Addis Ababa for peace talks mediated by former U.S. president Jimmy Carter. Shortly thereafter, Khartoum agreed to implement the November 1988 accords and schedule a September constitutional conference. The plan was nullified on June 30, when the Madhi regime was overthrown by a military coup led by Brig. Gen. Umar Hassan Ahmad al-BASHIR, who assumed the chair of a Revolution Command Council for National Salvation (RCC) and ultimately rejected the November 1988 treaty. The RCC immediately suspended the constitution, dissolved the Constituent Assembly, imposed emergency rule, and freed military leaders arrested on June 18 for allegedly plotting an earlier coup. Claiming that factionalism and corruption had led to economic malaise and an ineffective war effort, the military regime banned all political parties and arrested senior government and party leaders. On July 9 Bashir assumed the additional office of prime minister, heading a 21-member cabinet composed primarily of career bureaucrats drawn from the NIF and supporters of former president Numayri.

Despite claims that "peace through negotiation" was its first priority, the new government rejected the November 1988 treaty, suggesting instead that the sharia issue be decided by national referendum. However, the SPLA, which sought suspension of sharia while negotiations continued, resumed military activities in October.

A major cabinet reshuffle on April 10, 1990, was viewed as a consolidation of Islamic fundamentalist influence, and on April 24, a total of 31 army and police officers were executed in the wake of an alleged coup attempt the day before. Another reshuffle in January 1991 was followed by the introduction of a nine-state federal system (see Constitution and government, below), and on March 22 a new sharia-based penal code was instituted in the six northern states, prompting a strong protest from the SPLA.

On February 13, 1992, Prime Minister Bashir announced the appointment of a 300-member Transitional National Assembly, which met for the first time on February 24. Included in the assembly were all members of the RCC; a number of RCC advisors; all cabinet ministers and state governors; and representatives of the army, trade unions, and former political parties. The prime minister decreed that the assembly would sit for an indeterminate period, pending the selection of a permanent body as the final step of the new pyramidal legislative structure envisioned by the government.

In the wake of heavy fighting between his supporters and several SPLA breakaway factions in the south, Garang announced a unilateral cease-fire in late March 1993 in the conflict with government troops. Khartoum endorsed the cease-fire several days later, and peace talks with Garang representatives resumed in Abuja in late April. The government also initiated parallel negotiations in Nairobi, Kenya, with the SPLA dissidents, who had recently coalesced as the SPLA-United. However, both sets of talks were subsequently suspended when fighting between government forces and Garang's SPLA faction resumed near the Ugandan border by midyear.

On July 8, 1993, Prime Minister Bashir announced a cabinet reshuffle that was described as an "overt increase in NIF involvement." Subsequently, in a surprise, albeit essentially cosmetic, return to civilian control, the RCC dissolved itself on October 16 after declaring Bashir president and granting him wide authority to direct a transitional government. Bashir announced his administration's commitment to an undefined democratization program that would lead to national elections by the end of 1995. Nevertheless, the new cabinet, announced on October 30, appeared to further solidify NIF control and support the opposition's charges that the military-fundamentalist alliance had no true intention of loosening its stranglehold on political power.

In September 1993, the Inter-Governmental Authority on Drought and Development (IGADD, later the Inter-Governmental Authority on Development—IGAD), composed of representatives from Ethiopia, Eritrea, Kenya, and Uganda was established to mediate the Sudanese conflict. However, the talks ended in deadlock in late 1994 after the two sides had "adopted irreconcilable positions on southern self-determination and the relationship between state and religion."

On March 27, 1995, Bashir announced a unilateral two-month cease-fire to facilitate another peace initiative launched by former U.S. president Jimmy Carter. While the leading southern factions cautiously supported the truce, no progress was reported in resolving the conflict, despite a two-month extension of the cease-fire on May 25.

Widespread rioting broke out in several locations, including Khartoum and Port Sudan, in September 1995, bolstering observations of a weakened northern regime. The outbreaks, which appeared to be spontaneous, involved both student protesters and conservative elements angered by low salaries and food shortages. Further violence erupted in Khartoum in early January 1996 between police and Muslim fundamentalists calling for conversion of the country's Christians and animists to Islam.

In January 1996, the regime announced that elections would be held in March for president and a new 400-member National Assembly.

However, that balloting (conducted March 6–17) was boycotted by nearly all the major opposition groups, most of whom had coalesced under the banner of the National Democratic Alliance (NDA). Because political parties remained banned, candidates campaigned as independents. Most of the 275 elected assembly members were selected during the balloting, although in October President Bashir appointed eight legislators from constituencies in the south, where the civil war made voting impossible. When the assembly convened on April 1, the elected legislators were joined by 125 legislators who had been selected in January by representatives of local and state councils and numerous professional associations. Some 40 independent candidates contested the presidential balloting, and Bashir was elected to a five-year term on the strength of a reported 75.7 percent share of the vote. He was sworn in on April 1, and on the same day the new assembly convened and unanimously elected the NIF's Hassan Abdallah al-TURABI (long considered the dominant political leader in the country) as its president. On April 21, Bashir appointed a new cabinet, which excluded the signatories of a recent peace accord, the SPLA-United and the Southern Sudan Independence Movement (SSIM).

In January 1997, a major rebel offensive was reportedly launched by a more cohesive and potent NDA. In April the regime reached another agreement with the SSIM, the SPLA-United, and four SPLA breakaway groups, calling for suspension of sharia in the south and southern autonomy. With both the government and the SPLA claiming military success, IGAD proposed a "framework of principles" for a resumption of peace talks in July aimed to secure a self-determination plebiscite in the south. However, negotiations were quickly suspended until April 1998 and fighting continued.

Elections were held for ten southern gubernatorial posts in November 1997, and on December 1 the SSIM's Riak MACHAR was named head of a new Southern States' Coordination Council (SSCC) and given a four-year mandate to govern the south pending a decision on its permanent political status. However, the exercise was widely viewed as futile, considering Colonel Garang's depiction of the SSCC as a "sham."

A plane crash on February 12, 1998, killed First Vice President Maj. Gen. al-Zubayr Muhammad SALIH (one of the president's oldest and most trusted associates) and a number of other government officials. On March 8 Bashir finally settled on Ali Uthman Muhammad TAHA, considered second in authority in the NIF, to succeed Salih. In addition, the NIF had an enhanced presence in the extensively reshuffled cabinet, which also included dissident Umma members and representatives of southern rebels who had aligned with Khartoum.

In the face of heavy international pressure for political reform, the assembly, on March 28, 1998, approved the government's proposed new constitution, which authorized the legalization of political associations. The new basic law was endorsed by a reported 96.7 percent "yes" vote in a national referendum in late May and signed into law by President Bashir on June 30, 1998. On November 23 the assembly approved the Political Association Act, which established legal governance of party activity and registration of parties from January 1999.

As conflict rapidly escalated between Bashir and Turabi, Turabi proposed a series of constitutional amendments in November 1999 to curb Bashir's power. Bashir responded by announcing a three-month state of emergency and dissolving the National Assembly on December 12, 1999 (effective December 13). Bashir's declaration occurred a mere 48 hours prior to the scheduled National Assembly vote regarding Turabi's proposed amendments. The cabinet responded by formally issuing its resignation on January 1, 2000. Bashir appointed a new cabinet on January 25, retaining his backers in some ministry posts. The power struggle continued, however, because Turabi, while holding no official position, remained secretary general of the National Congress (NC), the successor to the NIF. Meanwhile, the government also was buffeted in February by the departure of Machar and his supporters due to the perceived failure of Bashir to implement the 1997 accord.

On March 12, 2000, the cabinet extended the state of emergency until the end of the year. Bashir consolidated power by removing Turabi as secretary general of the NC and replacing him with Ibrahim Ahmed OMAR. As part of an overall effort to enhance his regime's image, President Bashir announced an amnesty for his opponents in June 2000.

Despite seemingly positive negotiations between the government and the UP (see UP under Political Parties and Groups, below), the UP led an opposition boycott of assembly and presidential elections on December 13–23, 2000. Consequently, the NC secured 355 of the 360 contested assembly seats, while Bashir was elected to a second five-year term with a reported 86.5 percent of the vote. (After returning from 14 years in exile in May 1999, former president Numayri, as the candidate of the Popular Working Forces Alliance, finished second with 9.6 percent of the vote in the presidential poll.) DUP dissidents were included in the new cabinet named on February 23, 2001, as were UP dissidents in the reshuffle of August 19, 2002. Two DUP dissidents were also among those named to the cabinet in a reshuffle on November 30, 2002.

The political climate deteriorated when the state of emergency was again extended in January 2001, and Turabi and several of his associates were arrested in February after Turabi's Popular National Congress (PNC) had signed an accord with the SPLA to "resist" the government. (Most of the PNC members were released by presidential order in October, but Turabi remained under house arrest until October 2003. He was rearrested on March 31, 2004, along with ten military officers and seven PNC members for what government officials said was a plot to stage a coup. Some reports claimed that those arrested had links to rebels in the western province of Darfur [see below]. Turabi was released on June 30, 2005, when Bashir announced the release of all political detainees.)

Although elections were scheduled to occur in 2004, continued conflict between north and south and an unwillingness to relinquish power by the Bashir regime impeded the electoral process. Following the signing of the peace agreement in January 2005 between the government and the SPLM (see Current issues, below), a new 30-member power-sharing cabinet was announced on September 22, 2005. Fifteen posts went to the NC, 9 to the SPLM, and 6 to northern and southern opposition groups. On October 21, the first cabinet of the Government of South Sudan (GOSS) was appointed. The 22-member southern unity cabinet included 16 seats designated for the SPLM, 3 for the NC, and 3 for other south Sudan opposition groups. The peace agreement between north and south called for elections in 2009 and a referendum on the south in 2011. Meanwhile, the 450-member "national unity" assembly, which Bashir appointed by decree, convened for the first time on August 31, 2005, and members were selected according to a power-sharing quota.

Conflict between the leadership of the SPLM and the NC resulted in a cabinet reshuffle in October 2007, with a number of new appointments (see Political Parties and Groups). In December the two parties reached an agreement that allowed the SPLM members to rejoin the cabinet.

There were minor cabinet reshuffles in February and May 2008. In September a more substantial rearrangement accompanied the dismissal of Pagan AMUM of the SPLM, who had been minister of cabinet affairs, following Amum's highly public criticism of the government and the NC.

On February 17, 2009, the government and JEM signed a preliminary agreement on several areas of cooperation and an eventual cease-fire. The accord was brokered by the UN, AU, Arab League, and Qatar. In March Bashir was indicted by the ICC for his role in Sudan's ethnic conflict (see Current issues, below). Following the expulsion of international aid groups in response to Bashir's indictment (see Foreign relations, below), the JEM suspended further talks with the government.

Ahead of presidential elections in April 2010, the SPLM nominated Yasir ARMAN, the vice president of South Sudan, as its candidate. However, Arman withdrew in March, expressing concerns over the potential for fraud (see Current issues, below). With no other significant opposition, Bashir was reelected with 68.2 percent of the vote in April 11–15 balloting, which international observers cited for fraud and irregularities (see Current issues, below). In concurrent presidential balloting in the south, incumbent president Salva KIIR Mayardit (SPLM) won with 93 percent of the vote. The SPLM and other opposition parties also boycotted national legislative elections in most of the north. Consequently, the NC won a commanding 312 seats in the assembly polling April 11–15. The SPLM secured 99 seats, and no other party gained more than 4 seats. Bashir formed a new government in June that included the NC, SPLM, the UP, and the United Democratic Salvation Front (UDSF).

Under the terms of the comprehensive peace agreement, from January 9 to 15, 2011, a referendum was held on independence for South Sudan. Results showed that 98.8 percent voted in favor of independence. Following the vote, most of the SPLM ministers resigned from the government. On April 11, the assembly revoked the membership of legislators from the south. The removal of the SPLM deputies gave the NC near-total control of the assembly. When South Sudan achieved formal independence on July 9 (see entry on South Sudan), the remaining SPLM cabinet members resigned. On September 13 Bashir appointed Al-Hadj Adam YOUSSEF of the NC as vice president to replace Kiir, who resigned on July 9 to become the president of South Sudan. On December 10, Bashir appointed a government of national unity that included members of the opposition.

The cabinet was reshuffled on July 8, 2012. The minister of religion guidance and endowments was killed in a plane crash on August 19. He was replaced by Fatih Taj-al-Sir ABDALLAH in January 2013.

Constitution and government. The 1973 constitution provided for a strong presidential form of government. Nominated by the Sudanese Socialist Union for a six-year term, the president appointed all other executive officials and served as supreme commander of the People's Armed Forces. Legislative authority was vested in the National People's Assembly, a unicameral body that was partially elected and partially appointed.

The Southern Sudan Regional Constitution, abrogated by the June 1983 redivision, provided for a single autonomous region governed, in nonreserved areas, by the president of a High Executive Council (cabinet) responsible to a Regional People's Assembly. Each of the three subsequent regions in the south, like the five in the north, was administered by a centrally appointed governor, acting on the advice of a local People's Assembly. In a move that intensified southern dissent, President Numayri announced in June 1984 the incorporation into the north of a new province (Wahdah), encompassing territory theretofore part of the Upper Nile region, where oil reserves had been discovered.

Upon assuming power in 1985, the Transitional Military Committee (TMC) suspended the 1973 basic law, dissolved the central and regional assemblies, appointed a cabinet composed largely of civilians, and assigned military personnel to replace regional governors and their ministers. An interim constitution was approved by the TMC in October 1985. Assembly members chosen in April 1986 were mandated to draft a new basic law, although many southern districts were unrepresented because of rebel activity. The assembly's charge to act as a constituent body ceased with the call in April 1988 to convene a national constitutional conference.

In January 1987, the government announced the formation of a new Administrative Council for the South, comprising representatives of six southern political parties and the governors of each of the three previously established regions. The council, although formally empowered with only "transitional" authority, was repudiated by both the "unity" and "divisionist" groups. Subsequently, following the signing of a pro-pluralism "Transitional Charter" on January 10, 1988, to serve as an interim basic law, the council was suspended, and the administration of the southern provinces was assigned to the regional governors.

During negotiations between the Mahdi regime and southern rebels in early June 1989, an agreement was reached to open a constitutional conference in September. However, the Bashir junta rejected the June agreement and suspended the Transitional Charter. Subsequently, a national "political orientation" conference, held April 29–May 2, 1991, in Khartoum, endorsed the establishment of a pyramidal governmental structure involving the direct popular election of local councils followed by the successive indirect election of provincial, state, and national lawmaking bodies. On February 13, 1992, Prime Minister Bashir appointed a 300-member Transitional National Assembly, and he was named president on October 16, 1993, by the RCC, which then dissolved itself. Elections were held on March 6–17, 1996, to a new National Assembly, with concurrent nonparty balloting for president.

On February 5, 1991, the RCC announced the establishment of a new federal system comprising nine states—six (Central, Darfur, Eastern, Khartoum, Kordofan, and Northern) in the north and three (Bahr al-Ghazal, Equatoria, and Upper Nile) in the south. The states, each administered by a federally appointed governor, deputy governor, and cabinet of ministers, were given responsibility for local administration and some tax collection, although control over most major sectors remained with the central government. In early February 1994 President Bashir announced that the number of states had been increased from 9 to 26, new governors being appointed later in the month. A Southern States Coordination Council was named in December 1997 to govern the south pending final determination of the region's status, but authority of the new body remained severely compromised by the opposition of the main rebel group, the SPLA. In 2006 the state of West Kurdufan was merged with two others, reducing the number of states to 25. The 10 states of South Sudan became independent on July 9, 2011 (see Current issues, below), leaving the 15 northern states to constitute Sudan.

On March 22, 1991, a new penal code based on sharia went into effect in the north, the government announcing that the issue would be "open" in regard to the south, pending the outcome of peace negotiations. The new constitution, which went into effect on June 30, 1998, annulled most previous decrees by the Bashir regime, thereby permitting the reintroduction of a multiparty system. The new basic law described Islam as "the religion of the majority," while noting the "considerable number of Christians and animists" in the country and guaranteeing freedom of religion. The controversial issue of sharia, particularly as it might apply to the south, was skirted, the constitution stating only that the "religion, customs, and consensus of the Nation shall be the sources of legislation."

Following the peace agreement reached on January 9, 2005, between the government and the SPLM, an interim constitution was signed on July 9, 2005, allowing for power sharing during a six-year transitional period. Whether the south would continue under Khartoum's rule was to be determined by a referendum in 2011. The south was given a large degree of autonomy, with Garang being named president of the south, as well as first vice president of Sudan. (Salva KIIR Mayardit replaced Garang as president of the south and first vice president of Sudan on August 11, 2005, following the latter's death on July 30.)

In July 2007 the UN Security Council passed a resolution that included provisions for a joint AU-UN peacekeeping mission. Despite Khartoum's formal acceptance of the resolution, controversy over the size, troop competence, source countries, and command structure of the force delayed full deployment into 2008, while conflict continued unabated. However, in a gesture of cooperation, the government rescinded the old, "Islamist" currency, the dinar, in favor of the new Sudanese pound (see Current issues, below). The UN-AU mandate of operations in Sudan was scheduled to expire in June 2008, but the ongoing conflict resulted in extensions of operations through 2011.

In July 2009, the Permanent Court of Arbitration in the Netherlands granted control over most of the disputed oil-rich region of Abyei to the national government in Khartoum. The ruling was a defeat for the SPLM, which argued that the area should be part of the region included in the South's 2011 independence referendum.

On August 12, 2003, President Bashir issued a decree ending press censorship. Despite an increase in daily papers and online press, state media maintained control and censorship was evident. In 2008 it was reported that the government had quietly reinstituted media censorship. In its 2013 report on press freedom, Reporters Without Borders ranked Sudan a dismal 170th out of 179 countries.

Foreign relations. During much of the Cold War Sudan pursued a policy of nonalignment, modified in practice by changing international circumstances, while focusing its attention on regional matters. Prior to the 1974 coup in Ethiopia, relations with that country were especially cordial due to the prominent role Ethiopian Emperor Haile Selassie had played in bringing about a settlement in the initial southern rebellion. However, Addis Ababa later accused Khartoum of providing covert support to Eritrean rebels, while Sudanese leaders charged that SPLA camps were flourishing in Ethiopia with the approval of the Mengistu regime. Not surprisingly, relations between the two countries improved dramatically following the May 1991 rebel victory in Ethiopia; the presumed SPLA contingents were forced back into Sudan by Ethiopian troops and the Bashir regime became a vocal supporter of the new leadership in Addis Ababa. By contrast, the secular administration in Eritrea charged in early 1994 that Sudan was fomenting fundamentalist anti-government activity in the new nation of Eritrea, and in December it severed relations with Khartoum. After a period of improved relations, recent tension arose over border demarcation disputes between Sudan, Ethiopia, and Eritrea, where Sudanese troops are occupying Ethiopian lands to the north. Relations have since improved, as the Eritrean government played a significant role in mediating a peace agreement between Khartoum and eastern rebel groups (see Current issues, below).

Soon after taking power in 1969, Prime Minister Numayri forged close ties with Egyptian president Gamal Abdel Nasser within a federation scheme encompassing Sudan, Egypt, and the newly established Libyan regime of Colonel Muammar Qadhafi. Although failing to promote integration, the federation yielded joint Egyptian-Libyan military support for Numayri in defeating the communist insurgency of June 1971. However, Numayri was reluctant to join a second unity scheme—the abortive 1972 Federation of Arab Republics—because of Libyan-inspired conspiracies and opposition from the non-Arab peoples of southern Sudan. President Sadat's own estrangement from Qadhafi during 1973 led to the signing of a Sudanese-Egyptian agreement on political and economic coordination in February 1974. In subsequent years Sadat pledged to support Numayri against continued Libyan attempts at subversion, and Sudan followed Egypt into close alignment with the United States. While rejecting the Egyptian-Israeli peace treaty of 1979, Sudan was one of the few Arab states that did not break diplomatically with Cairo. Egypt's main strategic interest in Sudan focuses on water supplied from the Nile River via Sudan, which is currently governed by a 1959 treaty granting Egypt generous access to the Nile. Cairo supports the Comprehensive Peace Agreement CPA (see Current issues, below) but remains ambivalent towards the prospect of southern autonomy, which would require renegotiation of the water treaty.

In October 1988, Prime Minister Mahdi, reportedly desperate for arms, signed a unity proposal with Colonel Qadhafi that was denounced by the DUP and in January 1989 labeled "inappropriate" by the United States following reports that Libyan forces had used chemical weapons in attacks on SPLA forces. Concurrently, Washington, whose nonintervention policy had drawn criticism from international aid groups, announced its intention to supply aid directly to drought victims in areas under SPLA control rather than through allegedly corrupt government channels. Four months later Washington cut off all nonfamine relief support because of Khartoum's failure to service its foreign debt, lack of democratic commitment, and human rights record. Later in the year relations with the United States deteriorated even further when Sudan refused to join the UN coalition against Iraq, a decision that also cost Sudan financial support from Saudi Arabia and Egypt. In addition, many Arab states subsequently expressed concern over the growing influence of Islamic fundamentalism under the Bashir regime. However, Iran, anxious to support the fundamentalist cause, funded Sudanese economic and, according to some reports, military aid.

In August 1994, authorities in Khartoum seized terrorist Ilich Ramírez Sanchez (a.k.a. "Carlos"), who was flown to Paris for trial on charges stemming from a 1983 attack in the French capital. In return, France was reported to have persuaded the Central African Republic (CAR) to provide Sudanese military transit through CAR territory. In addition, Khartoum sought French assistance in restoring its relations with the United States following unexpectedly low aid grants from Iran.

Meanwhile, relations with other neighboring states deteriorated sharply. In September 1994 Egypt was accused of moving troops into Sudan's northern Halaib region, and relations deteriorated further in mid-1995 after President Mubarak had intimated that the NIF might have been involved in the failed attempt on his life in Addis Ababa on June 26. In the south, Uganda canceled a 1990 agreement providing for a military monitoring team on its side of their border, and in April 1995 it broke relations because of the alleged bombing of a Ugandan village by Sudanese government forces; however, relations were restored in mid-June as the result of talks between presidents Bashir and Museveni that were brokered by Malawian president Bakili Muluzi.

By late 1995, Sudan had come under widespread criticism for its alleged sponsorship of international terrorism, including possible involvement in the Mubarak assassination attempt. On December 19, foreign ministers of states belonging to the Organization of African Unity (OAU, subsequently the African Union—AU), met in Addis Ababa and called on Khartoum to extradite three Egyptians wanted for questioning in the Mubarak affair. On January 31, 1996, the UN Security Council instituted sanctions and adopted a unanimous resolution to the same effect. Earlier, as an expression of its displeasure, Ethiopia had ordered a reduction in Sudan's embassy staff to four, the closure of a Sudanese consulate, and a ban on nongovernmental organizations linked to the Sudanese regime.

In 1997 and early 1998, Eritrea, Ethiopia, and Uganda cooperated to restrict the spread of militant fundamentalism in the Horn of Africa, further straining relations with Sudan, which accused the other governments of supporting the SPLM and NDA. (Relations with Ethiopia subsequently improved, however, in conjunction with the outbreak of hostilities between that nation and Eritrea, which Khartoum charged was still backing Sudanese rebels.) Meanwhile, South African president Nelson MANDELA played a prominent role in efforts to bring the Bashir regime and its opponents together for peace talks under the aegis of IGAD.

In November 1997, Washington accused the Bashir government of supporting international terrorism and human rights abuses and imposed economic sanctions against Sudan. The friction that arose between the United States and Sudan after a meeting between U.S. secretary of state Madeleine Albright, Colonel Garang, and other NDA leaders in Uganda subsequently intensified when U.S. missiles destroyed a pharmaceutical plant in Khartoum on August 20, 1998, in response to bombings of the U.S. embassies in Kenya and Tanzania on August 7. Despite inconclusive evidence, Washington claimed the Sudanese facility had been producing nerve gas for the "terrorist network" of militant Islamic fundamentalist Osama bin Laden. The government in Khartoum, which had expelled bin Laden from the country in 1996 under U.S. pressure, strongly denied the U.S. accusations.

In 1999 and 2000, Sudan reestablished diplomatic relations with the United Kingdom, Kuwait, Ethiopia, Eritrea, Egypt, and Tunisia, and later requested that the UN Security Council lift the 1996 sanctions. The Security Council unanimously approved the request in September 2001.

Throughout 2004 and early 2005, the international response to human rights abuses in Darfur materialized slowly (see Current issues, below). In April 2005 the UN Security Council voted to refer 51 Sudanese—many of them said to be high-ranking NIF officials—for International Criminal Court (ICC) prosecution for crimes against humanity in Darfur. That same month, Western countries pledged $4.5 billion in urgent food aid for southerners displaced by the civil war. In response to food shortages, the Arab Authority for Agriculture and the Abu Dhabi Fund for Development in 2008 worked in conjunction with the Sudanese government to develop a large-scale agricultural program to mitigate food insecurity in Sudan by providing 28,000 hectares of free land for crop production.

In response to continuing attacks on Uganda by the Lords Resistance Army (LRA) from bases in Sudan, the newly installed Government of South Sudan signed a security protocol with Uganda in October 2005 calling for joint efforts to suppress the LRA. Recent reports indicate that despite a December 1999 accord, violence continued to occur as the LRA accused Sudanese troops of attacks by their forces on the Congo border, preventing peace meetings.

Relations with Chad worsened in 2005 as Chadian rebels launched a series of attacks from bases in Sudan. By December 2005 Chadian president Idriss Déby described the two countries as being in a state of "belligerency." In April 2007 Chad severed diplomatic ties with Sudan after a rebel movement springing from Darfur attacked N'Djamena (see entry on Chad). Through 2008 rebel activity by both Chadian rebels and Darfur rebels continued on the Sudan-Darfur frontier. On March 13, 2008, the two governments signed a nonaggression accord in Dakar, Senegal, but the rebels dismissed the accord and continued armed activity.

As an economic and military partner, China has been Sudan's closest ally and has done the most to protect the regime from UN sanctions. China is Sudan's largest trade partner and the largest investor in Sudan's oil industry, with almost 68 percent of Sudan's total export portfolio and 60 percent of Sudan's oil exports accounted for by trade with China since 2004. China has also supplied the Sudanese government with small arms, anti-personnel mines, howitzers, tanks, helicopters, and ammunition, in addition to constructing three arms factories in Sudan, despite a UN-sanctioned arms embargo on the region. The government also ordered new fighter jets from China in late 2005.

In 2006, China placed limited pressure on Khartoum to relieve international criticism before the 2008 Beijing Olympic Games. China voted in favor of the October 2006 resolution for a UN force in Darfur. Nonetheless, China continued its strong bilateral ties with Sudan. The October revelation that a hijacked freighter bound for South Sudan was carrying tanks and other weaponry with Kenyan licenses strained relations between Khartoum and Nairobi.

U.S. president George W. Bush authorized the transfer of vehicles and equipment for UNAMID in January 2009. In March, Sudan expelled 13 international aid agencies in retaliation for the ICC indictment of Bashir (see Current issues, below). The agencies were allowed to return in June. Unidentified aerial forces attacked a Sudanese weapons convoy en route to Egypt. The attack was reportedly conducted by Israeli forces to prevent the arms and munitions from being smuggled into Gaza. Sudan and Chad signed an agreement to normalize relations on May 3, following negotiations brokered by Qatar and Libya. However, the accord failed within weeks, and reports indicated that the JEM was establishing new bases in Chad for operations against the government in Khartoum. Meanwhile, reports throughout the year indicated that the Bashir government was buying an increasing number of arms and munitions from Iran. An international effort to convince firms to divest from Sudan secured a growing number of companies in 2009. In October the United States renewed sanctions against the Bashir regime because of the Sudanese government's actions in Darfur, and it offered new incentives to Sudan for resolving the Darfur conflict. In October, reports indicated that the Ugandan guerilla group, the

Lord's Resistance Army, had established new bases in Darfur (see entry on Uganda).

In February 2010, the presidents of Sudan and Chad held a new round of negotiations in an effort to revive the failed 2009 accord between the two countries. The two presidents agreed to stop supporting rebel groups.

Most foreign leaders and dignitaries boycotted Bashir's inauguration in May 2010. In July the ICC issued a new arrest warrant for Bashir on charges of genocide in Darfur. However, the AU announced its members should not arrest the Sudanese president. In July Bashir attended the Community of Sahel and Saharan States in Chad and then travelled to Kenya in August in defiance of the ICC warrants.

In September 2010, the Lord's Resistance Army conducted two attacks in the CAR from bases in Sudan, killing 16. The group also carried out a series of attacks on Sudanese villages, killing 15 and injuring more than 20.

On June 20, 2011, the governments of Sudan and South Sudan signed an agreement in Addis Ababa, Ethiopia, under the auspices of the AU, to demilitarize the border area around the contested town of Abyei (see Current issues, below). As part of the accord, Ethiopia agreed to deploy a 4,200-member peacekeeping force. The deployment was endorsed by the UN Security Council through Resolution 1990 on June 27.

Sudanese and Chinese officials signed a new agreement in June 2011 to allow Chinese firms to develop oil and gas fields in the country. In August Sudan recognized the new transitional government of Libya. Following continued fighting between Sudanese and South Sudanese forces in December, the UN Security Council adopted a resolution calling for both countries to demilitarize their joint border.

Fighting in Sudan in 2012 created a new wave of refugees with more than 100,000 fleeing to South Sudan and another 30,000 to Ethiopia in what reports described as a new round of ethnic cleansing. In February 2012, the northern branch of the SPLM released 29 Chinese construction workers who had been detained during fighting with government forces.

On September 27, 2012, the leaders of Sudan and South Sudan signed nine bilateral agreements to cover a range of issues remaining from the South's secession. The accords covered citizenship matters, the exchange of prisoners and reparation of refugees, the creation of a demilitarized border and, most significantly, the resumption of oil shipments from the South. Border crossings were reopened in October.

On October 24, 2012, Israeli launched an air attack that destroyed a weapons factory in Khartoum. Israel charged that the facility was operated by Iran to produce weapons for Palestinians in the Gaza Strip.

In February 2013, reports emerged that insurgents from Mali established bases in Darfur, following French-led military operations in Mali. Meanwhile, disputes over implementation of the 2012 agreements continued and led to a series of bilateral meetings between Bashir and Kiir under the auspices of the AU. Troops were finally withdrawn from the border regions in March 2013, and oil shipments from South Sudan resumed in April. However, in June, Khartoum threatened to shut off the pipelines, asserting that Juba was supporting rebel groups in the north. Shipments continued following mediation by the AU and China.

Current issues. Following the al-Qaida attacks in the United States in September 2001, the Sudanese government came under additional international scrutiny. One result was significant progress toward resolution of the southern conflict, which had led to the death of more than 1 million people (as casualties of either the fighting or related food shortages) and the dislocation of an additional 4 million. A tentative cease-fire was negotiated under U.S. mediation in January 2002. Although there was sporadic fighting in the first half of the year, with the NIF reportedly bombing civilians, a historic accord was signed in Kenya on July 20 by representatives of the government and the SPLM. The agreement, mediated by the IGAD, envisioned the establishment of a joint, six-year transitional administration for the south to be followed by a self-determination referendum in the region. The government also reportedly agreed that sharia would not be imposed in the south. The two sides signed a Comprehensive Peace Agreement (CPA) on January 9, 2005, in Nairobi, bringing to an end the 21-year war in the south and, ironically, making former enemies Garang and Bashir partners in a new government.

The agreement called for national elections within four years and a referendum on independence for the south to be held in six years. It also stipulated the sharing of power and a 50–50 split of oil profits between the north and the south. In addition, it called for a six-month "preinterim" period to draft a new constitution; a transitional government in Khartoum under Bashir; a separate administration in the south headed by a first vice president; a national assembly to be appointed within two weeks of the drafting of the interim constitution, with members divided roughly 70–30 north-south, with full legislative authority by 2011; and shared governance by the NC and SPLM of Kordofan and Blue Nile. The SPLM was authorized to keep its army in the south but agreed to withdraw from the east, while the regime agreed to withdraw its troops from the south by July 2007. Despite Bashir's insistence that 85 percent of troops had withdrawn from the region, in late August 2007 observers charged that 10,000 northern troops remained in the south, largely concentrated around the oil installations, and by January 2008 at least 18,000 northern troops still occupied the south. On May 20, 2008, conflict between northern and southern troops prompted a new deadline for northern withdrawal of June 2008. That deadline was also missed and northern troops continue to occupy the oil-rich regions of the south. As of October 2008, the UN planned to deploy more peacekeepers to the region. Critics of the regime argued that this constituted a small part of a general pattern of government backsliding on some terms of the CPA.

Meanwhile, a bloody struggle in the western region of Darfur continued unabated. The war, which erupted in February 2003, had been preceded by years of tribal clashes. Escalation occurred when the Darfur Liberation Front claimed in February 2003 to have seized control of Gulu, and government forces were sent to retake the village in early March. The conflict, fueled by the scarcity of water and grazing land, became an increasingly fierce rivalry between Arab tribesmen who raised cattle and needed the land, and black African farmers who relied on the water. The fighting intensified in 2004, as black Africans accused the government in Khartoum of using the mounted, Arab *Janjaweed* militias, sometimes accompanied by fighters in Sudanese military uniforms, to force people from their land.

While some 113,000 refugees fled across the border into Chad and fighting intensified, U.S. president George W. Bush called on the parties to negotiate. The insurgent groups—the Sudan Liberation Movement/Army (SLM/A) and the Justice and Equality Movement (JEM)—claimed that the government had neglected the impoverished areas for years.

In 2004 human rights workers charged that the government had used the *Janjaweed* to implement a policy resembling ethnic cleansing. Peace talks began in mid-July, as demanded by U.S. secretary of state Colin POWELL, but soon dissolved when Khartoum rejected the rebels' conditions, including a time frame for disarming the militias. On July 29 the UN Security Council threatened to enact punitive measures short of sanctions. In response, 100,000 people reportedly protested against a Security Council resolution in Khartoum, prompting rebel groups and government authorities to agree to meet in Nigeria for peace talks starting on August 23, 2004. However, the talks had broken down completely by August 8. The government refused to agree to stop aerial bombardment in Darfur and to disarm the *Janjaweed* militias, and the rebel groups refused to move into AU-designated confinement sites, arguing they would be too vulnerable to government attack. Powell declared on September 10 that the United States considered the killing, rape, and destruction in Darfur to be genocide and asked for urgent action by the Security Council.

On November 9, 2004, the government agreed to ban military flights over Darfur and signed two deals with the rebels after two weeks of talks in Nigeria. However, no agreement was reached on a long-term resolution to the fighting, and violence resumed within weeks. On March 23, 2005, the Security Council unanimously approved a resolution calling for 10,000 peacekeepers for Darfur and southern Sudan. However, resistance from the Sudanese government to a UN mission led to the continuation of the AU mission in Sudan. In May 2005 NATO agreed to assist the AU-led mission in Darfur with transport and other logistical aid, and Rwanda and Nigeria sent peacekeeping forces into Darfur in July. The AU force eventually numbered some 7,000. By September estimates of those killed in the conflict ranged from 70,000 to 300,000, and 2 to 3 million people were believed to have been displaced.

On another unsettling front, a tense military situation in eastern Sudan in the states of Kassala and the Red Sea Hills began to escalate in 2005 led by a group called the Eastern Front. This group came out of an alliance between the Beja Congress and the Rashaida Free Lions, which had also long complained about the government ignoring them. The conflict was widely resolved in late 2006 with aid from the Eritrean government, which mediated talks that led to the signing of the Eastern Sudan

Peace Agreement (ESPA) on October 14, 2006. The agreement granted the eastern states more representation in the national government and established the Eastern Sudan Reconstruction and Development Fund.

On July 10, 2005, Bashir ended the national state of emergency in all but three of Sudan's provinces: Darfur, Kasala, and Red Sea Hills. Bashir also ordered the release of hundreds of political prisoners, including Turabi. The SLM/A subsequently launched a new offensive in Darfur, and the AU initiated a new round of peace talks between the government and the SLM/A and the JEM in Abuja, Nigeria. The AU developed a comprehensive peace plan, which the Sudanese government accepted on April 30, 2006. On May 5, 2006, the Darfur Peace Agreement was created as a result of the peace talks in Abuja, Nigeria. The document was signed by a faction of the SLM/A as well as the Government of National Unity (GNU), which was the result of the 2005 CPA, but the primary rebel forces, a large faction of the SLM/A and JEM, did not sign the agreement. The plan called for the disarmament of the *Janjaweed* militias, elections within three years, and the provision of $500 million for the establishment and operation of an autonomous regional authority. Meanwhile, Sudan rejected a proposal from UN Secretary General Kofi Annan in April 2006 to replace the AU mission with a more expansive UN-led operation.

Unfortunately, the April 2006 peace agreement heightened tensions in Darfur, as rival rebel groups clashed and the government stepped up military offensives against the SLA/A and JEM. On October 20, 2006, the Sudanese government threw out the UN Special Envoy Jan Pronk, accusing him of undermining Sudan's armed forces and of trying to force the government to accept an August 2006 Security Council Resolution calling for 20,000 UN peacekeeping troops in Darfur. In December 2006 a proposal presented at the AU's Joint Ceasefire Commission in Addis Ababa called for a beefed up AU mission that would include only African troops with support staff of other nationalities. Bashir initially agreed in principle to the plan, but negotiation regarding details, such as the force's size, purpose, and command structure, were all subject to controversy, allowing the Sudanese government to stall the process.

In January 2007, Bill RICHARDSON, governor of the U.S. state of New Mexico, brokered a short-lived 60-day cease-fire agreement between the government and the main rebel groups, including the JEM and the SLA/A. In February 2007 the ICC formally accused two Sudanese of war crimes and crimes against humanity during the Darfur crisis, the first potential prosecutions since the UN Security Council referred cases to the ICC in April 2005. Formal indictments were made by June 2008, when arrest warrants issued on May 2, 2007, were pending against Ali Kushayb and Ahmad Haroun. In the same month, Luis Moreno-Ocampo, chief ICC prosecutor, complained of noncooperation with the ICC by the Sudanese government; ICC investigations found "no trace of Sudanese proceedings in relation to crimes in Darfur during the last three years. The Government itself has clarified that there were none." The ICC presented an application for the arrest of President Bashir for war crimes on July 14, 2008, but over two-thirds of council members were in favor of deferring the decision to arrest Bashir for one year. Nations such as China, Libya, and South Africa, as well as members of the Sudanese government and the AU, fear that Bashir's arrest would damage any progress made during the peace process. The Arab League has recommended that Sudan surrender the two Sudanese already indicted, and create a domestic court for judicial proceedings related to Darfur under the supervision of international bodies.

In 2007, the conflict was exacerbated by floods and resulting epidemics. A Security Council resolution passed in July 2007 authorized special envoys with the maximum authorized strength of approximately 26,000 military troops and police forces. The Sudanese government announced its formal acceptance of the plan, which outlines a joint AU-UN mission, with the majority of troops to come from African countries with logistical support from other UN member countries. Disagreement with the Sudanese government over the makeup of the mission slowed the implementation, with UN claims that many of the African troops that volunteered to take part in the mission did not meet UN peacekeeping standards in terms of training and equipment and needed to be supplemented with troops from other parts of the world. The government of Sudan and some AU leaders resisted this and argued that the African troops were capable of carrying out the UN mandate. Rebel leaders, government representatives, and international ministers and mediators prepared for peace talks in Tripoli, Libya. Talks began on October 27, 2007, and quickly collapsed. As of April 30, 2008, the AU and the UN had deployed 7,393 troops, 128 observers, and 1,716 police. The African Union/United Nations Hybrid Operation in Darfur (UNAMID) forces primarily come from Nigeria, Rwanda, South Africa, and Senegal.

By late 2007, the conflict in Darfur was attracting so much attention that the SPLM withdrew from the National Legislature, arguing that the concerns of south Sudan were being ignored. The SPLM withdrawal, announced by the party's secretary general, Pagan Amum, threatened to reignite the civil war between north and south Sudan. Peace between north and south was threatened by border disputes, which dictate oil revenue allocations between the two regions, and southern complaints that the NC did not adhere to the terms of the CPA. As a result of the SPLM withdrawal, Bashir reorganized the cabinet in December 2007 to appease the opposition.

In September 2008 the *New York Times* reported that an estimated 2.5 million people had been uprooted by the conflict in Darfur and that at least 200,000 had died. In October the government arrested the leader of a progovernment militia in Darfur, Ali Muhammad Ali ABD-AL-RAHMAN (Ali KUSHAYB), whom the ICC had indicted for war crimes. Although the government placed Kushayb in custody, it refused to turn him over to the ICC, and reports were that his arrest was a preventative measure designed to forestall his arrest by peacekeeping forces.

The ICC indicted Bashir on war crimes and crimes against humanity on March 4, 2009, and issued an international warrant for his arrest. The warrant was the first by the ICC for a sitting head of state. The government rejected the warrant and accused the court of "colonialism." In addition, African and Arab states refused calls to arrest Bashir, who openly made trips to Eritrea and Saudi Arabia and attended the Arab League Summit in Qatar. In April the National Election Commission announced that balloting would be held in February 2010 with 75 percent of the posts chosen by national balloting and the remaining 25 percent selected by state legislatures in indirect elections. The following month, fighting left at least 20 government soldiers and 40 JEM rebels dead in Darfur. Renewed fighting in South Sudan in June killed more than 1,000 and created more than 135,000 displaced persons. The strife originated in longstanding disputes among tribes over water rights and cattle-grazing areas. Opposition groups criticized the government census in August, arguing that the population count underestimated the inhabitants of southern Sudan. In December, the assembly approved legislation to enable the 2010 independence referendum on the south.

In January 2010, Bashir resigned from the military, as required by the constitution, to run for the presidency. Preelection violence reportedly killed more than 1,000 between January and April. Concerns over voter registration and potential fraud led opposition parties and international observers to request a delay in presidential and assembly polling scheduled for April. When the government refused to postpone the balloting, the SPLM, the UP, and other major opposition groups withdrew from the presidential elections and boycotted the assembly polling in the north. Nonetheless, the SPLM agreed to abide by the results of the balloting in exchange for assurances that the January independence referendum would take place as planned. In balloting that ran April 11–15, Bashir was reelected president, and the NC secured an overwhelming majority in the assembly. In balloting for president of the GOSS, Kiir was reelected, defeating Lam AKOL of the Sudan People's Liberation Army—Democratic Change (see Political parties, below). Following the balloting a militia commander attacked government posts in South Sudan in May. The fighting left 53 dead. In May Kiir appointed a new cabinet for the GOSS. Fighting in May in Darfur killed more than 600 and created a new wave of displaced persons. In July the JEM signed an accord with UNICEF to prohibit the use of child soldiers and remove underage fighters from areas of conflict.

The long-anticipated referendum on southern independence was conducted during January 9–15, 2011. Voters in the south overwhelmingly endorsed independence, with 98.8 percent of the vote in favor of separation from Sudan. Turnout was 97.6 percent. On February 21 Bashir announced that he would not seek reelection in 2015.

In May 2011, Sudanese forces attacked the disputed town of Abyei, killing more than 800 and creating an estimated 90,000 refugees. The oil-rich area was claimed by both Sudan and South Sudan. Under the CPA the region was supposed to conduct a referendum on independence, and reports indicated that the attack was an effort to ethnically cleanse the area. The AU mediated a settlement to demilitarize the region and deploy Ethiopian peacekeepers in June. Also in May, under the auspices of the UN, the Arab League, and the AU, a peace agreement for Darfur was signed in Doha. The accord called for the creation of a new regional government for the area. In September 2011, a number of political parties were suspended because their leaders had South Sudanese citizenship. In November 2011, the Sudan Revolutionary Front (SRF) was formed to unify the armed Sudanese opposition. The SRF united JEM, the northern branches of the SPLM/A (see Political Parties and Groups, below), and other smaller rebel groups. SRF forces secured a series of victories against Sudanese security forces in South Kordofan and the Blue Nile states in late 2011 and 2012.

In January 2012, South Sudan cut off the flow of oil to the north after charging that the north illicitly diverted more than $815 million in revenues due to Juba. This resulted in a 75 percent loss of revenue for the Bashir government (see entry on South Sudan). By July, the government had to cut popular subsidies on food, consumer goods, and fuel, leading to widespread protests. In addition, the inflation rate rose to more than 30 percent.

On February 8, 2012, the Darfur Regional Authority was created. The new body was tasked to implement the Doha peace accord. Nonetheless, renewed fighting in the region created an estimated 70,000 internal refugees by May 2012. Meanwhile, after Sudanese air attacks on South Sudan, SPLA forces captured the oil town of Heglig in April (they subsequently withdrew under international pressure).

The ICC issued an arrest warrant for Defense Minister Lt. Gen. Abdel-Rahim HUSSEIN, on March 1, 2012, indicting him on 20 charges of crimes against humanity and 21 charges of war crimes for his actions in Darfur in 2003 and 2004.

Sudan approved a smoking ban in interior public places such as schools and hospitals in September 2012. Tribal fighting in South Kordofan killed more than 200 during the winter of 2012–2013. Human rights groups criticized a government offensive in the Nuba mountains in the region, which left hundreds of civilians dead and prompted new allegations of war crimes against the regime.

In January 2013, the government and JEM signed a new peace framework that recommitted the group to the 2011 Doha agreement. Meanwhile, on January 5, the SRF and other opposition groups signed the New Dawn Charter, which pledged collaboration against the Bashir regime. In March, Bashir stated in two published interviews that he would not seek reelection. On April 1, Bashir announced a general amnesty for all political prisoners. Opposition groups were skeptical that the regime would release all detainees. Eleven military officers were convicted in April of plotting a coup in November 2012. Also in April, a donor conference pledged $3.65 billion for the reconstruction of Darfur, following the signing of a comprehensive peace treaty between JEM and the government. In May, the paramount chief of the Abyei region, Koul Deng KUOL, was assassinated while travelling in a UN convoy. Opposition figures accused the Bashir regime of orchestrating the killing.

Major flooding in Sudan in August 2013 killed more than 50 people and left more than 200,000 homeless. The floods also significantly damaged roads and other infrastructure.

POLITICAL PARTIES AND GROUPS

Following the 1969 coup, all political parties, except the Sudanese Communist Party (SCP), were outlawed. After the failure of the SCP coup in July 1971, the party was driven underground and its leaders were arrested. The following October, President Numayri attempted to supplant the existing parties by launching the Sudanese Socialist Union, modeled after the Arab Socialist Union of Egypt, the country's only recognized political group until its suspension by the TMC in April 1985. In 1986 the Union of Sudan African Parties (USAP) was formed with six parties representing the south of Sudan and the Nuba mountain region and won 36 seats in the assembly in 1986. The USAP was a founding member of the **National Democratic Alliance** (NDA), a loose antigovernment coalition. More than 40 parties were reported to have participated in the post-Numayri balloting of April 1986, although only the Umma Party (UP), Democratic Unionist Party (DUP), and National Islamic Front (NIF) obtained substantial legislative representation. The NDA called for a boycott of the March 1996 presidential and general elections. A joint NDA military command was established in October 1996 under the direction of the SPLM's Col. John Garang (for more on the NDA, see the 2012 *Handbook*).

The NDA suffered after the UP withdrew from the Alliance in March 2000 due to a preliminary agreement between Bashir and UP leader Sadiq al-Mahdi (see UP, below, for additional information). Speculations suggest Mahdi's discomfort with the authority of DUP leader and NDA, Chair Usman al-Mirghani, as well as the SPLM's military dominance within the Alliance. In May 2001 the UP declined an invitation to rejoin the NDA, although Mahdi and Mirghani subsequently met to devise a comprehensive peace plan. The UP and DUP tentatively endorsed the proposed accords between Khartoum and the SPLM in 2002, but the NDA was not officially included in negotiations. A January 2005 agreement between the government and the NDA made in Cairo reintegrated the NDA into politics.

In January 2007 the National Assembly passed the controversial Political Parties Bill, which allowed for the suspension or dissolution of any political party that the government deems to be carrying out activities contrary to the terms of the CPA, including preventing parties from participating in elections. The bill also prevents any member of security forces or government from joining any political party with the exception of President Bashir and Vice President Kiir, who are both military commanders, until the end of the CPA's transitional period. Following the announcement that elections would be held in February 2010, the government registered 37 new parties, bringing the number of official parties in Sudan to 72.

Government-Supportive Parties:

National Congress (NC). The NC is a partial successor to the National Islamic Front (*al-Jabhah al-Watani al-Islami*—NIF), which was organized prior to the April 1986 balloting by the leader of the fundamentalist Muslim Brotherhood, Dr. Hassan Abdallah al-Turabi, who as attorney general had been largely responsible for the harsh enforcement of sharia law under the Numayri government. The NIF won 51 legislative seats but refused to enter the government until May 1988 because of the UP commitment to revise the sharia system, which the NIF wanted to strengthen. The NIF gained a number of ministerial seats vacated by the DUP in December 1988, but withdrew from the coalition upon the latter's return in March 1989. Although Turabi was arrested in July 1989, along with the leaders of many other parties, he was released in December and soon became one of the new regime's most influential supporters. As it became more and more identified with fundamentalism, the Bashir government appointed numerous NIF adherents to key government posts, most observers agreeing that the Front had become a de facto government party. NIF/Muslim Brotherhood supporters also were reported to be directing the Islamic "security groups," which had assumed growing authority since 1990.

Turabi, one of the world's leading Islamic fundamentalist theoreticians, was routinely described as the country's most powerful political figure. A follower of Iran's late Ayatollah Khomeini, he called for the creation of Islamic regimes in all Arab nations, a position that concerned several nearby states (particularly Egypt) and major Western capitals. The NIF's "number two," Ali Uthman Muhammad Taha, was named foreign minister in February 1995 and first vice president in early 1998.

It was reported in 1996 that Turabi had directed that the NIF be renamed the National Congress (NC), to reflect a broader umbrella political organization open to all citizens, and to act as a quasi-institutional governing body. Subsequent news reports appeared to use the two names interchangeably, with the NIF rubric predominating. In January 1999 it was announced that a National Congress had been officially registered as a political party, while reports in March indicated similar status had been accorded to a National Islamic Front Party. It was not immediately clear what relationship, if any, the two groupings had to each other or the traditional NIF. Meanwhile, reports (officially denied) surfaced of friction between Turabi and party reformists as well as between Turabi and Sudanese President Bashir, who was named chair of the recently established NIF advisory council. Tensions between Turabi and Bashir resulted in the removal of Turabi as general secretary in May. Turabi subsequently formed a new party, the Popular National Congress (PNC, below), and Bashir's supporters formally used the NC rubric in the December 2000 elections.

The party held a general congress in October 2009 to determine candidates ahead of the 2010 elections. Although the ICC had indicted Bashir for his role in the country's genocide, he was the NC presidential candidate. Bashir was reelected president in April 2010. In addition, the NC won 312 seats in the assembly and dominated a unity government formed by Bashir in June and a new cabinet named in December. After Bashir announced that he would not seek reelection in 2015, reports indicated growing factionalism within the NC as possible successors jockeyed for influence.

Led by NC South Sudan chair Agnes Poni LUKUDU, the party's main leaders in the South defected to the SPLM in July 2012. Reports subsequently indicated that the NC was defunct in South Sudan.

After Bashir underwent surgery in November 2012, reports indicated that the president had been treated for throat cancer. The reports stirred speculation that Bashir might step down before scheduled presidential elections in 2015.

Leaders: Umar Hassan Ahmad al-BASHIR (President of the Republic and Chair of the Party's *Shura* [Council]), Ibrahim Ahmed OMAR (Secretary General), Ali Uthman Muhammad TAHA, Al-Hadj Adam YOUSSEF (Vice Presidents of the Republic).

Islamic Umma Party (*Hizb al-Ummah al-Islamiyah*—IUP). This small party split off from the mainstream Umma Party (see below) in 1985. In applying for recognition in early 1999, the IUP announced it would advocate sharia as the sole source of law while promoting "Mahdist" ideology and a nonaligned foreign policy. The IUP was officially registered in April 1999 and convened its first general congress with delegates from all parts of Sudan the same month. The IUP backed the NC in the 2010 balloting.

Leader: Wali al-Din al-Hadi al-MAHDI.

Umma (People's) Party (*Hizb al-Ummah*—UP). A moderate right-of-center formation, the UP has long been led by former prime minister Mahdi. Founded in 1945, UP receives its strongest support from Ansar Muslims of the White Nile and western Darfur and Kordofan provinces. It obtained a plurality of 100 seats at the 1986 assembly balloting. Members traditionally advocated the repeal of sharia law and were wary of NIF fundamentalism. Despite a historically pro-Libyan, anti-Egyptian posture, the party cultivated good relations with Western countries based, in part, on Mahdi's personal ties to Britain.

Prime Minister Mahdi and Idriss al-Banna were arrested shortly after the military coup in June 1989 (the latter being sentenced to 40 years in jail for corruption; Mahdi was released from prison and placed under house arrest in January 1990), amid rumors that the UP was considering some form of cooperation with the new regime. In light of growing fundamentalist influence within the Bashir government, the UP announced an alliance with the SPLM (see Other Groups, below) dedicated to overthrowing the government; ending the civil war; and reintroducing multiparty, secular democracy. The southern liaison notwithstanding, the UP membership was reported to be deeply divided following Mahdi's release from house arrest in May 1991. With southern groups tending more and more to support independence for their region, the UP in early 1994 was described as "open" on the question. Mahdi was rearrested in June 1994 on charges of plotting against the government and again in May 1995 for a three-month period. He was reportedly invited by the Bashir regime to join the new government formed in April 1996 but declined and eventually fled to Asmara, Eritrea, in December.

The UP was one of the first groups to seek recognition in early 1999, the pro-negotiation faction having apparently gained ascendancy. For his part, Mahdi in November concluded an agreement with Bashir known as the "Call of the Homeland Accord," which proposed a new, pluralistic constitution for Sudan and a four-year transitional period that would conclude with a self-determination referendum for the south. Consequently, in March 2000 Mahdi announced that the UP had withdrawn from the NDA, which he criticized for refusing to negotiate with the government, and directed the Umma militia to honor a cease-fire. Mahdi returned to the Sudan in November after four years of exile in Egypt, but the UP nonetheless boycotted the December legislative and presidential elections, arguing that the balloting should be postponed pending comprehensive "national reconciliation." The UP also declined Bashir's invitation to join the cabinet in February 2001, again on the premise that a "bilateral" agreement was not appropriate while other opposition groups remained in conflict with the government. Subsequent to leaving the NDA in 2000, the Umma Party split into several factions: the Umma Reform and Renewal faction, led by Mubarak al-FADIL al-Mahdi, a cousin of former prime minister al-Mahdi; the Umma General Leadership faction, also known as the Umma National Party, led by Dr. al-Sadiq al-Hadi al-MAHDI, another cousin of al-Mahdi; and the Federal Umma Party, led by Ahmed Babiker NAHAR. The Reform and Renewal splinter faction accepted ministerial posts in August 2002 and in the 2005 unity government. The party officially favors the deployment of a hybrid AU-UN peacekeeping force in Darfur. The party remains active but outside of the unity government. It complains that the CPA served to solidify the NC's hold on power, leaving little room for northern opposition parties to contest Bashir's power. Fadil was arrested in July 2007, together with 27 other opposition leaders, and was charged with plotting to overthrow the government, although he was subsequently released. In 2009 several prominent UP members defected to the newly formed SPLM-DC. In July the UP and the JEM signed an agreement of principles, which was criticized by the government and NC.

The UP National faction initially nominated former prime minister al-Mahdi as its presidential candidate in 2010, but the party withdrew from the presidential and legislative elections to protest alleged electoral irregularities. Nonetheless, al-Mahdi placed fifth in the polling, albeit with less than 1 percent of the vote. The faction also secured one seat in the assembly. Fadil of the Reform and Renewal faction received less than 1 percent of the vote in presidential balloting, and his grouping gained two seats in the assembly, despite participation in the boycott. The Federal faction secured three seats, and its leader, Nahar, was appointed to a cabinet position in the subsequent government.

In August 2011, the UP signed a memorandum of understanding with the government of South Sudan as part of an effort to foster political reconciliation. Both the Umma National faction and the Umma Reform and Renewal grouping received posts in the 2011 unity government.

The Umma National faction endorsed the series of agreements with South Sudan in 2012 and 2013.

Leaders: Dr. Sadiq al-MAHDI (Former Prime Minister and 2010 presidential candidate), Idris al-BANNA, Mubarak Abdullah al-MAHDI, Mubarak al-FADIL al-Mahdi (Umma Reform and Renewal Party Leader and 2010 presidential candidate), Sarrah NAGDALLA, Umar Nur al-DAIM (Secretary General), Ahmed Babiker NAHAR (Federal Umma Party Leader).

Democratic Unionist Party (*al-Hizb al-Ittihadi al-Dimuqrati*—DUP). The right-of-center DUP draws its principal strength from the Khatmiya Muslims of northern and eastern Sudan and is one of the parties that comprised the NDA. Based on its second-place showing at the 1986 poll, the DUP was the UP's junior partner in subsequent government coalitions, although internal divisions prevented the formulation of a clearly defined outlook. The faction led by party chair Usman al-Mirghani included pro-Egyptian traditionalists once linked to the Numayri regime, who were reluctant to repeal sharia until an alternative code was formulated. Younger members, on the other hand, urged that the party abandon its "semi-feudal" orientation and become a secular, centrist formation capable of attracting nationwide support. In early 1986, the DUP reunited with an offshoot group, the Democratic People's Party (DPP), and subsequently appeared to have absorbed the small National Unionist Party (NUP), which had drawn most of its support from the Khartoum business community (for more information on the history of the DUP, see the 2013 *Handbook*).

Despite significant divisions, the DUP was described by *Middle East International* in early 1994 as still officially opposed to independence for the South and "not adverse to some form of Islamic state" for Sudan. The latter issue apparently had contributed to the defection in 1993 of the DUP faction led by former deputy prime minister Sharif Zein al-Abidin al-HINDI, who advocated the separation of church and state despite his position as a religious leader. A possible change in the DUP's stance toward fundamentalism and Southern secession may have been signaled by the party's participation in subsequent NDA summits.

DUP Chair Mirghani described the guidelines adopted in late 1998 for legalization of parties as too restrictive, and his supporters did not submit a request for registration, although a splinter group reportedly sought recognition under the DUP rubric. Ahmad al-Mirghani returned from exile in November 2001, but Usman al-Mirghani, who had been elected chair of the NDA in September 2000, remained outside the country. Meanwhile, a DUP splinter faction, calling itself the DUP–General Secretariat, had accepted cabinet posts in the government in February 2001 and in the 2005 unity government. The mainstream DUP has since refused to take part in the unity government. Deputy Secretary General of the Party Ali Mahmoud Hassanein, was arrested in July 2007 at gunpoint with 27 other opposition politicians and charged with plotting to overthrow the government. The General Secretariat splinter faction, represented by Sharif Zein al-Abidin al-Hindi until his death in 2006, is now led by the former minister of industry, Jalal Yusuf Mohammed DIGAIR. The General Secretariat DUP continued to take part in the GNU government, in contrast to the Mirghani faction. Chair Mirghani's faction requested official representation in the cabinet but was rejected by the SPLM. The DUP suffered from a number of defections in 2008 and 2009. The Mirghani faction began to call itself the DUP—Original in 2010.

The DUP factions declined to join the opposition boycott of the 2010 elections. Hatim al-SIR was the DUP—Original's candidate in the presidential balloting. He received 1.9 percent of the vote, and the DUP—Original secured one seat in the assembly. Another faction, calling itself simply the DUP, secured four seats. The DUP—Original and the DUP refused to participate in the NC-led government of national unity after the balloting. In October, the DUP reportedly attempted to launch a new opposition coalition, the Broad National Front. The DUP and the DUP—Original both received ministries in the 2011 unity government. In 2013, the DUP signed a partnership agreement with the NC.

Leaders: Usman al-MIRGHANI (Symbolic Chair), Dr. Ahmad al-Sayid HAMAD (Former DDP Leader), Ali Ahmed al-SAYYED, Ali Mahmoud HASSANEIN.

The small grouping, the **Muslim Brothers,** led by Sheikh Sadiq Abdallah Abd al-MAJID, secured one seat in the assembly in the 2010 legislative elections.

Regional Interests, Opposition Parties, and Rebel Groups:

Sudanese People's Liberation Movement/Army (SPLM/A). The SPLM and its military wing, the Sudanese People's Liberation Army (SPLA), were formed in 1983 by Col. John Garang, who was an officer in the Sudanese army. Sent by the Numayri administration to negotiate with mutinous soldiers in the southern garrisons, Colonel Garang joined the mutineers, and under his leadership, the SPLA became the dominant southern rebel force. The SPLM and SPLA were supported by Libya prior to Numayri's ouster, when Tripoli endorsed the new regime in Khartoum. The SPLA called a cease-fire immediately following the coup but thereafter initiated military action against the Khartoum government after failing to win concessions on the southern question. Relying on an estimated 20,000–25,000 troops, the SPLA subsequently gained control of most of the nonurban south; sporadic negotiations with various northern representatives yielded several temporary cease-fires but no permanent solution to the conflict.

In 1986 the SPLM downplayed its Marxist-Leninist policies and supported a unified Sudan in which the south would be granted a larger voice in national affairs and a greater share of the nation's economic development programs. However, secessionist groups and SPLM's leaders in 1992 reportedly endorsed a division of Sudan into two autonomous, yet confederated, states, with the south operating under secular law and the north under sharia.

In August 1991, the SPLM was severely splintered when a group of second-tier leaders headquartered in the eastern town of Nasir announced their intention to wrest SPLA control from Garang, whom they accused of perpetrating a "dictatorial reign of terror." Long-standing tribal animosity also contributed to a split in the SPLA, where support for Nasir came primarily from the Nuer ethnic group, which has had a stormy relationship with Garang's Dinka supporters since the creation of the SPLA. Several months of fighting between the two factions left thousands dead, with Garang's supporters charging the dissidents with the "massacre" of Dinka civilians in January 1992. Although a temporary reconciliation between the SPLA factions was achieved at the Abuja peace talks with the government in June, sporadic fighting resumed later in the summer.

In September 1992, William Nyuon BANY conducted negotiations with the splinter group on behalf of Garang but defected to form his own faction, which in April 1993 coalesced with other anti-Garang groups as the SPLA-United (below). In early 1994 negotiations between the SPLA and the SPLA-United yielded a tentative cease-fire agreement, in which Garang reportedly agreed to support southern self-determination. Despite the possible reunification of southern forces, there was ongoing friction between Garang and the SPLA-United's Riak Machar.

In April 1994, some 500 delegates attended the first SPLA-SPLM conference since 1983. The conference was reportedly called to shore up Garang's authority in the face of competition from the SPLA-United. The SPLM leader was put in charge of the joint military command announced by the NDA in October 1996, after the SPLA-United and Machar's SSIM signed a peace accord with the Bashir government.

In late 2004, rumors of a "revolt" against Garang by secessionist SPLA officers who wanted Salva Kiir Mayardit to replace Garang as head of the SPLA surfaced, but Kiir feared a repeat of the 1991 uprising against Garang. On July 30, 2005, Garang died in a helicopter crash, an event that ignited rioting that led to the death of more than 100 people. He was succeeded as SPLM leader by his deputy Kiir. Kiir appointed Machar as vice president of the Government of Southern Sudan in August 2005.

Factions of the Southern Sudan Defense Force (SSDF) signed the Juba Declaration in 2006 in collaboration with the SPLA, but a splinter group of the SSDF still remains loyal to Gordon KONG and rejects the Juba Declaration and the CPA.

Throughout 2009, the SPLM endeavored to unite southern opposition groups under a single grouping in order to contest the 2010 elections. This effort was complicated by the emergence of a new rival party, the **SPLM–Democratic Change** (see the **Sudanese People's Liberation Army—United,** below). The SPLM nominated Yasir Arman as its presidential candidate but boycotted the elections. Arman's name had already been printed on the ballots, and he received 21.7 percent of the vote in spite of the boycott. The SPLM also refused to participate in assembly balloting in the northern provinces but still secured 99 seats in the legislature and joined the subsequent NC-led unity government. Kiir was reelected president of the GOSS, defeating Akom in balloting concurrent with the national elections. Kiir was sworn in on May 21.

The SPLM led the campaign for a "yes" vote in the January 2011 referendum on independence for South Sudan. After the referendum passed with 98.8 percent of the vote, several SPLM members of the government resigned. The remainder left office after formal independence on July 9. Kiir became president of the new country and named an SPLM cabinet.

For information on the SPLM after South Sudan's independence, please see the entry on South Sudan. The northern faction of the SPLM, the **SPLM-North** (SPLM-N) was outlawed by Bashir in October 2011. SPLM-N chair Arman was banned from Sudan.

AU-sponsored peace negotiations brought the SPLM-N and the government together in Addis Ababa beginning in April 2013, although little progress was reported.

Leaders: Yasir ARMAN (2010 presidential candidate and SPLM-N Chair), Abdel Aziz Adam el-HILU (SPLM-N Deputy Chair).

Sudanese People's Liberation Army—United (SPLA-United). The formation of the SPLA-United was announced in early April 1993 in Nairobi, Kenya, by SPLA dissidents who opposed the "one-man rule" of longtime SPLA leader John Garang. Included in the grouping was the Nasir faction (see SPLM, above); William Nyuon Bany's self-styled **Forces of Unity;** the so-called **Kerubino Group,** formed in February by Kerubino Kwanyin BOL; and several other dissidents who had escaped from a Garang prison in the fall of 1992.

Early in 1994, the SPLA-United faced heavy domestic and international pressure to reconcile with the SPLA, as fighting resulted in civilian casualties and exacerbated famine conditions in the south. Simultaneously, the SPLA-United's independence advocates gained widespread support. In 1995 the Nasir faction split from SPLA-United, where Riak Machar formed the Southern Sudan Independence Movement (SSIM). Concurrently, Nyuon Bany was expelled from the SPLA-United after being accused of collaboration with Khartoum, despite reports in 1996 of alliances with the north and Nyuon Bany resuming a pro-Garang posture within the SSIM. In April 1997 the SPLA-United and the SSIM signed an agreement with the government endorsing the preservation of Sudan's "known boundaries," thus relinquishing their drive for independence.

The SPLA-United, under Lam Akol, subsequently gained strength through a merger with the SSDF led by Machar. As a result, Machar was named head of the new Southern States Coordination Council (SSCC; see Political background, above). However, Machar later pulled out of the government, accusing President Bashir of failing to consult with him regarding governmental appointments. Machar subsequently became the USDF leader. Meanwhile, Akol served in Bashir's cabinet until August 2002, when he was dismissed for announcing that he intended to leave the NC and form a new party. By that time, Machar and his supporters had reintegrated into the SPLA and presented a unified front during peace negotiations. SPLA leader Akol was subsequently appointed foreign minister in the 2005 government of national unity. In October 2007 the SPLM, the political wing of the SPLA, withdrew from the National Legislature, demanding that the NC abide by the terms of the CPA and Akol be removed from government due to questionable loyalties, as Akol was developing closer ties with the NC. Bashir removed Akol from his position as foreign minister and appointed SPLM member Deng

Alor Kol in his place. By December 2007, SPLM legislature members were reappointed to their posts. In June 2009 Akol formed a new grouping, the **SPLM–Democratic Change,** to challenge the SPLM in the 2010 balloting. Akol was defeated by Kiir by an overwhelming margin in the April presidential elections. The SPLM–Democratic Change gained two seats in the National Assembly.

For information on the grouping after South Sudan's independence on July 9, 2011, see the entry on South Sudan. Meanwhile, the SPLA-North (SPLA-N) joined the rebel alliance, the Sudanese Revolutionary Front (Front), and continued to fight Sudanese forces in South Kordofan, Blue Nile, and Darfur. For more information on the grouping, see the entry on South Sudan.

Leaders: Lam AKOL (Commander in Chief), Deng ALOR Kol (Spokesperson), Pagan AMUM (Secretary General), Abdel Aziz Adam el-HILU (SPLA-N Commander).

United Democratic Salvation Front (UDSF). The UDSF is an outgrowth of the SSIM and was composed of southern Sudanese political figures and dissidents from the SPLA under the leadership of Riak Machar. The UDSF included representatives of rebel groups who had signed the 1997 peace accord with the government in Khartoum and was seen as a progovernment grouping that advocated a peaceful resolution of the North–South conflict. By 1999, the UDSF was fully operational, and in January 2000, Machar resigned as chair; he rejoined the SPLA in 2002. He was replaced by Elijah HON at a party congress. In September 2001, the party's general secretary, Ibrahim al-TAWIL, led a large group of UDSF members in a defection to the NC. In October 2001, in an effort to unify the party, new leadership elections were conducted, and Eng Joseph MALWAL was chosen chair. In March 2003, the UDSF signed a cooperation agreement with the NC and was subsequently included in successive cabinets, including the 2005 unity government. At a party congress in April 2009, the UDSF elected Gabriel Changson CHANG as its new leader. The UDSF supported Bashir in the 2010 presidential balloting and gained one cabinet post in the subsequent unity government. The USDF retained its cabinet post after the withdrawal of the SPLM cabinet members and the independence of South Sudan in July 2011 but lost the post in the December 2011 cabinet reshuffle. The UDSF subsequently emerged as a predominantly South Sudanese grouping (see entry on South Sudan).

Leaders: Gabriel Changson CHANG (Chair), Maj. Gen. (ret.) Albino AKOL (General Secretary).

Popular (People's) National Congress (*al-Mutamar al-Shabi*—PNC). The PNC is an Islamic fundamentalist organization that was formed by the Turabi faction of the NIF/NC. Turabi had earlier accused President Bashir of betraying the NC's Islamist tenets. Thus, Turabi claimed he was merely adding "Popular" to the original party's name and expelling members who had produced the crisis. Nevertheless, the PNC officially registered as a distinct party in July 2000. Turabi described the PNC as a "comprehensive *shura* organization," which indicated it would be outside the government. The PNC has few policy differences with the NC.

Turabi and several of his PNC supporters were arrested in February 2001 (see Current issues, above). Turabi was released in October 2003 and rearrested on March 31, 2004. The registrar of political parties issued a decree on April 1, 2004, to suspend the PNC's activities, following Turabi's arrest. Turabi was released as part of the general amnesty issued by Bashir in July 2005. Turabi has since refused to take part in the unity government and called for a popular uprising against the ruling party. He was arrested in January 2009 after he called on Bashir to surrender himself to the ICC. Turabi was released in March.

The PNC did not join the opposition boycott of the 2010 presidential and assembly elections. Abdullah Deng NHIAL was the presidential candidate of the PNC. He placed third in the balloting with 3.9 percent of the vote. The PNC secured four seats in the assembly and refused to join the NC-led unity government in June 2010. Meanwhile, Turabi was arrested again in May after his newspaper published an article that was critical of Sudan's foreign policy. Turabi was arrested on January 17, 2011, for criticizing the rising prices of food and commodities. He was released nine days later. In July 2012, the leader of the PNC's central committee, Kamal OMAR, was arrested. In 2012, the offices of the PNC party newspaper were raided and the publication suspended. The PNC was one of the signatories of the 2013 New Dawn opposition agreement.

Leaders: Hassan Abdallah al-TURABI, Ali al-Hajj MUHAMMAD (Secretary General).

Sudanese Communist Party (*al-Hizb al-Shuyui al-Sudani*—SCP). Founded in 1944 and a leading force in the struggle for independence, the SCP was banned under the Abbud regime and supported the 1969 Numayri coup, becoming thereafter the sole legal party until the abortive 1971 uprising, when it was again outlawed. During the 1970s the SCP was persecuted by the Numayri government with a series of quick trials that resulted in several executions of SCP members. The SCP resurfaced in the mid 1980s and campaigned as a recognized party in 1986, calling for opposition to Islamic fundamentalism; repeal of sharia; and the adoption of a secular, democratic constitution. It won three seats in the 1986 elections. The party displayed no interest in joining the government coalition in 1988 but accepted one cabinet portfolio in March 1989. Secretary General Muhammad Ibrahim NUGUD Mansur was arrested following the June 1989 coup, and in September four more party members were detained for alleged involvement in an antigovernment protest. Nugud was released from prison in February 1990 but was placed under house arrest until May 1991, at which time he was freed under what the government described as a blanket amnesty for all remaining political detainees. The SCP, operating primarily from exile, subsequently remained active in the anti-NIF opposition; with some NDA members complaining in late 1992 that the SCP's influence continued at a higher level than was warranted in view of communism's worldwide decline. The party leadership was reportedly critical in late 1998 and early 1999 of the closer ties apparently being established by UP leader Sadiq al-Mahdi with the NIF government. The SCP currently plays only a marginal role in national politics and opposes the secession of South Sudan from the federation. Nugud was the SCP's candidate in the 2010 presidential elections, but he received less than 1 percent of the vote. After the January 2011 referendum on South Sudan independence, the SCP called for an end to violence in the region. Nugud died in London on March 22, 2012, at age 82. The SCP was one of the parties of the New Dawn accord in 2013.

Leader: Muhammad Mukhtar Al-KHATIB.

Sudan Liberation Movement/Army (SLM/A). This group is a successor of sorts to the Darfur Liberation Front, a rebel group organized to combat repressive conditions in Darfur. The SLM/A was the main force for the 2003 Darfur based rebellion against the Sudanese government. The rebels split into two groups in 2004, as the SLM/A vehemently opposed Khalil Ibrahim, a radical opponent of Khartoum (see JEM, below). The SLM/A claimed to represent the region's black African farmers, who were angry over alleged government support for Arab militias. One faction of the SLM/A, known as the *Mani Arkoi* and led by Minni Minawi, was a nongovernment group that signed the AU-backed 2006 Darfur peace accord, but the main SLM/A body, led by party chair Abdallah Wahid Mohamed Ahmad Nur, rejected the agreement. After the signing in 2006, the SLM/A split further, with some factions joining the National Redemption Front and others joining with the JEM to form the Alliance of Revolutionary Force of West Sudan (ARFWS), though the ARFWS unification quickly ended after its formation in 2006. In August 2009 six factions of the SLM agreed to a unity accord ahead of the 2010 elections, although one group, led by Khamis Abdullah ABAKR, refused to reconcile.

In February 2010, new fighting broke out between the SLM/A and government forces. Reports indicated that more than 200 civilians had been killed and more than 10,000 had been displaced. In July an estimated 400 SLM/A fighters agreed to cease fighting as part of a UN initiative to reintegrate rebels into civil society. A new round of fighting broke out in June 2012, although the SLM/A officially endorsed a peaceful regime change. The SLM/A was one of the groups that formed the SRF in 2012. The SLM/A subsequently joined other SRF forces in a series of attacks on government areas.

Leaders: Abdallah Wahid Mohamed Ahmad NUR (Chair), Mustafa TIRAB (General Secretary), Minni MINAWAI (Leader of the *Mani Arkoi* faction).

Justice and Equality Movement (JEM). The JEM was founded in 2002 and commenced operations in 2003 after its split from the SLM in mid-2004. This split further complicated peace negotiations with Khartoum, with each of the groups at odds with the others based on tribal rivalries. It is reportedly supported by Islamists close to Hassan

Abdallah al-Turabi. Many JEM adherents reside in the Sudanese-Chad frontier region and the JEM also reportedly has the support of the Chadian government. In May 2006, the JEM refused to sign the AU-supported Darfur peace plan and helped create the **National Redemption Front** (NRF). The NRF was a short-lived coalition of rebel groups operating in Darfur and included the **Sudan Federal Democratic Alliance** (SFDA; for more on the SFDA, please see the 2012 *Handbook*).

The JEM supported the effort by the ICC to arrest President Bashir for genocide, along with the SPLM. The JEM attacked a Chinese oil-field on October 23, 2007, and kidnapped five Chinese workers with the intent of driving out foreign ownership. On May 10, 2008, the JEM carried out an attack on the Omdurman capital region of Sudan, demonstrating to the people of Darfur that the Sudanese government was potentially vulnerable to rebel reprisals. Meanwhile Bahar Idriss Abu GARDA, who was under indictment by the ICC for crimes against humanity, broke with the JEM and founded a new opposition grouping, the **United Resistance Front.** JEM signed a new cease-fire agreement with the government in February 2010. However, fighting between government forces and JEM groups continued through 2010.

In September 2011, JEM fighters rescued group leader Khalil Ibrahim Mohamed, who had been placed under house arrest in Tripoli by the Libyan government. Mohamed was subsequently killed in an air strike on December 22. Meanwhile, JEM was one of the founding groups of the SRF.

JEM led the effort to create the New Dawn Charter in January 2013. JEM and the government finalized a comprehensive peace accord in April. Meanwhile, in August, JEM prisoners in Khartoum's main jail launched a hunger strike to protest "cruel treatment."

Leader: Ahmed HUSSEIN.

Sudan Alliances Forces (SAF). The SAF is a rebel group operating in eastern Sudan, reportedly from bases in Ethiopia and Eritrea. In late 1996 it was described as a participant in the NDA, although its fighters were not believed to be under the direct command of the SPLA's Colonel Garang. The SAF currently engages in anti-fundamentalist activities from their offices outside of the Sudan, primarily in Poland. More than 40 fighters and 60 civilians were killed in combat between the SAF and SPLA in April and May 2009. In 2011, the SAF launched a new campaign in the Blue Nile state, forcing the evacuation of 1,400 civilians. In 2012, the group was estimated to have 500 fighters.

Leader: Brig. Gen. Abd al-Aziz Khalid OSMAN.

For information on the **Eastern Front** and the **East Democratic Party** (EDP), please see the 2012 *Handbook.*

Other Groups:

Other groups that have applied for, or been granted, recognition prior to the 2010 balloting include the **Alliance for People's Working Forces,** led by Kamal al-Din Muhammad ABDULLAH and former president Numayri; **Party of God** (*Hizb Allah* or *Hezbollah*), led by Sulayman Hasan KHALIL; **Future Party** (*Hizb al-Mustaqbal*), led by Abd al-Mutal Abd al-RAHMAN; **Islamic–Christian Solidarity,** launched under the leadership of Hatim Abdullah al-Zaki HUSAYN on a platform of religious harmony and increased attention to social problems; the **Islamic Path Party,** led by Hasab al-RASUL; the **Islamic Revival Movement,** led by Siddiq al-Haj al-SIDDIQ; the **Islamic Socialist Party,** led by Sabah al-MUSBAN; the **Liberalization Party;** the **Moderate Trend Party,** led by Mahmud JINA; the **National Popular Front,** led by Umar Hasan SHALABI and devoted to pan-Arab and pan-Islamic unity; the **National Salvation Party;** the **New Forces Association,** led by Abd al-Rahman Ismail KIBAYDAH; the **Popular Masses' Alliance,** founded by Faysal Muhammad HUSAYN in support of policies designed to assist the poor; the **Socialist Popular Party,** led by Sayyid Khalifah Idris HABANI; the **Sudanese Central Movement,** led by Muhammad Abu al-Qasim Haji HAMAD; the **Sudan Federal Party,** launched by Ahmed DIRAIGE (a leader of the Fur ethnic group) in support of a federal system; the **Sudan Green Party,** led by Zakaraia Bashir IMAN; the **Sudanese Initiative Party,** led by Jafar KARAR; the **Union of Sudan African Parties** (USAP), led by Joseph UKELLO; the **Sudan Labor Party,** led by James ANDERIA; the **South Sudan Democratic Front** (SSDF), led by Gordon BUAY; the **Covenant Democratic Party,** under Benjamin OCHAN; the **Sudanese National Alliance,** led by Abdel-Aziz KHALID; the **New National Democratic Party,** led by Munir Sheikh el-Din JALLAB; the **Sudanese Socialist Democratic Union,** under Fatima ABDEL-MAHMOOD; and the **United Democratic Front,** led by Peter Abdrhaman SULE. In February 2006 the **National Democratic Party** (NDP) was formed by a merger of several small groupings with leftist or nationalist orientations. On March 10, 2007, the **Socialist Union Party,** under the leadership of Fatimah Abd-al-MAHMOUD, was formed.

For more information on the now-defunct **National Movement for Reform and Development in Darfur**—NMRD, please see the 2008 *Handbook.* For information on the **Sudanese National Party** (*al-Hizb al-Watani al-Sudani*—SNP), see the 2009 *Handbook.* For further details on the **Baath Party**—BP (*Hizb al-Baath al-Sudan*), see the 2011 *Handbook.*

LEGISLATURE

The **National Legislature** currently comprises the Council of States and the National Assembly.

The **Council of States** comprises 50 members, 2 from each state, who are indirectly elected by state legislatures. Members serve five-year terms. The most recent elections to the council were held on May 11, 2010. The number of seats in the council was reduced to 32 following the independence of South Sudan on July 9, 2011.

Speaker: Lt. Gen. Adam Musa HAMID.

The **National Assembly** is composed of 450 members who are elected for five-year terms. In the most recent balloting, held April 11–15, 2010, the National Congress won 312 of seats; Sudan People's Liberation Movement, 99; Democratic Unionist Party, 4; Popular National Congress, 4; Federal Umma Party, 3; the Sudan People's Liberation Movement—Democratic Change, 2; Umma Reform and Renewal Party, 2; Umma National Party, 1; Democratic Unionist Party—Original, 1; Muslim Brothers, 1; independents, 3. (Eighteen seats remained vacant pending new balloting.) Following the independence of South Sudan on July 9, 2011, the number of seats in the assembly was reduced to 354.

President: Ahmed Ibrahim al-TAHIR.

CABINET

[as of August 15, 2013]

President and Prime Minister	Umar Hassan Ahmad al-Bashir (NC)
First Vice President	Ali Uthman Muhammad Taha (NC)
Second Vice President	Al-Hadj Adam Youssef (NC)
Ministers	
Agriculture and Forestry	Abdul Haleem Ismail Al-Mutafee (NC)
Antiquities, Tourism, and Wildlife	Mohamed Abdul Karim Al-Hud
Cabinet Affairs/Council of Ministers	Ahmed Sa'ad Omer Khidir (DUP)
Communications and Science	Essa Basheri
Culture and Information	Ahmed Bilal Osman
Defense	Lt. Gen. Abdel-Rahim Hussein (NC)
Education	Farah Mustafa Abdalla
Environment, Forestry, and Physical Development	Hassan Abdel Gadir Hilal (DUP)
Finance	Ali Mahmood Adbul-Rasool (NC)
Foreign Affairs	Ali Ahmed Karti (NC)
Foreign Trade	Osman Omer Al-Sharef (DUP)
Health	Bahar Idris Abu Garda
Higher Education and Scientific Research	Khames Kajo Kundah (NC)
Human Resources Development and Labor	Ishraqa Sayed Mahmoud (NC) [f]
Industry	Abdul Wahab Mohammed Osman

Interior	Ibrahim Mahmud Hamid (NC)
Justice	Mohamed Bushara Dousa (NC)
Livestock and Fishery	Faysal Hasan Ibrahim (NC)
Minerals	Kamal Abdul-Latif (NC)
Petroleum	Awad Ahmad Al-Jaz (NC)
Presidency	Lt. Gen. Bakri Hassan Salih (NC)
Religious Guidance and Endowments	Fatih Taj-al-Sir Abdallah
Roads and Bridges	Ahmed Babiker Nahar (Umma Reform and Renewal)
Water Resources and Electricity	Osama Abdalla Mohamed al-Hassan (NC)
Welfare and Social Development	Mashair Mohamed al-Amin (NC) [f]
Youth and Sports	Al-Fatih Tajal-Sir Abdalla (DUP—Original)

[f] = female

INTERGOVERNMENTAL REPRESENTATION

Ambassador to the U.S.: (Vacant).

U.S. Ambassador to Sudan: (Vacant).

Permanent Representative to the UN: Daffa-Alla Elhag Ali OSMAN.

IGO Memberships (Non-UN): AfDB, AU, Comesa, IOM, LAS, NAM, OIC.

SURINAME

Republic of Suriname
Republiek Suriname

Political Status: Former Netherlands dependency; granted internal autonomy on December 29, 1954, and complete independence on November 25, 1975; constitution of November 21, 1975, suspended on August 15, 1980, following military coup of February 25; present constitution approved by referendum of September 30, 1987.

Area: 63,036 sq. mi. (163,265 sq. km).

Population: 540,405 (2012E—UN); 566,846 (2013E—U.S. Census).

Major Urban Center (2011E—UN): PARAMARIBO (urban area, 278,000).

Official Language: Linguistically, Suriname is exceptionally diverse. The official language is Dutch, but English, Hindi, Javanese, Chinese, and Sranan Tongo (*Taki-Taki*), a Creole lingua franca, are widely spoken, while Spanish has been adopted as a working language to facilitate communication with Latin American neighbors. In the interior, a number of indigenous languages are also spoken.

Monetary Unit: Surinamese Dollar (market rate November 1, 2013: 3.27 dollars = $1US).

President: Désiré ("Dési") BOUTERSE (Mega Combination); elected by the National Assembly on July 19, 2010, and inaugurated on August 12 for a five-year term, succeeding Ronald (Runaldo) VENETIAAN (Suriname National Party).

Vice President and Chair of the Council of Ministers: Robert AMEERALI (independent); elected by the National Assembly on July 19, 2010, and inaugurated on August 12 for a term concurrent with that of the president, succeeding Ramdien (Ram) SARDJOE (Progressive Reform Party).

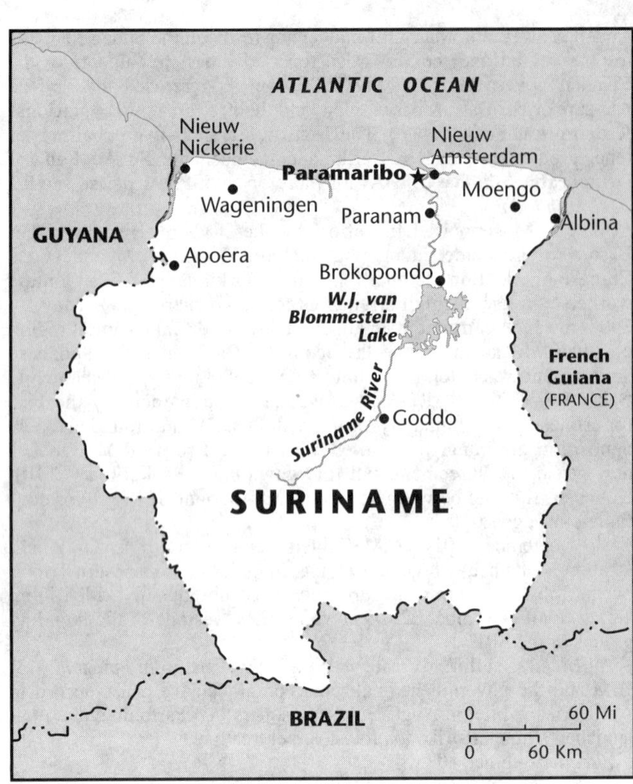

THE COUNTRY

Formerly known as Dutch Guiana, Suriname lies on the north-central coast of South America and is bordered by Guyana on the west, French Guiana on the east, and Brazil on the south. Because of the early importation of slave labor from Africa and contract labor from Asia, its society is one of the most ethnically varied in the world. The largest groups are Hindustanis (39 percent) and Creoles (31 percent), followed by Javanese (15 percent), Chinese (10 percent), black Africans, Amerindians, and various European minorities. Women constitute 41 percent of the workforce, according to the World Bank, and six female representatives serve in the current legislature.

The greater part of the land area is covered with virgin forest, although the coastal region is both flat and fertile. The tropical climate yields a wide range of agricultural products that include rice, various fruits, sugar, and coffee. Suriname ranks among the world's leading producers of alumina and bauxite that, together with aluminum, account for nearly 80 percent of the country's exports; however, the Australian-based BHP-Billiton, reportedly the world's largest bauxite mining company, announced in late 2008 that it would discontinue mining activities in Suriname by 2010 because of exhaustion of deposits at its three principal mines. By contrast, gold is increasingly becoming of economic importance.

Although long enjoying a higher standard of living than many of its neighbors, the country has experienced economic difficulty since 1980, due largely to reduced world demand for bauxite and the suspension of Dutch and U.S. aid in reaction to a wave of official killings in December 1982. Some aid programs resumed in 1988 but were subsequently stopped in 1993 because of unacceptable economic policies according to the International Monetary Fund (IMF).

Bolstered by increased gold production in recent years, Suriname was less affected than other countries by the global economic crisis. Annual GDP growth averaged 4.1 percent in 2009–2011, owing to "buoyant activity" in the mineral sector, according to the IMF. Higher food and fuel prices and substantial civil service pay increases contributed to a rise in inflation from 1.3 percent at the end of 2009 to 10.3 percent at the end of 2010. In January 2011, the authorities devalued the Surinamese dollar by 20 percent; at the same time, fuel taxes increased by 40 percent. Subsequently, inflation rose to 18.6 percent. Nevertheless, the IMF noted a favorable economic outlook for Suriname due to robust commodity prices and increased investment in the mineral and energy sectors and in infrastructure. This favorable outlook continued into 2012 as inflation dropped to 5 percent. Suriname's economy also saw a boost in foreign investment in its natural resource development, namely mining and oil. In 2013, GDP grew by 4.5 percent, and inflation was 4.8 percent.

GOVERNMENT AND POLITICS

Political background. First acquired by the Netherlands from Great Britain in 1667 in exchange for Manhattan Island, the territory now known as Suriname passed among Britain, France, and the Netherlands several times before Dutch authority was formally confirmed by the Congress of Vienna in 1815. It remained a dependency of the Netherlands until enactment of a Statute of the Realm in December 1954 that provided the country with a parliamentary form of government and the right of local constitutional revision, thereby according it full equality with the Netherlands and the Netherlands Antilles.

A substantial portion of Suriname's Hindustani population, which accounted for the bulk of the country's skilled labor force, opposed independence, fearing economic and political repression by the Creole-dominated government of Henck ARRON, who had become prime minister in 1973. More than 40,000 Surinamese, most of them Hindustanis, subsequently emigrated, the majority settling in the Netherlands, creating social and economic problems there, while leaving Suriname with gaps in commerce, medicine, and teaching. Because of the émigré problem, provisions guaranteeing certain Hindustani rights were incorporated into the independence constitution of 1975.

Prime Minister Arron was reconfirmed following a parliamentary election in October 1977 but was ousted in an armed rebellion of 300 noncommissioned officers on February 25, 1980, following government refusal to sanction trade union activity within the armed forces. On March 15 the leaders of the revolt, organized as a National Military Council (NMC), designated the politically moderate Dr. Henk CHIN A Sen as prime minister while permitting the essentially titular president, Dr. Johan H. E. FERRIER, to retain his office. On August 15 the constitution was suspended, with Ferrier dismissed and Chin named as his acting successor while continuing as prime minister. On December 3 Chin was confirmed as president, and the office of prime minister was abolished.

During 1981, differences arose between President Chin, who had called for a return to democratic rule, and Lt. Col. (formerly Sgt. Maj.) Dési BOUTERSE, who had emerged as the strongman of the NMC. As a result, Chin resigned on February 4, 1982, being replaced four days later, on an acting basis, by Lachmipersad F. RAMDAT-MISIER. In the wake of an unsuccessful uprising by right-wing military elements on March 10–11, martial law was declared, while in apparent response to foreign pressure, a new government headed by Henry N. NEYHORST in the reactivated post of prime minister was announced on March 31. Following the reported discovery of a new antigovernment conspiracy on December 8, Neyhorst also resigned, and the NMC ordered the execution of 15 leaders of a political group called the Association for Democratic Action, claiming that they had scheduled a coup for Christmas day. On February 26, 1983, Dr. Errol ALIBUX of the leftist Progressive Workers' and Farm Laborers' Union (PALU) was chosen to head a new cabinet dominated by PALU members. Austerity measures provoked a strike in December by bauxite workers, who were joined by electricity workers in early January 1984. The action forced the revocation of retroactive increases in income taxes, and on January 8 Colonel Bouterse announced the dismissal of the Alibux government. On February 3 an interim administration led by former Arron aide Willem (Wim) UDENHOUT was sworn in, pending "the formation of new democratic institutions." In December, the government announced a 27-month program for a "return to democracy" that included the establishment, on January 1, 1985, of an appointive 31-member National Assembly charged with the drafting of a new constitution.

On August 2, 1985, the Assembly formally designated Colonel Bouterse as "head of government," while reconfirming Ramdat-Misier as acting president. In early September it was announced that the Assembly had appointed a commission, structured on an essentially corporative basis (including representatives of the major unions and the Association of Surinamese Manufacturers), to draft a new basic law. Subsequently, a number of party leaders accepted an invitation from Colonel Bouterse to join the NMC in forming a Supreme Council (*Topberaad*) that would serve as the country's highest political organ. The new body approved the installation of a government headed by Pretaapnarain RADHAKISHUN on July 17, 1986, following the resignation of Prime Minister Udenhout on June 23. Radhakishun was in turn succeeded by Jules Albert WIJDENBOSCH on February 13, 1987.

Despite an earlier announcement that a general election would not be held until March 1988, Colonel Bouterse stated on March 31, 1987, that the balloting would be advanced to independence day, November 25, 1987, preceded by a September 30 referendum on the new constitution. The election yielded a landslide victory for the Front for Democracy and Development (FDO), a coalition of the three leading opposition parties, with Bouterse's recently organized National Democratic Party (NDP) winning only 3 of 51 legislative seats. On January 12, 1988, the new Assembly unanimously elected former agriculture minister Ramsewak SHANKAR to a five-year term as president, with former prime minister Arron designated as vice president and prime minister. Bouterse, however, remained commander in chief of the army and, because of a lack of constitutional specificity in regard to both the membership and functions of a revamped Military Council and a nonelective Council of State, appeared to have lost little capacity for the exercise of decisive political influence.

Of more immediate concern was the continued activity of a rebel Surinamese Liberation Army (SLA), led by former Bouterse aide Ronnie BRUNSWIJK, which had severely disrupted bauxite mining in the eastern region before a government counteroffensive that had driven it back to the border with French Guiana. In June 1988 the government reversed its long-standing position and announced that it would begin talks with the rebels, which did not commence until late October. Following a number of clashes between elements of the "Jungle Commando" and government militia units, the National Assembly approved an amnesty for the rebels on June 1, 1989, and ratified a formal agreement for terminating the conflict on August 8.

The four-year rebellion took a surprising turn on June 18, 1990, when Brunswijk appeared in Cayenne, French Guiana, stating that he had tired of the struggle and wished to seek asylum in the Netherlands. He then departed for Paris, leadership of the rebel group seemingly having been assumed by his deputy, Johan "Castro" WALLY. However, it soon appeared that the action had been a ruse to facilitate what proved to be unproductive talks with Dutch officials, followed by Brunswijk's return to Suriname in July.

Discussions between army and rebel representatives in October and November culminated in a request by Colonel Bouterse that the government withdraw several arrest warrants dating from the period of military rule. Bouterse was angered by the president's failure to offer assistance during a period of detention by Dutch authorities while on a European trip, and on December 22 the colonel resigned as military commander. His successor, Cdr. Iwan GRAANOOGST, mounted a Christmas Eve coup, which yielded Bouterse's reinstatement following the December 30 replacement, on an acting basis, of President Shankar by Johannes Samuel KRAAG and of Vice President and Prime Minister Arron by former prime minister Wijdenbosch.

In legislative balloting on May 25, 1991, what was now termed the New Front for Democracy and Development (NFDD) won 30 of 51 seats, while the army-backed NDP increased its representation from 3 seats to 10. After a lengthy impasse, during which no candidate was able to secure a presidential majority, a special United People's Assembly was convened (see Constitution and government, below) that on September 7 elected NFDD nominee Ronald (Runaldo) R. VENETIAAN as the new head of state; ten days later a cabinet headed by the vice president and prime minister, Jules R. AJODHIA, was announced.

On March 25, 1992, the National Assembly approved a number of constitutional amendments, including abolition of the political role of the army, which would thenceforth be limited to national defense and combating "organized subversion." On May 5, Brunswijk's SLA and another leading guerrilla group, the Amerindian *Tucayana Amazonicas,* agreed to suspend hostilities, and on August 8 signed a revised peace treaty with the government that included revival of the 1989 amnesty. Under the accord, members of the rebel groups would be permitted to join the police force for the interior, while the government was to give the region priority in economic development and social welfare programs.

On November 20, 1992, Colonel Bouterse, buffeted by reports that he had become the country's richest man by corrupt means, again resigned as army commander. However, on October 4, 1993, he returned to the limelight as leader of a mass demonstration in Paramaribo against government-mandated austerity measures and by mid-1995 appeared poised to reenter politics as NDP leader.

In an inconclusive general election on May 23, 1996, a four-party New Front (NF) coalition led by President Venetiaan's Suriname National Party (NPS) won 24 seats, contrasted with the NDP's second-place showing of 16. Thereafter, a series of failed efforts by Venetiaan to forge a majority with smaller parties prompted defections from the NF (see Political Parties, below) that yielded a bloc of 28 legislators supporting the NDP. However, the NDP's augmented strength fell short of the two-thirds needed to elect a president. A new United People's Assembly was therefore convened, which on September 5 named NDP Vice Chair Wijdenbosch to the presidency on a 437–407 vote. While Bouterse's party returned to power, the former dictator was himself barred from office at the insistence of the NDP's allies. Pretaapnarian (Pretaap) RADHAKISHUN, who had first served as cabinet head a decade earlier, became vice president and prime minister.

Through late 1997 and early 1998, a number of party realignments and defections took place, but the government succeeded in securing the support of 26 of the 51 legislators by late March.

On May 28, 1999, President Wijdenbosch dismissed his entire cabinet in the wake of an economic collapse that had triggered widespread popular demonstrations. On June 1 the National Assembly voted to remove the president from office, but he refused to comply on the grounds that such action required a two-thirds majority. Six weeks later, on July 16, a Dutch court sentenced Bouterse in absentia to 11 years' imprisonment and a $2.18 million fine for participating in smuggling drugs into the Netherlands between 1989 and 1997.

Before the election of May 25, 2000, Wijdenbosch left the NDP to form a group called the Democratic National Platform 2000. However, the new formation ran a poor third behind Venetiaan's New Front, which captured 47 percent of the vote, and an NDP-led Millennium Combination, which secured 15 percent. After lengthy interparty discussions, Venetiaan succeeded in securing a new mandate on August 4 and assumed office on August 12, with Ajodhia returning as vice president and prime minister.

In inconclusive balloting on May 25, 2005, the New Front lost a third of its National Assembly representation and failed to secure a necessary two-thirds majority for Venetiaan's reelection in two legislative ballots in July. Subsequently, the party concluded an alliance with the A-Combination, a recently formed Maroon-based coalition that yielded a third term for Venetiaan in a United People's Assembly poll on August 3.

Désiré Bouterse's Mega Combination secured 23 assembly seats at balloting on May 25, 2010, and with the support of Ronnie Brunswijk's A-Combination and the People's Alliance for Progress, obtained the two-thirds required for legislative designation of the former dictator as president.

The finance minister was replaced on June 10, 2011, and a subsequent major cabinet reshuffle occurred in May 2012 following the National Assembly's passage of the Amnesty Law. Three cabinet ministers were replaced in June and July 2013 (see Current issues, below).

Constitution and government. In the immediate wake of the 1990 coup, Commander Graanoogst promised an early return to civilian rule, a pledge that yielded the election of May 25, 1991. The 1987 constitution, under which the polling took place, sets forth a complex system of government within which the intended distribution of power is by no means clearly defined. A 51-member National Assembly, elected for a five-year term, selects a president and vice president for terms of the same duration; however, the action must be by a two-thirds majority, lacking which the choice is made by a simple majority of a United People's Assembly (*Vereinigde Volksvergadering*), comprised of the National Assembly members plus 289 local and regional councilors. The selection must be deferred until 30 days after the election to accommodate any disputed legislative contests. The president serves as chair of a nonelective State Council whose composition is "regulated by law" and whose purpose is to advise the government on public policy, ensuring that its actions are in conformity with the basic law; the president also chairs a Security Council, which is empowered to assume governmental authority in the event of "war, state of siege, or exceptional circumstances to be determined by law." The cabinet of ministers, on the other hand, is chaired by the vice president in a role equivalent to that of a prime minister serving under a "strong" president.

The Assembly may amend the constitution by a two-thirds majority or, lacking such a majority, by convening the equivalent of a presidential assembly. For electoral purposes the country is divided into ten districts.

In early 1992, the Assembly began debate on a variety of constitutional amendments, only one of which, a ban on political activity by the army, was subsequently approved. Other proposed changes would have limited the State Council to a purely advisory role, with no capacity to veto government decisions, and given the president the power of legislative dissolution, while permitting a two-thirds majority of the assembly to dismiss the president. In August 2012, the Senate Committee on Constitutional Reform issued a questionnaire to individuals, organizations, and institutions within Suriname to gather feedback at a hearing on possible revisions to the Constitution of 1987. The questionnaire addressed issues such as problems with the current constitution, individual freedoms, elections, and function of the branches of government.

Though freedom of expression is generally respected, libel remains a criminal offense and journalists practice self-censorship on sensitive issues. Suriname ranked 31st on the Reporters Without Borders annual press freedom index, reflecting the worsening relationship between the administration and the press following the passage of the 2012 amnesty legislation (see Current issues, below).

Foreign relations. Before the 1980 coup, Suriname's foreign relations turned on two main issues: long-standing border disputes with neighboring Guyana and French Guiana and the status of development assistance from the Netherlands. The border disputes resulted from Guyana's claim to a 6,000-square-mile tract reputedly rich in bauxite deposits and from France's claim to a 780-square-mile tract believed to contain deposits of gold; neither controversy has yet been resolved, although Suriname and Guyana agreed in mid-1995 to open negotiations on their dispute within the framework of a joint commission. The Dutch aid, exceeding $1.5 billion, was to have been disbursed over a period of 10–15 years to ensure the opposition's support for independence, raise the standard of living for the Surinamese people, and compensate for termination of the preindependence right of emigration from Suriname to the Netherlands.

Foreign policy uncertainty followed the first Arron overthrow, though a leftward thrust, led by the Bouterse faction and the NMC's pro-Cuban posture, emerged, prompting an increased flow of Surinamese to the Netherlands and the recall of the Dutch ambassador in March 1982. The subsequent withdrawal of Dutch aid (which had been the principal source of Suriname's relatively high standard of living) dealt a severe blow to the country's economy. In early 1983 it appeared that the fiscal shortfall might be alleviated by commitments from Cuba and Libya. However, on June 1, coincident with reports that the administration of U.S. president Ronald Reagan had considered a Central Intelligence Agency (CIA) plan to infiltrate and destabilize the self-proclaimed "socialist" regime, a substantial military and trade agreement was concluded with Brazil. Two weeks later, amid Dutch reports that Brazil had threatened to invade Suriname if efforts were not taken to curb Cuban influence, Colonel Bouterse announced that Sgt. Maj. Badressein SITAL, one of the most pro-Cuban members of the NMC, had been dismissed from both his Council and ministerial positions. In mid-October Bouterse visited the United States and later in the month, following the Grenada action, asked Cuba to withdraw its ambassador and sharply reduce its remaining diplomatic staff in Paramaribo.

In early 1984, the regime lodged official protests with the French and Netherlands governments over their alleged complicity in an invasion plot, and in March 1985 Suriname threatened to take the Netherlands to the International Court of Justice (ICJ) for discontinuance of its aid program under the 1975 independence accord. The latter pronouncement came in the wake of an adverse UN Human Rights Commission report on the 1982 killings. On the other hand, an announcement by the government that it would proceed with ICJ action appeared to be rendered moot by The Hague's positive response in 1988 to the balloting of the previous November. Subsequently, at the conclusion of a three-day visit to the Hague by President Venetiaan in June 1992, the Netherlands and Suriname signed a cooperation treaty that formally ended their lengthy estrangement, although Dutch financial assistance was again suspended in mid-1993 (see The Country, above).

A member of the UN and other international and regional organizations, Suriname was admitted to the Caricom in February 1995.

The aid issue was further exacerbated in September 1997 by a Dutch request that Interpol issue an international warrant for the arrest and extradition of Dési Bouterse on drug-trafficking and money-laundering charges. In a similar vein, the Netherlands appealed unsuccessfully for the arrest of Bouterse while the former dictator was on a private visit to Trinidad and Tobago in mid-1998. Bouterse went on trial in absentia in a Dutch court in March 1999 and four months later was convicted of the charge against him. Development aid from the Netherlands was again suspended in June 1999 before being resumed in early 2001, partly in response to the positive reaction of the Netherlands to the 2000 elections. Relations improved further in September 2001 when the Netherlands formally apologized for the practice of slavery in Dutch Guiana.

A new dispute with Guyana erupted in 2000 over an offshore oil concession by Guyana in disputed territory. The two countries filed claims with the UN in 2004, and in September 2007 issued the tribunal issued a ruling in favor of Guyana (for more, see the 2013 *Handbook*).

In early 2007, Suriname concluded an agreement allowing Venezuelan nationals to fish in its waters, if all of the catches were delivered to Paramaribo. However, the Surinamese government cited payment concerns in taking no immediate action to join PetroCaribe, under which Venezuela supplies oil and its byproducts to Caribbean countries on preferential terms.

Just one foreign head of state, Guyana's president Bharrat Jagdeo, attended Bouterse's inauguration.

Following the passage of the Amnesty Law (See Current issues, below), the Netherlands immediately withdrew its ambassador, while the Inter-American Court of Human Rights, the UN High Commissioner for Human Rights, and the European Union (EU) all took action in light of what they perceived to be interference with justice in a human rights case.

While France views the Amnesty Law as a negative action, it continues to push for good relations with Suriname and has recently held military exercises for its French Guyana soldiers in Suriname.

While relations with the Netherlands strained, ties with China strengthened. China is the second largest aid provider to Suriname. In 2011, illegal and legal Chinese immigrants reportedly constituted 10 percent of the population.

In November 2012, Suriname announced there were no plans to name an ambassador to The Hague, and the following month said there would be no rush to approve the reappointment of the Dutch ambassador. In March 2013, Suriname appointed its first ambassador to Turkey as part of an effort to strengthen economic ties between the two countries. An open skies agreement with the United States signed in July paved way for an increased economic relationship between the two countries.

Current issues. Prior to the 2010 poll, Désiré Bouterse, who was known to favor direct presidential elections, pledged to carry out "fundamental" political reforms. Following the election, he accepted "political responsibility" for the 1982 killings but insisted that he had not been personally involved. He stated that he would not intervene in the ongoing military trial, known as the December 8 trial, which reconvened on October 15 and then was postponed until November 19, but he subsequently appointed one of his codefendants as ambassador to France. Relations with the Netherlands worsened under Bouterse, with a Dutch spokesperson declaring that contacts would be restricted to "functional necessities."

In 2011, the president designated February 25, the anniversary of the 1980 coup, as a national holiday, and he added his wife to the government payroll with a salary of $4,000 a month for her role as first lady. The president also appointed his son Dino, a convicted cocaine and weapons dealer, to the country's new counterterrorism unit.

On April 4, 2012, the National Assembly passed a controversial piece of legislation designed to grant amnesty to the suspects of the 1982 political killings of opponents of the then military regime, which was led by current President Bouterse. A pro-Bouterse majority in parliament passed the Amnesty Law weeks before the verdict was to be delivered in the December 8 trial. Opposition parties and citizens across the country protested against the Amnesty Law. Prompted by internal opposition to the law, Bouterse dismissed eight ministers in a May 5 cabinet reshuffle. When the trial resumed on April 13, the defense called for the trial to be ended and for the lawsuit to be dismissed in light of the Amnesty Law. On May 11, the presiding judge, Cynthia Valstein-Motnor, suspended the trial in order to allow the constitutionality of the Amnesty Law to be examined by the Constitutional Court, which, though created in the 1987 Constitution, has never been established. While the Constitution of 1987 created the Constitutional Court, one has never been established. Though due to restart on December 12, the trial was further postponed while prosecutors await a ruling from the Constitutional Court. In January 2013, the International Commission of Journalists issued a statement voicing concern for the trial's delay. As of August 2013 it had yet to be established.

Cracks in the leading coalition came to light when AC leader Ronnie Brunswijk, whose support helped Bouterse win in 2010, announced at a rap concert in April 2013 that he plans to run for president in 2015. A Bouterse spokesperson shortly thereafter announced that Bouterse plans to seek a second term.

June and July 2013 saw three ministers replaced, part of an effort to root out corruption, nepotism, and to depoliticize the ministry of education.

POLITICAL PARTIES

Government Groups:

Mega Combination (*Mega Combinate*—MC). The MC was launched prior to the 2010 election as a four-party coalition supportive of Désiré Bouterse's bid for the presidency. In May 25, 2010, balloting, the coalition secured 40.2 percent of the vote and 23 assembly seats.

Leader: Désiré BOUTERSE (President of the Republic).

National Democratic Party (*Nationale Democratische Partij*—NDP). The NDP was formed before the 1987 election as a political vehicle for the supporters of Colonel Bouterse. As such, it succeeded the February 25 Movement, styled *Stanvaste* ("Steadfast") in Dutch, which had been characterized as a "movement, not a party" at its launching in 1984. Contrary to expectations, the NDP secured only three Assembly seats in 1987, two of which were subject to challenge and represented constituencies that had not been contested by Front nominees; the party's representation rose to 12 in 1991 and to 16 in May 1996.

Tension emerged in early 1999 between the rank-and-file of the NDP, described as supporters of Bouterse, and supporters (said to include most NDP legislators) of President Wijdenbosch. The president dismissed Bouterse as a presidential adviser in early April, Wijdenbosch subsequently forming the DNP 2000 (see under VVV, below).

An international arrest warrant was issued by a court in the Netherlands for Bouterse in 1997 on charges involving his alleged involvement in the smuggling of cocaine from Suriname to Europe. In June 2000 the Netherlands' court sentenced Bouterse in absentia to 11 years in prison in the case; however, Bouterse remained free in Suriname under protection of the Surinamese constitution, which prohibits extradition of nationals. (President Venetiaan proposed revision of the basic law to permit extradition in cases such as Bouterse's.) Meanwhile, prosecutors in the Netherlands in 2000 also attempted to pursue a case against Bouterse in connection with the execution of 15 political opponents in Suriname in 1982. The Netherlands High Court dismissed the charges in September 2001 on the ground that Netherlands had no jurisdiction in the case. However, similar charges were levied in Suriname (see Current issues, above).

For the 2000 campaign, the NDP served as the core component of an alliance styled the Millennium Combination (*Millenium Combatie*) that included the KTPI (below) and the DA'91 (below). Running alone in 2005, the NDP was legislative runner-up with 15 seats.

Bouterse relinquished the NDP chairmanship when he became president in 2010, saying that the two posts were incompatible; however, he resumed the post in March 2012.

Leaders: Lt. Col. Désiré (Dési) BOUTERSE (Chairman and President of the Republic), Ricardo PANKA (Mega Combination Faction Leader).

Party of National Unity and Solidarity (*Kerukunan Tulodo Pranatan Inggil*—KTPI). Formerly known as the Indonesian Peasants' Party (*Kaum-Tani Persuatan Indonesia*), the KTPI is a small, predominantly Javanese rural party founded in 1947. It joined the National Party Alliance before the 1977 election but withdrew in December 1978. As a participant in the New Front, it won seven seats in 1991 and five in 1996 before withdrawing to enter the Wijdenbosch government. It contested the 2000 balloting as part of the Millennium Coalition and joined the Mega Combination in 2010.

Leader: Willy SOEMITA.

Progressive Workers' and Farmers' Union (*Progressieve Arbeiders en Landbouwers Unie*—PALU). The only trade union to have retained a public role after many labor leaders were killed in December 1982, the left-wing PALU dominated the Alibux cabinet but was not represented in subsequent administrations. It won 4 Assembly seats from "war zone" constituencies in 1987, none in 1991 or 1996, and 1 in 2000. It joined the Megan Combination in 2010.

Leaders: Jim K. HOK (Chair), Henk RAMNANDANLAL (Vice Chair).

New Suriname (*Nieuw Suriname*—NS). The NS was founded in 2003.

Leader: Radjen Nanan PANDAY.

Government-Supportive Groups:

A-Combination (*A-Combinatie*—AC or A-Com). The AC was formed before the 2005 election as an alliance that included the **General Liberation and Development Party** (*Algemene Bevrijdings en Ontwikkelings Partij*—ABOP), led by former SLA leader Ronnie Brunswijk, and the **Brotherhood and Unity in Politics** (*Broederschap en Eenheid in Politiek*—BEP), led by Caprino Allendy. Celsius Waterberg assumed BEP leadership in September 2012.

An alliance with the NF in mid-2005 yielded the majority supporting Venetiaan's retention of the presidency, while its support of Bouterse in 2010 was crucial to legislative endorsement of the former dictator.

In April 2013, Burnswijk announced his intent to run for president in 2015.

Leaders: Ronnie BRUNSWIJK (ABOP), Celsius WATERBERG (BEP).

People's Alliance for Progress (*Volksalliante Voor Vooruitgang*—VVV). The VVV was formed before the 2005 campaign by former president Jules Wijdenbosch as a grouping of his DNP 2000, plus the KTPI and the two parties listed immediately below. It won five National Assembly seats in 2005, six in 2010.

Leaders: Salam Paul SOMOHARIO (Former Chair of the National Assembly), Jules WIJDENBOSCH (Former President of the Republic).

Democratic National Platform 2000 (*Democratisch Nationaal Platform 2000*—DNP 2000). The DNP 2000 was launched by Jules Wijdenbosch following his break with Colonel Bouterse in 1999. Closely affiliated with the group for the 2000 elections were **D21** (under A1, below) and the **Democratic Party** (*Democratische Partij*—DP), led by Frank PLAYFAIR. For the 1996 election the DP had joined the HPP (below) in forming the Alliance.

In the 2000 balloting, the DNP 2000 list won three National Assembly seats, one of which was taken up by Playfair.

Leaders: Jules Albert WIJDENBOSCH, Liakat Ali Errol ALIBUX.

Grassroots Party for Renewal and Democracy (*Basispartij voor Vernieuwing en Democratie*—BVD). Initially called the Movement for Freedom and Democracy (*Beweging voor Vriheid en Democratie*—BVD), the BVD is a Hindu party formed by a group of VHP dissidents in 1996. The movement participated in formation of the Wijdenbosch government in September and was subsequently registered as a party under its current name. Its former chair, Motilal MUNGRA, was dismissed as finance minister in August 1997 after accusing the president of extravagant expenditure, although the party retained its other cabinet posts. The BVD's Pretaapnarain RADHAKISHUN served as vice president and prime minister from 1996 until 2000. He died shortly after leaving office.

In the 2000 election, the BVD won 3.2 percent of the National Assembly vote but no seats.

In June 2010 the party ended its alliance with the PVF (below) as the latter was going to be focusing more on agriculture and the BVD "had other plans."

Leaders: Dilip SARDJOE (Chair), Dr. Tjanrikapersad (Tjan) GOBARDHAN.

Other Legislative Groups:

New Front for Democracy and Development (*Nieuw Front voor Democratie en Ontwikkeling*—NF). Initially a three-member coalition of traditional ethnic parties (NPS, VHP, SPA, below) styled the Front for Democracy and Development (*Front noor Democratie en Ontwikkeling*—FDO), the NF, augmented by the KTPI, gained 30 of 51 National Assembly seats in 1991, as contrasted with 40 won by the FDO in 1987. Its representation dropped to 24 after the election of May 23, 1996, and was reduced thereafter as a result of KTPI withdrawal and defections by VHP members in support of the Wijdenbosch presidency. The New Front recovered its majority in the May 2000 elections, the *Pertjajah Luhur* having joined the coalition to once again bring its membership to four parties. Its legislative representation dropped from 23 to 14 in 2010.

Leaders: Ronald (Runaldo) VENETIAAN (Former President of the Republic), Ruth WIJDENBOSCH.

Suriname National Party (*Nationale Partij Suriname*—NPS). A Creole grouping founded in 1946, the NPS was the leading advocate of independence from the Netherlands and the core party of the National Party Alliance before the 1980 coup. Its leader served as president from 1991 to 1996 and was returned to the office in 2000, when the NPS won 14 of the NF's 33 National Assembly seats, and again in 2005, despite reduction of the NF to a plurality of 23 seats. Gregory Allan Rusland succeeded Venetiaan as chair in June 2012.

Leaders: Gregory Allan RUSLAND (Chair), Ronald (Runaldo) VENETIAAN (Former President of the Republic).

Progressive Reform Party (*Vooruitstrvende Hervormde Partij*—VHP). Initially called the United Reform Party (*Verenigde Hervormings Partij*—VHP), and long the leading Hindu party, the left-of-center VHP originally opposed independence because of anticipated repression by the Creole-dominated Alliance. The VHP's legislative representation of 16 seats in 1987 dropped to 9 in 1991, all of which were retained in 1996 before the defection of a group styled the Movement for Freedom and Democracy (see BVD, under VVV, above). Cahndrikapersad Santokhi, who became chair in 2011, noted that the VHP is not committed to the NF in 2015.

Leader: Cahndrikapersad SANTOKHI (Chair).

Suriname Labor Party (*Surinaamse Partij van de Arbeid*—SPA). The SPA is a social democratic formation affiliated with the Centrale 47 trade union. It withdrew as a member of the New Front in July 2005 but subsequently returned, with its leader, Sigfried Gilds, being named minister of trade and industry. Gilds resigned his ministerial post in January 2006 after being accused of complicity in a money-laundering operation and was convicted and sentenced to 12 months in jail in early 2009. Meanwhile, the party named a new chair, Guno Castelen, a former Port Management director who was asked to step down for reasons described as "political considerations."

Leader: Guno CASTELEN (Chair).

Full Confidence Party (*Pertjajah Luhur*—PL). A splinter from *Pendawa Lima* (below), the *Pertjajah Luhur* joined the New Front before the 2000 legislative balloting. Its leader, Paul Somohardjo, was president of the National Assembly during the Venetiaan presidency.

Leader: Paul Slamet SOMOHARDJO.

Party for Democracy and Development in Unity (*Partij Voor Demokratie en Ontwikkeling Eenheid*—DOE). The DOE was formed in 1999. It secured one legislative seat in 2010. In 2001 party chair Carl Breeveld took his anticorruption campaign to Radio Nederland in Suriname, where he urged adoption of the country's draft anticorruption law, the first version of which had been introduced into parliament in 2008.

Leaders: Carl BREEVELD (Chair), Joany LANSDORF-WATKIN (Vice President), Paul BRANDON (Secretary).

Other Parties:

Alternative-1 (A-1). The A-1 was formed before the 2005 balloting as a coalition that included the three groups immediately below. It secured three seats in the 2005 poll.

Democratic ALTERNATIVE '91 (*Democratisch Alternatief '91*—DA'91). The DA'91 was launched before the 1991 election by Gerard BRUNINGS, an airline executive who urged a constitutional amendment precluding political activity by both labor and the military. At its inception the formation was a coalition of Brunings's **Alternative Forum** (*Alternatief Forum*—AF), which is now led by Ricardo (Rick) Otto van RAVENSWAAY; the Bushnegro Unity Party (*Bosneger Eenheids Partij*—BEP, see under AC, above), and two groups that withdrew before the 1996 election: the *Pendawa Lima* and the HPP (both below). The coalition won nine legislative seats in 1991, four in 1996, and two in 2000. Party leader Djagendre RAMICHELAWAN died in 2010.

Democrats of the 21st Century (*Democraten van de 21ste Eeuw*—D21). Organized in 1986, D21 was affiliated with DNP 2000 for the 2000 poll. In 2010 party leader Soewarto Moestadja was given a ministry post.

Leader: Soewarto MOESTADJA.

Political Wing of the Federation of Farmers and Farm Workers (*Politieke Vleugel van de Federatie van Agrariërs en Landarbeiders*—PVF, or Political Wing of the FAL). The PVF was organized in the late 1990s to advance the agenda of the FAL trade union, which opposed the Wijdenbosch government. In the 2000 National Assembly election it won two seats.
Leaders: Soedichand JAIRAM (Chair), Jiwan SITAL.

Prior to the 2010 election, two additional minor groups joined A-1: the **Amazone Party of Suriname** (APS), led by Kenneth VAN GENDEREN, and **Trepunt 2000** (T-2000), led by Arti JESSURUN.

Reformed Progressive Party (*Hernieuwde Progressieve Partij*—HPP). Formerly a member of the DA'91, the HPP is a predominantly Hindu social democratic formation that split from the VHP in 1975 and later participated in the pre-1980 National Party Alliance. For the 1996 election it joined the Democratic Party in forming The Alliance (*De Alliantie*), which secured three National Assembly seats. Also subsequently associated with the Alliance was the Christian democratic **Progressive People's Party of Suriname** (*Progressieve Surinaamse Volkspartij*—PSV) of W. WONG Loi Sing. In 2000 the HPP and the PSV registered separately.
Leader: Prim RAMTAHALSING (Chair).

Pendawa Lima. A predominantly Javanese party dating from 1975, the *Pendawa Lima* ("Five Sons of King Pandu") joined DA '91 in 1991, thereafter winning four parliamentary seats in its own right in 1996. Before the 2000 legislative poll, the *Pendawa Lima* split into two factions, with theretofore *Pendawa Lima* Chair Paul Somohardjo leading his faction into the New Front and subsequent government as the *Pertjajah Luhur.* (Both the rump *Pendawa Lima* and *Pertjajah Luhur* use the abbreviation "PL," causing confusion in some news reports.) Associated with *Pendawa Lima* in recent elections has been the **Progressive Bosneger Party** (PBP), led by Armand KANAPE. In January 2010 the party ended its alliance with the A1 due to differences with the PVF. Party leader Raymond Sapoen holds a ministry post.
Leader: Raymond SAPOEN.

Other parties include the **National Party for Leadership and Development** (*Nationale Partij voor Leiderschap en Ontwikkeling*—NPLO), led by Oesman WANGSABESARIE; the **National Reform Party** (*Nationale Hervormings Partij*—NHP), led by Kenneth MOENNE; the **New Choice** (*Naya Kadam*—NK), led by Waldo RAMDIHAL; the **Party for Progression, Justice, and Perseverance** (PPRS), led by Renee KAIMAN; the **Progressive Political Party** (PPP), led by Surinder MUNGRA; **Seeka**, led by Paul ABENA; and the **Union of Progressive Surinamers** (UPS), led by Sheoradj PANDAY.

Exile Group:

In January 1983, a Movement for the Liberation of Suriname was formed by exiles in the Netherlands under the leadership of former president Chin and former deputy prime minister André HAAKMAT. However, the Dutch government refused to recognize the group as a government in exile, and both subsequently declared their support for the Surinamese Liberation Army (see SLA, below).

Guerrilla Groups:

Surinamese Liberation Army (SLA). The largely *bosneger* SLA was formed in early 1986 by former army private Ronnie Brunswijk with the avowed aim of overthrowing Colonel Bouterse and "[restoring] the constitutional state" through free elections. The government charged Surinamese émigrés in the Netherlands with supporting the SLA, whose approximately 2,000 members launched a guerrilla campaign in the country's eastern and southern regions that appeared to have been largely contained by mid-1987. In the wake of the November election, the SLA's "Jungle Commando" was reported to have declared an unconditional truce, effective January 1, 1988. Sporadic conflict, interspersed by talks with government and army representatives, nonetheless continued, before the conclusion of a preliminary peace accord in a ceremony attended by Bouterse and Brunswijk on March 26, 1991, which was followed by a suspension of hostilities on May 5 and the conclusion of a formal peace treaty on August 1, 1992. The General Liberation and Development Party, led by Brunswijk, competed unsuccessfully in the 1996 and 2000 elections. Brunswijk was sentenced in absentia to eight years in prison by a court in the Netherlands in April 1999 following his conviction on charges of cocaine trafficking. He now heads the ABOP (under AC, above), the present status of the SLA being unclear.

Other guerrilla formations have included the **Union for Liberation and Democracy,** a radical derivative of the SLA led by Kofi AJONGPONG; the Saramaccaner *bosneger* **Angula** movement, led by Carlos MAASSI; the **Mandela Bushnegro Liberation Movement,** led by Leendert ADAMS ("Biko"); the Amerindian **Tucayana Amazonica,** led by Alex JUBITANA and Thomas SABAJO, which participated in the 1992 peace accords; and the previously unknown **Suriname Liberation Front,** led by Cornelius MAISI, which was routed by the army after a hostage seizure at a hydroelectric facility south of Paramaribo in March 1994.

LEGISLATURE

The former unicameral Parliament (*Staten*) was abolished on August 15, 1980. A constituent National Assembly (*Volksvergadering*) of 31 nominated members was established on January 1, 1985, as part of the government's "return to democracy" program. Balloting for the successor **National Assembly** (*Nationale Assemblee*) occurred on November 25, 1987, and, in the wake of the 1990 coup, on May 25, 1991. In the most recent election for 51 members on May 25, 2010, the seat distribution was as follows: Mega Combination, 23; New Front for Democracy and Development, 14; A-Combination, 7; People's Alliance for Progress, 6; and Party for Democracy and Development through Unity, 1.
President: Jennifer GEERLINGS-SIMONS.

CABINET

[as of August 1, 2013]

Chair	Robert Ameerali
Ministers	
Agriculture, Livestock, and Fisheries	Hendrik Setrowidjojo (VVV)
Defense	Lamuré Latour (NDP)
Education and Community Development	Ashwin Adhin
Finance	Adelien Wijnerman (NDP) [f]
Foreign Affairs	Winston Lackin (NDP)
Home Affairs	Soewarto Moestadja (VVV)
Justice and Police	Edward Belfort
Labor, Technological Development, and the Environment	Michael Miskin
Natural Resources	Jim Hok (PALU)
Planning, Land, and Forest Management	Steven Relyveld (NDP)
Public Health	Michael Blokland
Public Works	Rabin Parmessar (NDP)
Regional Development	Stanley Betterson (AC)
Social Affairs and Public Housing	Alice Amafo (AC) [f]
Trade and Industry	Raymond Sapoen (VVV)
Transport, Communication, and Tourism	Falisi Pinas (AC)
Youth and Sport	Ismanto Adna (KTPI)

[f] = female

INTERGOVERNMENTAL REPRESENTATION

Ambassador to the U.S.: Subhas Chandra MUNGRA.

U.S. Ambassador to Suriname: Jay Nicholas ANANIA.

Permanent Representative to the UN: Henry L. MacDONALD.

IGO Memberships (Non-UN): CARICOM, IADB, ICC, NAM, OAS, OIC, WTO.

SWAZILAND

Kingdom of Swaziland

Note: Following the legislative replenishments of September–October 2013, the king reappointed Prime Minister Sibusiso Dlamini on October 28, 2013, and a new cabinet (including a number of the incumbent ministers) was inaugurated on November 4.

Political Status: Independent monarchy within the Commonwealth since September 6, 1968.

Area: 6,703 sq. mi. (17,363 sq. km).

Population: 844,223 (2007C); 1,225,455 (2012E—UN); 1,386,914 (2012E—U.S. Census).

Major Urban Centers (2005E): MBABANE (administrative capital, 78,000), Lobamba (royal and legislative capital, 11,000), Manzini (33,000).

Official Languages: English, siSwati.

Monetary Unit: Lilangeni (official rate November 1, 2013: 10.17 emalangeni = $1US). The lilangeni is at par with the South African rand.

Sovereign: King MSWATI III; installed on April 25, 1986, succeeding (as Head of State) Queen Regent Ntombi THWALA.

Prime Minister: (*See headnote.*) Sibusiso Barnabas DLAMINI; appointed by the king on October 16, 2008, and sworn in on October 23 to succeed Absalom Themba DLAMINI. (Sibasiso Dlamini had also held the post in 1996–2003.)

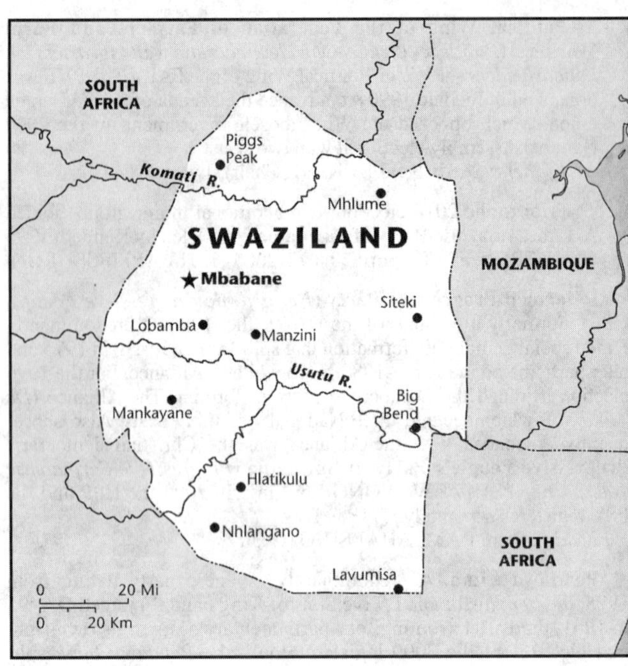

THE COUNTRY

Bordered on the north, west, and south by South Africa and on the east by Mozambique, Swaziland is the smallest of the three former British High Commission territories in southern Africa. The country comprises a mountainous western region (Highveld), a middle region of moderate altitude (Middleveld), an eastern lowland area (Lowveld), and the so-called Lubombo plateau on the eastern border. About 97 percent of the population is Swazi African, the remainder being of European and Eurafrican (mixed) stock. English is an official language, but siSwati (akin to Zulu) prevails among the indigenous population; Afrikaans is common among the Europeans, many of whom are of South African origin. Christianity is the religion of approximately half the people; there are a few Muslims, the remainder adhering to traditional beliefs. Women constitute about 37 percent of the workforce; female participation in government, with the exception of the former queens regent, has been minimal, although some women recently have been elected to the National Assembly and appointed to the cabinet. Overall, the influence of Swaziland's traditional culture (dominated by tribal chiefs) remains high, thereby compromising women's rights.

The economy is quite diversified given the country's small land area and population, although its composition, particularly in the mining sector, is changing. Production of iron ore, which had accounted for 25 percent of export earnings in 1967, virtually ceased by the end of the 1970s, while asbestos reserves, after 40 years of extraction, also approached depletion. Coal mining, on the other hand, underwent rapid development, while other minerals, such as tin, barites, and silica, were found in commercially exploitable quantities. Under normal conditions, water supplies are sufficient not only to support agriculture, which yields sugar (the main cash crop), forest products, and livestock, but also to provide a potential hydroelectric power base.

Growth of 3.5 percent was achieved in 2002, mainly due to expansion of the textile industry, which took advantage of reduced U.S. tariffs and quotas designed to assist developing African nations. However, the economy subsequently continued to suffer from high unemployment, persistent poverty, localized food shortages and, according to some international donors, irresponsible spending on the part of the royal family. In addition, Swaziland faced one of the highest rates of HIV/AIDS infection in the world; UN officials estimated in 2004 that 40 percent of adults were infected. After many years of seeming failure to implement a plan to combat the pandemic, the government in 2004 declared a national emergency regarding the issue and solicited international assistance in trying to halt the spread of the disease.

Little progress was subsequently made in reducing poverty, according to the International Monetary Fund (IMF), which cited, among other reasons, the high rate of HIV/AIDS infection, a prolonged drought, and factory closings that contributed to Swaziland's 30–40 percent unemployment rate. The IMF urged the government to reduce its budget deficit and increase privatization in order to attract investors. As the economic downturn spread across the globe, GDP growth registered an annual average of 1.2 percent in 2009–2010, far short of the 3.6 percent the IMF deemed necessary to prevent worsening poverty, said to affect as much as 70 percent of the population. In 2011 the IMF reported that the country was facing a "severe fiscal crisis," due to a sharp decline in revenue from the South African Customs Union (SACU), an unbudgeted 4.5 percent salary increase for civil servants and politicians, and spending "overruns" on defense. Among other things, the government was advised to slash 7,000 public-sector jobs and otherwise significantly reduce spending, measures that appeared increasingly difficult to enact in light of subsequent public protests (see Current issues, below). Growth was stagnant for 2011, and GDP contracted by 1.5 percent in 2012, while inflation rose to 9 percent for that year. Although a SACU "windfall" of $818 million in 2012 at least temporarily eased the fiscal crisis, international observers in 2013 continued to warn of potential budgetary collapse in light of the recent flight of foreign investment.

GOVERNMENT AND POLITICS

Political background. Swaziland came under British control in the mid-19th century when a Swazi ruler requested protection from his people's traditional enemies, the Zulu. Kept intact when the Union of South Africa was formed in 1910, the territory was subsequently administered under native rulers by the British high commissioner for South Africa. Preparations for independence began after World War II and culminated in the promulgation of internal self-government in 1967 and the achievement of full independence within the Commonwealth in 1968 under King SOBHUZA II, who subsequently exercised firm control of the country's political institutions. Following small gains by the semiradical Ngwane National Liberation Congress (NNLC) in a 1972 parliamentary election and frustration of his attempts to have an opposition MP deported, the king in April 1973 repealed the constitution, abolished the legislature, introduced a detention act, and banned all opposition political activity. On August 21, 1982, King Sobhuza died, having technically reigned from the age of one in 1899, although he had not been formally enthroned until 1921 and had not been recognized as paramount ruler by the British until 1966. He was succeeded as head of state by Queen Mother Dzeliwe SHONGWE, authorized to act as regent until a successor king was designated and reached maturity.

The naming of Prince Bhekimpi DLAMINI to succeed Prince Mabandla Fred DLAMINI as prime minister in March 1983 seemed to mark the ascendancy of conservative elements within the royal house. In August Queen Regent Dzeliwe was ousted from power, reportedly because she differed over the interpretation of her role with traditionalists within the *Liqoqo,* historically an advisory council of royal family members that had been elevated to the status of Supreme Council of State shortly before King Sobhuza's death. Queen Regent Dzeliwe was replaced by Ntombi THWALA, the mother of Prince MAKHOSETIVE, who was named successor to the former sovereign on August 10. Two months later, however, Prince Mfanasibili DLAMINI and Dr. George MSIBI, who were prominently involved in the palace coup that installed Queen Regent Ntombi, were dismissed from the *Liqoqo.*

On April 25, 1986, two years earlier than originally planned, Prince Makhosetive assumed the title of King MSWATI III in an apparent effort to halt the power struggle that had followed his father's death. The 19-year-old king, the world's youngest monarch, moved quickly to consolidate his control, temporarily disbanding the *Liqoqo* and appointing Prince Sotsha DLAMINI, a relatively obscure former police official, as prime minister on October 6.

After authorizing the arrest in May 1987 of 12 people allegedly involved in the palace intrigue of recent years, the king dissolved Parliament in September, one year early. Assembly elections were held in November, and the government was extensively reorganized at the end of the month. Although the king's bold action at the outset of his reign surprised some observers, most Swazis appeared to support his exercise of monarchical prerogative as a means of preserving stability.

The king formally assumed full executive authority at age 21 on April 19, 1989. Three months later he dismissed Prince Sotsha as prime minister, replacing him with Obed Mfanyana DLAMINI. The new prime minister was the founder and former secretary general of the Swaziland Federation of Trade Unions (SFTU), a background that appeared to strengthen the government's capacity to deal with a growing number of labor disputes.

On October 9, 1992, one month before the expiration of its term, the king dissolved Parliament and declared that, with the assistance of his cabinet (which would be restyled a Council of Ministers and act as a caretaker government), he would rule by decree until the adoption of a new constitution and the holding of elections. Balloting scheduled for November was postponed until 1993 to allow for the redefinition of constituencies and compilation of a voters' register. The monarch's action followed his approval of a draft charter that called for retention of the monarchy and the revival of multipartyism (banned in 1973 by King Sobhuza II).

Fearing a conservative backlash if the reform movement outpaced the prerogatives of the royal court and powerful traditional chiefs, the constitutional commission recommended that decisions regarding political parties be deferred. Consequently, candidates for the House of Assembly elections on September 18 and October 11, 1993, competed on a nonparty basis; nonetheless, the polling marked the first time that legislators had been popularly elected and royal family members had been prohibited from participating. Underscoring the change, Prime Minister Dlamini and all but three cabinet ministers lost their seats. As a result, on October 25 King Mswati named Andreas FAKUDZE as interim prime minister with responsibility for all 16 ministries. Ten days later the king appointed Prince Jameson Mblini DLAMINI, a conservative, to succeed Fakudze. Traditionalists hailed the monarch's choice, although the government named by Prince Jameson on November 10 included several reformists.

A follow-up round to the 1993 balloting was held on October 2, 1994, with voters selecting secretaries for the country's 55 regions (*Inkundla*). The new officials were described as links between legislators and their constituents, as well as coordinators of development activities in their areas.

The SFTU called a general strike (the most comprehensive in recent years) on March 13–14, 1995, to secure acceptance of a variety of demands, including the reinstatement of summarily dismissed state employees. The action was called off after the government appointed a select committee to consider the grievances. Subsequently, the SFTU called for another strike on July 17, which was called off after the House of Assembly imposed severe penalties for work stoppages. In mid-August the Senate endorsed a statement by King Mswati that Swazis did not want multiparty politics. Three months later, a well-attended opposition conference rejected the royal assessment in that matter.

On January 22–29, 1996, the SFTU organized a widely observed general strike, which was abandoned only after the king ordered the strikers back to work, threatening "to go to war" if necessary to end the action. Although some observers described the SFTU as "tarnished" by its capitulation to the monarch's threat, on February 16, three days before a scheduled resumption of the strike, King Mswati promised to reform the constitution and consider lifting the political party ban. Subsequently, the union suspended plans for renewed action; however, prodemocracy rallies continued.

On May 8, 1996, the king dismissed Prime Minister Dlamini, promising "concrete democratic changes." Subsequently, the king named Deputy Prime Minister Sishayi NXUMALO as acting prime minister, but Nxumalo immediately asserted that the Swazi people were not ready for political parties, which he described as ill-suited for the "close-knit, non-ethnic, traditional society." Nevertheless, on July 26 the king announced the creation of a 29-member Constitutional Reform Commission (CRC) with responsibility for drafting a new constitution. Concurrently, he named former finance minister and IMF executive director Dr. Sibusiso Barnabas DLAMINI as the new prime minister. The cabinet was reshuffled on November 13, the king pledging emphasis on economic development and the pursuit of foreign investment and trade.

In an apparent effort to quell increasingly vocal calls for reform from prodemocracy activists, the king abruptly dissolved the House of Assembly in August 1998. Observers attributed the low voter turnout in the October assembly elections to voter apathy and the prodemocracy forces' call for an electoral boycott. On November 13 the king reappointed Dlamini as prime minister, and on November 20 a new government was sworn in.

On May 31, 2003, the king dissolved the assembly and appointed a special council to act as a caretaker government until elections were held. Following the September–October elections, which were boycotted by most of the major opposition groups, the king appointed Absalom Themba DLAMINI as prime minister on November 14.

Unprecedented protests were reported in the run-up to the September 2008 assembly elections, as thousands demonstrated for the legalization of political parties. Commonwealth elections observers stated that they could not declare the results of the legislative poll credible because political parties were denied participation and the power of Parliament remained severely restricted. Following the elections, the first since the promulgation of a new constitution in 2006 (see Constitution and government, below), the king named Sibusiso Barnabas Dlamini to return to the premiership, which he had held in 1996–2003. Dlamini named a new government on October 24.

Suppression of political activists heightened in 2010 with the arrests of several union leaders and other prodemocracy demonstrators. In June a spate of bombings against government and opposition targets created "a sense of instability."

Attention turned in early 2011 to the country's severe financial crisis, as the finance minister ordered drastic budget cuts in February after warning that there might not be enough money to pay public employees. Despite the shortage of funds, the government stood firm on its plans to complete construction of a new airport—described as a pet project of the king and a "white elephant" by critics, who claimed the project already was over budget and, at nine years and counting, well behind schedule. Tensions heightened as economic conditions worsened, culminating in a mass protest in late March that led to the government agreeing to a 10 percent cut in ministers' salaries. In April thousands of teachers, students, and doctors, among others, rallied in protest against cuts to social spending and, perhaps inspired by popular uprisings elsewhere on the continent, to show their dissatisfaction with the monarchy. Police detained about 100 people, including journalists and labor leaders, in what was described as the largest security mobilization in Swaziland in decades. As pressure mounted on the political front, the government also faced a dire economic situation, prompting the king to issue an international plea for loans to prevent the country's total fiscal collapse. Both the IMF and the World Bank refused to provide short-term assistance, but in early August South Africa agreed to a tentative $355 million bailout conditioned on political and economic reforms, including the promotion of democracy, human rights, and good governance. Among other things, human rights advocates alleged that security forces had abused detainees in Swaziland by using torture and unjustified use of lethal force.

Constitution and government. For some years after independence, King Sobhuza II was reported to have been working on a revised Western-style constitution. However, in March 1977 he announced that he had abandoned the effort in favor of a form of traditional government based on tribal councils (*Tinkhundla*), which was formally introduced in October 1978. Under the *Tinkhundla* electoral system, polling was held without political campaigns or electoral rolls for an 80-member electoral college charged with naming four-fifths of a 50-member House of Assembly, which in turn named half of a 20-member Senate. Ten members of each were designated by the monarch, who also named the prime minister and other cabinet officials.

On February 14, 1992, a royal constitutional commission appointed by the king in late 1991 presented a draft charter for a multiparty electoral system, which was given preliminary approval by the monarch in October. The proposal called for a two-stage balloting process beginning with polling in the *Tinkhundla* for local representatives from among candidates chosen by the chiefs. In the second round of the secret balloting, the leading vote-getters from the first round were to compete for berths in an expanded House of Assembly and Senate of 55 and 20 members, respectively (the monarch having the right to appoint 10 additional members to each). The plan, while serving as a partial blueprint for the 1993 and 1998 polls, lacked formal approval, and its status remained distinctly uncertain.

A Constitutional Reform Committee (CRC) formed in 1996 proceeded haltingly. In January 2001 a draft constitution report from the CRC was criticized by the opposition and human rights groups as a "doctored document" and "not a truly representative report because group submissions were denied." The long-awaited new draft constitution was presented to the king in November 2003, but he did not sign it into law until July 26, 2005, after ordering the legislature to amend sections regarding religion and taxing the royal family. The new constitution promulgated on February 8, 2006, contained no specific language to legalize political parties and stipulated that candidates for election must run as individuals. Though the constitution included a bill of rights guaranteeing limited freedoms, the king retained ultimate authority, including appointment of the prime minister and the cabinet.

The judiciary, whose members are appointed by the king, encompasses a High Court, a Court of Appeal, and district courts. There are also 17 Swazi courts for tribal and customary issues. Swaziland is divided for administrative purposes into four districts, each headed by a commissioner appointed by the central government. There are ten partially elected town boards and councils (five each) and two fully elected municipal councils.

The government severely restricts press freedom, even though it is constitutionally guaranteed. Most major media outlets are state controlled (there is only one independent newspaper), and no criticism is permitted of the government or the king, who is included in the list of "Predators of Press Freedom" issued by Reporters Without Borders.

Foreign relations. Swaziland is a member of the United Nations (UN), the Commonwealth, and the African Union (AU, formerly the Organization of African Unity—OAU). It maintains close relations with South Africa as a result of geographic proximity, administrative tradition, and economic dependency (more than 80 percent of the kingdom's imports are from South Africa, and a substantial portion of its national income consists of remittances from Swazis employed in the neighboring state). Despite its ties to South Africa, Swaziland established diplomatic relations with Mozambique during 1976, prompted by a need to facilitate the movement of goods through the Mozambique port of Maputo (a security accord was concluded between the two countries in mid-1984).

Despite OAU strictures, Swaziland concluded a secret nonaggression pact with Pretoria in 1982 and subsequently strove to contain African National Congress (ANC) activity within its territory. However, a series of major raids on purported ANC strongholds by South African security forces in 1986 led to vehement protests by the Swazi government and a December visit by South African Foreign Minister Roelof "Pik" Botha, who reaffirmed his government's commitment to the 1982 pact and pledged that the incursions would cease. However, in July 1987 two top ANC officials and a Mozambican woman companion were killed in Mbabane. Two additional killings by alleged South African agents in August brought the total number of ANC deaths in 1987 to 11.

In September 1989 it was reported that Swaziland and South Africa had agreed on a border adjustment that would bring the largely Swazi-populated South African homeland of KaNgwane within the kingdom. However, no date was given for the formal transfer. (In 1994, KaNgwane was reintegrated into Transvaal in northern South Africa; Swaziland has continued to lay claim to the territory.)

In late 1997 relations between Swaziland and Mozambique were strained after it was reported that a Swazi prince leading a committee studying their shared border had asserted that Swazi territory legally encompassed all of Mozambique's Maputo Province. (The claim was dismissed by Maputo, which declared that it had never been formally contacted by Swaziland.)

In March 2005 the king and South African president Thebo Mbeki were scheduled to hold a summit, which activists had hoped Mbeki would use to push for reforms in Swaziland, but the meeting was postponed indefinitely. In May 2006, officials from Swaziland, Mozambique, and South Africa opened the Lubombo Tourism Route in what was described as "part of the ongoing cross-border initiatives" among the three countries.

Taiwan currently contributes $200 million per year in aid to Swaziland, one of Taiwan's few "allies" in Africa.

Current issues. Clashes broke out again in September 2011 between police and protesters in several cities as the government refused to accept a petition from civic groups calling for the introduction of multipartyism and reform of the judiciary. In the latter regard, the king, in an October cabinet reshuffle, replaced the justice minister, who had agreed that the judicial system was in crisis. An infusion of income from SACU late in the year eased the government's liquidity problem slightly, while some analysts argued that the king had unwisely sold off portions of various parastatal enterprises in order to secure short-term private financial backing. Meanwhile, negotiations with the IMF collapsed in mid-2012 over the government's disinterest in severe austerity measures, which many analysts concluded would have the immediate effect of further inflaming popular resentment. New strikes and protests in July–September again prompted harsh responses from authorities.

In October 2012 the assembly passed a nonconfidence motion against the government in the wake of questions about a recent contract for the nation's sole telephone provider. However, Prime Minister Dlamini, stating he served at the pleasure of the king, refused to resign, and a potential constitutional crisis arose when the king declined to dissolve the government. The assembly subsequently reversed the nonconfidence motion, thereby easing the immediate impasse, but not before it had become clear that legislative prerogatives still remained severely constrained. Most opposition groups subsequently joined organizations representing teachers, other public employees, students, and trade unions in calling for a boycott of the November local elections.

Protests over the extent of the king's authority continued in the first half of 2013, and opposition forces again supported a boycott of the September balloting for the House of Assembly, calling the poll "pointless." Nevertheless, a number of cabinet ministers and many other incumbent legislators were defeated in the poll, reflecting growing popular discontent with economic decline and perceived widespread corruption. Although the balloting was peaceful, international observers strongly lamented the political parties were still barred from formally presenting candidates.

POLITICAL GROUPS

During 1994, a number of groups, including Pudemo (below), joined with human rights and other groups to form a Confederation for Full Democracy in Swaziland (CFDS). (See the 2013 *Handbook* for additional information on the CFDS.) In early 1996 the CFDS appeared to have been superseded by the Swaziland Democratic Alliance (SDA), a coalition that included Pudemo; the Swaziland Federation of Trade Unions (SFTU), an 80,000 member grouping then led by Jan SITHOLE; and representatives of the Institute for Democracy and Leadership (Ideal), led by Dr. Jerry GULE. Organized to "try to force change," the alliance led a march on the prime minister's office and parliamentary building, which was noteworthy mainly for the paltry number of activists who participated. In early 1999 the SDA was bolstered by the addition of the NNLC (below) to its ranks, and in April the NNLC's Obed Mfanyan Dlamini (a former prime minister) was elected, along with Pudemo's Jerry NXUMALO and Sithole, to lead the reorganized alliance. However, in 2003 Obed Dlamini was elected to the assembly, even though other SDA members had called for a boycott of the elections. The conflict appeared to signal the collapse of the SDA.

Despite analysts' speculation about the freedom of association clause in the revised constitution allowing for the legal registration of political parties, in 2007 King Mswati declared that political parties remained banned. That pronouncement was reiterated in 2008 by the elections commissioner, and political parties were not allowed to participate in the September assembly elections.

The Swaziland United Democratic Front (SUDF) was launched in 2008 by Pudemo, trade unions, church groups, student activists, and other civic organizations. The SUDF, whose national coordinator is Wandile DLUDLU, served a prominent role in the 2011–2013 protests calling for economic and political reform. Most opposition groups called for a boycott of the September 2013 legislative poll, but former SFTU leader Sithole, now described as leader of the **Swaziland Democratic Party** (Swadepa), was elected to the assembly after changing course and deciding to pursue reform "from within."

Former Government Party:

Imbokodvo National Movement (INM). The *Imbokodvo* ("Grindstone") grouping dominated the political scene during the late 1960s and was the only political group permitted to function openly after 1973. The leadership of the party became vacant following the dismissal of Prince Mabandla Dlamini as prime minister in March 1983. Two royalist groups, formed as "cultural organizations" in 1996, were the *Sive Siyinqaba*, an offshoot of the INM led by Isaac SHABANGU and Zibuse SIMELANE, and the *Sibahle Sinje*, led by former assembly speaker Marwick KHUMALO. In 2000, the *Sive Siyinqaba* called on the king to lift the ban on political parties, while the *Sibahle Sinje* continued to back the no-party system. Khumalo, a member of the assembly, was described in 2012 as secretary general of a joint *Sive Siyinqaba–Sibahle Sinje*, which sent representatives to meetings of opposition groups promoting multipartyism, although *Sive Siyinqaba–Sibahle Sinje* argued that monarchical authority should be preserved. Khumalo was described as increasingly critical of the government in 2013.

Opposition and External Groups:

People's United Democratic Movement (PUDM or Pudemo). Initial reports about Pudemo surfaced in 1989 when the government accused the group of illegally circulating political pamphlets. In mid-1990 it was reported that after a period of inactivity, the group had resumed actively campaigning for electoral reform, multiparty democracy, and an end to corruption. The party unilaterally proclaimed its "legality" in February 1992.

In August 1993 party president Kislon Shongwe reportedly requested refuge at the UK's high commission in Mbabane after he was listed among opposition figures being sought for distributing "seditious pamphlets." In January 1996 Pudemo threatened to make the country "ungovernable" if the monarch failed to adopt a multiparty democratic system of government. Underscoring its more militant stance, Pudemo subsequently replaced Shongwe, who was described as "uncombative," and Secretary General Dominic MNGOMEZULU with Mario Masuku and Bonginkhosi DLAMINI, respectively. Masuku was named to the constitutional review commission established in May but later resigned on the ground that it had become apparent that the king had no intention of lifting the political party ban. In November 2000 Pudemo was among the forces of opposition to join the general strike called by the SFTU, during which Masuku was arrested along with other opposition leaders. Masuku was acquitted of sedition charges in August 2002.

In 2005 the king accused 13 Pudemo members of firebombing homes and offices of government officials; all were subsequently released. The government cracked down on a Pudemo rally in March 2006, arresting several party members, including Masuku (who was released the same day), and Bonginkhosi Dlamini (who was charged with high treason before being released later). Party leaders said they staged the protest to test the constitution's provision regarding political freedom. In August members of the party's youth wing, the Swaziland Youth Congress (Swayoco), were routed by police as the prodemocracy group marched near the capital.

In 2008 Pudemo called the assembly elections "a sham" and vowed to continue to press for political reforms. Party leader Masuku was charged in November under the country's new antiterrorism law and was temporarily sent to a maximum security prison. His arrest came in the wake of the prime minister's announcement that four political groups, including Pudemo and Swayoco, were deemed terrorist organizations and were therefore banned.

In May 2010 a leader of Swayoco died in police custody after his arrest at a May Day rally. Several other youth leaders were detained following a series of bombings in June. Participation in a prodemocracy rally in September resulted in the temporary detention of Masuku and party vice president Sikhumbuzo Phakathi.

In February 2011 the king refused an initiative suggested by Pudemo that would have led to opening a dialogue between the government and prodemocracy groups. Pudemo was at the forefront of protests that broke out later in the spring and continued sporadically into the fall of 2012 (see Current issues, above). Pudemo, insisting it eschewed violence in favor of peaceful dialogue, joined other opposition groups in calling for a boycott of the November 2012 local elections and the 2013 assembly poll. Swayoco secretary general Maxwell DLAMINI was reportedly charged with sedition in regard to protests prior to the 2013 balloting, while other reports indicated that Pudemo leader Masuku may also have been briefly detained.

Leaders: Mario MASUKU (President), Sikhumbuzo PHAKATHI (Secretary General), Jerry NXUMALO, Kislon SHONGWE.

Ngwane National Liberatory Congress (NNLC). The NNLC was at the forefront of opposition activities in the 1970s but thereafter was reported to have become temporarily moribund. At a meeting of the resuscitated body in December 1998, former prime minister Obed Mfanyana Dlamini was elected president of the congress, and in April 1999 he reportedly agreed to enter into the SDA (see introductory text to section on Political Groups, above). In the 2003 legislative elections, Dlamini was elected to the assembly after campaigning as a nonpartisan. In 2005 NNLC member Jimmy HLOPHE, running as an unaffiliated individual, won an assembly seat in a special election following the death of a member of the assembly. Earlier in 2005, requests to the high court by the NNLC and Pudemo to be involved in the constitutional review process were denied because, according to the judge, "in terms of the law they are nonexistent." The NNLC was among several political groups that protested the 2008 assembly elections.

In 2009 Obed Dlamini was appointed to the *Liquoqo* (the king's advisory council), his acceptance of the post generating strong criticism within the NLCC. In early 2012 the NLCC argued that Swaziland would become a "failed state" without democratic reforms.

Leaders: Alvit DLAMINI (President), Thamsanqa HLATSHWAYO (Secretary General).

African United Democratic Party (AUDP). References to the AUDP first appeared in 2006 in reports that it was taking its fight for registration to the courts. It was subsequently reported that the high court had ordered the government to register the AUDP in accordance with the revised constitution's freedom of association clause. However, King Mswati soon after confirmed that political parties remained illegal. The AUDP as of mid-2013 continued to be active in efforts to compel establishment of a multiparty system.

Leaders: Stanley MAUNDZISA (President), Sibusiso DLAMINI (Secretary General).

Swaziland National Progressive Party (SNPP). This party was referenced in 2000 as being affiliated with the SDA. In 2009 the SNPP condemned the prime minister's "attitude" following his remarks that those who were critical of the king's remarks at the opening session of Parliament could be charged with sedition. In supporting a teachers' strike in August 2012, the SNPP argued that the *Tinkhundla* system had failed the country and that cabinet ministers were self-serving.

Leader: Magadeyiwile MDLULI (President).

Swaziland Solidarity Network (SSN). Based in South Africa and led by a South African, Solly Mapaila, the SSN is a "pressure group" that has been critical of the Swaziland regime's alleged efforts to squelch prodemocracy activity. In October 1997 Mapaila, who was himself banned from Swaziland for allegedly fomenting unrest, accused the monarch of maintaining a list of ANC officials it sought to ban from entering the country. The SSN launched a campaign in 2000 calling for the international community to "isolate" Swaziland until political reforms were enacted. It renewed its calls for international action in 2005, citing the king's reported extravagant spending while most of the population lived in extreme poverty.

In 2008 the SSN backed the election boycott organized by Pudemo. Following the election, the SSN was among four political groups listed as "terrorist organizations" and banned by the prime minister. The SSN's response was that it was impossible for the government to ban the group because it is based in South Africa.

In June 2010 the SSN asserted that Swazi security forces were behind the spate of recent bombings and were using the attacks to cover up alleged illegal raids and arbitrary detentions of political activists.

Leaders: Solly MAPAILA (Chair), Lucky LUKHELE (Spokesperson).

Other political groups are the **Inhlava Party**, founded in 2006 by Mfomfo NKHAMBULE; the **Ngwane Socialist Revolutionary Party**, led by Thomas Vabula MAGAGULA; and the **National Congress for Democratic Change** (Nacodec), a breakaway from Pudemo. A group known as the **Swaziland People's Liberation Army** (*Umbane*), whose leadership remained "faceless," was reported in 2009 to be receiving financial backing and training for its members from the Sudanese People's Liberation Army. The group was declared a terrorist organization by Swaziland's prime minister.

The **Communist Party of Swaziland** (CPS) was launched in 2011 with the assistance of the South African Communist Party. CPS officials applauded recent reform activity on the part of Pudemo, Swayoco, and the SSN but called for an "intensified struggle." In addition to its antimonarchical stance, the CPS also opposed recent IMF demands as harmful to workers. The CPS called for a boycott of the September 2013 assembly poll, several of its members reportedly having been arrested in connection with recent protest demonstrations.

LEGISLATURE

On October 9, 1992, King Mswati dissolved the bicameral **Parliament** (*Libandla*) in preparation for new elections scheduled to follow the adoption of a new multiparty constitution in 1993. However, further deliberation on the draft charter was suspended, and the subsequent elections have been held on a nonparty basis.

Senate. The Senate is composed of 30 members (20 chosen by the monarch plus 10 elected via majoritarian vote by the House of Assembly), whose term of office is five years. The most recent balloting in the House of Assembly for the 10 elected members was held on October 23, 2013, and the king's appointments were announced on October 30.

President: Chief Gelane ZWANE.

House of Assembly. Enlarged by 15 seats following the 1992 elections, the assembly consists of 55 popularly elected members (1 for each electoral district), 10 monarchial appointees, and the speaker, who can be elected by the assembly from outside its membership and serve in an ex officio (nonvoting) capacity. (If popularly elected to the assembly, the speaker may vote but only to break a tie vote among the other members.) The term of office is five years, subject to dissolution by the king. Political parties are not permitted to participate in assembly elections, and all candidates run officially as independents. The most recent balloting for the 55 elected members was held on September 20, 2013, and the king's appointments were announced on October 5.

Speaker: Themba MSIBI.

CABINET

[as of September 1, 2013] (*See headnote.*)

Prime Minister	Sibusiso Barnabas Dlamini
Deputy Prime Minister	Themba Nhlanganiso Masuku
Ministers	
Agriculture	Clement M. Dlamini
Commerce, Industry, and Trade	Sen. Jabulile Mashwama [f]
Economic Planning and Development	Prince Hlangusemphi
Education and Training	Wilson M. Ntshangase
Finance	Majozi Sithole
Foreign Affairs and International Cooperation	Mtiti Fakudze
Health	Benedict Xaba
Home Affairs	Prince Gcokoma
Housing and Urban Development	Sen. Pastor Lindiwe Gwebu [f]
Information, Communications, and Technology	Winnie Magagula [f]
Justice	Chief Mgwagwa Gamedze
Labor and Social Security	Lutfo Dlamini
Natural Resources and Energy	Princess Tsandzile [f]
Public Service	Patrick Magwebetane Mamba
Public Works and Transport	Ntuthuko Dlamini
Sports, Culture, and Youth Affairs	Hlobisile Ndlovu [f]
Tinkhundia Administration and Development	Rogers Mamba
Tourism and Environmental Affairs	Mduduzi Dlamini

[f] = female

INTERGOVERNMENTAL REPRESENTATION

Ambassador to the U.S.: Abednego Mandla NTSHANGASE.

U.S. Ambassador to Swaziland: Makila JAMES.

Permanent Representative to the UN: Zwelethu MNISI.

IGO Memberships (Non-UN): AfDB, AU, Comesa, CWTH, IOM, NAM, SADC, WTO.

SWEDEN

Kingdom of Sweden
Konungariket Sverige

Political Status: Constitutional monarchy established on June 6, 1809; under revised constitution effective January 1, 1975.

Area: 173,731 sq. mi. (449,964 sq. km).

Population: 8,975,670 (2003C); 9,119,423 (2013E—U.S. Census).

Major Urban Centers (2007C): STOCKHOLM (788,000), Göteborg (490,000), Malmö (278,000), Uppsala (185,000).

Official Language: Swedish.

Monetary Unit: Krona (official rate November 1, 2013: 6.54 kronor = $1US).

Sovereign: King CARL XVI GUSTAF; succeeded to the throne September 19, 1973, following the death of his grandfather, King GUSTAF VI ADOLF.

Heir Apparent: Crown Princess VICTORIA Ingrid Alice Désirée, daughter of the king.

Prime Minister: Fredrik REINFELDT (Moderate Party); elected by the *Riksdag* on October 5, 2006, to succeed Göran PERSSON (Social Democrats) following the legislative elections of September 17; formed new government on October 6, 2006; formed new minority government on October 5, 2010, following the legislative elections on September 19.

THE COUNTRY

Situated on the Baltic side of the Scandinavian Peninsula and projecting north of the Arctic Circle, Sweden is the largest and most populous of the Scandinavian countries. The indigenous population, about 70 percent of which belongs (at least nominally) to the Evangelical Lutheran Church, is generally homogeneous except for some 400,000 Finns spread over the country and a Sámi (Lapp) minority in the north. In addition, there are more than 1 million resident aliens who have arrived since World War II. Early on, the resident aliens came mainly from Finland and Mediterranean countries

such as Greece, Turkey, and Yugoslavia. However, following Sweden's accession to the European Union (EU) in 1995, people from various EU countries have also immigrated to Sweden. In addition, Sweden has granted permanent residency to an increasing number of asylum-seeking refugees from Africa and Asia, including a large group from Iraq. Immigration has become an important political issue recently, in part in regard to the Muslim population (currently estimated at approximately 500,000).

In 2007, approximately 78 percent of women ages 25–64 were in the labor force, compared with close to 85 percent of men. Women won 45 percent of the seats in the *Riksdag* in 2010, making it one of the most gender-balanced parliaments in the world. Women are equally well represented in the cabinet.

Although only 7 percent of the land is cultivated and agriculture, forestry, and fishing contribute only 2 percent of GDP, Sweden is almost self-sufficient in foodstuffs, while its wealth of resources has enabled it to assume an important position among the world's industrial nations. A major producer and exporter of wood, paper products, and iron ore, Sweden also is a leading manufacturer of vehicles, pharmaceuticals, chemicals, and telecom equipment. The creative sector (including design, music, fashion, and gastronomy) is increasingly contributing to a healthy export income. Leading trading partners are Germany, Norway, and Denmark.

Despite socialist leadership throughout most of the post–World War II period, the private sector accounts for 80 percent of Sweden's output, although approximately 30 percent of jobs are in the public sector. The government provides generous benefits in education (universities are free), health care, and "social protection," and as a result, an estimated 44 percent of the average worker's labor costs are deducted in taxes.

The government decided in late 1997 that Sweden would not participate, despite meeting the economic prerequisites, in launching the EU's Economic and Monetary Union (EMU). Although the possibility of eventual membership remained open, Swedish voters again rejected adoption of the euro in a 2003 referendum.

Sweden's economy was hit hard by the global financial crisis in 2008, as exports weakened and investment declined significantly. In late 2008 the government approved a $2.4-billion cut in income taxes, $205 billion in aid to banks, and a three-year stimulus package, which included assistance to local municipalities and infrastructure development. GDP contracted by 5 percent in 2009, but the International Monetary Fund (IMF) praised the government for its "prompt and appropriate policy responses" to help ensure financial stability, and rapidly rising export demand (particularly from Germany and Asia) subsequently underpinned a remarkably swift economic recovery. Growth of 5.9 percent and 4.0 percent was achieved in 2010 and 2011, respectively, but the economy weakened significantly (only 0.8 percent growth) in 2012 under the influence of declining demand for Swedish exports from stagnant European economies and the conclusion of domestic stimulus measures. Meanwhile, unemployment, although down from a crisis-period high of 9 percent, remained troublesome at 7.5 percent.

GOVERNMENT AND POLITICS

Political background. A major European power in the 17th century, Sweden later declined in relative importance but nevertheless retained a significant regional position, including linkage with Norway in a union under the Swedish crown from 1814 to 1905. (Finland was a part of Sweden from the Middle Ages until 1809, when the two countries peacefully separated.) Neutrality in both world wars enabled Sweden to concentrate on its industrial development and the perfection of a welfare state under the auspices of the Social Democratic Labor Party (*Socialdemokratiska Arbetareparti*—SdAP, currently widely referenced as the Social Democrats), which was in power almost continuously from 1932 to 1976, either alone or in coalition with other parties.

In the *Riksdag* election of 1968 the Social Democrats under Tage ERLANDER won an absolute majority for the first time in 22 years. Having led the party and the country since 1946, Erlander was succeeded as party chair and prime minister by Olof PALME in October 1969. Although diminished support for the Social Democrats was reflected in the parliamentary elections of 1970 and 1973, the party maintained control until September 1976, when voters, disturbed by a climate of increasing labor unrest and inflation as well as declining economic growth, awarded a combined majority of 180 legislative seats to the Center Party (*Centerpartiet*), the Moderate Coalition Party (*Moderata Samlingspartiet*—MSP, currently referenced as the Moderates), and the Liberal People's Party (*Folkpartiet Liberalerna*—FpL, currently widely referenced as the Liberal Party or the Liberals). On October 8 a coalition government was formed under Center Party leader Thorbjörn FÄLLDIN. However, policy differences between the antinuclear Center Party and the pronuclear Moderates and FpL forced the government to resign in October 1978, providing the opportunity for Ola ULLSTEN to form a minority FpL government.

Following the election of September 16, 1979, a center-right coalition with a one-seat majority was formed by the Center Party, Moderates, and FpL, with the Center Party's Fälldin returning to the premiership. The Moderates withdrew from the coalition on May 4, 1981, in a dispute over tax reform, although they tacitly agreed to support the two-party government to avoid an early election and the likely return to power of the Social Democrats. Fälldin continued in office until the election of September 19, 1982, in which the Social Democrats obtained a three-seat plurality over nonsocialists, permitting Palme to return as head of a Social Democrats' minority administration supported in Parliament by the Left Party-Communists (*Vänsterpartiet-Kommunisterna*—VpK). Although the center-right FpL gained substantially at the balloting of September 15, 1985, the Palme government remained in power with the support of the VpK.

On February 28, 1986, Prime Minister Palme was assassinated in Stockholm by an unidentified gunman, the first postwar West European head of government to be killed while in office. (A drug addict was convicted of the crime in 1989, but he was subsequently freed by an appellate court.) Deputy Prime Minister Ingvar CARLSSON assumed interim control of the government and was confirmed as Palme's successor on March 12. The Social Democrats retained their dominant position in the election of September 18, 1988, with the conservative parties losing ground and the Green Ecology Party (*Miljöpartiet de Gröna*—MjP, widely referenced as the Greens) entering the *Riksdag* for the first time with 20 seats.

Prime Minister Carlsson resigned on February 15, 1990, after losing a key vote on an economic austerity plan that would have placed upper-middle-income taxpayers in a 72 percent bracket while freezing both prices and wages through 1991. However, he was returned to office 11 days later after accepting a substantially watered-down tax schedule that left most of the country's budgetary problems unresolved. As a result, the Social Democrats fell to a total of 138 seats out of 349 at triennial legislative balloting on September 15, 1991. Meanwhile, the aggregate strength of the four traditional "bourgeois" parties—the Center Party, Moderates, Liberals, and Christian Democratic Community Party (*Kristdemokratiska Samhällspartiet*—KdS)—rose to 170 seats, due mainly to gains by the Moderates and the Christian Democrats. While the Left Party (*Vänsterpartiet*, formerly the VpK) lost ground and the Greens disappeared from the *Riksdag,* the populist New Democracy (*Ny Demokrati*—NyD) party won a startling 25 seats in its first parliamentary race. The result was the installation of a four-party center-right administration under the Moderates' Carl BILDT that was 5 seats short of an assured parliamentary majority and therefore dependent on the NyD's external support.

Faced with the country's worst postwar economic crisis, Prime Minister Bildt and opposition Social Democratic leader Carlsson on September 20, 1992, concluded an unprecedented economic pact that called for tax increases and major public spending cuts over five years. However, the new cooperative spirit was badly dented in November, when the Social Democrats declined to support specific austerity measures, obliging the Swedish authorities to allow the krona to float and thereby to depreciate by 9 percent. Further welfare spending cuts mandated by the 1993–1994 budget ended the already frayed consensus.

Through 1993, the government relied on the NyD in critical parliamentary divisions, but in late March 1994 the NyD withdrew its support following the resignation the previous month of its leader, Count Ian WACHMEISTER. In campaigning for the fall legislative election, the ruling coalition derived some benefit from a modest economic upturn, but continuing high unemployment and uncertainty about the future of the welfare state gave the opposition Social Democrats powerful ammunition. Overhanging the campaign was the issue of Sweden's projected membership in the EU from January 1995, on which negotiations had been successfully concluded on March 1.

The outcome of the legislative balloting on September 18, 1994, was a decisive swing to the left, with the Social Democrats and the ex-Communist Left Party both gaining ground sharply and the left-oriented Greens reentering the *Riksdag* after a three-year absence. Of the outgoing coalition parties, the Moderates held their vote, but the other three lost seats, while the NyD disappeared from parliament altogether. Having rejected the Liberals' offer of a majority center-left coalition, the Social Democrats proceeded to form a minority one-party government headed by Carlsson, with qualified pledges of external support from the Left Party and the Greens.

Attention subsequently turned to the EU referendum set for November 13, 1994, with the pro-accession center-right parties, Social Democratic leadership, and business community countering a lively anti-EU coalition of the Left Party, the Greens, and many rank-and-file Social Democrats. The result, in a turnout of 82.4 percent, was a 52.2 to 46.9 percent vote in favor of accession.

On August 18, 1995, Prime Minister Carlsson unexpectedly announced that he would retire in March 1996, more than two years before the expiration of his government's mandate. Finance Minister Göran PERSSON was elected as chair of the ruling party on March 15, 1996, and he was sworn in as prime minister on March 17 to head a substantially reshuffled cabinet.

In the general election of September 20, 1998, the Social Democratic legislative representation fell from 161 to 131 seats, with the Moderates finishing second with 82 seats. The poor performance by the Social Democrats was largely seen as a result of voter dissatisfaction with the government's fiscally conservative policies and its willingness to make cuts in the welfare system. Once again relying on the qualified support of the Left Party and the Greens to avoid a legislative nonconfidence vote, Persson announced a reshuffled Social Democratic minority government on October 6.

The Social Democrats secured 144 seats in the September 15, 2002, legislative election, the legislative term of office having been permanently extended to four years. Running on a platform of tax cuts, including abolition of wealth and real estate taxes, the Moderates won only 55 seats, many Swedes having apparently concluded that the party's policies would endanger social benefits. Meanwhile, the Liberals made surprising gains, analysts attributing the increase, at least in part, to the party's call for a language test for citizenship. Persson immediately ruled out giving government positions to either the Left Party or the Green Party because of their opposition to adoption of the euro. However, the Social Democrats secured parliamentary support from the Left Party and the Moderates to form a minority government.

On September 10, 2003, Foreign Minister Anna LINDH, a key proponent in the pro-euro campaign, was assassinated in a Stockholm department store. On September 14, Swedish voters rejected adoption of the euro by 56 percent to 42 percent, despite the measure's strong backing by Prime Minister Persson.

In the September 17, 2006, parliamentary election, the Social Democrats won a plurality of 130 seats but lost power to the Alliance for Sweden (*Allians för Sverige*), whose member parties (the Moderates, Center Party, Liberals, and Christian Democrats) won a combined 178 seats. The chair of the Moderates, Fredrik REINFELDT, who was endorsed by all parties in the Alliance, was appointed prime minister on October 5. His new center-right coalition government named on October 6 included the four Alliance parties.

Tax cuts became a cornerstone of the governing coalition despite socialist concerns that the tax base supporting the welfare state would be eroded and thereby create a greater divide between rich and poor. The Alliance also embarked on a widespread effort to privatize state-owned assets by selling shares in some 50 publicly owned companies to raise revenue to pay down the public debt as well as to help create more jobs and foreign investment.

Following the influx of thousands of refugees from Iraq, the government in 2007 tightened its immigration policies, ruling that, in the case of asylum seekers from Afghanistan, Iraq, and Somalia, Sweden could legally deport immigrants unless it was proved that they would be threatened if they returned home. Additionally, the *Rikstag* approved legislation denying publicly funded health care to illegal immigrants. At the same time, relations with the global Muslim community were deeply strained by the publication in 2007 of a controversial cartoon by Swedish artist Lars VILKS depicting the prophet Mohammed. (Vilks claimed he meant to test the boundaries of speech and press freedoms in Sweden, not provoke Muslims.) Meanwhile, several Swedish newspapers republished the cartoon as a show of solidarity with Vilks and a defense of "Scandanavian values of openness."

Amid mounting concerns over potential terrorist attacks, the *Riksdag* in June 2008 narrowly passed one of the most comprehensive—and divisive—government surveillance laws in Europe. The law, effective January 1, 2009, authorized the defense department to scan all cross-border phone calls, e-mails, and faxes without a court order. The new security measures provoked outrage from the youth wings of the governing coalition parties as well as from journalists, who were not exempt from possible surveillance. The public backlash prompted the *Riksdag,* spurred by the Alliance, to adopt amendments in September providing for judicial oversight of the electronic surveillance. Meanwhile, though Sweden's military budget was cut significantly, the government dropped plans to disband several military units in the wake of security concerns related to Russia's military attacks in Georgia.

In March 2009 the government announced a major restructuring of the military starting in 2010. The plan called for an end within five years to the century-old practice of universal conscription in favor of a professional army as well as an increase in the number of Swedish troops by 50 percent, to 50,000. The Social Democrats criticized the plan, saying they didn't believe the military could meet its goals by voluntary conscription.

Prime Minister Reinfeldt formed a new minority government (comprising the four Alliance parties) on October 5, 2010, following the September 19 *Riksdag* balloting in which the Alliance parties won a plurality of 173 seats, followed by the Red-Green coalition (the Social Democrats, Left Party, and Greens) with 156 seats. For the first time in its history, the right-wing, anti-immigration Sweden Democrats won representation in parliament with 20 seats.

Constitution and government. The present Swedish constitution retains the general form of the old governmental structure, but the king is now a figurehead (formerly, as nominal head of government, he appointed the prime minister and served as commander in chief of the armed forces). In 1979 the *Riksdag* took final action on making women eligible for succession; thus the present king's daughter, VICTORIA, born in 1977, has become the heir apparent.

The chief executive officer, the prime minister, is nominated by the speaker of the *Riksdag* and confirmed by the whole house. The prime minister appoints other members of the cabinet, which functions as a policy-drafting body. Routine administration is carried out largely by independent administrative boards (*centrala ämbetsverk*). Legislative authority is vested in the *Riksdag,* which has been a unicameral body since 1971. The judicial system is headed by the Supreme Court (*Högsta Domstolen*) and includes 6 courts of appeal (*hovrätt*) and 100 district courts (*tingsrätt*). There is a parallel system of administrative courts, while the *Riksdag* appoints four *justitieombudsmen* to maintain general oversight of both legislative and executive actions. Any proposed amendment of the constitution must be approved twice by the *Riksdag* in successive legislative terms, requiring that a general election occur between the first approval and the second.

Sweden is administratively divided into 21 counties (including Stockholm) with appointed governors and elected councils and into

290 urban and rural communes with elected councils. The 20,000-strong Sámi (Lapp) community in the north has its own local assembly.

Under legislation approved in 1996, the Evangelical Lutheran Church was effectively disestablished as the Church of Sweden on January 1, 2000, terminating a legal and financial relationship between church and state that dated from the 16th century.

Under Sweden's Mass Media Act, which was implemented in January 1977, principles of noninterference dating to the mid-1700s and embodied in the Freedom of the Press Act of 1949 were extended to all media. Sweden is currently listed by Reporters Without Borders as one of the top countries in regard to press freedom.

Foreign relations. Sweden has not participated in any war nor joined any military alliance since 1814. Unlike Denmark, Iceland, and Norway, it declined to enter the North Atlantic Treaty Organization (NATO) in 1949, while its determination to safeguard its neutrality is backed by an impressive defense system. A strong supporter of international cooperation, Sweden participates in the United Nations and all its related agencies; in 1975 Sweden became the first industrial nation to meet a standard set by the Organization for Economic Cooperation and Development (OECD), allocating a full 1 percent of its GNP to aid for developing countries. Sweden also attaches importance to regional cooperation through the Nordic Council, while in 1960 it was a founding member of the European Free Trade Association (EFTA), although its membership in that body ceased upon its accession to the EU in 1995.

Stockholm's traditionally good relations with Moscow were strained during the 1980s and early 1990s by numerous incidents involving Soviet submarines in Swedish waters and intrusions of Russian planes into the country's airspace. However, during an official visit to Moscow by Prime Minister Carl Bildt from February 4–7, 1993, the long-standing controversy appeared to end when the Russians for the first time formally admitted to violations of Swedish territorial waters.

Citing the end of the Cold War and the need to improve its economy by means of increased trade, Sweden applied for membership in the European Community (EC, subsequently the EU) on July 1, 1991. To pave the way, it became a signatory of the European Economic Area (EEA) treaty between the EC and certain EFTA countries on May 2, 1992. Sweden also placed emphasis on post-Soviet regional cooperation, becoming a founding member of the ten-nation Council of the Baltic Sea States in March 1992 and of the Barents Euro-Arctic Council (comprising the five Nordic countries and Russia) in January 1993. Two months later Sweden modified its tradition of neutrality by agreeing to join a NATO military maneuver in August, and in May 1994, Sweden enrolled in NATO's Partnership for Peace program for the neutral and former communist states of Europe and the ex-USSR. Following referendum approval in November 1994 and *Riksdag* endorsement (by a vote of 278–36) in December, Sweden acceded to the EU on January 1, 1995.

Sweden became involved in Afghanistan in 2002 as a member of the International Security Assistance Force (ISAF), focusing primarily on humanitarian support. Meanwhile, following the U.S. invasion of Iraq in 2003, thousands of Iraqi refugees immigrated to Sweden, and Sweden adopted a prominent role in efforts to rebuild Iraq.

In 2008 Sweden deployed personnel to the NATO peacekeeping mission in Kosovo.

In May 2008 Denmark, Finland, Iceland, Norway, and Sweden met to discuss greater Nordic cooperation on defense matters, specifically agreements on a joint response to emergencies, as well as cooperation in defense procurement and coast guard activities. The arrangement was meant to respect each country's differing obligations to NATO and EU membership. Concern over Russia's conduct of foreign policy manners and its heavy use of the Baltic Sea for shipping prompted the talks.

Tensions heightened between Sweden and Russia in the wake of the latter's military intervention in Georgia in August 2008. Among other things, Sweden suspended all military cooperation with Russia (the two countries periodically had conducted joint military maneuvers). In 2009, Sweden negotiated with NATO, Norway, and Finland to collaborate on a Nordic air control operation (which Baltic states could later join) as a defense measure for the participating nations.

Belarus expelled Sweden's diplomatic corps in August 2012 after two Swedish citizens had organized an airdrop over Belarus of teddy bears carrying prodemocracy messages.

Current issues. Although Prime Minister Reinfeldt continued to receive credit for his handling of the effects on Sweden of the 2008 financial crisis, growth stagnated in 2012. Concern also focused on the possible impact on Sweden of the financial crisis in the eurozone, Reinfeldt expressing major reservations about the proposed deepening of EU economic and monetary integration as a means of stabilizing conditions. Reinfeldt argued that such measures would inappropriately penalize well-run countries such as Sweden.

Perhaps with an eye on the elections due by September 2014, the government introduced a stimulus plan in late 2012 that provided additional funds for infrastructure and other economic development while lowering corporate tax rates. Meanwhile, it appeared that the question of possible NATO accession would remain on the back burner until after the elections, although some observers suggested that the country's "defense readiness" had been deteriorating.

Nearly a week of riots in May 2013 in several suburbs of Stockholm that are heavily populated by immigrants severely jolted the nation and raised questions over the efficacy of immigrant absorption policies, previously heralded as a progressive model for the rest of the world. Prime Minister Reinfeldt attributed the unrest (triggered when a man, allegedly waving a machete, was killed in his home by police attempting to serve a warrant) to "hooliganism." However, others cited festering anti-police sentiment among young immigrants facing high unemployment and perceived racism as a contributing factor. Some analysts also noted that several decades of curtailment of previous "cradle-to-grave" social welfare benefits had resulted in rising income inequities.

POLITICAL PARTIES

In advance of the 2006 general election the Moderate Party, Center Party, Liberal People's Party, and Christian Democratic Party formed the Alliance for Sweden (*Allians för Sverige*). The parties in the coalition fielded their own candidates for the *Riksdag* but backed a single candidate, Fredrik Reinfeldt of the Moderates, for prime minister. After securing a slight majority (178 of 349 seats) among them in the legislative poll, the four parties served in the subsequent Reinfeldt-led center-right government. The Alliance won a plurality (173 seats) in the September 2010 *Riksdag* poll, which was also contested by the center-left Red-Green coalition of the Social Democratics, Left Party, and Greens (156 seats among the three parties). Reinfeldt subsequently formed a minority government of the four Alliance parties, and the Red-Green coalition dissolved.

Government Parties:

Moderate Party (*Moderate Partiet*—MP). This party was known as the Conservative Party before the 1968 election, after which it adopted the rubric Moderate Coalition Party (*Moderata Samlingspartiet*—MSP). However, it was subsequently widely referenced simply as the Moderate Party, that name being formally adopted in 2007. The party currently refers to itself as the Moderates (*Moderaterna*), a usage (rather than initials) that is widely employed in the media and government circles as well.

The party was originally organized as a vehicle for the financial and business communities and advocated tax cuts and reduced governmental interference in the economy. It favored a robust defense policy and strongly supported Sweden's accession to the EU. The MSP joined a center-left coalition government in 1976 but withdrew in 1981 after disagreeing with a tax reform plan. Its *Riksdag* representation dropped from 86 seats in 1982 to 66 in 1988 but rose again to 80 in 1991, when it formed a center-right coalition with the FpL, Center Party, and the Christian Democrats under the premiership of Carl Bildt. The MSP retained 80 seats in the 1994 national balloting (on a slightly higher vote share of 22.4 percent), but an overall electoral swing to the left returned the party to opposition. The MSP was unable to improve its position substantially in the September 1998 *Riksdag* election (82 seats and a 22.9 vote share), thwarting Bildt's determined campaign to return to the prime ministership. Bildt, a prominent EU/UN negotiator in Yugoslavia since 1995, resigned as party chair in mid-1999 and was succeeded by Bo LUNDGREN, a former minister of finance.

In the 2002 general election, the party's vote share dropped to 15.2 percent, good for 55 seats. As a result, Lundgren announced his resignation as party chair. Fredrik Reinfeldt replaced him in October 2003 and subsequently spearheaded the formation of the four-party Alliance for Sweden (see introductory text, above).

In a bid to capture the middle ground of Swedish politics prior to the 2006 election, the party dropped its call for radical tax cuts, instead emphasizing support for public services. It won 97 of the Alliance's 178 seats on a vote share of 26.2 percent in the legislative poll. Following Reinfeldt's installation as prime minister, the Moderate-led Alliance embarked on a plan to liberalize the economy through the privatization of state-owned assets and reform of the welfare system, including a reduction in employers' social security contributions, restrictions on access to unemployment and sick benefits, and efforts to boost employment.

The Reinfeldt administration was widely praised for its handling of the effects on Sweden of the global financial crisis of 2008–2009, and the Moderates improved to 107 seats (on a vote share of 30.1 percent) in the 2010 *Riksdag* balloting.

Leaders: Fredrik REINFELDT (Chair and Prime Minister), Per WESTERBERG (Speaker of Parliament), Anna Kinberg BATRA (Parliamentary Leader), Sten NORDIN (Mayor of Stockholm), Kent PERSSON (Secretary General).

Liberal People's Party (*Folkpartiet Liberalerna*—FpL). Originally formed as a parliamentary group in 1895, the first *Folkpartiet* merged with the Liberal Coalition Party in 1900. The two split in 1923 over alcohol issues and reunited in 1934 as the FpL. (The grouping has since usually been referred to simply as the Liberal Party or the Liberals.) The party draws support from rural free-church movements as well as from professionals and intellectuals. Favoring socially progressive policies that also strive to acknowledge individual responsibility, the FpL has sought the cooperation of the Center Party (below) on many issues, promoting "knowledge, work, and security" in its party platform. The FpL lost half of its parliamentary representation in the 1982 general election, and in July 1984 former prime minister Ola Ullsten resigned as chair "to make way for more dynamic influences."

In the September 1985 balloting, the FpL gained 30 additional *Riksdag* seats for a total of 51, but its representation fell in the next two ballots. Nevertheless, the party entered a four-party center-right coalition in 1991.

After another electoral setback in 1994 (26 seats on a 7.2 percent vote share), the Liberals reverted to opposition status, with Bengt WESTERBERG standing down as party chair. He was succeeded by Lars LEIJONBORG. In June 1996 the FpL announced a relaunch as a "bourgeois left" party emphasizing the fight against unemployment and ethnic separation. The party fell to 17 seats in the September 1998 general election but made dramatic gains in the 2002 election, winning 13.3 percent of the vote and 48 seats in the *Riksdag*.

The FpL secured 28 of the Alliance for Sweden's 178 seats in the 2006 *Riksdag* poll on a vote share of 7.5 percent. Leijonborg subsequently stepped down as party chair; he was succeeded by Jan Björkland, who was also named education minister in the subsequent four-party Alliance government. Under Björkland's leadership, the party moved toward what was described as conservative liberalism, taking tougher positions on crime, school, and discipline and strengthening its antidrugs stance. The party secured 24 of the Alliance's 173 seats in the 2010 *Riksdag* balloting on a vote share of 7.1 percent.

Leaders: Jan BJÖRKLUND (Chair), Johan PEHRSON (Parliamentary Leader), Nina LARSSON (Secretary General).

Center Party (*Centerpartiet*). Farmers' representatives first began breaking away from other parties to promote rural rights in 1910, and in 1922 they formally launched the Agrarian Party (the precursor to the Center Party). In return for agricultural subsidies, the party began to support the Social Democrats in the 1930s, occasionally serving as a junior partner in coalition with the Social Democrats. Since adopting its present name in 1958, the Center Party, campaigning for decentralization of government and industry and for reduced impact of government on the lives of individuals, has developed nationwide strength, including support from the larger urban centers. Opposition to nuclear power became another major party stance in the 1970s.

A major advance to 86 seats in the 1976 election enabled the Center Party to head a center-right coalition until 1978 under Thorbjörn Fälldin, who returned to the premiership in 1979 despite his party's 22-seat decline in that year's election. In opposition after a further slump to 56 seats in 1982, the Center Party continued to lose ground in 1985 (43 seats).

At a congress in June 1986, Karin SÖDER was elected as party leader to succeed Fälldin, who had resigned from the post six months earlier because of his party's poor showing in the 1985 election. However, Söder (Sweden's first female party leader) was forced to step down in March 1987 for health reasons. The party's fortunes continued to decline in 1988 (42 seats) and 1991 (31 seats). In the September 1994 election, the Center Party was reduced to 27 seats (on a vote share of 7.7 percent) and again went into opposition.

Party chair Olof JOHANSSON resigned in April 1998, and he was succeeded in June by Lennart DALÉUS, a staunch opponent of nuclear power who had led the party's successful 1980 referendum on decommissioning nuclear plants. Daléus promptly announced that the party would no longer cooperate with the Social Democrats and also voiced reservations about the Moderates. He hoped to be part of a centrist government following the September 1998 general election, but the Center Party fell to 18 seats on a vote share of 5.1 percent. Daléus was replaced as party leader by Maud Olofsson in 2001.

In the 2002 general election, the Center Party won 6.2 percent of the vote and 22 seats. It secured 29 of the Alliance for Sweden's 178 seats in the 2006 *Riksdag* poll on a vote share of 7.8 percent, and Olofsson was appointed enterprise and energy minister and deputy prime minister. With pressure mounting from coalition partners, Olofsson convinced the Center Party in February 2009 to reverse its long-standing position against nuclear power.

The Center Party declined to 23 seats in the 2010 *Riksdag* balloting on a vote share of 6.6 percent. Annie Lööf, 28, was elected party chair on September 23, 2011, and six days later she was named minister for enterprise, saying she wanted the party to focus on green issues and the underprivileged.

Leaders: Annie LÖÖF (Chair), Maud OLOFSSON, Anders W. JONSSON (Parliamentary Leader), Michael ARTHURSSON (Secretary General).

Christian Democrats (*Kristdemokraterna*—Kd). Also referenced as the Christian Democratic Party, this group was formed in 1964 as the Christian Democratic Coalition (*Kristen Demokratisk Samling*—KDS) to promote Christian values in politics. The group claimed a membership of more than 25,000 but for two decades was unable to gain *Riksdag* representation, although it secured a growing number of local and state seats. In September 1984 it entered into an electoral pact with the Center Party, thereby securing its first legislative seat in 1985 despite a marginal 2.6 percent vote share.

The KDS adopted the name Christian Democratic Community Party (*Kristdemokratiska Samhällspartiet*—KdS) in 1987. Excluded completely from representation in 1988, the KdS won 26 legislative seats in 1991 and joined a center-right coalition. Reduced to 15 seats (and 4.1 percent of the vote) in the 1994 balloting, the KdS went into opposition. In 1996 the party was renamed again, to the Christian Democratic Party, widely referenced simply as the Christian Democrats (Kd). Opposing adoption of the euro and stressing "cleaner politics," the Christian Democrats ran the most successful campaign in the party's history for the general election of September 1998, winning 42 seats (a gain of 27) on a vote share of 11.8 percent.

Göran Hägglund was elected party leader on April 3, 2004, succeeding Alf SVENSSON, who had been Sweden's longest-serving party leader, with 31 years in the post. In the 2006 legislative election it received 6.5 percent of the vote and 24 of the Alliance for Sweden's 178 seats.

Following the Alliance's announcement in September 2007 of increased fuel taxes (an effort to reduce greenhouse gases from emissions), the Christian Democrats were accused of betraying campaign promises to lower fuel prices. This criticism was spearheaded by their base of voters in rural areas, which had less access to public transportation.

Distancing his party from the growing popularity of the Sweden Democrats, Hägglund criticized that right-wing group in 2008, accusing the Sweden Democrats of being xenophobic and spreading Nazi ideology.

In April 2009, the Christian Democrats were the only party in parliament to dissent on a bill that legalized same-sex marriage. The party received 4.7 percent of the vote in the June European Parliamentary election, thereby retaining one seat. The Christian Democrats won 19 seats in the 2010 *Riksdag* poll on a vote share of 5.6 percent.

Leaders: Göran HÄGGLUND (Chair), Emma HENRIKSSON (Parliamentary Leader), Acko Ankarberg JOHANSSON (Secretary General).

Other Legislative Parties:

Social Democrats (*Socialdemokraterna*). The Social Democrats is currently the most widely used rubric for the party also referenced as the Social Democratic Labor Party (*Socialdemokratiska Arbetareparti*—SdAP) or the Social Democratic Party. Formed in the 1880s and long a dominant force in Swedish politics, the party has a "pragmatic" socialist outlook. During more than four decades of virtually uninterrupted power from 1932, it refrained from nationalizing major industries but gradually increased government economic planning and control over the business sector. When the party's representation in the *Riksdag* dropped to 152 seats in 1976, the Social Democrats were forced, despite their sizable plurality, to move into opposition. The party regained control of the government in 1982 and, despite a further reduction, maintained control in 1985 and 1988 with the aid of the VpK (see Left Party, below). There were few, if any, changes in party ideology and practice following the assassination of Prime Minister Olof Palme and the accession of his deputy, Ingvar Carlsson, to the prime ministership in March 1986. The Social Democrats were again forced into opposition in the legislative poll of September 1991, when the party's seat tally fell from 156 to 138. It staged a comeback in 1994, winning 161 seats and 45.3 percent of the vote.

Carlsson's surprise announcement in August 1995 of his impending departure as party leader and prime minister, combined with rapid public disenchantment with the EU, yielded a dramatic slump in support for the Social Democrats to only 28.1 percent in the September European Parliament balloting, when three of the seven Social Democrats elected were critical of EU membership. The leadership mantle subsequently passed to the finance minister, Göran Persson, who secured the position on March 15, 1996, two days before he was appointed prime minister.

Persson led the party to a strong showing in the September 2002 general elections, with the Social Democrats winning 39.8 percent of the vote and 144 seats (up from 131 seats on a vote share of 36.6 percent in 1998). The party was later thrown into confusion by the assassination of Foreign Minister Anna LINDH, who was considered by many to be the natural successor to Prime Minister Persson.

While the party officially was in favor of the EMU in 2004, several prominent party members, including Margot WALLSTRÖM, vice president of the European Commission, openly declared that they were against adoption of the euro.

Despite the healthy state of the Swedish economy, the Social Democrats did not win control of the parliament in the 2006 election, though it held the most seats (130 seats) of any single party, on a vote share of 34.9 percent. Following the election, Göran Persson stepped down as party leader, and former deputy premier Mona SAHLIN was elected party chair, becoming the first woman to hold that position in the party. Subsequently, eroding membership, especially among urbanites, became a cause for serious concern within the party.

The Social Democrats objected to but took few steps to stop the subsequent efforts of the Alliance for Sweden to pare back the social welfare system and privatize state-owned assets. In October 2008 Sahlin announced the formation of the Red-Green (*De Rödgröna*) alliance between the Social Democrats and the Greens. Sahlin pointedly excluded the former communist Left Party from the initial alliance, prompting criticism from trade unions and other sectors of the Social Democrats. Consequently, Sahlin reopened negotiations with the Left Party, and by December key differences over economic policy had been resolved, with all sides agreeing to a common economic proposal. The proposal included the Left Party's dropping its opposition to the maintenance of a state budget surplus and a spending ceiling.

The Social Democrats fell to 112 seats on a vote share of 30.7 percent in the 2010 *Riksdag* poll, barely maintaining the party's position as the leading legislative grouping. In the wake of the party's worst electoral performance in nearly 100 years, Sahlin relinquished her party leadership post at a special party congress in March 2011. New party leader Hakan JUHOLT vowed to restore left-wing policies, including ending child poverty, cutting youth unemployment, and reviewing the privatization of the energy and rail sectors.

Prominent labor union leader Stefan Löfven was elected party president in January 2012 following Juholt's resignation. The party's popularity subsequently rose, according to public opinion polls, as Löfven called for the easing of government austerity measures.

Leaders: Stefa LÖFVEN (Chair), Mikael DAMBERG (Parliamentary Leader), Carin JÄMTIN (Secretary General).

Left Party (*Vänsterpartiet*). Originally formed in 1917 as the Left Social Democratic Party (*Vänster Socialdemokratiska Partiet*—VSdP), the party was renamed the Communist Party (*Kommunistiska Partiet*—KP) in 1921 and the Left Party–Communists (*Vänsterpartiet–Kommunisterna*—VpK) in 1967. In May 1990 the party adopted its present name.

Long before the decline of communism in Eastern Europe, the party pursued a "revisionist," or "Eurocommunist," policy based on distinctive Swedish conditions. This posture provoked considerable dissent within the party before the withdrawal of a pro-Moscow faction in early 1977. Following the 1982 election, the party agreed to support a new government of the Social Democrats; the VpK's voting strength became crucial following the declining fortunes of the Social Democrats in 1985 and 1988. Having won 16 seats in the 1991 general election, the Left Party went into full opposition to the new center-right coalition government. In the 1994 balloting the party achieved its best result since 1948, winning 22 seats on a 6.2 percent vote share.

Having unsuccessfully opposed Sweden's accession to the EU, the Left Party advanced in the September 1995 European Parliament balloting and nearly doubled its parliamentary representation in the September 1998 elections, winning 43 seats on a vote share of 12 percent, its best showing since its formation. The party's legislative support subsequently remained crucial in the continuation of the minority government of the Social Democrats.

Gudrun SCHYMAN was leader of the Left Party between 1993 and 2003, promoting feminism as well as socialism. Lars OHLY replaced Schyman in a party election on February 20, 2004. Ohly's election highlighted a division between modernist and traditional wings of the party, with Ohly, a former railroad worker, representing the traditionalist wing. The party faced a possible split in January 2005, largely caused by Ohly's insistence (subsequently retracted) on calling himself a communist.

In the 2006 election, the Left Party won 5.8 percent of the vote, securing 22 seats. Efforts to modernize the party and address its communist past failed following an unsuccessful challenge to Ohly's leadership in June 2008 by Staffan NORBERG. In December the Left Party entered into the Red-Green coalition with the Social Democrats and the Greens (see Social Democrats, above, for details).

In the wake of the global economic recession, the Left Party in 2009 advocated an increase in state ownership and control of Swedish banks, including the proposed launch of a new state-owned investment bank.

Prior to the 2010 *Riksdag* balloting, the Left Party announced it would formally join a cabinet for the first time if the Red-Green coalition won a legislative majority. However, the Red-Greens fell short in that quest, securing 156 of 349 seats (19 seats for the Left Party on a vote share of 5.6 percent).

Ohly resigned as party chair in January 2012, and he was succeeded by Jonas Sjöstedt, a member of the *Riksdag* and former labor union leader.

In response to the riots near Stockholm in May 2013, Left Party leaders accused the government of having contributed to an erosion of social services, which had left the immigrant population segregated, "stigmatized," and bereft of opportunities for future advancement.

Leaders: Jonas SJÖSTEDT (Chair), Hans LINDE (Parliamentary Leader), Aron ETZLER (Secretary).

Green Party (*Miljöpartiet de Gröna*—MjG). Established in 1981, the Greens (as the party is most commonly referenced) benefited in the 1988 election from an upsurge of popular interest in environmental issues. The party advocated tax reduction for low-income wage earners, increased charges for energy use, and heightened penalties for pollution by commercial establishments and motor vehicle operators. It also called for the phasing out of nuclear-generated electricity and curtailment of highway construction. The party's parliamentary representation plummeted from 20 seats in 1988 to none in 1991 but recovered to 18 seats (on 5 percent of the vote) in 1994. The Greens opposed EU membership, which was approved in the November 1994 referendum.

The party declined to 16 seats in the 1998 general election on a vote share of 4.5 percent but agreed to continue to support the minority government of the Social Democrats on confidence motions. The Greens participated in negotiations with center-right parties after the election before deciding to renew its agreement with the Social Democrats. In the 2006 election the Greens won 19 *Riksdag* seats on 5.2 percent of the vote. It improved to 25 seats (third best party) in the 2010 *Riksdag* poll on a vote share of 7.3 percent as part of the Red-Green coalition led by the Social Democrats. The Greens subsequently resisted reported overtures from the Alliance for Sweden to participate in the new government.

Instead of leaders, the party has two spokespersons—a man and a woman.

Leaders: Åsa ROMSON and Gustav FRIDOLIN (Spokespersons); Gunvor G. ERICSON (Parliamentary Leader); Anders WALLNER (Secretary General).

Sweden Democrats (*Sverigedemokraterna*—Sd). A far-right, nationalist party that was established in 1988, the Sweden Democrats (considered by some to have links to neo-Nazi ideology) won 2.9 percent of the vote in the 2006 *Rikstag* election. The party platform included encouraging higher birthrates, stopping the development of a "multicultural society," promoting a robust national defense, and advocating harsher prison sentences. At the annual congress in May 2008, the Sweden Democrats called for an end to the special status rights of Sámi herders. However, the Sweden Democrats gained the most attention for the party's extreme anti-immigration stance, which called for a reduction in legal immigration by 90 percent. The party's harshest rhetoric was aimed at Muslims, party leader Jimmie Åkesson describing the growth of the Muslim population as Sweden's "biggest foreign threat since World War II."

In the 2010 *Riksdag* poll, the party entered the legislature for the first time with 20 seats (more than the Christian Democrats or the Left Party) on a vote share of 5.7 percent, sending a shockwave through the nation's political landscape. Although some analysts predicted that the Sweden Democrats might play a kingmaker's role in the formation of the next government, all of the other legislative parties denounced the platform of the Sweden Democrats and announced they would not work with that party.

In 2011 it was reported that the Sweden Democrats had adopted a more progressive stance on gay rights and had dropped its opposition to foreign adoptions and its support for the death penalty. In September, a member of parliament quit the party to serve as an independent, thus reducing the party's representation in the *Riksdag* to 19.

In mid-2013 the Sweden Democrats blamed the recent rioting in Stockholm's suburbs (see Current issues, above) on the government's "irresponsible" liberal immigration policies. At that time, the party was ranked third among all parties in public opinion polls.

Leaders: Jimmie ÅKESSON (Leader), Bjorn SÖDER (Parliamentary Leader and Secretary General).

Other Parties That Contested the 2010 Legislative Elections:

Feminist Initiative (*Feministiskt Initiativ*—FI). The FI was established in 2005, by, among others, former Left Party leader Gudrun Schyman, Ebba WITT-BRATTSTRÖM, and Stina SUNDBERG. (Witt-Brattström later became a vocal critic of the party, saying it was too far to the left and thus excluded some women.) The FI, which won close to 0.7 percent of the vote in the 2006 election, aims to achieve economic and social justice for women and eliminate societal complacency regarding violence against women. After the 2006 election, the FI decided to function as a feminist organization rather than a political party in order to accept state grant money for gender equality projects (Swedish law prohibits political parties from receiving state grants). However, in early 2008, the FI announced that it would reestablish itself as a political party to field candidates in upcoming local and general elections. The party won 2 percent of the vote in the June 2009 European Parliamentary election on a campaign that called for abortion to be a human right. The party won only 0.4 percent of the vote in the 2010 *Riksdag* election.

Leaders: Stina SVENSSON, Sissela Nordling BLANCO, Carl EMANUELSSON (Spokespersons).

Pirate Party (*Piratpartiet*—Pp). The Pp was founded by Rickard FALKVINGE in early 2006 to advocate for an open-information society in relation to the popular Internet-based file-sharing site Pirate Bay, which had recently been shut down by the government on charges of copyright infringement because it offered free downloads of films and music. Despite a rapidly growing membership, the Pp gained only 0.6 percent of the vote in the 2006 *Riksdag* election. The party's program mainly focused on fundamental reforms of copyright and patent laws and ensuring that citizens' rights to privacy were respected. Hence, it was a vocal opponent of the country's new far-reaching surveillance law, which permitted the government to identify people downloading material from the Internet.

The party won 7 percent of the vote and one of Sweden's 18 seats in the European Parliamentary election in June 2009, its support coming largely from males under age 30.

The Pirates secured only 0.6 percent of the vote in the 2010 *Riksdag* balloting. Meanwhile, the party announced plans to launch an Internet service provider that would not store the Internet addresses of its users and would thereby thwart government efforts to gain access to that information.

In January 2011, party founder Falkvinge announced that he was stepping down as leader to focus on promoting the party internationally. Party deputy Anna Troberg took over at the helm.

Leaders: Anna TROBERG (Chair), Jan LINDGREN (Secretary General).

Swedish Pensioners' Interest Party (*Sveriges Pensionärers Intresseparti*—SPI). Founded in 1987, the SPI seeks to secure higher social and financial status for retired people. The party won 0.5 percent of the vote in the 2006 *Riksdag* election and 0.2 percent in the 2010 legislative election. The party remains active at the regional level.

Leaders: Pelle HÖGLUND, Leif EKSTRÖM.

Health Care Party (*Sjukvårdspartiet*). Established in December 2005 by a merger of six local parties, the Health Care Party focused on people's need for appropriate health care. It gained only 0.2 percent of the vote in the 2006 parliamentary election but showed a strong regional following, in particular in the sparsely populated northern areas of Sweden. Following the 2006 elections, the local Stockholm Health Party joined the national party organization. The party received only a few votes in the 2010 *Riksdag* balloting.

Leader: Kenneth BACKGÅRD.

More than 25 other small parties participated in the 2010 *Riksdag* election, none securing more than 0.03 percent of the vote.

Other Parties:

The June List (*Junilistan*). *Junilistan*, described as mildly euroskeptic, was founded in 2003 by a group of economists led by Nils LUNDGREN, former head of the Swedish Central Bank. It surprised analysts by winning 14.4 percent of the vote (and 3 of Sweden's 19 seats) in the 2004 vote for the European Parliament. In 2006 the party won 1 of Sweden's 19 seats in the European Parliament. The June List supports Sweden's participation in the EU but rejects the idea of a European "supra-state," arguing that Sweden should retain control over Swedish national issues. In March 2008 Lundgren stepped down as party chair. He was succeeded in July by Sören WIBE. The party won only 3.6 percent of the vote in the 2009 European parliamentary elections. Party leader Wibe died in December 2010.

Leader: Brigitta SWEDENBORG.

LEGISLATURE

The unicameral ***Riksdag*** consists of 349 members serving four-year terms. (Before the 1994 election the term was three years.) Of the total, 310 are elected by proportional representation in a closed party-list system in 29 constituencies (2–34 seats each, depending on population). To gain representation a party must secure at least 4 percent of the nationwide vote or 12 percent of the vote within a constituency. The remaining 39 members are selected from a national pool designed to give absolute proportionality (based on the national vote) to all parties receiving at least 4 percent of the nationwide vote.

Following the most recent election on September 19, 2010, the seat distribution was as follows: the Social Democrats, 112; the Moderate Party, 107; the Green Party, 25; the Liberal People's Party, 24; the Center Party, 23; the Sweden Democrats, 20; the Christian Democrats, 19; and the Left Party, 19.

Speaker: Per WESTERBERG.

CABINET

[as of July 1, 2013]

Prime Minister	Fredrik Reinfeldt (MP)
Deputy Prime Minister	Jan Björklund (FpL)
Ministers	
Children and the Elderly	Maria Larsson (Kd) [f]
Culture and Sport	Lena Adelsohn Liljeroth (MP) [f]
Defense	Karin Enström (MP) [f]
Education and Research	Jan Björkland (FpL)
Employment	Hillevi Engström (MP) [f]
Enterprise	Annie Lööf (C) [f]
Environment	Lena Ek (C) [f]
European Union Affairs	Birgitta Ohlsson (FpL) [f]
Finance	Anders Borg (MP)
Financial Markets	Peter Norman (MP)
Foreign Affairs	Carl Bildt (MP)
Gender Equality	Maria Arnholm (FpL) [f]
Health and Social Affairs	Göran Hägglund (Kd)
Information Technology and Energy	Anna-Karin Hatt (C) [f]
Infrastructure	Catherine Elmsäter-Svärd (MP) [f]
Integration	Erik Ullenhag (FpL)
International Development Cooperation	Gunilla Carlsson (MP) [f]

Justice	Beatrice Ask (MP) [f]
Migration and Asylum Policy	Tobias Billström (MP)
Nordic Cooperation	Ewa Björling (MP) [f]
Public Administration and Housing	Stefan Attefall (Kd)
Rural Affairs	Eskil Erlandsson (C)
Social Security	Ulf Kristersson (MP)
Trade	Ewa Björling (MP) [f]

[f] = female

INTERGOVERNMENTAL REPRESENTATION

Ambassador to the U.S.: Sven Jonas HAFSTRÖM.

U.S. Ambassador to Sweden: Mark Francis BRZEZINSKI.

Permanent Representative to the UN: Mårten GRUNDITZ.

IGO Memberships (Non-UN): ADB, AfDB, CEUR, EBRD, EIB, EU, IADB, IEA, ICC, IOM, OECD, OSCE, WTO.

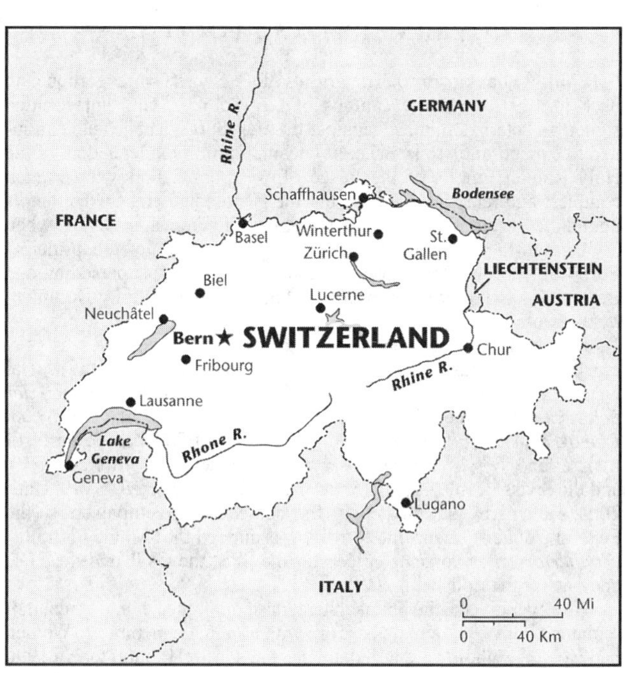

SWITZERLAND

Swiss Confederation
Schweizerische Eidgenossenschaft (German)
Confédération Suisse (French)
Confederazione Svizzera (Italian)
Confederaziun Svizra (Romansch)

Note: On December 4, 2013, the Federal Assembly elected Didier Burkhalter of the FDP.The Liberals as president of the confederation and Simonetta Sommaruga of the Social Democratic Party as vice president for a one-year term beginning January 1, 2014.

Political Status: Neutral confederation since 1291; equivalent of federal system embodied in constitution of May 29, 1874; current constitution, revising and reforming that of 1874, adopted April 18, 1999, effective January 1, 2000.

Area: 15,943 sq. mi. (41,293 sq. km).

Population: 8,036,900 (2012C). (After having conducted a standard full census every ten years since 1850, Switzerland in 2010 adopted a new system under which a census is completed each year using advanced methods of data collection and evaluation that rely on cantonal and communal population registers as well as a survey of approximately 5 percent of the population annually.)

Major Urban Centers (2005E): BERN (118,000), Zürich (327,000), Geneva (177,000), Basel (163,000), Lausanne (109,000).

Official Languages: German, French, Italian. Romansch is recognized as a national language but without full official status.

Monetary Unit: Swiss Franc (market rate November 1, 2013: 0.91 franc = $1US).

President of the Confederation and Chair of the Federal Council: (*See headnote.*) Ueli MAURER (Swiss People's Party); elected by the Federal Assembly on December 5, 2012, and inaugurated on January 1, 2013, for a one-year term to succeed Eveline WIDMER-SCHLUMPF (Conservative Democratic Party).

Vice President of the Confederation: (*See headnote.*) Didier BURKHALTER (FDP.The Liberals); elected by the Federal Assembly on December 5, 2012, and inaugurated on January 1, 2013, for a one-year term to succeed Ueli MAURER (Swiss People's Party).

THE COUNTRY

Situated in the mountainous heart of Western Europe, Switzerland has traditionally set an example of peaceful coexistence among different indigenous ethnic and cultural groups, although a post–World War II increase in the country's nonnative population was somewhat less than harmonious. The well-educated, politically sophisticated Swiss generally speak one of four languages: German (63.7 percent), French (20.4 percent), Italian (6.5 percent), and Romansch (0.5 percent). Roman Catholics account for 42 percent of the population, Protestants 33 percent, and Muslims 4 percent, while 11 percent claim no religious affiliation. The influx of foreign workers has ebbed in recent years, although they constitute 22 percent of the population, one of the highest rates in Europe. Women made up 46 percent of the employed labor force in 2008.

Switzerland's durable goods output is largely based on the production of precision-engineered items, pharmaceuticals, and special quality products that are not readily mass produced. The industrial sector as a whole contributes 28 percent of GDP, compared to only 1 percent for agriculture. (Raising livestock is the principal agricultural activity; the chief crops are wheat and potatoes.) Tourism and insurance are other major contributors to the economy, as is international banking, which has been under intense scrutiny in recent decades because of Switzerland's long-standing tradition of bank secrecy and consequential status as one of the world's biggest offshore tax havens. The country relies heavily on external transactions; foreign exchange earned from exports of goods and services, mostly to the European Union (EU), constitutes more than a third of the total national income. In 2007 Switzerland's GDP of $43,080 per capita (in terms of purchasing power parity) made it one of the world's richer countries.

In 2008 the global recession began to affect Switzerland significantly, and by the end of the first quarter of 2009, the economy was officially in recession. Consequently, GDP contracted by 1.9 percent in 2009 before rebounding to 2.7 percent growth in 2010 and 1.9 percent growth in 2011. In August 2011 the central bank cut interest rates in an effort to weaken the Swiss franc, after declaring that the currency was "massively overvalued" against the dollar and the euro. A month later the Swiss National Bank announced that the Swiss franc would not be permitted to appreciate any further than 1.2 Swiss francs = 1 euro, the eurozone debt crisis having continued to encourage investor flight into the perceived safety of the franc. Meanwhile, the financial sector faced growing demands for transparency, while major banks were required to beef up their capitalization significantly. As of the first half of 2013 the Swiss economy was performing better than most of the other European countries, and harsh austerity measures were avoided.

GOVERNMENT AND POLITICS

Political background. The origins of the Swiss Confederation date back to 1291, when the cantons of Uri, Schwyz, and Unterwalden signed an "eternal alliance" against the Hapsburgs. The league continued to expand until 1648, when it became formally independent of the Holy Roman Empire at the Peace of Westphalia. Following French conquest and reorganization during the Napoleonic era, Switzerland's boundaries were fixed by the Congress of Vienna in 1815, when Switzerland's perpetual neutrality was guaranteed by the principal European powers. The constitution adopted in 1874, superseding one from 1848, increased the powers conferred on the central government by the cantons.

For nearly five decades beginning in 1959, Switzerland was governed at the national level by a four-party coalition of the Social Democratic Party of Switzerland (*Sozialdemokratische Partei der Schweiz*—SPS), the Christian Democratic People's Party (*Christlich Demokratische Volkspartei*—CVP), the Radical Democratic Party of Switzerland (*Freisinnig-Demokratische Partei der Schweiz*—FDP), and the Swiss People's Party (*Schweizerische Volkspartei*—SVP). Until 2004 each party participated in the confederal executive body (the Federal Council), according to what was dubbed the "Magic Formula" (*Zauberformei*): two seats apiece for the SPS, the CVP, and the FDP, and one for the right-wing SVP.

However diverse the philosophical makeup of the Federal Council, it remained until 1984 a male bastion, with no female members. (Women had won the right to vote in federal elections in 1971, but it took a 1990 ruling by the Federal Supreme Court to end male-only voting in the half-canton of Appenzell-Innerrhoden, the last European jurisdiction to extend suffrage to women.) In October 1984, following a heated national debate, the bicameral Federal Assembly approved the FDP's nomination of Elisabeth KOPP, mayor of the Zürich suburb of Zumikon, as the first female member of the Federal Council. In so doing, the assembly appeared to have ensured that the position of nominal head of state would eventually fall to Kopp (due to the system of presidential rotation). However, she was obliged to resign her council post in December 1988 because of advice she improperly gave her husband, an officer of a company undergoing a formal money-laundering inquiry.

In August 1991, the country observed the 700th anniversary of the signing of its initial federal charter—the oldest such document known to exist—with minimal fanfare. In the October federal election the FDP, which had overtaken the SPS as the plurality party in 1983, again finished first but by a reduced margin of only three seats over the second-place SPS.

In May 1992, the government announced that it would apply for membership in the European Community (EC, subsequently the EU). Earlier that month Bern had signed a treaty providing for the creation of the European Economic Area (EEA) between the EC and the looser European Free Trade Association (EFTA), of which Switzerland was a founding member. The EEA treaty generated considerable public debate, culminating in a December 1992 referendum in which 50.3 percent of those voting (and 16 of 23 cantons) rejected ratification, despite having been urged to vote in favor by three of the four government parties, the centrist opposition parties, employers, trade unions, and the powerful banking sector. Opposing the measure were the most conservative government party (the SVP) and an uneasy coalition of ecologists and rightists. The voter turnout of 78.3 percent was the highest for any referendum since 1947; analysis showed that German and Italian speakers were decisively against the EEA, whereas the French-speaking Swiss voted overwhelmingly in favor.

In 1994 the government came under strong pressure to adopt tougher policies on immigration and crime. Swiss voters had already endorsed referendum proposals restricting immigration and making political asylum more difficult to obtain. In March the National Council voted to give the police increased powers to search and detain foreigners who lacked appropriate identification. The following month the government was embarrassed by an Amnesty International report asserting that some Swiss police officers were using unwarranted force against persons in custody, especially foreigners. As a result, government legislation that criminalized racial discrimination and racist propaganda was approved by referendum in September. More indicative of the popular mood, however, was a December referendum in which 73 percent of those voting endorsed tougher action against drug dealers and illegal immigrants.

The issue of proposed accession to the EU dominated the October 1995 federal lower house election, but the result was far from conclusive. The pro-EU Social Democrats achieved their best result ever (54 seats), mainly in the urban areas of Zürich, Basel, and Geneva. However, rural voters favored the strongly anti-EU SVP, which won 29 seats. The question of EU accession was subsequently deferred as both parties wished to preserve the ruling four-party coalition.

On January 1, 1999, Ruth DREIFUSS of the SPS became the first woman to hold the presidency of the confederation, while the most notable development at the national election in October was the rise of the SVP, which finished neck and neck with the SPS in total votes and moved into second place with 44 seats in the National Council.

In the National Council election of October 19, 2003, the SVP surpassed the SPS as the plurality party, winning 55 seats to 52 for the SPS, 36 for the FDP, and 28 for the CVP. As a consequence, the SVP, having threatened to go into opposition, successfully argued for a second seat on the Federal Council, with the CVP dropping to one, effective January 1, 2004. At that time the SVP's charismatic leader, Christoph BLOCHER, joined the Federal Council as councilor for justice and police.

Reflecting a rise in nationalistic, conservative sentiment, the SVP made further gains at the National Council poll on October 21, 2007, winning 29 percent of the vote and 62 seats, 19 more than the SPS. Nevertheless, the SPS, the CVP, and the Greens (*Die Grunë*) marshaled sufficient votes to replace the controversial Blocher on the Federal Council with the more moderate SVP parliamentarian Eveline WIDMER-SCHLUMPF. The SVP thereupon overturned Switzerland's four-party coalition formula, declaring that it would act as an opposition party. Consequently, in mid-2008 the SVP expelled Widmer-Schlumpf for accepting appointment to the Federal Council without the party's support. Widmer-Schlumpf and another expelled SVP member, the centrist Samuel SCHMID, subsequently formed the Conservative Democratic Party (*Bürgerlich-Demokratische Partei*—BDP). However, the SVP rejoined the government in January 2009, when party member Ueli MAURER was installed in the Federal Council as successor to Schmid, who, under pressure, had announced his resignation as defense councilor in November.

The SVP remained the largest party in the balloting for the National Council on October 23, 2011, although its vote total and representation declined. The five-party coalition subsequently remained intact.

Constitution and government. The 1874 constitution was revised by referendum on April 18, 1999, and a new constitution was put into legal force on January 1, 2000. The changes were primarily aimed at modernizing and updating the 1874 charter, which had been altered 140 times since it was written. The new constitution was approved by 59 percent of the vote; however, only 35 percent of eligible voters participated in the referendum. In addition to modernizing the document's language, the new constitution included new provisions pertaining to labor rights and equal opportunity for people with disabilities.

Under the constitution of 1999, Switzerland is (despite the retention of "confederation" in its official name) a federal republic of 23 cantons, 3 of which are subdivided into half-cantons. The cantons retain autonomy over a range of local concerns but lack the right to nullify national legislation. Responsibility for the latter is vested in a bicameral parliament, the Federal Assembly, both houses of which (the Council of States and the National Council) have equal authority. Legislation passed by the two chambers may not be vetoed by the executive nor reviewed by the judiciary. In addition to normal legislative processes, the Swiss constitution provides for the use of initiatives to amend the constitution and referendums to ratify or reject federal legislation. To go forward, the two require petitions bearing 100,000 and 50,000 signatures, respectively.

Executive authority is exercised on a collegial basis by the Federal Council, whose seven members are elected by the entire Federal Assembly. Each December the assembly elects two of the seven to serve for the following year as president of the confederation (in effect head of state) and vice president of the Federal Council (equivalent to deputy head of state). The president has limited prerogatives and serves as a first among equals. Although the Federal Council is responsible to the legislature, the council has increasingly become a nonpolitical body of experts from the leading political parties. Its members are usually reelected as long as they are willing to serve. A federal chancellor, elected by the Federal Assembly for a four-year term, heads the administrative arm of the Federal Council.

The Swiss judicial system functions primarily at the cantonal level; the only regular federal court is the Federal Supreme Court, which has the authority to review cantonal court decisions involving federal law. (Sublevels of the Supreme Court include a Federal Administrative Court, a Federal Patent Court, and a Federal Criminal Court.) Each canton has civil and criminal courts, a Court of Appeal, and a Court of Cassation.

Local government exists on two basic levels: the cantons and the approximately 3,000 communes (municipalities). In some of the larger cantons the communes are grouped into districts, which are headed by commissioners. There are two basic governing organs at the cantonal and communal levels—a unicameral legislature and, much like the federal system, a collegial executive. In five cantons and half-cantons (as well as in numerous smaller units) the entire voting population functions as the legislature, while in the others the legislature is elected. As at the federal level, initiatives and referendums may be used to propose, amend, or annul legislation within a canton.

After 30 years of separatist strife in the largely French-speaking, Roman Catholic region of Jura, Swiss voters approved cantonal status for most of the area in 1978. The creation of the 23rd canton, the first to be formed since 1815, was approved by over 82 percent of those voting in the national referendum. Jura's full membership in the confederation took effect on January 1, 1979. Southern Jura, predominantly Protestant and German-speaking, remained part of the Bern canton. The small German-speaking district of Laufental, having been cut off geographically from Bern by the creation of the Jura canton, voted on September 26, 1993, to be transferred from the Bern canton to the half-canton of Basel-Land.

In a constitutional referendum in March 1996, 76.1 percent of voters supported official recognition of Romansch, the 2,000-year-old language used, in five dialects, by approximately 50,000 inhabitants of the eastern canton of Graübunden (or Grisons). The measure enhanced the "national" status accorded by a 1938 referendum, obliging federal authorities to provide services to Romansch speakers in their own language. However, it did not grant Romansch the same "official" status given to German, French, and Italian; the law requires that all federal documents be issued in those languages.

The Swiss press is privately owned and free from governmental influence, although editors are accustomed to using discretion in handling national security information.

Canton and Capital	*Area (sq. mi.)*	*Population (2007E)*
Aargau/Argovie (Aarau)	542	569,000
Appenzell		
Ausserrhoden (Herisau)	94	53,000
Innerrhoden (Appenzell)	66	15,000
Basel/Bâle		
Basel-Land (Liestal)	165	265,000
Basel-Stadt (Basel)	14	189,000
Bern/Berne (Bern)	2,336	1,092,000
Fribourg (Fribourg)	645	254,000
Genève/Geneva (Genève)	109	431,000
Glarus (Glarus)	264	38,000
Graübunden/Grisons (Chur)	2,744	184,000
Jura (Delémont)	323	69,000
Luzern/Lucerne (Luzern)	576	353,000
Neuchâtel (Neuchâtel)	308	168,000
St. Gallen/St. Gall (St. Gallen)	778	451,000
Schaffhausen/Schaffhouse (Schaffhausen)	115	74,000
Schwyz (Schwyz)	351	138,000
Solothurn/Soleure (Solothurn)	305	249,000
Thurgau/Thurgovie (Frauenfeld)	391	231,000
Ticino/Tessin (Bellinzona)	1,085	328,000
Unterwalden		
Nidwalden (Stans)	106	43,000
Obwalden (Sarnen)	189	33,000
Uri (Altdorf)	416	35,000
Valais (Sion)	2,018	292,000
Vaud (Lausanne)	1,243	651,000
Zug/Zoug (Zug)	92	109,000
Zürich (Zürich)	667	1,276,000

Foreign relations. Swiss foreign policy has historically stressed neutrality and scrupulous avoidance of membership in military alliances. In the interest of maintaining that neutrality, Switzerland chose to remain outside the UN through the Cold War era, although it was accredited as a permanent observer to the organization. It also adhered to the statute of the International Court of Justice and belonged to many UN specialized agencies. In addition, foreign policy subsequently remained influenced by the principle of "solidarity," which holds that a neutral state is morally obligated to undertake social, economic, and humanitarian activities contributing to world peace and prosperity. Partly for this reason, Switzerland subsequently agreed to convert assorted debts owed by various developing nations into grants.

In 1984 both the National Council and the Council of States approved a government proposal that the country apply for UN membership; however, voters overwhelmingly rejected such action in a referendum in 1986. In contrast, in 1992 the electorate readily approved joining the IMF and World Bank.

In the aftermath of the December 1992 referendum that rejected participation in the EEA (see Political background, above), Swiss policy concentrated on limiting the negative effects of remaining outside that economic area. The government's strategy received a boost in May 1995 when Liechtenstein acceded to the EEA while retaining its 70-year-old economic and monetary union with Switzerland. As a result, Swiss exporters with outlets in Liechtenstein could benefit from the tariff concessions available under the EEA. The Swiss federal government also continued its legislative program to bring Swiss law into line with EEA/EU practice, although it was hindered by voters' rejection of attempts to ease existing restrictions on foreign ownership of property in Switzerland in a June 1995 referendum.

There were signs in 1995–1996 of a softening in Switzerland's stance of armed neutrality (usually referenced as dating from 1515 but formalized three centuries later by the Congress of Vienna). In June 1996 Flavio COTTI became the first Swiss foreign minister to address a meeting of the North Atlantic Treaty Organization (NATO); the Swiss government appointed a military attaché to an observer role in NATO soon thereafter. Despite opposition from conservative parties, in October the government announced plans to enter the NATO Partnership for Peace (PfP) program, while stressing that it had no intention of joining NATO itself. The government also pledged that it would abide by the June 1994 referendum decision precluding any armed participation in PfP peacekeeping exercises, although since December 1995 Switzerland had permitted NATO to fly over its territory and use its railways to supply peacekeeping operations in Bosnia.

The international image of Switzerland as a bastion of banking probity and humanitarian values was damaged in 1995–1997, particularly in the United States and Israel, when new developments emerged in the 50-year-old dispute over the assets of World War II Holocaust victims. The controversy centered on allegations that Swiss banks had knowingly accepted gold that had either been looted from the central banks of occupied countries or plundered from victims of the Holocaust by German Nazis. (U.S. officials argued that Germany had relied heavily on the sale of the gold to prolong its war effort.) Holocaust survivors and their heirs demanded a new investigation into the thousands of long-dormant Swiss bank accounts that they suspected contained assets of Nazi victims.

The Swiss commercial banks initially assumed an extremely conservative position on the inquiries, concentrating solely on dormant accounts for which complete documentation was available. By late 1997 they had identified some 16,000 such accounts, valued at about $54 million. It was agreed that the unclaimed money would be released through an independent panel; the banks also contributed to a government-sponsored voluntary fund of some $200 million that had been established to assist needy elderly survivors of the Holocaust. However, those measures failed to address the central question of looted gold, and pressure intensified on behalf of the plaintiffs in class-action suits against the banks.

In early 1998, an independent Swiss commission reported that some $450 million in Nazi gold had been received in Switzerland during the war, about 80 percent having been handled by the Swiss Central Bank and the remainder by private banks. (It was estimated that the gold was valued at about $4 billion in 1998, without interest.) Another commission concluded shortly thereafter that officials of the Central Bank had been aware that some of the gold had come from the Central Banks of countries overrun by the Germans. Jewish organizations demanded a settlement, without which a number of U.S. states threatened to discontinue their substantial dealings with Swiss financial institutions.

In April 1998 the three major Swiss commercial banks reversed themselves and announced they would pursue a "global settlement" of the claims, and a figure of $1.25 billion was reached in August. Most of the money was to be used to compensate victims (or their families) of the Holocaust for whom specific claims could not be documented—the so-called "rough justice" approach. The Swiss Central Bank notably refused to participate in the settlement, as the government argued that none of its actions as a neutral state during the war had been improper. That position partly reflected the sentiment of a growing segment of the population, which lashed out against the intense international scrutiny. (In November 1998, a government commission reported that the Holocaust debate had drawn attention to a degree of "latent Swiss anti-Semitism," creating "a political crisis concerning Switzerland's self-image.")

In late 1998, after four years of negotiations, Switzerland completed a trade agreement with the EU. A national referendum endorsed the measure in May 2000.

Swiss banks subsequently faced international scrutiny on several fronts beyond that of Nazi gold: for their role in providing services for apartheid South Africa during the international embargo; for their reluctance to disclose and freeze the money held by former Zairian president Mobutu Sese Seko; for their alleged involvement in money laundering by organized crime syndicates in Russia; and for "serious shortcomings" (according to a September 2000 report by the Federal Banking Commission) in accepting an estimated $500 million in deposits from Nigerian dictator Sani Abacha and his family. Meanwhile, in February 2001 the government identified the names on 21,000 accounts considered likely to have been owned by Holocaust victims between 1933 and 1945. Some 100,000 claims were expected to be filed for the dormant accounts.

In a referendum held in June 2001, Swiss voters narrowly approved (by 50.9 percent) permitting armed Swiss troops to participate in international peacekeeping missions. The vote also authorized training with NATO forces, although opponents of the proposal argued that Switzerland's traditional neutrality would be jeopardized. The government subsequently maintained its stance in favor of eventual accession to the EU, although in March 2001, 76.7 percent of voters rejected a referendum proposal to immediately apply for membership. However, the Swiss public finally endorsed UN membership in a March 2002 referendum with a yes vote of 54.1 percent, and Switzerland joined the UN in September.

Concerns about the influx of foreigners into Switzerland subsequently took on increasing political significance because many Swiss feared the loss of what they viewed as their unique culture. In November 2002, by a historically thin margin of 0.2 percent, voters defeated a measure (offered by the SVP) to restrict the country's asylum laws. However, in September 2004, provisions that would have made it easier for foreigners to become Swiss citizens were defeated. A proposal to ease procedures for citizenship for second-generation immigrants failed 56.8 percent to 43.2 percent, and a provision that would have guaranteed Swiss citizenship for third-generation immigrants at birth failed 51.6 percent to 48.4 percent.

In a referendum held in June 2005, 54.6 percent of voters supported joining the Schengen agreement, which provided for closer security cooperation with the EU and allowed persons from other Schengen countries (most of Europe) to enter Switzerland without passports. It also permitted signatories to share information, such as whether an asylum seeker has sought refuge in more than one country. (Switzerland became the 25th country to join the Schengen zone in December 2008.)

In another referendum, held in September 2005, 56 percent of voters approved a government-sponsored proposal to allow citizens of the ten new EU member states to live and work in Switzerland, provided they had jobs and were able to support themselves. Meanwhile, under an accord that had gone into force in July after 15 years of negotiations, Swiss banks agreed to withhold taxes on accounts belonging to depositors from EU and other countries. (In 2006 the new system yielded more than $500 million in tax revenue, three-quarters of which was handed over to EU countries whose residents held Swiss bank accounts.) However, Swiss-EU relations soured somewhat after the EU complained in December 2005 that low corporate tax rates in Switzerland violated the terms of their trade agreement.

U.S. objections to Switzerland's policy of strict bank secrecy resurfaced in 2008, when the U.S. Internal Revenue Service sued Swiss banking giant UBS for helping wealthy American account holders evade taxes. In February 2009 UBS admitted to helping U.S. taxpayers hide their accounts, and in August the bank agreed to provide the U.S. government with the names and account information for some 4,450 bank customers. The bank also agreed to pay $780 million in fines and penalties. In January 2010, however, the Swiss Federal Administrative Court ruled that lifting banking secrecy was illegal, necessitating ratification of the 2009 agreement by the Federal Assembly in June. Meanwhile, in September 2009, after completing a dozen bilateral double-taxation agreements to improve transparency and information exchange, Switzerland had been removed from the "grey list" of tax havens published by the Organization for Economic Cooperation and Development (OECD). Relations with the EU and Germany remained strained, however, over Switzerland's retention of generous corporate tax breaks, while contentious negotiations continued into 2013 on tax evasion issues (see Current issues, below).

Current issues. The banking sector continued to receive negative press in 2010 as, among other things, *Credit Suisse* agreed to pay $536 million to resolve U.S. claims that the bank had helped depositors evade sanctions on Iran and other countries. In a more positive light, legislation in 2011 permitted Swiss authorities to return money to countries whose previous heads of state had used Swiss accounts to loot their government coffers. The new law stipulated that the money was to be used "for the good of the people" in the countries involved.

In May 2011 the government abandoned plans to build any new nuclear reactors in the wake of the crisis at a nuclear plant in Japan following a tsunami in March. Pending approval by the legislature, the country's five existing reactors were to be decommissioned between 2019 and 2034, as they reach the end of their initial life spans.

The banking and nuclear issues apparently contributed to the improvement of the BDP and the Green Liberal Party (*Grünliberale Partei*—GLP), respectively, in the October 2011 balloting for the National Council, although the legislative results did not significantly alter the nation's political landscape. Attention in the first half of 2012 focused primarily on continuing efforts to prevent overvaluation of the Swiss franc (which threatened to undercut Swiss exports) and to resolve outstanding banking issues. In the latter regard, compromise bilateral agreements were announced between Switzerland and several major countries (including the United States, United Kingdom, and Germany) for the sharing of data and other measures to combat tax evasion.

In January 2013 Wegelin & Company, Switzerland's oldest private bank, pled guilty in a U.S. court to abetting tax evasion on the part of scores of U.S. citizens in 2002–2010. The bank agreed to pay $74 million in fines and restitution and subsequently announced it was going out of business. International pressure subsequently continued to mount on other Swiss banks, and in May 2013 the Federal Council announced support for a sweeping plan to permit banks to release information on foreign clients to aid in U.S. investigations into possible tax evasion by U.S. nationals. In conjunction with the proposed accord, Swiss banks were slated to pay $7–10 billion in fines, with the government agreeing to lend the banks money for some of those payments. In addition, the banks would have avoided additional indictments, as would have bank employees involved in the tax avoidance schemes. However, the National Council rejected the proposal in June as a broad spectrum of legislators expressed concern that the collapse of secrecy would put Swiss banks at a disadvantage versus other offshore havens not yet subject to greater transparency.

On other fronts in the first half of 2013, Swiss voters approved legislation granting shareholders greater control of the salaries and bonuses for corporate executives. Populist sentiment also appeared to contribute to the government's decision to eliminate tax incentives for foreign multinationals and to curb immigration from a number of EU countries.

POLITICAL PARTIES

The Swiss political scene was long characterized by a multiplicity of political parties; however, from 1959, it was dominated by a four-party coalition of the Swiss People's Party (SVP), the Social Democratic Party (SPS), the Radical Democratic Party (FDP), and the Christian Democratic People's Party (CVP) that controlled the majority of seats in both houses of the Federal Assembly. The SVP's December 2007 decision to move into opposition occasioned the creation of a new government party, the Conservative Democratic Party (BDP), founded by moderate former SVP members. In January 2009, the SVP returned to what thereby became a five-party government, which has continued intact following the 2011 legislative elections.

Government Parties:

Swiss People's Party (*Schweizerische Volkspartei*—SVP/*Union Démocratique du Centre*—UDC/*Unione Democratica di Centro*—UDC/*Partida Populara Svizra*—PPS). Formed in 1971 by a merger of the former Farmers', Artisans', and Citizens' Party with the Democratic Party, the SVP is a populist, right-wing party holding strong agrarian and socially conservative positions. Traditionally based in German-speaking cantons, it advocates a robust national defense as well as the protection of agriculture and small industry. The party appeared to be on the wane around 1990, but its fortunes began to improve thereafter. The SVP was the only government party to oppose the unsuccessful EEA accord in 1992. It increased its electoral support in 1995 to 14.9 percent, yielding 29 lower house seats (a gain of 4 over 1991), and improved to 44 seats in the 1999 poll, at which it secured approximately the same number of votes nationwide as the SPS (51 seats). The SVP's capture of 26.6 percent of the vote in 2003, largely in French-speaking Switzerland, for a plurality (55) of lower house seats led the governing coalition to grant the SVP a second seat on the Federal Council.

During the 2007 campaign, Christoph Blocher, a billionaire chemicals magnate serving as the nation's justice councilor, led the party's controversial calls to crack down on crimes committed by foreigners and prohibit the construction of minarets at Muslim places of worship. The SVP won 29 percent of the 2007 vote, more than any party since 1919, and 62 seats in the National Council, confirming it as Switzerland's strongest party. In an unprecedented move, Blocher's critics nominated Eveline Widmer-Schlumpf, a moderate SVP legislator, to run for the seat on the Federal Council theretofore held by Blocher. When she won, the SVP parliamentary group voted to exclude her and Samuel Schmid (the other SVP member of the Federal Council) from the party and threatened to act as an opposition party. Widmer-Schlumpf and Schmid subsequently affiliated with a new SVP spinoff, the BDP (see below).

Opinion polls showed waning support for the SVP after its formal move to the opposition in 2008. Among other things, business owners who had traditionally been SVP supporters criticized Blocher's call for capping executive pay at troubled Swiss banks *Crédit Suisse* and UBS and opposed SVP-backed efforts to curb the free movement of workers from EU countries. The party's return to the government in 2009, with former SVP leader Ueli Maurer replacing Schmid as defense minister, was seen as a victory for SVP moderates.

After 20 years of steady growth, the SVP's vote percentage fell to 26.6 percent in the 2011 elections, although it retained its plurality status (54 seats). Once again, the SVP had campaigned on a heavily anti-immigrant platform, officials decrying, among other things, what they perceived as the "Islamization" of the country.

Leaders: Toni BRUNNER (President), Christoph BLOCHER, Adrian AMSTUTZ (Leader of Parliamentary Group), Martin BALTISSER (General Secretary).

Social Democratic Party (*Sozialdemokratische Partei der Schweiz*—SPS/*Parti Socialiste Suisse*—PS/*Partito Socialista Svizzero*—PS/*Partida Socialdemocrata da la Svizra*—PS). Frequently referenced as the Socialist Party (SP/PS), the SPS, which was organized in 1888, is the most left-leaning governing party; it advocates direct federal taxation, a degree of state intervention in the economy, and accession to the EU. It adopted an essentially reformist social democratic program in 1982, and the party also has been influenced by the ecologist and feminist movements. In 1984, it came close to withdrawing from the government after its coalition partners rejected Christine BRUNNER for the Federal Council. SPS member Ruth Dreifuss joined the council in 1993 and became the first woman to hold the presidency of the federation in 1999.

Since 1992, the former *Partito Socialista Unitario* (PSU), now led by Manuele BERTOLI, has operated as an autonomous section of the national party, the ***Partito Socialista, Sezione Ticinese del PSS,*** in the Italian-speaking canton of Ticino.

In the 2007 lower house election, the SPS won 43 seats, a loss of 9 seats from 2003, though it remained the second largest party in the chamber, behind the SVP.

In 2010 the SPS was seen as having moved somewhat farther to the left after it presented a new manifesto calling for capitalism to be "transcended" and replaced by the "democratization" of the economy. The party secured 46 seats in the National Council in the 2011 election on a vote share of 18.7 percent.

Leaders: Christian LEVRAT (President); Andy TSCHÜMPERLIN (Leader of Parliamentary Group); Flavia WASSERFALLEN, Leyla GÜL (Co-secretary Generals).

FDP.The Liberals (*FDP.Die Liberalen*—FDP/*PLR.Les Libéraux-Radicaux*—PLR/*PLR.I Liberali*—PLR/*PLD.Ils Liberals*—PLD). The FDP.The Liberals was founded on February 28, 2009, upon the merger of the Radical Democratic Party (*Freisinnig-Demokratische Partei der Schweiz*—FDP/*Parti Radical-Démocratique Suisse*—PRD/*Partito Liberale-radicale Svizzero*—PLR/*Partida Liberaldemocrata Svizra*—PLD) and the Liberal Party (*Liberale Partei der Schweiz*—LPS/*Parti Libéral Suisse*—PLS/*Partito Liberale Svizzero*—PLS/*Partida Liberal-conservativa Svizra*—PLC). Leader of the historic movement that gave rise to the federated state, the FDP (also known as the Free Democrats) was liberal in outlook and advocated free-market policies and closer ties with the EU. The LPS was led by Pierre WEISS and had a political base among Protestants in the French-speaking part of the country. The FDP and LPS formed a legislative coalition (called the Radical and Liberal Union) in 2005 to strengthen their united front in parliament.

The FDP lost ground in 2007, winning 31 seats (15.8 percent of the vote) in the lower house, down from 36 in 2003, and 12 in the upper house, down from 14. As a result, it formally brought the Liberals into the party's ranks in an effort to increase popular support, in the process adding the Liberals' 4 lower house seats to the FDP total. The center-right FDP.The Liberals finished third in the balloting for the National Council in 2011 on a vote share of 15.1 percent. Analysts attributed the party's modest decline to its perceived association with the banking sector, which had been under intense public scrutiny for several years.

Leaders: Philipp MÜLLER (President), Gabi HUBER (Leader of Parliamentary Group), Stefan BRUPBACHER (General Secretary).

Christian Democratic People's Party (*Christlichdemokratische Volkspartei*—CVP/*Parti Démocrate-Chrétien*—PDC/*Partito Popolare Democratico*—PPD/*Partida Cristiandemocratica*—PCD). The CVP is a successor to the Swiss Conservative Party, formed in 1912 by elements long opposed to the centralization of national power; the party adopted its current name in 1970. Appealing primarily to Catholics, the party traditionally advocated cantonal control over religious education and supported taxes on alcohol and tobacco, while opposing direct taxation by the federal government. As its Catholic base subsequently dwindled, the CVP gained strength in Protestant areas by promoting less-conservative social policies and defining itself as a centrist party.

The CVP's lower-house representation declined gradually beginning in 1979, falling to a low of 28 seats in 2003 on a vote share of 14.4 percent. As a result, the CVP lost 1 of its 2 seats on the Federal Council to the SVP. In 2007, the party showed increased strength, winning 31 seats in the lower house, but its seat total declined to 28 in 2011 (on a vote share of 12.3 percent).

Leaders: Chrisophe DARBELLAY (President), Fillippo LOMBARDI (President of the Council of States), Urs SCHWALLER (Leader of Parliamentary Group).

Conservative Democratic Party (*Bürgerlich-Demokratische Partei*—BDP/*Parti Bourgeois Démocratique*—PBD/*Partito Borghese Democratico*—PBD/*Partida Burgais Democratica*—PBD). The BDP was founded on November 1, 2008, by former members of the SVP, including Eveline Widmer-Schlumpf and Samuel Schmid, "moderates" who had recently clashed with SVP hard-liners. Both politicians were elected in 2007 under the SVP banner but were subsequently expelled from the party after they opposed the reelection of SVP firebrand Christoph Blocher to the Federal Council. The BDP at that point held one seat in the upper house and five in the lower house. It lost one of its two representatives in the Federal Council when Schmid stepped down as defense minister on November 12, 2008.

Unlike the SVP, the BDP supports closer ties with the EU. However, it echoes the SVP in strictly defending Switzerland's neutrality.

The centrist BDP secured nine seats in the National Council in the 2011 poll on a vote share of 5.4 percent. Meanwhile, Samuel Schmid was reported to have formed a new, small party called the **Social Liberal Movement** (*Sozial-Liberale Bewegung*—SLB/*Mouvement Social-Libérale*—MSL/*Movimento Social-Liberale*—MSL).

Leaders: Martin LANDOLT (President), Hansjörg HASSLER (Parliamentary Leader), Nina SOSSO (Interim Secretary General).

Other Parliamentary Parties:

The Greens–Green Party of Switzerland (*Grüne–Grüne Partei der Schweiz/Les Verts–Parti Écologiste Suisse*—PES/*I Verdi–Partito Ecologista Svizzero/La Verda–Partida Ecologica Svizra*). The Swiss Federation of Green/Ecology Parties was founded in May 1983 by nine groupings, including two that had gained representation at the cantonal level in Zürich and Luzern the previous month and one that had gained a seat in the National Council in 1979. The federation obtained 3 National Council seats in 1983, 9 in 1987, and 14 in 1991. The party adopted its current name in 1993. Its National Council representation fell to 9 seats in 1995 when it received only 5 percent of the vote. The party sustained both its vote share and number of seats in the 1999 lower house elections, in which it worked jointly with the Green Alliance (*Grünes Bündnis/Alliance Verte*), an ecologist/feminist group, which subsequently merged with The Greens. The party increased its seat share in the lower house to 13 in 2003 and 20 in 2007, but its percentage of the vote declined to 8.4 percent (good for only 15 seats) in what was considered a "surprising setback" in the 2011 poll.

Leaders: Regula RYTZ, Adèle THORENS (Co-presidents); Maya GRAF (President of the National Council); Antonio HODGERS (Leader of Parliamentary Group); Miriam BEHRENS (Secretary General).

Green Liberal Party (*Grünliberale Partei Schweiz*—GLP/*Parti Vert-Libéral*—PVL/*Partito Verde-Liberale*—PVL/*Partida Verda-Liberala*—PVL). A centrist party, the GLP was founded on July 19, 2007, by four canton-level green parties; it called for measures to combat climate change and other threats to the environment, while otherwise maintaining a free-market, probusiness platform. In its first electoral test the GLP won 3 seats in the National Council and 1 in the Council of State in the 2007 balloting. The party capitalized on growing antinuclear sentiment to improve sharply to 12 seats (on a vote share of 5.4 percent) in the National Council in the 2011 balloting.

Leaders: Martin BÄUMLE (President), Tiana Angelina MOSER, Sandra GURTNER-OESCH (General Secretary).

Evangelical People's Party (*Evangelische Volkspartei der Schweiz*—EVP/*Parti Evangélique Suisse*—PEV/*Partito Evangelico Svizzero*—PEV/*Partida Evangelica de la Svizra*—PEV). Established in 1919, the EVP is committed to a program that advocates conservative Protestant positions on abortion and other social issues while adopting a more centrist approach to economic policy and supporting center-left goals on environmental protection and immigration. It retained its two seats in the National Council in the 2011 balloting on a vote share of 2.0 percent.

Leaders: Heiner STUDER (President); Maja INGOLD, Marianne STREIFF (Members of the National Council); Joel BLUNIER (General Secretary).

Christian Social Party (*Christlich-Soziale Partei*—CSP/*Parti Chrétien-Social*—PCS/*Partito Cristiano Sociale*—PCS/*Partida Cristian-Sociala*—PCS). A small center-left party, the CSP contested several National Council elections without success until it was able to secure one seat in 1995. It has held one seat ever since.

Leaders: Marius ACHERMANN (President), Karl VOGLER (Member of the National Council), Marlies SCHAFER-JUNGO (General Secretary).

Ticino League (*Lega dei Ticinesi*—*Lega*). The Ticino League, founded in 1991, is a right-wing formation that advocates greater autonomy for Ticino. It won two lower house seats in the 1991 balloting, after which it formed a parliamentary group with the Swiss Democrats. It secured one National Council seat in 1995, two in 1999, one in 2003 and 2007, and two in 2011 (on a vote share of 0.8 percent).

Giuliano BIGNASCA, the founder and primary financial backer of the Ticino League, died in March 2013. The following month the party won a vote share of 36 percent and three of seven seats in polling for the Lugano city council.

Leaders: Lorenzo QUADRI, Norman GOBBI (Secretary).

Citizens Movement of Geneva (*Mouvement Citoyens Genevois*—MCG). Founded in 2005, the right-wing MCG subsequently urged that restrictions be placed on the number of French commuters, estimated at 60,000, allowed to work in Geneva. The MCG argued that more jobs could be filled by Swiss nationals. After improving to 17 of 100 seats on the Grand Council of Geneva in the 2009 elections, the MCG secured its first seat (on 0.4 percent of the vote) in the National Council in the 2011 balloting.

Leaders: Eric STAUFFER (Founder), Mauro POGGIA (Member of the National Council).

Other Parties That Contested the 2011 Legislative Elections:

Federal Democratic Union (*Eidgenössisch-Demokratische Union*—EDU/*Union Démocratique Fédérale*—UDF/*Unione Democratica Federale*—UDF/*Uniun Democrata Federala*—UDF). The EDU is a fundamentalist Protestant, anti-immigration party founded in 1975. After holding at least one seat in the National Council since 1991, the EDU failed to secure representation in 2011.

Leaders: Hans MOSER (President), José LORENTE (Vice President), Andreas BRÖNNIMANN, Christian WABER (Secretary General).

Swiss Labor Party (*Partei der Arbeit der Schweiz*—PdA/*Parti Suisse du Travail–Parti Ouvrier et Populaire*—PST-POP/*Partito Svizzero del Lavoro*—PdL/*Partida Svizra de la Lavur*—PSdL). Organized in 1921 as the Swiss Communist Party, outlawed in 1940, and reorganized under its present name in 1944, the urban-based PdA long maintained a pro-Moscow position. The party removed all references to "communism" and "democratic centralism" from its statutes in September 1991 and the following month increased its representation in the National Council from one to three seats. It retained those seats in the 1995 balloting, after which its deputies affiliated with the Social Democratic parliamentary group.

In the 1999 lower house elections, the PdA gained 0.9 percent of the vote and won two seats, which it kept in 2003 with 0.7 percent of the vote. The PdA secured one lower house seat in 2007 but failed to gain representation in 2011 with a vote share of 0.5 percent.

Leader: Norberto CRIVELLI (President).

Freedom Party of Switzerland (*Freiheits-Partei der Schweiz*—FPS/*Parti Suisse de la Liberté*—PSL/*Partito Svizzero della Libertà*—PSL/*Partida Svizra da la Libertad*—PSL). Launched in 1985 as the Swiss Automobile Party (*Schweizer Auto-Partei*), a motorists' pressure group based in German-speaking Switzerland, the right-wing Freedom Party adopted its present name in 1994 but is still widely referred to as *Die Auto-Partei.* Its representation at the federal level peaked at eight National Council seats in 1991 after it had added an anti-immigration component to its manifesto. It fell back to seven seats in 1995 on a 4 percent vote share. Since 1999 its vote share has been under 1 percent.

Leaders: Jürg SCHERRER (President), Walter MÜLLER (Secretary).

Swiss Democrats (*Schweizer Demokraten*—SD/*Démocrates Suisses*—DS/*Democratici Svizzeri*—DS/*Democrats Svizers*—DS). The far-right SD emerged in 1961 as the National Action against Foreign Infiltration of People and Homeland (*National Aktion gegen Überfremdung von Volk und Heimat/Action Nationale contre l'Emprise et la Surpopulation Etrangéres*) and as of 1977 was known as the National Action for People and Homeland (*National Aktion für Volk und Heimat*—NA/*Action National*—AN). The group adopted its present name prior to the 1991 elections. It subsequently sought to reduce the number of resident foreign workers as well as the number of naturalizations. The party secured five seats in the National Council in 1991, but its share of the vote declined thereafter. It won three seats in 1995 and then only one in 1999 and 2003. The SD lost that seat in 2007 as former supporters apparently voted for the SVP. The SD again failed to gain representation in the 2011 balloting, at which it garnered 0.2 percent of the vote.

Leader: Bernhard HESS (President).

Swiss Pirate Party (*Piratenpartei Schweiz*—PPS/*Parti Pirate Suisse*—PPS/*Partito Pirata Svizzero*—PPS/*Partida da Pirats Svizra*—PPS). Based on the Swedish Pirate Party, the PPS was founded on July 12, 2009, by advocates of freedom of information; among other things, it has called for the elimination of patents and copyrights, perceived as a barrier to public access to information. The PPS secured 8.9 percent of the vote in local elections in Berlin in September 2011 but failed to

gain representation in the October balloting for the National Council on a 0.48 percent vote share.
Leader: Denis SIMONET (President).

Numerous other minor and fringe parties also presented candidates in 2011.

LEGISLATURE

The bicameral **Federal Assembly** (*Bundesversammlung/Assemblée Fédérale/Assemblea Federale*) consists of a Council of States and a National Council.

Council of States (*Ständerat/Conseil des Etats/Consiglio degli Stati*). The upper house consists of 46 members, 2 elected from each of the 20 cantons and 1 from each of the 6 half-cantons. Although election methods vary among the cantons, most of the elections are held on a two-round (if necessary) majoritarian basis. Following the elections of October 23–December 4, 2011, the Christian Democratic People's Party held 13 seats; the FDP.The Liberals, 11; the Social Democratic Party, 11; the Swiss People's Party, 5; The Greens–Green Party of Switzerland, 2; the Green Liberal Party, 2; the Conservative Democratic Party, 1; and independent, 1.
President: Fillippo LOMBARDI.

National Council (*Nationalrat/Conseil National/Consiglio Nazionale*). The lower house consists of 200 members elected for four-year terms by direct popular vote within each canton or half-canton, for the most part on a proportional representation basis, which varies among cantons. Seats are allocated to the cantons and half-cantons based on population. The Zurich canton has 34 seats, while the six half-cantons have only 1 seat each. (Majoritarian balloting is used in the six half-cantons.) The seat distribution resulting from balloting on October 23, 2011, was as follows: the Swiss People's Party, 54; the Social Democratic Party, 46; the FDP.The Liberals, 30; the Christian Democratic People's Party, 28; The Greens–Green Party of Switzerland, 15; the Green Liberal Party, 12; the Conservative Democratic Party, 9; the Evangelical People's Party, 2; the Ticino League, 2; the Citizens' Movement of Geneva, 1; and the Christian Social Party, 1. The next elections are due by September 2014.
President: Maya GRAF.

FEDERAL COUNCIL

[as of July 1, 2013] (*See headnote.*)

President	Ueli Maurer (SVP)
Vice President	Didier Burkhalter (FDP.The Liberals)
Department Heads	
Defense, Civil Protection, and Sports	Ueli Maurer (SVP)
Economic Affairs, Education, and Research	Johann Schneider-Ammann (FDP. The Liberals)
Environment, Transportation, Communications, and Energy	Doris Leuthard (CVP) [f]
Finance	Eveline Widmer-Schlumpf (BDP) [f]
Foreign Affairs	Didier Burkhalter (FDP.The Liberals)
Home Affairs	Alain Berset (SPS)
Justice and Police	Simonetta Sommaruga (SPS) [f]
Federal Chancellor	Corina Casanova (CVP) [f]

[f] = female

INTERGOVERNMENTAL REPRESENTATION

Ambassador to the U.S.: Manuel SAGER.

U.S. Ambassador to Switzerland: Donald Sternoff BEYER Jr.

Permanent Representative to the UN: Paul SEGER.

IGO Memberships (Non-UN): ADB, AfDB, CEUR, EBRD, EFTA, IADB, IEA, ICC, IOM, OECD.

SYRIA

Syrian Arab Republic
al-Jumhuriyah al-Arabiyah al-Suriyah

Political Status: Republic proclaimed in 1941; became independent on April 17, 1946; under military regime since March 8, 1963.

Area: 71,586 sq. mi. (185,408 sq. km).

Population: 21,898,000 (2013E—UN); 22,457,000 (2013E—U.S. Census).

Major Urban Centers (2005E, including suburbs): DAMASCUS (2,314,000), Aleppo (2,560,000), Homs (1,102,000).

Official Language: Arabic.

Monetary Unit: Syrian Pound (official rate November 1, 2013: 112.95 pounds = $1US). The Syrian pound, formerly pegged to the U.S. dollar, has been pegged to a basket of currencies since 2007.

President: Dr./Lt. Gen. Bashar al-ASSAD (Baath Party); sworn in for a seven-year term on July 17, 2000, and endorsed for a second seven-year term by a referendum held on May 27, 2007.

Vice Presidents: Farouk al-SHARAA (Baath Party); appointed by President Bashar al-ASSAD on February 11, 2006. Ms. Najah al-ATTAR (ind.); appointed by the president on March 23, 2006.

Prime Minister: Wael Nader AL-HALAQI (Baath Party), appointed by the president on August 9, 2012, following the defection of Riad HIJAB on August 6, 2012.

THE COUNTRY

The Syrian Arab Republic is flanked by Turkey on the north; the Mediterranean Sea, Lebanon, and Israel on the west; Jordan on the south; and Iraq on the east. Its terrain is distinguished by the Anti-Lebanon and Alawite mountains running parallel to the Mediterranean, the Jabal al-Druze Mountains in the south, and a semidesert plateau in the southeast, while the economically important Euphrates River Valley traverses the country from north to southeast. Ninety percent of the population is Arab; the most important minorities are Kurds, Armenians, and Turks. The Kurdish population, numbering 300,000, has faced discrimination in a variety of forms since the Baath Party came to power in 1963.

Islam is professed by 87 percent of the people, most of whom belong to the Sunni sect, which dominated the region for some 1,400 years prior to the assumption of power in 1970 by Hafiz al-ASSAD, an Alawite. About 13.5 percent of the population is Alawite, a Shiite offshoot that also draws on some Christian traditions and is viewed as "non-Muslim" by many Sunnis. Alawites have dominated governmental affairs under the regimes of Hafiz al-Assad and, more recently, his son, Bashar al-Assad. Arabic is the official language, but French and English are often spoken in government and business circles.

Syria is one of the few Arab countries with adequate arable land. One-fifth of the workforce is engaged in agriculture (more than half of the women work as unpaid family workers on rural estates). However, a lack of proper irrigation facilities makes agricultural production dependent on variations in rainfall. An agrarian reform law, promulgated in 1958 and modified in 1963, limits the size of individual holdings. Wheat, barley, and cotton are the principal crops, and Syria is one of the world's leading producers of olive oil. Major Syrian industries, the most important of which are food processing, tobacco, and textiles, are nationalized.

Despite experiencing 5.5 percent GDP growth in 2010, Syria's economic growth in 2011 dropped to approximately 1 percent because of social and political unrest in the country. In addition to lower than anticipated GDP growth, Syria's budget deficit surpassed 8 percent in 2011. Adding to the bleak economic news, direct foreign investment dropped during 2011 as well.

After more than 18 months of sustained internecine violence, Syria's GDP contracted significantly in 2012. Though violence and uncertainty obscured key economic data, the IMF reported that European Union (EU) sanctions on Syrian oil exports drove a severe downturn. In August, the Institute of International Finance projected that Syria's real GDP would contract 14–20 percent for the year. By June, the Syrian stock market had lost 50 percent of its January 2011 value, and the local currency had lost nearly the same percentage in black market trading. Agriculture output slipped drastically in 2012, while tourism and direct investment dried up almost completely. As the crisis in Syria entered its third year, the IMF reported that a dearth of economic data kept it from giving a reliable assessment of Syria's economy in 2013, or estimates for 2014.

GOVERNMENT AND POLITICS

Political background. Seat of the Umayyad Empire in early Islamic times before conquest by the Mongols in 1400, Syria was absorbed by the Ottoman Turks in 1517 and became a French-mandated territory under the League of Nations in 1920. A republican government, formed under wartime conditions in 1941, secured the evacuation of French forces in April 1945 and declared the country fully independent on April 17, 1946. Political development was subsequently marked by alternating weak parliamentary governments and unstable military regimes. Syria merged with Egypt on February 1, 1958, to form the United Arab Republic but seceded on September 29, 1961, to reestablish the independent Syrian Arab Republic.

On March 8, 1963, the Baath Arab Socialist Party assumed power through a military-backed coup. Gen. Amin al-HAFIZ became the dominant figure until February 1966 when a second coup led by Maj. Gen. Salah al-JADID resulted in the flight of Hafiz and the installation of Nur al-Din al-ATASSI as president. With Jadid's backing, the Atassi government survived war with Israel and the loss of the Golan Heights in 1967. Crises within the Baath Party precipitated by philosophical differences culminated in a coup led by Lt. Gen. Hafiz al-ASSAD in 1970. Assad became president and was subsequently elected secretary general of the party. The regime established a legislature, and in 1973, held the first national elections. The National Progressive Front (NPF), consisting of the Baath Party and its allies, won an overwhelming majority of seats in the People's Assembly. By 1981, all the seats were distributed among NPF members.

The Alawite background of Assad and some of his top associates triggered opposition among the country's predominantly urban Sunni majority, which experienced economic adversity as a result of the regime's socialist policies. The opposition turned into a rebellion led by the Muslim Brotherhood (see Political Parties, below) after Syria's 1976 intervention on the Maronite side in the Lebanese civil war. The struggle reached its climax in February 1982 in the northern city of Hama in a three-week uprising, which was suppressed with great bloodshed. By 1983, the seven-year insurgency had been decisively crushed, along with the Muslim Brotherhood's stated aim of establishing a fundamentalist Islamic state. (For information concerning the presidency of Hafiz Assad from 1983–1999, see the 2011 *Handbook*.)

After nearly 30 years in power, President Assad died on June 10, 2000. Vice President Abd al-Kalim KHADDAM assumed the position of acting president, although it was immediately apparent that careful plans had been laid for the swift succession of the deceased president's son, Bashar al-Assad. The international community had high hopes for the new president, a Western-trained ophthalmologist. Early in his regime, during what some called the Damascus Spring, Bashar Assad advocated greater media freedom, the release of hundreds of political prisoners, and a more active civil society. However, the emergency law, which was enacted when the Baath Party came to power in 1963, retained a ban on political opposition. The only reforms allowed to flourish were in the economic sector, which experienced an influx of private investment, particularly in Damascus. Nevertheless, the government remained hamstrung by Syria's national security challenges, conflict in Iraq, anti-Syrian ferment in Lebanon, and worsening relations with the United States. By 2003, with reform efforts foundering and relations with the United States turning sour, President Assad appointed Muhammad Naji al-UTRI as prime minister. In 2007, President Assad was endorsed for a second seven-year term, with a "yes" vote of 97.62 percent.

Bashar Assad was confident that Syria was immune from the type of sociopolitical discontent affecting significant portions of the Middle East during the Arab Spring of 2011. However, when what began in February of that year as weak street protests evolved into large-scale demonstrations by a faceless opposition, Assad alternated between ruthless, bloody suppression of dissent and a placating, rhetorical approach offering an array of what his critics described as disingenuous reforms.

In an effort to quell antigovernment protests, President Assad accepted the resignation of his entire cabinet on March 29, 2011. Assad announced on April 3 that he had appointed a new prime minister, Adel SAFAR. Legislation approved in July seemed to usher in a new political era, as it allowed for the licensing of new political parties as long as they were secular and respected "the rule of law."

Throughout 2011 Syria's opposition coordinated its activities by attending meetings in Istanbul to discuss strategy. These meetings spurred the formation of grassroots Local Coordination Committees, loose coalitions of activists intent upon coordinating diffuse pockets of antigovernment sentiment. The Committees, in turn, spawned the Syrian National Council, or SNC (see Political Parties, below). The Council—founded by a diverse set of secularists, Islamists, and Kurds—was intent upon bringing democratic pluralism to Syria. In October, the SNC called for Assad's demise and declared itself a government in exile. It also established a quasi-unified military—the Free Syrian Army (SFA) led by former Syrian Army colonel Riad al-ASAAD.

As fighting between the SFA and government forces intensified, the Arab League met in Cairo to force a ceasefire. Though Assad agreed to abide by a peace plan set forth by the League, his forces kept up their attacks. In response, the League voted to suspend Syria's membership. At an international Friends of Syria summit held in Tunis in February 2012, a group of 70 countries pressed for more sanctions aimed at Syria's leadership. In April, they met again, with Gulf state representatives asking for pledges that would be used to pay SFA salaries. Assad was also criticized by Human Rights Watch (HWR) as the perpetrator of crimes against humanity for relentless shelling of Homs and the torture of civilians and political prisoners. HRW urged the UN Security Council to refer Syria to the International Criminal Court.

Throughout the first half of 2012, the SFA and Syrian forces clashed throughout the country. In all cases Syrian forces held a superior advantage, from access to heavy munitions to a monopoly over airpower. In the midst of violence and instability, Syria managed to hold parliamentary elections, though many newly licensed opposition groups boycotted.

The Assad regime experienced many defections from the military and government in 2012, with the most significant defection being that of Prime Minister Riad HIJAB, who had been in office only two months. In July, a bomb targeting the heart of the regime's power in Damascus killed three top-level defense officials, including the defense minister. With a continuing wave of defections by key government members in early 2013, reports increasingly suggested that the regime was on the verge of collapse.

Constitution and government. According to the 1973 constitution, which succeeded the provisional constitutions of 1964 and 1969, Syria is a socialist popular democracy. Nominated by the legislature upon proposal by the Regional Command of the Baath Party, the president, who must be a Muslim, is elected by popular referendum for a seven-year term. The chief executive wields substantial power, appointing the prime minister and other cabinet members, military personnel, and civil servants; he also serves as military commander in chief. Legislative authority is vested in the People's Assembly (*Majlis al-Shaab*), which is directly elected for a four-year term. Only members of the Baath Party, or independents approved by the government, are allowed to run for an assembly seat. The judicial system, based on a blend of French, Ottoman, and Islamic legal traditions, is headed by the Court of Cassation and includes courts of appeal, summary courts, courts of first instance, and specialized courts for military and religious issues. Constitutional amendments may be proposed by the president but must secure the approval of two-thirds of the assembly.

For administrative purposes, Syria is divided into 13 provinces and the city of Damascus, which is treated as a separate entity. Each of the provinces is headed by a centrally appointed governor who acts in conjunction with a partially elected provincial council.

Government agencies or licensed political, religious, labor, and professional organizations issue most publications. The government controls broadcasting through the Syrian Arab Republic Broadcasting Service. In its 2013 index of freedom of the press, Reporters Without Borders ranked Syria 176th out of 179 countries. The same agency ranked Syria as the deadliest country for journalists in 2012. Once anti-government protests began in March 2011, press access to Syria was extensively curtailed. The UN Human Rights Council (UNHRC) reported that many members of the press have been detained and harassed by Syrian officials. In response to popular protest, in August 2011, the Syrian cabinet passed a new law, Legislative Decree No. 108, which criminalized all public forms of political dissent.

In February 2012, constitutional changes struck the provision that ensconced the Baath party's political dominance. However, in parliamentary elections held in May 2012, the Baath party and its affiliates in the National Progressive Front (NPF) continued their stranglehold on the government.

Foreign relations. Syrian foreign policy priorities are rooted in the fundamental objective of regime survival and center on four issues: Lebanon, the Arab-Israeli conflict, Syria's place in the Arab world, and relations with the United States.

Lebanon has been a problem and an opportunity for Syria since the emergence of the two independent states in the mid-1940s. France carved Lebanon out of Ottoman Syria to create a state containing a small Christian majority. From the standpoint of successive Syrian governments dating back some 50 years, a real "red line" issue is the specter of Lebanon falling altogether out of Syria's orbit and becoming a national security threat to the Damascus regime. (For discussion of Syria's relations with Lebanon from 1975–2000, see the 2013 *Handbook*.)

In 2004, Syria tried to strengthen its position in Lebanon by compelling the Lebanese parliament to adopt a constitutional amendment extending the term of President Emile Lahoud. However, the move fueled Lebanese resentment and drew international condemnation. The UN Security Council (UNSC) passed Resolution 1559, calling for the withdrawal of Syrian military and intelligence personnel and free elections in Lebanon. Rafiq al-Hariri, the former prime minister, was assassinated on February 14, 2005, prompting intense international pressure and massive Lebanese protests against Syria since Damascus topped the list of suspects. Syrian military forces withdrew from Lebanon in April 2005, and Lebanese elections in June produced a majority in parliament supportive of ending Syrian suzerainty. In 2008, Syria signed a formal agreement that for the first time recognized Lebanon's sovereignty, and the country established an embassy in Beirut.

Syria's hard-line policy toward Israel dates back to the first Arab-Israeli war in 1948. At the war's end, Syria alone among the Arab participants was in possession of land allotted to the Jewish state in the UN partition plan. Successive Syrian governments have employed anti-Zionist policies—including wars in 1967, 1973, and 1982—as an essential element of legitimacy within the country. Syrians have traditionally found the dispossession of the Palestinians, the occupation of the Golan Heights, and the willingness of other Arab states to make formal peace with Israel unacceptable and unjust. Yet Syrian policy has not been one of unremitting hostility toward Israel. Since 1974, Damascus has ensured that the cease-fire in the Golan Heights has remained in effect, and since the mid-1990s Syria has indicated its desire for conditional peace with Israel, provided the Israelis withdraw from the Golan Heights up to the boundary that separated Syrian and Israeli forces on the eve of war in 1967.

Since becoming president, Bashar al-Assad has publicly stated a willingness to resume negotiations with Israel, but Syria's alliance with Iran, its support of Hezbollah, and its sheltering of Hamas leaders have made both Israel and the United States skeptical of Syrian motives. Indeed, Syria's arms conduit to Hezbollah was an important factor in the July–August 2006 war between Israel and Hezbollah (see *Israel* entry).

Realizing the image and reality of an Arab-nationalist leadership role has traditionally been a Syrian foreign policy objective with important domestic political implications. The Baath Party founded the notion of pan-Arabism—a political philosophy that sought the unification of Arabs in a common cause. However, by the late 1970s, Syria had begun to recognize that the Arab nationalist movement had run its course. Indeed, Syria's decision to support Iran during the Iran-Iraq war placed it at odds with the entire Arab world, but the schism was mended by Iraq's 1990 invasion of Kuwait. The Iran–Syria alliance is vital to both parties and has taken on added significance in the wake of the 2006 summer war between Hezbollah and Israel. Hezbollah's ability to fight Israel and avoid defeat gave the Shiite organization a heroic image in the Sunni Arab streets, alarming the leaders of Egypt, Jordan, and Saudi Arabia. In their eyes, Syria had become Iran's junior partner and Tehran's tool to penetrate the Levant.

Syria's decisions to participate in the coalition that ousted Iraq from Kuwait and to join in the Arab-Israeli peace process launched at the 1991 Madrid Conference helped reconcile Damascus with Cairo and strengthened its relationship with Saudi Arabia, whose financial assistance was essential. At the same time, the Palestine Liberation Organization's (PLO) closeness to Iraq under Hussein and its decision to seek a separate peace with Israel only hardened the long-standing enmity between Assad and PLO chair Yasir Arafat and convinced Assad to pursue a peace process of his own.

In 1998, Turkey threatened to counter Syrian support of Kurdish nationalists by invading Syria. However, the two countries eventually found common ground on Kurdish separatism and overcame their differences over Euphrates River water and the Turkish province of Hatay, which Syria claimed.

(For information concerning U.S.–Syrian relations from 1990–2008, see the 2011 *Handbook*.) The Obama administration, which took office in January 2009, began to engage Syria diplomatically, and some analysts suggested that efforts by Assad to reorganize the Syrian government was an attempt to improve relations with the United States. However, the United States announced renewed sanctions against Syria in May, with President Barack Obama declaring that Syria was a serious threat to his country.

In 2010, Syria's foreign relations improved on a number of fronts. In March, Saudi Arabia extended development loans to help Syria finance infrastructure. Although Washington had rebuked Syria for sending long-range missiles to Hezbollah, the Obama administration eased exports of American telecommunications equipment to private U.S. firms working on projects in Syria. In addition, President Obama appointed Stephen FORD as the first U.S. ambassador to Syria since 2005. Initial American attempts to engage Syria, however, were dulled by Ford's reiteration of U.S. priorities in the region: reduction of Syrian support for Hamas and Hezbollah, as well as diminution of the relationship between Tehran and Damascus. This American pronouncement came soon after Iraq and Syria had reestablished diplomatic relations.

In 2011, Syria's foreign relationships were significantly affected by the public uprising against President Assad. The crackdown on protests resulted in numerous U.S. sanctions against Syrian officials. In August, President Obama called on Assad to step down—stopping short, however, of suggesting a military intervention. The United States supported UN attempts to stop Syrian violence, but unrelenting bloodshed prompted the Obama administration to recall Ambassador Ford and close its embassy. Intelligence community observers reported in 2012 that the United States was covertly supporting certain elements of the Syrian opposition movement. The United States criticized Russia over its relationship with Syria when reports surfaced that Russia would be shipping attack helicopters to Damascus. In light of statements made by an Assad regime official in August 2012 that the country's chemical weapons would be used in case of an external attack (the first-ever admission that Syria possessed such weapons), President Obama warned that the U.S. military would interpret the movement of such weapons as a provocation. Despite reservations about al-Qaida affiliated groups operating within the rebel fold, the Obama administration increased financial aid to the rebels and started to provide some weapons and munitions in September 2013.

In 2011, Russia and China scuttled all UN attempts to condemn the Syrian government. In March, a peace plan offered by the UN's special envoy to Syria—former UN secretary general Kofi Annan—authorized the deployment of UN observers to implement a ceasefire. The deployment, known as UN Supervising Mission in Syria (UNSMIS), could not stop the violence, but did bring about Annan's resignation. He was replaced by former Algerian foreign minister Lakhdar Brahimi. Intent upon implementing a ceasefire plan of his own, Brahimi tried to halt the violence in October 2012, but neither the government nor the rebels adhered to his plan. The UNHRC warned Syrian rebel groups that they would be prosecuted for crimes against humanity along with Assad if they were found guilty of atrocities in their prosecution of the war. Concern about human costs in the conflict, the UN appealed to member states in 2013 to raise $5 billion in order to give humanitarian aid to the estimated 6 million Syrians affected by the war.

EU officials announced an arms embargo against Syria in late 2011, and banned the importation of Syrian oil into Europe—Syria's biggest market. Anti-Assad groups requested North Atlantic Treaty Organization (NATO) intervention against the Assad regime, asking Alliance members to implement a no-fly zone over the country. However, NATO members ruled out such an action. After the Syrian army was accused of committing a massacre in the city of Houla, France, Germany, the UK, Italy, Spain, the Netherlands, Switzerland, and Bulgaria suspended diplomatic relations with Syria. In 2013 the EU also increased sanctions against the Assad regime and stepped up nonlethal support to the opposition.

Relations between Syria and Turkey began to deteriorate in 2011 and continued through 2013. At the outset of the uprising against Assad, Turkish Prime Minister Recep Erdogen announced his country's preference that Assad not be forced from power. The Turks pressed Assad to enact political reforms and to avoid bloodshed at all costs. However, Turkish troops were forced to guard their border repeatedly from 2011 through 2013, as the Syrian army besieged towns along the divide between the two countries. Turkey increased sanctions on Syria, and trade between the two countries slowed to a trickle. Istanbul also allowed Syrian exile groups to use Turkey as a base.

Turkish–Syrian relations were put to a severe test in June 2012, when Syrian air defense shot down a Turkish jet that had strayed into Syria's airspace. In October, Syrian mortar shells landed in a Turkish border village, killing five. In response, Turkish artillery shelled positions inside Syria for a week, an act representing the first direct military intervention in Syria during the crisis. Officials in Ankara asked NATO to develop a plan for the protection of Turkey in the event of a Syrian assault. Turkey's National Assembly voted to authorize force against Syria if national security was threatened by Assad. In a heightened state of vigilance, Turkish authorities forced a Syrian passenger plane flying from Moscow to Damascus to land in Ankara due to suspicions that it was carrying weapons for Assad's army. Both Syria and Turkey eventually closed their airspace to one another. Officials in Ankara reported that over 150,000 Syrian refugees had registered in Turkey and that it could not build camps to house them quickly enough.

Though Saudi Arabia at first said little about the situation in Syria, as violence increased during 2011 Riyadh voiced its displeasure. By February 2012, all six of the Gulf Cooperation Council (GCC) member states had recalled their diplomats and had expelled their Syrian counterparts. The Saudis and Qataris increased both financial and military aid to Syrian rebels, often indiscriminately. Acting with Turkey, the Gulf States attempted to coordinate the opposition's military operation by forming and arming a Supreme Military Council consisting of 30 allied rebel militias. In addition, Saudi intelligence chief Bandar bin Sultan offered to buy a massive amount of Russian arms if Moscow would abandon its ally Assad—a proposal rebuffed by President Vladimir Putin.

In response to the hundreds of thousands of Syrians crossing over the border into Lebanon, a leader of Lebanon's Future Block called upon Arab leaders to force Assad to stop his violent crackdown. However, Beirut's official stance on Syria was neutrality: In both UN and Arab League votes condemning the Assad regime, Lebanon either voted not to criticize its neighbor or abstained from voting. However, Lebanon's growing sectarian divide helped fuel conflict in Syria, as Shia Hezbollah militia members loyal to Assad and Sunni Salafi fighters loyal to the opposition fought inside Syria. In May 2013 Hezbollah's leadership declared it had joined an all-out battle to defeat anti-Assad forces, a move that increased the ranks of Sunni radicals drawn to fight in Syria. As a direct result, Shia-Sunni sectarian violence ramped up in Lebanon, and FSA leaders promised retribution against Hezbollah inside Lebanese territory. (See Lebanon entry.)

Observers noted that Israel's natural preference vis-à-vis the crisis in Syria was to deal with Assad rather than with an al-Qaida influenced successor regime. However, reacting to intelligence that Iranian weapons near Damascus were being shipped to Hezbollah in Lebanon, the Israeli air force bombed several Syrian targets in May 2013. In November 2011, Jordan's King Abdullah II called on Assad to quit, becoming the first Arab leader to make such a declaration. In retaliation, Assad loyalists attacked the Jordanian embassy in Damascus. In 2012, military units from Syria and Jordan exchanged gunfire near the Jordanian border cities of Al-Ramtha and Tel-Shihab. In response, officials in Amman started providing greater support for Syrian rebels, and requested sophisticated U.S. weaponry to bolster Jordan's border defenses.

In July 2011, Iran rebuked the Assad regime for failing to accede to legitimate demands of Syrians, and in September, President Mahmoud AHMADINEJAD strongly urged Assad to end civil strife and embrace the Syrian opposition. However, Iran provided diplomatic cover for Syria in the Organization of Islamic Cooperation (OIC), which sought to expel Syria in August 2012. Western and Israeli intelligence officers believe Tehran has provided Syria with materiel, personnel, intelligence, and funding since 2011. Members of the SFA reported that Iran's Revolutionary Guards forces had been active in Syria, and in September 2012, Iran confirmed that members of the Guard's elite Quds Force were helping the Assad regime as "counselors." In 2013 Iran continued to supply its allies in Damascus with materiel flown through Iraqi air space. Reports also revealed that the Iranians—working with Hezbollah—had established a 50,000 man "parallel army" designed to support the weary and increasingly depleted Syrian army.

As the war in Syria escalated, Iraq became concerned about refugee inflows: Border troops were reinforced and crossings into Syria randomly closed to limit immigration and maintain security. Iraq has accepted far fewer Syrian refugees than any of Syria's other neighbors. In 2013 Iraqi officials admitted that some parts of western Iraq bordering Syria were out of Tehran's control and were increasingly dominated by the region's al-Qaida franchise, the Islamic State in Iraq (ISI). Some ISI militias attacked Syrian troops that were forced over the border into Iraq by rebels, killing dozens.

Current issues. Throughout 2013 civil war continued to dominate life in Syria, bringing increasing loss of life, civil instability, and economic ruin. Fighting intensified, as Aleppo, Qusayr, Homs, Daraa, and the eastern suburbs of Damascus experienced extended sieges. In late 2012 the FSA was able to return its command center to the areas of Syria—mostly rural and in the north—under rebel control. It appeared as late as February 2013 that the rebels had gained tactical advantage over the Syrian army, which continued to experience defections and fatigue. The rebels successfully captured air force bases near Damascus and in the north but could not use the assets or hold their position as the Syrian Air Force continued to operate without opposition. An increased number of foreign fighters entered the country, with Hezbollah providing enough of an advantage to allow government forces to reclaim Qusayr. As government troops reasserted control over Homs, and the regime intensified bombing raids and the use of SCUD missiles, the tide of war turned to Assad's favor by July. After rebel groups started to fight each other over access to liberated territory, and international actors—most notably the United States—failed to respond to Assad's purported use of chemical weapons, observers asserted that the regime had reestablished the upper hand over a divided opposition (see below). Some analysts speculated that with staunch support from his allies Russia, Iran, and Hezbollah, it appeared that Assad was capable of continuing to fend off the challenge to his rule.

The UN concluded that by mid-2013, over 100,000 Syrians had died in 28 months of violence and warfare, and another 2 million people—half on them children—had sought refuge in neighboring countries. The economic toll on Syria has been devastating: factories and farmland have been wrecked and burned, oil fields plundered, and tourist spots vacated. According to unofficial reports, the national economy has contracted by 35 percent, personal savings have evaporated, the currency lost 85 percent of its value, and $15 billion of public infrastructure has been destroyed. Once a country proud of its low national debt, Syria has been forced to survive by borrowing from Russia, China, and Iran.

Reports also indicated that the opposition had become increasingly fractious, beset by ideological and religious differences. Though its headquarters returned to Syria, the FSA had only moderate influence on the plethora of militias financed by private donors with allegiances to hardline Salafi groups such as the Nusra Front (*Jabhat al-Nusra*). Led by Abu Muhammad al-JOULANI, Nusra has been in regular contact with the head of al-Qaida in Pakistan, Adman al-Zawahri. Western intelligence determined that another al-Qaida affiliate, *al-Qaida in Iraq*, became increasingly active in Syria during 2013, with reports that it may have merged with Nusra to form *al-Qaida in Iraq and the Levant* (*al-Shams*), or ISIS. Foreign fighters from as far away as Scandinavia were drawn to Syria as both Zawahiri and Jordanian Salafi cleric Abou Mohamad Tahawi released fatwas declaring jihad against Alawites.

Despite reports that Syrian rebels were becoming more radical and sectarian, Western states were active in helping the broad insurgency. Reports surfaced that the United States, the United Kingdom, and France continued to train rebels it vetted for ties to hardline Salafis. In addition, Saudi Arabia, Qatar, and Turkey continued to provide weapons and cash to certain rebel groups. However, by September 2013 news reports indicated that rebels groups were fighting and killing each other, either for ideological reasons—many Salafi groups viewed secular FSA troops as corrupt "sinners"—or to control spoils of conquest such as food supplies and oil fields.

The specter of chemical weapons use cast a long shadow over Iraq in 2013. Though Western leaders—particularly from the United States—continually warned Assad not to use such weapons, intelligence based upon isolated incidents indicated that either the regime or the rebels had used them in March and April. France and the UK informed the UN of evidence showing the use of sarin gas near Damascus, Homs, and Aleppo. The Assad regime blamed rebels, but the rebels implicated the regime. U.S. president Barack Obama said that Assad's use of chemical weapons would be a "game changer" that could lead to military intervention, though the next month the White House admitted that the regime had probably used them already.

On August 21, 2013, news agencies reported claims by rebels in eastern Damascus that gas attacks there had claimed hundreds of victims overnight. Videos posted on the Internet showed corpses of men, women, and children aligned in neat rows. In what was verified as the deadliest lethal gas attack since the 1980s (Saddam Hussein's gassing of Kurds in Halabja, Iraq), more than 1,400 people died from exposure to sarin gas delivered by rocket fire. Western leaders condemned the attack, promising dire consequences, while the Russians called for an investigation—insinuating that the attack might have be a "provocation" by the rebels. Syria denied involvement and also blamed the opposition.

Knowing that Russia and China would likely defeat a Security Council resolution authorizing a military response to Assad, UK and U.S. chief executives requested authorization to intervene in Syria from their legislatures. British Parliament declined to give Prime Minister David Cameron such license. In Washington President Obama lobbied Congress for such authority, but Congressional action was obviated when Russian President Vladimir Putin proposed a plan whereby the United States would forgo military action against Syria if the Assad regime would place its chemical arsenal under international control for eventual destruction. Critics pointed out that the act of securing approximately 1,000 tons of chemical stockpiles during the midst of a civil war might be impossible, while French and U.S. sources expressed concern about verification—especially if Russia were to play a lead role in facilitating the transfer process. Russia and the United States reached an agreement on September 14 that required Syria to enumerate its chemical weapons, transfer them to a UN-sponsored disposal team, and sign the Chemical Weapons Convention. According to U.S. officials, by mid-2014 all of the weapons and materials will have been collected. Though not formalized in the agreement, the United States reserved its right to act militarily should Assad not comply with the process.

POLITICAL PARTIES

Since the 1970s, Syria has been a single-party state. Though theoretically committed to pluralism, the Arab Baath Socialist party has dominated politics since the assent of its most dominant leader, Hafiz al-Assad. However, in July 2011, the country adopted legislation allowing new political parties to form—ostensibly in opposition to the Baath party. Though a dozen new groups have gained official party status, many more have preferred to remain unlicensed. Most true opposition parties and coalitions do not even operate in Syria, while many domestic entities recognized by the Assad regime as legitimate opposition parties are widely believed to be part of a pseudo-opposition fabricated by Assad loyalists.

Government Parties:

National Progressive Front (NPF). In 1972, President Hafiz al-Assad formed the NPF, a coalition of parties that has always been heavily dominated by the Syrian Baath. Following the death of Hafiz al-Assad in 2000, the other NPF components joined the Baath in endorsing his son, Bashar, as his presidential successor. Bashar al-Assad was elected that year. Subsequently, some previously outlawed parties were allowed to join the NPF as long as membership was not based on ethnicity or religion, including the **Syrian Social Nationalist Party**, which had been banned since 1955. Assad was reelected in 2007 for a second seven-year term. Minor parties that make up the remainder of the NPF are the **Arab Socialist Union Party**, **Arab Socialist Party**, **Syrian Communist Party**, **Union Socialist Party**, and **Union Socialist Democratic Party**.

Leaders: Bashar al-ASSAD (Chair), Sulayman QADDAH (Deputy Chair).

Baath Party. The Baath Party enjoyed de facto dominance of the Syrian political system since 1963, its long tenure partly attributable to its influence among the military. Formally known as the Baath (Renaissance) Arab Socialist Party (*Hizb al-Baath al-Arabi al-Ishtiraki*), the Baath Party is the Syrian branch of an international political movement that began in 1940. The contemporary party dates from a 1953 merger of the Arab Resurrectionist Party, founded in 1947 by Michel Aflak and Salah al-Din Bitar, and the Syrian Socialist Party, founded in 1950 by Akram al-Hawrani. The Baath Party philosophy stresses socialist ownership of the principal means of production, redistribution of agricultural land, secular political unity of the Arab world, and opposition to imperialism.

At the Baath Party's 2005 congress, younger members were elected to key committee positions, reflecting efforts by President Bashar al-Assad to give the party a more youthful look. Nevertheless, in terms of policy direction there was little substantive change from the party's core principles. Assad's regime resorted to more repressive measures after the 2005 Congress, leading to a consolidation of power before the 2007 elections. Nevertheless, the party has been challenged by violence and independent politicians calling for democratic change.

As President Assad turned to violent suppression of antigovernment demonstrations in 2011, some 230 party members—mostly from the region of southern Syrian surrounding Daraa—resigned their memberships. Commentators noted that these defections were best viewed in context as the party consisted of 2 million members nationwide. Observers pointed out that the majority of party members appeared to understand that the institution of significant political reforms would weaken Baath's monopolistic control of government. In 2012, most reports indicated that, despite some defections to the opposition, the vast majority of party members and leaders still supported President Assad. In July 2013 the party choose 16 new leaders to replace the existing leadership. One of the deposed leaders was Vice President Farouk al-SHARAA, who was retained in that post despite losing his position in the party. The speaker of the People's Assembly, Jihad al-Laham, and Prime Minister Wael al-Halaqi were among the new slate of leaders.

Leaders: Bashar al-ASSAD (President of the Republic, Secretary General of the Party, and Chair of the NPF), Jihad al-LAHAM, Wael Nader al-HALAQI.

Syrian Social Nationalist Party (*al-Hizb al-Suri al-Qawmi al-Ijtimai*—SSNP). Formally banned in the 1970s, the SSNP supports creation of "Greater Syria." In 2005, the SSNP was legalized and became the first official non-Arab, non-socialist political grouping.

The party secured two seats in the 2007 elections. Reports in 2009 alleged widespread dissatisfaction with party leader Asaad HARDAN among the rank-and-file members. When Prime Minister Safar assembled a new cabinet in April 2011, SSNP member and former minster of expatriates George SUWAYD was appointed minster of state.

Leaders: Asaad HARDAN (Party Chair), Issam al-MAHAYRI (Secretary General).

Opposition Groups:

Syrian Social Nationalist Party (*al-Intifada*). Though it shares the name of the party led by Asaad Hardan (see above), this unofficial party is led by regime stalwart and current minister of national reconciliation, Ali HAIDAR. Haidar merged his party into the National Committee for the Unity of Syrian Communists and combined forces to form the Popular Front for Change and Liberation in 2011 (see below). In 2012, the party joined the Coalition for Peaceful Change Forces, a large collection of unlicensed parties (see below). Haidar choose to run for parliament in May 2012 under the banner of the Popular Front for Change and Liberation, winning his seat.

The Arab Revolutionary Workers' Party. This socialist party has been active in the National Democratic Rally, while still participating in the Damascus Declaration for Democratic National Change (see below).

Leaders: Abdul Hafiz HAFIZ (Secretary-General), Tariq Abu al-HASSAN (Chair).

The Assyrian Democratic Organization—ADO. The largest Assyrian political organization in Syria, this party counts primarily Christians as members. It also was a founding member of the Damascus Declaration. As a party in exile, the ADO was also a founding member of the SNC in 2011.

Leader: Gabriel Moushe GAWRIEH (President).

The Communist Labor Party. As a far left opposition party, the Communist Labor Party has been in a plethora of coalitions simultaneously: the National Democratic Assembly, the Marxist Left Assembly, and the National Coordination Body for Democratic Change.

Leader: Fateh JAMOUS (Secretary-General).

The Democratic Arab Socialist Union—DASU. Though this party was originally established in 1964, it drifted toward an oppositional role in June 2011, when it helped found the National Coordination Body for Democratic Change. Party leader Hassan Abdul AZIM became the general coordinator for that coalition, yet the DASU officially parted way with the National Coordination Body in 2012.

Leader: Hassan Abdul AZIM (Secretary-General).

The Democratic Socialist Arab Baath Party. A splinter group from the ruling Baath party, this group has been in existence since 1970. In light of the 2011 uprising against President Assad, the party joined the National Coordination Body for Democratic Change.

The Syrian Democratic People's Party. This is an opposition party that is a member of both the National Democratic Assembly and the SNC. The party opposed the Damascus Declaration and allied itself loosely with other opposition groups in the banned opposition alliance, the Democratic National Gathering (DNG). A leading figure in the party, Georges SABRA, was arrested in June 2011 for the third time in three years and was held by Syrian security services until September 19, 2011.

Leaders: Giath Uyoun al-SOUD (Secretary-General), Riad al-TURK (Founder).

The Kurdish Democratic Union Party. A spin-off from the Turkistan Workers' Party outlawed by the Turkish government, this Syrian branch has not been well received by Damascus either. In 2011, the party chose not to join the largest Kurdish opposition block, the Kurdish National Council, instead opting for the smaller grouping in the Kurdish Patriotic Movement. Saleh Muslim MOHAMMED has led this party since 2010 and was reconfirmed as chair in 2012.

Leaders: Saleh Muslim MOHAMMED (Chair), Asiyah ABDULLAH (Cochair).

The Kurdish Democratic Party in Syria. This party helped found the Kurdish National Council and is closely allied with Kurdish movements outside of Syria—most notably, the Kurdish Democratic Party in Iraq. Observers agree that the Kurdish Democratic Party in Syria is the strongest of Syrian's Kurdish parties.

Leader: Abdul Hakim BASHAR (Secretary-General).

Kurdish Future Movement. Founded by Mashaal TAMMO in 2005, this group allied in 2011 with the smaller Yekiti and Azadi Kurdish parties to join the SNC. Tammo was assassinated in late 2011, with loyalists blaming either the Syrian government or members of the Kurdish Democratic Union Party for his death. Since Tammo's murder, internal leadership battles have weakened the Movement.

Leaders: Rezan Bahri SHAYKHMUS (Chair), Jangidar MUHAMMAD (Rival Chair).

The National Committee for the Unity of Syrian Communists (The Party of the Popular Will). This party is a splinter from one branch of the Syrian Communist Party (a member of the ruling NPF) and is led by Qadri JAMIL. In 2011, the party allied with Ali Haidar's al-Intifada branch of the Syrian Social Nationalist Party to form the Popular Front for Change and Liberation, which changed its name to Party of the Popular Will. Though it has not received official status as a party, Jamil decided to take his group into the larger Coalition of Peaceful Change Forces. In June 2012, Jamil was appointed deputy prime minister for economic affairs.

Leader: Qadri JAMIL (Chair).

National Development Party. Licensed by the Syrian government in 2012, observers question whether this secular party calling for a modern, democratic Syria is a true voice of opposition or merely a façade constructed by the Assad regime. Party leader Zaher Saadaldine announced the party's intention to field candidates in the May 2012 parliamentary elections but later joined a boycott against the polling.

Leaders: Zaher SAADALDINE (Founder), Mohammed SAMAAN (Spokesperson).

National Youth for Justice and Development. Though some observers have questioned whether this officially licensed party is a legitimate opposition party, it did run candidates in the 2012 parliamentary elections. However, it denounced the polling as fraudulent and asked the Supreme Constitutional Court to void the results. The party was not invited to take part in 2012's national reconciliation dialogue. Party president Berwyn Ibrahim is the only female political party leader in Syria.

Leader: Berwyn IBRAHIM (Secretary General).

Other newly licensed parties include **Syria the Homeland Party,** led by Ghatfan Hammoud and Majd Niazi; **Together for a Free and Democratic Syria,** represented by Munther Bader Halloum and Munther Khaddam; **National Democratic Solidarity Party,** led by Selim Al-Kharrat; **National Initiative Party**; **Syrian National Youth Party; Democratic Vanguard; Arab Democratic Solidarity Party; Partisans Party; Democratic Party;** and **National Development Party**.

Reform Party of Syria—RPS (*Hizb al-Islah al-Suri*). The RPS is a U.S.-based opposition party formed in 2001. It is opposes the Baath ideology of the Syrian government. In September 2011 the RPS criticized the administration of U.S. president Barack Obama for holding talks with the Syrian American Council, known supporters of the Muslim Brotherhood in Syria. The RPS suggested that the Obama administration was giving tacit support for the Brotherhood's aspirations to turn Syria into an "Islamic state instead of a democracy."

Leaders: Marc HUSSEIN (Secretary General), Farid GHADRY (Co-founder and Former President).

Muslim Brotherhood (*al-Ikhwan*). Founded in the 1940s, the Brotherhood is a Sunni Islamist movement that took part in parliamentary elections in its early history, winning 10 seats in 1961. The Brotherhood was banned by the Baath Party after the 1963 coup, and since then it has maintained an active underground campaign against the Baath Party and its leadership. It was charged, inter alia, with the massacres in Aleppo and Latakia in 1979 as well as the killing of a number of Soviet technicians and military advisers in 1980. In February 1982 it instigated an open insurrection in Hama that government troops quelled after three weeks of intense fighting that resulted in the devastation of one-fourth of the city and the deaths of more than ten thousand. Brotherhood members were among political prisoners released in 2000 with the advent of the so-called Damascus Spring. At the same time, the Brotherhood remained illegal, membership was punishable by death, and its leadership remained in exile.

Under Ali Sadr al-Din al-BAYANUNI, the Brotherhood intermittently negotiated with the Syrian government, stopped insisting on the right to use violence, no longer called for the introduction of sharia, and claimed to support a democratic system of government. It played a key role in drafting the Damascus Declaration. In 2005 the Brotherhood formed the National Salvation Front with other Syrian opposition members, but broke with the group in 2009.

In 2010, the Brotherhood elected a new secretary general, Riyadh al-SHAQFA, a leading figure in the group's military wing during the 1980s. Analysts believed the vote indicated the party's move toward a more aggressive stance against the Assad regime. In August al-Shaqfa announced that the Brotherhood's "truce" with the Assad regime had ended. In April 2011 the Brotherhood lent its rhetorical support to the antigovernment protestors and called upon all Syrians to unite for freedom. In addition, it helped establish the SNC, and in 2012, Brotherhood members held more than a quarter of the Council seats. Later in the year, Brotherhood political bureau chief Ali al-Bayanuni announced the group's intent to seek a license for its own—as yet unnamed—political party. In 2013 the Brotherhood started distributing a newspaper, *al-Ahed*, in areas occupied by rebel groups, and it became closely aligned with a coalition of antigovernment militias known as Shields of the Revolution.

Leaders: Riyadh al-SHAQFA (Comptroller General), Mohammad Farouk TAYFOUR (Deputy Comptroller General), Hatem al-TABSHI (Shura Council President).

Islamic Liberation Party (*Hizb al-Tahrir al-Islami*—ILP). The Islamic Liberation Party advocates the political and religious union of the entire Arab world. Hundreds of ILP members were reportedly detained by security forces in late 1999 and early 2000 in connection with a crackdown that coincided with fighting between Islamist militants and the Lebanese army in northern Lebanon. The ILP also strongly criticized the resumption of peace talks between Syria and Israel. Many of the ILP detainees were reportedly released in November 2000 under an amnesty issued by president Bashar al-Assad. In 2003 five ILP members were sentenced to prison terms ranging from eight to ten years. In July 2009 the ILP caused a stir in the United States when it held a conference in Chicago on the fall of capitalism and the rise of Islam.

Leader: Mohammad JABER.

Coalitions:

Damascus Declaration for Democratic National Change (DDDNC). Reformers had hoped Bashar al-Assad's pledge to promote greater openness during the Damascus Spring would translate into the formation of new parties. When it became apparent the promise of openness had been abandoned, the Damascus Declaration, signed by members of the opposition in October 2005, called for a nonviolent democratic overhaul of the Syrian government. In December 2007, coalition members met to elect the leadership of the group's National Council. Forty attendees were subsequently arrested, although most were released. In October 2008, 12 activists, including Secretary General Riad SEIF and chair of the National Council Fida al-HAWRANI, were found guilty of "weakening national feeling" and "spreading false news" and sentenced to 30 months in prison. Seif was released and left the Declaration. In 2011, the Declaration's members helped found the SNC (see below). The DDDNC organized a late 2012 meeting in Damascus that featured critics of the Assad regime calling for the president to step down.

Leaders: Samir NASHAR (Secretariat General president), Anas al-ABDEH (Secretariat General member).

The Syrian National Council—SNC. Though it operates in exile with headquarters in Turkey, the SNC is the largest political group opposing Bashar al-Assad's regime. However, its leadership has been in constant flux, and critics note its effectiveness has been muted by internal discord. Several subfactions exist within the SNC, and two of the most important are the Revolutionary Movement—represented by Hozan IBRAHIM—and the Bloc of Liberal Independents—led by former SNC chairman Burhan GHALIOUN. During 2012, both statements issued at the Friends of Syria conference and the actions of heads of state showed that the SNC's legitimacy as a government in exile was highly suspect.

National Coordination Body for Democratic Change. The goal of this loose coalition of unarmed opposition groups and parties is to provide the impetus for a new constitution, a democratic electoral system, the release of political prisoners, and—eventually—the prosecution of those responsible for Syria's political violence. However, members of the group decided not to attend the two Friends of Syria conferences held during 2012.

Leaders: Hassan Abdul AZIM (Chair), Haytham MANNA (Deputy Chairman).

The National Bloc. This coalition has featured a fluid and unstable membership list. In June 2012, the Bloc met in Rome and split into two factions: One was christened the Union of Democratic Coordination, and was led by Ahmad Ramadan; the other faction did not name itself but picked Radwan ZIADEH as its leader. An influential female leader, Basma Qodmani, left the Bloc in July 2012.

Leaders: Ahmad RAMADAN, Mutie al-BUTEIN, Tawfik DUNIA.

The Kurdish National Council in Syria—KNC. Another coalition operating in exile, this group was founded during late 2011 and is based in Iraq. At its high point in 2012, it attracted 11 Kurdish parties to its ranks, including groups formerly allied with the Kurdish Democratic Front.

Leaders: Abdul Hakim BASHAR (Chair), Khair al-Dien MURAD (Head of Foreign Relations).

The National Coalition for Opposition Forces and the Syrian Revolution—The Syrian National Coalition (SNC). The Syrian Nation Council, facing criticism that its exile status and unstable leadership made it difficult to attract international support, was convinced to join with activists and fighters based inside Syria in the National Coalition for Opposition Forces and the Syrian Revolution—an organization cobbled together at a November 2012 conference in Qatar. The new grouping is known as the Syrian National Coalition, and in addition to the members of the Syrian National Council, it includes representatives from local coordinating committees, Syrian human rights groups, academics, and citizens' groups. The fist leader was Moaz al-KHATIB, a well-known cleric. At the fourth Friends of Syria conference in December 2012, the SNC was formally recognized as the legitimate representative of the Syrian people, though nonattendees—notably, Russia and China—did not. The SNC went forward with installing a shadow government with a prime minister and a military command, though its effect on governance and the prosecution of the war within Syria was minimal. Its effectiveness was not helped by internecine squabbles, such as when the group elected as shadow prime minister Ghassan HITTO, a favorite of the Syrian Muslim Brotherhood, and the Coalition's military command leader, General Selim IDRISS, refused to recognize him.

Leaders: Ahmad JARBA (Secretary General), Riad SEIF (Vice President), Suheir ATASSI (Vice President).

LEGISLATURE

The **People's Assembly** (*Majlis al-Shaab*) is a directly elected, unicameral body presently consisting of 250 members serving four-year terms. In elections held in May 2012, the NPF (which is comprised of the Syrian Baath Party and six small parties) won 167 seats, and independents won 83 seats.

Speaker: Mohammed Jihad al-LAHAM (Baath Party).

CABINET

[as of September 1, 2013]

Prime Minister	Wael Nader al-Halaqi
Deputy Prime Minister for Economic Affairs	Qadri Jamil
Deputy Prime Minister for Foreign Affairs and Expatriates	Walid al-Muallem
Deputy Prime Minister for Local Administration	Omar Ibrahim Ghalawanji
Deputy Prime Minister for Economic Affairs	Qadri Jamil
Ministers	
Agriculture and Agrarian Reform	Ahmad al-Qadri
Communications and Technology	Imad Abdul-Ghani Sabbouni
Housing and Urban Development	Hussein Mohammad Farzat
Culture	Lubana Mushaweh [f]
Defense	Fahd Jassim al-Freij
Economy and Foreign Trade	Khodr Orfali
Education	Hazwan al-Wazz

Electricity	Imad Mohammad Deeb Khamis
Finance	Ismael Ismael
Health	Saad Assalam al-Nayef
Higher Education	Malek Ali
Industry	Kamal Eddin Touma
Information	Omran al-Zohbi
Interior	Mohammad Ibrahim al-Shaar
Internal Trade and Consumer Protection	Samir Izzat Kadi Amin
Justice	Najem Hamad al-Ahmad
Labor	Hassan Hijazi
Petroleum and Mineral Resources	Suleiman al-Abbas
Presidential Affairs	Mansour Fadlallah Azzam
Public Works	Hussein Arnous
Religious Trusts	Abdul-Sattar al-Sayed
Social Affairs	Kinda al-Shammat [f]
Tourism	Bisher Riyad Yazigi
Transport	Mahmoud Said
Water Resources and Irrigation	Bassam Hanna

Ministers of State

Environment	Nazira Sarkis [f]
National Reconciliation	Ali Haidar
Ministers of State	Hussein Mahmoud Farzat
	Joseph Suwayd
	Muhammad Turki al-Sayyid
	Hasseb Elias Shammas
	Abdullah Khalil Hussain
	Jamal Shaban Shaheen

[f] = female

INTERGOVERNMENTAL REPRESENTATION

Ambassador to the U.S.: (Vacant).

U.S. Ambassador to Syria: Robert S. FORD (located in Istanbul, Turkey).

Permanent Representative to the UN: Bashar JA'AFARI.

IGO Memberships (Non-UN): NAM, OIC, LAS.

TAJIKISTAN

Republic of Tajikistan
Jumhurii Tojikiston

Political Status: Designated autonomous republic within the Uzbek Soviet Socialist Republic on October 27, 1924; became constituent republic of the Union of Soviet Socialist Republics (USSR) on October 16, 1929; declared independence as Republic of Tajikistan on September 9, 1991; current constitution adopted by referendum on November 6, 1994.

Area: 55,250 sq. mi. (143,100 sq. km).

Population: 7,128,014 (2012E—UN); 7,768,385 (2012E—U.S. Census).

Major Urban Centers (2007E): DUSHANBE (670,168), Khujand (155,316).

Official Language: Tajik. Although the 1994 constitution accords Russian the status of a language of interethnic communication, a law passed in October 2009 requires all official government communication to be conducted in Tajik and states that all citizens should have a working knowledge of the language. Use of other languages in daily communication has not, however, been proscribed.

Monetary Unit: Somoni (official rate November 1, 2013: 4.77 somoni = $1US).

President: Emomali RAHMON (Imomali RAKHMONOV; People's Democratic Party of Tajikistan); designated by the Supreme Soviet on November 19, 1992, upon the resignation of Akbarsho ISKANDAROV (Islamic Renaissance Party); reelected by popular vote on November 6, 1994, and inaugurated for a five-year term on November 16; reelected for a seven-year term in 1999, November 6, 2006, and on November 18, 2006; most recently reelected on November 6, 2013.

Prime Minister: Oqil OQILOV (Akil AKILOV; originally identified with Communist Party of Tajikistan); appointed by presidential decree on December 20, 1999, succeeding Yakhyo AZIMOV (Communist Party of Tajikistan), who, as required by the constitution after a presidential election, had resigned on November 23 but remained in office during the interim; dismissed along with the entire cabinet on November 30, 2006, following the presidential election of November 6; reappointed on December 1 and confirmed by the Supreme Assembly on December 16; reappointed following parliamentary elections on February 28, 2010.

THE COUNTRY

Mountainous Tajikistan is bordered by Kyrgyzstan on the north, China on the east, Afghanistan on the south, and Uzbekistan on the west. Approximately 80 percent of the population is Tajik, 15 percent Uzbek, and only 1 percent Russian, as a consequence of a significant exodus of minorities in the 1990s. The dominant religion is Sunni Islam. Women make up about 44 percent of the active labor force, as well as 19 percent of the lower house and 14.7 percent of the upper house in parliament.

Although less than 10 percent of Tajikistan is arable, ample water supplies have helped make its farmland very productive, the leading crops being cotton, grains, vegetables, and fruits. The agricultural sector as a whole employs half of the workforce, and accounts for 21.4 percent of GDP. The industrial sector employs 12.8 percent of the active labor force but contributed 21.7 percent of GDP in 2011. Fueled by the country's extensive hydroelectric capacity, industry remains concentrated in such energy-intensive ventures as ore extraction and refining. Aluminum, by far the most important industrial product, is the leading national export, followed by hydroelectricity and cotton. Other mineral resources include gold, silver, and uranium. Leading manufactures include clothing and textiles, processed foods, and carpets. Turkey is the country's largest export partner at 30.5 percent, and China is the largest import partner at 42.3 percent of total.

Tajikistan was severely impacted by the 2009 international financial crisis moving from a respectable GDP growth rate of 7.9 percent in 2008 to 3.9 percent in 2009. A key factor in the slower growth rate was a drop in remittances from the millions of Tajiks working abroad, mainly in Russia. (Remittances typically amount to 30–40 percent of GDP.) Lower export earnings for cotton and aluminum also contributed to the slower expansion. The country recovered by 2010 with a GDP growth rate of 6.5 percent. In 2012 GDP grew by 8.0 percent, while inflation was 11.6 percent. For 2014 the World Bank ranked Tajikistan 143th out of 189 countries in its annual Doing Business index. GDP per capita rose slightly to $872 in 2012.

GOVERNMENT AND POLITICS

Political background. Most of the Tajik lands were conquered by Russia in the 1880s and 1890s. Popular uprisings in the wake of the 1917 Bolshevik Revolution were not completely suppressed until 1921. In 1924 the region was made an autonomous republic within the Uzbek Soviet Socialist Republic and in 1929 a constituent republic of the USSR.

On February 11, 1990, rioting erupted in Dushanbe when demonstrators, initially responding to reports that Armenian refugees were to be settled there, began calling for democratic reforms. A resultant state of emergency led to the suppression of the demonstrations, in part by Soviet soldiers. On August 25, with nationalism on the rise, a sovereignty declaration was issued asserting the precedence of the republic's constitution and laws over those of the USSR, and on November 30 the republic's legislature, the Supreme Soviet, voted to replace its chair with a president as head of state.

On August 25, 1991, in the wake of the failed Moscow coup against USSR president Mikhail Gorbachev, the Supreme Soviet ordered the nationalization of the assets of the Communist Party of the Soviet Union (CPSU) within the republic. On August 29 the Communist Party of Tajikistan (CPT) voted to withdraw from the CPSU, while the words "Soviet Socialist" were dropped from the republic's name. At the same time, anticommunist opposition groups, principally the Islamic Renaissance Party (IRP), the secular and pro-Western Democratic Party of Tajikistan (DPT), and the nationalist *Rastokhez* (Rebirth) movement, continued to organize demonstrations against the government.

On September 1, 1991, after losing a nonconfidence vote, the CPT's Qahhor MAHKAMOV (Kakhar MAKHKAMOV) resigned the presidency in favor of the Supreme Soviet chair, Kadreddin ASLONOV. On September 9 the legislature declared the independence of the Republic of Tajikistan, and on September 22 Acting President Aslonov issued a decree banning all CPT activities, despite the fact that the party had redesignated itself as the Tajik Socialist Party (TSP) the day before. On September 23 the ban was reversed and Aslonov resigned, being succeeded by former CPT first secretary Rakhman NABIYEV.

Nabiyev immediately imposed a state of emergency, but he lifted it on October 2, 1991. Opposition demonstrations continued, and on October 6 Nabiyev submitted his resignation, ostensibly to permit all candidates an opportunity to campaign on equal footing for a presidential election. On November 24, despite his reputation as a hard-line conservative, Nabiyev drew a 58 percent vote share in a field of seven candidates. Significantly, his closest competitor, Davlat KHUDONAZAROV of the DPT, received backing from the IRP, thus sealing an Islamic-prodemocracy opposition alliance that was to become a crucial factor in the unfolding civil conflict, which was based more on ethnic and regional differences than on ideology. In January 1992, Nabiyev named Akbar MIRZOYEV prime minister.

In March 1992 Maksud IKRAMOV, a prominent DPT member and chair of the Executive Committee (mayor) of Dushanbe, was arrested and charged with bribery. Coupled with an earlier dismissal of a minister from the Gorno-Badakhshan Autonomous Region, the action triggered widespread antiregime protests. Led by the IRP, the DPT, *Rastokhez,* and *Lali Badakhshan* (Badakhshan Ruby Movement, a nationalist formation organized by the Pamiri ethnic group of Gorno-Badakhshan), the demonstrators called for dissolution of the Supreme Soviet and the adoption of a new constitution. In late April, with the unrest continuing and the local army commander having indicated that his troops would not intervene, President Nabiyev organized a series of progovernment rallies in the capital, many of the demonstrators being communists from the southern Kulyab and northern Leninabad regions. In addition, Nabiyev secured legislative approval for a six-month period of direct presidential rule, including a suspension of civil liberties.

On April 22, 1992, the hard-line Safarali KENJAYEV resigned as chair of the Supreme Soviet. His reinstatement on May 3 triggered a fresh wave of protests, including a demonstration by upward of 100,000 persons on May 5. On May 10 security forces killed a reported 20 individuals gathered in front of the National Security Committee headquarters, where negotiations were taking place between government and opposition representatives. The next day, following intervention by the Muslim spiritual leader Kazi Ali Akbar TURAJONZODA of the IRP, Vice President Narzullo DUSTOV and a number of other hard-line officials resigned, and agreement was reached on a power-sharing arrangement whereby the opposition DPT and IRP would be awarded 8 of 24 cabinet posts. It was also agreed that an interim representative Assembly (*Majlis*) would be established, pending multiparty election of a permanent successor. However, the local soviets in Leninabad and Kulyab refused to accept the accord. Fighting between supporters and opponents of the agreement broke out in Kulyab and soon spread to the adjacent region of Kurgan-Tyube, where in August clashes between progovernment Kulyabi militiamen and Islamic-prodemocracy oppositionists reportedly cost hundreds of lives.

On August 30, 1992, Prime Minister Mirzoyev resigned and was succeeded on an interim basis by his deputy, Jamshed KARIMOV, while on September 7, President Nabiyev was forced to resign by opposition elements that had seized him during a melee in the Dushanbe airport. On September 24 Nabiyev's acting successor, Supreme Soviet chair Akbarsho ISKANDAROV, named Abdumalik ABDULLOJONOV to replace Karimov as the acting head of a coalition administration. Nevertheless, the conflict continued to intensify, with the new government losing effective control of Kulyab and Kurgan-Tyube to Nabiyev supporters led by Sangak SAFAROV. In early October former Supreme Soviet chair Kenjayev, who had organized a pro-Nabiyev Popular Front, tried to seize control of the capital from Islamic-prodemocracy forces. On November 19, Supreme Soviet chair Iskandarov stepped down in favor of Emomali RAHMON, leader of the pro-Nabiyev forces in Kulyab. Concurrent with Iskandarov's departure, the presidential system was abolished in favor of a parliamentary system, with the chair of the legislature again serving as head of state. Prime Minister Abdullojonov remained in office, but the cabinet was stripped of opposition appointees. On December 10, after a two-month blockade of the capital led by Kenjayev's militias, troops loyal to the successor government regained control of Dushanbe from Islamic-prodemocracy forces, most of which were eventually driven into the Afghan border region.

On April 3, 1993, the DPT's Maksud Ikramov was for the second time dismissed as mayor of Dushanbe, after having been reinstated to the position in late 1992. On April 11, former president Nabiyev died of an apparent heart attack, and on April 27 the Russian Supreme Soviet voted to send a peacekeeping force to Tajikistan to join contingents from Kazakhstan, Kyrgyzstan, and Uzbekistan that had been dispatched by the Commonwealth of Independent States (CIS). Two months later, on June 21, the Supreme Court banned the four leading opposition groups—the IRP, DPT, *Rastokhez,* and *Lali Badakhshan*—for engaging in assassination, kidnapping, and rebellion. By that time, the government had regained control over most of the country, and many opposition leaders, including the IRP's Turajonzoda, had gone into exile. The conflict nonetheless continued in the border region, with the Islamic forces reportedly receiving support from Afghan guerrillas.

Prime Minister Abdullojonov resigned in December 1993, at least in part because of the country's economic decline, and was succeeded by his deputy, Abdujalil SAMADOV. Subsequently, peace talks with opposition leaders were initiated in Moscow, despite the assassination in March 1994 of Deputy Prime Minister Mayonsho NAZARSHOYEV, who had been named to head the government delegation. The talks yielded an agreement to cooperate on aid to refugees and to seek national reconciliation through "political measures alone," but clashes continued to occur in areas along the Afghan frontier. Further UN-sponsored talks in Tehran, Iran, resulted in the signature of a cease-fire accord in September, seemingly without the government making any major concessions to the opposition. The cease-fire did little to reduce hostilities, however, with another deputy prime minister, Munavvarsho NASIRYEV, being killed by a land mine on the day of its notional implementation, October 20. Meanwhile, in July the Supreme Soviet had approved a draft constitution that was to be submitted to a popular referendum in conjunction with the first direct election of a state president, who would have expanded executive powers under the new constitution.

Held on November 6, 1994, the constitutional referendum and presidential election were boycotted by the Islamic opposition and the DPT, although some secular opposition parties backed the candidacy of former prime minister Abdullojonov. According to the official results, over 90 percent of the voters endorsed the constitution. In the presidential election the incumbent, Rahmon, received 58 percent of the votes cast, against some 35 percent for Abdullojonov, who complained of vote-rigging. On December 2, having been nominated by the president and endorsed by the legislature, Jamshed Karimov returned as prime minister to preside over a government that continued to be dominated by current or former communists.

Elections to the new 181-member Supreme Assembly, held in February–March 1995, were boycotted by most of the opposition parties, Islamic and secular. A majority of the winning candidates had no overt party allegiance, although about a third were declared communists.

Despite the presence since December 1994 of a small UN observer mission charged with monitoring the supposed cease-fire, fighting continued unabated between government and opposition forces. In a major flare-up in Gorno-Badakhshan in April 1995, hundreds died as government and CIS forces advanced on units of the Afghanistan-based IRP armed wing operating in alliance with Badakhshan separatists. By mid-year some 25,000 CIS peacekeeping troops were deployed in Tajikistan, the majority of them Russian.

Further peace talks took place in Kabul, Afghanistan, in May 1995 between President Rahmon and the IRP leader, Sayed Abdullo NURI, but no substantive progress was made on the opposition's demand for the legalization of all political parties, press freedom, release of political prisoners, amnesty for rebel leaders, and full autonomy for Gorno-Badakhshan. In June–July 1995 the government succeeded in bringing about a split in the DPT, with one faction accepting official registration and the other remaining in full opposition. During the latter part of 1995, notwithstanding an extension of the notional cease-fire, the civil war continued in the south and along the Afghan border.

An escalation of the conflict at the beginning of 1996 impelled President Rahmon to carry out a government reorganization in early February, with Karimov being replaced as prime minister by Yakhyo AZIMOV and with Mahmadsaid UBAIDULLOEV being dismissed as first deputy prime minister. The changes were reportedly made in response to demands by two rebel military leaders who had occupied the southern and western towns of Kurgan-Tyube and Tursunzade; troops loyal to one of the rebels, Col. Makhmud KHUDOBERDIYEV, an ethnic Uzbek from Leninabad, had briefly threatened the capital. Thereafter, fighting intensified in the central Garm and Tavil Dara areas.

The fall of Kabul to Taliban forces in September 1996 provided a spur to further peace efforts, and new negotiations between the government and the opposition were launched in October. At a meeting in Afghanistan on December 10–11, President Rahmon and the IRP's Nuri agreed to another cease-fire and to open formal peace talks in Moscow later in the month. Despite violations, the cease-fire appeared to contain the fighting, and on December 23 Rahmon and Nuri signed accords in the Russian capital providing for the establishment of a transitional National Reconciliation Commission (NRC), to be headed by a representative of the IRP-led United Tajik Opposition (UTO). The NRC would assume responsibility for overseeing reform of electoral laws and the reintegration of the opposition into normal life. Under the accords, opposition representatives were to be introduced into the structures of executive power, including central and local government and law enforcement agencies, in proportion to the representation of the parties on the NRC, taking regional balance into account. The commission would cease its work after the convocation of a new parliament and the formation of its ruling bodies.

Early in 1997, the secular National Revival movement, which had been organized in July 1996 by former prime ministers Abdullojonov, Karimov, and Samadov, staged protests against its exclusion from the peace process. At the same time, further negotiations between the government and the UTO were being overshadowed by kidnappings and battles among warlords and rogue military officers, most prominently Colonel Khudoberdiyev, who for a time controlled much of southern Tajikistan and again threatened the capital before being repulsed by government troops. Nevertheless, the cease-fire between the UTO and the government, which controlled little more than the capital region, continued to hold. When an assassination attempt on the life of President Rahmon failed in April, the UTO joined world capitals in condemning the attack.

On June 27, 1997, Rahmon and UTO leader Nuri signed a peace agreement in Moscow, officially ending the five-year civil war. The agreement provided for the eventual legalization of the UTO parties, the return of refugees and Afghan-based opposition forces, the integration of the latter within the regular army, and the granting to the UTO of 30 percent of government posts. The signatories also agreed that the NRC would have 26 members, 13 from the government and 13 from the UTO. Implementation of the peace was by no means assured, however, and in January 1998 the UTO briefly quit the NRC, citing government delays in meeting the terms of the agreement. Under pressure from the UTO, President Rahmon named five UTO members to his cabinet in February. In March he added as deputy prime minister the UTO's recently repatriated Ali Akbar Turajonzoda, who, however, failed to win formal parliamentary approval until November even though the position, which had previously carried supervisory responsibilities involving the economy, defense, and the interior, had been redefined to cover only economic and trade relations with CIS countries.

Sporadic fighting continued to break out throughout 1998. The combatants included troops loyal to the government, renegade field commands, UTO contingents (sometimes against each other), and unaffiliated militias. The most serious incident occurred in the northern city of Khujand (formerly Leninabad) on November 4–7, when forces under Colonel Khudoberdiyev staged a rebellion that claimed an estimated 300 lives and injured another 650 before being put down. Among those implicated in the rebellion were former prime minister Abdullojonov; his brother, Abdughani ABDULLOJONOV, who had previously served as mayor of Khujand; and a former vice president, Narzullo Dustov.

In the second half of 1999, progress accelerated toward fulfilling the terms of the 1997 peace accords. In June Nuri and President Rahmon had agreed to emphasize constitutional reform while continuing to decommission UTO forces, to integrate UTO troops into national military and security units, and to pursue the 30 percent target for UTO staffing of government positions. In early August Nuri announced that the military goals had been accomplished, which, under the terms of the June agreement, led the Supreme Court on August 12 to reinstate the four political groups that had been banned in 1993. In September 71.8 percent of those voting in a national referendum approved constitutional amendments that affected more than two dozen articles, included provisions permitting sectarian political parties, creating a bicameral parliament, and lengthening the presidential term to seven years. With the notable exception of President Rahmon's People's Democratic Party of Tajikistan (PDPT) and the IRP, most political parties had campaigned against the revisions, arguing that they would increase the current president's authority over legislation, regional administration, and the courts, and that the new upper house would slow down legislation and exacerbate regional tensions.

In October 1999 the UTO suspended its participation in the NRC and announced that it would boycott the November 6 presidential election, primarily because the Central Commission for Elections and Referendums had disqualified opposition candidates (technically, for having failed to obtain sufficient signatures to get their names on the ballot). Hours before the voting began, the UTO canceled the boycott, Nuri having received assurances from Rahmon regarding the conduct of upcoming parliamentary elections. With Rahmon's only opponent on the ballot, Davlat USMON of the IRP, having denounced the presidential contest as a sham, Rahmon secured 97 percent of the vote, and on November 16 he took the oath of office for another term. On November 23 Yakhyo Azimov and his cabinet resigned, as constitutionally mandated. The president named Oqil OQILOV (Akil AKILOV) as the new prime minister on December 20 and continued to make cabinet changes well into the new year.

With several of the smaller opposition parties having been declared ineligible, an election for the new lower house, the Assembly of Representatives, took place in February–March 2000. Amid accusations of campaign and voting irregularities, the PDPT and supporting parties captured more than two-thirds of the 63 seats. The Communists won only 13, and the IRP, 2. On March 23, indirect elections were held for the majority of the seats in the new upper house, the National Assembly, which was also expected to support President Rahmon's agenda.

In the next four years, amid numerous ministerial changes, President Rahmon consolidated his power, in part through passage in June 2003 of a referendum that removed a constitutional proscription against his seeking reelection in 2006. Similarly, the dominance of the PDPT was confirmed by the legislative elections of February–March 2005, which saw the opposition win only two seats in the National Assembly and six in the Assembly of Representatives. The Organization for Security and Cooperation in Europe (OSCE) described the elections as seriously flawed.

On November 6, 2006, President Rahmon won reelection with 79 percent of the vote against token opponents in a contest that was again criticized by objective international observers, as was the lower house election held on February 28, 2010 (with reballoting for one undecided seat occurring on March 14). Once again, the PDPT won overwhelmingly, taking 54 seats, while two government-supportive parties added another 4. The CPT and the IRP, with 2 seats each, were the only successful opposition parties. A minor cabinet reshuffle was undertaken on March 10, 2010. Another minor cabinet reorganization took place on January 4, 2012.

With the main opposition parties boycotting the November 6, 2013, presidential election, President Rahmon carried 83.6 percent of the vote, winning a constitutionally limited fourth seven-year term.

Constitution and government. The last of the ex-Soviet Central Asian republics to do so, Tajikistan adopted a post-Soviet constitution by referendum on November 6, 1994, with the new text coming into force immediately. It defines Tajikistan as a democratic, secular, and unitary state, and the people as the sole source of state power. Amendments approved by referendum in September 1999 included a provision permitting formation of sectarian political parties. In all, the referendum authorized changes to 27 articles of the basic law. Another referendum, passed on June 22, 2003, made 56 mostly minor changes (which voters had to accept or reject as a single package), with the most controversial provision being removal of a one-term limit for the presidency.

The 1999 revisions also replaced the unicameral legislature with a bicameral Supreme Assembly encompassing a National Assembly of indirectly elected and appointed members (plus former presidents of the republic) and an Assembly of Representatives, the latter directly elected from a combination of single-seat districts and national party lists. Parliamentarians serve five-year terms. The powers of the National Assembly, which must meet at least twice a year, include redefining territorial divisions and considering laws proposed by the lower house. The Assembly of Representatives, meeting in continuous session, is authorized to independently adopt the state budget and can override an upper house rejection of legislation with a two-thirds vote. The Supreme Assembly can override presidential vetoes of legislation with a two-thirds vote. Passage of constitutional amendments requires a two-thirds vote of both bodies and a three-fourths vote in the event of a presidential veto.

The president, described as the head of the executive branch and commander in chief, is now directly elected for up to two seven-year terms. His powers include appointing the prime minister and other ministers, as well as judges and other senior state and regional administrators, subject to legislative endorsement. He can also initiate referendums. The system of judicial authority is headed by a Constitutional Court and includes a Supreme Court, a Supreme Economic Court, and a Military Court.

Administratively, Tajikistan currently comprises the capital city of Dushanbe, the centrally administered Region of Republican Subordination (Nohiyahoi Tobei Jumhurii, formerly Karotegin), and three other regions (*viloyatho*): in the north, Sughd (formerly Leninabad); in the southwest, Khatlon, established in 1992 by the merger of the Kulyab (Kŭlob) and Kurgan-Tyube (Qŭrghonteppa) regions; and in the east, the Gorno-Badakhshan Autonomous Region (Badakhshoni Kŭhí Viloyati Avtonomii), which the 1994 constitution specifically defines as "an integral and indivisible part of Tajikistan." Regions, districts, and towns elect local assemblies that are chaired by presidential appointees, subject to the approval of the respective assemblies.

Press freedom is constrained in Tajikistan. The government controls most of the press and broadcast media. Reporters Without Borders ranked the country 123rd, down from 122nd in 2012, out of 179 countries in 2013.

Foreign relations. On December 21, 1991, Tajikistan became a charter member of the post-Soviet CIS. By early 1992 it had established diplomatic relations with a number of foreign countries, including the United States, and had been admitted to the Conference on (later Organization for) Security and Cooperation in Europe (CSCE/OSCE). It joined the United Nations in March 1992, the IMF in April 1993, and the World Bank in June 1993. As a predominantly Muslim country, Tajikistan also became a member of the Organization of the Islamic Conference. In February 2002 it formally joined NATO's Partnership for Peace program.

In March 1998 Tajikistan was admitted as a candidate member to the Central Asian Economic Union—renamed the Central Asian Economic Community in July 1998 and then the Central Asian Cooperation Organization (CACO) in February 2002—which had been established four years earlier by Kazakhstan, Kyrgyzstan, and Uzbekistan. In April 1998 a Tajik application to join Russia, Belarus, Kazakhstan, and Kyrgyzstan in the CIS Customs Union was approved, and formal entry occurred in February 1999. In 2005 the CACO merged into the Eurasian Economic Community (Belarus, Kazakhstan, Kyrgyzstan, Russia, Tajikistan, and Uzbekistan).

Relations with Moscow have remained close since independence. From 1993 until the mission's end in September 2000, Russia provided the bulk of troops for the CIS peacekeeping operation, which also included contingents from Kazakhstan, Kyrgyzstan, and Uzbekistan. Primarily to deter infiltration across the Afghan and Kyrgyz borders by such extremist groups as the Islamic Movement of Uzbekistan (IMU), Russian troops remain in Tajikistan. In June 2004, after lengthy negotiations, the Rahmon government granted Russia permission to establish a permanent military base for its troops and also agreed to permit unlimited Russian use of the Soviet-built space surveillance center in Nurek, one of the world's most sophisticated facilities for tracking satellites. In return, Russia reportedly agreed to forgo some $300 million in debt payments, to be offset by partial ownership of a hydroelectric power facility.

Postindependence relations between Tajikistan and Uzbekistan have been complicated by persecution of ethnic Tajiks in Uzbekistan and by nationalist resentment in Tajikistan over the prominence of ethnic Uzbeks in the state hierarchy. Although not espoused by the government, territorial claims by Tajik nationalists on Uzbek cities, including Samarkand and Bukhara, have also caused strains. In late 1998 President Rahmon accused the Uzbek government of complicity in the failed November revolt in Khujand. Captured rebels later claimed that members of the Uzbek special forces had helped train them, but Uzbek President Islam Karimov denied any involvement and subsequently accused Tajik officials of drug-trafficking.

Despite such tempestuous exchanges, in January 1999 Tajik prime minister Azimov met with President Karimov in Tashkent to discuss trade and economic cooperation. (Tajikistan remains dependent on Uzbekistan for almost all overland traffic.) Three months later the presidents of both countries joined their counterparts from Kazakhstan and Kyrgyzstan in signing a mutual security agreement intended to combat terrorism, Islamic extremism, and related threats. In June 2000 Tajikistan and Uzbekistan reached agreement on a protocol for delimiting their common border and signed a treaty of friendship.

Beginning in 1994 Tajikistan met regularly with the other members of the so-called Shanghai Five—China, Kazakhstan, Kyrgyzstan, and Russia—which focused their attention primarily on matters of regional stability and security. In 2001 Uzbekistan joined the grouping, which renamed itself the Shanghai Cooperation Organization (SCO); a formal SCO charter was signed in 2002 and a Secretariat was inaugurated in January 2004. Islamic militancy in Afghanistan and elsewhere in the region has been of particular concern.

Even before the October 2001 launch of U.S.-led strikes against al-Qaida and Afghanistan's Taliban regime, Tajikistan was believed to be aiding the anti-Taliban Northern Alliance, which was dominated by ethnic Tajiks. Special forces from the Ministry of the Interior were subsequently reported to be directly assisting the Northern Alliance in its march toward Kabul, and it was later confirmed that Tajikistan had permitted several of its air bases to be used by the United States and its allies in the campaign. In January 2002, apparently rewarding the Rahmon government for its cooperation, the United States lifted a 1993 restriction on the transfer of military equipment to Tajikistan.

In December 2003, Tajikistan joined China, Iran, Pakistan, Turkmenistan, and Uzbekistan in pledging to respect post-Taliban Afghanistan's sovereignty and to remain aloof from its internal affairs. In August 2007 President Rahmon and his Afghan counterpart, Hamid Karzai, inaugurated a bridge over the Pyranzh River. Built with funds from the United States, the cross-border bridge was expected to facilitate development of a major trade route. Tajikistan is also constructing a power transmission line to export hydroelectric power to Afghanistan and, eventually, Pakistan.

In July 2008, Tajik foreign minister Hamrokhon ZARIFI named Kazakhstan, Kyrgyzstan, Turkmenistan, Afghanistan, and Iran as key regional partners and Russia, China, and the United States as global partners. Zarifi particularly emphasized the Tajik-Russian relationship, noting the countries' cultural and political similarities. In July 2009 the presidents of Russia and Tajikistan attended the launching of Sangutdin-1 Hydropower Plant in Tajikistan, a joint venture in which Russia is the main shareholder.

In July 2011, the United States announced that it would construct a $10 million center to train Tajik security forces and counternarcotics officials. Tajikistan and China pledged greater bilateral cooperation on border security in August. In September Russia limited fuel exports to Tajikistan after Rahmon refused a request to allow additional Russian troops to be deployed along the Afghan-Tajik border. In November tension further increased when Russia deported 300 ethnic Tajiks. Meanwhile, Tajikistan agreed to accept a Russian proposal for a free trade area with the other CIS states in October. Also in October, Tajikistan and Belarus finalized a series of bilateral economic cooperation agreements.

In October 2012 Tajikistan granted a 30-year extension on the lease of Russian bases. Also in April, Uzbekistan suspended gas shipments to Tajikistan in a dispute over the Tajik construction of a hydroelectric plant that Uzbek officials claimed would cut water supplies to that country. Shipments resumed after two weeks under a short-term contract.

In January 2013 Tajikistan and Kyrgyzstan announced the delineation of 567 km of their 970 km joint border with plans to complete demarcation by the end of the year. In March Tajikistan was accepted as a full member of the World Trade Organization. In April the World Bank announced a $14.85 million grant to support agriculture in Tajikistan. In May Tajikistan and China announced a strategic partnership to further develop economic ties and toward mutual support concerning sovereignty and security. In October Tajikistan and Afghanistan signed agreements to cooperate on strengthening their economic ties and land mine removal.

Current issues. During 2009 and 2010, government forces continued to face militant opposition from two sources in the east: the IMU and former UTO commanders who oppose the Rahmon regime. In August 2009 a three-month campaign against IMU-linked militants concluded. Among those killed in the operation in the Tavil Dara Valley were Nemat AZIZOV and Mirzo ZIYOYEV, the latter a former minister of emergency situations and civil defense as well as a former UTO field commander. According to some reports, Ziyoyev had been facilitating the movement of IMU militants back and forth across the Afghan border, but some observers saw him as an assassination target because of his connections to other Rahmon opponents.

In September 2010, an ambush in the Rasht Valley killed 28 Tajik soldiers, part of a contingent that had been dispatched to the region following an August prison break by 25 inmates from a national security facility. All 25 had been convicted of links to the IMU, but the ambush was apparently engineered by opposition commanders, whose numbers include Sokh ISKANDAROV, Loudon DAVLAT, Abdullo RAHIMOV (aka Mullo Abdullo). A fourth commander, Mirzokhudzha AKHMADOV, reportedly surrendered in mid-October in return for amnesty.

Regionally, energy and water disputes continue to complicate relationships. Uzbekistan significantly reduced its export of natural gas to Kyrgyzstan and Tajikistan in mid-June 2009 as the two countries fell into arrears on their energy payments, and in November Uzbekistan announced it intended to withdraw from the regional electrical grid because of differences over transit tariffs with Tajikistan, which imports electricity from Turkmenistan via Uzbekistan. Tajikistan responded by threatening to withhold water, which, it claimed, would be needed to generate additional domestic hydroelectricity. Uzbekistan proceeded to stop transit of rail freight except for a two-week period in May 2010, when relief supplies were needed to overcome severe flooding in the south.

Parliamentary elections in February and March 2010 were criticized by international and domestic observers. Monitors from the OSCE and the European Parliament cited "serious irregularities" in polling, including proxy voting and ballot box stuffing.

On April 15, 2011, the insurgent leader Mullo Abdullo and 16 fighters were killed by Tajik security forces during a government offensive in the Rasht Valley. In August parliament approved legislation that placed significant restrictions on religious freedom, including a ban on youth under the age of 18 attending mosques. On August 2, First Deputy Prime Minister Asadullo GHULOMOV died in office; he was replaced by Matlubkhon DAVLATOV on January 4, 2012.

In May 2012 the government stopped exports of coal as part of a program to increase domestic use of the fuel. In July, following the assassination of a security official in Gorno-Badakhshan, Tajik security forces launched an offensive against a rebel group led by former warlord Tolib AYOMBEKOV. Twelve government troops and 30 insurgents were killed in the fighting.

In November 2013 President Rahmon solidified his presidency with a fourth seven-year term, winning 83.6 percent of the electorate. The election was widely seen as corrupt by the international community with the U.S. Department of State citing "a lack of pluralism and genuine choice." With the main opposition parties boycotting the election, widespread censorship by the state-controlled media and of the Internet, and alleged harassment of potential candidates by local authorities, Rahmon ran against five little-known candidates.

Also in November three earthquakes struck, destroying more than 100 homes and damaging more than 250 others. The earthquakes ranged from 4.0 to 6.2 on the Richter scale.

POLITICAL PARTIES

For most of the first decade after independence, political parties did not play a significant role in governance, although the Communist Party of Tajikistan (CPT) continued to be influential in the Supreme Assembly, and, as the 1990s drew to a close, President Rahmon's People's Democratic Party of Tajikistan (PDPT) became increasingly important.

In the wake of the June 1997 peace agreement that ended the civil war, Tajik politics was dominated by efforts to reintegrate the United Tajik Opposition (UTO) into government and the military. Established in Afghanistan in 1993 as the Islamic Revival Movement and renamed in 1996, the UTO included most opposition paramilitary organizations and four groups banned in 1993: the Islamic Rebirth Party (IRP), whose chair, Sayed Abdullo Nuri, served as principal negotiator in peace talks with the government; the Democratic Party of Tajikistan (the so-called Almaty wing of the DPT, following a party rupture in 1995); and two social organizations, the *Lali Badakhshan* and the *Rastokhez* movements. The *Lali Badakhshan,* led by Atobek AMIRBEK, had been formed in the late 1980s as a nationalist movement of the Pamiri people, who belong to the Ismaili Muslim sect and who demanded full autonomy for Gorno-Badakhshan. *Rastokhez* (Rebirth Movement) had been founded in 1990 as a nationalist/religious organization advocating the revival of Tajik culture and traditions. As a result of the 1996–1997 accords, the UTO and the government were equally represented on the National Reconciliation Commission (NRC). The IRP, DPT (Almaty), *Lali Badakhshan,* and *Rastokhez* had their legal standing restored in 1999.

In June 1999, a loose Consultative Council of Political Parties was formed in opposition to the constitutional amendments then being considered by the NRC. Parties associated with the council during the subsequent referendum campaign included the CPT, the so-called Tehran wing of the DPT, the Congress of People's Unity, Hakim MUHABBATOV's National Movement Party, the Agrarian Party, the Party of Justice, and the Party of Justice and Development (predecessor of the current Social Democratic Party of Tajikistan—SDPT). The ideological diversity of its members precluded the council's functioning as an electoral coalition in the 2000 legislative elections.

Meanwhile, the government had begun closing political parties on technical grounds, including the People's Unity Party (PUP), the Agrarian Party, and the Party of Justice (please see the 2012 *Handbook* for more information).

In April 2004 looking toward the 2005 elections, the IRP, the SDPT, and the Socialist Party of Tajikistan (SPT) agreed to cooperate in a loose For Fair and Transparent Elections alliance, which the DPT then joined in August. Given that a party must be formally registered for at least a year to contest an election, the only other parties eligible for the February 2005 balloting were the president's PDPT and the CPT. Two additional parties were registered in November 2005, bringing the total number of officially recognized parties to eight.

Presidential Party:

People's Democratic Party of Tajikistan—PDPT (*Hizb-i-Khalq-i-Demokrati Tojikiston*). Formed in 1993 as the People's Party of Tajikistan (PPT) by a group of northern business interests centered in Khujand, the PDPT includes in its membership many former Soviet-era Communists, including President Rahmon. Formally registered in December 1994, the PPT emerged from the 1995 Supreme Assembly election with only a handful of seats, but its representation subsequently swelled to about 90 with the addition of members who had run without declaring affiliations. The party adopted its present name in 1997.

President Rahmon officially joined the PDPT in March 1998 and was elected chair at a party congress in April. Described by a spokesperson at the time as a party of pragmatists and technocrats, the PDPT significantly expanded its base of support throughout the country as a result of the president's membership. In the election for the new lower house of the Supreme Assembly in February–March 2000, the PDPT won 15 of 22 party list seats on a 65 percent first-round vote share. In 2005 it won 52 of the lower house's 63 seats.

At the party's tenth congress, held in December 2009, most of the top leadership was replaced. In the subsequent lower house election, the PDPT won 54 seats. In assembly balloting on February 28, 2010, the PDPT won 54 seats. In August 2011, the PDPT launched an initiative to increase cooperation with the Communist Party of China.

President Rahmon also chairs the Central Council of a closely associated social movement, the **Movement for National Unity and Revival of Tajikistan** (frequently shortened to the National Unity Movement), which was established in 1997.

Leaders: Emomali RAHMON (President of the Republic and Chair of the Party), Safar SAFAROV (First Deputy Chair).

Other Parliamentary Parties:

Agrarian Party of Tajikistan (APT). The APT was formed in September 2005 and officially registered two months later. (An earlier Agrarian Party was permanently suspended in 1999.) In January 2006 the APT chair, Amir Qoraqulov, denied that his party intended to form a coalition with the PDPT before the November 2006 presidential election, in which he won 5.2 percent of the vote. Some opponents have asserted that the APT is a product of government efforts to split the opposition vote.

In 2010 the APT won two seats in the lower house, one on the basis of capturing 5.1 percent of the proportional vote.

Leaders: Amir QORAQULOV (Amirkul KARAKULOV, Chair), Rustum LATIPOV.

Communist Party of Tajikistan—CPT (*Hizb-i-Kommunisti Tojikiston*). Primarily based in the northern industrial region of Sughd (previously Leninabad) and in other areas of high ethnic Uzbek or Russian population, the CPT was the only registered party prior to the Tajik declaration of independence. In September 1991 it was banned by the Aslonov government, one day after it had decided to reorganize as the Tajik Socialist Party (TSP). The ban was immediately overturned but reimposed in October. Again functioning legally under its original name, the CPT regained its status as the dominant political group with the outlawing of its principal opponents in June 1993. In the February–March 1995 legislative balloting, at least a third of the elected candidates were acknowledged CPT members. It continued to advocate collective ownership and revival of a Soviet-based union of republics.

Claiming that a presidential victory by a Communist candidate would anger Russia, the CPT unexpectedly supported President Rahmon for reelection in 1999. It nevertheless remained within the opposition Consultative Council of Political Parties. The CPT won five party list seats, on a 20.6 percent vote share, in the Assembly of Representatives in the 2000 legislative election. In 2005 it won a total of four seats in the lower house. In 2006 its presidential candidate, Ismoil Talbakov, won 5.2 percent of the vote.

The February 2010 lower house election resulted in a loss of two seats. It won 7.0 percent of the party list vote. The CPT was highly critical of security operations in Gorno-Badakshan in 2012.

Leaders: Shodi SHABDOLOV (Chair), Ismoil TALBAKOV (Deputy Chair).

Islamic Rebirth Party—IRP (*Hizb-i-Nahzati Islom,* also translated into English as the Islamic Renaissance Party and the Islamic Revival Party). A rural-based grouping founded in June 1990, the IRP has indicated that its long-term objective is the conversion of Tajikistan into an Islamic republic, although it has rejected the label "fundamentalist." It supported the DPT's Davlat Khudonazarov for the presidency in 1991 but was banned in June 1993.

During 1992–1996 the armed Defense of the Fatherland wing of the IRP engaged in hostilities against government and CIS forces, drawing support from Tajiks who had fled to Afghanistan, from pro-Tajik Afghan mujahidin, and possibly from the Afghan government. Following the June 1997 peace agreement, the IRP remained at the center of the UTO.

Relegalized in August 1999, the IRP elected UTO leader Sayed Abdullo Nuri as chair and, in the interest of national unity, gave grudging support to the September constitutional referendum despite objections to particular provisions. For the November presidential election the IRP designated as its candidate Davlat Usmon, minister of economics and foreign economic relations. Usmon subsequently decided to boycott the election, but his name remained on the ballot and he won 2 percent of the vote.

Party and UTO deputy chair Ali Akbar Turajonzoda reportedly resigned both positions in October 1999 after being expelled from the IRP because he had broken party regulations and had described President Rahmon as worthy of reelection.

In the first-round legislative election of February 2000, the IRP won two party list seats on a 7.3 percent vote share. In September 2003 the party's fourth conference reelected Chair Nuri, who consistently denied the existence of any IRP connections to militant Islamic groups, particularly the Islamic Movement of Uzbekistan (IMU). Nuri also charged the government with persecuting the IRP in the guise of cracking down on another regional Islamic group, the *Hizb-ut-Tahrir.*

In May 2003 IRP deputy chair Shamsiddin SHAMSIDDINOV was arrested and subsequently charged with murder, forming an armed group, and other crimes dating back to the civil war. In January 2004 he was sentenced to a lengthy term in prison, where he died of natural causes in January 2008.

In the 2005 legislative elections the IRP again won two seats. Nuri died in 2006 and was succeeded by his deputy chair, Muhiddin Kabiri. The party refused to nominate a candidate for the 2006 presidential election. Kabiri was reelected party chair in September 2007.

In the February 2010 lower house election the IRP retained its two party-list seats by winning 8.2 percent of the proportional vote. It remains the only officially recognized Islamic party in Central Asia. In July 2012, Sabzali MAMADRIZOYEV, a member of the IRP presidium, was murdered.

Oinikhol BOBONAZAROVA, a female lawyer and human rights activist backed by IRP, failed to secure the 210,000 signatures needed to have her name on the 2013 presidential election ballot. Bobonzarova was widely seen as the only legitimate potential challenge for the election.

Leaders: Muhiddin KABIRI (Chair), Muhammadali HAIT (Deputy Chair), Hikmotulla SAYFULLOZODA, Sayidumar HUSAYNI.

Party of Economic Reforms (PER). Formation of the government-supportive PER was announced in September 2005, and it was officially registered in November. It was initially accused of attempting to split the opposition vote. In 2006 the party's chair, Olimjon BOBOEV, ran for president and finished second, with 6.2 percent of the vote. In 2009 he was named minister of transport and communication by the president.

In the February 2010 election the PER won two seats, one of them on the basis of taking 5 percent of the party-list vote.

Leaders: Mahmadsharif NOZIMOV, Sharofiddin SIROJOV.

Other Registered Parties:

Democratic Party of Tajikistan (DPT). Drawing its support largely from Gorno-Badakhshan, the strongly anticommunist DPT was launched in 1990 on a platform that called for Tajik sovereignty within a framework of confederal states. It was formally outlawed in June 1993.

Divisions between moderate and hard-line DPT factions led to an open split in June 1995, when Shodmon YUSUF was ousted from the leadership but refused to recognize the election of Jumaboy NIYAZOV as his successor. Claiming to be the authentic DPT leader, Yusuf approved terms with the government under which his faction was relegalized in July as the DPT, although it was thereafter often referenced as the DPT (Tehran Platform) to distinguish it from Niyazov's DPT (Almaty Platform). The latter entered into an opposition alliance with the IRP and functioned as part of the UTO. The peace agreement of June 1997 provided for the eventual legalization of the outlawed faction, and Niyazov was later named to the NRC's political committee.

Closely associated with the DPT during the civil war was the Coordinating Center for the Democratic Forces of Tajikistan, led by Otakhon LATIFI until his return from exile in 1997. The head of the NRC legal committee, Latifi was assassinated in September 1998.

At its third congress in July 1999 the DPT (Tehran) replaced Yusuf with Azam AFZALI and in September nominated a former presidential defense adviser, Zafar IKROMOV, as its candidate for the presidential election in November. When Ikromov withdrew, citing the election commission's failure to issue the papers needed to obtain the 145,000 signatures required for a place on the ballot, the party nominated in his stead Sulton Quvvatov. Along with two other opposition candidates, Quvvatov announced in early October that he would boycott the balloting because his campaign workers were being harassed and the news media were not providing impartial campaign coverage. The boycott became moot when the election commission disqualified Quvvatov because he had not met the deadline for obtaining the requisite signatures.

Meanwhile, in accordance with the June 1997 peace accords, the DPT (Almaty) had been legalized by the Supreme Court in August 1999, although the Ministry of Justice refused to register it because of a prohibition against two parties having similar names. At its fifth congress in late September the Almaty group replaced Jumaboy Niyazov with Mahmadruzi Iskandarov. Subsequently, the Supreme Court recognized the DPT (Almaty) as the official DPT, permitting its registration in time to contest the 2000 parliamentary election. With the DPT (Tehran) officially disbanded, Afzali and Quvvatov formed the *Taraqqiyot* (below).

Iskandarov was detained by Russian authorities in December 2004 at the request of the Tajik government, which accused him of terrorism and corruption. Shortly after his April 2005 release, he was abducted and delivered to Tajikistan, where in October he was convicted of terrorism, attempted murder, embezzlement, and weapons possession. He was sentenced to 23 years in prison.

In 2006 a *Watan* (Motherland) faction within the party was organized under the leadership of Masud Sobirov. In August Sobirov's supporters held an extraordinary congress that elected him party chair. Despite claims from the Iskandarov wing that the congress had been illegal, the Justice Department recognized Sobirov as DPT leader. Subsequently, however, a party congress ousted Sobirov for inadequate performance, including a failure to get the party's presidential candidate, Tabvardi ZIYOYEV, on the November ballot. In January 2007 Acting Chair Saidjaffar Ismonov, who had previously belonged to the PDPT and then the unregistered Party of Progressive Youth of Tajikistan, was confirmed as Sobirov's successor. Reconciliation efforts have not succeeded, with the result that the DPT remains split into three wings headed by Iskandarov, Ismonov, and Sobirov. The government continues to recognize the Sobirov wing as the official DPT. In the 2010 lower house election, it won only 1.0 percent of the party list vote.

Leaders: Masud SOBIROV (Chair of Registered DPT), Saidjaffar ISMONOV (Chair of Ismonov Wing), Mahmadruzi ISKANDAROV (Chair of Iskandarov Wing, in prison), Rahmatullo VALIYEV (Deputy Chair of Iskandarov Wing).

Social Democratic Party of Tajikistan (SDPT). The SDPT traces its origins to the Party of Justice and Development (*Adolat va Taraqqiyot*), formation of which was announced in 1998 by Rahmatullo Zoirov. Initially registered in February 1999, the party subsequently added "Social Democratic Party" to its name, but shortly thereafter the Ministry of Justice indicated that it intended to seek the party's closure for violating a proscription against membership by servicemen, law enforcement personnel, and judiciary staff. As a result, its registration was annulled. Zoirov subsequently served President Rahmon as senior adviser on legal policy from 2001 until resigning in 2003. Meanwhile, in December 2002, Zoirov had succeeded in registering the current SDPT. In 2005 he was a leading critic of how the legislative elections were conducted.

In November 2005 a deputy chair of the party, Hurinisso GHAFFORZODA, resigned from the SDPT to establish a social movement aimed at reviving cultural values. In the same month, Zoirov called for the opposition to name a joint candidate for the 2006 presidential election. When that effort failed, the SDPT chose not to contest the election. Earlier in the year, Zoirov accused the government of holding over 1,000 political prisoners, to which the regime warned him that he could face criminal charges unless he presented proof.

In the February 2010 lower house election the SDPT won only 0.8 percent of the party list vote. In December 2011, Zoirov was reelected party leader. In addition, reports indicated that party would change its name to the **National Social Democratic Party of Tajikistan.**

Leader: Rahmatullo ZOIROV (Chair).

Socialist Party of Tajikistan—SPT (*Hizb-i-Sotsialisti Tojikiston*). The SPT was organized in 1996 by former Supreme Soviet chair and Popular Front leader Safarali Kenjayev. In November 1998 the party reportedly expelled former vice president Narzullo Dustov for his alleged participation, earlier in the month, in the abortive revolt in the north. (Dustov went into exile.) Kenjayev, who had been serving as the head of the Supreme Assembly's Committee on Legislation and Human Rights, was murdered by unknown gunmen in March 1999.

The SPT advocates economic and social pluralism, decentralization of power, and secularism. It supported President Rahmon for reelection in November 1999 and won only 1.2 percent of the party list vote in the subsequent lower house election.

In August 2004 Mirhusayn NAZRIYEV was reelected chair, although he was opposed by members of a splinter group led by Abduhalim Ghafforov. In December, with both factions claiming to control the party, the Supreme Court ruled in Ghafforov's favor. In November 2006 Ghafforov won 2.8 percent of the presidential vote. In February 2010, the SPT finished last among the eight parties competing for lower house seats, winning only 0.5 percent of the proportional vote. Ghafforov campaigned unsuccessfully in a by-election in November 2011.

Leader: Abduhalim GHAFFOROV (Chair).

Unregistered Parties:

Progress Party (*Taraqqiyot*). Also translated into English as the Development Party, *Taraqqiyot* held its founding congress in the capital in May 2001. Committed to protecting the political rights of all citizens without regard to ethnicity, religion, language, or gender, the party has repeatedly tried to register without success. Virtually all of its initial membership had previously belonged to the disbanded DPT (Tehran). One of its founders, Sulton Quvvatov, was a former chair of the state tax committee and a prospective candidate for president in 1999 (see the DPT, above). Another founder, Azam Afzali, stated that the party would offer "constructive opposition" to the government (for more on the history of the party, please see the 2012 *Handbook*). In July 2004 the SDPT offered to reserve places for *Taraqqiyot* members, including Quvvatov, on its party list for the 2005 legislative elections. In June 2005 party leader Rustam Fayziyev was given a six-year prison sentence for insulting the president and stirring up ethnic hatred. Quvvatov died of natural causes on November 14, 2011.

Leaders: Rustam FAYZIYEV (Chair, in prison), Shodikhon KENJAYEV.

In March 2008 the Ministry of Justice, for the sixth time, rejected the registration application of the progovernment **Union Party** (*Vahdat*), led by Hikmatullo SAIDOV. In February 2012, Izzat AMON announced the formation of the **Taijkistan Youth Party.**

Banned Organizations:

Two banned Islamic organizations, the **Hizb-ut-Tahrir** and the **Islamic Movement of Uzbekistan** (IMU), have been active in Tajikistan. The IMU, now also known as the **Islamic Party of Turkestan,** has claimed responsibility for or been linked to numerous terrorist incidents in the Central Asian region and beyond, and both Kyrgyzstan and Uzbekistan have asserted that the group has operated from bases in Tajikistan, a charge that the government has denied. Reports in 2012 indicated renewed fighting between the IMU and government security forces. Members of the transnational *Hizb-ut-Tahrir* have been tried and sentenced to prison in Tajikistan, although the organization has not been as militant as the IMU.

LEGISLATURE

The 1994 constitution established a 181-member unicameral **Supreme Assembly** (*Majlisi Oli*). Constitutional amendments passed by referendum in September 1999 reconstituted the body as a bicameral legislature, all of whose members serve five-year terms.

National Assembly (*Majlisi Milli*). The upper chamber encompasses 25 indirectly elected members, 8 presidential appointees, and former presidents of the republic (currently one, Qahhor Mahkamov). The elected members are chosen by secret ballot of regional legislators in each of five equally weighted electoral districts: the country's four regions and Dushanbe. The most recent election was held March 25, 2010, with President Rahmon announcing his nominees on March 29.

Speaker: Mahmadsaid UBAIDULLOEV.

Assembly of Representatives (*Majlisi Namoyandagon*). The lower chamber encompasses 63 members: 41 deputies directly elected on a majority basis from single-seat districts, and 22 divided proportionally among eligible parties receiving at least 5 percent of the national vote. Following the most recent election of February 28, 2010, with runoff balloting in one constituency on March 14, the People's Democratic Party of Tajikistan held 54 seats; Agrarian Party of Tajikistan, 2; Communist Party of Tajikistan, 2; Islamic Rebirth Party, 2; Party of Economic Reforms, 2; independents, 1.

Speaker: Shukurjon ZUHUROV.

CABINET

[as of November 12, 2013]

Prime Minister	Oqil Oqilov
First Deputy Prime Minister	Matlubkhon Davlatov
Deputy Prime Ministers	Ruqiya Qurbonova [f]
	Murodali Alimardonov
Ministers	
Agriculture and Nature Protection	Qosim Qosimov
Culture	Mirzoshohrukh Asrori
Defense	Col. Gen. Sherali Khayrulloyev
Economic Development and Trade	Sharif Rahimzoda
Education	Abdujabbar Rahmonov
Energy and Industry	Shurali Gul
Finance	Safarali Najmuddinov
Foreign Affairs	Hamrokhon Zarifi
Health	Nustratullo Salimov
Internal Affairs	Ramazon Rakhimov
Justice	Rustam Mengliyev
Labor and Social Welfare	Mahmadamin Mahmadaminov
Land Improvement and Water Economy	Rahmat Bobokalonov
Transport	Nizom Hakimov
State Committee Chairs	
Environmental Protection	Khursandqul Zikirov
Investment and Management of State Property	Davlatali Saidov
National Security	Gen. Saimumin Yatimov

[f] = female

INTERGOVERNMENTAL REPRESENTATION

Ambassador to the U.S.: Nuriddin SHAMSOV.

U.S. Ambassador to Tajikistan: Susan M. ELLIOT.

Permanent Representative to the UN: Sirodjidin M. ASLOV.

IGO Memberships (Non-UN): ADB, CIS, EBRD, ICC, IOM, OIC, OSCE, SCO.

TANZANIA

United Republic of Tanzania
Jamhuri ya Muungano wa Tanzania

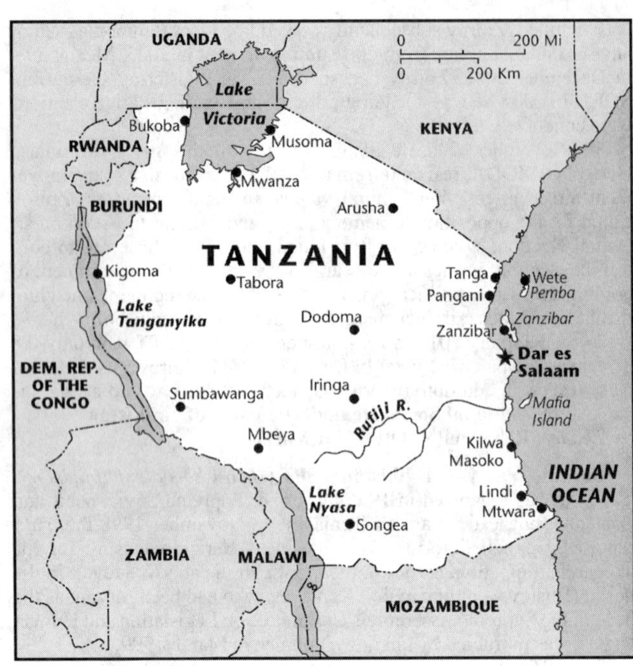

Political Status: Independent member of the Commonwealth; established in its present form on April 26, 1964, through union of the Republic of Tanganyika (independent 1961) and the People's Republic of Zanzibar (independent 1963); one-party constitution adopted April 25, 1977; multiparty system legalized June 17, 1992.

Area: 364,898 sq. mi. (945,087 sq. km), encompassing Tanganyika, 363,948 sq. mi. (942,626 sq. km) and Zanzibar 950 sq. mi. (2,461 sq. km), the latter including Pemba (350 sq. mi., 906 sq. km).

Population: 49,288,546 (2013E—UN); 48,261,942 (2013E—U.S. Census).

Major Urban Centers (2005E): DAR ES SALAAM (2,692,000), Mwanza (219,000), Zanzibar (town, 217,000), Tanga (190,000), Dodoma (169,000). The deadline for the transfer of government operations to a new capital in Dodoma has been extended numerous times. Although the National Assembly now sits in Dodoma, it remains uncertain when, or even if, full governmental relocation will occur.

Official Languages: English, Swahili.

Monetary Unit: Tanzanian Shilling (official rate November 1, 2013: 1,603.46 shillings = $1US).

President: Jakaya KIKWETE (Revolutionary Party of Tanzania); elected on December 14, 2005, and sworn in for a five-year term on December 21 to succeed Benjamin William MKAPA (Revolutionary Party of Tanzania); reelected on October 31, 2010, and sworn in on November 6.

Vice President: Mohamed Gharib BILAL (Revolutionary Party of Tanzania); elected concurrently with the president on October 31, 2010, and sworn in on November 6 to succeed Ali Mohamed SHEIN (Revolutionary Party of Tanzania).

Prime Minister: Mizengo PINDA (Revolutionary Party of Tanzania); appointed by the president and confirmed by the National Assembly on February 8, 2008, and sworn in on February 9, 2008, in succession to Edward LOWASSA (Revolutionary Party of Tanzania), who resigned on February 7; reappointed on November 16 and confirmed that day by the National Assembly.

President of Zanzibar: Ali Mohamed SHEIN (Revolutionary Party of Tanzania); elected on October 31, 2010, and sworn in on November 3 to succeed Amani Abeid KARUME (Revolutionary Party of Tanzania).

THE COUNTRY

The United Republic of Tanzania combines the large territory of Tanganyika on the East African mainland and the two islands of Zanzibar and Pemba off the East African coast. Tanzania's people are overwhelmingly African (primarily Bantu) stock, but there are significant Asian (largely Indian and Pakistani), European, and Arab minorities. In addition to the indigenous tribal languages, Swahili (Kiunguja is the Zanzibari form) serves as a lingua franca, while English and Arabic are also spoken. About 35 percent of the population on the mainland is Christian, 30 percent is Muslim, and the remainder adheres to traditional religious beliefs. Over 90 percent of the population on Zanzibar is Muslim, with Christian and traditional belief minorities. Women comprise nearly 50 percent of the labor force, with responsibility for over 70 percent of subsistence activities; Tanzanian women have a relatively high level of literacy and are represented in most levels of government and party affairs. After the 2010 elections, women held 126 of the 350 seats in the assembly (36 percent of the seats).

The economy is primarily agricultural. The most important crops on the mainland are coffee, cotton, and sisal, which collectively account for approximately two-fifths of the country's exports. The economies of Zanzibar and Pemba are based on cloves and coconut products. Industry, which accounts for about 24 percent of the GDP, is primarily limited to the processing of agricultural products and the production of nondurable consumer goods, although there is an oil refinery that is dependent on imported crude. For many years the country benefited from few extractive resources other than diamonds, but in 2006 Tanzania became Africa's third leading producer of gold. In addition, several international mining companies have recently begun exploration for uranium in several sites.

In April 2000 the IMF and World Bank agreed to support a comprehensive debt relief package for Tanzania, encouraged by reduction in the size of the public sector and greater influence of the free market (see the 2011 *Handbook* for information on the economy prior to 2000). GDP growth averaged about 6.8 percent annually between 2000 and 2008, based on expansion in the manufacturing, mining, and construction sectors. The IMF provided grants and loans under the fund's Poverty Reduction and Growth Facility (PRGF) initiative. Tanzania was also one of the countries approved for debt relief through the World Bank's Heavily Indebted Poor Country (HIPC) initiative. Growth was helped by a series of economic reforms, including privatization initiatives and anticorruption measures. The World Bank also committed $2.3 billion in 2006 in economic development assistance over a three-year period, and Japan canceled Tanzania's $580 million debt in 2007.

In 2008 the Millennium Challenge Account pledged $698 million to Tanzania for economic development. However, the global economic crisis that began in 2008 prompted the government to initiate a $1.3 billion stimulus package. The government's deficit rose to 13.3 percent of GDP in 2009. Meanwhile, foreign aid continued to contribute about 4 percent of the country's total GDP, and in August 2009 the EU announced more than $550 million in economic assistance for Tanzania. The IMF provided another $350 million. However, the UK reduced its aid for governmental budget support in 2008 and 2009 in response to the failure of the Tanzanian government to carry out agreed-upon reforms. In 2010 GDP grew at 6.5 percent, while inflation rose to 10.4 percent, and foreign aid accounted for 10 percent of GDP. Rising gold and commodity prices, combined with a new wave of foreign investment, helped spur the economy. In 2011, the United Kingdom cut its budgetary support to Tanzania by 30 percent, citing lack of progress in improving the business environment.

Despite the impacts of ongoing power shortages and the global economic situation, GDP grew by 6.9 percent in 2012 and 7 percent the next year. The government cut spending and tightened fiscal policy to curb rising inflation—caused by higher oil import prices and high food costs following a drought in the Horn of Africa—which reached 19 percent in late 2011 and declined to around 9 percent in 2013. Although Tanzania was ranked the second-best place to do business in Africa in 2007 by the World Bank, the country fell to tenth place on the continent, or 134th overall out of 185 countries. In May 2013 Brazil announced it would cancel Tanzania's $237 million debt.

GOVERNMENT AND POLITICS

Political background. The former British-ruled territories of Tanganyika and Zanzibar developed along separate lines until their union in 1964. Tanganyika, occupied by Germany in 1884, became a British-administered mandate under the League of Nations and continued under British administration as a United Nations trust territory after World War II. Led by Julius K. NYERERE of the Tanganyika African National Union (TANU), it became independent within the Commonwealth in 1961 and adopted a republican form of government with Nyerere as president in 1962.

Zanzibar and Pemba, British protectorates since 1890, became independent in 1963 as a constitutional monarchy within the Commonwealth. However, little more than a month after independence, the Arab-dominated government of Sultan Seyyid Jamshid bin Abdullah bin KHALIFA was overthrown by African nationalists, who established a People's Republic with Sheikh Abeid Amani KARUME of the Afro-Shirazi Party (ASP) as president.

Following overtures by Nyerere, the two countries combined on April 26, 1964, to form the United Republic of Tanganyika and Zanzibar, renamed the United Republic of Tanzania later in the same year. Nyerere became president of the unified state, and in September 1965 he was overwhelmingly confirmed in that position by popular vote in both sections of the country. Karume, in addition to becoming first vice president of Tanzania, continued to head the quasi-independent Zanzibar administration until April 1972, when he was assassinated. Nyerere thereupon appointed Aboud JUMBE to succeed Karume as first vice president and as leader of the ASP.

On February 5, 1977, TANU and the ASP merged to form the Revolutionary Party of Tanzania (*Chama Cha Mapinduzu*—CCM); subsequently, a new constitution was adopted on April 25, according the CCM a "dominant" role in the Tanzanian governmental system. On November 5, 1980, Prime Minister Edward SOKOINE announced his retirement for reasons of health, and two days later the president named Cleopa David MSUYA as Sokoine's successor. Sokoine returned as prime minister on February 24, 1983, but was killed in an automobile accident on April 12, 1984; he was succeeded 12 days later by Salim Ahmed SALIM. Earlier, on January 27, Vice President Jumbe had submitted his resignation in the wake of mounting secessionist agitation on Zanzibar, Ali Hassan MWINYI having been named his replacement on January 30.

Carrying out a pledge made in early 1984 to step down as head of state upon the expiration of his existing term, Nyerere withdrew from contention at the 1985 CCM congress in favor of Vice President Mwinyi, who was overwhelmingly nominated as the sole candidate for the October presidential balloting. Because of a constitutional prohibition against Zanzibaris occupying both presidential and prime ministerial offices, Prime Minister Salim was replaced following the October 27 poll by Justice Minister Joseph S. WARIOBA, who also assumed the post of first vice president; concurrently, Idris Abdul WAKIL, who had been elected president of Zanzibar on October 13, became second vice president, while Salim was named deputy prime minister and minister of defense.

Mwinyi's elevation to the presidency and his encouragement of private enterprise appeared to stem secessionist sentiment on Zanzibar. However, discord attributed to a variety of economic, religious, and political motives broke out again in late 1987. An apparent power struggle developed between Wakil and supporters of Chief Minister Seif Sharif HAMAD, a leader from the northern island of Pemba (where 90 percent of the islands' cloves are produced), after Hamad was dropped from the CCM Central Committee. On January 23, 1988, Wakil, claiming that dissidents were plotting a coup, suspended the Zanzibari government; three days later he announced a new administration in which Hamad was replaced by Omar Ali JUMA. In May Hamad and six of his supporters were expelled from the CCM for alleged "antiparty" activity. Observers reported a continued "undercurrent of rebellion" on the islands, however, and Hamad was arrested in May 1989 on charges of organizing illegal meetings, the government also accusing his supporters of forming a political group, *Bismallah* ("In the name of God"), dedicated to "breaking the union."

Mwinyi consolidated his authority during 1990; in March he ousted hard-line socialist cabinet members who opposed his economic policies, and, following Nyerere's retirement on August 17, he was elected CCM chair. On October 28 the president won reelection for a second five-year term, and on November 8 he named John S. MALECELA first vice president and prime minister, replacing Warioba. Meanwhile, on October 21 Salmin AMOUR had been elected president of Zanzibar and second vice president of the republic after Wakil had declined to seek reelection to the posts.

On June 17, 1992, President Mwinyi signed a bill legalizing opposition parties, following approval by the National Assembly and the Zanzibar House of Representatives, along with endorsement by the CCM. On July 1 the CCM became the first group to be officially registered under the new law, and by the end of August, 12 of the reportedly 35 parties that had requested application forms had been granted provisional registration.

In late 1992, the government scheduled multiparty elections, beginning with municipal and local balloting in 1993 and concluding with national elections in 1994–1995. Subsequently, the Civic United Front (CUF), a prominent opposition grouping, and four smaller parties threatened to boycott the polling, saying that the delays favored the CCM and calling instead for the convening of a constitutional conference before any elections were held.

In February 1993, Zanzibari membership in the Organization of the Islamic Conference (OIC) was categorized as "unconstitutional" and "separatist" by a Tanzanian parliamentary commission. (The membership was reportedly withdrawn in August 1993, although uncertainty on the question continued [see Membership in OIC].) The affair highlighted continued debate within the government over the two regions' respective roles, as well as a growing schism between Christians and Muslims, which was further evidenced by the anti-Muslim rhetoric of the increasingly popular Democratic Party leader, Rev. Christopher MTIKILA, and the militant activities of the Council for the Dissemination of the Koran in Tanzania (*Balukta*).

In April 1993, at the first balloting since the introduction of multipartyism, the CCM, aided by a CUF boycott, easily won two Zanzibari municipal by-elections. However, fiscal problems, coupled with the Muslim fundamentalist issue, continued to bedevil the ruling party. By late 1994, with less than a year remaining before the next presidential poll, its leadership had fallen into disarray, with former president Nyerere criticizing President Mwinyi as a political weakling and attacking Prime Minister Malecela and CCM Secretary General Horace KOLIMBA as "hooligans" who should resign their positions. The immediate upshot was an extraordinary event: a total ministerial boycott of a cabinet meeting called by the president. Mwinyi responded on December 4 by dissolving the National Assembly, and on December 5 he named a new government headed by former prime minister Cleopa Msuya. Meanwhile, the assembly, two days before the dissolution, had approved a constitutional amendment that created a furor on Zanzibar by specifying that henceforth the island president would no longer become a union vice president unless specifically elected as the president's running mate.

In preparation for the first nationwide multiparty elections, the CCM in July 1995 elected Minister of Science Benjamin William MKAPA as its presidential nominee, President Mwinyi being ineligible for a third term. The balloting of October 29 featured more than 1,300 legislative candidates, with nine opposition parties announcing that they would form a postelectoral coalition if it would give them a parliamentary majority. However, in results that were hotly disputed, Mkapa was credited with winning 61.8 percent of the valid presidential votes, while the CCM garnered 186 of 232 elective assembly seats. Earlier, in even more contentious Zanzibari balloting on October 22, the National Electoral Commission (NEC) had announced that President Amour had been reelected on a 52 percent vote share, with the CCM having been awarded 26 of 50 elective seats in the Zanzibar House of Representatives. Mkapa subsequently named former agriculture minister Frederick Tluway SUMAYE to head a new cabinet, which contained a majority of relatively young newcomers and excluded nearly all former ministers who had been tinged by charges of corruption.

Of 13 opposition parties that contested the 1995 election, only 4 obtained legislative representation. Their disappointing capture of only 24 percent of the seats on a near 40 percent share of the vote was attributed by many to the majority electoral system and by some to widespread electoral fraud, particularly in the Zanzibari balloting, in which the opposition's Seif Hamad was widely believed to have attracted more than the 48 percent vote share officially credited to him in the presidential poll.

Mkapa's economic and political reform efforts in 1996 drew broad praise. Such advances were overshadowed, however, by the political stalemate in Zanzibar where the CUF continued to boycott the legislature in protest over the CCM's alleged rigging of the 1995 elections. In addition, the government's anticorruption campaign was tarnished by the resignation of several ministers in late 1996 and early 1997 following bribery and abuse of power investigations, which also prompted a cabinet reshuffle in February 1997.

In January 1998, Commonwealth mediators introduced a seven-point plan to ease the tension in Zanzibar. However, both sides rejected the accord. In March the Commonwealth released another proposal that was subsequently reported to have been positively received by the CCM and CUF negotiators. The government continued its crackdown on alleged CUF militants in early 1999, but an agreement was finally signed by the CCM and the CUF providing for the return of the CUF to the National Assembly, the award of two additional assembly seats to the CUF, and the creation of an independent electoral commission to oversee the elections scheduled for October 2000. Each side subsequently charged the other with foot-dragging in implementing some provisions of the accord, and tension remained substantial on the island, exacerbated by the death in October 1999 of former president Nyerere, whose considerable domestic and international prestige and influence had been credited with holding the shaky union together. Attention in early 2000 focused on the attempt by Zanzibari president Amour to have the constitution amended to permit him to run for a third term. After reportedly "tumultuous" debate, the CCM rejected the appeal from Amour, who had been widely criticized on Zanzibar for hard-line tactics, including the arrest of prominent CUF members on treason charges (see CUF under Political Parties, below).

Balloting for the National Assembly and Zanzibar's House of Representatives, as well as for the presidencies of Tanzania and Zanzibar was held on October 29, 2000. However, reruns were required in 16 island constituencies on November 5 because of ballot problems in the initial poll. The CUF and many other opposition parties boycotted the reruns, arguing that new voting should have been ordered in all island constituencies. (See the 2012 *Handbook* for more information on the unrest and increasing tensions over Muslim fundamentalism that followed.) Final results showed President Mkapa securing a second five-year term with 71.7 percent of the vote against a fractured opposition. In addition, the CCM maintained its stranglehold on the assembly and a comfortable majority in the House of Representatives. Meanwhile, the CCM's Amani Abeid KARUME, the son of the first president of independent Zanzibar, was declared winner of the Zanzibari presidential poll with 67 percent of the vote. On November 23, President Mkapa reappointed Sumaye to head a reshuffled CCM cabinet.

The CCM candidate, Foreign Minister Jakaya KIKWETE, easily won the December 2005 presidential election in Tanzania with more than 80 percent of the vote, while the CCM increased its majority in the National Assembly. Edward LOWASSA was appointed prime minister on December 29, and a CCM cabinet was approved by the assembly on January 6, 2006. In October Kikwete conducted a major cabinet reshuffle in which ten ministers and eight deputy ministers changed positions.

In 2007 Foreign Minister Dr. Asha-Rose MIGERO was appointed as the UN's first deputy secretary general. She was succeeded as foreign minister by Bernard MEMBE.

On February 7, 2008, Lowassa resigned as prime minister following revelation of corruption charges linked to a scandal over illicit payments to an energy company. Nine other ministers were sacked as the president attempted to restore confidence in the government. Lowassa was replaced by the minister of state in the prime minister's office Mizengo PINDA, who was confirmed by the assembly on February 8. A new cabinet was approved on February 12. In response to the global economic crisis and in anticipation of legislative and presidential elections in 2010, the CCM government endeavored to enact broad economic reforms in 2009 in an effort to improve the economy (see Current issues, below). In June 2009, the UN announced that it would help conduct the 2010 balloting by providing technical assistance, monitors, and $23 million in support.

In balloting on October 31, 2010, Kikwete was reelected president, defeating six other candidates, including Willibrod Peter SLAA of Chadema, who placed second (see Current issues, below). Meanwhile national vice president Ali Mohamed SHEIN of the CCM was elected president of Zanzibar in concurrent polling. The CCM maintained a majority in the national parliament, although its numbers were reduced. On November 16 CCM member, Anna Semamba MAKINDA, was elected as the first female speaker of the Tanzanian assembly. Pinda was reappointed prime minister of Tanzania and sworn in on November 17. A reshuffled cabinet was named on November 24. Meanwhile, on November 18 Shein appointed a sixteen member coalition cabinet for Zanzibar which included ministers from the CCM and the CUF. Meanwhile in response to continuing government anticorruption efforts, a group of international donors who had withheld aid announced in November that they would release more than $700 million in assistance.

In April 2012 Kikwete conducted a major cabinet reshuffle following the publication of an audit that reported fraud and corruption in several ministries, including Energy and Minerals, which the president divided into two separate portfolios.

Constitution and government. An "interim" document of 1965 was replaced on April 25, 1977, by a "permanent" constitution, although the system of government was essentially unaltered. A number of amendments were adopted prior to the 1985 election; significantly, however, Tanzania remained a one-party state, with controlling influence exercised by the CCM at both national and regional levels. Legislation authorizing multiparty activity was approved in 1992 (see Political background, above).

The president is elected by universal suffrage for no more than two five-year terms. Since 1995 the vice president has also been elected as part of a national president/vice president ticket. (Previously Tanzania had two vice presidents: the president of Zanzibar [who served as first vice president if the president was from the mainland] and a presidentially appointed prime minister. The December 1994 constitutional amendment ending the automatic designation of the Zanzibar president as one of the two vice presidents left the insular region without mandated representation at the national executive level.) The prime minister is currently appointed by the president subject to confirmation by the National Assembly. Cabinet ministers are also appointed by the president.

The National Assembly, more than four-fifths of whose members are at present directly elected, sits for a five-year term, subject to presidential dissolution (in which case the president himself must stand for reelection). The judicial system on the mainland is headed by a High Court and includes local and district courts. In August 1979, a Tanzanian Court of Appeal was established to assume, inter alia, the functions of the East African Court of Appeal, which had ceased to exist with the collapse of the East African Community in 1977. All judges are appointed by the president.

Tanzania's 26 administrative regions (21 on the mainland, 3 on Zanzibar, and 2 on Pemba) are each headed by a regional commissioner appointed by the central government. Below the regional level there are 114 municipalities, town councils, and, in rural locations, area or district councils.

On October 13, 1979, a new constitution for Zanzibar was promulgated by its Revolutionary Council after having been approved by the CCM. Under the new system, designed to provide for "more democracy" without contravening the union constitution of Tanzania, the president of Zanzibar is directly elected for a five-year term and held to a maximum of two successive terms. There is also a largely elected House of Representatives endowed with the legislative authority previously exercised by the Revolutionary Council. The latter, however, has been retained as a "high executive council" of cabinet status, with members appointed by the president.

In 2000, the Thirteenth Amendment was ratified by a two-thirds majority in the National Assembly. The measure expanded presidential prerogatives to include the appointment of ten members to the National Assembly and permitted election of the president by a plurality instead of a majority of voters. The amendment also increased the percentage of seats reserved for women from 15 percent to 20 percent. In April 2002 the Zanzibari House of Representatives approved constitutional amendments that called for restructuring the national electoral commission to include opposition representation. In 2004 the Revolutionary Council on Zanzibar announced plans for a new flag, national anthem, and identity cards for the island.

In February 2005, the Fourteenth Amendment was ratified by the assembly. The measure had a number of provisions, including a section that allowed the prime minister to act as president in the absence of the president and vice president. It also loosened the rules about electoral campaigning.

In June 2009, the government announced plans to overturn laws that forbade dual citizenship and enact a new measure that would allow Tanzanians living abroad to retain, or regain, citizenship and participate in elections.

In a referendum in Zanzibar on July 31, 2010, voters approved a constitutional amendment which would allow political parties to form coalition governments by a margin of 66.4 percent in favor and 33.6 opposed.

There are few formal media restrictions in Tanzania. In 2006, Reporters Without Borders declared that Tanzania had the freest press in East Africa. In 2013, the group ranked Tanzania 70th out of 179 countries in freedom of the press (a decline from 36 the previous year, following reports of increased harassment of reporters and the murder of two prominent journalists).

Foreign relations. Tanzania belongs to the United Nations and most of its Specialized Agencies, the Commonwealth, and the African Union. In addition, it participated with Kenya and Uganda in the East African Community (EAC) until the organization was dissolved in mid-1977. Under President Nyerere's leadership, Tanzania pursued a policy of international nonalignment and of vigorous opposition to colonialism and racial discrimination, particularly in southern Africa, maintaining no relations with Pretoria and strongly supporting the effort of the Front-Line States to avoid South African trade routes. In addition, declaring South African destabilization efforts in nearby states to be a direct threat to Tanzania, the government in 1987 sent troops to Mozambique to assist Maputo in the fight against Renamo rebels. (The troops were withdrawn in December 1988, in part, reportedly, because of the cost of their maintenance.) Tanzania also gave asylum to political refugees from African countries, and various liberation groups were headquartered in Dar es Salaam.

Relations with Britain were severed from 1965 to 1968 to protest London's Rhodesian policy. Meanwhile relations with the United States were strained from the 1960s through the 1980s due to Tanzanian disagreement with U.S. policies on Africa.

Long-standing friction with Uganda escalated into overt military conflict in late 1978 (see entry on Uganda). After a six-month campaign that involved the deployment of some 40,000 Tanzanian troops, the forces of Ugandan president Idi Amin were decisively defeated, Amin fleeing to Libya. Subsequently, under an agreement signed with the government of Godfrey Binaisa, approximately 20,000 Tanzanians remained in the country to man security points pending the training of a new Ugandan army. During 1980 Kenya and Sudan were among the regional states expressing concern over the continuing presence in Uganda of the Tanzanian troops, the last of which were finally withdrawn in May–June 1981. (In 2007, Uganda paid Tanzania $67 million to retire debts that remained from the 1978 conflict.)

Relations with Kenya improved measurably upon the conclusion of a November 1983 accord among the two and Uganda on the distribution of EAC assets and liabilities. The border between Tanzania and Kenya, originally closed in 1977 to "punish" Kenya for allegedly dominating Tanzania's economy, was reopened, and the two countries reached agreement on a series of technical cooperation issues. Rapprochement was further enhanced in December, when the three former EAC members exchanged high commissioners in an effort "to facilitate expansion and consolidation in economic matters." (See Foreign relations in entry on Kenya for information regarding the recent reactivation of the EAC.)

In September 1995 Prime Minister Msuya appealed to the UN High Commissioner for Refugees (UNHCR) to aid in the repatriation of more than 800,000 Burundian and Rwandan refugees living in border area camps. In January 1996 the Tanzanian Army turned back an estimated 17,000 Rwandan Hutu refugees fleeing violence in Burundi; however, three days later the government reversed itself and reopened its border. In February relations between Tanzania and Burundi were enhanced by an agreement on border security and refugee repatriation; however, in March, as fighting in Burundi spilled over Tanzania's border, Dar es Salaam rejected the appointment of a Burundian ambassador for the second time.

Conditions deteriorated significantly toward the end of 1996 when large numbers of Hutu refugees crossed Burundi from Zaire (where Tutsis had destroyed Hutu camps and assumed control of the eastern part of the country) into Tanzania. Burundi's president Pierre Buyoya accused Tanzania of supporting Hutu "rebels" and criticized former Tanzanian president Nyerere for spearheading the regional economic sanctions against Burundi. (For more on the normalization of relations between the countries and the repatriation of refugees, see an earlier *Handbook*.) By February 2004, Tanzania had returned all identifiable Rwandan refugees; according to UN estimates, 20,000 remained in Tanzania illegally.

On August 7, 1998, 11 Tanzanians had been killed in Dar es Salaam when alleged militant Islamic fundamentalists set off simultaneous bomb blasts at U.S. embassies in Tanzania and Kenya. (For further details see entries on Kenya and Saudi Arabia, the latter containing a section on Osama bin Laden, whose terrorist network was suspected by U.S. officials of complicity in the bombings.)

The European Union (EU) provided $1.9 million in aid to support the 2001 peace accord between the government and the CUF and $14.82 million to assist Burundian refugees. Collaterally, relations between Tanzania and the United Kingdom (UK) improved significantly in the 1990s. The UK agreed in 2003 to provide assistance for Tanzania's refugee repatriation efforts, and in 2005 the UK announced that Tanzania would be the first African country to benefit from an initiative to write off the debt of poorer countries. Later in 2005, however, a diplomatic row occurred between the two countries when Tanzania unilaterally ended a $143.5 million water privatization project funded jointly by Britain and the World Bank. The Tanzanian government charged that the foreign companies involved in the project were not fulfilling their obligations.

In 2006, the United States granted Tanzania funds for an anticorruption campaign and a malaria suppression initiative on the heels of increasing its security assistance for counterterrorism efforts and launching a program to train personnel from the Bank of Tanzania to interdict financing of terrorist groups.

Reports surfaced in 2007 that China had delivered a number of shipments of arms and weapons to Tanzania, provoking criticism from the assembly over the secret nature of the transactions. The revelations coincided with a scandal in which a British arms firm was discovered to have paid $12 million to Tanzanian figures to secure the sale of a radar system to the country. (The firm BAE was forced to pay the Tanzanian government $47 million in 2011 in fines and fees because of the scandal.) On more positive notes, the UK in 2007 announced that it would provide $530 million over a ten-year period to finance improvements in Tanzania's educational system, and Switzerland granted Tanzania $15.5 million for poverty-reduction programs.

In March 2008 Tanzania commanded the 1,500 AU troops (750 of whom were Tanzanian) who deployed in the Comoros during a sovereignty dispute between the leader of Anjouan Island and the central government (see Comoro Islands entry). Tanzania also pledged to contribute troops to the UN peacekeeping mission in Darfur but strongly condemned the International Criminal Court's issuance of charges of genocide against Sudanese leader Umar Al-Bashir (see Sudan entry). In September Tanzania announced that it would grant citizenship to up to 76,000 Burundian refugees, many of whom had been in the country since 1972. More than 60,000 Burundians were repatriated between 2007 and 2008. The government subsequently announced the closure of most of the camps for the Burundians and threatened forcible repatriation for the remaining 36,000 refugees. In addition, an estimated 89,000 Congolese refugees remained in Tanzania in 2008. In October, Foreign Minister Bernard Membe announced the government intended to seek membership in the Organization of the Islamic Conference (OIC). The initiative was met with criticism from the opposition and Christian groups within Tanzania. No action was taken, although the government of Zanzibar subsequently sought permission to join the OIC on its own.

The government announced in March 2009 that it would increase efforts to reduce illegal fishing off its coastline and in its waters in Lake Victoria. Tanzania also joined a multilateral effort with South Africa, Kenya, and Mozambique to patrol waters for poachers of fisheries in the Indian Ocean. In November members of the EAC signed an agreement to create a common market in the region.

On April 16, 2010, the government announced that it would grant citizenship to the remaining Burundian refugees in Tanzania. In May, Tanzania, Ethiopia, Kenya, Rwanda, and Uganda, signed an accord which altered previous water-sharing agreements among the nations of the Nile River basin. The new accord was expected to create a more equitable distribution of water resources in the region. The EAC common market was formally launched on July 1.

Kikwete was one of five African presidents to participate in a joint mediation initiative in January 2011 to resolve the political crisis in Côte d'Ivoire (see the entry on Côte d'Ivoire). In April the government opened new areas offshore for drilling exploration following oil discoveries in the region by British Petroleum. In May the prime ministers of Tanzania and India signed a series of agreements on counterterrorism cooperation and the suppression of piracy. India also agreed to provide Tanzania with a $180 million line of credit to support infrastructure projects. The following month the United States announced it would provide $70 million to Tanzania to enhance agricultural production. In October Malawi requested African Union (AU) arbitration in a border dispute with Tanzania over disputed maritime boundaries on Lake Malawi (Lake Nyasa). The next month both nations agreed to new negotiations over the disputed areas.

In January 2013 Tanzania announced it would contribute troops to a UN peacekeeping force to be deployed to the Democratic Republic of the Congo (DRC). Kikwete and Chinese president Xi Jingping signed 16 economic cooperation agreements worth $800 million during the latter's state visit to Tanzania in March. The next month Malawi withdrew from maritime negotiations with Tanzania. Then in June Malawi protested a Tanzanian decision to allow passenger ships to travel in the disputed areas of Lake Malawi.

Current issues. In an effort to reduce the impact of the global economic slowdown and maintain the CCM's popularity ahead of elections in 2010, Kikwete announced a massive stimulus plan in July 2009. The package included tax breaks and support for sectors such as tourism and agriculture. However, unemployment continued to rise, especially in Zanzibar where unemployment in some regions reached approximately 40 percent, compared with the national average of 13 percent.

In national balloting on October 31, 2010, Kikwete was reelected with 61.1 percent of the vote. His closest challengers were Slaa of Chadema, who received 26.3 percent of the vote and Ibrahim Haruna LIPUMBA of the CUF who secured 8.1 percent. The CCM secured 185 seats, followed by Chadema with 28, and the CUF, with 18. No other party gained more than 5 seats. In voting for the Zanzibar assembly, the CCM secured 28 seats, and the CUF, 22. In presidential polling on Zanzibar, national vice president Shein of the CCM won with 50.1 percent of the vote, while Hamad of the CUF secured 49.1 percent. Hamad and the CUF subsequently agreed to join the CCM in a coalition government for Zanzibar. Foreign and domestic observers described the balloting on the mainland and Zanzibar as generally free and fair, although Chadema rejected the results and called for a recount. In December Kikwete pledged to support constitutional reforms that would limit the powers of the presidency.

In April 2011, in response to the increase in poaching throughout the country, Kikwete was prompted to order the deployment of security forces in national parks and game reserves. The president also called for increased penalties for poachers. Tanzania was plagued by power shortages throughout the summer and fall of 2011. In September, Kikwete denied that he had accepted a bribe from a Dubai-based company in 2005 while acting as foreign minister, an allegation revealed in a diplomatic cable released by the online group WikiLeaks.

Episodes of civil unrest gripped parts of the country throughout 2011–2012—a phenomenon some observers attributed to the combination of growing competition between the CCM and Chadema parties at the polls and a young, increasingly urban population that has not benefited much from mining-driven growth, which can be mobilized for demonstrations. Lowkassa frequently reiterated the need for youth employment and calls to remove the age limit for presidential candidates came from rising political stars Zitto KABWE, of Chadema, and the CCM's January MAKAMBA.

A series of corruption scandals dominated headlines in 2012. In March, after an annual report from the controller and auditor general blasted a handful of cabinet ministers for corruption and financial laxity, Kabwe launched a petition that threatened a vote of no confidence in the government, eventually gathering signatures from dozens of MPs across party lines. The parliamentary caucus of the CCM demanded the resignation of eight cabinet ministers in response. In May, Kikwete announced a cabinet reshuffling, replacing six ministers and transferring two.

After years of rising calls for a new constitution from civil society and opposition parties, Kikwete named on April 6 a 30-member team to recommend constitutional changes over a period of 18 months. Despite initial objections from opposition parties to Kikwete appointing the team's members, the media and public were reportedly supportive of the eventual nominees, which included politicians, academics, lawyers, and activists in different political parties from the mainland and Zanzibar. In May, however, Chadema's John MNYIKA called for a new constitution. He alleged that the ruling party was drafting the revisions behind closed doors.

The country's total estimated natural gas reserves nearly tripled following new finds in May and June 2012 off Tanzania's coast. In August, an assessment from the Economist Intelligence Unit predicted the dominance of Kikwete and the CCM would assure stability in the run-up to the October 2015 elections. In October two people died and dozens were injured, including a security officer, during proseparatist rioting in Zanzibar.

In May 2013 riots broke out following a general strike called to protest continuing economic inequality. At least nine protesters were killed and scores arrested in the violence. In reaction the government announced a series of major economic development projects estimated to be worth $500 million. Also in 2013 a wave of attacks against Christians on Zanzibar heightened concerns over the potential of Islamic extremism on the island. In June a new draft constitution was publicized by the constitutional review committee. Proposals included greater protections for civil liberties and the creation of separate regional governments for Tanzania and Zanzibar, with a union government. The new basic document was scheduled to be vetted through local and regional councils before its final ratification by a planned constitutional congress in 2014.

POLITICAL PARTIES

Constitutional amendments in 1992 allowed the formation of political parties other than the CCM. The first multiparty elections were held in 1995. In February 2003 opposition parties formed an electoral coalition to oppose the CCM in presidential and legislative balloting in October 2005. The coalition chose Bob Nyanga MAKANI of the Party for Democracy and Progress (*Chama Cha Demokrasia na Maendeleo*—Chadema) as its chair. The alliance failed to present a unified candidate list for the 2005 legislative balloting and could not unite behind a single candidate in the mainland presidential polling.

Four opposition parties (the CUF, TLP, Chadema, and NCCR-Mageuzi) signed an agreement in May 2007 to support a single candidate in the 2010 elections and field joint electoral lists. In December a similar agreement was concluded among five smaller parties, the CCD, the NLD, the Progressive Party of Tanzania (PPT-*Maendeleo*), Sauti Ya Umma (SAU), and Demokrasia Makini (*Makini*). The grouping adopted the Patriotic Front Parties (PFP) designation.

In June 2009, 12 opposition parties in Zanzibar formed an electoral alliance ahead of the 2010 balloting and agreed to support a single candidate in the island's presidential balloting. The parties included: the African Progressive Party of Tanzania (APPT-*Maendeleo*), Chadema, Jahazi Asilia, NCCR-Mageuzi, *Makini,* NLD, NRA, SAU, TLP, Tadea, the Union for Multiparty Democracy (UMD), and the UPDP. The grouping was named the Zanzibar Opposition Alliance.

Government Party:

Revolutionary Party of Tanzania (*Chama Cha Mapinduzi*—CCM). The CCM was formally launched on February 5, 1977, two weeks after a merger was authorized by a joint conference of the Tanganyika African National Union (TANU) and the Afro-Shirazi Party (ASP) of Zanzibar. During the January conference, President Nyerere had asserted that the new organization would be supreme" over the governments of both mainland Tanzania and Zanzibar. Subsequently, a National Executive Committee (NEC) was named by a process of hierarchical (indirect) election, with the NEC, in turn, appointing a smaller Central Committee, headed by President Nyerere.

Founded in 1954, TANU had been instrumental in winning Tanganyika's independence from Britain in 1961. It served after independence as the nation's leading policymaking forum, nominating the president and candidates for election to the National Assembly. Its program, as set forth in the 1967 Arusha Declaration and other pronouncements, called for the development of a democratic, socialist, one-party state.

The ASP, organized in 1956–1957 by Sheikh Abeid Amani Karume, had played a minor role in Zanzibari politics until the coup of 1964. Subsequently, it became the dominant party in Zanzibar and the leading force in the Zanzibar Revolutionary Council. Communist and Cuban models influenced its explicitly socialist program.

During the CCM's national conference in 1982, delegates approved a series of proposals advanced by the NEC to reestablish a separation of powers between party and state, particularly at the regional and local levels. Delegates to an extraordinary national party conference in

February 1992 unanimously endorsed the introduction of a multiparty system. At the party's fourth national conference, held in Dodoma on December 17–20, Ali Hassan Mwinyi, who had succeeded Nyerere as state president and party chair in 1985 and 1990, respectively, was reelected chair. In addition, delegates elected (then) Prime Minister Malecela and Dr. Salmin Amour, a Zanzibari, as vice chairs.

The first half of 1993 was marked by acrimonious debate between the party's mainland and island factions over the selection process for the vice presidency and military leadership. Furthermore, the party experienced rifts over how to respond to Christopher MTIKILA, the (then) prominent leader of the CCD (below).

In July 1995 Benjamin William Mkapa, then minister of science, education, and technology, defeated two opponents in intraparty balloting for designation as the CCM presidential nominee, and he was subsequently credited with a 61.8 percent vote share in the October–November general election. Underlining his commitment to a reform-minded agenda, Mkapa named only one senior CCM party official to his technocrat-dominated cabinet. Although observers praised the new president's early initiatives, a split emerged within the party between Mkapa's supporters and old guard members aligned with former first vice president and prime minister Malecela and former party secretary general Horace Kolimba.

At party balloting on June 22, 1996, Mkapa easily captured the party chair and, bringing his reform efforts to bear on the CCM, began to replace old guard members with his supporters. In February 1997 Horace Kolimba publicly denounced the new team of CCM leaders for their lack of "vision" (a charge that was promptly seconded by the CCM's Pius MSEKWA, speaker of the assembly). Furthermore, Kolimba accused the party of abandoning its "socialist" origins. The intraparty flap and public relations imbroglio arising from Kolimba's statements quickly dissipated in March after Kolimba died of a heart attack while defending his position to party officials. At a party congress in 1997, Mkapa was reelected to the party's top post by acclamation; meanwhile, Mkapa's continued efforts to infuse fresh blood into the CCM resulted in the election of a number of new faces to top posts. On the other hand, John Malecela's retention of the vice chair was described by observers as a reminder of the continued influence (albeit waning) of the party's old guard.

In 1998, the CCM experienced further intraparty tension when, after minimal consultation, Mkapa appointed a three-member CCM team to meet with Commonwealth officials in charge of the negotiations to end the Zanzibar stalemate. Several powerful CCM leaders were subsequently reported to be considering forming a breakaway group in reaction to the CCM-CUF agreement of early 1999. However, as the October 2000 national elections approached, the CCM exhibited greater unity and discipline. A March 2000 special congress rejected an intense effort by controversial Zanzibar president Amour to have the constitution amended to permit him to run for a third term. The CCM also subsequently agreed to delay further consideration of proposed constitutional amendments that had been condemned by opposition groups on both the mainland and Zanzibar.

At a June 2000 CCM congress, President Mkapa was selected without opposition to run for a second term in the October poll. Concurrently, Amani Abeid Karume, a longtime member of the Zanzibari cabinet, was chosen as the CCM candidate for president of Zanzibar from among four candidates, including one supported by Amour. Karume was widely viewed as a strong candidate for the post based on his anticorruption image and the fact that he was the son of Abeid Amani Karume, the first president of independent Zanzibar.

Mkapa was reelected party chair at the 2002 CCM party convention. At a party congress in May, Foreign Minister Jakaya Kikwete was chosen as the party's candidate for the mainland presidency. At a party congress in June 2006, Kikwete was elected party chair. In 2007 four senior CCM figures were suspended from the party for alleged misuse of funds, while five regional officials were removed for disobeying party regulations. The disciplinary actions were reported to be part of a larger program by the CCM to improve its national reputation prior to elections in 2010. Kikwete replaced Philip MANGULA with Yusuf MAKAMBA as the CCM secretary general at the party's November 2007 congress. Makamba was a close ally of the president and his choice was reported to be part of a larger effort by Kikwete to consolidate control of the party.

In June, two CUF members of Parliament defected to the CCM. In August, former APPT-*Maendeleo* presidential candidate Ana SENKORO joined the CCM along with a large number of members of the small party. Former Zanzibar chief minister Dr. Mohamed Gharib BILAL was chosen as Kikwete's vice presidential running mate for the 2010 presidential balloting.

Prior to the 2010 national elections, reports indicated a growing divide within the CCM between an anti-corruption wing, led by then house speaker Samwel SITTA and a status quo or "old guard" faction led by former prime minister Edward LOWASSA. In the October balloting, Kikwete was reelected president of the republic, while vice president Ali Mohamed SHEIN was elected president of Zanzibar. The CCM also secured a majority in the assembly and elected Anna Semamba MAKINDA as the nation's first woman speaker.

In June 2011, Lowassa and other senior CCM officials were forced to resign from the party's national executive committee because of the 2008 arms scandal, reportedly as part of an effort to bolster the image of the CCM prior to new elections in 2015. Other reports indicated that the dismissals were the result of intraparty strife. Lowassa retained the support of most of the CCM's youth wing and used young supporters to pressure CCM leaders. In August, Kikwete suspended an ally, Energy and Minerals Permanent Secretary David JAIRO, a month after CCM MP Beatrice MATUMBO SHELLUKINDO read aloud in Parliament a letter from Jairo soliciting money to ensure the smooth passage of the ministries' budgets. Shellukindo later reported receiving death threats. Observers described the rift in the CCM as increasingly bitter, while Kikwete, taking frequent trips abroad, remained aloof.

The CCM's elections to determine party leadership at a variety of local, regional, and national levels were scattered throughout 2012 in advance of the party's presidential nomination for the 2015 elections. The main contenders were Lowkassa and Sitta, along with Bernard Membe, Works Minister John MAGUFULI, and Asha-Rose MIGIRO. Under new rules instituted by Kikwete, district leaders—rather than regional leaders—will make up a greater proportion of NEC delegates, a change that was intended to empower grassroots supporters but that some observers said could open the door to widespread vote buying. In November 2012 Abdulrahman KINANA became secretary general of the party.

The CCM joined the Socialist International in February 2013. In June the CCM central committee endorsed the draft constitution.

Leaders: Jakaya KIKWETE (President of the Republic and Chair of the Party), Benjamin William MKAPA (Former President of the Republic), Philip MANGULA (Vice Chair, Mainland), Ali Hassan MWINYI (Former President of the Republic), Ali Mohamed SHEIN (President of Zanzibar), Mohamed Gharib BILAL (Vice President of the Republic), Mizengo PINDA (Prime Minister), Anna Semamba MAKINDA (Speaker of the National Assembly), Salim Ahmed SALIM (Member of the Executive Committee and Former Secretary General of the Organization of African Unity), Abdulrahman KINANA (Secretary General).

Opposition Parties:

Civic United Front (CUF). Also referenced as the People's Party (*Chama Cha Wananchi*—CCW), the CUF was founded in late 1991 by former NCCR-Mageuzi leader James MAPALALA, a lawyer who had also been instrumental in the February 1990 establishment of the Civil and Legal Rights Movement. Mapalala was reportedly arrested following the creation of the CUF, which was then deemed to be an illegal formation.

As in the case of other opposition groups, the CUF has been wracked by internal dissent; party chair Mapalala went so far in 1994 as to institute court action against his deputy, Seif Sharif Hamad, and Secretary General Shaaban MLOO. Although Hamad was officially declared runner-up to Salmin Amour in Zanzibar's 1995 presidential race, many observers felt he was the actual victor. Labeling the Amour government "illegal," the CUF refused to assume its Zanzibar parliamentary seats and accused the government of falsely arresting its members. Thereafter, despite a ban on its activities, CUF-directed unrest spread, with observers attributing incidents of arson and harassment to the group.

The split between the CUF's mainland and island wings widened dramatically in early 1997 when the former passed a resolution recognizing Amour's Zanzibar government. Intraparty dissension continued to plague the CUF throughout the year, and, in December, 14 members were arrested for their alleged roles in a coup plot in Zanzibar. In early 1998 further arrests of CUF dissidents were reported.

In May 1998, Mapalala broke with the CUF, announcing that he had formed a new group, the Justice and Development Party (below). Meanwhile, at Commonwealth-brokered negotiations with the Amour administration, CUF islanders agreed to participate in legislative proceedings, abandoning the position that Amour had to be removed prior to the representatives being seated.

The trial of the 18 CUF members (including four members of the House of Representatives) arrested in 1997–1998 formally opened in February 1999, the charge against them having been upgraded to treason, which carried a mandatory death sentence upon conviction. Proceedings were subsequently postponed until January 2000, when another short session resulted in further delay until at least August. Meanwhile, domestic and international human rights groups criticized the prolonged imprisonment of the defendants, whom Amnesty International described as "prisoners of conscience," and the apparent political nature of the charges.

At a general congress in early June 2000, Hamad was once again selected as the CUF candidate for president of Zanzibar in the balloting scheduled for October. The CUF candidate for president of Tanzania, Ibrahim Lipumba, finished second in the 2000 poll with 16.3 percent of the vote, while Hamad was credited with 33 percent of the vote in the controversial balloting for president of Zanzibar. Meanwhile, all of the 16 seats the CUF secured in the 2000 balloting for the Zanzibar House of Representatives came from CUF strongholds on Pemba. In the 2005 elections, Hamad was again the CUF's candidate for the presidency of Zanzibar. Hamad was defeated in controversial balloting in which he received 46.07 percent of the vote. (Only 32,000 votes separated Hamad from the winning candidate.)

In the legislative balloting in Zanzibar, the CUF increased its seats in the house to 19. Lipumba was also the CUF candidate for president of Tanzania in 2005, but he was again defeated, securing only 11.68 percent of the vote. The CUF remained the largest opposition party with 30 seats in the Tanzanian assembly.

In 2007 the CUF led efforts to create an electoral coalition of opposition parties ahead of the 2010 elections. The CUF undertook a boycott of the Zanzibar assembly in April 2008 in an effort to force the ruling CCM to create a unity government on the islands. After refusing to accept the results of the 2005 presidential balloting on Zanzibar, the CUF finally agreed in May 2008 to accept Amani Abeid Karume of the CCM as the legitimate leader of Zanzibar. Meanwhile, negotiations between the CUF and the CCM on a power-sharing arrangement in Zanzibar broke down during the summer.

The party's three top leaders, including Hamad, Lipumba, and Machano Khamis ALI, were reelected to their posts at a CUF congress in February 2009. Former CUF member of parliament and CUF deputy secretary general Wilfred LWAKATERE defected to Chadema in June, along with several hundred of his supporters after he lost his leadership position.

Lipumba placed third in balloting for president of Tanzania in October 2010, while Hamad placed second in polling for president of Zanzibar. In the direct legislative elections, the CUF increased its seats in the Zanzibar assembly to 22, but lost one seat in the national parliament to bring its total to 18. In September 2011, during a by-election, a CUF candidate was charged with election violations, accusations the party claimed were politically motivated.

In June 2013 the CUF organized a demonstration in Dar es Salaam against both rising crime and incidents of police brutality. Meanwhile, senior CUF leaders called on party members to support the proposed constitution.

Leaders: Seif Sharif HAMAD (1995, 2000, 2005, and 2010 candidate for President of Zanzibar and General Secretary), Ibrahim LIPUMBA (1995, 2000, 2005, and 2010 candidate for President of Tanzania and Chair of the Party), Machano Khamis ALI (Vice Chair).

Party for Democracy and Progress (*Chama Cha Demokrasia na Maendeleo*—Chadema). Chadema was launched in 1993 by former finance minister Edwin I. M. Mtei. It was awarded three elected assembly seats in 1995.

In 1997 Chadema stunned observers when it forwarded the controversial Rev. Christopher Mtikila as a candidate at a legislative by-election contest. (Described by *Africa Confidential* as a "fiery xenophobic evangelist," Mtikila, theretofore leader of the CCD, below, had been a staunch critic of the mainland's union with Zanzibar.)

Chadema supported the CUF candidate in the 2000 presidential poll; in concurrent legislative balloting the party improved its representation to four of the elected seats. The Chadema vice presidential candidate in the 2005 mainland elections died on October 27, 2005, causing a postponement of the balloting until December 14. The party's presidential candidate, Freeman Mbowe, placed third with 5.9 percent of the vote. Chadema secured five of the elected seats in the legislative polls. Chadema refused to participate in the CUF-led parliamentary boycott in Zanzibar, but it joined the CUF in an electoral coalition ahead of the 2010 balloting.

In 2009, a number of CUF members defected to Chadema and were rewarded with leadership posts within the party. Deputy Secretary General of Chadema Zitto Kabwe launched a campaign to take the party's top leadership post away from Mbowe in party elections scheduled for the fall. Chadema was instrumental in the formation of the Zanzibar Opposition Alliance in preparation for the 2010 elections. After losing a party primary in 2010, Chadema member Charles MWERA defected to the CUF, along with a number of other party members. Chadema secretary general Willibrod Peter SLAA was the party's 2010 presidential nominee. He placed second in the balloting. In legislative elections, Chadema dramatically increased its seats in the parliament to 28, overtaking the CUF as the largest opposition party. In August 2011 a by-election was postponed following a court challenge by Chadema that other candidates had violated election laws.

To many observers, the victory of Chadema candidate Joshua NASSARI in the April 1, 2012, Arumeru East by-election, seen as a key opener for the 2015 polls, signaled that the party could challenge the CCM's continued dominance and end its era of landslide victories. Following the election, some 300 young men, many armed, invaded a nearby gated estate that Nassari had identified for redistribution. On April 27, Ally BANANGA, who had been a member of CCM's National Central Committees, defected to the Chadema.

Beginning in February 2013, Chadema led a boycott of an assembly committee's investigation into misconduct by members of the assembly. On June 16 a bomb attack killed four at a Chadema rally in Arusha. Chadema officials claimed the attack was directed at party members who had defected from the CCM.

Leaders: Freeman MBOWE (2005 presidential candidate and Chair), Edwin I. M. MTEI (2000 presidential candidate), Willibrod Peter SLAA (2010 presidential candidate and Secretary General).

United Democratic Party (UDP). The UDP's John Cheyo ran fourth in the 1995 presidential race, with a 3.94 percent vote share; in the assembly balloting the party ran fifth, winning three elective seats. In 1997 the UDP added a fifth seat when Cheyo scored an upset victory in a by-election contest expected to be won by a NCCR-Mageuzi candidate. Cheyo secured 4.2 percent of the vote in the 2000 presidential poll. The UDP was a member of the opposition electoral coalition in the 2005 balloting and supported the CUF candidate in the presidential election. The party secured one seat in the assembly. In 2007, Cheyo emerged as one of the most vocal critics of government corruption. In June 2009 Cheyo was temporarily ejected from Parliament for his conduct during a debate on the government's response to pollution. Yahmi Nassoro DOVUTWA was the UDP presidential candidate in the 2010 elections. He placed sixth with less than 1 percent of the vote. The UDP did retain one seat in the assembly balloting.

Leaders: John CHEYO (Chair and 1995 and 2000 presidential candidate), Yahmi Nassoro DOVUTWA (2010 presidential candidate).

National Convention for Constitution and Reform–Mageuzi (NCCR-Mageuzi). The NCCR-Mageuzi was formed in the first half of 1991 as an outgrowth of the Steering Committee for a Transition Towards a Multiparty System, a broad-based organization comprising leading business owners and lawyers as well as political dissidents and student activists. Its initial chair, Abdallah Said FUNDIKIRA, and vice chair, James K. Mapalala, subsequently formed splinter organizations (below), although their successors vowed to keep the committee at the forefront of the "multiparty debate" and to push for its legalization. The party was again split in 1994 when Secretary General Prince Mahinja BAGENDA and several of his supporters withdrew to form the National Convention for Constitution and Reform–*Asili* (the Swahili word for "original").

In April 1995 Augustine Lyatonga MREMA, who had been dismissed as minister of labor and youth development in February for "indiscipline" and who withdrew from the CCM a month later, was selected as the NCCR-Mageuzi's standard-bearer for the presidential election in October. Mrema was credited with only 27.8 percent of the vote, while his party captured only 16 of 232 elective assembly seats.

Asserting that the current constitution unfairly hampered the opposition's electoral ambitions, the NCCR-Mageuzi announced in early 1997 that its top priority for the year would be to pressure the government into organizing a constitutional conference. However, in May the party's stated agenda was overshadowed when Mabere MARANDO, the NCCR-Mageuzi's secretary general, and Masumbuko LAMWAI, a NCCR-Mageuzi parliamentarian and former CCM member, attempted to oust Mrema, who had accused Marando of acting in complicity with the CCM. During the subsequent legal and political infighting, the Central Committee reportedly aligned behind Marando and his supporters and the National Executive Committee with Mrema. The reportedly irreconcilable nature of the split was underscored by the unwillingness of the two factions (styled the NCCR-Mrema and NCCR-Marando) to cooperate on by-election campaigns, thus, according to observers, costing the group winnable legislative seats. Furthermore, in October both factions sent representatives to an opposition summit.

After sustained legal and political infighting between the two camps, in April 1999, Mrema announced that he was leaving the NCCR-Mageuzi to join the TLP (see above). Lamwai subsequently rejoined the CCM. The NCCR-Mageuzi won only one elected seat in the 2000 legislative poll, while its proposed presidential candidate, Edith LUSINA, was precluded from running for failure to secure sufficient advance signatures of support.

In the 2005 presidential election, four parties, including the FORD, NRA, UMD, and the UPDP (see below), agreed to support the NCCR-Mageuzi candidate, Sengondo Mvungi. The NCCR-Mageuzi failed to gain any seats in the assembly. In 2007 the NCCR-Mageuzi became part of the CUF-led opposition electoral coalition. In September 2008 Mvungi was injured when violence erupted at a NCCR-Mageuzi rally. The NCCR-Mageuzi blamed the incident on pro-CCM youths. The NCCR-Mageuzi led the opposition to the government initiative to join the OIC in 2008–2009 (see Foreign relations, above).

Hashim Spunda RUNGWE was the party's 2010 candidate in the presidential balloting. He placed fifth in the voting with less than one percent of the votes. The NCCR-Mageuzi secured four seats in the national parliament in concurrent legislative elections. Ambar Haji KHAMIS was the NCCR-Mageuzi candidate in the Zanzibar presidential balloting. He also received less than 1 percent of the vote and the party did not gain any seats in the Zanzibar assembly. In by-election voting for the representative for the Igunga district, the NCCR-Mageuzi endeavored unsuccessfully to convince opposition parties to support a single candidate.

The party joined a Chadema-led boycott of an investigation into parliamentary misconduct in 2013, arguing that the inquiry was politically motivated.

Leaders: James MBATIA (Chair), Hashim Spunda RUNGWE (2010 presidential candidate), Sengondo MVUNGI (2005 presidential candidate), Hussein Mwaiseje POLISYA (Secretary General).

Tanzania Labour Party (TLP). This small party's profile grew significantly in 1999 when the leading opposition figure Augustine Mrema and over 1,000 of his followers joined after leaving the NCCR-Mageuzi. Mrema won 7 percent of the vote in the 2000 presidential poll, while the TLP secured three of the elected seats in concurrent assembly elections. In mid-2001 the TLP was reportedly riven by factions devoted to Mrema and party founder Leo LWEKAMWA. The TLP opposed the opposition coalition formed for the October 2005 election and decided to contest the balloting independently. Its candidate, Mrema, was placed fourth with less than 1 percent of the vote, and the TLP secured one seat in the assembly. In 2007 the TLP agreed to participate in the CUF-led electoral coalition. In October a court stripped TLP parliamentary deputy Phares KABUYE of his seat because he had defamed his rival in the 2005 balloting. In 2008 many TLP members reportedly defected to other parties. The party nominated Muttamwega Bhatt Mgaywa as its presidential candidate for Tanzania in 2010. He received less than 1 percent of the vote. On July 10, 2011, the party's central committee voted to suspend Deputy Secretary General Rajabu TAO after he allegedly submitted wrongful personal information about TLP candidates to the National Electoral Commission. The month before, Tao had alleged that Mrema had misappropriated party funds.

In 2013 Mrema was accused of corruption by fellow parliamentarians who sought to remove him from the chairmanship of the Local Authority Accounts Committee.

Leaders: Augustine MREMA (2000 and 2005 presidential candidate and Chair), Muttamwega Bhatt MGAYWA (2010 presidential candidate).

Other Parties That Contested the 2010 Election:

Tanzania Democratic Alliance Party (Tadea). The previously London-based Tadea was founded by Oscar Salathiel KAMBONA, a former TANU secretary general and Nyerere cabinet member who went into voluntary exile in 1967 after government authorities alleged he had been involved in a coup plot. Kambona was also one of the founders of the Tanzania Democratic Front (TDF), formed in London by a number of exile opposition groups to promote the introduction of a multiparty system. Tadea was registered in Tanzania in 1993. In 1996 Tadea was buffeted by allegations that its officials had misused publicly funded campaign finances.

The party joined the opposition alliance to contest the 2005 elections and supported the CUF mainland presidential candidate. In the October 2010 presidential elections in Zanzibar, Tadea secretary general Juma Ali KHATIB was the party's candidate. He placed fifth with less than 1 percent of the vote. Tadea competed unsuccessfully in a by-election for Bububu in September 2012.

Leaders: John D. LIFE-CHIPAKA (Chair), Juma Ali KHATIB (Secretary General and 2010 presidential candidate).

Union for Multiparty Democracy (UMD). The UMD was organized in late 1991 by Abdallah Said Fundikira, a well-known Tanzanian businessman, and others who had previously been involved in the NCCR. They proposed that a national conference be held to draft a new Tanzanian constitution that would permit multiparty activity. In addition, the UMD suggested that the union between the mainland and the islands of Zanzibar and Pemba be reevaluated. Following the formation of the UMD, Fundikira was arrested and released on bail after being charged with establishing an illegal organization. The UMD was nonetheless registered in 1993. The UMD supported the NCCR-Mageuzi candidate in the 2005 presidential elections and failed to gain any seats in the assembly. The UMD did not gain any seats in the 2010 legislative balloting. Reports in 2011 indicated that the party had become limited to a small number of areas.

Leaders: Chief Abdallah Said FUNDIKIRA (President of the Party and 1995 candidate for President of the Republic), Stephen M. KIBUGA (Vice President), Hussein Hassan YAHAYA (Secretary General).

National Reconstruction Alliance (NRA). Former industries and trade minister Kigoma Ali MALIMA resigned from the CCM on July 16 to become the NRA's 1995 presidential candidate; however, he died unexpectedly on August 5. Following the elections, the party reportedly faced an audit of its campaign financing practices amid allegations that it had misused public funds.

The NRA joined the electoral coalition that supported the NCCR-Mageuzi candidate in the 2005 elections. After being denied a permit for a demonstration in August 2008 in Zanzibar, the NRA filed a lawsuit against security forces. In presidential balloting on Zanzibar, the NRA candidate, Haji Khamis HAJI, placed fourth with less than one percent of the vote. Reports in 2013 indicated that the party might be defunct.

Leaders: Rashid MTUTA (Chair), Maoud RATUU (Secretary General), Haji Khamis HAJI (2010 presidential candidate).

Justice and Development Party (*Chama cha Haki na Usitawi*—Chausta). Chausta was launched in Zanzibar in May 1998 by former CUF leader James Mapalala. According to Mapalala, the new party was founded on the principle of development of the "individual." The party was officially recognized in late 2001. In August 2008 CCM youth disrupted a Chausta rally in Zanzibar. Chausta failed to win any seats in the 2010 legislative balloting and lost several by-elections in 2011.

Leaders: James MAPALALA (Chair), Joseph MKOMAGU (Secretary General).

Democratic Party (*Chama Cha Demokrasi*—CCD). The CCD was formed in late 1991 in anticipation of the introduction of a multiparty system. The CCD is sometimes referred to as the DP. Soon thereafter, the party was thrust into the national limelight by the August 1992 conviction of its leader, Christopher Mtikila, on charges of illegal assembly. The High Court subsequently dismissed the charges against Mtikila, whose nationalistic rhetoric had made him increasingly popular. However, in January 1993, Mtikila was arrested on charges of having fomented sedition and rioting by a speech in which he had accused the government of having "sold [Tanzania] to Arabs and Gabacholics [Asians]," urged Indo-Pakistanis, Arabs, Somalians, and Zanzibaris to emigrate, and warned that blood would flow if the alleged favoritism to foreigners continued. He was rearrested a number of times thereafter on a variety of charges, including the leadership of illegal demonstrations.

In 1997, Mtikila ran as a Chadema candidate in a legislative by-election, thus casting uncertainty on the future of the CCD, which had been unable to secure official recognition because of its unwillingness to accept Zanzibar as a legitimate part of the country. The CCD's candidate in the 2005 presidential election was Mtikila, who placed sixth in the balloting.

In 2008, the CCD joined with four other opposition parties in the Patriotic Front Parties coalition. The party did not gain any seats in the 2010 legislative elections.

Leaders: Christopher MTIKILA (2005 presidential candidate and Chair), Natanga NYAGAWA (Secretary General).

Other parties that contested the 2010 elections included the **African Progressive Party of Tanzania** (APPT-*Maendeleo*), formed in 2003 and led by Peter Kuga MZIRAY (Chair and 2010 presidential candidate); **Jahazi Asilia**, led by Abuu Juma AMOUR (Chair) and 2010 Zanzibar presidential candidate Kassim Bakar ALIY; the **Demokrasia Makini** (*Makini*), formed in 2001 and led by Godfrey HICHEKA and Georgia MTIKILA; and the **Sauti Ya Umma** (SAU), formed in 2005 and led by Paulo KYARA (2005 presidential candidate and Chair). These parties joined the Zanzibar Opposition Alliance in June 2009. None received more than 1 percent of the vote in the 2010 legislative balloting.

Other parties or groupings that participated in the 2010 balloting included: the **National League for Democracy** (NLD), led by Emmanuel MAKAIDI; the **United People's Democratic Party** (UPDP), led by Fahmi Nassoro DOVUTWA; the **Party of Associations** (*Chama Cha Kijamii*—CCK), led by Constantine AKITANDA, the former publicity secretary of the CCJ; the **Movement for Economic Change** (MEC); and the **Association of Farmer's Party** (*Chama Cha Wakulima*—AFP), formed in 2009 and led by Soud Said SOUD (Chair and 2010 Zanzibar presidential candidate).

Seven leaders of the Islamist and pro-Zanzibar independence group, **Association for the Awakening and Propagation of Islam in Zanzibar** (*Jumuiya ya Uamsho na Mihadhara ya Kiislamu Zanzibar—Uamsho*) were arrested for sedition in October 2012.

For information on the **Forum for Restoration of Democracy** (FORD), the **Patriotic Front Parties** (PFP), the **Zanzibar Organization,** the **Party of Society** (*Chama Cha Jamii*—CCJ); and the banned **Council for the Dissemination of the Koran in Tanzania** (*Balukta*), please see the 2010 *Handbook*.

LEGISLATURE

The Tanzania **National Assembly** (*Bunge*), also referenced as the Union Parliament, has a five-year mandate, barring dissolution. The current assembly includes 239 members directly elected in single-member constituencies (186 on the mainland and 50 on the islands). The constitution requires that women hold 20 percent of the assembly seats, an increase of 5 percent with the elections in 2000. Following every general election, parties in the assembly must nominate (according to the seats they hold) a number of women to fill any remaining seats of the 20 percent allotted them. The Zanzibar House of Representatives elects 5 of its members to the assembly, and the Tanzanian attorney general is entitled to a legislative seat. Another revision made in 2000 allows the president to appoint 10 members. At the most recent balloting of October 31, 2010, the Revolutionary Party of Tanzania (CCM) secured 186 of the directly elected seats; the Civic United Front (CUF), 24; the Party for Democracy and Progress (Chadema), 23; the National Convention for Constitution and Reform–Mageuzi (NCCR-Mageuzi), 4; the United Democratic Party (UDP), 1; and the Tanzania Labour Party (TLP), 1.

Speaker: Anne Semamba MAKINDA.

The Zanzibar **House of Representatives** is a 75-member body encompassing 50 elected members, 5 regional commissioners, 10 presidential nominees, and 10 members representing women and selected organizations. At the balloting of October 31, 2010, the Revolutionary Party of Tanzania won 28 of the elected seats, and the Civic United Front won 22.

Speaker: Pandu Amir KIFICHO.

CABINET

[as of November 15, 2013]

President	Jakaya Kikwete
Vice President	Mohamed Gharib Bilal
President of Zanzibar	Ali Mohamed Shein
Prime Minister	Mizengo Pinda
Ministers of State in the President's Office	
Good Governance	George Mkuchika
Public Relations and Coordination	Stephen Wassira
Public Service Management	Celina Kombani [f]
Ministers of State in the Vice President's Office	
Environment	Terezya Louga Hovisa [f]
Union Affairs	Samilia Suluhu Hassan [f]
Ministers of State in the Prime Minister's Office	
Investment and Empowerment	Mary Nagu [f]
Parliamentary Affairs	William Lukuvi
Regional Administration and Local Government	Hawa Abdulrahman Ghasia [f]
Ministers	
Agriculture, Food Security, and Cooperatives	Cristopher Chiza
Communications, Science and Technology	Makame Minyaa Mbarawa
Community Development, Women's Affairs, and Children	Sophia Simba [f]
Defense and National Service	Shamsi Vuai Nahodha
East African Cooperation	Samwel John Sitta
Education and Vocational Training	Shukuru Kawambwa
Energy and Mineral Resources	Sospeter Muhongo
Finance and Economic Affairs	William Mgimwa
Foreign Affairs and International Cooperation	Bernard Membe
Health and Welfare Development	Hussein Mwinyi
Home Affairs	Emmanuel John Nchimbi
Industries and Trade	Abdallah Kigoda
Information, Culture, and Sport	Fenella Mukangara [f]
Justice and Constitutional Affairs	Mathias Chikawe
Labor and Employment	Gaudentia Kabaka [f]
Lands, Housing, and Human Settlement	Anna Tibaijuka [f]
Livestock Development	Mathayo David Mathayo
Natural Resources and Tourism	Khamis Kagasheki
Transport	Harrison Mwakyembe
Water and Irrigation	Jumanne Maghembe
Works	John Pombe Magufuli
Without Portfolio	Mark James Mwandosya

[f] = female

INTERGOVERNMENTAL REPRESENTATION

Ambassador to the U.S.: Mwandaidi Sinare MAAJAR.

U.S. Ambassador to Tanzania: Alfonso E. LENHARDT.

Permanent Representative to the UN: Tuvako N. MANONGI.

IGO Memberships (Non-UN): AfDB, AU, Comesa, CWTH, ICC, IOM, NAM, SADC, WTO.

THAILAND

Kingdom of Thailand
Prathet Thai

Note: Considerable variation occurs in the English transliteration of Thai names. Where possible, Thai sources have been relied on, but these also present variations.

Political Status: Independent monarchy functioning under a constitution approved by popular referendum on August 19, 2007, validated by the Constitutional Drafting Assembly on August 21, and promulgated on August 24.

Area: 198,455 sq. mi. (514,000 sq. km).

Population: 67,598,735 (2012E—UN); 67,448,120 (2013E—U.S. Census).

Major Urban Center (2010E): BANGKOK (metropolitan area, 12,390,000).

Official Language: Thai.

Monetary Unit: Thai Baht (market rate November 1, 2013: 31.24 baht = $1US).

Sovereign: King BHUMIBOL Adulyadej (King RAMA IX); ascended the throne June 9, 1946; crowned May 5, 1950.
Heir Apparent: Crown Prince Maha VAJIRALONGKORN.

Prime Minister: YINGLUCK Shinawatra (For Thais Party); elected by the House of Representatives on August 5, 2011, and endorsed by the king on August 8, succeeding ABHISIT Vejjajiva (Democrat Party).

THE COUNTRY

The Kingdom of Thailand (known historically as Siam) is located in the heart of mainland Southeast Asia. Its immediate neighbors are Myanmar (Burma) in the west, Laos in the north and northeast, Cambodia in the southeast, and Malaysia in the deep south. Thailand is a tropical country of varied mountainous and lowland terrain. About 75 percent of its population is Thai; another 14 percent are ethnic Chinese, mostly urban residents prominent in commerce, banking, and manufacturing. Other minorities are of Malaysian, Indian, Khmer, and Vietnamese descent. Theravada Buddhism is professed by about 95 percent of the population, but religious freedom prevails and a number of other religions claim adherents. Women constitute approximately 51 percent of the labor force, primarily in agriculture; female participation in government, while increasing somewhat in recent years, remains low. Following the most recent elections in 2008 and 2011, women constituted 15.4 percent of the Senate and 15.8 percent of the House of Representatives, respectively. YINGLUCK Shinawatra became the first woman prime minister of Thailand in 2011.

Like most countries in Southeast Asia, Thailand is predominantly rural, with over 40 percent of its people still engaged in agriculture. Agriculture accounts for about 12 percent of GDP, compared to 43 percent for industry and 45 percent for services. Bulk and processed foodstuffs, especially rice, and other agricultural products, such as rubber, account for the majority of export earnings, but the growth of industrial output since the mid-1980s has raised earnings from manufactured goods that range from garments and electrical appliances to information technology items and vehicle components. Tourism is also a significant earner. The country's mineral resources include cassiterite (tin ore), tungsten, antimony, coal, iron, lead, manganese, molybdenum, and gemstones. Thailand's primary trade partners are Japan, China, the United States, the European Union, and the ASEAN region.

In 1999, GDP growth was 4.4 percent, rising to 6.1 percent by 2004 (for more on the economy prior to 1999, please see the 2012 *Handbook*). The Indian Ocean tsunami of December 2004—which according to official reports killed more than 100,000 people, left another 700,000 homeless, and caused $4.4 billion in property and infrastructure damage—combined with a drought, a weaker electronics market, and political unrest in the southern provinces reduced growth to 4.5 percent in 2005. Uncertainty following a military takeover in 2006, public demonstrations around the 2008 change of government, and the subsequent international financial crisis also depressed the growth rate, which was a recessionary –2.3 percent in 2009. In 2010, the IMF reported that GDP grew by 7.8 percent, but only by 0.1 percent in 2011, before rising by 6.4 percent in 2012. That year, inflation rose by 3 percent, and the official unemployment rate was 0.5 percent. GDP per capita in 2012 was $5,678. In its annual Doing Business survey in 2013, the World Bank ranked Thailand 18th out of 185 countries, a higher rating than that of more economically developed nations such as Germany or Japan.

GOVERNMENT AND POLITICS

Political background. Historical records indicate that the Thai people migrated to present-day Thailand from China's Yunnan Province about a thousand years ago. By the 14th century the seat of authority was established in Ayutthaya. Toward the end of the 18th century, Burmese armies conquered the kingdom but were eventually driven out by Rama I, who founded the present ruling dynasty and moved the capital south to Bangkok in 1782. Upon the conquest of Burma by the British in 1826, Rama III began the process of accommodating European colonial powers by negotiating a treaty of amity and commerce with Britain. Subsequent monarchs, Rama IV and V, by a combination of diplomacy and governmental modernization, avoided colonization by European powers in the 19th and early 20th century, the only Southeast Asian country to do so.

Thailand was ruled as an absolute monarchy until 1932, when a group of military and civilian officials led by Col. (later Field Mar.) Luang PIBULSONGGRAM (PIBUL Songgram) and PRIDI Phanomyong seized power in the first of a series of military coups. The Pibulsonggram dictatorship sided with the Japanese in World War II, but the anti-Japanese *Seri Thai* (Free Thai) movement, led by Pridi and SENI Pramoj, paved the way for reconciliation with the Allied powers at the war's end. Pridi dominated the first postwar government but was discredited and fled to China in 1947. Pibulsonggram ruled for the following decade, until overthrown by Field Marshal SARIT Thanarat, who in turn was succeeded in 1963 by Field Marshal THANOM Kittikachorn with the support of Gen. PRAPAS Charusathira, the army commander and national strongman.

Following promptings from the throne, the military regime in June 1968 promulgated a new constitution restoring limited parliamentary government. In the resultant 1969 election the Democrat Party (DP), led by Seni Pramoj, won all seats in the major urban centers of Bangkok and Chon Buri, but the government, through its vehicle the United Thai People's Party (UTPP), mustered sufficient strength elsewhere to retain control. The Thanom government in November 1971 dissolved the legislature, suspended the constitution, and banned all political parties except the government-sponsored Revolutionary Party. In October 1973, however, as a result of widespread student demonstrations and disapproval of the king, the Thanom government fell, and the rector of Thammasat University, SANYA Dharmasakti (Thammasak), was appointed prime minister. A period of civilian democratic rule, led successively by Sanya, Seni Promoj, and KUKRIT Pramoj, lasted until October 1976, when Adm. SANGAD Chaloryu reasserted military control. He was succeeded by Gen. KRIANGSAK Chamanan in 1977, and then Gen. PREM Tinsulanond in 1980.

In 1988 a period of civilian-led constitutionalism began. Leaders such as Maj. Gen. CHATCHAI Choonhavan and Gen. CHAOVALIT Yongchaiyut resigned their military commissions, joined political parties, and led civilian-dominated multi-party coalition governments. Subsequently, civilian party leaders, including the DP's CHUAN Leekpai and BANHARN Silpa-Archa of the *Chart Thai* (Thai Nation), emerged to win the prime minister's post by means of constitutional elections. (For details of the period 1970–2000 see the 2010 *Handbook.*)

A landmark election took place in January 2001, in which the *Thai Rak Thai* (Thais Love Thais) party, emerged into prominence by winning 248 seats in a 500-seat House of Representatives. Its founder, THAKSIN Shinawatra, who had amassed a fortune in the telecommunications industry and served as a minister in previous civilian governments, negotiated a coalition with the New Aspiration Party (NAP) and *Chart Thai* enabling him to claim the office of prime minister.

Prime Minister Thaksin's popularity in rural Thailand, coupled with a well-managed response to the December 2004 tsunami disaster, carried Thaksin to a further election victory in February 2005. *Thai Rak Thai* won a commanding 377 House seats, permitting Thaksin to form a one-party government. The opposition DP won only 96 seats.

During the following year, opposition to the prime minister's policies and alleged authoritarianism grew, especially among middle- and upper-class political elites in Bangkok, where in February 2006 an anti-Thaksin rally drew an estimated 100,000 protesters to Royal Plaza. A direct precipitant had been the tax-free sale by Thaksin's family of its 49 percent stake in the Shin Corporation, a telecommunications company, for $1.9 billion. Immediately after the anti-Thaksin rally, leaders from some 40 nongovernmental organizations and other groups announced formation of a People's Alliance for Democracy (PAD), which demanded Thaksin's resignation and a return to political reform. The PAD brought together a broad cross-section of predominantly urban interest groups, including nongovernmental organizations, academics, students, organized labor, businesses, and advocates for the poor. The PAD campaign, in addition to demanding Thaksin's resignation, hoped to rekindle the political reform movement that had brought down the government of SUCHINDA Kraprayoon in 1992. Critics of the PAD alleged, however, that it was covertly manipulated by the military and the Bangkok elite to derail the rural reforms proposed by the *Thai Rak Thai.*

Responding to the growing crisis of confidence in his administration, on February 26 Thaksin dissolved the House of Representatives and called an election for April 2. Opposition leaders ABHISIT Vejjajiva of the DP, former prime minister Banharn Silpa-Archa of *Chart Thai,* and SANAN Kachornprasart of *Mahachon* (Public Party) announced that they would boycott the election. Although Thaksin's party won 61 percent of the valid votes, 38 percent of voters abstained and about 12 percent of ballots were deliberately spoiled by voters. Consequently, on April 5 Thaksin announced that he was "taking some time off" and named Deputy Prime Minister CHITCHAI Wannasathit to act in his stead.

On April 25, 2006, in a nationwide address, King Bhumibol asked the nation's highest courts to resolve the country's "political mess." By that time, lawsuits had been filed requesting nullification of the April 2 results, and on May 8 the Constitutional Court did so by an 8–6 vote, primarily on technical grounds that voters' right to a secret ballot had been compromised by the positioning of voting booths and that the Electoral Commission had not allowed sufficient time between the late February dissolution of the sitting House of Representatives and the election date. The court by a 9–5 decision further ordered that new elections be held. On May 23 Thaksin reassumed his post, now as caretaker prime minister, and near the end of the month the Election Commission and the cabinet set October 15 as the new election date. As the election campaign intensified, Thaksin's opponents claimed he was corrupt, arrogant, favored cronies in his numerous cabinet shuffles, surrounded himself with "yes men," tried to manage the government as if he were CEO of a private business, and used his political power to curtail media critics.

In addition, the army commander-in-chief, Gen. SONTHI Boonyaratglin, a Muslim, objected to the Thaksin government's heavy-handed crackdown on the Muslim insurgency in the south. In January 2004 the government had declared martial law in the three Muslim-majority southern provinces in response to escalating attacks that targeted not only authorities but also school teachers, civil servants, and Buddhist monks. On April 30, a coordinated series of attacks against 11 police bases was met with a lethal response from the police and military, leaving over 100 Muslims dead, 30 of them killed during the storming of a mosque. An official inquiry concluded that excessive force had been used. In October, another deadly encounter ended with nearly 80 of some 1,300 detainees suffocating or dying of heat stroke while being transported in overcrowded trucks.

Although Thaksin established a National Reconciliation Commission (NRC) in March 2005 to formulate "peace-building" proposals for the south, in mid-July the cabinet approved an Emergency Powers Act that was promulgated by executive decree. The act, which was passed by both houses of the National Assembly in August, granted Thaksin authority to conduct wiretaps, ban media, conduct searches and detain suspects without warrants, censor news, and ban publications. In January 2006, with the death toll in the south having passed 1,000, Amnesty International accused the government and military of using arbitrary detentions, excessive force, and torture. In June the NRC, headed by former prime minister ANAND Panyarachun, reported that the underlying issues could not be resolved militarily. Instead, it recommended that indigenous Malay be adopted as a "working language" in the south, that the application of Islamic law be permitted in some situations, that a dialog be opened with militants, that a Fund for Healing and Reconciliation be created, and that mechanisms be established to allow greater local input in cultural and governmental matters.

On September 19, 2006, with Prime Minister Thaksin in New York for the opening of the UN General Assembly, the Thai military, led by General Sonthi, seized power in a bloodless coup, imposed martial law, suspended the constitution, dissolved the National Assembly, and banned political gatherings. On September 20 King Bhumibol appointed General Sonthi head of a Council for Democratic Reform in order "to create peace in the country" while the political impasse was resolved. Sonthi promised to install a civilian government and hold legislative elections under a new constitution by the end of the year. The coup leaders subsequently reconstituted the Council of Democratic Reform as the Council of National Security to advise the interim government. SURAYUD Chulanont, a retired general, was named interim prime minister of Thailand by royal decree on October 1. With the approval of the Council of National Security and in consultation with advisers to the monarchy, Surayud named a new cabinet, which was sworn in on October 9. The new cabinet enlisted a majority of civilian experts and notables; only three ministers were serving military officers, although others had reserve rank or were retired. Martial law was lifted in most provinces on January 27, 2007.

Following the April 2006 election, the Election Commission had recommended to the attorney general that five parties—*Thai Rak Thai,* the DP, and three minor formations—be dissolved for violating the constitution and the Political Party Act. Allegations included that *Thai Rak Thai* had bankrolled small parties to offer token competition, thereby illegally circumventing a requirement that a candidate in an uncontested race had to receive at least 20 percent of the vote to claim the seat. The DP was charged with paying bribes to elicit accusations that *Thai Rak Thai* had committed electoral fraud. The cases were heard by the Constitutional Tribunal, which ruled against *Thai Rak Thai* on May 28, 2007, dissolving the party and excluding 111 of its executives, including Thaksin, from political office for five years. The DP was cleared of electoral fraud, but the other three parties were also dissolved. In June corruption charges were brought against Thaksin and his wife, and many of their bank accounts were frozen.

With regard to the southern insurgency, the Thaksin government's harsh measures had been moderated in October 2006 by General Surayud, who apologized for his predecessor's wrongs, freed a number of detainees, and urged Thai security officials to engage with the

Muslim subjects. Nevertheless, the insurgency escalated, signaled by intimidation, arson, assassinations, beheadings, and ambushes of security forces. The government responded by reinforcing several local paramilitary formations, including the Ranger Force (*Thahan Phran*), the Volunteer Defense Corps (*Or Sor*), and the Village Defense Volunteers (*Chor Ror Bor*). Queen SIRIKIT sponsored a new Village Protection Force (*Or Ror Bor*). These militia were poorly trained and equipped, reported to be of dubious effectiveness save as reassurance to local Buddhists, and were allegedly implicated in extortion, beatings, and extrajudicial executions. Meanwhile, a mid-2007 report by Human Rights Watch put the number of deaths at the hands of the insurgents at 2,500, many of them victims of indiscriminate bombings and gruesome assaults (for more information, please see the 2013 *Handbook*).

With a new constitution having been approved in a referendum on August 19, 2007 (see Constitution and government, below), and with Sonthi, having retired from the military, being named deputy prime minister for security affairs in October, the interim government scheduled fresh elections for a reconstituted, 480-member House of Representatives. The December 2007 legislative election gave a plurality to the People Power Party (*Pak Palang Prachachon*—PPP), which was widely seen as the successor to *Thai Rak Thai.* A dozen seats short of a majority, SAMAK Sundaravej, the new leader of the PPP, invited five of the other six parties that had won seats in the House of Representatives to join in a coalition government. The new government, with Samak as prime minster, was sworn in on February 6, 2008. The DP took up the role of opposition in the House.

Subsequently, 11 members of the PPP accused of vote-buying lost their House seats and four PPP ministers were obliged to resign, two for electoral fraud, one because he allegedly insulted the king, and one because he made an unconstitutional agreement with Cambodia over a disputed temple at their common border (see Foreign relations, below). These events, compounded by Thaksin's brief return and subsequent flight to London, and the conviction (subsequently overturned) of his wife, KHUNYING Potjaman, for corruption, undermined the PPP's credibility and fuelled the PAD's protests.

The PAD also opposed Prime Minister Samak's alleged intent to amend the constitution to restore the 111 *Thai Rak Thai* executives to political eligibility, to forestall ongoing legal challenges to the PPP's existence, and to pardon Thaksin and his wife. The protests escalated in June and culminated in mass demonstrations and the occupation of the prime minister's office grounds in August. On September 2, 2008, Samak declared a state of emergency, empowering the military and police to ban gatherings of more than five people; to prevent media reporting that "causes panic, instigates violence, or affects stability"; and to hold suspects for up to 30 days without charge. The PAD persisted with demonstrations, in which one person was killed, and the Federation of State Enterprises, encompassing more than 40 labor unions, approved strikes that would cut off power and water to government buildings and disrupt public transportation and telecommunications. PAD demonstrations in August had already closed three airports in southern Thailand, stranding thousands of tourists.

On September 9, 2008, the Constitutional Court ordered Samak's resignation, having found him guilty of a conflict of interest for taking money for participating in two chef shows on commercial television. Deputy Prime Minister SOMCHAI Wongsawat, a brother-in-law of former prime minister Thaksin, became acting prime minister on September 9, was elected prime minister in his own right by the House on September 17, and was endorsed by the king on September 18. He presented his cabinet list to the king on September 24, whereupon it was approved. The PAD threatened not to accept the new government, which was dominated by many of the same PPP figures as the previous Samak-led government, but Somchai, having complied with the constitution and received a parliamentary majority and royal assent, vowed to carry on. Violent demonstrations erupted on October 9 and were broken up by the police at the cost of several deaths and numerous injuries among the protesters.

On October 20, 2008, at the request of Prime Minister Somchai, the House set up a 120-member assembly to redraft the constitution, but the opposition DP boycotted the session and the speaker of the Senate, 40 senators, and several academics spoke out against the redrafting project, which stalled. The PAD called new demonstrations, and on November 25 its followers occupied Bangkok's recently opened Suvarnabhumi International Airport, stopping all flights and stranding 7,000 passengers for a week. The Civil Court issued an injunction and Somchai declared a limited state of emergency, but the riot police did not move against the demonstrators. The crisis ended on December 2 when the Constitutional Court dissolved the PPP, *Chart Thai,* and Neutral Democratic parties and banned Somchai from holding office. Deputy Prime Minister CHAOVARAT Chanweerakul took over as acting prime minister. Democrat Party leader Abhisit commanded only 165 votes from his own party but attracted five other parties to form a coalition government that was sworn in on December 22. Among those rallying to Abhisit were former PPP legislators who established the Friends of Newin Group within the Proud Thais Party.

Elections for the house were conducted on July 3, 2011. The For Thais Party (*Phak Phuea Thai*—PPT), the successor to the PPP, led by Thaksin's sister, Yingluck Shinawatra, secured an absolute majority in the balloting, with 265 seats. Yingluck was elected prime minister by the house on August 5. She subsequently formed a six-party coalition government on August 10, which included the PPT, the Thai Nation Development Party (TNDP), the Thais United National Development Party (TUNDP), the Phalang Chon Party (PC), the Great People's Party (*Phak Mahachon—Mahachon*), and the New Democracy Party (NDP).

The king approved a cabinet reshuffle in January 2012. The new government included the PPT, the TNDP, the PC, and a number of independents. Several of the new appointees were longtime supporters of Thaksin. The cabinet was reshuffled in October 2012 and again on June 30, 2013.

Constitution and government. Thailand is a highly centralized constitutional monarchy whose governments in the modern era have been led by a prime minister and cabinet. Since 1932 the king has exercised little direct power but remains a popular symbol of national unity and identity and has played a pivotal indirect role in times of political crisis. He is advised by a Privy Council of his own appointees.

Since 1932 Thailand has had 17 constitutions, each reflecting the locus of political power of the day. An interim constitution approved by the monarch after the 1991 coup assigned a virtually unlimited "supervisory" role to the military-led National Peacekeeping Council (NPC). A new draft constitution was subsequently endorsed by the NPC-appointed National Legislative Assembly and, after being scrutinized by an assembly-appointed review committee, was declared in effect on December 9, 1991. Bicameralism was restored, with the House of Representatives being elected but the Senate remaining appointed.

On September 14, 1996, a joint session of the two legislative houses called for the election of an assembly to draft a new constitution. The assembly's new "open government" charter elicited intense debate and drew considerable opposition, for the most part from entrenched political groups. However, in view of large public demonstrations in support of the proposal, the new basic law was approved by the National Assembly (the collective term for the House and the Senate) on September 27, 1997. Changes included the expansion of the House of Representatives to 500 members, 400 to be elected on a single-member constituency basis and 100 by proportional representation from party lists. Other provisions called for the direct election of senators; guarantees regarding human rights, freedom of the press, and the right to assembly; and establishment of increased accountability on the part of officials, "with greater governmental transparency" overall. Senatorial powers include removal of ministers, members of the House, and justices.

The 1997 constitution was set aside by the military junta and an interim charter imposed by decree on September 27, 2006. Empowered by this charter, the junta appointed a 2,000-person National Assembly, which in turn appointed 200 candidates for a Constitution Assembly, which then selected a Constitution Drafting Committee of 25. The junta chose an additional 10 members for the committee, which set about drafting a new constitution according to guidelines set out by the junta. The draft constitution was submitted to the public in a constitutional referendum, Thailand's first, on August 19, 2007. The junta encouraged officials at all levels to advocate approval but outlawed campaigning against the draft constitution. The turnout was 57 percent and the approval rate was 58 percent, both lower than expected by the junta. The Constitution Drafting Assembly endorsed the outcome on August 20, 2007, and the constitution came into force on August 24, after obtaining the king's assent.

The thrust of the new constitution was to reduce the influence of populist political parties (such as the *Thai Rak Thai*) over the selection of legislators and to restrict the powers of the prime minister. Major changes from the 1997 constitution included the appointment rather than election of senators and a reduction in their number from 200 to 150, and the adoption of an electoral system for the House of Representatives of 400 single-member constituencies plus 80 selected by proportional representation. As before, the king was to appoint the political leader commanding a majority in the House to serve as prime minister, who in turn was to nominate the ministers and other members of the cabinet, subject to approval by the House. But the role of the prime minister was to be circumscribed by new provisions, including a two-term restriction, a reduction in the number of legislators necessary to launch a no-confidence debate, and a prohibition against a prime minister's leading a caretaker administration after the legislature was dissolved—all directed at preventing the alleged abuses of the Thaksin regime. Controversial provisions included the granting of amnesty to members of the junta that staged the 2006 coup, articles forbidding legislators from overseeing the work of bureaucrats or the military, and the designation of the military as the protector of the monarchy and constitution. However, passages protecting human rights and civil liberties remained as extensive in the new constitution as in its predecessor, and the practice of electing local government officials down to the subdistrict level was reaffirmed. The 2007 constitution prescribed no fundamental changes to the judiciary or the local administrative system.

The Thai judicial system is patterned after European models. The Supreme Court, whose justices are appointed by the king, is the final court of appeal in both civil and criminal cases; an intermediate Court of Appeals hears appeals from courts of first instance located throughout the country. The constitutionality of parliamentary acts, royal decrees, and draft legislation falls under the purview of a Constitutional Court, which may also rule on the appointment and removal of public officials and political party issues.

Administratively, the country is divided into 76 provinces, including Bangkok. Provincial governors are appointed by the minister of the interior, except for Bangkok, where the governor (often referred to as the mayor) is elected. Provincial subdivisions include districts (*amphoe*), communes (*tambons*), and villages (*mubans*). The larger towns are governed by elected municipal councils. Legislation passed in March 2000 authorizes direct election of municipal mayors and most local administrators.

Freedom of the press is curtailed in Thailand. In its 2013 index of media freedom, Reporters Without Borders ranked Thailand 135th out of 179 countries.

Foreign relations. One of the few Southeast Asian governments to depart from a neutralist posture, Thailand was firmly aligned with the United States and other Western powers after World War II and signed onto the Southeast Asia Collective Defense Treaty, which established the Southeast Asia Treaty Organization (SEATO) in Bangkok in 1954. From 1952 to 1972 Thailand received almost $1.2 billion in U.S. military aid, more than twice the value of U.S. economic assistance. The Thanom government approved the use of Thai air bases for U.S. military operations in Laos and South Vietnam, and the American buildup totaled 48,000 personnel in Thailand at its peak in 1969. The U.S. withdrawal from South Vietnam led to a corresponding reduction in Thailand, and by mid-1976, all remaining U.S. military installations were closed down. SEATO was declared inactive in 1977 and its Bangkok headquarters closed.

Various UN bodies functioning in East and Southeast Asia maintain headquarters in Bangkok, and Thailand has played a leading role in the establishment of several regional organizations, such as the Association of Southeast Asian Nations (ASEAN), of which Thailand became a charter member in 1967. More recently, Thailand has been active in the ASEAN Free Trade Agreement (AFTA), ASEAN Regional Forum (ARF), ASEAN Plus Three talks, the Asia-Pacific Economic Cooperation (APEC), and the East Asian Summit process begun in 2004. Thailand is second only to Singapore in its pursuit of free trade agreements with governments as diverse as New Zealand, Australia, China, the United States, India, and Bahrain. In 1999 Thailand dispatched some 1,500 troops as part of the international peacekeeping force sent to East Timor (now Timor-Leste) following the territory's independence vote in August and served as co-commander with Australia; from 2006 to the present Thailand has deployed a police team to the UN Integrated Mission in Timor-Leste.

Relations with Cambodia have traditionally been antagonistic, although Thailand joined with other ASEAN nations in recognizing the Pol Pot regime in mid-1975 and in calling for "the immediate withdrawal of all foreign troops" following the Vietnamese invasion of December 1978. While tacitly aiding *Khmer Rouge* forces in their opposition to the Vietnamese-backed regime of Heng Samrin, Thailand encouraged the noncommunist Khmer resistance to form a united front, an effort that contributed toward the organization of the Coalition Government of Democratic Kampuchea in June 1982.

As many as 250,000 Cambodians crowded into refugee camps in eastern Thailand during the Pol Pot era and the ensuing occupation by Vietnamese forces, and as late as 1998 the region continued to be a haven for those fleeing fighting between the Cambodian military and remaining *Khmer Rouge* guerrillas. Periodically, however, charges that Thailand provided sanctuary to fleeing *Khmer Rouge* strained relations with a number of countries, including the United States. Concern that arms might end up in guerrilla hands led Washington to terminate military aid and training under its 1995 Foreign Operations Act. Angered by the American action, Thailand joined Indonesia and Malaysia in opposing a request for the stationing of a "rapid response" flotilla of U.S. military supply ships in the Gulf of Thailand. Relations improved when Thailand received strong U.S. support in 1998 for its economic reforms.

In mid-2008 Thai-Cambodian relations soured over a dispute regarding ownership of land adjacent to the Preah Vihear temple. The International Court of Justice in 1962 had awarded this temple to Cambodia, but the status of surrounding land remained unresolved. Cambodia subsequently applied to register the temple and grounds with UNESCO as a World Heritage Site under Cambodian trusteeship. Thailand's minister of foreign affairs, NOPPADON Pattama, initially endorsed the application, but the Constitutional Court found that he had exceeded his authority and he was forced to resign. When UNESCO granted registration, in July 2008, Thailand moved troops onto the disputed land, and Cambodia reciprocated. In mid-October the armed confrontation erupted into a series of sporadic fire fights that left seven soldiers dead. Tension-reducing talks between the foreign ministers of Thailand and Cambodia were disrupted when Thaksin visited Phnom Penh in November 2009 at the invitation of Prime Minister Hun Sen, provoking Thailand to recall its ambassador to Cambodia and issue an extradition request. Cambodia in turn withdrew its ambassador to Thailand and rejected the extradition request, labeling it "politically motivated." In November 2010 the chief of the Thai-Cambodian Joint Border Commission VASIN Teeravechyan resigned amid criticism by the People's Alliance for Democracy that he was not pursuing Thailand's claim with sufficient vigor.

A history of uneven relations with neighboring Laos reached a low point in late 1987, when fighting broke out over disputed border territory. Bangkok subsequently adopted a conciliatory economic policy that facilitated a mutual troop withdrawal from border areas in March 1991. Five months later a border security and cooperation agreement provided for the repatriation of some 60,000 Laotian refugees from Thailand over a three-year period. More than 8,000 remained in 2008. In June Thai authorities repatriated 837 Hmong refugees, prompting concern by the UN High Commissioner for Refugees (UNHCR) that they would be persecuted by the Lao authorities.

Following an initiative by Prime Minister Chatchai Choonhavan in 1988 to turn Indochina "from a battleground into a market place," Thai policy toward Hanoi softened. In February 1993 Thai officials met in Hanoi with representatives of Cambodia, Laos, and Vietnam to chart a new framework of cooperation for developing the resources of the lower Mekong River. Subsequently, talks were also initiated with Laos, Myanmar, and China on development of the upper Mekong, which led to completion in April 2000 of a treaty governing navigation on the waterway.

In March 1996, Banharn Silpa-Archa became the first Thai prime minister in 16 years to visit Myanmar, with whose military leaders a border trade agreement was signed, while in 1998 the UN agreed to help protect some 100,000 Mon, Kayin (Karen), and other ethnic refugees from Myanmar who had taken refuge on the Thai side of the border. In March 1999 Myanmar's head of state, Than Shwe, joined Prime Minister Chuan for discussions on narcotics control and border tensions, but the cordiality ended in October when Thai authorities freed five dissidents who had taken 89 hostages at the Myanmar embassy in Bangkok the preceding day. Myanmar's military leaders immediately closed the Thai-Myanmar border. Bangkok, in turn, threatened to expel hundreds of thousands of illegal migrant workers from Myanmar. The border remained closed until late November. A second hostage incident occurred in January 2000 when members of an ethnic-minority militia called God's Army occupied a hospital in Ratchaburi, near the border, taking some 700 hostages. In contrast to the October incident, the Thai forces stormed the hospital on January 25, freed all the hostages, and killed all ten rebels, some, according to eyewitnesses, by summary execution, earning Yangon's approbation.

In February 2001, Thai troops engaged Myanmar forces that had reportedly pursued members of the Shan State Army across the border.

The encounter led to a series of bilateral meetings, in which the two governments agreed not only to work toward resolution of remaining border issues but also jointly to fight drug production and smuggling. Nevertheless, difficulties continued into 2002, with the border being closed from May until early October. In February 2003 Thaksin again traveled to Myanmar in furtherance of improved relations, and in July he announced that all dissidents from Myanmar would be moved to refugee camps near the border, of which nine had been established. The Thai government's preferred policy was voluntary repatriation, but continued political strife, ethnic warfare, and noncooperation by the authorities in Myanmar precluded this solution. In 2007 Thailand, with the help of the UNHCR, negotiated the removal of approximately 4,000 refugees, the majority from Myanmar, to third countries, led by the United States, and issued identity cards to up to 140,000 others, enabling them to work legally outside their camps. Thailand joined its ASEAN partners in urging the Myanmar junta to consult with the democratic opposition and take steps to resolve Myanmar's domestic disputes peacefully. In October Prime Minister Surayud proposed to UN special envoy Ibrahim Gambari that the UN organize regional talks including ASEAN, China, and India to address the crisis in Myanmar. Surayud also postponed the visit to Bangkok by Myanmar's new prime minister, Gen. Thein Sein. Relations improved in 2009 with Energy Minister WANNARAT Charnnukul's announcement on August 4 of a Thai-financed project to develop an offshore natural gas field in Myanmar's waters and import 300 million cubic feet of gas per day from Myanmar starting in 2013.

In January 1998, Malaysia took a stand against the Muslim separatists of southern Thailand when it quietly arrested several alleged Muslim insurgents from a faction of the Pattani United Liberation Organization (PULO) and returned them for trial in Bangkok. Malaysia, which is predominantly Muslim, had previously been a sanctuary for the separatists, who want independence for the 2.5 million Muslims residing in Thailand's southern provinces. The change in policy was seen as evidence of a new cooperativeness at a time when both countries faced the Asian Financial Crisis. In 1997 Thailand and Malaysia established a Joint Commission on Bilateral Cooperation to facilitate border control and enhance confidence and security-building measures. In 2004 they set up a Committee on Joint Development Strategy, and by 2007 they had implemented Joint Working Groups on Education, Employment, and Entrepreneurship tasked with raising standards of living of depressed communities on both sides of the border.

Even after the September 2001 al-Qaida attacks on the United States, and despite growing Islamic militancy in Thailand's southern provinces, Thai authorities routinely discounted the possible involvement of the Indonesia-based *Jemaah Islamiah* (JI) and al-Qaida in sporadic bombings and attacks against police stations. In June 2003, however, alleged JI members were among those arrested in connection with a plot to blow up two tourist resorts and the Bangkok embassies of Australia, Germany, Singapore, the United Kingdom, and the United States. Citing the urgency of the situation, in August 2003 the government bypassed the National Assembly and issued two antiterrorism laws by decree. In the same month the U.S. Central Intelligence Agency assisted Thai authorities in capturing Riduan Isamuddin (aka Hambali), an alleged JI leader with ties to al-Qaida.

Thailand has a warm relationship with China, exemplified by a plan jointly announced by their prime ministers in 2005 to develop a "strategic partnership" in a host of areas, including trade, security, and science and technology. China's cordial Olympics diplomacy and improved relations between Beijing and Taipei further reassured Bangkok, and bilateral trade grew to make China Thailand's second largest supplier of imports. But local producers remained skeptical of the growth of cheap goods allowed into the local market by the China-Thailand Free Trade Agreement of 2004 and a China-ASEAN agreement including Thailand that came into effect on January 1, 2010.

Relations with the U.S. administration of President George W. Bush were close. Thailand assisted in the U.S.-led invasion of Iraq, although its 440 medical and engineering personnel were withdrawn in August 2004. In 2003 the U.S. government designated Thailand a "major non-NATO ally." The U.S. government in 2006 and 2007 publicly urged the Thai military junta to lift martial law and restore democracy. Washington withheld over $35 million in economic aid, mainly for military training and assistance programs, but imposed no other sanctions, and continued programs related to development, democracy promotion, disaster assistance, counterterrorism, counternarcotics, human trafficking, and refugee assistance valued at $34 million. Full diplomatic, economic, and military relations were restored in 2008, and Secretary of State Hillary Clinton on July 23, 2009, reiterated the Barack Obama administration's commitment to work closely with Thailand on national, regional, and global issues. State Department reports in 2010 identified Thailand as a transit country for drug smuggling and human trafficking. Nevertheless, on May 13, Thailand was elected by the UN General Assembly to a three-year term on the Human Rights Council and on September 30 announced its candidacy for a seat on the UN Security Council.

The two governments began free trade agreement negotiations in 2004, but the talks stalled in mid-2006 over Bangkok's reluctance to grant legal protection to U.S. pharmaceutical companies and "national treatment" to U.S. multinational firms. The military coup of 2006 led to U.S. suspension of the talks. Despite officials-level consultations in June 2008 and March 2009, formal negotiations have not resumed.

In April 2011, renewed fighting between Thai and Cambodian soldiers in a disputed border region near the Preah Vihear temple killed 16 and wounded a score of others. Some 40,000 Thais and 20,000 Cambodians were displaced. A truce on April 30 ended the strife, followed by a more comprehensive cease-fire agreement on May 9. Meanwhile, Cambodia petitioned the International Court of Justice to revise its 1962 ruling on the disputed area.

On April 5, 2012, Thailand and Cambodia agreed to begin demining operations in the disputed area around Preah Vihear. In June, the United States announced it was abandoning the construction of a weather monitoring station in Thailand after the Yingluck government was unable to gain parliamentary approval for the plan. Following major flooding in Myanmar in August 2012, Thailand pledged financial and humanitarian assistance.

In January 2013 under pressure from China, Thailand announced that it would "invite" leaders of the banned Chinese religious group, the Falun Gong, to leave the country. Thailand and Mozambique finalized an agreement in February to ease restrictions on the import of minerals to Thailand. Thailand and the European Union (EU) initiated talks on a free trade agreement in March. Following more than 20 years of negotiations, Thailand and India signed an extradition treaty in May. In July, during a visit by Myanmar's President Thein Sein, three economic agreements were signed between Thailand and Myanmar.

Current issues. On October 22, 2008, the Constitutional Court found former prime minister Thaksin guilty of corruption in a land deal case, sentenced him to two years imprisonment, and issued a warrant for his arrest. The government revoked his Thai passport in April 2009, but Thaksin continued his travels on Montenegrin and Nicaraguan passports. Meanwhile, he continued to reject the Abhisit government's validity and to incite his followers by video broadcasts and by "tweets" through the social networking and blogging service Twitter. On March 31, 20,000 of his followers under the banner of the United Front of Democracy Against Dictatorship (UDD), also known as the Democratic Alliance Against Dictatorship (DAAD), and colloquially as the Red Shirts, forced the cancellation of a cabinet meeting in Bangkok. Further demonstrations took place on April 8 against Gen. Prem Tinsulanand, the king's chief privy counselor, and on April 11 when 10,000 protesters forced the cancellation of an ASEAN summit in Pattaya and obliged the government to fly visiting international leaders to safety by helicopter from their hotel venue. Pro-Thaksin supporters staged a major demonstration in September 2009 at which Thaksin spoke by videolink, and in November Thaksin visited neighboring Cambodia, further encouraging his supporters and angering the government.

Prime Minister Abhisit, in his December 2008 inaugural address, pledged to uphold the rule of law, tackle the economic downturn, and address such issues as rural poverty, healthcare, and microcredit schemes, all of which had made his predecessor Thaksin popular in the countryside. To address the economic slump the cabinet on January 13, 2009, approved an interim six-month budget of 115 billion baht (US$2.88 billion) to sustain employment and stimulate the economy. Proposals included free schooling for children up to 15 years of age and subsidies for rural infrastructure, low-income families, and small businesses. A package of tax cuts and overseas borrowing was added on January 20.

In April 2010, the ongoing confrontation between the Abhisit government (the Yellow Shirts) and the antigovernment United Front for Democracy against Dictatorship (UDD, or Red Shirts), allegedly incited and financed from exile by Thaksin, escalated. A military and police attempt on April 10–11 to dislodge the red shirts from their encampment in central Bangkok was repulsed with a loss of 25 lives and injuries to an estimated 850. A second attempt by the authorities ended in success on May 19, with the surrender of UDD leaders, including JATUPORN Prompam and NATTHAWUT Saikua. The authorities dismantled barricades and dispersed the protesters but at a cost of another 39 dead and 279 wounded, considerable property damage, and a diminution of foreign tourism.

In February 2011, seven leaders of the UDD were released as part of a reconciliation initiative. In August former prime minister Thaksin's sister, Yingluck Shinawatra, was elected prime minister of a coalition government following the July balloting, in which the PPT gained an absolute majority in the house. The coalition gave the Yingluck government the support of 300 members of the house. Meanwhile, throughout the campaign and her early period in office, Yingluck denied reports that her government was a front for Thaksin to reassert political power and influence.

Renewed fighting in the four southernmost provinces in August and September 2011 between Muslim insurgents and government security forces killed 53 and wounded more than 75. Widespread flooding inundated two-thirds of the country during the summer monsoon season. The floods killed more than 600 Thais and affected more than 3 million. Damage from the flooding was estimated to exceed $8 billion, in what many Thai officials described as the worst natural disaster in the nation's history. There was widespread domestic criticism of the Yingluck cabinet's response to the flooding, especially the government's initial refusal of foreign aid. In October, Doctors Without Borders announced it was suspending operations in the country after continued interference in its efforts to treat undocumented Burmese workers in Thailand. In December, the government restored Thaksin's passport. However, the former prime minister was disqualified from a royal amnesty that covered 26,000, meaning Thaksin still faced arrest if he returned to Thailand.

In February, Thai police arrested three Iranians in Bangkok for planning an attack on the Israeli embassy. Also in February, the cabinet approved the formation of a new constitutional assembly to draft a new basic law for the country. In June, the House of Representatives postponed controversial legislation on an amnesty for those involved in political fighting between 2005 and 2010. Meanwhile, the Supreme Court rejected a petition to declare the PPT illegal because of its efforts to revise the constitution (drafters of the petition argued that the PPT sought to weaken or even abolish the monarchy). However, the court also issued a stay on previously approved legislation to create the new constitutional assembly.

Yingluck easily survived a no-confidence vote on November 28, 2012, 308–159. The motion followed a contentious debate over a rice subsidy program in which the government paid farmers over-market prices for rice. Opposition parties alleged the program was rife with widespread corruption. In June 2013 the government announced it would reduce the subsidies by 20 percent after the program lost $4.4 billion when the government was unable to resell the rice to other governments. One result was that India and Vietnam surpassed Thailand as the leading international rice exporters.

On January 1, 2013, a new measure went into effect, setting the national minimum wage at 300 baht per day (approximately $9.55). The measure was highly popular among unions but opposed by business groups, which argued it would prompt companies to relocate outside of Thailand (for instance, Cambodia's daily minimum wage was $2.03). On March 24, a fire at a Karin refugee camp in Mae Hong Song province killed 37, injured 115, and temporarily left 2,300 without shelter. In July the Supreme Court ruled that a PPT bid to revise the constitution would require a referendum but that the legislature could adopt amendments without a national vote.

Antigovernment protests erupted through November and December 2013 against Prime Minister Yingluck Shinawatra and her attempt to pardon her brother, former Prime Minister Thaksin Shinawatra, of accusations of corruption. Prime Minister Shinawatra survived a no-confidence vote on November 27, only to dissolve the parliament on December 9 in an attempt to quell continuing protests. New elections were scheduled for February 2, 2014.

POLITICAL PARTIES

For the quarter-century preceding the 2001 election, Thailand's civilian governments typically featured shifting multiparty coalitions, with no single party being able to emerge from national elections holding a legislative majority. (For details on the political parties in coalition governments prior to 2001 see the 2010 *Handbook.*) Since 2001, three broad political groupings have maneuvered for power. The first was represented by the populist *Thai Rak Thai,* succeeded in 2007 by the People Power Party (PPP), which drew its support from poorer rural districts in the northeast. The second were urban civilian elites based in Bangkok, Songkhla, and other urban centers and in the southern Muslim provinces, who supported the Democrat Party. The third, a loose grouping of military officers, government officials, monarchist civilians, and business interests in central Thailand, was manifested by the *Chart Thai* party. Each was riven by factions. Numerous smaller parties formed around strong personalities or local interests, often originating in breakaway factions of the three main parties.

The January 2001 election saw 37 parties (out of some 60 registered) present lists for the 100 proportional seats and 400 constituency seats in the House of Representatives. The election produced a government that was dominated by Prime Minister Thaksin's *Thai Rak Thai* but that also included *Chart Thai* and the New Aspiration Party (NAP). *Tai Rak Thai* subsequently absorbed two other parties, *Seri Tham* and *Chart Pattana.* The election of February 2005 was swept by Thaksin and *Thai Rak Thai,* enabling formation of Thailand's first elected single-party government.

In the election of April 2006 28 parties were eligible, although many had minuscule memberships or existed primarily on paper; 18 ran in at least one district and 8 presented party lists for proportional seats. But the election was boycotted by the principal opposition parties, the Democrat Party (DP), *Chart Thai,* and *Mahachon.*

The Constitutional Court's banning of *Thai Rak Thai* in May 2007, and the exclusion of Thaksin and 111 party executives from political office or party leadership for five years, altered the political landscape. The DP emerged by default as the country's largest and most popular party. But *Thai Rak Thai* members and followers regrouped in the previously minor People Power Party (PPP) and reinvigorated it to the point where it overtook the DP as the country's most popular party. The PPP was reported to be financed by Thaksin from exile, and its leader, Samak Sundaravej, declared his intention to continue Thaksin's populist policies. In the election held December 23, 2007, only seven parties gained House seats out of 66 registered, the others failing either to win any of the 400 constituency seats or to reach the 5 percent threshold for one of the 80 proportional seats. The PPP led all parties, followed by the DP. On December 2, 2008, however, the Constitutional Court dissolved the PPP, the *Chart Thai,* and the Neutral Democratic Party for vote-buying in the 2007 election, which brought a six-party coalition, led by Abhisit and the DP, to power.

Government Parties:

For Thais Party (*Phak Puea Thai*—PPT). The PPT emerged in September 20, 2008, set up by 80 PPP members of the house who deserted the party ahead of its ban in December by the Constitutional Court. Its leaders included APIWAN Wiriyachai, former vice president of the house; CHALERM Yoobamrung, former health minister and PPP leader; and MINGKWAN Saengsuwan, formerly a minister of industry. Declining to endorse Abhisit as the new prime minister, the PPT in December called for an all-party national unity government to be led by Sanoh Thienthong of the Royalist People's Party. When that failed, the PPT called for the dissolution of the house and endorsed Pracha Promnok as a candidate for prime minister in a possible new government, but without success. Nevertheless, the January 2009 by-election victories in five constituencies and shifting party alliances enabled the PPT's strength in the house to grow to 189 out of 480 seats. In November 2010 executive board members WITTHAYA Buranasiri and SURAPONG Towichakchaikul resigned amid speculation that the Constitutional Court might dissolve the PPT. The PPT won 265 seats in the 2011 house elections, and Yingluck Shinawatra was elected prime minister by the house. In local balloting in 2012, the PPT lost seats in several strongholds with reports indicating that the losses were the result of voter displeasure over the government's handling of the 2011 floods. In October 2012 YONGYUTH Wichaidit resigned as both party leader and deputy prime minister after being implicated in a corruption scandal. He was replaced by then-Transport Minister JARUPONG Ruangsuwan.

Leaders: YINGLUCK Shinawatra (Prime Minister), JARUPONG Ruangsuwan (Leader), PHUMTHAM Wechayachai (Secretary General).

Thai Nation Development Party—TNDP (*Chart Thai Pattana*). The TNDP was founded on April 18, 2008, and became the new political home for members of the *Chart Thai* Party when the latter was dissolved in December 2008. The TNDP joined the Abhisit-led coalition and was awarded a deputy prime ministership; the tourism and sports, and energy ministries; and the deputy transport portfolio. The party had 25 seats in the house in 2010 and won 19 in the 2011 balloting. It joined the PPT-led coalition government following the balloting. Following a succession of cabinet reshuffles, the TNDP held two ministries in August 2013, while YUKOL Limlaemthong had been appointed deputy prime minister.

Leader: YUKOL Limlaemthong (Deputy Prime Minister and Minister of Agriculture).

Thais United National Development Party—TUNDP (*Ruam Jai Thai Chart Pattana*). The party arose from the formation of *Ruam Jai Thai* (variously translated as United Hearts Thai and Thais United), which was announced in late June 2007 by leaders including Pradit Phataraprasit. Although prohibited from active involvement because of his former standing in *Thai Rak Thai,* SOMKID Jatusripitak, a former deputy prime minister, was a key figure behind the organization.

In September 2007, *Ruam Jai Thai* leaders announced a merger with the *Chart Pattana* (National Development) group, led by SUWAT Liptapanlop, who, like Somkid, was prohibited from direct politicking. A possible merger with the *Pracharaj* and *Matchima* parties and the Bangkok 50 and *Saman Chan* groups was explored but was not consummated. The December 2007 election found the *Ruam Jai Thai* in sixth place, with nine seats. The party then joined the PPP-led coalition government and was awarded the positions of deputy finance minister and minister of energy. Following the fall of the Somchai government in December 2008, the TUNDP rallied to Abhisit's coalition, and the party's leader, Wannarat Channukul, was made minister for energy, and its secretary general was awarded the deputy finance portfolio in the new cabinet. In 2011 the party merged with **For the Motherland** (*Puea Pan Din*—PPD). The PPD emerged in September 2007 in the context of an ultimately unsuccessful merger effort by *Matchima, Pracharaj,* and other post–*Thai Rak Thai* groups (for more information on the PPD, see the 2011 *Handbook*).

The TUNDP secured seven seats in the house in the 2011 elections, and Wannarat Channukul was appointed minister of industry in the PPT-led cabinet but left the government following the January 2012 cabinet reshuffle. THEERA Wongsamut was elected party leader in March 2013.

Leaders: THEERA Wongsamut (Party Leader), PRADIT Phataraprasit (Secretary General).

Phalang Chon—PC. The pro-Thaksin, regional Phalang Chon party was formed in 2011 by former tourism minister SONTHAYA Kunplome. The party gained seven seats in the 2011 balloting, all from Chonburi Province, its home base. The PC joined the Yingluck coalition government in 2011.

Leaders: CHAO Maneewong, SONTHAYA Khunpluem (Minister of Culture).

Two other small parties joined the governing coalition: the **Great People's Party** (*Phak Mahachon—Mahachon*), a small grouping that was originally formed in 1998, which won one seat in the 2011 balloting, and the **New Democracy Party**—NDP, led by SURATHIN Pijarn, which also secured one seat in the 2011 elections.

Opposition Parties:

Democrat Party—DP (*Pak Prachatipat*). Organized in 1946, the DP is Thailand's oldest party. Traditionally a strong defender of the monarchy, it has derived much of its support from officials and urban professionals. It considers itself a left-of-center party but emerged as a right-of-center party as the popularity of Thaksin and the *Thai Rak Thai* shifted the political spectrum to the left. The fourth-ranked party in March 1992, it moved up to second with 86 seats in 1995 and similarly ranked with 123 seats in 1996.

In August 2000 the Constitutional Court convicted DP Secretary General Sanan Kachornprasart of having falsified an assets declaration and banned him from politics for five years. In the January 2001 election the party gained seats for a total of 128, but was far outdistanced by *Thai Rak Thai.* With former prime minister Chuan Leekpai having stepped aside as party leader, the April 2003 DP congress chose longtime party stalwart Banyat Bantadtan as leader. With his party having won only 96 seats in the February 2006 election, Banyat stepped down in favor of a younger leader, Abhisit Vejjajiva, who was unanimously confirmed as party leader in March.

After the banning of rival *Thai Rak Thai,* the DP emerged as the most popular party among Bangkok residents polled in November 2007, attracting 48 percent approval. Popular support was strongest in the capital's middle-class constituencies and in the conservative southern districts of the country. In the December election the DP again came in second to *Thai Rak Thai's* successor, the PPP, with 165 seats, and chose to sit in opposition and form a shadow cabinet rather than join the coalition government led by the PPP. In December 2008, the DP formed the core of a coalition government led by Abhisit and took 15 of the 24 cabinet posts. It won seven seats in the January 11, 2009, by-elections and, with defections from other parties, commanded 172 seats in the House. On April 5, 2010, the Electoral Commission made a preliminary finding that the Democrat Party had received 258 million baht illegally in 2005 and recommended the party be dissolved and its executives banned from politics for five years, but the finding was overturned on appeal. The June 2010 appointment of CHAIWUT Bannawat as industry minister and other personnel changes brought the number of DP members in the cabinet to 17 out of 24. On November 11 Abhisit announced that he would reappoint the party's secretary general SUTHEP Thaugsuban, recently elected to the House in a by-election, as deputy prime minister. Following the defeat of the DP in the legislative elections in July 2011, Abhisit resigned as DP leader. However, he was reelected as DP chair on August 6. Reports in September 2012 indicated that Abhisit was under investigation over his role in the 2010 Red Shirt crackdown.

In March 2013 the governor of Bangkok, DP member SUKHUMBHAND Paribatra, was reelected in a fierce campaign in which polls and pundits predicted his PPT opponent would win.

Leaders: ABHISIT Vejjajiva (Leader), KORN Chatikavanij (Deputy Leader), CHUAN Leekpai (Chief Adviser), BANYAT Bantadtan (Deputy Chief Adviser), SUTHEP CHALERMCHAI Sri-on (Secretary General).

Proud Thais Party—PTP (*Bhum Jai Thai*). Also called the Thai Pride Party, the PTP is an offshoot of the Neutral Democratic Party (below), which was dissolved by the Constitutional Court in December 2008. The PTP was founded on November 5, 2008, and on December 15 its members in the House joined with Abhisit's Democrat Party to form the current ruling coalition government. Characterized as a populist party, it shares many values with the rural populist parties spawned by Thaksin. (The NDP had entered into a coalition with the PPP in 2008.) With over 40 seats in the House, it viewed itself as a possible alternative to the currently dominant Democrats. It is divided by factions, including the Friends of Newin group (a fluid subcaucus led by banned politician NEWIN Chidchob who is identified by media commentators as the PTP's de facto leader), a smaller *Matchimathipatai* group, and the *Spra-at Klinpratoom* splinter. The PTP's House strength in 2010 stood at 32, and its members held the portfolios of commerce, interior, and transport in the Abhisit cabinet. In the July 2011 balloting, the party secured 34 seats in the house. In September 2012 ANUTHIN Chanweerakul was elected PTP leader, succeeding his father, CHAOVARAT Chanweerakul.

Leaders: ANUTHIN Chanweerakul (Leader), SAKSAYAM Chidchob (General Secretary).

Love Thailand Party (*Phak Rak Prathet Thai*—Rak Thailand). A protest party established by CHUWIT Kamolvisit in 2011, Rak Thailand campaigned against political corruption. It secured four seats in the 2011 house balloting.

Leader: CHUWIT Kamolvisit.

Motherland Party—MP (*Matubhum*). The MP's parent party, the Citizen's Party (*Rassadorn,* also translatable as Party of the People), was registered in 1986 by a largely military group whose leader, Gen. TIENCHAI Sirisamphan, had played a prominent role in the countercoup of September 1985. *Rassadorn* disbanded after failing to win any House seats in the November 1996 election, but in February 1999 it was reregistered by VATANA Asavahame, one of the *Prachakorn Thai* rebels who had defied the party leadership by supporting the Chuan administration. Nine more of the rebels subsequently joined *Rassadorn. Rassadorn* won only two House seats in January 2001. In July 2004, the party adopted the name *Mahachon* (Public Party—PP) after having been joined by former DP leader Sanan Kachornprasart and his followers.

In 2007 *Mahachon* claimed over two million members, mainly in the rural region centered on Nonthaburi district, but was weakened when Sanan and several other leaders decided to join *Chart Thai* and it won no seats in the December 2007 election. The party was revived under the *Rassadorn* label in February 2009 by Man Pattanotai, a former minister of information and communications technology in the Samak and Somchai governments. Its ranks included defectors from *Puea Pan Din* and the DP. Its three House members generally aligned with the governing coalition, while remaining formally independent. In June 2009 the *Rassadorn* leaders formally changed the party's name to *Matubhum.* The party secured two seats in the 2011 house balloting.

Despite being in the opposition, the MP's members of the House voted with the government in the November 2012 no-confidence vote.

Leaders: MAN Pattanotai, SOMSAK Wiwatanant.

The small **Rak Santi Party**—RSP, led by THAWIN Surachetpong, also secured one seat in the 2011 balloting.

Other Parties:

Social Action Party—SAP (*Kit Sangkhom*). A 1974 offshoot of the DP, the SAP is somewhat more conservative and free enterprise oriented than the parent group. It was the leading party in the 1983 balloting and served as the core of the Prem government coalition prior to the emergence of internal fissures, which prompted the resignation of longtime party leader Kukrit Pramoj in late 1985 and necessitated the legislative dissolution of May 1986. It was runner-up to the *Chart Thai* in 1988. Kukrit returned to the party leadership in August 1990. The party won 31 legislative seats in March 1992 and joined the Suchinda government in April; however, it left the promilitary alignment in June. It secured 22 seats in the September 1992 poll. Although it was a participant in the ensuing Chuan coalition, its leader, MONTRI Pongpanit, was not offered a cabinet portfolio because of allegations that he had become "unusually rich."

The party went into opposition in September 1993, subsequently joining the Chaovalit coalition after the 1996 election, after which it held 20 seats, down from 22 in 1995. Kukrit Pramoj died in October 1996, and two years later Montri announced that he was stepping down as formal party leader, in part as a gesture of responsibility for a scandal that had cost the party its health portfolio.

In July 1999 the SAP withdrew from the governing coalition as a result of a dispute between Deputy Prime Minister Suwit Khunkitti and RAKKIAT Sukthana over the party's cabinet seats. In March 2000 Suwit resigned his party leadership post, and in August he led a mass defection to *Thai Rak Thai.* (He later became leader of the new PPD.) With Rakkiat having joined *Seri Tham,* Montri having died in June, and Suwit having defected, the SAP's political life appeared limited, and it won one seat in the January 2001 house election. Nevertheless, under new leadership, the party registered for the December 2007 general election, but it did not win any seat. In mid-2008, however, Suwit left the PPP as a consequence of an intraparty dispute and returned to the SAP. The change of government in December 2008 and the by-election in January 2009 then offered the SAP a chance to revive by shifting its allegiance to the DP and joining Abhisit's coalition government, in which Suwit was awarded the portfolio of natural resources and environment. The SAP did not gain any seats in the 2011 house balloting.

Leaders: SUWIT Khunkitti, THONGPHLU Diphrai.

Thai Citizens (*Prachakorn Thai*—PT). *Prachakorn Thai* was launched prior to the 1979 election by the promilitary and charismatic populist Samak Sundaravej and displaced the Democrat Party to won a majority in Bangkok. From 1983 to 1986 it participated in a quadripartite governing coalition with the DP, the SAP, and the now-defunct National Democracy Party (*Chart Prachathipatai*), and in 1990 it entered the reshuffled Chatchai coalition.

Although the party won only three House seats in the 1992 election, it took 18 in 1995 and 18 again in 1996. Twelve of its MPs joined the governing coalition formed by Prime Minister Chuan in late 1997, for which they were expelled from the party. The Constitutional Court ruled the dismissal unconstitutional but the rebels declined to return to the PT. Nine subsequently joined the revived *Rassadorn, two* joined *Chart Pattana,* and one joined *Seri Tham.*

Samak won the Bangkok gubernatorial election in 2000, but the party failed to win any House seats in the elections of 2001, 2005, or 2006. In 2007 Samak moved to become leader of the PPP, leaving PT leadership to his brother Sumit. Despite putting up nearly 200 candidates in the December election, the party won no seats; nor did it secure representation in the 2011 house elections.

Leaders: SUMIT Sundaravej (President), SOMBOON Wesasunthornthaep (Secretary General).

Referendum Party (*Prachamati* Party—PP). Established September 25, 2007, the PP was considered close to *Matchimathipataya.* Its leader proposed that General Sonthi be named prime minister following the December election. Although the party fielded nearly 300 candidates, the PP was unsuccessful in capturing any House seats. It did not secure representations in the 2011 house balloting.

Leaders: PRAMUAN Ruchanaseree (Leader), WITHUN Naewphanich (Secretary General).

New Politics Party—NPP (*Karn Muang Mai*). The NPP was formally registered on June 2, 2009. An offshoot of the urban progovernment People's Alliance for Democracy, it contested the 2011 election to offset the popularity of the rural parties and movements mobilized by Thaksin's populist appeal. Labor leader Somsak Kosaisuuk was chosen as the NPP's inaugural leader. The NPP did not gain any seats in the 2011 house elections. A split emerged in the party afterward, with a faction led by SONDHI Limthongkul defecting from the NPP.

Leaders: SOMSAK Kosaisuuk, SURIYASAI Katasila (Secretary General).

For information on the **New Alternative**—NA (*Thang Luak Mai*), please see the 2012 *Handbook.* For information on the **Royalist People's Party**—RPP (*Pracharaj*), please see the 2013 *Handbook.*

Parties Dissolved in 2007:

Thais Love Thais (*Thai Rak Thai*—TRT). Thaksin Shinawatra, a leading figure in the telecommunications industry and a former leader of *Palang Dharma,* announced formation of *Thai Rak Thai* in July 1998. His platform included popular reforms such as debt relief for farmers and measures to promote business expansion. He was successful in recruiting senior members from the country's other parties, all vulnerable to factionalism. In the January 2001 election *Thai Rak Thai* won 248 seats, permitting Thaksin to claim the prime minister's office.

A series of mergers followed. In July 2001 *Thai Rak Thai* absorbed *Seri Tham* (also known as the Liberal Democratic Party); in March 2002 the **New Aspiration Party**—NAP (*Pak Kwam Hwang Mai*) disbanded, and its members joined Thai Rak Thai; and in August 2004 *Chart Pattana* (National Development Party) followed. (For more information on the NAP, see the 2011 *Handbook.*)

Internally, *Thai Rak Thai* was dominated by various faction leaders loyal to Thaksin, including SUDARAT Keyuraphan and SURIYA Jungrungreangkit. When his party was banned and 111 former senior party members were prohibited from direct involvement in party politics for five years after the military takeover in September 2006, Thaksin left Thailand and lived in exile thereafter, although he remained active in supporting the PPP (below) and other populist parties to which his followers transferred, and the Red Shirt movement. (For further details on *Thai Rak Thai* and the other banned political parties discussed below, see the 2010 *Handbook.*)

Other parties forced to dissolve in May 2007 for having committed electoral fraud were the **Pattana Chart Thai,** the **Progressive Democratic Party,** and the **Thai Ground Party.**

Parties Dissolved in 2008:

People Power Party (*Pak Palang Prachachon*—PPP). Previously a minor party established in 1998, the PPP attracted former members of the populist-welfare *Thai Rak Thai* (see above) after the latter was banned in 2007. The PPP, set up in August 2007, was led by veteran politician Samak Sundaravej, a former DP member and *Prachakorn Thai* founder. Notable new members included WICHIENCHOT Sukchotrat, a former member of the National Counter-Corruption Commission; former ambassador PHITTAYA Pukkamal; and WIKRAN Suphamongkol, nephew of former foreign minister KANTATHI Suphamongkol. Support was strongest in the poorer constituencies of the capital and in the north and northeast of the country, where former prime minister Thaksin enjoyed his greatest popularity.

The PPP was the clear winner of the December 2007 election, taking 199 out of 400 constituency seats and 34 out of 80 proportional seats. Eight seats short of clear majority in the House of Representatives, the PPP negotiated a coalition with five other parties, for a total of 316 seats, enabling it to form a government. The new cabinet, led by PPP leader Samak, was sworn in on February 6, 2008, with the PPP taking two-thirds of the 36 portfolios. Three of the female ministers were wives of banned executives of the disbanded *Thai Rak Thai.*

In July 2008 the Constitutional Court found Public Health Minister CHAIYA Sasomsup guilty of electoral reporting irregularities, ruled that Foreign Minister Noppadon Pattarna had violated the constitution in an agreement with Cambodia, and found House Speaker

YONGYUTH Tiyapairat guilty of vote-buying, obliging all three to resign. Large public demonstrations against Samak's government erupted in Bangkok in mid-2008, led by the People's Alliance for Democracy, which had agitated successfully against Thaksin's government in 2006. PPP was dissolved on December 2, 2008, by the Constitutional Court for vote-buying in the 2007 election and its leader and executives banned from holding office for five years.

Leaders: SAMAK Sundaravej (Party Leader and Former Prime Minister), SOMCHAI Wongsawat (Former Prime Minister), CHALERM Yoobamrung (Deputy Leader), SURAPHONG Suebwonglee (Secretary General).

Thai Nation (*Chart Thai*—CT). *Chart Thai* was regarded as the principal heir of the Thanom military regime's United Thai People's Party. In 1983 it merged with the Siam Democratic Party (*Prachatipat Siam*), a rightist monarchist group dating from 1981.

Following the 1988 election *Chart Thai* served as the core of two governing coalitions led by Gen. Chatchai Choonhavan until 1992, whereupon he was succeeded by retired air chief marshal SOMBOON Rahong. The choice triggered popular opposition to military domination of the government, and Somboon stepped down in favor of civilian leaders. In July 1995 *Chart Thai* momentarily became the largest legislative party, its representation rising from 77 to 92, but its strength in the House declined to 39 seats in 1996 and 41 seats in the January 2001 election. In the early 2000s leadership disagreements and defections to *Thai Rak Thai,* notably by SOMPONG Amornvivat, weakened *Chart Thai,* which then decided to join in coalition with *Thai Rak Thai.*

Chart Thai won 25 seats in the 2005 election for the House of Representatives but was not invited to join Prime Minister Thaksin's new government. It boycotted the April 2006 snap election (along with the DP and *Mahachon*) and demanded Thaksin's resignation.

In the December election, *Chart Thai* emerged as the third strongest party, winning 34 seats, and subsequently agreed to join the six-party coalition led by the newly formed PPP and won several cabinet posts. But on December 2, 2008, the Constitutional Court upheld indictments by the Electoral Commission and the attorney general that *Chart Thai* be disbanded for electoral fraud during the 2007 election.

Leaders: BANHARN Silpa-Archa (Leader), SOMSAK Prisananunthakul (Deputy Leader), SANAN Kachornprasart (Chief Adviser), WIRAI Wiriyakijja, PRAPHAT Bhothasuthon (Secretary General).

Neutral Democratic Party—NDP (*Matchimathipataya*). *Matchima* was formed in 2006 by SOMSAK Thepsuthin, a former *Thai Rak Thai's Wang Nam Yom* faction leader and cabinet minister. A populist party similar to *Thai Rak Thai, Matchima* pledged to establish nine million ponds in rural areas, reduce the price of tickets for public transport, and guarantee agricultural product prices. Factional disagreements in 2007 led to replacement of THANAPORN Sriyakoon by PRACHAI Leophairatana as leader and adoption of *Matchimathipataya* as the party's new name. In the December election NDP slipped to fifth place with only seven House seats, whereupon Prachai resigned and in February 2008 Anongwan Thepsuthin was chosen as leader. NDP subsequently joined the PPP-led coalition government but was banned by the Constitutional Court on December 2, 2008.

Leaders: ANONGWAN Thepsuthin (Leader), PORNTIWA Nakasa (Secretary General).

Insurgent Groups:

The insurgency dates back to 1960 with the formation of the **Barisan Revolusi Nasional** (BRN). This movement, based in *pondoks* or Islamic schools, produced three wings, the **BRN Ulema** to rally and coordinate Islamic clergymen, the **BRN Coordinate Group** to conduct agitation and sabotage, and the **BRN Congress**, a military formation. A recently formed BRN youth wing **Pemud**, and associated "small commando groups" known as the **Runda Kumpulan Kecil** (RKK) have been implicated in many attacks against civilians as well as the military since 2004, including August 2008 bombs in Sungai Kolok that killed two and a beheading of a local official in early September. In March 2013 the government opened a new round of negotiations with the BRN in Kuala Lumpur, Malaysia.

In parallel, the small **Pattani United Liberation Organization** (PULO), a secular organization, has fought since 1968 for an independent Islamic state carved from several southern provinces having Muslim majorities. In 1995 a "New PULO" militant splinter emerged. Also allegedly involved in carrying out escalating attacks against officials, teachers, and Buddhist leaders were the **Pattani Islamic Mujaheddin Movement** (*Gerakan Mujaheddin Islam Pattani*) and the **Patani Freedom Fighters** (*Pejuang Kemerdekaan Patani*). Connections to the international al-Qaida terrorist network and to *Jemaah Islamiah* have been alleged, particularly on the part of the **Jemaah Salafi,** founded in 1999 by Muhammad Haji JAEMING (Abdul Fatah) upon his return from training in a mujahidin camp in Afghanistan, but few substantial links have been verified. No group claimed responsibility for the rising tempo of attacks experienced in 2006 and 2007, and analysts believe they were carried out by decentralized territorial and mobile cells loosely inspired and supported by a loose network of secessionists and militant Muslim religious leaders. The widely varying locations, tactics, and weapons of the assaults suggest the absence of a central command despite the efforts since 1997 of an umbrella group, **Bersatu** (United), to coordinate the initiatives of the various antigovernment groups and movements.

LEGISLATURE

The 1991 basic law restored bicameralism in the form of a **National Assembly** (*Ratha Sapha*) encompassing an appointed Senate and an elected House of Representatives. The 1997 constitution provided for a directly elected Senate of 200 members not affiliated with political parties serving six-year terms. The House expanded to 500 seats in the January 2001 election, four-fifths directly elected from single-member constituencies and, for the first time, one-fifth chosen on a proportional basis from parties obtaining at least 5 percent of the national vote. Under the new constitution of August 2007, the legislature was to retain its two-chamber structure, but the number and method of selection of legislators were altered as described below.

Senate (*Woothi Sapha*). The first election to the new Senate was held March 4, 2000, with the successful candidates being a mix of unaffiliated political neophytes, reformers, and established figures. The Election Commission quickly disqualified 78 victors for vote-buying, fraud, and campaign offenses. All but 2 were, however, allowed to compete in a second round of balloting on April 29 for the vacated seats. Meanwhile, the term of the predecessor Senate had expired on March 21, and the Constitutional Court had ruled that the new body could not convene without the full complement of 200 senators. Sixty-six were elected on April 29, eight in a third round on June 4, three in a fourth round on July 9, and the final senator in a fifth round on July 22. The new Senate convened on August 1.

The election of April 19, 2006, was once again conducted amid numerous charges that some candidates circumvented proscriptions against campaigning or were too closely connected to political parties. By late July, 180 of the 200 potential senators had been endorsed by the Election Commission, but the commission ceased to function when its three remaining members were convicted of malfeasance and forced to resign. Meanwhile, the previous Senate continued to serve in an interim capacity until suspended by the military coup of September 19, 2006.

The 2007 constitution prescribed a Senate of 150 nonpartisan members. Seventy-six senators, one from each province, were to be directly elected. A Senate Selection Committee of seven officials and judges chaired by the president of the Constitutional Court was to select the remaining 74 senators from among nominees of professional, academic, public sector, and private sector associations. The last Senate elections were held on March 2, 2008. Seventy-four senators were appointed on February 14, 2008, by a seven-member committee headed by the chief of the Constitutional Court.

Speaker: NIKOM Wairatpanij.

House of Representatives (*Sapha Poothan Rassadorn*). The House of Representatives is composed of 500 seats, 375 members elected from 157 multiseat constituencies and 125 elected on a proportional party-list basis; members serve four-year terms. The last election on July 3, 2011, yielded the following results: For Thais Party, 265 (204 constituency and 61 party list); Democrat Party, 159 (115, 44); Proud Thais Party, 34 (29, 5); Thai Nation Development Party, 19 (15, 4); Thais United National Development Party, 7 (5, 2); *Phalang Chon*, 7 (6, 1); Love Thailand Party 4 (0, 4); Motherland (*Matubhum*), 2 (1, 1); Great People's Party (*Mahachon*), 1 (0, 1); New Democracy, 1 (0, 1); and Rak Santi, 1 (0, 1).

Speaker: SOMSAK Kiatsuranont.

CABINET

[as of August 1, 2013]

Prime Minister	Yingluck Shinawatra (PPT) [f]
Deputy Prime Ministers	Niwatthamrong Boonsongpaisan (PTT)
	Pracha Promnok (PPT)
	Kittirat na Ranong (ind.)
	Pongthep Thepkanjana (PTT)
	Yukol Limlaemthong (TNDP)
	Surapong Towichukchaikul (PTT)
	Plodprasob Surassawadeet (PPT)
Ministers	
Agriculture	Yukol Limlaemthong (TNDP)
Commerce	Niwatthamrong Boonsongpaisan (PTT)
Culture	Sonthaya Khunpluem (PC)
Defense	Yingluck Shinawatra (PPT) [f]
Education	Chaturon Chaisang (PPT)
Energy	Pongsak Raktapongpaisarn (PTT)
Finance	Kittirat na Ranong (ind.)
Foreign Affairs	Surapong Towichukchaikul (PPT)
Industry	Prasert Boonchaisuk (PTT)
Information and Communications Technology	Anudith Nakornthap (PPT)
Interior	Jarupong Ruangsuwan (PPT)
Justice	Chaikasem Nitisiri (PPT)
Labor and Social Welfare	Chalerm Yubamrung (PPT)
Natural Resources and Environment	Vichet Kasemthongsri (PPT)
Office of the Prime Minister	Santi Prompat (PPT)
	Warathep Ratanakorn (PPT)
Public Health	Pradit Sinthwanarong (PPT)
Science and Technology	Phiraphan Phalusuk (PPT)
Social Development and Human Security	Pavena Hongsakula (PPT) [f]
Tourism and Sports	Somsak Pureesrisak (TNDP)
Transport	Chatchachart Sitthiphan (PPT)

[f] = female

INTERGOVERNMENTAL REPRESENTATION

Ambassador to the U.S.: CHAIYONG Satjipanon.

U.S. Ambassador to Thailand: Kristie A. KENNEY.

Permanent Representative to the UN: Norachit SINHASENI.

IGO Memberships (Non-UN): ADB, APEC, ASEAN, IOM, NAM, WTO.

TIMOR-LESTE (EAST TIMOR)

Democratic Republic of Timor-Leste
República Democrática de Timor-Leste

Political Status: Independent republic established May 20, 2002; constitution approved by Constituent Assembly on March 22, 2002.

Area: 5,641 sq. mi. (14,609 sq. km).

Population: 1,219,992 (2012E—UN); 1,172,390 (2013E—U.S. Census).

Major Urban Center: (2010—Timor-Leste Census) DILI 228,559.

Official Languages: Portuguese, Tetum. A majority of Timorese are fluent in Bahasa Indonesia (a form of Malay); both it and English are "working languages."

Monetary Unit: U.S. Dollar (see U.S. entry for principal exchange rates).

President: José Maria VASCONCELOS, popularly known as Taur Matan RUAK) elected by popular vote on April 16, 2012; sworn in for a five-year term on May 20, succeeding José RAMOS-HORTA.

Prime Minister: Kay Rala Xanana (José Alexandre) GUSMÃO (leader of the National Congress of East Timorese Reconstruction); appointed by the president for a second term and sworn in on August 8, 2012, following the legislative election of July 7.

THE COUNTRY

Timor-Leste occupies the eastern half of the tropical island of Timor, near the eastern end of the Indonesian archipelago, plus the small islands of Ataúro (Pulo Cambing) and Jaco (Pulo Jako) as well as Oecussi (Ocussi Ambeno), an enclave on the northern coast of Indonesian West Timor. As a result of the 1859 division of the island by Portugal and the Netherlands, Timor-Leste shares its only land border with Indonesia. The nearest overseas neighbor is Australia to the south across the Timor Sea. The Timorese population is primarily of Malay and Papuan descent. About three-quarters spoke Bahasa Indonesia in 2000, but this proportion declined after the end of Indonesian rule. Less than one-quarter are fluent in Portuguese and one-fifth in English. Commonly spoken is Tetum, an Austronesian language that incorporated elements of Portuguese over the centuries. The vast majority of the population is Roman Catholic, with small Protestant, Muslim, Hindu, and Buddhist minorities. Equality of the sexes is guaranteed under the 2002 constitution. Twenty-five women won election to the current 65-member National Parliament, and 7 were appointed to the extended cabinet.

The leading occupations continue to be subsistence agriculture and fishing, which in 2012 accounted for 64 percent of employment and 26 percent of GDP. Principal crops include coffee (by far the leading export), grains, cassava, spices, coconut, vanilla, and tropical fruits. Small-scale manufacturing, accounting for 18 percent of GDP and 10 percent of employment, involves construction and the production of processed coffee, handicrafts, cloth, and a limited range of other consumables. Services, led by public administration, accounted for 57 percent of non-oil GDP and 26 percent of employment in 2012.

In 1999 violence perpetrated mainly by anti-independence militias, covertly supported by the Indonesian army, destroyed much of the country's infrastructure and precipitated refugee flows that together produced a 35 percent economic contraction in the first year of independence. Economic growth fluctuated thereafter, peaking at 12.7 percent in 2009, reflecting receipts of overseas aid, loans, and a multidonor UN Trust Fund for infrastructure and construction projects. Growth eased to 10 percent in 2012, and the IMF projects a similar growth rate in 2013 and 2014. Although per-capita income rose steadily in 2012, approximately two-fifths of Timorese remained below the poverty line, and one-fifth were unemployed. Much of the population had only limited access to education and basic infrastructure. Adult literacy was under 60 percent; only three-fifths of the population had safe drinking water, only one-fourth had electricity, the under 5 mortality rate was 54 per 1,000 live births, and the country ranked 134th (out of 187) on the Human Development Index.

Prospects for growth and development rest on tapping extensive offshore hydrocarbon reserves. Revenues from oil and gas exports and royalties, supplemented by export earnings from coffee, gold, manganese, and marble, generated a brief surplus in both external trade and the domestic budget, but the surpluses turned into deficits in 2013. The government's Petroleum Fund, in which oil and gas revenues are lodged, and which is invested in sovereign and European Union (EU) bonds and securities, reached $13.6 billion in June 2013. Timor-Leste's principal export partner is Australia and main source of imports is Indonesia.

GOVERNMENT AND POLITICS

Political background. Even though the bulk of the Indonesian archipelago came under Dutch control in the 17th century, the eastern end of the island of Timor and the enclave of Oecussi were claimed by Portugal, whose traders first arrived there in the early 1500s. In 1859 the

Netherlands and Portugal delineated the border between West and East Timor (although the resulting treaty was not ratified until 1904), and East Timor continued to be governed from Macao until reorganized as a separate colony in 1896. A local rebellion in 1910–1912 was repressed.

Following harsh Japanese occupation during World War II, East Timor returned to Portuguese control. Although Indonesia won independence from the Netherlands in 1949, a parallel struggle in East Timor failed. After a coup in Lisbon in 1974, the new democratic government of Portugal offered to conduct a referendum on the future of East Timor, designated an overseas territory since 1951. Although some organizations favored a continued relationship with Portugal or a gradual process of separation, by 1975 all the leading parties but one were advocating independence. Violence escalated, however, over what form of independent government should be established. On November 28 the left-wing Revolutionary Front for an Independent East Timor (*Frente Revolucionário do Timor-Leste Independente*—Fretilin) declared a "Democratic Republic," but this move was opposed by a number of anticommunist parties, including the Timorese Democratic Union (*União Democrática Timorense*—UDT) and the Timorese Democratic People's Association (*Associação Popular Democrática de Timor*—Apodeti). On December 7 Indonesian forces, with a tacit U.S. and Australian acquiescence, invaded to forestall an alleged communist takeover and restore order, ultimately driving Fretilin from the capital. Indonesia formally annexed East Timor on July 17, 1976, but Portugal and the United Nations refused to recognize the action.

The initial years of Indonesian rule were marked by political repression and a severe humanitarian crisis that saw an estimated 100,000 East Timorese succumb to starvation or what some observers characterized as genocidal violence by Indonesian forces intent on suppressing the Fretilin-led opposition. On November 12, 1991, Indonesian troops fired on demonstrators who had assembled in a Dili cemetery for the funeral of a student killed by the police two weeks earlier. More than 200 persons were shot or subsequently arrested and executed, and others beaten or tortured, provoking worldwide condemnation and a suspension of U.S. military training aid. The following November Fretilin's leader, Xanana GUSMÃO, was captured and later sentenced to life imprisonment. But resistance by Fretilin's military wing, the *Forças Armadas de Libertação Nacional de Timor-Leste* (Falintil), continued in the mountains.

Sporadic clashes between protesters and Indonesian security forces punctuated the next three years and became international news when in October 1996 two prominent Timorese pro-independence campaigners were awarded the Nobel Peace Prize. In its citation for Bishop Carlos Felipe XIMENES BELO (Roman Catholic prelate of East Timor) and José RAMOS-HORTA (a former journalist and leader of Fretilin campaigning in exile against Indonesian rule), the Norwegian Nobel committee accused the Suharto government of "systematically oppressing the people" of East Timor and also referred to estimates that under Indonesian occupation "one third of the population of East Timor have lost their lives due to starvation, epidemics, war, and terror." Fact-finding visits and critical reports by a U.S. human rights expert and a UN envoy followed.

In April 1998, 200 delegates of the All-Inclusive Intra-East Timorese Dialogue (AIETD) convened in Portugal and formed the National Council of Timorese Resistance (*Conselho Nacional de Resistência Timorense*—CNRT) to better coordinate the efforts of pro-independence groups such as the UDT and Fretilin. Xanana Gusmão and Ramos-Horta were named president and vice president, respectively, of the CNRT political committee.

Massive demonstrations in Jakarta led to President Sukarno's resignation in 1989 and the decision by his successor President Habibie to consider eventual independence for East Timor. Meeting in New York on May 5, 1999, the Portuguese and Indonesian foreign ministers agreed to hold a referendum on East Timor independence, and this agreement was endorsed by the UN Security Council, which set up the UN Assessment Mission in East Timor (UNAMET) to conduct the ballot. Pro-independence advocates warned that elements in the army were giving clandestine support to pro-integrationist militias, most prominently the Red and White Iron (*Besi Merah Putih*—BMP) and the Thorn (*Aitarak*). The referendum was held on August 30, with UNAMET reporting a 98.6 percent voter turnout, in which 78.5 percent favored independence and 21.5 percent favored autonomy within Indonesia. Pro-Indonesian militia leaders rejected the outcome and took to the streets in violent assaults on UN workers and journalists as well as East Timorese. The Indonesian military failed to intervene, and in subsequent days attacks, murders, and arson were reported throughout the territory, and 450,000 Timorese fled their homes.

On September 9, 1999, responding to international pressure by regional leaders meeting at the APEC summit in Auckland, New Zealand, and later by the UN Security Council, President Habibie agreed to allow a peacekeeping presence in East Timor, and on September 15 the UN Security Council unanimously approved formation of the International Force East Timor (INTERFET). Led by some 4,500 Australians and commanded by Maj. Gen. Peter Cosgrove, 8,000 peacekeepers from 30 countries began deploying on September 20. Seven days later, with most of the Indonesian armed forces having withdrawn, INTERFET formally assumed control and despite sporadic clashes with militia fighters moved into the hinterlands to restore order.

On October 19, 1999, Indonesia's supreme legislature, the People's Consultative Assembly, ratified the referendum results and revoked its 1976 integration decree, and three days later Gusmão flew into Dili, receiving a hero's welcome. On October 25, the UN Security Council was able to replace INTERFET with the United Nations Transitional Administration in East Timor (UNTAET), a multipurpose body including not only troops and police but also civilian specialists. Led by Special Representative Sergio Vieira de Mello, the UNTAET was assigned the task of administering East Timor during the transition to independence.

On December 1, José Ramos-Horta ended his 24-year exile, and on December 11 Vieira de Mello convened a 15-member advisory National Consultative Council (NCC), which included integrationists as well as CNRT representatives and UNTAET members.

On January 31, 2000, the Indonesian Commission to Investigate Human Rights Violations in East Timor asserted that members of the armed forces, the police, and the civil administration as well as the militias had conducted a postreferendum campaign of violence and destruction that it termed systematic and planned. The commission's report called for Jakarta to investigate further the actions of 33 individuals, including Wiranto and several other generals. On the same day a UN report on human rights abuses recommended creation of a war crimes tribunal, and in April the Indonesian attorney general named a 79-member investigative team to pursue the alleged "crimes against humanity."

On July 12, 2000, the NCC approved formation of a transitional government comprising João CARRASCALÃO, president of the UDT; Marí ALKATIRI of Fretilin; Fr. Filomeno JACOB; Mariano LOPES, head of the Public Service Commission; and four UNTAET members. Ramos-Horta joined as foreign minister on October 19. On October 23, 2000, Gusmão was elected president of the 36-member

UN-appointed interim legislature, the East Timor National Council (ETNC), but he resigned on March 28, 2001, because of dissatisfaction with the ETNC. His replacement, Ramos-Horta, was succeeded by Carrascalão on April 9.

On August 30, 2001, East Timor democratically elected the 88 members of a Constituent Assembly to supersede the ETNC and begin drafting a constitution. Fretilin dominated the election, winning 55 seats; the Democratic Party (*Partido Democrático*—PD) followed with 7 seats; the Social Democratic Party (*Partido Social Democrata*—PSD), 6; and the Timorese Social Democratic Association (*Associacão Social-Democrata Timorense*—ASDT), 6. As a result, Fretilin's secretary general, Marí Alkatiri, who had spent many years in African exile, was named chief minister of an interim East Timor Council of Ministers that included Fretilin, the PD, and a number of independents. Meanwhile, a UNTAET-sponsored court in Dili continued investigating militia-related crimes.

In January 2002, the Constituent Assembly voted to convert itself into a National Parliament and to adopt the constitution, both achieved on March 22. On April 14 Gusmão, who had severed his ties to Fretilin after the 1999 referendum, was elected to the presidency as an independent, capturing 82 percent of the vote against the token opposition of the ASDT's Francisco Xavier do AMARAL. Gusmão was inaugurated for a five-year term on May 20 in conjunction with the formal establishment of the Democratic Republic of Timor-Leste. On the same day Fretilin's Alkatiri was sworn in as Timor-Leste's first prime minister.

Independence day also marked the end of the UNTAET mission, which was succeeded by a United Nations Mission of Support in East Timor (UNMISET), whose mission was to enhance political stability, provide interim law enforcement while assisting the development of a domestic police service, and help maintain external security. UNMISET was replaced in May 2005 by a scaled-down UN Office in Timor-Leste (UNOTIL), subsequently recast in 2006 as the United Nations Integrated Mission in Timor-Leste (UNMIT).

On April 28, 2006, demonstrations in the capital supporting soldiers who had been dismissed from the army turned violent, precipitating two months of sporadic gang violence as well as clashes between elements of the police and armed forces that left nearly 40 people dead. The roots of the civil disorder can be traced to early February, when some 400 soldiers of the Timorese army (Falintil–*Forças de Defesa de Timor-Leste*—F-FDTL), led by Lt. Gastão SINHALA, left their barracks to protest alleged discrimination. The disgruntled troops from western districts of the country (*Loromonu*), whose numbers grew to about 600 later in the month, complained of favoritism toward the majority easterners (*Lorosae*), who had been more prominent and numerous in Falintil. The F-FDTL rebels were joined early in May by Maj. Alfredo REINADO and a contingent of military police. On May 24, Foreign Minister Ramos-Horta requested international aid, and the first of some 2,500 Australian, New Zealand, Malaysian, and Portuguese troops and police began arriving to restore a semblance of order to Dili and its environs. At the urging of the new government, the UN Security Council in August 2006 set up the UN Integrated Mission in Timor (UNMIT) to succeed UNOTIL and committed it to a two-year deployment, which was later extended. On May 29, 2006, President Gusmão convened the Council of State. And the next day he declared a 30-day state of emergency and, as commander in chief, assumed control of the F-FDTL and the Timorese police (*Policia Nacional de Timor-Leste*—PNTL), superseding the authority of Minister of the Interior Rogério LOBATO (Fretilin) and Secretary of State for National Defense Roque Félix RODRIGUES. Both cabinet members resigned on June 1, after which Ramos-Horta was assigned the defense portfolio in addition to his duties as foreign minister. Alkatiri and Lobato were charged with arming civilian supporters and inciting them to eliminate Alkatiri's opponents; charges against Alkatiri were dismissed in February 2007, but Lobato was convicted in March 2007 and given a prison sentence of seven and a half years.

On June 26, 2006, Prime Minister Alkatiri resigned under pressure brought to bear by supporters of the dismissed soldiers, the parliamentary opposition, and President Gusmão. Gusmão named José Ramos-Horta prime minister, and a reshuffled cabinet was sworn in on July 14.

In a role reversal Ramos-Horta was elected president for a five-year term in a two-way runoff on May 9, 2007, with 69.1 percent of votes. Gusmão, having chosen not to seek a second term as president, had assumed the leadership of a newly formed opposition party, the National Congress for Timorese Reconstruction (*Congresso Nacional de Reconstrução do Timor*—CNRT). His party won only 18 of 65 seats in the June 30 poll but was able to form a governing coalition, dubbed the Alliance of the Parliamentary Majority (*Aliança com Maioria Parlamentar*—AMP), with three other parties. Weeks of wrangling followed, with Fretilin failing in its attempts to form an alternative coalition. President Ramos-Horta appointed Gusmão as prime minister on August 6, and he assumed office two days later. In 2010, his coalition cabinet after adjustments included one CNRT leader holding two portfolios, three PSD ministers, one ASDT minister, a Fretilin Reform Group vice minister and six independents.

On February 11, 2008, rebels attempted to assassinate President Ramos-Horta, severely wounding him, and fired shots at Prime Minister Gusmão's motorcade. The rebels' leader, Reinado, was killed by Ramos-Horta's guards. Parliament declared a state of emergency, Australia dispatched 350 additional troops and police, and order was restored. On April 29, Reinado's second in command, Gastão SALSINHA, and 12 followers surrendered to the government, joining 15 others who had previously surrendered. Indonesia in May 2008 apprehended and turned over four rebels who had fled to West Timor. In all, 23 persons were sentenced to prison for terms ranging from 9 to 16 years.

Urban gang violence, which peaked in 2006, was also brought under control. Parliament, encouraged by a peace-building project sponsored by Oxfam, Concern, Action Asia, Yayasan Hak, and NGO Forum, in July 2008 passed a law to register and regulate "martial arts groups" (the core of many gangs) and in August 2008 brokered a "peace pact" between the two leading gangs, 7–7 and FSHT.

Corruption in government remained an obstacle to investment, as Timor-Leste declined from 123rd to 143rd in the Transparency International Index during the period 2006–2012 and Fretilin leaders accused the prime minister of awarding government contracts to political associates and family members. The government appointed Timor-Leste's first anticorruption commissioner, Aderito de Jesus SOARES, in February 2010 and in the following three years, he had investigated more than 150 cases of corruption among elected and appointed officials. However by 2012 Timor-Leste moved up to 113th on the corruption index, suggesting the effectiveness of remedial measures.

The appointment in March 2009 of Longuinhos MONTIERO as commander of the faction-ridden national police PNTL provoked objections by not only the Fretilin opposition but also the Brussels-based International Crisis Group in a December 2009 critique citing the lack of discipline and overly paramilitary style of the police. In October the government survived a vote of no confidence 38–25 brought by Fretilin leader Mari Alkatiri, who objected to the release of militia leader Martenus BERE to asylum in Indonesia.

Reforms in 2010 included the launch of a Civil Service Commission, a National Development Bank, a National Liberation Combatants (veterans) Consultative Council, and a Chamber of Commerce and Industry. In April the prime minister set Timor-Leste's development priorities as infrastructure, food security, human capital development, justice, good governance, and public security, and these were reflected in the 2012–2013 budget.

Constitution and government. The constitution drafted by the Constituent Assembly and approved in its final form on March 22, 2002, after a period of popular consultation, provides for freedom of speech and of the press, freedom of religion, the right of *habeas corpus,* and freedom of association (except that "armed, military or paramilitary associations, including organizations of a racist or xenophobic nature or that promote terrorism, shall be prohibited"). The chief executive, a popularly elected president serving a once-renewable five-year term, plays a largely ceremonial role. In the event no presidential candidate receives a majority on a first ballot, the constitution mandates a runoff between the top two contenders. Most executive power resides with the prime minister, who is appointed by the president but must command a parliamentary majority. The prime minister selects the members of the cabinet, who are then appointed by the president.

Prior to the 2007 election, the National Parliament altered the electoral law to reduce the number of representatives from 88 to 65, chosen by a mixed single-member constituency and party list electoral system. The National Parliament, which has a five-year term, may be dissolved prematurely and new elections held, but not within six months of the next scheduled election or within six months of the end of a presidential term. Among its powers, the legislature may amend the constitution by a two-thirds vote. The 2002 constitution also provides for a Council of State, an advisory body chaired by the president and encompassing all past presidents, the current prime minister and speaker of the National Parliament, five citizens selected by the legislature, and five designated by the president.

The independent judiciary is headed by a Supreme Court of Justice with authority to rule on the constitutionality of statutes and referenda and to certify "the regularity and validity of the acts of the electoral process." There is also a High Administrative, Tax, and Audit Court and provision for Military Courts. Below the national level, Timor-Leste is divided into 13 administrative districts. The constitution recognizes the enclave of Oecussi as meriting a "special administrative policy and economic regime." In 2009 the Indonesian-imposed law code was replaced by a civil law code based on the Portuguese system, and the criminal law code was likewise altered in 2011.

Foreign relations. Timor-Leste became the 191st member of the United Nations General Assembly on September 27, 2002, and subsequently joined a number of international organizations (see list below). It has participated in the ASEAN Regional Forum, a regional security consultative body, since 2005, and as an observer to both ASEAN and the Melanesian Spearhead Group, both of which it aspires to join. Since the outbreak of violence in 2006 Timor-Leste's security has been underpinned by the United Nations Integrated Mission in Timor-Leste (UNMIT). In August 2012 UNMIT was composed of 357 international civilian staff, 264 UN volunteers, and 1,269 police and military liaison officers from 39 countries and was supported by an International Stabilization Force of 390 Australian and 70 New Zealand troops. Reflecting an improved security situation, the UN Police command UNPOL in 2009 began transferring control of police posts and the police academy to the PNTL, the National Police of Timor-Leste, which in March 2011 assumed full control of security. UNMIT's mandate under UNSC Resolution 2037 was allowed to expire on December 31, 2012; by mid-2013 only a small number of foreign troops remained for training and liaison.

Even before independence, Timor-Leste's leaders favored close relations with its immediate neighbors, Australia and Indonesia. The Australian delegation to the independence festivities was led by Prime Minister John Howard, who joined President Gusmão in signing a Timor Sea Treaty that granted Timor-Leste 90 percent of revenue from a Joint Petroleum Development Area (JPDA). However, the neighbors remained at odds over delineation of their maritime boundary and eligibility for royalties from further oil exploitation development rights. Consequently, in 2003 Dili sought to revise the provision of the treaty that would give Timor-Leste only 20 percent of the larger Greater Sunrise field, which lies outside the JPDA in what Australia considers its territory, and was estimated to contain gas valued at $50 billion. Dili also wanted to redraw the maritime boundary with Australia in accordance with the Law of the Sea midpoint principle, but the Howard government argued for retaining the border as delineated by a 1972 agreement with Indonesia based on the continental shelf principle. Boundary talks, occasionally turbulent, led in January 2006 to the Treaty on Certain Maritime Arrangements in the Timor Sea (CMATS Treaty), ratified in February 2007, whereby final determination of the boundary was to be postponed for 50 years but Timor-Leste was to receive 50 percent of Greater Sunrise revenues in the interim. Exploitation of the Timor Sea oil field was expected to bring over $4 billion in royalties to Timor-Leste over the life of the project.

Australia remains Timor-Leste's principal security and trading partner as well as a source of aid and foreign investment. In February 2002 Timor-Leste and Australia signed two Memorandums of Understanding (MOUs) on combating illegal immigration and people smuggling, followed in August 2003 by an MOU on Cooperation to Combat International Terrorism. The two governments also signed an MOU in October 2006 on security arrangements within the JPDA. Australia funds and staffs training programs for the Timorese armed forces and police under its Defense Cooperation Program and Timor-Leste Police Development Program (TLPDP). Canberra in 2003 granted Timorese products duty-free access to the domestic market. Nevertheless, Australian Prime Minister Julia Gillard's proposal in July 2010 to set up and fund a regional refugee processing center in Timor-Leste provoked controversy; while President Ramos-Horta and Prime Minister Gusmão expressed initial interest, the National Parliament and the Fretilin party opposed the scheme, and it died in early 2011. On July 25, 2011, Timor Air, connecting Dili with Darwin, made its inaugural flight. In February 2012, Prime Minister Xanana Gusmão visited Canberra to meet his counterpart, Prime Minister Julia Gillard, and in May, Governor General Quentin Bryce and Minister for Veterans Affairs Warren Snowdon joined the celebrations of 10 years of independence in Dili. Defence Minister Stephen Smith visited in April 2013 to discuss security cooperation.

In May 2002, in a gesture of reconciliation, Indonesian president Megawati Sukarnoputri attended the independence ceremonies in Dili, prompting President Gusmão to announce that decades of repression and violence under Indonesian rule were to be relegated to "history and the past." In July Timor-Leste and Indonesia signed a joint communiqué establishing diplomatic relations, and in April 2005, during a visit by Indonesian president Susilo Bambang Yudhoyono, the two governments signed an agreement to begin demarcation of their 268 kilometer common border.

Relations with Indonesia were shadowed by the issue of justice for the victims of the militia violence of 1999. Indonesia refused to extradite persons indicted by Eeast Timor's Serious Crimes Unit, and in Jakarta, a handful of civilian and military figures convicted of crimes against humanity by an Indonesian Ad Hoc Human Rights Court were acquitted on appeal.

However the Indonesia Timor-Leste Joint Commission on Truth and Friendship, which reported in July 2008, found the Indonesian government, military, and police responsible for murder, rape, torture, and forced displacement of Timorese in 1999. The Indonesian president expressed "deep regret" and the Indonesian military chief Gen. Djoko Santoso stated that the 1999 mayhem "has become TNI's [the Indonesian military's] responsibility." Indonesian leaders and the president of Timor-Leste agreed that the report was a final authoritative account of "an unfortunate chapter" and pledged to forgo further recriminations or prosecutions in order to lay a foundation for future harmonious relations, a pledge that was renewed in August 2009 on the tenth anniversary of the independence referendum. (For further details on the indictments, trails, and reports relating to the 1999 violence, see the 2013 *Handbook*.) In 2012, President Susilo Bambang Yudhoyono attended the tenth anniversary ceremonies of East Timor's independence and renewed his support of East Timor's bid to join ASEAN.

China emerged as a leading benefactor, having been among the first to recognize the new state in 2002. In 2007 China was financing the construction of the presidential palace and a hospital, building barracks and providing uniforms for the armed forces, deploying police and medical aid personnel, training civil servants and farmers, and giving scholarships to students and officials to visit China. PetroChina won a contract to conduct a seismic survey and has expressed interest in developing offshore oil fields. In August 2008 President Ramos-Horta visited Beijing, where he was received by China's president, Hu Jintao, and in 2009 officials indicated that Timor-Leste would be purchasing two oil-fired power plants. In June 2010 Timor-Leste took command of two Jaco-class patrol boats purchased from China, which also trained 36 Timorese sailors to operate the vessels to counter fish poaching estimated to cost Timor-Leste $36 million annually. Wang Zhizen, vice-chair of the Chinese People's Political Consultative Conference National Committee, visited Dili in May 2012 to consult with officials and join the celebration of East Timor's 10th anniversary of independence.

The United States signed an agreement in 2009 for the U.S. Army to train Timor-Leste's marines alongside Indonesia's marines. U.S. aid, totaling over $30 million in 2012, focused on technical assistance to government prosecutors, legal aid institutions, media and journalists, civil society bodies, and security and health care. A delegation led by Secretary of State Hillary Clinton visited Dili for consultations in September. Other states and organizations maintaining supportive diplomatic, economic, and humanitarian relations include Portugal, Japan, and the European Union.

Current issues. Guided by the joint Strategic Development Plan 2012–2030, Australia pledged A$125.7 million during 2013–2014 for aid to good governance, agricultural production, clean water, mobile health clinics, classroom construction, and road rehabilitation. New Zealand in June 2013 pledged aid for the Community Policing Program and signed a Status of Forces Agreement with Dili. Relations with Indonesia were firmed up in 2011 by means of a memorandum of understanding on security and defense cooperation, foreshadowing establishment of a joint defense committee. Visits to Indonesia's president by Prime Minister Kay Rala Xanana Gusmão and President Taur Matan Ruak in March and June 2013, respectively, resulted in settlement of a disputed border segment (Delumi-Memo), establishment of three joint border-crossing posts, and a visa exemption agreement for diplomatic and service officials.

The presidential election of 2012 began in March with 12 candidates of which 2, Tuar Matan Ruak (independent) and Francisco GOMES (Aileba People's Liberty Party) proceeded to the runoff in April. Ruak won with 61.23 percent of the popular vote. The National

Parliament election of July 7 was contested by 21 political parties, of which 4 secured seats: CNRT, Fretilin, PD, and Reform Front (*Frenti-Mudança*), whereupon CNRT formed a coalition government with PD and Reform Front, leaving Fretilin again in opposition. President Taur Matan Ruak swore in the new government on August 8, with Xanana Gusmão of CNRT again as prime minister. The current cabinet has 55 members, including 31 CNRT leaders, 13 PD members, 5 Reform Front members, and 6 independents.

The U.S. State Department described the elections as "free and fair" but noted persistent human rights violations such as abuse of power by the police, an inefficient judiciary depriving citizens of expeditious trials, poor prison conditions, and social violence against women and children. Freedom House in 2013 rated Timor-Leste only "partly free" and below average on civil liberties, while Reporters Without Borders ranked the country 90th in press freedoms out of 179 countries surveyed.

The 2013–2014 budget of $1.6 billion was approved by the National Parliament on February 18, 2013; it projected increased allocations to rural infrastructure, the National Police, and the administration of justice.

POLITICAL PARTIES

Timor-Leste's oldest parties date from 1974, when local elites banded together to promote or resist movement toward independence. After the December 1975 Indonesian invasion, opposition to Indonesian annexation was led by the leftist Revolutionary Front for an Independent East Timor (Fretilin) and its military wing, Falintil. The anti-independence parties, such as the Timorese Democratic Union (UDT), accommodated the Indonesian authorities but later became disillusioned and opposed the occupation. In April 1998 Fretilin agreed to join other surviving parties in forming an umbrella National Council of Timorese Resistance (*Conselho Nacional de Resistência Timorense*—CNRT). The end of the Indonesian occupation in 1999 saw a proliferation of new parties, most of them small, personality based, and short-lived. In preparation for Timor-Leste's first election in August 2001, 16 parties registered candidate lists, and 12 won at least 1 seat in the Constituent Assembly. In the June 2007 parliamentary election 14 parties registered, but only 7 won seats, the rest failing to reach the threshold of 3 percent of the popular vote. Fretilin won the most seats, 21, but the next 3 finishers formed a coalition government, the Alliance of the Parliamentary Majority (*Aliança com Maioria Parlamentar*—AMP), under Xanana Gusmão, the leader of the National Congress for the Reconstruction of East Timor (CNRT), leaving Fretilin in opposition. In the July 2012 Parliamentary election, CNRT won 30 seats, followed by Fretilin with 25, PD 8, and Reform Front 2; no other party reached the threshold necessary to secure a seat.

Governing Coalition Parties:

National Congress for Reconstruction of Timor (*Congresso Nacional de Reconstrução do Timor*—CNRT). The CNRT is an indirect descendant of the National Council for Reconstruction of Timor (*Conselho Nacional de Resistência Timorense*—CNRT) that functioned as an umbrella body for resistance to Indonesian rule. Established in 1998, it lapsed following the country's independence. The current CNRT, with a modified name but same acronym, coalesced in early 2007 from elements dissatisfied with the existing political parties. It is centrist, moderate, and pragmatic in its ideology. Its organization is based on prominent personalities rather than a formal branch structure. Outgoing president Xanana Gusmão assumed leadership of the party in March 2007 and attracted many of his followers and supporters in the electorate. The party polled well in the June 2007 parliamentary election but did not succeed in gaining a majority, winning only 24 percent of the vote and 18 seats, placing second behind Fretilin, which won 21. As neither party could command a majority, in July Gusmão negotiated an agreement with the Timorese Social Democratic Association–Social Democratic Party alliance and the Democratic Party to forge a parliamentary majority. On August 6 Ramos-Horta requested that the CNRT form a government, appointing party president as prime minister. In government, CNRT has pursued an ambitious national development plan, funded by substantial withdrawals from the Petroleum Fund. No party won the majority seats in the 2012 election; CNRT led with 36.66 percent, negotiated a coalition with two other parties, PD and Reform Front, formed a new government, and took 31 cabinet posts.

Leaders: Xanana GUSMÃO (President), Deonisio da Costa Babo SOARES (Secretary General).

Democratic Party (*Partido Democrático/Parta Demokrat*—PD). Organized in June 2001 in preparation for the August Constituent Assembly election, the centrist PD advocates participatory democracy, an independent judiciary, and a market economy with selective intervention by the government. The PD is influenced by student and youth movement activists and former resistance figures. Based on an 8.7 percent vote share in the balloting, in 2001, it was awarded seven assembly seats. In the June 2007 legislative election, the PD won 11 percent of the vote and eight seats. Its leader, Fernando LASAMA de Araujo, who ran unsuccessfully for the presidency, and ten other PD members were awarded cabinet portfolios.

In March 2012, Araujo ran again for the presidency but came in fourth in the first round with 17.67 percent of the vote. In the parliamentary elections of 2012, the PD won 8 seats (10.31 percent of the vote) and entered a coalition with its ally CNRT, thereby being awarded 13 cabinet posts.

Leaders: Fernando de Araujo LASAMA (President and now Deputy Prime Minister and Coordinator of Social Affairs), Mariano Assanami Sabino LOPEZ (Secretary General).

Reform Front (*Frenti-Mudança*). From 2006 to 2011, this party was called Fretilin-Mudança (Revolutionary Front for an Independent East Timor—Change) to signal its leaders' disillusionment with the failure of the radical Fretilin leadership to adapt to the needs of a modernizing and pluralistic East Timor. As a faction in 2006, they tried to reform Fretilin from within. José Luis GUTERRES, formerly East Timor's UN ambassador, led a movement at the party congress to replace Marí Alkatiri as secretary-general but was outmaneuvered, and the faction members subsequently left Fretilin.

In the 2007 presidential election, Fretilin-Mudança activists supported José Ramos-Horta's candidature, and in the parliamentary election, they supported CNRT. José Luis Guterres was appointed vice-prime minister in the AMP government after the elections.

The group re-named itself Fretlin-Mudança (dropping the *i* for independent) to distinguish itself from the original Fretilin in order to register as a new political party for the 2012 elections. The Court of Appeal found the new name too similar to that of Fretilin and refused to approve it. A July 2011 resubmission with the new name Frenti-Mudança (Reform Front) was approved, although the party flag had to be changed to distinguish it from Fretilin's. Reform Front won two seats in the 2012 elections and was invited into the CNRT-led coalition government. It was awarded five cabinet posts, with Guterres appointed minister of foreign affairs.

Leaders: José Luis GUTERRES (President), Jorge da Conceição TEME (Secretary General).

Parliamentary Opposition Party:

Revolutionary Front for an Independent East Timor (*Frente Revolucionário do Timor-Leste Independente*—Fretilin). Founded in 1974 with a commitment to East Timorese independence from Portugal, the leftist Fretilin emerged from the Timorese Social Democratic Association (ASDT, above). It mounted an insurrection in 1975 and then declared formation of a Democratic Republic of East Timor on November 28. In December, however, it was forced from the capital by Indonesian forces.

Fretilin and its military wing, the Armed Forces of National Liberation of East Timor (*Forças Armadas de Libertação Nacional de Timor-Leste*—Falintil), led by Xanana Gusmão, continued to resist Indonesian annexation for more than two decades. In November 1992 Gusmão was captured by Indonesian forces, and in May 1993 he was sentenced to life in prison (subsequently reduced to 20 years, and then in 1999 to house arrest).

In the context of the UN intervention that followed the August 1999 independence referendum, Fretilin accepted a role in a UN-sponsored National Consultative Council (NCC). In July 2000 Fretilin's secretary general, Marí Alkatiri, joined a transitional government. Meanwhile, Gusmão had resigned from Fretilin after the 1999 referendum.

In the Constituent Assembly election of August 2001, Fretilin emerged with 57.3 percent of the popular vote and 55 of 88 seats, leading to Alkatiri's selection as chief minister in the second interim government and, ultimately, his assumption of the prime ministership at independence.

The April–July 2006 crisis strengthened a dissident group that sought Alkatiri's removal as party leader. In May his position was challenged at a party congress by José Luís Guterres, Timor-Leste's ambassador to the UN and the United States, who withdrew when Alkatiri engineered a change from secret ballot to a show of hands. On June 25 the Fretilin leadership backed his continuing as prime minister, but he stepped down the following day. He was replaced as president of the party by Francisco Guterres, while José Luís Guterres accepted the post of foreign minister in the Ramos-Horta cabinet. In 2007 José Luís Guterres's rebellious Fretilin *Grupo Mudança* (Fretilin Reform Group) supported the CNRT in the parliamentary election and its leader was subsequently named vice prime minister, provoking the mainstream leadership to expel the Reform Group members. In March 2009 prominent member Ana Maria Pessoa Pereira da SILVA PINTO was named prosecutor-general by the CNRT-led government and resigned her Fretilin membership, leaving Fretilin with 21 seats. In the 2012 election, Fretilin finished second with 29.87 percent of the vote and 25 seats, whereupon it continued as the sole opposition in Parliament. Its leader ran unsuccessfully for president in March 2012.

Leaders: Francisco ("Lu'Olo") GUTERRES (President), Jose dos REIS (Secretary General).

Other Parties Contesting the 2012 Elections:

Timorese Social Democratic Association (*Associação Social-Democrata Timorense*—ASDT). The current ASDT was formed in 2001 by one of the earliest Fretilin leaders, Francisco Xavier do Amaral, as a third-way Fretilin offshoot positioned between the parent party and more conservative elements. In 1974, Nicolau dos Reis LOBATO, Xavier do Amaral, José Ramos-Horta, and others had established the original ASDT, which was soon superseded by Fretilin. During Indonesian rule, Xavier do Amaral had resided in Jakarta, and he initially returned to East Timor as a proautonomy integrationist. He has also been associated with a more radical Fretilin offshoot, the CPD–RDTL.

In the 2001 Constituent Assembly election, the ASDT won 7.8 percent of the vote and six seats. Its leader Xavier do Amaral contested the 2002 and 2007 presidential elections without success.

Prior to the June 2007 parliamentary election, the ASDT negotiated an agreement with the PSD (see below) to cooperate in supporting each other's electoral campaign initiatives. The ASDT–PSD won 15.7 percent of the popular vote and 11 parliamentary seats, subsequently joining the CNRT and the PD in forming a coalition government. The party won 1.8 percent of the vote in 2012 and no seats but was awarded one ministerial post in the current cabinet.

Leaders: Joao Andre CORREIAL (President), Vicente dos SANTOS (Secretary General).

Social Democratic Party (*Partido Social Democrata*—PSD). Founded in September 2000 as a centrist alternative to Fretilin and the Timorese Democratic Union (see UDT, below), the PSD advocates consensus and formation of a national unity government. Its platform stresses social justice, better health care, participatory democracy, and Timor-Leste's membership in ASEAN. It would abolish the death penalty and establish a Timorese currency. In the 2001 election, it won 8.1 percent of the vote and six seats.

In 2007, its presidential candidate, Lúcia LOBATO, won 8.9 percent of the vote, for fifth place. In the run-up to the June 2007 legislative election, the PSD formed an electoral alliance with the ASDT that won 11 seats and then joined in establishing the governing coalition, gaining 3 cabinet posts. PSD won 2.15 percent of the vote in 2012.

Leaders: Zacarias de COSTA (President), Marito MAGNO (Secretary General).

Timorese Nationalist Party (*Partido Nacionalista Timorense—PNT*). Established in 1999 as a post-autonomy party, PNT was at one time a member of Fretilin, but its leader Abilio ARAUJO was expelled because of business links with the Suharto family of Indonesia. In the 2001 Constituent Assembly election, it won 2.2 percent of the votes and won 2.4 percent of the votes in the 2007 parliamentary election but no seats. PNT then joined a loose alliance with PDRT, PDC, PST, UDT, and PMD under the name Democratic Progressive League (Liga Democratica Progressiva—LDP).

Republic of Timor-Leste Party (*Partido Democrática Republica de Timor-Leste*—PDRT). The PDRT is supported by voters in the western districts of Timor-Leste and by those who sympathized with the 594 Group comprised of dissenting soldiers led by Maj. Alfredo Reinado. PDRT won 1.9 percent of the popular vote in the 2007 election. In the 2012 election, PDRT entered into a coalition with the PLPA (see below) but won no seats.

Aileba People's Liberty Party (*Partido Liberta Povo Aileba—PLPA*). The PLPA was founded in December 2009 and was officially registered in 2010. *Aileba* means carriers of wood and connotes itinerate peddlers. The party champions the rural poor and calls for better roads and access to clean water, schools, and health facilities in the rural districts. PLPA won 0.85 percent of the parliamentary vote and no seats in the 2012 election; its leader Francisco GOMES contested the presidential election but failed to make the run-off.

Leaders: Francisco GOMES (President), Gabriel FERNANDES (General Secretary).

Republican Party (*Partidu Repúblikanu*—PR). The PR was established in December 2005 by a leading academic and member of the Council of State, Joao Mariano Saldanha, who remains the party president. The party platform advocates popular democratic participation and emphasizes security, employment, education, health, and decentralization. Reflecting its promotion of gender equality and minority rights, the PR would establish a Ministry of Gender and Minority Affairs and wants to refocus the armed forces on peacekeeping. The party advocates making Tetum the primary official language.

The PR won 1.1 percent of the popular vote in the 2007 election and slumped to only 0.91 percent in the 2012 election.

Leaders: Joao Mariano SALDANHA (President), Belarmino F. NEVES (Secretary General).

Christian Democratic Party (*Partido Democrata Cristão/Partai Demokrasi Kristen*—PDC/PDK). The PDC was founded in 1998 in Portugal and in August 2000 in Dili as a largely Catholic party with links to churches in Australia and Portugal and to the Indonesian Christian Democratic Party. The PDC was briefly allied with the Christian Democratic Union of Timor (*União Democrata-Cristão de Timor*—UDC). Considered somewhat more left-leaning than the UDC, it attracted both Protestants and Catholics. In the 2001 election it won 1.9 percent of the vote and two Constituent Assembly seats, whereas the UDC won one seat on a 0.6 percent vote share. In 2006 the UDC and the PDC merged under the PDC title.

The PDC advocates Christian values, social justice, and a multilateral foreign policy free from great-power domination. In the June 2007 parliamentary election the PDC won 1.0 percent of the popular vote. The PDC president, António XIMENES, studied theology in Indonesia and directed the National Commission for Study on the Future of East Timor. PDC won 0.19 percent of the vote in 2012.

Leaders: António XIMENES (President), Julio PEREIRA (Secretary General).

Socialist Party of Timor (*Partido Socialista de Timor*—PST). The PST, a Fretilin splinter, leans toward Marxist-Leninism and has a small base of support among students and labor. In August 2001 it won one legislative seat on a 1.7 percent vote share but in 2007, gained no seat with 1.0 percent of the vote. Avelino Coelho da Silva, the party's secretary general, was named secretary of state for energy policy in the Gusmão government. In the July 2012 election, PST won 2.41 percent of votes and no seat, but the president of the party was appointed by Prime Minister Gusmão as the secretary of state for the Council Ministers of the current government.

Leaders: Avelino Coelho da SILVA (President), Pedro SARMENTO (Secretary General).

Timorese Democratic Union (*União Democrática Timorense*—UDT). The conservative UDT was established in 1974 as a predominantly Catholic, anticommunist formation that was initially open to federation with Portugal. Having opted for independence, the UDT was briefly allied with Fretilin, but the two were on opposite sides of the civil war that saw Fretilin's declaration of a republic in November 1975 and the subsequent invasion by erstwhile UDT ally Indonesia.

The UDT operated primarily from exile in Portugal and Australia during the period of Indonesian rule, although it again allied itself with Fretilin in 1986. It was revived in 1997 and participated in the CNRT, the NCC, and the transitional government of October 2000 before competing in the August 2001 Constituent Assembly balloting. In the election it won 2.3 percent of the vote, for two seats.

In the 2007 election, UDT obtained 0.9 percent of the popular vote and in the 2012 election gained 1.13 percent. The former leader of the party and East Timor ambassador to the Republic of Korea João Viegas CARRASCALÃO died in February 2012.

Leaders: Gilman EXPOSTO (President), Cipriano J. da Costa GONCALVES (Secretary General).

National Unity Party (*Partidu Unidade Nacional*—PUN). Founded in 2006, the PUN is a Christian democratic party committed to moral and family values, basic human needs, democracy, and human rights.

In the June 2007 parliamentary election, the PUN won three seats. Fernanda Borges was the parliamentary group leader and chaired the Parliamentary Committee on Constitutional Issues, Justice, Public Administration, Local Power and Government Legislation. In the 2012 election, PUN won no seats in national parliament with 0.68 percent of the vote.

Leaders: Fernanda Mesquita BORGES (President), Maria F. de DEUS (Secretary General).

Democratic Alliance (*Aliança Democratica*—AD). The AD was formed by the Association of Timorese Heroes (see KOTA, below) and the People's Party of Timor (see PPT, below) as a joint electoral front for the 2007 legislative elections. The grouping secured two seats. In the 2012 election, it received only 0.56 percent votes.

Association of Timorese Heroes (*Klibur Oan Timor Asuwain*—KOTA). Also known as the Sons of the Mountain Warriors, the KOTA was established in 1974 by Leão Pedro dos Reis Amaral and the late José MARTINS. The KOTA descended from the Popular Association of Monarchists of Timor (*Associação Popular Monarquia de Timor*—APMT), which represented traditional royalty. In 1975, the KOTA joined the UDT (see above) and Apodeti in actively opposing Fretilin's efforts to establish a leftist government and for a time backed the Indonesian intervention. Reemerging in the late 1990s, the KOTA backed independence, joined the CNRT, and participated in the 2001 Constituent Assembly election, in which it won 2.1 percent of the vote and two seats.

Prior to the 2007 legislative election, KOTA formed a coalition with the People's Party of Timor (PPT), called the Democratic Alliance (see DA, above).

Leaders: Manuel TILMAN (President), Maria Angela Freitas da SILVA (Secretary General).

National Democratic Unity of Timorese Resistance (*Unidade Nacional Democrática da Resistência Timorense*—Undertim). Undertim split from Fretilin in early 2005 and launched itself as a new party on August 30, 2005. Its leader was a prominent resistance fighter with Falintil for 20 years. The party platform stresses better housing, health, environment, and social security. It advocates compulsory military service, traditional justice in villages, and active engagement with Australia and Indonesia.

Undertim won two seats in the June 2007 election but gained no seat in the 2012 election, winning only 1.49 percent of the vote.

Leaders: Cornelio GAMA (President), Francisco Guterres MANUBUY (Secretary General).

National Development Party (*Partido Desenvolvimento Nacional*—PDN). Founded by a former secretary-general of PSD, Fernando Dias GUSMÃO, PDN was established on May 30, 2009. Gusmão was elected to the Constituent Assembly in 2001 and reelected to the National Parliament in 2007 as a PSD representative but left the party and resigned from the parliament in 2009 because of disenchantment with PSD's failure to implement its election policy promises.

In the July 2012 election, PND won 1.99 percent of the vote.

Leader: Lucas SOARES (Secretary General).

Enrich the National Unity of the Sons of Timor Party (*Partidu Kmanek Haburas Unidade Nasional Timor Oan*—Khunto). Khunto is a new party that was granted legal registration on June 22, 2011. Khunto won 2.97 percent of the votes in the 2012 election.

Leaders: Armanda Berta dos SANTOS (President), Antonio Verdial de SOUSA (Secretary General).

Liberal Democratic Party (*Partido Democrático Liberal*—PDL). The PDL originated as the Liberal Party (*Partai Liberal*), which was registered in 2001 and contested the Constituent Assembly elections in that year. Although the party consistently ran last in the voting, its 1.1 percent of the vote entitled it to one seat in the Assembly and also in the First National Parliament. In the 2012 election, PDL won 0.47 percent of the vote but no seat.

Leaders: Marito de ARAÚJO (President), Gaspar de ARAÚJO (Secretary General).

Timorese Democratic Party (*Partido Timorense Democratico*—PTD). This party, founded in 2011, contested the 2012 election but only won 0.54 percent of the vote.

Leader: Alianca da Conceicao ARAÚJO (President).

Popular Development Party (*Partido Desenvolvimento Popular*—PDP). This minor party won 0.40 percent of the vote in the 2012 parliamentary election.

Leaders: Antonio SOARES (President), Calistro das NEVES (Secretary General).

Millennium Democratic Party/East Timor National Republican Party (*Partidu Milénium Demokrátik*—PMD; *Partido Republika Nacional Timor Leste*—Parentil). PMD was founded in 2004 by pro-independence activist Herrmenegildo 'Kupa' LOPES and former members of the PSD. The party was registered in December 2005. PMD, a center party, calls for reconciliation and democracy. In the 2012 election, PMD formed a coalition with East Timor National Republican Party (*Partido Republika Nacional Timor Leste*—Parentil) called the Proclaimed Block, which won 0.66 percent of the parliamentary vote.

Leaders: Arlindo Francisco MARÇAL (President), Hermenegildo LOPES (Secretary General).

Timorese Popular Monarchy Association Party (*Associação Popular Monarquia Timorense*—APMT). This new party contested elections for the first time in 2012 and won only 0.84 percent of the vote.

Leaders: Pedro da Costa RAMALHO (President), Cesar Augusto dos Santos CARLOS (Secretary General).

LEGISLATURE

An 88-member Constituent Assembly (*Assembleia Constituinte*) was elected on August 30, 2001, superseding a 36-member interim body, the East Timor National Council, which had been appointed by UN administrators in October 2000. In 2002 the assembly was reconstituted as the **National Parliament** (*Parlamento Nacional*) and now comprises 65 members elected for a five-year term on a proportional basis.

In the July 7, 2012, election, the National Congress for Timorese Reconstruction (CNRT) won 30 seats; the Revolutionary Front for an Independent East Timor (Fretilin) 25 seats; the Democratic Party (PD), 8; and the Reform Front (Frenti-Mundaca), 2.

Speaker: Vicente da Silva GUTERRES (CNRT).

CABINET

[as of September 1, 2013]

Prime Minister	Kay Rala Xanana Gusmão (CNRT)
Deputy Prime Minister, Minister of Social Welfare and Sport	Fernando La Sama de Araújo (PD)
Ministers	
Minister of State, President of Council of Ministers	Hermenegildo Pereira Alves (CNRT)
Minister of Finance	Emília M. V. Pires (ind.) [f]
Minister of Foreign Affairs	José Luis Guterres (Reform Front)
Minister of Defense and Security	Cirilo José Cristovão (CNRT)
Deputy Minister of Foreign Affairs and Cooperation	Constâncio da Conceição Pinto (PD)
Minister of State Administration	Jorge da Conceição Teme (Reform Front)
Minister of Agriculture and Fisheries	Mariano Assanami Sabino (PD)
Minister of Justice	Dionisio C. Babo Soares (CNRT)
Minister of Health	Sergio Gama da C. Lobo (CNRT)
Minister of Education	Bendito dos Santos Freitas (CNRT)
Minister for Commerce, Industry and Environment	António da Conceição (PD)
Minister of Social Solidarity	Isabel Amaral Guterres (ind.) [f]
Minister of Public Works	Gastão Francisco de Sousa (PD)
Minister of Transport and Communications	Pedro da Silva Lay (ind.)

Minister of Natural Resources	Alfredo Pires (CNRT)
Minister of Tourism	Francisco Kalbuadi Lay (CNRT)

[f] = female

INTERGOVERNMENTAL REPRESENTATION

Ambassador to the U.S.: Constancio da Conceicao PINTO.

U.S. Ambassador to Timor-Leste: Karen Clark STANTON (nominated).

Permanent Representative to the UN: Sofia MESQUITA BORGES.

IGO Memberships (Non-UN): ADB, ICC, IOM, NAM.

TOGO

Republic of Togo
République Togolaise

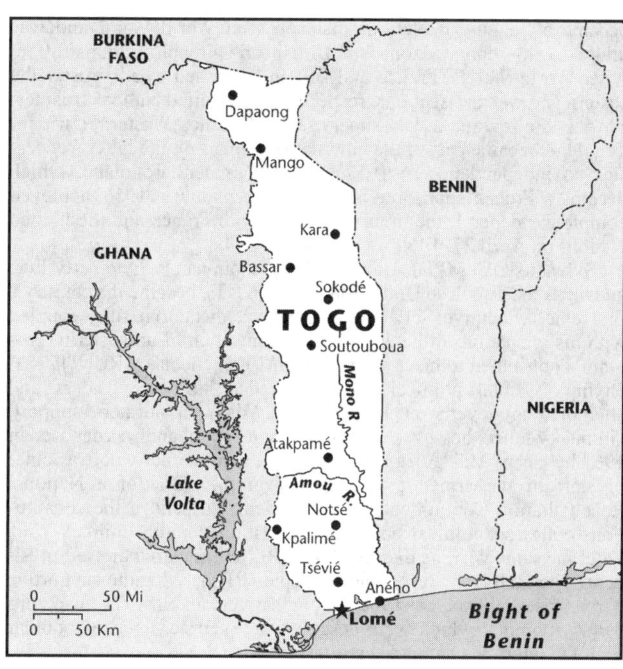

Political Status: Independent republic since 1960; personal military rule imposed in 1967; one-party state established November 29, 1969; Third Republic proclaimed on January 13, 1980, under constitution adopted in referendum of December 30, 1979; constitution suspended by a National Conference on July 16, 1991; multiparty constitution adopted by popular referendum on September 27, 1992.

Area: 21,622 sq. mi. (56,000 sq. km).

Population: 6,310,628 (2012E—UN); 7,154,237 (2013E—U.S. Census).

Major Urban Center (2010C): LOMÉ (837,437).

Official Language: French.

Monetary Unit: CFA Franc (official rate November 1, 2013: 486.52 francs = $1US). The CFA franc, previously pegged to the French franc, is now permanently pegged to the euro at 655.957 CFA francs = 1 euro.

President: Faure Essozimma GNASSINGBÉ (Union for the Republic, originally elected from the Rally of the Togolese People); elected on April 24, 2005, and inaugurated on May 4 following an extended constitutional crisis triggered by the death on February 5 of his father, Gen. Gnassingbé EYADÉMA (Rally of the Togolese People), who had been president since 1967; reelected on March 4, 2010, and inaugurated for a second term on May 3.

Prime Minister: Kwesi AHOOMEY-ZUNU (Pan-African Patriotic Convergence); appointed by the president on July 19, 2012, to succeed Gilbert HOUNGBO (Independent), following the latter's resignation on July 12; formed new government on July 31.

THE COUNTRY

Wedged between Ghana and Benin on Africa's Guinea Coast, the small Republic of Togo extends inland from a 31-mile coastline for a distance of 360 miles. Eighteen major tribal groups are located in its hilly, hot, and humid territory, the best known being the culturally dominant Ewe in the south, whose traditional homeland extends into Ghana; the Mina, another southern people; and the Kabiyé in the north, who staff most of the country's small army. Although French has been accorded official status, most people use indigenous languages, with Ewe being predominant in the south and Twi in the north. About 51 percent of the population adheres to traditional religious beliefs; the remainder embrace Christianity (29 percent, mainly Roman Catholicism) and Islam (20 percent). Somewhat more than half of adult women are in the work force, predominantly in the agricultural and trading sectors, but are generally underrepresented in the government and legislature. In the 2013 elections, women secured 14 seats in the assembly, or 15.4 percent of the total.

The economy depends primarily on subsistence agriculture, the three most important crops being cocoa, coffee, and cotton. Phosphate is the leading export, and oil refining, steel fabrication, and cement production are assuming increasing industrial importance. Smuggling has long been a source of contention with Ghana; as much as a third of Togo's cocoa exports originates in the neighboring state and are smuggled into Togo in exchange for luxury items that are much cheaper than in other parts of Africa.

GDP grew by an average of 2 percent from 2002 to 2008, fueled by increased agricultural output and expanded phosphate production. (For information on the Togolese economy prior to 2002, please see the 2012 *Handbook*.). The government's fiscal status was also improved by better tax collection procedures. However, most international donors continued to withhold assistance due to the Eyadéma regime's poor human rights record and failure to implement democratic reform. In 2004 the EU resumed aid after Togo met 22 preconditions, and in September 2005, the IMF followed suit. In April 2006 the World Bank included Togo among 11 countries that qualified for debt relief under the Heavily Indebted Poor Countries (HIPC) initiative.

Following the 2007 legislative elections, which were judged fair by international observers, Togo was granted additional economic aid. In 2008 the EU pledged an additional $190 million over a five-year period, while the World Bank agreed to write-off the arrears owed by Togo on past loans, some $135 million, and the Paris Club of creditor nations forgave $347 million in debt. In addition, the African Development Bank (AfDB) canceled 99 percent of Togo's $23.5 million debt to the institution. In November the IMF announced that Togo qualified for the HIPC program, which would allow the country to write off $2.2 billion in external debt if it completed the terms of the program. Togo's GDP grew by 4 percent in 2010, while inflation grew at 3.2 percent. In December 2010 the Paris Club agreed to cancel $203 million of Togo's debt, while the IMF and World Bank provided an additional $1.8 billion to Togo as part of the HIPC initiative (a reduction of 82 percent of Togo's foreign debt). Meanwhile, France eliminated $143 million of Togo's debt in May 2011, while Italy, Sweden, and Switzerland canceled an additional $84 million in debt in June. In 2011, GDP grew by 4.9 percent and 5 percent in 2012. That year inflation increased by 2.5 percent, and GDP per capita rose to $588. The government reported a deficit equal to 7.4 percent of GDP in 2013.

GOVERNMENT AND POLITICS

Political background. The present Republic of Togo is the eastern section of the former German Protectorate of Togoland, which became a League of Nations mandate after World War I and was divided into separate zones of British and French administration. After World War II, France and Britain continued to administer the eastern and western sections, respectively, as United Nations trust territories. Following a UN-supervised plebiscite, Western (British) Togoland became part of the new state of Ghana on the latter's accession to independence in 1957. Eastern (French) Togoland, which became a French-sponsored autonomous republic in 1956, achieved complete independence in an agreement with France and the United Nations on April 27, 1960.

Sylvanus OLYMPIO, leader of the predominantly Ewe party then known as the Togolese Unity Committee (CUT), became the country's first chief executive. Olympio's somewhat dictatorial rule, coupled with his alienation of the army by the imposition of an austerity program, contributed to his assassination in 1963. Nicolas GRUNITZKY, Olympio's chief political rival, succeeded him as president and attempted to govern on a multiparty basis with northern support. Grunitzky failed, however, to establish firm control and was deposed in 1967 by (then) Maj. Etienne EYADÉMA, a northerner who was chief of staff of the armed forces. Acting in the name of a National Reconciliation Committee (NRC), Eyadéma suspended the constitution, outlawed political activity, and instituted direct military rule. Later the same year, he dissolved the NRC and declared himself president. The Rally of the Togolese People (RPT), a regime-supportive party, was established in 1969 and, in that year and in 1971, made pro forma attempts (which were described as overruled by the "popular will") to return the nation to civilian rule.

A constitution drafted in 1969 was accepted by a reported 98 percent of the registered electorate on December 30, 1979, in balloting at which General Eyadéma (whose first name had been "Africanized" to Gnassingbé in 1974) stood as the sole candidate for a seven-year term as president. Concurrently, a unicameral general assembly was constituted on the basis of a single list of candidates presented by the RPT.

In September 1986, the government reported that it had rebuffed a coup attempt allegedly fomented in Ghana and Burkina Faso by supporters of the exiled sons of former president Olympio. However, some external critics suggested that the seriousness of the coup attempt may have been overstated by the Eyadéma regime to shift attention away from earlier reports of torture and illegal detention of political prisoners. On December 21, President Eyadéma was unopposed in election to a further seven-year term.

In early October 1990, the imposition of lengthy jail terms on two opposition figures for alleged antigovernment activity ignited a series of protests and strikes. On October 10, President Eyadéma responded by telling a RPT Central Committee meeting that the country's "apprenticeship in democracy" was complete and preparations should be made for a multiparty system. However, the establishment of a constitutional commission and scheduling of a referendum for late 1991 failed to appease government critics, with violent protests continuing into 1991.

In March 1991, ten opposition groups formed a Front of Associations for Renewal (FAR) under the leadership of Yawovi AGBOYIBO, and four days later, after a meeting with FAR representatives, the president agreed to accelerate reforms. In mid-April he authorized the legalization of opposition parties and pledged to hold multiparty elections within a year. Nevertheless, violent demonstrations continued, fueled by the discovery of the bodies of 30 slain protestors in a Lomé lagoon. Subsequently, in the course of negotiations with opposition leaders, Eyadéma agreed to transfer power to a prime minister to be elected by a National Conference on Togo's Future, which convened in Lomé on July 8. On July 16, the opposition-dominated conference declared its sovereignty, dissolved the National Assembly, abrogated the 1980 constitution, and stripped Eyadéma of all but ceremonial powers, thus prompting a government and army withdrawal from the proceedings. On July 23, the government rejoined the conference, and, at its close on August 28, the president publicly accepted most of its findings, including a diminished presidency, the election of Joseph Kokou KOFFIGOH as prime minister, and the replacement of the RPT-dominated National Assembly with an interim High Council of the Republic (HCR). However, Eyadéma's military supporters continued to reject both the conference's sovereignty claims and the new government, in particular Koffigoh's assumption of the defense ministry. Subsequently, military coup attempts on October 1 and 8 ended only after public appeals from Eyadéma that the troops return to their barracks.

In mid-October 1991, the HCR, under pressure from newly enfranchised party leaders to establish control of the government, formally ousted Eyadéma, and on November 26 the council banned the RPT on the eve of a party congress. The following day rebel troops surrounded Koffigoh's residence, and on December 2 the troops announced that they had "reclaimed" strategic points throughout Togo and had called on Eyadéma to name a new prime minister and dissolve the HCR. On December 3, Koffigoh was seized by the rebel soldiers and brought to Eyadéma, whereupon the prime minister announced his "surrender" and agreed to Eyadéma's request that he form a national unity government, assignments to which were announced on December 30.

On January 29, 1992, the government issued a revised electoral calendar that called for a constitutional referendum and municipal balloting in early April, a legislative poll in late May, and a presidential election in June. The schedule was subsequently abandoned because of widespread violence, including the May 5 wounding of opposition leader Gilchrist OLYMPIO, son of the former president, in an attack for which Capt. Ernest GNASSINGBÉ, the president's son, was implicated two months later. On August 13, negotiations between a presidential delegation and representatives of eight opposition parties on resumption of the transitional process were suspended, and on August 23 the government, citing ongoing unrest, canceled a constitutional referendum. Meanwhile, following extensive talks between the president and prime minister, at which the latter reportedly agreed to a number of concessions reversing earlier limitations on the president's power, the transition period, scheduled to expire on August 28, was extended to December 31.

On September 27, 1992, a new constitution was endorsed in a referendum by 99.09 percent of the voters. Concurrently, a new electoral calendar was released, which called for balloting to take place between October and December. However, the democratization process was halted on October 22 with seizure of the National Assembly building by pro-Eyadéma troops, who demanded the release of frozen RPT funds in return for the release of 40 legislative hostages. The crisis was resolved the following day when the HCR agreed to release the funds; however, Koffigoh declared the HCR's action invalid because it was performed under duress, while Eyadéma, who had supported earlier efforts to free the funds, called for sanctions against the intruders. Unappeased by the government's response, the opposition organized a general strike on October 26 to protest the military's action.

On November 11, 1992, Eyadéma, rejected as "unconstitutional" Koffigoh's dismissal of two propresidential cabinet ministers, one of whom had reportedly threatened to have the prime minister arrested. The United States responded on November 13 with suspension of $19 million in aid payments. Three days later Togolese unions, acting in concert with the Democratic Opposition Collective (COD-2), launched a general strike, which they warned would continue until the government agreed to the formation of a politically neutral security force, a new government, free and fair elections, prosecution of the troops implicated in the October National Assembly incident, and international monitoring of the transitional period. Meanwhile, Koffigoh's repeated compromises with Eyadéma appeared to have cost him the support of the COD-2, whose leaders, in early January 1993, refused to meet with him.

On January 13, 1993, Eyadéma dismissed Koffigoh, claiming that the transitional government's mandate had ended on December 31, 1992. However, five days later, in an action that the HCR described as "unconstitutional," he reappointed Koffigoh to his post. Tensions were further heightened on January 25 when security forces killed at least 20 people. Nationwide clashes between prodemocracy and government forces were subsequently reported, and at the end of the month, amid reports of rampaging soldiers and an imminent civil war, 300,000 Togolese fled to Benin and Ghana.

Negotiations opened on February 11, 1993, in Colmar, France, with representatives of the president, the government, the HCR, and the opposition in attendance; however, Eyadéma's delegation soon withdrew because of the opposition's demand for political neutralization of the armed forces. Three days later, following negotiations between the president and prime minister, during which the former reportedly pledged to keep troops loyal to him in their barracks, Koffigoh was named to head a "crisis government" dominated by presidential loyalists. The HCR rejected the legality of the new administration, calling it the product of a "constitutional coup d'état."

On March 25, 1993, Eyadéma's top military aide was among a number of military personnel reportedly killed when the president's residence came under attack from raiders who fled into Ghana.

Olympio, who was accused of planning the attack, countered by charging that the incident was part of a purge of army dissidents. Lending credence to his argument, over 140 former Eyadéma troops were reported to have fled Togo by early April, claiming that a presidentially sanctioned ethnic cleansing campaign was under way. An election timetable was subsequently released, which called for new presidential and legislative balloting. However, most of the opposition boycotted the long-deferred presidential poll of August 25 at which Eyadéma was credited with reelection amid increasing evidence that he had regained most of his pre-1991 powers.

In late September 1993, the COD-2 threatened to boycott legislative elections then scheduled for December unless the government agreed to provide access to state-controlled media, redefine voting constituencies, and increase the number of poll watchers. The balloting was further postponed until February following renewed fighting near Eyadéma's residence on January 5, 1994, which left more than 60 dead.

The multiparty poll, which was finally mounted on February 6 and 20, 1994, was marred by violence, with RPT militants accused of attacking opposition candidates. International observers nonetheless endorsed the results, which included a majority of 43 seats for the opposition Patriotic Front (FP) and 35 for the RPT. Subsequently, however, the Supreme Court, responding to petitions filed by the RPT, vacated 3 seats won by the opposition. Therefore, the FP's overall lead was imperiled, pending by-elections, which, having initially been scheduled for May, were deferred. Criticizing the Court's action, the FP's leading components (the Action Committee for Renewal—CAR and the Togolese Union for Democracy—UTD) threatened to boycott the National Assembly; however, the coalition's unanimity was sorely tested on April 22, when the president, in apparent violation of an earlier agreement, rejected CAR leader Yawovi Agboyibo as the FP's prime minister designate in favor of the UTD's Edem KODJO.

In mid-1994, a RPT characterization of the FP as a "facade of a coalition" seemed increasingly apt, as the CAR resisted UTD entreaties to join Kodjo's government. Earlier, on May 20, the CAR, which unlike the UTD had carried through on a legislative boycott, announced that it was abandoning the action, explaining that the regime's failure to mount by-elections by the legally mandated date of May 15 was tantamount to a confession that "conditions for legality, transparency, and security" had not been met. In December the CAR once again withdrew from the assembly, but in April 1995 President Eyadéma and Agboyibo reached an agreement on electoral reform, which called for equal representation for government and opposition parliamentary groups on all electoral commissions. As a result, the CAR rejoined the assembly in August; however, an alliance of RPT and UTD parliamentarians defeated the reform bill in February 1996.

Already strained relations between President Eyadéma and Prime Minister Kodjo deteriorated sharply in May 1996 when the Supreme Court supported Eyadéma's assertion that he alone controlled the appointment of senior administrative officials. For his part, Kodjo reportedly accused the president of establishing a "parallel government." Subsequently, following the RPT's capture of three assembly seats (and consequently a narrow legislative majority) in early August by-election balloting, Kodjo resigned on August 19, citing his desire to avoid the "legal war," which he described as likely to arise from the lack of an "obvious majority." The following day Eyadéma appointed Planning and Territorial Development Minister Kwassi KLUTSE as Kodjo's successor, and on August 27 the new prime minister announced the formation of a new government.

On December 3, 1996, the National Assembly voted to adopt a RPT-drafted document delineating the responsibilities of a new Constitutional Court. The poll was boycotted by the CAR, which had unsuccessfully sought to broaden the court's powers to include mediation of electoral disputes. (The new body was inaugurated in March 1997.) Thereafter, in September, the opposition boycotted an assembly vote on a new electoral code after attempts to persuade the legislature to include provisions for an independent electoral body were rebuffed. The code, approved unanimously by the propresidential legislators, provided for a nine-member commission (four from the propresidential forces and four from the opposition, in addition to an appointed chair).

Following presidential balloting on June 21, 1998, President Eyadéma was credited with a vote share of 52 percent and Gilchrist Olympio of the Union of Forces of Change (UFC) with 34 percent. The remainder of the tally was shared by four other candidates, led by Yawovi Agboyibo with 9.6 percent. However, the polling process was widely criticized by both domestic and international observers. Furthermore, two days after the polling, the chairperson of the electoral commission, Awa NANA, resigned, claiming that her efforts to prepare provisional electoral results had been blocked by "unidentified" individuals widely believed to be presidential supporters. Subsequently, the opposition, led by Olympio, who claimed that he had actually won the election with a 59 percent vote share, refused the president's offer to join a unity government and organized a number of demonstrations and work stoppages. Amid reports of mounting violence, on August 19 Prime Minister Klutse resigned; however, the president reappointed Klutse the following day, and on September 1 Klutse named a government that included a number of new members but no prominent opposition leaders.

In December 1998, government and opposition leaders announced that they had made progress in their efforts to organize a dialogue. Thereafter, however, the preparations ground to a halt as the two sides proved unable to agree on a venue for the proposed talks. Subsequently, in early 1999, the opposition announced its intention to boycott legislative polling then scheduled for early March. The Eyadéma administration rejected calls to delay the balloting until after interparty talks and proceeded with electoral preparations, albeit delaying the start of polling for two weeks.

Following legislative balloting on March 21, 1999, and two subsequent by-elections, the RPT, facing only limited competition from independent candidates and two minor parties, was credited with having won 79 of the 81 seats. On April 17, Klutse dissolved his government and offered his resignation, although he agreed to continue thereafter on a caretaker basis. On May 22, the president appointed Eugene Koffi ADOBOLI, a former official of the United Nations Conference on Trade and Development, as Klutse's successor. Facing continuing criticism for his inability to improve the economic condition, however, Adoboli resigned on August 25, 2000, one day after a vote of no-confidence against his government in the legislature. The president named Agbéyomé Messan KODJO of the RPT as Adoboli's successor on August 29.

Relations between the government and the opposition remained severely strained in late 2001 and the first half of 2002. Particularly galling to the opposition was an amendment to the electoral code approved by the assembly in February 2002 that required future presidential candidates to have resided in Togo for 12 consecutive months. Critics described the new law as designed to prevent another presidential run by the UFC's Gilchrist Olympio, who remained outside the country. The opposition parties also strongly objected to the government's offer of only five seats on the proposed 20-member electoral commission. In view of the impasse on that membership, the government in May appointed a committee of judges to oversee legislative elections which had already been twice postponed.

On June 27, 2002, President Eyadéma appointed Koffi SAMA of the RPT to replace Prime Minister Kodjo. (Kodjo was subsequently expelled from the RPT for criticizing the president; he later went into exile.) Sama was sworn in on June 30, and he announced his cabinet on July 5.

The RPT dominated the October 27, 2002, assembly balloting (72 of 81 seats), in part due to a boycott by most opposition parties. Sama was reappointed as prime minister on November 13. In December the RPT-controlled assembly approved a constitutional revision that removed the limit on the number of presidential terms for one person, thereby permitting Eyadéma to seek another term in the election scheduled for 2003. The assembly also lowered the eligibility age for presidential candidates from 45 to 35, a measure apparently designed to permit the eventual succession of Eyadéma's son, Faure Essozimma GNASSINGBÉ, who was only 37 years old at the time. Moreover, the basic law was changed to require presidential candidates to have resided in Togo for one year prior to the election. That provision prevented Gilchrist Olympio, who had been in exile in France, from contesting the election; he urged supporters to vote for Emmanuel BOB-AKITANI, the vice president of the UFC.

In the presidential poll of June 1, 2003, Eyadéma was credited with 58 percent of the vote, followed by Bob-Akitani (34 percent), and four minor candidates. Prime Minister Sama and his cabinet resigned on June 23, but the president reappointed Sama on July 1. On July 29 Sama formed a new cabinet that included a few members of minor opposition parties and, notably, Faure Gnassingbé.

President Eyadéma died of a heart attack on February 5, 2005. His son, Faure Gnassingbé, backed by the military and Sama, was immediately named interim president, although the constitution required the speaker of the assembly to fill a presidential vacancy. Because the current speaker, Fambaré NATCHABA, was out of the country at the time, the assembly, on February 6, elected Gnassingbé to replace Natchaba as speaker, and Gnassingbé was sworn in as president the following day to serve until the end of his father's term in 2008. The assembly also rescinded the constitutional provision that new presidential elections be held within 60 days in case of a vacancy. However, in the wake of intense domestic and international criticism, the assembly, on February 21, voted to reverse its decisions (see Foreign relations, below). Gnassingbé resigned as speaker and interim president on February 25 and was succeeded in both positions by Abbas BONFOH (hitherto the deputy speaker) pending new elections. In highly controversial balloting on April 24, Gnassingbé was credited with 60 percent of the vote and runner-up Bob-Akitani with 38.25 percent. After the Constitutional Court validated the results on May 3, Gnassingbé was sworn in on May 4. On June 9, the president appointed Edem Kodjo of the Pan-African Patriotic Convergence (*Convergence Patriotique Panafricaine*—CPP) as prime minister in an attempt to reach out to opposition groups. Kodjo's new cabinet, formed on June 20, comprised mostly members of the RPT, although several small opposition parties agreed to join. Efforts to form a broader unity government were initially rebuffed by the major opposition parties. However, in July, nine of the leading political parties signed a Comprehensive Political Accord, which established the framework for future elections. Provisions included the creation of an independent national electoral commission and the preparation of new voter rolls (to be used in conjunction with new identification cards). The UFC initially rejected the accord but later reversed itself after the government pledged to reform the nation's security forces.

As an outgrowth of the new pact, President Gnassingbé appointed opposition leader Agboyibo of the CAR as prime minister on September 16, 2006. Four days later, Agboyibo took office as head of a national unity government that included 16 new ministers. The RPT and its allies retained the majority of the ministries, but 16 posts were held by the opposition or independents, including members of the CAR, CPP, the Democratic Convention of African People, the Socialist Renewal Pact, and the Party for Democracy and Renewal.

In legislative balloting on October 14, 2007, the governing RPT won 50 seats, followed by the UFC with 27 seats and the CAR with 4 seats. Agboyibo resigned on November 13 and Komlan MALLY of the RPT was appointed prime minister on December 3. He named a cabinet composed of the RPT, with representation from some minor parties, including the Democratic Convention of African People (*Convention Démocratique des Peuples Africains*—CDPA) and independents. Both the UFC and the CAR refused to participate in the government. On September 5, 2008, Mally resigned following tensions with the president, who accused the prime minister of being ineffective. Mally was replaced two days later by Gilbert HOUNGBO, a political independent and former diplomat. Houngbo named a new cabinet on September 15 that was dominated by the RPT and did not include any members of the UFC or CAR. The size of the cabinet was increased from 22 to 26, and Mally was retained as minister of state for health. However, as part of the consolidation of power, the president's half-brother, Kpatcha, was not reappointed as minister of defense. Kpatcha was subsequently arrested for allegedly planning a coup (see Current issues, below).

Gnassingbé launched the Permanent Committee on Dialogue and Consultation (*Le Comité Permanent de Dialogue et de Concertation*—CPDC) in February 2009. The CPDC included the country's main political parties and served as a standing forum to develop consensus on issues such as elections, the constitution, and media rules. However, the CAR and the UFC initially boycotted the body. In June, the CPDC allocated seats for the national electoral commission in preparation for the 2010 presidential balloting. The president replaced the minister of primary and secondary education in March and created a new post, minister of state for water resources and village water, in May to oversee internationally funded improvements to the nation's water system.

In presidential balloting on March 4, Gnassingbé was reelected with 60.9 percent of the vote, defeating six other candidates. Jean-Pierre FABRÉ of the UFC placed second in the balloting with 33.9 percent of the vote. Houngbo was reappointed prime minister on May 7. The RPT and the UFC signed an agreement that on May 27 that paved the way for the creation of a coalition unity government (see Current issues, below). The new cabinet, including seven UFC ministers, was sworn in on May 28.

In March 2011, Gnassingbé conducted a minor cabinet reshuffle. In September, Togo's Truth and Reconciliation Commission began hearings for 250 victims of political and sectarian violence as part of a national reconciliation effort.

In April 2012 Gnassingbé dissolved the RPT to form a new grouping, the Union for the Republic (*Union pour la République*—UNIR) with himself as party president (see RPT, below). On July 11 Houngbo and the cabinet resigned (see Current issues, below). Former commerce minister Kwesi AHOOMEY-ZUNU (CPP) was appointed prime minister on July 19, and a new cabinet, including opposition UFC figures, was sworn in on July 31.

In long-delayed legislative balloting on July 25, 2013, the UNIR won a commanding majority (see Current issues, below).

Constitution and government. The 1979 constitution provided for a highly centralized system of government headed by a strong executive presiding over a cabinet of his own selection and empowered to dissolve a single-chambered National Assembly after consulting the Political Bureau of the RPT. It detailed a judicial system headed by a Supreme Court that included a Court of Appeal and courts of the first and second instance, with special courts for administrative, labor, and internal security matters.

On July 16, 1991, the National Conference on Togo's Future abrogated the 1979 basic law, transferred all but ceremonial presidential powers to a prime minister, and dissolved the legislature, with assignment of its powers to a High Council of the Republic (HCR), pending the promulgation of a new constitution and the holding of multiparty elections.

A draft constitution accepted by the HCR on July 2, 1992, called for a semi-presidential system with the head of state elected to a once-renewable five-year term and a prime minister chosen by the president from a parliamentary majority and responsible to the legislature, which would also have a five-year mandate. Other projected institutions included a High Court of Justice and a Supreme Court, in addition to a Constitutional Court, an Accounts Court, and an Economic and Social Council. On September 27, the new basic charter was approved by 99.08 percent of the participants in a referendum. In March 1997 a seven-member Constitutional Court was appointed to serve a seven-year term.

The country is divided for administrative purposes into five provinces, which are subdivided into 30 prefectures that were formerly administered by presidentially appointed chiefs and "special delegations" (councils) but are now subject to prefectural and municipal elections on the basis of direct universal suffrage.

For many years the media were almost exclusively government controlled. In early 2000 a new press bill further limited press freedom and made "defamation of the government" an offense subject to a prison sentence. A second repressive law was passed in 2002 and allowed fines of up to $7,500 and sentences of five years in prison for defaming the president and lesser penalties for defamation of other officials. However, many of the new measures were repealed in August 2004 as part of Togo's effort to restart international aid. In 2013 Reporters Without Borders ranked Togo 83rd out of 179 countries in freedom of the press.

Foreign relations. Togo's foreign policy has long been based on nonalignment, although historical links have provided a foundation for continued financial and political support from the West. Bowing to pressure from the Arab bloc, diplomatic relations with Israel were severed from 1973 to 1987.

Although one of the smallest and poorest of the African states, Togo has played a leading role in efforts to promote regional cooperation and served as the host nation for negotiation of the Lomé conventions between the European Community (EC) and developing African, Caribbean, and Pacific (ACP) countries. It worked closely with Nigeria in organizing the Economic Community of West African States (ECOWAS) in May 1975 and, having assumed observer status earlier with the francophone West African Economic Community (CEAO), joined the CEAO states in a Non-Aggression and Defense Aid Agreement (ANAD) in 1979. Its major regional dispute concerns the status of Western Togoland, which was incorporated into Ghana in 1957. A clandestine "National Liberation Movement of Western Togoland" has been active in supporting Togo's claim to the 75-mile-wide strip of territory and has called for a new UN plebiscite on the issue. There have been numerous incidents along the Ghanaian border, and the Eyadéma and Rawlings regimes regularly accused each other of destabilization efforts, including the "harboring" of political opponents. Heated exchanges occurred with Ghana and, to a lesser degree, Burkina Faso, following the reported coup attempt in Togo in

September 1986. However, Eyadéma avoided charging Accra and Ouagadougou with direct involvement in the plot, and relations were largely normalized by mid-1987, with Lomé calling for help from regional organizations to keep further enmity from developing. In December 1991 the Koffigoh administration announced that a comprehensive cooperation agreement had been reached with Ghana.

Togo's foreign affairs in 1992 and early 1993 were determined in great part by its domestic political turmoil. In early November 1992 both Benin and Ghana reported deaths of their nationals in border incidents involving Togolese security forces, although their complaints were relatively low-key in apparent support of the transitional government. On November 13 a deteriorating political situation led the United States to suspend all but humanitarian aid payments. Thereafter, in late January 1993, a French and German mediation effort was cut short when 20 prodemocracy demonstrators were killed by government forces outside the negotiation site. In mid-February, France, citing the death of the demonstrators and lack of progress toward democracy, announced restrictions on aid payments. France's decision came only weeks after its former president, Valéry Giscard D'Estaing, had written a controversial letter in support of Eyadéma.

Meanwhile, relations between Togo and Ghana continued to worsen. In March 1993 rebels who had attacked the Eyadéma compound retreated into Ghana, setting off an exchange of accusations between the two capitals. In early January 1994 Togo and Ghana were described as "close to war" after Lóme once again accused Accra of aiding alleged anti-Eyadéma insurgents in an attack on the president's residence. For its part, Ghana described the unrest in Togo as "the consequence of the government's refusal to establish a credible democratic process" and called on Lomé to resist always accusing Ghana "whenever there is an armed attack or political crisis." Such charges notwithstanding, relations between the two improved dramatically by midyear; on November 16 diplomatic ties were formally restored, and in December Eyadéma ordered the reopening of their shared border. Lomé's relations with Paris improved when France agreed to reschedule and forgive Togolese debt in May 1995.

In August 1998 the Togolese government reported that troops based near Lomé had been attacked by opposition-affiliated "terrorists" based in Ghana; however, the opposition countered that the fighters were actually government provocateurs who had attacked the headquarters and homes of UFC members. Collaterally, the incident proved to be a showcase for improved relations between Accra and Lomé (the two nations' presidents having signed cooperation agreements in Accra earlier in the year) because Ghana deployed forces to carry out a joint operation with Togolese troops pursuing the alleged "aggressors." However, conflicts over property rights were reported in 1999 along the border between Togo and Ghana, and in March 2001 Togo closed the border without explanation. The border was reopened and relations between the two sides improved dramatically with the election of John Kufuor as president of Ghana.

In 1998 Eyadéma helped mediate the conflict in Guinea-Bissau. Togolese troops also joined the international peacekeeping mission in Guinea-Bissau, and Eyadéma played a role in efforts to end the conflicts in Liberia and Sierra Leone. In addition, Togolese troops participated in the ECOWAS mission in Liberia and the UN mission in Sierra Leone. In light of Togo's importance to regional peacekeeping operations, the United States initiated joint training exercises with the Togolese military in April 2002.

Faure Gnassingbé's takeover in February 2005, following the death of his father, prompted regional organizations such as ECOWAS and the African Union (AU) to condemn the Togolese military for what was perceived as a coup. On February 9 the International Organization of the Francophonie suspended Togo's membership. On February 20 ECOWAS imposed a range of sanctions on Togo, including suspension of the country's membership, a travel ban on Togolese officials, and an arms embargo.

France was the first country to accept Faure Gnassingbé's controversial victory in the 2005 presidential election. In February 2006 Gnassingbé traveled to China to promote increased economic interaction between the two countries. (In 2005, trade between Togo and China was worth more than $500 million.)

Togo, Benin, and Nigeria entered into a pact in February 2007 to promote peace and economic development in the region. Subsequently, Togo, Ghana, and the UN signed a tripartite agreement in April to facilitate the voluntary return of Togolese refugees, many of whom had been in Ghana since the early 1990s. In June a cooperation framework was signed between Togo and Angola in an effort to overcome tensions that have lingered from Togo's past support of the Angolan rebel movement UNITA.

In December 2007, Togo and the United Arab Emirates established full relations as part of a broader effort by Togo to improve trade and political relations with countries in the Middle East. In January 2008 Togo announced that it would contribute 800 soldiers to the AU-led peacekeeping force in Darfur. In addition, in September, Togo and Belgium resumed diplomatic ties.

Togo and France signed a new defense accord in March 2009. Following meetings between Gnassingbé and German chancellor Angela Merkel in June, the Togolese president proclaimed a "new start" in relations between Togo and its former colonial power. Togo and Ghana launched an initiative in August to reduce cross-border crime, including joint border patrols. Also in August, the two governments signed an agreement in Accra whereby Ghana agreed to provide technical assistance during the 2010 elections. In December Togo expelled a French diplomat who was accused of interfering in national politics by supporting an opposition presidential candidate in upcoming presidential elections. France retaliated by expelling a Togolese diplomat.

During the Africa Cup of Nations, Angolan separatists attacked a convoy with the Togolese national soccer team and killed three, on January 8, 2010. Togo subsequently withdrew its team from the tournament. Fighting in Ghana in May prompted at least 3,500 refugees to flee into Togo. In November China granted Togo $25 million and offered technical assistance to improve the government's Internet and Web capabilities.

After clashes between rival tribes in northern Togo, Ghanaian authorities reported that more than 360 refugees had fled across the border in September 2011. Also in September, Togo recognized the transitional government of Libya. On October 24, Togo was elected for a two-year term on the UN Security Council.

In April 2012, Togolese and Nigerian officials held negotiations to speed the trials of 85 Nigerians under arrest in Togo. Reports were that as many as 800 Nigerians were in custody for various offenses in Togo, and the Nigerian government had expressed concern over the slow pace of judicial proceedings. In July, Togo and Sri Lanka agreed to establish diplomatic relations. In September India offered a $100 million incentive package to begin extracting rock phosphate from Togo for export as fertilizer. Togo and Sri Lanka established diplomatic relations in 2012.

In January 2013 Togo agreed to contribute troops to the AU-led military force fighting Islamist militants in Mali. Reports in 2013 indicated that Togo had increasingly become a route for the transshipment of illegal ivory, rhino horns, and animal skins. For instance, in July 2013, officials in Hong Kong intercepted more than two tons of illicit elephant tusks worth an estimated $2.5 million.

Current issues. Faure Gnassingbé's election in April 2005 (which the opposition and international observers described as fraudulent) triggered a new wave of violence and the flight of more than 30,000 people to neighboring countries. The UN reported that more than 500 people were killed in post-election violence, while property damage was estimated at $7 million. Turmoil continued throughout the summer, despite Gnassingbé's pledge to support new legislative elections if reconciliation could be achieved with the opposition. Gnassingbé undertook a range of actions to mollify the opposition, including the November 2005 release of 460 political prisoners.

The EU provided $18.7 million to support legislative balloting in 2007, while France pledged an additional $4.1 million. The elections were initially set for June but were postponed several times because of delays in voter registration and cost overruns. Foreign observers certified the elections on October 14 as free and fair, but the opposition challenged the balloting. On October 20 the constitutional court rejected the challenges and certified the results in which the RPT won a reduced majority. In November Gnassingbé met with exiled opposition leader Olympio in an unsuccessful effort to convince the UFC leader to have his party participate in the subsequent government. In April 2008 Gnassingbé launched a series of public meetings as part of a national truth and reconciliation process to heal lingering divisions.

On April 16, 2009, the president's half-brother Kpatcha GNASSINGBÉ and a number of military and civilian officials were arrested for planning a coup. Five people were killed in fighting between security forces and the rebels. Gnassingbé reshuffled several senior positions within the armed forces in response in an effort to shore up his support among the security forces. Kpatcha's supporters argued that his arrest was an effort by the president to remove a political rival ahead of the 2010 presidential election. In June Togo abolished the death penalty.

Gnassingbé was reelected president in balloting on March 4, 2010. Opposition parties challenged the results, but their complaints were dismissed by the Constitutional Court which affirmed the outcome on March 18. The RPT and the UFC subsequently formed a unity government in May, and Houngbo was reappointed prime minister. As a precondition for UFC involvement in the new government, the RPT agreed to support redrawing legislative districts and a new census. Floods in October left 21 dead and more than 80,000 displaced in the East and South of the country. Meanwhile a new 100-megawatt power plant that was funded by foreign donors opened in October and was expected to meet Togo's energy needs and allow the country to export electricity to neighboring states.

In March 2011, demonstrations against a new law restricting public protests resulted in 53 arrests and more than 50 injuries after security forces intervened. Protestors denounced the new measure, which instituted mandatory prison sentences for those involved in public protests that resulted in violence or property damage and that required government permission for demonstrations. On June 16, Gnassingbé replaced Health Minister Komlan Mally with Charles Condji AGBA after widespread strikes by health care workers over pay and working conditions. In September Kpatcha Gnassingbé and 32 others were sentenced to various prison terms for their role in the failed 2009 coup. In July Togo released the results of its first census in more than 29 years. The census revealed that the population had doubled since 1981.

Following widespread protests, Houngbo and the government resigned on July 18, 2012. Reports indicated Gnassingbé replaced the increasingly unpopular prime minister in an effort to reduce public discontent ahead of local and parliamentary elections, which were postponed until 2013.

Opposition groups decried legislation ahead of the 2013 Assembly elections, which expanded the Assembly from 81 to 91 seats as an effort by the ruling UNIR to increase its majority. Opposition groups also denounced the negotiations between the government and opposition groups, leading to the postponement of balloting from the original date of July 21 to July 25. In the polling, the UNIR won 62 seats, followed by the newly formed Let's Save Togo (*Collectif Sauvons le Togo*—CST) with 19, the Rainbow Alliance (*Coalition Arc-en-Ciel*—CAEC) with 6, and the UFC, 3. Opposition groups protested the results, alleging widespread fraud and voter intimidation. However the constitutional court confirmed the UNIR victory on August 12. Meanwhile opposition groups called for changes to the electoral law to transition to a system of proportional voting and the redrawing of districts as the opposition collectively received more votes than the UNIR in the balloting. The UNIR won 41.3 percent of the vote to the CST's 34.5 percent, the Rainbow Alliance's 11.2 percent, and 5.3 percent for the UFC.

POLITICAL PARTIES

Political parties were banned after the 1967 coup. Two years later, the official Rally of the Togolese People (RTP) was organized as the sole legitimate political party. However, in 1991, the RPT's 24-year-old monopoly was reversed, and opposition activities were coordinated by a Front of Associations for Renewal (*Front des Associations pour le Renouvellement*—FAR). In May the FAR was superseded by a Democratic Opposition Collective (*Collectif de l'Opposition Démocratique*—COD), which in turn gave way to the National Council for the Safeguard of Democracy (*Conseil National pour la Sauvegarde de la Démocratie*—CNSD) in late December. In July 1992 the CNSD was succeeded by a revived Democratic Opposition Collective (COD-2). In early 1993 the COD-2 appeared to split into two wings: a "moderate" faction aligned under the banner of the Patriotic Front (FP, below) and a "radical" component, the Union of Forces of Change (see UFC, below). (For more on political parties prior to 2002, please see the 2012 *Handbook.*)

In early 2002 a group of opposition parties formed The Front, which subsequently participated in the October launching of the Coalition of Democratic Forces (*Coalition des Forces Démocrates*—CFD) with other groups, including the Pan-African Patriotic Convergence and the UFC. The CFD sought to present a single candidate for the June 2003 election but ultimately boycotted that balloting due to perceived unwillingness on the part of the administration to permit full electoral participation by the opposition. Prior to the 2005 presidential election, six opposition parties agreed to support the candidacy of Bob-Akitani, including the UFC, the PDR, the **Action Committee for Renewal** (*Comité d'Action pour le Renouveau*—CAR), the **Democratic Convention of African People** (*Convention Démocratique des Peuples Africains*—CDPA), and the **Alliance of Democrats for Integrated Development** (*Alliance des Démocrates pour le Développement Intégré*—ADDI).

Ahead of presidential elections in March 2010, a new opposition coalition, the **Republican Front for Change in Power** (Front Républicain pour l'Alternance et le Changement—FRAC) was formed to support the candidacy of Jean-Pierre Fabré. The FRAC included the UFC, the ADDI, the **Socialist Renewal Pact** (*Pacte Socialiste pour le Renouveau*—PSR), the **Alliance** (*L'Alliance*), and **Sursaut Togo.**

In 2012 the **Union for the Republic** (*Union pour la République*—UNIR) was formed from the RPT as the main vehicle for Gnassingbé. Meanwhile opposition groups coalesced around two new coalitions, Let's Save Togo (*Collectif Sauvons le Togo*—CST) and the Rainbow Alliance (*Coalition Arc-en-Ciel*—CAEC).

Government Parties:

Union for the Republic (*Union pour la République*—UNIR). Initially formed as the **Rally of the Togolese People** (*Rassemblement du Peuple Togolais*—RPT), under President Eyadéma, the RPT was Togo's sole legal party until its constitutional mandate was abrogated by the National Conference in July 1991. In February 1994 the RPT captured 33 of the 57 seats decided in the first round of assembly balloting; however, the party subsequently fell short of an overall majority by winning only 2 second-round seats. The RPT's three victories in legislative by-election balloting in August 1996 left the party in control of 38 of 57 seats. It also claimed the vote of former interim prime minister Koffigoh and two former opposition legislators who held seats as independents. In November the RPT absorbed the **Union for Justice and Democracy** (*Union pour la Justice et la Démocratie*—UJD), a small grouping that controlled 2 assembly seats. At the RPT's congress on January 9–11, 1997, the party continued its recent swing back toward a hard-line posture and away from the proreform, youth movement that had characterized a 1994 congress. Evidencing the sea change were the appointments to the Central Committee of a number of old guard stalwarts. In November the party was bolstered by the addition of another minor party, the **Movement for Social Democracy and Tolerance.** The RPT captured 79 seats in the 1999 assembly balloting and 72 in 2002.

Following the death of President Eyadéma in February 2005, his son, Faure Gnassingbé, was elected RPT president. At the party's ninth congress in December 2006, Gnassingbé was reelected as RPT leader and Solitoki Esso was selected as secretary general. In the 2007 legislative elections the RPT secured 39.4 percent of the vote and 50 seats in the National Assembly.

Following the arrest of Kpatcha Gnassingbé after an alleged coup in April 2009, reports indicated divisions within the RPT along ethnic lines (Faure's mother was Ewe, from southern Togo, and Kpatcha's mother was Kabye, from the north). Nonetheless, president Gnassingbé was the RPT candidate in the 2010 balloting and easily won reelection with 60.9 percent of the vote. The RPT formed a new unity government in May.

At a RPT congress on April 14, 2012, the party voted to reconstitute itself as the Union for the Republic. Gnassingbé was elected party leader of the new formation. The UNIR won a supermajority in the 2013 Assembly balloting, granting it the ability to amend the constitution at will.

Leaders: Faure Essozimma GNASSINGBÉ (President of the Republic and the Party), Koffi SAMA (Former Prime Minister), Solitoki ESSO (Secretary General).

Opposition Parties:

Union of Forces of Change (*Union des Forces du Changement*—UFC). The UFC coalition is led by Gilchrist OLYMPIO, who has long been linked to the MTD (below). In July 1993 the Eyadéma government issued an arrest warrant that linked Olympio to an attack on the president's residence in March, and in early August, the UFC leader, who had been calling for a new electoral register, was disqualified from presidential polling for refusing to return to Togo for a medical checkup. Subsequently, the UFC spearheaded a successful boycott of the balloting by its (then) COD-2 partners; however its calls for a boycott of Assembly balloting in February 1994 were ignored. In December 1997 UFC Secretary General Jean-Pierre FABRÉ was arrested and briefly detained after he sought to investigate the alleged murder of opposition activists by government security forces.

Although officially declared the runner-up in June 1998 presidential balloting, Olympio, who had been blocked from entering Togo from his base in Ghana during the closing days of the campaign, claimed that he had received 59 percent of the vote, not the 34 percent with which he had been credited. Subsequently the UFC was at the forefront of the antigovernment actions that followed the polling, and in August UFC headquarters were attacked by unknown assailants. Although remaining critical of the French government's previous support of the Eyadéma regime, the UFC followed President Jacques Chirac's call for reconciliation and joined talks with the government in July 1999 along with the CAR and UTD.

The UFC helped form the antiregime CFD in 2002 but withdrew from the group in 2003. Olympio returned to contest the presidential election in 2003 but failed to meet the residency requirements. BOB-AKITANI ran as his proxy and placed second in the balloting. Bob-Akitani also finished second in the disputed April 2005 presidential poll. In September 2005 UFC member Gabriel Sassouvi DOSSEH-ANYROH was dismissed from the party after he accepted a cabinet post in the Gnassingbé government. The UFC subsequently declined to participate in the 2006 unity government, but party member Amah GNASSINGBÉ agreed to serve as a minister of state on a "personal basis," not as a representative of the party.

In the 2007 legislative elections, the UFC placed second with 37 percent of the vote and 27 seats. At the UFC's 2008 congress, Olympio was unanimously reelected president of the party and chosen as the UFC's 2010 presidential candidate. Jean-Pierre Fabré was reelected secretary general and Patrick Lawson was selected as first vice president. The UFC subsequently launched discussions with other opposition parties in an effort to rally them behind Olympio in the 2010 presidential balloting. Prior to the elections, Olympio was barred from campaigning by the electoral commission, reportedly for health reasons. Fabré became the UFC presidential candidate and the UFC formed the FRAC electoral coalition. Fabré placed second in the balloting but rejected the results. The UFC subsequently agreed to join the RPT-led government. Tensions between Fabré and Olympio over participation in the government prompted Fabré to withdraw from the UFC. Kokou AHOLOU was elected to replace Fabré as UFC general secretary on October 1. Also in October 2010 Fabré launched a new political party, the **National Alliance for Change** (*Alliance Nationale pour le Changement*—ANC). Several UFC ministers remained in the new government named in July 2012. The UFC unsuccessfully filed suit in 2013, challenging the results of the July Assembly balloting.

Leaders: Gilchrist OLYMPIO (Party President and 1998 presidential candidate), Kokou AHOLOU (Secretary General), Emmanuel BOB-AKITANI (2005 presidential candidate and Honorary President of the Party), Alexander AKAKPO (First Vice President).

Togolese Movement for Democracy (*Mouvement Togolais pour la Démocratie*—MTD). Prior to the legalization of political parties in April 1991, the MTD was a Paris-based organization. It disclaimed any responsibility for a series of bomb attacks in 1985 while charging that the Eyadéma regime had "unleashed a wave of repression" in their wake. In mid-1986 MTD Assistant Secretary General Paulin LOSSOU fled France in the face of a decision by authorities to expel him to Argentina for his "partisan struggle" against the Eyadéma regime. Several reported MTD members were imprisoned in 1986 for distributing anti-Eyadéma pamphlets, but all of their sentences were commuted by 1987.

The government accused the MTD of complicity in the September 1986 coup attempt, insisting that it planned to install Gilchrist Olympio, exiled son of the former chief executive, as president. Olympio, who was sentenced to death in absentia for his alleged role in the plot, described the charges as "preposterous," suggesting that internal dissent had generated the unrest. Olympio returned to Lomé on July 6, 1991, under an April 12 general amnesty, to participate in the National Conference. Although claiming no interest in avenging his father's death, Olympio described the existing regime as lacking "legitimacy." Subsequently, *Africa Confidential* cited his influence in Joseph Kokou Koffigoh's capture of the prime ministerial post.

In May 1992 Olympio was critically wounded in an assassination attempt that took the lives of four others, including MTD leader Eliot OHN. Following his return from rehabilitation in Europe, Olympio emerged as the opposition's most prominent spokesperson, and in early 1993 he reportedly suggested that ECOWAS establish a presence in Togo to counter the reemergence of pro-Eyadéma military factions as well as help facilitate the transitional process.

Leader: Gilchrist OLYMPIO (Party Leader).

Rainbow Alliance (*Coalition Arc-en-Ciel*—CAEC), The Rainbow Alliance was an opposition grouping formed in 2013 by the **Action Committee for Renewal** (*Comité d'Action pour le Renouveau*—CAR), the **Democratic Convention of African People** (*Convention Démocratique des Peuples Africains*—CDPA), and a number of small parties, including the **Union for Democracy and Solidarity–Togo** (*Union pour la Démocratie et la Solidarité–Togo*—UDS–Togo), the **Citizen Movement for Democracy and Development** (*Citoyen pour la Démocratie et le Développement*—MCD), and the **Democratic Pan-African Party** (*Parti Démocratique Panafricain*—PDP), whose presidential candidate, Bassabi KAGBARA, received less than 1 percent of the vote in the 2010 polling. The Alliance secured six seats in the 2013 Assembly balloting.

Leaders: Brigitte Kafui ADJAMAGBO-JOHNSON (2010 presidential candidate), Dodji APÉVON.

Action Committee for Renewal (*Comité d'Action pour le Renouveau*—CAR). The CAR was one of the leaders, along with the UTD, below, in the formation in October 1992 by "moderate" COD-2 parties of the Patriotic Front (*Front Patriotique*—FP), which sought to maintain links with the government despite the objection of other coalition partners. The FP boycotted presidential balloting in August 1993. However, dismissing calls from the more militant UFC for a second boycott, the FP split from its ally and participated in the February 1994 legislative balloting. The CAR captured 36 seats (2 of which were subsequently vacated); however, despite an earlier pledge, President Eyadéma refused to appoint Yawovi Agboyibo, the CAR's leader and presidential candidate, prime minister.

At a mid-March 1994 meeting, the FP, attempting to dispel rumors that dissension would render the coalition unable to assume a governing role, issued a communiqué demanding the right to form a cabinet. On March 26 the group agreed that the next prime minister would be a CAR member, and two days later it nominated Agboyibo as its choice for the post. Consequently, on April 22 the CAR denounced the appointment of the UTD's Edem Kodjo as prime minister as a "blatant and inadmissible violation" of the March agreement, called on Kodjo to "reconsider" his position, and declared that it would not participate in a UTD-led government, thereby effectively ending the Front's existence. Nevertheless, the following day Kodjo insisted that the FP was still viable and that he controlled a parliamentary majority (albeit a tenuous one in light of a Supreme Court ruling that had invalidated three FP electoral victories).

The CAR boycotted assembly by-election balloting in August 1996, thus conceding the loss of two more seats. Meanwhile, party officials complained that they had been the victim of a RPT-orchestrated "smear campaign." In October the party's legislative seat total dropped to 32 after a deputy defected to the RPT. (Earlier, two other CAR legislators had quit the party, switching their allegiances to the Eyadéma camp.)

The CAR reportedly organized a number of antigovernment demonstrations beginning in late 1996 and continuing through 1997. Furthermore, the group spearheaded concurrent legislative boycotts. In November 1997 Agboyibo, whom *Africa Confidential* described as seeming to "seek outright confrontation with the government," was attacked after attending a function at the U.S. embassy.

Following presidential elections in June 1998, Agboyibo reportedly asserted that the UFC's Olympio was the true top vote-getter. For his part, Agboyibo finished third in the balloting with 9 percent of the tally. The CAR joined the opposition boycott of the 1999 balloting. Agboyibo was found guilty of defamation charges in August 2001. Although a court of appeal nullified a six-month sentence against him in January 2002, he was held on additional conspiracy charges. In mid-March the president ordered his release for the "sake of national reconciliation." Agboyibo ran for the presidency in 2003 and placed third with 5.2 percent of the vote. In the 2005 presidential election, CAR supported the candidacy of Bob-Akitani. Agboyibo was appointed prime minister in September 2006, but resigned in November 2007, following legislative balloting in which the CAR received 8.2 percent of the vote and four seats in the National Assembly.

Agboyibo resigned as party president in October 2008 and was replaced by CAR Secretary General Dodji Apévon. Agboyibo was CAR's 2010 presidential candidate. He placed third in the balloting with 3 percent of the vote. In March 2011 Apévon began to participate in a series of regular meetings between President Gnassingbé and opposition leaders. Apévon called for the formation of a unified opposition bloc ahead of elections scheduled for October 2012. He was later instrumental in the creation of the Rainbow Alliance.

Leaders: Dodji APÉVON (President), Gahoun EGBOR (First Vice President), Yawovi AGBOYIBO (Former Prime Minister).

Democratic Convention of African People (*Convention Démocratique des Peuples Africains*—CDPA). In December 1989 CDPA members Godwin TETE and Kuevi AKUE were arrested for distributing antigovernment leaflets. Their sentencing in October 1990 led to violent protests, which in turn were followed by the government's decision to move toward a multiparty system. The CDPA was legalized in 1991.

In September 1992 the house of CDPA leader Nguessan Ouattara was bombed during a wave of political assassination attempts allegedly orchestrated by Eyadéma supporters. In 1993 the CDPA initiated the formation of the **Pan-African Social Democrats' Group** (*Groupe des Démocrates Sociaux Panafricains*—GDSP).

In August 1997 the CDPA's founder and secretary general, Léopold GNININVI, returned from a four-year, self-imposed exile, and in presidential elections in June 1998, he captured less than 1 percent of the vote.

The CDPA joined the boycott of the 2002 legislative elections and was one of the founding parties of both the CFD and The Front. In 2003 CDPA General Secretary Léopold Gnininvi registered to run in the presidential election, but he subsequently withdrew from the race. The CDPA joined the coalition that supported Bob-Akitani's candidacy in the 2005 presidential elections. The CDPA subsequently joined the unity governments in 2006 and 2007. In the 2007 legislative balloting, the CDPA placed fifth with 1.6 percent of the vote but no seats in the Assembly. The CDPA was part of the new government formed in 2008. However, opposition to participation in the coalition government led a number of members to publically quit the CDPA in 2008. Brigitte Kafui ADJAMAGBO-JOHNSON was the party's presidential candidate in the 2010 balloting and the nation's first woman presidential contender. She placed fifth with less than 1 percent of the vote.

Leaders: Nguessan OUATTARA, Léopold GNININVI (Secretary General and 1998 and 2003 presidential candidate), Brigitte Kafui ADJAMAGBO-JOHNSON (2010 presidential candidate), Emmanuel GU-KONU (First Secretary).

Let's Save Togo (*Collectif Sauvons le Togo*—CST). The CST was an opposition coalition formed in 2013 to contest that year's Assembly elections. The CST included: the **National Alliance for Change** (*Alliance Nationale pour le Changement*); the **Socialist Renewal Pact** (*Pacte Socialiste pour le Renouveau*—PSR); the **Alliance of Democrats for Integrated Development** (*Alliance des Démocrates pour le Développement Intégré*—ADDI), led by Nagbandja KAMPATIBE; the **Organization to Build a United Togo** (*Organisation pour Bâtir ans l'Uunion un Togo Solidaire*—OBUTS). led by former prime minister Agbéyomé KODJO, who secured less than 1 percent of the vote in the 2010 presidential balloting as the candidate for the coalition; and the **Workers' Party** (*Parti des Travailleurs*—PT), led by Claude AMENGAVI. The CST secured 19 seats in the 2013 Assembly balloting, becoming the largest opposition party in the legislature.

Leaders: Ata Messan Zeus AJAVON, Gérard ADJA.

National Alliance for Change (*Alliance Nationale pour le Changement*—ANC). The ANC was formed in October 2010 by Jean-Pierre FABRÉ and dissidents from the UFC. In November 2011 Fabré and eight other ANC members were removed from the legislature by the constitutional court, which ruled that they were ineligible to serve because they had been elected from the UFC. Fabré was arrested in March 2013, along with more than 30 others, following opposition demonstrations.

Leader: Jean-Pierre FABRÉ.

Socialist Renewal Pact (*Pacte Socialiste pour le Renouveau*—PSR). The PSR's 2003 presidential candidate placed fourth with 2.3 percent of the vote. The PSR was part of the six-party coalition that endorsed Bob-Akitani in the 2005 presidential polling. PSR leader Tchessa ABI broke with other opposition parties and joined the cabinet in June 2005. The PSR also participated in the 2006 unity government. The party did not gain any seats in the 2007 balloting and was not invited to join the 2008 government. The PSR joined the opposition coalition FRAC to support the UFC's Fabré in the 2010 presidential elections. The party sought to create a broad opposition front ahead of the October 2012 balloting.

Leader: Tchessa ABI (Party Leader).

Other Parties That Contested Recent Elections:

Pan-African Patriotic Convergence (*Convergence Patriotique Panafricaine*—CPP). The CPP was formed in August 1999 with the formal merger of the **Togolese Union for Democracy** (*Union Togolaise pour la Démocratie*—UTD); the **Party of Democrats for Unity** (*Parti des Démocrates pour l'Unité*—PDU); the **Democratic Union for Solidarity** (*Union Démocratique pour la Solidarité*—UDS); and the **African Party for Democracy** (*Parti Africain pour la Démocratie*—PAD).

On April 22, 1994, UTD leader and former secretary general of the Organization of African Unity, Edem Kodjo, was chosen by the president to head a new government. Kodjo subsequently led the negotiations to form the CPP (for more on the history of the UTD, please see the 2013 *Handbook*).

The CPP was among the main opposition groups that continued talks with the government in 2000 and 2001 and was subsequently active in the formation of the independent electoral commission and the CFD. CPP leader Kodjo was named prime minister in June 2005. He was replaced in September 2006 but was appointed minister of state in charge of the office of the presidency in the subsequent unity government. The CPP was given two other posts in the cabinet. In the 2007 balloting for the National Assembly, the CPP placed fourth with 1.9 percent of the voting, but no seats. At the CPP's 2009 congress, Kodjo initiated a reorganization of the party leadership. Kodjo also announced that he would soon retire from politics and not be a presidential candidate in 2010. In July, Kwesi AHOOMEY-ZUNU was appointed prime minister. The CPP failed to secure any seats in the 2013 Assembly balloting.

Leaders: Kwesi AHOOMEY-ZUNU (Prime Minister), Edem KODJO (President of the Party and Former Prime Minister), Jean-Lucien Savide TOVÉ (First Vice President), Cornelius AIDAM.

Other parties that remained active or participated in the 2007 balloting included the **Togolese Alliance for Democracy** (*Alliance Togolaise pour la Démocratie*—ATD), led by Adani Ifé ATAKPAMEVI, who was an independent presidential candidate in 1993; the centrist **Alliance of Democrats for the Republic** (*Alliance des Démocrates pour la République*—ADR), which contested successive legislative elections beginning in August 1996; and the **Party of Action for Democracy** (*Parti d'Action pour la Démocratie*—PAD), led by Francis EKOH; the **Party for Democracy and Renewal** (*Parti pour la Démocratie et le Renouvellement*—PDR), led by Zarifou AYEWA (who joined the cabinet in June 2005 and was appointed a minister of state in the 2006 unity cabinet, but not subsequent governments) and which received 1 percent of the vote in the 2007 legislative elections; the hard-line Marxist-Leninist **Pan-African Socialist Party** (*Parti Socialiste Panafricain*—PSPA), led by Francis AGBOBLI; the **National Front** (*Front National*—FN), led by Amela AMELA VI; the **Movement of Republican Centrists** (*Mouvement des Républicains Centristes*—MRC), led by Kabou Gssokoyo ABASS; the **Party for Renewal and Redemption**, whose leader, Nicholas LAWSON, won 1 percent of the vote in the 2005 presidential poll and less than 1 percent in the 2010 presidential balloting; and the **Party for Renewal and Social Progress** (*Parti pour le Renouveau et le Progrès Social*—PRPS), led by Agbessi MAWOU. In 2005, the **Initiative and Development Party** was formed by Adanu Kokou KPOTUI as the country's 63rd registered party.

Other newer parties include the **Union for Democracy and Solidarity–Togo** (*Union pour la Démocratie et la Solidarité–Togo*—UDS–Togo), led by Antoine FOLLY. Other new parties that contested the 2007 balloting but failed to secure seats were **The Nest** (*Le Nid*), **New Popular Dynamic** (*Nouvelle Dynamique Populaire*), and the **Regrouping of the Live Forces of Youth for Change** (*Regroupement des Forces Vives de la Jeunesse pour le Changement*). Among the parties formed since the 2007 balloting was **The Alliance** (*L'Alliance*), led by former National Assembly speaker and RPT official Dahuku PERE and a member of the 2010 opposition coalition, FRAC; **Sursaut Togo**, formed in 2010 by Kofi YAMGNANE; the **Action Bloc for Change**, formed in July 2011 by Thomas Kokou NSOUKPOÉ; and the **Mission for the Emergence of Togo in Memory of Eyadema** (METOME) was established by Badjo RAGOUTANTI-TIBA in April 2012.

For more information on the now-defunct **Coordination of Political Parties of the Constructive Opposition** (*Coordination des Partis de L'Opposition Constructive*—CPOC), see the 2008 *Handbook.* For information on the **Coordination of New Forces** (*Coordination des Forces Nouvelles*—CFN), see the 2010 *Handbook.*

For information on the **Rally for Support for Democracy and Development** (*Rassemblement pour le Soutien pour la Démocratie et le Développement*—RSDD), please see the 2012 *Handbook.*

LEGISLATURE

On July 16, 1991, the National Conference dissolved the existing National Assembly and subsequently transferred its powers to a High Council of the Republic (*Haut Conseil de la République*—HCR) for a transition period leading to multiparty elections. In early 1993 the HCR, already involved in a constitutional debate with the president over his efforts to reverse the prime minister's dismissal of two cabinet members, once again found itself in conflict with Eyadéma, who, in response to criticism of his dismissal and then reconfirmation of the prime minister, argued that the HCR's mandate had expired along with the transition period. Subsequently, after numerous postponements, Togo's first multiparty balloting took place over two rounds on February 6 and 20, 1994.

National Assembly (*Assemblée Nationale*). The National Assembly is composed of 91 members directly elected for five-year terms. In the most recent balloting on July 25, 2013, the Union for the Republic, 62; Let's Save Togo, 19; the Rainbow Alliance, 6; the Union of Forces of Change, 3; independents, 1.

President: Bonfoh ABBAS.

CABINET

[as of August 15, 2013]

Prime Minister	Kwesi Ahoomey-Zunu (CPP)
Ministers of State	
Primary and Secondary Education and Literacy	Solitoki Magnima Esso (RPT)
Foreign Affairs and Cooperation	Elliot Ohina (UFC)
Ministers	
Agriculture, Livestock, and Fisheries	Col. Ouro Koura Agadazi
Arts and Culture	Fiatuwo Kwadjo Sessenou
Civil Service and Administrative Reforms	Kokou Dzifa Adjeoda
Commerce and the Promotion of the Private Sector	Bernadette Léguézim-Balouki (RPT) [f]
Communication	Djimon Bro (UFC)
Defense	Faure Gnassingbé (RPT)
Development, Handicrafts, Youth and Youth Development	Victoire Sidemeho Tomegah-Togbé (RPT) [f]
Economic Affairs, Finance and Privatization	Adji Otheth Ayassor (RPT)
Environment and Forest Resources	Dédé Ahoéfa Ekoue (RPT) [f]
Government Spokesperson	Pascal Bodjona (RPT)
Health	Charles Condji Agba (RPT)
Higher Education and Research	Octave Nicoué Broohm (RPT)
Human Rights, Democracy, and Reconciliation	Doris Rita de Souza (UFC) [f]
Industry and Technical Innovation	François Agbéviadé Galley
Justice and Keeper of the Seals	Tchitchao Tchalim (RPT)
Labor, Employment and Social Security	Yacoubou Koumadjo Hamadou (RPT)
Office of the President, in Charge of Planning, Development and Territorial Management	Kokou Semondji
Post and Telecommunications	Cina Lawson (RPT) [f]
Public Works	Ninsao Gnofame (RPT)
Security and Civil Protection	Col. Damehane Yark (RPT)
Social Affairs and National Solidarity	Afi Ntifa Amenyo [f]
Sport and Leisure	Bakalawa Fofana (UFC)
Technical Education and Professional Training	Amadou Bouraïma Diabacaté (UFC)
Territorial Administration, Decentralization, Local Communities	Gilbert Bawara
Tourism	Padumhékou Tchao (RPT)
Transport	Dammipi Moupokou (RPT)
Urban Affairs and Housing	Komlan Nunyabu (UFC)
Water Resources, Sanitation, and Village Water Supplies	Bissoune Nabagou
Women	Patricia Dagban-Zonvide [f]
Ministers Delegate	
Minister of Agriculture, Livestock and Fisheries, in Charge of Rural Infrastructure	Godjigo Kolani (RPT)

[f] = female

INTERGOVERNMENTAL REPRESENTATION

Ambassador to the U.S.: Edawe Limbaye Kadanghe BARIKI.

U.S. Ambassador to Togo: Robert E. WHITEHEAD.

Permanent Representative to the UN: Menan KODJO.

IGO Memberships (Non-UN): AfDB, AU, ECOWAS, IOM, NAM, OIC, WTO.

TONGA

Kingdom of Tonga
Fakatu'i 'o Tonga

Political Status: Constitutional monarchy; independent within the Commonwealth since June 4, 1970.

Area: 289 sq. mi. (748 sq. km).

Population: 06,752 (2013E—UN); 106,322 (2013E—U.S. Census).

Major Urban Center (2005E): NUKU'ALOFA (39,300).

Official Languages: Tongan, English.

Monetary Unit: Pa'anga (official rate November 1, 2013: 1.83 pa'anga = $1US).

Head of State: King TUPOU VI; succeeded to the throne following the death of his father, King SIAOSI (GEORGE) TUPOU V, on March 18, 2012.

Crown Prince (*Heir to the Throne*): TUPOUTOU'A 'ULUKALALA (eldest son of the king).

Prime Minister: Lord TU'IVAKANO; appointed (upon the recommendation of the Legislative Assembly) by the king on December 21, 2010, to succeed Feleti SEVELE following the legislative elections of November 25.

THE COUNTRY

Located south of Samoa in the Pacific Ocean, Tonga (also known as the Friendly Islands) embraces some 200 islands that run north and south in two almost parallel chains. Only 45 of the islands are inhabited, the largest being Tongatapu, which is the seat of the capital and the residence of almost two-thirds of the country's population. Tongans (mainly Polynesian with a Melanesian mixture) constitute 98 percent

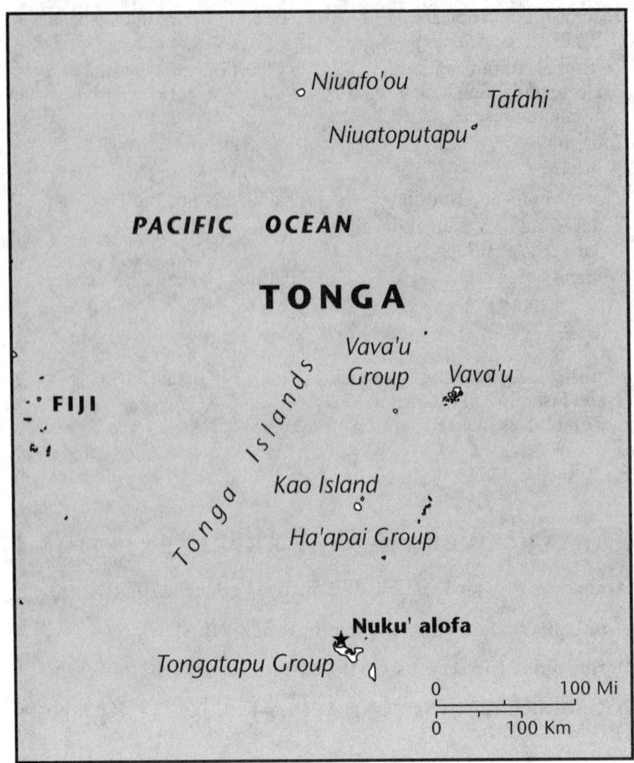

of the population, while Europeans and other Pacific islanders make up the remainder. The majority of the population is Christian, approximately 60 percent belonging to the Free Wesleyan Church of Tonga. The official female labor force participation rate is less than 14 percent, due in part to child-rearing demands in a society with an average of five children per family. There is one woman in the current cabinet; by virtue of that position, she also serves as an appointed member (the sole female) in the Legislative Assembly.

Primarily an agricultural country, Tonga produces coconuts and copra, bananas, vanilla, yams, taro, sweet potatoes, squash, pumpkins, and tropical fruits. Pigs and poultry are raised, while beef cattle (traditionally bred by Europeans) have assumed importance, thus reducing dependence on beef imports. Government-sponsored diversification efforts have focused on fishing and cultivation of specialty crops, including kava and mozuku (a type of edible seaweed). With the exception of some coconut-processing plants, no significant industries exist, although exploration for oil began recently. Donor aid and remittances from Tongans abroad (estimated at more than 50,000) provide "economic lifelines" in light of limited job opportunities in Tonga proper. Vast marine resources remain largely untapped in part due to the country's remoteness, while the tourism sector is still in its nascent stage.

The economy was negatively affected by prodemocracy riots in November 2006 that virtually destroyed the capital, Nuku'alofa. Subsequently declines in remittances and exports (associated with the global financial crisis) combined with a massive tsunami in September 2009 and a cyclone in February 2010 to dampen growth.

In October 2010 the World Bank pledged $50 million in grants over the next four years to promote recovery, stating that Tonga was at a "high risk of debt distress" and could not afford new borrowing. International institutions subsequently urged the government to assess incompetence (or perhaps even fraud) in state-owned enterprises and to combat money laundering. The reconstruction, financed by China, of the business section of Nuku'alofa contributed to GDP growth of about 2.9 percent in fiscal year 2010–2011, although that rate fell to 0.8 percent in fiscal year 2011–2012. The International Monetary Fund (IMF) in 2013 called upon the government to broaden the tax base to permit greater spending on infrastructure development, with the goal of encouraging foreign investment.

GOVERNMENT AND POLITICS

Political background. Christianized by European missionaries in the early 19th century, Tonga became a unified kingdom in 1845. British protection began in 1900 with the conclusion of a treaty of friendship and alliance whereby a British consul assumed control of the islands' financial and foreign affairs. New treaties with the United Kingdom in 1958 and 1968 gave Tonga full internal self-government in addition to limited control over its external relations, with full independence within the Commonwealth occurring on June 4, 1970.

In June 1989, the commoner (popularly elected) members of the Legislative Assembly for the first time forced rejection of a proposed government budget. Eight months later the country mounted its most intensely contested legislative election to date, with 55 candidates vying for the nine commoners' seats and 23 for the nine nobles' seats. While not organized as formal parties, two major groupings emerged: a prodemocracy movement headed by 'Akilisi POHIVA that criticized the islands' maldistribution of wealth and called for more responsible and efficient government; and a conservative group primarily concerned with economic development and the creation of new employment opportunities. Pohiva had been discharged from an education ministry post in 1985 after announcing in a radio broadcast that assemblymen had voted themselves 400 percent pay increases. Prior to the 1987 election (in which he successfully contested an assembly seat), Pohiva had launched a hard-hitting opposition newsletter, *Ko'e Kele'a,* and had instituted a suit for reinstatement to his former position. While the basic issue had become academic because of his assembly status, the Tongan Supreme Court handed down an unprecedented decision in mid-1988 awarding damages plus costs for unfair dismissal and a denial of free speech.

At the February 1990 poll, Pohiva's formation captured a majority of the commoner seats but remained a minority overall as the conservatives strengthened their control of the seats reserved for election by the nobles. Subsequently, the political ferment intensified, with the king of the predominantly Protestant country accusing both Pohiva and Tonga's Roman Catholic bishop of communist sympathies.

On August 21, 1991, the younger brother of King TAUFA'ANAU TUPOU IV, Prince Fatafehi TU'IPELEHAKE, stepped down after 26 years as prime minister, Deputy Prime Minister Baron VAEA being named his successor.

In November 1992 the prodemocracy movement organized a four-day public conference to indicate how the constitution could be amended to provide for greater popular participation in the political process. However the government declined to participate in the conference, prevented foreign invitees from entering the country to attend its sessions, and refused to broadcast news of the event on the grounds that it was not officially sponsored. Nonetheless, the movement appeared to grow, as evidenced by its capture of six of nine popularly elected seats in the 1993 legislative balloting and formation of the Tonga Democratic Party (TDP) under the auspices of the Friendly Islands Human Rights and Democracy Movement (FIHRDM, see under Democratic Party of the Friendly Islands [DPFI] in Political Parties, below) in August 1994. Prodemocracy candidates retained a majority of commoner seats at the January 1996 poll.

In September 1996, 'Akilisi Pohiva and two *Times of Tonga* editors were jailed for contempt after publication of a story that Pohiva intended to introduce a motion of impeachment against Justice Minister Tevita TUPOU for unauthorized attendance at the Atlanta Olympic games. The 30-day sentences yielded widespread protests by international media, and after 26 days the men were freed by the Supreme Court on procedural grounds. Although Pohiva and the Human Rights and Democracy Movement in Tonga (HRDMT, a successor to the TDP) expected to increase the representation of prodemocracy advocates in the March 1999 commoner balloting, only five were elected.

Crown Prince TUPOUTO'A was thought to have been the leading candidate to succeed Prime Minister Vaea upon the latter's retirement in early 2000, but he was passed over in favor of the king's youngest son, Prince 'ULUKALALA Lavaka Ata. The January 3, 2000, appointment was followed by a cabinet expansion and reorganization on January 25, 2001. In late September 2001 two cabinet ministers were forced to resign after being linked to the loss of millions in investments from the Tonga Trust Fund, into which income from the questionable sale of Tongan passports in 1983–1991 had been deposited.

In the legislative election of March 7, 2002, the HRDMT won seven of the nine popularly elected seats despite a controversy involving its recent publication in the *Times of Tonga* of a letter, possibly forged, that accused the king of holding $350 million in secret offshore accounts. On February 25 police had raided the HRDMT offices and briefly detained 'Akilisi Pohiva, who was among several politicians and journalists later charged with sedition and dealing in a forged document. Pohiva and two others were acquitted of the charges on May 19, 2003.

In the election of March 16–17, 2005, eight of the nine victorious commoners were HRDMT members. In an unprecedented move following the poll, King Taufa'ahau named two commoners to an expanded 16-member cabinet, one of whom, Feleti (Fred) SEVELE, became the first commoner to serve as prime minister.

Following his death on September 10, 2006, King Taufa'ahau was succeeded by his son, Crown Prince Tupouto'a, who assumed the title King SIAOSI (GEORGE) TUPOU V. However, the new king's coronation was postponed when, on November 16, 2006, a renewed prodemocracy demonstration quickly turned into a riot that destroyed some 80 percent of the capital's business district. By the end of the month, order had been restored with the help of 150 Australian and New Zealand troops and a pledge by the government of a new election in 2008, in which a majority of legislators would be selected by popular vote. However, Prime Minister Sevele announced in mid-2007 that the constitutional changes could not be enacted in time for the 2008 election but would be in place prior to another poll in 2010.

In the election of April 23–24, 2008, commoner representation under the FIHRDM banner was reduced to six seats, although Pohiva's endorsement by 11,290 voters was more than that of any other candidate. King Tupou V was finally coronated on August 1, 2008, having eagerly supported the diminution of his executive responsibilities as part of the country's democratization plans.

On April 15, 2010, a bill was passed that reduced the size of the Legislative Assembly to 26 members, of whom a majority of 17 would be popularly elected, while 9 would continue to be allocated to noble representatives. At the ensuing election of November 25, the FIHRDM-sponsored DPFI won 12 of the commoner seats, while independents won 5. Despite the anticipation that DPFI leader Pohiva would become the first commoner prime minister, the independents on December 21 joined the 9 nobles to elect Lord TU'IVAKANO as prime minister by a vote of 14–12 over Pohiva. The new cabinet inaugurated on January 14, 2011, included 2 members of the DPFI but not Pohiva (see DPFI under Political Parties for details). The cabinet was reshuffled on September 1.

King Tupou V died of natural causes on March 18, 2012. He was succeeded by his brother, former prime minister 'Ulukalala Lavaka Ata, who had been designated as heir to the throne in 2008. The new monarch assumed the title King TUPOU VI.

Constitution and government. Tonga is a hereditary constitutional monarchy whose constitution dates back to 1875. The executive branch has traditionally been headed by the Privy Council, including the king and a cabinet encompassing a prime minister, a deputy prime minister, other ministers, and the governors of Ha'apai and Vava'u. Prior to constitutional change in 2010, the unicameral Legislative Assembly included an equal number of elected hereditary nobles' and people's representatives, plus the cabinet members sitting ex officio. It is now composed of 17 people's representatives and 9 nobles (see Legislature, below, for details). The prime minister, appointed by the king from among the members of the assembly upon the recommendation of the assembly, may appoint up to 4 cabinet members from outside the legislature. Upon inauguration, those cabinet members become members of the assembly with full voting privileges except on no-confidence motions.

The judicial system is composed of a Supreme Court, magistrates' courts, and a Land Court. Ultimate judicial appeal is to the king, who appoints all judges. The 2010 constitutional revisions provided for an attorney general and a lord chancellor (appointed by the king) to assist in fostering legal transparency and independence of the judiciary.

Tonga is administratively divided into several groups of islands, the most important of which are the Tongatapu group, the Ha'apai group, and the Vava'u group. The governors of Ha'apai and Vava'u are appointed by the king on the advice of the prime minister.

Conditions regarding freedom of the press in Tonga are generally considered satisfactory, although several instances of government pressure on publishing enterprises have been reported recently.

Foreign relations. In 1900 Tonga and the United Kingdom signed a Treaty of Friendship and Protection, which provided for British control over financial and external affairs. Tonga became a member of the Commonwealth upon independence in 1970 and subsequently joined a number of UN-related organizations, including the Food and Agriculture Organization (FAO), the World Health Organization (WHO), and the United Nations Educational, Scientific, and Cultural Organization (UNESCO). It was admitted to the IMF in September 1985.

Relations with the United States were initially formalized in an 1888 treaty, which was largely revoked by Tongan authorities in 1920. A successor Treaty of Amity, Commerce, and Navigation was concluded during ceremonies marking the king's 70th birthday in July 1988. The most important component of the new accord was a provision guaranteeing transit of U.S. military vessels—including nuclear-armed craft—in the Tongan archipelago. The action was seen as underscoring a "tilt toward Washington" by a government that had failed to join a majority of its neighbors in ratifying the 1985 South Pacific Nuclear Free Zone Treaty (Treaty of Rarotonga).

Earlier, in October 1986, Tonga had served as the venue for the completion of negotiations that, after 25 months, yielded agreement on a tuna treaty between the United States and members of the South Pacific Forum (subsequently the Pacific Islands Forum) Fisheries Agency. The accord permitted access by the U.S. tuna fleet to nearly 8 million square miles of prime fishing grounds over a five-year period. Tonga became the final signatory to the pact in June 1989.

In late 1998 relations with Taiwan ended after the kingdom had switched recognition to the People's Republic of China, which had promised to extend both trade and aid. Tonga became the 188th member of the United Nations in September 1999.

In January 2008, a Nationality Act, approved in June 2007, came into effect. The act sanctioned dual citizenship for nonresident Tongans who had lost their native citizenship by being naturalized elsewhere.

In 2010 Prime Minister Sevele announced the deployment of 275 soldiers to Afghanistan under an agreement with Britain, which was to cover all first-year costs.

Tonga has been embroiled in a long-standing dispute with Fiji regarding sovereignty over the uninhabited Minerva Reefs, located some 900 miles north of New Zealand. The dispute intensified in mid-2011 when forces from the two countries reportedly squared off (without violence) near the reefs following the alleged destruction of a Tongan navigation beacon. Tensions with Fiji were also exacerbated by Tonga's apparent accommodation of Fijian oppositionists.

Current issues. Public opinion polls prior to the November 2010 legislative elections indicated that the major issues included crime, the role of women in government and society, and economic recovery. The success of the DPFI in the assembly poll was welcomed in all sectors as an important first step in the nation's democratization program. However, reformers were surprised by the failure of the DPFI leader 'Akilisi Pohiva to secure the prime ministership. Analysts attributed the elevation of Lord Tu'ivakano to the post to concern among independent legislators that a "party-based" government might prove divisive.

Lord Tu'ivakano, a former speaker and cabinet minister, pledged in early 2011 to focus on economic recovery, particularly in regard to agriculture and fishing and other private sector development. In March his administration finally lifted the state of emergency that had given the police broad authority since the 2006 riots. At midyear King Tupou initiated the "next stage" of reform by appointing an interim attorney general and interim lord chancellor (the latter being authorized to oversee the judiciary pending installation of a planned Judicial Appointments and Disciplinary Board).

Following the death of King Tupou V at the age of 63 in March 2012, domestic and international observers appeared unanimous in their praise for his role in Tonga's recent democratization process. Reformers called upon new King Tupou VI, described as deeply religious and conservative, to pursue further democratic changes, noting that the monarchy still retained broad appointment powers and the authority to veto legislation. The king's extensive political experience, including service as prime minister 2000–2006, was expected to be of use in addressing the nation's economic woes as well as ongoing political friction. One manifestation of the latter was the tabling (under the direction of opposition leader Pohiva) of a nonconfidence motion against the government in June. Although it initially appeared that the motion would succeed, a vote was delayed because of a lack of clarity in the new constitution on how to proceed. Subsequently a cabinet reorganization in early July and other developments served to rearrange the Assembly sufficiently to permit the government to survive by a margin of 13–11 when the vote was finally taken on October 8. Lawmakers then turned their attention to reform proposals aimed at, among other things, enhancing women's rights (only men are allowed to own land, and domestic violence has been a long-standing problem) and combating corruption.

POLITICAL PARTIES

Traditionally there were no political parties in Tonga, the initial equivalent of such a formation (see under DPFI, below) being an outgrowth of the Pro-Democracy Movement that sponsored the conference on democracy in November 1992.

Legislative Parties:

Democratic Party of the Friendly Islands (DPFI). The DPFI was launched prior to the November 2010 election by the Friendly Islands Human Rights and Democracy Movement (FIHRDM), which had been styled the Human Rights and Democracy Movement in Tonga (HRDMT) from 1998 to 2005. Earlier, the HRDMT was known as the People's Party (PP), which had initially been launched in August 1994 as the Tonga Democratic Party (TDP) by opposition MP 'Akilisi Pohiva.

Supporters of the HRDMT captured five of the nine commoner seats in the March 1999 balloting, disappointing prodemocracy activists, who had hoped to capture at least seven (and possibly all nine) and thereby generate momentum for the petition to the king to make all assembly seats subject to election by universal suffrage. Following the election, Pohiva argued that some voters had been swayed by progovernment television broadcasts and by misinformation concerning plans for land distribution in a "fully democratic" Tonga. In August 2001 the government turned down the group's application for registration as an incorporated society.

In the March 2002 legislative election, the HRDMT won seven seats. Subsequently, Pohiva was one of several persons charged with publication of a letter that accused the king of secreting some $350 million in offshore bank accounts; verdicts of acquittal were issued in May 2003. However, Pohiva was among those temporarily detained in early 2007 for perceived involvement in the riot of the preceding November.

Following constitutional revision to provide commoners with a majority of legislative seats, the DPFI won 12 of the 17 commoner seats in the November 2010 assembly poll. Although Pohiva's supporters expected that he would consequently become prime minister, the five independent legislators voted with the nobles to deny him the post. Pohiva initially indicated that he would accept the health portfolio in the cabinet proposed by the new prime minister, Lord Tu'ivakana, but Pohiva ultimately rejected the post, arguing that the DPFI should receive more than the two cabinet positions being offered and objecting to Lord Tu'ivakana's decision to offer posts to nonlegislators. On the other hand, 'Isileli PULU, previously described as Pohiva's "right-hand man," accepted the tourism portfolio (arguing it was best for reformers to "get started" in the new system), and another DPFI member, 'Uliti UATA, accepted the health portfolio. Pulu and Uata were among three ministers who resigned in late June 2012 in support of the no-confidence motion against the government (see Current issues, above).

Leaders: 'Akilisi POHIVA (General Secretary), Sitiveni HALAPUA (Deputy Leader).

Other Parties That Contested the 2010 Legislative Elections:

People's Democratic Party (PDP). The PDP was formed on April 15, 2005, by a group of HRDMT defectors with the announced goal of pursuing reform more aggressively than the parent group. On July 13 it became Tonga's first officially registered party. Although none of the PDP members had won a seat in the March 2005 legislative balloting, one of the party's founders, William Clive Edwards, won a by-election in 2006. After securing two seats in the 2008 assembly poll, the PDP was unsuccessful in 2010. However, Edwards was named to the January 2011 cabinet.

Leaders: Sione Teisina FUKO (President), William Clive EDWARDS (Minister of Justice), Semisi TAPUELUELU (Secretary).

Sustainable Development of the Land Party (*Paati Langafonua Tu'uola*—PLT). The PLT, calling for a moderate approach to political reform, was launched in August 2007 to recruit candidates for the Legislative Assembly, two of whom were elected in 2008. The party won no seats in 2010.

Leaders: Sione FONUA (President), Kamipeli TOFA (Secretary).

Tongan Democratic Labor Party (TDLP). The TDLP was organized by members of the Public Servants Association (PSA) who objected to a proposed amendment to Tonga's Public Service Act that would require government employees to resign before registering as electoral candidates. The TDLP ran a distant fourth with a 0.44 percent vote share in the 2010 assembly poll.

Leader: Mele AMANAKI (PSA General Secretary).

LEGISLATURE

Prior to the 2010 constitutional revision, the unicameral **Legislative Assembly** (*Fale Alea*) consisted, apart from the speaker, of nine nobles selected by the hereditary nobles of Tonga, nine people's representatives (commoners) elected by universal suffrage in single-round plurality voting, and the Privy Council, encompassing the king and his ministers. Under the 2010 changes, the number of people's representatives was increased to 17. The king appoints the speaker (upon the recommendation of the assembly) from among the nobles in the legislature. Any members of the cabinet (currently two) who are not elected legislators become members of the assembly upon their inauguration to the cabinet. They may vote on all matters except confidence motions. The king can dissolve the assembly and call for new elections at any time. No-confidence motions cannot be entertained in the assembly until 18 months have passed since the last election. In the most recent election of November 25, 2010 (prior to which the legislative term of office had been increased from three to four years), the Democratic Party of the Friendly Islands won 12 of the commoner seats and independents, 5. The next election was due by November 2014.

Speaker: Lord FAKAFANUA.

CABINET

[as of September 1, 2013]

Prime Minister	Lord Tu'ivakano
Deputy Prime Minister	Samiu Kuita Vaipulu
Ministers	
Agriculture, Food, Fisheries, and Forestry	Sione Sangster Saulala
Commerce, Tourism, and Labor	Viliami Uasike Latu
Defense	Lord Tu'ivakano
Education and Training	'Ana Maui Taufeulungaki [f]
Finance and National Planning	Lisiate 'Aloveita 'Akolo
Foreign Affairs and Trade	Lord Tu'ivakano
Health	Rev. Lord Tu'i'afitu
Information and Communications	Lord Tu'ivakano
Infrastructure	Samiu Kuita Vaipulu
Internal Affairs	Lord Vaea
Justice	William Clive Edwards
Lands, Environment, Climate Change, and Natural Resources	Lord Ma'afu
Police, Prisons, and Fire Services	Siosfia Tu'utafaiva
Public Enterprises	Sosefo Fe'ao Vakata
Revenue Services	Sosefo Fe'aomoeata Vakata
Attorney General	Neil Adsett
Lord Chancellor (Interim)	Albert Harison Waalkans
Governor of Ha'apai	Lord Havea Tu'iha'angana
Governor of Vava'u	Lord Fulivai

[f] = female

INTERGOVERNMENTAL REPRESENTATION

Ambassador to the U.S. and Permanent Representative to the UN: Mahe 'Uli'uli Sandhurst TUPOUNIUA.

U.S. Ambassador to Tonga: Frankie A. REED (resident in Fiji).

IGO Memberships (Non-UN): ADB, CWTH, PIF, WTO.

TRINIDAD AND TOBAGO

Republic of Trinidad and Tobago

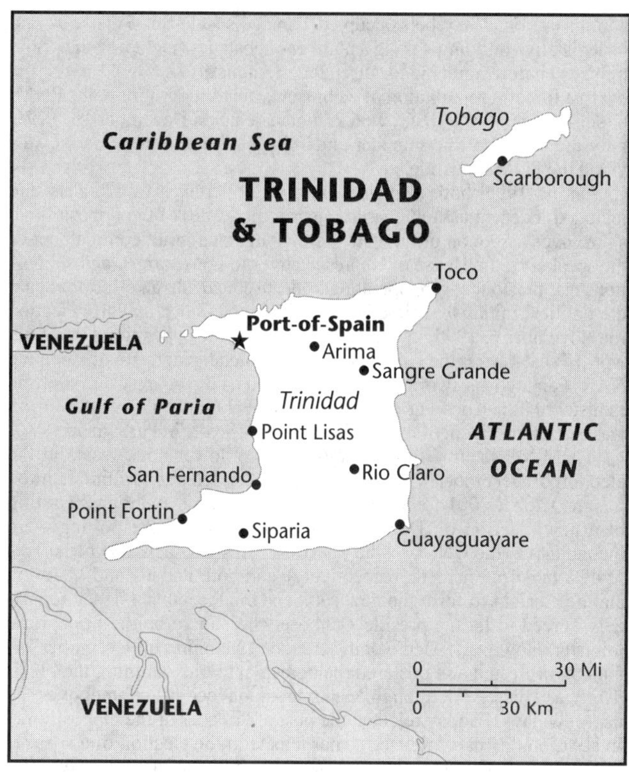

Political Status: Independent member of the Commonwealth since August 31, 1962; republican constitution adopted August 1, 1976.

Area: 1,980 sq. mi. (5,128 sq. km), of which Trinidad encompasses 1,864 sq. mi. (4,828 sq. km) and Tobago 116 sq. mi. (300 sq. km).

Population: 1,368,534 (2012E—UN); 1,225,225 (2013E—U.S. Census).

Major Urban Center (2011E): PORT-OF-SPAIN (66,000).

Official Language: English. On September 1, 2005, the government announced that Spanish would be adopted as an official language by 2020 to permit Trinidadians to compete more effectively in regional markets.

Monetary Unit: Trinidadian Dollar (market rate November 1, 2013: 6.42 dollars = $1US).

President: Anthony Thomas Aquinas CARMONA; elected by Parliament to a five-year term on February 15, 2013, and inaugurated on March 18, succeeding Dr. George Maxwell (Max) RICHARDS.

Prime Minister: Kamla PERSAD-BISSESSAR (United National Congress); appointed by the president and inaugurated on May 26, 2010, following general election on May 24, succeeding Patrick Augustus Mervyn MANNING (People's National Movement).

THE COUNTRY

The English-speaking state of Trinidad and Tobago, a pair of scenic tropical islands off the northern coast of South America, forms the southern extremity of the island chain known as the Lesser Antilles. Trinidad is the larger and more highly developed of the two islands, accounting for nearly 95 percent of the country's area and population and by far the greater part of its national wealth. Approximately 43 percent of the population are descendants of African slaves, while another 40 percent are descendants of East Indian indentured laborers brought in during the 19th century. Most of the former are presently concentrated in urban areas, while most of the latter are active as independent farmers. People of mixed ancestry, together with a few Europeans and Chinese, make up the rest of Trinidad's inhabitants, while Tobago's population is largely of African extraction. Roman Catholicism predominates, but Hinduism, Protestant Christianity, and Islam are also practiced.

The economy depends heavily on refined petroleum and related products derived from both domestically extracted and imported crude oil. Although domestic reserves were thought to be approaching exhaustion in the late 1960s, natural gas and oil deposits subsequently discovered off Trinidad's southeast coast gave new impetus to the refining and petrochemical industries, which now account for more than 90 percent of export earnings. Tourism is of growing importance, while agriculture plays a relatively minor role in the islands' economy. In late 2007 the government closed down its long-standing, but increasingly unprofitable, sugar industry in favor of a more balanced agricultural sector geared to domestic consumption.

Starting in 1973, soaring oil prices produced rapid growth, pushing per capita income by the early 1980s to about $7,000, the third highest in the Western Hemisphere. Between 1982 and mid-1990, on the other hand, real GDP declined by 30 percent, largely because of falling prices and markets for oil. While marginal recovery was registered from 1991 to 1998, it ultimately declined to 2.7 percent by 2002. Spurred by sales of recently discovered natural gas, growth averaged 9.3 percent per year in 2003–2007 but saw a sharp recession by 4.4 percent in 2009 with the global financial crisis. The economy was slow to recover, averaging a 0.66 percent annual decline over the next three years. The International Monetary Fund (IMF) expected GDP growth of 2 percent in 2013, reflecting the development of nonenergy sectors. Unemployment was low at 5.5 percent and inflation, 5.6 percent.

GOVERNMENT AND POLITICS

Political background. Discovered by Columbus and ruled by Spain for varying periods, Trinidad and Tobago became British possessions during the Napoleonic wars and merged in 1888 to form a single Crown Colony. Political and social consciousness developed rapidly during the 1930s, when the trade union movement and socialism began to emerge as major influences. The People's National Movement (PNM), the country's first solidly based political party, was founded in 1956 by Dr. Eric WILLIAMS and controlled the government without interruption for the next 30 years. Following participation in the short-lived, British-sponsored Federation of the West Indies from 1958 to 1962, Trinidad and Tobago was granted full independence within the Commonwealth on August 31, 1962.

After an initial period of tranquility, "black power" demonstrations broke out, resulting in the declaration of a state of emergency in April 1970 and later to an attempted coup by elements of the military. Subsequent political instability included a fresh wave of labor unrest that triggered a state of emergency in October 1971.

In October 1973, Prime Minister Williams announced his intention to retire from politics, but he reversed himself two months later, ostensibly at the request of his party, until steps had been taken to implement a republican constitution. In the legislative election of September 13, 1976, the PNM won 24 of the 36 House seats. Williams died unexpectedly on March 29, 1981, and was succeeded as prime minister and party leader by George M. CHAMBERS, who led the PNM to a 26–10 victory in parliamentary balloting on November 9.

Severe economic decline and the formation for the first time of a solid coalition of opposition groups—the National Alliance for Reconstruction (NAR)—led to reversal in 1986 of the PNM's theretofore uninterrupted control of the government, with the NAR winning 33 of 36 House seats in balloting on December 15, and Arthur N. R. ROBINSON succeeding Chambers as prime minister. The Robinson government proved no more successful in coping with fiscal adversity than its predecessor. In April 1989 a group of dissidents under the leadership of Basdeo PANDAY, who had been expelled from the NAR seven months earlier, organized the United National Congress (UNC), which secured a stunning by-election victory over both the NAR and PNM on May 1. An attempted coup by members of a militant, Black Muslim sect, the *Jamaat-al-Muslimeen,* on July 27, 1990, further embarrassed the administration. The rebels occupied Trinidad's state-run TV station and its legislative building, taking a number of hostages (including the prime minister) before agreeing to surrender on August 1.

In a forceful repudiation of Robinson's austerity program, the PNM, under Patrick MANNING, won 21 house seats on December 16, 1991; only the ousted prime minister and Tobago's other representative survived the PNM landslide.

During 1995, both leading parties were overtaken by scandals that included indecent assault charges against the leader of the opposition, a storm over demotion of the PNM foreign minister, brief confinement of the speaker of the House of Representatives to house arrest, and suggestions that the police were operating a "death squad." In an effort to regain the political initiative, Prime Minister Manning called an early election for November 6, 1995, in which the PNM and the opposition UNC both won 17 seats. After the UNC formed a "partnership agreement" with the NAR, Panday was sworn on November 9 in as the country's first prime minister of Indian descent. Subsequently, on February 14, 1997, Robinson was elected president of the republic in a 46–18 vote in Parliament.

The UNC secured a slim majority of 19 lower house seats in the election of December 11, 2000. However, the defection of three ministers in October 2001 forced a premature dissolution and the scheduling of a new election on December 10. The results of the polling were inconclusive (the UNC and the PNM won 18 seats each, on vote shares of 49.9 and 46.5 percent, respectively), and both Panday and Manning claimed a right to form the new cabinet. On December 17 they reportedly agreed to let the president choose who should be the next prime minister. However, when Robinson named Manning on December 24, Panday protested and declared the agreement void, claiming the president was "biased." Although Manning announced his cabinet over the next few days, Panday rejected the post of "Leader of the Opposition." In addition, his party refused to participate in the election of a speaker of the House of Representatives, which could not therefore formally convene, forcing an extended political stalemate.

On March 14, 2002, President Robinson requested that his term (expiring on March 18) be extended temporarily "in national interest," as Parliament remained unable to elect a successor. Despite Panday's protests, Manning approved the extension. On April 7, 2002, Robinson, on the advice of Manning, suspended the Parliament following yet another failed attempt to convene the House on April 5. Manning's subsequent attempt to convene the house in August also failed.

In a new election on October 7, 2002, the PNM secured a majority of 20 house seats and Prime Minister Manning was reappointed two days later. He was reelected to a third term on November 7, 2007, when the PNM gained 26 house seats by defeating a UNC-led party alliance. Manning called for a premature election on May 24, 2010, which the People's Partnership coalition, led by the UNC's new leader, Kamla PERSAD-BISSESSAR, won 29–12. There was speculation that Prime Minister Manning called for a snap election because he hoped to block the formation of precisely the opposition alliance (see PP, below) that led to his party's defeat. However the global recession, several local financial scandals, and a soaring crime rate led voters to favor the UNC.

Accusations of unethical and illegal behavior of government ministers led Prime Minister Persad-Bissessar to reshuffle the cabinet in June 2011, and she again made adjustments in June 2012.

Upon the expiration of President Max RICHARD's term, Parliament elected UNC nominee Anthony CARMONA on February 15, 2013. He was inaugurated on March 18. In September, Prime Minister Persad-Bissessar conducted a cabinet reshuffle—the third in as many years (see Current issues, below).

Constitution and government. Under the 1976 constitution, Trinidad and Tobago became a republic, with a president (elected by a majority of both houses of Parliament) replacing the former governor general. The functions of the head of state remain limited, executive authority being exercised by a prime minister and cabinet appointed from among the members of the legislature. Parliament consists of an appointed Senate, a majority of whose members are proposed by the prime minister, and a House of Representatives elected by universal adult suffrage. The judicial system is headed by a Supreme Court, which consists of a High Court and a Court of Appeal, while district courts function at the local level. There is also an Industrial Court and a Tax Appeal Board, both serving as superior courts of record. Judges are appointed by the president on the advice of the prime minister. In a waning anomaly among former British dependencies, Trinidad retains the right of ultimate appeal to the Judicial Committee of the UK Privy Council. The provision is designed to afford litigants access to a completely disinterested final court.

Rural administration is carried out on the basis of 9 counties on Trinidad, which are subdivided into 29 electoral wards, plus 1 ward for all of Tobago. Four municipalities (Port-of-Spain, San Fernando, Arima, and Point Fortin) have elected mayors and city councils.

After three years of debate, the House of Representatives in September 1980 approved a bill establishing a 15-member House of Assembly for Tobago with primarily consultative responsibilities. In January 1987 Tobago was granted full internal self-government, its House being given control of revenue collection, economic planning, and provision of services. In November 1996, a constitutional amendment was passed that enhanced the constitutional status of Tobago by creating an Executive Council to oversee its day-to-day affairs.

Press freedom is constitutionally guaranteed. Although there is legislation in place protecting freedom of information, the government has attracted criticism for trying to limit the categories of public information addressed by law. Reporters Without Borders ranked it 44th of 179 countries on the 2013 Press Freedom Index.

Foreign relations. In 1967, Trinidad and Tobago, which had joined the United Nations at independence, became the first Commonwealth country to be admitted to the Organization of American States (OAS). Its anticolonial but democratic and pro-Western foreign policy is oriented chiefly toward the Western Hemisphere and includes active participation in such regional organizations as the Caribbean Community and Common Market (Caricom). Since 1983, however, a number of disputes with fellow Caricom members over trade restrictions have tended to hinder regional cooperation. Trinidad and Tobago's objections to the U.S.-led invasion of Grenada in October 1983 also cooled relations with a number of Eastern Caribbean states, most notably Barbados, and strained traditionally cordial relations with the United States, with Prime Minister Chambers criticizing what he perceived as U.S. president Ronald Reagan's attempt to "militarize" the region. However, efforts have since been initiated to lower the government's profile both on trade and foreign policy issues. Relations with the People's Republic of China and the Soviet Union were established in 1974, while a broad trade agreement signed in August 1984 with China was hailed as a "major leap forward in China's relations with the Commonwealth Caribbean."

In August 1997 a long-simmering dispute erupted with Venezuela over oil drilling in the straits separating the two countries, with altercations between Trinidadian riggers and Venezuelan patrol boats becoming increasingly common. Subsequently, the government signaled its intention to supply gas to nearby islands, such as Martinique and Guadalupe, via undersea pipelines, and in 2003 a feasibility study was commissioned for an 1,800-mile line to Florida.

Meanwhile, friction arose with Barbados over a 1990 treaty between Trinidad and Venezuela, which was accused of awarding a large part of Barbados's and Guyana's maritime territory to Venezuela and Trinidad and Tobago. The dispute led to a ruling by the Permanent Court of Arbitration in The Hague in April 2006 that established a median line halfway between the exclusive economic zones of Barbados and Trinidad but allowed Barbados to exploit hydrocarbon resources up to 150 nautical miles beyond the line. Meanwhile the court stated that it lacked jurisdiction to rule on the right of Barbadian fishermen to operate in Trinidadian waters.

Trinidad and Tobago entered negotiations with Venezuela in January 2012 to share oil and natural gas deposits located on the maritime border between the two countries. Initial discussions on how to manage the resources were suspended in 2007, and another attempt ended inconclusively in 2010. Meanwhile, when the Trinidadian government awarded a $5.7 billion contract to a Saudi company to construct a petrochemical plant, several American bidders claiming they were unfairly bypassed, straining relations with the United States. In April 2012 maritime boundary talks with Grenada began because Trinidad launched a bidding round for offshore blocks that fall along the border between the two countries.

In recent years the Trinidad-based Caribbean Court of Justice (CCJ) has gained traction. Created in 2001 by the Organization of Eastern Caribbean States (OECS) as a Caribbean alternative to the London-based Privy Council, the CCJ is currently only used by three OECS states. Parliament did not approve a 2006 constitutional amendment to adopt the CCJ. The Persad-Bissessar administration maintains that, in light of the country's high crime rate, which more than doubled between 2001 and 2011, and the struggling economy, full membership with the CCJ is not a priority.

At a Caricom summit in February 2013, Prime Minister Persad-Bissessar proposed the creation of a regional security center based in Trinidad.

Current issues. Trinidad and Tobago has experienced an alarming increase in violent crime over the previous decade; 2011 saw 354 murders compared with just 151 in 2001. Confronted with the exceptionally high crime rate, Prime Minister Persad-Bissessar imposed a state of emergency from August 21 through December 5, the first use of the measure since an attempted coup in 1990.

Fissures within the People's Partnership emerged in early 2012, as a leading figure from the COP defected to the UNC in March and the Movement for Social Justice (MSJ) left the coalition in June. In an effort to ease tensions, Prime Minister Persad-Bissessar reorganized the cabinet to include two new COP appointments.

The parliament elected President Anthony Carmona on February 15, 2013, and he assumed office in March.

For the third time since March 2012, the PNM filed a no-confidence motion against the government in May 2013. The opposition presented several e-mails purportedly from high-level officials that allegedly demonstrated attempts by the Persad-Bissessar administration to undermine the judiciary and the media. The administration denounced the documents as fabrications, and the motion failed.

In September Persad-Bissessar conducted another cabinet reshuffle, the third in as many years, reportedly to reinvigorate her administration.

POLITICAL PARTIES

Government Coalition:

People's Partnership (PP). The PP was formed prior to the May 2010 election as a grouping of the parties below.

Leader: Kamla PERSAD-BISSESSAR (Prime Minister).

United National Congress (UNC). The UNC was formally launched on April 30, 1989, by the members of Club '88 (see under NAR, below) who had been formally expelled from the NAR in October 1988 after having campaigned against Prime Minister Robinson's style of leadership. The new group drew much of its support from former ULF members opposed to Robinson's IMF-mandated austerity policies. The UNC defeated both the NAR and the PNM in a local council by-election on May 1, 1989, but, while holding six parliamentary seats to the PNM's three, did not seek appointment as the official opposition until September 1990.

Although the UNC was unable to secure a plurality of seats in the 1995 balloting (it and the PNM winning 17 each), Party Leader Basdeo Panday formed a government on the basis of a "partnership agreement" with the NAR. The UNC won 19 seats in the December 2000 poll.

Relations between Prime Minister Panday and Ramesh MAHARAJ, the attorney general and UNC deputy leader, had long been strained by seeming slights. In early October 2001, Panday dismissed his rebellious colleagues, who promptly entered into an "alliance" with the opposition PNM. Subsequently, Maharaj claimed that his faction controlled the UNC and would place candidates in all 36 constituencies in the forthcoming election. Although Panday briefly registered a new formation—the United National Party (UNP)—in case the courts allowed the Maharaj faction to use the UNC rubric, both the Elections and Boundaries Commission and the High Court ruled in November in favor of Panday, prompting the Maharaj faction to leave the party to form a group styled Team National Unity (TNU), which won only 2.5 percent of votes in the December 2001 poll. Maharaj subsequently returned to the UNC.

The early legislative poll of December 10, 2001, yielded a stalemate with the PNM; in the subsequent balloting of October 7, 2002, UNC representation dropped to 16.

Charges of corruption against Panday while heading the UNC administration led to his brief imprisonment in mid-2005, and in October he moved from the post of party leader to that of chair, albeit with no apparent loss of party control. His successor as party leader, Winston Dookeran, resigned in September 2006 to form a new party, the Congress of the People (COP) (below).

For the 2007 election, the UNC was restyled the United National Congress–Alliance (UNC-A) as the leading component of a coalition that included the NAR and the NDP (below).

In February 2009, Deputy Leader Jack WARNER and (then) Chief Whip Ramesh Maharaj threatened to leave the UNC if Panday did not endorse internal leadership elections. A month later, Maharaj was fired as chief whip by Panday, who had warned that he would not tolerate public dissent within the party.

In January 2010, Kamla Persad-Bissessar became leader of the opposition after defeating Panday as leader of the UNC in December 2009. In the May 2010 elections, Persad-Bissessar led the PP coalition, with the UNC as its core component, to victory over the PNM with 29 seats.

Fissures quickly emerged within the coalition, with tensions growing with the COP. Meanwhile internal fractions with the UNC saw the defection of three party figures in 2013, including former minister of security Jack WARNER, who resigned amid a fraud inquiry and subsequently formed the **Independent Liberal Party** (ILJ—below).

Leaders: Kamla PERSAD-BISSESSAR (Prime Minister and Party Leader), Suruj RAMBACHAN (Deputy Party Leader), Roodal MOONILAL.

Congress of the People (COP). The COP was launched on September 10, 2006, by former UNC party leader Winston Dookeran, who had been threatened with expulsion from the UNC on the basis of claims that he was maintaining a parallel political organization.

In March 2012 San Fernando Mayor Marlene COUDRAY defected from the COP to join the UNC, sparking outrage within the COP. Prime Minister Persad-Bissessar, in an effort to ease tensions, appointed two new COP cabinet members in June.

Leaders: Prakash RAMADHAR (Political Leader), Carolyn SEEPERSAD-BACHAN (Chair), Nirad TEWARIE (General Secretary).

Tobago Organization of the People (TOP). The TOP is the result of a split within the Democratic Action Congress in 2008. It was launched as a coalition member of the People's Partnership prior to the Tobago poll of January 19, 2009, in which it won four seats.

Leader: Ashworth JACK (Party Leader).

National Joint Action Committee (NJAC). The NJAC was organized in 1969 by Geddes GRANGER as a political extension of the black power movement. Granger played a leading role in the black power disturbances of 1970 and was under detention from October 1971 to June 1972 before changing his name to Makandal Daaga. The group contested elections in 1981, when it secured 3.3 percent of the popular vote, and in 1986, when it won 1.5 percent. Although a member of the PP, the NIAC elected none of its own members in May 2010 and has historically been more active in local politics.

Leaders: Makandal DAAGA (Political Leader), Aiyegoro OME (President).

Opposition Party:

People's National Movement (PNM). Organized in 1956 by historian-politician Eric Williams, the PNM was the first genuinely modern party in the country's history and owed much of its success to its early formation, its founder's gift for leadership, and its comparatively high degree of organization. Although its support is predominantly African, its progressive and internationalist programs have been distinguished by their emphasis on national unity irrespective of ethnic origin. Following Williams' death on March 29, 1981, George M. Chambers was elected party leader.

After three decades of uninterrupted rule, the PNM was forced into opposition in December 1986, when it won only 3 of 36 lower house seats, a loss attributed to the inability of the Chambers administration to halt steady economic decline since 1982. Following the defeat, Chambers resigned as party leader and retired from politics (he died on November 5, 1997). Subsequently, the party's youth movement succeeded over the "old guard" by the naming of 40-year-old Patrick

Manning, one of the three successful House candidates, as the PNM's political leader. Manning led the party comeback in December 1991, when it captured 21 legislative seats. In 1995 the PNM secured a vote share of 48.8 percent (an increase of 3.7 percent from 1991) but tied in seats with the UNC, which was able to form a ruling coalition with the NAR. The PNM won 16 seats in legislative polling in December 2000, and 8 seats in the Tobago House of Assembly polling in January 2001. The party increased its representation to 18 in the December 2001 legislative polling, but the result was a stalemate, since the UNC also won 18 seats. In new balloting on October 7, 2002, the PNM secured a majority of 20 seats. It increased its majority to 26 of an enlarged house of 41 members in November 2007, and retained its 8 Tobago Assembly seats in balloting on January 19, 2009.

Its lower-house representation dropped to 12 at the premature general election of May 24, 2010. Three days later, Manning resigned as PNM leader in favor of Keith Rowley. In May 2011 former prime minister Manning was dismissed from parliament after being found guilty of contempt of parliament by the parliament's Privileges Committee, after he made serious accusations about actions taken by Prime Minister Persad-Bissessar.

In May 2013 the PNM filed its third no-confidence motion against the Persad-Bissessar administration, presenting in Parliament e-mails that purportedly demonstrated attempts of government officials to undermine the judiciary (see Current issues, above). The accusations embroiled the government in controversy, with the administration in July threatening Rowley with a defamation lawsuit.

Leaders: Keith ROWLEY (Political Leader and Leader of the Opposition), Orville LONDON (Deputy Political Leader for Tobago), Franklin KHAN (Chair), Ashton FORD (General Secretary).

Independent Liberal Party (ILJ). The ILP was launched in July 2013 by former international football official Jack WARNER, who left the UNC in April after he was accused of embezzlement during his tenure at an international football organization. In a by-election for his vacated parliamentary seat, Warner won a decisive victory with 69 percent of the vote.

Leader: Jack WARNER.

Other Parties:

National Alliance for Reconstruction (NAR). The NAR was launched in 1984 as a coalition of the United Labour Front (ULF), the Democratic Action Congress (DAC), and the Tapia House Movement (THM); all had participated in the 1981 campaign as members of the Trinidad and Tobago National Alliance (TTNA). In September 1985 the Organization for National Reconstruction (ONR) joined the new formation, which reorganized as a unified party in February 1986. (For more on the history of the four parties that formed the NAR, see the 2011 edition of the *Handbook.*)

The NAR's success in coalescing behind former PNM associate (and one-time heir apparent) of Prime Minister Williams, Arthur N. R. Robinson, and his ability to attract support from diverse ethnic and labor groups were considered major factors in the group's stunning victory in the December 1986 balloting. However, by early 1988 the alliance had encountered severe internal stress, culminating in the expulsion of a number of ULF dissidents led by Basdeo Panday, who had formed an anti-Robinson intraparty formation known as Club '88 ("Club" being an acronym for Caucus for Love, Unity, and Brotherhood). In April 1989 the Club '88 group reorganized as a separate party, the United National Congress (UNC, above).

The NAR retained only two lower house seats from Tobago in the December 1991 poll. Robinson resigned as party leader, the former minister of works, Carson Charles was named his successor at the NAR annual convention on March 29, 1992. The party retained overwhelming control of the Tobago House of Assembly on December 7, 1992, winning 11 seats to 1 for the PNM.

NAR leader Charles was replaced by Selby WILSON in early 1993, and Charles left the party to form the National Development Party (NDP). Wilson resigned the leadership in August 1994 after having denounced a by-election alliance between the NDP and the NAR.

In the 1995 election, the NAR again failed to secure representation in Trinidad. However, by keeping its 2 Tobago seats it was able to enter into a ruling alliance with the UNC. The NAR retained 10 of its 11 seats in the Tobago House of Assembly on December 9, 1996, the lost seat going to an incumbent who had resigned from the NAR in November and campaigned as an independent.

In October 1999, the NAR National Council named former party chair Anthony SMART as interim leader after "vacating of the post" by Nizam MOHAMMED, who insisted he had been dismissed and was subsequently reinstated. The NAR won one seat in the 2000 legislative election and four seats in the January 2001 Tobago House of Assembly poll. The party won no House of Representatives seats in 2001, 2002, or 2007. Carson Charles was reelected party leader on October 23, 2006.

During 2006 the NAR joined with a number of smaller parties in a series of shifting alliances. On April 20 a merger with the **Movement for National Development** (MND) and **Democratic Party of Trinidad and Tobago** was announced, which, without reference to the MND but with the addition of the DNA (below), was subsequently styled the Democratic National Alliance. However, the DNA withdrew on June 9, while in July the NDP (above) joined the grouping, which was restyled the National Democratic Alliance. The alliance subsequently fell apart after the 2007 election.

Leader: Carson CHARLES (Political Leader).

Democratic Action Congress (DAC). The DAC was launched in early 2003 by former NAR faction leader Hochoy Charles. The move was considered significant since the original DAC had been a founding component of the NAR; however, the party captured only one seat in the 2005 Tobago election. The party contested the 2007 election but only obtained 1.8 percent of the vote share. Following the 2007 election, most of the party members supported a merger that led to the creation of the TOP (above). Charles resisted the merger, however, claiming that the DAC was still its own political entity.

Leader: Hochoy CHARLES.

Democratic National Assembly (DNA). The DNA, an outgrowth of a number of groups, including Dr. Kirk Meighoo's Committee for Transformation and Progress, was launched in March 2006 and participated briefly in the Democratic National Alliance led by the NAR.

Leader: Dr. Kirk MEIGHOO.

Movement for Social Justice (MSJ). The MSJ, founded in 2009, is closely aligned with the country's trade unions. It withdrew from the People's Partnership in June 2012.

Leader: David ABDULAH.

National Vision Party (NVP). The NVP was formed in early 1994 by Yasin Abu Bakr, leader of the unsuccessful 1990 coup by the *Jamaat-al-Muslimeen.* It contested the 2010 election as the **New National Vision**, winning a vote share of 0.27 percent.

Leader: Fuad Abu BAKR.

LEGISLATURE

The national **Parliament** is a bicameral body consisting of an appointed Senate and an elected House of Representatives; Tobago has a unicameral **House of Assembly.**

Senate. The upper chamber consists of 31 members appointed by the president for a maximum term of five years: 16 are named on the advice of the prime minister; 6 on the advice of the leader of the opposition; and 9 at the president's discretion from religious, economic, and social groups.

President: Timothy HAMEL-SMITH.

House of Representatives. The lower chamber currently has 41 members directly elected for five-year terms, subject to dissolution. In the election of May 24, 2010, the People's Partnership won 29 seats (the United National Congress, 21; the Congress of the People, 6; the Tobago Organization of the People, 2) and the People's National Movement, 12. Following a by-election on July 29, 2013, the People's Partnership representation was reduced to 28 seats, and the Independent Labor Party held 1 seat.

Speaker: Wade MARK.

Tobago House of Assembly. Tobago's legislature consists of 15 members, 12 directly elected and 3 named by the majority party; its term is four years. In the most recent balloting of January 19, 2009, the People's National Movement won 8 of the elective seats and the Tobago Organization of the People, 4.

Chief Secretary: Orville LONDON.

CABINET

[as of September 15, 2013]

Prime Minister	Kamla Persad-Bissessar (UNC) [f]
Ministers	
Arts and Culture	Lincoln Douglas (COP)
Attorney General	Anand Ramlogan (UNC)
Communication	Gerald Hadeed
Community Development	Winston Peters (UNC)
Education	Dr. Tim Gopeesingh (UNC)
Energy and Energy Affairs	Kevin C. Ramnarine (UNC)
Environment and Water Resources	Ganga Singh (COP)
Finance	Larry Howai (UNC)
Food Production	Devant Maharaj (COP)
Foreign Affairs	Winston Dookeran (COP)
Gender, Youth, and Child Development	Clifton De Couteau (UNC)
Health	Dr. Fuad Khan (UNC)
Housing and Environment	Dr. Roodal Moonilal (UNC)
Justice	Emmanuel George (UNC)
Labor and Small and Micro-Enterprise Development	Errol McLeod (MSJ)
Lands and Marine Affair	Jairam Seemungal (UNC)
Legal Affairs	Prakash Ramadhar (COP)
Local Government	Marlene Coudray (UNC) [f]
National Diversity and Social Integration	Rodger Samuel (COP)
National Security	Gary Griffith (ind.)
Peoples and Social Development	Dr. Glenn Ramadharsingh (UNC)
Planning, Economic and Social Restructuring	Bhoendradatt Tewarie (COP)
Public Administration	Carolyn Seepersad-Bachan (COP) [f]
Public Utilities	Nizam Baksh (UNC)
Science and Technology	Dr. Rupert Griffith (UNC)
Sport	Anil Roberts (COP)
Tertiary Education and Skills Training	Fazal Karim (UNC)
Tobago Development	Delmon Baker (TOP)
Tourism	Chandresh Sharma (UNC)
Trade, Industry, and Investment	Vasant Bharath (UNC)
Transport	Stephen Cadiz (UNC)
Works and Infrastructure	Surujrattan Rambachan (UNC)
Ministers of State	
Environment and Water Resources	Ramona Ramdial (UNC) [f]
Finance and Economy	Rudranath Indarsingh (UNC)
Gender, Youth, and Child Development	Rasiah Ahmed (UNC) [f]
National Diversity and Social Integration	Embau Moheni (NJAC)
Peoples and Social Development	Vernella Alleyne-Toppin (TOP) [f]
Works and Infrastructure	Stacy Roopnarine (UNC) [f]

[f] = female

INTERGOVERNMENTAL REPRESENTATION

Ambassador to the U.S.: Neil Nadesh PARSAN.

U.S. Ambassador to Trinidad and Tobago: Margaret B. DIOP (acting).

Permanent Representative to the UN: Rodney CHARLES.

IGO Memberships (Non-UN): Caricom, CWTH, IADB, ICC, IOM, NAM, OAS, WTO.

TUNISIA

Republic of Tunisia
al-Jumhuriyah al-Tunisiyah

Political Status: Independent state since 1956; republic proclaimed July 25, 1957; under one-party dominant, presidential regime; interim government formed following civil unrest that resulted in the ouster of the president on January 14, 2011.

Area: 63,170 sq. mi. (163,610 sq. km).

Population: 10,837,703 (2012E—UN); 10,835,873 (2013E—U.S. Census).

Major Urban Centers (2005E): TUNIS (734,000), Sfax (Safaqis, 269,000), Ariana (252,000), Ettadhamen (116,000).

Official Language: Arabic; French is widely spoken as a second language.

Monetary Unit: Tunisian Dinar (market rate November 1, 2013: 1.65 dinars = $1US).

Interim President: Moncef MARZOUKI, elected by the Constituent Assembly on December 12, 2011, following the interim presidency of Fouad MBAZAÂ, named by the Constitutional Council on January 15, 2011, following a one-day interim presidency by Prime Minister Mohamed GHANNOUCHI, who succeeded President Gen. Zine El-Abidine BEN ALI (Democratic Constitutional Assembly), after the president fled the country on January 14 in the wake of massive antigovernment protests.

Interim Prime Minister: Ali LAARAYEDH (*Nahda*), appointed by interim president Moncef Marzouki on February 22, 2013, to succeed Hamadi JEBALI (*Nahda*).

THE COUNTRY

Situated midway along the North African littoral between Algeria and Libya, Tunisia looks north and eastward into the Mediterranean and southward toward the Sahara Desert. Along with Algeria and Morocco, it forms the Berber-influenced part of North Africa known as the "Maghreb" (West) to distinguish it from other Middle Eastern countries, which are sometimes referred to as the "Mashreq" (East). Tunisia's terrain, well wooded and fertile in the north, gradually flattens into a coastal plain adapted to stock-raising and olive culture, and becomes semiarid in the south. The population is almost exclusively of Arab and Berber stock, Arabic in speech (save for a small Berber-speaking minority), and Sunni Muslim in religion. Although most members of the former French community departed after Tunisia gained independence in 1956, French continues as a second language, and small French, Italian, Jewish, and Maltese minorities remain. Women, who constitute approximately 31 percent of the paid labor force, were the focus of relatively progressive national policies on equal rights, educational access for girls, and family planning. However women have faced increasing repression since the 2011 Jasmine Revolution.

About one-quarter of the working population is engaged in agriculture, which is responsible for about 13 percent of GNP; the main products are wheat, barley, olive oil, wine, and fruits. Petroleum has been a leading export, although there is also mining of phosphates, iron ore, lead, and zinc. Industry has expanded to more than 30 percent of GDP, with steel, textiles, and chemicals firmly established. Most development is concentrated in coastal areas, where tourism is the largest source of income; however, poverty is widespread in the subsistence farming and mining towns of the south (please see the 2013 *Handbook* for more information on the economy from the 1970s–2000s).

Strong performance in the energy sector in particular, as well as in agriculture, manufacturing, and services, contributed to average annual growth of 6 percent in 2005–2007, though unemployment remained at about 14 percent. The International Monetary Fund (IMF) commended

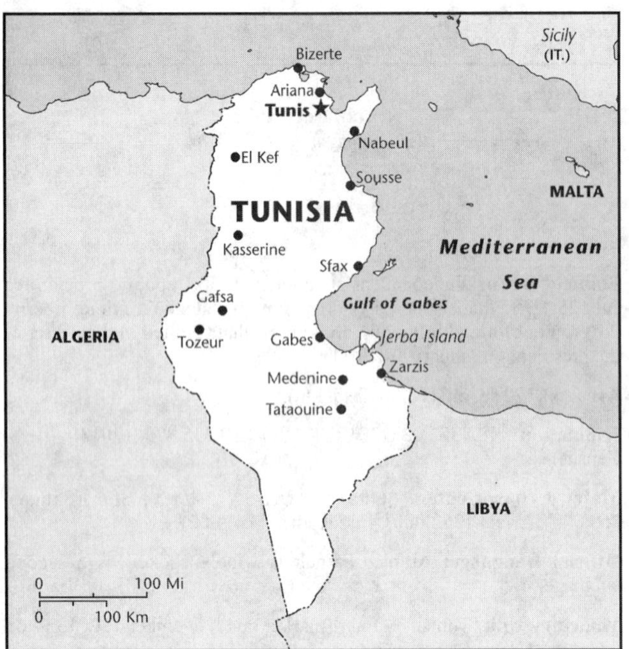

Tunisia for adopting banking reform measures and praised the country's efforts toward liberalizing trade and combating money laundering and the financing of terrorism. Despite the global economic recession, annual GDP growth of 3 percent was forecast for 2009, owing in large part to Tunisia's lower import costs and a fully implemented free-trade agreement with the European Union (EU). The economy continued to perform well in 2010, with annual GDP growth of 3.8 percent.

A state of uncertainty prevailed for most of 2011 following the ouster of the president in January. In May funding commitments of $500 million each were secured from the World Bank and the African Development Bank (AfDB), while the EU agreed to provide $367 million over three years. The economy was estimated to have contracted by 1.8 percent in 2011 on the heels of a 30 percent drop in tourism receipts and 25 percent decrease in foreign direct investment. Unemployment reached 19 percent (and youth unemployment hit 42 percent). Rapid credit growth was accompanied by a rise in headline inflation (from an average of 3.5 percent in 2011 to 5.7 percent by spring 2012).

Faced with an ailing economy, in 2012, the Tunisian government worked to steady its cash reserves and prop up its currency The IMF, which was working on a technical assistance program to strengthen bank regulation in Tunisia, predicted a gradual recovery. In 2012, GDP grew by 3.6 percent, while inflation was 5.6 percent, and unemployment, 18.9 percent. GDP per capita that year was $4,533.

Authorities were reportedly struggling to track down assets linked to the former regime's top officials, including foreign real estate, yachts, and bank accounts worth billions of dollars. By late August 2012, according to the *Financial Times*, officials had seized 550 buildings, 300 companies, 367 bank accounts, 48 boats, 223 cars, and 83 horses from Ben Ali's associates. Meanwhile officials began selling off hundreds of millions of dollars' worth of holdings in the automotive, telecommunications, construction, and financial sectors. In April 2013 officials were able to recover $28.8 million from a Lebanese bank account owned by the former president's wife. Meanwhile the IMF agreed to provide a $1.75 billion stability loan to Tunisia.

GOVERNMENT AND POLITICS

Political background. Seat of the Carthaginian empire destroyed by Rome in 146 BC, Tunisia was successively conquered by Romans, Arabs, and Turks before being occupied by France in 1881 and becoming a French protectorate under a line of native rulers (beys) in 1883. Pressure for political reforms began after World War I and in 1934 resulted in establishment of the nationalist Neo-Destour (New Constitution) Party, which spearheaded the drive for independence under the leadership of Habib BOURGUIBA. Nationalist aspirations were further stimulated by World War II, and an initial breakdown in independence negotiations led to the outbreak of guerrilla warfare against the French in 1952. Internal autonomy was conceded by France on June 3, 1955, and on March 20, 1956, the protectorate was terminated, with the country gaining full independence.

A national constituent assembly controlled by the Neo-Destour Party voted on July 25, 1957, to abolish the monarchy and establish a republic with Bourguiba as president. A new constitution was adopted on June 1, 1959, while Bourguiba's leadership and that of the party were overwhelmingly confirmed in presidential and legislative elections in 1959 and 1964.

Bourguiba was reelected in 1969, but his failing health precipitated a struggle for succession to the presidency. One-time front-runner Bahi LADGHAM, prime minister and secretary general of the party, was apparently too successful: the attention he received as chair of the Arab Superior Commission on Jordan and as effective executive during the president's absences led to a falling-out with an eventually rejuvenated Bourguiba; he was dismissed in 1970 and replaced by Hedi NOUIRA. President Bourguiba encountered an additional challenge from Ahmed MESTIRI, interior minister and leader of the liberal wing of the party. The liberals succeeded in forcing democratization of the party structure during the eighth party congress in October 1971, but Bourguiba subsequently reasserted his control over the party apparatus. Mestiri was expelled from the party in January 1972 and from his seat in the National Assembly in May 1973, while Bourguiba was named president for life on November 2, 1974.

In February 1980, Prime Minister Nouira suffered a stroke, and on April 24 Mohamed MZALI, the acting prime minister, was asked to form a new government. Mzali was reappointed following a general election on November 1, 1981, in which three additional parties were allowed to participate, although none secured legislative representation. Bourguiba dismissed Mzali on July 8, 1986, replacing him with Rachid SFAR, theretofore finance minister.

Gen. Zine El-Abidine BEN ALI was named to succeed Sfar on October 2, 1987, reportedly because of presidential displeasure at recent personnel decisions. Five weeks later, after a panel of doctors had declared the aged president medically unfit, Bourguiba was forced to step down in favor of Ben Ali, who designated Hedi BACCOUCHE as his prime ministerial successor.

Although widely termed a "bloodless coup," the ouster of Bourguiba and succession of Ben Ali were in accord with relevant provisions of the Tunisian constitution. Moreover, the takeover was generally welcomed by Tunisians, who had become increasingly disturbed by Bourguiba's erratic behavior and mounting government repression of the press, trade unions, legal opposition parties, and other sources of dissent, including the growing Islamic fundamentalist movement. (Following his deposition, Bourguiba retired from public view. He died at age 97 in 2000.)

Upon assuming office the Ben Ali government announced its commitment to domestic pluralism and launched a series of wide-ranging political and economic liberalization measures, which included the legalization of some political parties, the loosening of media restrictions, and the pardoning of more than 8,000 detainees, many of them fundamentalists. Additionally, in late 1988, the new regime negotiated a "national pact" regarding the country's political, economic, and social future with a number of political and labor groups. However, the Islamic Tendency Movement (*Mouvement de la Tendance Islamique*—MTI) refused to sign the accord, foreshadowing a steady deterioration in relations between the fundamentalists and the government.

Presidential and legislative elections, originally scheduled for 1991, were moved up to April 2, 1989, Ben Ali declaring they would serve as an indication of the public's satisfaction with the recent changes. No one challenged the popular Ben Ali in the presidential poll, but the legal opposition parties and fundamentalist independent candidates contested the House of Representatives balloting, albeit without success.

On September 27, 1989, Ben Ali dismissed Baccouche and named former Justice Minister Hamed KAROUI as prime minister. The change was reportedly precipitated by disagreement over economic policy, Baccouche having voiced concern over the "social effects" of the government's austerity program. Shortly thereafter, the government announced the formation of a "higher council" to oversee implementation of the national pact, although several opposition parties and MTI followers, now operating as the Renaissance Party (*Hizb al-Nahda*—generally referenced as *Nahda*) boycotted the council's meetings. Charging that the democratic process was in reality being "blocked" by the government, the opposition also refused to contest municipal elections in June 1990 or national by-elections in October 1991. Apparently in response to criticism that the government's enthusiasm for democratization had waned as its antifundamentalist fervor had surged, electoral law changes were adopted in late 1993 to ensure opposition parties of some legislative representation in the upcoming general election. Nevertheless, the Democratic Constitutional Assembly (RCD), officially credited with nearly 98 percent of the vote, won all 144 seats for which it was eligible in the balloting for a 163-member House on March 20, 1994. On the same date, Ben Ali was reelected without challenge, two potential independent candidates being stricken from the ballot by their failure to receive the required endorsement of at least 30 national legislators or municipal council presidents.

The RCD won control of all 257 municipal councils in local elections on May 21, 1995. While opposition candidates (standing in 47 municipalities) won only 6 of 4,090 seats, it was the first time since independence that the opposition had gained any such representation at all.

Ben Ali was reelected to a third full presidential term (then the constitutional limit) in balloting on October 24, 1999, securing more than 99 percent of the vote against two candidates presented by small opposition parties. Meanwhile, the RCD again secured all the seats for which it was eligible (148) in the concurrent legislative poll. Two days after being sworn in for his new term, President Ben Ali appointed Mohamed GHANNOUCHI, theretofore the minister for international cooperation and foreign investment, as the new prime minister.

Constitutional revision in 2002 removed the limit on the number of presidential terms, thereby permitting Ben Ali on October 24, 2004, to seek a fourth term, which he won with 95 percent of the vote against three other minor candidates. On the same date the RCD won all 152 seats contested on a district basis for an expanded assembly. Ghannouchi, who was retained as prime minister, headed a new government formed on November 10.

In the municipal election of May 8, 2005, to renew 264 councils comprising 4,366 seats, the RDC garnered 93.9 percent of the vote, while 4 opposition parties and 1 independent won representation with 6.1 percent of the vote. Three opposition groups whose candidates were barred from running boycotted the election. The RDC also dominated the new House of Advisers, which was established in balloting of July 3, 2005, in accordance with provisions adopted in the 2002 constitutional revision. The cabinet was reshuffled on August 17, 2005; January 25 and September 3, 2007; and August 29, 2008. One minister was replaced on October 10, 2009.

Ben Ali and the RCD swept the elections on October 25, 2009. Ben Ali secured 89.4 percent of the vote, defeating three other candidates, the closest challenger being Mohamed BOUCHIHA of the Popular Union Party (*Parti de l'Unité Populaire*—PUP) with 5 percent of the vote. The RCD won all 161 seats for which it was eligible in the enlarged, 214-member House of Representatives. Ben Ali was sworn in on November 12 and reshuffled the cabinet on January 14, 2010, retaining Ghannouchi as prime minister. In municipal elections in May the RCD won 75 percent of seats. Further changes to the cabinet were made on October 14, 2010, and on December 29, 2010.

As a result of escalating civil unrest in protest against perceived government corruption, youth unemployment, and other economic issues, President Ben Ali attempted to mollify demonstrators by dismissing the interior minister on January 12, 2011, and promising elections. However, the violent protests continued, and Ben Ali left the country on January 14. He was immediately succeeded as interim president by Prime Minister Mohamed Ghannouchi, who was replaced on January 15 by Fouad MBAZAÂ, the president of the House of Representatives, by appointment of the Constitutional Council. On January 17 Prime Minister Ghannouchi named a government of national unity, retaining several members of the previous regime and opposition leaders from the Renewal Movement (*Harakat Ettajdid/ Mouvement de la Rénovation*—MR), the Progressive Democratic Assembly (*Rassemblement Démocratique Progressiste*—RDP), and the Democratic Forum for Labor and Liberties (*Le Forum Démocratique pour le Travail et les Libertés*—FDTL). The following day, several ministers from the former opposition resigned in protest against RCD ministers having been retained in the cabinet. On January 19 the remaining RCD ministers and the prime minister resigned from the party. The foreign affairs minister resigned on January 27, and a further reshuffle of 20 ministers followed. On February 13, the newly appointed foreign affairs minister resigned. He was replaced on February 21. In the wake of more violent protests, Interim Prime Minister Ghannouchi resigned on February 27 and was immediately replaced by Beji Caid ESSEBSI, a former minister and diplomat. Five more ministers, who had been aligned with Ben Ali, resigned the same day. On March 7 Essebsi named a new interim cabinet, which did not include any members with ties to the previous regime. On March 9 a court ordered the dissolution of the former ruling RCD. The interior minister resigned on March 28 and was immediately replaced.

Hamadi JEBALI (*Nahda*) was named prime minister on December 14, 2011 (see Current issues, below). He resigned on February 19, 2013, after failing to form a government (see Current issues, below). Ali LAARAYEDH (*Nahda*) was named prime minister three days later and formed a *Nahda*-dominated coalition government on March 8.

Constitution and government. The constitution of June 1, 1959, endowed the Tunisian Republic with a presidential system backed by the dominant position of the (then) Neo-Destour Party. The president was given exceptionally broad powers, including the right to designate the prime minister and to rule by decree during legislative adjournments. In addition, the incumbent was granted life tenure under a 1975 amendment to the basic law. In the wake of President Bourguiba's ouster in 1987, the life presidency was abolished, the chief executive being limited to no more than three five-year terms.

A new constitution approved in a referendum on May 26, 2002, and promulgated on June 2, made provisions for an upper house, the House of Advisers; removed presidential term limits; and raised the age limit for a presidential candidate to 75 (from 70). The succession procedure was also altered, the president of the House of Representatives being designated to serve as head of state for 45–60 days, pending a new election, at which he could not present himself as a candidate. Other changes included reduction of the role of prime minister from leader of the government to "coordinator" of ministerial activities. Further constitutional amendments affecting the electoral code and expanding eligibility criteria for presidential candidates were promulgated on April 13, 2008. Following the civil unrest in January 2011, which resulted in the president's ouster, a state of emergency was declared. On January 17 the prime minister formed a Higher Political Reform Commission (HPRC) to oversee constitutional reform. On February 9 the legislature granted the prime minister broad authority to issue laws by decree.

The legislature was a unicameral body until 2005, with only a House of Representatives.

The House of Representatives (styled the National Assembly until 1981 and also referenced as the Chamber of Deputies) is elected by universal suffrage for a five-year term. Under Bourguiba it had limited authority and in practice was wholly dominated by the ruling party. Constitutional changes approved in July 1988 contained measures designed to expand the House's control and influence, although their impact has been minimal. The upper House of Advisers was seated after balloting on July 3, 2005. It comprises 126 members, 85 of whom are directly elected and 41 appointed by the president, all serving six-year terms, with half of the seats renewed every three years. Consultative bodies at the national level include a Social and Economic Council and a Higher Islamic Council. The judicial system is headed by a Court of Cassation and includes 3 courts of appeal, 13 courts of first instance, and 51 cantonal courts. Judges are appointed by the president.

Tunisia is administratively divided into 23 provinces, each headed by a governor appointed by the president. The governors are assisted by appointed government councils and 264 elected municipal councils.

Reporters Without Borders ranked Tunisia 138th out of 179 countries in 2013 as a result of intimidation of journalists, including arbitrary arrests and detention. In October 2012 the government refused opposition and media calls for a broad guarantee of freedom of the press in the draft constitution.

Foreign relations. Tunisia assumed a nonaligned posture at independence, establishing relations with both Eastern and Western countries, although placing particular emphasis on its relations with the West and with Arab governments. It became a member of the United Nations in 1956 and is active in all the UN-related agencies. It joined the Arab League in 1958 but boycotted its meetings from 1958 to 1961 and again in 1966 as a result of disagreements with the more "revolutionary" Arab states. As a signal of its support for peace negotiations (particularly the 1993 accord between Israel and the Palestine Liberation Organization), Tunisia exchanged low-level economic representatives with Israel in October 1994 in what was considered a possible precursor to eventual establishment of full diplomatic relations. However, Tunisia recalled those representatives from Israel in 1997 as part of the broad Arab protest over a perceived intransigence on the part of the Netanyahu administration in Israel.

Beginning in 1979, a series of agreements were signed with Algeria, culminating in a March 1983 "Maghreb Fraternity and Co-Operation Treaty," to which Mauritania acceded the following December. Relations with Libya, though reestablished in 1982 after a 1980 rupture over seizure of a southern town by alleged Libyan-trained insurgents, continued to be difficult. President Bourguiba's visit to Washington in June 1985 led to a mass expulsion of Tunisian workers from Libya, as well as reported Libyan incursions into Tunisia and efforts to destabilize its government. After suspending relations with Tripoli in September 1986, Tunis resumed relations a year later following a pledge by Libya to reimburse the expelled workers. Further economic and social agreements, including provisions for the free movement of people and goods between the two countries, were announced in 1988 as Tunisia stepped up its call for regional cooperation and unity, the latter bearing fruit with the formation of the Arab Maghreb Union in February 1989 (see article under Intergovernmental Organizations). Also in 1988, relations were reestablished with Egypt after an eight-year lapse.

The Iraqi invasion of Kuwait in August 1990 appeared to precipitate a change in Tunisia's theretofore unwavering pro-Western orientation. Although critical of the Iraqi occupation, Tunis strongly condemned the subsequent deployment of U.S. troops in Saudi Arabia and the allied bombing of Iraq in early 1991. However, security forces clamped down on large-scale pro-Iraqi demonstrations during the Gulf war, apparently out of concern that the situation might be exploited by Islamic fundamentalists.

President Ben Ali welcomed the antifundamentalist stance adopted by the Algerian military in early 1992, and Tunis was subsequently in the forefront of efforts among North African capitals to coordinate an "antiterrorist" campaign against Muslim militants. In October 1991, Tunisia recalled its ambassador from Sudan, charging Khartoum with fomenting fundamentalist unrest and providing sanctuary and financial support for groups intent on overthrowing the Tunisian government.

The EU, the focus of an estimated 80 percent of Tunisia's trade, and signed an association agreement with Tunis in 1995 that provided for the progressive reduction of tariffs (and elimination of many by 2008).

In 2006 Defense Secretary Donald Rumsfeld, on a visit to Tunis, discussed strengthening military ties with Tunisia while at the same time encouraging greater political reform. The United States provided $11 million to Tunisia for military training in 2006.

In October 2006, Tunisia closed its embassy in Doha, Qatar, after Qatar-based *Al Jazeera* television broadcast an interview with Moncef MARZOUKI, leader of the banned Congress for the Republic and former head of the Tunisian Human Rights League, in which he criticized the government and the lack of freedom in Tunisia.

In 2009, Tunisia, unlike many countries, agreed to the return of ten Tunisian detainees being held at the U.S. military prison in Guantánamo Bay, Cuba. In May Tunisia asked the United States to turn over two men who were being held on suspicion of being Islamist militants, both of whom had been convicted in absentia in Tunisian courts.

Following the Jasmine Revolution in Tunisia in January 2011, Western governments expressed concern over the violence but generally refrained from taking sides. In February thousands of Tunisian refugees fled to the Italian island of Lampedusa in the hope of gaining entry to the EU. Ultimately, the United States called on the interim prime minister to carry out democratic reforms, and French president Nicholas Sarkozy backed the protest movement as well, after denying Ben Ali refuge.

On February 24, 2012, Tunis hosted the Friends of Syria conference, which was attended by representatives from more than 70 countries and international organizations. The conference resulted in agreements to tighten sanctions and travel bans against Syrian president Bashir Assad and his senior aides and pledges of food and medicine for displaced Syrians. In November Libya announced it would provide $131 million in economic aid to Tunisia.

In March security forces and insurgents fought a series of battles along the border with Libya. In June the two countries announced a series of measures designed to improve border security. Meanwhile, a report found that 70 percent of the Tunisian workers who had fled Libya during that country's civil war had returned. In July, eight Tunisian soldiers were killed along the border between Tunisia and Algeria. The Tunisian government blamed insurgents based in Algeria for the attacks.

Current issues. The RCD dominated the May 2010 municipal elections, which were boycotted by the Progressive Democratic Assembly (*Rassemblement Démocratique Progressiste*—RDP). In June, the MR and the FDTL formed the Alliance for Citizenship and Equality, with what were described as two "nascent" groups—the Patriotic and Democratic Labor Party and the Reform and Development Movement—seeking a dialogue on a "transition to democracy," with little further explanation. In August, Amnesty International warned that an amendment to Tunisia's penal code was designed to further silence government critics and human rights activists. The amendment provides for imprisonment of up to 20 years, with a minimum sentence of five years, for those who contact foreign organizations "in order to harm Tunisia's vital interests." Tensions heightened in the repressive environment, and in December, after a street vendor set himself on fire in protest against his treatment by the police, demonstrators took to the streets for ten days in the town of Sidi Bouzid. Because of constraints on the media, little support emerged from other parts of the country. However, once news of the self-immolation appeared on the social media, protests spread to Tunis.

Following the death on January 5, 2011, of the street vendor, who had been visited in the hospital by President Ben Ali, promising reforms, the protests increased significantly, lawyers went on strike, and students and members of trade unions and political groups began demonstrating. The protests quickly spread across the country, focused on rising unemployment and inflation, government corruption and repression, and demands that Ben Ali leave. The president deployed the police to quell the protests after the army refused to fire on protesters—resulting in the dismissal of the army chief—but violence escalated, and scores of demonstrators were killed in what by then was termed the Jasmine Revolution. In a last-ditch effort to salvage the situation, President Ben Ali dismissed his interior minister, who had been accused of authorizing excessive force against protesters, and on January 14 he dissolved the entire government, declared a state of emergency, and called for early legislative elections. Later that day, however, Ben Ali handed over presidential authority to Prime Minister Ghannouchi and fled with his family to Saudi Arabia after having been refused entry into France. The following day, the president of the House of Representatives, Fouad Mbazaâ, ascended to the interim presidency by appointment of the Constitutional Council, and two days later Ghannouchi, as interim prime minister, named a caretaker unity government that included opposition leaders along with cabinet members from the RCD regime. The powerful General Union of Tunisian Workers (*Union Générale des Traivalleurs Tunisiens*—UGTT), which had initially refused to recognize the interim government, shifted its stance and supported Ghannouchi. However, mass protests continued daily, and opposition ministers began resigning in waves in protest against RCD members having been retained in the cabinet, prompting Mbazaâ and Ghannouchi to resign from the party and forcing a major reshuffle. The interior minister subsequently suspended the RCD and announced that the state of emergency would remain in place indefinitely. During the protests it was reported that nearly 150 protesters had died and 94 had been wounded. Later in the month the justice minister announced that Tunisia had issued an international arrest warrant against Ben Ali and several members of his family for allegedly stealing large sums of money from the government, among other charges.

Faced with continued violent protests, a police force crippled by mass desertions, a judiciary weakened by its ties to the former regime, and increasing political uncertainty, Ghannouchi resigned on February 27, 2011, and was immediately replaced by Beji Caid Essebsi, 84, who had held several ministerial posts over the years. Meanwhile, the president of the newly formed Higher Political Reform Commission (HPRC), Yadh BEN ACHOUR, who had been appointed by former interim prime minister Ghannouchi, announced that the constitutional deadline for holding new presidential elections within 60 days of Ben Ali's departure could not be met. On March 3 Interim President Mbazaâ said he would remain in office until July 24, the date set for the election of a constituent assembly, which would draft a new constitution. Shortly thereafter, Mbazaâ appointed a new interim government, this time with no members from the previous regime, reaffirming his commitment to "break with the past," lifting restrictions on the media, and releasing political prisoners. He also accused Ben Ali of high treason during the civil unrest. At the same time, the newly appointed interior minister, responding to a key demand of the protesters, announced the dissolution of the secret police and the state security system. On March 9, the former ruling RCD was abolished by court order. In the meantime, political groups were reorganizing, and new ones were forming as the interim government lifted the ban on political parties. Notably, Islamic fundamentalist *Nahda* party leader Rachid GHANOUCHI (no relation to the former prime minister), returned to Tunisia after 20 years in exile, and his party was subsequently legalized. However, other Islamist parties and religious groups were denied legal party status. The independent electoral commission set a new date of July 24 for the constituent assembly election to allow adequate time for preparation of electoral rolls and other organizational matters.

In April 2011, Tunisia requested the extradition of Ben Ali from Saudi Arabia to face dozens of charges, including voluntary manslaughter, drug trafficking, and conspiring against the state. Ben Ali was alleged to have ordered air strikes against Kasserine in the days before he fled the country. More than 350 property deeds of Ben Ali were confiscated, along with other assets. Meanwhile, a judge remanded to custody former RCD secretary general Abderrahmin ZOUARI on charges that he had misappropriated public funds and abused his position of power within the party. On April 15 hundreds of demonstrators protested outside the Saudi embassy in Tunis, demanding Ben Ali's extradition. As tensions and political debates continued to escalate, resulting in more clashes between demonstrators and the police and the arrest of hundreds of protesters, the interim prime minister imposed a night-time curfew in May, though it was soon lifted. In June Ben Ali and his wife Leila TRABELSI were convicted in absentia of embezzling state funds and unlawful possession of jewelry and artifacts, sentenced to 35 years each in prison, and fined $65 million. The following month Ben Ali was convicted in absentia of smuggling guns, drugs, and other artifacts and sentenced to more than 15 years in prison and fined $72,000. On June 8, the interim government accepted a recommendation from the electoral commission to postpone the election from July 24 to October 23. Meanwhile, the slow pace of reforms and reports that Ben Ali loyalists still had significant political influence fomented further civil unrest. More violent clashes with the police were reported in July, as well as Internet censorship and police beating of journalists. "The optimism and euphoria of January's revolution has given way to dread," *Africa Research Bulletin* reported. In early August, with the investigation of the previous regime still ongoing, the interim government seized 234 luxury cars that had belonged to Ben Ali's friends and relatives. In mid-August hundreds in Tunis protested the release of several former ministers facing corruption charges and called for judicial reforms, though the judiciary claimed it had been independent since Ben Ali's ouster. In September, the main parties agreed that the assembly would draw up a new constitution under which presidential and legislative elections would be held by October 2012. As the October 2011 constituent assembly election neared, at least 50 new parties were reportedly formed ahead of the poll.

In the October 23 election, which saw a turnout of about 52 percent, the *Nahda* party obtained around 40 percent of the vote and won 89 seats, making it by far the biggest single party. Of the 217 assembly seats, 42 went to women, thanks in part to a provision requiring parties to present an equal number of male and female candidates. The strictly proportional system ensured that at least 19 parties and 8 independent lists won representation, most often a single seat.

After the sweeping *Nahda* victory, party leader Rachid Ghanouchi called for cooperation with the other main parties, promising a new model of government that would fuse an Islamic character with the ideals of liberal democracy and repeating the party's campaign promise not to ban alcohol or impose a dress code on Western tourists.

On November 21 a three-party coalition pact was established between *Nahda*, the Democratic Forum for Labor and Liberties (FDTL), and the Congress for the Republic (CPR), confirming the deal to hold presidential and legislative elections under a new constitution in late 2012 or early 2013. The parties also agreed that Hamadi JEBALI, *Nahda*'s secretary general, would take over as prime minister in December and Moncef Marzouki of the CPR would succeed interim president Fouad Mbazaâ. On November 22, the Constituent Assembly held its inaugural session.

Throughout much of the following year, as parties struggled with defections and shifting alliances, the deep rivalries between secularists and ultraconservative Salafi Islamists were increasingly evident. On March 28, 2012, groups of liberal artists and Salafis both staged marches on Avenue Bourguiba, the central thoroughfare where the protests that had launched the Arab Spring began. Clashes ensued, with the ultraconservatives reportedly assaulting their rivals. The government subsequently announced a ban on marches there, but demonstrations continued. On April 5, the police first used teargas and batons on crowds after a group of unemployed demonstrators challenged the ban. Some liberal members of the assembly were reportedly beaten by police. Meanwhile, a string of confrontations between the dean of Tunis' Manouba University and Salafist student groups and their supporters, who demanded a prayer room and the right for female students to wear veils, occupied much of the national attention, feeding claims that the *Nahda*-dominated government was unwilling to confront ultraconservative Islamists. In May, Salafis burned police stations and bars in several towns. The police arrested 15 people, but moderates argued it was an all too rare response. Critics also took issue with a $1,500 fine levied against a TV executive for showing *Persepolis,* a film that offends some Muslims by depicting God, as well as the lack of investigative follow-up into attacks on the station and the executive's home.

In June 2012 Ben Ali was sentenced to life in prison for the killing of protesters, but Saudi Arabia refused to extradite him.

On August 13, 2012, thousands of women marched in Tunis to protest a provision in the new draft of the constitution that describes women as "complementary to men." On September 14 Salafist Islamic militants attacked the U.S. embassy in Tunis. Security forces killed 4 of the militants and injured 40. However sections of the embassy were burned or looted. The protest was in response to a U.S. film that was critical of Islam. Also in September the Ministry of Culture filed a series of lawsuits against Salafist groups that had disrupted cultural events and festivals. Violent protests led by the Tunisian General Labor Union in Siliana in December prompted the government to negotiate a truce that included pledges to spur job creation. These and other protests in December injured more than 250 protestors and 72 police officers.

On February 6, 2013, opposition leader Chokri BELAÏD (Democratic Patriots' Movement) was assassinated by three masked gunmen, creating a political crisis that resulted in the resignation of Prime Minister Jebali 13 days later. Most Tunisians blamed Salafist militants, and opposition leaders accused the government of not taking strong action to curb the extremists. A new government under Ali Laarayedh was installed in March and included a large number of independents. Also in March Kamel KEDHKADH, identified as one of Belaïd's assassins, was arrested in Algeria and extradited to Tunisia. Protests and demonstrations against the *Nahda*-led government continued through the summer and prompted the government to agree to new elections. Opposition leaders formally requested a UN inquiry into the murder, alleging that the government could not be trusted to investigate the crime. On July 25 opposition figure Mohamed BRAHMI was assassinated, leading to renewed protests and strikes. Meanwhile the growing crisis led the interim assembly to suspend its work in August after 60 deputies began a boycott of the body.

POLITICAL PARTIES

Although not constitutionally mandated, Tunisia was effectively a one-party state from the time the Tunisian Communist Party (PCT) was banned in January 1963 until its return to legal status in July 1981. (For more on the subsequent legalization of other historically significant parties, see an earlier *Handbook.*)

Following the civil unrest, referred to as the Jasmine Revolution, that began in early 2011, the ruling government party (RCD) was suspended by the interim government on February 6, and on March 9 a court in Tunis ordered the party's dissolution. The interim government also removed the ban on political parties, and by midyear more than 50 parties and 100 political associations had been formed. More than 80, including 3 religious groups, were denied authorization.

By mid-2012 observers highlighted a persistent imbalance between the organizational clout and cohesion of the well-organized *Nahda* party and the smaller, fractured secular parties as a challenge to the development of Tunisia's political sphere. The governing coalition, which controls 138 of the assembly's 217 seats, was also said to be a fragile "marriage of convenience" that was marked by mutual suspicions and showing signs of strain. Further tensions were highlighted by the July 27 resignation of Finance Minister Hussein Dimassi, reportedly over his feelings that a proposed compensation plan for political prisoners of the former regime, mostly Islamists from *Nahda,* was a reckless vote-buying tactic. Meanwhile, an effort by some secular parties to unite into a grand coalition proved short-lived, and a changing roster of small, shifting alliances predominated despite the many small parties that share similar ideologies and political incentives to join forces but nonetheless remain outside of coalitions. On August 14, the head of the drafting committee announced the new constitution would not be adopted by February 2013, which was seen as another hitch in the country's transition.

In 2012 press accounts described a tentative coalition formed between the PDP, Afek Tounes, and the Republican Party, a breakaway party from the PDM, led by Abdelaziz BELKHODJA.

Renaissance Party (*Hizb al-Nahda/Parti de la Renaissance*—PR or *Nahda*). Also known as the Renaissance Movement (*Harakat al-Nahda/Mouvement de la Renaissance*), *Nahda* was formed as the Islamic Tendency Movement (*Mouvement de la Tendance Islamique*—MTI) in early 1981 by a group of Islamic fundamentalists inspired by the 1979 Iranian revolution. Charged with fomenting disturbances, many MTI adherents were jailed during a series of subsequent crackdowns by the Bourguiba government. However, the MTI insisted that it opposed violence or other "revolutionary activity," and the Ben Ali government pardoned most of those incarcerated, including the movement's leader, Rachid Ghanouchi, shortly after assuming power. The new regime also initiated talks that it said were designed to provide moderate MTI forces with a legitimate means of political expression in order to undercut support for the movement's radical elements. As an outgrowth of that process, the MTI adopted its new name in early 1989; however, the government subsequently denied legal status to *Nahda,* ostensibly on the grounds that it remained religion based. Undaunted, the group quickly established itself as the government's primary opposition, its "independent" candidates collecting about 13 percent of the total popular vote (including as much as 30 percent of the vote in some urban areas) in 1989 legislative balloting.

Nahda boycotted higher council negotiations and municipal elections in 1990, Ghanouchi remaining in exile to protest the lack of legal recognition for the formation and the continued "harassment" of its sympathizers. Friction intensified late in the year following the arrest of three groups of what security forces described as armed extremists plotting to overthrow the government. Although the government alleged that some of those arrested had *Nahda* links, the party leadership strongly denied the charge, accusing the regime of conducting a propaganda campaign aimed at discrediting the fundamentalist movement in order to prevent it from assuming its rightful political role.

On October 15, 1991, the government announced that it had uncovered a fundamentalist plot to assassinate President Ben Ali and other government officials in order to "create a constitutional vacuum." However, *Nahda* leaders again denied any connection to violent antigovernment activity, reiterating their commitment to "peaceful methods" of protest and stressing that their vision for the "Islamization" of Tunisia was "compatible" with democracy and a pluralistic society. The disclaimers notwithstanding, the government flatly labeled *Nahda* "a terrorist organization" and intensified the campaign to "silence" it. Thousands of suspected *Nahda* sympathizers were detained, many later claiming that they had been tortured or otherwise abused in prison (a charge supported by Amnesty International). At a widely publicized trial in mid-1992, about 170 *Nahda* adherents were convicted of sedition. A number were sentenced to life imprisonment, including Ghanouchi and several other leaders who were tried in absentia. The government subsequently issued an international arrest warrant for Ghanouchi, who was living in London, but in mid-1993, the United Kingdom granted him political asylum. In 1994, Ghanouchi dismissed the recent Tunisian presidential and legislative elections as "a joke." Despite the "banned and fragmented" status of *Nahda,* Ghanouchi was described in 1996 as still the only possible "serious challenger" to Ben Ali. A number of *Nahda* adherents were released in November 1999 from long prison terms. In March 2001, Ghanouchi, in conjunction with **Democratic Socialist Movement** (*Mouvement des Démocrates Socialistes*—MDS) leader Mohamed Mouada, proposed establishment by *Nahda* and the legal opposition parties of a National Democratic Front to challenge the RCD, suggesting to some observers that *Nahda* hoped to return to mainstream political activity. However, *Nahda* remained relatively quiescent during the 2004 election campaign.

In March 2006, the government released 1,600 prisoners on the 50th anniversary of Tunisia's independence. Among those released were reportedly many political prisoners who had been jailed for 10 years because they were members of *Nahda*. Further, in November, President Ben Ali, marking his 19th year at the helm, pardoned 55 Islamists, all said to be members of *Nahda,* including leaders Habib ELLOUZE and Mohamed AKROUT, both of whom had received life sentences in 1992. In November 2008, Ben Ali pardoned and released another 21 PR members, some of whom had been serving life sentences. A former PR leader, Sadek CHOUROU was arrested in 2008 on charges of maintaining an outlawed organization. In 2009, an appeals court upheld his one-year prison sentence and subsequently extended it by one year to cover time the court said he should have served in the 1990s. Chourou was released in October 2010. In December, several Islamists were sentenced for trying to revive *Nahda* by holding meetings and trying to raise funds. Two were sent to jail for six months; others were convicted in absentia or given suspended sentences.

Party leader Ghanouchi (no relation to the former prime minister), who had been in exile in the United Kingdom for 20 years, returned to Tunisia on January 30, 2011, following the ouster of President Ben Ali and the interim government's decision to lift the ban on all political parties. *Nahda,* which Ghanouchi likened to Turkey's ruling Justice and Development Party (adhering to Islamist values in a secular state), was legalized on March 1.

Well-funded and the best-organized party, *Nahda* utilized its strong grassroots in the poorest areas during the run-up to the 2011 balloting for the assembly. Some of the support for *Nahda* was attributed to its credibility for opposing the former regime. It was also seen by supporters as more socially responsible and less likely to be corrupted.

During the campaign, the prospect of a strong *Nahda* showing divided the country, with women's groups and secularists mounting demonstrations against Islamist rule and a series of dramatic advertisements that suggested an Islamist win would scare off tourists and see women's rights curtailed.

On March 27, 2012, leaders announced the new constitution would not cite Islamic law as a source of legislation, a rejection of demands from ultraconservatives for an Islamic state. Some observers considered it a step toward delivering on the party's campaign promises not to overturn the secular order. Later, party officials complained of pressure from Salafist rivals to embrace more conservative positions. *Nahda* secured 89 seats in the assembly.

On February 22, 2013, Ali LAARAYEDH was appointed prime minister of a *Nahda*-led coalition government. Reports in 2013 indicated growing divisions within the party between moderates who sought negotiations and accommodations with the secular opposition and hard-liners, led by Ghanouchi.

Leaders: Rachid GHANOUCHI (Party President), Ali LAARAYEDH (Prime Minister), Noureddine BHIRI, Samir DILOU.

Congress for the Republic (*Le Congrès Pour la République*—CPR). Formed by activist Moncef Marzouki in July 2001, the political party was established to try to help create a democratic republic. Marzouki, who faced a year in prison for belonging to another illegal organization, lived in self-imposed exile in France for five years, returning to Tunisia in 2006 to encourage Tunisians to engage in peaceful demonstrations for human rights. Soon thereafter, Marzouki was charged with "incitement to civil disobedience." He returned to Tunisia from exile in France days after Ben Ali fled in January. The CPR has a history of past cooperation with *Nahda*. Some 40 members of the opposition in the assembly cast blank ballots to protest Marzouki's election as Tunisia's interim president, a position his critics said was largely powerless and meant to distract from the reality of Islamist control. The party subsequently showed signs of strain, with some members accusing Marzouki of putting his own ambition before the interests of the party. Twelve CPR representatives in the assembly seceded from the CPR and formed a new party on May 17, the **Independent Democratic Congress**, whose leaders include Abderraouf AYADI and Slim BOUKHDHIR.

The CPR secured 29 seats in the assembly. Reports in March 2013 indicated that CPR Secretary General Mohamed ABBOU had resigned and was forming a new party. He was replaced by Imed DAÏMI. CPR secured three cabinet posts in the coalition government announced in March.

Leaders: Moncef MARZOUKI (Interim President of the Republic), Imed DAÏMI (Interim Secretary General).

Popular Petition for Freedom, Justice and Development (*Pétition Populaire Pour la Liberté*—Popular Petition). Formed in March 2011 by Mohamed Hechim Hamdi, a London-based TV station owner, Popular Petition offered an ambiguous platform, and analysts said some of its campaign promises, including free health care for the elderly, were unrealistic. While the party came in third in the assembly elections, Hamdi postponed his return to Tunisia after an anticorruption commission published a letter he wrote in December 2009 to Ben Ali offering to produce television programs highlighting the country's "democratic developments." The Popular Petition secured 26 seats in the assembly. In January 2013 the party announced that Hamdi would be its presidential candidate in future elections.

Leader: Mohamed Hechim HAMDI.

Democratic Forum for Labor and Liberties (*Le Forum Démocratique pour le Travail et les Libertés—Ettakatol* or FDTL). Legalized in 2002, the FDTL had been active as an opposition group since it was organized in 1994. Its platform endorsed a commitment to "defending freedom, democracy, and social justice," among other things.

After the party failed to prevent passage of a constitutional amendment allowing Ben Ali to seek a fourth term in 2004, it called for a boycott of the 2004 elections and urged opposition parties to work toward cohesion. The FDTL was barred by the government from participating in the 2005 municipal elections, along with the RDP and the MR. The three groups had formed a loose alliance called the Democratic Coalition for Citizenship, which the government said did not abide by electoral regulations.

One of the party's leaders, Mustafa Ben Jafaar (formerly of MDS), who was highly critical of the 2008 constitutional amendment affecting presidential candidates, in June 2009 announced his bid for the presidency in the October general elections. However, he was ineligible to run under the new law that required a candidate to have been president of a party for two consecutive years. The party failed to win seats in the 2009 parliamentary elections.

In 2010, the party joined with the MR and two small groups in the prodemocracy Alliance for Citizenship and Equality.

Following the ouster of President Ben Ali in January 2011, Ben Jafaar was tapped as health minister in the interim government, but he quit in protest at the inclusion of RCD members in the cabinet.

In the run-up to the balloting on October 23, 2011, the party positioned itself as a challenger to the PDP (see below). The party secured 20 seats in the assembly. But, party leaders have been clear that the decision to join the governing "troika" was based on political expediency rather than ideological compatibility, and discontent has driven some defections from the party. In November 2011 Ben Jafaar was elected president of the Constituent Assembly. The FDTL received two ministries in the March 2013 coalition government.

Leader: Mustafa BEN JAFAAR (Secretary General, 2009 presidential candidate, and President of the Constituent Assembly).

Progressive Democratic Party (Parti Démocrate Progressiste—PDP). The PDP had been established as the Progressive Socialist Assembly (*Rassemblement Socialiste Progressiste*—RSP) by a number of Marxist groups in 1983. The pan-Arabist RSP was tolerated by the Bourguiba government until mid-1986. It formed a Democratic Alliance with the PCT and planned to field candidates for the 1986 balloting. However, the coalition boycotted the election after the government disqualified some of its candidates and sentenced 14 of its members to six-month jail terms for belonging to an illegal organization. The party was officially recognized in September 1988. The RSP did not secure any of the legislative seats reserved for opposition parties in 1994 or 1999, and it called for a boycott of the municipal elections of May 2000. The RSP changed its name to the Progressive Democratic Assembly (*Rassemblement Démocratique Progressiste*—RDP) in July 2001 in an effort to "broaden its ideological base." The RDP reportedly included many Marxists as well as moderate Islamists and liberals.

RDP Secretary General Ahmed Chebbi was blocked from contesting the 2004 presidential election because of a recent decree by President Ben Ali that candidates could be presented only by parties with legislative representation. The RDP consequently called for a boycott of the presidential balloting and withdrew its candidates from the legislative poll.

In 2006, May ELJERIBI was elected secretary general, replacing Chebbi, who had held the post for 23 years. Eljeribi became the first woman to head a political party in Tunisia. In 2007, Eljeribi went on a month-long hunger strike to protest alleged harassment against the party, specifically the party's newspaper, *al-Mawkif.* Two other party members, including Rachid KHECHANA, the paper's editor, began hunger strikes in April 2008 for the same reason.

Though the party had nominated Chebbi in early 2008 to be its 2009 presidential candidate, he was subsequently deemed ineligible under the new law that permitted only elected party leaders who had held the post for two consecutive years to contest presidential elections. The party failed to win seats in the 2009 parliamentary elections and subsequently boycotted the 2010 municipal elections.

Chebbi served in Tunisia's caretaker government after the revolution. Ahead of the 2011 Constituent Assembly elections, the RSP changed its name again and rebranded itself as a liberal party with a strong market orientation that would be a counterweight to *Nahda*, waging verbal attacks against its rival in the press. The party secured 16 seats in the assembly. The PDP led protests against the *Nahda*-led government through the summer of 2013.

Leader: Ahmed Néjib CHEBBI.

The Initiative (*L'Initiative/Al Moubadara*). Founded by Kamal Morjane, formerly a defense minister and foreign minister in Ben Ali's regime, the party secured five seats in the assembly. Like **The Homeland Party** (*Parti de la Patrie*/Al Watan Party)—founded in 2011 by Mohammed JEGHAM and Ahmed FRIAA, both interior ministers in the former regime—The Initiative absorbed members of the banned RCD. Unlike The Homeland, which contested the polls without success, The Initiative secured five seats in the assembly.

Leader: Kamal MORJANE.

Tunisian Aspiration (*Afek Tounes*). *Afek Tounes* is a center-left party seen as close to the PDP. It was founded in 2011 by Slim RIAHI, a businessman with real estate and oil interests in Libya, Britain, Qatar, and the United Arab Emirates. The party is close to the business community and shares some policies with the PDP and the pro-business regime of Ben Ali. The party secured four seats in the assembly.

Leader: Slim RIAHI.

Democratic Modernist Pole (*Pôle Démocratique Moderniste*—PDM). Formed in 2011, this coalition brought together left-wing groups. Its core is the Renewal Movement (*Harakat Ettajdid/ Mouvement de la Rénovation*—MR or Ettajdid). The Renewal Movement is heir to the Tunisian Communist Party (PCT), which was founded in 1934 as an entity distinct from the French Communist Party. The PCT was outlawed in 1963 and regained legality in July 1981. Historically of quite limited membership, the party secured only 0.78 percent of the vote in the 1981 legislative balloting. The party's new name was adopted at an April 1993 congress, with leaders announcing that Marxism had been dropped as official doctrine in favor of a "progressive" platform favoring "democratic pluralism." In 2010, the party joined with FDTL and two small groups in a coalition styled after the Alliance for Citizenship and Equality, which called for dialogue on "the transition to democracy."

Ahead of the 2011 assembly election, the party united a coalition of leftist groups around a secular, feminist platform as a counterweight to the Islamists. Other major centrist parties declined the party's call to unite against the Islamists, preferring to run on their own. The coalition secured five seats in the assembly.

Leaders: Riadh Ben FADL, Mustapha Ben AHMED, Ahmad IBRAHIM.

Party of Tunisian Communist Workers (*Parti des Ouvriers Communistes Tunisiens*—POCT). A formerly unrecognized splinter of the former PCT, the POCT is led by Hamma HAMMANI, who had been the director of the banned newspaper *El Badil* (The Alternative). Hammani was sentenced to eight years in prison in early 1994 on several charges, including membership in an illegal organization, his case being prominently cited in criticism leveled at the government by human rights organizations. Hammani and another POCT member who had been imprisoned with him were pardoned by President Ben Ali in November 1995. A number of POCT members were convicted in July 1999 of belonging to an illegal association, but most were released later in the year. Hammani and several associates were charged again in absentia in 1999 for having been members of an unrecognized group. In February 2002, they were retried and committed to various prison sentences. In September, however, Hammani and some of the others were released following a hunger strike that had attracted increasing international scrutiny to their case. Hammani called for a boycott of the 2004 elections.

During the popular uprisings in January 2011, Hammani was arrested at his home. Following the ouster of President Ben Ali, the interim government legalized the party on March 1. The party secured three seats in the assembly. In 2013 Hammani was reportedly one of the leaders of an opposition alliance, the Popular Front.

Leader: Hamma HAMMANI.

Democratic Socialist Movement (*Mouvement des Démocrates Socialistes*—MDS). Organized as the Democratic Socialist Group in October 1977 by a number of former cabinet ministers who sought liberalization of the nation's political life, the MDS was refused formal recognition in 1978, although its leader, Ahmed Mestiri, had served as an intermediary between the government and the trade union leadership in an attempt to resolve labor unrest. The new grouping was runner-up in the 1981 election but obtained only 3.28 percent of the vote, thus failing to secure either legislative representation or legal status. However, recognition was granted by President Bourguiba in November 1983.

Mestiri was arrested in April 1986 and sentenced to four months in prison for leading demonstrations against the U.S. bombing of Libya. The conviction automatically disqualified him from running for legislative office, the MDS thereupon becoming an early advocate of the November electoral boycott. (Under the amnesty program initiated by the Ben Ali government in late 1987, Mestiri was pardoned for the conviction.) The MDS fared poorly in the 1989 balloting, and Mestiri was criticized for rejecting the RCD's preelection offer of an electoral front with the MDS and other parties. Subsequently, Mestiri resigned as MDS secretary general, Assistant Secretary General Dali JAZI having earlier quit the party to join the government. Mestiri was reported to have left the party altogether in early 1992, as criticism grew of the "authoritarian" approach of its new leader, Mohamed MOUADA. Factionalization also contributed to the suspension by the MDS of another of its prominent leaders, Mustafa BEN JAFAAR.

The MDS supported President Ben Ali for reelection in 1994 but challenged the RCD in the national legislative balloting. Although no MDS candidates were successful on their own, ten were subsequently seated in the house under the proportional arrangement enacted to guarantee a multiparty legislature.

In October 1995 Mouada published a letter criticizing the "lack of political freedom" in Tunisia. Within days, he was arrested on charges of having had illegal contacts with representatives of the Libyan government, and in February 1996, he was sentenced to 11 years in prison. Mouada dismissed the charges as "obviously politically motivated," and his conviction was widely condemned by international observers. Khemais CHAMMARI, a member of the MDS as well as the House of Representatives, was also given a five-year sentence in July for "attacking state security." Both men were released in December, although Mouada was briefly detained again one year later. Meanwhile, an MDS congress in May 1997 had elected Ismaïl BOULAHIA to the new leadership post of secretary general, his discussion of the future of the "new MDS" apparently reflecting a diminution of Mouada's authority. However, Boulahia was not eligible to contest the 1999 presidential election because he had not held his MDS post the requisite five years, and he subsequently announced the MDS was supporting President Ben Ali for reelection. Meanwhile, the party secured 13 seats in the legislative balloting of 1999, again thanks solely to electoral law that guarantees regarding opposition representation.

Mouada was held under house arrest for one month in late 1999 on a charge of defaming the government, and he was sent to prison in June 2001 for violations in connection with his earlier release on the 1999 charge. Two months earlier, Mouada had issued a joint declaration with *Nahda* leader Rachid Ghanouchi calling for creation of a joint antigovernment front. However, apparently underscoring continued disagreement within the MDS regarding the extent of cooperation with the regime, Boulahia met with President Ben Ali in early 2001 and praised his commitment to "democratic values." In March 2002, Ben Ali pardoned Mouada. Meanwhile, Ben Jafaar joined the Democratic Forum for Labor and Liberties, continuing his heavy criticism of the administration.

The party supported Ben Ali in the 2004 presidential election and won representation in the municipal elections of 2005. Boulahia reiterated the party's support for Ben Ali in 2008, and the party endorsed the president's reelection bid in 2009. In the 2009 parliamentary elections, the MDS was the only party besides the RCD to field candidates in all constituencies. The party secured the second-highest number of seats (16) under the proportional representation system.

The party secured two seats in the 2011 Constituent Assembly election.

Leader: Mohammed AL-MOUADDA.

Other parties reported to have won seats in the assembly include **People's Progressive Unionist Movement** (MPPU), 2; **Maghrebin Liberal Party**, 1; the **Equity and Equality Party**, 1; the **Progressive Struggle Party**, 1; **Neo Destour Party**, 1; **Democratic Social Nation Party**, 1; **Cultural Unionist Nation Party**, 1; **Free Patriotic Union**, 1; **Democratic Patriots' Movement**, 1.

LEGISLATURE

Note: On February 8 and 9, 2011, in accordance with the constitution, both chambers of the legislature invested Interim President Fouad Mbazaâ with the authority to rule by decree, and the parliament was dissolved.

House of Representatives (*Majlis al-Nuwab/Chambre des Députés*). The lower house consists of 214 members serving five-year terms. Under a new system adopted for the 1994 election, most representatives are elected on a "winner-takes-all" basis in which the party whose list gains the most votes in a district secures all the seats for that district. (There are 25 districts comprising 2 to 10 seats each.) The remaining seats are allocated to parties that failed to win in any districts, in proportion to the parties' national vote totals.

From the establishment of the house in 1959 until 1994, members of the ruling party (RCD) occupied all seats. Although six opposition parties were permitted to offer candidates in the 1989 balloting and a number of independent candidates sponsored by the unsanctioned Renaissance Party also ran, the RCD won all seats with a reported 80 percent of the vote. RCD candidates also won all nine seats contested in October 1991 by-elections, which were boycotted by the opposition parties. The house was enlarged from 141 members to 163 for the 1994 election and to 182 for the 1999 balloting. The membership was expanded to 189 seats for the election on October 24, 2004, President Ben Ali decreeing that 43 seats be filled by women. The RCD won all 152 seats that were contested on a district basis (for the results of the most recent prerevolution balloting, see an earlier *Handbook*).

President: Fouad MBAZAÂ.

House of Advisers (*Majlis al-Mustasharin*). A referendum on May 26, 2002, provided for several constitutional changes, the creation of the upper house among them. The House of Advisers comprises 126 members, 85 of whom are indirectly elected by an electoral college of municipal and regional council members, and 41 appointed by the president, all serving six-year terms (half of the members are renewed every three years). The members include 14 from each of the 3 main professional unions and federations and 43 representatives from various regions of the country (for the results of recent prerevolution balloting, see an earlier *Handbook*).

Constituent Assembly. In the balloting of October 23, 2011, the seat distribution was as follows: *Nahda*, 89; Congress for the Republic, 29; Popular Petition, 26; Democratic Forum for Labour and Liberties (Ettakatol/FDTL), 20; Progressive Democratic Party (PDP), 16; The Initiative, 5; Modernist Democratic Pole (PDM), 5; Tunisian Aspiration, 4; Tunisian Workers' Communist Party (PCOT), 3; People's Progressive Unionist Movement (MPPU), 2; Movement of Social Democrats (MDS), 2; Maghrebin Liberal Party (PLM), 1; Equity and Equality Party, 1; Progressive Struggle Party, 1; Neo Destour Party, 1; Democratic Social Nation Party, 1; Cultural Unionist Nation Party, 1; Free Patriotic Union, 1; Democratic Patriots' Movement, 1; Independent lists, 8.

Speaker: Mustapha Ben JAFAAR.

INTERIM CABINET

[as of September 1, 2013]

Interim Prime Minister	Ali Laarayedh (*Nahda)*
Ministers	
Agriculture and the Environment	Mohamed Ben Salem (*Nahda*)
Communication Technology	Mongi Marzouk (*Nahda*)
Culture	Mehdi Mabrouk (ind.)
Development and International Cooperation	Amin Doghri (ind.)
Education	Salem Abyadh (ind.)
Employment and Vocational Training	Naoufel Jamali (ind.)
Equipment and the Environment	Mohamed Salmane (*Nahda*)
Finance	Elyes Fakhfkh (FDTL)
Foreign Affairs	Othman Jarandi (ind.)
Health	Abdellatif Mekki (*Nahda*)

Higher Education	Moncef Ben Salem (*Nahda*)
Human Rights and Transitional Justice	Samir Dilou (*Nahda*)
Industry and Technology	Mehdi Jomaa (ind.)
Interior	Lotfi Ben Jeddou (ind.)
Justice	Nadhir Ben Ammou (ind.)
National Defense	Rachid Sabbagh (ind.)
Regional and Local Development	Jameleddine Gharbi (*Nahda*)
Religious Affairs	Noureddine Khadmi (ind.)
Social Affairs	Khalil Zaouia (FDTL)
State Property	Slim Ben Hmidène (CPR)
Trade	Abdelwahab Matar (CPR)
Transport and Equipment	Abdelkarim Harouni (*Nahda*)
Tourism	Jamel Gamra (ind.)
Women's Affairs	Sihem Badi (CPR) [f]
Youth and Sports	Tarek Dhiab (ind.)

[f] = female

INTERGOVERNMENTAL REPRESENTATION

Ambassador to the U.S.: Mohamed Salah TEKAYA.

U.S. Ambassador to Tunisia: Jacob WALLES.

Permanent Representative to the UN: Othman JERANDI.

IGO Memberships (Non-UN): AfDB, AU, IOM, LAS, NAM, OIC, WTO.

TURKEY

Republic of Turkey
Türkiye Cumhuriyeti

Political Status: Independent republic established in 1923; parliamentary democracy since 1946, save for military interregna from May 1960 to October 1961 and September 1980 to November 1983; present constitution approved by referendum of November 7, 1982.

Area: 300,948 sq. mi. (779,452 sq. km).

Population: 75,217,838 (2012E—UN); 80,694,485 (2013E—U.S. Census).

Major Urban Centers (2007E): ANKARA (3,641,931), İstanbul (10,291,102), İzmir (2,651,568), Bursa (1,504,817), Adana (1,294,460), Gaziantep (1,136,281), Konya (932,589).

Official Language: Turkish. A 1982 law banning the use of the Kurdish language was rescinded in early 1991.

Monetary Unit: Turkish Lira (*Türk Lirası*—TL) (market rate November 1, 2013: 2.02 Turkish New Liras = $1US).

President of the Republic: Abdullah GÜL (Justice and Development Party); elected by the Grand National Assembly on August 20, 24, and 28, 2007, and sworn in for a seven-year term on the same day to succeed Ahmet Necdet SEZER (nonparty).

Prime Minister: Recep Tayyip ERDOĞAN (Justice and Development Party); appointed by the president on March 14, 2003; reappointed following early legislative elections on July 22, 2007, and formed new government on August 6; formed new government on August 29, 2007, following election of President Gül; formed a new government on July 6, 2011, following legislative elections on June 12.

THE COUNTRY

Guardian of the narrow straits between the Mediterranean and Black seas, present-day Turkey occupies the compact land mass of the Anatolian Peninsula together with the partially European city of İstanbul and its Thracian hinterland. The country, which borders on Greece, Bulgaria, Georgia, Armenia, the Nakhichevan Autonomous Republic of Azerbaijan, Iran, Iraq, and Syria, has a varied topography and is subject to extreme variation in climate. It supports a largely Turkish population (approximately 75 percent in terms of language) but has a substantial Kurdish minority of approximately 12 million, plus such smaller groups as Arabs, Circassians, Greeks, Armenians, Georgians, Lazes, and Jews. Some 99 percent of the populace, including both Turks and Kurds, are Muslim (the majority are Sunni). Islam remains a strong influence despite the secular emphasis of government policy since the 1920s.

Women constitute approximately 36 percent of the official labor force, with large numbers serving as unpaid workers on family farms. While only 10 percent of the urban labor force is female, there is extensive participation by upper-income women in such professions as medicine, law, banking, and education, with the government being headed by a female prime minister from 1993 to 1995. In the 2011 balloting for the assembly, women secured 78 seats, or 14.2 percent of the total.

Turkey traditionally has been an agricultural country, with about 30 percent of the population still engaged in agricultural pursuits. Grain (most importantly wheat), tobacco, cotton, nuts, fruits, and olive oil are the chief agricultural products; sheep and cattle are raised on the Anatolian plateau, and the country ranks among the leading producers of mohair. Natural resources include chrome, copper, iron ore, manganese, bauxite, borax, and petroleum. The most important industries are textiles, iron and steel, sugar, food processing, cement, paper, and fertilizer. State economic enterprises (SEEs) account for more than 60 percent of fixed investment, although substantial privatization has been implemented.

A financial crisis erupted in late February 2001, forcing a currency devaluation and other intervention measures (for information on the Turkish economy prior to 2001, see the 2010 *Handbook*). The resolution of the economic problems was considered a prerequisite to Turkey's long-standing goal of accession to the European Union (EU) (see Foreign relations, below, for details). With the aid of a $15.7 billion International Monetary Fund (IMF) "rescue package" in May 2001 and additional aid of up to $10 billion endorsed in November, the government narrowly avoided defaulting on its debt repayments.

Annual GDP growth averaged 4.7 percent in 2000–2008, while inflation averaged 24.9 percent (although the average inflation between 2004 and 2008 was 9.1 percent following a currency conversion). The economic stabilization was in large part due to banking reforms, privatization, and debt reduction.

In April 2006 parliament approved a long-sought social security reform bill, raising the retirement age to 65 and including measures to deter abuse. In 2009, the global economic crisis had a significant impact on the Turkish economy, most notably in a sharp drop in exports, as a result of which the unemployment rate rose to 14 percent. Meanwhile, GDP declined by 4.8 percent, although inflation remained low at 6.2 percent. The following year, GDP rebounded with 9 percent growth, mainly due to rising exports to the EU, but in 2012 GDP growth fell to 2.6 percent. In 2013 the economy grew by 3.4 percent. Inflation was 6.6 percent and unemployment, 9.4 percent.

GOVERNMENT AND POLITICS

Political background. Present-day Turkey is the surviving core of a vast empire created by Ottoman rule in late medieval and early modern times. After a period of expansion during the 15th and 16th centuries in which Ottoman domination was extended over much of central Europe, the Balkans, the Middle East, and North Africa, the empire underwent a lengthy period of contraction and fragmentation, finally dissolving in the aftermath of a disastrous alliance with Germany in World War I.

A secular nationalist republic was proclaimed on October 29, 1923, by Mustafa Kemal ATATÜRK, who launched a reform program under which Turkey abandoned much of its Ottoman and Islamic heritage. Its major components included secularization (separation of religion and state), establishment of state control of the economy, and creation of a new Turkish national identity. Following his death in 1938, Atatürk's Republican People's Party (*Cumhuriyet Halk Partisi*—CHP) continued as the only legally recognized party under his close associate, İsmet İNÖNÜ. One-party domination was not seriously contested until after World War II, when the opposition Democratic Party (*Demokrat Parti*—DP) was established by Celal BAYAR, Adnan MENDERES, and others.

Winning the country's first free election in 1950, the DP ruled Turkey for the next decade, only to be ousted in 1960 by a military coup led by Gen. Cemal GÜRSEL. The military justified the coup as a response to alleged corruption within the DP and the growing authoritarian attitudes of its leaders. Many of those so charged, including President Bayar and Prime Minister Menderes, were tried by martial courts and found guilty of violating the constitution, after which Bayar was imprisoned and Menderes and two of his ministers were executed.

Civilian government was restored under a new constitution in 1961, with Gürsel remaining as president until he suffered a stroke, and was replaced by Gen. Cevdet SUNAY in 1966. The 1961 basic law established a series of checks and balances to offset a concentration of power in the executive and prompted a diffusion of parliamentary seats among several parties. A series of coalition governments, most of them led by İnönü, functioned until 1965, when a partial reincarnation of the DP, Süleyman DEMİREL's Justice Party (*Adalet Partisi*—AP), won a sweeping legislative mandate.

Following its 1965 victory, the Demirel regime became the target of popular discontent. Although surviving the election of 1969, it was subsequently caught between left-wing agitation and military insistence on the maintenance of public order, a critical issue because of mounting economic and social unrest and the growth of political terrorism. The crisis came to a head in 1971 with an ultimatum from the military that resulted in Demirel's resignation and the formation of a "nonparty" government by Nihat ERİM. The new government amended the 1961 constitution, declared martial law in eleven provinces, arrested dissident elements, and outlawed the left-wing Turkish Workers Party (*Türkiye İşçi Partisi*—TİP) and the moderate Islamist National Order Party (*Millî Nizam Partisi*—MNP). The period immediately after the fall of the Erim government in 1972 witnessed another "nonparty" administration under Ferit MELEN and the selection of a new president, Adm. (Ret.) Fahri KORUTÜRK. Political instability was heightened further by an inconclusive election in 1973 and by both foreign and domestic policy problems stemming from a rapidly deteriorating economy, substantial urban population growth, and renewed conflict on Cyprus, which led to a Turkish invasion of the island in the summer of 1974.

Bülent ECEVİT was appointed prime minister in January 1974, heading a coalition of his own moderately progressive CHP and the smaller, more religious National Salvation Party (*Millî Selâmet Partisi*—MSP). Despite securing widespread domestic acclaim for the Cyprus action and for his insistence that the island be formally divided into Greek and Turkish federal regions, Ecevit was opposed by Deputy Prime Minister Necmettin ERBAKAN, who called for outright annexation of the Turkish sector and, along with his MSP colleagues, resigned, precipitating Ecevit's own resignation in September. After both Ecevit and former prime minister Demirel failed to form new governments, Sadi IRMAK, an independent, was designated prime minister on November 17, heading an essentially nonparliamentary cabinet. Following a defeat in the National Assembly only twelve days later, Irmak also was forced to resign, although he remained in office in a caretaker capacity until Demirel succeeded in forming a Nationalist Front coalition government on April 12, 1975.

At an early general election on June 5, 1977, no party succeeded in gaining a lower house majority, and the Demirel government fell on July 13. Following Ecevit's inability to organize a majority coalition, Demirel returned as head of a tripartite administration that failed to survive a vote of confidence on December 31. Ecevit then returned to his former position, organizing a minority government.

Widespread civil and political unrest throughout 1978 prompted a declaration of martial law in 13 provinces on December 25. The security situation deteriorated further during 1979, and, faced with a number of ministerial defections, Prime Minister Ecevit was obliged to step down again on October 16, with Demirel returning as head of an AP minority government on November 12.

Divided by rising foreign debt and increasing domestic terrorism, the National Assembly failed to elect a president to succeed Fahri Korutürk, despite casting over 100 ballots. Senate President İhsan Sabri ÇAĞLAYANGİL assumed the office on an acting basis at the expiration of Korutürk's seven-year term on April 6. On August 29 Gen. Kenan EVREN, chief of the General Staff, publicly criticized the assembly for its failure both to elect a new president and to promulgate more drastic security legislation, and on September 12 he mounted a coup on behalf of a five-man National Security Council (NSC) that suspended the constitution, dissolved the assembly, proclaimed martial law in all of the country's 67 provinces, and on September 21 designated a military-civilian cabinet under Adm. (Ret.) Bülent ULUSU. The junta banned all existing political parties, detaining many of their leaders, including Ecevit and Demirel; imposed strict censorship; and arrested upwards of 40,000 persons on political charges.

In a national referendum on November 7, 1982, Turkish voters overwhelmingly approved a new constitution, under which General Evren was formally designated as president of the Republic for a seven-year term. One year later, on November 6, 1983, the recently established Motherland Party (*Anavatan Partisi*—ANAP) of former deputy prime minister Turgut ÖZAL won a majority of seats in a newly constituted unicameral Grand National Assembly. Following the election, General Evren's four colleagues on the NSC resigned their military commands, continuing as members of a Presidential Council upon dissolution of the NSC on December 6. On December 7, Özal was asked to form a government and assumed office as prime minister on December 13.

Turkish voters rebuked Prime Minister Özal on March 26, 1989, when ANAP candidates ran a poor third overall, securing only 22 percent of the vote and losing control of the three largest cities. Özal refused, however, to call for new legislative balloting and, despite a plunge in personal popularity to 28 percent, utilized his assembly majority on October 31 to secure the presidency in succession to Evren. Following his inauguration at a parliamentary ceremony on November 9 that was boycotted by opposition members, Özal announced his choice of Assembly Speaker Yıldırım AKBULUT as the new prime minister.

Motherland's standing in the opinion polls slipped to a minuscule 14 percent in the wake of a political crisis that erupted in April 1991 over the somewhat heavy-handed installation of the president's wife, Semra Özal, as chair of the ruling party's İstanbul branch. Both Özals declared their neutrality in a leadership contest at a party congress in mid-June, but they were viewed as the principal architects of an unprecedented challenge to Prime Minister Akbulut, who was defeated for reelection as chair by former foreign minister Mesut YILMAZ.

Yılmaz called for an early election on October 20, 1991, "to refresh the people's confidence" in his government. The outcome, however, was a defeat for the ruling party, with former prime minister Demirel, now leader of the right-of-center True Path Party (*Doğru Yol Partisi*—DYP), negotiating a coalition with the left-of-center Social Democratic People's Party (*Sosyal Demokrat Halkçı Parti*—SHP) and returning to office for the seventh time on November 21, with the SHP's Erdal İNÖNÜ as his deputy.

Demirel's broad-based administration, which brought together the heirs of Turkey's two oldest and most prominent political traditions (the CHP and the DP), claimed greater popularity—50 percent voter support and more than 60 percent backing in the polls—than any government in recent decades. Thus encouraged, Demirel and İnönü launched an ambitious program to counter the problems of rampant inflation, Kurdish insurgency, and obstacles to full democratization.

On April 17, 1993, President Özal died of a heart attack, and on May 16 the Grand National Assembly elected Prime Minister Demirel head of state. The DYP's search for a new chair ended on June 13, when Tansu ÇİLLER, an economics professor, defeated two other candidates at an extraordinary party congress. On July 5 a new DYP-SHP coalition government, committed to a program of further democratization, secularization, and privatization, was accorded a vote of confidence by the assembly, and Çiller became Turkey's first female prime minister.

A major offensive against guerrillas of the Kurdistan Workers' Party (*Partîya Karkerén Kurdistan*—PKK) in northern Iraq was launched on March 20, 1995. Six weeks later the government announced that the operation had been a success and that all of its units had returned to Turkey. The popularity of the action was demonstrated in local elections on June 4, when the ruling DYP took 22 of 36 mayoralties on a 39 percent share of the vote. However, on September 20 a revived CHP, which had become the DYP's junior coalition partner after absorbing the SHP in February, withdrew its support, forcing the resignation of the Çiller government. (The SHP has since left the CHP.)

On October 2, 1995, Çiller announced the formation of a DYP minority administration that drew unlikely backing from the far-right Nationalist Action Party (*Milliyetçi Hareket Partisi*—MHP) and the center-left Democratic Left Party (*Demokratik Sol Parti*—DSP). However, the prime minister was opposed within the DYP by former National Assembly speaker Hüsamettin CİNDORUK, who resigned on October 1 and was one of ten deputies expelled from the party on October 16, one day after Çiller's defeat on a confidence motion. On October 31 President Demirel appointed Çiller to head a DYP-CHP interim government pending a premature election in December.

At the December 24, 1995, balloting the pro-Islamic Welfare Party (*Refah Partisi*—RP) emerged as the legislative leader, although its 158 seats fell far short of the 276 needed for an overall majority. Eventually, on February 28, 1996, agreement was reached on a center-right coalition that would permit the ANAP's Yılmaz to serve as prime minister until January 1, 1997, with Çiller occupying the post for the ensuing two years and Yılmaz returning for the balance of the parliamentary term, assuming no dissolution.

Formally launched on March 12, 1996, the ANAP-DYP coalition collapsed at the end of May amid renewed personal animosity between Yılmaz and Çiller over the former's unwillingness to back the DYP leader against corruption charges related to her recent premiership. The DYP then opted to become the junior partner in an alternative coalition headed by RP leader Necmettin ERBAKAN, who on June 28 became Turkey's first avowedly Islamist prime minister since the creation of the secular republic in 1923. Under the coalition agreement, Çiller was slated to take over as head of government in January 1998. However, on February 28, 1997, the military members of the National Security Council (*Milli Güvenlik Kurulu*—MGK) presented the civilian members of the council with a memorandum, reportedly expressing their concern that Erbakan's tolerance for rising religious activism would seriously threaten the country's secular tradition. Erbakan resigned on June 18, 1997, seemingly paving way for the leadership of his coalition partner, Çiller. However, on June 20 President Demirel bypassed Çiller, whose DYP had been weakened by steady defections, and selected the ANAP's Yılmaz to return as the next prime minister. A new coalition composed of the ANAP, the DSP, and the new center-right Democratic Turkey Party (*Demokrat Türkiye Partisi*—DTP) was approved by Demirel on June 30, and Yılmaz and his cabinet were sworn in on the following day.

The new coalition government in July 1997 proposed an eight-year compulsory education plan that included the closure of Islamic secondary schools, prompting weeks of right-wing and militant Islamic demonstrations.

The Yılmaz government collapsed on November 25, 1998, when he lost a vote of confidence in the Grand National Assembly following accusations of corruption against members of his cabinet. President Demirel asked Bülent Ecevit to form a new government on December 2, thereby abandoning the long-standing tradition of designating the leader of the largest party in the legislature as prime minister. (Such action would have put Recai KUTAN's moderate Islamist Virtue Party [*Fazilet Partisi*—FP] in power, an option opposed by the military.) When Ecevit proved unable to form a government, Demirel turned to an independent, Yalım EREZ, who also failed when former prime minister Çiller rejected his proposal that her DYP be part of a new coalition. After Erez abandoned his initiative on January 6, 1999, President Demirel again invited Ecevit to form the government. This time Ecevit succeeded in forming a minority cabinet made up of the DSP and independents; the DYP and ANAP agreed to provide external support.

Ecevit's cabinet survived a crisis that erupted in mid-March 1999, when the FP threatened to topple the government and joined forces with disgruntled members of parliament from various political parties who were not nominated for reelection. In balloting on April 18, 1999, Ecevit's DSP received 22 percent of the votes and became the largest party in the assembly, with 136 seats. On May 28 Ecevit announced the formation of a coalition cabinet comprising the DSP, MHP, and ANAP. Meanwhile, on May 16 Ahmet Necdet SEZER, chief justice of the Constitutional Court, was sworn in as the new president, following the legislature's rejection of President Demirel's request for constitutional revision that would have permitted him a second term.

In October 2001 the Grand National Assembly approved several constitutional amendments aimed at easing Turkey's path into the EU. The changes provided greater protection for political freedom and civil leaders, including protection for the Kurdish minority. Moreover, the number of civilians on the National Security Council was increased from five to nine, with the military continuing to hold five seats.

In January 2002 the Constitutional Court banned Justice and Development (AKP) leader Recep Tayyip ERDOĞAN from running for the legislature because of alleged seditious activities and ordered his removal from party leadership. In July Prime Minister Ecevit was forced to call early elections to the Grand National Assembly in the wake of the DSP-led coalition having lost its majority due to resignations. Subsequently, the DSP won only 1.2 percent of the vote and no seats in the November 3 election, as the AKP gained control with 34.3 percent of the vote and 363 seats. The CHP won 19.4 percent of the vote and 178 seats.

With Erdoğan prohibited from holding a seat in the assembly, the AKP's deputy leader, Abdullah GÜL, was appointed prime minister, though Erdoğan reportedly acted as de facto prime minister. Meanwhile, the AKP majority adopted constitutional changes that allowed Erdoğan to run for parliament, and in a March 9, 2003, by-election, Erdoğan won. Five days later he was appointed prime minister.

Also in March 2003 Turkey's Constitutional Court banned the People's Democracy Party (HADEP) from politics as a result of its alleged support for the PKK. In addition, 46 party members were individually banned from politics for five years. In September 2003 the PKK announced that it was ending its five-year cease-fire with the Turkish government. In a September 2004 offensive, the largest in five years, government troops killed 11 Kurdish rebels in the southeast province of Hakkari. The government blamed Kurdish rebels for a series of bombings in August and September.

The AKP further solidified its position with a strong showing in local elections on March 28, 2004, winning 42 percent of the vote, well ahead of the second-place CHP with 18 percent. Parliament adopted further reforms aimed at promoting Turkey's accession to the EU, including measures allowing broadcasting and education in Kurdish. Another law, enacted after an override of President Sezer's veto, allowed peaceful advocacy of an independent Kurdish state.

Prime Minister Erdoğan's nomination of Foreign Minister Gül as the AKP candidate for the May 2007 presidential election prompted widespread anxiety among secular elites and the military, who claimed that Gül's Islamist leanings made him unfit for office in Turkey's secular system. The military issued a memorandum publicly opposing Gül's candidacy and asserting that the military could not remain indifferent to the threat of an Islamist takeover. On April 27 and May 5, opposition parties boycotted presidential election votes, and Gül subsequently withdrew as a candidate. Meanwhile, the Constitutional Court ruled that a quorum of two thirds, or 367 members, was necessary for a legal presidential election. To overcome the deadlock, Erdoğan called for early general elections on July 22, a measure parliament unanimously approved. The assembly subsequently voted to amend the constitution to allow for direct popular election of the president, but the measure was vetoed by President Sezer. Another vote by parliament on June 1 produced the same result, and again Sezer rejected the measure, which would have required a national referendum to be held within 120 days. Parliament's vote to hold the constitutional referendum and then concurrent presidential and legislative elections was also vetoed by Sezer.

In the July 2007 early elections, the AKP secured a stunning victory, improving upon its 2002 return by 12 percent, with 46.7 percent of votes and 341 seats. The CHP and the MHP won 98 and 71 seats, respectively. Several smaller parties managed to circumvent the threshold and achieve small representation via coalitions or independent candidacies. Following the strong showing of the AKP, Gül, again nominated by Erdoğan, received 339 votes in parliament on August 28 to become president of the republic. Subsequently, a national referendum on the proposed constitutional changes was held in October, with 68.95 percent of voters registering approval for the amendments.

Controversy over the role of Islam in public life continued after the election, as in June 2008 the Constitutional Court annulled a constitutional amendment lifting a ban on women wearing headscarves on university campuses. A parliamentary majority had supported a constitutional amendment to lift the ban.

Following the poor performance of the AKP in the March 2009 municipal elections, Erdoğan reshuffled the cabinet on May 1. His appointments included his longtime foreign policy adviser Ahmet DAVUTOĞLU as foreign minister. Davutoğlu's appointment was seen by observers as a move toward enhancing Turkey's relations with the Middle East, among other things. In October, after years of declining electoral success, the ANAP merged with the DP (see Political parties and groupings, below).

On March 22, the AKP introduced a range of constitutional amendments designed to strengthen the powers of the government in relation to Turkey's traditionally secular institutions, including the military and the judiciary. The AKP failed to secure the needed two-thirds majority in the Parliament to adopt the amendments, forcing Erdoğan to present the measures in a national referendum. On July 7, the Constitutional Court rejected two of the amendments, but allowed 26 others to be put forward in a referendum on September 12. The constitutional changes were approved with 58 percent in favor (see Constitution and government, below). All of the major opposition parties opposed the amendments.

In legislative balloting on June 12, 2011, the AKP won a reduced majority in the 550-member assembly, with 327 seats. The majority fell short of the two-thirds needed to revise the constitution. On June 29, Erdoğan was reappointed prime minister of a reshuffled, smaller cabinet.

Erdoğan orchestrated a cabinet reshuffle in January 2013, replacing four ministers with close allies of the administration. Mass antigovernment protests erupted in Istanbul, Ankara, and towns around the country in June. On September 30 Erdoğan unveiled a broad set of reforms called the "democratization package." (For more on the protests and the reforms, see Current issues, below.)

Constitution and government. The 1982 constitution provided for a unicameral 400-member Grand National Assembly elected for a five-year term (the membership being increased to 450 in 1987 and 550 in 1995). The president, elected by the assembly for a five-year term, renewable once, is empowered to appoint and dismiss the prime minister and other cabinet members; to dissolve the assembly and call for a new election, assuming the concurrence of two-thirds of the deputies or if faced with a government crisis of more than 30 days' duration; to declare a state of emergency, during which the government may rule by decree; and to appoint a variety of leading government officials, including senior judges and the governor of the Central Bank. Political parties may be formed if they are not based on class or ethnicity, linked to trade unions, or committed to communism, fascism, or religious fundamentalism. Strikes that exceed 60 days' duration are subject to compulsory arbitration.

In 2003, the constitution was amended to change the membership and rules of operation of the country's National Security Council (*Milli Güvenlik Kurulu*-MGK), which has served as one of the most important levers for the control of Turkish politics by the military. The amendments reduced the number of council seats reserved for the military. For the first time in its history, the MGK had a civilian majority and a civilian secretary general.

Further amendments approved in 2007 provide for the direct election of the president every four years, reducing the presidential term from seven years to five, and allowing the president to stand for a second term (see Current issues, below). Amendments enacted in 2010 reduced the authority of the military to intervene in civilian affairs and made it easier for military officers to be charged by civilian authorities. The number of Constitutional Court justices was increased and Parliament was given greater control over the selection of judges. The measures also expanded civil liberties and made it more difficult to suspend political parties.

The Turkish judicial system is headed by a Court of Cassation (*Yargıtay*), which is the court of final appeal. Other judicial bodies include an administrative tribunal styled the Council of State (*Danıştay*), a Constitutional Court (*Anayasa Mahkemesi*), a Court of Accounts (*Sayıştay*), various military courts, and 12 state security courts.

The country is presently divided into 82 provinces, which are further divided into subprovinces and districts. Mayors and municipal councils have long been popularly elected, save during the period 1980–1984.

After decades of censorship, freedom of the press was largely restored in the first half of the 1990s. On July 21, 1997, the Council of Ministers accepted a draft granting amnesty to imprisoned journalists. Under current law, however, journalists still face prosecution and imprisonment for reporting on issues deemed sensitive by the government. Article 301 of the Turkish Penal Code, which punishes those who "publicly denigrate Turkishness or the Republic of Turkey," has been repeatedly invoked to allow persecution of journalists and intellectuals who express opinions contrary to official Turkish views on a number of political issues, such as the Armenian question. Hrant DİNK and Orhan PAMUK were targeted based on the code.

Concerns were raised in April 2008 over apparent government involvement in efforts to promote concentration of media ownership. Financial support of state banks to progovernment entrepreneurs to facilitate the purchase of the Sabah media group was seen as an overt government attempt to strengthen its grip over media.

The government's long-standing feud with the country's biggest media conglomerate, Dogan Media Group (*Doğan Medya Grubu*), attracted international attention following the levying of a $500 million tax fine against the group in February 2009. In October 2010 Turkey opened access to the Web site *YouTube* for the first time since 2008 but banned it again in November. A report by the EU indicated that Turkey continued to block more Web sites than any other European country. In 2013 the media watchdog group Reporters Without Borders ranked Turkey 154th out of 179 countries in terms of freedom of the press, and called the country "the world's biggest prison for journalists," estimating some 50 media professionals to be imprisoned. Reports of journalists being targeted by police with violence and arbitrary arrest during the Gezi Park protests in 2013 drew international criticism (see Current issues, below).

Foreign relations. Neutral until the closing months of World War II, Turkey entered that conflict in time to become a founding member of the United Nations and has since joined all of the latter's affiliated agencies. Concern for the protection of its independence, primarily against possible Soviet threats, made Turkey a firm ally of the Western powers, with one of the largest standing armies in the non-Communist world. Largely on U.S. initiative, Turkey was admitted to the North Atlantic Treaty Organization (NATO) in 1952 and in 1955 became a founding member of the Baghdad Treaty Organization, later the Central Treaty Organization (CENTO), which was officially disbanded in September 1979, following the Iranian and Pakistani withdrawals.

Relations with a number of Western governments stagnated in the 1960s, partly because of tensions over Cyprus. The dispute, with the fate of the Turkish Cypriot community at its center, became critical upon the island's attainment of independence in 1960 and nearly led to war with Greece in 1967. The 1974 Greek junta coup resulted in the temporary ouster of Cypriot president Makarios, and the subsequent Turkish invasion on July 20 yielded Turkish occupation of the northern third of the island. (For details, see the entries on Cyprus and Cyprus: Turkish Sector.)

Relations with the United States, strained by a congressional ban on military aid following the Cyprus incursion, were further undermined by a Turkish decision in July 1975 to repudiate a 1969 defense cooperation agreement and force the closure of 25 U.S. military installations. However, a new accord concluded in March 1976 called for reopening of the bases under Turkish control and substantially increased American military assistance. The U.S. arms embargo was finally lifted in September 1978, with the stipulation that Turkey continue to seek a negotiated resolution of the Cyprus issue.

While the Turkish government under Evren and Özal consistently affirmed its support of NATO and its desire to gain full entry to the EC (having been an associate member of the European Economic Community since 1964), relations with Western Europe deteriorated in the wake of the 1980 coup because of alleged human rights violations.

Ankara submitted a formal membership request to the EC, and in December 1989 the commission had laid down a number of stringent conditions for admission to the community, including an improved human rights record, progress toward improved relations with Greece, and less dependence on agricultural employment. Because of these concerns, Turkey remained outside the EU upon the latter's inception in November 1993, although, in an action viewed as linked to its EC bid, it had become an associate member of the Western European Union in 1992.

On March 6, 1995, Turkey and the EU agreed to a customs union, which entered into force on January 1, 1996. However, in July 1997 the EU Commission excluded Turkey from first-round enlargement negotiations scheduled for early 1998. Moreover, the commission recommended Cyprus for full membership, a decision that Turkey saw as controversial given the lack of a settlement of the Cyprus question. In light of improving Turkish/Greek relations, a December 1999 EU summit finally accepted Turkey as an official candidate for membership.

Apart from Cyprus, the principal dispute between Greece and Turkey has centered on territorial rights in the Aegean. In late 1984 Ankara rejected a proposal by Prime Minister Papandreou to assign Greek forces on Limnos to NATO, invoking a long-standing contention that militarization of the island was forbidden under the 1923 Treaty of Lausanne. The controversy revived in early 1989 with Turkey refusing to recognize insular sea and airspace limits greater than six miles on the premise that to do otherwise would convert the area into a "Greek lake." The dispute intensified in September 1994, with Greece declaring that it would formally extend its jurisdiction to 12 nautical miles upon entry into force of the UN Convention on the Law of the Sea on November 16. Turkey immediately warned that the move would be considered an "act of aggression," and on October 30 Athens announced that it would defer the introduction of what it continued to view as a "sovereign right." On June 8, 1995, the Turkish Parliament approved a declaration that an extension of Greek territorial waters in the Aegean to 12 miles would comprise a *casus belli* for Turkey, further straining bilateral relations with Greece.

Another territorial issue was addressed when Turkey concluded an agreement with Iraq in October 1984 that permitted the security forces of each government to pursue "subversive groups" (interpreted primarily as Kurdish rebels) up to a distance of five kilometers on either side of the border and to engage in follow-up operations for five days without prior notification.

However the Turkish government strongly supported UN-endorsed sanctions against Iraq in the wake of its invasion of Kuwait in August 1990. Despite considerable revenue loss, Turkey moved quickly to shut down Iraqi oil pipelines by banning ships from loading crude at offshore terminals. In September, despite opposition criticism, the legislature granted the administration special authority to dispatch troops to the Gulf and to allow foreign forces to be stationed on Turkish soil for non-NATO purposes (importantly, the stationing of F-111 fighter bombers at İncirlik air base to monitor the UN-sanctioned Iraqi no-fly zone north of the 36th parallel).

Turkey's attention refocused on maritime issues in 1994 as Ankara angered Moscow by seeking to impose restrictions on shipping through the Bosporus, despite the 1936 Montreux treaty, which provided complete freedom of transit through both the Bosporus and Dardanelles during peacetime. Turkey insisted that the new regulations were prompted only by technical considerations that had not existed at the time of the treaty's adoption.

During the 1992 conflict in Bosnia and Herzegovina, both the Bosnians and Turkish citizens of Bosnian descent appealed for action to oppose Serbian advances in Muslim areas; however, Atatürk's secularist heirs were reluctant to move in a manner that might be seen as religiously inspired. Urging limited military intervention, Turkey launched a pro-Bosnian campaign in various international venues, including the UN, the Conference on (subsequently the Organization for) Security and Cooperation in Europe (CSCE/OSCE), NATO, the Council of Europe, and the OIC.

Turkey commenced its own military action on March 20, 1995, targeting the Kurds in northern Iraq, provoking condemnation from West European governments. On April 10 the EU foreign ministers, while acknowledging Turkey's "terrorism problems," called on Ankara to withdraw its troops "without delay," and on April 26 the Parliamentary Assembly of the Council of Europe approved a resolution calling for suspension of Turkey's membership if it did not leave Iraq by late June. The Turkish government reacted angrily to an April 12 announcement that political exiles had established a Kurdish "parliament in exile" in the Netherlands. A renewed cross-border offensive was launched by some 30,000 troops on July 5–10. (See the 2013 *Handbook* for more on Kurdish relations in the mid-1990s.)

A major diplomatic dispute erupted in 1998 over Syria's alleged sheltering of PKK rebels, with Ankara warning Damascus in October of possible military action unless Syrian policy changed. The crisis was also colored by Syria's concern over the recent rapprochement between Turkey and Israel, which had produced a defense agreement and a recent visit by Prime Minister Yılmaz to Israel. Following intense mediation by several Arab leaders from the region, Syria subsequently agreed that it would not allow the PKK to set up "military, logistical, or financial bases" on Syrian territory. Collaterally, PKK leader Abdullah ÖCALAN was forced to leave Syrian-controlled territory in Lebanon. Öcalan moved to Russia, which, under insistent Turkish pressure, also refused him asylum. He then entered Italy, prompting a row between Rome and Ankara. Italy rejected Turkey's extradition request on the grounds that it could not send a detainee to a country that permitted the death penalty. Italy therefore attempted to negotiate Öcalan's transfer to Germany, where he also faced terrorism charges. However, Bonn, apparently fearing violence between its own Turkish and Kurdish minorities, declined to file an extradition request. Consequently, Öcalan was released from detention in Italy in mid-December and reportedly left that country in January 1999. In mid-February 1999, Öcalan was arrested shortly after he left the home of the Greek ambassador in Nairobi, Kenya. Despite the renewed animosity surrounding Öcalan's arrest, Turkish-Greek relations thawed noticeably in late 1999 when Greece lifted its veto on EU financial aid earmarked to Turkey and agreed to a European Council decision that gave Turkey the status of a candidate state for EU membership. In early 2000 the two countries agreed to establish a joint commission to "reduce military tensions" in the Aegean and to pursue cooperation in several other areas.

In 2003 Turkey's relationship with the United States faced a major challenge with Turkey's refusal to allow U.S. troops to use Turkish territory as a staging area for the invasion of Iraq in March 2003. Some observers attributed this refusal to a political power struggle taking place within Turkey. Relations with the United States also cooled because the Turkish government felt that Washington was indifferent to Kurdish terrorist activity in Turkey and northern Iraq. Indeed, in November 2004, Turkish newspapers published unconfirmed reports that the Turkish government had formulated a plan to move 20,000 Turkish troops into northern Iraq to prevent Kurds from taking complete control of Kirkuk. On January 26, 2005, a senior Turkish army general said bluntly that the Turkish military was prepared to intervene if clashes erupted in northern Iraq or if Iraqi Kurds attempted to form an independent state.

Iran and Turkey signed a security agreement on July 30, 2004, to place rebels opposed to either government on each government's list of terrorist organizations.

Relations with Russia have also been further strained by Turkey's ongoing efforts to control the passage of oil tankers through the Bosporus straits. Turkey has maintained that the increased number of oil tankers represented an environmental threat to its coastline and waterways and has imposed tighter regulations on passage, which Russia said added greatly to transit time and thus to costs. In August 2004 Turkey also proposed, and offered to help fund, construction of pipelines to reduce waterborne traffic. Apart from the issue of the Bosporus strait, however, Turkish relations with Russia have been generally good. Tourism between the two countries has increased significantly, as has bilateral commerce.

Turkey's relations with the EU reached a peak on December 17, 2004, when the European Council agreed to define October 3, 2005, as the starting date of EU-Turkey accession negotiations. However, accession to the EU by the Republic of Cyprus, and the political confusion caused by popular rejection of the European Constitution, downgraded Turkish membership on the EU agenda. Negotiations followed a rather slow pace in 2005, while the reform drive that had pleasantly surprised EU entities between 1999 and 2004 seemed to have been exhausted. In 2005 and 2006, however, European officials charged Turkey's government with backtracking on some reforms and slowing implementation of others. External observers, along with some Turks, voiced concern about the growing tensions between Islamic and secular forces inside Turkey. This was complicated by the opposition of Germany and France, two of the most influential EU member states, whose political leaders objected to full EU membership for Turkey and suggested a "privileged partnership" status instead. EU representatives in recent years have cited Turkey's failure to open air and sea connections with the Republic of Cyprus as a major hurdle to membership.

Iraq resurfaced as a contentious issue between Turkey and the United States in July 2006, when Turkey again called on the United States to crack down on Kurdish rebels in northern Iraq and made veiled threats to attack rebel bases if action was not taken.

Turkey's reputation in parts of the Middle East was enhanced when it offered in May 2008 to moderate peace negotiations between Syria and Israel, the dispute over the Golan Heights considered by Turkey easier to resolve than the dispute between the Israelis and the Palestinians. In addition, a September meeting in New York between President Gül and Iraqi president Jalal Talabani further improved relations between Turkey and Iraq. A visit by Mahmoud Ahmadinejad in August, the first such visit by an Iranian president in 12 years, was seen as paving the way toward improved relations between the two countries.

The fighting between Russia and Georgia in August 2008 over the latter's sovereignty underlined the complexity of Turkish policy toward the Caucasus. As Georgia's strongest regional strategic partner, Turkey's cooperation with Georgia has focused on the construction of oil and natural gas pipelines that circumvent Russia. However, with Russia as Turkey's second biggest trade partner, bilateral relations have significantly improved in recent years. Turkey thus condemned violation of Georgia's territorial integrity and the continuation of hostilities, while at the same time Ankara tried to avoid heightened tensions with Russia by refraining from joining NATO'S most outspoken critics. In an effort to balance its Russian interests, Turkey invoked the 1936 Montreux Treaty to prohibit the immediate passage of U.S. war vessels through the Turkish straits to the Black Sea. Interestingly, a significant part of Turkey's Caucasian diaspora, which had mobilized Turkish public opinion against Russia during the Chechnya crisis, justified Russia's military intervention in 2008 by objecting to Georgia's move to restore its sovereignty over the breakaway provinces of Abkhazia and South Ossetia.

The Georgian crisis provided an opening to Armenia, which had closed its borders with Turkey in 1993 during the Armenian-Azeri war in Nagorno Karabagh. Armenia was included in Turkey's new "Caucasus Alliance" initiative, and in September President Gül accepted, despite vehement objections from the opposition, an invitation from Armenian president Serzh Sarkisyan to visit Erivan. A subsequent meeting of the foreign ministers of Turkey, Armenia, and Azerbaijan in New York raised hopes for resolution of the Nagorno Karabagh question.

Turkish–Israeli relations suffered a serious diplomatic crisis in January 2009 when Prime Minister Erdoğan quarreled with Israeli President Shimon Peres during a discussion at the annual meeting of the World Economic Forum at Davos, Switzerland. Erdoğan lashed out against Israel's Gaza operations and abandoned the forum. He was welcomed in Istanbul by jubilant crowds, who approved of his anti-Israeli stance.

The visit of U.S. president Barack Obama to Turkey in May 2009 was seen as a big boost for Turkish foreign policy, as Obama aimed to restore relations with Turkey and further promote U.S. relations with the Islamic world. Shortly before his arrival, President Obama had reiterated support for Turkey's accession to the EU, causing a clash with French president Nicolas Sarkozy, a vocal opponent of Turkey's full EU membership. While Obama's visit helped improve the image of the United States in Turkey, it failed to produce solutions for a series of long-lasting disputes, including over Armenia and the status of Kurds in northern Iraq. In April 2009, Turkey and Armenia signed a "road map" for rapprochement between the two countries. The result was a historic accord, signed on October 10, 2009, establishing diplomatic relations between the two countries for the first time. The agreement also called for reopening the Turkish-Armenian border, which has been closed since 1993, and paved the way for resolution of the century-old dispute regarding the deaths of many Armenians in the final days of the Ottoman Empire through the creation of a joint committee of historians which would review Armenia's claims of genocide.

Turkey and China signed series of trade agreements worth more than $1.1 billion in January 2010. Also in January, the European Court of Human Rights released a report claiming that, of its signatories, Turkey was the single greatest violator of the European Convention of Human Rights during the period from 1960 to 2000. In February the European Parliament called on Turkey to withdraw its troops from Cyprus and engage in reunification negotiations over the island in order to accelerate EU membership discussions. The Erdoğan government rejected the call. Membership negotiations over eight areas of EU membership were suspended by the EU as a result of Turkey's unwillingness negotiate over Cyprus. Concurrently, EU member Cyprus announced it would prevent new negotiations with Turkey over EU membership in five additional areas.

In March 2010, Turkey withdrew its ambassador from the United States after the U.S. House of Representatives adopted a resolution recognizing Turkey's actions against Armenians in the early 1900s as genocide. The Swedish legislature passed a similar measure, prompting Turkey to also recall its ambassador from Sweden. Erdoğan threatened to expel an estimated 100,000 illegal Armenian immigrants if foreign governments continued to enact comparable resolutions.

On April 22, Armenia suspended ratification of the accord with Turkey, accusing the Turkish government of imposing additional conditions in exchange for approval of the agreement. Meanwhile, also in April, Gül hosted the leaders of Bosnia and Serbia in negotiations that resulted in the Istanbul Declaration, an agreement to settle a number of border and economic issues between the two countries. In June Turkey, Jordan, Lebanon, and Syria agreed to create a free trade zone by strengthening existing bilateral economic agreements.

During a raid on a convoy delivering aid to the Gaza Strip, eight Turkish activists were killed by Israeli security forces on May 31, 2010. Turkey recalled its ambassador in protest. On October 12 the assembly adopted a resolution to permit Turkish military forces to launch attacks into Northern Iraq to suppress the PKK.

On January 27, 2011, the European Court of Human Rights reported that Turkey had more human rights violations than any of the other 47 signatories to the European Convention on Human Rights. More than 10,000 Syrian refugees crossed into Turkey by the summer of 2011, fleeing growing strife in the country.

On February 18, 2011, the Erdoğan government strongly condemned U.S. ambassador Francis Ricciardone for criticizing restrictions on the Turkish press and the arrest of journalists. Tensions between Turkey and Israel also eroded United States–Turkish relations. In September 2011 Turkey expelled the Israeli ambassador and other senior diplomats and recalled its ambassador. It also suspended defense contracts with Israel for new weaponry. On September 12 Erdoğan announced publicly that he believed the May 2010 Israeli raid was a "cause for war," further heightening tensions. Also in September, Erdoğan condemned a joint Israeli–Greek Cypriot exploratory drilling venture off Cyprus (see entry on Cyprus).

Progress on EU membership slowed in 2011 as the Erdoğan government delayed implementation of reforms needed to join the organization.

Erdoğan conducted a diplomatic tour of Egypt, Libya, and Tunisia in September 2011 as part of a broader effort to increase Turkish influence in the Mediterranean. During the visits, Erdoğan reaffirmed Turkish support for Palestinian statehood. That same month, Turkey and the United States signed an agreement to deploy U.S. radar units as part of the NATO-backed missile defense system for Europe. In December, Erdoğan apologized for the deaths of 35 Kurdish youths who were killed in northern Iraq during a Turkish air strike. On December 22, Turkey recalled its ambassador and suspended bilateral relations with France after the French National Assembly voted to make it a crime to deny the Armenian Genocide.

In February 2012, Turkish aircraft bombed suspected PKK bases in Northern Iraq, prompting condemnation from the Iraqi government. Turkey and Turkmenistan signed a number of bilateral economic agreements in March. In May, Turkey negotiated a deal to import oil from the Kurdish region of Iraq. Baghdad opposed the arrangement and warned Turkey that it could damage bilateral relations.

On June 22, 2012, Syria shot down a Turkish plane that Damascus claimed had strayed into Syrian airspace. Ankara insisted that the plane was in Turkish airspace when it was attacked. Turkey condemned the downing and called for consultations with NATO. Relations with Syria soured further in October 2012, when Turkish civilians were killed by Syrian mortar fire along the border of the two countries. The incident prompted Turkish forces to fire into Syria for four days and deploy additional troops to the region.

In March 2013 Israeli Prime Minister Benjamin Netanyahu apologized to Erdoğan for the 2010 flotilla raid. Subsequently meetings were held to normalize ties between the two countries, but they stalled during the June protests (see Current issues, below), and relations have been slow to thaw.

Turkish involvement with the Syrian crisis deepened in 2013. On May 11 two car bombs killed 53 people in Reyhanli, near the Syrian border. Turkish officials arrested nine suspects with alleged links to the Assad regime. The incident heightened tensions toward Turkey's Syrian refugee population, which by October numbered more than 600,000, according to Turkish estimates. In August Erdoğan emerged as a vocal supporter of military intervention in Syria when President Obama weighed U.S. involvement (see the entry on the United States for more). Turkish military actions along the border increased in the autumn.

German Chancellor Angela Merkel sharply criticized the Turkish government's handling of antigovernment protests in June 2013 (see Current issues, below), causing further postponement of EU ascension talks that were slated to resume that month. In October it was announced negotiations would resume in November after a three-year hiatus.

In September Turkey announced plans to purchase a missile defense system from a Chinese company under U.S. sanctions for violating the North Korea, Iran, and Syria Nonproliferation Act, raising objections from the United States. Meanwhile NATO expressed concerns, citing compatibility of the system with those of other member countries.

Current issues. Competition between Prime Minister Erdoğan's AKP government and the secularist bureaucracy often resulted in conflict between the AKP government and President Ahmet Necdet Sezer. In early March 2006 tensions between Islamic and secular forces were evident in President Sezer's veto of the government's nominee for central bank governor. There was speculation that the Erdoğan administration had nominated Adnan BÜYÜKDENİZ, an economist and executive at an Islamic-style bank (which neither pays nor charges interest), in part, because of his religious convictions.

In 2007 there was a considerable rise in PKK activity and government operations in eastern and southeastern Turkey; on May 22 a suicide bomb in Ankara killed seven people, including the bomber, who was thought to be linked to the PKK.

The killing of a Catholic priest in Trabzon in February 2006 preceded a series of killings of Christians, including three Protestants in the eastern city of Malatya on April 18. These were followed by the killing of Hrant Dink, an ethnic Armenian journalist, in January 2007 in Istanbul; Dink's funeral became a large demonstration in favor of Turkey's democratization and protection of minorities.

Meanwhile, the formation of a "Republican Demonstration" (*Cumhuriyet Mitingi*) in Ankara in April 2007 by a number of secularist nongovernmental organizations (NGOs) met with considerable success, drawing millions to rallies in cities throughout the country in the spring of 2007, during which cries of "No to sharia (Islamic law)" were heard. The group was highly critical of Gül's presidential candidacy and feared a possible Islamization of the Turkish public sphere. The future of secularism became the focus of public concern. Another demonstration was held in May in İzmir.

Despite these expressions of discontent, the AKP retained power with 46.7 percent of the vote in the July 2007 parliamentary election by focusing on Turkey's economic growth, proposed constitutional amendments aimed at democratic reforms, progress toward EU accession, and removal of some Islamist candidates from its ballot. Further, the AKP enjoyed unprecedented electoral support in Kurdish regions as a result of reforms that promoted minority rights. The AKP's strong performance cleared the way for parliament's election of Gül as president of the republic, the scheduled election in May having been delayed as opposition parties boycotted the vote several times. The four-month political deadlock finally ended in August with Gül's election by 339 parliamentary votes. He assumed the office of president on August 28 and asked Erdoğan to form a new government (see Political background, above).

Meanwhile, the AKP, with the support of the Motherland Party (*Anavatan Partisi*—ANAP), in mid-2007 passed a law reducing from 120 to 45 the number of days required for holding a referendum on the AKP's amendment package, which was vehemently opposed by the military. On October 21, 69 percent of voters approved the constitutional amendments providing for the direct election of the president, reducing the presidential term from seven years to five, allowing the president to stand for a second term, holding presidential balloting every four years (instead of five), and reducing the parliamentary quorum to 184 members.

Domestic political tension continued to mount, however, following the government's decision in 2008 to press for another constitutional amendment to allow women to wear headscarves in universities. The proposal, which prompted strong secularist resistance, was nonetheless approved by a wide margin, owing to support from the AKP and the MHP. The CHP and the DSP appealed to the Constitutional Court, alleging that the amendment contravened the constitutional principle of secularism. The court overturned the amendment in June, effectively banning headscarves. Secular parties, fearing the Islamist leanings of the AKP, called for the party to be disbanded. In July the Constitutional Court ruled against the banning of the AKP, though it found the party guilty of "antisecularist activities."

Earlier in 2008, 33 people were arrested for their alleged participation in an organization accused of destabilizing the country through assassinations and bombings attributed to Islamist or Kurdish terrorists. Named after the mythical birthplace of the Turkish nation, "Ergenekon" reportedly intended to maximize polarization, wreak havoc in Turkish society, and, thus, precipitate a military coup. Those arrested included retired generals, journalists, and other figures allegedly connected to antidemocratic constituencies within the Turkish elite. More arrests took place on March 21, including the leader of the Workers' Party, Doğu Perinçek; the former rector of the University of Istanbul; and the chief editor of the secularist daily *Cumhuriyet.* The discovery of "Ergenekon" operations by the state prosecutor reinforced allegations of planned military coups in 2003 and 2004. On July 1, 2008, a new round of arrests included three retired generals; the chair of the Ankara Chamber of Commerce, and the Ankara bureau chief of the secularist *Cumhuriyet* daily. The arrests marked the first time retired generals had been taken into custody. Further arrests followed throughout 2008 and into 2009. Concern grew among some observers over the possible use of the Ergenekon investigation as a tool against government opposition.

The AKP suffered a blow in July 2008 when one of its most prominent members, former minister and member of parliament Abdülatif ŞENER, resigned and formed the Turkey's Party (*Türkiye Partisi*—TP) in 2009 (see Political Parties, below).

Despite winning most municipal elections in March 2009, the AKP lost several key cities and secured significantly fewer voters than in its landslide 2007 parliamentary victory (Its vote share was 38.9 percent, compared to 46.6 percent in the 2007 election.) Meanwhile, four opposition parties—the CHP, MHP, DTP, and Felicity Party (*Saadet Partisi*—SP)—made gains.

Security forces arrested more than 60 people suspected of ties to the PKK in raids across the country on January 21, 2010. The following day, nationwide raids resulted in the detention of 120 people believed to have ties with al-Qaida. On February 22, police arrested 49 current and retired senior military officers for involvement in an alleged coup. Eventually more than 196 were charged in the plot, known as "Sledgehammer." Government critics charged that the arrests were part of a government effort to reduce the independence of the military. In March General Saldiray BERK was arrested and charged with being the leader of the Ergenekon movement.

On March 8, a massive earthquake hit eastern Turkey, registering 6.0 on the Richter scale, and killing more than 60 people and displacing thousands. In May the government announced plans to construct the country's first nuclear power plant through an agreement with Russia.

In response to actions by security forces against suspected PKK members, the organization ended a unilateral cease-fire on June 1 (see Political parties and groupings, below, for further developments). As attacks on government and security personnel escalated through the summer, Turkish commandos launched raids into neighboring Iraq.

Major opposition figures and senior military and political officials boycotted the Republic Day, October 29, 2010, after Erdoğan announced his wife would attend the ceremonies wearing a traditional headscarf. On December 16 trials began for the 196 military officers charged in the alleged Sledgehammer plot.

The AKP won legislative elections in June 2011. During the balloting, a number of smaller parties had their candidates campaign as independents, reducing the number of groupings that formally participated from 27 to 15. In the balloting independent candidate Erol DORA became the first Christian to be elected to the assembly since 1960.

In March 2012 a controversial new education law ended prohibitions on attendance at single-sex Islamic schools by youths under 15. The new measure prompted widespread protests by secular groups. Also in March, two more former generals were arrested in connection with the Sledgehammer plot. Twenty-nine former military officers were arrested in April for their roles in the 1997 coup. In June, the high court decreed that President Gül could stand for reelection. Gül had been elected for a seven-year term to end in 2014, but constitutional changes in 2007 reduced the term of the president to five years.

In March 2013 jailed PKK leader Abdullah Öcalan called for a cease-fire and urged the withdrawal of Kurdish rebel fighters from Turkey. On April 25 the PKK announced that all forces would be withdrawn from the country by May 8, a step Ankara considered necessary for the progression of peace talks.

On May 28, 2013, a demonstration broke out against the demolition and redevelopment of Gezi Park, a public park in central Istanbul. The eviction of activists occupying the park by police on May 31 triggered a large-scale reaction with thousands taking to the streets of Istanbul and solidarity protests breaking out in some 80 towns and cities across Turkey. After clashes with police, demonstrators reoccupied the park on June 3, and protests were ongoing until police cleared the park on June 15. Protesters demanded the preservation of Gezi Park and restrictions on the use of teargas by police; however, the actions widened to represent general antigovernment sentiment. Clashes with police left at least 5 dead and some 8,000 injured. The Erdoğan government was criticized from abroad for the excessive use of teargas and brutality on behalf of police, and EU ascension talks were postponed as a result (see Foreign relations, above). In October a new political party registered as the Gezi Party.

The PKK halted the withdrawal in September, claiming the Turkish government had failed to take steps toward "democratization and the resolution of the Kurdish problem," though the cease-fire remained in place.

On September 30 Erdoğan unveiled a broad set of a reforms billed as the "democratization package." Though several measures addressed Kurdish rights—including allowing Kurdish language to be taught in private schools and decriminalizing characters found in the Kurdish but not Turkish alphabet—the PKK said the package was insufficient and did not resume the withdrawal. Other reforms included the scaling back of the head scarf ban and the opportunity for the parliament to debate the 10 percent electoral threshold.

POLITICAL PARTIES

Turkey's multiparty system developed gradually out of the monopoly originally exercised by the historic Republican People's Party (*Cumhuriyet Halk Partisi*—CHP), which ruled the country without serious competition until 1950 and which, under Bülent Ecevit, was most recently in power from January 1978 to October 1979. The Democratic Party (*Demokrat Parti*—DP) of Celal Bayar and Adnan Menderes, founded by CHP dissidents in 1946, came to power in 1950 and maintained control for the next decade but was outlawed following the military coup of May 27, 1960, with many of its members subsequently entering the conservative Justice Party (*Adalet Partisi*—AP). Other formations included an Islamic group, the National Salvation Party (*Millî Selâmet Partisi*—MSP); the ultra-rightist Nationalist Action Party (*Milliyetçi Hareket Partisi*—MHP); and the leftist Turkish Labor Party (*Türkiye İşçi Partisi*—TİP). All party activity was banned by the National Security Council on September 12, 1980, while the parties themselves were formally dissolved and their assets liquidated on October 16, 1981. In July 1992, the government lifted bans on all of the parties.

Government Party:

Justice and Development Party (*Adalet ve Kalkınma Partisi*—AKP). The AKP was launched in August 2001 by the reformist wing of the FP (see below) as a moderate religious, center-right formation. Out of the former parliamentarians from the FP and other parties, 53 later joined the AKP, making it the second-largest opposition party in the assembly (after the DYP). Some analysts noted that the AKP might prove to be a strong challenger to the coalition parties in the next legislative election.

In January 2002 the electoral commission ruled that AKP president Recep Tayyip Erdoğan was ineligible to run for office due to his imprisonment in 1999 on charges of having "incited hatred on religious grounds." In the November 2002 elections, the AKP won 34.3 percent of the vote and 363 legislative seats. Erdoğan's ineligibility was overturned when parliament approved a change to the constitution that allowed Erdoğan to run in a by-election in March 2003. A few days later, he was named prime minister.

The elections of July 22, 2007, gave Erdoğan the chance to shift the party toward the center. More than 150 members of parliament from the party's Islamist wing were removed from AKP candidate lists. The new party lists included prominent liberal secularists, academics, and young professionals. The crushing electoral victory, in which the party improved its margin of victory by more than 12 percent over the previous election, yielded 341 seats. (This seat share was less than in 2002 due to the electoral system but, nevertheless, consolidated the party's political dominance.)

On March 14, 2007, the chief prosecutor of the Court of Cassation sought to shut down the AKP because of the party's alleged antisecular activities. However, a ruling by the Constitutional Court in 2008 upheld the party's viability (see Current issues, above).

In municipal elections in March 2009, the AKP garnered 38.83 percent of the vote and 492 municipal seats. AKP candidates were elected in the country's biggest cities, Istanbul and Ankara. However, the results were perceived as less than satisfactory compared to the AKP's performance in the 2007 parliamentary elections.

In legislative balloting in June 2011 the AKP received 49.8 percent of the vote and secured 327 seats. Erdoğan was reappointed as prime minister. He was reelected AKP chair at the September 30, 2012, congress, his third and final term as party leader.

Leaders: Recep Tayyip ERDOĞAN (Prime Minister and President of the Party), Abdullah GÜL (President of the Republic), Haluk İPEK (Secretary General).

Opposition Parties:

Republican People's Party (*Cumhuriyet Halk Partisi*—CHP). The CHP is a left-of-center party founded in 1923 by Kemal Atatürk. It was dissolved in 1981 and reactivated in 1992 by 21 MPs who resigned from the Social Democratic People's Party (*Sosyal Demokrat Halkçı Parti*—SHP) to reclaim the group's historic legacy. The CHP absorbed the SHP on February 18, 1995. The CHP later absorbed the Party of Liberty and Change on June 8, 2007 (see below).

A member of the Socialist International, the SHP was formed in November 1985 by merger of the Populist Party (*Halkçı Parti*—HP), a center-left formation that secured 117 seats in the 1983 Grand National Assembly election, and the Social Democratic Party (*Sosyal Demokrat Parti*—SODEP), which was not permitted to offer candidates for the 1983 balloting. A leftist grouping that drew much of its support from former members of the CHP, SODEP had participated in the 1984 local elections, winning 10 provincial capitals. The SHP was runner-up to ANAP in November 1987, winning 99 assembly seats despite the defection in December 1986 of 20 of its deputies, most of whom joined the DSP. Its parliamentary representation was reduced to 82 upon formation of the People's Labor Party, whose candidates were, nevertheless, entered on SHP lists for the 1991 campaign. Subsequently, 18 of those so elected withdrew from the SHP, reducing its representation to 70.

On September 20, 1995, former CHP chair Deniz BAYKAL, who had been succeeded by the SHP's Hikmet CETİN at the time of the February merger, was reelected to his earlier post. Immediately thereafter he withdrew the party from the government coalition, thereby forcing Tansu Çiller's resignation as prime minister. In the resultant December election the CHP fell back to 49 seats on a 10.7 percent vote share. Baykal's CHP gave outside support to the Yılmaz-led ANAP-DSP-DTP coalition government of June 1998. However, amid accusations of corruption against various ministers, the CHP's call for a vote of no confidence against the Yılmaz cabinet brought the coalition down in November 1998. The CHP failed to surpass the 10 percent threshold in the April 18, 1999, elections, securing only 8.5 percent of the vote, and was therefore left out of the assembly. Baykal resigned from his chair's post on April 22. The CHP elected famous journalist and former tourism minister Altan ÖYMEN as its new leader on May 23; however, Baykal regained the post at an extraordinary congress in October 2000, defeating Öymen and two other minor candidates. The CHP's ranks were strengthened in 2002 by defections from the DSP.

In the November 2002 elections, the CHP won 19.3 percent of the vote and 178 legislative seats, thus becoming the main opposition party. In October 2004 the New Turkey Party (*Yeni Türkiye Partisi*—YTP) merged with the CHP. (The YTP had been formed in July 2002 by former DSP cabinet ministers, including Ismail Cem, among others.)

In January 2005 Baykal's presidency was challenged at a highly explosive CHP party congress by Mustafa SARIGÜL, the popular mayor of the İstanbul district of Şişli, who eventually lost his bid but vowed to continue his opposition. A few pro-Sarigül legislators left the party following the congress to join the SHP (see below). By mid-2005, rifts had developed within the party, resulting in the resignations of numerous dissidents (including legislators).The losses were reflected in the decline in the CHP's legislative seats, down to 154 by mid-2005.

The CHP spearheaded secularist reaction against the candidacy of Abdullah Gül, culminating in several large "Republican Demonstrations" in spring 2007. The party was consequently accused of swapping its leftist identity for a nationalist platform and identifying itself with the military establishment. On June 8, 2007, the Party of Liberty and Change (*Hürriyet ve Değişim Partisi*—HÜRPARTI) decided to merge into the CHP, and its leader Yaşar OKUYAN declared that he would not be a CHP candidate.

On the eve of the 2007 parliamentary elections, the party struck an alliance with the Democratic Left Party (*Demokratik Sol Parti*—DSP), and 13 members of that party ran under the CHP ticket. The party received 20.85 percent of the vote and 112 seats, which dropped to 99 when the 13 members withdrew from the CHP parliamentary group. In the aftermath of the elections, observers and party rank-and-file members expressed concerns about the CHP's future under Baykal's leadership.

The CHP continued its opposition by appealing to the Constitutional Court against AKP parliamentary decisions, such as the proposed constitutional amendment to allow women to wear headscarves in universities. CHP's identification with the most radical elements of the bureaucracy was revealed in its fierce opposition to the "Ergenekon" investigations, which it saw as an AKP ploy to rout political opponents.

In the March 2009 municipal elections, the CHP won 23.12 percent of the vote and the municipality of Izmir. At a party convention in May, Kemal KILIÇDAROĞLU was elected chair of the CHP. In May 2010 the short-lived Democratic Left People's Party (*Demokratik Sol Halk Partisi*—DSHP) voted to merge with the CHP (the DSHP had formed in November 2009). In legislative elections in June 2011 the CHP secured 26 percent of the vote and 135 seats. In July 2012, Kılıçdaroğlu was reelected party president.

Several CHP deputies participated in the protests that broke out over Istanbul's Gezi Park in June 2013. In September Prime Minister Erdoğan accused the CHP of being behind the mass antigovernment protests.

Leaders: Kemal KILIÇDAROĞLU (President), Haluk KOÇ (Deputy Chair).

Nationalist Action Party (*Milliyetçi Hareket Partisi*—MHP). Until 1969 the ultranationalist MHP was known as the Republican Peasant Nation Party (*Cumhuriyetçi Köylü Millet Partisi*—CKMP), formed in 1948 by conservative dissidents from the old Democratic Party. Dissolved in 1953, the grouping reformed in 1954, merging with the Turkish Villager Party in 1961 and sustaining the secession of the Nation Party in 1962.

The MHP dissolved following the 1980 military coup; in 1983 its sympathizers regrouped as the Conservative Party (*Muhafazakar Parti*—MP), which then was renamed the Nationalist Labor Party (*Milliyetçi Çalışma Partisi*—MCP) in 1985. (The MHP rubric was reassumed in 1992.) The MHP's extremist youth wing, members of which were known as the Grey Wolves (*Bozkurtlar*), remained proscribed, although similar activities were reportedly carried out under semi-official youth clubs. Holding 17 legislative seats as of September 1995, the MHP's 8.18 percent vote share on December 24 was short of the 10 percent required for continued representation. However, it subsequently acquired 2 seats from defections.

Historic MHP leader Alparslan TÜRKEŞ died in 1997. Following the election of Devlet Bahçeli as the new MHP president, members close to Türkeş's son and wife left the party to form the ATP and UBP.

The MHP won surprising support in the election of April 1999, gathering 18 percent of the votes and gaining 129 assembly seats. Some analysts noted that the party's popular support faded during its years in the coalition government from 1999 to 2002. The MHP suffered a major electoral blow in November 2002, when it received only 8.3 percent of the vote and no legislative seats. Although Devlet Bahçeli initially announced he would step down from his leadership position after the election, he ran for and won the party's presidency again in October 2003.

The party benefited from rising nationalist sentiment, which was bolstered by the Iraq crisis and deteriorating EU-Turkey relations. In the 2007 parliamentary elections, the party won 14.29 percent of the vote and 71 seats.

The MHP supported the constitutional amendment proposed by the AKP to allow women to wear headscarves in universities. While the party was less opposed to the AKP and avoided siding with the radical portion of the bureaucracy in its struggle against the AKP, it maintained a nationalist stance, notably in the country's disputes with Armenia and Cyprus. The MHP and CHP vehemently objected to President Gül's unofficial visit to Armenia in September 2008.

In the 2009 municipal elections, the MHP won 16 percent of the vote. This was perceived as a success, although hardly an indicator of the party's ability to become a major political contender. At a party congress in 2009, Bahçeli was reelected MHP president.

In May 2011 prior to national elections, a scandal involving alleged sex videos prompted the resignation of six senior MHP figures. In the assembly balloting, the MHP received 13 percent of the vote and 53 seats. In September, security forces arrested 36 MHP members. Defeating nine other candidates, Bahçeli remained party president in internal elections in November 2012.

Leaders: Devlet BAHÇELI (President), İsmet BÜYÜKATMAN (Secretary General).

Other Parties:

Democratic Left Party (*Demokratik Sol Parti*—DSP). Formation of the DSP, a center-left populist formation, was announced in March 1984 by Rahşan Ecevit, the wife of former prime minister Bülent Ecevit, who was barred from political activity prior to the constitutional referendum of September 1987. In the October 1991 election, the party attracted sufficient social democratic support to weaken the SHP (see below), although it won only 7 seats. It recovered in the December 1995 balloting, winning 76 legislative seats with 14.6 percent of the vote. The DSP became a junior partner in a Mesut Yılmaz–led coalition government, which also included the DTP (below), on June 30, 1998. After the Yılmaz–led coalition government collapsed in November 1998, Ecevit formed on January 12, 1999, a minority government, that ruled the country until the early elections of April 18. The DSP became the largest party in that balloting with 22 percent of the votes and 136 seats, and Ecevit subsequently formed a DSP-MHP-ANAP coalition cabinet.

In 2002 rifts within the party led some prominent members to resign to form the YTP. The DSP suffered a major electoral defeat in November 2002, receiving only 1.2 percent of the vote and no legislative seats. Bülent Ecevit resigned as party leader and nominated Zeki Sezer, a former cabinet minister, to replace him. Sezer was elected at the party's congress in July 2004.

The DSP struck an electoral alliance with the CHP on May 18, 2005. Thirteen DSP parliamentarians, including Sezer, were elected on the CHP ticket in the 2007 balloting. These members withdrew from the CHP during the first legislative session to form an independent DSP parliamentary group.

On May 18, 2009, Masum Türker defeated Sezer to become party president. In the March 2009 municipal elections, the DP garnered 2.78 percent of the vote. Ahead of the September 2010 referendum, a number of DSP members resigned to protest their party's opposition to the proposed constitutional changes. In the June 2011 national balloting the DSP received 0.25 percent of the vote.

Leaders: Masum TÜRKER (President), Hasan ERÇELEBİ (Secretary General).

Peace and Democracy Party (*Barış ve Demokrasi Partisi*—BDP). Formed in 2008, the BDP emerged as the successor party to the **Democratic Society Party** (*Demokratik Toplum Partisi*—DTP). Formerly known as the Democratic People's Party (*Demokratik Halk Partisi*—DEHAP), the DTP was launched in January 1999 by former members of the People's Democracy Party (*Halkin Demokrasi Partisi*—HADEP), the pro-Kurdish DTP (not to be confused with the Democratic Turkey Party [DTP]) was initiated by former legislators Leyla ZANA, Orhan DOĞAN, Hatip DİCLE, and Selim SADAK, who had joined the Democracy Party (*Demokrasi Partisi*—DEP) in 1994. The Turkish Grand National Assembly lifted the parliamentary immunity of these four Kurdish politicians, and they were arrested and jailed from 1994–2005. Based on concerns that the DEHAP would be banned by the Constitutional Court, the DTP was launched reportedly as a preemptive "successor" on November 9, 2005. Since then, all DEHAP mayors, members, and leaders have entered the DTP. While the DEHAP decided to dissolve itself in December 2005, the Constitutional Court continued to consider banning the party and started to address the case on July 13, 2006.

In an attempt to circumvent the 10 percent electoral threshold, which had prevented it from securing legislative representation in the past, the DTP decided to abstain from the July 22, 2007, elections and support party members who would formally resign their membership to run as independent candidates. Subsequently, 22 of these candidates were elected, and 20 of them formed the DTP parliamentary group in the first parliamentary session. The presence of DTP parliamentarians presented an opportunity to reconsider Turkey's Kurdish question.

On November 16, 2007, the chief prosecutor of the Court of Cassation sought to close the DTP because it was "a focal point of activities aiming to damage the independence of the state and the indivisible integrity of its territory and nation." As the DTP failed to draw a clear line between itself and the PKK, a rift developed between PKK sympathizers and social-democrats, who opposed terrorism. The party succeeded in restoring its electoral strength in southeastern and eastern Turkey in the March 2009 municipal elections.

On December 11, the Constitutional Court voted to ban the DTP because of its links to the PKK. The parliamentary deputies, and most members, of the DTP joined the BDP. However, 35 senior DTP officials were banned from politics for five years. In addition, some 80 members of the party were arrested,

In February 2010, Selahattin DEMIRTAŞ was elected leader of the BDP. In September Demirtaş was convicted of illegal propaganda on behalf of the PKK and sentenced to 10 months in prison. In the June 2011 legislative balloting 35 candidates supported by the BDP were elected as independents. In October, the BDP-affiliated deputies ended a boycott of parliament over the detention of six BDP members.

The BDP in October 2013 considered joining the People's Democratic Congress (*Halklarin Demokratik Kongresi*—HDK), an umbrella group uniting several leftist and Kurdish groups ahead of the 2015 parliamentary elections.

Leaders: Selahattin DEMIRTAŞ, Gülten KIŞANAK (Cochairs).

Great Unity Party (*Buyük Birlik Partisi*—BBP). A nationalist Islamic grouping, the BBP was launched in 1993 by a member of dissident MCP parliamentarians prior to the reactivation of the MHP in 1992. The party, whose members are known as "Turkish-Islamic Idealists" (*Türk-Islam ülkücüleri*), returned 13 deputies on the ANAP ticket in the 1995 election but subsequently opted for separate parliamentary status. The BBP won only 1.5 percent of the votes in the general election of April 1999. In November 2002 the party received 1.1 percent of the vote and no legislative seats.

While the party did not present candidates in the 2007 parliamentary elections, its leader, Muhsin YAZICIOĞLU, ran as an independent in the district of Sivas and was elected. On March 25, 2009, Yazıcıoğlu was killed in a helicopter crash near the city of Kahramanmaraş; party president Yalçın Topçu was elected as his successor.

In the 2009 municipal elections, the BBP won 2.24 percent of the vote. Members of the BBP were abroad the Gaza-bound convoy of ships that was attacked by Israeli forces in May 2010 (see Foreign affairs, above). In balloting in June 2011 the BPP secured 0.75 percent of the vote. The next month, Mustafa DESTICI was elected party leader.

Leader: Mustafa DESTICI.

Liberty and Solidarity Party (*Özgurlük ve Dayanışma Partisi*—ÖDP). Backed by many leftist intellectuals, feminists, and human rights activists, the ÖDP was launched after the December 1995 election as a broad alliance of various socialist factions together with elements of the once powerful Dev-Yol movement (see Extremist Groups, below). Some of the socialist groups, notably the United Socialist Party (*Birleşik Sosyalist Parti*—BSP), had contested the balloting as part of the HADEP bloc. The BSP had been formed as a merger of various socialist factions, including the Socialist Unity Party (*Sosyalist Birlik Partisi*—SBP), itself founded in February 1991 (and represented in the 1991–1995 assembly) as in large part successor to the United Communist Party of Turkey (*Türkiye Birleşik Komünist Partisi*—TBKP), led by Haydar KUTLU and Nihat SARGIN.

The TBKP had been formed in 1988 by a merger of the Communist Party of Turkey (*Türkiye Komünist Partisi*—TKP) and the Turkish Workers Party (*Türkiye İşçi Partisi*—TİP). Proscribed since 1925, the pro-Soviet TKP had long maintained its headquarters in Eastern Europe, staffed largely by exiles and refugees who left Turkey in the 1930s and 1940s. Although remaining illegal, its activities within Turkey revived in 1983, including the reported convening of its first congress in more than 50 years. The TİP, whose longtime leader, Behice BORAN, died in October 1987, had been formally dissolved in 1971 and again in 1980 but had endorsed the merger with TKP at a congress held on the first anniversary of Boran's death. Prior to the November 1987 election, the TKP and TİP general secretaries, Kutlu and Sargin, respectively, had returned to Turkey for the prospective merger but had been promptly arrested and imprisoned.

With the Constitutional Court subsequently confirming a ban on the TBKP in early 1990, former TBKP elements were prominent in the new ÖDP. The ÖDP fared poorly in the April 1999 elections, gaining less than 1 percent of the votes. Several constituent groups reportedly left the ÖDP in 2002. In November 2002 the party won 0.34 percent of the vote and no legislative seats.

In the July 22, 2007, elections, the party won 0.15 percent of the vote. However, ÖDP leader Ufuk URAS, in order to avoid the electoral threshold requirement, resigned from the party presidency in order to run as an independent. He was elected as a representative for Istanbul and was then reinstated in the party presidency. Due to its parliamentary representation, the ÖDP was able to attract more public attention and fulfill the role of a substantial social-democratic opposition party.

Growing discord between the party's liberal and socialist wings led to the resignation of Uras from the party and the formation of a new leftist liberal group. On June 22, 2009, Alper Taş was elected party president.

In the 2009 municipal elections, the ÖDP garnered 0.16 percent of the vote. The TIP reportedly reformed as a separate party in February 2010. ÖDP candidates ran as independents in the 2011 balloting but failed to secure any seats. In March 2012, the ÖDP led protests against Turkey's inclusion as part of NATO's missile defense system.

Leader: Alper TAŞ.

Democrat Party (*Demokrat Parti*—DP). Also known as the True Path Party (*Doğru Yol Partisi*—DYP), the center-right party was organized as a successor to the Grand Turkey Party (*Büyük Türkiye Partisi*—BTP), which was banned shortly after its formation in May 1983 because of links to the former Justice Party of Süleyman Demirel. The new group was permitted to participate in the local elections of March 1984 but won control in none of the provincial capitals. By early 1987, augmented by assemblymen of the recently dissolved Citizen Party (*Vatandaş Partisi*—VP), it had become the third-ranked party in the Grand National Assembly. The DYP remained in third place by winning 59 seats in the November 1987 balloting and became the plurality party, with 178 seats, in October 1991. In November it formed a coalition government under Demirel with the SHP (see below). A second DYP-SHP government was formed by the new DYP leader, Tansu Çiller, following Demirel's assumption of the presidency in May 1993. A new coalition was formed with the CHP in March 1995, following the latter's temporary absorption of the SHP. However, a CHP leadership change in September led to the party's withdrawal and the collapse of the Çiller government.

The DYP placed second in the December 1995 election (with 19.2 percent of the vote), eventually forming a coalition government with ANAP on March 12, 1996, that featured a "rotating" leadership under which the ANAP's Mesut Yılmaz became prime minister and Çiller was to return to the top post in January 1997. However, animosity between the DYP and ANAP leaders quickly resurfaced, with Çiller calling the prime minister a "sleaze ball" (for allegedly expediting press exposés of her questionable use of official funds as prime minister) and withdrawing the DYP's support for the coalition in late May. Overcoming its previous antipathy toward the RP, the DYP the following month entered a new coalition as junior partner of the Islamist party, with Çiller becoming deputy premier and foreign minister, pending a scheduled resumption of the premiership at the beginning of 1998. By mid-January 1997 a parliamentary inquiry had cleared the DYP leader of all corruption charges relating to her tenure as premier. After the DYP-RP coalition collapsed under emphatic pressure from the military and the secular political establishment in June 1997, the DYP remained in the opposition during the Yılmaz-led ANAP-DSP-DTP coalition. By backing CHP leader Deniz Baykal's proposal for a vote of no-confidence against the Yılmaz government, the DYP facilitated its collapse in November 1998. The DYP then gave outside support to Bülent Ecevit's minority government. DYP influence waned in the April 1999 elections, as it secured only 12 percent of the votes and 85 seats.

The DYP experienced a major electoral defeat in November 2002, receiving 9.5 percent of the vote and no legislative seats. This defeat prompted Tansu Çiller to resign following the election. With defections from other parties, the party had, by mid-2005, four legislative seats. In the run-up to the 2007 parliamentary elections, party leader Mehmet AĞAR announced an electoral alliance with the ANAP. Ağar and ANAP president Erkan Mumcu named their joint party the Democrat Party (*Demokrat Parti*—DP). However, the ANAP withdrew from the alliance after barely a month, and the DP ran in the elections on its own. The DP subsequently received 5.41 percent of the vote, 4.13 percent less than in the 2002 elections. This result led Ağar to resign from the presidency of the party and call for an extraordinary congress to elect a new leader.

The party maintained the rubric of the Democrat Party (*Demokrat Parti*—DP) and in 2008 elected Süleyman SOYLU as president. "Moral politics" and "moral democracy" were Soylu's guiding principles. Nonetheless, the party did not seem to attract significant political support. On May 16, 2009, the veteran politician Hüsamettin Cindoruk was elected party president. In the 2009 municipal elections, the DP won 3.72 percent of the vote. In October the ANAP merged with the DP (for more information on the ANAP, please see the 2009 *Handbook*). Namik Kemal Zeybek was elected party leader at a DP congress on January 15, 2011. In balloting for the national assembly on June 12 the DP won 0.65 percent of the vote. At a DP congress in May 2012, Gültekin UYSAL was elected party leader.

Leaders: Gültekin UYSAL (President), Mukhtar MAHRAMLI (Secretary General).

Party of the People's Rise (*Halkin Yükselişi Partisi*—HYP). The centrist HYP was established in February 2005 by Yaşar Nuri ÖZTÜRK, a former scholar of Islamic theology who became popular because of his "reformist" and modernist interpretations of religion. Öztürk is a former CHP legislator who left his party in April 2004 to protest Deniz Baykal's leadership style. In the 2007 parliamentary elections, the HYP collected 0.5 percent of the vote. At a November 2009 party conference, Ragıp Önder GÜNAY was elected president of the HYP. HYP candidates ran as independents in the 2011 assembly elections but failed to gain any seats.

Leader: Ragıp Önder GÜNAY (President).

Communist Party of Turkey (*Türkiye Komünist Partisi*—TKP). The TKP was launched in November 2001 as a merger of the Party for Socialist Power (*Sosyalist Iktidar Partisi*—SIP) and the Communist Party (*Komünist Partisi*—KP). The SIP was a continuation of the banned Party of Socialist Turkey (*Sosyalist Türkiye Partisi*—STP). The hard-line Marxist-Leninist SIP contested the 1995 election under the HADEP rubric. It secured less than 1 percent of the vote in 1999. The TKP was formed in July 2000 by former SIP members. In November 2002 the party won 0.2 percent of the vote and no legislative seats.

During 2007 legislative balloting, the party won 0.22 percent of the vote, while in the 2009 municipal elections, the BTP received 0.18 percent of the vote and in the June 2011 assembly polling, 0.15 percent of the vote.

Leaders: Erkan BAŞ (President), Kemal OKUYAN (General Secretary).

Felicity Party (*Saadet Partisi*—SP). The SP was formed in July 2001 by the traditionalist core of the Virtue Party (*Fazilet Partisi*—FP), which had been shut down by the constitutional court in June. The Virtue Party had been launched in February 1998, days before a constitutional court decision banned the Islamic-oriented Welfare Party, which was in the coalition government until June 18, 1997, on charges of undermining the secular foundations of the Turkish Republic.

The Welfare Party (*Refah Partisi*—RP) had been organized in 1983 by former members of the Islamic fundamentalist MSP. It participated in the 1984 local elections, winning one provincial capital. It failed to secure assembly representation in 1987.

Having absorbed Aydın MENDERES' faction of the Democrat Party (DP), the RP attained a plurality in the December 1995 election with 21.4 percent of the vote, but at that stage was unable to recruit allies for a government. However, the speedy collapse of an alternative administration brought the RP to office for the first time in June 1996, heading a coalition with the DYP. Under intense pressure from the military and secular political establishment, Prime Minister Necmettin ERBAKAN resigned on June 18, 1997, and the RP-DYP coalition failed. On February 22, 1998, the Constitutional Court banned the RP and barred some of its founders, including Erbakan, from political activity for five years. On March 6, 2002, Erbakan was sentenced to two years and four months in jail because he had embezzled more than $3 million from the fund of the banned RP. After several appeals, his sentence was converted to house arrest due to his ailing health.

Some 135 parliamentarians of the proscribed Welfare Party joined the FP, making it the main opposition party in the parliament. Although FP leaders denied their party was a successor to the RP, Turkey's secularists did not find the denial credible. The FP assumed the role of the main opposition party to both the Yılmaz-led ANAP-DSP-DTP coalition government that ended in November 1998 and to the Ecevit-led minority DSP government that was installed in January 1999. Although some analysts initially saw the FP as a likely winner of the general elections in April, the party secured only 15 percent of the votes and 111 seats. Recai Kutan was narrowly reelected as FP chair at the party congress in May 2000, fending off a challenge from a "reformist" wing led by Recep Tayyip Erdoğan (former mayor of Istanbul) and Abdullah Gül, which then broke away to launch its own formation, the Justice and Development Party (*Adalet ve Kalkınma Partisi*—AKP) in August 2001, following the banning of the FP in June. Further weakened by legislative defections and a marked shift of popular support to the AKP (see above), FP received an electoral setback in November 2002, winning only 2.5 percent of the vote and no legislative seats. In 2007 the party failed to provide a credible Islamist alternative to the ruling AKP and won just 2.34 percent of the vote.

On August 19, 2008, President Gül pardoned Erbakan and lifted his house detention. While AKP officials defended the decision on humanitarian grounds, secularists again became concerned about links between the AKP leadership and Islamists.

In the 2009 municipal elections, the SP garnered 5.16 percent of the vote. In October 2010 the SP elected the 84-year-old Erbakan as party president once again. Erbakan died on February 27, 2011. He was replaced by Mustafa Kamalak. The FP secured 1.3 percent of the vote in the 2011 national elections.

In January 2012, Kamalak visited Syria as part of an unofficial effort to maintain relations between the two countries.

Leaders: Mustafa KAMALAK (President), Tacettin ÇETİNKAYA (Secretary General).

Young Party (*Genç Parti*—GP). A populist, nationalist party, the GP was founded in 2002 by the controversial magnate Cem UZAN, who took control of the tiny Rebirth Party (*Yeniden Doğuş Partisi*—YDP), renaming it about two months before the November 2002 elections. His family controlled the substantial Uzan Holding, which counted a bank (İmar Bankası), a media group (Star), and Telsim, Turkey's second biggest mobile phone operator, among its assets. In the November 4, 2002, elections, the GP won 7.25 percent of the vote but secured no seats due to the 10 percent electoral threshold. Meanwhile, corruption and fraud charges against the Uzan family culminated in a lawsuit against Uzan by Motorola and Nokia, which accused him of defaulting on more than $2.5 billion worth of loans they had provided to Telsim. İmar Bankası was taken over by Turkish banking regulatory authorities, amid family complaints that the government was persecuting their businesses to neutralize Cem Uzan's political popularity. While Uzan's father, Kemal Uzan, and brother, Hakan Uzan, escaped abroad to avoid arrest, Cem Uzan remained in Turkey because he had no apparent personal involvement in corruption and fraud activities. The GP maintained its overtly populist and nationalist stance in the 2007 election campaign and won 3.03 percent of the vote.

On September 9, 2008, Uzan was convicted of insulting Prime Minister Erdoğan in a speech he gave in 2003. He was ordered by the court to enter an "anger management program" and read five books on "self development." Uzan subsequently fled to France following new charges of fraud and forgery. He was sentenced in absentia to 23 years in prison in April 2010. GP candidates ran as independents in the 2011 legislative balloting but failed to gain any seats. Uzan was reportedly in Jordan in 2012.

Leaders: Cem UZAN (President), Mehmet Ali AKGÜL (Secretary General).

Workers' Party (*İşçi Partisi*—IP). The Maoist-inspired IP, founded in 1992, is the successor of the Socialist Party (*Sosyalist Parti*—SP), which was launched in February 1988 as the first overtly socialist formation since the 1980 coup. The party called for Turkey's withdrawal from NATO and nationalization of the economy. The SP was deregistered by order of the Constitutional Court in June 1992, the IP securing less than 0.5 percent of the vote in 1995. Since 2000 the IP, self-described as "national leftist," has garnered public attention due to its staunchly nationalist and anti-EU stance.

In November 2002, the party received 0.5 percent of the vote and no legislative seats. In 2007 it received 0.36 percent of the vote. On March 21, 2008, Doğu Perinçek was arrested in connection with the "Ergenekon" investigation. In the 2009 municipal elections, the IP garnered 0.27 percent of the vote. In August 2010 Perinçek led a large protest over what he described as the government's arrest and detention of secularists in Istanbul. In balloting in June 2011 the party's candidates ran as independents and did not secure any seats in the assembly.

Leader: Doğu PERİNÇEK.

Other minor parties that participated in the 2011 elections were the **Turkey's Party** (*Türkiye Partisi*—TP), led by former AKP minister Abdülatif ŞENER; the **Labor Party** (*Emek Partisi*—EMEP), led by Selma GÜRKAN; the **Liberal Democrat Party** (*Liberal Demokrat Parti*—LDP), a free market grouping led by Cem TOKER; **Independent Turkey Party** (*Bağımsız Türkiye Partisi*—BTP), led by Haydar BAŞ; and the **People's Voice Party** (*Halkın Sesi Partisi*—HAS

Party), led by Numan KURTULMUŞ. (For more on the **Social-Democrat People's Party** [*Sosyaldemokrat Halk Partisi*], please see the 2012 *Handbook.*)

Extremist Groups:

Pre-1980 extremist and terrorist groups included the leftist **Revolutionary Path** (*Devrimci Yol*—Dev-Yol) and its more radical offshoot, the **Revolutionary Left** (Dev-Sol) (for more information on the Dev-Sol, please see the 2009 *Handbook*), both derived from the **Revolutionary Youth** (*Dev Genç*), which operated in the late 1960s and early 1970s; some of its members also joined the far leftist **Turkish People's Salvation Army** (*Türkiye Halk Kurtuluş Ordusu*—THKO). Other groups were the **Turkish People's Liberation Party Front** (*Türkiye Halk Kurtuluş Partisi-Cephesi*—THKP-C), the **Turkish Workers' and Peasants' Liberation Army** (*Türkiye İşçi Köylü Kurtuluş Ordusu*—TİKKO, below), and the **Kurdistan Workers' Party** (PKK, below). Armenian guerrilla groupings include the **Secret Army for the Liberation of Armenia** (ASALA), including a so-called Orly Group; the **Justice Commandos for the Armenian Genocide**; the **Pierre Gulmian Commando**; the **Levon Ekmekçiyan Suicide Commando**; and the **Armenian Revolutionary Army**. The activities of many of these groups have subsided, notable exceptions being Dev-Sol and the PKK.

Please see the 2012 *Handbook* for more on the extreme left groupings, the **Communist Party of Turkey-Marxist Leninist** (*Türkiye Komünist Partisi-Marksist-Leninist*—TKP-ML) and its armed wing, the **Turkish Workers' and Peasants' Liberation Army** (*Türkiye İşçi Köylü Kurtuluş Ordusu*—TİKKO), and the **Communist Labor Party of Turkey-Leninist** (*Türkiye Komünist Emek Partisi-Leninist*—TKEP-L).

Kurdistan Workers' Party (*Partîya Karkerén Kurdistan*—PKK). Founded in 1978, the PKK, under the leadership of Abdullah (Apo) Öcalan, was for a long time based principally in Lebanon's Bekaa Valley and northern Iraq. In southeast Anatolia, where it continues to maintain a presence, the party's 1992 call for a general uprising on March 21, the Kurdish New Year (Nevruz), was generally unheeded. Subsequently, a unilateral cease-fire declared by Öcalan under pressure from northern Iraq Kurdish leaders proved short-lived, and PKK terrorism re-escalated. In late July 1994 Turkish warplanes reportedly completely destroyed a PKK base in northern Iraq, and in mid-August a London court convicted three separatists of a number of attacks on Turkish property in the United Kingdom. Öcalan thereupon reiterated his call for a cease-fire as a prelude to the adoption of constitutional reforms that would acknowledge the "Kurdish identity." The government again failed to respond and in September charged the PKK with responsibility for the killing of a number of Turkish teachers in the southeastern province of Tunceli. Government military offensives against the Kurdish insurgents in 1995–1996 were combined with efforts to eradicate the PKK party organization.

Through 1997 and 1998, extensive Turkish military operations seriously undermined the PKK's ground forces. On April 13, 1998, the PKK's second-highest ranking commander, Şemdin SAKIK, who had left the organization a month earlier, was captured in northern Iraq by Turkish security forces. A more significant blow to the organization came with the arrest of party chair Öcalan by Turkish commandos in Nairobi, Kenya (see Foreign relations, above), in February 1999. The commander of the PKK's armed wing, the People's Liberation Army of Kurdistan (ARGK), Cemil BAYIK, had reportedly threatened Turkish authorities and foreign tourists on March 15, claiming that the whole of Anatolia "is now a battlefield." Some sources also reported a leadership struggle between Bayik and Abdullah Öcalan's brother, Osman ÖCALAN.

From February to July 1999, Kurdish militants engaged in various attacks, including suicide bombings, in response to their leader's arrest. A State Security Court accused Öcalan of being responsible for 30,000 deaths between 1984–1999. He was found guilty of treason and sentenced to death on June 29. During his defense, Öcalan argued that he could "stop the war" if the Turkish state would let him "work for peace" and spare his life. He apologized for the "sufferings PKK's actions may have caused," claiming that the "armed struggle had fulfilled its aims" and that the PKK would now "work for a democratic Turkey, where Kurds will enjoy cultural and linguistic rights." On August 2, Öcalan called on his organization to stop fighting and leave Turkish territory starting September 1. The PKK's "Presidential Council" quickly announced that it would follow its leader's commands, and during the PKK's congress in February 2000, it was announced that the party's political and armed wings would merge into a front organization called the People's Democratic Union of Kurdistan. Some analysts argued that the decision was in line with the PKK's decision to stop its armed struggle and seek Kurdish political and cultural rights within the framework of Turkey's integration with the European Union.

In 2001 a small group of renegade PKK members launched the Kurdistan Workers' Party-Revolutionary Line Fighters (*Partîya Karkarén Kurdistan-Devrimci Çizgi Savaşçıları*—PKK-DÇS) with the expressed aim to continue the armed struggle. In April 2002 the PKK decided to dissolve itself (announcing it had fulfilled its "historical mission") to launch a new organization called the Kurdistan Freedom and Democracy Congress (*Kongreya Azadî û Demokrasiya Kurdistan*—KADEK). The KADEK claimed to be against armed struggle, to have rejected fighting for an independent Kurdish homeland, and to have espoused a "political" line to press for cultural and linguistic rights for Turkey's Kurds as "full and equal members under a democratic and united Turkey." However, in May the EU announced it still considered the PKK a "terrorist organization." The Turkish government continued to claim that the PKK's transformation into KADEK was a "tactical ploy."

In September 2003 KADEK was restyled as the Peoples' Congress of Kurdistan (*Kongra Gelê Kurdistan*—Kongra-Gel). Several high-level defections occurred in the ranks, including that of Osman Öcalan, who reportedly joined a splinter group, the Democratic Solution Party of Kurdistan (*Partiya Welatparézén Demokratén Kurdistan*—PWDK) that was established in April 2004. In June 2004, Kongra-Gel announced that the cease-fire declared by Abdullah Öcalan in September 1999 was not respected by the Republic of Turkey and that they would return to "legitimate armed defense" to counter military operations against their "units." In April 2005 it was announced that PKK was reconstituted and the new formation was styled as the PKK–Kongra-Gel. Since the announcement, numerous sporadic clashes have been reported between the Turkish security forces and PKK–Kongra-Gel's armed wing, People's Defense Forces (*Hezen Parastina Gel*—HPG).

Since March 2005 a hitherto unknown group called "Kurdistan Freedom Falcons" (*Teyrêbazên Azadiya Kurdistan*—TAK) has taken responsibility for numerous car bomb explosions and other urban terrorist acts. Although some press reports claimed that TAK was one among many breakaway wings of PKK–Kongra-Gel, the organization quickly denounced any links with the group.

In 2007 there was a considerable rise in PKK activity (see Current issues, above), with numerous Turkish security staff and PKK members killed. On October 22, a Turkish military patrol was ambushed near Dağlıca by some 200 PKK militants. Twelve Turkish soldiers were killed, 16 were wounded, and 8 were taken hostage by PKK insurgents. A DTP committee negotiated their release on November 4. However, the released soldiers were prosecuted following their return to Turkey because of their failure to obey orders that would have prevented their capture. The Dağlıca incident was the largest PKK military attack on Turkish territory in many years, shocking the Turkish public.

Following reports of rifts within the PKK, Turkish forces invaded northern Iraq on February 21, 2008, attacking a PKK outpost and headquarters. Turkish troops withdrew eight days later. In July two bombs exploded in the Istanbul suburb of Gungören, killing 17 people and wounding more than 100. While the authorities accused the PKK of having been behind the attack, the evidence apparently was inconclusive. Investigation of the "Ergenekon" affair also led to speculation about possible links between the PKK and "Ergenekon."

In May 2009 in a newspaper interview, Murat Karayilan indicated the PKK had changed and was pursuing the promotion of Kurdish rights in Turkey without aiming to disrupt the unitary Turkish state. Further, he declared his readiness for armistice and dialogue with Turkey. Karayilan stressed that the solution he envisioned did not necessarily entail a federation, but greater local autonomy in accordance with a reform of the local authorities' law.

After negotiations with the government, the PKK declared a new unilateral cease-fire in August 2010 and pledged to maintain the truce through national elections scheduled in June 2011. However, in November, the TAK claimed responsibility for a bombing in Istanbul that wounded more than 30. The TAK asserted that it would not join the PKK cease-fire. The Turkish government subsequently announced the deployment of additional forces along the border with Iraq in an effort to stop cross-border incursions by Kurds based in Iraq. Meanwhile, in October 151 people, including 12 mayors, were arrested on suspicion of ties with the PKK.

On February 28, 2011, the PKK ended its unilateral truce after the government rejected a proposal to end the 10 percent threshold required for parties to gain seats in the assembly. In April an additional 35 political figures with suspected ties to the PKK were detained. In

November, Turkish security forces killed a PKK hijacker during an aborted ferry takeover.

In January 2012 more than 30 suspected PKK members were arrested in a security sweep in Turkey. In May, Ankara accused Syria of providing bases and military support for the PKK.

Leaders: Abdullah ÖCALAN (Honorary President), Zübeyir AYDAR (President), Murat KARAYILAN (Chair of the Executive Council).

Party of God (*Hizbullah*). *Hizbullah,* a militant Islamist Sunni group unrelated to the Lebanon-based Shiite *Hezbollah*, was active in southeast Anatolia in the early 1990s, when it launched a campaign of violence against PKK militants and pro-Kurdish lawyers, intellectuals, and human rights activists. On January 17, 2000, Hüseyin VELİOĞLU, reportedly a leader of the **Party of God** was killed and two of his associates were arrested in a shoot-out with police in İstanbul. Some unconfirmed press reports claimed that the group members were tolerated if not encouraged by the state security forces, which allegedly explained the fact that none of its members were caught until the shoot-out. During the months of January and February 2000, police arrested over 400 alleged members of *Hizbullah,* some reportedly civil servants. State security forces also found several safe-houses of the group, where they reportedly recovered mutilated bodies of dozens of victims, including famous moderate Islamic feminist Gonca KURİŞ, who was kidnapped in July 1998. In February 2012, 24 members of *Hizbullah* were convicted of terrorism charges.

Following the arrest of PKK leader Abdullah Öcalan in February 1999, a shadowy far-right group, **Turkish Avenger Brigade** (*Türk İntikam Tugayı*—TİT), issued death threats against pro-Kurdish activists and politicians and claimed responsibility for attacks on various HADEP buildings. Some unconfirmed reports suggest that the group is merely a facade for occasional "agent-provocateur" activities allegedly linked to factions within the Turkish security forces. Similar activities resurfaced with the rise of nationalist sentiment after 2004. On June 13, 2007, in a shanty house in the Istanbul neighborhood of Ümraniye, police discovered large quantities of explosives, hand grenades, and other ammunition, which were allegedly intended for use in terrorist attacks against minorities and liberal Turks. The discovery marked the unraveling of the "Ergenekon" affair. The subsequent investigation sought links with the aforementioned attacks.

In March 2013 imprisoned Kurdish leader Öcalan called for a cease-fire and the withdrawal of the PKK from Turkey.

(For information on the **Unity** [*Tevhid*], please see the 2012 *Handbook.*)

LEGISLATURE

The 1982 constitution replaced the former bicameral legislature with a unicameral 550-member **Turkish Grand National Assembly** (*Türkiye Büyük Millet Meclisi*) elected for a five-year term on a proportional basis (10 percent threshold).

Following the election of June 12, 2011, the seat distribution was as follows: Justice and Development Party, 327; Republican People's Party, 135; Nationalist Action Party, 53; and independents, 35. Members of the Democratic Society Party, Democratic Left Party, Liberty and Solidarity Party, and Great Unity Party ran as independents or on the tickets of other parties but reasserted their party affiliations following the assembly's first session.

Speaker: Cemil ÇİÇEK.

CABINET

[as of October 15, 2013]

Prime Minister	Recep Tayyip Erdoğan
Deputy Prime Ministers	Bülent Arınç
	Beşir Atalay
	Ali Babacan
	Bekir Bozdağ
Ministers	
Agriculture, Food and Animal Husbandry	Mehmet Mehdi Eker
Culture and Tourism	Ömer Çelik
Customs and Trade	Hayati Yazıcı
Development	Cevdet Yilmaz
Economy	Mehmet Zafer Çağlayan
Energy and Natural Resources	Taner Yıldız
Environment and Urban Planning	Erdoğan Bayraktar
European Union Affairs	Egeman Bağiş
Family and Social Policy	Fatma Şahin [f]
Finance	Mehmet Şimşek
Foreign Affairs	Ahmet Davutoğlu
Forestry and Water Works	Veysel Eroğlu
Health	Mehmet Müezzinoğlu
Industry, Science and Technology	Nihat Ergün
Interior	Muammer Güler
Justice	Sadullah Ergin
Labor and Social Security	Faruk Çelik
National Defense	İsmet Yilmaz
National Education	Nabi Avci
Transport	Binali Yıldırım
Youth and Sports	Suat Kılıç

[f] = female

Note: All ministers are members of the Justice and Development Party (AKP).

INTERGOVERNMENTAL REPRESENTATION

Ambassador to the U.S.: Namik TAN.

U.S. Ambassador to Turkey: Francis RICCIARDONE Jr.

Permanent Representative to the UN: Yasar Halit ÇEVİK.

IGO Memberships (Non-UN): ADB, AfDB, CEUR, EBRD, G-20, IEA, IOM, NATO, OECD, OIC, OSCE, WTO.

TURKMENISTAN

Republic of Turkmenistan
Tiurkmenostan Respublikasy

Note: In elections held on December 15, 2013, the governing Democratic Party of Turkmenistan won 47 seats while the recently created Party of Industrialists and Entrepreneurs won 14, trade unions won 33, women's groups 16, youth organizations 8, and citizens' groups 7. An observer mission from the Commonwealth of Independent States concluded that the elections were free, orderly, and competitive, but human rights campaigners dismissed them as a token gesture, noting that genuine opposition leaders are all in jail or in exile. Observers from the Organization for Security and Cooperation in Europe said that some improvements were made in the legal framework for elections but that choice was limited.

Political Status: Declared independence as Republic of Turkmenistan on October 27, 1991; new constitution adopted May 18, 1992; present constitution adopted September 26, 2008. First emerged as a political entity when the Turkmenian districts of the former Bukhara and Khorezm republics were added to the autonomous Turkistan Soviet Socialist Republic within the Russian Soviet Federative Socialist Republic on October 27, 1924; became a constituent republic of the Union of Soviet Socialist Republics (USSR) on May 12, 1925.

Area: 188,456 sq. mi. (488,100 sq. km).

Population: 5,209,408 (2012E—UN); 5,054,828 (2012E—U.S. Census).

Major Urban Center (2005E): ASHGABAT (Ashkhabad, 559,000).

Official Language: Turkmen.

Monetary Unit: Manat (market rate November 1, 2013: 2.85 new manats = $1US).

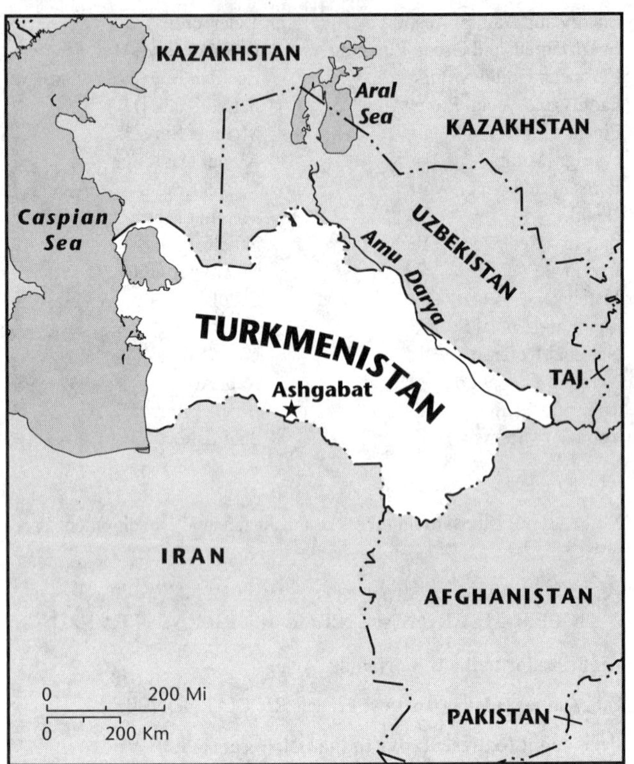

President and Prime Minister: Gurbanguly BERDIMUHAMMEDOV (Democratic Party of Turkmenistan); elevated from deputy prime minister to acting president and prime minister on December 21, 2006, following the death of Gen. Saparmurad Atayevich NIYAZOV (Saparmyrat NYYAZOW; Democratic Party of Turkmenistan); reelected on February 12, 2012, for a second five-year term.

THE COUNTRY

The southernmost republic of the former Soviet Union, Turkmenistan is bordered on the northwest by Kazakhstan, on the north and northeast by Uzbekistan, on the southeast by Afghanistan, on the south by Iran, and on the west by the Caspian Sea. The Kara Kum (Garagum) Desert occupies about 80 percent of the land area. Ethnic Turkmens, who are predominantly Sunni Muslims, account for approximately 77 percent of the population, followed by Uzbeks (9 percent), Russians (7 percent), and Kazakhs (2 percent). Turkmenistan is the most ethnically homogeneous of the five independent Central Asian republics to emerge out of the former Soviet Union in 1991, the other four being Kazakhstan, Kyrgyzstan, Tajikistan, and Uzbekistan. Women hold 17 percent of the seats in the current Assembly.

Industry, which contributes about 50 percent of the GDP and employs about 12 percent of the active labor force, is dominated by hydrocarbons. According to current estimates, Turkmenistan has the fourth largest reserve of natural gas in the world—8 trillion cubic meters, or more than 4 percent of the world's total gas reserves. Natural gas accounts for over half of the export earnings, with petrochemicals and other oil products adding another 30 percent.

Agriculture employs about 43 percent of workers, but its share of GDP is much smaller, approximately 8 percent, and is declining. A principal component of the country's irrigation network is a 500-mile Karakum canal that carries water from the Amu-Darya (Oxus) River, a major tributary of the Aral Sea. That diversion has contributed to an ecological catastrophe, the Aral Sea having lost 75 percent of its surface area and 90 percent of its water volume since the canal's completion in 1967. This has devastated fish stocks and created major public health hazards as newly dried-out saline seabeds have become contaminated with pesticides and fertilizer runoffs. Only about 4 percent of the country is arable land, and half of that is planted with cotton; in 2012, Turkmenistan was one of the world's top seven cotton producers. Apart from cotton, the country's other main crop is wheat, while in the livestock sector, it specializes in cattle meat, cow milk, and poultry production.

The breakup of the Soviet Union caused a dramatic decline in Turkmenistan's GDP in the mid-1990s, coupled with hyperinflation. However, growth has been constant since then due largely to the extensive development of its oil and natural gas resources. While foreign investment has grown steadily in recent years, corruption and the extremely tight grip the government maintains over the economy remain a disincentive to investors. Turkmenistan was ranked 170th out of 176 countries in Transparency International's 2012 Corruption Perceptions Index. Turkmenistan is currently both a net exporter, with oil and gas being its leading export commodity, and a net creditor.

GOVERNMENT AND POLITICS

Political background. Historic Turkestan occupied a vast area extending from the Caspian Sea in the west to the border of China in the east, and from the Aral Sea watershed in the north to Persia (Iran) and Afghanistan in the south. In 1924 what had been an autonomous republic of the Russian Soviet Federative Socialist Republic was split into (western) Turkmen and (eastern) Uzbek components, both of which became constituent republics of the USSR in 1925.

Following republican elections on January 7, 1990, Saparmurad NIYAZOV, the first secretary of the Turkmen Communist Party (TCP), was named chair of the Supreme Soviet (head of state). On August 23 the Supreme Soviet issued a declaration of Turkmenistan's "independent statehood," on the basis of which the adjectives "Soviet" and "Socialist" were dropped from the republic's official name and the Turkmen constitution and laws were assigned precedence over those of the Soviet Union. In a somewhat unusual move, the declaration identified Turkmenistan as a nuclear and chemical weapons–free zone. On October 27 Niyazov was unopposed in direct elections to the new post of executive president.

In August 1991 with democratic activists reportedly being arrested for alleging that Niyazov had supported the failed hard-liners' coup in Moscow against USSR president Mikhail Gorbachev, the president broke with the leaders of most fellow republics by not dismantling the Communist Party. Nevertheless, a referendum on independence was conducted on October 26 that yielded a 93.5 percent affirmative vote, and an implementing declaration was issued by the Supreme Soviet the following day. On December 16 the TCP was formally dissolved and immediately succeeded by the Democratic Party of Turkmenistan (DPT), which abandoned the Marxist-Leninist precepts of its predecessor while maintaining an absolute grip on power.

The Supreme Soviet approved a new constitution on May 18, 1992, and on June 26, Niyazov was reinvested as president after an election five days earlier in which he was again the sole candidate. On January 15, 1994, a reported 99.5 percent of voters favored exempting the president from having to stand for an additional term, while in elections to the lower house of the new legislature, held on December 11, only 1 of 50 seats was contested, with most of the returned candidates being DPT nominees.

During his tenure President Niyazov kept absolute control of Turkmenistan. He adopted the title *Turkmenbashi* (Leader of the Turkmen People), and the epithet "the Great" was routinely appended to his name in government press releases. He also took on the mantle of cultural protector, banning, for example, car radios, ballet, and opera. He developed a cult of personality around himself, ordering that the months of the year and days of the week be renamed in honor of famous Turkmen, including his mother and himself. His own books, called the *Ruhnama,* were used as historical texts, while his suppression of Islamic holy texts such as the Koran and hadith led Islamists to view him as a blasphemer. From 1991 to 2001 Niyazov implemented a massive urban renewal project in the capital, Ashgabat, that led to large-scale demolition of houses using forced evictions. Some of the evicted received neither financial compensation nor a new home.

The first evidence of popular unrest came in July 1995 when demonstrators in Ashgabat called for new presidential elections and an end to economic hardship and shortages. Authorities swiftly removed the demonstrators, and a number of political opponents subsequently were detained in prisons or psychiatric facilities. In mid-April 1998, at the urging of a visiting OSCE delegation, President Niyazov released several detainees incarcerated in connection with the July 1995 antigovernment demonstration. They included Durdymurat KHOJAMUKHAMMED, a leader of the opposition Democratic Progress Party (DPP), who had been held in a psychiatric hospital since 1996. Within days, however, exiled opposition leader and former foreign minister Avde KULIEV, having returned from Moscow, was placed under house arrest on charges that included extortion and trying to organize a coup in 1995. Kuliev was released on April 20, and he returned to Moscow on April 22.

In early November 2001 it was reported that the government had issued an arrest warrant for Boris SHIKHMURADOV, a former Western-oriented foreign minister who had most recently served as ambassador to China and was then in Russia. In addition to denying allegations that he had appropriated $25 million in state property, chiefly aircraft and armaments, and then sold them, Shikhmuradov responded by announcing that he was forming an opposition group, subsequently identified as the People's Democratic Movement of Turkmenistan (PDMT), to help depose Niyazov.

On November 25, 2002, gunmen fired on a presidential motorcade. Niyazov, who was uninjured, immediately attributed the attack to a number of former government officials who had aligned with Shikhmuradov, including former deputy prime minister Hudayberdi ORAZOW (Khudaiberdy ORAZOV) and the recently resigned ambassador to Turkey, Nurmuhammet HANAMOW (Nurmukhammed KHANAMOV), who subsequently emerged as a leader of the exiled opposition. A month later Shikhmuradov, who had secretly returned to Turkmenistan, announced on an opposition Web site that he intended to surrender to authorities in an effort to prevent further persecution of government opponents. Within days, Shikhmuradov was arrested, tried, convicted, and sentenced to life in prison. (In a taped confession Shikhmuradov admitted stealing state property, hiring mercenaries to assassinate the president, orchestrating a coup, using illegal drugs, and various other offenses. Professing rediscovered admiration for Niyazov, Shikhmuradov praised the president as "a gift from on high to the people of Turkmenistan.") By February 2003 more than 50 individuals had been convicted of involvement in the November plot.

The Assembly election of December 19, 2004, with runoff balloting on January 9, 2005, was once again conducted without international monitoring. All candidates were members of the DPT.

On December 21, 2006, President Niyazov died unexpectedly. Although the constitution specified that the speaker of the Assembly, Ovezgeldi ATAYEV, should serve as acting president pending the election of a successor, Atayev was relieved of his duties and charged with an unrelated criminal offense. (In February 2007 he was convicted of driving a prospective daughter-in-law to suicide.) As a result, the cabinet elevated Deputy Prime Minister Gurbanguly BERDIMUHAMMEDOV to the presidency. The following day, Akja NURBERDIYEWA was appointed acting speaker of the Assembly.

In an extraordinary session on December 26, 2006, the People's Council called a presidential election for February 2007 and amended the constitution, which had previously prohibited an acting president from seeking election to the presidency. The People's Council also endorsed Berdimuhammedov and five other presidential candidates, all from the DPT. In the February 11 election Berdimuhammedov was credited with 89 percent of the vote, and he was inaugurated on February 14.

Following constitutional reforms that expanded the size of the *Mejlis,* new elections were held on December 14 and 28, 2008, a year earlier than required by the constitution. All 125 members elected to the Assembly were members of the DPT or pro-presidential independents. The balloting marked the first time that foreign monitors were present as observers, although international groups criticized the elections for irregularities and because no opposition parties contested the elections In 2008 the new government initiated limited economic reforms, including the redenomination of the currency, reductions in state subsidies, and new incentives for foreign investment.

Constitution and government. The 1992 constitution featured a popularly elected strong president (head both of state and of government as well as commander-in-chief) whose powers include issuing laws, save those amending the constitution or revising the criminal code. Up until 2003, the country's highest representative body, the People's Council (*Khalk Maslakhaty*), typically met once a year with a mandate that included consideration of basic economic, social, and political policy; constitutional changes; ratification of intergovernmental treaties; and declarations of war and peace. The smaller Assembly (*Mejlis*) was chiefly responsible for enacting ordinary legislation. At the initiative of the president, in August 2003 the People's Council was restructured as a "fourth branch" of government, a "permanently functioning supreme representative body of popular government having the powers of supreme state authority and government." The body's membership was expanded to 2,507, encompassing executive, judicial, and legislative members as well as representatives of regional, local, civic, labor, party, and other groups.

In September 2008 the People's Council unanimously approved a new constitution touted as a step toward democracy and the free market. The document guarantees the right to free expression and the right to "receive information unless it represents a state secret or any other secret protected by law." The constitution adds, however, that the "execution of rights and liberties shall not violate the rights and freedoms of others, or contravene morality, law, public order, or national security." Changes from its predecessor include an endorsement of market economic principles. A strong presidency is retained, but an expanded Assembly may censure the president and amend the constitution, and it was given most of the powers of the People's Council, which was abolished.

The country is divided into five administrative regions, or *velayaty* (Akhal, Balkan, Dashkhovuz, Lebap, and Mary), which are subdivided into districts (*etraps*), towns, and urban settlements.

All media, including the Internet, are strictly controlled by the government. Reporters Without Borders, in its 2013 World Press Freedom Index, ranked Turkmenistan in bottom place, 179th, alongside North Korea and Eritrea. It said that "the official proclamation [in 2012] of a multiparty system and freedom of expression brought no changes whatsoever to the totalitarian rule in Turkmenistan." Only about 2 percent of Turkmen are connected to the Internet, while access to social media sites such as Facebook, Twitter, and YouTube is blocked, it noted.

Niyazov's successor, Gurbanguly Berdimuhammedov, had formerly been Niyazov's personal dentist before rapidly ascending the political ladder in the late 1990s. As health minister, he had implemented Niyazov's plan to close most of the country's medical facilities. After Niyazov died, he distanced himself from Niyazov's cult of personality and initially showed signs that he intended to reverse some of Niyazov's more draconian policies. He opened up the economy to greater foreign investment and called for educational and social reforms as well as restoring the pension benefits that Niyazov had withdrawn from 100,000 elderly people. To reassure Russia and Western Europe, he stated that Turkmenistan would honor all existing natural gas contracts. Rather than condemn the fundamentally undemocratic process by which Berdimuhammedov assumed the presidency, the United States and other Western countries chose to view the new president's pronouncements as positive steps that merited support (particularly given the potential for improved access to Turkmenistan's hydrocarbons). Berdimuhammedov has, however, continued his predecessor's practice of dismissing cabinet ministers, typically for "grave shortcomings" in their work, on a regular basis. When the Turkmen athletes failed to win any medals in the 2012 London Olympics, the president fired the sports minister. In October 2012 the authorities arrested a former minister, Geldymyrat Nurmuhammedov, after he openly criticized the government, and sent him to undergo six months of forced treatment for drug addiction, despite him having no history of drug use.

President Berdimuhammedov characterized adoption of the 2008 constitution as an important step in implementing his government's "New Revival," the process of democratic, economic, and cultural reform in the name of "government for the people." Critics abroad called it a superficial gesture toward the West. In May 2010 Berdimuhammedov encouraged the registration of a new party and directed the assembly leadership to draft a law on political parties to put the necessary procedures in place. In August 2012 he announced that a second political party, the Party of Industrialists and Entrepreneurs (PIE) would be allowed to compete with the DPT in subsequent elections. The move was immediately dismissed by Western analysts of the country, who noted that the new party was headed by Orazmammed MAMMEDOV, a close friend of the president.

Foreign relations. By early 1992 Turkmenistan had established diplomatic relations with a number of foreign countries, including the United States. On March 2, it joined the United Nations and on September 22 was admitted to the International Monetary Fund and the World Bank. As a predominantly Muslim country, it also joined the Organization of the Islamic Conference. It has attended summits of the Turkic-speaking states and in 1995 joined the Nonaligned Movement. In 1994 Turkmenistan became the first Central Asian republic to join NATO's Partnership for Peace program.

With "permanent neutrality" mandated by the 1992 constitution, the government's geopolitical priorities have focused on economic matters, particularly market access for its massive hydrocarbon reserves. Much of its diplomatic energies have been expended on negotiating the terms and conditions for the sale and transit of Turkmen gas through the surrounding countries' territories. In 1994 a dispute with Russia over pricing and barter arrangements led Moscow to cut off Turkmenistan's access to the sole natural gas pipeline that reached its European customers. Thereafter, Turkmenistan interrupted deliveries to Armenia, Georgia, and Ukraine because of payment arrears, while in 1997 Russia completely stopped the flow into the regional pipeline in retaliation for Turkmenistan's decision to dissolve the financially troubled joint venture the two countries had set up to export Turkmen gas.

In December 1997, President Niyazov and the new Iranian president, Mohammad Khatami, inaugurated a 125-mile-long pipeline carrying comparatively small quantities of natural gas to Iran. A second pipeline was completed in late 2009. In February 1998, Moscow and Ashgabat resolved their major disputes over Turkmen gas exports. An October 2000 visit by Ukraine president Leonid Kuchma resolved differences over payments arrears and future gas deliveries between those two countries. In 2006 Turkmenistan resolved another dispute with Russia over gas prices when Gazprom agreed to pay 54 percent more for Turkmen gas.

On the global security front, Turkmenistan became an increasingly significant actor due to its proximity to unstable countries and regions. In late 1996, the government took a more conciliatory line than neighboring republics toward the overthrow of the Afghan government by the Taliban militia, in part because the Islamic group had reportedly approved plans for a gas pipeline to Pakistan. However, the U.S. corporate sponsor of the venture withdrew following U.S. attacks in August 1998 on Afghan guerrilla bases. Following the September 2001 al-Qaida attacks on the United States and the consequent U.S.-led invasion of Afghanistan, Turkmenistan opened land and air corridors for the delivery of humanitarian aid to the Afghan people, and Niyazov indicated his support for a UN-led effort against international terrorism. He denied U.S. forces access to military facilities, however, citing his country's commitment to neutrality, but he was not averse to accepting U.S. military aid for training and equipment. The overthrow of the Taliban led to a May 2002 agreement with Pakistan and the interim Afghan government to conduct a new feasibility study for the pipeline project, which was approved in December 2002 at an initial projected cost of $2–3 billion.

In April 2006, during a visit to China, President Niyazov and Chinese officials approved a framework agreement for a natural gas pipeline to China via Uzbekistan and Kazakhstan. In December 2009 the presidents of the four countries met to inaugurate the recently completed 1,139-mile (1,833-kilometer) pipeline from Turkmenistan's Saman-Depe field. The new pipeline is due to reach its full capacity of 40 billion cubic meters by 2015, although China has already indicated it needs 60 billion cubic meters. Turkmenistan has, in addition, expressed interest in a possible Trans-Caspian gas pipeline called TANAP that would transit Azerbaijan and Georgia and then terminate in Turkey, thereby bypassing Russia and providing a new route to European customers. This project is also supported by the European Union (EU), which hopes that some of the Turkmen gas can ultimately be transported to European markets via another planned pipeline, Nabucco West, thereby making Europe less reliant on Russian gas. Previously, Turkmenistan relied heavily on Russia's natural gas giant, Gazprom, to distribute its gas, but President Berdimuhammedov wants to reduce this dependence by diversifying his country's export routes.

Another regional issue involves national claims to the Caspian Sea, which borders Azerbaijan, Iran, Kazakhstan, Russia, and Turkmenistan. Russia, Azerbaijan, and Kazakhstan have negotiated bilateral agreements dividing the seabed into territorial sectors, but Iran and Turkmenistan have argued for a more comprehensive approach. A joint task force continues to meet, but the basic issue remains unresolved and is a source of regional tension. Following the apparent attempt to assassinate President Niyazov in November 2002, relations with Uzbekistan worsened because of alleged Uzbek involvement, which Tashkent denied. In November 2004 President Niyazov met with Uzbek president Islam Karimov in Bukhara, Uzbekistan, where they signed a declaration of friendship and pledged closer cooperation in trade and a variety of other areas.

Relations between Turkmenistan and Russia deteriorated in 2009 following an explosion in one of the pipelines carrying Turkmen gas to Europe. The Turkmenistan government blamed Gazprom for the accident. In addition, Turkmenistan's agreement to supply China with 40 billion cubic meters of gas each year further alienated Moscow. Relations between the EU and Turkmenistan were normalized in April 2009, following years of strain over the country's human rights record. Concurrently, the EU Parliament approved a new trade agreement with Turkmenistan.

Current issues. The Turkmen economy continues to perform strongly due to increasing oil and gas exports. GDP growth for 2013 and 2014 is forecast to be 8 percent a year, while the country's GDP per capita, adjusted for purchasing power, has doubled since 2007, from about $5,000 to $10,000. The government continues to focus its efforts on concluding contracts with foreign energy companies—including from China, the United States, and the United Kingdom—to further develop its hydrocarbon sector. In May 2011 a British energy auditor reported that Turkmenistan had the world's second largest gas field: South Yolotan, which holds 14–21 trillion cubic meters and is bigger than the state of Luxembourg in size. The range of actual or potential customers for these gas supplies continues to broaden and now includes Afghanistan, India, Iran, Malaysia, Pakistan, South Korea, as well as Eastern and Western Europe. In July 2011 Turkmenistan opened its first offshore gas production plant at Kiyanli in the Caspian Sea. In September 2013 production began at an onshore gas field, Galkynysh, with the goal being for it to produce 30 billion cubic meters by the end of 2014.

The president has been trying to develop a Caspian-based tourism industry too by building a new resort city, Awaza, at a cost of $2 billion. In June 2013 the American pop star Jennifer Lopez raised eyebrows when she flew in to Awaza to perform for the president at his 56th birthday party, her trip having been organized by China's state-owned oil and gas company, China National Petroleum Corporation. Turkmenistan's record on political freedom and human rights continues to be heavily criticized. According to an April 2013 report from the advocacy group Human Rights Watch, the government is "among the most repressive in the world." The key problems, it said, are the government's imprisoning of political opponents, its refusal to allow journalists and human rights defenders to work openly, and arbitrary travel bans that it imposes on political activists and their relatives. There is no indication that the country is moving toward a genuinely pluralist political system despite the president having allowed a second party to form. Instead, he continues to exile people who fall out of favor and to arbitrarily interfere with citizens' ability to travel abroad. For example, in March 2011 an 80-year-old contributor to Radio Free Europe, Amangelen SHAPUDAKOV, was detained and forcibly confined in a psychiatric facility. Religion remains tightly controlled by the state, with all religious groups obliged to register to gain legal status, and the government continues to imprison Jehovah's Witnesses, who refuse to do military service on religious conscience grounds.

President Berdimuhammedov appears to be replacing the late President Niyazov's personality cult with one of his own. He is now known as "Arkadag" meaning "protector." His portrait features ubiquitously in schools, universities, hospitals, aircrafts, newspapers, and markets. He is praised endlessly by the state-controlled media, and he has built a grandiose new presidential palace, abandoning the one Niyazov built. In the February 2012 presidential elections, while seven other candidates were permitted to compete against him, news reports described them as token challengers drawn from government ministries and state enterprises. Several of them even praised Berdimuhammedov, and the president won reelection overwhelmingly, taking 97 percent of the vote. The Organization for Security and Co-operation in Europe (OSCE) refused to send election monitors on account of the conditions in the country, while the Russian head of an election observer mission from the Commonwealth of Independent States praised the ballot. A good illustration of his iron grip of the media was seen in April 2013 when he fell off his horse while competing in a horse race that appeared clearly choreographed to have him win. The thousands of spectators present observed the fall moments after he crossed the finish line. However the state-owned national broadcaster edited out the episode and made no reference to it in their extensive coverage of the event. Later, police checked computers, tablets, and mobile phones of departing passengers at airports to prevent footage of the fall being smuggled out.

Turkmenistan is also a major source country for men and women who are subjected to forced labor and prostitution, according to the U.S. State Department. Many are trafficked to Turkey, with some women subjected to forced prostitution and both men and women subjected to forced labor on construction sites, in textile sweatshops, and as domestic servants. The government has not made a serious effort to address the problem, nor is it trying to tackle the major overcrowding in Turkmen prisons, the report found. In September 2012, the country held the first-ever naval war games in its history, with warships and fighter jets staging attacks on an oil tanker in the Caspian Sea, maneuvers that were observed by the president. Most of the country's arms have been bought from Russia.

POLITICAL PARTIES

The Turkmen political system is dominated by the Democratic Party of Turkmenistan (DPT). A **National Movement "Revival"** (*Galkynysh*), chaired by the president, is a government-sponsored association of various associations and the DPT. Most political opponents currently operate from exile in Russia, Scandinavia, and Eastern Europe.

Government Party:

Democratic Party of Turkmenistan (DPT). The DPT is the successor to the Turkmen Communist Party, which was dissolved on December 16, 1991, after its 25th congress had admitted to "mistakes" during seven decades of Soviet rule. The DPT describes itself as the country's "mother party" and has been virtually unchallenged as the leading political force in the country. President Berdimuhammedov was elected chair of the party in August 2007. In the December 2008 elections to the expanded Assembly, all seats were claimed by DPT candidates or party-approved independents. Akja NURBERDIYEWA was reelected speaker of the chamber. In August 2013 Berdimuhammedov announced that he was stepping down as party leader in advance of the December 2013 parliamentary elections in order to give the country's two officially authorized parties an equal chance.

Leader: Kasymguly Babaev.

Government-Sanctioned Party:

Party of Industrialists and Entrepreneurs (PIE). This party was established in August 2012 after President Berdimuhammedov announced that a new party would be allowed to compete against his ruling DPT. The independence of the PIE immediately came under suspicion, with one news report noting that the party was inaugurated by a panel seated under a wall-sized picture of the president and that little was known about the new party's leader. It has since been reported that the leader is a close friend of President Berdimuhammedov. The PIE gained its first seat in parliament in June 2013 when its leader Orazmammed MAMMEDOV won a by-election in the eastern province of Lebap.

Leader: Orazmammed MAMMEDOV.

Unregistered Parties:

Unity (*Agzybirlik*). Originally formed in 1989 as a cultural and environmental forum, *Agzybirlik* was banned in 1990 and one of its founders, Shiraly NURMYRADOV, imprisoned, ostensibly for fraud. Released in 1992, Nurmyradov then relocated to Moscow. The party advocates adoption of a multiparty democracy.

In February 2000 another leader, Nurberdy NURMAMEDOV, was sentenced to five years in prison, reportedly for hooliganism and intent to murder. He had been arrested in January 2000 after criticizing the legislature's decision to permit the president more than two consecutive terms. He was released in January 2001 and attempted to run for president in 2007, but he was denied a place on the ballot. Nurmamedov remains the only significant opposition leader still living in Turkmenistan.

Leader: Nurberdy NURMAMEDOV.

Exile opposition groups have included the Vienna-based **Republican Party of Turkmenistan** (RPT), chaired by Nurmuhammet Hanamow, a former ambassador to Turkey, which was expressly forbidden from campaigning in the 2008 Assembly elections; the **United Democratic Opposition of Turkmenistan** (UDOT), led by former foreign minister Avde Kuliev until his death in Oslo in April 2007; and the **People's Democratic Movement of Turkmenistan** (PDMT, also identified as the National Democratic Movement of Turkmenistan), founded by former foreign minister Boris Shikhmuradov. Shikhmuradov and Hanamow were both accused of involvement in an alleged November 2002 assassination attempt against President Niyazov, and Shikhmuradov is serving a life sentence.

In October 2003, four opposition groups, all in exile, announced formation of a **Union of Democratic Forces of Turkmenistan** (UDFT). Founding members were the RPT; the UDOT; the **Socio-Political Movement *Watan*** (Motherland), now led by Hudayberdi ORAZOW (Khudaiberdy ORAZOV); and the **Socio-Political Movement "Revival,"** led by Nazar SUYUNOV. Earlier, in June 2002, various opposition formations had convened in Vienna, Austria, and had organized a "Roundtable of the Turkmen Democratic Opposition"; participants included *Agzybirlik,* the **Communist Party of Turkmenistan,** the **National Patriotic Movement of Turkmenistan,** the PDMT, Shirali NURMURADOV's **Popular Social Movement "Mertebe"** (Dignity), the **Social Democratic Party**, Turkmen communities from Russia and elsewhere, and a veterans' group.

Following President Niyazov's death, the RPT and *Watan* formed a **Democratic Coalition of Turkmenistan,** which nominated *Watan*'s Orazow as its 2007 presidential candidate. Orazow was not allowed on the ballot.

LEGISLATURE

Under the 1992 constitution, as amended, Turkmenistan had two national representative bodies: a quasi-parliamentary People's Council, which had among its powers establishing broad policy guidelines and amending the constitution, and a smaller Assembly performing ordinary legislative functions. The 2008 constitution abolished the People's Council and doubled the size of the Assembly.

Assembly (*Mejlis*). The *Mejlis* consists of 125 members elected for five-year terms from single-seat constituencies. The Supreme Soviet elected on January 7, 1990, became the *Mejlis* as of May 19, 1992. Elections were held on December 14, 2008, with run-off balloting on December 28 for districts in which no candidate had received more than 50 percent of the vote. One by-election was held on February 8, 2009, after an elected member declined to take his seat. All 287 candidates, including the 125 members elected to the *Mejlis,* were either members of the Democratic Party of Turkmenistan or independents who ran with state backing. The next elections were held on December 15, 2013; see headnote.

Chair: Akja NURBERDIYEWA.

CABINET

[as of September 1, 2013]

President	Gurbanguly Berdimuhammedov
Deputy Chair (Office of the President)	Yagsygeldi Kakayew
Deputy Chair (Office of the President)	Hojamuhammet Muhammedow
Office of the Chair of the Council of Ministers	Annamuhammet Gocyyew
	Bamyrat Hojamuhammedow
	Rashid Meredov
	Mammetniyaz Nurmammedov
	Byagul Nurmyradova
	Sapardurdy Toylyev
	Annageldy Yazmyradov
	Akmyrat Yegeleyev
Ministers	
Agriculture	Rejep Bazarov
Communications	Bayramgeldi Ovezov
Construction	Jumagelel Bayramow
Culture and the Media	Guncha Mammedova
Defense	Begenech Gundogdiyev
Economics and Development	Babamyrat Taganov
Education	Gulshat Mammedova [f]
Energy	Myrat Artykov
Environmental Protection and Natural Resources	Babageldi Annabayramow
Finance	Dovletgeldy Sadykov
Foreign Affairs	Rashid Meredow
Healthcare and Pharmaceutical Industry	Nurmuhammet Ammannepesov
Industry	Babanyyaz Italmazow
Interior	Iskander Mulikov

Justice	Murad Garryyew
Labor and Social Protection	Bekmyrat Mesrepowic Samyradow
National Security	Yaylim Berdiyew
Oil, Gas, and Mineral Resources	Mukhammetnur Khalylov
Railways	Bajram Annameredov
Road Transport	Mele Gurbandurdyev
Textile Industry	Saparmyrat Batyrov
Trade and Foreign Economic Relations	Batyr Abayew
Water Resources	Seyitmyrat Taganov

[f] = female

INTERGOVERNMENTAL REPRESENTATION

Ambassador to the U.S.: Meret Bairamovich ORAZOV.

U.S. Ambassador to Turkmenistan: Robert E. PATTERSON Jr.

Permanent Representative to the UN: Aksoltan T. ATAYEVA.

IGO Memberships (Non-UN): ADB, CIS, EBRD, IDB, NAM, OIC, OSCE.

TUVALU

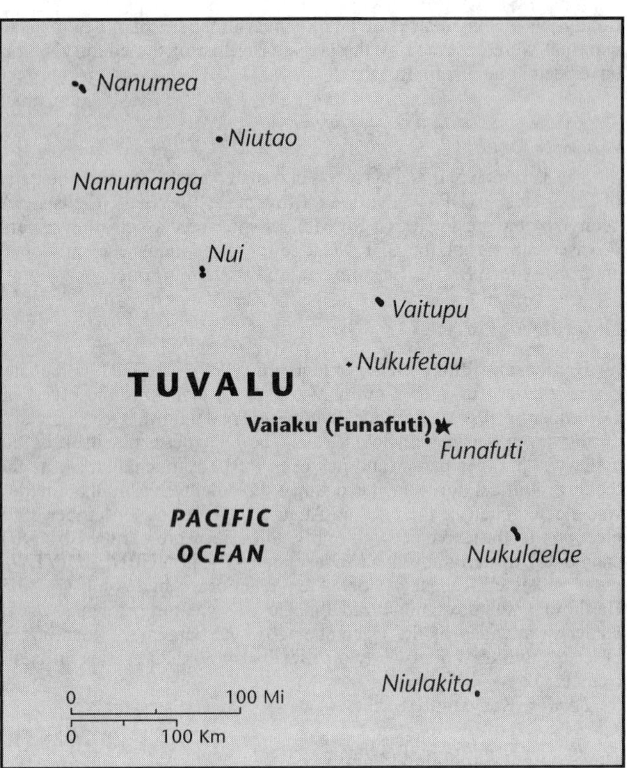

Constitutional Monarchy of Tuvalu
Fakavae Aliki-Malo i Tuvalu

Political Status: Former British dependency; independent with "special membership" in the Commonwealth since October 1, 1978.

Land Area: 10 sq. mi. (26 sq. km).

Resident Population: 10,619 (2012E—U.S. Census).

Major Urban Center (2005E): VAIAKU (Funafuti, 6,200).

Official Language: English (Tuvaluan is widely spoken).

Monetary Unit: Australian dollar (market rate November 1, 2013: 1.06 dollar = $1US). The Tuvaluan dollar, introduced in 1977, is used largely for numismatic purposes (market rate November 1, 2013: 1.06 dollar = $1US).

Sovereign: Queen ELIZABETH II.

Governor General: Iakopa ITALELI; sworn in on April 15, 2009, to succeed Rev. Filoimea TELITO.

Prime Minister: Enele SOPOAGA; elected by Parliament on August 4, 2013, succeeding Willy TELAVI, following a vote of no confidence on August 2.

THE COUNTRY

Formerly known as the Ellice Islands in the Gilbert group, Tuvalu consists of nine atolls stretching over an area of 500,000 square miles north of Fiji in the western Pacific. Only eight of the islands are considered inhabited for electoral purposes; activity on the ninth is confined to a copra plantation. With a total land area of 10 square miles, Tuvalu is one of the world's smallest countries, although its population density is the highest among South Pacific island nations and some 35 percent of its population is estimated to live beneath the poverty line. Its inhabitants are predominantly Polynesian and Protestant Christian. The soil is poor, with crops subject to variable rainfall, frequent cyclones, and increasing salinization. As a consequence, agricultural activity is confined largely to the coco palm and its derivatives, yielding a dependency on imported food. Women constitute 30 percent of the paid labor force, concentrated almost entirely in the service sector; female participation in politics and government has traditionally been minimal, although a woman entered the Paeniu cabinet in 1989.

Only about a third of Tuvaluans are formally employed, and the primary employer is the government. Much of the islands' revenue is derived from service-based industries and from remittances by Tuvaluans working abroad, primarily as merchant seamen or as phosphate miners on Nauru and Kiribati's Banaba Island. Since 1987, approximately one-third of the operating expenses have been covered by donations from foreign governments. In November 1999 a California-based firm agreed to pay Tuvalu $50 million over the ensuing decade for use of the country's Internet suffix ".tv," which would be licensed to Web address customers as an alternative to the ubiquitous ".com." The global depression brought a short period of significant economy growth to an end in 2009, when Tuvalu experienced a 1.7 percent decline. Since 2009, with the payment from the sale of the ".tv" designation being completed, the economy remained near stagnant. GDP grew by 1.3 percent in 2013, with inflation of 2.7 percent.

GOVERNMENT AND POLITICS

Political background. Proclaimed a protectorate with the Gilbert Islands (now independent Kiribati) in 1892 and formally annexed by Britain in 1915–1916, when the Gilbert and Ellice Islands Colony was established, the Ellice Islands were separated on October 1, 1975, and renamed Tuvalu. Independence on October 1, 1978, occurred only five months after the acquisition of full internal self-government, former chief minister Toalipi LAUTI becoming prime minister and Sir Fiatau Penitala TEO being designated Crown representative. On September 17, 1981, nine days after the country's first general election since independence, Lauti, on a 5–7 parliamentary vote, was obliged to yield office to Dr. Tomasi PUAPUA. Lauti's defeat was blamed largely on his controversial decision in 1979 to invest most of the government's capital with a California business that promised assistance in obtaining a $5 million development loan; the money, plus interest, was reported to have been returned by mid-1984.

Dr. Puapua remained in office as head of a largely unchanged administration after the election of September 12, 1985, but was forced to step down in favor of Bikenibeu PAENIU because of the loss of parliamentary seats by two cabinet members in the election of September 27, 1989.

Following legislative balloting on September 2, 1993, parliament found itself in a 6–6 tie between those who wished to retain Prime Minister Paeniu and supporters of his predecessor. The deadlock remaining after a second ballot, a new election was held on November 25. Thereafter, Puapua chose not to present himself as a candidate; Kamuta LATASI, a parliamentary backbencher and former private secretary to Governor General Toalipi Lauti, was chosen over Paeniu on a 7–5 vote. Latasi himself was on the losing end of a 7–5 nonconfidence vote on December 17, 1996, and was succeeded by Paeniu on December 23.

Following a campaign of exceptional bitterness, new balloting for parliament on March 26, 1998, returned Paeniu to his seat but not Latasi. Paeniu was reappointed for a new term as prime minister on April 8. However, he lost a vote of confidence by 7–4 on April 14, 1999, and the parliament on April 27 selected Ionatana IONATANA as his successor.

Prime Minister Ionatana died unexpectedly on December 8, 2000, and was succeeded by Deputy Prime Minister Lagitupu TUILIMU, in an acting capacity. On February 23, 2001, parliament elected Faimalaga LUKA as his successor, and he was sworn in at the head of a reshuffled cabinet the following day.

On December 13, 2001, the parliament elected Koloa TALAKE, a former minister of finance, as head of government. The previous week, Prime Minister Luka had lost a no-confidence motion when four legislators, including Talake, crossed the aisle to support the motion. (Named governor general on September 9, 2003, Luka retired in April 2005 and died on August 19.)

In balloting for an expanded 15-seat parliament on July 25, 2002, Talake, three other government ministers, and the speaker of parliament all lost their seats. On August 2 Saufatu SOPOANGA defeated the other candidate for prime minister, Amasone KILEI, by a vote of 8–7 and named a completely new cabinet.

Accused of misusing government property and money (charges he heatedly denied), Sopoanga lost a no-confidence vote (8–6) on August 25, 2004, and delayed the naming of a successor by resigning his legislative seat, thus forcing a by-election. Reelected on October 7, Sopoanga was named deputy prime minister by Maatia TOAFA following his election as the new prime minister on October 11. Toafa continued in office in mid-2005 after a crucial legislative by-election in which a progovernment candidate was chosen to replace a member who had resigned.

On August 14, 2006, Prime Minister Toafa was succeeded by Apisai IELEMIA following a general election on August 3, in which 8 of the 15 incumbent legislators lost their seats. Ielemia was, in turn, obliged to yield to Toafa, who formed his second administration after the election of September 29, 2010. After only three months in office, Prime Minister Maatia Toafa lost a confidence motion in Parliament on December 21, 2010, by one vote after Willy TELAVI, the minister for home affairs, withdrew his support from the government. Telavi was elected as the new prime minister on December 24 and subsequently named a new cabinet. On August 5, 2013, Enele SOPOAGA was sworn in after Telavi lost a confidence motion (see Current issues, below).

Constitution and government. The 1978 constitution (a substantially revised version of a preindependence document adopted three years earlier) provides for a governor general of Tuvaluan citizenship who serves a four-year term (or until age 65) and a prime minister who is elected by a unicameral parliament of 15 members. Should the office of prime minister become vacant with parliament unable to agree on a successor, the governor general may, at his discretion, name a chief executive or call for legislative dissolution. The government collectively reports to parliament, whose normal term is four years. The judiciary consists of a High Court, which is empowered to hear appeals from courts of criminal and civil jurisdiction on each of the eight inhabited islands as well as from local magistrates' courts. Appeals from the High Court may be taken to the Court of Appeal in Fiji and, as last resort, to the Judicial Committee of the Privy Council in London. Island councils (most of whose members are reportedly wary of centralized government) continue to be dominant in local administration.

In accordance with the results of a 1986 public poll that rejected republican status, the government announced that the link with the Crown would be retained, although constitutional changes would be introduced that would limit the governor general to a largely ceremonial role. However, the High Court in August 2003 ruled that the governor general retained the power to convene parliament in the face of a government effort to delay recall as a means of continuing in office. In early 2005 Prime Minister Toafa reopened the republican issue, declaring, over the apparent objection of his deputy, former prime minister Sopoanga, that he planned to hold a referendum on replacing Queen Elizabeth II with a president as head of state. Action in the matter was delayed, however, until April 2008, at which time a low turnout (22 percent) of the electorate rejected the change by a 2–1 majority.

Freedom of speech is constitutionally guaranteed, and the government generally respects freedom of the press. A semipublic company, the Tuvalu Media Corporation runs the country's only television and radio stations and also publishes a biweekly newspaper. Although external groups have criticized the company for failing to cover human rights issues, there have been no allegations of censorship.

Foreign relations. Upon independence Tuvalu elected to join Nauru as a "special member" of the Commonwealth, having the right to participate in all Commonwealth affairs except heads of government meetings. It was admitted to the United Nations as the world body's 189th member on September 5, 2000. At the regional level it participates in the Pacific Islands Forum (PIF) and the Pacific Community. Most contacts with other states are through representatives accredited to Fiji or New Zealand, although in 1984 formal relations, backdated to 1979, were established with former colonial partner Kiribati.

In early 1979 Tuvalu and the United States signed a treaty of friendship (ratified in June 1983) that included provision for consultation in the areas of defense and marine resources, with Washington acknowledging Tuvalu's sovereignty over four islands (Funafuti, Nukufetau, Nukulaelae, and Niulakita) originally claimed by the U.S. Congress in the so-called Guano Act of 1856.

In February 1986, Tuvalu, which had signed the antinuclear Treaty of Rarotonga in 1985, refused to sanction a "goodwill visit" by a French warship as a means of protesting continued nuclear testing in French Polynesia.

In December 1998 Prime Minister Paeniu visited Taiwan, whose battle with China for diplomatic support in the South Pacific had recently intensified. Taiwanese officials pledged development aid for Tuvalu's fishing industry. In 2001 Tuvalu supported UN membership for Taiwan. Taiwan is the only country in the world to maintain a resident ambassador in Tuvalu.

In March 2005 Tuvalu joined with Kiribati in seeking assistance from the PIF for wage arrears and repatriation of some 1,000 of their nationals who had been working for a decade as laborers in Nauru's phosphate mines. For its part, Nauru estimated that more than $2.3 million would be required for the repatriation effort.

In early 2008 Tuvalu became the 11th PIF member to ratify the Pacific Island Countries Trade Agreement (PICTA), which seeks the gradual reduction of import duties among participants. On June 24, 2010, Tuvalu became the 187th member of the International Monetary Fund.

On May 26, 2011, Tuvalu signed a communiqué with the Baltic nation Estonia establishing formal diplomatic relations, and in October, Russia and Tuvalu did the same. In March 2012, Tuvalu established diplomatic relations with Georgia's rebel Abkhazia government. Georgia had severed diplomatic relations the previous month.

In July 2012 Tuvalu was criticized by the United States for reflagging Iranian oil tankers, violating sanctions that were put in place to try to curb Iran's nuclear program. Tuvalu agreed to deregister the ships in August.

Tuvalu established diplomatic relations with Guyana in September 2012 and, the following year in July, did the same with Cyprus. In March Tuvalu opened its first embassy, one of just five overseas missions, in Taipei, Taiwan.

Current issues. Rising sea levels pose an imminent threat to the small island nation. Recent estimates suggest Tuvalu's land areas (most of which are little more than a meter above sea level) will be severely flooded within the next 15–20 years and will be completely submerged by the end of the century. Overtures to New Zealand and Australia about possible resettlement have produced mixed responses for the endangered island nation, which has already experienced shore erosion and increased salinity. Meanwhile Tuvalu adopted an ambitious $20 million plan to replace its imported fossil fuels with renewable solar energy and wind power by the year 2020. To facilitate the effort, it has installed a 40-kilowatt electrical system with help from Japan.

In September 2011 Tuvalu declared a state of emergency when the supply of fresh drinking water in the country was dramatically depleted from nearly a year without significant rainfall. New Zealand and Australia led the international charge, sending desalinization plants and emergency water tanks. Water donations alleviated the crisis by mid-November.

As opposition lawmakers prepared to table a no-confidence motion against Prime Minister Telavi's administration in July 2013, the speaker of the house blocked the action by suspending the house to await a by-election to fill a recently emptied seat. Controversy deepened when Governor General Iakopa ITALELI ordered Telavi's resignation; Telavi in turn wrote to Queen Elizabeth to inform her that he was dismissing Italeli. Ultimately on August 2 parliament voted 8–4 against Telavi. Enele Sopoaga was elected on August 4. He and his new cabinet took office on August 5.

POLITICAL PARTIES

Political affairs in Tuvalu are grounded in family ties and personalities, not ideology. In late 1992 it was reported that a group called the Tuvalu United Party (*Tama i Fulu a Tuvalu*) had been organized by Prime Minister Paeniu and his deputy, Dr. Alesana Kleis SELUKA, but the party has played no part in recent elections. While there have not been any political parties since, the 15 independent members who are elected to parliament do form loose coalitions consisting of government and opposition.

LEGISLATURE

Known prior to independence as the House of Assembly, the unicameral **Parliament** (*Palamente o Tuvalu*) consists of 15 members: 2 each from seven islands and 1 from the least populous inhabited island. The legislative term, subject to dissolution, is four years. In legislative balloting held on September 16, 2010, 5 new members, primarily senior civil servants, were among the 15 legislators elected.

Speaker: Kamuta LATASI.

CABINET

[as of October 1, 2013]

Prime Minister	Enele Sopoaga
Deputy Prime Minister	Vete Sakaio
Ministers	
Communication, Transport, and Public Utilities	Monise Lafai
Education, Youth, Sports, and Health	Fauoa Maani
Finance and Economic Development	Maatia Toafa
Foreign Affairs	Taukelina Finikaso
Home Affairs and Rural Development	Namoliki Neemia
Natural Resources	Pita Elisala
Public Utilities	Vete Sakaio

INTERGOVERNMENTAL REPRESENTATION

Ambassador to the U.S. and Permanent Representative to the UN: Aunese Makoi SIMATI.

U.S. Ambassador to Tuvalu: Frankie REED.

IGO Memberships (Non-UN): ADB, CWTH, PIF.

UGANDA

Republic of Uganda

Political Status: Independent member of the Commonwealth since October 9, 1962; republican constitution adopted on September 8, 1967; personal military rule (instituted on January 25, 1971) overthrown with establishment of provisional government on April 11, 1979; military regime installed on January 29, 1986; present constitution adopted on September 22,1995, with effect from October 8; amended by public referendum on July 28, 2005, to provide for multiparty system.

Area: 93,104 sq. mi. (241,139 sq. km).

Population: 35,738,345 (2012E—UN); 34,758,809 (2013E—U.S. Census).

Major Urban Center (2011E--UN): KAMPALA (metropolitan area, 1,533,000).

Official Language: English (Swahili and Luganda are widely used).

Monetary Unit: Ugandan Shilling (market rate November 1, 2013: 2,525.25 Ugandan shillings = $1US).

President: Lt. Gen. Yoweri Kaguta MUSEVENI (National Resistance Movement); sworn in on January 29, 1986, following the overthrow of Lt. Gen. Tito OKELLO Lutwa on January 27; popularly elected on May 9, 1996, and inaugurated for a five-year term on May 12; reelected for another five-year term on March 12, 2001; reelected in multiparty balloting on February 23, 2006, and inaugurated for another five-year term on May 12; reelected in multiparty balloting on February 18, 2011, and sworn in for another five-year term on May 12.

Vice President: Edward Kiwanika SSEKANDI (National Resistance Movement), appointed by the president on May 24, 2011, succeeding Gilbert Balibaseka BUKENYA (National Resistance Movement).

Prime Minister: Amama MBABAZI (National Resistance Movement), appointed by the president on May 24, 2011, succeeding Apolo NSIBAMBI (National Resistance Movement).

THE COUNTRY

Landlocked Uganda, located in east-central Africa, is bounded on the east by Kenya, on the south by Tanzania and Rwanda, on the west by the Democratic Republic of the Congo (DRC), and on the north by Sudan. The country is known for its lakes (among them Lake Victoria, the source of the White Nile) and its mountains, the most celebrated of which are the Mountains of the Moon (the Ruwenzori), lying on the border with the DRC. The population embraces a number of African tribal groups, including the Baganda, Banyankore, Basoga, and Iteso. For many decades a substantial Asian (primarily Indian) minority engaged in shopkeeping, industry, and other professions. In 1972, however, the Idi Amin government decreed the expulsion of all noncitizen Asians as part of a plan to put Uganda's economy in the hands of nationals, and at present only a scattering of Asians still reside in the country. Approximately 60 percent of the population is Christian and another 15 percent is Muslim, with the remainder adhering to traditional African beliefs. Women are primarily responsible for subsistence agriculture. The government is considered progressive regarding women's rights, with seats in the current parliament being reserved for women. Following the 2011 balloting, women held 135 seats in Parliament. One-third of the seats in local councils must, by law, also go to women.

Agriculture, forestry, and fishing contribute about one-third of Uganda's gross domestic product (GDP); industry, which is growing in importance, accounts for about 21 percent of GDP. Services account for the remainder. Coffee is the principal crop (Uganda is one of Africa's leading producers), followed by cotton, tea, peanuts, and tobacco.

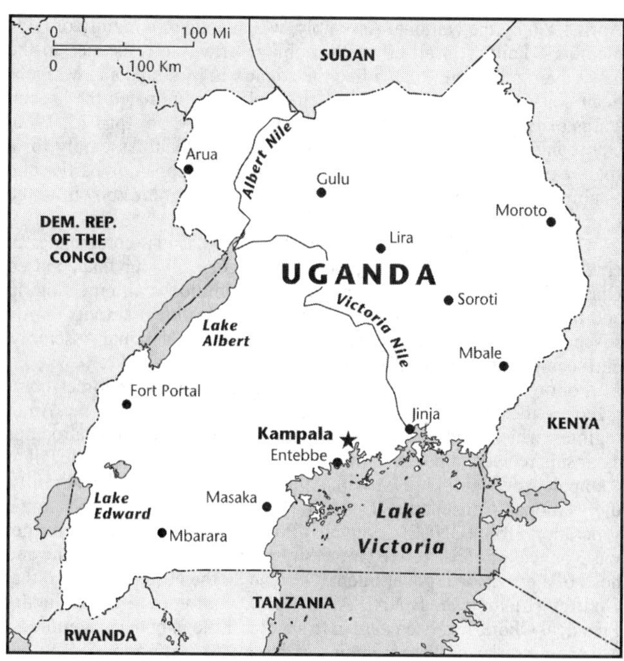

In May 2000 the IMF and World Bank announced that Uganda had qualified for $2 billion in debt service relief over the next 20 years based on the government's adherence to its comprehensive reform program and continued economic progress. (For information on Uganda's economy prior to 2000, please see the 2012 *Handbook.*) By mid-2005 GDP growth of 5.4 percent was offset by one of the highest population growth rates in the world and widespread poverty. Subsequently, the IMF in 2006 cited poverty reduction as the foremost economic issue for Uganda, and it urged reforms to curb corruption. Unhappy with alleged corruption in government spending and the country's slow progress toward democratization, the UK, traditionally Uganda's biggest donor, and three other donor countries canceled millions of dollars in aid to Kampala.

Oil was discovered in Uganda in 2009, though production plans were stalled by government claims that it was owed $434 million in capital gains tax by one of the interested oil companies (see Foreign relations, below). The economy was spared the worst effects of the global economic downturn, according to the IMF, and annual GDP growth averaged 6 percent in 2009–2011, owing in large part to increased investment. Fund managers advised Ugandan authorities to boost non-oil revenue, since anticipated oil revenue will last only a limited number of years. In 2011 severe food and water shortages due to drought affected 36 of 112 districts, particularly in the east. In 2012, Britain announced increased aid of $638 million through 2015 (see Foreign relations, below). GDP grew by 6.7 percent in 2011 and 2.6 percent in 2012. Inflation that year was 14.1 percent. GDP per capita was $547.

GOVERNMENT AND POLITICS

Political background. Uganda became a British protectorate in 1894–1896 and began its progress toward statehood after World War II, achieving internal self-government on March 1, 1962, and full independence within the Commonwealth on October 9, 1962. A problem involving Buganda and three other traditional kingdoms was temporarily resolved by granting the kingdoms semiautonomous rule within a federal system. The arrangement enabled Buganda's representatives to participate in the national government, and the king (*kabaka*) of Buganda, Sir Edward Frederick MUTESA II, was elected president of Uganda on October 9, 1963. The issue of national unity versus Bugandan particularism led Prime Minister Apollo Milton OBOTE, leader of the Uganda People's Congress (UPC) and an advocate of centralism, to depose the president and vice president in February 1966. A constitution eliminating Buganda's autonomous status was ratified in

April 1966 by the National Assembly, which consisted mainly of UPC members. Failing in an effort to mobilize effective resistance to the new government, the *kabaka* fled the country in May, and a new republican constitution, adopted in September 1967, eliminated the special status of Buganda and the other kingdoms. Earlier, on April 15, 1966, Obote had been designated president by the National Assembly for a five-year term. In December 1969 he banned all opposition parties and established a one-party state with a socialist program known as the Common Man's Charter.

On January 25, 1971, Maj. Gen. Idi AMIN Dada, commander in chief of the army and air force, mounted a successful coup that deposed Obote while the president was abroad at a Commonwealth meeting. In addition to continuing the ban on opposition political activity, Amin suspended parts of the constitution, dissolved the National Assembly, and secured his own installation as president of the republic.

Following an invasion by Tanzanian troops and exile forces organized as the Uganda National Liberation Army (UNLA), the Amin regime, which had drawn worldwide condemnation for atrocities against perceived opponents, was effectively overthrown with the fall of Kampala April 10–11, 1979, with Amin fleeing to Libya. Concurrently, the National Consultative Council (NCC) of the Uganda National Liberation Front (UNLF) designated Professor Yusuf K. LULE, former vice chancellor of Makerere University, as president of the republic and head of a provisional government. On June 20 the NCC announced that Godfrey Lukongwa BINAISA, a former attorney general under President Obote, had been named to succeed Lule in both capacities.

After a series of disagreements with both the NCC and the UNLF's Military Commission, Binaisa was relieved of his authority on May 12, 1980. (Binaisa died at age 90 in 2010.) On May 18 the chair of the Military Commission, Paulo MUWANGA, announced that a three-member Presidential Commission had been established to exercise executive power through a cabinet of ministers on advice of its military counterpart, pending a national election later in the year.

Former president Obote returned from Tanzania on May 27, 1980, and in mid-June agreement was reached between party and UNLF representatives on four groups that would be permitted to participate in the presidential/legislative campaign. Following balloting December 10–11, the UPC declared that it had secured a majority in the National Assembly, thus assuring Obote's reinvestiture as chief executive. Although the runner-up Democratic Party (DP) denounced the results as fraudulent, most victorious DP candidates took their legislative seats. The Uganda Patriotic Movement (UPM), led by former president Lule and his former defense minister, Yoweri MUSEVENI, refused to accept the one seat it had won. After shedding the party apparatus, Lule and Museveni formed a National Resistance Movement (NRM) and initiated a guerrilla campaign against Obote through the affiliated National Resistance Army (NRA).

During the next five years, while the UNLA achieved some success in repulsing the rebels, the NRA continued to hold the agriculturally important "Luwero triangle" north of Kampala, as well as its traditional strongholds in the Banyankore-dominated southwest. During the same period, many army actions against civilians were reported, including the harassment, wounding, or killing of DP members; by mid-1985, more than 200,000 were estimated to have died, either from army "excesses" or official counterinsurgency efforts.

On July 27, 1985, in a self-proclaimed attempt to "stop the killing," Brig. Basilio Olara OKELLO led a senior officers' coup against Obote, who had lost much international support and was again forced into exile. Two days later the constitution was suspended, and Obote's army chief of staff, Lt. Gen. Tito OKELLO Lutwa, was sworn in as chair of a ruling Military Council. On August 6 General Okello called for all guerrilla groups, including former Amin soldiers, to join his army, while naming Paulo Muwanga, who had served as Obote's vice president, as prime minister and DP leader Paul SSEMOGERERE as minister of the interior. Unlike most other resistance leaders, Museveni, the dominant NRM figure following Lule's death in January 1985, did not accede to Okello's call for "unity," citing continued abuses by army personnel who routinely failed to defer to Okello. In contrast, the NRA had a reputation for being well disciplined, relatively free of tribal rivalries, and far less brutal toward civilians.

By September 1985, when the first of a series of Kenyan- and Tanzanian-mediated peace talks began in Dar es Salaam, NRA forces had taken control of a number of strategic towns and supply routes, while another Obote associate, Abraham WALIGO, replaced Muwanga as prime minister. In November Museveni announced that "in order to provide services pending an agreement with the regime in Kampala," an "interim administration" was being established in rebel-held areas. A peace pact signed in Nairobi on December 17 gave Museveni the vice chair of the Military Council while providing for the dissolution of all existing armed units and the recruitment, under external supervision, of a new, fully representative force. However, the accord did not take effect. After failing to attend "celebrations" scheduled for January 4, 1986, Museveni, citing continuing human-rights abuses, launched a drive on Kampala, which culminated in the overthrow of the six-month-old Okello regime on January 27. Two days later, while NRA forces consolidated their control, Museveni was sworn in as president, thereafter appointing a cabinet that included as prime minister Dr. Samson KISEKKA, formerly the NRM's external spokesperson. In an attempt to prevent further civil war, Museveni also named representatives of other major political groups to his government. However, some UNLA units that had not disbanded fled to the north and the east, where they and other rebel groups continued to resist the NRA.

In mid-1986 Museveni absolved his immediate predecessor, General Okello, of atrocities committed by troops under his command. No such tender was made to former presidents Amin and Obote, with Museveni calling for their repatriation from exile in Saudi Arabia and Zambia, respectively, to face charges by a special commission of inquiry established to review the "slaughter" of Bantu southerners by their Nilotic followers. (Obote died in Zambia in October 2005.)

In February 1988 Museveni named three deputy prime ministers, including DP leader Ssemogerere, to assist the ailing Kisekka. In addition, the cabinet was reshuffled to include more representatives from the north and east, where rebel activity continued to impede national reconciliation. An even more drastic reshuffle was ordered in April 1989 coincident with conversion of the theretofore appointive National Resistance Council (see under Constitution and government, below) into a largely elective body. Six months later the council voted to extend the government's interim mandate (originally limited by President Museveni to four years) to January 1995. The action was justified by the minister of justice on the grounds that the country lacked the "essential political machinery and the logistics for the evolution of a democratic and a permanent stable government."

On January 22, 1991, Museveni appointed Kisekka to the new, largely ceremonial position of vice president, with George Cosmas ADYEBO, a 43-year-old economist, named prime minister. The government subsequently conducted a "final sweep" against rebel forces in the north and east, and in July Kampala reported that its troops had decimated the rebel forces, killing 1,500 insurgents between March and July (many, Amnesty International charged, after perfunctory military trials) and absorbing many others into the NRA. In August the government described the remaining rebels, predominantly from Joseph KONY's Uganda Democratic Christian Army, as "thugs" who had been reduced to raiding villages for food and whose earlier atrocities prevented their reintegration.

In January 1993 Museveni, who continued to reject domestic and international calls for the immediate introduction of multipartyism on the grounds that it would exacerbate religious and ethnic cleavages, announced plans for nonparty elections by the end of 1994. In February the NRC passed a constituent assembly bill that called for the delay of multiparty politics until at least the year 2000 (see Constitution and government, below).

Earlier, in what was described by critics as political repayment to the Baganda people for supporting the NRA struggle in the early 1980s, Museveni had begun negotiating with Baganda to restore its monarch. Consequently, on July 31, 1993, the son of Mutesa II, Ronald Muwenda MUTEBI, was crowned *kabaka,* an event described as a purely "ceremonial" action. Collaterally, pro forma recognition was granted to the coronation of Patrick David Matthew Olimi KABOYO II as monarch of the smaller Toro kingdom. (Kaboyo died on September 13, 1995, and was succeeded by his three-year-old son, Oyo Nyimba Kabamba IGURU IV.) On June 11, 1994, the oldest of Uganda's historic kingdoms was restored, with the crowning of Solon Iguri GAFABUSA I as king of the Bunyoro tribe. (The crowning of John BARIGYE as monarch of Uganda's Ankore kingdom was indefinitely delayed because of disputes within the clan leadership.) Meanwhile, on February 11, 1996, Henry Wako MULOKI, the Basoga's traditional leader, was reinstalled as *kyabazinga* (king) at a ceremony attended by Museveni.

On March 28, 1994, nonparty balloting was held to fill the 214-seat Constituent Assembly. As anticipated, NRM-affiliated candidates captured the majority of the seats (114), although the president's actual assembly supporters were reported as numbering only 93. In December the government announced that nonparty general elections would be held by late 1995; however, they were deferred until April–May 1996. Meanwhile, the Constituent Assembly on September 22 approved a new basic law that continued the ban on political campaigning and provided that the NRC would remain in existence for another five years. Upon promulgation of the document on October 8, the constituent body was dissolved.

At Uganda's first presidential balloting on May 9, 1996, President Museveni captured 74.2 percent of the vote, easily outpolling his two competitors, the DP's Ssemogerere (23.7 percent) and an Islamic candidate, Mohamed MAYANJA Kibirige (2.1 percent). Although Museveni controlled the media and local councils administering the polling, international observers described the polling as "fair. Thereafter, in "no-party" legislative polling staged between June 6 and 27, NRM candidates secured or were appointed to 271 of the 276 available posts. On July 6 Museveni named an enlarged cabinet that included only NRM members.

In early 1998 Museveni named his half-brother, Gen. Salim SALEH, as defense minister, a post held theretofore by the president himself. The appointment of Saleh, who had been credited with coordinating the government's highly successful offensives against its various rebel opponents in mid-1997, underscored Museveni's apparent dedication to a total rout of the Lord's Resistance Army (LRA—see Political Parties and Groups, below), whose call for a cease-fire in July had been rejected. (Saleh resigned in December after allegations of corrupt financial dealings were made against him.)

In May 1998 Museveni reshuffled the government and, following the retirement of Prime Minister Musoke, on April 6, 1999, the president named Apolo NSIBAMBI to head a substantially altered cabinet. In a referendum on June 29, 2000, 90 percent of the voters endorsed continuance of the no-party system.

On March 12, 2001, President Museveni was reelected to another five-year term, securing 69 percent of the vote compared to 28 percent for his nearest rival, Kizza BESIGYE, Museveni's former doctor and former military ally. Subsequently, the NRM retained its stronghold on the parliament in elections held on June 26. Although a dozen sitting cabinet members lost their legislative seats, most of them were defeated by other Museveni supporters. Following the elections, Museveni reappointed Prime Minister Nsibambi to head a significantly altered cabinet, which was sworn in on July 24. A constitutional referendum on July 28, 2005 (see Constitution and government, below), allowed for the registration of political parties, among other things, in advance of presidential and parliamentary elections on February 23, 2006. In the multiparty presidential election, Museveni defeated four challengers by garnering 59.26 percent of the vote. His nearest rival, Kizza Besigye, running as the Forum for Democratic Change (FDC) candidate, received 37.39 percent. The Democratic Party's John SSEBAANA Kizito won 1.58 percent, and the Uganda People's Congress (UPC) candidate, Miria OBOTE, widow of the former president, won less than 1 percent. In concurrent parliamentary elections, the NRM retained power, while five opposition parties also won representation. A reshuffled and enlarged cabinet, again led by Prime Minister Apolo Nsibambi, was sworn in on June 2, 2006.

The cabinet was reshuffled on February 16, 2009. In addition to naming 25 ministers, the new government appointed 44 ministers of state, including President Museveni's wife, Janet, as minister of state for the Karamoja region.

Former foreign minister and UN diplomat Olara Otunnu returned to Uganda in August 2009 after 23 years, most recently from exile in Zambia, to seek the presidential nomination of the UPC for the 2011 election. Despite a long career as an advocate for children's rights and international peace, Otunnu received what was described as a mixed reception by his party stemming from his role in Okello's military government in 1985. Museveni easily won a fourth consecutive term in the February 18, 2011, election, this time with 68.4 percent of the vote to Besigye's diminished 26 percent, while the DP's Norbert MAO finished a very distant third with 1.9 percent, and Otunnu was fourth with 1.6 percent. Four other candidates each received less than 1 percent. The NRM kept its stronghold in concurrent parliamentary elections, and all five parties previously represented retained small numbers of seats. Opposition leaders, including five presidential contenders, claimed the results were fraudulent because of alleged bribery, ballot stuffing, and harassment, and the European Union (EU) cited problems with the election as well. The government postponed local and mayoral elections from February 23 to March 14 after the electoral commission announced it had found evidence of fraud and subsequently dismissed 20 of its officials accused of participating in vote rigging. The minister of state for ethics and integrity resigned on March 15. He was one of nine ministers who had been suspended for contesting parliamentary elections as an independent in violation of a court ruling. Museveni was sworn in on May 12, and on May 24 he replaced both the vice president and the prime minister. Edward Kiwanika SSEKANDI was named vice president, and former security minister Amana MBABAZI was tapped as prime minister. The extensively reshuffled cabinet appointed on May 27 included 42 ministers of state and 10 women, and the president's wife was named to a ministerial post. Former vice president Gilbert Balibaseka BUKENYA, who had been appointed by the president on June 6, 2003, faced corruption charges in court on May 30.

The minister of foreign affairs, Sam KUTESA, was suspended on October 14, 2011, following allegations of corruption (see Current Issues, below). The cabinet was reshuffled on August 15, 2012, following the resignation of several ministers, and Kutesa was reinstated to his portfolio.

The first deputy prime minister, Eriya KATEGAYA, died on March 2, 2013. He was replaced during a broad cabinet reshuffle in May, in which the second and third deputy prime ministers were promoted.

Constitution and government. The 1962 constitution was suspended by Prime Minister Obote in February 1966. A successor instrument adopted in April 1966 terminated the federal system but was itself replaced in September 1967 by a republican constitution that established a president as head of state, chief executive, and commander in chief of the armed forces. While he did not formally revoke the 1967 constitution when he came to power, President Amin in February 1971 assumed judicial as well as executive and legislative powers. Subsequently, though martial law was never declared, military tribunals tried both civil and criminal cases and authorized numerous public executions. With but minor modification, the 1967 constitution was reinstated by the UNLF as the basis of post-military government in 1980; it was suspended by the Military Council in mid-1985 and remained inoperative thereafter.

On February 1, 1986, while in the process of organizing an interim government dominated by members of his NRM, President Museveni announced the formation of a National Resistance Council (NRC) to serve as an appointive surrogate for the former National Assembly. The NRC was converted into a largely elective body of 278 members in February 1989.

In early 1993 a 15-member commission, appointed by President Museveni in February 1989, released a report proposing the delay of multipartyism for seven years, during which time a largely elected Constituent Assembly would draft a new constitution. (Representatives of special interest groups, including the NRA, NRC, women, youths, and unions, were subsequently added to the 214-member parliament elected in March 1994.) However, the charter that emerged in September 1995 was promulgated without submission to a promised referendum. More importantly, it continued the ban on partisan activity (save behind closed party doors). In the wake of intense criticism from U.S. and British authorities, regime opponents sought to have the ban rescinded but were told that such action could be initiated only by the legislature elected under the constitution as adopted. The "no-party" system was subsequently endorsed by national referendum in June 2000.

In January 2004 the government initiated negotiations with opposition parties on the transition to multiparty politics and the future system of government. Six months later a court ruling invalidated (on a technicality) the 2000 referendum. Subsequently, as pressure for a multiparty system continued, parliament voted in May 2005 in favor of a national referendum on a multiparty political system, abolishing the two-term limit on the presidency, and granting the president the authority to dissolve parliament in case of a constitutional crisis. In balloting of July 28, 2005, the amendments were approved by 92.44 percent of voters.

Local government has assumed a variety of forms since 1971, the Amin and Lule governments both having reorganized the provincial and district systems. Currently, under initiatives adopted by the Museveni administration, local affairs are handled by several tiers of elected "resistance councils" ranging from village to regional levels. In August 2006 parliament approved 11 new districts, creating more seats for women (99) in advance of the August 28 elections for women district representatives.

On August 25, 2010, the Constitutional Court struck down Uganda's sedition law, ruling that it infringed on the right to freedom of speech guaranteed in Uganda's constitution. In 2013 Reporters Without Borders ranked Uganda 104 out of 179 countries in freedom of the press, a significant rise from 139 the year before.

Foreign relations. From independence, Uganda based its foreign policy on anticolonialism, retaining moderate Western support from its consistently nonaligned posture. However, reacting to criticism by the Amin regime of U.S. policies in Vietnam, Cambodia, and the Middle East, Washington terminated its economic assistance program in mid-1973 and subsequently closed its embassy because of public threats against officials and other Americans residing in the country. Three years later, in an event of major international import, Israeli commandos raided the Entebbe airport during the night of July 3–4, 1976, to secure the release of passengers of an Air France airliner that had been hijacked over Greece by Palestinian Arab guerrillas and flown to Uganda via Libya. Denying allegations that he had cooperated with the hijackers, Amin protested Israel's action and accused Kenya of aiding in its implementation.

Tensions with both Kenya and Tanzania resulted not only in the collapse of the tripartite East African Community (EAC) in June 1977 but ultimately in the Tanzanian military intervention of early 1979 (see Political background, above). The latter action came in the wake of an ill-conceived incursion into northern Tanzania in October 1978 by Ugandan troops, with effective Tanzanian withdrawal from Uganda not occurring until mid-1981 due to retraining requirements of the post-Amin Ugandan army. The two neighbors were critically involved in discussions between the short-lived Okello regime and the NRA, Kenyan president Daniel arap Moi being credited with brokering the December peace agreement between Okello and Museveni. Following Museveni's takeover in January 1986, both governments were quick to recognize the new regime, as was the United States. Nevertheless, relations with Kenya were subsequently strained by a series of border incidents, mutual accusations over the harboring of political dissidents, and Nairobi's displeasure at Ugandan links with Libya, particularly as manifested in an April 1989 trade accord. During a summit of the Ugandan, Kenyan, and Tanzanian presidents in Nairobi on November 22, 1991, the three declared an interest in reactivating cooperation efforts and appointed a three-member commission to draft an agreement.

Kampala concluded a security accord with Sudan in mid-1987 but subsequently charged that Khartoum was still aiding anti-Museveni rebel forces. Border tension intensified following the June 1989 coup in Sudan, precipitating the signing of another mutual nonaggression pact in April 1990, which provided for a Sudanese monitoring team on the Ugandan side of their border after Khartoum had accused Kampala of aiding the southern Sudanese rebels. Meanwhile, the Museveni administration accused former president Obote of training soldiers in Zambia, intimating that Lusaka was turning a blind eye to the activity.

Unrest in the Sudan and Zaire/Democratic Republic of the Congo (DRC) has dominated Uganda's regional relations since the early 1990s. In October 1992 Kampala warned its northern neighbor that it would mount an "appropriate response" against Sudanese troops crossing the border in pursuit of rebels, and in January 1993 it expressed its concern that a Sudanese plot to launch an Islamic fundamentalist movement in Uganda was under way. Meanwhile, the approximately 20,000 Sudanese refugees within Uganda's borders were joined by thousands of Zaireans fleeing unrest in their country.

In October 1994 Uganda canceled the 1990 agreement with its northern neighbor and ordered Sudan to withdraw its monitoring group, accusing it of activity incompatible with its mandate. In April 1995 Kampala severed relations with Khartoum, alleging improper activity by Sudanese diplomatic personnel and the sponsorship of a cross-border rebel attack on April 20. A subsequent agreement failed to bring an end to the border hostilities, with at least a limited number of Ugandan units operating in support of Sudanese rebels and the NRA conducting raids on Ugandan rebel bases inside Sudan.

Relations were restored with Kenya in January 1996 following a border summit between the two countries' leaders. The discussions also yielded mutual pledges to revive the dormant EAC. However, the continuing fragile nature of Ugandan-Kenyan ties was subsequently underlined by Nairobi's charge that the Museveni regime was supporting Kenyan rebels.

Meanwhile, rebel-related activities along their shared border continued to buffet Ugandan-Sudanese relations in 1996, but on September 9 diplomatic representatives from the two countries signed an agreement in Khartoum that reestablished ties. In December 1999 President Museveni signed an agreement with Sudanese authorities calling for mutual elimination of support for rebel movements, but in mid-2000 Museveni complained that Sudan was not living up to its end of the bargain. Relations between Sudan and Uganda appeared to improve in 2001, as Sudan reportedly permitted Ugandan forces to conduct military action in Sudan against rebels in the LRA. However, Uganda continued to accuse Sudan of helping the LRA, and rebel attacks—some targeting aid workers—continued.

Regional observers described Uganda as playing a crucial role in Laurent Kabila's ouster of the Mobutu government in Zaire (subsequently the DRC) in 1997. Kampala denied actively supporting Kabila, although admitting that its troops had crossed the border in pursuit of Ugandan rebels. Clashes occurred in August 1999 and the spring of 2000 between previously allied Ugandan and Rwandan troops in Kisangani in north-central DRC. A UN-sponsored disengagement agreement in June 2000 brought relative peace to the area, although tensions between Ugandan and Rwandan military forces remained high. Negotiations between senior levels of the two governments under British auspices in November 2001 failed to resolve the underlying strains between the two countries.

In July 2003 a tripartite agreement was signed among Uganda, Rwanda, and the office of the UN High Commissioner on Refugees, providing for the voluntary repatriation of some 26,000 Rwandans in refugee camps in western Uganda. In February 2004 the two countries signed a bilateral agreement to strengthen cooperation in several fields. Yet Uganda still accused Rwanda of aiding the rebel People's Redemption Army (PRA), said to operate in eastern Congo and West Nile. Uganda claimed the PRA was the armed wing of the new opposition group FDC and its exiled leader, retired colonel Kizza Besigye. The FDC claimed to know nothing of the PRA and accused the government of inventing the connection to discredit the FDC. Both Uganda and Rwanda were accused of meddling in the Ituri Province of the DRC, arming rebels there in exchange for minerals. Museveni and Rwandan president Paul Kagame tried to defuse the situation. In May 2005 three Ugandan soldiers were tried for spying against Rwanda, and months later, as tensions eased, Uganda and Rwanda signed an extradition treaty to crack down on criminals crossing the borders. Meanwhile, Uganda denied UN claims that it was trading weapons for minerals with the DRC.

Tensions in the region continued into 2006 following reports that Uganda had acknowledged issuing forged passports to Hutu rebels from Rwanda. The two countries subsequently began discussions to resolve the matter. Meanwhile, Uganda asked the UN to expel the DRC for allegedly harboring rebels intent on destabilizing Uganda. Upgrades to Uganda's airstrip at its borders with the DRC and Sudan raised concerns in those countries, but Ugandan authorities said the improvements were made to prepare for the November 2007 Commonwealth summit in Kampala. Some observers said the upgrades were designed to preempt surveillance flights out of the DRC and Sudan. On a more positive note, Kenya and Uganda reached an agreement to help curb illegal arms trafficking across their shared border, and in 2007 Rwanda and Uganda undertook the first steps toward demarcating disputed areas along their border.

China in 2006 boosted its arms sales to Uganda from $2.5 million to a contract for $1.5 billion over the next five years and agreed to provide training to the Ugandan military. Uganda also bought $4 million worth of weapons from Iran in 2007 for its "anti-insurgency" operation in the north.

In March 2007, in a move observers said was designed to strengthen relations with the United States, Uganda sent 1,600 peacekeeping troops to Somalia to help protect the interim government there and bolster U.S. efforts to prevent suspected al-Qaida terrorists from establishing a foothold there.

In 2008 a dispute between Uganda and the DRC over an oil-rich island in Lake Albert was resolved in Uganda's favor. The dispute dated to a violent confrontation between Congolese and Ugandan forces in 2007. Another territorial dispute, this one involving Kenya, over an island on Lake Victoria was set to be resolved by a panel of experts in Britain. Uganda has maintained ownership of Migingo island, a source for deep-water fish, and has had troops stationed there since 2004. When Uganda began charging residency fees to Kenyans, tensions heightened, leading to bilateral negotiations and an agreement in 2009 to have the panel resolve the issue. However, in May 2009 Kenya asked the UN to intervene in the dispute.

For the first time since 2003, the presidents of Uganda and the DRC met face-to-face in March 2009 following the discovery of oil in the region, amounting to 1 billion barrels, to discuss regional security and disputes over land.

In December 2009 the UN Security Council condemned the increasing attacks by the LRA across the region and for the first time called on all UN missions in the region to coordinate strategies and activities against the rebels in order to better protect civilians. The LRA was reported to have abducted nearly 1,000 children in the past year. The Security Council also reiterated its demand that the rebels surrender and disarm.

In May 2010 Uganda was among five Nile River basin countries that signed what was described as an historic agreement providing for equitable water-sharing among the signatories. In June, Uganda, as a nonpermanent member of the UN Security Council, voted to support a fourth round of sanctions on Iran prompted by its nuclear development program.

Also in May 2010 U.S. president Barack Obama signed into law the LRA Disarmament and Northern Uganda Recovery Act, which gave the administration the authority to coordinate a strategy to help Uganda, among other countries, disarm the LRA rebels. Critics said the strategy lacked details in its overall aims of protecting civilians and apprehending LRA leader Kony and his commanders or removing them from the battlefield.

In September 2010 the Ugandan army rejected LRA rebels' calls for renewed talks, saying they were waiting for Kony to sign a final peace agreement. In October the DRC, Central African Republic, and Sudan agreed to form a joint military force with Uganda to fight the rebels. The LRA was reported to be based in southern Darfur in late 2010.

On November 28, 2010, President Museveni traveled to Somalia—one of very few heads of state to travel to the dangerous region—to discuss security issues with President Sheikh Sharif Sheik Ahmed and other officials. Uganda and Burundi were the only countries providing troops for the AU peacekeeping force in Somalia.

In October 2011 the United States announced it was deploying 100 special operations forces to Uganda to help suppress the LRA and train Ugandan security forces. A short, highly critical film about the LRA, dubbed *Kony 2012*, became a viral Internet hit after its release in March 2012, with more than 90 million viewers. The film was credited with raising international awareness of the crimes of the LRA and prompted a U.S. Senate resolution supporting the deployment of U.S. special operations to Uganda.

The Irish company Tullow Energy finalized an oil production agreement with Uganda in March 2012. Estimates were that oil production would be worth up to $2 billion annually to Uganda. Meanwhile, in May Uganda agreed to increase its troop strength in Somalia by 2,000 troops, to a total of 8,000, in response to a request by the AU. In September a UN report accused Uganda of providing support for the M23 militants in the Democratic Republic of the Congo, including the transfer of weapons and the direct involvement of Ugandan troops alongside M23 fighters. In December the EU suspended approximately $300 million in aid, citing corruption (see Current issues, below).

In May 2013 Uganda was deemed to have been in breach of the East African Community (EAC) Treaty for denying entry to a Kenyan citizen in 2011. Also, in May, Uganda signed a trade treaty with Sri Lanka and became a signatory to the 2008 Convention on Cluster Munitions, which banned cluster bombs. In April Uganda suspended military operations in the Central African Republic against the LRA following a coup.

In April 2013 the UK's Commercial Court affirmed a Ugandan court's decision that Heritage Oil owed the Ugandan government $434 million in taxes as a result of that company's sale of oil rights to Tullow Energy.

Current issues. The plight of the Baganda people and the restoration of their kingdom became key issues as Ugandans' attention turned to the next presidential poll, scheduled for February 18, 2011. With the approaching elections, analysts said President Museveni aimed to cause a rift between Ronald Mutebi, the *kabaka* of the Baganda, and the Baganda people, an effort that began in 2009, when the government shut down the pro-Baganda radio station after the September riots, leaving the kingdom without an instrument to mobilize people against government policies. The government wanted to keep the radio station closed until after the election, observers said, to prevent the Baganda people from hearing about a controversial policy in which the government bought land from absentee landlords and gave it to Banyankore villagers.

In early 2010 four minor parties formed an electoral coalition, styled as Change 2011, and five opposition parties formed the Inter-Party Cooperation (IPC), an electoral coalition committed to backing a single presidential candidate and fielding joint candidates in parliamentary and local elections. The component parties—the UPC, Justice Forum (Justice, Education, Economy, Morality, African Unity—JEEMA), Conservative Party (CP), Social Democratic Party (SDP) and FDC—also agreed to form a coalition government if they were successful. The Democratic Party (DP), meanwhile, declined to join the IPC, saying its objectives were not clear. The DP's new president, Norbert Mao, overcame rifts in the party and became its flag bearer in March, while another party member, Samuel LUBEGA, chose to run as an independent. Meanwhile, former foreign minister and UN diplomat Olara Otunnu, who had returned to Uganda after 23 years, began to position himself in the political arena. Otunnu, the recipient of several major international awards for his work in advocating for children's rights and world peace, had had a role in the 1985 military government before leaving the country, but observers said once he returned he was the most well-known UPC member and garnered much media attention. Otunnu took over the helm of the party, despite detractors in the UPC who still had concerns about his role in the 1985 military government.

In March 2010 at least three people were killed by security forces when demonstrators turned out in protest of the destruction of the royal tombs of the four *kabakas,* a UN world heritage site in Kampala that was severely damaged by fire. The cause of the fire was undetermined.

In June 2010 five FDC members aligned with the IPC were jailed after they led a protest against the electoral commission, which they accused of incompetence. Their protest followed a pledge by the IPC to hold nationwide demonstrations against the commissioners, who had been reappointed by President Museveni in 2009 despite alleged irregularities in the 2006 elections that they supervised. Meanwhile, Otunnu was summoned by police for the third time for allegedly using "sectarian language" in radio broadcasts in which he alleged that President Museveni's troops had fomented war in northern Uganda; Otunnu refused to submit to questioning. Earlier in the month, during a rally of supporters, FDC leader Besigye was flogged by police and members of the country's notorious Kiboko—described as a "ragtag paramilitary"—wielding canes and led by Juma SEMAKULA. A number of opposition parties subsequently formed their own youth squads to counter Kiboko attacks. Meanwhile, that same month, the government established a registry and agreed to compensate some 10,000 people in northern Uganda who had been maimed by LRA rebels over the past two decades.

As politics continued to be the focus of attention, in July 2010 a former prominent member of the FDC, Beti Olive KAMYA, gained political registration for the Uganda Federal Alliance (UFA), which she had formed as a civil society in 2009 to promote a campaign to educate the Baganda people about their political rights.

A terrorist attack rocked Kampala on July 11, 2010, when suspected members of al-Shabbab killed 76 civilians while they were watching a television broadcast of the World Cup finals. In August 2010 the cohesion of the opposition broke down when the UPC withdrew from the IPC, citing "irreconcilable reasons." A rift had reportedly developed over how to proceed with the IPC's battle against the electoral commission, as the UPC opposed participation in any activities organized by the commission in preparation for the 2011 polls. UPC leader Otunnu subsequently became the flag bearer for his party, promising a new constitution if elected, and offering assurances to the Baganda people that there would be no restrictions on their movement. The day after the UPC's withdrawal, the IPC announced that its leader, Kizza Besigye of the FDC, would be the coalition's presidential candidate, as analysts had predicted. His nomination was said to have been conditioned on his signing an agreement to grant Baganda federal status and return its land if he was elected.

Meanwhile, the NRM was reported to have mended rifts within the party, and the president pressed to postpone prosecuting ministers implicated in the 2007 Commonwealth summit corruption scandal until after the 2011 election. Museveni was reported to have a large war chest and was accompanied to his campaign launch by his security chiefs in official dress, which some observers described as an intimidation tactic. Though Musevni was unopposed in his bid to be the NRM's flag bearer, the party vote reportedly was marked by violence and fraud in some parts of the country. The 2011 presidential poll, with seven candidates lined up to challenge Museveni, was predicted to be a test of the Baganda Kingdom's willingness to break with the current regime and support the opposition. Besigye, the IPC candidate, meanwhile, had the support of coalition members who championed Baganda interests.

In a landmark legal victory for Otunnu and others who had been arrested in the past months, the Constitutional Court on August 25, 2010, struck down the sedition law and said that the warrant against Otunnu had been unlawfully issued. Journalists hailed the ruling, which allowed them to freely criticize the government. The government immediately announced it would appeal the ruling. That same month the UN refugee agency called on Uganda to halt the forcible deportation of hundreds of Rwandans from refugee camps in the southwest of the country, saying the refugees did not feel safe returning to their homeland. The government said the deportations targeted illegal immigrants.

In September 2010 Uganda charged 32 people, including 4 Ugandans as alleged masterminds, in connection with the July terrorist attack. All were charged with 76 counts of murder, 10 counts of attempted murder, and committing acts of terrorism.

In a ruling hailed by the United States and others as a sign of judicial independence, the Constitutional Court on October 12, 2010, unanimously voted to dismiss the treason case against Kizza Besigye and ten others on grounds that the state had violated his constitutional rights by having him stand trial in a military court and a civilian high court at the same time. The ruling effectively protected Besigye from further prosecution ahead of the 2011 election. Besigye, for his part, called for the resignations of the chief prosecutor and the attorney general. Days before official campaigning began in November, the president announced the reopening of a Baganda radio station that the government had shut down in 2009, a move widely regarded as one of appeasement ahead of the elections. In December the government approved a huge supplementary budget, including $162 million for the president's office, the defense ministry, the police force, and the state house.

In early January 2011 police investigations of Otunnu and Besigye were reported, and DP members Annet NAMWANGA and her husband, journalist and former exile Lawrence KIWANUKA, were detained by the army for their alleged connection to a terrorist plot. Authorities said they had thwarted a grenade attack on a military base in Kampala.

Prior to the presidential and parliamentary elections in February 2011, the Constitutional Court ruled that it was illegal for independent members of parliament to contest the election on a party ticket and for members affiliated with a party to run as independents. The ruling called for independent members to vacate their seats before being nominated to stand in the election. Subsequently, 77 legislators whose term was due to expire in May left their seats and were forced to repay the salary they had received since their nominations in November 2010. The Supreme Court immediately granted an interim stay of the ruling. The day before the presidential election, the president signed a new law authorizing the tapping of phones and other communications equipment for security purposes. On the eve of the election, weeks after civil unrest had had a major impact in Egypt and Tunisia, Uganda's communication commissioner ordered mobile phone operators to block text messages with words referring to Egypt, dictator, and guns, among others. President Museveni made it clear there would be no revolution such as the one occurring in Egypt, in Uganda.

Following Museveni's overwhelming reelection, outcry over the fairness of the poll came not only from the opposition but also from election monitors. African Union (AU) observers said there was "an urgent need" to reform the electoral laws before the next election, and EU observers cited the use of state resources to turn the polling in Museveni's favor. According to the Inter-Parliamentary Union (IPU), a Ugandan nongovernmental organization reported "groups of people with sacks of money openly handing it out." *Africa Confidential* reported after the election that the government remained "unapologetic" about its use of party and state finances. Besigye, who claimed the polling was "fundamentally flawed," and five other presidential challengers alleged widespread bribery and vote rigging. Notwithstanding these allegations, some analysts pointed to the opposition's failure to unite ahead of the polls. The DP's Mao, the UPC's Otunnu, and Besigye called for peaceful protests. On March 9 demonstrators who gathered in Kampala to denounce the alleged fraud were dispersed by police firing shots into the air and using tear gas. Ten people were arrested. Unrest continued to mount, resulting in a series of Walk-to-Work protests in April against the escalating food and fuel prices. Besigye was arrested on the first day of the protests, April 11, for the fourth time in two weeks, though the walks attracted party leaders, members of parliament, and others who walked alongside "ordinary Ugandans" said to have been priced out of the transport system. Three days later Besigye was wounded by a rubber bullet, and as protests spread to other areas, there were reports of police brutality and the government halting live broadcasts of events. On April 18 opposition members who tried to walk from their homes in Kampala had their way blocked, and several party officials and local council leaders were arrested. Meanwhile, Besigye and Otunnu were charged with inciting violence. Mao was remanded to prison until May 2 after he refused to apply for bail. Among those said to be key to initiating the protests was a civil society coalition called Action for Change, run by political activists in Baganda. In response to the spreading protests, the government banned the social networks Facebook and Twitter.

President Museveni's inauguration on May 12, 2011, was spoiled somewhat by a simultaneous "people's inauguration" organized by Besigye, who had returned that morning from his medical treatment in Kenya for injuries he had sustained during protests the previous month. The opposition leader, who was subsequently placed under house arrest, agreed to conditional talks with the government but vowed to continue the prodemocracy protests. President Museveni accused the opposition of wanting to overthrow the government. On May 18 the president reshuffled the top army officers, reportedly removing the army chief because of his "born-again" Christian beliefs. A new government, composed largely of NRM loyalists, was sworn in on June 6, following the recent dismissal of the former vice president and the appointment of a new prime minister.

Domestic tensions remained high following the earlier protests, in which at least 300 people reportedly were arrested, 100 were wounded, and 9 people died. On June 9, 2011, police broke up a demonstration in Kampala organized by what was described as a new "pressure group," Free Uganda Now, comprising UPC, DP, and SDP members. In August police fired tear gas on thousands of demonstrators who had gathered in a show of support for Besigye one day after a court dismissed charges against Besigye stemming from his role in earlier protests.

Foreign minister Kutesa and two other government officials were voluntarily suspended on October 12, 2012, following charges that they accepted $22.6 million in bribes from foreign oil companies. Investigations by Ugandan and British police later proved the charges were false, and Kutesa was restored to office. Meanwhile, Tarsis KABWEGYERE, Museveni's choice to be the new minister of gender, labor, and social affairs after a cabinet reshuffle on August 15, was rejected by parliament on August 28.

Gay rights continue to be a significant issue in Uganda, where harassment and intimidation against homosexuals is common. Homosexuality remains illegal and same-sex marriage was banned in 2005. In 2009 legislation that would have imposed capital punishment for those repeatedly convicted of homosexuality was defeated after Western governments and international organizations threatened to suspend aid if the measure was enacted. However, in 2012, a similar measure was reintroduced and remained awaiting action in August 2013. On September 13 British Producer David CECIL was arrested for staging *The River and the Mountain,* a play about a young Ugandan who discloses the fact that he is gay to his family and colleagues. Cecil was released on bail four days later.

In December 2012 an internal auditor's report found that officials in the prime minister's office had misappropriated $13.4 million in foreign aid. Donors began to suspend assistance in response to the scandal. Uganda subsequently began refunding $4.2 million in aid to countries including Denmark, Norway, and Ireland.

Reports in May 2013 revealed that 11 senior military officers had been arrested and another 30 placed under surveillance for antigovernment activities, while Gen. (Ret.) David SEJUSA went into exile. From London, Sejusa announced his intention to overthrow Museveni.

POLITICAL PARTIES AND GROUPS

In 1986 President Museveni ordered the suspension of political party activity pending the adoption of a new constitution, although several parties were allowed to maintain offices and small staffs. The 1989 elections were conducted on a "nonparty" basis, even though members of at least four parties (the CP, the DP, UPC, and the Uganda Patriotic Movement [UPM]) ran for office with their affiliations obvious to voters. Several others, principally political wings of military groups that had been absorbed by the NRA, had by then been effectively dissolved.

In March 1990 the government extended the formal party ban until 1995, President Museveni continuing to question the advisability of restoring a full-fledged multiparty system. Museveni's official explanation for banning political party activity was that it would cause ethnic divisions within the country. NRM officials claimed the country operated under a no-party system, although the opposition charged that the NRM operated as a party even though it claimed not to be one. Originally the ban on all party activity was to last until 2000, when the question of a multiparty system would be addressed in a referendum. The announced result of that referendum was that voters had said yes to a continued "no-party" system with the NRM in control, although the legality of the election was questioned by the opposition. Ultimately, a court invalidated the referendum on a technicality, but the issue of multiparty activity persisted and was addressed in a referendum on June 28, 2005, and a number of political groups emerged in Uganda to address the reforms and to contest the 2006 elections.

Originally the referendum questions of a multiparty versus a no-party system and the extension of presidential term limits were to appear on the same ballot. A "yes" vote for multiparty activity would have also meant a "yes" for term-limit extensions. In a remarkable show of independence in June 2005, parliament voted to allow citizens to vote on each issue separately. Both amendments were approved by voters, though opposition groups—styled the G6 (the FDC, UPC, DP, CP, JEEMA, and the Free Movement)—boycotted the referendum, and turnout was low (officially 47 percent, though reports from exit polls put turnout at about 20 percent). Multiparty presidential and parliamentary elections were held for the first time in 20 years in February 2006. The UPC and the DP subsequently withdrew from the G6.

In August 2006 a dozen parties and groups reportedly merged to form The Parties Platform (TPP), chaired by Emmanuel TUMUSIIME, to present a united front to try to gain power. The groups opposed a proposal by President Museveni that only the parties that held seats in parliament could participate in drafting a code of conduct for inter-party cooperation. The parties of the TPP were: the Forum for Integrity in Leadership; the National Unity Party; the National Peasants Party; the Farmers Party of Uganda; the Movement for Democratic Change; the National Unity, Reconciliation, and Development Party; the Uganda People's Party; the Movement of Volunteers and Mobilizers; the Liberal Democratic Transparency; the People's United Movement; the National Convention for Democracy; and the Uganda Patriotic Movement.

Ahead of the 2011 presidential elections, an electoral coalition of minor parties called Change 2011 included the People's Development Party, National Coalition for Democracy, National Peasants Party, and Movement of Volunteers and Mobilizers. Another coalition, the Inter-Party Cooperation, which included JEEMA, CP, SDP, and FDC, backed coalition leader and FDC president Kizza Besigye for president.

Dominant Government Party:

National Resistance Movement—NRM. The NRM was formed following the controversial 1980 election by former president Yusuf K. Lule and Yoweri Museveni, the former directing the political wing from exile in London and the latter leading internal guerrilla activity through the National Resistance Army (NRA). Upon his assumption of the presidency in January 1986, Museveni declared that the NRM was a "clear-headed movement" dedicated to the restoration of democracy in Uganda. Despite the ineffectiveness of subsequent membership drives, Museveni on several occasions suggested that the NRM could become the centerpiece of a one-party or limited-party state in which wide-ranging political expression would be permitted but ethnic and religious sectarianism avoided.

In a dramatic turnaround, however, Museveni sponsored the motion in parliament in 2005 for a national referendum on a multiparty system versus a no-party system. Museveni championed multiparty political activity, observers said, to appease Western donors by assuring them of his intention to move toward a more democratic society. In addition, the multiparty ballot question was paired with a provision that would eliminate the two-term limit on the presidency, thus virtually assuring Museveni of a third five-year term.

In 2008 rifts were reported within the party between those who backed Museveni for another term and those who pressed for finding a successor, in addition to tensions resulting from Museveni's tightened control over the party. In September some 500 disaffected members of the FDC reportedly joined the NRM.

In advance of the 2011 general elections, in which Museveni said he would seek a fourth term, the NRM dominated local by-elections in 2009, winning in areas traditionally dominated by the opposition. The party, as expected, endorsed Museveni for the 2011 presidential bid, but the process was marred by irregularities and violence in some districts in the country. The party subsequently introduced biometric data registration to help eliminate fraud. Some 500 defectors, mainly from the UPC, reportedly joined the NRM late in 2010.

In a by-election in September 2012, 19-year-old Proscovia Alengot OROMAIT of the NRM was elected as the youngest member of parliament in the history of Uganda. Meanwhile, reports indicated a growing faction of the NRM supported the parliamentary speaker, Rebecca KADAGA, as the party's presidential candidate in 2016, although Museveni endeavored to garner support for his son, Brig. Kainerugaba MUHOOZI as his successor.

Reports in August 2013 indicated a growing number of defections from the NRM to the FDC.

Leaders: Lt. Gen. Yoweri MUSEVENI (President of the Republic and Chair of the Party), Moses KIGONGO (Vice Chair), Rebecca KADAGA (Speaker of the Parliament), Dorothy HYUHA (Deputy Secretary General), Amama MBABAZI (Prime Minister and Secretary General).

Other Legislative Parties:

Uganda People's Congress—UPC. The largely Protestant UPC was formed in 1960 with a stated commitment to "African socialism." It served as the ruling party under former president Apollo Milton Obote from independence until 1971 and again from late 1980 to 1985. Despite the inclusion of several UPC adherents in the initial Museveni administration, friction persisted between the government and Obote loyalists, particularly hardliners who launched splinters, such as the UPF, in response to the pro-Museveni posture of their former colleagues.

In February 1991 the **October 9 Movement,** an Obote-led UPC faction named after the date of Ugandan independence, was reportedly operating from a Nairobi-subsidized "training camp" along the Ugandan border in Kenya. Obote's chief of staff was identified as Lt. Col. John OGORE; also listed as movement leaders were Peter OTAI, former commander of the **Uganda People's Army** (UPA), and Peter OWILI, known as "the butcher of Nile Mansions" for the brutal interrogation methods he employed during Obote's presidency.

Despite living in exile in Zambia, Obote continued to control the UPC, and in June 1996 he ordered Assistant Secretary General Cecilia OGWAL not to participate in parliamentary elections. However, Ogwal, who had been credited with maintaining party unity after Obote's departure, defied his edict and captured a seat. Consequently, Obote dismissed her and named James RWANYARARE party spokesperson and chair of the UPC's Presidential Policy Commission (i.e., de facto party leader). For her part, Ogwal rejected Obote's authority to intervene and announced the formation of her own "task force," an act one observer described as an intraparty "coup" attempt. Her underfinanced splinter group was subsequently described as unlikely to challenge Rwanyarare, although she remained a controversial figure in the party. In 2005 Obote dismissed Rwanyarare and dissolved the Presidential Policy Commission, replacing it with a Constitutional Steering Committee. Ultimately, a court ordered the party to sort out its differences following the death of Obote in October 2005. The former president's widow, Miria Kalule Obote, was elected party leader in November 2005. She placed last in 2006 presidential balloting with less than 1 percent of the vote. (She was the first woman presidential candidate in Uganda and the first woman to lead a major political party.)

In January 2008 one faction within the party expressed its dissatisfaction with Miria Obote, but she refused to relinquish the presidency. Party veteran Joseph OTHIENO was vying to become party president in late 2009, as were numerous others, including former secretary general Peter Walubiri. Meanwhile, following an amendment to the party's constitution that reduces the president's term from seven years to five, Miria Obote said that she was ready to retire. In a subsequent move seen as Obote's way of ensuring that her son succeeded her, Obote reshuffled the party leadership in June 2009, replacing Walubiri and installing her son, Jimmy Akena, as vice chair. However, Akena's rein was short-lived, as in August 2009 former UN diplomat Olara Otunnu, a longtime critic of Museveni, returned to Uganda after an absence of 23 years. His return split the party, as opponents believed he had betrayed Obote and the UPC by siding with the 1985 coup plotters and subsequently accepting the post of foreign minister. Miria Obote fired at least one party official who met Otunnu upon his arrival at the airport. However, Otunnu's supporters prevailed, and he was elected party president on February 18, 2010.

Despite having initially agreed to join the IPC electoral alliance in advance of the 2011 general election, the UPC ultimately decided to field its own presidential and legislative candidates. Otunnu was tapped as the party's flag bearer and campaigned for sovereignty for the Baganda Kingdom and a federal system of government. He won a major legal victory in August when the Constitutional Court struck down the country's sedition law, nullifying the warrant against Otunnu, which the court ruled had been unlawfully issued. The ruling removed restrictions on freedom of expression, an important victory for Otunnu, who repeatedly took to the airwaves to criticize Museveni.

In October 2010 Apollo Milton Obote was posthumously awarded the country's independence medal on Independence Day.

Friction was reported within the party in November when youth members accused the financial wing of the party of sabotaging Otunnu's supporters.

In the 2011 presidential election Otunnu finished fourth with 1.6 percent of the vote. The party secured ten seats in concurrent parliamentary elections. In midyear, infighting escalated between Akena and Otunnu over claims by Akena that Otunnu was trying to suspend him.

In May 2012 eight UPC members of parliament sued Otunna over the president's unwillingness to call a special party congress to discuss fissures within the UPC. In July 2013 the UPC launched an unsuccessful effort to prevent the appointment of Gen. Aronda NYAKAIRIMA as interior minister, asserting that the former chief of the Ugandan defense forces should formally retire before joining the cabinet.

Leaders: Olara A. OTUNNU (Chair and 2011 presidential candidate), Miria Kalule OBOTE (2006 presidential candidate), Jimmy AKENA, Joseph BBOSA (Vice President), Akhbar Adoko NEKYON, Patrick MWONDHA (Treasurer), Chris OPOKA, John ODIT (Secretary General).

Democratic Party—DP. An advocate of centralization and a mixed economy, the DP draws on a solid Roman Catholic base and enjoys widespread support in southern Uganda. Officially, it ran second to the UPC in the post-Amin balloting of December 1980, winning 51 of 126 legislative seats, although the results were strongly challenged. The DP subsequently was weakened by defections to the UPC and sporadic harassment, killing, or detention of its leadership by the Obote government. While DP president Paul Ssemogerere joined the Okello cabinet, most DP leaders supported Museveni's NRA in continued guerrilla fighting. Several members of the DP executive committee were included in Museveni's first cabinet, and, despite reports of some deterioration in DP–NRM relations, Ssemogerere was named second deputy prime minister and foreign minister in February 1988; he retained both posts in the cabinet reorganization of July 1991.

In mid-1992 Ssemogerere was the reported leader of a cabinet revolt against Museveni's request for extension of the ban on political party activities; however, in May 1993 he advised party activists to curtail operations in the face of a presidential decree banning theretofore implicitly acceptable activities. In June 1995 the DP leader resigned as second deputy prime minister and minister of public service to position himself for the forthcoming presidential campaign.

In early 1996 the DP and the UPC forged an unofficial alliance, the Inter-Party Coalition (IPC), on the premise that in return for its support of DP candidates in the 1996 elections the UPC would be the opposition's standard-bearer at the next national elections. Subsequently, a number of UPC leaders made campaign appearances with Ssemogerere; however, following the DP leader's overwhelming electoral defeat, the UPC's Obote reportedly denied the coalition's existence. Collaterally, observers speculated that the alliance had cost Ssemogerere the votes of the Baganda people, who had been oppressed by Obote's regime and continued to resent him. Although Ssemogerere described the presidential polling as "rigged" in favor of the incumbent and subsequently boycotted the June legislative balloting, suggestions that the party would go into opposition were greeted with skepticism by observers, who cited the DP's history of participation in NRM governments. Subsequent to the June 2000 referendum (which the DP boycotted) on political party activity, Ssemogerere announced his intention to resign the party presidency, but he stayed on until his retirement in 2005. Factions within the party clashed in advance of the 2005 constitutional referendum but reportedly reunited a month later. John Ssebaana Kizito was elected party leader in November 2005, ending Ssemogerere's 25-year reign, and faction leader Hajji Ali Sserunjogi was elected vice president. Ssebaana finished third behind Museveni in the 2006 presidential election with 1.58 percent of the vote.

Dissension in the party was reported in 2007, resulting in the formation of a breakaway group, the Social Democratic Party (see Other Groups, below), and the demotion of Secretary General Lulume Bayiga to deputy secretary general. Subsequently, Bayiga served as acting secretary general until August 2008, when the party elected Mathias Nsubuga to fill the post. In September party vice president Hajji Ali Sserunjogi and chair Joseph Mukiibi were suspended because of their refusal to accept the appointment of Nsubuga. The two men disputed their suspension. Meanwhile, the party rejected joining the IPC electoral coalition that ultimately included the FDC and several other parties for the 2011 poll, as some DP members backed a regional party leader, Norbert Mao, to be the party's flag bearer. Mao was elected party chair at a conference in February 2010 that was boycotted by a faction led by Mukiibi and Lulume.

Mao, a former member of parliament, was among those who had tried to resolve the conflict between the government and the LRA by lobbying for a general amnesty.

In the 2011 presidential election Mao was third, with just 1.9 percent of the vote. Samuel Lubega, who had hoped for the party nod, ran for president as an independent and finished eighth with 0.4 percent. In concurrent parliamentary elections the party secured 12 seats. In September 2012 Nsubuga reportedly angered members of the party by declaring that he would support Rebecca KADAGA of the NRM in the next presidential election. In August 2013 the DP rejected a proposal to field a single opposition presidential candidate for the 2016 balloting.

Leaders: Norbert MAO (Party President and 2011 presidential candidate), John KAWANGA, Issa KIKUNGWE, Hajji Beswale KEZAALA, John SSEBAANA Kizito (2006 presidential candidate), Joseph MUKIIBI, Lulume BAYIGA, Mathias NSUBUGA (Secretary General).

Forum for Democratic Change—FDC. This opposition group was formed in July 2004 by a merger of the Reform Agenda, the Parliamentary Advocacy Forum, and the National Democratic Forum. The FDC's leader in exile, retired colonel Kizza Besigye, had challenged Museveni in the 2001 presidential election. Several opposition members of parliament previously affiliated with the UPC and DP reportedly joined the new group, which declared its intentions of becoming "a strong, democratic, mass organization."

Besigye returned from the United States in 2005 in order to participate in 2006 elections and drew large crowds at a number of rallies in areas that traditionally had supported Museveni. In what observers said was an attempt to prevent Besigye from challenging Museveni in the 2006 elections, Besigye was arrested in Kampala for allegedly supporting the rebel PRA based in the DRC and charged with treason. He was also charged with rape in connection with a 1997 case but was cleared of that charge in March 2006. Earlier, the FDC nominated him as the group's presidential candidate, and Besigye was freed on bail a month ahead of the 2006 presidential election. He came in a distant second to Museveni. Besigye subsequently was offered a seat in parliament by a newly elected delegate who reportedly calculated that the FDC leader would wield more power as leader of the opposition. However, Besigye turned down the offer.

In 2007 Besigye said he would step down as party leader in 2010 in advance of party preparations for the 2011 elections. Regan OKUMU, a member of parliament, soon declared his intention to contest the party presidency. A rift reportedly developed in the party in July 2008 during a meeting to determine a successor to Sulaiman KIGGUNDU, the party's national chair who had died a month earlier. John Butime was named acting national chair. In February 2009, however, Besigye defeated former army commander Gregory Mugisha MUNTU to retain leadership of the party. In April the FDC challenged the country's electoral commission, seeking to delay local by-elections with legal challenges accusing the commission of being unable to conduct fair elections.

In 2009 more than 100 NRM members defected to the FDC.

Ahead of the 2011 presidential election, in early 2010 the FDC was one of four parties that joined the electoral alliance known as the IPC, and Besigye was voted its flag bearer with the stipulation that he agree to sovereignty for the Baganda Kingdom. During the course of the campaign, he was beaten by security forces and the paramilitary Kiboko.

In October 2010 Besigye's treason trial was dismissed by the Constitutional Court, a ruling hailed as a sign of judicial independence and effectively protected him from further prosecution ahead of the 2011 election.

In the 2011 parliamentary poll the party won 34 seats. Following the concurrent presidential election, which Besigye claimed was rife with fraud after finishing a distant second, he organized a series of protests in April and was arrested several times. Injuries resulting from rubber bullets fired by the police during one of the protests resulted in his seeking medical treatment in Kenya. Upon his return, coinciding with the inauguration of President Musaveni in May, he participated in additional protests. In July Besigye announced that he would not run for the presidency in 2016, nor would he seek reelection as party president after his second term expires in 2014. In August charges against Besigye related to the protests were dismissed. In October 2012 he was arrested for holding a banned rally. In November Besigye resigned, and Maj. Gen. (Ret.) Mugisha MUNTU was elected party leader.

Leaders: Mugisha MUNTU (Party Leader), Dr. Kizza BESIGYE (2001, 2006, and 2011 presidential candidate), Salaami MUSUMBA (Vice President), Alice ALASO (Secretary General).

Conservative Party—CP. The CP is a small formation whose leader, prime minister of Baganda in 1964–1966, participated in the Okello and Museveni governments. CP has adopted to some extent the positions of the **Baganda Royalist Movement,** which has long sought restoration of the traditional Kingdom of Baganda.

In early 2005 rival factions divided the group, and a lengthy dispute over leadership ensued until May, when Mayanja Nkangi, on one side, reconciled with Yusufu Nsubuga Nsombu and John Ken Lukyamuzi on the other. Lukyamuzi, who supported the DP's Ssemogerere in the 1996 presidential election over Museveni, initially supported the FDC's Besigye in 2006, then said he would run for president but did not appear on the ballot. Lukyamuzi was forced to leave parliament in 2006 for allegedly breaking the law by failing to disclose his wealth. (Lukyamuzi petitioned the High Court to review the case.) Subsequently, a dispute over his leadership of the party remained unresolved. In 2008 Lukyamuzi continued to lead one faction of the party, while Nkangi claimed leadership of the "mainstream" CP faction. According to the inspector general for government (IGG), however, Lukyamuzi was ineligible for any leadership post for five years because of his earlier failure to reveal his assets.

In May 2008 the CP and other opposition parties called for electoral reforms, including banning representation of the army in parliament and establishing an impartial and independent electoral commission.

In 2010 the CP joined the IPC electoral coalition ahead of the 2011 presidential poll.

The party retained its single seat in the 2011 parliamentary election. In August 2012 Daniel Walyemera MASUMBA was elected president of the party. In 2013 the CP initiated coalition discussions with other opposition parties.

Leaders: Daniel Walyemera MASUMBA (President), Mubiru ALI (Vice President), Mukasa HUSSEIN (Secretary General).

Justice Forum (Justice, Education, Economy, Morality, African Unity—JEEMA). The Justice Forum was formed in October 1996 by Mohamed Mayanja Kibirige, who secured only 2.1 percent of the vote in the 1996 presidential election, to rally support for his candidacy in the 2001 presidential election. (Mayanja received just 1 percent of the vote in 2001.) In 2004 the group, which reportedly seeks a democratic, federal system of government, rejected a merger with the FDC.

Mayanja initially announced he would seek the presidency in 2006 but later withdrew.

JEEMA joined the IPC electoral coalition in advance of the 2011 general election. In June 2010 party leader Mayanja stepped down to make way for "a new breed of leaders." Nonetheless, he was elected party chair, with the presidency going to Asuman Basalirwa.

In the 2011 legislative election the party retained its seat. In 2013 JEEMA called for a constitutional amendment calling for the parliamentary speaker and deputy speaker to resign their seats after being elected and become ex officio members.

Leaders: Mohamed MAYANJA Kibirige (Chair and 1996 and 2001 presidential candidate), Asuman BASALIRWA (President), Diana OGWAL (Vice President), Yahya SSEREMBA (Spokesperson), Hussein KYANJO (Secretary General).

Other Groups:

Uganda Federal Alliance—(UFA). Established as a civil society in May 2009 by former FPC member Beti Olive Kamya, the group was registered as a political party in July 2010, three months after the electoral commission challenged the registration over ghost names on its party lists. At the time, UFA leaders claimed they were a civil society, not a political party, and therefore could not be deregistered by the electoral commission.

Kamya, a member of parliament, had formed the group to lobby for political rights for the people of the Buganda Kingdom. As the UFA's flag bearer in the 2011 election, Kamya—the only woman seeking the presidency—campaigned for a federal system of government, as well as a national public health plan, education reforms, and a guaranteed minimum wage.

In the 2011 presidential election Kamya won 0.7 percent of the vote, finishing fifth. In March 2012 the UFA threatened to sue the electoral commission, claiming the body did not do enough to allow Ugandans living outside the country to vote.

Leaders: Beti Olive KAMYA (President and 2011 presidential candidate), Aniba BONIFANS (Vice President), E. P. N. MAYEKU-MALESI (National Chair), Kavuma KAGGWA (Publicity Chair), Maj. Acikule NOAH.

Progressive Alliance Party—PAP. Established in April 2005 by Bernard KIBIRIGE, a former aide to Brig. Henry TUMUKUNDE, who was dismissed from his post as Uganda's military intelligence chief, the PAP has had a divisive history.

Its leaders deny that they are front men for Tumukunde, who was arrested in May 2005. (Tumukunde played a key role in Museveni's 1996 and 2001 elections, allegedly using "strong-arm" tactics and military intelligence to help the president.) Meanwhile, a rival intelligence chief and former supporter of Museveni, David Pulkol, left the FDC to join the PAP in September 2005, prompting accusations from Kibirige and other party members that Pulkol was sent by the NRM to spy on and "destroy" the party. Subsequently, however, Pulkol, who also had ties to Tumukunde, was elected party president and nominated as the party's presidential candidate for the 2006 election. Infighting in the party was blamed for his failing to meet the registration deadline, and in 2006 the group supported Kizza Besigye's FDC candidacy. A month before the election, about 100 PAP members linked to Tumukunde defected to the NRM and demanded Tumukunde's release. Reportedly, many of the defectors had been part of a "task force" organized by Tumukunde to support Museveni's 2001 bid, and they left the PAP in part because the party had no presidential candidate for 2006. Party secretary general Kibirige said in 2006 that he had quit politics to concentrate on business. In July 2013 the electoral commission requested that the high court deregister the PAP.

Leaders: David PULKOL (President), Dr. Kaddu MULINDWA (Interim Chair).

Other groups include the **Freedom Movement,** part of the so-called G6 group of opposition parties; **Forces for Change,** a splinter opposition group formed in March 2005 by Nasser Ntege SSEBAGALA and David Pulkol (who later joined the PAP); the **National Peasants Party,** led by Erias WAMALA; the **Republican Women and Youth Party,** led by Stella NAMBUYA; the **People's Independent Party,** led by Yahaya KAMULEGEYA and Amin SSENTONGO; **Movement for Democratic Change,** led by Paulsen KITIMBO; the **National People's Organization,** led by Abdu JAGWE; the **National Convention for Democracy,** led by Haji Jingo KAAYA; the **Farmers Party of Uganda,** led by Mudde Bombakka NSKIO; the **National Unity, Reconciliation, and Development Party,** led by Joseph NYANZI; and the **People's Progressive Party,** established in 2004 and led by Jaberi Bidandi SSALI, the party's 2011 presidential candidate; and the **People's Development Party,** whose leader, Dr. Abed BWANIKA, secured 0.6 percent of the vote in the 2011 presidential election. In November 2007 the **Social Democratic Party** (SDP) was formed by a group of dissidents from the DP, including Henry LUBOWA and Michael MABIKKE.

Guerrilla Groups:

Lord's Resistance Army—LRA. The LRA first emerged in the late 1980s as Lakwena Part Two, a small, predominantly Acholi successor group to the Holy Spirit Movement that had been led by "voodoo priestess" Alice LAKWENA from 1986 until her flight to Kenya in 1987 (Lakwena died in 2007). Under the leadership of Joseph Kony, the anti-NRA rebels remained active in northern Uganda, and in early 1991 the militants reportedly began referring to themselves as the Uganda Democratic Christian Army. Following inconclusive negotiations with government representatives in early 1994, Kony and his supporters launched a new offensive under their current name, claiming they were fighting "a holy war against foreign occupation" and seeking to install a government guided by the biblical Ten Commandments.

LRA bases in Sudan came under sustained attack by Sudanese rebel forces and the Ugandan Army beginning in April 1997, and in July LRA commanders reportedly called for a cease-fire (for more information on the history of the LRA prior to 1996, please see the 2012 *Handbook*). Subsequently, in the second half of 1997 Kony led his fighters in a series of cross-border raids, although the LRA had been forced to break into much smaller fighting cells than its usual 150–200 member units. Despite heavy casualties, according to government officials, the LRA continued to replenish its ranks by abducting teenage Ugandans and forcing them to march to Sudan for training and indoctrination.

In late 1998 a group of LRA dissidents led by Ronald Otim KOMAKECH reportedly split from the group following a dispute over the LRA's alleged targeting of civilians; subsequently, Komakech formed the **LRA–Democratic** and allied the splinter with the **Uganda National Rescue Front** (UNRF, below). The level of LRA activities actually increased after a December 1999 treaty between Sudan and Uganda ostensibly designed to end support for guerrilla groups. LRA activity subsided in 2000–2001, largely due to behind-the-scenes negotiations mediated by the U.S.-based Carter Center in Atlanta, which tried to initiate talks with LRA leader Kony and his backers, the Sudanese government. In February 2001, however, LRA rebels attacked a northern Ugandan town and abducted 40 people. In March Ugandan wildlife authorities suspended game-viewing activities in parts of the northwestern Murchison Falls National Park following an alleged LRA ambush in which at least 10 people were killed. In 2004 gains made by the Ugandan People's Defense Force (UPDF) against the rebels seemed to compel the LRA to seek a cease-fire. By mid-2005, however, talks had not made significant progress. Meanwhile, evidence of cooperation between Sudanese and Ugandan troops against the LRA raised hopes that combined pressure might force Kony's group into meaningful negotiations. In 2005 the ICC issued arrest warrants for Kony and other LRA leaders. Subsequently, the LRA leaders ensconced themselves in forested areas of the DRC and intermittently engaged in negotiations toward a permanent truce with the Ugandan government in 2006 and 2007.

Kony was reported to have executed his one-time deputy, Vincent Otti, in October 2007. Alfred James OBITA took over as leader of the LRA's negotiation team after David MATSANGA was dismissed in April 2008. Subsequently, it was reported that Matsanga had returned to replace Obita, whom Kony had dismissed. On August 4 the government granted amnesty to Obita and several other LRA and ADF rebels (see Current issues, above). Two of Kony's top commanders, Okot ODHIAMBO (whom Kony was reported to have killed in 2008) and Dominic ONGWEN, reportedly were killed or wounded in December when their hideout was attacked by a joint military operation from which Kony escaped. Subsequently, other unconfirmed reports surfaced that Odhiambo had defected from the Kony camp in 2009 and was requesting amnesty, and that Ongwen had moved from the DRC to South Sudan. Another top commander, Thomas KWOYELO, was said to have been captured on March 3, 2009. Also in 2010, the United States adopted a law aimed at developing a strategy to help disarm the LRA rebels and apprehend Kony.

Attacks continued as the LRA reportedly moved through the DRC, the Central African Republic, and Sudan. In late 2010 and early 2011 the LRA was reported to be based in southern Darfur. On May 12, 2012, Ugandan security forces captured Caesar ACHELLAM, a senior LRA leader. As a result of continued international efforts, by 2013, estimates were that the LRA had declined to approximately 250 fighters. Meanwhile, the United States offered a $5 million reward for the capture of Kony and other top LRA leaders.

Leaders: Joseph KONY, Oti LAGONY, Willy ORYEM, Yusuf ADEK.

Allied Democratic Forces—ADF. The ADF is reportedly composed of remnants of the late Amon BAZIRA's National Movement for the Liberation of Uganda, and Islamic militant fighters, styled the *Salaaf Tabliqs,* allegedly funded by the Sudanese government. ADF activity was first reported in 1995, but the group did not achieve prominence until 1997 when its numbers were reportedly swollen by the addition of former Zairean government forces and Rwandan Hutu *Inter-hamwé* fighters.

A government offensive in mid-1997 decimated the ADF's fighting strength and drove a majority of its fighters deep into the mountains of the Democratic Republic of the Congo (DRC). However, ADF militants were allegedly responsible for grenade attacks in Kampala in early 1998, and thereafter the ADF launched a series of attacks that claimed dozens of civilian lives. In February 1999 the ADF was accused of orchestrating a deadly bomb attack in Kampala. A number of ADF militants were killed in subsequent government raids, while the ADF was accused of killing both civilians and soldiers in several incidents throughout the rest of the year. In April 2000 the Ugandan government pulled out 2,000 soldiers from eastern DRC, claiming that the threat of cross-border ADF incursions was greatly reduced. Ugandan authorities in July arrested 28 ADF recruits accused of undertaking bomb attacks that have killed 67 people and injured 262 others since 1997. The ADF had resorted to urban terrorism after its ground insurgency was defeated in the mountains straddling Uganda's western border with the DRC. Some ADF rebel leaders and fighters allegedly were trained in terrorist Osama bin Laden's Afghan camps, and in December 2001 the United States listed the ADF as a terrorist organization. Clashes between Ugandan forces and ADF rebels continued into 2006, with security forces arresting and killing many suspected ADF members in the western forests of Uganda. The militants reportedly were fleeing the DRC following fighting between the Congolese army and UN peacekeeping forces. In 2007, the ADF's second in command, Balaya ISIKO, was killed in fighting with DRC soldiers. The ADF in western Uganda reportedly had been defeated by the Ugandan army.

In 2008 it was reported that the ADF was seeking peace talks with the Ugandan government. News reports said that the group had not been active in recent years. However, in July the Ugandan army claimed the ADF was regrouping and recruiting in the DRC. In 2009 the group's leader, Jamir Mukulu, was reported as saying he was ready to resume fighting if the Ugandan government did not commit to a peace process.

In July 2010 President Museveni appealed to ADF "remnants" in eastern Congo to give up their rebellion and return to Uganda. Meanwhile, Uganda increased its troops along the western border to counter possible further ADF attacks. In 2012 reports indicated that a new rebel grouping, the Revolutionary Forces for the Liberation of Uganda (RFLU), sought an alliance with the ADF. In 2013 Uganda launched a program to return child soldiers of the ADF to their villages.

Leaders: Jamir MUKULU, Yusuf KABANDA.

For information on other guerrilla groups that have largely been inactive in recent years, see earlier editions of the *Handbook.*

LEGISLATURE

The former National Assembly was dissolved following the July 1985 coup. Balloting for a new, formally recognized **Parliament** was held on a "no-party" basis in June 1996 (for more information on the legislature prior to 2011, please see the 2012 *Handbook*). In multiparty balloting on February 18, 2011 (the second following the 2005 constitutional revision), 237 seats were directly elected on a constituency basis; 112 additional district seats are reserved for women, and another 25 seats are reserved for representatives of youth, workers, and disabled persons and the Uganda People's Defense Force; 13 seats are filled on an ex-officio basis by cabinet ministers appointed by the president, and the number may vary according to the president's wishes. The seat distribution was as follows: National Resistance Movement (NRM), 263 (165 constituency, 85 district women, 13 indirectly chosen); independents, 44; Forum for Democratic Change, 34 (23 constituency, 11 district women); Democratic Party, 12; Uganda People's Congress, 10; Uganda People's Defense Forces, 10; Justice Forum, 1; Conservative Party, 1.

Speaker: Rebecca KADAGA.

CABINET

[as of August 15, 2013]

Prime Minister	Amama Mbabazi
First Deputy Prime Minister	Henry Kajura
Second Deputy Prime Minister	Gen. Moses Ali
Office of the President	Frank Tumwebaze
Prime Minister's Office	John Mwoono Nasasira
Ministers	
Agriculture, Animal Husbandry, and Fisheries	Tress Buchanayande
Attorney General	Peter Nyomi
Communications and Information Technology	John Mwoono Nasasira

Defense	Crispus Kiyunga
East African Affairs	(Vacant)
Education and Sports	Jessica Arupo [f]
Energy and Mineral Development	Irene Muloni [f]
Finance, Planning, and Economic Development	Maria Kiwanuka [f]
Foreign Affairs	Sam Kutesa
Gender, Labor, and Social Affairs	Mary Karooro Okurut [f]
Government Chief Whip	Justine Lumumba Kasule [f]
Health	Ruhakana Rugunda
Information and National Guidance	Rose Namayanja [f]
Internal Affairs	Gen. Aronda Nyakairima
Justice and Constitutional Affairs	Maj. Gen. Kahinda Otafiire
Karamoja Affairs	Janet Museveni [f]
Lands, Housing, and Urban Development	Daudi Migereko
Local Government	Adolf Mwesigye
Office of the Prime Minister	Tarsis Kabwegyere
Public Works	Abraham Byandaala
Relief and Disaster Preparedness	Hilary Onek
Security	Wilson Muruli Mukasa
Tourism and Wildlife	Maria Mutagamba [f]
Trade and Industry	Amelia Kyambadde [f]
Water and Environment	Ephraim Kamuntu
Without Portfolio	Richard Todwong

[f] = female

INTERGOVERNMENTAL REPRESENTATION

Ambassador to the U.S.: Oliver WONEKHA.

U.S. Ambassador to Uganda: Scott H. DELISI.

Permanent Representative to the UN: Richard NDUHUURA.

IGO Memberships (Non-UN): AfDB, AU, Comesa, CWTH, IOM, NAM, OIC, WTO.

UKRAINE

Ukrayina

Note: In an apparent response to heavy pressure from Russia, President Viktor Yanukovych in late November 2013 announced that Ukraine was not prepared to sign an association agreement and other accords designed to deepen Ukraine's economic ties to the European Union (EU). The decision triggered massive protests in Kiev by pro-EU demonstrators led by the major opposition parties. Russia, encouraging Ukraine to join the Russian customs union with Belarus and Kazakhstan, subsequently approved $17 billion in loans and sharply reduced the price of Russian gas exports to Ukraine.

Political Status: Formerly the Ukrainian Soviet Socialist Republic, a constituent republic of the Union of Soviet Socialist Republics; declared independence on August 24, 1991; new constitution adopted on June 28, 1996.

Area: 233,090 sq. mi. (603,700 sq. km).

Population: 46,174,076 (2012E—UN); 44,573,205 (2013E—U.S. Census).

Major Urban Centers (including suburbs, 2005E): KIEV (KYÏV, 1,771,000), Donetsk (Donèc'k, 4,644,000), Dnepropetrovsk (Dnipropètrovsk, 3,461,000), Kharkov (Charkiv, 2,837,000), Lvov (L'viv, 2,582,000), Odessa (Odèsa, 2,407,000).

Official Language: Ukrainian (replaced Russian in 1990). Following independence in 1991, the Council for Language Policy and the National Orthography Commission began working to restore syntax, style, and other aspects of Ukrainian to what they were before the 1930s, when Moscow ordered Ukrainian to be made more uniform with Russian. As proposed by the generally pro-Russian Ukrainian government installed in 2010, Ukrainian regions with Russian populations of more than 10 percent were authorized as of August 2012 to give official language status to Russian in addition to Ukrainian. Eight regions had reportedly done so by the end of the month.

Monetary Unit: Hryvna (official rate November 1, 2013: 8.17 hryvnas = $1US).

President: Viktor YANUKOVYCH (Party of Regions); elected in second-round balloting on February 7, 2010, and inaugurated for a five-year term on February 25, succeeding Viktor YUSHCHENKO ("Our Ukraine" Bloc).

Prime Minister: Mykola AZAROV (Party of Regions); nominated by the president on March 10, 2011, and approved by the Supreme Council on March 11 to succeed Yulia TYMOSHENKO (Yulia Tymoshenko Bloc), whose coalition government had collapsed on March 3 following a legislative nonconfidence vote; reappointed by the president on December 13, 2012, following the Supreme Council elections of October 28; formed new government on December 24, 2012.

THE COUNTRY

The third largest and second most populous of the former Soviet republics, Ukraine is bordered on the north by Belarus, on the east by Russia, on the south by the Black Sea and the Sea of Azov, and on the west by Moldova, Romania, Hungary, Slovakia, and Poland. The population is approximately 78 percent Ukrainian and 18 percent Russian, with no other group greater than 1 percent. The ethnic Russian population is located primarily in eastern and southern Ukraine, where there is significant sentiment in favor of the reestablishment of greater economic, political, and military integration with Russia. The population in western Ukraine is described in general as supportive of the country's orientation toward Western Europe. Most Ukrainians profess Eastern Orthodoxy, although there is a sizable Roman Catholic community and smaller numbers of Muslims and Jews.

The black-earth steppe of the south, one of the world's most productive farming regions, provided about one-quarter of the foodstuffs for the former Union of Soviet Socialist Republics (USSR). Agriculture currently accounts for about 12 percent of GDP and 15 percent of employment. The leading crop is wheat (Ukraine is one of the world's leading grain producers), followed by sugar beets, potatoes, and a wide variety of other vegetables and fruits. Natural resources, including iron, coal, bauxite, zinc, oil, and natural gas, have long supported a broad range of manufacturing activity, including metallurgy, machine building, and chemical production, which accounted for nearly a third of the Soviet Union's industrial output. Industry now contributes about 40 percent of Ukrainian GDP, primarily from mining and metallurgy, and employs some 25 percent of the labor force. Steel is the country's leading export.

The demise of the Soviet system yielded a 50 percent contraction in economic output in Ukraine in 1990–1994, accompanied by inflation that spiraled to more than 4,700 percent in 1993 before falling to 890 percent in 1994 and to under 100 percent in 1995. GDP also contracted from 1995 to 1997, albeit at a lower rate each year. A modest recovery appeared possible for 1998 until the economy was rocked by the Russian financial collapse of August, which constrained trade between the two countries and prompted a significant outflow of capital.

In 2000 the economy expanded for the first time since independence, achieving 6 percent growth. The International Monetary Fund (IMF), which had encouraged stabilization and liberalization measures, attributed the advance to exchange rate depreciation, unexpected economic resilience in Russia (Ukraine's principal trading partner), and an improved world market for Ukraine's exports, led by metals. However at the end of the year, virtually all the large Soviet-era state enterprises remained in government hands, while privatization and other market-oriented reforms continued to meet opposition from a Communist-Socialist-Agrarian parliamentary bloc.

On the right, politically well-connected entrepreneurs, the so-called oligarchs, also opposed many reform efforts, particularly in the energy sector, where the oligarchs benefited from a lack of transparency and informal barter arrangements among consumers, sellers, and suppliers.

GDP rose by more than 9 percent annually in 2001–2004, led by growth in the industrial sector and strong domestic consumer demand. However, Ukraine remained heavily dependent on imported energy products, particularly from Russia. In addition, the oligarchs retained a near monopoly on the industrial and financial sectors and were perceived as blocking reform of the tax system. The World Bank and IMF pledged additional aid in response to the government's action against money laundering, but the country was still viewed as a high risk by foreign investors.

Upon taking office in early 2005, President Yushchenko pledged to pursue free-market policies and to investigate the some 3,000 nontransparent privatizations that had been completed during the Kuchma administration. Foreign investors initially welcomed the market orientation brought on by the so-called Orange Revolution but were described as "unnerved" by the subsequent political turmoil. On a more positive note for supporters of proposed Ukrainian membership in the European Union (EU) and the World Trade Organization (WTO), the United States in December 2005 formally recognized Ukraine as a market economy, with the EU following suit in February 2006.

The Ukrainian economy was hit extremely hard by the global financial crisis that erupted in late 2008. In November the IMF approved $16.4 billion in emergency lending over the next two years to help stabilize the financial system, although conditions attached to the lending proved domestically controversial. Declines of more than 50 percent in the metal and chemical industries contributed to a shocking 15 percent drop in GDP for 2009, with unemployment climbing to more than 9 percent and annual inflation reaching 22 percent.

In August 2010 the IMF approved a new 29-month, $15.1 billion loan agreement, while the World Bank in September agreed to additional support for the financial sector, particularly the recapitalization of Ukrainian banks. The government also implemented a new tax code late in the year, although some 40 percent of business reportedly remained in the "shadow economy" and Ukraine continued to decline in corruption rankings. Increased demand for steel and other exports contributed to growth of 4.1 percent and 5.2 percent for 2010 and 2011, respectively, while inflation declined to 4.6 percent and unemployment fell to 7.9 percent by the end of 2011. However real GDP growth fell dramatically to 0.2 percent in 2012 due to severe drought (which compromised the wheat harvest) and deteriorating trade conditions (including a reduction in global demand for steel). The economy remained in recession for the first half of 2013, and short-term prospects were described as bleak. However significant longer-term improvement was projected as the result of a major new oilfield discovery in the east in July 2013 and the recent signing of a $10 billion agreement with Royal Dutch Shell for exploitation of the nation's massive shale gas reserves.

GOVERNMENT AND POLITICS

Political background. Under Polish rule in the 16th century, Ukraine experienced a brief period of independence in the 17th century before coming under Russian control in the 18th century. Ukraine again proclaimed independence following the overthrow of the Russian tsarist regime in 1917, with the region becoming a battlefield of conflicting forces that eventually yielded a Red Army victory and Ukraine's incorporation into the USSR as a constituent republic in 1922.

On July 16, 1990, the Ukrainian Supreme Soviet, under pressure from nationalist opposition forces, issued a sovereignty declaration that asserted the "indivisibility of the republic's power on its territory," its "independence and equality in external relations," and its right to countermand the utilization of its citizens for military service beyond its boundaries. In an equivocal vein, however, it failed to claim a right of secession from the Soviet Union and explicitly provided for dual Soviet and Ukrainian citizenship. The less than clear-cut nature of the declaration prompted widespread nationalist demonstrations, led primarily by student activists. On October 23 the chair of the council of ministers, Vitaliy A. MASOL, responded by submitting his resignation; he was succeeded by Vitold FOKIN.

Ukraine endorsed Soviet President Mikhail Gorbachev's union proposal in April 1991 but, in the wake of the subsequent failed hard-line coup against Gorbachev in Moscow, issued a formal declaration of independence on August 24. On August 31 the chair of the Ukrainian Supreme Soviet, Leonid KRAVCHUK, suspended the activities of the Communist Party of Ukraine (*Komunistychna Partiya Ukrainy*—KPU), and on September 4 the leader of the KPU legislative bloc announced that the group would disband. On December 1, in a vote held simultaneously with Kravchuk's reconfirmation in direct presidential balloting, Ukrainians overwhelmingly endorsed the August independence declaration. On December 8 the republic joined Belarus and Russia in announcing the demise of the Soviet Union, and on December 21 Ukraine became a founding member of the Commonwealth of Independent States (CIS).

Fokin, who had continued as prime minister upon reorganization of the council of ministers in May 1991, survived a confidence vote on July 1, 1992, following a decision to raise food prices, but he was forced to step down on September 30 amid uncertainty over the direction and pace of the republic's economic reform program. He was succeeded on an acting basis by First Deputy Prime Minister Valentin SIMONENKO, who yielded the office on October 27 to Leonid D. KUCHMA, the "technocrat" director of the former Soviet Union's largest arms production complex.

Increasingly battered by conservative parliamentarians opposed to his economic reform efforts, Prime Minister Kuchma submitted his resignation for the fifth time in as many months on September 9, 1993, with the Supreme Council voting acceptance of the resignation on September 21. Kuchma's deputy, Yukhym ZVYAHILSKIY, was named acting prime minister, although President Kravchuk assumed direct control of the government by decree on September 27. (Three days earlier the Supreme Council had averted a constitutional crisis by agreeing that parliamentary and presidential elections would be held in the first half of 1994.)

In an apparent overture to his pro-Russian critics, President Kravchuk, on June 16, 1994, appointed Vitaliy Masol as prime minister. Masol, now an independent, had served as prime minister under Soviet rule in 1987–1990.

In first-round presidential balloting on June 26, 1994, incumbent president Kravchuk won 37.7 percent of the vote, as contrasted with 31.3 percent for former prime minister Kuchma. However, at the runoff on July 10, Kravchuk lost to his opponent, 45.1 percent to 52.1 percent; critical factors in Kuchma's success were the endorsement of his candidacy by the revived KPU and support for him in the eastern industrialized areas with a heavy ethnic Russian population. At his inauguration on July 19 the new head of state promised gradual electoral reform and closer ties to Russia. Prime Minister Masol resigned in March 1995, reportedly over economic policy differences with President Kuchma, who was seeking more active reform. Masol was replaced by Col. Gen. Yevhen MARCHUK, theretofore a deputy premier and state security chair.

The 292–4 parliamentary passage on April 4, 1995, of a motion of nonconfidence backed by both Communist conservatives and reformers precipitated a major political crisis. President Kuchma reappointed Prime Minister Marchuk on April 8 and tabled proposals to strengthen the powers of the presidency pending the adoption of a new constitution (see Constitution and government, below). The Supreme Council's failure to ratify the changes on May 30 caused the president to threaten to call a referendum, whereupon the legislature, cognizant of the wide public support for the changes, on June 15 acceded to an interim "constitutional treaty" that granted most of the new powers sought by Kuchma. Conflict over economic reform nevertheless simmered between the legislature and the president, with Kuchma's determined pursuit of a market economy generating strains not only between the president and the KPU-led bloc but also within the mainly centrist political groups that provided the president's core support.

Prime Minister Marchuk was dismissed by President Kuchma on May 27, 1996, ostensibly for shortcomings in the conduct of economic policy, and was replaced by the first deputy prime minister, Pavlo LAZARENKO. Following the adoption in June of a new constitution that permanently extended presidential authority, Kuchma reshuffled the cabinet in October and again in February 1997 in an attempt to deal with corruption, stabilize the financial system, and press on with economic reforms. In June 1997 Prime Minister Lazarenko was replaced on an acting basis by First Deputy Prime Minister Vasyl DURDYNETS, ostensibly because of Lazarenko's failing health. However, Lazarenko had faced serious allegations of corruption and antireform sentiment, and his ouster had reportedly been ordered by Kuchma. In July the legislature approved Kuchma's nomination of Valeriy PUSTOVOYTENKO, minister of cabinet affairs and a member of the People's Democratic Party of Ukraine (*Narodno-Demokratychna Partiya Ukrainy*—NDPU), as the new permanent prime minister.

In late 1997 a new electoral law was adopted to increase the role of political parties in legislative elections by providing for half the legislators to be selected from party lists in nationwide balloting. New Supreme Council balloting was conducted under the revised system for the first time on March 29, 1998. Thanks to a strong performance in the proportional poll, the KDU improved its representation substantially. However, the KDU-led left-wing opposition was still unable to achieve a majority, with many of the independent candidates elected in the single-member districts representing business interests supportive of President Kuchma's economic reform efforts. Consequently, Prime Minister Pustovoytenko remained in office following the election, although the cabinet was extensively reshuffled in early 1999.

Thirteen candidates contested the presidential election of October 31, 1999, including Kuchma, KPU leader Petro SYMONENKO, Oleksandr MOROZ of the Socialist Party of Ukraine (*Sotsialtstychna Partiya Ukrainy*—SPU), and former prime minister Yevhen Marchuk, who was backed by a number of smaller parties. (In August, Moroz, Marchuk, and two other candidates had agreed that they would unite behind one of their number before the election, but Marchuk's selection as the consensus candidate on October 25 immediately led Moroz to assert that he would nevertheless remain in the race. A third member of the "Kaniv Four," Oleksandr TKACHENKO, chair of the Supreme Council and leader of the Peasants' Party of Ukraine [*Selyanska Partiya Ukrainy*—SelPU], withdrew in favor of Symonenko, not Marchuk.) The first round of presidential balloting ended with Kuchma claiming 36.5 percent of the vote, necessitating a November 14 runoff against the second-place Symonenko, who had won 22.2 percent. With third-place finisher Moroz and the other leftist candidates having thrown their support to Symonenko for the second round, Kuchma wielded his presidential prerogatives in an effort to secure the victory. On November 3 he dismissed the governors of three regions that had supported either Moroz or Symonenko, and on November 10 he named Marchuk head of the National Security and Defense Council in a bid to gain the 8.1 percent support Marchuk had received as fifth-place finisher in the first round. In the runoff election Kuchma took 57.7 percent of the vote. The Parliamentary Assembly of the Council of Europe and the Organization for Security and Cooperation in Europe (OSCE) were among the observer organizations citing flaws in the conduct of the second round.

Following President Kuchma's inauguration for a second term on November 30, 1999, the cabinet resigned, as required by the constitution. Kuchma quickly renominated the incumbent prime minister, but on December 14 the Supreme Council rejected Pushtovoytenko by a vote of 206–44. Two days later Kuchma nominated reformist Viktor YUSHCHENKO, the nonparty chair of the National Bank of Ukraine, who was confirmed and sworn in on December 22. The new prime minister came into office pledging a reform program that included "open" privatization, lower inflation, a balanced budget, cuts in the size of the government bureaucracy, payment of remaining wage and pension arrears, and restructuring of the agricultural sector. (President Kuchma had proposed converting the country's 10,000 collective farms into cooperatives and joint stock companies.) Subsequent cabinet changes included the appointment by Kuchma of three new deputy prime ministers, including Yulia TYMOSHENKO, a leader of Fatherland (*Batkivshchnyna*) and a former energy industry executive, who assumed responsibility for fuel and energy policy in January 2000.

On January 13, 2000, former president Kravchuk announced formation of a government-supportive parliamentary majority by 11 center-right factions, including his own Social Democratic Party of Ukraine (United) (*Sotsial-Demokratychna Partiya Ukrainy [Obyednana]*—SDPU[O]) and a number of independent deputies. The new Supreme Council majority immediately attempted to remove the SelPU's Tkachenko as parliamentary chair, but obstruction from the left initially prevented a vote. Convening in a nearby exhibition hall, the 239-member majority voted Tkachenko out of office on January 21, and on February 1 it elected in his place Ivan PLYUSHCH, who had previously served in the same capacity. The leftist opposition continued to meet in the Supreme Council chamber despite lacking a quorum, but a week later a group of majority deputies forced its way into the building. By February 15 the leftist opposition effort had lost its momentum, and regular parliamentary sessions resumed shortly thereafter.

Despite her earlier background in the energy sector, Deputy Prime Minister Tymoshenko vowed in 2000 to fight the sector's oligarchs and to end graft, insisting, for example, that electricity contracts specify transparent cash settlements instead of the barter arrangements that had left the industry open to profiteering and abuse. However, by mid-2000 Tymoshenko was drawing fire from President Kuchma, who was particularly critical of a natural gas deal Tymoshenko had initialed with Turkmenistan to reduce reliance on Russia's Gazprom, to which several of Ukraine's oligarchs had connections.

On November 28, 2000, SPU leader Moroz released to the public audiotapes implicating President Kuchma and others in a plot to "get rid of" independent journalist and presidential critic Heorhiy GONGADZE, who had gone missing in mid-September and whose headless body had been recovered near Kiev in early November. Kuchma, supported by the prosecutor general's office, insisted that the relevant recordings were fabrications, although participants in other conversations on the tapes attested to their authenticity. In response to the scandal, an anti-Kuchma National Salvation Forum (NSF) was organized in February 2001, including as a member former deputy prime minister Tymoshenko, who had been dismissed by Kuchma in January after being formally charged with corruption while head of Unified Energy Systems of Ukraine in 1996–1997.

Tymoshenko characterized her January 2001 removal from office as a reprisal carried out by Kuchma on behalf of "criminal clans of oligarchs." For its part, the prosecutor general's office justified Tymoshenko's detention in February–March by citing new evidence that she had paid nearly $80 million in bribes to former prime minister Lazarenko while he was in office. (Lazarenko, his immunity from prosecution having been lifted by the Supreme Council in 1999, also continued to face numerous charges [ranging from accepting bribes to ordering contract killings] in Ukraine.) Moreover in June 2000 he was convicted in Switzerland of money laundering during his earlier tenure as governor of Dnepropetrovsk. Lazarenko, not to be outdone, charged in 2000 that Kuchma and his aides had themselves embezzled and laundered hundreds of millions of dollars, including proceeds from IMF loans that were used to purchase high-yielding Ukrainian debt.

In early 2001 a philosophically incongruous coalition, ranging from Oleksandr Moroz's Socialist Party to the fascist Ukrainian National Assembly (*Ukrainska Natsionalna Asambleya*—UNA), continued to stage a series of militant "Ukraine Without Kuchma" rallies. Meanwhile, the NSF, led by Moroz, Tymoshenko (who had quickly donned the mantle of an anticorruption, proreform antagonist), and others, also pressed for President Kuchma's resignation or removal from office. In addition, there were indications that the loyalty of Ukraine's oligarchs, who had been among Kuchma's strongest supporters, might also be wavering. As a further complication, Kuchma and Prime Minister Yushchenko were not always in agreement, although they jointly condemned the NSF in a February 2001 statement that was also signed by Supreme Council Chair Ivan Plyushch.

The new center-right parliamentary majority having already dissipated, the country's oligarchs in early 2001 demanded formation of a new government that would better represent their interests. (The oligarchs' "fiefdoms" were being threatened by Prime Minister Yushchenko's reform policies.) From the opposite side of the political spectrum, the Communists and other leftists joined the oligarchic parties in calling for the market-oriented, centrist Yushchenko to be replaced. After Yushchenko lost a no-confidence vote in the Supreme Council, 263–69, he submitted his resignation on April 27, and a day later President Kuchma dismissed the cabinet, which remained in office in a caretaker capacity. On May 29 the Supreme Council confirmed Anatoliy KINAKH, a former first deputy prime minister, as Yushchenko's successor. Kuchma announced the final appointments to a revamped cabinet on July 10.

In the context of ongoing efforts by a frequently fractious opposition to force President Kuchma's resignation or to impeach him, Ukrainians elected a new Supreme Council on March 30, 2002. Former prime minister Yushchenko's "Our Ukraine" Bloc (*Blok Viktora Yushchenka "Nasha Ukraina"*—NU) finished with a plurality of 110 seats, followed by the pro-Kuchma "For a United Ukraine!" Electoral Bloc (*Vyborchiy Blok "Za Yedinu Ukrainu!"*—ZYU) with 101, and the KPU with 66. The NU and the KPU were joined by the Yulia Tymoshenko Bloc (*Blok Yuliyi Tymoshenko*—BYT) and the SPU as the principal opposition formations, which, despite their ideological differences, pledged to renew a joint effort to force Kuchma from office.

On November 16, 2002, President Kuchma nominated Viktor YANUKOVYCH, the governor of the Donetsk *oblast* (province) and leader of the recently formed pro-Russian Party of Regions (*Partiya Rehioniv*—PR), to be the new prime minister. The appointment was confirmed with 234 votes in the Supreme Council on November 21.

In October 2002 a senior judge opened a criminal investigation into alleged corruption and abuse of power on the part of the Kuchma administration. Although the Supreme Court subsequently ordered the investigation suspended, anti-Kuchma demonstrations were held in major cities in 2003 and 2004, the opposition claiming that inappropriate force was used by security forces to quell the protests. Consequently, Kuchma in early 2004 announced that he would not seek reelection, despite having been authorized to run by the Constitutional Court. The three major presidential contenders thereby became Prime Minister Yanukovych (Kuchma's preference as a successor), former prime minister Yushchenko, and Oleksandr Moroz of the SPU. The presidential campaign subsequently became one the world's most closely watched political developments, one major focus of attention being the apparent poisoning of reformist candidate Yushchenko, who nearly died as a consequence of what was initially described as an unknown illness. (He later claimed that he had been poisoned during a meeting in September with leaders of the Ukrainian security forces.) Tests subsequently appeared to verify that Yushchenko was suffering from dioxin poisoning, which among other things, had left his face severely disfigured. For many observers, the before and after photos of Yushchenko seemed to encapsulate the essence of the presidential contest—a corrupt, perhaps criminal, entrenched administration (represented by Prime Minister Yanukovych, President Kuchma's handpicked candidate as his potential successor) versus a rising tide of reformists determined to shake off the last vestiges of a communist past. Of course, such analysis was simplistic at best, as Yanukovych enjoyed substantial genuine support in industrialized areas of eastern and southern Ukraine, where much of the population spoke Russian and continued to prefer strong ties with Russia. He also appeared generally content with the economic role of the nation's oligarchs. Meanwhile, Yushchenko campaigned on a pro-Western platform that called, among other things, for Ukraine's eventual membership in the EU and North Atlantic Treaty Organization (NATO). Underscoring Ukraine's long-standing geographic schism in that regard, Yushchenko's support was strongest in central and western areas of the country.

The first round of balloting on October 31, 2004, produced a close race between Yanukovych (40.20 percent of the vote) and Yushchenko (39.01 percent) with observers reporting numerous violations of fair election practices. The government announced that Yanukovych won the November 21 runoff balloting with 49.46 percent of the vote, compared to 46.31 percent for Yushchenko, prompting protest demonstrations in major Ukrainian cities as well as an international outcry over perceived fraud on the government's part. The Supreme Council refused to ratify Yanukovych's victory and ordered a second runoff for December 26, at which Yushchenko, now the leader of an Orange Revolution (so named after his main campaign color) achieved a clear victory with 52 percent of the vote. Yanukovych initially refused to accept the results, but, in the face of intense international pressure, he resigned as prime minister on December 31, paving the way for Yushchenko's inauguration on January 23, 2005. The following day Yushchenko named Yulia Tymoshenko, his main Orange Revolution partner, as prime minister. Her appointment was confirmed on February 4 via 457 votes in the Supreme Council. Prime Minister Tymoshenko's new cabinet contained a number of "Our Ukraine" ministers as well as representatives of the SPU and the Party of Industrialists and Entrepreneurs of Ukraine; the legislators from the KPU provided the main opposition to her appointments. The new administration promised immediate reform in many areas, most notably in regard to combating corruption. Consequently, a number of investigations were reportedly launched into the recent spate of privatizations, which some observers had characterized as members of its Kuchma/Yanukovych administration having "looted" public resources.

In March 2005 the government relaunched the criminal investigation into the Gongadze case, President Yushchenko charging that the previous administration had covered up the facts in the matter. However momentum toward uncovering the details of the previous privatizations (another reform goal) was subsequently reported to have slowed. It appeared that enthusiasm for the review of the privatizations had waned in part due to concern expressed by foreign investors, who reportedly feared that their interests might be compromised by such scrutiny. Consequently, the government announced new guidelines designed to convince investors that property rights would henceforth be protected.

Reform efforts also subsequently appeared to be compromised by the growing friction between President Yushchenko and Prime Minister Tymoshenko. In April 2005, faced with gasoline prices that had soared by 30 percent, Tymoshenko imposed mandatory price caps. Perhaps in protest, Russian oil suppliers (responsible for 80 percent of Ukraine's oil needs) subsequently cut back on their distribution to Ukraine, causing significant shortages and consumer angst. Consequently, Yushchenko ordered that the price caps be removed, arguing that they ran counter to his administration's commitment to a market economy. Analysts thereafter noted additional problems, including personal rivalries, that were constraining the ability of the disparate elements behind the Orange Revolution to enact change. Overall, the lack of effective action was seen as eroding the government's credibility both domestically and internationally only six months after the new administration had been installed amid much optimism.

Mutual allegations of corruption from the supporters of Yushchenko and Tymoshenko contributed to Tymoshenko's dismissal as prime minister on September 8, 2005.

Tymoshenko immediately announced that she and her supporters were crossing over to the opposition. On September 9 Yushchenko nominated Yuriy YEKHANUROV, the governor of the Dnepropetrovsk region and a member of the NU, to be the next prime minister. However, the appointment was able to muster only an insufficient 223 votes of support in the Supreme Council on September 20, forcing Yushchenko to offer significant concessions to Yanukovych in order to get support from the PR, which subsequently agreed to endorse Yekhanurov, who was confirmed with 289 votes on September 23. The new cabinet announced on September 27–28 was dominated by the NU, although a number of posts were filled by nonparty technocrats.

In early January 2006 Russia reduced the flow of natural gas to Ukraine in the wake of several months of conflict over prices. An agreement was reached a few days later that permitted a resumption of full deliveries, but opponents of the accord claimed that Ukraine was being forced to double its payments as a punishment for the Orange Revolution. Popular discontent also was exacerbated by the lack of progress in the Gongadze case. (The trial of three police officers charged with involvement in the journalist's death was initially adjourned for the judge to assess if state secrets were involved, and trial proceedings continued slowly. The three officers were convicted in March 2008, although critics of the investigation charged that the masterminds of the crime remained at large.)

The Supreme Council on January 10, 2006, passed a motion of no confidence against the Yekhanurov government. However, the government remained in place pending balloting for a new Supreme Council, which, under recent constitutional revision, would be empowered to appoint most of the new cabinet.

The March 26, 2006, legislative balloting produced a surprising plurality for the PR, with the BYT and NU, which had been unable to forge an electoral coalition, splitting the Orange Revolution vote. Several attempts by the NU and BYT to form a coalition government foundered over the ensuing months, as did the PR's attempts to find enough partners to achieve a legislative majority. Conditions reached a critical point by July, with President Yushchenko facing the choice of calling for new elections or accepting an arrangement with his former arch-rival Yanukovych. Finally, on August 3 Yushchenko agreed to nominate Yanukovych to lead a new government dominated by the PR but also including members of the SPU, NU, and KPU. The proposed government was approved the following day with 271 votes in the Supreme Council. However, friction between Yushchenko and Yanukovych contributed to the resignation of four NU ministers in October and the NU's concurrent decision to officially move into opposition.

Conflict between President Yushchenko and Prime Minister Yanukovych subsequently continued unremittingly. In addition to disagreement on foreign policy (Yanukovych remaining much more oriented toward Russia than Yushchenko), the uncomfortable cohabitation was strained by the prime minister's effort (in conjunction with the PR-dominated Supreme Council) to wrest control of the foreign and defense ministries from the president's control. Various legislative and court maneuvers resulted in a standoff, and after the NU and the BYT had announced their joint opposition to Yanukovych's anticrisis coalition in February 2007, mass demonstrations by supporters of both camps rocked the capital at the end of March.

Charging Yanukovych with "unconstitutional behavior" in regard to the alleged solicitation of floor crossing by NU legislators in order to maintain a legislative majority for the government, Yushchenko in April 2007 ordered that new legislative elections be held in late June. However the Supreme Council continued to meet in defiance of Yushchenko's dissolution decree and refused to allocate funds for new elections. With government essentially paralyzed, 169 NU and BYT legislators resigned in June, providing the basis for Yushchenko to issue another dissolution decree on the grounds that the legislature no longer had two-thirds of its seats filled (a constitutional requirement for its continuation). Although many of the legal issues remained unresolved, a compromise was reached between the PR and the NU/BYT in late May for new legislative elections on September 30. Interestingly, the campaign focused less on international issues such as relations with Russia and NATO and more on domestic affairs. (All three leading electoral blocs [the PR, BYT, and Yushchenko's NU-NS] made what independent analysts considered unrealistic campaign pledges regarding financial assistance to the working class.)

The September 30, 2007, Supreme Council balloting again revealed a deeply divided electorate, as the PR secured a plurality, but the BYT and Yushchenko's Our Ukraine–People's Self-Defense (*Nasha Ukraina–Narodna Samooborona*—NU-NS) bloc combined for a slim majority. After extensive negotiations between the BYT and the NU-NS, Yulia Tymoshenko returned to the premiership on December 18 after being approved by the Supreme Council by the barest possible majority (226 votes in the 450-member council).

Considering the history of bickering between Yushchenko and Tymoshenko, it was not surprising that the Orange Revolution "redux" of late 2007 failed to usher in a period of political calm. Continued disputes with Russia also roiled the political waters in the first half of 2008, as did Yushchenko's insistence that the April NATO summit approve a membership action plan for Ukraine. (Large PR-led demonstrations against the NATO initiative were conducted in several cities.) Although Tymoshenko was perceived as less vehemently anti-Russian than Yushchenko in regard to Russia's actions in Georgia in August, most independent observers concluded that the schism between the two leaders was primarily personal, not ideological. Their mutual antipathy continued to dominate political affairs, and on September 3, ministers and legislators from the NU-NS announced that they were withdrawing their support for the coalition government led by Prime Minister Tymoshenko. When Tymoshenko and the BYT were subsequently unable to entice the NU-NS back into the coalition, the speaker of the Supreme Council on September 15 declared that the government had formally collapsed. Negotiations toward a new coalition government subsequently failed, and on October 8 President Yushchenko ordered the dissolution of the Supreme Council and announced that new legislative balloting would be held on December 7. However, under pressure from Tymoshenko, the Supreme Council challenged the dissolution decree and refused to approve funds for the elections, which Yushchenko subsequently postponed. On December 9 it was announced that a new majority coalition had been formed in the Supreme Council by the BYT, some 40 of the legislators from the NU-NS, and the Lytvyn Bloc, whose leader, Volodymyr LYTVYN, was elected speaker of the council with 244 votes, signaling that the coalition enjoyed sufficient legislative support to preclude immediate snap elections.

In April 2009 the Supreme Council, which had recently forced the dismissal of Foreign Minister Volodymyr OHRYZKO (one of President Yushchenko's two cabinet appointees), called for early presidential elections to be held on October 25. However, Yushchenko challenged that initiative, and in May, the Constitutional Court declared the legislative resolution invalid. The first round of the next presidential balloting was therefore scheduled for January 2010. (An attempt by Yanukovych and Tymoshenko to forge a BYT–PR coalition had collapsed at midyear over the long-standing issue of the division of authority between the president and the prime minister [see BYT, below, for additional information].)

Former prime minister Viktor Yanukovych of the PR finished first in the first round of presidential balloting on January 17, 2010, with 35 percent of the vote. Prime Minister Tymoshenko finished second with 25 percent of the vote, while incumbent president Yushchenko secured only 5 percent. Yanukovych defeated Tymoshenko in the runoff on February 7 by a vote of 48.95 percent to 45.47 percent ("Against All Candidates" was also a voting option). Tymoshenko, who alleged fraud in the poll, initially refused to resign the premiership as requested by Yanukovych in order for him to install a new government. However, in early March the Lytvyn Block withdrew from the BYT-led government, and Tymoshenko resigned after losing a confidence motion in the Supreme Council. On March 10 Yanukovych named the PR's Mykola AZAROV to head a government comprising members of the PR (supported legislatively by the KPU), the Lytvyn Block, and independents, Yanukovych having convinced the legislature to loosen regulations regarding the formation of coalition governments (see Constitution and government, below). Azarov was reappointed in December 2012 following the October legislative elections, in which the PR secured a plurality that, with the support of independents and the KPU, proved sufficient to form another PR-led government.

Political background (Crimea). In 1954 the Soviet leadership transferred the Crimean autonomous republic from Russian to Ukrainian administration, despite Crimea's largely ethnic Russian population. Subsequent moves to "rehabilitate" the original Crimean Tatars, who had been transported to Central Asia during World War II because of alleged collaboration with the Germans, yielded the return of some 250,000 Tatars to Crimea by the early 1990s. (It has been recently estimated that there are 1 million ethnic Russians, 600,000 Ukrainians, and 300,000 Tatars in Crimea.)

The status of Crimea became intertwined with postindependence political developments when the aspiration of the majority ethnic Russian population for union with Russia generated strains in Moscow-Kiev relations (see Foreign relations, below). Also complicating matters was disaffection among the peninsula's original Tatar inhabitants. Another source of friction was the long-running dispute over the ownership of the ex-Soviet Black Sea fleet based in the Crimean port of Sevastopol. In February 1992 Ukraine refused a Russian request for the retrocession of Crimea on the grounds that the CIS agreement included a commitment to accept existing borders, to which the Russian *Duma* responded in May by declaring the 1954 transfer of Crimea to Ukraine unconstitutional and void. The *Duma*'s action was in support of a declaration of independence from Ukraine by the Crimean Supreme Soviet, which the Crimeans repealed after the Ukrainians had voted to annul its content by an overwhelming margin. Subsequently, the Ukrainian foreign ministry issued a statement declaring that "the status of the Crimea is an internal Ukrainian matter which cannot be the subject of negotiation with another state."

In June 1992 an agreement in principle between President Kravchuk of Ukraine and President Boris Yeltsin of Russia provided for the Black Sea fleet of more than 800 ships, including auxiliary vessels, to be divided equally between the two countries. Differences nevertheless persisted, accompanied by periodic incidents involving naval personnel in Sevastopol and by nationalist opposition to compromise in both parliaments.

The election of Yuriy MESHKOV, leader of the secessionist Republican Movement of Crimea (*Republikanskve Dvizheniya Kryma*—RDK), as Crimean president on January 31, 1994, was seen in Kiev as a threat to the country's territorial integrity. On May 19 the Crimean legislature voted to restore its proindependence constitution of May 1992, with Sevastopol declaring in August that it had "Russian legal status." The Ukrainian Supreme Council consequently adopted legislation designed to curb Crimea's autonomy, enacting a measure in November providing for the automatic invalidation of any Crimean legislation in conflict with Ukrainian law. In March 1995, moreover, the Kiev legislature annulled Crimea's constitution and effectively abolished the Crimean presidency, with Ukrainian President Kuchma assuming direct control over the region from April 1. Meshkov denounced these actions as unconstitutional, although plans to hold a referendum on the separatist 1992 basic law were canceled at the end of May. In June 1995 Presidents Kuchma and Yeltsin reached a further accord, with Russia agreeing to buy part of the Ukrainian half of the Black Sea fleet, thus increasing its share to 81 percent. (Both sides retained naval bases in Sevastopol.)

Kuchma rescinded his direct rule over Crimea via decree in August 1995, while asserting that candidates for the Crimea premiership had to be approved by him. In February 1996 the appointment of Arkady DEMYDENKO as Crimean prime minister was so confirmed.

In May 1997 Russian president Yeltsin made a state visit to Ukraine to sign a 10-year friendship treaty and to resolve remaining differences over the Black Sea fleet. By virtue of a 20-year lease, the fleet was to be based primarily in Sevastopol. Both the Russian and Ukrainian navies were to use Streletskaya Bay, but the rest of the Black Sea would be used exclusively by Ukraine. Russia also would recognize Crimea and the city of Sevastopol as Ukrainian territory. In addition, the agreement would settle questions about Ukraine's bilateral debts and its claims on ships the Russians "inherited" upon the dissolution of the Soviet Union. (In February 1999 the Russian *Duma* ratified the treaty, which formally recognized, for the first time, Ukraine's sovereignty within its current borders.)

On June 3, 1997, Ukrainian president Kuchma approved the dismissal of Crimean prime minister Demydenko after the Crimean parliament had voted three times to sack Demydenko. Kuchma subsequently approved the appointment of Anatoli FRANCHUK, Kuchma's ally and a former Crimean premier (1994–1995), as Crimean prime minister; Franchuk's cabinet was approved by the Crimean parliament on June 19.

Elections to the Crimean Supreme Council were conducted on March 29, 1998, in conjunction with the balloting for the Ukrainian Supreme Council. Left-wing parties advanced in the Crimean Supreme Council, which elected Leonid HRACH of the Communist Party of Crimea (*Kommunisticheskaya Partiya Kryma*—KPK) as its new speaker. However, in an apparent reflection of the balance of power maintained at the national level, Kuchma named Serhiy KUNITSYN, the leader of the centrist factions in the Crimean Supreme Council, as the new Crimean prime minister on May 19. Subsequently, in January 1999, a new constitution was adopted for Crimea, which, among other things, was granted substantial budgetary authority.

Tensions between factions loyal to Hrach and Kunitsyn subsequently continued to play out, with Hrach repeatedly working through the legislature for Kunitsyn's dismissal. In September 2000 President Kuchma commented that he saw no need for the removal of Kunitsyn given the current balance of powers in the province, but on July 18, 2001, the Crimean legislature voted to dismiss Kunitsyn, who stepped down five days later. Kuchma then named Valeriy HORBATOV as Kunitsyn's successor. However, Kunitsyn returned to the Crimean prime minister's post in April 2002 following the March Crimean legislative elections, which were reportedly marred by numerous irregularities. (Horbatov had been elected to the Ukrainian Supreme Court.)

Tension between Crimea and the national government continued to simmer into 2004, as the Russian nationalists who dominated Crimea pressed for designation of Russian as an official language and for stronger military and political links with Russia. In the wake of the Orange Revolution at the national level in late 2004 and early 2005, Kunitsyn resigned as Crimean prime minister in April 2005, being described as the last major leader of the Kuchma era to leave office. He was succeeded by Anatoliy MATVIYENKO, a close associate of Ukrainian Prime Minister Tymoshenko and a member of the BYT. However, Matviyenko also fell victim to national politics a few months later when Tymoshenko and President Yushchenko became estranged. Anatoliy BURDYUHOV, a member of the NU, was named in September to replace Matviyenko as head of a Crimean government that included a number of bankers (including Burdyuhov) and increased representation for the Crimean Tatars.

Prior to the March 26, 2006, balloting for the Crimean Supreme Council, the region was described as still polarized along ethnic lines and suffering economic malaise. Not surprisingly, considering the fact that ethnic Russians constituted 60 percent of the Crimean population, the pro-Russian For Yanukovych Bloc won a strong plurality of 44 seats in the new council. With President Yushchenko's endorsement, Viktor PLAKYDA was selected in June as the new Crimean prime minister. Plakyda, the former director of the Crimean energy company, announced his intention to focus on economic development. However, political discord continued to dominate regional events as evidenced by major protests against the North Atlantic Treaty Organization (NATO) that forced cancellation of planned Ukrainian-U.S. military exercises in June as well as by ongoing calls from members of the Russian *Duma* for the reannexation of Crimea by Russia.

International attention focused on Crimea in August 2008 following the military conflict between Russia and Georgia over South Ossetia, observers wondering if the Russian hard line might also soon extend to Crimea. However Russian leaders, at least at the national level, continued to disavow any interest in regaining sovereignty over Crimea. Meanwhile, the Crimean Supreme Council in mid-September endorsed Russia's recognition of the independence of South Ossetia and Abkhazia.

Leaders of the Crimean Tatars in 2010 criticized the pro-Russian leanings of new Ukrainian president Yanukovych, particularly in regard to the new lease arrangement for the Russian Black Sea Fleet (see Current issues, below).

Crimean prime minister Plakyda resigned in March 2010, and he was succeeded by Vasyl DZHARTY, a former Ukrainian minister of the environment and natural resources who was described as having an open mind concerning Tatar legal efforts to reclaim land and property confiscated during World War II. When Dzharty died in August 2011, he was succeeded by Anatoliy MOHYLOV, who as chief of police in Crimea from 2007 to 2010 had overseen a crackdown on Tatar protest demonstrations.

Constitution and government. In mid-1990 the Council of Ministers was restructured as a Western-style cabinet headed by a prime minister. Coincident with his formal reinstallation as Ukrainian head of state on December 5, 1991, Leonid Kravchuk's title changed from chair of the Supreme Soviet to president of the republic. The draft of a new constitution published in October 1993 called for retention of most of the existing governmental structure, providing for a 450-seat Supreme Council and a Council of Ministers guided by a president directly elected for a five-year term.

Under the terms of the June 1995 interim "constitutional treaty," a Constitutional Commission completed work on the draft of a new constitution in March 1996. Despite some opposition to stronger presidential authority at the expense of the legislature, the Supreme Council in June adopted the new text; it granted significant new powers to the president, including the right to name the prime minister (with the concurrence of a parliamentary majority) and other officials, and recognized the right to own private property. In addition, the new basic law provided for the establishment of a National Security and Defense Council and for the holding of parliamentary and presidential elections in March 1998 and October 1999, respectively. It also specified that parliamentary deputies could not simultaneously hold government appointments. The parliament in September 1997 approved a mixed voting system for the Supreme Council, designating that half of the council members be directly elected from single-seat constituencies, with the remaining 225 seats being apportioned to parties that received at least 4 percent of all ballots cast in separate nationwide balloting.

In an April 2000 referendum voters overwhelmingly approved four Kuchma proposals that, if enacted, would have cut the number of legislative deputies from 450 to 300, added an appointive upper chamber to parliament to represent regional interests, limited legislators' immunity from prosecution, and given the president authority to dismiss the parliament if it went more than a month without a working majority or if it failed to pass the annual budget within three months of submission. Kuchma lobbied for the measures as a means of furthering "the systematic and efficient work of the legislature," whereas the majority of the Supreme Council saw the referendum as Kuchma's attempt to diminish the council's authority and to install a presidential system of government. In January 2001 the Supreme Council instead passed a bill adopting a strictly proportional party-list system for the next general election, with parties having to achieve 4 percent of the vote to obtain representation. The bill obviously favored the larger parties and factions and could have dramatically altered the balance of power in the Supreme Council. However, Kuchma promptly vetoed the electoral bill.

In August 2002 President Kuchma announced formation of a constitutional commission to study reforms in the hope of eliminating the administrative impasses that had characterized governance since independence. Among other things, he again called for establishment of a bicameral legislature. However, his lack of a legislative majority precluded progress.

A number of constitutional revisions were negotiated as part of the resolution of the presidential crisis of late 2004. Under the changes (which went into effect on January 1, 2006), significant authority previously exercised by the president was transferred to the Supreme Council. Although the president retained the formal right to nominate the prime minister, the Supreme Council acquired de facto control of the post. The Supreme Council was also given authority over all cabinet appointments except for the defense and foreign affairs portfolios, which remained under the president's purview. In addition, the Supreme Council was authorized to dismiss the prime minister and cabinet members. The basic law revisions also decreed that all 450 members of the Supreme Council would henceforth be elected by proportional voting.

In the midst of ongoing conflict between the president and the prime minister, the Supreme Council in December 2006 adopted additional legislation designed to further undercut presidential prerogatives. However, President Yushchenko refused to sign the new legislation, asking for a review by the Constitutional Court. The issue of the division of authority between the president and the prime minister/legislature subsequently remained contentious, although legislation was approved in May 2008 confirming that the foreign affairs and defense ministers were presidential nominees. Yushchenko presented his proposals to the Supreme Council in March 2009 for constitutional revision, based on recommendations from the National Constitutional Council he had established in late 2007. However, little attention was given to his proposals (including creation of a bicameral legislature and codification of substantial presidential authority) because of his diminished legislative clout.

Prior to trying to form a new government in March 2010, President Yanukovych successfully lobbied the Supreme Council to approve amendments to the laws regarding the formation of government coalitions. Previously, factions in the legislature were required to vote as blocs in regard to proposed governments. However, the revisions permitted individual legislators to vote for a coalition on their own, the change permitting Yanukovych to get legislative endorsement for the new government with the help of defectors from opposition parties (see Current issues, below).

In October 2010, at the urging of the Yanukovych administration, the Constitutional Court voided the constitutional changes (approved in 2004 and implemented in 2006) under which the Supreme Council had been given responsibility for most cabinet appointments and other previously presidential prerogatives. Under the 2010 changes, only the prime minister now requires legislative approval, not the other cabinet members. Electoral law revision in 2011 returned elections for the Supreme Council to a mixed proportional/majoritarian system.

A Supreme Court was installed in January 1997; there is also a Constitutional Court with members appointed by the president, legislature, and the bar association. In addition, the 2005 Code of Administrative Procedure provided for an additional court system headed by a High Administrative Court to deal with a variety of issues, including election-related cases.

Ukraine is divided into 24 provinces (*oblasts*), with Crimea administered as an autonomous republic. The metropolitan areas of Kiev and Sevastopol have special status. Local self-government functions in divisions and subdivisions.

Freedom of speech is guaranteed in the Ukrainian constitution, but prior to liberalization following the Orange Revolution, opposition publications were frequently subjected to official harassment and libel suits brought by government officials. Collaterally, domestic and international advocates for freedom of expression criticized the Ukrainian government for inadequately investigating the disappearance and murder of independent journalist Heorhiy Gongadze in 2000. The Parliamentary Assembly of the Council of Europe, for one, cited "intimidation, repeated aggressions, and murders" directed against journalists.

The Kuchma administration passed legislation in 2004 allowing the government to monitor Internet publications and e-mails, an initiative critics claimed was aimed at popular opposition Web sites. The hard line toward media freedom was perceived as partially responsible for the popular antigovernment sentiment that propelled the Orange Revolution in late December 2004, after which the Yushchenko administration pledged quick liberalization in favor of a Western-style media policy. The media were subsequently generally perceived as operating freely in regard to criticizing government officials. However, growing concern has been reported recently in regard to increased pressure on journalists by the Yanukovych administration. In 2011–2012 Reporters Without Borders announced that Ukraine had fallen dramatically in world rankings on press freedom, the journalistic watchdog organization citing a number of recent physical attacks on reporters.

Foreign relations. Although at the time not an independent country, Ukraine, like Byelorussia (now Belarus), was accorded founding membership in the UN in 1945 as a gesture to the USSR, which feared the world body would have an anti-Soviet bias. Theretofore not a member of the IMF or World Bank, independent Ukraine was admitted to both institutions in September 1992; earlier, it had become a member of the Conference on (subsequently Organization for) Security and Cooperation in Europe (CSCE/OSCE) following the demise of the Soviet Union and the creation of the CIS in December 1991.

Ukrainian leaders insisted following independence that they wished the country to become nuclear free, even though a substantial proportion of the former USSR's nuclear arsenal was located in Ukraine. Although Ukraine was a signatory of the 1992 Lisbon Protocol to the 1991 Strategic Arms Reduction Treaty (START I), which designated Russia as the sole nuclear power in the CIS, implementation was delayed by difficulties over the terms demanded by the Ukrainian government and the Ukrainian nationalist opposition. Not until November 1993 did the Ukrainian Supreme Council conditionally ratify START I, while indicating that it was not prepared to endorse the Nuclear Non-Proliferation Treaty (NPT) without substantial Western security guarantees, financial assistance for weapons dismantling, and compensation for nuclear devices transferred to Russia for destruction. The conditional ratification and statement of terms yielded speedy progress in January 1994 on a tripartite agreement, whereby the United States would provide assistance for the dismantling of nuclear weapons by Ukraine, with warheads being shipped to Russia for destruction. Eventually, Ukraine would also receive about $1 billion, via Russia, from the sale of reprocessed uranium from the warheads. In accordance with the agreement, Ukraine began shipping warheads to Russia in early March, and in December Ukraine formally acceded to the NPT, following parliamentary ratification the previous month. (On June 1, 1996, President Kuchma announced that Ukraine had completed the process of nuclear disarmament by transferring the last of its warheads to Russia.)

Ukraine acceded to NATO's Partnership for Peace program in February 1994, and in June it signed a partnership and cooperation agreement with the EU. An important aspect of the latter accord was the provision of EU aid for closure of the remaining nuclear reactors in Chernobyl, site of the world's worst nuclear accident (in 1986). Having been formally admitted to the Council of Europe in November 1995, Ukraine became a full member of the Central European Initiative (CEI) in May 1996 and was granted observer status within the Nonaligned Movement in September. In September 1997 Ukraine tentatively agreed to a plan by which it would join the Central European Free Trade Agreement (CEFTA, see Foreign relations in the entry on Poland), though no firm timetable was announced (Ukraine had not joined by late 2013). A new EU economic cooperation agreement with Ukraine took effect on March 1, 1998, committing each to increased trade and investment. Ukraine concurrently indicated that it eventually intended to apply for full EU membership.

As one of the largest recipients of U.S. foreign aid, Ukraine bowed to the pressure from the United States and Israel in March 1998 and declined to sell turbines for Russia to use in nuclear reactors destined for Iran. The agreement on commercial nuclear technology removed an impediment to improved relations with Washington at a time of sharply increased contacts between Ukraine and NATO officials. Despite the prospect of reprisals by Russia, which asked Kiev not to cancel the turbine contract, Ukraine tried to maintain the momentum it had gained in July 1997 when it had signed a cooperation charter with NATO. The agreement, reportedly modeled on the Russia-NATO Founding Act of May 1997, established a special relationship (short of membership) that included the exchange of military missions and the establishment of a NATO-Ukraine Commission, through which Ukraine could consult with NATO if it came under an external threat. In March 1998, clarifying its neutrality and its relationship with the Western alliance, Kiev said it did not rule out joining NATO in the future if membership would not jeopardize its relationship with neighbors, particularly Russia. President Kuchma also endorsed the expansion of NATO in March 1999 (again contrary to Moscow's wishes), although he condemned the subsequent NATO military campaign in the former Yugoslavia.

In June 1997 the presidents of Ukraine and Romania signed a treaty, subsequently approved by their respective parliaments, confirming existing borders and protecting the rights of national minorities. Meanwhile, the informal "Union of Three" alliance of Georgia, Ukraine, and Azerbaijan became identified through the abbreviation GUAM when Moldova joined the group in October. Earlier, in the fall of 1996, those former Soviet bloc nations had begun to strengthen their economic and political relationships based on a common pro-Western orientation, suspicion of Russia, and the prospects of collaborating on the exploitation of Azerbaijan's Caspian oil reserves. GUAM expanded to the GUUAM upon the accession of Uzbekistan in April 1999. (In May 2005 Uzbekistan withdrew from the grouping, which in May 2006 changed its name to the GUAM Organization for Democracy and Economic Development.)

Having received grant and loan pledges valued in the billions of dollars from the European Bank for Reconstruction and Development (EBRD) and other multilateral agencies as well as individual countries, Ukraine officially shut down the last operating nuclear reactor in Chernobyl on December 15, 2000. The financial and technical assistance was targeted for a range of projects, including construction of a more permanent sarcophagus around the highly radioactive reactor that was destroyed by the 1986 explosion. Other priorities included building replacement power facilities, upgrading safety at remaining nuclear plants, and aiding the local population.

A decade after the demise of the Soviet Union, delineation of Ukraine's borders with Moldova and Romania remained somewhat problematic. A treaty concluded with Moldova in 1999 provided the basis for border demarcation that began in late 2003. Meanwhile, negotiations with Romania continued over areas encompassing various arms of the Danube, the adjacent delta, the Black Sea continental shelf, and the minuscule Zmiyiny (Serpent) Island in potentially oil- and gas-rich waters in the Black Sea. (The question of Serpent Island and maritime delimitation in the Black Sea was submitted in 2004 to the International Court of Justice, which in February 2009 issued a ruling that awarded partial control to both countries but appeared to favor Romania by declining to classify the islet as qualifying for maritime demarcation.) Romania has long claimed Northern Bukovina and Southern Bessarabia, which it ceded to the Soviet Union in 1940, and fervent Romanian nationalists remained committed to incorporating the two areas into a Greater Romania.

Ukraine's foreign policy under President Kuchma was driven by two seemingly contradictory goals: to maintain friendly relations with Russia on the one hand and to open the door to Europe with a possible view to membership in the EU on the other. In reference to the former, in 2003 Kuchma was elected as chair of the CIS, becoming the first non-Russian to hold the post. In addition, treaties were signed in 2003 delineating the land boundary between Russia and Ukraine as well as resolving the status of the Sea of Azov as joint territorial waters. At the same time, the Kuchma administration sought to counterbalance its close relations with Russia through a policy of engagement with the United States and the EU. In pursuit of this opening to the West, Kuchma sent 1,650 troops to serve in Iraq in 2003, even though the Supreme Council had approved a motion condemning the U.S.-led intervention there. (The troops were withdrawn in 2005.)

The victory of Viktor Yushchenko in the controversial 2004 presidential race put a strain on Ukraine's relations with Russia, as Russian president Vladimir Putin had openly supported Yushchenko's main opponent, Viktor Yanukovych. However, Yushchenko's first foreign visit after his inauguration was to Moscow, where he pledged continued close relations. At the same time, Yushchenko intensified Ukraine's efforts to join the EU and endorsed eventual membership in NATO.

In what was seen as at least a symbolically significant initiative, in November 2005 the EU sent 70 police and customs personnel to help combat smuggling along the Ukrainian-Moldovan border. The EU also recognized Ukraine as having a market economy in February 2006, an important step toward further integration. However, the EU clearly remained skeptical of further membership expansion and as of late 2007 was only offering Ukraine additional economic cooperation, with accession remaining off the negotiating table for the immediate future. By that time it was also apparent that possible NATO membership had also receded from both Ukraine's and NATO's immediate concerns. Significantly, public opinion in Ukraine reportedly opposed NATO accession, particularly in view of Russia's strong objection to such an initiative. Russia was also distressed over the passage by Ukraine's Supreme Council in mid-2007 of legislation needed to proceed with Ukraine's WTO membership request. Analysts agreed that Moscow preferred that Ukraine not join the WTO unless Russia also gained admission; however, Ukraine acceded to the WTO in May 2008, Ukrainian officials indicating that they expected the WTO membership to enhance the country's EU membership prospects.

In late March 2008 the United States and Ukraine reached agreement on "strategic priorities" and additional trade cooperation. U.S. president Bush also urged the April NATO summit to approve a Membership Action Plan (MAP) for both Ukraine and Georgia despite Russia's continued strong objections. Although no MAPs were approved (primarily due to opposition from France and Germany), the summit appeared to endorse eventual memberships for Ukraine and Georgia. In the opinion of most analysts, the NATO issue contributed to Russia's intensifying hard line regarding regional security issues, culminating in the Georgian-Russian military conflict in August. Arguing that Crimea could be the next focus for Russia (despite Russia's insistence that it did not challenge Ukraine's current borders), President Yushchenko immediately called for Ukraine's accelerated integration into "Euro-Atlantic structures."

An acrimonious dispute erupted with Russia in January 2009 over the delivery of natural gas to Ukraine as well as the transshipment of gas through Ukraine to EU countries, several of which suffered shortages before resolution was achieved. Although the EU was critical of Ukrainian leaders (as well as those in Russia) in the matter, it nevertheless included Ukraine among the six post-Soviet countries invited in May to participate in the EU's Eastern Partnership. Subsequently, in June, new U.S. vice president Joseph Biden during a visit to Ukraine affirmed the U.S. administration's continued support for Ukraine's eventual NATO membership, despite recent U.S. efforts to improve U.S. relations with Russia. For his part, Russian president Medvedev in August accused Ukrainian president Yushchenko of pursuing "anti-Russian policies" and urged Yushchenko's defeat in the upcoming presidential poll. Following his election in early 2010, President Yanukovych initially appeared to steer Ukrainian foreign policy on a pro-Russian course that essentially precluded NATO accession. However, Yanukovych also pledged to continue to pursue further integration with the EU, and his relationship with Russian leaders was subsequently viewed as complicated. Among other things, Russian prime minister Putin objected to the prosecution of former Ukrainian prime minister Tymoshenko in regard to a ten-year Russian-Ukrainian gas contract signed in 2009. Putin in 2011 encouraged Ukraine to join the customs and trade union recently established by Belarus, Kazakhstan, and Russia. Yanukovych deflected consideration of such a move, analysts noting that Ukraine's full participation in the new union might interfere with further Ukrainian integration with the EU. (Putin had reportedly offered Ukraine a massive reduction in gas prices in return for Ukraine's commitment to the union.)

In the second half of 2011 the EU postponed completion of a significant trade and association agreement with Ukraine out of concern over Tymoshenko's arrest and conviction. Although the accord was ultimately initialed in March 2012, final approval remained suspended at least until the Eastern Partnership summit scheduled for November 2013, while Ukraine addressed EU concerns regarding "selective justice" and electoral deficiencies. (*See headnote.*)

Current issues. It was difficult to determine what was the most dramatic aspect of the presidential elections in early 2010—the remarkable reversal of fortune for Viktor Yanukovych after the fiasco of 2004 or the decline of President Yushchenko to only 5 percent of the vote in the first round of balloting. Meanwhile, although international observers characterized the poll as generally fair (despite a "bitter" campaign), Prime Minister Tymoshenko charged that vote-rigging had cost her victory in the second round. In forming a new government, Yanukovych benefited from revised regulations in regard to coalitions (see Constitution and government, above), which allowed six renegade legislators each from the BYT and the NU-NS to join independents and the deputies from the PR, KPU, and Lytvyn Bloc to provide 235 votes in the Supreme Council in support of new prime minister Mykola Azarov's "Stability and Reforms" coalition.

The new 2010 cabinet was all-male (drawing heavy criticism from feminist and other liberal groups) and dominated by prominent businessmen associated with the PR. Analysts described Azarov, a Russian-born former finance minister who had headed the tax administration under President Kuchma, as a "stern figure" who would focus primarily on economic recovery, leaving domestic and international political affairs to Yanukovych. In that regard, although Yanukovych pledged to pursue "equal relations" with Russia and the West, his initial pro-Moscow orientation quickly became clear. Perhaps most noteworthy was the signing in April of a lease extension under which Russia was given the right to base its Black Sea Fleet at Sevastopol until 2042 (the current lease had been scheduled to expire in 2017). Among other things, the extension effectively ended further consideration of Ukraine's possible accession to NATO, which forbids members to host military forces from non-NATO countries. Ukraine and Russia also announced new arrangements for the delivery of Russian natural gas as Russian president Dmitri Medvedev expressed his joy at "finally" having a "worthy Ukrainian partner."

In June 2010 President Yanukovych proposed major economic reforms, including reinvigoration of the stalled privatization of state-run enterprises, overhaul of the tax system, and introduction of various budget-tightening measures (including a controversial increase in the price paid by consumers for natural gas). As evidenced by the new IMF agreement in July, the international community appeared for the most part to endorse the new administration's economic policies. On the political front, however, assessments were more critical, particularly as Yanukovych adopted a Russian-style "managed democracy," under which the executive branch dominates. In the view of critics, the government's increasingly authoritarian bent was evidenced by increased pressure on journalists, the growing influence of politics within the judiciary, and constraints imposed on small parties in advance of the October 31 elections for mayoralties and provincial and municipal legislatures. (Western observers called those polls, in which the PR led all contenders by a wide margin, as a step backwards for democratization.) Many analysts also characterized the reopening of the bribery case (closed in 2005) against Tymoshenko and the arrest of several members of her recent government as politically motivated. Finally, prosecutors concluded their investigation into the Gongadze case by saying that the murder had been ordered solely by then interior minister Yury KRAVCHENKO, who himself had died mysteriously in March 2005 (authorities had ruled the death a suicide). The ruling appeared to close the case (except for the ongoing prosecution of the alleged hit man—Oleksiy PUKACH), and skeptics noted that it might preclude any action against officials from that era who are still alive. (In a surprising development, the prosecutor general's office in the first half of 2011 announced that former president Kuchma was being charged with "exceeding his authority" in the case, with the inference that he might have played an at least indirect role in the events leading up to Gongadze's murder. However, the case against Kuchma was dropped in December after the Constitutional Court ruled that the evidence against him had been illegally obtained through secret audio recordings. Subsequently Pukach was convicted in January 2013 and sentenced to life in prison.)

Former prime minister Tymoshenko was formally charged in December 2010 with abuse of power while in office. That charge involved the use of so-called carbon credits to pay state pensions. Additional charges were placed against her in April 2011 in regard to the 2009 gas contract signed with Russia. Investigations and trials involving former officials from Tymoshenko's government were also launched, and Tymoshenko gained widespread international support for her claim that the prosecutions were politically motivated. The EU was particularly critical of the administration's approach, characterizing it as a "contravention" of EU standards and suggesting that Tymoshenko's conviction might prove a hindrance to the proposed negotiation of an EU-Ukrainian trade deal.

Domestic critics of the government described the "political" trials of 2011 as part of a broader repression of democratic expression that had also affected journalists and numerous civic organizations. Several demonstrations also broke out to protest the spending cuts and other retrenchment (including pension reform) enacted by the Yanukovych administration at the request of the IMF.

In October 2011 Tymoshenko was sentenced to seven years in prison following her conviction for abuse of power in connection with the 2009 gas contract with Russia. The conviction and sentencing set off a firestorm of protest among her domestic supporters and the international community. Nonetheless, the verdict and sentence were subsequently upheld in the courts, and President Yanukuvych brushed aside calls for him to issue a pardon. In fact, prosecutors in April 2012 filed new charges of tax evasion against Tymoshenko, whose supporters alleged that she was being mistreated in prison. The issue damaged Ukraine's relationship with the EU (see Foreign Relations, above) and dominated the run-up to the October 2012 legislative poll, in which the PR faced strong competition from Tymoshenko's Fatherland and two surging groups—the right-wing Freedom (*Svoboda*) party and Vitali Klitschko's Ukrainian Democratic Alliance for Reform (UDAR).

The PR was credited with securing a plurality of 185 seats in the October 28, 2012, balloting for the Supreme Council, although voters also provided strong support for the opposition, which organized demonstrations in early November to protest alleged fraud surrounding the poll. Meanwhile, the OSCE argued that "democratic progress" appeared to have been reversed, citing the abuse of power and excessive role of money in general and extensive irregularities in the counting of the votes in the single-member constituencies in particular. The EU subsequently reaffirmed that the "erosion of democracy" was jeopardizing further integration with Ukraine, and in an apparent response, President Yanukovych in April 2013 pardoned two of the recently convicted opposition leaders. A possible agreement to permit Tymoshenko to leave jail to travel to another country for medical treatment was also reportedly under consideration in October.

POLITICAL PARTIES

As of early 2001, there were 110 officially registered parties in Ukraine. In January 2001 a reported 11 parties and 30 civic groups joined the Ukrainian Right-Wing (*Ukrainska Pravytsya*) alliance as a step toward consolidation of anti-Kuchma forces on the right. It was largely superseded, however, by formation in February of the National Salvation Front (NSF), which was organized as a "citizens' initiative," primarily by supporters of Yulia Tymoshenko. The NSF had as its goals coordinating activities with the "Ukraine Without Kuchma" movement, advancing a center-right legislative agenda, and marshaling diplomatic support for its anti-Kuchma stance. At the same time, other elements on the center-right coalesced around former prime minister Viktor Yushchenko, and in July they announced formation of an electoral bloc, "Our Ukraine" ("*Nasha* Ukraina"—NU).

In July 2001 the NSF formed an electoral committee that Tymoshenko indicated was prepared to engage in "peaceful coexistence or cooperation" with Yushchenko, but Yushchenko ultimately rejected any alliance with Tymoshenko. In early November the NSF was renamed the Yulia Tymoshenko Bloc (*Blok Yuliyi Tymoshenko*—BYT). Parties in the BYT initially included Fatherland, USDP, UNP *"Sobor,"* and URP. Meanwhile, in October the pro-Kuchma forces had established the third principal electoral bloc, "For a United Ukraine!" (*Vyborchiy Blok "Za Yedinu Ukrainu!"*—ZYU), which was chaired by Volodymyr LYTVYN, head of presidential administration. The parties in the ZYU included the Agrarian Party of Ukraine (APU), NDPU, PPPU, PR, and TU. (The ZYU finished second in the 2002 legislative balloting with 102 seats.) Forces on the left continued to be led by the Communist Party of Ukraine (KPU) and the Socialist Party of Ukraine (SPU).

Twenty-eight parties competed independently in the March 2006 legislative balloting, while another 50 parties participated in 17 electoral blocs, including a revamped NU and a slightly modified BYT. Under recent changes in the electoral law, parties were required to have been registered for at least one year to participate in the elections. Twenty-one parties or blocs presented candidates in the 2007 legislative poll, and 21 parties contested the proportional component of the 2012 elections, many small parties having opted to have their members included on a larger party's official slate. (Under electoral law changes approved in 2011, bloc lists, which had previously referenced multiple parties, were no longer permitted.)

Government and Government-Supportive Parties:

Party of Regions (*Partiya Rehioniv*—PR). The PR held its initial congress in March 2001 as the culmination of a process that began with the signing of a merger agreement by five centrist parties in July 2000. Connected to Donetsk financial and industrial interests, the nascent PR quickly formed a new parliamentary faction, Regions of Ukraine.

Of the PR's five founding organizations, the Labor Party of Ukraine (*Partiya Pratsi Ukrainy*—PPU) dated from late 1992, when it was organized by elements descended from Soviet-era official unions. Led by Valentyn LANDYK, the PPU participated in the 1998 general elections in the "Together" electoral alliance with the LPU (below). The Party of Regional Revival of Ukraine (*Partiya Rehionalnoho Vidrodzhennya Ukrainy*—PRVU), which won 0.9 percent of the proportional vote in the 1998 legislative election, was led by Donetsk's mayor, Volodymyr RYBAK, and Yukhym ZVYAHILSKIY. The other three founding parties were the recently formed Party "For a Beautiful Ukraine" (*Partiya "Za Krasyvu Ukrainu"*—PZKU), led by Leonid CHERNOVETSKIY; the All-Ukrainian Party of Pensioners (*Vseukrainskoi Partiya Pensioneriv*—VPP), led by Andriy KAPUSTA and Hennadiy SAMOFALOV; and the Party of Solidarity of Ukraine (*Partiya*

Solidarnosti Ukrainy—PSU), formed in July 2000 by the Solidarity (*Solidarnist*) parliamentary faction under Petro POROSHENKO.

In November 2000 the emerging grouping had adopted the unwieldy designation Party of Regional Revival "Labor Solidarity of Ukraine" (*Partiya Rehionalnoho Vidrodzhennya "Trudova Solidarnist Ukrainy"*). At the time, it was considered pro-Kuchma, while claiming to represent the interests of the regions within a unified state. At the March founding congress, Mykola Azarov, the chair of the State Tax Administration, was elected chair of the party, although he was quoted as saying he saw the position as temporary. Poroshenko, who had reportedly sought the chair's position, continued to lead the separate Solidarity faction in the Supreme Council and ultimately established the Solidarity Party. With the next legislative election in sight, Azarov resigned as PR leader in January 2002 to avoid charges of conflict of interest.

The PR was a principal forum for Viktor Yanukovych in the 2004 presidential elections. It was assisted in the 2006 legislative balloting by financial support from billionaire tycoon Rinat AKHMETOV, who was elected on the PR's list, along with a number of his business associates. Western campaign consultants also contributed to the PR's success (a plurality of 186 seats on a vote share of 32.1 percent). The PR advocated "strong ties" to the EU but opposed NATO membership. Yanukovych also pledged to pursue official language status for Russian and improvements in relations with Russia in general.

Yanukovych was named prime minister in the cabinet installed in August 2006, but the PR was forced into opposition status following the September 2007 legislative elections (despite having won a plurality of 175 seats on a vote share of 34.4 percent). The PR organized several mass protests in Kiev in April 2009 to protest government policies, particularly interaction with the IMF.

After withdrawing from a proposed grand coalition with the BYT in June 2009 (see Fatherland, below), Yanukovych, considered Russia's preferred candidate, and the PR called for increased wages and pension benefits (despite strong IMF objections) in his successful 2010 presidential bid, in which he finished first in the first round with 35.32 percent of the vote and won the runoff with 48.95 percent of the vote. Following his victory, Yanukovych turned over leadership of the PR to Mykola Azarov, who was named prime minister in March. The PR was credited with 36 percent of the nationwide vote in the October local elections. In 2012 Strong Ukraine (*Sylna Ukrayina*—SU), a centrist, middle-class party merged with the PR. The SU was previously known as the Ukrainian Labor Party, also referenced as the Working (*Trudova*) Party, which was launched in September 1999 by Mykhaylo SYROTA, a member of the legislature who had been instrumental in the adoption of the new Ukrainian Constitution in 1996. (That party should not be confused with the historical Labor Party of Ukraine, which was a founding member of the PR, or with Working Ukraine, below, with which Syrota had briefly been associated.) The Ukrainian Labor Party participated in the Lytvyn Bloc (see People's Party, below) in the 2007 legislative elections, securing 7 of that bloc's 20 seats. Syrota died in a car accident in August 2008. His son, Dmytro SYROTA, was subsequently elected as the SU's new leader.

Serhiy Tihipko, former leader of Working Ukraine, joined the Ukrainian Labor Party in 2009 and was elected party leader at the November congress, at which the SU rubric was adopted. Tihipko finished third in the first round of presidential balloting in January 2010 with 13.05 percent of the vote. He was reportedly offered the post of prime minister by Yulia Tymoshenko in return for his support in her bid in the presidential runoff, but he declined to endorse her. Tihipko was subsequently named deputy prime minister for the economy in the new PR-led cabinet.

The PR, campaigning on a platform of stability and emphasizing its government record, secured 30.0 percent of the proportional component of the 2012 legislative elections. Official PR candidates secured 185 seats overall, and most of the officially independent successful candidates ultimately joined the PR parliamentary faction.

Leaders: Viktor YANUKOVYCH (President of Ukraine and Honorary Party Leader), Mykola AZAROV (Prime Minister and Chair of the Party), Oleksandr YEFREMOV (Parliamentary Leader), Volodymyr RYBAK (Speaker of the Supreme Council).

Communist Party of Ukraine (*Komunistychna Partiya Ukrainy*—KPU). Formerly Ukraine's ruling party, the KPU was banned in August 1991 but was allowed to reregister in October 1993 (without regaining party property of the Soviet era); Petro Symonenko was elected party leader. Standing on a traditional platform of anticapitalism and antinationalism, the KPU secured a plurality of seats in the 1994 legislative balloting and subsequently served as the core of the parliamentary opposition to the economic restructuring efforts of President Kuchma.

The KPU's plurality rose in the 1998 legislative poll, the party performing particularly well in the nationwide proportional balloting, winning about 25 percent of the votes. First Secretary Symonenko finished second in the 1999 presidential poll, winning 22.2 percent of the initial vote and 38.8 percent in a runoff against the incumbent. KPU demands of the subsequent Yushchenko government included severance of ties to NATO, designation of Russian as an official language, commitment to a socialist economy, and central planning for state enterprises.

In 2000 it was reported that the KPU had split into two factions. The first was led by Symonenko and remained decidedly antimarket, anti-American, and pro-Russian. The second adopted the name **Communist Party of Ukraine (Reformed)**; its leader was reported to be Mikhail SAVENKO, a "progressive socialist" who was a member of the Working Ukraine faction in the Supreme Council.

At the March 2002 election the KPU took 66 seats, 59 of them on the basis of winning 20 percent of the proportional vote. It secured 21 seats in 2006 on a vote share of 3.7 percent and 27 seats in 2007 on a vote share of 5.39 percent. (The KPU [Reformed] won 0.29 percent of the vote in 2007.) The KPU continued its anti-NATO campaign in 2008.

In late 2009 Symonenko was named as the candidate of a KPU-led Bloc of Left and Center-Left Forces for the January 2010 presidential elections. Other groups in the bloc included the **Justice Party**, the SDPU, and the **Union of Left Forces**. Symonenko won 3.54 percent of the vote in the first round of balloting. The KPU subsequently supported the new PR-led government.

The KPU improved dramatically to 13.2 percent of the proportional vote in the 2012 legislative elections, good for 32 seats; none of its candidates won in the single-member constituencies, however. Symonenko announced after the balloting that the KPU would not necessarily support the PR in the future, but most KPU legislators voted with the government throughout the next year.

Leader: Petro SYMONENKO (First Secretary, Parliamentary Leader, and 2010 presidential candidate).

Ukraine-Forward! This party is a successor, at least in part, to the Ukrainian Social Democratic Party (*Ukrainska Sotsial-Demokratychna Partiya*—USDP), which was established in November 1998 by former justice minister Vasyl ONOPENKO, previously the leader of the Social Democratic Party of Ukraine (United). Onopenko finished eighth in the 1999 presidential election, with 0.5 percent of the vote. The USDP rain as part of BYT in the 2002, 2006, and 2011 legislative elections, securing 8 of the BYT's 155 seats in the latter poll.

In December 2011 BYT legislator Natalia Korolevska was elected leader of the USDP, considered a probusiness party. However, Korolevska was expelled from the BYT legislative faction in March 2012, faction leaders arguing that she had cooperated, against faction directives, in several instances with the Yanukovych administration. Two other USDP deputies withdrew from the BYT faction to protest her dismissal. Subsequently, the USDP changed its name to Ukraine-Forward!, positioned itself as between the opposition and the administration, and ran on its own in the 2012 legislative poll, securing 1.6 percent of the vote in the proportional component. Korolevska was named minister of social policy in the December 2012 cabinet, although it was not clear if the full party endorsed that decision.

Leaders: Natalia KOROLEVSKA, Andriy SHEVCHENKO.

Other Legislative Parties:

Fatherland (*Batkivshchyna*). The social-democratic Fatherland (also sometimes translated as Motherland) was established as a Supreme Council faction in March 1999 by Yulia Tymoshenko and other members of the All-Ukrainian Association *Hromada* (below) who objected to the parent party's support for Pavlo Lazarenko. Ironically, Tymoshenko had once been a close associate of Lazarenko, who had encouraged her to enter politics. Initially numbering about two dozen deputies, the Fatherland faction soon surpassed *Hromada,* which ultimately fell below the 14 adherents needed for official faction status.

In late December 1999 President Kuchma named Tymoshenko to the new Yushchenko cabinet as deputy prime minister for fuel and energy, but by mid-2000, she was already drawing criticism from Kuchma for her handling of the sector. Despite continuing support from the prime minister, she was dismissed from her cabinet post by Kuchma on January 19, 2001, four days after being formally charged with gas smuggling, tax evasion, and document forgery while head of Unified Energy Systems of Ukraine in 1996–1997.

In late 2001 Fatherland absorbed Stepan Khmara's Ukrainian Conservative Republican Party (*Ukrainska Konservatyvna Respublikanska Partiya*—UKRP). Intensely anti-Communist and anti-Russian, the UKRP had been formed in June 1992 by a radical wing of the URP (below) led by Khmara. (For additional information on the UKRP, see the section on Fatherland in the 2007 *Handbook.*)

Tymoshenko's supporters were instrumental in formation of the National Salvation Front (NSF) in 2001 and its successor, the Yulia Tymoshenko Bloc (*Blok Yuliyi Tymoshenko*—BYT) in 2002 (see introductory text, above, for additional information on the NSF and BYT [which won 22 seats in the 2002 legislative election]).

For the 2006 elections (at which it secured 129 seats on a vote share of 22.3 percent), the BYT comprised Fatherland, the USDP (see Ukraine-Forward!, above), and remnants of the Ukrainian People's Party Assembly (*Ukrainskoho Narodnoho Partiya "Sobor"*—UNP *"Sobor."*) The UNP *"Sobor,"* an anti-Kuchma party formed in 1999, had split in 2005 after a party congress voted to align with the BYT. (See URP *"Sobor,"* below, for additional information.)

The BYT was also aided in 2006 by the inclusion of Levko LUKYANENKO and his supporters from the URP (below), who had been left without affiliation following a split in the URP. The BYT campaigned on a platform of support for integration with Western Europe and opposition to the recently completed natural gas deal with Russia. Tymoshenko also maintained a populist stance that promised increased welfare spending and wide-ranging corruption investigations.

Having in 2006 declared its uncompromising opposition to the Yanukovych government and having subsequently aligned itself with the NU, the BYT finished second in the September 2007 legislative balloting. For that election the BYT also included the Reforms and Order Party (*Reformy I Poryadok Partiya*—RiP). The previously pro-Kuchma RiP had secured 3.1 percent of the national proportional vote in the 1998 legislative poll after negotiations for its inclusion in the Forward, Ukraine! alliance with the PKNS and UKhDP (see URP, below) had fallen through. In December 2000 it joined Hennadiy Udovenko's *Rukh* and the KUN in announcing formation of a center-right electoral bloc, which supported economic reform and greater integration of Ukraine with Western Europe. The RiP participated in the NU for the 2002 legislative poll but formed an alliance called the Civil Political Bloc (*Pora*—PRP) with the reformist It Is Time (*Pora*) Party for the 2006 legislative poll, winning 1.47 percent of the vote.

The BYT was credited with winning 155 seats in the 2007 legislative poll (165 for Fatherland, 9 for the RiP, 8 for the USDP, and 33 for "unaffiliated" candidates who ran on the BYT list). Following the election, the BYT formed a coalition government with the NU-NS that included Tymoshenko as prime minister, although friction between her and President Yushchenko subsequently continued to dominate the political scene. Meanwhile RiP leader Viktor Pynzenyk, a noted economist who had been named finance minister in the December 2007 government, resigned the post in early 2009, saying policy initiatives were being held "hostage to politics."

In the first half of 2009, the BYT appeared close to reaching a coalition agreement with the PR, the primary opposition party led by former prime minister Viktor Yanukovych. According to various reports, the proposed accord called for the groups to cooperate within parliament to amend the constitution to authorize parliament to elect the president (currently elected by popular vote), with Yanukovych slated to fill that position, while Timoshenko continued as prime minister (with expanded powers). However the proposed grand coalition collapsed in June when Yanukovych abruptly withdrew his support.

In October 2009 the BYT unanimously nominated Tymoshenko as its candidate for the January 2010 presidential election. She subsequently pledged, if elected, to pursue warmer relations with Russia (while also supporting additional cooperation with the EU) and to combat corruption (in part through judicial reform).

Tymoshenko finished second in the first round of presidential balloting in January 2010 with 25 percent of the vote and lost the subsequent runoff with 46 percent of the vote. Following the collapse of her government coalition in March, she became the leading voice of the opposition to new PR-led government and a key member of the new Committee to Protect Ukraine, formed in May to protest the pro-Russian policies of President Yanukovych. Prominent author Dmytro PAVLYCHKO was named coordinator of the new committee, which in addition to Fatherland and the RiP, included elements of the NU-NS, and the right-wing, nonparliamentary All-Ukrainian Union Freedom.

Tymoshenko and a number of former ministers from her government were arrested in 2011 in a crackdown the government attributed to its anticorruption campaign and Tymoshenko's supporters to a political lynching (see Current issues, above, for details). The BYT components and other opposition parties subsequently formed a Committee to Resist Dictatorship, which served as the foundation of cooperation for the 2012 legislative poll. Due to electoral law changes that had banned bloc formation for those elections, Tymoshenko allies were all presented on the Fatherland list. Included on the United Opposition Fatherland list were members of the RiP, the Popular Movement of Ukraine (*Rukh*, below), the People's Self-Defense Party (below), the **Front for Change, the Civic Platform, For Ukraine,** and the **Social Christian Party**.

The Front for Change, Civic Platform, and For Ukraine, were outgrowths of the NU-NS (see NSNU, below). The Front for Change was formed by Arseny Yatsenyuk, a former speaker of the Supreme Council, following the splintering of the NU-NS in late 2008. Yatsenyuk subsequently attracted significant support in public opinion polls by criticizing the prevalence of personal politics among the country's leading figures. Although he had initially professed a middle-of-the-road approach to Ukraine's main issues, Yatsenyuk, reportedly enjoying support among the oligarchs, campaigned for the presidency in 2010 on a platform that opposed NATO and EU membership. He won 6.96 percent of the first-round vote. Following the poll, the Front for Change declined to join the new-PR led government.

The Civic Platform was formed (following the NU-NS breakup) by former defense minister Anatoliy HRYTSENKO, who won 1.2 percent of the vote in the first round of the 2010 presidential election. (The European Party of Ukraine [*Evropeyska Partiya Ukraini*—EPU], another component of the NU-NS, merged into the Civic Platform in mid-2011.) For Ukraine, led by Byacheslav KRYLENKO, is a successor to the Party of Social Protection. The Social Christian Party was established in 2004 under the leadership of singer Oksana BILOZIR (a supporter of Viktor Yushchenko); the party secured 0.09 percent of the vote in the 2006 legislative elections. For the 2007 poll, it formed the Christian Bloc with the **All-Ukrainian Political Party of Ecology and Social Protection**.

The Fatherland list won 25.6 percent of the vote in the proportional component of the 2012 poll, good for 62 seats. For some of the single-member constituencies Fatherland cooperated with both the UDAR and Freedom, and those three parties formed a united front to protest what they claimed to be massive fraud in the counting of votes, particularly in the single-member constituencies.

Tymoshenko, having been sentenced to seven years in prison following her conviction in October 2011 on a charge of abuse of power, was barred from contesting the 2012 legislative election. Subsequently, in January 2013, she was also named as a suspect (along with Pavlo Lazarenko) in the case of the murder of a national legislator in 1996. She also continued to face tax evasion charges, although all proceedings against her were postponed due to her health issues.

In June 2013 it was announced that the RiP, *Rukh*, and the Front for Change had all formally merged into Fatherland, with Yatsenyuk being elected chair of the party. Fatherland subsequently called on all opposition parties to coalesce behind a single presidential candidate for 2015.

Leaders: Yulia TYMOSHENKO (Leader, in prison [as of October 15, 2013]), Arseny YATSENYUK (Chair and Parliamentary Leader), Oleksandr TURAHYNOV (Deputy Chair).

Popular Movement of Ukraine (*Narodnyi Rukh Ukrainy—Rukh,* or NRU). *Rukh* was organized in September 1989 as the Popular Movement of the Ukraine for Restructuring (*NRU za Perebudovu*). From the outset the grouping advocated Ukrainian independence, causing its critics among the anti-Communist groups to charge it with being more nationalist than democratic. Its founding chair, the writer Ivan DRACH, appealed to his colleagues to rally behind President

Kravchuk after the latter's break with the KPU. Another leader, Vyacheslav CHORNOVIL, who had secured a 25 percent vote share as the grouping's presidential candidate in 1991, insisted that *Rukh* should continue in opposition. Thereafter, the grouping remained deeply divided in regard to the president, although it agreed to fill two important positions (first deputy prime minister and economics minister) in the Kuchma administration. Having been formally registered as a party in 1993, *Rukh*, campaigning on a platform of market reform and opposition to CIS membership, won 20 seats in the 1994 legislative elections. The party called for Ukraine's integration into NATO and the EU and for other democratic and reformist parties to unite against the left.

Rukh was the second leading party in the 1998 legislative poll, being credited with about 10 percent of the vote in the nationwide proportional balloting. However, it continued to suffer from what one analyst described as a "crisis in direction," occasioned more by personality differences than policy disputes. In January 1999 Chornovil was ousted as chair in favor of Yuriy Kostenko, a former cabinet minister. Chornovil and his supporters subsequently formed a new parliamentary faction called the Popular *Rukh* of Ukraine-1, or *Rukh*-1. Chornovil died in a car accident in March, and Hennadiy UDOVENKO, a former foreign minister, was named acting chair of the new faction.

Kostenko and Udovenko both ran for president in 1999; the former, technically on the ballot as an independent, won 2.2 percent of the vote, and the latter took 1.2 percent. Following a court challenge over the use of the party name, the two factions were registered separately in January 2000, with Udovenko's party assuming the NRU designation and the Kostenko group taking the name Ukrainian Popular Movement (*Ukrainskyi Narodnyi Rukh—Rukh,* or UNR).

In November 2000, looking ahead to the next legislative election, Udovenko's NRU announced an electoral alliance with the Congress of Ukrainian Nationalists (KUN, below) and the RiP (see Fatherland, above). In early 2001 it appeared that the two *Rukh* parties could well be allies for the next Supreme Council balloting and might even reunite beforehand. However, although both joined the Yushchenko bloc, they failed to resolve their differences before the March 2002 election. Afterward, both branches continued to express an interest in reuniting. In 2004 Udovenko was replaced as head of his faction by Borys TARASYUK, while Kostenko and his supporters formed the UNP (below). Both branches participated in the NU-NS for the 2007 legislative balloting. After participating in the Fatherland list for 2012 legislative poll, Tarasyuk and his *Rukh* component formally merged with Fatherland in June 2013.

People's Self-Defense Party. This grouping is an outgrowth of Forward, Ukraine!, which had initially been formed for the 1998 legislative poll by the Centrist Christian Popular Union Party (*Partiya Khrystiyansko Noradniy Soyuz*—PKNS) and the Christian Democratic Party of Ukraine (*Khrystiyansko Demokratychnya Partiya Ukrainy*—KhDPU). The alliance secured 1.7 percent of the vote in that election. Forward, Ukraine! subsequently registered as a party in its own right and participated in the NU in the 2002 legislative poll. In 2003 the PKNS and KhDPU formed the Christian Democratic Union (*Khrystiyansko Demokratychnya Soyuz*—KDS) with the All Ukrainian Union of Christians. The KDS was reportedly a member of the NU Bloc for the 2006 legislative poll, although Forward, Ukraine! was listed as competing on its own in that poll, securing 0.02 percent of the vote.

Yuriy LUTSENKO, who was dismissed under pressure from the PR as interior minister in December 2006 and subsequently became an adviser to President Yushchenko, later established a civic movement called People's Self-Defense that included Forward, Ukraine! and the KDS. That movement formed an important component of the NU-NS in the 2007 legislative balloting, in which Forward, Ukraine! secured four of the NU-NS's 72 seats and the KDS secured. Lutsenko subsequently served as interior minister in the Tymoshenko cabinet from 2007–2010.

In February 2010 a Forward, Ukraine! congress voted to change the party's name to the People's Self-Defense Party, with Lutsenko as its leader. Lutsenko was arrested in December 2010 on embezzlement charges, his supporters characterizing the case as an element of a politically motivated campaign by the Yanukovych administration against Tymoshenko and her former ministers.

In February 2012 Lutsenko was convicted and sentenced to four years in prison, the verdict prompting broad criticism from the international community for its political overtones. He was pardoned by President Yanukovych in April 2013, and shortly thereafter, he launched a new opposition movement called the Third Republic. Meanwhile, the status of the People's Self-Defense Party remained unclear; the party's merger into Fatherland had been announced by Lutsenko in December 2011, but no formal action was subsequently reported in that regard by a party congress.

Ukrainian Democratic Alliance for Reform (UDAR). Headed by world heavyweight boxing champion Vitaliy KLITSCHKO (*Udar* translates as "Punch"), UDAR is an outgrowth of political support that coalesced around Klitschko for local elections in Kiev from 2006–2008. Klitschko's backers at the local level during that time included *Pora*, the RiP, *Rukh*, the USDP, and the small European Capital party, which changed its name to the New Country party in 2009 before formally adopting the UDAR rubric in April 2010. The center-right UDAR performed well in the 2010 Kiev municipal poll and, based on Klitschko's immense popularity, surged in national public opinion polls in the run-up to the October 2012 legislative balloting, for which it campaigned on a pro-Western, anticorruption platform. Although a degree of cooperation was reported between UDAR and Fatherland regarding single-member constituencies, friction between the two surfaced shortly before the balloting regarding final candidate selections. UDAR consequently declined to sign a proposed preelection coalition agreement with Fatherland and Freedom, the two other leading opposition parties. UDAR won 40 seats in the 2012 poll, including 34 on a vote share of 14.0 percent in the proportional poll, propelling the party and Klitschko into the forefront of national political affairs.

Leaders: Vitaliy KLITSCHKO (Chair and Parliamentary Leader), Vitaliy KOVALCHUK (Deputy Chair).

Freedom *(Svoboda).* A successor to the right-wing Social-National Party of Ukraine, Freedom is led by Oleh TYAHNYBOK, who has been described as having no serious rivals in the right flank. (Its strongest critics characterize Freedom as racist and anti-Semitic.) The party secured less than 1 percent of the vote in the 2006 and 2007 national legislative balloting but, promising to preserve the Ukrainian language and culture, had a greater impact in subsequent local elections, while Tyahnybok secured 1.43 percent of the vote in the first round of presidential balloting in January 2010.

Having softened its rhetoric, Freedom soared to 10.5 percent of the vote in the proportional component of the October 2012 legislative poll (good for 25 seats). It also captured 12 seats in the single-member constituencies, having cooperated with the Fatherland list in some of those races.

Leaders: Oleh TYAHNYBOK (Leader and Parliamentary Leader), Andry MOKHNYK (Deputy Leader).

United Center. This grouping was formed following the breakup of the NU-NS in late 2008 by former chief of staff Viktor Baloga, reportedly as an official successor to the Party of Private Property, which had not presented candidates in the 2007 legislative poll. As the result of defections from the NU-NS, United Center claimed control of six legislative seats as of mid-2010. Baloga joined the PR-led government in November 2010, and the United Center legislators generally supported the government in subsequent legislative votes. Running on its own, the United Center secured three seats in the voting for single-member constituencies in the October 2012 elections.

Leaders: Viktor BALOGA (Leader), Ihor KRIL.

People's Party (*Narodna Partiya*—NP). The NP is the rubric adopted in 2005 by the former Agrarian Party of Ukraine (*Ahrarna Partiya Ukrainy*—APU), which was established in 1996 to support farmers and which secured 3.7 percent of the proportional vote in the 1998 legislative balloting, just missing the 4 percent threshold necessary to be allocated proportional seats. The APU supported President Kuchma's reelection in the October–November 1999 balloting.

The APU was renamed the People's Agrarian Party of Ukraine in 2004, with Volodymyr Lytvyn, the speaker of the Supreme Council, becoming its leader. The NP rubric was adopted in 2005.

For the 2006 legislative balloting, the NP served as the core component of the Lytvyn Bloc, which also included the **Peasant Democratic Party,** and the small **Party of All-Ukrainian Union of the Left**

Justice. The bloc secured 2.44 percent of the vote in 2006 and failed to gain representation. However, the Lytvyn Bloc, performing well in rural areas and small towns in central Ukraine, won 20 seats on a vote share of 3.96 percent in the 2007 elections, when its primary components were the NP and the Ukrainian Labor Party (see under PR, above).

Lytvyn, the leader of the bloc, was again elected speaker of the Supreme Council in December 2008 as part of the formation of a new BYT-led coalition government, announcing he hoped to serve as a peacemaker in the nation's frayed political affairs. In declaring his candidacy for the January 2010 presidential election, Lytvyn lobbied for support from disgruntled former SPU members. After Lytvyn secured 2.35 percent of the vote in the first round of presidential balloting in January 2010, the Lytvyn Bloc defected from the Tymoshenko coalition, prompting its collapse in early March. The Lytvyn Bloc subsequently joined the new PR-led government.

After an initial plan for the NP's merger into the PR failed to materialize, the NP competed independently in the single-member constituencies in the October 2012 legislative poll, winning two seats.

Leaders: Volodymyr LYTVYN (Leader and Former Speaker of the Supreme Council), Kateryna VASHCHUK.

Union Party (*Partiya Soyuz*). Essentially a Crimean grouping that advocates creation of a union of Ukraine, Belarus, and Russia, this party secured 0.7 percent of the vote in the 1998 national proportional poll. In 2002 it ran as part of a Russian Bloc that also included the **For a United Russia Party** and the **Russo-Ukrainian Union Party**. In 2005 it formed the For Union Bloc with the **Socialist Ukraine Party,** the **Homeland Party,** and the **Slavic Party.** The bloc secured 0.20 percent of the vote in the 2006 legislative poll.

For the 2007 poll, the Union Party participated in the Election Bloc of Political Parties Kuchma (led by Oleksandr VOLKOV) with the **Center Party** (led by Viktor HOLOVKO). The Union Party, which holds seats in its Supreme Council of Crimea and in municipal bodies in Crimea, won one seat in the balloting for single-member constituencies in the 2012 national legislative balloting.

Leader: Lev MYRYMSKY.

Radical Party of Oleh Lyashko. This party is an outgrowth of the Ukrainian Radical-Democratic Party that was formed in September 2010 under the leadership of Vladislav TELIPKO. Oleh LYASHKO, who had been elected to the Supreme Council on the BYT lists in 2006 and 2007 but had been expelled from the BYT faction in October 2010 for his perceived cooperation with the PR-led government, subsequently joined the party, which in August 2011 adopted its current rubric and elected Lyashko as its leader. Lyashko was reelected to the Supreme Council in 2012.

Leader: Oleh LYASHKO.

Other Parties Contesting Both the Proportional and Majoritarian Components of the 2012 Legislative Elections:

People's Union "Our Ukraine" (*Narodni Soyus "Nasha Ukraina"*—NSNU). The propresidential, right-of-center NSNU was formed in early 2005 by supporters of President Yushchenko to, among other things, contest the 2006 legislative elections. It was considered to be a successor to "Our Ukraine" ("*Nasha Ukraina"*—NU), the electoral bloc that had been formed in 2001 to support Viktor Yushchenko's successful presidential campaign. Among the groups signing the 2001 NU accord were *Rukh*, the KUN, PKNS, RiP, LPU, Solidarity, the Republican Christian Party (RKP), and the Youth Party of Ukraine. Reports indicated that some 25 components of "Our Ukraine" participated in the launching of the NSNU. Described by some as the "next party of power," the NSNU nevertheless failed to attract a number of major Yushchenko allies.

Meeting in Kiev in March 2005, some 6,000 delegates to the NSNU's founding congress elected a 120-member Council and an Executive Committee. Deputy Prime Minister Roman BEZMERTNY was elected as head of the Council, while Yuriy YEKHANUROV was named head of the Executive Committee and Yushchenko was named as the party's honorary chair. The NSNU's 21-member presidium included 5 cabinet members.

Like its predecessor, the NSNU advocated market-driven economics and accelerated integration with Europe. It was initially reported that the NSNU planned to contest the 2006 elections in alliance with the BYT and the APU (see NP, above) but the NSNU ultimately served as the core component of the "Our Ukraine" bloc, which did not include the BYT or APU. The new bloc, which included the NSNU, *Rukh*, PPPU, KUN, KDS, and URP "*Sobor,*" finished third in the 2006 legislative election, securing 81 seats on a vote share of 13.95 percent.

Some members of the NU components joined the new cabinet that was installed in early August 2006, but most of them resigned as the NU formally went into opposition in October. The NU subsequently formed a pact with the BYT to coordinate their legislative activities.

For the 2007 poll, the NSNU served as the core component of the Our Ukraine–People's Self-Defense (*Nasha Ukraina–Narodna Samooborona*—NU-NS) bloc, which included *Rukh*, the UNP, URP "Sobor," Forward, Ukraine!, KDS, and *Pora*. Other components were the **European Party of Ukraine** (*Evropeyska Partiya Ukraini*—EPU), which was organized in 2006 under the leadership of Mykola KATERYNCHAK, and the **Party of Motherland Defenders** (*Partiya Zakhisnikiv Vitchizni*—PZV), led by Yuri KARMAZIN. Some NU-NS members subsequently lobbied for the members of the electoral bloc to merge into a single party, but the initiative failed to gain momentum. The NU-NS secured 14.15 percent of the 2007 vote, good for 72 seats (NSNU, 29; *Rukh,* 6; UNP, 6; Forward, Ukraine!, 4; EPU, 2; URP "Sobor," 2; KDS, 2; *Pora*, 1; PZV, 1; and 19 unaffiliated). Yuschenko subsequently negotiated a coalition agreement with BYT.

The NU-NS splintered in late 2008 when a majority of its legislators agreed to support the new BYT-led government despite objections from Yushchenko, whose relationship with Prime Minister Tymoshenko had deteriorated sharply. Some 17 NU-NS deputies, led by parliamentary leader Byacheslav Kyrylenko formed their own For Ukraine faction in parliament to support Yushchenko, while Arsensy Yatsenyuk (sacked in December as speaker of the Supreme Council) subsequently formed the Front for Change, former defense minister Anatoliy Hrytsenko launched a Civic Platform, and former chief of staff Viktor Baloga established the United Center. Although their groups initially remained nongovernmental organizations rather than parties, Yatsenyuk and Hrytsenko ran as candidates for the January 2010 presidential elections (see Front for Change and Civic Platform under Fatherland, above). Meanwhile, Yushchenko, reduced to single-digit support in public opinion polls, registered as an independent candidate in his reelection bid, although he was endorsed by the NSNU, described as "bankrupt" following the withdrawal of business-sector financial support for the president. Yushchenko secured only 5.45 percent of the vote in the first round of balloting in January 2010. A group of NU-NS deputies subsequently offered key legislative support to the new PR-led government. The NU-NS in 2011 announced that NU-NS deputies who cooperated with the government would be excluded from the NU-NS legislation faction.

Several key NU-NS splinters participated in the Fatherland list for the October 2012 elections to the Supreme Council, and the NU list (including members of the NSNU, UNP, and KUN) won only 1.1 percent of the proportional vote, with Yushchenko leading the list of candidates. In addition, none of the NU's 25 candidates was successful in the constituency balloting. It was reported in March 2013 that "Our Ukraine" had dissolved itself, although some members apparently attempted to continue party operations.

Ukrainian People's Party (*Ukrainska Narodna Partiya*—UNP). The UNP was formed in 2004 by Yuriy Kostenko and other members of the UNR faction of *Rukh.* The UNP reportedly won several mayoral races in the 2006 local elections.

In advance of the 2006 legislative elections, the UNP participated with other center-right parties in the launching of an electoral bloc called the Ukrainian National Bloc of Kostenko and Plyushch, which won 1.87 percent of the 2006 vote. (The bloc supported the UNP's Kostenko and parliamentarian Ivan Plyushch. Other components of the bloc included the Party of Free Peasants and Entrepreneurs of Ukraine.) The UNP secured 6 of the NU-NS's 72 seats in the 2007 legislative elections. Kostenko, who had won 2.2 percent of the presidential vote in 1999, secured only 0.22 percent of the vote in the first round of the presidential poll in 2010. After the UNP competed on the NU list in the 2012 legislative elections, there were reports that the UNP had been reabsorbed into *Rukh*.

Leader: Yuriy KOSTENKO (Leader).

Congress of Ukrainian Nationalists (*Konhres Ukrainskykh Natsionalistiv*—KUN). The KUN was founded in October 1992 as an electoral front of the émigré Organization of Ukrainian Nationalists (*Orhanizatsiya Ukrainskykh Natsionalistiv*—OUN), which had led the struggle against Soviet communism before being finally suppressed internally in the 1950s. In 1994 elements of the original OUN opposed to the formation of the KUN reestablished the OUN as a separate civic association.

Advocating Ukraine's exit from the CIS but divided between pro-capitalists and those favoring a state economic role, the KUN won five seats in the 1994 balloting, although its leader was prevented from standing in a Lviv constituency. The KUN participated in the National Front alliance with the Ukrainian Republican Party and Ukrainian Conservative Republican Party in the 1998 legislative poll. The KUN participated in the "Our Ukraine" bloc for the 2006 legislative poll but decided not to participate in the 2007 balloting. In 2012 its membership was represented on the NU list.

Leader: Steven BRATSIUN.

All-Ukrainian Association Community (*Vseukrainske Obyednannya Hromada*). Founded in September 1997, *Hromada* elected former prime minister Pavlo LAZARENKO as its first chair and joined the KPU and other leftist groups in blocking many initiatives proposed by the Kuchma/Pustovoytenko administration. The party's legislative stance appeared less founded in ideology than in Lazarenko's enmity toward Kuchma, who had insisted on Lazarenko's ouster as prime minister in the wake of corruption allegations. *Hromada* was credited with about 5 percent of the nationwide proportional vote in the 1998 legislative poll.

In December 1998 Lazarenko was arrested at the border by Swiss authorities on money laundering charges; he was subsequently released on bail of $2.6 million. Lazarenko left Ukraine for the United States in February 1999 after the Supreme Council had removed his immunity from prosecution and Ukrainian prosecutors had begun preparations to charge him with embezzlement and other malfeasance. The scandal surrounding Lazarenko split *Hromada*, with his supporters nominating him as the party's 1999 presidential candidate despite the corruption charges, while Lazarenko's opponents coalesced in a breakaway faction called Fatherland (above) under the leadership of Yulia Tymoshenko.

Lazarenko pleaded guilty to Swiss charges in June 2000. He received an 18-month sentence in absentia, and authorities confiscated $6.6 million from his accounts for return to Ukraine. In August 2006 Lazarenko was convicted for money laundering and other offences by a U.S. court and sentenced to nine years in prison.

Supporters of Lazarenko formed the Lazarenko Bloc for the 2006 legislative elections. In addition to *Hromada*, the bloc included the SDPU (below) and the **Social Democratic Union** (*Sotsial Demokratychnyy Soyuz*—SDS). The Lazarenko Bloc secured 0.30 percent of the vote in 2006. When the election commission refused to register Lazarenko as a candidate for the 2007 legislative elections, the Lazarenko Bloc refused to participate in that poll.

Hromada, running on its own, won 0.1 percent of the vote in the proportional component of the October 2012 legislative poll, Lazarenko again being barred from the party's candidate list. Lazarenko was released from U.S. prison in November and immediately applied for a U.S. residency permit, so he would not have to return to Ukraine, where charges against him remained outstanding.

Leader: Pavlo LAZARENKO (Former Prime Minister).

Liberal Party of Ukraine (*Liberalna Partiya Ukrainy*—LPU). Largely based in Donetsk, the LPU was formed in 1991 by Volodymyr SHCHERBAN, who subsequently served as the governor of the Sumy *oblast,* and Yevhen SHCHERBAN, who was assassinated in 1996. The LPU contested the 1998 legislative poll in the Together alliance with the Labor Party of Ukraine; the alliance won 1.9 percent of the national proportional vote.

In January 2005 Shcherban left office, and he subsequently reportedly fled Ukraine after an arrest warrant was issued charging him with corruption. (The former governor insisted the charges were politically motivated.) As a result of Shcherban's status, the LPU was not permitted to participate in the NU for the 2006 legislative poll. Running on its own, the LPU won only 0.04 percent of the vote. After boycotting the 2007 poll, the LPU secured 0.1 percent of the vote in the proportional component of the 2012 balloting.

Leader: Petro TSYHANKO (President).

Ukrainian National Assembly (*Ukrainska Natsionalna Asambleya*—UNA). Following its formation in the early 1990s, the UNA (also referenced as the UNA-Ukrainian People's Self-Defense—UNA-UNSO) pursued what was widely perceived as a neo-Nazi stance that emphasized Ukrainian nationalism and intense opposition to Russian policies, particularly in regard to ongoing Russian influence in areas such as Crimea. The party won three legislative seats in 1994, none in 1998, and one in 2002 (when it supported Viktor Yushchenko and the Orange Revolution). After securing no legislative seats in 2006 and not participating in the 2007 poll, the UNA-UNSO list won 0.08 percent of the vote in the proportional component of the 2012 balloting.

Leader: Yuriy SHUKHEVYCH.

Socialist Party of Ukraine (*Sotsialtstychna Partiya Ukrainy*—SPU). Although organized in 1991 by the former leader of the Communist legislative majority, the SPU was described as "not so much a successor to the Communist Party, as a party of economic populism." As such, it urged retention of a major state role in the economy while favoring priority for workers in privatization. It won 15 parliamentary seats in 1994 and attracted a further 12 independent deputies into its parliamentary group. In early 1996 two SPU deputies, Nataliya Vitrenko and Volodymyr Marchenko, were expelled from the party for criticizing the leadership for deviating from socialist ideals; they subsequently formed the PSP (below).

The SPU and the Peasants' Party of Ukraine (SelPU, below) formed an electoral bloc called For Truth, for the People, for Ukraine for the 1998 legislative poll, the alliance being credited with about 8 percent of the national proportional vote. SPU Chair Oleksandr Moroz, a former chair of the Supreme Council, finished third in the 1999 presidential election, taking 11.3 percent of the vote.

In November 2000 Moroz released secret tape recordings implicating President Kuchma in the disappearance of an independent journalist and then helped form the Ukraine Without Kuchma movement and the National Salvation Forum. At the March 2002 election, the SPU won 22 seats, 20 of them on the basis of a 6.9 percent share of the proportional vote.

The SPU joined the cabinet named in January 2005, and after winning 33 seats on a vote share of 5.7 percent in the March 2006 legislative poll, the party was initially perceived as a potential partner in a coalition government that would have included the NU and the BYT. However, Moroz switched allegiance to the PR, after which he was elected speaker of the Supreme Council, and the SPU joined the new PR-led cabinet. The SPU suffered a dramatic reversal (reflecting dissatisfaction among party members over Moroz's 2006 defection from the Orange Revolution) in the September 2007 balloting, securing only 2.86 percent of the votes and thereby losing all representation. Moroz, who had finished third in the three previous presidential elections, won only 0.38 percent of the vote as the SPU candidate in the first round of presidential balloting in January 2010. He was replaced as SPU leader in April 2012, and the SPU fell to 0.5 percent of the vote in the October legislative poll, the party's effort to merge with a number of other small leftist parties having been blocked by the government.

Leader: Petro USTENKO.

Other parties that ran unsuccessfully in both components of the 2012 legislative poll included: the **Russian Bloc** (0.3 percent of the vote in the proportional component), led by Olexandr SVISTUNOV; **New Politics** (0.1 percent), recently formed under the leadership of former PR legislator Volodymyr SEMYNOZHENKO; the **Ukrainian Party Green Planet** (0.4 percent); the **Party of Pensioners of Ukraine** (0.6 percent); the **Greens** (0.3 percent); the **Party of the Greens of Ukraine** (0.4 percent), led by Denys MOSKAL; **Ukraine of the Future** (0.2 percent), a liberal grouping led by Sviatoslav OLIYNK; the **People's Labor Union of Ukraine** (0.1 percent); and the **Political Union "Native Fatherland"** (0.2 percent).

Other Parties That Contested the 2007 Legislative Elections:

Ukrainian Republican Party "Assembly" (*Ukrainska Respublnkanska Partiya "Sobor"*—URP *"Sobor"*). The center-right URP *"Sobor"* was formed in December 2005 by former UNP *"Sobor"* leader Anatoliy MATVIYENKO and disaffected members of the Ukrainian Republican Party. The party participated in the NU-NS for the 2007 legislative balloting and unsuccessfully presented a small number of candidates in the single-member constituencies in 2012.

Leader: Pavlo ZHEBRIVSKY.

Progressive Socialist Party (*Prohresyvna Sotsialistychna Partiya*—PSP). Formed in 1996 by legislators recently expelled from the SPU, the PSP, considered the most radical of the country's leftist groupings, secured 4 percent of the national proportional vote in the 1998 legislative poll. Labeling herself a true Marxist, the party's 1999 presidential candidate, Nataliya Vitrenko, finished fourth in the balloting, with 11 percent of the vote.

For the 2002 election Vitrenko organized the Nataliya Vitrenko Bloc (*Blok Nataliyi Vitrenko*), which included the PSP and the **Party of Educators of Ukraine** (*Partiya Osvityan Ukrainy*—POU). The bloc won 3.2 percent of the proportional vote but no seats.

The PSP participated in the 2006 legislative poll in a People's Opposition Bloc of Nataliya Vitrenko (*Blok Nataliyi Vitrenko Narodna Opoziciya*) with the **Rus'-Ukrainian Union Party** (*Partiya Rus'ko-Ukrainsky Soyus*—RUS). The extremely pro-Russian and anti-American grouping opposed Ukraine's proposed membership in NATO, the EU, and the WTO and called for a new union of Belarus, Russia, and Ukraine. It won 2.93 percent of the vote, narrowly missing the threshold required to gain representation. Running on its own, the PSP won 1.32 percent of the vote in the September 2007 balloting. It did not participate in the 2012 poll.

Leaders: Nataliya VITRENKO, Volodymyr MARCHENKO.

Party of National Economic Development (*Partiya Natsionalno Ekonomichnoho Rozvytku Ukrainy*—PNERU). Led by banker Volodymyr Matviyenko, the PNERU won one seat in the 2002 legislative balloting but fell to a 0.23 percent vote share in the 2006 poll and 0.14 percent in 2007. It did not participate in the 2012 poll.

Leader: Volodymyr MATVIYENKO.

Election Bloc of Lyndmyla Suprun–Ukrainian Regional Activists. This grouping was formed for the 2007 legislative poll by the **People's Democratic Party** (led by Lyudmyla SUPRUN), the **Democratic Party of Ukraine** (led by Serhiy KOZACHENKO and Anna ANTONYEVA), and the **Republican Christian Party** (led by Volodymyr POROVSKY and Mykhaylo POROVSKY). (The People's Democratic Party and the Democratic Party had participated in the 2006 elections in a People's Democratic Party Bloc that also included the **Christian and Democratic Party** [led by the mayor of Kiev, Leonid CHERNOVETSKY].) The 2006 bloc secured 0.49 percent of the vote, and the 2007 bloc won 0.34 percent. As the candidate of the People's Democratic Party, Suprun secured 0.19 percent of the vote in the first round of presidential balloting in January 2010. Her party presented candidates unsuccessfully in the single-member constituencies in 2012.

Leader: Lyudmyla SUPRUN.

Party of Free Democrats. This center-right grouping was formerly known as *Yabluko* (Apple), which was formed in December 1999 to support Ukraine's capitalists and the middle class. A corresponding faction of about 14 deputies (the minimum required for recognition) formed within the Supreme Council. At the 2002 legislative election, however, *Yabluko* won only 1.2 percent of the proportional vote and no seats. The party's leader, Mykhaylo Brodskiy, announced in 2005 that *Yabluko* was merging with the BYT. However, *Yabluko* was revived in early 2007 following a rift between Brodskiy and Yulia Tymoshenko. The party adopted its new rubric in March; it secured 0.21 percent of the vote in the September legislative poll. Brodskiy won 0.06 percent of the vote as the party's candidate in the first round of presidential balloting in January 2010. The party competed (unsuccessfully) for only one seat in the single-member constituencies in the 2012 legislative election.

Leaders: Viktor CHAIKA, Mykhaylo BRODSKIY.

Party of Industrialists and Entrepreneurs of Ukraine (*Partiya Promislovtsiv i Pidpryyemtsiv Ukrainy*—PPPU). The PPPU was established by Prime Minister Anatoliy KINAKH in late November 2001. Previously the head of the Ukrainian Union of Industrialists and Entrepreneurs, Kinakh was elected to lead the new party at its February 2002 congress. The party's probusiness platform called for measures such as a significant reduction in the value-added tax and the adoption of policies favoring investment and the development of high-tech, export-oriented industry. Kinakh was named deputy prime minister in the January 2005 cabinet.

The PPPU participated in President Yushchenko's "Our Ukraine" (NU) bloc in the March 2006 legislative poll. However, Kinakh was named economics minister in the PR-led cabinet in March 2007, and most of the PPPU legislators concurrently switched allegiance to the PR's anticrisis coalition. (They were subsequently expelled from the NU.) Kinakh was elected to the Supreme Council in 2007 on the list of the PR, to which the PPPU had thrown its support.

Leaders: Lyudmyla DENYSYUK (Leader), Anatoliy KINAKH (Former Prime Minister).

Other parties and blocs that participated unsuccessfully in the 2007 legislative elections included the Agrarians Bloc Agrarian Ukraine, which included the **Ukrainian Peasant Democratic Party** (led by Valeriy VOSHCHEVSKIY); and the **All-Ukrainian Party of People's Trust**, which under the leadership of Andriy AZAROV, had secured 0.11 percent of the vote in the 2006 balloting.

Other Parties and Blocs That Contested the 2006 Legislative Elections:

Social Democratic Party of Ukraine (United) (*Sotsial-Demokratychna Partiya Ukrainy [Obyednana]*—SDPU[O]). Launched in 1990 by the minority leftist faction of the Ukrainian Social Democratic Movement (*Sotsial-Demokratychna Dvizheniya Ukrainy*—SDDU), the SDPU(O) was committed to democratic socialism in the tradition of the Second International, as exemplified by the prewar Ukrainian Social Democratic Workers' Party. The party's failure to win representation in the 1994 legislative poll strengthened those within it, favoring reunion with what was by then the SDPU.

Although the party included critics and prominent rivals of Kuchma, officials of the Kuchma government were also members. The SDPU(O) attempted a merger with the SDPU (below) late in 1997, but the negotiations failed. However, the SDPU(O) displayed surprising strength in the 1998 legislative election, attaining the required threshold of 4 percent to be allocated seats in the nationwide proportional voting. At the March 2002 election, the SPDU(O) won 6.3 percent of the proportional vote and 24 seats.

The SPDU(O) served as the core component of the Not Right Bloc (*Bloc Ne Tak)* that was formed in December 2005 by parties opposed to the Orange Revolution and Ukraine's proposed membership in Western organizations such as NATO and the EU. Other parties in the bloc (which won 1.01 percent of the vote in the 2006 legislative poll) included the **All-Ukrainian Political Union Women for the Future** (*Vseukrainske Politychne Obyednannya Zhinky za Majbutnie*—ZM), which won 2.1 percent of the proportional vote in the 2002 legislative elections under the leadership of Valentyna DOVZHENKO; the small, centrist **Republican Party of Ukraine,** launched in early 2005 by Yuriy BOYKO, a former head of the state gas company; and the **All-Ukrainian Union Center.**

The SPDU(O)'s Mykhaylo PAPIEV was named minister for labor and social policy in the August 2006 PR-led cabinet, and party Deputy Chair Nestor SHUFRYCH was appointed minister of emergency situations in December. Viktor MEDVEDCHUK, the SPDU(O) chair since 1998 and the head of the administration of President Kuchma in 2002–2005, resigned as party leader in July 2007. The new leaders subsequently announced that the SPDU(O) would not participate in the September legislative elections, describing them as unconstitutional. However, the party informally supported the PR in the balloting. The SPDU(O) presented (unsuccessfully) one candidate in a single-member constituency in the 2012 legislative poll.

Leaders: Yuriy ZAHORODNIY (Chair), Ihor SHURMA (Deputy Chair).

Peasants' Party of Ukraine (*Selyanska Partiya Ukrainy*—SelPU). Organized in January 1992 as the rural counterpart of the SPU, the SelPU was committed to land collectivization and opposed to rapid economic reform. By virtue of its strong support in the Soviet-era rural bureaucracy, it won 19 seats in the 1994 legislative balloting and subsequently attracted 31 independent deputies into its parliamentary group. Following the 1998 legislative poll (in which the SelPU competed in alliance with the SPU), Chair Oleksandr TKACHENKO, a strong opponent of IMF-requested economic reform, was elected chair of the Supreme Council. However, in early 2000 he was voted out in what was dubbed a "velvet revolution," by a pro-Kuchma majority. Since 2002 Tkachenko has been included on the KPU electoral list for national legislative balloting. The SelPU secured 0.31 percent of the vote in the 2006 legislative poll but did not participate in the 2007 or 2012 balloting.

Social Democratic Party of Ukraine (*Sotsial-Demokratychna Partiya Ukrainy*—SDPU). The SDPU was formed as the SDP by the majority moderate faction of the Ukrainian Social Democratic Movement, which split at its inaugural congress in May 1990. Likened to the German SPD, the party urged a complete break with Marxism but attracted only sparse support, winning two seats in 1994. In February 1995 the SDPU was reregistered following a merger with the Human Rights Party and, according to reports, the Ukrainian Party of Justice, although the latter contested the 1998 election as part of the Working Ukraine alliance. The SDPU received only 0.3 percent of the proportional vote in the 1998 legislative election. In the 2002 campaign it renewed its claim to being the only truly social democratic party in Ukraine, but it again attracted negligible vote support.

For information on other parties and blocs that presented candidates in the 2006 legislative elections, see the 2012 *Handbook*.

Other Parties:

It Is Time (*Pora*). The reformist *Pora* was formed in 2005 by members of youth organizations that had supported the Orange Revolution. It participated unsuccessfully in an electoral bloc with the RiP in the 2006 legislative elections before gaining one seat in the 2007 balloting as part of the NU-NS. It did not participate in the 2012 legislative elections.

Leader: Vladyslav KASKIV.

Liberal-Democratic Party of Ukraine (*Liberalno-Demokratychna Partiya Ukrainy*—LDPU). The LDPU was founded in Kiev in November 1990 on the premise that "socialism is incompatible with humanism and democracy." Its centrist orientation sharply distinguished it from the right-wing Russian Liberal Democratic Party. In the December 1991 presidential election the LDPU backed the candidacy of Volodymyr HRYNYOV. The LDPU participated in the European Choice electoral alliance with the USDP for the 1998 legislative balloting. The party was refused permission to participate in the 2006 legislative poll for technical reasons. It did not participate in the 2007 legislative elections but presented one candidate in a single-member constituency in 2012.

Leader: Andriy KOVAL.

Ukrainian Republican Party (*Ukrainska Respublikanska Partiya*—URP). The URP was launched during a congress of the Ukrainian Helsinki Union in April 1990, becoming Ukraine's first modern non-Communist party to receive official recognition. Its stated aim was the creation of a "parliamentary republic . . . [with] guaranteed freedom of activity."

In 1992 Mykhaylo HORYN, a cofounder of *Rukh,* joined the URP and was instrumental in organizing the Congress of National Democratic Forces (*Kongres Natsionalno–Demokratychnykh Syl*—KNDS), a coalition of some 20 organizations dedicated to working for national unity under President Kravchuk. The KNDS was credited with winning an aggregate of some 25 seats in the 1994 balloting, although the URP, weakened by the exit of a radical faction that became the Ukrainian Conservative Republican Party (UKRP, see Fatherland, above), won only 11 of those seats, one of its defeated candidates being Horyn. (He subsequently helped form the Republican Christian Party.) The URP led an unsuccessful effort to impeach President Kuchma in September 1997, accusing him of compromising the nation's sovereignty through the Black Sea treaty with Russia.

The URP contested the 1998 legislative election in a National Front (*Natsionalnyi Front*) alliance with the KUN (above) and the UKRP; however, the front won only 2.7 percent of the national proportional voting and therefore no proportional seats. The URP joined several other right-wing parties in supporting the 1999 presidential candidacy of former Security Service chief and prime minister Yevhen Marchuk, who won 8.1 percent of the vote, for fifth place in the October election.

In late 2001 the URP absorbed Oleksandr SERHIYENKO's Ukrainian Christian Democratic Party (*Ukrainska Khrystiyansko-Demokratychna Partiya*—UKhDP). Based in the Uniate Catholic population of Galicia, the UKhDP had been organized in April 1990 as the outgrowth of a Ukrainian Christian Democratic Front, formed in 1989. Its founders hoped to emulate the success of Bavaria's Christian Social Union before encountering a number of internal controversies that led in 1992 to the withdrawal of a moderate faction to form the Christian Democratic Party of Ukraine (*Khrystiyansko-Demokratychna Partiya Ukrainy*—KhDPU).

At an extraordinary session in October 2005, the URP split into two camps. One faction under the leadership of Levko LUKYANENKO retained the URP rubric, while a larger faction formed the URP *"Sobor"* (above). The rump URP was left without legal standing for the 2006 legislative poll. Consequently, Lukyanenko and several supporters were elected to the Supreme Council as part of the BYT. Following the elections, Lukyanenko launched the **URP-Lukyanenko**, which presented several unsuccessful candidates in the single-member constituencies in the 2012 legislative poll.

Leader: Levko LUKYANENKO.

Working Ukraine (*Trudova Ukraina*—TU). Working Ukraine (frequently translated into English as Labor Ukraine) was organized in March 1999 as a parliamentary faction. A 1998 electoral bloc of the same name, encompassing the Ukrainian Party of Justice (*Ukrainska Partiya Spravedlyvosti*—UPS) and the Civil Congress of Ukraine (*Hromadyanskiy Kongres Ukrainy*—HKU), had won 3 percent of the national proportional vote and one seat, held by the UPS's Andriy DERKACH, who joined the new faction.

Established as a party in June 1999, the TU was initially led by Mykhaylo SYROTA, who was subsequently associated with the Solidarity parliamentary faction. By that time, TU leadership had passed to former economic minister Serhiy TIHIPKO, a prominent banker. As of February 2001 the party's parliamentary faction comprised 48 deputies, second only to that of the KPU. Having called for formation of a coalition government, the TU subsequently campaigned to unseat Prime Minister Yushchenko.

One of the TU's stalwarts was Viktor PINCHUK, a son-in-law of former President Kuchma and representative of the powerful Dnepropetrovsk clan. The TU participated in the For a United Ukraine electoral bloc in 2002.

Tihipko, who managed the 2004 presidential campaign of the PR's Viktor Yanukovych, resigned as the TU leader in 2005. The party ran on its own in the 2006 legislative balloting, securing only 0.09 percent of the vote. In August 2007 TU leaders announced plans for the party's merger into the PR. Tihipko subsequently became the leader and 2010 presidential candidate of the SU (see PR, above).

Oleksandr PABAT secured 0.14 percent of the vote in the first round of presidential balloting in January 2010 as the candidate of the **People's Salvation Army**.

Regional Parties:

There are a number of active Crimean parties in addition to Crimean branches of many Ukrainian parties. The **Communist Party of Crimea** (*Kommunisticheskaya Partiya Kryma*—KPK), led by Leonid Hrach, was banned in 1991 but was permitted to reregister in 1993. The **National Movement of the Crimean Tatars** (*Natsionalyi Dvizheniya Krymskikh Tatar*—NDKT), led by Vashtiy ABDURAYIMOV, is the oldest of the Crimean Tatar groups, dating from the 1960s and formally established in April 1987. The **National Party** (*Milli Firka*—MF) is a radical Tatar group founded in August 1993 and named after the party that attempted to set up an independent Crimean Tatar republic in 1917–1918. The **Organization of the Crimean Tatar National Movement** (*Organizatsiya Krymskotatarskogo Natsionalnogo Dvizheniya*—OKND), the largest of the Crimean Tatar parties, urges exclusive jurisdiction for the Crimean parliament. The business-oriented **Party for the Economic Revival of Crimea** (*Partiya Ekonomicheskogo Vozrozhdeniya Kryma*—PEVK), which won one seat in the Ukrainian Supreme Council in 1994, has been led by Vladimir SHEVIOV (Volodymyr SHEVYOV). The secessionist **Republican Movement of Crimea** (*Republikanskoe Dvizheniya Kryma*—RDK) is led by Yuriy Meshkov, who was elected president of Crimea in January 1994. The **Russian Party of the Crimea** (*Russkoi Partiya Kryma*—RPK) was founded under the leadership of Sergei SHUVAINIKOV in September 1993 as a radical splinter of the RDK. The For Yanukovych Bloc was organized in Crimea in 2005 by supporters of former prime minister Viktor Yanukovych, while the Kunitsyn Bloc was launched by supporters of former Crimean prime minister Serhiy Kunitsyn. The former won 44 seats on a 33 percent vote share in the March 2006 balloting for the Crimean Supreme Council, while the latter secured 10 seats on a 7.6

percent vote share. The KPK finished fourth in the balloting with 9 seats. Reports in 2008 described the Russian Bloc, led by Vladimir TYUNIN, as the most powerful party in Crimea. Among other things, Tyunin called for Crimea to become part of Russia.

Other regional or ethnically based groups include the **Democratic Movement of the Donbas** (*Demokraticheskoe Dvizheniya Donbassa*—DDD); the **Union for Democratic Reforms** (*Obiednannia Demokratychnykh Peretvoren*—ODP), formed under the leadership of Serhiy USTYCH in December 1993 by former Soviet officials in the Transcarpathia region of western Ukraine; and the **Subcarpathian Republican Party** (SRP), which was established in 1992 to press for Transcarpathian autonomy. In 2008 the **Congress of the Carpathian Rusyns** called for creation of an ethnic Rusyn (or Ruthenian) state.

LEGISLATURE

Supreme Council (*Verkhovna Rada*). Formerly styled the Supreme Soviet, Ukraine's legislature is a unicameral body of 450 members. Under constitutional changes that went into effect in January 2006, all 450 members were selected in 2007 via proportional representation from a single nationwide constituency. The threshold to secure representation was 3 percent (reduced in 2006 from 4 percent); the term of office was four years. However constitutional amendments in early 2011 extended the term of the current legislature from four to five years and permanently fixed the term of office at five years. Later in the year, electoral law changes reintroduced a mixed proportional/single-member constituencies system (250 deputies elected via party-list proportional balloting in one nationwide constituency [5 percent threshold to gain representation] and 250 deputies elected via majoritarian [first-past-the-post] voting in single-member districts for which party and independent candidates were permitted). In addition, the formation of blocs (a previous fixture of the electoral landscape) was prohibited.

Following the balloting on October 28, 2012, the seats were distributed as follows: Party of Regions (PR), 185 (72 in the nationwide proportional balloting and 113 from single-member constituencies); Fatherland, 101 (62, 39); Ukrainian Democratic Alliance for Reform, 40 (34, 6); Freedom (*Svoboda*), 37 (25, 12); Communist Party of Ukraine, 32 (32, 0); United Center, 3 (0, 3); People's Party, 2 (0, 2); Union Party, 1 (0, 1); Radical Party of Oleh Lyashko, 1 (0, 1); independents, 43 (0, 43); and vacant, 5 (results were annulled in five single-member constituencies). Many of the independents subsequently aligned with the PR faction in the council. By-elections to fill 7 vacant seats were scheduled for December 15, 2013.

Speaker: Volodymyr RYBAK.

CABINET

[as of October 1, 2013]

Prime Minister	Mykola Azarov (PR)
First Deputy Prime Minister	Serhiy Arbuzov (ind.)
Deputy Prime Ministers	Yuriy Boyko (PR)
	Kostyantun Gryshchenko (ind.)
Ministers	
Agrarian Policy and Food	Mykola Prysyazhnyuk (PR)
Coal and Energy	Eduard Stavytsky (PR)
Culture	Leonid Novohatko
Defense	Pavlo Lebedev (PR)
Economic Development and Trade	Ihor Prasolov (PR)
Education and Science	Dmytry Tabachnyk (PR)
Environment and Natural Resources	Oleh Proskuriakov
Finance	Yuriy Kolobov (PR)
Foreign Affairs	Leonid Kozhara (PR)
Health	Dr. Raisa Bohatyriova (PR) [f]
Industrial Policy	Michael Korolenko
Infrastructure	Volodymyr Kozak (PR)
Internal Affairs	Vitaliy Zakharchenko (ind.)
Justice	Olena Lukash (PR) [f]
Regional Development, Construction, Housing, and Communal Services	Hennady Temnyk
Revenues and Fees	Oleksander Klymenko
Social Policy	Natalia Korolevska (Ukraine-Forward!) [f]
Youth and Sports	Ravil Safiullin

[f] = female

INTERGOVERNMENTAL REPRESENTATION

Ambassador to the U.S.: Olexander MOTSYK.

U.S. Ambassador to Ukraine: Geoffrey PYATT.

Permanent Representative to the UN: Yuriy SERGEYEV.

IGO Memberships (Non-UN): CEUR, CIS, EBRD, IOM, OSCE, WTO.

UNITED ARAB EMIRATES

al-Imarat al-Arabiyah al-Muttahidah

Political Status: Federation of six former Trucial States (Abu Dhabi, Dubai, Sharjah, Fujairah, Ajman, and Umm al-Qaiwain) established December 2, 1971; the seventh, Ras al-Khaimah, joined in 1972.

Area: 32,278 sq. mi. (83,600 sq. km).

Population: 4,106,427 (2005C), embracing (2009 estimates) Abu Dhabi (1,628,000), Dubai (1,722,000), Sharjah (1,017,000), Ras al-Khaimah (241,000), Ajman (250,000), Fujairah (152,000), and Umm al-Qaiwain (56,000); 8,315,686 (2013E—UN). Figures include noncitizens, who in 2010 constituted approximately 83 percent of the population, according to the government, which at that time estimated the total population at 8.2 million.

Major Urban Center (2005E): ABU DHABI (606,000).

Official Language: Arabic.

Monetary Unit: Emirati Dirham (market rate November 1, 2013: 3.67 dirhams = $1US).

Supreme Council: Composed of the rulers of the seven emirates (with dates of accession): Sheikh Khalifa ibn Zayed al-NAHYAN (Abu Dhabi, 2004), Sheikh Muhammad ibn Rashid al-MAKTUM (Dubai, 2006), Sheikh Sultan ibn Muhammad al-QASIMI (Sharjah, 1972), Sheikh Saud ibn Saqr al-QASIMI (Ras al-Khaimah, 2010), Sheikh Hamad ibn Muhammad al-SHARQI (Fujairah, 1974), Sheikh Humayd ibn Rashid al-NUAYMI (Ajman, 1981), and Sheikh Saud ibn Rashid al-MUALLA (Umm al-Qaiwain, 1981).

President: Sheikh Khalifa ibn Zayed al-NAHYAN (Ruler of Abu Dhabi); elected by the Supreme Council on November 3, 2004, to a five-year term, succeeding his father, Sheikh Zayed ibn Sultan al-NAHYAN, who died on November 2; reelected by the Supreme Council for a second five-year term on November 3, 2009.

Vice President and Prime Minister: Sheikh Muhammad ibn Rashid al-MAKTUM (Ruler of Dubai); named vice president and prime minister by the Supreme Council on January 5, 2006, succeeding his older brother, Sheikh Maktum ibn Rashid al-MAKTUM, who died on January 4.

THE COUNTRY

Formerly known as the Trucial States because of truces concluded with Britain in the 19th century, the United Arab Emirates (UAE)

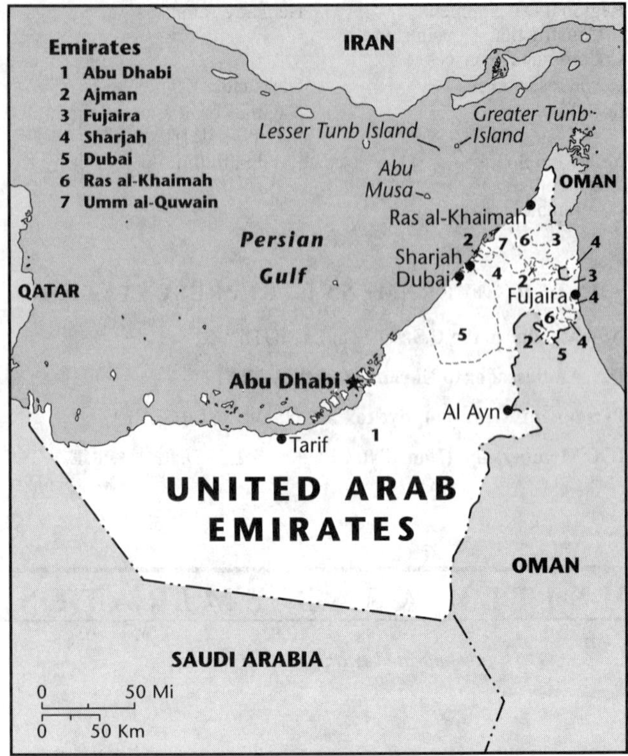

extends some 400 miles along the Persian Gulf from the southeastern end of the Qatar peninsula to the Gulf of Oman. (UAE territory separates Oman's governorate of Musandram, which overlooks the Strait of Hormuz, from the rest of Oman.) The UAE encompasses a barren, relatively flat territory characterized by extreme temperatures and sparse rainfall. The majority of the indigenous population is Arab and adheres to Islam (80 percent Sunni); there are also significant numbers of Iranians, Indians, Pakistanis, Baluchis, and descendants of former African slaves among the noncitizen population. (Some 100,000 descendants of immigrants are currently considered "stateless," despite having been born in the UAE.) Most UAE citizens are employed by the government, and they enjoy broad social benefits including subsidized housing and free health care and education. Tribal alliances contribute to long-standing support for the ruling families. The UAE has one of the most open societies in the Gulf region in terms of welcoming its huge foreign population and vast numbers of tourists without strictly enforcing many of its social laws among either group. Also, the UAE encourages women to participate in public life (20 percent of the seats in the consultative Federal National Council are reserved for women), and women may hold jobs. Although Arabic is the official language, English is commonly used in schools and among the diverse population; Farsi, Urdu, and Hindi are also spoken.

Traditionally, the area was dependent upon trading, fishing, and pearling. However, the discovery in 1958 of major oil reserves in Abu Dhabi and, subsequently, of smaller deposits in Dubai and Sharjah dramatically altered the economy. Oil wealth led to rapid infrastructural modernization, advances in education and health services, and a construction boom requiring a massive inflow of foreign labor. New industrial cities established at Jebel Ali in Dubai and Ruwais in Abu Dhabi gave rise to shipyards, cement factories, and other manufacturing sites. However, during the 1980s the UAE experienced a slowdown in economic growth because of reduced export revenues. As a result, the government moved to streamline the petroleum industry, which continued to account for 70 percent of government income, and began to develop marketing, refining, and petrochemical aspects of the oil trade.

Oil reserves are estimated at more than 95 billion barrels, approximately 8 percent of the world's total; approximately 90 percent of the UAE's known deposits are located in Abu Dhabi. The UAE government controls 60 percent of the energy sector, although it has permitted partial foreign ownership, thereby maintaining links with Western companies that have provided important ongoing infrastructure support. Moreover, the nation has firmly established itself as the region's leading trading center, partly on the strength of the Jebel Ali Free Trade Zone, where more than 350 companies operate. Dubai, in particular, has been effectively promoted as the region's trading and financial hub and as a major tourist destination.

The international financial crisis that developed in the second half of 2008 affected the UAE significantly, particularly in Dubai, where the recent rapid expansion of real estate prices and related construction came to a grinding halt. Real GDP in the UAE declined by more than 4 percent in 2009 as Dubai grappled with severe debt problems and oil receipts plummeted. Thanks to a major restructuring of Dubai's debt in 2010 and stimulus spending (including bank recapitalization and approval of funds for a massive new airport and other infrastructure improvements in Dubai) by the federal government, growth began to recover in 2010 and reached 4.3 percent in 2012. Concurrently the UAE regained its reputation as a safe haven for investors concerned about turmoil related to the Arab Spring elsewhere in the region. Other contributing expansionary factors in 2012 included higher oil prices, increased hydrocarbon production, and increased tourism.

GOVERNMENT AND POLITICS

Political background. Originally controlling an area known in the West as a refuge for pirates, a number of sheikhs in the eastern Persian Gulf first entered into agreements with the British in the early 19th century. After the failure of the initial treaty agreements of 1820 and 1835, a Perpetual Maritime Truce was signed in 1853. Relations with Britain were further strengthened by an Exclusive Agreement of 1892, whereby the sheikhs agreed not to enter into diplomatic or other foreign relations with countries other than Britain. In return, Britain guaranteed defense of the sheikhdoms against aggression by sea.

The treaty arrangements with Britain lasted until 1968, when the British announced their intention to withdraw from the Persian Gulf by 1971. An early attempt at unification, the Federation of Arab Emirates, was initiated in 1968 with British encouragement but collapsed when Bahrain and Qatar declared separate independence in 1971. Subsequently, the leaders of six of the Trucial States organized a new grouping, the UAE, which was formally constituted as an independent state on December 2, 1971, with Sheikh Zayed ibn Sultan al-NAHYAN of Abu Dhabi as president. The emirate of Ras al-Khaimah, which initially rejected membership, acceded to the UAE two months later after receiving assurances that the UAE would not relinquish claims on several islands in the Gulf recently occupied by Iran (see Foreign relations, below).

Apart from the death of Sheikh Khalid ibn Muhammad al-QASIMI (ruler of Sharjah) following an attempted coup in 1972, few major political developments occurred until the spring of 1979, when a series of disputes, principally between Abu Dhabi and Dubai over the extent of federal powers, led to the April 25 resignation of Prime Minister Sheikh Maktum ibn Rashid al-MAKTUM and his replacement five days later by his father, Sheikh Rashid ibn Said al-MAKTUM, ruler of Dubai, who also retained his position as vice president. In 1981 the emir of Ajman, Sheikh Rashid ibn Humayd al-NUAYMI, and the emir of Umm al-Qaiwain, Sheikh Ahmad ibn Rashid al-MUALLA, both of whom had ruled for more than 50 years, died and were succeeded by their sons, Sheikh Humayd ibn Rashid al-NUAYMI and Sheikh Rashid ibn Ahmad al-MUALLA, respectively.

On June 17, 1987, Sheikh Abd al-Aziz al-QASIMI seized power in Sharjah, accusing his brother, Sheikh Sultan ibn Muhammad al-QASIMI, of fiscal mismanagement. On July 20 Sheikh Muhammad was reinstated by the Supreme Council, which decreed that Sheikh Abd al-Aziz should thenceforth hold the title of crown prince and deputy ruler; however, Skeikh Abd al-Aziz was stripped of the title on February 4, 1990.

Following the death of Sheikh Rashid ibn Said al-Maktum on October 7, 1990, his son, Sheikh Maktum ibn Rashid, was named vice president. He also returned to his former position as prime minister.

In 1991 the UAE suffered a major blow to its international prestige by the midyear collapse of the Luxembourg-chartered Bank of Credit and Commerce International (BCCI), 77 percent of whose shares were owned by President Zayed and a group of financial associates. Ultimately, it was revealed that Sheikh Zayed had provided at least $1 billion to shore up the troubled institution since 1989. (For additional information, see the 2005–2006 *Handbook*.) A plan was approved in December 1995 under which BCCI creditors would be reimbursed $1.8 billion by the bank's major shareholders, observers estimating the paybacks would cover 20 to 40 percent of most deposits. The BCCI was formally liquidated by the UAE Central Bank in February 1996. (As of 2003 $5.7 billion had been authorized in paybacks to BCCI creditors, total claims having been estimated at $9 billion among some 80,000 depositors. The case, unprecedented in scope in British courts, went to trial in 2004, but liquidators dropped their case in 2005 in a move that shocked financial observers.)

The UAE cabinet submitted its resignation on March 17, 1997, and Sheikh Maktum was asked to form a new government, which was announced on March 25. The reshuffle, the first significant government change since 1990, was promoted as infusing "young blood" in the UAE policymaking process, although several important ministries remained in the hands of incumbents.

The president and vice president were reelected by the Supreme Council on December 2, 2001. The first cabinet reshuffle since 1997 took place on November 1, 2004; among the new cabinet members was the first female minister, a move in line with a stated government policy to involve more women in decision making. Sheikh Zayed, who had decreed the cabinet reshuffle, died on November 2; he was succeeded as president of the UAE and ruler of Abu Dhabi by his son, Sheikh Khalifa ibn Zayed al-NAHYAN.

In 2005 President Khalifa announced plans to hold limited elections as part of a package of political reforms. He proposed allowing half of the 40 members of the Federal National Council (FNC) to be elected by citizens appointed to electoral colleges in each emirate. The remaining 20 members of the FNC would continue to be appointed by the rulers of the 7 emirates (see Constitution and government, below).

Following the death of 62-year-old Sheikh Maktum on January 4, 2006, his younger brother, Defense Minister Sheikh Muhammad ibn Rashid al-MAKTUM, was named vice president and prime minister by the Supreme Council on January 5. He also succeeded his brother as ruler of Dubai.

Domestic attention in 2006 focused on the limited elections on December 16–20 for 20 members of the legislature. The elections were considered only a modest political reform since the rulers of the seven emirates chose those who could vote as members of an electoral college, and the actual number of electors was less than 7,000.

The global financial crisis that began in 2008 had major negative effects on the UAE, particularly in Dubai, where real estate prices fell by more than 30 percent and construction of many projects was suspended. The federal government first made $33 billion available to prop up banks in all seven emirates and then in February 2009 approved an additional $10 billion bailout for the financial sector in Dubai. However, Dubai World, the investment and management company that oversees much of the Dubai government's massive business interests, roiled international financial markets again in November by announcing plans to suspend payments on $23.5 billion of its debt for at least six months. However, Abu Dhabi in December agreed to another $10 billion bailout, which convinced the global financial community that Dubai was not headed for what many considered would have been a catastrophic default. Meanwhile, intense debt-restructuring negotiations continued, and in May 2010, seven leading creditors agreed to extend repayments on $14.4 billion of Dubai's debt over five to eight years at reduced interest rates. Nearly all the other creditors accepted new terms in September in a comprehensive restructuring plan that also called for Dubai World and affiliated bodies to sell some of their assets.

Sheikh Saqr ibn Muhammad al-QASIMI, who had ruled Ras al-Khaimah since seizing power from his brother in 1948, died on October 27, 2010, at the age of 92. He was succeeded by his son, Sheikh Saud ibn Saqr al-QASIMI, who had for a number of years been responsible for most governmental responsibilities in the emirate due to his father's advanced age. Sheikh Saud's half-brother, Sheikh Khalid ibn Saqr al-QASIMI, initially challenged the succession, announcing that he deserved consideration as the next emir despite having been deposed as crown prince in a 2003 family dispute. However, the UAE Supreme Council immediately endorsed Sheikh Saud's claim, and Sheikh Khalid reportedly left the country after security forces were deployed near his house.

Constitution and government. The institutions of the UAE were superimposed upon the existing political structures of the member states, which generally maintain their monarchical character. (Effective power within the federation remains in the hands of senior members of the ruling families of the seven emirates, led by Abu Dhabi, by far the most oil-rich emirate, and, to a lesser extent, Dubai, a major business center.) Under the federal constitution adopted in 1971 (designated an "interim" basic law until 1996), the rulers of the constituent states are members of the Supreme Council, which elects a president and vice president for five-year terms. Supreme Council decrees require the approval of the rulers of Abu Dhabi and Dubai and at least three other emirates. The president appoints a prime minister and a cabinet, and there is a consultative Federal National Council (FNC).

In July 1976 the FNC, following a failure to reach agreement on a new constitutional draft, voted to extend the life of the existing constitution for another five years beyond December 2. Further extensions were voted at five-year intervals thereafter until 1996, when the Supreme Council (May 20) and the FNC (June 18) approved an amendment removing "interim" from the language in the constitution, thereby effectively making it a permanent document.

In 2006 indirect elections were authorized for 20 of the 40 members of the FNC, all of whom were previously appointed by the rulers of the constituent emirates. Constitutional amendment in late 2008 empowered the FNC, previously confined to domestic affairs, to make recommendations on international matters as well.

Judicial functions have traditionally been performed by local courts applying Islamic law (sharia) and by individual decisions rendered by the ruling families. In June 1978 the president signed a law establishing four Primary Federal Tribunals (in Abu Dhabi, Ajman, Fujairah, and Sharjah) to handle disputes between individuals and the federation, with appeal to the federal Supreme Court (five judges appointed by the Supreme Council). However, a later decree of February 1994 specified that a variety of crimes (including murder, theft, adultery, and juvenile and drug-related offenses) would be tried in Islamic, rather than civil, courts.

The basic administrative divisions are the constituent states, each of which retains local control over mineral rights, taxation, and police protection. Abu Dhabi effectively controls the UAE's 65,000-member federal army.

While the constitution of the UAE guarantees freedom of the press, the government closely monitors Arabic-language media, although English-language media receive much less scrutiny. Meanwhile, journalism watchdogs have strongly criticized the UAE government recently for blocking politically charged Web sites and otherwise filtering Internet use. Bloggers and users of other social media were among those subjected to a sustained government crackdown in 2011–2013, the government in December 2012 enacting a new cyber crime law that critics argued was designed to suppress freedom of expression among netizens.

Foreign relations. The UAE is a member of the United Nations, the Arab League, the Organization of the Petroleum Exporting Countries (OPEC), and various regional groupings. Relations have been cordial with most countries, including the United States, although there have been territorial disputes with Iran, Oman, Qatar, and Saudi Arabia.

In 1971 Iran occupied Abu Musa, a small island in the Persian Gulf, and laid claim to the Greater and Lesser Tunbs, two uninhabited but potentially strategically important islands. Soon after, an agreement was reached between Tehran and the emir of Sharjah that provided for joint administration of Abu Musa and the sharing of revenue from offshore oil wells. However, no accord was reached regarding the Tunbs (claimed by Ras al-Khaimah). Following the establishment of diplomatic relations between Iran and the UAE in 1972, the issue remained relatively dormant before flaring up in 1992 (see below).

A dispute with Saudi Arabia and Oman concerned portions of Abu Dhabi, including the potentially oil-rich Buraimi Oasis, located at the juncture of the three states. Under the terms of an agreement reached in 1974, six villages of the oasis were awarded to Abu Dhabi and two to Oman; Saudi Arabia, in return for renouncing its claim, was granted a land corridor coterminous with the existing Abu Dhabi–Qatar border to the Persian Gulf port of Khor al-Adad. (The border demarcation issue resurfaced in September 1992 in the form of a clash between Saudi Arabian and Qatari forces [see Qatar: Foreign relations]. In June 2002 Oman and the UAE implemented an agreement to demarcate their border.)

In early 1981 the UAE joined with five neighbors—Bahrain, Kuwait, Oman, Qatar, and Saudi Arabia—in establishing the Cooperative Council of the Arab Gulf States (more commonly known as the Gulf Cooperation Council—GCC) to coordinate members' policies on security and stability in the area. Concern over the subsequent Iran-Iraq war led the UAE to participate in the GCC's annual Peninsula Shield joint military maneuvers. Although the hazards of the regional conflict did not preclude an increase in trade with Tehran, the UAE and the other GCC states became increasingly aware of their vulnerability to the potentially destabilizing effects of an Iranian-inspired Islamic revolution. Subsequently, in the wake of oilfield bombings by the Gulf combatants, including one by unidentified aircraft that killed eight people and destroyed two of five platforms in Abu Dhabi, the UAE took steps to purchase advance-warning systems from Britain, France, and the United States.

The UAE reacted nervously to Iraq's occupation of Kuwait on August 2, 1990, because it, like Kuwait, had been charged by

Baghdad with overproduction of oil. On August 19, having joined with other GCC governments in calling for Iraq's withdrawal from Kuwait, the UAE agreed to the deployment of foreign military units on its soil. It also cooperated with coalition forces during the confrontation that concluded with Iraq's defeat in February 1991. In April it was reported that the UAE had contributed nearly $3 billion to U.S. Gulf War costs.

With Iraqi belligerence still appearing to present a challenge to regional security, the Gulf states subsequently attempted to improve relations with Iran, and the UAE in July 1991 named its first ambassador to Tehran since the latter's 1979 revolution. However, in early 1992 Iran reignited the long-dormant Gulf dispute between the two nations by expelling some 700 UAE nationals from Abu Musa and seizing complete control of the island. After the GCC demanded in September that Iran repudiate its "annexation" of Abu Musa, Tehran reasserted its claim of sovereignty over the island as well as over the Greater and Lesser Tunbs, vowing that UAE forces would have to cross a "sea of blood" to retake the territory. Although the UAE subsequently sought international mediation of the dispute, Iran rejected the proposal, and tension between the countries continued.

In July 1994 the UAE became the fourth GCC country to conclude a military cooperation pact with the United States. The agreement, which provided for joint military exercises and the stationing of a U.S. naval task force on UAE territory, was reportedly signed because of the Emirates' perceived vulnerability to attack by Iran or Iraq.

As did its GCC neighbors, the UAE expressed concern in the 1990s over the security implications of growing Islamist militancy in North Africa and the Middle East. In March 2000 the UAE, as part of an ambitious defense program, signed a contract with the U.S.-based Lockheed Martin Corporation worth $6.4 billion for 80 F-16 fighters, having previously concluded a deal in 1998 for $3.5 billion for French planes. Concurrently the UAE announced plans to spearhead an $8 billion regional gas network in conjunction with other GCC members as well as Western energy companies. As a first stage of the 25-year project, Abu Dhabi negotiated a $3.5 billion agreement to develop gas fields in Qatar and ship gas from there, initially to the other emirates and Gulf states, such as Oman, and eventually to India and Pakistan. The project, the first such cross-border arrangement in GCC history, was considered an important element in establishing the UAE as the hub of a regional "energy security" network. At the same time, however, it brought increasing pressure from the international community on the UAE to establish procedures to ensure greater transparency and accountability in its financial sector. Critics charged that long-standing secrecy contributed to UAE banks being used for money laundering, while lack of oversight of business dealings permitted unnoticed transshipment of drugs and illegal weapons through UAE ports. The UAE's banking system and financial practices were further criticized after the September 2001 attacks in the United States when it became evident that close associates of Osama bin Laden had used the country's banks to transfer and receive money from several of the hijackers. Promising reform, the UAE in January 2002 adopted a series of policy changes to monitor banking practices and financial transactions and instituted new penalties to combat money laundering. The UAE also agreed to cooperate closely with the George W. Bush administration's war on terrorism. Among other measures, the UAE severed diplomatic relations with the Taliban administration in Afghanistan after it refused to hand over bin Laden.

In March 2003 the UAE president offered a vague plan for Iraqi president Saddam Hussein's permanent exile, defying the Arab League stance on noninterference in the internal affairs of a neighboring country. After the U.S. invasion and occupation of Iraq, the UAE, whose embassy in Baghdad had reopened in 2000, was among the first countries to send relief shipments.

In 2004 the commander of U.S. Central Command described U.S.-UAE military cooperation as among the strongest in the region. France's defense minister expressed similar sentiments, while the United Kingdom in 2005 announced its commitment to developing military and industrial cooperation with the UAE.

In 2006 the U.S. State Department set up offices in Dubai to enhance its ability to monitor Iran. Other countries made similar efforts, given Dubai's proximity to Iran and its popularity with Iranian businesspeople and tourists. As international concern regarding Iran's nuclear program increased, the UAE sought to balance its extensive commercial interests with Iran with its strong political ties to the United States.

DP World, a subsidiary of Dubai World, created a major political controversy in 2006 when it sought to manage terminal operations at six U.S. ports. The company sold its interests in the ports after what the *New York Times* described as "an unrelenting bipartisan attack" in the U.S. Congress over security concerns. Ironically, observers pointed out, the Dubai company's operations originated in Jebel Ali, the port outside the United States most often visited by the U.S. Navy and known for its state-of-the-art security. Soon after the DP World controversy, the Bush administration expressed security concerns over reported shipments of sensitive military technology from Dubai ports to Iran and Syria.

In April 2008 French president Nicolas Sarkozy visited the UAE, where he signed a deal to establish a permanent French military base in Abu Dhabi. On the same occasion, France and the UAE also signed a memorandum of understanding on cooperation in civil nuclear power projects. The UAE signed a similar nuclear deal with the United Kingdom in June 2008, while a nuclear cooperation pact was approved in January 2009 with the United States under which the UAE forswore uranium enrichment and plutonium reprocessing. The new U.S. administration of President Barack Obama accepted a plan in June for the UAE to buy fuel and materials for its nuclear power plants from the United States. The UAE subsequently signed a $20 billion agreement for a South Korean consortium to build four such plants, with the first scheduled to become operational in 2017.

In May 2009 the UAE announced that it would not participate in a proposed GCC monetary union, thereby appearing to doom the union's prospects.

International concern arose following the assassination of a Palestinian militant visiting Dubai in January 2010. Police in Dubai accused the Israel spy agency Mossad of the assassination and said many of the 26 attackers had used fake or stolen passports from European countries, who objected to Israel's actions and launched their own investigations into the passport situation.

The UAE continued in 2010 to voice its concern over Iran's nuclear program and Iran's support for militant Shiite groups in the Middle East. In May 2011 the government reportedly agreed to hire an American-led mercenary force of some 800 soldiers (mostly from Latin America) to provide additional security against the possibility of conflict with Iran or unrest among the Shiite population in the UAE.

In March 2011, following the outbreak of the Arab Spring in North Africa, the UAE (along with Saudi Arabia) deployed troops to Bahrain to support the Sunni-dominated government in Bahrain against Shiite protesters. Shiite-Sunni tensions also apparently contributed to renewed diplomatic conflict with Iran over the disputed Gulf islands when Iranian president Mahmoud Ahmadinejad visited Abu Musa in April 2012 and the Iranian military pledged a military response if its sovereignty claim was threatened. In June the UAE announced the opening of a new pipeline from the offshore oil fields of Dubai to Fujairah, thereby opening up 50 percent of UAE oil production to transshipment directly from the Gulf of Oman and avoiding the Strait of Hormuz, which could be blocked by Iran in case of conflict. Concurrent regional concerns for the UAE included the fighting in Syria (the UAE supported the opposition forces there and accused President Bashar al-Assad's government of "crimes against the Syrian people") and the ascendancy of to political dominance in Egypt of the Muslim Brotherhood, which the UAE accused of "exporting revolution."

In July 2013 the UAE expressed satisfaction over the ouster of Egyptian president Morsi and pledged $3 billion in aid to the new interim Egyptian administration. Meanwhile, still with a wary eye on Iran, the UAE agreed to buy 26 more U.S. F-16 warplanes (for $5 billion) as well as recently developed U.S. air-to-ground missiles.

Current issues. In March some 100 UAE reformers petitioned the government to install a genuine parliamentary democracy, with a fully elected legislature empowered to make law. With an apparent eye on developments in Egypt and Tunisia, the UAE government adopted a hard line, arresting five reformers. The federal government also announced a $1.5 billion investment program for its poorer northern emirates, mindful that economic disparities were playing a major role in the Arab Spring uprisings.

The number of UAE citizens eligible to vote in the electoral colleges was increased to nearly 130,000 for the September 2011 balloting for the Federal National Council, which was described as a "small nod" toward prodemocracy sentiment. However, the number of candidates remained limited, and turnout was low (about 28 percent).

The government arrested seven members of the *al-Islah* (Reform) society in December 2011 and stripped them of their UAE nationality for activities supporting "foreign agendas." Further arrests were reported throughout 2012 and into 2013, contributing to what Human

Rights Watch characterized as "an unprecedented crackdown on peaceful dissent." In the eyes of some analysts, the government's approach appeared unnecessarily heavy-handed, considering the fact that the Arab Spring had prompted little response among the UAE population, which was benefiting from the nation's renewed economic vigor. Nevertheless, nearly 70 defendants, including members of *al-Islah,* were convicted in July 2013 and sentenced to up to 15 years in jail after a mass trial on various security charges. Included were professors, lawyers, and other prominent members of society who argued that they were promoting reform (and, for some, a "more Islamic government"), not overthrow.

POLITICAL GROUPS

There are no political parties in the UAE.

Al-Islah (Reform). First organized in the 1970s, the Islamist *al-Islah* society was subsequently informally tolerated by the UAE government, and the organization gained influence in, among other areas, educational and judicial associations. The government reportedly adopted a more cautious approach toward *al-Islah* following the 2001 terrorist attacks in the United States, and in the wake of the Arab Spring uprisings in the region, a number of *al-Islah* members were among the petitioners calling in early 2011 for democratization in the UAE (see Current issues, above). The government responded with a crackdown that included the dissolution of *al-Islah*'s elected governing board and the replacement of *al-Islah* members in various associations with government appointees. In addition, in December a group of *al-Islah* members had their UAE nationality revoked over what the government described as matters of national security.

Sheikh Sultan ibn Kayed al-QASSIMI, described as the chair of *al-Islah*, was briefly detained in April 2012, and more members of the group were arrested later in the year, and in 2013, the government reportedly viewing *al-Islah* as a proxy in the UAE for the Muslim Brotherhood, whose recent rise to power in Egypt had generated concern in the Gulf sheikdoms. Leaders of *al-Islah*, claiming the support of 20,000 followers in the UAE, denied formal links with the Muslim Brotherhood.

LEGISLATURE

Federal National Council (*Majlis al-Watani al-Itihadi*). The UAE's consultative body currently consists of 40 delegates (8 each from Abu Dhabi and Dubai, 6 each from Sharjah and Ras al-Khaimah, and 4 each from Ajman, Fujairah, and Umm al-Qaiwain). Twenty are appointed by the rulers of the constituent states, and 20 are elected by electoral colleges (established in 2006) appointed by the rulers. The first elections were held in three rounds December 16–20, 2006, for 20 seats (one-half of the members in each emirate). The 20 elected and 20 appointed delegates were sworn in on February 12, 2007, for a two-year term, although the term was extended to four years in late 2008. The most recent balloting for the 20 elected delegates was held on September 24, 2011.

Speaker: Abdul-Aziz Abdallah al-GHURAIR.

CABINET

[as of September 1, 2013]

Prime Minister	Sheikh Muhammad ibn Rashid al-Maktum
Deputy Prime Minister (Interior)	Lt. Gen. Sheikh Saif ibn Zayed al-Nahyan
Deputy Prime Minister (Presidential Affairs)	Sheikh Mansur ibn Zayed al-Nahyan
Ministers	
Cabinet Affairs	Mohammed Abdullah al-Gergawi
Culture, Youth, and Community Development	Nahyan ibn Mubarak al-Nahyan
Defense	Sheikh Muhammad ibn Rashid al-Maktum
Development and International Cooperation	Sheikha Lubna bint Khalid al-Qasimi [f]
Economy	Sultan ibn Said al-Mansuri
Education	Hamaid Muhammad Obaid al-Qatami
Energy	Suhail Muhammad al-Mazrui
Environment and Water	Rashid Ahmad ibn Fahd
Finance	Sheikh Hamdan ibn Rashid al-Maktum
Foreign Affairs	Sheikh Abdallah ibn Zayed al-NAYHAN
Foreign Trade	Sheikha Lubna bint Khalid al-Qasami [f]
Health	Abdul Rahman Muhammad al-Owais
Higher Education and Scientific Research	Hamdan ibn Mubarak al-Nahyan
Justice	Hadef Jawan al-Zaheri
Labor	Saqr Ghabbash Said Ghabbash
Public Works	Abdullah ibn Muhammad al-Nuaimi
Social Affairs	Maryam Muhammad Khalfan al-Roumi [f]
Ministers of State	
Federal National Council Affairs	Anwar Muhammad Gargash
Financial Affairs	Ubayd Hamid al-Tayir
Foreign Affairs	Anwar Muhammad Gargash
Without Portfolio	Abdullah Ghubash
Without Portfolio	Rim Ibrahim al-Hashimi [f]
Without Portfolio	Sultan al-Jabir
Without Portfolio	Maytha Salim al-Shamsi [f]

[f] = female

INTERGOVERNMENTAL REPRESENTATION

Ambassador to the U.S.: Yousef Mana Saeed al-OTAIBA.

U.S. Ambassador to the United Arab Emirates: Michael H. CORBIN.

Permanent Representative to the UN: Lana Zaki NUSSEIBEH.

IGO Memberships (Non-UN): GCC, NAM, OIC, OPEC, WTO.

UNITED KINGDOM

United Kingdom of Great Britain and Northern Ireland

Political Status: Constitutional monarchy, under democratic parliamentary regime.

Area: 94,249 sq. mi. (244,104 sq. km), embracing England and Wales, 58,382 sq. mi. (151,209 sq. km); Scotland, 30,415 sq. mi. (78,775 sq. km); Northern Ireland, 5,452 sq. mi. (14,120 sq. km).

Population: 63,243,845 (2013E—UN); 63,395,574 (2013E—U.S. Census).

Major Urban Centers (2011E): *England:* LONDON (urban area, 9,787,000), Birmingham (1,085,000), Liverpool (552,000), Leeds (475,000), Sheffield (518,000), Bristol (536,000), Manchester (511,000); *Wales:* CARDIFF (335,000); *Scotland:* EDINBURGH (459,000), Glasgow (590,000); *Northern Ireland:* BELFAST (281,000).

Principal Language: English (Scottish and Irish forms of Gaelic are spoken in portions of Scotland and Northern Ireland, respectively, while Welsh is spoken in northern and central Wales).

Monetary Unit: Pound Sterling (market rate November 1, 2013: 0.63 pound = $1US).

Sovereign: Queen ELIZABETH II; proclaimed queen on February 6, 1952; crowned June 2, 1953.

Heir Apparent: CHARLES Philip Arthur George; invested as Prince of Wales on July 1, 1969.

Prime Minister: David William Donald CAMERON (Conservative Party); appointed by the queen on May 11, 2010, to lead a two-party coalition government following the election on May 6, succeeding James Gordon BROWN (Labour Party).

THE COUNTRY

The United Kingdom of Great Britain and Northern Ireland (UK) occupies the major portion of the British Isles, the largest island group off the European coast. The individual identity of its separate regions, each with distinctive ethnic and linguistic characteristics, is reflected in the complex governmental structure of the country as a whole. England, the heart of the nation, accounts for over half the total area and 83 percent of the total population. Wales, conquered in the Middle Ages, has its own capital, Cardiff, and a national language, Welsh, with which some 30 percent of the population have familiarity. Scotland, ruled as a separate kingdom until 1707, has long had its own legal and educational systems; its capital is Edinburgh. Conquered by the English in the Middle Ages, Ireland became part of the UK in 1800 but in 1921 was partitioned into Northern Ireland, whose Protestant majority opted for retention of British status, and the predominantly Catholic Irish Republic. Varieties of the Gaelic language are spoken in both Scotland and Northern Ireland. There are two established churches, the Church of England (Episcopalian or Anglican), with some 1.5 million active members, and the Church of Scotland (Presbyterian), with some 700,000 members. Nonestablished religions include Roman Catholicism, Islam, and Methodism. At the 2011 census, 59.3 percent of the population identified themselves as Christians, while 25.1 percent reported no religious affiliation. Apart from a legal prohibition on the monarch (who is head of the Church of England) or the heir to the throne becoming a Roman Catholic, religious freedom prevails.

In 2010 women comprised 50.8 percent of the paid (including part-time) workforce, concentrated in the retail, clerical, and human services sectors. Following the election of May 2010, women held 143 of the 650 seats in the House of Commons. Women also occupied 147 of the seats in the House of Lords and held 5 ministries in the new government.

Great Britain was the seat of the industrial revolution of the 18th century, and most of its urbanized and highly skilled population is engaged in manufacturing and service industries, mainly transport, commerce, and finance, with agriculture accounting for only 1 percent of GDP and employment. Machinery, basic manufactures, and agricultural products constitute the bulk of British imports. Machinery and transport equipment, basic manufactures, chemicals, and mineral fuels are the chief exports. Germany, the United States, and Japan rank as the leading trading partners.

The British economy experienced intermittent crises after World War II as the result of factors that included the wartime liquidation of most of the country's overseas assets and a lack of flexibility in management and labor practices. Emigration and immigration, featuring the "brain drain" of skilled professional personnel (mainly to the United States) and a concurrent influx of nonwhite labor from Africa, South Asia, the West Indies, and elsewhere, also produced unsettling economic and social effects, including racial tensions. The oil crisis of 1973–1974 was particularly damaging to the UK economy, but in the late 1970s fiscal constraint and increased exploitation of North Sea oil reserves yielded annual GDP increases of 2–3 percent, despite remaining structural problems. Under the post-1979 Conservative government, policies to increase productivity at first exacerbated the effects of international recession, causing unemployment to rise into the double digits and industrial output to fall. From 1983 the economy experienced something of a boom: Overall economic growth averaged over 3 percent a year from 1983 to 1989, corporate profits rose, productivity was second only to that of Japan, annual inflation fell to around 4 percent, and the government ran a budget surplus.

The "British economic miracle" foundered in the wake of the stock market crash of October 1989. Initially, the government sought recovery by increasing liquidity, but a rapid inflationary surge forced it to apply interest rates at record highs. In October 1990 the pound sterling was placed in the broad band of the European Community (EC) exchange rate mechanism (ERM), which in effect pegged it to the deutsche mark. By then, the economy had entered its deepest and longest recession since the 1930s, aggravated by similar difficulties in other industrial economies. In 1991–1992 overall output dropped by 3.6 percent and unemployment, having fallen to a ten-year low of 5.9 percent in 1989, rose to 10.5 percent by late 1992. In September 1992 massive speculation against the pound sterling forced its withdrawal from the ERM and, in effect, a 20 percent devaluation.

Clear signs of a rebound appeared in 1993, and by April 1994 the GDP had regained its pre-slump (1990) peak. The recovery continued in 1995–1997, with annual GDP growth averaging about 3 percent. A global slowdown held expansion to 2.2 percent in 1998 and 2.0 percent in 1999, although growth in the last three quarters of the latter year returned to an annualized rate of about 3 percent and helped vault the UK over France and into fourth place among the world's largest economies. Moreover, unemployment stood at only 4 percent, the lowest rate in a quarter of a century, while retail inflation remained below the target of 2.5 percent. Although the Labour administration that took office in 1997 had initially maintained the fiscal restraint imposed during the 18-year reign of the Conservatives, the budget for 2000–2001 proposed significant spending increases, with a focus on improving the national health system and education. GDP growth in 2000–2004 ranged between 2.0 percent and 3.2 percent annually.

In its 2005 report, the IMF praised the UK for a "remarkable performance" over the past decade, marked by sustained growth, low inflation, and steadily low unemployment. However, GDP growth for 2005 fell to 1.9 percent (the lowest in 13 years) and continued to fall as the global economic crisis spread. After contracting 4.4 percent in 2009, GDP crept upward, to 2.1 percent in 2010, only to fall back to 0.7 percent in 2011. Unemployment has risen, from 7.5 percent in 2009 to 7.9 percent in 2010, 8 percent in 2011, and 8.3 percent forecast for 2012. The new Conservative-led government elected in 2010 announced plans to restore confidence in the economy with a front-loaded proposal to cut spending and raise taxes, with the intention of balancing the budget by 2017. Instead, the UK entered its first double-dip recession (defined as consecutive quarterly drops in GDP before the economy has recovered from the latest recession) since 1975.

GOVERNMENT AND POLITICS

Political background. After reaching its apogee of global influence in the closing decades of the Victorian era, the UK endured the strains of the two world wars with its political institutions unimpaired but with sharp reductions in its relative economic strength and military power. The steady erosion of the British imperial position after World War II was only partially offset by the concurrent development and expansion of the Commonwealth, a grouping that continued to reflect an underlying British philosophy but whose center of gravity shifted to newly developed and developing nations. Despite continuing differences on many issues, the three traditional parties—Conservative, Labour, and Liberal (now the Liberal Democrats)—have in some respects drawn closer together.

The Labour Party, after winning the postwar elections of 1945 and 1950 under the leadership of Clement R. ATTLEE, went into opposition for 13 years while the Conservative Party governed under prime ministers Winston CHURCHILL (1951–1955), Anthony EDEN (1955–1957), Harold MACMILLAN (1957–1963), and Alec DOUGLAS-HOME (1963–1964). A Conservative defeat in the general election of October 1964 returned Labour to power under Harold WILSON. At the election of June 1970 the tide swung back to the Conservatives, who under Edward HEATH obtained a 30-seat majority in the House of Commons. In February 1974 the Conservatives outpolled Labour but fell 3 seats short of a plurality, Wilson returning to head the first minority government since 1929. A second election eight months later gave Labour an overall majority of 3 seats. In April 1976 Wilson unexpectedly resigned and was succeeded as prime minister by Foreign Secretary James CALLAGHAN, who saw Labour's fortunes plummet in the 1978–1979 "winter of discontent" that featured damaging public sector strikes.

In May 1979 the Conservatives obtained 339 seats (a majority of 44) in the House of Commons, enabling Margaret THATCHER to become the first female prime minister in British (and European) history. Benefiting from popular response to her handling of the Falkland Islands War (see Foreign relations, below), the Conservatives surged to a 144-seat majority at the election of June 1983. They retained control of the Commons with a somewhat diminished but still comfortable majority of 102 in June 1987, Thatcher becoming the first prime minister in modern British history to win three consecutive terms.

Following the introduction of a widely disliked community charge ("poll tax") in April 1990, the Conservatives' popularity took a downward turn that was only briefly reversed by public appreciation of Thatcher's firmness in response to the Persian Gulf conflict precipitated by Iraq's invasion of Kuwait in August. Amid a damaging series of by-election defeats for the Conservatives, a sense of crisis was generated by the resignation on November 1 of the deputy prime minister, Geoffrey HOWE, over the prime minister's lack of support for enhanced British participation in the EC. On November 13 the former defense secretary, Michael HESELTINE, reversing an earlier pledge, challenged Thatcher for the party leadership, and at an intraparty poll on November 20 he won sufficient backing to deny the prime minister a first-round victory. Two days later Thatcher announced her intention to resign. In the second-round ballot on November 27 Chancellor of the Exchequer John MAJOR defeated both Heseltine and Foreign Secretary Douglas HURD. Having abandoned the poll tax and moderated other aspects of "Thatcherite" policies that had enjoyed his keen support theretofore, Major led the Conservatives to a fourth successive election victory on April 9, 1992, despite economic recession and negative forecasts from opinion pollsters. Although Labour made significant gains, the Conservatives retained a working majority of 336 seats in the 651-member House of Commons.

The Danish referendum vote in June 1992 against the Maastricht Treaty on greater EC economic and political union caused divisions to surface within the Conservative Party between pro- and anti-EC factions, the latter being dubbed "Eurosceptics." Because of the government's modest majority, anti-EC Conservative MPs were able to mount protracted resistance to parliamentary ratification of the Maastricht Treaty until after reversal of the Danish negative vote in May 1993 (see Foreign relations, below).

The opposition Labour Party displayed its own internal fissures over the EC. However, its main task was to revitalize its leadership following the resignation of Neil KINNOCK, who had suffered defeat in two successive general elections. Elected leader in July 1992, John SMITH maintained Kinnock's moderate, pro-EC stance while initiating reviews of Labour's social and constitutional policies. A rapid Labour rise in the opinion polls in late 1992 was assisted by a series of major government reverses and blunders, amid a European currency crisis that forced the pound sterling out of the EC's ERM.

The withdrawal from the ERM represented a traumatic collapse of government economic policy. In March 1993 Chancellor of the Exchequer Norman LAMONT presented a "budget for jobs" and claimed that the recession was over, but a spiraling budget deficit obliged him to introduce tax increases effective in 1994, some in breach of Conservative election pledges. Major later sought to recover the initiative by launching a "back to basics" campaign, stressing traditional Conservative values on education, law and order, and other matters.

The issuance of the joint UK-Irish Downing Street Declaration on Northern Ireland in December 1993 yielded some political credit to Major (and led eventually to the historic cease-fire announcement by the Irish Republican Army [IRA] on August 31, 1994—see Northern Ireland entry). Conservative fortunes nevertheless continued their decline, and in June 1994 the party lost 16 of its 34 seats in the European Parliament. The clear victor in the balloting was the Labour Party, under the interim leadership of Margaret BECKETT following the sudden death of Smith on May 12. Subsequent Labour leadership elections, for the first time involving all individual party members, resulted in 41-year-old Tony BLAIR emerging an easy winner on July 22. Seeking to appeal to "middle England," Blair accelerated the modernization of Labour policies and structures.

Rocked by scandals, including the press revelation that certain Conservative MPs had accepted "cash for questions" (payment from outside interests for tabling parliamentary questions to ministers), the government continued to face bitter opposition from some of its own backbenchers. On November 28, 1994, eight Conservative Eurosceptics rebelled against a financing bill for the EU that the government had made an issue of confidence. The EU issue, the "sleaze factor" resulting from an unremitting flow of sex and financial scandals, and other divisions contributed to all-time low opinion-poll ratings for the Conservatives, who in local elections on May 4, 1995, suffered the party's heaviest postwar defeat.

Amid renewed speculation about his future, Prime Minister Major on June 22, 1995, announced his formal resignation from the party leadership, forcing critics to "put up or shut up" regarding his reelection. All but one cabinet minister declared support for the prime minister, the exception being John REDWOOD, who resigned as secretary for Wales in order to challenge Major on a strongly Eurosceptic platform. Major emerged the comfortable first-round victor on July 4.

Local elections in May 1996 dropped the Conservatives to third place, behind Labour and the Liberal Democrats, in terms of total local councilors. With allegations of improper financial conduct on the part of Conservative members of Parliament (including junior ministers) being supported by the Nolan Commission on Standards in Public Life, and with time running out on the five-year legislative term, the prime minister on March 17, 1997, asked for a dissolution of Parliament. The election held on May 1 resulted in one of the worst defeats for any governing party in the last century, as the Conservatives won only 165 seats, its losing candidates including 7 cabinet members. Labour swept to power by securing 418 seats on the strength of 44.4 percent of the vote. In keeping with his "centrist" stance, Blair named a mix of "old hands" and "New Labour modernizers" to the new cabinet appointed on May 7. Following the election, former prime minister Major announced his resignation as Conservative leader, with Eurosceptic William HAGUE defeating the pro-EU Kenneth Clarke in the subsequent contest to lead the party.

Carrying through on one of Labour's most prominent campaign pledges, the Blair government quickly pursued decisions in Wales and Scotland regarding devolution of regional authority. In a referendum on September 11, 1997, 74 percent of the voters in Scotland approved the proposed creation of a Scottish Parliament, while on September 18 a plan for establishment of a Welsh National Assembly was endorsed by 50.3 percent of the voters in Wales. (Elections for the two bodies—the first Scottish legislature since 1707 and the first ever in Wales—were held on May 6, 1999, with Labour emerging as the plurality party in both. The Scottish Parliament and Welsh National Assembly both held opening ceremonies on July 1, with Queen Elizabeth II in attendance in Edinburgh.)

The long process of negotiation and accommodation in Northern Ireland, which included the direct involvement of both British and Irish governments, led to the signing on April 10, 1998, of a multiparty peace accord, the Belfast (Good Friday) Agreement, followed on June 25 by the election of a Northern Ireland Assembly. Devolution of powers from London to the assembly and a power-sharing executive occurred on December 2, 1999.

In 1998–1999 the government issued white papers, or commission reports, addressing the future makeup of local government, various proportional representation schemes, campaign finance reform, freedom of information, and social service reform. At the same time, however, the Blair government downplayed any commitments that might entail substantial increases in spending or taxation, while encroaching even further on traditional Conservative territory by promoting "family values," social responsibility, citizenship, and a hard line on street crime. The "New Labour" program also attacked "something for nothing" welfare policies and proposed pension reform, despite considerable opposition from Labour traditionalists.

One of the most contentious issues during the early years of the Blair administration was if and when to adopt the EU's euro as a replacement for the pound sterling. Although the Blair government consistently supported eventual entry into the EMU, widespread public opposition forced the administration to review its strategy and adjust its timetable.

A lingering dispute over the disarming of the paramilitary IRA led London to reimpose direct rule in Northern Ireland on February 11, 2000. On May 30 power was again devolved, the IRA having agreed, earlier in the month, to put its arsenals under international supervision. Little progress was made in the following 16 months, despite repeated negotiating efforts by Prime Minister Blair, Irish Prime Minister Ahern, and others, as paramilitary arms decommissioning, police reform, and withdrawal of British forces continued to be at issue. On August 10, 2001, and again on September 22 London briefly suspended the assembly as a technical maneuver to avoid calling a new election. The devolved government was given new life by the IRA's October 23 announcement that it had begun decommissioning to "save the peace process," but revelations of IRA spying ultimately led London to reimpose direct rule from October 15, 2002 (see Northern Ireland entry for details).

The issues of immigration and political asylum also came to the fore in the late 1990s and early 2000s. With the Conservative Party calling for tough measures to discourage "economic migrants" posing as political refugees, Home Secretary Jack Straw in March 2000 called for a complete reexamination of the 1951 UN Convention on the Status of Refugees. An Immigration and Asylum Bill, passed in November 1999 with effect from April 1, 2000, instituted a voucher system instead of cash payments to asylum seekers and also authorized their dispersal around the country, over the objections of many local authorities.

At an early election called by Prime Minister Blair for June 7, 2001, Labour was overwhelmingly returned to office with 412 seats in the House of Commons (6 fewer than in 1997). A reshuffled cabinet was announced on June 8, and on the same day Conservative leader Hague stepped down despite modest gains by his party in simultaneous local elections. (Hague was succeeded in 2001 by Iain DUNCAN SMITH and in 2003 by Michael HOWARD. See section on the Conservative Party under Political Parties for details.)

In the wake of the September 11, 2001, terrorist attacks in the United States, the Blair government stood as the most steadfast supporter of the George W. Bush administration's October decision to launch military attacks against the al-Qaida network and the Taliban regime in Afghanistan. Earlier, Blair had called for tighter domestic security and had initiated steps to freeze assets of suspected terrorist organizations, monitor bank transactions, and introduce fast-track extradition. On December 14 an Anti-Terrorism, Crime, and Security Bill was enacted, although the Conservative majority in the House of Lords had exacted a number of tempering concessions beforehand.

At the poll of May 5, 2005, Labour, for the first time, registered its third consecutive victory in the House of Commons, albeit with a substantially reduced majority of 355 seats. Prime Minister Blair conducted a minor cabinet reshuffle on the following day.

The terrorist threat became a British reality in July 2005 with a series of London subway bombings in which 56 persons died and a subsequent second, albeit failed, series of attacks in three subway trains and a bus. The newly returned Blair government adopted a number of antiterrorist measures, including a catalog of offenses for which foreign militants could be deported. In September the government introduced new antiterrorism legislation calling, among other things, for an extension of the time a suspect could be held without charges being filed from 14 to 90 days. The following month a number of foreign-based Islamic groups were banned from operating in the UK on the government's assertion that they had ties to al-Qaida. These antiterrorism measures appeared to gain acceptance among the population and most political parties, but the more stringent initiatives fueled a growing debate over the extent to which civil rights and liberties should be curtailed in the name of national security.

Attention in early 2006 focused on the ongoing slide of the Labour Party (buffeted by a series of scandals and policy disputes) and the collateral emergence of the new Conservative leader, David CAMERON, as a dynamic actor on the political stage. Both appeared to contribute to the "meltdown" of Labour at the partial local elections in early May, as the government party suffered a third-place finish in vote percentage. Particularly costly (apparently) for Labour was the revelation that several wealthy businessmen who had secretly lent money to the party's 2005 campaign had been nominated by Blair for peerages, status that automatically includes appointment to the House of Lords. Popular discontent was also reported concerning the perceived lax enforcement of deportation laws for foreigners being released from prisons. Although Blair reportedly faced growing criticism from Labour backbenchers, his cabinet reshuffle (the biggest of his tenure) on May 5, 2006 (the day after an extremely poor performance by Labour in partial local elections) indicated his intention to pursue with vigor additional reform in areas such as education, energy, pensions, and health. At the same time, Blair pledged that he would resign the premiership in sufficient time to let Gordon BROWN (his presumed successor) establish himself as prime minister prior to the general election due by 2010. (In early September Blair announced that he would hand over the premiership within a year.) Meanwhile, Brown (the chancellor of the exchequer and an architect with Blair of "New Labour") began to speak out on a variety of issues outside the purview of his office, prompting some observers to suggest the Blair-Brown relationship was in effect an "undeclared shared premiership." For his part, Cameron focused on a determined effort to move the Conservatives toward the center on many topics in order to sustain the party's electoral momentum for, among other things, the elections scheduled for the spring of 2007 in Scotland and Wales.

By July 2006 public satisfaction with the way the government was running the country and with Blair as prime minister had dropped below 25 percent. An August report from the Home Office drew further attention to the simmering issue of immigration, reporting that almost 50,000 work applications from East Europeans had been approved in the second quarter of the year and that since 2004, when a number of East European countries had joined the EU, 427,000 Eastern Europeans had registered for work in the UK. Meanwhile, some cabinet ministers remained in open disagreement with Blair over his muted response to Israeli bombings in the Israeli-Lebanon war and his refusal to distance himself from Washington's pro-Israeli posture. On September 16, 8 junior aides resigned to protest Blair's refusal to set a definite date for his resignation, and an open letter from 17 Labour MPs called for Blair to step down. On the following day, Blair announced that he would leave within a year. However, Blair continued to be dogged by the "cash for peerages" scandal, in which the Labour Party received large loans from individuals later nominated for peerages. (Such loans, unlike direct donations, are not subject to strict public reporting requirements.) The suspicions of a quid pro quo got so close to Blair that he became the first prime minister interviewed by police in a criminal investigation. (In the end no one was charged with a criminal offense.) Blair also alienated members of the Labour Party in December 2006 when he urged that Britain's nuclear arms program be extended with a new generation of submarines. The March 2007 vote on the matter in the House of Commons produced the largest Labour Party rebellion since the Iraq war began; the measure passed only because of support from Conservatives.

The balloting for the Scottish Parliament on May 3, 2007, was most noteworthy for the advancement of the Scottish National Party (SNP) to a plurality status with 47 of 129 seats, compared to 46 for Labour. The SNP subsequently formed a minority government in Scotland, but the party's lack of a legislative majority was expected to preclude further movement (at least for the immediate future) toward its goal of full independence for Scotland. Meanwhile, Labour and *Plaid Cymru,* a Welsh nationalist party, formed a coalition government in Wales following the May elections to the Welsh National Assembly. Among other things, the coalition negotiations had apparently produced a pledge from Labour to support a referendum on *Plaid Cymru*'s call for the assembly to be given additional legislative authority.

After further losses by Labour and gains by Conservatives in May 3, 2007, local balloting and Labour's loss of plurality party status in the Scottish Parliament to the SNP on the same day, Prime Minister Blair announced on May 10 he would step down as party leader and prime minister before the end of June. When no viable challenge to the long anticipated leadership transfer to Gordon Brown emerged, Brown accepted the position as Labour leader on June 24 and as prime minister on June 27.

Confidence in Brown's leadership waned throughout his first year in office. The depth of the financial crisis, apparent since July 2007, led the government to nationalize Northern Rock bank in February 2008, after Brown failed to find a private-sector solution to the bank's impending failure. Further complicating matters for Brown, the government was able to secure only a 28-vote margin to stave off a Conservative Party attempt to force a public inquiry into decisions leading up to the invasion of Iraq, with 12 Labour backbenchers defecting from the government's position that such an inquiry should wait until the operations had ended. In June 2008 a vote on the government's bill to extend the maximum period terrorism suspects could be held without charge from 28 to 42 days (which was whittled back from the 90-day period Blair had proposed in 2005 and on which Blair had suffered his first defeat by parliament) passed by a mere 9-vote margin, supplied by 9 members of the Democratic Unionist Party as 36 Labour backbenchers defected.

Prime Minister Brown's leadership regarding the rescue of financial institutions in the fall of 2008 was generally well received by the public, and the double-digit lead the Conservatives had earlier held over Labour in opinion polls was cut to single digits. However, in May 2009 a major scandal erupted in the House of Commons involving expense account abuses. Although legislators from other parties were also cited, Labour appeared to suffer the greatest fallout from the scandal, especially since cabinet members and other Labour leaders were involved. The speaker of the House of Commons, Michael MARTIN (originally elected on the Labour ticket), announced his resignation from the speaker's post (effective June 21) after being harshly criticized for his handling of the issue. In addition, two Labour peers were suspended from the House of Lords (the first suspensions in 350 years), and two others were rebuked for allegedly seeking money in return for adding amendments to proposed legislation. Meanwhile, the harsh realities of the ongoing effects of the economic crisis had become apparent. The country's creditworthiness was downgraded, and government debt reportedly breached the level of 40 percent GDP, which Labour for many years had set as the maximum acceptable level. Consequently, Labour fell to third place in both the local elections and balloting for the European Parliament, held concurrently on June 4.

In an apparent attempt to counter anticipated challenges to his premiership, Brown reshuffled the cabinet on June 5, 2009. However, the government subsequently faced criticism on several policy fronts. In August the SNP government in Scotland returned a convicted Lockerbie bomber to Libya on compassionate grounds (the prisoner had been diagnosed with terminal cancer). Opposition parties and other critics charged that the Labour government in Westminster had been complicit in the decision and had bargained, in conjunction with the SNP, for oil and gas concessions from Libya (Brown denied that any deal had been made).

Despite polls showing that more than two-thirds of the public favored an early withdrawal of UK troops from Afghanistan, Brown declared in November 2009 that his government would not bow to the popular mood on the subject. Attention also focused on the Iraqi War Inquiry, some of whose opening witnesses in November questioned the bona fides of the intelligence on which the decision to participate in the U.S.-led invasion had been based. Others questioned the legitimacy (but not the legality) of the decision, given the lack of support from the UK populace and much of the international community. Former prime minister Blair testified in January 2010 and Brown in March.

Having never been in a strong enough position in public opinion polls to call for early elections, Brown did not seek dissolution of the House of Commons until April 2010 (the last possible moment since a new poll was constitutionally mandated by May). The month-long campaign focused on charges that 13 years of Labour government had gone too far in expanding the scope and role of the national government, infringed on too many civil liberties, and, in the end, been associated with the worst financial crisis since the depression of the 1930s. In balloting for the House of Commons on May 6, 2010, the Conservatives won 306 seats to Labour's 258 (neither major party securing an outright majority). In the early days after the election, Brown floated the idea of joining forces in government with the Liberal Democrats, but when this idea gained no traction, he resigned as Labour leader and prime minister on May 11. The same day the queen asked Conservative leader Cameron to form a government, which he did by announcing that the Conservatives and Liberal Democrats, which won 57 seats, would come together in the country's first coalition government since World War II, with Nick CLEGG of the Liberal Democrats as deputy prime minister.

In the balloting for the Scottish parliament on May 5, 2011, the SNP won an outright majority with 69 of the 129 seats. Alex Salmond, first minister and leader of the SNP, vowed to pursue Scottish independence from the UK and to hold a referendum on Scottish secession. In Wales the May 5 balloting resulted in a substantial loss for *Plaid Cymru*, which led the Labour Party to form a one-party minority administration.

Constitution and government. The UK is a constitutional monarchy that functions without a written constitution on the basis of statutes, common law, and long-standing but flexible traditions and usages, subject since 1973 to EC/EU membership and thus acceptance of the primacy of EC/EU law. Executive power is wielded on behalf of the sovereign by a cabinet of ministers drawn from the majority party in the House of Commons and, to a lesser degree, from the House of Lords. The prime minister is the leader of the majority party in the House of Commons and depends upon it for support. There is also a historically important Privy Council of government members and some 300 other individuals drawn from public life. Although superseded in importance by the cabinet, it retains an advisory role in some policy areas and continues to issue "orders in council," either under authority of the monarch, who presides over its meetings, or as authorized by Parliament. The Privy Council also reviews legislation passed by Crown dependencies (the Channel Islands and the Isle of Man).

Elected by universal adult suffrage, the House of Commons has become the main repository of legislative and sole repository of financial authority. The House of Lords retains the power to review, amend, or delay for a year legislation other than financial bills and takes a more leisurely overview of legislation, sometimes acting as a brake on the House of Commons. The lower house, which has a maximum term of five years, may be dissolved by the sovereign on recommendation of the prime minister if the latter's policies should encounter severe resistance or if the incumbent feels that new elections would increase the ruling party's majority.

Under legislation approved by the House of Lords 221–81, with Conservatives abstaining, on October 26, 1999, Labour's 1997 campaign pledge to end hereditary membership in the upper house moved forward. The bill, which received royal assent on November 11, authorized formation of an interim upper chamber to include among its members 92 hereditary peers. Meanwhile, the Wakeham Royal Commission appointed in October 1998 continued to draft proposals for a permanently restructured upper body. The final report, issued on January 20, 2000, proposed a chamber of 550 mostly appointed members but with a minority of 65, 87, or 195 to be elected through regional proportional representation. Law Lords (Lords of Appeal in Ordinary), lifetime appointees who have traditionally constituted the kingdom's highest court of appeal, would retain their seats. The existing 26 seats held by archbishops and bishops would be supplemented by 5 seats for representatives of non-Christian religions. Other life peers would be gradually phased out and replaced by a combination of appointed and elected members. A Labour white paper published in November 2001 offered an alternative proposal—abolition of all hereditary peers in a 600-member house encompassing 120 directly elected members, 120 appointees, 16 bishops, and most of the balance party nominees in proportion to vote shares in the most recent general election—but the plan was largely abandoned in May 2002, a number of party leaders insisting that a higher proportion of the upper house should be directly elected.

Following the developments of 2000–2002, the Blair administration called for abolition of the post of Lord Chancellor, the establishment of a Supreme Court, and, in the wake of devolution, absorption of the offices for Scotland and Wales by a department of constitutional affairs. Thus, in a mid-2003 cabinet reshuffle, the secretaries of state for Scotland and Wales, while retained, were assigned secondary status, with Lord FALCONER of Thoroton named secretary of state for constitutional affairs and invested as Lord Chancellor "for the transitional period."

In March 2004 the House of Lords referred the Constitutional Reform Bill to a special select committee, while the government abandoned plans for a bill to abolish the 92 seats held by remaining hereditary peers.

A year later, on March 25, 2005, royal assent was given to a revised Constitutional Reform Bill that provided for a Supreme Court separate from the House of Lords and, without abandoning the office itself, transferred the legislative functions of the Lord Chancellor to the Lord Speaker and the judicial functions to a President of the Courts for England and Wales.

In March 2007 the parliament took a series of free votes (no party obligation) on preferences for an elected House of Lords. Majorities in the House of Commons supported both an 80 and 100 percent elected composition. A majority in the House of Lords supported a wholly appointed body. Justice Secretary Jack STRAW announced in July that work on "fundamental" reform would continue. However, decisive action appeared unlikely before the next general election.

Apart from the newly established Supreme Court, which was inaugurated on October 1, 2009, the judicial system of England and Wales centers on a High Court of Justice for civil cases, with three divisions (Chancery, Family, and Queen's Bench); a Crown Court for criminal cases; and a Court of Appeal, with civil and criminal divisions.

Scotland has its own High Court of Justiciary (criminal) and Court of Session (civil), both including appeal courts, while Northern Ireland has a separate Supreme Court of Judicature, comprising a (civil) High Court of Justice, a (criminal) Crown Court, and a Court of Appeal. In relevant cases, UK citizens and groups have the right of appeal against national legal rulings to the European Court of Human Rights in Strasbourg, France.

Local government in England traditionally encompassed a two-tier structure of county and district (or borough or city) councils, but in recent years dozens of unitary authorities have been established. The traditional structure largely survives in 34 counties and more than 200 district councils, although some of the counties have seen unitary authorities established within their geographical boundaries. Under legislation enacted in 1994, Wales and Scotland, formerly with two tiers, moved on April 1, 1996, to a unitary system, with 22 and 32 elected councils, respectively. Northern Ireland has 26 district councils.

Since 1986, when the Greater London Council was abolished, the capital has been governed through 32 boroughs, each with its own elected council, and the Corporation of the City of London, its unique status reflecting its commercial rather than residential character. Additionally, at a referendum held on May 7, 1998, Londoners overwhelmingly approved direct election of a mayor and establishment of a 25-member London Assembly. The first mayoral and assembly elections were held in May 2000. (Subsequent mayoral and assembly elections were held in June 2004 and May 2008.)

The viability of the UK as a political entity has been a matter of major concern for three decades. The most intractable problem has been that of deep-rooted conflict in Northern Ireland between the majority Protestants, most of whom remain committed to the union with Great Britain, and a Catholic minority, substantial elements of which have long sought union with the Republic of Ireland. A multiparty peace accord, the Belfast (Good Friday) Agreement of April 10, 1998, was approved in Northern Ireland by referendum on May 22, with a new Northern Ireland Assembly being elected on June 25. Devolution of authority from London to the assembly and a Northern Ireland Executive occurred on December 2, 1999, although differences over the decommissioning of weapons held by the IRA resulted in reimposition of direct rule from February 11 to May 30, 2000. Upon devolution, the secretary of state for Northern Ireland retained authority in "excepted and reserved" areas, including law, criminal justice, and foreign affairs. Direct rule was again imposed for 24 hours in August and September 2001, and then for an indefinite period on October 15, 2002. In October 2006 talks involving the British government, the government of the Republic of Ireland, and all major parties in Northern Ireland produced the St. Andrews Agreement, which prompted new elections in Northern Ireland on March 7, 2007, and the restoration of the Northern Ireland Assembly on May 8 (see entry on Northern Ireland for details).

Although not characterized by the violence endemic in the Irish question, a powerful separatist movement has also developed in Scotland. Alarmed by the growing influence of the SNP, which won a third of the Scottish votes in the October 1974 general election, the Labour leadership, in a 1975 government paper, proposed the establishment of elected assemblies for both Scotland and Wales. Despite Conservative criticism that the departure would prove costly and contain "the danger of a break-up of Britain," pertinent legislation was completed in mid-1978. In March 1979, however, referendums yielded rejection of devolution in Wales and approval by an insufficient majority in Scotland. Successive Conservative administrations subsequently ruled out the creation of regional assemblies, although in March 1993 the government, in what was officially described as the first major review of the England-Scotland relationship since 1707, introduced measures to give the 72 Scottish MPs a larger role in decision making.

Immediately after taking power in May 1997, the new Labour government set out plans for new Scottish and Welsh devolution referendums. On September 11 the Scottish electorate voted by a substantial majority for an elected Parliament, and on September 18 Welsh voters approved creation of a National Assembly. Under the Government of Wales Act and the Scotland Act, both passed by the UK Parliament following the referendums, elections for the two new bodies were held on May 6, 1999, with formal transfer of devolved powers occurring on July 1. Although the UK Parliament retains ultimate authority to legislate on all matters, it will not routinely do so in devolved sectors, which include education, health, culture, local government, housing, transportation, and the environment. The Scottish Parliament cannot propose independence from the union, nor can it legislate in reserved areas, which include defense and treaty obligations. Because Wales has a closer legal association with England, the Welsh assembly has a more limited scope than the Scottish Parliament, with no authority to pass primary legislation governing, for example, the legal system or taxation. Both Scotland and Wales, like Northern Ireland, continue to be represented in the UK Parliament and in the Westminster cabinet. With regard to England, the Blair administration indicated its willingness to go beyond establishing the RDAs and the London Authority (mayor plus assembly) and to devolve powers from the UK government to English regional bodies as the demand arises.

Following the 1997 election, the Labour government began to examine proportional representation for use in British elections. The 1999 balloting for the new Scottish and Welsh legislatures utilized, for the first time, a combination system in which each voter cast two ballots, one for a constituency representative elected under the traditional "first-past-the-post" basis and the second for a party list from which "top-up" seats were allocated, thereby assuring that the makeup of the legislatures would better reflect each party's overall vote share. A proportional scheme was also introduced for the European Parliament elections held in June 1999. However, many members of the UK House of Commons, including a substantial number of Labour MPs, have not expressed enthusiasm for converting to a basically proportional system for the House, as proposed in the report of the Jenkins Commission on electoral reform in October 1998. In March 2008 Justice Secretary Jack Straw proposed consultation on whether the centuries-old "first-past-the-post" electoral system should be replaced by an "alternative vote" system, which would allow voters to express a first and second preference for candidates running in a constituency. Straw's proposal also asked whether voting should be designated a civic duty, thereby making voting mandatory, and whether elections should be conducted over a two-day weekend. A May 2011 referendum rejected the alternative-vote electoral system.

On October 28, 2011, all 15 Commonwealth countries approved a change to the rules of succession to abolish primogeniture and create equality between the sexes. Queen ELIZABETH II gave royal assent to the Succession to the Crown Bill on April 25, 2013. The change meant that the first child of the Duke and Duchess of Cambridge would assume the throne, regardless of sex. (Prince GEORGE of Cambridge was born on July 22, 2013.) In addition, marriage to a Roman Catholic will no longer remove an individual from the order of succession, although the monarch still must be a Protestant.

Freedom combined with responsibility represents the British ideal in the handling of news and opinion. The press, while privately owned and free from censorship, is subject to strict libel laws and is often made aware of government preferences with regard to the handling of news reports. In late 1989, faced with the prospect of parliamentary action to curb the excesses of the more sensationalist papers, publishers adopted an ethics code that limited intrusion into private lives, offered the objects of press stories reasonable opportunity for reply, provided for appropriately prominent retraction of errors in reporting, precluded payments to known criminals, and barred irrelevant references to race, color, and religion. In 1997 the Press Complaints Commission announced a revised code of conduct that widened the definition of privacy for individuals, prohibited "persistent pursuit" by photojournalists, and offered additional protections for children. A communications bill, which was first published in May 2002, replaced five regulatory bodies for the press, television, and radio with a single Office of Communications. A unanimous ruling in October 2006 by the Law Lords (Britain's highest court) tightened the provisions under which the press can be sued for libel. In July 2011 Prime Minister Cameron established a public inquiry to investigate ongoing allegations that reporters for the Rupert Murdoch–owned *News of the World* tabloid had hacked private phone calls and voice mails of a variety of public figures. Led by Lord Justice (Brian) Levenson, the inquiry has led to the arrest of *News* staff for hacking and bribing public officials. In March 2013 the three major political parties announced the creation of a new press regulatory body answerable to the queen, not parliament.

Reporters Without Borders ranked the United Kingdom 29 out of 179 countries in its 2013 Index of Press Freedom.

Foreign relations. Reluctantly abandoning its age-long tradition of "splendid isolation," the UK became a key member of the Allied coalitions in both world wars and has remained a leader in the Western group of nations, as well as one of the world's nuclear-armed powers. Postwar British governments have sought to retain close economic and military ties with the United States while maintaining an independent British position on most international issues. Britain has continued to play an important role in the United Nations and in collective security arrangements, such as the North Atlantic Treaty Organization (NATO), although after 1957 Britain's withdrawal of most military forces from the Far East and the Persian Gulf substantially diminished its weight in the global balance of power.

The UK's participation in the work of such institutions as the IMF, the General Agreement on Tariffs and Trade/World Trade Organization (GATT/WTO), and the Organization for Economic Cooperation and Development (OECD) reflects its continued central position in international financial and economic affairs as well as its commitment to assist in the growth of less-developed countries. (Similar concerns have also become a focus of the Commonwealth, which was formally established in 1931.) Unwilling to participate in the creation of the original three EC components (the European Economic Community [EEC], European Coal and Steel Community [ECSC], and European Atomic Energy Community [Euratom]), it took the lead in establishing the European Free Trade Association (EFTA) in 1960. Subsequently, Conservative and moderate Labour leaders began to urge British entry into the EC despite anticipated problems for the UK and other Commonwealth members. France, however, vetoed the British application for admission in 1963 on the grounds that the country remained too closely tied to the United States and the Commonwealth to justify close association with the continental nations. With the abandonment of French objections after President de Gaulle's resignation in 1969, a bill sanctioning entry was approved by the House of Commons in October 1971, and Britain was formally admitted to the EC on January 1, 1973. In a referendum held in June 1975, continued membership of the EC was endorsed by a two-thirds majority of participating voters, but enthusiasm for the European venture remained low in Britain over the subsequent two decades.

In late 1979 the Thatcher government won worldwide plaudits for its resolution of the seven-year Rhodesian civil war through a lengthy process of negotiation that culminated in independence under black majority rule in April 1980 (see Zimbabwe entry). In September 1981 Belize (formerly British Honduras) secured independence, as did Antigua and Barbuda in November. These were the latest territories to benefit from Britain's post-1957 imperial disengagement, which had seen 18 former possessions, protectorates, and colonies becoming independent during the 1960s, 10 in the 1970s, and 2 (including Zimbabwe) in 1980. Subsequently, St. Kitts and Nevis achieved independence in 1983, followed by Brunei in 1984.

The Falkland Islands War that erupted in April 1982 followed nearly two decades of sporadic negotiations between Britain and Argentina in a fruitless effort to resolve a dispute that had commenced in the late 18th century (see Falkland Islands under Related Territories, below). Following the Argentine defeat, the UN General Assembly renewed appeals for a negotiated solution to the sovereignty issue, and since 1984 the UN Committee on Decolonization has routinely passed Argentine-sponsored resolutions asking London to reopen negotiations on the matter. Two days of high-level talks in Madrid, Spain, in February 1990 produced a compromise settlement of conflicting claims to fishing rights and an agreement to restore a seven-year rupture in diplomatic relations, but the sovereignty issue remains unresolved.

In September 1984 Britain and China agreed that the latter would regain possession of Hong Kong in 1997, although the Conservative government continued to rebuff Spanish appeals for the reversion of Gibraltar, given manifest opposition to such a move by its inhabitants (see Special Administrative Region in China entry for information on Hong Kong, and Gibraltar under Related Territories, below).

While the Thatcher government had reservations about U.S. military intervention in Grenada in 1983, its generally close foreign policy alignment with Washington was demonstrated by endorsement of the U.S. bombing of Libya in 1986, as contrasted with the prevailing view of other EC countries. UK-U.S. cooperation was also a key factor during the Gulf crisis of 1990–1991, with British forces participating in the U.S.-led coalition that expelled Iraq from Kuwait.

In December 1991 the Major government was successful in negotiating various UK opt-outs from the EC's Maastricht Treaty on European union, notably from its commitment to a single European currency and from its jobs-imperiling social policy chapter. However, not until July 23, 1993, did the government obtain final parliamentary authority for its opt-out policy. This followed a stinging attack on the treaty by former prime minister Margaret Thatcher in the House of Lords, who cast her first vote in 34 years against her party's leadership, and came about only after Major had gained the reluctant support of his Conservative opponents in the House of Commons by making the decision a confidence motion. On July 30 a British court rejected the last legal challenge to the treaty, and on August 2 instruments of UK ratification were deposited in Rome.

In October 1997 the new Labour administration signaled a slightly more pro-European position by announcing that Britain would consider joining the EU's Economic and Monetary Union (EMU), but not immediately. Earlier, in May, the incoming foreign secretary had confirmed a Labour commitment to accept the social charter of the EU. In November 1998 the queen gave her assent to legislation that incorporated into British law the 1950 European Convention on Human Rights, with effect from October 2, 2000.

During 1992 UK diplomacy became increasingly preoccupied with the conflict in former Yugoslavia. Although some 3,400 British troops were committed to the UN humanitarian effort by 1994, the government firmly opposed any direct military intervention by external powers and backed both the UN arms embargo and the Vance-Owen diplomatic effort to obtain a negotiated settlement. Following major escalation of the Bosnian crisis in March 1995, London's policy underwent a significant shift. In addition to raising its troop contingent in the former Yugoslavia to 10,000, Britain agreed to contribute an additional 7,000 soldiers to a new NATO-led rapid reaction force charged with providing "enhanced protection" to the UN peacekeeping force. Subsequently, the British government was party to a NATO decision to step up air strikes around the Bosnian capital with the twin aims of relieving pressure on its inhabitants and of forcing Bosnian Serb acceptance of the latest peace plan. Britain gave its full support to the Dayton Accords of December 1995, which brought the conflict to a swift close. British troops remained part of the continuing UN peace force.

The Blair and Brown governments consistently supported the second U.S.-led incursion into Iraq, often at their political peril. A number of Blair's key aides resigned over the issue, including parliamentary leader Robin COOK in March 2003 and International Development Secretary Claire SHORT two months later. Even greater damage came from the fallout after the apparent suicide on July 13, 2003, of David KELLY, a ministry of defense weapons expert, who had been the source for alleged reports that Downing Street had "sexed up" a 2002 dossier on Iraqi weapons of mass destruction.

In 2009 Prime Minister Brown declared that some 9,000 UK troops would remain in Afghanistan, forming the second-largest contingent (behind that of the United States). In response to public discontent, in 2011 Prime Minister Cameron revealed plans to begin slowly drawing down the number of UK troops, but it would maintain its presence in Afghanistan with 9,000 troops until 2015. Cameron moved up the departure date to late 2014 following a meeting with U.S. president Barack Obama in March 2012. Prince Harry began a second deployment to Afghanistan on September 7.

In April 2004 Blair announced that he would call for a referendum on Britain's commitment to the EU after the next election. However, in June 2005 he said that the government would not proceed with a referendum bill, given the rejection of the EU constitution by the French and Dutch electorates. In mid-2006 the administration indicated that it might approve certain revisions in EU institutions on a "piece-by-piece" basis without a referendum. In December 2007 Prime Minister Brown signed the EU's Lisbon Treaty, which contains 96 percent of the language of the erstwhile EU constitution. The treaty, which amends rather than replaces previous EU treaties and would take effect no earlier than 2014, includes protocols and vetoes to protect UK interests in regard to security, foreign affairs, and social policy. The UK Parliament ratified the treaty in June 2008.

In November 2011 Prime Minister Cameron and French President Nicolas Sarkozy signed a treaty and agreed to strengthen cooperation and coordination between the two countries in areas of defense. Among other arrangements, the two countries planned to jointly build and deploy an unmanned drone, as well as coordinate information, equipment, and technology. In February, Cameron and Sarkozy announced a £500 billion contract to build a "next generation" nuclear power station. Cooperation between the two countries was set to last for 50 years, but following Sarkozy's reelection defeat in May, the new French defense minister, Jean-Yves Le Drian, announced Paris wanted to open the bilateral agreement to other countries.

The UK joined the United States and France in enforcing a no-fly zone in Libya and in the protection of Libyan citizens during the Libyan uprising of 2011. The decision to enter the conflict was supported by an overwhelming majority of MPs in the House of Commons.

Cameron has positioned himself as the face of opposition to increasing the EU's regulatory powers. He withdrew from talks about the EU fiscal pact in 2011 and declined to join the European Stability Mechanism in 2012. Eurosceptic Conservatives called for a referendum on EU membership in October 2011. The motion was rejected 483–111, including 81 Tory defectors, making it the biggest defeat Cameron had faced to date (see Current issues, below).

The UK held the rotating presidency of the G-8 in 2013, and Cameron hosted the annual leaders' summit in Northern Ireland in June. Cameron set three priorities for his term: advancing trade, ensuring tax compliance, and promoting greater transparency.

Current issues. The Conservative Party won 258 seats in the May 10, 2010, general elections but fell short of the 326 needed for a majority. David Cameron was appointed prime minister on May 11 and formed a coalition with the Liberal Democrats, which had 57 seats. The governing agreement (officially published on May 20) called for immediately addressing the budget deficit, finding a middle ground on immigration, creating a common policy regarding adoption of the euro, revising the manner in which UK parliamentary elections are conducted, resetting pension provisions, granting more local control over public education, and restoring civil liberties.

In particular, the deficit was to be attacked by spending reductions and tax increases. Immigration plans called for putting a cap on non-EU workers entering the country, while the point of agreement on the EU called for the UK not to join the eurozone.

The government moved quickly on its budget proposals by announcing plans to cut overall spending by nearly 20 percent, including 7.5 percent cuts in defense. The most severe tax increase in the government's package was a change in the value-added tax (VAT) from 17.5 to 20 percent. The only spending that was held safe was for health and international development assistance. In a reversal of the Conservative Party's campaign pledge, the withdrawal of the popular child benefit from middle-class families paying the 40 percent tax rate was included in the first round of announced cuts. Although labor union leaders promised a strong opposition to the cut, public reaction was muted.

Strains emerged in the governing coalition as the economic outlook took a turn for the worse. Cameron's austerity measures were called into question after it was revealed that the UK economy was not improving. The 2011–2012 budget included spending cuts and tax hikes and few measures to stimulate economic growth. Labour repeatedly insisted that the government needed to introduce some form of stimulus package to create jobs and growth.

Despite poor economic performance and some growing concerns over the government's continued austerity measures, the Conservatives fared well in the local elections on May 5, 2011, with overall gains in local council seats, and emerged as the winning party in the balloting. The opposition Labour Party also fared well, winning control of 57 local councils. The Liberal Democrats, in contrast, appeared to bear the brunt of voter frustrations and saw their vote share drop to its lowest level in 30 years. In a double defeat for the Liberal Democrats, the UK overwhelmingly voted against switching to the alternative-vote method of election in the referendum held on May 5 (67.9 percent of the voters voted against the proposal). Support for the Liberal Democrats had also fallen amid a controversial vote for raising university tuition (the party had campaigned against such an increase) and several other policy U-turns made by the party.

Meanwhile, the SNP gained an outright majority of seats in the May 5 balloting for the devolved Scottish parliament, in part driven by a poor performance by the Liberal Democrats. Under the leadership of Alex Salmond, first minister in the Scottish parliament, much of the party's previous administration was left intact. Salmond immediately announced his intention to work toward securing additional financial powers for the Scotland bill, already under consideration by the House of Commons, and pledged to hold a referendum on Scottish secession in the autumn of 2014. In light of the SNP's new majority, Cameron's government vowed to keep the UK intact while promising not to stop the referendum from occurring. The UK government also announced that it would consider changes in the Scotland Bill that would increase the borrowing power of Scotland.

Concurrent elections to the Welsh parliament produced Labour government that controlled exactly half of the seats (30 out of 60). Two months earlier, a referendum in Wales on whether to give the Welsh parliament the power to pass laws in the 20 devolved policy areas was approved by a strong majority (63.5 percent) of the voters. The clear "yes" vote implied increased power for the Welsh parliament and greater independence from the UK government, eliminating the need for negotiations between the two in order to pass policies in the devolved areas.

Cameron was put under fire again in August 2011 after the worst riots in 25 years broke out in London and subsequently spread to over 20 cities and towns while he was out of the country on holiday. The riots endured over several days and caused large-scale damage, while the police forces were restrained from engaging the rioters. The riots were quelled only after Cameron returned to the country and police activities increased. More than 3,000 people were arrested for looting, arson, and other offenses. In an intense questioning session in the House of Commons about the riots, Cameron reaffirmed his commitment to cut 16,000 police officers from the payroll.

On November 29, Chancellor of the Exchequer Osborne presented a gloomy budget update to the House of Commons. Unemployment stood at 8.1 percent, a 17-year high. He conceded that the government would not be able to eliminate the deficit by 2015, as promised, and more austerity measures were needed. Specifically, he imposed a 1 percent cap on pay raises for public-sector wages in 2012 and 2013, wages that had already been frozen in 2010–2011. With inflation running at 4.5 percent, this meant a cut in wages. He also raised the retirement age of civil servants from 60 for women and 65 for men to 68 for both. The next day, more than 2 million public workers staged a one-day strike, the largest since the 1970s.

The coalition also split over EU policy. In late 2011, leaders of the EU tried to hammer out a treaty that would enshrine fiscal discipline among all of its members. Greece, Ireland, and Portugal had already received financial bailouts to save them from bankruptcy, and German chancellor Angela Merkel and French president Sarkozy argued for a mechanism that would prevent countries from spending themselves into insolvency. Meeting in Brussels on December 8–9, the leaders of EU member states agreed to rewrite the Lisbon Treaty, the de facto EU constitution. Prime Minister Cameron shocked observers by vetoing the move when other members refused to make concessions to the London financial community. "For the first time since Britain joined the European Community in 1973," observed the *Guardian* newspaper, "a treaty that goes to the heart of how the EU works will be struck without a British signature."

A key part of Cameron's objection related to the proposed introduction of an EU financial transaction fee, known as a Tobin tax. He wanted veto power over any plan to transfer financial regulatory power from individual countries to the EU, insisted the European Banking Authority should remain in London, and opposed a regulation requiring that all euro-denominated transactions take place in countries that use the euro—which the UK does not.

When it became clear that even noneurozone countries planned to sign the new EU fiscal pact without the UK, Cameron argued against using the European Court of Justice to police national budgets, fearing that it might rewrite key EU policies without London's input.

Deputy Prime Minister Clegg insisted that the UK should sign the new treaty, arguing that Europe "can only address these problems by pulling together." Cameron appeared convinced by Clegg's plea and reversed his opposition regarding enforcement. His U-turn angered Tory Eurosceptics and prompted taunting from Labour. By July 2012, Cameron announced he had no plans to hold a referendum on ending Britain's EU membership; instead it would be interested in negotiating a new division of powers between London and Brussels.

The government's 2012–2013 budget registered little improvement. Presenting it to the House of Commons on March 21, Osborne conceded that the government would not be able to eliminate the deficit before 2016–2017 and declared the overriding necessity of protecting the UK's AAA credit rating. His proposed budget predicted a deficit of 7.6 percent of projected GDP (nearly double the EU ceiling) and anticipated unemployment peaking at 8.7 percent in 2012 before falling to 6.3 percent by 2016–2017.

The electoral reform proposals stalled admit party politics. The alternative-vote system was rejected in an April 2011 referendum. The proposal to reduce the size of the House of Commons to 600 floundered on disputes over redistricting. On August 6, Clegg denounced the Conservatives for backing out of a promise to reform the House of Lords into an elected body. "The Conservative Party is not honouring the commitment to Lords reform and as a result part of our contract has now been broken," he declared. "So I have told the prime minister that when, in due course, parliament votes on boundary changes for the 2015 election, I will be instructing my party to oppose them."

The UK put on two enormous celebrations in 2012. Queen Elizabeth II celebrated 60 years on the throne, and London played host to the 2012 Olympic Games. A series of jubilee events put the royal family on display to the world, while "Team GB" placed third in the medal count at the Olympics—the queen's granddaughter Zara Phillips even won a silver medal. While the jubilee and Games generated a swell of patriotism, they did little to dampen the country's increasingly dire financial situation. In fact, they may have even contributed to the economic woes. The government declared a national holiday on June 5, 2012, the culminating day of the jubilee celebration. However, analysts predicted that would cause economic output to fall by as much as £6 billion, which would not be fully offset by tourism revenue. The Olympic Committee suffered a major public relations setback in the final days before the Opening Ceremonies, when the security contractor announced that it could not provide enough staff; the government called on the armed forces to fill the gap. That news, as well as concerns over transportation bottlenecks, may have scared off some tourists, as many venues wound up with empty seats. The last-minute cost overruns and unsold tickets added to the $14 billion price tag for the Games, which Cameron insisted would be recouped in four years.

On September 4, with the jubilee, Olympics, and August break over, Cameron reshuffled almost his entire cabinet. One of the most high-profile changes involved Justine Greening, who was demoted from transport secretary to international development secretary. Greening's signature policy stance was opposition to adding a third runway to London's Heathrow airport. While business interests clamor for additional flights to ease congestion and add more flights to emerging markets, such as China, environmental groups have denounced expansion proposals. According to one commentator, "The cabinet reshuffle is a declaration of war on the environment." Environment secretary Caroline Spelman was sacked, along with Welsh secretary Cheryl Gillan and Sir George Young, leader of the Commons.

The changes undermined Cameron's promise to improve diversity within the Conservative Party and to have one-third of government posts be held by women by 2015. Two of the five women in the cabinet lost jobs altogether, and Baroness Sayeeda Warsi, a Muslim and the only nonwhite cabinet member, was moved to a nonvoting cabinet post. Only one of the 19 men in the cabinet was removed completely.

The British economy contracted in 2012, to a point that it was smaller than when Cameron took office in 2010. Wages have dropped 5.5 percent since 2010, when adjusted for inflation. GDP grew only 0.2 percent in 2012, and unemployment registered at 8.0 percent. As the economy continued to languish, Moody's downgraded the UK's AAA credit rating in February 2013. The 2013–2014 budget, announced in March 2013, predicted a deficit of 7 percent of GDP, far above the EU 3.0 percent ceiling.

In a speech delivered on January 23, Cameron reversed earlier statements by publicly committing to holding a referendum on continuing British participation in the EU before the end of 2017. While he would prefer to stay in a reconfigured EU, seeing it as an important tool for maintaining the country's global influence, his fellow Conservatives are split on the matter. Tory backbenchers warned they would vote against continued EU membership unless London was allowed to opt out of the fiscal ceiling, transaction tax, and other unpopular measures. Public opinion, according to a May 2013 poll, favored exit 43 percent to 37 percent. Labour and the Liberal Democrats have expressed interest in the referendum but argued for boosting the domestic economy first. Cameron had long resisted the idea of a referendum but changed course in a move calculated to tame the surging UKIP. However, his shift might have instead validated their demand.

Cameron wants certain EU powers returned to the state, although he has not announced exactly which ones. Devolution would require a new treaty and negotiations among all of the EU's 27 members, and leaders of these governments oppose the notion. In July 2012 the Conservative party, not the Conservative-led government, began an audit of EU regulations and their impact on the UK. Known as the Balance of Competences, the findings could become the basis of Cameron's proposal to restructure the EU.

Cameron delivered a major speech on immigration reform on March 25, announcing new regulations and screenings to prevent new arrivals from immediately accessing the country's extensive social safety net. Conservatives feared an influx of immigration from Romania and Bulgaria when the countries acceded to the EU's Schengen Area in January 2014. The hard line on immigration played well with the UKIP.

The UKIP and Greens fielded a record number of candidates in local elections on May 2, and both increased their representation. With 36 councils up for grabs, Labour took 29 percent of the vote, followed by the Conservatives (25 percent), UKIP (23 percent), and Liberal Democrats (14 percent). The balloting provided further evidence of the declining popular support for the junior government party. Going into the September Liberal Democrat annual conference, Clegg's popularity had sunk to 8 percent, and he faced many calls for his resignation.

Not only does Cameron face divisions within his government, he increasingly has run into resistance from within his party. Many backbenchers complain that he is more interested in liberal policies than traditional Conservative values. They cite his promotion of same-sex marriage (which was legalized in July 2013) and alternative energies as evidence. Disgruntled Tories have been attracted to the UKIP, whose popularity is rapidly rising. Fourteen major Conservative donors have given £500,000 to UKIP since 2010. In late September, Chancellor of the Exchequer Osborne ruled out a possible Tory-UKIP pact for the 2015 election.

On May 22, Pvt. Lee Rigby was walking near the Royal Artillery headquarters in London when a car jumped the curb and rammed into him. Two men jumped out of the car and hacked Rigby to death with knives and machetes. One attacker filmed part of the incident and was heard yelling Islamist sentiments. Cameron labeled the horrific incident an act of terrorism, prompting fears of more attacks against soldiers recently returned from Afghanistan.

The House of Commons dealt Cameron his worst defeat to date on August 29, when members refused to authorize military strikes against Syria, 285–272. Still smarting from poor intelligence that led Great Britain into war against Saddam Hussein in 2003, the parliament regarded intelligence reports about Syria warily. Miliband extracted a range of concessions from Cameron before the vote, but even the Labour leader's support for the bill was not enough for its passage.

As the Scottish independence referendum approached, *Plaid Cymru* called for a greater devolution of powers to Wales to match those exercised by Scotland and Northern Ireland. Party leader Leanne Wood also has demanded a role for Wales in any constitutional amendments that arise from the Scottish referendum.

POLITICAL PARTIES

Government Parties:

Conservative Party. Although in opposition during 1945–1951, 1964–1970, 1974–1979, and since 1997, the Conservative Party (formally the Conservative and Unionist Party, informally the Tory Party) dominated British politics through much of the 20th century, drawing support from business, the middle class, farmers, and a segment of the working class.

In February 1975 Margaret Thatcher, former secretary of state for education and science, was elected party leader, succeeding Edward Heath, under whom the Conservatives had lost three of the previous four elections. Following the party's return to power in May 1979, a rift developed between moderate members (derogatively styled "wets") and those supporting Thatcher's stringent monetary and economic policies; through the 1980s prominent wets were gradually dropped from the government, while others came to terms with "Thatcherism." The party's successful 1983 campaign manifesto called for, among other things, tough laws to curb illegal strikes and privatization of state-owned industry. The emphasis for the June 1987 election was on continued "positive reform" in such areas as fiscal management, control of inflation, greater financial independence for individuals, and improved health care.

Deepening divisions over European policy led in November 1990 to a leadership challenge by former cabinet minister Michael Heseltine, who obtained enough first-round votes to force Thatcher's resignation. But the succession went to the chancellor of the exchequer, John Major, who was regarded as the "Thatcherite" among the three second-round contenders but who quickly jettisoned his predecessor's more controversial policies. The Conservatives fought the April 1992 election on a platform of further privatization (including British Rail and the coal mines), financial accountability in the National Health Service, and freedom of choice in the state education sector. On a vote share of 41.9 percent, the party won its fourth consecutive term, taking 336 (out of 651) seats in the House of Commons, 40 fewer than in 1987.

Postelection difficulties caused a massive slump in the Conservatives' public standing, as evidenced by unprecedented local electoral trouncings in 1993–1994 and the concurrent loss in by-elections of several "safe" Conservative parliamentary seats to the Liberal Democrats. In June 1994 the party also fared badly in European Parliament balloting, falling from 34 to 18 seats (out of 87). Increasing intraparty criticism led Prime Minister Major to place his leadership on the line in June 1995. Reelected the following month with the support of 218 of the 329 Conservative MPs, he proceeded to elevate Heseltine to "number two" status in the Conservative hierarchy.

Additional by-election losses and several defections were followed by another rout in local elections in May 1996, even in the party's southern heartland. By the end of 1996, the government was perilously close to minority status in the House of Commons and reliant on the tactical support of Ulster Unionists to survive until the May 1997 election, at which Conservatives captured only 165 seats. The defeat was so extensive that Major resigned as party leader.

After three rounds of balloting, William Hague, former Welsh secretary, defeated former chancellor of the exchequer and EU advocate Kenneth Clarke to become (at 36) the youngest Conservative leader of the century. The EU issue flared up again later in the year when Clarke, Heseltine, and others objected to the decision by party leaders to maintain opposition to the EU's proposed single currency. Following through on a Hague commitment, in January 1998 the parliamentary delegation approved new procedures for selecting the party leader and challenging the incumbent. Under the new rules all party members, not just MPs, were empowered to vote for the leader.

At the annual party conference in October 1998, Hague reiterated his opposition to a single European currency, citing in support the results of a recently concluded referendum of party members. In February 1999 Heseltine, Clarke, and former prime minister Heath all voiced support for Prime Minister Blair's "national changeover plan" and later joined the cross-party "Britain in Europe" movement.

On December 2, 1998, Hague dismissed the party's leader in the upper house, Viscount CRANBORNE, for failing to consult with him before approving the so-called Cranborne compromise with Labour over the hereditary membership of an interim upper house of Parliament (pending full reform of the House of Lords) and over passage of a proportional representation scheme for the European Parliament elections in June 1999. Subsequently, Hague's apparent willingness to accept proportional representation for some elected bodies as well as an end to hereditary voting rights in a new upper chamber drew fire from hardline Conservatives, as did his initial support for a statement by (then) deputy leader Peter LILLEY in April 1999 that "the free market has only a limited role in improving public services like health, education, and welfare." The right interpreted the statement as further evidence of a retreat from Thatcherism.

As expected, the party fared poorly at the May 6, 1999, elections for the new Scottish Parliament and Welsh National Assembly, although it registered significant gains in simultaneous nationwide local elections. Conservatives took only 18 seats (all of them "top-up") in the 129-member Scottish legislature and 9 (8 "top-up") in the 60-member Welsh Assembly, but, following up on modest gains made locally in 1998, the party displaced the Liberal Democrats as the second largest party at the local level. A month later Conservatives outpolled Labourites at balloting for the European Parliament, winning 36 seats, more than reversing the party's losses in 1994. The trend continued in 2000, when a March by-election victory gave the party its first directly elected seat in the Scottish Parliament, with further gains recorded in May's local council elections.

In October 1999 Hague, in a retreat from an earlier attempt to delineate a "caring" conservatism, had outlined a "common sense revolution" that marked a clear return to Thatcherism. Over the next six months Hague elaborated on his call for tax cuts; repeated his "sterling guarantee" that the party would not adopt the euro during the next Parliament; took a strong Eurosceptic stance, including support for a proposal that the founding Treaty of Rome be renegotiated to permit members to opt out of EU policies unrelated to trade; accused the Labour administration of being soft on criminals, including sexual offenders; and opposed initiatives on homosexual rights. By mid-2000 the party's standing in public opinion polls had risen dramatically. Prior to the turnaround, many observers had expected Hague's leadership to be challenged by Michael PORTILLO, a former defense secretary under John Major who had returned to the House of Commons with a November 1999 by-election win. Hague, showing new confidence, nevertheless awarded Portillo the key role of shadow chancellor of the exchequer in February 2000.

Despite successes in local council elections, the Conservatives failed to make gains against Labour at the election of June 2001, winning 166 seats and 32.7 percent of the vote in England, Scotland, and Wales. As a consequence, Hague resigned on June 8. Although Portillo was initially regarded as his likely successor, the acrimonious leadership contest ultimately narrowed to a choice between Eurosceptic Iain Duncan SMITH and Kenneth Clarke, with Smith winning a clear victory on September 13. However, dissatisfaction subsequently arose over Duncan Smith's quiet and perceived unsure leadership, and he was forced to resign on October 29, 2003, after losing a vote of confidence among Conservative MPs. He was succeeded by Michael HOWARD on November 6. Howard himself resigned following the Conservative defeat in May 2005, although the Conservatives had improved their seat total to 197 on a vote share of 32.3 percent.

David Cameron, a youthful (39-year-old) "modernizer," was elected chair of the party in December 2005 by a two-to-one margin of party member votes over David DAVIS. Cameron immediately pledged to move the Conservatives toward the center for upcoming elections, promising a "more compassionate party" that would present a much larger percentage of female candidates (only four of the party's current MPs were women) and minority candidates. The new leader also emphasized environmental issues, called upon businesses to address "social concerns," and announced that it would undermine the party's credibility to pledge tax cuts during the next general election considering the national budget situation. Although the party's right wing reportedly objected to many of Cameron's centrist policies, the immediate results of the shift to the center included resounding success for the Conservatives in the May 2006 local elections (40 percent of the vote) and continued improvement in the party's position in public opinion polls. The Conservatives also secured 40 percent of the vote in the May 2007 local balloting and improved its representation by three seats in the London Assembly in May 2008 balloting. In the London balloting its mayoral candidate, Boris JOHNSON, defeated two-term incumbent and Labour candidate Ken Livingstone.

The Conservatives gained majority control of 26 of 27 county councils on a vote share of 38 percent in the June 2009 local elections. The party also won 25 of 69 seats in simultaneous balloting for the European Parliament on a vote share of 27.7 percent. A few weeks later Conservative MP John BERCOW was elected speaker of the House of Commons.

The Conservatives were the leading party in the May 2010 elections for the House of Commons, capturing 306 seats (20 short of a majority) on a vote share of 36.1 percent. Cameron subsequently formed a coalition government with the Liberal Democrats. The party lost 405 councilors in the May 2012 elections, while Labour picked up 823.

Lord STRATHCLYDE abruptly resigned as party leader in the House of Lords in January. After 25 years in the Lords he was reportedly weary of Liberal Democratic peers defecting to Labour on a number of issues.

The Conservatives won 1,116 council seats in the May 2013 local elections, down 335.

Leaders: David CAMERON (Prime Minister and Leader of the Party); George OSBORNE (Chancellor of the Exchequer); Sir George YOUNG (Party Leader in the House of Commons); Lord HILL OF OAREFORD (Party Leader in the House of Lords); Grant SHAPPS, Andrew FELDMAN (Cochairs).

Liberal Democrats. A federal organization of largely autonomous English, Welsh, and Scottish parties, the Liberal Democrats (also referenced as the Liberal Democratic Party) formed by merger of the Liberal and Social Democratic parties, as approved at conferences of the two groups on January 23 and 31, 1988, respectively. Initially called the Social and Liberal Democratic Party (SLDP), it adopted the shorter name in October 1989.

Reduced to a minority position by the rise of Labour after World War I, the Liberal Party (founded in 1859) continued to uphold the traditional values of European liberalism and sought, without notable success, to attract dissident elements in both of the main parties by its nonsocialist and reformist principles. Despite having won only 13 seats in the election of October 1974, the party played a crucial role in 1977–1978 by entering into a parliamentary accord with Labour, thus, for the first time in nearly 50 years, permitting a major party to continue in office by means of third-party support. In September 1982 the party voted to form an electoral alliance with the Social Democratic Party (SDP), which yielded an aggregate of 23 parliamentary seats in the 1983 election and 27 in 1987.

The SDP had been formally organized on March 26, 1981, by the "gang of four" right-wing Labour dissidents (Roy JENKINS, Dr. David OWEN, William RODGERS, and Shirley WILLIAMS), who strongly objected to the party's swing to unilateralist and anti-European positions. However, after a series of by-election successes in 1981–1982, the SDP lost impetus. Objecting to the proposed merger with the Liberals after the 1987 election, Owen resigned from the SDP leadership in August 1987 and in February 1988 announced the formation of a "new" SDP, which was ultimately dissolved in June 1990. Meanwhile, in July 1988 the merged Liberal Democrats had elected Paddy ASHDOWN as its leader.

At the April 1992 election the Liberal Democrats won 20 seats, which rose to 25 as a result of subsequent by-election victories. The May 1995 and May 1996 local elections saw the Liberal Democrats overtake the Conservatives as the second party (after Labour) in local government, its greatest strength being mainly in the south and west of England. In the May 1997 general election the party increased its representation to 46 seats, adding another with a by-election win in November. Having announced that it would cooperate with the new government, it subsequently agreed to participate in a special cabinet committee established by Prime Minister Blair for regular consultation in areas of "mutual interest."

In May 1999 the party finished fourth in balloting for the new Scottish and Welsh legislatures, but its 17 seats in the Scottish Parliament enabled it to emerge as the junior partner in a coalition administration in Scotland with Labour. As part of the agreement, David STEEL, former leader of the Liberal Democrats, was chosen to be speaker of the Scottish Parliament. In the May local council elections, Conservative gains dropped the Liberal Democrats back to third place in terms of total local seats.

On August 9, 1999, Charles KENNEDY was elected party leader, Ashdown having announced in January that he would step down following the June European Parliament elections. Under a proportional representation system, the Liberal Democrats saw their European Parliament seat total rise to ten, eight more than in 1994, despite a reduced vote share.

In March 2000 the party threatened to stop cooperating with the government if Labour reneged on its campaign pledge to pursue adoption of proportional voting for the House of Commons. The party also remained firmly committed to the EU and adoption of the euro.

In October 2000 the Liberal Democrats joined Labour in forming a coalition government in Wales. At the June 2001 election for the House of Commons, the party gained 6 seats, for a total of 52, although in local elections it lost the 2 local councils it had controlled. At the 2005 poll, the party gained 10 lower house seats for a total of 62 on a vote share of 22.1 percent.

Kennedy resigned as chair on January 7, 2006, after acknowledging an ongoing struggle with alcoholism. Walter Menzies ("Ming") CAMPBELL, a former Olympic sprinter and Scottish MP, became interim leader the same day and won the March 2 leadership contest in a three-way race. The Liberal Democrats subsequently remained opposed to British participation in the war in Iraq and expressed concern about the effect on civil rights of recent antiterrorism initiatives. The Liberal Democrats moved into second place (on a 27 percent vote share) behind the Conservatives in the May 2006 local elections.

Campbell resigned as party leader on October 15, 2007, after it became clear that new Prime Minister Brown did not intend to call for early elections. By that time, the Liberal Democrats were experiencing a decline in popularity polls, and party members had publicly expressed worries that Campbell's advanced age would be a detriment in leading the party into an election that was still two years away. Vincent Cable served as interim leader until Nick Clegg was elected as the party's new leader in December in a closely contested contest with Chris HUHNE.

The party suffered a setback in the May 2008 London Assembly elections, winning just 11.4 percent of the vote and three seats (a loss of two). Its candidate for mayor finished a distant third, with 9.6 percent of the first-preference votes. Although the party finished second in the June 2009 local elections with 28 percent of the vote, its seat total declined as it lost seats to the Conservatives. In concurrent balloting for the European Parliament, the Liberal Democrats finished fourth with 13.7 percent of the vote and 11 seats (down 1 from 2004).

The Liberal Democrats won 57 seats in the May 2010 elections for the House of Commons on 23.0 percent of the vote. The party subsequently joined a new coalition government (which included five Liberal Democrats) led by the Conservatives' David Cameron. The party lost 336 councilors in the May 2012 elections, dropping below 3,000 councilors for the first time in its history.

Energy secretary Chris Huhne was forced to resign on February 2, 2010, following allegations that he had conspired to have his wife take responsibility for a speeding ticket. The first cabinet minister to resign due to a criminal charge since 1721, Huhne was sentenced to eight months in prison in March 2013.

The party won 352 council seats in the May 2013 local elections, a loss of 124 seats.

Two factions emerged at the annual party conference in September. One faction, led by Clegg, wants to continue the alliance with the Conservatives for the 2015 parliamentary election and beyond. The other faction, led by Business, Innovations, and Skills Minister Vince CABLE, argues that the party should distance itself from the Tories and their damaging austerity policies now or face likely defeat in 2015.

Leaders: Nick CLEGG (Deputy Prime Minister and Leader of the Party), Simon HUGHES (Deputy Leader), Alistair CARMICHAEL (Party Chief Whip), Lord MCNALLY (Party Leader in the House of Lords), Tim FARRON (President).

Other UK Parliamentary Parties:

Labour Party. An evolutionary socialist party in basic doctrine and tradition, the Labour Party (founded in 1900) has moved to the center over the past decade but continues to reflect the often conflicting views of trade unions, doctrinaire socialists, and intellectuals, while seeking to broaden its appeal to the middle class and white-collar and managerial personnel. The trade unions traditionally constituted the basis of the party's organized political strength and provided the bulk of its income, although their influence over policy formulation and candidate selection has been reduced in recent years.

After periods of prewar minority government and participation in the wartime coalition, Labour won a large parliamentary majority in 1945 under Clement Attlee and between then and 1951 proceeded to create a comprehensive welfare state, while nationalizing some of the "commanding heights" of the economy. Returning to government in 1964 under Harold Wilson, Labour was unexpectedly defeated in 1970. However, it returned to power in February 1974 as a minority government, still under Wilson, who in a further election in October 1974 won a narrow victory. In early 1977 resignations and defections deprived the government of its majority, forcing Labour to conclude a parliamentary alliance with the small Liberal Party that lasted until late 1978. Meanwhile, James Callaghan succeeded Wilson as Labour leader and prime minister in April 1976.

Defeated by the Conservatives in the May 1979 balloting, Labour swung to the left and also changed its leadership selection procedure. Designated party leader in November 1980 under the old system of election by Labour MPs, Michael FOOT, a revered representative of Labour's "old left," presided over changes that in 1981 established an electoral college of affiliated trade unions, Labour MPs, and local constituency parties for selection of the party leader and deputy leader. This change, and a mainstream antipathy to the EC, caused a small number of right-wing, pro-EC MPs to break away in March 1981 and form the Social Democratic Party (see under Liberal Democrat Party, below). Foot fought the June 1983 election on a platform of withdrawal from the EC, unilateral nuclear disarmament, and socialist economic policies. Overwhelmingly defeated, he resigned the Labour leadership and was succeeded in October 1983 by Neil Kinnock. A disciple of Foot, Kinnock contested the June 1987 election on broadly the same policies as in 1983 and also suffered defeat. Thereafter, he initiated a radical policy review, which eventually resulted in Labour's dropping its hostility to the EC and to Britain's nuclear deterrent, while supporting market economics (subject to regulation). Kinnock continued Foot's policy of expelling Trotskyites of the "Militant Tendency."

Kinnock suffered a further election defeat in April 1992, although Labour's tally of 271 seats and a 34.4 percent vote share represented a significant gain over the 1987 results. He thereupon resigned and was succeeded by John Smith, a moderate who continued the "modernizing" thrust, notably by forcing through "one member, one vote" arrangements for the selection of Labour candidates and leaders. Smith led Labour to major advances in local balloting in 1993 and 1994 but died on May 12, 1994. He was succeeded in July, under the new voting arrangements, by another "modernizing" lawyer, Tony Blair. In the interim, Labour had won a major victory in the June European Parliament elections, taking 62 of the 87 UK seats with a 42.7 percent vote share, while the "Blair factor" boosted the party's electoral resurgence in subsequent parliamentary by-elections and in local balloting in May 1995. In a symbolic change to Labour's constitution, a special party conference on April 29 agreed to drop its celebrated "clause 4" commitment to "the common ownership of the means of production, distribution and exchange" in favor of a general assertion of democratic socialist aims and values. The trend toward "modernization" of the party continued with efforts to further reduce the role of union bloc votes. Moreover, Blair moved the party to the center by co-opting Conservative issues—a strategy often compared to that used by Democratic president Bill Clinton against the Republicans in the United States.

Labour's huge victory in the May 1997 balloting for the House of Commons (418 seats) included the election of 101 female Labour MPs, the party having purposefully presented "women only" lists in a number of safe constituencies. Following his accession to the prime ministership, Blair continued to promote "New Labour" in such areas as budget constraint and welfare reform while pressing ahead with promised initiatives on devolution of regional power in Wales and Scotland. Labour's "pro-yes" campaigns on the devolution referenda were conducted in alliance with the Liberal Democrats as well as *Plaid Cymru* in Wales and the Scottish National Party in Scotland.

In May 1998 the party's National Executive Committee (NEC) approved tightened procedures for vetting of parliamentary candidates, the main intention being to weed out those who had voted contrary to party policy or were otherwise deemed unsuitable. Six months later the NEC banned its members from leaking committee discussions and began requiring them to inform the Labour press office before making public comments on NEC matters. The measures offered opponents a further opportunity to label the Blairites as autocratic, as had a decision early in the year to expel two Labour members of the European Parliament, in part for attacking proposed welfare reforms and the leadership's control of the European Parliament candidate list.

Although failing to win a majority in either the new Scottish Parliament or the Welsh National Assembly, Labour emerged from the May 6, 1999, elections as the plurality party in both, taking 56 of 129 seats in Scotland and 28 of 60 in Wales. It entered into a coalition agreement on May 13 with the Scottish Liberal Democrats but in Wales chose to form a minority government under UK Secretary of State for Wales Alun MICHAEL. In a heated battle, Michael, relying on Prime Minister Blair's support, had defeated Rhodri MORGAN for leadership of Welsh Labour three months earlier. A year later, however, on February 9, 2000, Michael resigned as Welsh first minister shortly before the assembly passed a no-confidence motion, 31–27, largely because of his failure to distance himself from London. On February 15 the assembly confirmed Morgan as his successor. (The title of the office was subsequently changed to first secretary.)

At the European Parliament balloting of June 1999 Labour suffered its first major defeat since Blair's assumption of power, taking only 28 percent of the vote and 29 seats, a loss of 33. The defeat was largely explained by voters' opposition to Labour's pro-euro policy.

On February 20, 2000, Blair's preferred candidate for the new London mayoralty, former minister of health Frank DOBSON, won a narrow victory in a party electoral college, defeating leftist MP Ken LIVINGSTONE. The latter won 60 percent support from London party members and 72 percent from labor unions and societies, but Dobson prevailed on the strength of 86 percent support from the third, equally weighted electoral college bloc: Labor MPs, members of the European Parliament, and candidates for the Greater London Authority (GLA). To the chagrin of the party hierarchy, Livingstone ran as an independent and won the election on May 4. Despite Labour's previous strength in the capital, the party won only 9 seats on the 25-member GLA, equaling the Conservative total. In a further setback on May 4, Labour lost control of 16 of the 73 local councils it had previously held.

At the same time, intraparty disputes continued to surface over Prime Minister Blair's "command and control" managerial style (dubbed "control freakery" by opponents), his reliance on a small circle of advisers that critics dubbed "Tony's cronies," and his centrist "New Labour" programs. Peter KILFOYLE, who had resigned as under secretary of state for defense in January 2000, announced in February that he was forming a "heartlands group" of Labour MPs committed to the party's core supporters and traditional, left-of-center policies. Blair nevertheless remained firmly in control of Labour, which handily won the June 2001 House of Commons election, capturing 412 seats on a slightly reduced vote share of 42 percent.

The May 2005 poll was won by Labour with a Commons majority (55 percent) reduced for a number of reasons, including widespread disagreement over constitutional revision, Britain's role in the EU, and Blair's support of the U.S. position in Iraq. The prime minister subsequently faced growing criticism from left-wing backbenchers opposed to his ongoing reformist agenda. Following Labour's dismal performance in the May 2006 local elections (third place with only 26 percent of the vote), calls intensified for Blair to determine a timetable for his resignation in favor of Gordon Brown (the chancellor of the exchequer). At summer's end, Blair announced that he would step aside within a year. Eight months later, on the heels of another setback for Labour in the May 2007 local elections as well as in the Welsh Assembly and Scottish Parliament elections the same day, Blair said he would resign as party leader and prime minister by the end of June. By mid-May it was clear Gordon Brown would be the only leadership candidate with the required nomination support among MPs. Brown accepted the leader position unopposed at a party conference in Manchester on June 24. The same conference elected Harriet Harman as deputy leader over five others, including the odds-makers' preconference favorite and presumed Blair favorite, Alan JOHNSON. Brown was sworn in as prime minister on June 27.

The party subsequently found itself in the political doldrums. It lost a series of by-elections in early 2008, some in what had been strongly pro-Labour constituencies. The party was generally able to hold its own in the May 2008 London Assembly elections. However, its mayoralty candidate (Ken Livingstone, a two-term incumbent who had been expelled from the party in 2002 for his renegade run in 2000, only to be reinstated in the run-up to the 2004 mayoralty balloting) lost his reelection bid. By summer Labour's support had declined to 24 percent in public opinion polls, and it continued to fare poorly in by-elections. Plotting among Labour backbenchers to depose Brown as party leader subsequently became increasingly public, but the prime minister's standing rebounded in the wake of the support he received, at home and abroad, for his handling of the financial credit crisis.

Public discussion of removing Brown arose again in mid-2009 in the wake of a major scandal in the House of Commons over dubious expense account payments to MPs and the poor performance by Labour in the simultaneous balloting in June for local councils and the European Parliament. (Labour finished third in the local elections in the popular vote and won just 178 of the more than 2,300 seats on the councils, losing more than 60 percent of the seats it had previously held. The party also finished third in the European Parliament elections with 15.7 percent of the vote, good for only 13 seats [down from 22.6 percent of the vote and 19 seats in 2004].) Brown also faced the resignation of several cabinet ministers and outright revolt among some Labour members, although his leadership position remained intact at the September party conference.

The party was unable to overcome the decline in public favor before the May 2010 general election. Labour won just 29.0 percent of the vote in the House of Commons (its second-worst showing since rising to the status of one of two major British parties in the 1920s) and secured 258 seats. Five days after the election Brown resigned his premiership and his position as leader of the party. He was succeeded as leader on an interim basis by Harriet Harman until the party could hold an election. Four nominations for the leadership position were entered in late May, and, after a summer of maneuvering, Ed Miliband, a minister in Brown's former cabinet, emerged the winner in the final tally by edging out his brother, David MILIBAND (also a cabinet minister under Brown), by one percentage point in the fourth round of balloting.

Labour performed very well in the May 2012 council elections, taking 38 percent nationally compared to 31 percent for the Conservatives.

Labour picked up an additional 291 council seats in the May 2013 local elections. During the September party conference, Miliband announced that a Labour government would freeze energy prices for two years, raise taxes on big banks, and force urban landowners to use or lose their plots to ease the urban housing crunch.

Leaders: Ed MILIBAND (Party Leader and Leader of the Opposition), Harriet HARMAN (Deputy Leader), Ed BALLS (Shadow Chancellor of the Exchequer), Angela EAGLE (Shadow Leader in the House of Commons), Baroness ROYALL of BLAISDON (Shadow Leader in the House of Lords), David WATTS (Chair of Parliamentary Party).

Co-operative Party. Founded in 1917, the Co-operative Party operates largely through some 200 affiliated cooperative societies throughout Britain. Under a 1927 agreement with the Labour Party, it cosponsors candidates at local, national, and European elections, and it claims to have 32 Labour Co-ops currently in Westminster.

Leaders: Gareth THOMAS (Chair), Karin CHRISTIANSEN (General Secretary).

Scottish National Party (SNP). Founded in 1934, the SNP advocates Scottish independence within the EU. At the 1979 election it lost 9 of its 11 seats in the House of Commons and since then has managed to win no more than 6. The SNP aligned with Labour and the Liberal Democrats in support of a "yes" vote in the September 1997 referendum on creation of a Scottish Parliament.

As the May 6, 1999, elections for the new Parliament approached, Labour pulled away from the SNP in opinion polls, ending speculation that the nationalists could command a parliamentary majority. Although winning only 7 of 73 constituency seats despite a 28.7 percent first vote share (second to Labour's 38.8 percent), the SNP received an additional 28 "top-up" seats, making it the leading opposition party in the legislature.

At the party's annual conference in September 1999 party leader Alex Salmond predicted that Scotland would be independent by 2007, and in March 2000 the SNP put forward an independence referendum plan that it would pursue if it won the next Scottish election. Four months later Salmond announced that he would resign as SNP leader in September, at which time the party elected John SWINNEY, his deputy, to succeed him. Swinney had been challenged on the left by Alex NEIL.

At the June 2001 UK general election the SNP retained 5 of the 6 seats it had previously held. Amid criticism for ineffective election leadership and arguably disappointing results, Swinney resigned in June 2004. Salmond returned as leader following his election on September 3. The SNP returned to a representation of 6 in the House of Commons in 2005 on a vote share of 17.7 percent of the votes cast in Scotland, and the SNP became the largest party in the 129-seat Scottish Parliament when it won 47 seats in the May 3, 2007, balloting for that body. Salmond was elected first minister of Scotland on May 16 and was sworn in as leader of a minority government the next day.

The SNP retained its six seats in the House of Commons in 2010, securing 19.9 percent of the vote in Scottish constituencies. As 2010 drew to a close, Salmond continued to encourage the UK Parliament to make provisions for a referendum on possible additional devolution of powers to the Scottish Parliament, possibly even independence for Scotland. In the May 2011 elections the SNP gained its first ever majority in the Scottish parliament, prompting Salmond to schedule a referendum on Scottish independence for September 18, 2014. In October 2012 the SNP voted 394–365 to end its traditional opposition to an independent Scotland joining NATO.

Leaders: Alex SALMOND (Party Leader and First Minister of Scotland), Nicola STURGEON (Deputy Leader), Ian HUDGHTON (President), Angus ROBERTSON (UK Parliamentary Leader).

Plaid Cymru (literally, "Party of Wales," usually referred to by its Welsh name, or informally as the Welsh Nationalist Party). Founded in 1925, *Plaid Cymru* sought full self-government for Wales as a democratic socialist republic. In May 1987 it entered into a parliamentary alliance with the SNP to work for constitutional, economic, and social reform in both regions. It elected four MPs in 1992, when it gained 8.9 percent of the Welsh vote (partly through an alliance in six constituencies with the Welsh Green Party). In 1997 the party retained the four seats, and it joined the Labour Party and the Liberal Democrats in urging passage of the September referendum regarding establishment of a Welsh regional assembly.

Plaid Cymru finished second to Labour at balloting for the Welsh National Assembly on May 6, 1999, taking a 28.4 percent first-vote share and winning a total of 17 seats (9 constituency, 8 "top-up"). Labour subsequently backed the party's nominee as speaker of the new legislature, Lord Dafydd ELIS-THOMAS. In June 1999 *Plaid Cymru* won 2 seats in the European Parliament.

In May 2000, citing health reasons, the party's president, Dafydd WIGLEY, resigned. Ieuan Wyn Jones handily won election as his successor on August 3, and at the party's September annual conference he set 2003 as the target date for supplanting Labour as the foremost party in the Welsh National Assembly. At the June 2001 election for the House of Commons, *Plaid Cymru* retained its four seats. Three months later, at its annual conference, the party formally ended its demand for Welsh independence.

At the May 1, 2003, assembly election the *Plaid Cymru* lost 5 of its 17 seats and barely kept its position as the official opposition. Jones resigned as president and assembly leader within a week of the election. Folk singer and politician Dafydd IWAN was subsequently elected party president, with Jones winning reelection as assembly leader. *Plaid Cymru*'s representation in the House of Commons dropped to 3 in 2005 on a vote share of 12.6 percent of the votes in Wales. Jones subsequently warned party members at the *Plaid Cymru* annual conference that internal squabbling was compromising electoral effectiveness.

In the May 3, 2007, balloting for the Welsh assembly, *Plaid Cymru* improved by 3 seats to a total of 15. The party joined Labour in a coalition government that was installed on May 25, after negotiations had prompted a commitment from Labour to hold a referendum on *Plaid Cymru*'s proposal for additional law-making powers to be given to the assembly.

The party retained its three seats in the UK parliamentary balloting in May 2010 with an 11.3 percent vote share across Welsh constituencies. A month later, Iwan announced he would resign as president; he was succeeded by Jill Evans, who won the position in a June party vote. The UK government held a referendum on March 4, 2011, asking whether to increase the Welsh assembly's law-making powers on 20 devolved areas, including health and education. Some 63.5 percent of voters favored the motion.

Leaders: Leuan Wyn JONES (Party Leader and Deputy First Minister of Wales), Dafydd Trystan DAVIES (Chair), Jill EVANS (President), Elfyn LLWYD (UK Parliamentary Leader).

Green Party of England and Wales. Organized in 1973 as the Ecology Party, the Greens adopted their present name in 1985. (The semiautonomous Welsh branch is the **Welsh Green Party** [*Plaid Werdd Cym*].) The party addresses human rights issues in addition to problems affecting the environment.

The Greens have consistently polled less than 1 percent of the vote for the House of Commons. In June 1999, however, the Greens won two seats in the European Parliament on a 6.3 percent vote share. In November 1999 Lord BEAUMONT of Whitley, a life peer in the House of Lords, resigned from the Liberal Democrats and joined the Greens as their sole member in the UK Parliament. The party secured no lower house seats on a 1 percent vote share in 2005, and the death of Lord Beaumont in April 2008 meant the party went unrepresented in either chamber of parliament between 2008 and 2010. However, the party retained its two seats in the London Assembly in 2008 and its two seats (on a vote share of 8.6 percent) in the European Parliament in 2009. Also in 2008, the party switched from a collective leadership to a single leader, Caroline LUCAS. In the 2010 UK general election, Lucas became the first Green candidate to gain a seat in the UK parliament.

The Greens won 22 seats in the May 2013 local elections, adding 5 new constituencies.

Leaders: Natalie BENNETT (Leader), Will DUCKWORTH (Deputy Leader).

The Respect Party. Respect was launched in January 2004 by MP George Galloway, who had been expelled from the Labour Party in October 2003 after being found guilty of inciting UK troops in Iraq to disobey orders. Galloway, running as the candidate of Respect–The Unity Coalition, was reelected in 2005 by a constituency heavily populated by immigrants.

The party allows its members to hold memberships in other parties, most notably, until late 2007, the Socialist Workers Party. A schism emerged over Galloway's charge that the party was too disorganized to be effective, which drew the countercharge that he was willing to sacrifice principle for election. In the May 2008 London Assembly elections, the two factions ran on different lists, and both received less than 2.5 percent of the vote. Galloway decided to contest the 2010 balloting for the House of Commons in a new constituency, with another Respect member standing in his former constituency. Both candidates finished third in their respective contests. Galloway won a March 29, 2012, parliamentary by-election in Bradford Wells, a northern England constituency long regarded as a Labour stronghold. The party ran 12 candidates in the May 3, 2012, council elections, winning 5 seats.

Salma YAQOOB, the party's highly visible chair, resigned in September 2012 due to conflict with Galloway that was sparked by his comments about sexual assault charges levied against Julian Assage. Without Yaqoob, Galloway's bluster increasingly became a liability.

Leader: George GALLOWAY (Founder).

Note: For information on the Democratic Unionist Party, *Sinn Féin,* the Social Democratic and Labour Party, and the Alliance Party of Northern Ireland (all represented in the UK House of Commons), see Political Parties and Groups in the entry on United Kingdom: Northern Ireland.

Nonparliamentary Parties:

UK Independence Party (UKIP). The UKIP was created in 1993 by Alan SKED and members of the Anti-Federalist League (founded 1991) to oppose what it saw as the surrender of British sovereignty implicit in the terms of the EU's Maastricht Treaty; the party urged withdrawal from the EU and warned of the dangers posed by unrestricted immigration. It failed to win any parliamentary seats in 1997 but won 7 percent of the vote and 3 seats in the European Parliament balloting in June 1999. It fared even better in the European poll of June 2004, winning 12 of 75 seats in a third-place showing. Two members of the UKIP were elected to the London Assembly in 2004, but they subsequently defected to Veritas, a new party dedicated to the restoration of probity in public life, which had been founded in January 2005 by the UKIP's most celebrated MP, former talk show host Robert KILROY-SILK. Following the dissolution of Veritas, the two members of the assembly formed their own **One London** party. (They lost their seats in the assembly in 2008.)

In January 2007 three Conservative Party members of the House of Lords defected to the UKIP and thus gave the party its first parliamentary representation. The party claimed one seat in the House of Commons in April 2008 when Conservative member Bob SPINK declared his membership in the UKIP.

The UKIP recorded its best-ever electoral showing by finishing second (behind only the Conservatives) in the June 2009 balloting for the European Parliament, winning 13 seats on a vote share of 16.5 percent. However the members of the European Parliament (MEPs) have missed one-third of the votes in Strasbourg. In November Lord Pearson (Malcom Pearson) was elected as the new party leader, succeeding Nigel FARAGE, who had stepped down as party leader to concentrate on his membership in the European Parliament. Subsequently, Lord Pearson offered to keep the UKIP out of the general election due in 2010 if the Conservatives would pledge in writing that, if elected, they would hold a national referendum on the EU's Lisbon Treaty. However, Conservative leader David Cameron rejected the offer.

The UKIP vigorously contested the May 2010 general election, fielding 572 candidates for the House of Commons, and recorded its best performance to date with 3.1 percent of the vote. In the process, party leader Lord PEARSON did an about-face on his challenge to the Conservatives by campaigning on behalf of some of their candidates. He resigned his UKIP position in the summer, saying he was not cut out for party politics. Nigel FARAGE won a three-way contest for the leadership post on November 5.

The UKIP surged in popularity in 2013, with polling at 22 percent popularity at midyear, and the party won 147 local council seats in May. In a huge public gaffe, MEP Godfrey BLOOM referred to a group of women's activists as "sluts" during the party's annual conference. He was forced to quit the party's delegation in the European Parliament. Farage blasted Bloom for "destroying UKIP's national conference."

Leaders: Nigel FARAGE (Leader); Paul NUTTALL (Deputy Leader); Steve CROWTHER (Executive Chairperson).

British National Party (BNP). The BNP was founded in 1982 by a breakaway faction of the fascist National Front (NF) and advocates on behalf of "Native British" under attack from immigrants. In early 2006 BNP leader Nick Griffin was acquitted of charges of inciting racial hatred related to a speech he gave at a party conference in 2004 in which he reportedly made strongly anti-Muslim remarks. In the 2005 general election the BNP's 119 candidates secured 0.7 percent of the nationwide vote, up from 0.5 percent in 2001. The BNP doubled its seats in the local elections held in May 2006, performing well in the white working-class areas of east London, and held its own in the May 2007 local elections. The BNP claimed its first seat on the London Assembly when it won 5.4 percent of the party-list voting in the May 2008 balloting. In June 2009 the party won its first seats above the local level, securing two seats on 6.2 percent of the nationwide vote for the European Parliament. The Equality and Human Rights Commission sued the party in 2009 for violating race relation laws for its "Whites only" membership, employment, and services policies. The party dropped the rule because it could not afford a legal battle, but the EHRC says the policy continues in practice. Although the party fielded 338 candidates in the 2010 general election, no BNP candidate received as much as 15 percent of the vote in any constituency. It lost its seat on the London Assembly in the 2012 election. Andrew BRONS, one of two BNP MEPs, resigned from the party in late 2012, citing personal disagreements with Griffin.

Leader: Nick GRIFFIN (Chair).

The 2010 general election was contested by 135 parties, with only 10 receiving 0.5 percent or more of the nationwide vote and with many parties fielding a candidate in but a single constituency. Covering the full political spectrum, the small parties highlighted below are among those recently active.

On the left, the **Socialist Labour Party** (SLP) was launched in 1996 by miners' union leader Arthur SCARGILL to protest the perceived rightward drift of the Labour Party. The more militant **Socialist Workers' Party** (SWP), dating from 1950, has recently withdrawn its traditional support for Labour and until recently formed part of Respect–The Unity Coalition (see The Respect Party, above). Earlier, the SWP had formed an electoral coalition (the London Socialist Alliance) with the **Communist Party of Britain** (CPB) to support maverick Ken Livingstone's successful campaign for the capital's mayoralty in 2000. In 1997 the **Militant Labour** (ML, originally the Militant Tendency within the Labour Party) founded the Trotskyite **Socialist Party** (SP), led by Peter TAAFFE. An ML minority, led by the group's founder, Ted GRANT, remained within Labour as the Socialist Appeal, while the ML's Scottish branch, led by Tommy SHERIDAN, helped form a Scottish Socialist Alliance that, in turn, in 1998 established the autonomous **Scottish Socialist Party** (SSP), which is led jointly by Colin FOX and Frances CURRAN. In 1999 the SSP took one seat (won by Sheridan) in the new Scottish Parliament, and increased its numbers to six in the 2003 Scottish Parliament elections. However, it won no seats in 2007. The **Scottish Green Party** (SGP), led by Cllr Martha WARDROP (co-conveners), also won one seat in 1999, increased its representation to six in 2003, but fell back to two seats following the 2007 balloting. It currently has two members in the Scottish Parliament and 14 councilors. The **Socialist Party of Great Britain** (SPGB), a non-Leninist Marxist group founded in 1904, continues to maintain branches throughout the country but did not have a candidate in the 2005 or the 2010 UK general elections. Prior to the 2010 election, Dave NELLIST and Bob CROW organized the **Trade Unionist and Socialist Coalition** (TUSC), comprised of the SWP, SP, **Solidarity: Scotland's Socialist Movement**, and **Socialist Resistance.** TUSC also ran candidates in local elections in 2011 and 2012, receiving an average of 6.2 percent of the vote in 2012.

On the extreme left, the CPB, currently led by Robert GRIFFITHS, split in 1988 from the historical **Communist Party of Great Britain** (CPGB) to protest the CPGB's conversion to Eurocommunism. The CPGB was founded in 1920, briefly enjoyed parliamentary representation, and was influential in the trade union movement. However, it is now defunct, most of its remaining membership having reorganized in 1992 as the moderate **Democratic Left** (DL). The DL presented itself as an association rather than a party and so did not contest elections. In 1999, under the leadership of Nina TEMPLE, the DL membership voted to reorganize as the nondoctrinaire New Times Network. Other CPBG remnants include the Marxist-Leninist **New Communist Party** (NCP), formed by dissidents in 1977, and the **Communist Party of Scotland** (CPS). (Although the CPGB continues to pursue a reforging of the original CPGB, it is not officially registered as a party. Neither is the NCP or CPS.) The **Workers' Revolutionary Party** (WRP) has also undergone extensive splintering; the faction that has retained the WRP name is led by Sheila TORRANCE. A WRP offshoot includes the Trotskyite **Socialist Equality Party** (SEP, formerly the International Communist Party), which is led by Christopher Howard MARSDEN and serves as the British branch of the International Committee of the Fourth International. Other small groups include the Trotskyite **Alliance for Workers' Liberty** (AWL), led by Cathy NUGENT; the **Revolutionary Communist Group** (RCG); and the **Revolutionary Communist Party of Great Britain** (Marxist-Leninist), led by Chris COLEMAN.

On the extreme right, the **National Front** (NF), a fascist grouping founded in 1967, won a number of local council seats in the 1970s but largely disintegrated thereafter. Most of the NF defected in 1982 to what is now the BNP (above). In 1995 most remaining NF members regrouped under Ian ANDERSON as the **National Democrats** (ND). Under the leadership of Thomas HOLMES, the rump NF contested 17 constituencies in 2010. Founded in 1990 as the **Third Way** and registered in 2006 as the **National Liberal Party–the Third Way**, the party has roots in the NF but denounced national socialism in favor of worker participation in industry, adoption of Swiss-style democratic reforms, immigration restrictions, withdrawal from the EU and other multilateral groups, and an ecological agenda. The party is currently led by Daniel KERR. Extremist groups include the violent **Combat 18.**

Other formations include the **Christian People's Alliance** (CPA), launched in May 1999 as a Christian Democratic party and chaired by Alan CRAIG; the **Liberal Party** (currently led by Rob WHEWAY), which was formed by those who opposed the conversion of the historic party into what became the Liberal Democrats; **Mebyon Kernow** (literally, "Sons of Cornwall"), a Cornish separatist group formed in 1951 and currently led by Dick COLE; the **Islamic Party of Britain,** founded in 1989 and led by David Musa PIDCOCK; and the **Legalize Cannabis Alliance** (LCA), which voted in 2006 to deregister and continue as a pressure group. In addition, the anti-euro Democracy Movement, a self-described "non-party movement" led by Robin BIRLEY, was organized in 1999 as successor to the Referendum Movement, which began in 1994 as the Referendum Party of the late James GOLDSMITH.

Among the numerous British fringe groups are the **Natural Law Party** (NLP), founded in 1992 by practitioners of Transcendental Meditation and led by Dr. Geoffrey CLEMENTS (the NLP is no longer registered as a party); the **Official Monster Raving Loony Party,** led by Alan (Howling Laud) HOPE since the 1999 suicide of the party's founder, former rock singer (Screaming Lord) David SUTCH; and the **Make Politicians History Party** (led by Ronnie CARROLL), a successor to the individualist Rainbow Dream Ticket Party, which advocated abolishing Parliament and instituting government by home-based electronic referenda (the party voluntarily deregistered in 2009).

LEGISLATURE

The **Parliament** serves as legislative authority for the entire UK. Meeting in Westminster (London) with the queen as its titular head, until November 1999 it consisted of a partly hereditary, partly appointed House of Lords and an elected House of Commons (the real locus of power). Under the House of Lords Act 1999 the membership of the upper house was restructured (see below).

Following voter approval at separate devolutionary referendums held in Scotland and Wales in 1997, the UK Parliament passed legislation in 1998 that authorized creation of a Scottish Parliament and a Welsh National Assembly. Elections for both legislatures were held for the first time on May 6, 1999. Creation of a New Northern Ireland Assembly was approved by referendum on May 22, 1998, with the initial election occurring a month later, on June 25 (see the Northern Ireland entry). All three of the new legislative bodies are elected for four-year terms under a proportional representation system that combines single-member constituencies and "top-up" seats drawn from party lists.

House of Lords. Before reforms were instituted in 1999, the House of Lords had 1,330 members, of whom 751 were hereditary peers, either by succession or of first creation. The remaining members included the 2 archbishops and 24 other senior bishops of the Church of England, serving and retired Lords of Appeal in Ordinary (who constituted the nation's highest body of civil and criminal appeal), and other life peers. Only about 200–300 members of the House of Lords attended sessions with any degree of regularity. The House of Lords Act 1999 abolished the hereditary component and replaced it on an interim basis, pending more comprehensive reform, by 92 ex-hereditary members: 75 elected by all the hereditaries according to a predetermined party ratio, 15 house officers elected by the full membership, and 2 appointed royal office holders (the Earl Marshall and the Lord Great Chamberlain). The 75 peers elected on October 29 on a party basis comprised 42 Conservatives, 28 "crossbenchers" (independents), 3 Liberal Democrats, and 2 Labour members. The collateral election of house officers added 9 Conservatives, 2 Labour peers, 2 Liberal Democrats, and 2 crossbenchers.

Following the reforms, the full interim chamber had 670 members. The subsequent naming of new life peers—most of them Labour supporters, in an effort by the government to achieve political parity—plus the naming in April 2001 of 15 independent "people's peers" by an appointments commission, brought the total to 715 as of July 31, 2001. As of October 2010 the total current and qualified members was 744: Labour Party, 238; Conservative Party, 195; crossbenchers, 182; Liberal Democrats, 79; Democratic Unionist Party, 4; Ulster Unionist Party, 3; United Kingdom Independence Party, 2; Labour Independent, 1; Conservative Independent, 1; Independent Labour, 1; archbishops and bishops, 24; independents, 14. Seventeen others were on leave of absence, 15 were disqualified as senior members of the judiciary, and 1 was disqualified as a member of the European Parliament.

On June 28, 2006, the House of Lords for the first time elected its own leader as part of broader governmental changes proposed by the prime minister in 2003. The new Lord Speaker, who may serve a maximum of two five-year terms, assumed (effective July 4) the leadership role previously exercised by the Lord Chancellor (the prime minister's appointee and a member of the cabinet). Baroness Hayman of the Labour Party was elected as the first Lord Speaker, and, following the custom of the speaker of the House of Commons, she subsequently withdrew her party affiliation. Meanwhile, in March 2007 both houses of Parliament took a series of votes on a variety of possible alternatives for a popularly elected component for the House of Lords. In July 2008 the government submitted a white paper to the House of Commons proposing an 80 to 100 percent elected upper chamber.

Lord Speaker: Baroness D'SOUZA.

House of Commons. Following the general election of May 6, 2010, the House of Commons consisted of 650 members directly elected from single-member constituencies for terms of five years, subject to earlier dissolution. The strength of the parties was as follows: Conservative Party, 306 seats; Labour Party, 258; Liberal Democrats, 57; Democratic Unionist Party, 8; Scottish National Party, 6; *Sinn Féin,* 5 (seats not taken); *Plaid Cymru,* 3; Social Democratic and Labour Party, 3; Alliance Party of Northern Ireland, 1; Green Party of England and Wales, 1; speaker (running as "The Speaker Seeking Reelection"), 1. (According to long-standing convention, the speaker serves without party affiliation and votes only in case of a tie vote. The current speaker was initially elected to the House of Commons on the Conservative ticket in 2005.)

Speaker: John BERCOW.

Scottish Parliament. Party strength in the 129-member Parliament after the May 5, 2011, election was as follows: Scottish National Party, 69; Labour Party, 37; Conservative Party, 15; Liberal Democrats, 5; Scottish Green Party, 2; independent, 1.

Presiding Officer: Tricia MARWICK.

Welsh National Assembly (*Cynulliad Cenedlaethol Cymru*). Party strength in the 60-member National Assembly after the May 5, 2011, election was as follows: Labour Party, 30; Conservative Party, 14; *Plaid Cymru,* 11; Liberal Democrats, 5.

Presiding Officer: Rosemary BUTLER.

CABINET

[as of October 20, 2013]

Prime Minister and First Lord of the Treasury	David Cameron
Deputy Prime Minister	Nick Clegg (LD)
Secretaries of State	
Business, Innovations, and Skills	Vincent Cable (LD)
Cabinet Office	Francis Maude
Communities and Local Government	Eric Pickles
Culture, Olympics, Media, and Sport	Maria Miller [f]
Defense	Philip Hammond
Education	Michael Gove
Energy and Climate Change	Edward Davey (LD)
Environment, Food, and Rural Affairs	Owen Paterson
Foreign and Commonwealth Affairs	William Hague
Health	Jeremy Hunt
Home Department	Theresa May [f]
International Development	Justine Greening [f]
Justice	Chris Grayling
Northern Ireland	Theresa Villiers [f]
Scotland	Alistair Carmichael (LD)
Transport	Patrick McLoughlin
Wales	David Jones
Work and Pensions	Iain Duncan Smith
Chancellor of the Exchequer	George Osborne
Chief Secretary to the Treasury	Danny Alexander (LD)
Leader of the House of Commons	Andrew Lansley
Leader of the House of Lords	Lord Hill of Oareford
Lord Chancellor	Chris Grayling
Lord President of the Council	Nick Clegg (LD)
Lord Privy Seal	Andrew Lansley
Minister of the Civil Service	David Cameron
Minister for Women and Equality	Maria Miller [f]
Minister without Portfolio	Kenneth Clarke

[f] = female

Note: Except for those noted, all of the above are members of the Conservative Party.

INTERGOVERNMENTAL REPRESENTATION

Ambassador to the U.S.: Peter WESTMACOTT.

U.S. Ambassador to the UK: Matthew BARZUN.

Permanent Representative to the UN: Mark LYALL GRANT.

IGO Memberships (Non-UN): ADB, AfDB, CEUR, CWTH, EBRD, EIB, EU, G-8, G-20, IADB, IEA, ICC, IOM, NATO, OECD, OSCE, WTO.

RELATED TERRITORIES

All major, and many minor, territories of the former British Empire achieved full independence in the course of the last century, and most are now members of the Commonwealth, a voluntary association of states held together primarily by a common political and constitutional heritage and, in most cases, use of the English language (see "The Commonwealth" in Intergovernmental Organizations section). In conventional usage, the term Commonwealth also includes the territories and dependencies of the UK and other Commonwealth member countries. As of 2006 the UK retained a measure of responsibility, direct or indirect, for 3 Crown dependencies, 11 inhabited territories, 2 essentially uninhabited territories, and the so-called Sovereign Base Areas on Cyprus.

In September 1998, following up on a commitment made at the Dependent Territories Association conference in London the preceding February, the Blair government announced that it intended to introduce legislation that would supersede the 1981 British Nationality Act, which had excluded most colonial residents from British citizenship, and restore their "right of abode" in the UK, which had been revoked in 1962. The dependencies would be restyled British overseas territories. A white paper issued in March 1999 reaffirmed the government's intentions, although the government added that the Caribbean colonies would be required to introduce various criminal justice reforms—for example, abolishing the death penalty and decriminalizing consensual homosexual relations—before attaining the new status. Implementing legislation was passed in 2002, with British citizenship being conferred on citizens of all British overseas territories (except the Sovereign Base Areas) from May 21. Since 2005 many of the territories, with London's cooperation and encouragement, have been studying possible constitutional reforms.

Several of the Overseas Territories and Crown Dependencies were hit hard by the 2008 global financial crisis, prompting the UK's chancellor of the exchequer, Alistair DARLING, to commission a report on their need to improve standards of financial regulation and to find new methods for raising tax revenue. The report called upon UK related territories to put their government finances on firmer footing through more diversified tax systems, including the possible introduction of taxes on income, profits, capital gains, and sales. The report also called on territories with significant financial sectors to provide more help in tracking financial crimes. In May 2013 Prime Minister Cameron wrote the leaders of the Crown Dependencies, asking for their help in setting a new global standard for tax information exchanges and knocking "down the walls of company secrecy."

Crown Dependencies:

Though closely related to Great Britain both historically and geographically, the Channel Islands and the Isle of Man are distinct from the UK and are under the jurisdiction of the sovereign rather than the state.

Channel Islands.

Located in the English Channel off the northwest coast of France, the Channel Islands have been attached to the English Crown since the Norman Conquest in 1066. The nine islands have a total area of 75 square miles (198 sq. km) and a population (2010E) of 155,000. The two largest and most important are Jersey and Guernsey, each of which has its own parliament (the States) but is linked to the Crown through a representative who bears the title lieutenant governor and serves as commander in chief. While the Channel Islands control their own domestic affairs, defense policy and most foreign relations are administered from London. St. Helier on Jersey and St. Peter Port on Guernsey are the principal towns. Because of their mild climate and insular location, the islands are popular tourist resorts, and their low tax rate has attracted many permanent residents from the UK.

The government of Jersey is based in the "Assembly of the States," a 53-member elected body composed of 29 deputies, 12 constables (heads of parishes), and 12 senators, not counting 3 nonvoting ex officio members (attorney general, solicitor general, dean of Jersey) plus the lieutenant governor and a bailiff, who presides over the legislature. Deputies and constables serve three-year terms; senators serve six-year terms, with elections for half their number held triennially.

November 2005 marked a major change in Jersey's governmental structure. Under the States of Jersey Law 2005, the previous committee system of governance was replaced by a ten-member cabinet-style system headed by a chief minister. The other nine ministers are nominated by the chief minister from among the membership of the Assembly of the States, which then elects each minister individually. The authority of the lieutenant governor to veto resolutions of the states was abolished, and "orders in council," issued by the Privy Council in London, were henceforth to be referred to the States for review. On December 5 Sen. Frank WALKER was elected chief minister by a vote of 38–14 over Senator SYVRET.

Following Walker's election, the government launched two public consultations in 2007. Jersey residents were surveyed for their views on civil unions for homosexual and heterosexual couples, and also registered their preferences for alternative strategies to provide public services to an aging population in the face of a shrinking workforce.

Elections for senators were held October 15, 2008, with the balloting for deputies following on November 26. All winning senatorial candidates ran as independents, although three parties had candidates on the ballot: the **Jersey Democratic Alliance** (JDA), **Time 4 Change,** and **Jersey 2020.** The Centre Party, which had fielded senatorial candidates in 2005, changed its name to the **Jersey Conservative Party** (JCP) in 2007 but presented no candidates in 2008. Three JDA candidates won election as deputies, with the remaining 26 deputy seats being filled by independents. On December 9, 2008, Terry LE SUEUR, formerly a senator and theretofore deputy chief minister, was elected chief minister, 36 to 17, over senator Alan BRECKON. On the policy front, in October 2009 the assembly approved legislation to legalize civil partnerships, and the Law on Civil Partnerships came into effect on July 12, 2011.

The most recent senatorial election was October 19, 2011, and on November 14 Ian GORST defeated incumbent Sir Philip Bailhache, 27 to 24, to become chief minister. The Jersey Electoral Commission is in the process of formulating ways to restructure the assemblies, most likely to reduce the number of members to streamline operations.

The Organization for Economic Cooperation and Development commended Gorst in July 2013 for his government's efforts to increase tax transparency.

Guernsey is governed through its "States of Deliberation," which comprises 45 people's deputies elected from multi- or single-member districts every four years, 2 representatives from Alderney, 2 ex officio members (attorney general and solicitor general), and a bailiff. Prior to the election of April 21, 2004, the States had included 10 local (parish) representatives, but those seats were eliminated as part of a governmental reform process that also saw, from May 1, 2004, adoption of a ministerial administration. At that time, 43 separate committees were abolished in favor of a Policy Council, comprising a chief minister and 10 other ministers elected from and by the members of the States; 10 departments, each headed by a minister; and 5 "specialist" committees. The first Privy Council resigned en masse in February 2007 after revelations of an alleged rigged bidding process for a hospital construction project.

Peter HARWOOD was elected chief minister of Guernsey, 27 to 20, on May 1, 2012. A retired lawyer, Harwood entered the April 18 States election as a political novice, emphasizing that he would be "free of previous political baggage." He has prioritized improving the island's tax transparency requirements.

The small islands of Alderney, Sark, Herm, Jethou, Brecqhou, and Lihou are usually classified as dependencies of the Bailiwick of Guernsey, although Alderney and Sark have their own legislatures: the States of Alderney, encompassing a president and 10 deputies serving four-year terms (half elected every other year), and the Sark Court of Chief Pleas, comprising 40 hereditary "tenants" (landowners) and 12 deputies elected for three-year terms. Anticipating the need to dismantle the island's feudal political system in order to comply with the European Convention on Human Rights, voters in October 2006 approved the creation of a Chief Pleas Assembly, to comprise 28 elected and 2 ex officio members. The Chief Pleas approved the new law in February 2008, and elections were scheduled for the following December, pending approval from the British Privy Council. The election of 28 councilors (from 57 candidates) was held December 10, after which the councilors voted to assign themselves initial two- or four-year terms in order to permit the subsequent election of half the members every two years for staggered four-year terms.

Although the Channel Islands are not legally part of the EU, certain EU directives are deemed to apply to them, notably those relating to tariffs and agricultural policy. In February 1995 the Sark Court of Chief Pleas rejected the incorporation of relevant parts of the EU's Maastricht Treaty into Sark law. In November 1999, however, the court voted to rescind a 1611 law that had restricted property inheritance to men. In December the UK Privy Council approved the change, thereby preventing a future challenge in the European Court of Human Rights.

In November 1998 a report presented by the UK Home Office recommended that the Channel Islands and the Isle of Man, which between them have registered some 90,000 offshore businesses, require such operations to provide greater details about their ownership and activities. The report also proposed that the dependencies take additional steps to prevent money laundering and other financial offenses. The June 2000 decision of the OECD to include the Channel Islands and the Isle of Man among 35 international jurisdictions with harmful tax and investment regimes led the islands' administrations to assert that reform would be pointless unless other, larger jurisdictions, such as Switzerland and Luxembourg, also participated. In early August, however, the islands pledged to cooperate with OECD efforts to eliminate tax crimes perpetrated by offshore corporations, and in February 2002 they were removed from the blacklist.

In a February 2000 ruling with major implications for a number of UK institutions, the European Court of Human Rights determined that a Guernsey flower grower had been denied a fair trial when he appealed a planning decision denying him use of a packing shed as a residence. The original appeal had involved the bailiff of Guernsey, who held executive and legislative as well as judicial responsibilities, thereby calling into question his impartiality, according to the court. The decision increased the likelihood of future challenges against, for example, the UK's lord chancellor, particularly in cases based on policies that the chancellor helps administer.

In December 2007 an amendment to the Reform Law granting 16-year-olds the right to vote received Royal Sanction and was implemented ahead of the April 23, 2008, general election with all 45 members standing as nonpartisans. Guernsey's "Zero-10" tax strategy was also implemented in 2008, with income tax on company profits eliminated. The strategy singled out a minority of banking activities for a uniform 10 percent tax. However, the tax had to be modified in 2012 to make it EU compliant.

Lieutenant Governor and Commander in Chief of Jersey: John McCOLL.

Bailiff of Jersey and President of the Assembly of the States: Michael BIRT.

Chief Minister of Jersey: Ian GORST.

Lieutenant Governor and Commander in Chief of the Bailiwick of Guernsey and Its Dependencies: Air Marshal Peter WALKER.

Bailiff of Guernsey and President of the States of Deliberation: Richard COLLAS.

Chief Minister of Guernsey: Peter HARWOOD.

Isle of Man.

Located in the Irish Sea midway between Northern Ireland and northern England, the Isle of Man has been historically connected to Great Britain for over 700 years but remains politically distinct. It has an area of 227 square miles (588 sq. km) and at the 2006 census, a population of 80,058. The principal town is Douglas, and most income is derived from offshore banking and business services.

The island's self-governing institutions include the High Court of Tynwald (the world's oldest parliament in continuous existence), encompassing a president elected by the court, the Legislative Council, and the House of Keys, which is a 24-member body popularly elected for a five-year term. The Legislative Council includes a president, the lord bishop of Sodor and Man, a nonvoting attorney general, and eight others named by the House of Keys. The British monarch serves as head of state ("Lord of Man") and is represented by a lieutenant governor, who historically functioned as head of government and presided over an Executive Council. In 1986, however, the office of chief minister was created, and in 1990 a Council of Ministers replaced the Executive Council. Concurrently, the president of the Tynwald assumed many of the responsibilities of the lieutenant governor, who nevertheless still reserves important constitutional powers, including the authority to dissolve the House of Keys. The chief minister, elected by the legislature, nominates the other ministers.

The island levies its own taxes and has a special relationship with the EU, falling within the EU customs territory but remaining fiscally independent of it. In August 2000 the Manx administration joined the Channel Islands in agreeing to work with the OECD on tax harmonization, improved financial transparency, and information exchange.

At the election of November 22, 2001, independents won 19 seats in the House of Keys. Candidates affiliated with the **Alliance for Progressive Government** (APG), an identifiable political group but not an official party, won 3 seats, and the **Manx Labour Party** (MLP) won 2. The nationalist **Mec Vannin** (Sons of Mannin), which dates from 1962 and advocates republican independence, boycotts elections.

Following the 2001 polling the incumbent chief minister, Donald GELLING, was unanimously reelected to the post, but he stepped down a year later and was succeeded by Richard CORKHILL. In December 2004 Corkhill resigned because of a financial scandal, and on December 14 Gelling was returned as chief minister. James Anthony (Tony) Brown was elected chief minister on December 14, 2006, resigning, as required by law, his position of speaker of the house. Stephen Rodan was subsequently elected speaker. The November 23, 2008, balloting for the House of Keys resulted in the election of 21 independent members (1 affiliated with the APG), with the Liberal Vannin Party (LVP, founded in 2006) winning 2 seats and the MLP 1. Following elections on September 29, 2011, Allan BELL was elected chief minister. Bell commissioned an independent evaluation of government services in May 2012 in order to determine options for narrowing government-delivered services.

Lieutenant Governor: Adam WOOD.

President of the Tynwald: Clare CHRISTIAN.

Speaker of the House of Keys: Stephen RODAN.

Chief Minister: Allan BELL.

Inhabited Overseas Territories:

The territories described below remain directly subordinate to the UK, although a number of them enjoy almost complete autonomy in internal affairs. The term "colony" or "crown colony," a historical relic without contemporary legal import, is often still used in reference to these jurisdictions.

Anguilla.

One of the most northern of the Caribbean's Leeward Islands (see Antigua/Barbuda map, p. 52), Anguilla has a land area of 35 square miles (91 sq. km), exclusive of Sombrero's 2 square miles (5 sq. km), and a resident population (2010E) of 16,400. There is no capital city as such, apart from a centrally located sector known as The Valley. The main industries are tourism, offshore banking and finance, and construction. Overseas remittances from Anguillans living abroad are a substantial source of island revenue.

Anguilla was first settled by the British in 1632 and became part of the Territory of the Leeward Islands in 1956. Following establishment of the Associated State of St. Kitts-Nevis-Anguilla in early 1967, the Anguillans repudiated government from Basseterre, St. Kitts, and a British commissioner was installed following a landing by British security forces in March 1969. The island was subsequently placed under the direct administration of Britain, while a separate constitution that was enacted in February 1976 gave the resident commissioner (subsequently governor) authority over foreign affairs, defense, civil service, and internal security. Other executive functions are undertaken on the advice of an Executive Council that, in accordance with a 1982 constitution (amended in 1990), consists of a chief minister; three additional ministers; and the deputy governor and attorney general, ex officio. Legislative authority, save in respect of the governor's reserve powers, is the responsibility of a House of Assembly encompassing a speaker; seven elected members; two nominated members; and the deputy governor and attorney general, ex officio. An act of December 1980 formally confirmed the dependent status of the territory, which also includes the neighboring island of Sombrero.

Ronald WEBSTER, then leader of the People's Progressive Party, headed Anguilla's government after the separation from St. Kitts-Nevis in 1967 until 1977, when he was replaced by Emile GUMBS, then leader of what became the **Anguilla National Alliance** (ANA). Webster returned to power in 1980 as leader of the **Anguilla United Party** (AUP) but in 1984 was again replaced by Gumbs, who remained chief minister following the 1989 election until his retirement in February 1994 (by which time he was Sir Emile). Meanwhile, Webster had founded what became the **Anguilla Democratic Party** (ADP) but had reverted to the AUP for the 1989 election; subsequently, he formed the **Anguillans for Good Government** (AGG) party.

The March 1994 election failed to produce a clear winner, with the ANA (led by Eric REID), the ADP (led by Victor BANKS), and the

AUP (led by Hubert HUGHES) each winning two seats; an independent, one; and Webster's new party, none. The outcome was an AUP-ADP coalition under the chief ministership of the AUP leader. At the election of March 4, 1999, the ANA, led by Osbourne FLEMING, captured three house seats, but with the ADP and the AUP again winning two seats each, a renewal of the AUP-ADP coalition permitted Hughes to claim a second term as chief minister. Earlier, Hughes had stated that he hoped to move Anguilla closer to full internal self-government, citing Bermuda as a model and commenting that the present constitution placed ministers in "positions without power."

Within months of the election, a constitutional deadlock developed, Victor Banks having resigned as finance minister over Hughes's managerial style and his failure to consult the ADP. Banks then realigned his ADP with the ANA, and together they began a boycott of the house, leaving it without a quorum. Having failed to convince the High Court that the speaker of the house, a member of the ADP, should be forced to convene the legislature, in January 2000 Hughes asked the governor to call a new election. Held on March 3, the balloting returned all the incumbents to office, but with the **Anguilla United Front** (AUF) alliance of the ANA and the ADP controlling four seats; the AUP, two; and a former ADP member, now an independent, the seventh. On March 6 Osbourne Fleming assumed office as chief minister, with Banks again in charge of finance and economic development as well as investment and commerce.

At the election of February 21, 2005, the AUF retained its four seats; the **Anguilla National Strategic Alliance,** led by opposition leader Edison BAIRD, secured two; and Hubert Hughes's **Anguilla United Movement** (AUM) won one. Also competing in the election was the **Anguillan Progressive Party** (APP), led by Brent DAVIS.

Anguilla's process for constitutional review and reform, consistent with the 1999 white paper on overseas territories, was jump-started in 2006 with the appointment of a Constitutional and Electoral Reform Commission. The commission presented its report in August of that same year. Negotiations with UK officials over proposed constitutional changes, scheduled for July 2007, were delayed by Chief Minister Fleming in order to extend the period for public consultation. The government issued a press release on July 17, 2007, stating that Anguilla planned to seek "full internal self government" status from the UK.

On April 21, 2009, Alistair Harrison assumed the governorship from Andrew GEORGE, who retired. In a May address Harrison said he considered financial regulation of the off-shore financial industry his top priority. Of particular concern was Anguilla's inclusion on the OECD's so-called grey list of countries that have stated their intention to comply with rules for sharing tax information but have not yet done so.

In the February 15, 2010, balloting for the seven elected members of the assembly, the AUM won four seats, the AUF won two, and the APP won one, despite a vote distribution which had the AUF ahead of the AUM 39 to 33 percent. The next day the AUM's Hughes was sworn in as chief minister, named his cabinet, and announced the government would concentrate on restoring the economy.

Governor: Christina SCOTT.

Chief Minister: Hubert HUGHES.

Bermuda.

Named after Juan de Bermudez, a Spanish sailor who reached the islands in the early 1500s, Bermuda remained uninhabited for a century. Settled by the British and then established as a Crown colony in 1684, it consists of 150 islands and islets in the western Atlantic. It has a total land area of 21 square miles (53 sq. km) and a population (2010E) of 64,600, concentrated on some 20 islands. Blacks make up approximately 60 percent of the total population. The capital is Hamilton, with a population of about 3,000. The main economic activities are offshore business services (principally insurance and reinsurance), tourism, and light manufacturing. Over 10,500 international companies are registered, but only about 300 maintain a physical presence. Customs duties constitute the principal source of government revenue.

Under a constitution approved in mid-1967 (amended, in certain particulars, in 1979), Bermuda was granted a system of internal self-government whereby the Crown-appointed governor, advised by a Governor's Council, exercises responsibility for external affairs, defense, internal security, and police. The governor appoints as premier the majority leader in the lower chamber of the Parliament, the House of Assembly, which is popularly elected for a five-year term. (Formerly consisting of 40 members from 2-member constituencies, the representation was reduced to 36 single-member constituencies prior to the 2003 election.) The 11 members of the upper house, the Senate, are appointed by the governor, including 5 on recommendation of the premier and 3 on recommendation of the leader of the opposition.

The first general election under the new constitution, held in May 1968 against a background of black rioting, resulted in a decisive victory for the moderately right-wing, multiracial **United Bermuda Party** (UBP), whose leader, Sir Henry TUCKER, became the colony's first premier. The left-wing **Progressive Labour Party** (PLP), mainly black in membership, had campaigned for independence and an end to British rule, and its unexpectedly poor showing was generally interpreted as a popular endorsement of the existing constitutional arrangements.

At the election of October 5, 1993, the UBP (led since 1981 by Sir John SWAN) returned 22 members to the House of Assembly against 18 for the PLP (led by Frederick WADE), while the **National Liberal Party** (NLP; led by Gilbert DARRELL) lost the seat it had won in 1989. In February 1994, following an announcement that U.S. and UK forces would vacate Bermuda in 1995, the new legislature voted 20–18 in favor of holding a referendum on independence. The consultation eventually took place on August 16, 1995, with traditional party lines being partially reversed in that Sir John and some other UBP leaders (although not the party as such) urged a "yes" vote and the pro-independence PLP advocated abstention. Of a 58.8 percent turnout, 73.6 percent of the voters opposed independence, whereupon Sir John resigned from the premiership and UBP leadership and was replaced by Finance Minister David SAUL. The new premier moved to heal divisions within the UBP remaining from the bruising independence referendum and a subsequent conflict in the summer of 1996 over approval of a franchise license for a fast food chain. Three members who had rebelled against party leadership on both issues were returned to cabinet portfolios in January 1997, although the moves were insufficient to save the premier. On March 27 Saul was replaced by Pamela GORDON, the new leader of the UBP. Earlier, in December 1996, Jennifer SMITH had been elected leader of the PLP following the death of Frederick Wade.

Premier Gordon's decision to reshuffle her cabinet in May 1998 failed to prevent a dramatic victory by the PLP at the election of November 9. The PLP won for the first time, capturing 26 house seats versus 14 for the UBP, which had been in power for three decades. The victory was even more remarkable in that the winning party had run only 34 candidates for the 40 seats. Jennifer Smith was sworn in as premier on November 10 and shortly thereafter named a cabinet of 12 additional ministers, all but 1 black.

At the election of July 24, 2003, the PLP won 22 House seats and the UBP 14. Although reinstalled as premier, Smith had drawn criticism for an alleged "arrogant and secretive" leadership style and was forced to step down on July 28 in favor of Alex SCOTT.

In December 2004 the issue of independence was reopened by Prime Minister Scott, who announced the establishment of a Bermuda Independence Commission (BIC) that was instructed to hold public hearings on the subject in early 2005. While the current government favored independence, a July 2007 opinion poll indicated that 63 percent of Bermudans opposed it, with 25 percent in favor and 12 percent undecided.

At an October 2006 PLP delegate conference Dr. Ewart BROWN was elected party chair by a 107–76 vote over Scott. Brown was subsequently sworn in as premier on October 30. UBP leader Wayne FURBERT stepped down on March 31, 2007, and was replaced by Michael DUNKLEY on April 2 by a unanimous vote.

The Brown government's health minister resigned from the cabinet in February 2007 amid the opening of a criminal investigation into his business activities. In June the police arrested the former minister under theft and corruption charges. A new heath minister was sworn in on June 12.

At the election of December 18, 2007, in a replay of the previous balloting, the PLP won 22 House seats and the UBP 14. New UBP leader Michael Dunkley failed to win reelection from his constituency, leaving the party in disarray. Sir Richard Gozney was named governor in December in succession to Sir John VEREKER.

Ewart Brown's premiership subsequently continued to prove contentious with all parties, including his own. His standing among the public and his own party plummeted in 2009 when he accepted four Chinese Uighur detainees released from Guantánamo, telling neither his own cabinet ministers nor the British foreign office. Brown survived a motion of no confidence, but members of his own party took to the streets in protest, and polls showed his approval rating among the public was at an historic low. Brown resigned his premiership and his seat in the assembly in October 2010. The PLP elected Deputy Premier Paula Cox as Brown's successor.

In regularly scheduled elections on December 12, 2012, Cox and the PLP lost to the One Bermuda Alliance (OBA), 17 seats to 19. OBA formed in 2011 from the merger of the UBP and the short-lived Bermuda Democratic Alliance. After 14 years of PLP rule, the OBA hoped to reinvigorate Bermuda's economy and political scene. OBA's Craig CANNONIER was named premier.

Governor: George FERGUSSON.

Premier: Craig CANNONIER

British Indian Ocean Territory.

At the time of its establishment in 1965 the British Indian Ocean Territory consisted of the Chagos Archipelago, which had previously been a dependency of Mauritius, and the islands of Aldabra, Farquhar, and Desroches, which had traditionally been administered from the Seychelles (see Mauritius map, p. 868). The territory was created to make defense facilities available to the British and U.S. governments and was legally construed as being uninhabited, although in 1967–1973 some 1,800 Chagos Islanders (Ilois) were relocated from Diego Garcia in the Chagos group to make way for the construction of U.S. air and naval installations. Upon the granting of independence to the Seychelles in June 1976, arrangements were made for the reversion of Aldabra, Farquhar, and Desroches, the territory thenceforth to consist only of the Chagos Archipelago, with its administration taken over by the Foreign and Commonwealth Office. The total land area of the archipelago, which stretches over some 21,000 square miles (54,400 sq. km) of the central Indian Ocean, is 20 square miles (52 sq. km). At present, the only inhabitants are some 2,000 members of the British and U.S. military plus another 1,500 civilian personnel (mainly Filipinos and Sri Lankans) providing services for the Diego Garcia naval facility.

On March 3, 1999, the UK High Court ruled that the Chagos Refugee Group, led by Louis Olivier BANCOULT, could challenge the legality of the Ilois removal. The majority of the Ilois had settled in Mauritius, from where they have long pressed unsuccessful compensation claims. Appearing in the High Court in 2000, the claimants' counselor successfully argued that the 1971 Immigration Ordinance, which barred permanent residence in the archipelago, should be overturned, in part because it violated the European Convention on Human Rights. In 2004, however, the UK Privy Council issued orders in council that again placed visits to the islands under immigration control. On May 11, 2006, the High Court overruled the orders, calling the removal of the Chagossians "repugnant" and opening the possibility of their return. In late June the UK government indicated that it would appeal the decision. Meanwhile, in late March 102 islanders had set sail from Mauritius for a 12-day visit to the archipelago, the first such excursion permitted by the UK in more than three decades.

Under the joint usage agreements between the UK and the United States, the archipelago will be ceded to Mauritius when it is no longer needed for defense purposes.

The UK government began its appeal on February 5, 2007, of the High Court's 2006 decision overturning the removal order. In March Mauritian president Sir Anerood Jugnauth revealed that Mauritius was prepared to withdraw from the Commonwealth in order to bring the UK before the International Court of Justice (IJC) on behalf of the Chagossians. On May 23, 2007, the court of appeal upheld the previous decision and ordered the UK government to pay the Chagossians' legal fees and allow resettlement of all but Diego Garcia. The government appealed the decision to the House of Lords, and in October 2008 the lower court ruling was overturned, thereby barring the return of the Chagossians and removing any obligation for the UK government to pay further compensation.

On April 1, 2010, the British government established the Chagos Marine Reserve, a "fully no-take" marine reserve that banned commercial fishing. Environmental groups welcomed the declaration until diplomatic cables released by WikiLeaks in 2011 suggested the UK government added the no-fishing requirement to prevent the Chagossians from resettling the islands. Greenpeace, among others, condemned this policy as a "huge violation" of Chagossian rights.

Commissioner: Colin ROBERTS (resident in United Kingdom).

Administrator: John MCMANUS (resident in United Kingdom).

British Virgin Islands.

A Caribbean group of 46 northern Leeward Islands located some 60 miles east of Puerto Rico, the British Virgin Islands have a total area of 59 square miles (153 sq. km) and a population (2010E) of 29,000. Tourism and international business are the main industries, with the latter reportedly accounting for 90 percent of government revenue. The largest island, Tortola, is the site of the chief town and port of entry, Road Town (population 11,000 in 2002). The administration is headed by a governor. Representative institutions include a 15-member Legislative Council (13 elected members serving four-year terms; the attorney general, ex officio; and a speaker) and a 6-member Executive Council appointed and chaired by the governor. A chief minister is chosen from the legislature by the governor.

At the election of September 1986 the **Virgin Islands Party** (VIP), led by H. Lavity STOUTT, won five of nine Council seats, ousting the administration headed by independent member Cyril B. ROMNEY, who had been involved with a company undergoing investigation for money laundering. In March 1988 the deputy chief minister, Omar HODGE, was dismissed for attempting to delay the issuance of a report charging him with bribery; the following year he formed the **Independent People's Movement** (IPM). Stoutt remained in office following the balloting of November 2, 1990, at which the VIP won six seats; the IPM, one; and independents, two. The **United Party** (UP), led by Conrad MADURO, lost the two seats it had held since 1986.

In early 1994 a proposal by a UK constitutional review commission to expand the Legislative Council to 13 elective seats by adding four "at-large" members drew criticism from several islands parties. Chief Minister Stoutt led the attack on the plan, but to no avail. Balloting on February 20, 1995, for the 13 legislators yielded 6 seats for the VIP, 2 for the UP, 2 for Hodge's new **Concerned Citizen's Movement** (CCM), and 3 for independents. One of the independents sided with the VIP in return for a ministerial post, enabling Stoutt to begin a fifth successive term as chief minister. However, Stoutt died unexpectedly on May 16 and was succeeded by Deputy Chief Minister Ralph O'Neal. The opposition—numbering five members—received an unexpected boost when two supporters of the government temporarily switched sides in April 1997, coming close to bringing the government down. By June, however, the failure to unseat the government and dissatisfaction with the leadership of the UP's Maduro led three of the five opposition members to rebel, and in December 1997 Maduro was replaced as leader of the opposition by the leader of the CCM, Walwyn BREWLEY.

The VIP claimed a narrow election victory at balloting on May 17, 1999, winning seven seats in the Legislative Council to five for the recently formed **National Democratic Party** (NDP) and one for the CCM. Both the CCM and the UP took less than 10 percent of the total constituency and at-large votes, many of their previous supporters having switched allegiance to the NDP, led by Orlando SMITH.

At the election of June 16, 2003, the NDP won eight seats and the VIP five, permitting Smith to head the new government.

The Smith government won unanimous approval from the Legislative Council for its proposed draft of a new constitution in May 2007. The UK Privy Council ratified the bill and the new constitution came into force on June 15, 2007. Among the new powers of the British Virgin Islands government was the creation of a national security council.

The VIP regained control of the government at balloting on August 20, 2007, winning in a landslide with ten seats to two for the NDP, while the remaining elective seat went to an independent. Voter turnout was 66 percent. Ralph O'Neal headed the new government as First Premier under the new constitution (formerly the position was titled Chief Minister).

Power shifted in the November 7, 2011, election, as the NDP won 9 seats, VIP 4, and PPA none. NDP party chair Orlando SMITH was sworn in as premier following a campaign in which he pledged to protect the tourism and offshore financial services sectors while improving health care, education, and other services for residents.

Governor: William Boyd McCLEARY.

Premier: Orlando SMITH.

Cayman Islands.

Located in the Caribbean, northwest of Jamaica, the Cayman Islands (Grand Cayman, Little Cayman, and Cayman Brac) cover 100 square miles (259 sq. km) and have a population (2010E) of 61,000. George Town, on Grand Cayman, is the capital. The traditional occupations of seafaring and turtle and shark fishing have largely been superseded by tourism and other services. The islands have become one of the world's half-dozen largest offshore banking centers as well as a corporate tax haven. As of January 2000, 570 banks and trust companies, more than 2,200 mutual funds, some 500 insurance companies, and 47,000 other companies were registered. In mid-1999 the territory became the first government to request certification under the newly introduced UN Offshore Initiative. Accordingly, the UN Global Programme against Money Laundering had agreed to review the islands' banking and financial systems.

Discovered by Columbus in the early 1500s, the essentially uninhabited Caymans passed from Spain to England in 1670. Governed from Jamaica from the 1860s until 1959 and then briefly a part of the Federation of the West Indies, the islands were placed in 1962 under a British administrator (later governor), who chairs an Executive Council of 8 other members, including 3 ex officio and 5 chosen by and from among the Legislative Assembly. The latter body initially consisted of a speaker, 3 ex officio members, and 12 elected members. At balloting for an enlarged assembly on November 18, 1992, a National Team of government critics won 12 of the elective 15 seats, the remaining 3 going to independents. The outcome rendered uncertain a plan to introduce ministerial government, as the National Team had campaigned against it. However, after deliberations involving the governor and London, a ministerial system was introduced under a constitutional revision implemented in February 1994. Thus, the 5 elected members of the Executive Council now have ministerial responsibilities.

At a general election on November 22, 1996, the National Team secured nine seats, while two recently formed groupings, the **Democratic Alliance** and **Team Cayman,** took two and one, respectively, with independents winning three. In 1997 W. McKeeva Bush, now of the **United Democratic Party** (UDP), was ousted from the Executive Council following allegations that a bank of which he was a director had approved more than $1 billion in fraudulent loans.

In June 2000 George Town expressed astonishment at the decision of the international Financial Action Task Force (FATF) to place the Caymans on its list of 15 jurisdictions considered noncooperative with efforts to combat money laundering. In addition to having repeatedly asked the FATF to visit the Caymans, the government had recently been praised by the UK's Foreign and Commonwealth Office for its regulatory and enforcement efforts. In June 2001 Cayman Islands was delisted.

At the election held on May 11, 2005, after a six-month postponement because of damage from Hurricane Ivan in September 2004, the **People's Progressive Movement** (PPM), led by Kurt TIBBETTS, won 9 of the 15 elective seats, while the UDP won 5 and an independent, 1.

Following more than two years of discussion, a referendum on a new constitution was held alongside the general election in May 2009, at which the draft constitution received 63 percent support. Meanwhile, the UDP won nine seats, the PPM five, and independents one in the general election.

Newly elected assembly members were sworn in on Mary 27, 2009, with Bush returning to the post of Leader of Government Business. Throughout the remainder of the year the Bush administration struggled to deal with the deeply troubling government debt crisis and a much-threatened financial sector. He secured a $277 million loan from the UK government and pledged to cut spending, but Bush resisted calls from the UK to impose new taxes, claiming that they would negatively alter the islands' unique economic base. The new constitution entered into force on November 6, and Bush was sworn in as premier, the territory's first, the same day. As part of overall efforts to comply with international financial standards established by the OECD, the Bush administration over the next year negotiated bilateral agreements with a number of countries regarding the exchange of tax information.

In February 2011 Kurt Tibbets stepped down as leader of the PPM and was replaced as party leader and leader of the opposition by Alden McLaughlin. The Islands held a nonbinding referendum on July 18, 2012, on whether to adopt single-mandate constituencies. Although 64 percent of voters favored the change, turnout was so low that Bush proclaimed the results an indirect victory for the "no" side.

Bush was arrested in December 2012 and charged with corruption and mismanagement. Governor Duncan TAYLOR appointed Deputy Premier Juliana O'Connor-Connolly as interim premier. In parliamentary elections on May 22, 2013, the PPM won 9 of 18 seats; the UDP took only 3. Incoming Premier Alden MCLAUGHLIN (PPM) pledged to implement automatic exchanges of tax information regarding the islands' thriving financial sector. Helen KILPATRICK was appointed governor in September 2013.

Governor: Helen KILPATRICK.

Premier: Alden MCLAUGHLIN.

Falkland Islands.

Situated some 480 miles northeast of Cape Horn in the South Atlantic (see Argentina map, p. 56), the Falkland Islands currently encompasses the East and West Falklands in addition to some 200 smaller islands; the South Georgia and the South Sandwich islands ceased to be governed as dependencies of the Falklands in 1985. The total area is 4,700 square miles (12,173 sq. km), and the resident population, almost entirely of British extraction, was 2,478 at the 2006 census, excluding civilian employees of a British military base, who numbered 534 in 2001; most inhabitants live in the capital, Stanley, on East Falkland Island. The economy, traditionally dependent on wool production, has diversified in recent years, with fishing licenses now being the main source of revenue. Tourism has also increased in importance.

Under a constitution introduced in 1985 (replacing one dating from 1977), the governor is assisted by a Legislative Council that includes eight members elected on a nonpartisan basis (most recently on November 17, 2005) and by an Executive Council, three of whose members are selected by and from the elected legislators. In addition, both bodies have two ex officio members and a chief executive and a financial secretary, who are responsible to the governor. The attorney general and the commander of British forces may also attend Executive Council sessions.

The territory is the object of a long-standing dispute between Britain and Argentina, which calls it the Malvinas Islands (*Islas Malvinas*). Argentina's claim to sovereignty is based primarily on purchase of the islands by Spain from France in 1766; Britain claims sovereignty on the basis of a 1771 treaty, although uninterrupted possession commenced only in 1833. The Argentine claim has won some support in the UN General Assembly, and the two governments engaged in a lengthy series of inconclusive talks on the future disposition of the territory prior to the Argentine invasion of April 2, 1982, and the eventual reassertion of British control ten weeks later (see Argentina entry). The issue is complicated by evidence that significant oil and gas deposits may lie beneath the islands' territorial waters. In addition, Britain has taken the position that any solution must respect the wishes of the inhabitants. Thus, the current constitution refers explicitly to the islanders' right of self-determination.

In the wake of the 1982 war, Britain imposed a 150-mile protective zone, to which it added a 200-mile economic zone, effective February 1, 1987, although only a 150-mile radius was subsequently policed, principally to protect Falklands fisheries. As part of the 1990 Madrid agreement that led to the resumption of diplomatic relations with Argentina, Britain maintained its claim to a 200-mile economic zone but conceded that Argentine ships and planes could approach within 50 and 75 miles, respectively, of the islands without prior permission. In a further concession to Buenos Aires, London agreed in November 1990 to convert its 200-mile zone (exclusive of overlap with Argentina's own 200-mile limit) into an Anglo-Argentine cooperation area from which fishing fleets from other countries would be excluded.

In 1992 President Carlos Menem of Argentina pursued a dual policy of behind-the-scenes diplomacy and public assertions of the inevitability of Argentinean sovereignty over the Falklands. In November the first direct meeting between islanders' representatives and an Argentinean minister since 1982 took place in London. A major issue was Argentina's policy of reducing the cost of its fishing licenses in an attempt to lure foreign fleets into Argentinean waters and thus to deprive the Falklands government of its main source of revenue. In legislative elections on October 14, 1993, the eight elective seats were contested by 25 candidates, all independents, with those elected all rejecting unnecessary contact with Argentina until its sovereignty claim was dropped.

After the new Argentinean constitution promulgated in August 1994 repeated the claim to the islands, the UK government announced that the full 200-mile Falklands' economic zone would be policed even where it overlapped with the Argentinean zone. Talks in London in October at the foreign minister level made little progress on possible joint oil exploration in Falklands waters and other issues, while the collateral confirmation by President Menem that Argentina was prepared to pay substantial individual compensation to islanders in exchange for sovereignty did nothing to improve relations.

In October 1996 the Falklands administration issued oil exploration licenses to 13 companies, refusing only one application, from a consortium with Argentinean involvement. In a significant departure from previous policy, President Menem on December 30 suggested that sovereignty over the islands might be shared. His suggestion was immediately rejected by the UK government and by the Falkland Islands administration.

In April 1998 the UK announced that oil exploration of the Falklands coast had started, while in Argentina legislators introduced a bill to impose sanctions on commercial companies that failed to obtain Argentinean permission before operating in Falkland waters. The following October President Menem paid the first official visit to the UK by an Argentinean leader in nearly 40 years. Topics covered in a meeting with Prime Minister Blair included Falklands relations, while a subsequent letter from Menem to the islanders called for reconciliation "to heal old wounds." With secret talks reportedly under way on the territory's status, in January 1999 Buenos Aires offered to put in abeyance its sovereignty claim if the UK, in a largely symbolic gesture, would permit Argentinean flags to fly at selected locations, including the graveyard for its service-members killed during the Falklands war. Two months later Prince Charles visited both the Falklands and Argentina, where he laid a wreath at a monument to casualties of the conflict, as President Menem had done in England during his 1998 visit.

In May 1999 an Argentinean ministerial delegation met in London with members of the Falklands Legislative Council. Discussion topics included fishing and air connections. In the latter regard, in March Chile had announced a halt to Falklands flights—the only such contact between the islands and South America—to protest the continuing detention in London of former president Augusto Pinochet, pending resolution of a Spanish extradition warrant for human rights abuses during his reign. In July Buenos Aires and London agreed to permit air travel between Argentina and the islands, and Chile resumed flights with stopovers in Argentina.

In early 2004 Argentina granted its flagship airline two routes between Buenos Aires and Stanley. However, the islanders rejected the prospect of regularly scheduled flights from Argentina, and the recently installed Néstor Kirchner regime responded by denying permission for Chilean planes to fly through Argentine air space. Meanwhile, the Falkland economy, which had expanded 13-fold in the two decades after the war, was increasingly imperiled by a decline in sales of fishing licenses that was attributed to collapse in stocks of the previously abundant Ilex squid.

Relations between the UK and Argentina soured further in 2006 as President Kirchner, backed by the UN Special Committee on Decolonization and the Organization of American States, repeated his call for London to reopen negotiations on the territory's future status. Kirchner also indicated that he was considering taking a more hard-line approach on the issues of fishing rights and oil exploration. Upon his wife's investment in the presidency in 2007 (see Argentina entry), Cristina Fernández de Kirchner maintained Argentina's right to the islands. For its part, the British government reiterated that it had no intention to negotiate sovereignty in the absence of evidence that the islanders themselves sought a change.

A new constitution was announced for the islands in November 2008, effective January 1, 2009. In order to enhance internal self-government, the governor was required by the new constitution to abide by the advice of the Executive Council on most domestic policies. However, the governor retained veto power with respect to external, defense, and justice policies as well as when the governor deems the advice of the council to be contrary to the "the interests of good government." The new constitution also tightened rules for the acquisition of Falkland "status" (and thereby voting rights), installed the chief executive as head of the civil service, established a public accounts committee and a complaints commissioner in order to enhance transparency, and adopted provisions of the European Convention on Human Rights. The UK government emphasized that the constitutional revisions did not change the UK's commitment to the islands, nor the status of the islands as an overseas territory, nor the Falklanders' right to self-determination.

A new UK-Argentina dispute arose in February 2010 when UK-based oil company Rockhopper Exploration announced the discovery of a field, Sea Lion, believed to hold 320 million barrels of oil near the Falklands. The Argentinean government subsequently announced it would require permits for ships travelling through its waters and asked the UN to intervene. As U.S. and UK-based firms announced plans to buy stakes in Sea Lion, Argentina vowed to sue to prevent them from developing the field, and the capital city passed a law barring ships flying the British flag from using any of its ports. In a referendum on the political status of the islands held on March 10–11, 2013, 99.7 percent of voters indicated they preferred to remain an Overseas Territory of the United Kingdom. With a 92 percent turnout, only three valid no votes were recorded.

Governor: Nigel HAYWOOD.

Chief Executive: Keith PADGETT.

Gibraltar.

The territory of Gibraltar, a rocky promontory at the western mouth of the Mediterranean, was captured by the British in 1704 and ceded by Spain to the UK by the Treaty of Utrecht in 1713. It has an area of 2.1 square miles (5.5 sq. km), and its population numbers 29,800 (2010E), of whom about 21,000 are native Gibraltarians. The economy was long dependent on expenditures in support of its air and naval facilities; in recent years, however, tourism and financial services have grown in importance, and special status within the EC/EU has permitted it to transship foreign goods without payment of such duties as VATs. Financial services currently constitute about one-fifth of the economy, significantly more than UK defense expenditures.

British authority is represented by a governor. Substantial self-government was introduced in 1964 and further extended in 1969 by a new constitution that provided for a House of Assembly of 15 elected and 2 ex officio members (the attorney general and the financial and development secretary), plus a speaker appointed by the governor. Of the elected members, no more than 8 can represent the same party. The executive Gibraltar Council, chaired by the governor, has 4 additional ex officio members and 4 other members, including a chief minister, drawn from the elected members of the House of Assembly. The governor names as chief minister the majority leader in the assembly.

Gibraltar has been the subject of a lengthy dispute between Britain and Spain, which has pressed in the UN and elsewhere for "decolonization" of the territory and has impeded access to it by land and air. A referendum conducted by the British in 1967 showed an overwhelming preference for continuation of British rule, but Spain rejected the results and declared the referendum invalid. Spain's position was subsequently upheld by the UN General Assembly, which called in December 1968 for the ending of British administration by October 1, 1969. A month after promulgation of the 1969 constitution, which guarantees that the Gibraltarians will never have to accept Spanish rule unless the majority so desires, Spain closed its land frontier. In January 1978 Spain agreed to the restoration of telephone links to the city, but the border was not fully reopened until February 1985, following an agreement in November 1984 to provide equality of rights for Spaniards in Gibraltar and Gibraltarians in Spain; Britain also agreed to enter into discussions on the sovereignty issue.

At the election of March 1988 the **Gibraltar Socialist Labour Party** (GSLP) won the permissible maximum of eight legislative seats, its leader, Joe BOSSANO, becoming chief minister. Upon assuming office Bossano declared that most of the residents opposed the 1984 accord with Spain. Earlier, in December 1987, the assembly had rejected a UK-Spanish agreement on cooperative administration of the territory's airport. Quite apart from the impact of exclusive British control on the sovereignty issue, Spain has argued that the isthmus to the mainland, on which the airport is located, was not covered by the 1713 treaty.

The GSLP was again victorious at the election of January 16, 1992, retaining its majority with a vote share of 73 percent; the **Gibraltar Social Democrats** (GSD), led by Peter Caruana, won seven seats and the **Gibraltar National Party** (GNP), led by Dr. Joseph GARCIA, none. Following the election, Bossano insisted that his party's campaign for greater autonomy from Britain was not anti-Spanish, but rather "a clear expression of the desire for self-determination." Declining tourism and rising unemployment in 1993 caused further strains, with Bossano accusing Britain of neglecting Gibraltar's interests at the EU level.

The December 1994 round of UK-Spanish foreign ministers' talks on Gibraltar was snagged by heightened Spanish vigilance and consequential delays at the border crossing. Part of the Spanish concern was that Gibraltarians were increasingly supplementing traditional cigarette smuggling operations with drug trafficking and money laundering. In July 1995 UK pressure led the government to table a bill designed to stop money laundering and to bring Gibraltar's offshore banking into line with British and EU standards. Meanwhile, Chief Minister Bossano maintained his refusal to participate in the UK-Spanish talks, calling instead for direct discussions with Madrid on self-determination for Gibraltar.

A more flexible stance by the center-right GSD, which held that negotiations could proceed on any issue other than sovereignty, won the support of 48 percent of voters in a general election on May 16, 1996, with the GSLP slumping to 39 percent. The GSD secured eight assembly seats against seven for the GSLP, with the GNP again failing to win representation despite taking 13 percent of the vote. GSD leader Peter Caruana was sworn in as chief minister, pledging to participate in UK-Spanish talks.

In April 1998, in a shift of strategy, Madrid offered to open bilateral talks with Chief Minister Caruana regarding its recent proposal that Britain and Spain share sovereignty during a transitional period, with Gibraltar ultimately to achieve self-governing status under Spain—a proposal that Caruana and the Blair government dismissed. Later in the year both sides demonstrated a willingness to improve cooperation with regard to overflights of Spanish territory by Royal Air Force and NATO aircraft as well as the use and development of Gibraltar's airport. In 1999, however, a continuing dispute over fishing rights off Gibraltar for Spanish trawlers led Spanish customs officials to enforce strict, time-consuming border controls in retaliation. In October Caruana labeled bilateral talks on sovereignty between London and Madrid as "inappropriate and unacceptable." Instead, he proposed a "two flags, three voices" approach—the third voice being Gibraltar—which Spain has rejected.

In January 2000 Caruana surprised the opposition by calling an election for February 10, three months ahead of schedule. At the balloting his GSD increased its vote share to 58 percent and again claimed eight seats in the House of Assembly. An alliance of Bossano's GSLP and Joseph Garcia's small **Gibraltar Liberal Party** (successor to the GNP) won the other seven elective seats.

Two months later, on April 19, 2000, Spain and Britain announced that they had resolved differences over the territory's administrative status. Madrid's refusal to accept Gibraltar as a "competent authority" had delayed a range of EU business and economic initiatives. Spain agreed to recognize the validity of various documents issued by Gibraltar, including passports and identity cards. Britain agreed to act as a "postal box," relaying communications to and from Spain, which could thereby continue to avoid direct contact with the Gibraltar government. In addition, the agreement cleared the way for Britain to accede to parts of the EU's Schengen agreement on frontier controls, and it opened the way for Gibraltar-based financial corporations to compete throughout the EU. Chief Minister Caruana responded to the announcement of the agreement by saying, "Spain, Britain, and Gibraltar have all preserved their interests; there are no winners and no losers."

For the first time since December 1997, ministerial talks between Spain and the UK resumed on July 26, 2001, and by early 2002 it was clear that the two sides were moving closer toward a joint sovereignty arrangement. However, the prospect of any such arrangement was greeted with scorn by Caruana and generated, over the ensuing months, massive demonstrations by Gibraltarians.

Madrid and London nonetheless pressed ahead and by mid-2002 had reached agreement on joint rule, though differing as to its duration. The UK clearly viewed it as more than "transitional." In addition, Britain insisted that its military bases remain under its control. Caruana, meanwhile, refused to participate in the talks, save as an equal partner. Subsequently, on November 7, Gibraltar mounted a referendum in which 98.9 percent of the participants voted against shared sovereignty. In the November 28, 2003, general election, Caruana's Gibraltar Social Democrats retained its eight seats, while the GSLP-Liberal alliance again won seven.

After winning a challenge before the European Court of Human Rights to Gibraltar's exclusion from participating in elections to the European Parliament as part of the UK, Gibraltarians cast EU ballots for the first time in 2004 (as part of the South West England constituency). The UK's Conservative Party secured 69.5 percent of the vote in Gibraltar, reflecting dissatisfaction with the Labour government's joint sovereignty proposal as well as the significant attention (including an appearance by Conservative leader Michael Howard) voters in Gibraltar had received from the Conservatives.

In October 2004 Spain agreed, for the first time, to give Gibraltar a seat at the negotiating table, which led to the first three-party discussion in December. On February 10, 2005, the first session of a Trilateral Forum, with an open agenda, met in Malaga, Spain. Issues considered by the forum have included the airport and benefits for Spanish workers, but sovereignty has remained off the table.

On November 30, 2006, a referendum approved the new constitution, which was implemented on January 2, 2007. The updated constitution aimed to "modernize" relations with Britain, emphasize self-determination, and strengthen local autonomy, notably by increasing the number of legislative seats to 17, with the House of Assembly renamed the Gibraltar Parliament. The governor's veto powers were curtailed and those of the British foreign secretary were eliminated.

An August 12 collision between a Danish tanker, *Torm Gertrude,* and *New Flame,* a bulk carrier, prompted official complaints that Spanish beaches were being polluted. The Gibraltar government rejected these claims, but the incident emphasized the importance of coordination on maritime safety between the two neighbors.

In elections held October 11, 2007, the Gibraltar Social Democrats received 49 percent of votes; the Gibraltar Socialist Labour Party-Liberal coalition, 45 percent; the **Progressive Democratic Party**, 4 percent; the Parental Support Group, 1 percent; and the **New Gibraltar Democracy Party,** 1 percent. Turnout was 84.1 percent. (The **Progressive Democratic Party** [PDP] was launched in 2006, touting itself as a "positive alternative" for voters dissatisfied with the two major parties.) Caruana remained chief minister, with 10 seats in the Gibraltar Parliament, while the GSLP-Liberal alliance claimed 7.

Voters from Gibraltar showed their continued support for the UK Conservative Party by giving it 53.3 percent of the vote in the June 2009 balloting for the European Parliament. No other party received as much as 20 percent.

The general elections of December 8, 2011, dealt a loss to Caruana and the GSD, as the GSLP/LIB coalition took 48.88 percent of the vote and 10 seats. The GSD, which had governed the region since 1996, was awarded the remaining 7 seats. GSLP's Fabián PICARDO, who had become head of the party in April, was appointed chief minister on December 9.

Spain and Gibraltar became embroiled in a fishing rights dispute in early 2012, with skirmishes involving the British Royal Navy and Spanish police. Verbal conflict increased in August 2013, when Gibraltar dropped 70 concrete bocks into the sea to create an artificial reef but failed to alert Spain. Madrid stepped up border checks in response, prompting London to file a protest with the European Commission, saying the Spanish move impeded the flow of goods and people.

Governor and Commander in Chief: Sir Adrian JOHNS.
Chief Minister: Fabián PICARDO.

Montserrat.

A West Indian dependency in the Leeward Island group (see Antigua and Barbuda map, p. 53) with an area of 39.4 square miles (102 sq. km), Montserrat had a population (1996E) of 10,500 prior to large-scale evacuation (see below), which reduced the total to 4,482 in the 2001 census before recovering to an estimated 5,000 in 2010. Its principal sources of income are tourism, offshore business services, and export of machinery and transport equipment. Ministerial government was introduced in 1960, the territory currently being administered by an Executive Council comprising the chief minister, three additional elected ministers, and two ex officio members (attorney general and financial secretary) under the presidency of the London-appointed governor. The Legislative Council is composed of nine elected members plus the same two ex officio members. Elections are normally held every five years.

In August 1987 John OSBORNE of the **People's Liberation Movement** (PLM) was installed for a third five-year term as chief minister. In August 1989 a dispute arose between Osborne and Gov. Christopher TURNER over the latter's alleged failure to inform elected officials of police raids on banks suspected of illicit financial transactions. In late November, with most banking licenses having been canceled, the Organization of Eastern Caribbean States issued a statement condemning as "absolutely repugnant" an announcement by the UK Foreign and Commonwealth Office (FCO) that a proposed new constitution would transfer responsibility for offshore banking regulation to the governor. In return for Osborne's acceptance of the controversial change, the new basic law as implemented in February 1990 recognized Montserrat's right to self-determination and withdrew certain legislative powers formerly held by the governor.

Osborne's PLM retained only one seat in the balloting of October 8, 1991, after which a new administration was formed by the **National**

Progressive Party (NPP), led by Reuben MEADE, who had accused the Osborne administration of corruption and mismanagement. Efforts by the new Legislative Council to reestablish Montserrat as an offshore banking center failed. On February 2, 1993, after an investigation by Scotland Yard, Osborne and Noel TUITT, an associate, were cleared of the corruption charges, and in March 1994 Tuitt joined the NPP government following Meade's dismissal of David BRANDT as deputy chief minister. A partial eruption of long-dormant Chance's Peak volcano on July 19, 1995, precipitated the evacuation of some 5,000 people from their homes by late August. Further disruption was caused by a hurricane and tropical storm in September.

The eruptions continued intermittently in 1996, by the end of which the entire population of the southern part of the island, including the capital, Plymouth, had been evacuated; 800 were admitted to Britain under a special exemption from normally strict immigration rules, and the rest were housed in temporary accommodation in the north, where the second town, St. Peter's, became the de facto capital. With the island administration and the UK overseas aid program disputing how emergency aid grants should be used, the NPP retained only one seat in an election that was held on November 11 even though residents had fled four southern election districts. Two seats were won by the **Movement for National Reconstruction** (MNR), two by John Osborne's new **People's Progressive Alliance** (PPA), and two by independents. The outcome was an MNR-PPA coalition, MNR leader Bertrand OSBORNE being sworn in as chief minister on November 13.

In June 1997 the Soufrière Hills volcano erupted, claiming at least 19 lives and obliterating the capital. By the end of the year, only 3,400 of the original population were still on the island (with 500 living in temporary shelters), the remainder having either migrated to the UK or relocated to adjacent islands. The destruction slowed economic activity to a near standstill. As aid packages were caught up in London's governmental transition in May–June 1997 and the island administration was coping with abandoning the capital, simmering discontent grew among the islanders. On August 21, 1997, after four days of continuous demonstrations and protest, Chief Minister Osborne resigned and was replaced by independent David Brandt, who received the support of the MNR and NPP. Almost immediately, the new chief minister created conflict with London, alleging that aid packages for reconstruction and personal assistance, especially for off-island relocation, were insufficient to meet the emergency and that British policy was directed at depopulating the island. The criticism led London's secretary of state for international development to assert that the island was asking for "mad money" and "golden elephants next." A November 27, 1997, report by a Commons select committee placed blame for delays and maladministration on all parties, leading to a rationalization of the aid process and a gradual cooling of tensions.

On February 14, 1998, Robin Cook became the first FCO secretary to visit Montserrat. In May the UK government announced that all Montserratians who had not resettled elsewhere would be allowed to reside in Britain, while in June a draft development plan for the northern part of the island was announced. Despite continuing periodic volcanic activity and additional damage caused by Hurricane Georges in September, residents and businesses gradually began returning to the island's central zone. In 1999 the Blair administration announced that it would pay relocation travel costs for most Montserratians who wished to return to the island from Britain or Caribbean relocation sites. At the same time, the island administration moved forward with a proposal to build a new capital at Little Bay, on the northwestern coast, a project expected to take at least ten years to complete.

With the devastation in the south having made the parliamentary constituency system unworkable, in 2000 the government introduced legislation to facilitate adoption of a nine-member, at-large system for the 2001 election. By mid-2000 the resident population numbered about 5,000.

The collapse of Chief Minister Brandt's coalition in February 2001 precipitated an early election. At balloting on April 2 John Osborne's **New People's Liberation Movement** (NPLM) won seven of the nine seats in the Legislative Council, permitting him to reclaim the title of chief minister a decade after his last term in office. The NPP won the other two council seats.

Three parties and four independents contested the May 2006 legislative election. Although Rosalind CASSELL-SEALY's recently formed **Movement for Change and Prosperity** (MCAP) won four of the nine seats, Osborne's NPLM, which won three, formed a coalition administration with independent David BRANDT and Lowell LEWIS, the head of the **Montserrat Democratic Party** (MDP) and the leading vote-getter. Lewis stated after the election that the government's priorities would be the economy, housing, use of natural resources, and discussions with London about development projects, including a safe harbor and marina at Little Bay that would attract more visitors.

In June 2009 Chief Minister Lewis removed two cabinet ministers and called an election for September 8, two years earlier than required. The balloting produced a six-seat majority for the MCAP, and its leader, Reuben Meade, was sworn in as chief minister on September 9. The three remaining seats were won by independents, including Lewis.

After multiple rounds of talks with Montserratian and British officials, a new constitution came into force on September 27, 2011. The document grants the island more autonomy in international relations and strengthens human rights. Meade was sworn in as Montserrat's first premier on September 27, 2011.

Governor: Adrian DAVIS.

Premier: Reuben MEADE.

Pitcairn Islands.

Isolated in the eastern South Pacific and known primarily because of its settlement in 1790 by the *Bounty* mutineers, Pitcairn has been a British possession since 1838. Jurisdictionally encompassing the adjacent uninhabited islands of Ducie, Henderson, and Oeno, the dependency has a total area of 1.75 square miles (4.53 sq. km) and a declining population, which in 2010 totaled 53 persons. The only established community is Adamstown. The largest island of the group, Henderson, is a UNESCO World Heritage Site and wildlife sanctuary.

The British high commissioner to New Zealand serves as governor. Locally, the island is administered by an Island Council that also has judicial responsibilities. It consists of ten members: an elected island mayor, who serves a three-year term; the chair of the council, ex officio; four directly elected members; one member indirectly selected by the chair and the elected members; two members nominated by the governor, including the island secretary; and a commissioner, who serves as liaison, linking the mayor, council, and governor. All but the mayor and secretary serve one-year terms. The offices of mayor and council chair were established in 1999, prior to which the duties of both were performed by an island magistrate.

The main sources of income are sales of fruits, vegetables, and souvenirs to passing ships and online sales of honey, soaps, stamps, collectible coins, handicrafts, as well as *Bounty*-related souvenirs. Pitcairn has also begun licensing its Internet designation, "pn," an international abbreviation for "telephone." At present, the territory is accessible only by ship; the closest airport is in Mangareva, French Polynesia, some 310 miles away. The UK Department for International Development (DFID) has funded repairs to infrastructure and provision of limited television and Internet service, as well as telephone connections for each household.

In mid-2004 a scandal that had simmered for more than a decade erupted with charges of child rape, incest, and indecent assault against seven men, including the island mayor, Steve CHRISTIAN. Upon Christian's conviction in October, the Island Council designated his sister, Brenda CHRISTIAN, as interim mayor. On December 15 the islanders elected Jay WARREN, a former council chair and the only one of the seven to be acquitted, as her successor. In December 2007 Mike Warren defeated Jay Warren in a three-person mayoralty election.

Discussions in September 2009 produced an agreement between the UK government and the Pitcairn Council to establish the Pitcairn Constitutional Order 2010 as of March 2010. The new constitution included provisions to ensure protection of fundamental rights, obligated the governor to consult with the council before making laws, and clarified the independent role of Pitcairn courts. Elections to the island council were held on December 24, 2011. Councilors do not have party affiliations. DFID funded programs to reduce the sexual exploitation of children on Pitcairn in its 2011–2015 work plan.

Governor: Victoria TREADELL (resident in New Zealand).

Island Mayor: Mike WARREN.

St. Helena.

St. Helena and its dependencies, Ascension Island and the Tristan da Cunha island group, occupy widely scattered positions in the South Atlantic between the west coast of Africa and the southern tip of South

America. St. Helena, the seat of government, has an area of 47 square miles (122 sq. km) and a population (2010E) of 4,100. Its principal settlement is Jamestown. The economy currently depends on budgetary aid from the UK and on the sale of fishing licenses; small quantities of coffee are exported. Remittances from abroad also provide income, and a fish freezing facility has been established. With the final residence of the French Emperor Napoleon having been developed into a museum, St. Helena has potential as a tourist destination, but it remains largely inaccessible, with no airport or safe anchorage for small vessels.

Under a 1989 constitution the territory's governor presides over an Executive Council that includes 5 committee chairs drawn from the 12 elected members of the Legislative Council, who serve four-year terms; both councils also include, as ex officio members, the government secretary, attorney general, and financial secretary. The governor, represented by island administrators, holds executive and legislative powers for the dependencies.

Issues of immigration to the UK and citizenship in the mother country, along with local resentment over decisions by Gov. David SMALLMAN, led to disturbances in April 1997 over the governor's choice of a different social services committee chair than the nominee of the legislators. The approach of the July 9 Legislative Council elections also underscored the relatively limited power of the council compared to the reserve powers of the governor. Smallman retired in 1999.

The November 1999 breakdown of the island's only regularly scheduled cargo and passenger ship led to panic buying by Saints (as the islanders call themselves) concerned about running out of basic provisions. Although interim shipping arrangements were soon made, the temporary halt in the *St. Helena*'s bimonthly visits raised renewed concerns about the territory's isolation and led islanders to call for construction of an airport that would promote what has been termed "big earner" tourism. (Initial plans called for construction of an airport by 2010, but the UK government put the schedule on hold in light of the global recession of 2008–2009. However, in July 2010 the new British government announced it was overturning the previous Labour government's decision and committing £100 million for the project.)

In mid-2008 Gov. Andrew GURR proposed a new draft constitution for St. Helena, Ascension Island, and Tristan da Cunha that would, among other things, eliminate references to Ascension Island and Tristan da Cunha as dependencies of St. Helena, expand the authority of restructured elected councils on the islands, and incorporate a bill of rights. The new basic law was endorsed by the Legislative Council, submitted to the Queen, and came into force on September 1, 2009. General elections were held on November 4, leading to the election of 12 nonpartisan councilors. Funding for an airport was secured in late 2011; when the facility is finished in 2015 it is expected to transform the local economy.

Twelve nonpartisan councilors were elected in the July 17, 2013, general elections. All candidates came from a single constituency; in 2009 six councilors were selected from each of two constituencies.

Governor: Mark CAPES.

Speaker of the Legislative Council: Eric BENJAMIN.

Ascension Island. Encompassing an area of 34 square miles (88 sq. km) and with a 2010 population (excluding Royal Air Force personnel) of about 680, Ascension Island was annexed to St. Helena in 1922 and is presently the site of a major sea-turtle hatching ground, a BBC relay station, and a U.S. space-tracking station. During the Cold War it served as a signals intelligence base, and during the 1982 Falklands war it was a transit point for UK aircraft and ships. In March 1990 an Ariane telemetry reception station became operational under an agreement with the European Space Agency.

In mid-2000 a government study warned that the island's social structure was in danger of collapse without private sector development that could then fund such common services as education and health care. Otherwise, the island could become a "single-person's work-camp," with severe consequences not only for the permanent residents but also for the St. Helena citizens who earn their living there.

The first island government was introduced in April 2001, and an Island Council, chaired by the St. Helena governor, met for the first time in November 2002. Seven members are elected on a nonpartisan basis; two others (the attorney general and the director of financial services) serve ex officio. The governor later dissolved that council and called new elections in 2005. Claiming they were being used as bit players in a nonexistent democracy, six of the seven council members resigned in January 2007. The administrator announced in October 2010 that he was scheduling another election for February 2011, previously election attempts having failed because too few candidates were presented. Elections were held on February 25, 2011, with seven nominated candidates. Five of the candidates were subsequently elected and sworn in as councilors.

Administrator: Marc HOLLAND.

Tristan da Cunha. Annexed to St. Helena in 1938, Tristan da Cunha has an area of 38 square miles (98 sq. km), with a population in 2010 of 260. The dependency also includes the uninhabited islands of Inaccessible and Nightingale as well as Gough, a UNESCO World Heritage Site and residence of a South African meteorological team. The main island's entire population was evacuated because of a volcanic eruption in 1961 but was returned in 1963. Under the original 1985 constitution, the island administrator is advised by an Island Council of 11 members, with 8 elected for three-year terms (most recently in April 2010) and 3 appointed. The 2009 constitution reasserted the advisory role of the Island Council.

Administrator: Alex MITHAM.

Chief Islander: Ian LAVARELLO.

Turks and Caicos Islands.

The Turks and Caicos Islands, a southeastward extension of the Bahamas, consist of 30 small cays (8 inhabited) with a total area of 166 square miles (430 sq. km) and a population (2010E) of 31,200. The capital is Cockburn Town on Grand Turk. The principal industries are tourism, offshore banking and finance, and fishing. As of 1997, some 14,600 offshore businesses were registered in the islands.

Linked to Britain since 1766, the Turks and Caicos became a Crown colony in 1962 following Jamaica's independence. A constitution adopted in 1976 provided for a governor and an Executive Council comprising a chief minister, 5 additional ministers chosen by the governor from among elected legislators, and 3 ex officio members (governor, attorney general, chief secretary). A 20-member Legislative Council comprises 13 elected members, the 3 ex officio members of the Executive Council, 3 members appointed by the governor, and a speaker.

The former chief minister, Norman B. SAUNDERS, was obliged to resign after his arrest on drug-trafficking charges in Miami, Florida, in March 1985, Deputy Chief Minister Nathaniel J. S. FRANCIS being elected as his successor on March 28. Francis was also forced to resign following the issuance of a commission of inquiry report on arson, corruption, and related matters. The British government decided on July 25, 1986, to suspend the constitution and impose direct rule under the governor, with assistance from a four-member advisory council. Subsequently, a three-member constitutional commission was appointed to draft revisions in the basic law to inhibit corruption and patronage and promote "fair and effective administration."

At an election marking the islands' return to constitutional rule on March 3, 1988, the **People's Democratic Movement** (PDM), previously in opposition, won 11 of the 13 elective Legislative Council seats; by contrast, at the poll of April 3, 1991, the PDM (led by Derek TAYLOR) lost 6 seats to the **Progressive National Party** (PNP), whose total of 8 permitted Charles Washington MISICK to form a new government. In an election on January 31, 1995, Taylor and the PDM regained power, winning 8 seats against 4 for the PNP and 1 for Saunders standing as an independent, while the recently formed **United Democratic Party** (UDP), led by Wendal SWANN, failed to secure representation.

Resentment remaining from the 1986 constitutional suspension, objections to the reserve powers of the governor, and alleged British indifference to the islands found a focus in hostility to Gov. Martin BOURKE in April 1996. Among other things, he was charged with favoring one island (Providenciales, the center of the booming tourist industry) over the others in development. In addition, he caused concern by alleging both police corruption and a steady flow of drugs through the island chain. A petition for his removal from the island administration to the Foreign and Commonwealth Office was rejected in April 1996 after consultations with the islands, but in September, when his term expired, he was not reappointed.

At the election of April 24, 2003, the PDM secured seven of the elective seats on the Legislative Council, while the PNP took six. The PNP challenged the results in two closely fought constituencies and won both at by-elections on August 7. As a result, Taylor was obliged to resign in favor of Michael Misick.

A constitutional review process begun in 1999 concluded in 2006 with the adoption of a new constitution providing increased internal autonomy. The new document entered into force on August 9, at which time Misick was sworn in as the first premier of Turks and Caicos. The new constitution provides for a governor appointed by HM Queen Elizabeth II, a House of Assembly with 15 elective seats, and 6 seats appointed by the governor, including a speaker and attorney general. The cabinet consists of the governor, the premier, 6 other ministers, and the attorney general.

At the election of February 9, 2007, the PNP won a decisive majority by securing 13 of the elective seats on the Legislative Council, while the PDM, then led by Floyd SEYMOUR, took only 2.

In July 2008 (a month before leaving office), Gov. Richard TAUWHARE announced that a commission of inquiry had been launched to investigate allegations of government corruption in the islands. Premier Misick described the UK House of Commons report that had spurred the inquiry as "unbalanced" and based on false accusations.

By March 2009 the UK government had raised the possibility of temporarily suspending self-government in the islands and transferring governmental powers to the recently appointed governor, George WETHERELL. The inquiry commission subsequently reported that there were strong indications of "political immorality and immaturity and of general administrative incompetence," prompting Misick to resign his premiership. Galmo WILLIAMS was sworn in as premier on March 24. Misick sought to combat the charges in British courts, but by early summer he had exhausted his appeals. On August 14, 2009, under instructions from the UK Foreign Office, the governor imposed direct rule, which he said could last two years. Meanwhile, criminal investigation in the corruption charges against Misick and four of his cabinet ministers continued.

In June 2010 Douglas PARNELL was reelected as leader of the PDM. In August a PNP convention chose Clayton GREENE, a former speaker of the legislature, as the party's new leader. Although new elections had initially been scheduled for July 2011, the UK government in September 2010 postponed the balloting (and the return of local rule) indefinitely. PDM and PNP leaders strongly criticized the postponement, while also calling on the UK to increase funding to combat the recent upsurge in violent crime on the islands.

Shortly before leaving office in September 2011, Wetherell announced that the Commission of Inquiry report on possible corruption was recommending a criminal investigation by the police or others into the loan and land swap dealings of Misick. At his swearing-in ceremony on September 19 the newly appointed governor Ric Todd promised that elections would be held the following year. Interpol issued an arrest warrant for Misick, who asserted his innocence and moved to Brazil.

British direct rule ended with parliamentary elections held on November 9, 2012. The PNP won eight seats to the PDM's seven. Rufus EWING of the PNP was sworn in as premier on November 12.

Governor: Peter BECKINGHAM.

Premier: Rufus EWING.

Uninhabited Overseas Territories:

South Georgia and the South Sandwich Islands. South Georgia is an island of 1,387 square miles (3,592 sq. km) situated approximately 800 miles east-southeast of the Falklands; it was inhabited only by a British Antarctic Survey team at the time of brief occupation by Argentine forces in April 1982. The South Sandwich Islands lie about 470 miles southeast of South Georgia and were uninhabited until occupied by a group of alleged Argentine scientists in December 1976, who were forced to leave in June 1982. Formerly considered dependencies of the Falklands, the islands were given separate status in October 1985. The governor of the Falkland Islands also serves, ex officio, as territorial commissioner.

In 1993 concern over unregulated fishing led London to impose a 200-mile maritime zone and to increase efforts to manage the territory's fisheries, with particular emphasis on Patagonian toothfish, icefish, krill, and crab. On September 18, 1998, London announced that the 15-member military presence on South Georgia would be withdrawn in 2000, with territorial security to be assumed by troops stationed in the Falkland Islands.

In March 2004, in recognition of management practices that had been introduced to maintain sustainability, the South Georgia toothfish fishery became the first southern ocean fishery to be certified by the independent Marine Stewardship Council. Increased eco-tourism has brought more traffic to the islands in recent years, with indigenous species providing the greatest attractions. As ground-nesting birds have come under attack by a growing rodent population, the South Georgia Heritage Trust announced a plan to eradicate the rodents in 2011. In 2013 a reindeer eradication program began to protect the vegetation and avian residents.

Commissioner: Nigel HAYWOOD (resident in the Falkland Islands).

British Antarctic Territory. Formerly the southern portion of the Falkland Islands Dependencies, the British Antarctic Territory was separately established in 1962. Encompassing that portion of Antarctica between 20 degrees and 80 degrees west longitude, it includes the South Shetland and South Orkney Islands as well as the Antarctic Peninsula. Sovereignty over the greater portion of the territory is disputed by Great Britain, Argentina, and Chile, and its legal status remains in suspense in conformity with the Antarctic Treaty of December 1, 1959. Until June 30, 1989, the responsible British authority was a high commissioner, who served as governor of the Falkland Islands; on July 1 the administration was moved to the Foreign and Commonwealth Office, London, the head of the South Atlantic and Antarctic Department being designated commissioner. The British Antarctic Survey team, based year-round at Halley and Rothera stations, numbers roughly 40–50 in winter and 150 in summer, when stations at Fossil Bluff on Alexander Island and Signy in the South Orkneys are also manned. A number of other countries also maintain research facilities in the territory.

As of 2007, Britain planned to submit to the UN claims to areas of the Antarctic seabed, believed to be rich in energy reserves, based on UK sovereignty over the territory. Chile and Argentina could register competing petitions for rights to the seabed. Critics argued that the claims would undermine the 1959 Antarctic Treaty.

Commissioner: Peter HAYES (resident in the United Kingdom).

Sovereign Base Areas:

Akrotiri and Dhekelia. Under the 1960 Treaty of Establishment, which recognized Cyprus as an independent republic, the UK retained sovereignty over two Sovereign Base Areas (SBAs). Akrotiri (Western Sovereign Base Area) and Dhekelia (Eastern Sovereign Base Area) are to remain sovereign British territory "until the Government of the United Kingdom, in view of changes in their military requirements, at any time decide to divest themselves of the sovereignty or effective control over the SBAs or any part thereof." Although the SBA boundaries were drawn to exclude civilian population centers, the separation of the island into predominantly ethnic Greek and ethnic Turkish sectors in the mid-1970s led to a influx of civilians, and approximately 7,000 Cypriots now live within the SBAs. The UK resident population, military and civilian, numbers some 7,800. The UK Ministry of Defense owns approximately 20 percent of the 98 square miles (254 sq. km) that constitute the SBAs, as does the Crown, with the balance being privately held. Most of the private land is farmed.

Reporting to the Ministry of Defense rather than the Foreign and Commonwealth Office, the SBA administration, headquartered in Episkopi, is led by the commander of the British Forces Cyprus, who has executive and legislative powers comparable to those of a governor in a civilian overseas territory. Assisting the administrator are a chief officer, an attorney general, an administrative secretary, and two area officers. A Court of the Sovereign Base Areas adjudicates nonmilitary offenses. British concern over public finances in the wake of the 2008 international financial crisis and its aftermath has raised the possibility of withdrawing British troops from the bases, which would save £300 million annually.

Administrator: Air Vice Marshal Graham STACEY.

UNITED KINGDOM: NORTHERN IRELAND

Political Status: Autonomous province of the United Kingdom under separate parliamentary regime established in 1921 but suspended March 30, 1972; coalition executive formed January 1, 1974; direct rule reimposed May 28, 1974; consultative Northern Ireland Assembly elected October 20, 1982, but dissolved by United Kingdom June 19, 1986; devolution of limited self-rule to (new) Northern Ireland Assembly and multiparty power-sharing Northern Ireland Executive effected December 2, 1999; direct rule reimposed February 11–May 30, 2000, for one day on August 11, 2001, for one day on September 22, 2001, and from October 15, 2002, until the return of limited self-rule upon the convening of a new assembly and election of a new executive on May 8, 2007, in accordance with the St. Andrews Agreement of October 2006.

Area: 5,452 sq. mi. (14,120 sq. km).

Population: (Included in Ireland).

Major Urban Center (2011E): BELFAST (281,000).

Official Language: English.

Monetary Unit: Pound Sterling (market rate November 1, 2013: 0.63 pound = $1 US).

First Minister: Peter ROBINSON (Democratic Unionist Party); elected by the Northern Ireland Assembly on June 5, 2008, and reelected on May 5, 2011, succeeding Ian PAISLEY (Democratic Unionist Party), who had resigned on May 31, 2008.

Deputy First Minister: Martin McGUINNESS (*Sinn Féin*); elected by the Northern Ireland Assembly on May 8, 2007; reelected June 5, 2008, and again on May 5, 2011, on a joint ticket with First Minister Peter Robinson.

United Kingdom Secretary of State for Northern Ireland: Theresa VILLIERS; appointed on September 4, 2012, by UK Prime Minister David Cameron, succeeding Owen PATERSON.

THE COUNTRY

Geographically an integral part of Ireland, the six northern Irish counties (collectively known as "Ulster," although excluding three counties of the historic province of that name) are politically included within the UK for reasons rooted in the ethnic and religious divisions introduced into Ireland by English and Scottish settlement in the 17th century. As a result of this colonization effort, the long-established Roman Catholic population of the northern counties came to be heavily outnumbered by Protestants, who assumed a dominant political, social, and economic position and insisted upon continued association of the territory with the UK when the rest of Ireland became independent after World War I. Although a minority, Roman Catholics are strongly represented throughout Northern Ireland and constitute a rising proportion of the total population (40.3 percent according to the 2001 UK census, compared to 45.6 percent Protestant). Catholic complaints of discrimination, especially in regard to the allocation of housing and jobs and to limitation of the franchise in local elections, were the immediate cause of the serious disturbances that commenced in Northern Ireland during 1968–1969.

Despite recurring political violence, foreign investors have been drawn to Ulster by lucrative financial incentives and its proximity to the European market. After sharing in the UK recession of the early 1990s, Northern Ireland experienced an economic upturn in 1993. The signing of the multiparty Good Friday Agreement in April 1998 served as another spur to growth. A month later London announced a new $500 million economic aid package directed toward encouraging foreign investment, developing small businesses, easing unemployment, and improving labor skills. Tourism was also targeted for growth.

Northern Ireland's primary trading partners are Great Britain and the rest of the European Union. For 2010–2011, sales to Great Britain represented 46.0 percent of total sales, while France, Germany, and the Netherlands comprised 58.6 percent of sales to the rest of the EU. In addition to clothing and textiles, food and beverages, and machinery, growth industries include pharmaceuticals, software, telecommunications, and electronics. The creative media sector, which includes television, radio, film, animation, and computer games, is growing, and efforts are being made to locate and train workers with appropriate skillsets.

Women made up 45.6 percent of the active labor force in 2007, and the ratio of male/female hourly wage rates was virtually at parity. Women hold 20 of 108 seats in the Northern Ireland Assembly, 3 of 13 cabinet posts, 4 of the 18 seats at Westminster, and 21 percent of local councilor–elected posts.

Gross value added (GVA) per capita (the UK measure of economic prosperity) is only 79 percent of the UK as a whole. Meanwhile, unemployment, which had improved steadily over the past decade to 4.0 percent in 2007, rose steadily to 8.0 percent in 2011 as the effects of the global financial crisis took hold. However, the rate dipped to 6.9 percent for the first half of 2013, which is less than the UK average of 7.7 percent.

GOVERNMENT AND POLITICS

Political background. Governed as an integral part of Ireland, and therefore of the UK, throughout the 19th and early 20th centuries, Northern Ireland acquired autonomous status in 1921 as part of a general readjustment necessitated by the success of the Irish independence movement in the rest of Ireland. The Government of Ireland Act of 1920 provided for a division of Ireland as a whole into separate northern and southern sections, each with its own legislature. Enshrined in the December 1921 Anglo-Irish treaty, this arrangement was reluctantly accepted by the Irish nationalist authorities in Dublin but embraced in Northern Ireland as the best available means of continuing as an integral part of the UK. The new government of Northern Ireland was dominated from the beginning by the pro-British, Protestant interests controlling the Ulster Unionist Party (UUP), with militant elements becoming known as "loyalists." Ties with Britain were sedulously maintained, for both religious and historic reasons and because of accompanying economic benefits, including social services and agricultural subsidies. Opposition Catholic sentiment in favor of union with the Irish Republic represented a continuing but long-subdued source of tension.

Catholic-led "civil rights" demonstrations against political and social discrimination erupted in 1968, evoking counterdemonstrations by Protestant extremists and leading to increasingly serious disorders, particularly in Londonderry (known to Catholics as Derry). In November 1968 the government of Terence O'NEILL proposed a number of reform measures that failed to halt the disturbances and yielded an erosion of support for the prime minister within his own government and party. Parliament was accordingly dissolved, with a new election in February 1969 producing the usual unionist majority but failing to resolve an internal UUP conflict. In April mounting disorder and acts of sabotage led the Northern Ireland government to request that British army units be assigned to guard key installations. Although O'Neill persuaded the UUP to accept the principle of universal adult franchise at the next local government elections, he resigned as party leader on April 28 and as prime minister three days later. His successor in both offices, Maj. James D. CHICHESTER-CLARK, an advocate of moderate reform, was chosen by a 17–16 vote of the UUP over Brian FAULKNER, an opponent of the O'Neill reform program. The government promptly announced an amnesty for all persons involved in the recent disturbances and received a unanimous vote of confidence on May 7.

After renewed rioting in Belfast, Londonderry, and elsewhere during the first half of August 1969, Chichester-Clark agreed on August 19 that all security forces in Northern Ireland would be placed under British command; that Britain would assume ultimate responsibility for public order; and that steps would be taken to ensure equal treatment of all citizens in Northern Ireland in regard to voting rights, housing, and other issues. The subsequent deployment of regular British soldiers in the province was at first welcomed by the Catholic population as affording protection from Protestant incursions into their localities. However, under the influence of the Provisional Irish Republican Army (Provisional IRA or the "Provos"), many Catholics quickly came to see the British troops as an occupying force, and their alienation increased as the result of the internment without trial of several hundred Catholics in August 1971. Growing polarization was highlighted by the formation in 1971 of the ultra-loyalist Democratic Unionist Party (DUP) by a hard-line faction of the UUP led by Dr. Ian PAISLEY.

The situation turned sharply worse on "Bloody Sunday," January 30, 1972, when a prohibited Catholic civil-rights march in Londonderry was infiltrated by hooligan elements, and 14 unarmed civilians died as the result of clashes with British troops. A wave of violence and hysteria followed. Unable to act in agreement with the Belfast regime of Prime Minister Brian Faulkner, who had succeeded Chichester-Clark in March 1971, British Prime Minister Edward Heath announced that he would reimpose direct rule. The Northern Ireland Parliament was prorogued rather than dissolved, and William (subsequently Viscount) WHITELAW was designated to exercise necessary authority through the newly created office of secretary of state for Northern Ireland. With the backing of the three leading British parties, these changes were quickly approved by the British Parliament and became effective, initially for a period of one year, on March 30, 1972. The 1972 death toll from political violence reached 478, the highest annual total during the post-1969 "Troubles."

A plebiscite on the future of Northern Ireland was held on March 8, 1973, but was boycotted by the Catholic parties. An unimpressive 57.4 percent of the electorate voted for Ulster's remaining within the UK, while 0.6 percent voted for union with the Republic of Ireland and the remainder abstained. The British government subsequently organized the election on June 28 of a Northern Ireland Assembly of 80 members to serve a four-year term. This step was formalized on July 18 by passage of a parliamentary bill permitting the devolution of powers to the assembly and an executive, and on November 27 Brian Faulkner was named chief of an executive-designate that included representatives of both Protestant and Catholic factions.

In a meeting in Sunningdale, England, on December 6–9, 1973, that was attended by members of the Irish and UK governments as well as the executive-designate of Northern Ireland, agreement was reached on the establishment of a tripartite Council of Ireland to oversee changes in the relationship between the northern and southern Irish governments. On January 1, 1974, direct rule was terminated. While the (mainly Catholic) Social Democratic and Labour Party (SDLP) endorsed the agreement, the bulk of the Unionist Party rejected it, forcing Faulkner's resignation as party leader on January 7 and as chief executive on May 28, in the wake of which direct rule was again imposed.

In July 1974 the UK Parliament passed the Northern Ireland Act of 1974, which authorized the election of a Constitutional Convention. At balloting on May 1, 1975, the United Ulster Unionist Coalition (UUUC), a grouping of largely "anti-Sunningdale" parties, won 45 of 78 convention seats. On September 8 the UUUC convention members voted 37–1 against the participation of republicans in a future Northern Ireland cabinet, and on November 20 the convention concluded its sitting with a formal report that embraced only UUUC proposals. The convention was reconvened on February 3, 1976, in the hope of reaching agreement with the SDLP and other opposition parties, but it registered no further progress and was dissolved a month later.

The UUUC was itself dissolved on May 4, 1977, following the failure of a general strike called by its more intransigent loyalist components, acting in concert with the Ulster Workers' Council (UWC) and the Ulster Defense Association (UDA), the largest of the Protestant paramilitary groups. With the level of violence having declined, Secretary of State for Northern Ireland Roy MASON proposed in late November that a new attempt be made to restore local rule. The effort was abandoned, however, because of intensified violence in the first quarter of 1978, which prompted the House of Commons in late June to extend the period of direct rule for another year. In the absence of a political settlement, the order was renewed annually thereafter.

Following the failure of another attempt at constitutional talks in early 1980 and a further escalation of violence, seven republican inmates of the Maze prison near Belfast began a hunger strike on October 27 in support of a demand for "political" status. While the strike was called off on December 18 following government promises of improvement in prison conditions, the action was widely publicized and was renewed in March 1981, with ten prisoners ultimately dying, including Bobby SANDS and Kieran DOHERTY, who had won election to, respectively, the UK and Irish parliaments shortly before their deaths. The most significant diplomatic development of the year was a meeting in London on November 6 at which UK Prime Minister Margaret Thatcher and Irish Prime Minister Garret FitzGerald agreed to set up an Anglo-Irish Intergovernmental Council (AIIC) to meet on a periodic basis to discuss matters of common concern.

In early 1982 the Thatcher government secured parliamentary approval for the gradual reintroduction of home rule under a scheme dubbed "rolling devolution." The initiative assumed substantive form with balloting on October 20 for a new 78-member Northern Ireland Assembly. For the first time the Provisional *Sinn Féin* (the political wing of the Provisional IRA) participated in the process, obtaining five seats. The poll was accompanied, however, by an upsurge of terrorist activity, with both the Provisional *Sinn Féin* and the SDLP boycotting the assembly session that convened on November 11 to formulate devolution recommendations.

During a meeting in Hillsborough Castle, Northern Ireland, on November 15, 1985, Prime Ministers Thatcher and FitzGerald concluded an Anglo-Irish Agreement that established an Intergovernmental Conference (IGC) within the context of the AIIC to deal on a regular basis with political and security issues affecting the troubled region. Subsequently, in reaction to unionist maneuvering, the small nonsectarian Alliance Party joined *Sinn Féin* and the SDLP in boycotting the Northern Ireland Assembly, while the 15 unionist MPs resigned their seats in the UK House of Commons to force by-elections as a form of referendum on the Hillsborough accord. (One unionist seat fell to the SDLP.) On June 19, 1986, the UK government dissolved the assembly, which had become little more than an anti-accord forum for unionists. The dissolution, which signaled the failure of London's seventh major peace initiative in 14 years, did not, however, abolish the body, leaving open the possibility of future electoral replenishment.

In February 1989 agreement was reached on the functions and membership of another joint undertaking provided for in the Anglo-Irish accord: a British-Irish Inter-Parliamentary Body of 25 MPs from each country, including minority party representatives. The first meeting of the new group opened in London on February 26, 1990, but two seats reserved for unionist parliamentarians remained vacant because of their continued opposition to the 1985 accord.

In March 1991 continued tension in the province was momentarily eased by the announcement of agreement on new talks in three "strands": first, discussions between the Northern Ireland "constitutional" parties, focusing on devolution and power sharing, chaired by Secretary of State Peter BROOKE; second, "North-South" talks between the Northern Ireland parties and the UK and Irish governments; and third, "East-West" talks between London and Dublin on replacing the 1985 Anglo-Irish Agreement. Any agreement reached under the talks would be put to referendums in both Northern Ireland and the Republic of Ireland.

Although preliminary first-strand talks opened on schedule on April 30, 1991, the so-called Brooke initiative quickly ran into procedural and political obstacles. Not until June 17 was it possible for full first-strand discussions to begin in Belfast, marking the first formal inter-party talks in Northern Ireland in 16 years. However, it became apparent that Brooke had overestimated the willingness of the parties to seek common ground, with the unionist parties remaining resolutely opposed to any formula that appeared to give Dublin a role in Northern Ireland's affairs.

A July 1991 breakdown in the talks was followed by an escalation of sectarian violence, and by January 1992 the number of British troops assigned to the province had risen to 11,500. The conflict nonetheless continued, with the number of killings attributed to Protestant paramilitary groups, principally the Ulster Volunteer Force (UVF) and the Ulster Freedom Fighters (UFF), reportedly approaching those perpetrated by the IRA.

The talks were formally suspended by Brooke on January 27, 1992, pending the outcome of the UK election on April 9. In that contest the 17 Northern Ireland constituencies returned 13 Unionists, while the SDLP increased its representation in the House of Commons to 4 by gaining the West Belfast seat held since 1983 by the *Sinn Féin* president, Gerard (Gerry) ADAMS. In the postelection reshuffle Brooke was replaced as Northern Ireland secretary by Sir Patrick MAYHEW, who on April 17 announced his intention to resume the talks.

On June 30, 1992, representatives of the four leading Ulster formations met in London with an Irish government delegation, the first time since Ireland became independent in 1921 that hard-line unionists had met with Irish officials. On July 1 the participants agreed to undertake sustained negotiations on the North-South relationship, but deadlock soon emerged, in part over the Republic of Ireland's continuing constitutional claim to the whole of Ulster. The talks formally concluded without agreement in early November, whereupon meetings of the IGC resumed. Meanwhile, sectarian violence continued unabated. On August 10, 1992, the UK government announced the banning of the loyalist UDA, bringing the number of proscribed organizations in Northern Ireland to ten.

The advent of a *Fianna Fáil*/Labour coalition government in the Republic of Ireland in January 1993 heralded a more accommodating line by Dublin, and despite continuing IRA bombings in England, the quest for a negotiated settlement appeared to gain momentum. During April and May 1993, SDLP leader John HUME held a series of meetings with *Sinn Féin* leader Adams in what was characterized by Hume as an effort to bring about "a total cessation of all violence." On May 27 Irish President Mary Robinson conferred in London with Queen Elizabeth II in the first such meeting between the two countries' heads of state. Most significantly, on December 15, 1993, Prime Ministers John Major and Albert Reynolds issued their Downing Street Declaration. Aiming to bring about the end of hostilities in the province, the declaration acknowledged that "the people of the island of Ireland" might wish to opt for unification but reiterated that "it would be wrong to attempt to impose a united Ireland in the absence of the freely given consent of the majority of the people of Northern Ireland." The declaration thereby raised the possibility that Dublin would take steps to delete its constitutional claim to the North; it also stated that if IRA violence were brought to "a permanent end," *Sinn Féin* could expect to participate in all-party talks. Reaction to the new document was decidedly cool among the unionists, while *Sinn Féin* declined to give an immediate response, preferring instead to call for "clarifications."

The 25-year-old logjam in Northern Ireland appeared to be broken by an IRA announcement on August 31, 1994, that from midnight that day "there will be a complete cessation of military operations" by all IRA units. Noting that "an opportunity to secure a just and lasting settlement has been created," the statement called for "inclusive negotiations." Received with great rejoicing in Northern Ireland, especially among Catholics, the IRA announcement prompted London to take the position that if the cease-fire proved to be a permanent renunciation of violence, *Sinn Féin* would be invited to participate in future negotiations. In Dublin Prime Minister Reynolds took speedier action, receiving Adams on September 5 to discuss the convening of a "forum of peace and reconciliation." Unionist spokespersons, however, described the cease-fire as a public relations ploy and demanded that the IRA surrender its weapons and explosives prior to meaningful talks. On October 13 the three main loyalist paramilitary organizations also declared a cessation of hostilities but made it clear that they would not surrender their weapons until the IRA had done so.

The position of *Sinn Féin,* however, was that arms decommissioning should be dealt with at the talks rather than before and should be part of a complete "demilitarization" of Northern Ireland, including the withdrawal of British troops. This basic impasse persisted, despite the progressive upgrading of the UK government's contacts with *Sinn Féin.* The first public talks between the two sides took place in December 1994 in Belfast, while Adams and Secretary of State Mayhew finally met on May 24, 1995, on the margins of a Washington conference aimed at promoting investment in Northern Ireland.

Meanwhile, the UK and the Irish government, now headed by Prime Minister John Bruton, continued to clarify their positions. A joint "framework document" issued on February 22, 1995, envisaged the creation of a North-South council with "executive, harmonizing or consultative functions" and the restoration of self-government to Northern Ireland under a power-sharing formula. The document also recorded the Irish government's pledge to introduce a constitutional amendment deleting any territorial claim to Northern Ireland, while the UK government would propose constitutional legislation enshrining its commitment to uphold the democratic wish of the Northern majority. Reactions to the document were predictable: conditional approval from Adams, who noted that "its ethos is for one Ireland," but strong condemnation from unionist leaders, with Paisley of the DUP describing it as "Ulster's death warrant."

In early July 1995 violence resurged in conjunction with the annual "marching season," during which Protestant fraternal orders hold upward of 3,000 marches, some through Catholic neighborhoods, chiefly to mark the July 1690 defeat of the Catholic King James II by the Protestant William of Orange at the Battle of the Boyne. Amid fears that the peace process was losing momentum, on July 24 the UK and Irish prime ministers issued a three-part plan under which the disarmament of paramilitary groups would be supervised by an international commission, a target date would be set for the opening of all-party talks, and early release dates would be set for some of the 1,000 republican and loyalist paramilitaries currently serving prison sentences. The timing of decommissioning remained a sticking point, however, with London continuing to insist on paramilitary disarmament as a precondition for all-party discussions. While attempting to persuade London to modify its stance, the Dublin government went ahead with its "forum of peace and reconciliation," in which *Sinn Féin,* the SDLP, and a large number of others (but not the main unionist parties) set out their positions on the issue and the constitutional future. In September the UUP elected a new leader, David TRIMBLE, who had come to prominence in July by defying a police blockade and leading an Orange Order march through the Catholic neighborhood of Drumcree, near Portadown.

Intensive UK-Irish negotiations in October–November 1995 attempted to confront the decommissioning issue and thereby prepare the way for multiparty negotiations. As a result, on December 15 an international commission headed by former U.S. senator George Mitchell began to address the disarmament question, while a tentative date of February 1996 was set for opening interparty talks. In January 1996 the Mitchell panel proposed that all parties adhere to six principles, including the renunciation of political violence and a commitment to eventual, full decommissioning under international supervision.

Blaming what it labeled British intransigence, the IRA abruptly ended its cease-fire on February 2, when a massive bomb exploded in London, killing two men and causing damage later estimated at up to $300 million. The bombing appeared to catch even *Sinn Féin* off guard, casting doubt on the extent of its influence over the IRA. Security measures in Northern Ireland, which had been relaxed, were rapidly stepped up, and on February 28 both governments demanded an immediate and unequivocal restoration of the cease-fire, pending which *Sinn Féin* would be excluded from talks.

After individual discussions with Northern Ireland parties started in March (the uninvited *Sinn Féin* representatives being turned away), the UK government enacted legislation authorizing election of a consultative Northern Ireland Forum for Political Dialogue. Balloting took place on May 30, returning 90 members from 18 constituencies and a further 20 members from the 10 parties securing the largest shares of the popular vote. Although *Sinn Féin* participated in the election, winning 17 seats on a larger-than-expected vote share, it remained aloof from the forum. Moreover, the SDLP, with 21 seats, soon withdrew, preferring to concentrate on direct talks. Thus, the forum was left to the two main unionist parties, the UUP (30 seats) and the DUP (24 seats), and to various smaller groupings. The latter included the Ulster Democratic Party (UDP) and the Progressive Unionist Party (PUP), which were described as "close to the thinking of" the leading loyalist paramilitaries, the UDA and the UVF, respectively.

With the forum effectively sidelined by the absence of the nationalist parties, attention turned to the multiparty negotiations, which opened on June 10, 1996, in Stormont Castle, the seat of the direct-rule administration. Both governments and all of the main parties except *Sinn Féin,* whose leaders were again turned away, took part, although the proceedings were initially stalled by unionist objections to the proposal that former senator Mitchell be the chair. In July the traditional Protestant marches again provoked sectarian altercations, while the IRA and a splinter, the Continuity Army Council, or Continuity IRA, continued their attacks into the autumn and beyond. In October the UUP and the SDLP finally agreed on a full agenda for the Stormont negotiations, while in November the SDLP and *Sinn Féin* requested, among other things, a guarantee that *Sinn Féin* would be admitted to the talks if the IRA declared another cease-fire. Britain and Ireland disagreed, however, on the precise terms for *Sinn Féin*'s participation.

Talks resumed in January 1997 but were suspended in March to await the UK election of May 1, in which the UUP took 10 of Northern Ireland's 18 seats in the House of Commons, followed by the SDLP with 3, and the DUP and *Sinn Féin* with 2 each. Under Prime Minister Tony Blair the new UK Labour government moved swiftly to place Northern Ireland high on the political agenda, with Dr. Marjorie (Mo) MOWLAM assuming office as secretary of state for Northern Ireland. Despite another round of hostilities associated with the Protestant marching season, on July 19 the IRA announced a resumption of the August 1994 cease-fire, opening the way for *Sinn Féin* to join the multiparty talks when they began again in mid-September. Although *Sinn Féin* had explicitly endorsed the six Mitchell principles, which also included a commitment to abide by the terms of any negotiated peace settlement, the unionists, objecting to *Sinn Féin*'s presence, boycotted the opening session. In late September, however, in a precedent-shattering shift of policy that drew the wrath of hard-line loyalists, the UUP's Trimble agreed to rejoin the talks despite *Sinn Féin*'s presence. Thus, representatives of eight parties—the UUP, SDLP, *Sinn Féin,* UDP, PUP, the Alliance Party of Northern Ireland (APNI), the Northern Ireland Women's Coalition, and the Labour Coalition—gathered in Stormont in October, the principal absentee being Paisley's DUP. In tandem, an Independent International Commission on Decommissioning (IICD), chaired by a retired Canadian general, John de Chastelain, broached the disarmament issue.

In October 1997 Tony Blair met with Gerry Adams, the first such meeting between a UK prime minister and *Sinn Féin* in more than 70 years, while in November the new Irish prime minister, Bertie Ahern, conferred with the UUP's Trimble. Despite such confidence-building steps, little progress was achieved before the Christmas break, during which the leader of the paramilitary Loyalist Volunteer Force (LVF), Billy WRIGHT, was murdered inside the Maze prison by members of the Irish National Liberation Army (INLA). Retaliations ensued, and on January 9, in a spectacular political gambit, Secretary Mowlam met in the Maze with loyalist prisoners and earned their support for continued peace discussions.

Although provocations by paramilitaries on both sides continued, Prime Ministers Blair and Ahern issued a brief framework for peace titled "Propositions on Heads of Agreement" on January 12, 1998. The outline proposed "balanced" constitutional change by both the UK and Ireland; establishment of a directly elected Northern Ireland legislature and a North-South ministerial body; formation of British-Irish "intergovernmental machinery"; and adoption of "practical and effective measures" concerning such issues as prisoners, security, and decommissioning. The constitutional changes put forward by the prime ministers included excision of the Irish Republic's territorial claim to Northern Ireland, coupled with revision of British constitutional legislation dealing with the UK's authority over affairs in the North. *Sinn Féin* initially evinced little enthusiasm for the proposal, which fell significantly short of the party's long-standing demand for reunification with the South, while unionists expressed concern that creation of a North-South organ would in fact pave the way for reunification.

Early in 1998 the UDP and *Sinn Féin* were separately suspended from the multiparty talks because of cease-fire violations committed by their paramilitary associates, the UFF and the IRA, respectively, but in March both parties were readmitted to Stormont. On March 25 Mitchell set a 15-day deadline for the two governments and the eight participating parties to achieve a final peace plan, which was concluded on April 10 (a day late) following a marathon negotiating session. The Belfast Agreement, which quickly became better known as the Good Friday Agreement, called for the following: (Strand One) creation of a Northern Ireland Assembly with full authority to legislate "in devolved areas," an Executive Committee (Northern Ireland Executive) of ministers drawn from the legislature and headed by a first minister and a deputy first minister, a consultative Civic Forum of community and business leaders, and a continuing role for the secretary of state for Northern Ireland in matters not devolved to the new institutions; (Strand Two) creation of a North-South Ministerial Council; and (Strand Three) establishment of a British-Irish Council with representatives from Ireland and all the British isles, including devolved institutions in Scotland and Wales. In addition to requiring removal from Ireland's constitution of the claim to Northern Ireland, the agreement mandated adherence to human rights and equal opportunity, full decommissioning by May 2000, normalization of security arrangements in Northern Ireland (including the withdrawal of the roughly 17,500 British troops), and formation of an independent commission to review policing procedures. Finally, an assessment of the criminal justice system was to include "an accelerated programme for the release of prisoners" affiliated with those organizations maintaining a "complete and unequivocal" cease-fire. Accompanying the Good Friday Agreement was a new British-Irish Agreement, superseding the 1985 Anglo-Irish Agreement and committing London and Dublin to carrying through on the peace arrangements.

With an island-wide referendum—the first such vote since partition—scheduled for May 22, supporters and opponents of the Good Friday Agreement quickly began campaigning. In April David Trimble convinced the UUP as a whole to back the agreement despite vehement opposition from six of his party's ten MPs, the DUP, the small United Kingdom Unionist Party (UKUP), and the fraternal Orange Order. Meeting in Dublin on May 10, a special *Sinn Féin* conference also endorsed the agreement and authorized members to sit in the proposed Northern Ireland Assembly. In the end, the referendum passed with a 71 percent affirmative vote in the North, on a turnout of 81 percent. Balloting for the new 108-member assembly took place on June 25, with 16 parties offering candidates. The UUP obtained a plurality of 28 seats, followed by the SDLP with 24, the DUP with 20, and *Sinn Féin* with 18. In all, opposition unionists claimed 28 seats, just short of the number that would have enabled them to tie up legislation (see Constitution and government, below, for a discussion of rules governing passage of measures requiring "cross-community support").

On July 1, 1998, the new Northern Ireland Assembly elected the UUP's Trimble as first minister and the SDLP's Seamus MALLON as deputy first minister, John Hume having declined the latter nomination. Already, however, a major stumbling block to full formation of the power-sharing Executive Committee, and thus to devolution, had emerged. Whereas Trimble demanded that the IRA begin decommissioning its arms before he would allow *Sinn Féin* to take up any ministerial positions, Gerry Adams argued that the Good Friday Agreement contained no such stipulation.

Once again, the Protestant marching season brought with it a series of violent incidents, including the torching of ten Catholic churches on July 2–3, 1998. Following a ruling by an independent Parades Commission that the traditional Orange Order parade in Drumcree would not be allowed to pass through a Catholic neighborhood, more than 5,000 Orangemen protested at the barricades. A month later, on August 15, in the worst carnage since the "Troubles" began, a car bomb exploded in Omagh, killing 29 and injuring more than 200 others. A recently formed IRA splinter, the "Real IRA," claimed responsibility for the attack, which even the INLA and the Continuity IRA condemned. The bombing provoked Prime Ministers Blair and Ahern to introduce in their respective legislatures antiterrorism measures that Ahern characterized as "extremely draconian." Both parliaments passed similar bills in early September.

On September 10, 1998, for the first time, Trimble and Adams met privately in Stormont, but they made no progress on the decommissioning dispute. Trimble, responding to the announcement on October 16 that he and John Hume had won the Nobel Peace Prize for their efforts, expressed the hope that the decision had not been "premature." On October 31 the negotiators missed the deadline set by the Good Friday Agreement for creation of the "shadow" (predevolution) Executive Committee and the North-South Ministerial Council. The stalemate appeared broken on December 18 with the announcement in Stormont of a further agreement covering formation of ten government departments and six cross-border bodies, the principal goal being British transfer of authority to the Northern Ireland Assembly and Executive Committee in February 1999. The new agreement provided for the UUP and the SDLP to head three departments each, with *Sinn Féin* and the DUP being responsible for two each. Ministerial nominations would await progress on disarmament. Although the LVF on the same day became the first paramilitary group to turn in some of its weapons, the IRA refused to reciprocate, calling the LVF action a "stunt."

In January 1999 Trimble set February 15 as the date for inaugurating the Executive Committee, while Secretary of State Mowlam established March 10 as the date for transferring powers to the assembly. However, neither deadline was met. On February 16 the assembly voted 77–26 in favor of the December power-sharing accord and also approved creation of the Civic Forum, the North-South Ministerial Council, the British-Irish Council, and the cross-border bodies. Nevertheless, the decommissioning issue remained unresolved, even after the UUP and *Sinn Féin* held their first party-to-party session the following day. Despite personal efforts by Prime Ministers Blair and Ahern, Secretary of State Mowlam announced on March 9 that she was postponing devolution again, until April 2, Good Friday.

Although all the principal paramilitary groups continued to adhere to cease-fires (despite a notable increase since late 1998 in the number of "punishment beatings" inflicted by gangs against members of their own communities), a prominent nationalist civil rights lawyer, Rosemary NELSON, was killed by a car bomb on March 15, 1999. The apparent perpetrator, the recently organized loyalist Red Hand Defenders (RHD), was quickly added by Secretary of State Mowlam to the list of banned organizations, as was another new loyalist paramilitary group, the Orange Volunteers (OV). At the end of March, Blair and Ahern made another attempt to resolve the decommissioning impasse. They proposed in the Hillsborough Declaration that the UUP, SDLP, *Sinn Féin,* and DUP nominate their members of the Executive Committee and that within one month, in a "collective act of reconciliation," the paramilitaries voluntarily "put beyond use" various arms.

Upon IICD certification of the decommissioning, the assembly could confirm the nominees to the Executive Committee. The "changed security situation" would also permit "further moves on normalisation and demilitarisation." On April 13, however, *Sinn Féin* rejected the declaration, reiterating that all parties should adhere to the letter of the Good Friday Agreement, which specified only that decommissioning occur by May 2000. On April 20 Ahern and Blair met in London with UUP, SDLP, and *Sinn Féin* leaders, to no avail. In mid-May London and Dublin set a new deadline of June 30 for formation of the Executive Committee, but further attempts by Blair and Ahern to broker an agreement proved fruitless. On July 14 Trimble reaffirmed that the UUP would not sit with *Sinn Féin* in a devolved government until decommissioning had begun, prompting Deputy First Minister-elect Mallon to resign on July 15 and Blair to announce that devolution would be further postponed.

Through August 1999, unionists and *Sinn Féin* verbally skirmished over whether the IRA had broken its cease-fire. Meanwhile, former U.S. senator Mitchell had agreed to chair a review of the peace process that opened on September 6 in Belfast and moved on October 12 to London, where the newly appointed secretary of state for Northern Ireland, Peter MANDELSON, insisted that the negotiators had no alternative but to meet the terms of the Good Friday Agreement. "There is no Plan B," he asserted. "It's that or nothing." An effort by both the UUP and *Sinn Féin* to temper their rhetoric prompted Mitchell to extend negotiations beyond an October 23 deadline, and in early November he held meetings with U.S. President Clinton as well as the British and Irish prime ministers. Shortly thereafter, *Sinn Féin* reported that the IRA was prepared to establish contact with General de Chastelain. On November 15–16, in a sequence of carefully worded, coordinated statements, Mitchell, Trimble, and Adams separately endorsed the continuance of devolution and decommissioning. On November 17 the IRA confirmed that, following establishment of the institutions outlined in the Good Friday Agreement, it would name a representative to "enter into discussions" with de Chastelain. In a secret ballot on November 27, 58 percent of the UUP's governing council backed Trimble's cautious acceptance of the IRA initiative. Thus, the UUP gave up its demand that decommissioning had to begin before it would sit with *Sinn Féin* on the power-sharing Northern Ireland Executive.

On November 29, 1999, the Northern Ireland Assembly approved ten nominees to serve in the executive under Trimble and Mallon. The latter had been reaffirmed as deputy first minister by a 71–28 vote of the assembly, thereby negating his July resignation through a legally questionable maneuver that was challenged by the DUP and other hard-liners. (The stratagem circumvented having to jointly reelect Mallon and First Minister Trimble, who probably would not have secured the necessary 30 unionist votes.) On December 1 the UK Parliament authorized devolution, and on December 2 London formally transferred power to the assembly and the executive; however, the cabinet convened minus the two DUP ministers, who refused to sit with the two *Sinn Féin* ministers. On the same day, Dublin formally promulgated the constitutional changes that ended the Irish Republic's claims to the North, and on December 2–3 IRA representatives met for the first time with General de Chastelain. On December 13 the North-South Ministerial Council held its inaugural meeting, and on December 17 representatives of Ireland, the UK, the Channel Islands, the Isle of Man, and the devolved governments of Northern Ireland, Scotland, and Wales gathered in London for the first session of the Council of the Isles.

The IRA's subsequent failure to begin disarming led the UK government to reimpose direct rule on February 11, 2000. In a last-minute effort to salvage the power-sharing government, the IRA had told General de Chastelain that it was prepared to address putting its arms and explosives "beyond use," but the offer came too late to forestall the reimposition. In response, on February 15 the IRA suspended further contacts with de Chastelain.

While attending talks in Washington in mid-March 2000, Trimble indicated that he might consider reinstituting the power-sharing government prior to any actual arms decommissioning by the IRA. The statement catalyzed his opponents within the UUP, and at a March 25 session of the party's governing council he faced a leadership challenge by the Rev. Martin SMYTH. Although Trimble managed to win 57 percent of the council vote, Smyth's supporters, including the influential hard-liner Jeffrey DONALDSON, succeeded in linking restoration of the government to a highly charged symbolic issue: retaining the name of the territory's controversial police agency, the Royal Ulster Constabulary (RUC). On September 9, 1999, Chris Patten, a former UK governor of Hong Kong, had released a report on RUC reform that proposed, among a list of 175 recommendations, changing the force's name to the Police Service of Northern Ireland (PSNI). Unionists had immediately denounced the proposal as well as suggestions that the police oath and insignia be revised to remove all association with the UK. (*Sinn Féin* had responded to the report by repeating its long-held position that the RUC should be abolished.)

Despite a series of diplomatic meetings and public negotiations, little substantive progress on resolving the armaments impasse occurred until May 6, 2000, when the IRA announced that it would accept international inspection of its arms stockpiles and would "completely and verifiably" put its weapons beyond use. As inspectors it nominated Martti Ahtisaari, former president of Finland, and Cyril Ramaphosa, former secretary general of South Africa's ruling party, the African National Congress. London and Dublin quickly proposed that power-sharing be resumed on May 22, but on May 18 Trimble, fearing defeat, postponed a crucial meeting of the UUP governing council. In an effort to defuse the RUC issue, Secretary of State Mandelson agreed to amend pending legislation on RUC reform, adding, for example, mention of the RUC to the legal description of the police service. On May 27, by a vote of 459–403, Trimble again prevailed over the UUP hard-liners, despite the opposition of Deputy Leader John TAYLOR, who viewed Mandelson's concessions as inadequate.

On May 30, 2000, London returned authority to the Northern Ireland Assembly and Executive. In early June Mandelson made additional concessions to garner republican support for the RUC reform legislation, but he left the name-change issue unresolved. At the same time, the new home rule government faced differences over other symbolic issues—principally, the refusal of the *Sinn Féin* ministers to fly the Union Jack over their offices.

On June 25 the IRA stated that it had reopened discussions with de Chastelain's IICD, and on June 26 arms monitors Ahtisaari and Ramaphosa reported that they had conducted their first inspections of IRA stockpiles. In further fulfillment of the Good Friday Agreement, authorities by late July had released more than 425 paramilitary prisoners, loyalist and republican alike, from prison, although Johnny ADAIR, a former leader of the UFF, was returned to prison on August 22 following renewed feuding between loyalist paramilitary groups in July–August. Responding to the outbreak of violence, Secretary of State Mandelson ordered British troops onto the streets of Belfast.

On October 28, 2000, First Minister Trimble overcame another challenge to his leadership when the UUP governing council rejected a hard-line proposal that the party withdraw from the government if the IRA failed to actively begin disarmament by November 30. Trimble instead proposed that he prohibit the executive's two *Sinn Féin* ministers from participating in official North-South meetings until the IRA actively engaged with the IICD. Trimble's decision drew immediate criticism not only from Gerry Adams, but also from Deputy First Minister Mallon. Meanwhile, in the last week of October weapons inspectors Ahtisaari and Ramaphosa conducted their second inspection of IRA stockpiles, as a result of which they described the IRA as "serious about the peace process."

During the first half of 2001 no significant progress was made in resolving three linked issues: IRA decommissioning, as demanded by the unionists; departure of the UK military, as demanded by the republicans; and reform of the RUC, as demanded by both (though with seemingly irreconcilable goals). Renewed negotiating efforts by Prime Ministers Blair and Ahern failed, leading First Minister Trimble to announce in May 2001 that he would resign his office on July 1, in the absence of concrete action by the IRA.

As predicted by Trimble himself, hard-liners made notable gains in the general election of June 7, 2001. Whereas his UUP lost 3 of its 9 seats in the UK House of Commons (having already lost 1 to the DUP at a September 2000 by-election) and 31 of its 185 local council seats, Ian Paisley's DUP gained 2 seats in the House of Commons, for a total of 5, and 40 additional council seats, for a total of 131. The SDLP held steady, retaining its 3 parliamentary seats and losing only 3 of its 120 local council seats, while *Sinn Féin* saw its membership in the House of Commons rise from 2 to 4 and its local council representation increase from 74 to 108.

With a backdrop of renewed sectarian rioting, centered on a Roman Catholic school in a predominantly Protestant area of Belfast, Trimble, as he had threatened, resigned on July 1, 2001. His action automatically vacated the office of deputy first minister. A diplomatic scramble ensued as Ireland and the UK attempted to reinvigorate the peace process before six weeks had passed, after which a new first minister had to be elected, a Northern Ireland Assembly election called, or direct rule reimposed. On August 6 the IICD released a statement confirming that the IRA had accepted a method for putting its weapons "completely and verifiably" beyond use, but in the absence of a timetable and at least a minimal surrender of weapons, the unionists dismissed the agreement as inadequate. Nevertheless, believing that a breakthrough might be near, London decided to exploit a legal loophole and reset the six-week clock by imposing direct rule for a single day beginning at midnight on August 11. The move by Secretary of State for Northern Ireland John REID angered the IRA, however, and it withdrew from its agreement with the IICD. The situation was further complicated by the arrest in Colombia of three alleged IRA members who, according to Colombian authorities, had been assisting the principal leftist guerrilla organization, the Colombia Revolutionary Armed Forces (*Fuerzas Armadas Revolucionarias de Colombia*—FARC). (Gerry Adams subsequently denied accusations that at least one of the men was acting as a *Sinn Féin* representative.) Meanwhile, the sectarian violence in Belfast again worsened, leading Reid to announce on October 12 that the government no longer recognized the cease-fires with the UDA/UFF and the LVF.

Facing increasing international pressure following the September 11, 2001, attacks by Islamic terrorists in the United States, the IRA stated on September 20 that it would renew and accelerate its talks with the IICD. Collaterally, London heralded a breakthrough based on the decisions of the SDLP and then the UUP and DUP (but not *Sinn Féin*) to participate in the formation of a cross-community Northern Ireland Policing Board as part of a new Police Implementation Plan. (The RUC was formally renamed the PSNI on November 4.) Citing these positive developments, on September 21, with the second six-week period about to expire, London announced another direct-rule interregnum that began at midnight on September 22 and concluded 24 hours later.

On October 18, 2001, the UUP and DUP ministers withdrew from the executive after the assembly had rejected a unionist demand that the two *Sinn Féin* ministers be excluded. Shortly thereafter, Adams and his deputy, Martin McGUINNESS, for the first time explicitly called upon the IRA to begin disarming, and on October 23 both the IRA and the IICD released statements announcing that a quantity of arms had in fact been decommissioned. In response, Trimble announced that the UUP would return to the executive and that he would seek reelection as first minister.

At the assembly's first vote on November 2, two members of the UUP voted against Trimble, leaving him one vote short of the necessary unionist majority, despite unanimous nationalist support. On November 6 he achieved the necessary margin when the assembly allowed three members of the Alliance Party to temporarily redesignate themselves as unionists. However, the DUP was incensed by the maneuver, which led to scuffles outside the assembly.

An additional IRA decommissioning occurred in April 2002, but continuing sectarian violence in Belfast prompted Trimble, in early July, to threaten the withdrawal of the UUP from the assembly if authorities did not take corrective measures. Although he accused the IRA of fomenting the rioting, loyalist paramilitaries appeared to be equally culpable. The annual marching season once again led to repeated clashes, and in late July London vowed to stiffen its response to security violations. A week earlier, on July 16, the IRA had issued an unprecedented public apology to the families of its innocent victims.

On October 4, 2002, the *Sinn Féin* offices in Stormont were raided by authorities investigating alleged IRA spying, and two days later Denis DONALDSON, a *Sinn Féin* administrator, was arrested and charged with possessing some 1,200 documents of potential use to paramilitaries. The unionists immediately demanded the resignations or dismissal of the *Sinn Féin* ministers. On October 15, in an effort to forestall the collapse of the peace process, London reimposed direct rule for the fourth time.

Despite the continuation of direct rule, elections to the suspended Northern Ireland Assembly were held on November 26, 2003. The results suggested that resumption of the peace process might prove impossible. For the Protestants, Ian Paisley's DUP, which strongly opposed the 1998 Good Friday Agreement, displaced Trimble's UUP to become the largest party, with 30 seats. For the Catholics, in a similar reversal of the 1998 results, *Sinn Féin* won 24 seats, as opposed to the SDLP's 18.

Despite the 2003 electoral results, multiparty talks were resumed on February 3, 2004, with the DUP and *Sinn Féin* communicating through intermediaries. Subsequently, UK Prime Minister Blair and Irish Prime Minister Ahern held a series of meetings that yielded no consensus on power-sharing, while in December Paisley announced a hardening of the DUP position by insisting on photographic evidence of IRA arms decommissioning.

In early 2005 the peace process reached a new point of collapse with the IRA being blamed for an armed attack on Belfast's Northern Bank in December 2004 and thereafter withdrawing its offer to decommission. On April 7 *Sinn Féin* leader Adams drew no response in urging the IRA to abandon its "armed struggle," while an appeal by Blair and Ahern for the IRA to end "all paramilitary and criminal activity" was equally unproductive until late July when, in a potentially historic development, the IRA pledged to lay down its arms and oppose British rule in the future only through peaceful political involvement. Specifically, the IRA announced that it had "formally ordered an end to the armed campaign" and would pursue a "purely political and democratic program through exclusively peaceful means." Promises were also made that the IRA's massive stockpiles of arms (reportedly buried in bunkers throughout Northern Ireland) would be quickly dismantled.

The May 5, 2005, local elections reinforced the shifts in unionist and nationalist party success. The DUP gained more than 50 additional councilors; *Sinn Féin* improved by 18; the UUP dropped by 39 to fall behind the DUP in number of unionist councilors region-wide; and the SDLP dropped by 16 seats to fall behind *Sinn Féin* in number of nationalist councilors. However, a single party gained majority control in only 2 of 18 councils (the DUP in Ballymena and Castlereagh).

Prime Minister Blair labeled the IRA announcement a step of "unparalleled magnitude," and in August 2005 the UK indicated that it would cut its troop level (then 10,000) in Northern Ireland in half by 2007 in view of the improved security outlook. In addition, in September General de Chastelain said the IICD was satisfied with the decommissioning of the IRA weapons. However, DUP leader Paisley condemned the UK response as "premature," calling for the "dissolution" of the IRA. He and other Protestant leaders also accused the British and Irish governments of "disregarding" loyalist concerns. Consequently, the DUP continued to refuse to meet directly with *Sinn Féin* when Blair and Ahern relaunched negotiations toward another power-sharing government.

In February 2006 the Independent Monitoring Commission (IMC), established by the UK and Ireland in 2004 to monitor armed groups in Northern Ireland, concluded that the IRA was no longer "engaged in terrorism," while Protestant militants had been responsible for more than 20 killings in the fall of 2005. Encouraged by the IRA's "progress," Blair and Ahern subsequently appeared to focus on pressuring the DUP to adopt a more positive negotiating role. In April the two prime ministers declared a deadline of November 24 for the assembly parties to agree on formation of a new executive, without which a "new way to govern" Northern Ireland would be pursued. Analysts suggested that the deadline posed a "veiled threat" to the DUP, as it implied that the alternative to a power-sharing government could be greater control by the Irish Republic. Adams welcomed the announcement, and in May he proposed that Paisley be named as first minister of the proposed new government. However, the offer was emphatically rejected by Paisley (described as *Sinn Féin*'s "most intractable foe"), and little progress was reported through the summer, despite the establishment of a multiparty Preparation for Government Committee and the reconvening of the Northern Ireland Assembly (see Legislature, below).

Prime Minister Blair and Ahern managed to organize "last ditch" negotiations that brought the two chief protagonists (Ian Paisley of the DUP and Gerry Adams of *Sinn Féin*) and leaders of other parties together for a series of meetings in St. Andrews, Scotland, on October 11–13, 2006. Tentative agreement was reached for the restoration of self-rule the following spring, assuming that final details were successfully negotiated for the proposed power-sharing arrangements. In addition, final approval was required from *Sinn Féin* regarding the acceptance of and support for the police force and the criminal justice system. (Theretofore, *Sinn Féin* supporters had refused to recognize the authority of the PSNI, which the nationalists believed was dominated by the unionists.)

Although neither the DUP nor *Sinn Féin* expressly endorsed the St. Andrews Agreement by the November 10, 2006, deadline, the British and Irish governments deemed the parties' statements of intent to be sufficient to continue. Consequently, on November 22 Westminster approved the enabling legislation required for the agreement to go into effect. Two days later, the Northern Ireland Assembly that had been elected in 2003 met to receive nominations from the DUP and *Sinn*

Féin (expected to finish first and second, respectively, in the upcoming assembly balloting) for the two principal executive positions. Adams nominated *Sinn Féin*'s Martin McGuinness for deputy prime minister, but Paisley deferred acceptance of the post of first minister pending *Sinn Féin*'s formal agreement to participate in the police force and criminal justice system. After a *Sinn Féin* conference on January 28, 2007, Blair and Ahern announced on January 30 that new assembly elections would be held as planned..

In the assembly balloting on March 7, 2007, DUP increased its seat representation from 30 to 36, while *Sinn Féin* advanced from 24 to 28. Paisley and Adams met on March 26 and agreed upon the nominations of Paisley and McGuinness to head the new executive. Those appointments were approved when the new assembly convened on May 8, as were the remaining cabinet appointments. (Under the unique system in Northern Ireland whereby cabinet posts are assigned according to assembly representation, DUP was accorded 5 of the 12 cabinet posts; *Sinn Féin,* 4; the UUP, 2; and the SDLP, 1.)

Despite widespread concerns over the potential stability of the new government, it survived without major incident throughout 2007. Symbolic of the cooperative working relationship between Paisley and McGuinness was their joint visit to the United States in December, at which time President George W. Bush congratulated all parties in the decades-long dispute for having apparently put violence behind them in favor of a "more hopeful chapter."

A leading indicator that Ian Paisley's time as first minister may have been nearing its end came with his January 2008 resignation as leader of the Free Presbyterian Church. He also announced on March 4 that he would resign as DUP party leader. Although his age (82) and recent resignation of his son from a junior ministerial position likely weighed in his decision, the main impetus appeared to be dissatisfaction among church and party leaders with Paisley's facilitation of the peace process and cooperation with McGuinness.

On April 14, 2008, Peter Robinson, theretofore deputy leader of DUP, was elected unopposed as Paisley's successor as DUP leader. Cooperation between DUP and *Sinn Féin* was expected to diminish under Robinson's leadership, and, when Paisley officially vacated the office of first prime minister on May 31, interparty tensions reemerged. *Sinn Féin* initially threatened to prevent Robinson from replacing Paisley as first minister by refusing to renominate McGuinness on the joint ticket unless DUP took action on the issues of policing, justice, and the Irish Language Act. However, negotiations led by UK prime minister Gordon Brown, as well as officials from the U.S. and Irish governments, succeeded in getting *Sinn Féin* to lift its threat. On June 5 Robinson was elected as first minister and McGuinness was reelected as deputy first minister. However, three months of stalemate followed, as *Sinn Féin* blocked all efforts for the executive to meet on other business until DUP agreed to a date for transferring policing and justice powers to local ministers. Progress in that regard was achieved in October when Paul GOGGINS, minister of state in the UK Northern Ireland office, clarified that the transfer of the related responsibilities to the Northern Ireland Assembly would not include access to sensitive national security information, such as secret files on IRA informers. Consequently, the assembly in November met for the first time since June and forged a compromise to create a justice ministry. The plan called for the justice minister to be chosen from outside the ranks of DUP or *Sinn Féin,* although both parties would have a veto over the appointment. (It was believed that a member of the Alliance Party was likely to be named to the post.)

No firm timetable was set for inauguration of the Department of Justice, and throughout 2009 progress toward a final agreement was slow. On the republican side, some opponents of the transfer resorted to violence. The Real IRA claimed responsibility for the March 2009 murder of two British soldiers, the first such murders in the province since 1997. Two days later, members of the Continuity IRA (CIRA) claimed responsibility for the murder of a police constable in Amagh. On a more positive note, three unionist paramilitary groups (the UVF, RHC, and UDA) voluntarily decommissioned their weapons in June. On the unionist side, the strength of DUP's resolve to see the process through came into doubt on the heels of two political developments. In the June balloting for the European Parliament, the newly formed Traditional Unionist Voice (TUV), created by a DUP dissident, cut substantially into DUP's vote support while running on a platform objecting to joining in a government in which participation by *Sinn Féin* was mandated. Unionist voters also appeared upset over revelations of unseemly personal expense charges to the public by DUP leaders (see DUP, below). Even an October pledge of £800 million by UK prime minister Brown to fund Northern Ireland's takeover of policing and justice functions left DUP unmoved.

In early January 2010 DUP leader Robinson found himself in deep personal political difficulty as the media published scandalous details of alleged sexual and financial improprieties on the part of his wife, Iris Robinson. On January 9 Iris Robinson was expelled from DUP for financial misconduct, and, with speculation swirling that the first minister had been aware of his wife's alleged fiscal misdeeds, Peter Robinson took three weeks' leave from his formal duties on January 11. Arlene FOSTER (DUP minister for enterprise, trade, and investment) stepped in as interim replacement under an arrangement whereby Robinson would continue to lead negotiations over the unresolved policing and justice issue and Foster would oversee day-to-day matters. Robinson returned to office on February 3, and the next day *Sinn Féin* and DUP announced they had reached agreement on the creation of the Department of Justice. On March 9 the assembly endorsed the proposal by a vote of 88–17, with only the UUP in dissent. In accordance with the agreement, the new department was established on April 12, and, as long expected, David FORD, leader of the nonsectarian APNI, was installed as minister. Ominously, less than a half hour after the transfer of powers, a bomb exploded at the Northern Ireland headquarters of the British M15 security forces, with the Real IRA claiming responsibility.

The year-long anticipation of a sharp decline in DUP's political standing proved ill-founded, at least as recorded in the May 5, 2010, balloting for the UK House of Commons. DUP held on to eight of its nine seats and outpolled the upstart TUV by better than a six-to-one margin. The one loss was noteworthy, however, inasmuch as DUP leader Peter Robinson was defeated in his reelection bid for the UK parliamentary seat he had held for 31 years. His poor electoral showing immediately provoked questions about whether he should remain as party leader and first minister. These questions were pushed aside in short order; five days after the election DUP unanimously endorsed his continuing service in both positions.

Just over a month after his election to the UK premiership in May 2010, David Cameron presented the long-awaited report on the 12-year investigation into the 1972 Bloody Sunday killings. The report found that all those shot by British soldiers were unarmed and that the shootings were both unjustified and unjustifiable. New Northern Ireland justice minister Ford was left with the responsibility to decide whether to prosecute any of the soldiers involved.

Terrorist incidents increased in 2010 compared with the previous year. Some observers attributed this escalation of violent activities to the province's poor economic condition, as Northern Ireland was targeted for stringent cuts by the UK government's austerity measures in the midst of an already faltering economy. Against this backdrop, a climate of peace and negotiation characterized the province's official politics. In response to the murder of a Catholic constable in the Police Service of Northern Ireland (PSNI) in April 2001, McGuiness called for nationalists to inform on the attackers. This call marked a reversal in the position of McGuiness on the issue, who had previously declined to call for nationalists to provide information on dissident republicans. Around the same time, the power-sharing executive of Northern Ireland successfully completed the entire four-year term. The National Assembly was dissolved in March, and with no noticeably controversial issues on the agenda, the parties embarked on an electoral campaign described by commentators as uneventful. Voting behavior was expected to fall along sectarian lines, and the balloting on May 5 resulted in few changes to the composition of the National Assembly. DUP gained two seats, while *Sinn Féin* and the APNI each gained one. The UUP and the SDLP each lost two seats, while the Green Party maintained its one seat. Of note in an otherwise unremarkable election was the success of the upstart TUV in its attempt to capture a seat in the assembly. Robinson and McGuinness were reelected as first minister and deputy minister, respectively, shortly after the election on May 12, and David Ford of the APNI was reinstated as minister of policing and justice. The new cabinet was a mix of new and old faces among the five parties, with *Sinn Féin* now heading the ministries of Agriculture, Education, and Culture, the UUP heading the Department of Regional Development, and the APNI heading the Department of Employment and Learning.

Constitution and government. The Government of Ireland Act of 1920 gave Northern Ireland its own government and a Parliament empowered to act on all matters except those of "imperial concern" (e.g., finance, defense, foreign affairs) or requiring specialized technical input. The royal authority was vested in a governor appointed by the Crown and advised by ministers responsible to Parliament; in practice, the leader of the majority party was invariably designated as prime minister. Parliament consisted of a 52-member House of Commons, directly elected from single-member constituencies, and a Senate, whose 26 members (except for 2 serving ex officio) were elected by the House of Commons under a proportional representation system. Voting for local government bodies was subject to a property qualification that excluded an estimated 200,000 adults, including a disproportionate number of minority Catholics. The effective disenfranchisement of a substantial portion of the Catholic population precipitated the original disturbances in 1968–1969.

Until 1998 British efforts to bring about agreement on a form of coalition government acceptable to both Protestants and Catholics failed to bear fruit. The Northern Ireland Constitution Act of 1973 abolished the office of governor and provided for a regional assembly and executive; however, the executive functioned only in 1974, and the assembly and its successor in 1973–1974 and 1982–1986. A Constitutional Convention in 1975–1976 failed to produce agreement, and the only major constitutional developments for more than a decade thereafter involved the extension of a consultative role to the Irish government by means of various bilateral accords. Accordingly, direct rule, in effect since 1972 (save for January–May 1974), continued through the UK secretary of state for Northern Ireland. Under direct rule local government encompassed 26 elected city, district, and borough councils with very limited responsibilities for refuse collection, street cleaning, recreational facilities, environmental health, and consumer protection.

Following completion of the Belfast Agreement of April 10, 1998 (familiarly called the Good Friday Agreement but also referenced in some official documents as the Multi-Party Agreement), and pending approval of the agreement by referendum on May 22, the British Parliament passed legislation authorizing election of a New Northern Ireland Assembly, the term "New" being dropped upon formal devolution of authority to the body. Elected on June 25, the legislature comprised 108 members from 18 constituencies.

Under the terms of the Good Friday Agreement and the Northern Ireland Act of 1998, which Parliament passed in November 1998 and which repealed the Government of Ireland Act of 1920, assembly members individually defined themselves as a "designated unionist," a "designated nationalist," or "other." Decisions requiring "cross-community support"—for example, standing orders, budget allocations, and election of the assembly chair—required either majority approval, including support from a majority of both nationalists and unionists, or assent by a weighted majority of 60 percent, with affirmative votes from at least 40 percent of unionists and 40 percent of nationalists. To further protect the minority, the cross-community provision could be triggered on any other matter if 30 or more assembly members presented a "petition of concern."

Assembly members were to be elected for five-year terms, subject to early dissolution by a vote of two-thirds of the entire membership. Devolved legislative authority extended to such areas as agriculture, economic development, tourism, and education, while "excepted and reserved matters" remaining in the hands of the UK Northern Ireland secretary included international relations, defense, security, criminal justice, taxation, regulation of financial services, national insurance, and regulation of broadcast and telecommunication services. Under devolution, executive authority resided in an Executive Committee of ministers chosen from the leading assembly parties in proportion to their membership in the body. The assembly selected a first minister and a deputy first minister, who stood for election jointly and were required to secure majority support from both nationalists and unionists. In addition to heading the executive, which might have up to ten additional members, the two leaders jointly nominated ministers and junior ministers to two principal intergovernmental bodies, the North-South Ministerial Council and the British-Irish Council (also known as the Council of the Isles), both of which were established under treaties concluded by the UK and Ireland on March 8, 1999.

The North-South Ministerial Council had as its mandate bringing together "those with executive responsibilities in Northern Ireland and the Irish Government, to develop consultation, co-operation, and action within the island of Ireland," on both an island-wide and a cross-border basis. Decisions required agreement by both sides. The British-Irish Council, which was to meet at the summit level twice a year and in other formats "on a regular basis," included representatives from Scotland, Wales, the Channel Islands, and the Isle of Man in addition to Great Britain, Northern Ireland, and Ireland, the purpose being "to promote the harmonious and mutually beneficial development of the totality of relationships among the peoples of these islands." Two additional treaties signed on March 8 authorized formation of various implementing bodies and of a British-Irish Intergovernmental Conference, the latter replacing the Anglo-Irish Intergovernmental Council and the Intergovernmental Conference of 1985.

Northern Ireland is represented in the UK House of Commons, currently with 18 seats (increased from 17 in 1997). It also has 3 seats in the European Parliament.

The UK government reimposed direct rule on Northern Ireland on October 15, 2002. However, limited self-rule was restored on May 8, 2007 (see Political background, above).

Northern Ireland's press, radio, and television are organized along the same lines as in Great Britain.

Current issues. September 28, 2012, marked the centennial of the Ulster Covenant against Home Rule. Over 500,000 persons signed the document, rejecting London's proposal to have Northern Ireland ruled from Dublin. A year of exhibitions, lectures, and other public events revisited the event and tried to accurately portray both sides of the dispute. Celebrations were to culminate with a massive parade in Belfast. However, officials became alarmed over the possibility of violence following three days of sectarian rioting at the beginning of September. Police used water cannons to separate rival republican and loyalist gangs in the worst violence in seven years. The riots, which injured more than 60 police officers, reacted to an incident on July 12, when the Royal Black Institution had marched past St. Patrick's church in Belfast playing an anti-Catholic song. Tensions eased when the institution issued an apology to the church, saying it was not the direct target of its demonstration. Subsequently, more than 30,000 people marched peacefully in the Covenant Day parade.

A new round of sectarian conflict began when the Belfast City Council voted on December 3 to stop flying the Union flag over city hall on a daily basis, as it had since 1906. Instead, it would be raised only on 17 significant days. Council members from *Sinn Féin*, the SDLP, and the APNI backed the measure. Outraged loyalists began nightly protests that grew in size and lasted through February. As tensions escalated, bricks, gasoline bombs, rubber bullets, and water cannons were used. Dozens of police were injured and more than 200 protestors arrested as the violence spread to other cities. Business leaders complained that the violence had ruined the Christmas shopping season and cost them £15 million in lost sales.

The protests were led by a younger generation and organized via social media. Instead of former paramilitaries, the people throwing bricks at police tended to be underemployed, frustrated, and detached from the community. The demographics of Belfast are in flux, with Protestants leaving and East European immigrants moving in. The region needs investment to create jobs, but televised scenes of street riots have deterred investors.

Prime Minister David Cameron hosted the G-8 summit in Enniskillen on June 17–18. Despite the high level of security surrounding the conference center, leaders cited the event as a sign of increased stability in the region. Others suggested it was a way for London to emphasize that Northern Ireland is undeniably part of the United Kingdom, given the secessionist tendencies in Scotland. Shortly before the summit, Westminster announced an economic pact that would create enterprise zones in Northern Ireland, £20 million to develop an aerospace industry, housing and to rid Belfast of the "peace walls" dividing Protestant and Catholic neighborhoods.

Northern Ireland's political leaders are watching Scotland's latest moves toward independence very closely. Should Scotland separate from the UK, it could trigger a redefinition of Ulster's relations with London. Deputy First Minister Martin McGuinness has stated that he plans to introduce a motion on independence during the next session of the NI Assembly, possibly by 2016. First Minister Robinson has called on all Unionist parties to combine into one strong party to defend the UK from separatism.

POLITICAL PARTIES AND GROUPS

Parties Represented in the Cabinet:

Democratic Unionist Party (DUP). The DUP was founded in 1971 by a hard-line loyalist faction of the UUP, attracting working-class Protestant support for its strongly anti-Catholic, anti-Dublin position. It was consistently the runner-up to the parent party, winning 21 seats in the 1982 assembly election and 3 UK House of Commons seats in June 1983, all of the latter being retained in 1987. The party was represented at the 1988 Duisburg talks by Deputy Leader Peter Robinson, who urged the creation of an alternative to the 1985 Anglo-Irish accord.

A growing schism between the DUP's older and younger members was, in part, responsible for the party leader's decision in May 1990 to agree to political negotiations. The older faction, led by Ian Paisley, had long adhered to a "no negotiation" policy, while the more youthful faction, exemplified by Robinson, advocated the creation of a political and religious dialogue. At the same time, the party mainstream was moving from an "integrationalist" to a "devolutionist" posture that favored a provincial government with relatively strong legislative and executive powers.

The DUP retained its three Westminster seats in the UK balloting of April 1992, after which the failure of yet another round of constitutional talks left the party's internal divisions unresolved. In the forum elections of May 1996 the party fell into third place, with 19 percent of the vote, and in the May 1997 UK election it lost the constituency of Mid Ulster to *Sinn Féin.*

The DUP strongly opposed *Sinn Féin*'s presence at the Stormont negotiations of 1997–1998 and refused to participate. It campaigned against the Good Friday Agreement and won 20 of the 28 seats captured by unionist oppositionists at the June Northern Ireland Assembly election. Allotted two portfolios in the Northern Ireland Executive, the DUP adopted obstructionist tactics to protest *Sinn Féin*'s presence in the body.

In a September 2000 by-election for a seat in the UK House of Commons, the DUP captured the district from the UUP, prompting Paisley to declare that First Minister Trimble "is finished, absolutely finished." In the UK general election of June 2001 the DUP won 5 seats, a gain of 2. In simultaneous local balloting the party added 40 council seats, for a total of 131.

In the Northern Ireland Assembly balloting of November 2003, the DUP outpolled the UUP for a plurality of 30 seats. The DUP also won 1 of 3 Northern Ireland seats in the June 2004 elections to the European Parliament. In the House of Commons election of May 2005, the DUP increased its representation from 5 to 9, securing 33.7 percent of the vote in Northern Ireland and consolidating its status as the dominant unionist party with a similar advance in the simultaneous local elections. The DUP remained the plurality party in the March 7, 2007, balloting for the Northern Ireland Assembly, securing 36 seats on a 30.1 percent share of first-round votes. As the largest party, the DUP was able to nominate Paisley for the position of first minister in the subsequent coalition government with *Sinn Féin.* The power-sharing coalition and Paisley's overtly friendly relationship with Deputy First Minister McGuinness subsequently created strains in party ranks. Amid controversies over power sharing and his son's property dealings, Paisley announced in March 2008 that he would resign as party leader at the end of May. His longtime adviser and confidant, Peter Robinson, won election to the party leader post in April, assumed the leadership position on May 31, and was elected first minister on June 5.

Although Robinson's subsequent approach to the DUP's power-sharing arrangements with *Sinn Féin* was less friendly and less accommodating than Paisley's, hard-line unionist elements still remained skeptical, thereby creating a possible source of a permanent fracture within the party. In addition, Robinson found himself in political trouble over reports in April 2009 that he, his wife, and other DUP members were "double dipping" on salaries and claiming large expense reimbursements. (Robinson and his wife, each of whom held positions as representatives in both the UK Parliament and the Northern Ireland Assembly, reportedly were paid more than one-half million pounds in annual salaries and expenses.)

The DUP's vote share fell to 18.1 percent in the June 2009 elections to the European Parliament, down dramatically from 32 percent in 2004. In what was initially thought to be an ominous sign for the DUP's long-term political standing, most of the defecting voters appeared to turn to the TUV (below), a new hard-line unionist alternative. Nevertheless, the DUP held onto 8 of its 9 seats in the May 6, 2010, UK parliamentary balloting. The one lost seat was the one previously held by Peter Robinson, with the loss being attributed to his personal difficulties more so than DUP shortcomings. (See Recent developments, above, for information on the issues surrounding Robinson and also on his retention of both his party leadership post and his position as first minister of Northern Ireland.) The other noteworthy change came as a result of former leader Ian Paisley deciding not to seek reelection. He was succeeded by his son (Ian Paisley Jr.), who won handily, and in June Ian Paisley Sr. was named to a peerage in the UK House of Lords.

In the May 2011 National Assembly elections the DUP won 38 seats, an increase of 2, with 30.6 percent of first-preference votes.

Leaders: Peter ROBINSON (First Minister of Northern Ireland and Party Leader), Nigel DODDS (Deputy Leader), James McCLURE (President), Maurice MORROW (Chair), David SIMPSON (Vice President).

Sinn Féin. The island-wide *Sinn Féin* (see also Ireland: Political Parties) serves as the legal political wing of the outlawed IRA (see Former and Current Republican Paramilitary Groups, below). In addition to advocating improved living and working conditions for its primarily Catholic, working-class constituency, throughout the 1970s and 1980s it consistently called for the disbanding of British security forces, the withdrawal of Britain from Northern Ireland's government, and the negotiation of a political settlement through an all-Ireland constitutional conference.

Its president, Gerard (Gerry) Adams, was *Sinn Féin*'s only successful candidate in the 1987 UK general election, but, as in 1983, he refused to occupy his seat in the Commons. In early 1988 the SDLP (below) attempted to forge ties with *Sinn Féin,* but its interest waned in April when *Sinn Féin* refused to "repeal its commitment to limited guerrilla warfare." A second attempt at linkage was broken off in September following the resumption of IRA bombings in downtown Belfast.

Responding to comments made by UK Secretary of State Peter Brooke, in April 1990 Adams said that the IRA might be persuaded to cease terrorist activities if London established a dialogue with *Sinn Féin.* However, *Sinn Féin*'s continued refusal to renounce IRA violence led to its exclusion from the April 1991 talks. In April 1992 Adams lost his Westminster parliamentary seat to the SDLP.

The IRA cease-fire declaration of August 31, 1994, yielded enhanced international stature and negotiating prominence for Adams and other *Sinn Féin* leaders. However, the IRA renewed hostilities in February 1996 while continuing to press for unconditional talks. Though successful in both the 1996 Forum elections (winning 15 percent of the vote) and in the May 1997 UK general elections (winning two seats), the party still chose to remain aloof from either political process. Renewal of the IRA cease-fire in July 1997 and *Sinn Féin*'s affirmation of its commitment to the six Mitchell principles, including full decommissioning and rejection of political violence, enabled Adams to join the Stormont multiparty peace talks in September. In response, a hard-line faction left the party and formed the 32 County Sovereignty Committee (below).

At a special party session convened in Dublin on May 10, 1998, and attended by a number of furloughed nationalist inmates from prisons in Northern Ireland and Britain, Adams won overwhelming endorsement of the Good Friday peace plan and permission for *Sinn Féin* members to take up seats in the new Northern Ireland Assembly. In balloting for the assembly in June, the party won 18 seats, sufficient for it to claim 2 positions on the governing Executive Committee upon devolution.

In June 2000 Cathal CRUMLEY became the first member of *Sinn Féin* to be elected mayor of a Northern city, Londonderry, since partition. Earlier in the year the UK government had introduced a bill in the House of Commons that would permit a member of any UK legislature, including the Northern Ireland Assembly, to hold simultaneously a legislative seat in the Republic of Ireland. The Disqualifications Bill, which passed Parliament on November 30, was widely regarded as a "sweetener" for *Sinn Féin* as it permitted the party's assembly members, particularly Gerry Adams, to seek election to the *Dáil.*

In the UK general election of June 2001, *Sinn Féin* doubled its representation in the House of Commons, to 4 seats. It also made gains locally, adding 34 council seats to the 74 it had previously held.

On October 4, 2002, the *Sinn Féin* offices in Stormont were raided by authorities investigating IRA spying, and two days later Denis Donaldson, the party's office administrator, was arrested and charged with possessing some 1,200 documents of potential use to paramilitaries. The revelations ultimately contributed to London's reimposition of direct rule on October 15. (The case took a surreal turn in December 2005 when the charges against Donaldson were dropped and Donaldson acknowledged that he had in fact been a British agent for 20 years.)

The party won 24 seats in the Northern Ireland Assembly election of November 2003.

In August 2004 Adams, in an effort to counter the DUP's objection to revival of the peace talks, called publicly for the disbanding of the IRA as a paramilitary force.

Sinn Féin gained one of Northern Ireland's three seats in the 2004 European Parliament elections and secured five seats (including one by

Adams) in the May 2005 UK House of Commons balloting on a share of 24.3 percent of the votes in Northern Ireland. Shortly thereafter, Adams intensified his call for the renunciation of violence, and the IRA subsequently announced its historic pledge to disarm. (Adams has never acknowledged having played a leadership role in the IRA, although many observers have ascribed such status to him.)

In January 2007 *Sinn Féin* formally endorsed the provisions for police services in the St. Andrews Agreement of the previous November, thereby permitting plans for new assembly elections to proceed in March. *Sinn Féin* won 28 seats (finishing second to the DUP) in that balloting on a 26.2 percent share of first-preference votes. The party also retained its 1 seat from Northern Ireland in the June 2009 European Parliament elections with a first-place vote total of 26.3 percent and remained the leading nationalist party in the May 2010 balloting for the UK House of Commons. In the May 2011 National Assembly elections *Sinn Féin* increased its seat share by 1, bringing the total number of seats under the party's control to 29 with 26.9 percent of first-preference votes. This time the party's representatives did not include Adams, who had resigned his seat in the National Assembly in order to contest, and ultimately win, a parliamentary seat in the Republic of Ireland.

Leaders: Gerard (Gerry) ADAMS (President), Martin McGUINNESS (Deputy First Minister of Ireland), Declan KEARNEY (Chair), MaryLou McDONALD (Vice President), Dawn DOYLE (General Secretary).

Ulster Unionist Party (UUP). The UUP, historically Northern Ireland's dominant party, was split by the 1973 Sunningdale Agreement, the anti-Sunningdale majority becoming known as the Official Unionist Party (OUP). The formation of a "joint working party" between the OUP and the DUP (above) was announced in August 1985 to protect "Ulster's interests within the UK." Throughout 1986 the working party attempted to disrupt local government in protest of the Anglo-Irish Agreement of 1985. By contrast, joint OUP-DUP publications in 1987 called for all Northern Ireland parties to negotiate an alternative to the 1985 accord in a spirit of "friendship, cooperation, and consultation." In addition, the OUP, DUP, and the now-defunct Ulster Popular Unionist Party (UPUP) of James KILFEDDER agreed to present only one unionist candidate from each constituency in the 1987 House of Commons elections, at which they retained 13 of 14 seats. The OUP continued to issue conciliatory statements during 1988, but the party's demand that the Anglo-Irish accord be rescinded before any substantive negotiations could take place between unionists and republicans helped derail initiatives advanced at a meeting of the OUP, DUP, Alliance Party, and Social Democratic and Labour Party (SDLP, below) in October in Duisburg, West Germany.

In May 1990 OUP leaders softened their position, reportedly agreeing to tripartite talks between the province's parties and the British and Irish governments in return for "de facto" (temporary) suspension of the bilateral pact. Subsequently, in April 1991, OUP and DUP representatives attended the opening of the Ulster talks as joint unionist negotiators despite the incompatibility of the DUP's "devolutionist" position and the OUP's "integrationalist" call for increased linkage between Ulster and Britain. The Official Unionists won 9 of the 17 Northern Ireland seats in the UK election of April 1992, by which time they had officially adopted the UUP designation to signify continuity with the historic party.

Having held the party leadership since 1979, James MOLYNEAUX stood down in August 1995 and was succeeded by David Trimble, a leading UUP critic of the concessions being made to Dublin in the peace process. Two years later, in a remarkable turnaround, Trimble agreed to sit at the same negotiating table as *Sinn Féin,* and on April 10, 1998, UUP representatives signed the multiparty Good Friday Agreement. Fighting off intraparty opponents, including 6 of the party's 10 members of Parliament, Trimble secured UUP approval of the peace plan, and in the June 25 election the party won a plurality of 28 seats in the 108-seat Northern Ireland Assembly. On July 1 the assembly elected Trimble first minister of the Executive Committee, and in October 1998 he shared the Nobel Peace Prize with the SDLP's John Hume.

On October 9, 1998, a faction within the UUP formed Union First in opposition to the Good Friday Agreement and the presence of *Sinn Féin* in the government. Thereafter, criticism of Trimble continued to grow. Resentment over what hard-line unionists viewed as ill-advised concessions to *Sinn Féin* culminated in a March 25, 2000, challenge to his leadership by the Rev. Martin Smyth. Although the party's governing Ulster Unionist Council (UUC) gave Trimble 57 percent of the vote, Union First's Jeffrey Donaldson and Deputy Leader John Taylor were both considered to be likely future challengers. On May 27, having threatened to resign in the event of a negative vote, Trimble gained only 53 percent endorsement of the UUC (459–403) to accept the IRA's offer to permit international monitoring of its arms stockpiles.

On October 28, 2000, the UUC reconvened to consider a Donaldson proposal that the UUP withdraw from the government unless the IRA began decommissioning by November 30. Trimble countered by asserting that, as first minister, he would not authorize the government's two IRA ministers to participate in official North-South meetings until the IRA actively engaged with General de Chastelain's IICD. Trimble again won the council's support, 445–374.

Trimble resigned as first minister effective July 1, 2001. A month earlier the UUP had seen its support at the polls decline, costing it 3 of its 9 seats in the UK House of Commons and 31 of its 185 local council seats. Trimble was reelected first minister on November 6, 2001, although he had failed to obtain the needed majority of nationalist votes four days earlier when two UUP members, Peter WEIR and Pauline ARMITAGE, voted against him. Weir was subsequently expelled from the party and joined the DUP in April 2002; Armitage's membership was suspended.

The UUP lost its plurality to the DUP in the Northern Ireland Assembly election of November 26, 2003, and in late December Trimble's most severe intraparty critic, Jeffrey Donaldson, announced that he was quitting the UPP and aligning himself with the DUP. The UUP member of the European Parliament, Jim NICHOLSON, retained his seat in the 2004 balloting for that body, as the UUP came in third in votes (behind the DUP and *Sinn Féin*). At the UK general election of May 5, 2005, the UUP lost four of its five seats in the House of Commons, including the one held by Trimble, on a share of only 17.7 percent of the votes in Northern Ireland. The UUP also declined in the concurrent local elections, and Trimble, who had apparently suffered from the voters' perception that he and the UUP had been "too soft" regarding *Sinn Féin* and the IRA, promptly resigned as party leader. He was succeeded on June 24 by Reg Empey. While Trimble officially remained a UUP member of the suspended Northern Ireland Assembly through 2007, he was named as a member of the House of Lords in April 2006 and sat on that body as a crossbencher. In April 2007 Trimble announced he had joined the Conservative Party.

The UUP won 18 seats in the March 2007 elections for the Northern Ireland Assembly on a 14.9 percent share of first-preference votes. With 9 fewer seats than it had won in 2003, the UUP fell from second to third largest party in the assembly. Throughout 2008 UUP and UK Conservative Party leaders held discussions on reestablishing their once strong relationship, with an eye toward the UUP regaining lost support and the Conservatives broadening their geographical appeal. In November the parties announced an agreement to field candidates jointly for the June 2009 European Parliament elections and the 2010 balloting for the UK Parliament under the rubric of the **Ulster Conservative and Unionists–New Force.** The alliance finished third with 17.0 percent of the vote in the European Parliament poll, with the UUP incumbent retaining his seat. Prior to the May 2010 balloting for the UK House of Commons the UUP's one incumbent in that body left the party. He won as an independent, while none of the official UUP candidates were successful. In the May 2011 National Assembly elections the UUP held onto 16 of its seats with 13.2 percent of first-preference votes.

Leaders: Mike NESBITT (Party Leader), Lord EMPEY (Chair).

Social Democratic and Labour Party—SDLP (*Páirtí Sóisialta Daonlathach an Lucht Oibre*). Founded in 1970 and a member of the Socialist International, the SDLP is a largely Catholic, left-of-center party that has championed the reunification of Ireland by popular consent, with Catholics being accorded full political and social rights in the interim. Its longtime leader, Gerard FITT, participated in the post-Sunningdale Faulkner government and subsequently became the only non-unionist to hold a seat in the UK House of Commons. Fitt resigned as party leader in November 1979 after the SDLP constituency representatives and executive had rejected the government's working paper for the 1980 constitutional conference on devolution. The SDLP won 14 assembly seats in 1982 but joined *Sinn Féin* in boycotting sessions. It won 3 UK House of Commons seats in 1987 on a platform that attacked the Thatcher government on employment, housing, education, and agricultural policies.

In addition to supporting the 1985 Anglo-Irish Agreement and resultant UK-Irish cooperation on Northern Ireland, the party became an enthusiastic participant in the 1991 Brooke initiative and its successor talks. Seeking a framework for peace, in April and May 1993 SDLP leader John Hume undertook an unprecedented series of meetings with

Sinn Féin leader Gerry Adams and subsequently helped negotiate the 1994 IRA cease-fire.

The SDLP had mixed results at the polls during the 1990s, picking up 1 seat in the 1992 UK general election but returning just 3 MPs in 1997. A year earlier it had won a somewhat disappointing 21 seats in balloting for the Northern Ireland Forum. A strong supporter of the 1998 Good Friday Agreement, the party carried 24 seats, second to the UUP, in the subsequent election for the Northern Ireland Assembly. The party's deputy leader, Seamus Mallon, was elected deputy first minister of the Executive Committee, the position having been turned down by the overtaxed Hume, who served in the European Parliament as well as the UK House of Commons.

Hume received the 1998 Nobel Peace Prize, not only for his contribution to the Good Friday Agreement, but also for having been, over several decades, "the clearest and most consistent of Northern Ireland's political leaders" in the search for peace. In August 2000 Hume announced that he intended to resign his assembly seat but would retain his other positions. On September 17, 2001, however, he indicated that he would step down as party leader, and a day later Mallon made a similar announcement. At a November party conference Mark Durkan was named to replace Hume. Hume retired from public life in February 2004.

In balloting for the European Parliament in June 2004, the SDLP failed to win any of Northern Ireland's 3 seats. At the May 2005 balloting for the UK House of Commons, the SDLP retained its 3 seats with 17.5 percent of the votes in Northern Ireland. The party finished fourth in the March 7, 2007, elections for the Northern Ireland Assembly, securing 16 seats on a 15.2 percent share of first-preference votes. It also came in fourth (only 1 percent behind the UUP/Conservative alliance that won the third and final seat) in the June 2009 balloting for the European Parliament. Mark DURKAN stood down as party chair in September 2009, and Margaret Ritchie was elected as the first female leader of a major Northern Ireland party. The party retained its 3 seats in the May 2010 UK parliamentary election. In the May 2011 National Assembly elections the SDLP lost 2 of its previously held seats for a new total of 14, winning 14.5 percent of first-preference votes.

Leaders: Alasdair McDONNELL (Party Leader), Dolores KELLY (Deputy Leader).

Alliance Party of Northern Ireland (APNI). A nonsectarian and nondoctrinaire group founded in 1970 in reaction to growing civil strife, the Alliance Party, like the SDLP, participated in the post-Sunningdale Faulkner government. It won ten assembly seats in 1982 and was the only non-unionist party to participate in that body's subsequent proceedings. For lack of alternative proposals, the party in 1987 announced continued support of the 1985 Anglo-Irish Agreement, although it called for the additional enactment of a bill of rights for Northern Ireland. It has achieved occasional success in local elections but has never won a seat in the UK House of Commons.

The Alliance was one of the four Ulster parties represented at talks between unionists and republicans in Duisburg, West Germany, in October 1988. Alliance officials attended the opening of the interparty Ulster talks on April 30, 1991, and, although sympathetic to the unionist position, indicated that they would support the SDLP.

Party leader Dr. John ALDERDICE was nominated to the House of Lords in 1996, giving the Alliance representation in the UK Parliament for the first time. It backed the Good Friday Agreement of 1998 but won only six seats at the subsequent assembly election, a performance that led Lord Alderdice to resign the party leadership. UK Secretary of State for Northern Ireland Mo Mowlam immediately named him as initial presiding officer of the assembly.

Party Leader Sean NEESON announced on September 6, 2001, his decision to step down in favor of "a fresh face," with David Ford then being elected in October as his successor. A month later, in a maneuver designed to secure David Trimble's reelection as first minister and thereby avert a collapse of the power-sharing government, Ford and two other Alliance assembly members temporarily redesignated themselves as unionists. As a result, Trimble was able to secure a bare majority of unionist votes, permitting his return to office.

The party retained its existing six seats at the 2003 assembly election. Although it improved to seven seats in 2007, that level of representation was not sufficient for it to be accorded any portfolios in the original formation of the multiparty cabinet (determined by a formula that does not guarantee posts to smaller parties). The party's nonsectarian standing proved instrumental later, however, as Ford was the cross-community consensus candidate to head the newly created Department of Justice in April 2010. One month later, the party won its first-ever seat in the UK House of Commons when its candidate defeated DUP leader Peter Robinson. In the May 2011 National Assembly elections the party increased its seat share to seven, with 7.7 percent of first-preference votes, and Ford was reconfirmed as the head of the Department of Justice.

APNI voted to remove the Union flag from Belfast city hall in December 2012, prompting death threats and attacks on party leaders' homes.

Leaders: David FORD (Party Leader), Naomi LONG (Deputy Leader), Billy WEBB (President), Andrew MUIR (Chair), Kellie ARMSTRONG (Vice Chair), Gerry LYNCH (Executive Director).

Other Parties Winning Seats in the 2011 Assembly Elections:

Green Party in Northern Ireland (GPNI). A left-leaning branch of the Irish Green Party, the GPNI emphasizes environmental concerns and an integrationist perspective on the governance of Northern Ireland. In the 1998 assembly balloting the party placed last in first-preference votes, and in the 2003 assembly balloting its first-preference support was only 0.4 percent of the total votes. After the party won only three local council positions in 2005, a party conference on December 4, 2006, chose to replace its constitution by taking on the status of a regional grouping with direct association with the Irish Green Party and enhanced ties to green parties in Scotland, England, and Wales. The GPNI won one seat in the May 2011 National Assembly elections, with 0.9 percent of first-preference votes.

Leader: Steven AGNEW (Party Leader).

Traditional Unionist Voice (TUV). The TUV was established in October 2007 by James (Jim) Allister, who had been elected to the European Parliament on the DUP ticket in 2004. Allister had resigned from the DUP in March 2007 in disagreement over the DUP's willingness to accept the requirement that *Sinn Féin* be included in a power-sharing arrangement. The TUV holds essentially the same positions as the DUP with regard to strong bonds with the UK and traditional family values. However, the TUV more stridently opposed putting police powers under the control of the Northern Ireland Assembly. It also completely rejects any form of devolution arrangement that requires a unionist and republican coalition. (The TUV does not formally oppose the possible formation of such a coalition but argues that it should not be mandated.)

Allister lost his seat in the European Parliament in the June 2009 balloting, as the TUV finished fifth with 13.5 percent of the vote and thereby did not qualify for any seats. However, the party appeared ready to continue to press its policy principles, having attracted many disaffected UUP voters. Allister subsequently stated his intention to contest the new UK House of Commons elections (2010) and Northern Ireland Assembly balloting (2011) as a candidate in the unionist stronghold of North Antrim, Ian Paisley's constituency. He was unsuccessful in the former, finishing a distant second (with 17 percent of the vote) to Ian Paisley Jr. (46 percent), but successful in the latter, winning the North Antrim seat with 10 percent of first-preference votes.

Leaders: James (Jim) ALLISTER (Leader), William ROSS (President), Ivor McCONNELL (Chair).

Other Parties Contesting the 2011 Assembly Elections:

Progressive Unionist Party (PUP). The PUP emerged out of the loyalist paramilitaries, in this case the Ulster Volunteer Force (UVF). The PUP's former leader, David ERVINE, served in the UVF and was imprisoned for five years for possession of explosives. The party is distinctive in that, while it is part of the unionist camp, it also champions working-class causes without regard to sect, and the party leader speaks openly of parallels in policy to British Labour. With a definition of unionism based more on the idea of citizenship than on religion, the party has appeared the most flexible in the unionist camp. It signed the 1998 Good Friday Agreement and won two seats in the June Northern Ireland Assembly election, one of which was lost in 2003.

In the wake of the renunciation of violence by the IRA in 2005, Ervine came under increasing pressure to facilitate similar action on the part of the UVF (see below). Meanwhile, in May 2006 Ervine formed a controversial alliance with the UUP in the assembly in an attempt to secure an executive position for unionist forces. However, the assembly speaker ruled that the maneuver violated assembly rules.

Ervine died unexpectedly in early January 2007. He was succeeded as party leader by Dawn PURVIS, who also was chosen to defend (successfully) Ervine's assembly seat in the March 2007 balloting for the Northern Ireland Assembly. Purvis resigned in June 2010 after the UVF was linked to a murder, despite its previous commitments to decommission its weapons. She said she could not lead a party that maintained relations with the UVF. Brian Ervine, brother of the late David Ervien, took over as party leader until the October 2011 party conference elected Billy Hutchinson.

Leader: Billy HUTCHINSON (Party Leader).

Six other registered parties fielded candidates in the 2011 assembly elections without success: **UK Independence**, led by Nigel FARAGE; the **Workers' Party**, led by Michael FINNEGAN; the **People Before Profit Alliance**; the **Socialist Party**; **Procapitalism,** led by Charles SMYTH; and the **British National Party**, led by Nick Griffin.

Other Parties and Groups:

Northern Ireland Conservatives (NI Conservatives). This grouping is the Northern Ireland branch of the UK Conservative Party. Its branch affiliation previously was with the UUP, which sat with the Conservatives in Westminster until disagreement over the 1973 Sunningdale Agreement split the UUP and severed the UUP's bond with the UK Conservatives. The Conservatives NI fielded candidates in the 1998, 2003, and 2007 Northern Ireland Assembly elections, its best showing being in 2007, when it won 0.5 percent of the first-preference votes. In July 2008 UK Conservative Party Leader David Cameron announced exploratory talks that could lead to recementing relations with the UUP. Among other things, Cameron promised to include a UUP MP in a ministerial post in a future Conservative government in Westminster. The Conservatives NI formed an electoral alliance with the UUP later in the year. On June 14, 2012, the party relaunched as NI Conservatives a "fresh, pro-Union, center-right party, which is proudly and distinctly Northern Irish." In its new form, the party is fully part of the UK Conservative Party but responsible on devolved issues.

Leader: Irwin ARMSTRONG (Chair).

United Unionist Assembly Party (UUAP). The UUAP, now formally registered as the United Unionist Alliance, was established with effect from September 21, 1998, by three unionists who had been elected to the Northern Ireland Assembly as independents. In April 2000 one of the three, Denis Watson, a leader of the Orange Order who had been expelled from the UUP for opposing the Good Friday Agreement, was reported to have joined the DUP. However, he remains listed as the UUP leader in the official party registry. The UUAP currently has two members serving as local councilors.

Leader: Denis WATSON (Leader).

Northern Ireland Women's Coalition (NIWC). The NIWC emerged in time for the forum elections of May 1996, although it won only about 1 percent of the vote. The movement was strongly nonpartisan, with candidates from a range of political persuasions, and nonsectarian. It signed the 1998 Good Friday Agreement and won two assembly seats in 1998 and none in 2003. The NIWC formally disbanded in May 2006. Its cofounder and former leader, Monica McWILLIAMS, is the current chief commissioner of the Northern Ireland Human Rights Commission.

32 County Sovereignty Movement (32 CMA). This *Sinn Féin* splinter was formed in September 1997 as the 32 County Sovereignty Committee by ardent nationalists opposed to Gerry Adams's decision to support the Mitchell principles and join the multiparty negotiations in Stormont. One of its organizers, Bernadette SANDS-McKEVITT, is the sister of Bobby Sands, a leader of the Maze prison hunger strikes who died in 1981. The Movement is believed to be affiliated with the paramilitary Real IRA (below), which claimed responsibility for the August 1998 Omagh bombing. In June 2000 the Movement condemned the IRA's decision to permit international inspections of its arms stockpiles as "the first stop in a decommissioning surrender process." The U.S. State Department, describing the 32 CMA as an "alias" for the Real IRA, has designated the 32 CMA as a terrorist organization.

Numerous parties based in the Republic of Ireland also have branches in Northern Ireland. (See the entry on Ireland for information on those parties.)

For information on the following de-registered parties—the **United Kingdom Unionist Party** (UKUP), the **Northern Ireland Unionist Party** (NIUP), and the **Ulster Democratic Party** (UDP)—please see the 2013 *Handbook*.

Former and Current Republican Paramilitary Groups:

Irish Republican Army (IRA). In the late 1960s arguments escalated between the dominant socialist faction in the Republican Clubs, as the (illegal) Northern Ireland section of *Sinn Féin* was then known, and traditional nationalist elements wanting to organize an armed defense of Catholic areas under attack from police and Protestant gangs. The dispute led to the creation in 1969 of a breakaway "Provisional" Army Council that set about rebuilding the IRA, which had withered away since its last terrorist campaign in 1956–1962. The "Provisional" IRA, supported by the "Provisional" *Sinn Féin,* quickly became a large and effective guerrilla organization, defining its aims as British withdrawal from Northern Ireland and the reunification of Ireland as a socialist republic. (Although in frequent use into the 1990s, the term "Provisional" had become redundant in the early 1980s, when the "Official" rump of the *Sinn Féin* became the Workers' Party—see the discussion of *Sinn Féin* in the Republic of Ireland entry.)

Especially active in 1971–1976, when it carried out more than 5,000 bombings, a similar number of armed robberies, and more than 15,000 shootings, resulting in many hundreds of security-force and civilian deaths, the IRA was banned under the 1978 Emergency Provisions Act. It continued its activities in Northern Ireland, Britain, and sometimes continental Europe almost without interruption until 1994.

On August 31, 1994, following secret contacts with the British government, the IRA instituted a cease-fire with the aim of making it possible for *Sinn Féin,* which after 1981 had developed a strong electoral following, to take part in negotiations with the British and Irish governments and with regional parties. With *Sinn Féin* remaining marginalized by demands from most parties and the government that the IRA surrender its weapons, the IRA resumed its military activities in February 1996 by exploding a massive bomb in the financial district of London.

The cease-fire was renewed on July 19, 1997, which opened the way for *Sinn Féin* to join the peace negotiations in Stormont two months later. The IRA gave qualified support to the Good Friday Agreement of April 1998 but at the time refused to link decommissioning of its arms to formation of a devolved government for Northern Ireland, as demanded by the plurality UUP. In December 1998 senior IRA leaders elected a seven-member Army Council headed by hard-liner Brian KEENAN, reinforcing the possibility that the cease-fire might be rescinded were *Sinn Féin* to be excluded from the Northern Ireland Executive.

The IRA's continuing refusal to begin disarming before the inauguration of the power-sharing executive delayed devolution until December 2, 1999, shortly after the IRA had indicated that it was willing to discuss disarmament with Gen. John de Chastelain of the IICD. Nevertheless, no tangible progress was made in the following two months. On February 11, 2000, the IRA offered, in the words of a report from de Chastelain, "to consider how to put arms and explosives beyond use," but the proposal was too late to prevent London's reimposition of direct rule. On May 6, however, the IRA announced that it would accept international monitoring of its arsenals and would "completely and verifiably" put its weapons beyond use. The breakthrough and a subsequent positive UUP response led London, on May 30, to return authority to the Northern Ireland Assembly and Executive. On June 25 the IRA stated that it had reopened discussions with de Chastelain's IICD, and on June 26 arms inspectors reported that they had completed their first visits to IRA caches. Another inspection occurred in May 2001, although the IRA still refused to consider a firm timetable for decommissioning. In early August the IICD announced an agreement on how decommissioning might proceed, but a week later the IRA rescinded its approval because of the August 11 suspension of the power-sharing government. In mid-September it agreed once again to move forward on discussions with the IICD, and on October 23 the IRA announced its first confirmed decommissioning of weapons. An additional, larger decommissioning occurred in April 2002, and on July 16 the IRA issued its first public apology to the families of its innocent victims.

In October 2002 the discovery of alleged IRA spying in official offices in Stormont led to demands from UK Prime Minister Blair, among others, that the IRA reject violence and fully commit itself to peace. The reimposition of direct rule from London on October 15 led the IRA, two weeks later, to discontinue talks with the IICD.

The IRA's alleged involvement in the December 2004 robbery of Belfast's Northern Bank yielded a breakdown in what had appeared to be a promising outcome for the lengthy peace talks. However, momentum returned in mid-2005 when the IRA, following the encouragement of *Sinn Féin* leader Gerry Adams, renounced the use of violence and vowed to disarm. There have been few reports of IRA activity recently in the wake of cross-community political progress (see Recent developments, above). The Independent Monitoring Commission (IMC), a group organized by the UK and Irish governments to evaluate paramilitary activities, reported in September 2008 that the IRA leadership and terrorist structure were no longer operational and thus no longer posed a security threat.

Irish National Liberation Army (INLA). Formed in 1975 by dissident members of the "Official" IRA after that group had adopted a policy of nonviolence, the INLA was banned in 1979 after assassinating a close associate of Margaret Thatcher. A number of INLA members joined the Maze hunger strikes of 1980–1981. Other members of the INLA and its political front, the **Irish Republican Socialist Party** (see Ireland: Political Parties), were killed in internal feuds, in disputes with the IRA, or in attacks allegedly related to the involvement in the drug trade of the INLA itself and a splinter group, the **Irish People's Liberation Organization** (IPLO). The INLA declared a cease-fire on August 22, 1998, in the wake of the Omagh bombing, and reaffirmed it in early August 1999. In March 2000 the INLA stated that it had delivered to the principal loyalist paramilitary groups, the UDA and UVF, a paper on maintaining the cease-fire even in the face of political impasse. The INLA announced in 2010 that it had decommissioned its weapons.

Continuity IRA (CIRA). Adamantly opposed to the peace process, including the IRA cease-fire announced in 1994, the CIRA (also referenced as the Continuity Army Council—CAC) in 1996 claimed responsibility for a number of attacks in Northern Ireland. Some reports characterized the CIRA as an armed wing of the Republican *Sinn Féin* (RSF) party (see Ireland: Political Parties), although the RSF denied any such linkage. Although itself responsible for bombings and killings, the CIRA condemned the August 1998 Omagh bombing as an unjustified "slaughter of the innocents." Believed to number at that time only about 30, the group may have attracted additional members following the cease-fire declared by the Real IRA (below) in September 1998. The CIRA remained the only republican group not to have declared a cease-fire, and in the first seven months of 2000 it claimed responsibility for a number of bombings in Northern Ireland and England. Some antiterrorism agencies suspected, however, that other groups, particularly the Real IRA, may have been using the CIRA as a cover name. In March 2009 the CIRA, declared a terrorist organization by the United States, claimed responsibility for the murder of a Catholic PSNI officer.

Real IRA. Apparently organized in October 1997 in opposition to the renewed IRA cease-fire and *Sinn Féin*'s participation in the Stormont peace talks, the Real IRA probably numbered no more than 100–150 members. It was believed in some quarters to be serving as the military wing of the 32 County Sovereignty Movement, whose leaders have denied any connection.

In June 1998 reports surfaced that the Real IRA, the Continuity IRA, and the INLA had held a summit in Dundalk, Ireland, and may have agreed to unify their forces. Following the August Omagh bombing, however, the Continuity IRA and the INLA distanced themselves from the attack, for which the Real IRA claimed responsibility. On August 18, three days after the car bombing, the Real IRA announced a "complete cessation of all military activity." On September 8, reportedly after its leaders received personal visits from the IRA, it declared a "permanent" cease-fire, although it was implicated in subsequent bombings, including a number in England. In May 2000 it warned that it was preparing a renewed bombing campaign. Two months later the Real IRA was implicated in a failed effort to smuggle a shipment of explosives and weapons from Croatia, and in September it was branded as the probable perpetrator of two attacks on security bases in the North. In March 2001 authorities implicated the Real IRA in a car-bomb explosion outside the West London offices of the British Broadcasting Corporation (BBC). Other bombings in May and August were also attributed to the Real IRA. In May 2002 three Real IRA members pleaded guilty to conspiracy and other charges and received 30-year sentences.

Michael McKevitt, the leader of the Real IRA, was convicted in 2003 of the charge of heading a terrorist organization; he was sentenced to a 20-year prison term. (The verdict was handed down by a nonjury Special Criminal Court authorized to adjudicate terrorism cases following the 1998 Omagh bombing.) In March 2009 the Real IRA claimed responsibility for the murder of two UK soldiers, apparently in the hope of forestalling the policing and justice negotiations (see Recent developments, above). The group also claimed responsibility for the detonation of a bomb at British security headquarters in Northern Ireland within 30 minutes of the opening of the new Department of Justice.

Leader: Michael McKEVITT (in prison).

Former and Current Loyalist Paramilitary Groups:

Ulster Defense Association (UDA). Formed in 1971 by the amalgamation of loyalist paramilitary groups, mainly in greater Belfast and Londonderry, the UDA was initially a mass-membership organization involved in street protests and rallies, including the political strike and accompanying intimidation that brought down the power-sharing administration in 1974. It became increasingly involved in sectarian violence, using such cover names as **Ulster Freedom Fighters** (UFF) and "Ulster Young Militants" to claim responsibility for several hundred killings, the vast majority being noncombatant Catholics. From the mid-1970s the UDA also became deeply enmeshed in racketeering in Northern Ireland, while in the late 1980s it obtained significant material support from the apartheid regime in South Africa.

The UFF was banned in 1973, but the UDA remained legal until 1992, when it was proscribed after a British Army intelligence agent operating in the UDA high command was convicted of conspiracy to murder. The case highlighted allegations that the loyalist paramilitaries had benefited extensively from collusion with members of the police, the army, and the intelligence services. In the interim, the UDA had established a political front, the **Ulster Democratic Party** (UDP), which remained legal.

In 1991 the UDA/UFF joined the Ulster Volunteer Force and the Red Hand Commando (below) in forming a Combined Loyalist Military Command (CLMC) to coordinate paramilitary activities. The CLMC declared a brief cease-fire in 1991 and then an indefinite cease-fire (subsequently violated) in October 1994, four months after the IRA had done so. In October 1997 conflict within the CLMC broke into the open, and the UDA announced its withdrawal, leading to reports that the joint command had disbanded. Within days sporadic intraloyalist violence was reported, without, however, threatening the cease-fire.

Cease-fire violations attributed to the UFF led to suspension of the UDP from the Stormont peace talks in January–March 1998, but on April 25 the UDA announced its support for the Good Friday Agreement. It may now number only several hundred members, although it claimed the support of as many as 40,000 at its peak in the 1970s. In September 1999 UFF leader Johnny Adair was released from prison in accordance with the peace agreement, having served 4 years of his 16-year term for terrorism.

On June 20, 2000, members of the UFF threatened to break its cease-fire, "reserving the right" to defend Protestant homes in the context of "ethnic cleansing" and "intimidation" perpetrated by nationalists. Three days later, however, it retracted its warning. Two months later, Adair's early release was suspended in the context of violent clashes between the UFF/UDA and the UVF/PUP in Belfast. Altercations continued for several more months. On December 15 the UDA, the UVF, and the Red Hand Commando agreed to a truce.

On October 12, 2001, responding to a renewed wave of violence and rioting, Secretary of State for Northern Ireland John Reid declared an end to the government's cease-fire with the UDA/UFF. Adair, having completed his sentence, was released from prison on May 15, 2002.

The UDA formally renounced violence and disbanded its armed units in November 2007 and in 2009 announced the decommissioning of its weapons.

Ulster Volunteer Force (UVF). The UVF was founded in 1966 and was quickly banned after allegedly killing two Catholics. It was restored to legal status in 1974 to encourage it to become involved in politics through the Volunteer Political Party (later reconstituted as the Progressive Unionist Party—PUP, above). Banned again after several murders in October 1975, the UVF conducted a protracted campaign of sectarian assassinations designed to put pressure on the IRA to halt its activities, the most active UVF units being based in Belfast, Armagh, and Tyrone.

In general, the UVF held to the CLMC cease-fire of 1994, despite differences with the UDA that reportedly led to the UVF's expulsion from Londonderry in November 1997. A splinter group, the Loyalist Volunteer Force (below), left the UVF in 1996, and infighting between the two persisted. In January 2000 a UVF commander, Richard JAMESON, was assassinated, with suspicion immediately falling on the LVF. The parent group may now number a few hundred members, compared to 1,500 in the 1970s.

In July and August 2000 a renewed feud with the UFF for control of loyalist territory (and possibly drug trafficking) in Belfast resulted in the redeployment of UK troops in the capital. In December 2000 the UVF joined the UDA and the Red Hand Commando in a truce.

The UK government charged that the UVF was significantly involved with "loyalist riots" that broke out in Belfast in September 2005, and the UVF was also blamed for several murders in connection with its ongoing feud with the LVF. Consequently, the UK signaled that it no longer considered the UVF to be honoring the cease-fire. In mid-2006 the UVF was pressured to disband (as the LVF had), but it refused to "clarify" its stance. Although the UVF announced in 2009 that it would decommission its arms, the Independent Monitoring Commission linked the group to the shooting of a loyalist in June 2010.

Red Hand Commando (RHC). Formed in 1972 and proscribed since 1973, the small RHC was frequently linked to the UVF, with some reports describing it as nothing more than a cover name for the larger group. The RHC agreed to the December 2000 truce between the UVF and the UDA. In 2009 the RHC joined the UVF and UDA in agreeing to the decommissioning of their weapons.

Loyalist Volunteer Force (LVF). Apparently dating from about 1994, the LVF formed within the UVF around the leadership of Billy Wright, who opposed the 1994 cease-fire and any concessions to nationalists. The LVF withdrew from the UVF in 1996 and was banned a year later. On December 27, 1997, Wright was murdered in Maze prison by INLA inmates, after which the LVF was implicated in a number of apparently retaliatory sectarian killings. (Collaterally, unconfirmed reports suggested that the group was permitting UFF paramilitaries to use the LVF name as a cover.)

The LVF declared a unilateral cease-fire on May 15, 1998, but also urged a "no" vote at the May 22 referendum on the Good Friday Agreement. Three months later it called for an "absolute, utter" end to terrorism and made its cease-fire permanent, thereby qualifying its incarcerated members for early release under the peace accord. On December 18, 1998, the LVF became the first paramilitary organization to decommission some of its weapons, a gesture that the IRA labeled a "stunt."

In November 2005 it was reported that the LVF had disbanded after directing its members to discontinue all operations. The decision was described as a "direct response" to the IRA's recent decision to decommission its arms.

Orange Volunteers (OV). Reviving the name of a major loyalist paramilitary group of the 1970s, the Orange Volunteers emerged in 1998 in opposition to the Good Friday Agreement and the cease-fires declared by other loyalist organizations. It subsequently conducted a small number of sectarian attacks. Its membership, apparently numbering no more than a few dozen individuals disaffected from the UDA/UFF and the LVF, may have overlapped that of the Red Hand Defenders (below). In 2000 both groups were added to the U.S. government's annual list of organizations suspected of terrorism.

Red Hand Defenders (RHD). Like the OV, the RHD was formed in 1998 by loyalist rejectionists. In March 1999 it claimed responsibility for the car bombing that killed prominent lawyer Rosemary Nelson. Two days later, Frankie CURRY, a reputed RHD member, was killed in what some officials characterized as an ongoing conflict between loyalist groups engaged in organized crime. The RHD blamed the UVF for Curry's death but denied that he was a member. In January 2002, following the shooting of a postal worker, the RHD indicated that it was disbanding at the request of the UFF, but another shooting in April was attributed to the group. Some analysts argued that the RHD was a cover name for the UDA/UFF.

LEGISLATURE

The former bicameral Northern Ireland Parliament was replaced by a unicameral Northern Ireland Assembly under the Northern Ireland Constitution Act of July 1973. The assembly and a Northern Ireland Executive functioned in 1973–1974, while a 1982 act of Parliament led to the election of another assembly, initially with consultative powers, in November 1982. With its tasks unfulfilled, the assembly was dissolved in June 1986, although subject to legislative provision that it could be reactivated. On May 30, 1996, provincial elections were held for a 110-member Northern Ireland Forum for Political Dialogue, a nonlegislative body designed to provide a platform for discussion and to assist in choosing delegates to the coming peace talks.

A 108-member body, initially termed the New Northern Ireland Assembly, was elected for a five-year term on June 25, 1998, but was suspended upon the reintroduction of direct rule on October 15, 2002. New assembly balloting was conducted on November 25, 2003, although the body remained under suspension.

The assembly convened "without power" on May 15, 2006, for the first time in three-and-a-half years as part of the revived effort to resolve the governmental impasse, and assembly committees continued to meet throughout the summer. The St. Andrews Agreement of November 2006 provided for the return of self-rule to Northern Ireland, and balloting was held for a **Northern Ireland Assembly** on March 7, 2007. The most recent balloting occurred on May 5, 2011, resulting in the following distribution of seats: the DUP, 38; *Sinn Féin,* 29; the UUP, 16; the SDLP, 14; the Alliance Party of Northern Ireland, 8; the Green Party in Northern Ireland, 1; the TUV, 1; and independents, 1. (The 108 members of the assembly [6 from each of 18 constituencies] are elected via universal suffrage under a single-transferable vote system for five-year terms, subject to dissolution.)

Speaker: William HAY.

CABINET

[as of October 21, 2013]

First Minister	Peter Robinson (DUP)
Deputy First Minister	Martin McGuinness (SF)
Ministers	
Agriculture and Rural Development	Michelle O'Neill (SF) [f]
Culture, Arts, and Leisure	Carál Ní Chulín (SF) [f]
Education	John O'Dowd (SF)
Employment and Learning	Stephen Farry (APNI)
Enterprise, Trade, and Investment	Arlene Foster (DUP) [f]
Environment	Mark H. Durkan (SDLP)
Finance and Personnel	Sammy Wilson (DUP)
Health, Social Services, and Public Safety	Edwin Poots (DUP)
Justice	David Ford (APNI)
Regional Development	Danny Kennedy (UUP)
Social Development	Nelson McCausland (DUP)

[f] = female

UNITED STATES

United States of America

Political Status: Independence declared on July 4, 1776; federal republic established under constitution adopted on March 4, 1789.

Area: 3,732,396 sq. mi. (9,666,532 sq. km); includes gross area (land and water) of the 50 states, excluding Puerto Rico and other territories. These totals are somewhat higher than earlier ones because of a 1990 change in the method of calculating interior waters.

Population: 327,859,492 (2012E—UN); 316,668,567 (2013E—U.S. Census). Does not include the U.S. Territories.

Major Urban Centers:

City Proper	*Population* (2012E)	*Metro Area* (2012E)
Washington, D.C.	632,323	5,860,342
New York, N.Y.	8,336,697	19,831,838
Los Angeles, Calif.	3,857,799	13,052,921
Chicago, Ill.	2,714,856	9,522,434
Houston, Texas	2,160,821	6,177,035
Philadelphia, Pa.	1,547,607	6,018,800
Phoenix, Ariz.	1,488,750	4,329,534
San Antonio, Texas	1,382,951	2,234,003
San Diego, Calif.	1,338,348	3,117,063
Dallas, Texas	1,241,162	6,700,991
San Jose, Calif.	982,765	1,894,388
Austin, Texas	842,592	1,834,303
Jacksonville, Fla.	836,507	1,377,850
Indianapolis, Ind.	834,852	1,928,982
San Francisco, Calif.	825,863	4,455,560
Columbus, Ohio	809,798	1,944,002
Fort Worth, Texas	777,992	2,274,380
Charlotte, N.C.	775,202	2,296,569
Detroit, Mich.	701,475	4,292,060
El Paso, Texas	672,538	830,735
Memphis, Tenn.	655,155	1,341,690
Boston, Mass.	636,479	4,640,802
Seattle, Wash.	603,535	3,552,157
Denver, Colo.	634,256	2,645,209
Nashville, Tenn.	624,496	1,726,693
Baltimore, Md.	621,342	2,753,149

Principal Language: English. In the 2010 census approximately 80.1 percent spoke only English; 12.2 percent Spanish; 7.7 percent other.

Monetary Unit: Dollar (selected market rates November 1, 2013: $1US = 2.26 Brazilian real, 6.10 Chinese yuan renmimbi, 0.74 euro, 62.33 Indian rupee, Japanese yen, 13.08 Mexican peso, 10.17 South African rand, 0.63 UK pound, 98.77).

President: Barack H. OBAMA (Democratic Party); elected on November 4, 2008 (technically, by the electoral college on December 15), and inaugurated on January 20, 2009, for a four-year term, succeeding George W. BUSH (Republican Party); reelected on November 6, 2012.

Vice President: Joseph R. BIDEN Jr. (Democratic Party); elected on November 4, 2008, and inaugurated on January 20, 2009, for a term concurrent with that of the president, succeeding Richard B. CHENEY (Republican Party); reelected on November 6, 2012.

THE COUNTRY

First among the nations of the world in economic output, the United States ranks third in area (behind Russia and Canada) and also third in population (after China and India). Canada and Mexico are the country's only contiguous neighbors. Most of U.S. territory ranges across the North American continent in a broad band that encompasses the Atlantic seaboard; the Appalachian Mountains; the Ohio, Mississippi, and Missouri river valleys; the Great Plains; the Rocky Mountains; the deserts of the Southwest; and the narrow, fertile coastland adjoining the Pacific. Further contrasts are found in the two noncontiguous states: Alaska, in northwestern North America, where the climate ranges from severe winters and short growing seasons in the north to equable temperatures in the south; and Hawaii, in the mid-Pacific, where trade winds produce a narrow temperature range but extreme variations in rainfall.

Regional diversity is also found in economic conditions. Industrial production is located mainly in the coastal areas and in those interior urban centers with good transportation connections, as in the Great Lakes region. Agricultural products come primarily from the far western, plains, midwestern, and southeastern states. The median household income varies considerably from state to state, with a national median of $50,054 in 2012, a 1.5 percent decline from the previous year.

The nation's ethnic diversity is a product of large-scale voluntary and involuntary immigration, much of which took place before 1920. According to Census Bureau estimates, the population in 2010 was 72.4 percent white, 12.6 percent black, 4.5 percent Asian and Pacific Islander, and 0.9 percent American Indian and native Alaskan. In addition, Hispanic Americans (a nonexclusive category) constituted 16.3 percent in 2010 (up from 12.5 percent in 2000), thereby becoming the country's largest minority group.

In 2009 83.1 percent of adults identified themselves as religious, of whom Protestants constituted 51.3 percent; Roman Catholics, 23.9 percent; Jews, 1.7 percent; and Orthodox Christians, 0.6 percent. Although English is the principal language, Spanish is the preferred tongue of sizable minorities in New York City (largely migrants from Puerto Rico), in Florida (primarily Caribbean expatriates), and in the Southwest and California (mainly from Mexico and Central America). Other languages are spoken among foreign-born and first-generation Americans.

In 2012 women constituted 53 percent of the labor force and were concentrated in management, professional, sales, and office occupations. Women earned approximately 84 percent of the median male wage. As a result of the November 2012 national election, female representation in the incoming 113th Congress climbed to a record 20 seats in the Senate and 77 seats in the U.S. House of Representatives. Women governors led five states following the 2012 balloting.

Owing to a historic transfer of population from farm to city (now seemingly at an end, with migration to rural areas fluctuating close to a reversal in 1990–2000), only a small proportion of the population is engaged in agriculture, which nevertheless yields a substantial proportion of U.S. exports. As of 2011 agriculture employed 1.2 percent of the population. By contrast, 19.2 percent of the labor force was engaged in mining, manufacturing, and construction and 79.6 percent in service activities. Of increasing importance to the administration of the nation's Social Security system is the aging of the population; the percentage of those age 65 and older rose from approximately 4 percent in 1900 to 13.5 percent in 2011.

The United States has experienced long-term economic growth throughout most of its history, with marked short-term fluctuations in recent years. During 1960–2005 the real per capita rise in GDP averaged 3.7 percent. December 2000 marked the 127th consecutive month of economic expansion, the longest period of peacetime growth in U.S. history. Federal budget surpluses were recorded from 1998 through 2001, but government spending went into deficit thereafter.

GDP expanded by approximately 1.7 percent in 2001. However, due to the Federal Reserve Bank's lowering interest rates and collateral government tax cuts, a fairly rapid recovery followed, with average annual growth of about 3 percent reported for 2002–2005. Growth cooled to an average of 2.1 percent in 2006–2007. A significant decline of 1.9 percent was registered in 2008 following the dramatic downturn in the housing market and the stock market and the collapse of several large financial institutions, in what many observers described as a "great recession" (see Political Background, below). The government responded with varying public and private capital injections that dramatically increased the deficit and national debt.

In 2009 GDP decreased by 3 percent as a result of declines in investments and exports. GDP rose by 2.4 percent in 2010 and 1.8 percent in

2011, according to the IMF. Inflation almost doubled from 1.6 percent in 2010 to 3.1 percent the next year, while unemployment declined from 9.6 percent to 9 percent. Gross government debt rose from 98.6 percent of GDP to 102.9 percent over those two years. In 2013 GDP growth of 1.9 percent was charted, with inflation of 1.8 percent. Unemployment was 7.7 percent—dipping below 8 percent for the first time since the financial crisis.

GOVERNMENT AND POLITICS

Political background. Beginning as a group of 13 British colonies along the Atlantic seaboard, the "United States of America" declared themselves independent on July 4, 1776, gained recognition as a sovereign state at the close of the Revolutionary War in 1783, and in 1787 adopted a federal constitution that became effective on March 4, 1789. George WASHINGTON took office as the first president of the United States on April 30. Westward expansion, colonization, judicious purchase, and annexation during the ensuing 100 years found the nation by 1890 in full possession of the continental territories that now make up the 48 contiguous states. Alaska, purchased from Russia in 1867, and Hawaii, annexed in 1898, became the 49th and 50th states, respectively, in 1959.

The constitutional foundation of the Union has been severely threatened only by the Civil War of 1861–1865, in which the separate confederacy established by 11 southern states was defeated and reintegrated into the Federal Union by military force. The U.S. political climate has been characterized by the alternating rule of the Republican and Democratic parties since the Civil War, which initiated a period of industrial expansion that continued without major interruptions through World War I before being temporarily checked by the Great Depression of the early 1930s.

The modern era of administrative centralization and massive federal efforts to solve economic and social problems began in 1933 with the inauguration of Democratic president Franklin D. ROOSEVELT. The onset of direct U.S. involvement in World War II on December 7, 1941, brought further governmental expansion. Following the defeat of the Axis powers, efforts supporting European reconstruction and attempting to meet the challenge posed by the rise of the Soviet Union as a world power dominated the administration of Harry S. TRUMAN, the Democratic vice president who succeeded Roosevelt upon his death on April 12, 1945, and was elected in 1948 to a full four-year term. Newly armed with atomic weapons, the United States abandoned its traditional isolation to become a founding member of the United Nations (UN) and the leader of a worldwide coalition directed against the efforts of the Soviet Union and, after 1949, the People's Republic of China, to expand their influence along the periphery of the communist world. A series of East-West confrontations over Iran, Greece, and Berlin culminated in the Korean War of 1950–1953, in which U.S. forces were committed to large-scale military action under the flag of the UN.

Dwight D. EISENHOWER, elected president on the Republican tickets of 1952 and 1956, achieved a negotiated settlement in Korea and some relaxation of tensions with the Soviet Union, but efforts to solve such basic East-West problems as the division of Germany proved unavailing. Whereas Eisenhower's attempts to restrict the role of the federal government met only limited success, his eight-year incumbency witnessed a resumption of progress toward legal equality of the races—after a lapse of 80 years—pursuant to the 1954 Supreme Court decision declaring segregation in public schools unconstitutional. An economic recession developed toward the end of Eisenhower's second term, which also saw the beginning of a substantial depletion of U.S. gold reserves. In spite of a resurgent economy, balance-of-payments problems persisted throughout the succeeding Democratic administrations of presidents John F. KENNEDY (1961–1963) and Lyndon B. JOHNSON (1963–1969).

The assassinations of President Kennedy in 1963 and civil rights advocate Martin Luther KING Jr. and Sen. Robert F. KENNEDY in 1968 provided the most dramatic evidence of a deteriorating domestic climate. To counter sharpening racial and social antagonisms and growing violence on the part of disaffected groups and individuals, Congress, at President Johnson's urging, passed laws promoting equal rights in housing, education, and voter registration and establishing programs to further equal job opportunities, urban renewal, and improved education for the disadvantaged. These efforts were in part offset by the negative domestic consequences of U.S. involvement in the Vietnam War, which had begun with limited economic and military aid to the French in the 1950s but by the mid-1960s had become direct and massive. Disagreement over Vietnam was also largely responsible for halting a trend toward improved U.S.-Soviet relations that had followed the Cuban missile crisis of 1962 and had led in 1963 to the signing of a limited nuclear test-ban treaty. Moved by increasing public criticism of the government's Vietnam policy, President Johnson on March 31, 1968, announced the cessation of bombing in most of North Vietnam as a step toward direct negotiations to end the war, and preliminary peace talks with the North Vietnamese began in Paris on May 13.

Richard M. NIXON, vice president during the Eisenhower administration, won the election on November 5, 1968, in a three-way race against Democratic nominee and Vice President Hubert H. HUMPHREY and former Alabama governor George C. WALLACE, a dissident Democrat who ran under the segregationist American Independent Party. Nixon took 43.4 percent of the national popular vote, the lowest of any victorious candidate since 1912, while Humphrey secured 42.7 percent and Wallace, 13.5 percent, the largest total for a third-party candidate since 1924.

As president, Nixon embarked on a vigorous foreign policy campaign while selectively limiting the nation's external commitments in Southeast Asia and elsewhere. Domestically the Nixon administration became increasingly alarmed at the growing antiwar movement and reports of radical extremist activity, and in April 1970 it initiated a program of surveillance of militant left-wing groups and individuals. In May the president's decision to order Vietnamese-based U.S. troops into action in Cambodia provoked an antiwar demonstration at Kent State University, in the course of which the Ohio National Guard killed four students. Final agreement on a peace treaty in Vietnam was not obtained until January 27, 1973 (see Foreign relations, below), by which time the "youth rebellion" that had characterized the late 1960s was in pronounced decline.

Nixon was reelected in a landslide victory over an antiwar Democrat, Senator George S. McGOVERN of South Dakota, on November 7, 1972. Winning a record-breaking 60.7 percent of the popular vote, Nixon swept all major electoral units except Massachusetts and the District of Columbia, although the Democrats easily retained control of both houses of Congress. Within a year, however, the fortunes of Republican executive leaders were quickly reversed. On October 10, 1973, Spiro T. AGNEW resigned as vice president after pleading no contest to having falsified a federal income-tax return. He was succeeded on December 6 by longtime Michigan representative

Gerald R. FORD, the first vice president to be chosen, under the 25th Amendment of the Constitution, by presidential nomination and congressional confirmation. On March 1, 1974, seven former White House and presidential campaign aides were charged with conspiracy in an attempted cover-up of the Watergate scandal (involving a break-in at Democratic National Committee headquarters at their Washington, D.C., building on June 17, 1972), while President Nixon, because of the same scandal, became on August 9 the first U.S. chief executive to tender his resignation. Vice President Ford, who succeeded Nixon on the same day, thus became the first U.S. president never to have participated in a national election.

In the election of November 2, 1976, the Democratic candidate, former Georgia governor Jimmy CARTER, defeated President Ford by a bare majority (50.6 percent) of the popular vote. Ford thus became the first incumbent since 1932 to fail in a bid for a second term. Carter also became a one-term president on November 4, 1980, as his Republican opponent, Ronald REAGAN, swept all but six states and the District of Columbia with a popular vote margin of 10 percent and a near ten-to-one margin in the electoral college. In congressional balloting the Republicans ended the Democrats' 28-year control of the Senate and registered substantial gains in the House of Representatives, the two bodies for the first time since 1916 being controlled by different parties.

The 1980 outcome was hailed as a "mandate for change" unparalleled since the Roosevelt landslide of 1932. Accordingly, President Reagan moved quickly to address the nation's economic problems by a combination of across-the-board fiscal retrenchment and massive tax cuts. Only the military establishment received significant additional funding to redress the perception of a widening gap between U.S. and Soviet tactical and strategic capabilities. Part of the so-billed New Federalism involved sharply curtailed aid to the states, passing to state governments responsibility for social programs that had long been funded directly from Washington, D.C. While most liberals decried the new administration's commitment to economic "realism," the country made significant progress in lowering interest rates and slowing inflation.

Despite the onset of a severe economic recession that the administration sought to counter with a series of "hard-line" fiscal and monetary policies, the midterm elections of November 2, 1982, yielded no significant alteration in the domestic balance of power. The Democrats increased their majority in the House of Representatives by 26 seats to 269–166. However, Republican control of the Senate remained unchanged at 54–46.

On November 6, 1984, President Reagan won reelection by the second-largest electoral college margin (97.6 percent) in U.S. history, nearly equaling the record of 98.5 percent set by President Roosevelt in 1936. His Democratic opponent, Walter F. MONDALE, won only in his home state of Minnesota and in the District of Columbia. The Republicans also retained control of the Senate (53–47), while the Democrats retained control of the House with a reduced majority of 253–182.

Over the 18 months following Reagan's second inauguration on January 21, 1985, the administration followed on campaign promises regarding taxes with sweeping changes that ultimately emerged as the Tax Reform Act of 1986, marked by a reduction in the number of tax brackets and a lowering of the top rate, with families at or below the poverty line freed of any obligation. The package was to be paid for, in part, by the elimination of many deductions and loopholes, with little measurable gain for individuals in the middle-income range. During the same period, while inflation and unemployment remained at moderate levels, the nation recorded massive trade deficits, despite steady erosion in the value of the U.S. dollar, which declined by more than 20 percent in trade-weighted terms from December 1984 to March 1986. As a result the Reagan administration, steadfastly maintaining its commitment to free trade, called for measures to counter what it perceived as a "protectionist upsurge" on the part of many of its trading partners.

In the nonpresidential balloting of November 4, 1986, the Democrats increased their margin in the House to 258–177 while regaining control of the Senate, 55–45. At the state level they suffered a net loss of 8 governorships, retaining a bare majority of 26.

On November 8, 1988, Republican George H. W. BUSH became the first sitting vice president since Martin Van Buren in 1836 to win the presidency, defeating his Democratic opponent Michael S. DUKAKIS by securing 54 percent of the popular vote and 79 percent of the electoral college vote. The Democrats, however, marginally increased their control of the House (260–175), with no change in the composition of the Senate and a net gain of 1 gubernatorial office over the 27 held immediately before the election.

Following the midterm balloting of November 6, 1990, the Democrats held 267 House seats (a net gain of 8 over the preelection distribution) and 56 Senate seats (a net gain of 1), while retaining a total of 28 governorships (a net loss of 1). One House seat in 1990 was won by Bernard SANDERS, an independent Vermont socialist, and the remaining 167 by the Republicans, who retained 44 Senate seats and 20 governorships, with 2 of the state houses being filled by independents. In the presidential poll of November 3, 1992, Arkansas governor William CLINTON denied Bush reelection by winning 43 percent of the popular and 69 percent of the electoral college votes, as contrasted with percentages of 38 percent and 31 percent for the incumbent. Business owner H. Ross PEROT, running as an independent, secured no electoral college support despite capturing 19 percent of the popular vote (the best showing by a third candidate since 1912). In congressional balloting the Democrats retained control of the Senate by an unchanged majority of 57; they also retained control of the House of Representatives by a reduced majority of 259 seats, 175 being won by Republicans and Sanders retaining his seat from Vermont. At the state level the Republicans gained a single governorship from the Democrats, the resultant distribution being 27–21–2. A record number of voters (more than 104 million) cast ballots in 1992, although the 55.9 percent turnout of those eligible fell short of the 60.8 percent reported in 1968.

Five days after Clinton's inauguration on January 20, 1993, the president named his wife, Hillary Rodham CLINTON, to head a task force on health care reform, for which he campaigned vigorously in the months that followed. The president's proposals were challenged as administratively burdensome and far too costly. Other legislative matters included a struggle (ultimately successful on November 30, 1993) to secure passage of the so-called Brady bill, requiring a waiting period for the purchase of a handgun, and a bitterly contested budget and deficit reduction plan that secured final approval on August 6.

By early 1994 the president's agenda was becoming increasingly hostage to the Whitewater scandal, involving a failed property venture in which the Clintons had a substantial interest. At the president's request, a special prosecutor was appointed on January 20, 1994, to investigate the affair, which also became the subject of congressional hearings. To add to the president's troubles, Paula JONES, a former Arkansas state employee, filed a sexual harassment suit against Clinton on May 6. Despite such distractions, the president in late August finally secured congressional approval for his centerpiece crime bill, approving (but not authorizing) expenditure of $30 billion over six years on anticrime measures and banning certain categories of assault weapons.

The midterm election of November 8, 1994, yielded disastrous setbacks for the Democrats, who lost control of the Senate for the first time since 1986 by a margin of 52–48 and, far more unexpectedly, of the House for the first time since 1954 by a margin of 230–204, with Sanders again returning as an independent. Astonishingly, no Republican incumbent at either the gubernatorial or congressional levels was defeated. The day after the November poll, Alabama senator Richard C. SHELBY switched his allegiance from Democrat to Republican. Far more embarrassing to the Democrats was the defection of Colorado senator Ben Nighthorse CAMPBELL, a Native American, on March 3, 1995, leaving the Republicans with an upper house majority of 54.

A chastened President Clinton accepted responsibility for the congressional defeat and called for a "partnership" between the executive and legislative branches of government. The appeal drew a guardedly favorable response from Republican Senate leader Robert J. (Bob) DOLE, while the more flamboyant incoming House speaker, Newt GINGRICH, indicated that cooperation with the president would take second place to implementation of a ten-point "Contract with America," which called for, among other items, a balanced-budget amendment to the Constitution, a presidential line-item veto of budget legislation, welfare reform, and the introduction of congressional term limits. The balanced-budget and term-limits amendments subsequently were defeated, while nine other proposals were approved in the House and pending in the Senate. (On May 27 the Supreme Court ruled that action by the states to impose term limits on federal legislators was unconstitutional.)

In the aftermath of the country's worst domestic bombing attack, the destruction of a federal office complex in Oklahoma City on April 19, Congress approved several administration proposals designed to inhibit and punish terrorist attacks on U.S. property or personnel at home and abroad.

Buffeted by continuing legal problems but buoyed by public opinion polls that showed Clinton leading Republican challenger Dole by as much as 20 points, the president accepted renomination by the Democrats and went on to defeat Dole on November 5, 1996, by a popular vote margin of 49–41 percent, with third-party candidate Perot winning 8 percent. In the electoral college the race was substantially more unbalanced; Clinton secured 379 of the 538 votes, whereas Dole won 159. Despite the president's victory, the Republicans retained control of both houses of Congress by substantial margins (55 of 100 Senate and 227 of 435 House seats). The biennial congressional balloting of November 3, 1998, yielded an unchanged Senate division, but the Democrats scored an upset by gaining 5 seats in the House despite the president's mounting personal difficulties and conventional wisdom regarding midterm elections.

On December 19, 1998, President Clinton became the second U.S. president (after Andrew Johnson in 1868) to be impeached by the House of Representatives. The principal charges against him were perjury in testimony before a grand jury regarding a sexual relationship with a former White House intern, Monica LEWINSKY, and obstruction of justice in seeking false testimony from Lewinsky in the sexual harassment case brought by Paula Jones. On February 12, 1999, Clinton was acquitted, the Senate having failed to register the two-thirds majority needed for conviction on largely party-line votes of 45–55 and 50–50, with 10 Republicans defecting on the first count and 5 on the second.

In the presidential election of November 7, 2000, exit polls that initially gave Florida to the Democratic nominee, Vice President Al GORE, changed to favor Texas governor George W. BUSH (son of the 41st president), and then suggested a race "too close to call." Subsequently, a recount of 45,000 disputed ballots was halted by Florida's secretary of state, resumed by order of the state supreme court, suspended by the U.S. Supreme Court, and then effectively terminated by the Court on December 12. Bush won the Florida contest by only 537 votes of 6 million cast. As a result Bush was declared the victor by an electoral college count of 271–266, although he trailed Gore in the popular count. Meanwhile the Senate was evenly split (50–50) for the first time in 120 years, while the Republican House majority fell to its narrowest since 1954: 221 against 212 for the Democrats, with 2 independents. On June 6, 2001, however, the Democrats assumed control of the Senate following a decision by Republican Sen. James JEFFORDS of Vermont to sit as an independent and vote with Democrats on most matters. This marked the first time in U.S. history that the balance of power in a house of Congress shifted because of a midterm change in party allegiance.

On the morning of September 11, 2001, the United States suffered the most devastating terrorist attack in its history when two hijacked commercial airliners were deliberately flown into the upper floors of the World Trade Center's twin 110-story towers in New York City. The towers collapsed shortly after impact, destroying neighboring buildings as well, killing some 2,800 people. Meanwhile hijackers steered a third airliner into one side of the Pentagon, the headquarters of the U.S. Department of Defense, near Washington, D.C., costing an additional 184 lives. A fourth hijacked flight crashed in rural Pennsylvania, killing the 44 passengers and crew, some of whom, having been alerted by mobile phone to the fate of the other three aircraft, had attempted to overpower the hijackers. In response to the terrorist assaults, the White House ordered all civilian flights in U.S. airspace grounded and temporarily closed the country's borders.

Attention immediately focused on the al-Qaida terrorist network of Osama bin Laden, and within days the government confirmed that all 19 hijackers had connections to al-Qaida. The Bush administration subsequently demanded that the Taliban regime in Afghanistan, which had afforded safe harbor to bin Laden, hand him over and eliminate his terrorist training camps. The Taliban refused. On October 7 aerial forces from the United States and the United Kingdom, supported on the ground by the opposition Northern Alliance, launched a military assault to unseat the Taliban, capture or kill bin Laden, and destroy the al-Qaida bases. The Taliban succumbed in December, and late in the month an interim government was established in Kabul (see the entry on Afghanistan). Military action against pockets of al-Qaida and Taliban resistance continued as the U.S. government contemplated additional steps in what it characterized as a worldwide "war on terrorism."

In late October 2001 the U.S. Congress passed the USA PATRIOT Act, a cornerstone of the Bush administration's domestic response to the terrorism threat. The act expanded the government's authority to wiretap, conduct Internet surveillance, combat money laundering, and detain foreign nationals. Additional legislation strengthened airport security, while an executive order of November 13 authorized secret military tribunals for foreign nationals. By the end of the year 1,200 individuals were being detained in connection with the September 11 events, and the government had begun "voluntary" questioning of 5,000 noncitizens.

The U.S. economy, already in a slump, also suffered significant damage from the September 11 attacks, which the hijackers, most of them Saudi nationals, had aimed at the heart of the U.S. financial and business district. The New York Stock Exchange experienced a massive, but temporary, sell-off upon reopening on September 17, consumer confidence flagged, unemployment rose, and the U.S. airline industry registered losses that threatened bankruptcy as business and tourist travel declined precipitously. The government acted quickly to shore up the airlines, supplement defense appropriations, provide tens of billions of dollars for homeland security and for relief and recovery efforts in New York City, and stimulate the economy. One consequence was a swift end to the brief era of budget surpluses recorded during the final years of the Clinton administration.

In the midterm elections of November 5, 2002, the Republican Party recaptured control of the U.S. Senate by a 51–48 margin (Senator Jeffords remained an independent) and added 6 seats in the House, its majority rising to 229. On November 25 President Bush signed legislation creating a cabinet-level Department of Homeland Security and then named Tom RIDGE, then director of the White House Office of Homeland Security, as its head. Two days later he approved the establishment of an independent ten-member commission to investigate intelligence failures leading up to the attacks of September 11, 2001.

In his State of the Union address on January 29, 2002, President Bush grouped Iraq, Iran, and North Korea in an "axis of evil" intent on developing weapons of mass destruction (WMD) and, in the case of Tehran and Baghdad, supporting international terrorism. In October Congress authorized President Bush to take preemptive military action against Iraq if all other means failed to deter the Saddam Hussein regime from an alleged buildup of WMD. Given the Bush administration's view that Hussein had not adequately complied with UN Security Council Resolution 1441 of November 8, 2002, to begin disarming, U.S. forces launched an attack (code-named Operation Iraqi Freedom) on March 20, 2003. On May 1 Bush announced that combat operations had ended, despite resistance that took on an increasingly complex character in the following three years (see the entry on Iraq).

In the 2004 presidential election, President Bush won a second term with 286 electoral college votes on a popular vote share of 50.7 percent, versus 252 electoral college votes for his Democratic opponent, Sen. John KERRY of Massachusetts. In the congressional poll Republicans secured a majority in both chambers (55–44 in the Senate and 232–202 in the House of Representatives). Following the election, the Republicans held 29 governorships versus the Democrats' 21. Bush subsequently won congressional approval for the creation of an overarching director of the nation's 15 spy agencies, tapping former UN ambassador John D. NEGROPONTE for the post.

In late 2005 a controversy erupted over President Bush's authorization that allowed the National Security Agency (NSA) to conduct eavesdropping on telecommunications between U.S. citizens and foreign nationals. The administration argued that the monitoring was key to prosecuting the war on terror, was within the president's authority as commander in chief, and had been authorized by a congressional resolution to use "all necessary and appropriate force" in response to the September 2001 terror attacks. Critics of the policy, including the Republican chair of the Senate Judiciary Committee, Arlen SPECTER of Pennsylvania, countered that it violated the 1978 Foreign Intelligence Surveillance Act (FISA) and had not been authorized by Congress. (In August 2007, Congress passed the FISA Amendment Act, clarifying the FISA court's oversight responsibility with respect to domestic and foreign eavesdropping.)

Throughout 2006, the war in Iraq continued to dominate the political front. The rapid U.S. military ouster of Saddam Hussein and the dismantling of his Sunni regime had been followed by several years of unremitting sectarian violence, mostly between Shiite and Sunni factions, as well as attacks from diverse sources—remnants of the prior regime, militias loyal to Islamic clerics and tribal leaders, Iraqi nationalists, al-Qaida recruits, and foreign nationals—against U.S. military forces and their newly trained Iraqi counterparts.

In the November 2006 midterm elections, Democrats won control of the House of Representatives by a margin of 31 seats (233–202) and, somewhat unexpectedly, of the Senate, where a 49–49 tie was broken by two pro-Democratic independents. Following the polling, the Democrats also held 28 of 50 governorships, effectively reversing the Republican Party's gains in 2004. At the start of the 110th Congress in January 2007, Democrat Nancy PELOSI of California, a severe critic of the Bush administration, was elected Speaker of the House, becoming the first woman to hold that position.

Economic problems mounted in the second half of 2007, with spiraling energy costs; a record trade deficit; an increase in foreclosures in the housing market, accompanied by a wave of major financial institutions losing unprecedented amounts of money as fallout from a subprime mortgage-lending crisis; and a drop in the value of the dollar to its lowest level in 25 years. The housing market declined further in 2008 as house prices fell dramatically and foreclosures mounted. This trend was exacerbated by a tightening of credit as banks reported huge losses linked to the mortgage-backed securities. Several large investment firms went bankrupt or were taken over, and unemployment reached a five-year high of 5.8 percent for the year. Congress approved a revised version of a Bush administration proposal for a $700 billion emergency bailout to buy up "toxic" mortgage assets and stabilize the economy in response to the most serious crisis since the Great Depression. The Treasury Department announced plans to invest up to $250 billion into nine of the largest U.S. banks, a measure designed to help ease the credit crunch.

Insurgent attacks in Iraq declined significantly in 2007 and 2008 as a result of the U.S. troop "surge," which had been initiated in February 2007. The United States began withdrawing the additional troops in 2008, though many U.S. politicians complained that the Iraqi government had failed to meet many of the benchmarks that had been established.

Beginning in mid-2007, the 2008 presidential campaign dominated the political scene. Early in the contest, Hillary Clinton, the junior senator from New York, and Barack Obama, the junior senator from Illinois, became the Democratic Party front-runners. Obama, 47, claimed victory on June 3, 2008, becoming the first African-American to win the nomination of either major party. Meanwhile, Republican senator John McCain of Arizona, a prisoner of war during the Vietnam War, overcame a wave of Republican opposition to immigration legislation he sponsored in 2007 and emerged from a large field of primary contenders to claim victory as the party's nominee on March 4. McCain surprised political pundits and the public at large with his subsequent selection of Alaska governor Sarah PALIN as his running mate. Palin, a virtual unknown outside of her home state, appeared to energize the Republican Party with her conservative values. McCain's campaign focused on government reforms, national security, and the economy.

Obama named a veteran legislator, Senator Joseph BIDEN of Delaware as his running mate. Obama, campaigning on a broad platform of change, pledged to withdraw all troops from Iraq within 16 months of taking office and to raise taxes on wealthier citizens and reduce taxes for the middle class. Meanwhile, a surge in violence along the Pakistan-Afghanistan border prompted both U.S. presidential candidates to support military efforts to oust Taliban supporters of al-Qaida in the region.

In the general elections on November 4, 2008, Obama was elected president with 365 electoral college votes and 52 percent of the popular vote, defeating McCain, who received 173 electoral votes and 46 percent of the popular vote. Democrats substantially increased their standing in Congress and with a majority in the House and Senate were able to pass a number of legislative victories, including a massive overhaul of the American health care system, a series of economic stimulus bills, and reform of the U.S. financial sector (see Current issues, below).

The 2010 midterm elections on November 2 were a Republican landslide in the U.S. House. Republicans gained 66 seats, bringing the GOP ranks to 242. In the U.S. Senate the GOP took 6 additional seats, bringing its total to 47, thereby slimming the Democratic majority to 3 seats. The election was widely viewed as a referendum on the economy, which had seen few gains in employment, and on health care reform, which Republicans had criticized. The 2010 midterms were the electoral debut of Tea Party candidates in the GOP, whose populist message railed against spending, particularly in areas of social services and economic stimulus, and against health care reform. In a number of high-profile cases Tea Party candidates defeated GOP-endorsed candidates in primary elections. Tea Party candidates went on to win 3 seats in the Senate and as many as 60 GOP seats in the House. Tea Party successes in Congress and in state races increased pressure on Republicans to move farther to the right. Republicans also captured 11 additional governorships, bringing their total to 29, compared with 20 for the Democrats, along with 1 independent. Republican John BOEHNER of Ohio was elected speaker of the House of Representatives on January 5, 2011.

By 2011 the GOP controlled 28 state legislatures, the Democrats, 15, with 6 divided between the two parties (Nebraska's legislature is non-partisan). This gave the Republicans additional power over redistricting political boundaries prior to the 2012 elections.

Mitt ROMNEY captured the Republican presidential nomination for the 2012 election and named Wisconsin House member Paul RYAN, a leading fiscal conservative, as his running mate. Obama, unopposed, was renominated. The national campaign was highly negative as outside interest groups (commonly known as "super PACs," with no limits on their ability to raise and spend funds) combined with the major parties to spend more than $6 billion on national, state, and local polling. The Obama campaign sought to portray the wealthy Romney as an archconservative who favored the rich. The Romney organization was highly critical of the president's management of the economy and major policy initiatives, including health care reform.

On November 6, 2012, Obama was reelected with 50.6 percent of the vote and 332 electoral votes to Romney's 47.8 percent and 206 electoral votes. In concurrent congressional balloting, Democrats gained two seats in the Senate, to bring their total to 55, including two independents who caucus with the party, while Republicans were reduced to 45 seats. The GOP maintained a majority in the House with 233 seats to 201 Democrats. Republicans gained one additional governorship, North Carolina, in the 2012 balloting, bringing their total to 30, compared with 20 held by Democrats.

Constitution and government. The Constitution of the United States, drafted by a Constitutional Convention in Philadelphia in 1787 and declared in effect on March 4, 1789, established a republic in which extensive powers are reserved to the states, currently 50 in number, that compose the Federal Union. The system has three distinctive characteristics. First, powers are divided among three federal branches—legislative, executive, and judicial—and between the federal and state governments, themselves each divided into three branches. Second, the power of each of the four elements of the federal government (the presidency, the Senate, the House of Representatives, and the federal judiciary) is limited by being shared with one or more of the other elements. Third, the different procedures by which the president, senators, and members of the House of Representatives are elected make each responsible to a different constituency.

Federal executive power is vested in a president who serves for a four-year term and, by the 22nd Amendment (ratified in 1951), is limited to two terms of office. The president and vice president are formally designated by the electoral college, composed of electors from each state and the District of Columbia. Selected by popular vote in numbers equal to the total congressional representation to which the various states are entitled, the electors are pledged to vote for their political parties' candidates and customarily do so. Presidents are advised by, and discharge most of their functions through, executive departments headed by officers whom they appoint but who must have Senate approval. Presidents may, if they desire, use these officers collectively as a cabinet having advisory functions. In addition, presidents serve as commanders in chief, issuing orders to the military through the secretary of defense and the Joint Chiefs of Staff of the Army, Navy, Air Force, and Marine Corps, who also serve the chief executive collectively as an advisory body.

Legislative power is vested in the bicameral Congress: The Senate has two members from each state chosen by popular vote for six-year terms, with renewal by thirds every two years; the House of Representatives, elected by popular vote every two years, has a membership based on population, although each state is entitled to at least one representative. The two houses are further differentiated by their responsibilities: For example, money bills must originate in the House, whereas the advice and consent of the Senate is required for ratification of treaties and appointment of top government officials such as cabinet members. In practice no major legislative or financial bill is considered by either chamber until it has been reported by, or discharged from, one of many standing committees. By custom the parties share seats on the committees on a basis roughly proportional to their legislative strength. Within the parties preference in committee assignments has traditionally been accorded on the basis of seniority (continuous service in the house concerned), although departures from this rule are becoming more common. The Senate (but not the House) permits "unlimited debate," a procedure under which a determined minority may, by filibustering, bring all legislative action to a halt unless three-fifths of the full chamber elects to close debate. Failing this, a bill objectionable to the minority will eventually be withdrawn by the leadership. A presidential veto may be overridden by separate two-thirds votes of the two houses.

Congress has created the General Accountability Office (formerly the General Accounting Office) to provide legislative control over public funds and has established 66 agencies, boards, and commissions—collectively known as independent agencies—to perform specified administrative functions.

The federal judiciary is headed by a nine-member Supreme Court and includes courts of appeal, district courts, and various special courts, all created by Congress. Federal judges are appointed by the president, contingent upon approval by the Senate, and serve during good behavior. Federal jurisdiction is limited, applying most importantly to cases in law and equity arising under the Constitution, to U.S. laws and treaties, and to controversies arising between two or more states or between citizens of different states. Jury trial is prescribed for all federal crimes except those involving impeachment, which is voted by the House and adjudicated by the Senate.

In early July 2005 Supreme Court Justice Sandra Day O'CONNOR, the Court's first female justice, announced her retirement, providing President Bush with his first opportunity to influence the Court's direction. To replace O'Connor, who in recent years had been a prominent swing vote on a range of conservative-versus-liberal issues, including abortion rights, Bush selected a conservative, John ROBERTS, who was a judge on the Court of Appeals for the District of Columbia Circuit. As Senate and media investigations into Roberts's background were getting under way, the court's chief justice, William REHNQUIST, died on September 3, with Bush then nominating Roberts to succeed Rehnquist. Roberts was quickly confirmed by the Senate and sworn in on September 29. Bush's new pick to succeed O'Connor was more controversial. Samuel ALITO's opposition to abortion and his support for expanding presidential powers while serving as a judge on the Third Circuit Court of Appeals sparked considerable opposition, but not enough to block Senate confirmation. Alito was sworn in on January 31, 2006.

After Justice David SOUTER, a centrist on the Court, announced his retirement in April 2009, President Obama selected Sonia SOTOMAYOR, a judge of Puerto Rican descent on the Court of Appeals for the Second Circuit. Though some critics objected to earlier comments that she had made alluding to what she had termed the superior judicial insights of a "wise Latina woman," the Senate confirmed Sotomayor's appointment. She was sworn in on August 6, becoming the first Hispanic justice to serve on the Supreme Court. In April 2010 Supreme Court Justice John Paul STEVENS announced his retirement, leading to the August appointment of then solicitor general Elena KAGAN, who brought female representation on the court to an unprecedented three seats.

The federal Constitution and the institutions of the federal government serve generally as models for those of the states. Each state government is made up of a popularly elected governor and legislature (all but one bicameral) and an independent judiciary. The District of Columbia, as the seat of the national government, was traditionally administered under the direct authority of Congress; however, in May 1974 District voters approved a charter giving them the right to elect a mayor and city council, both of which took office on January 1, 1975. Earlier, under the 23rd Amendment to the Constitution (ratified in 1961), District residents had won the right to participate in presidential elections, and in 1970 they were authorized by Congress to send a nonvoting delegate to the House of Representatives. An amendment to give the District full congressional voting rights was approved by both houses of Congress in 1978 but not ratified by the requisite 38 of the 50 state legislatures.

In practice, the broad powers of the federal government, its more effective use of the taxing power, and the existence of many problems transcending the capacity of individual states have tended to make for a strongly centralized system of government. Local self-government is a well-established tradition, based generally on English models, with approximately 87,500 municipalities, townships, counties, or other substate entities. Education is a locally administered, federally subsidized function.

Freedom of the press is constitutionally guaranteed, and the media are broad based and multifaceted. Several media outlets, including newspapers such as the *New York Times* or the *Wall Street Journal* and broadcasters such as the Cable News Network (CNN), have international markets. The press and broadcasting media are privately owned and enjoy editorial freedom within the bounds of state libel laws. There is no legal ban on the ownership of broadcasting facilities by the press. The Federal Communications Commission (FCC) has, however, been under some pressure to deny relicensing under potentially monopolistic circumstances. In its 2012 report on freedom of the press, the media watchdog group Reporters Without Borders ranked the United States 32nd out of 179 countries.

State and Capital	*Area (sq. mi.)*	*Population (2012E)*
Alabama (Montgomery)	51,705	4,822,023
Alaska (Juneau)	591,004	731,449
Arizona (Phoenix)	114,000	6,553,255
Arkansas (Little Rock)	53,187	2,949,131
California (Sacramento)	158,706	38,041,430
Colorado (Denver)	104,091	5,187,582
Connecticut (Hartford)	5,018	3,590,347
Delaware (Dover)	2,045	917,092
Florida (Tallahassee)	58,664	19,317,568
Georgia (Atlanta)	58,910	9,919,945
Hawaii (Honolulu)	6,471	1,392,313
Idaho (Boise)	83,564	1,595,728
Illinois (Springfield)	56,345	12,875,255
Indiana (Indianapolis)	36,185	6,537,334
Iowa (Des Moines)	56,275	3,074,186
Kansas (Topeka)	82,277	2,885,905
Kentucky (Frankfort)	40,410	4,380,415
Louisiana (Baton Rouge)	47,752	4,601,893
Maine (Augusta)	33,265	1,329,192
Maryland (Annapolis)	10,460	5,884,563
Massachusetts (Boston)	8,284	6,646,144
Michigan (Lansing)	58,527	9,883,360
Minnesota (St. Paul)	84,402	5,379,139
Mississippi (Jackson)	47,689	2,984,926
Missouri (Jefferson City)	69,697	6,021,988
Montana (Helena)	147,046	1,005,141
Nebraska (Lincoln)	77,355	1,855,525
Nevada (Carson City)	110,561	2,758,931
New Hampshire (Concord)	9,279	1,320,718
New Jersey (Trenton)	7,787	8,864,590
New Mexico (Santa Fe)	121,593	2,085,538
New York (Albany)	49,108	19,570,261
North Carolina (Raleigh)	52,669	9,752,073
North Dakota (Bismarck)	70,702	699,628
Ohio (Columbus)	41,330	11,544,225
Oklahoma (Oklahoma City)	69,956	3,814,820
Oregon (Salem)	97,073	3,899,353
Pennsylvania (Harrisburg)	45,308	12,763,536
Rhode Island (Providence)	1,212	1,050,292
South Carolina (Columbia)	31,113	4,723,723
South Dakota (Pierre)	77,116	833,354
Tennessee (Nashville)	42,144	6,456,243
Texas (Austin)	266,807	26,059,203
Utah (Salt Lake City)	84,899	2,855,287

Vermont (Montpelier)	9,614	626,011
Virginia (Richmond)	40,767	8,185,867
Washington (Olympia)	68,139	6,897,012
West Virginia (Charleston)	24,232	1,855,413
Wisconsin (Madison)	56,153	5,726,398
Wyoming (Cheyenne)	97,809	576,412
Federal District		
District of Columbia	69	632,323

Foreign relations. U.S. relations with the world at large have evolved subject to the changing conditions created by the growth of the country and its international influence. An initial policy of noninvolvement in foreign affairs, which received its classical expression in President Washington's warning against "entangling alliances," gradually gave way to one of active participation in the concerns of international community. At the same time, the nation has evolved from a supporter of revolutionary movements directed against the old monarchical system into a predominantly conservative influence, with a broad commitment to the support of traditional democratic values.

U.S. policy in the Western Hemisphere, the area of most historical concern, continues to reflect the preoccupations that inspired the Monroe Doctrine (of President James Monroe) of 1823, in which the United States declared its opposition to European political involvement and further colonization in the Americas and in effect established a political guardianship over the states of Latin America. Since World War II this responsibility has become largely multilateral through such bodies as the UN and the Organization of American States (OAS), and direct U.S. intervention in Latin American affairs has typically been limited to instances in which a Central American or Caribbean country appeared in immediate danger of falling into chaos or under leftist control.

Overseas expansion during the late 19th and early 20th centuries resulted in the acquisition of American Samoa, Hawaii, and, following the Spanish-American War of 1898, the Philippines, Puerto Rico, and Guam; in addition, the United States secured a favored position in Cuba in 1902–1903, obtained exclusive rights in the Panama Canal Zone in 1903, and acquired the U.S. Virgin Islands by purchase in 1917. The country did not, however, become a colonial power in the European sense and was among the first to adopt a policy of promoting the political evolution of its dependent territories along lines desired by their inhabitants. In accordance with this policy, the Philippines became independent in 1946; Puerto Rico became a commonwealth freely associated with the United States in 1952; Hawaii became a state of the Union in 1959; measures of self-government have been introduced in the Virgin Islands, Guam, and American Samoa; and the Canal Zone was transferred to Panama on October 1, 1979, although the United States retained effective control of 40 percent of the area through 1999. Certain Japanese territories occupied during World War II were provisionally retained for strategic reasons, with those historically of Japanese sovereignty, the Bonin and Ryukyu islands, being returned in 1968 and 1972, respectively. The greater part of Micronesia (held by Japan as a League of Nations mandate after World War I) became, by agreement with the UN, the U.S. Trust Territory of the Pacific. In 1986, following the conclusion of a series of compacts of association with the Commonwealth of the Northern Mariana Islands, the Federated States of Micronesia (FSM), the Republic of the Marshall Islands, and the Republic of Palau (Belau), the UN Trusteeship Council indicated that it would be appropriate to terminate the trusteeship. All were eventually approved by the UN Security Council by October 1, 1994.

Globally, U.S. participation in the defeat of the Central Powers in World War I was followed by a period of renewed isolation and attempted neutrality, which, however, was ultimately made untenable by the challenge of the Axis powers in World War II. Having played a leading role in the defeat of the Axis, the United States joined with its allies in assuming responsibility for the creation of a postwar order within the framework of the UN. However, the subsequent divergence of Soviet and Western political aims, and the resultant limitations on the effectiveness of the UN as an instrument for maintaining peace and security, impelled the United States during the late 1940s and 1950s to take the lead in creating a network of special mutual security arrangements that were ultimately to involve commitments to more than four dozen foreign governments. Some of these commitments, as in the North Atlantic Treaty Organization (NATO), the Australia, New Zealand, United States (ANZUS) Security Treaty Pact, and the Inter-American Treaty of Reciprocal Assistance (Rio Pact), are multilateral in character; others involve defense obligations toward particular governments, such as those with Thailand, the Philippines, and the Republic of Korea.

The United States also exercised leadership in international economic and financial relations through its cosponsorship of the International Monetary Fund (IMF) and World Bank, its promotion of trade liberalization efforts, and its contributions to postwar relief and rehabilitation, European economic recovery, and the economic progress of less-developed countries. Much of this activity, like parallel efforts put forward in social, legal, and cultural fields, has been carried on through the UN and its related agencies.

The United States has pursued international agreements on measures for the control and limitation of strategic armaments. Agreements and bilateral talks with the Soviet Union on disarmament stretched from 1969 under Nixon into the Reagan administration nearly 20 years later through, for instance, the strategic arms limitation treaties (SALT I and SALT II), the strategic arms reduction talks (START), and the intermediate-range nuclear forces (INF) negotiations (see below and the 2010 *Handbook* for more details).

U.S. military forces, operating under a UN mandate, actively opposed Communist-sponsored aggression in the Korean War of 1950–1953. Other U.S. forces, together with those of a number of allied powers, assisted the government of South Vietnam in combating the insurgent movement that was actively supported by North Vietnamese forces for nearly two decades. By 1965 this assistance had become a major U.S. military effort, which continued after the initiation of peace talks in 1968. The lengthy discussions, involving U.S. Secretary of State Henry A. KISSINGER and North Vietnamese diplomat Le Duc Tho as the most active participants, resulted in the conclusion of a four-way peace agreement on January 27, 1973, that called for the withdrawal of all remaining U.S. military forces from Vietnam, the repatriation of American prisoners of war, and the institution of political talks between South Vietnam and its domestic (Viet Cong) adversaries. The U.S. withdrawal was followed, however, by a breakdown in talks, renewed military operations in late 1974, and the collapse of the South Vietnamese government on April 30, 1975.

In a move of major international significance, the United States and the People's Republic of China announced on December 15, 1978, that they would establish diplomatic relations as of January 1, 1979. The United States met all three of China's long-sought conditions: severance of U.S. diplomatic relations with Taipei, withdrawal of U.S. troops from Taiwan, and abrogation of the Republic of China defense treaty. However the United States indicated that it would maintain economic, cultural, and other unofficial relations with Taiwan.

In the Middle East, Secretary Kissinger embarked on an eight-month-long exercise in "shuttle diplomacy" following the Arab-Israeli "October War" of 1973. U.S. economic interests were, for the first time, directly undermined as a result of an Arab embargo instituted in October 1973 on all oil shipments to the United States and the Netherlands, and on some shipments to other Western European states. The embargo was terminated by all but two of the producing nations, Libya and Syria, in March 1974, following the resumption of full-scale diplomatic relations (severed since 1967) between the United States and Egypt. Kissinger brokered an Israeli-Egyptian disengagement agreement in January 1974 and a second in September 1975. Meanwhile Kissinger brought about a limited Golan Heights disengagement between Israel and Syria in May 1974, followed a month later by a renewal of diplomatic relations between the United States and Syria (also suspended since 1967). In September 1978 President Carter, hosting a Camp David summit, was instrumental in negotiating accords that led to the signing of a peace treaty between Egypt and Israel in Washington, D.C., on March 26, 1979.

Despite a recognized danger to U.S. diplomatic personnel, the Carter administration permitted the deposed shah of Iran to enter the United States in October 1979 for medical treatment. On November 4 militants stormed and occupied the U.S. embassy compound in Tehran, taking 66 hostages. Iranian leader Ayatollah Khomeini announced on November 17 that female and black hostages would be released because they had experienced "the oppression of American society." Thirteen hostages were released; the militants demanded the return of the shah in exchange for the remaining 53. Although condemnations of the seizure were forthcoming from the UN Security Council, the General Assembly, and the World Court, neither their nor personal pleas by international diplomats were at first heeded by the Islamic Republic's leadership, which vilified the United States as "the great Satan." President Carter aborted a rescue mission by a U.S. commando force in April 1980 after early mishaps. Eventually, however, negotiations that commenced on the eve of the 1980 U.S. election culminated in the freeing of the hostages on Reagan's presidential inauguration day (January 20, 1981).

The Reagan administration viewed the conclusion of the 1988 INF treaty as the result of consistent (and largely successful) pressure on U.S. European allies to maintain a high level of military preparedness as compared with the Soviet Union. In the Middle East the Reagan administration attempted to negotiate a mutual withdrawal of Israeli and Syrian forces from Lebanon in the wake of the Israeli invasion of June 1982 and the subsequent evacuation of Palestinian Liberation Organization (PLO) forces from Beirut, for which the U.S. government provided truce supervision assistance. In 1987, despite the risk of a major confrontation with Iran, the Reagan administration mounted a significant naval presence in the Persian Gulf to protect oil tankers from seaborne mines and other threats stemming from the Iran-Iraq conflict. In Asia, the United States provided substantial military assistance to Pakistan and Thailand in response to Soviet intervention in Afghanistan and communist operations in Cambodia, respectively, while strongly supporting the post-Marcos regime in the Philippines. In the Caribbean, the United States provided the bulk of the forces that participated in the 1983 postcoup intervention in Grenada, and it welcomed the 1986 ouster of Haitian dictator François Duvalier. In Central America, the Reagan administration attempted to contain Soviet-Cuban involvement in Nicaragua and to help the Salvadoran government defeat leftist guerrilla forces. Overall, in keeping with a 1980 campaign pledge, President Reagan sought to restructure both the military and civilian components of the nation's foreign aid program so as to reward "America's friends," whatever their domestic policies, in an implicit repudiation of his predecessor's somewhat selective use of aid in support of global human-rights objectives.

Seven months after the nullification of Panama's May 1989 presidential balloting, Gen. Manuel Noriega assumed sweeping powers to deal with what was termed "a state of war" with the United States. On December 20 the George H. W. Bush administration intervened militarily (for more, see the 2013 *Handbook*).

In 1990 the Bush administration became preoccupied with the international crisis generated by Iraq's seizure of Kuwait on August 2 and the remarkable prodemocracy upheaval in Eastern Europe that had been triggered by Gorbachev's reforms in the Soviet Union. Five days after the fall of Kuwait, the United States announced the deployment of ground units and aircraft to defend Saudi Arabia, and on November 29 the UN Security Council approved the use of "all necessary means" if Iraq did not withdraw from Kuwait by January 15, 1991. On January 12 the U.S. Congress authorized military action against Iraq, and on January 16 "Operation Desert Storm" began, yielding the liberation of Kuwait on February 26–27 by a U.S.-led multinational force.

Four decades of superpower confrontation formally ended on November 21, 1990, with the adoption of a treaty reducing conventional forces in Europe at a Paris summit of the Conference on Security and Cooperation in Europe (CSCE). Agreement eight months later on final details of the long-sought START paved the way for signing by Bush and Gorbachev at a Moscow summit on July 30–31, 1991. Under the accord, 50 percent of the Soviet and 35 percent of the U.S. ballistic missile warheads were slated for destruction.

Following the Gulf War President Bush identified resolution of the Arab-Israeli dispute as the top priority of his administration. In pursuit of this objective, Secretary of State James BAKER painstakingly negotiated a conference involving Israel, Syria, Lebanon, and a joint Jordanian-Palestinian delegation, convened in Madrid, Spain, in October 1991 under the joint auspices of the United States and Soviet Union. Additional bilateral and multilateral talks were held over the ensuing months, with no substantive results.

Following the failed Moscow coup of August 1991, the United States welcomed the achievement of independence by the Baltic states, and in December, after the legal collapse of the Soviet Union, Congress moved to recognize Ukraine, followed later by recognition of the remaining former Soviet republics as well as the former Yugoslavian republics of Croatia, Slovenia, and Bosnia and Herzegovina. President Bush and Russia's Boris Yeltsin signed an unprecedented extension of the 1991 START accord during their first formal summit on June 16–17. Under START II, each nation would be limited to 3,000–3,500 long-range weapons (down from 11,000–12,000 on the eve of START I), while all land-based multiple warhead missiles would be banned. Another summit highlight was an agreement on reciprocal most-favored-nation trade status.

On November 24, 1992, the United States completed its military withdrawal from the Philippines (see the entry on Philippines), ending a presence that had existed since 1898, save for three years during World War II. Ten days later, in an operation termed "Restore Hope," President Bush ordered the dispatch of 28,000 U.S. soldiers to Somalia to ensure the safe delivery of international relief supplies to the country's starving population (see the entry on Somalia).

Trade issues occupied center stage during the waning months of the Bush administration. The North American Free Trade Agreement (NAFTA), which had been concluded on August 12, 1992, by the United States, Canada, and Mexico after 14 months of negotiation, was formally signed on December 17. It secured U.S. legislative approval in November 1993 and came into force on January 1, 1994.

The foreign policy highlight of Clinton's first year was the formal signing at the White House on September 13, 1993, of a historic agreement between Israel and the PLO on Palestinian self-rule in Jericho and the Gaza Strip (see the entries on Israel and PLO following the country listings). Other 1993–1994 concerns included a deteriorating situation in Somalia, where 18 U.S. soldiers were killed in October 1993, due in large part to the refusal by Defense Secretary Les ASPIN to provide more tanks and armored vehicles. Aspin subsequently admitted his mistake, and on December 15, President Clinton announced Aspin's resignation. On February 3, 1994, William J. PERRY was sworn in as the new defense secretary. By March 31, 1994, all but a small number of U.S. troops were withdrawn from Somalia.

In the face of a somewhat wavering posture regarding events in Bosnia and Herzegovina, the Clinton administration in early 1994 issued a new set of guidelines for peacekeeping and related activities that would preclude U.S. military involvement short of a clear threat to international security, a major natural disaster, or a gross violation of human rights. From February 1994 the launching of UN-approved NATO air strikes against Serbian positions in Bosnia eased U.S.-European differences on how to respond to the conflict in former Yugoslavia, where deployment of U.S. ground troops continued to be confined to the UN/CSCE observer contingent in Macedonia. Thereafter, the genocidal Rwandan crisis that erupted in April elicited a substantial U.S. humanitarian effort in neighboring countries and the dispatch of 200 U.S. troops to help run Kigali airport, although participation in UN peacekeeping was ruled out. These measures, however, failed to prevent widespread bloodshed.

On June 2, 1994, the Clinton administration called for international economic sanctions against North Korea to force disclosure of that country's nuclear weapons capacity (see the entry on Democratic People's Republic of Korea); following the death of North Korean leader Kim Il Sung on July 8, a U.S.-North Korean agreement signed on August 12 met some of the concerns of the international community.

In July 1994 U.S. Middle East diplomacy registered a major success when President Clinton on July 25 supervised the White House signing of a peace declaration between King Hussein of Jordan and Prime Minister Rabin of Israel.

During 1994 the Clinton administration worked to implement a 1993 agreement providing for departure of the military junta and the return of exiled President Jean-Bertrand Aristide in Haiti. On September 19 an advance contingent of 20,000 troops landed on Haitian soil under a UN mandate to oust the incumbent regime. On October 13 junta leader Gen. Raoul Cédras left aboard a U.S. flight to Panama, and on October 15 Aristide returned to Haiti (see the entry on Haiti). Meanwhile, large numbers of Haitian "boat people" had been picked up and transported to the U.S. Guantánamo Bay Naval Base in Cuba, with Cuban refugees (in a change of policy) being accorded like treatment as of August 19. In another policy shift on May 2, 1995, the United States agreed to admit Cuban, but not Haitian, detainees remaining at Guantánamo, with all subsequent refugees being returned to their homeland. Meanwhile, the U.S. Senate on December 1, 1994, ratified the 1993 GATT accord establishing the World Trade Organization (WTO).

In 1996, the Clinton administration, which for some time had indicated its displeasure with UN Secretary General Boutros Boutros-Ghali, vetoed his reelection by the Security Council. At issue was Boutros-Ghali's alleged failure to reform the world body, in response to which Congress continued to withhold dues of more than $1 billion. On December 13 a lengthy confrontation with France over Boutros-Ghali's successor ended with the selection of Kofi Annan, a Ghanaian and longtime UN civil servant who had earned high marks for directing peacekeeping operations in Bosnia.

On October 26, 1997, Jiang Zemin began a nine-day state visit to the United States, the first by a Chinese head of state since 1985, with President Clinton reciprocating in June 1998. Shortly thereafter, Clinton failed to win "fast track" trade authority, a practice precluding Congress from partial amendment of trade legislation, even though it had been extended to every other president since 1974 (and would be granted to Clinton's successor, George W. Bush, in August 2002).

In 1998 President Clinton ordered cruise missile attacks on Afghanistan and Sudan in response to the August 7 terrorist bombings of U.S. embassies in Kenya and Tanzania. He also ordered air strikes against Iraq in mid-December after Baghdad had failed to honor a November 14 pledge to resume full cooperation with UN weapons inspectors.

On March 24, 1999, following a year of escalating ethnic fighting between the Kosovo Liberation Army (KLA), a group of ethnic Albanians, and Serb and Yugoslav security forces, U.S.-led NATO air strikes began. At the same time, Clinton pledged that no U.S. ground troops would be sent to Kosovo. By June, however, Clinton said he would send as many as 7,000 ground troops to assist NATO in peacekeeping operations.

In April 1999 relations with China were sorely tested by the NATO bombing of the Chinese embassy in Belgrade, Yugoslavia, which the United States attributed to a mapping error. In August the Senate, by a 51–48 vote, refused to ratify the Comprehensive (nuclear) Test Ban Treaty (CTBT).

Talks began in Geneva in April 2000 on a START III accord, following Russian ratification of START II, while the House on May 24 approved the China trade bill, thus paving the way for Chinese admission to the WTO. On August 22 President Clinton signed a controversial measure providing upward of $1.3 billion to aid Colombia's war on drug traffickers. On October 12, 17 U.S. sailors were killed and 37 wounded in a terrorist attack on the USS *Cole,* a destroyer docked in Aden, Yemen.

Before leaving office on January 20, 2001, President Clinton, voicing reservations, signed a treaty to establish an International Criminal Court (ICC) to succeed the ad hoc international war-crimes tribunals in The Hague (an action for which the succeeding Bush administration promptly withdrew support). Concurrently, Senator Helms, the Senate's leading critic of UN financing, agreed to the release of $582 million in back dues to the world body under a deal providing for reduction of the U.S. share in the annual $1.1 billion administrative budget to 22 percent (down from 25 percent) and of its contribution to the peacekeeping budget to 26 percent (down from 31 percent) by 2004.

The second war in the Persian Gulf, launched by President George W. Bush on March 20, 2003, proved far more divisive and much more costly than the first. While the United States expressed regret that the UN Security Council would not issue a resolution specifically authorizing military action against Iraq, it insisted that Resolution 1441 provided sufficient authority. However, the chief UN weapons inspector, Hans Blix, had, on March 7, given a decidedly mixed assessment of Iraq's compliance with the 2002 resolution, and at midyear an administration spokesperson conceded that the President Bush had relied on "incomplete and possibly inaccurate" intelligence in having declared in his January State of the Union address that Saddam Hussein had attempted to secure uranium from Africa. Subsequent evidence that Iraq apparently possessed no WMDs at the outset of hostilities damaged the credibility of the administration. By early 2005 more than a dozen countries participating in the U.S.-led military coalition had decided to pull out or reduce their forces in Iraq, with more following in 2006 and 2007.

In November 2007, Arab leaders, including Syria's foreign minister, accepted an invitation by the United States to attend a broadly inclusive Middle East peace summit. Although the summit issued a statement of "joint understanding," further progress proved unobtainable after the collapse of a five-month-old cease-fire in Gaza in November 2008 and renewed border fighting between Israel and the Palestinians.

Tension heightened between the United States and Russia in August 2008, after Russia invaded the former Soviet state of Georgia in response to that country's deployment of troops in South Ossetia. The United States and the EU called for a halt to fighting, and NATO deployed ships to the Black Sea carrying U.S.-supplied humanitarian aid to Georgia. NATO suspended interaction with Russia in alliance bodies.

In October 2008 the United States removed North Korea from its list of states that sponsor terrorism, citing North Korea's recent agreement on measures to verify its nuclear program. In November President Bush, in his final days in office, called Libyan leader Col. Muammar Abu Minyar al-Qadhafi, marking the first conversation ever between the Libyan leader and a U.S. president. However, the August 2009 release from a Scottish prison of a terminally ill, convicted perpetrator of the 1988 Lockerbie attack, and his hero's welcome home in Libya prompted a souring of U.S.-Libyan relations.

In October 2009 the Norwegian Nobel committee awarded president Obama the Nobel Peace Prize, just 263 days after taking office.

Obama's Afghan strategy was hampered by a resurgence of Taliban attacks, weakening resolve by allied forces to engage in combat missions, and dwindling confidence in Afghan president Karzai. In January 2010 Obama committed to sending 30,000 additional U.S. troops to Afghanistan, raising the total there to nearly 100,000, as part of a strategy to stabilize the country and train Afghan security forces in preparation for a U.S. exit. In November NATO and U.S. officials agreed to hand security over to Afghan forces by the end of 2014, with some allied forces remaining in a support role beyond that date. Obama declared an end to the American combat mission on August 31, 2010, in Iraq, leaving some 50,000 troops to "advise and assist" Iraqi security forces.

The Obama administration sought a new policy of engagement with Pakistan to counter the Taliban and al-Qaida forces in the Pakistani border regions with Afghanistan. In March 2009 the administration unveiled the "Af-Pak" strategy to treat the border region as part of a single theater, linking stability in Afghanistan with the disruption of militant "safe havens" within tribal areas of Pakistan. To gain Pakistan's support the U.S. approved a $7.5 billion aid package to Pakistan in October, tripling non-military aid to the country. A failed car bombing on March 1, 2010, in Times Square, New York, was linked to the Pakistani Taliban. U.S. Secretary of State Hillary Clinton asserted there would be "severe consequences" for Pakistan if a successful terrorist attack in the United States were traced to that country.

After Iran rejected an offer to have uranium shipped out of the country for enrichment, the Obama administration in June 2010 led efforts at the United Nations Security Council to impose a fourth round of sanctions on Iran. Meanwhile, Obama focused efforts on the signing of a new Strategic Arms Reduction Treaty (START) with Russia by the end of the year, despite stiff resistance from Senate Republicans. In late November NATO members and Russia agreed to set up a "working group" on a missile defense system that would protect Europe and North America through mobile and sea-based radars and interceptors, a departure from a Bush-era proposal to set up fixed bases in Poland and the Czech Republic. However, tensions over missile defense continued, and in 2011 Russia threatened to target U.S. antimissile bases in Europe. The group WikiLeaks released more than 200,000 internal and classified state department and military documents at the end of 2010. Allegedly obtained from a U.S. soldier, the releases exposed diplomatic and military activities, intelligence reports and assessments, and correspondence between U.S. officials.

The Obama administration endeavored to maintain a delicate balance during the Arab Spring movements that swept through North Africa and the Middle East beginning in January 2011. The popular uprisings toppled regimes in Egypt and Tunisia and threatened other U.S. allies such as Morocco and Bahrain. The United States publicly backed the spread of democracy, although concerns were raised over instability in the region and the potential for the spread of Islamic extremism.

The Obama administration deployed U.S. military forces to support an international coalition that intervened in Libya in March 2011 in order to enforce the UN no-fly zone over the country, which was in the midst of a civil war. The United States and other powers conducted air and cruise missile attacks against the regime of Libyan leader Muammar Qadhafi, who was overthrown and eventually killed by rebels on October 20, 2011. Obama faced domestic criticism for deploying the U.S. military in combat operations without congressional authorization.

Al-Qaida leader Osama bin Laden was killed by U.S. special operations forces on May 2, 2011, during a raid on his compound in Abottabad, Pakistan. The discovery that bin Laden had lived near one of Pakistan's main military academies reinforced U.S. concerns over Islamabad's commitment to suppress al-Qaida and the Taliban. Tensions between the two countries were exacerbated by U.S. drone attacks on suspected terrorist targets in Pakistan. In July 2011 the Obama administration suspended $800 million in military aid to Pakistan.

Negotiations over a continued U.S. military presence in Iraq broke down in October 2011. Consequently, all U.S. forces withdrew from Iraq in December. During 2012 an increase in attacks on NATO troops

by Afghan security forces (known as "blue-on-green" attacks) prompted U.S. military leaders to suspend joint operations with their Afghan counterparts in September. Meanwhile, through 2012 the Obama administration continued to attack suspected Taliban and al Qaeda leaders in Pakistan, Yemen, and Somalia with aerial drone strikes. Growing civilian and military casualties from the drone attacks prompted Pakistan to suspend NATO convoy routes for six months from January to July 2012 (see entry on Pakistan).

In November 2011 Hillary Clinton became the first U.S. secretary of state to visit Myanmar since 1955. U.S. sanctions were relaxed following significant political reforms in the country (see entry on Myanmar). A free trade agreement with South Korea was ratified by the U.S Senate in October 2011 and went into effect in March 2012.

Throughout 2012 the Obama administration pressed for increased economic sanctions against Iran in an effort to pressure Tehran into abandoning its nuclear weapons program. The United States also attempted, less successfully, to increase pressure on the Syrian regime to end an ongoing civil war. However, efforts to foster international sanctions or other measures were frustrated at the UN by China and Russia (see entry on Syria).

On September 11, 2012, militants attacked the U.S. consulate in Benghazi, Libya. Ambassador Chris Stevens and three other Americans were killed in the attack. The Obama administration initially asserted that the incident was caused by anti-U.S. sentiment over a film that lampooned Islam. The administration was criticized for its response when intelligence revealed that the attack was likely a preplanned terrorist attack (see Current issues, below).

Among the files released by Edward SNOWDEN in the May 2013 NSA leak (see below) was documentation of a U.S. surveillance program targeting EU offices as well as 38 embassies of U.S. allies including France, Japan, India, and more. The revelations surfaced in late June and early July and stirred anger from longtime allies in Europe and Asia, generating calls from the European Parliament to veto data-sharing agreements with the United States.

The affair proved particularly stressful for U.S.-Russian relations when Snowden, who initially fled to Hong Kong following the leaks, flew to the Moscow airport to avoid an extradition request filed by the United States in late June. Russia granted Snowden's request for temporary asylum on August 1, rejecting repeated requests from U.S. authorities to turn him over to face charges. Already strained by the ongoing conflict in Syria, relations further deteriorated as the United States threatened to withdraw from upcoming high-profile summits, including the September G-20 in St. Petersburg.

An unspecified threat in early August caused the State Department to close 21 U.S. embassies across the Middle East and North Africa, some for up to a week.

On August 21 a poison gas attack was reported to have taken place in Syria, almost exactly one year after President Obama warned that the use of chemical or biological weapons by the Assad regime was a "red line." Obama on September 1 announced that he would seek congressional approval for a "limited" military strike on Syria. On October 9 Russian Foreign Minister Sergey Lavrov proposed a negotiated compromise that Damascus could turn over its chemical weapons stockpiles to avoid a military strike. Obama subsequently changed course, and talks between U.S. and Russian officials begun in Geneva on September 12 yielded agreements for disarmament framework and, on September 26, a UN Security Council resolution.

Current issues. After his January 2009 inauguration, President Obama called for the closure of the controversial Guantánamo Bay prison camp and overseas secret prisons set up by Bush for suspected terrorists. The closure of the Guantánamo prison was deferred when Congress refused to fund it due to fears that some of the detainees, who could not be tried because the evidence provided in their cases could compromise covert agents, were nevertheless deemed too dangerous to be released or transferred to U.S. prisons. Obama was able to convince several allies to take a number of the prisoners. The first detainee from the camp to be transferred to U.S. soil, Tanzanian national Ahmed Ghailani, was tried in New York City on charges involving the bombing of U.S. embassies in Africa and convicted of conspiracy on November 17, 2011.

The recession, the deepest since the 1930s, continued to worsen in the first half of 2009, as corporations collapsed and unemployment rose. The new administration responded in February with the American Recovery and Reinvestment bill, a stimulus package to temper the growing unemployment rate—which reached a 26-year high of 10.2 percent in the fourth quarter of 2009. Obama signed the $789 billion measure into law on February 17. Other large-scale measures to stabilize the financial sector and counter home foreclosures were announced that month.

In March 2009 American International Group (AIG), a major insurer of the troubled banks, announced the largest loss in U.S. corporate history, prompting the administration to provide it with $30 billion in emergency funding to stem further threats to the financial system. It assumed shares in both General Motors and Chrysler in June after the two auto giants filed for bankruptcy. (In June 2011 the Treasury sold its shares in Chrysler to Italian automaker Fiat.)

Obama then called on Congress to pass legislation before the end of the year extending health insurance to almost all Americans, almost 50 million of whom had no coverage, barring private insurers from refusing coverage to individuals with "preexisting conditions," and creating a new, government-sponsored health insurance plan that consumers could choose instead of private insurance. The proposal sparked a contentious debate between Democratic supporters and Republican opponents, who characterized it as "socialized medicine" or "Obamacare." Independent and conservative voters, meanwhile, focused on the plan's impact on the ballooning budget deficit, which was projected to expand by a trillion dollars in addition to existing debt from 2010–2019 if the plan was passed.

Democrats in Congress pushed through the final version of the health care reform package in March 2010 with near unanimous opposition from Republicans and a sizable minority of conservative Democrats. The Patient Protection and Affordable Care Act and the Health Care and Education Reconciliation Act were designed to be implemented in stages, the most far-reaching of measures, which mandated that all Americans obtain health insurance through reforms in the private insurance market, or pay a penalty, to begin taking effect in 2014.

Also in March 2010 Obama reversed a campaign pledge and announced a major expansion in oil and gas exploration in coastal waters in an effort to win conservative support for a forthcoming bill on climate change. However, Obama's stance quickly changed when on April 20 a deep-water oil drilling rig in the Gulf of Mexico caught fire and sank, causing a massive gusher of oil that continued for 86 days until the well's operator, British Petroleum, capped it. The BP Deepwater Horizon spill represented the world's largest accidental release of oil into marine waters in history, resulting in untold environmental damage and prompting Obama, who faced public critique over his handling of the disaster, to announce new environmental safeguards for oil and gas exploration.

In May Obama won another key element of his legislative agenda with Senate approval of a bill to reform the U.S. financial system. The Restoring American Financial Stability Act put additional restraints on bank activities and empowering regulators to act on risks inherent in the financial system. In June Obama accepted the resignation of Gen. Stanley McCHRYSTAL after the four-star general and commander of forces in Afghanistan made disparaging remarks about the president and top aides in a magazine article. McChrystal was replaced by Gen. David PETRAEUS, who previously commanded forces in Iraq. In other staff changes Obama's chief of staff Rahm EMANUEL resigned to run for mayor of Chicago and was replaced by bank executive William DALEY, and Council of Economic Advisers chair Christine ROMER resigned in September with analysts attributing the turnover as an effort by Obama to gain a fresh start going into the midterm elections.

In the November 2010 balloting, the Democrats suffered historic losses. Party members in centrist or right-leaning districts had the greatest losses, as the Republicans regained control of the House of Representatives and numerous state legislatures and governorships, and picked up seats in the Senate. The lame-duck 111th Congress managed to pass three major measures after the elections: (1) Senate ratification of the U.S.-Russian START treaty (see Foreign relations, above), (2) an extension of Bush-era tax cuts and unemployment benefits, and (3) the repeal of the "Don't Ask, Don't Tell" policy prohibiting homosexuals from serving in the military.

The White House announced several staff changes in early 2011: Gene SPERLING, an adviser to Treasury Secretary Geithner, succeeded Larry SUMMERS as chair of the National Economic Council; General Electric executive Jeff IMMELT took the helm of a new jobs and competitive council; and Biden assistant James "Jay" CARNEY replaced Robert GIBBS as press secretary. Later in the year retiring Defense Secretary Robert GATES was replaced by CIA director Leon PANETTA, who was, in turn, succeeded by General Petraeus.

Differences between congressional Republicans, who emphasized spending cuts to reduce the deficit, and Democrats, who supported tax increases to cut spending created a stalemate over an increase to the federal debt ceiling. A last-minute compromise averted a government shutdown in August. The deal included the creation of a bipartisan supercommittee charged with forging a deal to obtain $1.5 trillion in deficit reductions over a ten-year period. Failure to obtain an agreement would result in $1.2 trillion in automatic spending cuts. Meanwhile, in response to concerns over the ability of the United States to address its growing debt and deficit, the credit agency Standard & Poor's downgraded the creditworthiness of Treasury bonds for the first time since the initial rating in 1917. By August the U.S. debt reached $14.58 trillion, or more than 100 percent of the nation's $14.53 trillion GDP, while the federal deficit was 8.7 percent of GDP in 2011, down from 8.9 percent the year before. On November 21 the committee reported that it was unable to reach an agreement.

White House chief of staff Daley resigned on January 27, 2012, and was replaced by Jacob J. LEW, formally the director of the Office of Management and Budget. Voters in North Carolina approved a state constitutional amendment on May 8 banning same-sex marriage. The next day, Obama became the first U.S. president to endorse same-sex marriage.

On June 5, 2012, Wisconsin governor Scott WALKER became the first incumbent to win a gubernatorial recall election in U.S. history. He received 53 percent of the vote. Democrats sought to turn Walker out of office after he oversaw an effort that reduced collective bargaining rights in the state. Commerce secretary John BRYSON resigned on June 21 following two car accidents and a period of medical leave. He was replaced by his deputy on an acting basis.

In a major reversal of U.S. immigration policy, on June 15, 2012, Obama issued an executive order that halted the deportations of illegal immigrants under the age of 30 and allowed them to defer deportment and apply for work permits under certain conditions. The measure was harshly criticized by Republicans who argued it was an attempt by the president to bolster his share of the Latino vote ahead of the November balloting.

Meanwhile, on June 28, 2012, a divided Supreme Court upheld the major provisions of Obama's health care reform but granted states the option of whether or not to participate in the program's expanded Medicaid initiative. On the same day, attorney general Eric HOLDER became the first cabinet member to be held in contempt of Congress in response to his refusal to turn over documents related to the "Fast and Furious" scandal (a controversial program that supplied Mexican drug cartels with U.S. weapons in an effort to track the flow of the arms). Concurrently, the Obama administration exerted executive privilege to avoid the release of additional information.

Through the summer of 2012 the United States experienced its worst drought in 55 years, affecting 29 states. On July 20, 2012, a gunman killed 12 and injured 58 at a cinema in Aurora, Colorado. Both Obama and Romney temporarily suspended their political campaigns, but the mass shooting did not prompt renewed debate over the country's gun laws.

In national balloting on November 6, 2012, Obama was reelected, while Democrats expanded their majority in the Senate, and Republicans kept control of the House. In the polling, Tammy BALDWIN of Wisconsin became the first openly gay person elected to the Senate. In state ballot initiatives, voters in Maine, Maryland, and Washington endorsed same-sex marriage, while Washington and Colorado voted to decriminalize the possession of small amounts of marijuana. Oklahomans passed a measure to eliminate affirmative action.

In the midst of continuing congressional investigations into the death of ambassador Chris Stevens in Benghazi, General Petraeus resigned on November 9 after it was revealed that he had engaged in an extramarital affair.

On December 14, 2012, a gunman entered an elementary school in Newtown, Connecticut, and killed 20 children and 6 adults. Following the shooting, President Obama sought a ban on assault weapons. The measure was abandoned in March 2013 when it didn't secure the necessary 60 votes in the Senate.

A tense fiscal debate between Democrats and Republicans ended in the late hours of December 31, when the House voted 257–167 in support of the American Taxpayer Relief Act, on the eve of automatic tax increases and large spending cuts known as the "fiscal cliff." The bill, which had passed the Senate with overwhelming support less than a day earlier, raised taxes on high-earning Americans, the first tax hike in two decades.

Barack Obama was inaugurated for his second term on January 21, 2013.

On April 15 two bombs exploded near the finish line of the Boston Marathon, killing 3 and injuring more than 140 people. A three-day manhunt ensued for Chechen immigrant brothers Tamerlan and Dzhokhar Tsarnaev. Tamerlan was killed in a shoot-out by police. Dzhokhar, a naturalized U.S. citizen, was arrested on April 19 and later charged with using weapons of mass destruction.

Revelations that the U.S. Internal Revenue Service (IRS) disproportionately evaluated conservative groups associated with the Tea Party movement led to the resignation of acting IRS director Steve MILLER in May.

In response to an article published in the UK's *Guardian* newspaper the day before, the U.S. federal government confirmed on June 6 two separate surveillance operations: a seven-year program collecting and monitoring phone records within the United States and an overseas Internet surveillance effort that began six years earlier, known as Prism. Officials defended the classified programs, saying they were known to Congress and helped to thwart more than 50 potential terrorist events. Former CIA employee Edward Snowden, whose subsequent flight to Moscow strained U.S-Russian relations (see Foreign relations, above), was revealed to be responsible for the leaks, part of a massive disclosure of some 50,000 documents. Domestic and international fallout from the leaks continued as fresh details were released through the summer and fall.

In two landmark rulings handed down on June 26, 2013, the Supreme Court ruled that same-sex married couples were entitled to federal benefits and struck down a key section of the 1965 Voting Rights Act.

Because lawmakers in Congress were unable to reach agreement on a new budget in September, a partial government shutdown began on October 1. The Democratic-led Senate and Republican-led House failed to negotiate the key point of contention—a GOP demand that federal government funding come on the condition of a one-year delay in the implementation of health care reforms.

The political crisis deepened as the looming debt ceiling threatened to cause the country to default on public debt. After weeks of bitter negotiations, on October 17 Congress passed a bill ending the shutdown, raising the debt ceiling until February 7, and authorizing current spending levels through January 15.

POLITICAL PARTIES

Although the U.S. Constitution makes no provision for political parties, the existence of two (or occasionally three) major parties at the national level has been a feature of the U.S. political system almost since its inception. The present-day Democratic Party traces its origins back to the Democratic-Republican Party led by Thomas JEFFERSON during George Washington's administration, whereas the contemporary Republican Party, though not formally constituted until the 1850s, regards itself as the lineal descendant of the Federalist Party led by Alexander Hamilton during the same period.

The two-party system has been perpetuated by tradition, by the practical effect of single-member constituencies as well as a single executive, and by the status accorded to the second main party as the recognized opposition in legislative bodies. The major parties do not, however, constitute disciplined doctrinal groups. Each is a coalition of autonomous state parties—themselves coalitions of county and city parties—that come together chiefly in presidential election years to formulate a general policy statement, or platform, and to nominate candidates for president and vice president. Control of funds and patronage is largely in the hands of state and local party units, a factor that weakens party discipline in Congress. Policy leadership is similarly diffuse, both parties searching for support from as many interest groups as possible and tending to operate by consensus.

For at least a quarter of a century, popular identification with the two major parties was remarkably stable. From 1960 to 1984, according to surveys by the University of Michigan, between 40 and 46 percent of the voters considered themselves Democrats, whereas 22–29 percent identified with the Republicans. During the same period, 23–35 percent viewed themselves as independents (the higher figure occurring in the mid-1970s, when younger voters tended to dissociate themselves from partisan politics). In a subsequent poll conducted in early 1995, 37 percent of respondents called themselves independents, 30 percent Republicans, and 29 percent Democrats, with nearly 60 percent of voting-age individuals voicing their preference for a tripartite system.

Since 1932 the rate of voter participation has averaged 55.7 percent in presidential elections, ranging from a low of 49.0 percent for Bill

Clinton in 1996 to a high of 64 percent for Barack Obama in 2008 (turnout was 57.5 percent in 2012). The turnout in nonpresidential years has been substantially lower, averaging between 30 and 40 percent. In the 2010 mid-term election, voter turnout averaged 40.3 percent, slightly higher than the previous two mid-term election years.

Congressional Parties:

Democratic Party. Originally known as the Democratic-Republican Party, the Democratic Party counts Thomas Jefferson, Andrew JACKSON, Woodrow WILSON, Franklin D. Roosevelt, John F. Kennedy, Lyndon B. Johnson, and Bill Clinton among its past presidents. Its basis has traditionally been an unstable coalition of conservative politicians in the southeastern states, more liberal political leaders in the urban centers of the Northeast and the West Coast, and populists in some towns and rural areas of the Midwest. The party was weakened in 1968 by the conservative secessionist movement of southern Democrats led by George C. Wallace and the challenge to established leadership and policies put forward by senators Eugene J. McCarthy and Robert F. Kennedy, both of whom had sought the presidential nomination ultimately captured by Hubert H. Humphrey. The party was further divided by the nomination of Sen. George S. McGovern, a strong critic of the Vietnam policies of both presidents Johnson and Nixon, as Democratic presidential candidate in 1972.

The party benefited from the circumstances surrounding the resignations of Vice President Spiro Agnew in 1973 and of President Nixon in 1974, scored impressive victories in both the House and Senate in 1974, recaptured the presidency under Jimmy Carter in 1976, and maintained substantial congressional majorities in 1978. In 1980 it retained control of the House by a reduced majority while losing the Senate and suffering a decisive rejection of President Carter's bid for reelection. The party's strength in Congress was largely unchanged in 1984, despite the Reagan presidential landslide, and in 1986 it regained control of the Senate; it retained control of both houses, despite the defeat of its presidential candidate, Michael Dukakis, in 1988. Led by Clinton of Arkansas, the Democrats regained the White House in 1992 while preserving their congressional majorities, but, in a startling reversal, the party lost control of both houses in 1994. Although unable to regain control in 1996 or 1998, the Democrats countered expectations by registering marginal recovery in 1998. Denied the presidency in 2000, despite a popular majority for Vice President Al Gore, the party drew even with the Republicans in the Senate, whereas a ten-seat gain in the House was insufficient to win control. In June 2001, the Democrats assumed control of the Senate with the support of Sen. James Jeffords of Vermont, who had left the Republican Party to sit as an independent.

The disappointing results of the November 2002 balloting, in which the party was unable to win either house of Congress, were attributed by many observers to the Democrats' inability to present clear policy alternatives to the Republican agenda. Following the election, Richard A. GEPHARDT of Missouri, the House minority leader, resigned his post and was succeeded by Nancy Pelosi of California, the first woman to head either party in Congress.

In 2004 the party was even less successful than in 2000, failing to gain the White House for its standard-bearer, Sen. John Kerry of Massachusetts, and losing further ground in both the Senate and House.

On February 12, 2005, the party elected former Vermont governor Howard Dean as its national chair.

The lengthy presidential primary campaign got under way following the midterm elections in November 2006, with candidates stumping in earnest by early 2007. Those vying for the party's nomination, in addition to Hillary Rodham Clinton, Barack Obama, and Joseph Biden, were Christopher DODD, senator from Connecticut; Mike GRAVEL, former senator from Alaska; Dennis KUCINICH, congressman from Ohio; Bill RICHARDSON, governor of New Mexico; and Tom VILSACK, former governor of Iowa. Senator Clinton's early lead tapered into 2008, until she conceded the closely fought race four days after Obama won the party's nomination on June 3.

The Democratic Party's presidential nominee, Barack Obama, secured 365 electoral college votes and 52.9 percent of the popular vote in November 2008 to become the first presidential candidate since Carter to receive more than a 50 percent vote share.

The Democrats captured significant majorities in the Senate and the House in the 2008 elections but initially fell 2 seats short of the 60-seat powerful majority in the upper house. On April 30, 2009, Republican Arlen Specter of Pennsylvania switched to the Democratic Party, and on June 30 the Minnesota Supreme Court upheld the decision of a lower court to recognize the narrow victory of Democrat Al FRANKEN over Republican incumbent Norm COLEMAN, ending the Republicans' ability to filibuster to defeat legislation. Following Massachusetts Senator Edward M. KENNEDY's August 25 death,, Republican Scott BROWN was elected, reducing the party's majority to 59 seats.

In June 2010 West Virginia Senator Robert BYRD, the longest serving member of Congress in history and a Democratic leader, died in office. In the November midterm elections, the Democrats lost more than 60 House seats in the biggest shift in power since 1948. After losing the majority, disgruntled House Democrats reportedly sought a change in leadership, although Hoyer's stated refusal to run against Pelosi secured her victory in caucus elections on November 17 in a 150–43 vote. In December 2010 the House censured long-serving Democratic Representative Charles RANGEL of New York for financial misconduct in filing inaccurate tax papers and other improprieties.

In May 2012 the trial of former Democratic senator and 2004 vice-presidential candidate John Edwards on six counts of campaign fraud ended in a mistrial.

Obama faced no formal opposition in his bid for the Democratic presidential nomination in 2012. However, significant percentages of voters in southern states, including Arkansas, Kentucky, and North Carolina, voted "uncommitted" rather than endorse the president. An intricate and comprehensive "get-out-the-vote" effort generated a large turnout among the party's base. Obama won the balloting, while Democrats gained two seats in the Senate, although the GOP maintained control of the House of Representatives. Results at the state level were mixed, as Democrats gained control of state legislatures in Minnesota and Maine but lost both houses in Arkansas. Democrats gained a supermajority in the California legislature.

In a May 2013 special election to fill a vacant South Carolina House seat, Democrat Elizabeth COLBERT BUSCH lost to GOP candidate former governor Mark SANFORD.

Leaders: Barack H. OBAMA (President), Joseph R. BIDEN Jr. (Vice President), Harry M. REID (Senate Majority Leader), Patrick LEAHY (Senate President Pro Tempore), Richard (Dick) DURBIN (Senate Majority Whip), Nancy PELOSI (House Minority Leader), Steny H. HOYER (House Minority Whip), James E. CLYBURN (Assistant House Minority Leader), Debbie Wasserman SCHULTZ (National Chair).

Republican Party. Known informally as the "Grand Old Party" (GOP), the present-day Republican Party was founded as an antislavery party in the 1850s and includes Abraham LINCOLN, Theodore ROOSEVELT, Dwight D. Eisenhower, Richard Nixon, and Ronald Reagan among its past presidents. Generally more conservative in outlook than the Democratic Party, the Republican Party traditionally drew its strength from the smaller cities and from suburban and rural areas, especially in the Midwest and parts of New England. In recent years Republicans have tended to advocate welfare and tax reforms, including a simplified tax system and revenue-sharing to relieve the burden of local property taxes; the achievement of a "workable balance between a growing economy and environmental protection;" and military preparedness sufficient to preclude the nation's becoming a "second-class power." The party's base has shifted primarily to the South and West.

Following a hard-fought campaign, with results not clear until December 12, the party's presidential candidate in 2000, George W. Bush, secured a bare majority of electoral votes. The Senate was split 50–50, while the Republicans retained control of the House with a reduced majority of 221 seats. In June 2001 the Republicans lost control of the Senate when Jeffords of Vermont became an independent, but they regained it in the November 2002 election and held it for the ensuing four years.

Charged with violating Texas campaign laws, House Majority Leader Tom DeLAY stepped down in January 2006 and was replaced by John Boehner on February 2. In the presidential primary campaign, which began in early 2007, the following Republican candidates sought the party's nomination, in addition to McCain: Michael D. (Mike) Huckabee; Mitt Romney; Fred THOMPSON, former senator from Tennessee; Duncan HUNTER, congressman from California; Ron PAUL, congressman from Texas; and Rudolph Giuliani. Mitt Romney was the most serious challenger to McCain until the latter's campaign surged ahead in mid-2008.

In the 2008 elections Republican representation declined by 21 House seats and 8 Senate seats. In the presidential election, Senator

John McCain received 173 electoral votes and 45.7 percent of the popular vote as the Republican nominee. After Sen. Arlen Specter's defection to the Democratic Party in 2009, the Republicans lost the ability to filibuster in the Senate.

The GOP faced its greatest internal challenge in the form of a populist revolt from the "Tea Party." The movement opposed federal spending initiatives, including so-called "pork barrel" riders on legislation that drove money home to districts. Loosely organized by chapters, the Tea Party toppled a number of GOP favorites in the 2010 primary, including Utah's long-standing incumbent Senator Robert BENNETT. In Delaware, Tea Party candidate Christine O'DONNELL, who defeated the GOP's preferred Senate candidate in the primary, former governor Michael CASTLE, rankled voters with revelations of financial troubles and a well publicized admission that she had once "dabbled into witchcraft," while Sharron ANGLE, running against Democratic Senator Harry Reid in Nevada, raised concerns because of her unorthodox views that the Department of Education should be eliminated, the United States should withdraw from the United Nations, and a disbelief that the U.S. Constitution mandates the separation of church and state. Both were defeated in November.

Historic gains in the House gave the GOP a strong majority in that chamber, while the Republicans also increased their seats in the Senate and made sizable gains at the state and local levels. The new House speaker, John BOEHNER, vowed to cut government spending, reduce the size of government, and repeal the health care reforms. There were eight major contenders for the Republican Party's presidential nomination for the 2012 election: Texas governor Rick Perry, former Massachusetts governor Mitt Romney, Texas representative and former Libertarian presidential candidate Ron Paul, Minnesota representative and congressional Tea Party leader Michele Bachmann, former pizza chain executive Herman Cain, former house speaker Newt Gingrich, former Pennsylvania Senator Rick Santorum, and former Utah governor and ambassador to China Jon Huntsman. Romney quickly emerged as the frontrunner, but many conservatives and Tea Party activists opposed his nomination. Several candidates were able to challenge Romney, including Santorum who won the Iowa Caucus, and Gingrich, but Romney's funding advantages eroded the field, and the former governor had a commanding delegate lead by March. Romney lost the general election to incumbent president Obama on November 6, 2012. Republicans did maintain control of the House of Representatives and took control of the legislature in Arkansas for the first time since Reconstruction. The GOP also gained control of the state senates in Alaska and Wisconsin but lost their majorities in both houses in Minnesota and Maine and in at least one chamber in Colorado, New Hampshire, New York, and Oregon.

In a May 2013 special election the GOP retained the South Carolina House seat vacated by Tim SCOTT, who was appointed to the state's vacant Senate seat in January, when former governor Rick Sanford, who had resigned as chair of the Republican Governors Association in 2009 amid scandal, defeated Democrat Elizabeth Colbert Busch.

Leaders: John BOEHNER (Speaker of the House), Eric CANTOR (House Majority Leader), Kevin McCARTHY (House Majority Whip), Mitch McCONNELL (Senate Minority Leader), John CORNYN (Senate Minority Whip), Mitt ROMNEY (2012 presidential candidate and Former Governor of Massachusetts), Reince PRIEBUS (National Chair), Sharon DAY (Cochair).

Other Parties:

Although third parties have occasionally influenced the outcome of presidential balloting, the Republican Party in 1860 was the only such party in U.S. history to win a national election and subsequently establish itself as a major political organization. The third parties having the greatest impact have typically been those formed as largely personal vehicles by prominent Republicans or Democrats who have been denied nomination by their regular parties, such as Theodore Roosevelt's Progressive ("Bull Moose") Party of 1912 and the American Independent Party organized to support the 1968 candidacy of George C. Wallace.

The only nonparty candidates in recent history to attract significant public attention were former Democratic senator Eugene J. McCARTHY, who secured 751,728 votes (0.9 percent of the total) in 1976; former Republican representative John B. ANDERSON, who polled 5,719,722 (6.6 percent) in 1980; and Texas entrepreneur H. Ross PEROT, who won 19,237,247 (19 percent) in 1992 and whose substantial support gave rise to subsequent attempts to establish a credible third party before his **Reform Party**'s far less impressive showing of 8 percent in 1996. Thereafter, despite a 1998 Minnesota victory for the party's gubernatorial candidate, former professional wrestler Jesse VENTURA, the party declined further, winning only 0.4 percent of the vote in 2000 under longtime Republican conservative Patrick J. BUCHANAN. In a marginally more impressive showing, **Green Party** nominee Ralph NADER obtained 2.7 percent of the vote, whereas the **Natural Law Party** candidate, Harry BROWNE, secured 0.4 percent. Nader ran as an independent in 2004, winning only 0.3 percent of the vote, and in 2008.

Third-party candidates in 2012 were **Libertarian Party** (LP) nominee Gary JOHNSON, a former Republican governor of New Mexico; Green Party nominee Jill STEIN; **Constitution Party** (CP) nominee Virgil GOODE, a former Virginia member of the House of Representatives who served as both a Democrat (1997–2000) and Republican (2000–2009); **America's Party** (formally **America's Independent Party**) nominee Tom HOEFLING; **Peace and Freedom Party** nominee Roseanne BARR, an actress; and former mayor of Salt Lake City and **Justice Party** nominee Rocky ANDERSON.

Other minor parties, none of national significance in recent elections, have included the **Alaskan Independence Party** (AKIP), led by Lynette CLARK; the **American Independent Party** (AIP), led by Mark SEIDENBERG; the **American Nazi Party** (ANP), led by Rocky SUHAYDA; the **Communist Party of the United States of America** (CPUSA), led by Sam WEBB; the **Concerned Citizens** (CC), Connecticut affiliate of the **Constitution Party**, led by Jim CLYMER; the **Conservative Party** (CP), led by Sam A. GALLO and based in Louisiana with affiliates in 21 other states; the Rhode Island–based **Cool Moose Party,** led by Robert J. HEALEY Sr.; the **Corrective Action Party** (CAP), led by Bernard PALICKI; the **Democratic Socialists of America** (DSA), which is a member of the Socialist International and led by Maria SVART; the **Expansionist Party of the United States** (XP), which seeks expansion of the United States into an eventual world union, led by L. Craig SCHOONMAKER; the **Independent Party** (IP); the **Independent American Party** (IAP), led by Kelly GNEITING; the Latino **La Raza Unida** (People United) **Party** (LRUP); the **Liberal Party** (L); the **Liberty Union Party** (LU) of Vermont; the **Light Party,** led by Da VID; the **Mountain Party** (MP) of West Virginia; the **National Democratic Policy Committee** (NDPC), which has supported dissident Democrat, Lyndon LAROCHE, as a presidential candidate; the white supremacist **National Patriot Party** (NPP), which was formally launched in April 1994, mainly by former supporters of Perot; the now-defunct **National Unity Party** (NUP), which in 1984 endorsed John Anderson for a second presidential bid; the **New Federalist Party** (NFP), organized in 1975 "to promote the principles of George Washington and the Federalist founders of this nation"; the **Pacific Party** (PP); the **Pansexual Peace Party** (PPP); the feminist and socialist **Peace and Freedom Party** (PFP), based in California; **Politicians Are Crooks** (PAC); the now-defunct **Populist Party of America** (PPA), an outgrowth of the middle-class "America First" movement of the 1930s; the **Progressive Party** (PR); the Marxist **Progressive Labor Party** (PLP); the **Right to Life Party** (RLP), based in New York; the **Social Democrats USA** (SDUSA), a member of the Socialist International; the **Socialist Labor Party** (SLP); the **Timesizing.com Party** (TCP), based in Massachusetts; the **United States Pacifist Party** (USPP); the **Vermont Grassroots Party** (VGP); the **Veterans Industrial Party** (VIP), led by Ernest Lee EASTON; the **Working Families Party** (WFP); and the **World Socialist Party of the United States** (WSPUS).

LEGISLATURE

Legislative power is vested by the Constitution in the bicameral **Congress of the United States.** Both houses are chosen by direct popular election; one-third of the Senate and the entire House of Representatives are elected every two years. Congresses are numbered consecutively, with a new Congress meeting every second year. The last election (for the 112th Congress) was held on November 2, 2010.

Senate. The upper chamber consists of 100 members—2 from each state—elected on a statewide basis for six-year terms. Following the most recent balloting on November 6, 2012, the Democrats controlled 55 seats (including 1 independent) and the Republicans, 45.

President: Joseph R. BIDEN Jr. (Vice President of the United States).
President Pro Tempore: Patrick J. LEAHY.

House of Representatives. The lower house consists of 435 voting representatives, with each state entitled to at least 1 representative and the actual number from each state being apportioned periodically on the basis of population. The size and shape of congressional districts are determined by the states themselves; however, the Supreme Court has ruled that such districts must be "substantially equal" in population and must be redefined when they fail to meet this requirement. Resident commissioners from the District of Columbia, Guam, Puerto Rico, and the Virgin Islands were traditionally nonvoting delegates; however, in January 1993, over unanimous Republican opposition, they were given the right to vote in the body's Committee of the Whole, though not in the (usually pro forma) final passage of legislation. The right was revoked by the new Republican majority in January 1995; Democrats restored the privilege when they retook House control following the 2006 elections. In 2009 the resident commissioner of the Northern Marianas joined the ranks of nonvoting delegates, bringing their total to six, all of whom were Democrats or pledged to caucus with the Democrats. In the most recent elections on November 6, 2012, Democrats won 201 seats, and Republicans won 233.

Speaker: John BOEHNER.

CABINET

[as of September 26, 2013]

President	Barack H. Obama
Vice President	Joseph R. Biden Jr.
Secretaries	
Agriculture	Thomas J. Vilsack
Commerce	Penny Pritzker [f]
Defense	Chuck Hagel (R)
Education	Arne Duncan
Energy	Ernest Moniz
Health and Human Services	Kathleen Sebelius [f]
Homeland Security	Rand Beers (acting)
Housing and Urban Development	Shaun L. S. Donovan
Interior	Sally Jewell [f]
Justice	Eric H. Holder Jr.
Labor	Thomas Perez
State	John Kerry
Transportation	Anthony Foxx
Treasury	Jack Lew
Veteran's Affairs	Eric K. Shinseki
Cabinet-Level Aides	
Administrator, Environmental Protection Agency	Gina McCarthy [f]
Chief, Council of Economic Advisers	Jason Furman
Director, Office of Management and Budget	Sylvia Burwell [f]
United States Trade Representative	Michael Froman
White House Chief of Staff	Denis McDonough

[f] = female

Note: Except where noted, all of the above are members of the Democratic Party.

INTERGOVERNMENTAL REPRESENTATION

The various U.S. ambassadors to foreign governments, as well as the various foreign ambassadors accredited to the United States, are given at the end of the relevant country entries.

Permanent Representative to the UN: Samantha POWER.

IGO Memberships (Non-UN): ADB, AfDB, APEC, EBRD, G-8, G-20, IADB, IEA, IOM, NATO, OAS, OECD, OSCE, WTO.

RELATED TERRITORIES

The United States never acquired a colonial empire of significant proportions. Among its principal former overseas dependencies, the Philippines became independent in 1946, Puerto Rico acquired the status of a commonwealth in free association with the United States in 1952, and Hawaii became the 50th state of the Union in 1959. In addition to Puerto Rico, the United States now exercises sovereignty in the Virgin Islands, Guam, American Samoa, the Commonwealth of the Northern Mariana Islands, and an assortment of smaller Pacific and Caribbean islands, including the Midway Islands and Navassa. On January 6, 2009, President George W. Bush established the Pacific Remote Islands Marine National Monument, which encompasses Johnston, Palmyra and Wake atolls; Howland, Baker, and Jarvis islands; and Kingman Reef—a total of 86,888 square miles (225,040 sq. km). The Department of the Interior supervises the monument, the components of which are all national wildlife refuges.

Numerous other small insular territories have historically been claimed by the United States, including Christmas Island in the Indian Ocean, which passed from British to Australian administration in 1958. Quita Sueño, Roncador, Serrana, and Serranilla, a group of uninhabited islets in the western Caribbean, were turned over to Colombia under a 1972 treaty that the U.S. Senate failed to ratify until 1981 because of conflicting claims by Nicaragua.

Under the so-called Guano Act of 1856, the United States claimed jurisdiction over 58 Pacific islands ostensibly discovered by American citizens and presumed to contain extractable resources, principally phosphate. In 1979 the United States concluded a treaty with the newly independent state of Tuvalu whereby it renounced all claims under the act to the four southernmost of the country's nine islands. The following September the U.S. government concluded a similar treaty with Kiribati under which, in addition to surrendering Canton (subsequently Kanton) and Enderbury (theretofore under joint British and American administration), the United States relinquished claims to the eight Phoenix Islands, the five Southern Line Islands, and Christmas (subsequently Kiritimati) Island in the Northern Line group. In June 1980 a treaty was concluded with New Zealand whereby U.S. claims to four islands in the northern Cook group were also abandoned. The treaties were ratified by the U.S. Congress in 1983 over strong conservative opposition.

Until October 1, 1979, the United States held administrative responsibility for the Panama Canal Zone (see Panama: Panama Canal Zone), while U.S. administration of the Trust Territory of the Pacific Islands was effectively terminated with the independence of Palau on October 1, 1994. (For a discussion of the Trust Territory see the 1993 *Handbook,* pp. 946–948.)

Major Caribbean Jurisdictions:

Puerto Rico. Situated in the Caribbean between the island of Hispaniola in the west and the Virgin Islands in the east, the Commonwealth of Puerto Rico is composed of the large island of Puerto Rico together with Vieques, Culebra, and many smaller islands. Its area is 3,515 square miles (9,103 sq. km). According to the 2010 U.S. census, the population of Puerto Rico was 3,725,789 (99 percent Hispanic). Despite a falling birth rate, population density remains among the highest in the world, amounting in 2010 to 1,088 persons per square mile (420 per sq. km). San Juan, with a population of 381,931 in 2010, is the capital and principal city. Spanish blood and culture are dominant, with an admixture of Native American, African, and other immigrant stock, largely from Western Europe and the United States. Most Puerto Ricans are Spanish-speaking and Roman Catholic, although religious freedom prevails. Both English and Spanish served as official languages from 1902 to 1991, when a bill was approved requiring that all government proceedings take place in Spanish, with official bilingualism being reestablished in 1993. The economy, traditionally based on sugar, tobacco, and rum, advanced dramatically after 1948 under a self-help program known as Operation Bootstrap that stressed diversification and the use of incentives to promote industrialization through private investment, both local and foreign. Subsequently, industry surpassed agriculture as a source of income. Despite marked economic and social gains, however, the commonwealth has been burdened by high public debt and a high unemployment rate that has consistently been in the double digits (14.2 percent in 2012). Reflecting a significant maldistribution of wealth, 45.6 percent of the population was listed in 2011 as below the poverty line.

Ceded by Spain to the United States under the 1898 Treaty of Paris, Puerto Rico was subsequently governed as an unincorporated U.S. territory. The inhabitants were granted U.S. citizenship in 1917, obtaining in 1947 the right to elect a chief executive. The present commonwealth status, approved by plebiscite in 1951, entered into effect on July 25, 1952; under its terms, Puerto Rico now exercises approximately the same control over its internal affairs as do the 50 states, but residents, though U.S. citizens, do not vote in U.S. presidential elections and are represented in the U.S. Congress only by an elected resident commissioner in the House of Representatives. The resident commissioner has voting privileges in House committees (except for the House's Committee of the Whole) but not on the House floor. In November 1997 the Puerto Rican Supreme Court recognized the existence of Puerto Rican, in addition to U.S., citizenship. Federal taxes do not apply in Puerto Rico except by mutual consent (for example, Social Security taxes). The commonwealth constitution, modeled on that of the United States but incorporating many social and political innovations, provides for a governor and a bicameral Legislative Assembly (consisting of a 27-seat Senate and a 51-seat House of Representatives) elected by universal suffrage for four-year terms. An appointed Supreme Court heads the independent judiciary.

Puerto Rican politics was dominated from 1940 through 1968 by the **Popular Democratic Party** (*Partido Popular Democrático*—PPD) of Governor Luis MUÑOZ Marín, the principal architect of Operation Bootstrap and of the commonwealth relationship with the United States. While demands for Puerto Rican independence declined sharply after 1952, a substantial movement favoring statehood continued under the leadership of Luis A. FERRÉ and others. In a 1967 plebiscite 60.4 percent opted for continued commonwealth status, 39 percent for statehood, and 0.6 percent for independence. Following shifts in party alignments in advance of the 1968 election, Ferré was elected governor as head of the pro-statehood **New Progressive Party** (*Partido Nuevo Progresista*—PNP). Four years later the PPD, under Rafael HERNÁNDEZ Colón, regained the governorship, while the PNP, under San Juan mayor Carlos ROMERO Barceló, returned to power in 1976. Romero served until January 1985, when Hernández Colón began the first of two additional terms. The PNP's Pedro ROSSELLÓ was elected governor in 1992 and reelected in 1996.

The anti-statehood PPD secured an upset victory at the election of November 7, 2000, sweeping the governorship, both legislative houses, and most city halls. Its standard-bearer, Sila María CALDERÓN, who on January 7, 2001, became the commonwealth's first female governor, obtained 49 percent of the vote. The pro-statehood PNP candidate, Carlos PESQUERA, won 46 percent, with Rubén BERRÍOS Martínez of the **Puerto Rican Independence Party** (*Partido Independentista Puertoriqueño*—PIP) finishing a distant third.

A disputed gubernatorial poll in 2004 generated a recount that lasted two months, followed by a bitter court battle. The PPD's Aníbal ACEVEDO-VILÁ was declared the winner over former president Pedro Rosselló by 3,500 votes out of 2 million cast. In the Senate and House races, however, the pro-statehood forces secured majorities.

In 2008 Acevedo-Vilá sought another term despite a federal indictment against him on corruption charges, which he insisted were politically motivated. Though acquitted in early 2009, the charges contributed to his defeat in the November poll by the PNP's Luis FORTUÑO, theretofore Puerto Rico's representative (resident commissioner) in the U.S. Congress, who captured 52.8 percent of the vote. Acevedo-Vilá won 41.3 percent, followed by Rogelio FIGUEROA of the **Puerto Rico for Puerto Ricans Party** (*Partido Puertoriqueños por Puerto Rico*—PPR) with 2.8 percent and the PIP's Edwin IRIZARRY Mora with 2 percent. The PNP also won overwhelming majorities in both houses of the Legislative Assembly. (See below for information on the 2012 elections.)

A small but frequently violent independence movement became active in the 1920s, when the radical Nationalist Party was formed by Pedro ALBIZU Campos. On November 1, 1950, a group of *nacionalistas* attempted to assassinate President Harry S. Truman, while on March 1, 1954, another group wounded five U.S. members of Congress on the floor of the House of Representatives. (In 1979 President Jimmy Carter commuted the sentences of the four Puerto Ricans still serving sentences for the two attacks, despite Governor Romero Barceló's strong objection.) Currently, the separatist movement is directed by the PIP and the Marxist **Puerto Rican Socialist Party** (*Partido Socialista Puertoriqueño*—PSP), which collectively have won no more than a combined 6 percent of the vote in recent elections. The most militant organization advocating independence was the **Armed Forces for National Liberation** (*Fuerzas Armadas de Liberación Nacional*—FALN), which engaged in terrorist activities in New York City as well as in San Juan from the mid-1970s to the mid-1980s. In late 1979, three other terrorist groups—the **Volunteers of the Puerto Rican Revolution,** the **Boricua Popular Army** (*Ejército Popular Boricua,* also known as the *Macheteros*), and the **Armed Forces of Popular Resistance**—claimed joint responsibility for an attack on a busload of U.S. military personnel that killed two and left ten injured. In 2000 President Bill Clinton offered clemency to 16 FALN members who had been convicted of terrorist acts more than two decades earlier. A month later, 11 of the prisoners were released, despite a 311–41 House vote that condemned the president's action. The FALN leader, Carlos Alberto TORRES, having served nearly 30 years in prison, was released in July 2010.

In September 1978 the UN Decolonization Committee endorsed a Cuban resolution that labeled Puerto Rico a colony of the United States and called for a transfer of power before any referendum on statehood. On December 13, 1998, in a nonbinding referendum, 50.8 percent of Puerto Ricans voted for no change in status, while 46.5 percent favored statehood, and 2.5 percent, independence. (See below for information on the 2012 referendum.)

The status of the island of Vieques, two-thirds of which had long been used as a bombing range by the U.S. Navy, came to a head after the killing of a civilian security guard during a bombing run in April 1999. Numerous protests erupted in the ensuing months.

On June 14, 2001, President Bush announced that all exercises on Vieques would end by May 2003, but Vieques residents on July 29 voted by a 2–1 margin for immediate closure of the naval facility. The U.S. Congress insisted that the range was needed for war on terrorism related tests, but the PIP threatened to mount a general strike. Accordingly, the navy withdrew on May 1, 2003, turning about 14,500 acres over to the U.S. Fish and Wildlife Service. Since then, with oversight from the Environmental Protection Agency, contract workers have been clearing the site of unexploded munitions. Some 7,000 of the island's more than 9,000 residents have filed claims for illnesses from pollutants released during the period of live-fire exercises.

In June 2011 Barack Obama became the first U.S. president since John F. Kennedy in 1961 to make an official visit to Puerto Rico. A two-part nonbinding referendum on November 6, 2012, asked voters if they wanted to change the current Commonwealth status and which of three alternatives (statehood, sovereign free association [informally referenced as "enhanced commonwealth," which would provide greater autonomy], or independence) they preferred. According to initial results, 54 percent answered yes to the first question, while in response to the second question 61 percent endorsed statehood, 33 percent sovereign free association, and 5 percent independence. Consequently, a request for statehood was expected to be forwarded to the U.S. Congress. In concurrent balloting, Alejandro GARCIA Padilla, the candidate of the PPD, was elected governor by a narrow margin over Fortuño, a statehood advocate. Following his election, Garcia said that a constituent assembly should be convened to prepare another plebiscite on the statehood matter for 2014.

Some observers suggested that Fortuño's defeat reflected the recent increase in violent crime and ongoing economic difficulties. Though Fortuño's austerity program was credited with a return to financial stability following four years of economic contraction, it was unpopular among many Puerto Ricans. Meanwhile, the PPD secured strong majorities in Puerto Rico's Senate and House of Representatives in the November 6 poll as well as a majority of mayoralties. Garcia was sworn in on January 2, 2013.

In May 2013 Resident Commissioner Pedro PIERLUISI introduced legislation in Congress that would offer statehood to Puerto Rico. The measure would ask Puerto Rican voters if they support statehood, and with majority approval, the president would submit legislation to Congress for admission as a state. As of October 1 the bill had not faced a vote.

Governor: Alejandro GARCIA Padilla.

Resident Commissioner (member of the U.S. House of Representatives): Pedro PIERLUISI.

Virgin Islands. Situated 40 miles east of Puerto Rico and just west and south of the British Virgin Islands, the U.S. Virgin Islands (formerly known as the Danish West Indies) include the large islands of St. Croix, St. Thomas, and St. John, and about 50 smaller islands. The total area, including water surfaces, is 132 square miles (342 sq. km); the population was 106,405 at the 2010 census. The capital, Charlotte

Amalie on St. Thomas, is the sole substantial town. Two-thirds of the people are of African origin, and approximately one-quarter are of Puerto Rican descent. English is the principal language, although Spanish is widely spoken. The people are highly religious, with most being either Baptist or Roman Catholic.

Purchased by the United States from Denmark in 1917, the Virgin Islands, an unincorporated territory, were initially administered by the U.S. Navy and then, from 1931 to 1971, by the Department of the Interior. Residents were made U.S. citizens in 1927 and were granted a considerable measure of self-government in the Revised Organic Act of 1954, which authorized the creation of an elected 15-member Senate. Under a New Organic Act of 1968, executive authority was vested in a governor and a lieutenant governor, both of whom since 1970 have been popularly elected. Since 1973 the territory has sent one nonvoting delegate to the U.S. House of Representatives. (The delegate can vote in House committees but not on the House floor.) Elected governors were Melvin EVANS (to 1975), a Republican; Cyril KING (1975–1978) of the **Independent Citizens' Movement** (ICM), who died in office; Juan F. LUIS (1978–1987), also of the ICM; and Alexander FARRELLY (1987–1995), a Democrat.

In a referendum held October 11, 1993, 90 percent of those voting favored continued or enhanced U.S. territorial status, while the options of full integration with the United States and independence each attracted about 5 percent. The 27.4 percent turnout fell short of the required 50 percent plus one to validate the outcome.

In November 1994 Dr. Roy SCHNEIDER, a Republican standing as an independent, was elected governor, defeating the former lieutenant governor, Derek HODGE, a Democrat. In November 1998 retired university professor Charles TURNBULL, a Democrat, defeated Schneider, criticized for overspending. Turnbull won reelection on November 5, 2002, and a fellow Democrat, John de JONGH Jr., succeeded him in a runoff poll on November 21, 2006.

On June 12, 2007, voters chose 30 delegates for a constitutional convention. (Voters rejected previous constitutional efforts in 1964, 1971, 1979, and 1981.) After two years of often contentious negotiations, the convention forwarded a draft proposal to Governor de Jongh in late May 2009. However, the governor refused to submit the proposal to U.S. president Barack Obama and the U.S. Congress for consideration on the grounds that some of its provisions were outside the framework of the U.S. constitution and thereby unacceptable. Among other things, the proposal failed to recognize the supremacy of the U.S. constitution and offered extra rights (including property tax exemptions) to "native" Virgin Islanders.

On November 2, 2010, Governor de Jongh easily won reelection. Following the November 6, 2012, elections, the Democrats held 10 seats in the Senate; independents, 4; and the ICM, 1.

Governor: John de JONGH Jr.

Delegate to the U.S. House of Representatives: Donna CHRISTENSEN.

Major Pacific Jurisdictions:

American Samoa. Located in the South Pacific just east of the independent state of Samoa, American Samoa includes the six Samoan islands (Annuu, Ofu, Olosega, Rose, Tau, Tutuila) annexed by the United States pursuant to a treaty with Great Britain and Germany in 1899, and also the privately owned Swain's Island (currently with 4–30 inhabitants, at various times), 200 miles to the north and west, which was annexed in 1925. The land area of 77 square miles (199 sq. km) is inhabited by a population almost entirely of Polynesian ancestry that more than doubled from 27,159 at the 1970 census to 57,291 at the 2000 census but fell to 55,519 at the 2010 census. Fagatogo village, on Tutuila's Pago Pago Harbor, is the administrative capital. The social structure is based on the same *matai* (family chief) system that prevails in neighboring Samoa. Although educational levels are comparatively high, subsistence farming and fishing remain the predominant way of life. U.S. government spending, fish canning, and tourism are the main sources of income, and the government is the territory's single largest employer. About one-third of all high school graduates leave Samoa for the U.S. mainland.

Constitutionally, American Samoa is an unincorporated territory. Indigenous inhabitants are nationals but not U.S. citizens and therefore cannot vote in U.S. presidential elections. Administered until 1951 by the U.S. Navy and then by the Department of the Interior, the territory held its first gubernatorial elections in November 1977. Its bicameral legislature (*Fono*) consists of an 18-member Senate chosen by clan chiefs and subchiefs, and a popularly elected, nonpartisan, 20-member House of Representatives, exclusive of a nonvoting member from Swain's Island. The judiciary consists of five district courts and a High Court, although a Court of Appeals in San Francisco ruled that the U.S. District Court for Hawaii has jurisdiction over federal crimes committed in American Samoa. Appointed district governors head the territory's three political districts.

Between January 1981 and January 1997 the Republican Peter Tali COLEMAN and the Democrat A. P. LUTALI alternated four-year terms as governor. In 1996 Coleman, in poor health, chose not to run again, while Lutali placed third in the first round of nonpartisan voting on November 5. Lutali's lieutenant governor, Tauese P. F. SUNIA, emerged victorious in the November 19 runoff. He was reelected in 2000. Lieutenant Governor TOGIOLA T. A. Tulafono became governor following Sunia's death in March 2003 and was reelected to full terms in 2004 and 2008.

In December 2006 a Future Political Status Study Commission recommended continuation of the island's "unorganized and unincorporated" status, enactment of legislation to strengthen the *matai* system and prevent further alienation of communal land, and the imposition of new restrictions on the entry and residence of aliens. However, in June 2010 a constitutional convention called for greater autonomy from the federal government. The proposed 34 changes to American Samoa's constitution were put before the voters on November 2 despite objections from many that they were faced with an up-or-down, all-or-nothing ballot question. The package lost by a 70 percent to 30 percent vote.

Governor Togiola in the first half of 2012 again called for the territory to explore options for greater autonomy. Traditional chiefs argued that the 2010 referendum had settled the matter. Togiola also suggested a referendum be held on his proposal that members of the Senate (currently selected by the chiefs) be chosen through direct popular election in the future.

Six candidates contested the first round of gubernatorial balloting on November 6, 2012, Togiola being precluded by term limits from seeking reelection. LOLO Matalasi Moliga, an independent who had recently resigned as president of the Development Bank of American Samoa to run for the post, and Lieutenant Governor FAOA Aitofele Sunia, a Democrat, proceeded to a November 20 runoff. Lolo won with 52.9 percent of votes and took office on January 3, 2013. In a concurrent referendum, voters rejected by a near two to one majority a proposed constitutional amendment that would authorize the *Fono* to override a governor's veto instead of the U.S. secretary of the interior, who is currently so empowered.

Governor: LOLO Matalasi Moliga.

Delegate to the U.S. House of Representatives: FALEOMAVAEGA Eni Hunkin.

Guam. The unincorporated U.S. territory of Guam is geographically the southernmost and largest of the Mariana Islands in the west-central Pacific. Its area of 209 square miles (541 sq. km) supports a population that numbered 159,358 at the 2010 census, inclusive of U.S. service members and their dependents. The capital, Hagåtña (formerly Agaña), has a civilian population of about 1,100. The islanders, predominantly of Chamorro (Micronesian) stock and Roman Catholic faith, have a high level of education, with a literacy rate of more than 90 percent. The economy depends largely on military spending and tourism (over 1 million arrivals a year, mostly from Japan and South Korea).

Acquired from Spain by the 1898 Treaty of Paris, the island is the responsibility of the U.S. Department of the Interior. Guamanians were made U.S. citizens by an Organic Act of 1950; although they do not vote in U.S. presidential elections, they have since 1973 sent a delegate to the U.S. House of Representatives. (The delegate has voting rights in House committees but not on the House floor.) Under the Guam Elective Governor Act of 1968, since November 1970 the governor and lieutenant governor have been popularly elected for four-year terms. The legislature, reelected every two years, was reduced from 21 to 15 members in 1998. A Federal District Court heads the judicial system. Local government in 19 municipalities is headed by elected district commissioners.

In 1982 voters, by a three-to-one margin, expressed a preference for a commonwealth rather than statehood, and in an August 8, 1987, referendum, approved 10 of 12 articles of a Commonwealth Act; on November 7 the remaining articles, providing for the recognition of indigenous Chamorro rights and local control of immigration (both bitterly opposed by non-Chamorros) were also approved. In 1992 the end of protracted talks between Guam's Commission on

Self-Determination and a Bush administration task force achieved a "qualified agreement" on a commonwealth bill. Although endorsed by Democratic presidential candidate Bill Clinton at the party's 1992 convention, the measure was not introduced in the U.S. Senate until November 1997; by then, President Clinton, under pressure because of congressional unwillingness to sanction a Chamorro-only franchise, or line-item veto power over federal legislation, had reversed himself, and the measure did not pass.

Early elected governors were Republican Carlos G. CAMACHO (to January 1975), Democrat Ricardo J. BORDALLO (1975–1979 and 1983–1987), Republican Paul McDonald CALVO (1979–1983), and Republican Joseph F. ADA (1987–1995). In 1987 Bordallo was convicted for influence peddling; although he secured partial suspension of his prison sentence in October 1988, he committed suicide in 1990, immediately before he was to serve out the remainder of the sentence.

On November 8, 1994, Democrat Carl GUTIERREZ defeated Tommy TANAKA, the Republican nominee, by a comfortable 54.6 percent majority; concurrently, the Democrats also bucked a national trend by retaining legislative control with a slightly reduced majority of 13–8. In 1996, on the other hand, Republicans regained legislative control for the first time since 1980 by a razor-thin margin of 11–10. In a comeback effort, former governor Ada failed to turn back Gutierrez's reelection on November 3, 1998, even though the Republicans surged to a 12–3 majority in the downsized legislature.

In the November 5, 2002, election Republican Felix CAMACHO won the governorship over Democrat Robert UNDERWOOD, taking 55.2 percent of the vote. In the legislative election, Democrats won 9 seats, while Republicans took the other 6. There was no shift in the legislative balance at the next election, held November 2, 2004, but on November 7, 2006, the Republicans won an 8-to-7 majority. Collaterally, Camacho won reelection by again defeating Underwood, but the margin of victory was narrow, 50.3 percent to 48.0 percent. The Democrats regained their legislative majority by securing 10 of the 15 seats on November 4, 2008.

Term limits precluded Governor Camacho from seeking reelection in November 2010. Republican nominee Eddie B. CALVO won a narrow victory over former governor Gutierrez. Meanwhile Democrats maintained a legislative advantage, winning nine seats.

A significant improvement in Guam's economy is expected as the result of a decision reached in 2006 for the eventual relocation of many U.S. servicemen and their dependents from the Japanese island of Okinawa to Guam and other Pacific territories. Initially, it was estimated that some 8,600 servicemen and perhaps as many at 9,000 of their dependents would be moved to Guam. However, as negotiations regarding the final parameters (including the start date) of the initiative continued in the fall of 2012, it was reported that the number of servicemen moving to Guam would be reduced to about 5,000, some on a rotational basis that would reduce the number of dependents to about 1,300.

In balloting on November 6, 2012, the Democrats retained their 9–6 advantage in the legislature, while Madeleine BORDELLO, a Democrat, was reelected as delegate to the U.S. House of Representative.

Governor: Eddie B. CALVO.

Delegate to the U.S. House of Representatives: Madeleine BORDELLO.

Commonwealth of the Northern Mariana Islands (CNMI). Located north of the Caroline Islands and west of the Marshalls in the western Pacific, the Marianas (excluding Guam) constitute an archipelago of 16 islands with a land area of 184 square miles (477 sq. km). The population of 53,883 at the 2010 census (down 22 percent from 2000) resides on six islands, including Saipan (the administrative center), Tinian, and Rota. Classed as Micronesian, the people are largely Roman Catholic.

In 1972 a Marianas Political Status Commission initiated negotiations with Washington that resulted in the 1975 signing of a covenant to establish a Commonwealth of the Northern Mariana Islands in political union with the United States. The covenant was approved by the U.S. Senate on February 24, 1976, and signed by President Gerald Ford on March 24. In January 1978 a government consisting of the commonwealth's first governor, Democrat Carlos S. CAMACHO, and a Northern Marianas Commonwealth Legislature was established. The bicameral legislature encompasses a 9-member Senate elected for staggered four-year terms and a 20-member (formerly 14-member) House of Representatives elected biennially. Under U.S. and local law, the commonwealth ceased to be a component of the Trust Territory of the Pacific Islands on November 3, 1986, with its residents becoming U.S. citizens on the same day. (According to a census report, the percentage holding U.S. citizenship had dropped to 50.3 in 2008.) The change in status under international law came with formal removal from trusteeship by vote of the UN Security Council on December 22, 1990. Since 2009 the commonwealth has been represented in the U.S. House of Representatives by a delegate who has voting rights in House committees but not the House floor.

Governor Camacho was succeeded by Republican Pedro Pangelinan ("Teno") TENORIO (1982–1990), who was in turn followed by another Republican, Lorenzo (Larry) I. De Leon GUERRERO. Governor Guerrero lost a reelection bid in 1993 to his Democratic opponent, Froilan C. ("Lang") TENORIO, although the Republicans retained majorities in both legislative houses. In the election of November 1997 Tenorio and Lt. Gov. Jesus C. BORJA ran on separate tickets (the latter technically as an independent), thus splitting the Democratic vote and enabling former Republican governor Pedro Tenorio to win with 45.6 percent of the vote. A subsequent judicial challenge to his victory on the basis of a two-term limit adopted in 1986 was rejected on the grounds that the change could not be applied retroactively.

In the election of November 3, 2001, Juan BABAUTA, a Republican, captured the governor's office with 42.8 percent of the vote, defeating Benigno R. Fitial of the **Covenant Party** (CP, recently formed by Fitial), the Democrat Borja, and Froilan Tenorio, now of the **Reform Party.** Republicans also retained control of both legislative chambers.

A four-way gubernatorial race on November 5, 2005, pitted Governor Babauta against Speaker of the House Fitial, Froilan Tenorio, and independent Heinz HOFSCHNEIDER. The contest was so close, however, that the outcome remained unclear until more than 1,200 absentee ballots were counted two weeks later. In the end, Fitial won by 99 votes over Hofschneider. In simultaneous legislative balloting, no party won a majority in either house. In the Senate, the CP and the Republicans each held three seats, the Democrats, two, and one independent; in the House, the CP and the Republicans each won seven seats, followed by the Democrats and independents with two each.

In contrast, Republicans dominated the November 3, 2007, election for an expanded House, winning 12 of the 20 seats. The CP won 4; the Democrats, 1; and independents, 3. Of the 3 Senate seats up for election, a member of the CP, a Democrat running as an independent, and an independent each won.

In early 2009 former chief justice Jose S. DELA CRUZ predicted likely bankruptcy for the commonwealth if changes were not made in a land alienation rule that discourages foreign investment. The assessment came in the wake of a sharp decline in tourism (expected to continue because of the exclusion of Chinese and Russians from the federal visa waiver process) and U.S. congressional approval of measures to federalize labor and immigration controls that would severely affect the status of "guest workers." The "federalization" transition was subsequently postponed at least until the end of 2014.

Governor Fitial was reelected to another five-year term in runoff balloting on November 23, 2009, in which Hofschneider, the Republican candidate, lost by 370 votes despite having narrowly led the first round. In December 2010 Fitial announced the planned merger of the CP and the Republican Party (his original party), but leaders of both parties objected, and the initiative was dropped. After Fitial rejoined the Republican Party in early 2012, he continued to face criticism in the CNMI House of Representatives from members of the CP and so-called Independent Republicans. The anti-Fitial bloc in September tabled a 16-count impeachment resolution accusing Fitial of corruption and neglect of duty in regard to, among other things, recent government contracts. The impeachment resolution was defeated by a 10–9 October House vote.

Twelve independents, four Republicans, and four CP members were elected to the House in balloting on November 6, 2012, while two independents and one Republican were elected in the partial Senate replenishment. Sixteen of the House members were described as anti-Fitial, and his opponents vowed to introduce another impeachment motion soon, although Fitial argued that they would be better off focusing on economic problems. Meanwhile, Gregorio Kilili SABLAN, an independent who caucuses with the Democrats, was reelected as the CNMI delegate to the U.S. House of Representatives with 80 percent of the vote. He pledged to ask the federal government to investigate possible corruption in the CNMI and endorsed proposed immigration reform that would permit foreign workers, many who have arrived without legal status, to remain in the Commonwealth under new visa protocols, as requested by business leaders and CNMI officials.

On February 11, 2013, the House impeached Fitial for charges of corruption and failure to perform duties. The governor resigned on February 20, before the impeachment proceedings were considered in the Senate, and lieutenant governor Eloy INOS took office.

Governor: Eloy INOS.

Delegate to the U.S. House of Representatives: Gregorio Kilili Camacho SABLAN.

Pacific Remote Islands Marine National Monument:

Johnston Atoll. Encompassing Johnston, Sand, North, and East islands, Johnston Atoll lies about 700 miles southwest of Hawaii. The islands have a combined area of about 1.0 square mile (2.7 sq. km), most of which was engineered by dredging and filling. The population of Johnston Island was 1,387 (primarily government personnel) in 1994; the other islands are officially uninhabited. Annexed in 1858, the atoll was under the joint administration of the U.S. Defense and Interior departments after World War II and continues to be managed by the U.S. Air Force.

During 1990 a number of island governments, including those of American Samoa, the Marshall Islands, and the Northern Marianas, complained to the federal government of the incineration of dangerous chemicals (including nerve gas) and armaments on Johnston Island, arguing that there was a danger of the jet stream carrying pollutants not only to their shores but "around the world." Subsequently, during an October summit meeting with Pacific leaders in Hawaii, President George H. W. Bush indicated that the Defense Department would proceed with disposal of the materials already on the island but had no plans to continue the practice thereafter. In early 1999 the U.S. Army announced that its Johnston Island Atoll Chemical Disposal System (JACADS) would be closed. It was subsequently reported that the destruction of chemical weapons on Johnson had been completed in 2004, and the U.S. Environmental Protection Agency in 2009 certified that the facility had been properly cleaned and closed. (Since 1926 the U.S. Fish and Wildlife Service has been responsible for the area as a wildlife refuge, but it remains closed to the public.)

Palmyra Atoll. A group of about 50 islets situated on a horseshoe-shaped reef about 1,000 miles south of Honolulu, Palmyra became a U.S. territory upon the annexation of Hawaii in 1898. It was placed under civil administration of the Interior Department by the Hawaii Statehood Act of 1959. Privately owned by the Fullard-Leo family of Hawaii from 1922, the atoll, covering 4 square miles (10.44 sq. km), was occupied during World War II by the U.S. Navy, which built an airstrip subsequently used by the U.S. Air Force until 1961. In early 2000 the U.S.-based Nature Conservancy announced that it had launched a $37 million fund-raising campaign to buy the atoll, which is home to 20 bird species and has five times as many coral species as the Florida Keys. The sale, concluded in November 2000, led to the construction of a $1.5 million wildlife research station.

Wake Atoll. Consisting of three islets with a combined area of 3 square miles (7.8 sq. km) with no indigenous population, Wake Atoll lies roughly midway between Hawaii and Guam. It was formally claimed by the United States in 1900.

Although Wake falls under the jurisdiction of the Department of the Interior, activities have long been administered by the U.S. military. An air and naval station was established before World War II, during which Wake was occupied by Japanese forces. It is also the site of a U.S. Missile Defense Agency facility. In August 2006 the remaining military personnel, numbering fewer than 200, were evacuated in advance of one of the central Pacific's most powerful storms, Typhoon Ioke, which caused an estimated $88 million in damage on the island. Subsequently, upwards of 100 people, mainly civilian contractors, were engaged in restoring services. The airfield remains available for emergency landings by civilian as well as military aircraft.

Howland, Baker, and Jarvis Islands. Uninhabited, with a combined land area of about 3.8 square miles (9.84 sq. km), Howland, Baker, and Jarvis are widely scattered islands situated more than 1,300 miles south of Honolulu. Claimed by the United States in 1936, all three were designated national wildlife refuges in 1974, and in late 2007 the U.S. Fish and Wildlife Service announced the availability of a number of conservation plans for their management over the next 15 years.

In May 1999 President Teburoro Tito of Kiribati claimed that the three islands were geographically part of Kiribati and should come under its jurisdiction; there has been no indication, however, that Washington was prepared to consider the claim.

Kingman Reef. The uninhabited Kingman Reef, surrounding a lagoon 932 miles southwest of Honolulu, has no permanent land. It was annexed in 1922 and subsequently administered by the Department of the Navy. Characterized by the Scripps Institution of Oceanography in early 2008 as "one of the planet's most pristine coral reefs," Kingman has been a national wildlife refuge since 2001.

Other Insular Possessions:

Midway Islands. Consisting of Eastern and Sand islands (not to be confused with Johnston Atoll's Sand Island, above), the Midway Islands have a combined area of 2 square miles (5.2 sq. km). Located at the northwestern end of the Hawaiian chain, the Midway Islands were annexed in 1867 and are best known as the site of a major U.S. naval victory against Japan in 1942. Administered by the Department of the Navy until 1996, Midway was then taken over by the Department of the Interior. The largely military population of about 2,500 (1994) was withdrawn.

On June 15, 2006, President George W. Bush turned a 200,000 square mile tract of ocean including the Midway Islands into the world's largest marine sanctuary, the Northwestern Hawaiian Islands Marine National Monument. Renamed the Papahanaumokuakea Marine National Monument in March 2007, it is home to approximately 7,000 wildlife species, a number of which are endangered by plastic debris and lead paint flakes from former military buildings, prompting extensive cleanup operations scheduled for completion by 2017.

Navassa. Situated between Jamaica and Haiti and claimed by the United States in 1916, Navassa is a small island of 2 square miles (5 sq. km) that served as the site of a lighthouse maintained by the U.S. Coast Guard until 1996. In July 1981 six U.S. Marines were temporarily deployed on Navassa to thwart a semi-official attempt by Haitians to lay claim to the island. The island is currently administered by the Department of the Interior.

URUGUAY

Oriental Republic of Uruguay
República Oriental del Uruguay

Political Status: Independent state proclaimed in 1825; republic established in 1830; presidential-congressional system reinstated on March 1, 1985, supplanting military-controlled civilian government in power since February 1973.

Area: 68,037 sq. mi. (176,215 sq. km).

Population: 3,518,729 (2012E—UN); 3,324,460 (2013E—U.S. Census).

Major Urban Center (2011E): MONTEVIDEO (1,672,000).

Official Language: Spanish.

Monetary Unit: Uruguayan Peso (market rate November 1, 2013: 21.43 pesos = $1US).

President: José Alberto MUJICA Cordano (Progressive Encounter—Broad Front); elected on November 29, 2009, and inaugurated on March 1, 2010, for a five-year term, succeeding Tabaré Ramón VÁZQUEZ Rosas (Progressive Encounter—Broad Front); named a new government on March 2, 2010.

Vice President: Danilo ASTORI (Progressive Encounter–Broad Front); elected on November 29, 2009, and inaugurated on March 1, 2010, for a term concurrent with that of the president, succeeding Rodolfo NIN Novoa (Progressive Encounter–Broad Front).

THE COUNTRY

Second smallest of South American countries, Uruguay has historically been among the best performers in terms of education, per capita income, and social welfare. Its official designation as the Oriental (Eastern) Republic of Uruguay derives from its position on the eastern bank of the Uruguay River, which forms its frontier with Argentina and opens into the great estuary of the Rio de la Plata, on which both Montevideo and the Argentine capital of Buenos Aires are situated. From its 120-mile Atlantic coastline, Uruguay's rolling grasslands gently climb to the Brazilian boundary in the northeast. More than half of the population, which is almost entirely of Spanish and Italian origins, is concentrated in Montevideo, the only large city. While Uruguay was once a popular destination for immigrants, the flow of people has reversed. An estimated one-fifth of the population lives abroad, mostly in Europe or the United States. According to the World Bank, 56 percent of women are in the labor force. Currently, 16 women serve in the legislature.

Although cattle- and sheep-raising were the traditional basis of the economy, crop farming has increased in recent years, and a sizable industrial complex (primarily food processing) has developed around the capital. Textiles, meat, wool, and leather goods are currently the leading exports, while industrial promotion and foreign investment laws instituted in the early 1980s encouraged production of electrical equipment and minerals.

GDP growth averaged 3.2 percent annually throughout the 1990s but the economy entered a protracted recession from 1999 through 2002, contracting by 3.9 percent annually through the period. A principal cause of the downturn was declining world commodity prices for Uruguayan exports, but in late 2001 the economy was thrown into a tailspin by the financial crisis in Argentina. Economic recovery and a resumption of growth led to a significant expansion of 5.7 percent annually from 2003 to 2008. GDP fell to 2.4 percent in 2009, owing in large part to a decline in commodity prices and the global financial crisis. Inflation and unemployment declined to about 7 percent each from double-digit highs at the turn of the century. Overall, the country was among the few able to avoid a recession during the global economic downturn, according to the International Monetary Fund, which cited recent financial system reforms, robust growth in exports, and lower poverty rates. Robust GDP growth of 8.9 percent in 2010 slowed to 5.7 percent in 2011 and fell further in 2012 to 3.8 percent, where it remained in 2013. Inflation was 7.3 percent and unemployment 6.5 percent.

GOVERNMENT AND POLITICS

Political background. Before the 20th century Uruguay's history was largely determined by the buffer-like position that made it an object of contention between the colonial powers Spain and Portugal and, later, between Argentina and Brazil. Uruguay proclaimed its independence in 1825 and was recognized by its two neighboring countries in 1828, but both continued to play a role in the internal struggles of Uruguay's Colorado and Blanco parties following the proclamation of a republic in 1830. The foundations of modern Uruguay were laid during the presidency of José BATLLE y Ordóñez, who took office under the Colorado banner in 1903 and initiated the extensive welfare program and governmental participation in the economy for which the nation was subsequently noted. Batlle y Ordóñez and the Colorado Party were also identified with a method of government characterized by a presidential board, or council, employed from 1917 to 1933 and again from 1951 to 1967. The Colorados, who had controlled the government continuously from 1865, were finally ousted in the election of 1958 but were returned to power in 1966, when voters also approved a constitutional amendment returning the country to a one-person presidency.

The first of the presidents under the new arrangement, Oscar Diego GESTIDO (Colorado), took office in March 1967 but died nine months later and was succeeded by Vice President Jorge PACHECO Areco (Colorado). Faced with a growing economic crisis, rising unrest among workers and students, and increasing activity by *Tupamaro* guerrillas, both presidents sought to enforce economic austerity and resorted to emergency security measures. Economic and political instability continued after the election of Juan María BORDABERRY Arocena (Colorado) in November 1971, and worsening circumstances culminated in military intervention on February 8, 1973. Under the direction of Gen. César Augusto MARTÍNEZ, José PÉREZ Caldas, and Esteban CRISTI, the military presented a 19-point program that emphasized economic reform, reducing corruption by officials, and greater military participation in political life. President Bordaberry accepted the program on February 13, with governmental reorganization commencing almost immediately. A National Security Council was created to oversee the administration, Congress was dissolved and replaced by a Council of State, and municipal and local councils were supplanted by appointed bodies. Opposition to the increasing influence of the military was met by coercion: a general strike by the National Confederation of Workers (*Confederación Nacional de Trabajadores*—CNT) resulted in the group's proscription, while several opposition political leaders were placed in temporary detention during July and August. The National University of Montevideo was closed in October, and the Communist-led *Frente Amplio,* in addition to numerous minor leftist groups, was banned in December. Subsequently, as many as 400,000 Uruguayans were reported to have fled the country.

In early 1976 President Bordaberry, whose constitutional term was due to expire, butted heads with the military because he wished to remain indefinitely in office as head of a corporativist state within which normal political activity would be prohibited. The military, on the other hand, preferred a Brazilian-style "limited democracy," with the traditional parties gradually reentering the political process over the ensuing decade. On June 12 the military view prevailed: Bordaberry was deposed, and Vice President Alberto DEMICHELLI was named as his interim successor. On July 14 a newly constituted Council of the Nation (incorporating the Council of State, the three heads of the armed services, and other high-ranking officers) designated Dr. Aparicio MÉNDEZ Manfredini as president for a five-year term commencing September 1.

In August 1977 the government announced that President Méndez had accepted a recommendation by the military leadership that a general election be held in 1981, although only the Colorado and National (Blanco) parties would be permitted to participate. Subsequently, it was reported that a new constitution would be promulgated in 1980, while all parties would be permitted to resume their normal functions by 1986.

The proposed basic law, which would have given the military effective veto power within a context of "restricted democracy," was rejected by more than 57 percent of those participating in a referendum held November 30, 1980. The government promptly accepted the decision while announcing that efforts toward "democratic institutionalization" would continue "on the basis of the current regime."

Following designation by the Council of the Nation, the recently retired army commander, Lt. Gen. Gregorio Conrado ALVAREZ Armellino, assumed office on September 1, 1981, as "transition" president for a term scheduled to end upon reversion to civilian rule in March 1985. Fourteen months later, on November 28, 1982, a nationwide election was held to select delegates to conventions of three legally recognized groups, the Colorado and Blanco parties and the Civic Union, whose leaders were to participate in the drafting of a constitution to be presented to the voters in November 1984. The balloting, in which antimilitary candidates outpolled their promilitary counterparts within each party by almost five to one, was followed by a series of talks between the regime and the parties, which broke down in July 1983 over the extent of military power under the new basic law. The impasse yielded a period of instability through mid-1984, with escalating public protests (including Chilean-style "banging of the pots"), increased press censorship, and arrests of dissidents (most prominently the respected Blanco leader, Wilson FERREIRA Aldunate, upon his return from exile on June 16). Government statements that adherence to the declared electoral timetable (which called for balloting on November 25) would be "conditional" upon the cooperation of the civilian parties yielded further protests, while deteriorating economic conditions prompted a series of work stoppages.

After talks resumed in July 1984 between the army and a multiparty grouping (*Multipartidaria*) consisting of the legal parties (excluding the Blancos, who had quit the group in protest at the imprisonment of their leader) and a number of formations that were still nominally illegal, an agreement was reached on August 3 confirming the November 25 election date and establishing a transitional advisory role for the military until late 1985. The signing of the pact was followed by a relaxation of press censorship and the legalization of a number of additional parties that, in concert with the Communist Party (*Partido Comunista*—PC), which remained outlawed at the time, reactivated the 1971 Broad Front (*Frente Amplio*—FA) coalition (see Political Parties, below).

Despite the Blanco Party's condemnation of the August 1984 agreement as an "acceptance of dictatorship," the party rejoined the *Multipartidaria* after the group had initiated talks with business and union leaders on a peaceful transition to civilian rule. However, because of the continued proscription of both the Blanco leader and *Frente Amplio*'s Gen. Liber SEREGNI, the Colorado candidate, Julio María SANGUINETTI Cairolo, enjoyed a considerable advantage in the presidential race, gaining a 38.6 percent vote share at the November balloting while his party won a slim plurality in both houses. The new Congress convened on February 15, 1985, followed by Sanguinetti's inauguration on March 1. To avoid public embarrassment at the swearing-in ceremony (the president-elect having indicated an aversion to accepting the presidential sash from a military ruler), President Alvarez had resigned on February 12, Supreme Court President Rafael ADDIEGO Bruno being named his interim replacement. In further attempts to remove the legacy of the military regime, the Sanguinetti government, with broad support from the public and opposition parties, released all political prisoners, including former *Tupamaro* guerrillas, and permitted the return of an estimated 20,000 exiles. Subsequently, a 1986 decision to declare an amnesty for military members charged with human rights abuses generated strong dissent, although Uruguayan voters failed to reverse the action in a referendum conducted in April 1989.

While the Blanco right-wing candidate, Luis Alberto LACALLE Herrera, won the presidency in November 1989, the party's inability to win more than a plurality of legislative seats necessitated the formation of a National Agreement (*Coincidencia Nacional*) with the Colorados under which the latter were assigned four portfolios (later three) in the government that took office on March 1, 1990. Lacalle terminated the de facto coalition in the course of a cabinet reshuffle in January 1993, albeit with two right-wing Colorados being retained until mid-May 1994.

The election of November 27, 1994, returned Sanguinetti Cairolo to the presidency, but in the legislature the vote share was split nearly three ways by the Colorado, Blanco, and recently launched Progressive Encounter (*Encuentro Progresista*—EP) groupings. Earlier, in a plebiscite conducted on August 28, a number of reforms that had been expected to pass easily (including a measure that would have sanctioned "ticket-splitting") were overwhelmingly rejected. Given the Colorados's narrow legislative plurality, President Sanguinetti emulated his predecessor in organizing a coalition government with 6 of 13 cabinet posts awarded to members of three other parties: 4 from the Blancos and 1 each from two nonlegislative groups, the Civic Union (*Unión Cívica*—UC) and the People's Government Party (*Partido por el Gobierno del Pueblo*—PGP) (see Political Parties, below).

In the election of October 31, 1999, the left-wing Progressive Encounter—Broad Front (EP-FA) captured pluralities in both legislative chambers. In a presidential runoff on November 28, however, the EP-FA candidate, Tabaré VÁZQUEZ Rosas, saw his first-round lead of 38.5 percent overcome by the Colorado candidate, Jorge BATLLE Ibáñez, who had also received Blanco's backing following the third-place finish of Lacalle Herrera in the initial balloting. Installed as Sanguinetti's successor on March 1, 2000, President Batlle named a coalition cabinet of Colorados and Blancos.

In late October 2002, with Uruguay in the throes of a serious economic crisis, the five Blanco ministers announced their intention to resign, and on November 3 a party convention supported the decision, although the Blancos, despite some dissent, indicated that they would continue to work with the government in the legislature.

In presidential balloting on October 31, 2004, the EP-FA's Tabaré VÁZQUEZ Rosas secured 51.7 percent of the vote to become the first left-wing chief executive in Uruguay's history. The Blanco's Jorge LARRAÑAGA was a distant second with 35 percent of the vote; 6 other challengers garnered no more than 11 percent each. In the concurrent parliamentary election, the EP-FA won 53 of the 99 seats in the Chamber of Representatives and 17 of 30 seats in the senate, ending 170 years of control by the Blanco and Colorado parties. In a constitutional referendum the same day, 62.75 percent of voters approved an amendment providing for public ownership of the water supply and sanitation services, the provision describing them as "fundamental human rights."

President Vázquez was inaugurated on March 1, 2005, and appointed the country's first leftist cabinet on March 2.

Former president Bordaberry was arrested in 2006 in connection with the assassination of two lawmakers in Buenos Aires, after a judge ruled that alleged killings outside Uruguay were not covered under the country's amnesty laws. Due to ill health, Bordaberry was allowed to serve his prison term under house arrest. In 2008 Bordaberry was charged in connections with the murder of two opposition members and the disappearance of nine others.

The cabinet was reshuffled on March 1, 2008, when President Vázquez replaced six ministers in advance of the 2009 presidential elections. Ministers with leading roles in political parties were removed to ensure that government work was not interrupted by party activities.

In the run-up to the 2009 general election, a major rift developed in the governing coalition as President Vázquez denounced an EP-FA dissenter's attempt to seek an unprecedented constitutional amendment to allow the president to seek reelection. (For more information, see the 2011 *Handbook*.) Vázquez, who said he would not seek reelection, supported Danilo ASTORI, his former finance minister and a senator from the more conservative wing of the coalition in the primaries, but the nomination went to the EP-FA's José Alberto MUJICA Cordano, a former guerilla leader of the MLN who had spent 14 years in prison. In recent years, Mujica, who was serving as a senator for the MPP (Movement of Popular Participation, below) at the time of his nomination, adopted the moderate policies of the coalition. Subsequently, Astori agreed to be Mujica's running mate. Mujica's main challengers were former president Luis Alberto Lacalle of Blanco and Pedro Bordaberry, son of the former president, of the Colorado party. In parliamentary balloting on October 25, the EP-FA retained its majority in both houses. Two measures in concurrent referenda failed; one would have repealed a general amnesty for military and law enforcement officials involved in human rights abuses during the dictatorship between 1973 and 1985. A week ahead of the election the Supreme Court voted unanimously in ruling the amnesty law unconstitutional. The referendum, which 47 percent of voters approved, would have annulled the law that was confirmed in a 1989 plebiscite. The other measure defeated in 2009 was one that would have allowed absentee ballots.

Neither Mujica nor Lacalle won a majority in first-round balloting on October 25, 2009, forcing a runoff on November 29, in which Mujica secured 52.4 percent of the vote to Lacalle's 43.5 percent. Though voting is compulsory in Uruguay, turnout of only 89 percent was recorded.

On February 10, 2010, the Supreme Court sentenced former president Bordaberry to 30 years in prison for his role in the 1973 military coup.

When members of the new parliament took their seats on February 15, 2010, it marked the first time in Uruguay's history that both chambers were presided over by women—but only temporarily, as control of the senate was handed over to Vice President Astori after he was sworn in on March 1. President Mujica, pledging to maintain the moderate-left ideology of the preceding administration, was inaugurated on March 1, 2010, and named a new government on March 2 that included four members of the Movement of Popular Participation (*Movimiento de Participación Popular*—MPP), as well as representatives of six other parties in the EP-FA.

Constitution and government. The present governmental structure is modeled after that of the 1967 constitution. Executive power is vested in the president who appoints the cabinet, while legislative authority is lodged in a bicameral General Assembly. Both the president and the legislature were elected, before 1996, through a complex system of electoral lists that allowed political parties to present multiple candidates, with the leading candidates within each of the leading lists being declared the victors. However, on December 8, 1996, voters narrowly approved a constitutional amendment that provided for internal party elections for presidential candidates. Under the change, a runoff between the two leading candidates is required if one does not win 40 percent of the vote with a 10 percent lead over the runner-up. The judicial system includes justices of the peace, courts of first instance, courts of appeal, and a Supreme Court. Subnationally Uruguay is divided into 19 departments, which were returned to administration by elected officials in November 1984.

In accordance with "Institutional Act No. 19" (the August 1984 agreement between the Alvarez regime and the *Multipartidaria*), the army, navy, and air force commanders participate in an advisory National Security Council (*Consejo Nacional de Seguridad*), which also includes the president, the vice president, and the defense, foreign, and interior ministers. The council's actions are subject to the approval of the General Assembly. Other provisions of the act require the president to appoint military commanders from a list presented by the armed forces, limit the scope of military justice to crimes committed by members of the armed forces, and preclude the declaration of a state of siege without congressional approval.

Freedom of expression is constitutionally guaranteed, and there are few violations of press freedom. In the 2013 Press Freedom Index, Reporters Without Borders ranked Uruguay 27 of 179 countries.

On October 31, 2004, a constitutional amendment, approved in a national referendum, provided for public ownership of the water supply and sanitation services, describing them as "fundamental human rights."

Foreign relations. A member of the United Nations, the Organization of American States (OAS), the Latin American Free Trade Association, Mercosur, and other Western Hemisphere organizations, Uruguay has been a consistent supporter of international and inter-American cooperation and of nonintervention in the affairs of other countries. Not surprisingly, the former military government maintained particularly cordial relations with neighboring rightist regimes, while vehemently denying accusations of human rights violations by a number of international bodies. As a result, military and economic aid was substantially reduced under U.S. President Jimmy Carter. Although marginal increases were permitted during the Ronald Reagan's first administration, a campaign led by the exiled Ferreira Aldunate tended to isolate the Méndez and Alvarez regimes internationally, while the January 1984 accession of Raúl Alfonsín in Argentina substantially inhibited relations with Buenos Aires.

Before his initial assumption of office, President Sanguinetti met with Alfonsín and other regional leaders. His inauguration, attended by 500 representatives of more than 70 countries, featured a carefully staged but largely unproductive meeting between U.S. Secretary of State George Shultz and Nicaraguan President Daniel Ortega. Diplomatic relations with Cuba, broken in 1974 at the request of the OAS, were restored in late 1985, while in an effort to stimulate economic revitalization, trade accords were negotiated with Argentina, Brazil, Mexico, Paraguay, and the Soviet Union. During a 1988 regional summit with Presidents Alfonsín of Argentina and Sarney of Brazil, President Sanguinetti pledged his government's accession to protocols of economic integration adopted by the neighboring states in December 1986; after reaffirmation of the pledge in November 1989, on May 22, 1991, the Uruguayan senate unanimously approved entry into what had become known as the Southern Cone Common Market (*Mercado Común del Cono Sur*—Mercosur). By early 2000, however, Uruguay had joined Paraguay in complaining of "creeping bilateralization" of Mercosur decision-making, with the smaller partners being pressured to accept agreements reached between Argentina and Brazil. As a result, a number of concessions were made for the minor participants.

Relations with Argentina have been strained since early 2006 because of the construction of two pulp mills by Spanish and Finnish firms in Uruguay across the Uruguay River from Gualeguaychú, Argentina. In July the International Court of Justice (ICJ) rejected Argentina's request that the construction work be suspended. Meanwhile, President Vázquez filed a new complaint against Argentina at the ICJ over roadblocks erected by environmental protesters to block tourists bound for Uruguay's coast. The Spanish company abandoned its plan to build on the Uruguay River and instead decided to construct a mill on the River Plate. (The Finnish mill was completed in 2007.) Movement toward concessions in 2007 was disrupted when in early 2008 Argentine environmentalists, supported by the Entre Rios provincial government, pledged to block traffic twice a week. Tensions eased in July when the Argentine and Uruguayan foreign ministers agreed to establish a binational commission to study the environmental impact, but protests continued. Consequently, Uruguay vetoed the nomination of former Argentine president Nestor Kirchner as president of the Union of South American Nations (UNASUR). Meanwhile, several Uruguayan politicians revived the long-standing dispute over the value of the country's participation in Mercosur, given alleged "hegemonistic" behavior by its two largest members.

In 2009, as part of a move to demonstrate close relations, Uruguay provided vital support to Venezuela in its efforts to launch its first satellite in cooperation with the Chinese government. This was underscored in August when Uruguay, along with six other South American nations, contributed to the founding of *Banco del Sur* (Bank of the South), a development bank intended to rival the power of U.S. banks in the region. Despite cooperation with Venezuela's controversial president, Hugo Chávez, President Vázquez joined the United States in expressing concern over the recent increase in arms purchases by Venezuela that year.

On April 20, 2010, the ICJ handed down a final ruling on the paper-mill dispute between Argentina and Uruguay, ruling that Uruguay had breached its procedural obligations but not its substantive obligations under a previous treaty signed by the two countries. An Argentine federal tribunal ruled in June that the roadblock would be lifted. In July the two countries agreed to joint environmental monitoring for the mills and in November signed a technical agreement that guaranteed joint supervision and monitoring of environmental and water quality of the river by the two countries' scientists.

At a meeting of Mercosur heads of state in December 2010, member countries signed agreements to standardize national policies on trade, immigration, and investment.

Brazil's president, Dilma Rousseff, visited Uruguay on an official state visit in May 2011. Rousseff signaled that Brazil would move to enroll Uruguay as a strategic partner. The two sides also signed eight accords that spelled out deepening connections in exchanging energy and technology as well as bilateral efforts to improve education and health care. In August Mujica signed more bilateral treaties with his Argentine counterpart, Cristina Fernández, demonstrating the warming relations between the two countries, and a transnational passenger rail line that had been out of service for three decades was restarted.

In September 2011, Uruguay announced plans to open an embassy in Hanoi, Vietnam. Uruguay also sought deeper bilateral relations with Iran and China. Signifying a radical shift in Uruguay's financial standing over the past decade, the head of the Central Bank's Economic Advisory said in November that Uruguay had become a net creditor to the IMF.

In December 2011 Uruguay sponsored a proposal to ban vessels under the flag of the Falkland Islands from docking in ports of Mercosur countries, signifying Mujica's commitment to regional diplomatic solidarity. The measure was adopted as the debate between Argentina and the United Kingdom over the long-disputed territory resurfaced. The ban chiefly affects fishing vessels from the Falklands, though it also inconveniences British ships bound for the islands that stop off in the port of Montevideo. Several Spanish shipping associations took issue with the ban as their vessels are under the Falklands flag.

Relations with Argentina inflamed in April 2013 when Mujica, accidentally speaking in front of a live microphone, insulted Argentine president Fernández, calling her worse than her predecessor and late husband.

Inaction within Mercosur relating to the June 2012 suspension of Paraguay led Uruguayan leaders to seek independent bilateral trade relations. In May, Mujica visited China to strengthen ties, and in June, Vice President Astori moved to create links, in hopes of eventual integration, with the Pacific Alliance trade bloc (including Mexico, Colombia, Chile, and Peru).

Current issues. In what Vice President Astori deemed a "wake-up call" for the EP-FA, the Blanco Party dominated the May 9, 2010, municipal elections, winning 12 of 19 departments. The ruling EP-FA held control of Montevideo's regional government, seen as the second-most important elected office after the presidency, and two other regional governments, but the poll clearly pointed to dissatisfaction with the EP-FA.

In August 2010 the Navy commander resigned after his nephew was indicted in a corruption scandal that involved selling military procurements for personal gain. Four officers were implicated in fraud amounting to some $5 million dating to the period between 2006 and 2009. The defense minister ordered an audit of all transactions back to 1985. Quick action and transparency by the administration and the judiciary were hailed by observers as another example of why Uruguay had recently been categorized as the second-most stable state in the region, behind only Chile, in the Fund for Peace's Failed States Index.

Triggered by President Mujica's criticism of bureaucracy and power of unions, a dozen trade unions went on strike and took other protest actions for higher wages and better benefits in November 2010.

The government announced in early 2011 that it would move 1,000 soldiers into the ranks of the national police to bolster public security efforts, prompted by public perception that the country had grown more dangerous. (Uruguay had one of the lowest homicide rates in the region at 6.6 per 100,000.) The military's image as a tool of repression during the dictatorship era had been rehabilitated by the predominant role it had come to play in UN operations around the world, becoming the tenth largest contributor to the international community's peacekeeping missions.

The EP-FA moved to dismantle the amnesty law in 2011. The effort received more fuel with a second Supreme Court decision ruling the law unconstitutional in November 2010 and a trial in the Inter-American Court of Human Rights (IACHR) on charges brought by María Macarena Gelman García against Uruguay for the death of her mother, dissident Maria Claudia García Iruretagoyena de Gelman. The IACHR ruled in March that the government of Uruguay should open an investigation into the deaths of the plaintiff's mother and pay her $180,000 as compensation. In April the senate narrowly voted (by 16–15) to repeal several articles of the amnesty law. Opposition legislators slammed the vote as having no respect for the will of the people as embodied in the two previous referenda votes. Mujica opposed the annulment of the law—which the more left-wing constituents of his coalition favored on the grounds that the choice of the country had already been made in the referenda—while simultaneously saying that he would not veto it if it passed through the legislature. However after 14 hours of debate in May, those in favor of repealing the law were unable to secure a majority, and it continued to remain in effect.

Concerned with the concentration of rural land among few owners, Mujica pushed for high taxes on large landowners in 2011. Despite a rift with Vice President Astori, who believed the tax should be based instead on farm profitability, the measure passed in November. In February 2013 the Supreme Court struck down the tax as unconstitutional and redundant, prompting the administration to introduce a revised version of the law in April.

In a May 2012 interview with an Argentinean newspaper, Uruguay's first lady, Senator Lucía TOPOLANKSY, called for the military to be "loyal" to the ruling FA coalition, sparking friction between the armed forces and the administration. The administration's uneasy relationship with the military branch was aggravated later in the month when the commander of the navy resigned, at Mujica's urging, over his links to the 2010 corruption scandal that prompted his predecessor's departure.

Mujica unveiled a controversial new security plan in June 2012 calling for the "regulated and controlled legalization of marijuana." The proposal suggests combating drug-related violence by creating a state-run industry in which the government controls the importation, production, sale, and distribution of the drug. Other regional leaders have discussed legalization as a method of tackling narcotics-related violence throughout Central and South America, but the United States strongly opposes the strategy. The bill was introduced to the Chamber of Representatives in November 2012 and, after 13 hours of debate, was approved in July 2013 with the support of all 50 FA members in the 96-member body. The measure, expected to pass the Senate, prompted a warning from the International Narcotics Control Board that the law would "be in complete contravention to the provisions of the international drug treaties to which Uruguay is party."

In October 2012 the Senate approved a FA-supported bill to legalize abortion, 17–14, after it was approved 50–49 in the lower house in September. The Blanco and Colorado Parties opposed the bill. Several lawmakers on both sides of the debate allowed substitutes to vote in their places because they were unwilling to support their party line. Antiabortionists called for a referendum; however, in consultation balloting in June 2013, the measure received support of 9 percent of the electorate, short of the 25 percent needed to authorize a referendum.

POLITICAL PARTIES

In 2004 the leftists, for the first time, won majorities in both the presidential and congressional balloting. Their representation remained virtually unchanged after the 2009 elections.

Presidential Coalition:

Progressive Encounter–Broad Front (*Encuentro Progresista–Frente Amplio*—EP-FA). Encompassing a number of left-wing groups, plus a group of Blanco dissidents, the EP was launched before the 1994 election. While running third in the November poll, the alliance was only marginally eclipsed by the second-place Blancos, thus effectively terminating Uruguay's traditional two-party system. Tabaré Vázquez, the popular former mayor of Montevideo who had been the EAP standard-bearer in 1994, easily won the EP's 1999 presidential nomination, securing 82 percent of the votes in the April primary. Although winning a plurality of 38.5 percent in October 1999, he was defeated in second-round balloting by Colorado-Blanco nominee Jorge Batlle Ibáñez. However, in 2004 Vázquez received slightly more than 50 percent of the first-round vote to win election as president.

Originally a Communist-led formation of 11 members that included the Uruguayan Socialist Party (*Partido Socialista del Uruguay*—PSU), Christian Democratic Party (*Partido Demócrata Cristiano*—PDC), and Oriental Revolutionary Movement (*Movimiento Revolucionario Oriental*—MRO), the FA contested the 1971 election but was subsequently proscribed by the military regime, while its presidential candidate, retired general Líber Seregni, was imprisoned and stripped of his military rank. Seregni was released in March 1984 but was banned from political activity, thus unable to serve as the November nominee of the Front, which had attracted a number of dissidents from the Colorado and Blanco parties. In the 1984 balloting, Front candidate Juan CROTTOGINI won 20.4 percent of the vote, while the coalition won 21 Chamber seats (almost as many as the Blancos) and 6 senate seats. In early 1985 a split developed between the group's Marxist and social democratic legislators over the degree of support to be given to the Sanguinetti administration, although in May the president, in a gesture to the Front, decreed that Seregni's military rank be restored. Subsequently a noncommunist "Lista 99" faction joined with elements of the PDC and PSU in a "Triple Alliance" that contested elections in student and labor organizations, winning the leadership of the leading student federation in July.

Throughout 1986 the Front was solidly opposed to the military amnesty program, joining the call for a plebiscite to decide the issue, although it initially rejected a membership bid by the like-minded MLN (see under MPP, below). Meanwhile the "Lista 99" group became increasingly identified as the People's Government Party (PGP), which, before the 1989 balloting, joined the PDC and Civic Union in a coalition styled the New Space (*Nuevo Espacio*) (below), with the MLN subsequently becoming a Front member.

By 1992 the Socialists had displaced the long-dominant Communists as the leading component of the Front, but the Socialists failed to control the group's plenum, with the highly popular mayor of Montevideo, Vázquez, threatening in late 1993 to withdraw from the 1994 presidential race if internal party elections were not held; however, in March 1994 Vázquez was proclaimed the group's standard-bearer for the presidential campaign.

On February 5, 1996, Seregni resigned as FA president because of irreconcilable differences over electoral reform (primarily in regard to Seregni's willingness to endorse second-round presidential balloting in return for abolition of the *ley de lemas*). In late 1996, following the interim leadership of a 12-member executive, Tabaré Vázquez was elected Seregni's successor; however, he resigned in September 1997 because of opposition to his support of the privatization of a Montevideo hotel complex. Seregni died on July 31, 2004.

At the time of the 2004 election, the EP-FA (sometimes referenced as EP-FA-NM [*Nueva Mayoría*]) encompassed the groups listed below. The New Space Party (*Nuevo Espacio*) joined the EP-FA following the election, and the 26th of March Movement (*Movimiento 26 de Marzo*—M26M) withdrew in mid-2008. Despite President Vázquez's endorsement of Danilo Astori in the 2009 primary elections the party's nomination was won by former MLN rebel leader and senator José Mujica, who was supported by the party's former guerrilla and communist factions. Mujica also picked up the endorsement of Argentine president Cristina Fernández, who gave some 100,000 Uruguayans living in Argentina two days off to return home to cast their votes. Argentine Peronism movement leaders also campaigned for Mujica, who won the presidency in second-round balloting on November 29, 2009.

The coalition began to strain before May 2010 regional elections, when several of the parties vied for seats in races across the country; the Communist Party (*Partido Comunista*—PCU), PSU, and MPP fought for the mayorship of Montevideo, which the EP-FA ultimately won. In some races, generally in rural areas, support for the coalition declined by as much as 10 percent compared to previous years, raising calls for reforming the coalition's candidate selection process.

Former president Vázquez of the PSU and coalition leaders signaled in early 2011 that he would be the EP-FA's presidential candidate in 2014. The coalition faced questions about its future election prospects after it went ahead with a plan to repeal the country's long-standing military amnesty law (see Current issues, above), even though the electorate had twice voted in referenda 20 years apart to keep the law. Using a large sum of political capital in early 2011, the legislative leaders enforced coalition discipline to get the repeal measures passed through the lower house and did the same in the senate, though the bills failed in the upper chamber. The leader of the coalition's CAP-L (Current Thought-Action and Freedom, below) and a former prison cellmate of Mujica's, Eleuterio FERNÁNDEZ Huidobro, resigned his senate seat in protest against the coalition's push to repeal the amnesty law in 2011. He was replaced by an EP-FA alternate but was appointed by Mujica in July to become Uruguay's defense minister.

By July 2011 Mujica appeared to be indecisive; cabinet ministers began openly criticizing him. The PCU voiced anger over the lack of pressure from the president to move on redistributing wealth to deal with Uruguay's income gap, while the more centrist FLS (Liber Seregni Front, below) and PSU pushed for policies to preserve economic stability. In August elements of the coalition, including Mujica's MPP, were working on introducing legislation that would limit foreign ownership of Uruguayan land, a quarter of which was found to be in the hands of interests from abroad in 2011. Mónica XAVIER of the PSU emerged victorious in a four-way contest for the FA presidency in May 2012. Land reform policy continued to be divisive within the coalition, with Vice President Astori heading the moderate FA faction that opposed Mujica's land tax. Renewed divisions emerged in early 2013 when Astori described inflation as the country's greatest challenge, a claim immediately dismissed by Mujica. In February Mujica announced that he would not modify his socially progressive economic policies despite internal tensions. Vázquez confirmed his candidacy in August 2013 for the 2014 presidential election.

Leaders: José ("Pepe") MUJICA (President of the Republic), Mónica XAVIER (President of the Coalition), Ivonne PASSADA, Rafael MICHELINI, and Juan CASTILLO (Vice Presidents).

Liber Seregni Front (*Frente Liber Seregni*—FLS). The center-left coalition, named after the FA founder, the FLS was founded in August 2009 ahead of the October general elections by vice-presidential candidate Danilo Astori of the Uruguayan Assembly (Asamblea Uruguay—AU), as well as the leaders of New Space (*Nuevo Espacio*—NE) and the Progressive Alliance (*Alianza Progresista*—AP). As moderates in the coalition, the FLS in 2011 pushed the EP-FA to adopt strategies that would bolster economic stability and investment in education and infrastructure. In July 2012, Astori clashed with Mujica over their positions on the admittance of Venezuela to Mercosur.

Leader: Danilo ASTORI (Vice President of the Republic).

New Space (*Nuevo Espacio*—NE). The NE was founded following a struggle within the *Frente Amplio* nominees for the 1989 presidential balloting. The Marxist wing wished to renominate General Seregni as the coalition's sole candidate, while social democrats within the party supported PGP leader Hugo BATALLA, or, alternatively, both contenders under an electoral law provision permitting multiple nominees. As an agreement between the factions proved impossible, the PGP and PDC withdrew from the *Frente Amplio* in March 1989, subsequently joining the Civic Union (see below) in launching *Nuevo Espacio* as a tripartite formation with Batalla as its standard-bearer.

Prior to the 1994 balloting, the PGP's Batalla agreed to campaign as a vice-presidential contender on a ticket with Sanguinetti, the Colorados' presidential candidate. The PDC joined the Progressive Encounter, and the Civic Union withdrew to campaign separately, with a rump group of PGP members remaining within a reorganized *Nuevo Espacio.* The latter ran fourth in the presidential race. After the 2004 election the party decided to join the EP-FA and was accepted in November 2005.

Leaders: Rafael MICHELINI (President), Jorge POZZI (Deputy), Héctor PÉREZ Piera (Former President).

Uruguayan Assembly (Asamblea Uruguay—AU), Founded in 1994 by then senator Danilo Astori, the social democratic AU developed a reputation for pragmatism in developing successful legislation supported by ideologically diverse parties. The AU's Carlos Baráibar was elected president of the Chamber of Representatives in 1997.

Leaders: Danilo ASTORI (Vice President of the Republic and President of the Party), Carlos BARÁIBAR (Senator and former President of the Chamber of Deputies).

Progressive Alliance (*Alianza Progresista*—AP). This social-democratic party was founded in 1999 by Rodolfo Nin Novoa and subsequently joined the EP-FA.

Leader: Rodolfo NIN Novoa (Former Vice President).

Uruguayan Socialist Party (*Partido Socialista del Uruguay*—PSU). Founded in 1910, the PSU has participated in the Broad Front since its inception in 1971. The PSU fell into a period of uncertainty when President Tabare Vazquez resigned from his own party while still in office in protest over the platform to legalize abortion. Following the EP-FA's presidential win in 2009, PSU members were named to two cabinet posts. In 2011 the party began a reelection campaign for former President Vázquez, whose reform plan included nine points to alter the coalition's ideological foundation and looked to a consultative process to draw in other member parties of the EP-FA. Vazquez confirmed his candidacy for the 2014 election in August 2013.

Leaders: Reinaldo GARGANO (President), Yerú PARDIÑAS (Secretary General).

Movement of Popular Participation (*Movimiento de Participación Popular*—MPP). Commonly referred to as the Tupamaros (after Túpac Amaru, an 18th-century Inca chief who was burned at the stake by the Spaniards), the MPP is an outgrowth of the National Liberation Movement (*Movimiento de Liberación Nacional*—MLN), a longtime clandestine guerrilla group that used violence and charges of political corruption in an attempt to radically alter Uruguayan society. Its last recorded clash with the police was in Montevideo in April 1974; six years later, in 1980 MLN founder Raúl SENDIC Antonaccio was sentenced to 45 years' imprisonment after having been held without trial since 1972. A number of others were sentenced for "subversion" in late 1983 at the height of the antidissident campaign. Many Tupamaros were among the hundreds who returned to Uruguay at the end of 1984, while the core of the group, including Sendic, was released when all political prisoners were freed in March 1985. At the MLN's first legal convention in December 1985, an estimated 1,500 delegates established a 33-member central committee and endorsed the abandonment of armed struggle in favor of nonviolent electoral politics. Its bid to join the Broad Front was rebuffed in 1986, reportedly due to PDC objection, but approved before the 1989 poll. The MLN was one of the leading opponents of the government's controversial military amnesty program, attracting an estimated 17,000 for its first political rally in December 1986. Sendic died in Paris in April 1989, reportedly from a neurological condition occasioned by his years of imprisonment The Movement campaigned as a Front member during the ensuing electoral campaign.

In 1991 relations with other Front members reportedly cooled, with the MLN's Eleuterio FERNÁNDEZ calling for General Seregni's resignation and an internal election to determine "who are the real leaders of the Uruguayan Left."

MPP candidates attracted nearly one-third of the EP-FA votes in the 2004 balloting. In 2009 MPP leader José Mujica won the presidential primary for the EP-FA, and Astori, who had the support of President Vázquez, agreed to be his running mate. Mujica quit the MPP after the primary election so as not to be tied to a particular group within the coalition.

Leaders: Lucía TOPOLANSKY Saavedra (President), Edison Eduardo BONOMI Varela (Party Co-founder and Interior Minister).

Christian Democratic Party (*Partido Demócrata Cristiano*—PDC). Currently left-democratic in orientation, the PDC was founded in 1962 by dissidents from the predecessor of the current Civic Union (below). Banned at the time of the primary balloting in November 1982, the PDC operated negatively as a "fourth party" by calling on its followers for blank ballots, 84,000 of which were cast. The ban was lifted in August 1984. Before joining the *Nuevo Espacio* in 1989 the PDC operated as the "moderate" tendency within the *Frente Amplio*. It participated in forming the Progressive Encounter before the 1994 poll. The party is a member of the Christian Democratic International. A party convention was held in October 2006, during which the PDC confirmed its complete support for the government of President Vázquez.

Leaders: Héctor LESCANO (President), Juan A. ROBALLO (Secretary General).

Workers' Party (*Partido de los Trabajadores*—PT). The PT is a small, extreme left-wing formation founded in 1980.

Leaders: Juan Vital ANDRADE (1984 presidential candidate), Rafael FERNANDEZ.

Additional EP-FA components that secured cabinet posts in the Mujica administration were the **Artiguist Source** (*Vertiente Artiguista*—VA), led by Mariano ARANA; **Current Thought-Action and Freedom** (*La Corriente de Acción y Pensamiento-Libertad*—CAP-L), led by Eleuterio Fernández Huidobro; and the **Communist Party** (*Partido Comunista*—PCU), led by Eduardo LORIER.

Other parties in the EP-FA in 2004 were the **Blanco Popular and Progressive Movement** (*Movimiento Blanco Popular y Progresista*—MBPP); the **Left Front of Liberation** (*Frente Izquierda de Liberación*—Fidel); the **Leftist Current** (*Corriente de Izquierda*—CI); the **Nationalist Action Movement** (*Movimiento de Acción Nacionalista*—MAN); the **Party for the Victory of the People** (*Partido por la Victoria del Pueblo*—PVP); the **Pregon Group** (*Grupo Pregón*—GP); and the **26th of March Movement** (*Movimiento 26 de Marzo*—M26M), which announced its departure from the EP-FA in March 2008, citing ideological differences.

Other Legislative Parties:

Colorado Party (*Partido Colorado*—PC). Founded in 1836 and in power continuously from 1865 to 1958, the largely urban-based PC has emphasized liberal and progressive principles, social welfare, government participation in the economy, and inter-American cooperation.

For some years the party's leading faction, as heir to the policies of former president José Batlle y Ordóñez, was the *Unidad y Reforma,* led by a longtime opponent of the military establishment, Jorge Batlle Ibáñez. However, the group was formally headed by Dr. Julio María Sanguinetti because of the personal proscription of Batlle Ibáñez under the military regime. *Unidad y Reforma* obtained 45 percent of the vote in the November 1982 election and successfully advanced Sanguinetti as its presidential candidate in 1984. Other factions included the promilitary *Unión Colorado Batllista* (*pachequista*) group led by former president Jorge Pacheco Areco, who ran as a minority presidential candidate in 1984; the *Libertad y Cambio,* led by former vice president Enrique Tarigo; and the antimilitary *Batllismo Radical* and *Corriente Batllista Independiente.*

In 1986 the party strongly endorsed the military amnesty urged by President Sanguinetti, while continuing to promote coalition efforts with elements of the Blanco Party. Runner-up in the 1989 balloting, the PC was awarded four portfolios in the Lacalle administration of March 1990, an alliance that effectively ended in January 1993, although two Colorado ministers retained their portfolios until May 1994.

By 1992 *Unidad y Reforma* had split into two components, the *Batllismo Unido* (subsequently *Batllismo Radical*), headed by Batlle Ibáñez, and the *Foro Batllista,* led by Sanguinetti. Also active were the *Unión Colorado Batllista* and *Cruzada 94,* led by Pablo MILLOR. Batlle Ibáñez captured 54 percent of the votes within the PC's presidential primary in April 1999, earning the nomination over Luis HIERRO López (45 percent), who had the support of President Sanguinetti. With the additional backing of the Blancos, Batlle won the November runoff against the *Frente Amplio*'s Tabaré Vásquez and took office as president in March 2000.

The party placed third in the 2004 presidential poll with only 10.3 percent of the vote, while losing two-thirds of its congressional representation. A call for renewal began after the PC's poor showing, which in 2007 crystallized into a new faction calling itself *Vamos Uruguay* under the leadership of Juan Pedro BORDABERRY Herrán. At the PC's national convention in September 2009, Bordaberry, son of former president Bordaberry, was chosen as the Colorado presidential candidate for the October 2009 general elections. At the same meeting it was also decided that two former presidents, Julio María Sanguinetti and Jorge Batlle, would not participate in the National Executive Committee, breaking a forty-year tradition.

Pedro Bordaberry won 17 percent of the vote and placed third in the 2009 presidential election. The party won 17 seats in the Chamber of Representatives and 5 seats in the senate in concurrent legislative elections. The party saw a resurgence of support during the 2010 regional elections.

In early 2011 the PC and the PN presented a unified front of opposition to the EP-FA–driven attempt to dismantle the country's longstanding amnesty law, which eventually failed. With rising youth criminality becoming a political issue, the party in August 2011 began collecting signatures to hold a plebiscite during the 2014 general election on lowering the age of sentencing from 18 to 16 years.

In August 2013 the PC and PN took steps toward creating an alliance to compete in the 2015 Montevideo municipal elections.

Leaders: Max SAPOLINSKI (Secretary General), Juan Pedro BORDABERRY Herran (2009 presidential candidate), Guillermo STIRLING (2004 presidential candidate).

Blanco (National) Party (*Partido Nacional*—PN). Traditionally representing conservative, rural, and clerical elements but now largely progressive in outlook, the *Partido Nacional* won the elections of 1958 and 1962, subsequently failing to win either the presidency or a legislative plurality until November 1989. Its longtime principal grouping, the centrist *Por la Patria,* was led, before his death in March 1988, by Wilson Ferreira Aldunate, who was in exile at the time of the 1982 balloting. His absence did not prevent the *ferreiristas* from obtaining 70 percent of the party vote in 1982; other antimilitary factions in 1982 included the *Consejo Nacional Herrerista (Herrismo),* heir to a grouping formed in 1954 by Luis Alberto de Herrera, and the conservative *Divisa Blanca,* led by Eduardo Pons Etcheverry.

Ferreira returned to Uruguay in June 1984 and was promptly arrested, along with his son, Juan Raúl, who had led an exile opposition group known as the Uruguayan Democratic Convergence. After officially rejecting the August "Institutional Act No. 19" and refusing to participate in the election campaign, the main faction, at Ferreira's urging, offered Alberto Zumarán as its presidential candidate. Zumarán won 32.9 percent of the vote, while the Blancos obtained 35 seats in the Chamber of Deputies and 11 senate seats. Released from prison five days after the November poll, Ferreira was elected party president in February 1985. Although he initially criticized the reported "deal" between the military and the Colorados to thwart the initiation of human rights trials, he vowed to "let the president govern" and supported the military amnesty program in 1986. The issue split the party, however, as the left-leaning *Movimiento Nacional de Rocha* faction, led by Carlos Julio Pereyra, called for a referendum to defeat the measure. The smaller, right-leaning *Divisa Blanca* not only supported the amnesty but also reportedly urged coalition with the Colorados.

Both Pereyra and Zumarán presented themselves as Blanco candidates in the 1989 presidential poll, which was won by Luis Alberto de Herrera's grandson, Luis Alberto Lacalle, with Gonzalo Aguirre Ramírez of the *Renovación y Victoria* faction as his running mate. The coalition forged by Lacalle with the Colorados was effectively terminated as the result of a midterm cabinet reshuffle in January 1993, with the last two Colorado ministers resigning in May. At the 1994 poll, four Blancos presented themselves as presidential candidates: Aguirre Ramírez, party chair Carlos Julio Pereyra, former interior minister Juan Andrés Ramírez (favored by President Lacalle), and state power utility head Alberto Volonté.

Lacalle, the candidate of the party's right-wing, secured the Blanco nomination for the 1999 presidential election by winning 49 percent of the votes in the April primary, but he ran third in the first-round poll of October 31. To prevent a possible victory by the Left, the Blancos threw their support in the runoff of November 28 to the Colorado's Batlle Ibáñez, who then formed a coalition government in which the Colorados participated until withdrawing in November 2002.

In 2003 Cristina MAESO, leader of a *Basta y Vamos* ("Enough–Let's Go") faction, became the first woman to contend (albeit unsuccessfully) for a major party's presidential nomination.

The party ran second in the 2004 presidential race with a 36.9 percent vote share, while increasing its lower house representation from 22 to 34.

The Blancos unified behind Luis Alberto Lacalle de Herrera as its 2009 presidential candidate. He finished second in the October balloting, with 29.1 percent of the vote, and lost by nearly 9 percentage points in the November runoff to José Mujica. The Blancos lost representation in both chambers of the General Assembly, securing 9 seats in the senate and 30 in the Chamber of Representatives. The party was the recipient of strong voter support in the 2010 regional elections, particularly in rural areas.

In early 2011, the PN and the PC presented a unified front of opposition to the EP-FA–driven attempt to dismantle the country's long-standing amnesty law, which eventually failed. In June Lacalle resigned as president of the party, calling on the PN to renew and reform itself in order to take on the EP-FA. He signaled that the party would look to taking up a more centrist position in Uruguay's political spectrum and reaching out to a broader segment of the population.

The PN led the opposition of the legalization of abortion in 2012 (see Current issues, above). In May 2013, the party selected Luis LACALLE POU, the son of the former president Lacalle, as 2014 presidential candidate.

Leaders: Luis Alberto HEBER Fontana (President), Gustavo PENADÉS (Secretary General), Luis Alberto LACALLE Herrera (Former President of the Republic and 1999 and 2009 presidential candidate), Gonzalo AGUIRRE Ramírez (Former Vice President of the Republic and leader of *Renovación y Victoria*).

Independent Party (*Partido Independiente*—PI). The small centrist PI was formed in 2003 and won a single seat in the Chamber of Representatives in the 2004 general election. The PI chose Pablo Andrés Mieres Gomez as its 2009 presidential candidate. He placed fourth with 2.49 percent of the vote. Concurrently, the party won two seats in the Chamber of Representatives.

Leaders: Pablo Andrés MIERES Gomez (Party President and 2009 presidential candidate), Iván POSADA (2009 vice-presidential candidate).

Other Party That Contested the 2009 Elections:

Popular Assembly (*Asamblea Popular*—AP). The left-wing AP was formed in 2006.

In the 2009 presidential election, José Raúl Rodriguez da Silva finished fifth with 0.67 percent of the vote. The AP remained active through 2011 at the local-advocacy level, organizing marches for trade unions and to further human rights goals.

Leaders: José Raúl RODRIGUEZ da Silva (2009 presidential candidate), Helios SARTHOU.

Other Parties:

Anti-imperialist Unitary Commissions (*Comisiones Unitarias Antiimperialistas—COMUNA*). COMUNA was formed is 2008 through the unification of the Oriental Revolutionary Movement (*Movimiento Revolucionario Oriental*—MRO) and various defectors from the FA coalition. The MRO is a pro-Cuban former guerrilla group that participated in the FA's launching in 1971. It made headlines (and embarrassed other Front groups) in late 1991 by characterizing a follower who had been arrested for robbery as a "social fighter." It was expelled from the FA in 1993 after some of its leaders had urged a return to "armed revolutionary struggle for Latin America."

Leader: Mario ROSSI Garretano (Founder and President of the Party).

For information on the **Civic Union** (*Unión Cívica*—UC) party, see the 2010 edition of the *Handbook.*

LEGISLATURE

The bicameral Congress (*Congreso*), dissolved in June 1973 and replaced under the military regime with an appointive Council of State, reconvened for the first time in 12 years on February 15, 1985, following the election of November 25, 1984. The two houses, now styled collectively as the **General Assembly** (*Asamblea General*), are elected simultaneously on a proportional basis, both for five-year terms.

Chamber of Senators (*Cámara de Senadores* o *Senado*). The upper house consists of 30 elected members and one ex-officio member (the vice president). Following the October 25, 2009, election, the seat distribution was as follows: the Progressive Encounter–Broad Front, 16; Blanco (National) Party, 9; and Colorado Party, 5.

President: Danilo ASTORI.

Chamber of Representatives (*Cámara de Representantes*). The lower house comprises 99 members. Following the election of October 25, 2009, the seat distribution was as follows: the Progressive Encounter–Broad Front, 50; Blanco (National) Party, 30; Colorado Party, 17; and Independent Party, 2.

President: Germán CARDOSO.

CABINET

[as of August 15, 2013]

President	José Alberto Mujica Cordano (EP-FA—MPP)
Vice President	Danilo Astori (EP-FA–FLS)
Ministers	
Agriculture, Livestock, and Fisheries	Tabaré Aguerre (EP-FA—ind.)
Economy and Finance	Fernando Lorenzo (EP-FA–FLS)
Education and Culture	Ricardo Ehrlich (EP-FA–MPP)
Foreign Affairs	Luis Almagro (EP-FA–MPP)
Housing, Territorial Planning, and Environment	Francisco Beltrame (EP-FA–MPP)
Industry, Energy, and Mining	Roberto Kreimerman (EP-FA–PSU)
Interior	Edison Eduardo Bonomi Varela (EP-FA–MPP)
Labor and Social Welfare	Eduardo Brenta (EP-FA–VA)
National Defense	Eleuterio Fernández Huidobro (EP-FA—CAP-L)
Public Health	Susana Muniz (EP-FA–PCU) [f]
Social Development	Daniel Olesker (EP-FA–PSU)
Tourism and Sport	Liliam Kechichian (EP-FA–FLS) [f]
Transport and Public Works	Enrique Pintado (EP-FA–FLS)

[f] = female

INTERGOVERNMENTAL REPRESENTATION

Ambassador to the U.S.: Juan Carlos PITA Alvariza.

U.S. Ambassador to Uruguay: Julissa REYNOSO.

Permanent Representative to the UN: José Luis CANCELA.

IGO Memberships (Non-UN): IADB, ICC, IOM, Mercosur, OAS, WTO.

UZBEKISTAN

Republic of Uzbekistan
Ozbekiston Respublikasi

Political Status: Eastern portion of Turkistan Soviet Socialist Republic detached on October 27, 1924, to form Uzbek Soviet Socialist Republic within the Russian Soviet Federative Socialist Republic (RSFSR); became constituent republic of the Union of Soviet Socialist Republics (USSR) on May 12, 1925; declared independence as Republic of Uzbekistan on August 31, 1991; present constitution adopted on December 8, 1992.

Area: 172,740 sq. mi. (447,400 sq. km).

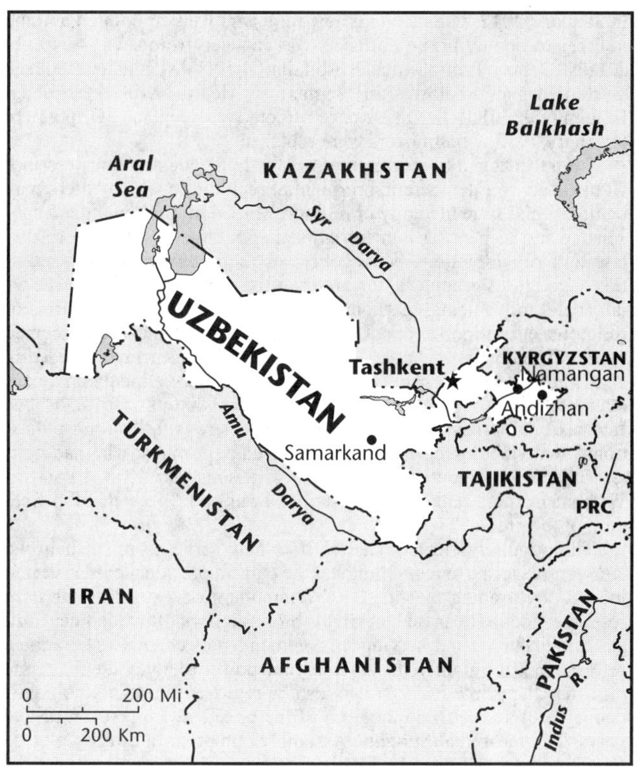

Population: 28,337,880 (2012E—UN); 28,661,637 (2013E—US Census).

Major Urban Centers (2011E—UN): TASHKENT (2,137,218), Namangan (391,297), Samarkand (361,339), Andijan (338,366).

Official Language: Uzbek. Russian remains the principal everyday language.

Monetary Unit: Uzbekistani som (market rate November 1, 2013: 2,173.96 som = $1US).

President: Islam A. KARIMOV (Liberal Democratic Party); elected to the new office of president by the Supreme Soviet on March 24, 1990; reconfirmed for a five-year term by popular election on December 29, 1991; granted three-year term extension (to December 31, 1999) by referendum of March 26, 1995; reelected on January 9, 2000; term extended by the Supreme Assembly to 2007, in accordance with a referendum passed on January 27, 2002; reelected on December 23, 2007.

Prime Minister: Shavkat MIRZIYOYEV (MIRZIYAYEV) (National Revival Democratic Party); appointed by the president and confirmed by the Supreme Assembly on December 11, 2003, succeeding Otkir SULTONOV; reconfirmed on January 28, 2005, and on January 27, 2010.

THE COUNTRY

The Central Asian state of Uzbekistan—the region's most populous—is bordered on the north and west by Kazakhstan, on the northeast by Kyrgyzstan, on the southeast by Tajikistan, and on the south, save for a short frontier with Afghanistan, by Turkmenistan. The national territory also includes several small exclaves in Kyrgyzstan, the largest being the town of Sokh. The principal ethnic groups are Turkic-speaking Uzbeks (approximately 76 percent); Russians (6 percent); Tajiks (5 percent), Kazakhs (4 percent), and Tatars (2 percent). The vast majority of citizens are Sunni Muslims, but there is also a small Shiite population; Eastern Orthodoxy predominates among the Russians. Women make up slightly less than half of the workforce and constitute 22 percent of the current lower house and 15 percent of the current upper house.

Crops include cotton (Uzbekistan remains one of the world's top cotton fiber exporters), rice, wheat, tobacco, sugarcane, and a wide variety of vegetables and fruits. The agricultural sector contributes 21.9 percent of GDP and employs 44 percent of workers. Uzbekistan also ranks as one of the world's leading producers of gold, the leading export; other extractable resources include oil, coal, uranium, copper, molybdenum, tungsten, zinc, and natural gas. As a whole, industry accounts for 37.7 percent of GDP. A growing source of income has been remittances and other transfers (7 percent of GDP in 2012) from some of the 5.5 million Uzbek citizens working abroad. (For information on the economy prior to 2000, please see the 2012 *Handbook*.)

Government figures, which are historically unreliable and difficult to verify, put GDP growth at 9 percent in 2008, driven by trade, transport, services, communications, and industry, before dropping to an estimated 2.5 percent in 2009 due to recession in export markets and a sharp decline in remittances. In late 2008 the government undertook a stimulus package that included a guarantee of bank deposits, relaxed tax penalties, and increased investment opportunities for exporters. GDP growth rebounded in 2010 to 8.5 percent, 8.3 percent in 2011, and 7.9 percent in 2012. Inflation in 2012 was 12.1 percent. GDP per capita that year was $1,737. In its 2013 survey on the Doing Business survey, the World Bank ranked Uzbekistan 154 out of 179 countries, far behind neighboring states such as Kazakhstan (49) or Kyrgyzstan (70) because of endemic corruption.

GOVERNMENT AND POLITICS

Political background. Astride the ancient caravan routes to the Orient, Uzbekistan is one of the world's oldest civilized regions. In the 14th century what is now its second city, Samarkand, served as the hub of Tamerlane's vast empire. In the 19th century, after a lengthy period of decay, much of its territory was conquered by Russia. In 1920 it became part of the Turkistan Soviet Socialist Republic within the Russian Soviet Federative Socialist Republic. Separated from Turkmenia in 1924, Uzbekistan entered the USSR as a constituent republic in 1925. In 1929 its eastern Tajik region was detached and also accorded the status of a Soviet republic.

On March 24, 1990, at the opening of a recently elected Uzbek Supreme Soviet, Islam A. KARIMOV was elected by secret ballot to the new post of Supreme Soviet president. The following November, as part of a government reorganization, the chair of the Council of Ministers, Shakhrulla MIRSAIDOV, was named vice president. In August 1991, in the wake of a failed Moscow coup against USSR president Mikhail Gorbachev, President Karimov resigned from the Politburo of the Communist Party of the Soviet Union, and the property of the Uzbek Communist Party (UCP) was nationalized. On August 28 Uzbekistan assumed control of all union enterprises within its territory and declared its intention to conduct its own foreign policy. Three days later the Supreme Soviet issued a declaration of independence and announced a change of name to Republic of Uzbekistan. In November the UCP was replaced by the People's Democratic Party of Uzbekistan (PDP), and on December 29 independence was endorsed, by a 98.2 percent vote, in a popular referendum. In a parallel poll, Karimov, as the PDP candidate, won confirmation as president with an 86 percent share of the vote, as contrasted with the 12 percent garnered by Muhammad SALIH of the opposition Freedom (*Erk*) grouping. Following the poll, Abdulhashim MUTALOV of the PDP was named independent Uzbekistan's first prime minister. A month later, the vice presidency was abolished.

Although the 1992 constitution enshrined a commitment to multiparty democracy, Uzbekistan remained effectively a one-party state under the PDP. Genuine opposition parties, such as the nationalist Unity (*Birlik*) movement and the more moderate *Erk,* experienced systematic harassment leading to outright proscription, while the authorities encouraged the formation of new parties broadly supportive of the government.

Elections to a new 250-member legislature, held in three rounds in December 1994 and January 1995, were contested by two parties, the PDP and the government-aligned Progress of the Fatherland, with the PDP winning a large majority of the seats claimed by party nominees. In a March referendum President Karimov further consolidated power by securing what most observers regarded as an implausible 99.6 percent endorsement for a three-year extension of his existing five-year term, due to expire at the end of 1996. In December the Supreme Assembly confirmed Otkir SULTONOV as prime minister in succession to the demoted Mutalov, who three months later was dismissed from the cabinet altogether. Meanwhile, critics of the regime, including former vice president Mirsaidov, continued to accuse the government of authoritarianism and one-party rule.

In November–December 1997 an outbreak of violence in Namangan precipitated a government crackdown against alleged Islamic activists, and between May 1998 and January 1999 several dozen were convicted of terrorism and anticonstitutional acts. A series of at least six bomb blasts shook Tashkent on February 16, 1999, killing 15 and injuring more than 120. Hundreds of Islamic activists and government critics were arrested in succeeding weeks. Between June and August more than two dozen individuals were sentenced to death or lengthy prison terms on related charges that included attempted assassination of the president. Most of those arrested in the wake of the bombings were subsequently released, after months in detention.

For the Supreme Assembly elections of December 1999 *Birlik* and *Erk* were denied registration. The PDP again won more seats than any of its competitor parties, but its predominance was challenged by the National Democratic Party "Self-Sacrificers" (*Fidokorlar*), formation of which had been announced, with President Karimov's imprimatur, in December 1998. In January 2000 Karimov, officially nominated by *Fidokorlar* but also backed by the rest of the political establishment, easily won reelection as president, capturing 92 percent of the vote against the PDP's token candidate, Abdulkhafiz JALOLOV, who stated on election day that he, too, had cast his ballot for the incumbent.

In a January 27, 2002, referendum a reported 92 percent of those voting approved extending the presidential term to seven years, while 94 percent endorsed introducing a bicameral legislature, as had been proposed by President Karimov in May 2000. The Supreme Assembly subsequently passed implementing legislation, effective from the next legislative election. In December 2003 the Supreme Assembly confirmed President Karimov's selection of Shavkat MIRZIYOYEV, governor of Samarkand and an agricultural specialist, as successor to Prime Minister Sultonov, who was retained as a deputy prime minister.

On March 28–April 1, 2004, a series of explosions in Bukhara and Tashkent claimed nearly 50 lives, the majority of them suspected terrorists. On July 30 three coordinated suicide bombings occurred outside the U.S. and Israeli embassies and at the prosecutor general's office. A then unknown group called the Jihad Islamic Group (JIG), a splinter from the Islamic Movement of Uzbekistan (IMU), claimed responsibility for the attacks. Dozens of individuals were ultimately tried, convicted, and sentenced to between 3 and 18 years in prison for the spring incidents.

In the first election for the new 120-seat Legislative Chamber, held on December 26, 2004, with runoff balloting on January 9, 2005, the recently organized Liberal Democratic Party of Uzbekistan (LDP) won a plurality of seats, ahead of the PDP and *Fidokorlar.* Elected members of the new Senate were chosen indirectly by regional bodies on January 17–20.

On May 13–14, 2005, the eastern city of Andijan erupted in mass protest against civil rights abuses and widespread poverty. In response, troops reportedly fired indiscriminately into crowds of mostly unarmed civilians numbering in the low thousands. The government, which put the death toll at 187, blamed the unrest on terrorists and Islamic extremists associated with the IMU and another banned organization, the *Hizb-ut-Tahrir.* Human rights groups put the death toll at 500–750 and charged that many had been massacred in the streets. Hundreds fled across the Kyrgyz border. Tashkent refused to allow an independent inquiry, as called for by the UN and others, leading the European Union (EU) to impose sanctions that included banning the import of arms or equipment that could be used in state repression.

President Karimov easily won reelection on December 23, 2007. Two of the other three presidential candidates on the ballot represented government-supportive parties, while the third, Akmal SAIDOV, nominated by a citizens' initiative group, was a legal scholar, member of the Legislative Chamber, and former ambassador. The Organization for Security and Cooperation in Europe (OSCE) determined that the elections failed to meet international standards, but the Russian-led Commonwealth of Independent States (CIS) called the vote legitimate.

In the two-stage Legislative Chamber election held December 27, 2009, and January 10, 2010, once again only progovernment parties were permitted to offer candidates. The LDP won a leading 53 of the 150 seats in the expanded lower house, followed by the PDP with 32, the new *Milliy Tiklanish* Democratic Party with 31, and the Justice (*Adolat*) Social Democratic Party of Uzbekistan with 19. Fifteen reserved seats were indirectly filled by the Ecological Movement of Uzbekistan (EMU). In March 2010 the cabinet was shuffled under the continuing leadership of Prime Minister Mirziyoyev. Between December 2010 and November 2011, three ministers were replaced. Another minor cabinet reshuffle took place in January 2012 when several new ministers were appointed and the number of deputy prime ministers was reduced from seven to six. In August Deputy Prime Minister Abdulla ORIPOV was dismissed (see Current issues, below). In September Health Minister Adham Ilkhamovich IKROMOV was promoted to replace Oripov. In February 2013 two ministers were replaced.

Constitution and government. The 1992 constitution describes Uzbekistan as a democratic presidential republic in which "there may be no official state ideology or religion." Freedom of thought and conscience and respect for human rights are guaranteed, although a 1998 law set stringent requirements governing the reregistration and activities of religious groups, which are prohibited from engaging in sectarian social movements, missionary work, proselytizing, most forms of religious education, and publication of religious materials deemed extreme, chauvinistic, or separatist. Formal press censorship ended in 2002, but the government continues to dominate the media and exert overwhelming pressure on nongovernment outlets. (In 2008 the International Crisis Group concluded that there were "strong indications" that Uzbek security forces murdered a journalist who had written extensively about torture in Uzbek prisons.) In 2013, Reporters Without Borders ranked Uzbekistan 164 out of 179 countries in freedom of the press.

The popularly elected head of state may serve no more than two consecutive terms, a restriction that the current president circumvented in 2007 by arguing that the 2002 referendum on extending his term reset the clock. The president wields broad authority that includes initiating legislation, and serving as commander in chief. Constitutional reforms in 2011 granted the assembly the power to nominate the prime minister (the prime minister can also be removed through a no-confidence vote) and reduced the term of the president from seven to five years. The bicameral Supreme Assembly comprises a directly elected Legislative Chamber and a Senate that is largely chosen by and from among regional and local councils but also includes presidential appointees. The Senate has authority to approve certain government officials (e.g., ambassadors and Supreme Court justices) as well as limited powers to delay or block bills passed by the Legislative Chamber.

At its highest level the independent judiciary includes a Constitutional Court, a Supreme Court, and a High Economic Court. Administratively, Uzbekistan encompasses 12 regions (*wiloyatlar*), the autonomous republic of Karakalpakstan (Qoraqalpoghiston), and the capital city (Tashkent). Subdivisions include more than 160 districts and over 110 cities and towns. The president appoints regional governors (*khokims*) as well as lower court judges.

Foreign relations. On December 21, 1991, Uzbekistan became a sovereign member of the CIS. By early 1992 it had established diplomatic relations with a number of Western countries, including the United States. In March it was admitted to the United Nations and in September became a member of the International Monetary Fund and the World Bank. It joined the Conference on (later Organization for) Security and Cooperation in Europe (CSCE/OSCE) in 1992 and subscribed to the NATO-sponsored Partnership for Peace program in July 1994. In June 1996 Tashkent signed a partnership and cooperation agreement with the EU.

The Uzbek government has maintained close relations with Russia. A March 1994 economic integration agreement led in July 1995 to the signing of 15 detailed accords covering economic and military cooperation. During a visit by President Karimov to Russia in May 1998, he and President Boris Yeltsin agreed to coordinate their efforts to control the spread of fundamentalism, with President Imomali Rakhmonov of Tajikistan concurring. In October Yeltsin paid a return visit to Uzbekistan, at which time the two chiefs of state promised mutual aid in the case of an attack on either country, presumably by Afghanistan's Taliban or its allies. In 2006 Uzbekistan joined the Collective Security Treaty Organization (CSTO), seven years after having announced its withdrawal from the predecessor Collective Security Treaty (CST).

In January 1994 Uzbekistan joined with Kazakhstan and Kyrgyzstan to form the Central Asian Economic Union (CAEU), which was later extended to cover defense, foreign policy, and social affairs. In July 1998, with Tajikistan having joined as a candidate member in March, the CAEU adopted the name Central Asian Economic Community, which was then reconfigured in March 2002 as the Central Asian Cooperation Organization (CACO). Russia became the fifth member in October 2004. In January 2006 Uzbekistan was admitted to the Eurasian Economic Community (EurAsEc) of Belarus, Kazakhstan, Kyrgyzstan, Russia, and Tajikistan, which at the same time decided to absorb the redundant CACO. In November 2008 the Uzbek government confirmed its intention to withdraw from EurAsEc and to pursue closer relations with non-Eurasian countries.

In June 2001 Uzbekistan joined China, Kazakhstan, Kyrgyzstan, Russia, and Tajikistan in establishing the Shanghai Cooperation Organization (SCO), which had begun as the so-called Shanghai Five in the mid-1990s. The principal mandate of the SCO is to ensure regional stability, with a particular focus on containing Islamic militancy. The SCO has also played an increasingly important role in determining oil and natural gas production development and diversification throughout the region. The organizations tenth annual summit convened in Tashkent on June 11, 2010.

Uzbekistan's overriding concern with Islamic militancy can be traced to the Afghan civil war of the 1990s, when the Uzbek government, despite its denials, was widely reported to be providing weapons and financial assistance to the anti-Taliban militia led in the north by Gen. Abdul Rashid Dostam, an ethnic Uzbek. In July 1999, as a member of the "Six-Plus-Two" contact group on Afghanistan, Uzbekistan hosted UN-sponsored peace talks between the Taliban and its principal opponents. The Tashkent meeting produced no significant progress in resolving the Afghan civil war, although the Six-Plus-Two partners (China, Iran, Pakistan, Russia, Tajikistan, Turkmenistan, and the United States as well as Uzbekistan) reaffirmed their ban on military assistance to all belligerents in the conflict. In late 2001, following the September terrorist attacks on the United States, the Karimov government agreed to support the United States and its allies in their effort to oust the Taliban.

In April 2000 the presidents of Kazakhstan, Kyrgyzstan, Tajikistan, and Uzbekistan signed a mutual security agreement providing for joint action against terrorism, political and religious extremism, organized crime, and other threats.

In January 1998 Presidents Karimov of Uzbekistan and Rakhmonov of Tajikistan signed several bilateral agreements covering, among other things, the resolution of debt issues and joint antidrug activities. The meeting also apparently indicated Karimov's grudging acceptance of proposed Islamist participation in the Tajik government. Later in the year, however, relations grew heated when Rakhmonov asserted that Uzbekistan had allowed leaders of a failed revolt in northern Tajikistan to enter the country and that Uzbekistan aimed "to take the whole of Tajikistan under its control." Shortly thereafter, captured rebels reportedly admitted that members of the Uzbek special forces had helped train them. In addition to denying the allegations, Karimov later accused Tajik officials of involvement in drug trafficking. In August 1999, in an effort to root out ethnic Uzbek militants, government aircraft bombed camps across the Tajik border. Some of the bombs hit Tajik villages, provoking an outcry from Dushanbe. In June 2000, however, Uzbekistan and Tajikistan signed a friendship treaty and agreed to demarcate their border, although the alleged persecution of ethnic Tajiks in Uzbekistan and claims by Tajik nationalists to Uzbek territory continue to cause strains.

In August 1999 fundamentalists associated with the IMU seized hostages in southern Kyrgyzstan and reaffirmed their intention to create an Islamic state in Central Asia. Uzbekistan joined Russia and Kazakhstan in providing military assistance to the Kyrgyz government, which negotiated the release of the final hostages in October. In 2000 Uzbekistan unilaterally began mining its borders with Tajikistan and Kyrgyzstan as part of its efforts to stop incursions by militants and to halt the flow of illegal drugs. The mining of the border remained a sore point into 2004, when Tashkent announced that it would remove the explosives. A terrorist bombing along the Uzbek-Kyrgyz border in May 2009 and Kyrgyzstan's agreement to host a second Russian military base, potentially located near its border with Uzbekistan, further complicated the relationship, as did the flight in June 2010 of some 400,000 ethnic Uzbek refugees across the border from southern Kyrgyzstan, where they and their property had been subjected to unrestrained violence by elements of the Kyrgyz community. By the end of the month, however, civil order had been restored and many Uzbeks were already returning.

Water rights have long been a source of regional disputes. Tensions over water supplies erupted in a demonstration in July 1997 on the Kazakh-Uzbek border when Tashkent decided to reduce the amount of water flowing through its territory to southern Kazakhstan. Meanwhile, Kyrgyzstan debated how much to begin charging Uzbekistan and Kazakhstan for water from Kyrgyz reservoirs. In September the three nations agreed with Turkmenistan and Tajikistan to set up a fund to try to save the Aral Sea by alleviating the damage caused by overuse of the Amu-Darya and Syr-Darya rivers for irrigation. More recently, in March 2008, the Uzbek government held an international conference on the Aral Sea crisis, as the volume of the sea had dropped to a tenth of its 1977 levels. In October 2010 Uzbekistan announced that it had spent more than $1 billion in the previous ten years on efforts to save the Aral Sea.

The U.S.-led "war on terrorism" provided the Karimov regime with an opportunity to exploit its strategic location in Central Asia. In October 2001 Karimov granted U.S. forces access to the former Soviet air base in Khanabad—the largest such facility in Central Asia—as part of a "qualitatively new relationship" with the United States. Although the initial announcement indicated that the base would be used for launching search and rescue missions and for funneling humanitarian aid to the Afghani people, Khanabad was soon being used for offensive staging by U.S. and, later, NATO forces. In March 2002 Karimov met with President George W. Bush at the White House, and Karimov and U.S. Secretary of State Colin Powell signed five cooperation agreements, one of which stated that the United States would "regard with grave concern any external threat" to Uzbekistan. U.S. operations in Afghanistan aimed at defeating the Taliban were also directed at IMU elements present in Afghanistan and elsewhere in the region. For its part, Uzbekistan promised to move forward with its political and economic transformation. In July 2005, however, hard U.S. criticism of the events in Andijan may have contributed to Tashkent's demand that U.S. forces vacate the Khanabad base in 180 days. The United States completed its withdrawal on November 21.

In February 2009 the Uzbek government agreed to allow U.S. supplies transit through Uzbek territory from Russia and Kazakhstan to NATO forces in Afghanistan. Gen. David Petraeus, then the head of the U.S. military's Central Command, visited Uzbekistan in mid-August 2009 and signed a military cooperation agreement with the government. In December Uzbekistan and the United States finalized an accord to increase technology cooperation between the two countries. Meanwhile, in October 2011 the United States ended a limited arms embargo on Uzbekistan that had been put in place to protest the nation's human rights record.

In April 2011, during a visit to China, Karimov signed a series of investment agreements worth $5 billion. On October 18 Russia proposed a free trade agreement with other CIS states, but Uzbekistan, along with Azerbaijan and Turkmenistan, asked for additional time before accepting the offer. In November Uzbekistan and Kyrgyzstan finalized an agreement for the former to supply electricity to the latter.

In March 2012 Uzbekistan and the United States signed an agreement to allow U.S. military air and land shipments to cross the country on their way to Afghanistan. The initiative was designed to reduce U.S. dependency on Pakistan as a supply route for forces in Afghanistan (see entry on Pakistan). On April 1 Uzbekistan suspended gas shipments to Tajikistan in response to the Tajik construction of a hydroelectric plant on the Amu Darya River. Uzbek officials claimed the facility would seriously limit the water flow into their country. Shipment was resumed after two weeks under a temporary contract following pledges by Tajikistan to reenter into negotiations on the issue. In May Uzbekistan announced that it would join the proposed CIS free trade area.

Border incidents in January 2013 between Uzbekistan and Kyrgyzstan led to reciprocal temporary blockades against ethnic enclaves in each country. Both nations pledged a joint investigation into the episodes. In February Uzbekistan and China finalized a range of agreements on the transfer and sale of plants and agricultural products. In April Uzbekistan and Russia signed new investment and immigration accords during a visit by Karimov to Moscow. The U.S. State Department gave Uzbekistan its lowest rating in combatting human trafficking and child labor in June 2013. Uzbekistan had been upgraded in 2008.

Current issues. The Legislative Chamber election in December 2009–January 2010 attracted scant media coverage or public interest, belying the 88 percent reported turnout for the first round. Prior to the election the government conducted what has become a regular preelection crackdown directed against political opponents and rights activists, confining many to house arrest. There were also reports of beatings and other forms of intimidation. The OSCE's Office for Democratic Institutions and Human Rights, having concluded that sending even a limited election monitoring team to Uzbekistan would not be "meaningful," declared, in what can only be viewed as an understatement, that "the current political spectrum does not offer the electorate a genuine choice between competing political alternatives."

The United States and EU countries have refrained from harsh criticism of Uzbekistan's human rights record, apparently because of the country's willingness to allow supplies to pass through its territory to NATO troops in Afghanistan. In addition, European countries view imports of Uzbek natural gas as an alternative energy source that could reduce their dependence on Russia. Germany in particular has pursued deeper engagement with Uzbekistan since the EU relaxed sanctions that were imposed following the 2005 Abidjan massacre.

Energy and water disputes continue to complicate regional relationships. Uzbekistan significantly reduced its export of natural gas to Kyrgyzstan and Tajikistan in mid-June 2009 as the two countries fell into arrears on their energy payments, and in November it announced it intended to withdraw from the regional electrical grid because of differences over transit tariffs with Tajikistan, which imports electricity from Turkmenistan via Uzbekistan. Tajikistan responded by threatening to withhold water. Uzbekistan proceeded to stop transit of rail freight. In contrast, in December 2009 the presidents of Uzbekistan, Turkmenistan, Kazakhstan, and China met to inaugurate a recently completed 1,139-mile (1,833-kilometer) Turkmenistan-China natural gas pipeline that passes through Uzbekistan and Kazakhstan.

Questions have recently arisen over who might succeed President Karimov, who is 73. Some speculation has focused on a daughter, Gulnora KARIMOVA, while other reports indicated the successor may be Prime Minister Mirziyoev or First Deputy Prime Minister Rustam AZIMOV.

In March 2012 Karimov announced that legislative elections would be held in December 2014. The government launched a major privatization initiative in May. The program sought to sell off 500 state enterprises over a two-year period. In July Karimov approved an increase to the salaries of local and regional government employees as part of an effort to reduce graft and corruption. In response to international pressure, the government banned the use of child labor in cotton harvests in August.

In September 2012 two major telecommunications scandals prompted the dismissal of Deputy Prime Minister Abdulla Oripov. The first involved the telecommunications giant Uzdunrobita, which had its license revoked for tax evasions, leaving 40 percent of Uzbek mobile phone owners without service. Courts subsequently ordered the confiscation of the company's $700 million in assets in what independent media outlets described as a "shakedown." Meanwhile, Western reports alleged that a Nordic telecommunications company had been forced to improperly pay $320 million to obtain licenses to operate in Uzbekistan.

POLITICAL PARTIES

The political system remains dominated by the People's Democratic Party of Uzbekistan (PDP), successor to the Soviet-era Uzbek Communist Party. Although authorities permitted a small number of other parties to form, the government routinely banned true opposition parties. All six of the progovernment parties and organizations discussed below were established with President Karimov's participation or approval. (For more on political parties prior to 2004, please see the 2012 *Handbook.*)

Progovernment Parties and Organizations:

Liberal Democratic Party of Uzbekistan—LDP (*Ozbekiston Liberal-Demokratik Partiyasi*—OzLiDeP). Aiming to attract businesses, entrepreneurs, and industrial workers, the LDP held its founding congress in November 2003, a month after receiving the imprimatur of President Karimov. The only new party to have been registered since the 1999 Supreme Assembly election, the LDP contested the December 2004–January 2005 balloting for the new lower house of the Supreme Assembly, finishing first, with 41 seats. The party's original chair, Qobiljon TOSHMATOV, resigned in May 2004, ostensibly for health reasons, although some reports indicated that he had earned President Karimov's displeasure at a recent session of the Supreme Assembly.

In preparation for the upcoming national election, the LDP held its fifth congress in November 2009. In the Legislative Chamber election of December 2009–January 2010 the party won a leading 53 seats. Reports in 2012 indicated a significant increase in efforts to expand local LDP chapters.

Leaders: Islam KARIMOV (President of the Republic), Muhammadyusuf TESHABOYEV (Chair), Baxtiyor YOQUBOV (Leader in the Legislative Chamber).

People's Democratic Party of Uzbekistan—PDP (*Ozbekiston Xalq Demokratik Partiyasi*). The PDP was organized in November 1991 as successor to the former Uzbek Communist Party, whose activities had been suspended in August. Officially committed to promarket reform and multi-party democracy, the PDP has nevertheless backed the Karimov government's cautious line on both fronts. In June 1996 President Karimov resigned as party chair and PDP member. His successor, Abdulkhafiz Jalolov, contested the January 2000 presidential race, with Karimov's approval, but won only 4.2 percent of the vote and subsequently retired from politics. A month earlier the PDP had won 48 Supreme Assembly seats, down from the 69 it had claimed in the balloting of December 1994–January 1995.

In the December 2004–January 2005 election for the new lower house the PDP won 28 seats, with another 8 being captured by party members who had been nominated by independent citizens' groups. In December 2007 the party's presidential candidate, Asliddin Rustamov, finished second, with 3.3 percent of the vote. In the 2009–2010 Legislative Chamber election the PDP won 32 seats.

Reports in 2011 indicated that a number of PDP members had defected to join a new grouping, the Social Democratic Party of Workers and Farmers.

In April 2013 at a party congress, Hotamjon KETMONOV became party chair.

Leaders: Hotamjon KETMONOV (Central Committee Chair and First Secretary), Asliddin RUSTAMOV (2007 presidential candidate), Latifjon GULOMOV (Leader in the Legislative Chamber).

National Revival Democratic Party (*Milliy Tiklanish Demokratik Partiyasi*—MTDP). The MTDP was formed in June 2008 by the merger of the National Democratic Party "Self-Sacrificers" (*Fidokorlar*) and the National Revival Party (*Milli Tiklanish Partiyasi*—MTP).

Established at a congress in December 1998, *Fidokorlar* (sometimes translated as "Patriots") was created in response to President Karimov's call a month earlier for a new party of uncorrupted, more youthful, future leaders. *Fidokorlar* won 34 seats in the December 1999 national election, and in January 2000 President Karimov was reelected under the party's banner. In April 2000 *Fidokorlar* and Progress of the Fatherland (*Vatan Tarrakiyeti*—VT) announced a merger, with the new group retaining *Fidokorlar* as its name. The VT, founded in 1992, was a promarket party broadly supportive of the Karimov government. In the 2004–2005 national election *Fidokorlar* won 18 seats, not counting 1 won by a party member nominated by an independent group of citizens.

The MTP, based in the Uzbek artistic and intellectual community, was founded in June 1995. It won 10 Supreme Assembly seats in 1999 and 11 in 2004–2005. The party chair, Xurshid DOSTMUHAMMAD, was nominated for the presidency in 2007, but he was kept off the ballot after failing to obtain the required number of supporting signatures (5 percent of the electorate).

The MTDP, which held its second congress in November 2009, won 31 seats in the subsequent Legislative Chamber election. In May 2013 Sarvar OTAMURADOV was elected party chair.

Leaders: Shavkat MIRZIYOYEV (Prime Minister), Sarvar OTAMURADOV (Chair), Ulegbek MUHAMMADIYEV (Leader in the Legislative Chamber).

Justice Social Democratic Party of Uzbekistan (*Adolat Sotsialdemokratik Partiyasi*). *Adolat* was relaunched in February 1995 as a progovernment grouping, having in a previous incarnation been a grouping of Muslim dissidents that was banned shortly after its formation in 1992. Adopting a left-of-center economic and social program, the new party claimed the support of some 50 deputies in the new Supreme Assembly and subsequently obtained official registration. It won 11 Supreme Assembly seats in 1999 and 8 in the 2004–2005 election, not counting 2 seats claimed by party members nominated by independent citizens' groups.

In 2007, the party's leader at the time, Dilorom Tashmukhamedova, became the first woman to stand for president in Uzbekistan. She finished third in the December 2007 presidential election, capturing 3.0 percent of the vote, and is the current speaker of the lower house, in which *Adolat* holds 19 seats. Narimon UMAROV, chair of the State Committee for Nature Protection, was elected party leader in June 2013.

Leaders: Narimon UMAROV (Chair of the Party's Political Council), Dilorom TASHMUKHAMEDOVA (Speaker of the Legislative Chamber).

Ecological Movement of Uzbekistan—EMU (*Ozbekiston Ekologik Harakati*). Formed in August 2008 and sponsored by the government, the EMU focuses on environmental and public health issues.

Aslan MAVLYANOV, the director of the Institute of Hydrology and Geological Engineering under the State Committee on Geology, initially led the group, whose members are primarily scientists and medical professionals. Under a law passed in December 2008, the EMU now holds 15 reserved seats in the Legislative Chamber. The EMU led the 2012 opposition to the proposed Tajik hydroelectric plant on the Amu Darya River and opposition in 2013 to a Tajik aluminum plant.

Leader: Boriy ALIXONOV (Chair).

Unregistered Groups:

Birlik Popular Movement Party (*"Birlik" Xalq Harakati Partiyasi*). The *Birlik* Party, which held its founding congress in August 2003, traces its origin to the Popular Movement of Uzbekistan "Unity" (*Ozbekiston "Birlik" Xalq Harakati—Birlik*), a nationalist and secular formation launched in 1988 on a platform that urged secession from the Soviet Union. Presumed to be the strongest of the opposition groups (although weakened by the formation of *Erk,* below), it was not permitted to contest the presidential balloting of December 1991 and was banned by the Supreme Assembly for "antigovernment activities" the following year. Most of its principal leaders were subjected to beatings, imprisonment, and other forms of harassment by the Karimov regime.

Having failed to obtain reregistration as a party, *Birlik* did not contest the 1994–1995 election and held a congress in exile in Moscow in July 1995. Since again being denied party status in 1999, *Birlik* has continued as a nongovernmental social movement. Hoping to finally achieve recognition as a party, in 2003 *Birlik* members organized the *Birlik* Party, which was equally unsuccessful in its effort to register. The organization has close ties to the *Ezgulik* human rights society headed by Vasila Inoyatova. However, while *Ezgulik* condemned the EU's decision in 2007 to ease sanctions against the Uzbek government, *Birlik* leadership supported the EU's move. *Birlik* leaders also asked the EU to demand their party be allowed to participate in the 2009 parliamentary elections. On November 21, 2010, party leader Abdurahim PULAT (Abdurakhim PULATOV) died in exile in the United States.

Leaders: Vasila INOVATOVA (Secretary General), Pulat AXUNOV (Deputy Chair).

Freedom Democratic Party of Uzbekistan (*Ozbekiston "Erk" Demokratik Partiyasi*). *Erk* was organized in April 1990 by a group of *Birlik* dissidents who called for economic and political autonomy for Uzbekistan within a Soviet federation. Its chair, Muhammad Salih, a prominent poet, was a distant runner-up to the Islam Karimov, then representing the PDP, in the 1991 presidential poll and in July 1992 resigned from the legislature (and left the country) after being denied an opportunity to speak. At a joint meeting the same month, *Erk* and *Birlik* representatives committed themselves to common action against the Karimov regime.

In October 1993 *Erk* failed to meet a deadline for reregistration as a party because it had no address, its offices having been declared a fire risk. A brother of the *Erk* chair was reported in August 1995 to have been jailed for five years for activism in the Association of Young Democrats of Turkistan, an *Erk* affiliate.

Karimov accused Salih of being behind the February 1999 bombings in Tashkent, despite an absence of convincing evidence. Salih was convicted of terrorism in November 2000 and sentenced, in absentia, to 15 years in prison.

Erk was permitted to hold its first party congress in ten years in October 2003, but it remained unregistered. An internal dispute saw a number of party members, led by Samad MUROV, argue for replacement of the party leadership—an effort that Secretary General Otanazar Oripov characterized in February 2004 as a government effort to undermine the party. In May 2006 a National Salvation Committee, newly established among exiles in Kyrgyzstan, proposed Salih as a presidential candidate for 2007. Reports in October 2012 indicated that several *Erk* members had been detained.

Leaders: Muhammad SALIH (SOLIH, SOLIKH; aka Salay MADAMINOV) (Chair, in exile), Polat OXUNOV (Deputy Chair), Otanazar ORIPOV (Secretary General).

Free Peasants' Party (*Ozod Dehqonlar*—OD). At its founding congress in December 2003, the OD called for agricultural reform and limitations on presidential powers. The party failed to achieve legal status in 2004, and in September 2008 held a meeting in Tashkent to discuss economic issues. Among those invited were four human rights activists from the Jizakh region, who were detained at a Tashkent hotel by antiterrorism officials but released after a few hours. Other rights activists saw the arrests as an attempt to intimidate the organizers.

In April 2005 the OD announced formation of an opposition coalition called **Sunshine Uzbekistan** (*Serquyosh Ozbekistonim*). The Sunshine Coalition, as it is also known, is headed by Sanjar UMAROV, who in March 2006 was given a ten-year prison sentence for theft. After visiting him in July 2008, family members sent a letter to President Karimov pleading for his release, citing health concerns. Another of the group's leaders and sister to the general secretary, Nodira HIDOYATOVA, received a ten-year sentence but was released in May 2006. Umarov was finally released in November 2009, after which he left for the United States. In July 2012 party leader Hidoyatova fled Uzbekistan claiming she was about to be arrested.

Leader: Nigora HIDOYATOVA (Nigara KHIDOYATOVA).

Solidarity (*Birdamlik*). *Birdamlik* is an opposition movement led from the United States and committed to nonviolent change. In March 2007 it attempted to stage small protests in Tashkent, but these were disrupted by the authorities. It later called for a peaceful demonstration on the anniversary of the 2005 Andijan protest. Its leader, Bahodyr Choriev, has stated that *Birdamlik* hopes to unify all democratic Uzbek opposition parties. He was expelled from Uzbekistan in December 2009, only two months after having returned from abroad. An attempt to hold a constituent assembly in November was canceled when the government prevented delegates from attending. Three *Birdamlik* leaders were arrested in June 2012 for leading anti-Kyrgyz protests. They were released though given large fines. Reports in December 2012 indicated that *Birdamlik* held an illegal protest in Tashkent.

Leaders: Bahodyr CHORIEV, Dilorom SHAKO.

Banned Groups:

Islamic Movement of Uzbekistan (IMU). The militant IMU, which has also been known since 2001 as the **Islamic Party of Turkestan,** advocates creation of an Islamic republic under religious law. Some of its members may have participated in the Justice (*Adolat*) Movement that was banned in 1992, but the IMU itself did not emerge until 1999. In May 2000 a U.S. State Department report labeled it as one of the world's most dangerous terrorist organizations and alleged that it had been behind the February 1999 Tashkent bombings and an August–October hostage situation in Kyrgyzstan. Later reports indicated that at least some members were moving from bases in Tajikistan to Afghanistan, where many of its members were apparently trained at al-Qaida camps.

In August 2000 two IMU incursions from across the Tajik border occurred. Operations against the 100 or so militants continued into September. Two months later the Supreme Court found IMU leaders Tahir YOLDASH (Tohir YOLDOSHEV) and Juma NAMANGONIY guilty, in absentia, of terrorism and imposed death sentences. In November 2001 Namangoniy was killed in Afghanistan, where IMU forces suffered heavy losses as allies of the Taliban. Policy differences within the IMU over whether to focus on opposing the Karimov regime or expanding its support for Islamic militancy throughout Central Asia and elsewhere apparently led to formation in 2002 of the Islamic Jihad Union (below). In May 2005 the Uzbek government assigned blame for the Andijan unrest to the IMU and *Hizb-ut-Tahrir* (below).

In January 2008, Yoldash, in a video, declared jihad on the Pakistani government and its security forces. In July, Pakistan premier Yousaf Raza Gillani asserted that the IMU was behind a spike in violence in his nation's tribal areas. In September 2009 Pakistan stated that the 5,000 IMU operatives in the country's tribal areas constituted the area's largest foreign militant group. In August 2010 the IMU confirmed that Yoldash had been killed in August 2009 by a U.S. drone attack in Pakistan's northwest. Six suspected IMU militants were killed in a U.S. drone strike in July 2012 in Pakistan. In June 2013 Afghan officials asserted that IMU militants were increasingly active in the country and fighting alongside Taliban forces.

Leader: Usman ODIL.

Islamic Jihad Union—IJU (*Ittehad-e-Jihad Islamic;* aka Jihad Islamic Group—JIG). Believed to have been established in March 2002 by the most militant faction of the IMU after the IMU was severely weakened by the U.S.-led war in Afghanistan, the IJU claimed responsibility for a series of terrorist acts in Uzbekistan in March–July 2004. The organization also took responsibility for a foiled terrorist plot against the U.S. military base in Ramstein, Germany, in September 2007 and for two terrorist attacks in May 2009, one taking place at a post along the Uzbek-Kyrgyz border, and another in Andijan. The IJU claims to have hundreds of members operating in Europe. In April 2012 an Uzbek citizen was arrested in Philadelphia in the United States for supporting the IJU. Reports in April 2013 revealed that U.S. law enforcement officials were investigating links between the IJU and Tamerlan and Dzhokhar Tsarnaev, two brothers who carried out the Boston Marathon bombing (see entry on the United States).

For more on the banned *Hizb ut-Tahrir* (Liberation Party), please see the 2012 *Handbook.*

LEGISLATURE

The Supreme Assembly (*Oliy Majlis*) was initially established as a unicameral legislature of 250 directly elected members. Constitutional revisions passed by referendum in February 2002 called for the establishment of a bicameral Supreme Assembly encompassing a Senate and a Legislative Chamber, with the members of both serving five-year terms. A law passed in December 2008 disqualifies independent candidates from contesting seats in the Legislative Chamber.

Senate (*Senati*). The Senate comprises 100 members: 16 presidential appointees in addition to 84 representatives (6 from each of the country's 12 regions, 6 from the capital, and 6 from the Karakalpakstan autonomous republic), chosen by and from among regional "representative bodies of state power. The initial presidential appointees included several cabinet members, judges, academics, heads of civil organizations, and industrialists. Elected members were most recently chosen on a nonpartisan basis on January 20 and 22, 2010.

Speaker: Ilgizar SOBIROV (Ilgizar SABIROV).

Legislative Chamber (*Konunchilik Palatasi*). The lower chamber comprises 150 members, 135 directly elected and 15 chosen to represent the Ecological Movement of Uzbekistan. The most recent election was held December 26, 2004, with runoff balloting in 39 constituencies on January 10, 2010, produced the following results: Liberal Democratic Party of Uzbekistan, 53 seats; People's Democratic Party of Uzbekistan, 32; *Milliy Tiklanish* Democratic Party, 31; and Justice (*Adolat*) Social Democratic Party of Uzbekistan, 19.

Speaker: Dilorom TASHMUKHAMEDOVA.

CABINET

[as of August 1, 2013]

Prime Minister	Shavkat Mirziyoev
First Deputy Prime Minister	Rustam Azimov
Deputy Prime Ministers	
Chair of the Women's Committee	Elmira Basitkhanova [f]
Chair State Committee for Architecture and Construction	Batir Zakirov
Culture, Education, Healthcare, and Social Security	Adham Ilkhamovich Ikromov
Industrial Sector	Ulugbek Rozukulov
Marine Geology, Fuel and Energy, Chemical, Petrochemical and Metallurgical Industries	Gulomjon Ibragimov
Ministers	
Agriculture and Water Resources	Zafar Ruziev
Culture and Sports	Minhojiddin Hojimatov
Defense	Kabul Berdiyev
Economics	Galina Saidova [f]
Emergency Situations	Tursinkhon Khudayberganov
Finance	Rustam Azimov
Foreign Affairs	Abdulaziz Kamilov
Foreign Economic Relations, Investments, and Trade	Elyor Ganiev
Higher and Secondary Specialized Education	Bakhodir Khodiev
Internal Affairs	Bahodir Matlubov
Justice	Nigmatilla Yuldoshev
Labor and Social Security	Aktam Khaitov
Public Education	Inoyatov Ilyasovich
Public Health	Anvar Alimov
Secretary, National Security Council	Murod Atayev
Chairs of State Committees	
Customs	Zokhid Dusanov
Demonopolization and Development of Competition (Acting)	Umar Turdiev
Geology and Mineral Resources (Acting)	Ilkhomboy Turamuratov
Land Resources, Geodesy, Cartography, and Real Estate	Saidqul Arabov
Nature Protection	Nariman Umarov
State Property Management (Acting)	Aziz Abduhakimov
Statistics	Botir Turaev
Taxes	Botir Parpiyev

[f] = female

INTERGOVERNMENTAL REPRESENTATION

Ambassador to the U.S.: Bakhtiyar GULYAMOV.

U.S. Ambassador to Uzbekistan: George KROL.

Permanent Representative to the UN: Dilyor KHAKIMOV.

IGO Memberships (Non-UN): ADB, CIS, EBRD, NAM, OIC, OSCE, SCO.

VANUATU

Republic of Vanuatu
République de Vanuatu (French)
Ripablik blong Vanuatu (Bislama)

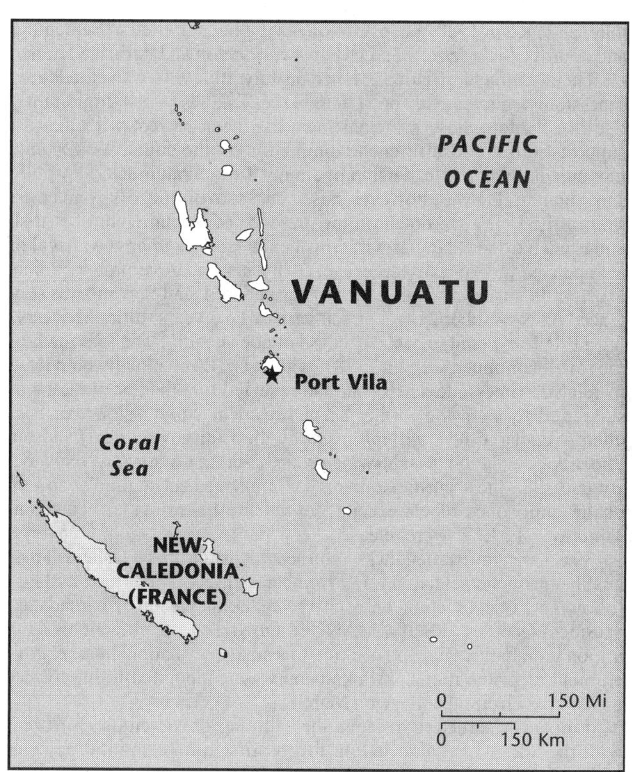

Political Status: Formerly the New Hebrides; became the Anglo-French Condominium of the New Hebrides in 1906; present name adopted upon becoming an independent member of the Commonwealth on July 30, 1980.

Area: 4,647 sq. mi. (12,035 sq. km).

Population: 252,792 (2012E—UN); 227,574 (2012E—U.S. Census).

Major Urban Center (2011E): VILA (Port Vila, 47,600).

Official Languages: English, French, Bislama. The last, a pidgin dialect, is recognized constitutionally as the "national language," and efforts are currently under way to accord it equal status with English and French as a medium of instruction.

Monetary Unit: Vatu (official rate November 1, 2013: 95.55 vatu = $1US).

President: Iolu Johnson ABIL (Party of Our Land); elected by the electoral college on September 2, 2009, and inaugurated the same day for a five-year term in succession to Kalkot MATASKELEKELE Mauliliu, whose term of office had expired on August 16. (Maxime CARLOT Korman, the speaker of Parliament, served as acting president from August 16, 2009, to September 2.)

Prime Minister: Moana CARCASSES Kalosil (Vanuatu Green Party); elected by parliament and sworn in on March 23, 2013, following the resignation of Sato KILMAN (People's Progressive Party).

THE COUNTRY

An 800-mile-long archipelago of some 80 islands, Vanuatu is situated in the western Pacific southeast of the Solomon Islands and northeast of New Caledonia. The larger islands of the group are Espiritu Santo, Malekula, Tanna, Ambrym, Pentecost, Erromanga, Aoba, Epi, and Efaté, on which the capital, Vila, is located. Over 90 percent of the inhabitants are indigenous Melanesians; the remainder encompasses small groups of French, English, Vietnamese, Chinese, and other Pacific islanders. Approximately 85 percent are Christian, Presbyterians constituting the largest single denomination, followed by Roman Catholics and Anglicans. Approximately three-quarters of adult women have been described as "economically active," most of them in agricultural pursuits; female participation in government, on either the village or national level, is minimal.

The bulk of the population is engaged in some form of agriculture. Coconuts, taro, and yams are grown for subsistence purposes, with copra, kava, timber, cocoa, and beef constituting the principal exports. In 1981 a national airline was established, while maritime legislation was enacted to promote Vanuatu as "a flag of convenience." The country also emerged as an offshore financial center, with well over 1,000 companies (including more than 60 banks as of 2000) incorporated in Port Vila yielding close to $1.5 million annually in revenue.

In June 2000 Vanuatu was threatened with economic sanctions by the Organization for Economic Cooperation and Development (OECD) for "harmful" policies related to its offshore financial services. Although the government subsequently pledged its cooperation in fighting money laundering and other financial crimes, in 2001 it insisted that it had the right to set its own tax policies and would not share information about nonnational accounts with foreign tax authorities. Further action regarding Vanuatu's international tax status served as the nucleus of a dispute with Australian authorities in early 2008.

Vanuatu has remained one of six Pacific island countries on the OECD list of money-laundering venues.

Although Vanuatu was formally characterized by the United Nations as a "least developed country," tourism, forestry projects, and the discovery of promising mineral deposits, including gold and manganese, offer potential for long-term economic growth. From 1990 to 1999, however, the annual real change in GNP averaged 2.5 percent. Renewed expansion of 2.8 percent occurred in 2000, with further improvement thereafter to an annual average of 6.4 percent for 2004–2008. The economic progress led the UN to announce in July 2006 that Vanuatu would likely qualify for "developing country" status by 2013, a change rejected by the Edward NATAPEI administration in mid-2009, since it would entail a reduction in foreign aid. Growth slowed to 3.5 percent in 2009 and, in the face of challenging economic times worldwide, averaged 2 percent through 2012. In 2013 GDP grew by 4.3 percent, reflecting growth in the tourism sector and new investment projects. Inflation was 1.7 percent.

GOVERNMENT AND POLITICS

Political background. Settled during the first half of the 19th century by a variety of British and French nationals, including a sizable contingent of missionaries, the New Hebrides subsequently became the scene of extensive labor recruitment by plantation owners in Fiji and Queensland. Following a series of unsuccessful efforts to stem the frequently inhumane practice of "blackbirding," Britain and France established a Joint Naval Commission in 1886 to safeguard order in the archipelago. Two decades later, faced with competition by German interests, the two governments agreed to form a cumbersome but reasonably serviceable condominium structure that entailed dual instruments of administration at all levels, including two police forces, two resident commissioners, and two local commissioners in each of the territory's four districts.

A 42-member Representative Assembly (replacing an Advisory Council established in 1957) convened for the first time in November 1976 but immediately became embroiled in controversy as to whether 13 members not elected by universal suffrage (4 representing tribal chiefs and 9 representing economic interests) should be required to declare party allegiance. Condemning what they termed the "present unworkable system of government," the 21 representatives of the Party of Our Land (*Vanua'aku Pati*—VP) boycotted the second assembly session in February 1977, prompting the colonial administrators to call a new election, the results of which were voided because of another VP boycott.

In the assembly election of November 14, 1979, the VP won 26 of 39 seats, and on November 29 party leader Fr. Walter Hadye LINI was designated as chief minister. Earlier, the colonial powers had agreed to independence in 1980, a constitution having been drafted in September and approved in a series of notes between London and Paris in October.

The attainment of independence on July 30, 1980, was clouded by secessionist movements on a number of islands, most importantly Espiritu Santo, whose principal town had been seized, with indirect support from the local French community, by the cultist *Na-Griamel* movement under the leadership of Jimmy Tupou Patuntun STEVENS. The Vanuatu flag was, however, raised on Santo on July 30 by an emissary of the Lini government in the presence of a contingent of British and French troops that was withdrawn on August 18 upon the arrival of a Papua New Guinean force backed by central government police. Most of the insurgents subsequently surrendered, and Stevens was sentenced on November 21 to a prison term of 14.5 years (ultimately serving 11, before being released because of poor health). The aftermath of the revolt continued well into 1981, with over 700 eventually convicted of related crimes. Stevens's trial had revealed that the insurgency was supported by both the former French resident commissioner (subsequently declared *persona non grata* by the Lini government) and the Phoenix Foundation, a right-wing group based in Carson City, Nevada. By late 1981 the security situation had improved substantially, and all of the imprisoned rebels except Stevens and his principal lieutenant, Timothy WELLES, were released.

The Lini government was returned to office in the islands' first postindependence election on November 2, 1983. Three months later, following his conviction on a charge of nonpayment of a road tax, President George Ati SOKOMANU resigned. Despite voicing his frustration with Father Lini and offering to lead a new "national unity" government as prime minister, Sokomanu was reappointed to his former post by the electoral college on March 8.

Lini was returned to office in the balloting of November 30, 1987, with the VP's vote share falling for the first time below 50 percent, while the opposition Union of Moderate Parties (*Union blong Moderet Pati*—UMP) increased its showing to 42 percent, compared with 33 percent in 1983.

Following the 1987 election a leadership dispute erupted between Lini and party ideologue Barak SOPE Ma'au Tamate, who mounted an unsuccessful bid for the prime minister position and was subsequently charged with instigating a major riot in Vila on May 16, 1988. In the wake of the disturbance, Sope was dismissed from the cabinet, stripped of his longtime post as party secretary general, and, along with four associates, expelled from the party after endorsing a no-confidence motion against the administration. On July 25 the "Gang of Five" was also ousted from Parliament under a 1983 Vacation of Seats Act that precluded alteration of party affiliation by members. In response to the action, 18 members of the opposition UMP initiated a legislative boycott and on July 27 were also expelled for violating a parliamentary ban on three consecutive absences. Ironically, the Vanuatu Court of Appeal on October 21 ruled the 1983 act unconstitutional and reinstated the Sope parliamentarians (who had regrouped as the Melanesian Progressive Party—MPP) while upholding the ouster of the UMP members.

Five days after by-elections on December 13, 1988, for the vacated UMP seats, which neither the UMP nor the MPP contested, President Sokomanu attempted to dissolve Parliament and name an "interim" government headed by Sope. Lini reacted by arresting Sope and his "ministers," with the Supreme Court ruling on December 19 that the president's action had been unconstitutional because it had not been undertaken with the support of two-thirds of the legislators and the advice of the prime minister. On January 12, 1989, Sokomanu was dismissed from office for "gross misconduct," and on January 30 Health Minister Fred TIMAKATA was designated by the electoral college as his successor. Subsequently, Sokomanu was convicted of incitement to mutiny and sentenced to a six-year prison term, while Sope and UMP leader Maxime CARLOT received five-year sentences for seditious conspiracy and treason. The sentences were dismissed in April by an appeals tribunal of jurists from Tonga, Papua New Guinea, and Vanuatu, although the convictions were allowed to stand.

In the wake of severe criticism from key party leaders for dismissing dissident party members and numerous other purges of government personnel (the prime minister at one point was reported to be holding more than 50 portfolios), Lini was replaced by General Secretary Donald KALPOKAS as VP president at a special party congress on August 7, 1991. On September 6, after President Timakata had denied a request that Parliament be dissolved, Lini was also ousted as prime minister, with Kalpokas designated his successor. Lini and a number of supporters thereupon organized the National Unity Party (NUP), which, by splitting the traditional VP vote in the election of December 2, gave a plurality to the francophone UMP. On December 16, in an action he characterized as stemming from a "pact with the devil," the UMP's CARLOT (the honorific "Korman" subsequently being added to his name) formed a governing coalition with the NUP and a small regional formation, *Fren Melanesia.*

Initially withdrawing to the status of a parliamentary backbencher, Lini precipitated a government crisis in mid-1993 by reportedly demanding appointment as deputy prime minister and minister of justice. Rebuffed in the matter, Lini and five legislative colleagues withdrew their support for the government, thereby causing a rupture with a progovernment NUP faction led by Sethy John REGENVANU, which subsequently reorganized as the People's Democratic Party (PDP). The ensuing reduction in Carlot Korman's parliamentary majority to 24 of 46 seats made it impossible to reach the two-thirds majority in the electoral college needed to elect a new president at the expiration of the incumbent Timakata's term on January 31, 1994. It was not until March 2 that a compromise government nominee, Jean-Marie LEYE Lenelgau, was able to secure election through a decision by the VP, which held 9 legislative seats, to support his candidacy. As a result of its action the VP was expelled from the opposition coalition, with Barak Sope succeeding the VP's Kalpokas as leader of the opposition.

In September 1994, as the result of a Decentralisation Act approved four months earlier, the country's 11 local government councils were abolished to pave the way for elected bodies in six newly defined provinces. For the ensuing provincial council balloting of November 15, the opposition consisted, on the one hand, of Lini's NUP and, on the other, of a Unity Front (UF) coalition encompassing the VP, the MPP, the Tan Union, and a relegalized *Na-Griamel* under the leadership of its founder's son, Frankie STEVENS (although the younger Stevens was also serving as the leader of government business in Parliament). The result was a three-way split, with the UMP, NUP, and UF winning two provinces each, although the UF secured an overall plurality of 41 seats, as contrasted with 34 and 20 for the UMP and NUP, respectively.

In the general election of November 30, 1995, Kalpokas's UF secured a plurality of 20 legislative seats, while Carlot's UMP won 17 and Lini's NUP, 9. Meanwhile, a deep intra-UMP split had developed between Carlot and the party president, Serge VOHOR, with the UF seeking an alliance both with the Vohor faction and with the NUP. Intense negotiation then ensued, with Vohor eventually concluding a pact with the NUP that yielded his installation as Carlot's successor on December 24.

In early February 1996 a number of Carlot's supporters joined the UF in a motion of no confidence in Vohor, whose resignation averted the need for a vote and permitted Carlot to form a new government in coalition with the UF. The dispute between Carlot and Vohor intensified in March, with Vohor convening a UMP congress (on his home island of Santo) at which Carlot and his supporters were expelled from the party. Two months later, anti-Vohor faction leader Amos ANDENG called for a retaliatory congress (in Carlot's home village of Erakor) that declared the action of the Santo meeting invalid and named Carlot to succeed Vohor as UMP president.

In mid-1996 the Carlot administration was rocked by the issuance of an ombudsman's report charging that the country faced bankruptcy because of an alleged scam involving issuance of letters of guarantee signed by Carlot and his finance minister, Barak Sope. While denying any wrongdoing, the prime minister shuffled his cabinet on August 5, reassigning Sope to the Ministry of Commerce and Trade. Having refused to accept the demotion, Sope was dismissed from the government on August 12. Concurrently, Carlot cited the MPP leader for "disloyalty" in withdrawing his party from the UF in favor of a new alliance with the Tan Union and *Fren Melanesia,* styled the MTF. The government coalition thus being effectively reduced to his UMP faction and the VP rump of the UF, Carlot succumbed to a no-confidence vote on September 30 and was immediately succeeded by party rival Vohor, who named Sope as his deputy.

On October 12, 1996, while Vohor was visiting French Polynesia, striking members of the paramilitary Vanuatu Mobile Force (VMF) abducted President Leye and flew him to the northern island of Malekula for talks at gunpoint with Acting Prime Minister Sope, who promised that payment would be forthcoming to the VMF for long overdue arrears of $980,000. Thirteen days later Sope and three MTF ministerial colleagues were sacked in a cabinet shakeup that brought the VP into the government as a coalition partner of Vohor's UMP faction and the NUP. In late May 1997 Vohor and Carlot were apparently

reconciled, with Carlot and his UMP-Natora faction joining Vohor's UMP group, Sope's MPP, and the NUP in a new government coalition, the VP's Kalpokas again becoming leader of a one-party opposition. However, the friction between Carlot and Vohor soon resurfaced, with the former filing a no-confidence motion in November against the prime minister, whose government had been the target of numerous corruption allegations. President Leye immediately dissolved the legislature and ordered new elections, which, following a January 1998 Court of Appeal ruling upholding his decision, were held on March 6. The balloting produced no significant alteration in the party makeup of the Parliament, and intense negotiations were reportedly required before the VP and the NUP, longtime rivals, agreed to form the next government. On March 30 the VP's Kalpokas returned to the prime ministerial post he had held in the early 1990s, while the NUP's Lini was named deputy prime minister.

On October 19, 1998, Kalpokas dismissed Lini and expelled his NUP from the ruling coalition because of the party's participation in drafting a no-confidence motion against the government. Kalpokas then formed a new alliance with a faction of the UMP headed by Willie JIMMY and the John Frum Movement (JFM).

Nearly two dozen candidates competed in the 1999 presidential race. Not surprisingly, no one received the required support in the first round of balloting of the electoral college in mid-March. Following apparently intense negotiations, Fr. John Bernard BANI, an Anglican minister and Kalpokas ally, was elected on March 25 with the reported support of all parties except the NUP, even though he had received only two votes on the first ballot.

The government lost its parliamentary majority in by-elections in August 1999 and, facing the loss of a no-confidence vote, Kalpokas resigned on November 25. MPP leader Barak Sope was immediately elected his successor, appointing a coalition administration that included members of the JFM, the NUP, the UMP, the Vanuatu Republican Party (VRP), and *Fren Melanesia Pati* (FMP).

Divisions within the UMP, including the departure in early 2001 of Willie Jimmy's faction, were followed in late March by Serge Vohor's decision to withdraw what was left of the UMP from the government and side with the VP, now headed by Edward Natapei, leader of the opposition. Without UMP support, Prime Minister Sope could no longer command a parliamentary majority, but he failed to convince President Bani to dissolve Parliament and schedule a new general election. In early April, Parliament Speaker Paul Ren TARI of the NUP refused to permit legislative debate on a no-confidence motion filed by the opposition, which turned to the courts for redress. With the country's chief justice having threatened to cite Tari for contempt if he failed to let debate proceed, the no-confidence motion passed 27–18 on April 13, immediately after which Natapei was elected prime minister at the head of a VP-UMP coalition.

In the parliamentary election of May 2, 2002, Natapei's VP secured 14 seats and its coalition partner, the UMP, won 15, thereby ensuring the reelection of Natapei as prime minister when the new Parliament convened on June 3. His tenure ended with an inconclusive election on July 6, 2004, that yielded the third designation of the UMP's Serge Vohor on July 29. Vohor subsequently became embroiled in a dispute over his decision in early November to establish diplomatic relations with Taiwan, and his government fell on December 11, followed by the election of Ham LINI as head of a nine-party coalition administration.

In the election of September 2, 2008, the VP won a plurality of 11 seats, and Natapei was again designated to lead a coalition government that included Lini as his deputy prior to a reshuffle in November 2009 in which the ministers from the NUP and VPR were dropped from the cabinet and members of the opposition, including Sato KILMAN, theretofore the leader of the opposition, were added.

In mid-2009 Maxime Carlot Korman abandoned his post as deputy opposition leader to support the Natapei administration, while Natapei's deputy, Ham Lini, expelled the parliamentary speaker, George WELLS, from the NUP for alleged involvement in negotiations to topple the coalition government. Subsequently, Carlot Korman replaced Wells as speaker but was obliged to return the office to his predecessor in January 2010. In December 2010 the Natapei government lost a vote of no confidence, resulting in his dismissal as prime minister. Parliament immediately elected Deputy Prime Minister Sato Kilman as the next prime minister; he defeated former Prime Minister Vohor by a vote of 29–23. Kilman's tenure ended with a no-confidence motion on April 24, 2011, passed 26–25. Parliament subsequently elected Serge Vohor to a fourth term as prime minister, though his term was voided by a May 13 Court of Appeals ruling that by winning half of parliamentary votes, Vohor had failed to secure the constitutionally mandated clear majority.

The office thus returned to its previous holder, Sato Kilman. Shortly thereafter, however, the Chief Justice of Vanuatu voided Kilman's initial 2010 election on the grounds that it was not conducted by the appropriate secret balloting prescribed by the Constitution, and Edward Natapei was appointed to head an interim government. On June 26, 2011, Kilman was elected for technically his first term as prime minister.

Legislative elections were held on October 30, 2012. Sixteen parties secured seats, and the ensuing three weeks saw a scramble to piece together a ruling coalition, ultimately won by Kilman. The victory was short-lived, however, as he resigned in March 2013, and Moana CARCASSES Kalosil of the Vanuatu Green Party (VGP) was elected on March 23 (see Current issues, below).

Constitution and government. Under the independence constitution, Vanuatu's head of state is a largely titular president designated for a five-year term by an electoral college consisting of all members of the Parliament and the presidents of the six provincial councils. Executive power is vested in a prime minister elected by secret legislative ballot; both the prime minister and other ministers (whom the prime minister appoints) must hold legislative seats. Members of the unicameral Parliament are elected from multimember constituencies through a partially proportional system intended "to ensure fair representation of different political groups and opinions." The legislative term is four years, subject to dissolution. There is also a National Council of Chiefs, whose members are designated by peers sitting in District Councils of Chiefs. The National Council is empowered to make recommendations to the government and Parliament on matters relating to indigenous custom and language. A national ombudsman is appointed by the president after consultation with the prime minister, party leaders, the president of the National Council of Chiefs, and others. The judicial system is headed by a four-member Supreme Court, the chief justice being named by the president after consultation with the prime minister and the leader of the opposition; of the other three justices, one is nominated by the speaker of Parliament, one by the president of the National Council of Chiefs, and one by the six council presidents. A Court of Appeal is constituted by two or more Supreme Court justices sitting together. Parliament is authorized to establish village and island courts, as deemed appropriate.

President Kalkot MATASKELEKELE wrote a formal letter to Prime Minister Lini in June 2006 repeating a recommendation he had made earlier that Vanuatu adopt a republican system of government with a popularly elected president who would be the head of state and the head of government with the power to appoint a cabinet whose members would not necessarily be members of Parliament. Lini responded by acknowledging that the country needed to engage in a review of the national constitution but stopped short of endorsing a presidential system.

The six provinces created in 1994 bear names that are acronyms of those of their principal islands. Stretching roughly from north to south they are Torba (Torres, Banks), Sama (Espiritu Santo, Malo), Penama (Pentecost, Ambae, Maéwo), Malampa (Malakula, Ambrym, Paama), Shefa (Shepherds, Epi, Efaté), and Tafea (Tanna, Anatom, Futuna, Erromango, Aniwa).

Freedom of speech is constitutionally protected, and the government generally respects freedom of the press. There is one government-owned newspaper, in addition to several privately owned ones. Vanuatu has just one television station.

Foreign relations. Although Vanuatu was not admitted to the United Nations until the fall of 1981, it became, at independence, a member both of the Commonwealth and the *Agence de Coopération Culturelle et Technique,* an organization established in 1969 to promote cultural and technical cooperation within the French-speaking world. Regionally, it is a member of the Pacific Community and the Pacific Islands Forum (PIF), while in 1984 both the Asian Development Bank and the Economic and Social Commission for Asia and the Pacific established regional headquarters in Port Vila. Diplomatic relations were established with the Soviet Union in July 1986 and with the United States the following October, although Vanuatu maintains no embassies abroad, save for the appointment in late 2007 of an ambassador to the European Union in Brussels as part of an effort to secure enhanced development aid. In addition, Vanuatu established a diplomatic office in Fiji, which opened on March 29, 2011.

Under the francophone UMP, Vanuatu's prior policy of supporting liberation struggles and actively attacking remaining pockets of colonialism in the Pacific subsided, particularly with regard to the French territory of New Caledonia. (For information about Vanuatu and the South Pacific Nuclear-Free Zone, see the 2013 *Handbook.*)

In a highly unusual move, Prime Minister Vohor announced on November 3, 2004, that Vanuatu had established relations with Taiwan, asserting that the country could continue to maintain existing relations with the People's Republic of China (a position to which the PRC took immediate exception). Vohor's own cabinet voted twice against the action. On November 16 Vohor dismissed Foreign Minister Barak Sope, who had led the opposition to it. Vohor was oustered on December 11 and "all agreements made by Vohor with Taiwan" were repealed by the new government's foreign minister, Sato Kilman. Subsequently, Prime Ministers Lini and Natapei lauded Beijing's one-China policy in meetings with PRC officials in 2005 and 2010, respectively. In December 2012 China agreed to fund and construct a $14.3 million convention center in Vanuatu.

In a similar move, the Kilman administration announced in May 2011 that it was formally recognizing Abkhazia, a disputed region within Georgia that claims to be a sovereign state, becoming one of six countries to do so. In May 2013 Georgian media reported that the island nation had revoked its recognition of Abkhazia. Vanuatu and Georgia established official diplomatic ties in July, seemingly confirming the revocation, though Abkhazia continued to report that ties had not been severed.

Likewise, Vanuatu officially began diplomatic relations with South Korea in June 2011.

Vanuatu is a member of the Melanesian Spearhead Group (MSG), a South Pacific island regional bloc that includes Fiji, Papua New Guinea, and the Solomon Islands. The MSG was formed in 1986 to promote economic development and sustainable growth, good government, preservation of Melanesian cultures, and regional cooperation and security among members, and in the 1990s was a force supporting decolonization movements in New Caledonia.

Membership in the PIF has increased Vanuatu's support for greater regional and international labor mobility as a means for improving the local economy, especially in regard to greater access to Australia and New Zealand labor markets for its citizens. More recently, Vanuatu in early 2008 completed domestic requirements for inclusion in the Pacific Island Countries Trade Agreement (PICTA).

Vanuatu has recently sought to formally restart talks for accession to the World Trade Organization (WTO). Talks had been suspended in 2001, in part over Vanuatu's unwillingness to expose its retail, telecommunications, and services sectors to rapid liberalization. In furtherance of its independence in trade policy, Vanuatu continued to withhold negotiation on WTO entry until April 2009, when discussions resumed after most of its concerns had apparently been resolved. The WTO welcomed Vanuatu as a new member on October 26, 2011, and the government had until December 31 to approve the accession package. Parliament passed the legislation, and President Abil signed on in June 2012.

Tensions escalated between Vanuatu and Australia after a senior advisor to Prime Minister Kilman was arrested in May 2012 at Sydney Airport for his part in an international tax scam. In response to what the administration interpreted as international humiliation, Vanuatu's foreign office expelled 12 Australian Federal Police (AFP) officers, who had been stationed in Port Vila as part of Australia's policing expansion through the Pacific region. Following talks in early 2013, Vanuatu in February agreed on the return of AFP officers.

Current issues. In an election overseen by an interim Edward Natapei-led government, Sato Kilman was elected prime minister over Serge Vohor by a vote of 29–23 on June 26, 2011. This election marked the technical beginning of Kilman's first term as prime minister since his previous tenures had been voided by the courts. Kilman restored all of his cabinet ministers from the June 2011 term.

Organizational failures plagued the run-up to the October 30, 2012, balloting. More than 70 candidates, including Kilman, were left off the initial ballot list because of outstanding government debts.

Nearly 350 candidates from over 30 parties, a record high, contested. Sixteen parties secured representation. No single group secured more than 10 seats (the VP, with 8, won the largest presence), and a scramble to create a ruling coalition ensued. Kilman, uniting his PPP with groupings, including the NUP and VGP, scraped together the 29 votes needed to confirm him for a second term on November 21. His administration immediately faced a no-confidence motion, charges of electoral irregularities, and a lawsuit charging Kilman's ineligibility due to outstanding debt (dismissed by the Supreme Court in late January). By mid-March parliamentary opposition had reportedly gathered 33 supporters for a no-confidence motion. Kilman resigned on March 21 to avoid the motion. Moana Carcasses Kalosil of the VGP was elected with 34 votes on March 23 and appointed his cabinet the same day.

POLITICAL PARTIES

Government Parties:

Vanuatu Green Party (VGP). Vincent BOULEKONE and Paul TELUKLUK organized the Vanuatu Greens, sometimes called the Green Confederation, after leaving the UMP (see below) in early 2001. Boulekone had previously helped found the Tan Union, also a splinter from the UMP, before the December 1988 election but subsequently rejoined the parent party. His 2001 departure coincided with that of Willie Jimmy and was generally regarded as reflecting leadership rather than ideological differences with the UMP's Serge Vohor faction. The Greens won three parliamentary seats in May 2002; the seats were retained in 2004 by a **Green Confederation** (GC) that included the VGP and the **Vanuatu Green Alliance** (VGA). The Greens lost one seat in the 2008 balloting, but upon the election of Edward Natapei as prime minister, the VGP left the opposition and joined the government as party leader Moana Carcasses was appointed minister of internal affairs. In 2011 the VGP entered into an alliance with Prime Minister Sato Kilman's PPP and two other parties. In October 2012 balloting, the VGP secured three seats. The party initially joined the coalition led by Kilman following the elections. Following Kilman's March 2013 resignation, Carcasses made a successful bid for prime minister and assembled a cabinet.

Leaders: Moana CARCASSES Kalosil (Prime Minister and Party President), John TERRY (Secretary General).

Party of Our Land (*Vanua'aku Pati*—VP). Long at the forefront of the drive for independence and the return of indigenous lands, the VP was formed in 1972 as the New Hebrides National Party. Its boycott of a Representative Assembly election in 1977 led to cancellation of the results. It won 26 of 46 legislative seats in November 1987, a reduction, proportionally, from 24 of 39 in 1983. In an unexpected contest in December 1987, Secretary General Barak Sope challenged Fr. Walter Lini for the party leadership but was defeated by a near 2–1 vote. Sope was expelled from Parliament on July 25, 1988, after having been dismissed from the cabinet and the party for reportedly instigating a riot in Vila in mid-May. He and four other former VP members responded by announcing the formation of a rival Melanesian Progressive Party (MPP, below), whose members refused to accept court-sanctioned legislative reinstatement on October 21. In early 1989, Sope was convicted of sedition after having been named head of the anti-Lini "interim government" by President Sokomanu in mid-December. The VP won all of the 5 vacant seats filled by special elections in 1989 because of boycotts by the MPP and UMP.

The VP split as a result of the 1991 ouster of its longtime leader, Father Lini, who subsequently formed the NUP. Prior to the November 1994 provincial elections the party joined the MPP and the Tan Union in a coalition called the Unity Front (UF), which won a plurality of 20 seats in the general election of November 1995 but became effectively moribund upon withdrawal of the MPP and Tan Union in August 1996.

The VP returned to government in October 1996, moved into opposition in May 1997, and in March 1998 joined with the NUP in forming an administration under Donald Kalpokas that lasted until November 1999. Shortly thereafter, Kalpokas was replaced as party leader by Edward Natapei, who became prime minister in April 2001 and retained the post after the May 2002 election, in which the party won 14 seats. Natapei was forced to resign after the election of June 2004, in which the VP was reduced to 8 seats, but was named Lini's deputy prime minister in July 2007. He returned as prime minister in September 2008 after the VP secured a plurality of votes. A leadership struggle erupted within the VP in early 2010 led to the suspension from membership of Natapei's rival, Harry IAUKO. In 2010 Natapei lost a vote of no confidence, which resulted in his dismissal as prime minister. In June 2011 he was named the leader of the opposition in a coalition with the UMP. With 8 seats, the VP was the biggest vote-getter in October 2012 balloting, however initial attempts to form a ruling coalition failed and the

VP was relegated to the opposition. Following Kilman's March 2013 resignation, the VP supported a VGP-led government.

Leaders: Edward NATAPEI (Party President), Joe NATUMAN (Vice President), Sela MOLISA (Secretary General).

Melanesian Progressive Party (MPP). The MPP was organized by Barak Sope and four other VP members after the former VP secretary general had been expelled from the party in mid-1988. In April 1989 ousted President George Sokomanu formally joined the new group after he, Sope, and two others had been released from prison by reversal of their sedition convictions.

During 1989 both the Vanuatu Independent Alliance Party (VIAP) and the National Democratic Party (NDP) merged with the MPP. The VIAP was a Santo-based group formed in June 1982 by two dismissed VP ministers, Thomas Reuben SERU and George WOREK; for the 1983 campaign it adopted a platform based on "free enterprise capitalism and anticommunism," losing all three of its existing parliamentary seats. The NDP was formed in late 1986 by John NAUPA, transport minister in the Lini government from 1980 to 1983; it was critical of the administration's handling of the economy and insisted that foreign policy should concentrate on the maintenance of good relations with Britain and France.

Following Prime Minister Sope's ouster in April 2001, it appeared likely that the MPP and the other leading opposition party, the NUP, would establish a coalition or merge. Instead, an MPP faction led by Sato Kilman split off (see PPP, above) in August. The MPP won only three seats in the 2002 election and an equal number in 2004. It declined further to one seat in 2008. In 2011 Witeu SOPE, the younger brother of party President Barak Sope, defected from the party and joined the Vanuatu Labor Party (see below). It won two seats in the October 2012 election. Though initially joining Kilman's coalition, the MPP threw its support behind Carcasses in March 2013. Party leader Esmon SAIMON was appointed to the VGP-led cabinet.

Leader: Esmon SAIMON.

Land and Justice Party (*Graon mo Jastis Pati*—GJP). The GJP, created in November 2010 by former independent MP Ralph Regenvanu, is centered on the ideas of land and justice, and it represents what it calls "four legs": the church, chiefs, women, and youth. In October 2012 balloting, the GJP won 4 seats. Attempts to form a ruling coalition with the VP and the UMP failed in November. However, the GJP joined the ruling government formed under Carcasses in March 2013.

Leaders: Ralph REGENVANU (Party President and Founder), Anthea TOKA (Secretary).

Union of Moderate Parties (*Union des Partis Moderés*—UPM/ *Union blong Moderet Pati*—UMP). The UMP is the successor to the New Hebrides Federal Party, which was organized in early 1979 as an alliance of predominantly pro-French groups, including Jimmy Stevens's *Na-Griamel.* Following the deportation of two Federal Party MPs to New Caledonia in 1982 for involvement in the Santo rebellion, the non-secessionist elements of the party regrouped under the present label, winning 12 seats in the 1983 election and 19 seats in 1987. Party leader Vincent Boulekone was ousted from Parliament in 1986 for missing meetings but was ordered to be reinstated by the Supreme Court, which ruled that ill health excused the absences. Following the 1987 balloting, Boulekone was replaced by Carlot.

On July 27, 1988, 18 UMP members were dismissed from Parliament after having walked out in protest at Barak Sope's expulsion, the party refusing to recontest the seats in by-elections on December 13. Carlot was among those convicted of sedition after having been named deputy prime minister in the abortive Sope government of December 18. The Tan Union, a now-defunct breakaway UMP faction headed by Boulekone, contested the December balloting, becoming the official opposition upon winning six legislative seats.

Following the December 1991 election, in which it won a plurality of 19 seats, the UMP joined with Lini's NUP to form a coalition government under Carlot. Most of the Lini group went into opposition in mid-1993. A new UMP-NUP coalition was concluded after the November 1995 balloting, although the UMP was by then divided into factions led by Carlot and Vohor. Carlot left the UMP in early 1998 to launch the VRP, and the party was further split by the decision of a faction led by Willie Jimmy to support the VP-led Kalpokas government in October. Vohor and Jimmy, rivals for the party leadership, reached a short-lived accommodation at a November 2000 party congress, but in early 2001 Jimmy announced his resignation from the UMP. Meanwhile, Vohor's decision to leave the Barak Sope government led to the no-confidence motion that ended Sope's tenure in April 2001, with Vohor then being appointed deputy prime minister in the Natapei VP-UMP administration. The UMP won a plurality of 15 seats at the May 2002 parliamentary election, seven of which were lost in July 2004. Seven of the remaining seats were retained in September 2008.

Vohor was temporarily elected prime minister in 2011, but the election was later voided by the courts.

In October 2012 elections, the UMP won five seats, and subsequently, unsuccessfully, attempted to form a ruling coalition with the VP and the GJP. The party's representation was reduced to four with the defection of Silas YATAN to the VGP. Three party members were appointed to the Carcasses cabinet in March 2013.

Leader: Serge VOHOR (Party President).

People's Progressive Party (PPP). Formation of the PPP was announced in August 2001 by Sato Kilman, previously a faction leader of the MPP. Kilman indicated that the party's focus would be on development of agriculture, commerce, communications, and tourism. The party won four parliamentary seats in 2004 and participated in the Lini government until forced out in mid-2007 because of alleged involvement in a financial scandal. Its legislative representation was unchanged in 2008. In 2009 the PPP again joined the government when Kilman defected from the opposition and was appointed deputy prime minister in Edward Natapei's VP-led coalition government. In 2011 Kilman replaced Natapei as prime minister. In October 2012 balloting, the PPP secured six seats and Kilman negotiated a ruling coalition of HOW MANY parties, thereby confirming his continued leadership. Strong opposition immediately challenged the tenuous coalition, and in March, facing a no-confidence motion, Kilman resigned as prime minister. Subsequently, one PPP parliamentarian, David TOSUL, was appointed to the Carcasses cabinet.

Leaders: Sato KILMAN (Party President), Dunstan HILTON (Vice President), Willie LOP (Secretary General).

Natatok Indigenous People's Democratic Party (NIPDP). Launched in July 2011, the NIPDP is a modern formation of a 1979 political group led by Efate leaders. The party secured two seats in October 2013 elections. Under the Carcasses government formed in March 2013, one NIPDP member held a cabinet post.

Leader: Jonas JAMES (Minister of Justice).

Parliamentary Parties:

National Unity Party (NUP). The NUP was organized by Fr. Walter Lini following his ouster as VP president on August 7, 1991, and his defeat on a parliamentary no-confidence motion on September 6. Third-ranked with nine seats, after the 1995 election, the NUP reentered the government as the UMP's junior partner. Excluded from the Carlot government of February 1996, the NUP returned as a participant in the second Vohor administration in late October 1996, although Lini did not enter the cabinet until succeeding his estranged sister, Hilda LINI, as justice minister in November.

Prior to his dismissal in October 1998, Walter Lini served as Prime Minister Kalpokas's deputy in a VP-NUP coalition. He died on February 21, 1999. Ten months later the NUP was a leading participant in formation of Barak Sope's five-party government. In the 2002 parliamentary election, the NUP declined from 11 to eight seats, but it rebounded to a plurality of 10 seats in July 2004, with Lini's brother, Ham, forming a coalition government on December 11. It retained the eight seats but lost its plurality to the VP in the September 2008 poll. A participant in the subsequent Natapei administration, it was obliged to go into opposition by the cabinet reshuffle of November 2009. The UNP returned to government, however, with the election of Sato Kilman as prime minister in June 2011. Kilman named Ham Lini as deputy prime minister and appointed two other NUP members to the cabinet. The NUP won three seats in October 2013 balloting. A party split subsequently emerged as Ham Lini signed an agreement to join Kilman's alliance, while party vice president Mokin STEVENS penned an agreement with the VP and the UMP.

Leaders: Ham LINI (Party President), Mokin STEVENS (Vice President), Ambae James BULE (Secretary General).

Na-Griamel Movement. *Na-Griamel* was founded by Jimmy Stevens, whose secessionist rebellion on Espiritu Santo was crushed in 1980. Stevens was released from 11 years' imprisonment in August 1991 and died on February 28, 1994, the leadership of *Na-Griamel* passing to his son, Frankie. Elected to Parliament in 1991, the younger

Stevens served briefly as deputy opposition leader before defecting to the government in early 1994. *Na-Griamel* was permitted to reopen its headquarters for the first time in 14 years the following August. Despite the ambiguous role of its leader, *Na-Griamel* participated in the UF for the 1994 provincial poll before formally rejoining the government in February 1995. It secured one legislative seat in 1995, and none thereafter until 2008, when it again captured one seat. In October 2011 *Na-Griamel* signed a solidarity agreement with the VGP. In October 2012 balloting *Na-Griamel* won three seats.

Leader: Maxim George (Secretary General).

Vanuatu Republican Party—VRP (*Ripablikan Pati blong Vanuatu*). The formation of the VRP was announced in January 1998 by Carlot, who had previously led a UMP faction opposed to Prime Minister Vohor. The VRP won three seats at the May 2002 legislative election, four in 2004. A split within the party emerged in June 2009, when Carlot crossed the aisle to support the government, thereby relinquishing his position as deputy leader of the opposition. However, most VRP legislators eventually endorsed the action by Carlot, who thereafter served as speaker of Parliament until his party returned to opposition in the cabinet reshuffle of November 2009. Carlot returned to the office of speaker in December 2010, when Natapei was defeated as prime minister following a vote of no confidence. In April 2011 the VRP saw a major split within the party, resulting in the defection of four MPs from the VRP to other parties in Parliament. Carlot defected from the party ahead of the October 2012 balloting, launching the **Vanuatu Democratic Party** (VDP—below). The VRP won one seat in October 2012.

Leaders: Maxime CARLOT Korman (President), Jean-Yves CHABOD (Vice President), Jossie MASMAS (Secretary General).

Reunification Movement for Change (*Namangi Aute*—RMC). The RMC secured three seats in the October 2012 balloting.

Leaders: Charlot SALWAI, Paul TELUKLUK.

Iauko Group (IG). Founded by VP defector Harry IAUKO ahead of the October 2012 elections, the new grouping secured three seats in the balloting. The party's presence was reduced to two with Iauko's sudden death in December, but his son, Pascal Sebastien IAUKO, filled the seat in a by-election held in May 2013.

Leader: Pascal Sebastien IAUKO.

Other parties that secured one seat in the 2012 parliamentary elections include the **Peoples Service Party** (PSP); the **Vanuatu National Party** (VNP); the **Vanuatu Liberal Democratic Party** (VLDP); and the **Vanuatu Progressive Development Party** (VPDP).

Other Parties and Groups:

Vanuatu Labour Party (VLP). A trade-union grouping launched in 1986, the VLP captured one parliamentary seat in 2008. In early 2011, after the eventually voided election of Serge Vohor as prime minister, the VLP joined the government when VLP president and MP, Joshua Kalsakau, was named deputy prime minister. The VLP unsuccessfully contested the 2012 elections

Leader: Joshua KALSAKAU (President).

A record 32 parties contested the 2013 elections, including the newly formed **Vanuatu Democratic Party** (VDP), the **Vanuatu Progressive Republican Farmers' Party**, the **Vanuatu Presidential Party**, and **Makitotsan**. Parties that contested the 2008 elections include the **National Community Association** (*Association de la Communauté Nationale*—NCA) and the **People's Action Party** (*Parti de L'Action Populaire*—PAP). (See the 2013 *Handbook* for more.)

LEGISLATURE

The Vanuatu **Parliament** is a unicameral body currently consisting of 52 members elected for four-year terms, subject to dissolution. Balloting was most recently held on October 30, 2012, with results as follows: Party of Our Land, 8 seats; People's Progress Party, 6; Union of Moderate Parties, 5; National Unity Party, 4; Land and Justice Party, 4; Greens Confederation, 3; *Na-Griamel* Movement, 3; Melanesian Progressive Party, 2; Natatok Indigenous People's Democratic Party, 2; People's Service Party, Vanuatu National Party, Vanuatu Liberal Democratic Party, Vanuatu Progressive Development Party, and Vanuatu Republican Party, 1 each; and independents, 4.

Speaker: Philip BOEDORO.

CABINET

[as of October 1, 2013]

Prime Minister	Moana Carcasses Kalosil (GC)
Deputy Prime Minister	Edward Nipake Natapei (VP)
Ministers	
Agriculture, Quarantine, Forestry, and Fisheries	David Tosul (PPP)
Education	Bob Loughman (VP)
Finance and Economic Management	Maki Simelum (VP)
Foreign Affairs, External Trade, and Telecommunications	Edward Nipake Natapei (VP)
Health	Serge Vohor (UMP)
Internal Affairs and Labor	Patrick Crowby (UMP)
Justice	Jonas James (NIPDP)
Lands and Natural Resources	Ralph Regenvanu (GJP)
Planning and Climate Change Adaptation	Thomas Laken (GC)
Public Utilities and Infrastructure	Esmon Saimon (MPP)
Sports and Youth	Tony Wright (UMP)
Trade, Tourism, Commerce, and Ni-Vanuatu Business Development	Toara Daniel Kalo (GC)

INTERGOVERNMENTAL REPRESENTATION

Ambassador to the U.S.: Vanuatu does not maintain an embassy in Washington.

U.S. Ambassador to Vanuatu: Walter NORTH.

Permanent Representative to the UN: Eric Belleay KALOTTI (chargé d'affaires).

IGO Memberships (Non-UN): ADB, CWTH, NAM, PIF.

VATICAN CITY STATE

Stato della Città del Vaticano

Political Status: Independent sovereign state, under papal temporal government; international status governed by the Lateran Treaty with Italy of February 11, 1929; constitution of June 7, 1929, superseded by a New Fundamental Law signed by the pope on November 26, 2000, with effect from February 22, 2001.

Area: 0.17 sq. mi. (0.44 sq. km).

Population: 832 (2012E—UN); 836 (2013E—U.S. Census). There are numerous lay workers, most of them Italian citizens, who live outside the Vatican.

Official Language: Latin (Italian is the working language).

Monetary Unit: Euro (market rate November 1, 2013: 0.74 euro = $1US). On December 29, 2000, the Vatican and Italy signed an agreement permitting Vatican adoption of the euro, authorization having already been granted in principle by the European Union. Since introduction of euro notes and coins in 2002, the Vatican has been permitted to mint its own euro coins, which are issued in small quantities for collectors, as was true of Vatican lire.

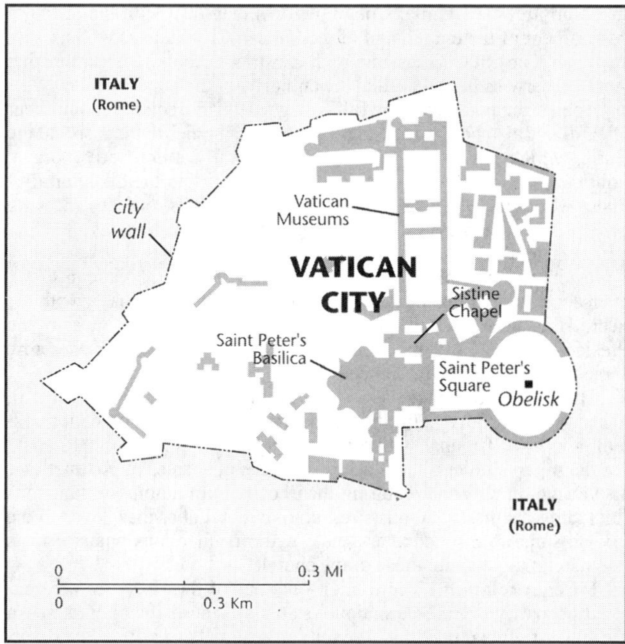

Sovereign (Supreme Pontiff): Pope FRANCIS (Jorge Mario BERGOGLIO); elected to a life term by the College of Cardinals on March 13, 2013, and invested as pope on March 19, succeeding Pope BENEDICT XVI (Josef RATZINGER), who resigned on February 28, 2013.

Secretary of State of the Roman Curia and Papal Representative in the Civil Government of the Vatican City State: Cardinal Pietro PAROLIN; appointed by Pope Frances on August 31, 2013, and took office on October 15, succeeding Cardinal Tarcisio BERTONE, who resigned on June 3, 2013.

Secretary for Relations with States: Archbishop Dominique François Joseph MAMBERTI; appointed by Benedict XVI on September 15, 2006, succeeding Cardinal Jean-Louis Pierre TAURAN.

President of the Pontifical Commission for the Vatican City State and President of the Governatorate of the Vatican City State: Cardinal Giuseppe BERTELLO; appointed by Pope Benedict XVI on October 1, 2011, succeeding Cardinal Giovanni LAJOLO.

THE COUNTRY

An enclave surrounding the Basilica of Saint Peter and including 13 other buildings in and around the city of Rome, the Vatican City State, the smallest independent entity in the world, derives its principal importance from its function as the world headquarters of the Roman Catholic Church and official residence of its head, the pope. The central administration of the church is customarily referred to as the Holy See (*Santa Sede*), or more informally as the Vatican. The Vatican City State is the territorial base from which the leadership of the church exercises its religious and ecclesiastical responsibilities for a worldwide Catholic population of more than 1.2 billion people and over 400,000 Catholic priests. The city state's population, predominantly of Italian and Swiss extraction, is limited mainly to Vatican officials and resident employees and their families. Italian is the language of common use, although Latin is employed in the official acts of the Holy See.

The Vatican's income is based on contributions from Roman Catholic congregations around the world; the sale of postage stamps and souvenirs; and substantial investments in real estate, bonds, and securities. The Administration of the Patrimony of the Apostolic See (*Amministrazione del Patrimonio della Sede Apostolica*) manages its holdings, while the Institute for Religious Works (*Istituto per le Opere di Religione*—IOR) acts as a bank for monies held by affiliated religious orders. The Vatican's financial status long remained confidential and hence the object of intense speculation, until a 1979 announcement revealed that the church's operations would be $20 million in deficit for that year.

Strong investment performance buoyed Vatican finances in the 1990s (for more on the Vatican's finances, please see the 2013 *Handbook*), but the weakening dollar contributed to the return of deficits in most of the early 2000s, exceeding $14 million in 2007. (Although the euro is its official currency, the Holy See has substantial investments in U.S. dollars and receives generous contributions from the church in the United States.) The global financial crisis, a corresponding decline in donations, and a major overhaul of the Vatican's telecommunications infrastructure were blamed for deficits of $1.28 million in 2008 and $5.1 million in 2009. Vatican finances bounced back in 2010, registering a surplus of $14.5 million, but they were back in the red by $19 million in 2011, one of the worst budget deficits in years. In 2012 the Vatican had a small surplus of $2.8 million; however, worldwide donations declined. For instance, donations to the Peter's Pence Collection, fell from $69.7 million to $65.9 million, a 12 percent drop.

GOVERNMENT AND POLITICS

Political background. Italy's recognition of the Vatican City State in the Lateran Treaty of 1929 terminated a bitter political controversy that had persisted since the unification of Italy in 1860–1870. Before that time the popes had exercised political sovereignty over the city of Rome and substantial portions of the Italian peninsula, where they ruled as territorial sovereigns in addition to performing spiritual and administrative functions as heads of the Catholic Church. The absorption of virtually all territorial holdings by the new Italian state and the failure of Pope PIUS IX to accept the legitimacy of the compensation offered by the Italian Parliament left the Holy See in an anomalous position that was finally regularized after a lapse of two generations. In addition to the Lateran Treaty, by which Italy recognized the independence and sovereignty of the Vatican City State, a concordat was concluded that regulated the position of the church within Italy, while a financial convention compensated the Holy See for its earlier losses. The status of the Vatican City State as established by the Lateran Treaty has since been recognized, formally or tacitly, by a great majority of the world's governments.

Pope Paul VI (Giovanni Battista MONTINI), who had been elected on June 21, 1963, died on August 6, 1978, and was succeeded on August 26 by Pope JOHN PAUL I (Albino LUCIANI), who in turn succumbed on September 28 after the shortest pontificate since that of Pope LEO XII in 1605. His successor, Cardinal Karol WOJTYŁA, archbishop of Kraków, Poland, who assumed the title Pope JOHN PAUL II, became pope on October 16, 1978, the first non-Italian to be elected since Pope ADRIAN VI in 1522.

The papal term of John Paul II was one of the longest and most significant in modern history. Among other things, he was the most widely traveled pope of any era, and he commanded worldwide veneration, even as he moved the church away from the liberal direction of the Second Vatican Council, opened in 1962 during the papacy of Pope JOHN XXIII. Following John Paul II's death on April 2, 2005, he was succeeded on April 19 by Cardinal Josef RATZINGER, who became Pope BENEDICT XVI. Ratzinger, a close confidant of John Paul II, had served since 1981 as head of the Congregation for the Doctrine of the Faith (once known as the Holy Office of the Inquisition), the Vatican office responsible for maintaining orthodox doctrine throughout the Roman Catholic communion.

Since 2001 the Vatican has struggled to deal with the repercussions of a major scandal in the United States and elsewhere involving child sexual abuse by clergy and the institutional church's perceived longstanding indifference to the problem. On November 21, 2001, John Paul II voiced an apology to the victims, and in January 2002 the Vatican issued new procedures for handling alleged abuse, including trying accused clergy in secret ecclesiastical courts but without precluding civil and criminal action by secular authorities. In subsequent statements John Paul II called pedophilia "grievously evil" and, during a summit of all U.S. cardinals in Rome in April, both a crime and an "appalling sin." Such statements did not, however, quell the outcry from much of the laity. Moreover, individual dioceses, which are generally responsible for their own financial affairs, faced millions of dollars in settlements to victims, and several were forced to file for bankruptcy protection. The Vatican's immunity from U.S. prosecution, under the Foreign Sovereign Immunity Act, was challenged in June 2006, when a U.S. district judge ruled that a lawsuit brought against the Vatican for allowing a priest who was a known child molester to be transferred from city to city could proceed.

Pope Benedict XVI was initially perceived as showing ambivalence in this matter. One of his earliest acts as pope was to meet with Cardinal Bernard Francis Law, former archbishop of Boston, who had been forced to resign because of his lack of action against pedophile priests. However, in May 2006 Benedict asked the Rev. Marcial Maciel Degollado, founder of the conservative Legionaries of Christ and the target of multiple molestation charges, to leave the ministry for a life of "prayer and penitence." In 2012 the Vatican launched an investigation into seven Legion priests over allegations of sexual abuse of minors dating back decades. It also defrocked a Roman Catholic monk who had sexually abused boys at an abbey and school in London. In 2008 Benedict met with victims of abuse during his American visit in April and on World Youth Day in July in Sydney, Australia. His demeanor during the U.S. trip helped soften an image that had been considered rigid. He met with President George W. Bush and addressed the UN, stressing the need for religious freedom.

In his January 2006 first encyclical, viewed as an inclusive and conciliatory message, Pope Benedict XVI affirmed the importance of charity and love, including sexual intimacy, as fundamental expressions of Christian faith. During his first year in office, however, Benedict XVI mostly lived up to his reputation for conservatism in doctrinal matters, continuing his predecessor's affirmation of traditional teachings on such matters as papal primacy and infallibility, the exclusion of women from the priesthood (while at the same time acknowledging that the church has long marginalized and discriminated against women), and opposition to birth control and gay marriage.

From the first month of his pontificate, Pope Benedict XVI spoke out forcefully against a proposed measure to legalize gay marriage in Spain, urging Catholics to work and vote against it. In 2012 Benedict was critical of the failure of the European Union (EU) to mention Europe's Christian roots in the proposed EU constitution.

On February 28, 2013, Benedict became the first pope since 1415 to resign (see Current issues, below). Cardinal Jorge Mario BERGOGLIO, the archbishop of Buenos Aires, was elected on March 13 to succeed Benedict. The new pope was the first from the Western Hemisphere and the first Jesuit. He became Frances I on March 19.

In an effort to democratize the Church, Pope Frances on April 13, 2013, established an eight-member advisory council that included cardinals with substantial reformist credentials. On August 30, Archbishop P. Fernando Vérgez ALZAGA was appointed secretary general of the Vatican.

Constitution and government. On November 26, 2000, Pope John Paul II signed a new constitution intended to "harmonize in a legal manner" various governmental changes that had been introduced since promulgation of the preceding basic law on June 7, 1929. As in the past, the Vatican City State retains the form of an absolute monarchy. Supreme legislative, executive, and judicial power is vested in the pope in his capacity as bishop of Rome; the pope, who is elected for life, serves concurrently as supreme pontiff of the Universal Church, primate of Italy, archbishop and metropolitan of the Province of Rome, and sovereign of the Vatican City State. Assisting the pope in the exercise of his varied responsibilities are the members of two major organs, the College of Cardinals and the Roman Curia (*Curia Romana*).

Members of the College of Cardinals, who numbered 212 as of March 1, 2012, are named by the pope and serve as his chief advisers and coadjutors during his lifetime; upon the pope's death, those under the age of 80, of which there were 125 as of July 1, 2012, meet to elect his successor, which is their right as titular clergymen in the city of Rome. The meeting of the college to elect a pope is still referred to as a conclave from the Latin *cum clave* (with a key), which refers to the locked room where the cardinals meet. Reforms instituted by John Paul II in February 22, 1996, in an "Apostolic Constitution" entitled *Universi Dominici Gregis,* ended the practice of detaining the electors in a locked room until a result emerged, although strict secrecy of the voting process has been maintained. Also, prior to 1996 a candidate for pope (usually a cardinal but not necessarily even a bishop) required a majority of two-thirds (or two-thirds plus one, depending on the number of electors). However, the 1996 reforms authorized election by a simple majority in the event of a protracted deadlock. The 1996 revisions also eliminated the options of election by universal acclamation or by delegation to an electoral subcommittee. On June 11, 2007, Benedict XVI modified the election procedures established in *Universi Dominici Gregis,* phasing out the possibility of election by simple majority even in the case of a protracted deadlock. Future elections under any circumstances will require a two-thirds majority. While the papacy is vacant, the full college (meeting in General Congregation) or subcommittees (Particular Congregations) may deal with the ordinary government of the church and of the Vatican City State as well as with any emergency matters arising, with the strict exception of matters that would otherwise be reserved to the authority of the pope.

Apart from conclaves, the full college meets infrequently. A number of cardinals also hold positions on the various bodies that constitute the Curia, which serves as the church's central administrative organ. Political responsibilities have devolved primarily to the Secretariat of State, which in 1988 was divided into two sections, one dealing with general affairs and the other addressing relations with states. A secretary of state heads the Secretariat. A Pontifical Commission, headed by a president (essentially functioning as the "mayor" of Vatican City), oversees civil administration of the Vatican and works closely with the Secretariat. The current president of that commission is also the President of the Governatorate of Vatican City State and is therefore sometimes informally referenced as the Vatican's "governor."

The Vatican City State has its own security force (the Swiss Guard), postal service, coinage, utilities, department store, communication system, and local tribunal with a right of appeal to higher ecclesiastical courts. A papal edict issued in July 1995 set out "rules of conduct" for all Vatican employees, requiring them, on pain of automatic sanctions (including dismissal), to observe Catholic moral doctrines "even in the private sphere" and not to associate with organizations whose "goals are incompatible" with those of the church.

Foreign relations. The foreign relations of the Holy See are centered primarily on its international status as seat of the church, set in the context of its position as a sovereign entity. Its activities as a sovereign state continue to be governed by the Lateran Treaty and related agreements with the Italian government, which enable it to enter into international agreements and bilateral diplomatic relations in its own right. Worldwide, such diplomatic linkages now total well over 100 (supplemented by unofficial representation in other countries), while the Holy See has permanent observer status at the United Nations, with, as of July 2004, all rights of full membership except that of voting. It is also a full member of certain specialist agencies at the UN, and it participates in the Organization for Security and Cooperation in Europe (OSCE).

The Vatican's close relations with Italy were threatened in the 1980s by the revelation of links between the IOR, otherwise known as the Vatican bank, and Italy's Banco Ambrosiano, which collapsed in August 1982. The Vatican and the Italian government subsequently appointed a joint commission to investigate the matter, and in May 1984 the IOR agreed "in recognition of moral involvement," but without admission of culpability, to pay 109 creditor banks up to $250 million of a $406 million settlement against Banco Ambrosiano's successor institution.

Earlier, in February 1984, negotiations were concluded on a new Italian-Vatican concordat. Provisions included the abandonment of Roman Catholicism as Italy's state religion and of mandated religious instruction in public schools, although secular authorities would continue to accord automatic recognition to church marriages and full freedom to Catholic schools.

John Paul II exemplified a concerted effort to use the papal position to improve relations, not only with non-Catholic Christian entities but also with some non-Christians. The historic breach with Protestant Christendom, dating to the 16th century, was partly overcome in 1982, when the Vatican established full diplomatic relations with the United Kingdom and with the Lutheran countries of Denmark, Norway, and Sweden.

In contrast, major differences with the Orthodox Christian hierarchy continued to affect the Vatican's relations with a number of countries. In 1992 the Orthodox Church severely criticized Rome for seeking converts in "Orthodox" territory, as signified by Pope John Paul II's 1991 creation of new dioceses in the former Soviet Union. The ecumenical patriarch, Bartholomew I (representing 15 churches, with 170 million adherents), made a first official visit to the Vatican in June 1995, while a trip by John Paul II to Romania in May 1999 marked the first visit in 1,000 years by a Roman Catholic pope to a country having an Orthodox majority. It was followed in May 2001 by a first visit to Greece, where the pope met with Archbishop Christodoulos of the Greek Orthodox Church. At that time John Paul II apologized for the sacking of Constantinople in 1204. The pope subsequently undertook groundbreaking visits to Ukraine (June 2001), Kazakhstan and Armenia (September 2001), and Azerbaijan and Bulgaria (May 2002). Benedict XVI continued John Paul II's outreach to the Orthodox Church by visiting with Bartholomew I during Benedict's trip to Turkey (November 2007). In December 2009 Russian president Dmitry

Medvediv visited the Vatican and agreed to establish full diplomatic relations and exchange ambassadors.

In January 1984 formal relations at the ambassadorial level were reestablished with the United States after a lapse of 117 years, and a wide range of other linkages followed during the ensuing decade. In the first meeting between a pope and a Soviet head of state, Mikhail Gorbachev was accorded a private audience at the Vatican in December 1989; the meeting served as a prelude to the establishment of official contacts in March 1990. Earlier, in July 1989, relations had been reestablished with Poland after a rupture of more than four decades. Further reflecting the tide of change in Eastern Europe, relations were reestablished with Hungary in February 1990, with Czechoslovakia in April, and with Romania in May. The Vatican established relations with most of the other former Soviet republics during 1992. Speedy recognition was extended to the predominantly Catholic former Yugoslav republics of Croatia and Slovenia in January 1992 and to Muslim-dominated Bosnia and Herzegovina in August.

In addition, relations with Mexico (broken in 1861) were normalized in September 1992, following the deletion of anticlerical clauses from the country's 1917 constitution. As a result of the changes, the church was authorized to own property and operate schools, while priests and nuns were enfranchised and permitted to wear clerical garb in public. John Paul II had a special fondness for the country and visited it four times during his pontificate (1979, 1990, 1993, and 1999). On August 21, 2009, Bolivia and the Vatican signed the Treaty of Inter-Institutional Cooperation, which was meant to improve relations between the two states and reflect the important role the church plays in providing social services in Bolivia.

In March 2009 Pope Benedict visited Cameroon and Angola, discussing peace, reconciliation, democracy, and human rights. Particularly noteworthy was his meeting in Llunda on women, where he lamented the adverse conditions to which women have been subjected and affirmed their right to "equal dignity." Far more controversial was his comment that AIDS "cannot be overcome by the distribution of prophylactics." This assertion provoked the Belgian parliament to "condemn the unacceptable statements of the pope." The Vatican deplored the condemnation and maintained that it was an attempt to intimidate the pope from teaching the church's doctrine. The pope appeared to reverse this stance in November 2010, when he declared that the use of condoms is permissible as a means to prevent the spread of AIDS. He did not, however, change the church's prohibition of birth control, enshrined in *Humanae Vitae*, the encyclical of PAUL VI, which condemned artificial means of birth control.

In September 1993 a senior member of the Vatican's Congregation for the Oriental Churches became the highest-ranking Catholic official to visit China since the Communist takeover in 1949. Ostensibly responding to an invitation to attend China's National Athletic Games, the emissary reportedly met with government officials amid indications of a possible end to the lengthy estrangement. Further discussions took place between 1996 and 1998, but the Vatican's continuing recognition of the Taiwanese government prevented normalization with Beijing. The Vatican has long been troubled by the existence of the Chinese Catholic Patriotic Association (CCPA), a Catholic organization that observers view as a creation of the Beijing government. Although the CCPA claims that it wants to maintain a "religious connection" with the Vatican, it rejects the pope's power to govern the Chinese Church, saying that the Vatican's assertion of authority in China amounts to political interference. In a letter to the Chinese people dated May 27, 2007, Benedict XVI objected to the ordination of bishops without the approval of the Vatican while maintaining that the Vatican had no desire to meddle in Chinese politics. Tensions with Beijing increased again in 2012 when the Vatican excommunicated a Chinese bishop ordained without papal approval.

In February 2000 John Paul II became the first pope to visit Egypt, and a month later he made the first pilgrimage to the Holy Land by a pope since 1964, visiting Jordan and Israel, including Palestinian-controlled Bethlehem, where he recognized the Palestinians' "natural right to a homeland." In May 2009 Pope Benedict undertook an 11-day trip to Jordan, the Palestinian territories, and Israel. The pope hoped to build better relations with Muslims and Jews, to defend the rights of Christians living in the Holy Land, and to encourage peace between Israel and its neighbors. He reiterated the Vatican's position that both Israelis and Palestinians have a right to their own states, and he also stressed that members of all three religions are children of Abraham and should show mutual respect for each other. At the request of Israeli Prime Minister Benjamin Netanyahu, Benedict affirmed Israel's right to exist in view of Iran's hostility.

In January 1998 John Paul II made a highly publicized trip to Cuba, the only Latin American country that he had not previously visited. In addition to calling upon the government to introduce pluralism, he criticized the long-standing U.S. economic sanctions against Fidel Castro's regime as "unjust and ethically unacceptable." During his 2012 visit to the country, Pope Benedict XVI urged the Cuban government to introduce economic and political reforms, called for an end to Cuba's isolation in the world, and criticized the U.S. trade embargo against Cuba.

On March 12, 2000, Pope John Paul II delivered a far-reaching but nonspecific apology for sins committed by Catholics, the church's "children," over the two preceding millennia. Without mentioning the Crusades, the Inquisition, or the Holocaust, church leaders cited such offenses as intolerance and discrimination against women, minorities, indigenous peoples, Jews, and the poor. The apology, an "act of repentance," according to the Vatican, came two years after release of a long-awaited report from the Vatican on the role of the church during the Nazi era.

In relations with the non-Catholic world, Pope Benedict XVI has had a mixed record. He has been largely unsuccessful in improving Jewish-Catholic relations, despite the dramatic change in the church's attitude toward Jews, who have gone from being called "perfidious" in the old Good Friday service to being referred to as "our elder brothers" by John Paul II. As Cardinal Ratzinger, Benedict XVI had played an important role in articulating a new theological position for the church toward Jews and other non-Catholics. However, he was criticized by Jewish leaders when he failed to explicitly condemn anti-Semitism during a May 2006 visit to the Nazi death camp Auschwitz-Birkenau in Poland. (See the article in the 2011 *Handbook* for background on the relationship between the Vatican and Israel.)

Although the Vatican normalized diplomatic ties with the predominantly Muslim nation of Malaysia in July 2011, papal relations with Islam were volatile during Benedict XVI's tenure. The most controversial event of his pontificate thus far was his speech at the University of Regensburg, given on September 13, 2006, in which he quoted a 14th-century Byzantine emperor, who claimed that Islam was "evil and inhuman." Continued fallout from the speech threatened to sour Benedict XVI's visit to Turkey in November 2006, but he was warmly greeted by the Turkish prime minister at the airport and received favorable coverage on Turkish television.

Pope Benedict's visit to Beirut in September 2012 was marred by unrelated demonstrations against an anti-Islamic film. The protests left one dead and scores injured.

In March 2013, during a meeting with Francis, Argentine President Cristina Fernándz de Kirchner asked the pontiff to help initiate bilateral discussions with the United Kingdom over the status of the Falkland Islands.

In an effort to curb money laundering, the Vatican Bank closed accounts for foreign diplomats in October 2013 after reports emerged that Iranian, Iraqi, and Indonesian officials were using the bank to move large sums of cash.

Current issues. In 2009 there was another temporary setback in Catholic-Jewish relations. Benedict lifted a ban on four bishops of the Society of St. Pius X, a schismatic group that does not recognize the Second Vatican Council. Unbeknownst to the pope, one of the bishops, Richard Williamson, had denied the mass murder of the Jews during World War II. The scandal strained the relationship between the Chief Rabbinate of Israel and the Vatican. Subsequently the pope denounced Holocaust deniers and wrote a letter of apology.

On July 7, 2009, Benedict issued a third encyclical, *Caritas in Veritate* (Charity in Truth), the first encyclical on social teaching in 20 years, issued in part as a response to the economic crisis that had gripped the world for the last year. Perhaps the most controversial suggestion was its call for reforming the United Nations into a stronger institution that could protect the vulnerable nations of the developing world as well as regulate the world economic system, while recognizing national sovereignty. In 2011 the Vatican once again addressed the economic crisis, calling for an overhaul of the world's financial systems and proposing the establishment of a supranational authority to oversee the global economy in order to bring more democratic and ethical principles to an out-of-control market.

In June 2010 Vatican officials criticized the government for raiding the headquarters of the Roman Catholic Church in Belgium while investigating the church after the bishop of Bruges resigned in April for allegedly sexually abusing a child 25 years before. The case was only one of a number that caused the church a great deal of embarrassment in Europe. There were two shocking government reports on sexual abuse in Ireland, and numerous allegations in Germany, Switzerland, Austria, and the Netherlands. The scandals caused five bishops to resign. The Vatican also suffered a setback in the United States, when the Supreme Court refused to hear a Vatican appeal claiming that as a sovereign nation, it is immune from prosecution. The case involved a boy in Oregon who was allegedly abused in the 1960s.

In addition to issuing apologies for the abuses, in July 2010 the Vatican released a revision of the 2001 norms dealing with clerical sexual abuse, which streamlined the procedures dealing with accusations of abusive priests and extended the statute of limitations to 20 years after the victim's 18th birthday. In November the Vatican announced that it was preparing new guidelines for bishops dealing with such cases.

In September 2010 Benedict visited the United Kingdom. It was his fourth international trip in the past year, having previously visited Cyprus, Malta, and the Czech Republic. During the trip he again apologized four times for the Church's failure to have dealt more forcefully in the past with the problems of sexual abuse, but in a major speech to the British people he addressed the role of religion in modern secular societies, which he argued can provide a moral compass for making decisions that affect the common good. The reception he received was positive. The press too was mostly positive.

On May 1, 2011, before the biggest crowd since his investiture, Pope Benedict presided over a mass celebrating the life of John Paul II and beatified him, making him an object of public veneration.

Far less positive was an assessment of the Vatican's role in dealing with the sexual abuse scandal in Ireland, historically one of the world's most predominantly Catholic societies. A scathing criticism of the Vatican's behavior in allegedly covering up child abuse by priests, issued in July 2011 by Prime Minister Enda Kenny, won widespread popular acclaim, but it prompted the Vatican to recall its ambassador. In September 2011 two U.S. advocacy groups asked the International Criminal Court in The Hague to investigate Pope Benedict XVI and three cardinals for alleged crimes against humanity by sheltering Roman Catholic clergy who were guilty of sexually abusing children.

In December 2010, after the IOR came under investigation for money laundering, the Vatican issued norms to comply with European Union banking transparency standards. The new law was required under a 2009 monetary agreement with the EU, which allowed the Vatican to adopt the euro as its currency. In April 2012 the president of the IOR, Ettore Gotti Tedeschi, was dismissed by the bank's board because of poor job performance, erratic behavior, and chronic absence from board meetings. In June the director of the famously secretive bank met with a few dozen journalists to highlight the bank's serious efforts at fighting money laundering and to stress its internal and external financial controls.

The dismissal of Tedeschi happened amid a growing scandal—dubbed "Vatileaks" by the Italian press—over leaked Vatican documents, which involved periodic releases of correspondence that laid bare discord within the Holy See, including internal allegations of cronyism and corruption. The IOR board suggested that Tedeschi might have himself leaked some of the documents. A few days after Tedeschi's ouster, Pope Benedict's butler, Paolo GABRIELE was arrested for allegedly leaking the pope's confidential correspondence.

One of the most prominent clashes involved Archbishop Carlo Maria Viganò, the second-ranking official in the part of the Curia that administers Vatican City. In letters to the pope and Vatican Secretary of State Cardinal Tarcisio Bertone, Viganò claimed he had made enemies within the Curia and beyond after ferreting out corruption and financial misconduct. He requested permission to continue cleaning up the Holy See's financial affairs but was instead removed from his post and, in August 2011, named the papal nuncio, or ambassador, to the United States. A Vatican spokesman insisted the appointment of Viganò was, contrary to press reports, "proof of unquestionable respect and trust."

In April 2012 the Vatican appointed Joseph TOBIN, an American bishop, to rein in the largest and most influential group of Catholic nuns in the United States, saying that the group had "serious doctrinal problems." The Leadership Conference of Women Religious, in the Vatican's assessment, had challenged church teaching on homosexuality and the male-only priesthood and promoted "radical feminist themes incompatible with the Catholic faith." The sisters were also scolded for making public statements that contradicted the bishops. Six weeks later, the 21 national board members of the group announced their rejection of the Vatican's judgment and their intention to send their president and executive director to Rome to open a dialogue with Vatican officials. On October 6 former papal butler Gabriele was convicted by a Vatican court of theft and leaking confidential documents and sentenced to 18 months in prison.

Citing age and poor health, Pope Benedict stunned Catholics with his decision to resign in February 2013. Benedict continued to live in the Vatican and was granted the title "pope emeritus." His successor, Jorge Mario Bergoglio, chose the papal name Frances, in honor of St. Frances of Assisi. The new pontiff's humility and personal warmth contrasted significantly with the reserved and "aloof" Benedict. Once in office, Frances undertook a number of steps to reduce tensions within and outside of the Church, including directing Church leaders to "act decisively" against abusive priests. On October 1 the Vatican announced that Pope John XXIII and Pope John Paul II would be canonized in a ceremony on April 27, 2014.

THE ROMAN CURIA

[as of September 15, 2013]

Secretariat of State

Secretary of State	Cardinal Pietro Parolin
Substitute for General Affairs	Archbishop Giovanni Angelo Becciu
Secretary for Relations with States	Archbishop Dominique Mamberti
Official of the Secretariat of State	Archbishop Marco Dino Brogi

Governatorate of Vatican City State

President	Archbishop Giuseppe Bertello
Secretary General	Archbishop P. Fernando Végez Alzaga
Deputy Secretary General	(Vacant)

Note: In addition to the bodies noted below, which have political and administrative functions relating to the Vatican as a state, there are numerous other bodies within the Curia with mainly ecclesiastical, theological, ecumenical, disciplinary, cultural, or pastoral functions, including congregations, tribunals, councils, commissions, and committees. The major bodies are referred to as dicasteries of the Roman Curia.

INTERGOVERNMENTAL REPRESENTATION

Apostolic Nuncio to the U.S.: Archbishop Carlo Maria VIGANÒ.

U.S. Ambassador to the Holy See: Ken HACKETT.

Permanent Observer to the UN: Archbishop Francis Assisi CHULLIKATT.

IGO Memberships (Non-UN): OSCE.

VENEZUELA

Bolivarian Republic of Venezuela
República Bolivariana de Venezuela

Political Status: Independence originally proclaimed in 1821 as part of Gran Colombia; independent republic established in 1830; federal constitutional system restored in 1958. Current constitution approved by referendum on December 15, 1999.

Area: 358,850 sq. mi. (916,445 sq. km).

Population: 27,229,930 (2011C); 29,718,357 (2013E—UN); 28,459,085 (2013E—U.S. Census).

Major Urban Centers (2011E): CARACAS (1,942,652), Maracaibo (1,898,700), Valencia (1,380,000), Barquisimeto (936,000).

Official Language: Spanish.

Monetary Unit: Bolívar (market rate November 1, 2013: 6.29 bolívares fuertes = $1US). [Note: devalued February 2013.]

President: Nicolás MADURO (United Socialist Party of Venezuela) inaugurated on April 19, 2013, for a five-year term, following the death of Lt. Col. (Ret.) Hugo Rafael CHÁVEZ Frías (United Socialist Party of Venezuela) on March 5, 2013.

Executive Vice President: Jorge ARREAZA (United Socialist Party of Venezuela), appointed by Maduro on April 19, 2013. Maduro was appointed by Chavez on October 10, 2012, to succeed Elías JAUA Montano (United Socialist Party of Venezuela).

THE COUNTRY

Situated on the northern coast of South America between Colombia, Brazil, and Guyana, the Republic of Venezuela is made up of alternating mountainous and lowland territory drained, for the most part, by the Orinoco River and its tributaries. Two-thirds or more of the rapidly growing population, most of it concentrated in coastal and northern areas, is of mixed descent, the remainder being Caucasian, Negro, and Amerindian. Roman Catholicism is the dominant faith, but other religions are tolerated. Women constitute about one-third of the paid labor force, concentrated in the clerical and service sectors.

One of the world's leading oil producers, Venezuela has one of the highest per capita incomes in Latin America. Oil exports generate 96 percent of all export revenue. Oil revenues have spurred a dramatic increase in government spending, which in turn has resulted in a somewhat more equitable distribution of wealth. The poverty rate fell from 49 percent in 2002 to 29 percent by 2011.

The industrial sector, which includes iron and natural gas, employs about one-fourth of the labor force and contributes 37 percent of GDP. By contrast, agriculture now accounts for only 4 percent of GDP; rice, corn, and beans are the principal subsistence crops, while coffee and cocoa are exported, along with some sugar, bananas, and cotton. Under government sponsorship Venezuela has been attempting to regain its historic position as a major stock-raising country, while diversification has become the keynote of economic planning, in part to reduce a dependence on oil sales.

In January 2010 the government devalued the Venezuelan bolívar, setting one exchange rate for imported goods and a lower one for essential goods, such as staple foods, which are heavily subsidized. The devaluation, intended to make Venezuelan exports more competitive abroad, threatened to stimulate further inflation and rampant black market currency trading. Growth contracted significantly, reportedly making Venezuela the region's worst performer in 2010. Annual GDP of about 4 percent in 2011 rebounded to 5.5 percent in 2012, owing in large part to increased government spending. Unemployment averaged 8 percent in between 2009 and 2012.

GOVERNMENT AND POLITICS

Political background. Homeland of Simón BOLIVAR, "the Liberator," Venezuela achieved independence from Spain in 1821 and became a separate republic in 1830. A history of political instability and lengthy periods of authoritarian rule culminated in the dictatorships of Gen. Juan Vicente GÓMEZ from 1908 to 1935 and Gen. Marcos PÉREZ Jiménez from 1952 to 1958, the interim being punctuated by unsuccessful attempts to establish democratic government. The ouster of Pérez Jiménez by a military-backed popular movement in January 1958 prepared the way for subsequent elected regimes.

The return to democratic rule was marked by the December 1958 election of Rómulo BETANCOURT, leader of the Democratic Action (AD) party and of the non-Communist Left in Latin America. Venezuela made considerable economic and political progress under the successive AD administrations of Betancourt (1959–1964) and Raúl LEONI (1964–1969), with Cuban-supported subversive efforts being successfully resisted. The election and inauguration of Dr. Rafael CALDERA Rodríguez of the Social Christian Party (COPEI) in 1969 further institutionalized the peaceful transfer of power. As the first Christian Democratic president in Venezuela and the second in Latin America (following Eduardo Frei Montalva of Chile), Caldera adhered to an independent pro-Western policy while seeking to "normalize" Venezuelan political life through such measures as legal recognition of the Communist Party, appeals to leftist guerrilla forces to lay down their arms, and the broadening of diplomatic contacts with both Communist and non-Communist regimes.

Venezuela's politics were dominated by its two leading parties during the administrations of the AD's Carlos Andrés PÉREZ (1974–1979), Luis HERRERA Campíns of COPEI (1979–1984), and Jaime LUSINCHI of AD (1984–1989). (See the entry in the 2010 *Handbook* for details.)

Although economic conditions steadily worsened under Lusinchi, the AD retained the presidency in the election of December 4, 1988, as Carlos Pérez became the first Venezuelan president to be elected for a second term; the AD, on the other hand, lost its congressional majorities, winning only 23 of 49 elective seats in the Senate and 97 of 201 seats in the Chamber of Deputies. (For more on Pérez's "economic shock program" and the riots it precipitated, see the 2012 *Handbook*.)

On February 4, 1992, the president escaped assassination during an abortive coup by junior officers, including a prominent paratrooper named Hugo CHÁVEZ, which included an attack on his official residence. On June 11 COPEI's two representatives resigned from the "National Unity" government they had joined only three months before, and on June 29, in accepting the resignations of 11 cabinet members, Pérez implemented a previously announced plan to slash cabinet-rank personnel by two-thirds. Despite a second major coup attempt on November 27, state and local elections were held on December 6, in which the AD lost further ground.

In March 1993 the attorney general applied to the Supreme Court for a ruling as to whether President Pérez should be charged with the embezzlement of $17 million in state funds that the chief executive said had been expended for secret security and defense purposes, but that opponents insisted had been diverted to campaign and other nonofficial uses. After the court responded in the affirmative, the Senate on May 21 suspended the president, who was constitutionally succeeded, on an interim basis, by the Senate president, Octavio LEPAGE, on May 22. On June 5 the Congress named a highly respected, pro-AD independent, Sen. Ramón José VELASQUEZ, to complete the final eight months of the Pérez presidency.

On December 5, 1993, former president Caldera, who had been expelled from COPEI in June for refusing to support its presidential candidate, Oswaldo ALVAREZ Paz, was elected to a second term as the nominee of a recently organized, 17-party National Convergence (CN) coalition. Although credited with only 30.5 percent of the vote, he was but one contender in a record field of 18.

On June 24, 1994, in the face of continued economic and political problems that had sparked rumors of a possible coup, President Caldera adopted wide-ranging powers that included a suspension of six constitutional guarantees, five of which were restored by Congress on July 21. Among the financial difficulties was a liquidity crisis that resulted in 13 banks being brought under state control by mid-August.

Although no respite from the recession was evident, President Caldera suspended his remaining emergency powers on July 6, 1995, promulgating instead a financial emergency law that authorized him to intervene in the economy without having to abrogate constitutional rights.

Considerable social unrest preceded the accord finally concluded with the IMF in April 1996, which called for accelerated privatization and flotation of the bolívar. Thereafter, on May 30, the Supreme Court handed down a guilty verdict against former president Pérez, who was, however, released from 28 months of detention on September 19 and then returned to the political arena by campaigning successfully for his old Senate seat in November 1998.

On December 8, 1998, the February 1992 coup leader, Hugo Chávez Frías, gained an impressive victory in presidential balloting over Henrique SALAS Römer, the nominee of both traditional rival parties, with former beauty queen Irene SÁEZ a distant third. Following his election, Chávez pledged to pursue constitutional revision to lay "the foundations of a new republic," and at a Constituent Assembly poll on July 25, 1999, candidates from his Patriotic Pole coalition won 121 of 128 contested seats.

The assembly created a "judicial emergency commission" to restructure the nation's court system on August 19, 1999, and on August 30 stripped the opposition-controlled Congress of its remaining powers. The Assembly then drafted a new basic law (see below), which was approved by 71.2 percent of the participants in a December 15 referendum.

At its concluding session on January 30, 2000, the Constituent Assembly named its president, Chávez's political mentor Luis MIQUILENA, to head a transitional National Legislative Commission, pending the election of a National Assembly on May 28. However, the balloting was subsequently postponed for technical reasons until July 30, when President Chávez was elected to a new six-year term and his Fifth Republic Movement (*Movimiento Quinta República*—MVR) and its allies won a majority of the 165 seats in the new National Assembly.

In November 2000 Chávez secured legislative approval of an enabling law granting him decree powers for a year. Further enhancing his power was voter approval of rigid labor controls in a December 3 referendum. Having already alienated organized labor, Chávez exacerbated a growing rift with the military leadership in February 2001 by naming a longtime associate, José Vicente RANGEL, as Venezuela's first civilian minister of defense. In June, in an effort to consolidate his support among leftists and the poor, he authorized formation at the neighborhood level of Bolivarian Circles (*Círculos Bolivarianos*) committed to advancement of the "Bolivarian revolution."

On November 13, 2001, using his decree powers, President Chávez promulgated 49 laws involving economic, financial, infrastructural, and social policies. The most controversial measures permitted expropriation of underutilized farmland, in the name of an "agrarian revolution," and required that joint hydrocarbon ventures include majority government participation. Oil royalties were also increased. In response, the Venezuelan Federation of Chambers of Commerce and Industry (*Federación Venezolana de Cámaras y Asociaciones de Comercio y Producción—Fedecámaras*), supported by the country's largest labor union group, the Venezuelan Workers' Confederation (*Confederación de Trabajadores de Venezuela*—CTV), announced that it would mount a nationwide one-day strike in December.

In March 2002 managerial staff of the state petroleum company, *Petróleos de Venezuela* (PDVSA), with support from the industry's union, the *Federación de Trabajadores Petroleros* (*Fedepetrol*), began a job action, which was followed on April 9 by a general strike organized by the CTV and *Fedecámaras.* Two days later, with 150,000 anti-Chávez protesters massed outside the presidential palace, more than a dozen demonstrators were killed by gunfire from, apparently, members of the Bolivarian Circles.

On April 12, 2002, senior military officers, led by Gen. Luis RINCON, the armed forces commander, announced that Chávez had resigned, although it quickly became apparent that a coup had been mounted against him. With Chávez in custody, the military named Pedro CARMONA, president of *Fedecámaras,* as provisional president. Acting by decree, Carmona attempted to dissolve the National Assembly and the Supreme Court and to suspend the constitution, but wide popular support for the government takeover failed to materialize as advocates of democracy joined Chávez loyalists in the streets. Carmona subsequently resigned, and on April 13 the National Assembly elevated Vice President Diosdado CABELLO to the presidency. Cabello, in turn, returned the presidency to Chávez on April 14. (In 2009, Cabello was serving as the Chávez government's minister of public works.)

In late 2002 and early 2003 major business and labor sectors staged a general strike over several months that crippled the economy, severely reducing oil production. In the end, the strike's proponents were forced to call off their action in the face of rising public anger.

In 2003 the opposition was confident that it could remove Chávez by means of a popular referendum, campaigning for which was launched on November 21. The recall ballot on August 26, 2004, was endorsed by only 40.7 percent of the participating voters. The president and his allies were further strengthened on October 31 by winning 20 of 23 state governorships (15 of which had been held by *antichavistas*), as well as the mayoralty of Caracas. The leading opposition parties boycotted the December 4, 2005, legislative balloting, resulting in a 75 percent abstention rate and an assembly with almost no opposition representation.

The administration advanced proposals for a constitutional change that permitted Chávez to run, successfully, for a third term on December 3, 2006. The opposition united behind a single candidate, endorsing Zulia state governor Manuel ROSALES under the New Time (*Un Nuevo Tiempo*—UNT) banner. Chávez defeated Rosales by a 62–37 percent margin in voting that was internationally judged to be free and fair. No other candidate received more than 0.04 percent of the vote. On January 8, 2007, just before his inauguration, Chávez replaced nearly every minister in his cabinet and named a new vice president, former National Electoral Council president Jorge RODRÍGUEZ. Another cabinet reshuffle occurred on January 3–4, 2008, with the naming of a new vice president, retired Col. Ramón CARRIZALEZ, and nine new ministers.

In 2007 Chávez began to take Venezuela in a markedly more radical direction toward "21st Century Socialism," as the National Assembly approved a second "enabling law" allowing him to rule by decree for 18 months. Though he suffered a setback with the December constitutional referendum proposing central control over states and municipalities, the president pushed through a host of reforms by other means, including decrees and laws that easily passed the assembly.

In February 2008 Venezuela's pro-Chávez comptroller-general, citing corruption and misuse of funds, banned 272 individuals, nearly all of them opposition politicians, from contesting municipal and state gubernatorial elections later in the year. Ultimately, the governing United Socialist Party of Venezuela (*Partido Socialista Unido de Venezuela*—PSUV) won 17 of 23 governorships, a slightly weaker showing than in 2004. The opposition won the governorships of the three most populous states and mayoral races in Caracas and Maracaibo.

Ostensibly to increase "participatory democracy," Chávez moved to bolster the funding of thousands of "community councils," citizen groups accountable to the presidency that take on functions formally under the purview of local governments. An April 9, 2008, decree started the process of consolidation of 126 regional or municipal police forces into a single national force. Chávez also removed authority from Venezuela's central bank, placing monetary policy under presidential control.

The president's 18-month decree authority expired on July 31, 2008. On that day, Chávez issued 26 decrees, including a restoration of the "Geometry of Power" proposal for central control over states and municipalities, which had been defeated in the December 2007 referendum. Another decree increased the state's ability to regulate the production, distribution, import, and export of food.

Following President Chávez's victory in a February 2009 constitutional referendum to abolish term limits (see Constitution and government, below), he reshuffled the cabinet, consolidating some ministries and giving Vice President Carrizalez the additional portfolio of defense minister.

In September 2009 Chávez restructured the Council of Ministers, giving six cabinet ministers the additional title of "vice president" with responsibility for broader policy issues. Vice President Carrizalez assumed the title of first vice president.

Several ministers resigned on January 24, 2010. Following the resignation of Vice President Carrizalez on January 25, Agriculture Minister Elías JUAU Milano was named to replace him on January 26.

More cabinet changes were made in February, April, May, June, July, and October.

In the National Assembly elections held on September 26, 2010, the PSUV secured the most seats but failed to retain its two-thirds majority.

Since 2009 the Chávez government has moved forward with plans to nationalize key sectors, including banking, energy and hydrocarbon, and gold. The expropriations, along with the arrests of some wealthy businessmen, resulted in a significant decline in foreign investment. The economy slid into a recession, which continued through the first half of 2010 and was compounded by a severe drought. Adding to the tension was the nation's spiraling homicide rate, as more than 16,000 suspected murders were recorded for the year. Analysts said Venezuela's persistent economic inequality, insufficient national police force, and increasingly politicized judicial system were hampering the government's ability to improve security.

Attention in 2010 turned to the National Assembly elections, the first held under a new law passed in 2009, which observers said favored the major parties and their candidates. Another law adopted around the same time allowed the election commission to redraw electoral districts at any time. In 2010 the districts were drawn to give more representation to states that were pro-Chávez, and the percentage of seats filled by proportional representation was reduced. The opposition Democratic Unity Table (*Mesa de la Unidad Democrática*—MUD) coalition, consisting of several dozen national and regional parties with diverse ideologies, nevertheless managed to win 65 seats, while the PSUV and its allies won 98, short of a two-thirds majority by 12 seats.

Virtually all significant legislation enacted since January 2011 has been by decree of President Chávez. Among the laws he issued are those that gave the government the rights to take over all "idle and underused land and buildings" and impose a profit tax on oil sales over $40 per barrel.

In June Chávez flew to Cuba for emergency surgery to treat a "pelvic abscess." He remained in Cuba for several weeks, undergoing additional surgery and chemotherapy. He returned to Venezuela in October and declared himself cured of cancer. However, rumors abounded that Chávez's cancer had spread and was more virulent than had previously been reported.

On November 1, 2011, Chávez announced the nationalization of a subsidiary of the UK-owned agricultural company Vestey Group, following failed talks between the government and the company over compensation. Meanwhile, the government introduced price controls on many basic goods in order to curb the 27 percent annual inflation rate. On November 11 Juan Carlos Fernandez, Chile's consul in Venezuela, was abducted while leaving a Caracas hotel. During a two-hour hostage ordeal, Fernandez reportedly suffered a gunshot wound before he was released. One week later Chávez announced that the government was deploying up to 3,650 troops in Caracas and surrounding areas to bolster police forces in their fight against violent crime.

On January 6, 2012, Chávez appointed General Henry Rangel SILVA, whom the U.S. government had formerly accused of being a drug kingpin, as the new defense minister, prompting speculation that Chávez was trying to shore up support within the military.

In a sign of the most energized and unified opposition in years, a group of parties held a joint primary on February 12 for voters to decide on a MUD unity candidate to oppose Chávez in the October 7 general elections. The 39-year-old former Miranda governor Henrique CAPRILES, of the Justice First party, won the primary by a decisive margin. However, he faced long odds in the general election, given Chávez's control over the entire state apparatus to promote his campaign and a massive increase in government spending on social programs to attract voters during the run-up to the election. Capriles touted his administrative successes as governor, vowing to continue the fight against poverty, but with better management skills.

Many voters were said to be anxious about losing their jobs or government benefits if they voted for Capriles, especially after the introduction of a new electronic voting system that some feared might be used by the government to track who voted against the president.

Chávez easily won re-election on October 7, securing 55.14 percent of the vote to Capriles's 44.24 percent, although Capriles took more votes from than any past Chávez challenger. Three days later, Chávez selected Foreign Minister Nicolás MADURO to be his vice president.

Gubernatorial elections were held on December 16, with the ruling PSUV winning 20 or 23 races. Capriles held onto his seat, defeating former vice president Elías Jaua Milano.

Chávez vowed to take Venezuela farther down the road of "21st century socialism," but his health began to rapidly deteriorate. He returned to Cuba for additional surgeries in November and December and announced on December 8 that his cancer had returned. He also addressed the people of Venezuela on television, instructing them to "elect Nicolás Maduro as president of the republic." Chávez was too ill to be inaugurated on January 10, 2013, prompting speculation over who was actually running the country. Chávez returned to Venezuela on February 18 and passed away on March 5 at age 58. Maduro won election to formally succeed Chávez and was inaugurated on April 19, 2013. (See Current Issues for more information.)

Constitution and government. Under its constitution of January 23, 1961, Venezuela was designated a federal republic. It now encompasses 23 states (the newest, Vargas, created with effect from January 1, 1999), a Federal District, and 72 Federal Dependencies (islands in the Antilles). Executive power was vested in a president who was elected by universal suffrage for a five-year term and until mid-1992 (when a one-term ban was imposed on all future incumbents) could be reelected after a ten-year interval. The legislative body (Congress of the Republic) consisted of a Senate and a Chamber of Deputies, both elected by universal suffrage for five-year terms concurrent with that of the president. The states were administered by popularly elected governors; had their own elected, unicameral legislative assemblies; and were divided into county-type districts with popularly elected mayors and municipal councils.

Among the numerous changes introduced by the 1999 basic law, the presidential term was extended to six years with the possibility of one immediate renewal; executive authority vis-à-vis the economy was substantially enhanced; the bicameral legislature was abandoned in favor of a unicameral National Assembly; public administration was drastically reorganized; oil production was to remain vested in the state; the rights of indigenous peoples were affirmed; and the country was renamed *República Bolivariana de Venezuela* in honor of the independence hero.

In May 2004 the Supreme Court was enlarged from 20 to 32 members.

In October 2008 constitutional reforms were approved that allow the president to appoint officials, popularly referred to as "viceroys," empowered to carry out most of the functions of elected mayors and governors. On February 15, 2009, a referendum to remove the two-term limit on the president, mayors, governors, and National Assembly members was approved by a vote of 54.9 percent.

The Venezuelan media transmits a broad range of political views, and private media remain occasionally critical of the government, but threats to revoke broadcast licenses have resulted in widespread self-censorship. The Radio and Television Social Responsibility Act prohibits any programming viewed as an incitement to antistate violence and requires broadcasters to air government material for up to 70 hours a week.

In August 2009 the government closed 32 radio stations and 2 regional television stations, nearly all of them opposition-leaning, claiming that they were broadcasting illegally. Reporters Without Borders ranked Venezuela 117th out of 179 countries in its 2013 Index of Press Freedom, citing arbitrary closures of media outlets and 170 instances of violence against journalists.

Foreign relations. A member of the United Nations and its related agencies, the Organization of Petroleum Exporting Countries (OPEC), the Organization of American States (OAS), the Latin American Integration Association, the Union of South American Nations (UNASUR), and other hemispheric organizations, Venezuela was traditionally aligned with the West in both inter-American and world affairs. During the presidencies of Betancourt and Leoni, it was subjected by the Cuban regime of Fidel Castro to repeated propaganda attacks and armed incursions. Although it consequently took a particularly harsh line toward Cuba, it was equally critical of right-wing dictatorships in the Americas and for some years refused to maintain diplomatic relations with governments formed as a result of military coups. This policy was modified during the 1960s by the establishment of diplomatic relations with Argentina, Panama, and Peru as well as with Czechoslovakia, Hungary, the Soviet Union, and other Communist countries, while in December 1974, despite earlier differences, a normalization of relations with Cuba was announced.

A long-standing territorial claim to the section of Guyana west of the Essequibo River has caused intermittent friction with that country, Venezuela declining in June 1982 to renew a 12-year moratorium on unilateral action in the dispute and subsequently refusing to sanction submission of the controversy to the International Court of Justice. In September 1999 the issue was revived by the Venezuelan foreign minister, who rejected the century-old award to the former UK dependency.

A Venezuelan claim to tiny Bird Island (*Isla de Aves*) to the west of Dominica has periodically strained relations with its Caribbean neighbors. While the island, on which Venezuela is reportedly constructing a scientific station, is of little intrinsic importance, the Organization of Eastern Caribbean States (OECS) has expressed concern that it might serve as the basis of a claim by Caracas to a 200-mile-wide exclusive economic zone.

For more than three decades Caracas has been engaged in a dispute with Colombia regarding sovereignty over the Gulf of Venezuela (Gulf of Guajira). Other disagreements have arisen over the smuggling of foodstuffs, drug trafficking, and alleged attacks by Colombia's guerrilla and paramilitary groups on the Venezuelan national guard and Venezuelan citizens. Over the years the two countries have concluded a number of agreements aimed at combating drug traffickers, but an "open border" has made interdiction of drug shipments difficult.

The Chávez government's ties with the United States have deteriorated steadily, with some of the first problems brought about by an August 2000 visit by President Chávez to Iraq (the first by a head of state since the first Gulf war), a visit to Caracas by Fidel Castro in late October, the conclusion of a military cooperation treaty with Russia in May 2001, and subsequent criticism of the U.S. bombing of Afghanistan as "fighting terror with terror." Relations deteriorated following the failed April 2002 coup attempt, which, it is widely believed, occurred with strong U.S. backing and support.

In December 2004 Chávez embarked on a tour of countries viewed as potential buyers of Venezuelan oil, including the People's Republic of China. Earlier, Venezuela concluded an agreement with Cuba to supply Havana with cut-rate oil in return for a medical assistance program valued at over $750 million. Venezuela has been Cuba's closest ally during the 2000s, with President Chávez the only foreign leader routinely granted audiences with the Castro brothers. Out of the Cuba-Venezuela relationship sprang the Bolivarian Alliance for the Americas (ALBA), an organization of left-leaning Latin American and Caribbean nations that Chávez proposed as an alternative to the proposed Free Trade Area of the Americas.

A major rupture in Colombian-Venezuelan relations followed Colombian security forces' abduction from Caracas of Rodrigo Granda, a Colombian citizen considered to be the "foreign minister" of Colombia's largest guerrilla group, the Revolutionary Armed Forces of Colombia (FARC), in early 2005. Tensions heightened as top Colombian officials, including Defense Minister Juan Manuel Santos, accused Venezuela of harboring and assisting Colombian guerrillas on Venezuelan territory. For his part, Chávez continued to be an ardent critic of "Plan Colombia" and other U.S. programs in the Andes. Venezuela also objected to Colombia's decision to grant asylum to Pedro Carmona, the business leader briefly named to Venezuela's presidency during the abortive April 2002 coup.

Venezuela's relations with Peru soured in 2006, when Chávez openly endorsed Peruvian presidential candidate Ollanta Humala. Humala did not win, in part because opponents, including the eventual victor, Alán García, portrayed him as a Chávez puppet. Relations between Chávez and García remained rocky.

A similar election-year dynamic that year damaged relations between Venezuela and Mexico, with Chávez and Mexican president Vicente Fox engaging in a series of bitter verbal exchanges. Relations with Fox's successor, Felipe Calderón, improved somewhat, and Venezuela sent an ambassador to Mexico City in September 2007.

In 2006 Venezuela failed to win a nonpermanent seat on the UN Security Council. After 47 rounds of voting, neither Venezuela nor U.S.-backed Guatemala was able to win the two-thirds of General Assembly votes necessary to fill the seat normally reserved for a Latin American country. The position eventually went to Panama.

In August and September 2007, relations with Colombia appeared to improve as President Uribe invited Chávez to facilitate possible peace and prisoner-exchange dialogues with the FARC. However, relations broke down after Uribe abruptly "fired" Chávez from this role on November 22. The two leaders engaged in months of name-calling.

South America's worst security crisis in decades was triggered by a March 1, 2008, Colombian raid into Ecuadorian territory that killed Raúl Reyes, one of the FARC's most senior leaders. In response to what he viewed as a serious violation of Ecuador's sovereignty, Chávez warned Colombia that he would respond to a similar operation in Venezuela with fighter jets, and ordered his military to deploy ten tank battalions—about 9,000 troops—to Venezuela's border with Colombia. The threat of hostilities was defused by a March 7 meeting of the region's leaders in Santo Domingo, at which the leaders agreed to reinstate their ambassadors.

Tensions remained very high, however, as files recovered from Reyes's computer appeared to indicate that guerrilla leaders and key Venezuelan government officials had been discussing the possibility of material support for the FARC's cause. While Venezuela denied any wrongdoing and challenged the files' authenticity, Chávez's Colombia rhetoric toned down substantially over the following months. On June 8 Chávez surprised nearly all observers by publicly calling on the FARC to release all of their hostages and to abandon the armed struggle. Tensions with Colombia did not flare up again for the remainder of 2008.

On September 11, 2008, after Bolivia expelled its U.S. ambassador, Venezuela declared U.S. Ambassador Patrick Duddy *persona non grata* in an act of "solidarity." The U.S. government responded by expelling Ambassador Bernardo Álvarez HERRERA. A few days later, the U.S. Treasury Department added Ramón RODRÍGUEZ CHACÍN, who had just vacated his post as Venezuela's interior minister, to its list of major international narcotrafficking figures, citing indications of links to Colombia's FARC that appeared on recovered guerrilla computers.

The U.S. government has placed a series of sanctions on Venezuela for failing to cooperate on initiatives against drugs and terrorism, and for violating religious freedom, making it impossible for Caracas to receive U.S. aid or to purchase weapons with U.S.-made components. In October 2008 the Venezuelan government expelled two researchers for Human Rights Watch from the country. The move prompted a sharp rebuke from the European Parliament.

President Chávez sought warmer relations with countries that are generally cool to the United States. A 2008 visit to China resulted in a host of new investment agreements, including increased Chinese access to Venezuelan oil. Ties with Russia have warmed significantly. Venezuela is one of a very few countries to recognize the breakaway Georgian regions of Abkhazia and South Ossetia. Venezuela has made many arms purchases from Russia, including a fleet of tanks and help from the Medvedev government in establishing a nuclear energy program.

President Chávez offered more conciliatory language to incoming U.S. president Barack Obama in early 2009. The two presidents exchanged cordial public greetings at the April Summit of the Americas in Trinidad and Tobago. In June the two countries reinstated their ambassadors.

Venezuela's relations with Peru deteriorated in April 2009, when the government of Alán García granted asylum to President Chávez's chief political rival, former presidential opponent Manuel Rosales. Venezuelan authorities had ordered Rosales's arrest on corruption charges.

President Chávez and Colombian president Uribe met in January 2009, pledging greater economic cooperation. In April Chávez, speaking at a joint press conference with Uribe, again called on the FARC guerrillas to negotiate and plan to disband.

In mid-July, when the Colombian media revealed that Bogotá would allow U.S. military personnel to use bases on Colombian soil, Chávez responded by freezing relations with Colombia. The Uribe government parried by revealing that it had recovered several Swedish-made rocket launchers from the FARC that had originated in Venezuela. Chávez recalled his ambassador and announced plans to cut annual trade with Colombia and to expropriate Colombian businesses in Venezuela. Tensions increased following the U.S.-Colombia defense agreement signing on October 30, as Chávez instructed the Venezuelan military to "prepare for war" with Colombia.

Chávez cultivated closer ties with Iran during a visit to Tehran in April 2009, when he became one of the first foreign leaders to visit following President Ahmadinejad's crackdown on protests against alleged electoral fraud. The leaders discussed sales of Venezuelan uranium for Iran's nuclear program. Chávez's September visit to Iran was part of a so-called "rogue states" tour that included Libya, Syria, Algeria, Turkmenistan, and Belarus, among others.

In July 2010 Colombia's ambassador to the OAS formally accused Venezuela of sheltering 1,500 Colombian guerrillas. President Chávez severed relations and ordered a military alert. However, the incoming Colombian president, Juan Manuel Santos, declared his willingness to resolve the conflict. On August 10, three days after his inauguration, Santos met with Chávez, and the two leaders agreed to restore full relations.

In September 2010 President Chávez refused to allow entry to the new U.S. ambassador, Larry Palmer, due to some comments Palmer had made to a U.S. senator, including allegations that the Chávez administration had ties to Colombian rebels. The United States subsequently revoked the visa of Venezuela's ambassador.

On September 9, 2011, the U.S. government named four officials close to President Chávez in its drug "kingpin" list and imposed sanctions against Venezuela, including freezing assets and prohibiting U.S. citizens from conducting business deals in Venezuela.

On January 8, 2012, the United States ordered the expulsion of Livia Acosta NOGUERA, Venezuela's consul general in Miami, following accusations that she had discussed the possibility of orchestrating cyber attacks against the U.S. government while serving in Venezuela's embassy in Mexico City. On January 16 Venezuela announced that it was withdrawing its remaining diplomatic and consular officials from Miami.

On June 13, 2012, Chávez confirmed that Venezuela was building unmanned aerial drones in cooperation with China, Russia, and Iran.

The Netherlands concluded a trade agreement with Venezuela in June 2013 that will provide greater economic cooperation between the two countries. Venezuela is the closest neighbor of Aruba, Curaçao, and St. Maarten in the Dutch Caribbean.

The March 8 funeral for Chávez provided an opportunity for heads of state to signal their continued interest in Venezuela. Some 33 heads of state attended, including Cuba's Raúl Castro and Iran's Ahmadinejad. The United States sent a token delegation, especially after then-Vice President Maduro suggested that Washington had infected Chávez with the fatal cancer and on March 5 expelled to U.S. diplomats for allegedly encouraging the Venezuelan military to overthrow the Chávez government. On March 11 the United States expelled two Venezuelan diplomats.

Current issues. The Venezuelan constitution specifies that presidential elections had to be held within 30 days of Chávez's death. Maduro became acting president and appointed Jorge ARREAZA as acting vice president. Arreaza was minister for science and technology as well as Chávez's son-in-law. He had been the family spokesperson during the president's long illness. On April 14 Madura narrowly defeated Capriles for the presidency, 50.61 percent to 49.12 percent. While Chávez beat Capriles by 1.6 million votes in 2012, Maduro's margin was less than 250,000. When Capriles demanded a recount, Maduro initially agreed then reversed himself, sparking protests from both sides. When opposition legislators refused to acknowledge Maduro's victory, Cabello, the speaker of the National Assembly, refused to let them speak and seized their paychecks, sparking fistfights. The Supreme Court later fined Capriles for challenging the results.

As he struggled to consolidate his legitimacy, Maduro lashed out at critics at home and abroad. When the United States, Chile, and Peru declined to recognize Maduro's election, he denounced U.S. President Barack Obama as the "grand chief of devils." Peru's Foreign Minister Rafael Roncagliolo urged him to adopt a "climate of dialogue, tolerance, and mutual respect," but Maduro called the advice "the mistake of his life." The president also accused several Colombian political leaders of trying to assassinate him. The PSUV is reportedly fracturing, with Cabello leading the anti-Maduro camp.

Meanwhile the economy rapidly declined. The government had spent 40 percent more than in took in in 2012, and Maduro devaluated the currency twice in early 2013 as inflation passed 30 percent. Shortages, including food, increased throughout the year. In September power failures caused blackouts in 70 percent of the country. Maduro accused the United States of supporting plots to sabotage the power grid and expelled three diplomats, including the chargé d'affaires, in October. He also requested special powers to rule by decree in order to "fight against corruption and the economic war declared by the bourgeoisie against the people."

POLITICAL PARTIES

It is a sign of Chávez's profound influence that even after his death, Venezuela's political party system can be divided into in two broad categories: pro-Chávez and anti-Chávez. The **United Socialist Party of Venezuela** (*Partido Socialista Unido de Venezuela*—PSUV) has dominated the political scene for over a dozen years, and it has created alliances with like-minded smaller parties ahead of elections. These include the Patriotic Pole (*Polo Patriótica*—PP) in 2000, the **Block for Change** (*Bloque para el Cambio*) in 2005, the **Patriotic Alliance** (*Alianza Patriótica*) in 2008, and the **Great Patriotic Pole** (*Gran Polo Patriótica*—GPP) for the 2012 presidential election. These alliances are often fleeting—the GPP included 35,000 parties, collectives, and social movements in December 2011 and was defunct by November 2012. The anti-Chávez camp is led by the **Democratic Unity Table** (*Mesa de la Unidad Democrática*—MUD). Eleven parties formed MUD in June 2009 and by the 2010 election that number had grown to more than 50 groups.

Presidential Party:

United Socialist Party of Venezuela (*Partido Socialista Unido de Venezuela*—PSUV). Before the 2000 election, a Patriotic Pole (*Polo Patriótica*—PP) of 14 pro-Chávez parties included the MVR and MAS (below). A year later, the MAS withdrew, leaving the MVR as the coalition's only major component. For the 2005 poll, the pro-Chávez group reorganized as the Block for Change (*Bloque para el Cambio*).

Following his 2006 reelection victory, President Chávez pressured all government-supportive parties to form a single party instead of, in his words, "an alphabet soup that is fooling the people." Instead of a ruling coalition of 21 groups as before, the president declared that all of his supporters must join the new party and cease to exist as independent entities, or be considered political adversaries. The PSUV held its inaugural congress on January 12, 2008, and became the dominant pro-Chávez force. Three coalition members—For Social Democracy (*Podemos*), Fatherland for All (PPT), and the Communist Party of Venezuela (PCV)—remained independent, but allied, parties. The still-forming PSUV united with smaller progovernment parties to compete in the 2008 municipal and state elections as the Patriotic Alliance (*Alianza Patriótica*), a designation that by 2009 was no longer used.

In May 2010 the party conducted primary votes in which roughly 2.5 million members (more than one-third of the party's registered membership) chose nominees for the 110 National Assembly seats elected by district. It was reportedly the largest intraparty election in Venezuelan history. Party leaders, including President Chávez, selected the state-based candidates for the seats elected by proportional representation. Meanwhile, some leading *chavistas* complained about the degree of control exercised by the government over the party.

The PSUV won 95 seats in the September 26 legislative election with 46 percent of the vote. Its three allied parties (PCV, COPEI, and the indigenous Foundation for Training, Integration, and Dignity) each took a single seat, giving the PSUV control over 98 of 165 seats, 12 short of a majority.

Going into the October 7, 2012, presidential election, the PSUV anchored a new alliance, the **Great Patriotic Pole** (*Gran Polo Patriótica*—GPP) formed exclusively to support Chávez's reelection. Chávez easily won with 55.14 percent of the vote, although he was too ill to take the oath of office in January.

Following the death of President Chávez in March 2013, Nicolás MADURA replaced him as president of the country and the PSUV. The party reportedly fractured in late 2013 into a Madura faction and one loyal to Diosdado CABELLO, the president of the National Assembly. Madura announced plans to reactivate the GPP for upcoming elections.

Leaders: Nicolás MADURA (President of the Republic), Diosdado CABELLO (First Vice President of the Party).

Fifth Republic Movement (*Movimiento Quinta República*—MVR). The MVR was launched in July 1997 by presidential aspirant Hugo Chávez Frías, who had previously been associated with the outlawed Revolutionary Bolivarian Movement–200 (*Movimiento Bolivariano Revolucionario–200*—MBR-200), an intensely nationalist formation composed largely of former military figures opposed to the alleged corruption and social disparity occasioned by government economic policies. Chávez, having been arrested following the February 1992 revolt and then released from prison in March 1994 as part of a conciliatory gesture by President Caldera toward the military, had indicated that the MBR-200 would be converted into a political formation. In 2002 the MVR saw some Chávez opponents leave to form the Solidarity Party (below) and the Revolutionary Transparency Party (TR).

For the 2005 legislative poll, all MVR candidates were designated by the party's "National Tactical Command," with nearly a quarter of sitting members of the National Assembly deemed insufficiently loyal to be given an opportunity for reelection.

Unity of Electoral Victors (*Unidad de Vencedores Electorales*—UVE). The UVE, founded in 2005, was one of several pro-Chávez parties competing within the Block for Change coalition. The group appeared to be indistinguishable from the MVR, even using the same logo; critics alleged it was part of a strategy to increase the progovernment bloc's majority by adding to the proportional representation. The group won four National Assembly seats in the 2005 legislative elections; immediately afterward, however, its deputies joined the MVR.

People's Electoral Movement (*Movimiento Electoral del Pueblo*—MEP). The MEP was founded in 1967 by a left-wing faction of the Democratic Action (AD, below) that disagreed with the party's choice of a presidential candidate for the 1968 election. It won three lower house seats in 1978, none thereafter. In 1987 the party selected Edmundo CHIRINOS, rector of the Central University of Venezuela, as its 1988 presidential nominee, who, in addition to being supported by the Communist Party, received the endorsement of the Independent Moral Movement (*Movimiento Moral Independiente*—MMI), a small left-wing group formed in 1986. Based on nationwide polling results, the MEP was granted one seat in the Chamber of Deputies after the November 1998 election. In 2005 the MEP won one National Assembly seat. That legislator joined the PSUV, but the MEP refused to dissolve.

Leader: Wilmer NOLASCO (Secretary General).

Venezuelan Popular Unity (*Unidad Popular Venezolana*—UPV). The UPV was founded in February 2004 as a "radical and ruthless" pro-Chávez leftist party. It won one seat in the December 2005 National Assembly election. In 2007 its leader, Lina Ron, indicated that the party would accept President Chávez's dictate that supporting parties unite as the PSUV, given that Chávez is "the messiah God sent to save the people." Ron died suddenly in 2011 at age 51.

Several other parties and groups in the pro-Chávez coalition with no legislative representation joined the PSUV as well. They include the **Independent Solidarity Movement** (*Movimiento Solidaridad Independente*—MSI or SI), organized in early 1997 to support the interests of the middle class and led by Paciano PADRON and Luis EDUARDO Ortega; the **Union Party** (*Partido Unión*—PN), launched in May 2001 as a social democratic alternative to the AD and COPEI by Lt. Col. (Ret.) Francisco ARIAS Cárdenas; the **Agriculturalist Action** (*Acción Agropecuaria*—AA), led by Hiram GAVIRIA and Gustavo BASTIDAS; the **Emergent People** (*Gente Emergente*—GE), founded in 1991 in opposition to the "irresponsible power elite" and led by Fernando ALVAREZ Paz and Lazaro CALAZÁN; the **Independents for the National Community** (*Independientes por la Comunidad Nacional*—IPCN), which was organized by Antonio GONZÁLEZ to foster community development; the Moral Force (Fuerza Moral—FM), formed in 1998 by Hernán GRÜBER Odreman, a former rear admiral who participated in the abortive coup of November 1992 and was appointed governor of the Federal District by Chávez in January 1999; and the **New Democratic Regime** (*Nuevo Régimen Democrático*—NRD), which was launched in 1997 by Guillermo GARCÍA Ponce, Manuel ISIDRO Molina, and Pedro MIRANDA. In addition, by 1998 an **Independence Movement** (*Movimiento Independencia*—MI), headed by J. A. COVA Sosa, had evolved from The Notables (*Grupo Notables*), a group of well-known public figures who had supported the 1992 coup attempts. One of The Notables was José Vicente Rangel, the 1983 presidential candidate of the New Alternative (*Nuevo Alternative*—NA), a coalition that had included, among other groups, the pro-Moscow faction of the MIR (see **Movement to Socialism** [*Movimiento al Socialismo*—MAS] below).

Pro-Government Parties in the National Assembly:

Communist Party of Venezuela (*Partido Comunista de Venezuela*—PCV). Founded in 1931, the PCV was proscribed in 1962 but relegalized in 1969 following its renunciation of the use of force. The party lost its three seats in the assembly after endorsing the 1988 presidential candidacy of the MEP's Edmundo Chirinos. In 1997 it expelled its only MP, Ricardo GUTIÉRREZ, who subsequently became a leader of *Podemos*.

The PCV won eight National Assembly seats in 2005; all but three deputies subsequently defected to the PSUV. The party joined in an electoral alliance with the PSUV for the 2010 legislative elections and won one seat.

Leaders: Jerónimo CARRERA (President), Pedro EUSSE, Oscar FIGUERA (Secretary General).

National Indian Council of Venezuela (*Consejo Nacional Indio de Venezuela*—CONIVE). Founded in 1989 to defend indigenous rights, this pro-Chávez party won all three National Assembly seats reserved for indigenous communities in the 2000 elections and won two of three seats in the 2005 elections. Both CONIVE deputies later joined the PSUV. The party contested the 2010 National Assembly elections in alliance with the PSUV and received one seat.

Leaders: Noeli POCATERRA, Raúl TEMPO (Executive Secretary).

Fatherland for All (*Patria para Todos*—PPT). The leftist-revolutionary PPT was organized in late 1997 by a dissident faction of *La Causa Radical* (below). In December 2005 it won 11 seats in the National Assembly. While it was a member of the Patriotic Alliance in the 2008 local elections, the PPT's remaining five deputies declined to join the PSUV. In early 2010 Henri FALCON, the governor of Lara state, defected from the PSUV to join PPT. The PPT leadership subsequently announced it would not join in coalition with PSUV for the 2010 legislative elections, in light of the president's drift toward authoritarian rule. The party won two assembly seats in 2010 but was not part of either electoral alliance.

Leader: Rafael UZCÁTEGUI (Secretary General).

Opposition Parties in the National Assembly:

Democratic Unity Table (*Mesa de la Unidad Democrática*—MUD). The National Unity (*Unidad Nacional*—UN) was the principal opposition coalition participating in the November 2008 regional elections. It was formed with the signing of an agreement in January 2008 by the leaders of 11 member parties. Several more parties joined in February. The coalition won five states and four of the five Caracas mayors' offices.

On June 8, 2009, all of the same major opposition parties—plus *Podemos* (For Social Democracy, below), the only coalition member with legislative representation—came together to form the MUD. The coalition included a total of 50 major and minor parties. Despite some infighting, the coalition assembled a common slate of candidates to challenge the PSUV in the September 2010 legislative elections, with one main opposition candidate in most districts. The grouping won 65 seats on a 48 percent vote share, compared with the PSUV's 46 percent vote share and 98 seats. The vote distribution was attributed to the way the districts were defined for the polling.

In the 2012 presidential contest, the MUD backed Henrique Capriles, who won 44 percent of the vote to Chávez's 54 percent. Capriles ran for president again in April 2013, following the death of Chávez, winning 49.12 percent to Maduro's 50.61 percent. Capriles' demands for a recount were rejected by the National Election Council.

Leader: Ramón AVELEDO (Executive Coordinator).

Justice First (*Primero Justicia*—PJ). The PJ traces its origins to a civil association formed in 1992 by a Supreme Court justice, Alirio ABREU Burelli, to promote legal reform. It was constituted as a political party in 2000 and went on to win five seats from the state of Miranda in the National Assembly election. It was the second largest vote getter of the 44 parties in the coalition that supported Manuel Rosales's failed 2006 opposition presidential bid.

The PJ won 10 seats as part of the MUD coalition in the 2010 assembly elections. Henrique CAPRILES Radonski, governor of Miranda, was the opposition presidential candidate in 2012 and 2013, finishing second both times.

Leaders: Julio BORGES (National Coordinator), Henrique CAPRILES Radonski (2012, 2013 Presidential Candidate).

A New Time (*Un Nuevo Tiempo*—UNT). The Zulia-based UNT movement was founded in 1999 by regional dissidents from the Democratic Action Party. Manuel Rosales, an outspoken Chávez opponent from a social-democratic background, was a longtime member of Democratic Action.

In 2006 a coalition of 44 opposition groups, including all of Venezuela's dominant pre-1998 political parties, joined behind the UNT standard to support one presidential candidate, Rosales, to challenge Chávez. Subsequently, the UNT ceased to play a formal leadership role in the opposition, as the coalition's member parties remained autonomous. The **Democratic Left** (*Izquierda*

Democrática—ID), a group of former communists opposing what they perceived as Chávez's lack of commitment to democracy, folded their membership into the UNT in 2007. As a single party, UNT was the largest of several opposition parties participating in the 2008 municipal and gubernatorial elections under the National Unity banner.

In April 2009 Rosales, then the mayor of Maracaibo, went into exile in Peru to avoid arrest on corruption charges he claimed were politically motivated.

The UNT won 10 seats as part of the MUD coalition in the 2010 legislative elections.

Leaders: Omar BARBOZA (President), Manuel ROSALES, Enrique OCHOA.

Democratic Action (*Acción Democrática*—AD). Founded in 1937, the AD was forced underground by the Pérez Jiménez dictatorship but regained legality in 1958 and held power for ten years thereafter. An advocate of rapid economic development, welfare policies, and Western values, it won an overwhelming victory in 1973, capturing the presidency and both houses of Congress. Although it lost the presidency in 1978, it remained the largest party in the Senate and tied the Social Christians for representation in the Chamber of Deputies. In 1983 it regained the presidency and won majorities in both houses of Congress. By 1987, with its popularity waning because of continued economic crisis, the AD was deeply divided in the selection of its candidate for the 1988 presidential poll, former interior minister Octavio LEPAGE Barretto. Handpicked by President Lusinchi as his successor, he was ultimately defeated in party electoral college balloting by former president Carlos Andrés Pérez, who, following his election on December 4, returned to office on February 2, 1989.

The party suffered a major setback in state and municipal balloting in December 1992, and its candidate finished second with 23.6 percent of the vote in the presidential poll of December 1993, although it won pluralities in both houses of Congress on the latter occasion.

In November 1998 presidential hopeful Luis ALFARO Ucero was expelled by the party but nevertheless pursued his quest as an independent supported by an assortment of small parties, including the URD (Democratic Republican Union, below). The AD, which had retained both its congressional pluralities earlier in the month, backed the PRVZL's Salas Römer (Project Venezuela, below) in the December presidential race. Alfaro Ucero received 0.4 percent of the vote for a fourth-place finish.

AD/ABP ("Bravo People" Alliance, below) candidate Antonio LEDEZMA defeated his PSUV opponent in the November 2008 elections for the mayoralty of Caracas. Shortly afterward, President Chávez moved to strip the mayor's office of most of its powers.

The AD won eight seats as part of the MUD coalition in the 2010 legislative elections.

Leaders: Isabel CARMONA de Serra (President), Henry RAMOS Allup (Secretary General).

Social Christian Party (*Comité de Organización Política Electoral Independiente*—COPEI) is a Christian-democratic party that has been active in Venezuelan politics since its creation in 1946. COPEI produced two presidents of Venezuela, including party founder Rafael CALDERA Rodríguez (1969–1974) and Luis HERRERA Campis (1979–1984) and was a strong national presence until the rise of Hugo Chávez. COPEI won five legislative seats in 2000 but did not run in 2005. The COPEI won five seats as part of the MUD coalition in the 2010 legislative elections.

Leader: Roberto Enríquez (Chair).

For Social Democracy (*Por la Democracia Social—Podemos*). The center-left *Podemos* was formed in November 2002, primarily by former members of MAS (Movement to Socialism, below) who remained loyal to President Chávez. In 2005 it finished a distant second to the MVR in the National Assembly election, winning 15 seats. Though it lost some deputies to the PSUV, its six remaining legislators resisted joining the new party. Former party president Ramon MARTINEZ received asylum in Peru in January 2010 in the wake of corruption charges against him in Venezuela. *Podemos* won two seats as part of the MUD coalition in the 2010 legislative elections. In June 2012 a faction led by Secretary General Ismael GARCÍA broke away to help establish the **Advanced Progressive** party.

Leaders: Didalco BOLIVAR (President), Baudillo REINOSO (Vice President).

Parties receiving one seat each in the National Assembly in the 2010 legislative elections as part of MUD included: **The Radical Cause** (*La Causa Radical or Causa R*), a far-left group strongly established in Bolívar state since the 1980s; **Clear Accounts** (*Cuentas Claras*), a center-progressive party based in Carabobo state; **Project Venezuela** (*Proyecto Venezuela*—PRYZL), another center-right party based in Carabobo state; and the **Zulia State Autonomous Indigenous Movement**.

Movement to Socialism (*Movimiento al Socialismo*—MAS). Originating as a radical left-wing group that split from the PCV in 1971, the MAS subsequently adopted a "Eurocommunist" posture and became the dominant legislative party of the left by capturing 2 Senate and 11 Chamber seats in 1978. It supported José Vicente Rangel for the presidency in 1978 but, with the exception of a small group of dissidents, was deeply opposed to his 1983 bid as leader of the left-wing New Alternative coalition. Having responded positively to the mid-1981 appeal from AD leader Carlos Andrés Pérez for a "synchronization of the opposition," it appeared to be adopting a democratic-socialist rather than a rigidly Marxist orientation. In late 1987 the majority, anti-Moscow faction of the Movement of the Revolutionary Left (*Movimiento de Izquierda Revolucionaria*—MIR), led by Moisés MOLEIRO, was reported to have merged with the MAS. (The MIR, which was founded by radical students in 1960, engaged in urban terrorism from 1961 to 1964 and thereafter conducted guerrilla operations from a rural base. Legalized in 1973, it won 4 Chamber seats in 1978 before splitting into two factions, the smaller being a pro-Moscow group led by party founder and 1978 presidential candidate Américo MARTIN.)

In March 1996 the MAS formed an alliance with the anti-Caldera legislative bloc, while insisting, somewhat inconsistently, that by so doing it was asserting its independence rather than going into opposition. Teodoro Petkoff resigned from the MAS in July 1998 over its decision to support Chávez.

The party began distancing itself from the government coalition in May 2001 in the wake of reports that the president was considering a declaration of emergency that would permit him to rule by decree. Five months later Chávez stated that the MAS was "no longer an ally of the Bolivarian revolution" and called on it to leave the coalition. In late November a dissident group formed *Podemos*.

The MAS joined the MUD coalition ahead of the 2010 assembly elections but did not win any seats.

Leaders: Felipe MUJICA (President), José Antonio ESPAÑA, Nicolás SOSA.

Other parties in the MUD coalition include **Democracy Renovated** (*Democracia Renovadora*—DR), led by José Gregorio GARCÍA Urquiola; **Liberal Power** (Fuerza Liberal—FL), led by President Haydée DEUTSCH; **Venezuela Vision** (*Visión Venezuela*—VV), led by Omar ÁVILA; the **Platform for Social Encounter** (*Plataforma de Encuentro Social*—PES), founded in 2008 by Globovisión television host Augusto URIBE; **Only One People** (*Un Solo Pueblo*—USP), founded in 2002 and led by Director General Enrique ARTEAGA; **Independent Solidarity** (*Solidaridad Independiente*—SI), led by Juan de Dios RIVAS Velásquez; the **Republican Movement** (*Movimiento Republicano*—MR), led by President Carlos PADILLA; **Red Flag** (*Bandera Roja*—BR), led by Gabriel PUERTA Aponte.

Other Parties:

For information on the **Humanist Popular Front** (*Frente Popular Humanista*—FPH), a faction in the 2005–2010 National Assembly, the **New Revolutionary Way** (*Nuevo Camino Revolucionario*—NCR), the **Venezuelan Ecological Movement** (*Movimiento Ecológico Venezolano*—MOVEV), the **"Bravo People" Alliance** (*Alianza Bravo Pueblo*—ABP), and the **Democratic Republican Union** (*Unión Republicana Democrática*—URD), please see the 2013 *Handbook*.

Armed Groups:

The Pebble (*La Piedrita*). This small, far-left, Caracas-based group launched a series of tear-gas attacks on the offices of opposition political parties, media outlets and the Catholic Church in 2008 and 2009. Its leader, Valentín Santana, gained notoriety for threatening to kill the head of the RCTV network that lost its broadcast license in 2007.

Though the roughly 50-member group claims to be ardently pro-Chávez, the president asked the attorney-general's office to arrest Santana in February 2009. He remained a fugitive in late 2013.

Leader: Valentín SANTANA.

Bolivarian Liberation Forces (*Fuerzas Bolivarianas de Liberación*—FBL). This group, which has operated sporadically in Colombian border zones since the early 2000s, is believed to work closely with Colombia's FARC guerrillas. It has allegedly killed members of the security forces, prompting President Chávez to order the dissolution of the group, which claims to support him. In May 2013 it released a video on YouTube threatening any group that opposed the election of President Maduro.

Leader: Eleazar JUÁREZ (National Coordinator).

LEGISLATURE

Under the former constitution, the Venezuelan legislature was a bicameral Congress of the Republic (*Congreso de la República*) consisting of a 46-member Senate (*Senado*) and a 189-member Chamber of Deputies (*Cámara de Diputados*), both with additional nominated members to compensate for party underrepresentation. The Congress was effectively superseded by the Constitutional Assembly elected on July 25, 1999, and was formally dissolved on January 4, 2000. On January 30, the assembly delegated its legislative powers to a 21-member National Legislative Commission that served until the National Assembly election of July 30.

National Assembly (*Asamblea Nacional*). The current legislature is a unicameral body of 167 members, including 3 representing indigenous peoples. An August 2008 electoral reform law increased, from 60 to 70 percent, the number of deputies elected directly, with the number chosen by proportional representation dropping from 40 to 30 percent.

In the most recent elections on September 26, 2010, the United Socialist Party of Venezuela and its allies won 98 seats; Democratic Unity Table, 65; and Fatherland for All, 2.

President: Diosdado CABELLO.

CABINET

[as of October 19, 2013]

President	Nicolás Maduro Moros
Executive Vice President	Jorge Arreaza
Vice President for Planning	Jorge Giordani
Vice President for Territorial Development	Rafael Darío Ramírez Carreño
Vice President for Economic Affairs	Nelson Merentes
Vice President for Political Affairs	Elias Jaua Milano
Vice President for Social Affairs	Héctor Rodríguez Castro
Ministers	
Agriculture and Lands	Iván Gil
Commerce	Alejandro Antonio Fleming Cabrera
Communes and Social Protection	Reinaldo Iturriza
Communications and Information	Ernesto Villegas Poljak
Culture	Fidel Barbarito
Defense	Carmen Teresa Meléndez Maniglia [f]
Education	Maryann del Carmen Hanson Flores [f]
Electricity	Jesse Chacón
Energy and Petroleum	Rafael Darío Ramírez Carreño
Environment	Dante Rivas
Finance	Nelson José Merentes Diaz
Food	Félix Osorio Guzmán
Foreign Affairs	Elias Jaua Montano
Health	Isabel Iturria [f]
Higher Education	Pedro Calzadilla
Housing and Habitats	Ricardo Antonio Molina Penaloza
Indigenous Peoples	Aloha Nuñez [f]
Industry	Ricardo José Menéndez Prieto
Interior and Justice	Miguel Rodríguez Torres
Labor and Social Security	María Cristina Iglesias [f]
Penitentiary Services	Maria Iris Varela Rangel [f]
Planning and Finance	Jorge Giordani
President's Office	Carmen Melendez [f]
Public Banking	Rodolfo Marco
Science, Technology, and Intermediate Industry	Manuel Fernández Melendez
Sports	Alejandra Benítez
Tourism	Andrés Izarra
Transportation, Air, and Water	Herbert García Plaza
Transportation and Land	Haiman El Troudi
Women's Affairs and Gender Equality	Andreína Tarazón [f]
Youth	Héctor Rodríguez Castro

[f] = female

INTERGOVERNMENTAL REPRESENTATION

Ambassador to the U.S.: Bernardo Álvarez HERRERA (visa revoked by the United States in 2010).

U.S. Ambassador to Venezuela: (Vacant).

Permanent Representative to the UN: Samuel MONCADA.

IGO Memberships (Non-UN): IADB, ICC, IOM, Mercosur, NAM, OAS, OPEC, CO, WTO.

VIETNAM

Socialist Republic of Vietnam
Cộng Hòa Xã Hội Chủ Nghĩa Việt Nam

Political Status: Communist republic originally proclaimed September 2, 1945; Democratic Republic of Vietnam established in the north on July 21, 1954; Republic of Vietnam established in the south on October 26, 1955; Socialist Republic of Vietnam proclaimed on July 2, 1976, following surrender of the southern government on April 30, 1975; present constitution adopted on April 15, 1992.

Area: 128,402 sq. mi. (332,561 sq. km).

Population: 90,939,819 (2012E—UN); 92,477,857 (2013E—U.S. Census).

Major Urban Centers (metropolitan areas, 2009C, preliminary): HANOI (6,448,837), Ho Chi Minh City (formerly Saigon, 7,123,340), Haiphong (1,837,302), Can Tho (1,187,089), Da Nang (887,069).

Official Language: Vietnamese.

Monetary Unit: Dông (market rate November 1, 2013: 21,110.00 dông = $1US).

President: TRUONG TAN SANG; elected by the National Assembly on July 25, 2011, succeeding NGUYEN MINH TRIET.

Vice President: NGUYEN THI DOAN; elected by the National Assembly on July 25, 2007, succeeding TRUONG MY HOA; reelected on July 25, 2011.

Prime Minister: NGUYEN TAN DUNG; elected by the National Assembly on June 27, 2006, succeeding PHAN VAN KHAI; reelected on July 25, 2007; reelected on July 26, 2011.

General Secretary of the Vietnamese Communist Party: NGUYEN PHU TRONG; appointed by the Central Committee on January 19, 2011, succeeding NONG DUC MANH.

THE COUNTRY

A tropical land of varied climate and topography, Vietnam extends for roughly 1,000 miles along the eastern face of the Indochina Peninsula between the deltas of its two great rivers, the Red River in the north and the Mekong in the south. To the east, the country borders on the Gulf of Tonkin and the South China Sea; in the west, the mountains of the Annamite Chain separate it from Cambodia and Laos. A second mountainous region in the north serves as a partial barrier between Vietnam and China, which historically exercised great influence in Vietnam and provided its name, "Land of the South."

The Vietnamese population is of mixed ethnic stock and includes numerous highland tribes as well as Chinese, Khmer, and other non-Vietnamese peoples. The Viet (Kinh) constitute some 86 percent of the population. Although religion is not encouraged by the state, most Vietnamese are nominally Buddhist—there is a state-sponsored Buddhist Church of Vietnam—or Taoist, with a significant Roman Catholic minority (approximately 7 percent of the total population), particularly in the south. Vietnamese is the national language, while French was long the preferred second language. Women constitute 49 percent of the active labor force, but their participation in party and governmental affairs has traditionally been much less. Women hold 122, or 24.4 percent, of the seats in the current National Assembly.

Northern Vietnam was traditionally a food-deficient area, dependent on supplementary rice and other provisions from the south. It developed a considerable industrial economy, however, based on substantial resources of anthracite coal, chromite, iron, phosphate, tin, and other minerals. About 54 percent of the country's employed labor force works in the agricultural sector, which contributes about 21 percent of GDP, compared with 41.1 percent for industry and 38 percent for services. Manufacturing and mining account for about 15 percent of the employed workforce. As of 2012, crude oil constituted Vietnam's leading export, followed by marine products (mainly frozen seafood), footwear, and electronic goods and components. Wood and wood products, rubber, coffee, and coal have steadily increased in importance. In 2012 Vietnam was the world's largest exporter of rice.

Decentralization of economic planning yielded only marginal overall growth, however, and in 1986 Vietnam enacted a political and economic "renovation" (*Đổi Mới*) program, reportedly modeled after the Soviet Union's perestroika (for an overview of the economy prior to the 1980s, see the 2011 *Handbook*). Radical reforms included fiscal and monetary austerity, a shift away from public sector control of the economy, and an opening of markets to international trade. As a result, the average annual GDP growth rate was about 9 percent for 1992–1997.

For 2000–2008 GDP growth averaged about 7.5 percent annually, but it fell to 5.3 percent in 2009 as a consequence of the international recession. GDP grew by 6.8 percent in 2010 and 5.9 percent the following year. In 2011 inflation more than doubled to 18.7. GDP rose by 5 percent in 2012, while inflation declined to 9.1 percent. GDP per capita that year was $1,527. In its 2012 Doing Business survey, the World Bank ranked Vietnam 99th out of 185 countries.

GOVERNMENT AND POLITICS

Political background. Vietnam's three historic regions—Tonkin in the north, Annam in the center, and Cochin-China in the south—came under French control in 1862–1884 and were later joined with Cambodia and Laos to form the French-ruled Indochinese Union, more commonly called French Indochina. The Japanese, who occupied Indochina in World War II, permitted the establishment on September 2, 1945, of the Democratic Republic of Vietnam (DRV) under HO CHI MINH, the Communist leader of the nationalist resistance movement then known as the Vietminh (*Việt Nam Độc Lập Đồng Minh Hộội,* or Vietnamese Independence League). Although the French on their return to Indochina accorded provisional recognition to the DRV, subsequent negotiations broke down, and in December 1946 the Vietminh initiated military action against French forces.

While fighting with the Vietminh continued, the French in 1949 recognized BAO DAI, former emperor of Annam, as head of state of an independent Vietnam within the French Union. Treaties conceding full Vietnamese independence in association with France were initialed in Paris on June 4, 1954; in practice, however, the jurisdiction of the Bao Dai government was limited to South Vietnam as a consequence of the military successes of the Vietminh, the major defeat suffered by French forces at Dien Bien Phu in May 1954, and the armistice and related agreements concluded in Geneva, Switzerland, July 20–21, 1954. The Geneva accord provided for a temporary division of Vietnam near the 17th parallel into two separately administered zones—Communist in the north and non-Communist in the south—pending an internationally supervised election to be held in 1956. These arrangements were rejected, however, by the Bao Dai government and by the republican regime that succeeded it in South Vietnam in 1955. Vietnam thus remained divided between a northern zone administered by the Communist-ruled DRV and a southern zone administered by the anti-Communist government of the Republic of Vietnam.

Within North Vietnam, a new constitution promulgated in 1960 consolidated the powers of the central government, and elections in 1960 and 1964 reaffirmed the preeminence of Ho Chi Minh, who continued as president of the DRV and chair of the Vietnam Workers' Party (VWP), successor in 1954 to the Indochinese Communist Party (ICP). Ho Chi Minh died in 1969, his party position remaining unfilled in deference to his memory. The political leadership passed to LE DUAN, who had been named first secretary of the VWP nine years earlier.

Communist-led subversive and terrorist activity against the government of South Vietnam resumed in the late 1950s by Vietcong (Vietnamese Communist) resistance elements in a continuation of the earlier anti-French offensive, now supported and directed from the north. Within the south, these operations were sponsored from 1960 onward by a Communist-controlled political organization called the National Front for the Liberation of South Vietnam, or simply the National Liberation Front (NLF). Despite the initiation of U.S. advisory assistance to South Vietnamese military forces in 1954, guerrilla operations by Vietcong and regular North Vietnamese units proved increasingly disruptive.

In 1961 the growth of the Communist-supported insurgency forced NGO DINH DIEM (who had assumed the South Vietnamese presidency following the ouster of Bao Dai in 1955) to assume emergency powers. Popular resentment of his increasingly repressive regime led, however, to his death in a coup d'état that was secretly supported by the United States and directed by Gen. DUONG VAN MINH ("Big Minh") on November 1, 1963. A period of unstable military rule followed. Leadership was held successively by General Minh (to January 1964), Gen. NGUYEN KHANH (to February 1965), and Gen. NGUYEN VAN THIEU, who assumed the functions of head of state in June 1965. The powerful post of prime minister went to Air Marshal NGUYEN CAO KY. By then, concerned that the south was facing military defeat, the United States had begun air operations against selected military targets in the north and was ordering large contingents of its ground forces into action in the south.

In response to U.S. pressure, a new constitution was promulgated on April 1, 1967. Thieu and Ky were elected president and vice president, respectively, on September 3.

On January 31, 1968, a holiday marking the Vietnamese lunar new year (*Tết Nguyên Đán*), Communist forces launched an audacious offensive throughout the south, including in Saigon and other urban centers. Although viewed by most historians as unsuccessful in strictly military terms, the Tet offensive had deep political consequences. In the United States it served to crystallize growing antiwar sentiment and contributed to the decision of U.S. president Lyndon Johnson not to seek reelection. On March 31 Johnson announced a cessation of bombing in all but the southern area of North Vietnam, adjacent to the demilitarized zone straddling the 17th parallel. The action proved more successful than a number of earlier bombing halts in paving the way for peace talks. Preliminary discussions between U.S. and North Vietnamese representatives were initiated in Paris on May 13, while expanded talks began in Paris on January 18, 1969. It was not until September 1972, however, following major U.S. troop withdrawals and the failure of another major Communist offensive, that Hanoi agreed to drop its insistence on imposing a Communist regime in the south and accepted a 1971 U.S. proposal for a temporary cease-fire.

A peace agreement was concluded on January 27, 1973, on the basis of extensive private discussions between U.S. secretary of state Henry Kissinger and DRV negotiator LE DUC THO. (Although the two were jointly awarded the Nobel Peace Prize in October 1973, Le Duc Tho declined the award, stating that peace had not yet been achieved.) The agreement provided for a withdrawal of all remaining U.S. forces and for political talks between the South Vietnamese and the Vietcong aimed at the establishment of a National Council of National Reconciliation and Concord (NCNRC). The Saigon government and the Provisional Revolutionary Government of South Vietnam failed, however, to reach agreement on the council's composition.

Despite North Vietnam's formal support of the peace accord, it was estimated that as of May 1974 some 210,000 North Vietnamese troops were fighting in the south, as compared to 160,000 at the time of the 1972 cease-fire. A new Communist offensive, launched in late 1974, resulted in the loss of Phuoc Long Province, 70 miles north of Saigon, in early January 1975. By late March, in the wake of a near total collapse of discipline within the South Vietnamese army, the cities of Hué and Da Nang had fallen. On April 21, as the Communist forces neared Saigon, President Thieu announced his resignation, and Vice President TRAN VAN HUONG was sworn in as his successor. Huong himself resigned on April 28 in favor of Gen. Duong Van Minh, who called for a cease-fire and immediate negotiations with representatives of the North Vietnamese and the NLF's military wing, the People's Liberation Armed Forces (PLAF). The appeal was rejected, and on April 30 Communist forces entered Saigon, and the South Vietnamese government surrendered.

On June 6, 1975, the Provisional Revolutionary Government under the nominal presidency of HUYNH TAN PHAT was invested as the government of South Vietnam, although real power was exercised by PHAM HUNG, fourth-ranked member of the VWP Politburo and secretary of the party's South Vietnamese Committee. On April 25, 1976, a reunified Vietnam held an election for an enlarged National Assembly, which on July 2 proclaimed the Socialist Republic of Vietnam. On the same day it named TON DUC THANG, the incumbent president of North Vietnam, as head of state, and it appointed two vice presidents: NGUYEN LUONG BANG, theretofore vice president of the DRV, and NGUYEN HUU THO, leader of the southern NLF. PHAM VAN DONG, previously the DRV premier, was designated to head a cabinet composed largely of former North Vietnamese ministers, with the addition of six South Vietnamese. On December 20 the VWP concluded a congress in Hanoi by changing its name to the Vietnamese Communist Party (VCP) and adopting a series of guidelines designed to realize the nation's "socialist goals."

Under a revised constitution, a new National Assembly was elected on April 26, 1981, and a five-member collective presidency (Council of State) designated on July 4. The second-ranked member of the VCP Politburo, TRUONG CHINH, was named council chair (thus becoming nominal head of state). The third-ranked Pham Van Dong continued as chair of the Council of Ministers.

Longtime party leader Le Duan died in July 1986. The VCP Central Committee named Truong Chinh as his successor. However, in a remarkable change of leadership at the Sixth VCP Congress in December, NGUYEN VAN LINH was named general secretary, with Chinh, Dong, and Tho being among those retired from the Politburo. A major governmental reorganization followed. In June 1987 Gen. VO CHI CONG succeeded Chinh as chair of the Council of State, and Hung replaced Dong as chair of the Council of Ministers. Following Hung's death in March 1988, Sr. Gen. VO VAN KIET, theretofore a deputy chair of the Council of Ministers, was named acting chair. In an unprecedented contest in June, the nominee of the party's Central Committee, DO MUOI, was forced to stand against Vo Van Kiet for election as permanent chair, winning the office by only 64 percent of the National Assembly vote.

Another major restructuring of the party leadership occurred at the Seventh VCP Congress in June 1991, when 7 of 12 Politburo members were dropped and Do Muoi succeeded Nguyen Van Linh as general secretary. The party shake-up was paralleled by sweeping government changes when the Eighth National Assembly met for an unusually lengthy 9th session in July and August. A new Council of State was named (albeit with Vo Chi Cong continuing as chair), as well as a new Council of Ministers under Vo Van Kiet. The legislature also initiated debate on a new constitution, the draft of which was completed at the body's 10th session in December and approved at the 11th session in April 1992. In September the National Assembly named Sr. Gen. LE DUC ANH and NGUYEN THI BINH to the newly created posts of president and vice president, respectively, while reappointing Vo Van Kiet as head of government, with the new title of prime minister.

In September 1997 the National Assembly chose TRAN DUC LUONG and PHAN VAN KHAI to succeed Le Duc Anh and Vo Van Kiet as president and prime minister, respectively. In December the VCP Central Committee elected the decidedly more conservative Lt. Gen. LE KHA PHIEU as general secretary in place of Do Muoi.

Meeting at its Ninth Party Congress, the VCP on April 22, 2001, replaced Le Kha Phieu with economic reformer NONG DUC MANH, a member of the northern Tay ethnic minority and theretofore chair of the National Assembly. No major changes in the government occurred until a new cabinet was installed on August 8, 2002, during the opening session of the expanded, 498-seat National Assembly, which had been elected on May 19. President Luong and Prime Minister Khai were reelected on July 24 and 25, respectively, by the legislature, which chose TRUONG MY HOA as vice president.

The Tenth Congress of the VCP, held April 18–25, 2006, marked the departure from the party leadership of President Tran Duc Luong and Prime Minister Phan Van Khai. On June 27, as expected, the National Assembly elected NGUYEN MINH TRIET as president (to complete the remaining year in Tran's term) and confirmed NGUYEN TAN DUNG as prime minister. Following the National Assembly election of May 20, 2007, the legislature reelected the president and prime minister on July 24 and 25, respectively.

At the 11th Congress of the VCP from January 12 to 19, 2011, NGUYEN PHU TRONG was elected party chair, and TRUONG TAN SANG was selected as president. Following the assembly election of May 22, the legislature formally elected Sang president on July 25. Dung was reappointed as prime minister by the president on July 25 and reelected by the assembly the following day.

Constitution and government. Upon reunification in 1976, the DRV constitution of January 1, 1960, was put into effect throughout the country pending adoption of a new basic law that on December 18, 1980, received unanimous legislative approval. The 1980 document defined the Socialist Republic as a "state of proletarian dictatorship" advancing toward socialism, and identified the Communist Party as "the only force leading the state and society." A unicameral National Assembly, the highest organ of state authority, was mandated to elect a Council of State as the state's collective presidency; administrative functions were to be directed by a Council of Ministers, appointed by and responsible to the assembly.

Under the 1992 constitution the Council of State was abolished in favor of a president who is elected by and from within the assembly. The chief executive nominates a vice president, a prime minister, a chief justice of the Supreme Court, and a head of the Supreme People's Inspectorate, all of whom must be approved by the assembly. The party continues to define overall state policy but no longer conducts its day-to-day implementation. In 2001 the National Assembly approved 24 constitutional amendments, including recognition of private enterprise as a legitimate economic sector. Another change permits the National Assembly to consider no-confidence motions against government leaders.

The judicial system is headed by the Supreme People's Court and the procurator general of the Supreme People's Organ of Control. People's Courts, Military Tribunals, and People's Organs of Control operate at the local level. Economic courts to adjudicate business disputes were authorized in 1993, while the country's first comprehensive civil code entered into effect in 1996.

All communications media are controlled and operated by the government, the Communist Party, or subordinate organizations. A 2006 Decree on Cultural and Information Activities requires prepublication review of articles and sets fines for using anonymous sources, defaming unspecified "national heroes," distributing "reactionary ideology," and revealing "party secrets, state secrets, military secrets, and economic secrets." Internet access is closely monitored, and postings deemed adverse to state interests may also result in prosecution. In 2013 the media watchdog group, Reporters Without Borders ranked Vietnam 172nd out of 179 in terms of freedom of the press.

For administrative purposes the country is divided into 59 provinces and 5 centrally administered municipalities (Can Tho, Da Nang, Haiphong, Hanoi, and Ho Chi Minh City); subdivisions include districts, towns, and provincial capitals. Each administrative unit elects a People's Council, which then selects a People's Committee to serve as an executive.

Foreign relations. Prior to reunification, North Vietnamese external policy combined traditional Vietnamese nationalism with Communist ideology and tactics. Relations with most other Communist nations were close, and aid from the People's Republic of China, the Soviet Union, and Eastern Europe was essential to both the DRV's industrial development and its military campaigns in the south. Consequently, the DRV avoided commitments to either side in the Sino-Soviet dispute.

An application submitted by North Vietnam in 1975 to join the UN was blocked by U.S. action in the Security Council, as was a second application submitted on behalf of the newly unified state in 1976. In May 1977 the United States withdrew its objection after Hanoi agreed to provide additional information on the fate of missing U.S. servicemen, and the socialist republic was admitted to the world body in September.

The DRV had long been involved in the internal affairs of both Laos and Cambodia (Kampuchea), where it supported insurgent movements, partly as a means of keeping open its supply routes to South Vietnam. Following reunification, Hanoi concluded a number of mutual cooperation agreements with Laos that some observers viewed as leaving that country little more than a province of Vietnam. Collaterally, relations with the *Khmer Rouge*–led government of Democratic Kampuchea deteriorated sharply, resulting in numerous military encounters along the two countries' common frontier and a severance of diplomatic relations in December 1977. The clashes escalated through 1978 and prompted a Vietnamese invasion of its neighbor at the end of the year. In January 1979 Phnom Penh fell to the Vietnamese, supported by a small force of dissident Khmers, and a pro-Vietnamese People's Republic of Kampuchea was proclaimed under Heng Samrin, a former member of the Kampuchean General Staff. Some 200,000 Vietnamese troops remained in the country.

Chinese forces invaded northern Vietnam on February 17, 1979, and occupied a number of border towns, suffering heavy casualties before withdrawing in mid-March. The incursion was described by Beijing as a "limited operation" designed to "teach Hanoi a lesson" after failure to resolve a number of long-standing disputes—primarily, the validity of late-19th-century border agreements between France and the Chinese empire, jurisdiction over territorial waters in the Gulf of Tonkin, and sovereignty over the Paracel and Spratly islands in the South China Sea. The last island group (also claimed in whole or in part by Brunei, Malaysia, Philippines, and Taiwan) was considered particularly important because of its strategic location astride shipping lanes and the possibility (subsequently confirmed) of oil and gas reserves in its vicinity. Peace talks undertaken by Hanoi and Beijing in April 1979 were broken off by the Chinese in March 1980. Intermittent border conflicts continued thereafter.

In January 1989 Hanoi dispatched a delegation to Beijing for the first high-level discussions between the two governments in eight years. On September 26, 1989, Vietnam announced that it had withdrawn all its troops from Cambodia, a claim disputed by China. In November 1991 high-level talks resulted in normalization of Vietnam-China relations after a 20-year estrangement, although it was not until October 1993 that the two countries agreed to negotiations aimed at resolving their various territorial disputes.

Following the Communist collapse in Eastern Europe and the 1991 dissolution of the Soviet Union (on which Vietnam had remained heavily dependent for economic assistance), regional relations with Japan, South Korea, Thailand, Brunei, and Malaysia improved. In 1992 Australia and Japan formally renewed aid to Vietnam. Relations also improved with the United States, which eased its long-standing trade embargo. In December U.S. President George H. W. Bush authorized U.S. companies to initiate commercial relations with Vietnam. Less than two years later, in February 1994, U.S. President Bill Clinton announced an end to the 19-year U.S. economic embargo in view of "significant and tangible results" in the search for American servicemen missing in action.

In 1995 there were more than 46,000 Vietnamese expatriates in numerous detention camps, from Thailand to Hong Kong. In mid-March representatives of 30 countries met in Geneva and agreed that 40,000 "boat people" in Hong Kong and Southeast Asia would be returned by early 1996, triggering riots by detainees in Hong Kong, Malaysia, and the Philippines. An aid program sponsored by the European Union assisted some 50,000 returnees before concluding in 1999.

Declaring that it was time to "bind up our own wounds," U.S. President Clinton extended full diplomatic recognition to Vietnam on July 11, 1995. (In November 2000 Clinton became the first U.S. president to visit the unified Vietnam, and in June 2007 Nguyen Minh Triet became the first president of the socialist republic to visit the United States.) Vietnam's admission to the Association of Southeast Asian Nations (ASEAN) was formalized a month later. In 1996 Vietnam officially applied to join the Asia-Pacific Economic Cooperation (APEC) forum, to which it was formally admitted in 1998.

In October 1998 Vietnam and China announced their intention to resolve land and Gulf of Tonkin boundary disputes by the year 2000. The two signed a land border treaty on December 30, 1999, and a maritime agreement in December 2000, although the latter did not resolve the Spratly and Paracel disputes. (Actual demarcation of the land border was finally concluded in 2008.) On November 4, 2002, China and the ten ASEAN members signed a voluntary Declaration on the Conduct of Parties in the South China Sea that, while not a formal code of conduct, pledged to seek nonviolent solutions to the competing territorial claims.

In December 1998 South Korea's President Kim Dae Jung apologized for sending some 300,000 troops to supplement U.S. forces during the Vietnam War. Prime Minister Khai, noting that Vietnam required neither an apology nor reparations, called instead for a "progressive and future-oriented bilateral relationship."

In September 2000 Vietnam and Russia reached agreement on settling Soviet-era debts, with Hanoi pledging to repay $1.7 billion over 23 years, mostly through business concessions. In February 2001 Russian President Vladimir Putin became the first Russian head of state to visit Vietnam.

Vietnam's accession to the World Trade Organization (WTO) was given the highest priority by the Communist government. In May 2006 Vietnam overcame the last major hurdle: completion of a new bilateral trade and investment agreement with the United States. In addition to opening up Vietnam's banking, securities, and insurance markets to foreign companies, the pact also ended U.S. quotas on the importation of Vietnamese garments, cut Vietnamese tariffs, and cleared the way for foreigners to participate in wholesale and retail trade. On November 7 the WTO voted to admit Vietnam, which ratified the accession protocol on November 28. On January 10, 2007, Vietnam officially became a member.

On October 31, 2010, the prime ministers of Vietnam and Japan signed an agreement to construct two nuclear reactors in Ninh Thuan province. Also in October, Vietnam demanded the release of a fishing vessel and its crew after Chinese naval units detained the fishermen in the disputed waters of the Paracel Islands.

In February 2011 Thailand announced the closure of the last refugee center for Montagnards who fled Vietnam. On May 26 an incident between a Chinese naval vessel and a Vietnamese survey ship highlighted tensions over the disputed Spratly and Paracel Islands. There were large protests outside the Chinese embassy in Hanoi, and the Vietnamese navy conducted drills in the area of the disputed islands. In June Vietnam and the United States initiated joint programs to remove or destroy unexploded ordnance from the Vietnam conflict and to restore areas damaged by the defoliant Agent Orange. In October Vietnam and India signed a number of economic agreements in an effort to boost trade between the two countries. The following month, Russia agreed to provide an $8 billion loan to construct nuclear power plants.

Twenty-one Vietnamese fishermen were detained by Chinese naval forces for operating in Chinese-claimed waters near the Paracel Islands in March 2012. They were released the following month. In June the Vietnamese legislature enacted a law reaffirming the country's sovereignty over the Paracel and Spratly Islands. The measure was condemned by China. Meanwhile, Vietnam protested a Chinese call for proposals from foreign oil companies for exploratory drilling in the disputed waters.

On March 20, 2013, a Chinese naval vessel fired on four Vietnamese fishing boats, sinking one, in the waters near the Paracel Islands. Following a visit to Vietnam by Russia's defense minister, reports indicated that Moscow sought a new lease for a naval base at Cam Ranh Bay. Also in March, Japan announced it would provide $2 billion in development assistance to Vietnam. Furthermore, in August, Japan and Vietnam agreed to increase law enforcement cooperation, including training and police intelligence collaboration. Meanwhile, in 2013, Vietnam made substantial progress on free trade treaties with the EU and South Korea, with expectations to finalize both accords in 2014.

Current issues. In October 2009 nine individuals were convicted and sentenced to between two and six years in prison for engaging in activities deemed harmful to national security—in this case, hanging prodemocracy banners, passing out leaflets, writing articles critical of the government, and posting similar material on the Internet. All were accused of participating in Bloc 8406, a prodemocracy group founded in 2006 (see Opposition Movements, in the Political Parties section, below). Another prominent dissident, LE CONG DINH, a prodemocracy and human rights lawyer, had been arrested in June 2009 on charges of colluding with other dissidents and foreigners to subvert the government. He and three other activists were convicted of subversion in January 2010 and sentenced to between 4 and 16 years in prison. A week later another court handed down a four-year sentence to PHAM THANH NGHIEN for providing propaganda to "overseas reactionary websites."

The release of Fr. Nguyen Van Ly from prison in March 2010 did little to assuage critics of Vietnam's human rights record in the U.S. Congress. A number of leading senators and representatives called for Vietnam to be relisted as a "country of particular concern" for violations of religious freedoms. On the whole, however, cordial relations between Vietnam and the United States continued. In August the two countries conducted their first joint naval exercises. In December a conference of donor states and organizations, including the World Bank, pledged $7.9 billion in economic development for Vietnam.

On May 6, 2011, Vietnamese security forces clashed with Hmong protestors in Dien Bien. Reports indicated that more than 60 Hmong were killed and several hundred arrested. Flooding in June and July killed 28, destroyed 2,000 homes, and damaged more than 72,000 hectares of crops in the northern regions of the country. In August 10,535 prisoners, including political detainees, were granted amnesty to celebrate the country's independence day.

On March 30, 2012, nine executives of Vietnam's largest shipbuilding corporation, including its chairman PHAN THANH BINH, were convicted of fraud and mismanagement after the company accumulated debts of more than $4.5 billion and defaulted on a $600 million loan payment. Binh was an ally of Prime Minister Dung. In August, another Dung ally, banking mogul NGUYEN DUC KIEN, was arrested for financial mismanagement of the country's largest bank. The arrests and uncertainty over the economy led to a dramatic $4 billion decline in the stock market and a spike in inflation, prompting calls for further economic reforms.

In January 2013, 14 dissidents were convicted of sedition for online posts and blogs and sentenced to between three and 13 years in prison. The government also contended that they belonged to the exile group the Vietnam Reform Party (see Political Parties, below).

Beginning in March 2013, the government allowed citizens to post comments and suggestions in an online forum on a draft constitution. The initiative was an effort to demonstrate more openness, but reports indicated that those who posted highly critical commentaries or who advocated for radical changes faced fines and harassment. A committee to draft a new constitution began work in August with a goal of submitting recommendations in October. In May the finance minister was replaced, reportedly as part of an effort to accelerate economic growth.

POLITICAL PARTIES

The Communist party apparatus of North Vietnam operated for many years as the Vietnam Workers' Party—VWP (*Đảng Lao Động Việt Nam*). The VWP was formed in 1954 as successor to the Indochinese Communist Party (founded in 1930 and ostensibly dissolved in 1954) and was the controlling party of North Vietnam's National Fatherland Front (NFF). In South Vietnam, the core of the Provisional Revolutionary Government formed in 1969 was the National Front for the Liberation of South Vietnam (*Mặt Trận Giải Phóng Miền Nam Việt Nam,* or the National Liberation Front—NLF), which had been organized in 1960 by some 20 groups opposed to the policies of President Diem.

In 1976 representatives of the NFF, the NLF, and other organizations met in Hanoi to organize an all-inclusive **Vietnam Fatherland Front**—VFF (*Mặt Trận Tổ Quốc Việt Nam*), which was formally launched during a congress held in Ho Chi Minh City on January 31–February 4, 1977. In addition to the Vietnamese Communist Party (VCP), the front includes various trade union, peasants', women's, youth, and other mass organizations. Under an electoral law approved by the National Assembly in 1980, the VFF is responsible for nominating candidates in all constituencies, in consultation with local groups.

Leading Party:

Vietnamese Communist Party—VCP (*Đảng Cộng Sản Việt Nam*). The VCP is structured on traditional Communist party lines. A party Congress meets at five-year intervals to select a Central Committee, a Politburo that functions as the executive body, and an administrative Secretariat. The ruling party's present name was adopted by the VWP at its Fourth Congress in 1976. In 1996 the Eighth Party Congress created a five-member Standing Board to replace the larger Secretariat, but the Secretariat was reinstituted at the Ninth Party Congress in 2001.

At a party plenum in June 1997 the Central Committee chose Phan Van Khai to replace Vo Van Kiet as prime minister (pending assembly approval) and voted to limit local officials to two five-year terms (the appointments were previously for life). The committee members were unable, however, to decide on a replacement for President Le Duc Anh, who, along with Vo Van Kiet, had been left off the candidate list for the National Assembly elections due in July. Subsequently, the Committee gave the nod to Tran Duc Luong, and in September its choices were approved by the National Assembly.

In December 1997 the Central Committee elected Lt. Gen. Le Kha Phieu as the party's new general secretary, replacing Do Muoi, who joined Le Duc Ahn and Vo Van Kiet in resigning from the Politburo. All three were subsequently named advisers to the VCP Central Committee.

In January 1999 the party expelled TRAN DO, a retired general and a Central Committee member, for advocating open elections and freedom of expression. His subsequent request to publish a newspaper was denied. He died in August 2002.

The Ninth Party Congress was held April 19–22, 2001. Reportedly, the outgoing Politburo had recommended a second term for General Secretary Le Kha Phieu but was resisted by the Central Committee, which settled on the chair of the National Assembly, Nong Duc Manh.

Meeting April 18–25, 2006, the 1,176 delegates to the Tenth Party Congress elected a 160-member Central Committee (plus 21 alternate members), a Politburo of 14, and an 8-member Secretariat. Although Nong Duc Manh stayed on as general secretary, President Tran Duc Luong, Prime Minister Phan Van Khai, and National Assembly Chair NGUYEN VAN AN all retired from the leadership, signaling their imminent departure from government.

At the 11th Party Congress from January 12 to 19, 2011, the 1,400 delegates elected Nguyen Phu Trong to replace Manh, who retired, and Truong Tan Sang as president. The Congress approved an expanded Central Committee with 175 members. The Committee subsequently elected the 14 members of the Politburo, including Tong Thi Phong, only the second woman elected to the body. The Secretariat was enlarged to ten members. In May 2012 the central committee began a series of meetings on constitutional reforms designed to privatize the public sector and reduce corruption in government and industry.

In August 2013 reports emerged that LE HEIU DANG, a dissident member of the party who had left the VCP along with others to form a new grouping, the **Social Democratic Party.**

General Secretary: NGUYEN PHU TRONG.

Other Members of Politburo: LE HONG ANH, LE THANH HAI (Chair, Ho Chi Minh City People's Committee), TRUONG TAN SANG (State President), NGUYEN SINH HUNG (Chair, National Assembly), NGUYEN TAN DUNG (Prime Minister), PHAM QUANG NGHI (Chair, Hanoi People's Committee), Gen. PHUNG QUANG THANH (Minister of National Defense), TO HUY RUA (Chair of the Central Information and Education Committee), TONG THI PHONG (Deputy Chairwoman of the National Assembly), TRAN DAI QUANG (Deputy Minister of Public Security), NGO VAN DU (Chair, Inspectorate Commission), DINH THE HUYNH (Chief of the Committee for Propaganda and Education), NGUYEN XUAN PHUC (Chair of the Government Office).

Secretariat: NGUYEN PHU TRONG, TRUONG TAN SANG, LE HONG ANH, TO HUY RUA, NGO VAN DU, DINH THE HUYNH, NGO XUAN LICH, TRUONG HOA BINH, HA THI KHIET, NGUYEN THI KIM NGAN.

Opposition Movements:

The government actively suppresses prodemocracy movements and rigorously prosecutes their most outspoken proponents. On April 8, 2006, a total of 118 prodemocracy supporters signed a "Manifesto 2006 on Freedom and Democracy for Vietnam," which gave birth to the **Bloc 8406.** Signers included PHAN VAN LOI and Nguyen Van Ly, the Catholic priest who was imprisoned in March 2007 for distributing material deemed antigovernment by the state. In 2006 a dissident **Democratic Party of Vietnam**—DPV (*Đảng Dân Chủ Việt Nam*), named after an earlier party that had been disbanded in 1988, was founded by HOANG MINH CHINH, who died in 2008. Activists associated with the DPV have also been prosecuted by the government. DPV vice secretary NGAI NGUYEN met with U.S. president Obama in March 2012.

Expatriate Vietnamese in the United States, Europe, and elsewhere have established numerous political groups, many of which claim insurgent or other support within Vietnam. Examples include the **Vietnam Populist Party** (*Đảng Vì Dân*—DVD, also known as the For the People Party) is based in Houston, Texas, and the international **Vietnam Reform Party** (*Việt Nam Canh Tân Cách Mạng Đảng—Việt Tân*), chaired by DO HOANG DIEM. The *Việt Tân* dates from 2004, when it succeeded the National United Front for the Freedom of Vietnam (NUFLV).

LEGISLATURE

The present **National Assembly** (*Quốc Hội*) is a unicameral body of 500 members serving five-year terms. For the most recent election of May 22, 2011, the Fatherland Front approved 827 candidates, including about 117 nonparty candidates and 15 described as self-nominated. The Vietnam Communist Party won 458 seats, with nonparty candidates winning 38 and self-nominees winning 4.

Chair: NGUYEN SINH HUNG.

CABINET

[as of September 15, 2013]

Prime Minister	Nguyen Tan Dung
Deputy Prime Ministers	Hoang Trung Hai
	Nguyen Xuan Phuc
	Nguyen Thien Nhan
	Vu Van Ninh
Ministers	
Agriculture and Rural Development	Cao Duc Phat
Construction	Trinh Dinh Dung
Culture, Sports, and Tourism	Hoang Tuan Anh
Education and Training	Pham Vu Luan
Finance	Dinh Tien Dung
Foreign Affairs	Pham Binh Minh
Industry and Trade	Vu Huy Hoang
Information and Communication	Nguyen Bac Son
Internal Affairs	Nguyen Thai Binh
Justice	Ha Hung Cuong
Labor, War Invalids, and Social Welfare	Pham Thi Hai Chuyen
National Defense	Gen. Phung Quang Thanh
Natural Resources and Environment	Nguyen Minh Quang
Planning and Investment	Bui Quang Vinh
Public Health	Nguyen Thi Kim Tien
Public Security	Gen. Tran Dai Quang
Science and Technology	Nguyen Quan
Transport	Dinh La Thang
Chair, Committee of Ethnic Minorities	Giang Seo Phu
Director, Government Office	Vu Duc Dam
Governor, State Bank	Nguyen Van Binh
Inspector General	Huynh Phong Tranh

INTERGOVERNMENTAL REPRESENTATION

Ambassador to the U.S.: NGUYEN Cuong Ouoc.

U.S. Ambassador to Vietnam: David SHEAR.

Permanent Representative to the UN: LE Hoai Trung.

IGO Memberships (Non-UN): ADB, APEC, ASEAN, IOM, NAM, WTO.

YEMEN

Republic of Yemen
al-Jumhuriyah al-Yamaniyah

Political Status: Independent Islamic Arab republic established by the merger of the former Yemen Arab Republic (North Yemen) and the People's Democratic Republic of Yemen (South Yemen) on May 22, 1990.

Area: 205,355 sq. mi. (531,869 sq. km), encompassing 75,290 sq. mi. (130,065 sq. km) of the former Yemen Arab Republic and 195,000 sq. mi. (336,869 sq. km) of the former People's Democratic Republic of Yemen.

Population: 25,645,365 (2012E—UN); 25,408,288 (2013E—U.S. Census).

Major Urban Center (including suburbs, 2005E): SANA (1,625,000).

Official Language: Arabic.

Monetary Unit: Yemeni Rial (market rate November 1, 2013: 214.80 rials = $1US).

President: Abd Rabbo Mansour HADI (General People's Congress), elected to an interim two-year term on February 21, 2012.

Vice President: (vacant)

Prime Minister: Mohammed Salem Basindwa (General People's Congress); appointed by vice president Hadi on November 27, 2011.

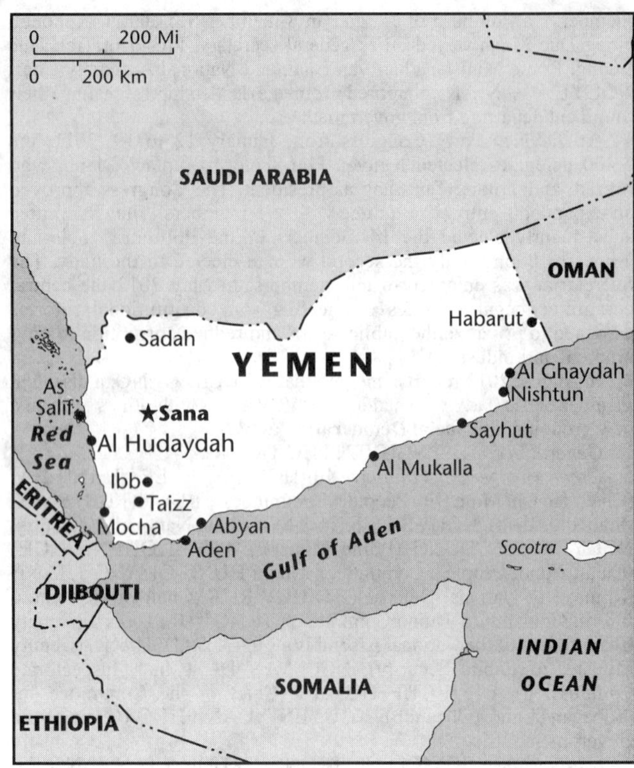

THE COUNTRY

Located at the southern corner of the Arabian Peninsula, where the Red Sea meets the Gulf of Aden, the Republic of Yemen shares a lengthy but until recently largely undefined northern border with Saudi Arabia and a narrow eastern border with Oman (formally demarcated in 1992). Hot, semidesert terrain separates the Red Sea and Gulf coasts from a mountainous interior. The people are predominantly Arab and are divided into two Muslim religious communities: the Zaidi of the Shiite sect in the north and east and the Shaffii community of the Sunni sect in the south and southwest. Tribal influences remain strong, often taking priority over formal governmental activity outside of urban areas. The annual population growth rate was an estimated 2.8 percent between 2005 and 2010, and the fertility rate was 5.3 children per woman. A third of Yemen's workforce is unemployed, and more than 40 percent of the population survives on under $2 a day.

As a result of topographical extremes, Yemeni farmers produce a variety of crops, including cotton (the leading export), grains, fruits, coffee, tobacco, and *qat* (a mild narcotic leaf, which is chewed daily by an estimated 90 percent of the northern population and is estimated to account for nearly 50 percent of GDP). However, the crops do not adequately feed the population.

Yemen is marked by conservative religious views that have limited women's participation in civil affairs. However, these viewpoints have waxed and waned in accordance with political and social developments. In the former Yemen Arab Republic, purdah (the seclusion of women) precluded public life for women; by contrast, the Marxist government of the former People's Democratic Republic of Yemen emphasized women's rights. Prior to the 1990 Iraqi invasion of Kuwait, a labor shortage created by the exodus of more than a million Yemeni men to work outside the country increased women's responsibility in subsistence agriculture. The latest constitution granted women suffrage, but observers subsequently cited a turn to conservative Islam that led, inter alia, to the legalization of polygamy and the adoption of conservative Muslim dress by women in the previously more liberal south. In recent years, Yemen has made progress in construction, transportation, and trade in the non-oil sector, facilitated by privatization laws, a bank reform plan, and the establishment of an anticorruption authority. Nevertheless, millions of dollars in international aid have been withheld because of little progress in rooting out corruption.

In 2011, protests against President Salih and the political stalemate that ensued brought Yemen's economy to the brink of collapse, as the country faced shortages of fuel, food, water, electricity, and internal security. The IMF reported that GDP decreased 10.5 percent for the year, with Yemen's combination of crises and shortages costing the economy approximately $5 billion. Of special concern was the availability and cost of water: since the start of the political crisis in February 2011, the price of water increased by up to 1,000 percent. General inflation for 2011 was 17.6 percent. Adding further injury to a bleak economic landscape, oil production capacity was diminished from 2011 through 2013 as saboteurs blew up pipelines and damaged oil production facilities.

Civil discord significantly diminished after President Hadi took office in February 2012, but security remained elusive. As a result the economy continued to contract, albeit at a slower rate than 2011. The IMF concluded that Yemen's 2012 GDP declined by 0.09 percent, while inflation moderated slightly to 17.1 percent. Using its Rapid Credit Facility, the IMF approved an emergency loan of $94 million to Yemen in 2012, and Saudi Arabia donated $2 billion worth of fuel. Oil minister Hisham ABDALLAH reported in July 2012 that attacks on the country's oil production infrastructure had cost Yemen over $4 billion in revenue. IMF economists reported modest GDP growth for 2013 of 4.4 percent, and an easing of inflation to 7.5 percent. The economic forecast for 2014 was a GDP increase of 5.4 percent, and an inflation increase of 8.7 percent.

GOVERNMENT AND POLITICS

Political background. ***Yemen Arab Republic (YAR).*** Former site of the Kingdom of Sheba and an early center of Near Eastern civilization, the territory subsequently known as North Yemen fell under the rule of the Ottoman Turks in the 16th century. The withdrawal of Turkish forces in 1918 made it possible for Imam YAHYA Muhammad Hamid al-Din, the traditional ruler of the Zaidi religious community, to gain political supremacy. The imamate persisted until September 1962 when a series of uprisings against the absolute regime of the imams culminated in the installation of a group of army officers under Col. (later Field Marshal) Abdallah al-SALAL. Modern governmental institutions were established with the adoption of a new constitution in late 1970 and the election of the Consultative Council in early 1971—which later morphed into the Presidential Council. On July 17, 1978, the four-member Presidential Council appointed Maj. Ali Abdallah SALIH president of the republic, while Abd al-Aziz Abd al-GHANI remained prime minister.

Salih's early presidency was tested by continuing conflicts between republican and traditional groups, and the incursion in early 1979 of South Yemeni forces who were joined by the rebel leftist National Democratic Front (NDF). A mediation agreement brokered by the Arab League brought about a cease-fire and the withdrawal of southern troops. Unification talks between Sana and Aden began soon after (see Republic of Yemen, below, for information on negotiations leading to unification with the People's Democratic Republic of Yemen and political developments from 1990 to the present).

People's Democratic Republic of Yemen (PDRY). British control of South Yemen began with the occupation of Aden in 1839 and gradually extended into what came to be known as the Western and Eastern Protectorates. Aden was ruled as part of British India until 1937, when it became a separate Crown colony. On November 30, 1967, Britain handed the territory over to the area's strongest political organization, the left-wing Nationalist Front (NF). The country rapidly emerged as a center of left-wing revolutionary nationalist agitation in South Arabia, and the country's name was changed in December 1970 to the People's Democratic Republic of Yemen. Procommunist factions subsequently held power through 1978, when the NF was reorganized and retained political control as the Yemeni Socialist Party (YSP). In February 1986 the YSP Central Committee named Ali Salim al-BEIDH as its secretary general.

Republic of Yemen. In the fall of 1981 unification talks between North Yemen's President Ali Abdallah Salih and his South Yemen counterpart, Ali Nasir MUHAMMAD, culminated in an agreement signed in Aden on December 2 to establish a Yemen Council that would promote political, economic, and social integration. On December 1, 1989, a draft joint constitution called for an integrated multiparty state headed by the five-member Presidential Council. The new basic law was implemented on May 22, 1990, after ratification by the constituent states' respective parliaments. Newly promoted General Salih assumed the presidency of the Republic of Yemen, and the PDRY's al-Beidh was named vice president for what was initially proclaimed a 30-month transitional term.

The first general elections on April 27, 1993, handed Salih's General People's Congress (GPC) a majority; it formed a coalition with the conservative Yemeni Congregation for Reform (*Islah*) and the YSP, and the parties shared seats on the new Presidential Council. In February 1994 sporadic fighting between military units representing the north and south broke into a full-fledged war, as Salih declared a state of emergency on May 5. On May 21 al-Beidh announced the south's succession from the union and the formation of an independent Democratic Republic of Yemen, although no international recognition was forthcoming. Northern forces secured control of Aden on July 7, effectively ending the short-lived succession.

In September 1994 the House of Representatives elected Salih to a new five-year presidential term, and in October Salih appointed Maj. Gen. Abdurabu Mansour HADI as vice president and named former YAR prime minister al-Ghani as prime minister of the first postwar government. Peaceful parliamentary elections held in April 1997 were broadly viewed as an important step toward improving Yemen's image as a stable country genuinely committed to democracy. Among other things, the participation of women as candidates and voters earned praise from the West.

In the country's first direct presidential election on September 23, 1999, Salih won 96.3 percent of the vote, though only one challenger was sanctioned under controversial electoral regulations. Subsequently, a national referendum on February 20, 2001, extended the presidential term from five to seven years, extended the legislature's term from four to six years, and enlarged the Shura Council (see Constitution and government, below).

In legislative elections on April 27, 2003, the GPC significantly increased its majority, winning 238 seats in comparison to the YSP's 7 and *Islah*'s 46. Some accusations of vote fraud surfaced, and polling-day violence resulted in 3 dead and 15 injured. Thereafter, a major cabinet reshuffle included the creation of a new ministry of human rights, headed by a woman.

In 2005 President Salih announced that he would not seek reelection in 2006, claiming he would turn leadership over to "young blood." A major cabinet reshuffle on February 11, 2006, replaced 16 members, resulting in a cabinet in which all ministers were members of the GPC. Despite his earlier pledge, Salih ultimately registered as a presidential candidate in 2006 and in September was reelected to a third term with 77.2 percent of the vote. Next among the president's challengers was Faisal bin SHAMLAN, a former oil minister and nominee of the Joint Meeting Parties (JMP), a coalition of oppositional parties (see Political Parties and Groups, below). Salih was sworn in for a seven-year term on September 27. The following year President Salih appointed Electricity Minister Ali Muhammad MUJAWAR of the GPC as prime minister. Mujawar named a new cabinet on April 4 and was sworn in along with the new government on April 7, 2007.

The country's first election of provincial governors in May 2008—whereby governors were indirectly elected by members of the municipal councils—resulted in the GPC winning the governorship of Sana and 16 other provinces, while independents were elected in three provinces. The opposition JMP boycotted the election and called for direct, public voting in future polls. Progress toward electoral reform appeared to advance in August when the JMP agreed to proposed amendments to Yemen's electoral law. The amendments called for reducing the presidential term from seven years to five, shortening legislative terms from six years to four, reserving 15 percent of seats in both chambers of the legislature for women, and establishing a 15-member electoral commission. Opposition groups objected to the proposed formulation of the electoral commission, pressing for representation from more political parties and criticizing the GPC for trying to dominate the commission. Ultimately, the GPC agreed to include opposition party representatives in the electoral commission.

JMP members secured a pledge from President Salih in February 2009 that he would help push through reforms and ensure fair elections. Shortly thereafter, an agreement was reached between the GPC and the JMP, and parliament approved postponing the House of Representatives elections for two years until April 2011 so electoral reforms could be discussed and implemented. The postponement appeased the opposition's concerns about vote rigging. After lengthy delay, in July 2010 the GPC and JMP agreed to start multiparty "national dialogue" to discuss political and electoral reform.

However, substantive progress on proposed reform was not forthcoming, and the government realized that the time to implement the necessary election mechanisms for the April 2011 polling had past. In early January 2011 the House of Representatives passed an election reform amendment that reduced the president's term from seven to five years but allowed for more than two successive terms. Opposition MPs, who mostly abstained from voting, feared that the amendment would be used by President Salih to strengthen his hold on power while subverting the popular will.

Public discontent with the new electoral amendments, antigovernment sentiment fueled by public uprisings against autocratic regimes in Tunisia and Egypt, adverse public reaction to the arrest of a prominent female political activist and Islah member Tawakul KARMAN (who would go on to win the Nobel Peace Prize in October 2011), and the continuance of sectional tensions in the North and South combined to spawn countrywide protests against President Salih's leadership beginning in January 2011. In February the protestors demanded the president's resignation, and protests grew in number as "day of rage" events drew tens of thousands of people to the streets—first in Sana and then across the country—the protests growing in size and intensity, as well as becoming increasingly violent. When the government announced the arrest of a Southern Movement leader (see Political Parties and Groups, below), it appeared that secessionists in the South had joined the antigovernment uprising. Demonstrations against the Salih regime in northern Saada province suggested the Huthis—Zaidi Shiites with ties to Iran—had joined the revolt as well.

In February 2011 Salih approached the JMP to discuss "legitimate" governing demands, as well as the establishment of a new unity government, but was rebuffed. The JMP countered with a proposal for the president to leave office by the end of the year, which Salih promptly rejected. Meanwhile, some GPC members resigned from the party due to the regime's "excessive" violence against the protestors.

In the wake of widespread civil strife, the president dismissed the entire cabinet and pushed a new state-of-emergency law through the House of Representatives. However, the president's actions could not prevent the defection of his brother-in-law, top army commander general Ali Mohsen al-AHMAR, to the growing array of political actors aligned against him. Evidence of the erosion of Salih's effective authority came when Huthi militiamen took de facto control over the Saada governorate on March 24.

As the frequency and intensity of antigovernment protests continued, reports surfaced that members of the armed forces—especially those loyal to General al-Ahmar—had backed the opposition in anti-government protests. Meanwhile, diplomats from the Gulf Cooperation Council (GCC) countries presented President Salih with a power-sharing plan to end the political stalemate. Several times in 2011 Salih rejected the plan, even as more and more southern territory was liberated from government control by militias affiliated with al-Qaida in the Arabian Peninsula (AQAP).

Broadly viewed, Yemen's security situation has deteriorated rapidly since 2004, with some observers suggesting that the country was becoming the world's next failed state. The southern secessionist movement, restless Huthi rebels in the north, and growing support for al-Qaida have detracted from Yemen's ability to develop and use its few natural resources. Groundwater supplies fail to meet the demands of a growing population, and observers warn that Sana could be the first world capital to run out of water. The country also has one of the highest malnutrition rates in the world with an estimated one-third of the population suffering from chronic hunger.

Current security concerns can be traced to 2008, when hostilities between the government and Huthi rebels escalated, resulting in the deaths of several Huthi militiamen. The conflict, which dates to a 2004 uprising by popular Shiite cleric Husayn al-HUTHI and his Organization of Believing Youth (*al-Shabab al-Mumin*), has taken hundreds of lives in clashes with the Yemeni army that have displaced nearly 350,000 people. The government renewed its offensive against the Huthis in August 2009 after President Salih accused Iran of aiding the rebels. For their part, the Huthis blamed Saudi Arabia for supporting the Yemeni army. In November, as fighting pressed against the border, the Saudis positioned ground troops along the frontier and launched air strikes into northern Yemen.

Sensing President Salih's weakness during 2011, the Huthis attacked an army base in the northern town of Dahrah—embarrassing the army unit commandeered by Salih's son, Ahmed Salih. The Huthis announced in 2012 that they would not participate in the national dialogue, nor would they honor President Hadi's request that they disband their militias. Throughout 2012 sporadic violence occurred between rebels and government forces. However, observers noted that conflict in the north had taken on a sectarian dimension as more and more skirmishes involved Salafi groups taking up arms against the Huthis, resulting in scores of deaths and injuries.

Another security concern in recent years has been the growing separatist movement in several southern provinces, which has fomented demonstrations, confrontations, and calls for independence. By 2009 the situation in South Yemen had deteriorated to the point that journalists were banned from the region, and a broad government crackdown on the media ensued. Meanwhile, Nasir al-WAHISHI, the leader of AQAP, declared his group's support for the uprising.

In the restless southeast of Yemen, a surging AQAP kept the region embroiled in conflict. The towns of Jaar and Zinjibar came under attack as AQAP forces attempted to take control of the territory. However, when U.S. drones killed top AQAP target Anwar al-AWLAKI in October, the rebels were temporarily sidelined.

Even after President Salih stepped down in February 2012, AQAP intensified its activity in the south. The Ansar al-Sharia Brigade of al-Qaida took responsibility for March 2012 attacks in Zinjibar in which 175 Yemeni forces were killed. Counterattacks by the army pushed AQAP fighters out of central Zinjibar, but in May al-Qaida struck back with a car bomb at a military parade ground in Sana that killed more than 100 recruits and injured hundreds. The attack targeted new defense minister Mohammed Nasir AHMED, who was unharmed. In May 2012 the army began a concentrated effort to drive AQAP out of the major towns in Abyan province, and by June they had pushed the militants completely out of both Zinjibar and Jaar.

Salih was finally pressured into accepting the GCC power-sharing agreement in late 2011. However, the civilian death toll of the uprising against him had claimed almost 2,000 lives. Salih's departure promoted Abd Rabbo Mansour Hadi to the presidency until he was duly elected by national referendum in March 2012. Hadi was tasked with assembling a unity government equally representing the GPC and the JMP (see Political Parties and Groups, below). Salih was to receive immunity from future prosecution, but only if he quit political activity in Yemen. Hadi's term was limited to two years, during which time new electoral laws could be passed, a national reconciliation dialogue held, and a new constitution written.

Despite the agreement he signed when vacating the presidency, Salih continued to be a force in Yemeni politics throughout 2012 and 2013. A chorus of criticism arose from the general population regarding the immunity deal Salih received, with many voices calling for his arrest and prosecution, and JMP members began referring to Salih as the shadow president. Salih was forced to quit the chairmanship of the GPC, but not until the U.S. ambassador and UN special envoy applied significant pressure. Though former president Salih was not named explicitly, the UN passed a resolution in June 2012, condemning all actors who sought to undermine Yemen's political, social, and economic transition.

Constitution and government. The 1990 constitution of the Republic of Yemen stipulated that the Islamic legal code (sharia) was "one source" of Yemeni law (the wording was later changed to "the source"). A legislative branch was established, including the 301-member popularly elected House of Representatives, which was given the power to appoint the five-member Presidential Council that selected from its members a chair and vice chair, who effectively served as the republic's president and vice president. Additionally, the transitional government appointed a commission to redraw the boundaries of local provinces, some of which tribal chiefs had ruled as virtual fiefdoms.

In the aftermath of the civil war, the House of Representatives in September 1994 revised the basic law, providing for an elected chief executive, limited to two five-year terms, with broadened powers, including the right to name the vice president and prime minister.

In 1997 President Salih established the 59-member Consultative Council, an advisory body. In a 2001 constitutional referendum, the council was replaced with the new Shura Council, whose 111 presidentially appointed members had some decision-making responsibilities. The referendum also extended the presidential term of office to seven years. On April 27, 2008, the country's local authorities law was amended to allow members of municipal councils in each province to indirectly elect all 20 provincial governors, who had previously been appointed by the president.

As stipulated in the power-sharing agreement signed by former president Salih and members of the GPC and JMP in November 2011, Yemen must revise its electoral laws to accommodate pluralistic politics and must construct and ratify a new constitution that protects basic human rights.

Press freedom in Yemen underwent considerable liberalization following unification in 1990, resulting in a blossoming of newspapers and other periodicals. However, censorship was re-imposed at the outbreak of the 1994 civil war: harassment and prosecution of journalists is a common occurrence. The Committee to Protect Journalists reported that the Yemeni High Judicial Court had established a "special press court" to handle media and publishing offenses and in 2010 noted that the court had been used to punish views critical of the government. In light of secessionist activity in the south during 2011, media freedom was further curtailed by the Salih government. Reporters Without Borders ranked Yemen 169th out of 179 countries in its 2013 World Press Freedom Index.

Foreign relations. The Republic of Yemen's foreign policy agenda was dominated throughout the second half of 1990 and early 1991 by Iraq's incursion into Kuwait. (For information regarding foreign relations of the YAR and PDRY, see the 2011 *Handbook*.) Yemen was the sole Arab UN Security Council member to vote against the resolution to use "all necessary means to uphold and implement" the council's earlier resolutions concerning Iraq. Instead, Yemen called for a peaceful, Arab-negotiated settlement. Consequently, in January 1991 the United States announced it would withhold aid promised to Yemen; the Gulf states also withheld aid. Tension between Yemen and Saudi Arabia was described as being at an all-time high in mid-1992, their border conflict having taken on greater significance in view of new oil discoveries in the region.

During the 1994 civil war the United States endorsed unity, and thereby the northern cause, and pressured Arab countries to forgo plans to recognize the Republic of South Yemen, thereby hastening the secessionist regime's collapse. Saudi Arabia's "quiet" financial and military support for the southern forces exacerbated tension with Sana, and sporadic clashes were reported in late 1994 between Saudi and Yemeni troops in the contested border region.

Yemen became the focus of intense international attention in 2000 following the bombing of the destroyer USS *Cole* while it was refueling in Aden harbor on October 12. Five years later, a Yemeni court jailed four people in the bombing, considered by the United States to have been an al-Qaida attack. Relations with Washington improved following the al-Qaida attacks on the United States in September 2001, with Salih announcing that his government would cooperate with the subsequent U.S.-led global "war on terrorism." With several hundred suspected al-Qaida members jailed as of March 2005, the United States praised the government's crackdown on terrorists. At the same time, analysts suggested that Salih faced a difficult job balancing cooperation with the United States and growing public sentiment critical of Israel and the United States. Relations with the United States were strained in 2007–2008 following Sana's refusal to accede to a U.S. request to extradite Jamal al-BADAWI, a member of al-Qaida who had been found guilty of organizing the attack on the *Cole*.

In 2006 members of the GCC agreed to help bolster Yemen's economy in order to secure membership candidacy for the GCC. In December 2008 Yemen was admitted to four GCC bodies, and in March 2009 it was admitted to the GCC's Chambers of Commerce. However, Yemen has not been granted full council membership.

In May 2009 U.S. officials held talks with their Yemeni counterparts regarding cooperation in the U.S. war against terrorism. Earlier in the year Yemen had rejected a U.S. bid to send Yemeni detainees held at the U.S. military prison at Guantánamo Bay, Cuba, to a rehabilitation program in Saudi Arabia. The Yemeni government said it would take in the men—who comprise the largest group of prisoners in Guantánamo—after building its own rehabilitation center. In July 2010, the United States and Yemen revisited the issue, and although no formal agreement was reached, the first Yemeni detainee was released.

A failed suicide bomb on Christmas Day 2009 aboard a U.S. airliner en route from Amsterdam to Detroit, Michigan, provoked renewed U.S. interest in Yemen's security situation. The "underwear bomber," Nigerian national Umar Farouk Abdulmutallab, allegedly attended an al-Qaida training camp in Yemen's mountainous east and plotted the attack with operatives there. In January 2010 the United States blamed the airline plot on AQAP, and moved swiftly to reinforce ties with the Yemeni government. U.S. counterterrorism officials ranked Yemen as one of their top concerns, following only Afghanistan and Pakistan.

The United Kingdom hosted an international summit in late January 2010 on combating Islamic radicalization in Yemen. Attendee U.S. Secretary of State Hillary Clinton commended Yemen for making a "brutally honest" assessment of its economic and security problems. Participants pledged to support Yemen in fighting al-Qaida, and in February a donor conference was held in Riyadh. In October the world witnessed the ability of AQAP to plan international terror operations from within Yemen, as aviation authorities discovered explosives hidden in the cargo of two U.S.-bound airplanes. (The planes were intercepted and searched, one in the UK and one in Dubai.) The explosive material found on the two planes was the same as found on Umar Abdulmutallab in December 2009. Security officials in the Middle East, Europe, and the United States accused the American-born Muslim cleric Anwar al-Awlaki of instigating the failed bombing.

As the political crisis of 2011 unfolded, some key actors in Yemen's foreign relations orbit changed course. Saudi Arabia's long-held preference for keeping Yemen weak was certainly realized by the political stalemate in Sana. However, as central authority weakened and both the Huthis and al-Qaida extended their influence, the Saudis lost faith in Salih's ability to tamp down threats to the kingdom. When Gen. Ali Mohsen al-AHMAR broke with the president, the Saudis put their full backing behind GCC diplomatic initiatives and cut off money transfers to Yemeni elites.

The United States, meanwhile, exerted its greatest effort confronting the threat posed by an unrestrained AQAP. Visiting Sana in early January, Hillary Clinton reminded Salih that the U.S. military would continue to conduct joint operations with the Yemeni military. By April, however, U.S. officials had rescinded military aid payments to Yemen and applied diplomatic pressure on Salih to hasten his departure from power. U.S. airstrikes using drone aircraft intensified throughout the summer, with multiple attacks against AQAP targets occurring throughout the year.

Iran, a constant worry to Yemen because of its backing of the Shiite Huthis, voiced its objection over Salih's violence toward antigovernment demonstrators. In March 2011 intelligence reports indicated that the Quds Force, an elite branch of the Islamic Revolutionary Guards Corps, was actively involved with supplying arms and materiel to the Huthi rebels. In July 2012 President Hadi rebuked Iran for "meddling" in Yemeni domestic affairs, his public denouncement coming days after the government discovered an Iranian "spy ring" operating in North Yemen.

When Hadi took office, his first trip abroad was to Saudi Arabia where he met with King Abdullah. The two leaders discussed security issues with the kingdom's intelligence chief but also touched on Yemen's fuel crisis. In March the Saudis were forced to close their consulate in Aden when one of its diplomats was kidnapped by AQAP gunmen. A Friends of Yemen Conference held in Riyadh in May elicited pledges of more than $4 billion to start Yemen's economic and social restoration project, with $3.25 billion coming from the Saudis. In October, China, France, Russia, the UK and the United States pledged an additional $2.5 billion.

Yemeni relations with the United States in 2012 were mostly positive. The Pentagon and State Department announced $159 million in new aid—$112 million of which was military aid. The Pentagon also announced it would again provide advisors on the ground in Yemen. Thanks to the help of both Yemeni and Saudi Arabian security agents, the United States was able to foil an AQAP plot to blow up American airliners on the first anniversary of Osama bin Laden's death. Close cooperation between the United States and Yemen in targeting and eliminating al-Qaida militants earned the public praise of the Obama administration, highlighted by President Obama's willingness to meet with Hadi when the Yemeni president attended the UN General Assembly in August 2012. However, Yemenis reacting to an anti-Muslim film produced in the United States by an Egyptian expatriate and distributed via the Internet attempted to attack the American embassy in Sana on September 12, 2012. Yemeni security killed one protestor, and kept the rest at bay with water canon.

Yemeni-Iranian relations hit a low point after a series of events in 2012 and 2013. With observers noting Yemen's status as the site of proxy wars between Saudi Arabia and Iran, President Hadi was openly critical of Tehran when boats carrying weapons bound for the Huthi militia were detained on the southern coast. Iran has strategic interests in Yemen that go beyond its geographical proximity to the vital shipping lanes of the *Bab Al Mandab*: Yemen is an important *entrepot* for Iranian weapons that traverse East Africa on their way to Hamas and Hezbollah stockpiles. Hadi also accused the Iranians of aiding the southern secessionist movement known as *Hirak*. Meanwhile, reports indicated that the Saudis continued to give material support to the Sunni followers of Abdullah Bin Hussayn Al AHMER, leader of the Hashid confederation that has tried to counter Huthi influence in the north since 2009.

The United States also implicated Iran for fomenting secessionist activity in the south, singling out Hezbollah as one group helping the south-Yemen independence movement both materially and through coordination of communication efforts. Western intelligence sources believe Hezbollah gives support to the Huthis as well, citing Yemeni security reports that military technicians from Beirut have instructed Huthis how to manufacture and deploy short-range rockets.

Saudi Arabia increased its Fund for Development commitment—aimed at increasing productive capacity in Yemen—by $275 million in 2013. At the same time, the kingdom embarked upon a deportation program that affected 20,000 Yemenis, a move that prompted demonstrations at the Saudi embassy in Sana. In an unrelated incident, a Saudi diplomat was assassinated in Yemen's capital, an act attributed to either AQAP or Huthi rebels. Throughout 2012 and 2013 Saudi fighter planes continued to aid U.S.-led missions against AQAP targets in south Yemen. Sources reported that more than 300 al-Qaida personnel had been killed by U.S.-Saudi airstrikes in 2012 alone, with the pace in 2013 matching the previous year.

Due to August 2013 intelligence reports of coordination between al-Qaida's top leader, Ayman Al ZAWAHRI, and the leader of AQAP, Nasir Al Wahishi, that could lead to attacks on Western interests, the United States, Germany, the UK, and France closed their embassies in Sana for over a week. The U.S. State Department also advised American citizens to leave Yemen. Meanwhile, the United States continued to provide Yemen with $350 million in aid in 2013, mostly as a hedge against AQAP and Iranian provocations in the region.

Current issues. Three issues loomed large in Yemen during 2013: political reconciliation, erosion of national unity, and continued threats from AQAP.

The primary vehicle for reconciling Yemen's competing political and geographic factions was the National Dialogue Conference, which commenced in March. A gathering of 565 representatives from established parties, coalitions, and public interests met for months to resolve differences and allow for the drafting of a new constitution for the post-Salih era. However, differences were hard to overcome, and progress was limited. A primary fissure was the issue of southern separatism: Many key actors from *Hirak* either choose not to attend the conference, or predicated all discussion upon recognition of the South's former status as an independent country. In August the government in Sana issued a blanket apology to southerners (and to Huthis) for Salih's military campaigns against them. Mostly, the apology failed to sway people outside of Sana that the Hadi administration or the central government sought genuine reconciliation or meaningful change. Even a plan to create five or six subnational states in a federal system that would shift significant autonomy away from Sana failed to attract sufficient interest. By September many of the southern representatives suspended their participation in the Dialogue, complaining that Sana preferred to maintain the status quo.

The extent to which national unity can exist in Yemen, as espoused by leaders in the central government, appeared to lose all credibility in 2013. In Aden and its region of south Yemen, secessionist sentiment was omnipresent, and observers questioned whether Sana continued to exercise actual authority there. In the north, Huthis were in de facto control of Saada and its environs. Salafi militias challenged Huthis rebels throughout the north and contested the control of certain mosques there. In Sana, members of *Islah*—whose Muslim Brotherhood orientation clashes with Huthi-dominated Zaidi-Shiite Islam—protested violently with Zaidis attempting to rest control of mosques in the capital. Government security forces killed 10 protestors in Sana when Huthis attacked a security headquarters there, demanding that detainees from Saada—some of them drug and weapons smugglers—be released.

Though President Hadi successfully reorganized the military's leadership ranks to lessen the influence of Salih-era appointees, the steepest challenge facing security forces in Yemen continued to be AQAP. Hundreds of military officers and staff members were assassinated in 2012 and 2013. Targeting killing of al-Qaida fighters and leaders carried out by the Yemeni military, U.S. drones, and Saudi fighter pilots also resulted in hundreds of al-Qaida deaths—including second-in-command Saeed AL-SHIHRI. President Hadi rejected a truce offered by AQAP that did not come with a provision for disarmament, and after several al-Qaida attacks on military bases in the southeast and a call by AQAP for bounties of up to $23,000 for the killing of American soldiers and diplomatic personnel, the Yemeni army launched an offensive against al-Qaida strongholds in Hadramaut province.

POLITICAL PARTIES AND GROUPS

Under the imams, parties in North Yemen were banned, political alignments determined largely by tribal and religious loyalties. The successor Republic of Yemen legalized some 70 groups and in April 1993 allowed multiparty elections that gave rise to opposition politics.

In 2006, in advance of presidential elections scheduled for September, six opposition groups formed a coalition known as the Joint Gathering or the Joint Meeting Parties (JMP). The six groups were the Yemen Socialist Party (YSP), Islah, Baath, the Nasserite Unionist People's Party (NUPP), the Union of Popular Forces (UPF), and *al-Haqq*. (The Baath later withdrew from the JMP following disputes on a number of policies.) The JMP's nominee for president was former oil minister Faisal bin Shamlan, the main challenger to Salih. (For information about the National Council of Opposition Forces [NCOP], see the 2011 *Handbook*.)

In 2008–2009 the JMP, chaired by Hasan Muhammad ZAYD of *al-Haqq*, was instrumental in pressing for fair elections. The coalition had threatened to boycott the elections if they were held as originally scheduled, claiming vote rigging ahead of the poll. The 2009 legislative elections were postponed first until 2011 and then indefinitely as a result of the political stalemate of 2011–2012. During the 2011 protests against the Salih regime, the JMP sought to direct the zeal of public discontent toward political action but drew criticism from various youth movement leaders who claimed that JMP coalition members were co-opting "their revolution" for crass political ends.

Government Party:

General People's Congress—GPC (*Mutamar al-Shabi al-Am*). Encompassing 700 elected and 300 appointed members, the GPC was founded in 1982 in the YAR. Longtime YAR president Ali Abdallah Salih relinquished his position as secretary general of the GPC upon assuming the presidency of the Republic of Yemen in May 1990; however, the group continued as one of the parties (along with the YSP, below) responsible for guiding the new republic through the transitional period culminating in the 1993 legislative election.

The GPC won a plurality, 123 seats, in the April 1993 House of Representatives balloting, its support coming primarily from northern tribal areas. Although a coalition government with the YSP was announced on May 30, the two leading parties grew increasingly estranged prior to the onset of the 1994 civil war. Following that conflict, the GPC announced the formation of a new government in coalition with Islah (see below). At its fifth congress, held in 1995, the GPC reelected all incumbent party leaders, including Salih as chair.

The GPC, aided by a YSP boycott, won a majority of 187 seats in the April 1997 House balloting, and Islah joined the opposition. In the balloting of April 2003 the GPC won 238 seats. Islah negotiated, though ultimately unsuccessfully, to avoid splitting the antigovernment vote.

President Salih was reelected party president in 2005 and nominated as the party's 2006 presidential candidate. Following Salih's reelection in September coupled with the party's success in concurrent local elections, the GPC solidified its dominant position. Its stronghold was further enhanced in May 2008 when the party dominated elections for provincial governors, and six party members were named to a reshuffled cabinet.

In 2009–2010 the GPC struggled to govern the country in the face of growing criticism of its handling of deepening civil unrest. Demonstrations in April by opposition parties called for an end to "repressive policies," and "arbitrary arrests" increased in southern towns as the economy worsened. U.S. military operations aimed at al-Qaida targets sparked another wave of protests in June over perceived violation of Yemeni sovereignty.

As a result of the antigovernment protests of 2011, nine GPC members of the House of Representatives resigned in late February over concerns that the government response to street protests was too violent. President Salih formally dismissed the all-GPC cabinet in March, reducing it to a caretaker role until a new slate of ministers could be appointed at an unspecified future date. In April some former GPC ministers and MPs formed their own political grouping—the Justice and Development Bloc.

As the country's political crisis intensified in 2011, the party oversaw multiple negotiations with JMP members, aimed at achieving a settlement that would transfer power to a broader base of Yemeni political actors once President Salih was persuaded to resign the presidency. After Salih was forced to leave the country in June after the attack on his life, Vice President Hadi became the lead voice articulating GPC preferences and negotiating the details of a future unity government (see Current issues).

In August 2011 former GPC prime minister and acting speaker of the Shura Council al-Ghani succumbed to the injuries he sustained in June's mosque attack. The same month party assistant secretary general Sultan al-Barakani implicated *Islah* party member Hamid al-AHMAR as the main suspect in that attack, though the government neither revealed any evidence nor made formal charges against him. In April 2012, after having stepped down as president, Salih resigned from the chairmanship of the GPC, relinquishing the position to Abdel Karim al-Iryani. Though observers speculated that Hadi would assume the position of party chair at the GPC's 30th anniversary conference in September, the president chose not to attend, and the chairmanship remained al-Iryani's. In 2013 Salih reinserted himself into the GPC's leadership. Though he was not assigned a formal position, he was once again the de facto head of the party and led the GPC's delegation in the NDC. However, voices in the party resent Salih's continued involvement, especially in light of threats by the UN Security Council to sanction the former president for "attempting to derail political reconciliation in the country."

Leaders: Abdel Karim al-IRYANI (Chairman), Abd al-Qadir Abd al-Rahman BAJAMMAL (Secretary General), Sultan al-BARAKANI (Assistant Secretary General).

Other Legislative Parties:

Yemeni Congregation for Reform (*al-Tajammu al-Yamani lil-Islah*). Also referenced as the Yemeni *Islah* Party (YIP), *Islah* was launched in September 1990 under the leadership of influential Northern tribal leader Sheikh Abdallah ibn Husayn al-AHMAR, formerly a consistent opponent of unification. The party subsequently campaigned against the 1990 constitution in alliance with several other groups advocating strict adherence to sharia. (For details regarding the party from 1993 to 2003, see the 2012 *Handbook*.)

In the elections of April 27, 2003, *Islah* garnered 46 seats, and al-Ahmar was reelected as speaker of the House of Representatives. In 2005 some in the party reportedly agreed to allow women to participate in elections, which would presumably strengthen party results, though there was no official pronouncement on the subject. (In 2009 there were reportedly female members on the *Islah* Shura Council, among them the president of Women Journalists Without Chains, Tawakul KARMAN.)

In 2005 Yemen asked the United States to remove Abd Al-Maguid-ZINDANI, the chair of the *Islah* governing council, from its list of suspected terrorists. The United States had previously accused al-Zindani of working with Osama bin Laden. Party leader Sheikh al-Ahmar, who heads former president Salih's tribe, said he personally supported Salih's 2006 reelection bid, though his preference was "not binding" on the party. The party, as part of the JMP coalition, officially supported Faisal bin SHAMLAN in the election.

In February 2007 the party replaced al-Zindani as its spiritual leader but urged the government to continue to press Washington to remove al-Zindani's name from its list of suspected financiers of terrorism. In March al-Ahmar was reelected party president, and al-Zindani was named to the party's supreme panel. Muhammad Ali al-Yadoumi, formerly vice chair of the party, was named chair in January 2008 to succeed Sheikh al-Ahmar, who died in December 2007.

In May 2009 a regional party leader indicated his intent to form a new southern "reform" movement, and as civil unrest deepened, the party became increasingly critical of the governing GPC. In December *Islah* secretary general Abd al-Wahab Ali al-UNSI accused the GPC of fomenting unrest in the country with "extremist policies" so it could act as mediator and thereby cement power.

In January 2011 *Islah* leaders and MPs rejected proposed amendments to the constitution that would have allowed President Salih to stay in office indefinitely. The same month Salih criticized the opposition parties—and *Islah* in particular—for threatening to boycott the April parliamentary elections—elections that did not take place as scheduled.

Taking a cue from the spontaneous antigovernment street protests of 2011, *Islah*—working in concert with its JMP partners—promoted "Day of Rage" rallies on Fridays. However, the youth movement organizers of the popular protests accused the established opposition parties of hijacking the youths' revolutionary goals.

In June *Islah* MP Ali ASHSHAL accused President Salih of exaggerating the threats to national security posed by domestic al-Qaida elements in order to remain in power. At the same time, armed tribesmen loyal to *Islah* were engaged in conflict with Yemeni security forces north of Sana. Later in July the party accused the Salih government of attempting to assassinate *Islah* president Mohammed YADOUMI by firing at his car.

In August, *Islah* member Hamid al-AHMAR called on Western countries to freeze the assets of President Salih. Prior to 2011, al-Ahmar's name had been mentioned often as a possible candidate to replace Salih as president of Yemen in 2013 if the scheduled election was to take place. However, the election of Hadi as president in February 2012 ended such speculation. As a JMP member, *Islah* became part of the national reconciliation government assembled by Prime Minister Basindwa in compliance with the GCC power-sharing agreement. During 2012 *Islah* took a hard line against the Huthi rebellion, and some of its members in Aden clashed with members of the Southern secessionist group *Hirak*. One *Islah* camp in the South was even stormed by armed members of the Southern Movement. In June 2013 *Islah* MPs suspended their party's participation in the House due to conflicts with GPC MPs over governing procedures laid down by the Gulf Initiative power-sharing agreement.

Leaders: Muhammad Ali al-YADOUMI (Chair), Muhammad Ali AJILAN (Chair of *Islah* Governing Council), Sheikh Abd al-Wahab Ali al-ANSI (Secretary General).

Yemeni Socialist Party—YSP (*al-Hizb al-Ishtiraki al-Yamani*). (For information about the YSP prior to 1993, see the 2011 *Handbook.*) The YSP won 56 seats in the April 1993 House of Representatives election, and party leaders announced a potential merger with the GPC. However, with substantial opposition to the plan having reportedly been voiced within the YSP's 33-member Politburo, no progress toward the union ensued, and the YSP on its own was allocated 9 cabinet seats in the government formed in May.

Personal animosity between YSP secretary general Ali Salim al-Beidh and Yemeni president Salih was considered an important element in the subsequent North-South confrontation, which culminated in the 1994 civil war. However, al-Beidh and his supporters attributed the friction to the inability of security forces to protect YSP members. An estimated 150 YSP members were assassinated between May 1990 and early 1994.

Following the collapse of the YSP-led People's Democratic Republic of Yemen (PDRY) in July 1994, the party appeared to be in disarray. Al-Beidh announced from exile that he was "retiring from politics," although some of the other secessionist leaders who had fled the country pledged to pursue their goal of an independent South. Meanwhile, in September the YSP rump in Yemen elected a new Politburo comprising 13 Southerners and 10 Northerners. Aware that a significant portion of the YSP had opposed the ill-fated independence movement, President Salih announced that the reorganized party would be allowed to keep its legal status. However, he declared al-Beidh and 15 other separatist leaders to be beyond reconciliation and subject to arrest for treason should they return to Yemen. Subsequently, when the GPC/YIP coalition government was formed in October, the YSP announced it was assuming the role of "leading opposition party." The party subsequently continued to challenge the GPC's stranglehold on power, and the YSP strongly opposed the 2001 constitutional amendments that lengthened the presidential and legislative terms of office.

In 2003 Salih reconciled with al-Beidh and pardoned YSP members who had been sentenced to death. The party secured eight seats in the 2003 elections. In a move toward further cooperation, YSP leaders began talks with the GPC in 2005 to bridge the gap between them.

In July 2008 the party's MPs boycotted the legislative session to protest proposed constitutional amendments recommended by the president. YSP leaders said the amendments did not address the release of political prisoners, among other issues. The same month the YSP's agreement to enter into a national dialogue with the GPC raised the possibility of eventual YSP appointments to prominent government positions.

In March 2011 Abu Bakr Batheeb, the party's assistant secretary general, emphasized the need to ratify the power-sharing initiatives in the proposal put forward by the GCC countries. Batheeb and the rest of his party were vindicated when Salih stepped down, and as a JMP member the YSP joined the reconciliation government as partners with the GPC in 2012. During 2012 the YSP advocated a national apology to the people of the former PDRY, calling for the reinstatement of former security officers and the repatriation of seized property. However, YSP leader Yassin Numan issued steady criticism of the Southern Movement, accusing the *Hirak* groups of trying to undermine the "historical" achievements of the YSP in the region. Perhaps in response to his strong rhetoric, gunmen made an attempt on Numan's life in late August 2012.

Leaders: Yassin Said NUMAN (Former Speaker of the House of Representatives and Secretary General), Yahya Abu ASBU (Deputy Secretary General), Abu Bakr BATHEEB (Assistant Secretary General).

Arab Socialist Baath Party—ASBP (*Hizb al-Baath al-Arabi al-Ishtiraki*). The Yemen branch of this secularist pan-Arab party fielded seven successful candidates in the April 1993 legislative elections, and party member Mujahid Abu SHAWARIB was subsequently named a deputy prime minister in the cabinet formed in May. However, *Baath* leaders announced that the party would sit in opposition, with Abu Shawarib serving essentially as an independent rather than a *Baath* representative. The grouping secured two seats in the 1997 house elections and two seats in the 2003 elections. In 2006 the party announced its support for President Salih in the presidential election. In December 2009 *Baath* president Abd al-Wahhab MAHMUD became president of the JMP.

The party condemned the January 2011 arrest and detention of Naif al-QANIS, head of its National Relations chair and a leader in the JMP. In August al-Qanis spoke on behalf of the JMP when he rejected the addition of GPC amendments to the GCC initiative that would alter the timetable for transitioning to a new government. In 2012 al-Qanis continued his criticism of the power-sharing agreement, specifically the provision granting Salih immunity from future criminal prosecution. ASBP members were instrumental in organizing protests calling for the former president to be charged for the deaths of civilians during the 2011–2012 uprising. Al-Qanis noted that the GCC agreement granted immunity only if Salih disengaged from Yemeni politics permanently—a condition the former president has never fulfilled.

Leaders: Abdullah al-AHMAR (Assistant Secretary General), Muhammad Al-ZUBAIRY (Secretary General and JMP President), Abd al-Wahhab MAHMUD, Dr. Qasim SALAM.

Nasserite Unionist People's Party—NUPP (*al-Tanthim al-Wahdawi al-Shabi al-Nasri*). Formed in 1989 and the largest of the nation's Nasserite groupings, the NUPP won one seat in the 1993 legislative balloting, three in 1997, and three in 2003. The party is a member of the opposition coalition JMP, and in 2009 party leader Abdul Malik al-Makhlafi was named a member of the national committee in charge of implementing the terms of the cease-fire with Huthi rebels in Saada Province (see Current Issues above).

In July 2010 an exiled Nasserite leader, Abdel-Raqib AL-QERSHI, was shot by an unknown gunman when he returned to Yemen following an amnesty offer by President Salih. Al-Qershi had fled the country in 1978 to escape the death penalty for his alleged involvement in an armed rebellion to topple the Salih government. In 2012 party leader Mohammed al-Sabri advocated for a national committee that would investigate the Salih regime's crimes, a step that party members considered crucial for true reconciliation to occur.

Leaders: Mohammed al-SABRI, Abdul Malik al-MAKHLAFI, Sultan al-ATWANI (Secretary General).

Other Parties and Groups:

Truth Party (*al-Haqq*). Founded by Islamic religious scholars in late 1991, *al-Haqq* won two seats in the 1993 parliamentary balloting. Although *al-Haqq* had no successful candidates in the 1997 elections, party leader Ibrahim al-WAZIR was named minister of justice in the new GPC-led cabinet formed in May. He was replaced after the 2003 reshuffle. Sheikh Ahmad ibn Ali SHAMI, the secretary general of *al-Haqq,* was named minister of religious guidance in the May 1998 reshuffle, although he left the post in September. The government has accused the group of backing the rebellion of cleric and former Truth leader Husayn al-Huthi. In December 2009 Truth Party secretary general Hasan Muhammad Zayd stepped down as president of the JMP.

In February 2010 *al-Haqq* rejected the Yemeni government conditions to end the Huthi conflict in Saada Province. In July Zayd warned that a new war with Saudi Arabia might result because of an alleged Saudi attack on a mosque in the province.

In April 2011 Zayd described the role of antigovernment street protesters as purely revolutionary in nature and concluded that the youth movement should not have a role in Yemini politics, a statement that angered many of the youth protest organizers and deepened the divide between them and the political parties. In July Zayd was prevented by Yemeni intelligence services from boarding a flight to Saudi Arabia for the alleged offense of being a "spy for Iran." His brief detention drew condemnation from human rights organizations, as well as calls from JMP members that further harassment of opposition figures would not be tolerated. In March 2012 the party's Executive Committee announced the dismissal of Zayd from the secretary general post for allegedly conducting party business without consulting the Committee, though later he was reinstated. In January 2013 the party conducted the first General Conference in its history in preparation for the National Dialogue.

Leaders: Hasan Muhammad ZAYD (Secretary General), Muhammad ibn Muhammad al-MANSUR (Vice President), Ibrahim al-WAZIR, Sheikh Ahmad ibn Ali SHAMI.

League of the Sons of Yemen (*Rabibat Abna al-Yaman*—RAY). Founded in 1990 to represent tribal interests in the South, the league campaigned against the proposed constitution for the new republic because it did not stipulate sharia as the only source of Yemeni law. The party offered 92 candidates in the 1993 general elections, none of whom were successful. League leader Abdul Rahman al-Jafari, born in Yemen but a citizen of Saudi Arabia, was named vice president of the breakaway Democratic Republic of Yemen in 1994. Following the separatists' defeat, al-Jafari moved to London, where he served as chair of the Yemeni National Opposition Front. Al-Jafari maintained that he was also still the leader of the League of the Sons of Yemen, but members remaining in Yemen had voted to dismiss him from his post. A small league rump participated in the 1997 elections without success.

The League's Executive Committee in March 2000 called for national reconciliation through dialogue with the Salih government and subsequently suspended its antigovernment activities. Al-Jafari announced in 2006 that he would return to Yemen to support Salih's reelection bid. Speaking on *al-Jazeera* in June 2009, al-Jafari called for a two-council parliament that would better represent regional interests and advocated improved training of army and security forces.

In terms of his party's vision of a political settlement that would end the stalemate of 2011, Mohsen Mohammad Bin Fareed, secretary general of the party, noted that in 2008 his party put forth a proposal that Yemen be divided into five states, with Sana as the political capital and Aden as the trading capital. Throughout the year he continued to advocate for a political solution that would preserve Yemen in a united but decentralized manner—even by allowing significant sovereignty for the separatist elements in South Yemen. Though RAY had little influence at the NDC sessions, its prior suggestion of a federalized government structure was widely discussed at the conference.

Leaders: Abdul Rahman al-JAFARI, Mohsen Mohammad Bin FAREED (Secretary General).

Other parties include the **Liberation Party**; the **Democratic Nasserite Party**, led by 2006 presidential candidate Yasin Abdu SAID; the **Liberation Front Party,** established in South Yemen in the 1970s by Abdul Fattah ISMAIL; the **National Social Party,** led by Abd al-Azziz al-BUKIR; the **Popular Liberation Unity Party**; and the **Popular Unity Party**.

The so-called **Southern Movement** (*Hirak*) is a loose coalition of at least seven identifiable separatist groups located in the south of the country: **Higher National Forum for the Independence of the South**; **Higher National Council for the Liberation of the South**, led by Hasan Baoum and Mohammed Salih TAMMAH; **Movement of the Southern Peaceful Struggle**, led by Salah al-SHANFARA and Nasser al-KHUBBAJI; **Union of the Southern Youth**, led by Fadi Hasan BAOUM; **National Forum for the Southern Peaceful Struggle**, led by Salih Yahya SAID; **Council for Leading the Peaceful Revolution**, led by Tariq al-FADHLI; and **Council of the Peaceful Movement to Liberate the South**, established in 2010 as an umbrella organization for all Southern opposition groups, and led by Hasan BAOUM and Tariq al-FADHLI.

The **Aden-Abyan Islamic Army** claimed responsibility for the December 1998 kidnapping of 16 Westerners in Southern Yemen. Zein al-Abidine al-MIHDAR, described as one of the leaders of the group, reportedly called for strikes against U.S. installations and an end to U.S. "aggression" against Iraq. Mihdar and several others went on trial in April 1999. (For information on the group's activities from 1999 to 2008, see the 2011 *Handbook*.)

In 2009 the government arrested 10 members of the Aden-Abyan Islamic Army for alleged jihadist activities. However, the government later ordered the release of a number of Army members on the recommendation of clerics, who said the fighters had repented their extremist views. In April 2010 three members of the Army were arrested, accused of killing two policemen and blowing up an official's vehicle in the southern province of Abyan.

New Parties:

Al-Rashad Union Party. Also known as the Yemeni Rashad Union, this party was formed in March 2012 with the intention of uniting Yemen's Salafis in one party, jointly calling for implementation of sharia law while also rejecting Western democracy. Rashad differentiated itself from *Islah*—Yemen's dominant Islamist party—by excluding women from political life. Despite its theme of unification, many Salafi groups have rejected Rashad. The party sent seven representatives to the NDC in 2013.

Leaders: Mohamed Al-BAIDANI (Cofounder), Abdallwahab Al-HOMAIQANI (Secretary General).

Nation Party (*Hizb al-Omma*). Founded by a former leader of the al-Haqq Party, Mohammed Muftah, Omma is closely associated with the political goals espoused by the Huthis of North Yemen, with some observers speculating that the party has been influenced by Tehran. Omma called for a boycott of the February 2012 presidential election won by the CGP's Hadi.

Justice and Building Party. Formed in early 2012 by former GPC members, this party has attracted disaffected members of the 2011 revolution—specifically women and young men who identify as part of the "revolutionary youth."

Leader: Mohammed ABULAHOUM (President).

The Justice and Development Bloc. Originally formed by estranged GPC members, this group came together shortly after the uprising against former president Salih began in 2011.

Leaders: Mohamed Abdulelah al-KADI (Founding Member), Abdulaziz JUBARI (Party Spokesman).

Future Democratic Party (*Hizb al-Mustaqbal al-Dimuqrati*). Billed as a nonideological party, Future party leaders has attracted former GPC members, revolutionary youth, and women—the latter group representing 35 percent of party membership.

Leaders: Saleh Al-JALAAE (Secretary General), Ammar MOHAMMED, and Nabeel ABDULLA.

Arab Spring Party. The first Yemeni party established and led exclusively by a woman, the Arab Spring has attracted many members of the revolutionary youth.

Leaders: Amal Lutf al-THAWR (Founder and Chair), Alawi al-HUTAMI.

National Solidarity Party. This party was founded by Sheikh Hussein al-Ahmar, who also serves as party chair. Al-Ahmar's wealth garnered influence when NDC seats were being distributed in March 2013, as the party earned 31 seats at the Dialogue sessions.

Other new parties include **Free Yemen Party,** led by Awsan Mohammed AQLAN; **al-Watan Party,** formed by members of the Civic Coalition of Revolutionary Youth and led by cofounder Husam al-SHARJABI; the **Youth Justice and Development Party**; the **Social Peace Party,** led by Mohammed al-BASHIRI; the **Youth National Democratic Development Party;** and the **Freedom and Justice Party.**

LEGISLATURE

Shura Council (*Mali's al-Shura).* The largely advisory Shura Council was established in accordance with constitutional amendments approved in a national referendum on February 20, 2001. The president appointed all 111 members of the advisory body, including some from the opposition, on April 28.

Speaker: (Vacant).

The transitional **House of Representatives** (*Mali's al-Nowak*) is a 301-member body installed in 1990 to include the 159 members of the former YAR Consultative Assembly, the 111 members of the former PDRY Supreme People's Council, and 31 people named by the government to represent opposition groups. On April 17, 1993, the house was directly elected by universal suffrage. A national referendum on February 20, 2001, approved a constitutional amendment increasing the legislative term of office from four to six years.

Following the most recent elections, on April 27, 2003, the seats were distributed as follows: the General People's Congress, 238; the Yemeni *Islah* Party, 46; the Yemeni Socialist Party, 8; the Nasserite Unionist People's Party, 3; the Arab Socialist *Baath* Party, 2; independents, 4.

Elections originally scheduled for 2009 were postponed until April 2011, and then postponed indefinitely (see Government and Politics, above).

Speaker: Yahya Ali al-RAEE.

CABINET

[As of September 27, 2013]

Prime Minister	Mohammed Salem Basindwa (JMP)
Deputy Prime Minister for Cabinet Affairs	Jawara Hamud Thabit (JMP)
Deputy Prime Minister for Economic Affairs	(Vacant)
Deputy Prime Minister for Interior Affairs	(Vacant)
Ministers	
Agriculture and Irrigation	Farid Ahmad Mujawwar (GPC)
Communications and Information Technology	Ahmad Ubayd bin Daghir (GPC)
Culture	Abdallah Awabil Manthuq (JMP)
Defense	Muhammad Nasir Ahmad Ali (GPC)
Education	Abd al-Razaq al-Ashwal (JMP)
Electricity and Energy	Salih Hasan Sumiya (JMP)
Expatriate Affairs	Mujahid al-Qahali (GPC)
Finance	Sakhir Abbas al-Wajih (JMP)
Fisheries	Awadh al-Suqutri (GPC)
Foreign Affairs	Abu Bakr Abdallah al-Qirbi (GPC)
Higher Education and Scientific Research	Yahya al-Shuaybi (GPC)
Human Rights	Huriya Ahmad Mashur (JMP)
Industry and Trade	Saad al-Din Ali Salim bin Talib (JMP)
Information and Government Spokesperson	Ali Ahmed al-Amrani (JMP)
Interior	Abdul-Qadir Qahtan (JMP)
Justice	Murshid Ali al-Arshani (JMP)
Labor and Social Affairs	Amat al-Razaq Ali Hamad (GPC) [f]
Legal Affairs	Mohammed Ahmed al-Mikhlafi (JMP)
Local Administration	Ali al-Yazidi (JMP)
Oil and Mineral Resources	Hisham Sharaf Abdallah (GPC)
Planning and International Cooperation	Mohammed al-Saadi (JMP)
Public Health and Population	Ahmed Qasim al-Anisi (GPC)
Public Works and Roads	Umar Abdallah al-Karashmi (GPC)
Religious Endowments and Islamic Affairs	Hamoud Mohammed Ubad (GPC)
Shura Council and Parliamentary Affairs	Rashad Ahmad al-Rasas (GPC)
Social Security and Civil Service	Nabil Abdu Shamsan (GPC)
Technical Education and Vocational Training	Abd al-Hafiz Numan (JMP)
Tourism	Qasim Sallam (GPC ally)
Transportation	Waid Abdullah Ba Thib (JMP)
Water and Environment	Abd al-Salaam Razaz (JMP)
Youth and Sport	Mu'ammar al-Iryani (GPC)
Ministers of State	
Director of the Office of the Prime Minister	Muhammad Saeed Zafir
Minister of State	Shayif Azi Saghir (GPC)
Minister of State	Hasan Ahmed Sharaf al-Din

[f] = female

INTERGOVERNMENTAL REPRESENTATION

Ambassador to the U.S.: (Vacant).

U.S. Ambassador to Yemen: Gerald FEIERSTEIN.

Permanent Representative to the UN: Jamal Abdullah al-SALLAL.

IGO Memberships (Non-UN): IOM, NAM, OIC.

ZAMBIA

Republic of Zambia

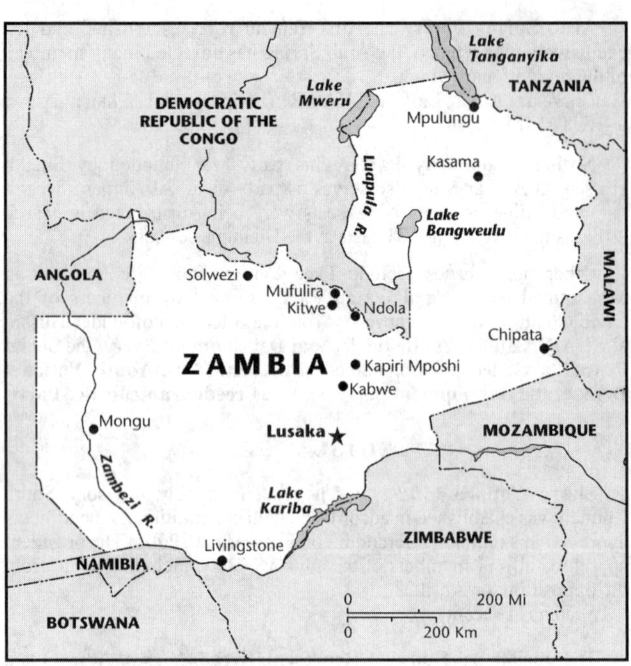

Political Status: Independent republic within the Commonwealth since October 24, 1964; under one-party, presidential-parliamentary system from 1972 to adoption of multiparty constitution on August 29, 1991.

Area: 290,584 sq. mi. (752,614 sq. km).

Population: 14,222,233 (2013E—UN); 14,222,233 (2013E—U.S. Census).

Major Urban Center (2005E): LUSAKA (metropolitan area, 1,647,000).

Official Language: English.

Monetary Unit: Kwacha (official rate November 1, 2013: 5.50 kwachas = $1US). On January 1, 2013, the Zambian kwacha was revalued, with 1 new kwacha equal to 1,000 of the old kwachas.

President: Michael SATA (Patriotic Front); popularly elected on September 20, 2011, and inaugurated for a five-year term on September 23, succeeding Rupiah BANDA (Movement for Multiparty Democracy).

Vice President: Guy SCOTT (Patriotic Front); appointed by the president on September 29, 2011.

THE COUNTRY

Landlocked Zambia, the former British protectorate of Northern Rhodesia, is bordered by the Democratic Republic of the Congo, Tanzania, and Malawi on the north and east, and by Angola, Namibia, Zimbabwe, and Mozambique on the west and south. Its terrain consists primarily of a high plateau with abundant forests and grasslands. The watershed between the Congo and Zambezi river systems crosses the northern part of the country. The bulk of the population belongs to various Bantu tribes, the most influential being the Bemba in the north and the Lozi, an offshoot of the Zulu, in the southwest. (Tribal influences remain highly influential in political affairs.) Nonindigenous groups include a small number of whites (mainly British and South African), Asians, and persons of mixed descent concentrated in the Copperbelt in the north. Nearly three-quarters of native Zambians are nominally Christian, almost equally divided between Catholics and Protestants; the remainder adheres to traditional African beliefs. The official language is English, but Afrikaans and more than 70 local languages and dialects are spoken. Women comprise approximately one-third of the labor force, not including unpaid agricultural workers. Although a number of women involved in the independence struggle achieved positions of influence in the former ruling party, female representation is minimal in politics. Following the 2011 elections, women held 18 of 157 seats in the Assembly (11.5 percent).

Zambia is one of the world's largest producers of copper and cobalt. The former accounts for 75 percent of export earnings, but Zambia's share of the world copper market has declined significantly in the wake of a nearly 80 percent decline in production, attributed in large part to mismanagement of state-owned mines. Zinc, coal, cement, lime, sulphur, and magnetite are among other minerals being extracted. Agriculture employs two-thirds of the labor force, with maize, peanuts, tobacco, and cotton constituting the chief commercial crops. Because of a booming copper industry, Zambia, until the early 1970s, enjoyed one of Africa's highest standards of living, with rapid development of schools, hospitals, and highways. However, a subsequent decline in copper prices yielded infrastructural decay, rising unemployment within the rapidly growing and highly urbanized population, a foreign exchange shortage, an external debt of more than $6 billion, and the erosion of social services. Although the government had exercised budgetary restraint and relaxed its control of the economy in accordance with International Monetary Fund (IMF) strictures dating to the mid-1970s, rioting over price increases in late 1986 prompted Lusaka to abandon austerity measures and break with the IMF. However, economic reform measures were reinstated in 1998, paving the way for renewal of relations with international lenders and donors. In 1992 the Chiluba government launched a privatization program; however, market reform was subsequently seen as having failed to help the nation's poor (an estimated 83 percent of the population). Funds for education and health remained severely constrained at a time when about one-fifth of the population was believed to be HIV-positive. The IMF and World Bank continued to approve loans (Western aid accounted for one-half of the government's budget), and Zambia was included on the list of countries eligible for the international community's new debt-relief program. However, donors expressed concern over the apparent pervasive nature of corruption in government affairs at all levels. Among other things, the economic distress contributed to the emergence of a degree of political instability that was unusual by Zambian standards.

Severe drought in 2002 caused a decline in agricultural production that left 25 percent of the population temporarily dependent on food aid. Collaterally, the pace of economic reform slowed, prompting the temporary suspension of IMF and World Bank assistance. However, real GDP growth averaged 4.8 percent a year in 2004 and 2005, in part due to soaring copper prices and the investment of $1 billion by mining companies. In addition, the Group of Eight in 2005 canceled Zambia's $2.5 billion debt. GDP growth of 6 percent was reported for 2006, bolstered by expansion in the mining sector and a recovery in agricultural production. Zambia also qualified for $3.8 billion in debt relief from the IMF. Meanwhile, the Zambian administration's program for combating HIV/AIDS, including free drugs, resulted in significantly reduced death rates in its first two years and was hailed internationally as a success.

In 2008–2009 annual GDP growth averaged 5.8 percent. Owing in large part to the global economic crisis, demand for copper fell dramatically, mining companies cut thousands of jobs, and inflation increased to 15.2 percent as food costs soared. Subsequently, mining companies successfully lobbied for the abolishment of the windfall tax of 47 percent that had been approved at the height of the copper boom. On a positive note, in May the IMF approved $330 million in financial aid to help Zambia's economic recovery.

The economy began to recover in 2010, with annual growth of 7 percent continuing in 2011 due to a resurgence in the mining industry and the agriculture sector. The IMF urged the government to restore the windfall mining tax in order to pay for social and public investment. Meanwhile, fund managers commended the Zambian authorities for raising electricity tariffs to recover costs and attract more private investment. A rail line linking Zambia and Malawi that was completed in 2010 after more than 30 years was hailed as a boost to trade. In June 2011 the IMF approved the final installment of $29.3 million in a three-year loan program. Significant increases in copper and cobalt revenues continued to bolster the economy. Growth remained high in 2012 as

GDP expanded by 7.3 percent. GDP was estimated to grow by 7.8 percent in 2013, as copper exports increased by 6 percent. Inflation was projected to be 6.7 percent in 2013, according to the IMF, which recommended reforms to promote inclusive growth, including improving access to financial services and boosting agriculture. In its 2013 report on Doing Business, the World Bank ranked Zambia 94th out of 185 countries or seventh among sub-Saharan African countries.

GOVERNMENT AND POLITICS

Political background. Declared a British sphere of influence in 1888, Northern Rhodesia was administered jointly with Southern Rhodesia until 1923–1924, when it became a separate British protectorate. From 1953 to 1963, it was linked with Southern Rhodesia and Nyasaland (now Malawi) in the Federation of Rhodesia and Nyasaland, which was dissolved at the end of 1963 in recognition of the unwillingness of the black majority populations in Northern Rhodesia and Nyasaland to continue under the political and economic domination of white-ruled Southern Rhodesia. A drive for Northern Rhodesia's complete independence, led by Harry NKUMBULA and Kenneth D. KAUNDA, concluded on October 24, 1964, when the territory became an independent republic within the Commonwealth under the name of Zambia (after the Zambezi River). Kaunda, as leader of the majority United National Independence Party (UNIP), became head of the new state; Nkumbula, whose African National Congress (ANC) had trailed in the preindependence election of January 1964, became leader of the opposition. The political predominance of Kaunda and his party was strengthened in the general election of December 1968, Kaunda winning a second five-year term as president and the UNIP again capturing an overwhelming legislative majority. In December 1972 Kaunda promulgated a law banning all parties except the UNIP and introduced what was termed "one-party participatory democracy." In December 1978 he was reelected for a fourth term following disqualification of Nkumbula and former vice president Simon M. KAPWEPWE.

On August 27, 1983, the president dissolved the National Assembly to pave the way for an October 27 election, in which, as sole presidential candidate, he garnered 93 percent of the vote and was returned to office for a fifth five-year term. Two years later Kaunda transferred both the prime minister and the UNIP secretary general to diplomatic posts; Defense Minister Alexander Grey ZULU was chosen to head the party, while Prime Minister Nalumino MUNDIA was replaced by Minister of Education and Culture Kebby MUSOKOTWANE.

Following a UNIP restructuring that was generally interpreted as enhancing his personal control of both party and government, Kaunda, again the sole candidate, was elected for a sixth presidential term on October 26, 1988, with a reported 96 percent "yes" vote. On the other hand, eight cabinet members were defeated in assembly elections held the same day, apparently reflecting increased opposition to government policy. Shortly after the election, Kaunda reshuffled the cabinet, and on March 15, 1989, he named Gen. Malimba MASHEKE to replace the young and popular Musokotwane as prime minister; the subsequent posting of Musokotwane to a diplomatic mission lent credence to the view that he had become a political threat to Kaunda.

In early 1990 the regime rejected a number of proposals for liberalization of the Zambian political system. However, by midyear the government had grudgingly agreed to implement reforms in an attempt to appease increasingly vociferous critics, particularly among the trade and business communities. In the wake of a coup attempt in June and price riots in July, Kaunda agreed to a voter registration drive and the freeing of a number of political prisoners. In September, following a series of major prodemocracy rallies, the president announced plans for multiparty elections by October 1991. On December 4 the National Assembly legalized the formation of political parties, and on December 30 the Zambian Congress of Trade Unions (ZCTU) aligned itself with the leading opposition group, the Movement for Multiparty Democracy (MMD).

In 1991 the regime's practices, including strict control of the media, drew MMD condemnation and led to violent clashes between MMD and UNIP supporters. Nevertheless, on August 2 the National Assembly approved a new multiparty constitution, and, following its formal signing on August 29, the president dissolved the legislature and allowed the state of emergency decree to lapse for the first time since independence. On October 31, in balloting supervised by former U.S. president Jimmy Carter and representatives of the Commonwealth and the Organization of African Unity (OAU, subsequently the African Union—AU), the MMD's Frederick CHILUBA won 74 percent of the presidential vote and the movement's candidates captured 125 of 150 assembly seats.

The MMD secured a vast majority of the 1,190 local council seats contested on November 30, 1992; however, the ruling party's victories were tainted by a lack of competition in approximately 400 councils, coupled with voter apathy (less than 10 percent of eligible voters reportedly having participated). Observers attributed the apparent growing disenchantment among voters to the effects of a severe economic austerity program compounded by the perception of unmitigated governmental corruption.

On March 4, 1993, the administration's prestige was further damaged when Chiluba declared an indefinite state of emergency and 25 UNIP members, including three of former president Kaunda's sons, were arrested on charges relating to an alleged coup plot. On March 9 the president shortened the detention without trial period from 28 to 7 days, apparently seeking to combat domestic and international charges that his administration had overreacted to reports about the alleged plot, and on May 25 the state of emergency was lifted.

In August 1993 15 prominent MMD officials resigned from the government and National Assembly because of the Chiluba administration's alleged unwillingness to investigate corruption and drug trafficking charges against powerful cabinet ministers; the MMD defectors, citing a "critical national crisis of leadership and governance," launched the National Party (NP). Chiluba dismissed the resignations as the "teething problems" of democratic reform; however, in December international aid donors meeting in Paris voted to withhold aid payments until Lusaka investigated the allegations, and on January 6, 1994, the ZCTU called on the Chiluba administration to dissolve the government. Consequently, on January 11, 1994, Chiluba reshuffled his cabinet, claiming to have ousted tainted ministers, and in March the World Bank agreed to release suspended aid payments despite opposition protestations that the president had shielded corrupt ministers while dismissing two who had sought to expose malfeasance.

On July 3, 1994, Vice President Levy MWANAWASA resigned, citing alleged irresponsibility and greed among his colleagues. On the following day Chiluba named Brig. Gen. Godfrey MIYANDA, theretofore a minister without portfolio, to replace Mwanawasa.

In October 1994 former president Kaunda officially announced that he would end his retirement to campaign for early presidential elections, saying "there is a crisis in Zambia... I have accepted the call to come back." In February 1995, Kaunda, who had been under surveillance since August 1994 because of allegations that his return was being financed by foreign backers, was charged with attempting to hold an illegal political party meeting. Meanwhile, the MMD sought to block his presidential eligibility by pressing for a constitutional amendment that would disqualify anyone not born in Zambia of Zambian-born parents (Kaunda's parents having been born in Malawi). Such an amendment, as well as a second amendment disqualifying any person who had already been twice elected president, were included in a draft document issued on June 16. The proposed charter was released despite the objections of an independent constitutional review commission, which had declared the amendments "rubbish" and accused the MMD of having bribed its authors.

On May 16, 1996, the National Assembly approved the Constitution of Zambia Amendment Act 1996, and 12 days later the president sanctioned the measure, thus officially banning Kaunda from future elections. Subsequent opposition efforts to have the constitutional changes suspended and the upcoming balloting held in accordance with the 1991 document were dismissed in September by the president and High Court, respectively. On the other hand, in an effort to dampen mounting opposition charges that electoral preparations were being "rigged," Chiluba agreed to provide opposition representatives with equal access to the media and oversight of vote tabulation. On October 19 Chiluba dissolved the assembly and announced that presidential and legislative elections would be held on November 18. (The opposition's subsequent charge that the government's mandate would expire on October 31 and that any of its actions thereafter would be illegal were dismissed by the regime as "immature.") On October 23 Kaunda announced that the UNIP would boycott the November elections to protest the constitutional changes and the government's alleged manipulation of the voter registration drive.

As anticipated, President Chiluba and the MMD secured landslide victories in polling on November 18, 1996, with the former capturing 69.5 percent of the vote and his party 131 of the 150 seats contested. Their victories were marred, however, by alleged electoral irregularities and by what one observer described as a "revolt of MMD voters" in high-profile contests won by independents and opposition candidates.

Thereafter, amid widespread opposition calls for a campaign of civil disobedience to force the government to hold fresh elections, Chiluba put the military on alert on November 28. On December 2 Chiluba named a new cabinet that was described as "tribalist" because of the preponderance of members from the Northern and Luapula regions (Chiluba is from the latter).

Tensions remained high in Lusaka throughout the first half of 1997 as the Chiluba administration, now reportedly under the direction of MMD hard-liners, was sharply denounced by both domestic and international observers for introducing legislation that would strictly regulate both the media and nongovernmental organizations. (In March the latter law went into effect, but in April the government suspended the controversial Press Council Bill.) In early August antigovernment demonstrations in Lusaka turned into rioting, and, at an illegal opposition rally on August 23, Kaunda and Roger CHONGWE, leader of the Liberal Progressive Front, were shot and wounded in what Kaunda described as an assassination attempt.

On October 28, 1997, a group of junior military officers led by Capt. Steven LUNGU (a.k.a. "Captain Solo") took over a government radio station and declared that they had established a "National Redemption Council" and were prepared to overthrow the government. Within hours the reportedly drunken rebels were overpowered by forces loyal to the president; nevertheless, the government declared a state of emergency, and in the following weeks more than 80 mid-level officers and dozens of opposition members were detained, with a number of others reportedly fleeing the country amid reports that those arrested were being tortured.

On December 2, 1997, Chiluba demoted his vice president, Brig. Gen. Godfrey Miyanda, to the education ministry and named as his replacement Lt. Gen. Christon TEMBO. Furthermore, Chiluba drastically reshuffled both the government and the military leadership.

In late April 2001 a fractured MMD congress agreed to seek constitutional revision to permit President Chiluba to run for a third term, prompting massive protest demonstrations and significant external condemnation. Under heavy pressure, Chiluba finally declared he would not seek reelection. However, on May 4 he dissolved the cabinet, permitting him to appoint a new government on May 6 that pointedly did not include theretofore Vice President Tembo and some 11 other MMD members who had opposed the third-term initiative. Former vice president Mwanawasa became the surprise MMD candidate in the December 27, 2001, presidential balloting, securing, according to official results, a narrow victory (28.69 percent to 26.76 percent) over the second-place finisher, Anderson K. MAZOKA of the United Party for National Development (UPND). However, opposition parties charged that the balloting had been rigged and demanded a court review. (The Supreme Court launched a review of the charges but closed the case in November 2004.) Meanwhile, the MMD was also credited with pluralities in the concurrent assembly and municipal elections, the UPND easily outdistancing the other contenders to secure its position as the dominant opposition grouping. Not surprisingly, considering the electoral challenge, no opposition parties were represented in the cabinet appointed by Mwanawasa on January 7, 2002. However, Mwanawasa appointed members of the UNIP and the Forum for Democracy and Development (FDD) to junior cabinet positions in a May 28, 2003, reshuffle. He also named Nevers MUMBA, a prominent pastor and leader of the National Citizens' Coalition (NCC), as vice president. Mumba was in turn succeeded by Lupando MWAPE of the MDD on October 4, 2004, and by 2005 it was reported that the non-MDD cabinet members had been replaced by MDD stalwarts.

On April 5, 2006, the assembly adopted a controversial electoral reform bill establishing the president's authority to set election dates and requiring only a plurality in a single-round election to decide presidential balloting, among other provisions (see Current issues, below). The bill was promulgated on May 19, and on July 26 President Mwanawasa dissolved Parliament and called for early tripartite elections on September 28, 2006. President Mwanawasa won reelection with a plurality of 43 percent of the vote, defeating main challengers Michael SATA of the Patriot Front (PF) with 29 percent, and Hakainde HICHILEMA of the United Democratic Alliance (UDA) with 25 percent. Two other candidates, including former vice president Godfrey Miyanda, received less than 2 percent of the vote. In legislative balloting the MMD remained the largest parliamentary party with 73 seats, though it lacked a clear majority without the 8 presidentially appointed members. The opposition PF, however, made a stunning comeback with 43 seats (it had won 1 seat in 2001). The newly formed United Democratic Alliance (see Political Parties, below) secured 26 seats. On October 9 the president named Rupiah BANDA of the UNIP as vice president to replace Mwape, who lost his seat in the parliamentary elections. Banda and the new cabinet were sworn in on October 10. Three cabinet ministers were replaced in early 2007.

President Mwanawasa died at age 59 on August 19, 2008, following complications of a stroke weeks earlier. A by-election to choose a successor to serve the remaining three years of Mwanawasa's term was held on October 30. The acting president, Vice President Rupiah Banda (MDD), secured 40.09 percent of the vote, narrowly defeating Michael Sata of the PF, who garnered 38.13 percent. The remaining challengers, Hakainde Hichilema (UPND) and Godfrey Miyanda of the Heritage Party (HP), trailed far behind.

On November 14, 2008, President Banda appointed Legal Affairs Minister George Kunda as vice president, while still allowing Kunda to retain his cabinet post. Banda reshuffled the cabinet the same day.

A minor cabinet reshuffle was announced on March 24, 2009. The communications and transport minister, Dora SILIYA, resigned on April 21, 2009, after she was accused of wrongdoing for allegedly ignoring advice from the attorney general in a contract matter. An appeals court subsequently cleared Siliya of the charges, and on June 17 she was reappointed as education minister in a minor cabinet reshuffle.

The cabinet was reshuffled on January 5, 2010, and in May, a UNIP member was appointed to the post of minister of home affairs. Three ministers were reshuffled on September 28.

The minister for works and supply was replaced on February 24, 2011. On September 20 concurrent presidential, parliamentary, and local elections were held (see Current issues). On September 22 violence erupted in several areas in the country's north because of delayed publication of the final results. The next day official results showed Sata had won 42.24 percent to Banda's 35.63 percent. Voter turnout was 53.65 percent. Sata was inaugurated on September 23 and unveiled his new cabinet on September 29. Significantly, Sata appointed Guy SCOTT as his vice president; Scott was the only white man besides South Africa's P. W. Botha to reach the level of vice president in a modern, democratically elected African government. In December, Sata named a number of MND members to the cabinet as deputy ministers.

Constitution and government. Zambia's 1964 constitution was superseded by the adoption at a UNIP conference in August 1973 of a constitution of the "second republic" that reaffirmed the introduction in 1972 of a one-party system and further provided for the sharing of authority between the party and traditional organs of government. To further emphasize the role of the UNIP, its secretary general (rather than the prime minister) was designated the nation's second-ranking official.

On August 2, 1991, the National Assembly adopted a new constitution that provided for multiparty elections, a two-tiered parliament, abandonment of the post of prime minister in favor of a revived vice presidency, and a presidentially appointed cabinet. In 1993 President Chiluba named a 22-member commission to revise the 1991 document. Draft amendments, released in June 1995 in expectation of a constituent assembly and national referendum, were approved by the National Assembly on May 16, 1996, and by President Chiluba on May 28. The Constitution of Zambia Amendment Act 1996 limits participation in presidential polling to Zambian-born citizens whose parents were also born in Zambia and disqualifies traditional chiefs and anyone who has lived abroad during the previous 20 years. The chief executive is limited to two five-year terms.

The judiciary embraces a Supreme Court, a High Court, and various local courts. Administratively, the country is divided into nine provinces, including the city of Lusaka and its environs, which are subdivided into 55 districts.

Zambia has a relatively free press, and in 2013 Reporters Without Borders ranked the country 72nd out of 179 in media freedom.

Foreign relations. While pursuing a generally nonaligned foreign policy (an 18-year coolness with Britain having been ended by a Kaunda state visit to London in 1983), Zambia consistently opposed racial discrimination in southern Africa and provided sanctuary for numerous exile groups engaged in guerrilla operations against white-controlled territories. Prior to the constitutional changes in South Africa, Zambia's prestige among Front-Line States was pronounced. In the wake of treaties concluded by Angola and Mozambique with South Africa, Lusaka became the headquarters of the African National Congress (ANC), making it a target for bomb attacks in May 1986 by South Africa forces, which also crossed the border on a "reconnaissance mission" in April 1987 that left several persons dead. Kaunda assumed the chair of the Front-Line grouping in early 1985, vowing to promote increased mutual support among member governments. In

1986 he denounced the United States and the United Kingdom for "conspiring" to support the South African government, warning they would share responsibility for the impending anti-apartheid "explosion." Zambia was also in the forefront of a regional plan to lessen reliance on South African trade routes that included rehabilitation of the Benguela Railway in Angola and the Tanzania-Zambia (Tanzam) link to Dar es Salaam. In other regional affairs, troops were at times deployed in border clashes with Malawi and Zaire, the latter agreeing in 1986 to a joint review and demarcation of disputed territory that yielded a settlement in 1989. (Disputes continued to erupt in 2005 at the border of the renamed Democratic Republic of the Congo, reportedly notorious for illegal crossings and smuggling.) In November 1989 a joint security commission was established with Mozambique in an attempt to thwart cross-border guerrilla activity.

Since its ascension to power in October 1991, the Chiluba government's foreign policy agenda was topped by relations with international creditors. In late 1991 the government negotiated a release of the aid allocations suspended in September when the Kaunda regime had allowed debt repayment and austerity programs to lapse. The government's decision to sever diplomatic ties with Iran and Iraq for their alleged financing of coup plotters against Chiluba was described in *Africa Confidential* as owing more to "fundamentalist Christian and anti-Muslim" tendencies within the administration than to substantive evidence of foreign involvement. Furthermore, the Chiluba government experienced slow progress in establishing relations with regional neighbors, many of whom were Kaunda supporters and had expressed distrust of the new administration's criticism of the ANC as well as of its links to South African commercial interests.

The Zambian assembly's approval of a controversial constitutional amendment bill in May 1996 provoked widespread disapproval from Zambia's Western donors, and in June a number of them suspended aid payments. Regionally, however, the Southern African Development Community (SADC) was described by observers as having adopted a "passive" position after the Chiluba government rebuffed its initial intervention efforts, and South Africa, the only SADC member considered powerful enough to influence Lusaka, refused to assume a leadership role.

Aid donors remained unwilling to restart payments through the first half of 1997; however, in July the suspension was partially lifted. Negotiations on further relaxation of payment restrictions were postponed after Lusaka imposed a state of emergency from October until March 1998. In May 1998 the World Bank agreed to a new aid package contingent on Lusaka enacting economic and political reforms; in particular, the bank pressed the government to speed privatization efforts and improve its human rights record.

Zambian-Angolan relations deteriorated in early 1999 as Luanda threatened military action against Zambia if Lusaka continued its alleged support for Angolan rebels. Thereafter, in a thinly veiled reference to Luanda, the Chiluba administration blamed "external forces" for a series of bombings in Lusaka. Later agreements between Luanda and Lusaka appeared to ease the tension, however, although a large Angolan refugee population subsequently continued to create difficulties for the Zambian government, as did an influx of refugees from fighting in the Democratic Republic of the Congo (formerly Zaire). A joint UN-Zambian program to repatriate Angolan refugees subsequently had substantial success, although there continued to be sporadic raids by Congolese rebels into Zambia. In response, the government increased border patrols.

In November 2004 the Zambian military launched a series of training exercises overseen by French military experts. The operations were part of a larger regional initiative through which France hoped to promote military cooperation among Tanzania, Zambia, and Zimbabwe that could lead, among other things, to joint regional humanitarian operations.

The final repatriation of some 34,500 Angola refugees was reported to be under way in 2005, though many were still living in camps in remote areas of Zambia in 2006.

Zambian opposition leader and 2006 PF presidential candidate Michael Sata was refused entry into Malawi in March 2007, reportedly on suspicion that he intended to help former Malawi president Elson Bakili Muluzi reorganize his former ruling United Democratic Front party. Sata denied the allegations. In June the Zambian government began revoking the refugee status of some 6,000 Rwandans who fled their war-torn country in the mid-1990s. Another 10,000 refugees from the Democratic Republic of the Congo also were urged to leave.

Chinese companies stepped up their investments in copper mining in Zambia in 2007, signing multimillion-dollar deals in exchange for significant tax concessions from the government. However, tension existed in relations at the popular level. In February workers at a Chinese-based company planned a large demonstration against China's president, resulting in his visit being canceled.

In 2008 Russia stepped up its economic interest in Zambia as three firms engaged in talks with President Mwanawasa over the possibility of investing $2 billion in Zambian mining projects. If successful, according to news accounts, this would amount to the country's single largest direct investment by a foreign entity.

Cordial relations with Malawi were marked in 2010 by cooperation meetings between the two countries' foreign ministers. China and Zambia agreed to "elevate" their bilateral relationship after a meeting in Beijing. Michael Sata rose to fame in 2006 on a tide of strong anti-Chinese rhetoric. But his tone has since softened, reportedly after the Chinese Embassy encouraged some companies to donate to the PF's 2011 campaign.

In August 2012 Zambia and Mozambique finalized a border demarcation project that clarified a number of disputed areas. The agreement was designed to improve border security and decrease the illegal movement of Zambians into Mozambique.

In April 2013 Zambia and Angola signed a defense cooperation agreement, following three years of negotiations. The accord called for increased intelligence cooperation and joint military maneuvers. In August, more than 1,000 workers from the Tanzania-Zambia Railway Authority were dismissed following a strike that stopped the flow of valuable minerals, including copper and magnesium.

Current issues. In what was described as a landmark trial in August 2009, former president Chiluba was acquitted on all corruption charges. (He had been convicted by a London court in 2007 of stealing $46 million in public funds from Zambia.) His wife, who had been sentenced in March 2009 to 42 months in prison, was released on bail and later rearrested for allegedly having received money and property stolen by her husband when he was in office. Both Chiluba and his wife protested the charges.

In a move that was seen as potentially affecting the 2011 elections, the National Constitutional Conference in late June 2010 released another draft constitution, this one providing for a majoritarian system for electing a president—a system that had been rejected by the MMD in 2006. Meanwhile, Banda found himself facing criticism not only from the opposition but also from within the MMD. Much of the opposition focused on the president's ties to Chiluba, who, despite his earlier acquittal, was widely regarded as having stolen state funds. Opposition members claimed Banda's alliance with Chiluba effectively put a halt to anticorruption efforts. Dissension over the role of Chinese companies and workers escalated in October following an incident in which Chinese mine managers shot and wounded Zambian workers who were protesting against the conditions at a mine. Local residents have been concerned about loss of jobs to the immigrants following Chinese investment of more than $1 billion in the country. Presidential hopeful Michael Sata was said by observers to be courting the thousands of jobless youths in mining towns, where some 80 percent of voters lived. Late in the year three new political parties emerged as a platform from which their leaders launched presidential bids (see Other Parties and Groups under Political Parties, below).

Violence broke out in January 2011 when protesters and police clashed in a town west of the capital as the demonstrators demanded restoration of an agreement granting "half-independence" to the western province formerly known as the Barotseland. Sata, for his part, vowed to restore the Barotseland agreement of 1964 if elected. Meanwhile, the opposition was riven by fighting between the PF and the UPND, which failed to agree on supporting a single presidential candidate. In midyear Banda was spending significant amounts of money not included in the 2011 budget on roads and other infrastructure and in the poorest areas, which traditionally were strongholds of Sata and the PF. The death in June of former president Chiluba was seen as a blow to the Banda campaign, which was already marred by power struggles that resulted in the defections to the PF of several high-profile party members. It was not until July 28 that Banda announced the official date of September 20 for concurrent presidential, parliamentary, and local balloting, thus allowing only about 50 days of campaigning. In August the drawn-out process of writing a new constitution came to a halt after the new draft failed to win parliamentary approval. Observers cited the proposed majoritarian system for electing a president as among the key reasons for its demise.

In the run-up to the election, Banda was widely expected to be able to swing the vote. The MMD borrowed heavily to finance its campaign, which featured entertainers, lollipops, and thousands of free bicycles. Michael Sata ran on an anticorruption platform. The registration of 1.2 million new voters—overwhelmingly young and struggling—was believed to have played a significant role in the outcome. The participation of some 9,000 observers deployed by the Civil Society Election Coalition to monitor polls across the country played another. Analysts say the fact that Sata is Catholic, while Banda had fallen out with the Roman Catholic Church, also contributed. Sata defeated Banda in the balloting, and the PF won a plurality in the Assembly.

After the election, Sata set out to make good on campaign pledges to root out the massive corruption he alleged was going on under his predecessor and promised he would reinstate anticorruption measures that Banda's government had dismantled. He ordered police to confiscate the MMD's elections materials, including thousands of bicycles, until they could prove ownership and show they had paid taxes on them. He also put to work a new legal team, and the government finally registered the London High Court's $58 million judgment against Chilupa and his associates. Sata fired his senior private secretary after an envelope stuffed with $2,000 was discovered in his office. And investigators began looking into officials who had been connected to the privatization of Zamtel, the state-owned telecommunications network. The discovery of roughly $400,000 buried on the farm of Austin LIATO earned the former labor minister a two-year prison sentence. But other than that, investigators did not turn up much proof of the widespread looting that Sata had railed against, and analysts subsequently warned that he was at risk of losing public confidence as events unfolded throughout the spring.

In early March 2012 on the heels of efforts to reassure shareholders in foreign-owned mining companies that the new government would not nationalize the mines or increase its stake in them, Mines Minister Wylbur SIMUUSA stated that the government would raise its stakes in the mines to 35 percent. In response, the global ratings agency Fitch downgraded Zambia's outlook and Simuusa was quickly sacked.

On March 14, 2012, the MMD was stripped of its legal status for failing to pay registration fees over the last two decades, an amount totaling roughly $70,000. The move was widely seen as engineered by Sata as a means to intimidate the MMD, and opposition officials complained of "an assault on democracy." In solidarity with the MMD, the UPND threatened to withdraw its 29 legislators from the parliament. On March 15, the MMD won a decision from the High Court to stay the cancelation of its registration.

On March 29, 2012, the BBC reported that the Barotse royal household and other Barotse leaders were demanding independence, accusing the government of ignoring a deal that granted the region semiautonomy. Government officials reportedly labeled the demand for independence "treason," even though Sata had initially claimed he would restore the agreement.

In September 2012 the government conducted a successful bond auction worth $750 million. The auction for the ten-year bonds demonstrated continued investor confidence in Zambia and provided funds for infrastructure and economic development programs. Meanwhile, Sata ended popular subsidies for fuel and corn in response to pressure from the World Bank.

In March 2013 the Assembly removed former president Banda's immunity from prosecution. Banda was subsequently arrested on corruption charges related to an oil arrangement with Nigeria. He was released on bail after his initial incarceration. Critics accused the government of targeting opposition leaders for arrest and intimidation. His trial was repeatedly delayed.

POLITICAL PARTIES

In December 1972 the United National Independence Party (UNIP) became the country's only legal political party. During the late 1980s reformists called for a multiparty system, with President Kaunda repeatedly dismissing the idea as unworkable because of "too many tribal conflicts." However, in September 1990 he bowed to mounting pressure and agreed to termination of the UNIP monopoly. Three months later, the president signed a National Assembly bill legalizing the formation of political parties, and in August 1991 a multiparty constitution was adopted. Thereafter, on October 31 the UNIP, the Movement for Multiparty Democracy (MMD), and 12 smaller parties participated in the first multiparty balloting since 1968.

Several parties formed electoral alliances in advance of the 2006 presidential and parliamentary elections. The UPND, the UNIP, and the FDD formed the United Democratic Alliance (UDA). A coalition of smaller parties, styled the National Democratic Focus (NDF), included the ZRP, Zadeco, and the ZDDM.

Government Party:

Patriotic Front—PF. The PF was formed in 2001 by disgruntled former MMD members, including Michael Sata, who resigned as MMD secretary general in September to protest what he described as the irregular method of selection of Levy Mwanawasa as the MMD's standard-bearer. Sata was credited with 3.35 percent of the vote in the 2001 presidential poll.

In 2005 Sata, a staunch critic of President Mwanawasa, was charged with alleged espionage for supporting striking mine workers, and in 2006 Sata and party secretary general Guy Scott were charged with defaming the president after Sata allegedly leaked a letter written by President Mwanawasa. Sata claimed the letter was a forgery and a "trap."

Sata's supporters engaged in violent protests when initial reports of his 2006 presidential victory were determined to be wrong. Riots occurred mainly in the Copperbelt, where Sata was regarded as a hero because of his battle for the rights of miners. Sata made headlines during the campaign by saying that if elected he would expel Chinese investors from the mining industry in Zambia and would promote ties with Taiwan, angering Chinese officials. In December 2006 Sata was arrested on charges of "false declaration of assets" in connection with documents he had filed in his election bid. The charges were dropped a few days later.

In 2008 the Supreme Court nullified three of the PF's parliamentary seats following a ruling that the seats had not been won fairly. In the run-up to the 2008 presidential by-election, a rift in the party developed in May after Sata dismissed some 20 party members who had attended a government-sponsored conference on proposed revisions to the constitution, which the PF officially opposed. The disaffected PF members were said to have joined the camp of Peter MACHUNGWA, a former minister in the Chiluba government, who had rejoined the PF in 2006. Presidential candidate Sata ruled out a proposed electoral alliance with the UPND to back the candidacy of Hakainde Hichilema, saying the PF was strong enough to win on its own. Two days before the October 30 by-election, 300 members of the PF reportedly resigned to join the MMD.

However, in advance of the 2011 elections, the PF and the UPND in 2009 agreed to an electoral alliance to challenge the MMD.

In February 2009 Secretary General Edward MUMBI resigned from the party in the wake of what he called "weird allegations" against him leveled by Sata. Following the 2008 elections, Sata had accused Mumbi of accepting a bribe to derail the PF's presidential campaign. Mumbi, for his part, said Sata failed to provide donated resources to rural areas to ensure PF success in the election, and he blamed Sata for the party's loss.

In advance of the 2011 elections, party members were pressing for Sata to be their presidential candidate, despite the PF's alliance with the UPND. Meanwhile, Mumbi accused the party of being connected to the "red card" campaign (see Current Issues, above), but party officials denied it. The party secured 60 seats in the 2011 balloting, and Sata won the presidency. He chose Guy SCOTT, a well-known moderate within the party, as his vice president. Scott was barred from succeeding Sata since he was not born in Zambia, leading observers to speculate that the president chose Scott so he could ensure that the vice-president did not emerge as a future political rival.

Party secretary general Wynter Kabimba, one of Sata's closest confidants, is reportedly working to build a base in the party, seeking to take over its leadership in 2016. Opposition parties accused Kabimba of attempting to create a one-party state after he launched an aggressive campaign to lure opposition lawmakers to the PF.

Leaders: Michael SATA (President of the Republic and 2001, 2006, 2008, and 2011 presidential candidate), Guy SCOTT (Vice President of the Republic), Given LUBINDA (Spokesperson), Wynter KABIMBA (Secretary General).

Other Legislative Parties:

Movement for Multiparty Democracy—MMD. Formed in mid-1990 as a loose alliance of anti-UNIP groups in support of a voter registration drive, the MMD applied for legal party status immediately following legislative approval of a multiparty system in December. Among other things, the group issued a manifesto declaring its commitment to a free-market economy.

In June 1991 the MMD denounced a proposed draft constitution on the grounds that it would advance an excessively powerful presidency; the party threatened to boycott upcoming elections if it were adopted. Consequently, President Kaunda met in July with MMD leaders to forge a compromise document. Meanwhile, violent clashes between MMD and UNIP supporters continued, and in September the MMD complained that limiting the campaign period to two months favored the incumbents. Nevertheless, in the October 31 balloting Frederick Chiluba of the MMD defeated Kaunda's bid for reelection, with the MMD also winning an overwhelming majority of National Assembly seats. Subsequently, in sparsely attended balloting in late November 1992, the party captured nearly 75 percent of 1,190 local council seats.

In early 1993 a growing interparty chasm was reported between those members urging faster governmental reform and a second, reportedly more influential faction, which was concerned less with reform and more with "strengthening the political and financial interests of the... commercial class." Founding member and party chair Arthur Wina was one of 14 prominent MMD officials who withdrew from the grouping in August to protest the dismissal of cabinet ministers identified as having exposed corruption and drug trafficking by their colleagues. Thereafter, more members left the party as its popularity plummeted amid allegations that top officials were sheltered from the effects of the government's economic austerity program. On the other hand, in November 1993 Enoch Kavindele, leader of the United Democratic Party, dissolved his party and joined the MMD, claiming that he and Chiluba shared similar development strategies.

Internal friction, based in part on tribal differences as well as the personal ambition of various MMD leaders, was reported throughout the rest of the 1990s, although the party retained solid political control at both the national and local levels. Fractionalization reached its apex in early 2000 when it became apparent that President Chiluba's supporters were intent on constitutional revision that would permit him a third term. Some 400 delegates walked out of the MMD congress in Lusaka at the end of April to protest the initiative; however, the remaining delegates dutifully endorsed Chiluba as the MMD candidate in the upcoming presidential race, calling for a national referendum on the proposed constitutional change. In the wake of massive protest demonstrations, Chiluba several days later announced he had decided not to seek a third term, but at the same time more than 20 senior members of the MMD (including some 11 cabinet members) were expelled from the party, some of them subsequently helping to form new opposition parties.

In August 2001 Levy Mwanawasa, a prominent attorney and former vice president of the republic, was selected as the new MMD standard-bearer. Critics initially described Mwanawasa as Chiluba's hand-picked successor, but tension was apparent between the two MMD leaders following Mwanawasa's controversial victory in the national balloting, the new president, among other things, reportedly rejecting Chiluba's suggestions for cabinet appointments. In 2002 Chiluba was forced to resign as party president, resulting in Mwanawasa becoming acting president. According to some reports, Mwanawasa subsequently was unanimously elected as party president on the understanding that he would not prosecute Chiluba. After thousands of protesters demanded that Parliament lift Chiluba's immunity, the president made the same request. Following Chiluba's arrest on corruption charges in 2003, his supporters defected from the MMD and formed the PUDD (below).

The National Citizens' Coalition (NCC), sometimes referred to as the National Christian Coalition, merged with the MDD after the MDD's leader, prominent pastor Nevers Mumba, was appointed vice president in 2003. (Mumba had run for the presidency in 2001 but had received only 2.2 percent of the vote.) In October 2004 Mumba was dismissed as vice president following his comments accusing opposition parties of taking funds from foreign sources. He was forced to leave the party in 2005 after he reportedly accused President Mwanawasa and his wife of using government money to buy party convention votes, and subsequently supported opposition candidate Michael Sata of the PF in the 2006 presidential election.

Although Mwanawasa won the party leadership by a landslide in 2005, providing him a mandate to seek a second term as president of the republic in 2006, rifts in the party were reported among rivals who campaigned against him. Following Mwanawasa's decisive victory in 2006, the party appeared to rally behind Mwanawasa and the reforms he proposed.

Former ZRP Secretary General Sylvia MASEBO, then minister of local government and housing, defected to the MMD in June 2006.

Rifts in the party reappeared in 2008 as Mwanawasa lay ill in a Paris hospital. While some in the party suggested that a search for a successor begin, the idea was soundly rejected by others. The party had no vice president to tap as a successor to Mwanawasa (the party congress having canceled an election for the seat in the wake of reports of alleged vote-buying by candidates). Additionally, some of the party's other possible contenders, specifically Michael Mabenga and Katele Kalumba, the latter a finance minister under former President Chiluba, were tainted by allegations of corruption. The party was also divided over the selection of a presidential candidate, as 19 members sought to be the standard-bearer. Ultimately, Vice President Rupiah Banda, a former member of the UNIP, who, MMD leaders claimed, had joined the MMD "a long time ago," was chosen on September 5 as the party's presidential nominee over six others, including Finance Minister Ngandu Magande.

Despite President Banda's weak victory over the PF's Michael Sata in the October 2008 by-election, in June 2009 the party endorsed Banda for reelection in the 2011 poll. Banda pledged to strengthen the party in advance of the elections, however, corruption and infighting marked events in 2010. National Secretary Kalumba was convicted, along with two others, of corruption and sentenced to five years in prison, and former defense minister George Mpombo and former finance minister Magande were forced to resign after their alleged "outbursts" against President Banda. Magande subsequently formed a new party, the National Movement for Progress (below).

Ahead of the 2011 presidential election, Banda, under pressure from his sons, fired his longtime friend and ally, Vernon MWAANGA, as his campaign manager after Mwaanga nominated two people for party posts in opposition to the two nominees Banda preferred. The firing of Mwaanga, the defection to the PF of several high-ranking party members in protest against Mwaanga's sacking, and the death in June of former president Chiluba were seen as considerable blows to Banda's reelection effort. Within party circles Henry and James Banda, the president's sons, received much of the blame for their father's defeat in the 2011 elections. Following the balloting, several MND deputies in the Assembly defected to the PF, prompting a wave of by-elections.

Leaders: Rupiah BANDA (Former President of the Republic), Michael MABENGA (National Chair), Lupando MWAPE (Former Vice President of the Republic), Dora SILIYA (Spokesperson), Boniface KAWIMBE, Chembe NYANGU (Deputy National Secretary), Richard KACHINGWE (National Secretary).

United Party for National Development—UPND. Described as representing the interests of urbanized Zambians, the UPND was launched on December 1998 under the leadership of business leader Anderson Mazoka, who had recently left the MMD. The party quickly became a major opposition grouping, winning four of the six legislative by-elections it had contested as of mid-2000. Mazoka, running with the support of the National Party, secured an official 26.76 percent of the vote in the 2001 presidential balloting, although his supporters charged he had actually won the election and challenged the results in court. Meanwhile, the UPND easily became the leading opposition party by securing 49 seats in the concurrent legislative balloting.

Following Mazoka's death in 2006, a rift developed in the party, with members from the Southern Province backing Mazoka's widow as successor while party officials approached ZCTU president Leonard HIKAUMBA over the party's acting president, Sakwiba SIKOTA. After the party's divisive and chaotic convention in July, in which Lusaka businessman (and Mazoka protégé) Hakainde Hichilema was elected president, Sikota resigned (along with party vice president Robert SICHINGA and secretary general Logan SHEMENA), and he subsequently formed the United Liberal Party (below). Sikota blamed "tribalism and violence" for the party's election upheaval, though the election was declared fair by the Foundation for Democratic Process (FODEP). Sikota's departure reportedly left the party in disarray, with party vice president for economic and political affairs Patrick Chisanga trying to mend fences. Following Hichilema's failed bid for the presidency in 2006, the UDA faced a rift with FDD leader Edith Nawakwi over whether Hichilmena would automatically be the UDA's candidate for the next presidential election in 2011.

The UPND was unsuccessful in persuading the PF's Michael Sata to participate in an electoral alliance with the UPND and back Hichilema in the 2008 by-election. Meanwhile, Hichilema caused a rift in the party as a result of his trip to China in May to sign a cooperation agreement with the Chinese Communist Party, since China was seen as being a key supporter of the MMD government.

In 2009 the UPND called on parliament to repeal a public procurement act adopted a year earlier and replace it with one that had stronger anti-corruption measures. Though the UPND and the PF had agreed to an electoral alliance to challenge the MMD in the 2011 presidential election, rifts developed in 2010 over who should be the standard-bearer, with Hichilema unwilling to give ground to the PF's Sata and declaring himself a candidate. Further, some 250 members were said to have defected to the MMD.

In March 2011 it was reported that the UPND had entered into an alliance with the small APC (below). Ahead of the September election, Hichilema pledged to create more jobs, invest in education, and uphold the public trust. He placed third in the balloting with 18.4 percent of the vote. In 2013, Hichilema was charged with a series of crimes, including corruption and unlawful assembly.

In February 2013 the UNDP expelled Assembly deputy Greyford MONDE after he became deputy agriculture minister in the PF-led government.

Leaders: Hakainde HICHILEMA (President of the Party and 2006, 2008, and 2011 presidential candidate), Richard KAPITA (Vice President), Charles KAKOMA (Spokesperson), Winston CHIBWE (Secretary General).

United National Independence Party—UNIP. The UNIP was formed as a result of the 1958 withdrawal of Kenneth D. Kaunda, Simon M. Kapwepwe, and others from the preindependence African National Congress (ANC), led by Harry Nkumbula. The UNIP was banned by the British in March 1959, reconstituted the following October, and ruled Zambia from independence until October 1991.

On May 29, 1990, in announcing that the National Council had approved the holding of a referendum on multipartyism, President Kaunda stated that it would be "stupid" for the party not to explain to the public that approval of such a system would be equivalent to "courting national disaster." Nevertheless, at the 25th meeting of the UNIP National Council on September 24, 1990, Kaunda announced that referendum plans would be canceled and a multiparty constitution adopted prior to the 1991 poll.

At an extraordinary party congress held August 6–7, 1991, Kaunda faced a leadership challenge from businessman Enoch Kavindele; however, under pressure from party stalwarts, Kavindele withdrew his bid, and Kaunda won unanimous reelection as party president. Thereafter, in nationwide balloting on October 31, both Kaunda and the UNIP suffered resounding defeats, the former capturing only 24 percent of the presidential vote and the latter being limited to 26 assembly seats. In the wake of his electoral defeat, Kaunda resigned as party leader on January 6, 1992, but reversed himself four months later.

Fueled by the defection of a number of party members to Kavindele's newly formed United Democratic Party (UDP) and the UNIP's poor showing in local elections in November 1992, speculation mounted in early 1993 that Kebby Musoktwane, who had been elected party president at an extraordinary congress on October 1, would be supplanted by Maj. Wezi Kaunda, head of the UNIP's military wing and son of the former president. However, Wezi Kaunda, along with his two brothers, Tilyenji Kaunda and Panji KAUNDA, were among approximately 25 people, including 7 UNIP central committee members, arrested in March 1993 on charges stemming from an alleged coup plot. For its part, the party denied charges that it had planned to overthrow the Chiluba administration, with Musoktwane insisting that he had aided the government in exposing the plot.

In June 1993 former president Kaunda resigned from the party, citing a desire to become "father" to all Zambians and complaining that he had been denied a pension by the Chiluba government. In March 1994 approximately 85 members of the now defunct UDP rejoined the UNIP. (Prior to its dissolution in late 1993 UDP membership had been dominated by UNIP defectors.) In June 1994 the UNIP was instrumental in the formation of the Zambia Opposition Front (Zofro), an opposition umbrella organization that included the **Independent Democratic Front** (IDF), led by Mike KAIRA; the **Labour Party** (LP), led by Chipeza MUFUNE; the **National Democratic Alliance** (NDA), led by Yonam PHIRI (the NDA was reportedly deregistered in 1998); the **National Party for Democracy** (NPD), led by Tenthani MWANZA; and the **Zambia Progressive Party** (ZPP).

Although Kaunda's decision in May 1995 to return to political life was coolly received by Musoktwane and his youthful supporters, the former president encountered little difficulty in being reelected to the UNIP presidency on June 28. Kaunda continued to enjoy broad party support throughout 1995 and the first half of 1996 despite intensive government efforts to discredit him. However, in June 1996 former party secretary general Benjamin Mibenge called for an extraordinary UNIP congress to elect a new leader, asserting, according to *Africa Confidential,* that it was time to break "the myth that Dr. Kaunda can forever lead the party." Meanwhile, the government arrested seven people (including Kaunda) with ties to the UNIP, charging them with complicity in a wave of bombings and bomb threats allegedly masterminded by a terrorist group called *Black Mamba,* Kaunda's nickname during Zambia's independence drive.

In early October 1996 Zofro announced it would back single candidates in the upcoming legislative balloting. Meanwhile, Kaunda declared his intention of running for president again despite the recent controversial amendment that appeared to have disqualified him. However, later in the month the UNIP announced plans to boycott the legislative balloting, citing what it described as the "mismanagement" of the voter registration drive and charging the government with manipulating the constitution. Furthermore, Kaunda asserted that the continued imprisonment of six prominent party members on treason charges had undermined the UNIP's electoral preparations. The charges were dropped on November 1. (Charges against Kaunda had been dismissed earlier.)

In April 1997 a simmering intraparty rivalry between Kaunda's supporters and members opposed to his continued domination exploded into public view as the two groups clashed at a UNIP function. Internecine concerns were subsequently overshadowed, however, by violent encounters between the UNIP and supporters of the Chiluba government. In June the UNIP and its opposition allies called for foreign intervention to ease the political and social "crisis" gripping Lusaka. Two months later Kaunda accused the government of attempting to assassinate him and Roger Chongwe, leader of the **Liberal Progressive Front** (LPF), a small party allied with the UNIP.

In January 1998 Kaunda was indicted by the government for his alleged role in the October 1997 coup attempt. The UNIP president was held under house arrest until June 1, when the government, under intense international pressure, dropped the charges. In June Kaunda said he would retire from the UNIP, although he agreed to serve as party president on an acting basis until his successor was elected. Subsequently, members of the UNIP's youth wing were reported to have rallied behind the succession ambitions of Wezi Kaunda. However, Wezi died in November 1999 after being attacked by gunmen in his driveway.

Kenneth Kaunda officially retired from the UNIP presidency at the beginning of an extraordinary congress in Ndola in May 2000. He was succeeded by Francis NKHOMA, a former central bank governor, although severe factionalization was subsequently still reported in the party, particularly in regard to the new president's positive comments about potential cooperation with the MMD, of which he had been a member from 1990 to 1994. Tilyenji Kaunda was elected to the UNIP presidency in April 2001 and won 9.96 percent of the votes in the December presidential election. In 2003 the UNIP announced it would cooperate with the ruling MMD, and UNIP legislators were appointed to junior cabinet posts. Following President Mwanawasa's reelection in 2006, he appointed former UNIP representative in Europe and former cabinet minister Rupiah Banda as vice president of the republic.

The party claimed in September 2008 that Vice President Rupiah Banda had never officially resigned from the UNIP, even though Banda was on the ballot as the MMD's candidate for president. However, Kaunda threw his support behind Banda's candidacy because, observers said, he felt Banda would be more sympathetic to the UNIP than would Sata. In mid-October the party officially announced its endorsement of Banda's candidacy.

In April 2009 the UNIP and the UPND condemned the PF's plans for a protest demonstration against job losses in the Copperbelt, arguing that the demonstration would not resolve the issue, and that it was not necessary to blame the government when the global economic downturn was the cause. Secretary General Alfred Banda resigned from the party in 2009 in a dispute regarding the UNIP's not having held a national congress.

In 2010 some 100 members defected to the PF. Meanwhile, party leader Kaunda announced that he would seek the presidency in the 2011 poll and subsequently secured the party's nomination. He placed fifth in the balloting with less than 1 percent of the vote, while the UNIP secured 28 seats in the Assembly.

Leaders: Tilyenji KAUNDA (President and 2001 and 2011 presidential candidate), Njekwa ANAMELA (Vice Chair), Jemima BANDA (Secretary General).

Forum for Democracy and Development—FDD. Reportedly enjoying support among students and other urban dwellers, the FDD was launched in 2001 by former MMD members opposed to efforts by President Chiluba to run for a third term. Party founders included Lt. Gen. Christon Tembo, who had been dismissed as vice president of the republic by Chiluba in May. Tembo finished third in the 2001 presidential balloting, securing 12.96 percent of the vote according to the official results. The FDD expelled four members in 2003 after they accepted cabinet posts in the MMD-led government. Several other FDD members subsequently left the party and joined the MMD. Former finance minister Edith Nawakwi was elected party president in 2005.

The FDD did not participate in the 2008 by-election, and in March 2009, Tembo died.

In 2010 party vice president Chifumu Bandu was chair of the country's National Constitutional Commission when it released its draft charter for public review. In March the party chastised Nawakwi for her repeated verbal attacks against President Banda, stating that they were her personal views and not those of the party. Nawakwi was the party's 2011 presidential candidate. She received less than 1 percent of the vote. The party secured one seat in the 2011 elections.

Leaders: Edith NAWAKWI (Party President and 2011 presidential candidate), Chifumu BANDA (Vice President), Levy NGOMA (Youth Chair).

Alliance for Democracy and Development—ADD. The ADD was established by independent member of parliament Charles MILUPI in May 2010 with the aim of "entrenching real democracy." Milupi placed third in the presidential election in 2011, and the party secured one seat in the Assembly polling.

Leader: Charles MILUPI (Chair and 2011 presidential candidate).

Other Parties That Contested the 2011 Elections:

United Liberal Party—ULP. Former UPND acting president Sakwiba Sikota formed the United Liberal Party in July 2006 after his failed bid to become UPND president. He broke away with several other senior officials of UPND, accusing the latter party of corruption and tribalism. Many of his supporters were reported to be from his home Western Province.

The party backed Rupiah Banda in the 2008 and 2011 presidential elections. It received less than 1 percent of the vote in Assembly balloting.

Leaders: Sakwiba SIKOTA (President), Chrispin SHUMINA (Secretary General).

Zambia Republican Party—ZRP. The formation of the ZRP was announced in February 2001 as a merger of the Zambia Alliance for Progress (ZAP, see below), the Republican Party (RP), and the small National Republican Party.

The RP, with support centered in the Copperbelt, had been founded in mid-2000 by wealthy businessman Ben Mwila and a number of his supporters following their expulsion from the MMD. (Mwila had incurred the wrath of other MMD leaders by indicating a desire to run for president of the republic while a possible third term for President Chiluba was still under consideration.)

Both Mwila and Dean MUNGOMBA of the ZAP announced their presidential ambitions prior to the creation of the ZRP, and friction quickly materialized between the two. Consequently, Mungomba announced that he and his supporters were withdrawing from the ZRP to resume ZAP activity, although a number of former ZAP members remained in the new grouping.

Mwila was officially credited with 4.84 percent of the vote as the ZRP candidate in the 2001 presidential poll. Among other things, the ZRP platform called for increased privatization of state-run enterprises and the extension of agricultural subsidies.

In June 2006 a faction that included about 15 members, led by party secretary general Shirley Masebo, defected to the MMD.

Reports in 2011 indicated that Mwila ran unsuccessfully as an independent in that year's Assembly balloting.

Leaders: Benjamin Yorum MWILA (President and 2001 presidential candidate), Ben KAPITA (Chair).

Zambia Direct Democracy Movement—ZDDM. The ZDDM joined the NDF in 2006. In 2008 party leader Edwin Sakala urged a government of national unity prior to the October 30 by-election.

The party turned its focus in 2010 to fighting poverty and disease and began its own "white card" campaign to promote national progress.

Party leader Edwin Sakala withdrew from the national presidential race in August 2011. The ZDDM received less than 1 percent of the vote in the 2011 Assembly balloting.

Leaders: Edwin SAKALA (Chair), Maurice CHOONGO (Spokesperson).

Heritage Party—HP. The HP was formed in 2001 by Brig. Gen. Godfrey Miyanda, a former MMD stalwart and former vice president of the republic, who had left the ruling party in the dispute over a proposed third term for President Chiluba. He rejected pressure to join with the FDD; subsequently, some FDD and MDD members reportedly defected to the HP in 2001. Miyanda secured 7.96 percent of the vote in the 2001 presidential balloting, according to official results, and the party gained 4 seats in the legislative balloting. In 2006 the HP and the AC entered into an alliance in which the AC agreed not present a presidential candidate and to support the candidate put forth by the HP. Also, candidates in parliamentary and local elections in 2006 ran under the HP banner, according to the agreement between the HP and the AC.

Miyanda was tapped as the party's flagbearer for the 2011 presidential election. He received 0.17 percent of the vote, while the HP secured just 0.02 percent of the vote in concurrent legislative polling.

Leader: Brig. Gen. Godfrey MIYANDA (Former Vice President of the Republic and 2001, 2006, 2008, and 2011 presidential candidate).

All People's Congress—APC. Formed in 2005, the APC's stated goal was to "set the Zambian political life on a new course for the future," striving for economic progress and social justice. The APC briefly joined the NDF in March 2006 but subsequently withdrew over reported tribal differences. Some reports said that APC leader Ken NGONDO was expelled from the NDF.

Ngondo, a businessman and former member of Parliament, finished last in the 2006 presidential balloting with less than 1 percent of the vote.

The APC backed Rupiah Banda in the 2008 presidential election. Party leader Ngondo died in November 2010.

In 2011 the APC failed to secure any seats in the Assembly balloting.

Leaders: Chozi NGUNI (President), Maggy NGONA.

New Generation Party—NGP. Former FDD youth leader Humphrey Siulapwa formed the NGP in 2003 to address issues of youth, in particular. Siulapwa registered as a presidential candidate in 2006 but subsequently withdrew because of the high entry fee required. The party fielded parliamentary candidates in 2006 but failed to win any seats.

The NGP endorsed Banda in the 2008 and 2011 elections. It received less than 1 percent of the vote in the 2011 legislative balloting.

Leader: Humphrey SIULAPWA.

Other parties participating in the 2011 elections were the **Citizens Democratic Party** (CDP); **Zambians for Empowerment and Development** (ZED), led by Frederick MUTESA, who received 0.08 percent of the vote in the presidential balloting; the **National Revolution Party** (NRP), headed by Cosmo MUMBA, formerly of the NGP, and Kelly WALUBITA; the **New Generation Party** (NGP); the **United Party for Democracy and Development** (UPDD), formed by dissidents from the UPND and led by Felix SENKA; the **Federal Democratic Party**; the **New Generation Party**, led by Cosmo MUMBA; and the **Zambia Conservative Party** (ZCP), led by Joseph CHIPILI and Peter SIMPEMBA.

Three parties or groupings that formed ahead of the 2011 elections and provided platforms for their leaders to run for president are: the **National Restoration Party** (NAREP), founded in March 2010 by Elias CHIPIMO Jr. with the goal of providing quality services to all Zambians; and the **National Movement for Progress** (NMP), founded in September 2010 by former finance minister Ngandu Magande, a fierce critic of Banda, after Magande was expelled from the MMD. The **Mega Combination** *(Mega Combinate*—MC) was launched prior to the 2010 election as a four-party coalition supportive of Désiré BOUTERSE's bid for the presidency.

Other Parties and Groups:

Agenda for Change—AC. Established in 2006 by a U.S.-based professor, Henry KYAMBALESA, this small party entered into an electoral agreement with the HP in advance of the presidential and parliamentary elections.

In 2010 party leader Kyambalesa objected to an article in the proposed constitution promoting Christian values and principles on the basis that such wording was inconsistent with upholding an individual's right to freedom of religion.

Leader: Henry KYAMBALESA.

National Leadership for Development—NLD. The NLD was launched in mid-2001 by Yobert Shamapande, a former United Nations (UN) official and relative newcomer to domestic politics. Running on a platform that emphasized education, poverty reduction, gender balance in government, and better health services, Shamapande won 0.5 percent of the vote in the 2001 presidential balloting. Thereafter, Shamapande pledged his support to President Mwanawasa's policies. The NLD was reportedly defunct.

Leader: Yobert SHAMAPANDE (President and 2001 presidential candidate).

Barotse Patriotic Front—BPF. References to the BPF first appeared in 1998 in regard to calls for independence or autonomy for a portion of western Zambia that had, along with regions in what are now Namibia and Botswana, been known as Barotseland. That kingdom of Lozi-speakers had enjoyed what one journalist called "half-independence" under British colonial rule. The area in Zambia became part of that country at independence in 1964 under an autonomy agreement with the UNIP under which the tribal chieftain was to retain significant powers, particularly in regard to control of land and resources. Lozi leaders subsequently claimed that UNIP had abrogated the agreement by stripping the chief of many of his powers.

The BPF in 1999 supported the secessionist activities of the Caprivi Liberation Front, which represents Lozi-speakers in Namibia (see Illegal Groups in the entry on Namibia for details). The BPF also called for a self-determination vote in western Zambia, prompting the detention of BPF leader Imasiku Mutangelwa on sedition charges. The BPF has acted in concert with a Barotse Cultural Association, while a Forum for the Restoration of Barotseland in July 2001 petitioned the OAU and the UN to conduct a self-determination referendum. In 2004 the BPF renewed its call to restore the name Barotseland to the Western Province and for the constitution of Zambia to uphold the 1964 agreement. Reports in 2013 indicated that the BPF was defunct.

Leaders: Imasiku MUTANGELWA (President), Pumulo YUSIKU (Executive Secretary).

Minor parties include the **Common Cause Democracy** (CCD), led by James MTONGA; the **New Congress Party** (NCP), led by Cosmas MWALE and Secretary General John CHIBOMA; the **Progressive Parties Alliance** (PPA), led by Paul BANDA; the **United Nationalist Party** (UNP), led by Achim NGOSA; the **United Poor People of Zambia Freedom Party** (UPPZFP), led by Alex MULIOKELA; and the **People's Democratic Party** (PDP), formed in 2013 and led by George MPOMBO.

For more information on the **United Democratic Alliance**—UDA, which participated in the 2006 and 2008 elections but is now defunct, please see the 2013 *Handbook.* Please also see the 2013 *Handbook* for more details on the defunct **National Democratic Focus**—NDF, an alliance of smaller parties, initially referenced as the National Democratic Front and formed prior to the 2006 presidential election.

LEGISLATURE

The current **National Assembly** is a unicameral body consisting of 150 elected members, 8 presidentially appointed members, and the speaker, who is elected by the members of the assembly from outside their membership. The term of office is five years. Prior to the 1991 election, candidates were required to be members of the United National Independence Party (UNIP) and endorsed by that party's Central Committee. In the most recent elections on September 20, 2011, the seat distribution was as follows: the Patriotic Front, 60; the Movement for Multiparty Democracy, 55; the United Party for National Development, 28; Alliance for Democracy and Development, 1; Forum for Democracy and Development, 1.

Speaker: Patrick MATIBINI.

CABINET

[as of November 15, 2013]

President	Michael Sata
Vice President	Guy Scott
Ministers	
Agriculture and Cooperatives	Emmanuel Chenda
Chiefs and Traditional Affairs	Inonge Wina [f]
Commerce, Trade, and Industry	Robert Sichinga
Community Development and Social Services	Joseph Katema
Defense	Geofrey Mwamba
Education, Science, Vocational Training and Early Education	John Phiri
Finance and National Planning	Alexander Chikwanda
Foreign Affairs	Wylbur Simuusa
Health	Joseph Kasonde
Home Affairs	Edgar Lungu
Information and Broadcasting	Mwansa Kapeya
Justice	Wynter Kabimba
Labor and Social Security	Fackson Shamenda
Lands, Natural Resources and Environmental Protection	Harry Kalaba
Local Government, Housing, Early Education and Environmental Protection	Nkandu Luo [f]
Mines, Energy and Water Development	Christopher Yaluma
Sport, Youth, and Child Development	Chishimba Kambwili
Tourism and the Arts	Sylvia Masebo [f]
Transport, Works, Supply and Communications	Yamfwa Mukanga

[f] = female

Note: All of the above are members of the Patriotic Front.

INTERGOVERNMENTAL REPRESENTATION

Ambassador to the U.S.: Palan MULONDA.

U.S. Ambassador to Zambia: Eric T. SCHULTZ (nominated).

Permanent Representative to the UN: Mwaba Patricia KASESE-BOTA.

IGO Memberships (Non-UN): AfDB, AU, Comesa, CWTH, IOM, NAM, SADC, WTO.

ZIMBABWE

Republic of Zimbabwe

Political Status: Became self-governing British Colony of Southern Rhodesia in October 1923; unilaterally declared independence November 11, 1965; white-dominated republican regime proclaimed March 2, 1970; biracial executive established on basis of transitional government agreement of March 3, 1978; returned to interim British rule on basis of cease-fire agreement signed December 21, 1979;

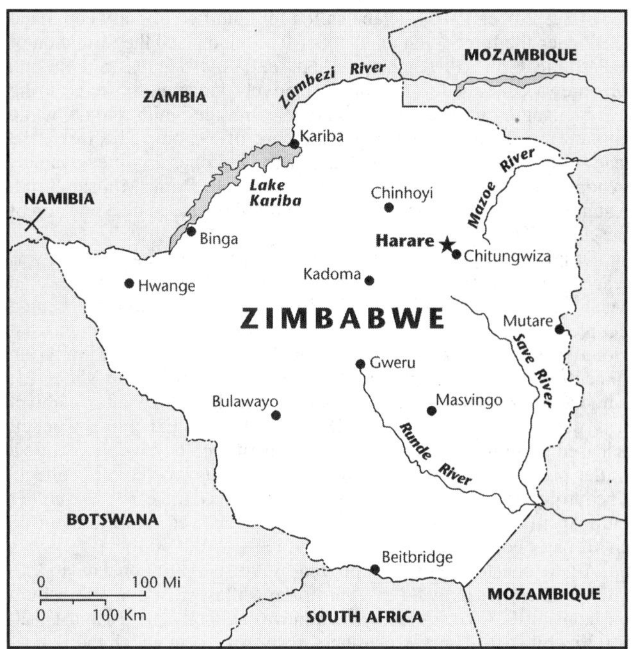

achieved de jure independence as Republic of Zimbabwe on April 18, 1980; new constitution approved by referendum on March 16, 2013, and adopted on May 22.

Area: 150,803 sq. mi. (390,580 sq. km).

Population: 13,099,108 (2012E—UN); 13,182,908 (2013E—U.S. Census).

Major Urban Center (including suburbs, 2009E—UN): HARARE (formerly Salisbury, 1,513,173).

Official Language: English (Shona and Sindebele are the principal African languages).

Monetary Unit: Zimbabwe Dollar (official rate November 1, 2013: 361.90 dollars = $1US). Although the Zimbabwe dollar has an official exchange rate, the currency was suspended in 2009 because of hyperinflation. By 2011 a one-trillion Zimbabwean dollar bill had a street value of about $5. The South African rand, the U.S. dollar, and the British pound are now commonly used.

President: Robert Gabriel MUGABE (Zimbabwe African National Union-Patriotic Front); sworn in as prime minister on April 18, 1980, following legislative election of February 14 and 27–29; reconfirmed following election of June 30 and July 1–2, 1985; elected president by parliament on December 30, 1987, and inaugurated for an anticipated six-year term on December 31, succeeding the former head of state, Rev. Canaan Sodindo BANANA; reelected for a six-year term, following constitutional revision, by popular vote March 28–30, 1990; reelected for another six-year term March 16–17, 1996; reelected for another six-year term March 9–11, 2002; reelected in a disputed runoff on June 27, 2008, and sworn in for a five-year term on June 29; reelected in disputed balloting on July 31, 2013, and sworn in for another five-year term on August 22.

Vice President: Joyce MUJURU (Zimbabwe African National Union-Patriotic Front); appointed by the president on December 6, 2004, to succeed Simon MUZENDA, who died on September 20, 2003; reappointed by the president on October 13, 2008, and sworn in the same day; reappointed by the president on September 11, 2013, and sworn in the same day.

THE COUNTRY

Bordered by Botswana, Zambia, Mozambique, and South Africa, Zimbabwe occupies the fertile plateaus and mountain ranges between southeastern Africa's Zambezi and Limpopo rivers. The population includes approximately 11.5 million Africans, mainly Bantu in origin; some 200,000 Europeans; and smaller groups of Asians and people of mixed race. The Africans may be classified into two multitribal groupings, the Shona (about 82 percent) in the north, and the Ndebele, concentrated in the southern area of Matabeleland. Shona-Ndebele rivalry dates to the 19th century and has contributed to a pronounced north-south cleavage. The majority of the European population is Protestant, although there is a substantial Catholic minority. The Africans include both Christians and followers of traditional religions; the Asians are a mixture of Hindus and Muslims.

In 1982 a Legal Age of Majority Act significantly enhanced the legal status of women (including the right of personal choice in selecting a marital partner, the right to own property outright, and the ability to enter into business contracts); it has, however, been unevenly utilized because of its conflict with traditional law. In 2008 about 47.5 percent of the paid labor force was estimated to be female; black women are responsible for most subsistence agriculture (cash-crop production had been undertaken mainly by some 4,500 white farmers who at one time owned more than 70 percent of the arable land); white and Asian women are concentrated in the clerical and service sectors. In the 2013 legislative balloting, women secured 85 of 270 seats (31.5 percent), including 60 reserved for women.

Zimbabwe was endowed with natural resources that historically yielded a relatively advanced economy oriented toward foreign trade. Zimbabwe exported maize and other food crops to shortage-plagued neighbors. Despite international trade sanctions on Zimbabwe (then Rhodesia), its economy prospered for much of the 1970s because of continued access to trade routes through South Africa, which became the conduit for up to 90 percent of Rhodesian imports and exports. The lifting of sanctions at the end of 1979 further stimulated the economy, although budget deficits and inflation persisted. In addition, unemployment was aggravated by a growing pool of workers seeking better jobs because of rapid educational advances by blacks.

Zimbabwe has suffered from severe deterioration of economic, social, and political conditions, in large part due to the government's controversial land redistribution program (see Political background, below). The government has also been buffeted by allegations of corruption and broad mismanagement of the economy, marked by a bloated and inefficient civil service, massive budget deficits, and, at times, a soaring inflation rate. Severe poverty has remained widespread. Conditions steadily worsened from 2005 to 2007. During that period, inflation and infant mortality rates were estimated to be among the highest in the world, and millions of people were said to be suffering from food shortages. The government introduced emergency reforms, issuing new currency and seizing cash from citizens and businesses in an effort to curtail black-market trade.

In mid-2007 price controls were introduced to help regulate the market. Inflation was reported to be 100,000 percent. The International Monetary Fund (IMF) expressed "deep concern over the deteriorating economic and social conditions" and Zimbabwe's $129 million in arrears to the fund's poverty reduction program. The fund subsequently tabled its review to consider restoring Zimbabwe's voting rights.

In 2008 as the nation's reserve bank printed excess money without restraint to bankroll government spending, Zimbabwe was reported to have among the world's highest rates of inflation and debt-to-GDP ratio. GDP contracted by 14 percent, according to the IMF. Contributing to deteriorating conditions were severe food shortages and a cholera epidemic that killed more than 4,000 people. Also in 2008 the government enacted legislation which mandated that 51 percent of all businesses be owned by indigenous Zimbabweans in a policy known as "indigenization." The measure was unevenly applied to foreign firms, but it severely constrained foreign investment (see Current issues, below).

The government began to control hyperinflation in January 2009 when it abandoned the domestic currency in favor of the U.S. dollar and the South African rand. Following the establishment of the unity government in February, inflation contracted to nominal rates, and the food shortage eased. Bilateral development aid remained frozen due to donor concerns over economic mismanagement and human rights violations. However, in August and September the IMF released $500 million in reserves to Zimbabwe, marking the nation's first loan from an international financial institution in nearly a decade. An annual GDP growth of 9 percent was recorded in 2010, but the nation's external debt remained high and unemployment was estimated at 95 percent. On a positive note, the IMF restored Zimbabwe's voting rights and began the process of removing the freeze on the nation's general reserve account.

Due to the impact of drought on agricultural production, GDP growth slowed to 4.4 percent in 2012. Inflation that year was 3.7 percent, and

GDP per capita was $755. The IMF noted the government had a mixed record of success at implementing past reforms, and, while mining revenues are high, investment "appears hampered by uncertainties related to the indigenization policy and the political process." The IMF also noted significant risks ahead from political instability. In its 2013 annual Doing Business survey, the World Bank ranked Zimbabwe a dismal 173rd out of 185 countries.

GOVERNMENT AND POLITICS

Political background. Originally developed and administered by the British South Africa Company, Southern Rhodesia became an internally self-governing British colony in 1923 under a system that concentrated political power in the hands of its white minority. In 1953 it joined with Northern Rhodesia (now Zambia) and Nyasaland (now Malawi) in the Federation of Rhodesia and Nyasaland. However, Southern Rhodesia reverted to separate status in 1963 when the federation was dissolved and Northern Rhodesia and Nyasaland prepared to claim their independence. A new constitution granted to Southern Rhodesia by Britain in December 1961 contained various provisions for the benefit of the African population, including a right of limited representation in the Legislative Assembly. However, the measure failed to resolve a sharpening conflict between African demands for full political equality based on the principle of "one-person, one-vote" and white Rhodesian demands for permanent white control.

In view of the refusal of Britain to agree to independence on terms that would exclude majority rule, the colonial government under Prime Minister Ian D. SMITH on November 11, 1965, issued a Unilateral Declaration of Independence purporting to make Rhodesia an independent state within the Commonwealth. Britain repudiated the action, declared the colony to be in a state of rebellion, and invoked financial and economic sanctions; however, it refused to use force against the Smith regime.

Rhodesia approved a new constitution on June 20, 1969, declaring itself a republic; subsequently, Britain suspended formal ties with the separatist regime.

On December 8, 1974, an agreement was concluded in Lusaka, Zambia, by Bishop Abel MUZOREWA of the African National Council (ANC), Joshua NKOMO of the Zimbabwe African People's Union (ZAPU), Ndabaningi SITHOLE of the Zimbabwe African National Union (ZANU), and James CHIKEREMA of the Front for the Liberation of Zimbabwe (Frolizi), whereby the latter three, representing groups that had been declared illegal within Rhodesia, would join an enlarged ANC executive under Bishop Muzorewa's presidency for a period of four months to prepare for negotiations with the Smith regime aimed at transferring power to the majority. Three days later Prime Minister Smith announced that, upon the receipt of assurances that insurgents within Rhodesia would observe a cease-fire, all black political prisoners would be released and a constitutional conference would be held without preconditions. On December 15, however, Smith again reiterated his government's opposition to the principle of majority rule.

In March 1975 Sithole, who had returned to Salisbury in December, was arrested by Rhodesian authorities on charges of plotting to assassinate his rivals in order to assume the ANC leadership. He was released a month later, following the intervention of Prime Minister Balthazar Johannes Vorster of South Africa. On December 1, 1975, Nkomo and Prime Minister Smith concluded a series of meetings by signing a declaration of intention to negotiate a settlement of the Rhodesian issue, but the agreement was repudiated by external ANC leader Bishop Muzorewa (then resident in Zambia) and by ZANU leader Sithole.

Early 1976 witnessed an intensification of guerrilla activity by Mozambique-based insurgents under the leadership of former ZANU secretary general Robert MUGABE, and a breakdown in the talks between Nkomo and Smith on March 19. In September, Smith announced that he had accepted a comprehensive package tendered by U.S. secretary of state Henry Kissinger, calling for a biracial interim government and the establishment of majority rule within two years. Britain responded to the Kissinger-Smith accord by convening a conference in Geneva between a white delegation led by Smith and a black delegation that included Nkomo, Mugabe, Muzorewa, and Sithole. However, the conference failed to yield a settlement, with the black leaders rejecting the essentials of the Kissinger plan by calling for an immediate transfer to majority rule and the replacement of the all-white Rhodesian army by contingents of the nationalist guerrilla forces.

In September 1976 Mugabe called for a unified military command of all guerrilla forces, and on October 9 he announced the formation of a Patriotic Front (PF) linking ZANU and ZAPU units. Sithole and Muzorewa continued to assume a relatively moderate posture during 1977, engaging in sporadic negotiations with the Smith regime, while Nkomo and Mugabe constituted the core of a more radical external leadership. During 1977 a number of British proposals were advanced in hopes of resolving the impasse on interim rule. Prime Minister Smith resumed discussions with Muzorewa and Sithole based on a revision of the earlier Kissinger package.

Despite the opposition of the PF to these talks, an agreement was reached on March 3, 1978, by Smith, Muzorewa, Sithole, and Mashona Chief Jeremiah S. CHIRAU of the Zimbabwe United People's Organization (ZUPO) to form a transitional government that would lead to black rule by the end of the year. Accordingly, an Executive Council comprising the four was established on March 21, while a multiracial Ministerial Council to replace the existing cabinet was designated on April 12. On May 16 the Executive Council released preliminary details of a new constitution that would feature a titular president elected by parliament sitting as an electoral college. The projected national election was postponed in early November until April 1979, following the failure of a renewed effort to convene an all-party conference.

A new constitution was approved by the assembly on January 20, 1979, and endorsed by 84 percent of the white voters in a referendum on January 30. A lower-house election was held on April 10 and 17–20 for 20 white and 72 black members, respectively, in which the UANC won 51 seats in the face of a boycott by the PF parties. Following a Senate election on May 23, Josiah GUMEDE of the UANC was elected president of Zimbabwe/Rhodesia, and on May 29 he requested Bishop Muzorewa to accept appointment as prime minister.

Following renewed guerrilla activity by PF forces in mid-1979, talks between representatives of the Muzorewa government and the Patriotic Front commenced on September 10 and ran for 14 weeks. These discussions yielded a constitutional agreement, an interim administration agreement, and a cease-fire agreement on December 5 that called for Britain to reassume full administrative authority for an interim period, during which a new and carefully monitored election would be held as a prelude to the granting of legal independence. In December the terms of the agreement were approved by parliament, and Lord SOAMES was appointed colonial governor, with Sir Anthony DUFF as his deputy. On December 12 Lord Soames arrived in Salisbury, where he was welcomed by members of the former government of Zimbabwe/Rhodesia, who, one day earlier, had approved a parliamentary bill terminating the Unilateral Declaration of Independence and transferring authority to the British administration.

White and common roll elections were held in February 1980, the Rhodesian Front winning all 20 white seats and Mugabe's ZANU-PF winning a substantial overall majority in the House of Assembly. Accordingly, Mugabe was asked by Lord Soames on March 4 to form a cabinet that included 16 members of ZANU-PF, 4 members of Nkomo's Patriotic Front–ZAPU, and 2 members of the RF. The new government was installed during independence day ceremonies on April 18 following the inauguration of Rev. Canaan Sodindo BANANA, a Mugabe supporter, as president of the republic.

The period immediately after independence was characterized by persistent conflict between armed forces of ZANU-PF and PF-ZAPU (units of Mugabe's Zimbabwe African National Liberation Army [ZANLA] and Nkomo's Zimbabwe People's Revolutionary Army [ZIPRA], respectively). To some extent the difficulties were rooted in ethnic loyalties, with most ZANLA personnel having been recruited from the northern Shona group, while ZIPRA had recruited primarily from the Ndebele people of Matabeleland. The government announced in November 1981 that a merger of the two guerrilla organizations and the former Rhodesian security force into a 50,000-man Zimbabwean national army had been completed. However, personal animosity between Mugabe and Nkomo continued, threatening the viability of the coalition regime. On February 17, 1982, Nkomo and three other ZAPU government members were dismissed from the cabinet, Nkomo declaring that his group should thenceforth be construed as an opposition party. From 1982 to 1987, Mugabe's infamous Fifth Brigade, trained in North Korea, led a terror campaign called "Gukurahundi" to intimidate dissident Ndebeles in Matabeleland and the Midlands, resulting in thousands of deaths, burning of villages, and other atrocities.

After a series of postponements, the first postindependence legislative elections were held in mid-1985. Smith's party, renamed the

Conservative Alliance of Zimbabwe (CAZ), rallied to regain 15 of the 20 white seats on June 27, while in common roll balloting held July 1–4, Mugabe's ZANU-PF won all but 1 of the non-Matabeleland constituencies, raising its assembly strength to 64 as contrasted with ZAPU's 15. Although the results fell short of the mandate desired by Mugabe for introduction of a one-party state, ZAPU members, including Nkomo, responded to overtures for merger talks, which eventually yielded an agreement on December 22, 1987, whereby the two parties would merge, with Nkomo becoming one of two ZANU-PF vice presidents. Three months earlier, following expiration of a constitutionally mandated seven-year entrenchment, the white seats in both houses of parliament had been vacated and refilled on a "non-constituency" basis by the assembly. On December 31 Mugabe, having secured unanimous assembly endorsement the day before, was sworn in as executive president; concurrently, Simon MUZENDA was inaugurated as vice president, with the post of prime minister being eliminated. On August 2, 1990, 21 of 26 ZANU-PF Politburo members voted against Mugabe's appeal for a constitutional amendment to institutionalize the one-party system that was now in place on a de facto basis.

The Senate was abolished prior to the balloting of March 28–30, 1990, in which Mugabe won 78 percent of the presidential vote and ZANU-PF swept all but four seats in the House of Assembly. Following the election, a second vice presidency was established by constitutional amendment, with Nkomo being named to the post.

On May 1, 1993, the government released a list of 70 farms, encompassing approximately 470,000 acres, which it planned to purchase for redistribution under authority of the 1992 Land Acquisition Act. Subsequently, the powerful Commercial Farmers' Union (CFU), representing approximately 4,000 white farmers, denounced the government for violating its pledge to buy only "derelict and underutilized" properties. Following the revelation in early 1994 that a majority of the parcels appropriated under the act had been granted on cheap leases to senior government officials and civil servants, Mugabe suspended that specific program in April.

At presidential balloting held March 16–17, 1996, President Mugabe captured a third term. The president's victory was tarnished, however, by the withdrawal of his only two competitors, Sithole and Muzorewa, during the week prior to balloting. Both men complained of being harassed by government security forces, and they charged that the electoral system unfairly favored the incumbent. Furthermore, voter turnout was reported to have been only 32 percent. Thus, even with an official 92 percent vote share (Sithole's and Muzorewa's names remained on the ballot, and both garnered votes), Mugabe was rumored to have secured only 28.5 percent of the potential vote, far from the mandate for which he had campaigned.

A possible settlement appeared in the making in early 1999 concerning the incendiary question of land redistribution. According to the plan, the Zimbabwean government was to buy land from the dominant white farmers for use by black farmers, while the international community was to provide substantial aid for the development of infrastructure related to agriculture. However, the government's true intentions remained obscure as President Mugabe continued to threaten to expropriate the white farms, and donor countries demanded significant economic reform on the part of the administration before releasing the promised financial assistance. Consequently, Mugabe attempted to secure authority to seize white farms through proposed constitutional revision. The amendment proposed by the government would have made Mugabe president for life, given him the power to dissolve parliament, and endorsed the administration's land redistribution program. In January 2000, Mugabe added a further proposal requiring Britain to pay compensation for all land that the government acquired compulsorily for resettlement. Underscoring growing internal discontent, 55 percent of those voting in a national referendum held on February 12–13, 2000, rejected the proposed changes in the basic law.

When the February 2000 national referendum rejected the measure, blacks, many from influential war veterans' groups, began expropriating land. Collaterally, the administration, according to a rising chorus of domestic and international critics, launched a campaign of intimidation against opposition parties and dissidents. Opposition forces had coalesced in 1999 as the Movement for Democratic Change (MDC), which lobbied strongly against the constitutional revision. In April 2000 parliament passed a constitutional amendment that incorporated the land clause that Mugabe had inserted into the draft constitution in January 2000. The clause allowed the regime to forcibly acquire land without paying compensation, which was made the responsibility of the British government. The Supreme Court's ruling in November 2000 that the land invasions were illegal was ignored.

ZANU-PF barely withstood an electoral challenge from the MDC in flawed assembly balloting held June 24–25, 2000, securing 62 of the 120 elective seats. The assembly in January 2002 approved the Public Order and Security Act banning public gatherings without police approval to undercut the MDC challenge to Mugabe in the March presidential poll. Mugabe won another term in that election, defeating Morgan TSVANGIRAI of the MDC, 56 percent to 42 percent. The MDC rejected the results as fraudulent (a court rejected the charge of voter fraud in 2006).

Zimbabwe's worsening economic situation was accelerated by Mugabe's land redistribution. The lack of expertise among black farmers who had received land and the disinterest of many of those who had acquired large commercial farms combined with drought conditions and the lack of government-subsidized inputs to undermine food security. The government allegedly used food to buy votes in the March 31, 2005, assembly elections, in which ZANU-PF won 78 seats, which, coupled with its 30 appointive seats, gave the president's party a two-thirds majority. The MDC won 41 seats, and 1 seat went to an independent candidate. In the first polling for the newly reestablished Senate seats on November 26, 2005, the ZANU-PF won 43 seats and the MDC won 7. The election was boycotted by the Tsvangirai faction of the MDC, the larger of the two factions into which the MDC had split in October 2005 (see Political Parties, below).

Further exacerbating the declining economic and social conditions, the government in May 2005 launched Operation Murambatsvina ("drive out rubbish") purportedly to rid urban areas of informal market traders and shantytowns. As a result, 700,000 people were displaced. The MDC charged that the program was meant to punish the urban dwellers who voted in March against the ZANU-PF. Critics claimed that by dispersing urban dwellers, the government reduced the possibility of an uprising and drove people back to rural areas in the aftermath of the economic collapse precipitated by the land redistribution program. With inflation escalating out of control in 2007, Mugabe ordered all shops and businesses to cut their prices by half and deployed troops to monitor compliance. By the end of July, some 8,500 shop owners and executives had been arrested, and shortages linked to the price-cut directive further encouraged black market demand.

In the parliamentary elections of March 29, 2008, the MDC became the largest party in the House of Assembly with 99 of 207 seats. The ZANU-PF retained its standing as the largest party in the Senate with 30 seats. In concurrent presidential balloting both Mugabe and Tsvangirai claimed victory, despite each having secured less than a clear majority. Results were not published by the constitutional deadline of April 19 for holding a runoff, as the electoral commission reported it was investigating irregularities. In official results announced on May 2, neither Mugabe nor Tsvangirai had secured the 50 percent threshold to avoid a runoff. Violence ensued, with Tsvangirai claiming some 86 MDC supporters were killed and 200,000 displaced ahead of the runoff set for June 27. Tsvangirai subsequently withdrew from the runoff, citing the violence and voting irregularities. The poll proceeded, and Mugabe was declared the winner; he was sworn in on June 29. Elections to fill 3 seats in the assembly were held concurrent with the runoff, resulting in the MDC having an edge with 100 seats while the ZANU-PF secured 99. The MDC-M, the faction headed by Arthur MUTAMBARA, won 10 seats.

On July 18, 2008, Mugabe signed an agreement with Tsvangirai and Mutambara to prepare for unity talks. The agreement stipulated that all parties refrain from convening parliament or establishing a government outside of the talks. However, on August 19 Mugabe announced that he would convene parliament, which opened its first session on August 25, some six months after the election. Yielding to international pressure, Mugabe agreed to talks with the MDC and the MDC-M mediated by South African president Thabo Mbeki. On September 15 all three groups signed the Global Political Agreement, which provided for Mugabe to remain president and tapped Tsvangirai as prime minister. Disputes over the allocation of ministerial authority remained unresolved until January 27, 2009. Tsvangirai was sworn in as prime minister on February 11. A new government was formed on February 13 with the ZANU-PF holding 15 ministerial posts and the MDC and MDC-M together holding a total of 16. The ministry of home affairs was jointly held by a ZANU-PF member and an MDC member. The deputy agriculture minister, Roy BENNETT, a senior aide to the prime minister, was arrested on February 13 and charged with treason, a charge later altered to inciting insurgency. Bennett was released on March 12 but was blocked from taking office. One of the two vice presidents, Joseph MSIKA, died on August 6. John NKOMO of the ZANU-PF was sworn in on December 14 to succeed him.

In a cabinet reshuffle on June 23, 2010, all seven posts affected went to members of Prime Minister Tsvangirai's MDC-T faction. A ministry for national healing and reconciliation was established in December.

Minor cabinet changes were made in January, August, and September 2011. Vice President Nkomo died on January 17, 2013, but was not replaced.

A new constitution was approved in a national referendum on March 16, 2013, with 94.5 percent of the vote. Both the ZANU-PF and the MDC supported the new basic law, which was also approved overwhelmingly by parliament (see Current issues, below). It came into force on May 22. Mugabe called for national elections on July 31 to implement the terms of the new constitution (see Current issues, below). In the balloting, Mugabe was reelected, while the ZANU-PF won a commanding majority in the legislature. Opposition groups denounced the results and unsuccessfully challenged the outcome in court. Mugabe named a ZANU-PF cabinet on September 10.

Constitution and government. The constitution that issued in 1979 was amended numerous times (see the 2013 *Handbook*). The Global Political Agreement accepted by ZANU-PF and the two MDC formations on September 15, 2008, called for a transitional power-sharing government with executive power divided between the president and prime minister. The agreement required the inclusive government to prepare a new draft constitution within 18 months to be voted on in a national referendum. The process of constitutional reform began in April 2009 with the formation of the Constitutional Parliamentary Committee. Referendums were postponed repeatedly and finally conducted on March 16, 2013.

The 2013 constitution reduced the term of the president from six to five years, renewable once (although the restrictions did not apply to incumbent President Mugabe). The basic law abolished the office of prime minister and gave the president the power to appoint the cabinet. The legislature is bicameral, with an 80-member Senate and 210-member National Assembly, both elected for five-year terms (see Legislature, below). The new constitution devolved powers to the provinces and established an independent electoral commission, as well as a peace and reconciliation commission. The measure also forbade legal challenges to the seizure of white-owned land. The existing Supreme Court was replaced by a Constitutional Court, while the judicial system has both general and appellate divisions, and includes magistrate courts at the local level.

The country is divided into ten provinces: West, Central, and East in Mashonaland; North and South in Matabeleland; Midlands; Manicaland; Masvingo; Harare; and Bulawayo (though the latter two are cities, they have provincial status). Each is headed by a centrally appointed provincial governor and serves, additionally, as an electoral district for senate elections. Local government is conducted through town, district, and rural councils.

Zimbabwe has a lengthy record of limiting press freedom. On March 15, 2002, Mugabe signed a law that made it a crime for journalists to practice without a government-approved license. Foreign journalists have been jailed. Following the formation of the unity government, press freedom improved. A new independent newspaper was published in June 2010, marking the end of the progovernment newspaper's seven-year monopoly. The 2013 constitution guaranteed freedom of the press. In 2013, Reporters Without Borders ranked Zimbabwe 133rd out of 179 in freedom of the press.

Foreign relations. Zimbabwe became a member of the Commonwealth upon achieving de jure independence in April 1980; it was admitted to the OAU (subsequently the African Union—AU) the following July and to the UN in August. In January 1983 it was elected to a seat on the UN Security Council, where its representatives assumed a distinctly anti-American posture. The strain in relations with the United States culminated in 1986 with Washington's withdrawal of all aid in response to strongly worded attacks from Harare on U.S. policy regarding South Africa. Despite (then) Prime Minister Mugabe's refusal to apologize for the verbal onslaughts, the aid was resumed in August 1988.

In regional affairs, Harare occupied a leading position among the front-line states bordering South Africa, concluding a mutual security pact with Mozambique in late 1980 and hosting several meetings of the Southern African Development Coordination Conference (now the SADC). For more on Zimbabwe's support for Mozambique's anti-insurgency campaign, see an earlier *Handbook*.

The Zimbabwean government initially declined, for the sake of its own domestic "reconciliation," to provide bases for black nationalist attacks on South Africa. However, the anti-apartheid African National Congress (ANC) continued to operate from Zimbabwean territory, its cross-border attacks yielding retaliatory incursions by South African troops into Zimbabwe.

In February 1997 Zimbabwe and South Africa signed a defense agreement; however, their ties were subsequently strained by what Harare asserted were unfair South African trade practices and Pretoria's crackdown on illegal Zimbabwean immigrants. In February 1998 Zimbabwe, South Africa, and Namibia signed an extradition treaty.

In mid-1998 President Mugabe dispatched troops to the Democratic Republic of the Congo (DRC) to shore up the presidency of Laurent Kabila, from whose administration Harare reportedly sought mining concessions. At the peak of the conflict, an estimated 12,000 Zimbabwean troops were in the DRC, President Mugabe also strongly endorsing the succession of Joseph Kabila to the DRC presidency after the death of Laurent Kabila in early 2001. The support from Zimbabwe was considered crucial to the lasting power of the DRC administration, although the economic drain on scarce Zimbabwean resources contributed to growing anti-Mugabe sentiment. The last contingent of Zimbabwean troops left the DRC in November 2002.

In December 2003, the Commonwealth Heads of Government Meeting in Nigeria suspended Zimbabwe, citing continued human rights violations. Zimbabwe responded by withdrawing from the organization.

In 2005 Zimbabwe was reelected to the UN Human Rights Commission, drawing sharp criticism from Western countries, among others, which cited Zimbabwe's appalling human rights record.

Most Western donors froze development aid and imposed an arms embargo after Mugabe enacted his controversial land redistribution program. Zimbabwe increasingly turned to South Africa and China for financial aid as economic conditions worsened. South Africa loaned $470 million to bail Zimbabwe out of IMF and humanitarian crises in 2005, and China signed a $1.3 billion energy deal with the Mugabe government in 2006.

In 2007 China halted aid to Zimbabwe, citing the impact of hyperinflation on investment.

The disputed 2008 reelection of President Mugabe drew harsh rebukes from the international community. Botswana, Kenya, Sierra Leone, and Zambia called for punitive action against Mugabe, but the AU ultimately pressed for power-sharing talks. SADC pressure was instrumental in gaining MDC leader Morgan Tsvangirai's consent to form a government of national unity in February 2009.

The United States and the European Union (EU) kept "targeted" sanctions in place after the installation of the new government, citing continued violations of the rule of law. Prime Minister Tsvangirai traveled to Europe and North America in June 2009, meeting with U.S. president Barack Obama and other leaders but failing to persuade them to restart nonhumanitarian aid. EU officials refused to consider renewing aid in the absence of full implementation of the Global Political Agreement.

In February 2011 the EU extended its sanctions against Zimbabwe for another year over concerns of political violence (see Current issues, below). In March China agreed to $700 million in loans to Zimbabwe aimed at protecting Chinese companies from the indigenization program.

In December 2012 Zimbabwean troops were deployed along the border with Mozambique after incursions were reported by Mozambican rebel groups (see entry on Mozambique).

In March 2013 the EU suspended some sanctions as a reward for the successful conduct of a constitutional referendum. In June, South Africa announced it would provide $100 million to conduct national elections in July. When Zimbabwe refused to allow Western election observers to monitor polling in July, the EU, United States, and other international bodies rebuffed calls to lift remaining sanctions (including those that had been suspended). Following the balloting, the United States and other Western powers were critical of the government's oversight of the elections.

Current issues. Negotiations on political reforms broke down in July 2011 when no agreement was reached on a road map for elections. The suspicious death in August 2011 of Ret. Gen. Solomon Mujuru, leader of an influential ZANU-PF faction who had been seen by many as a likely successor to Mugabe, strengthened Mugabe's position in the party. Many analysts, as well as some MDC leaders, accused the ZANU-PF of killing Mujuru, who was the husband of Vice President Joyce Mujuru. By November the level of violence was reportedly so intense that many observers believed that the power-sharing deal was in jeopardy. On a positive note for the country's economy, international diamond regulators agreed to let Zimbabwe trade some $2 billion in diamonds. The country had been under sanctions since 2009 as the result of noncompliance with the Kimberley Process, which certifies that the source of rough diamonds is free from conflict.

Throughout 2011 and 2012 ZANU-PF stepped up attacks and intimidation against the MDC, including the reported arrest, assault, or murder of MDC officials.

Throughout the fall the failures of the Indigenization and Economic Empowerment Act became increasingly clear: Minister of Economic Development Tapiwa MASHAKADA warned the act made it impossible to attract investment into the country; economic consultant John ROBERTSON went so far as to suggest it was part of a ZANU-PF scheme to derail the economic recovery in order to prevent the MDC from benefiting politically.

The inquest into the death of General Solomon Mujuru closed on February 6, 2012, without turning up hard evidence of foul play, despite ongoing speculation. The court denied the family's request to exhume his body for examination by a forensics expert.

On February 19 Mugabe reaffirmed that he would call elections in 2012. Tsvangirai launched spirited rallies, somewhat dampening criticism of his party for giving in to Mugabe's call for elections.

In May 2012 a visit from UN human rights commissioner Navi PILLAY proved to be a public debacle. She had been invited by Justice Minister Patrick Chinamasa, who at the last minute switched the venue for her appearance without giving adequate notice to anyone but ZANU-PF members. But the tactic backfired when Pillay showed up at the original venue instead and then held a press conference in which she stated that without reform the disasters of the 2008 election would be repeated.

In early August 2012 ZANU-PF's Politburo began meeting to consider the draft constitution drawn up by a select committee. The public expectation was that any changes would be minor and the resulting draft would be ready for a plebiscite by late fall. Instead the party's revisions, announced in late August, constituted a radical rewrite that stripped away virtually all progressive measures included in the draft, removing checks and balances and dramatically tightening the powers of the president and his party over the government. In response, Welshman Ncube said he was "astonished at the sheer scale of disrespect, contempt and audacity exhibited." For instance, the new draft allowed the president to designate his successor, subject to approval by parliament, if he left office before the completion of his term. Nonetheless, the MDC officially supported the new basic law, which reduced the president's term of office and limited the chief executive to two terms (although the term limit applied to the next president, not Mugabe). There were other limitations on executive power, including restrictions on the ability of the president to issue decrees, declare emergency rule, or dissolve parliament. The draft constitution also contained a bill of rights and permitted dual citizenship. The constitution was approved by referendum in March 2013 and came into force in May.

Meanwhile, in January 2013, the head of the nation's human rights commission, Reginald AUSTIN, resigned in protest over the body's lack of independence and dearth of resources. Opposition groups bitterly decried Mugabe's decision in May to hold elections on July 31, 2013, arguing that there was not enough time to organize campaigns and that promised reforms to the electoral system had not been enacted. In addition, while Mugabe permitted election observers from the AU and neighboring states, he forbade monitors from the EU or other international bodies. Mugabe asserted that he was responding to a constitutional court decision calling for balloting when the parliament's term ended in June.

In the balloting, Mugabe secured 61 percent of the vote and defeated three other candidates. Tsvangirai placed second with 34.9 percent of the vote. In legislative balloting, ZANU-PF won 160 seats, followed by the MDC with 49, in the Assembly. In the Senate, ZANU-PF secured 37 seats to 21 for the MDC and 2 for the MDC-M. Reports indicated a number of problems with the balloting, and opposition groups challenged the outcome. For instance, in ZANU-PF strongholds the number of eligible voters on the rolls often outnumbered the population. On August 20, the high court rejected opposition challenges to the results.

POLITICAL PARTIES

At a convention of the Zimbabwe Congress of Trade Unions (ZCTU) in Harare in late February 1999, the ZCTU announced that it had coalesced with the anti-regime civic organization, the National Constitutional Assembly (NCA), as well as 30 other civic groups and a number of human rights, trade, and student organizations to form a political movement dedicated to pressuring the Mugabe government to enact economic, electoral, and constitutional reforms. Morgan Tsvangirai and Gibson Sibanda, leaders of both the ZCTU and the new coalition, had emerged in 1998 as point men for the anti-Mugabe forces. The NCA subsequently served as a major force in the creation of the nation's first and only effective opposition party, the Movement for Democratic Change (below).

By 2000 the MDC had emerged as the chief opposition party to Mugabe's ZANU-PF. Both ZANU-PF and the MDC are divided into factions, with alliances shifting as the inclusive government formulates policy and all sides prepare for Mugabe's eventual departure from power. ZAPU was revived as an independent party in 2009 (see below).

Governing Parties:

Zimbabwe African National Union–Patriotic Front (ZANU-PF). ZANU was formed in 1963 as a result of a split in the Zimbabwe African People's Union (ZAPU), an African nationalist group formed in 1961 under the leadership of Joshua Nkomo. Nkomo had in 1957 revived the dormant ANC, which was banned in 1959. He then was elected from exile as the president of a new National Democratic Party, which was declared illegal in 1961, leading to the formation and quick banning of ZAPU. ZANU, led by Ndabaningi Sithole and Robert Mugabe, was also declared illegal in 1964, and both ZANU and ZAPU initiated guerrilla activity against the Rhodesian government announced in November 1965.

In December 1974 ZANU President Sithole agreed to participate (along with ZAPU) in the enlargement of the African National Council to serve as the primary organization for negotiating with the Smith government (see Political background, above). However, Mugabe opposed such discussions and went into exile in Mozambique, from where he contested Sithole's dominance in ZANU. By late 1976 Mugabe was widely recognized as ZANU's leader, and he concluded a tactical (Patriotic Front—PF) agreement with Joshua Nkomo of ZAPU, although a minority of the ZANU membership apparently remained loyal to Sithole. The PF alliance broke down prior to the 1980 assembly election, Nkomo's group campaigning as PF-ZAPU and Mugabe's as ZANU-PF. Both parties participated in the government formed at independence, although ZANU-PF predominated with 16 of 22 ministerial appointments.

At ZANU-PF's third ordinary congress held in December 1989, the Politburo was enlarged from 15 to 26 members, the Central Committee was expanded from 90 to 150 members, a national chair was created, and ZAPU was formally incorporated into the party (despite rejection of its demands for a sole vice presidency filled by Nkomo and an expunging of the group's Marxist-Leninist tenets). Further, the party's socialist orientation was redefined to emphasize the Zimbabwean historical, cultural, and social experience. Ultimately, on June 22, 1991, the party agreed to delete all references to Marxism, Leninism, and scientific socialism from its constitution.

At a party congress in December 1995, Mugabe loyalists blocked efforts to open a party-wide dialogue on the question of presidential succession. The ruling party's preference for centralized power was upheld in December 1997; the Central Committee urged the president to forge ahead with plans to seize white-owned properties, in defiance of international donors and ZANU-PF moderates. Despite the schisms within ZANU-PF, Mugabe was reelected without opposition as party president in 1999. Subsequently, in controversial balloting, ZANU-PF retained a narrow majority in the assembly in June 2000, and Mugabe was reelected to another term as president in March 2002.

With the rise of factionalism within ZANU-PF, party solidarity began to disintegrate in 2004. Five party officials were arrested on espionage charges (three of the officials were later convicted of spying for South Africa), and a purge of the party targeted members who had been involved in the Tsholotsho meeting on November 18, 2004, and who opposed Mugabe's choice of Joyce Mujuru as vice president of the republic. Mujuru was appointed in December 2004 over house speaker Emmerson Mnangagwa, regarded by many as the president's likely successor until the political fallout from the failed palace coup attempt to make Mnangagwa the replacement for the late Simon Muzenda.

In December 2006, Mugabe declared at the ZANU-PF congress that only "God" could remove him from office, though a constitutional amendment would be required for an extension of his term. The Mujuru and Mnangagwa factions refused to support the motion, and no vote was taken on the resolution. The Mujuru and Mnangagwa factions united for a brief time to oppose Mugabe's attempt to remain in power.

The ZANU-PF Central Committee decided on March 30, 2007, that Mugabe would be the party's only presidential candidate and backed a proposal for parliamentary elections, which were not due until 2010, to be held concurrently with the presidential election in 2008. The Mnangagwa faction supported Mugabe, but the Mujuru faction (headed by Mujuru's husband Solomon Mujuru, a retired army general) backed former ZANU-PF member Simba MAKONI, who ran as an independent after being expelled from the party by Mugabe. The subsequent mysterious death of her husband was believed to have weakened Mujuru's alliances.

The party's internal battle over succession intensified after it lost exclusive control of Zimbabwe's government in 2009. The Mujuru faction appeared to have jockeyed successfully for the upper hand, as Joyce Mujuru was nominated by a majority of provinces to remain senior vice president of the party and of the republic. John Nkomo, loyal to the Mnangagwa faction, was elected vice president to succeed Joseph Msika, who died in August 2009. At the ZANU-PF national congress in December, Mugabe was reelected party president. At the ZANU-PF congress in December 16–18, 2010, Mugabe was tapped as the party's flagbearer for national presidential elections, which had tentatively been set for 2011 but were ultimately put off. Through 2011–2012 the party was said to be increasingly consumed by factionalism and roiled by the release from WikiLeaks of unredacted U.S. diplomatic cables that exposed ZANU-PF sources who had talked freely with American officials. In advance of the party's December 2011 congress, Chairman Simon Khaya MOYO also complained of a situation in which government had come to be "above the party," a dynamic he said he would be reversed.

Mugabe was reelected president in 2013, and the ZANU-PF won a majority in both houses of the legislature. Subsequent party infighting over the speaker's position highlighted the continuing division of the ZANU-PF between the Mnangagwa and Mujuru factions. Pro-Mnangagwa member Jacob MUDENDA was elected speaker on September 2013.

Leaders: Robert Gabriel MUGABE (President of the Republic and President of the Party), Joyce MUJURU (Vice President of the Republic and Vice President of the Party), Emmerson MNANGAGWA, Simon Khaya MOYO (National Chair), Didymus MUTASA (Secretary).

Movement for Democratic Change (MDC). Launched in September 1999, the MDC was an outgrowth of the ZCTU/NCA (see above), its core components including workers, students, middle-class intellectuals, civil rights activists, and white corporate executives opposed to the perceived corruption of the ZANU-PF government as well as its management of the economy. Many of the MDC adherents were former members of the Forum Party of Zimbabwe, which had been established in 1993 under the leadership of Enoch DUMBUTSHENA (a retired chief justice) and David Coltart (see 1999 *Handbook* for details on the Forum Party).

In a rapid rise, the MDC secured 57 of 120 elected seats in the 2000 assembly balloting. MDC leaders claimed fraud on the part of the government in some 37 of the 62 seats secured by the ZANU-PF. The MDC was the first opposition party to have broad inter-ethnic appeal and challenge the ruling party for every elected seat. Party leader Morgan Tsvangirai narrowly lost to President Mugabe in the controversial 2002 presidential election. On February 25, 2002, days before the presidential election in March, Tsvangirai was charged with treason for allegedly plotting to assassinate President Mugabe. He was acquitted in October 2004 but in the following month was charged with treason in connection with his call in 2003 for street protests to remove Mugabe. The government withdrew the treason charge in August 2005 without giving reasons.

In October 2005 the MDC split, leaving the lawful leadership of the party in question. Tsvangirai maintained he was still in charge of the party despite dissidents claiming he had been expelled. Prior to the November 2005 senate election, the MDC was deeply divided over whether to participate. Arthur Mutambara led the faction (MDC-M) that contested the election. Tsvangirai's faction, MCD-T, opposed participation, while a faction led by party secretary general Welshman Ncube planned to field candidates. Subsequently, 26 members who had been expelled by Tsvangirai stood for election, with only 7 winning Senate seats.

At the MDC-T party congress in March 2006, Tsvangirai was reelected president.

Ncube's faction appointed former MDC vice president Gibson Sibanda as acting president. The Ncube group held a congress in February 2006 and elected former student activist Arthur Mutambara as party president and Sibanda as vice president, with Ncube retaining the post of secretary general. The following month, however, Mutambara said it was wrong for MDC members to have contested the Senate elections, and he urged those who were elected to resign. Further, he proposed reconciling with Tsvangirai's faction, and in July the leaders of both factions vowed to work together to unseat the ZANU-PF.

After the torture and beatings of MDC members, including Tsvangirai, in Harare on March 11, 2007, the factions agreed in April to contest the 2008 elections as a coalition. It was agreed that Tsvangirai would be the coalition's president and Mutambara its vice president and that the factions would respect each other's autonomy and equality. Nevertheless, at a May 19 meeting, Tsvangirai tried to install Thokozani Khupe, his deputy, as second vice president and demanded that a panel of 30 from each faction select parliamentary candidates. In July, the Mutambara faction announced it would field its own candidates in 2008.

Meanwhile, Simba Makoni, the former ZANU-PF member who had announced his candidacy as an independent in the 2008 presidential election, received the backing of Mutambara. Ahead of the elections, violence against the MDC increased, resulting in Tsvangirai's seeking shelter in the Dutch embassy in Harare. Ultimately, the MDC won the most seats (by one) in the assembly, despite weakening party alliances and alleged intimidation by the ZANU-PF.

Following the signing of the Global Political Agreement (GPA) on September 15, 2008, by Mugabe, Tsvangirai, and Mutambara, many MDC leaders, including government ministers, faced trial on what were widely deemed to be politically motivated charges. Six months after establishment of the unity government, many rank-and-file MDC-T members, frustrated at what they perceived as bad faith on the part of the ZANU-PF and continued use of repressive measures against the MDC, advocated the party's withdrawal from the coalition. In October 2009 Tsvangirai announced his faction was suspending its participation in the government and would boycott cabinet meetings, but he reversed his stance three weeks later.

Numerous MDC members, including parliamentarians and cabinet ministers, continued to be harassed and arrested. The home of Finance Minister and party secretary general Tendai Biti was bombed, and his office was attacked.

Tensions heightened between MDC factions in 2011, as Welshman Ncube, elected president of the MDC-M faction at its January congress, announced that he would assume the deputy prime minister's post, but Mutambara refused to stand down. In February Mutambara declared Ncube expelled from the party. While the case went to court, Mutambara retained his government post. The Tsvangirai faction was involved in violent clashes with supporters of competing provincial leaders ahead of the MDC-T's April congress in Bulawayo. Most of the national party leaders were reelected, including Tsvangirai, who was unopposed in his leadership bid.

By the spring of 2012 MDC secretary general Tendai Biti, whose performance as finance minister earned him a degree of credibility at both the domestic and international levels, was "seen as the natural successor to the more pedestrian, gaffe-prone Morgan Tsvangirai," according to *Africa Confidential*.

Reports indicated that the continuing rivalry between Tsvangirai and Ncube contributed to the MDC's poor showing in the 2013 balloting. In those elections, Tsvangirai placed second in the presidential contest with 34.9 percent of the vote, while Ncube, as the candidate of the MDC-M, was third with 2.7 percent. Speculation emerged after the balloting that Tsvangirai would step down as leader of the MDC.

Leaders: Morgan TSVANGIRAI (President of the MDC-T faction and Former Prime Minister), Thokozani KHUPE (Vice President), Roy BENNETT (Treasurer); Welshman NCUBE (President of the MDC-M and Former Deputy Prime Minister), Arthur MUTAMBARA (MDC-M), Nelson CHAMISA, Tendai BITI (MDC-T Secretary General).

Other Parties That Contested Recent Elections:

Zimbabwe African National Union–Ndonga (ZANU-Ndonga). Led by Ndabaningi Sithole from its formation ahead of the 1980 election until his death in December 2000, the ZANU-Ndonga's main electoral base has been the small ethnic group the Ndau, who are concentrated in Chipinge in Manicaland Province.

Its sole parliamentary representative for Chipinge, who had been elected in 1985 and re-elected in 1990, was killed in an automobile accident in October 1994, but Sithole recaptured the seat in a by-election held December 19–20. In the 1995 election, the Chipinge constituency was divided into two electoral districts. Sithole was elected to represent Chipinge South and Wilson Khumbula, to represent Chipinge North. ZANU-Ndonga was the only opposition party to be represented in the 1995 parliament, the other opposition seat held by independent Margaret Dongo.

In October 1995 Sithole was charged with participation in a plot to assassinate President Mugabe. Sithole, who had been released on bail, announced his candidacy in the 1996 presidential election but later withdrew from the race in March 1996, charging that security forces were harassing his supporters. In late 1997 he was found guilty of treason and sentenced to two years in prison. Sithole died in December 2000, his appeal of his 1997 sentence never having been heard.

In the June 2000 election, Wilson Khumbula won the only house seat secured by ZANU-Ndonga. He received 1 percent of the vote in the 2002 presidential election. In March 2005 Khumbula lost the seat and the party failed for the first time since 1985 to have any representative in the House of Assembly. The party sought representation in the November 2005 senate election but secured only 1.81 percent of the votes.

Khumbula supported Simba Makoni in the 2008 presidential election. Semwayo supported the MDC's Tsvangirai in the 2013 presidential election. It did not win any seats in concurrent parliamentary balloting.

Leaders: Gondai Paul VUTUZA (President of the Party), Reketayi SEMWAYO (National Chair), Wilson KHUMBULA (2002 presidential candidate).

Zimbabwe African People's Union—Federal Party (ZAPU-FP). In 2002 this Matabeleland-based breakaway party from Agrippa Madhlela's ZAPU party (below) was led by Paul SIWELA. The party supported federalism and full regional autonomy for Matabeleland. Siwela ran without ZAPU's endorsement in the 2002 presidential race after the party decided not to contest the 2002 presidential election, instead supporting the candidacy of the MDC's Morgan Tsvangirai.

ZAPU-FP contested the 2005 Senate election, securing just 0.03 percent of the vote.

In September 2007 the MDC and the ZAPU-FP agreed to form an alliance ahead of the 2008 elections, resulting in Siwela's expulsion from ZAPU-FP. Siwela subsequently formed a new party, the Federal Democratic Union (FDU), which became inactive and subsequently defunct after failing to win any seats in the 2008 legislative election.

Leader: Sikhumbuzo DUBE (Acting President).

Zimbabwe African People's Union (ZAPU). The new incarnation of ZAPU constitutes a reconfiguration of Zimbabwe's oldest political party. Originally led by Joshua Nkomo, ZAPU was formed in 1961 and played a leading role in the popular struggle against colonial rule in Rhodesia. The party and its Zimbabwe People's Revolutionary Army (ZIPRA) drew their strength primarily from the Ndebele people of Matabeleland and the Midlands. Conflict between ZAPU and ZANU intensified after independence was achieved, culminating in the Gukurahundi massacres perpetrated by ZANU-PF forces that claimed the lives of thousands of Ndebele civilians in the mid-1980s. In part to put a stop to these clashes, ZAPU agreed to the unity accord of December 22, 1987, whereby its party infrastructure was absorbed into that of ZANU-PF. Former ZIPRA fighters and ZAPU members retained a separate and subordinate party identity.

In December 2008 a national conference of ZAPU members declared that the party was pulling out of the unity accord, asserting that ZANU-PF had violated the spirit of the agreement and reneged on its commitments. Former ZANU-PF politburo member Dumiso Dabengwa was named the party's interim chairperson. A preliminary ZAPU party congress in Bulawayo on May 16, 2009, attended by more than 1,000 delegates, ratified the withdrawal. The party's ranks swelled as thousands defected from ZANU-PF in Matabeleland and other parts of the country. President Mugabe dismissed the new formation as an illegitimate endeavor by "rogue" elements within the ruling party; in response, Dabengwa claimed that ZAPU remained the nation's authentic liberation movement.

The ZAPU used the constitutional outreach process to campaign for devolution of power into five regions, including Matabeleland, and proportional representation in parliamentary elections, vowing to reject any final document that omitted these two planks. Dabengwa accused the MDC of aping the corrupt practices of ZANU-PF now that it shares government power, suggesting that the difference between the two top parties had become minimal. At the ZAPU national congress in Bulawayo in August 2010, Dabengwa was elected president on a slate of new leaders.

In March 2011 Dabengwa distanced himself from the Matabeleland secessionists (see Matabeleland Liberation Front, below), affirming that ZAPU is a nationalist party. In July a serious rift developed when Cyril NDEBELE, a former speaker of parliament who had headed ZAPU's Council of Elders, claimed the presidency of the party. Joining him was Canciwell NZIRAMASANGA, who had been interim deputy chairperson until he was defeated at the party congress by Emilia Mukaratirwa. Ndebele and Nziramasanga accused Dabengwa of running the party despotically and fanning ethnic tensions, and they vowed to create a parallel national structure for the breakaway faction.

Dabengwa was the ZAPU candidate in the 2013 presidential elections. He received 0.7 percent of the vote. The party did not secure any seats in parliament in the concurrent legislative balloting.

Leaders: Dumiso DABENGWA (President of the Party), Emilia MUKARATIRWA (Vice President), Ralph MGUNI (Secretary General).

Additional parties that participated in the 2008 or 2013 elections include, among others: the **Zimbabwe Youth in Alliance** (ZIYA), led by Chawaona KANOTI and Moses MUTYASIRA; **Zimbabwe Progressive People's Democratic Party** (ZPPDP), formed in 2007 by Tafirenyika MUDUANHU; **Zimbabwe Development Party** (ZDP), led by former ZANU-PF member Kisinoti MUKWAZHE and Rev. Everisto CHIKANGA (Mukwazhe was the party's 2013 presidential candidate, but withdrew prior to the balloting); **Peace Action Is Freedom for All,** led by Abel NDLOVU; **Voice of the People/Vox Populi** (VP), formed in 2006 by Moreprecision MUZADZI with the support of Zimbabweans living in regions such as Botswana and South Africa; **ZURD,** led by Madechiwe COLLIAS; **Patriotic Union of Matabeleland** (PUMA), established in 2006 by Leonard NKOLA, a former member of ZANU-PF, to unify Matabeleland and seek autonomy for the region; **Christian Democratic Party** (CDP), formed by William GWATA in 2008; **Freedom Front,** formed in 2013 by Cosmas MPONDA; **Alliance Khumbula Ekhaya** (AKE), launched in 2013; the **FreeZim Congress;** the **People's Democratic Union;** and the **Mavambo/Kusile/Dawn,** founded by Simba MAKONI. None receive more than 1 percent of the vote in the 2013 balloting.

Other Parties:

Democratic Party (DP). Launched by Zimbabwe Unity Movement (ZUM) expellees (including Emmanuel MAGOCHE) in 1991, the DP held its inaugural congress in September 1992. DP President Wurayayi Zembe had been a leading member of the NCA committee, which included parties aligned to the NCA that embraced the cause for a new democratic constitution. At the annual general meeting of the NCA held in Harare, Zembe was nominated to the NCA chair but withdrew from the race. Lovemore MADHUKU was reelected after the NCA's constitution had been amended to allow for a third term.

The DP has claimed resource constraints have prevented the party from having held any congresses. The party has boycotted all elections since 1995 on the grounds that a new democratic constitution is necessary before free and fair elections can be held. The DP blasted the formation of a constitutional committee in parliament in April 2009, declaring the process illegitimate and proposing an inclusive constitutional conference facilitated by the UN, AU, and SADC. On April 30, 2009, Zembe was arrested outside the office of the national government in Harare and reportedly forced to stand at gunpoint under a water tap for 15 minutes before being released. The DP opposed the 2013 constitution.

Leader: Wurayayi ZEMBE.

Zimbabwe People's Party (ZPP). The ZPP was formed in August 2007, claiming to stand for "genuine democracy" and calling on Zimbabweans to fight poverty. There was some speculation that the ZPP was sponsored by Zimbabwe's Central Intelligence Organization to split the opposition vote in the 2008 elections, but the interim party president, Justin Chiota, denied the rumors.

In August 2008 Chiota, who was excluded from participation in elections for reportedly submitting his nomination papers past the deadline, voiced strong opposition to the March elections. The Supreme Court later ruled that the decision to exclude him from the first round of presidential balloting was invalid. Chiota's subsequent bid to overturn the presidential election was rejected by the high court. Chiota also argued that power-sharing talks between the MDC and ZANU-PF were unconstitutional. On November 22, 2011, Chiota killed his estranged wife and then committed suicide. Subsequently, the party reportedly went defunct.

Leader: Justin CHIOTA.

Matabeleland Liberation Front (or Mthwakazi Liberation Front—MLF). Launched in Bulawayo in December 2010 by a group of Zimbabwean exiles in South Africa, the members' mission was to advocate for regional power while organizing for the liberation, autonomy, or secession of Matabeleland.

Party leaders Paul Siwela, formerly of the defunct Federal Democratic Union (FDU), John Gazi, and Charles Thomas were arrested in March 2011 after distributing pamphlets calling for Zimbabweans to join the Arab Spring and demanding the dissolution of the Mugabe regime. All three were charged with treason. Gazi and Thomas were bailed out with funds from the MDC's Ncube faction. Siwela was released after 90 days in solitary confinement and banned from participating in political activity. In April four party leaders handed in a petition to the Zimbabwean embassy in South Africa demanding the secession of Matabeleland and the Midlands provinces. They also burned Zimbabwe flags to underscore their demands.

In November 2011 Siwela claimed that security forces stormed and searched his house. MLF boycotted the 2013 national elections.

Leaders: Paul SIWELA, John GAZI, Charles THOMAS.

Other parties include the **Zimbabwe People's Democratic Party** (ZPDP), led by Isabel MADANGURE, who died in 2011 (she was one of the first women to form a political party in the 1980s); the **Zimbabwe Integrated Party** (ZIP), formed in 2008 by Fanuel ZIMIDZI (a separate entity from Heneri Dzinotyiwei's ZIP, which joined the MDC on June 28, 2006); the **United Democratic People's Constitution** (UDPC), formed in February 2008 by Tasunungurwa MHURUVENGWE; and the **Zimbabwe National Congress** (ZNC), formed in 2009 by Ibbo MANDAZA and Kudzai MBUDZI.

For more information on other small parties, see the 2009 *Handbook.* For information on the **Multi-People's Democratic Party** (MPDP), please see the 2013 *Handbook.*

LEGISLATURE

Zimbabwe has had seven legislatures since 1980. The first two were bicameral (for details see the 1989 edition of the *Handbook*). In February 1990 the upper house (Senate) was abolished, the legislature thereupon becoming a unicameral body, the House of Assembly. A bicameral legislature was reinstituted in 2005, following a constitutional amendment approved by the house on August 30 to establish a Senate. The Constitutional Amendments No. 18, which was passed unanimously by the house on September 18, 2007, and the Senate on September 26, and No. 19, approved by both chambers on February 5, 2009, provided for changes in the number of house and Senate members (see Constitution and government, above). Under the provisions of the 2013 constitution, the lower house was renamed the National Assembly.

Senate. The Senate comprises 80 members. All serve five-year terms. As of 2013, 62 members are directly elected (6 from each of the 8 provinces and the two municipalities, and two to represent the disabled community). The remaining members are the 2 heads of the Council of Chiefs, and 16 traditional chiefs.

In the most recent balloting on July 31, 2013, the seat distribution was as follows: The Zimbabwe African National Union–Patriotic Front, 37; the Movement for Democratic Change, 21; and the Movement for Democratic Change–Mutambara, 2.

President: Edna MADZONGWE.

National Assembly. There are 210 members in the Assembly all of them directly elected.

Following the most recent balloting on July 31, 2013, the seat distribution was as follows: the Zimbabwe African National Union–Patriotic Front, 160; the Movement for Democratic Change, 49; and independent, 1.

Speaker: Jacob MUDENDA.

CABINET

[as of September 11, 2013]

President	Robert Gabriel Mugabe
Vice President	Joyce Mujuru [f]
Ministers	
Agriculture, Mechanization, and Irrigation Development	Joseph Made
Defense	Sydney Sekeramayi
Energy and Power Development	Dzikamai Mavhaire
Environment, Water, and Climate	Savior Kasukuwere
Finance	Patrick Chinamasa
Foreign Affairs	Simbarashe Mumbengegwi
Health and Child Welfare	David Parirenyatwa
Higher and Tertiary Education, Science and Technology Development	Olivia Muchena [f]
Home Affairs	Kembo Mohadi
Industry and Commerce	Mike Bimha
Information Communication Technology, Postal and Courier Services	Webster Shamu
Justice, Legal Affairs, and Parliamentary Affairs	Emmerson Mnangagwa
Lands and Land Resettlement	Douglas Mombeshora
Local Government, Public Works, and National Housing	Ignatius Chombo
Media, Information, and Broadcasting Services	Jonathan Moyo
Mines	Walter Chidhakwa
Presidential Affairs	Didymus Mutasa
Primary and Secondary Education	Lazarus Dokora
Public Service, Labor, and Social Welfare	Nicholas Goche
Small and Medium Enterprise Development	Sithembiso Nyoni
Sports, Arts, and Culture	Andrew Langa
Tourism	Walter Mzembi
Transport and Infrastructural Development	Obert Mpofu
Women's Affairs, Gender, and Community Development	Oppah Muchinguri [f]
Youth Development, Indigenization, and Empowerment	Francis Nhema
Ministers of State	
Senior Minister of State	Simon Khaya Moyo
Education and Vocational Training	Josiah Hungwe
Presidential Affairs	Flora Buka [f]
Vice President's Office	Sylvester Nguni

[f] = female

Note: All of the above are members of the Zimbabwe African National Union–Patriotic Front.

INTERGOVERNMENTAL REPRESENTATION

Ambassador to the U.S.: Machivenyika Tobias MAPURANGA.

U.S. Ambassador to Zimbabwe: David Bruce WHARTON.

Permanent Representative to the UN: Chitsaka CHIPAZIWA.

IGO Memberships (Non-UN): AfDB, AU, Comesa, IOM, NAM, SADC, WTO.

PALESTINIAN AUTHORITY/PALESTINE LIBERATION ORGANIZATION

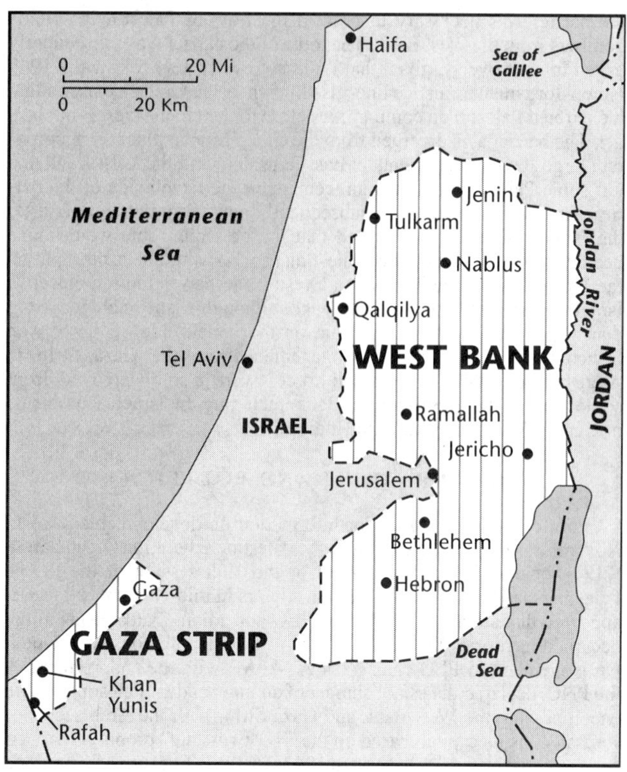

Political Status: Declaration of Principles establishing a "Palestinian authority" to assume partial governmental responsibility in Gaza and portions of the West Bank signed by Yasir Arafat (chair of the Palestine Liberation Organization) and Israeli prime minister Yitzhak Rabin on September 13, 1993; agreement reached on May 4, 1994, between Arafat and Rabin for formal launching of the withdrawal of Israeli troops from certain occupied territories and inauguration of the first Palestinian Authority (PA, or Palestinian National Authority [PNA]) on July 5; extension of limited Palestinian self-rule to additional territory approved in Israeli-Palestinian accord on September 24, 1995; elected civilian government inaugurated February–May 1996 to govern most of Gaza and portions of the West Bank; mixed presidential–prime ministerial system adopted for Palestinian self-rule areas on March 10, 2003; Israeli settlements in Gaza dismantled and all Israeli forces withdrawn unilaterally from Gaza in August–September 2005; control of Gaza taken over in June 2007 by the Islamic Resistance Movement (Hamas), with the PNA retaining control of Palestinian self-rule territory in the West Bank.

Population: 4,402,135 (2013E—UN); 4,440,127 (West Bank: 2,676740; Gaza: 1,763,387) (2013E—U.S. Census).

President: Mahmoud ABBAS (Fatah/Palestine Liberation Organization); directly elected on January 9, 2005, and inaugurated for a four-year term on January 15 to succeed Yasir ARAFAT (Fatah/Palestine Liberation Organization), who had died on November 11, 2004. (President Abbas's term was subsequently extended indefinitely pending new elections, which had not been held as of the end of 2013.)

Prime Minister: Rami HAMDALLAH (nonparty); appointed by the president on June 2, 2013, to succeed Salam Khaled Abdallah FAYYAD, who had been serving in a caretaker capacity since his resignation was accepted on April 13; formed government on June 6, 2013; reappointed by the president on August 13, 2013; and formed government (identical to the previous government) on September 19, 2013. (Ismail HANIYEH [Islamic Resistance Movement], who had been dismissed by the president [along with his entire cabinet] on June 14, 2007, but had refused to accept the dismissal, continued as of October 1, 2013, to head a de facto government in Gaza.)

GEOGRAPHY

Gaza Strip. The Gaza Strip consists of that part of the former League of Nations' Mandate for Palestine contiguous with the Sinai Peninsula that was still held by Egyptian forces at the time of the February 1949 armistice with Israel. Encompassing some 140 square miles (363 sq. km), the territory was never annexed by Egypt and since 1948 has never been legally recognized as part of any state. In the wake of the 1967 war, nearly half of its population of 356,100 (1971E) was living in refugee camps, according to the United Nations (UN) Relief and Works Agency for Palestinian Refugees in the Near East (UNRWA). The population was estimated by Palestinian officials to be 934,000 prior to a census conducted in late 1997, the results of which indicated an increase to about 1,022,000. (The population in Gaza was estimated at 1,640,000 in 2012.)

Most of Gaza was turned over to Palestinian administration under the Israeli-Palestinian accord of May 4, 1994, with Israel retaining authority over Jewish settlements and responsibility for external defense of the territory. On February 20, 2005, the Israeli cabinet by a vote of 17 to 5 endorsed a plan for unilateral disengagement from Gaza to begin on August 15 of that year. The plan required the dismantling of all Israeli settlements in the Gaza Strip, the evacuation of 8,000 Jewish settlers, and the closure of Israeli military bases. The withdrawal was completed on September 12, marking the end of 38 years of Israeli rule over the territory. However, Israel retained offshore maritime control as well as control of airspace over Gaza.

West Bank. Surrounded on three sides by Israel and bounded on the east by the Jordan River and the Dead Sea, the West Bank encompasses what was the Jordanian portion of the former League of Nations' Mandate for Palestine between 1948 and 1967. It has an area of 2,270 sq. mi. The Palestinian population in the West Bank (including East Jerusalem) was estimated at 2,650,000 in 2012, while the Jewish settler population (including East Jerusalem) had grown to an estimated 500,000.

The West Bank was occupied by Israel following the 1967 Arab-Israeli war. In July 1988 King Hussein of Jordan announced that his government would abandon its claims to the West Bank and would respect the wishes of Palestinians to establish their own independent state in the territory.

Under the Israeli–Palestinian accord of May 4, 1994 (an extension of the September 13, 1993, Oslo Agreement [see Political background, below]), the West Bank enclave of Jericho was turned over to Palestinian administration on May 13. Palestinian control was extended to six more West Bank towns (Bethlehem, Jenin, Nablus, Qalqilya, Ramallah, and Tulkarm) in late 1995 as the result of the second major "self-rule" accord, signed on September 28, 1995. Concurrently, civic authority in more than 450 villages in the West Bank was also turned over to the Palestinians, although Israeli forces remained responsible for security in those areas. In January 1997 Israeli troops withdrew from all but about 20 percent of the West Bank town of Hebron. In addition, an agreement was announced for additional redeployment of Israeli troops from other West Bank areas in three stages over the next 18 months.

It was generally expected in 1997 that the withdrawals would occur relatively quickly from most of the villages already under Palestinian civic authority, with as yet ill-defined redeployment from the rural areas in the West Bank to follow. However, none of the withdrawals had occurred by March 1998, as negotiations between Palestinian representatives and the Israeli government collapsed. A new series of withdrawals was authorized by the Wye agreement of October 1998, but only the first of those stages was implemented. The subsequent "effective state of war" between the Palestinians and Israelis precluded further resolution as Israeli forces occupied many of the areas previously turned over to Palestinian control.

In June 2002 Israel began constructing a barrier to separate the West Bank from Israel. The Israeli government stated that the construction of the barrier was necessary to prevent the flow of Palestinian suicide bombers from the West Bank. The route of the barrier was subsequently mired in controversy, given that it did not completely follow the 1949 Israeli-Jordanian armistice line, also known as the Green Line, and that it encircled Palestinian communities close to the Israel–West Bank border. The barrier also diverged from the Green Line in places to incorporate large Jewish settlements in East Jerusalem and the West Bank and left some Palestinian population centers on the Israeli side of the barrier. The Israeli government subsequently approved a new route after the Israeli Supreme Court ruled that the previous route would have been disruptive to the lives of Palestinians who would have been put on the Israeli side of the barrier. As a result, the new route ran closer to Israel's boundary with the West Bank, although it still included more than 6 percent of West Bank land on the Israeli side of the barrier. Concomitant with Israeli disengagement from the Gaza Strip in August–September 2005, Israeli forces were also redeployed from some areas in the northern West Bank, including the Israeli settlements of Ganim, Kadim, Sa-Nur, and Homesh.

GOVERNMENT AND POLITICS

Political background. (For information on developments prior to November 1988, see the section on the Palestine Liberation Organization [PLO], below.) Upon convocation of the 19th session of the PLO's Palestine National Council (PNC) in Algiers in mid-November 1988, it appeared that a majority within the PLO and among Palestinians in the occupied territories favored "land for peace" negotiations with Israel. On November 15 PLO chair Yasir ARAFAT, with the endorsement of the PNC, declared the establishment of an independent Palestinian state encompassing the West Bank and Gaza Strip, with the Arab sector of Jerusalem as its capital, based on the UN "two-state" proposal that had been rejected by the Arab world in 1947. The PLO Executive Committee was authorized to direct the affairs of the new state pending the establishment of a provisional government.

In conjunction with the 1988 independence declaration, the PNC adopted a new political program that included endorsement of the UN resolutions that implicitly acknowledged Israel's right to exist. The PNC also called for UN supervision of the occupied territories pending final resolution of the conflict through a UN-sponsored international conference. Although Israel had rejected the statehood declaration and the new PLO peace initiative in advance, many countries (more than 110 as of April 1989) subsequently recognized the newly proclaimed entity. The onrush of diplomatic activity following the PNC session included a speech by Arafat in December to the UN General Assembly, which convened in Geneva for the occasion because of U.S. refusal to grant the PLO chair a visa to speak in New York. A short time later, after a 13-year lapse, the United States agreed to direct talks with the PLO, Washington announcing it was satisfied that Arafat had "without ambiguity" renounced terrorism and recognized Israel's right to exist.

On April 2, 1989, the PLO's Central Council unanimously elected Arafat president of the self-proclaimed Palestinian state and designated Faruk QADDUMI as foreign minister of the still essentially symbolic government. Israel remained adamantly opposed to direct contact with the PLO, however, proposing instead that Palestinians end their intifada (uprising) in return for the opportunity to elect non-PLO representatives to peace talks.

During the rest of 1989 and early 1990, the PLO appeared to make several significant concessions, despite growing frustration among Palestinians and the Arab world in general over a perceived lack of Israeli reciprocity. Of particular note was Arafat's "conditional" acceptance in February 1990 of a U.S. plan for direct Palestinian-Israeli peace talks, theretofore opposed by the PLO in favor of a long- discussed international peace conference. However, the Israeli government, unwilling to accept even indirect PLO involvement, rejected the U.S. proposal, thus further undercutting the PLO moderates. By June the impasse had worsened, in part because of PLO protests over the growing immigration to Israel of Soviet Jews, many of whom settled in the West Bank. Moreover, Washington decided to discontinue its talks with the PLO because of a lack of PLO disciplinary action against those claiming responsibility for an attempted commando attack in Tel Aviv.

Subsequently, the PLO leadership and a growing proportion of its constituency gravitated to the hard-line, anti-Western position being advocated by Iraqi president Saddam Hussein, a stance that created serious problems for the PLO following Iraq's invasion and occupation of Kuwait in August 1990. Despite anti-Iraq resolutions approved by the majority of Arab League members, Arafat and other prominent PLO leaders openly supported President Hussein throughout the Gulf crisis. As a result, Saudi Arabia and the other Gulf states suspended their financial aid to the PLO (estimated at about $100 million annually), while Western sympathy for the Palestinian cause eroded. Following the defeat of Iraqi forces by the U.S.-led coalition in March 1991, the PLO was left, in the words of a *Christian Science Monitor* correspondent, "hamstrung by political isolation and empty coffers." Consequently, the 20th PNC session in Algiers in late September agreed to a joint Palestinian-Jordanian negotiating team with no official link to the PLO for the multilateral peace talks inaugurated in Madrid, Spain, in October.

As the peace talks moved into early 1992, Arafat and his Fatah component of the PLO faced growing criticism that concessions had produced little in return, and fundamentalist groups such as the Islamic Resistance Movement (Hamas) benefited from mainstream PLO defections in the West Bank and Gaza. Consequently, it was widely believed that Arafat would face yet another strong challenge at the PLO's Central Council meeting scheduled for April. However, circumstances changed after the PLO leader's plane crashed in a sandstorm in the Libyan desert on April 7, with Arafat being unaccounted for, and widely presumed dead, for 15 hours. Panic reportedly overcame many of his associates as they faced the possible disintegration of a leaderless organization. Thus, when Arafat was found to be alive, a tumultuous celebration spread throughout the Palestinian population, reconfirming his preeminence. As a result, even though the succession issue remained a deep concern, Arafat's policies, including continued participation in the peace talks, were endorsed with little opposition when the Central Council finally convened in May. Negotiations were put on hold, however, until the Israeli election in June, after which PLO leaders cautiously welcomed the victory of the Israel Labor Party as enhancing the peace process.

Although peace talks resumed in August 1992, they failed to generate any immediate progress, and criticism of Arafat's approach again intensified. In September the PLO's Democratic Front for the Liberation of Palestine (DFLP), the PLO's Popular Front for the Liberation of Palestine (PFLP), Hamas (not a PLO member), and a number of other non-PLO groups established a coalition in Damascus to oppose any further negotiations with Israel.

Israel's expulsion of some 400 Palestinians from the occupied territories to Lebanon in late December 1992 further clouded the situation, the PLO condemning the deportations and ordering Palestinian representatives to suspend their participation in the peace negotiations. Even after the talks resumed in mid-1993, they quickly appeared deadlocked, and rancorous debate was reported within the PLO leadership on how to proceed. By that time, with Hamas's influence in the occupied territories continuing to grow, onlookers were describing the PLO and its aging chair as "fading into oblivion" and "collapsing." However, those writing off Arafat were unaware that PLO and Israeli representatives had been meeting secretly for nearly eight months in Oslo, Norway, and other European capitals to discuss mutual recognition and the beginning of Palestinian self-rule in the occupied territories. Although initial reports of the discussions in late August were met with widespread incredulity, an exchange of letters on September 9 between Arafat and Israeli prime minister Yitzhak Rabin confirmed that the peace process had indeed taken a hopeful turn. For his part, Arafat wrote that the PLO recognized "the right of the State of Israel to exist in peace and security" and described PLO Charter statements to the contrary to be "inoperative and no longer valid." The chair also declared that the PLO renounced the "use of terrorism and other acts of violence." In return, Rabin's short letter confirmed that Israel had "decided to recognize the PLO as the representative of the Palestinian people and commence negotiations with the PLO within the Middle East peace process."

For all practical purposes the initial round of direct PLO-Israeli negotiations had already been completed, and the mutual recognition letters were quickly followed by unofficial but extensive reports of a draft Declaration of Principles regarding Palestinian autonomy. The PLO Executive Committee endorsed the draft document on September 10, 1993, and the stage was set for a dramatic ceremony on September 13 in Washington, D.C., that concluded with the signing of the declaration by Arafat and Rabin. The Declaration of Principles authorized a "Palestinian authority" to assume governmental responsibility in what was projected to be a gradually expanding area of the occupied territories from which Israeli troops were to withdraw. Among other things, the accord proposed the establishment of an interim Palestinian government in the Gaza Strip and the West Bank town of Jericho and committed Israel and the PLO to negotiating a permanent settlement on all of the occupied territories within five years. However, mention of the agreement was rarely made without immediate reference to the many obstacles in its path, including strong opposition from Israel's *Likud* Party and, on the Palestinian side, from Hamas, the DFLP, and the PFLP. There was also widespread concern that militant activity could sabotage the peace agreement. In addition, many details remained to be resolved before the Declaration of Principles could be transformed into a genuine self-rule agreement. Finally, there still appeared to be a wide, and possibly unbridgeable, gulf between the Israeli and PLO positions on the future of Jerusalem, the status of Palestinian refugees, and whether a completely independent Palestinian state would ultimately be created. Nevertheless, the remarkable image, flashed via television to a transfixed world, of Arafat and Rabin shaking hands at the Washington ceremony seemed to persuade even the most skeptical observers that a historic corner had been turned. For the PLO chair, the agreement represented an extraordinary personal triumph, his enhanced status being reflected by a private session with U.S. president Bill Clinton after the signing ceremony and by a meeting the next day with UN secretary general Boutros Boutros-Ghali.

International donors quickly expressed their enthusiasm for the September 1993 agreement by pledging $2.4 billion to promote economic development in Gaza/Jericho over the next five years. Shortly thereafter, the PLO's Central Committee approved the accord by a reported vote of 63–8. However, the declaration's projection that Israeli troops would begin their withdrawal by mid-December 1993 proved unrealistic, and extended negotiations were required on issues such as the size of the Jericho enclave and the control of border crossings.

Amid growing international concern that the peace plan could unravel, negotiations resumed in April 1994, and, at a May 4 ceremony in Cairo, Arafat and Rabin signed a final agreement formally launching Israeli troop withdrawal and inaugurating limited Palestinian self-rule. The Israeli pullout, and concurrent assumption of police authority by PLO forces, was completed in Jericho on May 13 and in most of Gaza on May 18. (Israeli troops remained stationed in buffer zones around 19 Jewish settlements in Gaza.)

The 1994 accord provided for all government responsibilities in Gaza/Jericho (except, significantly, for external security and foreign affairs) to be turned over to the "Palestinian authority" for a five-year interim period. Negotiations were to begin immediately on the second stage of Israeli redeployment, under which additional West Bank territory was to be turned over to Palestinian control, while a final accord on the permanent status of the occupied territories was to be completed no later than May 1999.

On May 28, 1994, Arafat announced the first appointments to the Palestinian National Authority (PNA), with himself as chair of the cabinet-like body. (The PLO leader subsequently routinely referred to himself as "president" of the PNA. However, the title, and indeed the Palestinian insistence on including "National" in the PNA's name, was not sanctioned by the Israeli government, which remained officially opposed to the eventual creation of a Palestinian state. Meanwhile, the media was split on the matter, with some referencing the PNA and others the Palestinian Authority [PA].) With most PLO offices in Tunis having been closed, Arafat entered Gaza on July 1, setting foot on "Palestinian soil" for the first time in 25 years. It was initially assumed that the PNA's headquarters would be in Jericho, where the PNA, which had already held several preliminary sessions, was formally sworn in before Arafat on July 5. However, Arafat and most government officials subsequently settled in Gaza City. Internal security initially proved to be less of a concern than anticipated within the autonomous areas, and the PNA focused primarily on efforts to revive the region's severe economic distress. The World Bank, designated to manage the disbursement of the aid pledged by international donors the previous fall, announced plans to distribute about $1.2 billion over the next three years, primarily for infrastructure projects. On the Palestinian side, coordination of such assistance fell to a recently established Palestinian Economic Council for Development and Reconstruction (PECDAR).

In late August 1994 Israeli officials announced they were turning educational responsibilities for Palestinian areas in the West Bank over to the PNA as the beginning of an "early empowerment" program. The PNA was also scheduled to assume authority throughout the West Bank soon in four additional areas—health, social welfare, taxation, and tourism. On the political front, the PNA proposed that elections to a Palestinian Council be held in December. However, no consensus had been reached by September either between the PLO and Israel or among Palestinians themselves on the type, size, constituency, or mandate of the new legislative body.

Pessimism over the future of the self-rule plan deepened in the fall of 1994 as security matters distracted attention from political and economic discussions. Under heavy pressure from Israel, the PNA authorized the detention of several hundred members of Hamas after that grouping had claimed responsibility for a gun and grenade attack in Jerusalem on October 9. Ten days later a Hamas suicide bomber blew up a bus in Tel Aviv, killing 22 people and prompting Israel to close its borders with the West Bank and Gaza and implement other new security measures. In addition, Palestinian police arrested nearly 200 members of the militant group Islamic Jihad (*al-Jihad al-Islami*) after it claimed responsibility for a bombing in Gaza in early November that left three Israeli soldiers dead. The tension culminated on November 18 in the killing of 13 people as Palestinian police exchanged gunfire with Hamas and Islamic Jihad demonstrators in Gaza, some observers suggesting that the Palestinians were on the brink of a civil war. Further complicating matters for the PLO/PNA, a meeting of the PLO Executive Committee called by Arafat in November failed to achieve a quorum when dissidents refused to attend. Among other things, the PLO chair had hoped that the committee would formally rescind the sections in the organization's National Covenant that called for the destruction of Israel.

Another Islamic Jihad suicide bombing on January 22, 1995, killed more than 20 people in the Israeli town of Netanya. Israel responded by suspending negotiations with the PNA until stronger measures were taken to prevent such attacks from the West Bank and Gaza. Consequently, Arafat authorized the creation of special military courts in February to deal with "issues of state security" and thereby permit a crackdown on militants. While the action appeared to appease Israel, it was criticized by human rights activists and non-PLO Palestinian organizations. As a result, facing yet another test of his leadership, Arafat called for a PLO Executive Committee meeting, the absence of the proposed covenant change from the agenda apparently facilitating the achievement of a quorum. Although reportedly facing intense scrutiny from the Executive Committee, which was seen as attempting to recover some of the influence it had lost to the PNA, the PLO chair nevertheless emerged from the meeting with a mandate to pursue negotiations with Israel.

Following a further intensification in April 1995 of the PNA campaign against "terrorists," peace talks regained momentum, 100-member negotiating teams from each side sequestering themselves in the Egyptian resort of Taba for several months. Finally, after six consecutive days of direct negotiations between Arafat and Israeli foreign affairs minister Shimon Peres, agreement was reached on September 24, 1995, on the next phase of Israeli troop redeployment and the extension of Palestinian self-rule to much of the West Bank. Israeli troops were to start withdrawing immediately from certain towns and villages in the West Bank, with the PNA assuming control therein. Temporary joint responsibility was arranged for rural areas, while Israeli troops were to continue to guard the numerous Jewish settlements in the West Bank and Gaza. Upon completion of the Israeli redeployment, elections were to be held, under international supervision, to a new Palestinian Council. Provision was also made for a 25-member "executive authority," whose head would be elected in separate balloting. It was estimated that self-rule would initially be extended to about 30 percent of the West Bank, with additional territory (up to a 70 percent total) to be ceded following the proposed Palestinian elections. In support of the accord, Israel pledged a three-stage release of thousands of Palestinian prisoners, while the PLO agreed to revoke the anti-Israeli articles in its covenant within two years.

The Israeli-Palestinian Interim Agreement on the West Bank and Gaza (informally referred to as "Oslo II") was signed by Arafat and Prime Minister Rabin at another White House ceremony on September 28, 1995, the attendees including King Hussein of Jordan and President Husni Mubarak of Egypt. Israel and the PLO agreed that Israeli troops would begin immediately to withdraw from six more West Bank towns while negotiations continued on the contentious issue of the town of Hebron, home to a small but highly vocal group of ultrareligious Jewish settlers. The agreement also envisioned the turning over of authority to Palestinians in more than 450 additional villages in the West Bank, followed by Israeli withdrawal from most other rural areas. Although many details of the latter withdrawal were left unspecified, it was agreed that it would be conducted in three stages—6 months, 12 months, and 18 months after the election of the Palestinian Council, which was designated to succeed the PNA as the primary Palestinian governmental body. It was estimated that the council would be responsible for more than 70 percent of the West Bank following the proposed Israeli withdrawal, with Israel maintaining control of the Jewish settlements and its numerous military installations in the West Bank.

Although "less mesmerizing" than its 1993 predecessor, the 1995 signing was considered no less consequential since the 400-page accord delineated in "intricate detail" most of the substantive aspects of the Israeli-Palestinian "divorce." On the other hand, very contentious issues remained to be resolved, including the rights of several million Palestinian refugees in countries such as Jordan, Lebanon, and Syria, many of whom hoped to return "home" to the West Bank and Israel. Talks were scheduled to begin in May 1996 on that question as well as the future status of Jerusalem, the eastern portion of which Palestinians claimed as their "capital." Difficult negotiations were also forecast regarding the estimated 140,000 Jewish settlers in Gaza and the West Bank, many of whom vowed never to leave the region to which, in their opinion, "Greater Israel" had a biblically ordained right. A final agreement on these and all other outstanding issues was due no later than May 1999, at which point the Palestinian Council was scheduled to turn over authority to whatever new governmental organs had been established. It was by no means clear what the final borders of the Palestinian "entity" would be or, for that matter, what official form of government it would assume. Although Israeli officials maintained their formal opposition to an independent Palestine, Arafat described the 1995 agreement as leading to "an era in which the Palestinian people will live free and sovereign in their country." However, in a decision that was to have major repercussions, the Israeli and PLO negotiators postponed further discussions of the contentious issue of the proposed withdrawal of Israeli troops from Hebron.

Despite concerns that the assassination of Israeli Prime Minister Rabin in November 1995 would interfere with the implementation of the recent agreement, Israeli withdrawals from the six additional towns proceeded even more quickly than expected and were completed by December 30, 1995. Consequently, with the formal encouragement of the PLO Executive Committee, Arafat subsequently attempted to convince Hamas and theretofore "rejectionist" PLO factions to participate in the upcoming Palestinian elections. Although those discussions initially appeared promising, Hamas and a number of major PLO components (most notably the DFLP and the PFLP) ultimately urged their supporters to boycott the balloting on the grounds that electoral regulations were skewed in favor of Arafat's Fatah at the expense of smaller formations. Nevertheless, the elections on January 20, 1996, for the Palestinian Council and separate balloting for the head (or "president") of the council's "executive authority" were still viewed as a major milestone in the self-rule process. Only one person (Samihah Yusuf al-Qubbaj KHALIL, an opponent of the Oslo peace agreements) challenged Arafat for the latter post. The PLO chair garnered 87.1 percent of the votes in balloting that was widely construed (in conjunction with Fatah's success in the legislative poll) as confirming strong support for him personally and majority endorsement of his peace policies. Arafat was inaugurated in his new position in ceremonies in Gaza City on February 12, 1996, and on May 9 he announced the formation of a new cabinet, technically the "executive authority" of the Palestinian Council but widely referenced as the "new" PNA, which continued the semantic PNA/PA controversy. The government won a vote of confidence in the Palestinian Legislative Council (PLC, as the new body had widely become known) by 50–24 on July 27.

Militant opposition to the Oslo accords moved even further to the forefront of concerns in late February and early March 1996 when bomb attacks left some 60 Israelis dead in Jerusalem and Tel Aviv. Temporary closure of the borders of the self-rule areas by Israeli forces generated pressure upon Arafat from within the Palestinian population, while the additional security issues were seen as a substantial political problem for Israeli prime minister Shimon Peres, facing an early election in May. Arafat implemented several measures apparently designed to help Peres, including the arrest of a number of militants from Hamas and other groups and the banning of some six Palestinian "militias." In addition, the PLO chair convened the 21st session of the PNC (now reported as comprising 669 members) in Gaza City on April 22–24 to consider formal revision of the National Covenant to reflect recent understanding of the issue. The PNC session, the first to be held on "Palestinian" soil since 1966, agreed by a vote of 504–54 that all clauses in the covenant that contradicted recent PLO pledges were to be annulled. In general, the changes would recognize Israel's right to exist and renounce "terrorism and other acts of violence" on the part of the PLO. Final language on the revisions was to be included in a new charter, which the PNC directed the Central Council to draft.

The "final talks" on Palestinian autonomy officially opened on May 5, 1996, but substantive negotiations were postponed until the Israeli election of May 29. Following the surprising *Likud* victory in that balloting, resulting to some extent from security concerns within the Israeli populace arising from the recent bomb attacks, progress slowed on the Palestinian front. No agreement was quickly forthcoming regarding Hebron, which became the focus of Israeli right-wing attention, and the planned three-stage withdrawal of Israeli troops from rural areas in the West Bank was not implemented. Israeli-PLO talks resumed in late July, but no progress ensued, even after face-to-face discussions between Arafat and new Israeli prime minister Benjamin Netanyahu in early September. International concern that the autonomy plan was deteriorating and growing criticism from moderate Arab states also seemingly failed to move the Netanyahu government (a tenuous coalition that included several ultraconservative groupings). Rising pressure finally erupted in fighting between Palestinians and Israelis in late September. U.S. president Bill Clinton quickly summoned Arafat, Netanyahu, and Jordan's King Hussein to a "crisis summit" in Washington, which appeared to reduce tensions, albeit without any apparent resolution of the underlying issues, particularly the status of Hebron, described as a "powder keg" that seemingly had assumed a psychological importance well out of proportion to its intrinsic significance.

As Netanyahu continued to resist redeployment of Israeli troops from Hebron throughout the rest of 1996, Arafat warned of the risk of the spontaneous resumption of the intifada. Finally, under apparent heavy U.S. pressure, Netanyahu accepted an agreement in early January 1997 that essentially reaffirmed the provisions of Oslo II. Among other things, the new accord (approved by the PLO Executive Committee on January 15) provided for Palestinian control to be extended to about 80 percent of Hebron, with Israeli withdrawal from additional rural West Bank areas to occur in stages from March 1997 through mid-1998. Assuming satisfactory progress on that front (not a certainty considering differing Israeli and Palestinian views on how much territory would ultimately be ceded to Palestinian rule), final talks were to be conducted on the still highly charged issues of the status of Palestinian refugees throughout the region, the nature of permanent governmental structures for the Palestinian "entity," and disposition of sovereignty claims to East Jerusalem.

Chair Arafat convened a "national dialogue" meeting in February 1997 in an effort to involve the formerly dissident PLO factions as well as non-PLO Palestinian groups in adopting a consensus on Palestinian proposals should final status talks be launched with Israel. However, Arafat's "national unity" conference in August appeared primarily aimed not at negotiations but rather at portraying solidarity in the face of perceived Israeli intransigence. The presence of Hamas and Islamic Jihad at the session lent weight to Arafat's assertions that military resistance (including resumption of the intifada) was a growing possibility. Meanwhile, the PNA itself had come under heavy domestic and international criticism, one corruption commission suggesting that more than $300 million in aid had been mishandled. The PLC demanded in late 1997 that President Arafat replace the cabinet with a new government comprising experts in their various fields rather than political appointees. It also called upon him to address allegations that Palestinian police and security forces had been responsible for widespread human rights abuses.

In February 1998 the PLO Executive Committee deferred a final decision on the proposed new PLO charter, eliciting Israeli concern that the 1996 action by the PNC remained insufficient as far as guaranteeing Israel's security was concerned. In addition, when agreement could not be reached on the extent of the next Israeli withdrawal, the Israeli government approved highly controversial Jewish settlement construction in East Jerusalem. Meanwhile, attention within the PLO focused on the question of a successor to Arafat, whose health was believed to be in decline. No dominant candidate had emerged, once again spotlighting the difficulties that would be faced if Arafat were unable to continue as the champion of the Palestinian cause.

In July 1998 Israeli and Palestinian negotiators met for the first time in over a year, and in October Netanyahu traveled to the United States to meet with Arafat and Clinton at the Wye Plantation in Maryland. After ten days of reportedly "tortuous" negotiations (capped off by a surprise visit from ailing King Hussein of Jordan), Netanyahu and Arafat signed an agreement on October 23 that proposed a three-month timetable for the next withdrawals of Israeli forces from the West Bank.

It was envisaged that negotiations would then begin regarding the third (and last) withdrawal phase and the other outstanding issues.

In addition to the geographic expansion of Palestinian autonomy, Israel also agreed in the 1998 Wye accords to release a number of Palestinian prisoners, permit the opening of the Gaza airport, and proceed with the establishment of a transit corridor for Palestinians from the West Bank to Gaza. For their part, Palestinian leaders pledged expanded security measures and additional repudiation of the anti-Israeli sections of the PLO Covenant. The first redeployment (centered around the northern West Bank town of Jenin) occurred on November 20, and international donors, signaling support for the resumption of progress, subsequently pledged some $3 billion in additional aid for development in the autonomous areas. However, Netanyahu faced significant opposition within his cabinet over the accord and appeared to place numerous barriers in the way of further implementation by, among other things, authorizing the expansion of Jewish settlements in the West Bank and demanding that Palestinian officials adopt a comprehensive weapons collection program, refrain from anti-Israeli "incitement," and drop their plans to unilaterally declare statehood on May 4, 1999. Clinton visited Israel and the self-rule territories on December 12–15 in an effort to reinvigorate the Wye plan, attending the session of the PNC in Gaza that endorsed the requested Covenant changes. However, the Netanyahu coalition finally collapsed in the ensuing days, and further implementation of the Wye provisions was suspended pending new Israeli national elections (later scheduled for May 1999).

Following his inauguration in July 1999, new Israeli prime minister Ehud Barak called for a comprehensive peace settlement with the Palestinians, Syria, and Lebanon within 15 months. On September 4 he and Arafat signed an agreement in Sharm al-Shaikh in Egypt that provided for the "reactivation" of the 1998 Wye accord via the immediate transfer to Palestinian control of additional territory in the West Bank and the release of some Palestinians under Israeli arrest in return for the Palestinian leadership's "zero tolerance" of terrorism. So-called final status negotiations were subsequently launched on the very difficult issues of Jewish settlements in the occupied territories, the eventual status of Jerusalem (which both sides envisioned as their capital), and the future of some 3.6 million Palestinian refugees seeking a return to Israel. Little progress was achieved by the spring of 2000, however, except for some redeployment of Israeli forces in the West Bank (bringing about 43 percent of the West Bank under complete or partial Palestinian control). In April, Barak appeared to accept the eventual creation of "an independent Palestinian entity" (he avoided using the word "state") comprising Gaza and 60–70 percent of the West Bank. However, he indicated a "majority" of the Jewish settlers in the disputed areas would remain under Israeli sovereignty. Hopes for a resolution declined further in May when sporadic violence broke out in Gaza and the West Bank, fueled by Palestinian anger over the lack of progress in negotiations.

Faced with a collapsing coalition in Israel, Barak attended a "make-or-break" summit with Arafat and U.S. president Clinton at Camp David in July 2000. Although agreement appeared close on several issues, the summit ended unsuccessfully when common ground could not be found regarding the status of Jerusalem and sovereignty over holy sites there, notably Temple Mount (*Haram al-Sharif*), a sacred location for both Jews and Muslims. (Clinton criticized Arafat for being unwilling to make the "difficult decisions" required to conclude a pact.)

Serious rioting on the part of Palestinians erupted in late September 2000 following a visit by hard-line *Likud* leader Ariel Sharon to Temple Mount that was viewed as unnecessarily "provocative" by many observers. Although Barak subsequently indicated a willingness to endorse the establishment of two separate "entities" in Jerusalem, negotiations collapsed in October in the face of the "second intifada" and heavy reprisals by the Israeli military that included the use of assault helicopter and rocket attacks. By the end of December more than 350 people had been killed and 10,000 injured in the violence. In addition, Israel had banned Palestinian workers from entering Israel and had imposed other economic sanctions such as the withholding of tax payments to the PNA.

At the end of 2000 President Clinton, attempting to cap his eight-year tenure with a "last hurrah" Middle East breakthrough, proposed a settlement under which all of Gaza and some 95 percent of the West Bank would be placed under Palestinian control, although some West Bank settlements would remain Israeli. The proposed accord also reportedly called for Palestinian sovereignty over certain areas of East Jerusalem, the return of a "small number" of Palestinian refugees, and a "mutual accommodation" regarding Temple Mount. Barak reportedly approved the compromise, but Arafat in early 2001 raised a number of objections, particularly in regard to the refugee issue. (The Palestinian position—that all refugees and their descendants be permitted to return to Israel—had been rejected as an impossibility by most Western capitals and, of course, Israel, on the grounds that the Jewish Israeli electorate would be overwhelmed politically by the returnees.)

Barak's defeat by hard-liner Sharon in the February 2001 special prime ministerial balloting in Israel appeared to doom prospects for any settlement soon of the Palestinian questions, particularly in view of the fact that President George W. Bush's new administration in Washington had announced it did not consider itself in any way bound by the "parameters" endorsed by Clinton. For his part, Sharon pledged that Jerusalem would remain "whole and unified" under Israeli sovereignty and that no Jewish settlements would be dismantled. Consequently, the rest of the year was marked by escalating violence that included numerous suicide bombings by Palestinian militants and massive retaliation by Israel in the form of missile attacks and tank incursions. However, late in the year President Bush expressed his support for the eventual establishment of a Palestinian state and called for the withdrawal of Israeli forces from the areas previously under Palestinian control. Peace advocates also saw a glimmer of hope when Arafat, whose compound was besieged by Israeli troops, subsequently called upon all Palestinian groups to honor a cease-fire and indicated "flexibility" on the refugee question. However, suicide bombings continued unabated in early 2002, and Israel in April launched an offensive of unprecedented scale that left it in control of most West Bank towns. When that initiative failed to restrain the suicide bombers, the Sharon government announced at midyear that it would begin to construct a "security fence" around the West Bank. Positions subsequently remained hardened as Sharon called Arafat an "enemy" and demanded a change in the Palestinian leadership.

Meanwhile, criticism in Palestinian circles of Arafat's government continued, although it was muted somewhat by an apparent desire within the Palestinian community to present a unified front in the face of renewed Palestinian-Israeli violence. In response to the discontent, in the spring of 2002 Arafat, whose compound in Ramallah had been under siege by Israeli forces for months as part of the broad Israeli incursion, reportedly admitted "errors" in peace negotiations as well as in the administration of the PNA, and he promised significant reform efforts. He also subsequently pledged to conduct new presidential and legislative elections when Israeli forces were withdrawn from areas previously under Palestinian control. However, concerned over the number of suicide bombings and other attacks on Israeli citizens, President Bush called for the "removal" of Arafat, portraying the Palestinian leader as unable or unwilling to combat terrorism. (Many analysts had concluded by that time that Arafat had little control over the attacks being claimed by Hamas and Islamic Jihad.)

Arafat trimmed his cabinet on June 9, 2002, although he was unable to convince the so-called rejectionist groups (notably Hamas, Islamic Jihad, the PFLP, and the DFLP) to participate in the new government. Arafat also subsequently promised reform in social sectors and indicated support for the eventual establishment of the post of prime minister, who would theoretically assume some of the authority heretofore exercised by Arafat.

In late 2002 Arafat declared that new elections would be postponed indefinitely due to Israel's continued occupation of territory formerly under Palestinian control. However, under heavy international pressure, Arafat in early 2003 formally endorsed the proposed installation of a Palestinian prime minister. The PLC on March 10 officially established the new position, although power-sharing arrangements vis-à-vis the president were left vague. (Among other things, Arafat retained control over peace negotiations with Israel.) Mahmoud ABBAS was nominated to the premiership, and his new cabinet was installed on April 29. Abbas promised to combat corruption, disarm militants, and pursue additional reform in Palestinian institutions. However, it quickly became clear that Abbas and Arafat were locked in a power struggle, and Abbas resigned on September 6. He was succeeded on September 10 by Ahmad QURAY, the speaker of the PLC.

At the end of April 2003 the Middle East Quartet (the European Union [EU], Russia, the UN, and the United States) presented a "road map" toward the eventual establishment of an "independent, democratic, and viable" Palestinian state. The first steps would be an immediate and unconditional cease-fire and a freeze on new Israeli settlements. The plan also envisioned completion of a new Palestinian constitution, in the hope that Palestinian elections could be held by the end of the year. The major component of the second phase of the road map would be the convening of an international conference that would, among other things, help determine provisional borders for the new state. Final negotiations were slated for completion by the end of 2005, assuming Palestinian institutions had been "stabilized" and Palestinian security forces had proven adequate in combating attacks against Israel. Israeli prime minister Sharon offered qualified support for the road map, as did the Israeli *Knesset,* although the latter insisted that it be made clear that Palestinian refugees would not be guaranteed the right to return to their former homes in Israel.

In the wake of renewed heavy violence, the *Knesset* in September 2003 endorsed the potential expulsion from the Palestinian territories of Arafat, whom Sharon and Bush blamed for the ongoing stalemate. Significantly, in February 2004 Sharon announced that he intended to order the unilateral disengagement of Israel from the Gaza Strip in light of the lack of progress regarding the road map.

Apparently in response to the growing reform tide, Arafat in mid-2004 once again acknowledged that he had "made mistakes," indicating that he was prepared to lead a renewed negotiation initiative. However, by that time it was clear that his health had failed to a point of unlikely recovery, and attention mostly focused on ensuring a smooth transition to the new PNA and PLO leaderships.

In July 2004 Prime Minister Quray threatened to resign unless the PLC granted him greater authority, particularly in regard to security. His request was partially granted, and the issue became mostly moot when Arafat died of an unknown illness at a hospital near Paris on November 11. (The French inquiry into Arafat's death was reopened in 2012 after Arafat's widow claimed that a radioactive toxin was discovered on his clothes that had been returned to her.) Mahmoud Abbas was quickly named to replace Arafat as chair of the PLO executive committee, while PLC speaker Ruhi FATTUH assumed presidential authority on an acting basis.

With Hamas and Islamic Jihad boycotting the presidential balloting on January 9, 2005, on the grounds that their involvement would have implied acceptance of the 1993 Oslo accords. Abbas won the presidency with 62 percent of the vote. His nearest rival (20 percent of the vote) was Moustafa BARGHOUTI, a secular independent associated with neither the PLO nor Hamas. Abbas was sworn in on January 15, and he invited Quray to form a new government. The international community welcomed the installation of a new Palestinian regime, and President Bush called Abbas "a man of courage."

Despite its boycott of the January 2005 presidential balloting, Hamas competed in the municipal elections held in the Palestinian territories in December 2004–January 2005 and in May and September 2005. Hamas performed strongly in all of those polls, underscoring the growing disenchantment among Palestinians with Fatah's governance.

In February 2005 President Abbas appointed a new cabinet consisting mainly of technocrats, again under the leadership of Quray. The appointments were seen as an effort to reduce the influence of the Fatah "old guard" that had been closely aligned with Yasir Arafat. Meanwhile, Ariel Sharon pushed ahead with his plan to evacuate the Gaza settlements and to disengage militarily from the Gaza Strip, overcoming opposition from within his own governing coalition. The disengagement was achieved in August–September. Although Sharon and Abbas subsequently agreed on a cease-fire and Hamas itself declared a period of "calm," violence continued throughout 2005 as little progress was made in negotiations. Sporadic conflict also broke out between Palestinian security forces and Islamist militants. President Abbas visited President Bush twice in 2005, but Abbas's positive international stature did not have much impact on Palestinian dissatisfaction with political and economic conditions.

Hamas scored a stunning victory in balloting for the PLC on January 25, 2006, securing 74 of 132 seats, compared to 45 seats for Fatah. Ismail HANIYEH of Hamas was inaugurated on March 29 to lead a new government that included only Hamas members and several independents, Fatah having declined to join the cabinet.

The United States and European states greeted the formation of the Hamas-led cabinet by suspending financial aid to the PNA and demanding that Hamas pledge to cease violence and recognize the state of Israel. Israel also halted the transfer of customs tax revenues to the PNA, causing severe economic distress for a large part of the Palestinian population, especially those employed by the PNA.

In May 2006 three people were killed when armed supporters of Hamas clashed with Abbas loyalists in Gaza. The fighting escalated over the next few weeks as Hamas deployed a militia of some 3,000 fighters to Gaza. However, Hamas subsequently withdrew its "implementation force" from Gaza to calm tensions. Shortly thereafter, Abbas called on Hamas to endorse a national accord that had been drawn up by prisoners detained in Israel, including Fatah leader Marwan BARGHOUTI. The plan called for acceptance of the pre-1967 boundaries for a Palestinian state (with Jerusalem as its capital), the establishment of a national unity government to include Hamas and Fatah, and PLO negotiations with Israel toward a two-state solution. Furthermore, Abbas issued an ultimatum to Hamas to recognize Israel or else he would call for a referendum on the proposed accord. Hamas consented to many of the articles of the document, with the notable exception of negotiations that would lead to the recognition of Israel. However, any potential for a peace initiative was squashed after two Israeli soldiers were killed and another kidnapped by Palestinian militants who had tunneled under the border from Gaza. While rival Palestinian factions still called for a government of national unity, Abbas tabled further negotiations on the subject because of the "sensitivity" of the most recent event. Meanwhile, Hamas demanded that Israel fully withdraw from the occupied territories, turn over tax revenues owed to the Palestinians, and immediately release all Palestinian ministers and lawmakers (including the speaker of the PLC) arrested in the months following the June abduction of the Israeli soldier.

Some analysts perceived a softening of Hamas's stance regarding potential recognition, or at least "acceptance," of the Israeli state during national unity negotiations between Fatah and Hamas in September 2006. Hamas also implied it might consider a "long-term truce" with Israel. However, Ehud Olmert (who had become prime minister of Israel in the wake of Ariel Sharon's stroke in January) subsequently authorized additional construction of Jewish settlements in the West Bank. Israel also maintained its economic blockade of Gaza and initiated several military offensives into Gaza in response to rocket attacks into Israel. Meanwhile, Palestinian workers went on strike in September to demand back wages, the Hamas-led government responding that it was being crippled by Israel's refusal to release tax revenues. Hamas also charged Fatah with promoting the demonstrations.

Israel withdrew its forces from Gaza in early November 2006, and a cease-fire was announced at the end of the month between Israel and most of the militant Palestinian groups. (Significantly, Islamic Jihad did not accept the agreement.) Olmert also urged "dialogue" that would lead to "an independent and viable Palestinian State," while Arab nations and Iran agreed to contribute financially to the PNA.

Factional Hamas–Fatah fighting intensified in December 2006, and President Abbas threatened to call early elections unless a national unity government could be established. Nevertheless, violence continued in January 2007, spreading from Gaza into several major cities in the West Bank.

President Abbas on February 8, 2007, signed an agreement with the Hamas leadership for a new "national unity" government. Among other things, the new coalition pledged to pursue a settlement with Israel based on a 2002 "land-for-peace" proposal from King Abdullah of Saudi Arabia that had recently been reendorsed by the Arab League. Consequently, Haniyeh and his cabinet resigned on February 15, although Abbas immediately reappointed Haniyeh to form a new government. On March 17 the PLC approved the new cabinet (which included ten ministers from Hamas, six from Fatah, three from recently formed smaller groups, one from the DFLP, and five independents) by a vote of 83–3. However, Israel, still vehemently opposed to any negotiations with Hamas, called the new PNA a "step backwards" and continued its hard-line approach by arresting Hamas leaders and supporters in the West Bank.

Severe factional infighting broke out between Fatah and Hamas in May 2007 in Gaza, and in June Hamas took over complete control of Gaza. President Abbas on June 14 dissolved the PNA in light of what he called the "military coup" in Gaza and declared a one-month state of emergency. On June 17 Abbas appointed a new "emergency" government headed by Salam FAYYAD, theretofore the PNA's finance minister. The emergency cabinet resigned on July 13, but most of its members were included in the "caretaker" or "transitional" government appointed the following day. However, Haniyeh disputed the legitimacy of Abbas's actions, arguing that a new government required approval of the PLC. Consequently, Haniyeh continued to lead a five-member cabinet in Gaza that he described as the legitimate Palestinian government.

Western donors immediately resumed aid to Abbas's PNA following the installation of the emergency government in the West Bank in June 2007. Also with the goal of supporting Abbas in his conflict with Hamas, Israel subsequently released tax revenues to the PNA and called for renewed peace talks. At the same time, Israel continued its daily attacks on what it called rocket-launching sites in Gaza.

In October 2007, as part of ongoing talks on the "fundamental issues," Israeli prime minister Olmert indicated that Israel might consider a division of Jerusalem as part of a potential final peace settlement. That and other initiatives were discussed at a U.S.-led peace conference in Annapolis, Maryland, at which Olmert and Abbas agreed to resume formal negotiations with the goal of reaching agreement within a year. However, Hamas called Abbas a "traitor" for participating in the conference, while Olmert faced significant opposition in Israel for his perceived concessions to the Palestinians.

Deadly conflict continued in Gaza in late 2007 and early 2008 between Hamas and Fatah and between Hamas supporters and Israeli security forces. In mid-January 2008 Israel, responding to rocket attacks from Gaza into Israel, launched a major incursion into Gaza and closed Gaza's borders. Palestinians destroyed a border fence into Egypt later in the month, permitting them to rush into Egypt to buy much-needed fuel, food, medical supplies, and other necessities constrained by the Israeli blockade.

A suicide bombing in Israel in early February 2008 (the first in more than a year) prompted another Israeli air strike in Gaza, and tit-for-tat violence intensified into the summer. Israel and Hamas finally announced a cease-fire in June, with Israel agreeing to ease its controversial blockade. Meanwhile, President Abbas called for a "national dialogue" between Fatah and Hamas with the goal of new national elections. (In the opinion of many analysts, the initiative reflected an acknowledgment that Hamas had solidified its control in Gaza by, among other things, replacing judges and prosecutors with Hamas supporters and by expanding the Hamas network of social services and business connections.) Nevertheless, Fatah–Hamas discord continued, and the prospects for a comprehensive settlement with Israel before the end of the year dimmed in the face of political chaos in Israel. Meanwhile, Haniyeh expanded the Hamas cabinet in Gaza at midyear.

Hamas formally declared the six-month cease-fire with Israel ended as of December 19, 2008, arguing that Israel had not lived up to its agreements regarding the truce, which Hamas reportedly had also sporadically violated. (Hamas argued that Israeli had reneged on its pledge to lift the economic blockade on Gaza and had contravened the accord through the arrest of Hamas members in the West Bank.) After Hamas rocket attacks from the Gaza Strip into Israel intensified, Israel, on December 27 launched a series of massive air strikes (Operation Cast Lead) against suspected Hamas security compounds in Gaza. In the face of additional rocket and mortar attacks into southern Israel, Israeli ground forces entered the Gaza Strip on January 3, 2009, to at least neutralize, if not topple, Hamas through "all-out war" if necessary. More than 1,500 Palestinians were killed (including some 900 civilians) during the offensive, which also destroyed or damaged 21,000 houses and otherwise decimated the infrastructure in Gaza before Israel declared a cease-fire on January 17. Hamas, which had continued to fire rockets and mortars into Israel during the conflict, declared its own unilateral cease-fire the same day, although it reserved the right to resume military activity unless Israeli troops were withdrawn quickly.

Most Arab states strongly condemned the late 2008–early 2009 Israeli offensive in Gaza (Egyptian president Hosni Mubarak characterized it as "savage aggression"), and most Western capitals expressed concern over the intensity of the Israeli campaign. A UN report later in the year criticized both sides in the conflict, citing the ongoing Hamas rocket attacks. However, the report's strongest language was reserved for the Israeli military, accused of a "disproportionate attack" that leveled "collective punishment" against civilians. The UN called for further investigation of possible war crimes, including Israel's alleged use of white phosphorous against mostly civilian targets and the alleged execution of Palestinian civilians. Israel, which rejected the report as biased, accused Hamas of having used civilians as human shields. Human rights groups also charged Hamas with arresting, torturing, and in some cases, executing alleged Palestinian "collaborators" following the conflict.

In early March 2009 international donors pledged some $4.5 billion to assist in reconstruction in Gaza over the next two years, although delivery of the aid was subsequently compromised by donor insistence that it not be used to prop up Hamas. The international community also called for Hamas and Fatah to negotiate a resolution to their political stalemate.

Prime Minister Fayyad announced the resignation of his transitional cabinet on March 9, 2009, in anticipation of the formation of a Hamas-Fatah national unity government. However, when negotiations in that regard collapsed, President Abbas on May 19 appointed a new government (again led by Fayyad) that included a number of independents, several members of Fatah, and one member each from the DFLP, PFLP, and the Palestinian Democratic Union (PDU). Meanwhile, discussions between the Abbas administration and Israel toward resumption of formal peace talks foundered when newly installed Israeli prime minister Benjamin Netanyahu, despite some conciliatory rhetoric, resisted heavy U.S. pressure to halt the construction of Jewish settlements in East Jerusalem and the West Bank.

After new U.S. President Barack Obama in June described the stateless status of Palestinians as "intolerable," Netanyahu endorsed the proposed "two-state" solution to the impasse, although the conditions he attached on Palestinian sovereignty appeared to doom prospects immediately. Frustrated by the lack of progress, President Abbas, in scheduling new presidential elections for January 2010, announced that he might not run for reelection. For its part, Hamas did not endorse the proposed election schedule, and in December the balloting was postponed indefinitely, the terms of Abbas and the legislators being extended until new elections were held.

In March 2010 President Abbas agreed to so-called proximity talks with Israel under U.S. mediation, the PLO having endorsed the initiative. However, Israel shortly thereafter announced it had approved new settlement construction in East Jerusalem and the West Bank, delaying the new talks until early May. At that time, Palestinian negotiators indicated that direct talks could take place only if Israel imposed a freeze on all construction, the ten-month "restriction" announced by Netanyahu in November 2009 having done little to alleviate Palestinian concerns.

In late May 2010 Israeli commandos intercepted (in international waters) the six-ship Gaza Freedom Flotilla, which was attempting to deliver what organizers characterized as purely humanitarian supplies to Gaza. Nine activists were killed in the attack, which the international community widely condemned. (A subsequent UN report accused Israel of "an unacceptable level of brutality," but Israeli officials claimed their forces had been fired upon first.)

U.S. Secretary of State Hillary Clinton hosted face-to-face talks between Abbas and Netanyahu in early September 2010, but Israeli settlement construction resumed apace later in the month, scuttling prospects for further meaningful negotiations. Later in the year Abbas asked the UN Security Council to consider declaring the construction of Jewish settlements in the West Bank as illegal. Fourteen members of the council voted "yes" on the request in February 2011, but the United States vetoed the resolution. Meanwhile, the Arab League endorsed Abbas's decision to suspend talks with Israel until a settlement freeze was imposed.

Fayyad and his cabinet resigned on February 14, 2011, in the wake of anti-administration demonstrations, but Fayyad was reappointed the same day. Fayyad's proposed continuation as prime minister proved to be a sticking point in implementing the April reconciliation agreement between Fatah and Hamas (see Current issues, below). With negotiations on the proposed national unification government sputtering, President Abbas, on May 16, 2012, reappointed Fayyad to head another West Bank government that included members of Fatah, the DFLP, and the PDU, as well as independents. On September 2, Prime Minister Haniyeh announced a reshuffle of the Hamas cabinet in Gaza.

Prime Minister Fayyad resigned on April 13, 2013, but he remained in a caretaker capacity until Rami HAMDALLAH succeeded him on June 6. Questions over authority within Hamdallah's administration prompted him to offer his own resignation only two weeks later, but he was subsequently again asked by President Abbas to form a government, which was installed on September 19.

Current issues. In late April 2011 representatives from Hamas and Fatah announced that agreement had been reached for their reconciliation. The accord, signed on May 4 in Cairo by Abbas and Hamas leader Khalid MISHAL, called for the formation of a transitional unity government pending new balloting for the PLC and installation of a permanent government. Abbas described the agreement as ending "four black years," while Mishal said Hamas would "pay any price" to achieve unity. Not surprisingly, Prime Minister Netanyahu denounced the agreement, reaffirming Israel's continued opposition to any peace negotiations involving Hamas.

In October 2011 President Abbas attracted significant international attention by formally requesting UN recognition of Palestinian statehood and full UN membership for Palestine. However, the Security Council's admissions committee subsequently reported that no more than 8 of the council's 15 members appeared ready to endorse the proposal, which therefore was not presented to the full council. (Even if the accession request had received the required nine votes in the council, the United States had promised to veto it.)

President Abbas and Hamas leader Mishal met again in November 2011 and announced that presidential and legislative elections would be held in May 2012, assuming successful negotiation of the proposed national unity government. In that regard, the two leaders in February 2012 tentatively agreed that Abbas himself would head a new government of "independent technocrats" who would oversee preparations for the elections while also addressing the dire economic conditions in Gaza. However, agreement on the ministerial appointments proved elusive, prompting Abbas in May to reappoint the new Fayyad-led government to attend to the administration of affairs in the West Bank.

Meanwhile, a UN report argued that Gaza might not be "a livable place" by 2020 without immediate attention to rampant unemployment and an increasing shortage of classrooms, hospital beds, food, water, and basic services. Hamas prime minister Haniyeh called upon his new cabinet (installed in September) to concentrate on such problems, adding that he still preferred the eventual appointment of a joint Fatah–Hamas government. By that time, many Palestinians appeared to blame the split between the two factions for the lack of economic progress. Among other things, demonstrators in September conducted a week-long protest, primarily directed at Prime Minister Fayyad, over rising prices and other hardships in the West Bank. In a possibly related vein, voter antipathy was apparent in the October 21 local elections, the first Palestinian election of any kind since 2006. (Hamas boycotted the elections, and no polls were held in Gaza.)

In early November 2012 Israel, claiming it was responding to a surge in rocket attacks into southern Israel, initiated an air assault (Operation "Pillar of Defense") on numerous targets inside Gaza, prompting Hamas and other militant groups to launch hundreds of retaliatory rockets. Israeli forces appeared poised to initiate a ground campaign as well, but a cease-fire was brokered by Egypt and the United States eight days after the outbreak of hostilities. Despite massive infrastructure damage and the death of more than 160 Palestinians, Hamas declared a "victory of resistance."

In late November 2012 the United Nations General Assembly overwhelmingly voted to upgrade Palestine's UN status to "nonmember observer state" ("state" being the key word). Among other things, the change gave Palestinians access to various UN-affiliated bodies, such as the International Criminal Court (where Palestinians could press claims against Israel). In what was widely perceived as a manifestation of its objection to the UN decision, Israel in early December announced that it was withholding tax revenues scheduled to be paid to the PNA (ostensibly to pay areas in the PNA's utility bill).

Jewish settlement activity also ramped up in early 2013, apparently contributing to further warming in relations between Hamas and Fatah. Among other things, Hamas was given permission to conduct rallies in the West Bank, while similar privilege was granted to Fatah in Gaza.

The resignation in April 2013 of Prime Minister Fayyad, whose government had received broad international praise for its competence, was attributed, at least in part, to an ongoing power struggle between the PNA and Fatah's old guard. Some observers predicted that the resignation might facilitate formation of a unity government between Abbas and Hamas (which had strongly criticized Fayyad for being aligned too closely with the United States). However, Hamas remained opposed to peace negotiations with Israel, prospects for which had reportedly been gaining background momentum under the leadership of U.S. Secretary of State John Kerry, thereby dooming the chances for a unity administration. New prime minister Hamdallah, the president of a West Bank university, announced that his government would continue to pursue the policies espoused by Abbas.

Although public opinion polls indicated that neither the Palestinian nor the Israeli populations held out much hope for success, direct talks between Palestinian and Israeli officials resumed in mid-August 2013 without preconditions (i.e., no freeze on Jewish settlement activity or agreement regarding the pre-1967 borders as a starting basis). A nine-month deadline was envisioned for a final agreement, although the first few months of the initiative produced no signs of progress.

POLITICAL PARTIES AND GROUPS

Palestine Liberation Organization (PLO). Establishment of the PLO was authorized on January 17, 1964, during an Arab summit held in Cairo, Egypt. Largely through the efforts of Ahmad SHUQAIRI, the Palestinian representative to the Arab League, an assembly of Palestinians met in East Jerusalem the following May 28–June 2 to draft a National Covenant and General Principles of a Fundamental Law, the latter subsequently serving as the constitutional basis of a government-in-exile. Under the Fundamental Law, the assembly became a 315-member Palestinian National Council (PNC) comprised primarily of representatives of the leading *fedayeen* (guerrilla) groups, various Palestinian mass movements and trade unions, and Palestinian communities throughout the Arab world. An Executive Committee was established as the PLO's administrative organ, while an intermediate Central Council (initially of 21 but eventually of 100 members) was created in 1973 to exercise legislative-executive responsibilities on behalf of the PNC between PNC sessions.

In its original form, the PLO was a quasi-governmental entity designed to act independently of the various Arab states in support of Palestinian interests. Its subordinate organs oversaw a variety of political, cultural, and fiscal activities as well as a Military Department, under which a Palestine Liberation Army (PLA) was established as a conventional military force of recruits stationed in Egypt, Iraq, and Syria.

In the wake of the 1967 Arab-Israeli war, the direction of the PLO underwent a significant transformation. Shuqairi resigned as chair of the Executive Committee and was replaced in December 1967 by Yahia HAMMUDA, who was in turn succeeded in February 1969 by Yasir Arafat, leader of Fatah (below). At that time the PNC adopted a posture more favorable to guerrilla activities against Israel, insisted upon greater independence from Arab governments, and for the first time called for the establishment of a Palestinian state in which Muslims, Christians, and Jews would have equal rights. In effect, the PLO thus tacitly accepted a Jewish presence in Palestine, although it remained committed to the eradication of any Zionist state in the area.

In 1970–1971 the PLO and the *fedayeen* groups were expelled from Jordan, and Lebanon became their principal base of operations. Fearing that Jordan might negotiate on behalf of Palestinians from the occupied territories following the Israeli victory in the October 1973 war, the PLO in June 1974 formally adopted a proposal that called for the creation of a "national authority" in the West Bank and Gaza as a first step toward the "liberation" of historical Palestine. This tacit recognition of Israel produced a major split among the PLO's already ideologically diverse components, and on July 29 a leftist "rejection front" was formed in opposition to any partial settlement in the Middle East.

In December 1976 the PLO Central Council voiced support for establishment of an "independent state" in the West Bank and Gaza, which was widely interpreted as implying acceptance of Israel's permanent existence. Shortly thereafter, contacts were established between the PLO and the Israeli left.

On September 1, 1982, immediately after the PLO withdrawal from West Beirut (see the entry on Lebanon), U.S. president Ronald Reagan proposed the creation of a Palestinian "entity" in the West Bank and Gaza, to be linked with Jordan under King Hussein. The idea was bitterly attacked by pro-Syrian radicals during a PNC meeting in Algiers in February 1983, with the PNC ultimately calling for a "confederation" between Jordan and an independent Palestinian state, thus endorsing an Arab League resolution of five months earlier that implicitly entailed recognition of Israel. Over radical objections, the Algiers meeting also sanctioned a dialogue with "progressive and democratic" elements within Israel, i.e., those favoring peace with the PLO. Subsequently, in an apparent trial balloon, Fatah's deputy chair, Salah KHALAF, declared that the group would support the Reagan peace initiative if the United States were to endorse the principle of Palestinian self-determination. The meeting's final communiqué, on the other hand, dismissed the Reagan proposal as not providing "a sound basis for a just and lasting resolution of the Palestinian problem."

PLO chair Arafat met for three days in early April 1983 with King Hussein without reaching agreement on a number of key issues, including the structure of a possible confederation, representation of Palestinians in peace negotiations with Israel, and the proposed removal of PLO headquarters to Amman. Soon after, amid evidence of growing restiveness among Palestinian guerrillas in eastern Lebanon, the PLO Executive Committee met in Tunis to consider means of "surmounting the obstacles" that had emerged in the discussions with Hussein.

In mid-May 1983 Arafat returned to Lebanon for the first time since the 1982 Beirut exodus to counter what had escalated into a dissident rebellion led by Musa Awad (also known as Abu Akram) of the Libyan-backed Popular Front for the Liberation of Palestine–General Command (PFLP-GC), a splinter of the larger PFLP. In late June Arafat convened a Fatah meeting in Damascus to deal with the mutineers' insistence that he abandon his flirtation with the Reagan peace plan and give greater priority to military confrontation with Israel.

On June 24, 1983, Syrian president Hafiz al-Assad ordered Arafat's expulsion from Syria after the PLO leader had accused Assad of fomenting the PFLP-GC rebellion, and a month later Arafat ousted two senior commanders whose promotions had caused tension within the ranks of the guerrillas in Lebanon's Bekaa Valley. The PLO infighting nonetheless continued, and in early November one of Arafat's two remaining Lebanese strongholds north of Tripoli fell to the insurgents. Late in the month the PLO leader agreed to withdraw from an increasingly untenable position within the city itself, exiting from Lebanon (for the second time) on December 20 in a Greek ferry escorted by French naval vessels.

Arafat strengthened and formalized his ties with Jordan's King Hussein in an accord signed in February 1985. The agreement, described as "a framework for common action towards reaching a peaceful and just settlement to the Palestine question," called for total withdrawal by Israel from the territories it had occupied in 1967 in exchange for comprehensive peace; the right of self-determination for the Palestinians within the context of a West Bank/Gaza/Jordan confederation; resolution of the Palestinian refugee problem in accordance with UN resolutions; and peace negotiations under the auspices of an international conference that would include the five permanent members of the UN Security Council and representatives of the PLO, the latter being part of a joint Jordanian-Palestinian delegation.

In reaction to the February 1985 pact with Jordan, six PLO-affiliated organizations formed a Palestine National Salvation Front (PNSF) in Damascus to oppose Arafat's policies. Differences over peace initiatives also erupted during a November meeting in Baghdad of the PNC's Central Council. Disagreement turned mainly on whether to accept UN Security Council Resolutions 242 and 338, which called for Israeli withdrawal from the occupied territories and peaceful settlement of the Palestine dispute in a manner that would imply recognition of Israel. Shortly thereafter, Arafat attempted to reinforce his image as "peacemaker" with a declaration denouncing terrorism. His "Cairo Declaration" was issued after lengthy discussions with Egyptian president Husni Mubarak on ways to speed up peace negotiations. Citing a 1974 PLO decision "to condemn all outside operations and all forms of terrorism," Arafat promised to take "all punitive measures against violators" and stated that "the PLO denounces and condemns all terrorist acts, whether those involving countries or by persons or groups, against unarmed innocent civilians in any place."

The PLO sustained a major setback at the hands of Shiite Amal forces that besieged two Palestinian refugee camps in Lebanon during May and June 1985. From Tunis an extraordinary session of the Arab League Council called for an end to the siege, which was accomplished by Syrian mediation in mid-June. One effect of the action was to temporarily heal the rift between pro- and anti-Arafat Palestinian factions.

By early 1986 it had become apparent that the Jordanian-PLO accord had stalled over Arafat's refusal, despite strong pressure from King Hussein and other Arab moderates, to endorse UN Resolutions 242 and 338 as the basis of a solution to the Palestinian issue. Among the PLO's objections were references to Palestinians as refugees and a failure to grant them the right of self-determination. On the latter ground, Arafat rejected a secret U.S. tender of seats for the PLO at a proposed international Middle East peace conference. In February Hussein announced that the peace effort had collapsed and encouraged West Bank and Gaza Palestinians to select new leaders. He underscored the attack on Arafat during ensuing months by proposing an internationally financed, $1.3 billion development plan for the West Bank, which he hoped would win the approval of its "silent majority." The PLO denounced the plan, while describing Israeli efforts to appoint Arab mayors in the West Bank as attempts to perpetuate Israeli occupation. The rupture culminated in Hussein's ordering the closure of Fatah's Jordanian offices in July.

King Hussein's overture elicited little support from the West Bank Palestinians, and by late 1986, it was evident that Arafat still commanded the support of his most important constituency. Rather than undercutting Arafat's position, Hussein's challenge paved the way for unification talks between Fatah and other PLO factions that had opposed the accord from the outset. Following initial opposition from the PNSF in August, the reunification drive gained momentum in early 1987 with indications that Georges Habash of the PFLP (the PNSF's largest component) might join leaders of the DFLP and other groups in trying to rescue the PLO from its debilitating fractionalization. Support was also received from PLO factions in Lebanon that had recently coalesced under Fatah leadership to withstand renewed attacks by Amal forces. Indeed, Syria's inability to stem the mass return of heavily armed Fatah guerrillas to Lebanon was viewed as a major contribution to Arafat's resurgence within the PLO. Meanwhile, King Hussein also attempted to mend relations with the PLO by announcing that the Jordanian-PLO fund for West Bank and Gaza Palestinians, suspended at the time of the February 1986 breach, would be reactivated. Subsequently, the fund was bolstered by new pledges totaling $14.5 million from Saudi Arabia and Kuwait.

Although hard-line factions continued to call for Arafat's ouster, the PLO leader's more militant posture opened the way for convening the long-delayed 18th session of the PNC (its membership reportedly having been expanded to 426) in Algiers on April 20–26, 1987. Confounding critics who had long predicted his political demise, Arafat emerged from the meeting with his PLO chair intact, thanks in part to a declared willingness to share the leadership with representatives of non-Fatah factions. Thus, although several Syrian-based formations boycotted the Algiers meeting, Arafat's appearance at its conclusion arm-in-arm with former rivals Habash of the PFLP and Nayif Hawatmeh of the DFLP symbolized the success of the unity campaign.

During the last half of 1987 there were reports of secret meetings between the PLO and left-wing Israeli politicians to forge an agreement based on a cessation of hostilities, a halt to Israeli settlement in Gaza and the West Bank, and mutual recognition by the PLO and Israel. However, nothing of substance was achieved, and by November it appeared that interest in the issue had waned, as evidenced by the far greater attention given to the Iran-Iraq war at an Arab League summit in November.

The Palestinian question returned to the forefront of Arab concern in December 1987 with the outbreak of violence in the occupied territories. Although the disturbances were believed to have started spontaneously, the PLO, by mobilizing grassroots structures it had nurtured throughout the 1980s, helped to fuel their transformation into an ongoing intifada (uprising).

In an apparent effort to heighten PLO visibility, Arafat demanded in March 1988 that the PLO be accorded full representation (rather than participation in a joint Jordanian-Palestinian delegation) at any Middle Eastern peace conference. However, the prospects for such a conference dimmed in April when the PLO's military leader, Khalil al-WAZIR (also known as Abu JIHAD), was killed, apparently by an Israeli assassination team. Whatever the motive for the killing, its most immediate impact was to enhance PLO solidarity and provide the impetus for a dramatic "reconciliation" between Arafat and Syrian president Assad. However, that rapprochement soon disintegrated, as bloody clashes broke out between Fatah and Syrian-backed Fatah dissidents (see Fatah Uprising, below) for control of the Beirut refugee camps in May. However, elsewhere in the Arab world, the position of the PLO continued to improve. A special Arab League summit in June 1988 strongly endorsed the intifada and reaffirmed the PLO's role as the sole legitimate representative of the Palestinian people. In addition, a number of countries at the summit reportedly pledged financial aid to the PLO to support continuance of the uprising.

On July 31, 1988, in a move that surprised PLO leaders, King Hussein announced that Jordan would discontinue its administrative functions in the West Bank on the presumption that Palestinians in the occupied territories wished to proceed toward independence under PLO stewardship. Although Jordan subsequently agreed to partial interim provision of municipal services, the announcement triggered extensive debate within the PLO on appropriate policies for promoting a peace settlement that would yield creation of a true Palestinian government. (For information on developments from 1988 to 1998, see Political background, above.)

The peace process appeared to have been relaunched by the Wye accords of October 1998, as part of which the PLO Central Council met on December 10 to consider Israeli requests regarding the PLO covenant. Arafat and other Palestinian representatives had argued that no further action was required, claiming that the PLO chair's earlier letter to President Clinton had made it clear that articles in the covenant had been voided by the PNC in 1996. However, the Central Council endorsed the particulars in Arafat's letter, and on December 14 the PNC reaffirmed the covenant changes by a nearly unanimous show of hands. In addition, under heavy international pressure, the Central Council in late April 1999 endorsed Arafat's recent decision to postpone the unilateral declaration of Palestinian statehood, which had been planned for May 4, 1999. Following the Sharm al-Shaikh agreement of September 1999, the PLO Central Council extended the deadline for statehood declaration until September 2000. Meanwhile, by early 2000 the PFLP and the DFLP had resumed participation in the council's deliberations. Another positive development, at least for Palestinians, was a meeting in February 2000 between Arafat and Pope John Paul II at which the Vatican reportedly recognized the PLO as the legitimate voice of Palestinian sentiment and endorsed eventual "international status" for Jerusalem.

Prior to the "make or break" summit between Arafat and Israeli prime minister Barak (who faced growing opposition within Israel to his peace efforts) in the United States in July 2000, the PLO Central Council indicated its solid support for Arafat and authorized him to declare statehood on September 13. However, when the U.S. summit collapsed, the Central Council, under intense international pressure, agreed at a meeting on September 9–10 to postpone the declaration once again. (Arafat had traveled to some 40 countries to solicit support for the declaration. The United States, EU, and many others resisted the idea, however, in part because of the prevailing sentiment in many capitals that Arafat had missed a significant opportunity at the U.S. summit. The PLO chair had reportedly been offered substantial concessions by Barak but had ultimately rejected terms regarding the status of holy sites in Jerusalem as well as the return of Palestinian refugees and their descendants to Israel.)

Although the PLO was not one of the groups demanding the creation of the post of prime minister to share PNA responsibilities with Arafat, Fatah dutifully approved the cabinet installed under new Prime Minister Mahmoud Abbas (the secretary general of the PLO Executive Committee) in April 2003. Subsequently, differences within Fatah and the PLO seemed to mirror those in the PLC and PNA over the power struggles between Arafat and Abbas and between Arafat and Abbas's successor, Ahmad Quray. PLO reformists pressed for significant power sharing and implementation of genuine anticorruption measures, while Arafat's long-standing backers in the organization supported his demand for his retention of the responsibility for peace negotiations and control of Palestinian security forces.

Abbas was elevated to the chair of the PLO Executive Committee only hours after Arafat's death on November 11, 2004. In addition, Faruk Qaddumi was named chair of the Fatah Central Council with no apparent tumult.

Following a funeral in Cairo (his birthplace), Arafat was buried in Ramallah, where he had lived under virtual Israeli siege for three years. (Israel refused Arafat's request to be buried in Jerusalem.) The Cairo ceremony was attended by many Arab leaders and dignitaries from around the world, while public demonstrations in Ramallah and elsewhere illustrated the deep grief felt by the Palestinian population at the loss of the only leader the PLO had known for 35 years. At the same time, the occasion appeared even sadder to many observers because of their belief that Arafat had missed several opportunities in the past decade to see much of his Palestinian dream accomplished prior to his death. For their part, the United States and Israel focused on the transition to new Palestinian leaders as an opportunity to revive the peace process.

Following Abbas's election as president in January 2005 and Prime Minister Quray's formation of a new cabinet, the two leaders indicated a desire to establish a clear "separation" between the "political" PLO and the "governmental" PNA. Plans were also announced to expand, restructure, and revitalize the PNC. In addition, at midyear Abbas called for negotiations with Hamas and Islamic Jihad toward their possible membership in the PLO. Moreover, Abbas launched talks with the hitherto "rejectionist" PLO factions with the goal of having them participate in a new PNA following the anticipated unilateral withdrawal of Israeli forces from Gaza in August.

Following Hamas's resounding victory in the January 2006 legislative elections, tensions increased within the PLO, Fatah having lost its majority in the legislature and thus some of its power base. Among other things, newly elected Fatah members of the PLC walked out after Hamas canceled all decisions made by the outgoing PLC. Abbas, though still holding executive authority, was now part of what was described as a "two-headed administration" in a power struggle with the ruling Hamas government. (See Political background and Current issues, above, for subsequent developments.)

In December 2009 the PLO Central Council postponed new elections for the PLC and president of the PNA indefinitely, pending resolution of the conflict with Hamas. The council extended the mandates of the current legislators and President Abbas until the new balloting could be conducted. In October 2010 the council voted to suspend negotiations with Israel until Israel agreed to a settlement freeze in the West Bank and disputed areas of Jerusalem.

In 2011, the PLO established a reform committee to consider changes in PLO structures in the wake of the Fatah–Hamas reconciliation agreement, with possibilities including the eventual incorporation of Hamas and Islamic Jihad into the PLO. Although the reconciliation remained unfulfilled as of late 2013, the committee agreed that the PLO's PNC should eventually become an elected body of 350 members, 200 to be elected by Palestinians in foreign countries.

Many (if not all) of the non-Fatah PLO components reportedly objected to the resumption of negotiations with Israel in August 2013.

Executive Committee: Mahmoud ABBAS (Chair and Head of the Political Department), Zakaria al-AGHA (Refugees), Ali ISHAQ (Youth and Sports), Mahmud ISMAIL, Taysir KHALID (Expatriate Affairs), Riyad al-KHUDARY (Higher Education), Abd al-Rahim MALLOUGH (Arab Relations), Muhammad Zudi al-NASHASHIBI (Palestinian National Fund), Yasir Abed RABBO (Secretary), Dr. Assad Abd al-RAHMAN, Ghassen al-SHAKAA (International Relations), Hassan ASHRAWI, Hanna AMIRA (Social Affairs), Saeb EREKAT, Ahmad QURIA (Jerusalem Affairs), Ahmed MAJDALANI, Salih RAAFAT, Ziad AMR, Wasel ABU-YOUSEF.

Fatah. The term Fatah (Arabic for "opening") is a reverse acronym of *harakat al-tahrir al-watani al-filastini* (Palestine Liberation Movement). Fatah was established mainly by Gulf-based Palestinian exiles in the late 1950s. The group initially adopted a strongly nationalist but ideologically neutral posture, although violent disputes subsequently occurred between traditional (rightist) and leftist factions. Although Fatah launched its first commando operations against Israel in January 1965, it remained aloof from the PLO until the late 1960s, when divisiveness within the PLO, plus Fatah's staunch (though unsuccessful) defense in March 1968 of the refugee camp in Karameh, Jordan, contributed to the emergence of Yasir Arafat as a leading Palestinian spokesperson. Following Arafat's election as PLO chair in 1969, Fatah became the PLO's core component.

Commando operations in the early 1970s were a primary responsibility of *al-Asifa*, then the formation's military wing. Following expulsion of the *fedayeen* from Jordan, a wave of external (i.e., non-Middle Eastern) operations were conducted by Black September terrorists, although Fatah never acknowledged any association with such extremist acts as the September 1972 attack against Israeli athletes at the Munich Olympics. By early 1973 the number of "external" incidents had begun to diminish, and during the Lebanese civil war of 1975–1976 Fatah, unlike most other Palestinian organizations, attempted to play a mediatory role.

As the result of a Fatah leadership decision in October 1973 to support the formation of a "national authority" in any part of the West Bank it managed to "liberate," a hard-line faction supported by Syria broke from Fatah under the leadership of Sabry Khalil al-Banna and his Revolutionary Council of Fatah. Smaller groups defected after the PLO's defeat in Beirut in 1982.

Internal debate in 1985–1986 as to the value of diplomatic compromise was resolved in early 1987 by the adoption by Fatah of an essentially hard-line posture, a decision apparently considered necessary to ensure continuance of its preeminence within the PLO. However, Fatah's negotiating posture softened progressively in 1988 as Arafat attempted to implement the PNC's new political program. Thus, Fatah's fifth congress, held August 3–9, 1989, in Tunis, Tunisia, strongly supported Arafat's peace efforts, despite growing disappointment over the lack of success in that regard to date. The congress, the first since 1980, also reelected 9 of 10 previous members to an expanded 18-member Central Committee and elected Arafat to the new post of Central Committee Chair.

Prior to the September 1993 signing of the PLO-Israeli peace settlement, it was reported that the Fatah Central Committee had endorsed its content by a vote of 12–6. As implementation of the accord proceeded in 1994, some friction was reported between formerly exiled leaders returning to Gaza/Jericho and Fatah representatives who had remained in those regions during Israeli occupation. In part to resolve such conflict, new by-laws were proposed under which Fatah "would operate more like a normal party" with numerous local branches and national committees led by elected chairs. Meanwhile, as would be expected, many of those named to the new Palestinian National Authority (PNA) and other governmental bodies were staunch Fatah supporters.

Fatah presented 70 candidates (reportedly handpicked by Arafat) in the January 1996 Palestinian legislative elections; about 50 of these "official" Fatah candidates were successful. However, a number of Fatah dissidents ran as independents and secured seats. In concurrent balloting for president of the PNA, Arafat was elected with 87.1 percent of the vote, further cementing Fatah's dominance regarding Palestinian affairs. However, Arafat and Fatah were subsequently subjected to intense legislative scrutiny (surprisingly rigorous in the opinion of many observers) over perceived governmental inefficiency, or worse.

Following the outbreak of the second intifada (or the *al-Aqsa* intifida, a reference to a mosque on Temple Mount in Jerusalem) in 2000 and the collapse of Israeli-Palestinian peace negotiations, "deep dialogue" was reported within Fatah regarding the military and political future for Palestinians. A new guerrilla formation, the *al-Aqsa* Martyrs' Brigade, was reportedly organized as an offshoot of Tanzim, the grassroots Fatah militia in the West Bank. *Al-Aqsa* claimed responsibility for a number of attacks against targets within Israel in the first few months of 2002, and the United States placed the group on its list of terrorist organizations. Marwan Barghouti, the reported leader of Tanzim and generally considered the second most popular Palestinian leader after Arafat, was arrested by Israeli security forces in April 2002 and charged with terrorism. At about the same time, *al-Aqsa* announced it would not carry out any attacks on civilians in Israel but reserved the right to attack military targets and Jewish settlements in Gaza and the West Bank.

On the political front, a number of Fatah members were among reformists who pressured Arafat in 2002 to combat perceived corruption and mismanagement within the PNA and to appoint a prime minister to share executive authority. Fatah subsequently endorsed the appointments of Mahmoud Abbas and Ahmad Quray to the new prime ministership in March 2003 and September 2003, respectively. Meanwhile *al-Aqsa* claimed responsibility for a number of attacks on Israeli soldiers and suicide bombings in 2002–2004. (To some observers Fatah appeared at best dysfunctional at that point because some of its members were regularly perpetrating attacks while others in the government and police forces were attempting to establish "security.")

Following Arafat's death in November 2004, Faruk Qaddumi was named to succeed him as chair of Fatah's Central Council. Subsequently, Fatah successfully presented Mahmoud Abbas as its presidential candidate in the January 2005 balloting. (Barghouti, sentenced to life in prison in mid-2004 on the terrorism charges, had initially expressed an interest in running for president from jail, observers suggesting he would have had a good chance of success. However, his supporters apparently chose unity over confrontation, and Barghouti withdrew from contention.)

In February 2005 reformist elements in Fatah reportedly blocked efforts by Fatah's old guard to retain dominance in the new Palestinian cabinet. Among other things, the reformists argued that Fatah was losing popular support to Hamas because of perceived ties of many Arafat loyalists to long-standing corruption.

Following what was described as Fatah's "stunning" defeat by Hamas in the January 2006 legislative elections, violent demonstrations in Gaza on the part of hundreds of Fatah supporters demanded the resignation of the Fatah leadership, prompting a trip to the area by President Abbas, who called on Hamas to participate in a national unity government. However, Fatah continued to be at odds with the Hamas-led government, seeking to have PLO members named to the cabinet and pressuring the PNA to endorse a national accord document proposed by Marwan Barghouti and other Palestinians prisoners in Israel. (See Political background and Current issues, above, for information on subsequent Fatah-Hamas conflict.)

Fatah held its sixth congress (the first in 20 years and the first to be held in Palestinian-controlled territory) in mid-2009 amid reports of severe generational divisions and disagreement regarding negotiations with Israel and Hamas. Abbas was reelected as Fatah's leader by a show of hands among the 2,300 delegates, although a number of reform advocates (including the imprisoned Barghouti) were elected to the new 18-member Central Council. The congress's final document essentially reconfirmed the movement's previous policy positions, including the right to resistance "in all its forms" to Israeli occupation. For his part, Abbas urged peaceful civil disobedience as the preferred tactic and called for an agreement with Hamas on a new national unity government.

In early 2012 the Fatah leadership ejected a number of members from the party for running in the upcoming municipal elections as independents after they were left off the official Fatah states. Fatah maintained control of most major municipalities in the October 21 poll, although independent states presented by the former Fatah members won in Nablus and Jenin. Under the direction of Abbas, Fatah endorsed the revival of peace negotiations with Israel in August 2013. It also supported the recent ouster by the military of Egyptian president Morsi.

Leaders: Mahmoud ABBAS (Chair); Mohammad GHNEIM; Ahmad QURAY (Former Prime Minister of the Palestinian National Authority); Nabil SHAATH, Marwan BARGHOUTI (imprisoned in Israel), Mohammad DAHLAN, Saeb EREKAT, Muhammad ISHTAYYIH, Jibril RAJOUB, Zakaria al-AGHA, Naser al-KIDWA (Members of the Central Council); Azzan Al-AHMED, Amin MAKBOUL (Secretary General).

Palestine People's Party (PPP). A Soviet-backed Palestine Communist Party (PCP) was formed in 1982 to encompass Palestinian communists in the West Bank, Gaza Strip, Lebanon, and Jordan with the approval of parent communist organizations in those areas. Although it had no formal PLO affiliation, the PCP in 1984 joined a campaign to negotiate a settlement among sparring PLO factions. As part of the reunification program approved in April 1987, the PNC officially embraced the PCP, granting it representation on PLO leadership bodies. The PCP, which was technically illegal but generally tolerated by Israel in the occupied territories, endorsed the creation of a Palestinian state adjacent to Israel following withdrawal of Israeli troops from occupied territories. In late 1991 the PCP changed its name to the PPP.

In September 1993 the PPP endorsed the PLO-Israeli accord on the condition that substantial "democratic reform" be implemented within the PLO. Although it was subsequently not represented in the PNA formed in 1994, the PPP was described as an "effective ally" of Fatah and PLO chair Arafat in the fledgling Palestinian self-rule process.

The PPP contested the January 1996 Palestinian legislative elections, albeit without success. However, PPP general secretary Bashir al-Barghuthi was named minister of industry in the Palestinian cabinet named in May. The PPP's presidential candidate, Bassam al-Salhi, secured 2.7 percent of the vote in the January 2005 presidential balloting. In 2006 the PPP urged a government of national unity and, along with Fatah and the PFLP, sought to have the PLO recognized as the only legitimate representative of the Palestinian people.

Leaders: Bashir al-BARGHUTHI, Bassam al-SALHI (Secretary General).

Arab Liberation Front (ALF). The ALF has long been closely associated with the Iraqi branch of the Baath party. Its history of terrorist activity included an April 1980 attack on an Israeli kibbutz. Subsequently, there were reports of fighting in Beirut between the ALF and pro-Iranian Shiites. ALF leader Ahmed ABDERRAHIM died in June 1991, and the status of the front's leadership subsequently remained unclear. Although the ALF was reported to have considered withdrawing from the PLO following the September 1993 agreement with Israel, it was apparently persuaded to remain as part of the "loyal opposition." In 1995, however, the front was reported to have split into two factions over the question. In the early 2000s the ALF reportedly distributed Iraqi money to relatives of suicide bombers.

In 2006 the group refused to participate in legislative elections, saying there could be no democracy under occupation.

Leaders: Mahmud ISMAIL, Rakad SALIM (Secretary General, jailed in Israel).

Democratic Front for the Liberation of Palestine (DFLP). Established in February 1969 as a splinter from the PFLP (below), the DFLP was known as the Popular Democratic Front for the Liberation of Palestine (PDFLP) until adopting its present name in 1974. In 1973 the PDFLP had become the first Palestinian group to call for the establishment of a democratic state—one encompassing both banks of the Jordan—as an intermediate step toward founding a national entity that would include all of historic Palestine. Its ultimate goal, therefore, was the elimination of both Hashemite Jordan and Zionist Israel. The DFLP subsequently advocated a form of secular nationalism rooted in Marxist-Leninist doctrine, whereas

Fatah initially envisaged a state organized on the basis of coexistent religious communities. Despite their political differences, the PDFLP/DFLP and Fatah tended to agree on most issues after their expulsion from Jordan in 1971. However, unlike Fatah, the DFLP supported the Islamic left in the Lebanese civil war of 1975–1976.

The DFLP, which since 1984 had taken a middle position between pro- and anti-Arafat factions, played a major role in the 1987 PLO reunification. In addition, its close ties with the PFLP, reduced in 1985 when the DFLP opted not to join the PFLP-led Palestine National Salvation Front (PNSF), were reestablished during the unity campaign. The DFLP endorsed the declaration of an independent Palestinian state by the PNC in November 1988, although its leaders interpreted the new PLO political position with less moderation than PLO chair Arafat, declaring they had no intention of halting "armed struggle against the enemy." Subsequently, differences were reported between supporters of longtime DFLP leader Nayif Hawatmeh, who opposed granting any "concessions" to facilitate peace negotiations, and supporters of Yasir Abed Rabbo, a DFLP representative on the PLO Executive Committee, who called for a more "realistic" approach and became one of the leading PLO negotiators attempting to implement the PNC's proposed "two-state" settlement. In early 1990 the DFLP Political Bureau reported it was unable to resolve the internal dispute, which was symptomatic of disagreement among Palestinians as a whole. After his supporters had failed to unseat Hawatmeh at a party congress late in the year, Rabbo formed a breakaway faction in early 1991. Both factions were represented on the new PLO executive committee late in the year, although Hawatmeh continued to criticize Arafat's endorsement of the U.S.-led Middle East peace talks. He also called for formation of a "collective" PLO leadership to reduce dependence on Arafat.

Rabbo's wing subsequently continued to support Arafat, but the main DFLP faction remained dedicated to a "no negotiations" stance. Not surprisingly, Hawatmeh and his followers rejected the September 1993 peace accord with Israel, and the DFLP leader described the May 1994 Cairo Agreement as "not binding on the people of Palestine." Meanwhile, Rabbo was given the culture and arts portfolio in the new PNA, and he was subsequently described as a leader of the recently formed PDU (see below).

In January 1994 the DFLP joined with other PLO groupings (including the PFLP, PLF, PPSF, and the PNSF) plus Hamas and Islamic Jihad to form a loosely knit coalition known as the Alliance of Palestinian Forces. Earlier, in October 1993, the same groups had reportedly formed a National Islamic Front, the subsequent name change appearing to reflect concern among secularist PLO factions over participation in an "Islamic" organization. In any event, the Alliance of Palestinian Forces was based on the opposition of its constituent groups to the accord negotiated by PLO chair Arafat with Israel in September 1993. The alliance pledged to "confront and resist" the Gaza/Jericho agreement and to pursue an independent Palestinian state and the return of Palestinian refugees to Israel. A 10-member Executive Committee was announced, and 20 members of what was expected eventually to be a larger Central Council were appointed. Although policy coordination was envisioned, it was reportedly agreed that each component of the alliance would determine how to proceed with its own "resistance" activities. However, the alliance subsequently collapsed, apparently due to the "incompatibility" of its leftist and Islamic elements.

Several DFLP "lieutenants" were reported in mid-1995 to have relocated from Damascus to Gaza, prompting speculation that the grouping might participate in the proposed election of a Palestinian Council. Although the DFLP ultimately boycotted that balloting, it encouraged its supporters to register as voters in anticipation of municipal elections that were expected to be held following the completion of the proposed Israeli withdrawal from the West Bank. The DFLP attended Palestinian conferences chaired by Arafat in February and August 1997, indicating that it was hoping to have a say in the proposed negotiations with Israel concerning the final status of Palestinian autonomy. However, in early 1998 it was reported that a plenary session of the DFLP in Damascus had agreed to draw up new strategies, apparently out of conviction that the current peace process was moribund.

In August 1999 DFLP leaders met with Arafat for the first time since 1993, and the DFLP resumed participation in the PLO's Central Council later in the year. In October the United States dropped the DFLP from the U.S. list of terrorist organizations. However, the DFLP claimed responsibility for an attack in mid-2001 in Gaza that left three Israeli soldiers dead. The DFLP later blamed Israel for a car bombing in Gaza in February 2002 that killed several DFLP members.

The DFLP joined the PFLP in mid-2004 in denouncing the fledgling unilateral disengagement plan being considered by Israeli prime minister Sharon, and the groups announced that the "armed struggle" would continue. The DFLP participated in the January 2005 presidential elections (its candidate, Taysir Khalid, won 3.4 percent of the vote), but in 2006 the DFLP declined to participate in the PNA following the unilateral withdrawal of Israeli forces from Gaza.

Leaders: Nayif HAWATMEH (Secretary General, in Syria); Taysir KHALID (2005 presidential candidate); Talal Abu ZAREEFA, Abu LAILA (Members of the Politburo).

Popular Front for the Liberation of Palestine (PFLP). The leftist PFLP was established in 1967 by merger of three main groups: an early Palestine Liberation Front, led by Ahmad Jabril; and two small offshoots of the Arab Nationalist Movement—the Youth for Revenge and Georges Habash's Heroes of the Return. However, Jabril and some of his followers quickly split from the PFLP (see PFLP-GC, below). The PFLP favored a comprehensive settlement in the Middle East and resisted the establishment of a West Bank state as an intermediate strategy. Its ultimate goal was the formation of a Palestinian nation founded on scientific socialism, accompanied by the PFLP's own evolution into a revolutionary proletarian party.

After the failure of efforts to achieve PLO unity in 1984, the PFLP played a key role in formation of the anti-Arafat PNSF. The PFLP endorsed the 1987 reunification in light of Fatah's increased militancy, but its delegates to the 1988 PNC session voted against the new PLO political program. Habash subsequently announced that his group, the second-largest PLO faction (after Fatah) would accept the will of the majority "for the sake of unity." However, he added that he expected the peace initiatives to fail and vowed continued attacks by PFLP fighters against Israeli targets. In early 1990 Habash was described as in "open opposition" to Arafat's acceptance of a U.S. plan for direct talks between Palestinian representatives and Israel, calling instead for increased military confrontation. The PFLP reportedly suspended its membership in the PLO executive committee in late 1991 to protest the negotiations.

During its December 1992 congress in Syria, the PFLP vowed to return to "radical action" in order to "regain credibility" among Palestinians. Consequently, Habash condemned the peace accord of September 1993, urging an "intensification" of the struggle for an independent state with Jerusalem as its "capital." However, the PFLP remained represented in the new PLO executive committee named in April 1996, although several subsequent shootings of Israeli settlers (which prompted the arrest by Palestinian police of some 30 PFLP members) apparently indicated continued resistance to the current peace process on the part of at least some of the PFLP faithful. By 1997 the PFLP was described in general as interested in participating with Arafat's Fatah and other PLO factions in establishing a consensus position to present in proposed "final status talks" with Israel, should the peace process develop that far. Meanwhile, in November 1997 a breakaway group reportedly formed as the Palestinian Popular Forces Party (PPFP) under the leadership of Adnan Abu NAJILAH.

In late April 2000 Habash announced his retirement; he was succeeded by his longtime deputy, Mustafa al-ZIBRI (Abu Ali Mustafa), who had returned to the West Bank in 1999 after 32 years in exile. (Habash died of a heart attack in January 2008.) Al-Zibri was killed by rockets fired at his Ramallah office by an Israeli helicopter in August 2001, thereby becoming the highest-ranking Palestinian leader to die in such an attack. The PFLP subsequently claimed responsibility for four bomb explosions in Jerusalem in September 2001 and the assassination of Israeli tourism minister Rechavam Ze'evi in October. A number of PFLP adherents, including Secretary General Ahmed Saadat, were subsequently arrested by Palestinian security forces, and the PFLP military wing was reportedly "banned" from Palestinian self-rule areas.

The PFLP claimed joint responsibility with Fatah for an attack on Israeli soldiers in February 2003, and several PFLP members were killed in subsequent Israeli reprisals. Although PFLP leaders joined other dissident PLO factions in meeting with Palestinian president Abbas in mid-2005, they reported that "no real coalition" had been formed and complained of ongoing Fatah domination of PLO affairs.

In 2006 Secretary General Saadat was arrested by Israeli forces after they stormed a prison in Jericho where he and other Palestinian activists were being held. Saadat faced 19 charges in Israel, including arms dealing and inciting violence. Two PFLP members were sentenced to life imprisonment in early 2008 following their convictions on charges relating to the 2001 Ze'evi assassination. Meanwhile, the Israeli prosecutor ruled that there was insufficient evidence against Saadat in regard to the assassination, although Saadat remained in jail (serving a life sentence on other charges) as of late 2013.

Leaders: Ahmed SAADAT (Secretary General, jailed in Israel), Jamil MAJDALAWI, Nasser IZZAT, Mahir al-TAHER, Abdel Rahim MALOUH, Kayed al-GHOL, Jamil MIZNER, Rabah MUHANNA, Khalida JARRAR.

Palestine Liberation Front (PLF). The PLF emerged in 1976 as an Iraqi-backed splinter from the PFLP-GC. In the early 1980s the group itself split into two factions—a Damascus-based group led by Talaat YACOUB, which opposed PLO chair Yasir Arafat, and a Baghdad- and Tunis-based group led by Muhammad ABBAS (Abdul Abbas), who was sentenced in absentia to life imprisonment by Italian courts for his alleged role in masterminding the hijacking of the cruise ship *Achille Lauro* in 1985, which resulted in the killing of an American tourist. Although Arafat had vowed that Abbas would be removed from his seat on the PLO Executive Committee because of the conviction, Abbas was granted "provisional" retention of the position at the 1987 PNC unity meeting, which was supported by both PLF factions.

Reconciliation within the PLF was subsequently achieved, at least nominally: Yacoub was named secretary general, while Abbas accepted a position as his deputy. However, Yacoub died in 1988, leaving control largely in Abbas's hands. In May 1990 the PLF accepted responsibility for a failed attack on Tel Aviv beaches by Palestinian commandos in speedboats, an event that precipitated a breakdown in the U.S.-PLO dialogue because of a lack of subsequent disciplinary action against Abbas. Apparently by mutual agreement, Abbas was not included in the new PLO Executive Committee selected in September 1991.

In March 2004 it was reported that Abbas had died of "natural causes" while in "unexplained U.S. custody in Iraq." New PLF secretary general Umar SHIBLI said he hoped to reintegrate the PLF into PNA activity. In 2006 the PLF was one of several factions that blamed Fatah and Hamas for increasing conflict in Gaza.

Leader: Wasel ABU-YOUSEF (Secretary General).

Palestinian Democratic Union (PDU). The PDU (also referenced as FIDA ["sacrifice" in Arabic], which is also a reverse acronym for the group's Arabic name, *al-ittihad al-dimuqrati al-filastini*) was launched in early 1993, not as a challenge to the PLO (then headquartered in Tunisia) but, in the words of a spokesperson, as a means of "moving the center of gravity" of the Palestinian opposition to "the occupied territories." Although some of the group's organizers were described as members of the DFLP, the PDU identified itself as nonideological and committed to the Middle East peace process. Operating under the reported leadership of Yasir Abed Rabbo (a longstanding Arafat loyalist), the PDU was one of the few non-Fatah groupings to contest the January 1996 elections to the Palestinian Legislative Council, securing one seat. Rablo left the PDU in 2002. In 2004 the group called on Hamas and Islamic Jihad to join the Palestinian leadership.

Leaders: Siham al-BARGHUTHI, Zuheira KAMAL, Jamil SALHUT, Saleh RAFAT (Secretary General).

Palestine Popular Struggle Front (PPSF). The PPSF broke from the PFLP while participating in the Lebanese civil war on behalf of the Islamic left. Although the PPSF was represented at the 1988 and 1991 PNC sessions, it denounced that council's political initiatives on both occasions and was not subsequently represented on the PLO Executive Committee. In 1995 it was reported that the PPSF had split into several factions, one of which had expressed support for PLO chair Arafat and the PNA. Longstanding PPSF leader Samir GHOSHEH died in 2009.

Leaders: Anwar Abu MAWAR, Khalid Abd al-MAJID, Ahmed MAJDALANI (Secretary General).

Islamic Resistance Movement (Hamas). Hamas rose to prominence in 1989 as a voice for the Islamic fundamentalist movement in the occupied territories and as a proponent of heightened conflict with Israeli authorities. It subsequently confronted mainstream PLO elements, particularly Fatah, over leadership of the intifada as well as Palestinian participation in Middle East peace negotiations. Capitalizing on the initial lack of progress in those talks, Hamas scored significant victories in various municipal and professional organization elections in the occupied territories in the first half of 1992. In addition, the movement's military wing—the *Izz al-Din al-Qassam* Brigades—was believed to be involved in fighting with Fatah supporters and to be responsible for the execution of Palestinians suspected of cooperating with the Israeli authorities. Hamas founder Sheikh Ahmed YASSIN, arrested in 1989, was sentenced to life imprisonment by an Israeli court in October 1991 for ordering several such killings of alleged Palestinian "collaborators." Breaking with a long-standing insistence on the annihilation of Israel, Mousa Abu Marzouk, one of the group's leaders (then based in Syria), stated in April 1994 that peace was possible if Israel withdrew from the occupied territories.

In June 1995 Israeli authorities arrested 45 Hamas militants on suspicion of plotting attacks on civilian targets, and in August it took steps to secure the extradition of Marzouk, who had been detained as a suspected terrorist upon entering the United States a week earlier. (The United States in 1997 "expelled" Marzouk to Jordan, from which he again relocated to Syria after the Jordanian government ordered the closure of all Hamas offices in Jordan in late 1999.)

In 1995 and 1996 Hamas was described as deeply divided between those favoring continued violence against Israel and those believing it was time to join the peaceful political process unfolding in the Palestinian self-rule areas. Palestinian leader Yasir Arafat met with Hamas leaders in late 1995 in what was described as a determined effort to win the movement's participation in upcoming Palestinian elections. After initially wavering on the proposal, Hamas announced it would boycott the balloting.

In January 1996 Yahya AYYASH, a Hamas militant (known as "The Engineer") who had been blamed by Israeli officials for a number of bomb attacks, was assassinated in Gaza by a bomb that was widely attributed to Israeli security forces. Subsequently, Hamas militants calling themselves the "Yahya Ayyash Units" claimed responsibility for several suicide bombings in Israel in February and March. Following the blasts, Marzouk (in a interview from his U.S. jail) said that the Hamas political wing had little direct control over the "militias" in the occupied and previously occupied territories. Meanwhile, Arafat outlawed the *al-Qassam* Brigades but continued his political dialogue with Hamas moderates, mindful that the grouping retained significant popular support among Palestinians, built, in part, upon Hamas's network of schools, health services, and other social programs.

Sheikh Yassin was released from prison on October 1, 1997, apparently as part of the "price" Israel agreed to pay after the bungled assassination attempt of Hamas militant Khaled Meshal in Jordan the previous month. Yassin went to Jordan for medical treatment and then to his home at Gaza, where he was welcomed as a hero by ecstatic crowds. He subsequently maintained an apparently deliberately vague position on developments regarding Palestinian autonomy, at times reverting to previous fiery rhetoric exhorting holy war against Israeli forces while at other times appearing conciliatory toward Arafat and the PNA, despite the fact that an estimated 80 influential Hamas leaders remained in PNA detention.

According to some reports, Hamas was approached by Arafat about joining the Palestinian cabinet in mid-1998. Although that overture was rejected, Yassin in April 1999 attended a PLO Central Council meeting as an observer, suggesting a growing degree of "accommodation" between the two groups. On the other hand, Palestinian security forces arrested some 90 Hamas activists in Gaza in August.

In December 2000 Hamas warned of a return of a campaign of suicide bombings in view of renewed Palestinian-Israeli violence, and the grouping subsequently claimed responsibility for a number of car bomb and suicide bomb attacks in Israel. In February 2003 Yassin urged Muslims around the world to attack "Western interests" in the event of a U.S.-led invasion of Iraq. Yassin also rejected the "road map" peace proposal offered by the Middle East Quartet in April and vowed that attacks on Israeli targets would continue.

International attention focused intently on Hamas when Yassin was killed by Israeli missiles in March 2004. Israeli prime minister Sharon dismissed Yassin as an "arch-terrorist," although the assassination of the blind, wheelchair-bound Hamas leader was viewed with dismay in many areas of the world. Such consternation had little effect on Israeli policy, however, and Abd al-Aziz RANTISI, who had succeeded Yassin as the leader of Hamas, was himself killed in an Israeli attack in April.

Throughout 2005 Hamas slowly grew in popularity to become a formidable rival to Fatah. In successive municipal elections Hamas won the majority of seats in several local councils, including West Bank towns, such as Nablus, that had been Fatah strongholds. A watershed moment for Hamas came in January 2006 when it won a clear majority of seats (74 out of 132) in balloting for the Palestinian Legislative Council, capitalizing on Palestinian anger against the PLO and PNA over corruption and poor delivery of services as well as public disillusionment with the overall process of negotiations with Israel (the withdrawal from Gaza notwithstanding). Subsequent to the election and the formation of a Hamas-dominated cabinet, the group faced immense Western pressure to commit itself to a two-state solution and to renounce violence.

Following the collapse of the unity government in mid-2007 in the wake of severe Hamas-Fatah conflict, Ismail Haniyeh insisted that his Hamas-led cabinet remained legitimate, although its de facto control was limited to Gaza. Hamas solidified its dominance in Gaza over the ensuing year as it arrested a number of Fatah leaders and otherwise suppressed opposition. (Many of the Hamas leaders in the West Bank were similarly detained by Fatah.) Egypt attempted to broker a reconciliation between Hamas and Fatah that envisioned the installation of a new joint transitional cabinet, new presidential and legislative elections in 2009, and the inclusion of Hamas and Islamic Jihad in the PLO. However, the talks were suspended indefinitely in November 2008. Meanwhile, the leaders of Hamas reiterated their willingness to "accept" (but not formally recognize) the state of Israel in return for establishment of a Palestinian state based on the 1967 borders and further negotiations regarding the rights of Palestinian refugees.

Following the devastating Israeli offensive in Gaza in December 2008–January 2009 (in which a number of Hamas leaders were killed or arrested), talks between Hamas and Fatah towards a possible national unity government opened in February 2009. However, no progress was achieved, and the relationship between the two groups reportedly remained "venomous." Subsequently, Khalid Mishal, who had been reelected as chair of the Hamas Political Bureau in May, announced that Hamas hoped to be a participant in negotiations toward a peace settlement with Israel, although he rejected official recognition of Israel, offering only a "long-term truce." Meanwhile, several reports in the fall of 2009 focused on the perceived struggle within Hamas between the current leadership and Islamic fundamentalists pushing for stricter adherence to Islamic law in Gaza.

Mahmoud al-MABHOUH, described as a senior *al-Qassam* military commander who had been living in Damascus, was murdered in a Dubai hotel in January 2010, reportedly by Israeli agents using passports from several European countries. Mabhouh had been accused by Israel of killing two Israeli soldiers in 1989.

Ismail Haniyeh, the head of the de facto Hamas government in Gaza, announced in late 2010 that Hamas was prepared to accept any negotiated settlement with Israel (even on terms contrary to Hamas's goals) if a majority of Palestinians throughout the world endorsed the settlement in a global referendum.

Despite the much-publicized reconciliation agreement between Hamas and Fatah in mid-2011, Hamas's stance was vague in regard to President Abbas's application to the UN in September for recognition of Palestinian statehood. Hamas officials reportedly complained that they had not been consulted in the matter.

Mishal and other Hamas leaders moved their headquarters from Damascus to Qatar in early 2012 after Hamas members appeared to offer support for rebels trying to oust Syrian president Bashar al-Assad. Among other things, Hamas lost financial support from Iran for abandoning Assad, although Qatar subsequently pledged $400 million to assist the Hamas-led government in Gaza.

Ahmed JABARI, described as the leader of *al-Qassam*, was killed in the eight-day Israeli assault in Gaza in November 2012. Hamas also reportedly suffered significant degradation of its military capability, although Hamas, whose survival was considered by some to be at risk at the beginning of the conflict, held "victory" celebrations following the cease-fire. Islamist supporters of the region's Arab Spring also appeared to rally behind Hamas.

In December 2012 Hamas leader Mishal traveled to Gaza for the first time, and he subsequently reaffirmed his support for reconciliation with Fatah and eventual formation of a unity government. However, Hamas hard-liners continued to oppose that initiative, which receded in likelihood in August 2013 when PLO leader Abbas agreed to reopen negotiations with Israel, Hamas describing such talks as "absurd." Meanwhile, by that time Hamas was suffering financially and psychologically from the repercussions of the military's ouster of Egyptian president Morsi, whose Muslim Brotherhood–led government had been a strong Hamas supporter.

Leaders: Khalid MISHAL (Chair of the Political Bureau, in Qatar), Ismail HANIYEH (Prime Minister of the De Facto Hamas Government in Gaza and Former Prime Minister of the Palestinian Authority), Abdel Aziz DUWAIK (Speaker of the Palestinian Legislative Council, released from Israeli prison in 2009), Ahmed BAHAR (Deputy Speaker of the Palestinian Legislative Council), Khalil al-HAYEH (Member of the Political Bureau), Nizar AWADALLAH (Member of the Political Bureau), Mousa Abu MARZOUK, Mahmud al-ZAHHAR (Member of the Political Bureau), Ghazi HAMAD, Ziyad Al-ZAZA.

Palestinian National Initiative (PNI). The PNI is a movement founded by Moustafa Barghouti in 2002 as a democratic "third force" alternative to both the PLO and Hamas. The base of the PNI included secular, left-leaning intellectuals, many of whom, such as Barghouti, had been prominent in the Palestinian nongovernmental organization community. Barghouti finished second in the January 2005 presidential elections, winning 20 percent of the vote. In the January 2006 legislative elections, the PNI won three seats with 2.7 percent of the vote.

Leader: Mustafa BARGHOUTI.

Islamic Jihad (*al-Jihad al-Islami*). Islamic Jihad is considered a Palestinian extension of Egypt's Islamic Jihad, which was originally launched as a splinter of Egypt's Muslim Brotherhood (see entry on Egypt). Islamic Jihad has been linked to a number of bomb attacks against Israeli soldiers both in the occupied territories and within Israel. Fathi SHAQAQI, described as the leader of Islamic Jihad, was assassinated in Malta in October 1995, reportedly by Israeli secret agents. It was subsequently reported that Ramadan Abdullah Shallah, a "Gaza-born militant" who had helped form Islamic Jihad, had assumed leadership of the grouping. Like Hamas, the other leading "rejectionist" grouping in the occupied and previously occupied territories, Islamic Jihad boycotted the 1996 Palestinian elections. Following the bomb attacks in Israel in early 1996, the Islamic Jihad military wing was one of the groups formally outlawed by Palestinian leader Arafat.

Islamic Jihad boycotted the February 1997 "national dialogue" meeting convened by Arafat but, in what was seen as a potentially significant shift, attended the August unity conference, which was also chaired by the Palestinian president. Nevertheless, leaders of Islamic Jihad were careful to point out that the group had not renounced the use of violence against Israel, and Islamic Jihad claimed responsibility for some of the attacks on Israeli civilians in 2001–2005. Islamic Jihad did not participate in the January 2005 Palestinian presidential elections or the January 2006 legislative elections. Some of the rocket and mortar attacks into Israel in late 2008 and early 2009 were attributed to Islamic Jihad. In 2010 leaders of the group reportedly described any potential negotiated settlement with Israel as "forbidden religiously and politically." However, Islamic Jihad in 2011 endorsed the tentative reconciliation agreement between Hamas and Fatah.

Islamic Jihad, considered by many observers to have Iranian backing, claimed responsibility for a number of rocket and missile attacks on Israel in March 2012. As Hamas subsequently distanced itself from the regime of Syrian president Assad, Iranian support appeared to grow even further for Islamic Jihad, which maintained its headquarters in Damascus.

Leaders: Ramadan Abdullah SHALLAH (Secretary General, in Syria), Abdallah al-SHAMI (Spokesperson), Muhammad al-HINDI, Sheikh Bassam SADI.

Popular Front for the Liberation of Palestine–General Command (PFLP-GC). Although the General Command broke from the parent front in late 1967, both organizations fought on the side of the Islamic left in the Lebanese civil war. The PFLP-GC was one of the founding members (along with the PFLP, PLF, PPSF, *al-Saiqa,* and Fatah Uprising) of the Palestine National Salvation Front (PNSF), launched in February 1985 in Damascus in opposition to the policies of PLO chair Arafat. Following the reconciliation of the PFLP and the PLF with other major PLO factions at the 1987 PNC meeting, PFLP leader Georges Habash declared that the PNSF had been dissolved, but the remaining "rejectionist" groups continued to allude to the PNSF umbrella.

The PFLP-GC, headquartered in Damascus, was reported to have influenced the uprisings in the West Bank and Gaza Strip in late 1987 and 1988, having established a clandestine radio station, the Voice of Jerusalem, that attracted numerous listeners throughout the occupied territories. U.S. and other Western officials reportedly suspected the PFLP-GC of complicity in the December 1988 bombing of a Pan American airliner over Lockerbie, Scotland, although PFLP-GC officials vehemently denied that the group was involved.

In May 1991 the PNSF, by then representing only the PFLP-GC, *al-Saiqa,* and Fatah Uprising (the PPSF having attended the 1988 PNC meeting), negotiated a preliminary "unity" agreement of its own with the mainstream PLO under which each PNSF component was to be given representation in the PNC. The proposed settlement was generally perceived as an outgrowth of a desire by Syria, the primary source of support for the PNSF, to normalize relations with the PLO and thereby enhance its influence in projected Middle East peace talks. However, negotiations with Fatah ultimately proved unproductive, yielding a PNSF boycott of the 1991 PNC session.

In September 1993 PFLP-GC leader Ahmad Jabril warned that Arafat had become an appropriate target for assassination because of the peace settlement with Israel. In mid-1996 the PFLP-GC was described as the primary conduit for the transfer of Syrian weapons to Hezbollah guerrillas in southern Lebanon, where Jabril's son, Jihad JABRIL, was reportedly in charge of a PFLP-GC "training center."

The PFLP-GC declined to join the PFLP in resuming activity in the PLO's Central Council in early 2000. In April 2002 the PFLP-GC claimed responsibility for rocket attacks from Lebanon into the Golan Heights and Israel, and Jihad Jabril was killed in a car bomb attack in Beirut the following month. (His father attributed the attack to Israeli agents.) In mid-2005 Ahmad Jabril announced that the PFLP-GC was not yet ready to commit to participation in the Palestinian government following the planned withdrawal of Israeli forces from Gaza, although he agreed to join negotiations on the matter. In 2006, following Hezbollah's cross-border attack from Lebanon on Israeli soldiers, Israel reportedly targeted a PFLP-GC stronghold in eastern Lebanon. Severe fighting among PFLP-GC factions was reported in a Palestinian military camp in Lebanon in April 2010.

The PFLP-GC reportedly endorsed the tentative reconciliation agreement between Hamas and Fatah in 2011. Although some Palestinians in Syria by the fall of 2012 had reportedly aligned with rebel groups attempting to overthrow Bashar al-Assad, the PFLP-GC reaffirmed its allegiance to the embattled president and pledged in September 2013 to "retaliate" if the United States attacked Syria.

Leaders: Talal NAJI, Musa AWAD, Khalid JIBRIL (military leader), Ahmad JABRIL (Secretary General).

Al-Saiqa. Established in 1968 under the influence of the Syrian Baath Party, *al-Saiqa* ("Thunderbolt") came into conflict with Fatah as a result of *al-Saiqa*'s active support for Syrian intervention during the Lebanese civil war. The group's longtime leader, Zuheir MOHSEN, who served as the PLO's chief of military operations, was assassinated in Paris in July 1979, his successor being a former Syrian air force general. Denouncing the decisions of the November 1988 PNC session, *al-Saiqa* leaders said they would attempt to get the PLO back on its original revolutionary course of "struggle."

In 2006 the group opposed President Abbas's proposed national accord referendum.

Leaders: Issam al-KADE, Mohamed KHALIFAH.

Fatah Uprising. An outgrowth of the 1983 internal PLO fighting in Lebanon, the Uprising (a Fatah splinter group) drew its membership from PLO dissidents who remained in Beirut following the departure of Yasir Arafat. One of the most steadfast of the anti-Arafat formations, it waged a bitter (and largely successful) struggle with mainstream adherents for control of Beirut's refugee camps in May–July 1988. It condemned the PNC declaration of November 1988 as a "catastrophe" and in early 1990 called for attacks on U.S. interests worldwide "because America is completely biased towards the Zionist enemy." The group also called for the assassination of Arafat in the wake of the PLO's September 1993 agreement with Israel.

In 2006 the group reportedly was involved in the smuggling of arms into Lebanon and was reportedly reinforced by forces from Damascus in its clashes with the Lebanese army near the border with Syria.

Leaders: Saed MUSA (Abu MUSA), Muraghah Abu-Fadi HAMMAD (Secretary General).

Revolutionary Council of Fatah. The Revolutionary Council (also known as the Abu Nidal Group) was held responsible for more than 100 terrorist incidents in over 20 countries after it broke away from Fatah in 1974. Targets included Palestinian moderates as well as Israelis and other Jews, and the group's predilection for attacks in public places in Europe and Asia led to allegations of its involvement in the assaults on the Vienna and Rome airports in December 1985. The shadowy organization, which operated under numerous names, was formed by Sabry Khalil al-BANNA, better known as Abu Nidal, one of the first PLO guerrillas to challenge the leadership of Yasir Arafat. Nidal reportedly plotted to have Arafat killed soon after their split, prompting Nidal's trial in absentia by the PLO, which issued a death sentence. Somewhat surprisingly, the Revolutionary Council of Fatah sent representatives to the preparatory meeting for the April 1987 PNC session, although they walked out during the first day of the regular session.

After its Syrian offices were closed by President Assad in 1987, the council transferred the bulk of its military operations to Lebanon's Bekaa Valley and Muslim West Beirut, with Abu Nidal and other leaders reportedly moving to Libya. Fierce personal rivalries and disagreements over policy were subsequently reported within the group, apparently prompting Abu Nidal to order the killing of about 150 dissidents in Libya in October 1989. Consequently, several former senior commanders of the organization fled to Algiers and Tunis, where they established an "emergency leadership" faction opposed to the "blind terrorism" still espoused by Abu Nidal's supporters. The internecine fighting subsequently spread to Lebanon, where in June 1990 the dissidents were reported to have routed Nidal's supporters with the aid of fighters from Arafat's Fatah.

In July 1992 Walid KHALID, described as Abu Nidal's top aide, was assassinated in Lebanon, apparently as part of a series of "score settling" killings by rival guerrilla groups. In November 1995 Palestinian police arrested a group of reported council members in connection with an alleged plot against Arafat's life.

In mid-1998 it was reported that an ailing Abu Nidal was being detained in Egypt after having crossed the border from Libya, possibly as the result of a falling out with Libyan leader Muammar al-Qadhafi. However, Egyptian officials denied that report, and U.S. officials subsequently suggested Abu Nidal may have relocated to Iraq. In August 2002 Iraqi security forces reported that Abu Nidal had committed suicide during their attempt to arrest him in connection with an alleged plot to overthrow the regime of Saddam Hussein. Although uncertain of the circumstances, Western analysts accepted the fact of Abu Nidal's death, noting that it presumably meant the formal end of the Revolutionary Council, for which no activity had been reported since 1996.

Army of Islam. A small faction in Gaza led by prominent clan leader Mumtaz DOGMUSH, the Army of Islam was the focus of a crackdown by Hamas in September 2008. The grouping had earlier claimed responsibility for several kidnappings reportedly conducted in association with the so-called Popular Resistance Committees (see below), led by another branch of the Dogmush clan. Israeli air strikes in Gaza killed several reputed Army of Islam leaders in 2010.

Israeli officials alleged that members of the **Popular Resistance Committees** (PRC) operating out of Gaza had been responsible for an August 2011 attack that killed a number of Israelis and prompted, among other things, a dispute between Israel and Egypt (see Foreign relations in the entry on Israel for details). Representatives of the PRC denied involvement but said they approved of the attack. PRC leader Awad Kamal al-NEIRAB was killed in a retaliatory Israeli air strike; he was succeeded by Zuhir al-QAISI, who died in another Israeli attack in March 2012, which triggered a barrage of rocket attacks from Gaza into Israel.

LEGISLATURE

Palestinian Legislative Council. The September 1995 Interim Agreement on the West Bank and the Gaza Strip (the second of the Palestinian "self-rule" accords between Israel and the PLO) provided for the election of a Palestinian Council to exercise legislative and executive authority in those areas of the previously occupied territories to which Palestinian autonomy had been or was about to be extended. The agreement initially established the size of the council at 82 members, but the membership was increased to 88 late in the year by mutual consent of Israeli and Palestinian representatives. Sixteen electoral districts were established in the Gaza Strip, West Bank, and East Jerusalem, and all Palestinians who were at least 18 years of age and had lived in those districts for at least three years were declared eligible to vote.

Nearly 700 candidates, including over 400 independents and some 200 representatives of small parties and political factions, reportedly contested the initial council elections conducted on January 20, 1996. However, balloting was dominated by Yasir Arafat's Fatah faction of the PLO, most other major groupings (including Hamas, Islamic Jihad, the Democratic Front for the Liberation of Palestine, the Popular Front for the Liberation of Palestine, and other PLO factions opposed to the current peace negotiations) having boycotted the election. According to *Middle East International,* Palestinian officials reported that the successful candidates included 50 of the 70 "official" Fatah nominees, 37 independents (including 16 Fatah dissidents), and 1 member of the Palestinian Democratic Union.

The council (by then routinely referenced as the Palestinian Legislative Council, or PLC) convened for the first time on March 7, 1996, in Gaza City. Ahmad Quray was elected speaker by a vote of 57–31 over Haidar Abd al-SHAFI, a critic of Arafat and the recent accords with Israel. In addition to serving as leader of the new council, the speaker was also envisioned as the person who would assume the position of head of the council's executive authority in the event of the incapacitation or death of the person in that position. Regarding such matters, the council proposed a Basic Law of Palestine, which would serve as a "constitution" until the completion of the "final talks" with Israel. The council fell into conflict with Arafat in 1997 over his failure to sign the Basic Law or to pursue other reforms the council had recommended, including the replacement of the current cabinet with a technocratic government better able to deal with the myriad Palestinian economic and development needs. Late in the year the council suspended its sessions to put pressure on the Palestinian leader, who agreed to reorganize the government.

Following the death of Arafat in November 2004 and installation of new Palestinian leadership in early 2005, new PLC elections were scheduled for July 2005. However, they were later postponed as deliberations continued on, among other things, whether a proportional representation system should be established. In preparation for the upcoming elections, the council was expanded from 88 members to 132. Half the seats, or 66, would be elected through proportional representation, while the remaining 66 would be elected from 16 constituencies, whose number of seats would be determined by population. Six seats in the council were also reserved for Christians.

Hamas, running as "Change and Reform," won 74 seats in the January 25, 2006, balloting for the PLC. Fatah finished second with 45 seats. (Although Hamas scored only 3 percentage points higher than Fatah overall, it won 45 of the 66 seats elected on a constituency basis. Meanwhile, Fatah won 28 seats elected by proportional representation and 17 on a constituency basis.) Of the 13 remaining seats, the Popular Front for the Liberation of Palestine (running as the Martyr Abu Ali Mustafa List) won 3 seats; The Alternative (a coalition of the Democratic Front for the Liberation of Palestine, the Palestinian People's Party, and the Palestine Democratic Union) won 2; the Palestinian National Initiative won 2; the Third Way (founded by Hanan Ashrawi and former Palestinian finance minister Salam Fayyad) won 2, and independents won 4.

In December 2009 the PLO Central Council extended the mandate of the current legislators indefinitely pending new elections. The tentative Hamas-Fatah reconciliation agreement of mid-2011 called for such elections to be held following the planned installation of a transitional "unity" government. However, implementation of that agreement had not been achieved as of November 2013.

Speaker: Abdel Aziz DUWAIK.

CABINET

[as of October 1, 2013]

Prime Minister	Rami Hamdallah (ind.)
Deputy Prime Minister	Ziad Abu Amr (ind.)
Deputy Prime Minister (Economic Affairs)	Muhammad Mustafa
Ministers	
Agriculture	Walid Assaf (Fatah)
Cabinet Secretary General	Fawaz Aqel
Culture	Anwar Abu Eisheh
Economy	Jawad Harzallah (Fatah)
Education and Higher Education	Ali Abu Zuhri (Fatah)
Finance	Shukri Bishara
Foreign Affairs	Riyad al-Malki
Health	Dr. Jawad Awwad
Interior	Said Abu Ali (Fatah)
Jerusalem Affairs	Adnan al-Husseini (Fatah)
Justice	Ali Muhanna (Fatah)
Labor	Ahmad Majdalani
Local Government	Saed al-Kawni
Minister of State for Planning	Mohammed Abu Ramadan (ind.)
Prisoner Affairs	Issa Qaraqe (Fatah)
Public Works and Housing	Maher Ghneim (Fatah)
Religious Affairs and Awqaf	Mahmoud al-Habbash (ind.)
Social Affairs	Kamal al-Sharafi
Telecommunications and Information Technology	Safa Nasser Eddin (ind.) [f]
Tourism and Antiquities	Rula Maayah (Fatah) [f]
Transportation	Nabil Dameidi
Women's Affairs	Rabiha Diab (Fatah) [f]

[f] = female

Note: Hamas, which controls the Gaza Strip, continued to operate its own de facto cabinet for that territory under the leadership of Prime Minister Ismail Haniyeh as of October 2013. Other members of the cabinet (all members of Hamas) included Mazen HANIYEH (Justice), Yusef Sobhi AGHREVZ (Housing and Public Works), Ismail RADWAN (Religious Affairs), Ziyad al-ZAZA (Finance and Deputy Prime Minister), Abd al-Aziz al-TIRSHAWI (Agriculture), Mufiz al-MAKHALATI (Health), Mohammed Jawad al-FARRA (Local Government), Fathi HAMMAD (Interior), Osman al-MUZAYNI (Education), and Mahmud al-ZAHAR (Foreign Affairs).

INTERGOVERNMENTAL REPRESENTATION

Ambassador to the Permanent Observer Mission of Palestine to the UN: Riyad H. MANSOUR.

INTERGOVERNMENTAL ORGANIZATIONS

AFRICAN UNION (AU)

Established: By charter of the predecessor Organization of African Unity (OAU) adopted May 25, 1963, in Addis Ababa, Ethiopia; Treaty Establishing the African Economic Community (AEC)—the Abuja Treaty—adopted June 3, 1991, by the OAU heads of state and government in Abuja, Nigeria, and entered into force May 12, 1994; Constitutive Act of the African Union (AU) adopted July 11, 2000, by the OAU heads of state and government in Lomé, Togo, and entered into force May 26, 2001. (The OAU remained in existence during a one-year transitional period ending July 8, 2002; the Abuja Treaty remains a cornerstone of the AU.)

Purpose: To "achieve greater unity and solidarity" among African states; to "accelerate the political and socio-economic integration of the continent"; to "promote and defend African common positions"; to "promote peace, security and stability"; to "promote democratic principles and institutions, popular participation and good governance"; to assist in Africa's effort "to play its rightful role in the global economy and in international negotiations"; and to "promote sustainable development at the economic, social and cultural levels."

Headquarters: Addis Ababa, Ethiopia.

Principal Organs: Assembly of Heads of State and Government; Executive Council; Peace and Security Council (15 members); Permanent Representatives Committee; Pan-African Parliament; Economic, Social, and Cultural Council; Commission; Court of Justice.

Web site: www.au.int

Chair of the Commission: Nkosazana Dhlamini Zuma (South Africa).

Membership (54): Algeria, Angola, Benin, Botswana, Burkina Faso, Burundi, Cameroon, Cape Verde, Central African Republic, Chad, Comoro Islands, Democratic Republic of the Congo, Republic of the Congo, Côte d'Ivoire, Djibouti, Egypt, Equatorial Guinea, Eritrea, Ethiopia, Gabon, Gambia, Ghana, Guinea, Guinea-Bissau (suspended since April 2012), Kenya, Lesotho, Liberia, Libya, Madagascar, Malawi, Mali, Mauritania, Mauritius, Mozambique, Namibia, Niger, Nigeria, Rwanda, Sahrawi Arab Democratic Republic, Sao Tome and Principe, Senegal, Seychelles, Sierra Leone, Somalia, South Africa, South Sudan, Swaziland, Tanzania, Togo, Tunisia, Uganda, Zambia, Zimbabwe.

Official Languages: Arabic, English, French, Kiswahili, Portuguese, Spanish, and any other African language.

Origin and development. The OAU was the most conspicuous result of the search for unity among the emerging states of Africa, a number of whose representatives participated in the first Conference of Independent African States in April 1958 in Accra, Ghana. It remained in existence, with mixed success, until 2000. For a fuller discussion of the OAU, see the AU article in the 2010 *Handbook.*

The Algiers OAU summit of July 12–14, 1999, marked the return of Libya's Colonel. Muammar al-Qadhafi, who had not attended OAU heads of state meetings in more than 20 years and who now proposed that an extraordinary summit be held to consider establishing a "United States of Africa." As a result, on September 8–9, 1999, the heads of state and government reconvened in Sirte, Libya, and agreed to the formation of the AU as successor to the OAU. Following subsequent negotiations, African leaders signed the Constitutive Act of the AU at the OAU summit on July 10–12, 2000, in Lomé, Togo.

Based loosely on the model of the European Union (EU), the AU was conceived as building on existing elements of the OAU—for example, the AEC and the Mechanism for Conflict Prevention, Management, and Resolution—but with a stronger institutional structure. It was also expected to serve as a means of achieving faster sustainable economic development and integration and as a better vehicle for representing unified African positions in international forums and organizations.

At the OAU's fifth extraordinary summit, held March 1–2, 2001, in Sirte, the OAU declared the AU to be established. The OAU remained in existence for a one year transition period, during which technical arrangements were worked out and the remaining protocols for various AU organs drafted.

The OAU's 37th and final full summit convened July 9–11, 2001, in Lusaka, Zambia. On the economic front, the summit launched the New Africa Initiative (NAI) with the goal of ending poverty, war, and disease in Africa by 2015 through better governance, foreign investment in a more open marketplace, and sustainable development. Having attracted widespread support from the developed world and from the UN Economic Commission for Africa, the plan was renamed the New Partnership for Africa's Development (NEPAD) at an October 23, 2001, OAU meeting in Abuja, Nigeria.

On July 9–10, 2002, the heads of state and government, meeting in Durban, South Africa, inaugurated the AU. Among the actions taken by the July 2002 inaugural summit was the adoption of the Protocol Relating to the Establishment of the Peace and Security Council (PSC) of the AU. On December 26, 2003, Nigeria became the 27th AU state to deposit its instrument of ratification, thereby bringing the protocol into force.

At the second extraordinary session of the assembly, meeting February 27–28, 2004, in Sirte, Libya, the Common African Defense and Security Policy (CDSP) was adopted, as called for in the Constitutive Act and the PSC protocol. The CDSP defined defense as encompassing "both the traditional, military, and state-centric notion of the use of the armed forces of the state to protect its national sovereignty and territorial integrity, as well as the less traditional, non-military aspects which relate to the protection of the people's political, cultural, social and economic values and ways of life."

After becoming operational in 2003, one of the first tasks of the PSC was to organize the African Standby Force (ASF) planned to be fully operational by 2015. This force intends to incorporate police and civilian components as well as military personnel, in keeping with its broad mission, which includes possible preventive deployment, peacekeeping, and postconflict disarmament and demobilization. The Southern Africa Brigade, the first component of the ASF, was established in August 2007.

At the January 30–31, 2005, summit in Abuja, Nigeria, the African Union Non-Aggression and Common Defense Pact was adopted, and it came into effect December 18, 2009, with the last of the 53 countries signing the document on February 2. The fifth regular summit, held July 4–5, 2005, called for a full cancellation of all African countries' debts and for "the abolition of subsidies that stand as an obstacle to trade"—an initiative passed by the G-8 summit in July 2005 and approved by both the IMF and the World Bank in September 2005.

The AU's peacekeeping efforts in Darfur were complicated by Sudan's bid at the sixth AU summit (held January 23–24, 2006, in Khartoum, Sudan) to assume the organization's presidency for the year. Amid accusations of genocide in the Darfur conflict, Sudan withdrew in favor of the Republic of the Congo, but with suggestions that it might renew its bid in 2007. The AU's 7,000-strong peacekeeping force in Darfur, funded by the United States and the EU, had little success in stopping the violence. The peacekeeping force continued to operate nonetheless, and after months of negotiation with the government of Sudan, a mid-August 2007 resolution of the UN Security Council called for the establishment of a peacekeeping force of 26,000 under joint UN and AU command, consisting only of troops from Africa.

The July 2–4, 2007, summit, held in Accra, raised once again the issue of a single government for Africa. Most participants favored stronger economic union but had no appetite for complete political union. Col. Qadhafi—who had called for the immediate establishment of a single government, foreign policy, and army for Africa—left the summit early.

Throughout 2007 and 2008, the AU was preoccupied with crises in several member states. The joint UN/AU peacekeeping force began operations on December 31, 2007, but was seriously undermanned and poorly equipped. In August 2008 the UN Security Council extended the force's mandate for another year. Only then did Sudan promise to allow its full deployment. On June 30 the AU and UN appointed Djibril Yipene Bassole, foreign minister of Burkina Faso, as joint chief mediator. His task was complicated by the efforts of the International Criminal Court to bring Sudanese government officials to trial for genocide, an action the AU condemnedas working against the peace process.

In late February 2008 the Comoro Islands central government rejected an AU proposal of sanctions against Anjouan, peace talks broke off, and by late March AU troops arrived to assist in an attack to retake Anjouan. This operation, the AU's first offensive military operation, was successful, and in June 2008 Anjouan held an election to replace its deposed president.

The AU peacekeeping force in Somalia, sanctioned by the UN Security Council as the African Union Mission to Somalia (AMISOM), received six-month extensions to its mandate on August 20, 2007; February 20, 2008; and August 20, 2008. Like its counterpart in Darfur the Somalia mission was seriously undermanned, but suffered much more from guerrilla attacks. On July 1, 2008, the AU announced that it would continue the difficult mission in its present form through the end of the year but urged the UN to take it over. On August 19, 2008, the two main Somali factions, the Transitional Federal Government (TFG) of Somalia and the Alliance for the Re-Liberation of Somalia (ARS), signed a peace agreement under AU auspices.

The AU was most successful in mediating a resolution of the disputed December 27, 2007, presidential election in Kenya and its violent aftermath. By the end of February, AU chair Jakaya Kikwete and former UN secretary general Kofi Annan were in talks with all parties involved to ensure that a power-sharing agreement took hold. Their efforts were successful and the AU gained a great amount of prestige.

The AU's role in the disputed March 2008 Zimbabwe elections received less praise. AUC Chair Jean Ping, first visited Zimbabwe in early May. Further action took the form of electoral monitoring and a vote at the July 1–2, 2008, summit disapproving of Zimbabwean president Mugabe's actions. On July 22, 2008, Mugabe and Morgan Tsvangirai, his rival, signed an agreement to begin negotiations on sharing power, an agreement that the AU welcomed.

In other business at the Sharm-el-Sheikh summit, the organization endorsed the concept of an all-African government, though there was no consensus how that might be achieved. Another decision from the meeting was to merge the African Human and Peoples' Rights Court and the African Court of Justice into one body.

On August 8, 2008, a military coup overthrew the government of Mauritania. AU mediation, coupled with sanctions and with pressure from other international groups, ended in a presidential election in July 2009. This election, certified by the AU as fair, returned the coup leader, General Mohamed Ould Abdelaziz, to office as a civilian president.

In September 2008 Chad, long involved in an undeclared war with neighboring Sudan, signed the AU's non-aggression pact. In November the AU brokered restoration of diplomatic relations between the two countries. For more on activities and developments since 2008, see "Recent Activities" below.

Structure. The Assembly of Heads of State and Government, the supreme decision-making organ of the AU, meets twice annually in ordinary session to define overall AU policy and to supervise the activities of the other AU organs. Substantive decisions are made by consensus or, failing that, a two-thirds majority. A simple majority suffices on procedural questions.

The Executive Council, comprising the foreign ministers or other designated representatives of all member states, meets at least twice a year to confer on preparation for meetings of the assembly, the implementation of assembly decisions, the AU budget, and matters of intra-African cooperation and general international policy. Assisting the Executive Council is the Permanent Representatives Committee, made up of ambassadors accredited to the AU. An advisory Economic, Social, and Cultural Council (ECOSOCC) was launched in March 2005.

Consisting of 15 members elected with due regard for "equitable regional representation and rotation," the PSC includes in its mandate supervision of a planned African Standby Force equipped to intervene in crisis situations.

The Pan-African Parliament, established under a protocol to the AEC treaty, is envisaged as evolving into a directly elected organ with full legislative powers. Initially, however, it comprises five representatives chosen by and from the member states' legislatures and reflecting "the diversity of political opinion in each." The inaugural parliamentary session was held on March 18–20, 2004, in Addis Ababa.

The AU Commission replaced the OAU's Secretariat. The Commission chair, who is elected by the assembly for a four-year term, is assisted by a deputy and eight elected commissioners. The commission oversees the work of the AU in many administrative and policy areas. For a list of the responsibilities of the individual commissioners, see *Political Handbook of the World* 2012. In addition, the Commission services the Conference on Security, Stability, Development, and Cooperation in Africa (CSSDCA), which was established by the 2000 OAU summit in Lomé and has a primary role in regional monitoring and evaluation.

The chair of the entire AU, as distinct from the AU Commission, rotates annually, by vote of the Assembly, among the heads of state of member countries.

The Constitutive Act additionally called for the formation of eight specialized technical committees: Rural Economy and Agricultural Matters; Monetary and Financial Affairs; Trade, Customs, and Immigration Matters; Industry, Science, and Technology; Energy, Natural Resources, and the Environment; Transportation, Communication, and Tourism; Health, Labor, and Social Affairs; and Education, Culture, and Human Rights. The assembly may create additional specialized technical committees.

Three new financial institutions are also mentioned in the founding act: the African Central Bank, the African Monetary Fund, and the African Investment Bank. At the eighth Ordinary Session of the Executive Council, held January 16–17, 2006, in Addis Ababa, the first members of the African Court on Human and People's Rights were elected. Creation of this body was proposed in a protocol to the 1981 African Charter on Human and People's Rights. The Court of Justice was merged with the African Court on Human and People's Rights on July 1, 2008. The Court of Justice is responsible for serving as a criminal court for Africa and is largely charged with handling cases pertaining to human rights violations. The Court of Justice also serves as the legal branch of the AU.

Related specialized agencies, all previously associated with the OAU, include the African Accounting Council, the African Civil Aviation Commission (AFCAC), the African Telecommunications Union (ATU), the Pan-African Institute of Education for Development, the Pan-African News Agency (PANA), and the Pan-African Postal Union (PAPU).

Recent Activities. The 12th summit, held January 26–February 3, 2009, in Addis Ababa, was most notable for the Executive Council electing Muammar Qadhafi as chair, succeeding Jakaya Kikwete of Tanzania. Qadhafi again announced that he wanted to turn the AU into a "United States of Africa." As a compromise, the group commissioned a study to consider restructuring the Commission as an "Authority." Qadhafi had previously stated that multi-party democracy in Africa led to tribalism and bloodshed, and should be replaced by one-party systems such as his own. At the June Ordinary Session of the Executive Committee, held in Sirte, Qadhafi proposed immediate dissolution of all organs of the AU, and creation of the United States of Africa. Commission chair Ping said that more urgent matters needed attention, and they should wait for the reaction of the July 1–3 session of the AU Assembly. The latter meeting adopted the notion of transforming the AU Commission into the African Union Authority. The Authority would have broader powers than the Commission, and would be responsible for creating common defense, diplomacy, and trade policies. Libyan media, perhaps too hopefully, stated that the chair of the Commission would become "Africa's first president." The change would, however, first have to be ratified by all the AU member states.

The 12th summit also called on the International Criminal Court (ICC) to reconsider indicting Sudanese president Omar al-Bashir on charges of war crimes and crimes against humanity in Darfur. The ICC issued an arrest warrant for Bashir in March 2009. By August 2009 the commander of UNAMID forces in Sudan declared that the war was essentially over, with fighting reduced to banditry and inconsequential local disputes.

On March 17, 2009, a military coup in Madagascar forced out President Marc Ravalomanana, and installed Andry Rajoelina in his place. The AU suspended Madagascar from participation in its activities, and relocated the July summit from Madagascar to Libya. Tensions on the island grew worse throughout the summer, and the AU decided that military intervention, such as its actions in the Comoro islands, was not feasible. In August 2009 the AU assisted in brokering a power-sharing arrangement, but the cabinet named by Rajoelina in early September contained few of his opponents, and opposition parties cried foul.

In May 2009 Zimbabwean prime minister Morgan Tsvangirai urged the AU and the SADC (see article on Zimbabwe) to help make the power-sharing between President Mugabe and himself work (see separate article on Zimbabwe).

AU peacekeeping operations continued in Somalia, though without much success. At the July 2009 Summit Commission chair Ping said that the AU with its 4,000 peacekeepers had essentially abandoned Somalia to its fate. At least 8,000 were needed, he said. The heads of state agreed to look for more troops among the AU member states. In January 2010 the AU extended its mandate in Somalia, but had difficulty finding more troops, and indeed had difficulty in persuading member states to fulfill their existing pledges. At the July 2010 summit the group pledged 2,000 more troops, also changing the peacekeeping force's rules of engagement to improve efficiency and morale. AU peacekeepers would now be able to shoot first if they faced imminent attack. The conference however rejected a call from Ugandan president

Museveni for the AU to go on the offensive against the Al-Shabaab Islamist rebels in Somalia. Several member states, particularly Muslim ones, objected.

At the January 31–February 2, 2010, Addis Ababa summit, Libyan president Qadhafi failed in an attempt to stay on for a second year as the organization's chair. He was succeeded by Bingu wa Mutharika, president of Malawi.

In February 2010 an AU delegation visited NATO headquarters in Belgium, to discuss closer cooperation between the two groups in Africa's new strategic environment. AU–U.S. talks opened in Washington for the first time in April. They ended with a pledge of more U.S. cooperation with the AU.

The 15th summit was held July 19–27, 2010, in Kampala, Uganda. It came only a few days after Al-Shabaab terrorists killed more than 70 people in three separate bombings. At the summit Guinea announced that it would send troops to join the peacekeeping forces in Somalia.

Between the two summits there was a military coup in Niger, which the AU condemned, and it suspended that country from membership. On March 16, 2011, following the successful completion of a new parliamentary election in Niger, the PSC voted to lift the suspension. Similarly, a highly contested election in Cote d'Ivoire resulted in the AU suspending the country in November 2010. The AU subsequently sent a commission of 20 individuals into the country to help the two sides come to a peaceable agreement. After five months of negotiating, the election dispute was resolved with the assistance of the AU officials, and the country was reinstated on April 21, 2011.

The 16th summit occurred in January 2011 at the UN Conference Center in Addis Ababa, Ethiopia. The meeting discussed the necessary steps toward the transition of the AUC into the African Union Association. The meeting also endorsed Mauritius's claim to the Chagos Archipelago, a territory disputed by the British.

In July the 17th summit focused largely on the political conflict in Libya. In a resolution approved by the assembly, the AU declared that a political situation was the only acceptable solution, and urged the UN to support the efforts of the AU rather than using force. A framework agreement submitted by an ad hoc committee on the Libya situation was approved and sent to the Libyan government.

Also in July 2011, the newly formed Republic of Sudan became the 54th member of the African Union.

The continued fighting and unrest in Libya was a major concern of the AU throughout the latter half of 2011. The PSC kept a close monitor on the situation, as did a high level ad hoc committee formed at the request of the AUC. The AU continually emphasized its commitment to the people of Libya and called for a peaceful resolution of the situation. Following the ouster and death of Colonel Qadaffi in October, the PSC recognized the government of the National Transitional Council and allowed the NTC to assume Libya's seat in the AU. The AU also organized a liaison office in Tripoli to assist with the peaceful transition of power and rebuilding of the Libyan infrastructure.

The 18th summit held in January 2012 largely centered on African integration. One such measure was the full establishment of the Pan African University. The PAU was formally created in December 2011, but the January summit started the organization of the university by authorizing permanent institution sites and the hiring of faculty and staff. The meeting also saw measures taken to speed up the full economic integration of the continent by creating an action plan for integration and establishing the framework of the economic union. It set a 2017 deadline for the full implementation of a free trade continent.

In January 2012, a group of rebels began an attack against the government of Mali. On March 22, Mali President Amadou Toure was removed from office in an armed coup. Mali was suspended from the AU the next day. Similarly, a military coup in Guinea-Bissau in early April resulted in the suspension of that country from the AU, pending the restoration of a constitutional government. Suspensions were lifted on October 24, 2012.

The 19th summit was held in July 2012. During the weeklong summit, the member states focused on the Arab-Israeli conflict through a series of resolutions and declarations. The member states reaffirmed its support for Palestine and its UN membership, while calling for Israel's immediate withdrawal from PLO territory. The member states also were greatly concerned by the expulsion of African nationals from Israel. Another major area of concern was the growing political unrest in Mali. The most significant action of the summit, however, was the election of Dr. Nkosazana Clarise Dhlamini Zuma of South Africa as AUC Chairperson. Dr. Dhlamini-Zuma is the first woman to be elected to the post and is the first representative of a southern African nation to hold the high office since the formation of the OAU in 1963. She replaced Dr. Jean Ping as AUC Chairperson.

The year 2013 marked the 50th anniversary of the OAU/AU. The January summit met under the theme of "Pan-Africanism and African Renaissance." The meeting saw the group emphasize the importance of maternal health, institutional reforms, and unity among the region.

In honor of its golden anniversary, the organization's May summit was tied to the main anniversary celebration. The 21st summit was significant for its adoption of the 50th Anniversary Solemn Declaration. The declaration recalled its great heritage and the progress that it has made over the last 50 years, and pledged its continued work to advance pan-Africanism and unity within the member states. The declaration identified the eight core priorities to be used in drafting the Agenda 2063, which include a pledge to end wars in Africa by 2020 and a commitment to work toward swift implementation of the Continental Free Trade Agreement. Also at the meeting, the group announced its Agenda 2063 effort, which is a pan-African attempt to craft a set of 50-year development goals. The Agenda 2063 website was launched in September to allow the public to provide suggestions for the development goals. The draft of the Agenda is to be discussed at the January 2014 summit.

On July 3, 2013, the Egyptian government suspended its constitution, which had been ratified in December 2012, and overthrew their president Mohamed Morsi, who was elected in a June 2012 national referendum. In light of these events, the PSC called a special meeting on July 5 to discuss the situation. At that meeting, the PSC authorized the expedited creation of a high-level team to assist Egypt in its transition back to a democratic government and constitutional order.

The AU lifted its sanctions against Madagascar on September 2013 in light of the country's progress and scheduled elections.

An extraordinary summit of the Assembly of the AU was held in October 2013 to discuss the relationship between the AU and the ICC. The summit yielded a declaration from the organization stating that no sitting head of government shall be prosecuted before an international tribunal or court, and the AU affirmed that it would not require an AU head of government to appear. This meeting came as a response to the ICC's investigation of the sitting Kenyan president and vice president. The AU has issued an appeal to the UN Security Council and ICC to delay the indictment, but as the AU Assembly Chairman noted, the ICC has never responded positively to an AU request for deferral.

ARAB LEAGUE

al-Jami'a al-'Arabiyah

Official Name: League of Arab States.

Established: By treaty signed March 22, 1945, in Cairo, Egypt.

Purpose: To strengthen relations among member states by coordinating policies in political, cultural, economic, social, and related affairs; to mediate disputes between members or between members and third parties.

Headquarters: Cairo, Egypt.

Principal Organs: Council of the League of Arab States (all members), Economic and Social Council (all adherents to the 1950 Collective Security Treaty), Joint Defense Council (all adherents to the 1950 Collective Security Treaty), Permanent Committees (all members), General Secretariat.

Web site: www.arableagueonline.org

Secretary General: Nabil Al Arabi (Egypt).

Membership (22): Algeria, Bahrain, Comoro Islands, Djibouti, Egypt, Iraq, Jordan, Kuwait, Lebanon, Libya, Mauritania, Morocco, Oman, Palestine, Qatar, Saudi Arabia, Somalia, Sudan, Syria, Tunisia, United Arab Emirates, Yemen.

Official Language: Arabic.

Origin and development. A long-standing project that reached fruition late in World War II, the league was founded primarily on Egyptian initiative following a promise of British support for any Arab organization that commanded general endorsement. In its earlier years the organization focused mainly on economic, cultural, and social cooperation, but in 1950 a Convention on Joint Defense and Economic Cooperation was concluded that obligated the members in case of attack "immediately to take, individually and collectively, all steps available, including the use of armed force, to repel the aggression and restore security and peace." In 1976 the Palestine Liberation Organization (PLO), which had participated as an observer at all league conferences since September 1964, was admitted to full membership. Egypt's participation was suspended from April 1979 to May 1989 because of its peace agreement with Israel.

After many years of preoccupation with Arab-Israeli issues, the league's attention in 1987 turned to the Iraq-Iran conflict as Arab moderates sought a united front against Iran and the potential spread of militant Islamic fundamentalism. An extraordinary summit conference held November 8–11 in Amman, Jordan, condemned "the Iranian regime's intransigence, provocations, and threats to the Arab Gulf States" and called for international "pressure" to encourage Iran to accept a UN-sponsored cease-fire.

The prospect for effective cooperation was severely compromised by Iraq's takeover of Kuwait on August 2, 1990, which split the league into two deeply divided blocs. On August 10, the majority voted to send a pan-Arab force to guard Saudi Arabia against a possible Iraqi attack; several members (most notably Egypt and Syria) ultimately contributed troops to the U.S.-led liberation of Kuwait in early 1991. The minority included members overtly sympathetic to Baghdad and those that were adamantly opposed to U.S. military involvement.

In the mid-1990s, prospects for institutional reform were constrained by financial difficulties: only four members (Egypt, Jordan, Saudi Arabia, and Syria) had paid their full dues in 1996, while the remaining members were a combined $80 million in arrears. As a consequence, the league was forced to close several foreign offices and reportedly had difficulty meeting its payroll at times.

In November 1997, despite the league's financial troubles, 17 members agreed to proceed with the establishment of the Arab Free Trade Zone in 1998, with the goal of cutting customs duties by 10 percent a year until their elimination at the end of 2007. In other activity during the year, the Arab League foreign ministers, meeting in March in Cairo, recommended that members reactivate the economic boycott against Israel and cease all activity geared toward normalizing relations with that country given the stalled peace process.

The Amman, Jordan, summit of March 27–28, 2001, marked the first regular summit since 1990, with Iraq in attendance as a full participant. The league ended up calling once again for an end to the sanctions against Iraq and also for Baghdad to work out its differences with the UN over inspections and related issues. Two months later, on May 16, Amr Mahmoud Moussa, previously Egypt's foreign minister, began his tenure as the league's new secretary general.

With regard to the "road map" for peace in the Middle East that was formally introduced April 30, 2003, by the European Union, the UN, Russia, and the United States, the Arab League expressed its cautious support.

On March 22–23, 2005, only 13 of 22 leaders attended the league summit in Algiers, Algeria, and the resolutions adopted "were of comparatively little significance," according to The New York Times. However, plans were unveiled for an Arab common market by 2015 and a regional security system. The participants also approved the establishment of an interim Arab Parliament, which met for the first time on December 27, 2005, in Cairo, Egypt. The Parliament has 88 representatives, 4 from each Arab League member, but it has no legislative authority, leaving its responsibilities unclear apart from serving as a forum on Arab issues. It was decided that this interim legislature would move to Syria, meeting twice a year with the aim of creating a permanent Arab legislature by 2011. Mohammad Jassim al-Saqr, a Kuwaiti described as a liberal, was elected its speaker.

The Arab League's response to the landslide victory of the militant group Hamas in the January 2006 Palestinian Authority elections was mixed. Secretary General Moussa said Hamas should renounce violence against Israel and recognize its right to exist if it expects to function as a legitimate government. On the other hand, at its March 28–29, 2006, summit in Khartoum, the league pledged to contribute $55 million a month toward the operation of the Palestinian Authority.

The 2006 summit, like its predecessor, was not attended by the heads of several member states, for reasons including poor security and Sudan's position on the Darfur crisis. In addition to its commitment to the Palestinian Authority, the league pledged $150 million to support the mission of African Union peacekeepers in Darfur. The years 2006 and 2007 saw continuing Arab League involvement in efforts to broker peace between the Hamas and Fatah factions of the Palestinian Authority. When Hamas seized control of the Gaza Strip in June 2007, however, the Arab League joined in the policy of the U.S. and Israel of supporting the rump Palestinian Authority government of the Fatah-led faction in the West Bank.

The 2007 summit, held March 28–29 in Riyadh, Saudi Arabia, produced a renewed call for Israel to negotiate on the basis of the 2002 "land for peace" proposal. In April 2007 the league set up a contact group, consisting of Jordan and Egypt (countries having diplomatic relations with Israel), to deal directly with Israel on the proposal. On July 25, 2007, the foreign ministers of those countries went to Israel and met Israeli prime minister Ehud Olmert. By September 2007, however, the league began to say that Israel was not taking the dialogue seriously, regarding it only as an exercise in public relations.

The Arab League was actively involved in the troubles of Iraq and Lebanon throughout 2007 and 2008. In September 2007 the league turned down a Syrian government request to establish a fund in aid of Iraqi refugees in Syria. In January 2008, however, the league tried to reestablish itself as a mediator in Iraq after almost a year of absence, but with little success. Lebanon (see separate article) was in a prolonged and sometimes violent state of unrest after its president's term ended in November 2007, and parliament failed to elect a successor. Many blamed pro-Syrian factions for the stalemate, and the Iranian-backed Hezbollah movement temporarily took over much of Beirut in early May 2008. The Arab League was deeply involved in negotiations that led to a compromise, with Hezbollah's official standing much increased, and the Lebanese parliament finally elected a president on May 28, 2008.

By mid-2008 the primary matter of concern for the Arab League was the situation in Darfur, in particular the prospect of the International Criminal Court (ICC) issuing an arrest warrant for Sudanese president Omar al-Bashir, charging him with genocide. The league's aim was to postpone or defuse the potential crisis, and in any case not to support Bashir's arrest. On July 19 it passed a resolution declaring that there was no need for an international trial, but that a Sudanese court was capable of trying Bashir. The matter dragged on until March 4, 2009, when an ICC arrest warrant was finally issued. Bashir defiantly attended the March 28–29 league summit in Doha, Qatar, and received the united support of the attendees.

In late-August 2008 a league representative visited Iraq, looking for ways for friendly Arab states to build their influence with the government there. For more information on developments since 2008, see "Recent Activities" below.

Structure. The principal political organ of the league is the Council of the League of Arab States, which meets in regular session twice a year, normally at the foreign ministers level. Each member has one vote in the council; decisions usually bind only those states that accept them, although a two-thirds majority vote on financial and administrative matters binds all members. The council's main functions are to supervise the execution of agreements between members, to mediate disputes, and to coordinate defense in the event of attack. There are numerous committees and other bodies attached to the council, including permanent committees dealing with finance and administration, legal affairs, and information.

The council has also established an Administrative Court, an Investment Arbitration Board, and a Higher Auditing Board. Additional ministerial councils, attended by relevant ministers or their representatives, are held in a dozen areas including transport, justice, health, telecommunications, and environmental affairs.

Three additional bodies were established by the 1950 convention: a Joint Defense Council to function in matters of collective security and to coordinate military resources; a Permanent Military Commission, comprised of representatives of the general staffs, to draw up plans for joint defense; and an Economic Council, comprised of the ministers of economic affairs, to coordinate Arab economic development. The last was restructured as an Economic and Social Council in 1977. An Arab Unified Military Command, charged with the integration of strategy for the liberation of Palestine, was formed in 1964.

The General Secretariat is responsible for internal administration and the execution of council decisions. It also administers several agencies, including the Bureau for Boycotting Israel (headquartered in Damascus, Syria).

Membership in the league generally carries with it membership in an array of specialized agencies, including the Arab Bank for Economic Development in Africa (BADEA) and the Arab Monetary Fund (AMF), as well as a variety of other bodies dealing with economic, social, and technical matters.

Many Arab Summit Conferences have been held since the first one met in 1964. Summit resolutions give direction to the work of the council and other league organs, although the organization's charter did not provide a framework for convening summits.

Recent Activities. The conflict between Israel and Hamas in Gaza and the massive destruction that it caused was responsible for a serious rift between league members. In January 2009 two rival conferences were held simultaneously on the question: a meeting of Arab League foreign ministers in Kuwait and a "Pan-Arab" meeting in Doha, called by the emir of Qatar. Saudi Arabia and Egypt in particular disapproved of the Doha meeting, fearing that would undercut Egyptian attempts to broker an end to the Gaza attacks. The rift continued through the March summit in Doha, which Egyptian president Mubarak did not attend.

On April 8, 2009, president of the (Greek) Republic of Cyprus Demetris Christofias met in Cairo with Secretary General Moussa, and announced that his country would accredit an ambassador to the Arab League. Moussa declared that the Cyprus problem should be solved in accordance with UN resolutions. In May 2009 league foreign ministers met in Cairo to work out how to restart "serious and direct" talks between the Palestinians and Israel. All parties subsequently visited Washington, D.C., but there was little immediate progress. Arab League influence on the peace process since has been marginal.

In late June 2010 Libya and Yemen floated a proposal to turn the Arab League into an Arab Union, but without success. The same meeting, held in Sirte, Libya, produced a series of proposals to make the league more effective in economic and trade cooperation. These proposals came at a time when many members felt that the league should be drastically reorganized, if it was to be in any way effective.

In mid-2010, Moussa announced that he would leave the organization when his ten-year term as secretary general expired in May 2011, presumably to run for the Egyptian presidency. A dispute arose as to whether his successor should be an Egyptian, as was customary. In an unprecedented effort to express discontent with the traditional Egyptian dominance of the League, Qatar, in addition to Egypt, nominated a candidate for the secretariat upon Moussa's retirement. Realizing the dissatisfaction many countries felt about the Egyptian candidate, Egypt replaced its candidate with the Egyptian foreign affairs minister, Nabil Al Arabi. Upon Al Arabi's nomination, a move that was welcomed by the entire Arab League, Qatar withdrew its candidate, and Al Arabi was unanimously elected on May 15, 2011, as the seventh secretary general of the Arab League.

In February 2011 Secretary General Moussa issued a statement recognizing the legitimacy of the claims of reform and change in Libya and voiced his opinion that it was time for Colonel Qadhafi to leave office. In March the Arab League voted to recognize the Libyan revolutionary government and called for a no-fly zone over Libya to be enforced by the UN as a measure to prevent further human rights violations by the Qadhafi regime. The Arab League opposed all UN military intervention in Libya, claiming that it is a violation of the no-fly zone. Qadhafi was captured by members of the National Liberation Army in October 2011, and subsequently killed.

On July 14, 2011, the Arab League voted unanimously to endorse the Palestinian plan for UN membership, which was expected to be voted on in the fall. The UN Security Council opted to postpone the vote, claiming that Palestinian statehood lacked support. The Arab League has been a proponent of Palestinian land claims from its inception as an organization. The Arab League also has a long history of anti-Israeli policies and actions.

Following the Arab spring revolts of 2011, Syria has become increasingly unstable as it finds itself in the midst of a multi-year civil war. Protestors have beencalling for the resignation of President Bashar al-Assad, who, despite increasing violence, vows to remain in power despite the formation of an opposition movement.

The March 2012 annual summit was held in Baghdad, Iraq, with only 10 of the 22 member states represented. The low attendance was the result of a growing split within the Arab League over how to handle the situation in Syria. The Arab League states have differing opinions on whether or not the league should withdraw its observer mission from the politically torn country. With low attendance at its annual summit, the Arab League voted to turn the situation over to the United Nations Security Council to consider. The Arab League noted that the UNSC is the only global body with binding authority. In July 2012, President Assad agreed to the terms of the UN-Arab League Special envoy's peace settlement.

The 2013 summit was held in Doha from March 21–27 in the midst of great turmoil in the Arab world on the whole. The organization continued its long-time support of Palestine by announcing the creation of a new economic assistance fund worth $1 billion (US) to finance conservation projects that protect Arab identity in Jerusalem and assist the Palestinians in their efforts against the Israelis. Furthermore, in light of the ongoing political unrest in Syria, the Arab League took a major step by replacing the Syrian government's seat in the Arab League with a representative from the Syrian National Council. The League also called on its member states to enact legislation that would open the door for economic integration in the region.

On August 21 the Arab League accused the Syrian government of carrying out chemical weapons attacks outside of Damascus that killed hundreds. As the situation further deteriorated, the Arab League called a special meeting in Cairo in early September to further discuss the situation. At that meeting, the members expressed their support of Russian president Vladimir Putin's plan to put Syria's chemical weapons under the control of international monitoring. This plan came to fruition, when on September 28, the UN Security Council unanimously adopted a resolution to secure and destroy Syria's chemical weapons. The UN-Arab League envoy to Syria, Lakhdar Brahimi, and Secretary General Al Arabi were also two of the major players in the attempt to hold a second Geneva peace conference on the Syria issue.

ASIA-PACIFIC ECONOMIC COOPERATION (APEC)

Established: At a meeting of foreign and economic ministers of 12 nations November 6–7, 1989, in Canberra, Australia; objectives and principles set forth in Seoul Declaration approved during ministerial meeting November 12–14, 1991, in Seoul, South Korea; Declaration of Institutional Arrangements adopted September 10–11, 1992, in Bangkok, Thailand.

Purpose: To provide a forum for discussion on a variety of economic issues and to promote multilateral cooperation among the region's market-oriented economies.

Headquarters: Singapore.

Principal Organs: Economic Leaders' Meeting, Ministerial Meeting, Senior Officials' Meeting, Budget and Management Committee, Committee on Trade and Investment, Economic Committee, Secretariat.

Web site: www.apec.org

Executive Director: Dr. Alan Bollard (New Zealand).

Membership (21): Australia, Brunei, Canada, Chile, China, Hong Kong, Indonesia, Japan, Republic of Korea, Malaysia, Mexico, New Zealand, Papua New Guinea, Peru, Philippines, Russia, Singapore, Taiwan ("Chinese Taipei"), Thailand, United States, Vietnam.

Observers: Association of Southeast Asian Nations, Pacific Economic Cooperation Council, Pacific Islands Forum.

Official Language: English.

Origin and development. In early 1989, Australian Prime Minister, Robert Hawke proposed that a permanent body be established to coordinate economic relations among market-oriented nations on the Pacific Rim, with particular emphasis to be given to dialogue between Western Pacific countries and the United States. The proposal was endorsed by the Pacific Economic Cooperation Conference (PECC; a group of business, academic, and government representatives who had held informal discussions since 1980), and the first APEC meeting was held November 6–7 in Canberra, Australia. Ministers from 12 nations—Australia, Brunei, Canada, Indonesia, Japan, Republic of Korea, Malaysia, New Zealand, Philippines, Singapore, Thailand, and United States—attended the inaugural session, with debate centering on how to proceed in adopting formal APEC arrangements.

Due to concern among some members of the Association of Southeast Asian Nations (ASEAN; see separate article) that they might be overwhelmed by such economic giants as Canada, Japan, and the United States, the Canberra session decided to keep APEC as a loosely defined, informal grouping officially committed only to an annual dialogue meeting. As regional economic cooperation gained momentum in other areas of the world, pressure grew within APEC for a more structured format. Consequently, the Ministerial Meeting in November 1991 in Seoul, South Korea, adopted a declaration outlining APEC's objectives; established additional organizational structure; and approved the membership of China, Hong Kong, and Taiwan.

The "institutionalization" of APEC was completed during a Ministerial Meeting September 10–11, 1992, in Bangkok, Thailand, with the decision to establish a permanent Secretariat in Singapore as of January 1, 1993. The November 1992 Ministerial Meeting directed APEC's new permanent Secretariat to establish an electronic tariff database for the region, survey members regarding investment regulations, and study ways to harmonize customs procedures and reduce impediments to "market access" among members.

Mexico and Papua New Guinea were admitted into APEC in November 1993, while Chile's membership application was approved effective November 1994. The latter was the subject of debate within APEC, as some officials suggested that admission of South American countries could cost the organization its focus. Consequently, a moratorium on any additional APEC members was declared until at least 1996

Hoping to impel integrationist sentiment in the region (which controls more than one-half of the world's economy and accounts for nearly one-half of all global trade), the APEC finance ministers met for the first time March 18–19, 1994, in Honolulu, Hawaii. Among other things, plans were endorsed to double the capital of the Asian Development Bank, to promote cross-border investment, and to study ways of facilitating finance for large infrastructure projects.

A potentially historic step was taken at the second APEC summit, held November 15, 1994, in Bogor, Indonesia, with the adoption of a "declaration of common resolve" to pursue "free and open trade and investment" over the next quarter century. The loosely worded accord called on the region's developed nations to dismantle their trade barriers by 2010 and for developing nations to follow suit by 2020. Differences of opinion regarding the appropriate pace and intensity for implementing the 1994 action agenda were readily apparent at the next summit, held in November 1995 in Osaka, Japan. After much discussion it was agreed that many APEC stipulations, at least for the time being, would be implemented on a voluntary basis.

The central issue of the November 1997 summit, held in Vancouver, Canada, was the Asian economic crisis, which prompted several APEC members to seek assistance from the International Monetary Fund (IMF). Japan proposed creating a separate Asian fund to help resolve the crisis, but that idea was rejected at an ASEAN meeting held earlier in November in Manila, where it was agreed that the IMF would play the central role in promoting economic stabilization.

Political events in East Timor, Indonesia, provided a backdrop to the September 12–13, 1999, Economic Leaders' Meeting in Auckland, New Zealand, where the APEC foreign affairs ministers supported the formation of a United Nations (UN) multinational military presence to restore order to the troubled jurisdiction. The summit noted progress toward economic recovery in Asia, approved APEC Principles to Enhance Competition and Regulatory Reform, and called for an improved "international framework" for the flow of trade and investment capital.

The timing of a new round of trade negotiations proved to be a contentious topic at the November 15–16, 2000, summit, which was held in Bandar Seri Begawan, Brunei. The United States, Japan, and Canada pressed for a rapid start, whereas Malaysia and many of the smaller economies preferred a more deliberate pace. In its final declaration the summit opted for a carefully worded compromise in which the leaders agreed "that a balanced and sufficiently broad-based agenda that responds to the interests and concerns of all WTO members should be formulated and finalized as soon as possible in 2001 and that a round be launched in 2001."

The October 19–21, 2001, Economic Leaders' Meeting, held in Shanghai, China, offered general support for U.S.-led efforts to combat terrorism, including cutting off funding for terrorist groups. The summit declaration did not, however, specifically address U.S. military response to the September terrorist attacks on New York and Washington.

During 2002, rather than proposing new initiatives, APEC concentrated its efforts on previously established goals, including improved business management and evaluation, peer review, structural reforms, and transparency. All were in keeping with the three goals emphasized in the 1994 Bogor Declaration, namely, trade and investment liberalization, business facilitation, and economic and technical cooperation. At the October 26–27 Economic Leaders' Meeting in Cabo San Lucas, Mexico, attendees endorsed a Trade Facilitation Action Plan aimed at reducing transaction costs by 5 percent over five years; a Statement to Implement APEC Transparency Standards; several counterterrorism measures, including an APEC Energy Security Initiative and a proposal for Secure Trade in the APEC Region (STAR); and a Statement to Implement APEC Policies on Trade and the Digital Economy. The summit also urged the WTO to complete its current round of trade negotiations by January 2005.

In the first half of 2003, planned APEC activities were overshadowed by the onset of the Severe Acute Respiratory Syndrome (SARS) outbreak. Precautions against the spread of the newly identified viral illness led to the cancellation of some 30 APEC-sponsored meetings in March–July. Meeting on June 2–3, in Khon Kaen, Thailand, the APEC Ministers Responsible for Trade, recognizing the severe economic repercussions of SARS for the region, pledged to restore business confidence in trade, investment, travel, and mobility by endorsing a plan of action that focused on the need to establish principles for health screenings, the timely exchange of information on the outbreak, and cooperation in prevention and treatment.

The 2003 Economic Leaders' Meeting, held October 19–21 in Bangkok, endorsed the SARS Action Plan and a Health Security Initiative, but with the outbreak contained, greater attention was directed toward economic matters. A principal focus was on "free and open trade and investment," including the need for bilateral, regional, and multilateral accords to be "complementary and mutually reinforcing." Along the same lines, the participants called for a renewed commitment to WTO liberalization negotiations and efforts to extend the perceived benefits of globalization to a broader spectrum of people and societies.

The APEC annual summit, held November 19–21, 2004, in Santiago, Chile, adopted the Santiago Initiative for Expanded Trade in APEC and also received a study from the APEC Business Advisory Council outlining the dimensions of a possible Free Trade Area of the Asia-Pacific region. In addition to highlighting trade and investment liberalization as a path toward advancing development, the closing declaration stressed the issues of energy security, public health, and ending corruption by ensuring transparency.

As in 2003, U.S. President George W. Bush devoted much of his time to discussing with other heads of government North Korea's nuclear program. The summit participants also noted the need to improve security through adoption of antiterrorist conventions and implementation of measures intended, for example, to cut off terrorist financing. Some critics have asserted, however, that expanding the scope of APEC discussions to includematters of security and governance has diminished APEC's importance as an economic forum.

At the Ministerial Meeting on November 15–16, 2005, in Busan, Korea, APEC adopted Busan Roadmap, a document outlining a strategy for reaching the organization's original goals in the light of a decade of globalization and change in world economic relationships, while maintaining sustainable development practices. The national leaders issued a separate statement in support of a successful conclusion to the WTO's sixth Ministerial Meeting in Hong Kong, China, and agreed to confront pandemic health threats and continue to fight against terrorism.

The APEC summit, held in Hanoi, Vietnam, on November 18, 2006, took place in the shadow of North Korea's recent nuclear test, but the conferees were not able to come up with a completely unified approach to the problem. Summit participants also acknowledged for the first time that the APEC area contained too many bilateral trade agreements, to the point of being an impediment to free trade.

Australia became the 2007 host for APEC, and the Australian government announced initiatives to strengthen the organization. These initiatives would include increasing its budget by 30 percent and making the Secretariat stronger and more centralized, with the position of executive director not rotating each year.

The September 8–9, 2008, APEC summit was held in Sydney, Australia. It had been expected to move forward with India's application to join the group. At the event the United States and New Zealand opposed India's accession, which Australia had strongly supported. The meeting decided to extend a moratorium on admitting new members until 2010.

On environmental matters, the summit made a commitment to the "aspirational goals" of increasing energy efficiency 25 percent from

2005 levels by 2030 and increasing forest cover in the region by at least 20 million hectares (approximately 8.1 million acres) by 2020. The summit also called, again, for a rapid conclusion to the long-stalled Doha round of trade talks. It was announced that the United States would host the summit in 2011 and Russia in 2012. Russian president Vladimir Putin had said that he felt APEC to be one of the most effective and useful international organizations, though some commentators felt that such a high-level meeting producing so few concrete results was a sign that APEC was irrelevant.

In June 2008 a meeting of APEC trade ministers in Arequipa, Peru, agreed to cut tariffs among APEC members to zero by 2020. The matters that dominated APEC in 2008 and 2009, however, were the world economic crisis and the organization's direction after the apparent failure of the Doha round of free-trade negotiations. The November 19–20, 2008, ministerial meeting, as well as the November 22 summit, both held in Lima, Peru, focused on the world financial crisis and the perceived need to avoid a return to protectionism. The meetings reaffirmed APEC's desire to complete the Doha round, and worked towards an action plan to make that happen. They also approved the change of the executive secretary's tenure from annual rotation to a three-year term. For more information on developments since 2008, see "Recent Activities," below.

Structure. APEC's governing body is the annual Ministerial Meeting, the chair of which rotates each year among the members. Decisions are reached by consensus. Since 1993 overall guidance has been provided by the Economic Leaders' Meeting, an informal gathering of APEC heads of state and/or government that immediately follows the yearly Ministerial Meeting. In addition, sectoral ministerial meetings have been held (some annually) regarding various issues.

Responsibility for policy implementation rests primarily with a Senior Officials' Meeting (SOM), which convenes as necessary. There are four standing committees: Budget and Management; Trade and Investment, which is assisted by more than a dozen subcommittees and expert groups; Economic, assisted by an Economic Outlook Task Force; and the SOM Committee on Economic and Technical Cooperation.

The APEC Secretariat is the main organ responsible for the day-to-day activities of the organization. A team of program directors that are nominated by the member economies assists the executive director in the operational and organizational administration of APEC. Beginning in 2010, the position of executive director was changed to a three-year term, open to any qualified citizen of a member country. The position was previously designated to be an ambassador of the country that was currently presiding over the organization. Other organs include several topical special task groups that address concerns related to anti-corruption and transparency, counterterrorism, electronic commerce, gender, health, social safety nets, and emergency preparedness. There are also 11 working groups: Agricultural Technical Cooperation, Energy, Fisheries, Human Resources Development, Industrial Science and Technology, Marine Resources Conservation, Small and Medium Enterprises, Telecommunications and Information, Tourism, Trade Promotion, and Transportation. Since 1996 the APEC Business Advisory Council, comprising up to three senior business executives from each member country, has met to discuss APEC action plans and other business issues.

Recent Activities. By July 2009, with the global economic crisis far from over, APEC trade ministers were compelled to take a stand against a rising desire for protectionism. They declared that they would develop an "inclusive growth" strategy to deter protectionism during Japan's 2010 tenure in the organization's chair.

The November 14–15, 2009, summit, held in Singapore, was U.S. President Barack Obama's first opportunity to engage with leaders of the entire Asia-Pacific region. He expressed that the United States, as a Pacific nation, would be a strong and enduring partner for the region. The group's leaders dropped any attempt to reach accord on remediating climate change ahead of the December 2009 Copenhagen meeting. They also resolved (vainly) to conclude the Doha Round of global trade talks in 2010.

The November 13–14, 2010, summit held in Yokohama, Japan, called for the group to concentrate on its core mission, the creation of a seamless Asia-Pacific trading area. President Obama called on APEC nations not to rely exclusively on exports to the United States for economic growth. Countries with a large trade surplus must take steps to boost domestic demand, he said, clearly referring to China and Japan clearly. Chinese president Hu Jintao said his country was trying to increase domestic consumption, but held out no prospect of large or immediate readjustments in the value of his currency.

The November 12–13, 2011, summit in Honolulu, Hawaii, centered on talks regarding the Trans-Pacific Partnership (TPP), an existing free trade agreement between Brunei, Chile, New Zealand, and Singapore. Continuing in a similar vein to the 2010 summit, APEC members sought to take the TPP trade agreement "to the next level." Australia, Malaysia, Peru, Vietnam, Japan, and the United States are existing APEC members seeking to enter the TPP. Such a partnership would be nearly 40 percent larger than the European Union. The effort to expand the TPP, spearheaded by the United States, has been criticized as being overly ambitious and impractical. Additionally, several APEC nations are hesitant to lift the existing trade tariffs, as would be required for entry into the TPP. The summit also discussed strategies to minimize negative effects from the European debt crisis. This included plans to reduce tariffs on environmentally friendly goods to 5 percent by 2015, as well as plans to double exports in five years.

At a June 2012 meeting of the APEC Finance Ministers, the group reiterated the call of the APEC Leaders to reduce bilateral trade agreements in order to promote the creation of a Free Trade Asia-Pacific Agreement. They also called on the member states to work with the WTO to promote economic growth in the field of information technology. This meeting came on the coattails of a new report that indicated the APEC member states remained the fastest growing economies in the world in 2012.

The 2012 summit, held in Vladivostok, Russia, focused on the key issues of institutional progress within APEC, enhancing cooperation as a means of producing growth, strengthening its efforts concerning food security, and liberalizing its trade and investment policy within the framework of broader regional integration. Both the ministers and economic leaders emphasized international trade as a key component of economic growth, job creation, and recovery from the global depression experienced over the past few years. Like many other economic organizations, APEC noted the importance of small and medium-sized enterprises for fostering further growth. The meeting also saw the appointment of Dr. Alan Bollard as the new executive director of the APEC Secretariat.

The year 2013 saw progress of several major initiatives under way in APEC. A preliminary progress report in April noted that APEC was on target to meet its goal of a 10 percent increase in supply chain performance by 2015. A special ministerial meeting pertaining to women and small and medium size enterprises, held in August 2013, noted the efforts currently being undertaken to promote economic growth in the region. The meeting emphasized the continued importance of gender equity in business as a means for job creation and development.

The 2013 summit, held in Bali, Indonesia, focused primarily on the steps necessary for the developing countries to achieve the Bogor Goals by 2020. These efforts include steps to reduce tariffs on environmental goods, enhance sustainable growth practices, promote integration within the region through physical and institutional connectivity, and increase efforts in economic growthand equity among nations and people. In addition to outlining steps still to be taken, the ministers and economic leaders noted the progress that has been made in several other key areas, including partnership with other organizations, supply chain performance, and progress in development of the secretariat's strategic growth plan.

ASSOCIATION OF SOUTHEAST ASIAN NATIONS (ASEAN)

Established: By foreign ministers of member states August 9, 1967, in Bangkok, Thailand.

Purpose:"To accelerate economic growth, social progress and cultural development in the region . . . to promote active collaboration and mutual assistance on matters of common interest in the economic, social, cultural, technical, scientific, and administrative fields . . . to collaborate more effectively for the greater utilization of [the member states'] agriculture and industries, the expansion of their trade, including the study of problems of international commodity trade, the improvement of their transport and communication facilities and raising the living standards of their people."

Headquarters: Jakarta, Indonesia.

Principal Organs: ASEAN Heads of State and Government, ASEAN Ministerial Meeting, ASEAN Community Councils, ASEAN Standing Committees.

Web site: www.aseansec.org

Secretary General: Le Luong Minh (Vietnam)

Membership (10): Brunei, Cambodia, Indonesia, Laos, Malaysia, Myanmar (Burma), Philippines, Singapore, Thailand, Vietnam.

Official Language: English.

Origin and development. ASEAN was part of a continuing effort during the 1960s to create a framework for regional cooperation among the non-Communist states of Southeast Asia. Earlier efforts attempts included the Association of Southeast Asia (ASA), established in 1961 by Malaya, the Philippines, and Thailand; and the short-lived Maphilindo association, created in 1963 by Indonesia, Malaya, and the Philippines. The change of government in Indonesia in 1966 opened the way to a broader association, with plans for ASEAN broached at an August conference in Bangkok, Thailand, and implemented a year later with Indonesia, Malaysia, Philippines, Singapore, and Thailand as founding members.

The first ASEAN-sponsored regional summit conference was held February 1976 in Pattaya, Thailand.

Although economic cooperation has long been a principal ASEAN concern, progress has been slowed by such factors as differing levels of development among member countries and similarity of exports. By contrast, the association generally demonstrated political solidarity in its early years, primarily through an anticommunist posture that yielded strong condemnation of Vietnam's 1978–1989 military involvement in Cambodia.

In 1982, Sri Lanka's application for admission was denied on geographic grounds in 1982, while Brunei was admitted following its independence in 1984.

ASEAN convened its first summit in a decade on December 14–15, 1987. Meeting in Manila, Philippines, the heads of state called for a reduction in tariff barriers between members and a rejuvenation of regional economic projects.

ASEAN's dominant concern in 1988 remained the situation in Cambodia. ASEAN members met with representatives of the Vietnamese and warring Cambodian factions in July 1988 and February 1989 in Jakarta, Indonesia, in an effort to negotiate a settlement. When Vietnam withdrew its last troops in September 1989, ASEAN continued to play an important role in talks aimed at producing a permanent political resolution to the Cambodian conflict.

Another major issue for ASEAN was the formation of the Asia-Pacific Economic Cooperation (APEC) forum, which now includes seven ASEAN members plus 14 other countries (see article on APEC). Apparently concerned that their interests could be slighted in a grouping involving global economic powers, the ASEAN countries were initially seen as resisting efforts to formalize the APEC, which was inaugurated in November 1989, beyond regular meetings of foreign and trade ministers.

Concerned that economic integration in North America and Europe might negatively affect the Far East, the January 27–28, 1992, ASEAN Summit in Singapore created the ASEAN Free Trade Area (AFTA). In July 1993 the ASEAN foreign ministers decided the association would host a regional security forum designed, among other things, to facilitate the peaceful resolution of disputes and promote regional stability. The forum—now comprising the ASEAN members, Australia, Canada, China, the EU, India, Japan, Democratic People's Republic of Korea, Republic of Korea, Mongolia, New Zealand, Pakistan, Papua New Guinea, Russia, and United States—was perceived by some as an Asian equivalent of the Conference on (later Organization for) Security and Cooperation in Europe (CSCE, OSCE), although its eventual structure and purview remained vague.

The ASEAN Regional Forum (ARF) met for the first time July 25, 1994, during the ASEAN Ministerial Meeting in Bangkok, Thailand. Substantive talks were reported on a variety of concerns, including North Korea's nuclear posture, the region's escalating arms race, claims by a number of countries to the potentially oil-rich Spratly Islands in the South China Sea (see article on Vietnam), and the need for the other ARF members to engage China in a "genuine security dialog." However, no formal agreements were reached regarding conflict resolution mechanisms, and most attendees cautioned that they expected the ARF to proceed slowly.

Meanwhile, at their 1995 annual meeting, the ASEAN foreign ministers endorsed a proposal to move up the final implementation date for AFTA from 2003 to 2000. (The original target date of 2008 had already been changed to 2003 the previous year.) Vietnam, admitted as a full ASEAN member at the meeting, was given until 2006 to comply with the AFTA tariff reductions.

The ASEAN foreign ministers meeting on July 20–21, 1996, appeared to be at odds with the United States and other Western nations regarding the extent to which international bodies should interfere in the domestic affairs of members. The ASEAN leaders suggested that issues such as human rights and government corruption should not be addressed by the upcoming first ministerial meeting of the World Trade Organization (WTO). The question came into even sharper focus for ASEAN two days later at the third session of the ARF, attended for the first time by India and Myanmar. The presence of the latter was the source of much discussion considering the heavy pressure Western capitals had exerted on Myanmar regarding human rights and political repression.

Laos and Myanmar were admitted to ASEAN on July 23, 1997, the day before the 30th annual meeting of foreign ministers was held in Kuala Lumpur, Malaysia. The West, as expected, objected to Myanmar's accession, and at the July 27 meeting of the ARF the Western nations and Japan criticized Myanmar's human rights record.

The ASEAN Summit held on December 15–16, 1998, in Hanoi, Vietnam, was marked by disagreement over Cambodia's prospective membership; Hanoi, backed by Indonesia and Malaysia, pushed hard for Cambodia's immediate accession, but the other members insisted on further delay to assess the new Cambodian government's stability. (Cambodia was ultimately admitted to ASEAN at a special ceremony April 30, 1999, in Hanoi.) Prior to the summit, the ASEAN foreign and finance ministers agreed to bring AFTA's launch date forward to 2002 for the original ASEAN partners.

An informal summit held November 27–28, 1999, in Manila, overlapping meetings of the ASEAN foreign and finance ministers, discussed developments in East Timor and also proposed a code of conduct regarding the disputed Spratly Islands, but the session was dominated by economic developments. With China, South Korea, and Japan participating, in a format dubbed "ASEAN plus three" (ASEAN +3), the session reached agreement on a nonspecific framework for East Asian economic cooperation, which was hailed as a major advance toward wider regional integration. The ASEAN leaders also advanced the target date for elimination of all import duties from 2015 to 2010 for all members except Cambodia, Laos, Myanmar, and Vietnam, which saw their target moved from 2018 to 2015.

The 33rd annual Ministerial Meeting was held July 24–25, 2000, in Bangkok, with the most notable development being a decision to establish an informal ministerial troika that would serve as a rapid response team in the event of a regional emergency. Consisting of the current ministerial chair, his predecessor, and his successor, the troika would have limited ability to act, given the noninterference principle and the need to consult all ASEAN members beforehand. The foreign ministers' meeting was once again followed by a session of the ARF, which for the first time included North Korean participation. At this meeting the EU agreed to reopen its dialogue with ASEAN three years after suspending the talks in protest of Myanmar's accession.

The annual summit held November 5–6, 2001, in Bandar Seri Begawan, Brunei, was also attended by leaders of China, Japan, and South Korea. Two major developments were a commitment to oppose terrorism, despite some differences over the U.S.-led military intervention in Afghanistan, and an agreement to support a Chinese proposal for an eventual ASEAN-China free trade area (FTA). With regard to the latter, Malaysia, in particular, expressed concerns about the ability of ASEAN products to compete directly against Chinese manufacturers.

The November 3–5, 2002, summit in Phnom Penh, Cambodia, was also attended by Chinese president Zhu Rongji and the Indian prime minister, Atal Bihari Vajpayee. At the meeting the ten ASEAN members signed a framework agreement on establishing a FTA by 2010, although the poorer ASEAN states—Myanmar, Cambodia, Laos, and Vietnam—were given an additional five years to eliminate specified tariff barriers. The ASEAN leaders also created a task force for drafting an FTA framework agreement with India. Significant progress was also made regarding competing territorial claims in the South China Sea, although the summit's joint declaration on the issue did not contain the formal code of conduct that ASEAN states had sought. In other business, the summit formally approved the appointment of Ong Keng Yong of Singapore as the organization's next secretary general, effective January 2003.

The second quarter of 2003 was dominated by the Asian outbreak of the new viral disease Severe Acute Respiratory Syndrome (SARS). An emergency meeting of the ASEAN +3 health ministers on April 26 in Kuala Lumpur was quickly followed by a Special ASEAN Leaders' Meeting on SARS (and a parallel ASEAN-China session) April 29 in Bangkok. The meeting noted the outbreak's "serious adverse impact" and emphasized the importance of "strong leadership, political commitment, multisectoral collaboration and partnership" in overcoming the economic and societal consequences.

Meeting October 7–8, 2003, in Bali, Indonesia, the ASEAN leaders endorsed creation of an ASEAN Community by 2020. The Bali Concord II plan called for a free trade agreement and greater security and social cooperation, but significant barriers remain to be overcome, including the economic disparities among members.

On July 2, 2004, in Jakarta, Indonesia, the ARF admitted Pakistan to its membership, following the withdrawal of Indian objections. The ARF session, which was immediately preceded by ASEAN foreign minister and ASEAN +3 meetings, covered in its discussions North Korea's nuclear weapons program, international terrorism, improved maritime security, the need to increase export controls on technology and materials that could be used in producing weapons of mass destruction (WMD), and the political situation in Myanmar. The November 27–30 summit in Vientiane, Laos, appeared to indicate a return to the principle of noninterference in members' internal matters. Major developments in the economic sphere were discussed, including a decision to accelerate by three years the schedule for introducing the ASEAN FTA. Additionally, Brunei, Indonesia, Malaysia, Philippines, Singapore, and Thailand committed to ending internal tariffs by 2007, with Myanmar, Cambodia, Laos, and Vietnam following suit by 2012. Also at the summit, Chinese prime minister Wen Jiabao and the ASEAN leaders signed a trade agreement eliminating tariffs on many agricultural and manufactured goods by 2010.

At the foreign ministers' meeting held in Cebu, Philippines, on April 9–12, 2005, Malaysia, Philippines, and Singapore reportedly led a movement exerting pressure on Myanmar to bypass its turn to chair ASEAN. Although the Myanmar government previously resisted any such suggestion, the foreign ministers announced July 25 that Myanmar would in fact "relinquish" the chair for 2006 in favor of the Philippines, ostensibly because it wanted to maintain its focus on reconciliation and democratization at home.

The early months of 2006 were marked by efforts to arrange an ASEAN fact-finding mission to Myanmar to investigate the human rights situation there. After several delays, the Myanmar government agreed to a visit by Malaysian foreign minister Syed Hamid Albar at the end of March. He made the visit, but returned one day early on March 24, apparently because he was not allowed to meet with prodemocracy leader Aung San Suu Kyi, who was under house arrest. Hamid subsequently issued a statement that Myanmar's inflexibility was holding its neighbors hostage, and that ASEAN could not be expected to continue shielding Myanmar from criticism.

After a November 17, 2006, meeting in Kuala Lumpur, ASEAN promised increased cooperation with the United States in virtually all areas of mutual concern. The ASEAN summit held January 11–15, 2007, on the Philippine island of Cebu, notable for the presence of a Chinese delegation, produced an agreement to open up some service sectors of the participants' economies by July 2007. This would be a first step in creating a China-ASEAN free trade area by 2015. The meeting also produced the Cebu Declaration, which called for the accelerated creation of the ASEAN Community, moving the date up from 2020 to 2015.

During 2007 and 2008 several interrelated issues dominated ASEAN affairs. A July 20, 2007, ministerial meeting in Manila approved a draft charter for the organization. The charter, for the first time, gave legal status to ASEAN and imposed binding rules on its members. In general, the charter strengthens the secretary general's position. Among other things, it provides for a commission to monitor human rights in the region. The military rulers of Myanmar came close to not signing the charter document, but the organization formally adopted the draft at its November 18–22, 2007, summit in Singapore. On October 21, 2008, Indonesia became the last country to do so, and the charter was formally launched on December 15, 2008.

In general, ratification of the charter was the occasion for much comment that, while ASEAN had long talked about being an organization for its countries' peoples, it had never achieved much in that regard. Unfortunately for ASEAN's reputation, July 2008 brought an armed standoff between Cambodian and Thai forces over the disputed site of the Preah Vihear temple. Conflict over the temple, which sits on the Cambodian-Thai border, was provoked by the UN's approval of Cambodia's request to classify the building as a World Heritage site. Cambodia asked ASEAN to mediate, but ASEAN foreign ministers declined, saying that the "bilateral process must be allowed to continue" between Thailand and Cambodia. For more on activities since 2008, see "Recent Activities," below.

Structure. While the ASEAN Heads of State and Government is the organization's highest authority, the annual Ministerial Meeting, comprised of the foreign ministers of the member states, ordinarily sets general policy. Continuing supervision of ASEAN activities is the responsibility of the Standing Committee, which is located in the country hosting the Ministerial Meeting and includes the directors general of the ASEAN departments within each member country's foreign ministry. The foreign minister of the host country acts as chair, and the ASEAN secretary general also participates.

Sectoral ministerial meetings convene in more than a dozen fields, including agriculture and forestry, economics, energy, environment, finance, information, investment, labor, law, rural development and poverty alleviation, science and technology, transportation, and tourism. Nearly 30 committees and more than 120 working groups offer support. In addition, the heads of the ASEAN countries' diplomatic missions in various countries—Australia, Belgium, Canada, China, France, India, Japan, Republic of Korea, New Zealand, Pakistan, Russia, Switzerland, United Kingdom, and United States—meet to confer on matters of external relations. The Secretariat is headed by the secretary general, who serves a five-year term.

Most recently, ASEAN created three councils in 2009 as part of the governance for the ASEAN Community. The ASEAN Community Councils are responsible for overseeing and developing policy guidelines for each of the three "communities": the Political-Security Community, the Economic Community, and the Socio-Cultural Community. The sectoral ministerial meetings were also placed under the oversight and jurisdiction of the appropriate ASEAN Community Council.

ASEAN has also established a number of specialized bodies, including centers for Agricultural Development Planning, Biodiversity Conservation, Earthquake Information, Energy, Management, Specialized Meteorology, Poultry Research and Training, Rural Youth Development, Timber Technology, Tourism Information, and University Network.

Recent Activities. A meeting of ASEAN finance ministers was held February 26–March 1, 2009, in Thailand. This meeting was in preparation for the 14th ASEAN summit, originally planned for December 2008, but rescheduled for April 10–12, 2009, due to massive antigovernment unrest. At the Finance Ministers' Meeting ASEAN signed a free trade agreement with Australia and New Zealand. The April 2009 summit had to be aborted. Antigovernment protesters broke through police cordons at the Thai resort of Pattiya while the meeting was in progress. The ASEAN participants were airlifted to safety. Before the summit's collapse, China had offered a $10 billion investment fund to ASEAN for cooperation on infrastructure construction, energy resources, and communication.

ASEAN had always been devoted—to a fault, many said—to noninterference in its members' internal affairs. However, in August 2009, in an almost unprecedented move, ASEAN condemned Myanmar for putting the prodemocracy leader Aung San Suu Kyi on trial, and sentencing her to a further period of house arrest, after an apparently deranged American swam to the house where she was under detention.

Also in August 2009 ASEAN and India signed a free trade agreement after more than six years of talks. The October 2009 summit, this time held in Thailand without incident, signed the ASEAN Intergovernmental Commission on Human Rights into existence. There was a general sense that, as the ASEAN Charter approached its first anniversary, its new structure was working well.

On January 1, 2010, a free trade agreement between China and ASEAN came into force. Vietnam, as president of the group for the year, announced that its focus would be on regional integration. While arranging to put the topic at the forefront of the April 2010 summit, Vietnam also insisted on discussion of Chinese assertiveness about its territorial claims in the South China Sea. The summit also called for free elections in Burma, in a statement unusually blunt for ASEAN. In August 2010 Burma set November 7 as the date for its first general election since 1990.

The October 2010 summit, also held in Vietnam, while it worked to advance regional integration, was held in the shadow of a dispute over some islands currently controlled by Japan, but claimed by China. In reaction to this dispute China had stopped exporting rare earth minerals (essential for producing electronic components) to Japan. Japan subsequently announced that it would work with Vietnam to develop sources of rare earth minerals in that country.

On March 4, 2011, East Timor formally applied for membership in ASEAN. Indonesia supported immediate admission, but other ASEAN members endorsed a period of transition. On May 7–8 ASEAN members met in Jakarta at the group's 18th summit but were unable to reach a consensus on East Timor's membership. The group endorsed the creation of a common platform on global affairs by 2022 and the establishment of an ASEAN Institute for Peace and Reconciliation. Meanwhile, ASEAN pledged to support efforts to resolve a continuing border dispute between Cambodia and Thailand. At ASEAN's 19th summit in Bali, the group praised Myanmar's decisions to reregister the prodemocracy National League for Democracy and to allow the group to participate in future elections.

At the 20th ASEAN Summit meeting held in April 2012 in Phnom Penh, Cambodia, the member states reaffirmed their commitment to the establishment of the ASEAN Community by 2015. The Phnom Penh Declaration expressed a continued effort to move forward on the various aspects of the ASEAN Community, including human rights, government legitimacy, and trade and economic measures. The summit also saw an increased effort to meet the deadline for establishing a drug-free ASEAN by 2015. The Secretary General also issued a request to strengthen the power of the secretariat, arguing that it was vital for the continued success of the organization and its soon-to-be-established community. Sultan Bolkiah of Brunei spoke in overwhelming support for this position and encouraged others to do the same.

At the 21st Summit, also held in Phnom Penh, in November 2012, several major documents were produced by the organization—the ASEAN Human Rights Declaration and the Bali Concord III Plan of Action. Furthermore, the heads of state reaffirmed their commitment to launching the ASEAN Economic Community by 2015. At this meeting, the organization also elected Le Luong Minh of Vietnam as the next secretary general of the organization.

Under the chairmanship of Brunei, the 22nd summit was held in April 2013. The meeting saw the leaders of the ASEAN states further reiterate their commitment to economic union by approving the ASEAN Roadmap and the ASEAN Economic Community Blueprint. These two documents will provide the structure necessary to guide the organization toward its implementation date of 2015. The meeting also yielded the authorization to begin negotiations in May on the regional economic cooperation partnership.

At the October 2013 ASEAN summit meeting, the organization announced that Myanmar would be awarded the 2014 chairmanship of ASEAN. This will mark Myanmar's first time holding this position since joining the organization in 1997. Myanmar was scheduled to assume the chairmanship in 2006, but was passed over (see above). Occurring alongside the summit were several ASEAN summits with specific nations, including Japan, China, India, and for the first time, the United States. ASEAN and China discussed the possibility of working out disputes concerningnavigation in the South China Sea, but despite pressure from Washington, the two sides were unable to reach any agreement. In its meeting with ASEAN, India announced plans to sign a free trade agreement with the organization by the end of 2013 and build a separate ASEAN mission in Jakarta.

CARIBBEAN COMMUNITY AND COMMON MARKET (CARICOM)

Established: August 1, 1973, pursuant to the July 4, 1973, Treaty of Chaguaramas (Trinidad), as successor to the Caribbean Free Trade Association.

Purpose: To deepen the integration process prevailing within the former Caribbean Free Trade Association, to enable all member states to share equitably in the benefits of integration, to operate certain subregional common services, and to coordinate the foreign policies of the member states.

Headquarters: Georgetown, Guyana.

Principal Organs: Heads of Government Conference, Community Council of Ministers, Secretariat.

Web site: www.caricom.org

Secretary General: Irwin LaRocque (Dominica).

Membership (15): Antigua and Barbuda, Bahamas (member of the community but not the common market), Barbados, Belize, Dominica, Grenada, Guyana, Haiti, Jamaica, Montserrat, St. Kitts-Nevis, St. Lucia, St. Vincent and the Grenadines (member of the community but not of the common market), Suriname, Trinidad and Tobago.

Associate Members (5): Anguilla, Bermuda, British Virgin Islands, Cayman Islands, Turks and Caicos Islands.

Official Language: English.

Origin and development. The formation of the Caribbean Free Trade Association (Carifta) in 1968 followed several earlier attempts to foster economic cooperation among the Commonwealth countries and territories of the West Indies and Caribbean. Antigua, Barbados, and Guyana signed the initial agreement December 15, 1965, in Antigua, while an amended accord was approved February 23, 1968, in Georgetown, Guyana, by those governments, Trinidad and Tobago, and the West Indies Associated States. Jamaica joined in June 1968 and was followed later in the month by the remaining British-associated islands, which had previously agreed to establish their own Eastern Caribbean Common Market. Belize was accepted for membership in June 1970.

At an eight-member conference of heads of state of the Caribbean Commonwealth countries in April 1973 in Georgetown, the decision was made to replace Carifta with a new Caribbean Community and Common Market (Caricom) that would provide additional opportunities for economic integration, with an emphasis on obtaining greater benefits for the less-developed members. The new grouping was formally established July 4, 1973, in Chaguaramas, Trinidad, by the prime ministers of Barbados, Guyana, Jamaica, and Trinidad. Although the treaty came into effect August 1, 1973, Carifta was not formally superseded until May 1, 1974, by which time all former Carifta members except Antigua and St. Kitts-Nevis-Anguilla had acceded to the new group. Antigua joined July 5, 1974, and St. Kitts-Nevis-Anguilla acceded on July 26, with St. Kitts-Nevis continuing its membership after the United Kingdom resumed responsibility for the administration of Anguilla in late 1980. After a lengthy period of close cooperation with the grouping, the Bahamas formally acceded to membership in the community (but not the common market) in July 1983. Suriname was admitted in 1995, thereby becoming the first Caricom member whose official language was not English. Haiti, a long-standing observer, was invited to join at the July 1997 Caricom summit, with final terms for full accession set two years later. Deposit of an accession instrument followed ratification by the Haitian Parliament in May 2002.

The 1973 treaty called for a common external tariff (CET) and a common protective policy vis-à-vis community trade with nonmembers, a scheme to harmonize fiscal incentives to industry and development planning, and a special regime for the less-developed members of the community. However, in the wake of unfavorable economic developments during the mid-1970s, progress toward economic coordination and integration stagnated.

As early as 1984 Caricom leaders had agreed to impose a CET on certain imports, but over the next decade deadlines for introducing a comprehensive CET were repeatedly missed. The first CET, with a 30–35 percent maximum, was finally instituted in 1993 and then lowered, in two additional phases, to 0–25 percent, although members were permitted considerable flexibility with regard to application. At the same time, Caricom moved forward on a 1989 pledge to create a unified regional market in "the shortest possible time." Goals for the market included elimination of any remaining trade barriers between members, free movement of skilled labor, abolition of passport requirements, development of regional air and sea transport systems using the resources of existing carriers, and rationalization of investment incentives throughout the community. Adoption of a single currency was also discussed. In furtherance of economic and political integration, in 1989, the heads of government established the West Indian Commission that, in 1992, proposed formation of the broader Association of Caribbean States, a larger organization designed to address economic cooperation in the Caribbean as a whole.

Recognizing the need for collateral, organizational reform, in October 1992 the Caricom heads of government authorized formation of a task force whose work ultimately led to adoption in February 1997 of Protocol I amending the Treaty of Chaguaramas. The first of nine related protocols, Protocol I significantly restructured Caricom's organs, principally by creating the Community Council of Ministers as the second highest Caricom organ and authorizing formation of supportive ministerial councils. Five months later at the annual summit held in Montego Bay, Jamaica, the Caricom leaders called for establishing the Caricom Single Market and Economy (CSME) by 1999. The official launch of the CSME occurred in January 2006 and became fully operational in 2013.

Regional integration and development lie at the center of Caricom's activities, but the organization has also negotiated agreements with neighboring countries and sought a common voice in various international forums, particularly those involving trade and globalization. With regard to the broader issue of positioning itself to compete in the global economy, in 1997 Caricom created a Regional Negotiating Mechanism (RNM) to outline a strategy for international trade and economic negotiations, although the RNM soon ran into "serious financial problems" because of funding shortfalls.

At the July 1998 Caricom summit, held in St. Lucia, community leaders approved plans to form the new Caribbean Court of Justice (CCJ) to function as a court of final appeal (replacing the United Kingdom's Privy Council in the case of the 12 Caricom states with historical ties to the United Kingdom) and settle disputes arising from the Treaty of Chaguaramas.

The 20th summit, held July 4–7, 1999, in Port-of-Spain saw further progress toward establishing the CCJ, despite objections from some who saw the proposed displacement of the UK Privy Council as an effort to reintroduce capital punishment. The Heads of Government Conference also addressed another controversy—namely, the threat of sanctions by the Organization for Economic Cooperation and Development (OECD). The OECD included 11 Caricom members (the exceptions being Bahamas, Guyana, Suriname, and Trinidad and Tobago) on its list of jurisdictions having "harmful" tax policies.

On July 15–16, 2000, shortly after the 2000 annual conference, Caricom convened in Castries to discuss the OECD tax policy issue and the recent report of the Group of Seven's Financial Action Task Force (FATF), which labeled Bahamas, Dominica, St. Kitts-Nevis, and St. Vincent as "uncooperative" in efforts to combat money laundering. In response, the Bureau of the Conference set up the Caribbean Association of Regulators of International Business, which was assigned the initial task of evaluating the FATF criteria. In June 2001 the FATF removed Bahamas from its noncompliance list, although Grenada was added in September. St. Kitts was removed in June 2002, as were Dominica in October 2002, Grenada in February 2003, and St. Vincent in June 2003.

In furtherance of introducing the CSME, the July 3–6, 2001, Heads of Government Conference agreed in principle to phase out the remaining restrictions on the free movement of capital, goods, and services, while in August Caricom joined with the International Monetary Fund and the UN Development Program in announcing the establishment of a Caribbean Regional Technical Assistance Center (Cartac) in Bridgetown to provide technical assistance and training in economic and financial management issues. With additional funding from Canada, the Caribbean Development Bank (CDB), the Inter-American Development Bank, the United Kingdom, the United States, and the World Bank, Cartac opened in November.

Meeting July 2–5, 2003, in Montego Bay, the heads of government signed several documents required for inaugurating the CCJ, to be sited in Trinidad and Tobago, in November. They included the Protocol on the Privileges and Immunities of the Caribbean Court of Justice and the Regional Judicial and Legal Services Commission and the Agreement Establishing the Caribbean Court of Justice Trust Fund. The latter measure permitted the CDB to begin raising some $100 million to capitalize the trust fund. In the area of external trade, the attendees discussed anticipated negotiations with the EU related to an Economic Partnership Agreement, continuing plans for the proposed Free Trade Area of the Americas, and ongoing World Trade Organization negotiations.

The CCJ was inaugurated on April 16, 2005, even though only Barbados and Guyana approved its jurisdiction over civil and criminal appeals. In general, the Caricom members favored letting the court review issues related to the revised Treaty of Chaguaramas and the anticipated CSME, but most had not resolved reservations about the court's appellate status. The CCJ began hearing its first case, an appeal of a libel verdict from Barbados, in August 2005.

Haiti was suspended from active participation in Caricom after the ouster of its president, Jean-Bertrand Aristide, in February 2004. After the February 26, 2006, victory of Rene Preval in the Haiti presidential elections, Caricom was quick to invite Haiti to return to full participation in the organization. President Preval was welcomed at the 11th Heads of State Conference held on July 3–6, 2006, in St. Kitts-Nevis. Much of 2007 and 2008 were dominated by controversy over the Economic Partnership Agreement (EPA) between the Cariforum (Caricom plus the Dominican Republic) and the European Union (EU), originally scheduled for signing by December 31, 2007. The EPA was duly initialed in December 2007, but its ratification by the Caricom states, first scheduled for April 2008, was postponed several times. October 31, 2008, a deadline specified by the EU, was the last date mentioned. The agreement was widely criticized throughout the region as exposing Caricom members to job losses and competition from EU products and services. On October 30, 2008, all Cariforum members except Guyana and Haiti signed the EPA. The president of Guyana, Bharrat Jagdeo, declared that his country would be prepared to sign a goods-only version of the EPA. Otherwise, he prophesied complete EU domination of the region within 20 years. Haiti was not ready to sign the agreement at all. For more on developments since 2008, see "Activities" below.

Structure. Policy decisions under the Treaty of Chaguaramas are assigned to the Heads of Government Conference, which meets annually and is the final authority for all Caricom forums. Each participating state has one vote and most decisions are taken unanimously. The chair of the conference rotates biannually among the members. Until 1998 the Common Market Council dealt with operational aspects of common market activity, but, as part of the Protocol I restructuring, it was replaced by the Community Council of Ministers. The council, the organization's second-highest organ, consists of community affairs ministers and any others designated by each member state. Its responsibilities include strategic planning and coordination of economic integration, functional cooperation, and external relations.

Also assisting the Conference and the Council of Ministers are four ministerial councils: Council for Finance and Planning (COFAP), Council for Foreign and Community Relations (COFCOR), Council for Human and Social Development (COHSOD), and Council for Trade and Economic Development (COTED). In addition, there are legal affairs, budget, and central bank governors committees. The Secretariat, Caricom's principal administrative organ, is headed by a secretary general and includes several administrative directorates in support of the Ministerial Councils. A deputy and various assistant secretaries general oversee numerous subsidiary offices.

The Assembly of Caribbean Community Parliamentarians (ACCP), whose creation was endorsed at the 1989 Caricom summit, was established in mid-1994 after a sufficient number of member states ratified the related agreement. A consultative body, the new assembly was designed to promote public and governmental interest in Caricom.

Caricom has established or sponsors several other community institutions, such as the Caribbean Agricultural Research and Development Institute, the Caribbean Environmental Health Institute, and the Caribbean Meteorological Organization (for a complete listing of Caricom-sponsored organizations, see the 2011 *Handbook*). Associate institutions include the CDB in St. Michael, the University of Guyana, the University of the West Indies, the Caribbean Law Institute, and the Secretariat.

Recent Activities. The Caribbean Regional Negotiating Machinery (CRNM) had taken the lead on EPA negotiations, and was widely criticized by Caricom members who did not favor the deal. At Caricom's inter-sessional Heads of Government Meeting, held March 12–13, 2009, in Belmopan, Belize, it was decided to phase out the CRNM, and integrate its functions into the Caricom secretariat since there were questions concerning the authority of the CRNM and its legal role under the treaty. The March meeting, dominated by the world financial crisis and its implications for the region, also considered the practicalities of implementing the EPA with Europe, and the status of negotiations with Canada on a new trade agreement.

The economic crisis continued to take a toll on prospects for Caribbean unity. In May 2009 Prime Minister Ralph GONSALVES of St. Vincent declared that his fellow citizens were being discriminated against in some Caricom countries, and that it might be better for St. Vincent to withdraw from the CSME. In May also came complaints of discrimination by the government of Antigua and Barbuda against other Caricom nationals, with stories of midnight raids and deportations.

Global economic conditions cast a general malaise over Caricom. In July 2009 Jamaican prime minister Bruce GOLDING spoke in favor of creating a permanent institution, so that important community decisions need not wait for a semi-annual conference. Debate continued as to whether an unelected directorate, on the EU model, would be suitable for Caricom.

The year 2010 showed modest progress for Caricom's organizational objectives. In June the United States and Caricom celebrated the start of a major regional security partnership, the Caribbean Basin Security Initiative (CBSI). This partnership aimed to use U.S. funds to combat crime, both internal and transnational, in the area. Most observers saw the July 4 opening of the 31st summit as a lackluster affair, with several heads of state absent, and Secretary General Carrington calling for members not to despair in the face of economic and natural disasters. In August Carrington announced that he would resign at the end of the year; he had been in office for 18 years.

In June 2011, the heads of government elected Ambassador Irwin LaRocque of Dominica as the new secretary general of Caricom. La Rocque had served Caricom as the assistant secretary general for Trade and Economic Integration since 2005. Ambassador LaRocque replaced Lolita Applewhaite of Barbados, who had been serving as the acting secretary general after Carrington's resignation December 31, 2010. La Rocque formally began his tenure as secretary general on August 15.

At the 32nd summit, held July 1–4, 2011, the Caribbean Regional Public Health Association (CARPHA) was created as the final part of the 2001 Nassau Declaration, designed to improve public health in the region. CARPHA will merge five existing regional health organizations to increase access to health care in the Caribbean. The 2011 summit also focused on agriculture, transportation, and arms limitations to increase security.

In early March 2012, the heads of government met for an intersession summit. One of the most significant moves to come out of that meeting was the initial plan to restructure the Caricom Secretariat. This move to restructure came after an outside consulting company commissioned to study the organization in 2010 released it reports noting that Caricom was facing serious crises that could put the continued existence of Caricom in question. The Secretary General began the process by hiring a change facilitator to help with the new reform actions. The 33rd summit, held July 4–6, 2012, saw a continued move forward in the reform process. The summit leaders also advanced the plans for its January 2013 inauguration of CARPHA. Despite hopes to be ready for January implementation, CARPHA launched on July 2 in conjunction with the 2013 annual summit. Another significant initiative that came out of the summit were plans for a study to analyze the feasibility of adding French and Dutch in addition to English as the official languages of Caricom.

The year 2013 was notable for Haiti in regard to Caricom matters. Haiti assumed the chairmanship of Caricom for the first time since becoming a member in 2002. In February, the country hosted its first Caricom meeting (the inter-sessional meeting of the Caricom Heads of State) since joining the organization. Both events are evidence of the great strides made by Haiti in overcoming the devastating earthquake of 2010.

The inter-sessional meeting in February focused largely on broader issues of regional crime and security. U.S. Attorney General Eric Holder was in attendance as a special guest, and was actively involved in the discussions about strengthening security and crime prevention in the Caribbean region. The meeting also expressed the need for an arms trade treaty and expressed its desire to have a Caricom-U.S. Summit within the next year.

At a meeting of the Council for Trade and Economic Development in May, Secretary General LaRocque suggested that the committee strongly consider adding representatives from the private sector. LaRocque noted the significant role played by the private sector in generating economic growth in his exhortation.

The 2013 summit was held in early July in Trinidad and Tobago. One of the major decisions to come out of the meeting was the creation of a Caricom Reparations Commission designed to address the issue of reparations for native genocide and slavery. The commission will be composed of the chairs of the National Reparations Committees in each member state. The Community also decided to consider the request of Haiti to hold a special meeting on individuals with disabilities.

COMMON MARKET FOR EASTERN AND SOUTHERN AFRICA (COMESA)

Established: By treaty signed November 5, 1993, in Kampala, Uganda; effective as of December 8, 1994.

Purpose: To promote wide-ranging regional economic cooperation, particularly in the areas of agriculture, industry, transportation, and communications; to facilitate intraregional trade through the reduction or elimination of trade barriers and the establishment of regional financial institutions; to establish a common external tariff and internal free trade zone; and to pursue "economic prosperity through regional integration."

Headquarters: Lusaka, Zambia.

Principal Organs: Authority of Heads of State and Government, Council of Ministers, Committee of Governors, Intergovernmental Committee, Court of Justice, Secretariat.

Web site: www.comesa.int

Secretary General: Sindiso Ngwenya (Zimbabwe).

Membership (19): Burundi, Comoro Islands, Democratic Republic of the Congo, Djibouti, Egypt, Eritrea, Ethiopia, Kenya, Libya, Madagascar, Malawi, Mauritius, Rwanda, Seychelles, Sudan, Swaziland, Uganda, Zambia, and Zimbabwe.

Origin and development. Comesa is the successor organization to the Preferential Trade Area for Eastern and Southern African States (PTA), founded in 1981, and endorsed by the United Nations' Economic Commission for Africa and the Organization of African Unity (OAU).

At the January 1992 PTA heads of state meeting, delegates conceded that the organization had little to show for its first ten years of existence. Toward that end, PTA officials proposed a merger with the Southern African Development Community (SADC), whose overlapping membership and objectives were producing a "parallel existence" between the two groups that was seen as counterproductive. However, the SADC, historically much more successful in attracting international financial support because of its highly visible face-off with apartheid-era South Africa, rejected the proposed union.

Many of the PTA's original tasks were expanded in the treaty establishing the Common Market for Eastern and Southern Africa (Comesa), which was signed during the PTA's 12th summit on November 5, 1993, in Kampala, Uganda. Shortly after ratification on December 8, 1994, officials and journalists began to refer to Comesa as the successor to the PTA, even though some PTA members—Lesotho, Mozambique, and Somalia—ultimately opted not to join, and two nonmembers of the PTA—Democratic Republic of Congo and Egypt—did join. The renamed Eastern and Southern Africa Trade and Development Bank continues to be known less formally as the PTA Bank, and the autonomous *Compagnie de Réassurance de la Zone d'Echanges Préférentiels* (ZEP-RE) is similarly styled the PTA Reinsurance Company in English.

The initial Comesa summit was held December 7–9, 1994, in Lilongwe, Malawi; however, of the 22 signatories it had only been ratified by 12. Although plans were discussed for eventual cooperation in the areas of customs, transportation, communications, agriculture, and industry, formal arrangements remained incomplete, partly because of uncertainties over the relationship between the PTA/Comesa and the SADC. (Most SADC members seemed to prefer distinguishable north and south zones of economic cooperation.)

The outlook for Comesa was further clouded in late 1995 when South Africa announced it did not intend to join. At the end of 1996 Mozambique and Lesotho announced their withdrawal from Comesa, and speculation arose that Namibia might follow suit. Also that year the SADC countries once again vetoed Comesa's offer to merge as a single trade zone. Kenya, Tanzania, and Uganda considered turning away from Comesa activity in favor of the proposed reactivation of their old East African Community (EAC). In fact the EAC was revived, but Kenya, Tanzania, and Uganda remained members of both groups.

In late January 1997, Secretary General Bingu Mutharika was suspended during an investigation into the recent management of funds within the Secretariat. Mutharika resigned in April (although he continued to deny any wrongdoing), and Erastus Mwencha of Kenya succeeded him in an acting capacity.

Mwencha officially replaced Mutharika at the third Comesa summit, held in mid-1998 in Kinshasa, Democratic Republic of Congo. Summit participants agreed to eliminate tariffs and visas within the group by 2000 and to admit Egypt as the first North African member. Egypt officially became a member after ratifying the Comesa treaty later that year, but progress toward the removal of tariffs was slower than expected. In other activities, the Comesa Court of Justice, established under the Comesa treaty, held its first session in September 1998, and the PTA Development Bank decided to invite countries from outside the region to become members in an effort to increase the bank's capital.

Speaking at the fourth Comesa summit May 24–25, 1999, Kenyan president Daniel arap Moi called for greater subregional cooperation, which he described as crucial for achieving high economic growth rates and attracting investment capital. Otherwise, he warned, the Comesa countries would face being marginalized by ongoing economic globalization and competition from other trading blocs. As a key step toward further integration, the summit established a committee charged with preparations to introduce a Free Trade Area (FTA).

Arguably the most significant event in the organization's history occurred at an extraordinary summit in Lusaka, Zambia, on October 31, 2000, when nine Comesa members—Djibouti, Egypt, Kenya, Madagascar, Malawi, Mauritius, Sudan, Zambia, and Zimbabwe—inaugurated Africa's first FTA, enabling duty-free trade in goods, services, and capital and eliminating other nontariff trade barriers for the participants. Political concerns in several states, including Burundi, Rwanda, and Eritrea, delayed their participation, and Namibia's and Swaziland's membership in the Southern African Customs Union (SACU) made their entry into Comesa's FTA problematic. Moreover, in what was generally acknowledged to be a major setback, Tanzania withdrew from Comesa in September 2000, citing the need to streamline its international memberships and preferring to remain in the SADC because of the latter's emphasis on building capacity for the production of goods.

Later in 2001 Comesa launched the African Trade Insurance Agency (ATIA) in Nairobi, with funding from the World Bank group, the European Union (EU), and Japan, to protect investors against political risks. In addition, on October 29 Comesa and the United States signed a significant Trade and Investment Framework Agreement.

The May 23–24, 2002, summit in Addis Ababa, Ethiopia, saw the reappointment of Secretary General Mwencha. The attendees also authorized the return of the Comesa Trade and Development Bank to Bujumbura and signed a protocol for establishing the Fund for Cooperation, Compensation, and Development.

The organization's eighth summit, held March 17, 2003, in Khartoum, Sudan, focused on the anticipated introduction of the customs union and accompanying Common External Tariff (CET) in December. Meanwhile, Secretary General Mwencha reported, intra-Comesa trade had expanded at a rate of 30 percent per year since the 2000 launch of the FTA. The summit also called for further development of basic infrastructure; discussed food security, particularly in light of recurrent crises in the Horn of Africa; and emphasized the need to strengthen regional peace and security. With regard to trade, Comesa agreed to adopt a regional approach in pursuit of an Economic Partnership Agreement with the EU. In other business, the summit received a request for membership from Libya.

Rwanda and Burundi announced in 2003 that they were preparing to join the FTA, as did Namibia and Swaziland, assuming that remaining issues involving their SACU memberships were resolved. Namibia, however, left Comesa in July 2003, intending to concentrate on its relationship with the SACU. On January 1, 2004, Burundi and Rwanda joined the FTA.

The ninth summit was held June 7–8, 2004, in Kampala, Uganda. Trade and investments within the community were discussed, as was the plan to move to a customs union by the end of the year. For the first time a business summit ran concurrently with the heads of state and government meeting, attracting more than 600 delegates. At the tenth summit June 2–3, 2005, in Kigali, Rwanda, Comesa admitted Libya. The eleventh summit was held November 15–16, 2006, in Djibouti, with the main theme being to strengthen the group through the projected customs union. Also in 2006, the projected year for monetary union was accelerated from 2025 to 2018. The Monetary Cooperation Programme consists of four stages. The first two concern the consolidation of existing currencies and the creation of a replacement. Stage 3 requires that a formal exchange rate and central monetary institution be created. The final stage, to be completed in 2018, is full monetary cohesion among all Comesa nations and a Central Bank.

In January 2007 Comesa recognized global climate change as "a major threat to sustainable growth and development in Africa" and outlined multiple goals to address the issue. Among the goals discussed were to have a more unified vision for Africa's role on climate change, to promote regional and national cooperation on the issue, to improve the institutional capacities of COMESA to address climate change challenges, and to establish guidelines for an African BioCarbon Facility.

At the 12th summit, held May 22–23, 2007, in Nairobi, all Comesa states were urged to join the FTA as soon as possible. This was to facilitate launch of the customs union and the CET by December 2008. Thirteen states were members at that time. Rivalry between Comesa and SADC intensified in 2007, spurred by the World Trade Organization (WTO) rule that no country can be a member of more than one customs union. As Comesa and SADC each intended to create a customs union, member countries were forced to choose between the organizations. By late 2007 Angola had left Comesa for the SADC. In November 2007 Comesa signed a Regional Integration Support Mechanism (RISM) with the EU, granting the bloc 78 million euros (U.S. $100 million) over five years to offset harm done to poorer member countries by the customs union.

By January 2008 several African trade blocs were showing concern about agreements with the EU. Comesa had been negotiating with the EU under the Eastern and Southern Africa (ESA) platform, but several member states had signed individual agreements with Brussels. In February 2008 a meeting of Comesa trade ministers endorsed a proposal for a unified FTA among Comesa, the SADC, and East African Community (EAC) states. The attitude seemed to be that membership in multiple trade blocs might, after all, be acceptable. In May 2008 it was announced that Comesa had set September 2008 as the cut-off date for member states to submit their national tariff schedules, as agreed under the CET.

At a July 2008 extraordinary summit meeting in Sharm-el-Sheikh, Egypt, Sindiso Ngwenya of Zimbabwe was chosen as secretary general in place of Erastus Mwencha, who had resigned to take a job with the African Union secretariat. Ngwenya announced that in October 2008 Uganda would convene a meeting between Comesa, SADC, and EAC representatives to discuss the harmonization of trade. On October 22 representatives of the three groups, meeting in Kampala, agreed to form a free trade zone of all their members—an area stretching along the east side of Africa from Egypt to South Africa. For more on activities since 2008, see "Recent Activities," below.

Structure. The apex of Comesa comprises the Authority of Heads of State and Government, which establishes by consensus fundamental policy and directs subsidiary organs in pursuit of the common market's objectives. The Council of Ministers monitors and reviews the performance of administrators and financial managers in addition to overseeing the organization's programs and projects. The Intergovernmental Committee, comprising permanent secretaries from the member countries, develops and manages cooperative programs and action plans in all sectors except finance and monetary policy, which is the domain of the separate Committee of Governors of the members' central banks. There are also several technical committees and the Secretariat, which comprises five divisions: Administration; Trade, Customs, and Monetary Harmonization; Investment and Private Sector Development; Infrastructure Development; and Information and Networking. The secretary general serves a once-renewable, five-year term. The Court of Justice is responsible for interpreting the Comesa treaty and for adjudicating related disputes between members.

The PTA Bank is the most prominent of various Comesa-established autonomous institutions, which also include the Comesa Bankers' Association (BAPTA), the Comesa Metallurgical Industries Association (Comesamia), the Comesa Telecommunications Company (Comtel), the Eastern and Southern Africa Business Association (ESABO), the Federation of National Associations of Women in Business (Femcom), the Leather and Leather Products Institute (LLPI), and the Pharmaceutical Manufacturers of Eastern and Southern Africa (Pharmesa).

Recent Activities. At the Comesa summit held June 7–8, 2009, in Victoria Falls, Zimbabwe, Sudanese president Omar al-Bashir was in attendance. The meeting called on the International Criminal Court (ICC) to suspend the arrest warrant against him. The summit approved the launch of a Comesa Customs Union. This launch was marred by Ugandan president Yoweri Museveni telling the summit that while East African Community (EAC) members in Comesa supported the concept of the customs union, they needed to reevaluate their participation, since they were close to completing a customs union of their own. Shortly thereafter, the EAC members, more than half of Comesa, opted out.

In October 2009 the Democratic Republic of the Congo expressed interest in joining the Comesa FTA and customs union. In the same month the Government of Southern Sudan (see Sudan article) expressed a similar interest. During 2010 non-tariff trading barriers (including such things as cumbersome quality inspection rules or excessive transit charges) came under increasing scrutiny. By October 2010 rules were prepared to penalize countries that used such practices. Egypt was a particular subject of complaint.

On August 31, 2010, World Trade Organization (WTO) secretary general Pascal Lamy addressed Comesa's 14th summit, held in Lozitha, Swaziland. He called for increased regional integration as a means to development. He also called for a speedy conclusion to the Doha Round of trade talks (see WTO article).

At the October 14–15, 2011, summit, the council of ministers declared approval of a Grand Tripartite Free Trade Area, proposed in 2001, which would encompass half the continent. The summit also turned its focus to improving maternal health by investing in science and technology.

In December 2011, Comesa officially launched a new programme geared toward climate change. The programme is focused on increasing renewable energy, carbon efficient agricultural practices, and more linkage between agriculture, forestry and land use. In July 2012, the programme was approved for joint implementation in a tripartite agreement between Comesa, the EAC, and the SADC.

The tripartite agreement set a five-year goal for implementation of all components of the climate change programme.

At a June 2012 meeting of the Science, Technology, and Innovation Ministers of the member states, the group voted to establish a Comesa Innovation Council to increase the importance of science and technology in the community, as well as promote the growth of both resources and progress in those fields throughout the region.

At the November 2012 Heads of State and Government meeting held in Kampala, the organization adopted a plan for increased regional trade that had been adopted by the Council of Ministers. The plan is another step in the completion of the tripartite FTA. Also at the meeting, Ugandan President Museveni suggested that integration should have two components: economic integration and political integration. Museveni noted the limitations of such political integration at this time, but noted it was a realistic goal for the future.

Uganda joined the FTA in November 2012, and in January 2013, COMESA began the second phase of the preparatory stage, which focuses on trade in services and special trade issues such as intellectual property. In April 2013, COMESA officially launched its COMESA Innovation Council. This new council is composed of ten highly respected scholars. As an outgrowth of the new Innovation Council, COMESA put forth a draft of a new Intellectual Property Policy in May. According to a COMESA news release, the new draft policy emphasizes "capacity building in institutions and human resources for intellectual property innovation."

THE COMMONWEALTH

Established: By evolutionary process and formalized December 31, 1931, in the Statute of Westminster.

Purpose: To give expression to a continuing sense of affinity and to foster cooperation among states presently or formerly owing allegiance to the British Crown.

Commonwealth Center: The Secretariat is located in Marlborough House, London, which also serves as the site of Commonwealth meetings in the United Kingdom.

Principal Organs: Meeting of Heads of Government, Secretariat, Commonwealth Ministerial Action Group.

Web site: www.thecommonwealth.org

Head of the Commonwealth: Queen Elizabeth II.

Secretary General: Kamalesh Sharma (India).

Membership (53, with years of entry): Antigua and Barbuda (1981), Australia (1931), Bahamas (1973), Bangladesh (1972), Barbados (1966), Belize (1981), Botswana (1966), Brunei (1984), Cameroon (1995), Canada (1931), Cyprus (1961), Dominica (1978), Fiji (1970, reentered 1997, suspended 2009), Ghana (1957), Grenada (1974), Guyana (1966), India (1947), Jamaica (1962), Kenya (1963), Kiribati (1979), Lesotho (1966), Malawi (1964), Malaysia (1957), Maldives (1982), Malta (1964), Mauritius (1968), Mozambique (1995), Namibia (1990), Nauru (1999), New Zealand (1931), Nigeria (1960), Pakistan (1947, reentered 1989), Papua New Guinea (1975), Rwanda (2009), St. Kitts-Nevis (1983), St. Lucia (1979), St. Vincent and the Grenadines (1979), Samoa (1970), Seychelles (1976), Sierra Leone (1961), Singapore (1965), Solomon Islands (1978), South Africa (1931, reentered 1994), Sri Lanka (1948), Swaziland (1968), Tanzania (1961), Tonga (1970), Trinidad and Tobago (1962), Tuvalu (2000), Uganda (1962), United Kingdom (1931), Vanuatu (1980), Zambia (1964).

Working Language: English.

Origin and development. A voluntary association that gradually superseded the British Empire, the Commonwealth traces its origins to the mid-1800s, when internal self-government was first introduced in the colonies of Australia, British North America (Canada), New Zealand, and part of what was to become the Union of South Africa. The increasing maturity and independence of these overseas communities, particularly after World War I, eventually created a need to redefine the mutual relationships between the United Kingdom and the self-governing "dominions" that were collectively coming to be known as the British Commonwealth of Nations. The Statute of Westminster, enacted by the British Parliament in 1931, established the principle that all members of the association were equal in status, in no way subordinate to each other, and united by allegiance to the Crown.

The original members of the Commonwealth, in addition to the United Kingdom, were Australia, Canada, the Irish Free State, Newfoundland, New Zealand, and the Union of South Africa. In 1949 the Irish Free State became the Republic of Ireland and withdrew from the Commonwealth. In the same year Newfoundland became a province of Canada. South Africa ceased to be a member upon becoming a republic in 1961 because of the opposition of the other Commonwealth countries to Pretoria's apartheid policies; however, it was readmitted June 1, 1994, following the installation of a multiracial government. Pakistan withdrew in 1972 but rejoined in 1989. Because of political instability, its status has changed or come into question several times. Likewise, Fiji's status has often been in jeopardy because of political unrest.

The ethnic, geographic, and economic composition of the Commonwealth has been modified fundamentally by the accession of former colonial territories in Asia, Africa, and the Western Hemisphere. This infusion of racially nonwhite and economically less developed states had significant political implications, including modification of the Commonwealth's unwritten constitution to accommodate the desire of many new members to renounce allegiance to the British Crown and adopt a republican form of government. In 1949 the pattern was set when Commonwealth prime ministers accepted India's formal declaration that, on becoming a republic, it would accept the Crown as a symbol of the Commonwealth association and recognize the British sovereign as head of the Commonwealth. The movement toward a multicultural identity was solidified by the Declaration of Commonwealth Principles adopted by the heads of government at their 1971 Singapore summit. In addition to acknowledging the organization's diversity, the Singapore declaration enumerated a set of common principles, including the primacy of international peace and order; individual liberty regardless of racial, ethnic, or religious background; people's "inalienable right to participate by means of free and democratic processes in framing the society in which they live"; opposition to "colonial domination and racial oppression"; and the "progressive removal" of wide disparities in wealth and living standards.

The new thrust was further evidenced by a North-South summit in October 1981, which reflected that most Commonwealth members were developing countries. Subsequently, a 1982 report, *The North-South Dialogue: Making It Work,* proposed many institutional and procedural reforms to facilitate global negotiations on development and related issues, and a 1983 document, *Towards a New Bretton Woods,* proposed short-, medium-, and long-range changes to enhance the efficiency and equity of the international trading and financial system.

A declaration in October 1987 that Fiji's Commonwealth status had lapsed followed two successive coups, abrogation of the country's constitution, and proclamation of a republic. Readmission required the unanimous consent of the Commonwealth members, and Fiji's application remained blocked until mid-1997 by India. Fiji was finally readmitted effective October 1, 1997, but its membership was suspended in May 2000 following displacement of the elected government. Full participation was restored in late 2001, following democratic elections in August through September.

The October 1991 summit in Harare, Zimbabwe, was noteworthy for the adoption of a declaration redefining the Commonwealth's agenda. The Harare Declaration, drafted under the guidance of a ten-member High Level Appraisal Group, committed all Commonwealth countries, regardless of their political or economic conditions, to promote democracy, human rights, judicial independence, equality for women, educational opportunities, and the principles of "sound economic management."

During the 1980s and early 1990s, the Commonwealth was most prominently identified by its efforts to end apartheid in South Africa, although debate frequently raged within the organization over tactics, especially the imposition of sanctions. Accordingly, the formal readmission of South Africa in midyear was the highlight of 1994.

In a departure from precedent, membership was granted on November 13, 1995, to Mozambique, even though it had never been a British colony and was not at least partly English speaking. A "unique and special" case regarding Mozambique had been presented by its Anglophone neighbors because of regional trade concerns.

The Commonwealth Heads of Government Meeting (CHOGM) held November 8–13, 1995, in Auckland, New Zealand, was dominated by discussion of the excesses of Sani Abacha, the military ruler of Nigeria, who executed the internationally known author and nonviolent activist Ken Saro-Wiwa while the conference was in progress. This resulted in the suspension of Nigeria's membership and the launching of efforts (ultimately largely unsuccessful) by the Commonwealth to influence the actions of the military regime in Abuja.

Nigeria was also a major topic at the 1997 CHOGM held in Edinburgh, Scotland. While praising the role Nigeria played in the Liberia conflict, the summit decided to continue Nigeria's suspension because of ongoing human rights abuses and the suppression of democracy. Sierra Leone was also suspended (until the restoration of President Tejan Kabbah's government in March 1998), and the summit called on Commonwealth members to support the sanctions imposed by the United Nations (UN) and the Economic Community of West African States on that country.

Another focus of attention at the summit was the promotion of economic prosperity. The heads of government adopted the Edinburgh Commonwealth Economic Declaration, which called for continued global economic integration, with greater attention to the smaller, less developed countries that believed they were being left behind. To assist the smaller countries, the Commonwealth leaders agreed to support efforts to develop a successor to the Lomé Convention (see European Community section of European Union article), to offer duty-free access to certain markets, and to establish a Trade and Investment Access Facility.

In October 1998 CMAG concluded that the Nigerian government had taken enough steps toward democracy to warrant the lifting of sanctions and resumption of Nigerian participation in some Commonwealth activities. Full participation was restored May 29, 1999, following presidential elections the previous February.

At the November 12–15, 1999, Commonwealth summit in Durban, South Africa, the organization established a ten-member High-Level Review Group (HLRG) comprising the heads of government of Australia, India, Malta, Papua New Guinea, Singapore, South Africa, Tanzania, Trinidad and Tobago, United Kingdom, and Zimbabwe. The HLRG was assigned the task of recommending how the Commonwealth could best meet the challenges of the 21st century.

Also occurring in 1999, Nauru became the 53rd full member of the Commonwealth after 31 years as a special member, and Tuvalu, a special member from 1978, became the 54th full member in 2000. In 2005 Nauru resumed its status as a special member, a category of membership available to very small countries.

At a 2000 meeting, the heads of government confirmed Pakistan's suspension from Commonwealth activities in the wake of the previous month's coup in Islamabad. Similarly, in March 2002 Zimbabwe's participation in Commonwealth meetings was suspended as a consequence of a widely condemned presidential election earlier in the month.

The CHOGM held December 5–8, 2003, in Abuja, Nigeria, was dominated by the Zimbabwe issue. Although many African states argued that the Mugabe government could best be engaged by lifting the suspension, the opponents prevailed. The Commonwealth proceeded to form a balanced committee of leaders from Australia, Canada, India, Jamaica, Mozambique, and South Africa to pursue "national reconciliation" in Zimbabwe and a rapid return of that country to full participation, but Zimbabwe's governing party quickly voted to terminate membership in the Commonwealth on December 7. In acknowledging the withdrawal, Secretary General McKinnon expressed his hope that Zimbabwe would rejoin "in due course, as have other members in the past."

Four and a half years after the military coup that brought Gen. Pervez Musharraf to power, Commonwealth ministers decided to restore full membership to Pakistan at a May 2004 meeting in London.

The marriage of Prince Charles, Queen Elizabeth's son and heir to the throne, to Camilla Parker Bowles in April 2005 had implications for the Commonwealth. The British Department of Constitutional Affairs stated on March 21 that Parker Bowles would automatically become queen when Charles became king, despite Charles's declarations to the contrary, unless the parliaments of the UK and the Commonwealth countries of which the UK monarch was head of state all agreed to a change in the law. On March 23 the Commonwealth Secretariat announced that Charles would not automatically succeed Queen Elizabeth as head of the Commonwealth when he became king. Instead, the various Commonwealth heads of government would elect the next head of the Commonwealth. Appointing anyone other than the British monarch to this symbolic position would mark a substantial shift away from the organization's British and imperial roots.

In December 2006 Fiji was suspended from some privileges of Commonwealth membership following a military coup. Also in that month Rwanda formally applied to join the Commonwealth. Subsequently, Burundi also expressed an interest. When the 2007 CHOGM took place in Kampala, Uganda, November 23–25, the president of Rwanda was present as an observer, and Rwanda's application was again on the agenda. An outcome of the meeting was a clarification of the rules, spelling out the right of countries that had never been under British rule to join the Commonwealth, if on examination they met the appropriate democratic standards.

In November 2007 the Commonwealth suspended Pakistan from full membership because President Musharraf had not ended the state of emergency, released political prisoners, and stepped down as army chief of staff as he had promised. The suspension was lifted in May 2008, democratic elections having been held in Pakistan, and Musharraf having resigned from the army.

A conference on Rwanda's proposed accession was subsequently held in August 2008, in Kigali, Rwanda. Rwanda, which in October 2008 mandated English as the language of education instead of French, received widespread support for its bid. Rwanda's application was approved at the 2009 CHOGM, held in Trinidad and Tobago, November 27–29. Rwanda thus became the second Commonwealth member, along with Mozambique, that had never been part of the British Empire. For more on activities since 2008, see "Recent Activities," below.

Structure. One of the least institutionalized intergovernmental organizations, the Commonwealth was virtually without permanent machinery until the establishment of its Secretariat in 1965. The ceremonial head of the organization is the reigning British monarch, who serves concurrently as constitutional sovereign in those member states that still maintain their traditional allegiance to the British crown. Since World War II, the heads of government have held biennial meetings, and specialized consultations occur periodically among national ministers. National finance ministers normally convene in the nearest convenient Commonwealth site on the eve of the annual fall meetings of the International Monetary Fund and World Bank to discuss monetary and economic issues.

The Secretariat organizes meetings and conferences, collects and disseminates information on behalf of the membership, and is responsible for implementing collective decisions. The secretary general, who currently serves a four-year term, is assisted by three deputies with responsibilities for political affairs, economic and social development, and development cooperation. Since its reorganization in 2002, the Secretariat has encompassed nine divisions.

The Secretariat's divisions oversee Commonwealth activities. Among the most prominent, the Political Affairs Division participates in organizing Commonwealth Heads of Government Meetings (CHOGMs), conducts research, aids various committees in their tasks, and monitors political issues and developments of importance to Commonwealth members. Since 1990 its observer missions have also monitored election campaigns, preparations for balloting, and elections in some two dozen Commonwealth countries around the globe. In 1999 it drafted a "Framework for Principles for Promoting Good Governance and Combating Corruption." The Economic Affairs Division conducts research and analysis and supports expert groups in areas such as North-South economic relations, protectionist tariffs, reform of the international financial system, debt management, and youth unemployment. Its purview also includes environmental concerns and sustainable development. In the area of technical assistance and development, the Commonwealth Fund for Technical Cooperation provides training, expertise, and advice in the promotion of economic growth, public sector reform, poverty alleviation, infrastructural and institutional development, and capacity building. A Commonwealth Youth Program likewise funded through voluntary contributions is an effort to encourage youth participation in economic and social development.

In addition, a Commonwealth Equity Fund, designed to encourage private sector investment in the emerging stock markets of developing countries, was launched in 1990 and was followed in 1995 by formation of a Commonwealth Private Investment Initiative (CPII). The latter was established to help geographic regions attract capital for small- and medium-size ventures and for former state enterprises that were being privatized. On the political front, a Commonwealth Ministerial Action Group (CMAG) was created in November 1995 to provide guidance toward "good governance" in countries undergoing transition to democracy.

The autonomous Commonwealth Foundation, the formation of which was authorized by the Commonwealth heads of government in 1965, supports nongovernmental organizations, professional associations, and other such bodies. The Commonwealth of Learning, likewise authorized by the heads of government and located in Vancouver, Canada, was established in 1987 to promote distance learning and thereby improve access to education and training. Some three dozen additional Commonwealth associations, institutes, councils, and other groups were also established over the years, largely to promote development or disseminate information in such fields as forestry, health, telecommunications, education, journalism, law, and sports. Most are based in London.

Recent Activities. By the start of 2009 there was concern about India's progress in building the facilities to host the 2010 Commonwealth Games. In March 2009 the Commonwealth gave Fiji six months to make progress toward holding elections, with expulsion from the organization as the alternative. In September 2009 Fiji's suspension, though not expulsion, was reaffirmed. In March the Commonwealth also celebrated its 60th anniversary.

According to a July 2009 survey, commissioned as part of an effort to rejuvenate and "re-brand" the Commonwealth, interest in the group seemed to differ sharply among its members. Populations of the older, predominately white, members showed less interest, with Britons the least interested, and only one third of Australians and Canadians strongly opposed to leaving the Commonwealth. Members of developing countries, to the contrary, valued the Commonwealth much more highly, and South Africans thought more of the Commonwealth tie than of relations with the United States.

Now being a member, Rwanda received a Commonwealth observer group to monitor its August 9, 2010, presidential election. The group pronounced the election, which gave President Paul Kagame a new term, to be reasonably free and fair.

In September 2010 CMAG met for its biannual meeting, during which time the group focused largely on the political situation in Fiji. The group reiterated its support for Fiji and vowed to continue helping them restore their constitutional government. The Commonwealth is currently working with the interim government in Fiji to ensure that the island is able to peaceably restore democracy.

In 2011 the Commonwealth was asked to oversee elections in two African countries—Uganda and Nigeria—after both had been plagued by political instability. In both cases the Commonwealth representatives found the elections to be free and fair. The biennial CHOGM meeting was held in Perth, Australia, October 28–30, 2011. The meeting brought about several key decisions concerning administrative reform and management of the Commonwealth. Perhaps most notably, the Commonwealth members agreed to draft a charter for the organization, a step that would help the group move toward a more traditional intergovernmental organization structure. The meeting also discussed South Sudan's entrance into the Commonwealth and authorized the Secretary General to move forward with admissions procedures. The meeting also addressed issues such as food security, the economy, migration, and greater involvement.

The February 2012 resignation of Maldives' President Nasheed created turmoil and political unrest in Maldives. The CMAG visited the island in mid-February, and at its bi-annual meeting later in February determined that the resignation of Nasheed was constitutionally questionable. Further actions by the government, such as the disruption of the opening parliamentary session, led the Commonwealth to actively pursue measures to end the political unrest in Maldives. Upon the urging of the CMAG, Maldives established a Commission of National Inquiry in June to investigate the February transition of power. The Commonwealth remained actively involved in the political situation in Maldives throughout 2012 and 2013, and welcomed the progress made in that country since the 2012 coup and was an observer to their October 2013 elections.

The Commonwealth Charter, first proposed at the 2011 CHOGM meeting, was drafted over the course of 2012. The document codified the governing principles of the Commonwealth and expressed the core principles of democracy, human rights, and the rule of law that serve to guide the actions of Commonwealth members. The charter was approved by the secretariat in December 2012. On Commonwealth Day 2013, Her Majesty Queen Elizabeth II signed the historic document, marking its full, official implementation.

The year 2013 saw a concerted focus on youth in the Commonwealth. In addition to its normal youth programs, the ministerial meeting of Commonwealth Youth Ministers identified youth as a commonwealth priority and a key to creating sustainable development and growth. As a result, the Commonwealth createdthe Commonwealth Youth Council, sponsored special awards for youth, and launched its new Youth Development Index.

In October 2013, Gambia, a member since 1965, formally withdrew from the Commonwealth. The secretariat expressed hope that Gambia would one day rejoin the organization once the social and political unrest has been resolved. Also in October, the Commonwealth and South Africa reached a landmark agreement concerning principles of debt management. As part of the agreement, the South African National Treasury will host a group of financial advisors from the Commonwealth who will provide assistance to the member states in the region. South Africa will also send local debt management experts to the Commonwealth secretariatto assist local member states in that region. This is the first agreement of its kind within the Commonwealth.

COMMONWEALTH OF INDEPENDENT STATES (CIS)

Sodruzhestvo Nezavisimykh Gosudarstv (SNG)

Established: By the Alma-Ata Protocol, signed by 11 of the former constituent states of the Union of Soviet Socialist Republics in Alma-Ata (now Almaty), Kazakhstan, on December 21, 1991.

Purpose: To assist in the orderly transfer of governmental functions and treaty obligations of the former Soviet Union to its independent successor states, to promote coordinated policies in disarmament and national security, and to work toward economic unity among members.

Administrative Center: Minsk, Belarus.

Principal Organs: Council of Heads of State, Council of Heads of Government, Ministerial Councils, Interparliamentary Assembly, Joint Chiefs of Staff, Executive Committee, Secretariat.

Web site: www.cisstat.com (Site has a comprehensive English section.)

Executive Secretary: Sergei Lebedev (Russia).

Membership (11): Armenia, Azerbaijan, Belarus, Kazakhstan, Kyrgyzstan, Moldova, Russia, Tajikistan, Ukraine, Turkmenistan, Uzbekistan.

Origin and development. Following acceptance on September 6, 1991, of the Baltic states' withdrawal from the Soviet Union, a proposal was advanced for the creation of an economic commonwealth of the remaining Soviet republics. The plan was endorsed by all 12 republics during a meeting on October 1–2 in Alma-Ata (now Almaty), Kazakhstan, although four states (Azerbaijan, Georgia, Moldova, and Ukraine) abstained from signing a formal treaty in Moscow on October 18. Less than a month later, on November 14, agreement was reached on the formation of the Union of Sovereign States, which its principal advocate, USSR president Mikhail Gorbachev, characterized as a "union of confederal democratic states." However, the seven republican delegations that attended the November 25 meeting decided not to initial a draft treaty, returning it to their Supreme Soviets for more consideration. Ukraine's absence from the discussions cast further doubt as to the treaty's viability.

In a referendum December 1, Ukrainians voted overwhelmingly for independence, and one week later, in a highly symbolic meeting in Brest, Belarus, the Russian Federation and Belarus joined Ukraine in proclaiming the demise of the Soviet Union and the establishment of the Commonwealth of Independent States (CIS). On December 13 the five Central Asian republics of Kazakhstan, Kyrgyzstan, Tajikistan, Turkmenistan, and Uzbekistan agreed to join the CIS, and on December 21 they were joined by Armenia, Azerbaijan, and Moldova in Alma-Ata, Kazakhstan. In December 1993 Georgia decided to join the Commonwealth.

The Azerbaijan legislature voted against ratification of the accord in October 1992 but reversed its position the following June upon a government change in Baku. Azerbaijan's membership was formalized at the CIS summit in September. Georgia's membership was ratified by the Georgian Supreme Council in March 1994. Moldova's parliament ratified CIS membership in April 1994, reversing a negative vote on the question taken the previous August.

After the first six months of its existence, the viability of the CIS appeared in question because little effective action had been taken in economic, political, or military affairs. In seeming contradiction to their stated goal of cooperation, CIS members were preparing to introduce their own national currencies and had instituted numerous cross-border trade restrictions. The commonwealth had also proved ineffective in resolving the fighting between Armenia and Azerbaijan over Nagorno-Karabakh, ethnic conflict in Moldova, and secularist-Islamic fundamentalist disputes in Central Asian republics.

Tension remained high between Russia and Ukraine over the status of Crimea and control of the Black Sea fleet. Ukraine was one of five countries (the others being Azerbaijan, Belarus, Kyrgyzstan, and Moldova) that declined to sign a CIS collective security treaty at a May 1992 summit in Tashkent, Uzbekistan. However, the June agreement between Russia and Ukraine on the Black Sea fleet dispute (see separate article on Ukraine) eased tensions, enabling the CIS to function more effectively.

In March 1992, CIS members (except Azerbaijan, Moldova, and Ukraine) endorsed the creation of a joint CIS military command, which moved into the former Warsaw Treaty Organization headquarters in Moscow. CIS leaders also backed establishing CIS peacekeeping forces to act within and between member states, and in May most signed the Treaty on Collective Security. However, de facto control of both nuclear and regular forces remained in national hands. In 1993 the participating CIS defense ministers ended the joint military command, preferring less structured and, at least from the Russian perspective, less expensive efforts at military cooperation. The CIS did, however, set up an integrated air defense network in 1995 under Russian control and financing and has since continued joint exercises.

In July 1993 Belarus, Russia, and Ukraine agreed in principle to establish their own "single economic space," reflecting an apparent acknowledgment that effective CIS activity remained a distant prospect. Central Asian states also voiced concern over the commonwealth's future, and in 1994 Kazakhstan, Kyrgyzstan, and Uzbekistan formed the Central Asian Economic Union (CAEU).

Supporters of genuine economic cooperation were buoyed by the signing of a customs union between Belarus and Russia during the May 1995 CIS summit in Minsk. Meeting in Moscow in November, CIS heads of government signed integration agreements covering gas supplies, external relations, and scientific research but failed to resolve CIS members' energy supply debts to Russia. On March 29 the presidents of Russia, Belarus, Kazakhstan, and Kyrgyzstan, meeting in Moscow under CIS auspices, signed a treaty to create a CIS customs union.

The next CIS summit was finally held on March 28, 1997. Once again plans were endorsed by CIS members (with the exception of Georgia) for accelerated integration. The prime ministers of six CIS states also signed an agreement in early October called the Concept for the Integrated Economic Development of the CIS, but little hope for implementation was provided at the CIS summit, held October 23 in Chişinău, Moldova. Blocs included the Belarus-Russia union; the CIS Customs Union of Belarus, Kazakhstan, Kyrgyzstan, and Russia; the Central Asian Economic Community (CAEC, successor to the CAEU) of Kazakhstan, Kyrgyzstan, Tajikistan, and Uzbekistan; and the so-called GUAM grouping of Georgia, Ukraine, Azerbaijan, and Moldova. (Tajikistan joined the CIS Customs Union in February 1999. The GUAM became the GUUAM for a short time with Uzbekistan's admission in April 1999, but returned to its former name when Uzbekistan suspended membership in June 2002. In February 2002 the participants of the CAEC agreed to reshape it as the Central Asian Cooperation Organization [CACO].)

In 1999 six members of the CIS Collective Security Council—Armenia, Belarus, Kazakhstan, Kyrgyzstan, Russia, and Tajikistan—renewed their commitment to collective defense for an additional five years. The January 20, 2000, Moscow summit voiced support for the 1972 Anti-Ballistic Missile Treaty, which CIS saw as threatened by efforts in the United States to implement a national missile defense system. Later that year, on November 30–December 1, CIS leaders met in Minsk to establish an antiterrorism center in Moscow.

On October 10, 2000, the five constituent states of the CIS Customs Union signed a treaty in Astana, Kazakhstan, authorizing conversion of the organization into the Eurasian Economic Community (EAEC), effective April 2001. Initial goals of the EAEC, which is modeled on the European Economic Community, were to harmonize tariff and taxation policies, employment regulations, and visa regimes. Armenia, Moldova, and Ukraine have observer status in the EAEC. Uzbekistan joined at a January 2006 summit in St. Petersburg and the EAEC decided to absorb the CACO to eliminate institutional duplication.

Meeting in Yerevan, Armenia, May 25, 2001, the presidents of the six states of the CIS Collective Security Council agreed to move ahead on formation of a 3,000-troop rapid reaction force to be headquartered in Bishkek, the Kyrgyz capital, in response to heightening concerns over drug trafficking, organized crime, terrorism, and Islamist militancy. The session was followed by a full CIS summit on May 31–June 1 in Minsk, where the focus of attention was progress toward establishment of a much-delayed free trade zone.

The organization's focus turned once again to terrorism in the wake of the September 11, 2001, al-Qaida attacks against the United States. Particular emphasis was given to closer coordination on counterterrorism and border security. The most significant shift in policy, however, may have been Russian acquiescence in the positioning of U.S. forces in Central Asia to root out terrorist bases in Afghanistan and oust the Taliban regime. Uzbekistan and Kyrgyzstan permitted the entry of U.S. contingents, but a number of other CIS member states objected to the U.S. military presence. In August 2005, the United States was ordered to vacate its bases in Uzbekistan.

In April 2002 the six parties to the Collective Security Treaty met in Almaty, Kazakhstan, to strengthen joint efforts against terrorism, drug smuggling, and illegal immigration. The session concluded with agreement on establishing a more formal security structure and was immediately followed by military exercises involving the Collective Rapid Reaction Forces. Plans for the new security organization were further advanced at the October 6–7, 2002, CIS summit in Chişinău, where the treaty participants signed a charter for the organization.

Meeting on April 28, 2003, in Dushanbe, Tajikistan, the presidents of Armenia, Belarus, Kazakhstan, Kyrgyzstan, Russia, and Tajikistan formally established the Collective Security Treaty Organization (CSTO) with headquarters in Moscow and named Nikolai Bordyuzha of Russia as its first secretary general. One of the organization's principal assignments was identified as management of the rapid reaction forces.

A CIS summit on September 18–19, 2003, in Yalta, Ukraine, saw the presidents of Belarus, Kazakhstan, Russia, and Ukraine reach agreement on the formation of a single economic space (SES) that would ultimately harmonize customs, tariff, transport, and related regimes. However, as the SES initiative moved forward in 2004, various disputes arose over the adoption of a single economic agreement for the CIS. Ultimately, the CIS decided to adopt 61 separate agreements to be reviewed at a summit in Yalta in September, at which time several were signed.

The CIS heads of government met in April 2004 and supported creation of the CIS Reserve Fund, which would help member states in the event of natural disasters. The following month CIS defense ministers met in Armenia and agreed to form a CIS peacekeeping force, and in June they drafted a document that encouraged the CIS and NATO to cooperate in managing a peacekeeping force under United Nations (UN) mandate. Because of increasing concerns about terrorism and border control (and to bolster military cooperation among members), the Secretariat of Defense Ministers was increased from 10 members to 21 in August 2005.

The 38th CIS summit on September 16, 2004, in Astana, Kazakhstan, focused primarily on security and economic issues; the group issued a statement on the fight against international terrorism and vowed to step up the work of the CIS antiterrorist center. A summit on August 16, 2005, in Kazan, Russia, included adoption of antiterrorism documents but also marked the departure of Turkmenistan from full membership. Turkmenistan, which expressed its preference for establishing its international neutrality, remained an associate member. Meanwhile, dramatic changes of government in the region—the "rose revolution" in Georgia in 2003, the "orange revolution" in Ukraine in 2004, and the "tulip revolution" in Kyrgyzstan in 2005—did not bode well for the organization's future. President Putin increasingly seemed to see the West as a rival trading power rather than a partner and began to exploit politically Russia's position as a supplier of oil and natural gas. During the winter of 2005–2006, huge increases in the price of natural gas caused outrage and recrimination in the European Union (EU) and such Western-leaning CIS members as Ukraine.

Georgia withdrew from the CIS Council of Defense Ministers in February 2006 with aims to join the North Atlantic Treaty Organization (NATO). In May 2006 Georgia, Moldova, and Ukraine threatened to leave the CIS as tension increased with Russia over energy prices and a Russian ban on Moldovan and Georgian wine. The relationship steadily worsened that year as Georgia demanded the withdrawal of Russian peacekeepers from secessionist South Ossetia under accusations that Russia was propping up the separatist regime. After Georgia arrested four Russian military officers on spying charges, Russia slapped transport blockades on Georgia and visa restrictions on Georgian citizens.

In June 2006, Uzbekistan upgraded its membership to full member status.

Tensions rendered several 2006 CIS meetings unproductive, with the commonwealth unable to serve as an effective negotiating forum. Georgian and Ukrainian presidents were conspicuously absent at a July meeting of heads of state. The CIS summit on November 28, 2006, in Minsk, scheduled to coincide with a NATO summit meeting, produced few results. The summit was held to address "questions on the effectiveness and improvement of the Commonwealth" and to sign an agreement delimiting state borders between CIS members, thereby completing the process of turning administrative borders into national borders. Amidst continued rancor, the subject of reform was put off until the following year.

In the meantime, alienated CIS member states continued seeking other avenues for economic, energy, and military cooperation. GUAM was formalized as an international agency committed to a "pro- European" path at a May 2006 meeting in Kiev. The member nations signed a new charter pledging to uphold democratic values and foster mutual economic development and cooperation. Its immediate goals were to reduce dependence on Russian energy and boost relations with the United States as a way to resolve conflicts in their regions. GUAM nations also signed a protocol to implement a free trade zone within member nations' borders. In the same year, member states began discussing the creation of a peacekeeping force that could work under UN mandates, potentially with the aim to replace Russian peacekeepers in the separatist regions of Georgia and Moldova.

On the pro-Russian side, EAEC members—Russia, Belarus, and Kazakhstan—signed the legal framework to establish a customs union immediately following the October 5, 2007, CIS summit in Dushanbe, Tajikistan. At the summit, CSTO members signed agreements enhancing the organization's military power by allowing member states to purchase Russian arms at lower Russian domestic prices. The CSTO also agreed to create an international peacekeeping force, although the Russian foreign minister denied that it would be used in conflicts involving the breakaway Georgian areas of Abkhazia and South Ossetia.

The 2007 CIS summit produced several outcomes. A reform plan was adopted calling for a "qualitatively new level of interaction" among member states. It included the appointment of national coordinators to monitor compliance with decisions adopted by CIS governing bodies. Georgia and Turkmenistan refused to sign and Azerbaijan did so with reservations, while Georgia's president suggested that CIS membership had done nothing to counter Russia's retaliatory trade and travel sanctions. A common migration policy for member states was also adopted, emphasizing regulation and coordination of worker's movements to ensure legal migration and greater social protections for migrants.

In April 2008 the president of Turkmenistan, Gurbanguly Berdymukhammedov, attended a NATO summit in Romania. This led to speculation that Turkmenistan might be moving closer to NATO, perhaps under the cover of an agreement worded to maintain its official neutrality.

In July 2008 the presidents of three of the countries in the Western-leaning GUAM group (Georgia, Ukraine, Azerbaijan, and Moldova), held their annual summit in Batumi, Georgia. The presidents of Lithuania and Poland, both NATO members, were present as observers. The group issued a statement calling for the peaceful resolution of regional disputes, specifically addressing Azerbaijan's breakaway region of Nagorno-Karabakh. The meeting also discussed a project to build an oil pipeline from Odessa, Ukraine, to Poland, which would circumvent Russia in moving Caspian oil to Europe.

The informal CIS summit in Saint Petersburg on June 6–7, 2008, served to demonstrate some CIS members' recognition of Russia's resurgence. Moldova, in particular, seemed concerned with adopting a more conciliatory approach to Russia than in the past.

At a conference of CIS prime ministers in Minsk on May 16, 2008, Belarus assumed the rotating presidency of the organization. The meeting adopted a draft convention on migration. After the meeting the president of Belarus, Alexander Lukashenko, declared that it was time to address issues of integration within the CIS more seriously.

In 2008 relations between Russia and Georgia slid toward collapse, with Russia offering overt support of the breakaway Georgian regions of Abkhazia and South Ossetia. In May 2008 Russia sent peacekeeping forces into Abkhazia under CIS auspices. In the same month, a Russian fighter aircraft shot down a Georgian spy drone over Abkhazia. Georgia protested, but stopped further drone flights. In June NATO urged that Russia remove troops from Abkhazia, but on June 19 there was a standoff between Georgian and Russian forces on the border, solved only after a tense telephone conversation between the two countries' presidents. Medvedev publicly warned Georgia of the most serious consequences if it persisted in trying to join NATO. On August 8 Georgian troops assaulted the South Ossetian capital of Tskhinvali, and Russia responded with a military thrust into Georgia proper. After a French-brokered cease-fire, Russian forces began slowly to withdraw from captured Georgian territory. On August 13, Georgian president Mikhail Saakashvili announced that Georgia was withdrawing from the CIS and urged other members, particularly Ukraine, to do likewise. On August 19 the CIS Secretariat said that it had received official notice of Georgia's withdrawal, which would become effective, under the CIS constitution, one year from that date. Georgia further announced that it was withdrawing from all peacekeeping agreements with Russia, going back to 1994. Russia recognized Abkhazia and South Ossetia as independent states, and on September 12 Abkhazia applied to join the CIS.

In general, Russia's influence within the CIS seemed to be waning. At the October 10, 2008, CIS summit in Bishkek, Kyrgyzstan, the presidents of Ukraine and Azerbaijan did not attend. Georgia was told that the door was open for it to return to the CIS. Moldova was designated to hold the rotating presidency of all CIS organizations in 2009. For more on developments since 2008, see "Recent Activities," below.

Structure. The Council of Heads of State (the supreme CIS body) and the Council of Heads of Government are required to meet at least every six and three months, respectively. In addition, CIS discussions regarding foreign affairs, defense, transportation, energy, the environment, and other areas have been regularly conducted at the ministerial level. Preparation for the various CIS meetings is the responsibility of a permanent administrative staff located in Minsk, Belarus.

Creation of the Interparliamentary Assembly was approved by seven CIS states (Armenia, Belarus, Kazakhstan, Kyrgyzstan, Russia,

Tajikistan, and Uzbekistan) in April 1992. Azerbaijan, Georgia, Moldova, and Ukraine joined later. The assembly meets in St. Petersburg and is assisted by its own secretariat.

In April 1999 the CIS Executive Secretariat was reorganized as the Executive Committee; the executive secretary was given the collateral title of chair of the Executive Committee. Many other organs were subsumed by the new committee, including the Interstate Economic Committee.

Recent Activities. In May 2009 Medvedev said he hoped that Ukraine would abandon its increasingly pro-Western policies. He also declared that CIS countries should better coordinate their economies for mutual support. Relations with Belarus remained tense, however, and in June Kyrgyzstan announced that NATO could use an airbase on its soil for shipment of supplies to troops in Afghanistan.

When Georgia's withdrawal from the CIS took effect in August 2009, it became clear that Georgia's association with the group was far from over. Public opinion surveys showed that most Georgians wanted some continued connection, and the Georgian government asked that most of its multilateral treaties with the CIS remain in force.

The October 9–10, 2009, CIS summit, held in Chişinău, was considered less than successful. The presidents of Kazakhstan, Tajikistan, and Turkmenistan did not attend. Russian president Medvedev cited a tight schedule as a reason for not meeting Ukrainian president Viktor Yushchenko, who declared that the CIS had lost its relevance, and that it was "like an old woman who is waiting for her death."

In March 2010 UN secretary general Ban Ki-Moon visited Moscow, and signed a declaration recognizing the CSTO as a legitimate partner with the UN in "fighting global challenges and threats." Moon had previously signed such a declaration with NATO, and his present visit was a step toward Medvedev's announced goal of making the CSTO a worthy competitor of NATO. In May 2010 Russian foreign minister Sergei Lavrov, while addressing the Russian parliament, warned NATO and the EU against interfering in the affairs of CIS member states. At the same time some Russian commentators welcomed NATO activities in Afghanistan, saying that NATO was doing something that the CSTO might otherwise be forced to do.

The September 3, 2011, summit in Dushanbe, Tajikstan, focused on the assessment of CIS activity over the past 20 years and creation of a plan for future development. The presidents of Uzbekistan, Azerbaijan, and Belarus were not in attendance and were instead represented by their prime ministers.

In October 2011, the CIS heads of state agreed to the terms of a CIS free trade zone between member states. Azerbaijan, Uzbekistan, and Turkmenistan all requested more time to decide on whether or not to enter the trade union. Russian Prime Minister Vladimir Putin was the driving force behind the negotiation of the trade agreement. The free trade zone entered into affect on January 1, 2012. Uzbekistan acceded to the free trade agreement in March 2012.

Newly elected Russian President Vladimir Putin also hosted two CIS events in May 2012. The CSTO met to celebrate its tenth anniversary and discuss the progress it has made. The heads of state also held a casual meeting focused on the newly instituted CIS free trade zone.

At its December summit, CIS leaders produced the Declaration of the Heads of States—members of the Commonwealth of Independent States on the further development of all-round cooperation. The document stresses the importance of the organization as a regional organization for humanitarian, economic, and security purposes and called for further efforts at deeper integration. The group also opted to focus on ecology, environment, and culture in 2013. The emphasis on culture is reflective of Armenian and Belarusian priorities for the year.

In May, the Council of Heads of Government met in Minsk. The most important result of the meeting was the approval of the protocol of agreement for Uzbekistan to join the free trade area, becoming the ninth member. The meeting also saw a new agreement concerning atomic energy, in which all parties agreed work toward the development of sustained atomic energy states.

In August, the EAEC's principal organ, the Eurasian Economic Commission, completed its draft agreement for the Eurasian Economic Union, which would deepen the existing level of economic integration in the region. The effort at deeper integration in the region, despite hesitancy from some CIS member states, is a major initiative of Russia's Vladimir Putin. These efforts have led some observers to question Putin's motives and fear that Putin is trying to re-create the Soviet "buffer zone" of the Cold War era.

In September 2013, Ukraine announced its accession to the CIS' anti-terrorism agreement, which the organization drafted in 1999.

COUNCIL OF EUROPE

Conseil de l'Europe

Established: By statute signed May 5, 1949, in London, England, effective August 3, 1949; structure defined by General Agreement signed September 2, 1949.

Purpose: To work for European unity by strengthening pluralist democracy and protecting human rights, seeking solutions to the problems facing European society, and promoting awareness of European cultural identity.

Headquarters: Strasbourg, France.

Principal Organs: Committee of Ministers, Parliamentary Assembly, Secretariat, Congress of Local and Regional Authority, the European Court of Human Rights, Commissioner for Human Rights, Conference of INGOs.

Web site: www.coe.int

Secretary General: Thorbjørn Jagland (Norway).

Membership (47): Albania, Andorra, Armenia, Austria, Azerbaijan, Belgium, Bosnia and Herzegovina, Bulgaria, Croatia, Cyprus, Czech Republic, Denmark, Estonia, Finland, France, Georgia, Germany, Greece, Hungary, Iceland, Ireland, Italy, Latvia, Liechtenstein, Lithuania, Luxembourg, Macedonia, Malta, Moldova, Monaco, Montenegro, Netherlands, Norway, Poland, Portugal, Romania, Russia, San Marino, Serbia, Slovakia, Slovenia, Spain, Sweden, Switzerland, Turkey, Ukraine, United Kingdom.

Observers States (6): Canada, Holy See, Israel, Japan, Mexico, United States.

Official Languages: English, French, German, Italian, and Russian.

Origin and development. In 1946 Winston Churchill put forward his plan for a "United States of Europe," and former European resistance fighters subsequently drew up an implementing program in Hertenstein, Switzerland. International groups were quickly established, and one of the most important of these, the Union of European Federalists, joined Churchill's United Europe Movement, the Economic League for European Cooperation, and the French Council for United Europe to form an International Committee of Movements for European Unity. Under the leadership of Duncan Sandys of the United Kingdom, the committee organized the first Congress of Europe in The Hague, Netherlands, in May 1948, and called for the establishment of a European Assembly and other measures to unite Western Europe. These combined efforts came to fruition on May 5, 1949, when the foreign ministers of Belgium, Denmark, France, Ireland, Italy, Luxembourg, Netherlands, Norway, Sweden, and the United Kingdom met in London to sign the Statute of the Council of Europe.

The organization was conceived as an instrument for promoting increased unity in Western Europe through discussion and, where appropriate, common action in the economic, social, cultural, scientific, legal, and administrative areas, and in the protection of human rights. Except for matters of national and regional defense, the Council of Europe and the Parliamentary Assembly of the Council of Europe (PACE) conduct activities in every conceivable aspect of European political, social, and cultural life. For example, deputies responsible to the Council of Ministers participate in a plethora of rapporteur groups, working parties, and committees concerned with, among other issues, human rights, democratic stability, administrative and budgetary matters, legal cooperation, social and health questions, education and culture, institutional reforms; and relations with the European Union (EU), the Organization for Security and Cooperation in Europe (OSCE), and the Organization for Economic Cooperation and Development (OECD).

In response to overtures from Eastern European countries, the Parliamentary Assembly in May 1989 created a Special Guest of the Assembly status, which, following the collapse of communism and the breakup of the Soviet Union and Yugoslavia, became an intermediate stage toward full membership for most ex-Communist states, although the admission of some proved contentious because of issues related to human rights and regional conflicts. Hungary became a full member in 1990, followed by Czechoslovakia and Poland in 1991;

Bulgaria in 1992; Romania, Estonia, Lithuania, Slovenia, the Czech Republic, and Slovakia in 1993 (the last two as successors to Czechoslovakia); Latvia, Albania, Moldova, Ukraine, and Macedonia in 1995; the Russian Federation and Croatia in 1996; Georgia in 1999; Armenia and Azerbaijan in 2001; and Serbia and Montenegro in 2003. Andorra was admitted in 1994.

Of the remaining nonmember European states, Belarus has applied for full membership but was suspended from special guest status in January 1997 because of its perceived undemocratic tendencies. A 1998 application for membership by Monaco was not approved because the principality's lack of a parliamentary opposition complicated its ability to guarantee a pluralist delegation. Election law changes followed by elections in February 2003 remedied the situation, and Monaco was admitted as a member on October 5, 2004.

Among the most significant achievements of the council are the drafting and implementation of the European Convention for the Protection of Human Rights and Fundamental Freedoms. Signed in November 1950 and entering into force in September 1953, the convention set up the European Commission of Human Rights, composed of independent lawyers from member states, to examine alleged violations by signatories and to attempt to broker negotiated settlements between the involved parties. A European Court of Human Rights was also established to consider cases in which those negotiations fail. The Council of Ministers approved the creation of a new post of commissioner for human rights in May 1999, after abolishing the Commission of Human Rights.

Other landmark conventions include the European Cultural Convention (which entered into force in 1955), the European Convention for the Peaceful Settlement of Disputes (1958), the European Social Charter (1965), the European Convention on the Suppression of Terrorism (1978), the European Convention for the Prevention of Torture and Inhuman or Degrading Treatment or Punishment (1989), the Convention on Laundering, Search, Seizure, and Confiscation of Proceeds From Crime (1993), the Framework Convention for the Protection of National Minorities (1998), the Convention on Human Rights and Biomedicine (1999), and the European Convention on the Exercise of Children's Rights (2000).

Much of the council's attention in recent years has focused on defining its role among the continent's often overlapping organizations, particularly in regard to the former Soviet-bloc countries of Eastern Europe. It became the official coordinator of human rights issues for the Conference on Security and Cooperation in Europe (CSCE, subsequently the OSCE) following that body's institutionalization in 1990; it also assisted with the establishment of a CSCE Parliamentary Assembly in 1992, in accordance with the council's earlier proposal for an all-European representative forum. In addition, the council's program on democratic institutions has provided assistance to the emerging European democracies in the field of constitutional, legislative, and administrative reform. On the proposal of President Mitterrand of France in May 1992, the council held its first summit meeting of heads of state and government October 8–9, 1993, in Vienna, Austria, to consider structural reform of the organization.

Minority and political rights remained prominent council concerns in 1996, particularly in connection with new accessions to full membership. Opposition to Russia's admittance in the Parliamentary Assembly (over the Chechnya military operation and then the Communist victory in the December 1995 State Duma election) was eventually overcome early in 1996 on the strength of various Russian promises. The required two-thirds assembly majority was marshaled in January, with the Committee of Ministers moving swiftly to admit Russia the following month. Even more controversial was Croatia's application, which was approved by the assembly in April but, in an unprecedented move, deferred by the Committee of Ministers in light of concerns about the democratic credentials of the Tudjman government and its commitment to the Dayton peace agreement for Bosnia and Herzegovina. On the basis of assurances from Zagreb, Croatia was accorded formal membership in November.

The second summit of the council's heads of state and government was held October 10–11, 1997, in Strasbourg to pursue the "consolidation of democracy" on the continent and to reaffirm the council's standard-setting role in areas such as human rights. The summit's final declaration called on the Committee of Ministers to propose structural reform within the council to promote, among other things, social cohesion, cultural diversity within the context of respect for democratic values, and the security of citizens, via programs designed to combat organized crime, government corruption, and terrorism.

In January 1999 Lord Russell-Johnston, a former leader of the Scottish Liberal Democratic Party, was elected to a three-year term as president of the Parliamentary Assembly. The UK's Terry Davis was also nominated as the council's next secretary general, but in the June election he lost by two votes to Walter Schwimmer of Austria. Davis was elected secretary general in 2004.

During the first half of 2000 renewed fighting in Chechnya not only generated a decision by the Parliamentary Assembly to suspend Russia's voting rights but also called for Russia's suspension from the full council. Moscow, in turn, threatened to withdraw from the organization. Admission of special guests Armenia and Azerbaijan proved almost as contentious, although both were formally welcomed in early 2001. At the same time, PACE restored Russia's voting rights, although Moscow has continued to be criticized not only for its actions in Chechnya but also for a widely perceived failure to adhere to principles of free speech and free press.

On June 21–22, 2001, the council hosted the first world congress on abolition of the death penalty. The council has repeatedly criticized the United States, in particular, for executing convicted criminals, and in mid-2001 threatened both the United States and Japan with suspension of their observer status if they did not take steps toward ending capital punishment. On July 1, 2003, Protocol No. 13 to the European human rights convention entered into effect, thereby making prohibition of capital punishment absolute. The council continues to condemn executions under the death penalty in the US and Japan.

The 109th session of the Committee of Ministers convened November 7–8, 2001. Immediately following the September 11 terrorist attacks on the United States, the council had vowed its support for the fight against terrorism and indicated that it would consider updating the European Convention on Suppression of Terrorism. On September 25, however, PACE offered a word of caution to the United States, describing the September 11 attacks as "crimes" rather than acts of war and urging Washington to seek United Nations (UN) Security Council approval before initiating reprisals. PACE also proposed that the remit of the International Criminal Court (ICC), which the United States has not joined, be expanded to cover international terrorism.

The Convention on Cyber-Crime was opened for signature November 23, 2001. More than two dozen member states (plus the United States, Japan, Canada, and South Africa) immediately signed the convention, which entered into force in July 2004.

Five months after the admission of Bosnia and Herzegovina on April 24, 2002, PACE voted 122–6 in favor of admitting Yugoslavia as soon as its two constituent republics had completed ratification of a new constitution. Accordingly, the new "state union" of Serbia and Montenegro was admitted April 3, 2003. In June 2006 Montenegro declared independence and was admitted as a separate member in May 2007.

On the agenda for the June 23–27 PACE session was a report on the rights of prisoners held by the United States in Afghanistan or at its Guantanamo Bay, Cuba, base. Also in May 2003, the anticipated amendment to the suppression of terrorism convention was opened for signature.

During 2005 and 2006 the council became involved in the controversy over reports that the United States was moving people suspected of terrorism for interrogation into countries in which torture was practiced and that some Eastern European countries were cooperating with the U.S. Central Intelligence Agency (CIA) by holding such people in secret prisons. The council's special rapporteur, Dick Marty of Switzerland, declared that at least 14 European governments were to some degree cooperating with, or at least turning a blind eye to, this program of "extraordinary rendition." His report stated that there was clear evidence of aircraft bearing such prisoners flying over and landing in Europe for rendition operations, with the UK, Portugal, Ireland, and Greece as "stop-off points."

On May 15, 2006, Russia rotated into the six-month chair of the council's Committee of Ministers. This caused controversy, as many believed Russia's record on observing human rights and the rule of law was too weak to justify this position. Russia also complained that the council was trying to impose a pro-Western position on Belarus. The council's affairs in late 2006 and 2007 were marked by tensions between a pro-EU tendency and the resurgence of Russia. In October 2006 Russia objected to any expansion of the North Atlantic Treaty Organization (NATO) eastward.

The former Soviet republics of the Caucasus and beyond continued to be the council's main focus in late 2007 and into 2008. Secretary General Davis visited Armenia in November 2007 to discuss the dispute with Azerbaijan over the region of Nagorno-Karabakh. He promised council involvement in the peace process, but declined to compare the region's status to that of Kosovo. The March 2008 presidential election in Armenia was criticized, both by council and OSCE observers, and violence followed. In April the Parliamentary Assembly adopted a resolution urging an open dialog between opposing groups, and criticized the Armenian government for its lack of response.

Council of Europe monitors denounced the December 2007 Russian presidential election as unfair, a charge that Russian election managers angrily denied, accusing Western observers of bias.

In January 2008 the council's rapporteur on Belarus recommended a measured reopening of contacts with that country. However, the council was forced to condemn Belarus in February for carrying out three executions.

The council was involved to some extent in mediating an end to the August 2008 military clash between Georgia and Russia. After a visit to the region, secretary general Davis condemned Russia's unilateral recognition of the Georgian regions of Abkhazia and South Ossetia as independent states. Other nations and international organizations joined in this condemnation.

Subsequent PACE resolutions were critical of both Russia and Georgia. In November 2008 Davis visited Moscow to help Russia "overcome any difficulties that may arise in carrying out its commitments to the Council of Europe." The main points of contention were Russia's deteriorating record on civil liberties, its frequent failure to carry out decisions of the European Court of Human Rights, and its failure to ratify the 2004 Protocol 14 to the European Convention on Human Rights, which seeks to streamline and speed up the court's work. Russia, while not signing the protocol, continues to declare support for its aims, and for the Council of Europe in general.

In December 2008 the European Court of Human Rights unanimously declared that indefinite retention of the DNA and fingerprint records of persons who have been arrested but not convicted is illegal. This ruling was expected to have a large impact in the UK, where such retention is standard practice. In September the council's commissioner for human rights, Thomas Hammarberg (Sweden), criticized new UK procedures for handling people who had requested asylum. For more information on activities since 2008, see "Activities," below.

Structure. The Committee of Ministers, comprised of the foreign ministers of all member states, considers all actions required to further the aims of the council. The decisions of the committee take the form either of recommendations to governments or of conventions and agreements, which bind the states that ratify them. The committee normally meets twice a year in Strasbourg. Most of its ongoing work, however, is performed by deputies who meet collectively almost weekly. Overall policy guidance has recently been provided by meetings of the heads of state and government.

The Parliamentary Assembly, the deliberative organ, can consider any matter within the purview of the council. Its conclusions, if they call for action by governments, take the form of recommendations to the Committee of Ministers. The members of the assembly are drawn from national parliaments and apportioned according to population, the states with the smallest populations having 2 seats and those with the largest, 18. (Countries granted Special Guest of the Assembly status have held seats, although without voting power.) The method of delegate selection is left to the national parliaments. Within the assembly all members participate not as state representatives but as individuals or as representatives of political groups; each delegation includes spokesmen from both the government and the opposition.

Assembly committees cover culture, science, and education; economic affairs and development; environment, agriculture, and local and regional affairs; equal opportunities for women and men; honoring of obligations and commitments by member states; legal affairs and human rights; migration, refugees, and demography; political affairs; rules of procedure and immunities; and social, health, and family affairs. In addition, a joint committee comprises, in equal numbers, members of the assembly and a representative from each member government. A standing committee comprises the chairs of national delegations, the chairs of the general assembly committees, and the Bureau of the Assembly (the assembly president, 18 vice presidents, and leaders of the political groups). The president of the assembly is elected annually for a renewable term; normally he serves a total of three years.

Part of the council's work is carried out by specialized institutions, such as the European Court of Human Rights, the Commissioner for Human Rights, the European Youth Foundation, the European Center for Global Interdependence and Solidarity (the North-South Center), the Social Development Fund, and the Congress of Local and Regional Authorities of Europe.

The council's many parliamentary, ministerial, and governmental committees and subsidiary groups are serviced by a Secretariat staffed by some 1,800 recruits from all member countries. The secretary general is elected by the assembly for renewable, five-year terms from a list of candidates proposed by the Committee of Ministers.

Recent Activities. The June 2009 Parliamentary Assembly, meeting in Strasbourg, saw one of the most serious disagreements in the organization's history. With the term of office of the current secretary general, Terry Davis, due to expire on August 31, the assembly was presented with two candidates chosen by the Committee of Ministers. In the past the assembly had always chosen its own candidates. Declining to vote on the Committee of Ministers' nominees, the assembly struck the election of a new secretary general from its agenda, and the meeting ended with no replacement for Davis selected. At the same meeting the assembly agreed to reinstate the special guest status of Belarus, if that country agreed to a moratorium on executions. Fruitless discussions with Belarus continued through 2010. A new Secretary General was not elected until September 29, 2009, in the person of Thorbjørn Jagland of Norway.

In early 2010 Russia finally ratified Protocol 14, which came into force on June 1 of that year. Russia also called for the breakaway Georgian regions of Abkhazia and South Ossetia to become members of the Council of Europe, before Council monitors could operate there. In May Macedonia took over the presidency of the council, with Greece objecting to Macedonia, calling its role the "Macedonian Presidency." In December 2010 the Council hosted a special conference in Istanbul on "Prevention of Terrorism." The purpose of the two-day meeting was to get Council members to reflect on improving efforts to combat terrorism and fight against the human rights atrocities committed by terrorists. Similarly, in April 2011 the Council of Europe hosted a special meeting of the UN Security Council on terrorism. The meeting focused on international efforts to end terrorism, preventative policies, and the increased utilization of law enforcement and criminal justice to stop terrorism.

In keeping with its emphasis on human rights, 2011 brought about several opportunities for the Parliamentary Assembly to discuss violations of its key premises. Belarus continues to use the death penalty and remains on suspension for failure to institute a moratorium on the death penalty. The execution of two Belarusian terrorists in November prompted another outcry from the Parliamentary Assembly. Similarly, the late 2011 confirmation of a secret CIA-run prison in Romania has prompted many in the Parliamentary Assembly to call for justice and action against those responsible for the cover up of the prison.

The emphasis on Human Rights was continued through the British chairmanship of the Council of Europe's Committee of Ministers from November 2011 to May 2012. On several occasions, human rights were named as the primary concern of the British chairmanship. This priority was evident through the high level conference held in April 2012 to address the future of the Human Rights Court and ways to reform it so as to give it more power and called on member states to create a national human rights institution in each state. At the May 2012 Committee of Ministers biannual meeting, the British chair again advocated human rights as a primary concern by taking many of the ideas from the April conference and enacting them to ensure that the European Convention on Human Rights remains strongly enforced across the entire council. In June 2012, Albania announced that during its six-month tenure as chair of the Committee of Ministers, it too was going to pursue a human-rights-focused agenda.

In addition to human rights, Albania also focused its efforts on unity throughout the region. At a November 2011 conference entitled "Diversity in Europe," Albania emphasized the importance of educating youth about the strengths of diversity and the opportunities for dialogue with the Mediterranean states. Albania also took steps to promote democratic societies and the rule of law within Europe.

During its chairmanship, Andorra continued the conversation about education started by Albania. From November 2012 to May 2013, the Council of Europe held three education-related conferences, discussing issues of democratic civic education, educational competencies, and the role of government in education. Also during Andorra's tenure, the organization passed the 15th protocol of the European Convention on the Protection of Human Rights. The protocol was opened for signatures in June 2013. As of October 2013, the protocol has been signed by 23 states and ratified by 1.

Picking up with the progress made by Andorra, Armenia welcomed the efforts of PACE to pass Protocol No. 16 of the Convention on the Protection of Human Rights, which was passed by the Committee of Ministers in July. Protocol No. 16 was opened for signatures on October 2. The Committee of Ministers has drafted a Convention against Trafficking in Human Organs, which is under consideration of PACE.

In October 2013, PACE welcomed the UN decision concerning chemical weapons in Syria, but expressed concern that it did nothing to stop the actual war. It also noted that all of those guilty of committing crimes against humanity in Syria should be brought to justice, including being brought before the ICC if necessary.

ECONOMIC COMMUNITY OF WEST AFRICAN STATES (ECOWAS)

Communauté Économique des États de l'Afrique de l'Ouest
Comunidade Económica dos Estados da África Ocidental
(CEDEAO)

Established: By Treaty of Lagos (Nigeria), signed May 28, 1975; amended by Treaty of Cotonou (Benin), signed July 24, 1993; entry into force of the latter announced July 30, 1995.

Purpose: "To promote cooperation and integration leading to the establishment of an economic union in West Africa in order to raise the living standards of its peoples, and to maintain and enhance economic stability, foster relations among member states and contribute to the progress and development of the African Continent."

Headquarters: Abuja, Nigeria.

Principal Organs: Authority of Heads of State and Government, Council of Ministers, Community Parliament, Economic and Social Council, Specialized Technical Commissions, Community Court of Justice, ECOWAS Bank for Investment and Development, ECOWAS Commission.

Web site: www.ecowas.int

ECOWAS Chair: Alassane Ouattara (Côte d'Ivoire).

Commission President: Kadré Désiré Ouedraogo (Burkina Faso).

Membership (15): Benin, Burkina Faso, Cape Verde, Côte d'Ivoire, Gambia, Ghana, Guinea, Guinea-Bissau, Liberia, Mali, Niger, Nigeria, Senegal, Sierra Leone, Togo.

Official Languages: English, French, Portuguese, and "all West African languages so designated by the Authority."

Origin and development. The Economic Community of West African States (ECOWAS) received its greatest impetus from discussions in October 1974 between Gen. Yakubu Gowon of Nigeria and President Gnassingbé Eyadéma of Togo. The two leaders advanced plans for a more comprehensive economic grouping than the purely francophone West African Economic Community (*Communauté Economique de l'Afrique de l'Ouest*—CEAO), which had been recently launched by Côte d'Ivoire, Dahomey (later Benin), Mali, Mauritania, Niger, Senegal, and Upper Volta (later Burkina Faso). The treaty establishing ECOWAS was signed by representatives of 15 West African states on May 28, 1975, in Lagos, Nigeria, and by the end of June had been formally ratified by enough signatories (seven) to become operative. However, it took until November 1976 for an agreement to be worked out on protocols to the treaty. The delay resulted in part from Senegal's effort to make its ratification dependent upon a broadening of the community to include Zaire (later Democratic Republic of the Congo), and several other francophone states of Central Africa. Ultimately, it was decided that any such expansion would be unrealistic. Cape Verde joined in 1977.

Despite beginning with purely economic concerns, ECOWAS shifted its focus with its controversial involvement in the civil war that broke out in Liberia in August 1990. The ECOWAS Monitoring Group (ECOMOG) was formed and sent to Liberia to facilitate a cease-fire, organize an interim government, and oversee the holding of new national elections. A tenuous cease-fire was finally negotiated at an extraordinary summit in late November, but the political situation in Liberia remained chaotic.

In the midst of the Liberian civil war efforts, a special committee was established in 1991 to propose revisions to the ECOWAS treaty. By July 1993 a peace accord (negotiated with United Nations [UN] assistance) was signed by Liberia's warring factions. This appearance of success produced an atmosphere of enthusiasm during the ECOWAS summit in Cotonou, Benin, July 22–24. Hoping to capitalize on the newfound cohesion, the summit signed the Treaty of Cotonou, the special committee's revision of the original Lagos treaty. The new accord was designed to speed up implementation of a regional common market, which would include, progressively, a monetary union, an internal free trade zone (providing for the free movement of people, goods, services, and capital), and a common external tariff and trade policy. This quicker implementation occurred by making summit decisions binding on all members and expanding ECOWAS's political mandate. In addition, a number of new bodies, such as the Community Parliament and the Economic and Social Council, were authorized.

At the conclusion of a summit on July 28–29, 1995, ECOWAS announced that sufficient ratifications had been received for the treaty to enter into effect, although the Community Parliament and Community Court of Justice were not inaugurated until 2000 and 2001, respectively.

The October 1998 ECOWAS summit saw the group of nations move more toward promoting peace and stability in the region. Toward this end, the summit participants agreed to ban the trade in, and manufacture of, small arms throughout ECOWAS and called on other parts of Africa to do the same. The summit also approved a peace accord that ECOWAS representatives had helped negotiate in Guinea-Bissau and that committed the community to providing peacekeeping forces in that country as of early 1999. In what was perhaps the boldest move at the summit, ECOWAS also endorsed a conflict resolution mechanism authorizing it to intervene in the internal affairs of its member states if the security of the region was threatened.

Meanwhile, Mauritania, apparently objecting to moves toward greater military and monetary integration, announced in December 1999 its intention to withdraw from the organization, effective December 2000.

Although ECOWAS failed to achieve a common external tariff by its target of January 2000, in April the English-speaking countries, Gambia, Ghana, Guinea, Liberia, Nigeria, and Sierra Leone, plus Portuguese-speaking Cape Verde, reached an agreement on establishing by 2003 a new West African monetary union in parallel to the francophone West African Economic and Monetary Union (*Union Economique et Monétaire Ouest-Africaine*—UEMOA). In February 2000, apparently setting aside what ECOWAS chair and president of Mali, Alpha Oumar Konare, termed the "anglophone/francophone distractions" that had long impeded economic integration, ECOWAS and the UEMOA agreed to a joint action plan that envisaged, in part, a merger of the UEMOA and the proposed second monetary union into a single zone by 2004. The 2005 summit, however, postponed plans to introduce a common currency by July 1, 2005.

In early July, following the failure of yet another negotiated cease-fire in Liberia, ECOWAS agreed to dispatch several thousand troops to Monrovia, and the resultant ECOWAS Mission in Liberia (ECOMIL) was deployed in August.

In March 2005 ECOWAS launched the Regional Market Systems and Traders' Organizations in West Africa in an effort to improve regional cooperation in trade, with a particular focus on agriculture. The program was seen as the first step toward development of an ECOWAS common agricultural policy. Progress was also reported in regard to the proposed common external tariff for ECOWAS, a key component of the planned free trade area. Meanwhile, on the political front, ECOWAS was active in early 2005 in helping resolve the turmoil in Togo; the community also subsequently assisted in Liberia and Côte d'Ivoire.

At the April 12, 2006, summit, held in Niamey, Niger, the ECOWAS heads of state approved organizational changes to turn its secretariat into a commission to increase efficiency and productivity. ECOWAS leaders approved various efforts to improve members' economies and infrastructure, including moves toward a common airline and a common standard for mobile telephones. On April 12, 2006, the group's trade ministers met in Abuja to evaluate progress toward the second phase of negotiations with the EU on an Economic Partnership Agreement (EPA). This prospective agreement would lead to the creation of a free trade area between the two regions. At that meeting it was also announced that India had extended a $250 million line of credit, repayable over 25 years, for development projects within the group.

At a July 2006 meeting, ECOWAS finalized plans to transform the Executive Secretariat into the Executive Commission. The group would now have a president, a vice president, and seven commissioners, with a limited and well-defined role for each commissioner. Member states would be expected to cede some of their powers to the commission in the interest of faster decision making. The same restructuring was intended to make the Community Parliament more powerful by making its decisions binding on member states. The new arrangement came into effect in February 2007.

In June 2007 ECOWAS leaders met in Abuja to discuss ways of speeding up the group's transition (now long behind schedule) into a border-free zone, and the group set 2020 as a target for full regional integration. In October 2007 the group's Convergence Council commissioned a study on ways to bring about a single currency for West Africa. The ECOWAS standby force, successor to ECOMOG, came into being at the end of 2007, with the appointment of a Nigerian general, Hassan Lai, as chief of staff in November and the holding of maneuvers in Senegal in December.

Late 2007 and early 2008 saw controversy over ECOWAS states signing the proposed EPA with the EU. The original deadline was the end of 2007, but several member states and individual politicians objected, calling the proposed agreement a bad one for the region. They felt that the EPA, rather than helping the region's economies, would open them up to subsidized European goods. At the January 18, 2008, summit in Ouagadougou the matter was put on hold until 2009. An interim agreement was signed in late November 2008, but a full EPA continues to remain stalled as of mid-2013.

The group envisioned travel and migration between ECOWAS states as being relatively free of restriction. In 2008 the ECOWAS passport was close to full implementation, but on several occasions trouble arose between migrant groups and residents of countries. Nevertheless, ECOWAS passports are currently issued by 10 of the 15 member countries: Benin, Côte d'Ivoire, Ghana, Guinea, Liberia, Niger, Nigeria, Senegal, Sierra Leone, and Togo. For more on activities since 2008, see "Recent Activities," below.

Structure. The basic structure of ECOWAS consists of the Authority of Heads of State and Government; the Council of Ministers comprised of two representatives from each member; the ECOWAS Commission, which is headed by a commission president that is assisted by a vice president and fifteen commissioners; the Community Court of Justice, which settles disputes arising under the treaty; the Economic and Social Council; and eight specialized technical commissions. These commissions are Administration and Finance; Food and Agriculture; Environment and Natural Resources; Human Resources, Information, and Social and Cultural Affairs; Industry, Science and Technology, and Energy; Political, Judicial, and Legal Affairs and Regional Security and Integration; Trade, Customs, Taxation, Statistics, Money, and Payments; and Transport, Communications, and Tourism. The ECOWAS Community Parliament of 120 national representatives began its inaugural session in November 2000 in Abuja. The Community Court of Justice was inaugurated in January 2001. The Council of Elders was formed in July 2001.

The Treaty of Lagos authorized creation of the Fund for Cooperation, Compensation, and Development (FCCD), supported by members' contributions, the revenues of community enterprises, and grants from non-ECOWAS countries. In addition to financing mutually approved projects, the fund, headquartered in Lomé, Togo, was established to compensate members who suffered losses due to the establishment of community enterprises or the liberalization of trade. Upon ratification of treaty changes approved by the heads of state in December 2001, the FCCD was reconfigured as the ECOWAS Bank for Investment and Development (EBID), which has the broader mission of financing private investment in infrastructure and such public sector activities as poverty reduction.

Recent Activities. In more recent developments, a special summit held January 10, 2009, condemned the December coup in Guinea, and suspended that country from all ECOWAS meetings until constitutional order was restored. It appeared that discussions between ECOWAS and the Guinea regime were being fruitful. But the group's chair-in-office, Nigerian president Umaru Musa Yar'Adua, called on member states to avoid working at cross-purposes in helping Guinea.

ECOWAS had been active in trying to maintain constitutional peace in Guinea-Bissau since the November 2008 attempted assassination of that country's president João Bernardo Vieira. Following a successful attempt on Vieira's life by renegade soldiers in March 2009, an ECOWAS mission visited Guinea-Bissau, where senior military officers assured them that the murder was not part of a coup. Commission president Mohammed ibn Chambas noted that "the lack of serious security sector reform" had long been a major problem in Guinea-Bissau, and Chambas hoped the issue would now be comprehensively addressed.

The June 21, 2009, summit, held in Abuja, was noteworthy in that it incorporated a special ECOWAS-Spain summit. Spanish prime minister Jose Luis Zapatero led a delegation to discuss strengthening cooperation between Spain and ECOWAS, a situation that would be "to the mutual benefit of both the sub-region and the Kingdom of Spain given its proximity to Africa." The ECOWAS summit otherwise called on all member states to work harder on regional economic integration. Yar'Adua also called on member states to continue pushing forward the peace process in Guinea and Guinea-Bissau. He noted that thanks to ECOWAS efforts, elections would shortly be held in Guinea-Bissau, and later, he hoped, in Guinea.

In June 2009 ECOWAS announced that a Common Mining Code for its members would be in place by the end of 2012. In October 2009 ECOWAS suspended Niger after its president, Mamadou Tandja, held an election widely regarded as illegal. In December ECOWAS declared it no longer recognized Tandja as Niger's president. Tandja was subsequently removed by a military coup, with presidential elections set for January 2011. Under ECOWAS pressure Guinea held elections in June 2010.

In August defense chiefs of ECOWAS and the Community of Portuguese-Speaking Countries (CPLP) announced a plan to help Guinea-Bissau become more stable. In May 2010 ECOWAS was able to congratulate Togo on a presidential decree that, after long negotiation, set up an inclusive government.

The February 15, 2010, summit, held in Abuja, appointed Victor Gbeho of Ghana to replace Mohammed Ibn Chambas as president. Chambas had resigned to take another job, and Beyu was to fill out his term, ending in December 2010. Acting Nigerian president Goodluck Jonathan presided over the meeting, in place of President Umaru Yar'Adu who, due to ill health, could not host the summit in person.

Much of the March 2011 summit, held in Abuja, Nigeria, centered on the situation in Libya, the progress toward democracy made by several member states (namely Guinea, Niger, and Burkina Faso), and, most significantly, the stalled progress of the EPA between ECOWAS and the EU. The ECOWAS Commission used 2011 as an opportunity to emphasize the importance of monetary integration and further improvements to both the financial progress of the member states and the safety and progress of nations' infrastructures.

In January 2012, a group of rebels began an attack against the government of Mali. On March 22, Mali President Amadou Toure was removed from office in an armed coup. Mali was suspended from ECOWAS on April 2, and a mediator was appointed by the organization to help seek a peaceful transition of power. Following the signing of the April 6 framework agreement on the transition back to constitutional order in Mali, the sanctions were lifted. Similarly, a military coup in Guinea-Bissau in early April resulted in sanctions being levied by ECOWAS at an emergency session of the Heads of State held in late April to deal with the burgeoning situations in Guinea-Bissau and Mali.

The June summit meetingprimarily focused on security concerns in the region. While they lifted their sanctions on Guinea Bissau, they still expressed concern over Mali. The situation in Mali remained a major priority as the Authority voted in support of accelerating the deployment of its standby force to the country. The continual terrorist attacks in Mali also resulted in new sanctions being placed on those hindering the ECOWAS work in Mali. Another decision to come from the summit was a move to expand the ECOWAS Commission from nine commissioners to twelve.

At its semi-annual meeting held February 27–28, the ECOWAS Authority again focused on security concerns and political unrest, namely in Mali and Guinea-Bissau. In regard to the still ongoing terrorist attacks, ECOWAS further denounced them and reinforced its commitment to the troops for around the region that are deployed in Mali to help stabilize the region. They also announced their continued support for the efforts made by the transitional government to move the country toward elections. Concerning Guinea Bissau, the Authority echoed its call for the government to produce a roadmap for transition and extended their transitional period until the end of the year. They also asked for the African Union to lift their sanctions on the transitional state. Also occurring at the meeting, the heads of state again voted to expand the Commission from 12 to 15. The summer meeting of the authority was again concerned with issues in Guinea Bissau and Mali, but expressed its support and commendation for upcoming elections in both states.

Efforts to bring ECOWAS under a common currency within a common economic union continue to progress and were discussed at both meetings of the Authority in 2013. A decision, however, by the ECOWAS Convergence Council called on the organization to revise its timetable for full integration of the single currency.

EUROPEAN FREE TRADE ASSOCIATION (EFTA)

Established: By convention signed January 4, 1960, in Stockholm, Sweden, effective May 3, 1960; updated convention signed June 21, 2001, in Vaduz, Liechtenstein, with entry into force on June 1, 2002.

Purpose: Initially, to promote economic expansion, full employment, and higher standards of living through elimination of barriers to nonagricultural trade among member states; more recently, to expand trade and other cooperation relations with external countries and to further European integration through a single European Economic Area, extending not only to free trade, but also to deregulation, removal of technical and nontariff barriers to trade, and cooperation with the European Union in the service and agricultural sectors as well as industry.

Headquarters: Geneva, Switzerland.

Principal Organs: Council, EFTA Council Committees, Consultative Committee, EFTA Surveillance Authority, EFTA Court, Secretariat.

Web site: www.efta.int

Secretary General: Kristinn F. Árnason (Iceland).

Membership (4): Iceland, Liechtenstein, Norway, Switzerland.

Working Language: English.

Origin and development. EFTA was established under British leadership in 1959–1960 as the response of Europe's so-called outer seven states (Austria, Denmark, Norway, Portugal, Sweden, Switzerland, United Kingdom) to the creation of the original six-state European Economic Community (EEC). With the breakdown of negotiations to establish a single, all-European free trade area encompassing both groups, the seven decided to set up a separate organization that would enable the non-EEC states both to maintain a unified position in further bargaining with the "inner six" and to carry out a modest liberalization of trade within their own group, provided for in the establishment of the 1960 EFTA Convention (the Stockholm Convention). Finland became an associate member of EFTA in 1961; Iceland joined as the eighth full member in 1970. At the start of 1973, however, Denmark and the United Kingdom withdrew upon joining the European Community (EC).

Unlike the EEC, EFTA was not endowed with supranational features. It was not designed to establish a common market or common external tariff, but merely to eliminate internal trade barriers on nonagricultural goods. This objective was met at the end of 1966, three years ahead of schedule. A second goal, a comprehensive agreement permitting limited access to EC markets, led to completion of various trade pacts, the first of which became effective January 1, 1973, concurrent with the initial round of EC expansion.

Following enlargement of the EC, a further range of activity was unofficially added to the EFTA agenda, and cooperation was extended to more diverse economic matters than the trade concerns specified in the Stockholm Convention, including such areas as raw materials, monetary policy, inflation, and unemployment.

Organized outside EFTA's institutional framework, the first summit in 11 years convened in May 1977 in Vienna, Austria, and adopted the Vienna Declaration, which prescribed a broad framework for future activities. It included, for example, a resolution calling upon EFTA to become a "forum for joint consideration of wider European and world-wide economic problems in order to make a constructive contribution to economic cooperation in international fora." In pursuit of this goal, a multilateral free trade agreement between the EFTA countries and Spain was signed in 1979 in Madrid, while in 1982 concessions were extended to permit Portugal to expand its industrial base prior to joining the EC. Cooperation between EFTA and the EC/European Union (EU) continued to grow based on general guidelines promulgated in the 1984 Luxembourg Declaration, which endorsed the development of a European Economic Space (EES) including all EFTA and EC countries. The accord called for the reduction of nontariff barriers; more joint research and development projects; and exploratory talks in such areas as transportation, agriculture, fishing, and energy. In an effort to reduce border formalities, EFTA reached agreement with the EC on the use of a simplified customs form, the Single Administrative Document (SAD), to cover trade within and between the two groups. The SAD convention was the first direct agreement between EFTA and the EC. Both the SAD accord and a related convention on common transit procedures became effective on January 1, 1988.

Two years earlier, at the start of 1986, Portugal had left EFTA to join the EC, at which time Finland rose to full EFTA membership. Liechtenstein, which previously participated as a nonvoting associate member by virtue of its customs union with Switzerland, was admitted as a full member in May 1991.

An EFTA summit in June 1990 again strongly endorsed the EES concept, and formal EC-EFTA discussions immediately began, but the negotiations proved much more difficult than anticipated. The major sticking points were EFTA's request to exempt many of its products from EC guidelines and an inability to agree on a structure through which EFTA could influence EC decision making. Some progress, particularly in regard to the exemptions issue, was reported at a special December session called to "reinvigorate" talks on the European Economic Area (EEA), as the EES had been renamed at the EC's request. In addition, negotiations in early May 1991 resolved many of the remaining disagreements, with a preliminary accord being signed in October. However, the European Court of Justice mandated the omission of a proposed EEA legal body from the agreement, and a new pact was signed in May 1992.

The EEA was scheduled to go into effect on January 1, 1993, but its final ratification proved contentious. For EFTA the most surprising problem was the rejection of the EEA by a Swiss referendum on December 6, 1992. Despite this, the other EFTA members agreed to pursue the EEA without Switzerland. A protocol to accommodate the change was signed on March 17, 1993, in Brussels, and by late 1993 all the EC states and the remaining EFTA countries had completed their ratification procedures. As finally launched on January 1, 1994, the EEA provided for greatly expanded freedom of movement of goods, services, capital, and labor among the (then) 17 participating nations, home to a population of some 372 million. After negotiating amendment of its customs and monetary union with Switzerland that caused deferred membership, Liechtenstein became the 18th EEA member on May 1, 1995.

For four EFTA member states the EEA arrangement was regarded as a stepping stone to full EU membership, Austria having submitted its application as early as July 1989, with Finland, Norway, and Sweden following suit in 1991–1992. Negotiations with all four applicants were completed by early 1994, and referendums later in the year in Austria, Finland, and Sweden approved EU membership. However, Norwegian voters voted "no" on the proposal, as they had once before in 1972. Consequently, an EFTA ministerial session in December 1994 in Geneva decided that EFTA would continue to function, even though its membership was to fall as of January 1, 1995, to four countries with a total population of scarcely more than 11 million.

In addition to its focus on the EEA, EFTA has devoted considerable energy to expanding other external ties. An EFTA ministerial session in June 1995 saw representatives of the three Baltic republics (Estonia, Latvia, and Lithuania) express interest in negotiating free trade agreements, which formally entered into effect in 1996–1997. EFTA already had similar arrangements with Bulgaria, the Czech Republic, Hungary, Israel, Poland, Romania, Slovakia, Slovenia, and Turkey. Additional free trade agreements were reached with Morocco and the Palestine Liberation Organization (PLO) in 1997 and 1998, respectively.

Meeting in June 1999 in Lillehammer, Norway, the EFTA ministers called for the Stockholm Convention to be updated in order to consolidate the EEA regime and a set of agreements between the EU and Switzerland that was about to be concluded.

Work on the proposed convention revisions continued through 2000 and into 2001, with the EFTA Council signing the revised EFTA Convention during its ministerial session in Vaduz, Liechtenstein, on June 21–22, 2001. The Vaduz Convention entered into force on June 1, 2002.

EFTA signed several additional free trade agreements with Macedonia in June 2000, Mexico in November 2000, Croatia and Jordan in June 2001, Singapore in June 2002, and Chile in June 2003 (with effect from February 2004). The agreements with Morocco, the PLO, and Jordan were noteworthy in that they marked a clear decision by the EFTA Council to expand the organization's relationships throughout the Mediterranean region, while the agreement with Mexico marked EFTA's first transatlantic venture, and that with Singapore, the first into the Far East.

Attention in 2002 and the first half of 2003 largely focused on the planned expansion of the EU to 25 members in May 2004. Under the EEA Agreement, all ten new EU members (Cyprus, Czech Republic, Estonia, Hungary, Latvia, Lithuania, Malta, Poland, Slovakia, and Slovenia) were required to negotiate EEA participation. Two principal stumbling blocks quickly emerged: (1) the EU's request that the three EFTA EEA members increase their contributions toward eliminating economic and social disparities in the poorer EU countries (the ten prospective members plus Portugal, Spain, and Greece), and (2) the need to adjust tariff arrangements affecting Poland's significant fishmeal processing industry. Poland argued that a loss of tariff-free fish imports from Iceland and Norway would devastate its fishmeal industry. The EU, however, insisted that a uniform tariff regime had to be maintained.

The final agreement called for Iceland, Liechtenstein, and Norway to provide some $1.4 billion in 2004–2009 for the poorer EU countries, down from the $3 billion that had initially been requested. Poland was forced to concede the tariff issue.

The increasingly integrated relationship between EFTA and the EU advanced in other respects in the early 2000s. At the same time, EFTA ministers also have focused attention on expansion of free trade with non-EU countries. EFTA and the EU have also worked together on a "European Neighborhood Policy," designed to reach out to Eastern European and Mediterranean countries that are currently outside the EEA, and to try to prevent the formation of new barriers. The collapse of World Trade Organization (WTO) talks in late 2006, and difficulties since then in reviving them, led to an increased interest by EFTA in forming bilateral free trade agreements (FTAs) with non-European countries. For more on activities since 2008, see "Recent Activites," below.

Structure. The EFTA Council, the association's principal political organ, consists of one representative from each member state and normally meets two times a year at the ministerial level, twice a month at lower levels. Its responsibilities include supervising the implementation and operation of various free trade agreements and managing relations with the EU. Decisions are generally reached by consensus. Assisting the Council are various standing organs, including the Committee on Customs and Origin Matters, the Consultative Committee (comprising representatives from government and private economic organizations in the member states), the Committee on Technical Barriers to Trade, the Committee of Members of Parliament of EFTA Countries, the Committee of Trade Experts, and the Committee on Third-Country Relations. The latter two and the Council are aided by a number of Expert Groups that provide advice on state aid; public procurement; intellectual property; price compensation; trade procedures; legal issues; and services, investment, and establishment. The EFTA Secretariat opened an office in 1988 in Brussels to facilitate cooperation with the EC. In addition, an Office of the EFTA Statistical Adviser is located in Luxembourg.

EFTA also participates in various bodies in connection with the EEA. The EEA Joint Committee, which brings together EFTA, EU, and European Commission representatives, is the main EEA decision-making organ, while an EEA Council of EU and EFTA ministers offers overall direction. A Standing Committee of the EFTA States (Switzerland participates as an observer) consolidates the position of EFTA members regarding incorporation of EU laws, regulations, and procedures into the EEA. The committee is itself assisted by five subcommittees (Free Movement of Goods, Free Movement of Capital and Services, Free Movement of Persons, Flanking and Horizontal Policies, Legal and Institutional Matters) and some 40 working groups. The EEA Joint Parliamentary Committee, which serves as a forum for EEA issues, brings together 12 members from parliaments of the EEA states and 12 members of the European Parliament. The EEA Consultative Committee focuses on social matters. EFTA has also established its own Brussels-based Surveillance Authority, which monitors implementation of the EEA agreement, and an EFTA Court, sitting in Geneva, as final arbiter of legal disputes.

Recent Activities. At a ministerial meeting on June 22, 2009, in Hamar, Norway, EFTA signed a free trade agreement with the Gulf Cooperation Council, which includes the oil-producing states of Saudi Arabia, Kuwait, United Arab Emirates, Oman, Dubai, Qatar, and Bahrain. The agreement covered goods, services, and government procurement. Additionally, the ministers opened FTA negotiations with Hong Kong and agreed to consider initiating talks with Vietnam and Russia, although Russia's FTA was not expected to be finalized until after WTO accession.

As of October 2009, the EFTA had concluded 18 FTAs with nations and groupings outside the EU. Besides the GCC agreement, the most recent FTAs have been with Columbia in November 2008 and Canada, whose agreement went into force in July, 2009. The Canadian pact centered primarily on exchanging goods. However, it was opposed by the Canadian shipbuilding industry, which feared competition from Norway's strong maritime sector. To cushion the impact, the agreement included a 15-year phase-out of Canadian shipbuilding duties.

Additionally, the EFTA was in talks with Albania, Algeria, India, Indonesia, Peru, Serbia, Thailand, and Ukraine in 2009.

Trade talks with India were launched in 2008 and focused on liberalizing the movement of service suppliers, at India's request, and ensuring intellectual property rights for Swiss pharmaceutical companies. Although initially projected to conclude in 2009, negotiations were extended by disputes over subjecting India's low-cost generic pharmaceutical market to intellectual property restrictions. Norway withdrew from talks, reportedly in protest against Swiss insistence that India abide by stricter rules than those required by the WTO. Nevertheless, trade talks with India continued in September 2009 with a fourth round that focused on agricultural and industrial goods.

EFTA's 2009 annual status report stated that its four nations comprised the world's fifth largest provider of commercial services and the EU's third largest trading partner.

In December 2009 Serbia signed an FTA with EFTA, as did Ukraine in June 2010, for a total of 20 agreements with entities outside the EU. In July Malaysia and EFTA signed a Joint Declaration on Economic Cooperation, considered to be a first step toward a full FTA. In June 2010 Iceland began negotiations for entrance to the EU; on entering the EU it would presumably reduce EFTA to three members.

After Icelandic voters rejected a second referendum to reimburse the Netherlands and the United Kingdom for a $5.44 billion loan after the failure of Iceland's banks (see article on Iceland) on April 9, 2011, the two countries threatened to take Iceland before the EFTA Surveillance Court. The following month, Iceland reported to the EFTA court that assets recovered from bankrupt banks would be used to compensate the two nations. In June EFTA signed an FTA with Hong Kong and China. At EFTA's November summit, the organization finalized an FTA with Montenegro and initiated negotiations with Costa Rica, Honduras, and Panama on similar accords. For 2012 EFTA's operating budget was $20.1 million.

In June 2012, EFTA held its summer ministerial meeting in Gstaad, Switzerland. At the meeting, the ministers of the four member states placed heavy emphasis for the ongoing trade negotiations with various states across the globe. Also at the June meeting, EFTA signed a new joint declaration on cooperation with Georgia. This joint declaration makes Georgia the fortieth country with which EFTA has established a preferential or free trade agreement.

At the November meeting of the EEA Council, most of the group's discussion focused on the continuing financial crisis in Europe. The council reaffirmed its support for ongoing discussions between the EU and EFTA to keep the EEA current with financial legislation in Europe. The group also called on Europe to continue its policies of responsibility and solidarity to weather the crisis. Also at the meeting, the council welcomed Croatia's application for accession to the EEA, which coincides with its July 1, 2013, entry into the EU.

At the summer ministerial meeting, EFTA announced the signing of new free-trade agreements with Bosnia and Herzegovina and several Central American states, including Panama and Costa Rica. In addition, the ministers reaffirmed their commitment to ongoing negotiations with Russia, Belarus, Kazakhstan, Vietnam, Malaysia, and Serbia. The ministers, while expressing continued concern about the economic situation in Europe, also noted its support of the joint efforts between EFTA and the EU to keep the EEA current and effective. They congratulated the organization on the 500 legal acts that were incorporated into the EEA in 2012 alone.

In 2013, more than 300 new legal acts were added to the EEA Agreement. These acts included new regulations and directives concerning issues such as the implementation of the new ".eu" web domain, trading illegally harvested timber, vehicle emissions, clean air, air travel, veterinary issues, the transfer of defense-related products, and business registration. EFTA's operating budget for the year was $22.3 million.

THE EUROPEAN UNION (EU)

Established: European Coal and Steel Community (ECSC) created by treaty signed in Paris, France, April 18, 1951, effective July 24, 1952; European Economic Community (EEC) and European Atomic Energy Community (Euratom) created by Treaties of Rome, signed March 25, 1957, in Rome, Italy, effective January 1, 1958; common institutions of the three European Communities (EC) established by Merger Treaty signed April 8, 1965, in Brussels, Belgium, effective July 1, 1967; European Union (EU) created by Treaty on European Union, initialed by the heads of state and government of the 12 members of the EC on December 11, 1991, in Maastricht, Netherlands, signed by the ECforeign and finance ministers on February 7, 1992, and entered into force November 1, 1993. (The ECSC terminated upon expiry of its founding treaty on July 23, 2002.)

Purpose: To strengthen economic and social cohesion; to establish an economic and monetary union, including a single currency; to implement a common foreign and security policy; to introduce a citizenship of the European Union; to develop close cooperation on justice and home affairs.

Headquarters: Brussels, Belgium. (Some bodies have headquarters elsewhere.)

Principal Organs: European Council (heads of state or government of all members), Council of the European Union (all members), Commission of the European Communities (referred to in all but legal and formal contexts as the European Commission—27 members), European Parliament (736 elected representatives), Court of Justice of the European Communities (informally, the European Court of Justice—27 judges and 8 advocates general), Court of Auditors (27 members, including its president plus a secretary general), European Central Bank.

Web site: http://europa.eu/index_en.htm

Presidency of the Council of the European Union: Rotates every six months among the member states, with the full presidency being formed from a trio of three consecutive presidencies (Ireland, from January 2013; Lithuania, from July 2013; Greece, from January 2014; Italy, from July 2014).

President of the European Council: Herman Van Rompuy (Belgium).

President of the European Commission: José Manuel Durão Barroso (Portugal).

President of the European Parliament: Martin Schulz (Germany).

President of the European Court of Justice: Vassilios Skouris (Greece).

President of the Court of Auditors: Vitor Manuel da Silva Caldeira (Portugal).

President of the European Central Bank: Mario Draghi (Italy).

Members (27): Austria, Belgium, Bulgaria, Cyprus, Czech Republic, Denmark, Estonia, Finland, France, Germany, Greece, Hungary, Ireland, Italy, Latvia, Lithuania, Luxembourg, Malta, Netherlands, Poland, Portugal, Romania, Slovakia, Slovenia, Spain, Sweden, United Kingdom.

Official Languages (23): Bulgarian, Czech, Danish, Dutch, English, Estonian, Finnish, French, German, Greek, Hungarian, Irish, Italian, Latvian, Lithuanian, Maltese, Polish, Portuguese, Romanian, Slovak, Slovenian, Spanish, Swedish.

Note: The European Union (EU) is the most recent expansion of a process of European integration that was first formalized by the creation of the European Coal and Steel Community (ECSC) in 1952 and then expanded in 1958 by the launching of the European Economic Community (EEC, also known as the Common Market) and the European Atomic Energy Community (Euratom). Especially after entry into force in 1967 of the Merger Treaty, which established "Common Institutions" for the three European Communities, they were referred to as a singular European Community (EC). On November 1, 1993, the Treaty on European Union (also known as the Maastricht Treaty) added two new "pillars" of cooperation—foreign and security policy, and justice and home affairs—to the original pillar created by establishment of the EEC. At that time "EU" became the familiar designation for all three pillars. The Maastricht Treaty also amended the EEC's founding document to replace the term "European Economic Community" with the more encompassing "European Community," reflecting the first pillar's evolution beyond economic matters. The ECSC was terminated when its treaty expired July 23, 2002, but the EC (that is, what was originally the EEC) continues to exist (as does Euratom) and in fact remains legally distinct from the EU despite sharing organs. Thus, references to EC activity are still correct (and even required) in some legal and other formal situations, but common practice has favored the use of "EU" as an umbrella, particularly given what EU officials themselves have described as "the difficulties of delineating what is strictly EC or EU business." The Treaty of Lisbon (Reform Treaty) signed in December 2007 and effective December 2009, brings the three pillars even closer together, as suggested by a provision that renames the 1958 founding treaty of the EC as the Treaty on the Functioning of the European Union.

Origin and development. The formation of the European Communities was one of the most significant expressions of the movement toward European unity that grew out of the moral and material devastation of World War II. For many Europeans, the creation of a United States of Europe seemed to offer the best hope of avoiding a repetition of that catastrophe. Other influences included fear of aggression by the Union of Soviet Socialist Republics (USSR) and practical experience in economic cooperation gained by administering Marshall Plan aid through the Organization for European Economic Cooperation (OEEC).

These elements converged in a 1950 proposal by French foreign minister Robert Schuman that envisaged a common market for coal and steel that would, among other things, serve as a lasting guarantee of European peace by forging an organic link between France and Germany. Although the United Kingdom declined to participate in the project, the governments of France, the Federal Republic of Germany, Italy, Belgium, the Netherlands, and Luxembourg agreed to put the Schuman Plan into effect through the ECSC treaty, which they signed April 18, 1951, in Paris, France, and which entered into effect July 24, 1952. The original institutional structure of the ECSC, whose headquarters was established in Luxembourg, included a council of ministers, an executive high authority, a parliamentary assembly, and a court of justice.

The ECSC pioneered the concept of a European common market by abolishing price and transport discrimination and eliminating customs duties; quota restrictions; and other trade barriers on coal, steel, iron ore, and scrap. Common markets for coal, steel, iron ore, and scrap were established in 1953 and 1954. Concurrently, steps were taken to harmonize external tariffs on these products. In addition, community-wide industrial policy was facilitated through short- and long-term forecasts of supply and demand, investment guidance and coordination, joint research programs, and regional development assistance. These activities were financed by a direct levy on community coal and steel, the level being fixed by the commission in consultation with the European Parliament.

The next decisive stage in the development of the European Communities was reached with the signature on March 25, 1957, in Rome, Italy, of the Treaties of Rome, which established as separate organizations the EEC and Euratom, effective January 1, 1958. (By convention, "Treaty of Rome," in the singular, references just the EEC; for a detailed discussion of Euratom, see the end of the EU article.) Two types of national linkage to the EEC were detailed: full membership, under which an acceding state agreed to the basic principles of the Treaty of Rome, and associate membership, involving the establishment of agreed reciprocal rights and obligations in regard to such matters as commercial policy.

Although Euratom and the EEC from their inception shared the Assembly and Court of Justice already operating under the ECSC, they initially had separate, albeit similar, councils of ministers and commissions. Subsequently, a treaty establishing a single Council of Ministers (formally renamed as the Council of the European Union in 1993) and commission for all three communities was signed by the (then) six member governments (Belgium, France, Federal Republic of Germany, Italy, Luxembourg, Netherlands) on April 8, 1965, in Brussels, Belgium. However, application of the treaty's provisions was delayed by prolonged disagreement about selecting a president to head the newly merged commission. The choice of Jean Rey of Belgium was ultimately approved, and the new institutions were formally established as of July 1, 1967.

During this period the central issues of the communities—the sharing of authority by member governments and the communities' main administrative organs, and expansion through admission of additional European states—could be most clearly observed in the EEC, whose rapid development included a series of crises in which the French government, with its special concern for national sovereignty and its mistrust of supranational endeavors, frequently opposed the other members.

The crucial issue of national sovereignty versus community authority was tested by a year-long French boycott of all three communities that ended after an intergovernmental understanding was accepted that restricted the independent authority of the commission to establish and execute community policy.

The membership issue had first been brought to the forefront by the decision of the United Kingdom in July 1961 to apply for admission to the EEC on condition that arrangements could be made to protect the interests of other Commonwealth states, the other members of the European Free Trade Association (EFTA), and British agriculture. France initially blocked the bid in early 1963 on the general ground that the United Kingdom was too close to the United States and not sufficiently European in outlook. A formal UK application for membership in the three communities was submitted in May 1967, with similar bids subsequently being advanced by Ireland, Denmark, and Norway. Action was again blocked by French opposition, despite support for British accession by the commission and the other five member states. Further negotiations for British, Irish, Danish, and Norwegian membership opened in June 1970, and on January 22, 1972, the treaty of accession and accompanying documents, which provided for expansion to a ten-state organization, were signed in Brussels. Accession was approved by referenda in Ireland (May 11) and Denmark (October 2). However, Norwegian voters, insufficiently placated by concessions offered for the benefit of their state's agricultural and fishing interests, rejected accession in a national referendum held September 24–25. In the case of the United Kingdom, legislation permitting entry was approved by parliament and entered into force October 17, the three accessions becoming effective January 1, 1973. In February 1976 the EC foreign ministers stated that, in principle, they endorsed Greece's request for full membership (an agreement of association was approved in 1962), and a treaty of admission was signed May 28, 1979. Accordingly, Greece became the community's tenth member January 1, 1981.

Negotiations concerning Portuguese and Spanish membership began in October 1978 and February 1979, respectively, but were delayed due to apprehension about their ability to accelerate industrial diversification as well as the projected impact of their large agricultural sectors on the EC's Common Agricultural Policy (CAP; see below). Thus, Portugal and Spain were not formally admitted until January 1, 1986.

From the beginning, the EEC assumed the task of creating a community-wide customs union that would abolish all trade restrictions and establish freedom of movement for all goods, services, labor, and capital. A major part of this task was accomplished by July 1, 1968, a year and a half ahead of the schedule laid down in the Treaty of Rome. All customs duties on community internal trade had been gradually removed, and a common external tariff was ready to be applied in stages. At the end of the community's "transition period"—December 31, 1969—workers became legally free to seek employment in any member state, although in practice the freedom had already existed.

The Treaty of Rome provided steps toward a full economic union of the member states by stipulating common rules to ensure fair competition and coordinated policies governing agriculture, transport, and foreign trade. CAP, centrally financed from a conjoint fund, was put into effect July 1, 1968. The product of extremely complex negotiations, it involved common marketing policies with free trade throughout the community, common price levels for major products, a uniform policy for external trade in agricultural products (including export subsidies), and a program to increase the efficiency of community farming. CAP became, however, a constant source of controversy over ever-growing funding costs. Failed compromise packages of agricultural and budgetary policy reforms—including budget rebates demanded by the United Kingdom—caused the breakup of both the December 1983 and the March 1984 meetings of the ministerial council. European leaders meeting in June 1984 in Fontainebleau, France, finally reached accord on budgetary policy, which included for Britain a guaranteed rebate of two-thirds its net contribution to the community in future years, with EC revenues being enhanced by an increase from 1 percent to 1.4 percent of the value-added tax received from member states.

Agreement was reached in July 1978 for the establishment of a European currency association to include a joint reserve fund to prevent currency fluctuations between member states and a mechanism by which intra-community accounts could be settled by use of European Currency Units (ECUs). The resultant European Monetary System (EMS), which included an Exchange Rate Mechanism (ERM) to limit currency fluctuations, came into effect March 13, 1979. In its first decade the ECU became an attractive medium for the issue of bonds by private and public financial institutions, placing it behind only the U.S. dollar and the German deutsch mark in popularity on the international bond market.

In 1985 the European Commission proposed almost three hundred regulations and directives to eliminate fiscal, physical, or technical barriers to trade. Late in the year the European Council approved a number of reforms, most of which were ultimately included in the Single European Act, which amended the Treaty of Rome in ways intended to streamline the decision-making process, open up more areas to EC jurisdiction, and reinvigorate the movement toward European economic and political cooperation. With tariff barriers to trade among members largely eliminated by 1985, the Single European Act sought to eliminate nontariff barriers when it went into effect on July 1, 1987, following ratification by each EC member state. With an overarching goal of establishing a single internal market by the end of 1992, the act's "1992 program" sought to remove most barriers to the free movement of goods, services, people, and capital within the community, resulting in a single market that would be larger, in terms of population and aggregate gross product, than that of the United States. The powers of the European Parliament also were expanded and a permanent secretariat, headquartered in Brussels, was established to assist the presidency of the Council of the European Communities in implementing a framework of European political cooperation.

Even as the community created a single market, EC summits in July and December 1987 broke up without resolution of a spending deficit that exceeded the members' total budgeted contributions of $35 billion by an additional $6 billion. Disagreement continued to center on the controversial CAP subsidies and large-scale storage of surplus food, which accounted for some 70 percent of EC spending. Britain refused to increase its EC contribution until "financial discipline" had been instituted.

In view of the problems involved, an emergency summit in February 1988 in Brussels, Belgium, achieved remarkable results. The participants established a budget ceiling of 1.3 percent of the EC's GNP, set a cap on future growth of agricultural subsidies, approved cuts in the intervention price for surplus farm commodities, and agreed to double aid to the EC's southern members over a five-year period.

With the agricultural and financial crises averted, the EC turned its attention to the single market plan. Subsequent rapid progress in that regard generated a surprisingly intense "Euro-enthusiasm," but in London, the Margaret Thatcher government continued to serve as a brake on EC momentum, particularly in regard to the monetary union plan proposed in April 1989 by a committee headed by European Commission president Jacques Delors of France. The monetary union proposal, which was distinct from the "1992 program," called for EC members to endorse a three-stage program that would include, among other things, the creation of a regional central bank in the second stage and a common currency in the third stage. Despite strong support from most of the other EC countries, UK resistance necessitated a compromise at the summit held in June in Madrid, Spain. Consensus could be reached only on the first stage of the plan, under which EC members agreed to harmonize certain monetary and economic policies beginning in July 1990. Prime Minister Thatcher agreed to allow preparations to proceed for an EC conference on the much more controversial second and third stages of the plan but, on another matter, she opposed a draft EC charter of fundamental social rights that was supported by the 11 other national leaders, claiming it contained unacceptable "socialist" overtones.

In June 1989 the EC was asked to coordinate Western aid to Poland and Hungary from the Organization for Economic Cooperation and Development (OECD), a program (Poland/Hungary Aid for Restructuring of Economies—PHARE) that was later opened to other Eastern European states. In November, emphasizing the community's expanding political role, a special one-day EC summit in Paris expressed its "responsibility" to support the development of democracy throughout Eastern Europe. At a December summit in Strasbourg, France, EC leaders endorsed German unification provided it included recognition of Europe's postwar borders. In addition, the summit supported the proposed creation of the multibillion-dollar European Bank for Reconstruction and Development (EBRD; see separate article) to assist economic transformation throughout Eastern Europe. In 1991, as a further measure to promote economic and political reform in the countries that emerged from the collapse of the USSR, the EC introduced Technical Assistance to the Commonwealth of Independent States (TACIS).

The EC heads of state met for two-day summits in late April and June 1990 in Dublin, Ireland, to delineate further the community's future role in the "new architecture" of Europe. They declared that East Germany would be incorporated into the EC automatically after the creation of a single German state, gave "qualified" support to West German chancellor Helmut Kohl's call for up to $15 billion in economic assistance to the Soviet Union (seen as a means of reducing Soviet objections to unified Germany's membership in the North Atlantic Treaty Organization), and endorsed a sweeping environmental protection statement. In October 1990 the two Germanies formally unified.

During their December 1990 summit in Rome, the EC heads of state and government formally opened two parallel conferences: one to consider wide-ranging proposals for EC political union and the other to oversee negotiations on the more fully developed monetary union plan. Based on consensus proposals from both conferences, the heads of state and government initialed a Treaty on European Union and numerous related protocols and documents at a pivotal summit on December 9–11, 1991, in Maastricht, Netherlands. The Maastricht Treaty called for establishment of a single currency and regional central bank by 1999 and committed the signatories to the pursuit of "ever closer" political union by adding to the EC two new "pillars": common foreign and security policies, and justice and home affairs. The Maastricht Treaty also authorized the European Council, which had been established in 1974 as an informal forum for discussions among the heads of state or government of the EU members, to provide political guidelines for EU development.

The plans for economic and monetary union were by far the most specific of the treaty's elements. The EU leaders agreed to launch a European Monetary Institute (EMI) on January 1, 1994, directing that the advisory powers of the EMI would eventually be transformed into the formal authority of a European Central Bank (ECB). It was initially envisaged that both the bank and the proposed single currency be operational as early as January 1, 1997, for those countries meeting certain economic criteria and wishing to proceed. However, if that timetable could not be achieved, the single currency was to be established January 1, 1999, and the ECB six months later for qualifying states. A separate "opt-out" protocol gave the United Kingdom the right to make a final decision later on adoption of the single currency, while Germany entered a similar stipulation in ratifying the treaty.

The articles on political union in the Maastricht Treaty were vaguer, although the treaty introduced the concept of EU "citizenship," designed to confer a variety of rights and responsibilities on all nationals of member states. However, in response to growing European concern about turning too much control over to Brussels, draft references to the union's "federal" nature were dropped from the final text of the treaty, which emphasized instead the notion of subsidiarity, under which all decisions would be "taken as closely as possible to the citizens." Regarding the proposed common foreign and security policies, the treaty, in one of its most widely discussed provisions, called for the strengthening of the Western European Union (WEU, see separate article in *Political Handbook of the World* 2011) to "elaborate and implement" defense decisions.

Included in the protocols affiliated with the treaty was a social policy charter that required all EU states (except the United Kingdom) to guarantee a variety of workers' rights. Those provisions were deleted from the treaty proper at the United Kingdom's insistence, with Prime Minister John Major threatening to repudiate the accord otherwise. Negotiations were also required with Greece, Ireland, Portugal, and Spain to ensure their endorsement of the treaty through promises of a substantial expansion of development aid to the so-called poor four.

The EC foreign and finance ministers formally signed the Maastricht Treaty on February 7, 1992, the expectation being that it would proceed smoothly through the required national ratification process in time for its scheduled January 1, 1993, implementation. However, the optimism proved unjustified as Danish voters rejected the treaty by a narrow margin in its first electoral test June 2. Following a strong "yes" majority in the Irish referendum June 18, the treaty was approved without substantial opposition by Greece's and Luxembourg's parliaments in July; however, its future was once again clouded by the September 20 French referendum, which endorsed ratification by only 51 percent. The community was also severely shaken in September by a currency crisis that prompted the United Kingdom and Italy to drop out of the ERM.

Facing an apparent crisis of confidence, the EC leaders convened an emergency summit October 16, 1992, in Birmingham, England, to express their continued support for the Maastricht Treaty while reassuring opponents that some of its more ambitious goals were reduced in scope. Parliamentary approval of the treaty was subsequently achieved by the end of the year in Belgium, Italy, Germany, Netherlands, Portugal, and Spain. Germany's formal ratification was delayed pending the outcome of a constitutional challenge. In addition, the prospect for a reversal of the Danish position improved when the December 1992 EC summit in Edinburgh, Scotland, agreed to extend Denmark several "opt-out" concessions, most importantly regarding the monetary union plan. The EC leaders also agreed to postpone consideration of controversial proposals regarding the free movement of people within the community. Nevertheless, by the target date of January 1, 1993, it was estimated that approximately 80 percent of the provisions of the "1992 program" for establishing a single internal market had been implemented by the member states.

Danish voters accepted the Maastricht accord in a second referendum on May 18, 1993. With the treaty awaiting only UK ratification, the June 1993 EC summit focused on the community's economic woes, which were contributing as much as any of the other problems to a growing "Euro-pessimism." In particular, the summit proposed measures designed to reduce unemployment, which was above 10 percent in the community. Although French president Mitterrand attempted to portray the session as marking a "psychological recovery" for the EC, the community shortly thereafter experienced another currency crisis. Faced with a possible total breakdown of the ERM, the EC agreed in early August to let the franc and the six other non-German currencies still in the system float more freely against the mark.

UK ratification, albeit by a very narrow margin, occurred in July 1993, and a favorable ruling in the German court case in early October finally cleared the way for implementation of the treaty. The EC heads of state and government held a special summit October 29 in Brussels to celebrate the completion of the ratification process, and the EU was launched when the treaty officially went into force November 1.

The first EU summit was held December 11–12, 1993, in Brussels. The EU heads of state and government turned to the region's economic problems, particularly that of continued high unemployment. The summit adopted an economic recovery plan that appeared to represent a compromise between those advocating activist labor policies and those convinced that government influence was already too great in economic affairs. For the first camp, the summit approved a six-year public works program designed to create jobs in, among other areas, the transportation, energy, environmental, and telecommunications sectors. For those looking to the free market to resolve unemployment, the summit called for a reduction in "rigidities" in the European labor market, proposing that minimum wages be lowered and that labor costs supporting European social welfare programs be significantly reduced.

In other activity, the European Council endorsed negotiations toward a "stability pact" for Central and Eastern European nations seeking EU membership. The pact would attempt to establish agreement on the protection of minority rights in those countries and create mechanisms for the peaceful resolution of border disputes. Among other things, it was hoped that such an initiative would prevent a repetition of the breakdown that had occurred in the former Yugoslavia, the EU having been criticized for its seeming paralysis in dealing with that situation.

The European Council once again emphasized economic affairs during its June 24–25, 1994, summit in Corfu, Greece, one formal highlight of which was the signing of the Partnership and Cooperation

Agreement with Russia. Nevertheless, media reports centered on the union's latest political difficulty—the failure of the council to agree on a successor to commission president Delors, who announced his retirement effective January 1, 1995. After the United Kingdom rejected the nomination of Belgian prime minister Jean-Luc Dehaene, whom it deemed as too "federalist," a special summit was convened on July 15 in Brussels to approve a compromise nominee—Jacques Santer, the prime minister of Luxembourg. Nominees to the new commission subsequently faced intense confirmation hearings in the parliament, reflecting divisions between those in favor of rapid integration and an increasingly vocal group of "Euro-skeptics."

As members of the EFTA participating in the European Economic Area (EEA) with the EU, Austria, Finland, Norway, and Sweden had been formally invited in the spring of 1994 to join the EU at the beginning of 1995. Austria's membership was endorsed by a 66 percent "yes" vote June 12, 1994, while a positive vote also was obtained in the Finnish referendum October 16 and in Swedish balloting November 13. In contrast, Norway voted decisively against EU accession in its referendum during November 27–28. Switzerland's membership remained on file after Swiss voters rejected EEA membership in a 1992 referendum. More recently, in May 2001, Swiss voters decisively rejected applying for EU membership, although the country had entered into various economic agreements with the EU.

The focus of the December 9–10, 1994, summit in Essen, Germany, was on enlargement, with the heads of state of Austria, Finland, and Sweden participating in preparation for the accession of those countries January 1, 1995. The leaders of Bulgaria, the Czech Republic, Hungary, Poland, Slovakia, and Romania also attended the summit to discuss in greater detail the criteria for eventual admission. However, despite the obvious external fervor for the EU, enthusiasm within the union subsequently appeared to wane, particularly in regard to the common currency proposal. Turbulence in the financial markets contributed to an acknowledgment by the European Council, which met June 26–27, in Cannes, France, that the proposed single currency would not be launched in 1997. The summit held December 15–16, 1995, in Madrid reaffirmed the EU's commitment to a 1999 final target date, although it was emphasized that the required economic standards would not be diluted for participation in the monetary union. The EU leaders also agreed that the new currency would be called the euro.

The December 1995 summit also gave formal approval for creation of an intergovernmental conference (IGC) that was authorized to propose revisions to the EC/EU founding treaties. Issues to be addressed included the possible elimination of the unanimity requirement for decisions involving the EU's two new pillars—foreign and security policy, and justice and home affairs. Potentially extensive structural changes were also to be considered in the hope that such bodies as the commission and the parliament could become less unwieldy, particularly given the anticipated admission of new members to the union. In addition, ardent integrationists hoped institutional reforms would convince a still largely skeptical European population that the EU was prepared to deal effectively with basic day-to-day concerns such as unemployment, environmental degradation, and internal security.

Although the IGC was launched in March 1996, little progress was apparent by the time of the June 21–22 summit in Florence, Italy. EU leaders reportedly hoped to provide a boost for the initiative at the summit, but the session was instead dominated by the conflict between the United Kingdom and its EU partners over the EU's March ban on exports of UK beef and beef products following the outbreak of bovine spongiform encephalopathy (BSE, the so-called mad-cow disease) in UK herds. A compromise was quickly reached. Much more problematic, however, was the strong UK response to the ban, the government of John Major having instituted a policy of "noncooperation" in May under which the UK veto was briefly used to block all EU action requiring unanimity.

Attention subsequently focused on negotiations regarding the monetary union. German leaders indicated that the entire concept was in jeopardy unless other nations were willing to accept enforceable budgetary discipline as a means of keeping the euro "strong." Bonn's proposed "stability and growth pact" on the matter reportedly met with strong French resistance prior to the EU summit held December 13–14, 1996, in Dublin. However, a compromise favoring the German position was negotiated whereby participants in the monetary union would be subject to mandatory heavy financial penalties for breaching fiscal guidelines. Agreement also was reached on the creation of a new exchange rate mechanism to determine the relationship of the euro to the currencies of the countries that postponed entry into the monetary union.

A special heads of government summit May 23, 1997, in Noordwijk, Netherlands, was buoyed by the presence of the new UK prime minister, Tony Blair, whose Labour government was decidedly more enthusiastic about the EU than its Conservative Party predecessor. A meeting of the European Council on June 16–17, in Amsterdam, Netherlands, endorsed wide-ranging amendment of the various EC and EU treaties in the interest of broadening the purview of the EU and speeding up the decision-making process. Among other things, the proposed Amsterdam Treaty provided for formal inclusion in the EC/EU treaty structure of (1) the Social Charter (previously relegated to protocol status); (2) a new employment chapter; (3) the Schengen Accord regarding free movement of people and goods across internal EU borders; and (4) the stability and growth pact, designed to enforce budgetary discipline on those countries joining the Economic and Monetary Union (EMU). The treaty also removed several policy areas from national control in favor of "common" EU authority, while some additional areas already governed by the EU were moved into the category of requiring approval by Qualified Majority Voting (QMV) rather than unanimous national consent. Agreement also was reached, in principle, on giving the European Parliament additional authority and on limiting the size of the commission following expansion of EU membership.

Despite the perceived weakness of the Amsterdam Treaty, its completion did permit the EU to turn to its two other pressing issues: enlargement and the monetary union. Regarding the former, a December 12–13, 1997, summit in Luxembourg invited five ex-communist states—the Czech Republic, Estonia, Hungary, Poland, and Slovenia—as well as Cyprus, to begin formal membership discussions in March 1998. The inclusion of Cyprus among the "first-wave" countries was controversial, particularly because Turkey was pointedly excluded. EU officials said they hoped that both the Cypriot and Turkish communities on Cyprus would participate in the membership negotiations, although the government of the Turkish Republic of Northern Cyprus declined.

Ireland approved the Amsterdam Treaty via national referendum in late May 1998, and Danish voters followed suit shortly thereafter with a 55 percent endorsement. The latter was considered an important test in light of the problems caused in 1993 by the initial Danish rejection of the Maastricht Treaty.

On March 26, 1998, Germany had officially endorsed the January 1999 EMU launching, despite the German Bundesbank's having questioned the "sustainability" of the financial status of several countries, with Belgium and Italy drawing particular attention because of their high level of official debt. In April the European Parliament called for treaty revisions to ensure the "accountability" of the incoming ECB, suggesting that a monitoring body (including several parliament members) be established to review ECB decisions and activity. An EU summit May 1–3 in Brussels formally agreed that the ECB would open June 1 and would assume responsibility at the start of 1999 for monitoring policy (including setting interest rates) for the countries adopting the euro.

Thus the currencies of the 11 participating countries—Austria, Belgium, Finland, France, Germany, Ireland, Italy, Luxembourg, Netherlands, Portugal, and Spain—were permanently linked with the initiation of the EMU on January 1, 1999, at which time the participants also began issuing debt in euros. The formal launch was marked by great fanfare, with supporters describing it as representing the "biggest leap forward" since the Treaty of Rome. Two years later, Greece, which had initially failed to qualify on the basis of economic performance, became the 12th EMU member. On January 1, 2002, euro banknotes and coins for public use were introduced in the 12 EMU members—plus Andorra, Monaco, Montenegro, San Marino, and the Vatican—and commercial use of the old national currencies was discontinued by the end of February 2002. During the ten months following the launch of the Euro, the most significant problem facing a number of euro-zone members was keeping fiscal deficits within targeted limits. In November France, Germany, and Portugal were all cited for failure to reduce deficits to 3 percent, as required by the EMU's stability and growth pact. In 2003, Swedish voters rejected adoption of the euro. On January 1, 2007, Slovenia became the 13th EMU member. In 2007 the European Council noted that Cyprus and Malta had fulfilled the convergence criteria and legal requirements to adopt the euro and could do so on January 1, 2008. The eurozone broadened to 16 states with Slovakia's adoption of the euro on January 1, 2009.

Meanwhile, one of the EU's most serious crises to date had begun to develop over allegations of fraud and corruption in EU budgetary matters. In November 1998 the EU Court of Auditors had reported uncovering serious "mismanagement," and commission president Santer created an internal anti-fraud unit. In mid-January 1999 the European Parliament appeared poised to approve a censure motion that would have forced the resignation of the European Commission. The motion was ultimately defeated (293–232), but only after a "peace package" was negotiated under which the commission agreed to the establishment of an independent panel of experts to assess the situation. In March the panel reported that substantial fraud, mismanagement, and nepotism had "gone unnoticed" by the commissioners, many of whom had "lost control" over spending within their areas of responsibility. Consequently, the commission resigned en masse on March 16, and EU leaders convened in a special summit March 24–26 in Berlin to designate Romano Prodi, former prime minister of Italy, as the next president of the commission. Shortly after the summit, the French legislature ratified the Amsterdam Treaty, paving the way for its entry into force on May 1.

The elections to the European Parliament, held between June 10 and 13, 1999, in the differing venues, were notable in that they led to formation of a 233-seat, center-right bloc by the European People's Party and the European Democrats (EPP-ED), thereby unseating the Party of European Socialists (180 seats) as the plurality grouping. On September 15 the legislature confirmed Prodi as the head of a new European Commission scheduled to serve out the remainder of its predecessor's term and to start a new five-year term beginning in January 2000.

A special two-day session of the heads of government held October 15–16, 1999, in Tampere, Finland, focused on matters related to the EU's third pillar, justice and home affairs, including immigration, asylum, and organized crime. The summit also marked a change in strategy regarding enlargement, with leaders agreeing that negotiations on accession should be opened with six additional prospective members—Bulgaria, Latvia, Lithuania, Malta, Romania, and Slovakia—early in the new year. The decision received the assent of the European Council during its summit December 10–11 in Helsinki, putting the six countries on the same footing as the six that were regarded as "fast-track" entries: Cyprus, Czech Republic, Estonia, Hungary, Poland, and Slovenia. The council also formally approved Turkey as a candidate for admission, despite reservations regarding its human rights record, and unspoken misgivings about Turkey being a Muslim, if secular, country.

During the same period the EU was moving steadily toward establishing its own military capability. On June 3–4, 1999, a European Council meeting in Cologne, Germany, selected (then) NATO secretary general Javier Solana Madariaga of Spain as the first EU high representative for foreign and security policy, a position authorized by the Treaty of Amsterdam, which also provided for the use of combat forces for "crisis management." The heads of state and government also agreed to begin formalizing a much-debated joint security and defense policy, under which the EU would assume the WEU's defense role and its "Petersberg tasks" (named for the official German guesthouse near Bonn where, in 1992, the WEU defined its future military responsibilities): peacekeeping, humanitarian and rescue missions, and military crisis management.

An unprecedented joint meeting of EU foreign and defense ministers November 15, 1999, in Brussels confirmed Solana's WEU appointment and, drawing on the experiences of the conflicts in Bosnia and Kosovo, discussed how to handle future altercations. A central component of the EU strategy was formation of an EU rapid reaction force (RRF) that would be independent of NATO and the United States. A month later, at the Helsinki summit, the European Council authorized formation by 2003 of a 60,000-member RRF that could respond to crises that did not involve NATO as a whole. As the plan continued to evolve over the following year, the EU agreed to work closely with NATO, thereby mitigating U.S. objections. It also agreed to invite the participation in EU-led missions of non-EU states that were NATO members—most particularly, Turkey—as well as non-NATO European countries, such as Russia. Formation of the RRF was given a further go-ahead by the foreign and defense ministers' meeting November 20, 2000, in Brussels, although Denmark exercised its right to opt out. The ministers also agreed to assume the WEU's operational role. Earlier in the year, in April, the WEU/EU Eurocorps, which was inaugurated in November 1993, undertook its most significant mission to date, namely command of the NATO-led Kosovo Force (KFOR) in Yugoslavia.

During 2000 several important developments occurred in the economic sphere. A special heads of government summit March 23–24 in Lisbon introduced a ten-year program, dubbed the Lisbon Strategy, to develop the EU into "the world's most competitive and dynamic knowledge-driven economy," with attendant goals that included improving the employment rate from 61 percent to 70 percent and achieving an average annual growth rate of 3 percent. One of the core elements of the strategy was the creation of a European Research Area (ERA). In the ERA, researchers, technology, and knowledge would circulate as freely as possible—presumably without jeopardizing the EU's strong intellectual property protections. Research initiatives would also be implemented and funded at the European level.

Interim reports, the most recent a May 2007 "green paper," indicated that the EU was falling short of its ambitious goals of research integration. The slow pace of developing new pharmaceuticals, of which only a handful were commercialized in the EU in 2007, was a particular concern. Additionally, while the Lisbon goal was to match innovation in the United States by 2010, rising economic powers such as China and India were also becoming increasingly competitive. As a result, the "Ljubljana Process" was launched at a ministerial meeting on April 14–15, 2008, in Ljubljana, Slovenia, that set five new initiatives to be achieved by 2020 in the following areas: improving mobility of researchers, a legal framework to aid the development of pan-European research infrastructures, management of intellectual property rights, joint programming for research programs across the EU, and a common policy for international science and technology cooperation. Additionally, a consensus between member states on a new framework for governance of the ERA was commissioned for presentation by the end of 2009.

In July 2000 the EU finance ministers named a committee headed by former EMI president Alexandre Lamfalussy to examine the operation of EU securities markets and to propose changes in current practices and regulations. In September the Paris, Brussels, and Amsterdam stock exchanges merged as Euronext, and in 2002 Euronext acquired the London-based derivatives market LIFFE and merged with the Portuguese exchange. Already second only to London in terms of listings and market capitalization, Euronext anticipated becoming "the first fully integrated cross-border European market for equities, bonds, derivatives, and commodities." In April 2007, the New York Stock Exchange acquired Euronext and the merger of the two created the world's largest stock exchange.

In December 2000 the EU's comprehensive review of institutional reform, which included a special summit October 12–15 in Biarritz, France, drew to a close. Meeting on December 7–11, 2000, in Nice, the European Council agreed to significant restructuring of EU institutions, primarily to accommodate 12 new member countries. (The 13th potential member, Turkey, was excluded from the calculations, given that it had not yet begun formal accession negotiations.) Requiring ratification by the European Parliament and all 15 current member countries, the resultant Treaty of Nice bowed to German insistence that the expanded European Parliament and the QMV system give greater weight to the populations of the member states.

The Treaty of Nice, which was signed by the members' foreign ministers February 26, 2001, in Brussels, hit its first roadblock June 8 when some 54 percent of Ireland's voters rebuffed it. EU leaders insisted, however, that expansion plans would proceed and that efforts would be made to address the Irish public's concerns. These included the impact of expansion on Ireland's standing and the status of its military neutrality in the context of the EU's new military capabilities. Ultimately, the Irish voters were satisfied, and in an October 20, 2002, referendum, 62.9 percent endorsed the Treaty of Nice, permitting its entry into force February 1, 2003.

The ratification process for the Treaty of Nice coincided with a continuing debate over the EU's long-term purpose and structure. German leaders, on the one hand, called for even closer integration, including adoption of a federal structure. France, on the other hand, continued to oppose such a model, which it saw as threatening national constituencies. Another area of contention was the Charter of Fundamental Rights, which was drawn up in September 2000 and formally approved by the heads of government at the Nice summit. The charter's firmest opponent, the United Kingdom, argued that its incorporation into the EU treaty was unnecessary because all EU members had already acceded to the European Convention on Human Rights.

In a significant development for the EU's external relations, the first summit of Balkan states and the EU was held November 24, 2000, in Zagreb, Croatia. The EU pledged €4.7 billion ($3.9 billion) in aid during

2000–2006 to support "reconstruction, democratization, and stabilization" in Albania, Bosnia and Herzegovina, Croatia, Macedonia, and Yugoslavia. Most Balkan states had already expressed an interest in eventual EU membership.

During their February 25–26, 2001, meeting in Brussels, the EU foreign ministers agreed to abolish virtually all trade barriers for 48 of the least developed countries, including 39 members of the EC-affiliated ACP group. Dubbed the Everything But Arms Proposal, the initiative made trade in all manufactured and agricultural goods, except armaments, duty- and quota-free, although phase-in periods were established for bananas (to 2006), rice (2009), and sugar (2009)—three commodities that had caused major trade disputes in recent years.

Meeting in mid-June 2001, in Göteborg, Sweden, the EU heads of government established 2004 as the firm entry date for the next expansion, although it remained uncertain exactly how many of the eligible countries would be ready for admission at that time.

In the immediate aftermath of the September 11, 2001, terrorist attacks on the United States, the EU heads of government held an emergency meeting September 21 in Brussels, where they extended full support to Washington. An informal summit, which convened October 19 in Ghent, Belgium, focused on the economic and political consequences of the attacks and of the recently launched U.S. "war on terrorism." Subsequent related actions included endorsement of a uniform arrest warrant and a May 2002 decision to freeze the assets of 11 suspected terrorist organizations. Developments at a June 21–22 summit in Seville, Spain, included acceptance of a plan to counter illegal immigration, adopt a common asylum policy, and introduce a common border force. Cooperation declined after the initiation of the Iraq War in 2003, typified by EU reluctance to accept cleared detainees from the U.S. military prison at Guantanamo Bay in 2009. In November that year, the EU also objected to an antiterrorism plan that would allow U.S. law enforcement to access EU citizen's financial data, but it ultimately signed a deal that limited the scope to terrorism inquiries.

Meeting on December 14–15, 2001, in Laeken, Belgium, the heads of government agreed to establish a constitutional convention, to be chaired by former French president Valéry Giscard d'Estaing, and to map out a more efficient and democratic structure for the union. On February 28, 2002, the convention began its task. A "skeleton draft" of the proposed constitution for a "union of European states" was published October 28, 2002, but the 46-article document deliberately avoided controversial issues that had yet to be resolved. It did, however, propose reserving powers not specifically conferred by the constitution on EU institutions to the member states. This was seen as an effort to restrain the growth and power of the European Commission in particular.

On March 23, 2002, responding to a U.S. decision to impose unilateral steel tariffs of between 8 and 30 percent, the EU announced retaliatory tariffs against up to 300 U.S. products. The steel products were manufactured by previously state-owned French, German, Italian, Spanish, Swedish, and UK companies that received subsidies before being privatized. The WTO proceeded to address the complex issue, while in December the EU and the United States, at a Paris meeting sponsored by the Organization for Economic Cooperation and Development (OECD), agreed to open negotiations on reducing or eliminating steel subsidies.

Meanwhile, the ECSC's founding treaty had expired on July 23, 2002, resulting in the closure of the European Coal and Steel Community. Perhaps its most significant accomplishment, apart from serving as a model for creation of the EEC, was a decades-long, painful reduction of overcapacity in the community's steel industry. The process introduced production quotas, banned state subsidies, closed obsolete facilities and modernized others, restructured the market, and expanded retraining funds and other support for former steelworkers. By 1999 the steel workforce had declined to 280,000 (from 870,000 in 1975), and some 63 million tons of capacity had been eliminated since 1980. In July 2002 all ECSC assets and liabilities were transferred to the EU. In the interim, ECSC net assets, which were valued at some $1.6 billion at that time, were to be managed by the European Commission and then, after completion of the community's liquidation, to be designated as Assets of the Research Fund for Coal and Steel. Matters related to the coal and steel industries are now addressed within the EU framework.

Proposed changes to CAP and a parallel Common Fisheries Policy (CFP) drew considerable attention in 2002. France and Spain, two principal beneficiaries of the existing CAP, voiced objections. Spain also expressed concern over efforts under the CFP to reduce fleet sizes and better manage fish stocks. A December 2002 decision to limit catches of Atlantic cod, haddock, and whiting also angered British fishermen.

Problems also persisted with regard to establishing the RRF as part of a comprehensive European Security and Defense Policy (ESDP). The first anticipated RRF mission, to assume control in October 2002 of peacekeepers in Macedonia, required the approval of NATO, but Turkey wanted assurances that the RRF would not undertake missions in the Aegean and locations near Turkey. At a summit held December 12–13, 2002, in Copenhagen, Denmark, the EU formally completed a "comprehensive agreement" resolving the dispute with Turkey over the RRF. Under the pact, only EU members and candidates that also are members of NATO or participants in the NATO Partnership for Peace (PfP) program have access to NATO facilities. Accordingly, Malta and Cyprus are excluded.

The most significant action taken at the summit, however, was the approval of the admission of ten new members: the Czech Republic, Cyprus (excluding the Turkish Republic of Northern Cyprus), Estonia, Hungary, Latvia, Lithuania, Malta, Poland, Slovakia, and Slovenia. Accession treaties were signed at an informal European Council session on April, 16, 2003, with formal admission, following the necessary ratifications, then occurring on May 1, 2004.

The EU has relationships with special territories associated with its member states that vary based on their level and type of participation in EU policy areas and programs, spelled out in the European Community Treaty of 2002. Among them are the Spanish Canary Islands, which remain outside the European Value-Added Tax (VAT) areas but submit to EU policy in all other respects. The French islands of Guadeloupe and Martinique in the Caribbean, French Guiana on the northern coast of South America, and Reunion in the Indian Ocean are outside the Schengen and VAT areas, but carry the euro as legal tender and are part of the EU Customs Union.

The Overseas Countries and Territories (OTCs) are a grouping of 20 territories linked to Denmark, France, the Netherlands, and the United Kingdom whose nationals are in principle EU citizens, although they are not directly subject to EU law but rather benefit from association agreements, most of which pertain to trade. Bermuda is listed in the European Community Treaty, but the arrangements for association are not applied to it because of the wishes of the government. Development assistance from the EU for the OTCs amounts to $429 million in 2008–2013. In March 2009 the Indian Ocean island of Mayotte voted to become part of France, thereby reversing its status as an overseas collectivity and effectively joining the EU.

The European Council met in emergency session February 17, 2003, to discuss the looming crisis regarding the United States and Iraq, but a deep divide separated France and Germany, which opposed military action, from the United Kingdom, Spain, and Italy, the most vocal supporters of the Bush administration's stance against the Saddam Hussein regime. French president Chirac subsequently criticized statements supporting intervention made by the eight Eastern European prospective members, plus candidate countries Romania and Bulgaria. Iraq policy remained on the agenda at the regular council session March 20–21, which also addressed progress toward achieving the Lisbon Strategy goals for economic competitiveness.

On April 25, 2003, four opponents of the month-old invasion of Iraq met to discuss defense cooperation. At that time Belgium, France, Germany, and Luxembourg decided to establish a headquarters for planning joint military operations, although some critics, especially the United Kingdom, viewed the decision as contrary to a prior pledge not to compete with NATO's collective defense mission. A compromise was reached in November, with France and Germany withdrawing their headquarters plan and the United Kingdom agreeing to formation of a joint military planning unit independent of NATO. In addition, the EU foreign ministers agreed that common consent would be required to initiate any EU peacekeeping or humanitarian mission, and then only if NATO chose not to act. At the December 2003 council summit, the defense plan received the approval of the EU leaders. In February France, Germany, and the United Kingdom announced their support for forming joint battle groups, each with 1,500 personnel, within the RRF. The first such units (the total number was subsequently set at 13) were ready for deployment in January 2007. In June 2004 the EU foreign ministers approved establishment of the European Defense Agency (EDA), with responsibilities that included improving joint defense capabilities, promoting related research and development, and advancing development of a competitive defense market within the EU. In 2005 the EDA absorbed the functions of the Western European Armaments Group (WEAG), a subsidiary body of the WEU.

Meeting in regular session on June 19–20, 2003, in Salonika, Greece, the council received a draft constitution from the Convention on the Future of Europe and assigned preparation of a final text to an IGC, which was to begin its work in October. In other business, the council indicated its willingness to aid in Iraqi reconstruction and endorsed a statement by the EU foreign ministers on the possible use of military force to prevent the spread of weapons of mass destruction (WMD). Shortly thereafter, an EU-U.S. extradition treaty was signed. The EU members retained the right to refuse extradition in death penalty cases.

When the IGC on the constitution convened in October 2003, differences over many provisions still required resolution, principal among them the makeup of the European Commission and voting procedures in the proposed Council of Ministers. The draft text called for reducing the commission to 15 members beginning in 2009, but most of the smaller member countries argued that each should continue to be represented by at least one commissioner. With regard to the Council of Ministers, the constitutional text specified a "double majority" system under which passage of a measure would require support from a majority of ministers representing, collectively, at least 60 percent of the total EU population. An EU summit December 13 failed to resolve the issues, but the attendees managed to agree on the 2007 admission of Bulgaria and Romania to the union. The meeting also accepted the Former Yugoslavian Republic of Macedonia as a candidate country.

In January 2004 the European Commission asked the ECJ to rule on the validity of a November 2003 decision by the EU finance ministers to suspend the stability and growth pact (SGP), thereby avoiding the imposition of penalties against France and Germany for failing to keep their budget deficits in check. In April 2004, with the ECJ not yet having ruled, the commission issued warnings to Greece, Italy, the Netherlands, and Portugal over their deficits. Three months later the ECJ determined that the finance ministers had exceeded their authority in suspending the SGP, but the judges also ruled they could not force the ministers to carry through on the commission's recommendations regarding sanctions. As a consequence, the issue of sanctions was thrown into the political arena, and reform of the SGP became an even more contentious issue.

The March 25–26, 2004, European Council summit was dominated by the March 11 terrorist bombings in Madrid and the subsequent election of a new Spanish government. In addition to appointing a new EU counterterrorism coordinator, the summit participants stated that they intended to act jointly, including with military force, in response to terrorist attacks, and they approved a 50-point plan of action.

In late April 2004, the justice and home affairs ministers sought consensus on another volatile issue: setting minimum standards for treating those seeking political asylum under a proposed Common European Asylum System (CEAS). The CEAS proposal was not, however, universally welcomed, with the UN's high commissioner for refugees, Ruud Lubbers, describing the plan as intended to reduce standards and to "deter or deny protection to as many people as possible."

As scheduled, the EU's enlargement from 15 to 25 members took place May 1, 2004, with the election of a new European Parliament following on June 10–13. As had been expected following the expansion, the voters returned the center-right European People's Party/European Democrats as the plurality grouping. Somewhat unexpectedly, however, the leading governing parties in 23 of the 25 member states won smaller vote shares than they had in the most recent national elections.

At a June 17–18, 2004, summit of EU leaders, a spirit of compromise resolved the remaining disputes over the text of the 350-article EU constitution, which required ratification by all 25 member countries. Predictably, the final draft was immediately attacked by both proponents of a unified Europe and those fearing the loss of national sovereignty and identity. Under the constitution, which was to supersede existing EU treaties, EU law would have primacy over national law in specified areas, when the objectives could best be achieved at the EU level. The European Council would elect an EU president for a once-renewable term of two and a half years and would also choose a minister for foreign affairs. The European Commission would retain the formula of one commissioner per state for one five-year term, after which the number of commissioners would be reduced to two-thirds the number of member states, filled by rotation. The Council of Ministers would meet in various configurations, depending on the sector involved (e.g., agriculture, transport). The European Parliament, comprising no more than 750 members (a maximum of 96 and a minimum of 6 per country), and the Council of Ministers would jointly "exercise legislative and budgetary functions." Unless otherwise specified in the constitution, European Council decisions would continue to be by consensus. In the Council of Ministers, unanimity would be required in such sensitive areas as foreign policy, defense, and tax law. Otherwise, a "double majority" QMV system would apply, generally requiring support from 55 percent of the ministers, representing at least 65 percent of the EU population.

Although the Charter of Fundamental Rights was incorporated into the constitution, its application was to be limited to matters of EU law, with the interpretation of guaranteed rights allowing for national differences based on, for example, tradition. The complete constitution also encompassed 36 protocols, including one amending the Euratom treaty, and 50 Declarations Concerning Provisions of the Constitution. Meeting October 29 in Rome, the EU heads of government and their foreign ministers signed a constitutional treaty to advance its ratification in all member countries, by referendum or legislative act, by November 2006.

Meanwhile, on July 22, 2004, the new parliament had approved the nomination of Portuguese prime minister José Manuel Barroso to serve as president of the European Commission for 2005–2010.

A November 4–5, 2004, EU summit adopted a new five-year Hague Program on freedom, justice, and security that addressed terrorism and organized crime, basic rights and citizenship, and the CEAS. The Hague Program, a follow-up to a plan that was adopted at the 1999 Tampere summit, did not, however, resolve deep divisions over the proposed common asylum plan, especially the use of extraterritorial holding centers. There also were fundamental differences over whether asylum seekers who entered the EU would be deported to the centers or whether the centers would be used only to house those who had been intercepted while in transit to EU countries.

The EU summit of December 16–17, 2004, was highlighted by the announcement that accession talks with candidate country Croatia would begin March 17, 2005, provided that the Zagreb government fully cooperated with the International Criminal Tribunal for the former Yugoslavia (ICTY) in The Hague. The summit also confirmed that accession talks with Turkey would begin on October 3, 2005, but several EU members, including France and Italy, had already indicated their likely opposition to admitting the predominantly Asian and Islamic country. Questions also persisted regarding Turkey's stance toward Cyprus and its human rights record.

On February 22, 2005, President Bush visited institutions of the EU. U.S.-European relations had been strained considerably by the U.S.-led invasion of Iraq in 2003. Moreover, U.S. administration officials had made several statements that caused some in Europe to believe that the United States was no longer supportive of an integrated Europe, especially one that took stances counter to U.S. policy. Bush's trip was widely seen as an effort to allay such concerns.

In February 2005 President Barroso announced his commission's economic program, as well as its social and environmental agenda. The economic program recommended market liberalization, deregulation, and, most controversially, extension of the single market concept to services as well as goods. The goal was to meet Lisbon Strategy targets, which projected 3 percent annual growth and the creation of 6 million new jobs during the 2005–2010 term.

At a summit March 22–23, 2005, the EU leaders focused on reforming the stability and growth pact, which had largely been disregarded since the 2002 decision of the finance ministers not to impose economic penalties on France and Germany for noncompliance. At the summit the members retained the pact's principal benchmarks—keeping national budget deficits under 3 percent of GDP and public debt to less than 60 percent of GDP—but basically exempted countries experiencing low or negative growth. They excluded from the budget ceiling expenditures for education, defense, foreign aid, and research and extended the time limits for offending countries to make the necessary adjustments. France, Germany, Italy, and Spain, each of which failed to adhere to the original criteria, were among the countries backing the revisions, which critics described as rendering the pact worthless.

On January 12, 2005, the European Parliament overwhelmingly endorsed the proposed EU constitution, although most UK, Polish, and Czech MEPs voted in opposition. On February 20 Spanish voters became the first to approve the constitution by referendum, but its prospects for unionwide ratification suffered a major blow in late May and early June when French and Dutch voters rejected the constitution by 54.7 percent and 61.5 percent, respectively. Analysts interpreted the French vote in large part as dissatisfaction with the current French government, while in the Netherlands it was a fear of a loss in national sovereignty and identity because of the rapid pace of enlargement and an influx of immigrants from the East. Despite the French and Dutch results, many supporters of the constitution urged that the ratification process continue, although the EU leaders, meeting June 16–17, instead called for a "period of reflection." While 16 countries had ratified the new constitution as of August 2007, seven other EU members postponed consideration. If, in the end, five or fewer states failed to ratify the constitution, it could be reconsidered rather than scrapped. In mid-2006, European public opinion seemed to be turning more strongly against the constitution, but its supporters inside the EU structure were still enthusiastic about keeping it alive without substantial modification. The inability of the member states to ratify the EU Constitution led to the passage of the Lisbon Treaty (see Recent Activities, below).

During the same period, a crisis erupted over the 2007–2013 EU budget when the United Kingdom refused to accept a reduction in its budget rebate (which was instituted in 1984 when the United Kingdom's economic position was much weaker) unless the reduction was accompanied by additional reforms, particularly with regard to CAP. In June 2003 the EU agricultural ministers approved further "decoupling" of CAP subsidies from productivity and redirected the program toward giving farmers flat payments related to rural development and environmental protection. Since then, the number of excluded or partially affected agricultural products has been reduced. Nevertheless, several EU members supported the UK argument that a continuing budgetary emphasis on agriculture was misdirected. France, the largest recipient of CAP support and a leading opponent of maintaining the UK budget rebate, disagreed. After protracted negotiations, a compromise was reached in December 2005 on the 2007–2013 EU budget. The United Kingdom agreed to give up approximately 20 percent of its rebate during the coming budget period, while the European Commission was asked to hold a "full and wide-ranging" review of all EU spending, including CAP and the UK rebate, and to draw up a report in 2008–2009. Additional substantial cuts in annual CAP subsidies are anticipated after 2013.

In February 2006 the European Parliament passed a bill authorizing an internal market for services, which, after subsequent revisions, resulted in the EU Services Directive that was adopted by the end of the year.

In another move to extend the internal market, 22 EU governments in May 2006 agreed to an informal code of conduct to open competition to nonnational EU members in the €30 billion ($38 billion) defense market. Spain, Hungary, and Denmark chose not to participate, Spain and Hungary because they thought that their own firms would not be competitive, and Denmark because it has an opt-out from EU military cooperation.

On December 21, 2007, the Schengen area of the EU, where there are no internal border posts or passport checks for EU citizens (thereby promoting the free movement of people), was expanded to include 9 of the 10 countries that joined the EU in 2004. Zone membership thereby increased to 24 of the 27 EU member states, plus non-EU members Iceland and Norway (EU members Ireland and the United Kingdom do not participate).

The new countries included the Czech Republic, Estonia, Hungary, Latvia, Lithuania, Malta, Poland, Slovakia, and Slovenia. Cyprus, which joined the EU in 2004, had not met the technical requirements to join as expected in late 2009. Bulgaria and Romania were on track in 2010 to gain Schengen membership by 2011. On December 12, 2008, Switzerland became the 25th country to join the Schengen area with the lifting of land border controls, followed by the removal of airport controls for Schengen passport holders in March 2009.

On January 1, 2007, Russia interrupted its supply of gas to the EU after a conflict with Ukraine about gas prices. Although the EU has been attempting to diversify its sources, it currently gets a quarter of its gas from Russia. Gazprom, Russia's state-controlled gas monopoly, has been unwilling to open its pipeline network to independent companies and other gas-producing states such as Kazakhstan and Turkmenistan, arguing, among other things, that the network is already stretched to capacity to meet its commitments for the next 20 years. Regular energy talks between the EU and Russia have taken place since 2000. At the October 2007 annual summit, energy discussions centered on security of supply. EU officials were hoping to resume talks concerning Russian gas supplies and opening that country's energy sector to west European investors at a conference in June 2008, although there were concerns that member EU nations had no coordinated foreign policy platform on Russia. The EU has also called for Russian membership in the WTO, despite ongoing concerns about human rights in Russia.

In another foreign policy area, members of the EU have played a central role in negotiating with Iran regarding its production of weapons-grade uranium. In June 2006, as he had in 2003, Javier Solana delivered to Iran a proposal offering a package of incentives not to produce weapons-grade material. Iran rejected the overture. Thus, in 2007 Solana and the member states continued to pressure Iran through such measures as sanctions. In May 2008 Iran presented a counter package of proposals to EU officials outlining a different strategy to address security issues regarding the spread of nuclear powers but refused to suspend its own enrichment program. Relations with Iran deteriorated in 2009. Following Iran's detention of local staff from the British embassy in Tehran, the United Kingdom requested that EU members pull out their ambassadors. Iran maintained that the EU had disqualified itself from nuclear talks because it had interfered with Iran's disputed presidential election.

In 2007, following two years of reflection generated by the French and Dutch rejection of the proposed EU Constitution, the EU formally called a halt to plans for amending the document. The European Council session in Brussels in June 2006 had proposed reaching a decision on institutional reform by the end of 2008. Further impetus toward drawing up a framework for reform emerged from the informal Berlin summit held on March 25, 2007, to mark the 50th anniversary of the signing of the Treaty of Rome. On June 23 an IGC was given a detailed mandate to draw up a new reform treaty by the end of 2007. The European Parliament and the European Commission also participated in the deliberations, leading to council approval of a treaty text on October 19. It was later signed by the heads of state or government in Lisbon on December 13.

The Lisbon Treaty, also known as the Reform Treaty, echoed many of the institutional changes proposed in the failed constitution and required ratification by all 27 EU members. It amends existing EU and EC treaties, with the EC's 1958 founding treaty being renamed the Treaty on the Functioning of the European Union. Many of the new treaty's institutional reforms echo those originally proposed in the failed constitution: the president of the European Council (now an official institution within the EU by virtue of the treaty) is to be elected for a once-renewable term of two and a half years; the European Parliament will comprise a maximum of 750 seats, with no more than 96 and no fewer than 6 per country; the number of commissioners in the European Commission will be reduced, beginning in November 2014, to two-thirds the number of member states, filled by rotation; and, in the Council of the European Union a "double majority voting" (or DMV) system (55 percent of the members, representing at least 65 percent of the EU population) will apply to most policy areas, also beginning in 2014. In addition, the selection of a commission president was to be linked to the results of parliamentary elections, and a new high representative for the union in foreign affairs and security policy was to be named, with the officeholder also serving as commission vice president. For the first time, specific provisions have been included for the withdrawal of a member state from the union.

The Reform Treaty also stipulates that legal force be given to the Charter of Fundamental Rights, which was formally signed on December 12, 2007, by the presidents of the European Council, the European Commission, and the European Parliament. However, the charter is addressed to EU institutions, bodies, and agencies, not to national governments, legislatures, or courts when they enact, implement, or interpret national laws.

The treaty gives the European Parliament greater influence over legislation, the budget, and international agreements, thereby placing it on a more equal footing with the Council of the European Union. At the same time, under the principle of subsidiarity, national parliaments should be better able to monitor the union's institutions to ensure that they act only when the policy goals are best attained at the union level. In the realm of policy, the new treaty could enhance the union's ability to act in a number of key areas, including security and justice, energy, climate change, globalization, public health, research, space, and humanitarian assistance. The treaty also includes a provision for citizens' initiatives, whereby a proposal having the support of at least 1 million citizens from a number of states can be presented to the European Commission for discussion.

On December 18, 2007, Hungary became the first member state to ratify the treaty. However, a number of setbacks delayed its passage. In March 2008 Poland's legislature postponed ratification as the main opposition party argued that the country might be forced to accept same-sex civil partnerships and that Germany might reclaim property lost after World War II. Finland, too, hesitated because of an internal legislative dispute over representation in the European Parliament. Additionally, the United Kingdom witnessed a legal challenge over whether ratification had to be put to a public referendum. This challenge ultimately proved unsuccessful. Conservative Czech parliamentarians, meanwhile, asked for their supreme court to rule on whether multiple provisions within the treaty were compatible with the country's constitution. All four countries eventually accepted the treaty.

Of all the countries considering ratification, only Ireland was constitutionally required to put the Lisbon Treaty to a referendum. Irish activists campaigned hard against the treaty ahead of polling on June 12, 2008, when 53.4 percent of Irish voters rejected it, preventing its ratification. EU leaders were thus thrust into a crisis over how to proceed. Meanwhile, the Polish and Czech presidents refused to ratify the treaty before an Irish approval, and Germany's ratification was slowed by a constitutional court case assessing the treaty's compatibility with domestic law. For more on activities since 2008, see "Recent Activities," below.

Structure. The Treaty on European Union established two new pillars—a common foreign and security policy (CFSP), and justice and home affairs (JHA)—while also amending, but not superseding, EC treaties. Accordingly, the EC continues as the EU's first pillar—the "community domain" of common policies and laws decided by the "community method," involving the European Commission and two legislative organs, the Council of the European Union and the European Parliament. In reaching decisions involving the community domain, the Council of the European Union usually uses a QMV system.]In contrast, decisions involving the second and third pillars are usually made by unanimous vote of the Council of the European Union, although the Treaty of Amsterdam provided for use of QMV in some areas not involving the military or defense. The Treaty of Amsterdam also renamed the JHA pillar as the Police and Judicial Cooperation in Criminal Matters (PJCC) and transferred some of that pillar's original tasks to the EC.

The EU founding treaty authorized the European Council (comprising the heads of state or government of the member states) to "provide the Union with the necessary impetus for its development" and to "define the general political guidelines" for the grouping. The council typically meets four times a year, chaired by the head of state or government of the member state holding its presidency. The remaining institutional framework of the EU has the same basic components as those originally allotted to the individual communities: the Council of the European Union (originally called the Council of Ministers) to provide overall direction and to legislate, the representative European Parliament with colegislative responsibilities, the executive and administrative European Commission charged with the initiation and implementation of EU policies, and the Court of Justice to adjudicate legal issues. A Court of Auditors was added in 1977.

Depending on the subject under discussion, EU states can be represented on the Council of the European Union by their foreign ministers, as is usually the case for major decisions, or by other ministers. As a result of the Luxembourg compromise in 1966, the principle of unanimity is retained for issues in which a member feels it has a "vital interest." However, changes approved in 1987 reduced the number of areas subject to such veto, the use of QMV in the council being increased to speed up integration efforts. The distribution of votes is as follows: France, Germany, Italy, and the United Kingdom, 29 each; Poland and Spain, 27 each; Romania, 14; Netherlands, 13; Belgium, the Czech Republic, Greece, Hungary, and Portugal, 12 each; Austria, Bulgaria, and Sweden, 10 each; Denmark, Finland, Ireland, Lithuania, and Slovakia, 7 each; Cyprus, Estonia, Latvia, Luxembourg, and Slovenia, 4 each; and Malta, 3. Under QMV, passage of a proposal typically requires 255 of the 345 votes (73.9 percent), representing a majority of the member states. If challenged, however, those in the majority must demonstrate that they collectively represent at least 62 percent of the total EU population.

The Maastricht Treaty altered the required makeup of the European Commission and the method of its selection, eliminating country representation, per se, and stipulating only that the commission must include at least one and no more than two individuals from each EU state. However, the 20-member commission that took office in January 1995 preserved the established distribution of two members from each of the "big five" (France, Germany, Italy, Spain, and the United Kingdom) and one each from the smaller states. In November 2004, the commission was expanded to 25 members, one from each state, after a six-month period in which interim commissioners from the ten new states worked alongside those who were serving out their five-year terms. In a complicated selection process, the member states first nominate a commission president and then, in consultation with that person, nominate the full commission. The president and the rest of the commission are subject to confirmation (or possible rejection) by the European Parliament and final appointment "by common accord" of the member states. In general, the commission mediates among the member governments in community matters, exercises a broad range of executive powers, and initiates community action. Its members are completely independent and are forbidden by treaty to accept instructions from any national government. Decisions are made by majority vote, although in practice most are adopted by consensus.

In 2007 the commission was expanded to 27, one commission member from each of the member states. Below is a list of its members and the principal subject or subjects of their portfolios. A 28th commissioner was added in July 2013 upon Croatia's accession to the EU (See recent activities, below).

José Manuel Barroso (Portugal)	President
Catherine Ashton [f] (United Kingdom)	Vice President, High Representative of the Union for Foreign Affairs and Security Policy
Viviane Reding [f] (Luxembourg)	Vice President; Justice, Fundamental Rights, and Citizenship
Joaquín Almunia (Spain)	Vice President, Competition
Siim Kallas (Estonia)	Vice President; Transport
Neelie Kroes [f] (Netherlands)	Vice President, Digital Agenda
Antonio Tajani (Italy)	Vice President; Industry and Entrepreneurship
Maroš Šefčovič (Slovakia)	Vice President; Inter-Institutional Relations and Administration
Janez Potočnik (Slovenia)	Environment
Olli Rehn (Finland)	Economic and Monetary Affairs
Andris Piebalgs (Latvia)	Development
Michel Barnier (France)	Internal Market and Services
Androulla Vassiliou [f] (Cyprus)	Education, Culture, Multilingualism, and Youth
Algirdas Ŝemeta (Lithuania)	Taxation and Customs Union, Audit, and Anti-Fraud
Karel De Gucht (Belgium)	Trade
Tonio Borg (Malta)	Health
Neven Mimica (Croatia)	Consumer Policy
Maíre Geoghegan-Quinn (Ireland)	Research, Innovation, and Science
Janusz Lewandowski (Poland)	Financial Programming and Budget
Maria Damanaki [f] (Greece)	Maritime Affairs and Fisheries
Kristalina Georgieva [f] (Bulgaria)	International Cooperation, Humanitarian Aid, and Crisis Response
Günter Oettinger (Germany)	Energy
Johannes Hahn (Austria)	Regional Policy
Connie Hedegaard [f] (Denmark)	Climate Action
Štefan Füle (Czech Republic)	Enlargement and European Neighborhood Policy
Cecilia Malmström[f] (Sweden)	Home Affairs
Dacian Cioloş (Romania)	Agriculture and Rural Development
Lázló Andor (Hungary)	Employment, Social Affairs and Inclusion

[f] = female

The European Parliament is an outgrowth of the consultative parliamentary assembly established for the ECSC and subsequently mandated to serve in the same capacity for the EEC and Euratom. The parliament's authority has gradually increased over its history, but has remained quite limited relative to other EU organs. Many initiatives that would emanate from a national parliament instead emanate, in the case of the EU, from the European Commission and its professionals in the commission's directorates general in Brussels.

Under a 1975 treaty the parliament was empowered to participate in formulation of the annual EC budget and even reject it by a two-thirds vote—save for deference to the Council of Ministers regarding agricultural spending, the largest item in the community's budget. The Single European Act, the Treaty on European Union, and the Treaty of Amsterdam further extended parliament's budgetary powers and legislative purview. In addition, the parliament, previously only authorized to dismiss the entire commission (but not individual members) by a vote of censure, can now reject nominees for individual posts. The parliament, which meets annually (normally in Strasbourg, France) and has a five-year term, must also approve EU treaties, as well as the admission of new EU members. (The Reform Treaty further increases the parliament's powers.)

The move to direct elections in all member states in 1979 was followed by the Maastricht Treaty's direction that the parliament should draw up plans for future elections to take place under uniform voting procedures and constituency arrangements. Some progress was made in this regard for the 1994 elections, notably in that for the first time all EU citizens could vote in their EU country of residence.

Under the Treaty of Nice, as amended after the accession treaties with Bulgaria and Romania, the number of members of parliament reduced from 785 to 736 for the 2009–2014 parliamentary term.

Additionally, following the most recent parliamentary election in 2009, all political groups in the European Parliament must include members from at least seven member states with a minimum of 25 members. The statute of members, which was adopted in 2005, entered into force on the first day of the new term on July 14, 2009, and made the terms of conditions of a member's work more transparent and introduced a common salary for all members.

The most recent election was held June 4–7, 2009, and membership was allocated as follows: Austria, 17; Belgium, 22; Bulgaria, 17; Cyprus, 6; the Czech Republic, 22; Denmark, 13; Estonia, 6; Finland, 13; France, 72; Germany, 99; Greece, 22; Hungary, 22; Ireland, 12; Italy, 72; Latvia, 8; Lithuania, 12; Luxembourg, 6; Malta, 5; Netherlands, 25; Poland, 50; Portugal, 22; Romania, 33; Slovakia, 13; Slovenia, 7; Spain, 50; Sweden, 18; United Kingdom, 72. Upon accession to the EU in 2013, Croatia was allocated 12 seats. Members sit not by nationality, but by political affiliation. As of October 2013, the makeup of the political groups was as follows:

European People's Party (EPP), 275

Austria	Austrian People's Party (ÖVP), 6
Belgium	Christian Democratic and Flemish (CD&V), 3
	Christian Social Party–*Europäische Volkspartei* (CSP-EVP), 1
	Democratic Humanist Center (CDH), 1
Bulgaria	Citizens for European Development of Bulgaria (GERB), 5
	Blue Coalition (SDS-DSB), 2
Croatia	Croatian Democratic Union (HDZ), 5
Cyprus	Democratic Rally (Disy), 2
Czech Republic	Christian and Democratic Union–Czech People's Party (KDU-ČSL), 2
Denmark	Conservative People's Party (C), 1
Estonia	Fatherland Union (IRL), 1
Finland	National Coalition Party (Kok), 3
	Christian Democrats-True Finn (KD-PS), 1
France	Union for a Popular Movement (UMP), 24
	Union of Democrats and Independents (UDI), 4
	New Center (NC), 1
	Radical Party (PR), 1
Germany	Christian Democratic Union (CDU), 34
	Christian Social Union (CSU), 8
Greece	New Democracy (ND), 7
Hungary	Federation of Young Democrats–Christian Democratic People's Party (FiDeSz-KDNP), 14
Ireland	*Fine Gael*, 4
Italy	People of Freedom (PdL), 22
	Union of Christian and Center Democrats (UDC), 6
	Brothers of Italy—the Center-Right National Party (FI-CN), 2
	Union of Democrats for Europe (UDE), 1
	Future and Freedom for Italy (FLI), 1
	South Tyrol People's Party (SVP), 1
	Independent Candidate, 1
Latvia	Unity (V), 4
Lithuania	Homeland Union Christian Democrats (TS-LKDP), 4
Luxembourg	Christian Social People's Party (CSV), 3
Malta	Nationalist Party (PN), 2
Netherlands	Christian Democratic Appeal (CDA), 5
Poland	Civic Platform (PO), 25
	Polish People's Party (PSL), 4
Portugal	Social Democratic Party (PSD), 8
	Popular Party (PP), 2
Romania	Democratic Liberal Party (DLP), 11
	Hungarian Democratic Union (UDMR), 3
Slovakia	Slovak Democratic and Christian Union (SDKÚ-DS), 2
	Christian Democratic Movement (KDH), 2
	Party of the Hungarian Coalition (SMK), 2
Slovenia	Slovenian Democratic Party (SDS), 3
	New Slovenia–Christian People's Party (NSi), 1
Spain	Popular Party (PP), 24
	Democratic Union of Catalonia (UDC), 1
Sweden	Moderate Coalition Party (MSP), 4
	Christian Democratic Party (KD), 1

Progressive Alliance of Socialists and Democrats (S&D), 194

Austria	Austrian Social Democratic Party (SPÖ), 5
Belgium	Socialist Party (PS), 3
	Socialist Party–Differently (SP.A), 2
Bulgaria	Coalition for Bulgaria (BSP), 4
Croatia	Socialist Party Hrvatske (SPH), 5
Cyprus	Movement of Social Democrats EDEK (KS), 1
	Democratic Comma (DK), 1
Czech Republic	Czech Social Democratic Party (ČSSD), 7
Denmark	Social Democratic Party (A), 5
Estonia	Social Democratic Party (SDE), 1
Finland	Finnish Social Democratic Party (SSDP), 2
France	Socialist Party (PS), 13
Germany	Social Democratic Party of Germany (SPD), 23
Greece	Panhellenic Socialist Movement (PA.SO.K), 8
Hungary	Hungarian Socialist Party (MSzP), 4
Ireland	The Labour Party, 2
Italy	Democratic Party (PD), 21
	Italy of Values-List of Peter (IdV), 1
Latvia	Alliance of Political Parties "Harmony Center" (PPA "SC"), 1
Lithuania	Lithuanian Social Democratic Party (LSDP), 3
Luxembourg	Socialist Workers' Party of Luxembourg (LSAP), 1
Malta	Malta Labour Party (MLP), 4
Netherlands	Labor Party (PvdA), 3
Poland	Democratic Left Alliance (SLD)/Union of Labor (UP), 7
Portugal	Portuguese Socialist Party (PSP), 7
Romania	Party of Social Democrats- Conservative Party (PSD-PS), 11
Slovakia	Direction (*Směr*), 5

Slovenia	Slovenian Democrats (SDS), 2
Spain	Spanish Socialist Workers' Party (PSOE), 22
	Socialist Party of Catalonia (PSC-PSOE), 1
Sweden	Social Democrats(s), 6
United Kingdom	Labour Party, 13

Alliance of Liberals and Democrats for Europe (ALDE), 85

Austria	Independent Candidate, 1
Belgium	Flemish Liberals and Democrats (VLD), 3
	Reformist Movement (MR), 2
Bulgaria	Movement for Rights and Freedoms (DPS), 3
	National Movement for Stability and Progress (NDSV), 2
Denmark	Liberal Party (V), 3
Estonia	Independent Candidate, 2
	Estonian Reform Party (ER), 1
Finland	Finnish Center (*Kesk*), 3
	Swedish People's Party (SF), 1
France	Democratic Movement (MoDem), 5
	Citizenship Action Participation for the 21st Century (CAP), 1
Germany	Free Democratic Party (FDP), 12
Greece	Democratic Alliance (DA), 1
Ireland	Fianna Fáil (FF), 3
	Independent Candidate, 1
Italy	Italy of Values-List of Peter (IdV), 4
	Independent Candidate, 1
Latvia	Latvia's First Party-Latvian Way (LPP-LC), 1
Lithuania	Darbo Party (DP), 1
	Lithuanian Republican Liberals (LRLS), 1
Luxembourg	Democratic Party (DP), 1
Netherlands	People's Party for Freedom and Democracy (VVD), 3
	Democrats 66 (D66), 3
Romania	National Liberal Party (PNL), 5
Slovakia	People's Party-Movement for a Democratic Slovakia (L'S-HZDS), 1
Slovenia	Liberal Democracy of Slovenia (LDS), 1
	For Real (*Zares*), 1
Spain	Basque Nationalist Party (PNV), 1
	Democratic Convergence of Catalonia (CDC), 1
Sweden	Liberal People's Party (FP), 3
	Center Party (CP), 1
United Kingdom	Liberal Democrats (LD), 12

Group of the Greens/European Free Alliance, 58

Austria	The Greens, 2
Belgium	Ecologists (ECOLO), 2
	Green!, 1
	New Flemish Alliance (N-VA), 1
Denmark	Socialist People's Party (SF), 1
Estonia	Independent Candidate, 1
Finland	Green League (*Vihr*), 2
France	Europe Écologie, 15
	Party of the Corsican Nation (PNC), 1
Germany	Alliance '90/The Greens, 14
Greece	Ecologist Greens (OP), 1
Latvia	For Human Rights in United Latvia (PCTVL), 1
Luxembourg	The Greens, 1
Netherlands	Green Left (GL), 3
Portugal	Independent Candidate, 1
Spain	Galician Nationalist Block (BNG), 1
	Initiative for Catalonia-Green (ICV), 1
Sweden	Green Ecology Party (MpG), 2
	Pirate Party, 2
United Kingdom	Green Party, 2
	Scottish National Party (SNP), 2
	Plaid Cymru, 1

European Conservatives and Reformists Group (ECR), 56

Belgium	Libertarian, Direct, Democratic Party (LDD), 1
Croatia	Croatian Party of Rights (HSP), 1
The Czech Republic	Civic Democratic Party (ODS), 9
Denmark	Independent Candidate, 1
Hungary	Independent Candidate, 1
Italy	Conservatives for Social Reform (CSR), 1
	Independent Candidate, 1
Latvia	For Fatherland and Freedom (TB-LNNK), 1
Lithuania	Electoral Action of Poles in Lithuania(AWPL), 1
Netherlands	Christian Union (CU), 1
Poland	Law and Justice (PiS), 6
	Poland is the Most Important (PJK), 3
	Independent Candidate, 2
United Kingdom	Conservative Party (Cons.), 26
	Ulster Conservatives and Unionists (UUP), 1

European United Left/Nordic Green Left (GUE/NGL), 35

Croatia	Croatian Labor (HL-SR), 1
Cyprus	Progressive Party of the Working People (AKEL), 2
The Czech Republic	Communist Party of Bohemia and Moravia (KSČM), 4
Denmark	People's Movement against the European Union (FmEU), 1
France	Left Front (FG), 4
	Alliance of the Overseas (AOM), 1
Germany	The Left, 8
Greece	Communist Party of Greece (KKE), 2
	Coalition of the Radical Left (SY.RIZ.A.), 1
Ireland	Socialist Party (SP), 1
Latvia	Harmony Center (SC), 1
Netherlands	Socialist Party (SP), 1
	Independent Candidate, 1
Portugal	Portuguese Communist Party (PCP), 2
	Left Block (BE), 2
Spain	United Left (IU),1
Sweden	Left Party (Vp), 1
United Kingdom and Northern Ireland	*Sinn Féin*, 1

Europe of Freedom and Democracy (EFD), 32

Belgium	Independent Candidate, 1
Bulgaria	People for Real, Open and United Democracy (PROUD), 1
Denmark	Danish People's Party (O), 1
Finland	Christian Democrats-True Finn (KD-PS), 1
France	Movement for France-Hunting,Fishing, Nature, Tradition (MPF—CPNT), 1
Greece	Popular Orthodox Rally (LA.O.S.), 2
Italy	Northern League (LN), 7
	I Love Italy (LAI), 1

Lithuania	Order and Justice Party (TT), 2
Netherlands	Christian Union-Reformed Political Party, 1
Poland	Several Poland (SP), 4
Slovakia	Slovak Nationalist Party (SNS), 1
United Kingdom	United Kingdom Independence Party (UKIP), 10

Unattached, 31

Austria	Freedom Party of Austria (FPÖ), 2
	List of Hans-Peter Martin "For Democracy, Control, Justice," 1
	Alliance Future Austria, 1
	Independent Candidate, 1
Belgium	Flemish Interest, 1
Bulgaria	National Democratic Party, 1
France	National Front (FN), 3
Hungary	Movement for a Better Hungary (JMM), 3
Ireland	Labour Party, 1
Italy	Northern League (LN), 1
	Independent Candidate, 1
Netherlands	Party for Freedom (PVV), 4
	Article 50 (A50), 1
Romania	Greater Romania Party (PRM), 2
	Social Democrat Party (PSD), 1
Spain	Union, Progress and Democracy (UPyD), 1
United Kingdom	We Demand a Referendum, 1
	United Kingdom Independence Party (UKIP), 2
	British National Party (BNP), 1
	Democratic Unionist Party (DUP), 1
	British Democratic Party (BDP), 1

The Court of Justice of the European Communities (less formally, the European Court of Justice—ECJ), encompassing 27 judges and 8 advocates-general, sits in Luxembourg. In 1989 a Court of First Instance was established to help the ECJ deal with its increasingly large workload. The 27 members of each court are appointed for six years by agreement between the governments of the member states. The judges themselves appoint a president of their prospective court who serves a three-year term. Both courts can sit in plenary session or in chambers of three or five judges. Since the 2004 EU enlargement, instead of convening in a plenary session, 13 ECJ judges can sit as a Grand Chamber. The ECJ can sit in plenary session when a member state or an EU/EC institution that is party to the proceedings so requests or in particularly complex or important cases. A European Civil Service Tribunal, comprised of seven judges, is under the Court of First Instance.

Recent Activities. EU policy supports gradual and carefully managed enlargement. However, debate continues over how large the EU should become and whether prospective nations should reflect core European values. The classification of Turkey as a candidate country has been particularly controversial because of issues such as immigration, political Islam, human rights standards, and its shared border with Iraq and Syria. Although Turkey has a small piece of territory in continental Europe, many argue that it belongs to Asia Minor.

Turkey first applied for membership in 1987 (at that time to the EEC). The European Council finally accepted its eligibility in 1997. Accession talks began in 2005, and as of mid-2010 only 1 of the 35 chapters, or policy areas, had been provisionally closed, with Turkey meeting conditions concerning science and research. Another 18 chapters have been opened, but the process has been stymied by Turkey's refusal to open ports to Greek Cypriot ships and planes, as well as the continued objections of France.

Turkey's prospects have been dimmed by slow progress on political reforms and by the growing political influence of far-right and anti-immigrant parties in the European Parliament after the elections in June 2009. The country is not expected to satisfy all qualifications for membership within the decade. Given this outlook, there has been discussion about granting Turkey and other aspiring countries a special EU partnership that would be short of membership. Turkey has rebuffed alternatives to full integration.

In 2004 an EU "Neighborhood Policy" plan was launched with the aim of giving countries immediately bordering Europe by land or sea intermediary levels of EU benefits following bilateral agreements on "action plans" for political and economic reforms. Agreements were signed in 2005 with Israel, Jordan, Moldova, Morocco, the Palestinian Authority, Tunisia, and Ukraine; in 2006 with Armenia, Azerbaijan, and Georgia; and in 2007 with Egypt and Lebanon. Other countries reportedly on the list but without agreed upon action plans as of late 2009 included Algeria, Belarus, Libya, and Syria. A progress report filed by the Commission in April 2009 enunciated the difficulties of advancing the program because of the recent violent conflicts in Georgia and in Gaza, the slow pace of democratic reforms, and the global financial crisis, among other stated reasons.

Other partnerships with EU's surrounding countries have also been advanced in recent years. The Union for the Mediterranean, formerly known as the Barcelona Process, was launched in July 2008 between the EU and 16 countries in the southern Mediterranean and Middle East and identified priority projects, including ridding pollution from the Mediterranean. Additionally, on May 8, 2009, in Prague, the EU launched an "Eastern Partnership" initiative with post-Soviet states to "accelerate political association and further economic integration" with the EU but without the prospect of eventual EU membership. Signatories included the EU along with Armenia, Azerbaijan, Belarus, Georgia, Moldova, and Ukraine. The initiative will establish free trade areas and offer EU economic aid, technical expertise, and security consultations in exchange for obligations by the six former Soviet states to commit to democracy, the rule of law, and human rights policies. Russia accused the EU of carving out a new sphere of influence.

In late 2007 Bosnia and Herzegovina signed stabilization and association agreements with the EU, a first step toward membership, while Serbia's stalled talks resumed after it agreed to arrest and extradite remaining fugitives wanted by the war crimes tribunal. Meanwhile, the EU council in February 2008 launched a crisis management mission to the newly declared country of Kosovo. The EU Rule of Law Mission in Kosovo is charged with assisting in the formation of "independent and multi-ethnic" law enforcement and judicial systems. Kosovo signed a pre-accession assistance agreement in May that provided $83 million for infrastructure and financial stabilization projects, although its future membership was considered uncertain given that four EU countries that would have to ratify its accession had not recognized Kosovo as an independent state. Additionally, in July 2009 the EC recommended visa-free access for Macedonians, although no date had been set for EU membership talks because of election violence and widespread corruption.

Croatia is expected to become the 28th country to join the EU, in 2011. Negotiations were slowed in 2008 by Slovenia's veto of accession talks as a result of a longstanding border dispute. Talks resumed in September 2009 following Slovenia's agreement to handle the dispute separately. Montenegro submitted an application in December 2008, followed by Albania in April 2009.

At an EU summit in Brussels on March 13–14, 2008, an agreement was reached on greenhouse gas emissions and renewable energy to meet targets for a 20 percent reduction in emissions by 2020. The plan was approved by the European Parliament on December 17 despite objections by Eastern European countries that the measures would raise energy costs and be overly burdensome during an economic recession. Nevertheless, the plan gave each nation and sector mandated emission limits, while creating an auction system on emissions from industrial sources (currently free of charge) beginning in 2013, and set 20 percent targets for better energy efficiency and renewables in the EU's energy mix.

In one of the first concrete signs of defense cooperation between EU member states, the EU announced plans in November 2008 to build a pan-European military aircraft transport fleet. Expected to be operational within a decade, the European Air Transport Fleet would be housed by member nations and made available for humanitarian and peacekeeping missions.

In November 2008 the EU officially slipped into economic recession, its first since the creation of the eurozone in 1999. The downturn quickly became the single greatest challenge facing the union, with the Baltic states, Spain, and the United Kingdom especially exposed by inflated real estate markets. Countries with large current account deficits, notably Greece and Hungary, also suffered. Germany's economy also declined because of its heavy reliance on exports.

In response, EU institutions took unprecedented actions to salvage the block's financial industries. Initially injecting $270 billion into the

EU banking system in August 2007, efforts were doubled a year later. Throughout the fall of 2008 and into 2009, the European Central Bank repeatedly cut interest rates in coordination with the central banks of member countries and the U.S. Federal Reserve. It was also announced that members that breached the budget deficit threshold of 3 percent of GDP would be given time to bring their spending in line before penalties would be imposed.

Meanwhile, in October and December 2008 the EU took directed action with the IMF and World Bank to assist Hungary and Latvia, whose currencies had dramatically depreciated. In November the EC outlined a $257 billion stimulus package for member states, equivalent to approximately 1.5 percent of the EU's GDP, to be drawn from member governments and from within EU budgets. The stimulus plan was passed in December and was viewed with skepticism, particularly by Germany, which resisted a return to large-scale deficit spending after having made painful strides in recent years to balance its own budget. Other analysts said the plan's combination of tax cuts and accelerated regional spending was not sufficiently targeted to provide immediate relief.

In March 2009 EU leaders, led by Germany, rejected a proposal for a special aid package to non-eurozone countries, although Hungary warned of a new "Iron Curtain" descending. However, soon after, at a leadership summit in Brussels, assistance available to non-eurozone countries was doubled to $68 billion and a $5 billion stimulus measure was directed toward green technology and digital communication projects. EU leaders rejected pressure from the United States to raise the size of their economic stimulus plans in favor of restraining budget deficits. Following the collapse of Iceland's banking industry, Iceland's parliament (*Althing*) narrowly voted in July 2009 to apply for EU membership in the hopes of achieving lasting economic stability. The decision was received warmly by EU leaders, although Iceland's entry was not assured because of likely differences over EU quotas that could affect its fish industry. The Netherlands and the UK were also said to be ready to veto Iceland's accession unless Iceland paid compensation for their citizens who had lost money in the collapse of the online bank Icesave.

A cornerstone of the EU response to the recession has been to impose stricter regulation on financial markets. In February and March 2009 the EU announced new regulatory requirements for credit-rating agencies and additional oversight over hedge funds. Additionally, in September the EU called for limits on executive bonuses as part of G-20 discussions on an overhaul of the global financial system.

The June 4–7, 2009, parliamentary election ushered in a smaller body dominated by center-right groups. The size of parliament decreased from a record of 785 members to 736, while center-left parties failed to articulate a socialist response to the ongoing economic recession. Populist parties and some environmental formations made some inroads, while in Hungary the far-right nationalist Jobbik party took third place. The election registered a new low in voter turnout at 43 percent, with Central and Eastern European countries displaying the most voter apathy. The resulting body split into a number of new formations. The largest remained the European People's Party, which dropped the suffix "European Democrats" after a 54-strong contingent led by the UK Conservatives dropped out and formed the European Conservatives and Reformists Group. The Party of European Socialists changed its name to Progressive Alliance of Socialists and Democrats to signify that it was not a rigidly socialist formation.

Following the election an EU summit in Brussels on June 18–19 resulted in a package of legal guarantees addressing policy areas important to Ireland to safeguard against a second Irish refusal of the Lisbon Treaty in a referendum to be held in October. Additionally, countries agreed to establish a "European system of financial supervisors" by 2010 that would consist of three new authorities with oversight powers of the banking, insurance, and securities sectors. The agreement represented a compromise solution between a contingent led by France that called for much stricter regulation over the financial industry and the United Kingdom, which worried that additional supervision would drive companies out of the country.

Meanwhile, in July 2009 four EU countries (Austria, Bulgaria, Romania, and Hungary) completed a deal with Turkey to cede territory for the construction of the Nabucco pipeline to bring stable gas supplies from the Caspian Sea to Europe, but the source of the supplies was not assured as Azerbaijan refused to commit its gas reserves to Europe, instead cooperating with Russia in building a rival pipeline. Repeated disruptions in winter deliveries of Russian gas to EU countries, the result of Russian disputes with Ukraine, have intensified the EU's efforts to find an alternative supplier to Russia, which currently provides one-quarter of the EU's gas supplies.

On September 16, 2009, Barroso was reelected to a second five-year term of office with the unanimous support of all members and no opposing candidate. However, he faced criticism for favoring large member states, such as Germany, France, and the United Kingdom.

At an earlier EU summit on June 18–19, 2009, the European Council approved a set of "legal guarantees" pertaining to the Lisbon Treaty that affirmed that Irish policies on taxation, abortion, education, family, workers' rights, and military neutrality would be addressed to "the mutual satisfaction of Ireland and the other member states." Upon the insistence of Ireland, the measures were to become protocol, meaning they would be incorporated into EU treaties, although several EU countries were uneasy about the designation because it would need to be ratified by all EU national parliaments. However, it was agreed this would be done as part of the next accession agreement, expected upon Croatian membership in 2011.

Irish voters approved the treaty by 67 percent in a referendum on October 2, 2009, thereby removing the last major hurdle to the treaty's implementation. Despite the strong margin of victory, analysts attributed the treaty's passage to Irish economic despair and fear over losing ties to the EU rather than genuine enthusiasm for the treaty. The president of the Czech Republic, Václav Klaus, ratified the treaty on November 23 following the resolution of legal questions surrounding its compatibility with the Czech constitution. Poland's president, Lech Kaczyński, had signed the treaty on October 10. Polish and Czech ratification allowed for implementation of the treaty on December 1, 2009, which began with the appointment of the Belgian prime minister, Herman Van Rompuy, as the permanent president of the European Council, for a term of two and a half years, and with the selection of Catherine Ashton, of the UK Labour Party, as the High Representative for Foreign Affairs.

Most of 2010 was dominated by an ongoing crisis involving the sovereign debt of several eurozone countries with weak economies, and with related speculative runs on the euro. Greece and Ireland both came close to default, Greece between February and May, Ireland in October and November. Both countries required support from the entire EU community and the International Monetary Fund (IMF, see separate article). Severe austerity measures and riots ensued in both countries. Italy, Spain, and Portugal were also mentioned as likely to have economic problems. Some commentators went as far as to wonder if the euro could survive in its present form. Significant German money went into the Greek bailout, causing the German public's dissatisfaction with the EU and with the euro to rise. The non-eurozone UK, the majority of whose citizens already dislike the EU, also contributed to the rescue of Ireland.

An October 2010 Council summit set in place stringent new rules designed to protect the euro. A rainy-day fund was proposed to protect the euro in times of crisis. The EU budget was to increase by only 2.9 percent annually. A serious disagreement ensued in November with the parliament, which wanted a 6 percent increase. Failing resolution, the 2011 budget would remain at 2010 levels.

On June 17, 2010, the European Council decided to open accession talks with Iceland. Icelandic membership would give the EU more standing in future negotiations concerning the Arctic. Formal negotiations began in July 2011. In October 2010 Serbia's application was seen as back on track, since it had given up its demand that the EU consider Kosovo as part of Serbian territory. Montenegro was also progressing toward membership. Meanwhile in June 2011 the EU finalized negotiations with Croatia on membership and announced in September that the nation would join the EU on July 1, 2013.

On January 31, 2011, the EU imposed a series of sanctions on Belarus following government repression of protests in the aftermath of disputed presidential balloting (see entry on Belarus). In recognition of Myanmar's elections in November 2010, the EU in April 2011 suspended a series of sanctions against figures in the new government (see entry on Myanmar).

In January 2011 Estonia joined the euro zone. The following month, in response to continuing concerns over the debt crisis in Greece, Ireland, Portugal and Spain, the euro zone leaders agree to establish a €500 billion emergency fund, the European Stabilization Mechanism. In May Portugal became the next European nation to request EU financial assistance. A €78 billion rescue package was subsequently negotiated. Meanwhile, a second, €109 billion package was finalized for Greece. Both Spain and Italy had to adopt austerity budgets to contain spiraling debt costs. In December EU leaders launched talks on a new fiscal policy treaty designed to prevent excessive debts and deficits among the 27 members of the Union. However, Hungary and the United Kingdom objected to constraints that the agreement would place on national governments and subsequent negotiations centered on the 17 members of the Eurozone. The remaining 25 members of the EU, including the 17 members of the Eurozone, agreed to a Treaty on Stability, Coordination, and Governance in the Economic and Monetary Union at a special summit held in Brussels in January 2012. The treaty accomplished the goals of the proposed treaty from December 2011 that had been rejected by the UK. The treaty was fully ratified by all of the member states by December 12, 2012, and entered into effect on January 1, 2013.

By February, the situation in Greece had further deteriorated to the point that the EU and IMF (see separate article, under UN Specialized Agencies) agreed to a second bailout of the Greek economy for a total of €230 billion. This deal, even larder than the first one, was designed to reduce Greece's national debt from 160 percent of the GDP to 120 percent by 2020. The bailout agreement called on Greece to accept a permanent representative from the troika—the EU, IMF, and ECB—and make additional budget and spending cuts of €3.3 billion. The austerity measure passed the Greek legislature after heated debate, but resulted in wide spread anger and mass resignations from within the government, as many Greek citizens and officials claimed that the EU and IMF had treated them too harshly.

As the EU remained focused on the debt crisis, the European Parliament issued a February green paper that called on the EU member states to approve the creation and sale of Eurobonds. The European Economic and Social Committee echoed this sentiment during a June 2012 meeting. One of the biggest supporters of the Eurobond position is French president Francois Hollande (see below), while German Chancellor Angela Merkel remains the largest opponent of the position. Merkel remains committed to her position that austerity measures are the only way to safely handle the crisis.

French and Greek elections held in May both resulted in the election of anti-bailout opposition parties within each state. This proved to further complicate matters in reaching a comprehensive debt reduction solution at a special May meeting of the European Commission. The new French President, Francois Hollande, of the French Socialist Party, called for a re-negotiation of the January 2012 EMU treaty. Furthermore, the party change in Greece resulted in some discussion at the May commission meeting of possibly removing Greece from the Eurozone if the new leaders did not soon implement the already approved austerity measures.

Further signaling an economic spiral downward, Spain requested a bank bailout of its own in May 2012, amounting to the sum of €100 billion. Like the other countries that have received a bailout, Spain was expected to implement a series of austerity measures that involve reducing debt, cutting spending, and increasing revenue. Also, the European Financial Stability Facility (EFSF), a fund created by the January EMU treaty to assist with the economic bailout, was given the authority to purchase Spanish bonds as a means of reducing debt. Spain became the fourth Eurozone country to accept a bailout of its banking industry. The bailout was finalized in July 2012.

At a June 2012 meeting of the European Council, the heads of state and government agreed to a new plan to help combat the debt crisis—the Compact on Growth and Jobs. The new agreement aims to ease the crisis by reinvigorating the economy, deepening its commitments to overall job creation, and working to increase Europe's competitiveness in the global market. The council also approved a series of member-specific recommendations for debt reduction and improvements in financial security. The council also discussed ways to save the EMU and prevent the total collapse of the Eurozone. A full report is expected in the fall.

On a slightly different note, the May 2012 plenary session of the European Parliament resulted in the passage of a new Financial Transaction Tax (FTT) that would apply to all security and stock transactions. The new tax has been the topic of legislative discussions since early 2011, but was tabled in a late-2011 session. The bill creating the FTT also placed a series of preventative measures to curtail tax evasion.

In November the EU and 10 Latin American states signed an agreement ending their dispute over bananas. The agreement lowered the EU's import tariff on bananas and established annual maximum tariff rates until 2017. The banana dispute, settled within theWTO framework, had been ongoing since 1992.

In December the European Council approved a new initiative designed to streamline innovation in Europe with the creation of a unitary patent. The new EU patent will be accepted in all EU member states, will be more cost efficient and easier, and will be obtained through the European Patent Office in Munich. Also at the meeting, the Council approved its roadmap agreement for the completion of the Economic and Monetary Union. The roadmap calls for immediate action concerning the completion, strengthening, and implementation of enhanced economic governance and the adoption of the Single Supervisory Mechanism on banking. The roadmap also called for further mechanisms to be put in place by the end of 2013.

On December 10, 2012, the European Union was awarded the Nobel Peace Prize for its role in advancing security and reconciliation in Europe.

In February the United States and European Union announced that they were beginning discussions to negotiate a bilateral trade agreement between the two parties. The agreement will have three main components: market access; regulatory issues and non-tariff barriers; and rules, principles, and new modes of cooperation to address shared global trade challenges and opportunities. Transatlantic trade currently amounts for 47 percent of the world GDP. The trade deal could yield annual GDP increases of 0.5 percent for the EU and 0.4 percent for the United States. At the G-8 meeting in May, UK Prime Minister David Cameron hailed this as the "biggest bilateral trade deal in history, a deal that will have greater impact than all the other trade deals on the table put together."

In March the EU announced negotiations of a new Free Trade agreement between the two parties. Official negotiations began in April.

In June the European Commission approved Latvia's entry into the Eurozone. Having achieved high levels of sustainable economic convergence with the euro area, Latvia will officially enter the Eurozone and make the Euro its official currency effective January 1, 2014.

At a meeting of the European Council in late June, the Council took further measures to advance the completion of the EMU. The council adopted country-specific recommendations concerning policy changes and approved the multiannual financial framework for 2014–2020. The MFF will guide the EU's budgetary and spending process until 2020 by representing its political priorities with financial backing. The meeting also saw a decision concerning the troubling situation with youth unemployment. The Council encouraged the creation of new programs to promote employment and authorized the January 1, 2014, implementation of the Youth Employment Initiative (YEI). The YEI will provide economic assistance to states with higher than 25 percent unemployment in their youth sector.

On July 1, 2013, Croatia became the 28th member of the European Union after a decade-long accession process. Croatia voted on its 12 European Parliament members in April, who took their seats at the July plenary session of the EP.

Later in July, the European Commission proposed the creation of a European Public Prosecutor's Office. According to Commission President Barroso, the new position will build upon the EU's "commitment to upholding the rule of law; it will decisively enhance the protection of taxpayers' money and the effective tackling of fraud involving EU funds." According to the EU website, "The European Public Prosecutor's Office will make sure that every case involving suspected fraud against the EU budget is followed up and completed, so that criminals know they will be prosecuted and brought to justice."

EUROPEAN ATOMIC ENERGY COMMUNITY

(Euratom)

Communauté Européenne de l'Energie Atomique (CEEA)

Established: By Treaty of Rome (Italy), signed March 25, 1957, effective January 1, 1958.

Purpose: To develop research, to disseminate information, to enforce uniform safety standards, to facilitate investment, to ensure regular and equitable distribution of supplies of nuclear material, to guarantee that nuclear materials are not diverted from their designated uses and to exercise certain property rights in regard to such materials, to create a common market for the free movement of investment capital and personnel for nuclear industries, and to promote the peaceful uses of atomic energy.

Membership: (See European Union.)

Web site: http://euratom.org

Origin and development. Euratom was established in response to the assessment that atomic power on a large scale would be urgently needed to meet the growing energy requirements for economic expansion. The original six European Steel and Coal Community (ECSC) member states also sought to reduce the lead that Britain, the Soviet Union, and the United States had acquired in the field of peaceful uses of nuclear energy. To this end, the members decided to pool their efforts, as the area was too complex and expensive to be dealt with nationally. Structurally, the Treaty of Rome provided for a council, a commission, and the sharing of the assembly and court of justice already operating under the ECSC.

In December 1969 it was agreed to reshape Euratom so that it could conduct nuclear research under contract for community clients and extend its activities to other scientific research projects, especially those involving noncommunity states. The council also resolved to streamline the community's management, making its operations more flexible and ensuring more effective coordination of its nuclear activities. These reforms took effect in 1971.

In 1981 an agreement came into force between the community, France, and the International Atomic Energy Agency (IAEA) regarding safeguards on certain nuclear materials, and officials signed long-term agreements establishing conditions for the sale and security within the EC of nuclear materials supplied by Australia and Canada. In November 1995 Euratom and the United States completed negotiations on a controversial new agreement concerning "nuclear cooperation" to replace an accord set to expire at the end of the year. The most contentious element of the pact was a provision giving Euratom members greater latitude in selling plutonium originating from the United States. Previously, Washington had held a veto power over any such transactions; however, the new agreement permitted Euratom members to trade the plutonium within EU borders without U.S. approval. In 2000 the United States and Euratom reached a cooperative agreement that covers fusion as well as fission research.

Given that approximately one-third of the EU's energy is nuclear, Euratom continues to be involved in efforts to prevent a disruption of nuclear fuel supplies. Since 1960 a Euratom Supply Agency operating under the commission has coordinated all of Euratom's contracts for the supply of fissionable material. Inspections of installations that use these supplies are conducted on a regular basis to ensure that nuclear materials are not diverted from peaceful uses and are otherwise maintained under appropriate safeguards.

Because of diminished popular support for nuclear energy, triggered in part by the 1986 Chernobyl disaster in the Soviet Union, the European Commission stopped approving new loans for construction of nuclear power plants within member countries. In June 2004, however, the commission approved a proposal for a Finnish plant, the first in the EU in over a decade and the world's first "third-generation" (post-2000) facility, which has new safety, reliability, and cost-saving features. In June 2004 the commission approved a loan of €224 million ($275 million) for construction of a reactor in candidate country Romania. Loans for safety and modernization efforts were also extended to other Eastern European countries, including Russia and Ukraine, where the last Chernobyl reactor was permanently shut down in December 2000. The Finnish plant currently has two operational reactors with construction to begin on the third reactor by 2015. By January 2006, France and the Czech Republic had announced plans to build more nuclear plants, and Belgium, Italy, Germany, and Sweden had all begun reconsideration of the nuclear power moratorium.

Concurrently, scientists have intensified research on thermonuclear fusion, which many believe could provide power without most of the safety risks and environmental problems associated with fission reactors. The long-term goal of the EU Fusion Program is "the joint creation of prototype reactors which will lead to electric power plants that meet society's needs: operational safety, respect for the environment, economic viability." Since the first half of the 1980s, fusion research has been conducted at the Joint European Torus (JET), a research and development facility in Culham, United Kingdom. On January 1, 2000, the new European Fusion Development Agreement (EFDA) became operational to govern use of JET to coordinate fusion technology projects within the EU and to oversee EU participation in outside endeavors. These endeavors include the international thermonuclear experimental reactor (ITER) project initiated in 1988 by Japan, Russia, and the United States, for which a design was completed in 2001. China and South Korea also are participating in the $12 billion project. In June 2005 the partners announced that ITER would be built in Cadarache, France, with a target completion date of 2015.

In December 2002 the European Court of Justice (ECJ), ruling in a dispute brought by the European Commission against the Council of the European Union, stated that Euratom, as well as the individual member countries, had competence with regard to broader nuclear safety concerns. In a declaration accompanying the Act of Accession to the 1994 global Convention on Nuclear Safety, the council had erred, according to the ECJ, by overly limiting Euratom's role to workplace-related protections and emergency planning, whereas the organization was also competent in safety matters related to siting facilities, design and construction, and operations. In May 2005, confirming a 2004 proposal by the commission, the council extended Euratom competence to two international conventions adopted in 1986, the Convention on Early Notification of a Nuclear Accident and the Convention on Assistance in the Case of a Nuclear Accident or Radiological Emergency.

Meanwhile, during the constitutional debates of the Convention on the Future of Europe, the question of Euratom's future role became a significant issue. In the end, in 2003 the drafting convention left the Euratom treaty intact. Later, the European Parliament, which has long sought greater control over Euratom activities, urged the intergovernmental conference (IGC) on the constitution "to convene a Treaty revision conference in order to repeal the obsolete and outdated provisions of that Treaty, especially those relating to the promotion of nuclear energy and the lack of democratic decision-making procedures." The governments of Austria, Germany, Hungary, Ireland, and Sweden also called for convening a special IGC on Euratom and related nuclear matters, as they also did in a declaration attached to the Treaty of Lisbon in 2007. That treaty, ratified in 2009, includes Euratom's expenditures and revenues in the EU budget, excluding the Euratom Supply Agency and joint undertakings.

Euratom has its own "framework program" for nuclear research and training activities that is managed by common EC institutions. Euratom's Seventh Framework Program (FP7), which calls for spending €2.8 billion ($3.6 billion) during 2007–2011 encompasses two categories of research. "Indirect actions," which are managed by the commission's Directorate General for Research, involve fusion energy, nuclear fission, and radiation protection. "Direct actions," undertaken by the Joint Research Center (JRC), cover three themes: nuclear waste management; environmental impact; and basic knowledge, nuclear safety, and nuclear security. The JRC was established by Euratom and has become a leading European institute for nuclear research.

Pressure to expand nuclear power in EU borders, particularly in the East, has grown in recent years, although Euratom's role remains controversial. Despite safety concerns brought by activists, the EC in December 2007 approved construction of a new two-unit Russian-designed nuclear power plant in Belene in northern Bulgaria, paving the way for an application for a sizable Euratom loan, which would be the agency's first in 20 years. By late 2007 the Belene project was plagued with uncertainties, including corruption allegations and difficulties in attracting funding even as Euratom guaranteed a $780 million loan. In 2007 the European Commission authorized the creation of a new group—the European Nuclear Energy Forum (ENEF). The ENEF is composed of representatives from each member state, representatives from various EU Institutions, and nuclear industry representatives. The ENEF is designed to promote an environment more conducive to discussing the risks and opportunities of nuclear energy.

In February 2008 the European Council of Ministers updated Euratom statutes by shrinking its advisory committee from 75 to 56 members to improve the body's efficiency. The agency was also given approval to build a multinational nuclear fuel reserve to provide a backup supply of enriched uranium to be used if supplies from outside the EU were cut off for political reasons.

Recent Activities. In March 2009 the EC announced its intent to advance a nuclear nonproliferation framework for bilateral agreements with nuclear countries seeking to have significant nuclear trade with EU countries or industries. Euratom would negotiate bilateral agreements and provide expertise in nuclear energy in exchange for commitments to use nuclear energy for entirely peaceful purposes.

Upon an EC directive in November 2008, Euratom drafted a Nuclear Safety Directive that established legally binding rules for safety standards on nuclear installations within EU member states and enhanced the powers of national regulatory bodies. The EC approved the directive on June 25, 2009.

On December 22, 2009, the EU Council approved a mandate for the Commission to negotiate a full nuclear cooperation agreement with Russia. It was estimated that about 45 percent of all enriched uranium in the EU came from Russia, either directly or from the nuclear power plants of EU countries that were formerly in the Soviet orbit. In May 2010 the commission called for a "sustainable framework" for the funding of ITER. ITER's costs had experienced explosive growth. On November 2, 2010, the U.S. National Nuclear Security Administration (NNSA) announced that it had signed an agreement with Euratom to promote greater cooperation in nuclear security and nonproliferation.

In 2011 Euratom estimated that one-third of the 144 nuclear reactors then in operation in the EU would need to be decommissioned by 2025. To support the decommissioning of aged nuclear plants, the EC approved €500 million to shut down plants in Bulgaria, Lithuania, and Slovakia. In September the EC enacted new regulations requiring Euratom to standardize the manner in which it reported on energy projects.

In May 2012, the European Commission approved a new series of safety guidelines for nuclear power plants designed to increase the community's protection from the effects of nuclear radiation. The legislation is the third measure of its kind since March 2011, marking a definite commitment from the European Commission to safeguard the EU citizens from any form of nuclear radiation.

At its June 2012 meeting in Bratislava, the European Nuclear Energy Forum discussed the progress made in the ongoing stress tests of the nuclear reactors in EU member states. The stress tests have currently completed phase two of three and the self-assessments of each facility are undergoing peer review from a team of nuclear energy experts from across the EU countries. The forum also discussed the financial and security concerns and advantages that are presented by nuclear power in the context of the Energy Roadmap 2050.

In May 2013 the European Nuclear Energy Forum encouraged member states to increase their investments in the energy sector, noting that there was a greater need for sustainable and renewable energy but a lack of funds for the research necessary to bring about the solutions. The ENEF also agreed that while individual member states should continue to control the mix of energy sources, there needs to be a collective look toward the future of energy in Europe. The organization suggested the need for a new energy outlook plan that would forecast to 2030 or 2050.

In June 2013 Euratom issued a proposed revision to the 2009 nuclear safety directive to be voted upon by the entire European Commission. The revisions introduced new safety objectives, established a European system of peer review, increased transparency, and added new provisions for emergency response.

In September Euratom and the IAEA signed a memorandum of understanding in which the two sides agreed to cooperate in their efforts. Under the new memorandum of understanding, the two organizations will benefit from the work of the other organization and undertake initiatives to reduce duplication of projects.

GROUP OF EIGHT

Established: Originally formed as the Group of Seven (G-7) during the San Juan, Puerto Rico, summit of leading industrial democracies held on June 27–28, 1976; first met as the kindred Group of Eight (G-8) after the addition of Russia as a formal participant at the May 15–17, 1998, G-7 summit in Birmingham, United Kingdom.

Purpose: To discuss problems relating to "geopolitical and security issues, the partnership with Africa in its dual political and economic dimensions, and subjects of common interest to the G-8 countries, facing specific challenges."

Principal Organs: The G-8 has one formal organ as such—the presidency. There are also annual summits, twice-a-year (and ad hoc) meetings of finance ministers and central bank governors, and other meetings of government ministers and officials.

Web site: http://www.g8.utoronto.ca (The G-8 has no formal website. The G-8 Research Group at the University of Toronto maintains this website with G-8 information.)

President: David Cameron (United Kingdom).

Membership (8): Canada, France, Germany, Italy, Japan, Russia, United Kingdom, United States.

Observers: The European Union is a permanent observer. China and India are also generally invited to G-8 meetings as observers.

Origin and development. The origins of the G-7 and G-8 can be traced back to 1962 and the founding of the informal Group of Ten (G-10) by Belgium, Canada, France, the Federal Republic of Germany, Italy, Japan, the Netherlands, Sweden, the United Kingdom, and the United States.

Later in the decade finance ministers and sometimes central bank governors from France, the Federal Republic of Germany, Japan, the United Kingdom, and the United States began to meet as an additional informal caucus that became known as the Group of Five (G-5). As a consequence of discussions at the July 30–August 1, 1975, Helsinki Conference on Security and Cooperation in Europe, the heads of state or government of the G-5 plus Italy convened in November 1975 in Rambouillet, France, to address various economic and financial concerns, including growth, inflation, exchange rates, monetary reform, oil prices, and unemployment. Canada joined as the seventh participant in the San Juan, Puerto Rico, summit in 1976, at which time the assembled leaders agreed on the utility of holding annual sessions. Thus the G-7 was born.

The agendas of the 1976 summit and then the May 7–8, 1977, summit in London, United Kingdom, were broadened to include such concerns as balance-of-payments problems and North-South relations. Also, beginning with the 1977 summit, the European Community (EC, subsequently the European Union—EU) was included in discussions. At the next summit, held July 16–17, 1978, in Bonn, West Germany, the G-7 issued an unprecedented statement denouncing aircraft hijacking that was widely recognized as the group's first political declaration. Developments at the 1979 summit in Paris included the establishment of the Financial Action Task Force (FATF), which was asked to identify and promote policies that would combat money laundering. The agendas at succeeding summits expanded to arms control, the environment, political reform, and terrorism. During the second half of the 1980s the G-7 focused on such matters as rectifying trade imbalances, stabilizing exchange rates, combating protectionism, and relaxing debt repayment pressure on the world's poorest countries.

The issue of how best to encourage free-market reform in the Soviet Union and its former satellites in Eastern Europe dominated the G-7 summit July 15–17, 1991, in London, which was attended by Soviet leader Mikhail Gorbachev. Some observers predicted that the meeting might lead to creation of a Group of Eight, a possibility that U.S. president George H. W. Bush then broached at the 1992 summit in Munich, Germany, which Russian president Boris Yeltsin attended. By the 1994 summit in Naples, Italy, Russian participation in most non-financial discussions had become the norm, resulting in the designation Political-8 (P-8). Russia's formal inclusion at the May 15–17, 1998, summit in Birmingham, United Kingdom, marked the birth of the G-8.

In the first half of the 1990s, G-7 discussions often centered on how best to support the fledgling free market systems in the former Communist world. The breakup of Yugoslavia and the attendant crises in the Balkans, Russian action in Chechnya, and the Mexico peso crisis of 1994–1995 also were among the most pressing topics during this period. Terrorism moved to the forefront of the agenda at the June 28–29, 1996, summit in Lyon, France, which took place only a week after the bombing of a U.S. military base in Saudi Arabia. At the urging of U.S. president Bill Clinton, the G-7 leaders approved a 40-point plan to combat crime and terrorism.

Meeting in February 1999, the finance ministers and bank governors approved a plan to establish a Financial Stability Forum (FSF), its primary purpose being to prevent economic crises by improving oversight of, and information exchange within, the world's financial systems. The forum comprised representatives of the G-8 countries, the Netherlands, Australia, Hong Kong, Singapore, Switzerland, the European Central Bank, the Bank for International Settlements (BIS), the International Monetary Fund (IMF), the OECD, the World Bank, the Basel Committee on Banking Supervision, the International Accounting Standards Board, the International Organization of Securities Commissions, the International Association of Insurance

Supervisors, the Committee on the Global Financial System, and the Committee on Payment and Settlement Systems.

Steps were also taken to include developing countries in discussions related to reform of global financial systems. Largely at the instigation of President Clinton at the November 1997 Asia-Pacific Economic Cooperation (APEC) summit in Vancouver, Canada, a temporary Group of 22 (G-22) took shape. In addition to the G-8 countries, G-22 participants included Argentina, Australia, Brazil, China, Hong Kong, India, Indonesia, South Korea, Malaysia, Mexico, Poland, Singapore, South Africa, and Thailand. The grouping held its first meeting in April 1998. Less than a year later, on March 11, 1999, a successor Group of 33 (G-33) met for the first time in Bonn, Germany, with a second session convening April 25 in Washington, D.C.

The G-33 was superseded September 26, 1999, by a new Group of 20 (see separate article) comprising representatives of the EU and the IMF/World Bank, as well as the G-8 members and the following 10 countries: Argentina, Australia, Brazil, China, India, Republic of Korea, Mexico, Saudi Arabia, South Africa, and Turkey.

The G-8 summit held July 20–22, 2001, in Genoa, Italy, took place amid disruptions caused by antiglobalization protests. In addition to the troubled state of the world economy, discussions centered on topics such as cutting emission of greenhouse gases, implementing a development plan for Africa, and overcoming the "digital divide." The session also approved a $1.3 billion fund to help combat AIDS, tuberculosis, and malaria.

Canada hosted the June 26–27, 2002, summit in Kananaskis, Alberta—sufficiently removed from the nearest large city, Calgary, to ease security concerns. Despite disagreements on particular issues—for example, U.S. tariffs directed against steel and softwood lumber imports and U.S. president George W. Bush's call for Palestinians to replace Yasir Arafat as leader of the Palestinian Authority—several initiatives were approved. The G-8 agreed to a ten-year aid package of $20 billion (half from the United States) to assist Russia and other countries of the former Soviet bloc in securing their remaining nuclear materials. The leaders also agreed to provide additional debt relief under the HIPC (Heavily Indebted Poor Countries) initiative, but the $1 billion commitment was far less than some advocates had sought. Similar criticism greeted the G-8 African Action Plan, which confirmed an earlier commitment of $6 billion per year, beginning in 2006, in support of the African Union's New Partnership for Africa's Development (NEPAD).

In 2003, at a February meeting of finance ministers and central bankers, some participants had criticized the Bush administration for its large tax cuts and projected fiscal deficits. In February 2004 Japan and the European G-8 members expressed, with greater urgency, their concern about the consequences of a recent steep fall in the value of the U.S. dollar, which the Bush administration, facing a fall election, appeared willing to accept in the expectation that a weak dollar would spur export sales, encourage manufacturing, and create jobs.

Following President Bush's call in April 2004 for more engagement with China in the rich countries' economies, China was invited to participate for the first time in a meeting of the finance ministers and central bank governors at a G-8 meeting on October 1 in Washington, D.C. Meanwhile, some of the G-8 countries continued to be at odds with the United States and Britain over financing peacekeeping missions in Iraq, the topic dominating the June 8–10, 2004, summit in Sea Island, Georgia, with Iraqi interim president Sheikh Ghazi Ajil al-Yawar in attendance.

In 2005 G-7 ministers met often early in the year, struggling to come to terms with debt relief for Africa and many other of the poorest countries. On June 11, in what was described as a "landmark deal" brokered by Britain, the G-8 leadersagreed to pay to relieve 18 of the poorest countries—most of them in Africa—of some $40 billion in debt. The agreement, the basis of which was hammered out by President Bush and British prime minister Tony Blair a week earlier, would also benefit another nine countries, bringing the total debt reduction tab to some $55 billion. By the end of 2005, the developing world energy shortage was engaging G-8 attention, as were ways to combat international terrorism.

The July 15–17, 2006, summit was the first to be hosted by Russia. The summit was supposed to deal primarily with energy security from the standpoint of both consumer and producer nations. The conference was dominated, however, by fighting in Lebanon between Israel and Hezbollah. The conference produced a statement that called for restraint.

The value of the yuan and increasing concerns about the U.S. economy's health increasingly occupied G-7/G-8 attention during 2007. These concerns were in evidence at the June 6–8 summit in Heligendamm, Germany, but the main emphasis was on climate change. The meeting produced an agreement to "consider seriously" cutting carbon dioxide emissions by 50 percent by 2050, but no specifics were laid out.

The July 7–8, 2008, summit in Hokkaido, Japan, was held amid sharply growing concerns about climate change. Tony Blair, now no longer the British prime minister, addressed the G-20 meeting in March 2008. He asked for revolutionary climate action by G-8 and other nations. In April Japanese Prime Minister Yasuo Fukuda met with EU representatives, promising to push for strong measures at the G-8 summit. By June, however, Fukuda was trying to lower expectations for results. He said the mission of the G-8 meeting was "to send out messages pointing to solutions," and the UN, rather than the G-8, should come up with medium-term goals for reducing emissions. The climate change discussions effectively ended in an impasse among the G-8 countries. The summit agreed only to work toward halving greenhouse emissions by 2050, but without giving any specifics on how this could be achieved. After the meeting U.S. president George W. Bush declared that the United States would take no concrete steps towards reducing emissions during his presidency. For more on developments since 2008, see "Recent Activities" below.

Structure. The G-8 is administered by a presidency of the organization. The presidency rotates from country to country in one-year terms in the following order: France, the United States, the United Kingdom, Russia, Germany, Japan, Italy, and Canada. The presidency is responsible for organizing and hosting the annual summit, and handles all communication for the G8. The presidency also handles international relations with non–G-8 members and NGOs. Activities coalesce around annual summits of the members' heads of state or government, joined by the president of the European Council and the European Commission. National delegations also include finance and foreign ministers and a personal representative of each president, prime minister, or chancellor. Summits typically include a day of private, informal bilateral and multilateral discussions among the leaders.

Throughout the year high-level meetings can be held by the members' foreign ministers; by finance ministers and central bank governors; or by ministers responsible for the environment, justice and interior, labor, development, and other areas. Ad hoc task forces and working groups also have been established.

Recent Activities. The 2009 summit, scheduled for July 8–10 in Maddalena, on the Italian island of Sardinia, was moved to the mainland town of L'Aquila. The conference was described as extremely disorganized, and its ability to deal with matters of pollution and climate change was reduced by Chinese president Hu Jintao's decision to leave early to deal with domestic unrest. The conference pledged, without offering specifics, that by 2050 average global temperatures should not rise more than two degrees Celsius above the year 1900 levels. The summit also pledged $20 billion for a three-year initiative to help poor countries develop their own agriculture. The sum was larger than many observers had expected, and the plan was felt likely to be more effective than if it had simply involved sending food.

After the L'Aquila summit questions grew about the G-8's continued usefulness. It had become clear that the world's balance of power had shifted, at least as far as economic matters were concerned, and that such countries as China, India, and Brazil could not be ignored. Thus, many felt that the G-20 meeting, which would be held September 24–25 in Pittsburgh, Pennsylvania, would be much more significant.

Canada was said to be particularly interested in keeping the G-8 alive, feeling that its influence would be diluted in a G-20 setting. To this end it was fortunate that Canada was able to host the 2010 G-8 summit June 25–26 in Muskoka, Ontario, immediately prior to the G-20 summit in Toronto June 26–27.

The 2011 summit was held May 26–27 in Deauville, France. The summit most notably produced the G-8 Declaration: Renewed Commitment for Freedom and Democracy. The declaration addressed issues such as the situation in Japan following the 2011 earthquake, the significance and role of the Internet in global affairs, world economics, environmental protection, nuclear power, climate change, and international development and security. At the summit the G-8 also produced the Deauville Partnership, a two-part plan of action and statement regarding the Arab Springs, and a joint declaration between the G-8 and Africa on the development of African nations.

In June, upon the recommendation of G-8 president Nicolas Sarkozy, the G-8 hosted a summit on nuclear safety in light of the situation in Japan following the earthquake. The summit produced several recommendations that were discussed at the 2011 International Atomic Energy Agency (see article, UN: Related Organization) Conference June 24–25.

At a September 2011 meeting of the G-8 finance ministers, the Deauville Partnership was fully implemented with the launch of the economic component. Through the use of regional development banks, the G-8 finance ministers are overseeing economic strategies to support sustainable and inclusive growth.

The 2012 G-8 summit, hosted by the United States, was held at Camp David, Maryland, in May. The summit produced the Camp David Declaration, which called on the G-8 countries to continue their work to aid in the recovery of the global economy, seek ways to promote the effective use of alternative energy sources, and work to fight global poverty and food shortages. The G-8 announced the creation of the New Alliance for Food Security and Nutrition to aid in increased flow of money and resources to African countries struggling with food security issues and poverty. The summit also discussed different measures to promote security, stability, and economic recovery in the Middle East, especially in Afghanistan.

In 2013 the G-B operated under the presidency of the United Kingdom. Prime Minister David Cameron announced that his priorities for the UK presidency were to advance trade, ensure tax compliance, and promote greater transparency. These priorities set the stage for the 2013 summit held in Lough Erne, Northern Ireland, June 17–18. The Lough Erne Declaration reinforced many of these principles by expressing the G-8's commitment to openness, shared information, and reduced tariffs. The meeting also identified job growth as the group's top priority and the key to ending the global economic recession. In order to achieve progress, the G-8 stressed the importance of sound fiscal policies and investment in small-medium sized enterprises. The group also issued a new policy on open data.

Perhaps the biggest announcement to come out of the summit, however, was the announcement that the United States and European Union were beginning discussions to negotiate a bilateral trade agreement between the two parties. Discussing the significance of this, Cameron noted that it could have an impact of $160 billion on the EU economy, $128 billion on the U.S. economy, and $136 billion on the economy in the rest of the world.

GROUP OF TWENTY

Established: September 25, 1999, at a Washington, D.C., session of the G-7 finance ministers. The Group of Twenty (G-20) consists of 19 larger-economy countries and the European Union, in addition to representatives of the International Monetary Fund and the World Bank. The group's finance ministers and central bank governors began meeting in 1999, and since that time have met every fall. G-20 heads of state or government began meeting in November 2008 (see below) and this elevation of status seems to represent the G-20's future.

Purpose: "A new mechanism for informal dialogue in the framework of the Bretton Woods institutional system, to broaden the dialogue on key economic and financial policy issues among systemically significant economies and to promote cooperation to achieve stable and sustainable world growth that benefits all."

Principal Organs: The G-20 has no permanent organs. There is a meeting of its members' finance ministers and central bank governors each fall, with occasional meetings of deputies and seminars at other times. Recently the heads of state or government of G-20 countries have also met. Arrangements are principally in the hands of the country that chairs the group in any particular year. (See below under Structure.)

Web site: www.g20.org. This site has recently become the official site of the G-20. It is managed by the host state in connection with its chairing of the group. The University of Toronto also maintains a very complete record of G-20 activities at www.g8.utoronto.ca/g20.

Membership (20): Argentina, Australia, Brazil, Canada, China, European Union, France, Germany, India, Indonesia, Italy, Japan, Mexico, Russia, Saudi Arabia, South Africa, South Korea, Turkey, United Kingdom, United States.

Origin and development. Reflection on the Asian economic crisis of the late 1990s caused the finance ministers of the G-7 countries (Canada, France, Germany, Italy, Japan, United Kingdom, and United States) to suggest establishing a larger group, inviting the participation of a wider range of countries whose economic importance was growing. The enlarged group held its inaugural meeting in Berlin, December 15–16, 1999.

The communiqué from the group's kickoff meeting, held in Berlin on December 15–16, 1999, stated the G-20's intent, as a group of "systemically significant economies," to meet for informal dialogue within the framework of the Bretton Woods system(see the discussion of the International Bank for Reconstruction and Development in the article on United Nations Specialized Agencies). The G-20 expressed relief that economic conditions were improving, worldwide and particularly in Asia, and hoped it might be useful in guiding the world's economies into an era of humane globalization.

The third meeting, November 16–17, 2001, in Ottawa, Canada, was held in the shadow of the September 11, 2001, attacks. The G-20 condemned these attacks not only as acts of terrorism but as an assault on global economic confidence and security. It resolved to fight terrorism by attacking the sources of funds for terrorist organizations.

The October 26–27, 2003, meeting in Morelia, Mexico, took as its first topic the prevention and resolution of financial crises. The group showed an increased concern for social safety nets for those not benefiting from the new financial order, as well as the importance of institution building and financing for development. And for the first time it considered the consequences of living in a world where countries other than the United States were becoming significant engines of economic growth.

The November 19–21, 2004, meeting in Berlin set some guidelines for the future in an Accord for Sustained Growth. It also announced a Reform Agenda, an account of what several member countries planned to do with their own economies. The United States, for example, was "determined to reduce its public budget deficit, to continue reforming health insurance and the pension system, and to raise private savings."

In 2006 the G-20 finance ministers met in Melbourne, Australia, November 18–19. After "spirited discussion" the group agreed to remain in close touch with the ongoing process of reform within the World Bank and the International Monetary Fund (IMF). The G-20 called for, among other things, more representation for smaller countries and a more transparent process for the selection of management in those bodies.

The 2007 meeting was held in Kleinmond, South Africa, November 17–18. The group expressed optimism for continued growth in the world economy, if at perhaps a slower rate than in the past. The final communiqué also noted that "recent events [troubles in the U.S. mortgage market] have emphasized the need for greater effectiveness of financial supervision and the management of financial risks." It called for a better understanding of the way in which financial shocks are transmitted around the world.

The 2008 annual summit, held in São Paulo, Brazil, November 8–9 was unique in that the difficulties in global credit markets had reached the point where lending had almost ceased, and a recession unparalleled since World War II was under way. The finance ministers blamed the crisis on excessive risk taking and faulty risk management practices in financial markets. They welcomed the fact that the problem was being elevated to a meeting of G-20 heads of state or government, to be held in Washington D.C. in a few days, and essentially deferred to that meeting. The emergency Washington summit took place on November 14–15. Never before had the heads of such a large group of emerging nations participated with the traditional financial powers in making economic policy for the world. The summit agreed that all member countries would take steps to stimulate their economies. The World Bank and the IMF were to do their part and the G-20 nations were to make sure that the IMF had sufficient funds for the purpose. Finance ministers were to produce a more specific plan by March 31, 2009. For more since 2008, see "Recent Activities," below.

Structure. The G-20 has no permanent staff. The G-20 chair rotates between members, and is selected from a different regional grouping of countries each year. The chair is part of a revolving three-member management Troika consisting of immediate past, present, and immediate future chairs. The Troika is intended to ensure continuity in the G-20's work and management through the years. The incumbent chair establishes a temporary secretariat for the duration of its term. This body coordinates the group's work and organizes its meetings. The latest Troika consists of Mexico (2012), Russia (2013), and Australia (2014).

Recent Activities. The G-20 leaders committed themselves to meeting again by April 30, 2009, to review progress. They actually met in London on April 1–2. This summit meeting declared that "prosperity is indivisible," that it must reflect the interest of all people, in all countries for present and future generations, in "an open world economy based on market principles, effective regulation, and strong global institutions." The G-20 agreed to triple the resources immediately available to the IMF to $750 billion, to support at least $100 billion in additional lending by the Multilateral Development Banks, and to authorize gold sales by the IMF. The group also agreed to abolish the Financial Stability Forum (FSF, see article on the Group of Seven/Group of Eight) in favor of an expanded Financial Stability Board, to consist of all existing FSF members, all G-20 countries, Spain, and the European Commission. This new board was to work closely with the IMF to give early warning of macroeconomic and financial risks, and to offer ways to avoid them. The G-20 agreed to bring regulation to all "systemically important" financial institutions and markets, including hedge funds. The FSF's recent issuing of new principles on executive pay and compensation were to be endorsed and implemented. The G-20 also declared that "the era of banking secrecy is over." It promised to move aggressively in applying sanctions against countries that would not cooperate in making bank account information available when needed. It also promised to go after tax havens, of which the Organization for Economic Cooperation and Development (OECD, see separate article) had recently produced a list. Also, the G-20 proposed to bring registration and regulatory oversight to credit rating agencies, to ensure their practices did not involve conflicts of interest with the institutions whose products they were being asked to rate. Such conflicts of interest were widely believed to have played a part in the collapse of credit in the United States. Finally, the G-20 countries pledged to reach agreement at the December 2009 climate change conference, to be held in Copenhagen, Denmark.

The London summit was generally considered a success. It was marred by demonstrations, to which the London police reacted with a degree of violence that many considered unacceptable.

The G-20 leaders met again in Pittsburgh, Pennsylvania, September 24–25, 2009. Their judgment on what they did the previous April was that "it worked." Conditions were somewhat better, the leaders said, but there was no room for complacency. The general consensus was that the London goals had been at least partly met. The group of leaders agreed to meet again in Canada in June 2010, in South Korea in November 2010, and annually thereafter, beginning with a meeting in France in 2011. They also pledged to complete the Doha round of trade negotiations by the end of 2010. The Pittsburgh declaration thus completed the G-20's transformation from a relatively informal gathering of finance ministers into what is likely to be, for the foreseeable future, the most powerful public instrument for setting world financial policy.

G-20 finance ministers, meeting in Washington, D.C., in April 2010 and in Korea in June, declared that the global recovery was proceeding faster than expected, thanks to the efforts of G-20 countries. The ministers praised the EU's efforts to rescue the Greek economy, and called for renewed efforts to cut budget deficits worldwide. The June 26–27 summit in Toronto, Canada, met amid the sense that the worldwide recovery was proceeding, but was still fragile. A second, "double-dip" recession was not impossible. China refused to commit to raising the value of its currency. Many Canadians criticized the lavish arrangements that their government had made in hosting the gathering.

G-20 summits have long included meetings of some of the world's prominent business leaders, but South Korea worked to expand and institutionalize this aspect of the gathering, which it hosted November 11–12 in Seoul. South Korea was the first G-20 host country that is not also a member of the G-8. The preceding meeting of finance ministers agreed on a series of steps to reform the IMF, making it more sensitive to the needs of poor countries. Both the finance ministers and the heads of government were concerned about world trade and currency imbalances. The summit agreed to work to avoid competitive currency devaluation, but without producing a firm plan. China again resisted any upward revaluation of the yuan, which some estimate is overvalued by as much as 25 percent.

In February 2011 the G20 finance ministers met for their annual meeting, at which time they addressed major issues facing the world in the midst of challenging economic times. The meeting called for increased surveillance of the IMF to strengthen the international monetary system, a plan that was discussed in more detail at its March conference on the international monetary system. The conference also stressed the need for implementation of international standards and regulations for banks and long-term investment in agriculture.

The importance of agriculture remained a major issue in 2011 as the French president and G-20 chair Nicolas Sarkozy called a meeting of G-20 agriculture ministers in June 2011. The agriculture ministers drafted an "Action Plan on Food Price Volatility and Agriculture" that detailed their plans for how to help the struggling agricultural industry in G-20 countries. The action plan was approved by the heads of government at the November 2011 Summit. The November 2011 Summit in Cannes also saw the approval of a similar action plan for global promotion of growth and jobs. The summit leaders also increased and reaffirmed their commitment to assist the IMF in establishing a stronger international monetary system; the group also committed to further assisting global efforts to improve development in order to achieve the millennium development goals.

The largest issue facing the G-20 in 2012 was the financial crisis and problems in the Eurozone, as was evident at the 2012 G-20 Summit in Los Cabos, Mexico. The June summit made the financial crisis in the Euro Area a major point of discussion, and the member countries agreed to focus more time and effort to achieve stability in the area, with G-20 member states from the EU pledging to take all necessary measures to restore the stability of the Eurozone and hopefully prevent such a crisis from happening again. The 2012 summit also brought about the Los Cabos Growth and Job Action Plan. The plan laid out an 8-step process to address the near-term risks that are hindering growth and a 6-step process for strengthening the long-term foundations for growth and job creation. The summit also examined major issues such as food security, challenges facing the financial sector, government corruption, and environmental protection.

When G-20 leaders met for the 2013 summit, held in St. Petersburg, Russia, on September 5–6, they faced a slightly better global economic situation than they had a year earlier. In celebration of five years since the 2008 summit in Brazil, G-20 leaders reaffirmed their commitment to act together to promote sustainable economic growth and future prosperity. The biggest result of the summit was the St. Petersburg Action Plan. This plan—hailed by Vladimir Putin as the fulfillment of Russia's priorities as president of the G-20—established a series of medium-term goals to reduce budget deficits and implement comprehensive structural reforms in each country. The meeting also adopted the St. Petersburg Development Strategy, which defined the organization's main priorities for assisting low-income countries. The group also continued to stress the importance of job creation, sustainable economic growth, and fiscal responsibility.

INTERNATIONAL CRIMINAL COURT (ICC)

Cour Pénale Internationale (CPI)

Established: On July 1, 2002, founded by the Rome Statute of the International Criminal Court treaty.

Purpose: "The International Criminal Court (ICC) is an independent, permanent court that tries persons accused of the most serious crimes of international concern, namely genocide, crimes against humanity and war crimes.

"The ICC is a court of last resort. It will not act if a case is investigated or prosecuted by a national judicial system unless the national proceedings are not genuine, for example if formal proceedings were undertaken solely to shield a person from criminal responsibility. In addition, the ICC only tries those accused of the gravest crimes."

Headquarters: The Hague, Netherlands.

Principal Organs: Assembly of States Parties, Presidency, Judicial Divisions, Office of the Prosecutor, Registry, Office of Public Council for Victims, Office of Public Council for Defense.

Web site: www.icc-cpi.int

President: Judge Sang-Hyun Song (South Korea).

Membership (122). As of July 2013, the following states had ratified the Rome Statute, which establishes the court: Afghanistan, Albania, Andorra, Antigua and Barbuda, Argentina, Australia, Austria, Bangladesh, Barbados, Belgium, Belize, Benin, Bolivia, Bosnia and Herzegovina, Botswana, Brazil, Bulgaria, Burkina Faso, Burundi, Cambodia, Canada, Cape Verde, Central African Republic, Chad, Chile, Colombia, Comoros, Congo, Cook Islands, Costa Rica, Côte d'Ivoire, Croatia, Cyprus, Czech Republic, Democratic Republic of the Congo, Denmark, Djibouti, Dominica, Dominican Republic, Ecuador, Estonia, Fiji, Finland, France, Gabon, Gambia, Georgia, Germany, Ghana, Greece, Grenada, Guatemala, Guinea, Guyana, Honduras, Hungary, Iceland, Ireland, Italy, Japan, Jordan, Kenya, Latvia, Lesotho, Liberia, Liechtenstein, Lithuania, Luxembourg, Macedonia, Madagascar, Malawi, Maldives, Mali, Malta, Marshall Islands, Mauritius, Mexico, Moldova, Mongolia, Montenegro, Namibia, Nauru, Netherlands, New Zealand, Niger, Nigeria, Norway, Panama, Paraguay, Peru, Philippines, Poland, Portugal, Republic of Korea, Romania, Saint Kitts and Nevis, Saint Lucia, Saint Vincent and the Grenadines, Samoa, San Marino, Senegal, Serbia,Seychelles, Sierra Leone, Slovakia, Slovenia, South Africa, Spain, Suriname, Sweden, Switzerland, Tajikistan, Tanzania, Timor-Leste, Trinidad and Tobago, Tunisia, Uganda, United Kingdom, Uruguay, Vanuatu, Venezuela, Zambia.

Official Languages: English, French.

Origin and development. During the latter half of the 20th century there was an increasing interest in prosecuting what came to be called crimes against humanity. The Nuremberg trials of prominent Nazis after World War II and the Tokyo trials of wartime Japanese leaders were the first such prosecutions. Instances of mass murder and "ethnic cleansing" during the breakup of Yugoslavia in the 1990s, as well as the Rwandan genocide of 1994, revived a desire for a supranational court to try those responsible. The United Nations (UN) established ad hoc courts to try accused criminals in both of these conflicts and eventually addressed the matter of a permanent court at a conference held in Rome in 1998. The resulting treaty, the Rome Statute of the International Criminal Court, was adopted on July 17, 1998, by a 120–7 vote, with 21 countries abstaining. Opposed were China, Iraq, Israel, Libya, Qatar, the United States, and Yemen. After 60 signatories had ratified the treaty in April 2002, it came into force on July 1 of that year, and work commenced on setting up the court.

After its initial opposition, the United States signed the treaty, but on May 5, 2002, the George W. Bush administration withdrew its signature, to the outrage of human rights organizations worldwide. Its justification was that the treaty would undermine U.S. judicial authority. There was also concern in U.S. military circles that accession to the treaty might lead to U.S. military personnel being tried by the court for their actions abroad. South African judge Richard Goldstone, the first chief prosecutor at the War Crimes Tribunal for the former Yugoslavia, called the U.S. decision a "backwards step," adding, "the U.S. have really isolated themselves and are putting themselves into bed with the likes of China, Yemen and other undemocratic countries." Russia, also a signatory to the treaty, declared that it would not ratify it unless the United States did so.

The Rome Statute is fully binding only on those states that have ratified it and have become parties to the statute. Participating states are obligated to detain a person for whom the court has issued an arrest warrant if that person is found on its territory. A state that is not a party to the statute but that is a member of the United Nations might be obliged to detain someone wanted in a case that originated with the UN Security Council.

The ICC functions as a court of last resort. When governments are unable or unwilling to prosecute fairly, the ICC tries those accused of the gravest crimes. Several criteria are considered while determining which cases will be brought before the court. The scale, nature, manner, and impact of crimes are the areas that are assessed. Once a case meets the minimum requirements, the question of gravity is raised. Due to resource restrictions, the court is unable to investigate and prosecute all potential crimes, therefore a case of sufficient gravity will merit further action by the court.

As of late 2013 seven states that are parties to the Rome Statute had identified and referred to the ICC cases of alleged criminality that took place inside their territories. In addition, the Security Council has referred to the court the situation in Darfur, Sudan. Sudan is not a party to the Rome Statute. Cases stemming from these referrals have been developed and are in progress.

Structure. The ICC exists to receive complaints of human rights abuses, to investigate them, and if necessary to issue arrest warrants in preparation for a trial. It can receive complaints from state actors, from the UN Security Council, or from private individuals. It can only accept cases concerning events that occurred after July 1, 2002, when it came into existence.

The Assembly of States Parties is the management, oversight and legislative body of the International Criminal Court. It is composed of representatives of the states that have ratified and acceded to the Rome Statute. The Assembly of States Parties has a Bureau, consisting of a president, two vice presidents, and 18 members, elected by the assembly for a three-year term. The Bureau is intended to represent all parts of the world equitably, as well as represent the world's principal legal systems. In September 2003 the Assembly of States Parties established its own Permanent Secretariat. The assembly determines the budget and oversees the election of judges, prosecutor, and deputy prosecutor(s). Decisions are made by consensus or by vote if consensus is not possible. The Assembly of States Parties has also established a Trust Fund for the benefit of victims of crimes within the jurisdiction of the court and the families of victims.

The Presidency is responsible for the overall administration of the court, with the exception of the Office of the Prosecutor, and for specific functions assigned to it in accordance with the statute. The Presidency is composed of three judges of the court, elected by their fellow judges, for a term of three years.

The Judicial Divisions consist of 18 judges, organized into the Pre-Trial Division, the Trial Division, and the Appeals Division. The judges of each division are responsible for conducting the proceedings of the court at different stages. Assignment of judges to divisions is made depending on the functions that each division performs and the qualifications and experience of the judge. This is done in a manner ensuring that each division benefits from an appropriate combination of expertise in criminal law and procedure and international law.

The Office of the Prosecutor is responsible for receiving referrals and any substantiated information about crimes within the court's jurisdiction, examining them, and conducting investigations and prosecutions. The office is headed by the Prosecutor, who is elected by the Assembly of States Parties for a term of nine years.

The Registry is responsible for the non-judicial aspects of the administration of the court. The Registrar is the principal administrative officer of the court and reports to the president of the court. The Registrar is elected by the judges for a term of five years.

The court also includes a number of semi-autonomous offices such as the Office of Public Counsel for Victims and the Office of Public Counsel for Defense. While part of the Registry, they function as wholly independent offices.

Although the ICC maintains its headquarters in The Hague, it can meet anywhere, and has frequently operated in Africa. The ICC should not be confused with the International Court of Justice (ICJ) or the International Criminal Tribunal for the former Yugoslavia (ICTY), both of which also have their headquarters in The Hague. The ICJ hears civil disputes between sovereign countries, while the ICTY is a temporary body, established by the United Nations to prosecute crimes committed during the wars in the former Yugoslavia. The ICTY is best known for its apprehension and prosecution of Slobodan Milošević, the former president of Yugoslavia and Serbia. The ICTY's connection with Milošević is perhaps what most causes it to be confused with the ICC.

Recent Activities. In July 2004 the ICC began a formal investigation into alleged human rights abuses committed in the low-level civil war that had been in progress in Uganda since the 1980s. It especially looked at charges against the rebel group the Lord's Resistance Army (LRA), which was accused of rape, mutilation, and using abducted children as fighters. In October 2005 the court issued arrest warrants for five LRA leaders, all of whom went into hiding in either Sudan or the lawless eastern Democratic Republic of the Congo. One suspect has since been confirmed dead; the others remain at large.

In late March 2005 the Security Council authorized the ICC to begin collecting evidence against the Sudanese government and opposition militias that have been accused of committing mass killings, torture, rape, and other atrocities in the country's Darfur region. The ICC immediately began an investigation. The court indicted Bahr Idriss Abu Garda, the former commander of a group in Darfur that was fighting the Sudanese government. He voluntarily turned himself in to the court, declaring his innocence. The case against him was dismissed on February 8, 2010. In May 2007 the ICC also issued arrest warrants for

Sudan's Minister of State for Humanitarian Affairs, Ahmed Haroun, and militia leader, Ali Muhammad Al Abd-Al-Rahman; in July 2008 it issued a warrant for Sudanese president Omar al-Bashir. Bashir has denied any part in the genocide and refuses to acknowledge the court's jurisdiction. He has since traveled abroad to friendly countries, including some that are under the obligation to arrest him, but has not been detained. Bashir has likewise refused to allow warrants to be served on the other two accused Sudanese citizens. In May 2010 the ICC took the unprecedented step of reporting Sudan to the Security Council over the outstanding warrants.

The ICC has had more success in apprehending and trying suspects from the Democratic Republic of the Congo (DRC). In April 2005 Congolese president Joseph Kabila asked the ICC to investigate alleged war crimes in the eastern part of his country, where he exerted little authority. The result was four arrest warrants, with three people under detention in The Hague as of December 2010 and one at large.

In October 2010 the court agreed, after legal maneuvering, to pursue a trial of Jean-Pierre Bemba, a Congolese citizen who is accused of leading militias in neighboring Central African Republic (CAR) in 2002 and 2003. These militias are accused of wide-scale murder and rape. Mr. Bemba was arrested in Belgium in 2008 and extradited to The Hague. The trial began in November 2010.

The ICC's actions have received mixed, but generally favorable, reviews. States that are sympathetic to the Sudanese government—particularly Chad—have denounced it as biased against Africa. The UN Secretary General, Ban Ki-moon, has praised it for changing national governments' attitudes for the better. The United States (not a signatory to the treaty) and the United Kingdom (a signatory) regard it as an impediment to the actions of their peacekeeping forces around the world.

In November 2011, former Côte d'Ivoire president Laurent Gbago was arrested and detained by the ICC on four counts of crimes against humanity, including murder, rape, and persecution. The charges levied against Gbago resulted from a string of violent actions taken by his administration from December 2010 to April 2011. In a February 2012 hearing, the ICC elected to expand the investigation of Gbago to include a series of war crimes dating back to 2002. The Confirmation of Charges Hearing occurred in February 2013. In June Pre-Trial Chamber I adjourned the hearing and asked the prosecution to provide further evidence or consider further investigation of the charges presented against Gbago. Gbago is the most prominent suspect thus far to be brought before the ICC.

In January 2013 the ICC's Office of the Prosecutor opened an investigation into crimes committed in Mali. The situation was referred to the court by the government of Mali in July 2012. In March 2013 Bosco Ntaganda voluntarily surrendered and was placed in the custody of the ICC. Ntaganda is one of six accused of war crimes executed in the Democratic Republic of the Congo. His pre-trial hearing occurred in late March, and the confirmation of charges hearing is scheduled for February 2014.

The ICC has 18 open cases regarding seven situations worldwide as of 2013. Formal investigations have been launched regarding the situations in Libya, Kenya, Côte d'Ivoire, Democratic Republic of Congo, Uganda, Central African Republic, Mali, and Sudan.

INTERNATIONAL ENERGY AGENCY (IEA)

Established: By the Agreement on an International Energy Program, which was signed by the Council of Ministers of the Organization for Economic Cooperation and Development (OECD) November 15, 1974, in Paris, France.

Purpose: To coordinate the responses of participating states to the world energy crisis and to develop an oil-sharing mechanism for use in times of supply difficulties; to coordinate national energy policies, share relevant information on energy supplies and markets, and establish closer relations between petroleum-producing countries and consumer states.

Headquarters: Paris, France.

Principal Organs: Governing Board, Standing Groups, Committee on Energy Research and Technology, Committee on Non-Member Countries, Executive Director.

Web site: www.iea.org

Executive Director: Maria van der Hoeven (The Netherlands).

Membership (28, with year of entry)**:** Australia (1979), Austria (1974), Belgium (1974), Canada (1974), Czech Republic (2001), Denmark (1974), Finland (1992), France (1992), Germany (1974), Greece (1977), Hungary (1997), Ireland (1974), Italy (1978), Japan (1974), Republic of Korea (2002), Luxembourg (1974), Netherlands (1974), New Zealand (1977), Norway (participates under a special agreement), Poland (2008), Portugal (1981), Slovakia (2007), Spain (1974), Sweden (1974), Switzerland (1974), Turkey (1981), United Kingdom (1974), United States (1974).

Observers: All other OECD members, as well as the Commission of the European Communities, may participate as observers.

Origin and development. Created as a response by OECD member states to the energy crisis of 1973–1974, the IEA began provisional operation on November 18, 1974, with signatory governments given until May 1, 1975, to deposit instruments of ratification. Norway, one of the original sponsors, did not immediately participate as a full member because of fear that sovereignty over its own vast oil resources might be impaired. Spain, Austria, Sweden, and Switzerland applied for membership, although the last three reserved the right to withdraw if IEA operations interfered with their neutrality. New Zealand was admitted in 1975, and a later agreement with Norway gave it a special status close to full membership. Subsequently, Australia, Greece, and Portugal joined. France and Finland cooperated with the agency until becoming members in 1992. The Czech Republic joined in February 2001, as did South Korea the following year, and Poland in 2008.

In the event of an oil shortfall of 7 percent or more, the Governing Board can invoke oil-sharing contingency plans and order members to reduce demand and draw down oil reserves. Participating countries agree to maintain oil stocks equal to 90 days' worth of the previous year's net imports. A system of complementary Coordinated Emergency Response Measures, dating from 1984, may be invoked by the Governing Board under circumstances that do not necessarily constitute a full emergency.

Over the years, the IEA has broadened the scope of its activities to include analyses of various energy sectors as well as Country Reports that review energy policies, prices, and developments in key nonmembers as well as in member states.

Regular publications include the *World Energy Outlook* and annual statistical analyses of the oil, natural gas, electricity, and coal industries. Through Implementing Agreements, the IEA also helps fund cooperative research efforts involving such areas as alternative energy sources (ocean power, wind, solar, battery, hydro, hydrogen, geothermal, biomass), clean coal technology, hybrid vehicles, energy efficiency, superconductivity, heat pump and heat exchange technology, and nuclear fusion.

Apart from the energy crisis of the 1970s, the most perilous events for the IEA have been the Iran-Iraq war of the 1980s and the Gulf crisis of 1990–1991. In 1984 IEA members discussed plans to be implemented should the Strait of Hormuz be closed because of the Iran-Iraq war. Members agreed to early use of government-owned or -controlled oil supplies to calm the market in cases of disruption.

A week after the Iraqi invasion of Kuwait on August 2, 1990, the IEA Governing Board met in emergency session, urging efforts to avert a possible oil crisis. Another IEA emergency session on January 11, 1991, unanimously approved a contingency plan to ensure "security of supply." Two days after the January 16 launching of Operation Desert Storm against Iraq, the plan was activated and IEA members were directed to make an additional 2.5 million barrels per day of oil available to the market. The IEA reported that 17 countries subsequently released oil from stockpiles during the war, helping to keep supplies and prices relatively stable.

In 2003 the IEA issued its first *World Energy Investment Outlook,* which concluded that some $16 trillion was needed in energy-related investment by 2030, half of it for transportation and distribution systems. During the biennial International Energy Forum, held in September 2002 in Osaka, Japan, the IEA, OPEC ministers, and other key participants appeared increasingly comfortable about holding discussions in the open rather than behind closed doors. The IEA's contention that suppliers and consumers both benefit from collaborative planning was subsequently reinforced when a confluence of circumstances—the aftermath of a general strike in December in Venezuela, Japan's decision to temporarily shut down nuclear plants because of security concerns, unrest in Nigeria, and the March 2003 invasion of Iraq—could have precipitated a major supply crisis. Instead, with the IEA, its members, oil corporations, and OPEC working in concert, no significant supply shortages or price spikes occurred.

By the 2005 Governing Board meeting, held on May 3 in Paris, the effect on the oil market of rapid economic growth in China and India had become increasingly evident. The final report warned against a business-as-usual approach to energy, stressing the need for more investment and more creative thinking to ensure adequate supplies and reduce the rise in greenhouse gases. During 2005 and 2006, gasoline prices rose substantially throughout the developed world, with no promise of a return to previous levels. In addition to increased demand, real or perceived instability in major producer countries, notably in Iran and Nigeria, caused irregularity in energy markets. In its November 2006 *World Energy Outlook,* the IEA declared that nuclear power must be an important part of any attempt to maintain the world's energy supply and to combat global warming. In June 2007 the IEA praised Germany for its environmental policies, but urged it to end plans to phase out nuclear energy.

In May 2008 the United States urged China and India to join the IEA, saying that membership would help them better manage their energy supplies. The United States' action was widely perceived as an admission that the IEA would become much less effective without the participation of these two emerging industrial giants.

In September 2008 the IEA for the first time surveyed the energy policies of the entire European Union (EU) as opposed to only those countries that are IEA members. In September also the IEA called on India to abolish fuel subsidies, as a way to reduce demand. In the same month Poland was admitted to the IEA, 14 years after it had first applied to join. For more on activities since 2008, see "Recent Activities," below

Structure. The IEA's Governing Board is comprised of ministers of member governments. The board is assisted by three standing groups (Emergency Questions, Long-Term Cooperation, and the Oil Market) and two committees (Energy Research and Technology and Non-Member Countries). Decisions of the Governing Board are made by a weighted majority except in the case of procedural questions, when a simple majority suffices.

A Coal Industry Advisory Board reports to the Standing Group on Long-Term Cooperation. There also is an Industry Advisory Board on Oil. Working parties reporting to the Committee on Energy Research and Technology (CERT) focus on fossil fuels, renewable energy technologies, and end-use technologies; a Fusion Power Coordinating Committee also reports to the CERT. The office of the Executive Director includes an Emergency Planning and Preparations Division, which helps carry out the work of the Standing Group on Emergency Questions.

Recent Activities. Historically, the IEA has been mostly concerned with the supply of oil and gas. In January 2009 the international group Energy Watch went so far as to claim that the IEA was obstructing the world's switch to renewable energy. The group claimed that the IEA had consistently underpredicted the growth of renewable energy.

The global economic crisis took the price of crude far down from its June 2008 peak of $124.52 per barrel to near $40 in early 2009. This period brought a variety of calls from the IEA about oil's future direction, though with an increasing sense that as the world economy seemed to stabilize late in 2009, the price of oil might rise again. A February 2009 IEA report predicted a worldwide oil shortage again in 2010, on the assumption that the global recession would be largely over by then.

The IEA *World Energy Outlook 2009,* published in November of that year, stressed the importance of converting as much as possible to biomass-based fuels, whose production emits less carbon than fossil fuels. It declared that current trends were unsustainable, and blamed transportation for approximately 97 percent of the projected increase in energy demand by 2030. The IEA believed that in the short term the worldwide recession would lessen the increase in carbon emissions. But some observers believed that the IEA's projection of future demand was too low, and of supply too high, favoring business-as-usual policies in its member states.

But perhaps no report had anticipated the growth in China's use of energy. In March 2010 the IEA reported that Chinese oil consumption had jumped by an "astonishing" 28 percent in January 2010 compared with January 2009. A July 2010 IEA report stated that for the first time China, rather than the United States, was the world's leading consumer of energy. A Chinese official denied this. However in August the Chinese government ordered over 2,000 factories—mostly heavy industry—to close, because they were wasting too much energy.

In the *World Energy Outlook 2010,* the IEA highlighted removal of government subsidies for fossil fuels as the fastest way of attacking the world's rising demand for energy.

In April 2011 the IEA released its first *Clean Energy Progress Report*. The report cited continued reliance on fossil fuels as a major challenge to clean energy and called on member countries to continue to assess their energy policies in an effort to make them less harmful to the environment. It also heralded the successes that have been experienced with regard to clean energy, such as the increased use of solar energy and wind energy since 2000. Another IEA report was released in May that focused on increasing use of clean energy sources in home construction as a means of reducing carbon dioxide and energy emissions.

In response to the political and military situation in Libya, the IEA authorized the release of 60 million barrels of oil in June 2011 to offset the decreased supply that has resulted from oil not being produced in Libya. This action, combined with a sharp rise in OPEC (see separate article) oil production, helped meet the demands of the market and lower the price of oil.

The *World Energy Outlook 2011* noted that the rising costs of oil in the global market were largely due to increasing transportation costs. To combat the "end of cheap oil," the report called for an increased turn to renewable energy and nuclear power. It also called for Russia to increase its oil and natural gas production, while decreasing its consumption.

The year 2012 saw major changes in the price of oil, with oil reaching record highs during the month of March before costs began to subside. The volatile oil-market was the IEA's top concern for most of 2012. The January 2012 Symposium on Energy Outlook, a joint seminar between the IEA, the International Energy Forum, and OPEC (see separate article), was entirely focused on solutions to deal with the rapidly increasing oil prices and the subsequent impact on the global oil market. The March 2012 quarterly meeting was entirely focused on gas and oil prices; the IEA member states expressed great concern about the impact oil prices were having on their already struggling economies. In October 2012 the IEA announced a new initiative calling on its member states to work together to double hydroelectricity production by 2050.

In February 2013 Executive Director Maria vanderHoeven announced that IEA would begin to increase its cooperation with emerging economies outside the IEA membership. This partnership between the IEA and major emerging economies (including China, Russia, Brazil, India, Indonesia, and South Africa) has been termed an Association, while the organization looks at how to deepen their cooperation with these nations. In June 2013 the IEA announced its prediction that renewable energy, which has increased by 40 percent over the last five years, will surpass gas as the primary energy source by 2016. They also announced a projection of increased gas consumption in 2014.

INTERNATIONAL ORGANIZATION FOR MIGRATION (IOM)

Organisation Internationale pour les Migrations
Organización Internacional para las Migraciónes
(OIM)

Established: On December 5, 1951, in Brussels, Belgium, as a provisional movement to facilitate migration from Europe; formal constitution effective November 30, 1954; present name adopted in November 1989.

Purpose: To advance understanding of the causes and effects of migration; to collect, analyze, and disseminate information on migrant rights and welfare; to provide a forum for discussion of practical solutions to migration issues; to assist states in managing migration through resettlement, immigration, and the return and reintegration of migrants, refugees, displaced persons, and former combatants.

Headquarters: Geneva, Switzerland.

Principal Organs: Council (all members and observer states), Executive Committee (33 members), Director General's Office.

Web site: www.iom.int

Director General: William Lacey Swing (United States).

Membership (151): Afghanistan, Albania, Algeria, Angola, Antigua & Barbuda, Argentina, Armenia, Australia, Austria, Azerbaijan, Bahamas, Bangladesh, Belarus, Belgium, Belize, Benin, Bolivia, Bosnia and Herzegovina, Botswana, Brazil, Bulgaria, Burkina Faso, Burundi, Cambodia, Cameroon, Canada, Cape Verde, Central African Republic, Chad, Chile, Colombia, Comoros, Democratic Republic of the Congo, Republic of the Congo, Costa Rica, Côte d'Ivoire, Croatia, Cyprus, Czech Republic, Denmark, Djibouti, Dominican Republic, Ecuador, Egypt, El Salvador, Estonia, Ethiopia, Finland, France, Gabon, Gambia, Georgia, Germany, Ghana, Greece, Guatemala, Guinea, Guinea-Bissau, Guyana, Haiti, Holy See (The Vatican City State), Honduras, Hungary, India, Iran, Ireland, Israel, Italy, Jamaica, Japan, Jordan, Kazakhstan, Kenya, Republic of Korea, Kyrgyzstan, Latvia, Lesotho, Liberia, Libya, Lithuania, Luxembourg, Madagascar, Malawi, Maldives, Mali, Malta, Mauritania, Mauritius, Mexico, Federated States of Micronesia, Moldova, Mongolia, Montenegro, Morocco, Mozambique, Myanmar, Namibia, Nauru, Nepal, Netherlands, New Zealand, Nicaragua, Niger, Nigeria, Norway, Pakistan, Panama, Papua New Guinea, Paraguay, Peru, Philippines, Poland, Portugal, Romania, Rwanda, Saint Vincent & the Grenadines, Senegal, Serbia, Seychelles, Sierra Leone, Slovakia, Slovenia, Somalia, South Africa, South Sudan, Spain, Sri Lanka, Sudan, Suriname, Swaziland, Sweden, Switzerland, Tajikistan, Tanzania, Thailand, Timor-Leste, Togo, Trinidad and Tobago, Tunisia, Turkey, Uganda, Ukraine, United Kingdom, United States, Uruguay, Vanuatu, Venezuela, Vietnam, Yemen, Zambia, Zimbabwe.

Observers (12): Bahrain, Bhutan, China, Cuba, Indonesia, Macedonia, Qatar, Russian Federation, San Marino, Sao Tome and Principe, Saudi Arabia, Turkmenistan.

Official Languages: English, French, Spanish.

Origin and development. A Provisional Intergovernmental Committee for the Movement of Migrants from Europe was established by delegates to a 16-nation International Migration Conference in 1951 in Brussels, Belgium. The Intergovernmental Committee for European Migration (ICEM) was based on a constitution that came into force November 30, 1954.

Since the ICEM operations began, more than 13 million migrants and refugees in more than 125 countries have been assisted with travel, placement, orientation, medical payments, vocational and language training, and other resettlement or repatriation services. Overall, the IOM has engaged in programs affecting every inhabited continent. Beginning in 1965, the organization carried out a Selective Migration Program to facilitate a transfer of technology from Europe to Latin America through the migration of highly qualified individuals. More than 27,000 European professionals, technicians, and skilled workers were relocated through the 1970s. Beginning in 1971 the organization also participated in the emigration of hundreds of thousands of Jews from the Soviet Union, and it assisted in the resettlement of more than 1 million refugees from Indochina after 1975.

In November 1980 the group's name was changed to the Intergovernmental Committee for Migration (ICM), "European" being deleted from its name due to the broadened scope of the organization's activities. On May 20, 1987, a number of formal amendments to the ICM constitution, including another change of name to the International Organization for Migration (IOM), were approved to better reflect the worldwide nature and expanding mandate of ICM activity. The amendments came into effect on November 14, 1989, after being ratified by two-thirds of the member states.

In the second half of the 1990s, it began a countertrafficking program in Cambodia and Thailand and also assisted in reintegrating demobilized soldiers in Angola and Guatemala. In 1996–1999 it undertook a Return of Qualified Nationals program to assist Bosnia and Herzegovina in encouraging the return of professionals and other skilled emigrants. The IOM also has participated in numerous efforts to address the problem of skilled workers leaving developing countries, most recently with a focus on Africa. An estimated 70,000 African professionals now emigrate to the West annually.

During 2001 the IOM drew on its earlier experiences in Bosnia and Herzegovina to organizean Out-of-Kosovo Voting Program that registered more than 125,000 Kosovars living outside the province. The IOM also has been directly involved in the German Forced Labor Compensation Program, which has sought to identify and compensate victims of slave and forced labor during the Nazi era, and in implementing the settlements won in the Holocaust Victim Assets Litigation against Swiss banks.

In 2003, following the U.S.-led ouster of the Saddam Hussein government, the IOM introduced an Iraq Transition Initiative to help Iraqi refugees, internally displaced peoples, and former combatants. The IOM also responded to unrest in Côte d'Ivoire by helping repatriate individuals from neighboring states who were stranded in the region. The IOM has also been active in the response to the devastating earthquake of October 2005 in Pakistan; the Indian Ocean tsunami of December 26, 2005; the Indonesian government's efforts to build peace in the troubled province of Aceh; the May 2006 earthquake on the island of Java; and the disastrous cyclone of May 2008 in Myanmar.

Since 1998 IOM membership has more than doubled, and relations have been established or strengthened with dozens of other intergovernmental organizations. There has been a corresponding increase in the IOM budget, which leapt from $242 million in 1998 to more than $1.2 billion in 2013.In March 2007 it opened a liaison office in Beijing, China—a country greatly affected by migration from country to city. Of particular concern in 2007 and 2008 was the rise of migration or attempted migration, often under desperate conditions, from Africa to Europe. The IOM is working in Africa to deter this migration through propaganda campaigns and programs to help stranded migrants go home. The problem of human trafficking continued to be a focus, with the IOM looking at trafficking to the Gulf States, and the Central Asian republics of the former Soviet Union.

William Lacey Swing (United States), a diplomat with U.S. and UN experience, was elected Director General at the June 2008 council meeting and assumed his post on October 1, 2008. At the same meeting India and Somalia were welcomed as full members, their status being upgraded from that of observers. For more on developments since 2008, see "Recent Activities," below.

Structure. The Council, which normally meets once a year, is comprised of representatives of all member and observer states. The 23-member Executive Committee, which meets twice a year, is elected by the Council for a two-year term. A Subcommittee on Budget and Finance assists the Council. The Standing Committee on Programmes and Finance is open to all member states and meets biennially to discuss and assess the effectiveness of IOM's programs and budget.

The Director General's Office oversees the daily operations of IOM headquarters, provides management coordination, and assists with policy formulation and program development. The director general is elected for a five-year term by the Council. Administrative divisions at IOM headquarters include External Relations; Administrative Support (Department of Budget and Finance, Department of Human Resources and Common Services Management); Information Technology and Communications; Migration Policy, Research, and Communication; Program Support, which includes the Donor Relations Division, the Emergency and Post-Crisis Division, and Project Tracking; Special Programs (Compensation Programs); and Migration Management Services (MMS). Also linked to the Director General's Office in Geneva are the Office of the Inspector General, Legal Services, Media and Public Information, and a Meetings Secretariat.

In the field, the IOM relies on its Manila and Panama Administrative Centers, which between them have additional responsibilities for information technology, security, and administration; 18 other Missions with Regional Functions scattered around the globe; some 225 Country Missions and suboffices; and short-term emergency Special-Purpose Missions. These centers interact with the IOM's field offices, providing project support and training in the core areas of movement (resettlement, repatriation, and transportation), assisted voluntary returns and integration, counter-trafficking, labor migration, mass information, migration health, and technical cooperation. Most of the organization's more than 7,000 staff work at the field level.

Activities. In May 2009 the IOM sent rapid response teams to assist Pakistanis displaced by fighting in that country's northwest region. It also provided shelter for Pakistani families displaced by the August 2010 floods. In August 2009 the IOM opened a Labor Migration Center in a South African town bordering Zimbabwe, to help Zimbabweans find properly credentialed work in South Africa.

There was some good news in 2010, although the problems described above continued. The IOM reported that as many as 2 million internally displaced people had returned to their homes in Southern Sudan since the signing of a peace agreement between the north and south in 2005. Also fewer people were now fleeing their homes in Iraq, although returnees were finding living conditions very difficult.

In August 2010 Trinidad and Tobago became the 127th member of the organization and were followed by five additional countries in November: Botswana, Central African Republic, Lesotho, Swaziland, and Timor-Leste. After the political uprising of the Arab Spring revolutions in early 2011, over 200,000 refugees, primarily from Libya, were able to return home with the help of the IOM.

The 100th Session of the IOM Council met in December 2011. At that meeting, the IOM approved the membership of 14 new states, four of which had previously been observers: Djibouti, Chad, Ethiopia, Maldives, Guyana, Nauru, Comoros, Antigua & Barbuda, the Holy See, Micronesia, South Sudan, Mozambique, Seychelles, and Vanuatu. The session also approved the creation of a new Migration Emergency Fund Mechanism. The fund is intended to increase the IOM's ability to respond to emergency situations and global migration crises.

In May 2012, the IOM helped facilitate the migration of many South Sudan refugees that were being held in Khartoum, Sudan, after the Sudanese government closed the major thoroughfares from Sudan to South Sudan.

At the November 2012 meeting of the IOM Council, the organization approved the membership of St. Vincent and the Grenadines and Malawi, while also upgrading the membership of Papua New Guinea from Observer State to full member. In June 2013 the IOM Council voted to approve the membership of two new member states—Malawi and Suriname. At the meeting, the Council also unanimously re-elected William Lacy Swing to a second five-year term as Director General.

With increasing violence and turmoil in Syria, the IOM has been actively involved in the relocation of Syrian refugees. Iraq opened its borders to Syrian refugees in August 2013, and as of September 1, over 195,000 Syrian refugees have been relocated to the Kurdish regions of Iraq. There are also an additional 100,000 refugees in Lebanon, over 200,000 in Jordan, and over 130,000 in Turkey. The crisis in Syria has been one of the IOM's primary concerns since early 2012.

NON-ALIGNED MOVEMENT

Established: Through the course of an increasingly structured series of conferences comprising states that describe themselves as not aligned with either one of the world's great powers (originally perceived as the Soviet Union and United States), the first of which met September 1–6, 1961, in Belgrade, Yugoslavia.

Purpose: To promote a "transition from the old world order based on domination to a new order based on freedom, equality, and social justice and the well-being of all"; to pursue "peace, achievement of disarmament, and settlement of disputes by peaceful means"; to search for "effective and acceptable solutions" to world economic problems, particularly the disparities in the level of global development"; to support self-determination and independence "for all peoples living under colonial or alien domination and foreign occupation"; to seek "sustainable and environmentally sound development"; to promote "fundamental rights and freedom"; to contribute to strengthening "the role and effectiveness of the United Nations" (Final Declaration, Belgrade, 1989).

Headquarters: None.

Principal Organs: Conference of Heads of State, Meeting of Foreign Ministers, Coordinating Bureau (25 members).

Web site: None. Malaysia, which chaired the NAM from 2003–2006, now sponsors the NAM News Network www.namnewsnetwork.org as its "gift to NAM."

Chair: Hassan Rouhani (Iran).

Membership (120): Afghanistan, Algeria, Angola, Antigua and Barbuda, Azerbaijan, Bahamas, Bahrain, Bangladesh, Barbados, Belarus, Belize, Benin, Bhutan, Bolivia, Botswana, Brunei, Burkina Faso, Burundi, Cambodia, Cameroon, Cape Verde Islands, Central African Republic, Chad, Chile, Colombia, Comoro Islands, Democratic Republic of the Congo, Republic of the Congo, Côte d'Ivoire, Cuba, Djibouti, Dominica, Dominican Republic, Ecuador, Egypt, Equatorial Guinea, Eritrea, Ethiopia, Fiji, Gabon, Gambia, Ghana, Grenada, Guatemala, Guinea, Guinea-Bissau, Guyana, Haiti, Honduras, India, Indonesia, Iran, Iraq, Jamaica, Jordan, Kenya, Democratic People's Republic of Korea, Kuwait, Laos, Lebanon, Lesotho, Liberia, Libya, Madagascar, Malawi, Malaysia, Maldives, Mali, Mauritania, Mauritius, Mongolia, Morocco, Mozambique, Myanmar, Namibia, Nepal, Nicaragua, Niger, Nigeria, Oman, Pakistan, Palestine (represented by the Palestinian Authority), Panama, Papua New Guinea, Peru, Philippines, Qatar, Rwanda, St. Lucia, St. Kitts and Nevis, St. Vincent and the Grenadines, Sao Tome and Principe, Saudi Arabia, Senegal, Seychelles, Sierra Leone, Singapore, Somalia, South Africa, Sri Lanka, Sudan, Suriname, Swaziland, Syria, Tanzania, Thailand, Timor-Leste, Togo, Trinidad and Tobago, Tunisia, Turkmenistan, Uganda, United Arab Emirates, Uzbekistan, Vanuatu, Venezuela, Vietnam, Yemen, Zambia, Zimbabwe.

Observer States (17): Argentina, Armenia, Bosnia-Herzegovina, Brazil, China, Costa Rica, Croatia, El Salvador, Kazakhstan, Kyrgyzstan, Mexico, Montenegro, Paraguay, Serbia, Tajikistan, Ukraine, Uruguay.

Origin and development. The first Conference of Nonaligned Heads of State, at which 25 countries were represented, was convened in September 1961 in Belgrade, largely through the initiative of Yugoslavian president Josip Tito, who had expressed concern that an accelerating arms race might result in war between the Soviet Union and the United States. The precursor of the Non-Aligned Movement is traced back to the Bandung Asian-African Conference in Indonesia, April 18–24, 1955. Subsequent conferences, which attracted more and more third world countries haveconvened in Egypt, Zambia,Algeria, Sri Lanka, Cuba, India, Zimbabwe, Serbia, Colombia, South Africa, Egypt, and Iran.

The 1964 conference in Cairo, with 47 countries represented, featured widespread condemnation of Western colonialism and of the retention of foreign military installations. Thereafter, the focus shifted away from essentially political issues, such as independence for dependent territories, to the advocacy of occasionally radical solutions to global economic and other problems. Thus, in 1973 in Algiers there was an appeal for concerted action by the "poor nations against the industrialized world"; this became a basis of debate within the UN for a New International Economic Order (NIEO) and led to the convening of an inconclusive Conference on International Economic Cooperation in late 1975 in Paris, France.

At the 1979 Havana meeting, political concerns resurfaced in the context of an intense debate between Cuban president Fidel Castro, who was charged with attempting to "bend" the movement in the direction of the "socialist camp," and President Tito of Yugoslavia, who urged that it remain true to its genuinely nonaligned origins. In search of a compromise, the Final Declaration of the Havana Conference referred to the movement's "non-bloc nature" and its opposition to both "hegemony" (a euphemism used in reference to presumed Soviet ambitions) and all forms of "imperialism, colonialism, and neocolonialism." In addition, the conference reiterated an earlier identification of "Zionism as a form of racism."

The eighth NAM summit in Zimbabwe in 1986 marked the 25th anniversary of the movement. The site was chosen to underscore the group's main concern: the South African government's policy of forced racial segregation. A final declaration called on nonaligned nations to adopt selective, voluntary sanctions against South Africa pending the adoption of comprehensive, mandatory measures by the UN Security Council. The members demanded international pressure to eliminate apartheid, Pretoria's withdrawal from Namibia (Southwest Africa), and an end to aggression against neighboring states.

Some of NAM's most radical members (including Cuba, Iran, and Iraq) stayed away from the 1989 Belgrade summit after preparatory talks revealed that most members favored fewer polemics and a return to the group's original posture of neutrality. Consequently, the meeting's final declaration was markedly less anti-American and anti-Western than previous ones. Instead, the summit emphasized the need to "modernize" and develop a "realistic, far-sighted, and creative" approach to international issues. The declaration also praised Washington and Moscow for their rapprochement, which, by reducing tensions in many areas of the world, had created a "window of opportunity for the international community."

NAM emerged somewhat revitalized from its tenth summit, held in 1992 in Jakarta, Indonesia. At the conclusion of the meeting NAM declared its intention to project itself as a "vibrant, constructive, and genuinely independent component of the mainstream of international relations." With anti-Western rhetoric kept to a minimum, NAM asked developed nations to give "urgent priority" to establishing "a more equitable global economy" and to assist developing nations in resolving the problems of low commodity prices and "crushing debt burdens." The summit agreed to establish a broad-based committee of experts to devise a debt reduction approach. The Jakarta Message also called for extended South/South trade and investment cooperation. In addition, NAM said it would press for a restructuring of the UN that would include the diminution or elimination of the veto power of the five permanent members of the Security Council and an expansion of council membership.

Also at the summit, action on politically sensitive membership applications from Macedonia and Russia was deferred indefinitely. However, South Africa was welcomed to the NAM ranks following the installation of a multiracial government in Pretoria.

NAM continued to press for UN restructuring at its 11th summit, held October 18–20, 1995, in Cartagena de Indias, Colombia. It also argued that UN peacekeeping efforts should be cut so more resources could be used for combating poverty. The summit's communiqué strongly criticized the United States for continuing its heavy economic pressure against Cuba and urged the industrialized nations to adopt a more "just" system of world trade.

The 12th NAM summit, held September 2–3, 1998, in Durban, South Africa, was expected to concentrate on economic issues, but the ongoing fighting in the Democratic Republic of the Congo diverted attention. The summit also condemned terrorism, insisting that it be countered in accordance with UN principles, not by unilateral initiatives, and expressed regret that the Middle East peace process remained at a standstill—a situation it attributed to Israeli intransigence.

NAM was divided over the Kosovo crisis of 1999, with Muslim member states supporting intervention on behalf of the Kosovars and predominantly backing the U.S.-led NATO air war against Yugoslavia in March–June. The division came in the context of a more fundamental concern that the movement was being eclipsed by the then 133-member Group of 77, which had gained increasing recognition as an effective voice for the economic interests of developing countries.

The organization's 13th Meeting of Foreign Ministers convened April 8–9, 2000, in Cartagena, where the topics under discussion included barring participation by military regimes that had overthrown democratically elected governments. Championed by India, the proposal was generally viewed as an effort to establish democracy as the norm for all members, but observers also noted that New Delhi was clearly targeting Pakistan for exclusion.

The 13th summit was planned for October 2001 in Bangladesh, but the meeting was postponed because of preparations for that country's October 1 national election. The venue was subsequently changed to Amman, Jordan, but instability in the Middle East ultimately led the Coordinating Bureau, meeting in April 2002 in Durban, to designate Malaysia as the host. Thus the 13th summit convened on February 24–25, 2003, in Kuala Lumpur.

Attended by some 60 heads of state or government, the first day of the summit included an address by Malaysian prime minister Mahathir bin Mohamad, who lambasted the West for using undemocratic means to force democracy on other countries. Among the specific issues debated at the summit were the threat of war against Iraq and the nuclear crisis in North Korea. In a "Statement Concerning Iraq," the movement warned against the dangers of preemptive action by the United States and its allies, but it also advised the Saddam Hussein regime to comply with UN Security Council resolutions. With regard to North Korea's nuclear program, the summit ultimately supported Pyongyang's contention that a solution would best be found if the U.S. would agree to negotiate directly instead of insisting on multilateral involvement. In addition, as at previous summits, the participants voiced support for the Palestinian people and condemned Israeli actions and alleged human rights abuses in the West Bank and Gaza.

In keeping with its overall theme of "Continuing the Revitalization of the Non-Aligned Movement," the 2003 summit approved the Kuala Lumpur Declaration. Among other things, the declaration urged the wider international community to ensure that globalization led to the "prospering and empowering of the developing countries, not their continued impoverishment and dependence." In addition, the declaration called upon member states to improve the effectiveness and efficiency of the movement and to enhance unity and cohesion "by focusing on issues that unite rather than divide us."

The 14th Conference of Heads of State took place from September 11–16, 2006, in Havana, Cuba. This meeting, coupled with Cuba's chairing of NAM in 2007 and statements of mutual encouragement between NAM members Venezuela and Iran, caused the United States to look on NAM with increasing disfavor. In June 2007 U.S. secretary of state Condoleezza Rice addressed the U.S. India Business Council and declared that NAM had "lost its meaning"—an opinion quickly contested by Indian foreign minister Pranab Mukherjee. In July 2007 David C. Mulford, the U.S. ambassador to India, put forth a different opinion, stating that "India has played a major role in Non-Aligned Movement over the years and still continues (to do so) in many cases."

Several commentaries, however, have suggested that while the ideal of nonalignment remains as important as ever, NAM might not be useful in its present form. Because NAM has no central headquarters, it has perhaps suffered in recent years from lack of an official, external face. During its period as chair of the group (2003–2006), Malaysia addressed this problem with a very comprehensive Web site, or E-Secretariat, which not only documented Malaysia's leadership of the organization, but also thoroughly recorded all aspects of the movement's work. Unfortunately, such initiatives have not continued under subsequent NAM presidencies.

NAM involvement, led by Cuba, in the UN continued. In November 2007 Cuba spoke for NAM against a resolution that condemned North Korea for its record on human rights, declaring that exploitation of this issue "for political purposes should be prohibited." In February 2008 a NAM-sponsored resolution in the UN Security Council condemning Israel for the situation in the Gaza Strip failed to pass. This led to an unpleasant exchange between the Israeli and Cuban delegates. In February also, the NAM ambassadors voted unanimously in favor of a resolution at the International Atomic Energy Agency (IAEA), supporting Iran in its peaceful development of nuclear power. In May 2008 NAM condemned the Sudanese rebel Justice and Equality Movement and voiced its support for Sudan's territorial integrity, while calling on all parties to the Darfur conflict to reach a peaceful solution.

In July 2008 Iran hosted a NAM foreign ministerial meeting, at which Iran asked for NAM support in its bid for a seat on the UN Security Council. Iran was chosen to host the organization's 16th summit, to be held in 2012. For more on activities since 2008, see "Recent Activities," below.

Structure. By convention, the chief executive of the country hosting the most recent Conference of Heads of State serves as NAM's chair. Foreign ministers' meetings are generally held annually between conferences, which are usually convened every three years. A Coordinating Bureau, established at the 1973 conference, currently numbers 25 (including the chair; a rapporteur-general; and, on an ex officio basis, the immediate past chair) with the following regional distribution: Africa, 10; Asia, 9; Latin America and the Caribbean, 4; Europe, 2. In addition to a Political Committee, an Economic and Social Committee, and a Committee on Palestine, NAM has created various working groups over the years.

Recent Activities. At the July 2009 Sharm-el-Sheik summit Egypt took over the organization's presidency from Cuba. The meeting took place amid a general sense that NAM needed a new role, possibly using the world financial crisis to address the distribution of global wealth. There was some feeling that, while the dangers of the Cold War era had passed, nonaligned nations needed to protect themselves from the bad effects of global capitalism. Russian president Dmitry Medvedev declared that Russia, a guest state, was ready to take a more active role in NAM's business. The conference condemned the ICC, which had by now issued an arrest warrant for Sudanese president Al-Bashir, and reiterated its support for a peaceful nuclear program in Iran. NAM support for Iran was evident at a March 2010 meeting of the IAEA board of governors. The Iranian representative declared himself satisfied with the result.

In March 2010 the Special Ministerial Meeting of the Non-Aligned Movement on Interfaith Dialogue and Cooperation for Peace and Development (SNAMMM) was held in Manila, Philippines. This meeting adopted a declaration of the value of tolerance, diversity, and mutual understanding in promoting world peace.

On May 23–27, 2011, at the 16th Ministerial Summit in Bali, Indonesia, Fiji and Azerbaijan were recognized as NAM members. In addition to confirming new NAM members, the Bali Declaration was adopted. The Bali Declaration is a 2007 IPCC (Intergovernmental Panel on Climate Change) report confirming the existence of global climate change, and it asserts with 90% certainty that it is mostly due to human activity. Member states agreed to a more robust NAM role in addressing international issues, in support for an independent Palestine, and in the promotion of nuclear disarmament, international security and stability, and the inalienable right of all states to pursue the peaceful use of nuclear energy.

On May 7–9, 2012, the 17th Ministerial Summit was held in Egypt as that country concluded its three-year term in the rotating presidency. The ministers of the 120 heads of state focused largely on the role of developing countries in the world. In this regard, it called for increased UN authority in the realm of global governance to ensure that developing countries are represented fairly and equally. The ministers also condemned the United States' sanctions against Syria, and condemned several Israeli practices aimed at Palestine. The ministers called on the UN and the rest of the global community to bring an end to the Israeli occupation of Palestinian territory.

The 16th NAM summit was help in Teheran, Iran, in September 2012. Despite objections from many of the Western nations, including the United States, the summit was still attended by over 100 heads of state and UN Secretary General Ban Ki Moon, among others. The summit called for a changing approach to global conflict resolution, advocating the main themes of peace and justice. The summit noted that in today's global climate, the UN is the most effective means of handling disputes, but is in need of reform. Concerning the civil war in Syria, the organization condemned the American sanctions against Syria and welcomed the efforts being undertaken by the Un and Arab League. The group also expressed its continued support of Palestinian sovereignty and condemned Israeli actions in the area. The group also expressed its support of the Iranian nuclear program, declaring it an issue of state authority to develop, research, and use atomic energy. Venezuela was selected to be the host of the 17th NAM Summit to be held in 2015.

Following the Iranian elections of June 2013, Hassan Rouhani became chair of the Non-Aligned Movement after assuming the Iranian presidency beginning August 1. In conjunction with a meeting of the UN General assembly in September 2013, NAM called a Ministerial Meeting on Cooperation for the Rule of Law at the International Level. The meeting continued to urge the program of UN reform outlined at its 16th summit.

NORTH ATLANTIC TREATY ORGANIZATION (NATO)

Organisation du Traité de l'Atlantique Nord (OTAN)

Established: September 17, 1949, by action of the North Atlantic Council pursuant to the North Atlantic Treaty signed on April 4, 1949, in Washington, D.C., and effective as of August 24, 1949.

Purpose: To provide a system of collective defense in the event of armed attack against any member by means of a policy based on the principles of credible deterrence and genuine détente; to work toward a constructive East-West relationship through dialogue and mutually advantageous cooperation, including efforts to reach agreement on militarily significant, equitable, and verifiable arms reduction; to cooperate within the alliance in economic, scientific, cultural, and other areas; and to promote human rights and international peace and stability.

Headquarters: Brussels, Belgium.

Principal Organs: North Atlantic Council (all members), Nuclear Planning Group (all members), Military Committee (all members), International Staff.

Web site: www.nato.int

Chair of the North Atlantic Council and Secretary General: Anders Fogh Rasmussen (Denmark).

Membership (28): Albania, Belgium, Bulgaria, Canada, Croatia, Czech Republic, Denmark, Estonia, France, Germany, Greece, Hungary, Iceland, Italy, Latvia, Lithuania, Luxembourg, Netherlands, Norway, Poland, Portugal, Romania, Slovakia, Slovenia, Spain, Turkey, United Kingdom, United States.

Partnership for Peace Participants (22): Armenia, Austria, Azerbaijan, Belarus, Bosnia and Herzegovina, Finland, Georgia, Ireland, Kazakhstan, Kyrgyzstan, Macedonia, Malta, Moldova, Montenegro, Russia, Serbia, Sweden, Switzerland, Tajikistan, Turkmenistan, Ukraine, Uzbekistan.

Official Languages: English, French.

Origin and development. The postwar consolidation of Western defenses was undertaken in light of the perceived hostility of the Soviet Union as reflected in such actions as the creation of the Communist Information Bureau (Cominform) in October 1947, the February 1948 coup in Czechoslovakia, and the June 1948 blockade of West Berlin. U.S. willingness to join Western Europe in a common defense system was expressed in the Vandenberg Resolution adopted by the U.S. Senate on June 11, 1948, and subsequent negotiations culminated in the signing of the North Atlantic Treaty on April 4, 1949, by representatives of Belgium, Canada, Denmark, France, Iceland, Italy, Luxembourg, Netherlands, Norway, Portugal, the United Kingdom, and the United States.

The treaty did not prescribe the nature of the organization that was to carry out the obligations of the signatory states, stipulating only that the parties should establish a council that, in turn, would create a defense committee and any necessary subsidiary bodies. The outbreak of the Korean War on June 25, 1950, accelerated the growth of the alliance and led to the appointment in 1951 of Gen. Dwight D. Eisenhower as the first Supreme Allied Commander in Europe. Emphasis on strengthened military defense of a broad area, reflected in the accession of Greece and Turkey to the treaty in February 1952, reached a climax later that month at a meeting of the North Atlantic Council in Lisbon, Portugal, with the adoption of goals calling for a total of 50 divisions, 4,000 aircraft, and strengthened naval forces. Subsequent plans to strengthen the alliance by rearming the Federal Republic of Germany (FRG) as part of a separate European defense community collapsed, with the result that the FRG was permitted to establish its own armed forces and, in May 1955, to join NATO.

NATO's gravest problem during the mid-1960s was the estrangement of France over matters of defense. French resistance to military integration under NATO reached a climax in 1966 when President de Gaulle announced the removal of French forces from consolidated commands and gave notice that all allied troops not under French command had to be removed from French soil by early 1967. These stipulations necessitated the rerouting of supply lines for NATO forces in Germany; transfer of the alliance's European command from Paris, France, to Casteau, Belgium; and relocation of other allied commands and military facilities. Thereafter, France participated selectively in NATO's operations, although it rejoined the Military Committee in 1996.

During the 1970s NATO suffered from additional internal strains. Early in 1976 Iceland threatened to leave the organization because of a dispute with Britain over fishing rights off the Icelandic coast. Disputes between Greece and Turkey, initially over Cyprus and subsequently over offshore oil rights in the Aegean Sea, resulted in Greece's withdrawal from NATO's integrated military command and a refusal to participate in NATO military exercises. In October 1980, five months after Greece threatened to close down U.S. bases on its territory, negotiations yielded an agreement on its return as a full participant. However, relations between Greece and Turkey subsequently remained tenuous. For instance, in October 2000 Greece withdrew from a NATO exercise in Turkey when Ankara objected to the flight of Greek aircraft over disputed Aegean islands.

In June 1980 U.S. president Jimmy Carter reaffirmed his administration's conviction that Spanish membership in NATO would significantly enhance the organization's defensive capability. The Spanish government originally made its application contingent upon Britain's return of Gibraltar and the admission of Spain to the European Community, but Madrid later decided that it could negotiate both issues subsequent to entry. Therefore, following approval in late October by the Spanish courts, the government formally petitioned for NATO membership, with a protocol providing for Spanish accession being signed by the members in December 1981. A referendum in March 1986 ensured Spain's continued participation with three domestic stipulations: the maintenance of Spanish forces outside NATO's integrated command; a ban on the installation, storage, and introduction of nuclear weapons; and a progressive reduction in the U.S. military presence. In November 1996 the Spanish parliament endorsed Spain's full participation in NATO's military structure, which occurred in 1999.

The structure of East-West relations was irrevocably altered by the political whirlwind that swept through Eastern Europe during late 1989 and early 1990, with the demolition of the Berlin Wall (described by one reporter as the "ultimate symbol of NATO's reason for existence") dramatically underscoring the shifting security balance. The dramatic changes in the European political landscape that accompanied the fall of the Berlin Wall and the demise of the Soviet Union substantially altered NATO's perception of its role on the continent. With superpower rapprochement growing steadily, U.S. officials in early 1990 suggested that U.S. and Soviet troop levels could be sharply cut. NATO also endorsed Washington's decision not to modernize the short-range missiles in Europe and agreed to reduce the training and state of readiness of NATO forces.

A Warsaw Pact summit in Moscow in early June and a NATO summit in London in early July confirmed the end of the Cold War. Suggesting that "we are no longer adversaries," Western leaders proposed that a NATO–Warsaw Pact nonaggression agreement be negotiated. NATO's London Declaration also vowed a shift in military philosophy away from forward defense, involving heavy troop and weapon deployment at the East-West frontier, and toward the stationing of smaller, more mobile forces far away from the former front lines. The allies agreed that the Conference on (later Organization for) Security and Cooperation in Europe (CSCE/OSCE) should be strengthened as a forum for pan-European military and political dialogue and urged rapid conclusion of a conventional arms agreement so that talks could begin on reducing the continent's reliance on nuclear weapon systems. They also insisted that Germany remain a full NATO member upon unification, a condition initially resisted by Moscow but ultimately accepted as part of the German-Soviet treaty concluded in mid-July.

As the Warsaw Pact continued to disintegrate, NATO pursued its own military retrenchment and reorganization. In May 1991 the NATO defense ministers approved the most drastic overhaul in the alliance's history, agreeing to reduce total NATO troop strength over the next several years from 1.5 million to 750,000 (including a cutback of U.S. troops from the existing 320,000 to 160,000 or fewer). In addition, it was decided to redeploy most of the remaining troops into seven defense corps spread throughout Western and Central Europe. The new plan also called for the creation of an Allied Rapid Reaction Corps (ARRC) of 50,000–70,000 troops to deal quickly with relatively small-scale crises, such as those that might arise from the continent's myriad ethnic rivalries. At the same time, NATO nuclear weapons were retained in Europe as a hedge against a sudden shift in Soviet policy.

Other issues addressed by NATO in 1991 included a proposed charter change that would permit "out-of-area" military activity (the alliance's participation in the recent Gulf war having been constrained by the restriction against its forces being sent to a non-NATO country) and the security concerns of former Soviet satellites in Eastern Europe, several of which had inquired about admission to NATO. Although all such overtures were rejected as premature, the ministers called for the development of a "network of interlocking institutions and relationships with former communist-bloc nations." The impulse led to the establishment in December of the North Atlantic Cooperation Council (NACC) as a forum for dialogue among the past NATO–Warsaw Pact antagonists. Participating in the NACC were the 16 NATO countries plus Albania, Armenia, Azerbaijan, Belarus, Bulgaria, Czech Republic, Estonia, Georgia, Hungary, Kazakhstan, Kyrgyzstan, Latvia, Lithuania, Moldova, Poland, Romania, Russia, Slovakia, Tajikistan, Turkmenistan, Ukraine, and Uzbekistan. Austria, Finland, Malta, Slovenia, and Sweden had NACC observer status.

The NACC, which worked in liaison with various NATO bodies and met regularly in conjunction with the North Atlantic Council, played a growing role in implementing the new strategic concept endorsed at the November 1991 NATO summit. While reaffirming the essential military dimension of the alliance, the heads of state agreed that a political approach to security would become increasingly important in Europe. Consequently, the summit called for additional reductions in NATO's conventional and nuclear forces beyond those proposed in May.

The NATO leaders also endorsed a larger role for such organizations as the CSCE, the European Community (EC, later the European Union—EU), and the Western European Union (WEU) defensive and political alliance in dealing with the continent's security issues. Significantly, however, the 1991 summit continued to insist that proposed pan-European military forces would complement rather than supplant NATO. As further evidence of the alliance's intention to remain active in European affairs, the NATO foreign ministers in May 1992 agreed to make forces available on a case-by-case basis for future peacekeeping missions necessitated by ethnic disputes or interstate conflict on the continent.

In November 1992 NATO agreed to use its warships, in conjunction with WEU forces, to enforce the UN naval blockade against the truncated Federal Republic of Yugoslavia. In April 1993 the alliance authorized its jets to monitor the UN ban on flights over Bosnia and Herzegovina. Otherwise, NATO appeared to be locked in a somewhat paralyzing debate on how to deal with the fighting in that country. In May 1993 U.S. president Bill Clinton suggested that NATO forces be used to create "safe havens" for Bosnian Muslims, but agreement could not be reached within the alliance on the proposal. In midsummer Clinton, who had previously been criticized for not taking a more active role in the Bosnian controversy, suggested that U.S. planes might be used to bomb areas in Bosnia under Serbian control, if requested by the UN. Prodded by the new U.S. assertiveness, the NATO defense ministers endorsed the Clinton position and discussed plans for a 50,000-strong NATO peacekeeping force that could be used in the event of a permanent Bosnian cease-fire.

At the same time the EC was evolving what it initially called a Common Foreign and Security Policy as part of the Maastricht Treaty, which brought the EU into existence in November 1993. In response to these events, NATO began developing a framework for Combined Joint Task Forces (CJTFs), which were envisaged as multinational, multiservice contingents that could be quickly deployed for humanitarian, peacekeeping, or defense purposes. Implementation of the CJTF concept began in 1999, and by 2004 three CJTF commands were established, two land based and one naval.

A NATO summit held January 10–11, 1994, in Brussels struck a compromise regarding expansion by launching a highly publicized Partnership for Peace (PfP) program, which extended military cooperation but not full-fledged defense pacts to the non-NATO countries. By mid-1996, 28 nations (including previous Warsaw Pact members, former Soviet republics, and several longtime "neutral" states) had signed the PfP Framework Document. Among other things, the PfP states pledged to share defense and security information with NATO and to ensure "democratic control" of their armed forces. In return NATO agreed to joint training and planning operations and the possible mingling of troops from PfP states with NATO forces in future UN or OSCE peacekeeping missions. NATO ambassadors in February 1994 agreed to conduct air strikes against certain Serbian targets if requested by the UN. Later in the month, in the first such direct military action in the alliance's history, NATO aircraft shot down four Serbian planes that were violating the "no-fly" zone in Bosnia and Herzegovina. In addition, NATO planes bombed several Serbian artillery locations around Sarajevo in April.

Two issues dominated NATO affairs over the next year—the continued conflict in Bosnia and planning for the expected accession of Eastern and Central European countries to the alliance. Regarding the former, NATO responded to growing aggressiveness on the part of Bosnian Serbs by launching a bombing campaign against Serbian positions on August 30, 1995, near Sarajevo. The Serbians subsequently agreed to withdraw their heavy guns from the area as demanded by NATO, the alliance's hard-line approach also apparently contributing to an intensification of peace talks among the combatants in Bosnia. Consequently, NATO tentatively approved the proposed deployment of some 60,000 troops (including 20,000 from the United States) to take over peacekeeping responsibilities from UN forces in Bosnia should a permanent cease-fire go into effect.

By that time a degree of progress had been achieved regarding the alliance's membership plans as well. Among other things, NATO said that applicants would have to display a commitment to democracy and human rights, foster development of a free-market economy, establish democratic control of the military, and not become mere "consumers of security." It also was agreed that new members would not have to accept the stationing of NATO forces or nuclear weapons in their territory.

In the autumn of 1995 NATO members were greatly concerned over a scandal involving Secretary General Willy Claes. Claes, who had succeeded the late Manfred Wörner of Germany in October 1994, was investigated in a corruption case involving a helicopter contract awarded while he was Belgium's economic affairs minister in 1988. He resigned from his NATO post on October 20, 1995. The subsequent selection process for a new candidate degenerated into a public dispute. The first candidate announced by the European NATO members, Ruud Lubbers (former prime minister of the Netherlands), was vetoed by the United States, apparently because of a lack of consultation beforehand. France then blocked Uffe Ellemann-Jensen from Denmark, whom the United States supported, reportedly due in part to the candidate's less-than-satisfactory mastery of French. (Many NATO observers also noted that Ellemann-Jensen had recently criticized French nuclear testing.) As a compromise, Javier Solana Madariaga, a prominent member of Spain's Socialist government since 1982, was appointed to the post on December 5. The new secretary general's announced priorities included the expansion of NATO and the promotion of a peace pact in Bosnia. Regarding the latter, the NATO foreign and defense ministers, meeting in joint session on December 5, formally approved the establishment of the peacekeeping force for Bosnia and Herzegovina (called the Implementation Force, or IFOR) to oversee the recently signed Dayton Accord. IFOR began its mission on December 20 (see article on Bosnia and Herzegovina for details).

The other major development at the December 1995 NATO session was an announcement from France that it planned to rejoin the NATO military structure after an absence of nearly three decades. However, it subsequently became apparent that the French decision was contingent on controversial restructuring that would provide greater European control of military affairs on the continent. A degree of progress on that question was perceived at the meeting of NATO foreign ministers on June 2–3, 1996, the United States agreeing that, under some circumstances, the European countries could conduct peacekeeping and/or humanitarian missions on their own under the command of an expanded WEU. However, even though the French defense minister was formally welcomed by his NATO counterparts at their session on June 13, Paris soon after threatened to reverse its recent decision unless Washington agreed to relinquish control of NATO's Southern Command to a European. The United States resisted that demand, primarily because of the prominence of the U.S. Sixth Fleet in the Southern Command.

The U.S.-French debate subsequently deteriorated into public insults prior to the meeting of NATO foreign ministers on December 10–11, 1996, at which Paris appeared to back away from its threat to block NATO expansion unless it got its way regarding the Southern Command. Meanwhile, on a more positive note, the NATO ministers endorsed the creation of a new mission for Bosnia and Herzegovina (the 31,000-strong Stabilization Force, or SFOR), scheduled to take over at the end of the month from IFOR. The Bosnian mission had been widely viewed as a major success for NATO, as had the PfP program, many of whose members had lent troops to IFOR. The streamlined SFOR included troops from the United States, Russia, and some 23 other NATO and non-NATO countries, including, significantly, Germany, whose commitment of 2,000 soldiers marked the first time that combat-ready FRG ground troops had been deployed outside NATO borders since World War II.

It also was agreed at the December 1996 session that NATO would make its long-awaited announcement regarding the admission of new members at the summit scheduled for July 8–9, 1997, in Madrid, Spain. Russia immediately denounced any such plans as "completely inappropriate," and the topic dominated NATO affairs in early 1997. While describing expansion as "inevitable," U.S. representatives were reportedly hoping that a special relationship could still be established between the alliance and Russia that would make Moscow less "antagonistic" to the NATO decision. While Russia strongly preferred that Europe abandon NATO and instead focus on strengthening the OSCE, Moscow ultimately accepted NATO enlargement.

Following months of intense negotiations, NATO and Russia signed a Founding Act on Mutual Relations, Cooperation, and Security on May 27, 1997, in Paris, France. Both sides committed to stop viewing each other as "adversaries" and endorsed "a fundamentally new relationship." NATO also stated it had no intention of stationing nuclear weapons or "substantial combat forces" within the borders of new members. In addition, a NATO-Russia Permanent Joint Council (PJC) was established to discuss security issues, which appeared to satisfy Moscow's goal of having a say in NATO decision making, although NATO officials made it clear that Russia would not be able to veto any of the alliance's decisions. Collaterally, Western leaders promised Russia an expanded role in the Group of Seven and other major international forums.

Although Russia remained officially opposed to any expansion of NATO, the new accord permitted NATO to extend membership to the Czech Republic, Hungary, and Poland in 1999. A number of NATO leaders, led by French president Chirac, had supported the inclusion of Romania and Slovenia in the first round as well but deferred to the U.S.-UK position after a statement from NATO Secretary General Solana that Romania, Slovenia, and the three Baltic states were "strong candidates" for the second round of expansion.

Progress regarding the new members at the Madrid summit served to distract attention from the ongoing conflict between France and the United States. Washington once again refused Paris's demand that a European be put in charge of the Southern Command, and France therefore declined to return to the integrated military command. Meanwhile, at the conclusion of the summit, NATO signed an agreement with Ukraine that established a NATO-Ukraine Commission and provided for cooperation and consultation on a wide range of issues. In other activity in 1997 the alliance replaced the NACC with the Euro-Atlantic Partnership Council (EAPC), which was designed to enhance the PfP program and permit cultivation of broader political relationships among the "partners" and full NATO members. NATO also unveiled a new military command structure, scheduled to be in effect by April 1999. Subsequently, in early 1998, NATO announced it would keep its forces in Bosnia past June, with SFOR's mission now to include civil security. (At the 2004 Istanbul summit, NATO announced it would end the SFOR Mission at the end of that year.)

Events in 1998 were dominated by NATO's admonitions to Yugoslavia's Serbian leaders regarding their policies in the province of Kosovo, where actions against ethnic Albanian separatists had begun in late February. In June a newly authorized Euro-Atlantic Disaster Response Coordination Center (EDRCC) began operating, its first assignment being to assist Kosovar refugees. In June and August, with the cooperation of PfP members Albania and Macedonia, NATO held military exercises near Yugoslavia's borders, while in October continuing hostilities led NATO to warn Belgrade of imminent air strikes. In response, Yugoslavia agreed to admit OSCE observers and to begin military and security withdrawals from the province. To provide the 2,000-member observer force with air surveillance, NATO placed a coordination unit in Macedonia, where an additional command center was sited in November. Widespread hostilities in Kosovo nevertheless resumed in January 1999. In February peace talks opened in Rambouillet, France, cosponsored by France and the United States, but discussions came to an abrupt halt on March 19 when the Serbian delegation continued to reject one of the proposed peace plan's key provisions, namely the presence of NATO peacekeepers on Serbian soil. On March 24, 1999, NATO forces initiated Operation Allied Force—the first intensive bombing campaign in the organization's history—which in the following weeks extended throughout Yugoslavia (see article on Serbia and Montenegro for additional details).

The Kosovo situation dampened the alliance's 50th anniversary summit, which was held on April 23–25, 1999, in Washington. Highlights of the summit were the welcoming of the accession of the Czech Republic, Hungary, and Poland (which had been formally admitted at a ceremony at the Truman Library in Missouri on March 12) and the approval of a new Strategic Concept, including a European Security and Defense Identity (ESDI) within the alliance. The summit communiqué acknowledged that the WEU, using "separable but not separate NATO assets and capabilities," could conduct defensive operations without direct U.S. participation. It also noted "the resolve of the European Union to have the capacity for autonomous action" in military matters that did not involve the full alliance. Despite U.S. pressure for NATO to adopt a more global posture, the Strategic Concept continued to limit NATO's purview to the "Euro-Atlantic area," with the communiqué reiterating the primacy of the UN Security Council in international peace and security matters. The summit also saw issuance of a Membership Action Plan (MAP) for future enlargement and the launch of a Defense Capabilities Initiative (DCI), the latter of which emphasized the need for interoperability in command and control and information systems, particularly given the likelihood that future missions would require rapid deployment and sustained operations outside alliance territory. Finally, NATO agreed to build new headquarters in Belgium, at a cost of about $800 million. Construction began in 2008, with completion scheduled for 2012.

On August 5, 1999, NATO approved the appointment (effective the following October) of UK Secretary of State for Defense George Robertson (subsequently Lord Robertson of Port Ellen) as the successor to Secretary General Solana.

During the same period NATO was negotiating cooperative military agreements with Russia, other former Soviet republics, and a number of Eastern and Central European nations under the PfP program. In May 2000 Croatia became a PfP partner and announced that it would ultimately seek full NATO membership. Also that month, the foreign ministers of nine Eastern and Central European PfP countries—Albania, Bulgaria, Estonia, Latvia, Lithuania, Macedonia, Romania, Slovakia, and Slovenia—agreed to apply collectively for NATO membership in 2002.

Although NATO was criticized by United Nations (UN) secretary general Kofi Annan, among others, for circumventing the UN in launching the air campaign against Yugoslavia in March 1999, the June 10 Security Council resolution that established the UN Interim Administration Mission in Kosovo also included a provision for the NATO-led Kosovo Force (KFOR). By April 2001 KFOR encompassed some 50,000 troops, the bulk of them from NATO and PfP countries, although command had passed a year earlier to the WEU/EU's Eurocorps, consisting of German, French, Spanish, Belgian, and Luxembourgian units. (For additional information on KFOR, see the entries on Serbia and Montenegro.)

Having been involved since the height of the Cold War in attempts to reduce conventional as well as nuclear forces, NATO in April 1999 launched an Initiative on Weapons of Mass Destruction (WMD) and authorized the creation of a WMD Center within the International Staff in Brussels. In 2001 the U.S. George W. Bush administration unilaterally decided to proceed with the development of a National Missile Defense (NMD), despite strong objections from most European allies, as well as Russia. Bush's plan was the major topic of discussion at a special one-day NATO summit held on June 13, 2001, in Brussels, the U.S. president declaring that the Anti-Ballistic Missile Treaty, which prohibits the deployment of new missiles, was a "relic of the past" and needed to be scrapped. The summit, mostly given over to informal discussion among the NATO leaders, was seen as a success for Bush in that many of his European counterparts reportedly agreed to maintain an "open mind" on the NMD, although France and Germany remained explicitly opposed to it. Some allies also were reportedly reassured by Bush's pledge that Washington would unilaterally reduce the number of U.S. offensive nuclear weapons and would attempt to negotiate a new missile treaty with Russia. Further heartening the European leaders, Bush unequivocally endorsed the European Security and Defense Policy and the "new options" offered by "a capable European force, properly integrated with NATO."

On August 22, 2001, responding to a request for assistance from the government of Macedonia, NATO began Operation Essential Harvest, a 30-day mission by approximately 3,500 troops to help disarm ethnic Albanian groups in that Balkan state. In September NATO authorized Operation Amber Fox, encompassing 700–1,000 personnel, primarily to protect international monitors overseeing implementation of the Macedonian peace plan. On December 16, 2002, Operation Amber Fox was in turn succeeded by a new mission, Operation Allied Harmony, to minimize any further risk of ethnic destabilization. This mission was to be of short duration, with NATO contingents being replaced in 2003 by elements of the EU's newly authorized Rapid Reaction Force.

The day after the September 11, 2001, terrorist attacks on the United States, the North Atlantic Council (NAC) invoked the collective self-defense provisions of the founding treaty. The unprecedented decision was followed in October by authorization for specific steps requested by the United States in its efforts to confront international terrorism. These included access to military facilities and intelligence information and the deployment of NATO's airborne early-warning squadron to the United States. NATO also dispatched its Standing Naval Force Mediterranean to the Eastern Mediterranean to support the U.S.-led military operation in Afghanistan and to deter terrorism.

Meeting on November 20–22, 2002, in Prague, Czech Republic, the NATO heads of state extended membership invitations to Bulgaria, Estonia, Latvia, Lithuania, Romania, Slovakia, and Slovenia, with formal admission anticipated for 2004. At the same time, the summit approved establishment of a mobile, rapidly deployable NATO Response Force (NRF). Earlier in the year, on May 28, the NATO heads of state had signed the Rome Declaration, which institutionalized a closer working relationship with Moscow through creation of a NATO-Russia Council (NRC) as successor to the NATO-Russia PJC. The NRF was inaugurated on October 15, 2003. The force numbered 9,000 troops and was initially placed under the command of British general Sir Jack Deverell. The NRF was designated fully operational with 25,000 available troops at the 2006 Riga summit. Since 2003, the NRF has undertaken five operations, including security missions to protect the 2004 Athens Olympics and elections in Iraq. In 2008 and 2010 the composition and organization of the NRF was revised to ensure the unit could be staffed in light of the continuing deployments of NATO forces in Afghanistan.

In its first major military operation outside the transatlantic region, in August 2003 NATO assumed command of the International Security Assistance Force (ISAF) authorized by the UN in Afghanistan. NATO oversaw 5,500 peacekeeping troops in the Kabul region. Efforts to expand the NATO-led mission to more remote regions of the country were constrained by the unwillingness of members and allies to contribute more troops to the ISAF. This inability of the alliance to deploy additional forces demonstrated the growing strain on European member states as the allies tried to maintain operations in areas such as the Balkans, Afghanistan, and Iraq. However, NATO agreed to provide 2,000 additional troops to provide security during the 2004 Afghan elections. In addition, at the 2004 Istanbul summit, NATO leaders agreed to provide troops for at least five provincial reconstruction teams in the Afghan countryside. At the June 2006 Brussels summit NATO leaders announced that the alliance would increase its forces in Afghanistan to 17,000, allowing the United States to reduce its troop strength from 20,000 to 16,000. NATO also announced at the summit that the United States would succeed British command of the NATO-Afghan mission in 2007.

During the winter of 2002–2003, the United States asked individual NATO states to contribute forces to the anti-Iraq coalition. Belgium, France, Germany, and Luxembourg strongly resisted the U.S. initiative, which was supported by other members, such as the United Kingdom, Netherlands, Italy, and Spain. The divide threatened the cohesiveness of the alliance in February 2003 after the antiwar allies blocked a request from Ankara for NATO to provide surveillance aircraft and antimissile batteries to protect Turkey in the event of armed conflict with Iraq. The deadlock was resolved on February 16 by having the Defense Planning Committee (of which France was not a member) resolve the dispute. NATO subsequently authorized the deployment of both early-warning aircraft and antimissile systems.

NATO did not formally participate in the March 2003 invasion of Iraq, but a number of individual NATO members, including the United Kingdom and Poland, contributed troops to the invasion force and to the postwar peacekeeping coalition that the UN authorized.

On January 29, 2003, seven NATO aspirants (Bulgaria, Estonia, Latvia, Lithuania, Romania, Slovakia, and Slovenia) began formal accession negotiations with the alliance. On March 26, 2003, the protocols were signed, and the ratification process began. On March 29, 2004, the seven nations became full members of NATO. The new members were expected to change the internal dynamics of NATO. All seven supported the U.S.-led invasion of Iraq and favored NATO as the cornerstone of European security, placing them at odds with other NATO members such as France and Germany, which sought a greater security role for the EU.

On September 22, 2003, NATO approved the appointment (effective January 5, 2004) of Dutch foreign minister Jaap de Hoop Scheffer as successor to Secretary General Lord Robertson. As was the case with many of his predecessors, de Hoop Scheffer's appointment was the result of compromises among the allies. Candidates such as Norway's defense minister Kristin Krohn and Portugal's António Vitorino (an EU commissioner) were rejected by France because of their countries' support of the U.S.-led invasion of Iraq, while the United States vetoed Canadian finance minister John Manley because of his country's opposition to the Iraq War.

At the June 2004 summit in Istanbul, interim Iraqi prime minister Iyad Allawi requested additional NATO aid. However, the prewar divide continued, and NATO leaders could only reach a compromise whereby alliance forces would train the Iraqi military and police forces. (NATO deployed 300 troops for the training mission, although Belgium, France, Germany, Greece, Luxembourg, and Spain declined to participate.) Nonetheless, the mission marked the second major non-transatlantic security operation by NATO. Also, in its June 28 communiqué following the summit, NAC affirmed support for Poland's command of the coalition's multinational division in Iraq.

Anders Fogh Rasmussen of Denmark succeeded de Hoop Scheffer as NATO secretary general on August 1, 2009. Rasmussen's appointment was initially blocked by Turkey because of the former Danish prime minister's defense in 2006 of the publication of newspaper cartoons depicting the Prophet Mohammed that many Muslims found offensive. Turkish officials reportedly opposed the nomination because of concerns that Rasmussen's appointment could serve as a focal point for Islamic extremists, but dropped their opposition in exchange for several senior appointments within the alliance.

In June 2006 Putin warned NATO against further expansion to states such as Ukraine; nonetheless, the alliance continued discussions with Ukraine and other states, including Croatia, Georgia, Armenia, and Azerbaijan. NATO also sought to strengthen ties with nonmembers, and in April 2006 the alliance announced plans for regular security forums with states such as Australia, Finland, Japan, New Zealand, South Korea, and Sweden. Proposals for a global version of PfP were also endorsed.

In April 2009 France rejoined the Defense Planning Committee (DPC) after withdrawing from the body in 1966. The DPC, which dated from 1963, focused on a range of matters related to collective defense planning and also offered guidance to military leaders. The DPC typically met at the permanent representative level but also convened twice a year as a meeting of defense ministers. Following a review of all NATO structures, the decision was made to dissolve the DPC and absorb its functions into the NAC in June 2010.

At the NAC meeting in June 2006 in Brussels, the alliance's defense ministers decided to require all member states to devote 2 percent of their GDP to defense, replacing a longstanding "gentleman's agreement" regarding the 2 percent threshold that only 7 of the 26 NATO members reached in 2005. (The average expenditure per NATO country in 2005 was 1.8 percent.) At the same meeting, NAC agreed to reorient the alliance so that it could simultaneously conduct six medium-size operations (of up to 20,000 troops each) and two major missions (of up to 60,000 troops each). The change was designed to better reflect NATO's contemporary range of operations.

At the alliance's November summit in Riga, NATO invited Bosnia and Herzegovina, Montenegro, and Serbia to join PfP. By October 2006 NATO-led ISAF had completed its expansion so that it had a presence in the four main geographic regions of Afghanistan. NATO then initiated a countrywide stabilization program that included increased humanitarian projects and development initiatives, as well as new military operations against Taliban forces.

NAC extended the term of NATO secretary general de Hoop Scheffer by two years in January 2007. De Hoop Scheffer remained in office through 2009 to provide continuity as the alliance commemorated the 60th anniversary of its formation that year.

Alliance troops launched NATO's largest offensive in the southern provinces of Afghanistan, Operation Achilles, in March 2007. More than 4,500 NATO, and 1,000 Afghan, soldiers participated in the anti-Taliban strikes that began in March. By the summer more than 33,000 soldiers from 37 NATO and allied countries were participating in ISAF. Nonetheless, Taliban attacks and other antigovernment activity continued to increase in remote areas of the country. In June NATO agreed to provide strategic airlift and other support for the AU Mission in Somalia (AMISOM) through 2007.

U.S. plans to deploy a missile defense system in Europe created strife within NATO and renewed tensions with Russia in 2007. At a defense ministers' meeting in Brussels in June, NATO agreed to continue efforts to develop an alliance-based theater missile defense system while launching a broad assessment of the U.S. initiative.

NATO and Russia reiterated their commitment to cooperation at a series of events that commemorated the fifth anniversary of the NATO-Russia Council in June 2007. However, Russia announced plans to unilaterally withdraw from the Conventional Forces in Europe Treaty (CFE) in July, and NAC responded by reaffirming its commitment to the CFE and urging the Russian government to reconsider and open a dialogue on the agreement. In December 2007 Russia stopped exchanging information with NATO about its troop movements, a development about which NATO expressed "deep regret" but no intention of retaliating. The second half of 2007 had seen conditions less and less conducive to good relations between Russia and NATO. Kosovo was a source of tension, with Russia strongly opposing it becoming an independent state, and the West tending to favor it. The former Soviet republics of Ukraine, Azerbaijan, and Georgia were all moving toward NATO membership, with Georgia's intentions a special irritant to Moscow.

By everyone's admission, the NATO operation in Afghanistan was having difficulties. At a December 2007 NATO foreign ministers' conference in Edinburgh, Scotland, both the U.S. and UK defense ministers declared that not enough NATO countries were deploying their troops where there was fighting. Germany was particularly mentioned in this context. Individual national force contributions to the Afghanistan mission dominated the February 2008 Vilnius meeting of NATO defense ministers, and Canada threatened to withdraw part of its forces unless other alliance members increased their presence. At the April 2008 Bucharest summit, French president Nicholas Sarkozy announced the deployment of an additional 1,000 troops, with other NATO states and partner countries dispatching smaller increases. The April deployment of an additional 2,400-troop U.S. Marine expeditionary unit allowed ISAF to undertake Operation Azada Woza in the Helmand region of Southern Afghanistan to suppress Taliban forces and heroin production. By 2008 ISAF numbered 52,700, its highest level. Nonetheless, the Taliban continued a series of aggressive attacks. In June, for the first time, more coalition troops died in Afghanistan (45) than in Iraq (31).

Also at the 2008 Bucharest summit, the United States led an unsuccessful effort to invite Georgia and Ukraine to join NATO. Concerns over Russian reaction led France and Germany to oppose membership. Albania and Croatia were invited to begin accession discussions, and formal membership protocols were signed in July. Meanwhile, initial membership talks were launched with Bosnia and Herzegovina and Montenegro. In addition, Malta announced that it would rejoin PfP. At the summit, NATO heads of state endorsed a U.S. proposal for a missile defense system. In June NATO's Science for Peace and Security program completed the destruction of 1,300 tons of toxic, Soviet-era missile fuel in Azerbaijan. In August, in response to the Russian invasion of Georgia, NATO suspended meetings of the NATO-Russia Council. NATO also agreed to create the NATO-Georgia Commission to prepare Georgia for eventual membership in the alliance. For more on major activities since 2008, see "Recent Activities" below.

Structure. NATO's complex structure encompasses a civilian component, a military component, and a number of partnership organizations. At the apex is the NAC, the principal decision-making and policy organ. It normally meets twice a year at the ministerial level to consider major policy issues, with the participation of the member states' ministers of foreign affairs and/or defense. It also may meet as a summit of heads of state and government. Between ministerial sessions the NAC remains in permanent session at NATO headquarters, where permanent representatives, all of whom hold ambassadorial rank, convene. Decisions at all levels must be unanimous.

The civilian structure includes the Nuclear Planning Group (NPG), which consists of the defense ministers of the alliance. Its purview extends from nuclear safety and deployment to such related matters as proliferation and arms control. Like NAC, the NPG may call on a host of committees and other bodies, the most prominent of which are the Senior Political Committee and the Defense Review Committee, to provide expert advice, to assist in preparing meetings, and to follow through on decisions.

The secretary general, who is designated by NAC, serves as chair of NAC, the NPG, the EAPC, and the Mediterranean Cooperation Group (MCG), as well as joint chair of the NRC and the NATO-Ukraine Commission. As NATO's chief executive, the secretary general has an important political role in achieving consensus among member governments and also can offer his or her services in seeking solutions to bilateral disputes. Former Danish prime minister Anders Fogh Rasmussen became secretary general on August 1, 2009. At the 2002 Prague summit, NAC approved a reorganization of NATO's civilian headquarters structure, known as the International Staff. The new system created a deputy secretary general post and six main divisions (later expanded to nine), each led by an assistant secretary general. The new divisions were Defense Investment, Defense Policy and Planning, Emergency Security Challenges, Executive Management, Operations, Political Affairs and Security Policy, Resources, Public Diplomacy, and the NATO Office of Security (headed by a director).

The highest military authority is the Military Committee, which operates under the overall authority of NAC and NPG. At its top level the Military Committee is attended by the members' chiefs of defense, although, as with the NAC, it is typically in continuous session attended by permanent military representatives from all members. The Military Committee is chaired by a non-U.S. officer of at least four-star rank. The current chair is General Knud Bartels of Denmark. The committee furnishes guidance on military questions, including the use of military force, both to NAC and to subordinate commands. It also meets with PfP partners on matters of military cooperation. The Military Committee is supported by the International Military Staff (IMS), which includes some 380 military personnel from the member states and 85 civilian personnel. The IMS is led by a three-star officer, currently Lt. Gen. Jürgen Bornemann of Germany.

Until 1994 the NATO military structure embraced three main regional commands: Allied Command Europe (ACE), Allied Command Atlantic (ACLANT), and Allied Command Channel. However, in 1994 Allied Command Channel was disbanded, and its responsibilities were taken over by ACE. In addition, in 2002 NAC agreed to dissolve ACLANT as an operational command. It was replaced by Allied Command Transformation (ACT). Each command is responsible for developing defense plans for its area, for determining force requirements, and for the deployment and exercise of its forces. Except for certain air defense squads in Europe, however, the forces assigned to the various commands remain under national control in peacetime.

After it absorbed the Allied Command Channel responsibilities in 1994, ACE had three major subordinate commands: Northwest (led by a designee of the United Kingdom), Central (led by a designee of Germany), and Southern (led by a designee of the United States). In 1997 NATO defense ministers agreed to reduce the number of command headquarters from 65 to 20 by 1999. On September 1, 2003, ACE was transformed into Allied Command Operations (ACO). The reorganized ACO initially incorporated two major subordinate commands, Allied Forces North Europe and Allied Forces South Europe, which had a total of seven subregional commands between them, as well as separate air and naval component commands. No fewer than nine other commands and staffs fell under ACO, most of them encompassing rapid reaction forces established in the 1990s. In 2004 ACO was again reorganized and the two subordinate commands divided into Allied Joint Force Command HQ Brunssum, Allied Joint Force Command HQ Naples, and Allied Joint Force Command Lisbon. Other major subordinate structures under ACO include, among others, the Standing Naval Force Atlantic, a Striking Fleet Atlantic, and a Submarine Allied Command Atlantic. There also is a separate Canada–United States Regional Planning Group, originally created in 1940 and incorporated into the NATO command structure in 1949. Its principal task is to recommend plans for the defense of the U.S.-Canada region.

ACO headquarters, known formally as Supreme Headquarters Allied Powers Europe (SHAPE), is located in Casteau, Belgium. The Supreme Allied Commander Europe (SACEUR) has traditionally been designated by the United States and serves concurrently as commander in chief of U.S. forces in Europe (CINCEUR). In April 2013 General Phillip Breedlove of the U.S. Air Force was named SACEUR, replacing U.S. admiral James G. Stavridis. Stavridis had been the first naval officer to be SACEUR.

ACT, with headquarters in Norfolk, Virginia, is headed by the Supreme Allied Commander Transformation (SACT), who is designated by the United States. In September 2009 French admiral Stéphane Abrial became the first non-U.S. SACT (see CAP activities, below). ACT includes the Joint Warfare Center in Stavanger, Norway; the Joint Force Training Center in Bydgoszcz, Poland; the Undersea Research Center in La Spezia, Italy; the Joint Analysis and Lessons Learned Center in Lisbon, Portugal; the Maritime Interdiction Operational Training Center in Crete; and the NATO School in Oberammergau, Germany. ACT's main mission is to transform NATO's military capabilities to respond more efficiently to new threats and operations.

The NATO Parliamentary Assembly is completely independent of NATO but constitutes an unofficial link between it and parliamentarians of the 28 member countries. It was founded in 1955 as the NATO Parliamentarians' Conference and was subsequently known, until 1998, as the North Atlantic Assembly. PfP partners have associate delegation status in the assembly. By keeping alliance issues under constant review and by disseminating knowledge of NATO policies and activities, the assembly encourages political discussion of NATO matters. During the 1990s its mandate was broadened to include European security as a whole, plus economic, environmental, social, and cultural issues relevant to Central and Eastern Europe. The assembly meets twice a year in plenary session, with various committees and study groups convening throughout the year.

Political dialogue also takes place within the 50-member EAPC, which comprises the 28 NATO members plus the 22 PfP partners, the NRC, the NATO-Ukraine Commission, and the MCG. Established in 1997, the MCG grew out of a Mediterranean Dialogue proposed by NATO in 1994 and initiated in 1995, when Egypt, Israel, Jordan, Mauritania, Morocco, and Tunisia agreed to join. Algeria became the seventh non-NATO member in 2000. The MCG is intended to promote mutual understanding and to serve as a forum on security and stability in the Mediterranean region. At the Istanbul summit in June 2004, NAC decided to expand security cooperation in the Middle East based on the pattern of success of the MCG. Modeled on the PfP, the Istanbul Cooperation Initiative (ICI) was designed to improve military and intelligence cooperation between NATO and Middle Eastern and Persian Gulf states and standardize equipment and operational guidelines. Bahrain, Kuwait, Qatar, and the United Arab Emirates joined the ICI. In 2006 NATO ministers began searching for a host country in which to establish a joint NATO-MCG training center. In addition to formal structures, NATO also has significant relationships with a number of other countries. Australia, Japan, New Zealand, and South Korea were designated as Contact Countries following the 2006 Riga summit. NATO and these nations developed annual work programs and collaborated closely on military operations, training, and logistics.

NATO has established more than three dozen subsidiary and related organizations, agencies, and groups that undertake studies, provide advice, formulate policies for referral to NAC or other NATO decision-making structures, manage specific programs and systems, and provide education and training. Many of these bodies are NATO Production and Logistics Organizations (NPLOs) concerned with technical aspects of design, production, cooperation, and management in communication and information systems; consumer logistics (pipelines, medical services); and production logistics (armaments, helicopters, other aircraft, missiles). Other bodies are concerned with standardization, civil-emergency planning, airborne early warning, air traffic management, electronic warfare, meteorology, and military oceanography. The Science for Peace and Security program was launched in 2006 to enhance scientific and technical cooperation between NATO and partner countries. The initiative provides funding and assistance for research and national projects ranging from environmental clean-up and protection to cybersecurity. In June 2007 NAC agreed to create a new agency to facilitate the alliance's Strategic Airlift Capability (SAC). Under SAC, 15 NATO members and two PfP states would have access to strategic airlift assets acquired by and managed by the alliance. In 2008 the SAC participants agreed to purchase three C-17 aircraft and to station the assets at Papa Airbase in Hungary.

Recent Activities. In response to growing civilian casualties in Afghanistan, NATO issued a new tactical directive in January 2009 that implemented a number of new measures to minimize collateral damage during attacks. On April 3–4, NATO leaders met in Strasbourg, France. Rasmussen was formally designated the next NATO secretary general. France reentered NATO's integrated military structure following an agreement whereby the United States agreed that a non-U.S. military officer would be appointed SACT. French admiral Abriel was subsequently appointed to the post (see Structure, above). On April 7 Albania and Croatia officially joined the alliance. The NATO-Russia Council resumed meetings on April 29 and the exchanges marked the formal resumption of interaction following the Georgian war. The following day two Russian diplomats were expelled for espionage. However, neither the incident nor subsequent NATO-led military exercises in May and June affected relations with Russia. In August a suicide bomber attacked ISAF headquarters in Kabul, killing seven and wounding more than 100, in a strike that was seen as part of a broader effort to disrupt the Afghan presidential and provincial elections that were held on August 20. On September 4 a NATO airstrike killed more than 90 civilians prompting a NATO apology and new guidelines on the conduct of aerial attacks. In December the United States announced that it would commit an additional 30,000 troops to the NATO-led mission in Afghanistan as part of a "surge" designed to enhance security while Afghan forces were being trained. Other contributors to ISAF deployed a further 7,000 troops.

In May 2010 a high level panel led by former U.S. secretary of state Madeleine Albright recommended that NATO develop a new strategic concept to better reflect changes in the international environment. In July the web group WikiLeaks released more than 91,000 documents on the conflict in Afghanistan. Information in the documents detailed covert operations and both civilian deaths and casualties from friendly fire. The controversial files undermined already declining public support in Europe and the United States for the mission in Afghanistan. At a summit in Lisbon in November, NATO heads of state agreed to withdraw combat forces from Afghanistan by 2014 (although the alliance would continue training and support operations). NAC endorsed the creation of a ballistic missile defense system in Europe. NAC also approved a new strategic concept that reaffirmed the alliance's collective defense mission and committed NATO to developing new capabilities to address emerging security threats such as missile attacks or cyber warfare. In addition, NATO announced that it would reduce the number of military headquarters from eleven to seven and consolidate non-military agencies and bureaus to reduce redundancies. At Lisbon, the NATO-Russia Council met for its third summit and endorsed cooperation on missile defense between the former Cold War enemies.

In November 2010 NATO reaffirmed its commitment to Afghanistan by signing the Declaration of Enduring Partnership with the Middle Eastern nation. The declaration established a framework for future political assistance and enhanced cooperation. The biggest area addressed in the document was NATO's commitment to assist Afghanistan in matters of national security with regard to both policy reforms and officer development.

In response to a political uprising that occurred in Libya in February 2011, the UN Security Council passed a resolution (Resolution 1973) that placed an arms embargo and a no-fly zone on Libya. Four weeks after passing the initial resolution, the UN Security Council passed a second resolution on Libya, authorizing regional IGOs to handle enforcement of the UN sanctions. On March 23 NATO launched an arms embargo on Libya, and the next day it voted to enforce the no-fly zone over the country. On March 27 Operation Unified Protector began as NATO decided to assume responsibility for the entire military operation enforcing the UN Security Council Resolution 1973. NATO assumed sole command of international airborne and maritime efforts on March 31.

Operation Unified Protector consisted of a series of air strikes that were targeted at military and air defense sites in Libya to ensure that the no-fly zone was observed by the Libyan dictator Colonel Qaadhafi. The air raids were also targeted at groups of advancing Libyan troops and their equipment in a preventative move to stop Colonel Qadaffi's further oppression of the Libyan people. Naval forces were charged with the task of preventing naval attacks and preventing any arms from reaching the country.

NATO voted on June 1 to extend its mission by another 90 days. After numerous successes on both the aerial and the naval fronts, NATO leaders chose to continue their pressure until such time as Qadhafi leaves power. The move was hailed as a sign of continued support for the Libyan citizens and an end to Qadhafi's oppressive regime. On July 13 the NAC met with the Libyan Transitional National Council and agreed upon the desire to begin working toward a political solution, but troops remain in the region despite the decision. Qadaffi was forced out of Tripoli in August 2011, and the National Transitional Council (NTC) took power. In September, the NAC voted to continue its military in Libya, pledging to stay the course until "threats to civilians" no longer persist. The NTC forces captured and killed Qadaffi on October 20, 2011, and NATO announced the end of Operation Unified Protector on October 31.

In June 2011 President Barack Obama (United States) announced plans to begin the withdrawal of U.S. troops in Afghanistan. This move was part of a NATO plan to remove troops and turn security over to the Afghanis by 2014. Just a few weeks after the announcement that the United States would begin withdrawing troops from Afghanistan, the NATO efforts in that country experienced another major change. General David Petraeus announced his resignation as commander of the ISAF forces in Afghanistan to accept the position as director of the U.S. Central Intelligence Agency. Petraeus, who had been in that position since 2010, was replaced by General John Allen. In December 2011 at a conference on Afghanistan held in Bonn, the NATO leaders agreed to extend their commitment to Afghanistan beyond 2014, ensuring that the country would have international support after the full transition of security leadership. As of May 2012, plans have been made for transition to full security leadership in each of the provinces in Afghanistan by July 2013. At the July 2012 Tokyo Conference on Afghanistan, NATO reaffirmed its financial commitment to help train and assist the Afghan security forces that took control of security in Afghanistan's Bamyan province on July 17, 2011. NATO also called on the rest of the international community to participate in the financial support of Afghanistan's self-reliance in security matters.

In May 2012, NATO held its biannual summit in Chicago. The summit was focused on three main goals: the future of Afghanistan, a stronger NATO defense system, and increasing partnerships between NATO and other world countries to achieve global progress. These goals were evident as NATO outlined a reaffirmed support for the 2014 transition in Afghanistan. In regard to NATO defense, the successful creation of an interim ballistic missile defense system was announced, marking the completion of the first stages of the 2010 Lisbon summit decision. NATO also expressed a great deal of appreciation for its partners across the world and their continued support for NATO initiatives.

In November NATO received a request from Turkey asking for the installation of Patriot missiles as a defensive safeguard to augment the Turkish Air Force in light of continuing violence along the Turkish border. NATO Foreign Ministers approved the request on December 4, and the United States, Germany, and the Netherlands (the three states with Patriot missiles) officially deployed the missiles in late December.

In February 2013 General Allen was replaced as commander of ISAF forces in Afghanistan by General Joseph Dunford Jr. Allen was nominated for the post of SACEUR, but respectfully declined in favor of retirement from the military. General Phillip Breedlove was then appointed SACEUR.

On June 18, Afghanistan's President Karzai announced the transition of the fifth and final group of Afghani cities, provinces, and districts. The announcement was hailed by Secretary General Rasmussen as a major step in the completion of the roadmap set forth at the Lisbon Summit. Rasmussen noted that the ISAF would soon begin to transition from a combat mission to a support mission, and he continued to reinforce the end of the NATO combat mission by 2014.

The civil war in Syria continued to be an especially problematic event in international affairs, particularly after the discovery of chemical weapons in late August. The North Atlantic Council convened a special meeting on August 28 to discuss the situation. At that meeting, the council condemned the use of chemical weapons and expressed its support of the UN investigation into the atrocities being committed in Syria. The council also reaffirmed its commitment to protecting the security of its southeastern border in Turkey. An extraordinary session of the NATO-Russia committee was called on September 17 to discuss the U.S.-Russia framework for eliminating the Syrian chemical weapons. The leaders of that committee expressed their full support for the U.S.-Russian framework calling for the surrender of chemical weapons to be placed under UN control. The committee called on the UN Security Council to quickly implement the framework and emphasized the grave danger of delay. The framework was approved at a Security Council meeting on September 27.

ORGANIZATION FOR ECONOMIC COOPERATION AND DEVELOPMENT (OECD)

Organisation de Coopération et de Développement Economique (OCDE)

Established: By convention signed December 14, 1960, in Paris, France, effective September 30, 1961.

Purpose: "To help member countries promote economic growth, employment, and improved standards of living through the coordination of policy [and] . . . to help promote the sound and harmonious development of the world economy and improve the lot of the developing countries, particularly the poorest."

Headquarters: Paris, France.

Principal Organs: Council (all full members plus the European Commission), Executive Committee (14 members), Economic Policy Committee, Development Assistance Committee, Secretariat.

Web site: www.oecd.org

Secretary General: Ángel Gurría (Mexico).

Membership (34): Australia, Austria, Belgium, Canada, Chile, Czech Republic, Denmark, Estonia, Finland, France, Germany, Greece, Hungary, Iceland, Ireland, Israel, Italy, Japan, Luxembourg, Mexico, Netherlands, New Zealand, Norway, Poland, Portugal, Republic of Korea, Slovakia, Slovenia, Spain, Sweden, Switzerland, Turkey, United Kingdom, United States.

Limited Participant: European Commission.

Official Languages: English, French.

Origin and development. The OECD replaced the Organization for European Economic Cooperation (OEEC), whose original tasks—the administration of Marshall Plan aid and the cooperative effort for

European recovery from World War II—had long been completed, although many of its activities had continued or had been adjusted to meet the needs of economic expansion. By the 1960s the once seemingly permanent postwar shortage of dollar reserves in Western European countries had disappeared, many quantitative restrictions on trade within Europe had been eliminated, and currency convertibility had been largely achieved. This increased economic interdependence suggested the need for an organization in which North American states could also participate on an equal footing. Thus, the OEEC, of which Canada and the United States had been only associate members, was transformed into the OECD. The new grouping also was viewed as a means of overseeing foreign aid contributions to less-developed states. It later expanded to include virtually all the economically advanced free-market states. Japan became a full member in 1964, followed by Finland in 1969, Australia in 1971, and New Zealand in 1973. The membership remained static until Mexico's accession in 1994. Subsequently, the Czech Republic (1995), Hungary (1996), Poland (1996), South Korea (1996), and Slovakia (2000) joined. Chile, Israel, and Slovenia joined in 2010. Russia is currently in the process of finalizing its accession, but has been stagnant since May 2012. Membership is limited to countries with market economies and pluralistic democracies and is granted by invitation only. New countries must be approved by each existing member, giving each country veto power. The OECD Center for Cooperation with Non-Members promotes dialogue with more than 70 nonmember countries, which are invited to subscribe to OECD agreements and treaties and benefit from policy and economic recommendations.

The key to the OECD's major role in international economic cooperation has long been its continuous review of economic policies and trends in member states, each of which submits information annually on its economic status and policies and is required to answer questions prepared by the Secretariat and other members. This confrontational review procedure has led to very frank exchanges, often followed by recommendations for policy changes. OECD analyses, generated in part through the use of a highly sophisticated computerized model of the world economy, are widely respected for being free of the political concerns that often skew forecasts issued by individual countries. Furthermore, the OECD has been in the forefront of efforts to combat unstable currencies, massive trade imbalances, third world debt, and high unemployment in industrialized countries.

A degree of controversy developed during the 1989 Council meeting over a recent U.S. citation of Japan, Brazil, and India as "unfair traders" subject to possible penalties. Japan challenged the U.S. decision as a threat to the "open multilateral trading system" and asked for an OECD statement criticizing Washington. The final communiqué, while not specifically mentioning the United States, condemned any "tendency toward unilateralism."

On another controversial topic, the OECD, after having completed an extensive review of the cost of farm support, called for the elimination of all agricultural subsidies by wealthier producers. Attempts to overcome substantial differences among members regarding agricultural policy continued at the 1990 Council meeting, the ministers giving the "highest priority" to completing agreements on farm subsidies and other outstanding issues in the Uruguay Round of the General Agreement on Tariffs and Trade. Other activity during 1990 included the opening of the Center for Cooperation with European Economies in Transition, designed to advise and guide Central and Eastern European countries as they moved toward free market economies.

In mid-1994 the OECD released the results of a two-year study on the structural causes of unemployment among members. Noting the high rate of unemployment in Europe (about 12 percent) as opposed to the United States (about 6 percent), the report urged European governments to introduce a new flexibility in their labor markets. Other recommendations were greeted cautiously by government officials, who feared changes would erode social benefits and the overall standard of living.

Mexico became the first new OECD member in 23 years when, with strong U.S. and Canadian backing, it acceded in May 1994. The OECD signed a cooperation agreement with Russia at the June 1994 ministerial session, pledging to assist Moscow with legal, structural, and statistical reforms to promote Russia's integration into the global economy, an effort that U.S. officials described as the "best investment we can make in our security."

At the 1996 ministerial meetings, a preliminary agreement was reached regarding corruption in the developing world. Negotiations subsequently continued on the proposed plan to make the bribing of foreign officials a criminal offense, and in November 1997 the treaty was finalized. (The treaty entered into force on February 15, 1999, following its ratification by 12 signatories.)

In January 1998 the OECD established the Center for Cooperation with Non-Members as its "focal point" for discussions on policy and to encourage dialogue with emerging market economies. At the April 1998 Council meeting, negotiations on the multilateral investment agreement, which had been seen as promising, were suspended. The negotiations came to an end later that year following France's withdrawal from them, reportedly because it would lose the ability to protect its domestic movie and television markets under the proposed agreement.

In 1999 the OECD established guidelines for corporate governance, which were considered surprisingly progressive for their time. However, by late 2002 OECD officials urged that the guidelines be toughened in light of the increasing corporate scandals. Among other things, the OECD argued that independent oversight bodies needed to be established because self-regulation had failed, particularly in the auditing sector. The OECD also called for the development of guidelines for pension fund administrators.

Another major focus of OECD attention in recent years has been the harmful effect on international trade and investment of so-called tax havens around the globe, which provide foreign depositors with the opportunity to deposit large sums of money with little or no tax consequence. Additional momentum in pursuing reform in the havens developed following the terrorist attacks on the United States in September 2001, at which time the George W. Bush administration called on all banks to help identify and seize accounts that might be linked to terrorist organizations or activity. OECD accords with several Caribbean countries in early 2002 appeared to stifle cohesive resistance, and by the end of the year, only seven countries (Andorra, Liberia, Liechtenstein, Marshall Islands, Monaco, Nauru, and Vanuatu) were still considered uncooperative on the matter.

The OECD tax haven initiative has been conducted alongside efforts by the Financial Action Task Force to combat money laundering through the use of another "name-and-shame" blacklist. By the end of 2001, 23 countries and territories were on the money-laundering blacklist. By October 2007 all the countries had been delisted.

A major OECD tax initiative hit a wall in 2003 when some member states were reluctant to join in the establishment of a comprehensive exchange system of banking information to prevent money laundering by terrorist organizations and tax evasion by individuals and corporations. In September 2003 Switzerland and Luxembourg balked at the OECD's 2006 deadline for entrance into the system, seeking to preserve their nations' well-established practice of banking secrecy. The two nations blocked an agreement among the member countries, marking the first time member states had used a veto inside the governing Council.

In October 2006 the OECD was one of the organizations involved in trying to restart the stalled Doha Round of trade talks but with little ultimate success. In its November 2006 *Economic Outlook* publication, it criticized the Russian government for its tendency to reintroduce state control of the economy by taking majority positions in the directorate of many companies that had previously been privatized.

In May 2007 the organization invited five new countries to discuss membership: Russia, Estonia, Chile, Israel, and Slovenia. By December 2007 accession talks were beginning. The OECD also suggested that Brazil, China, India, Indonesia, and South Africa, all increasingly powerful economies, could be invited in the near future. In June 2007 South Africa became the first African country to sign the OECD's antibribery convention.

In March 2008 Taiwan complained that China was trying to interfere with its participation in the OECD. Also in March the OECD rejected suggestions from U.S. and EU quarters that Sovereign Wealth Funds (SWFs)—funds that are controlled by a cash-rich nation-state, most often in Asia or the Middle East—should be more transparent. Secretary General Gurría said he saw no problem as long as profit, rather than politics, drove the funds' strategies.

In June 2008 the Estonian foreign minister said that his country should be ready to join the OECD by the end of 2009. Later in 2008 and through 2009 the OECD, like many other international organizations, was occupied by the global economic crisis. It went from forecasting an economic slowdown in August 2008, to a forecast of a protracted slowdown in November, to warnings about the U.S. economy in December, to a statement in June 2009 that the recession was "near bottom," and a declaration in August 2009 that the economies of rich countries were generally stabilized. The OECD also noted (in October 2008) that income inequality had risen sharply in rich countries where statistics were available. For more information on activities since 2008, see "Recent Activities," below.

Structure. The Council, the principal political organ, convenes at least once a year at the ministerial level, although regular meetings are held by permanent representatives. Generally, acts of the Council require unanimity, although different voting rules may be adopted in particular circumstances. Supervision of OECD activities is the responsibility of the 14-member Executive Committee, whose members are elected annually by the Council and usually meet once per week. The secretary general, who chairs the regular Council meetings, is responsible for implementing Council and Executive Committee decisions with the assistance of a Secretariat that employs some 2,500 people. The current annual budget is approximately €354 million ($479 million), 22 percent of which is contributed by the United States. Japan is the next leading contributor.

Probably the best known of the OECD's subsidiary organs is the Development Assistance Committee (DAC), which evolved from the former Development Assistance Group and now includes most of the world's economically advanced states as well as the Commission of the European Communities. DAC oversees members' official resource transfers. The Economic Policy Committee, another major OECD organ, is responsible for reviewing economic activities in all member states. The OECD includes more than 200 committees that produce data, analyses, guidelines, or recommendations affecting policy in every major area of development. The number of committees continues to grow each year. The Committee on International Investment and Multinational Enterprises was responsible for formulating a voluntary code of conduct for multinational corporations, which was adopted by the OECD in 1976. In addition, high-level groups have been organized to investigate commodities, positive adjustment policies, employment of women, and many other issues.

To complement the work of DAC, an OECD Development Center was established in 1962. Its current priorities emphasize working to meet the basic needs of the world's poorest people, with a focus on rural development and appropriate technology in Africa, Asia, and Latin America. Twenty-six members and nonmembers (including Argentina, Brazil, Chile, and India) participate in the center's activities. The Center for Educational Research and Innovation (CERI), established in 1968, works toward similar goals.

Recent Activities. In analyzing the world recession's effects, the OECD had a particularly gloomy view of Russia's prospects. The OECD saw a declining world demand for oil as stopping Russia's economic growth, while leaving it prey to the underlying problems of too much bureaucracy and too much political interference in business. On June 24, 2009, Russia launched its formal bid for membership in the OECD.

The OECD continues to work against tax havens and other kinds of international malfeasance. In December 2008 Israel became the first Middle Eastern state to sign on to the OECD antibribery convention, thus putting it one step closer to membership in the organization. In April 2009 the OECD removed the last four countries—Costa Rica, Malaysia, the Philippines, and Uruguay—from its blacklist of tax havens. In August the organization reported that all OECD countries were in compliance with its convention on the exchange of bank data for tax purposes, and that Hong Kong and Macao had agreed to pass legislation to the same end.

In 2010 Chile, Israel, and Slovenia joined the organization. Chile's accession caused concern among the Group of 77 coalition of developing countries, of which it was also a member. Nothing prohibited Chile belonging both to a group of developing countries and a group of developed countries, but to many it seemed inappropriate. Accession talks with Israel were contentious. The OECD demanded that Israeli official statistics exclude territories that the OECD does not consider part of Israel. There was also concern that Israel was not fully living up to the antibribery convention, and that Israel was not complying with the OECD's intellectual property standards, particularly in respect to generic drugs. Estonia also finalized its membership December 9, 2010.

In May 2010 Russia agreed with the OECD on a schedule of consultations on its accession to the antibribery convention.

OECD reports in 2010 declared the global recession to be over, giving different estimates of growth as the year progressed. The general conclusion was that recovery would be slow, but that there would be no so-called double-dip recession. The 2011 report, however, noted that while government stimulus money was declining in the global economy and the private sector was beginning to recover, new outside factors have emerged that could be problematic if countries do not remain committed to economic improvement. The 2011 annual report also indicated concern over the economic imbalances that exist from country to country. Likewise, the report prompted the OECD to increase its work on creating jobs and finding unemployment solutions.

The year 2011 also saw the emergence of a new plan for global development. The OECD Strategy for Development calls for an increase in sustainable growth in as many countries as possible. To achieve this goal, the OECD has committed itself to more integration and collaboration on the subject, particularly with the underdeveloped countries desiring to improve their economic situations. The effort will focus largely on finding sustainable growth programs and mobilizing natural resources within the states. The plan also calls for a new OECD Tax and Development program to assist countries interested in reforming their tax codes. In November 2011, the OECD invited Colombia to join the working group of the antibribery convention, marking the beginning of its accession process to the convention.

In February 2012, Russia completed its nearly 2-year accession process to the OECD's antibribery convention. Russia became the 39th country to sign the convention. In May 2012, Russia was invited to join the OECD's Nuclear Energy Association. These actions are major steps toward finalizing Russia's accession into the OECD as a full member, which Russian leaders hope to have completed by late 2013.

The financial crisis in the Euro zone, beginning in late 2011 and extending into 2012, was of major concern to the OECD. The OECD played an active role in advising struggling countries, such as Greece and Italy, in regard to policy options for handling the situation. The OECD welcomed the Greek debt reduction agreement, and by May 2012, reported in its *Economic Outlook* that the crisis in the euro zone seems to have been averted. The report did note, however, that if diligent efforts to reform policies and correct the economic imbalances were not enacted, the crisis might worsen. The report also noted that while the global crisis had been mostly averted, growth would remain subdued going forward.

At the May 2013 ministerial meeting, OECD members approved invitations for Colombia and Latvia to begin the accession process; roadmaps for each nation's accession process were finalized by the organization later in the year. If the accession process moves at the projected pace, both states will be admitted as full members by December 2015. At that same ministerial meeting, the group also approved a plan to open accession talks with Costa Rica and Lithuania in 2015 and outlined the need for member states to implement job creation programs, having noted that unemployment is the largest problem facing the global economy.

In the 2013 edition of its annual *Economic Outlook*, the OECD noted that the global economy, particularly in the most advanced nations, should experience growth beginning in mid-2013 through 2014. It did predict, however, that the Euro zone would continue to struggle with lingering effects of the financial crisis. The organization suggested the Euro zone continue its slow process of structural consolidation, construct and implement a full-fledged banking union, and ease their monetary policies. In light of the partisan political struggles going on in the United States throughout 2013, the OECD warned against the sequestration tactics that issued across the board cuts and was critical of the October government shutdown for the impact it could have upon the global economy.

ORGANIZATION OF EASTERN CARIBBEAN STATES (OECS)

Established: By treaty signed June 18, 1981, in Basseterre, St. Kitts, effective July 4, 1981.

Purpose: The Mission of the Organization of Eastern Caribbean States is to be a **Center of Excellence** contributing to the sustainable development of OECS Member States by supporting their strategic insertion into the global economy while maximizing the benefits accruing from their collective space.

Headquarters: Castries, St. Lucia.

Principal Organs: Authority of Heads of Government of the Member States, OECS Assembly, Council of Ministers, Economic Affairs Council, and the OECS Commission.

Web site: www.oecs.org

Director General: Dr. Len Ishmael (St. Lucia).

Membership (7): Antigua and Barbuda, Dominica, Grenada, Montserrat, St. Kitts and Nevis, St. Lucia, St. Vincent and the Grenadines.
Associate Members (2): Anguilla, British Virgin Islands.

Official Language: English.

Origin and development. The seven full participants in the OECS were formerly members of the West Indies Associated States, a pre-independence grouping established in 1966 to serve various common economic, judicial, and diplomatic needs of British Caribbean territories. The attainment of independence by four of the members—Dominica, Grenada, St. Lucia, and St. Vincent—during 1974–1979 and the impending independence of Antigua on November 1, 1981, gave impetus to the formation of a subregional body.

Meeting in 1979 in Castries, St. Lucia, the prospective members called for establishment of the OECS as a means of strengthening relations between the seven least-developed members of the Caribbean Community and Common Market (Caricom; see separate article). Following nearly a year and a half of negotiations, an OECS treaty (the Treaty of Basseterre) was concluded and came into force July 4, 1981. A dispute over location of the new organization's headquarters was settled by agreement that its central secretariat would be located in Castries (administrative center of the former associated states), while its economic affairs secretariat would be located in St. John's, Antigua, where the Secretariat of the Eastern Caribbean Common Market (ECCM) was sited.

To further cooperation and integration in the Caribbean, the OECS established the Eastern Caribbean Central Bank (ECCB) on October 1, 1983, in accordance with its decision in July 1982 to upgrade the Eastern Caribbean Currency Authority. The major functions of the ECCB are administering the EC dollar and exchange control, making currency rate adjustments, regulating credit policies, fixing interest rates, and establishing reserve requirements for members' commercial banks.

Following the U.S.-led invasion of Grenada in October 1983 to overthrow a pro-communist government, a Regional Security System (RSS) was established in cooperation with the United States to ensure the political stability of the OECS members.

In the mid-1980s, at the urging of Prime Minister John Compton of St. Lucia, the OECS considered forming a political union to counter nationalism and promote integration. When serious differences among the member states prevented significant progress, the four Windward countries (Dominica, Grenada, St. Lucia, and St. Vincent) indicated they might proceed toward their own political union, which would be open to accession by the Leeward states if they so wished. In 1990 the Windward group set up a widely representative Regional Constituent Assembly (RCA), which in January 1992 approved a draft constitution. By then, however, domestic political concerns had dampened enthusiasm for the project, and the RCA's final recommendations were never presented to the national legislatures and electorates. The OECS was also involved in establishing the independent Eastern Caribbean Telecommunication Authority (ECTEL) in Castries, with members Dominica, Grenada, St. Kitts and Nevis, St. Lucia, and St. Vincent and the Grenadines. ECTEL was described at its opening in October 2000 as the world's first regional telecommunications regulatory body. A year later the OECS launched in St. Kitts the Eastern Caribbean Securities Exchange, the first regional securities market in the hemisphere.

A report from the Organization for Economic Cooperation and Development in June 2000 labeled all the OECS members except Montserrat as "tax havens" and threatened to impose sanctions if steps were not taken to tighten regulation of their offshore financial industries. At the same time the independent Financial Action Task Force on Money Laundering included Dominica, St. Kitts and Nevis, and St. Vincent on its list of "noncooperative" jurisdictions, to which Grenada was subsequently added. The accusations drew heated denials from several OECS governments, some asserting that they had a sovereign right to establish their own banking and financial policies without external interference. Nevertheless, by 2003 all had taken sufficient action to be removed from both lists.

A special meeting of the heads of government in Grenada in April 2001 reviewed the organization's mission, structure, and financing. Despite previous restructuring and streamlining, budgetary problems continued to plague the group, with participants therefore naming the Technical Committee on the Functioning and Financing of the OECS Secretariat to develop a strategy for resolving financial arrears and also to consider additional reconfiguration. The 34th OECS summit, held July 25–26, 2001, in Dominica, received the report of the technical committee, which recommended maintaining the existing secretariat structure, writing off some arrears, and adopting a two-year strategy for member states to remit the balance of their outstanding commitments.

At the same time, summit participants moved forward on two major initiatives. First, the authority set a January 2002 date for instituting the free movement of nationals, including the elimination of restrictions on work and residency permits, throughout the member states. A task force was established to work out the details of the plan, which had been discussed for more than a decade, and also to address adoption of a common passport and ID (eventually abandoned). Member governments signed free movement legislation by the middle of 2002. Second, the heads of government authorized another task force to work toward establishing an OECS economic union modeled on the EU.

Meeting on January 31–February 1, 2002, in The Valley, Anguilla, the heads of government endorsed the economic union concept. (At least initially, associate members Anguilla and the British Virgin Islands were not expected to participate.) The authority cited the need for a "single economic space" to compete in the era of globalization and trade liberalization. The union was seen as a way to promote economic diversification and growth, increase export competitiveness, expand employment opportunities, further human resource development, and speed up free movement of people, goods, services, and capital.

With regard to the proposed Free Trade Area of the Americas (FTAA), a report prepared by the United Nations (UN) Economic Commission for Latin America and the Caribbean had concluded that the FTAA would be of little advantage to the OECS members. According to the report, an FTAA could, however, have a negative impact on trade within the 15-member Caricom, in which all the OECS members participate.

The anticipated inauguration of Caricom's (see separate article) Single Market and Economy (CSME) provided a focus for the 41st OECS heads of government meeting, which was held June 16–17, 2005, in Roseau, Dominica. Many OECS businesses opposed the CSME, fearing the subregion's relative disadvantages versus the larger Caricom economies. At the same time, the authority continued to advance subregional integration, including the final drafting of the OECS Economic Union Treaty.

On June 23, 2006, the seven OECS heads of government signed a declaration of intent to place the Economic Union Treaty before their countries' legislatures. At the same event, an OECS flag was unveiled. At a meeting in September 2007, trade experts met in Dominica to harmonize tariffs prior to the December 31 deadline for completing an Economic Partnership Agreement (EPA) with the EU, in conjunction with the rest of Caricom. The agreement was completed as scheduled.

Regional integration ran into further trouble in 2008, as the proposal for the economic union stalled. An important aspect of the treaty was that some decisions of the OECS Authority would now be binding on member states, where previously decisions were purely a matter of consensus.In August 2008 Trinidad and Tobago and three OECS Member States (Grenada, St. Lucia and St. Vincent and the Grenadines) reached an accord to pursue an Economic Union by 2011 and deeper political integration by 2013. In September the OECS issued a statement supporting this move and a task force, was set up to consider the proposal's merits. For more on developments since 2008, see "Recent Activities" below.

Structure. Normally meeting in biennial summits, the Authority of Heads of Government of the Member States is the highest OECS policymaking organ. It is supported by the OECS Commission (formerly known as the OECS Secretariat), which is headed by a director general and encompasses four divisions: functional cooperation, external relations, corporate services, and economic affairs. The functional cooperation division oversees several specialized units related to areas such as the environment, education, commerce, and aviation (for a full listing of the specialized units see *Political Handbook of the World 2012*). The

External Relations Division maintains missions in Brussels, Belgium, Geneva, Switzerland, and Puerto Rico. In general, the OECS Commission prepares reports, extends administrative and legal expertise, and provides supervision for the organization.

The Revised Treaty of Basseterre (2010) added three additional organs to the structure of the OECS. The OECS Assembly is a legislative body composed of five members of parliament from each the member states and three members of parliament from each of the associate members that reports to the OECS Authority. The Assembly has binding legislative power in matters pertaining to the actions of the OECS and, by virtue, its individual members. The Economic Affairs Council is composed of ministers from each member state and is responsible for the administration of the OECS Economic Union (see below). The Council of Ministers is composed of ministers from each of the member states and reports to the OECS Authority. The Council of Ministers has the power to enact Acts of the Organization upon the recommendations of the OECS Commission.

Recent Activities. OECS leaders originally welcomed the April 2009, decision of the G-20 countries to inject relief money into financial institutions as a response to the world financial crisis, but by May 2009 some in the group were having second thoughts. Caribbean countries were among the world's most heavily indebted, and it did not seem clear how the G-20's action would benefit them.

On June 2, 2009, the Trinidad and Tobago task force recommended that that country should be allowed to join the OECS. The Trinidadian opposition party was however opposed to joining without a referendum, and worried, as did many observers, about a negative effect on Caricom.

In November 2009 the OECS gathered for its 50th meeting of the OECS Authority. The meeting focused largely on solutions to the tourism and economic slumps, steps to increase agricultural production, plans for the OECS Economic Union, and the growing problem with crime in OECS member states.

New diplomatic relations were established in 2010. Both Finland and Germany began diplomatic relations with the OECS in early 2010. Furthermore, at the 51st summit, held in June 2010, the OECS members joined together in an agreement, the Revised Treaty of Basseterre, to create an economic union. The economic union would help promote growth in the Eastern Carribbean nations and would be the first step in removing the economic barriers that separate the member states. The accord also provided a framework for an OECS Commission: an executive body with decision-making capability. With Antigua and Barbuda being the first country to ratify the Revised Treaty of Basseterre, the OECS Economic Union was officially created January 21, 2011. The Revised Treaty of Basseterre also provided for the creation of several new principal organs of the OECS—the OECS Assembly, the Council of Ministers, the Economic Affairs Council, and the OECS Commission

In addition to the creation of the Economic Union, the decision for the integration of the OECS states by allowing free movement of people and goods through the country from other OECS member states was finalized at an OECS summit in January 2011. The free movement of people became effective August 1. The OECS also voted at the January 2011 meeting to establish a legislative body similar to the structure of European parliamentary systems that would be located in Antigua and Barbuda. The OECS Assembly has binding legislative authority over all states of the OECS

Much of 2011 was focused on tourism. In March, tourism ministers from the OECS member states adopted a new Common Tourism Policy, which was finalized in October. The new policy primarily focuses on tourism development throughout the region. At the 53rd summit of the OECS, held in May 2011, the OECS moved forward with its January decision to establish the free movement of people and goods throughout the OECSby June 1, 2013 to be. Another major milestone for the OECS was reached in October 2011 with the establishment of diplomatic relations with the United States. In December 2011, the OECS's High Commission in Canada was closed, after the decision to close was approved by the member states in June. The decision to close the foreign embassy was the result of increasing financial strains pn the member states.

The OECS held its 54th annual summit in January 2012. At that meeting, the discussions centered largely on the transition into a new governance structure with the creation of the new principal organs under the Revised Treaty of Basseterre. The summit also discussed new issues arising with the economic union, such as electronic transactions and maritime commerce and governance. In February 2012, the Chief Justice of the Eastern Caribbean Supreme Court (ECSC) Hugh Anthony Rawls announced his resignationeffective August 1. Dame Janice Pereira, who was appointed by Queen Elizabeth II on September 28 and sworn into office on October 24, succeeded Rawls. Pereira became the first woman to be named chief justice of the ECSC.

The OECS held its 55th annual summit in June 2012. The meeting was mostly focused on the inauguration of the OECS Assembly, procedural matters necessary to appoint a new Chief Justice of the ECSC and the commencement of free circulation of goods within the economic union, which took effect July 1, 2013. The OECS Assembly was inaugurated on August 10, 2012, formally launching the new organ of the OECS. The first official sitting of the Assembly was held March 26, 2013, with a second sitting to be scheduled by the end of 2013.

In June 2013 the OECS Authority held its 57th summit. The meeting largely focused on the draft of the OECS Development Strategy, a document compiled by the Secretariat outlining the priorities for continued regional growth in all the major sectors. The summit also called for increased cooperation between governments and the private sector to boost development in the region, particularly in regard to renewable energy. The heads of state also endorsed a proposal for all OECS member states to join the Advisory Center on the WTO Law.

ORGANIZATION FOR SECURITY AND COOPERATION IN EUROPE (OSCE)

Established: As the Conference on Security and Cooperation in Europe (CSCE) on July 3, 1973, by meeting of heads of states and other representatives of 35 nations in Helsinki, Finland; Helsinki Final Act adopted August 1, 1975; Charter of Paris for a New Europe adopted November 21, 1990; current name adopted at Heads of State or Government Summit on December 5–6, 1994, in Budapest, Hungary.

Purpose: "To consolidate respect for human rights, democracy, and the rule of law, to strengthen peace, and to promote unity in Europe."

Headquarters: Vienna, Austria.

Principal Organs: Heads of State or Government Meeting (Summit), Ministerial Council, Senior Council, Permanent Council, Conflict Prevention Center, Forum for Security Cooperation, Office for Democratic Institutions and Human Rights, High Commissioner on National Minorities, Office of the Representative on Freedom of the Media, Parliamentary Assembly, Secretariat.

Web site: www.osce.org

Secretary General: Lamberto Zannier (Italy).

Membership (57): Albania, Andorra, Armenia, Austria, Azerbaijan, Belarus, Belgium, Bosnia and Herzegovina, Bulgaria, Canada, Croatia, Cyprus, Czech Republic, Denmark, Estonia, Finland, France, Georgia, Germany, Greece, Hungary, Iceland, Ireland, Italy, Kazakhstan, Kyrgyzstan, Latvia, Liechtenstein, Lithuania, Luxembourg, Macedonia, Malta, Moldova, Monaco, Montenegro, Mongolia, Netherlands, Norway, Poland, Portugal, Romania, Russia, San Marino, Serbia, Slovakia, Slovenia, Spain, Sweden, Switzerland, Tajikistan, Turkey, Turkmenistan, Ukraine, United Kingdom, United States, Uzbekistan, Vatican City State.

Official Languages: English, French, German, Italian, Russian, and Spanish.

Origin and development. The creation of a forum for discussion of East-West security issues was first proposed in the late 1960s. The Soviet Union, in particular, supported the idea as a means of establishing dialogue between the North Atlantic Treaty Organization (NATO) and the Warsaw Treaty Organization (Warsaw Pact) and formalizing the post–World War II status quo in Europe. Talks in 1972 led to the establishment of the CSCE on July 3, 1973, in Helsinki, Finland, by the foreign ministers of Canada, the United States, and 33 European countries. At a summit July 30–August 1, 1975, the heads of state and government signed the Helsinki Final Act, which declared the inviolability of national frontiers in Europe and the right of each signatory "to choose and develop" its own "political, social, economic, and cultural systems."

The act called for ongoing discussion of three thematic "baskets"—security, economic cooperation, and human rights—and provided for periodic review of progress toward implementation of its objectives, although no provision was made for a permanent CSCE headquarters or staff. Consequently, the conference operated in relative obscurity and had little impact beyond the establishment of so-called Helsinki Groups in the Soviet Union and other Eastern European nations to monitor human rights.

The third CSCE review conference, held in Vienna, Austria (1986–1989), laid the groundwork for negotiations that produced the Treaty on Conventional Armed Forces in Europe (CFE), through which NATO and Warsaw Pact members agreed to substantial arms reductions. The CFE treaty was signed at the second CSCE summit on November 19–21, 1990, in Paris. The NATO and Warsaw Pact members also signed a joint document declaring they were "no longer adversaries." In addition, the summit adopted the Charter of Paris, which significantly expanded the CSCE mandate and established a permanent institutional framework.

The November 1990 CSCE summit was viewed by many of the 34 national leaders in attendance as a landmark step toward the establishment of a pan-European security system, a long-standing goal that had seemed unattainable until the dramatic improvement in East-West relations. However, despite the formal opening of the CSCE Secretariat in Prague in February 1991 and a Conflict Prevention Center in Vienna in March, the euphoria over the CSCE's prospects faded somewhat by the time the Council of Foreign Ministers met in June. In light of the perceived potential for instability within the Soviet Union and ongoing ethnic confrontation elsewhere on the continent, Western leaders had recently reaffirmed NATO as the dominant body for addressing their defense and security concerns. In addition, some observers wondered if the CSCE would prove too unwieldy, as its decisions required unanimity and it lacked any enforcement powers.

Although most prominently identified since 1990 with its field operations and with election-related activities, the OSCE's agenda has expanded to include a wide range of crucial issues facing its membership. Through various seminars, workshops, conferences, conventions, reports, and projects, it continues to address concerns in what it defines as three "dimensions": politico-military, human, and economic. More specifically, the OSCE has been involved in promoting human and minority rights; development of democratic institutions and procedures, including an independent judiciary and a free press; the participation of women in economic and political life; economic and environmental matters; and efforts to halt money laundering, organized crime, the financing of terrorism, human trafficking, and drugs.

Under the Charter of Paris and, later, the Helsinki Document, the CSCE took on an increasingly prominent role in conflict management; peacekeeping; the promotion of democratic standards; and the monitoring of political, legal, and other developments in Europe and Central Asia. In its first effort at mediation, in July 1991 the CSCE dispatched a mission to Yugoslavia that had no success in curtailing the violent ethnic conflicts resulting from that country's breakup. The latter missions, with never more than 20 international personnel, had as their mandate promoting dialogue between the Belgrade government and the ethnic communities in the three regions, but the rump Yugoslavia terminated the missions' memorandum of understanding in 1993. Technically, the regional missions remained in existence until 2001, when Yugoslavia welcomed a new undertaking—the OSCE Mission to Serbia and Montenegro—with a mandate to promote "democratization, tolerance, the rule of law, and conformity with OSCE principles, standards, and commitments." On June 29, 2006, following the separation of Serbia and Montenegro into independent countries, the mission was, in effect, divided into two: the OSCE Mission to Montenegro and the OSCE Mission to Serbia.

Albania joined the CSCE in June 1991 and was followed in September by Estonia, Latvia, and Lithuania. Russia subsequently assumed the former USSR seat. The other ten members of the Commonwealth of Independent States (CIS) joined in early 1992, the CSCE having decided to include the five Central Asian republics because of their former inclusion in the Soviet Union. Croatia, Georgia, and Slovenia were admitted in March, followed shortly thereafter by Bosnia and Herzegovina. The Czech Republic and Slovakia were admitted in 1993 following the dissolution of Czechoslovakia, while Macedonia joined the renamed OSCE in October 1995, after Greece lifted its veto. Andorra's accession in 1996 brought the OSCE's active membership up to 54. Yugoslavia (subsequently Serbia and Montenegro) returned to active status in November 2000, Belgrade's membership having been suspended in July 1992. Montenegro joined in June 2006, and the former Serbia and Montenegro membership now officially represents Serbia alone.

The fourth CSCE follow-up session, held from March to July 1992 in Helsinki, focused on reformulating the organization's aims and structures. Its recommendations were adopted as the Helsinki Document by the third CSCE summit, held in the Finnish capital July 9–10. The text specified that the CSCE's task was now "managing change"; that summit meetings should "set priorities and provide orientation"; that the Council of Foreign Ministers was "the central decision-making and governing body of the CSCE"; and that the Committee of Senior Officials (CSO) was responsible for ongoing "overview, management, and coordination" of CSCE activities. The summit also decided in principle that the CSCE should have its own peacekeeping capability, which should operate in conformity with United Nations (UN) resolutions and in concert with NATO, the CIS, the European Community, and the Western European Union.

A number of other OSCE missions became operational in 1992–1993. Missions to Estonia and Latvia were concerned with institution-building; the inculcation of OSCE principles and, in the case of Estonia, promotion of integration and intercommunal understanding between ethnic Estonians and ethnic Russians. Both missions concluded at the end of 2001. In December 1992 a new civilian-military mission to Georgia was directed to promote negotiations with secessionists in South Ossetia and, secondarily, to assist the UN in its similar efforts with regard to Abkhazia. The Mission in Georgia later took on such additional tasks as building democratic institutions, promoting human rights, and encouraging development of a free press. These missions in the Caucasus came to an end in 2009 (see below). It is important to note that OSCE missions can be established only by consensus among the member countries.

Also in 1992, the Minsk Process was fashioned to convene a conference in Minsk, Belarus, that would resolve the Nagorno-Karabakh conflict between Armenia and Azerbaijan. Although the conference has yet to be held, an Initial Operation Planning Group (IOPG), dating from May 1993, was superseded in December 1994 by a High-Level Planning Group (HLPG) that continues to meet in Vienna. The ongoing Minsk Process is cochaired by France, Russia, and the United States and includes eight other countries in addition to the principals. Separate from the Minsk Process, the OSCE launched a seven-person Office in Yerevan (Armenia) in February 2000 and a six-person Office in Baku (Azerbaijan) in July 2000.

Two other OSCE missions date from 1993. The Mission to Moldova facilitated the formation of a peace plan that envisaged substantial autonomy for the Transdnestr region; the plan was accepted by the Moldovan government in 1994. In December 1993 the council also established a Mission to Tajikistan because of the civil war. Deployed in February 1994, the handful of staff members helped secure a peace pact in 1997. In November 2002 the mission was redesignated the Center in Dushanbe (the Tajik capital) with a staff of 16 mandated to "promote the implementation of OSCE principles and commitments."

Throughout 1994 Russia continued to press for a strengthening of the CSCE, hoping to position it rather than NATO as the preeminent security organization for the "new Europe." Although bluntly dismissive of the notion that it would supplant NATO, Western leaders did agree that the grouping needed, in the words of one participant, "more heft." Thus, the CSCE became the OSCE during the Heads of State or Government Summit on December 5–6 in Budapest, Hungary.

In 1995 the OSCE, with the goal of further integrating all five Central Asian members into the organization, established an OSCE liaison office in Central Asia in Tashkent, Uzbekistan. In July 1998 the OSCE decided to open individual offices in Kazakhstan, Turkmenistan, and Kyrgyzstan. Currently, the OSCE has separate offices in each of the Central Asian republics.

Under the November 1995 Dayton peace agreement for Bosnia and Herzegovina the OSCE was allotted a key role, notably in organizing elections.

In October 1998 the OSCE, with the approval of the United Nations, undertook its largest mission to date, the Kosovo Verification Mission (KVM). The KVM was authorized for one year and was supposed to verify that all sides of the conflict were in compliance with UN resolutions. It was also directed to monitor elections and help establish a police force and other institutions in Kosovo. Despite the presence of the KVM and several attempts at negotiating an end to the fighting, the violence in Kosovo continued, and the mission had to be withdrawn in March 1999 before NATO initiated its bombing campaign against Yugoslavia. The OSCE returned to Kosovo following the conclusion in June of a comprehensive peace plan that included establishment of a UN Interim Administration Mission for Kosovo (UNMIK), with the OSCE Mission in Kosovo to be responsible for implementing democratic reforms and building governmental institutions.

The Office for Democratic Institutions and Human Rights (ODIHR) has reviewed electoral laws and observed elections in more than two-dozen member countries. Frequently, its reports have highlighted deficiencies in electoral processes, and, on occasion, the OSCE refuses to send monitoring teams.

In other field activities, the OSCE has been assisting since 1994 in implementing Russian-Latvian and Russian-Estonian agreements on military pensioners. The OSCE also provided a representative in 1995–1999 to another bilateral agreement between Russia and Latvia regarding the temporary operation and dismantling of the Skrunda Radar Station in Latvia.

The OSCE Heads of State or Government Meeting held on December 2–3, 1996, in Lisbon, Portugal, resolved in favor of a negotiated revision of the 1990 CFE Treaty, as demanded by Russia in light of its perceived need to deploy additional forces in unstable border regions.

The major event of 1999 was a summit convened on November 18–19 in Istanbul, Turkey. Despite concerns over Russia's renewed offensive in Chechnya, criticism of which led to Russian president Boris Yeltsin's early departure from the meeting, the summit managed to conclude two major agreements. All 54 active member countries signed the new European Security Charter, which, in part, reinforced various agreements dealing with security and human rights and called for more rapid response to requests for assistance from member states, particularly with regard to conflict prevention and crisis management. In addition, the 30 states belonging to NATO or the defunct Warsaw Pact signed a revised CFE Treaty, in which all signatories accepted verifiable ceilings for such military equipment as tanks, artillery, and combat aircraft and agreed not to deploy forces outside their borders without approval by the affected country.

A heightened emphasis on opposing terrorism was well in evidence at the December 3–4, 2001, Ministerial Council session in Bucharest, Romania, and at the December 6–7, 2002, session held in Porto, Portugal. As part of an OSCE Strategy to Address Threats to Security and Stability in the Twenty-first Century, the session also called for establishment of a Counter-Terrorism Network to coordinate counter-terrorism measures; share information; and "strengthen the liaison" among OSCE delegations, government officials, and the new Action against Terrorism Unit (ATU) in the Secretariat.

The 2003 ministerial session endorsed an Action Plan to Combat Trafficking in Human Beings, which called for adding a related special unit in the Secretariat and the appointment of a special representative.

Moscow claimed the OSCE had taken an "intrusive" interest in the affairs of the former Soviet Union, particularly with regard to the monitoring of elections and borders. Russia continued to refuse to uphold its commitment made to the OSCE in 1999 to remove its troops from Georgia and Moldova, and prepared to contest the monitoring of the Georgian border. When the disputed March 2005 Kyrgyz elections resulted in the ouster of the government, the OSCE called for harmony among the country's new leaders and declared that the ousted president, Askar Akayev, should not attempt to return from Russia, whence he had fled. The OSCE's position prevailed, and an election to elect a new president was held in July.

The OSCE, best known for monitoring elections in countries where democracy is relatively new, broke new ground by announcing that it would monitor the 2005 British general election—not with the expectation of finding fraud but as a way to assess the issues around ballot security and postal voting in developed countries. In November 2004 it had conducted a "targeted observation" of legislative and presidential balloting in the United States, and in 2006 it sent teams to both Canada and Italy.

At the October 2006 OSCE foreign ministers' meeting in Brussels, Russian rhetoric reminded some observers of Cold War days. Foreign minister Sergei Lavrov suggested divorcing humanitarian concerns from the OSCE, and perhaps establishing a special organization to deal with such concerns exclusively. He said that each country could make its own decision about membership in such an organization.

In September 2007, when Georgia accused a Russian aircraft of entering its airspace and firing a missile, the OSCE played an important part in keeping channels of communication open between the two countries, perhaps preventing the crisis from worsening. But observers noted that the incident showed that the OSCE needed a faster procedure for reacting to such events.

Poll-watching during Russia's resurgence occupied the OSCE well into 2008. In September 2007 Poland, now a member of the EU and NATO, refused to admit OSCE observers to its October parliamentary elections, saying that it was now a democracy needing no such monitoring. OSCE monitoring of the December 2, 2007, Russian parliamentary elections faced difficulties not encountered in the elections of 2003. At first Russia would allow only a much smaller number of observers than before, so ODIHR canceled the mission in mid-November, saying that it had been denied the necessary visas. In the end OSCE observers went to Russia, and OSCE branded the election—won decisively by President Vladimir Putin's party—as "not fair."

Differing U.S. and Russian agendas for the OSCE were apparent at the November 29–30, 2007, annual ministerial council meeting held in Madrid. Russia seemed to win the debate over allowing Kazakhstan, a close ally sometimes criticized for its record on human rights, to assume the OSCE presidency in 2010. However, Russia made no progress in its efforts to rein in the ODIHR. Russia continued to push, against the United States, for an OSCE charter.

The OSCE criticized the December 2007 parliamentary elections in Kyrgyzstan, in which the president's party won every seat. The OSCE likewise criticized the Uzbek presidential election in the same month, but a U.S. member of the mission called the criticism "nonsense," saying that ODIHR monitors often wrote their reports without leaving their hotels. ODIHR finally boycotted Russia's March 2008 presidential election after acrimonious disagreement with Russia about the size and duration of its mission. Russia called ODIHR's position a further reason for reforming the organization.

The seventeenth annual session of the Parliamentary Assembly met June 29–July 3, 2008, in Astana, Kazakhstan. It called for increased transparency in the OSCE and for the ODIHR and the Parliamentary Assembly to work more closely together to assure effective monitoring of elections. The Astana Declaration came close to seeking an OSCE charter.

The remainder of 2008, as well as 2009, was dominated by the threat of renewed fighting between Russia and Georgia after the August 2008 conflict was mediated to a close. In September 2008 talks about increasing the OSCE monitoring contingent came to a halt because Russia objected to monitors also working in the breakaway Georgian regions of South Ossetia and Abkhazia. Russia regards these regions as independent states. On December 21, 2008, at the OSCE Permanent Council meeting in Vienna, Russia objected to any extension of the mission's mandate, unless the OSCE set up separate missions for South Ossetia and Abkhazia. Plans were put in place to end the Georgia mission by June 30 of that year. Negotiations continued, but on May 21, 2009, the Greek chair of the OCSE suspended them indefinitely, citing lack of progress. The mission's mandate thus expired, though an EU mission remained in place. For more on activities since 2008, see "Recent Activities," below.

Structure. Prior to the signing of the Charter of Paris in November 1990, the CSCE had little formal structure, operating as what one correspondent described as a "floating set of occasional negotiations." The charter provided for Heads of State or Government Meetings (Summits) and established a Council of Foreign Ministers to meet at least once a year as the "central forum for political consultations within the CSCE process." A Committee of Senior Officials was empowered to carry out the decisions of the council. The charter also authorized the establishment of a Conflict Prevention Center in Vienna, for which a separate secretariat was created, and an Office for Free Elections in Warsaw. The latter body was subsequently renamed the Office for Democratic Institutions and Human Rights (ODIHR).

In 1992 the CSCE also established a Forum for Security Cooperation (for negotiations on further arms control, disarmament, and confidence-building measures) and a High Commissioner on National Minorities. It also adopted a Convention on Conciliation and Arbitration, which led to establishment of a Court of Conciliation and Arbitration to which signatories of the convention could submit disputes. Furthermore, the NATO and former Warsaw Pact members signed an Open Skies Treaty that permitted aerial reconnaissance. (The treaty entered into effect in

January 2002.) In July 1992 the inaugural meeting of the CSCE Parliamentary Assembly took place in Budapest, Hungary.

In addition to adopting the OSCE designation, the December 1994 summit in Budapest enacted several structural changes designed to convey a greater sense of permanency. Thus, the Committee of Senior Officials was renamed the Senior Council and was mandated to meet at least three times a year (once as the Economic Forum). The Ministerial Council (formerly the Council of Foreign Ministers) was mandated to meet in non-summit years. While the Senior Council was given broad responsibility for the implementation of OSCE decisions, day-to-day operational oversight was assigned to a Permanent Council. OSCE members are generally represented on the Permanent Council by their ambassadors in Vienna, where the offices of the main Secretariat are located. (The Secretariat also maintains an office in Prague, Czech Republic.)

In 1997 OSCE members approved a plan to create within the Secretariat the post of coordinator of economic and environmental activities as part of an effort to "strengthen the ability of the Permanent Council and the OSCE institutions to address economic, social and environmental aspects of security." An Office of the Representative on Freedom of the Media was added in 1998. Although the 1994 summit called for upgrading the authority of the OSCE secretary general, the position subsequently remained to a large part subordinate to the organization's chair-in-office (CiO), a post held by a foreign minister of a member country for a one-year term.

Recent Activities. In July 2009 the OSCE monitored presidential elections in Albania and Kyrgyzstan. It described the Albanian election as fair, but was less satisfied with the election in Kyrgyzstan.

Kazakhstan's 2010 presidency of the OSCE was controversial. Many said that its civil rights record ("worse than Russia's") was deteriorating even as it led an organization supposedly devoted to civil rights. Kazakhstan in turn touted the fact that, as a member of the Collective Security Treaty Organization (CSTO), an organ of the Commonwealth of Independent States (CIS, see separate article), it was well placed to bridge the divide between East and West. Kazakhstan announced that its presidency would be devoted to combating terrorism, resolving conflicts, and reconstruction in Afghanistan, with correspondingly less emphasis on democracy. However in February 2010 a Kazakh court overturned a ruling that prevented the media from publishing criticism of President Nursultan Nazarbayev's son-in-law. The main initiative of the oil-rich country's presidency was to be the calling of an OSCE summit in Almaty in December 2010, the first such since 1999. The aim was to produce an important document that defined, or redefined, the organization's purpose.

In April 2010 Kyrgyzstan suffered a bloody popular revolution, in which President Kurmanbek Bakiyev was deposed and left for Kazakhstan on April 15. On April 16 the interim government announced that it would renew a lease on the U.S. air base at Manas—a critical transit point for personnel and supplies going to Afghanistan. The OSCE declared the conduct of the Kyrgyz constitutional referendum of June 2010 generally acceptable. The new constitution would transfer much power from the president to parliament. In May 2011 the independent Kyrgyzstan Inquiry Commission, led by representatives of the OSCE, issued a report that criticized the role played by the current Kyrgyz government in the violence that occurred in the aftermath of the demise of the previous regime. The report prompted antigovernment protests in Kyrgyzstan.

The OSCE cited a range of problems in balloting in Azerbaijan on November 7, 2010, including media bias and electoral fraud. However, the group praised the legislative elections in Moldova on November 28.

On July 1, 2011, Lamberto Zannier, a career diplomat from Italy, became the new OSCE secretary general, replacing Marc Perrin de Brichambaut of France. In September negotiations resumed to resolve the conflict between Moldova and the separatist Dneister region. (Earlier talks had been suspended in 2006.) The OSCE, the EU, the United States, Russia, and Ukraine formed a mediating group to help facilitate negotiations, dubbed the "5 + 2" talks.

At its December 2011 ministerial meeting, the OSCE committed to strengthen its commitment and efforts to assist Afghanistan in its transition to a full Afghani-led security force. The OSCE ministers also adopted a decision calling on its member states to increase their efforts to remove the barriers preventing gender equity in the economic sphere. That included encouraging shared roles in both the business and domestic spheres. The summit also issued a strong declaration in which the member states committed to end human trafficking of all kinds. Also at the summit, Mongolia submitted its application to become a participating state of the OSCE.

The OSCE observed the March 2012 Russian election in which former president and current Prime Minister Vladimir Putin was reelected as president. The OSCE observer mission called the elections "skewed in favour of one of the contestants, Valdimir Putin." The observer mission also declared that the whole election process was unfair from the beginning. In June 2012, the OSCE also observed the Serbian elections in Kosovo. Unlike the Russian election report, the Serbian elections were declared open and fair, although the observer mission did note that more transparency is still needed.

At the July 2012 annual session of the OSCE Parliamentary Assembly, the group adopted several resolutions. The most significant was the adoption of the Monaco Declaration. The Monaco Declaration calls for OSCE member states to release all political prisoners, and calls on leaders to revise the requirements of military information sharing. At the session, the group also voted to approve a bill banning OSCE member states from approving the visas of anyone associated with the death of Russian lawyer Sergei Magnitsky, who was killed by Russian officials after discovering a massive Russian government tax fraud.

On November 21, Mongolia acceded to the OSCE as the 57th member of the organization, having been a long-time Asian Partner for Cooperation.

On December 6, the OSCE ministers gathered for the annual meeting. The meeting, held in Dublin, was most noted for its passage of the Helsinki +40 Agreement. The political agreement established a framework to advance the OSCE through 2015 by setting clear goals for the vision of the organization's future and calling on the next three chairs of the organization to work in close cooperation to meet the goals set forth. The Dublin conference also saw the passage of a Declaration on Good Governance, which emphasized the importance of good governance in the member states, called for a renewed pledge to combat corruption, terrorism, and money laundering, and reiterated the role of the private sector in promoting growth.

In March, the ministerial council voted to extend the mandate of the OSCE Representative on Freedom of the Media. What might have normally been a relatively insignificant action was further compounded by Russia's attached statement calling for a revision of the original mandate, placing more explicit definitions of media into the mandate in light of the ever-changing social media society. The United States also issued a statement, in which it disagreed entirely with the Russian government's position.

In April, the Belarusian OSCE delegation made a statement during a meeting of the permanent council condemning the US military prison at Guantanamo Bay, Cuba. The proclamation by the Belarusian minister called the prison a violation of human rights and supported the UN resolution calling on the United States to immediately close the site. An OSCE delegation visited Guantanamo Bay in August to investigate the issue further.

In keeping with the spirit of the Helsinki +40 Agreement, a special meeting of the Permanent Council was held in July 2013 to discuss the priorities of the OSCE in 2014 and 2015 under Swiss and Serbian leadership, respectively. Among the priorities listed were dialogue in the South Caucasus, modernizing military transparency arrangements, arms control, respecting human rights in the fight against terrorism, and cooperation in the Western Balkans.

ORGANIZATION OF AMERICAN STATES (OAS)

Organisation des Etats Américains
Organização dos Estados Americanos
Organización de los Estados Americanos
(OEA)

Established: By charter signed April 30, 1948, in Bogotá, Colombia, effective December 13, 1951.

Purpose: To achieve "an order of peace and justice, promoting solidarity among the American states; [to strengthen] their collaboration and [defend] their sovereignty, their territorial integrity, and their independence . . . as well as to establish . . . new objectives and standards for the promotion of the economic, social, and cultural development of the peoples of the Hemisphere, and to speed the process of economic integration."

Headquarters: Washington, D.C., United States.

Principal Organs: General Assembly, Meeting of Consultation of Ministers of Foreign Affairs, Permanent Council, Inter-American Council for Integral Development, Inter-American Juridical Committee (11 jurists from member states), Inter-American Commission on Human Rights (seven members), Inter-American Court of Human Rights (seven jurists from member states), Specialized Conferences, Specialized Organizations, General Secretariat.

Web site: www.oas.org

Secretary General: José Miguel Insulza (Chile).

Membership (35): Antigua and Barbuda, Argentina, Bahamas, Barbados, Belize, Bolivia, Brazil, Canada, Chile, Colombia, Costa Rica, Cuba, Dominica, Dominican Republic, Ecuador, El Salvador, Grenada, Guatemala, Guyana, Haiti, Honduras, Jamaica, Mexico, Nicaragua, Panama, Paraguay, Peru, St. Kitts and Nevis, St. Lucia, St. Vincent and the Grenadines, Suriname, Trinidad and Tobago, United States, Uruguay, Venezuela.

Permanent Observers (68): Albania, Algeria, Angola, Armenia, Austria, Azerbaijan, Belgium, Benin, Bosnia and Herzegovina, Bulgaria, China, Croatia, Cyprus, Czech Republic, Denmark, Egypt, Equatorial Guinea, Estonia, European Union, Finland, France, Georgia, Germany, Ghana, Greece, Holy See, Hungary, Iceland, India, Ireland, Israel, Italy, Japan, Kazakhstan, Latvia, Lebanon, Lithuania, Luxembourg, Malta, Macedonia, Monaco, Morocco, Netherlands, Nigeria, Norway, Pakistan, Philippines, Poland, Portugal, Qatar, Republic of Korea, Romania, Russia, Saudi Arabia, Serbia, Slovakia, Slovenia, Spain, Sri Lanka, Sweden, Switzerland, Thailand, Tunisia, Turkey, Ukraine, United Kingdom, Vanuatu, Yemen.

Official Languages: English, French, Portuguese, Spanish.

Origin and development. The foundations of the OAS were laid in 1890 at an International Conference of American States in Washington, D.C., where it was decided to form an International Union of American Republics to serve as a permanent secretariat. The name of the organization itself was changed in 1910 to Union of American Republics, and the secretariat was renamed the Pan American Union.

The experience of World War II encouraged further development of the still loosely organized "inter-American system." An Inter-American Conference on Problems of War and Peace, meeting in February–March 1945 in Mexico City, concluded that the American republics should consider adoption of a treaty for their mutual defense. Through the Inter-American Treaty of Reciprocal Assistance (Rio Treaty), which was opened for signature on September 2, 1947, in Rio de Janeiro, Brazil, they agreed an armed attack originating either within or outside the American system would be considered an attack against all members, and each would assist in meeting such an attack. (In September 2002 Mexico renounced the Rio Treaty, which it described as obsolete in the post–Cold War era.) Organizational streamlining was undertaken by the Ninth International Conference of American States, which met in March–May 1948 in Bogotá, Colombia, and established the 21-member OAS.

The adoption by Cuba of a Marxist-Leninist ideology generally was viewed by other member governments as incompatible with their fundamental principles, and the Eighth Meeting of Consultation of Ministers of Foreign Affairs, held January 23–31, 1962, in Punta del Este, Uruguay, determined that Cuba, in effect, had excluded itself from participation in the inter-American system. The trade and diplomatic quarantine against Cuba was ultimately lifted at a special consultative meeting on July 29, 1975, in San José, Costa Rica, although the resolution did not lift Cuba's exclusion from formal participation in OAS activities until 2009.

Evidence of the organization's increasing economic and social concerns was manifested by the adoption of the Act of Bogotá, a program of social development, by a special OAS conference in September 1960. On August 17, 1961, an Inter-American Economic and Social Conference adopted the Charter of Punta de Este, a ten-year program designed to implement the provisions of the U.S.-sponsored Alliance for Progress, while a code of conduct for transnational corporations was approved in July 1978.

On July 18, 1978, the nine-year-old Convention on Human Rights entered into force. The agreement provided for an Inter-American Court of Human Rights, composed of seven judges elected by the OAS assembly, to serve in a private capacity. Most members ratified the convention with reservations, so the court's impact has been limited. The Inter-American Commission on Human Rights has been more active.

The Falkland Islands crisis of 1982, which began with an Argentinean invasion on April 2, yielded an extended special session of the OAS during April and May. The participants passed a resolution that supported Argentina's claim to the Falklands (called Las Malvinas by Argentina), condemned the British effort to regain the island colony, and considered a possible U.S. breach of the 1947 Rio pact because of Washington's assistance to Britain.

The Falklands conflict pointed to a growing rift between, on the one hand, the United States and the English-speaking Caribbean members of the OAS and, on the other, most Latin American members. Following the U.S. intervention in Grenada in October 1983, most OAS members attending a special session on October 26 condemned the U.S. action. Washington and its Caribbean allies countered that the United States had not violated the Rio Treaty, but instead had tried to bring order to Grenada.

A special foreign ministers' meeting convened on December 2, 1985, in Cartagena, Colombia, to consider proposed amendments to the OAS charter. The resulting Protocol of Cartagena, which entered into force in November 1988, modified admission rules to permit the entry of Belize and Guyana, previously ineligible because of territorial disputes with OAS members Guatemala and Venezuela, respectively. Under the new criteria, all American states that were members of the UN as of December 10, 1985, plus specified non-autonomous territories (Bermuda, French Guiana, Guadeloupe, Martinique, and Montserrat, but not the Falkland Islands) would be permitted to apply. The protocol also increased the authority of the secretary general, permitting him, on his own initiative, to bring to the attention of the assembly any matter that "could affect the peace and security of the continent and development of its member countries." At the same time, the Permanent Council was authorized to provide peacekeeping services to help ameliorate regional crises.

Despite initial opposition from the United States, the OAS played an active role in the Central American peace negotiations initiated in early 1987 by former Costa Rican president Oscar Arias, with efforts directed toward conflicts in El Salvador and Guatemala, as well as Nicaragua. In 1989 attention turned to Panama. Despite the diplomatic failure, 20 OAS members approved a resolution in December that "deeply deplored" the U.S. invasion of Panama and called for the immediate withdrawal of U.S. troops.

Canada, which had long avoided active participation in the OAS because of perceived U.S. dominance, finally joined as a full member in 1990. The complement of member states grew to 35 with the accession of Belize and Guyana in 1991. Meanwhile, Washington continued to insist that Cuban eligibility for reintegration into regional activity had to be preceded by democratic elections.

During its June 1991 General Assembly, the organization adopted Resolution 1080, which authorized an emergency meeting of the Permanent Council following a coup or other threat to democracy in any member country. The resolution reflected that, for the first time in OAS history, all active members had democratically elected governments. The first test of the resolution was the military overthrow of the Haitian government of Fr. Jean-Bertrand Aristide on September 30, 1991. Haiti remained a focus of attention throughout 1992 and into 1993 as OAS observers attempted to monitor the human rights situation in that nation during UN negotiations.

The OAS also met in special sessions to address the seizures of dictatorial power by democratically elected leaders in Peru in 1992 and in Guatemala in May 1993, condemning both events but rejecting any specific action. The Inter-American Council for Integral Development (*Consejo Interamericano para el Desarrollo Integral*—CIDI) came into existence in 1996. Particular CIDI concerns are trade, social development, and sustainable development.

A major OAS concern in the first half of 1994 was Washington's preparation for a possible invasion of Haiti, as diplomatic measures and economic sanctions failed to sway the Haitian military leaders. The OAS General Assembly in June endorsed a tightening of sanctions but took no position on the use of military force, several leading members having argued against such intervention. Consequently, Washington looked to the UN for international approval of its Haitian policy, and in late July the UN Security Council authorized "all necessary action," including use of a U.S.-led multinational force, to return civilian government to Port-au-Prince.

In 1995 one major priority was the new OAS Unit for the Promotion of Democracy, mandated to observe national elections, provide special training for the staffs of national legislatures, create mechanisms to expand the dissemination of information on governmental activities, and establish courses for the armed forces and police regarding human rights protection.

The 1996 creation of CIDI came about largely in response to a perception that the earlier donor-recipient model of technical assistance needed to be replaced by a structure entailing cooperation of equal partners on well-defined programs devoted to economic and social development. CIDI replaced the Inter-American Economic and Social Council and the Inter-American Council for Education, Science, and Culture. In 1997 the General Assembly eliminated the Inter-American Nuclear Energy Commission, which had not been funded since 1989.

The addition of the IACD in 1999 continued the process of rationalizing the OAS's economic and development structures; in addition to serving as the principal agency responsible for promoting and organizing cooperative ventures, the IACD offers training programs and facilitates technical exchanges.

In 1998, through the Inter-American Drug Abuse Control Commission, the OAS instituted a Multilateral Evaluation Mechanism for evaluating antidrug programs and coordinating members' responses to the illicit trade in drugs. In recent years the OAS also has increasingly taken on the role of broker in bilateral disputes, including border issues involving El Salvador and Honduras, Honduras and Nicaragua, and Guatemala and Belize. To finance negotiations and such related activities as compliance monitoring, in 2000 the General Assembly authorized the establishment of a Fund for Peace. Additional security-related efforts have included the adoption of the Inter-American Convention against the Illicit Manufacturing of and Trafficking in Firearms, Ammunition, Explosives, and Other Related Materials, which entered into force in 1998, and the adoption and ratification of the Inter-American Convention on Conventional Arms Acquisitions in 1999.

On September 11–12, in a special session in Lima, Peru, the OAS adopted a charter that authorizes sanctions against a member state that experiences "an unconstitutional interruption of the democratic order or an unconstitutional alteration of the constitutional regime that seriously impairs the democratic order."

The special session coincided with the September 11, 2001, terrorist attacks on the United States, which led a September 19 emergency session of the Permanent Council to invoke the Rio Treaty and thereby authorize assistance to Washington in its "war on terrorism."

An Intra-American Convention against Terrorism was opened for signature at the 2002 General Assembly session, which met June 2–4 in Bridgetown, Barbados. The meeting's closing declaration called for a "multidimensional" approach to hemispheric security, which "encompasses political, economic, social, health, and environmental factors." At the subsequent session, held June 9–10, 2003, in Santiago, the General Assembly issued the Declaration of Santiago on Democracy and Public Trust. In addition to characterizing the Inter-American Democratic Charter as the "principal hemispheric benchmark" for promoting and defending democratic principles and values, the summit identified "greater efficiency, probity, and transparency" as central to good governance. A month later, the Convention against Terrorism entered into force, 30 days after having obtained a sixth ratification.

A Special Summit of the Americas met January 12–13, 2004, in Monterrey, Mexico, to focus attention on economic growth, social and human development, and democratic governance. The OAS also hosted a series of meetings on drafting an American Declaration on the Rights of Indigenous Peoples. The OAS assistant secretary general acknowledged that much more needed to be done.

At the OAS General Assembly on June 7, 2004, in Quito, Ecuador, former Costa Rican president Miguel Angel Rodríguez was elected as the new secretary general. Rodríguez, who was favored by the United States, announced his resignation October 8, 2004, after allegations surfaced of financial corruption during his time in office in Costa Rica. Rodríguez was just two weeks into his five-year term in the OAS post, having been sworn in September 23.

Negotiations and debate over Rodríguez's successor occupied OAS leaders for the next six months, with the group deadlocking 17–17 through five rounds of voting on April 11, 2005. Finally, on May 2, 2005, Insulza, a socialist, was elected in what was viewed as a setback for the United States. Insulza's election marked the first time in OAS history that a candidate opposed by the United States had become secretary general.

2006 was a time of financial difficulty for the OAS. The secretary general noted that while no member states were in arrears in their dues, inflation and the need to meet UN guidelines on staff compensation meant that many of the organization's programs would have to be funded privately. IAnother major turning point in OAS history occurred in July 2006 when Brazil took over the chair of the Inter-American Defense Board—the first time that responsibility had left the United States in the organization's history.

The year 2007 was marked by the actions of Venezuelan president Hugo Chávez and the organization's response. Amid widespread protests in Venezuela and beyond, the Chávez government refused to renew the license of a television station well known for criticizing the government. The United States condemned Venezuela and asked the OAS to intervene, but the only result was a general OAS call to respect media freedom. The OAS also complied when Venezuela demanded that it remove from its Web site a report from the Berlin-based organization Transparency International criticizing the amount of graft in Venezuela.

The March 1, 2008, raid by Colombia against a Revolutionary Armed Forces of Colombia (FARC) rebel camp inside Ecuador caused the OAS to set up a five-member commission to investigate. By March 18 the OAS had passed a resolution deploring the Colombian incursion and calling it "a clear violation of articles 19 and 21 of the OAS charter," but it noted that Colombia had already apologized and promised no more such incidents would occur. The resolution was seen as a defeat for the United States, who had wanted the resolution to recognize the raid as a legitimate act of self-defense. In June 2008 Colombia and Ecuador restored diplomatic relations at a low level.

At the June 1–3, 2008, meeting of the General Assembly, of which the nominal theme was "Youth and Democratic Values," the representative from Antigua and Barbuda made a strong plea for the organization to work against greenhouse gas emissions, which he called a "clear and present danger" to the hemisphere. For more on developments since 2008, see "Recent Activities" below.

Structure. As the principal political organ of the OAS, the General Assembly meets annually to set policy, discuss the budget, and supervise the work of the organization's specialized agencies. The Permanent Council meets throughout the year to oversee the organization's agenda and has the authority to form committees and working groups. In addition to a General Committee, current committees include Administrative and Budgetary Affairs, Hemispheric Security, Juridical and Political Affairs, Inter-American Summits Management, and Civil Society Participation in OAS Activities. Under the Rio Treaty, the Meeting of Consultation of Ministers of Foreign Affairs discharges the organization's security functions and is convened to consider urgent problems.

The General Secretariat, headed by a secretary general who serves a five-year term, encompasses more than two dozen offices, departments, units, and agencies. It also oversees two cultural institutions, the Art Museum of the Americas and the Columbus Memorial Library, both based in Washington.

Reporting to the General Assembly, the CIDI comprises a ministerial-level representative from each member state; it meets annually on a regular basis but also may convene in special session or at a sectoral level at other times. In addition to a Permanent Executive Committee, it has an Executive Secretariat for Integral Development that operates within the overall OAS General Secretariat.

Affiliated in various ways with the OAS are many specialized agencies, bodies, and other organizations, many predating the establishment of the OAS itself (for a complete listing, see the 2011 *Handbook*).

Recent Activities. The election of Barack Obama as U.S. president in November 2008 caused the OAS to think once more about readmitting Cuba to full membership and ending the U.S. trade embargo against that country. In April 2009 former Cuban president Fidel Castro called for the forthcoming fifth Summit of the Americas to end Cuba's isolation. At this meeting, held April 17–19 in Port of Spain, Trinidad and Tobago, U.S. secretary of state Hillary Clinton admitted that the U.S. policy toward Cuba had failed and welcomed Cuban overtures for a new dialogue. President Obama attended the summitand declared that the United States sought a "new beginning" with Cuba. At the 39th regular session of the OAS General Assembly, meeting June 2–3, 2009, in San Pedro Sula, Honduras, the organization voted to rescind Cuba's 1962 banishment. On June 4 Ricardo Alarcon, the Speaker of the Cuban parliament, welcomed the decision, but said that Cuba might not necessarily want to rejoin the OAS immediately.

Also in June 2009 the Honduran army expelled President Manuel Zelaya, accusing him of aiming at perpetual office, and replaced him with Roberto Micheletti, the Speaker of Congress. The OAS suspended Honduras from full membership, refusing to recognize the November election of Profirio Lobo as president. On June 1, 2011, in a special session called to address the Honduran situation, the General Assembly voted to lift the country's suspension. Honduras was immediately reinstated.

A conference of many Latin American and Caribbean states met February 22–23, 2010, in Cancun, Mexico, and agreed to set up a new regional bloc that excluded the United States and Canada. This new organization was to be an alternative to the OAS, and its existence would call into question the relevance of the OAS. Observers were particularly critical of the OAS parliamentary procedures, which tended toward vote by consensus and frequently produced what was characterized as a "lowest common denominator" resolution. Insulza responded with a statement that the organization was still relevant and that its processes could be reformed.

On July 22, 2010, Colombia called an extraordinary meeting of the Permanent Council, complaining that Venezuela was sheltering Colombian rebels on its territory. The next day Venezuelan president Chávez cut diplomatic ties with Colombia.

In November 2010 the OAS urged Nicaragua and Costa Rica to withdraw their forces from a disputed border region. Costa Rica, which had brought the matter before the Permanent Council, agreed, but Nicaragua, supported by Venezuela, did not. Costa Rica claimed a diplomatic victory.

The June 2011 meeting of the OAS assembly was largely focused on security issues, human rights, and illegal trafficking in OAS states. Most notably, the assembly produced the Declaration of San Salvador on Citizen Security in the Americas, which recognized the need for increased OAS efforts on security and called for the secretariat to develop a plan of action and encouraged the member states to increase security policies in their individual countries. The OAS also voted at the summit to readmit Honduras, who had been suspended since a 2009 coup.

The year 2011 also marks the 10th anniversary of the creation of the Inter-American Democratic Charter (IADC). In honor of the occasion the OAS has undertaken a review of the IADC and has considered methods to increase its participation in encouraging democracy throughout the Americas.

Three states were added as permanent observers to the OAS in 2011: Macedonia (May), Albania (October), and Malta (September).

The sixth Summit of the Americas (held every three years) was held in April 2012. While no major decisions resulted from the meeting, the heads of state engaged in an extended discussion of drug trafficking, particularly noting dissatisfaction among Central and South American states with the United States' policy of deporting drug traffickers out of the US and into the other American states.

The 42nd annual OAS General Assembly was held in Cochabamba, Bolivia in June 2012. The overarching theme of the meeting was food security with sovereignty. The delegates at the assembly signed the Declaration of Cochabamba, which was a set of principles concerning agricultural growth in the American States. The declaration included an appeal to all of the member states to put greater emphasis on sustainable, agricultural development. The assembly also dealt with disputed territory in the Maldivian Islands, increased maritime access for Bolivia, and a new report produced by the Inter-American Commission for Human Rights. In light of the report, the OAS passed a series of declarations designed to encourage greater human rights and equality for women, as well as increase the amount of education about the importance of human rights throughout the region.

In September 2012, the OAS joined the World Economic Forum's Partnering for Cyber Resilience Initiative, which was launched in January 2012. The move was reflective of the organization's continued emphasis on cyber security in the 21st century.

One of the biggest needs identified for 2013 by Secretary General Insulza was improved prioritization of OAS projects. Insulza noted that the OAS has too many projects for its limited resources, and will only be effective moving forward if it prioritizes the projects in which it is involved. This need was further highlighted in a bipartisan recommendation from the U.S. Senate.

On March 22, 2013, the OAS convened an extraordinary General Assembly meeting for the purpose of concluding the two-year review and reform of its human rights protocols. The meeting approved by acclamation a resolution authorizing the IACHR to strengthen its operations through further legislation, committing to fully fund the efforts of the IACHR for the future, and urging all member states to accede to all components of the OAS human rights program.

At its regular summit in June, the OAS General Assembly produced several key decisions. The main document of the meeting, the OAS Declaration of Antigua, Guatemala, calls on member states emphasize "public health, education, and social inclusion" while working to prevent organized crime and promote regional development. Likewise, the OAS approved two new conventions, the Inter-American Convention against Racism, Racial Discrimination, and Related Forms of Intolerance and the Inter-American Convention against All Forms of Discrimination and Intolerance. Both conventions are designed at promoting equality for all throughout the region. The meeting also called for new approaches to deal with the global drug trade, which is particularly problematic in Latin America. The meeting also saw the creation of a hemispheric cooperation mechanism for effective public management designed to strengthen public administration within the region. The object of the new mechanism is to promote effective public administration as a means of strengthening democracy in the hemisphere.

ORGANIZATION OF ISLAMIC COOPERATION (OIC)

Munazzamat al-Mu'tamar[Ta'aavon] [al-Alam al-Islami]
Organisation de la Coopération Islamique (OCI)

Established: By agreement of participants at the Conference of the Kings and Heads of State and Government held September 22–25, 1969, in Rabat, Morocco; charter signed at the Third Islamic Conference of Foreign Ministers, held February 29–March 4, 1972, in Jiddah, Saudi Arabia.

Purpose: To promote Islamic solidarity and further cooperation among member states in the economic, social, cultural, scientific, and political fields.

Headquarters: Jiddah, Saudi Arabia.

Principal Organs: Conference of Kings and Heads of State and Government (Summit Conference), Conference of Foreign Ministers, General Secretariat.

Web site: www.oic-oci.org

Secretary General: Ekmeleddin İhsanoğlu (Turkey).

Membership (57): Afghanistan, Albania, Algeria, Azerbaijan, Bahrain, Bangladesh, Benin, Brunei, Burkina Faso, Cameroon, Chad, Comoro Islands, Côte d'Ivoire, Djibouti, Egypt, Gabon, Gambia, Guinea, Guinea-Bissau, Guyana, Indonesia, Iran, Iraq, Jordan, Kazakhstan, Kuwait, Kyrgyzstan, Lebanon, Libya, Malaysia, Maldives, Mali, Mauritania, Morocco, Mozambique, Niger, Nigeria, Oman, Pakistan, Palestine, Qatar, Saudi Arabia, Senegal, Sierra Leone, Somalia, Sudan, Suriname, Syria (suspended since August 2012), Tajikistan, Togo, Tunisia, Turkey, Turkmenistan, Uganda, United Arab Emirates, Uzbekistan, Yemen. Nigeria's government approved that nation's admission into the OIC in 1986, but the membership was formally repudiated in 1991 in the wake of intense Christian opposition; the OIC has not recognized the latter decision.

Observer States (5): Bosnia and Herzegovina, Central African Republic, Russia, Thailand, Turkish Republic of Northern Cyprus.

Official Languages: Arabic, English, French.

Origin and development. Although the idea of an organization for coordinating and consolidating the interests of Islamic states originated in 1969 and meetings of the conference were held throughout the 1970s, the Organization of the Islamic Conference (OIC) only began to achieve worldwide attention in the early 1980s. From a base of 30 members in 1969, the grouping has doubled in size, with the most recent member, Côte d'Ivoire, being admitted in 2001. The OIC is the world's second-largest IGO, after the United Nations.

During the 1980s three lengthy conflicts dominated the OIC's agenda: the Soviet occupation of Afghanistan, which began in December 1979 and concluded with the final withdrawal of Soviet troops in February 1989; the Iran-Iraq war, which began in September 1980 and ended with the cease-fire of August 1988; and the ongoing Arab-Israeli conflict. At their August 1990 meeting, the foreign ministers described the Palestinian problem as the primary concern for the Islamic world. However, much of the planned agenda was disrupted by emergency private sessions concerning Iraq's invasion of Kuwait on

August 2. Most attending the meeting approved a resolution condemning the incursion and demanding the withdrawal of Iraqi troops. In addition to other ongoing conflicts among conference members, the Gulf crisis contributed to the postponement of the heads of state summit that normally would have been held in 1990.

When the sixth summit was finally held December 9–11, 1991, in Dakar, Senegal, more than half of members' heads of state failed to attend. Substantial lingering rancor concerning the Gulf crisis was reported at the meeting, while black African representatives asserted that Arab nations were giving insufficient attention to the problems of sub-Saharan Muslims. On the whole, the summit was perceived as unproductive.

In the following three years much of the conference's attention focused on the plight of the Muslim community in Bosnia and Herzegovina. The group's foreign ministers repeatedly called on the UN to use force, if necessary, to stop Serbian attacks against Bosnian Muslims, but the conference stopped well short of approving creation of an Islamic force to intervene on its own, as reportedly proposed by Iran and several other members. OIC efforts to improve the international image of Islam continued in 1995, in conjunction with ceremonies marking the organization's 25th anniversary.

The renewed Palestinian uprising and the Israeli response to it provided a principal focus for OIC meetings in 2000. These included the June 27–30 Conference of Foreign Ministers in Kuala Lumpur, Malaysia, and the ninth summit November 12–13 in Doha, Qatar, which devoted its first day to discussing "the serious situation prevailing in the Palestinian occupied territories following the savage actions perpetrated by the Israeli forces."

Meeting June 25–29 in Bamako, Mali, the regular 28th Conference of Foreign Ministers reiterated a call for member countries to halt political contacts with the Israeli government, sever economic relations, and end "all forms of normalization." In other areas, the conference urged member states to ratify the Statute of the International Islamic Court of Justice, called for formation of an expert group that would begin drafting an Islamic Convention on Human Rights, condemned international terrorism, noted the progress made toward instituting an Islamic Program for the Development of Information and Communication (PIDIC), and cautioned that care must be taken to ensure that the economic benefits of globalization were shared and the adverse effects minimized.

Immediately after the September 11, 2001, terrorist attacks against the United States, the OIC secretary general, Abdelouahed Belkeziz, condemned the terrorist acts, as did an extraordinary Conference of Foreign Ministers session in Doha. The Doha session did not directly oppose the ongoing U.S.-led military campaign against al-Qaida and the Taliban regime in Afghanistan, although it did argue that no state should be targeted under the pretext of attacking terrorism. The session also rejected as counter to Islamic teachings and values any attempt to justify terrorism on religious grounds.

The impending U.S.-led war against the Saddam Hussein regime in Iraq generated a second extraordinary session of the Islamic Summit Conference on March 5, 2003, in Doha. The meeting included an exchange of personal insults by the Iraqi and Kuwaiti representatives and a warning from the secretary general that a U.S. military campaign would lead to occupation and foreign rule. The session concluded with a call for the elimination of all weapons of mass destruction (WMD) from the Middle East.

In response to subsequent international developments, the secretary general praised improved cooperation between Iran and the International Atomic Energy Agency; condemned the November 2003 terrorist attacks against synagogues in Istanbul, Turkey, and a housing complex in Riyadh, Saudi Arabia; and welcomed Libya's decision to end the development of WMD. On February 25, 2004, the OIC argued before the International Court of Justice in The Hague, Netherlands, that the security wall being constructed by Israel on Palestinian land was illegal.

The OIC subsequently continued to condemn acts of terrorism around the world, including the March 2004 bombings in Madrid, Spain; the attacks against London's transit system in July 2005; and the explosions at the Egyptian resorts of Sharm El-Shiekh and Naama Bay later the same month. With regard to developments in Iraq, in August 2005 the OIC urged "prudence and consensus" during deliberations on the draft Iraqi constitution. In particular, the OIC advocated a policy of inclusion, cautioning that the exclusion of any component of the population (implicitly, the Sunni minority) would ill serve "the creation of commonly desired conditions of democracy, stability, peace, and welfare in this important member of the OIC."

A third extraordinary session took place December 7–8, 2005, in Jiddah to address the violent worldwide Islamic outrage following publication in a Danish newspaper of cartoons critical of the Prophet Mohammad. The conference condemned violence, saying that Islam was in a crisis, and offered an ambitious ten-year plan to "revamp Islamic mindsets." Symbolic of this decision was the intention to reorganize the OIC itself and to build a new headquarters in Saudi Arabia.

The 33rd meeting of OIC foreign ministers, held June 19–22, 2006, in Baku, Azerbaijan, reinforced the message of moderation in the Islamic world. Later events, however, may have pushed the OIC some distance away from its traditionally moderate stance. In early August 2006 the OIC held a crisis meeting in Kuala Lumpur on the fighting between Hezbollah and Israel. It condemned Israel's attacks on civilians in Lebanon, calling for an immediate cease-fire, which was to be supervised by a UN force. Malaysia promised troops.

In 2007 the OIC was one of several bodies involved with the UN in efforts to resolve the Darfur crisis, but it was noted that the UN Human Rights Council (UNHRC) had been thwarted in its efforts to pass any resolution against Sudan by the OIC and various African countries since its opening session in June 2006. In July 2007 OIC secretary general Ekmeleddin İhsanoğlu of Turkey issued a statement rejecting an election in the secessionist Nagorno-Karabakh region of Azerbaijan, declaring that "the OIC fully recognizes the sovereignty and territorial integrity of Azerbaijan." Azerbaijan, not surprisingly, went on record in February 2008 as opposing any recognition of Kosovo's independence.

The March 13–14, 2008, OIC summit, held in Dakar, Senegal, adopted a revised charter. The new charter was intended to render decision-making within the organization more effective and the OIC more productive in promoting humanitarian efforts around the world. İhsanoğlu went on record as favoring the European Union (EU) as a model for any large multinational organization. He stated that a joint effort between the OIC and the West could bridge the gap between the Muslim and Western worlds. The new charter may have signaled a more activist line on the part of an organization once renowned for its moderate tone. This new tone was most evident in a free-speech resolution introduced with the OIC's backing at the UN in November 2008, declaring defamation of religion to be a violation of international law.

In other matters, in July 2008 the OIC opened an office in Iraq. In September Kosovo appealed to the OIC for support for its declaration of full independence from Serbia. Few OIC countries supported independence however, and Iran announced that it would block Kosovo from joining the OIC. For more on events since 2008, see "Recent Activities" below.

Structure. The body's main institution is the Conference of Foreign Ministers, although a summit of members' heads of state and government is held every five years. Sectoral ministerial conferences have also convened in such areas as information, tourism, health, and youth and sports.

Over the years many committees and departments have evolved to provide input on policy decisions and to carry out the OIC's executive and administrative functions. The organization's secretary general, who serves a four-year, once-renewable term, heads the General Secretariat and is aided by four assistant secretaries general—for science and technology; cultural, social, and information affairs; political affairs; and economic affairs—and a director of the cabinet, who helps administer various departments. The secretariat also maintains permanent observer missions to the United Nations (UN) in New York City, United States, and Geneva, Switzerland, and an Office for Afghanistan was recently established in Islamabad, Pakistan. Other OIC organs include the al-Quds (Jerusalem) Committee, the Six-Member Committee on Palestine, the Standing Committee for Information and Cultural Affairs (COMIAC), the Standing Committee for Economic and Trade Cooperation (COMCEC), the Standing Committee for Scientific and Technological Cooperation (COMSTECH), and various additional permanent and specialized committees.

To date, the OIC has established four "specialized institutions and organs," including the International Islamic News Agency (IINA, founded in 1972); the Islamic Development Bank (IDB, 1974); the Islamic States Broadcasting Organization (ISBO, 1975); and the Islamic Educational, Scientific, and Cultural Organization (IESSCO, 1982). Of the organization's eight "subsidiary organs," one of the more prominent is the Islamic Solidarity Fund (ISF, 1977). The founding conference of the Parliamentary Union of the OIC Member States was held in June 1999.

Activities. In April 2009 an OIC official indicated that the organization wanted to establish a peacekeeping force; no further details were available. In June at the UN, OIC member states opposed the UN establishing a Special Rapporteur to monitor laws that discriminate against women.

In September 2009 the OIC appointed a special representative to Kashmir—a move condemned by the Indian government, which said the organization had no standing to be involved in the dispute.

Sudanese president Omar al-Bashir accepted, then later declined, Turkey's invitation to attend the OIC's Standing Committee for Economic and Commercial Cooperation (COMCEC) meeting November 5–9, 2009, in Istanbul. The Turkish government had said that Bashir, the subject of an arrest warrant from the International Criminal Court, would not be arrested in Turkey. But pressure from the EU may have caused both Turkey and Bashir to think again. At the conference Turkey and Malaysia agreed to work together to develop Halal food standards for the OIC; this to pave the way for the OIC to enter a market currently dominated by non-Muslim countries.

In May 2010 U.S. president Obama appointed Rashad Hussain, a deputy associate counsel at the White House and "a respected member of the American Muslim community," the second U.S. envoy to the OIC. At the OIC's 37th Council of Foreign Ministers meeting in Dushanbe, Tajikistan, the group issued the Dushanbe Declaration, which called for a renewed dialogue between Islamic and non-Islamic nations and new efforts to combat prejudice and Muslim stereotypes.

During the Arab Spring, beginning in February 2011, the OIC supported the implementation of a no-fly zone over Libya but opposed any direct military intervention. The OIC subsequently recognized the new Libyan government on September 5, after the overthrow of the previous regime. The OIC also called for an end to ongoing violence in Syria. At the OIC's 38th meeting of the Council of Foreign Ministers in June, the group called for international recognition of Palestine. The foreign ministers also approved changing the name of the group to the Organization of Islamic Cooperation, a proposal first put forward in 2007 by Secretary General İhsanoğlu, who argued that the word *conference* suggested a one-time meeting.

Throughout 2012, the OIC stressed the importance of interfaith harmony. As a serious of bombings and attacks against Christians in Nigeria took place in the first half of the year, the secretary general called on OIC member states to seek peace between the various faiths. The OIC was also involved in a March meeting at the Vatican to discuss Arab-Israeli peace and the need for peaceful relations between the different religions.

In April 2012, Kazakhstan formally ratified the OIC Charter. At a June 2012 meeting, the Executive Committee of the OIC recommended the suspension of Syria from the organization in light of the ongoing political violence and civil war. The full Council of Foreign Ministers is scheduled to vote upon the recommendation in November. Later in June, China expressed interest in becoming an observer state of the OIC. While no formal application has been submitted as of yet, the Chinese government requested information on several OIC projects in order to examine possible funding.

In light of the violence of the civil war in Syria, the OIC voted to suspend Syria's membership in the organization at an extraordinary summit held in August 2012.

At the 2013 Islamic Summit held in February, the OIC was primarily focused on several grave situations occurring within their mandate. Noting the continuing escalation of conflict in Syria, the OIC called for those in Syria to seek a peaceful solution. While urging the UN Security Council to act, they noted their sincere hope that a Syrian-led resolution of the conflict could be achieved. The meeting also yielded a resolution on Palestine, in which the organization condemned the Israeli attacks on the Gaza Strip in November 2012, commended the UN for upgrading the PLO to status as an observer state, and continued to urge its member states to push for international recognition of Palestine. The meeting also called for member states to recognize Kosovo, expressed a desire to collectively take efforts to promote economic growth and job creation, and strongly condemned the terrorist activity in Mali.

In regard to the ever-worsening situation in Syria, Secretary General İhsanoğlu endorsed the plan put forth in September 2013 to place Syria's chemical weapons, which were first discovered in late-August, under international control. İhsanoğlu also reiterated its call for the UN Security Council to take actions to end the violence and bloodshed in the war-torn state.

ORGANIZATION OF THE PETROLEUM EXPORTING COUNTRIES (OPEC)

Established: By resolutions adopted September 14, 1960, in Baghdad, Iraq, and codified in a statute approved by the Eighth (Extraordinary) OPEC Conference, held April 5–10, 1965, in Geneva, Switzerland.

Purpose: To coordinate and unify petroleum policies of member countries; to devise ways to ensure stabilization of international oil prices to eliminate "harmful and unnecessary" price and supply fluctuations.

Headquarters: Vienna, Austria.

Principal Organs: Conference, Board of Governors, Economic Commission, Secretariat.

Web site: www.opec.org

Secretary General: Abdalla Salem El-Badri (Libya).

Membership (12, with years of entry): Algeria (1969), Angola (2007), Iran (1960), Iraq (1960), Kuwait (1960), Libya (1962), Nigeria (1971), Qatar (1961), Saudi Arabia (1960), United Arab Emirates (Abu Dhabi in 1967, with the membership being transferred to the UAE in 1974), Venezuela (1960). Ecuador, which joined OPEC in 1973, withdrew on January 1, 1993, and rejoined in October 2007. Iraq currently does not participate in OPEC production quotas.

Official Language: English.

Origin and development. A need for concerted action by petroleum exporters was first broached in 1946 by Dr. Juan Pablo Pérez Alfonso of Venezuela. His initiative led to a series of contacts in the late 1940s between oil-producing countries, but it was not until 1959 that the first Arab Petroleum Conference was held. At that meeting Dr. Pérez Alfonso convinced the Arabs, along with Iranian and Venezuelan observers, to form a union of producing states, with OPEC being formally created by Iran, Iraq, Kuwait, Saudi Arabia, and Venezuela on September 14, 1960, during a conference in Baghdad, Iraq.

The rapid growth of energy needs in the advanced industrialized states throughout the 1960s and early 1970s provided OPEC with the basis for extracting ever-increasing oil prices. However, OPEC demands were not limited to favorable prices; members also sought the establishment of an infrastructure for future industrialization, including petrochemical plants, steel mills, aluminum plants, and other high-energy industries as a hedge against the anticipated exhaustion of their oil reserves in the 21st century.

The addition of new members and negotiations with petroleum companies on prices, production levels, and tax revenues dominated OPEC's early years, with prices remaining low and relatively stable. However, largely because of OPEC-mandated increases, prices soared dramatically from approximately $3 for a 42-gallon barrel in the early 1970s to a peak of nearly $40 per barrel by the end of the decade. Thereafter, a world glut of petroleum, brought on by overproduction, global recession, and the implementation of at least rudimentary energy conservation programs by many industrialized nations subsequently reversed that trend. The influence of formal OPEC price setting waned as the organization began to increasingly depend on negotiated production quotas to stabilize prices.

In December 1985, as spot market prices dropped to $24 a barrel and production dipped to as low as 16 million barrels per day, OPEC abandoned its formal price structure to secure a larger share of the world's oil market. By mid-1986, however, oil prices had dropped by 50 percent or more to their lowest levels since 1978, generating intense concern among OPEC members with limited oil reserves, large populations, extensive international debts, and severe shortages of foreign exchange. As a result Saudi Arabia increased its output by 2 million barrels per day in January 1986 to force non-OPEC producers to cooperate with the cartel in stabilizing the world oil market.

During their December 1987 meeting in Vienna, OPEC oil ministers attempted to reimpose discipline, but the talks became embroiled in political considerations stemming from the Iran-Iraq war. The meeting concluded with 12 members endorsing the $18-per-barrel fixed-price concept and agreeing to a 15-million-barrels-per-day production quota, Iraq's nonparticipation leaving it free to produce at will. However, widespread discounting quickly forced prices down to about $15 per barrel.

In the wake of the Gulf cease-fire, OPEC cohesion seemed to return. In their first unanimous action in two years, the members agreed in late November 1988 to limit production to 18.5 million barrels per day as of January 1, 1989, while maintaining a "target price" of $18 per barrel. Responding to the organization's apparent renewal of self-control, oil prices rose to nearly $20 per barrel by March 1989. However, contention broke out again at the June OPEC session, with Saudi Arabia resisting demands for sizable quota increases. Although a compromise agreement was concluded, Kuwait and the UAE immediately declared that they would continue to exceed their quotas.

In November 1989 OPEC raised its official production ceiling from 20.5 to 22 million barrels per day, allowing Kuwait a quota increase from 1.2 to 1.5 million barrels per day. However, the UAE, whose official quota remained at 1.1 million barrels per day, did not participate in the accord and continued, as did Kuwait, to produce close to 2 million barrels per day. Pledges for restraint were again issued at an emergency meeting in May 1990, but adherence proved negligible. Consequently, in July Iraq's president Saddam Hussein threatened to use military intervention to enforce the national quotas. While the pronouncement drew criticism from the West, several OPEC leaders quietly voiced support for Hussein's "enforcer" stance and, mollified by the Iraqi leader's promise not to use military force to settle a border dispute with Kuwait, agreed on July 27 to Iraqi-led demands for new quotas. However, on August 29, in a dramatic reversal prompted by Iraq's invasion of Kuwait on August 2 and the ensuing embargo on oil exports from the two countries, the organization authorized producers to disregard quotas to avert possible shortages. OPEC's action legitimized the 2-million-barrels-per-day increase already implemented by Saudi Arabia and dampened Iraq's hope that oil shortages and skyrocketing prices would weaken the resolve of the coalition embargo. In December production reached its highest level in a decade, while prices fluctuated between $25 and $40 in response to the continuing crisis.

In early March 1991, following Iraq's defeat in the Gulf War, OPEC agreed to cut production from 23.4 to 22.3 million barrels per day for the second quarter of the year. In June OPEC rejected Iraq's request to intercede with the United Nations to lift the Iraqi oil embargo.

In September 1991 OPEC agreed to raise its collective production ceiling to 23.6 million barrels per day in preparation for normal seasonal increases in demand. However, Iran and Saudi Arabia remained in what analysts described as a "trial of strength" for OPEC dominance: the former lobbying for lowered production ceilings and higher prices and the latter resisting production curbs or any challenge to its market share. Consequently, on February 15, 1992, OPEC members agreed to their first individual production quotas since August 1990, with the Saudis grudgingly accepting a 7.8-million-barrels-per-day quota. In April and May the organization extended the February quotas despite reports of overproduction, citing the firm price, albeit lower than desired, of $17 per barrel.

Prices remained low for the rest of 1992 as the global recession undercut demand and overproduction continued to plague OPEC; meanwhile, Kuwait attempted to recover from the economic catastrophe inflicted by the Gulf crisis by pumping oil "at will." With a relatively mild winter in the Northern Hemisphere having further reduced demand, a February 1993 emergency OPEC meeting sought to reestablish some sense of constraint by endorsing a 23.5-million-barrels-per-day limit on its members.

Actual levels continued at more than 25 million barrels per day, however, and a more realistic quota of 24.5 million barrels per day was negotiated in September 1993. The new arrangement permitted Kuwait's quota to rise from 1.6 million to 2.0 million barrels per day, while Iran's quota grew from 3.3 million to 3.6 million. Meanwhile, Saudi Arabia agreed to keep its production at 8 million.

The November 1994 conference also agreed to maintain the current quota of 24.5 million barrels per day for at least one more year. However, pressure for change grew in 1995, particularly as non-OPEC production continued to expand. Secretary General Rilwanu Lukman (Nigeria) and oil ministers from several OPEC countries argued that non-OPEC nations' failure to curb production could lead to serious problems for all oil producers.

The announcement of Gabon's impending withdrawal from OPEC (having been a member since 1973) was made at the ministerial meeting held June 5–7, 1996. Among the reasons cited for the decision were the high membership fee and the constraints imposed by OPEC production quotas.

In late 1997 OPEC decided to increase production by 10 percent to 27.5 million barrels per day for the first half of 1998. However, the organization reversed course sharply when the price fell to $12.80 per barrel, a nine-year low, in March 1998. Saudi Arabia and Venezuela (joined by nonmember Mexico) immediately announced a reduction of 2 million barrels per day in their output. When prices failed to rebound, OPEC announced a further reduction of 1.3 million barrels per day in July. Overall, OPEC's revenues in 1998 fell some 35 percent from the previous year, raising questions about the organization's ability to control prices on its own.

Oil prices fell to less than $10 per barrel in February 1999, prompting an agreement in March under which OPEC cut production by 1.7 million barrels per day while Mexico, Norway, Oman, and Russia accepted a collective reduction of 400,000 barrels per day. Prices subsequently rebounded to more than $26 per barrel late in the year and more than $30 per barrel in early 2000. Consequently, from March to October 2000, OPEC increased production four times by a total of 3.4 million barrels per day before prices, which reached a high of $37.80 per barrel in September, fell in December to $26 per barrel, safely within the OPEC target range of $25–$28 per barrel.

The heads of state of the OPEC countries met for only their second summit in history (the first was in 1975) in Venezuela in September 2000 amid intensified concern over the impact of high oil prices on the global economy. Among other things, OPEC leaders criticized several European countries for imposing high taxes on oil products, thereby driving up consumer energy costs.

Declining economic conditions in the first eight months of 2001 sharply reduced the demand for oil, and OPEC responded with production cuts in February, April, and September totaling 3.5 million barrels per day. Prices for the most part remained within the target range for that period. However, the September 11, 2001, terrorist attacks in the United States severely undercut demand, in part because of plummeting air travel, and prices fell below $17 per barrel by November. OPEC demanded that non-OPEC producers again assist in reducing production, and Russia reluctantly agreed to cut its production by 150,000 barrels per day beginning in January 2002, in conjunction with an additional OPEC cut of 1.5 million barrels per day. Prices rose to nearly $30 per barrel in the fall of 2002, despite evidence that many OPEC countries were producing above the quotas established in late 2001. OPEC leaders argued that prices were artificially inflated because of fears over a possible U.S. invasion of Iraq and concern emanating from other Middle East tensions.

To address the potential for disturbances in the global oil market from the strikes by oil workers in Venezuela, OPEC agreed in January 2003 to raise the quota to 24.5 million barrels per day. However, by April discussion turned to what was viewed as an "unavoidable" production cut. Complicating factors included the potential for the full return of Iraqi oil to world markets following the toppling of the Saddam Hussein regime. In that regard Iraq sent a delegation to OPEC's September session, at which quotas were cut by 900,000 barrels per day.

Despite rising prices, OPEC declined to increase production in January 2004 and, citing the upcoming seasonal dip in demand, reduced quotas again in February. Consequently, the United States warned OPEC that the cuts might harm an already fragile global economy. By March oil prices peaked at $37.45 per barrel, and some non-OPEC countries (such as Mexico) snubbed OPEC's request for production constraint.

Terror attacks on the oil infrastructures in Iraq and Saudi Arabia contributed to continual price increases in mid-2004, finally prompting OPEC to expand its production quotas. Nevertheless, "spare" oil capacity remained at its lowest in decades. The Group of Eight issued a stern warning about the effects of rising oil prices, which reached a 21-year high in July of more than $43 per barrel. By October the price peaked at more than $55 per barrel; it then declined by 23 percent by the end of the year.

In December 2004 OPEC announced a production cut to stem the slide in oil prices. Meanwhile, it was estimated that OPEC members were enjoying their highest oil revenue ever in nominal terms. OPEC informally relaxed quota compliance in March 2005, and prices hovered at about $50 per barrel. However, the International Monetary Fund and the United States called for significant additional OPEC production increases to, among other things, provide a more substantial cushion against unforeseen oil shocks. OPEC agreed to that request in June, but the per-barrel price subsequently grew to almost $60.

In 2005 and 2006 the world's demand for oil seemed finally to be straining the producing countries' ability to supply, with some saying that this was the long-predicted first sign that the world was running out of oil. Rapid economic growth in China, and to a lesser extent in India, was also said to be a factor. Tensions between the United States and Iran pushed prices to more than $75 per barrel for periods in May and June 2006.

Financial and political conditions remained disturbed through 2006 and 2007. The U.S. dollar, the currency in which OPEC trades, remained weak, with little sign of recovery, and China and India's appetite for oil and bilateral purchase arrangements increased. In March 2007 Angola joined OPEC—a move calculated to boost that country's international standing, but a disappointment to Western countries that had hoped to keep Angola's oil reserves outside the OPEC cartel. Ecuador indicated that it wanted to rejoin OPEC, and did so in October 2007. In May 2007 Ecuador and Venezuela agreed to an exchange of Ecuadorian crude oil for Venezuelan refined product.

In May 2008 Indonesia announced that it would withdraw from OPEC by the end of the year because the country had become a net importer of oil.

OPEC held a summit meeting November 17–18, 2007, in Riyadh, Saudi Arabia, with oil prices continuing to rise and a general expectation that the organization would not raise production quotas. At the meeting Iranian president Mahmoud Ahmadinejad suggested that the organization no longer trade in U.S. dollars, but Saudi Arabia opposed this idea. At both its December 2007 and March 2008 extraordinary meetings, OPEC declined to raise production quotas. In January 2008 the price of crude oil reached $100 per barrel, and by June 2008 approached $140. This caused the price of gasoline to rise to more than $4 per gallon in the United States, with corresponding increases elsewhere in the world's developed economies. Many observers began to feel that OPEC was not in control of world oil prices, with commodity speculation and international instability overriding the basic considerations of supply and demand. Gas prices led to changing habits, and demand for oil eased by 800,000 barrels per day in the first half of 2008. Crude oil prices declined, and were approaching $100 by September 2008. The worldwide economic crisis of late 2008 caused the price of crude oil to fall precipitously, reaching around $50 per barrel by early December. An October 24 OPEC production cut of 1.5 million barrels per day had no effect on the decline. A meeting on December 17, 2008, produced an agreement to cut production by 2.2 million barrels a day—the largest cut in OPEC history. The price stabilized around $40 per barrel, some $35 less than they had hoped, and then gradually rose to around $70 per barrel by late 2009. For more information on activities since 2008, see "Activities" below.

Structure. The OPEC Conference, which normally meets twice per year, is the supreme authority of the organization. Comprising the oil ministers of the member states, the conference formulates policy, considers recommendations from the Board of Governors, and approves the budget. The board consists of governors nominated by the various member states and approved by the conference for two-year terms. In addition to submitting the annual budget, various reports, and recommendations to the conference, the board directs the organization's management, while the Secretariat performs executive functions. Operating within the Secretariat are a research division and departments for administration and human resources, data services, energy studies, petroleum market analysis, and public relations and information. In addition, the Economic Commission, established as a specialized body in 1964, works within the Secretariat's framework to promote equitable and stable international oil prices. The Ministerial Monitoring Committee was established in 1982 to evaluate oil market conditions and to make recommendations to the conference.

The OPEC Fund for International Development has made significant contributions to developing countries, mostly Arabian and African, in the form of balance-of-payments support; direct financing of imports; and project loans in such areas as energy, transportation, and food production. All current OPEC members plus Gabon are members of the fund. As of 2008 more than $5 billion in loans were approved for nearly 1,200 operations in the public sector and about $850 million for private sector operations. In addition, grants totaling $433 million were approved for more than 1,000 operations.

Recent Activities. Russia attended OPEC's March 2009 meeting with a proposal for closer cooperation—in fact for setting up a Russian liaison office at OPEC headquarters—but declined, for the time being, an invitation to become a full member.

In April 2009 Brazil announced that it was again considering an invitation to join OPEC, but it ultimately decided not to do so. Previously Brazil had concentrated on exporting refined, rather than crude, oil products. The September 9, 2009, OPEC meeting saw the group agreeing to maintain current production levels, with the price of oil slowly rising as the world economy appearing to come out of the worst of the recession. Production quotas remained unchanged through the rest of 2009 and most of 2010, with Iran denying that it was cheating. Prices were relatively stable around $80 per barrel for most of 2010, but with a tendency to rise toward $90 in the late summer and fall as many world economies recovered somewhat.

Longer-term prospects were uncertain, however. OPEC's *World Oil Outlook 2010* acknowledged that the global economic crisis was different from anything seen in recent times, making predictions about oil much riskier. It looked to transportation as the most likely sector for growth in oil consumption, but saw little room for growth in OPEC production capacity in the medium term.

On the other hand a January 2010 U.S. Geological Survey report predicted that Venezuela might have much larger oil reserves than previously thought, 513 billion barrels as opposed to Saudi Arabia's proven 260 billion barrels. The effect of Iraq's renewed full production was also an imponderable. In January 2010 the Brazilian government announced that it was taking much firmer control of newly discovered offshore deposits.

In October 2010 it was announced that Iran would hold the OPEC presidency in 2011 for the first time since before its 1979 Islamic revolution. At its biannual meeting in December 2010 in Ecuador, OPEC discussions focused largely on the impact economic uncertainty would have upon the oil market. In the face of lower demand growth and a fragile economy, the group decided to maintain oil production levels. The organization also stressed its plea for cooperation from nonmember states to effectively manage oil prices in an uncertain economy.

The year 2011 saw that cooperation increase as OPEC worked with several other IGOs on energy and oil–related endeavors. The International Energy Agency (IEA) and the International Energy Forum (IEF) worked with OPEC for a symposium on energy outlooks in the year. Likewise, OPEC ministers met with EU officials for its eighth meeting to discuss the current energy situation and the future of the oil market in providing energy solutions.

At the December 2011 conference, the organization announced that it would maintain its 30-million-barrel-per-day quota, despite the increasingly volatile oil prices. This decision was made in part because the group attributed the rapidly fluctuating prices to geopolitical tension and overspeculation in the commodities market, not to supply and demand. The conference also expressed concern about the economic downturn and reaffirmed its commitment to take the appropriate measures to ensure reasonable oil prices.

The year 2012 saw oil consumption increase slightly. Oil prices also increased early in 2012, but the increase was short lived as prices began decreasing in mid-2012. In June 2012, OPEC met for its 161st Conference in Vienna. Despite an increase in oil consumption, OPEC decided to maintain its production levels, since more oil was being consumed from non-OPEC exporters. Most of the conference, however, was concerned with the recently decreasing price of oil, a welcome change as many of the geopolitical tensions that had driven prices up began to subside. Even with oil prices dropping, OPEC did express continued apprehension about the economy and asked the Secretary General to maintain close supervision of the fluctuating global economy.

In October OPEC again joined forces with the IEA and IEF to host its first joint symposium on gas and coal market outlooks. The meeting was the outgrowth of a request from the 2011 G-20 Summit in Cannes (see separate article). In December OPEC gathered for its 162nd summit under the chairmanship of Iraq. The meeting stressed the importance of continued work on climate control and discussed the future of the oil market moving into 2013. Expecting non-OPEC production to increase, OPEC leaders predicted a slight decrease in demand from the OPEC states. The conference asked the secretariat for continued monitoring of the market to ensure adequate supply, and extended the secretary general's term for another year.

In March 2013 OPEC continued its recent cooperation with the IEA and IEF in hosting a workshop on the relationship between the physical and financial oil markets. In May OPEC convened for its 163rd biannual conference in Vienna. At the meeting, leaders recognized the significance of steady oil prices throughout the first part of 2013 as a sign of adequate supply. They also noted that current production levels were, therefore, adequate and could see an easement of OPEC fundamentals in the latter half of the year.

PACIFIC ISLANDS FORUM (PIF)

Established: As the South Pacific Forum by a subgroup of the South Pacific Commission meeting August 5, 1971, in Wellington, New Zealand; current name adopted October 3–5, 1999, effective October 2000.

Purpose: To facilitate cooperation among member states, to coordinate their views on political issues of concern to the subregion, and to accelerate member states' rates of economic development.

Headquarters: Suva, Fiji.

Principal Organs: The Forum, Pacific Islands Forum Secretariat.

Web site: www.forumsec.org

Secretary General of Forum Secretariat: Tuiloma Neroni Slade (Samoa).

Membership (16): Australia, Cook Islands, Federated States of Micronesia, Fiji, Kiribati, Marshall Islands, Nauru, New Zealand, Niue, Palau, Papua New Guinea, Samoa, Solomon Islands, Tonga, Tuvalu, Vanuatu.

Associate Members (2): New Caledonia, French Polynesia

Observers (3): Timor-Leste, Tokelau, Wallis and Futuna.

Official Language: English.

Origin and development. Since the South Pacific Commission (SPC, now the Pacific Community) was barred from concerning itself with political affairs, representatives of several South Pacific governments and territories decided in 1971 to set up a separate organization, the South Pacific Forum (SPF), in which they might speak with a common voice on a wider range of issues. At a meeting of the forum in April 1973, representatives of Australia, Cook Islands, Fiji, Nauru, New Zealand, Tonga, and Western Samoa signed the Apia Agreement, which established the South Pacific Bureau for Economic Cooperation as a technical subcommittee of the committee of the whole. The Gilbert Islands (now Kiribati), Niue, Papua New Guinea, Solomon Islands, Tuvalu, and Vanuatu subsequently acceded to the agreement. In 1975 the bureau was asked to serve as secretariat, although it was not reorganized and renamed the Forum Secretariat until 1988.

The Marshall Islands and the Federated States of Micronesia, formerly observers, were granted membership in 1987 after Washington, in late 1986, declared their compacts of free association with the United States to be in effect. Palau, formerly an SPF observer, became a full member in 1995 following resolution of its compact status.

The SPF-sponsored South Pacific Regional Trade and Cooperation Agreement (SPARTECA), providing for progressively less restricted access to the markets of Australia and New Zealand, came into effect in 1981. The process culminated in 1985 with approval by Canberra and Wellington of the elimination of all duties for most products from other SPF members.

Following a decision at the 15th annual SPF meeting, the delegates to the 16th annual meeting in 1985 concluded the Treaty of Rarotonga (Cook Islands), which established the South Pacific Nuclear-Free Zone (SPNFZ). The treaty forbids manufacturing, testing, storing, dumping, and using nuclear weapons and materials in the region. It does, however, allow each country to make its own defense arrangements, including deciding whether or not to host nuclear warships. The treaty became operative in December 1986 when Australia became the eighth SPF member to tender its ratification. Those countries known to possess nuclear weapons were asked to sign the treaty's three protocols, the SPF having added an "opt-out" provision that would permit adherents to withdraw if they believed their national interests were at stake. The Soviet Union and China both ratified the protocols in 1988. France, the United Kingdom, and the United States, after years of declining to support the treaty, signed the protocols March 25, 1996. France, the object of intense SPF criticism for its nuclear tests in the region in late 1995 and early 1996, ratified the SPNFZ on September 20, 1996, as did the United Kingdom on September 19, 1997. In May 2011, U.S. president Barack Obama called on the Senate to ratify the treaty, but it has yet to do so. During the first half of the 1990s, environmental concerns became an increasingly important focus for the forum. Among other things, it called for the abolition of drift-net fishing; argued that global warming could cause sea levels to rise and inundate such low-lying countries as Kiribati and Tuvalu; objected to the planned incineration of chemical weapons on Johnston Atoll, an unincorporated territory about 700 miles southwest of Hawaii controlled by the U.S. military since 1934; and announced in 1994 an attempt to negotiate region-wide logging and fishing agreements that would sharply curtail access and protect fragile ecosystems while providing for sustainable development.

In January 1992 five of the smallest SPF members (Cook Islands, Kiribati, Nauru, Niue, and Tuvalu) formed the Small Island States (SIS) to address mutual concerns such as fishing rights, global warming, and airspace issues. The SIS members also began to explore the possible creation of their own development bank. The Marshall Islands became the sixth SIS member in 1997.

At the August 24–25, 1998, summit, which was held in the Federated States of Micronesia, the SPF endorsed the establishing of a South Pacific whale sanctuary, criticized India and Pakistan for testing nuclear devices, and granted New Caledonia observer status for the next summit.

The 30th SPF summit was held October 3–5, 1999, in Koror and endorsed the concept of a Pacific free trade area (FTA) that might eventually include Australia and New Zealand. (In 1993 the Melanesian Spearhead Group of Papua New Guinea, Solomon Islands, and Vanuatu introduced their own FTA, which Fiji later joined.) As envisaged, free trade would be introduced in stages over the next decade, with the six SIS countries and other least developed countries (LDCs) joining a bit later. The forum also decided to adopt the name Pacific Islands Forum, following a one-year transition period. At the 31st forum session, held October 27–30, 2000, in Tarawa, Kiribati, the renamed organization approved (with immediate effect) and opened for ratification the new Agreement Establishing the Pacific Island Forum Secretariat.

Hosted by Nauru, the August 16–18, 2001, forum session marked the organization's 30th anniversary with one of its most notable accomplishments: the opening for signature of the Pacific Island Countries Trade Agreement (PICTA) and the Pacific Agreement on Closer Economic Relations (PACER). PICTA was signed by all the 12 Forum Island Countries (FICs) except the Marshall Islands, Micronesia, and Palau, which were given additional time to sign because of complexities related to their status with the United States. PICTA anticipated the creation of an FTA by 2010, although the SIS members and LDCs do not have to eliminate their intracommunity tariffs until 2012. Tuvalu signed on to PICTA in April 2010, joining Cook Islands, Fiji, Niue, Samoa, Solomon Islands, and Vanuatu, These countries were by then trading under PICTA terms and conditions. In addition, "excepted imports" are protected until 2016. PACER outlines a framework for future trade relations between PICTA states and the much larger economies of Australia and New Zealand. PACER contains provisions for "trade facilitation" and increased financial and technical assistance to the FICs, but it also offers assurances to Australia and New Zealand that they will not be disadvantaged by any external trade agreements negotiated by the PICTA group.

Following ratification by six signatories, PICTA entered into force in April 2003, at which time all nontariff barriers to trade were eliminated. PICTA signatories have as long-range goals the creation of a single market to cover trade in services as well as goods and free movement of capital and labor. PACER, which entered into effect in October 2002, following ratification by seven signatories, provides for future trade negotiations but does not mandate a forum-wide FTA.

Meeting on August 14–16, 2003, in Auckland, the forum elected Australia's Greg Urwin as secretary general, a post that was traditionally awarded to an FIC national. The election came at a time of increasing regional involvement by Australia.

The 2004 meeting of the Pacific Islands Forum was held August 3–10, 2004, in Apia, Samoa. The chief subject of the meeting was discussion and endorsement of the forum's emerging multiyear Pacific

Plan, an instrument for encouraging the forum's vision of sustainable growth and integration in the Pacific region. The forum endorsed the plan as thus far developed and looked for more specifics in the future.

In 2006 and 2007 the Pacific Islands Forum was concerned with unrest among some of its members. In August 2006 Tonga asked to be excused from hosting the October summit because the king's health was deteriorating. He died in September 2006. The summit was eventually held in Suva and was notable for complaints about Australian heavy-handedness in its leadership of the peacekeeping force in the Solomon Islands. In February 2007 the Solomon Islands government asked the forum to discuss an "exit strategy."

In December 2006 there was a military coup in Fiji, followed by a partial return to civilian government in January 2007. The Fijian interim government first promised elections and a full democracy in 2010. The forum and Fiji established a working group to create a joint approach to restoring democracy, with the forum aiming for elections within two years. In July 2007 Samoa declared that Fiji should be allowed to attend the coming October summit, even if the coup leader came. However, in August 2007 Australian prime minister Alexander Downer declared that the leader of the Fiji coup and interim prime minister, Frank Bainimarama, would not be welcome at the forthcoming meeting. Bainimarama attended the meeting anyway, held October 16–17, 2007, in Vava'u, Tonga. He made a definite commitment to hold elections in early 2009 and to abide by their outcome.

Also in October 2007 Taiwan's six allies in the forum—Solomon Islands, Marshall Islands, Kiribati, Nauru, Palau, and Tuvalu—declared that Taiwan's status should be upgraded to that of a regular dialogue partner.

In March 2008 a meeting of forum foreign ministers in Auckland expressed concern that Fiji's interest in a so-called people's charter might get in the way of the promised early 2009 elections. In April the forum sent two representatives to observe elections in Nauru at the request of the Nauru government.

In May 2008, Greg Urwin resigned as secretary general of the forum for health reasons. Deputy Secretary General Dr. Feleti Sevele of Vanuatu was named acting secretary general. In August 2008 Urwin died, and later that month Tuiloma Neroni Slade of Samoa was chosen as his permanent replacement. The 2008 summit focused on economic issues and the world financial crisis weighing heavily on the economically weak Pacific islands. For more on developments since 2008, see "Recent Activities" below.

Structure. The Pacific Islands Forum has no constitution or codified rules of procedure. Decisions are reached at all levels by consensus.

The forum meets annually at the heads of government (summit) level but also convenes at other times on a ministerial basis to discuss particular concerns and prepare proposals for summit action. In recent years the member states' ministers of foreign affairs, economy, and education, for example, have held meetings. In addition, forum summits have been followed by post-forum dialogue meetings since 1989. There are currently 14 dialogue partners; Canada, China, the European Union (EU), France, India, Indonesia, Italy, Japan, Malaysia, Philippines, Republic of Korea, Thailand, United Kingdom, and United States. Taiwan applied for dialogue status in the early 1990s, but the forum sidestepped the issue by permitting individual members to establish the requested dialogue relationship without formal SPF involvement.

The Pacific Islands Forum Secretariat, headed by a secretary general, reports to the Forum Officials Committee, which includes representatives from all 16 member countries. The secretariat encompasses four divisions—corporate services; development and economic policy; political, international, and legal affairs; and trade and investment. The PIF also has a number of affiliated organizations (for a complete listing of affiliated organizations, see the 2011 *Handbook*). In addition, the forum's secretary general chairs the eight-member Council of Regional Organizations in the Pacific (CROP), which includes the Secretariat of the Pacific Community and the South Pacific Regional Environment Programme among its participants.

Recent Activities. In late 2008 Fiji made some moves to re-engage with the forum. However by January 2009, with little progress made toward the restoration of democracy, the forum called on Bainimarama to set a specific date in 2009 for elections, and to do that by May 1. When Bainimarama failed to honor the deadline, Fiji was suspended from the forum. The group's headquarters in Fiji continue to function, however.

The August 2009 summit, held in Cairns, Australia, called for serious action on climate at the forthcoming Copenhagen conference. Australia prime minister John Howard pointed out that roughly 50 percent of the Pacific islands' population lived within 1.5 kilometers of the ocean, and that many small islands were in danger of being literally washed away by the rising sea level. Papua New Guinea and the Solomon Islands tried unsuccessfully to have Fiji restored to full membership in the organization. Following this meeting a new round of trade and integrations discussions, know as PACER Plus, commenced.

Problems with Fiji continued. In July 2009 Bainimarama announced that Fiji would have a new constitution in 2013, with elections in 2014. In November Fiji expelled Australian and New Zealand diplomats, a move that caused immediate retaliation in kind. The Fiji regime again expelled Australia's acting High Commissioner in July 2010, just before the Forum summit. Bainimarama then convened a meeting, called "Engaging the Pacific," as a rival to the Forum. Neither Australia nor New Zealand was invited to participate and the meeting exhibited a strong anti-colonialist theme.

The August 2010 summit, held in Port Vila, Vanuatu, saw New Caledonia expressing interest in full membership. The meeting commended progress of the PACER Plus negotiations. It also renewed its call for action on carbon dioxide emissions and for a return to democracy in Fiji.

The year 2011 marked the 40th anniversary of the creation of the PIF. In honor of that occasion, the Forum hosted an anniversary lecture series that focused on the Pacific Plan, the Forum's plan for future development. The PIF also hosted a series of competitions, such as an art competition for high school students, to encourage citizens of the PIF member states to be a part of the anniversary celebration.

In July 2011, the Forum's Economic Ministers held their annual meeting in Samoa. The meeting produced the Forum Economic Action Plan 2011, which called for broadening the IGO's economic base, strengthening the commitment to coordinating development funds, and improving access to the funds designated for climate change efforts. The PIF's annual summit was held September 7–8, 2011, in Auckland, New Zealand. The summit encouraged the Forum's continued discussion of economic sustainability and development, fishing and agricultural policies, and climate change. The Forum's heads of state also discussed continued assistance to Fiji to promote a return to parliamentary democracy. The Forum also agreed to allow Fiji to participate in a limited capacity in meetings concerning the PACER.

The 2011 Pacific Plan Annual Report reported growth and progress on completing its goals of increased cooperation and integration in the region. Major growth occurred in fisheries, climate change, and education. The majority of the main regional institution reforms of the Pacific Plan were also enacted in 2011, most notably the creation of the Secretariat of the Pacific Community.

In January 2012, Fiji announced the end of the Public Emergency Regulation, a move greatly welcomed by the PIF. The end of the emergency regulations marks the first step toward Fiji's transition back to a democratic regime. The PIF continues to assist and encourage Fiji to seek peace and democracy.

In May 2012, the Marshall Islands announced the approval of a new trade policy framework that would pave the way for its inclusion and accession into PICTA and PACER. The PIF has been encouraging and working with the Marshall Islands over the last several months to develop such a policy.

In late August the forum met for its annual meeting. At the meeting, the leaders of the member states approved the Pacific Leaders Gender Equality Declaration. The declaration outlined the dangers and problems associated with gender inequity and called on member states to enact a program based on equal rights legislation, economic empowerment, ending violence against women, and promoting health and education for women. The forum also produced agreements concerning the status of the Pacific Plan, climate change, and fishing and ocean rights. The group also nominated a committee to oversee the 2013 review of the Pacific Plan.

In January the review committee began the work of reviewing the Pacific Plan. The committee was composed of six individuals, and chaired by form prime minister of Papua New Guinea Sir Makere Morauta. The committee held consultations with the forum members and other non-state actors to assess the progress and effectiveness of the plan.

In September, the review committee presented its preliminary findings at the annual meeting of the Forum. The full finding of the committee is due to the secretariat by the end of October. In addition to discussing the review of the Pacific Plan, pacific leaders also discussed the situation in Fiji, expressing optimism that the state would soon be able to rejoin the forum and have their suspension lifted. The group also released the Majuro Declaration on Climate Leadership. The declaration outlined broad climate control goals, and identified specific action items for each state to work on implementing.

REGIONAL DEVELOPMENT BANKS

Regional development banks are intended to accelerate economic and social development of member states by promoting public and private investment. The banks are not meant, however, to be mere financial institutions in the narrow sense of the term. Required by their charters to take an active interest in improving their members' capacities to make profitable use of local and external capital, they engage in such technical assistance activities as feasibility studies, evaluation and design of projects, and preparation of development programs. The banks also seek to coordinate their activities with the work of other national and international agencies engaged in financing international economic development. The five major regional development banks are discussed below.

African Development Bank

(AFDB)

Banque Africaine de Développement

(BAD)

Web site: www.afdb.org

The Articles of Agreement of the AfDB were signed August 4, 1963, in Khartoum, Sudan, with formal establishment of the institution occurring in September 1964 after 20 signatories had deposited instruments of ratification. Lending operations commenced in July 1966 at the bank's headquarters in Abidjan, Côte d'Ivoire.

Until 1982 membership in the AfDB was limited to states within the region. At the 1979 annual meeting, the Board of Governors approved an amendment to the bank's statutes permitting nonregional membership as a means of augmenting the institution's capital resources; however, it was not until the 17th annual meeting, held in May 1982 in Lusaka, Zambia, that Nigeria announced withdrawal of its objection to the change. Non-African states became eligible for membership December 20, 1982, and by the end of 1983 more than 20 such states had joined the bank.

The bank's leading policymaking organ is its Board of Governors, encompassing the finance or economic ministers of the member states; the governors elect a bank president, who serves a five-year term and is chair of a Board of Directors. The governors are empowered to name 18 directors, each serving a three-year term, with 12 seats to be held by Africans. The bank's African members are the same as for the African Union (AU), save for the inclusion of Morocco (no longer a member of the AU).

While limiting the bank's membership to African countries was initially viewed as a means of avoiding practical difficulties and undesirable political complications, it soon became evident that the major capital-exporting states were unwilling to lend funds without having a continuous voice in their use. In response to this problem, an African Development Fund (ADF) was established in November 1972 as a legally distinct intergovernmental institution in which contributing countries would have a shared managerial role. The ADF Board of Governors encompasses one representative from each state as well as the AfDB governors, ex officio; the 12-member Board of Directors includes six nonregional designees. Nonregional contributing countries—all of whom, except the United Arab Emirates, are now AfDB members—are Argentina, Austria, Belgium, Brazil, Canada, China, Denmark, Finland, France, Germany, India, Italy, Japan, the Republic of Korea, Kuwait, the Netherlands, Norway, Portugal, Saudi Arabia, Spain, Sweden, Switzerland, Turkey, the United Kingdom, and the United States. In addition, in February 1976 the bank and the government of Nigeria signed an agreement establishing a Nigeria Trust Fund (NTF) with an initial capitalization of 50 million Nigerian naira (about $80 million). Unlike the ADF, the NTF is directly administered by the AfDB. Together, the AfDB, the ADF, and the NTF constitute the African Development Bank Group.

Earlier, in November 1970, the AfDB participated in the founding of the International Financial Society for Investments and Development in Africa (*Société Internationale Financière pour les Investissements et le Développement en Afrique*—SIFIDA). Headquartered in Geneva, Switzerland, with the International Finance Corporation (IFC) and a large number of financial institutions from advanced industrial countries among its shareholders, SIFIDA is authorized to extend loans for the promotion and growth of productive enterprises in Africa. Another related agency, the Association of African Development Finance Institutions (AADFI), inaugurated in March 1975 in Abidjan, was established to aid and coordinate African development projects, while the African Reinsurance Corporation (Africa-Re), formally launched in March 1977 in Lagos, Nigeria, promotes the development of insurance and reinsurance activity throughout the continent. The AfDB holds 10 percent of Africa-Re's authorized capital of $50 million.

At the bank's 1988 annual meeting, U.S. officials surprisingly announced that Washington was now willing to support concessional interest rate rescheduling for the "poorest of the poor" African countries. However, African representatives called for additional debt measures, such as extension of maturities and pegging repayment schedules to a country's debt-servicing "history" and "capacity." Following up on discussions initiated at the annual meeting, the bank announced late in the year that the countries involved faced suspension of existing loan disbursements and would not be eligible for new loans until the arrears were cleared.

During the 1989 annual meeting and 25th anniversary celebration, at which the bank was described as "probably the most successful of the African multinational institutions," the Board of Governors pledged that lending activity would continue to accelerate. On the topic of debt reduction, the bank praised the initiatives launched at the recent Group of Seven summit but called for further measures, including more debt cancellations by individual creditor nations.

A dispute between regional and nonregional members regarding the bank's future continued at the May 1993 AfDB annual meeting as Western nations continued to press for a stricter policy on arrears, better evaluation of project performance, and greater support for private sector activity. In addition, at the insistence of donor countries, an independent task force was established, chaired by former World Bank vice president David Knox, to review all bank operations. The task force report, released shortly before the AfDB's May 1994 annual meeting, strongly criticized the bank for keeping poor records, maintaining a top-heavy bureaucracy, and emphasizing the quantity of lending at the expense of quality. The report also supported the contention of donor countries that the accumulation of arrears (more than $700 million) had become a threat to the bank's future. The nonregional members subsequently proposed that regular AfDB lending be limited to "solvent" nations, but African members rejected their advice.

Fractious debate continued at the May 1995 annual meeting. Further tarnishing the bank's image, the governors were unable to elect a successor to outgoing AfDB Presiden Babacar N'Diaye, with regional and nonregional members backing different candidates. However, at a special meeting in Abidjan in late August, the Board of Governors finally chose Omar Kabbaj, a one-time official of the International Monetary Fund (IMF), as the new AfDB president. Shortly thereafter, Kabbaj announced that an external committee would be established to evaluate the bank's operations, internal structures, and fiscal status. The new president also pledged that the AfDB would immediately begin to give greater emphasis to private sector loans, one issue on which regional and nonregional members appeared in agreement. Meanwhile, talks on the ADF replenishment remained suspended pending Kabbaj's restructuring proposals, expected by the end of the year.

Under the leadership of Kabbaj, the AfDB cut approximately 240 employees (20 percent of the staff) and otherwise restructured the bank's operations, paving the way for an infusion of new capital. At the annual meeting held May 21–22, 1996, the ADF was replenished with $2.6 billion, though this entailed a cut from prior levels. When ADF lending resumed shortly thereafter, the AfDB adopted guidelines recommended by the World Bank under which the number of states eligible for new loans was reduced from 53 to 12.

Although those changes were widely perceived as representing genuine progress, the AfDB governance report released in 1996 delineated several continuing problems. The report argued that further "stark" measures needed to be taken to prevent the bank from being relegated to the role of a minor player on the continent. Specific issues to be addressed included "incompetence" in some bank operations, low morale among the remaining employees, and a lack of "financial credibility" stemming from arrears of $800 million amassed by 25 out of 53 recipients.

In July 1996 a special summit was held in Libreville, Gabon, to discuss issues raised in the report and to plot the future of the bank, particularly in regard to the contentious issue of control. Led by Nigeria, some African countries opposed giving nonregional members additional decision-making power, despite the bank's weakened condition. The governance report outlined several alternatives, ranging from a 50–50 split of control between nonregional and African nations, to no change at all (which might have meant the cessation of Western contributions).

A compromise was reached in March 1998 when it was agreed that a capital increase of about 35 percent ($7.65 billion) would be implemented, with the nonregional share being set at 40 percent. Significantly, while the African members were allowed to retain control of 12 of the 18 seats on the Board of Directors, future discussions would require 70 percent (at least one nonregional vote) endorsement by that board on "crucial" issues.

Under Kabbaj's leadership, significant structural reforms were implemented during the late-1990s, contributing to improved international credibility for the bank. A vision statement approved by the Board of Governors in 1999 gave greater emphasis to reducing poverty and increasing productivity, with other concerns including good governance, regional cooperation and development, gender mainstreaming, and environmental sustainability. Operationally, the AfDB rededicated to meeting client needs through strategic planning and compliance monitoring. An executive restructuring in early 2002 included the establishment of two additional vice presidencies, raising the total to five. The five vice presidencies included: planning, policy, and research; operations in the Central and Western regions; operations in the Northern, Eastern, and Southern regions and the private sector; corporate management; and finance. The reorganization also involved establishing two operational complexes: sector departments, with responsibility for project management; and country departments, with responsibility for such broader areas as macroeconomic analyses, lending policy, and public sector management.

In February 2003 the AfDB temporarily moved its headquarters from Abidjan to Tunis, Tunisia, because of the outbreak of civil war in Côte d'Ivoire. International institutions (led by the Group of Eight) subsequently announced plans for the AfDB to manage a new fund slated to provide as much as $10 billion a year to improve infrastructure in Africa. After numerous ballots that weeded out several candidates, in 2005 the Board of Governors elected Donald Kaberuka, the finance and economy minister from Rwanda, over Olabisi Ogunjobi, a Nigerian who had worked at the bank since 1978. It was widely reported that Kaberuka had enjoyed the support of most of the bank's Western members. In 2010 Kaberuka was appointed for a second five-year term.

In May 2006 the organization was embarrassed that, for the first time, its external auditor was unable to approve its accounts without qualification. Effective July 2006, a new organizational structure was introduced, principally affecting the operational complexes and the Office of the Chief Economist. In May 2007 the AfDB caused some controversy by holding its 47th annual meeting in Shanghai, China. At this meeting Chinese premier Wen Jiabao rejected criticism that China was only interested in Africa as a potential supplier of raw materials. In November 2007 the bank canceled Liberia's debt.

In December 2007 the bank won a three-year replenishment for the ADF of $8.9 billion, a 57 percent increase over the previous three-year replenishment.

The bank's 2008 annual meeting, held May 14–15 in Maputo, Mozambique, welcomed Turkey as the 25th nonregional member. At this meeting the bank also pledged an extra $1 billion to combat the food crisis in Africa. The 2009 annual meeting, held May 14–15 in Dakar, Senegal, had as its theme "Africa and the Financial Crisis: An Agenda for Action." The AfDB had previously given input to the April 2009 G20 conference in London (see separate article). Kaberuka declared that, while six months had wiped out much of Africa's recent economic progress, the fact was that Africa's GDP was still growing, while that of the developed countries was generally declining.

The 2010 AfDB annual meeting was held May 27–28 in Abidjan, Côte d'Ivoire. While participants heralded their return to Côte d'Ivoire, they did not feel quite ready to move the headquarters back. Consequently, use of the Tunis facility was extended through May 2011. (In November 2011 a new agreement was signed between the AfDB and Côte d'Ivoire to relocate the headquarters in the future.) At the meeting the bank's governors approved the bank's sixth general capital increase, tripling its capital resources to almost $100 billion.

Total bank group approvals reached $6.3 billion in 2010, a decline from $12.4 billion in 2009. The decrease was indicative of the stabilization of the region's economy. As of the end of 2010, cumulative disbursements since 1967 reached $86.1 billion for 3,526 loans and grants. In its 2011 annual report the AfDB found that the economy accelerated on the continent, with total GDP growing by 4.9 percent, up from 3.1 percent the previous year, while overall inflation fell from 10 to 7.7 percent.

Total bank group approvals have continued to decline since 2010, reaching only $5.72 billion in 2011. At the 2012 annual meeting held in Tanzania, the AfDB Governors expressed great satisfaction with the progress made by Africa in 2011, noting that most of the African countries had grown by 5.1 percent over the course of the year. The most significant event of the 2012 meeting was the approval of South Sudan's request to become a member of the bank. The bank president, Donald Kaberuka, also laid out a more detailed plan for the bank's transition back to its headquarters in Côte d'Ivoire.

Bank group approvals once again declined for 2012, only totaling $4.25 billion. This decline is largely attributed to several nations having reached their borrowing limit. At the 2013 annual meeting of the Board of Governors, President Kaberuka unveiled a new Ten-Year Strategy, outlining the AfDB's new objectives of inclusive growth and the transition to green growth. In June 2013, the AfDB successfully returned to its headquarters in Côte d'Ivoire, having been temporarily located in Tunisia for a decade.

Asian Development Bank
(ADB)

Web site: www.adb.org

Launched under the auspices of the United Nations (UN) Economic Commission for Asia and the Far East (ESCAFE), subsequently the Economic and Social Commission for Asia and the Pacific (ESCAP), the ADB began operations December 19, 1966, in its Manila, Philippines, headquarters as a means of aiding economic growth and cooperation among regional developing countries. Its original membership of 31 has since expanded to 67, including 48 regional members: Afghanistan, Armenia, Australia, Azerbaijan, Bangladesh, Bhutan, Brunei, Cambodia, China, Cook Islands, Fiji, Georgia, "Hong Kong, China," India, Indonesia, Japan, Kazakhstan, Kiribati, the Republic of Korea, Kyrgyzstan, Laos, Malaysia, Maldives, Marshall Islands, Federated States of Micronesia, Mongolia, Myanmar, Nauru, Nepal, New Zealand, Pakistan, Palau, Papua New Guinea, Philippines, Samoa, Singapore, Solomon Islands, Sri Lanka, Tajikistan, "Taipei, China," Thailand, Timor-Leste, Tonga, Turkmenistan, Tuvalu, Uzbekistan, Vanuatu, and Vietnam; and 19 nonregional members: Austria, Belgium, Canada, Denmark, Finland, France, Germany, Ireland, Italy, Luxembourg, Netherlands, Norway, Portugal, Spain, Sweden, Switzerland, Turkey, the United Kingdom, and the United States. The People's Republic of China acceded to membership March 10, 1986, after the ADB agreed to change Taiwan's membership title from "Republic of China" to "Taipei, China." Taiwan thereupon withdrew from participation in bank meetings for a year, although continuing its financial contributions, before returning "under protest." North Korea applied for membership in 1997, but the United States and Japan, in particular, remain opposed.

Each member state is represented on the Board of Governors, which selects a 12-member Board of Directors (eight from regional states) and a bank president who chairs the latter. Four vice presidents and a managing director general assist the president in managing the bank.

ADB resources are generated through subscriptions; borrowings on capital markets; and income from several sources, including interest on undisbursed assets. Most funds are in the form of country subscriptions. Leading shareholders as of 2010 were Japan (17.7 percent), China (7.3 percent), India (7.2 percent), Australia (6.6 percent), Indonesia (6.2 percent), the United States (5.9 percent), Canada (5.9 percent), the Republic of Korea (5.7 percent), and Germany (4.9 percent). In all, about 71.4 percent of subscribed capital is provided by regional members.

In June 1974 an Asian Development Fund (ADF) was established to consolidate the activities of two earlier facilities, the Multi-Purpose Special Fund (MPSF) and the Agricultural Special Fund (ASF), whose policies were criticized because of program linkages to procurement in donor countries. The ADF, which provides soft loans, receives most of its funding from voluntary contributions by the industrialized ADB members, who also support a Technical Assistance Special Fund (TASF). A Japan Special Fund for technical assistance grants was set up in 1988 to aid in economic restructuring and facilitating new investment; a Currency Crisis Support Facility was added in 1999. The ADB Institute Special Fund supports the ADB Institute, which was established in 1997 to examine development issues and to offer related training and assistance.

In the mid-1980s there was intense debate within the ADB regarding proposed changes in lending policies. Western contributors called on the bank, which in the past provided loans almost exclusively for specific development projects, to provide more "policy-based" funding, under which the recipient country would have spending discretion as long as certain economic reforms were implemented. A compromise agreement was reached in 1987 to allocate up to 15 percent of annual outlays to such loans. Also in partial response to Western demands, the ADB in 1986 established a private sector division to provide private enterprise loans that would not require government guarantees. During the same year, after potential loan recipients complained that ADB requirements were too stringent, the ADB adopted an adjustable lending rate system.

Extensive debate on the bank's direction and strategies for the next decade was generated by a report from an expert external panel submitted in early 1989. The report echoed many of the recommendations of an earlier internal task force that urged greater support for social programs. The report also called for expanded private sector activity, attention to the role of women in development, and additional environmental study in connection with all bank projects. In May the Board of Governors endorsed many of the proposed initiatives, especially those concerned with poverty alleviation and the environment.

As negotiations began in 1993 on a proposed doubling of the bank's authorized capital, an independent task force was established to review ADB operations. The task force recommended the bank shift from an "approval culture," in which quantity of lending was the major criteria, to a focus on "project quality." The bank also agreed to stricter guidelines regarding arrears.

Those proposed refinements notwithstanding, it was widely agreed that the bank's past performance was satisfactory, and the Board of Governors in May 1994 approved an increase in ADB subscribed capital to $48 billion, with the replenishment expected to support lending for the next eight to ten years. Although members with combined 94 percent of the board's voting power supported the increase, China and other members reportedly voiced strong protest over the insistence of Western nations that future lending be tied to "good governance" and that additional emphasis be given to social and environmental development.

Some behind-the-scenes controversy attended a subsequent effort by the ADB to prepare a 2001–2015 Long-Term Strategic Framework, with recipient countries resisting pressure by donor countries for greater say in development plans and for making loan approvals partially dependent on such considerations as good governance.

Under the leadership of bank president Tadao Chino, who was reelected to a second term in September 2001, the ADB undertook a partial administrative reorganization. As part of the 15-year strategic plan, greater emphasis was to be given to sustainable development, private sector participation (a Private Sector Operations Department was created), environmental considerations, and poverty reduction. Projects involving social infrastructure such as health facilities and programs, education, and water supplies were to receive greater support.

The ADB was criticized in the early 2000s for a perceived failure to allocate sufficient resources for poverty reduction. Perhaps as a consequence, the bank announced it would begin offering grants (as opposed to loans) to its poorer members. That decision was made after donors agreed to a $7 billion replenishment of the ADF for the four-year period through 2008. Bank officials estimated that about one-fifth of ADF assistance in the future would consist of grants.

Haruhiko Kuroda of Japan was installed as the ADB's new president in February 2005. In early 2005 the ADB established a $600 million fund to assist victims of the recent devastating tsunami. At a donors' conference of November 19, 2005, the ADB pledged $1 billion to help Pakistan recover from a major earthquake and to provide winter support to its victims.

At its 2005 annual meeting, held May 4–5 in Kyoto, Japan, the ADB came under attack for not doing more to abate environmental degradation and for doing little to prevent the growing disparity between rich and poor countries in the region. Against this background, the ADB began considering a role change in an Asia no longer uniformly poor and shiftedits focus from the alleviation of poverty to promoting sustainable development.

Criticism of the ADB's direction dominated the organization's 2007 annual meeting, held May 3–4 in Madrid, Spain. The U.S. representative alone voted against the bank's long-term strategy, protesting that China and India, now with huge cash reserves, should no longer be given huge loans to fight poverty.

ADB's response to the world economic crisis has been to increase lending and to enhance its own liquidity. At its annual meeting, held May 4, 2009, in Bali, Indonesia, the bank announced a $120 billion crisis fund to boost liquidity. The economic ministers at the forum denied that the fund was an attempt to circumvent IMF rules that would have forced member countries to make unpopular economic reforms.

In June 2009 China criticized the ADB for funding a flood-management project in the northeastern Indian state of Arunachal Pradesh, which China claims. The bank responded that it does not take sides in territorial disputes. The May 1–4, 2010, annual meeting, held in Tashkent, Uzbekistan, concentrated on increasing domestic demand in Asia. ADB also announced an Asia Solar Energy Initiative to develop large capacity solar projects, intended to generate some 3,000 MW of solar power by 2012.

At the 2011 annual meeting, held in Hanoi, Vietnam, ADB focused on rising commodity prices, infrastructure, and climate change. The Board of Governor's also considered a new report on where Asia will be in 2050, which estimates that Asia will account for nearly half of the world's economy.

The 2012 annual meeting in the Philippines was predominately concerned with the sustainable development of all of Asia and creation of different response measures to economic disaster and downturn. The biggest issue facing the ADB, according to a new institutional report, is the lack of equal growth across Asia and the South Pacific. This challenge led the ADB to increase its contribution to the Asian Development fund by nearly 10 percent. The global economic downturn has also impacted the ADB. To counter the economic problems, the Association of Southeast Asian Nations (ASEAN) announced that it was doubling the funds available under the Chiang Mai Initiative Multilateralization, a financial pool used for economic emergencies.

In April 2013 the ADB Board of Governors elected a new bank president, Takehiko Nakao. Nakao had previously served as Japan's Vice Minister of Finance for International Affairs and Minster to the United States. At the 2013 annual meeting in India, ADB leadership issued a call for increased innovation and integration within the region. These themes were identified as being key to the region's further growth, continued reduction of poverty, and successful completion of the Millennium Development Goals.

European Bank for Reconstruction and Development
(EBRD)
Banque Européenne pour la Reconstruction et la Développement
(BERD)

Web site: www.ebrd.com

The idea of a multibillion-dollar international lending effort to help revive the economies of Eastern European countries and assist their conversion to free-market activity was endorsed by the heads of the European Community (EC, subsequently the European Union—EU) in December 1989, based on a proposal from French president François Mitterrand. After several months of negotiation in which most other leading Western countries were brought into the project, a treaty to establish the EBRD with initial capitalization of $12.4 billion was signed by 40 nations, the EC, and the European Investment Bank (EIB) on May 29, 1990, in Paris, France. London was chosen as the headquarters for the bank, which proponents described as one of the most important international aid projects since World War II. Mitterrand's special adviser, Jacques Attali, who first suggested such an enterprise, was named to direct its operations. The bank officially opened April 15, 1991.

According to the bank's charter, its purpose is to "promote private and entrepreneurial initiative" in Eastern European countries "committed to applying the principles of multiparty democracy, pluralism, and market economics." Although the United Kingdom and the United States originally pressed for lending to be limited entirely to the private sector, a compromise was reached permitting up to 40 percent of the EBRD's resources to be used for public sector projects, such as roads and telecommunications. The bank operated using the basket of the currencies of EC member states known as the European Currency Unit (ECU) until January 1, 1999, when the euro came into existence, replacing the ECU at par.

Although Washington initially opposed its participation, the Soviet Union was permitted to become a member of the EBRD on the condition that it would not borrow more from the bank than it contributed in capital for at least three years, at which point the stipulation would be reviewed. The restriction was imposed because of fears that Soviet needs could draw down most of the EBRD resources and because of U.S. arguments that Moscow had yet to meet the criteria of democracy and market orientation. Despite the "net zero" limitation, Moscow was reportedly eager to join the organization because it would be its first capitalist-oriented membership in an international financial institution, and in March 1991 the Supreme Soviet endorsed participation by a vote of 380–1. The net zero condition was eliminated following the breakup of the Soviet Union, with the bank declaring the newly independent former Soviet republics to be eligible for up to 40 percent of total EBRD lending.

The United States is the largest shareholding member, with 10.1 percent of the capital, followed by Germany, France, Japan, Italy, and the United Kingdom, each with 8.6 percent as of December 31, 2010. At the launching of the EBRD, the Soviet Union held a 6 percent share, two-thirds of which was subsequently allocated to Russia and the remainder to the other 14 former Soviet republics, all of which (Armenia, Azerbaijan, Belarus, Estonia, Georgia, Kazakhstan, Kyrgyzstan, Latvia, Lithuania, Moldova, Tajikistan, Turkmenistan, Ukraine, and Uzbekistan) joined the bank in 1992. At the end of 2007, Russia held 4 percent of shares, while the EU itself and the EIB each held 3 percent. In addition to these 23 members, 42 other states are bank members: Albania, Australia, Austria, Belgium, Bosnia and Herzegovina, Bulgaria, Canada, Croatia, Cyprus, Czech Republic, Denmark, Egypt, Finland, Greece, Hungary, Iceland, Ireland, Israel, Jordan, Republic of Korea, Liechtenstein, Luxembourg, Macedonia, Malta, Mexico, Mongolia, Montenegro, Morocco, Netherlands, New Zealand, Norway, Poland, Portugal, Romania, Serbia, Slovakia, Slovenia, Spain, Sweden, Switzerland, Tunisia, and Turkey.

Apart from ordinary resources, the EBRD also administers 11 special funds: the Baltic Investment Special Fund and the Baltic Technical Assistance Special Fund, to aid private sector development of small- and medium-sized enterprises (SMEs) in Estonia, Latvia, and Lithuania; the Russian Small Business Investment Special Fund and the Russian Small Business Technical Cooperation Special Fund; the Balkan Region Special Fund and the EBRD SME Special Fund, to assist, respectively, in reconstruction and in development of SMEs in Albania, Bosnia and Herzegovina, Bulgaria, Croatia, Macedonia, Romania, and Yugoslavia; the EBRD Technical Cooperation Fund, to aid in financing technical cooperation projects; the Financial Intermediary Investment Special Fund, to support financial intermediaries in all countries of operation; the Italian Investment Special Fund, to aid modernization, restructuring, expansion, and development of SMEs in selected countries; the Moldova Micro Business Investment Special Fund, to target SME development in Moldova; and the SME Finance Facility Special Fund, to aid SME financing in Bulgaria, Czech Republic, Estonia, Hungary, Latvia, Lithuania, Poland, Romania, Slovakia, and Slovenia. Some 16 countries—including non-EU members Canada, Iceland, Japan, Norway, Switzerland, "Taipei, China," and the United States—have pledged an aggregate of €311 million to the 11 funds. At the end of 2013 the EBRD was operating with €30 billion in capital assets.

The first EBRD loans were approved in late 1991. At the first annual meeting of the Board of Governors in April 1992, bank officials reported that 20 loans totaling ECU 621 million (about $770 million) were thus far approved. However, some East European leaders described the bank's impact as marginal, and it was widely accepted that lending was restrained by problems in finding reliable borrowers for specific projects. EBRD president Attali reportedly suggested that the bank consider making loans in support of long-term economic restructuring, but the idea was quickly vetoed by the United States as beyond the EBRD mandate.

At the second Board of Governors' meeting in April 1993, it was announced that the bank approved 54 investment projects in 1992, involving a total EBRD contribution of ECU 1.2 billion (about $1.5 billion), although actual disbursements for the year totaled only ECU 126 million (about $156 million). The meeting was overshadowed by earlier press disclosures that EBRD disbursement up to the end of 1992 was only half the level of the bank's expenditure on its London offices, staff salaries, travel expenses, and administrative costs. Amid widespread criticism of his style of management, Attali announced his resignation on June 25, and was succeeded In August by, Jacques de Larosiére of France, a former managing director of the International Monetary Fund (IMF).In November the Board of Governors approved internal spending reforms proposed by Larosiére.

At the March 1994 Board of Governors' meeting, it was announced that the EBRD earned an approximate $4.5 million profit in 1993, compared to a loss of $7.3 million the previous year. De Larosiére told the April 1995 annual meeting, however, that he expected the bank's capital base to be exhausted by the end of 1997 under the current rate of lending. Although it was widely conceded that the bank made significant improvement in its "budgetary discipline," Western donors reportedly were awaiting further reform in bank operations before agreeing to launch replenishment talks.

At the EBRD's annual meeting held in mid-April 1996 in Sofia, Bulgaria, de Larosiére called on Eastern European nations to strengthen their banking regulations and supervision since the failure of private banks to follow "basic banking procedures" was contributing to economic difficulties in many Eastern European nations. The shareholders also agreed to double the EBRD's authorized capital from ECU 10 billion to ECU 20 billion (about $25 billion at exchange rates then prevailing) to accommodate a proposed lending increase that went into effect in April 1997. Forty-eight of the 60 members deposited their instruments of subscription to the capital increase by the end of the year. President de Larosiére said the additional resources would ensure the EBRD would continue to operate "on the cutting edge" of the economic transition in Europe.

With the EBRD emerging in the post-Soviet era as the single largest source of private sector financing in Russia, that country's financial crisis in August 1998 resulted in a loss of ECU 261 million ($283 million) for the year. At the end of 1998, Russia accounted for about 25 percent of the EBRD's disbursed outstanding loans, but despite the crisis and its profound impact throughout the region, only four Russian loans were classified as nonperforming. Overall financing for 1998 totaled ECU 2.37 billion for 96 projects, down from 108 in 1997. The EBRD returned to profitability in 1999 earning €42.7 billion as the region recovered more rapidly than expected.

EBRD president de Larosiére announced his retirement in January 1998 and was succeeded in July 1998 by Horst Köhler, president of the German Savings Bank Association. Köhler, who resigned after 20 months in office to become managing director of the IMF, was in turn succeeded in July 2000 by Jean Lemierre, a French financial official.

In recent years the bank has shifted attention from the more developed economies of Central Europe toward the east. In its November 2001 Transition Report, the EBRD, looking ahead to the eventual EU accession of ten bank members, urged that all 27 countries of operation continue to receive assistance. Otherwise, the bank feared a "Brussels lace curtain"—the financial and economic equivalent of the Iron Curtain—might divide the EU from the rest of the continent.

In April 2004 the EBRD announced plans for substantial expansion of lending to its seven poorest members (Armenia, Azerbaijan, Georgia, Kyrgyzstan, Moldova, Tajikistan, and Uzbekistan). In particular, the bank said it would direct support to the private sector in those countries.

The years 2005–2007 also marked a period of relative success in achieving the bank's aims. At the end of 2007, the Czech Republic was slated to be the first recipient country to "graduate," meaning that it had achieved "an advanced state of transition" and would receive no more EBRD investment. In March 2007 the bank announced that net profit had increased by 57 percent to a record €2.4 billion in 2006 from a year earlier, an increase largely caused by gains from stock investments. In September 2007 a project was announced (to be administered by the EBRD) to cover the site of the Chernobyl nuclear disaster in a giant steel protective casing.

In May 2008 the EBRD issued a $1 billion global bond, its first benchmark issue since 2004. In May Thomas Mirow of Germany was named president, succeeding Lemierre at the end of his two four-year terms. Mirow's appointment was controversial. Some were concerned with a lack of transparency while others argued that he was Germany's candidate. This was a concern since the German government was known to be interested in merging the EBRD with the European Investment Bank. Also in May 2008 Turkey applied for full membership in the bank, becoming a full country of operations as well as a shareholder in November of that year. In November 2008 the bank announced that it would boost investment in 2009, particularly in Central and Eastern Europe, to combat the growing international financial crisis. The year 2009 saw the bank making loans to many smaller enterprises in Eastern Europe and Western and Central Asia.

Lending commitments in 2009 totaled €7.9 billion for 311 projects, compared to €5.1 billion for 302 projects in 2008. The 2008 commitments, affected by the world financial crisis, represented a 9 percent decrease from the 2007 level of €5.6 billion for 353 projects. Of the 2009 commitments, 48 percent went to "early and intermediate transition countries," while 31 percent went to Russia and 21 percent went to "advanced transition countries.

The bank's focus in late 2009 and throughout 2010 was to mitigate the effects of the global recession on the fragile economies of Eastern Europe. In early May Mirow was particularly concerned that the Greek debt crisis might spill over into Greece's southeastern European neighbors. Shortly thereafter, and ahead of the May 14–15 annual meeting, held in Zagreb, Croatia, Russia promised an addition €40 million in capital to the bank and guaranteed an additional €360 million in case of need. At the meeting the bank's governors approved a 50 percent increase in its authorized capital, €20 billion to €30 billion. That would enable it to increase its annual financing activities to €8.5 billion—€9 billion in 2011–2014—from the €5–6 billion currently available.

In 2010 the EBRD had 1,541 employees in 33 regional offices and operations in 29 countries. That year the bank initiated 386 new projects worth €9.1 billion. The largest commitments were in the financial sector, which accounted for 34 percent of new investments, followed by the corporate sector, 25 percent, and energy, 21 percent. The year 2010 also marked the resumption of economic growth in the region, which posted growth of 4.2 percent. In January 2011 Jordan and Tunisia joined the EBRD. The EBRD Board Of Governor's voted in favor of expanding bank membership to Southern and Eastern Mediterranean region following a request by the Group of 8 nations for the bank to expand its operations in North Africa and the Middle East. The bank is focusing its Mediterranean expansion in Jordan, Tunisia, Egypt and Morocco. In 2011, the bank continued its levels of commitment from 2010, with 380 new projects and commitments totaling €9.1 billion with €6.7 billion in annual disbursements.

At the 2012 annual meeting, the Board of Governor's elected a new bank president, Sir Suma Chakrabarti. Sir Chakrabarti, a senior British Justice minister, succeeded Thomas Mirow, who had been serving as president since 2008. The Board of Governor's called for the EBRD to continue its historic emphasis in Europe, while continuing to increase its involvement in the Mediterranean.

In 2013 the EBRD was operating 393 projects in 35 countries and employed over 2,000 people. The EBRD's projects range from local infrastructural development to its Chernobyl Site Transformation Initiative. At the 2013 Board of Governor's annual meeting, the organization announced a renewed effort to promote growth in its countries of operation, which has dropped to just 2.2 percent over the last year. The bank also announced plans to focus on small and medium size enterprises in its future funding given the success of these enterprises at creating jobs and promoting economic growth.

European Investment Bank
(EIB)

Web site: www.eib.org

The EIB is the European Union (EU) bank for long-term finance. It was created by the Treaty of Rome, which established the European Economic Community (EEC) on January 1, 1958. The bank, headquartered in Luxembourg, has as its basic function the balanced and steady development of EU member countries, with the greater part of its financing going to projects that favor the development of less-advanced regions and serve the common interests of several members or the whole community. Although industrial modernization remains important in the context of an expanded community and its transformation into the EU, emphasis has shifted more toward projects involving communications infrastructure, urban development, the environment, energy security, regional development, and cross-national industrial integration. Most recently, projects in health and education have taken on greater importance.

The EIB membership is identical to that of the EU: Austria, Belgium, Bulgaria, Cyprus, Czech Republic, Denmark, Estonia, Finland, France, Germany, Greece, Hungary, Ireland, Italy, Latvia, Lithuania, Luxembourg, Malta, Netherlands, Poland, Portugal, Romania, Slovakia, Slovenia, Spain, Sweden, and the United Kingdom. Each has subscribed part of the bank's capital of €232 billion, although most funds required to finance its operations are borrowed by the bank on international and national capital markets. Capital shares range from 0.4 percent of the total for Malta to 16.2 percent each for France, Germany, Italy, and the United Kingdom. Only 5 percent of capital is paid in. Outstanding loans are limited to 2.5 times the subscribed capital.

EIB activities were initially confined to the territory of member states but have gradually been extended to other countries under terms of association or cooperation agreements. Current participants include 10 countries in the Mediterranean region (Algeria, Egypt, Israel, Jordan, Lebanon, Morocco, Serbia, Syria, Tunisia, and Turkey) and the 77 African, Caribbean, and Pacific (ACP) signatories of the Lomé IV Convention and its successor, the Cotonou Agreement of 2000.

The bank is administered by a 27-member Board of Governors (one representative—usually the finance or economy minister—from each EU state) and a 28-member Board of Directors (one from each member state and one representing the European Commission). The president of the bank, appointed by the Board of Governors, chairs the Board of Directors, heads a Management Committee that encompasses eight vice presidents, and oversees the 2,000-plus EIB staff. Other organs include a Management Committee, an Audit Committee, a General Secretariat, a General Administration Office, and five directorates (Lending Operations in Europe, Lending Operations Outside Europe, Finance, Projects, and Risk Management).

The EIB's lending rose rapidly in the 1990s in response to the "buoyant level of investment" in the member countries, financial requirements arising from the EU single market, and more flexible lending conditions. Within the community itself, the EIB was directed by the European Council in December 1992 to assist in the development of the economic and monetary union envisioned by the Maastricht Treaty. In addition, in connection with the launching of the EU in November 1993, the EIB was asked to concentrate on trans-European projects (particularly those in the communications, energy, environmental, and transportation sectors) and small- and medium-sized enterprises (SMEs). Some of that activity was directed through a new European Investment Fund (EIF) launched in mid-1994 to provide loan guarantees to projects deemed valuable for "strengthening the internal market." The EIB also participated in the creation of the European Bank for Reconstruction and Development (EBRD, above) to assist in implementing economic reforms and support political democratization throughout Eastern Europe.

In line with a March 2000 decision of the European Council to further increase support for SMEs, the EIB Board of Governors established an EIB Group comprising the EIB and the EIF. The EIB was directed to increase its shares in the latter from the original 40 percent to 60 percent, with the balance held by the European Commission (30 percent) and various European financial institutions (10 percent). The reorganization was intended to improve the group's ability to approve and administer loans, venture capital investments, and SME guarantees.

The EIB Group constituted a core component of the EIB's Innovation 2000 Initiative (i2i), which earmarked for the following three years €12–15 billion for loans involving SMEs and such sectors as health, education, research and development, and information and communications technology. Under President Philippe Maystadt, the bank continued to shift its emphasis toward projects involving human resources and advanced technology.

The annual value of signed EIB financing contracts rose incrementally throughout the 1990s, reaching, in the last year of the decade, €31.8 billion. The total increased by 13 percent in 2000 to €36 billion and to €36.8 billion in 2001.

Although the impending expansion of the EU drew considerable attention to the EIB's pre-accession assistance, its additional partners around the world also continued to avail themselves of EIB resources. For example, under the 2000 Cotonou pact, total EU aid to the ACP countries for 2002–2006 was set at €15.2 billion: €11.3 billion as grants from EU members, €2.2. billion to be managed by the EIB through an Investment Facility, and some €1.7 billion in loans from EIB resources.

In 2001 the EIB agreed to permit lending to Russia for environmental projects in regions that border EIB member states. Subsequently, the bank expanded its authorized capital in 2002–2003 to facilitate the inclusion of ten new members in 2004.

In March 2005 the bank announced plans to expand private sector lending in the southern Mediterranean and to resume lending in Palestinian areas.

Activity in 2007 concentrated on energy and climate-change matters. The EIB and the World Bank created a carbon-credit fund for Europe, and in June 2007 the EIB, long criticized for a lack of interest in such matters, formulated in its 2007–2009 operational plan a priority of "sustainable, competitive and secure energy."

The bank's 2009 annual report rolled out an operational plan for the years 2009–2011. This plan called for a significant increase in lending, especially to SMEs, to counter the global recession. The bank's intention was to increase its total lending volume by approximately 30 percent in 2009 and 2010. Lending approvals in 2010 totaled €83.2 billion, compared to €103.9 billion in 2009. Among external projects supported by EIB in 2010 were utility infrastructure improvements in the Dominican Republic and water supply enhancements in South Africa.

The year 2011 saw a record high contribution to the real economy of the Eurozone and the rest of the world as the EIB contributed €61 billion in disbursements. The EIB financed 485 projects in 70 countries in 2011, and continued to focus many of its projects on alternative, environmentally safe forms of energy.

In June 2012, the EIB launched a new initiative—the EIB Institute. The EIB Institute is designed to organize the bank's community engagement measures in efficient and transparent way. The Institute will be focused on promoting social and economic development through new programs designed to increase knowledge through education about the EIB and its economic policies among the region's citizens. The bank saw a slight drop in its investments in 2012, approving only €52 billion of disbursements. Despite lower investment, the organization still financed over 400 projects in 60 countries.

In June 2013 the EIB announced the successful completion of its ten year goal of a €10 billion capital increase and launched a new "Investment Plan." The new investment plan calls for the EIB to increase its investments in SMEs that promote job creation and skill training for the growing youth population of Europe. The needs for more support for SMEs and programs to combat youth unemployment were identified by the Board of Governors as the two largest issues facing the EIB in 2013. In August the EIB signed the necessary framework agreement with Azerbaijan to begin financing projects in that country. Azerbaijan is the sixth Eastern European nation to sign such an agreement with the EIB.

Inter-American Development Bank
(IADB)
Banco Interamericano de Desarrollo
(BID)

Web site: www.iadb.org

Following a reversal of long-standing opposition by the United States, the IADB was launched in 1959 after acceptance of a charter drafted by a special commission to the Inter-American Economic and Social Council of the Organization of American States (OAS). Operations began October 1, 1960, with permanent headquarters in Washington, D.C.

The current members of the IADB are Argentina, Austria, Bahamas, Barbados, Belgium, Belize, Bolivia, Brazil, Canada, Chile, China, Colombia, Costa Rica, Croatia, Denmark, the Dominican Republic, Ecuador, El Salvador, Finland, France, Germany, Guatemala, Guyana, Haiti, Honduras, Israel, Italy, Jamaica, Japan, the Republic of Korea, Mexico, the Netherlands, Nicaragua, Norway, Panama, Paraguay, Peru, Portugal, Slovenia, Spain, Suriname, Sweden, Switzerland, Trinidad and Tobago, the United Kingdom, the United States, Uruguay, and Venezuela.

The purpose of the IADB is to accelerate economic and social development in Latin America, in part by acting as a catalyst for public and private external capital. In addition to helping states in the region coordinate development efforts, the bank provides technical assistance; borrows on international capital markets; and participates in cofinancing with other multilateral agencies, national institutions, and commercial banks. Loans typically cover a maximum of 50–80 percent of project costs, depending on the level of development of the country in which the projects are located; poverty-reduction projects in the least-developed countries may be eligible for 90 percent financing. In the wake of criticism that the bank had not supported regional integration and had neglected the area's poorest nations, major contributors agreed in December 1978, after eight months of intense negotiations, to adopt a U.S.-sponsored policy that would allocate less assistance to wealthier developing nations—such as Argentina, Brazil, and Mexico—and, within such countries, would focus primarily on projects aimed at benefiting the neediest economic sectors.

Each IADB member is represented on the Board of Governors, the bank's policymaking body, by a governor and an alternate, who convene at least once a year. Administrative responsibilities are exercised by 14 executive directors. The Board of Executive Directors is responsible for day-to-day oversight of operations. The bank president, elected by the governors, presides over sessions of the Board of Executive Directors and, in conjunction with an executive vice president and a vice president for planning and administration, is responsible for the management of various offices as well as 13 departments. These departments cover such issues as regional operations, development effectiveness and strategic planning, the private sector, sustainable development, research, information technology and general services, human resources, budget and corporate procurement, integration and regional programs, finance, and legal. An Office of Evaluation and Oversight reports directly to the Board of Executive Directors. In addition, the IADB has established the Institute for Latin American and Caribbean Integration (*Instituto para la Integración de América Latina y el Caribe*—INTAL), founded in 1964 and headquartered in Buenos Aires, Argentina; and the Inter-American Institute for Social Development (*Instituto Interamericano para el Desarrollo Social*—INDES), which opened in 1995 in Washington, D.C.

IADB voting is on a weighted basis according to a country's capital subscription; leading subscribers as of December 31, 2010, were the United States (30 percent), Argentina and Brazil (10.6 percent each), Mexico (6.9 percent), Venezuela (5.7 percent), Japan (5 percent), and Canada (4 percent). Non-American members held about 16 percent of the voting shares. Total subscribed capital is $170 billion as of 2013.

In November 1984 the Inter-American Investment Corporation (IIC) was established as an autonomous affiliate of the IADB to "encourage the establishment, expansion, and modernization of small- and medium-sized private enterprises" (SMEs) by extending long-term loans and otherwise assuming equity positions in such projects, helping to raise additional resources, and offering advisory services. The first joint meeting of the Boards of Governors of the IADB and the IIC was held in March 1987, with the IIC making its initial disbursements in late 1989.

In 1993 the IIC approved loans and equity investments totaling $124 million for 31 projects, but approvals fell to $42.7 million for 14 projects in 1994 due to a "period of consolidation" precipitated by calls for a review of the corporation's performance to date. Based on the recommendation of an external committee of international experts, the IIC staff was halved to approximately 60 employees in 1994 and additional efficiency measures were instituted. In 2005, Governors agreed to increase the IIC debt to equity ratio to 3:1, thereby permitting lending to increase to $600 million based on the corporation's subscribed capital of $200 million. The governors also agreed to open IIC membership to nonmembers of the IADB, a measure designed to permit the accession of Taiwan, which has strong economic ties with many Latin American countries. As of 2001, however, all nonregional members were IADB members. In 2000 the IADB Board of Governors approved a capital increase to $700 million for the IIC.

Another IADB affiliate, the Multilateral Investment Fund (MIF), was formally launched in January 1993. Together, the IADB, IIC, and MIF are identified as the IADB Group. Unlike the IIC, which supports individual projects directly, MIF attempts to improve the investment climate in the region in general by financing management training and developing local financial institutions designed to assist small-scale entrepreneurs. The fund also provides grants to help countries formulate policies designed to alleviate the "human and social costs" of structural adjustment. Like the IIC, MIF is an autonomous operation, although it uses IADB technical and administrative resources. About $1.3 billion was pledged (including $500 million each from Japan and the United States) for MIF's first five years. In 1994, MIF's first full year of operation, 29 projects totaling $64 million were approved. The IADB also serves as administrator of more than 50 trust funds.

Relations within the IADB between the United States and some Latin members have been tense on occasion. The bank called for a $25 billion replenishment in 1986, but a dispute ensued when the United States asked for greater influence, including virtual veto power over loans. Although willing to accept the U.S. proposal to link some loans to economic reforms, Latin American and Caribbean members objected strongly to the veto request. The conflict was seen as central to the February 1988 resignation of Antonio Ortiz Mena of Mexico after 17 years as IADB president. Uruguay's foreign minister, Enrique Iglesias, was named president effective April 1, and, shortly thereafter, a high-level review committee was established that in December called for wide-ranging reform of the bank's procedures and organization.

In early 1989 the IADB reported that 32 loans were approved in 1988 totaling $1.7 billion, down significantly from $2.4 billion in 1987 and $3.0 billion in 1986, and the lowest total since 1976. The decline was attributed to the replenishment impasse as well as the difficulty many bank members faced in undertaking new projects because of the continued regional economic crisis. However, the bank's prospects improved significantly when an 11th-hour compromise was reached on the proposed replenishment at the March 1989 Board of Governors meeting. The agreementauthorized a $26.5 billion capital increase (bringing total authorized capital to $61 billion), designed to permit aggregate lending of $22.5 billion in 1990–1993. Although the United States was not given the blanket veto power it sought, a system of "staggered delays" was established under which challenges to specific loans would be reviewed before release of funds.

In conjunction with the replenishment, the Board of Governors for the first time directed that some bank resources be used to support national economic policy changes via so-called sector adjustment loans. The bank also agreed, as part of its "revival," to a thorough internal reorganization designed to enhance effectiveness and boost the IADB's capacity to transfer resources. As a result, several new divisions were created to reflect the bank's new priorities of regional economic integration, environmental protection, the financing of micro-enterprises, development of human resources, and additional channeling of nonregional funds (from Japan, in particular) to the region.

Stemming in part from resolution of the replenishment issue, lending approvals in 1989 grew to $2.6 billion for 36 loans involving 29 projects in 15 countries. Approvals in 1990 jumped to $3.9 billion for 45 loans. Continuing its rapid expansion, the bank approved $5.3 billion in loans in 1991 and $6 billion in 1992 and 1993.

After 16 months of negotiations, agreement was reached in April 1994 on the bank's next replenishment, under which subscribed capital grew to $100 billion. Bank officials announced an expanded mandate for lending through the end of the century, with consideration to be given for the first time to the "modernization of the state" through reform, for example, of legislative and judicial institutions. In addition, a projected 40 percent of the replenishment was to be earmarked for health services, education, poverty alleviation, and other "social commitments."

The IADB also made it clear it would continue to assist governments establish policies designed to encourage free-market activity, while at least 5 percent of the replenishment would be used for direct loans to the private sector. That emphasis was apparently underscored at the request of donor countries, particularly the United States, which were to have voting power virtually equal to that of borrowing countries. The bank was also given a lead role, in conjunction with the OAS, in following up on the recommendations of the Summit of the Americas, held in December 1994 in Miami, Florida. Among other things, the 34 nations represented at the summit agreed to work toward creation of a Free Trade Area of the Americas by 2005. To that end, the OAS and the IADB signed an agreement in mid-1995 to coordinate their policies and activities to promote regional economic integration. At the second Summit of the Americas, held in April 1998 in Santiago, Chile, IADB president Iglesias pledged that the bank would develop a training facility to improve its members' bargaining skills in matters of international trade and provide $40 billion in loans in the next five years, including $5 billion for education and $500 million for micro-enterprises.

IADB lending approvals dropped to $5.3 billion in 1994 before rebounding to a record level in 1995 of $7.3 billion for 82 projects in 22 countries. Mexico was the leading recipient of new loans, partly because of the economic crisis it suffered beginning in late 1994. Approvals totaled $6.8 billion in 1996 and $6 billion in 1997 before jumping to $10 billion in 1998. Lending in 1999 totaled $9.5 billion. In May that year the IADB and the World Bank committed a combined $5.3 billion toward a $9 billion reconstruction package for Central American countries devastated by Hurricane Mitch in October 1998.

The annual IADB meeting in late March 2000 in Washington, D.C., served to refocus attention on the effectiveness of bank lending strategies. Addressing the meeting, U.S. secretary of the Treasury Lawrence Summers proposed that the IADB reassess its programs, increase interest charged to the more affluent borrowing countries, and accelerate the move from large-scale projects—for example, power generation infrastructure—toward smaller ones designed to help alleviate poverty. His remarks, which were supported by Iglesias, came in the context of mounting evidence that despite rapid regional economic growth in the 1990s as a whole, the percent of the population in abject poverty had not changed over the decade. According to the United Nations (UN) Economic Commission for Latin America and the Caribbean (ECLAC), 15 percent of the population in borrowing countries remained in extreme poverty, with about 40 percent living on $2 a day or less. President Iglesias noted that various economic adjustment policies, although largely successful, had not adequately confronted social problems, and he warned that resultant discontent could ultimately erode democracy in the region.

In 2004 the IADB announced its support for the proposed Central American Free Trade Agreement (CAFTA) and began to allocate resources to projects designed to prepare for it. The bank also committed itself to providing greater assistance to small- and medium-sized businesses and generally to simplifying procedures for lending to businesses. The subject receiving the most attention in the first half of 2005 was China's request for membership. The United States continued to oppose China's application, officially because of Washington's belief that a country should not join a development bank as a donor if it owes money to another development bank (China has outstanding World Bank loans). Complicating the issue was the fact that ten IADB shareholders maintained diplomatic ties with Taiwan. Also in 2005, Luis Alberto Moreno of Colombia was elected to succeed Iglesias as IADB president. Moreno was elected to a second term in 2010.

At the bank's March 2007 annual meeting in Guatemala City, the United States withdrew its previous objections to China's membership. At this meeting the bank also announced that Bolivia, Guyana, Haiti, Honduras, and Nicaragua, five of the poorest countries in Latin America, were to have their debts to the bank, a sum of more than $4 billion, forgiven. Concurrently, it was announced that remittances from Latin American emigrants now exceeded all foreign investment and aid to the region.

On January 12, 2009, China officially joined the bank as its 48th member. During 2009 the bank was discussing a significant capital increase, its first in fifteen years. In July 2009 the bank eliminated a rule known as the Policy-Based Lending Authority in order to allow Canada to increase its callable (but not paid-in) capital available for lending. In August Canada temporarily increased its callable capital by $4 billion, the increase to last for between five and eight years. The IADB actually posted a record year in 2009, with a successful strategy of providing countercyclical financing to Latin American and Caribbean countries during the global economic crisis.

Loan approvals and guarantees totaled $15.5 billion in 2010. In July 2010 the IDB's board agreed to increase its capital by $70 billion by 2015. During 2010 about 46 percent of IADB financing was to support poverty reduction, while 34 percent went to small or underdeveloped nations and 23 percent for climate change mitigation and sustainable energy.

In 2011, the IADB successfully completed its goals for the capital increase approved in 2010. The IADB approved 167 projects in 2011, totaling $10.1 billion in commitments. The bank's actual disbursements for the year reached $8.6 billion. In late-2011, the IADB signed an agreement with China Eximbank to create an equity platform that would aid in the development of Latin America. The fund is expected to be operational by late 2012. In 2012, IADB President Luis Moreno announced the creation of a new fund that will be used to assist member states in their efforts to curtail crime and violence. The creation of this fund is the result of rising crime in Latin America and the Caribbean. The year 2012 saw a slight increase in commitments from 2011, with the IADB approving 169 projects totaling $11.4 billion.

At the 2013 annual meeting in Panama City, Panama, the Board of Governors authorized the creation of a reform proposal for restructuring the bank's private sector operations. The decision comes as another step to improve the bank's efficiency and transparency within its operations. In May 2013 the IADB released the book from its latest study, "More Than Revenue: Taxation as a Development Tool." The study found that many Latin American nations have missed out on potential economic development because of their outdated tax codes and called for member states to update and revise their tax codes. In August 2013, Moreno announced a new IADB emphasis on road safety, noting that road safety improvements would be given priority in all new transportation project funding requests.

SHANGHAI COOPERATION ORGANIZATION (SCO)

Shanghai Hezuo Zuzhi
Shankhayskaya Organizatsiya Sotrudnichestva

Established: By declaration of the heads of the member states, meeting in Shanghai, China, on June 15, 2001. The body's structure was formalized in a charter signed on June 7, 2002, in Moscow, Russia, and came into full effect September 19, 2003.

Purpose: To strengthen mutual trust, friendship, and good relations between the member states; to maintain peace, security, and stability in the region and to promote a new democratic, fair, and rational political and economic international order; to counteract terrorism, separatism, and extremism in all their manifestations; to fight against illicit narcotics and arms trafficking and other types of criminal activity of a transnational character, as well as illegal migration; to encourage efficient regional cooperation in such spheres as politics, trade and economy, defense, law enforcement, environment protection, culture, science and technology, education, energy, transportation, and credit and finance.

Headquarters: Beijing, China.

Principal Organs: Heads of State Council, Heads of Government Council, Council of National Coordinators, Secretariat, Regional Counter-Terrorism Structure.

Web site: www.sectsco.org

Secretary General: Dmitry Fedorovich Mezentsev (Russia).

Membership (6): China, Kazakhstan, Kyrgyzstan, Russia, Tajikistan, Uzbekistan.

Observers (5): Afghanistan, India, Iran, Mongolia, Pakistan.

Dialogue Partners (3): Belarus, Turkey, Sri Lanka.

Official Languages: Chinese, Russian.

Origin and development. The Shanghai Cooperation Organization (SCO) grew out of a less formal grouping, the so-called Shanghai Five, comprised of China, Kazakhstan, Kyrgyzstan, Russia, and Tajikistan, whose heads of state had been meeting annually since April 1996. This association was concerned with improving mutual trust in their border regions, as well as coordinating policy on other military and security topics. In July 2000 the president of Uzbekistan, Islam Karimov, attended a Shanghai Five meeting as an observer. When the SCO was founded in 2001, Uzbekistan joined as a full member.

An aim of the SCO from its earliest days, unstated but recognized on all sides, was to counteract the influence of the United States in the region. The June 2001 meeting endorsed the Anti-Ballistic Missile (ABM) Treaty, which the U.S. government wanted to scrap. The anti-American tendency was initially most noticeable in China. The anti-American sentiment of the SCO members was disrupted almost immediately after the SCO's formation by the September 11, 2001, terrorist attacks in New York and the Washington, D.C., area. The first meeting of the SCO, held September 13–14, condemned the September 11 attacks and declared its willingness to work with all countries to counter the global threat of terrorism.

When the group's foreign ministers met in Beijing on January 2, 2002, U.S. forces were already in Afghanistan and some Central Asian SCO members were giving them logistical support. At a June 7, 2002, summit in Moscow, the heads of state adopted the SCO Charter. This document formally established the SCO as an international organization with definite aims and a permanent secretariat.

From August 8 to 12, 2003, all SCO states except Uzbekistan held joint antiterrorism exercises. The 2004 summit was held on June 17 in Tashkent, Uzbekistan. Hamid Karzai, Afghanistan's president, attended the meeting as an observer. The SCO pledged itself to help in rebuilding Afghanistan. It also adopted agreements to combat narcotics trafficking. Similarly, the 2005 summit was held on July 5 in Astana. This was the first summit at which representatives of the observer states were officially present. The meeting attendees urged the United States to set a timetable for removing its bases from SCO member countries.

By 2006 the SCO was attracting increasing international attention, and debate began about whether it might turn into a military alliance—a Central Asian version of the North Atlantic Treaty Organization (NATO). Proponents of this idea pointed to the antiterrorism exercises already held and the plans announced in April 2006 for the entire group to hold war games in Russia. Some maintained that the SCO had adequate economic reasons for existing and a military focus was unnecessary. While Russia might be interested in the bloc as a military counterweight to the United States, Chinahad little such concern.

As a result of the 2006 summit, where Mahmoud Ahmadinejad, president of Iran, attended as an observer, Iran began expressing interest in having full membership in the organization. The meeting approved establishment of the SCO Business Council and Interbank Consortium.

By March 2007 both India and Pakistan were seeking full membership in the SCO. It was also becoming clear that although Russia was very interested in promoting the military side of SCO, other member states were not. The chief of the Russian general staff complained of this lack of interest on the eve of the SCO war games that were held in Russia on August 17, 2007. The games took place at the same time as the 2007 summit, which was held in Bishkek.

In March 2008 Iran formally applied for full membership in the SCO. A meeting of SCO foreign ministers on July 18, 2008 failed to address Iranian membeship or consider ending the moratorium on new full members. Reasons were not clear, but presumably Russia, China, or both, did not approve. The 2008 summit was held August 28 in Dushanbe. It proved a diplomatic setback for Russia, as the meeting failed to endorse Russia's military action in Georgia. For more on activities since 2008, see "Recent Activities," below.

Structure. The SCO exists as a forum for its heads of state to attempt to coordinate policy. The grouping initially concentrated on border, defense, and security policy, but more recently moved into wider economic, social, and geopolitical concerns. It maintains no kind of parliamentary representation, having instead a top-down structure in which the Heads of State Council (HSC) is the highest decision-making body. The HSC meets annually, as does the Heads of Government Council (HGC). Among other functions, the HGC adopts the SCO's annual budget. Among the representatives of the member countries who meet with their peers from time to time are speakers of parliament, secretaries of security councils, foreign ministers, and ministers of defense. There are also meetings of ministers from various sectors, as well as meetings of specialized groups, such assupreme courts. The Council of National Coordinators (CNC) is in charge of coordinating SCO interaction among the member states. The SCO has two permanent bodies: the Secretariat in Beijing and the Regional Antiterrorism Structure in Tashkent, Uzbekistan. The secretary-general is appointed by the HSC for a period of three years. The office rotates among the member states, alphabetically by the Russian alphabet.

Recent Activities. On March 27, 2009, the SCO organized a conference on Afghanistan. The conference, which took place in Moscow, was also attended by UN secretary-general Ban Ki-moon and a delegation from the United States. The SCO members and observers expressed a desire to play a larger part in solving Afghanistan's problems. In mid-April 2009 SCO members conducted a military exercise in Tajikistan, simulating a response to a terrorist attack from Afghanistan.

The 2009 SCO summit was held in Yekaterinburg, Russia, from June 15–16. As a response to the global economic crisis, China promised a $10 billion loan to Kazakhstan, Uzbekistan, Kyrgyzstan, and Tajikistan. SCO also welcomed Sri Lanka as a new Dialogue Partner.

Over winter 2009–2010 Pakistan reiterated its interest in becoming a full member of SCO. At the June 10–11 summit, held in Tashkent, leaders from the observer states were for the first time included in a restricted meeting of the SCO Heads of State Council. Among other things, the summit discussed ways in which SCO might help stabilize the situations in Afghanistan and Kyrgyzstan. The meeting also addressed qualifications for membership. SCO was an open organization, though membership was restricted to countries from the SCO region. No country could gain full membership if UN sanctions were outstanding against it. Hence Iran could only be an observer.

By late 2010 some felt that SCO was becoming less relevant. Medvedev attended the November 20 NATO summit in Lisbon. There he signed a declaration that Russia and NATO were no longer a threat to each other and agreed to cooperate with NATO's program to build an antimissile defense system. This system would protect against attack from Iran and North Korea.

On June 15, 2011, the heads of state met to discuss the possibility of increasing economic integration in the future. The November 2011 annual summit, held in Saint Petersburg, Russia, saw further discussion of the global economy, emerging technology, and further security cooperation among the member states and other neighboring states.

In June 2012, the heads of state met in Beijing to discuss several initiatives, such as increased cooperation in the field of agriculture and the advancement of multilateral economic and financial cooperation in the region. The heads of state also called for continued progress on setting up the SCO Development Bank. At that meeting, Dmitry Fedorovich Mezentsev was selected as the next Secretary-General of SCO. Mezentsev began his three-year term January 1, 2013.

SCO has recently sought to expand its membership. A committee has been established to discuss expansion procedures and met regularly during 2013. SCO decided at its June 2012 summit to admit Afghanistan as an observer state and Turkey as a dialogue partner. Afghanistan joined effective immediately. Turkey formally joined in April 2013. Even though Turkey was admitted as a dialogue partner, they were not invited to attend the 2013 summit held in Bishkek in September. The annual summit was primarily focused on major world issues occurring outside the SCO mandate area. The most pressing issue was in regard to Syria. The organization expressed its commitment to the plan presented by Russian President Vladimir Putin for ridding Syria of chemical weapons. Also at the meeting, India asked to be considered for full membership.

SOUTH ASIAN ASSOCIATION FOR REGIONAL COOPERATION (SAARC)

Established: By charter signed December 8, 1985, in Dhaka, Bangladesh.

Purpose: "[T]o promote the welfare of the peoples of South Asia and to improve their quality of life; . . . to promote and strengthen collective self-reliance among the countries of South Asia; . . . to promote active collaboration and mutual assistance in the economic, social, cultural, technical and scientific fields; . . . and to co-operate with international and regional organizations with similar aims and purposes."

Headquarters: Kathmandu, Nepal.

Principal Organs: Meeting of Heads of State or Government, Council of Ministers, Standing Committee, Programming Committee, Technical Committees, Secretariat.

Web site: www.saarc-sec.org

Secretary General: Ahmed Saleem (Maldives).

Membership (8): Afghanistan, Bangladesh, Bhutan, India, Maldives, Nepal, Pakistan, Sri Lanka.

Observers (9): Australia, Myanmar, China, European Union, Iran, Japan, Mauritius, South Korea, United States.

Origin and development. Prior to the formation of SAARC, South Asia was the only major world region without a formal venue for multigovernmental collaboration. The association was launched on December 8, 1985, in Dhaka, Bangladesh. The summit was convened by recommendation of the ministerial South Asian Regional Cooperation Committee (SARC), formed on August 1983 in New Delhi, India, with subsequent meetings in July 1984 in Malé, Maldives, and in May 1985 in Thimbu, Bhutan. At the conclusion of SAARC's founding session, the participants issued a charter setting forth the objectives of the new grouping and directed that decisions would be made by unanimous vote at annual summits, at which "bilateral and contentious" issues would be avoided.

In light of SAARC's formal repudiation of involvement in purely bilateral concerns, the 1986 summit in Bangalore, India, did not officially address the major conflicts within the subcontinent. Instead, the summit was devoted to discussion of proposed SAARC institutions that would serve to reduce regional tensions through cooperation in such areas as communication, transport, and rural development.

Little SAARC progress was achieved in 1989 and 1990, as national and international conflicts continued to hold center stage in the region. The 1989 summit, scheduled for November in Sri Lanka, was postponed as the result of widespread ethnic violence there, coupled with increased tension between Colombo and New Delhi over the presence of Indian troops. SAARC subsequently attempted to convene the meeting in March 1990, but intensified Indian-Pakistani friction over Kashmir necessitated another postponement. The summit was finally held in November in Malé, although substantive action was limited because India, Nepal, Pakistan, and Sri Lanka had recently installed new governments, and internal turmoil broke out in the other three countries that were members at the time.

The sixth summit eventually convened December 21, 1991, with the heads of state agreeing to "suppress terrorism" while also committing themselves to support "civil and political rights" and to combat poverty in the region. In addition, an intergovernmental group was created to consider ways to dismantle long-standing barriers to trade between SAARC members. Meanwhile a SAARC development fund was discussed, with proponents arguing that "trade and business unity" would help reduce political cleavage in the region.

Unsettled conditions in the region continued to plague SAARC, and the summit scheduled for January 1993 was postponed at the request of Prime Minister Rao. When the summit was finally held April 10–11 in Dhaka, Bangladesh, it was marred by mass demonstrations against Rao and his government's handling of the Hindu-Muslim conflict. The most significant development at the summit was the initialing of a plan to establish the South Asian Preferential Trade Agreement (SAPTA) for reducing or eliminating intraregional trade barriers.

No SAARC summit was held in 1994, primarily because of ongoing turmoil in India (where the meeting was scheduled to be held) and continued friction between SAARC members. When SAARC leaders finally met May 2–4, 1995, in New Delhi, they agreed to proceed with the SAPTA launching, with more than 200 products identified for lower tariff rates. Following ratification by all SAARC states, SAPTA formally went into effect December 8, concurrent with the commemoration of the grouping's tenth anniversary. However, it was widely agreed that SAPTA represented only a modest beginning, and SAARC established an "expert working group" to begin immediately on plans to expand it into the South Asian Free Trade Agreement (SAFTA).

The political question of integration reemerged at the ninth SAARC summit, held May 12–14, 1997, in Malé. The seven heads of state or government agreed that a process of informal political consultations would help their efforts to foster better relations and faster economic integration. Although still officially opposed to a political component within SAARC, India nonetheless reached a bilateral agreement with Pakistan on May 12 within the "SAARC setting." SAARC leaders also agreed to move the formation of SAFTA forward to 2001 from 2005. At that time, approximately 20 percent of the world's population lived within SAARC's borders, but intraregional trade accounted for only 1 percent of the global total.

Following India's and Pakistan's tests of nuclear devices in May 1998, Pakistan again attempted to introduce a political element into SAARC at the tenth summit, held in late July 1998 in Colombo. Pakistani Prime Minister Nawaz Sharif offered changes to the SAARC charter that would allow for bilateral negotiations and establish a regional peace council, but the other members rejected the proposed changes. Although the prime ministers of India and Pakistan met during the summit for the first time since the nuclear tests, the talks were not considered successful. Another focus of the summit was economic integration. SAARC reaffirmed its intention to complete and implement SAFTA in 2001. However, a group of eminent persons appointed by SAARC reported that 2008 was a more realistic date for launching SAFTA.

The 11th SAARC summit, scheduled for November 1999 in Kathmandu, was postponed at India's request following the October coup in Pakistan, and little progress on the organization's major concerns was accomplished in the following two years. A third special session of the Standing Committee met August 9–10, 2001, in Colombo, at which time they adopted a schedule for negotiating additional SAPTA concessions; drafting the SAFTA treaty; and holding meetings (some at the ministerial level) concerned with culture, the environment, health, information, media, telecommunications, and poverty alleviation.

As a further indication of the political differences impeding progress toward SAARC's regional goals, in October 2001 the organization abandoned its efforts to draft a unified statement condemning terrorism and the September 11 attacks against the United States. Once again, India and Pakistan strongly disagreed: India insisted the proposed statement condemn terrorism in Kashmir, whereas Pakistan rejected any such explicit reference to the disputed region.

The 11th SAARC summit was finally held January 5–6, 2002, in Kathmandu, Nepal, the attendees reaffirming their commitment to SAFTA and adopting a convention on preventing trafficking in women and children. However, renewed tension between India and Pakistan prompted postponement of the 12th summit scheduled for January 2003 until January 2004, at which time a new protocol was approved in regard to combating terrorism. SAARC leaders also endorsed tentative draft guidelines for SAFTA, which, fully established, would encompass approximately 20 percent of the world's population. (SAFTA came into force January 1, 2006.) Although the 2004 summit (which also adopted a new social charter) was deemed successful, political considerations again interrupted regional progress in early 2005 when the 13th summit was postponed because of turmoil in Nepal and Bangladesh.

The 13th summit was held November 8–13, 2005, in Dhaka. The participants declared the decade 2006–2015 the SAARC Decade of Poverty Alleviation and decided to establish the SAARC Poverty Alleviation Fund (SPAF) with contributions both voluntary and assessed, as was to be agreed upon in future discussions. Some commentators felt that dealing with trade and economic concerns was SAARC's best way forward, given the intractable political differences between some of its members.

During 2006 and 2007, China, the European Union, Japan, South Korea, and the United States all applied for observer status with SAARC. All five entities were represented at the April 3–4, 2007, summit in New Delhi. Additionally, Afghanistan was admitted as a member. The representatives of India and Pakistan declared that it was time to move beyond their historic antagonism, ending the summit with a feeling of renewed energy in the group and hopes for future South Asian economic and customs unions.

In April 2008 it was announced that SAARC would be creating a database on terrorism and narcotics trafficking, modeled after the Interpol database. The services sector was also said to be ready for inclusion in SAFTA in the near future. In May 2008 Myanmar, formerly known as Burma, applied for full membership in SAARC, as Australia had recently done. Both applications were approved at the organization's 15th summit, held August 2–3 in Colombo. The meeting (for which the Tamil Tiger rebels had proclaimed a truce) also pledged several efforts to speed up regional economic growth. For more on activities since 2008, see "Recent Activities," below.

Structure. General policies are formulated at the annual meeting of heads of state and, to a lesser extent, at the semiannual meetings of the Council of Ministers. Sectoral ministerial meetings may also convene. The Secretariat was established in January 1987 in Kathmandu. Six technical committees address agriculture and rural development, health and population activities, women and youth, science and technology, transportation, and the environment. The committees report to the Standing Committee of foreign secretaries, which prepares recommendations for the Council of Ministers. The Programming Committee was established to assist the Standing Committee, which also oversees SAARC's regional centers. For more details about the SAARC Regional Centers, see the full listing in *Political Handbook of the World* 2012.

Activities. In October 2008 the Afghan representative announced that his country was interested in hosting some SAARC meetings in the near future. In February 2009 the Maldives, scheduled to host the 2009 summit, declared that it would not be able to do so before October, if at all. As a result no summit took place in 2009.

The 16th SAARC summit took place in Thimphu, Bhutan, April 28–29, 2010. Many observers felt that SAARC's 25 years had been a disappointment, with little economic integration achieved. The summit concluded by adopting a 36-point Thimphu Silver Jubilee Declaration that endorsed Bangladesh's proposal for a Charter of Democracy for regional cooperation aimed at strengthening good governance. Under the subtitle of "Building Bridges" the 2011 SAARC summit was held in Addu, Maldives, and attended by all eight member nations. In addition to continued support for the full creation of SAFTA by 2016, four agreements were signed: (1) the Agreement on Rapid Response to Natural Disasters, (2) the Seed Bank Agreement, (3) the Agreement on Multilateral Arrangement on Recognition of Conformity Assessment, and (4) the Agreement on Implementation of Regional Standards. Nepal is slated to host the 18th summit in 2012.

While SAFTA has been functional since 2006, several barriers still exist that prevent it from being as effective as the SAARC ministers would like. At its February 2012 meeting, the SAFTA Ministerial Council called on all of its member states to strive to remove more of the products on their sensitive lists. The sensitive list is a list of items that have a higher tariff in a given country. The higher tariffs on some items result in non-competitive and preferential trading within the region. In March 2012, Ahmed Saleem was elected by the ministerial council to succeed Fathimath Dhiyana Saeed as secretary general of SAARC.

The Eighteenth SAARC summit in Nepal was scheduled for 2013. Despite the efforts taken by the Nepali Government, political conflict in Maldives and upcoming elections in Nepal have forced the meeting to be postponed until at least early 2014. Before the summit can be held, a meeting of the SAARC Interior Ministers must occur, which is set to be hosted in Maldives and has been postponed multiple times. At that meeting of the Inter-Summit in Maldives, the date will be officially set for the conference and Nepal will announce the appointment of the next SAARC Secretary General. In regard to progress on SAFTA implementation, the SAFTA Ministerial Council met in September 2013 to discuss the possibility of a complete economic union and a SAARC Development Bank that would replace the SAARC Development Fund.

SOUTHERN AFRICAN DEVELOPMENT COMMUNITY (SADC)

Established: By the Treaty of Windhoek, signed August 17, 1992, in Windhoek, Namibia, by representatives from the ten members of the former Southern African Development Coordination Conference (SADCC); Agreement Amending the Treaty signed August 14, 2001, in Blantyre, Malawi.

Purpose: To achieve self-sustaining development and economic growth based on collective self-reliance and interdependence; to achieve sustainable use of natural resources while protecting the environment; to promote and defend regional peace and security; to enhance the standard of living through regional integration, including establishing a free trade area.

Headquarters: Gaborone, Botswana.

Principal Organs: Summit Meeting of Heads of State and Government; SADC Tribunal; Council of Ministers; Organ on Politics, Defense and Security Cooperation; Sectoral/Cluster Ministerial Committees; SADC Secretariat; Standing Committee of Senior Officials; SADC National Committees.

Web site: www.sadc.int

Executive Secretary: Dr. Stergomena Lawrence Tax (Tanzania).

Membership (15): Angola, Botswana, Democratic Republic of the Congo, Lesotho, Madagascar, Malawi, Mauritius, Mozambique, Namibia, Seychelles, South Africa, Swaziland, Tanzania, Zambia, Zimbabwe.

Working Languages: English, French, Portuguese.

Origin and development. The SADC originated as the Southern African Development Coordination Conference that convened in July 1979, in Arusha, Tanzania, by Angola, Botswana, Mozambique, Tanzania, and Zambia (the "Front-Line States" opposed to white rule in southern Africa). As a follow-up to the Arusha meeting, the SADCC was formally established during a summit of the heads of state or government of nine countries (the original five plus Lesotho, Malawi, Swaziland, and Zimbabwe) that convened April 1, 1980, in Lusaka, Zambia. Namibia joined the SADCC after achieving independence in 1990.

The SADCC was considered one of the most viable of the continent's regional groupings, although its actual accomplishments were modest compared to its members' development needs. During its first six years, the SADCC concentrated on the rehabilitation and expansion of transport corridors to permit the movement of goods from the interior of the region to ocean ports without the use of routes through South Africa. In 1986, however, SADCC leaders concluded that such infrastructure development would not reduce dependence on South Africa sufficiently unless accompanied by broad, long-term economic growth in the region. Consequently, the SADCC announced that additional emphasis would be given to programs and projects designed to increase production within the private sector and in enterprises with government involvement. It also sought to expand intraregional trade, support national economic reform, and encourage international investment. The program of action eventually encompassed some 500 projects, ranging from small feasibility studies to large port and railway construction projects.

Throughout the 1980s the conference called for the international community to impose comprehensive, mandatory sanctions against Pretoria, South Africa, to protest apartheid. However, consensus was not attained on regional action, such as the severance of air links with Pretoria, primarily because of objections from Lesotho and Swaziland, members whose economies were most directly linked to South Africa.

At their tenth anniversary summit in August 1990, the SADCC leaders discussed proposals to expand the conference's mandate and influence, in part by enhancing the authority of the secretariat. The heads of state, concerned with the region's stagnant export revenue and mounting debt burden, emphasized the need to increase intraregional trade over the next decade. In addition, they endorsed automatic membership for South Africa once apartheid was dismantled.

While participants in the 1991 summit urged that sanctions be continued against Pretoria pending further democratic progress, they endorsed preliminary discussions with representatives of the liberation movements in South Africa regarding future coordination of economic policies. In addition to possible resolution of the South African issue, peace initiatives in Angola and Mozambique were cited by SADCC officials as cause for hope that after three decades of violence the region might be headed for a sustained period of peace. With this in mind, the Treaty of Windhoek was signed on August 17, 1992, transforming the SADCC into the SADC, through which members were to seek development and integration in several areas, leading to a full-fledged common market. Arrangements for the free movement of goods, capital, and labor among members were to be made at an undetermined date. The most ardent SADC integrationists also suggested the community might eventually pursue political union, perhaps through a regional parliament, and security coordination.

One immediate concern for the SADC was its relationship with the Preferential Trade Area for Eastern and Southern African States (PTA), established in 1981 with many of the same goals as those adopted by the SADC. In late 1992, with eight of the (then) ten SADC members also belonging to the PTA (with Botswana and Namibia as exceptions), the PTA called for a merger of the two organizations. Not surprisingly, the SADC Executive Secretariat opposed the proposal, and at a January 1993 meeting the SADC, reportedly concerned over the PTA's history of ineffectiveness, rejected the overture. However, the SADC indicated it would try to avoid duplicating PTA activities, suggesting that the PTA could assume full responsibility for economic cooperation among the 11 "northern," or non-SADC, countries, with the SADC doing the same for its members.

In one of a summer-long series of remarkable international events precipitated by the democratic transition in Pretoria, the SADC accepted South Africa as its 11th member at a summit held in late August 1994 in Gaborone, Botswana. Although they welcomed South Africa to their ranks, the other SADC members reportedly expressed concern they might be overwhelmed by its economic might. The summit also began to weigh greater security responsibilities, addressing such proposals as the creation of a mechanism for the peaceful resolution of conflicts among members and the establishment of regional peacekeeping and defense forces. Thus, the SADC defense ministers in November endorsed the concept of a regional deployment force, which would not be a permanent army but one available for quick mobilization from standing national armies.

The dominant concern for the SADC in 1995 remained the dual membership problem regarding the PTA, an issue further complicated by the recent signing of a treaty establishing the Common Market of Eastern and Southern Africa (Comesa). Although most SADC members signed the treaty, several postponed ratification, while South Africa and Botswana indicated their lack of interest in the alignment. Consequently, the SADC summit held August 28 in Johannesburg, South Africa, called for an immediate joint summit between the SADC and PTA/Comesa to resolve the matter. Meanwhile, SADC leaders endorsed the proposed elimination of trade barriers between SADC members and the establishment of a common SADC currency. The summit also signed a protocol for cooperation in water management and launched negotiations on similar protocols in the areas of tourism and energy. Mauritius became the 12th SADC member in August 1995.

During the summit held August 23–24, 1996, in Maseru, Lesotho, the SADC again declined to merge with Comesa and instead reemphasized its own goal of establishing a Southern Africa Free Trade Area within eight years. (Lesotho and Mozambique subsequently announced they did not intend to ratify the Comesa treaty, and Tanzania eventually dropped out in favor of continued membership in the SADC.) The Seychelles and Democratic Republic of the Congo became the 13th and 14th members on September 8 and 9, 1997, respectively.

The Organ on Politics, Defense, and Security, launched at the 1996 summit, was at the center of controversy during the September 1997 summit, particularly because of its relative independence from the other SADC institutions. South African president Nelson Mandela, chair of the summit, insisted on bringing the organ under the direct control of the summit, while Zimbabwean president Robert Mugabe, chair of the organ, opposed such a move. Mandela also surprised the summit by proposing the SADC punish members via sanctions if they did not adopt the democratic values central to the organization.

An SADC summit in late July 1998 in Namibia attempted to refocus the community's attention on economic cooperation. Attendees pledged to eliminate tariffs and other restrictions on 90 percent of intra-community trade by 2005. However, security matters, particularly the recent outbreak of fighting in the Democratic Republic of the Congo (DRC), returned to the fore at the SADC summit September 13–15 in Mauritius. The SADC summit, at DRC President Laurent Kabila's insistence, refused to meet with the representatives of Rwanda and Uganda (apparent supporters of the DRC rebels) who traveled to Mauritius to discuss the matter.

The SADC's role in domestic affairs became even more clouded shortly after the summit, when first South African and then Botswanan troops entered Lesotho to quell unrest generated by anger over the May election, which was followed by a mutiny within the Lesotho Defense Force (LDF). By May 1999 an advisory team mandated to help retrain and restructure the LDF replaced the troops.

The August 6–7, 2000, summit in Windhoek drew widespread international criticism for a decision to support the Mugabe government's expropriation of white-owned land in Zimbabwe. The summit's final communiqué also focused on such economic concerns as rising external debt, a regional cereal deficit, the HIV/AIDS crisis, and continuing poverty.

The March 9, 2001, summit in Windhoek, in addition to approving the organizational changes called for in a report on restructuring (see Structure, below), elected Mauritian Prega Ramsamy executive secretary as successor to Namibian Kaire Mbuende, who was dismissed in 2000. Held in Blantyre, Malawi, the August 12–14 annual summit again focused on regional security issues, but also formally approved a package of treaty amendments to accommodate the previously accepted structural reforms. In September 2001 South Africa became the first SADC country to implement the free trade protocol signed in 1996 in Maseru. By then, however, the original free trade target date for the community as a whole was pushed back to 2008, when "substantially all" intra-SADC trade was to become tariff free. Exceptions were to be permitted on a country-by-country temporary basis for "sensitive products." Looking further ahead, the SADC introduced a customs union in 2010 and plans on introducing a full common market in 2015.

A January 14, 2002, extraordinary summit in Blantyre focused on conflicts and security matters in the DRC, Angola, and especially Zimbabwe. At the October 2–3, 2002, summit in Luanda, Angola, the SADC took no substantive action with regard to Zimbabwe, the main issue under discussion being drought and a resultant food crisis that was severely affecting Lesotho, Malawi, Mozambique, Swaziland, Zambia, and Zimbabwe.

In 2003, the Seychelles, citing its inability to pay its annual membership fee, announced its intention to withdraw as of mid-2004. By the August 25–26, 2003, summit in Dar es Salaam, Tanzania, the food crisis had abated, and the SADC turned its focus to economic and social planning, adopting a blueprint called the Regional Indicative Strategic Development Plan (RISDP). The summit also adopted the SADC Charter on Fundamental Social Rights, the Strategic Indicative Plan for the Organ (SIPO), and a mutual defense pact. The defense pact provided for collective action against armed attack and denied support to groups seeking the destabilization of other members, but it continued to uphold the principle of nonintervention in members' internal affairs.

A meeting of the Council of Ministers March 12–13, 2004, in Arusha, Tanzania, officially launched the RISDP, which included among its economic concerns food security, sustainable growth, trade promotion, regional integration, and development of transport and communications infrastructure. To further emphasize the importance given to combating food shortages and chronic malnutrition, the SADC scheduled an extraordinary summit on agriculture and food security for May 2004. In mid-2004, Madagascar expressed its interest in joining, and the 2005 summit welcomed it as its 14th member.

In the wider international sphere, the SADC and the European Union (EU) continue to hold biennial ministerial meetings. Negotiations on an SADC/EU Economic Partnership Agreement opened in 2004 in Windhoek. These discussions took a different direction in March 2006 when the SADC asked the EU to negotiate a bilateral agreement with the SADC, as opposed to holding discussions about joining a larger agreement between the EU and less-developed countries.

At the August 2005 summit in Gabarone, Botswana, Tomaz Augusto Salomao of Mozambique was appointed as the new SADC executive secretary. Other activity included the appointment of the first five members of the SADC tribunal. Also in 2005 the SADC activated the first of five planned standby brigades of SADC peacekeeping forces.

As negotiations with the EU and Africa's several economic blocs began to intensify in 2006, membership by some countries in multiple, competing blocs became a significant issue. The EU would not allow a country to be a part of more than one Economic Partnership Agreement (EPA), and membership in multiple customs unions could cause great difficulties. Salomao declared that all members must decide to which bloc they would belong by 2010, when the SADC customs union comes into effect. In March 2007 the SADC signed a Memorandum of Understanding with the United States, paving the way for increased U.S. aid and consultancy to help the SADC implement a free trade area by 2008.

At the 27th summit of SADC heads of state, held in Lusaka, Zambia, August 16–17, 2007, the Seychelles was readmitted to membership. But in September 2007, Rwandaannounced that it was no longer interested in joining SADC, preferring to work instead with Comesa.

A pressing problem facing the SADC in 2007 and 2008 was the deteriorating situation in Zimbabwe. In March 2007 SADC appointed South African president Thabo Mbeki to mediate between government and opposition parties in Zimbabwe. Mbeki met with Zimbabwean president Robert Mugabe numerous times in late 2007 and throughout the electoral crisis of 2008 (see separate article on Zimbabwe), but had little success in stopping the violence. In July 2008 a "reference group" of senior diplomats was created to help Mbeki.

The SADC as an organization also received much criticism for its failure to confront Mugabe with more energy. Mugabe walked out of the August 2007 Lusaka summit after exchanging harsh words with Zambian president Levy Mwanawasa when the latter tried to put the situation in Zimbabwe on the meeting's agenda. Mugabe did not attend an SADC meeting that Mwanawasa organized in April 2008, complaining that representatives of the Zimbabwean opposition parties had been invited. As chair of SADC, Mwanawasa rejected attempts to expel Zimbabwe, but in June 2008 described the SADC's failure to take a firmer line with Mugabe as "scandalous." Negotiations at the August 16–17, 2008, summit in Sandton, South Africa, failed to move talks of power-sharing in Zimbabwe forward. Botswana president Ian Khama boycotted the meeting because Mugabe was present, calling Mugabe's presidency "illegitimate."

On January 1, 2008, the SADC Free Trade Area (FTA) came into effect, and most goods were able to move between SADC countries without import duties. Some smaller SADC countries worried that the FTA would cause their economies to be swamped by the regional powerhouse South Africa.

The SADC continued contacts with Mugabe. In September 2008 Mbeki and the SADC mediated a power-sharing agreement, with Mugabe to be president and Tsvangirai prime minister. This agreement only marked the start of many months of wrangling about the allocation of cabinet posts. A meeting on November 9 in South Africa between the rivals and the SADC produced a ruling that Tsvangirai's party must share control of the Home Affairs ministry, including the police, with Mugabe's party. Mugabe would remain in control of the army and security services. The unity government was finally formed at the end of January 2009, but wrangling continued late into the year. For more on activities since 2008, see "Recent Activities," below.

Structure. Under the terms of the Lusaka Declaration issued in 1980, individual members of the SADCC were assigned coordinating roles over specified economic concerns. Thus, in July 1980 the conference's first operational body, the Southern African Transport and Communications Commission, was formed under Mozambique's leadership. For a listing of the other state assignments, see the 2013 *Handbook*. When the SADC was established to replace the SADCC in 1992, it was decided to keep the existing SADCC structure intact for the time being, with a few additional or reassigned sectorial responsibilities. Other changes were made in response to the community's post-apartheid regional security concerns, which led in mid-1996 to creation of the Organ on Politics, Defense, and Security. The objectives of the organ included fostering cooperation with regard to issues of law and order, defending against external aggression, and promoting democracy. The organ was also authorized to mediate domestic disputes and conflicts between members.

At an extraordinary summit held March 9, 2001, in Windhoek, the SADC approved a report on restructuring that called for phasing out within two years the nearly two dozen sector coordinating units and replacing them with four directorates: trade, finance, industry, and investment; infrastructure and services; food, agriculture, and natural resources; and social and human development and special programs. The structural reform was viewed as essential to advancing regional integration and strategic planning, efficient use of available resources, and equitable distribution of responsibilities.

Under the reorganization, the SADC's chief policymaking organ, the Summit Meeting of Heads of State or Government, convenes at least once per year, with the position of chair rotating annually. Between summit meetings, policy responsibility rests on a troika of the SADC chair, his predecessor, and his successor, with other national leaders co-opted as needed. The Organ on Politics, Defense, and Security Cooperation was given a rotating chair, with the organ's internal structure and functions detailed in a Protocol on Politics, Defense, and Security Cooperation that was signed at the August 2001 summit. The Council of Ministers remains responsible for policy implementation and organizational oversight. The Standing Committee of Senior Officials, comprising a permanent secretary from each member country, serves as a technical advisory body to the council, with an emphasis on planning and finance.

In addition, the restructuring called for creation of the Integrated Committee of Ministers (ICM) to ensure "proper policy guidance, coordination and harmonization of cross-sectoral activities." The ICM, replacing the Sectoral Committee of Ministers, is primarily responsible for overseeing and guiding the work of the new directorates. It answers to the council and includes at least two ministers from each SADC state. To provide policy coordination, particularly with regard to interstate politics and international diplomacy, a new body, the Ministers of Foreign Affairs, Defense, and Security, was subsequently added to the SADC structure.

Duties of the Executive Secretariat, which is headed by an executive secretary, include strategic planning, management of the comprehensive SADC program of action, and general administration. At the individual state level, representatives of government, the private sector, and civil society meet as SADC national committees to provide input to the central SADC organs and to oversee programs within each jurisdiction.

During the 2000 summit, SADC leaders signed a protocol establishing an SADC tribunal, as provided for in the founding treaty. The tribunal has responsibility for interpreting the treaty and subsidiary documents and for adjudicating disputes between members.

Recent Activities. In other Zimbabwean affairs, Mugabe continued to seize white-owned farms during 2009. A group of 79 white farmers appealed to the SADC tribunal, which supported them. On September 2 Zimbabwe announced that it would not be bound by tribunal decisions.

In economic news, the SADC came to an agreement on October 22, 2008, with the East African Community (EAC) and Comesa to create a 26-nation free-trade zone, stretching uninterrupted from Egypt to South Africa.

The matter of the white Zimbabwean farmers continued into 2010. In January a Zimbabwean court rejected the SADC tribunal's judgment. The farmers appealed to the tribunal again in March. The tribunal ruled in their favor, and the South African authorities handed the ownership documents of a Cape Town house belonging to Zimbabwe's government to the farmers. The house was to be sold if the government of Zimbabwe did not pay the farmers' legal fees. On June 2 the farmers again approached the tribunal, asking that Zimbabwe be suspended or expelled from the SADC for ignoring the tribunal's rulings. The tribunal declared Zimbabwe in contempt and referred the matter to the August 16–17 SADC summit, held in Windhoek.

However, on August 3, prior to the summit, the South African Justice and Constitutional Affairs Minister asked for a legal opinion on the legal reach of SADC tribunal rulings, both in South Africa and Zimbabwe. The summit later ordered a six-month review of the "role, functions and terms of reference" of the tribunal. There were rumors that the tribunal judges' terms would not be renewed, and the tribunal effectively disbanded. In November the SADC's actions in respect to the tribunal came under legal challenge in South Africa. Whatever the outcome, many felt that the SADC had shown itself unwilling to stand up to Robert Mugabe, and that the group's standing was seriously compromised.

The 31st summit was held in Luana, Angola August 17–18, 2011. The summit opened with new elections for several SADC organs. Angola's president, Jose Eduardo dos Santos, and Armando Emilio Guebuza, president of Mozambique, were elected as SADC Chair and Deputy Chair, respectively. Additionally, Jacob Gedleyihlekisa Zuma, president of South Africa, was elected as chair of the SADC Organ on Politics, Defense and Security Cooperation. The summit also voiced support for ongoing discussions that started in June 2011 for the Tripartite Free Trade area between Comesa, EAC, and SADC.

Political unrest in Madagascar between the eleven competing factions has consumed the attention of the SADC in much of 2011 and 2012. SADC appointed a special mediator to help the various parties come to a consensus about restoring constitutional order. In March 2011, eight of the smaller factions signed an SADC negotiated agreement that called for a new government with the goal of new elections in 2012. The agreement excluded the main opposition parties, however, and failed to solve many problems. In September 2011, ten of the competing groups signed a roadmap agreement that called for a new national unity government to be in place by November. Despite the agreements, progress remained stalled, and at a June 1, 2012, extraordinary session of the Heads of State or Government focused on regional security issues, SADC placed a July 31 deadline on the country to set a date for the new elections. SADC hosted a meeting between the two opposing sides of the government to settle disputes over elections on July 24–25, but no decision was finalized.

In July 2012, SADC approved a tripartite agreement on the Comesa (see separate article) Climate Control Programme for joint implementation between Comesa, the EAC, and the SADC. The tripartite agreement set a five-year goal for implementation of all components of the climate change programme, including increasing renewable energy and expanding environmentally friendly agricultural practices.

From summer 2012 into 2013, much of the SADC's focus was on issues of regional security and democracy. In August, the SADC convened for its annual summit in Mozambique, which largely focused on the political unrest in the region. The SADC called for an end to the violence in the Democratic Republic of the Congo and approved a mission to Rwanda to help bring about a negotiated end to Rwandan assistance of the armed rebels. In Madagascar, the organization called for the Malagasy people to implement the roadmap fully and continue its progress toward elections in May. Concerning Zimbabwe, the group noted the progress that had been made toward adopting a new constitution and called on the international community to fully lift its sanctions on the state. The meeting also discussed progress in areas of economics, HIV and AIDS prevention, and food security.

The political unrest in the DRC, Madagascar, and Zimbabwe continued to be a priority for the SADC. Two extraordinary summits of the Heads of State or Government were held, one in December 2012 and another in May 2013, to address these situations. In regard to Madagascar, both summits urged the transition government to diligently pursue legitimate elections and called on former presidents to withdraw their candidatures for the sake of moving forward. In regards to the DRC, the summits continued to condemn the violence in that state and issued an urgent call for humanitarian relief from the rest of the international community. An SADC Intervention Brigade was deployed to the DRC in February under a UN mandate as a peacekeeping operation. In Zimbabwe, the organization commended the progress made by the state concerning the implementation of the Global Political Agreement and implementing a new constitution.

The 2013 annual summit met in August under the chairmanship of the Malawi government. The meeting continued to see an emphasis on political unrest, noting the urgent need for continued action in the DRC, but expressing commendation for the progress made in Madagascar and Zimbabwe. The summit also noted with great concern the July removal of the constitutional government in Egypt. The summit also discussed the deteriorating economic performance and called for member states to take strides toward economic growth and increased food production. In addition to policy matters, SADC also elected a new executive secretary, Dr. Stergomena Lawrence Tax of Tanzania.

SOUTHERN CONE COMMON MARKET (MERCOSUR/MERCOSUL)

Nemby Nemuha
Mercado Común do Cono Sur
Mercado Comum de Cone Sul

Established: By treaty signed March 26, 1991, in Asunción, Paraguay, by the presidents of Argentina, Brazil, Paraguay, and Uruguay.

Purpose: To establish a regional "common market of the southern cone" through the harmonization of policies in agriculture, industry, finance, transportation, and other sectors; to promote economic development through expanded extraregional trade and the pursuit of foreign investment.

Headquarters: Montevideo, Uruguay.

Principal Organs: Council of the Common Market, Common Market Group, Joint Parliamentary Commission, Secretariat.

Web site: www.mercosur.int (in Spanish and Portuguese only)

Secretary General: None—Secretary General Samuel Pinheiro Guimarães resigned in the middle of the 2012 Annual summit, and as of October 2013, no successor has been named.

Membership (6): Argentina, Brazil, Bolivia, Paraguay, Uruguay, Venezuela.

Associate Members (6): Chile, Colombia, Ecuador, Guyana, Peru, Suriname.

Observer (2): Mexico, New Zealand.

Official Languages: Guaraní, Portuguese, Spanish.

Origin and development. The idea of a regional common market was first advanced in the late 1980s by Argentina and Brazil, which had signed a series of bilateral agreements that they hoped could be extended to other countries. Supporters of the concept also argued that a regional bloc would be helpful in taking advantage of the Enterprise for the Americas Initiative recently announced by U.S. president George H. W. Bush. Paraguay and Uruguay responded positively to the integration overtures from their larger neighbors, but Chile, expressing concern about the volatility of Brazil's economy, declined to join the grouping.

The Treaty of Asunción was signed March 26, 1991, with ratification by the members' legislatures completed by September. Membership discussions continued thereafter with Bolivia and Chile, one proposal being that they be given associate status pending expiration of a five-year moratorium on new memberships.

Although negotiations during Mercosur's first year of existence on a proposed common external tariff were unproductive, significant progress was achieved in reducing intraregional tariffs. By the end of 1992 annual intraregional trade had jumped by an estimated 50 percent, although a substantial portion of the increase resulted from a vast influx of Brazilian goods into Argentina. The December Mercosur summit accepted further cuts in intraregional tariffs.

At their fifth summit, held January 17, 1994, in Montevideo, Uruguay, the Mercosur heads of state again expressed their confidence in the common market's future. No immediate progress was reported on what became the major sticking point in Mercosur negotiations—the common external tariff. With Brazil apparently standing firm in its demand for substantial tariffs on such products as computers, telecommunications equipment, and petrochemicals, some negotiators predicted that external tariff arrangements could not be completed by the January 1, 1995, target date. However, intensive negotiations later in the year yielded sufficient agreement for the Mercosur presidents to sign the Protocol of Ouro Prêto on December 17 in Ouro Prêto, Brazil, providing for the launching of the intraregional free trade zone and common external tariff on January 1. Free trade within Mercosur was established for approximately 85 percent of the products under consideration, with the other items scheduled to decline to zero within four to five years. In regard to the common external tariff, duties of from 0 to 20 percent were applied to most imports from outside the region. Plans were also endorsed for further discussions toward monetary integration and the coordination of industrial and agricultural policies.

Mercosur subsequently attracted substantial interest from other regional groupings. The European Union (EU) signed a cooperation agreement in December 1995 with Mercosur, pledging to pursue a reduction in EU-Mercosur tariffs as well as broader economic, scientific, and social consultation.

Meanwhile, Chilean officials continued to pursue duty-free trade with Mercosur countries that would not affect Chilean tariffs on products from other nations, and on October 1, 1996, Chile became an associate member of Mercosur, subject to intraregional free trade provisions but excluded from Mercosur's external tariff arrangements. Bolivia's eligibility was complicated by its participation in the Andean Group (subsequently the Andean Community of Nations—CAN) because the Treaty of Asunción forbids dual regional affiliations. Despite this, Bolivia was accorded observer status in 1994 and became an associate member in January 1997.

Throughout 1997 Mercosur engaged in a series of meetings with Andean countries to create a free trade zone between the two groupings. A Mercosur summit in late July 1998 in Argentina reaffirmed its commitment to the proposed South American free trade zone. However, Mercosur was unable to resolve two issues for its own members: how to regulate the regional automobile market and how to settle Brazil's complaint over Argentina's tariffs on Brazilian sugar. On the political front, the presidents pledged to keep the region free of weapons of mass destruction and signed the Ushuaia Protocol on July 14, which committed the members to appropriate standards of democratic governance and threatened expulsion for noncompliance.

The June 30, 2000, summit in Buenos Aires was broadly viewed as an effort to revitalize Mercosur. Chile, despite reservations about what it regarded as the group's high external tariff, announced that it intended to seek full membership. On September 1, at a meeting of South American presidents in Brasília, Brazil, participants called for introduction of a South American free trade area in the "briefest term possible." The year concluded with a December 8 Mercosur summit in Florianópolis, Brazil, where the major news was a decision to suspend membership talks with Chile, given that country's decision to pursue a bilateral trade accord with the United States.

The tenth anniversary Mercosur summit convened June 20–21, 2001, in Asunción. Highlights included an agreement to cut the common external tariff by one point, to 12.5 percent, by January 1, 2002, and to establish a disputes tribunal. Also at the summit, Venezuelan president Hugo Chávez formally submitted his country's application for associate membership.

At the July 4–5, 2002, summit in Buenos Aires, Mercosur voiced firm support for Argentina's efforts to overcome its economic crisis, criticized the United States for a lack of attention to the needs of Latin America, and welcomed to the session Mexican president Vicente Fox, who argued for a Mexican-Mercosur tariff-free zone. Trade negotiations with the Andean Community continued to gain momentum. At the 23rd summit, held December 5–6 in Brasília, a framework agreement with CAN was signed, although some quarters expressed frustration that a detailed pact had yet to be concluded.

At the end of 2002, Brazil's president-elect Luiz Inácio da Silva called for strengthening Mercosur through such measures as raising Bolivia and Chile to full membership and creating a directly elected Mercosur parliament.

At the June 18–19, 2003, summit in Asunción, Mercosur set 2006 as the target date for establishing the parliament. The parliament actually opened in May 2007. Peru concluded an associate agreement in August 2003 and officially became the third associate member in December 2003.

The 25th summit, held December 16–17, 2003, in Montevideo, was highlighted by completion of a ten-year free trade agreement with CAN members Colombia, Venezuela, and Peru. The session also marked Peru's entry as an associate member of Mercosur, an agreement to that effect having been concluded August 25. In 2005 Venezuela officially petitioned to become a full Mercosur member.

Conflict between Argentina and Uruguay over the construction on the Uruguayan side of the Uruguay River of two cellulose plants has been a central issue for Mercosur since 2005. The plants represent the largest foreign investment in Uruguay's history (approximately $1.7 billion) and are funded by European investors. The Argentines object to the plants on environmental grounds. Uruguay believes the matter should be settled via the conflict resolution mechanisms of Mercosur, while Argentina claims it is a bilateral matter that should be settled in The Hague. Argentina formally filed papers at The Hague in early May 2006.

The prospect of Venezuela's accession, and that country's increased involvement with the organization, caused an immediate leftward turn in Mercosur politics. By the time of the January 19, 2007, meeting in Rio de Janeiro, the bloc's new direction became more apparent, with Chávez proposing a shift in policy toward helping the region's poor and developing a "Socialism for the 21st century." Also at this time, Bolivia and Ecuador, both countries with suspicions about free trade, were said to be interested in gaining full membership in Mercosur.

In April 2007 the first South American energy summit was held in Venezuela. At this meeting it was agreed that work should start on merging Mercosur and the Andean Community (see separate article) into a bloc to be known as the Union of South American Nations (UNASUR), with headquarters in Quito, Ecuador. Uruguay continued to criticize Mercosur's new political direction, even as a new Mercosur parliament opened in Montevideo in May 2007. In early July Chávez declared that Venezuela was not interested in full membership unless the organization was prepared to break with "U.S.-style capitalism." Mexico (an observer state) had expressed interest in closer association, but in July da Silva said that would be difficult as long as Mexico was a member of the North American Free Trade Association (NAFTA).

During the December summit Mercosur asked the EU to relax its trading rules to encourage a better dialogue. At the same time the EU agreed to donate €50 million ($33 million) to the organization. The summit ended with a declaration committing the organization to speeding up Venezuela's accession to full membership. In December 2007 Mercosur and Israel signed an agreement liberalizing trade between them.

The July 2, 2008, summit, held in Tucumán, Argentina, focused on the rising prices of energy and food. At the summit Hugo Chávez offered to create an agricultural development fund for the region, donating one dollar for every barrel of oil that Venezuela sold at over $100 per barrel. The summit also saw the group united in indignation over a new EU law concerning illegal immigration. This law, which came into effect in 2010, allows for illegal immigrants to be detained for up to 18 months and to be banned from reentry on any terms for five years. The Mercosur heads of state issued a joint statement condemning "every effort to criminalize irregular migration and the adoption of restrictive immigration policies, in particular against the most vulnerable sectors of society, women and children."

The December 16–17, 2008, summit, held in Costa do Sauipe, Brazil, addressed, but failed to resolve, one the group's most vexing problems, that of double taxation of goods that are imported from outside Mercosur, then passed from one member state to another. While all concerned recognized that charging customs duties inside the group violated the principle of a common market, it proved impossible to work out the modalities of distributing the cost of the external tariff around the member countries. For more on activities since 2008, see "Recent Activities," below.

Structure. The Council of the Common Market, comprised of members' foreign and economic ministers, is responsible for policy decisions. Negotiations with third parties are carried out under the auspices of the Common Market Group (*Grupo Mercado Común*), comprised of four regular members and an equal number of deputy members from each country. Working under the direction of the ministers of foreign affairs, the group is assisted by the Mercosur Trade Commission, which also sees to the enforcement of "common trade policy instruments for the operation of the customs union." The Mercosur parliaments are represented in the Joint Parliamentary Commission, and there also is an Economic-Social Consultative Forum. The administrative Secretariat, assisted by several technical committees, was established in 1992 in Montevideo, Uruguay.

Recent Activities. The July 2009 summit, held July 23–24 in Paraguay, came amidst general acknowledgment that on economic matters the group was making very slow progress. Various bilateral disputes between members persisted. Matters moved faster on the political front, where the member states refused to recognize the regime that had ousted the president of Honduras, as well as promising not to recognize the results of any future potentially fraudulent elections in that country. In December 2009 it disavowed the recent presidential elections in that country. Mercosur also recognized Guaraní, the indigenous language of Paraguay, as one of its three official languages. Venezuela's application for full membership made little progress, several Mercosur members being unsure of Venezuela's democratic credentials. In late 2009 the Brazilian Senate ratified Venezuela's admission, but in January 2010 Paraguay declined to move on ratification. There the matter rests.

In June 2010 the EU moved to reopen trade negotiations with Mercosur. There was progress, in spite of protests both from Argentina and France about food imports from the other side. The Mercosur region's economic growth over the preceding years had made it a less unequal negotiating partner, however, and by late September EU officials were expressing confidence in an early agreement. In August 2010 Mercosur signed a trade agreement with Egypt, after six years of negotiation.

The August 3, 2010, summit in San Juan, Argentina, witnessed the signing of a customs agreement binding on all members. Some said this agreement effectively turned Mercosur into a customs union.

An October 19 meeting of Mercosur foreign ministers agreed to revitalize and democratize the languishing Mercosur parliament by reassigning its seats on a basis of proportional representation. This redistribution was to be complete by 2015. The presidents of the Mercosur member states met in Foz de Iguaco, Brazil, December 14–16, 2010. The leaders signed a range of agreements, including measures to create standard policies on immigration, financial markets, and automobile manufacturing.

In June 2011 Mercosur issued a statement that rejected British commitments to maintain sovereignty over the Falkland Islands. At its December summit in Montevideo, Uruguay, Mercosur agreed to allow member states to individually raise tariffs on goods imported from outside the trade bloc in an effort to protect domestic industries. Mercosur also signed a free trade agreement with the Palestinian Authority. At the meeting the bloc's leaders renewed their call for Paraguay's legislature to approve Venezuela's membership. The summit was marred by the apparent suicide of Argentine deputy foreign trade minister Ivan Heyn during the conference.

At the December 2011 summit, Argentina assumed the presidency of Mercosur. The heads of state voted at the summit to raise import tariffs to thirty-five percent in an effort to keep trade within Mercosur to help the struggling economies of the Mercosur states. The summit also yielded a resolution to prevent any British ships coming from the Falkland Islands to enter any port within a Mercosur state. This resolution is significant because it agrees to enforce this policy by using all measures possible.

The year 2012 saw increased tension between Uruguay and Mercosur as a whole. Argentina gradually installed a series of trade restrictions that the Uruguayan government feels are targeted at decreasing exports from Uruguay to Argentina. Then in April, Uruguay announced that it did not agree with the blockade of the Falkland Islands, and stated that it would still trade with the islands. In May, three former Uruguay presidents admitted that Mercosur had failed and left Uruguay trapped. This came just two weeks after Uruguay Vice President Danilo Astori claimed that Mercosur was going through its worst time in history.

In June 2012, Mercosur gathered in Mendoza, Argentina, for its biannual summit. In light of recent political disorder in Paraguay after the removal of President Fernando Lugo in early June, Mercosur voted to suspend Paraguay from membership and its summit meeting. The members also voted to approve Venezuela's application for full membership, making them the fifth Mercosur member state. Venezuela's membership became effective July 31. Perhaps the most significant action of the Mercosur summit was the surprise resignation of Secretary General Samuel Pinheiro Guimaraes. Pinheiro Guimaraes resigned after a major disagreement with the Brazilian foreign minister and what he expressed as the member states' failure to consider his proposals.

In December 2012 the presidents of the member states approved Bolivia's accession to Mercosur. Bolivia became the sixth member of Mercosur, although Paraguay remained on suspension.

At their 2013 biannual summit meeting, held in Montevideo, Uruguay, the heads of state voted to restore Paraguay's membership and terminate the suspension in light of successful elections. The organization also approved the applications of Guyana and Suriname to become associate members. Furthermore, the organization condemned the United States for international espionage, and called for the matter to be considered by the UN Security Council, citing American actions as a violation of international law. The heads of state also spent a great deal of time discussing the necessary steps to move forward with political and economic integration within the Mercosur realm.

UNITED NATIONS (UN)

Established: By charter signed June 26, 1945, in San Francisco, United States, effective October 24, 1945.

Purpose: To maintain international peace and security; to develop friendly relations among states based on respect for the principle of equal rights and self-determination of peoples; to achieve international cooperation in solving problems of an economic, social, cultural, or humanitarian character; and to harmonize the actions of states in the attainment of these common ends.

Headquarters: New York, United States.

Principal Organs: General Assembly (all members), Security Council (15 members), Economic and Social Council (54 members), Trusteeship Council (5 members), International Court of Justice (15 judges), Secretariat.

Web site: www.un.org

Secretary General: Ban Ki-Moon (South Korea).

Membership (193): See Appendix C.

Official Languages: Arabic, Chinese, English, French, Russian, Spanish. All are also working languages.

Origin and development. The idea of creating a new intergovernmental organization to replace the League of Nations was born early in World War II and first found public expression in an Inter-Allied Declaration signed on June 12, 1941, in London, England, by representatives of five Commonwealth states and eight European governments-in-exile. Formal use of the term United Nations first occurred in the Declaration by United Nations, signed on January 1, 1942, in Washington, D.C., on behalf of 26 states that subscribed to the principles of the Atlantic Charter (August 14, 1941) and pledged their full cooperation for the defeat of the Axis powers. At the Moscow Conference on October 30, 1943, representatives of China, the Union of Soviet Socialist Republics (USSR), the United Kingdom, and the United States proclaimed that they "recognized the necessity of establishing at the earliest practicable date a general international organization, based on the principle of the sovereign equality of all peace-loving states, and open to membership by all such states, large and small, for the maintenance of international peace and security." In meetings at Dumbarton Oaks in Washington, D.C., between August 21 and October 7, 1944, the four powers reached agreement on preliminary proposals.

Meeting from April 25 to June 25, 1945, in San Francisco, California, representatives of 50 countries participated in drafting the United Nations Charter, which was formally signed June 26. Poland was not represented at the San Francisco Conference but later signed the charter and is counted among the 51 "original" UN members. Following ratification by the five permanent members of the Security Council and most other signatories, the charter entered into force October 24, 1945. The General Assembly, which convened in its first regular session January 10, 1946, accepted an invitation to establish the permanent home of the organization in the United States; privileges and immunities of the UN headquarters were defined in a Headquarters Agreement with the U.S. government signed June 26, 1947.

The membership of the UN, which increased from 51 to 60 during the period 1945–1950, remained frozen at that level for the next five years as a result of U.S.-Soviet disagreements over admission. The deadlock was broken in 1955 when the superpowers agreed on a "package" of 16 new members: four Soviet-bloc states, 4 Western states, and 8 "uncommitted" states. Since then, states have normally been admitted with little delay. The exceptions are worth noting. The admission of the two Germanies in 1973 led to proposals for admission of the two Koreas and of the two Vietnams. Neither occurred prior to the formal unification of Vietnam in 1976, and action in regard to the two Koreas was delayed for another 15 years. On November 16, 1976, the United States used its 18th veto in the Security Council to prevent the admission of the Socialist Republic of Vietnam, having earlier in the same session, on June 23, 1976, employed its 15th veto to prevent Angola from joining (the United States subsequently relented, and Angola gained admission). In July 1977 Washington dropped its objection to Vietnam's membership.

With the admission of Brunei, the total membership during the 39th session of the General Assembly in 1984 stood at 159. The figure rose to 160 with the admission of Namibia in April 1990, fell back to 159 after the merger of North and South Yemen in May, advanced again to 160 via the September admission of Liechtenstein, and returned to 159 when East and West Germany merged in October. Seven new members (Democratic People's Republic of Korea, Estonia, Federated States of Micronesia, Latvia, Lithuania, Marshall Islands, and Republic of Korea) were admitted September 17, 1991, at the opening of the 46th General Assembly. Eight of the new states resulting from the collapse of the Soviet Union (Armenia, Azerbaijan, Kazakhstan, Kyrgyzstan, Moldova, Tajikistan, Turkmenistan, and Uzbekistan) were admitted March 2, 1992, along with San Marino. Russia announced the previous December that it was assuming the former USSR seat. Three of the breakaway Yugoslavian republics (Bosnia and Herzegovina, Croatia, and Slovenia) were admitted May 22. Capping an unprecedented period of expansion, Georgia became the 179th member on July 31.

The total increased to 180 with the dissolution of Czechoslovakia on January 1, 1993, and the separate entry of the Czech Republic and Slovakia on January 19. On April 8 the General Assembly approved the admission of "the former Yugoslav Republic of Macedonia," the name being carefully fashioned because of the terminological dispute between the new nation and Greece (see separate article on Macedonia). Monaco and newly independent Eritrea were admitted May 28, followed by Andorra on July 28. Palau, which achieved independence following protracted difficulty in concluding its U.S. trusteeship status (see section on Trusteeship Council), became the 185th member December 15, 1994. Kiribati, Nauru, and Tonga were admitted September 14, 1999, and Tuvalu joined September 5, 2000.

A change of government in October 2000 led to the November 1, 2000, admission of the Federal Republic of Yugoslavia (FRY). On September 22, 1992, the General Assembly, acting on the recommendation of the Security Council, decided the FRY could not automatically assume the UN membership of the former Socialist Federal Republic of Yugoslavia. The assembly informed the FRY that it would have to apply on its own for UN membership, and such an application was submitted the following day. However, no action on the request was taken by the assembly because of concern over the Federal Republic's role in the conflict in Bosnia and Herzegovina and, later, its actions regarding the ethnic Albanian population in the Yugoslavian province of Kosovo. As a consequence, the FRY was excluded from participation in the work of the General Assembly and its subsidiary bodies. Throughout this period, however, the UN membership of the Socialist Federal Republic of Yugoslavia technically remained in effect. A certain ambiguity, apparently deliberate, surrounded the issue, permitting the FRY and others to claim that it was still a member, although excluded from active participation, while some nations argued that the membership referred only to the antecedent Yugoslavian state. In any event, the flag of the Socialist Federal Republic of Yugoslavia, which was also the flag of the FRY, continued to fly outside UN headquarters with the flags of all other UN members, and the old nameplate remained positioned in front of an empty chair during assembly proceedings. In October 2000 the Security Council, in a resolution recommending admission of the FRY, acknowledged "that the State formerly known as the Socialist Federal Republic of Yugoslavia has ceased to exist." A representative of the FRY took up the empty seat, and a new FRY flag replaced that of the former Yugoslavia.

On September 10, 2002, the UN admitted Switzerland, which had long maintained a permanent observer mission at UN headquarters and had actively participated as a full member of the various UN specialized and related agencies. The Swiss government, having concluded that UN membership in the post–Cold War era would not jeopardize its long-standing international neutrality, sought admission after winning majority support from Swiss voters at a March 2002 referendum. Timor-Leste became the 191st member on September 27.

In 2003 the FRY became the "state union" of Serbia and Montenegro, which dissolved in June 2006, following a successful independence referendum in Montenegro. Accordingly, on June 28 the world's newest independent state, Montenegro, was admitted as the UN's 192nd member. Serbia, as the successor state to the state union, retained the UN seat held to that point by the FRY.

The Holy See (Vatican City State) has formal observer status in the General Assembly and maintains a permanent observer mission at UN headquarters. In July 2004 the UN granted the Holy See the full range of membership privileges, with the exception of voting.

In July 2007 Taiwan formally applied for membership in the UN. The application marked the first effort by the island nation to gain membership as Taiwan and not the Republic of China. The bid was rejected by the UN legal affairs office on the grounds that General Assembly Resolution 2758 granted sole representation for China to the People's Republic of China. The General Assembly subsequently approved by consensus the recommendation of the legal affairs office in September. After 16 consecutive annual failures, in September 2009 Taiwan announced that it would not seek membership in the UN.

Following its self-declared independence from Serbia in February 2008, Kosovo sought membership in the UN (see "Security Council"). However, in September Serbia, which considered the Kosovar declaration of independence to be illegal, asked the General Assembly to refer Kosovo's status to the International Court of Justice (ICJ). In a vote on the Serbian motion on October 9, 77 members supported the proposal, 6 opposed it, and 74 abstained. In July 2010 the ICJ ruled in favor of Kosovar independence, declaring that it did not violate international law (see "ICJ"). The General Assembly subsequently approved an EU-sponsored resolution that called for renewed dialogue between Serbia and Kosovo prior to further negotiations on UN membership.

On January 12, 2010, 83 UN staff and employees died during an earthquake in Haiti in the largest loss of life in a single day in the history of the world body (see "Secretary General").

The Republic of South Sudan formally seceded from Sudan on July 9, 2011, as a result of an internationally monitored referendum held in January 2011 and was admitted as the 193rd member by the United Nations General Assembly on July 14, 2011. Meanwhile, in May, the European Union (EU), a permanent observer, was given additional powers in the General Assembly, including the right to participatein debatesand submit proposals.

On September 23, 2012, Palestine requested full membership in the UN (see the 2013 *Handbook* for more information on Palestine's status prior to 2012). The United States threatened to veto the bid, and negotiations continued into 2012. Meanwhile, the United Nations Educational, Scientific and Cultural Organization (UNESCO) voted to admit Palestine as a full member (see "UNESCO") on October 31. On November 29, the General Assembly voted 138 to 9, with 41 abstentions, to grant the Palestine National Authority status as a non-member observer state over opposition by Israel, Canada and the United States, among others. The new designation gave Palestine the same same status as the Vatican. Under pressure from the United States, Palestine subsequently agreed not to press for full UN membership until April 2014 in order to continue negotiations with Israel (see entry on Israel).

Structure. The UN system can be viewed as comprising (1) the principal organs, (2) subsidiary organs established to deal with particular aspects of the organization's responsibilities, (3) a number of specialized and related agencies, and (4) a series of ad hoc global conferences to examine particularly pressing issues.

The institutional structure of the principal organs resulted from complex negotiations that attempted to balance both the conflicting claims of national sovereignty and international responsibility and the rights of large and small states. The principle of sovereign equality of all member states is exemplified in the General Assembly; that of the special responsibility of the major powers, in the composition and procedure of the Security Council. The other principal organs included in the charter are the Economic and Social Council (ECOSOC), the Trusteeship Council (whose activity was suspended in 1994), the International Court of Justice (ICJ), and the Secretariat.

UN-related intergovernmental bodies constitute a network of Specialized Agencies established by intergovernmental agreement as legal and autonomous international entities with their own memberships and organs and which, for the purpose of "coordination," are brought "into relationship" with the UN. While sharing many of their characteristics, the International Atomic Energy Agency (IAEA) remains legally distinct from the Specialized Agencies; the World Trade Organization, which emerged from the UN-sponsored General Agreement on Tariffs and Trade (GATT), has no formal association with the UN.

The proliferation of subsidiary organs was caused by many complex factors, including new demands and needs as more states attained independence; the effects of the Cold War and its end; a greater concern with promoting economic and social development through technical assistance programs (almost entirely financed by voluntary contributions); and a resistance to any radical change in international trade patterns. For many years, the largest and most politically significant of the subordinate organs were the United Nations Conference on Trade and Development (UNCTAD) and the United Nations Industrial Development Organization (UNIDO), which were initial venues for debates, for conducting studies and presenting reports, for convening conferences and specialized meetings, and for mobilizing the opinions of nongovernmental organizations. They also provided a way for less developed states to formulate positions in relation to the industrialized states. During the 1970s both became intimately involved in activities related to program implementation, and on January 1, 1986, UNIDO became the UN's 16th Specialized Agency.

One of the most important developments in the UN system has been the use of ad hoc conferences to deal with major international problems. (Conferences are discussed under General Assembly: Origin and development and within entries for various General Assembly Special Bodies or UN Specialized Agencies.)

GENERAL ASSEMBLY

Membership (193): All members of the United Nations (see Appendix C).

Observers (77): African, Caribbean, and Pacific Group of States; African Development Bank; African Union; Agency for the Prohibition of Nuclear Weapons in Latin America and the Caribbean; Andean Community of Nations; Asian-African Legal Consultative Organization; Asian Development Bank; Association of Caribbean States; Association of Southeast Asian Nations; Black Sea Economic Cooperation Organization; Caribbean Community; Central American Integration System; Collective Security Treaty Organization; Common Fund for Commodities; Commonwealth of Independent States; Commonwealth Secretariat; Community of Portuguese-Speaking Countries; Community of Sahelo-Saharan States; Conference on Interaction and Confidence Building Measures in Asia; Cooperation Council for the Arab States of the Gulf; Council of Europe; East African Community; Economic Community of Central African States; Economic Community of West African States; Economic Cooperation Organization; Energy Charter Conference; Eurasian Development Bank; Eurasian Economic Community; European Organization for Nuclear Research; European Union; Global Fund to Fight AIDS, Tuberculosis, and Malaria; GUUAM; Hague Conference on Private International Law; Holy See; Ibero-American Conference; Indian Ocean Commission; Inter-American Development Bank; Inter-Parliamentary Union; International Center for Migration Policy Development; International Committee of the Red Cross; International Criminal Court; International Criminal Police Organization; International Development Law Organization; International Federation of Red Cross and Red Crescent Societies; International Fund for Saving the Aral Sea; International Hydrographic Organization; International Institute for Democracy and Electoral Assistance; International Olympic Committee; International Organization for Migration; International Organization of Francophones (*Organisation Internacionale de la Francophonie*); International Seabed Authority; International Tribunal for the Law of the Sea; International Union for the Conservation of Nature and Natural Resources; Islamic Development Bank; Italian–Latin American Institute; Latin American Economic System; Latin American Integration Association; Latin American Parliament; League of Arab States; Organization for Economic Cooperation and Development; Organization for Security and Cooperation in Europe; Organization of American States; Organization of Eastern Caribbean States; Organization of the Islamic Conference; Organization of Petroleum Exporting Countries Fund for International Development; Pacific Islands Forum; Palestine (formerly designated as the observer mission of the Palestine Liberation Organization); Partners in Population and Development; Permanent Court of Arbitration; Regional Center on Small Arms and Light Weapons in the Great Lakes Region, the Horn of Africa and Bordering States; Shanghai Cooperation Organization; South Asian Association for Regional Cooperation; South Center; Southern African Development Community; Sovereign Military Order of Malta; University for Peace; World Customs Organization.

Origin and development. The General Assembly can consider any matter within the scope of the charter or relating to the powers and functions of any organ provided for in the charter. It can also make corresponding recommendations to the members or to the Security Council, although it cannot make recommendations on any issue the Security Council has under consideration unless requested to do so by that body.

The General Assembly's prominence in the UN system results from the vigorous exercise of its clearly designated functions and to its assertion of additional authority in areas (most notably the maintenance of peace and security) in which its charter mandate is ambiguous. Since all members of the UN participate in the assembly on a one-country–one-vote basis, resolutions passed in the organ have varied considerably as the membership has changed. Thus, while the assembly's early history was dominated by Cold War issues, the rapid expansion of the membership to include less developed and developing countries—which now comprise an overwhelming majority—led to a focus on issues of decolonization and, more recently, development.

As the colonial period ended, UN attention focused increasingly on problems of colonialism and racial discrimination in certain southern African territories, including the Portuguese dependencies of Angola, Mozambique, and Portuguese Guinea (subsequently Guinea-Bissau); Southern Rhodesia (Zimbabwe); and Namibia. During the 1960s the assembly moved from general assertions of moral and legal rights in this area to condemnations of specific governments, accompanied by requests for diplomatic and economic sanctions and threats of military sanctions. In 1972 the assembly "condemned," for the first time, violations by the United States of Security Council sanctions against importing chrome and nickel from Southern Rhodesia. In December 1976 the assembly took the unprecedented action of passing a resolution endorsing "armed struggle" by Namibians. Subsequently, a number of peace proposals were discussed, culminating in a 1978 UN plan for Namibian independence, which would take another 12 years to achieve. In December 2000 the General Assembly marked the 40th anniversary of the 1960 decolonization declaration by declaring 2001–2010 to be the Second International Decade for the Eradication of Colonialism. The resolution passed by a vote of 125–2 (the United Kingdom and the United States in opposition), with 30 abstentions.

The assembly's work in development formally began with a proposal by U.S. president John F. Kennedy that the 1960s be officially designated as the UN Development Decade. The overall objective of the decade was the attainment in each less developed state of a minimum annual growth rate of 5 percent in aggregate national income. To this end, the developed states were asked to make available the equivalent of 1 percent of their income in the form of economic assistance and private investment. By 1967 it had become clear that not all objectives would be achieved by 1970, and a 55-member Preparatory Committee for the Second UN Development Decade was established by the General Assembly in 1968 to draft an international development strategy (IDS) for the 1970s. While the publicity surrounding the demand for a new international economic order (NIEO), particularly at the 1974, 1975, and 1980 special sessions of the General Assembly, tended to overshadow the IDS, the latter maintained its effectiveness, establishing quantitative targets for the Second Development Decade and on other issues such as human development, thus remaining the single most comprehensive program of action for less developed states. The Third Development Decade began January 1, 1981.

During the Second and Third Development Decades, the assembly increasingly concentrated on North-South relations, with an emphasis on economic links between advanced industrialized countries (often excluding those having centrally planned economies) and less developed countries. Major discussion topics, all of them integral to the NIEO, included international monetary reform and the transfer of real resources for financing development; transfer of technological and scientific advances, with specific emphasis on the reform of patent and licensing laws; restructuring of the economic and social sectors of the UN system; expansion of no-strings-attached aid; preferential and nonreciprocal treatment of less developed states' trade; recognition of the full permanent sovereignty of every state over its natural resources and the right of compensation for any expropriated foreign property; the regulation of foreign investment according to domestic law; supervision of the activities of transnational corporations; a "just and equitable relationship" between the prices of imports from and exports to less developed states ("indexation"); and enhancement of the role of commodity-producers' associations. Efforts were also made to launch a comprehensive discussion of development issues through global negotiations. Although several UN special sessions have been held on this topic, advanced and developing countries have disagreed on the necessity, scope, and utility of such talks.

In 1990 the General Assembly acknowledged widespread failure in reaching many of its 1980 goals, blaming "adverse and unanticipated developments in the world economy," which had "wiped out the premises on which growth had been expected." In launching the Fourth UN Development Decade (effective January 1, 1991), the assembly warned that major international and national policy changes were needed to "reactivate" development and reduce the gap between rich and poor countries. The plan called for priority to be given to the development of human resources, entrepreneurship, and the transfer of technology to the developing countries. Because the earlier targets had proven unrealistic, the new strategy established "flexible" objectives that could be revised as conditions warranted.

The charter entrusts both the General Assembly and the Security Council with responsibilities concerning disarmament and the regulation of armaments. Disarmament questions have been before the organization almost continuously since 1946, and a succession of specialized bodies was set up to deal with them. Among those currently in existence are the all-member Disarmament Commission, established in 1952 and reconstituted in 1978, and the 65-member Conference on Disarmament (known until 1984 as the Committee on Disarmament), which meets in Geneva, Switzerland. The UN played a role in drafting the Treaty Banning Nuclear Weapon Tests in the Atmosphere, in Outer Space, and Under Water (effective October 1963), as well as the Treaty on the Non-Proliferation of Nuclear Weapons (effective March 1970). The Second Special Session on Disarmament, held June–July 1982 at UN headquarters, had as its primary focus the adoption of a comprehensive disarmament program based on the draft program developed in 1980 by the Committee on Disarmament. Although the session heard messages from many of the world's leaders, two-thirds of the delegations, and almost 80 international organizations, no agreement was reached on the proposal.

The assembly met in special session May–June 1988 in another attempt to revise and update its disarmament aims and priorities. As in 1982, however, no consensus was reached on a final declaration. "Irreconcilable differences" were reported between Western countries and developing nations (usually supported by the Soviet bloc) on several issues, including conventional arms controls in said nations, proposed curbs on space weapons, nuclear-weapon-free zones, and nuclear arms questions pertaining to South Africa and Israel. However, negotiations were successfully completed in September 1992 during the Conference on Disarmament on a Convention on the Prohibition of the Development, Production, Stockpiling and Use of Chemical Weapons and on Their Destruction. The convention was endorsed by the General Assembly in November, was opened for signature in January 1993, and entered into effect April 29, 1997, six months after the 65th ratification. Accordingly, the Organization for the Prohibition of Chemical Weapons (OPCW), based in The Hague, Netherlands, began operations to oversee implementation of the convention. The highest OPCW organ, the Conference of States Parties, met for the first time in May 1997; responsibility for the organization's day-to-day activities has been delegated to a 41-member Executive Council. As of September 2013 instruments of ratification or accession had been deposited by 189 states.

Negotiations on a Comprehensive Nuclear-Test-Ban Treaty (CTBT) began in 1993 and concluded with its adoption on September 10, 1996, by the General Assembly. The CTBT was opened for signature September 24, and the five declared nuclear powers—China, France, Russia, the United Kingdom, and the United States—were among the initial signatories. A notable exception was India, which had exploded its first nuclear device in 1974 and whose August decision to reject the treaty was strongly condemned. As of September 2013, 183 countries had signed the CTBT, but its rejection by the U.S. Senate in October 1999 left the treaty in limbo: 161 countries have ratified it, including 36 of the 44 states having nuclear power or research reactors, but all 44 must ratify the treaty for it to enter into effect, at which time a Comprehensive Nuclear-Test-Ban Treaty Organization (CTBTO) would begin operations.

On December 3, 1997, in Ottawa, Canada, the Convention on the Prohibition of the Use, Stockpiling, Production, and Transfer of Anti-Personnel Mines and on Their Destruction (the Ottawa Convention) was signed. Although a protocol of the 1981 Conventional Weapons Convention had established limits on land mines, it had not called for an outright ban on their use. The Ottawa Convention entered into force March 1, 1999, sufficient signatory states having deposited their ratifications. As of September 2013 the United States was not one of the 161 countries to have ratified the document, in large part because of what it continued to see as the necessity of land mine use in the frontier between North and South Korea. As of September 2013, 25 nations were declared to be mine-free under the convention's certification process.

UN activity in regard to human rights also dates virtually from the organization's founding. The assembly's 1948 adoption of the Universal Declaration of Human Rights marked perhaps the high point of UN action in this field. Subsequently, the Commission on Human Rights directed efforts to embody key principles of the declaration in binding international agreements. These efforts culminated in two human rights covenants—one dealing with economic, social, and cultural rights, and the other with civil and political rights—both of which came into force in January 1976.

On October 3, 1975, concern for human rights was, for the first time, explicitly linked with nationalism in the form of a resolution contending that Zionism is a form of "racism and racial discrimination." After considerable parliamentary maneuvering, the resolution passed November 10 by a vote of 72–35, with 32 abstentions. Sixteen years later, in only the second such reversal in its history, the assembly voted 111–25, with 13 abstentions, to revoke the Zionism resolution.

The Commission on Human Rights sponsored a World Conference on Human Rights June 14–25, 1993, in Vienna, Austria. It was attended by a reported 5,000 delegates from 111 countries and numerous intergovernmental and nongovernmental organizations. The conference's final declaration encouraged the General Assembly to appoint a commissioner for human rights. The proposed creation of the Office of the UN High Commissioner for Human Rights (OHCHR) generated considerable controversy at the 1993 General Assembly session. China and several developing countries, many of which had been accused of human rights violations in the past, initially attempted to block the Western-led initiative. A compromise was eventually reached under which the assembly unanimously agreed to establish the office while leaving the extent of the new commissioners authority "purposely vague." In February 1994 Secretary General Boutros Boutros-Ghali of Egypt appointed José Ayala Lasso of Ecuador as the first high commissioner, a choice criticized by some human rights advocates because Ayala Lasso had served as a foreign minister under the military regime in Ecuador in the late 1970s. He was succeeded in 1997 by Mary Robinson, former president of Ireland, who in May 2001 was reelected for an additional year, until September 2002. She had declined renomination for a second four-year term after complaining the office lacked the power needed to effectively advance human rights. On September 12, 2002, she was succeeded by Brazilian diplomat Sergio Vieira de Mello, who had most recently served as a special representative of the UN secretary general in Kosovo and then in East Timor. Vieira de Mello was killed in August 2003 while temporarily serving as a special representative of the secretary general in Iraq. His successor, Louise Arbour, had previously served as a justice of the Canadian Supreme Court. She assumed the office on July 1, 2004, and was replaced by Navanethem Pillay of South Africa on September 1, 2008, who was renewed for a second term to begin on September 1, 2012.

Questions relating to outer space are the province of a 69-member Committee on the Peaceful Uses of Outer Space, established by the General Assembly in 1960 to deal with the scientific, technical, and legal aspects of the subject. In addition to promoting scientific and technical cooperation on many space endeavors, the committee was responsible for the adoption of the Treaty on Principles Governing the Activities of States in the Exploration and Use of Outer Space Including the Moon and Other Celestial Bodies (entered into force October 10, 1967), and the Agreement on the Rescue of Astronauts, the Return of Astronauts and the Return of Objects Launched into Outer Space (entered into force December 3, 1968). Three additional treaties have since been adopted. The General Assembly has also adopted five sets of "Legal Principles" based on the committee's work, which cover use of satellites for television broadcasting, nuclear power sources in outer space, remote sensing, and international cooperation in the exploration and use of outer space. Beginning in 2007 the committee became increasingly involved in the promotion of outer space technologies to address climate change, including monitoring and measurement of resources.

Oceanic policy has also become a major UN concern. In 1968 the General Assembly established a 42-member Committee on the Peaceful Uses of the Seabed and the Ocean Floor. Detailed and controversial negotiations in this area ensued, most notably in conjunction with the Third UN Conference on the Law of the Sea (UNCLOS), which held 11 sessions during 1973–1982 devoted to the formulation of a highly complex UN Convention on the Law of the Sea. The convention addressed a wide range of issues, such as territorial rights in coastal waters, freedom of passage through strategic sea routes, and the exploitation of seabed resources. Delegates to the tenth session (August 1981) in Geneva reluctantly agreed to discuss several sensitive issues about which the U.S. Ronald Reagan administration had expressed reservations. Although the 440 articles of the proposed treaty had received consensual approval during previous UNCLOS sessions, the United States demanded that such items as the regulation of deep-sea mining and the distribution of members for a proposed International Seabed Authority (ISA) be reexamined before it would consider approving the document.

Following a year-long review of the proposed treaty, Washington ended its absence with the presentation of a list of demands and revisions to be discussed at the 11th session. Although compromises were reached in several disputed areas, other differences remained unresolved, including the rights of retention and the entry of private enterprises to seabed exploration and exploitation sites, mandatory technology transfers from private industry to the ISA, and amending procedures. On April 30, 1982, the treaty was approved by 130 conference members, with 17 abstentions and 4 voting against, including Israel, Turkey, the United States, and Venezuela. The treaty was opened for ratification and signed by 117 countries on December 10.

The Preparatory Commission was charged with establishing the two main organs of the convention—the ISA and the International Tribunal for the Law of the Sea. In addition, the General Assembly in 1983 created the Office of the Special Representative of the Secretary General for the Law of the Sea, whose functions included carrying out the central program on law of the sea affairs, assisting states in consistently and uniformly implementing the convention's provisions, and providing general information concerning the treaty.

China, France, India, Japan, the Republic of Korea, and Russia (as successor to the Soviet Union) were registered by the Preparatory Commission as the initial "pioneer investors" under a program established to recognize national investments already made in exploration, research, and development work related to seabed mining. Pioneer investors were entitled to explore allocated portions of the international seabed but had to wait until the convention entered into force to begin commercial exploitation.

Led by the United States, many states that had not signed the convention won a renegotiation in 1994 of the contentious section authorizing the proposed ISA to control seabed mining and allocate profits from it. Washington subsequently signed the agreement concerning seabed mining and indicated that it was prepared to sign the convention itself. (As of 2012, however, the United States was the only major maritime country that was still a provisional member of the ISA and not a party to the convention.) The convention finally entered into effect November 16, 1994, one year after receiving the required 60th ratification from among its 159 signatories. On the same date the International Seabed Authority was formally launched at its headquarters in Kingston, Jamaica. It was agreed that an assembly comprising all authority members would be the supreme organ of the ISA. The assembly is authorized to select a 36-member council, which serves as an executive board; a secretary general; and the 21 judges of the International Tribunal for the Law of the Sea, designated to rule on disputes regarding provisions of the convention.

Elections for the 21 judges of the tribunal were held August 1, 1996, and they were sworn in the following October in Hamburg, Germany. On November 16, 1998, the ISA terminated the membership of all provisional members (then eight countries, including, notably, the United States, which had yet to become parties to the convention), thereby reducing the authority's membership to 130. The status of the former provisional members was downgraded to that of observer to the assembly. Both the ISA and the tribunal subsequently completed agreements with the UN whereby they became autonomous organizations with close ties to the UN. As of September 2013, the ISA had 166 members and 34 observer states.

The UN Convention on the Law of the Sea also established the Commission on the Limits of the Continental Shelf (CLCS) in New York, with 21 members elected by the parties to the convention. The first members were elected in March 1997 for five-year terms. The commission's purpose is to review members' plans to expand activities on the continental shelf beyond 200 miles off their shores.

Structure. All members of the UN, each with one vote, are represented in the General Assembly, which now meets for a full year in regular session, normally commencing the third Tuesday in September. Special sessions (convenable, contrary to earlier practice, without formal adjournment of a regular session) may be called at the request of the Security Council, of a majority of the member states, or of one member state with the concurrence of a majority. Twenty-eight such sessions have thus far been held: Palestine (1947 and 1948); Tunisia (1961); Financial and Budgetary Problems (1963); Review of Peace-Keeping Operations and Southwest Africa (1967); Raw Materials and Development (1974); Development and International Economic Cooperation (1975, 1980, and 1990); Disarmament (1978, 1982, and 1988); Financing for UN Forces in Lebanon (1978); Namibia (1978 and 1986); the Economic Crisis in Africa (1986); Apartheid in South Africa (1989); Illegal Drugs (1990 and 1998); Follow-up on the 1992 Earth Summit (1997); Population and Development (1999); Small Island Developing States (1999); Women: Gender Equality, Development, and Peace for the Twenty-First Century (2000); Social Development (2000); Implementation of the Habitat Agenda (2001); HIV/AIDS (2001); Children (2002); and Commemoration on the 60th Anniversary of the Liberation of the Nazi Concentration Camps (2005). The General Assembly may convene a follow-up to a special session. For instance, in 2007, a plenary meeting was held to follow up on the 2002 session that created the "A World Fit for Children" action plan. The 2007 session issued a new declaration on the protection of children that was subsequently adopted by 140 countries.

Under the "Uniting for Peace" resolution of November 3, 1950, an emergency special session may be convened by nine members of the Security Council or by a majority of the UN members in the event that the Security Council is prevented, by lack of unanimity among its permanent members, from exercising its primary responsibility for the maintenance of international peace and security. The seventh, eighth, and ninth such sessions dealt, respectively, with the question of Palestine (July 22–29, 1980), negotiations for Namibian independence (September 3–14, 1981), and the occupied Arab territories (January 29–February 5, 1982). The tenth, on Israeli actions in the occupied territories, opened on April 24–25, 1997, and has reconvened repeatedly, most recently in January 2009.

The General Assembly elects the ten non-permanent members of the Security Council; the members of ECOSOC; and, together with the Security Council (but voting independently), the judges of the International Court of Justice. On recommendation of the Security Council, it appoints the secretary general and is empowered to admit new members. The assembly also approves the UN budget, apportions the expenses of the organization among the members, and receives and considers reports from the other UN organs.

At each session the General Assembly elects its own president and 21 vice presidents; approves its agenda; and distributes agenda items among its committees, which are grouped by its rules of procedure into three categories: Main, Procedural, and Standing.

All member states are represented on the six Main Committees: First Committee (Disarmament and International Security), Second Committee (Economic and Financial), Third Committee (Social, Humanitarian, and Cultural), Fourth Committee (Special Political and Decolonization), Fifth Committee (Administrative and Budgetary), and Sixth Committee (Legal). Each member has one vote; decisions are taken by a simple majority. Resolutions and recommendations approved by the Main Committees are returned for final action by a plenary session of the General Assembly, where each member again has one vote but where decisions on "important questions"—including recommendations on peace and security questions; election of members to UN organs; the admission, suspension, and expulsion of member states; and budget matters—require a two-thirds majority of the members present and voting. Agenda items not referred to a Main Committee are dealt with directly by the assembly in plenary session under the same voting rules.

There are two Procedural (Sessional) Committees. The General Committee, which is comprised of 28 members (the president of the General Assembly, the 21 vice presidents, and the chairs of the six Main Committees), draws up the agenda of the plenary meetings, determines agenda priorities, and coordinates the proceedings of the committees. The Credentials Committee, which consists of nine members, is appointed at the beginning of each assembly session and is responsible for examining and reporting on credentials of representatives.

The two Standing Committees deal with continuing problems during and between the regular sessions of the General Assembly. The Advisory Committee on Administrative and Budgetary Questions (16 members) handles the budget and accounts of the UN as well as the administrative budgets of the Specialized Agencies; the Committee on Contributions (18 members) makes recommendations on the scale of assessments to be used in apportioning expenses. The members of each Standing Committee are appointed on the basis of broad geographical representation, serve for terms of three years, retire by rotation, and are eligible for reappointment.

The General Assembly is also empowered to establish subsidiary organs and ad hoc committees. Apart from the Special Bodies, dozens of such entities of varying size presently deal with political, legal, scientific, and administrative matters. Those of an essentially political character (with dates of establishment) include the UN Conciliation Commission for Palestine (1948), the Special Committee of 24 on Decolonization (1961), the Committee on the Elimination of Racial Discrimination (1965), the Special Committee on Peacekeeping Operations (1965), the Special Committee to Investigate Israeli Practices Affecting the Human Rights of the Palestinian People and Other Arabs of the Occupied Territories (1968), the Ad Hoc Committee on the Indian Ocean (1972), the Special Committee on the Charter of the United Nations and on the Strengthening of the Role of the Organization (1975), the Committee on the Exercise of the Inalienable

Rights of the Palestinian People (1975), the Committee on Information (1978), the Advisory Board on Disarmament Matters (1978), the Disarmament Commission (1978), the Conference on Disarmament (1978), the Committee on the Elimination of Discrimination against Women (1982), the Committee against Torture (1984), the Trade and Development Board (1995), the UN Open-ended Informal Consultative Process on Oceans and the Law of the Sea (UNICPO, 1999), and the United Nations Peacebuilding Commission (2005). Subsidiary groups dealing with legal matters include the International Law Commission (1947); the Advisory Committee on the UN Program of Assistance in Teaching, Study, Dissemination, and Wider Appreciation of International Law (1965); the UN Commission on International Trade Law (1966); the Committee on the Rights of the Child (1989); the Ad Hoc Committee on Terrorism (1997); and the Ad Hoc Committee on a Comprehensive and Integral International Convention on Protection and Promotion of the Rights and Dignity of Persons with Disabilities (2002). Those dealing with scientific matters include the Committee on the Peaceful Uses of Outer Space (1959) and the UN Scientific Committee on the Effects of Atomic Radiation (1955). Subsidiary groups dealing with administrative and financial matters include the Board of Auditors (1946), the Investments Committee (1947), the International Civil Service Commission (1948), the UN Administrative Tribunal (1949), the UN Joint Staff Pension Board (1948), the Panel of External Auditors (1959), the Joint Inspection Unit (1966), the Working Group on the Financing of the UN Relief and Works Agency for Palestinian Refugees in the Near East (UNRWA, 1970), the Committee on Relations with the Host Country (1971), and the Committee on Conferences (1974).

There are also a number of "open-ended" Working Groups considering the following: the Question of Equitable Representation and Increase in the Membership of the Security Council (1993), the Financial Situation of the United Nations (1994), the Causes of Conflict and the Promotion of Durable Peace and Sustainable Development in Africa (1999), the Integrated and Coordinated Implementation and Follow-up to the Major UN Conferences and Summits in the Economic and Social Fields (2003), and the Ad Hoc Working Group on the Revitalization of the General Assembly (2010).

In March 2006 the General Assembly established a Human Rights Council (UNHRC) as a subsidiary body of the General Assembly and made it directly accountable to and elected by the full membership of the UN. It replaced the controversial Commission on Human Rights, which had been one of ECOSOC's Functional Commissions. However, through 2012, the UNHCR had condemned only one country, Israel, for human rights abuses and remained unable to pass proposed resolutions on human rights violations in a number of other states, although it expressed "concern" over Sudan. This led many critics to contend that the body was no more effective than its predecessor. Beginning in 2008, the UNHRC began conducting a periodic review of all member states. The first round of reviews was scheduled to take four years. In March 2009 the United States announced it would be a candidate for election to the UNHRC, marking a reversal of the policy of the administration of President George W. Bush. The United States was subsequently elected to the UNHRC for a three-year term in May. On September 15, 2009, the UNHRC issued its final report on the 2008–2009 Gaza Conflict. The report determined that both Israeli security forces and Palestinian militias, including Hamas, had been guilty of crimes against humanity. The report called for those suspected to have been involved in the war crimes to be turned over to the International Criminal Court for prosecution. On March 21, 2013, the UNHRC approved on a vote of 25 to 13, with 8 abstentions, a resolution that was critical of Sri Lanka's actions during the final period of that country's civil war which ended in May 2009 (see entry on Sri Lanka).

Activities. The 55th session, which opened on September 11, 2000, was preceded by the Millennium Summit, held September 6–8 and attended by some 150 heads of state and government in the largest such gathering in history (for activities prior to 2000, please see the 2010 *Handbook*). Described as a "working summit," the meeting provided an opportunity for bilateral talks between government leaders as well as for the signing of various treaties and conventions. The summit's final declaration reaffirmed the role of the United Nations and its charter as "indispensable foundations of a more peaceful, prosperous, and just world" and committed the signatories to honor "fundamental" values: freedom, equality, solidarity, tolerance, respect for nature, and a shared responsibility for economic and social development.

Presided over by Harri Holkeri of Finland, the 55th regular session focused on globalization, authorized a June 2001 special session on HIV/AIDS, adopted resolutions on measures to eliminate international terrorism and on severing the link between illicit trade in diamonds and armed conflict, examined East Timor's ongoing transition to full independence, admitted Tuvalu as the 189th UN member, and accepted the Federal Republic of Yugoslavia as a full participant in the General Assembly. The long-standing issue of U.S. dues arrears and the scale of assessments for the regular budget ($2.54 billion for the 2000–2001 biennium) reached an apparent resolution in December. The U.S. share having been reduced from 25 percent to 22 percent of the budget (with the resultant 2001 shortfall to be offset by a voluntary contribution of some $34 million from Ted Turner), Washington agreed to begin paying its $1.3 billion in arrears. A new, complicated formula for funding peacekeeping operations was also accepted; the U.S. contribution would initially drop from 30 percent to 27 percent.

Major developments also occurred with regard to the International Criminal Court (ICC), the first permanent international tribunal with jurisdiction to try individuals for genocide, war crimes, and crimes against humanity. (For a discussion of existing nonpermanent courts, see Security Council: International Criminal Tribunals.) By the end of 2000, 139 states had signed the ICC Statute (also known as the Rome Statute), including the United States. Washington nevertheless remained concerned about removing its soldiers and officials from the court's jurisdiction, and the new George W. Bush administration was not expected to submit the treaty for Senate ratification. Indeed, on May 6, 2002, the Bush administration formally withdrew the U.S. signature from the Rome Statute. A month earlier, on April 11, the minimum 60 ratifications had been surpassed, and on July 1 the founding statute entered into effect and the ICC became a reality. Meeting on September 3–10, the Assembly of States Parties to the statute took a host of actions, including adopting rules of evidence and procedure; reviewing the specific genocidal crimes, crimes against humanity, and war crimes laid out in the Rome Statute; confirming procedures for the election of judges to the court; and approving an initial budget.

The court was inaugurated March 11, 2003. In February the 89 states that had ratified the founding treaty elected 18 judges to varying initial terms of three, six, and nine years. (Of the five permanent members of the Security Council, only France and the United Kingdom had completed ratifications.) The judges proceeded to elect a president, Philippe Kirsch of Canada, and two vice presidents, and on April 21 the Assembly of States Parties elected Luis Moreno-Ocampo of Argentina as chief prosecutor. On September 12 the ICC assembly established a Permanent Secretariat, with the UN Secretariat therefore concluding its services to the assembly at the end of the calendar year.

Meanwhile, the United States continued exerting financial pressure on signatory countries to exempt U.S. citizens from being turned over to the ICC. By July 2003 more than 40 ICC members had signed bilateral agreements to that effect with Washington, which threatened to suspend military aid to three dozen other countries, many in Latin America.

An agreement defining the court's continuing relationship with the UN was concluded by Judge Kirsch and Secretary General Kofi Annan on October 4, 2004. Among other things, it set forth the terms for cooperation between the UN and court prosecutors and provided for the Security Council to refer to the court matters within its purview. Accordingly, in March 2005 the Security Council referred the conflict in Darfur, Sudan, which led the prosecutor to open in June an investigation into allegations of genocide and crimes against humanity. Other referrals involved events in the Central African Republic, Democratic Republic of the Congo, and Uganda. As of September 2013, the court had 122 state parties. In March 2009 Sang-Hyun Song of South Korea was elected to replace Kirsch.

On July 9–20, 2001, a UN Conference on the Illicit Trade in Small Arms and Light Weapons in All Its Aspects convened in New York. The most contentious UN-sponsored gathering of the year, however, was the August 31–September 7, 2001, World Conference Against Racism, Racial Discrimination, Xenophobia, and Related Intolerance, held in Durban, South Africa. Among the topics drawing heated debate were the Middle East and slavery. On September 3 the United States, Canada, and Israel withdrew their delegations because of what U.S. secretary of state Colin Powell labeled "censure and abuse" directed at Israel. In the end, the conference's lengthy closing declaration included a statement on Palestinian-Israeli matters that was less strident than Washington had feared. While expressing concern about "the plight of the Palestinian people under foreign occupation" and recognizing the right of Palestinians to self-determination and statehood, the document also recognized "the right to security for all States in the region, including Israel." On the matter of slavery and the slave trade, a number of

European delegations had expressed concern the final declaration might, at least indirectly, call for reparations. A compromise was ultimately reached on the relevant passages, one of which asserted that "slavery and the slave trade are a crime against humanity and should always have been so."

The 56th General Assembly session began on September 12, 2001, its opening having been delayed by a day because of the September 11 terrorist attacks in the United States. The start of the annual two-week general debate, presided over by Han Seung Soo of the Republic of Korea, was postponed from September 24 and reduced to a single week, November 10–16. A special General Assembly session on children (a follow-up to the 1990 World Summit for Children) was also postponed until May 8–10, 2002. Not surprisingly, the 2001 general debate focused on terrorism, but such perennial issues as globalization, development, and poverty reduction also occupied the agenda. Among other actions, 118 states signed an International Convention for the Suppression of the Financing of Terrorism. On October 12 the UN in general and Secretary General Annan in particular were awarded the Nobel Peace Prize in recognition of their work "for a better organized and more peaceful world." On June 29 the UN had unanimously elected Annan to a second term as secretary general.

On February 12, 2002, the Optional Protocol to the Convention on the Rights of the Child on the Involvement of Children in Armed Conflict, which had been passed by the General Assembly in May 2000, entered into effect, having been ratified by the specified minimum of 14 countries. On December 18 the General Assembly adopted another optional protocol, this one to the 1989 UN International Convention against Torture, by a 127–4 vote. Countries in opposition were the Marshall Islands, Nigeria, Palau, and the United States.

An International Conference on Financing for Development met May 18–22, 2002, in Monterrey, Mexico. Perhaps most notably, donor countries established as a goal 0.7 percent of GDP for Official Development Assistance, considerably more than either the United States or the European Union (EU), for example, were providing. At an International Conference on Sustainable Development, held in Johannesburg, South Africa, on August 26–September 4, long-standing North-South differences continued to be argued. The developed world urged adoption of a cautious approach favoring environmentally conscious sustainable development, while most of the developing country delegations placed greater emphasis on rapid expansion of trade and development opportunities.

The 57th General Assembly session, presided over by Jan Kavan of the Czech Republic, held its general debate September 12–20, 2002. Areas of focus included peace and security, terrorism, globalization, HIV/AIDS, sustainable development, and the mounting crisis in Iraq (see "Security Council"). Specific measures included adoption of the New Partnership for Africa's Development (NEPAD), a broad, multilateral approach to African development (see the article on the African Union).

The 58th General Assembly session held its general debate on September 23–October 2, 2003, under the presidency of Julian Hunte of St. Lucia. Secretary General Annan's opening address and annual report stressed the difficulty presented by the doctrine that individual states had the right to act preemptively and unilaterally against perceived threats. Annan warned that such a doctrine could result in a "proliferation of the unilateral and lawless use of force." He proposed instead a "common security agenda" that addressed the threats posed to international order not only by weapons of mass destruction and terrorism but also by poverty, deprivation, and civil war. Partly in response to a failure of diplomacy prior to the March 2003 U.S.-led invasion of Iraq, Annan later named a High-Level Panel on Threats, Challenges, and Change to review the role of the UN. Among the panel's 16 members were Chinese, Russian, and U.S. officials.

Continuing subjects of debate at the 2003 session included global warming, HIV/AIDS, and protectionist trade measures and debt as impediments to achieving the principal Millennium Development Goal of halving poverty by 2015. Delegates passed a resolution on "Revitalization of the Work of the General Assembly" with a view toward improving cooperation with the Security Council and the Economic and Social Council. Another resolution expressed "deep concern" over escalating threats to the safety and security of humanitarian and UN personnel. The General Assembly also endorsed a December 9–12 meeting in Merida, Mexico, that saw 95 countries sign a Convention against Corruption. It failed to reach agreement, however, on an even more controversial subject, namely a ban on human cloning, and in early November voted to postpone further action for two years.

Jean Ping of Gabon was named president of the 59th session, from September 21–30, 2004, and the session was followed on October 4–5 by discussions related to strengthening the UN and revitalizing the General Assembly. In early December the High-Level Panel on Threats, Challenges, and Change submitted its report, which included 101 recommendations on matters as varied as Security Council reform, terrorism and nuclear proliferation, sustainable development, and use of force to protect human rights. On March 21, 2005, drawing on the panel's work, Secretary General Annan submitted to the General Assembly a report on reform, which called for expanding the Security Council to 24 members, streamlining the General Assembly agenda, and replacing the controversial UN Commission on Human Rights with a Human Rights Council.

On April 13, 2005, the General Assembly adopted an International Convention for the Suppression of Acts of Nuclear Terrorism, which was opened for signature during the September 14–16 World Summit of national leaders, who gathered to mark the UN's 60th anniversary. The summit concluded with a final declaration covering UN reform and the Millennium Development Goals that had been adopted in 2000, but a number of proposals advocated by Secretary General Annan—most significantly those related to nuclear disarmament and nonproliferation—were dropped from the document or weakened in order to reach consensus. The declaration broke new ground with its assertion that the UN had the right to intervene if "national authorities manifestly [fail] to protect their populations from genocide, war crimes, ethnic cleansing and crimes against humanity." With Jan Eliasson of Sweden as president, the regular 2005 session was highlighted by the December approval of a resolution to create a Peacebuilding Commission. The 31-member advisory body, including national representatives from the Security Council, ECOSOC, and peacekeeping missions, was designed to focus on methods for stabilizing and rebuilding countries in the post-conflict period. The General Assembly also voted to reconfigure the Central Emergency Revolving Fund as the Central Emergency Response Fund (CERF) for humanitarian disasters. Plans called for supplementing the preexisting $50 million revolving fund with a $450 million facility that could provide grants and loans.

On March 15, 2006, the General Assembly, by a vote of 170–4, approved creation of the Human Rights Council (UNHRC) to serve as the main UN forum for dialogue and cooperation on human rights. Israel, the Marshall Islands, Palau, and the United States voted against the resolution, and Belarus, Iran, and Venezuela abstained. The negative U.S. vote largely reflected concern that seats on the council, like those on the ECOSOC's Commission on Human Rights, would be filled on a regional basis. Election of the UNHRC's 47 members—a cohort considerably larger than had been envisaged by Secretary General Annan—took place on May 9, and its first session was held June 19. The General Assembly approved a series of reforms for UN management, procurement, and enhanced information technology efforts in July 2006. Annan was granted $20 million to implement the reform package. In August the sixteenth biennial AIDS Conference was held in Toronto. The gathering drew 20,000 participants. During the meeting, the UN's special envoy on HIV/AIDS to Africa, Stephen Lewis, accused the G-8 nations of failing to follow through on pledges made in 2005 to support enhanced access to drugs and treatment. (As of the Toronto conference, the UN had collected only $525 million to combat HIV/AIDS, tuberculosis, and malaria against a goal of $5.8 billion.) Partially in response to such criticism, the General Assembly launched the UNITAID, a multilateral program to purchase drugs to treat HIV/AIDS, tuberculosis, and malaria and redistribute them to 94 countries in Africa, Asia, Latin America, and the Caribbean. By 2010 UNITAID had 35 member states and an annual budget of more than $400 million.

Haya Rashed Al Khalifa of Bahrain was elected president of the 61st General Assembly session, becoming the third woman chosen for the post. The theme of the session was "Implementing a Partnership for Global Development." On September 13, 2006, the General Assembly approved the Declaration on the Rights of Indigenous Peoples. The nonbinding document articulated the rights of native peoples to unique cultures, languages, and traditions, and prohibited discrimination against them. Australia, Canada, New Zealand, and the United States were the only countries to vote against the declaration, which passed with 113 votes in favor and 11 abstentions.

The closing session of the 61st General Assembly was notable for anti-U.S. speeches by the presidents of Iran and Venezuela. At the time, Venezuela was campaigning for seat on the UN Security Council, and the harsh rhetoric used was reported to have undermined the effort and led to the selection of Panama as a compromise candidate for the seat.

During the assembly's meetings in September 2006, South Korean foreign minister Ban Ki-Moon emerged as the leading candidate to succeed Annan after a series of informal polls of the Security Council. Ban's reputation for quiet diplomacy garnered him the support of the United States, China, and Russia, which collectively sought a less-activist secretary general than Annan. On October 13 the General Assembly appointed Ban as the eighth UN secretary general after the Security Council recommended his appointment in Resolution 1715. Annan announced in October that the UN Foundation, founded by Turner, had exceeded its $1 billion goal. Meanwhile, the High-Level Panel on UN Systems-Wide Coherence, formed in February 2006 to recommend internal reforms, released a report that contended duplication and inefficiency could be reduced by 20 percent by the creation of a single board or commission to coordinate the activities of the UN's agencies and bodies. On December 13 the General Assembly adopted the Convention on the Protection and Promotion of the Rights and Dignity of Persons with Disabilities, which opened for signatures on March 30, 2007, and was immediately signed by 81 countries and the EU, a record number for a UN convention.

The General Assembly adopted a resolution that condemned denial of the Holocaust on January 26, 2007. The resolution was in response to statements by the president of Iran that appeared to question the reality of the atrocities. The assembly also approved a reform proposal by Ban that included the division of the body's peacekeeping operations into two bodies: a department of peace operations and a department of field support.

In May 2007 the assembly elected Srgjan Kerim of Macedonia as the president of the 62nd session. Some delegations condemned Ban's decision to convene a September meeting of world leaders on climate change under the auspices of the Security Council, arguing that the General Assembly was the better forum for such an event. In June the General Assembly approved Ban's proposed reform of UN peacekeeping operations (see "Secretariat"). Meanwhile, in October the General Assembly held the High-Level Dialogue on Interreligious and Intercultural Understanding and Cooperation for Peace in an effort to promote interaction among diverse groups and cultures. In November the General Assembly designated September 15 of each year as International Democracy Day.

Miguel d'Escoto Brockmann was elected president of the 63rd session of the General Assembly on June 4, 2008. The session's debate theme was "The Impact of the Global Food Crisis on Poverty and Hunger in the World as Well as the Need to Democraticize the United Nations." Brockmann called on the world body to enhance the power of the General Assembly by diluting the power of the Security Council and moving toward a system of "one country, one vote" in which all member states would be equal. In late October, Brockmann called on the international community to help reform the global financial system, in the wake of widespread economic turmoil. The General Assembly also declared 2008 the International Year of Sanitation and directed agencies to develop reports and recommendations to ensure that the 2015 Millennium Development Goals on sanitation were met.

On June 10, 2009, Ali Abdussalem Treki of Libya was elected president of the 64th session of the General Assembly, which subsequently began on September 15. During the session, the assembly approved a draft resolution on the Alliance of Civilizations, an initiative that sought to promote a culture of peace throughout the world. The body also called on the secretary general to develop specific programs to support the Alliance of Civilizations. A resolution that pledged UN support for new, and newly restored, democracies was also approved. United States president Barack Obama, in his first speech before the General Assembly, pledged a more cooperative foreign policy and called for a new international treaty to ban nuclear weapons. His remarks were seen as a foreshadowing of reduced tensions between the United States and the UN. On October 19 the assembly voted to grant observer status to the International Olympic Committee. For the 18th consecutive year, the assembly called on the United States to end its economic embargo on Cuba on a vote of 187 in support, 3 opposed (the United States, Israel, and Palau), and 2 abstentions (Micronesia and the Marshall Islands). The assembly designated July 18 as Nelson Mandela International Day in honor of the accomplishments of the South African freedom fighter and leader.

The General Assembly voted unanimously on July 2, 2010, to establish a new bureau to promote women's rights, the UN Entity for Gender Equality and the Empowerment of Women (UN Women). The new organization combined four existing bodies: the Division for the Advancement of Women, the International Research and Training Institute for the Advancement of Women, the Office of the Special Adviser on Gender Issues and the Advancement of Women, and the UN Development Fund for Women. Michele Bachelet, the former president of Chile, was appointed the first head of UN Women on September 14. On July 29 the assembly enacted a resolution affirming that access to clean water and sanitation was a basic human right. Joseph Deiss of Switzerland was elected president of the 66th session of the General Assembly. The session included high level meetings to reduce the loss of biodiversity and new strategies to improve development among small island states. The assembly also engaged in a debate on Security Council reform, but an agreement on revising the number or composition of the permanent members of the body remained elusive. The 2010–2011 UN budget was approved by the General Assembly at the session. The $4.2 billion budget was an increase of 0.5 percent over the previous cycle.

At the opening of the 65th General Assembly on September 23, 2010, Deiss warned that the UN was in danger of being marginalized "as other actors emerge on the international scene." Enlargement of the Security Council came under consideration, as a way to dilute its influence relative to the General Assembly.

On March 3, 2011, the General Assembly ejected Libya from the Human Rights Council in reaction to President Qadhafi's suppression of protestors. On June 21 the General Assembly overwhelmingly elected Ban to a second five-year term, beginning January 1, 2012. On September 23, Palestine requested full membership and was granted non-member observer state status in November.

To mark the 20th anniversary of the 1992 Rio Conference ("Earth Summit"), the UN Conference on Sustainable Development ("Rio + 20") was held in June 2012 and included representatives from 192 countries and a range of international organizations. Differences among the attendees prevented the adoption of any binding agreements; however, participants endorsed a proposal that the UN Environmental Program would be the lead international environmental authority.

The 66th session of the General Assembly began on September 13, 2011. With her September 22 speech, Brazilian president Dilma Rousseff became the first woman to open the general debate. Nassir Abdulaziz Al-Nasser of Qatar was elected president of the session, which included high-level meetings on the prevention and control of noncommunicable diseases, desertification, and sustainable development. In December the General Assembly approved a $5.15 billion budget for 2012–2013.

The 67th session of the General Assembly opened on September 18, 2012. Vuk Jeremićof Serbia was elected president of the session whose theme was "Bringing about adjustment or settlement of international disputes or situations by peaceful means," and which was dominated by discussions of the ongoing civil war in Syria.

On April 2, 2013, the General Assembly voted 154 to 3, with 23 abstentions, to adopt the Arms Trade Treaty. Voting against the accord were Iran, North Korea, and Syria, while China, India, and Russia were among those states that abstained. The treaty regulated the global trade in conventional weapons by requiring states to assess the impact of arms imports and exports on areas such as their potential to contribute to human rights violations, organized crime or terrorism, as well as tracking the status of imported waepons. The accord will not enter into force until it has been ratified by 59 countries. By October 2013, 113 states had signed the treaty, while 7 had ratified it.

John W. Ashe of Antigua and Barbuda was elected president of the 68th session of the General Assembly, which began on September 17, 2013. The session included high-level meetings and sustainable development, the impact of the Millennium Development Goals, and nuclear disarmament.

GENERAL ASSEMBLY: SPECIAL BODIES

Over the years, the General Assembly has created a number of semiautonomous Special Bodies, two of which (UNCTAD, UNDP) deal with development problems, three (UNHCR, UNICEF, UNRWA) with relief and welfare problems, and two (UNEP, UNFPA) with demographic and environmental problems.

In addition to the United Nations University (UNU), which alone sponsors or cosponsors some dozen Research and Training Centers and Programs, a number of other specialized bodies for conducting research and providing training have been established. These include the United Nations Institute for Training and Research (UNITAR) and the United Nations Research Institute for Social Development (UNRISD) (both discussed below); the UN Institute for Disarmament

Research (UNIDIR), located in Geneva; the UN Entity for Gender Equality and the Empowerment of Women (UN Women), based in New York; and the UN Interregional Crime and Justice Research Institute (UNICRI), based in Turin, Italy.

United Nations Children's Fund
(UNICEF)

Established: By General Assembly resolution of December 11, 1946, as the United Nations International Children's Emergency Fund. Initially a temporary body to provide emergency assistance to children in countries ravaged by war, the fund was made permanent by General Assembly resolution on October 6, 1953, the name changed to United Nations Children's Fund while retaining the abbreviation UNICEF.

Purpose: To give assistance, particularly to less developed countries, in the establishment of permanent child health, educational, protective, and welfare services.

Headquarters: New York, United States.

Principal Organs: Executive Board (36 members), Program Committee (Committee of the Whole), National Committees, Secretariat. Membership on the Executive Board rotates on the following geographical basis: Africa, 8; Asia, 7; Latin America and the Caribbean, 5; Eastern Europe, 4; Western Europe and other, 12.

Web site: www.unicef.org

Executive Director: Anthony Lake (United States).

Activities. UNICEF has long been actively involved in programs dedicated to maternal and child health, nutrition, education, and social welfare. In keeping with the intent of the Child Survival and Development Revolution (CSDR), which was adopted in 1983 to provide "a creative and practical approach" to accelerating progress for children, UNICEF added emphasis on the problems of children affected by armed conflicts, exploitation, abandonment, abuse, and neglect. Increased attention was also given to the role of women in economic development, problems specific to female children, the need for family "spacing," and the provision of better water and sanitation facilities. In all the areas it covers, UNICEF's goal is to foster community-based services provided by workers selected by the community and supported by existing networks of government agencies and nongovernmental organizations.

UNICEF's activities are supported exclusively by voluntary contributions, approximately two-thirds of which are donated by governments and much of the remainder raised by its 36 National Committees, based primarily in more affluent countries. In addition to its New York headquarters, UNICEF maintains major offices in Tokyo, Japan, and Brussels, Belgium. The crucial Supply Division operates out of Copenhagen, Denmark. In addition, its Innocenti Research Center, located in Florence, Italy, focuses on child development and advocacy. Seven regional offices around the globe help support 190 country offices. UNICEF reports indirectly to the General Assembly through the Economic and Social Council (ECOSOC).

For information on UNICEF prior to 2007, see the 2013 *Handbook.* In January 2007 UNICEF initiated an effort to raise $635 million to address 33 ongoing humanitarian crises around the world, with the largest share designated for the Darfur region of Sudan. In the previous year, the body raised $513 million for 53 emergencies through the year. UNICEF and the French government cosponsored a conference in February to eliminate the use of child soldiers. At the event, 58 nations agreed to take steps to disarm child soldiers and undertake steps to reintegrate the fighters into society. UNICEF director Ann Veneman noted that there were an estimated 250,000 underage soldiers involved in conflicts around the world. UNICEF used June 16, the AU-sponsored Day of the African Child to launch an initiative to draw attention to the problem of child trafficking. Meanwhile, UNICEF offered support to expand the Measles Initiative, at that time focused on Africa, into India and Pakistan. The goal of the initiative was to reduce deaths from measles by 90 percent from 2000 levels by 2010. In its 2007 report, *State of the World's Children: Women and Children, the Double Dividend of Gender Equality,* UNICEF highlighted continuing discrimination against women and outlined steps through which repression could be alleviated to benefit both women and children. The report also asserted that improvements in gender equality would add to progress toward the UN's Millennium Development Goals. One offshoot of the report was a UNICEF partnership with the UN Fund for Population Activities (UNFPA) to launch a $44 million program to reduce female genital mutilation (see "United Nations Fund for Population Activities").

UNICEF reported in September 2007 that the number of children who died annually dropped below 10 million in 2005 for the first time since the organization began keeping records. On November 5, UNICEF called on governments to ban the use and stockpiling of cluster munitions that the body argued disproportionately affected women and children. UNICEF specifically denounced their use in the 2006 conflict in Lebanon.

In 2008 UNICEF and the World Health Organization released the report of a Joint Monitoring Program that examined sanitation and access to safe drinking water around the world. The report found that the world was on track to meet the Millennium Development Goals on water and sanitation by 2015, but that 2.5 billion people, 38 percent of the world's population, still lacked access to safe water. UNICEF announced a range of programs to teach sanitation practices and improve access to safe water. UNICEF's *State of the World's Children 2008: Child Survival* called for increased measures to cut child mortality. It reported that 26,000 children under the age of five die every day, and that almost half of all child mortality occurred in sub-Saharan Africa.

In response to a global economic crisis, UNICEF and the Overseas Development Institute held a conference in November 2009 to highlight the impact of the worldwide recession on children. Meanwhile, UNICEF undertook a leading role in disaster relief following tsunamis that affected areas such as Indonesia, the Philippines, and Samoa, and it launched a program with WHO to better prepare countries for the H1N1 influenza through public education and preparedness campaigns. Its report, *State of the World's Children 2009: Maternal and Newborn Health,* noted that approximately 1,500 expectant mothers died every day and called for global action to reduce maternal and neonatal mortality. It also reported that women in developing countries were 300 percent more likely to die during pregnancy or childbirth than women in developed states.

In 2009 UNICEF endeavored to more closely link its efforts with other UN operations. The organization reported that in 2009, 85 percent of its missions were aligned with the UN Development Assistance Framework and the Millennium Development Goals. Also in 2009, UNICEF created a liaison office with the AU. Among UNICEF's more notable accomplishments was a polio vaccination effort in Afghanistan, India, Nigeria, and Pakistan. In all, UNICEF purchased and distributed more than 3 billion vaccines, ranging from polio to measles to influenza. UNICEF's rehabilitation and reintegration for children in armed conflict was able to remove 12,600 children in nine countries from armed groups. Contributions to UNICEF declined by about 2 percent in 2009, and the organization's budget for the year was $3.3 billion. On September 6 James Elder, UNICEF spokesperson in Sri Lanka was expelled from the country over comments that were critical of the government's treatment of Tamil refugees.

In May 2010 Anthony Lake of the United States became the new executive director of UNICEF. In response to a cholera outbreak in Haiti UNICEF initiated a two-fold program to educate the population about prevention and to provide additional medical supplies to local hospitals and clinics. Shortage of funds hampered UNICEF's response to the natural and human-made disasters of 2010 and 2011. The organization remained active in Haiti and also operated in Pakistan, where monsoon floods both in 2010 and 2011 caused widespread devastation.

In 2012, in response to the ongoing conflict in Syria (see entry on Syria), UNICEF increased efforts to provide aid to families and children fleeing to neighboring states such as Jordan. In July 2012 UNICEF reported that 8 million people remained at risk of malnutrition in Somalia, Ethiopia, and Kenya because of drought. Through the summer, UNICEF coordinated the disbursement of $405 million in humanitarian aid to the region. In August UNICEF announced that a joint program with the Angolan government had resulted in a year without any new polio cases in that country. In September a joint UNICEF-WHO report found that the child mortality that been dramatically reduced since the 1990s. In 2011 an estimated 6.9 million children died beforethe age of five, compared with 12 million in 1990. Developing countries which received significant foreign aid to supportimmunization and health programs had the most significant decreases in childhood mortality.

In 2013 UNICEF's executive board approved a budget of $2.1 billion for 2014–2017 to support a strategic plan that emphasized "linking resources to results" by establishing clear goals and objectives for projects and increasing oversight of programs. In a March report, "Syria's Children: A Lost Generation?," UNICEF highlighted the extreme danger facing Syrian children as a result of the ongoing civil war. UNICEF programs in Syria vaccinated more than 1.3 million children, and provided regular access to healthcare for 421,700 women and children. However, the conflict has affected more than 2 million children, including 500,000 who were refugees in 2013. UNICEF's appeal for $195 million in emergency funding for Syria had not been fulfilled by October 2013.

United Nations Conference on Trade and Development (UNCTAD)

Established: By General Assembly resolution of December 30, 1964.

Purpose: To promote international trade with a view to accelerating the economic growth of less developed countries, to formulate and implement policies related to trade and development, to review and facilitate the coordination of various institutions within the United Nations system in regard to international trade and development, to initiate action for the negotiation and adoption of multilateral legal instruments in the field of trade, and to harmonize trade and related development policies of governments and regional economic groups.

Headquarters: Geneva, Switzerland.

Principal Organs: Conference; Trade and Development Board (151 members); Commission on Trade in Goods and Services, and Commodities; Commission on Investment, Technology, and Related Financial Issues; Commission on Enterprise, Business Facilitation, and Development; Secretariat.

Web site: www.unctad.org

Secretary General: Mukhisa Kituyi (Kenya).

Membership (194): All UN members, plus Holy See (Vatican City State). A number of intergovernmental and nongovernmental organizations have observer status.

Activities. UNCTAD's quadrennial conference of governmental, intergovernmental, and nongovernmental representatives is considered the world's most comprehensive forum on North-South economic issues. Over the years it has addressed many of the economic and developmental difficulties faced by the developing world and the least developed countries (LDCs), although not always successfully (for information on UNCTAD's activities prior to 2007, please see the 2013 *Handbook*).

UNCTAD's 2007 budget was $50 million, with an additional $25 million available for technical aid to individual countries. In an effort to standardize the manner in which information and communication technology statistics were reported by governments, UNCTAD issued the *Manual for the Production of Statistics on the Information Economy* in February. The publication was designed to serve as the basis for UN training courses on information technology. UNCTAD reported in its 2007 annual trade and development index, which combines trade with economic and social standards, that the United States led developed countries for a second year in a row. The United States was followed by Germany and Denmark, while Singapore led developing countries, with South Korea in second place and China in third. In October UNCTAD commenced an EU-funded program to increase Angola's international trade through training in sustainable development and intergovernmental cooperation in economic policy.

UNCTAD XII was held in April 2008 in Accra, Ghana, and resulted in the Accra Accords. Through the accords, UNCTAD pledged to assist developing countries narrow the gaps among nations in economic development, with a special focus on small island developing nations. UNCTAD also committed itself to developing methods to reduce rising food and commodity prices that disproportionately affected poorer countries. Finally, the accords noted the range of difficulties developing states faced and called for new development strategies, including increased aid and foreign investment and more technology transfers from developed nations. UNCTAD also launched a new database on global trade that provided governments with comparative statistics on more than 235 products in 130 countries. UNCTAD's annual trade and development index noted that the global financial crisis was estimated to reduce economic growth to 3 percent in 2008, down 1 percent from the year before, but that the major impact would be on developing countries. The report also argued that official development assistance would have to be increased by $50 billion to $60 billion per year for the world to meet the 2015 Millennium Development Goals.

UNCTAD's 2009 trade and development report, *Responding to the Global Crisis, Climate Change Mitigation and Development,* focused on the responses of both developed and developing countries addressing the worldwide economic crisis. The report specifically highlighted the dangers of deregulation of financial markets and called for a range of government reforms. The publication also explored how efforts to mitigate global climate change would affect trade networks and development strategies. Other notable publications during the year were *Development and Globalization: Facts and Figures 2008* and the *UNCTAD Handbook of Statistics 2008.* UNCTAD also launched a new database to provide information on creative goods and services. The new source contains statistics for 130 countries and covers 1996–2006, with plans to update the database as information becomes available. In July Supachai Panitchpakdi of Thailand was reappointed for a second four-year term as UNCTAD's secretary general.

UNCTAD's 2009 budget was $95 million in 2009, including $35 million in voluntary contributions from states and other organizations, and $60 million from the UN regular budget. During the year, UNCTAD funded, or participated in, 255 programs in 81 countries, including efforts to enhance e-government capabilities and trade capabilities. The UNCTAD study *Economic Development in Africa Report 2009: Strengthening Regional Economic Integration for Africa's Development* analyzed a variety of economic development strategies and recommended new methods to improve integration among African countries in order to make them more competitive in the global economy. UNCTAD also produced a range of studies on climate issues, including the development of biofuels and e-tourism, and the launch of a new annual survey, the *Least Developed Countries Report 2010.* UNCTAD's *World Investment Report 2009* highlighted the decrease in foreign direct investment (FDI) from $1.7 trillion in 2008 to $1.2 trillion, although there was a significant increase in FDI to developing countries, which received 43 percent of the investments in 2009. As the world economic crisis persisted, UNCTAD issued a report in September 2010 that urged investment managers worldwide to behave responsibly. "All institutional investors [should] be encouraged to formally articulate their stance on responsible investment to all stakeholders," it said. At the November 2010 G-20 summit in Seoul, South Korea, UNCTAD was given the task, among others, of developing quantifiable indicators for increased economic value and job creation arising from private sector investment, to develop policy recommendations to further such value addition.

In March 2011 UNCTAD proposed a "new modality of inclusive, cooperative and South-centered global development." In April it chose as the theme of UNCTAD XIII "Development-centered globalization: Towards inclusive and sustainable growth and development" for the conference in April in Doha, Qatar. At the session, members endorsed efforts to mainstream sustainable development as part of overall economic development practices. In May it issued a set of proposed principles for the responsibilities of borrowers and lenders of sovereign debt. In its 2011 *World Investment Report,* UNCTAD reported that FDI for 2010 was $1.24 trillion. This was a rise from the previous year but remained 15 percent lower than 2007. In 2011 UNCTAD approved a budget for 2012–2013 of $143.1 million.

On September 1, 2013, Mukhisa Kituyi of Kenya became the new secretary general of UNCTAD. In its 2013 *World Investment Report*, UNCTAD found that global FDI continued to decline, falling by 18 percent in 2012. That year, for the first time FDI to developing countries exceeded that to developed states (developing coutnries accounted for 52 percent of FDI inflows). FDI was expected to rise to $1.6 trillion in 2014 and $1.8 trillion in 2015.

United Nations Development Program (UNDP)

Established: By General Assembly resolution of November 22, 1965, which combined the United Nations Expanded Program of Technical Assistance (UNEPTA) with the United Nations Special Fund (UNSF).

Purpose: To coordinate and administer technical assistance provided through the UN system, in order to assist less developed countries in their efforts to accelerate social and economic development.

Headquarters: New York, United States.

Principal Organs: Executive Board (36 members), Committee of the Whole, Regional Bureaus (Africa, Arab States, Asia and the Pacific, Europe and the Commonwealth of Independent States, Latin America and the Caribbean), Bureau for Resources and Strategic Partnerships, Bureau for Development Policy. Membership on the Executive Board rotates on the following geographical basis: Africa, 8; Asia, 7; Latin America and the Caribbean, 5; Eastern Europe, 4; Western Europe and other, 12.

Related Organs. The following special funds and programs are administered by the UNDP: the UN Capital Development Fund (UNCDF), established in 1960 but administered by the UNDP since 1972; the United Nations Volunteers (UNV), formed in 1971; the Program of Assistance to the Palestinian People (PAPP), authorized by the General Assembly in December 1978; the UN Development Fund for Women (UNIFEM), formerly the Voluntary Fund for the UN Decade for Women, established in 1976 and reconstituted in 1984; the Global Environment Facility (GEF), established in 1991 in conjunction with the UN Environment Program (see the UNEP article) and the World Bank; the Drylands Development Center (DDC), established in 2002 in Nairobi, Kenya, as successor to the Office to Combat Desertification and Drought (UNSO, from the original UN Sudano-Sahelian Office); and the UN Office for Project Services (UNOPS), created in 1994 to assist other UN bodies and member states by providing management and support services for projects. In 2001 the Executive Board closed the UN Revolving Fund for Natural Resources Exploration (UNRFNRE), which had been established in 1974, and the UN Fund for Science and Technology for Development (UNFSTD), which had been set up in 1979, initially as an Interim Fund.

Web site: www.undp.org

Administrator: Helen Clark (New Zealand).

Activities. UNDP works in partnership with 177 governments, dozens of intergovernmental agencies, and increasingly with civil society organizations and the private sector to promote "sustainable human development" throughout Africa, Asia, Latin America, the Middle East, and parts of Europe. In its early decades the organization focused its attention on five main areas: (1) surveying and assessing natural resources having industrial, commercial, or export potential; (2) stimulating capital investments; (3) training in a wide range of vocational and professional skills; (4) transferring appropriate technologies and stimulating the growth of local technological capabilities; and (5) aiding economic and social planning. In addition, in the 1980s the General Assembly assigned the UNDP three special mandates: the International Drinking Water Supply and Sanitation Decade (1981–1990), the Women in Development program, and implementation of the new international economic order (NIEO). During the 1990s priorities were redefined to encompass poverty elimination, good governance, environmental considerations, and women's development. For the first decade of the 21st century five "Communities of Practice" were identified: democratic governance, poverty reduction, energy and the environment, HIV/AIDS, and crisis prevention and recovery. Gender issues, information and communication technology, and capacity development cut across all five.

In mid-1999 Administrator James G. Speth, one of the highest-ranking UN officials from the United States, retired from his post. His replacement was Mark Malloch Brown of the United Kingdom, who had previously served with the World Bank. Malloch Brown immediately had to confront a loss of confidence in the agency's abilities and a related drop in donor funding. In an effort to reverse the trend, the UNDP introduced a 2000–2003 business plan that significantly restructured the organization's operations, adopted a Multi-Year Funding Framework (MYFF), and cut headquarters staff. Innovations included the establishment of nine subregional resource facilities (SURFs) for Arab states, the Caribbean, Central and Eastern Africa, Europe and the Commonwealth of Independent States countries, Latin America, the Pacific and North and Southeast Asia, Southern Africa, West and South Asia, and Western Africa. Each SURF supports the activities of country offices by making available policy specialists, expert referrals, technical support, and access to a global network of pertinent information. At the same time, the UNDP stepped up efforts to bring civil society organizations, foundations, and the private sector into partnership with donor countries, recipients, and intergovernmental organizations. To facilitate this process the UNDP created a Bureau for Research and Strategic Partnerships. In addition, "thematic trust funds" were established to utilize special donations for the UNDP's program emphases. Other changes included establishment of a Bureau for Crisis Prevention and Recovery as successor to the Emergency Response Division.

The UNDP has been designated as the UN coordinating agency for achieving the Millennium Development Goals (MDGs) arising from the September 2000 Millennium Summit in New York. In addition to the broad goal of developing a global partnership for development, principal targets for 2015 include halving the billion-plus people living on less than $1 a day, guaranteeing completion of primary education by all children, eliminating gender disparities at all educational levels, reducing by two-thirds the mortality rate for children under five, cutting by three-fourths the number of women who die in childbirth, ensuring environmental sustainability, and reversing the spread of HIV/AIDS as well as reducing the incidence of malaria and other major diseases. To assist developing countries in meeting the MDGs, the UNDP launched Capacity 2015 at the World Summit for Sustainable Development, held August 26–September 4, 2002, in Johannesburg, South Africa. With its focus on capacity building, particularly through linking local sustainable development with national and international initiatives, Capacity 2015 expanded on the UNDP's earlier Capacity 21, which advanced the Agenda 21 goals set forth by the June 1992 UN Conference on Environment and Development in Rio de Janeiro, Brazil.

Since 1990 the UNDP has issued an annual *Human Development Report,* containing an index that incorporates data on infant mortality, life expectancy, literacy, education expenditure, and individual purchasing power. Using what has been described as "unusually direct language," various reports have called for a drastic reduction in military spending, the promotion of human rights and gender equality as an integral component of economic development, curtailment of government corruption, and steps to overcome a growing global income disparity. (For information on UNDP prior to 2007, please see the 2013 *Handbook.*)

In October 2007 the UNDP agreed to oversee the disbursement of $150 million in loans from the Japan Bank for International Cooperation to the Iraqi government to aid in reconstruction of electricity networks. The funds were the first disbursement in a $3.5 billion pledge made by Japan in 2005. The agreement was touted by the UNDP as a model for future aid arrangements. The following month, the UNDP and the Mohammed bin Rashid Al Maktoum Foundation, the largest private Arab charity, launched a $20 million program to promote education in the Middle East and Persian Gulf. Progress would be measured by an annual UNDP report, the *Arab Knowledge Report.*

The 2008 *Human Development Report—Fighting Climate Change: Human Solidarity in a Divided World* analyzes the nexus of development and climate change and provides recommendations for countries on how to pursue economic growth in a sustainable manner. The report also includes various visual and interactive materials on carbon emissions in an effort to make the document more accessible to a broader audience. In September the UNDP sponsored a week-long series of meetings on the Millennium Development Goals to support the meeting on these goals convened by the secretary general for heads of state. The UNDP brought together business leaders, private groups, and government officials to discuss progress and to devise new strategies to achieve the UN's objectives. Norway, Spain, and the United Kingdom subsequently pledged $275 million in additional funding to help meet the Millennium Development Goals.

On March 31, 2009, the UN General Assembly unanimously elected former New Zealand prime minister Helen Clark as the new administrator for UNDP. For the 2008–2009 biennium the UNDP projected its budget to be $10.7 billion, of which $8.67 billion would be spent on programs and activities, with the remainder devoted to operational and support costs. The 2009 *Annual Report: Living Up to Commitments* highlighted the need for governments, nongovernmental organizations, and private volunteer groups to continue to support programs to aid the needy and disadvantaged during the international recession. The UNDP's 2009 human development index ranked Norway, Iceland, and Australia first, second, and third, respectively, in human development.

The January 2010 earthquake in Haiti destroyed the UNDP office in that country, but the organization was designated as the lead UN agency in the crisis and quickly launched a massive aid program that included the creation of 95,700 temporary jobs. UNDP published the 20th anniversary edition of its *Human Development Report* in 2010. Titled *The Real Wealth of Nations: Pathways to Human Development,* the study provided a historical overview of development issues and introduced new methods to calculate the UNDP's human development, besides the traditional human development index. For instance, the inequality index accounted for dramatic inequities among societies. Under this measure, states with widespread inequality fell by an average of 22 percent in the standings. The human development index ranked Norway first and Zimbabwe last among 169 countries. In July the UNDP main office in Colombo, Sri Lanka, was closed following protests against the UN. The demonstrators demanded an end to a UN panel investigating human rights abuses in Sri Lanka.

In December 2010 UNDP delivered ballots to Juba, Sudan, for the referendum on southern Sudan's proposed secession from the Khartoum-governed country. In February 2011 it announced a series of new measures to fight fraud and misuse of funds intended for fighting pandemic diseases in developing countries. In May its Community of Practice on Electoral Assistance for the Arab Region met in Cairo, Egypt, to offer assistance with the post-Hosni Mubarak elections. Through 2011 UNDP provided assistance to more than 100 countries in anticorruption programs, while more than 120 nations received aid in democratic governance initiatives.

UNDP's annual human development report, *Sustainability and Equity: A Better Future for All,* called for efforts to combine sustainability and equity programs. In its annual human development index of 187 countries for 2011, Norway retained the top spot, while the United States fell from fourth to twenty-third and the Democratic Republic of the Congo ranked last.

The 2013 UNDP human development report, *The Rise of the South: Human Progress in a Diverse World* highlighted the growing economic progress of developing countries. The publication found that more than 500 million people had risen out of poverty as the result of sustained economic growth in 40 developing countries. The report also estimated that by 2030 approximately 80 percent of the world's "middle class" would reside in developing states. In 2013, the UN Capital Development Fund, overseen by the UNDP, provided ongoing funding for microfinance programs in 48 countries and supported more than 7,300 volunteers in the UN Volunteers initiative promoted "peace and development" in more than 60 countries.

United Nations Environment Program (UNEP)

Established: By General Assembly resolution of December 15, 1972, as the outgrowth of a United Nations Conference on the Human Environment held June 6–16, 1972, in Stockholm, Sweden.

Purpose: To facilitate international cooperation in all matters affecting the human environment; to ensure that environmental problems of wide international significance receive appropriate governmental consideration; and to promote the acquisition, assessment, and exchange of environmental knowledge.

Principal Organs: Governing Council (58 members), Committee of Permanent Representatives, High-Level Committee of Ministers and Officials, Secretariat. Membership on the Governing Council rotates on the following geographical basis: Africa, 16 seats; Asia, 13; Latin America and the Caribbean, 10; Eastern Europe, 6; Western Europe and other, 13.

Web site: www.unep.org

Headquarters: Nairobi, Kenya.

Executive Director: Achim Steiner (Germany).

Activities. In addition to distributing both technical and general information, notably through its "state of the environment" reports, UNEP acts as a catalyst within the UN system on environmental matters. Recent priorities have included climate change (particularly global warming), freshwater resources, deforestation and desertification, protection of wildlife and flora, handling of hazardous wastes and toxic chemicals, preservation of oceans and coastal areas, the effect of environmental degradation on human health, and biotechnology. UNEP also supports a broad range of public education programs designed to combat the mismanagement of natural resources and to build environmental considerations into development planning. Regional offices are located in Bangkok, Thailand; Geneva, Switzerland; Manama, Bahrain; Mexico City, Mexico; Nairobi, Kenya; and Washington, D.C., United States.

UNEP has been at the forefront of efforts to negotiate international agreements on environmental issues and has provided an institutional framework for administering various conventions. The Ozone Secretariat, which services the 1985 Vienna Convention for the Protection of the Ozone Layer, is headquartered in Nairobi, while the allied Multilateral Fund Secretariat for the Implementation of the (1987) Montreal Protocol on Substances That Deplete the Ozone Layer is based in Montreal. Other secretariats are responsible for administering the 1973 Convention on International Trade in Endangered Species of Wild Fauna and Flora (CITES); the 1979 Bonn Convention on the Conservation of Migratory Species of Wild Animals; the 1989 Basel Convention on the Control of Transboundary Movements of Hazardous Wastes and Their Disposal; the 1992 UN Framework Convention on Climate Change, which the UNEP drafted in conjunction with the World Meteorological Organization (WMO); the Convention on Biological Diversity, which came into force in December 1993; the Convention to Combat Desertification in Countries Experiencing Serious Drought and/or Desertification, Especially in Africa, adopted in June 1994; the Regional Seas program, including the Global Program of Action for the Protection of the Marine Environment from Land-Based Activities, adopted in November 1995; the Rotterdam Convention on the Prior Informed Consent (PIC) Procedure for Certain Hazardous Chemicals and Pesticides in International Trade, adopted in September 1998; and the Stockholm Convention on Persistent Organic Pollutants, which entered into effect in May 2004.

UNEP provides the secretariat for the Scientific and Technical Advisory Panel (STAP) of the Global Environment Facility (GEF), which UNEP administers in conjunction with the UNDP and the World Bank. It also maintains a Global Resource Information Database (GRID), a Global Environment Information Exchange Network (Infoterra), and an International Register of Potentially Toxic Chemicals. In 1993 it launched an International Environmental Technology Center in Osaka, Japan. In partnership with the UN Office for the Coordination of Humanitarian Affairs (OCHA), it maintains a Joint UNEP/OCHA Environment Unit to respond to environmental emergencies. In 2000 the previously independent World Conservation Monitoring Center, which had been organized in 1988 with UNEP support, was reorganized as a UNEP "collaborating center" in Cambridge, England. Other recent partnerships include the UNEP Risø Center on Energy, Climate, and Sustainable Development (URC) in Roskilde, Denmark, and the UNEP Collaborating Center on Water and the Environment (UCC Water) in Hørsholm, Denmark. In 2001 the UNEP Post-Conflict Assessment Unit was established in Geneva on the strength of work performed in the Balkans (primarily Kosovo) since 1999. In 2003 a secretariat for the UNs multiagency Environmental Management Group became fully operational, also in Geneva.

A highlight of UNEP activities during the 1990s was the UN Conference on Environment and Development (UNCED, also informally referred to as the Earth Summit), held June 3–14, 1992, in Rio de Janeiro, Brazil. The conference was viewed as a "mixed success" by most environmentalists, although the sheer number of prominent attendees—at the time, the largest-ever gathering of world leaders—highlighted the extent to which environmental issues had risen on the world's political agenda. Formal action taken at UNCED included issuance of the Rio Declaration, a nonbinding statement of broad principles for environmentally sound development, and the signing (by 153 nations) of the legally binding Biological Diversity Convention and the Framework Convention on Climate Change. The United States, however, refused to sign the former, and the latter was approved only after specific targets for reducing carbon dioxide emissions had been deleted at Washington's insistence.

By consensus, the summit also endorsed a statement on Forest Principles, designed to reduce deforestation; however, resistance from timber-exporting nations precluded its adoption as a binding convention. In addition, UNCED issued an 800-page document titled *Agenda 21,* which outlined plans for a global environmental cleanup and proposed measures to assure that third world nations pursue development policies compatible with environmental protection. *Agenda 21* also called for enhancement of UNEP's role in the areas of environmental monitoring, research, education, and the creation of international environmental law. It endorsed the creation of a new UN Commission on Sustainable Development to assess compliance with the summit conventions and proposed a doubling of GEF resources to help developing nations meet environmental targets (for UNEP activities between 1992 and 2000, please see the 2010 *Handbook*).

The UN World Conference on Climate Change, which met November 13–25, 2000, in The Hague, Netherlands, ended in failure because of a disagreement between the United States and members of the European Union (EU) over greenhouse gas reductions. The conference had been expected to conclude a treaty that would meet the requirements of the 1997 Kyoto Protocol, under which 38 industrialized nations would by 2012 reduce such emissions to an average 5.2 percent below the 1990 levels. However, many EU member states objected to U.S. efforts to achieve the target not by an absolute reduction in emissions from fossil fuels, but by "supplementary, flexible" measures that would include transferring cleaner-burning technology to the developing world and earning credits "calculated for carbon sinks"—forests capable of absorbing carbon dioxide from the atmosphere. Talks were scheduled to resume in Berlin, Germany, in mid-2001, but in March the new U.S. president, George W. Bush, announced that the United States would insist on renegotiating the Kyoto Protocol, in part because it did not include standards for developing countries.

Meeting under UNEP auspices December 4–11, 2000, in Johannesburg, South Africa, delegates from 122 countries agreed to ban 12 toxic chemicals known as persistent organic pollutants (POPs). POPs break down slowly, travel easily, are readily absorbed by animals, and have been linked to birth defects and other abnormalities in humans. The targeted "dirty dozen" included dioxins, polychlorinated biphenyls (PCBs), and various pesticides, although 25 developing countries would be permitted to continue use of DDT in their fight against malaria. The new convention was signed in May 2001 in Stockholm, Sweden, and entered into force in May 2004, three months after deposit of a 50th ratification.

From October 29–November 10, 2001, representatives from 164 countries met in Marrakesh, Morocco, to complete the legal text for the Kyoto Protocol. Because protocol approval requires the ratification of countries accounting for at least 55 percent of global greenhouse gas emissions, the Kyoto standards suffered a potentially fatal blow in September 2003 when Russia, during a World Conference on Climate Change in Moscow, indicated that it would not commit to ratification. Without support by either the United States or Russia, the 55 percent goal could not be achieved.

During the 2001 Marrakesh meeting, UNEP released a report warning that global warming could reduce the output of rice, maize, and wheat by one-third during the next half-century. Earlier in the year, UNEP's second *Global Environment Outlook* report had focused on problems related to the world's supply of fresh water, including pollution and scarcity, and emphasized the need to embrace environmental considerations in economic planning, particularly given the accelerating pace of globalization. The report also noted that some 3 million people die annually from diarrhea attributable to contaminated water, that each year polluted water contributes to the deaths of millions of children under five years of age, and that poor management of water systems is a significant factor in the spread of malaria and other insect-borne diseases. The UNEP also reported in 2001 significantly greater loss of coral reefs and forests than had previously been estimated. The third *Global Environment Outlook* cautioned that as of 2002 half of all rivers were polluted or seriously depleted and that by 2032 over half of the world's population could be living in "water-stressed" areas.

With the 1999 General Assembly session having endorsed creation of an annual, high-level environmental gathering, the UNEP responded by converting what had been biennial Governing Council sessions into annual meetings of the Governing Council/Global Ministerial Environment Forum (GMEF), which met for the first time May 29–31, 2000, in Malmö, Sweden. (In odd-numbered years the Governing Council/GMEF convenes in regular session; meetings in alternate years are designated as special sessions.) At the Seventh Special Session of the Governing Council/GMEF, held February 13–15, 2002, the board adopted a report on International Environmental Governance that called for an expanded UNEP role in coordinating environmental aspects of sustainable development and in assisting countries with capacity building and training. The session, held in Cartagena, Colombia, also devoted attention to preparations for the August 26–September 4 World Summit on Sustainable Development, held in Johannesburg.

The 22nd Regular Session of the Governing Council/GMEF met at UNEP headquarters on February 3–7, 2003. One focus of attention was mercury pollution, although the U.S. George W. Bush administration effectively blocked efforts to begin drafting a global protocol that would define mandatory restrictions.

The Eighth Special Session of the Governing Council/GMEF met March 29–31, 2004, in Jeju, South Korea, where issues related to water and sanitation were preeminent. A total of 158 countries sent representatives to the meeting, which considered such topics as water shortages, overfishing, and the recent increase in the number and severity of dust storms in Northeast Asia. Collaterally, UNEP released the *Global Environment Year Book 2003,* which called attention to the growing problem of "dead zones"—oxygen-depleted ocean areas caused by the runoff from nitrogen fertilizers, sewage, and industrial pollution. Also coming under scrutiny was solid waste and sewage disposal for small island countries, which often have neither the space nor the money for proper disposal. According to UNEP, some 90–98 percent of sewage from Pacific and Caribbean islands enters coastal waters untreated. Perhaps the most controversial proposal discussed at the March session involved conducting research on how environmental problems and pressures contribute to international conflict.

On November 18, 2004, reversing its previous stance, Russia completed formal ratification of the Kyoto Protocol, which went into effect on February 16, 2005. Meanwhile, in 2012, Canada became the first country to withdraw from the Kyoto Protocol. As of October 2013, a total of 191 countries and dependent territories plus the EU had ratified the protocol, the notable exception, apart from the United States, being Australia.

In March 2005 UNEP published the *Millennium Ecosystem Assessment,* the result of work by 1,300 authors and scientists from 95 countries. The report focused on the consequences, both positive and negative, of changes in ecosystems in preceding decades and on the requirements for preventing further degradation. While acknowledging the human benefits in terms of economic development and general well-being that have accrued from some ecosystem changes, the report found that 60 percent of the areas examined had been substantially degraded or overused—a rate of deterioration that could result in dire consequences for future generations if sustained. Suggested corrective actions included education, changes in consumption patterns, technological advances, and factoring into production costs environmental considerations. Follow-up reports were scheduled to be released every five years.

In 2006 UNEP released *Marine and Coastal Ecosystems & Human Well-being: Synthesis,* which examined the loss of coastal marine resources and tied those degradations to human activities, such as overfishing, habitat loss, climate change, pollution, and poor land use. For example, the report found that 75 percent of the fish stocks studied were in need of management programs to reverse declines and stabilize populations. UNEP's budget for the year was $105 million.

UNEP proclaimed 2007 the Year of the Dolphin and launched a global effort to increase awareness of the threats facing different species. The Intergovernmental Panel on Climate Change (IPCC) issued its fourth assessment report on climate change in February 2007. The study was composed of four main reports and found that "global warming was unequivocal" and caused mainly by human activities and the production of greenhouse gases. It warned that temperatures would continue to rise for centuries even if current production of pollutants was curtailed.

In February 2007 at a conference in Paris, French president Jacques Chirac called for UNEP to be absorbed into a new, strengthened body to be titled the United Nations Environment Organization (UNEO). Chirac's proposal was endorsed by 46 countries, but opposed by the United States, Russia, and China. No action was taken on the plan. In October UNEP published the *Global Environment Outlook: Environment for Development* (GEO-4). GEO-4 was described as the most comprehensive review of the changes in the global ecosystem since 1987 and was the work of more than 300 scientists. It identified climate change, loss of biodiversity, and degradation of the world's oceans as the main environmental threats facing the world. UNEP also announced that it had met its goal of hiring women for half of its professional staff in 2007.

For its work on climate change, the IPCC was awarded the 2007 Nobel Peace Prize, along with former U.S. vice president Albert Gore Jr., a leading advocate for action against global warming. In November UNEP chartered the International Panel for Sustainable Resource Management. The new body was charged with examining the impact of biofuels and recycling on the environment.

In 2008 UNEP announced that it had fallen short of its 2007 target of $72 million in contributions to the Environment Fund by $2.8 million. Building on GEO-4, UNEP developed a series of intermediate objectives, highlighted in the 2008 publication *UNEP Medium-Term Strategy 2010–2013: Environment for Development.* The report named six areas of focus: "climate change; disasters and conflicts; ecosystem management; environmental governance; harmful substances and hazardous waste; and resource efficiency—sustainable consumption and production." The publication also set measurable goals for each area and emphasized the transition of UNEP into a results-oriented organization with a goal of becoming the world's foremost environmental body. UNEP created a new strategic partnership with the Democratic Republic of the Congo to assist the country in developing its resources in an environmentally friendly manner. The arrangement was seen as a prototype for future relationships with individual states. UNEP also created the Poverty and Environment Facility to oversee the disbursement of aid under the joint UNEP-UNDP Poverty and Environment Initiative.

UNEP's staff increased to 597 in 2009, mainly in response to the need to oversee and coordinate new environmental programs across the globe. UNEP budgeted $171 million in expenditures for the Environment Fund that year. Through 2009, UNEP prepared for the Seal the Deal summit in Copenhagen in December 2009. The meeting was designed to bring together heads of state and other leaders to finalize strategies to address climate change and develop a successor agreement to the Kyoto Protocols. Meanwhile, UNEP's *Global Trends in Sustainable Energy Investment 2009* was produced in an effort to influence the Copenhagen meeting by providing information on best energy practices and encouraging the use of renewable resources. The Copenhagen Summit, December 7–16, 2009, was widely regarded as a failure since delegates were unable to agree on specific country commitments to reduce greenhouse emissions. Instead, delegates "noted" the nonbinding Copenhagen Accord, drafted by the United States, Brazil, China, India, and South Africa, through which countries could offer voluntary reductions. The agreement also pledged that developed states would provide up to $100 billion to developing nations to mitigate the impact of climate change.

In April 2010 Achim Steiner of Germany was reelected UNEP director for a second four-year term. Published in 2010, UNEP's 2009 annual report, *Seizing the Green Opportunity,* highlighted the growth in green technologies and industries and called for new investments in these sectors. More than 170 countries participated in UNEP's Billion Tree Campaign, which resulted in the planting of more than 7.4 billion trees worldwide. Parties to the 1992 UN Framework Convention on Climate Change met in Bonn, Germany, on May 31–June 11 to craft a new agreement to limit global warming. The new accord went further than relying on the pledges from the Copenhagen Summit and called on developed states to reduce greenhouse gas emissions by 25–40 percent by 2020, with further cuts by 2050.

The 2010 annual report, *A Year in Review*, noted that the *Global Environmental Outlook* was being reworked to emphasize solutions. It mentioned significant progress in setting and coordinating the UN's environmental agenda and noted the completion of an internal reform program. This program was to improve the synergy between different UNEP operations, as well as increasingly incorporating gender concerns into the agency's work.

For 2010–2011 UNEP's budget was $448 million. UNEP's 2011 annual report noted that 15 of 21 reforms recommended in 2008 had been completed. Meanwhile, UNEP had dispersed more than $200 million to support clean energy projects. The report also found that the elimination of lead in gasoline had saved the world $2.4 trillion in health costs and prevented 1.2 million premature deaths. In November 2012 UNEP published *Emissions Gap Report 2012*, which warned that greenhouse gas emissions into the atmosphere would rise to 58 billion gigatons annually by 2020, far above the 44 billion gigaton maximum to avert a 2 degree Celsius temperature rise.

In 2013 the General Assembly approved a UNEP budget for 2014–2015 of $631 million, a 2.6 percent increase. The budget included plans to reduce staffing costs by 30 percent and reallocate funding to operations. In January 2013 under the auspices of UNEP, negotiations on a treaty to limit mercury in manufacturing and mining were finalized. The Minmata Convention on Mercury was presented for adoption at a conference in October.

United Nations Institute for Training and Research
(UNITAR)

Established: By General Assembly resolution of December 11, 1963. The inaugural meeting of the Board of Trustees was held March 24, 1965, and the institute became operational the following year.

Purpose: "To enhance the effectiveness of the United Nations through training and research in the maintenance of peace and security and in the promotion of economic and social development."

Headquarters: Geneva, Switzerland.

Principal Organ: Board of Trustees (up to 30 members appointed by the UN secretary general), of whom one or more may be officials of the UN Secretariat and the others governmental representatives. The UN secretary general, the president of the General Assembly, the president of the Economic and Social Council, and the institute's executive director are ex-officio members.

Web site: www.unitar.org

Executive Director (Interim): Sally Fegan-Wyles (Ireland).

Activities. UNITAR provides practical assistance to the UN system, with particular emphasis on the problems of less developed countries. The institute is also concerned with the professional enrichment of national officials and diplomats dealing with UN-related issues and provides training for officials within the UN system. Seminars, courses, and symposia have dealt with multilateral diplomacy, economic development, international law, and UN documentation.

Despite years of declining pledge contributions and a decision in the late 1980s to reorient its programs toward training and away from research, UNITAR ended the decade with the General Assembly having reaffirmed the "validity and relevance" of UNITAR's mandate. In 1991 a high-level report on the future role of UNITAR was presented to the General Assembly, which endorsed a strengthening of UNITAR's training mandate, provided the institute avoided duplicating the work of other UN bodies. As a result, the Board of Trustees in mid-1992 approved a proposal from Secretary General Boutros-Ghali that UNITAR focus on these training areas: multilateral diplomacy; negotiations training for conflict resolution; economic and social development on selected matters in which UNITAR has a "competitive advantage" over other UN agencies; environmental and natural resource management training; peacekeeping, peacemaking, and peacebuilding; and the application of information systems. Training programs would be open to UN and non-UN diplomats, representatives from intergovernmental and nongovernmental organizations, national officials, and even the private sector.

In April 1993 the General Assembly approved a resolution providing for the shift of UNITAR's headquarters from New York City, New York, in the United States, to Geneva, Switzerland, and directed that the institute's future activities would have to be financed completely by voluntary contributions or special purpose grants. New York and Hiroshima, Japan, continue to host UNITAR offices.

In March 2007 Carlos Lopes of Guinea-Bissau was appointed UNITAR's executive director (for information on UNITAR prior to 2007, please see the 2013 *Handbook*). Lopes announced in November that UNITAR was undergoing a major transition to focus its efforts on standardizing methodologies between governments as the main goal of its training programs. The new director also noted that UNITAR had developed relationships with Columbia University, New York, United States; the University of Cape Town, Cape Town, South Africa; and the Ecole Libre des Sciences Politiques (Sciences Po), Paris, France, and that these academic partners would certify future training and educational initiatives.

As of 2008 the number of UNITAR staff members engaged in training and capacity-building programs had increased to about 80. The majority were engaged in the following areas: decentralized cooperation (local action) for development, chemicals and waste management, climate change, environmental law, foreign economic relations, HIV/AIDS, international affairs management, international migration policy, legal aspects of debt and financial management, needs of women and children in conflict and postconflict zones, peacekeeping operations instruction, peacemaking and preventive diplomacy, and technology and information systems for sustainable development. In April UN secretary general Ban initiated a new UNITAR lecture series in Geneva on global challenges. The series was designed to engage the public and increase awareness of the major issues facing the UN and the global community. UNITAR announced that it would reconfigure its peacekeeping training to better address challenges and to make better use of new training technologies, including Web-based programs.

UNITAR reinitiated its global migration program in 2009 and became the chair of the interagency body, the Global Migration Group. UNITAR saw a 57 percent increase in its biennial operating budget in 2009, mainly due to a rise in funding from donor states. Through the year, UNITAR increased the activities of the UN Operational Satellite Applications Program (UNOSAT). The program used satellite imagery to produce maps and data to support UN activities and research. UNOSAT launched discussions with the European Space Agency over cooperative ventures and was involved in disaster mapping of 34 incidents in 2009, including the Samoan tsunami and flooding in the Philippines and Vietnam. UNOSAT's increased activities were made possible by a rise in funding from Denmark, Norway, and Sweden.

UNOSAT also became engaged in monitoring pirate activity around the Horn of Africa and was able to map a decline in the success rate of attempted hijackings from 40 percent in 2008 to 23 percent in 2009 as a result of increased international naval patrols in the region. A 2009 report concluded that Africa was the main beneficiary of UNITAR's programs, receiving 40.3 percent of the organization's funding, followed by Asia and the Pacific, 21.4 percent, and Latin America and the Caribbean, 19.9 percent. UNOSAT continued to monitor natural disasters, including the 2010 flooding in Thailand and the impact of Cyclone Giri that same year. In November 2010 UNITAR began training at its Nairobi office, designed to make UN peacekeeping missions greener. It noted that UN Field Missions globally account for 56 percent of the total UN greenhouse gas emissions.

In March 2011 UNITAR began publishing satellite maps of Libya and the surrounding countries to track the movements of refugees from the Libyan civil war. UNOSAT's fourth monitoring report on internal refugees in Somalia revealed that in 2012 there was a 45 percent increase in the number of displaced persons or sites from the previous year. A similar analysis of Syrian refugee sites in Turkey also indicated an increase. In September 2012 Sally Fegan-Wyles of Ireland became interim executive director of UNITAR. UNITAR's budget for the 2012-2013 period was $44.8 million. That year UNITAR completed more than 400 training projects that included 23,000 participants.

UNOSAT was praised for its ability to provide rapid mapping of disaster incidents in September 2013 at a forum sponsored by the UN Office for the coordination of Humanitarian Affairs (OCHA). UNOSAT maps on average 35–40 emergenceis per year and 35 percent of its mapping projects support OCHA operations. In October, UNOSAT began providing regular data to the UN Operations and Crisis Center.

United Nations Office of High Commissioner for Refugees (UNHCR)

Established: By General Assembly resolution of December 3, 1949, with operations commencing January 1, 1951, for a three-year period; five-year extensions subsequently approved through December 31, 2008.

Purpose: To provide protection, emergency relief, and resettlement assistance to refugees, and to promote permanent solutions to refugee problems.

Headquarters: Geneva, Switzerland.

Principal Organs: Executive Committee, Standing Committee.

Web site: www.unhcr.org

High Commissioner: António Guterres (Portugal).

Membership of Executive Committee (87): Algeria, Argentina, Australia, Austria, Azerbaijan, Bangladesh, Belgium, Benin, Brazil, Bulgaria, Cameroon, Canada, Chile, China, Colombia, Congo, Côte d'Ivoire, Costa Rica, Croatia, Cyprus, Democratic Republic of the Congo, Denmark, Djibouti, Ecuador, Egypt, Estonia, Ethiopia, Finland, France, Germany, Ghana, Greece, Guinea, Holy See (Vatican City State), Hungary, India, Iran, Ireland, Israel, Italy, Japan, Jordan, Kenya, Republic of Korea, Lebanon, Lesotho, Luxembourg, Macedonia, Madagascar, Mexico, Moldova, Morocco, Mozambique, Namibia, Netherlands, New Zealand, Nicaragua, Nigeria, Norway, Pakistan, Philippines, Poland, Portugal, Romania, Russia, Rwanda, Serbia, Slovenia, Somalia, South Africa, Spain, Sudan, Sweden, Switzerland, Tanzania, Thailand, Togo, Tunisia, Turkey, Turkmenistan, Uganda, United Kingdom, United States, Venezuela, Yemen, Zambia. Membership on the Executive Committee is permanent following approval by the Economic and Social Council and the General Assembly.

Activities. The UNHCR, financed partly by a limited UN subsidy for administration but primarily by contributions from governments, nongovernmental organizations, and individuals, attempts to ensure the treatment of refugees according to internationally accepted standards. In all, the UNHCR maintains 259 offices in 126 countries, with a total staff of 7,685.

The UNHCR promoted the adoption of the UN Convention on the Status of Refugees in 1951 and an additional protocol in 1967 that together provide a widely applicable definition of the term "refugee," establish minimum standards for treatment of refugees, grant favorable legal status to refugees, and accord refugees certain economic and social rights. (As of October 2013 there were 145 parties to the convention, and 146 to the protocol.) In addition, the UNHCR conducts material assistance programs that provide emergency relief (food, medicine) and supplementary aid while work proceeds on the durable solutions of (in order of priority) the voluntary repatriation of refugees, their integration into the country where asylum was first sought, or their resettlement to a third country. Activities are often conducted in cooperation with other UN agencies, national governments, regional bodies, and private relief organizations (for more information on the activities of the UNHCR prior to 2003, please see the 2013 *Handbook*).

During 2003 the U.S.-led invasion of Iraq did not generate a major refugee exodus, as had been feared, but caused considerable internal displacement. As of May 2004 the UNHCR was preparing to help in the "phased return" of some 500,000 Iraqis to their homes, beginning as soon as the security situation stabilized. At the same time, the organization was facing renewed difficulties in Sudan's Darfur region, where hostilities in late 2003 led some 120,000 refugees to scatter just across the remote border with Chad.

In 2004 the UNHCR reported that the number of asylum applications in 36 developed countries dropped by 20 percent in 2003 to 471,000, down from 587,000 the previous year and the lowest number in six years. While the UNHCR attributed the improvement to more stable situations in Afghanistan, the Balkans, and Iraq, an additional factor was the rise of intolerance and anti-asylum measures in Europe and elsewhere. However, the UNHCR reported that the number of "people of concern" rose to 19.2 million in 2005 after declining to 17 million in 2004. In 2005 there was a worldwide decrease in the number of refugees, from 9.54 million to 8.39 million. This capped a five-year decrease of 31 percent and brought the overall number of refugees to its lowest level since 1980. Among refugee populations, the largest was some 1.1 million Afghans living in Pakistani camps, although the UNHCR projected that an additional 1.5 million Afghans were probably residing outside camps where there were no UNHCR services. The largest IDP population was 2 million in Colombia. In Iraq, the number of IDPs increased to 1.2 million. Sudan accounted for 840,000 IDPs and 150,000 refugees.

High Commissioner Lubbers resigned in February 2005 after he was accused of sexual harassment by women employees. He was succeeded by former Portuguese prime minister António Guterres, who initiated a series of reforms in budgeting and crisis management.

By January 2007 the UNHCR estimated that there were 32.86 million asylum seekers, refugees, or IDPs worldwide. The largest number was in Asia, 14.91 million, followed by Africa with 9.72 million, and Europe with 3.43 million. The UNHCR announced a partnership with the Clinton Global Initiative in an effort to raise $220 million to provide educational programs for 9 million refugee children. Among the UNHCR's major operations in 2007 were the resettlement of Roma refugees in Hungary, Kosovo, and Montenegro, and the closure of the last major temporary refugee camp in Kosovo. The body also undertook a major initiative to provide supplies for 160,000 refugees in Kenya who were displaced by flooding. In cooperation with the Afghan government, the UNHCR oversaw the return of 200,000 Afghan refugees from Pakistan and undertook major missions to support displaced persons in Somalia and Sudan. In July the UNHCR doubled its aid to $123 million annually to support the estimated 2.2 million externally displaced Iraqis in neighboring states and the 2 million internal refugees. The UNHCR also called on the United States to increase the number of Iraqi asylum seekers admitted from the 8,000 granted refuge in 2006. During 2007, the UNHCR signed an agreement with Morocco to enhance its presence in the country and an accord with Kazakhstan to facilitate operations in that country.

On April 29, 2008, the UN General Assembly voted to increase the membership of the executive committee from 72 to 76 states. In June the UNHCR report *2007 Global Trends: Refugees, Asylum-Seekers, Returnees, Internally Displaced and Stateless Persons* noted that by the end of 2007, the number of IDPs was 51 million, including 26 million displaced by conflict and 25 million displaced as the result of natural disasters. Of the two categories, at least 31.7 million were in the UNHCR's areas of operations, a decline of 3 percent from the previous year. The report also found that 80 percent of refugees remained in the region of their origin and that more than half resided in urban areas. In the publication the UNHCR changed the way it counted refugees and IDPs. Those who had been resettled through host country programs for periods of five to ten years, depending on the country, were no longer classified as refugees. The report found that the number of refugees and IDPs rose for the second consecutive year, after annual declines from 2001–2005.

Between October 2007 and 2008 the UNHCR assisted more than 250,000 Afghans in their return, mainly from Iran and Pakistan. In addition, the UNHCR aided the government of Tanzania in beginning the return of an estimated 110,000 Burundians to their homes and in consolidating Tanzania's 11 refugee camps into 5. The initiative was part of a cooperative program with other UN agencies to provide training and resources so that refugees and IDPs were able to transition back into their local economies. In another example, as part of an effort to return Hutu refugees to Rwanda, the UNHCR launched a construction program to build new housing for the returnees.

The UNHCR's 2009 budget was a record $2 billion. Completed in 2008, UNHCR's global service center in Budapest became the organization's second largest office in 2009, with a staff of 180 (behind only its headquarters in Geneva with 740). The center was created to consolidate a number of smaller regional offices and centralize functions as part of a broader reform effort to reduce costs and increase efficiency. In May the UNHCR responded when fighting between the Taliban and Pakistani government forces created more than 200,000 refugees in northwestern Pakistan. The agency's annual report noted that there were approximately 15.2 million refugees (including 4.7 million in UN-administered camps in the Middle East), which represented an 8 percent reduction from the previous year. The agency also noted that there were about 26 million internally displaced persons, including 14.4 million under the care of the UN. This figure was stable from the previous year but included new displaced populations in Colombia, Pakistan, the Philippines, Somalia, Sri Lanka, and Sudan. Colombia, Iraq, and Sudan remained the countries with the largest numbers of internally displaced persons.

UNHCR's budget in 2010 increased dramatically to a record $3.1 billion. The organization reported that although the total number of refugees decreased, UNHCR provided care to a larger percentage of at-risk populations. At the beginning of 2010, there 10.5 million refugees, of which 4.6 million received some assistance from the UNHCR (not including those under the care of the UNRWA). There were also 14.5 million IDPs under the care of the organization. The UNHCR estimated that there were more than 12 million stateless people around the globe, but noted that countries such as Bangladesh and Sri Lanka had seen the number of stateless persons decline dramatically. The largest number of refugees and IDPs were in Asia, followed by Africa. In April Guterres was reelected the UNHCR high commissioner by the General Assembly. In addition, the UNHCR executive board was increased to 79 members.

The UNHCR's annual report for 2010 stated that 25.2 million were receiving some form of protection. Approximately 12 million were stateless. Pakistan hosted the largest number of refugees, followed by Iran and Syria. Approximately 7.2 million refugees had little prospect of returning home, the highest number since 2001. The agency's 2011 budget was $3.32 billion.

In 2011 UNHCR reported 10.5 million refugees of concern, a minor decrease from the previous year. The number of IDPs rose to 27.5 million, 14.7 million of whom received aid from UNHCR. The largest number of IDPs were in Africa, some 11.1 million. UNHCR's budget continued to increase, rising to $3.6 billion in 2012, and $4.3 billion, the following year.

In 2013 the UNHCR reported another small decrease in the number of refugees of concern, down to 10.4 million. Approximately 50 percent of refugees were in Asia, with Africa accounting for about 28 percent. The number of IDPs again increased, rising to 28.8 million, with 6.5 million newly displaced IDPs. Conflicts in Syria and the Democratic Republic of the Congo (DRC) accounted for roughly half of the new IDPs (2.4 million in Syria and 1 million in the DRC). The UNHCR provided services or care for approximately15.5 million IDPs.

United Nations Population Fund
(UNFPA)

Established: By the secretary general in July 1967 as the Trust Fund for Population Activities; name changed in May 1969 to United Nations Fund for Population Activities (UNFPA), with administration assigned to United Nations Development Program (UNDP); became operational in October 1969; placed under authority of the General Assembly in December 1972; became a subsidiary organ of the assembly in December 1979; name changed to United Nations Population Fund in December 1987, with the UNFPA designation being retained.

Purpose: To enhance the capacity to respond to needs in population and family planning, promote awareness of population problems in both developed and developing countries and possible strategies to deal with them, assist developing countries in dealing with their population problems in the forms and means best suited to their needs, and play a leading role in the UN system in promoting population programs and reproductive health.

Principal Organ: Executive Board (same membership as the UNDP Executive Board).

Web site: www.unfpa.org

Headquarters: New York, United States.

Executive Director: Babatunde Osotimehin (Nigeria).

Activities. The UNFPA continues to be the largest source of multilateral population assistance to less developed areas (for UNFPA activities prior to 2002, please see the 2010 *Handbook*). A major issue for the UNFPA has been hostility from the United States, which has not committed funds to the organization since mid-2002. The George W. Bush administration has continued to cite abortion and sterilization policies in China as justification, although a report by its own investigators showed no link between such policies and the UNFPA. Critics have asserted that the withdrawal of U.S. funds represents an effort to appease religious conservatives among the U.S. electorate.

Despite the U.S. failure to contribute funds, in 2005 the UNFPA had a record year in funding, with 172 countries and a range of nongovernmental and private organizations contributing $565 million, compared with $506 million in 2004. Expenditures, including programs in 148 developing countries, were $523 million.

In 2007 UNFPA initiated a joint program with the UN Children's Fund (UNICEF) to reduce female genital mutilation by 40 percent in 16 countries by 2015. The ultimate goal of the program was to end the practice entirely within 20 years through increased education and government action.

In the *State of World Population 2007: Unleashing the Potential of Urban Growth,* UNFPA noted that in 2008, for the first time in history, more than half of the world's population, or 3.3 billion people, lived in urban areas, marking the first time in history that city-dwellers outnumber their rural counterparts. By 2030, a projected 60 percent of the world's population would be urban. The report stated that the benefits of urbanization outweighed the negative consequences, especially in regard to reproductive healthcare and infant mortality rates. Nonetheless, the study also found that the population living in slums in urban areas doubled to 200 million, or 72 percent of the urban population, by 2005 in sub-Saharan Africa, compared with 56 percent of the urban population in South Asia.

In 2008 the UNFPA had programs in 158 countries and offices in 112 nations with 1,031 staff members, 44 percent of whom were women. To increase efficiency, the UNFPA developed and implemented a new strategic plan to guide the organization through 2011. The plan identified three main areas at the core of the UNFPA's mission: "population and development, reproductive health and rights, and gender equality." The agency also carried out a reorganization that established new regional offices in Bangkok, Bratislava, Cairo, Johannesburg, and Panama City, with six additional, new sub-regional offices. The UNFPA also reorganized its technical division and created a new program division to develop and oversee individual projects. The *State of World Population 2008: Reaching Common Ground; Culture, Gender and Human Rights* asserted the universality of human rights and the need to ensure the application of global frameworks to all countries. It presented an overview of strategies to implement culturally sensitive development plans that both promoted human rights and respected local traditions and mores. The UNFPA also launched the Maternal Health Trust Fund to provide assistance to mothers and newborns in 2008. Through 2009, the program was active in 61 countries.

In 2009 the UNFPA had 129 offices and was active in 155 countries with a budget of $783.1 million, of which $469.4 million was provided by donor countries and organizations, an increase of $40 million over the previous year. In October the UNFPA sponsored the fourth international parliamentarians conference on the action program from the 1994 International Conference on Population and Development (ICPD). Legislators from 115 countries attended the summit and reaffirmed commitments to reproductive health and access to medical services. The UNFPA also expanded its family planning programs to include efforts in 72 countries, including the distribution of more than 50 million female condoms in 2009. The UNFPA 2010 annual report highlighted the fact that as the population aged, less developed countries were not well prepared to deal with the consequences. Income increased to $870 million for the year, with much of the increase coming from voluntary contributions. Expenditures amounted to $801.4 million. The agency was deeply involved in Haitian earthquake relief.

In 2011 UNFPA increased its operations to 156 countries and had a record budget of $934 million. In its annual report, UNFPA highlighted the birth of the world's 7th billion person and the implications of population growth on resource use and sustainable development. In its 2011 annual report, the UNFPA highlighted that there were 1.8 billion people in the world from the ages of 10 to 24, the "largest youth cohort in human history." Concurrently, advances in medicine and care mean that there were more people over the age of 60, some 900 million, than ever before.

The UNFPA budget continued to increase, rising to anotherrecord, $963.2 million for 2012. *The State of the World Population 2012: By Choice, Not by Chance* highlighted the negative affects of unintended-pregnancies and underscored the need for greater access to family planning in developing states. The report found that 222 million women lacked access to family planning, and that there were an estimated 80 million unintended pregnancies in 2012. In July, the UNFPA, the United Kingdom, and the Bill and Melinda Gates Foundation held a conference that raised $2.6 billion for family planning.

United Nations Relief and Works Agency for Palestine Refugees in the Near East (UNRWA)

Established: By General Assembly resolution of December 8, 1949; mandate most recently extended through June 30, 2011.

Purpose: To provide relief, education, and health and social services to Palestinian refugees (i.e., people [and later the descendants of people] who resided in Palestine for a minimum of two years preceding the Arab-Israeli conflict in 1948 and who, as a result of that conflict, lost both their homes and their means of livelihood).

Headquarters: Gaza and Amman, Jordan. (Most of the operations, previously in Vienna, Austria, were moved to Gaza in July 1996. The remainder were relocated to the agency's other longstanding headquarters in Amman.)

Web site: www.unrwa.org

Commissioner General: Filippo Grandi (Italy).

Advisory Commission: Comprised of representatives of the governments of Australia, Belgium, Canada, Denmark, Egypt, Finland, France, Germany, Ireland, Italy, Japan, Jordan, Kuwait, Lebanon, Luxembourg, the Netherlands, Norway, Saudi Arabia, Spain, Sweden, Switzerland, Syria, Turkey, the United Kingdom, and the United States. The Palestinian National Authority, the European Union, and the League of Arab States are observers.

Activities. As of January 2013 approximately 5.2 million people who met the established definition of Palestinian refugee were registered with the UNRWA, a 3 percent increase over the previous year. About 1.5 million of that number lived in 58 refugee camps, many of which had in effect become permanent towns; the remainder lived in previously established towns and villages in the areas served by UNRWA—Jordan, Lebanon, Syria, the West Bank, and Gaza. The UNRWA's original priority was to provide direct humanitarian relief to refugees uprooted by the fighting that followed the creation of Israel. In the absence of a peaceful settlement to the Palestinian question, the UNRWA's attention shifted to education (it runs about 660 schools attended by approximately 491,000 students) and the provision of public health services (it operates 139 health centers) to a basically self-supporting population. The UNRWA employs some 30,300 people, including 19,600 educators and 4,100 medical personnel.

Some Israelis and members of the U.S. Congress, among others, have accused the UNRWA of allowing refugee camps to be used for terrorist training and activities. A 2006 audit by the U.S. General Accounting Office concluded that no money provided by the United States—the source of some 30 percent of UNRWA funds—could be linked to terrorist activities in the refugee camps. (For information on UNRWA prior to 2006, please see the 2013 *Handbook.*)

In 2007 the UNRWA's budget was $487.1 million. The United States, the European Commission, Sweden, Norway, and the United Kingdom were the agency's largest donors for the year. In February the EU announced that it would increase support for the UNRWA by 7 percent between 2008 and 2010 with total funding during that period at €264 million ($379.1 million). Fighting in the Nahr al-Bared refugee camp in Lebanon between security forces and Islamic militants forced most of the 31,000 inhabitants of the settlement to flee. The UNRWA estimated that it would take three years to rebuild the camp. Meanwhile, fighting between Hamas and Fatah in June created a new refugee crisis and led the UNRWA to issue an appeal for $246.15 million in emergency funding. Through November, the UNRWA had collected $111 million in emergency relief.

The UNRWA's 2008 budget was $541.8 million, and the agency's main donors were, in order of contributions, the United States, the European Commission, Sweden, the United Kingdom, Norway, and the Netherlands. The continuing refugee crisis in Gaza and the West Bank led the UNRWA to again request emergency donations. For 2008, the UNRWA sought $263.4 million. However, by October 2008 the agency had received only about 60 percent of that amount. At the same time, the UNRWA's appeal for emergency funding for refugees in Lebanon exceeded its goal of $54.8 million as the organization had secured $57.2 million by October. In June the UNRWA and the UAE Red Crescent launched a major initiative to rebuild and refurbish some of the oldest refugee camps that had 60-year-old facilities. The first phase of the project was the construction of a new health clinic and 140 housing units in the Neirab Camp, the largest of the UNRWA's facilities in Syria. Also in June the UNRWA began reconstruction of the Nahr al-Bared camp in Lebanon. In September the UNRWA issued a flash appeal for $43 million to cover temporary operations in the camp during the rebuilding work.

For 2009 the UNRWA's budget remained flat at $541 million, but by May it was estimated that falling donations would result in an operating deficit of $125 million for the year. The United States was the largest contributor to the UNRWA that year, providing $268 million for the regular operating budget and for emergency appeals. The EU was second, at $232.7 million. Efforts to reduce expenditures at some camps led to protests by refugees through the summer. The UNRWA launched the Gaza quick response program in 2009 as an effort to coordinate all of the emergency funding appeals into a single initiative for the region. The UNRWA sought $371.3 million but had raised only $192.6 million through August. A similar effort for the West Bank performed even more poorly, securing only $31 million of the requested $90 million. Nonetheless, the UNRWA provided emergency food assistance to more than 1.2 million people through 2009. In October the UNRWA began the da'am (support) program, which was designed to better identify the needs of the most disadvantaged groups and provide assistance more efficiently. Eight communities were initially involved in the project, which was expected to be expanded throughout the system in late 2010. A UNRWA employment program provided 1.7 million work days in Gaza and the West Bank, employing 30,891 people.

In 2010 the UNRWA completed a three-year reform program designed to improve the organization's internal management of human resources, strengthen individual program oversight, and streamline organizational procedures. Meanwhile the organization completed repairs to the 51 UNRWA facilities that had been damaged during fighting in 2008 and finished work on 4,921 temporary shelters in case of future fighting. The UNRWA also finalized work to repair and expand the water and sewage systems in eight of its camps in the West Bank. The UNRWA 2010–2011 regular biennial budget was $1.23 billion, of which more than 50 percent was allocated to education. Through October 2010, the agency's emergency appeals totaled $323.3 million.

UNRWA expenditures in 2011 totaled $655 million of which approximately half was allocated for education and training and $118 million for health care. The United States was the largest donor to UNRWA in 2011 with $239 million, followed by the EU at $175 million. Following the outbreak of fighting in Syria, the UNRWA began additional deliveries of food and medical supplies to Syrian camps in August 2012.

In 2012 the UNRWA's regular budget was $675.3 million. In addition the agency raised $300 million through emergency appeals, with a significantportion of the funding used to address deteriorating conditions in Syria. In 2012 the UNRWA launched a broad reform process across its programs. In 2013 the agency's health centers in Lebanon and Gaza implemented reforms to improve efficiency through the use of electronicrecords, an e-appointment system, and a team approach to healthcare delivery. The reforms were scheduled to be put into place in Jordan, Syria, and the West Bank by 2015. Educational reforms, including more stringent teacher certification requirements and updated curriculums were also scheduled to be implemented by 2015.

United Nations Research Institute for Social Development (UNRISD)

Established: July 1, 1964, by means of an initial grant from the government of the Netherlands, in furtherance of a General Assembly resolution of December 5, 1963, on social targets and social planning.

Purpose: To conduct research into the "problems and policies of social development and relationships between various types of social and economic development during different phases of economic growth."

Headquarters: Geneva, Switzerland.

Principal Organ: Board of Advisors, consisting of a chair appointed by the UN secretary general and ten individual members nominated by the Commission for Social Development and confirmed by the Economic and Social Council. There are also seven ex-officio members—a representative of the UN Secretariat; two representatives (in rotation) from the FAO, ILO, UNDP, UNESCO, UNHCR, UNU, and WHO; the executive secretary of the Economic Commission for Western Asia; the directors of the Latin American Institute for Economic and Social Planning and the African Institute for Economic Development and Planning; and the institute director.

Web site: www.unrisd.org

Director: Sarah Cook (United Kingdom).

Activities. The focus of UNRISD activities has shifted over the years to reflect current concerns in social development and public policy. Thus, in 1988 the board approved redefinitions of priority research areas to include food policy in the world recession, refugees and returnees, and the social impact of the economic crisis. Subsequent areas of research interest included participation and changes in property relations in communist and post-communist societies; integrating gender into development policy; and the environment, sustainable development, and social change. The institute currently considers eradicating poverty, promoting democracy and human rights, establishing gender equity, examining the effects of globalization, and ensuring environmental sustainability as "overarching concerns" in all UNRISD efforts.

Current research emphases include civil society and social movements; democracy, governance, and human rights; identities, conflict, and cohesion; social policy and development; and technology, business, and society. Ongoing projects include, for example, examination of grassroots movements and land reform initiatives, public sector reform in crisis-ridden countries, HIV/AIDS and development, the interaction of information technologies and social development, and social policy and "late industrializers" in Africa, Latin America, and the Middle East.

In 2007 the UNRISD launched a major research project on poverty reduction, scheduled to be completed and published in 2009 (for information on UNRISD prior to 2007, please see the 2013 *Handbook*). To facilitate the research, the UNRISD sponsored a series of conferences around the world to bring together scholars and policymakers. The agency announced that its other research programs for the next two years would be organized into five broad areas: social policy and development; markets, business, and regulation; civil society and social movements; identities, conflict, and cohesion; and gender development. Through 2008 the UNRISD supported 118 researchers in 40 countries examining social policy and economic development. The UNRISD's core funding was $3.3 million, an increase from $2.8 million in the prior year, and its project funding was $859,479 versus $1.2 million in the previous year.

The UNRISD's operating budget for 2009 increased to approximately $4 million. In September 2009 UNRISD sponsored a major conference in Seoul, South Korea, on poverty reduction programs. Meanwhile, Sarah Cook of the United Kingdom was appointed the director of UNRISD in November, following the resignation of Thandika Mkandawire of Sweden in April. From 2006 through 2009, UNRISD commissioned more than 40 research papers to support the flagship report *Combating Poverty and Inequality: Structural Change, Social Policy and Politics,* published in 2010. The report explored the impact of the global economic crisis on the ability to achieve the MDG, especially the reduction of poverty. It noted that for the first time in history, the number of malnourished people in the world rose above 1 billion and that even if the MDG objective of reducing poverty by 50 percent by 2015 was met, more than 1 billion people would remain in poverty. However, the report also concluded that economic growth in Asia had helped reduce the number of people living on less than $1.25 worldwide from 1.8 billion to 1.4 billion in 2009. The report suggested, even if not explicitly stating, that the MDG might not be met.

In 2010 the organization's expenditures totaled approximately $3.4 million. Expenditures increased slightly in 2011 to $3.9 million, but fell in 2012 back to $3.4 million. The 2012 policy brief, *Gendered Impacts of Globalization: Employment and Social Protection,* reviewed existing literature on women's participation in the labor force and inequality in pay and benefits. The report called for pension reform to include noncontributory retirement systems and increased maternity and care leave.

Following the May 2013 UNRISD conference, "Potential and Limits of Social and Solidarity Economy (SSE)," UN agencies, including, UNRISD, the FAO, and the ILO, created the Inter-Agency Task Force on Social and Solidarity Economy in September. SSE refers to organizations that have both a social and an economic impact but are not part of the traditional for-profit sector. For example, UNRISD noted that in the United Kingdom, "social enterprises" employed more than 800,000 people and added $37.1 billion to the economy. The interagency grouping was charged with "mainstreaming" SSE in economic and public policy considerations.

United Nations University (UNU)

Established: By General Assembly resolution of December 11, 1972; charter adopted December 6, 1973; began operations September 1, 1975.

Purpose: To conduct action-oriented research in fields related to development, welfare, and human survival, and to train young scholars and research workers.

Headquarters: Tokyo, Japan.

Principal Organs: University Council (comprising 24 educators, each from a different country, in addition to the UN secretary general, the director general of UNESCO, the executive director of UNITAR, and the university rector, ex officio); Boards and Advisory Committees overseeing Research and Training Centers and Programs (RTC/Ps).

Web site: www.unu.edu

Rector: David M. Malone (Canada).

Activities. In July 1997 UN Secretary General Kofi Annan addressed the role of the UNU and other research bodies in his plan for overall UN reform. Annan argued that research institutes sometimes appeared to be living "in a world of their own, largely removed from the work and concerns of the United Nations." Furthermore, he wrote, these institutes rarely communicated among themselves and sometimes duplicated each other's work. In September new UNU Rector Hans van Ginkel of the Netherlands urged the UNU to tie its own proposed reforms to those of the UN in general and to increase cooperation with other UN entities, such as the UNDP, UNESCO, UNEP, UNICEF, and WHO. He also suggested that new UNU research concentrate on two program areas—peace and governance, and environment and sustainable development.

A mission statement adopted in 1999 defines the UNU's purpose as contributing "through research and capacity building, to efforts to resolve the pressing global problems that are the concern of the United Nations, its peoples and its Member States." Accordingly, the university considers as its principal functions fostering an international community of scholars; providing a bridge between the UN and the academic community; serving as a think tank for the UN; and aiding capacity building, especially in the developing world. Scholars affiliated with and contracted by the UNU conduct research and address needs in five general thematic areas: peace and security (international relations, the UN system, human security, armed conflicts); good governance (democracy and civil society, leadership, human rights, and ethics); development and poverty reduction (globalization and development, growth and employment, poverty and basic needs, urbanization); science, technology, and society (innovation, information technology and biotechnology, software technology, food and nutrition); and the environment and sustainability (resource management, sustainable industry and cities, water, global climate, and governance).

Much of the UNU's work is conducted through 13 RTC/Ps located around the world. In 1985 the university established its first RTC, the

World Institute for Development Economics Research (UNU-WIDER) in Helsinki, Finland. UNU-WIDER currently directs its programs toward conducting multidisciplinary research and analysis on how structural changes affect the world's poorest populations, training scholars and government officials in economic and social policy, and providing a forum on issues related to equitable and environmentally sustainable growth. In 1987 the council approved the creation of the Institute for Natural Resources in Africa (UNU-INRA) with the goal of strengthening scientific and technological capacities in such areas as land use, water management, energy resources, and minerals development. After being temporarily housed in Nairobi, Kenya, the UNU-INRA moved into permanent headquarters in Accra, Ghana, in 1993. (For more information on the centers and research operations of the UNU, please see the 2013 *Handbook.*)

In August 2007 Konrad Osterwalder of Switzerland became rector of the UNU, replacing van Ginkel. The European Commission asked the UNU to examine the issue of recycling electronic waste (e-waste) and develop a report, published in November, on how best to increase recycling of e-waste such as cellular phones, old computing equipment, and household appliances. The UNU also produced *Accountability and the United Nations System* (Policy Brief Number 8, 2007) in an effort to guide UN reforms and enhance financial and managerial accountability in the world body.

The UNU and the University of Tokyo created a joint initiative in July 2008 to facilitate research in the science of sustainability. The UNU and the government of Japan launched a pilot program through the Hiroshima Peacebuilders' Center to train people in conflict mediation and prevention. The training program also involved other UN bodies, including the UNHCR, UNDP, and UNICEF. The UNU documentary film *Voices of the Chichinautzin,* about the challenges faced by indigenous people of the Chichinautzin region of Mexico, won the best feature award at the Moondance International Film Festival.

In 2009, the system produced more than 800 publications, ranging from books to policy and technical briefs, and it sponsored more than 350 public events, including conferences, seminars, lectures, and presentations. The UNU articulated a new vision through the publication of the *United Nations University Strategic Plan, 2009–2012,* which called for the university to become a globally recognized research institution by reorganizing and reinvigorating its core functions and engaging in a sustained outreach program. The UNU's 2008–2009 biennial budget was $101.8 million, generated from donors and investment income (the UNU does not receive funding from the regular UN budget). In 2010 the UNU launched a new graduate program in sustainability, development, and peace at its Tokyo facility. The agency received $36.9 million in contributions during 2010.

UNU's 2010–2011 budget was $108 million. In 2011 UNU had faculty from 75 countries. That year the university launched a new master's degree in environmental governance with a specialty in biodiversity. In addition, two new centers were planned, the UNU International Institute for the Alliance of Civilizations and the UNU Institute for Integrated Management of Material Fluxes and Resources.

The UNU's budget for 2012–2013 biennium was $142.8 million. That year, the UNU staff numbered 679, along with 224 fellowship recipients, and 166 interns. In 2012 the UNU had 1,387 publications and conducted 275 public events. More than 5,500 students attended 146 training courses, with 110 held in developing countries. On March 1, 2013, David M. Malone of Canada was appointed rector of UNU.

SECURITY COUNCIL

Permanent Membership (5): China, France, Russia, United Kingdom, United States. (The other permanent members in late December 1991 accepted Russia's assumption of the seat previously filled by the Union of Soviet Socialist Republics.)

Nonpermanent Membership (10): Terms ending December 31, 2013: Azerbaijan, Guatemala, Morocco, Pakistan, and Togo. Terms ending December 31, 2014: Argentina, Australia, Luxembourg, Rwanda, and South Korea.

Web site: www.un.org/en/sc

Origin and development. In declaring the primary purpose of the UN to be the maintenance of international peace and security, the charter established a system for collective enforcement of the peace based on unity among the five permanent members of the Security Council. Peace efforts of the council are effective only to the degree that political accord is possible in relation to specific international disputes and only when the parties to such conflicts are willing to allow the UN to play its intended role.

The only instance of an actual military operation undertaken under UN auspices in response to an act of aggression was the Korean involvement of 1950–1953. The action was possible because the Soviet Union was boycotting the Security Council at the time and was thus unable to exercise a veto. The United States, which had military forces readily available in the area, was in a position to assume direction of a UN-established Unified Command, to which military forces were ultimately supplied by 16 member states. As of December 2002 the UN command remained in South Korea, with troops from the United States constituting the only foreign contingent. In 1975 the U.S. representative to the UN proposed, in a letter to the president of the Security Council, that the command be dissolved, with U.S. and South Korean officers as "successors in command," if North Korea and China would first agree to continue the armistice. However, no such agreement was subsequently concluded.

In certain other instances, as in the India-Pakistan War of 1965 and the Arab-Israeli War of 1967, the positions of the major powers have been close enough to lend weight to Security Council resolutions calling for cease-fires. The Security Council endorsed the use of "all necessary means" to liberate Kuwait from occupying Iraqi forces in early 1991; however, unlike the 1950 Korean deployment, the Desert Storm campaign was not a formal UN operation, the United States preferring to maintain military control rather than defer to an overall UN command.

The NATO-led air campaign against Yugoslavia's repression of the ethnic Albanian population in Kosovo during March–June 1999 was, again, initiated without direct Security Council backing, the United States and its NATO allies knowing full well that Russia and probably China would have vetoed a call for direct military action. On May 14 the Security Council did, however, pass a resolution urging support for humanitarian relief efforts to aid Kosovar refugees and internally displaced persons. The resolution also called for a political solution in line with principles put forward on May 6 by Canada, France, Germany, Italy, Japan, Russia, the United Kingdom, and the United States. A June 10 resolution authorized a United Nations Interim Administration Mission in Kosovo (UNMIK) and a NATO-led Multinational Force in Kosovo (KFOR), the latter to maintain security pending a handover to an UNMIK-established civilian police corps.

The Kosovo mission was the most comprehensive ever undertaken under Security Council auspices, going well beyond peacekeeping, and was followed only four months later by a similarly all-encompassing effort, the United Nations Transitional Administration in East Timor (UNTAET), which had as its task nation-building in preparation for East Timor's full independence. On May 17, 2002, with that goal accomplished, the Security Council authorized formation of a United Nations Mission of Support in East Timor (UNMISET) as a successor to the UNTAET. The new mission was mandated to ensure East Timor's domestic and international security and to offer support to the government of the new state. On May 21, 2005, UNMISET was succeeded by the United Nations Office in Timor-Leste (UNOTIL), which had been established by Security Council resolution as a special political mission to be directed by the UN Department of Peacekeeping Operations. In view of civil disorder in Timor-Leste, UNOTIL's one-year mandate was extended to August 20, 2006. There was general acknowledgment, however, that UNMISET had been withdrawn too hastily and that a comparable new mission was required to assist the new state (see the article on Timor-Leste).

The 1990s also saw the Security Council assume a leading role in establishing venues for prosecuting and trying alleged war crimes. It authorized creation of an International Criminal Tribunal for the former Yugoslavia in 1993 and an International Criminal Tribunal for Rwanda in 1994, as well as the special court for Sierra Leone in 2002, and the special tribunals for Cambodia in 2003 and Lebanon in 2005.

Structure. Originally comprising 5 permanent and 6 nonpermanent members, the council was expanded on January 1, 1966, to 15, including 10 nonpermanent members elected by the General Assembly for two-year terms. The charter stipulates that in the election of the nonpermanent members due regard must be paid to the contribution of members to the maintenance of international peace and security and to the other purposes of the organization, and also to equitable geographic distribution. The presidency of the Security Council rotates monthly.

Council decisions on procedural matters are made by an affirmative vote of any nine members. Decisions on all other matters, however, require a nine-member affirmative vote that must include the concurring votes of the permanent members; the one exception is that in matters involving pacific settlement of disputes, a party to a dispute must abstain from voting. It is the requirement for the concurring votes of the permanent members on all but procedural questions that enables any one of the five to exercise a veto, no matter how large the affirmative majority.

In discharging its responsibilities the Security Council may investigate the existence of any threat to peace, breach of the peace, or act of aggression, and in the event of such a finding may make recommendations for resolution or decide to take enforcement measures to maintain or restore international peace and security. Enforcement action may include a call on members to apply economic sanctions and other measures short of the use of armed force. Should these steps prove inadequate, the Security Council may then take such military action as is deemed necessary.

The charter established a Military Staff Committee, composed of the permanent members' chiefs of staff (or their representatives), to advise and assist the Security Council on such questions as the council's military requirements for the maintenance of peace, the regulation of armaments, and possible disarmament. In the absence of agreements to place armed forces at the council's disposal, as envisaged by the charter, the committee has not assumed an important operational role.

In addition to the Military Staff Committee, the Security Council currently has three Standing Committees—the Committee on the Admission of New Members, the Committee of Experts on Rules of Procedure, and the Committee on Council Meetings away from Headquarters—each composed of representatives of all council members. There is also a UN Compensation Commission, which was established in 1991 to pay damages to governments, individuals, and businesses injured by the Gulf War. On September 28, 2001, responding to the September 11 terrorist attacks on the United States, the Security Council authorized creation of a new ad hoc Counter-Terrorism Committee. On April 28, 2004, Resolution 1540 authorized creation of another ad hoc committee concerned with preventing the proliferation of weapons of mass destruction (WMD) and their delivery. Resolution 1673, passed unanimously on April 27, 2006, authorized the 1540 Committee to also focus on preventing "non-state actors" from acquiring WMD.

The Security Council is also empowered to establish so-called sanctions committees, ten of which were functioning as of 2009. Most were established to oversee arms embargoes—against, for instance, Somalia (since 1992) and Sudan (since 2004)—and/or to freeze assets or impose travel restrictions on government officials or other individuals. In some cases, the original mandate of a sanctions committee has been expanded or redefined. In December 2000, for example, the Security Council expanded the mission of the Afghanistan committee, which it had created in 1999 primarily in response to Afghanistan's failure to extradite suspects in the 1998 bombings of U.S. embassies in Kenya and Tanzania. Initially assigned to monitor air travel restrictions and a freeze on the Afghan Taliban regime's financial assets, the committee's mandate was extended to include monitoring an air and arms embargo and the freezing of funds of Osama bin Laden and associates. In 2002, following the demise of the Taliban regime, several additional resolutions further modified the terms of the sanctions.

The council has created a number of working groups to address peacekeeping operations, conflict prevention and resolution in Africa, and improving the effectiveness of sanctions. In February 2001 the Working Group on General Issues on Sanctions issued dozens of recommendations for more effective use of sanctions, including monitoring their impact, providing incentives to lift them, and setting time limits for them. The committee also proposed that the Security Council consider imposing secondary sanctions on countries that fail to adhere to direct sanctions. The committee's final report was issued in 2006.

Activities. Peacekeeping activities include observation, fact-finding, mediation, conciliation, and assistance in maintaining internal order. UN observer groups to supervise cease-fire lines, truce arrangements, and the like have functioned in Africa, the Balkans, Indonesia, the Middle East, Kashmir, and former Soviet republics. On a larger scale, the UN Operation in the Congo (UNOC) was initiated in 1960 and continued until 1964 in an attempt to stabilize the chaotic situation in that state (subsequently Zaire and, since mid-1997, the Democratic Republic of the Congo). Since 1964 the UN Force in Cyprus (UNFICYP) has attempted to alleviate conflict between the Greek and Turkish elements in the Cypriot population under a mandate subject to semiannual renewal.

There have been several peacekeeping operations in the Middle East. A UN Emergency Force (UNEF) was interposed between the military forces of Egypt and Israel in the Sinai and Gaza areas from early 1957 until its withdrawal at the insistence of Egypt in 1967. The UNEF was reconstituted in October 1973 to supervise a cease-fire along the Suez Canal and to ensure a return of Israeli and Egyptian forces to the positions that they held on October 22, 1973. Soon after the signing of the Egyptian-Israeli peace treaty in March 1979, it became clear that the Soviet Union—on behalf of its Arab friends—would veto an extension of the force when its mandate expired on July 25. Faced with this prospect, the United States concluded an agreement with the Soviet Union to allow monitoring of the treaty arrangements by the UN Truce Supervision Organization (UNTSO), established in 1948 to oversee the Arab-Israeli cease-fire. Other forces currently serving in the Middle East are the UN Interim Forces in Lebanon (UNIFIL), established in 1978, and the UN Disengagement Observer Force (UNDOF), deployed in Syria's Golan Heights since 1974. (For organizational details on existing peacekeeping forces, see the next section.)

As a body that meets year-round and is frequently called upon to respond to world crises, the Security Council is often the most visible of the UN organs. Given its composition and the nature of its duties, political considerations typically dominate its deliberations. In the 1980s the council tended to focus on problems in the Middle East, Central America, and southern Africa. During 1986 it debated resolutions condemning Israel for continued military activity in southern Lebanon, the alleged violation of the sanctity of a Jerusalem mosque, and the interception of a Libyan airliner in the search for suspected terrorists. The resolutions failed as the result of vetoes by the United States, itself the subject of condemnation resolutions later in the year. Other Western-bloc council members joined the United States in defeating a measure denouncing the U.S. bombing of Libya in April, while the United States cast the only vote against a resolution seeking to ban military and financial aid to contra rebels fighting the government of Nicaragua.

The major topics of debate in 1987 were the proposed imposition of mandatory sanctions against South Africa for its apartheid and Namibian policies, Israeli actions in Gaza and the West Bank, and the Iran-Iraq war. U.S. and UK vetoes continued to block the imposition of sanctions against South Africa, although the council late in 1987 unanimously condemned the "illegal entry" of South African troops into Angola. In December the council approved (with the United States abstaining) a resolution "deploring Israeli practices and policies" during recent outbreaks of violence in the occupied territories. The council also urged a reactivation of UN leadership in Middle East peace negotiations.

In September 1987 the council approved a peace plan that provided the framework for termination of the Iran-Iraq war in August 1988. In conjunction with that agreement, the council established the UN Iran-Iraq Military Observer Group (UNIIMOG) to supervise the cease-fire and monitor the withdrawal of troops to internationally recognized boundaries. (UNIIMOG's mandate was terminated in early 1990 following the successful completion of its mission.) Other UN groups mobilized in 1988 and 1989 were the UN Good Offices Mission in Afghanistan and Pakistan (UNGOMAP—terminated in March 1990 after monitoring the withdrawal of Soviet troops from Afghanistan); the UN Angola Verification Mission (UNAVEM); the UN Transition Assistance Group (UNTAG), established to supervise the withdrawal of South African troops from Namibia and the transition to Namibian independence; the United Nations Observer Group in Central America (*Grupo de Observadoresde las Naciones Unidas en Centroamérica*—ONUCA); and the UN Observation Mission for the Verification of Elections in Nicaragua (*Observadores de Naciones Unidas para la Verificación de las Elecciones en Nicaragua*—ONUVEN).

The Security Council's prominent role in conflict resolution was widely perceived as having significantly enhanced the global reputation of the peacekeeping forces (which were awarded the 1988 Nobel Peace Prize), the Secretariat, and the United Nations as a whole. Improved relations within the council were attributed to the reduction in East-West tension, UN secretary general Javier Pérez de Cuéllar praising Washington and Moscow for permitting the body to become "more responsive [and] collegial." Building upon the unqualified successes of UNTAG and ONUVEN (the first UN force to supervise an election in an established nation), the permanent members of the council in early 1990 endorsed an Australian proposal that a peacekeeping force be deployed to help resolve the long-standing conflict in Cambodia and supervise the election of a new national government. In addition, the council in late April approved a peace plan for the Western Sahara under which a UN group would oversee a referendum in the territory. The council also considered creating a small UN observer force to monitor the treatment of Palestinians in the occupied territories, but the United States vetoed the measure in May.

The Security Council moved even further to the forefront of the global stage by assuming a major role in an international response to Iraq's invasion of Kuwait on August 2, 1990. Launching what would eventually be perceived as a historic series of resolutions (most adopted unanimously) through which "the teeth" of the UN Charter were bared with rare decisiveness and speed, the council condemned the takeover within hours of its occurrence and demanded the withdrawal of Iraqi troops. Several days later the council also imposed comprehensive economic sanctions on Iraq and established a special committee to monitor the sanctions process. In addition, the council endorsed a naval blockade of Iraq and approved UN aid for "innocent victims" of the crisis as well as countries adversely affected by the trade embargo. Finally, in its most dramatic decision, the council on November 28 authorized U.S.-led coalition forces to use "all necessary means" to implement previous resolutions and "to restore international peace and security in the area" if Iraq did not withdraw from Kuwait by January 15, 1991, thereby providing the basis for launching Operation Desert Storm on January 16, 1991.

Following the liberation of Kuwait and the announcement of a suspension of military operations by allied forces in late February 1991, the council adopted a permanent cease-fire plan on April 3 demanding that Iraq return all Kuwaiti property, accept liability for the damage it caused during the war, and destroy all its chemical and biological weapons, as well as its long-range ballistic missiles. After Iraqi acceptance of the conditions on April 6, the council established the UN Iraq-Kuwait Observation Mission (UNIKOM) to monitor a demilitarized zone between the two countries. The council also remained deeply involved in efforts to resolve refugee problems associated with the conflict, especially in regard to Iraq's Kurdish population.

Tension between the council and Iraq continued throughout the ensuing year, particularly over what were perceived as attempts by Baghdad to undermine UN supervision of the destruction of plants and equipment related to nuclear, chemical, and biological weapons. With some Western nations reportedly considering a resumption of military action, the Security Council in the spring of 1992 warned that "grave consequences" would ensue if Iraq interfered any further with UN oversight activity.

Even without the extraordinary burden of the Gulf crisis, the council would have encountered a busier schedule than usual in 1990–1991. Following extended debate prompted by the death of a number of Palestinians in the occupied territories in October 1990, the council approved a carefully worded resolution rebuking Israel and asking the UN secretary general to monitor the status of Palestinian civilians "under Israeli occupation." In addition, the council reaffirmed its support for a UN-sponsored Middle East Peace Conference. Other activity in late 1990 included negotiations on the final framework for a comprehensive settlement of the Cambodian situation and the creation of a UN observer group to help monitor elections in Haiti.

Discussions also continued toward finalization of the Western Saharan peace plan, with the council in April 1991 authorizing a UN Mission for the Referendum in Western Sahara (*Mission des Nations Unies le Référendum dans le Sahara Ouest*—MINURSO). A month later the council approved a United Nations Observer Mission in El Salvador (*Observadores de las Naciones Unidas en El Salvador*—ONUSAL) as part of a continuing effort to foster a peace settlement in that country's long-standing civil war. Initially, ONUSAL's mandate was limited to verifying adherence to a human rights agreement signed by the government and the rebels in 1990, but the council expanded the mission's mandate in January 1992 to include monitoring the permanent cease-fire.

In February 1992 the council authorized two of its largest operations to date, the UN Protection Force (UNPROFOR) to help implement and monitor a cease-fire in eastern Croatia, and the UN Transitional Authority in Cambodia (UNTAC). Two months later the council also established the UN Operation in Somalia (UNOSOM) in an effort to mediate an end to the civil war in that country and permit the delivery of much-needed food relief. Other April activity included the declaration of an air and arms embargo against Libya because of Tripoli's refusal to permit the extradition of two of its nationals suspected of complicity in the 1988 airplane bombing over Lockerbie, Scotland.

In June 1992 UN Secretary General Boutros Boutros-Ghali proposed a number of changes to improve the peacemaking and peacekeeping abilities of the Security Council. The most striking recommendation was for "as many countries as are willing" to make 1,000 of their troops available for immediate council deployment, thereby establishing, in essence at least, the long-debated UN standing army. Boutros-Ghali said such forces would be instrumental in implementing the "preventative diplomacy" strategy endorsed at a Security Council summit in New York in January. The meeting, the first ever of the heads of state of the permanent and nonpermanent council members, had agreed that greater effort should be made to identify trouble spots in advance so intervention could be ordered before the outbreak of violence.

Throughout 1992 and the first half of 1993, the Security Council became more focused on the former Yugoslavia, particularly after authorizing UNPROFOR troops to enter Bosnia and Herzegovina for humanitarian purposes. Some 40 resolutions were approved in response to conflicts in the region. Included were the imposition of sanctions against the Federal Republic of Yugoslavia, condemnation of "ethnic cleansing" and myriad human rights violations in Bosnia, approval of an International Criminal Tribunal for the former Yugoslavia, and a number of generally unsuccessful or unimplemented peacemaking efforts, such as the imposition of no-fly zones and the establishment of "safe areas" for Bosnian Muslims. Following the collapse of talks launched by the European Community, the council also found itself responsible for efforts to negotiate an end to the complex Bosnian conflict.

Concurrently, the council's UNOSOM II resolution of March 1993 introduced a controversial "nation-building" element to UN intervention. Although credited with having brought food relief to the starving population and having pacified most of the country, UNOSOM troops, acting in conjunction with a U.S. rapid deployment force, found themselves locked in deadly combat with the supporters of clan leader Gen. Mohamed Farah Aidid in Mogadishu. As losses mounted within the UNOSOM and U.S. contingents, council members began to consider a more "realistic" attitude toward what it could accomplish in such situations.

In other activity during 1992–1993, the council fought in what was described as a "war of nerves" with Baghdad concerning UN monitoring of Iraqi weapon sites. The council also expressed its concern over the renewal of fighting in Afghanistan, condemned the Israeli deportation of about 400 Palestinians from the occupied territories in December 1992, and demanded the withdrawal of Armenian forces from Azerbaijan in August 1993.

Peacekeeping operations over the next year continued the recent pattern of occasional successes mixed with inconclusive or seemingly failed missions. UNTAC was disbanded in November 1993 following elections and installation of a coalition government in Cambodia, while ONUSAL was widely praised for its contribution to the completion of elections in El Salvador in early 1994. In addition, Mozambique conducted its first multiparty elections in October 1994 with the assistance of the UN Operation in Mozambique (*Opération des Nations Unies au Mozambique*—ONUMOZ). However, positive results were scarce in the former Yugoslavia, Somalia, Angola, and Liberia, while the council was embarrassed by the refusal of the military regime in Port-au-Prince to permit the deployment of the UN Mission in Haiti (UNMIH). Consequently, the council's permanent members continued to reassess the limits of peacekeeping endeavors, and in early May 1994 new guidelines were established. Future missions would require a "clear political goal" reflected in a "precise mandate," a cease-fire among combatants, and the integration, if possible, of forces from regional peacekeeping organizations.

The council's new caution was reflected in its response to the genocide in Rwanda. The United States resisted the call for large-scale reinforcement of the UN Assistance Mission for Rwanda (UNAMIR) in April 1994 (see article on Rwanda for details.) Although 5,500 additional troops were eventually authorized, the council was strongly criticized in many quarters for the delay. Late in the year, amid mounting evidence of widespread atrocities, the Security Council authorized creation of an International Criminal Tribunal for Rwanda.

The Rwandan situation also underscored the ongoing need for the council to develop rapid deployment capability. UN Secretary General Boutros-Ghali announced in early 1994 that some 15 countries had pledged troops and/or equipment to the proposed standby force. Nevertheless, he argued that rhetorical backing for peacekeeping operations, which cost an estimated $3.2 billion in 1993, was still not matched by sufficient tangible support.

In February 1995 UNOSOM withdrew from Somalia, having failed in its goal of fostering political stability there. Success also remained elusive in former Yugoslavia, where beleaguered UNPROFOR forces would be replaced by U.S.-led NATO troops in Bosnia and Herzegovina following a permanent cease-fire. (UNPROFOR's responsibilities in Croatia and Macedonia had been delegated in March to two new missions—the UN Confidence Restoration Operation in Croatia [UNCRO] and the UN Preventive Deployment Force [UNPREDEP].) On the positive side, ONUMOZ and ONUSAL were disbanded after successfully completing their missions in Mozambique and El Salvador, respectively. In addition, the UNMIH deployed its forces in Haiti following the return of the civilian government to Port-au-Prince. Hope also grew for a resolution of the protracted conflict in Angola; some 7,000 UNAVEM III troops were authorized to help implement the most recent cease-fire.

The new UN Mission of Observers in Tajikistan (UNMOT) was very limited in scope as the Security Council deferred to a large peacekeeping force provided by Russia under the aegis of the Commonwealth of Independent States. This arrangement was considered significant in regard to future peacekeeping efforts, particularly given that UN resources were, in the words of Secretary General Boutros-Ghali, "overstretched and underfinanced."

The Security Council's reassessment of its peacekeeping limitations continued throughout 1995, particularly in light of UNPROFOR's ineffectiveness and NATO's bombing campaign in late summer against Bosnian Serb aggressiveness. Its military assertiveness having contributed to the conclusion of a U.S.-brokered comprehensive peace agreement in November, NATO for all practical purposes assumed full responsibility in December for overseeing the cease-fire through, among other things, the deployment of some 60,000 troops (see entries on Bosnia and Herzegovina and NATO for details). Concurrently, UNPROFOR was disbanded (effective January 31, 1996), having been deemed a failure for the most part. The counterpoint between NATO action and the UN's previous impotence came into even sharper focus as the cease-fire held throughout 1996 and the complicated new electoral process was completed successfully in Bosnia under NATO supervision.

The Security Council also closed down UNAMIR in August 1996, the mission having had no impact on the raging Hutu-Tutsi ethnic conflict in Rwanda. Significantly, when related violence intensified in Zaire in the fall, the proposed international responses focused on regional or Western-led intervention forces, not a UN operation. A growing "go-it-alone" attitude had also been apparent in the unilateral action taken by the United States in Iraq in September when Washington launched cruise missiles against Iraqi positions without seeking Security Council endorsement (see article on Iraq).

Attention in the council during the second half of 1996 was focused on the acrimonious selection of the next UN secretary general. Washington's implacable opposition to a second term for Boutros-Ghali eventually resulted in council endorsement of Kofi Annan. In other activity, the council's long-delayed "oil-for-food" proposal to Iraq was implemented in mid-December, thereby permitting Baghdad to sell Iraqi oil to fund the importation of civilian food and medicine. Later in the month a permanent cease-fire was concluded in Guatemala thanks in large part to UN negotiators. The UN Human Rights Verification Mission in Guatemala, deployed in 1994, defused numerous potential threats to the cease-fire. (That verification mission was augmented for several months in the first half of 1997 by some 155 military observers, although the deployment had been delayed temporarily at the insistence of China, which objected to Guatemala's diplomatic recognition to Taiwan.)

No major new peacekeeping missions were launched in 1997, although small successor operations were authorized for Angola, Haiti, and Croatia. Meanwhile, the limited UN Observer Mission in Liberia (UNOMIL) closed down following the installation of an elected civilian government in Monrovia, the Security Council having left most of the peacemaking and peacekeeping activity there in the hands of regional forces directed by the Economic Community of West African States (ECOWAS). The council also deferred to ECOWAS regarding the turmoil in Sierra Leone, although it formally condemned the May 1997 military coup and endorsed the forced reinstallation of the civilian government in March 1998.

Meanwhile, discussion continued on proposed enlargement of the council. A special panel called in 1997 for the council to be expanded to 24 members, including 5 new permanent members who, however, would not have veto power. The panel suggested that two new permanent members come from the industrialized countries (probably Germany and Japan) and one each from Africa, Asia, and Latin America. However, the proposed expansion was viewed with little enthusiasm by the current permanent council members, who expressed concern that the body might become unwieldy.

The council's agenda in 1997 and early 1998 was dominated by its efforts to compel Iraq to cooperate fully with the weapons inspection program instituted earlier in the decade but still subject to a "cat-and-mouse" approach by Baghdad. Following a negative report from the UN Special Commission (UNSCOM), which was responsible for oversight of the inspections, the Security Council in mid-1997 formally rebuked Iraq for noncompliance and interference with UNSCOM's work and threatened to impose additional sanctions. Baghdad responded provocatively, ordering all U.S. members of UNSCOM out of the country on the grounds that they were involved in intelligence-gathering activity beyond the purview of UNSCOM. Although the United States and United Kingdom adopted a hard line and urged consideration of the use of force against Iraq, the other Security Council members declined to endorse such action. Consequently, when Iraq declared in early 1998 that certain sites were off limits to inspectors (who by then had reincorporated the U.S. personnel), Washington, backed by London, announced it would proceed independently against Baghdad and ordered a significant buildup of troops, planes, and ships in the region. The Security Council authorized Annan to negotiate a settlement with Iraqi president Saddam Hussein. Following the last-minute success of Annan's mission in late February, the Security Council threatened Iraq with the "severest consequences" if further violations of the inspection protocols ensued.

The Annan agreement of early 1998 provided only a temporary break in the conflict between the Iraqi government and the Security Council. Baghdad continued to impede the work of UNSCOM throughout the rest of the year. Tensions came to a head in December following another unfavorable review of Iraqi compliance by UNSCOM. Arguing that previous council resolutions gave them the authority to do so, the United States and United Kingdom bombed Iraq for four days in an effort to force the Iraqi government to resume cooperating with the weapons inspectors. The attack seemed to have backfired, however, when Baghdad refused to allow UNSCOM personnel, who had been withdrawn from the country prior to the attack, to reenter Iraq unless sanctions were lifted.

On December 17, 1999, after months of negotiations, the Security Council approved—with China, France, Malaysia, and Russia abstaining—UNSCOM's replacement by the UN Monitoring, Verification and Inspection Commission (UNMOVIC). The council offered the possible suspension of sanctions in exchange for Iraqi compliance, but Iraq immediately rejected the attendant conditions as "impossible to fulfill." Although the International Atomic Energy Agency (IAEA) was permitted to renew limited inspections beginning in January 2000, Iraq refused entry to UNMOVIC personnel.

Meanwhile, much of the Security Council's attention had been diverted to the Balkans. In 1998 it had passed resolutions calling for an end to arms sales to Yugoslavia and for a cease-fire in that country's province of Kosovo. In October the council had also endorsed the establishment of an Organization for Security and Cooperation in Europe (OSCE) mission for the purpose of verifying that the Yugoslav federal government was abiding by these resolutions, but the mission ended in failure with the withdrawal of the OSCE monitors and the subsequent bombing of Yugoslavia by NATO in March–June 1999. Formation of the UNMIK was authorized upon suspension of the air campaign on June 10.

In February 1999 the UNPREDEP mission in Macedonia and a UN Observer Mission in Angola (*Mission d'Observation des Nations Unies en Angola*—MONUA) both came to an end, the former successfully and the latter as a failure. The Security Council had authorized the MONUA in June 1997 to assist in national reconciliation and demobilization, but the peace between the Angolan government and the National Union for the Total Independence of Angola (UNITA) never took hold. With the government making gains on the battlefield, Luanda concurred in the decision to terminate the MONUA. On October 15, however, the Security Council authorized establishment of a United Nations Office in Angola (UNOA), its mandate being to pursue opportunities for peace and to assist with humanitarian efforts, capacity building, and human rights.

The protracted conflict in the neighboring Democratic Republic of the Congo (DRC) led the council in late November 1999 to authorize a United Nations Organization Mission in the Democratic Republic of the Congo (*Mission de l'Organisation des Nations Unies en République*

Démocratique du Congo—MONUC) in the hope that a July cease-fire signed by Angola, Namibia, Rwanda, Uganda, and Zimbabwe, as well as the DRC and rebel forces, would hold. Also in Africa, a small UN Observer Mission in Sierra Leone (UNOMSIL), which the council had authorized in June 1998 primarily to monitor security and human rights conditions, gave way in October 1999 to a much larger UN Mission in Sierra Leone (UNAMSIL).

The last of several follow-up efforts in Haiti—the UN Civilian Police Mission in Haiti (*Mission de Police Civile des Nations Unies en Haïti*—MIPONUH)—concluded in March 2000, and the UNMOT effort in Tajikistan drew to a close two months later. A UN Mission in the Central African Republic (*Mission des Nations Unies en République Centrafricaine*—MINURCA), which had been authorized by a Security Council resolution in March 1997 to facilitate stability and security in the wake of a mutiny within the country's armed forces, was succeeded in February 2000 by a UN Peacebuilding Support Office under the UN secretary general. Another Security Council peacekeeping effort, the UN Mission in Ethiopia and Eritrea (UNMEE), came into existence in June 2000, in cooperation with the Organization for African Unity (OAU), following a cease-fire in the Horn of Africa.

A Panel on United Nations Peace Operations, chaired by Algerian Lakhda Brahimi, issued its report in August 2000, with the Security Council then establishing a working group in October to consider the recommendations in Brahimi's report. In a resolution passed unanimously on November 13, the council endorsed the report's conclusion that peacekeeping missions needed clear, credible, and achievable mandates, as well as the capacity to present a believable deterrent in hostile circumstances. The report also called for expansion and restructuring of the Secretariat's Department of Peacekeeping Operations, a greater reliance on intelligence gathering, adoption of means for responding more rapidly to potential crises, and allocation of additional resources.

During the Millennium Summit at UN headquarters in New York, the heads of state and government of the Security Council members convened for only the second time in UN history, with nine presidents, five prime ministers, and one foreign minister in attendance. The council unanimously adopted a September 7 resolution endorsing the body's continuing role in maintaining peace even while recognizing that poverty, infectious disease, and illegal trade in diamonds and other natural resources were among the social and economic pressures most linked to peace and stability.

The Security Council called in a July 2000 resolution for UN member states to consider voluntary HIV testing and counseling for their troops undertaking peacekeeping missions. January was labeled the "month of Africa" as the council considered a host of Africa-related concerns, while an October meeting examined the role of women in peace and security. Following the resumption of the Palestinian intifada (uprising) in September, an October 7 resolution (the United States abstaining) "deplored the provocation" caused by the visit of future Israeli prime minister Ariel Sharon to the Temple Mount (Haram al-Sharif) in September. In mid-December the council considered an additional resolution that would have authorized creation of an observer force of police and military for the occupied Palestinian territories, but the measure fell a single vote short of the nine needed for approval when seven council members abstained. A renewed effort to approve an observer force met with a U.S. veto on March 28, 2001.

Against a backdrop of the September 11, 2001, al-Qaida assault on the United States, on September 12 and 28 the Security Council unanimously condemned the attacks and requested all states to deny terrorists access to bases and financing, and to aid in bringing the perpetrators to justice. Resolution 1373, passed on September 28, also authorized formation of the ad hoc committee on counterterrorism.

Despite firm support for U.S.-led efforts to forge an international coalition to combat terrorism, protracted debate slowed a subsequent U.S. push against the Saddam Hussein regime and its alleged WMD. On September 16, 2002, UN secretary general Kofi Annan announced that Iraq had unconditionally offered entry to UNMOVIC teams, which, Baghdad claimed, would confirm that it harbored no biological, chemical, or other sanctioned weapons. The United States and its chief ally on the Security Council, the United Kingdom, quickly dismissed the offer as a probable ruse. Washington also asserted that Iraq had ties to the al-Qaida terrorist network, but most members of the Security Council found the evidence less than compelling. Meanwhile, U.S. and UK aircraft continued their latest in a series of air assaults against military targets within Iraq's southern no-fly zone.

On November 8, 2002, the Security Council unanimously approved Resolution 1441, which threatened "serious consequences" if Iraq failed to disarm. Although the compromise resolution stopped short of the broad imprimatur that Washington and London had sought, it was interpreted by the United States as not requiring further Security Council approval before launching military action—a prospect that seemed increasingly likely as the year drew to a close. Responding to Iraq's December 8 delivery to the UNMOVIC of a 12,000-page Iraqi weapons declaration, U.S. secretary of state Colin Powell asserted that it "totally fail[ed]" to meet the Security Council's demands for a comprehensive, accurate accounting of WMD. At the end of the year inspectors from both the UNMOVIC and the IAEA were continuing their work despite only marginal Iraqi compliance.

Also during 2002 the United States, having withdrawn its signature in May from the treaty establishing the International Criminal Court (ICC), insisted that its troops on council-sponsored peacekeeping missions be exempted from the ICC's jurisdiction. In June the Security Council rejected a U.S. resolution that would have exempted all UN peacekeepers. Washington then attempted, again unsuccessfully, to exempt peacekeepers in Bosnia and Herzegovina, where the NATO-led Stabilization Force (SFOR) included some 4,000 U.S. military personnel. A compromise resolution on July 12 specified that the troops of states that had not joined the ICC would be granted a one-year exemption, renewable upon request. The decision was made largely moot when the council decided to terminate the Bosnian mission at the close of 2002. December 2002 also saw the completion of a much smaller operation, the United Nations Mission of Observers in Prevlaka (UNMOP), which had been established in 1996 to monitor demilitarization of the Prevlaka peninsula based on a 1992 agreement between Croatia and Montenegro.

In January 2003 UNMOVIC Executive Chair Hans Blix reported that Iraq might have misinformed the UN about Iraqi weapons' programs and called for greater cooperation from the Saddam Hussein regime. Soon afterward, Blix indicated that Iraq had indeed become more forthcoming, and he asked the Security Council to allow the UNMOVIC a number of additional months to verify Iraq's compliance with Resolution 1441's provisions regarding chemical and biological weapons. In addition, Director General Mohamed El Baradei of the IAEA asked for more time for his inspectors to assess the possible presence of nuclear weapons in Iraq. However, in late February the United States, the United Kingdom, and Spain introduced a resolution calling for Security Council authorization of military action against Iraq unless immediate steps were taken by the Hussein regime to prove its submission to Resolution 1441. After some of the bitterest debate in the council since the end of the Cold War, Russia joined France and Germany in blocking the resolution, adamantly insisting that the UNMOVIC needed more time to complete its inspections. UNMOVIC inspectors left Iraq in mid-March, however, when it became clear that a U.S.-led invasion of Iraq was imminent.

Despite the rancor of the prewar debate, the antiwar members of the council in May 2003 joined the rest of the members in authorizing the allied forces to occupy Iraq and to proceed with planned reconstruction. To assist in the rebuilding, the council agreed to discontinue its sanctions against Iraq and to phase out the "oil-for-food" program, with a view toward ramping up oil production. (In 2004 the council welcomed Secretary General Annan's appointment of a high-level committee to investigate charges of corruption in regard to the "oil-for-food" program. See the discussion of the Secretariat for further details.) Given the radically changed circumstances in Iraq, the UNIKOM mandate concluded on October 6. The council also endorsed the interim government established in Iraq in 2004 and approved the allies' schedule for the transition to an elected government.

In 2003–2004, the council endorsed the "road map for peace" regarding the Israeli-Palestinian conflict, declared any acts of violence against civilians to be "unjustifiable," voted to discontinue sanctions against Libya after Tripoli renounced its controversial weapons programs, and passed a resolution (at the request of the United States) requiring all UN members to adopt legislation designed to prevent terrorists from gaining possession of WMD. The council also faced a significantly increased demand for peacekeeping forces, particularly in Africa, where extensive missions were approved for Burundi, Côte dIvoire, Liberia, and Sudan. In 2003 the Security Council imposed an arms embargo and other restrictions on various foreign and Congolese groups and militias operating in the Democratic Republic of the Congo. These sanctions were followed by establishment of a sanctions committee, expansion of the embargo in 2004, and implementation of an associated travel ban in 2005. Also in 2004, the Security Council imposed an arms embargo on Côte d'Ivoire; froze assets of, and instituted a travel ban on, various Ivorian officials; and authorized creation of a corresponding sanctions committee. Resolution 1556 imposed an arms embargo on "all non-governmental entities and individuals" operating in North, South, and West Darfur, Sudan. The Darfur embargo was expanded in March 2005, when asset and travel restrictions were also imposed and a sanctions committee was created. (In April 2006 the travel ban and assets freeze were expanded to additional individuals.)

In early 2005 when Secretary General Annan proposed increasing the membership from 15 to 25 as part of his recommendations for broad UN reform and restructuring. Brazil, Germany, India, and Japan, known as the G-4, intensified their campaign to gain permanent council membership. The G-4 proposal called for six new permanent seats, including two seats for African countries, as well as for the addition of four new nonpermanent members. Although the case for expansion appeared to gain momentum when the G-4 dropped their demand for veto power, in August 2005 the African Union voted to reject the proposal primarily because the new permanent members would not have the veto. The expansion question was discussed at the September General Assembly session, although support among the current permanent members of the Security Council was reportedly lukewarm at best.

In May 2005 UNOTIL began operations in Timor-Leste as the second currently functioning "political or peacebuilding" mission. The first was the United Nations Assistance Mission in Afghanistan (UNAMA), which had been established in March 2002 to advise on the peace process, promote human rights, provide technical assistance, and manage UN relief and development aid. Although authorized by Security Council resolutions, both missions function under the Department of Peacekeeping Operations within the Secretariat. A third such operation, the United Nations Integrated Office in Sierra Leone (UNIOSIL), succeeded the UNAMSIL when that mission's mandate expired on December 31, 2005. Two months earlier, the Security Council had established its most recent sanctions committee in connection with the February assassination of former Lebanese prime minister Rafiq Hariri. Resolution 1636 authorized the imposition of travel restrictions and financial measures directed against Syrians and Lebanese suspected of involvement in the assassination.

The increasing burden of peacekeeping operations was highlighted in February 2006 by New York University's annual review of global operations. The review, which gave additional support to the idea of creating emergency standby arrangements, noted that in the previous six years the number of UN peacekeeping personnel had grown from under 13,000 to more than 60,000. Also in February, Under Secretary General for Peacekeeping Operations Jean-Marie Guéhenno reported that the number of sexual abuse complaints directed against peacekeeping personnel had fallen since introduction of a new reporting system in 2005, although he characterized the number, 295, as still unacceptable.

In response to fighting in Southern Lebanon between Israel and Hezbollah forces in July 2006, the Security Council adopted Resolution 1701, which called for an end to combat and the withdrawal of combatants from the region. The resolution also authorized an increase of the United Nations Interim Force in Lebanon (UNIFIL) to 15,000 troops and expanded the mandate of the mission (see "United Nations Interim Force in Lebanon").

The Security Council launched an effort to reform its working methods in 2006. It reconvened the ad hoc Working Group on Documentation and Other Procedural Questions and tasked the body to examine practices and recommend changes to improve transparency and efficiency. The group's recommendations were approved in July and included a range of minor reforms including increased communication between the Security Council and the General Assembly, more documentation from the council, and enhanced open meetings. The success of the group led the Security Council to authorize it for another year.

Ban Ki-Moon of the Republic of Korea was unanimously recommended by the Security Council in October 2006 to replace Annan as the new UN secretary general. Also in October, the Security Council adopted Resolution 1718, which placed economic sanctions on North Korea following that country's nuclear tests. The sanctions helped prompt renewed diplomacy, which led to an agreement whereby North Korea agreed to dismantle its nuclear weapons program. Meanwhile, the success of the United Nations Operation in Burundi (*Opération des Nations Unies au Burundi*—ONUB) in facilitating a peace accord between rebels and the government led the Security Council to replace the mission with the smaller United Nations Integrated Office in Burundi (*Bureau Intégré des Nations Unies au Burundi*—BINUB).

In 2006 the United States vetoed two resolutions, both calling for the Israeli withdrawal from Gaza, while in 2007 China vetoed a draft resolution calling on Myanmar's government to release political prisoners and stop repressive measures enacted in response to a prodemocracy movement. Also in 2007 Venezuela sought to gain a nonpermanent seat on the Security Council but was opposed by the United States, which instead supported Guatemala. The result was a deadlock that lasted through 47 votes before a compromise was reached through which Venezuela and the United States agreed to support Panama, which was subsequently elected to the body. Concern over Iran's noncompliance with UN nuclear inspectors and the possibility that the country had undertaken a nuclear weapons program prompted the Security Council to adopt Resolution 1737 in December 2006 in an effort to prompt a peaceful settlement of the growing crisis. The resolution imposed limited sanctions on Iran. Divisions between the United States, France, and the United Kingdom, all of which endorsed more stringent measures, and China and Russia, which opposed tougher action, prevented substantive further action through 2007.

In February 2007 UN representative Martti Ahtisaari recommended to the Security Council that the Serbian province of Kosovo be granted eventual independence under the supervision of the UN. However, independence was opposed by both Serbia and Russia. Negotiators from Russia, the United States, and the EU launched a new round of talks with Serb and Kosovar leaders with the goal of developing a new proposal for the Security Council in December 2007. Meanwhile, efforts to forge a common policy on Sudan were stymied by Chinese opposition. While a joint peacekeeping force between the AU and the United Nations Mission in Sudan (UNMIS) had been approved, Sudanese opposition to the deployment of non-African troops limited the size and scope of the operation. In May the United States imposed new economic sanctions on Sudan and developed a draft resolution that would increase pressure on the Sudanese government to end interference with the UNMIS. Subsequently, however, the United States agreed to delay its resolution to allow Ban time to negotiate a new agreement. The secretary general held a ministerial meeting in September which brought together representatives from 20 countries, but the meeting failed to break the impasse over the expanded UN mission in Sudan. The Security Council extended the mandate of the UNMIS through 2007.

The Security Council conducted its first open debate on climate change in April 2007. The session was initiated by the United Kingdom, which, along with other members of the council, asserted that global warming had significant security implications, including increased competition for resources. However, countries such as China and Pakistan criticized the forum and argued that there were other agencies within the UN that were better suited to discuss climate change. Meanwhile, in June, the council voted in Resolution 1762 to end the UNMOVIC mission in Iraq.

To protect the growing number of refugees in the region, estimated at 230,000, and to deter attacks by Sudanese rebel groups in the area, the Security Council authorized the creation of the United Nations Mission in the Central African Republic and Chad (*Mission des Nations Unies en République Centrafricaine et au Tchad*—MINURCAT) in September 2007.

A report delivered to the Security Council by the Stockholm International Peace Research Institute (SIPRI), published in November 2007, questioned the efficiency of UN arms embargoes. The report found that since 1990 only one-fourth of the 27 arms embargoes had been effective. The study did conclude that the presence of UN peacekeepers, however, dramatically increased the likelihood that the sanctions would be successful. SIPRI recommended that the Security Council increase the frequency of reviews of embargo regimes. It also advocated that the council work to have more countries criminalize violations of UN sanctions and prosecute nationals who contravene the embargoes.

In February 2008, following Kosovo's unilateral declaration of independence, the Security Council conducted an emergency session at the request of Serbia and Russia, both of which sought to block the Kosovar bid. No resolution was reached and Russia then circulated a draft resolution to the Security Council in March that would have preserved the territorial integrity of Serbia. However, Russia gained the support of only 6 of the council's 15 members. Serbia then requested that the issue of Kosovar independence be adjudicated through the ICC. The General Assembly voted in favor of the Serbian initiative in October 2008 (see General Assembly).

On June 19, 2008, the Security Council adopted Resolution 1820, which called on the world body to take greater steps to protect women and children in zones of conflict and specifically requested that the secretary general adopt stronger rules to ensure "zero tolerance of sexual exploitation and abuse in UN peacekeeping operations." On June 24 the undersecretary general for security and safety, Sir David Veness, resigned in the aftermath of a car bomb attack that killed 17 UN personnel at the world body's main office in Algiers. Partially in response to the attack, the Security Council adopted Resolution 1822, which called on all nations to work together to cut funding for such terrorist organizations as al-Qaida. In August Ban named Andrew Hughes of Australia as the new chief of UN police missions to replace Mark Kroeker of the United States, who resigned in April.

The Security Council was briefed by the special prosecutor for Sudan of the International Criminal Court (ICC) in June 2008 on allegations that the government was not cooperating with the court. The ICC later charged Sudanese president Omar al-Bashir with genocide for his role in the humanitarian crisis (see article on Sudan). Pressure by the United States for the Security Council to take stronger action regarding the conflict in Darfur was repeatedly blocked through 2008, though the council did extend the mandate of UNMIL through 2009.

In May 2008 China and Russia vetoed a Security Council resolution condemning the government of Zimbabwe for violence against its opposition groups and leaders in the aftermath of elections in that country. In response to demands by Eritrea that the UN Mission in Ethiopia and Eritrea (UNMEE) reduce its staff and limit helicopter flights, along with fuel blockages, the Security Council ended the operation on July 31.

Following an October 2008 report by the International Atomic Energy Agency that Iran continued to block inspectors' access to its nuclear facilities, the Security Council unanimously adopted Resolution 1835, which reaffirmed existing sanctions on Iran and called on the government to immediately suspend its uranium-enrichment program. Meanwhile, in response to increased piracy off of the coast of Somalia, the Security Council adopted Resolution 1838 in October, calling on states to work with Somalia's interim Transitional Federal Government to use air and naval resources to end the attacks on merchant and humanitarian shipping. Also in October, former UN envoy Ahtisaari won the Nobel Peace Prize for his work with the world body, including his efforts to resolve the status of Kosovo.

On January 14, 2009, the Security Council extended the mandate of MINURCAT and authorized an increase in the number of peacekeeping forces, up to 5,200 troops. The council subsequently extended a number of other UN operations, including those in Burundi, Liberia, and the Western Sahara. In January the Security Council also passed a resolution calling on Eritrea and Ethiopia to peacefully settle an ongoing border dispute between the two nations. The Security Council unanimously adopted Resolution 1874 on June 12. The measure increased sanctions on North Korea, following that country's second nuclear weapons test. On June 15 Russia vetoed a Security Council resolution to extend the UN observer mission in Georgia and Abkhazia. On September 24 the council, represented by 14 heads of state, including U.S. president Obama, adopted Resolution 1887, which reaffirmed the UN's commitment to the Non-Proliferation Treaty and called on member states to support counter-proliferation efforts and reduce nuclear weapons stockpiles. Meanwhile, on September 30 the Security Council unanimously approved Resolution 1888, which called on all actors in a conflict to take measures to protect vulnerable populations, including women and children, from sexual violence. On October 15 Nigeria, Gabon, Lebanon, Brazil, and Bosnia and Herzegovina were elected as nonpermanent members of the Security Council in a rare round of uncontested balloting. Resolution 1907, enacted on December 23, imposed sanctions on Eritrea that included a travel ban for officials, an arms embargo, and the freezing of some assets, as a result of Eritrea's support for armed groups in Somalia.

On June 9, 2010, the Security Council adopted Resolution 1929, which enacted new sanctions against Iran for its continued nuclear program. The measure was a compromise between council members the United States, France, and the United Kingdom, which sought tougher sanctions, and Russia and China, which resisted new restrictions. Meanwhile, on June 15 the Republic of Korea asked the Security Council to investigate and censure the Democratic People's Republic of Korea in response to the sinking of a Republic of Korea naval vessel and the loss of 46 sailors. China, a traditional ally of the Democratic People's Republic of Korea, resisted council intervention. The council issued a statement deploring the loss of life and urged the two countries to engage in a dialogue. On December 31 MINURCAT's mission ended and UN forces were withdrawn. Also on December 31, BINUB's mandate expired and the mission transitioned to the UN Office in Burundi (*Bureau des Nations Unies au Burundi*—BNUB).

The Council voted sanctions and the creation of a no-fly zone against Libya in March 2011 (see entry on Libya). In October 2011 and again in February 2012 China and Russia vetoed Security Council resolutions calling on Syria to abide by an Arab League peace proposal. Meanwhile, former secretary general Annan was appointed as a special envoy to Syria (see "Secretariat"). Following the eruption of new fighting between Sudan and South Sudan, the council adopted resolution 2046 in May 2012, which called for an end to the violence and a withdrawal of military forces in disputed border areas. The council also extended the mandate of the UN Interim Security Force for Abyei (UNISFA) in the region. In May the Security Council imposed new sanctions on North Korea, following that nation's failed rocket launch on April 13.

The UN Supervision Mission in Syria (*Mission de supervision des Nations Unies en Syrie*—MISNUS), established in April 2012, was suspended on June 16, 2012, as a result of increasing violence in Syria. UN efforts to reduce strife and allow the redeployment of MISNUS failed, and the mission's mandate was terminated on August 19.

Rwanda's election to the Security Council in October 2012 was highly controversial in the aftermath of a UN report that accused Kigali of supporting the M23 militia in the Democratic Republic of the Congo (see entry on the Democratic Republic of the Congo). In December, the UN Integrated Mission in Timor-Leste (UNMIT), launched in 2006, ended (please see the 2013 *Handbook* for more detail on UNMIT).

In January 2013 the Security Council expanded existing sanctions on North Korea after Pyongyang launched another rocket in violation of previous UN restrictions. On March 7 the Security Council condemned North Korea's third nuclear test and imposed additional sanctions on the country (see entry on North Korea). On April 25 the Security Council unamiously adopted Resolution 2100, which authorized the creation of a 12,600-member peacekeeping force, UN Multidimensional Integrated Stabilisation Mission in Mali (*Mission Multidimensionnelle Intégrée des Nations Unies pour la Stabilisation au Mali*—MINUSMA), to replace the existing African Union operation (see below). The Security Council passed Resolution 2106 which called for greater efforts to end "impunity for sexual violence against women."After two years of significant debate and allegations of inaction, the UN Security Council on September 28, 2013, unanimously adopted a U.S.-Russian resolution calling on Syria to end its chemical weapons program and to allow international inspectors access to suspected chemical weapons facilities. The resolution followed the dispatch of a UN inspection team to investigate alleged chemical weapons attacks.

SECURITY COUNCIL: PEACEKEEPING FORCES AND MISSIONS

In addition to the forces and missions listed here, the United Nations Command in Korea (established on June 25, 1950) remains technically in existence. The only UN member now contributing to the command is the United States, which proposed in June 1975 that it be dissolved. As of 2012 no formal action had been taken on the proposal (see Security Council: Origin and development).

United Nations/African Union Hybrid Operation in Darfur (UNAMID)

Established: By Security Council resolution of July 31, 2007; modified by Security Council resolution on July 30, 2013.

Purpose: To protect civilians; provide security for humanitarian assistance; verify the implementation of peace agreements and facilitate a political settlement to ongoing conflicts; and monitor the borders between Sudan and Chad and the Central African Republic.

Headquarters: El Fasher, Darfur.

Force Commander: Lt. Gen. Paul Ignace Mella (Tanzania).

Composition: As of August 31, 2013, 14,481 troops, 347 military observers, and 4,720 civilian police from Bangladesh, Burkina Faso, Burundi, Cambodia, Cameroon, China, Côte D'Ivoire, Djibouti, Egypt, Ethiopia, Gambia, Germany, Ghana, Indonesia, Iran, Jordan, Kenya, Kyrgzstan, Lesotho, Madagascar, Malawi, Malaysia, Mali, Mongolia,

Namibia, Nepal, Nigeria, Pakistan, Palau, Peru, Republic of Korea, Russia, Rwanda, Senegal, Sierra Leone, South Africa, Tajikistan, Tanzania, Thailand, Togo, Uganda, Yemen, Zambia, and Zimbabwe.

United Nations Disengagement Observer Force
(UNDOF)

Established: By Security Council resolution of May 31, 1974.

Purpose: To observe the cease-fire between Israel and Syria following the 1973 Arab-Israeli War.

Headquarters: Camp Faouar (Syrian Golan Heights). (A UNDOF office is located in Damascus, Syria.)

Force Commander: Maj. Gen. Iqbal Singh Singha (India).

Composition: As of August 31, 2013, 1,166 troops from Fiji, India, Ireland, Nepal, and the Philippines.

United Nations Force in Cyprus
(UNFICYP)

Established: By Security Council resolution of March 4, 1964, after consultation with the governments of Cyprus, Greece, Turkey, and the United Kingdom.

Purpose: To serve as a peacekeeping force between Greek and Turkish Cypriots.

Headquarters: Nicosia, Cyprus.

Force Commander: Major General Chao Liu (China).

Composition: As of August 31, 2013, 849 troops and 69 civilian police from Argentina, Australia, Austria, Bosnia-Herzegovina, Brazil, Canada, Chile, China, Croatia, Hungary, India, Ireland, Italy, Lithuania, Montenegro, Serbia, Slovakia, Ukraine, and the United Kingdom.

United Nations Interim Administration Mission in Kosovo
(UNMIK)

Established: By Security Council resolution of June 10, 1999, which also authorized formation of a Multinational Force in Kosovo (Kosovo Force—KFOR).

Purpose: To promote significant autonomy and self-government in Kosovo; to provide civilian administrative functions, including holding elections; to maintain law and order while promoting human rights and ensuring the safe and voluntary return of Kosovar refugees and displaced persons; and to ultimately oversee a transfer of authority to civilian institutions established under a political settlement. KFOR was authorized to establish and maintain a secure environment in Kosovo until such time as the UNMIK Civilian Police could assume this task on a region-by-region basis. In December 2008 the EU Rule of Law Mission in Kosovo (EULEX) took over most of UNMIK's duties in terms of civilian police and security, allowing a substantial reduction in UN personnel.

Headquarters: Priština, Kosovo, Serbia.

Head of Mission: Farid Zarif (Afghanistan).

Operational Framework: Four "pillars"—peace and justice, civil administration, democratization and institution-building under the direction of the Organization for Security and Cooperation in Europe; reconstruction and economic development under the European Union. KFOR is now under NATO/EU command.

Composition: As of August 31, 2013, 8 police officers and 9 military liaisons from Croatia, Czech Republic, Germany, Hungary, Italy, Norway, Moldova, Pakistan, Poland, Portugal, Romania, Russia, Turkey, and Ukraine, in addition to the NATO-led peacekeeping and monitoring force.

United Nations Interim Force in Lebanon
(UNIFIL)

Established: By Security Council resolution of March 19, 1978, and augmented by subsequent Security Council resolution on August 11, 2006.

Purpose: To confirm the withdrawal of Israeli troops from Lebanon, to restore peace and help ensure the return of Lebanese authority to southern Lebanon, to extend access to humanitarian support for the civilian population, to facilitate the return of displaced persons, to establish a zone free of weapons and armed personnel other than those of the Lebanese security forces and UNIFIL, and to aid the government of Lebanon in securing its borders.

Headquarters: Naqoura, Lebanon.

Force Commander: Maj. Gen. Paulo Serra (Italy).

Composition: As of August 31, 2013, 10,555 troops from Armenia, Austria, Bangladesh, Belarus, Belgium, Brazil, Brunei, Cambodia, China, Croatia, Cyprus, El Salvador, Finland, France, FYR of Macedonia, Germany, Ghana, Greece, Guatemala, Hungary, India, Indonesia, Ireland, Italy, Kenya, Malaysia, Nepal, Nigeria, Qatar, Republic of Korea, Sierra Leone, Slovenia, Spain, Sri Lanka, Tanzania, and Turkey.

United Nations Military Observer Group in India and Pakistan
(UNMOGIP)

Established: By resolutions adopted by the United Nations Commission for India and Pakistan on August 13, 1948, and January 5, 1949; augmented and brought under the jurisdiction of the Security Council by resolution of September 6, 1965, in view of a worsening situation in Kashmir.

Purpose: To assist in implementing the cease-fire agreement of January 1, 1949.

Headquarters: Rawalpindi, Pakistan (November–April); Srinagar, India (May–October).

Chief Military Observer: Maj. Gen. Young-Bum Choi (Republic of Korea).

Composition: As of August 31, 2013, 42 military observers from Chile, Croatia, Finland, Philippines, Republic of Korea, Sweden, Thailand, and Uruguay.

United Nations Mission for the Referendum in Western Sahara
Mission des Nations Unies pour le Référendum dans le Sahara Ouest
(MINURSO)

Established: By Security Council resolution of April 29, 1991.

Purpose: To enforce a cease-fire in the Western Sahara between Morocco and the Polisario Front, to identify those eligible to vote in the proposed self-determination referendum in the region, and to supervise the referendum and settlement plan.

Headquarters: Laayoune, Western Sahara.

Force Commander: Maj. Gen. Imam Mulyono (Indonesia).

Composition: As of August 31, 2013, 6 civilian police from Chad, Egypt, Jordan, and Yemen; 27 troops and 199 military observers from Argentina, Austria, Bangladesh, Brazil, China, Croatia, Egypt, El Salvador, France, Ghana, Guinea, Honduras, Hungary, Ireland, Italy, Malawi, Malaysia, Mongolia, Nepal, Nigeria, Pakistan, Paraguay, Peru, Poland, Republic of Korea, Russia, Sri Lanka, Togo, Uruguay, and Yemen. An additional 2,200 troops and observers were authorized but not deployed because of the lack of progress in referendum negotiations.

United Nations Mission in Liberia
(UNMIL)

Established: By Security Council resolution of September 19, 2003; modified by Security Council resolution on September 17, 2012.

Purpose: To support implementation of the recent cease-fire agreement in Liberia, to support humanitarian and human rights activities, and to assist in training national police and the proposed restructured military.

Headquarters: Monrovia, Liberia.

Force Commander: Maj. Gen. Leonard Muriuki Ngondi (Kenya).

Composition: As of August 31, 2013, 5,760 troops, 127 military observers, and 1,456 civilian police from Argentina, Bangladesh, Benin, Bolivia, Bosnia and Herzegovina, Brazil, Bulgaria, China, Croatia, Denmark, Ecuador, Egypt, El Salvador, Ethiopia, Fiji, Finland, France, Gambia, Germany, Ghana, India, Jordan, Kenya, Kyrgyzstan, Lithuania, Malaysia, Montenegro, Namibia, Nepal, Niger, Nigeria, Norway, Pakistan, Paraguay, Peru, Philippines, Poland, Republic of Korea, Romania, Russia, Rwanda, Senegal, Serbia, Sri Lanka, Sweden, Switzerland, Thailand, Togo, Turkey, Uganda, Ukraine, United States, Uruguay, Yemen, Zambia, and Zimbabwe.

United Nations Mission in the Republic of South Sudan
(UNMISS)

Established: By Security Council resolution of July 9, 2011.

Purpose: When South Sudan became independent of Sudan on July 9, 2011, the United Nations Mission in the Sudan (UNMIS, see 2011 *Handbook*) was terminated, being replaced by UNMISS. UNMISS was to operate for one year, with its mandate subsequently renewed.

Headquarters: Juba, South Sudan.

Force Commander: Maj. Gen. Johnson Sakyi (Ghana).

Composition: As of August 31, 2013, 6,806 troops, 146 military observers, and 664 civilian police from Argentina, Australia, Bangladesh, Belarus, Benin, Bolivia, Bosnia and Herzegovina, Brazil, Cambodia, Canada, China, Denmark, Ecuador, Egypt, El Salvador, Ethiopia, Fiji, Gambia, Germany, Ghana, Guatemala, Guinea, India, Indonesia, Japan, Jordan, Kenya, Kyrgyzstan, Malaysia, Mongolia, Namibia, Nepal, the Netherlands, New Zealand, Nigeria, Norway, Papua New Guinea, Paraguay, Peru, Philippines, Poland, Republic of Korea, Romania, Russia, Rwanda, Samoa, Senegal, Sierra Leone, South Africa, Sri Lanka, Sweden, Switzerland, Tanzania, Timor-Leste, Togo, Turkey, Uganda, Ukraine, United Kingdom, United States, Yemen, Zambia, and Zimbabwe.

United Nations Operation in Côte d'Ivoire
Opération des Nations Unies en Côte d'Ivoire
(ONUCI)

Established: By Security Council resolution of February 27, 2004; augmented by Security Council resolution on July 30, 2013.

Purpose: To facilitate implementation of the peace agreement signed by the parties to the conflict in Côte d'Ivoire. (The ONUCI was a successor to the United Nations Mission in Côte d'Ivoire [*Mission des Nations Unies en Côted'Ivoire*—MINUCI], a political mission that had been established by the Security Council in May 2003.)

Headquarters: Abidjan, Côte d'Ivoire.

Force Commander: Maj. Gen. Iqbal Asi (Pakistan).

Composition: As of August 31, 2013, 6,945 troops, 192 military observers, and 1,555 civilian police from Argentina, Bangladesh, Benin, Bolivia, Brazil, Burkina Faso, Burundi, Cameroon, Canada, Central African Republic, Chad, China, Democratic Republic of the Congo, Djibouti, Ecuador, Egypt, El Salvador, Ethiopia, France, Gambia, Ghana, Guatemala, Guinea, India, Ireland, Jordan, Madagascar, Malawi, Moldova, Morocco, Namibia, Nepal, Niger, Nigeria, Pakistan, Paraguay, Peru, Philippines, Poland, Republic of Korea, Romania, Russia, Rwanda, Senegal, Serbia, Tanzania, Togo, Tunisia, Turkey, Uganda, Ukraine, Uruguay, Yemen, Zambia, and Zimbabwe.

United Nations Organization Stabilization Mission in the Democratic Republic of the Congo
Mission de l'Organisation des Nations Unies en République Démocratique du Congo
(MONUSCO)

Established: By Security Council resolution of May 28, 2010, as a successor to the United Nations Organization Mission in the Democratic Republic of the Congo (MONUC, see 2011 *Handbook*). MONUSCO was to concentrate its activities in the eastern DRC while keeping a reserve force capable of operating elsewhere.

Purpose: The effective protection of civilians and humanitarian personnel, as well as the protection of UN personnel, facilities, installations, and equipment. Monusco would also assist the government, along with international and bilateral partners, in strengthening its military; support the reform of the police; develop and implement a multi-year joint UN justice support program in order to develop the criminal justice system; and support the Congolese government in consolidating state authority in the territory freed from armed groups.

Headquarters: Kinshasa, Democratic Republic of the Congo. Liaison offices are maintained in Addis Ababa, Ethiopia; Bujumbura, Burundi; Harare, Zimbabwe; Kampala, Uganda; Kigali, Rwanda; Lusaka, Zambia; and Windhoek, Namibia.

Force Commander: Lt. Gen. Carlos Alberto dos Santos Cruz (Brazil).

Composition: As of August 31, 2013, 18,766 troops, 504 military observers, and 1,418 civilian police from Algeria, Bangladesh, Belgium, Benin, Bolivia, Bosnia and Herzegovina, Burkina Faso, Cameroon, Canada, Central African Republic, Chad, China, Côte d'Ivoire, Czech Republic, Djibouti, Egypt, France, Ghana, Guatemala, Guinea, India, Indonesia, Ireland, Jordan, Kenya, Madagascar, Malawi, Malaysia, Mali, Mongolia, Morocco, Nepal, Niger, Nigeria, Pakistan, Paraguay, Peru, Poland, Romania, Russia, Senegal, Serbia, South Africa, Sri Lanka, Sweden, Switzerland, Tanzania, Togo, Tunisia, Turkey, Ukraine, United Kingdom, United States, Uruguay, Yemen, and Zambia.

United Nations Stabilization Mission in Haiti
Mission des Nations Unies pour la Stabilisation en Haïti
(MINUSTAH)

Established: By Security Council resolution of April 30, 2004; expanded by Security Council resolution on October 13, 2009, and again on June 4, 2010; modified by Security Council resolution on October 12, 2012. (MINUSTAH assumed the authority previously exercised by the Multinational Interim Force [MIF] that had been authorized by the Security Council in February 2004.)

Purpose: To support the constitutional and political process underway in Haiti; to help maintain security and stability; to assist with the restoration and maintenance of the rule of law, public safety, and public order; to assist the transitional government in Haiti in reforming the Haitian national police; to assist in the disarmament and demobilization of armed groups; to provide support for the holding of free and fair elections; and to assist in the post-disaster recovery and reconstruction following the January earthquake.

Headquarters: Port-au-Prince, Haiti.

Force Commander: Lt. Gen. Edson Leal Pujol (Brazil).

Composition: As of August 31, 2013, 6,233 troops and 2,457 civilian police from Argentina, Bangladesh, Benin, Bolivia, Brazil, Burkina Faso, Burundi, Cameroon, Canada, Central African Republic, Chad, Chile, Colombia, Côte d'Ivoire, Croatia, Ecuador, Egypt, El Salvador, France, Grenada, Guatemala, Guinea, India, Indonesia, Jordan, Mali, Nepal, Niger, Nigeria, Norway, Pakistan, Paraguay, Peru, Philippines, Republic of Korea, Romania, Russia, Rwanda, Senegal, Spain, Sri Lanka, Thailand, Togo, Turkey, United States, Uruguay, and Yemen.

United Nations Truce Supervision Organization
(UNTSO)

Established: By Security Council resolution of May 29, 1948.

Purpose: To supervise the cease-fire arranged by the Security Council following the 1948 Arab-Israeli War. Its mandate was subsequently extended to embrace the armistice agreements concluded in 1949; the Egyptian-Israeli peace treaty of 1979; and assistance to other UN forces in the Middle East, specifically the UNDOF and UNIFIL.

Headquarters: Jerusalem, Israel.

Chief of Staff: Maj. Gen. Michael Finn (Ireland).

Composition: As of August 31, 2013, 154 military observers from Argentina, Australia, Austria, Belgium, Canada, Chile, China, Denmark, Estonia, Finland, France, Ireland, Italy, Nepal, Netherlands, New Zealand, Norway, Russia, Serbia, Slovakia, Slovenia, Sweden, Switzerland, and the United States.

United Nations Interim Security Force for Abyei
(UNISFA)

Established: By Security Council resolution of June 27, 2011; augmented by Security Council resolution on May 29, 2013.

Purpose: To supervise the withdrawal of Sudanese and South Sudanese forces from Abyei; facilitate the delivery of humanitarian aid to the region; secure the region's oil infrastructure; and protect civilians from violence.

Headquarters: Abyei Town, Sudan.

Chief of Staff: Maj. Gen. Yohannes Gebremeskel Tesfamariam (Ethiopia).

Composition: As of June 30, 2012, 3,788 troops,101 military observers, and 15 police officers from Benin, Brazil, Cambodia, Ecuador, Ethiopia, Ghana, Guatemala, India, Mongolia, Namibia, Nepal, Nigeria, Paraguay, Peru, Philippines, Russian Federation, Rwanda, Sierra Leone, Tanzania, Uruguay, Zambia, and Zimbabwe.

United Nations Multidimensional Integrated Stabilisation Mission in Mali
Mission Multidimensionnelle Intégrée des Nations Unies pour la Stabilisation au Mali
(MINUSMA)

Established: By Security Council resolution of April 25, 2013.

Purpose: The stabilization of key population centers and support for the reestablishment of state authority throughout the country; support for the implementation of the transitional roadmap, including the national political dialogue and the electoral process; the protection of civilian sand UN personnel; the promotion and protection of human rights; and support for humanitarian assistance, cultural preservation, and national and international justice.

Headquarters: Barnako, Mali.

Force Commander: Maj. Gen. Jean Bosco Kazura (Rwanda).

Composition: As of August 31, 2013, 6,010 troops and 809 civilian police from Bangladesh, Belgium, Benin, Burkina Faso, Burundi, Cambodia, Cameroon, Canada, Chad, Chile, Colombia, Côte d'Ivoire, Egypt, Finland, France, Germany, Ghana, Guinea, Italy, Jordan, Liberia, Mauritania, Niger, Nigeria, Rwanda, Senegal, Sierra Leone, Sweden, Togo, Thailand, Togo, United Kingdom, and United States.

SECURITY COUNCIL: INTERNATIONAL CRIMINAL TRIBUNALS

Lacking a permanent international court with jurisdiction to prosecute and try cases involving accusations of war crimes, genocide, and crimes against humanity, the Security Council established the International Criminal Tribunal for the former Yugoslavia (ICTY) in 1993 and the International Criminal Tribunal for Rwanda (ICTR) in 1994. Meeting in Rome, Italy, in 1998, a UN conference approved formation of a permanent International Criminal Court (ICC), which by April 2002 had obtained sufficient ratifications for its establishment in July (see the General Assembly section).

As of August 2013 the ICTY indicted 161 individuals, including those who had been acquitted and those whose cases had been withdrawn. Proceedings had been concluded against 136 persons and there were 19 individuals serving sentences, while 46 had completed their sentences; 25 cases were still proceeding, including 21 appeals, and 18 were acquitted. The last two indicted individuals remaining at large, RatkoMladić, formerly commander of the Bosnian Serb army and Goran Hadžić, formerly president of the Republic of Serbian Krajina, were arrested on May 26, 2011, and July 20, 2011, respectively.

On November 2, 2002, Biljana Plavšić, former president of the Serb Republic of Bosnia and Herzegovina, pleaded guilty to one count of a crime against humanity for political, racial, and religious persecution, and on February 27, 2003, she was sentenced to 11 years in prison. By far the most prominent figure turned over to the court by national forces was former Yugoslav president Slobodan Milošević, who died on March 11, 2006, during his trial. The former president of the Republic of Srpska, Radovan Karadžić, was arrested on July 18, 2008, and turned over to the ICTY on July 30. Karadžić refused to recognize the authority of the ITCY and avoided entering a plea until a not guilty plea was entered on his behalf in March 2009. His trial began in October 2009. By August 2013 the trials of Mladić, Hadžić, Karadžić, and Vojislav Šešelj, the president of the Serb Radical Party, were the last remaining ongoing cases, although appeals were still being heard in other cases.

As of August 2013 the ICTR had brought public indictments against some 95 individuals and had arrested more than 50 people, while 4 individuals remained at large; 75 trials had reached their conclusion (with 47 convictions and 12 acquittals), and one trial was in progress (along with 16 appeals). Thirty cases had been passed to Rwandan national courts for adjudication. The highest-ranking defendant, former Rwandan prime minister Jean Kambanda, pleaded guilty to genocide in 1998 and was sentenced to life in prison. In 2008 three of the remaining high-level indictees were arrested, including Callixte Nsabonimana, Dominique Ntawukulilyayo, and Augustin Ngirabatware. In June the ICTR requested a one-year extension from the Security Council to complete its trial work, partially as a result of the three arrests. In 2009 and 2010 the ICTR requested additional time to complete all trials. In 2013 the Security Council requested that the tribunal complete all work by December 31, 2014.

In August 2000 the Security Council unanimously indicated its support for forming a third war crimes tribunal, for Sierra Leone, which began its proceedings in 2003, although not as a subsidiary body of the Security Council. Former Liberian president Charles Taylor was the highest-ranking defendant tried by the court. He was convicted of 11 counts of war crimes on April 26, 2012, and sentenced to 50 years in prison. The conviction was hailed by human rights groups. A similar joint criminal tribunal in Lebanon began in 2005, and in 2007 a tribunal began in Cambodia to prosecute and try former Khmer Rouge regime members. The Special Tribunal for Lebanon issued indictments for five individuals through 2013, but all remained at large and their trials had not begun. Through August 2013, the Cambodia Tribunal (officially known as the Extraordinary Chambers in the Courts of Cambodia), had indicted five individuals. Khmer Rouge leader Kang Kek Lewwas convicted of crimes against humanity in July 2012, and sentenced to 35 years in prison. One indictee died during his trial, while another was declared mentally unfit for trial. Two other trials remained ongoing.

International Criminal Tribunal for the Former Yugoslavia
(ICTY)

Formal Name: International Tribunal for the Prosecution of Persons Responsible for Serious Violations of International Humanitarian Law Committed in the Territory of the Former Yugoslavia since 1991.

Established: By Security Council resolution of May 25, 1993.

Purpose: To prosecute and try persons who allegedly committed serious violations of international humanitarian law on the territory of the former Yugoslavia since 1991, the subject offenses being genocide, crimes against humanity, and violations of the 1949 Geneva Conventions and the laws or customs of war.

Headquarters: The Hague, Netherlands.

Chief Prosecutor: Serge Brammertz (Belgium).

Permanent Judges: Theodor Meron (United States, President), Carmel A. Agius (Malta, Vice President), Jean-Claude Antonetti (France), Guy Delvoie (Belgium), Christoph Flügge (Germany), Mehmet Güney (Turkey), Burton Hall (Bahamas), Khalida Khan (Paksitan), O-gon Kwon (Republic of Korea), Liu Daqun (China), Bakone Justice Moloto (South Africa), Howard Morrison (United Kingdom), Alphonsus Martinus Maria Orie (Netherlands), Fausto Pocar (Italy), Arlette Ramaroson (Madagascar), Patrick Lipton Robinson (Jamaica), William Hussein Sekule (Tanzania), and Bakhtiyar Tuzmukhamedov (Russia). There are also 4 *ad litem* judges.

Registrar: John Hocking (Australia).

Web site: www.icty.org

International Criminal Tribunal for Rwanda
(ICTR)
Tribunal Pénal International pour le Rwanda (French)
Urukiko Nshinjabyaha Mpuzamahanga
Rwagenewe u Rwanda (Kinyarwanda)

Formal Name: International Criminal Tribunal for the Prosecution of Persons Responsible for Genocide and Other Serious Violations of

International Humanitarian Law Committed in the Territory of Rwanda and Rwandan Citizens Responsible for Genocide and Other Such Violations Committed in the Territory of Neighboring States, between 1 January 1994 and 31 December 1994.

Established: By Security Council resolution of November 8, 1994.

Purpose: To prosecute crimes allegedly committed by Rwandans and others in Rwanda, and by Rwandans in neighboring states, between January 1, 1994, and December 31, 1994, the subject offenses being violations of the 1949 Geneva Conventions, genocide, and crimes against humanity.

Headquarters: Arusha, Tanzania. The office of the prosecutor is located in Kigali, Rwanda.

Chief Prosecutor: Hassan Bubacar Jallow (Gambia).

Permanent Judges: Vagn Joensen (Denmark, President), Florence Rita Arrey (Cameroon, Vice President), Khalida Rachid Khan (Pakistant), Arlette Ramarosen (Madagascar), Solomy Balungi Bossa (Uganda), Lee Gacugia Muthoga (Kenya), Seon Ki Park (Republic of Korea), Robert Fremr (Czech Republic), Mpparany Rajohnson (Madagascar), Patrick Robinson (Jamaica), Carmel Agius (Malta), Mehmet Güney (Turkey), Liu Daqun (China), Theodor Meron (United States), Fausto Pocar (Italy), William Sekule (Tanzania), Bakhtiyar Tuzmukhamedov (Russia), Gderdao Gustave Kam (Burkino Faso), and Andrésia Vaz (Senegal). There are also 12 *ad litem* judges.

Registrar: Adama Dieng (Senegal).

Web site: www.unictr.org

ECONOMIC AND SOCIAL COUNCIL

(ECOSOC)

Membership (54): Albania, Austria, Belarus, Benin, Bolivia, Brazil, Bulgaria, Burkina Faso, Cameroon, Canada, China, Colombia, Croatia, Cuba, Denmark, Dominican Republic, Ecuador, El Salvador, Ethiopia, France, Gabon, Haiti, India, Indonesia, Ireland, Japan, Kuwait, Kyrgyzstan, Latvia, Lesotho, Libya, Malawi, Mauritius, Mexico, Nepal,Netherlands, New Zealand, Nicaragua, Nigeria, Pakistan, Qatar, Republic of Korea, Russia, San Marino, Senegal, South Afirca, Spain, Sudan, Sweden, Tunisia, Turkey, Turkmenistan, United Kingdom, United States. One-third of the members rotate annually on the following geographical basis: Africa, 14 seats; Asia, 11; Latin America and the Caribbean, 10; Eastern Europe, 6; Western Europe and others, 13.

Web site: www.un.org/ecosoc

President of the 2013 Session: Néstor Osorio (Colombia).

Origin and development. Initially, the activities of ECOSOC were directed primarily to the twin problems of relief and reconstruction in war-torn Europe, Asia, and, after 1948, Israel. By the mid-1950s, however, the problems of less developed states of Africa, Asia, and Latin America began to claim primary attention.

Substantially increased activity has occurred under the auspices of ECOSOC subsidiary organs as UN operations have proliferated in the economic and social fields. At the direction of the General Assembly, ECOSOC in 1987 established a special commission to identify ways to simplify UN structures and functions in those areas. In May 1988, however, the commission announced that it was unable to reach a consensus, its chair citing "political concerns" within the international community and "vested interests" within the UN as hindering effective reorganization. Nevertheless, ECOSOC continued to attempt to streamline and "revitalize" its own operations. As part of that effort, the council in mid-1991 agreed to discontinue its practice of holding two or more sessions each year in various locations in favor of a single four- to five-week substantive session annually (alternating between New York and Geneva), preceded by a number of organizational sessions.

In mid-1992 ECOSOC once again found itself immersed in debate on the proposed restructuring of UN bodies dealing with economic and social issues, pressure having grown to eliminate overlapping mandates and provide "more efficient and cost-effective" services. Secretary General Boutros Boutros-Ghali, a major force behind the streamlining efforts, said he hoped ECOSOC would achieve the same "relevance" to economic and social development in the world that the Security Council had recently achieved regarding peacemaking and peacekeeping. Under Boutros-Ghali and his successor, Kofi Annan, ECOSOC underwent considerable reorganization, including a reduction in the number of Standing Committees and Commissions.

Structure. By a charter amendment that entered into force in 1965, the membership of ECOSOC was increased from 18 to 27 in order to provide wider representation to new states in Africa and Asia. Similarly, membership was raised to 54 as of September 1973. One-third of the members are elected each year for three-year terms, and all voting is by simple majority; each member has one vote.

Much of ECOSOC's activity is carried out through its eight Functional and five Regional Commissions (described in separate sections) and a number of Standing Committees and Commissions that currently include the Commission on Human Settlements (established in 1977), the Committee on Negotiations with Intergovernmental Agencies (1946), the Committee on Non-Governmental Organizations (1946), and the Committee for Program and Coordination (1962). In 2000 ECOSOC established the United Nations Forestry Forum (UNFF) to promote conservation and sustainable development. Membership in the UNFF is open to all UN member states. In addition, there are assorted ECOSOC Expert Bodies, such as the Ad Hoc Group of Experts on International Cooperation in Tax Matters; the Committee for Development Policy; the Committee of Experts on Public Administration; the Committee of Experts on the Transport of Dangerous Goods and on the Globally Harmonized System of Classification and Labeling of Chemicals; the Committee on Economic, Social, and Cultural Rights; the Permanent Forum on Indigenous Issues; and the United Nations Group of Experts on Geographical Names. In 2001 ECOSOC created two Ad Hoc Advisory Groups On African Countries Emerging From Conflict, one for Burundi and the other for Guinea-Bissau. These were followed in 2004 by the reactivation of the Ad Hoc Advisory Group on Haiti, which had been active in 1999. In 2006 the advisory group on Burundi was terminated, as was the group on Guinea-Bissau the following year, when the newly created Peace Building Commission was tasked to oversee the countries.

Because of the scope of its responsibilities, ECOSOC has complex relationships with a number of UN subsidiary and related organs. It participates in the Chief Executives Board (CEB, formerly the Administrative Committee on Coordination [ACC]), which comprises the secretary general and the heads of the Specialized Agencies and the International Atomic Energy Agency (IAEA), and elects the members of the independent International Narcotics Control Board (INCB), three from nominees proposed by the World Health Organization and ten from other nominees offered by UN members and parties to the 1961 Single Convention on Narcotic Drugs. It also elects the executive boards of the United Nations Development Program/United Nations Population Fund and the United Nations Children's Fund, the Executive Committee of the United Nations Office of High Commissioner for Refugees, half of the members of the UN/FAO Intergovernmental Committee of the World Food Program, 10 board members of the United Nations Research Institute for Social Development, and the 22 members of the Program Coordination Board for the Joint UN Program on HIV/AIDS (UNAIDS).

Activities. ECOSOC produces or initiates studies, reports, and recommendations on international economic, social, cultural, educational, health, and related matters; promotes respect for, and observance of, human rights and fundamental freedoms; negotiates agreements with the UN Specialized Agencies to define their relations with the UN; and coordinates the activities of the Specialized Agencies through consultations and recommendations.

For information on ECOSOC activities before 2001, see the 2010 *Handbook*. ECOSOC drew international notice at its early May 2001 organizing session when, in secret balloting, the United States lost its seat on the Commission on Human Rights and on the International Narcotics Control Board, effective January 1 and March 1, 2002, respectively. The United States had been represented on both the commission and the board continuously since their formation. The outcome of the votes drew predictable ire from members of the U.S. Congress, who threatened to retaliate, in part by withholding $582 million in back UN dues. Many observers described the slight as an indication of dissatisfaction within the UN over stances taken by the George W. Bush administration, particularly its opposition to formation of the International Criminal Court and its withdrawal from the Kyoto Protocol, which was aimed at reducing emissions of greenhouse gases (see the article on the UN Environment Program). Further controversy broke out in July 2002 when ECOSOC endorsed a plan for a system of regular inspections of prisons and detention centers throughout the world to combat the abuse of prisoners. Washington opposed that measure, apparently unwilling to permit such scrutiny of U.S. facilities in the United States and elsewhere. Nevertheless, the United States was returned to the Commission on Human Rights in 2003.

In early 2003 ECOSOC announced plans to coordinate its activities more closely with the IMF, World Bank, and the WTO in order to implement the goals set at the 2002 International Conference on Financing for Development. The council also subsequently indicated a desire to become more involved with "practical activities on the ground" as directed by the Security Council. Among other things, ECOSOC cited "expanded investment in health and education as a critical component in the UN's recently enhanced peacebuilding role." Collaterally, the council reported that the plight of poor countries as of 2005 had improved very little despite much attention given to the issue during the first half of the decade. ECOSOC pledged to intensify its oversight of the many commissions and agencies under its purview as part of proposed overall UN reform geared toward enhancing efficiency and effectiveness.

In accordance with the March 2006 General Assembly resolution creating the UN Human Rights Council, ECOSOC abolished the Commission on Human Rights on June 16. In addition, the ECOSOC voted to increase the membership of its Commission on Science and Technology for Development from 33 to 43 members beginning in February 2007 in order to broaden participation in the body.

In accordance with a proposal accepted at the 2005 World Summit, ECOSOC conducted its first Annual Ministerial Review (AMR) in July 2007 in Geneva. The AMR brought together national delegations and representatives from the UN and private sector to assess goals related to sustainable development in line with the theme of the meeting, "Strengthening Efforts to Eradicate Poverty and Hunger, Including through the Global Partnership for Development." In July the ECOSOC launched the Development Cooperation Forum (DCF), a biennial meeting to facilitate progress on the Millennium Development Goals. The DCF was designed to draw together participants from individual countries and representatives from various UN bodies, as well as the World Bank, IMF, and business sector. The initial meeting of the group was held in New York in June 2008.

The 2008 AMR, conducted in July in New York, focused on "Implementing the Internationally Agreed Goals and Commitments in Regard to Sustainable Development." The AMR included sessions on the UN's development agenda, implementing global development goals on a national basis, and the integration of the Millennium Development Goals with other initiatives. In addition, Belgium, Finland, Luxembourg, and the United Kingdom reported on national efforts to promote development. At ECOSOC's 2008 substantive session, the council passed 9 resolutions and 3 decisions, the most ever at one of its annual meetings. The resolutions included a condemnation of sexual violence against humanitarian and aid workers, an expression of concern over the growing number of people affected by natural disasters, and a call for joint action to lessen the impact of rising food and commodity prices.

ECOSOC's third AMR was conducted in July 2009 in Geneva. The event was centered on three goals: reviewing the UN's development initiatives, analyzing the main global challenges and opportunities surrounding public health, and examining potential new ECOSOC programs. Bolivia, China, Jamaica, Japan, Mali, Sri Lanka, and Sudan each gave national presentations on development issues. Among the resolutions adopted at ECOSOC's substantive session in Geneva in July was a call for the UN development programs to try to achieve gender balance in their personnel.

The fourth AMR took place at the UN headquarters in New York from June 28 to July 1, 2010. Thirteen countries provided national presentations. The session focused on the challenges faced by women in economic development and endorsed the declaration *Implementing the Internationally Agreed Goals and Commitments in Regard to Gender Equality and Empowerment of Women.* The document reaffirmed the commitment of the world body to the recommendations from the 1995 Beijing Summit and recommitted ECOCOS to ending gender-based discrimination and barriers to economic development. The second DCF was conducted on June 29–30, 2010, in New York. The final report from the event highlighted the need to develop a coherent and cross-agency approach to development and called for the UN to develop an "economic architecture" that permitted the nexus of migration, trade, and finance to be addressed. At the same July meeting the administration of U.S. president Barak Obama pushed for ECOSOC to accredit the International Gay and Lesbian Human Rights Commission for consultative status, so that it could have a presence at the UN Recognition. In the culmination of a three-year campaign, accreditation was granted.

In May 2011 ECOSOC renewed Iran's membership, in spite of objections from the United States and Canada. Amid questions about the organization's role and future direction, Swiss president Micheline Calmy-Rey proposed that ECOSOC reinvent itself as the United Nations' lead organization to manage the challenges of global sustainability.

The theme of the 2012 AMR, held in July in New York, was "Promoting Productive Capacity, Employment, and Decent Work to Eradicate Poverty in the Context of Inclusive, Sustainable, and Equitable Growth at All Levels for Achieving the MDGs." At the session, ECOSOC presented growth models that had weathered the global economic downturn in a sustainable and equitable fashion. The meetings' final declaration warned of the dangers to economic development posed by the global financial crisis and called for more active efforts to achieve gender equity in the labor force.

In July 2013 ECOSOC launched an initiative to review progess on implementing commitments made by member states at the 1995 Beijing World Conference on Women. In September, the UN announced it planned to replace the Commission on Sustainable Development with a high level political forum of world leaders that would meet every four years, beginning in 2016, to discuss sustainable development. ECOSOC was charged with coordinating annual meetings of the group at the ministerial level. The theme for the 2013 AMR was "Science, Technology, and Innovation (STI) and Culture for Sustainable Development and the Millennium Development Goals."

ECONOMIC AND SOCIAL COUNCIL: FUNCTIONAL COMMISSIONS

ECOSOC's Functional Commissions prepare reports, evaluate services, and make recommendations to the council on matters of economic and social concern to member states. Participants are elected for terms of three or four years, depending on the particular commission. Selection is made with due regard for geographical distribution; in the case of the Commission on Narcotic Drugs, emphasis is also given to countries producing or manufacturing narcotic materials. The Commission on Narcotic Drugs has a Subcommission on Illicit Drug Traffic and Related Matters in the Near and Middle East, and four regional Heads of National Drug Law Enforcement Agencies (HONLEA).

Commission on Crime Prevention and Criminal Justice

Established: February 6, 1992.

Purpose: To provide policy guidance on crime prevention and criminal justice, including the treatment of offenders, and to facilitate the activities of UN and other international programs in those areas. (Commission mandates are implemented by the Center for International Crime Prevention [CICP] of the Office for Drug Control and Crime Prevention [ODCCP].)

Membership (40): Algeria, Argentina, Austria, Bahamas, Belarus, Brazil, Cameroon, China, Colombia, Croatia, Cuba, Czech Republic, Democratic Republic of the Congo, Germany, Indonesia, Iran, Italy, Japan, Kenya, Mauritius, Mexico, Namibia, Nigeria, Norway, Pakistan, Peru, Republic of Korea, Russia, Saudi Arabia, Sierra Leone, South Africa, Switzerland, Thailand, Tunisia, Uganda, United Arab Emirates, United Kingdom, United States, Uruguay.

Commission on Narcotic Drugs

Established: February 16, 1946.

Purpose: To serve as the UN's principal policymaking body on drugs and to advise the council on matters related to the abuse and control of narcotic drugs. (Commission mandates may be implemented through the UN International Drug Control Program [UNDCP] within the Office for Drug Control and Crime Prevention [ODCCP].)

Membership (53): Afghanistan, Algeria, Angola, Australia, Austria, Belgium, Benin, Bolivia, Brazil, Cameroon, Canada, China, Colombia, Croatia, Cuba, Czech Republic, Democratic Republic of the Congo, Denmark, Egypt, France, Germany, Guatemala, Hungary, India, Indonesia, Iran, Israel, Italy, Japan, Kazakhstan, Mexico, Namibia, the Netherlands, Nigeria, Pakistan, Peru, Poland, Republic of Korea,

Russia, Spain, St. Vincent and the Grenadines, Suriname, Tajikistan, Tanzania, Thailand, Togo, Turkey, Turkmenistan, Ukraine, United Kingdom, United States, Uruguay, Zimbabwe.

Commission on Population and Development

Established: October 3, 1946, as the Population Commission. Current name adopted in 1994.

Purpose: To study and advise the council on population issues and on integrating population and development strategies. As of 1996 the commission has also been charged with monitoring, reviewing, and implementing the International Conference on Population and Development Program of Action (1994) at the national, regional, and international levels.

Membership (47): Algeria, Angola, Bangladesh, Belgium, Belarus, Brazil, China, Côte d'Ivoire, Cuba, Democratic Republic of the Congo, Ecuador, Egypt, El Salvador, Gabon, Georgia, Germany, Ghana, Guatemala, Haiti, Hungary, India, Indonesia, Iran, Israel, Jamaica, Japan, Luxembourg, Malawi, Malaysia, Moldova, Norway, Pakistan, Philippines, Portugal, Russia, Rwanda, St. Lucia, Senegal, Spain, Switzerland, Tanzania, Turkmenistan, Uganda, United Kingdom, United States (two vacancies).

Commission on Science and Technology for Development

Established: April 30, 1992.

Purpose: To promote international cooperation in the field of science and technology for development; to formulate guidelines for the harmonization of UN scientific and technological activities and to monitor those activities.

Membership (43): Austria, Brazil, Bulgaria, Cameroon, Central African Republic, Chile, China, Costa Rica, Cuba, Dominican Republic, Finland, France, Germany, Hungary, India, Iran, Japan. Latvia, Lesotho, Liberia, Malta, Mauritius, Mexico, Nigeria, Oman, Peru, Philippines, Portugal, Russia, Rwanda, Saudi Arabia, Sri Lanka, Sweden, Switzerland, Tanzania, Togo, Tunisia, Turkey, United States, Zambia (two vacancies).

Commission for Social Development

Established: June 21, 1946, as the Social Commission; renamed the Commission for Social Development on July 29, 1966.

Purpose: To advise the council on all aspects of social development policies, including, recently, an increased emphasis on policies aimed at increasing the equitable distribution of national income.

Membership (46): Albania, Andorra, Austria, Bangladesh, Belarus, Brazil, Burkina Faso, Cameroon, China, Cuba, Dominican Republic, Ecuador, Egypt, El Salvador, Ethiopia, Gabon, Germany, Haiti, Iran, Italy, Japan, Lesotho, Liberia, Mauritania, Mauritius, Mexico, Mongolia, Nepal, Netherlands, Nigeria, Peru, Philippines, Qatar, Republic of Korea, Russia, Spain, Sudan, Sweden, Switzerland, Ukraine, United States, Venezuela, Vietnam, Zimbabwe (two vacancies).

Commission on the Status of Women

Established: June 21, 1946.

Purpose: To report to the council on methods to promote women's rights; to develop proposals giving effect to the principle that men and women should have equal rights.

Membership (45): Argentina, Bangladesh, Belarus, Belgium, Brazil, Burkina Faso, Central African Republic, China, Comoros Islands, Cuba, Democratic Republic of the Congo, Dominican Republic, Ecuador, El Salvador, Estonia, Finland, Gambia, Georgia, Germany, Indonesia, Iran, Israel, Jamaica, Japan, Lesotho, Liberia, Libya, Malawi, Malaysia, Mongolia, Netherlands, Niger, Pakistan, Paraguay, Philippines, Republic of Korea, Russia, Spain, Swaziland, Switzerland, Thailand, Uganda, United States, Uruguay, Zimbabwe.

Commission on Sustainable Development

Established: February 12, 1993.

Purpose: To monitor implementation of agreements reached at the 1992 UN Conference on Environment and Development; to oversee the integration of those two areas throughout the UN system.

Membership (53): Algeria, Antigua and Barbuda, Argentina, Australia, Bangladesh, Belgium, Belarus, Benin, Brazil, Canada, China, Colombia, Costa Rica, Côte d'Ivoire, Cuba, Democratic Republic of the Congo, Denmark, Eritrea, Estonia, Ethiopia, France, Gabon, Germany, Israel, Kazakhstan, Kyrgyzstan, Latvia, Libya, Luxembourg, Malaysia, Malawi, Mauritius, Mongolia, Namibia, Netherlands, Nigeria, Norway, Pakistan, Panama, Peru, Philippines, Romania, Russia, Saudi Arabia, Switzerland, Thailand, Togo, Ukraine, United Arab Emirates, United Kingdom, United States, Uruguay, Venezuela.

Statistical Commission

Established: June 21, 1946.

Purpose: To develop international statistical services, to promote the development of national statistics and to make them more readily comparable, and to assist the UN Secretariat and Specialized Agencies in their statistical work.

Membership (24): Australia, Barbados, Botswana, Bulgaria, Cameroon, China, Colombia, Cuba, Czech Republic, Dominican Republic,Germany, Hungary, Italy, Japan, Mongolia, Morocco, Netherlands, Niger, Norway, Oman, Russia, Tanzania, United Kingdom, United States.

ECONOMIC AND SOCIAL COUNCIL: REGIONAL COMMISSIONS

The primary aim of the five Regional Commissions, which report annually to ECOSOC, is to assist in raising the level of economic activity in their respective regions and to maintain and strengthen the economic relations of the states in each region, both among themselves and with others. The commissions adopt their own procedural rules, including how they select officers. Each commission is headed by an executive secretary, who holds the rank of undersecretary of the UN, while their Secretariats are integral parts of the overall United Nations Secretariat.

The commissions are empowered to make recommendations directly to member governments and to Specialized Agencies of the United Nations, but no action can be taken in respect to any state without the agreement of that state.

Economic Commission for Africa
(ECA)

Established: April 29, 1958.

Purpose: To "initiate and participate in measures for facilitating concerted action for the economic development of Africa, including its social aspects, with a view to raising the level of economic activity and levels of living in Africa, and for maintaining and strengthening the economic relations of countries and territories of Africa, both among themselves and with other countries of the world."

Headquarters: Addis Ababa, Ethiopia. Subregional Development Centers are located in Tangier, Morocco, for Northern Africa; Kigali, Rwanda, for Eastern Africa; Yaoundé, Cameroon, for Central Africa; Niamey, Niger, for Western Africa; and Lusaka, Zambia, for Southern Africa.

Principal Subsidiary Organs: Conference of African Ministers of Finance, Planning and Economic Development; Sectoral Ministerial Conferences; Technical Preparatory Committee of the Whole; Follow-up Committee on the Conference of Ministers; seven expert-level committees (Women in Development, Development Information, Sustainable Development, Human Development and Civil Society, Industry and Private Sector Development, Natural Resources and Science and Technology, Regional Cooperation and Integration); Secretariat. The Secretariat includes an Office of Policy Planning and Resource Management and six substantive divisions: African Center for Gender and Development, Development Information Services, Development Policy Management, Economic and Social Policy, Sustainable Development, and Trade and Regional Integration.

Executive Secretary: Carlos Lopes (Guinea-Bissau).

Membership (54): Algeria, Angola, Benin, Botswana, Burkina Faso, Burundi, Cameroon, Cape Verde Islands, Central African Republic, Chad, Comoro Islands, Côte d'Ivoire, Democratic Republic of the Congo, Djibouti, Egypt, Equatorial Guinea, Eritrea, Ethiopia, Gabon, Gambia, Ghana, Guinea, Guinea-Bissau, Kenya, Lesotho, Liberia,

Libya, Madagascar, Malawi, Mali, Mauritania, Mauritius, Morocco, Mozambique, Namibia, Niger, Nigeria, Republic of the Congo, Rwanda, Sao Tome and Principe, Senegal, Seychelles, Sierra Leone, Somalia, South Africa, South Sudan, Sudan, Swaziland, Tanzania, Togo, Tunisia, Uganda, Zambia, Zimbabwe. (Switzerland also participates in a consultative capacity.)

Web site: www.uneca.org

Activities. Recent ECA initiatives have included sponsorship of African Development Forums, the first of which convened in Addis Ababa in October 1999 (for activities prior to 2006, see the 2013 *Handbook*).

In its publication *Economic Report on Africa 2007: Accelerating Africa's Development through Diversification,* the ECA noted that African countries had an average GDP growth rate of 5.7 percent in 2006. The report also asserted that diversification was the most important factor in sustained economic growth. In June 2007 the ECA, the African Development Bank, and the AU cosponsored a conference that approved the African Charter on Statistics, which aimed to standardize the collection and dissemination of data. The ECA also cooperated with the Central Bank of Nigeria to launch the Africa Finance Cooperation (AFC) in March. The AFC provided funding for projects to support the New Partnership for Africa's Development (NEPAD) and had an initial capitalization of $2 billion.

In March 2008 the ECA conducted a symposium in New York on the commission's support for NEPAD. The symposium called for the ECA to better coordinate UN efforts on behalf of NEPAD. A follow-up meeting was held in September in Addis Ababa. In the *Economic Report on Africa 2008: Africa and the Monterrey Consensus, Tracking Performance and Progress,* the ECA noted that Africa's economic growth rate was 5.7 percent in 2007 and that inflation remained generally low, though some countries, most notably Zimbabwe, had unsustainable levels of inflation. While income growth exceeded 3 percent between 2001 and 2006, the publication noted that growth would have to increase dramatically to close the gap between Africa and the developed countries of the North. The report also highlighted the changing nature of direct foreign investment in Africa, as Asia, and particularly China, had significantly increased investment in the continent over the past five years.

At the second ECA-sponsored annual joint meeting of the African ministers of economy, finance, and planning, held in Addis Ababa in June 2009, the ministers issued a call for swift and innovative action on the part of member states to address the global economic crisis. The *Economic Report on Africa 2009: Developing African Agriculture Through Regional Value Chains* was divided into two main parts. The first section examined recent global economic patterns and trends, while the second part explored methods to enhance regional agricultural markets and supply chains. The report noted that GDP expansion in Africa contracted from 5.7 percent in 2007 to 5.1 percent in 2008 and was expected to fall to 2 percent in 2009. In addition, the ECA identified rising fuel and energy prices as the greatest threats to economic stability on the continent. The ECA also published the *African Women's Report 2009,* which included the African Gender and Development Index (AGDI) designed to provide a tool to measure women's equality on the continent. The first AGDI measured 12 countries, including Benin, Burkina Faso, Cameroon, Egypt, Ethiopia, Ghana, Madagascar, Mozambique, South Africa, Tanzania, Tunisia, and Uganda, chosen to represent the five regions of Africa. Of the test states, Madagascar ranked highest in gender development, followed by Egypt and South Africa, while Benin ranked last.

In its March 2011 Economic Report on Africa the ECA broke new ground by advocating a middle course between the neoliberal economic doctrines prevalent in the West and the African preference for heavy state control. A September 2011 conference in which ECA representatives participated also called for a new approach to development in Africa. It was generally admitted that no African country would achieve its Millennium Development Goals. In its 2012 economic report on Africa, the ECA noted that the continent's GDP growth rate had slowed to 2.7 percent in 2011 as a result of the global economic crisis. However, the publication predicted that GDP would grow by 5.1 percent in 2012.

The 2012 report *Illicit Financial Flows from Africa: Scale and Developmental Challenges* asserted that foreign multinationals had transferred as much as $1.5 trillion annually from Africa to developed nations. Also in 2012, South Sudan became the 54th member of the ECA. That year the ECA launched a number of reforms to streamline the organization. Meanwhile, Carlos Lopez of Guinea-Bisseau, who had been the director of the UN Staff College and had a reputation as a reformer, was appointed executive director of the ECA.

The 2013 ECAEcomic Report on Africa, *Making the Most of Africa's Commodities: Industrializing for Growth, Jobs and Economic Transformation,* noted that economic growth on the continent had exceeded 5 percent in 2012, and forecast growth of 4.8 percent in 2013. The publication also highlighted Africa's considerable resources, including 42 percent of the world's gold, and 12 percent of the globe's oil reserves, but called on countries to diversify their economies. The report also asserted that several African countries lacked the "capacity" to carry out economic reforms.

Economic Commission for Europe
(ECE)

Established: March 28, 1947.

Purpose: To promote economic cooperation, integration, and sustainable development among member countries.

Headquarters: Geneva, Switzerland.

Principal Subsidiary Organs: Committee on Economic Cooperation and Integration; Committee on Sustainable Energy; Committee on Environmental Policy; Committee on Housing and Land Management; Committee on Trade, Industry and Enterprise Development; Conference of European Statisticians; Inland Transport Committee; Timber Committee; Secretariat.

Web site: www.unece.org

Executive Secretary: Sven Alkalaj (Bosnia-Herzegovina).

Membership (56): Albania, Andorra, Armenia, Austria, Azerbaijan, Belarus, Belgium, Bosnia and Herzegovina, Bulgaria, Canada, Croatia, Cyprus, Czech Republic, Denmark, Estonia, Finland, France, Georgia, Germany, Greece, Hungary, Iceland, Ireland, Israel, Italy, Kazakhstan, Kyrgyzstan, Latvia, Liechtenstein, Lithuania, Luxembourg, Macedonia, Malta, Moldova, Monaco, Montenegro, Netherlands, Norway, Poland, Portugal, Romania, Russia, San Marino, Serbia, Slovakia, Slovenia, Spain, Sweden, Switzerland, Tajikistan, Turkey, Turkmenistan, Ukraine, United Kingdom, United States, Uzbekistan. (Israel's long-standing application for membership, based on its "fundamental economic relations" with the European Community and the United States, was approved by ECOSOC in July 1991. The Holy See also participates in the work of the commission in a consultative capacity.)

Activities. In December 2005 the ECE established the Economic Cooperation and Integrated Division (ECID). ECID was tasked to develop strategies to enhance competitiveness through increased innovation (for information on the ECE prior to 2005, please see the 2013 *Handbook*).

At its February 2006 meeting the member states proposed initiatives to increase economic cooperation and integration. In response to rising fuel costs, the ECE tasked one of its expert groups to explore energy efficiency, costs, and resources. It also decided to include the issue of energy security in its annual meetings. In November the Committee on Sustainable Energy voted to undertake an intergovernmental dialogue on energy. Meanwhile, the Committee on Trade adopted a new mandate to develop joint programs with other UN bodies and agencies. The ECE also initiated a project to identify and remove nontariff trade barriers between Europe and the countries of Central Asia, in cooperation with Special Program for the Economies of Central Asia (SPECA). The joint ECE-SPECA program endorsed 28 projects through 2007. It also conducted two high-level conferences, the first, Focus on Asia, in May in Almaty, Kazakhstan, and the second, Focus on Europe, in November in Berlin, Germany. In addition, in 2007 the ECE signed a memorandum of understanding with the Inter-Parliamentary Assembly of the Eurasian Economic Community to promote deeper integration of the regions.

The ECE's ministerial conference in Belgrade, Serbia, in October 2007 was titled "Environment for Europe" and concentrated on issues such as energy efficiency and sustainability. In February 2008 the ECE launched an initiative to help transitioning economies develop public-private partnerships. A pilot program was scheduled to begin in Moscow in October to better train officials and members of the private sector on issues related to public-private ventures. In August, in response to continuing problems in the United States and European housing markets, the ECE created a new advisory body, the Real Estate

Market Advisory Group. The new group was formed to work with the existing Working Party on Land Administration to develop new guidelines for the regulation of real estate markets and financing, as well as develop programs with individual countries to increase housing capacity in an environmentally friendly manner.

Through 2008 the ECE undertook 60 technical cooperation programs with 18 countries in Central and Eastern Europe and Central Asia. These initiatives were designed to enhance economic and technical knowledge and increase the competitiveness of countries in transition. The ECE undertook environmental performance reviews of the legal and official policy frameworks of Kazakhstan, Kyrgyzstan, and Ukraine. In response to recommendations developed in 2006, the ECE finalized a series of internal reforms that were designed to streamline the governing structure of the organization and increase transparency. The reforms were meant to bolster the relationship between the secretariat and the individual member states. Meanwhile, former Slovak foreign minister and former secretary general of the OSCE Ján Kubiš was appointed executive secretary of the ECE in December.

At its annual meeting in 2009, the ECE proposed a tax on carbon emissions with the proceeds to be distributed to developing states. The body also called for reforms in the transportation sector, which accounted for 13 percent of all greenhouse gas emissions, to reduce emissions and improve efficiency.

In 2010 the ECE and the Eurasian Development Bank finalized a memorandum of understanding to facilitate cooperation between the two bodies in promoting the Millennium Development Goals. Also, the UNE launched the third Wood Energy Enquiry to document the use of wood as an energy source in Europe. The two previous reports demonstrated a growing use of wood and found that wood was the main renewable energy source used in the region, accounting for just over half of all renewable energy use between 2005–2007.

The year 2011 saw increasing interest in water conservation and management, particularly among ECE members that were formerly part of the Soviet Union. Among other initiatives, the EU Water Initiative National Policy Dialogue on Integrated Water Resource Management took place in March in Tbilisi, Georgia. A second meeting was held in October in Dushanbe, Tajikistan.

On March 8, 2012, Sven Alkalaj was appointed executive secretary of the ECE. In its 2012 annual report, the ECE stressed the need for green technologies to lead Europe's economic recovery and to alleviate poverty. In 2012 the ECE launched Astana Water Action, a program with 75 specific goals for nations to improve the management of water and water resources.

The ECE conducted a conference in July 2013 to promote public private partnerships (PPP) in sectors such as transport, energy management, and schools and health. The ECE charged its Public-Private Partnership Center of Excellence with developing standards and recommendations on PPPs for governments. In October at an ECE meeting, ministers from 55 countries agreed on a regional strategy on sustainable housing and land management. The initiative had 15 objectives, supported by 36 goals, and was designed to cut energy consumption through new investments in technology and better management of multifamily housing developments.

Economic Commission for Latin America and the Caribbean (ECLAC)

Comisión Económica para America Latina y el Caribe (CEPAL)

Established: February 25, 1948, as the Economic Commission for Latin America; current name adopted in 1984.

Purpose: To "initiate and participate in measures for facilitating concerted actions for... raising the level of economic activity in Latin America and the Caribbean and for maintaining and strengthening the economic relations of the Latin American and Caribbean countries, both among themselves and with other countries of the world."

Headquarters: Santiago, Chile. Subregional headquarters are located in Mexico City, Mexico, and Port of Spain, Trinidad and Tobago, with offices in Bogota, Columbia, Buenos Aries, Argentina, Brasilia, Brazil, Montevideo, Uruguay, and Washington, D.C., United States.

Principal Subsidiary Organs: Caribbean Development and Cooperation Committee, Central American Economic Cooperation Committee, Committee of High-Level Government Experts from Developing Member Countries for Analysis of the Achievement of the International Development Strategy in the Latin American Region, Conference on the Integration of Women into the Economic and Social Development of Latin America and the Caribbean, Latin American and Caribbean Institute for Economic and Social Planning (*Instituto Latinoamericano y del Caribe de Planificatión Económica y Social*—ILPES), Latin American Demographic Center (*Centro Latinoamericano y Caribeño de Demografía*—CELADE), Statistical Conference of the Americas of ECLAC, Secretariat. The Secretariat includes ten divisions: Economic Development, Economic and Social Planning, Gender Development; Sustainable Development and Human Settlements, International Trade and Integration, Natural Resources and Infrastructure, Population and Development, Productive Development and Management, Social Development, and Statistics and Economic Projections.

Web site: www.eclac.org

Executive Secretary: Alicia Bárcena (Chile).

Membership (44): Antigua and Barbuda, Argentina, Bahamas, Barbados, Belize, Bolivia, Brazil, Canada, Chile, Colombia, Costa Rica, Cuba, Dominica, Dominican Republic, Ecuador, El Salvador, France, Germany, Grenada, Guatemala, Guyana, Haiti, Honduras, Italy, Jamaica, Japan, Mexico, Netherlands, Nicaragua, Panama, Paraguay, Peru, Portugal, Republic of Korea, St. Kitts and Nevis, St. Lucia, St. Vincent, Spain, Suriname, Trinidad and Tobago, United Kingdom, United States, Uruguay, Venezuela.

Associate Members (8): Anguilla, Aruba, British Virgin Islands, Cayman Islands, Montserrat, Puerto Rico, Turks and Caicos, United States Virgin Islands.

Activities. For ECLAC activities prior to 2006, see the 2011 *Handbook.* In July 2006 ECLAC predicted that economic growth in the region would exceed 5 percent for the year but urged member states to implement economic safeguards against rising energy prices. ECLAC conferred membership on Japan and associate membership on the Turks and Caicos in 2006 and full membership on the Republic of Korea in 2007. For 2007 ECLAC and Germany launched the program Toward a More Just and Equitable Globalization to cooperate on tax reform, government technology, and renewable energy. The accord covered a three-year period and was designed to support projects in individual countries. The program was undertaken in tandem with ECLAC's 2007–2008 cooperation program with the Swedish International Development Cooperation Agency (SIDA) titled "Enhancing Economic and Social Conditions and Opportunities of Vulnerable Groups in Latin America."

ECLAC estimated that the region's economic growth would be 4.7 percent in 2008, despite rising food and energy prices. Notably, ECLAC found that direct foreign investment in Latin America and the Caribbean exceeded $100 billion for the first time in 2007 and was likely to continue to grow through 2008. In the report *Economic Survey of Latin America and the Caribbean, 2007–2008,* ECLAC urged the nations of the region to consolidate their economic development and take steps to prevent wide fluctuations in economic performance. In cooperation with UNDP and 12 other UN agencies, ECLAC produced *Millennium Development Goals: Progression Toward the Right to Health in Latin America and the Caribbean* in 2008. The report highlighted the accomplishments and challenges of the region as it worked toward the health-related goals of the UN in areas such as malnutrition, access to health care, and poverty reduction programs.

In the publication *Preliminary Overview of the Economies of Latin America and the Caribbean 2008,* ECLAC noted that 2008 was the sixth year of overall GDP growth in the region, with expansion averaging 5 percent between 2003 and 2008. However, the report also warned that growth would fall to less than 2 percent in 2009, with unemployment increasing from a regional average of 7.5 percent to more than 8 percent, although inflation was expected to fall from 8.5 percent to 6 percent. Through 2009 ECLAC produced reports on the policies that governments in the region undertook in response to the global economic crisis. Separate research predicted that regional trade would decline by 13 percent through the year. In September 2009 ECLAC hosted the Second Latin American and Caribbean for Negotiations on Climate Change in Santiago, Chile. The session was designed to promote common positions on climate change issues within the region ahead of the December UN climate change conference in Copenhagen.

ECLAC published the *Environmental Indicators of Latin America and the Caribbean* in 2010. The study found both positive and negative environmental trends. For instance, between 1990 and 2007, the total amount of territory preserved for biodiversity increased from 9.5 percent to 19.5 percent, however, during the same period deforestation decreased the amount of forest coverage from 48.8 percent to 44.9 percent of the total area (a loss of 78 million hectares of forests). ECLAC's economic studies indicated that poverty in the region in 2010 had returned to levels comparable to the pre-global crisis. ECLAC found that 32.1 percent of the population (180 million people) of the region lived in poverty, with 12.9 percent (72 million people) in extreme poverty. These rates equaled those in 2008.

A September 2010 assessment of the region's progress toward meeting MDGs suggested that it was in much better shape than other less developed parts of the globe. Their chief lack of progress, however, was toward the goal of environmental sustainability. Statements from the group in 2011 seemed to echo the ECA's interest in structural change, with governments displaying a less passive attitude toward business. A June 9 statement encouraged food-exporting Latin American states to take advantage of high world food prices to lift their citizens out of poverty.

ECLAC's 2012 *Macroeconomic Report on Latin American and the Caribbean* forecast growth of 3.7 percent in 2012, led by Chile, Mexico, Peru, and Venezuela. Meanwhile, regional urban unemployment declined to a record low of 6.5 percent. Tax reforms in a number of countries led to increased government revenues. Although foreign trade slowed in 2011, tourism rose sharply.

ECLAC's 2013 report, *A Sluggish Postcrisis, Mega Trade Negotiations and Value Chains: Scope for Regional Action*, forecast that exports from Latin America and the Caribbean will rise by only 1.5 percent. Meanwhile, the 2013 *Economic Survey of Latin America and Caribbean: Three Decades of Uneven and Unstable Growth* found that unemployment in the region in the first quarter of 2013 was 6.7 percent, while inflation was 6 percent.

Economic and Social Commission for Asia and the Pacific (ESCAP)

Established: March 28, 1947, as the Economic Commission for Asia and the Far East; current name adopted in 1974.

Purpose: To facilitate cooperation in economic and social development within the region, to provide technical assistance and serve as an executing agency for operational projects, to conduct research and related activities, to offer advisory services as requested by governments, and to serve as the principal forum for the region within the UN system.

Headquarters: Bangkok, Thailand. A Pacific Operations Center opened in Port Vila, Vanuatu, in 1984, and then relocated to Suva, Fiji in 2005.

Principal Subsidiary Organs: Advisory Committee of Permanent Representatives and Other Representatives Designated by ESCAP Members; Asian and Pacific Center for Agricultural Engineering and Machinery (Beijing, China); Asian and Pacific Training Center for Information and Communication Technology for Development (Incheon, Republic of Korea); Asian and Pacific Center for Transfer of Technology (New Delhi, India); Committee on Emerging Social Issues; Committee on Managing Globalization; Committee on Poverty Reduction; Regional Coordination Center for Research and Development of Coarse Grains, Pulses, Roots, and Tuber Crops in the Humid Tropics of Asia and the Pacific (Bogor, Indonesia); Special Body on Least Developed and Landlocked Developing Countries; Special Body on Pacific Island Developing Countries; Statistical Institute for Asia and the Pacific (Chiba, Japan); Secretariat. The Secretariat includes an Office of the Executive Secretary, an Office of the Deputy Executive Secretary, the United Nations Information Services, the Pacific Operations Center, and nine divisions, two of them largely administrative (Program Management and Administration) and the other seven substantive: Emerging Social Issues; Environment and Sustainable Development; Information, Communication, and Space Technology; Poverty and Development; Statistics; Trade and Investment; and Transport and Tourism.

Executive Secretary: Noeleen Heyzer (Singapore).

Web site: www.unescap.org

Membership (53): Afghanistan, Armenia, Australia, Azerbaijan, Bangladesh, Bhutan, Brunei, Cambodia, China, Democratic People's Republic of Korea, Federated States of Micronesia, Fiji, France, Georgia, India, Indonesia, Iran, Japan, Kazakhstan, Kiribati, Kyrgyzstan, Laos, Malaysia, Maldives, Marshall Islands, Mongolia, Myanmar, Nauru, Nepal, Netherlands, New Zealand, Pakistan, Palau, Papua New Guinea, Philippines, Republic of Korea, Russia, Samoa, Singapore, Solomon Islands, Sri Lanka, Tajikistan, Thailand, Timor-Leste, Tonga, Turkey, Turkmenistan, Tuvalu, United Kingdom, United States, Uzbekistan, Vanuatu, Vietnam.

Associate Members (9): American Samoa, Commonwealth of the Northern Mariana Islands, Cook Islands, French Polynesia, Guam, Hong Kong, Macao, New Caledonia, Niue. Switzerland participates in a consultative capacity.

Activities. ESCAP is the largest of the five ECOSOC Regional Commissions, with its member countries encompassing about 60 percent of the world's population. It operates with a general staff of nearly 400, as well as 200 professionals, advisers, and project personnel. The various divisions of the Secretariat (see Principal Subsidiary Organs) carry out the projects and programs formulated by the organization's policymaking committees. To strengthen its role in helping South Pacific island nations and territories, ESCAP inaugurated a Pacific Operations Center in Vanuatu in 1984. In 1993 ESCAP signed an agreement with the Asian Development Bank (ADB) that delineates 11 areas of common interest in which closer cooperation will be pursued. The two organizations agreed to prepare joint studies, develop and carry out projects together, and conduct ESCAP/ADB workshops and conferences. ESCAP remains a source of highly respected economic analyses, including its annual *Economic and Social Survey of Asia and the Pacific.*

For the first time in its history, in 2006 ESCAP initiated a work program that concentrated solely on Pacific issues, including efforts to integrate urban and regional planning based on the recommendations of the 2004 Pacific Urban Agenda. The agenda called for the reduction of urban poor by half by 2015 and improvements in housing and land development. (For information on ESCAP prior to 2006, please see the 2013 *Handbook.*)

In conjunction with humanitarian and labor organizations, in September 2008 ESCAP held a series of training sessions to promote better data collection as one means to reduce child labor. Also in 2008 ESCAP created a Transportation Committee to facilitate multinational cooperation on transport networks and capabilities. Following huge earthquakes in China, ESCAP announced a joint program to help China and other East Asian states reduce vulnerabilities to natural disasters. In October ESCAP and the Republic of Korea announced a joint $200-million, five-year initiative to promote low-carbon and environmentally friendly economic growth as part of the broader East Asia Climate Partnership created by the Republic of Korea.

In 2009 ESCAP began efforts to create three more regional offices, one each for East and Northeast Asia, North and Central Asia, and South and Southwest Asia. ESCAP's publication, *Economic and Social Survey of Asia and the Pacific 2009: Addressing Triple Threats to Development,* identified the global economic recession, volatility in commodities markets, and climate change as the three main obstacles to continued growth and stability. The report also highlighted the continuing disparity in economic growth rates among developed and developing states. GDP growth among developing states was 5.8 percent, while GDP among developed countries was–0.4 percent. In November ESCAP held the first Asia-Pacific Trade and Investment Week, which included conferences, summits, and workshops designed to promote balanced trade.

ESCAP published *Women in Asia-Pacific: Challenges and Priorities Data Sheet* in 2010. The report highlighted a range of challenges that women in the region face, including under-representation in political bodies, gender discrimination and exploitation, and lack of health and social protections. The study called for greater progress on gender equality. ESCAP's 2009 *Statistical Yearbook,* published in 2010, reported that the population growth rate for the region had fallen to 1 percent per year, the lowest level among the five regions. Growth was highest among the landlocked developing countries at 1.7 percent, and lowest among the developed economies at 0.3 percent. The Asia-Pacific's aggregate GDP was $17.7 trillion, second only to Europe at $19.7 trillion, led by China's 11 percent annual average growth rate.

ESCAP's 2012 *Statistical Yearbook* reported that 4.2 billion people lived in the Asia-Pacific region in 2012 but that population growth rates had declined by 1.5 percent per year to 1 percent. Meanwhile, the more developed states faced stagnant or declining GDPs as a result of the economic slowdowns in Europe and the United States. GDP among these nations fell by 4.1 percent, although regionally GDP grew by 0.5 percent. In June ESCAP hosted the first Regional Integrated Early Warning System (RIMES) conference where 21 countries pledged to support regional early warning efforts for natural disasters such as typhoons or tsunamis.

To better facilitiate South-South discussions on sustainable development, ESCAP created a network to disseminate best practices among governments in Southeast Asia in 2013. ESCAP's 2013 annual report was titled *Building a Resilient, Inclusive and Sustainable Asia and the Pacific: Because People Matter* and found that there were only 65 employed women for 100 employed men. To reduce this gap, ESCAP launched a series of dialogues and seminars.

Economic and Social Commission for Western Asia (ESCWA)

Established: August 9, 1973, as the Economic Commission for Western Asia; current name adopted in 1985.

Purpose: To "initiate and participate in measures for facilitating concerted action for the economic reconstruction and development of Western Asia, for raising the level of economic activity in Western Asia, and for maintaining and strengthening the economic relations of the countries of that area, both among themselves and with other countries of the world."

Headquarters: Beirut, Lebanon.

Principal Subsidiary Organs: Preparatory Committee; Advisory Committee; seven specialized committees (Energy, Liberalization of Foreign Trade and Economic Globalization, Social Development, Statistics, Transport, Water Resources, Women); Secretariat. The Secretariat includes seven divisions: Administrative Services; Program Planning and Technical Cooperation; Economic Analysis, Information and Communication Technology; Globalization and Regional Integration; Social Development; and Sustainable Development and Productivity. There are also a Statistics Coordination Unit and an ESCWA Center for Women.

Web site: www.escwa.un.org

Executive Secretary: Rima Khalaf (Jordan).

Membership (14): Bahrain, Egypt, Iraq, Jordan, Kuwait, Lebanon, Oman, Palestine, Qatar, Saudi Arabia, Sudan, Syria, United Arab Emirates, Yemen.

Activities. The most important procedural event in the commission's history was the 1977 decision to grant full membership to the Palestine Liberation Organization (PLO)—the first non-state organization to achieve such standing in a UN agency—despite a fear on the part of some UN members that the PLO would use its membership to gain full membership in the General Assembly. Israeli-Palestinian agreements, beginning with the 1993 Declaration of Principles, led to the redesignation of the PLO membership as, simply, Palestine, even though no de jure Palestinian state existed (for information on ESCWA's activities prior to 2005, please see the 2013 *Handbook.*)

The ESCWA released a report in June 2005, *Social and Economic Situation of Palestinian Women, 1990–2004,* that specifically criticized Israel for the erosion of living standards among women in the Palestinian territories. In July 2006 the ESCWA protested the Israeli incursion into Lebanon, including attacks on UN facilities. The ESCWA's Sustainable Management of the Environment Team increased its efforts to support sustainable development through 2007. The team worked with a number of ESCWA members to create national sustainable development strategies and to harmonize environmental regulations across borders. ESCWA reported that foreign direct investment in the region exceeded $62 billion, the highest figure in the area's history. For 2007, ESCWA estimated that economic growth for Western Asia would be 5.4 percent.

On January 16, 2008, ESCWA held the first meetings of its newly formed technical committee, a body created to bolster integration and coordination among the national representatives of ESCWA. In July ESCWA, Germany and the government of Iraq sponsored a series of meetings and training seminars for Iraqi officials on water-dispute resolution tactics and strategies. As part of its ongoing effort to enhance foreign trade and direct investment, ESCWA conducted the "Third Forum on Arab Business Community and the WTO Agreements," in Beirut, Lebanon, to discuss the Doha round of trade negotiations with senior political and business leaders. Sudan joined ESCWA on August 15, becoming the 14th member of the group.

ECSWA convened a conference on land management and sustainable development in March 2009 as a means to identify and promote best practices for rural development. In addition to regional leaders and ministers, the event brought together experts from organizations such as the UN University, the UN Development Program, and the Food and Agriculture Organization. In July ECSWA launched a yearlong celebration of the 35th anniversary of the creation of the organization. Meanwhile, research by ECSWA found that foreign direct investment into the region had declined by 6.3 percent in 2008, mainly as the result of the global economic crisis and falling energy prices. Saudi Arabia, the United Arab Emirates, and Egypt were the main recipients of foreign investment and accounted for 76 percent of the total flows into the region.

In 2010 Rima Khalaf of Jordan was appointed executive secretary of ECSWA to succeed Bader Al-Dafa of Qatar. ESCWA's 2009 annual report, published in 2010, found that after dramatic economic growth in 2008, with average GDP growth among member states reaching 7.5 percent per year, in 2009 average GDP growth slowed to 3.2 percent. The decline in energy prices caused Kuwait, Saudi Arabia, and the United Arab Emirates to experience negative growth for the year. The report also found that stock exchanges in the region lost 44 percent of their value in 2008, but rose by 11 percent the following year. In an effort to coordinate national responses to the global recession, ESCWA organized a number of conferences and summits, including a high-level meeting of senior government officials in Damascus in May 2009.

In March 2010 an ESCWA report estimated youth unemployment in the Arab world at an average 30 percent, as opposed to 15 percent globally. In July it held a workshop for Arab parliaments on eliminating all forms of discrimination against women, with special reference to women as holders of positions of power. In July 2011 ESCWA held a Beirut conference on supporting the transition to a green economy in Arab countries.

In 2012 ESCWA reported that economic growth for the region during the previous year was 4.8 percent, mainly due to continuing high energy prices. Oil production among ESCWA states was 19.5 million barrels per day, an increase from 18 million barrels per day in 2009. However, political instability and uncertainty were likely to constrain future economic growth, as were increasingly large government deficits and debts.

ESCWA's 2013 *Survey of Economic and Social Developments in the Arab Region, 2012–2013,* found that GDP rose in the Arab region in 2012 by 4.8 percent, while inflation was 5.5 percent and the regional unemployment rate was 11.1 percent. Exports from the Arab world increased by 7.8 percent, with 51.4 percent of those products going to the Asia-Pacific region. Oil production rose to 23.5 million barrels per day, as Libyan production tripled from the year before.

TRUSTEESHIP COUNCIL

Web site: www.un.org/en/mainbodies/trusteeship

Membership (5): *Permanent Members of the Security Council:* China, France, Russia, United Kingdom, United States. China, previously not an active participant in Trusteeship affairs, assumed its seat at the May 1989 session.

Structure. Under the UN Charter the membership of the Trusteeship Council includes (1) those UN member states administering Trust Territories, (2) those permanent members of the Security Council that do not administer Trust Territories, and (3) enough other members elected by the General Assembly for three-year terms to ensure that the membership of the council is equally divided between administering and non-administering members. These specifications became increasingly difficult to meet as the number of Trust Territories dwindled. In consequence, no members have been elected to the council since 1965. (The Trusteeship Council formally suspended its operations on November 1, 1994.)

Activities. The Trusteeship Council is the organ principally responsible for the supervision of territories placed under the International Trusteeship System. Originally embracing 11 territories that had been either League of Nations mandates or possessions of states defeated in

World War II, the system was explicitly designed to promote advancement toward self-government or political independence. By 1976 ten of the former Trust Territories (British Togoland, French Togoland, British Cameroons, French Cameroons, Ruanda-Urundi, Somaliland, Tanganyika, Nauru, northern New Guinea, and Western Samoa) had become independent, either as sovereign states or through division or merger with neighboring states in accordance with the wishes of the inhabitants.

The last Trust Territory was the U.S.-administered Trust Territory of the Pacific Islands, which had undergone several administrative reorganizations, the most recent yielding four groupings: the Northern Mariana Islands, the Federated States of Micronesia, the Marshall Islands, and Palau. In 1975 the Northern Mariana Islands voted for commonwealth status in political union with the United States. In 1983 the Federated States of Micronesia and the Marshall Islands approved "compacts of free association" providing for internal sovereignty combined with continued U.S. economic aid and control of defense. A similar compact was endorsed by majorities in several plebiscites in Palau, but the Palauan Supreme Court ruled in 1986 that a collateral revision of the Palauan constitution to permit facilities for nuclear-armed U.S. forces had to first secure 75 percent approval.

In addition to the Palauan question, termination of the territory's trust status remained clouded until the late 1980s by opposition from the former Soviet Union, then a permanent member of both the Trusteeship and Security Council. Since the Trust Territory of the Pacific Islands, unlike other trust territories, was designated a "strategic area" at its inception, a supervisory role, according to the UN Charter, was "exercised" by the Security Council, implying that its approval was required for termination of the trusteeship.

At its 53rd session, held May 12–June 30, 1986, the Trusteeship Council endorsed by a three-to-one vote the position that the United States had satisfactorily discharged its obligations and that it was appropriate to terminate the trusteeship. The majority argued that UN missions sent to observe the plebiscites had concluded that the results constituted a free and fair expression of the wishes of the people. In casting its negative vote, the Soviet Union was highly critical of U.S. policy regarding economic development and potential military use of the territory. Subsequently, Washington declared the compacts with the Marshall Islands and the Federated States to be in effect from October 21 and November 3, 1986, respectively, with inhabitants of the Commonwealth of the Northern Mariana Islands acquiring U.S. citizenship on the latter date. Thus, Palau remained—under U.S. law—the one remaining component of the Trust Territory.

Amid growing violence and political turmoil, referendums were held in Palau in August 1987 that led the Palauan government to declare the constitutional issue resolved and the compact approved. However, in April 1988 the Supreme Court of Palau declared the voting invalid. Subsequently, at its May meeting the Trusteeship Council recommended by a vote of three to one that the compact be approved as soon as possible, with disagreements of interpretation to be left to bilateral Palau-U.S. negotiations. The dissenting vote was cast by the Soviet Union, which continued to charge the United States with "anticharter" activity in the handling of the Trust Territory.

Similar sentiments were expressed at the May 1989 council meeting, which was most noteworthy for the return of Chinese representatives. China joined France, the United Kingdom, and the United States in endorsing the compact as the appropriate vehicle for resolution of Palau's political status. The council's report to the Security Council noted that a recent mission to Palau had concluded that "an overwhelming majority" of its citizens endorsed the compact and that criticism of U.S. spending on economic and social development by some islanders "reflected tactical considerations" aimed at "obtaining additional concessions." The United States subsequently pledged further aid to Palau, but a seventh vote on the compact, held in February 1990, again failed to achieve 75 percent approval.

In light of the continuing diminution of East-West tension, the Soviet Union in late 1990 withdrew its objection to the formal termination of UN involvement in those trusteeship areas whose permanent political status had been resolved. Consequently, upon the recommendation of all five Trusteeship Council members, the Security Council on December 22 voted to terminate the Trusteeship Agreements for the Marshall Islands, the Federated States of Micronesia, and the Northern Mariana Islands. The vote was reportedly facilitated by a U.S. pledge not to expand its military presence in the region.

The Trusteeship Council met in May 1991 to discuss the Palauan situation, which remained unresolved despite hopes that changes in U.S. policy in the region would break the long-standing "logjam." During the May 1992 meeting (at which Russia assumed the former USSR seat) U.S. officials said that Palau was facing its last chance to approve the proposed compact of free association. In November a national referendum approved an amendment to the Palauan constitution to permit ratification of the compact by a simple majority. Consequently, the eighth (and final) vote on the issue was held November 9, 1993, with the compact receiving a 68 percent endorsement.

Palauan and U.S. officials subsequently announced the implementation of the compact effective October 1, 1994, after all possible legal challenges to the final vote had been exhausted. Therefore, on November 1 the Trusteeship Council formally suspended its operations, and on November 10 the Security Council declared that the applicability of the Trusteeship Agreement regarding Palau had been terminated. However, the Trusteeship Council was not dissolved, an action that would have required a change in the UN Charter. Instead, the council remained in existence with the proviso that it would henceforth meet "only on an extraordinary basis, as the need arises." Also in 1994, a proposal was submitted for the Trusteeship Council to have oversight of the areas of the world outside of national boundaries, including the majority of the world's oceans. However, no action was taken.

In 1997 Secretary General Kofi Annan proposed that the UN consider reconstituting the council as a forum for UN members to "exercise their collective trusteeship for the integrity of the global environment and common areas such as oceans, atmosphere and outer space." Later, in 2005, he proposed the abolition of the council. Neither proposal was acted upon. Options continue to be discussed as part of an overall review of the UN Charter.

INTERNATIONAL COURT OF JUSTICE

(ICJ)

Cour Internationale de Justice (CIJ)

Established: By statute signed as an integral part of the United Nations Charter in San Francisco, United States, June 26, 1945, effective October 24, 1945.

Purpose: To adjudicate disputes referred by member states and to serve as the principal judicial organ of the United Nations; to provide advisory opinions on any legal question requested of it by the General Assembly, Security Council, or other organs of the United Nations and Specialized Agencies that have been authorized by the General Assembly to make such requests.

Headquarters: The Hague, Netherlands.

Web site: www.icj-cij.org

Composition: 15 judges, elected by the UN General Assembly and Security Council for terms ending on February 5 of the years indicated below.

Parties to the Statute (193): All members of the United Nations (see Appendix C).

Official Languages: English, French.

Peter Tomka (President)	Slovakia	2012
Bernado Sepúlveda Amor (Vice President)	Mexico	2015
Hishashi Owada	Japan	2012
Ronny Abraham	France	2018
Mohamed Bennouna	Morocco	2015
Joan Donoghue	United States	2015
Christopher Greenwood	United Kingdom	2018
Kenneth Keith	New Zealand	2015
Xue Hanqin	China	2012
Leonid Skotnikov	Russia	2015
Antonio Augusto Cançado Trindade	Brazil	2018
Abdulqawi Yusuf	Somalia	2018
Dalveer Bhandari	India	2012
Julia Sebutinade	Uganda	2012
Georgio Gaja	Italy	2012

Origin and development. The International Court of Justice (ICJ), often called the World Court, is the direct descendant of the Permanent Court of International Justice (PCIJ). Created in 1920 under the Covenant of the League of Nations, the PCIJ, which between 1922 and 1938 had 79 cases referred to it by states and 28 by the League Council, was dissolved on April 19, 1946, along with the other organs of the league.

The Statute of the International Court of Justice was adopted at the San Francisco Conference in June 1945 as an integral part of the UN Charter and, as such, entered into force with the charter on October 24, 1945. Except for a few essentially formal changes, the statute is identical to that of the PCIJ. All members of the UN are automatically parties to the statute. States that are not UN members are entitled to become parties to the statute (under conditions to be determined in each case by the General Assembly upon the recommendation of the Security Council) or to appear before the court without being a party to the statute (under conditions to be laid down by the Security Council). Only states may be parties to cases before the court, whose jurisdiction extends to all cases that the parties refer to it and all matters specifically provided for in the UN Charter or other existing treaties. In the event of a dispute as to whether the court has jurisdiction, the matter is settled by a decision of the court itself. The General Assembly or the Security Council may request the ICJ to give an advisory opinion on any legal question; other UN organs or Specialized Agencies, if authorized by the General Assembly, may request advisory opinions on legal questions arising within the scope of their activities.

States adhering to the statute are not required to submit disputes to the court, whose jurisdiction in a contentious case depends upon the consent of the disputing states. In accordance with Article 36 of the statute, states may declare that they recognize as compulsory, in relation to any other country accepting the same obligation, the jurisdiction of the court in all legal disputes concerning (1) the interpretation of a treaty; (2) any question of international law; (3) the existence of any fact which, if established, would constitute a breach of an international obligation; and (4) the nature or extent of the reparation to be made for the breach of such an obligation. However, declarations under Article 36 have often been qualified by conditions relating, for example, to reciprocity, the duration of the obligation, or the nature of the dispute. The United States, in accepting the court's compulsory jurisdiction in 1946, excluded matters of domestic jurisdiction "as determined by the United States of America." This exception, often called the Connally Amendment, has been something of a model for other states.

Structure. The ICJ consists of 15 judges elected for renewable nine-year terms by separate majority votes of the UN General Assembly and the Security Council, one-third of the judges being elected every three years. Candidates are nominated by national groups in the Permanent Court of Arbitration (PCA) and national groups appointed by non-PCA UN members, with the General Assembly and Security Council assessing the nominees according to the qualifications required for appointment to the highest judicial offices of their respective states. Due consideration is also given to ensuring that the principal legal systems of the world are represented. No two judges may be nationals of the same state, and no judge may exercise any political or administrative function or engage in any other occupation of a professional nature while serving on the ICJ. As a protection against political pressure, no judge can be dismissed unless, in the unanimous opinion of the other judges, he or she has ceased to fulfill the required conditions for service. If there are no judges of their nationality on the court, the parties to a case are entitled to choose ad hoc or national judges to sit for that particular case. Such judges take part in the decision on terms of complete equality with the other judges.

The procedural rules of the ICJ have been adopted without substantial change from those of the PCIJ, the court itself electing a president and a vice president from among its members for three-year terms. In accordance with Article 38 of the statute, the court in deciding cases applies (1) international treaties and conventions; (2) international custom; (3) the general principles of law "recognized by civilized nations"; and (4) judicial decisions and the teachings of the most highly qualified publicists, as a subsidiary means of determining the rules of law. All questions are decided by a majority of the judges present, with nine judges constituting a quorum. In the event of a tie vote, the president of the court may cast a second, deciding vote.

The Registry of the Court is headed by a registrar (currently Philippe Couvreur of Belgium, reelected for another seven-year term on February 8, 2007), who maintains the list of cases submitted to the court and is the normal channel to and from the court.

Activities. From 1946 through 2013 the ICJ heard 154 cases, issued 94 judgments, and rendered 40 advisory opinions. Among the most celebrated of the advisory opinions was its determination in July 1962 that the expenses of the UN Operation in the Congo and the UN Emergency Force in the Middle East were "expenses of the Organization" within the meaning of Article 17 of the UN Charter, which stipulates that such expenses "shall be borne by the members as apportioned by the General Assembly." (For information on the court prior to 1979, please see the 2012 *Handbook.*)

In November 1979 the United States, claiming violation of several international treaties and conventions, asked the court to order Iran to release the 53 U.S. hostages who were being held in the U.S. Embassy in Tehran; in December the court unanimously upheld the U.S. complaint. In May 1980 the court issued its formal holdings in the case, which ordered Iran to release all of the hostages immediately and warned its government not to put them on trial; the court also held that Iran was liable to pay reparations for its actions. However, in April 1981, following the release of the hostages, the United States requested that the court dismiss its claim against Iran for payment of damages and a special Iran-United States Claims Tribunal was set up to attempt to resolve approximately 3,000 cases from U.S. companies and individuals filing for damages from Iran's government (see article on Permanent Court of Arbitration). In May 1992 the tribunal ruled that Iran was entitled to compensation for nonmilitary assets frozen in the United States following the embassy seizure, although the amount of reimbursement was yet to be determined.

In November 1992 Iran initiated another suit against the United States for damages caused by the U.S. Navy when it attacked Iranian oil platforms in the Persian Gulf during 1987–1988. Iran claimed that such action violated the 1955 Iran-United States Treaty of Amity, Economic Relations, and Consular Rights. Despite U.S. objections, the court ruled that it had jurisdiction over the matter. In 1997 the United States submitted a counterclaim stating that Iran, by attacking shipping in the Persian Gulf during its war with Iraq, had "breached its obligations to the United States" under the treaty in question. The United States asked the court to grant it restitution for the resultant damages. On November 6, 2003, the court ruled that the U.S. action had not been justified but that both countries' requests for reparations were invalid because the treaty was inapplicable.

In October 1984 the court ruled on a dispute between the United States and Canada over possession of some 30,000 square nautical miles of the Gulf of Maine southeast of New England and Newfoundland. The ruling awarded about two-thirds of the area in question to the United States and the remainder to Canada. The court also settled a long-standing border dispute between Mali and Burkina Faso with a decision in December 1986 that divided the contested area into roughly equal parts.

One of the court's most publicized cases in the 1980s involved a suit brought by Nicaragua challenging U.S. involvement in the mining of its harbors. During preliminary hearings, begun in April 1984, Nicaragua charged that the action was a violation of international law and asked for reparations. The United States sought, unsuccessfully, to have the case dismissed on the ground that Nicaragua's failure to submit an instrument of ratification of the court's statutes prevented it from appearing before the court. In May the ICJ rendered an interim decision that directed the defendant to cease and refrain from mining operations and to respect Nicaraguan sovereignty. In November the court ruled that it had a right to hear the case, but in early 1985 Washington, anticipating an adverse ruling, stated it would not participate in further proceedings on the ground that it was a political issue, over which the court lacked jurisdiction. In June 1986, citing numerous military and paramilitary activities, the court ruled the United States had breached international law by using force to violate Nicaragua's sovereignty. In a series of 16 rulings, each approved by a substantial majority, the court directed the United States to cease the activities cited and to pay reparations to Nicaragua. The judgment was nonenforceable, however, as the United States had previously informed the court that it would not submit to ICJ jurisdiction regarding conflicts in Central America.

In 1986 Nicaragua also filed suit against Honduras and Costa Rica for frontier incidents and attacks allegedly organized by anti-Sandinista forces. Honduras announced it did not consent to the court's jurisdiction in the matter, although in February 1987 it agreed to refer to the ICJ a dispute with El Salvador involving both land border demarcation and maritime jurisdiction. Later in the year, as negotiations on a proposed Central American peace plan proceeded, Nicaragua dropped the suit against Costa Rica and "postponed" its action against Honduras. Deliberations in the latter suit resumed in late 1988 but were again suspended as part of the peace plan negotiated by the presidents of five Central American nations in late 1989.

In April 1988, at the request of the General Assembly, the court was brought into the dispute between the UN and the United States over U.S. attempts to close the UN observer mission of the Palestine Liberation Organization (PLO). The United States had ordered the closing because recent legislation classified the PLO as a "terrorist" organization, but the General Assembly strongly denounced the U.S. action as a violation of the 1947 "host country" treaty. The court ruled that the United States must submit the issue to binding international arbitration, although it was unclear whether the United States would accept the decision. The issue became moot later in the year when a U.S. district court declared that the government had no authority to close the mission and the U.S. Justice Department announced it would not appeal that decision.

The likelihood of an expansion in the court's calendar grew in early 1989 when the Soviet Union announced its recognition of ICJ jurisdiction over "interpretation and application" of five international human rights agreements. Washington also appeared to be supporting a broader mandate for the court after several years of aloofness triggered by the 1986 ruling on the Nicaraguan suit. In August the two superpowers agreed to give the ICJ jurisdiction in resolving disputes stemming from the interpretation of seven treaties on the extradition and prosecution of terrorists and drug traffickers.

Washington underscored its new attitude in 1989 by permitting the ICJ to rule on a long-standing investment dispute with Italy and by agreeing to defend itself in a suit filed by Iran for financial compensation for those killed when an Iranian jetliner was shot down by the USS *Vincennes* over the Persian Gulf in July 1988 (see article on the International Civil Aviation Organization). UN secretary general Pérez de Cuéllar strongly welcomed the heightened respect being accorded to the ICJ, describing the court as a "crucial component of the UNs recent attempt to prove its ability to function as the guardian of world security." To further the ICJ's role in the peaceful settlement of bilateral disputes, Pérez de Cuéllar announced late in the year that a trust fund would be established to help pay the legal expenses of poorer nations appearing before the court.

The most publicized ICJ case in the first half of 1992 involved Libya's request for the court to block the U.S.-UK attempt to force the extradition of two Libyans for trial in connection with the 1988 bombing of a Pan Am airliner over Scotland. Libya asked the court to declare sanctions imposed by the Security Council in the matter to be illegal, but the court ruled 11 to 5 that it did not have the authority to block compliance with the council's decision. Libya ultimately agreed to have the accused tried under Scottish law at a court in the Netherlands, but the ICJ still had before it jurisdictional questions relating to the 1971 Montreal Convention for the Suppression of Unlawful Acts against the Safety of Civil Aviation. In September 2003, however, improved relations led the three parties to request that the proceedings be discontinued, and the ICJ obliged.

In April 1993, acting on a request from Bosnia and Herzegovina, the court ordered the Federal Republic of Yugoslavia to "take all measures within its power to prevent the commission of genocide" against the Bosnian Muslim community. In August Bosnia and Herzegovina asked it to overturn the Security Council arms embargo and to declare that any partitioning of Bosnia would be illegal. Although the court rejected both requests in September, it demanded the "immediate and effective" implementation of its April genocide order, the decision being described as an "implicit rebuke" to Yugoslavia and a political boost to the Bosnian cause.

In February 1994 the ICJ ruled in favor of Chad in its long-standing dispute over the border territory known as the Aozou Strip (see entries on Chad and Libya). Other subsequent ICJ activity included the formation of a seven-member Chamber of Environmental Matters to assist in what was expected to be a growing caseload in that area. The court also urged that greater use be made of its ability to offer "advisory opinions" as part of the UN's overall preventative diplomacy strategy.

Cases related to nuclear weapons dominated the ICJ calendar in late 1995, beginning with a request from New Zealand (supported by a number of smaller island states) for a court injunction against the resumption of French nuclear testing in the South Pacific. The ICJ declined the request, ruling that its authority from a 1973 case extended only to above-ground nuclear tests. The court also heard about three weeks of widely publicized testimony in November 1995 regarding an advisory opinion sought by the General Assembly on whether the threat or use of nuclear weapons was a violation of international law. In July 1996 the ICJ ruled by an 8–7 vote that "generally" the use of such weapons would be contrary to international law, although the court equivocated on their use in self-defense. In the face of "legal uncertainty" the ICJ urged the international community to resolve the question permanently through disarmament negotiations.

On September 25, 1997, the court issued its ruling on a dispute between Hungary and Slovakia over the construction of two dams on the Danube River, finding that both were guilty of breaching a treaty originally signed in 1977, Hungary for failing to build one dam and Slovakia for diverting flow of the Danube through another it built in 1992. In early 1998 Hungary and Slovakia reached agreement on where a new dam on the Danube was to be built in accordance with the decision, but Budapest subsequently backed away from the agreement, stating that an assessment of the project's impact on the environment had to be completed before the Hungarian legislature could consider the accord. Consequently, in September 1998 Slovakia filed a request for an additional judgment. Bilateral negotiations subsequently resumed, and the court has therefore not ruled on the case.

In the first, although indirect, death penalty case before the ICJ, in 1999 Germany accused the United States of violating international legal obligations when it failed to inform two German citizens, Walter and Karl LaGrand, of their right to contact the German consulate following their U.S. arrest. Both defendants were ultimately convicted of murder and executed without the United States having provided, according to Germany, "effective review of and remedies for criminal convictions impaired by a violation of the rights under Article 36" of the Vienna Convention on Consular Relations. The United States acknowledged the failure of "competent authorities" to adhere to the convention, and in June 2001 the court ruled for Germany. In a similar case, *Mexico v. United States,* in 2004 the court ruled in favor of Mexico, which in 2003 had charged the United States with a failure to avail some 50 Mexican nationals of their consular rights. The court proposed as a remedy that the United States undertake a "review and reconsideration" of the convictions and sentences.

In October 1999 the Democratic Republic of the Congo (DRC) filed a case against Uganda for invasion, human rights violations, and the plunder of natural resources. In a July 2000 interim ruling, the court urged Uganda to withdraw its troops in accordance with a June UN resolution that had called for the removal of all foreign troops from the country. A final ruling had not been made as of mid-2007. In 1998 Guinea had filed a case against the DRC on behalf of an expatriate businessman who had been imprisoned, stripped of his assets, and expelled; that case also remained open. Earlier in the year, the court ruled that it did not have jurisdiction in a case brought by the DRC against Rwanda in 2002.

Many of the court's most recent judgments have concerned territorial disputes. In December 1999 the court ruled in Botswana's favor and against Namibia in a case involving competing claims to Kasikili (Sedudu) Island in the Chobe River. A boundary dispute between Bahrain and Qatar was concluded in March 2001, when the judges awarded the Huwar Islands and adjacent shoals to Bahrain and the contested Zubarah strip to Qatar. In October 2002 the court addressed issues of land and maritime boundaries between Cameroon and Nigeria; although neither disputant won a complete victory, the complex decision largely favored Cameroon, which was awarded oil-rich Bakassi Peninsula. Two months later the court ruled that Malaysia, not Indonesia, held sovereignty over Pulau Ligitan and Pulau Sipadan in the Celebes Sea. In July 2005 the court settled a frontier dispute between Benin and Niger.

In its first advisory ruling in five years, the court announced on July 9, 2004, its opinion that the construction of a wall by Israel in the occupied Palestinian territory was "contrary to international law." In addition to ruling that affected Palestinians should receive reparations from Israel and that part of the security barrier should be torn down, the court referred the matter to the General Assembly and Security Council for further action. The lone dissenting vote in the 14–1 nonbinding ruling was cast by Judge Thomas Buergenthal of the United States.

On December 15, 2004, the court unanimously dismissed eight cases that had been brought by the Federal Republic of Yugoslavia (now the separate states of Serbia and Montenegro) against individual NATO countries (Belgium, Canada, France, Germany, Italy, Netherlands, Portugal, and the United Kingdom) in connection with the legality of the 1999 NATO air campaign during the Kosovo conflict. The cases, filed under the 1948 UN Convention on the Prevention and Punishment of the Crime of Genocide, initially numbered ten, but the court had immediately dismissed those against Spain and the United States because Madrid and Washington had signed the 1948 convention with the proviso that they could refuse court jurisdiction. In 2004 the eight outstanding cases were rejected by a majority of the judges on the grounds that at the time the Federal Republic of Yugoslavia filed its complaints it had not yet formally been admitted to the United Nations (and was therefore not a party to the ICJ Statute), following the breakup of the former Socialist Federal Republic of Yugoslavia in the early 1990s. As of July 2006 Serbia and Montenegro remained party to separate Genocide Convention cases brought against Yugoslavia by Bosnia and Herzegovina in 1993 and by Croatia in 1999.

In February 2005 the court ruled that it could not settle a dispute between Liechtenstein and Germany over property that had been confiscated during World War II by Czechoslovakia but that had subsequently come into German possession. The court ruled that it did not have jurisdiction because the conflict dated to 1945, and the applicable convention on the peaceful settlement of disputes had not entered into force between Germany and Liechtenstein until 1980.

As of August 2006, 12 cases remained before the court, including the Hungary-Slovakia case, 2 involving the DRC, and 2 involving Serbia and Montenegro. Four of the remaining 7 were territorial disputes. Nicaragua filed in 1999 against Honduras over a shared maritime border and in 2001 against Colombia "concerning title to territory and maritime delimitation" in the western Caribbean. Cases filed in 2003 concerned rival claims by Malaysia and Singapore to Pedra Branca/Pulau Batu Puteh, Middle Rocks, and South Ledge, and a Congolese-French dispute over the latter's judicial actions against Congolese officials charged with torture and crimes against humanity. In 2004 Romania submitted a claim against Ukraine over their shared maritime boundary in the Black Sea.

In May 2006 Argentina filed suit against Uruguay to stop the construction of two pulp mills on the Uruguay River, asserting that the mills would do irreparable environmental damage. (In July, the ICJ declined to order construction stopped until the case was tried.) In August France consented to the court's jurisdiction in a case brought by Djibouti, which had charged France with violating a bilateral treaty and a bilateral convention.

On January 23, 2007, on a vote of 14 to 1, the court declined Uruguay's request to issue an order for Argentina to end blockades of roads and bridges to the construction sites in the pulp mills case. In February the ICJ reaffirmed in *Bosnia and Herzegovina vs. Serbia and Montenegro* that the court had jurisdiction under Article IX of the Convention on the Prevention and Punishment of the Crime of Genocide when one country alleged genocide by another. In May the court ruled on an issue of diplomatic protection for Ahmadou Sadio Diallo related to his role in two private companies in a dispute with the Democratic Republic of the Congo.

In January 2008 Peru initiated a suit against Chile over the maritime boundary between the two countries. The countries were given until 2010 to enter their initial briefs. Ecuador filed suit against Colombia in April over the use of aerial herbicides to destroy illicit drugs near the two countries' border. In June Mexico asked for clarification in the 2004 case *Mexico v. United States.* Mexico argued that the United States was required to reexamine past cases in which Mexican nationals were convicted by U.S. courts. After collecting evidence and briefs from both sides, the court was still deliberating over the case as of October 1, 2009. On October 10 the UN General Assembly asked the ICJ to rule on Kosovo's unilateral declaration of independence. In December the ICJ heard oral arguments in an advisory case on Kosovar independence.

In February 2009 in *Belgium v. Senegal,* the ICJ was asked to rule on whether or not Senegal was obligated to either prosecute or extradite former Chadian president Hissène Habré. Habré had been in exile in Senegal since 1990 and had been arrested for crimes against humanity in 2000. However, a Senegalese court dismissed the charges since the country did not at the time have statutes expressly prohibiting crimes against humanity. Senegal did amend its legal code to include genocide and crimes against humanity in 2007. Meanwhile, a Belgian national filed charges in Belgium against Habré in 2005, and the country issued an international arrest warrant for the former president. In its 2009 motion Belgium asked the court to determine if Senegal should prosecute Habré under its new laws or turn him over to Brussels. Also in 2009 Honduras brought suit before the ICJ after the former president of Honduras, Manuel Zelaya, was given refuge in the Brazilian embassy. Honduras claimed that Brazil's action amounted to illegal interference in the domestic affairs of the country (the suit was dropped in May 2010, see article on Honduras).

On July 22, 2010, the ICJ issued an opinion, on a vote of ten-to-four, that the 2008 Kosavar declaration of independence did not violate international law. Three new cases were initiated before the court in 2010. Australia brought suit against Japan in June, alleging that in violation of international conventions Japan illicitly continued to hunt whales under the guise of scientific research. In July Burkina Faso and Niger jointly requested that the court adjudicate a long-standing border disagreement. Costa Rica filed suit against Nicaragua in November after troops from the latter occupied territory that was claimed by both nations. Costa Rica had already gained a decree from the OAS calling on Nicaragua to withdraw. Also in November, the ICJ was asked to provide an advisory opinion in a disagreement over the dismissal of an employee between the International Fund for Agricultural Development and the Administrative Tribunal of the International Labor Organization.

In April 2011 the court dismissed a suit brought by Georgia against Russia alleging racial discrimination in the two countries' dispute over South Ossettia. On July 19 the court ordered both Thailand and Cambodia to withdraw their troops from the disputed plot around a 12th-century Hindu Shiva temple, which the UN had declared a World Heritage Site. The court was reconsidering a 1962 ruling that awarded the site to Cambodia. In September Turkey announced that it would challenge Israel's blockade of the Gaza Strip before the court. The court was expected to rule on the long-standing dispute between Greece and the Former Yugoslav Republic of Macedonia. The case concerned Greece's objection to the latter country's name.

In December 2011 Nicaragua brought suit against Costa Rica, asserting that a Costa Rican construction project along the border of the two countries will cause significant environmental damage to the ecosystem of the San Juan de Nicaragua River. The court determined that initial filings had to be complete by December 2013 in the case.

On February 3, 2012, the court ruled in favor of Germany in a case against Italy and Greece. Italian courts had issued a series of decisions that asserted Germany had lost its state immunity from lawsuits related to atrocities commited during World War II because the crimes commited had violated international law. Although Germany had paid reparations and concluded treaties with Italy and other states, plaintiffs contendedthat the reparations did not compensate all victims of German actions. In a 12 to 3 decision, the ICJ found that Germany retained its state immunity, which could not be voided by national courts, no matter the severity of crimes or actions. The court did note that Germany could still be liable for reparations through other means. The court applied its ruling to the Italian cases and a similar tort brought forward by Greece.

In September 2013 Nicaraugua initiated new proceedings against Colombia by asking the court to delineate the extent of Nicaragua's continental shelf beyond a 200-nautical-mile zone, following a November 2012 decision, in which the ICJ settled the maritime boundary between the two countries within that 200 mile limit.

SECRETARIAT

Secretary General	Ban Ki-Moon (Republic of Korea)
Deputy Secretary General	Jan Eliasson (Sweden)
Senior Management Group	
Chief of Protocol	Desmond Parker (Trinidad and Tobago)
Chief of Cabinet	Susanna Malcorra (Argentina)
Children and Armed Conflict	Leila Zerrougui (Algeria)
Conference on Trade and Development	Mukhisa Kituyi (Kenya)
Development Program	Helen Clark (New Zealand)
Disarmament Affairs	Angela Kane (Germany)
Economic and Social Affairs	Wu Hongbo (China)
Economic Commission for Africa	Carlos Lopes (Guinea-Bisseau)
Economic Commission for Europe	Sven Alkalaj (Bosnia-Herzegovina)
Economic Commission for Latin America and the Caribbean	Alicia Bárcena (Chile)
Economic and Social Commission for Asia and the Pacific	Noeleen Heyzer (Singapore)
Economic and Social Commission for Western Asia	Rima Khalaf (Jordan)
Field Support	Ameerah Hag (Bangladesh)

Gender Equality and Empowerment of Women	Phumzile Mlambo-Ngcuka (South Africa)
General Assembly and Conference Management	Tegegnework Gettu (Ethiopia)
High Commission for Refugees	António Guterres (Portugal)
Human Rights	Navanethem Pillay (South Africa)
Human Settlements Program	Joan Clos (Spain)
Least Developed Countries, Landlocked and Small Island Developing States	Gyan Chandra Acharya (Nepal)
Legal Affairs	Miguel de Serpa Soares (Portugal)
Management	Yukio Takasu (Japan)
Office for the Coordination of Humanitarian Affairs and Emergency Relief Coordinator	Valerie Amos (United Kingdom)
Office of Internal Oversight Services (Reports to the General Assembly)	Carmen Lapointe (Canada)
Peacebuilding Support	Judy Cheng-Hopkins (Malaysia)
Peacekeeping Operations	Herve Ladsous (France)
Policy Planning and Strategic Coordination	Robert Orr (United States)
Political Affairs	Jeffrey D. Feltman (United States)
Population Fund	Babatunde Osotimehin (Nigeria)
Public Information	Peter Launsky-Tieffenthel (Austria)
Safety and Security	Kevin Kennedy (United States)
Sexual Violence in Conflict	Zainab Hawa Bangura (Sierra Leone)
Special Advisor on Africa	Maged Abdelaziz (Egypt)
Special Advisor on Change Implementation	Kim Wan-soo (Republic of Korea)
Special Advisor on Myanmar	Vijay Nambiar (India)
Special Advisor on the Prevention of Genocide	Adama Dieng (Senegal)
UN Children's Fund	Anthony Lake (United States)
UN Environment Program (Executive Director)	Achim Steiner (Germany)
UN Office in Geneva (Director General)	Kassym-Jomart Tokayev (Kazakhstan)
UN Office in Nairobi (Director General)	Sahle-Work Zewde (Ethiopia)
UN Office in Vienna, Office on Drugs and Crime	Yury Fedotov (Russia)
World Food Program	Ertharin Cousin (United States)

Other Senior Officers

Executive Director, Counter-terrorism	Jean-Paul Laborde (France)
UN Ombudsman	Johnston Barkat (United States)

Special/Personal Representatives or Envoys of or Advisers to the Secretary General

Africa	Maged Abdelaziz (Egypt)
African Union	Haile Menkerios (South Africa)
Alliance of Civilizations	Nassir Abdulaziz al-Nasser (Qatar)
Avian and Human Influenza	David Nabarro (United Kingdom)
Burundi	Parfait Onanga-Anyanga (Gabon)
Central Africa	Abou Moussa (Chad)
Central African Republic	Babacar Gaye (Senegal)
Children and Armed Conflict	Leila Zerrougui (Algeria)
Côte d'Ivoire	Aïchatou Mindaou Souleymane (Niger)
Democratic Republic of the Congo	Martin Kobler (Germany)
Disaster Reduction	Margareta Wahlström (Sweden)
Equatorial Guinea and Gabon	Nicholas Michel (Switzerland)
Financing for Development	Philippe Douste-Blazy (France)
Food Security and Nutrition	David Nabarro (United Kingdom)
Gender Issues and Advancement of Women	Rachel N. Mayanja (Uganda)
Global Education	Gordon Brown (United Kingdom)
Great Lakes Region	Mary Robinson (Ireland)
Guinea-Bissau	José Ramos-Horta (Mali)
HIV/AIDS in Africa	Speciosa Wandira-Kasibwe (Uganda)
HIV/AIDS in Asia	Prasada Rao V.R. Jonnalagadda (India)
HIV/AIDS in the Caribbean	Edward Greene (Guyana)
HIV/AIDS in Eastern Europe	Michel Kazatchkine (France)
Least Developed Countries, Landlocked Developing Countries, and Small Developing Island States	Gyan Chandra Acharya (Nepal)
Liberia	Karin Landgren (Sweden)
Libya	Tarek Mitri (Lebanon)
Malaria	Ray Chambers (United States)
Mali	Albert Gerard Koenders (Netherlands)
Migration	Peter Sutherland (Ireland)
Millennium Development Goals	Jeffrey Sachs (United States)
Prevention of Genocide	Adama Dieng (Senegal)
Post-2015 Development Goals	Amina Mohammed (Nigeria)
Sahel	Romani Prodi (Italy)
Sexual Violence in Conflict	Zainab Hawa Bangura (Sierra Leone)
Sierra Leone	Jens Anders Toyberg-Frandzen (Denmark)
Somalia	Nicholas Kay (United Kingdom)
Sport for Development and Peace	Wifried Lemke (Germany)
Sudan	Haile Menkerios (South Africa)
Sudan/Abyei	Maj. Gen. Yohannes Gebremeskel Tesfamariam (Ethiopia)
Sudan/Darfur	Mohamed Ibn Chambas (Ghana)
South Sudan	Hilde Johnson (Norway)
United Nations International School	Michael Adlerstein (United States)
Violence Against Children	Marta Santos Pais (Portugal)
West Africa	Said Djinnit (Algeria)
Western Sahara	Wolfgang Weisbrod-Weber (Germany)
World Summit on Information Society	Nitin Desai (India)
Youth	Ahmad Alhendawi (Jordan)

Web site: www.un.org/sg

Structure. The Secretariat consists of the secretary general and the UN staff, which, since early 1998, includes a deputy secretary general. The secretary general, who is appointed for a five-year term by the General Assembly on recommendation of the Security Council, is designated chief administrative officer by the charter, which directs him to report annually to the General Assembly on the work of the UN, to appoint the staff, and to perform such other functions as are entrusted to him by the various UN organs. Under Article 99 of the charter, the secretary general may bring to the attention of the Security Council any matter that in his opinion may threaten international peace and security. Other functions of the secretary general include acting in that capacity at all meetings of the General Assembly, the Security Council, the Economic and Social Council, and the Trusteeship Council, and presenting any supplementary reports on the work of the UN that are necessary to the General Assembly.

The charter defines the "paramount consideration" in employing staff as the necessity of securing the highest standards of efficiency, competency, and integrity, with due regard to the importance of recruiting on as wide a geographical basis as possible. In the performance of their duties, the secretary general and the staff are forbidden to seek or receive any instructions from any government or any other authority external to the UN. Each member of the UN, in turn, is bound to respect the exclusively international character of the Secretariat's responsibilities and not to seek to influence it in the discharge of its duties.

In addition to its New York headquarters, the UN maintains offices in Geneva, Switzerland; Nairobi, Kenya; and Vienna, Austria. Personnel of various specialized and subsidiary organs are also headquartered in New York or other UN sites around the globe.

The regular budget of the organization is financed primarily by obligatory contributions from the member states, as determined by a scale of assessments that is based on capacity to pay and currently varies from 0.001 percent of the total for the poorest members to 22 percent for the United States. Collectively, eight Western industrialized countries (Canada, France, Germany, Italy, Japan, Spain, United Kingdom, and the United States) contribute approximately 61 percent of the budget. China is the largest contributor among developing states and provides 5.1 percent of the budget, followed by Brazil at 2.9 percent. Activities outside the regular budget, including most peacekeeping activities and technical cooperation programs, are separately financed, partly through voluntary contributions.

Activities. The level of international political activity undertaken by various secretaries general has depended as much on the political environment and their own personalities as on charter provisions. Prior to the breakup of the Soviet Union in the early 1990s, the most important factor was often the acquiescence of the superpowers. This was vividly demonstrated by the Soviet challenge to the Secretariat during the Belgian Congo crisis of 1960. UN intervention in the Congo, initiated on the authority of the Security Council in the summer of 1960, led to sharp Soviet criticism of Secretary General Dag Hammarskjöld and a proposal by Soviet Chair Nikita Khrushchev in September 1960 to abolish the Secretariat and substitute a tripartite executive body made up of Western, communist, and neutral representatives. Although the proposal was not adopted, the USSR maintained a virtual boycott of the Secretariat up to the time of Hammarskjölds death in September 1961 and imposed a number of conditions before agreeing to U Thant of Burma as his successor. U Thant was in turn succeeded in 1971 by Kurt Waldheim of Austria.

In December 1981, in the wake of decisions by Waldheim and Salim A. Salim of Tanzania to withdraw from consideration, Javier Pérez de Cuéllar, a relatively obscure Peruvian diplomat, was selected by a closed session of the UN Security Council as the recommended candidate for UN secretary general. The full UN General Assembly unanimously elected Pérez de Cuéllar on December 15, and his five-year term as the fifth secretary general began January 1, 1982. Despite earlier hints that he might not seek a second term because of budget problems, Pérez de Cuéllar, upon the unanimous recommendation of the Security Council, was reelected by the General Assembly in October 1986 for an additional five years beginning January 1, 1987.

In September 1987 Pérez de Cuéllar launched an intensive campaign to win support from Iran and Iraq for a Security Council plan to settle the war between them. Further underscoring his heightened visibility in international diplomacy, the secretary general in October was selected to serve on the committee charged with verifying compliance with the recently negotiated Central American peace plan. The Secretariats peacemaking role continued to grow throughout 1988 as cease-fires were negotiated in the Iran-Iraq and Western Saharan conflicts in August and agreements were signed by Angola, Cuba, and South Africa in December that permitted implementation of the long-delayed UN plan for the independence of Namibia.

To take advantage of the "extraordinary improvement in the world political climate," Pérez de Cuéllar in 1989 suggested further extension of the UNs peacekeeping role, calling upon countries to designate standby troops for that purpose out of their national armies. He also urged the United Nations to assemble a more sophisticated information gathering system so that it could monitor "incipient conflicts" and possibly prevent them from erupting. The Secretariat, hoping to build upon its role in the highly successful Namibian settlement, pursued negotiations in Cambodia, Cyprus, El Salvador, and the Western Sahara, while also sending a delegation in June 1990 to review progress toward the dismantling of apartheid in South Africa.

Other topics addressed by Pérez de Cuéllar as his second term neared completion included the "old, stubborn problems, unrelated to the cold war," such as "grave" global economic disparity, third world debt, and environmental degradation. The secretary general was also highly visible in international efforts to negotiate a withdrawal of Iraqi forces from Kuwait in late 1990 and early 1991, prior to the launching of the U.S.-led military campaign.

As expected, the widely respected Pérez de Cuéllar declined to stand for a third term, and in the fall of 1991 the General Assembly, acting upon the recommendation of the Security Council, unanimously elected Boutros Boutros-Ghali, the Egyptian deputy prime minister for foreign affairs, as the UNs sixth secretary general, effective January 1, 1992. Boutros-Ghali, the first Arab and the first African to hold the post, rose to prominence as part of the Egyptian team that negotiated the Camp David peace treaty with Israel.

Because he was well known in UN circles and familiar with the organization's bureaucracy, the new secretary general was able to institute a significant restructuring of the Secretariat in February 1992 as part of ongoing streamlining throughout the UN system. Most operations were consolidated into four major new departments, permitting a reduction in the number of under secretaries general and assistant secretaries general while also providing a more direct and, it was hoped, a more efficient chain of command. One of the new departments was devoted to peacekeeping, an area in which Boutros-Ghali suggested UN influence could be expanded even further.

In June 1992 Boutros-Ghali outlined an Agenda for Peace, which called upon UN members to make armed forces available to the Security Council on a permanent on-call basis. The secretary general also suggested that the council's long-dormant Military Staff Committee be reactivated to assume authority over what would essentially become the UN's standby army. A wider role in "preventative diplomacy" was also urged, Boutros-Ghali asking regional organizations to seek UN intervention before disputes escalated into warfare.

Boutros-Ghali's recommendations were initially endorsed in many quarters. However, disillusionment was apparent a year later, stemming from the failure of UN efforts in Bosnia and Herzegovina, ongoing difficulties in Somalia and Angola, and the inability of fact-finding missions in Azerbaijan, Georgia, and Tajikistan to prevent bloodshed. For his part, Boutros-Ghali argued that the United Nations was being asked to take on more than it could handle, especially considering the "chasm" that existed between its assignments and the money member states were willing to provide. The secretary general was also facing resistance both from member states and from UN employees in his efforts to further revamp the Secretariat and other UN bureaucracies, despite general agreement that the organization remained highly inefficient in many areas. However, a new Office for Inspections and Investigations (OII) was established in 1993 to combat waste and mismanagement and to address allegations of corruption within the UN system. A year later, the office was replaced by an Office of Internal Oversight Services, which is headed by an assistant secretary general who has operational independence.

As a counterpoint to his 1992 Agenda for Peace, Boutros-Ghali unveiled an Agenda for Development in May 1994. Despite the "distorted perception" throughout the world that peacekeeping was being emphasized at the expense of other areas, the secretary general stressed that "development is still the major activity of the UN." However, Boutros-Ghali argued that new levels of coordination were required within the UN and between the UN and other international organizations to combat donor fatigue and to mobilize public opinion in support of development assistance. Progress also depended on the ability of developing nations to find "the right blend" of governmental influence and private initiative for maximum economic growth.

In late 1994 and 1995, Boutros-Ghali consistently criticized UN members for failing to meet their financial obligations, especially those for peacekeeping operations. The secretary general reported that arrears had reached $3.24 billion as of September 1995, making it "impossible for us to do our job." Boutros-Ghali also argued, however, that the United Nations retained a "moral obligation" to go into crisis areas, whatever the financial and/or political limitations might be. In a related vein, the secretary general was reported to be somewhat at odds with the Security Council, which he described as being too involved with the conflict in Bosnia and Herzegovina at the expense of problems in other sections of the world. Underscoring his determination to focus attention on "underdog conflicts," Boutros-Ghali made a week-long trip across Central Africa in mid-1995. The secretary general's concern for his home continent was further highlighted in March 1996 when he launched the ten-year, $25 billion UN System-wide Special Initiative on Africa, described as one of the largest cooperative operations ever attempted by UN agencies and other regional organizations.

In June 1996 the United States issued a surprisingly strong statement pledging to veto a second term for Boutros-Ghali, arguing that he was ill-suited to implementing the reforms Washington was demanding in return for payment of some of its $1.3 billion in arrears. Representatives from many countries rushed to the defense of the secretary general, pointing out that he had reduced UN staffing by some 10 percent and had attempted to restructure the UN's bureaucratic maze of agencies. Nevertheless, at the first round of balloting in the Security Council on November 19, the United States cast the lone dissenting vote against Boutros-Ghali's reelection, forcing the consideration of other candidates.

The four primary contenders to emerge were Kofi Annan of Ghana, then the under secretary general for peacekeeping operations; Amara Essy, the foreign minister of Côte dIvoire; Hamid Algabid of Niger, then the secretary general of the Organization of the Islamic Conference; and Mauritanian diplomat Ahmedou Ould Abdallah. Several straw votes in the Security Council in early December effectively reduced the choices to Annan (backed by the United States) and Essy. Although France, an ardent supporter of Boutros-Ghali, reportedly threatened to veto Annan to protest Washingtons heavy-handedness in the selection process, Annan was finally approved on December 13, with the General Assembly making the appointment official four days later.

Upon taking office on January 1, 1997, Annan, the first black African to hold the job, called for "a time for healing" and pledged to pursue UN reform. Among the most important reforms approved by the General Assembly late in the year was the creation of the position of the deputy secretary general, Louise Fréchette of Canada becoming in January 1998 the first person to hold the position. Other changes included the formation of a cabinet-like Senior Management Group, the creation of the Department of Disarmament Affairs, the merger of three departments into the newly created Department of Economic and Social Affairs, the reorganization of the UN Drug Control Program (UNDCP) and the Center for International Crime Prevention (CICP) under the new Office for Drug Control and Crime Prevention (ODCCP) in Vienna, the consolidation of the Geneva-based Center for Human Rights under the Office of the High Commissioner for Human Rights (UNHCHR), and a proposed reduction in administrative costs of at least $200 million over four years.

In April 1998 Annan issued a wide-ranging report on African issues, particularly the wars being fought across the continent and the lack of economic development. Exhibiting a growing willingness to address such issues bluntly, he criticized African leaders for relying on military rather than political approaches to problems and for their failure to attend to good governance. In September 1998 Annan questioned the U.S. bomb attacks on suspected terrorist sites in Afghanistan and Sudan, arguing that "individual action by member states" was not the solution to the "global menace" of terrorism.

In subsequent speeches and reports, the secretary general staked out a clear position in support of UN intervention to prevent a recurrence of the genocidal events in Rwanda and Kosovo during the 1990s. In addition to urging the Security Council to respond faster to the outbreak of civil wars, Annan countered ardent advocates for the primacy of national sovereignty by arguing that "nothing in the Charter precludes a recognition that there are rights beyond borders," particularly when a state was violating human rights within those borders. He also strongly supported establishment of a permanent International Criminal Court (ICC; see General Assembly) and chastised the United States for its objections to such a court, as well as for its unwillingness to provide more than transport and logistical support to peacekeeping ventures in Africa.

The April 2000 secretary general's report focused on development issues. Annan called for efforts to reduce youth unemployment and to "bridge the digital divide" between technologically advanced and developing states. He also urged the developed world to provide debt relief and to drop tariffs on commodities from developing countries, thereby helping them increase the export earnings needed to finance development. In addition, Annan advocated greater involvement by private sector partners in humanitarian relief efforts. In December 2000 he named a high-level panel of financial experts, chaired by former Mexican president Ernesto Zedillo, to propose steps to help speed development in poor countries. With a special UN session on HIV/AIDS approaching in June 2001, Annan subsequently called for creation of a Global AIDS and Health Fund.

On June 29, 2001, the General Assembly unanimously elected Annan to a second term, which began January 1, 2002. On October 12 Annan and the UN were awarded the Nobel Peace Prize.

In late 2002 not only the Security Council but also the General Assembly and Secretariat became increasingly tied up in the debate over weapons inspections in Iraq and a threatened U.S. invasion of that country. From then until the actual launch of hostilities in March 2003, Secretary General Annan argued for adherence to the international rule of law and the need to address matters of peace and security in the context of "the unique legitimacy provided by the UN Security Council." He subsequently incurred Washington's wrath, not to mention that of right-wing U.S. media outlets, by branding the war "illegal" and by asserting that going to war had not made the world safer. He also opposed the George W. Bush administration's efforts to keep U.S. peacekeeping troops exempt from prosecution by the new ICC.

A major shake-up in the UN security structure followed a suicide truck bombing at UN headquarters in Baghdad, Iraq, on August 19, 2003. Twenty-two people died in the blast, including Annans special representative to Iraq, Sergio Vieira de Mello of Brazil, and the former UN chief of protocol, Nadia Younes of Egypt. An independent report published in March 2004 faulted administrators for having failed to conduct a security review of the facility, in the mistaken assumption that UN personnel would not be targeted by insurgents. As a consequence, Secretary General Annan fired his security coordinator, Tun Myat of Myanmar, and demoted other personnel. Annan refused, however, to accept the resignation of Deputy Secretary General Fréchette, who had headed a committee that recommended a UN return to Iraq. On January 13, 2005, Annan named David Veness, an assistant commissioner of Londons Metropolitan Police Service and an antiterrorism expert, to head a newly created Department of Safety and Security.

Meanwhile, the secretary general was drawing increasing criticism in connection with the $64 billion "oil-for-food" program, which had permitted Iraq to sell oil and use the income to meet humanitarian needs. An investigation initiated by the secretary general in April 2004 into bribery and illicit payments led to the revelation that Annan's son, Kojo Annan, had been paid by a Swiss contractor, Cotecna Inspection Services, which had been responsible for monitoring Iraqi compliance with the program. February and March 2005 interim reports by the Independent Inquiry Committee, headed by former chair of the U.S. Federal Reserve Paul Volcker, exonerated Kofi Annan of involvement in awarding the contract to Cotecna but found procedural errors and procurement violations dating back to Boutros-Ghali's term as secretary general. The committee also criticized Annan's former chief of cabinet, Syed Iqbal Riza of Pakistan, for having shredded documents relevant to the case. The first UN staffer held criminally culpable in the "oil-for-food" scandal was Aleksandr Yakovlev of Russia, who in August 2005 pleaded guilty to taking some $1.3 million in bribes while heading a procurement department.

The Volcker committee report issued on September 7, 2005, indicted the UN for "illicit, unethical and corrupt behavior" as well as inadequate auditing and overall bureaucratic inefficiency. During the 1996–2003 "oil-for-food" program, the Saddam Hussein regime illicitly pocketed billions of dollars while paying bribes to some 270 politicians and journalists. Although Annan accepted responsibility for the "deeply embarrassing" shortcomings documented in the report, he rejected calls for his resignation and vowed to press ahead with his reform agenda.

On March 21, 2005, drawing on the work of a High-Level Panel on Threats, Challenges, and Change that he had named in November 2003, Secretary General Annan submitted to the General Assembly his long-awaited report on reform, "In Larger Freedom: Toward Development, Security, and Human Rights for All." Among other things, the secretary general called for expanding the Security Council to better reflect a geopolitical balance; streamlining the General Assembly agenda; making the Secretariat more flexible, transparent, and accountable; and replacing the controversial UN Commission on Human Rights with a Human Rights Council elected by the General Assembly. He asked all developing countries to improve governance, target corruption, and uphold the rule of law while striving to meet the Millennium Development Goals set forth in 2000. At the same time, he urged developed countries to significantly increase their amount of development assistance and debt relief and to permit duty-free and quota-free imports from the least developed countries. He cautioned, however, that sustainable development required due attention to environmental factors and concerns about the depletion of natural resources. In the area of security he emphasized the importance of working in concert to control terrorism, end weapons proliferation, and stop civil wars. He also urged collective action against genocide, ethnic cleansing, and crimes against humanity if individual countries were unable or unwilling to act.

In January 2006 eight UN officials, including Andrew Toh, the assistant secretary general for central support services, were suspended in connection with more than 200 alleged instances of fraud in the purchase of equipment for peacekeeping missions. The allegations resulted from an inquiry into procurement practices that led Chief of Staff Mark Malloch Brown, speaking to the Security Council in

February, to confirm the need for reform, particularly in the awarding of contracts. Also in February, Secretary General Annan announced the formation of a senior 15-member panel to propose methods to enhance collaboration and cooperation between agencies. The panel was one of the recommendations from the UN 60th anniversary summit. It suggested changes as part of Annans broader reform program and focused on the UNs role in environmental, humanitarian, and development policies. In March, in addition to naming Malloch Brown as successor to Deputy Secretary General Fréchette, Annan announced additional specific reforms, including increased training for UN staff and improvements in technology, communications, and records. Annan also called for relocating some UN agencies from New York and Geneva to less expensive locations as a means of reducing expenditures.

A report on sexual misconduct by UN peacekeeping forces released in August 2006 detailed 313 investigations and noted that the inquiries had resulted in the dismissal of 17 UN peacekeepers and the forced repatriation of 161 others. In September the UN's first all-female peacekeeping unit was deployed to UNMIL. The force consisted of 125 woman officers from India. Women comprised less than 4 percent of the personnel of all UN peacekeeping missions as of 2008.

In informal polling in September and October 2006 among Security Council members to determine the next secretary general, Foreign Minister Ban Ki-Moon of the Republic of Korea emerged as the leading candidate among seven contenders mostly from Asia. Ban was the favored candidate of the United States and China, but France and the United Kingdom initially sought a more activist candidate. However, after Ban won the fourth informal poll on October 2, all of the other candidates withdrew. He was unanimously recommended by the Security Council and appointed by the General Assembly on October 13.

Once in office, Ban replaced two-thirds of the body's senior management team. He named Asha-Rose Migiro of Tanzania as the new deputy secretary general. She was the third person to hold the post and the first non-Westerner. Throughout the senior management, the new secretary general increased the number of appointments from the developing world. Ban also detailed five priorities for his term in office. First, he called for the UN to strengthen its traditional core pillars of security, development, and human rights. Second, he declared his intent to restore confidence in the office of the secretary general. Third, Ban wanted to improve the efficiency of the UN management system, particularly its human resource system. Fourth, the new secretary general sought to set higher ethical and professional standards for all UN employees and agencies, including the adoption of annual performance reviews. Fifth and finally, Ban declared his intent to revolutionize the relationship between the Secretariat and UN member states. In order to demonstrate his earnestness about ethical reform, Ban released his personal financial disclosure form for external review and promised to continue to do so each year. His deputy secretary general has also adopted this practice. In June 2007 the UN's peacekeeping structure was divided into two departments, peacekeeping operations and field support, as part of a broader reform effort proposed by Ban in January to increase efficiency through greater specialization. Each of the new departments was headed by an undersecretary general.

In November Ban became the first UN secretary general to make an official visit to Antarctica. While touring the region, Ban called for greater action to slow global warming. He also announced the launch of a system-wide UN campaign to combat violence against women. Ban's initiative was scheduled to last through 2015 and mandate that the General Assembly include at least one agenda item per year to address gender violence. The secretary general also pledged to reform UN agencies to better address violence against women, particularly during peacekeeping operations. In 2008 Ban released a report that showed attacks on UN staff had increased dramatically in the preceding year, and that deaths of UN workers due to attacks had increased by 38 percent.

Following attacks on UN workers, including the bombing of UN offices in Algiers in December 2007, Ban pledged to better protect UN staffers, and in 2008 convened the Independent Panel on Safety and Security to develop recommendations on how to better secure UN facilities and personnel. Meanwhile, throughout 2008, Ban continued to undertake a series of reforms at the world body. He appointed a chief information officer to oversee the UN's information technology systems, and he altered the UN's procurement system to ensure greater transparency and efficiency. He also shortened the hiring process for new UN staffers.

In response to rising food prices, in April 2008 Ban established the High Level Task Force on the Global Food Security Crisis to identify problems and develop strategies, as well as to coordinate the UN response. Ban brought together more than 100 world leaders at the High Level Event on the Millennium Development Goals in New York in September and was able to secure pledges of more than $16 billion in additional funding for poverty reduction efforts and an additional $3 billion to combat malaria and other diseases. In October Ban reported that an independent review of the $500-million Central Emergency Response Fund (CERF) found the reserve had been largely successful in its mission of providing assistance for natural disasters, and he urged members to annually contribute to CERF. Also in October, Ban conducted a high-level meeting of the heads of 17 major pharmaceutical and medical companies and received pledges that the firms would expand research and increase access to drugs and medicines in developing countries. In November Ban issued an urgent appeal for all member states to pay their dues. At the time, member states owed $756 million to the regular budget and $2.9 to the peacekeeping budget.

An investigation into the UNs handling of an inquiry into the death in 2000 of a British contractor working for UNDP led to the creation of the five-member Internal Justice Council (IJC). After Joe Comerford died, the UN refused his widow compensation until 2008 when she was awarded £143,000. The world body engaged in behavior that was later described by investigators as "reckless and callous" toward the widow. The IJC was formed to be an independent, judicial body for arbitration within the UN.

In 2008 Ban initiated the program UNiTE to End Violence Against Women. The program sought by 2015 to have nations adopt national legislation that mirrored international conventions and to institute plans to curb gender violence. UNiTE also promoted the development of global data collection and analysis of violence against women. The initiative was developed in response to a 2006 report that highlighted trends in gender violence and was in response to a 2007 General Assembly resolution that called for greater progress in the elimination of violence against women.

On Janaury 31, 2009, Ban's special representative to Myanmar, Ibrahim Gambari, visited the country for a series of meetings in an effort to persuade the military government to restore democracy. The sessions were unsuccessful, although Gambari was able to meet with opposition leader Aung San Suu Kyi, who remained under house arrest. Ban launched the We Must Disarm (WMD) campaign on June 13. The WMD initiative was a multimedia effort to promote nuclear disarmament and increase awareness of the dangers of weapons proliferation. The secretary general worked with actor Michael Douglas, a UN messenger of peace, in the campaign, which culminated in the International Day of Peace on September 21. The secretary general convened the UN Climate Change Summit in September. The event brought together more than 100 world leaders and was a precursor to the Copenhagen conference on climate change later that year. U.S. president Obama pledged that the country would recommit itself to involvement in global efforts to reduce greenhouse gases and address climate change.

In September 2009 Ban removed Peter Galbraith as a UN deputy special representative to Afghanistan. Galbraith had a public dispute with the senior UN figure in Afghanistan, Kai Eide, over the management of run-off balloting following a disputed presidential election in August.

Following a massive earthquake in Haiti in January 2010, Ban launched a widespread appeal for humanitarian aid, noting that more than 1.2 million Haitians needed emergency food and shelter. Ban appointed former U.S. president Bill Clinton as a special envoy for Haiti to raise awareness of the disaster. However, John Holmes, the UN emergency relief coordinator at the time, noted in a leaked e-mail that the UN response was "poorly coordinated and resourced." In April the secretary general appointed Norman Girvan of Jamaica as a special representative in an effort to resolve a long-standing border dispute between Guyana and Venezuela. Talks between the two nations had been suspended since 2007. In July the media reported that the outgoing under-secretary general of the Office of Internal Oversight Services (OIOS), Inga-Britt Ahlenius, had written a highly critical memo about Ban, accusing the secretary general of unwarranted interference in operations of the UN watchdog agency. Ban subsequently appointed Carmen Lapointe of Canada as the new head of the OIOS.

In August 2010 Ban created a ten-member advisory council to increase global "awareness" of the issues faced by the world's 49 least developed states (LDCs) ahead of the fourth UN Conference on LDCs scheduled for May 2011. Also in August, Ban sent Assistant Secretary General Atul Khare of India to the Democratic Republic of the Congo to investigate reports of mass rape by Rwandan Hutu rebels in Luvungi, and charges that UN peacekeepers at a nearby post failed to take action to prevent the attacks.

In June 2011 Ban was unanimously reelected for a second term as secretary general. Following his reappointment, Ban reshuffled his senior management team. In January 2012 Ban announced a five-year agenda, "The Future We Want." The plan called for increased global efforts to combat malaria and polio and the designation of Antarctica as a global nature preserve. In response to widespread fighting in Syria, Ban appointed former secretary general Annan as a special peace envoy. Annan developed a six-point peace plan that was endorsed by the Security Council and initially accepted by the Syrian government. However, renewed strife precluded the implementation of the initiative (see entry on Syria). On March 2, Ban appointed Jan Eliasson of Sweden as deputy secretary general. In December Ban appealed for $2.2 billion from international donors to support a WHO initiative to eliminate cholera in Haiti by 2022.

Ban appointed Tegegnework Gettu of Ethiopa as under-secretary for the General Assembly and conference management in 2013. In June of that year, Ban appointed Jean-Paul Laborde of France as executive director of the UN's counterterrorism directorate. In September Ban announced that he had secured $1.5 billion to launch a new program, Education First, desgined to support global education efforts. On October 1, Ban opened the annual session of the General Assembly by calling on world leaders to take stronger action to end the civil war in Syria, which he described as a "regional calamity with global ramifications." The secretary general also urged continued action on climate change.

UNITED NATIONS: SPECIALIZED AGENCIES

The United Nations has designated 16 organizations as Specialized Agencies, 13 of which are discussed here. This edition of the *Handbook* does not include separate articles on the UN World Tourism Organization (UNWTO), or 2 agencies whose activities are largely technical: the Universal Postal Union (UPU), which traces its origins to the 1874 Treaty Concerning the Establishment of a General Postal Union (the Berne Treaty), and the World Meteorological Organization (WMO), successor to the International Meteorological Organization (founded in 1878). Appendix C lists the members of all 16 Specialized Agencies.

FOOD AND AGRICULTURE ORGANIZATION OF THE UNITED NATIONS

(FAO)

Established: By constitution signed in Quebec, Canada, October 16, 1945. The FAO became a UN Specialized Agency by agreement with the Economic and Social Council (approved by the General Assembly on December 14, 1946).

Purpose: "To promote the common welfare by furthering separate and collective action... for the purpose of: raising levels of nutrition and standards of living... securing improvements in the efficiency of the production and distribution of all food and agricultural products; bettering the condition of rural populations; and thus contributing toward an expanding world economy."

Headquarters: Rome, Italy.

Principal Organs: General Conference (all members), Council (49 members), Secretariat.

Web site: www.fao.org

Director General: José Graziano da Silva (Brazil).

Membership (194, plus 2 Associate Members, and 1 member organization, the EU): See Appendix C.

Official Languages: Arabic, Chinese, English, French, German, Spanish.

Working Languages: Arabic, Chinese, English, French, Spanish.

Origin and development. The 34 governments represented at the UN Conference on Food and Agriculture held May 18–June 3, 1943, in Hot Springs, Virginia, agreed that a permanent international body should be established to deal with problems of food and agriculture. The Interim Commission on Food and Agriculture submitted a draft constitution that was signed October 15, 1945, in Quebec, Canada, by the 30 governments attending the first session of the FAO General Conference. The organization, which inherited the functions and assets of the former International Institute of Agriculture in Rome, Italy, was made a Specialized Agency of the United Nations effective December 14, 1946.

In November 1991 the conference admitted the European Community (subsequently the European Union—EU) as a regular FAO member, marking the first time such an organization had joined a UN Specialized Agency. The EU's rights are somewhat circumscribed, however, in that it cannot vote in elections or hold office, and it may otherwise participate as an alternative to, not in addition to, its individual member states. The November 1993 General Conference readmitted South Africa, which had withdrawn in 1964. FAO membership rose to 188 in December 2003 with the admission of Micronesia, Timor-Leste, Tuvalu, and Ukraine; to 189 members in 2006 with the addition of the Russian Federation; and by 2010 to its current 192 members.

FAO responsibilities were significantly broadened in 1963 when, following a suggestion by the United States, the UN/FAO World Food Program (WFP) began operations to provide food aid in furtherance of economic and social development, to offer relief services in the event of natural and man-made disasters, and to promote world food security. Subsequently, as part of its effort to avoid overlapping mandates, the General Assembly in 1995 authorized the FAO and the WFP to absorb the responsibilities of the World Food Council (WFC), a special body of the assembly that was disbanded in May 1996. The vast majority of the FAO's 10,600 employees serve in the field.

Structure. The General Conference, which normally meets at Rome once every two years, is the organization's major policy-making organ; each member has one vote. Its responsibilities include approving the FAO budget and program of work, adopting procedural rules and financial regulations, formulating recommendations on food and agricultural questions, and reviewing the decisions of the FAO Council and subsidiary bodies.

The FAO Council's 49 members are elected for three-year rotating terms by the conference from seven regional groupings (Africa, 12 seats; Asia, 9; Europe, 10; Latin America and the Caribbean, 9; Near East, 6; North America, 2; Southwest Pacific, 1). The council meets between sessions of the conference and acts on its behalf as an executive organ responsible for monitoring the world food and agriculture situation and recommending any appropriate action. Assisting the council are three elected managerial committees that deal with program, finance, and constitutional and legal matters. Committees on commodity problems, fisheries, agriculture, forestry, and world food security address specialized issues and are open to all members.

Responsibility for implementing the FAO program rests with its Secretariat, which is headed by a director general serving a six-year term of office. Its headquarters staff has 1,956 full-time employees, while 1,735 are assigned to regional and subregional offices and field projects. There were 2,670 field program projects in 2012, of which 444 were emergency operations. The regional offices are located in Accra, Ghana (Africa); Bangkok, Thailand (Asia and the Pacific); Cairo, Egypt (Near East); Rome, Italy (Europe); and Santiago, Chile (Latin America and the Caribbean). Liaison offices are maintained at UN headquarters in New York and Geneva; in Yokohama, Japan; in Brussels, Belgium (for the EU); and in Washington, D.C.

The FAO's work programs are divided among seven departments, which typically encompass a varying number of divisions, each with its own mandate and programs. The Agriculture and Consumer Protection Department includes the Animal Production and Health Division, FAO/International Atomic Energy Agency (IAEA) Joint Division for Nuclear Techniques in Food and Agriculture, the Land and Water Development Division, the Plant Production and Protection Division, the Rural Agriculture and Agro-Industries Division, and the Nutrition and Consumer Protection Division. The Economic and Social Development Department has three divisions: Agricultural and Development Economics, Commodities and Trade, and Statistics. The Fisheries and Aquaculture Department includes three divisions: Economics and Policy, Management, and Fish Products and Industry. The Forestry Department has divisions titled Forestry Economics and Policy, Forest Management, and Forest Products and Industries. The Natural Resources Management and Environment Department includes four divisions: Environment, Climate Change and Bioenergy, the Land

and Water Division, and the Research and Extension Division. The Technical Cooperation Department encompasses the Policy Assistance Division, the Investment Center, the Field Operations Division, and the Emergency Operations and Rehabilitation Division. The other FAO department is Corporate Services, Human Resources, and Finance. The latter is responsible for issuing the FAO's numerous publications, which include the annual *State of Food and Agriculture* and, since 1999, the annual *State of Food Insecurity in the World.* It also maintains a number of databases, most prominently the International Information System for the Agricultural Sciences and Technology (AGRIS) and the Current Agricultural Research Information System (CARIS).

Other FAO services are offered through the administrative Office of Program, Budget, and Evaluations. An FAO legal office is responsible for providing in-house legal services, advising member states, and assisting in preparation of relevant treaties.

The FAO sponsors some 30, mostly regional, commissions concerned with, for example, agricultural statistics, forestry, fisheries, plant protection, and pests and diseases (including desert locusts, African animal sleeping sickness, and foot-and-mouth disease). The joint FAO/World Health Organization (WHO) Codex Alimentarius Commission, established in 1962 and now numbering 170 member countries, assists in the preparation, publication, and updating of international food standards.

The WFP is supervised by a 36-member executive board (half elected by the Economic and Social Council of the United Nations and half by the FAO Council), which succeeded the Committee on Food Aid Policies and Programs in January 1996. Its executive director, currently Ertharin Cousin of the United States, is jointly named by the UN secretary general and the FAO director general.

Activities. To fulfill its stated purposes of raising living standards and securing improvement in the availability of agricultural products, the FAO collects, analyzes, interprets, and disseminates information relating to nutrition, food, and agriculture. It recommends national and international action in these fields, furnishes such technical assistance as governments may request, and cooperates with governments in organizing missions needed to help them meet their obligations.

The FAO's work is supported through the Regular Program budget and through the separate Field Program of technical assistance. The Regular Program, with mandatory contributions from member states, covers the costs of Secretariat operations but also includes as one component the Technical Cooperation Program (TCP). The TCP constitutes the portion of the regular budget contributed to field projects, which are primarily funded through trust funds established by donor countries. Other international institutions also participate. The 2010–2011 regular budget was $1 billion with voluntary contributions of $1.2 billion.

In 1994 the FAO established the Special Program for Food Security (SPFS), which focuses on helping low-income food-deficit countries (LIFDCs) improve agricultural productivity and output on an environmentally sound, economically sustainable basis. As of 2011, at least 57 countries had SPFS projects, which are primarily funded through extra-budgetary means, in some stage of development. Other special programs include the Global Information and Early Warning System (GIEWS), which began operations in 1975, and the Emergency Prevention System (EMPRES) for Transboundary Animal and Plant Pests and Diseases, founded in 1994. The GIEWS attempts to gauge future food supplies in order to forestall food emergencies, while the EMPRES focuses on the control and eradication of targeted diseases and pests (desert locusts, rinderpest, and animal sleeping sickness).

At the November 12–23, 1999, General Conference, the FAO reelected Director General Jacques Diouf to a second term despite opposition from the United Kingdom and some other industrialized countries. It also approved a strategic framework for 2000–2015 that established three overarching goals: "access of all people at all times to sufficient nutritionally adequate and safe food"; the "continued contribution of sustainable agricultural and rural development, including fisheries and forestry, to economic and social progress and the well-being of all"; and the conservation, improvement, and sustainable use of national resources, "including land, water, forests, fisheries and genetic resources." The framework goals also repeated the WFS target of halving the number of undernourished by 2015.

The World Food Summit: Five Years Later, which was postponed from November 2001 because of security concerns following the September 11, 2001, attacks on the United States, convened June 10–13, 2002, in Rome. Although the summit was attended by 74 heads of state or government, few leaders of industrialized countries participated.

A year later, the 2003 *State of Food Insecurity in the World* made it clear that without a significant acceleration in food production and distribution, the goal of halving the undernourished population by 2015 remained unattainable. Although hunger decreased in the first half of the 1990s, the overall trend was reversed in the second half of the decade, according to the report, leaving 840 million people undernourished in 1999–2001. Reasons for the lack of progress included insufficient resources for distributing food, conflicts in central and western Africa, a severe drought in southern Africa, and the spread of HIV/AIDS.

In response to this setback, the FAO called for wide adoption of an anti-hunger program that combines increased agricultural productivity in rural communities with immediate access to food for the hungry. The FAO emphases include improving rural infrastructure and market access; using available water resources and irrigation more effectively; utilizing both chemical and organic fertilizers; and adopting integrated biological controls to help combat pests, insects, and plant diseases. The FAO has also emphasized, despite continuing criticism from some quarters, greater use of biotechnology.

On June 29, 2004, the FAO-sponsored International Treaty on Plant Genetic Resources for Food and Agriculture entered into effect. Among other things, the treaty provides for the Multilateral System for Access and Benefit Sharing to streamline procedures and reduce transaction costs for plant breeders, farmers, and researchers seeking access to the genetic resources of over 60 of the world's most important food and forage crops. In addition, some 600,000 genetic samples held by the 16 research centers of the Consultative Group on International Agricultural Research (CGIAR) come under the terms of the treaty, and the Global Crop Diversity Trust was established to support gene conservation and assist developing countries.

In October 2006, the agency issued a warning that in the ten years following the World Food Summit pledge to halve world hunger, little to no progress had been made. A 2007 FAO brief, *The State of Food and Agriculture,* reported widespread waste in the processing and shipping of food aid by donor countries.

The FAO commissioned the first-ever independent evaluation of itself, and in July 2007 a draft form was released. "FAO: The Challenge of Renewal" gave a harsh review of the 60-year-old organization, calling for a three-to-four year immediate action plan to address long-standing management and budget failings. The report, finalized later in the year, called the FAO's governance "weak" and noted a lack of clear priorities, insufficient trust and mutual understanding between member states and the Secretariat, declining budget resources, and needed re-appraisal of the FAO's development efforts. The report urged the FAO to shift its focus from food production to employment as a means of income generation and food access and warned that failure to do so would cause the FAO to fade into insignificance. Director General Diouf declared that he "welcomed" the report as "a significant and historic effort to improve the organization's work," adding that the report "recognizes that change is a shared responsibility of the (FAO) secretariat and the member countries." The FAO conference of November 2007 established an elaborately structured committee, or set of working groups, to address the report's recommendations. These working groups reported back late in 2008.

Meanwhile the FAO was forced to respond to the steep rise in food prices in 2008. In advance of a June 4, 2008, FAO conference on world food security, to be held in Rome, President Abdoulaye Wade of Senegal lashed out at the FAO and his fellow countryman Jacques Diouf. Wade called the FAO an "inefficient money-gobbler" that should be abolished. He also threatened to sue the FAO for deducting, as he claimed, 20 percent of all funds collected to alleviate the food crisis.

In September 2008 Diouf said that the number of hungry people worldwide had risen from 850 million to 925 million in 2007, and that he could see the number reaching one billion by the end of 2008. He called for an annual investment of $30 billion to double world food production. On November 20, 2008, the FAO adopted a plan of reform. The plan spent $42.6 million over three years, roughly half of it in 2009, to effect "reform with growth." Among other things, the plan reduced the agency's 120 directorships by one third, freeing up $17.4 million to be spent on technical assistance programs. Director-General Diouf said, "We must build a new FAO," promising a "sweeping overhaul of the way FAO works."

The year 2009 saw a reduction in world food prices from their peaks of the previous year, but prices still remained a concern, particularly in poor countries. The FAO remained critical of biofuels because they compete with food production. UN aid to Colombia's extensive biofuel program was suspended. By June 2009 the FAO stated that the number

Headquarters: Rome, Italy.

Principal Organs: Governing Council (all members), Executive Board (18 members), Secretariat.

Web site: www.ifad.org

President: Kanayo F. Nwanze (Nigeria).

Membership (172): See Appendix C.

Official Languages: Arabic, English, French, Spanish.

Origin and development. The creation of the International Fund for Agricultural Development is regarded as one of the most significant recommendations approved by the November 1974 World Food Conference, which set a 1980 target for agricultural development of $5 billion to be disbursed either directly or indirectly through the fund. At the Seventh Special Session of the General Assembly, held in September 1975, it was agreed that the fund should have an initial target of 1 billion Special Drawing Rights (SDRs), a basket of several world currencies that many inter-governmental organizations use as a medium of exchange, or about $1.25 billion. Until that sum was pledged and the IFAD agreement was ratified by 36 states—including 6 developed, 6 oil-producing, and 24 developing states—the fund took the form of a preparatory commission. The Governing Council first convened December 13, 1977, and IFAD approved its first projects in April 1978.

At its 12th annual session in January 1989 (for information on IFAD prior to 1989, please see the 2012 *Handbook*), the Governing Council experienced difficulty in agreeing on a proposed third replenishment of funding, with OPEC countries arguing that the five-year decline in oil prices had curtailed their ability to contribute. After extensive negotiations, the council reconvened in early June and approved a third replenishment of $532.9 million, well below the $750 million sought. Non- oil-producing developing countries pledged $52.9 million, OPEC countries $124.4 million, and OECD countries $345.6 million to the replenishment, which extended through June 30, 1992. The replenishment was expected to permit the fund to maintain annual lending levels of about $250 million. To address the growing threat of widespread famine in Africa, the Executive Board in January 1991 endorsed a second phase of the Special Program for Sub-Saharan African Countries Affected by Drought and Desertification, which had been initiated in 1986.

Negotiations on a fourth replenishment initially stalled because of ongoing differences between the OECD and OPEC countries regarding their relative contributions, mounting uncertainty as to the fund's role among overlapping UN bodies, and Western concern that IFAD administrative costs were too high. Consequently, the 17th Governing Council, held January 26–28, 1994, in Rome, established a 36-member special committee to "scrutinize" current arrangements and propose "substantive changes" to the council. The committee's recommendations for a significant IFAD restructuring were subsequently approved by the January 1995 council. The council agreed that the voting power of members would be tied in the future to the size of their contributions. The council scheduled implementation of the new structure upon completion of the $460 million fourth replenishment, which was approved in February 1997. (For information on subsequent replenishments, please see "Activities.")

Structure. The Governing Council, which normally meets annually but can convene special sessions, is the fund's policymaking organ, with each member state having one representative. The council may delegate certain of its powers to the 18-member Executive Board, comprised of delegates from eight developed (List A), four oil-producing (List B), and six non-oil-producing developing (List C) states (two each from sublists C1, Africa; C2, Europe, Asia, and the Pacific; and C3, Latin America and the Caribbean). Decisions of the council are made on the basis of a complex weighted voting system under which a member's voting power is partly determined by their past and present contributions.

IFAD administers most of its programs through three departments: External Affairs, Program Management, and Finance and Administration. The Program Management Department, which runs the fund's overall lending program, encompasses five regional divisions: Near East and North Africa, Asia and the Pacific, Latin America and the Caribbean, Western and Central Africa (Africa I), and Eastern and Southern Africa (Africa II). It also includes the Technical Advisory Division, which offers expertise in, and manages technical assistance grants for, agronomy, livestock, rural infrastructure, rural finance, institutions, natural resource management, the environment, gender issues, public health and nutrition, household food security, irrigation, livestock, rural finance, household food security, and sustainable livelihoods. IFAD has a total staff of about 500.

IFAD also serves as the "housing institution" for the Global Mechanism, which was established in October 1997 by the First Conference of Parties to the Convention to Combat Desertification. The Global Mechanism serves primarily as a coordinating program for financing antipoverty and anti-desertification efforts in Africa. IFAD also houses the International Land Coalition, a global consortium of multilateral, bilateral, and civil society organizations that emerged from the IFAD-sponsored Conference on Hunger and Poverty in November 1995. Called the Popular Coalition to Eradicate Hunger and Poverty until its present name was assumed in February 2003, the International Land Coalition reflects the view that the rural poor can best achieve empowerment through land reform and increased access to productive assets, especially "common-property resources," and through active involvement in decision making at all levels of governance. Other participating organizations include the Food and Agriculture Organization (FAO), the World Food Program (WFP), the Inter-American Development Bank (IADB), the World Bank, and the European Commission. In 2001 IFAD was also designated as an executing agency for the Global Environment Facility (GEF), which is administered by the UN Development Program (UNDP), the UN Environment Program (UNEP), and the World Bank. In 2006 the Farmer's Forum was started as a way to feed information from small farmer and rural producers' organizations into IFAD. It meets biannually in conjunction with IFAD Governing Council meetings.

Activities. The fund was the first international institution established exclusively to provide multilateral resources for agricultural development of rural populations. IFAD-supported projects have often combined three interrelated objectives: raising food production, particularly on small farms; providing employment and additional income for poor and landless farmers; and reducing malnutrition by improving food distribution systems and enhancing cultivation of the kinds of crops the poorest populations normally consume. In its first quarter-century, specific emphases included access to land, water, and other productive resources; sustainable rural production; water management and irrigation; rural financing; rural microenterprises; storage and processing of agricultural output; access to markets; small-scale rural infrastructure; capacity-building for small producer groups and organizations; and research, extension, and training.

The bulk of the fund's resources are made available in the form of highly concessional loans. Outright grants are limited to 7.5 percent of each year's budget. Low-income countries are eligible for loans repayable over 40 years (including a ten-year grace period) with no interest and only a 0.75 percent annual service charge. Those countries with moderately higher per capita GNPs are extended loans on intermediate terms, while the rest may borrow on ordinary terms. Many projects receiving IFAD assistance have been cofinanced with the Asian Development Bank, the African Development Bank, the IADB, the World Bank, UNDP, the OPEC Fund, the Islamic Development Bank, the Arab Fund for Economic and Social Development, and other international funding sources. Activity during the February 1998 meeting of the Governing Council included the establishment of an IFAD Trust Fund to aid the poorest countries in taking advantage of the World Bank–led Heavily Indebted Poor Countries (HIPC) debt-reduction initiative. The countries in which IFAD projects are located also often contribute financially.

Apart from replenishments, IFAD supports programs and projects through a number of other means. During 2002, supplementary funds were used, for example, to enhance the role of women in various projects, to provide short-term technical assistance, to mitigate the impact of HIV/AIDS in eastern and southern Africa, and to assist with irrigation in northern Africa. Donors to these and other projects included Canada, Germany, Italy, Japan, Netherlands, Portugal, Switzerland, and the United Kingdom.

In early February 2001 IFAD released its *Rural Poverty Report 2001,* which noted that poverty reduction was proceeding at less than one-third the rate needed to reduce by half the number of people in poverty by 2015, the target set by the World Food Summit in 1996 and repeated at the September 2000 Millennium Summit at UN headquarters. Under present conditions, the effort was doomed to fail, according to the report, in part because the real value of agricultural aid had dropped by two-thirds between 1987 and 1998, even though three-fourths of the world's poor continue to live off the land.

IFAD's Strategic Framework for 2002–2006, which focused on how the organization could best contribute to achieving the Millennial Development Goals (MDGs) set forth at the Millennium Summit, restated IFAD's overall mission in simple terms: "enabling the rural poor to overcome their poverty." Emphasis was placed on strengthening the capacity of the poor and their organizations, improving equitable access to resources and technology, and increasing access to financial assets and markets. During 2002 IFAD joined various other UN organs and specialized agencies as a leading participant in the International Conference on Financing for Development, held in Monterrey, Mexico, in March; the World Food Summit: Five Years Later, held in Rome in June; and the World Summit on Sustainable Development, held August–September in Johannesburg, South Africa.

In June 2006 it was announced that IFAD would launch a microfinance strategy targeting some remote and mountainous areas of China. In partnership with other international donor agencies in 2007, IFAD also created the African Enterprise Challenge Fund to support rural businesses and entrepreneurship beginning in 2008 and the $10 million Financing Facility for Remittances to assist foreign workers in transferring money back to rural families.

Effective July 31, 2007, Australia withdrew from IFAD. In introducing related legislation in the Federal Parliament in June 2004, the Australian government had cited IFAD's "limited relevance" to the country's overall aid program and its focus on Southeast Asia and the Pacific. The government also noted the failure of the IFAD senior managers to address Australia's concerns.

In 2007 and 2008 IFAD was active in projects to bring the economic benefits of mobile telephone service to poor rural areas in the developing world. Creative uses of mobile phones range from a greater ability for farmers to negotiate prices to safe and inexpensive ways to move money. In October 2007 IFAD reported that in 2006 remittances from migrants sent to family members in their home countries amounted to more than all international aid given to developing countries, approximately $300 billion as against approximately $270 billion.

In April 2008, in response to the worldwide rise in food prices, IFAD made up to $200 million available to help poor farmers plant more crops in the forthcoming season. In June UN secretary general Ban praised IFAD as having one of the UN's most successful development programs.

With food prices down from their peak in 2008, but still high; the world in a serious economic recession; and agricultural production continuing to fall, there was what amounted to competition between developing and developed countries to provide IFAD's next president. Many representatives of developing countries said that the agency's presidents had always come from developed countries and that, no disrespect to past presidents, it was time for a change. When IFAD's Governing Council met in Rome February 18–19, 2009, it elected Kanayo Nwanze of Nigeria to replace Sweden's Lennart Båge. Nwanze was vice president of IFAD.

Among the loans made by IFAD in 2009 was a $31 million loan to China to help reduce rural poverty in a remote tea-growing area. IFAD publications continued to stress the importance of remittances. An October 2009 report, "Sending Money Home to Africa," emphasized the point and called on African countries to make the process easier and less costly for their expatriates.

In its *Rural Poverty Report 2011,* IFAD noted that increases in commodity prices, including fuel costs, had caused food prices to double between 2006 and 2008. The global recession did lead to a subsequent decline in costs, nonetheless, the organization predicted that food prices would continue to rise substantially over the next decade, especially in light of population increases. To contain prices, diminish malnutrition, and meet demand, IFAD estimated that food production would have to increase by 70 percent by 2050. Through 2012 IFAD had provided $13.7 billion in funding for 892 projects since its inception.

A January 2011 report, issued jointly with the FAO and the International Labour Organization (see "ILO") pointed out that women in rural areas were suffering disproportionately from the economic downturn. Nevertheless, in February IFAD's Office of Evaluation reported that the organization had done well with its efforts to remove gender disparity. In May 2011 The United States Department of State joined with IFAD in a new initiative to assist the flow of investment from international migrants to reduce rural poverty and improve food security in their home countries. IFAD efforts continued to encourage smallholder farming as opposed to larger-scale operations, and an October 2011 report declared that agricultural cooperatives were a key to reducing hunger and poverty.

In its 2011 annual report, IFAD noted that it had increased its new grant and loan commitments to almost $1 billion for 2011, an 18 percent increase over the previous year. At year's end, IFAD had 240 ongoing projects worth $4.6 billion. In 2011 IFAD completed negotiations over its ninth replenishment, totaling $1.5 billion. The sum was expected to finance operations through 2015. The organization also announced a plan to increase its number of country offices to 40 by 2013 and a long-term goal to reduce rural the number of poor and hungry by 50 percent by 2015.

In February 2012 South Sudan became the latest UN member to join IFAD. In 2012 IFAD trained 4.8 million people in agricultural best practices, with an additional 1.5 million provided education in entrepreneurship and business management. In addition, IFAD allocated 14 percent of its portfolio to rural finance projects, and had 4.3 million borrowers, 69 percent of whom were women.

INTERNATIONAL LABOUR ORGANIZATION

(ILO)

Established: By constitution adopted April 11, 1919; instrument of amendment signed in Montreal, Canada, October 9, 1946, effective April 20, 1948. The ILO became a UN Specialized Agency by agreement with the Economic and Social Council (approved by the General Assembly on December 14, 1946).

Purpose: To promote international action aimed at achieving full employment, higher living standards, and improvement in the conditions of labor.

Headquarters: Geneva, Switzerland.

Principal Organs: International Labour Conference (all members); Governing Body (28 governmental, 14 employer, and 14 employee representatives); International Labour Office.

Web site: www.ilo.org

Director General: Guy Ryder (United Kingdom).

Membership (185): See Appendix C.

Official Languages: English, French, Spanish.

Origin and development. The International Labour Organization's original constitution, drafted by a commission representing employers, employees, and governments, formed an integral part of the 1919 post–World War I peace treaties and established the organization as an autonomous intergovernmental agency associated with the League of Nations. The ILO's tasks were significantly expanded by the 1944 International Labour Conference in Philadelphia, which declared the right of all human beings to pursue their "material well-being and their spiritual development in conditions of dignity, of economic security and equal opportunity." The Declaration of Philadelphia was subsequently appended to the ILO's revised constitution, which took effect June 28, 1948.

In 1946 the ILO became the first Specialized Agency associated with the United Nations. Since then, the organization's considerable growth has been accompanied by numerous changes in policy and geographical representation. While improved working and living conditions and the promotion of full employment remain central aims, the ILO also deals with such matters as migrant workers, child labor, the working environment, and the social consequences of globalization.

In 1970 one of the first official acts of Director General Wilfred Jenks of the United Kingdom was to appoint a Soviet assistant director general. The hostile reaction of the American Federation of Labor–Congress of Industrial Organizations (AFL-CIO) led the U.S. Congress to temporarily suspend payment of U.S. contributions to the organization. The ire of Congress and the AFL-CIO was again aroused in 1975 when the ILO granted observer status to the Palestine Liberation Organization (PLO). Finally, on November 5, 1975, the United States filed its intention to withdraw from the ILO, objecting to a growing governmental domination of workers' and employers' groups and what it considered the ILO's "appallingly selective concern" for human rights as well as other philosophical differences. On November 1, 1977, U.S. president Jimmy Carter formally announced his country's withdrawal, effective November 5. Shortly thereafter, however, U.S. secretary of labor F. Ray Marshall strongly hinted that the United States might reconsider. Thus, the Carter administration carefully watched events at subsequent annual conferences, and in February 1980 Carter announced that the United States would return to the organization.

In early 1988 the United States, after a 35-year hiatus, ratified two ILO conventions. One of the documents, relating to mandatory consultation on ILO standards, was also the first non-maritime convention it had ever endorsed. The improvement in the U.S.-ILO relationship was further underscored at the 1988 annual session of the conference when the United States expressed its "common views and interests" with the ILO.

At the 1998 ILO conference the organization adopted the Declaration on Fundamental Principles and Rights at Work, which called on members to respect the principles embodied in the ILO constitution, the Declaration of Philadelphia, and conventions on fundamental rights, even if the countries had not ratified particular conventions. Those fundamental rights encompass the abolition of forced labor, child labor, and employment discrimination, plus the right to collective bargaining and freedom of association.

Structure. The ILO is unique among international organizations in that it is based on a tripartite system of representation that includes not only governments, but also employer and employee groups.

The International Labour Conference, which meets annually, is the ILO's principal political organ; all member states are represented. Each national delegation to the conference consists of two governmental delegates, one employer delegate, and one employee delegate. Each delegate has one vote, and split votes within a delegation are common. Conference duties include approving the ILO budget, electing the Governing Body, and setting labor standards through the adoption of conventions. Most important items require a two-thirds affirmative vote.

The Governing Body normally meets three times per year. Of the 28 governmental delegates, 10 represent the "states of chief industrial importance"; the other 18 are elected for three-year terms by the governmental representatives in the conference. The 14 employer and 14 employee representatives are similarly elected by their respective caucuses. The Governing Body reviews the budget before its submission to the conference, supervises the work of the International Labour Office, appoints and reviews the work of the various industrial committees, and appoints the director general.

The International Labour Office, headed by the director general, is the secretariat of the ILO. Its responsibilities include preparing documentation for the numerous meetings of ILO bodies, compiling and publishing information on social and economic questions, conducting special studies ordered by the conference or the Governing Body, and providing requested advice and assistance to governments and to employer and employee groups.

ILO subdivisions include the following, each headed by an executive director: Standards and Fundamental Principles and Rights at Work, Employment, Social Protection, Social Dialog, Management and Administration, and Regions and Technical Cooperation (with regional offices for Africa, the Americas, Arab states, Asia and the Pacific, and Europe and Central Asia). Additional offices, programs, and institutes report directly to the director general. These include the International Institute for Labour Studies, which was founded in 1960 in Geneva. The International Training Center of the ILO, which was established in 1964 in Turin, Italy, as the International Centre for Advanced Technical and Vocational Training, initially provided residential training programs to those in charge of technical and vocational institutions, although it now offers postgraduate work and high-level in-service programs.

Activities. The ILO is charged by its constitution with advancing programs to achieve the following: full employment and higher standards of living; the employment of workers in occupations in which they can use the fullest measure of their skills and make the greatest contribution to the common well-being; the establishment of facilities for training and the transfer of labor; policies (in regard to wages, hours, and other conditions of work) calculated to ensure a just share of the fruits of progress to all; the effective recognition of the right of collective bargaining; the extension of social security benefits to all in need of such protection; the availability of comprehensive medical care; the provision of adequate nutrition, housing, and facilities for recreation and culture; and the assurance of equality of educational and vocational opportunity. In addition, the ILO has established an International Program for the Improvement of Working Conditions and Environment (*Programme International pour l'Amélioration des Conditions et du Milieu de Travail*—PIACT). PIACT activities include studies, tripartite meetings, clearing-house and operational functions, and the setting of standards.

The ILO's chief instruments for achieving its constitutional mandates are conventions and recommendations. Conventions are legal instruments open for ratification by governments; while not bound to ratify a convention adopted by the conference, member states are obligated to bring it to the attention of their national legislators and also to report periodically to the ILO on relevant aspects of their own labor law and practices. Typical ILO conventions include Hours of Work, Industry (1919); Underground Work, Women (1935); Shipowners' Liability, Sick and Injured Seamen (1936); and Abolition of Forced Labor (1957). (For an overview of conventions enacted prior to 2000, please see the 2012 *Handbook.*) Recommendations only suggest guidelines and therefore do not require ratification by the member states. In both instances, however, governments are subject to a supervisory procedure—the establishment of a commission of inquiry—that involves an objective evaluation by independent experts and an examination of cases by the ILO's tripartite bodies to ensure the conventions and recommendations are being applied. There is also a widely used special procedure whereby the Governing Body investigates alleged governmental violations of trade unionists' right to "freedom of association."

A number of recent ILO reports and actions have been more controversial. A 2000 report on labor rights listed Oman, Saudi Arabia, and the United Arab Emirates as states barring labor unions, and cited Bahrain and Qatar for imposing severe restrictions. The report also discussed the cases of murdered trade unionists in Colombia, the Dominican Republic, Ecuador, Guatemala, and Indonesia, and noted that arrests and detentions had recently occurred in more than 20 other countries.

On November 16, 2000, in an unprecedented action, the ILO Governing Body urged member states and fellow UN agencies to apply sanctions against Myanmar (Burma) for its continued use of forced labor and threatened to send its dossiers to the International Criminal Court to prosecute members of the ruling junta. The 1999 conference had already barred Myanmar from participating in ILO sessions and programs. Estimates suggested 800,000 or more Myanmar workers might have been forced to work in agriculture and construction by the country's military regime. The ILO's demands for basic labor rights in Myanmar continued in 2007 when the ILO won a concession from the government to allow victims of forced labor to bring complaints to the agency without retaliatory action. The 12-month trial agreement postponed legal sanctions even as the Commission on Inquiry noted at the June 2007 ILO conference that none of its recommendations to Myanmar on stemming forced labor had been implemented.

The *World Employment Report 2001,* published in January 2001, examined "Life at Work in the Information Economy." It saw "hopeful signs" that new information technology would have a positive effect on employment despite a "digital divide" not only between developed and developing countries, but within even the most technologically sophisticated societies. The report also projected that 500 million additional jobs would be needed during the next decade to reduce by half global unemployment while keeping up with the flow of new workers into the labor force. In 2004 the ILO began investigating Belarus for impeding workers' rights to establish independent trade union organizations and formed 12 recommendations with a June 2005 compliance deadline. After continued violations of workers' freedom of association, the European Union (EU) in June 2007 withdrew Belarus from the union's generalized system of trade preferences—thereby forcing certain manufacturers to pay higher export tariffs to EU countries—in an effort to force ILO compliance. This situation still existed in late 2011, although Belarus remained in negotiations with the ILO to gain compliance.

In February 2004, two years after being launched by the ILO, the World Commission on the Social Dimension of Globalization released its final report. Having been established to consider how economic, social, and environmental objectives could be combined while spreading the benefits of globalization to all, the commission warned of "deep-seated and persistent imbalances in the current workings of the global economy, which are ethically unacceptable and politically unsustainable." It claimed "wealth is being created, but too many countries and people are not sharing in its benefits." As a consequence, the world risked "a slide into further spirals of insecurity, political turbulence, conflicts and wars." Chaired by the presidents of Finland and Tanzania, the commission echoed the ILO's call for "decent work" as a global goal.

The report led to the ILO adopting the Decent Work Agenda, which serves as a framework within the agency and in its international policy goals to discuss and define adequate working conditions, rights, and opportunities. Since 2005 the agenda has included decent work programs in many member states to support initiatives and laws that better working conditions, and international forums have been hosted on a number of related topics, such as globalization and working conditions in African and Asian states. The agenda has also served as a basis for declarations of support by such international bodies as the Group of Eight, which promised in June 2007 to use "decent work" and ILO labor standards in bilateral trade agreements. Earlier in the year, the ILO and the United Nations Development Program signed an agreement to coordinate development efforts toward decent work policy goals.

Delegates to the 92nd International Labour Conference, held June 1–19, 2004, continued to debate the social and economic consequences of globalization. They also maintained the ILO's recent emphasis on children by focusing on child domestic labor.

The 95th conference, held May 31–June 16, 2006, focused on occupational health and safety, violence in the workplace, and, again, on the changes wrought by globalization. The 96th conference, held May 30–June 15, 2007, was named the Work in Fishing Convention and ended with the adoption of standards promoting medical care at sea and social security protection for fishing industry workers. Speaking at the 97th conference, held June 9–13, 2008, Director General Somavía called for urgent measures to address "globalization without social justice." In September 2008 the ILO issued a more hopeful report entitled "Green Jobs: Towards Decent Work in a Sustainable, Low-Carbon World." This report said that the emerging green economy could create "tens of millions of new green jobs."

The organization celebrated its 90th anniversary in April 2009 against what Director General Somavía called "the frightening backdrop of the crisis with rising unemployment and underemployment, business closures, deteriorating conditions of work, growing inequality, poverty and insecurity, and the undermining of respect for rights at work." The ILO warned against a crippling worldwide rise in the rate of unemployment, also stating that the crisis was partly responsible for a global rise in human trafficking and forced labor. An ILO report stated that forced labor was present in the supply chain of virtually every country, advanced or not.

The 98th conference, held June 3–19, 2009, adopted a Global Jobs Pact, which called on all concerned to respond to the crisis, and promote recovery from it, in a way that would advance decent and humane working conditions. In October 2009 the ILO and the World Trade Organization (WTO, see separate article) jointly issued a report titled *Globalisation and Informal Jobs in Developing Countries*. This report pointed out an increase in the informal workforce as a result of unfettered free trade and marked a step toward the ILO and WTO cooperating in new ways. Previously, the ILO dealt exclusively with workforce issues and the WTO with matters of trade. The ILO's position in late 2009 was that, for the majority of the world's workers at least, the crisis was far from over.

In a 2010 report sponsored by the ILO entitled *Trade and Employment in the Global Crisis,* the authors note that real wages declined globally even for those workers who were able to retain their jobs. This finding was underscored by the ILO's *Global Employment Trends,* which found that unemployment had also reached its highest level ever, at 212 million in 2009 (6.6 percent of the world's labor force), an increase of 34 million over the prior year. Unemployment grew most in the EU, rising to 8.4 percent from 6 percent, and Latin America and the Caribbean, up to 8.2 percent from 7 percent. In June the ILO removed Colombia from its list of states that failed to meet international labor standards.

In November 2010 the ILO experienced a strike by its own staff in Geneva. The staff union complained about censored communications and interference with rights of association. Director-general Somavía agreed to outside mediation, and matters were resolved. In December the publication "Global Wage Report 2010/11—Wage policies in times of crisis" stated that the economic crisis had cut growth of wages in half worldwide.

In January 2011 the organization warned that the global recovery was not translating into jobs and that world unemployment remained at a record 205 million. But in February it reported that sub-Saharan Africa, on which it had not been able to gain reliable statistics for several years, had outperformed even the most advanced economies, achieving a wage growth of 6.5 percent between 2004 and 2008—well above the global average of 4.5 percent.

The ILO held its 100th annual meeting June 15–17, 2011, amid calls for a "new era of social justice." In particular, it adopted a new set of labor standards that, for the first time, covered domestic workers. On September 30, 2011, Somavía announced that, for family reasons, he would leave office one year from that date, a few months ahead of schedule.

In its *Global Employment Trends 2012: Preventing a Deeper Jobs Crisis,* the ILO reported that since the global economic crisis began in 2007, more than 27 million people had lost their jobs. To reduce current unemployment and accommodate new workers entering the labor force, 400 million new jobs would have to be created by 2022. However, the employment-to-population ratio has declined from 61.2 percent in 2007 to 60.2 percent in 2010 as businesses have increased productivity and reduced the need for new workers, a trend expected to continue into the near future.

On October 1, 2012, Guy Ryder of the United Kingdom was elected to replace Somavia as director general of the ILO. Once in office, Ryder launched an ambitious program to reform the ILO's administrative structure. The reforms streamlined decision-making by reducing the overall size of the administrationand reduced redundancies. To oversee the effort, a deputy director general for management and reform was appointed. In 2013 the ILO warned of a "scarred generation" of youth who were unable to find adequate employment. In 2012 more than 73 million youth worldwide (12.6 percent of the population) were unemployed, an increase of 3.5 million since 2007.

INTERNATIONAL MARITIME ORGANIZATION

(IMO)

Established: March 17, 1958, as the Inter-Governmental Maritime Consultative Organization (IMCO) on the basis of a convention opened for signature on March 6, 1948. IMCO became a UN Specialized Agency as authorized by a General Assembly resolution of November 18, 1948, with the present designation being assumed on May 22, 1982, upon entry into force of amendments to the IMCO convention.

Purpose: To facilitate cooperation among governments "in the field of governmental regulation and practices relating to technical matters of all kinds affecting shipping engaged in international trade; to encourage the general adoption of the highest practicable standards in matters concerning maritime safety, efficiency of navigation and the prevention and control of marine pollution from ships; and to deal with legal matters" related to its purposes.

Headquarters: London, United Kingdom.

Principal Organs: Assembly, Council (40 members), Legal Committee, Maritime Safety Committee, Marine Environment Protection Committee, Technical Cooperation Committee, Secretariat.

Web site: www.imo.org

Secretary General: Koji Sekimizu (Japan).

Membership (170, plus 3 Associate Members): See Appendix C.

Official Languages: Arabic, Chinese, English, French, Russian, Spanish.

Working Languages: English, French, Spanish.

Origin and development. Preparations for the establishment of the Inter-Governmental Maritime Consultative Organization were initiated shortly after World War II but were not completed for well over a decade. Meeting in Washington, D.C., in 1946 at the request of the UN Economic and Social Council, representatives of a group of maritime states prepared a draft convention that was further elaborated at the UN Maritime Conference held in early 1948 in Geneva, Switzerland. Despite the strictly limited objectives set forth in the convention, the pace of ratification was slow, primarily because some signatory states were apprehensive about possible international interference in their shipping policies. Canada accepted the convention in 1948 and the U.S. Senate approved it in 1950, but the necessary 21 ratifications were not completed until Japan deposited its ratification on March 17, 1958. Additional difficulties developed at the first IMCO Assembly, held January 1959 in London, England, due to claims by Panama and Liberia that, as "major shipowning nations," they were eligible for election to the Maritime Safety Committee. Panama and Liberia were widely regarded as "flags of convenience" for shipowners wishing to avoid more serious regulation elsewhere. An affirmative ruling by the International Court of Justice paved the way for a resolution of the issue at the second IMCO Assembly, held in 1961.

The thrust of IMCO activities during its first decade involved maritime safety, particularly in regard to routing schemes. Adherence was voluntary until 1977, when the Convention on the International Regulations for Preventing Collisions at Sea (1972) went into force. In 1979 the (1974) International Convention on the Safety of Life at Sea (SOLAS), specifying minimum safety standards for ship construction, equipment, and operation, received the final ratification needed to bring it into force, effective May 1980.

Problems of maritime pollution were the subject of a November 1968 special session of the assembly, which led to the establishment of the Legal Committee and the scheduling of the first of several major conferences on marine pollution. In 1978 sufficient ratifications were finally received for the 1969 amendments to the International Convention for the Prevention of Pollution of the Sea by Oil (1954) to come into force, while the International Convention on Civil Liability for Oil Pollution Damage (1969) and the International Convention on the Establishment of an International Fund for Compensation for Oil Pollution Damage (1971) entered into force in 1975 and 1978, respectively. In January 1986 amendments formulated in 1984 to the International Convention for the Prevention of Pollution from Ships (1973), as modified by a 1978 protocol, became binding. This treaty is regarded as the most important in the area of maritime pollution as it is concerned with both accidents and spills resulting from normal tanker operations.

By 1974 the tasks of the organization had so expanded beyond those originally envisioned that the assembly proposed a number of amendments to the original IMCO convention, including a new statement of purpose and a new name, the International Maritime Organization (IMO).

Of importance in the area of maritime travel and transport was the entry into force in 1979 of a convention establishing the International Maritime Satellite Organization (Inmarsat). Inmarsat faced increasing competition from the private sector for satellite communication services, and became private itself in 1999. It was later renamed the International Mobile Satellite Organization (IMSO); the IMO retains oversight and enforcement powers over the IMSO.

A new procedure was introduced in 1986 to facilitate the adoption of most amendments to conventions. Originally, positive action by two-thirds of the contracting parties to a convention was required. Under the new "tacit acceptance" procedure, amendments are deemed to be accepted if less than one-third take negative action for a period generally set at two years (in no case less than one), assuming that rejections are not forthcoming from parties whose combined fleets represent 50 percent of the world's gross tonnage of merchant ships.

In 1988 the IMO approved the Convention for the Suppression of Unlawful Acts against the Safety of Maritime Navigation, promoted by several countries directly or indirectly affected by the hijacking of the Italian cruise ship *Achille Lauro* in 1985. It came into effect in 1992.

Structure. The IMO Assembly, in which all member states are represented and have an equal vote, is the principal policymaking body of the organization. Meeting in regular session every two years (occasional extraordinary sessions are also held), the assembly decides upon the work program of the IMO, approves the budget, elects the members of the Council, and approves the appointment of the secretary general. The IMO Council normally meets twice a year and is responsible, between sessions of the assembly, for performing all IMO functions except those under the purview of the Maritime Safety Committee (MSC) and the Marine Environment Protection Committee (MEPC). The Facilitation Committee, which is primarily concerned with reducing documentation requirements for port entry and departure, became a formally institutionalized Committee of the Organization only in January 2009, although its origins go back to 1972 as a subsidiary committee of the council.

There are currently 40 members on the IMO Council, comprising three groups: 10 members representing "states with the largest interest in providing international shipping services," 10 having "the largest interest in providing international seaborne trade," and 20 elected from other countries with "a special interest in maritime transport and navigation and whose election... will ensure the representation of all major geographic areas of the world."

The organization's technical work is largely carried out by the following seven subcommittees of the MSC and the MEPC: Human Element, Training, and Watchkeeping, Implemention of IMO Instruments, Navigation, Communications, and Search and Rescue, Pollution Prevention and Response, Ship Design and Construction, Ship Systems and Equipment, and Carriage of Cargoes and Containers.

The IMO's Technical Cooperation Committee provides training and advisory services to help developing countries establish and operate their maritime programs in conformity with international standards. Such activities are often linked to UN Development Program (UNDP) projects and to the World Maritime University, established by the IMO in Malmö, Sweden, in 1983 to train high-level administrative and technical personnel. In 1988 the IMO inaugurated the International Maritime Law Institute at the University of Malta. By 2013 the IMO had five regional coordinators, in Côte d'Ivoire, Ghana, Kenya, Philippines, and Trinidad and Tobago.

Activities. The IMO's programs fall under five major rubrics: maritime safety, technical training and assistance, marine pollution, facilitation of maritime travel and transport, and legal efforts to establish an international framework of maritime cooperation. In most of these areas, IMO activity is primarily devoted to extensive negotiation, review, and revision of highly technical conventions, recommendations, and guidelines. The IMO also regulates unique and permanent identification numbers on commercial ships, although the identification and assigning of numbers is maintained by the company Lloyd's Register-Fairplay in the United Kingdom. An IMO regulation that took effect in 2009 mandates unique identification numbers for shipping companies and registered owners.

On February 1, 1992, the Global Maritime Distress and Safety System (GMDSS), adopted in 1988 as an amendment to the 1974 SOLAS Convention, entered into force. Hailed by the IMO as the "biggest change to communications at sea since the introduction of the radio," the GMDSS requires the use of satellite communications during international voyages undertaken by ocean-going ships of 300 gross tons or more. Fully implemented as of February 1999, the GMDSS was intended to eliminate outdated radiotelegraphy or radiotelephony technology for transmitting location and distress information.

In mid-1993 an amendment to the 1973 convention on pollution from ships went into effect that requires new oil tankers to be fitted with double hulls or some other equally secure method of protecting the cargo. Under an amendment approved by the MEPC in December 2003, in part because of the sinking of the oil tanker *Prestige* off the coast of Spain in November 2002, virtually all single-hull tankers were to be phased out by 2010.

Concern was expressed at the 18th IMO Assembly meeting, held October–November 1993 in London, that some shipowners were neglecting appropriate repairs and maintenance for economic reasons. Secretary General William A. O'Neil of Canada, who was reelected at the meeting for a second four-year term, urged governments, particularly those that provided "flags of convenience" to ships from other nations, to enforce IMO regulations vigorously so that international standards would not be jeopardized. In what appeared to be a related matter, Liberia, which registers more ship tonnage than any other nation, was rebuffed in its attempt to win a seat on the IMO Council.

In 1995 significant new design requirements were proposed for "roll-on, roll-off" ferries (ships where vehicles enter through large doors at one end and leave through similar doors at the other) by an expert panel appointed to investigate the September 1994 capsizing of the ferry *Estonia,* in which 859 people died. In November 1995 the IMO approved a somewhat diluted version of the new "roll-on, roll-off" safety standards, while asking national governments to adopt even stricter controls on a voluntary basis.

In 1996 the International Convention on Salvage (1989) entered into force, and the IMO adopted the International Convention on Liability and Compensation for Damage in Connection with the Carriage of Hazardous and Noxious Substances (HNS) by Sea. The allied HNS Protocol on Preparedness, Response, and Cooperation to Pollution Incidents was approved in 2000. In 2001 the International Convention on the Control of Harmful Anti-fouling Systems on Ships was opened for ratification, as was the International Convention on Civil Liability for Bunker Oil Pollution Damage. In February 2004 the IMO adopted the International Convention for the Control and Management of Ships' Ballast Water and Sediments. By October 2010, 27 countries had ratified the convention. Meanwhile, the Convention on the Removal of Wrecks in May 2007 resulted in a set of uniform international rules to ensure the prompt and effective removal of shipwrecks beyond and within territorial waters, including making shipowners financially liable for wreck removal by requiring they post a form of financial security.

The November 19–30, 2001, assembly session was dominated by a renewed emphasis on security occasioned by the September 11, 2001, al-Qaida assaults on the United States. During the next year the MSC and its inter-sessional working group rapidly prepared measures designed to tighten ship and port security, and at the December 9–13, 2002, Conference of Contracting Governments to the 1974 SOLAS Convention the delegates, meeting at IMO headquarters, approved a series of major amendments. These included adoption of the new International Ship and Port Facility Security Code (ISPS Code) specifying mandatory security requirements for governments, port authorities, and shipping companies, and various nonmandatory guidelines for meeting those requirements. Earlier in the month the MSC had adopted additional SOLAS amendments to improve the safety of bulk carriers.

The 23rd session of the assembly, which met November 24–December 5, 2003, endorsed establishment of a voluntary audit scheme intended to promote safety and environmental protection by determining member state compliance with convention standards. The assembly also adopted new guidelines on refuge for ships needing assistance when lives were not at risk, approved guidelines on ship recycling, and confirmed the appointment of Efthimios Mitropoulos of Greece as successor to Secretary General William O'Neill, who had served in that capacity for 14 years.

The 24th session of the assembly, meeting November 21–December 2, 2005, called on member states to use naval and air forces to combat piracy off the coast of Somalia. It endorsed continuation and expansion of the long-term antipiracy effort which had begun in 1998. To that end the IMO contributed towards the May 2006 opening of an antipiracy center in Mombasa, Kenya. As the Somali piracy problem continued into 2007, the IMO and the World Food Program issued a joint call for the UN Security Council to arrange for foreign naval ships to patrol the coastline.

On July 1, 2006, a new convention came into force regarding treatment of people rescued at sea. This convention was partly inspired by the increasing number of people attempting to migrate in overcrowded, unseaworthy boats, and, among other things, it spells out a ship captain's absolute responsibility to rescue people whose lives are in danger, irrespective of the wishes of the ship's owner.

In recent years, the IMO has also shown increased concern for the shipping industry's impact on global climate change. In May 2000 the IMO prohibited the use of toxic fluorocarbons on board ships. Also in 2000 the IMO published a study on the contribution of ships to global warming emissions that identified options for ship design changes to reduce those emissions. Interim guidelines on carbon dioxide indexing were approved by the MEPC in 2005.

In November 2007 the IMO participated in a UN Security Council committee meeting on boosting border security and detecting illegal arms shipments to better deal with terrorist threats. The meeting resulted in plans to streamline information sharing and coordination between member organizations on border control and security matters.

The IMO has also changed shipping routes in recent years in an effort to preserve ocean wildlife, including labeling a basin off the coast of Nova Scotia as an "area to be avoided" seasonally by commercial shipping in order to protect the endangered right whale.

In 2008 the IMO began to implement a satellite tracking system, the Long Range Information and Tracking (LRIT) of Vessels, to reduce collisions and serve as a rescue tool. All ships constructed after December 31, 2008, are mandated to include the system, and it is being phased in for earlier vessels.

The most serious matter before the IMO, and the shipping community as a whole, in 2008 was piracy. This menace reemerged in the waters off Southeast Asia and Indonesia, and particularly off the coasts of Nigeria and East Africa. Most attacks were launched from Somalia, and according to the IMO roughly 80 percent of world food assistance to that country arrived by sea. Because of pirate attacks, the number of ships willing to deliver food to Somalia had declined by half in 2007.

In April 2008 the IMO states of East Africa began working on a regional agreement for patrol of their seas. In the meantime Western naval forces continue to guard the region. In June the IMO welcomed a Security Council resolution allowing foreign ships to enter Somali waters at will in pursuit of pirates. In September Yemen announced plans to build a regional antipiracy center to assist ships attacked by pirates, but some observers complained that the world's navies were not doing enough about the problem. Another problem facing the world's shippers in 2008 was a lack of crew, particularly of officers. In November 2008 the IMO announced a "Go to Sea" campaign, in cooperation with the ILO and private industry groups, to encourage recruitment into the merchant marine and to improve the industry's image.

On March 2, 2009, the IMO launched a partnership between itself, the UN Development Programme (UNDP), and several large shipping companies to tackle the problem of marine bio-invasions caused by the transfer of alien plants and animals in ships' ballast tanks.

The Hong Kong International Convention for the Safe and Environmentally Sound Recycling of Ships, 2009, was adopted at a conference held there in May 2009. The convention was felt to be of added importance because the worldwide recession was causing more ships to be retired and broken up. On July 27, 2009, the MPEC produced a package of energy efficiency measures for ships but could not come to a decision about raising the cost of ships' fuel and using the money to help poor nations tackle climate change.

The IMO budget for 2010–2011 (the latest available) is $94.5 million and its staff number just over 300. In June 2010 the IMOP announced that it was awarding the 2009 International Maritime Prize to Johan Franson of Sweden who served as chairman of the IMO council from 2005–2009. Also in 2010 the IMO announced its support for a new code for ships that transverse polar regions and called on its member states to adopt the measure. In its annual summary of piracy and maritime armed robbery for 2009, the IMO reported that the number of incidents had increased to 406, a 24.6 percent increase over the previous year. The greatest rise in attacks occurred in East Asia and Asia. In East Africa alone, the number of acts of piracy increased from 134 to 222. More than 770 crew members were taken hostage during the year, with 8 killed, 59 wounded, and 32 missing. The IMO also reported that despite a rise in shipping, the number of vessels lost to accidents or negligence fell to its lowest level on record.

Piracy and environmental concerns dominated the IMO's attention in 2011. In January the UN Secretary-general's special adviser on piracy even declared that the pirates were winning. Pirates' technological and business sophistication was increasingly a match for their victims. Moreover, 90 percent of all pirates captured by national navies were released because no states were prepared to accept them and no jurisdiction was prepared to prosecute them. In February the IMO stated that an unacceptably high proportion of ships sailing across the Gulf of Aden and the western Indian Ocean were not following IMO anti-piracy best practices. Such ships "are not registered with the Maritime Security Centre Horn of Africa; are not reporting to United Kingdom Maritime Trade Operations (UKMTO) Dubai; show no visible deterrent measures and are not acting upon the navigational warnings to shipping promulgating details of pirate attacks and suspect vessels." In March 2011 the United Arab Emirates signed on to the IMO anti-piracy code. In September the IMO issued new guidelines for the employment of armed private contractors aboard merchant ships—a practice that it recognized, but did not fully endorse.

On June 28, 2011, Koji Sekimizu of Japan was elected secretary general of the organization, to take office at the end of the year, when the term of Efthimios Mitropoulos expired. In July the IMO published, for the first time, energy efficiency standards for global shipping. The fuels used by large vessels are some of the world's dirtiest. On September 8 Palau became the organization's 170th member state.

In May 2012 the IMO signed a range of new antipiracy cooperation agreements with other UN agencies and the EU. The agreements included intelligence sharing and joint efforts to enhance antipiracy capabilities of countries around the Horn of Africa. In June Mozambique became the 20th state to sign the IMO's antipiracy code. Meanwhile, Indonesia announced it would ratify several IMO conventions, including the International Convention on Search and Rescue and the accord on the Prevention of Pollution from Ships. The IMO budget for 2012 was $48.8 million. The top contributors to the IMO in 2012, based on the tonnage of their merchant fleets, were Panama, Liberia, the Marshall Islands, and the United Kingdom.

Amendments to the 1978 International Convention on Standards of Training, Certification and Watchkeeping for Seafarers(STCW) which had been approved in 1995, came into force in 2012, following the adoption by the requisite number of parties. By 2013, 157 parties had signed the STCW, representing more than 99 percent of the world's merchant ships. In 2013, internal reforms consolidated and reduced the number of subcommittees of the MSC and MEPC from nine to seven groups. The IMO budget for 2013 was $50.7 million.

INTERNATIONAL MONETARY FUND

(IMF)

Established: By Articles of Agreement signed at Bretton Woods, New Hampshire, United States, July 22, 1944, effective December 27, 1945; formal operations began March 1, 1947. The IMF became a UN Specialized Agency by agreement with the Economic and Social Council (approved by the General Assembly on November 15, 1947).

Purpose: "To promote international monetary cooperation through a permanent institution which provides the machinery for consultation and collaboration on international monetary problems. To facilitate the expansion and balanced growth of international trade, and to contribute thereby to the promotion and maintenance of high levels of employment and real income and to the development of the productive resources of all members as primary objectives of economic policy. To promote exchange stability, to maintain orderly exchange arrangements among members, and to avoid competitive depreciation. To assist in the establishment of a multilateral system of payments in respect of current transactions between members and in the elimination of foreign exchange restrictions which hamper the growth of world trade. To give confidence to members by making the Fund's resources temporarily available to them under adequate safeguards, thus providing them with the opportunity to correct maladjustments in their balance of payments without resorting to measures destructive of national or international prosperity... [and] to shorten the duration and lessen the degree of disequilibrium in the international balance of payments of members."

Headquarters: Washington, D.C., United States.

Principal Organs: Board of Governors (all members), Board of Executive Directors (25 members [24 elected by member countries or groups of countries plus the IMF managing director, who serves as chair of the board]), International Monetary and Financial Committee (24 members), Managing Director and Staff.

Web site: www.imf.org

Managing Director: Christine Lagarde (France).

Membership (188): See Appendix C.

Origin and development. The International Monetary Fund is one of the two key institutions that emerged from the July 1–22, 1944, UN Monetary and Financial Conference in Bretton Woods, New Hampshire: the International Bank for Reconstruction and Development (IBRD) was established to mobilize and invest available capital resources for the reconstruction of war-damaged areas and for the promotion of general economic development where private capital was lacking; the IMF was created with the complementary objectives of safeguarding international financial and monetary stability and of providing financial backing for the revival and expansion of international trade.

Following ratification by the required 28 states, the Articles of Agreement of the bank and fund went into effect December 27, 1945, and formal IMF operations commenced March 1, 1947, under the guidance of Managing Director Camille Gutt (Belgium). While the membership of the IMF expanded rapidly over the next three decades, most communist countries, including the Soviet Union, remained nonmembers. However, the pressures of external debt to the West mounted rapidly for some participants in the Soviet-bloc Council for Mutual Economic Assistance (CMEA) in the late 1970s, and in 1981 Hungary and Poland, both CMEA members, applied for IMF membership (Romania was previously the only Eastern European participant). Hungary became a member in 1982, but Poland's admission was deferred pending resolution of questions regarding its existing debt and international payment obligations. In December 1984 the United States, with the largest proportion of voting power, lifted all objections concerning Poland, thus opening the way for its entry in June 1986. Angola joined in 1989, while Bulgaria, Czechoslovakia, and Namibia joined in 1990. Mongolia joined in 1991.

In a move that surprised many observers, the Soviet Union formally applied for IMF membership in July 1991. In conjunction with the World Bank, the IMF in October approved a special associate status for the USSR, but the action proved of little practical consequence as the country's dissolution occurred shortly thereafter. In 1992 the IMF offered regular membership to the former Soviet republics, all of which were admitted by September 1993. In December 1992 the IMF's Board of Executive Directors declared Bosnia and Herzegovina, Croatia, Macedonia, Slovenia, and the new Federal Republic of Yugoslavia to be successors to the assets and liabilities of the former Socialist Federal Republic of Yugoslavia and established their respective shares. In January 1993 the board made a similar ruling regarding the former Czechoslovakia. Membership was quickly approved for the Czech Republic, Slovakia, Croatia, Macedonia, and Slovenia, but unsettled conditions in Bosnia and Herzegovina postponed its membership until December 1995. In addition, it took until December 2000 for the board to conclude that the rump Federal Republic of Yugoslavia had fulfilled the necessary requirements to become a member. Montenegro joined the IMF in 2007, followed by Kosovo in 2009, and Tuvalu in 2010.

The development of the IMF has occurred in four phases, the first spanning from Bretton Woods until about 1957. Under the managing directorships of Camille Gutt and Ivor Rooth (Sweden), the fund was seldom in the news, and its activity, in the form of "drawings" or borrowings, was light. During much of this period, the U.S. Marshall Plan was providing the needed balance-of-payments support to the states of Europe because the IMF lacked the capital to perform such a massive task.

At the end of 1956, when Per Jacobsson (Sweden) was named managing director, the fund entered a more active phase, the outstanding example being large drawings by the United Kingdom, partly as a result of the 1956–1957 Suez crisis.

The third phase of development can be dated from Jacobsson's death in 1963. His successor, Pierre-Paul Schweitzer (France), managed the IMF during a period in which its activities were directed increasingly toward the needs of developing states. Also, by the mid-1960s the need for reform of the international monetary system had become more evident. Thus, beginning in 1965, the IMF became increasingly involved in talks regarding the creation of additional "international liquidity" to supplement existing resources for financing trade. Discussion between the Group of Ten (see separate entry) and the fund's executive directors led in 1967 to the development of a plan for creating new international reserves through the establishment of special drawing rights (SDRs) over and above the drawing rights already available to fund members. In general, SDRs may be allocated to IMF members proportionate to their IMF quotas, subject to restrictions relating to the allocation and use of such rights.

The U.S. suspension of the convertibility of the dollar into gold in August 1971 compounded the previous need for reform. By 1972 many states were "floating" their currencies and thus fundamentally violating the rules of the fund, which were based on a system of fixed exchange rates normally pegged to the U.S. gold price. That year, the United States decided not to support Schweitzer's reelection bid, largely because of his outspoken criticism of the U.S. failure to "set its own economic house in order" and control its balance-of-payments deficits.

When H. Johannes Witteveen (Netherlands) took over as managing director in 1973, his chief task was to continue reform of the international monetary system while enhancing the role of the IMF. Consequently, Witteveen proposed creation of an IMF oil facility that was established in June 1974 and served, in effect, as a separate borrowing window through which members could cover that portion of their balance-of-payments deficits attributable to higher imported oil prices. This facility provided 55 members with SDR 802 million until its termination in 1976. Three months later the fund set up an "extended facility" to aid those members with payments problems attributable to structural difficulties in their economies. In addition, as part of the accords reached at the January 1976 session of the Interim Committee, one-sixth of the fund's gold was auctioned for the benefit of less developed countries. The sales, which began in June 1976, continued until April 1980, with profits of $1.3 billion transferred directly to 104 countries and with another $3.3 billion placed in a trust fund to assist poorer countries. The final loan disbursement from the fund upon the latter's discontinuance in March 1981 yielded a cumulative total of SDR 2.9 billion committed to 55 members. Trust fund repayments have subsequently been used to support other IMF assistance programs.

Another plateau was reached when, at the end of April 1976, the Board of Governors approved its most comprehensive package of monetary reforms since the IMF's establishment. Taking the form of a second amendment to the Articles of Agreement, the reforms entered into force April 1, 1978. Their effect was to legalize the system of "floating" exchange arrangements, end the existing system of par values based on gold, and impose upon members an obligation to collaborate with the fund and with each other in order to promote better surveillance of international liquidity. In addition, the requirement that gold be paid into the fund was lifted.

The fourth phase of development was initiated with the entrance into office on June 17, 1978, of Jacques de Larosière (France). Aided by a massive increase in IMF funds, Larosière addressed the major problems of the fund's members: burdensome debts for non-oil- producing developing countries, inflation and stagnant economic growth among the developed members, and balance-of- payments disequilibria for virtually all. In order to assist the non-oil-producing third world countries, the fund further liberalized its "compensatory facility" (established in 1963) for financing temporary export shortfalls, extended standby arrangements through the creation in 1979 of a "supplementary financing facility," and expanded the activities of the trust fund to provide additional credits on concessional terms.

To support the drain on its resources, the IMF has relied on periodic quota increases; the Eighth General Review of Quotas came into effect in January 1984 and additional increases were also approved in 1990, 1997, and 2009 (see "Activities").

Structure. The IMF operates through the IMF Board of Governors, the IMF Board of Executive Directors, the International Monetary and Financial Committee (known until September 1999 as the Interim Committee on the International Monetary System), and a managing director and staff of some 2,600 persons. Upon joining the fund, each country is assigned a quota that determines both the amount of foreign exchange a member may borrow under the rules of the fund (its "drawing rights") and its approximate voting power on IMF policy matters. As of 2012 the largest contributor, the United States, had 16.47 percent of the voting power, while the smallest contributors held considerably less than 1 percent each.

The Board of Governors, in which all powers of the fund are theoretically vested, consists of one governor and one alternate appointed by each member state. In practice, its membership is virtually identical to that of the Board of Governors of the IBRD, and its annual meetings are actually joint sessions (which similarly include the governing boards of the International Development Association and the International Finance Corporation). One meeting in three is held away from Washington, D.C.

The Board of Executive Directors, which has 25 members (including the managing director as chair) generally meets at least once a week and is responsible for day-to-day operations; its powers are delegated to it by the Board of Governors. Each of the five members having the largest quotas (currently the United States, the United Kingdom, Germany, France, and Japan) appoints a director. Appointment privilege is also extended to each of the two largest lenders to the fund, providing they are not among the countries with the five largest quotas. Consequently, Saudi Arabia, the largest lender, has appointed a director since 1978. The other directors are elected biennially by the remaining IMF members, who are divided into 18 geographic groupings, each of which selects one director. (China and Russia constitute geographic entities by themselves and therefore the "election" by each of a director, in practical terms, amounts to an appointment.) Each elected director casts as a unit all the votes of the states that elected him.

The managing director, who is appointed by the Board of Executive Directors and serves as its chair, conducts the ordinary business of the fund and supervises the staff. In the first major management restructuring since 1949, the number of deputy managing directors was increased from one to three in 1994.

There are several other ministerial-level committees and groups that routinely interact with the fund, usually in conjunction with joint IMF-World Bank sessions. One is the Development Committee, which was established in 1974 by the IMF and the World Bank to report on the global development process and to make recommendations to promote the transfer of real resources to developing countries. The committee, whose structure mirrors that of the Interim Committee, generally issues extensive communiqués prior to IMF–World Bank meetings.

Regular statements are similarly issued by the Group of Ten, the Group of Seven, and the Group of 24. The latter group, which receives secretariat support from the fund, represents the interests of the developing countries in negotiations on international monetary matters.

Activities. The IMF's central activity is to assist members in overcoming short-term balance-of-payments difficulties by permitting them to draw temporarily upon the fund's reserves, subject to established limits and conditions with respect to the amount of drawing rights, terms of repayment, etc. Assistance may take the form of standby credits (credits approved in advance), which may or may not be fully utilized. A member can also arrange to buy the currency of another member from the fund in exchange for its own.

A second major IMF responsibility has been to supervise the operation of the international exchange-rate system in order to maintain stability among the world currencies and prevent competitive devaluations. In part because stable exchange-rate patterns depend on economic stability, particularly the containment of inflationary pressures, the fund since 1952 has regularly consulted with member states about their economic problems, the formulation and implementation of economic stabilization programs, and the preparation of requests for standby IMF assistance.

In the area of assistance to less developed states, the fund participates in many of the consultative groups and consortia organized by the IBRD. It also conducts a separate program of technical assistance—largely with reference to banking and fiscal problems—utilizing its own staff and outside experts through a training program organized by the IMF Institute at Washington, D.C.

Beginning in the early 1980s, the fund encountered growing demands from the developing world for reform in its procedures. In particular, a number of states objected to the imposition of the IMF's so-called standard package of conditionality, which often required, for example, that a country reduce consumer imports, devalue its currency, and tighten domestic money supplies in return for standby credit. Subsequently, the issue continued to be a constant center of controversy for the IMF. Non-oil-producing developing countries struggling under massive balance-of-payments deficits called for greater fund access but with fewer domestically unpopular restrictive conditions attached. At the same time, industrialized countries, adversely affected by high unemployment, inflation, and economic stagnation, demanded stricter structural adjustment clauses and called for increased reliance on the private sector as a source of aid and development capital for all but the poorest of the developing countries.

With the third world's debt crisis worsening, the Board of Governors in October 1985 approved the creation of the Structural Adjustment Facility (SAF) to provide low-income countries with concessional loans in support of national policy changes designed to resolve persistent balance of payments problems. The SAF, funded by SDR 2.7 billion in reflows from the discontinued trust fund, was formally established in March 1986, offering ten-year loans with a 0.5 percent interest charge and a five-and-one-half-year grace period Pressure for further IMF initiatives continued throughout 1986 and 1987. (For more information, please see the *Political Handbook of the World 2012*.)

Soon after his appointment as IMF managing director in January 1987, Michel Camdessus called for a complete review of IMF conditionality and a tripling of SAF funding. Following endorsement of the latter at the October 1987 joint IMF-World Bank annual meeting, the fund announced the establishment of an Enhanced Structural Adjustment Facility (ESAF) funded by SDR 6 billion from 20 countries, led by Japan (SDR 2.8 billion) and West Germany (SDR 1 billion), but not including the United States. The new facility generally offered the same terms and followed the same procedures as the SAF. (In February 1994 the IMF launched an enlarged and extended ESAF; in late 1999 the ESAF was renamed the Poverty Reduction and Growth Facility [PRGF] and given an expanded mandate to include poverty reduction and promotion of sustainable development.)

The April 1988 interim committee meeting approved additional changes, including the launching of an external contingency mechanism to assist borrowers in case of external "shocks" such as collapsing commodity prices or higher interest rates in world markets. However, borrowers facing unforeseen sharp drops in export earnings were required to engage in rigorous domestic action to qualify for the new relief program.

By the time of the joint annual meeting with the World Bank held September 1988 in West Berlin, a consensus was emerging that debt reduction, not simply more restructuring, was required. The issue was brought into sharper focus in April 1989 when the Interim Committee, while praising recent announcements by several large creditor nations that they would forgive portions of government-to-government debts, called for "urgent considerations" of proposals for reducing the much larger debt owed by developing nations to commercial banks. The IMF and the World Bank subsequently approved the use of their resources to support debt reduction, especially by providing incentives to commercial banks.

In line with the Brady Plan proposed by the United States, the new strategy was designed to produce partial write-offs of debts, additional rescheduling of remaining debts for longer terms and/or lower interest rates, and an infusion of new loans from the banks. Countries "with a strong element of structural reform" were permitted to apply up to 25 percent of their access to fund resources to support principal reduction and an additional 15 percent for interest support. Moreover, in another major policy change, the IMF agreed that its funds could be released prior to conclusion of a commercial bank financing arrangement. By 1994 about 80 percent of the commercial bank debt had been restructured, leading some observers to declare the debt crisis, as far as commercial banks were concerned, to be over.

A major IMF issue appeared resolved when a 50 percent quota increase was approved in the first half of 1990 to raise the quota total from SDR 90 billion to SDR 135 billion (nearly $180 billion). A logjam in negotiations was broken when the United States endorsed the action after other IMF members had accepted the U.S. demand that a stricter policy be adopted regarding countries in arrears on payments.

The quota increase was made contingent on the approval of an amendment to the IMF Articles of Agreement that would permit the Board of Executive Directors to suspend the voting rights and certain related rights of members that failed to fulfill their IMF obligations. The amendment had been accepted by the required number of IMF members by November 1992, at which time the new quotas, now totaling SDR 146 billion (about $217 billion) because of the addition of new members, took effect.

As negotiations on a tenth quota increase were being conducted, some members called for a substantial enlargement in anticipation of a heavy draw on IMF resources by the former Soviet republics and former Soviet satellites as they switched from centrally planned to free-market economies. In April 1993 the IMF established a temporary systemic transformation facility (STF) to assist such transitional nations in their balance of payment problems and help them pay for much-needed imports such as spare parts to modernize their industries. About $5 billion had been allocated from the STF by the end of 1994, the date initially established for terminating the facility; however, the IMF agreed to extend STF operations.

In June 1993 the IMF approved what was expected to be the most important STF arrangement—a $3 billion credit to Russia. However, in September, with almost half of the loan disbursed, the IMF halted the flow because of Russia's failure to limit inflation and implement other economic reforms prescribed by the fund.

Russia was a major topic of discussion at the September 1993 IMF-IBRD annual meeting, with supporters of Russian president Boris Yeltsin arguing that he needed backing in his battle with the Russian parliament, which had resisted many of the IMF reforms. With criticism of its "rigidity" in the matter having intensified, the IMF finally released the remaining $1.5 billion to Russia in April 1994, fund officials crediting Moscow's economic reforms with, among other things, having brought previously runaway inflation down to a manageable level. A $6.8 billion standby loan was approved for Russia in 1995 and another $10.2 billion loan in 1996. In return, the Russian government pledged to reduce its budget deficit and cut tariffs on imports, but in October the IMF briefly suspended disbursements of the loan because of slow progress in revenue collection. The lending resumed in December when a new Russian tax commission agreed, among other things, to close loopholes in its collection system.

In February 1995 the IMF approved a $17.8 billion standby loan to assist in the U.S.-led "bailout" of Mexico, whose financial markets had recently experienced severe turmoil. The fund subsequently announced it would require borrowers to provide better financial data on a monthly basis to help prevent such "meltdowns" in the future. Among other things, stricter economic surveillance was expected to preclude national governments from "hiding" negative developments in their infancy, a practice that often sabotages the market's corrective mechanisms until it is too late. Managing Director Camdessus also endorsed a proposal from the Group of Seven that the IMF establish a $50 billion emergency fund to assist countries caught in circumstances such as Mexico's.

The other primary focus of attention for the IMF in the second half of 1996 was approval (in cooperation with the World Bank and the Group of Seven) of a new debt relief program, the Heavily Indebted Poor Countries (HIPC) Initiative, which was expected to lead to the eventual forgiveness of some $5.6–$7.7 billion of the debt owed by 20 of the world's poorest countries. The plan, formally endorsed at the joint IMF–World Bank meeting in September, was to permit forgiveness of up to 100 percent of debt owed to the IMF and World Bank by the eligible countries, provided they met certain criteria regarding free-market influence, the encouragement of foreign investment, and attention to basic social needs. Concurrently, the Paris Club of creditor nations agreed to forgive up to 25 percent of the debt owed to them by the countries concerned.

In February 1997 the IMF Executive Board approved the creation of a trust fund to serve as a conduit for dispersal of resources to the new debt relief fund. Subsequently, 41 countries were identified as eligible for aid, with Uganda, Bolivia, Burkina Faso, and Guyana receiving quick approval for assistance. Thereafter, IMF concerns quickly turned to the financial crisis gripping Southeast Asia. In August the IMF announced that it would extend a $3.9 million loan to Thailand as part of a $16 billion rescue package, which also included pledges from leading regional economic powers, the United States, and the World Bank. In November a $10 billion loan was offered to Indonesia, and in December South Korea received a $21 billion standby credit from the IMF, the largest ever approved for an IMF member at that time. According to the IMF's director, the economic reform requirements attached to the loan packages were markedly different from their predecessors in their insistence that the recipients enact structural reforms in their finance sectors with the aim of increasing transparency and reducing corruption.

Despite the rhetorical emphasis on good governance, the IMF in early 1998 decided to continue lending to Russia even though Moscow had failed to meet fund-mandated tax collection targets. An additional $11.2 billion in support for Russia was approved at midyear in connection with renewed pledges from Russian leaders that significant reform was in the offing. Meanwhile, extensive crisis lending proceeded smoothly for South Korea and Thailand, although disbursements for Indonesia were compromised by political developments in that country. In addition, in December the IMF agreed to $18 billion in emergency support as part of a $41.5 billion rescue package endorsed by the international financial community for Brazil. The fund also in late 1998 resumed lending to Pakistan, whose testing of a nuclear device earlier in the year had led to a suspension of IMF support.

In late 1998 the U.S. House of Representatives agreed, after substantial initial reluctance, to provide U.S. funding for the IMF quota increase that had been proposed in 1997. Consequently, the 45 percent quota increase went into effect in January 1999, the fund having accepted U.S. insistence on greater transparency in the IMF decision-making process. Subsequently, in November, Managing Director Camdessus, who had been appointed to a third five-year term in 1997, announced his intention to resign, effective February 2000. However, the selection of his successor proved surprisingly difficult as the United States pushed for a conservative candidate who would return the IMF to its initial limited mission, Japan suggested its own candidate, and developing nations demanded a role in the selection process. A compromise was finally reached on Horst Köhler of Germany, the president of the European Bank for Reconstruction and Development best known for his role in the reunification of East and West Germany while a member of the German cabinet. Following Köhler's appointment, the IMF and World Bank agreed to reduce the overlap in their objectives, with the fund concentrating on the promotion of global economic stability while letting the bank attend to the "institutional, structural, and social dimensions" of development.

Managing Director Köhler also indicated a desire to establish a more "consultative" relationship with recipient countries in order to ease domestic political pressure often felt by national governments forced to implement IMF-mandated reforms. At the same time, the IMF addressed recent conservative criticism of its policies by agreeing to reduce the length of its loans and charge higher interest rates. In the eyes of many observers the fund turned a significant psychological corner in December 2001 when it refused additional support for Argentina, thereby permitting that country to slide into default. The IMF in 2002 continued to resist pressure to assist the Argentinian government on the grounds that it had failed to adopt necessary reforms, especially in its banking sector. However, as part of an effort to combat the "contagion" affect of the Argentinian crisis on neighboring countries, the IMF in September 2002 approved substantial new credits for Brazil.

In January 2004 the IMF issued a surprisingly harsh critique of U.S. fiscal policy, describing the U.S. foreign debt as reaching record-breaking proportions that could threaten the stability of the global economy. The fund called upon the George W. Bush administration to reverse its recent tax cuts in order to reduce the U.S. budget deficit.

In March 2004 Köhler resigned as managing director in order to run for the presidency of Germany. He was succeeded by Rodrigo de Rato y Figaredo, who, while serving as Spain's finance minister, had been credited with balancing the Spanish budget and halving unemployment. A year later de Rato announced that he favored selling some $7 billion of the IMF's gold reserves to assist in the global effort to reduce the debt burdens of developing nations.

The communiqué following the IMF's September 24, 2005, annual meeting warned against an increasing gap between rich and poor nations, while it commended many poor countries on the economic progress they had made. It also warned against increasing oil prices as a potential cause of inflation, which it felt was otherwise under control, and it encouraged oil-producing and oil-consuming nations to work together to combat this problem.

In answer to widening concerns about the U.S. trade deficit with China, the IMF was given a greater role in leading multilateral consultations with relevant member nations to correct major trade imbalances. The decision at the April 2006 IMF–World Bank meeting also included the establishment of a surveillance unit to monitor trade deficits, surpluses, and currency exchange rates. It was agreed that the IMF would be able to force groups of countries to the table to discuss their economic policies and reach agreement on changes as problems surfaced. However, little progress was made amid criticisms that the countries involved showed little interest in concrete policy adjustments.

By the IMF–World Bank meeting in September 2006, demands for giving growing economies greater contributory quotas (and thereby greater voting shares) in IMF decision making were answered. Member states increased the voting shares of China, South Korea, Mexico, and Turkey and agreed to devise a new quota formula for other IMF members, including African nations, in 2008. The process was expected to be contentious because of Western countries' reluctance to concede influence in the body.

In late 2007, as fallout from the U.S. mortgage crisis and a global credit crunch roiled international financial markets, the IMF faced increasing pressure to shore up global economic stability. Developing countries publicly railed against the IMF for failing to rein in speculative lending practices in advanced economies, while the United States and other Western countries leaned on the IMF to correct major trade imbalances with China by forcing an appreciation of the renminbi. When pressed at the spring 2007 meeting, China agreed to make its exchange rate more flexible "in a gradual and controlled manner" and cut tax rebates on its exports. In June, the IMF announced the first overhaul of its surveillance policy in 30 years, largely seen as directed towards China. The agency set up a more rigorous system to scrutinize and expose exchange rate policies in individual countries. Regardless of the intentions of a government, if its economic policy resulted in "fundamental exchange-rate misalignment" or "large and prolonged current account deficits or surpluses," it could be labeled as an exchange rate manipulator.

Growing criticism about the IMF's relevance and effectiveness was a backdrop to much of its activities in 2007. With indebted countries paying back IMF loans ahead of schedule and emerging economies relying on their own foreign exchange reserves rather than IMF funds for financial security, the agency ended its fiscal year 2007 in tight financial straits.

An expert panel of outside economists recommended it sell some of its gold reserves to shore up its financial profile. In May, the Independent Evaluation Office (IEO) said the IMF's advice on foreign exchange rate policy was ineffective and inadequate, blaming the agency management for failing to provide clear direction and incentives to countries.

Further discussions about internal IMF reform continued as de Rato announced his resignation in June 2007. The managing director's vacancy came amidst calls for a non-European to fill the post, but former French finance minister and economics professor Dominique Strauss-Kahn was appointed in November, pledging to make IMF financing a priority by adopting a new income model. The aims of the model were to make the fund less dependent on lending, increase representation of large developing countries in the body, and continue aiding low-income countries despite calls that such work should be left to its sister organization, the World Bank.

Strauss-Kahn also agreed to press ahead with agency goals to scrutinize sovereign wealth funds, which have become increasingly influential in world markets despite a lack of transparency. These government-held funds, many developed by oil-rich nations, have come to control as much as $2.5 trillion in investments, often by targeting the strategic assets of developed nations. However, the funds do not routinely disclose their size or asset allocations. Under pressure from the United States, Strauss-Kahn said the IMF would develop a set of best-practices guidelines for sovereign wealth funds, which would include restrictions on fund holders' interference in a host country's politics. During 2008 the IMF negotiated a voluntary code of conduct with 26 countries that have sovereign wealth funds. The deal was up for approval at the October 2008 World Bank–IMF meeting.

The IMF's record as an economic prognosticator in 2008 was mixed. Early in the year, while warning of the risks of inflation and a global economic slowdown, the IMF paid relatively little attention to problems in the world's credit markets. By April it revised its estimate of world economic growth downwards and admitted it had not warned about the credit situation insistently enough or early enough. Yet by mid-May the IMF saw the worst of the economic crisis as past. On July 17 it raised its world economic forecast again, but by July 28 was saying that the credit crisis was getting much worse and was likely to spread from developed to less developed economies. On September 28, 2008, Strauss-Kahn suggested that the IMF could act as a kind of watchdog and "honest broker" for world financial markets during difficult times. During the late fall of 2008 the IMF issued increasingly dire statements about the world economy, culminating in an October 12 warning that it stood at "the brink of systemic meltdown." The IMF activated special rules for emergency lending to countries whose economies were in danger of collapse, rules last used in the Asian financial crisis of 1997. In late 2008 and into 2009 several countries applied for, and were granted, emergency loans, including Iceland, whose banks had collapsed from exposure to international subprime mortgage securities.

On October 26, 2009, the IMF board "admonished" Strauss-Kahn for unprofessional behavior and bad judgment, although clearing him of charges of abuse and sexual harassment and allowing him to keep his job. Many female IMF staffers had been uncomfortable with Strauss-Kahn's behavior. He apologized to the staff in general and specifically for a brief affair with an IMF senior economist, who had since left the organization.

The G-20 meeting held in London in early April 2009 enhanced the IMF's role in responding to the crisis. The group agreed that the IMF should triple the amount it borrows to ensure that it has enough funds to lend to countries in need. This new money was to be guaranteed by the financially stronger member countries. The intention was that an IMF member could seek IMF assistance when it saw trouble on the horizon, rather than when disaster was imminent. Such IMF help would become a regularly accepted part of the world financial scene and would have less chance of causing panic in the affected country than a last-minute IMF intervention. The London meeting also gave the IMF and the World Bank much increased authority to carry out G-20 policies, developing an early-warning system against the kind of crisis that the world was presently suffering and perhaps ultimately acting as a world financial regulator. The IMF was charged with reporting progress by late 2009.

In April 2010 the IMF initiated a review of its quotas as part of the 14th General Review. The result was an agreement in November to recalculate the quota system and shift about 6 percent of the shares from developed states to major developing countries. The transition was in recognition of the growing economic importance of emerging markets and made China the third largest member of the IMF. The IMF also doubled its quotas from SDR 238.4 billion to 476.8 billion (about $755.7 billion). The doubling gave each member state, at a minimum, a 100 percent increase in its quota. One result of the reforms was an increase in borrowing capacity to $550 billion.

At the joint IMF–World Bank meeting in April 2010, the IMF proposed two new taxes on banks to support future financial bailouts. At the October meeting of the IMF and World Bank, reports indicated that an impasse remained between China and developed economies led by the United States, the United Kingdom, and the eurozone over China's "artificial" manipulation of its currency to keep its value low in an alleged effort to make its exports more attractive. The IMF's *World Economic Outlook,* published in October, forecast that global economic growth would average 4.8 percent in 2010 and 4.2 percent in 2011. Developing economies were expected to lead economic growth with China's GDP growth estimated to be 10.5 percent in 2010 and 9.6 percent in 2011, while India's GDP would rise to 9.7 percent in 2010 and 8.4 percent in 2011. Meanwhile, GDP growth by the United States would be 2.6 percent in 2010 and 2.3 percent in 2011. Throughout 2010 the IMF worked with the EU to develop a series of financial rescue plans for EU member states, including a €110 billion package for Greece (see entry on Greece), in exchange for reforms to financial sectors and social welfare systems in the affected countries.

In February 2011 a report from the IMF's Independent Evaluation Office blasted the agency for failing to give adequate warning ahead of the 2008 world financial crisis. "Weak internal governance, lack of incentives to work across units and raise contrarian views, and a review process that did not 'connect the dots' or ensure follow-up... played an important role, while political constraints may have also had some impact," the report said. Strauss-Kahn described the report as "humbling."

At the Spring 2011 joint meeting of the World Bank and IMF the IMF position was that it saw no imminent threat to recovery of the world's economy, though, in addition to Europe's debt problems, it warned about continued inflation in China, and the possibility of a "boom and bust" cycle in Asia as a whole. It called on European banks to strengthen their capital position.

On May 15 Strauss-Kahn was arrested in New York on the charge of sexually assaulting a hotel housekeeper. He denied the charge, declaring that the encounter had been consensual. He was held in jail for several days, before being released on bail under very restrictive conditions. While in jail he resigned from the IMF. By late August prosecutors had lost faith in the credibility of Strauss-Kahn's accuser, and the charges were dropped. By mid-June the list of candidates to replace him had narrowed to two: Agustin Carstens, governor of the Mexican central bank, and Christine Lagarde, the French finance minister. While the managing director of the IMF has traditionally been a European, many member countries felt that times had changed enough for other parts of the world to be considered. Nevertheless, on June 28 Lagarde was elected with support from the U.S., Europe and such emerging market nations as China, India and Brazil.

Lagarde immediately pledged to give emerging economies greater influence at the IMF, and just a few days after taking office appointed Zhu Min, of China, to the new position of second deputy managing director. Zhu was the first Chinese national to be a deputy managing director.

In July 2011, the IMF warned Italy to take seriously its commitment to spending cuts, if it was to avoid a sovereign debt crisis such as was affecting Greece, and said that Greece would need at least an additional €100 billion in aid from the EU and from private sources. It also deferred Greece's return to the capital markets to 2014. In July the IMF again warned China that it must "rebalance" its economy, warning that inflation, property speculation, and the currency were dangerous to sustainable growth. It declared that the yuan was undervalued by between 3 percent and 23 percent, depending on how it was measured.

In September the IMF's *World Economic Outlook* warned of a possible "lost decade" of growth in the advanced economies but stated that there was still time—just—for governments to take concerted action. On September 25 Lagarde warned that it might not have the funds to bail out the larger eurozone countries, like Italy, Spain, and possibly even France, if the crisis continued to spread. To discourage a new recession, countries that were able to do so should consider delaying or even reversing budget cuts.

By late October the "troika" of European Commission, the European Central Bank, and the IMF presented to an EU summit a report saying that Greece would need another bailout, with private banks taking significant losses on their Greek debts. The G20 summit, held in Cannes, France, November 3–4, 2011, produced a general statement of intent to rebalance the world economy, but with no details on how the group might help the eurozone by increasing the IMF's funding. French president Nicolas Sarkozy said that specific steps would be agreed by February 2012.

By 2012 the IMF staff numbered 2,610, from 154 countries. The organization had a portfolio, including pledges and committed resources, of over $1 trillion, with annual quotas from member states totaling $364 billion. Through August 2012 the IMF had committed $247 billion in new loans for the year, of which $189 billion had been accessed. Greece, Portugal, and Ireland were the largest borrowers as a result of the IMF participation in bailout programs for the three eurozone members. In addition, Mexico and Poland both received significant precautionary loans in 2012 to prevent financial crises. At the IMF's annual meeting in October 2012, the group warned that the two greatest dangers to the world economy were the continuing Eurozone sovereign debt crisis and the failure of the United States to adopt deficit reduction measures. Representatives of emerging economies were critical of the failure to approve quota reforms at the meeting.

In January 2013 the executive board submitted recommendations for significant reforms to the quota formula. Those findings were were scheduled to be acted on in January 2014. On April 30, 2013, Cyprus approved a controversial and precedent-setting EU-IMF rescue plan that included a one-time tax on bank deposits of more than €100,000 in exchange for $13.6 billion in additional bailout funding (see entry on Cyprus). The IMF's July *World Economic Outlook* forecast that the global economy would grow by 3 percent for 2013, led by growth in emerging and developing economies, while the Eurozone would remain in recession until 2014.

INTERNATIONAL TELECOMMUNICATION UNION

(ITU)

Established: By the International Telecommunication Convention signed in Madrid, Spain, December 9, 1932, effective January 1, 1934. The ITU became a UN Specialized Agency by agreement with the Economic and Social Council (approved by the General Assembly on November 15, 1947).

Purpose: To foster international cooperation for the improvement and rational use of telecommunications.

Headquarters: Geneva, Switzerland.

Principal Organs: Plenipotentiary Conference (all members), World and Regional Conferences on International Telecommunications, Council (46 members), General Secretariat.

Web site: www.itu.int

Secretary General: Hamadoun Touré (Mali).

Membership (193): See Appendix C.

Official Languages: English, French, Spanish.

Working Languages: Arabic, Chinese, English, French, Russian, Spanish.

Origin and development. The beginnings of the ITU can be traced to the International Telegraph Union founded May 17, 1865, in Paris, France. The International Telegraph Convention concluded at that time, together with the International Radiotelegraph Convention concluded in Berlin in 1906, was revised and incorporated into the International Telecommunication Convention signed in 1932 in Madrid, Spain. Entering into force in 1934, the Madrid convention established the ITU as the successor to previous agencies in the telecommunications field. A new convention adopted in 1947 took account of subsequent advances in telecommunications and also of the new position acquired by the ITU as a UN Specialized Agency. Conventions have since been periodically revised to address changing standards and needs as radio communication and telecommunication continue to evolve.

Structure. The ITU's complicated structure is a reflection of its long history and growth. As international telecommunications expanded, new organs and functions were typically grafted onto the preexisting ITU structure, producing a plethora of conferences, assemblies, organs, and secretariats, and necessitating a major reorganization in the early 1990s. At an extraordinary Plenipotentiary Conference in Geneva, Switzerland, in December 1992, the ITU adopted its current constitution, which rationalized the organization's structure, effective March 1993. In 2011 South Sudan became the 193rd member of the ITU.

The Plenipotentiary Conference remains the principal political organ of the ITU. Regular sessions are held every four years to make any necessary revisions in the conventions, determine general policy, establish the organization's budget, and set a limit on expenditures until the next conference. Each member has one vote on the conference, which elects the Council, as well as the secretary general and the deputy secretary general. The Council, comprised of 46 members from six administrative regions (Africa, Americas, Asia, Australasia, Eastern Europe, and Western Europe), supervises the ITU between sessions of the parent body. Meeting annually at the organization's headquarters, it reviews and approves the annual budget and coordinates the work of the ITU with other international organizations.

Under the 1993 restructuring, the Plenipotentiary Conference can approve the convening of World and Regional Conferences on International Telecommunication. There are three types of global conferences, corresponding to the ITU's three program sectors: Radiocommunication Conferences, generally held every two to three years in conjunction with technically oriented Radiocommunication Assemblies; Telecommunication Standardization Assemblies, typically held every four years; and Telecommunication Development Conferences, also held at four-year intervals.

The General Secretariat, headed by the elected secretary general, administers the budget, directs the ITU's sizable research and publishing program, and otherwise provides administrative support. Each of the three sectors—Radiocommunication, Telecommunication Standardization, and Telecommunication Development—has its own administrative bureau headed by a director.

Activities. The general aims of the ITU are to maintain and extend international cooperation for the improvement and rational use of radiocommunication and telecommunication and to aid developing countries in obtaining appropriate technologies and establishing needed services. In addition, the ITU undertakes studies, issues recommendations and opinions, and collects and publishes information for the benefit of its members.

The Radiocommunication Sector (ITU-R) was established by consolidation of the International Radio Consultative Committee (founded in 1927) and the International Frequency Registration Board (IFRB), the latter of which had been responsible since 1947 for allocating and recording frequency assignments and for handling interference disputes. These tasks currently fall under the purview of the ITU-R's 12-member Radio Regulations Board, which maintains the Master International Frequency Register (MIFR) for radio services—everything from ham radio to high-definition television. The Radiocommunication Sector's basic mission is to ensure "rational, equitable, efficient and economical use of the radiofrequency spectrum by all radiocommunication services, including those using satellite orbit."

The Telecommunication Standardization Sector (ITU-T) has as its mission ensuring "an efficient and on-time production of high quality standards covering all fields of telecommunications except radio." It relies on more than a dozen study groups to formulate recommendations, which are nonbinding standards covering, for example, network interconnectivity and electromagnetic compatibility.

The purpose of the Telecommunication Development Sector (ITU-D) is to "facilitate and enhance telecommunication development worldwide by offering, organizing, and coordinating technical cooperation and assistance activities." The ITU recognized this need even before the 1993 reorganization, having authorized creation of the Telecommunication Development Bureau in 1989. In 2003 ITU secretary general Yoshio Utsumi called for a heightened global policy perspective to increase access to information and communication technology (ICT) to the developing world, asking for a "concerted global effort" to "eliminate the gap between rich and poor when it comes to access to information."

The ITU's first World Telecommunication Development Conference (WTDC) was held in March 1993 in Buenos Aires, Argentina, amid widespread concern the "telecommunications gap" was still widening between rich and poor countries. U.S. vice president Al Gore called for creation of a "planetary information network," built primarily by the private sector, to foster economic growth and political liberalization. The second WTDC took place in Valletta, Malta, in March 1998 and adopted an action plan that paid particular attention to the telecommunication needs of the world's least developed countries (LDCs). That theme was bolstered at the third WTDC held in 2002 in Istanbul, Turkey, at which delegates adopted an action plan to close the "digital divide" between rich and poor countries and to aid in the transition to the modern telecommunication and ICT environment. The action plan included six programs: regulatory reform; expanding access to developing countries; applying Internet networks to government, health, and education sectors; enhancing private sector investment; human resources development; and a special program to assist LDCs. The most recent WTDC was held May 24–June 4, 2010, in Hyderabad, India.

The first World Radiocommunication Conference (WRC) convened October 23–November 17, 1995, in Geneva, Switzerland. The primary purpose of the WRC is to review and revise the Radio Regulations, the international treaty governing the use of the radio-frequency spectrum and the geostationary-satellite and non-geostationary-satellite orbits. The conference also discussed the ever-increasing problem of allocation of the radio-frequency spectrum, pressure in that area having grown particularly intense in regard to mobile satellite communications. The ITU-R administers the organization's International Mobile Telecommunications-2000 (IMP-2000) program, which establishes standards governing third-generation (3G) wireless communications via satellite and wireless terrestrial links. At a WRC meeting June 9–July 4, 2003, in Geneva, delegates placed a heavy emphasis on the further allocation of spectrum in regard to wireless access services, broadband wireless services aboard airplanes and ships, and satellite data services.

The 2000 World Telecommunication Standardization Assembly (WTSA) in Montreal, Quebec, Canada, adopted many varied resolutions emphasizing collaboration among ITU sectors and also established ground rules for associate membership and accounting rate principles for international telephone services. The October 5–14, 2004, meeting in Florianopolis, Brazil, adopted a four-year plan focused on setting global standards for network security, compatibility of old and new network systems, and transitions to new technologies. Internet governance and next-generation networks (NGNs) were prominent issues, prompting the ITU to create a new study group on NGNs. The WTSA also adopted a series of Internet resolutions to counter spam and to increase ITU involvement in the debate over internationalized domain names.

Additionally, the ITU took a lead role, along with the UN secretary general, in organizing the two-phase World Summit on the Information Society. The first phase took place in Geneva in December 2003 and adopted a declaration of principles and a plan of action to expand universal access to the Information Society. The second phase took place November 16–18, 2005, in Tunisia. Discussions about freedom of use and universal access to the Internet dominated the second phase, with China in particular arguing for a state's right to place some restrictions in the name of national security.

The two summits led to the adoption of the Doha Action Plan in March 2006 at the ITU's World Telecommunication Development Conference. The Doha plan spelled out a strategy to develop telecommunications infrastructure for use in underserved areas and with marginalized populations. In response to a series of natural disasters, including the 2004 tsunami in Southeast Asia, the Doha plan also targeted poor countries and small island nations for emergency telecommunications development.

Governance of the Internet again became a topic at the first ever Internet Governance Forum in November 2006, during which Secretary General Utsumi pressed for greater worldwide influence in overseeing Internet functions. The U.S. government refused to cede control of computers directing Internet traffic but later announced it would relax oversight over the Internet Corporation for Assigned Names and Numbers (ICANN), the private agency that controls domain names and other key functions.

The 17th Plenipotentiary Conference in Antalya, Turkey, held November 6–24, 2006, saw renewed commitments to the implementation of the World Summit on the Information Society (WSIS) and Doha Action Plan goals for universal access as well as discussions on internationalized Internet domain names, Internet interoperability, and convergence. The conference also appointed a new secretary general, Mali-born Hamadoun Touré, then director of the ITU's Telecommunications Development Sector.

Touré caused a stir in early 2007 when he seemed to back away from the union's previously stated position on global Internet governance, stating he did not see the ITU becoming the governing body. He said his priorities instead were to bridge the so-called information divide between rich and poor countries and curb Internet-related crime. In May that year, the ITU announced the two-year Global Cybersecurity Agenda to address issues of network security, financial fraud, identity theft, virus attacks, spam, and child pornography.

In June 2006 the ITU helped negotiate an agreement between 101 nations in Europe, Africa, and the Middle East to introduce a standardized digital system for radio and TV broadcasts. In October 2007 the ITU and the African Development Bank cohosted the Connect Africa Summit and raised investment commitments of $55 billion from private industry and government sources (to be completed by 2012) to provide widespread access to broadband communication technology in Africa. Also in October 2007 the Radiocommunication Assembly endorsed WiMAX, a wireless phone signal standard used heavily in emerging markets.

In December 2007 the ITU made a presentation at the UN Conference on Climate Change in Bali, Indonesia. It pointed out that improved telecommunications could be part of the solution to climate change, but that, as they produced high-tech garbage, they were also part of the problem. In July 2008 the ITU created the new Focus Group on Information and Communication Technologies (ICTs) and Climate Change. The group had an aggressive work plan to be completed by April 2009.

In March 2008 the ITU deployed 25 satellite terminals to parts of Zambia that had been cut off by flooding. In May it deployed 100 such terminals to China after a disastrous earthquake there. In June it called on all countries to adopt a single standardized telephone number, 116.111, for children to use if they needed any kind of help. In September the organization predicted that there would be four billion mobile phones in use by the end of the year. In October 2008 the ITU held its first ever Global Standards Symposium, in Johannesburg, South Africa. This meeting called for the "bewildering" array of global telecommunication standards and protocols to be simplified. At this meeting and elsewhere concern was voiced that the EU was trying to develop its own set of standards, usurping the ITU's traditional role in this regard.

In March 2009 the ITU opened headquarters for its Global Cybersecurity Agenda on the outskirts of Kuala Lumpur, Malaysia. In October the organization approved a new, and energy-efficient, universal charger that would work with any mobile telephone. The ITU estimated that currently 51,000 tons of obsolete chargers added to the world's pollution each year. On November 3, 2009, the ITU introduced a "standards conformity and interoperability program," designed to give potential buyers of communications equipment a better idea of how their purchase might (or might not) work with the rest of the world.

In 2010 the ITU estimated that there were 5.3 billion mobile phone subscriptions around the world, although the rate of growth in new users fell to a 1.6 percent increase. In addition text messaging tripled between 2007 and 2010, growing from 1.8 trillion to 6.1 trillion, or approximately 200,000 per second in 2010. The number of Internet users doubled between 2005 and 2010, rising to above 2 billion, with China the largest Internet market (420 million users). However, there continued to be widespread disparity between the developed and the developing world, with 71 percent of the population in developed countries online, while only 21 percent of the developing world had internet access. In an effort to address the imbalance, the ITU partnered with private industry to open a new Internet training facility in Togo, the 80th facility of its kind in the developed world. The ITU issued recommendations in 2010 calling on the information and communications technology sector to better address issues of climate change by reducing emissions and improving energy efficiency, and playing a greater role in tracking changes in worldwide weather patterns.

In March 2011 the ITU deployed satellite telephones and related equipment to Japan, to help with communications and the search for survivors after the earthquake and tsunami. In May it signed an agreement with the European Patent Office, agreeing to share information and co-operate in developing worldwide technical standards. On October 5 South Sudan joined the ITU, raising its membership to 193.

Data released by the ITU in June 2012 highlighted the growth in mobile-cellular usage and the disparities in mobile-broadband access. By the end of 2011 there were almost 6 billion cellular subscriptions, an 86 percent global usage rate. Developing countries accounted for 80 percent of new subscriptions. In India alone, 142 million new cellular subscriptions were added in 2011, more than Europe and the Middle East combined. There were 105 countries in which there were more cellular phone subscriptions than inhabitants, including Botswana, Gabon, and South Africa. However, in Africa as a whole, there were fewer than 5 mobile-broadband subscriptions per 100 inhabitants, whereas in some developed countries such as Singapore and the Republic of Korea, there were more mobile-broadband subscriptions than inhabitants. At the December 2012 World Conference on International Telecommunications (WCIT), the ITU approved expanded governance of the internet by the agency. The controversial reforms were opposed by the United States, Canada, the United Kingdom, and many EU stateswhich argued the changes could limit the free flow of information and legitimize filtering of the internet.

The IRU report, *The State of Broadband 2013: Universalizing Broadband* found that there were 7 billion mobile subscriptions in 2013 and that the number of such subscriptions would overtake the global population in 2014. In March 2013 the ITU called on member states to adopt plans to ensure gender equality in broadband access by 2020.

UNITED NATIONS EDUCATIONAL, SCIENTIFIC, AND CULTURAL ORGANIZATION

(UNESCO)

Established: By constitution adopted in London, England, November 16, 1945, effective November 4, 1946. UNESCO became a UN Specialized Agency by agreement concluded with the Economic and Social Council (approved by the General Assembly on December 14, 1946).

Purpose: To contribute to peace and security by promoting collaboration among states in education, the natural and social sciences, communications, and culture.

Headquarters: Paris, France.

Principal Organs: General Conference (all members), Executive Board (58 members), Secretariat.

Web site: www.unesco.org

Director General: Irina Bokova (Bulgaria).

Membership (195, plus 8 Associate Members): See Appendix C.

Official Languages: Arabic, Chinese, English, French, Russian, Spanish. French and English are working languages.

Origin and development. UNESCO resulted from the concern of European governments-in-exile over the problem of restoring the educational systems of Nazi-occupied territories after World War II. Meetings of the Allied Ministers of Education began in London, England, in 1942, and proposals for a postwar agency for educational and cultural reconstruction were drafted in April 1944; the constitution of UNESCO, adopted at a special conference in London, November 1–16, 1945, came into force a year later, following ratification by 20 states.

The 1974 General Conference voted to exclude Israel from the European regional groups of UNESCO, thus making that country the only member to belong to no regional groups. At the same session a motion was passed to withhold UNESCO aid from Israel on the ground that it had persisted "in altering the historical features" of Jerusalem during archaeological excavations. At the 1976 General Conference, Israel was restored to full membership in the organization; however, the conference voted to condemn Israeli educational and cultural policies in occupied Arab territories, charging that the latter amounted to "cultural assimilation." The adoption of this resolution was reported to be part of the price demanded by Arab and Soviet-bloc member countries for agreeing to Israel's return to the regional group. In November 1978 the organization again voted to condemn and cut off funds to Israel, charging that Arab monuments in Jerusalem had been destroyed in the course of further archaeological activity.

Debate at the 21st General Conference in 1980 raged over a resolution calling for the establishment of the New World Information and Communication Order (NWICO). Western delegates objected to the proposal, which called for an international code of journalistic ethics, on the ground that it might restrict freedom of the press. At the fourth extraordinary session of the General Conference, held in Paris in late 1982, the NWICO was included as a major component of the proposed medium-term UNESCO work plan for 1985–1989. The conference finally adopted a compromise plan for the NWICO that entailed the deletion of passages unacceptable to the industrialized countries, the rejection of a proposed study of Western news agencies, and the addition of material calling for freedom of the press and referencing its role as a watchdog against abuses of power.

Debate over the NWICO continued in 1983. Despite the compromise seemingly accepted at the 1982 Paris meeting, the document presented at a symposium on the news media and disarmament in Nairobi, Kenya, in April called for "national news agencies" and "codes of conduct" for journalists, with no mention of the right of news organs to operate freely. It also called for a study of the obstacles to circulation in industrialized countries of information produced in developing countries. In response, a number of industrial nations, including the United States, indicated that they would withhold funds from the organization, forcing it to appeal to external sources to meet its projected 1984–1985 budget of $328.8 million.

Subsequently, the organization came under even greater attack from members alleging unnecessary politicization of UNESCO activities and mismanagement by Director General Amadou Mahtar M'Bow of Senegal. The United States, at the forefront of the critics, called for major reforms in 1984. Rebuffed in the effort, it withdrew from membership, with the United Kingdom and Singapore following suit in 1985.

The controversial director general announced in late 1986 that he would not seek reelection upon expiration of his second term in November 1987, but, at the urging of the Organization of African Unity, subsequently reversed his position. Several additional Western nations threatened to withdraw from UNESCO in the event of M'Bow's reelection, and acrimony dominated efforts by the October meeting of the Executive Board to determine its nominee for the post. After four ballots, M'Bow withdrew, it having become apparent that the Soviet bloc planned to cast its decisive votes for his opponent, Federico Mayor Zaragoza of Spain. The board thereupon nominated Mayor, although 20 (mostly African) members voted against him.

The General Conference in November formally elected Mayor, who promised to restructure and reinvigorate the organization in hopes of bringing the United States and the United Kingdom back into its fold. In March 1988 Mayor reported extensive budget austerity measures had been introduced and a month later urged UNESCO to "talk less and less about political issues and more and more about education, culture, and science." The 1989 General Conference also attempted to mollify the United States by calling for a "free, independent, pluralistic press" throughout the world and by deferring a membership request from the Palestine Liberation Organization. Acting against the recommendations of a panel of distinguished Americans, who reported that UNESCO was making "clear and undeniable progress," the United States announced in April 1990 that it would not rejoin the organization.

The 1991 General Conference continued to urge the United States and the United Kingdom to reconsider their positions regarding UNESCO. Mayor intensified the lobbying campaign to get the former members to rejoin in the spring of 1992, noting that sharp cutbacks in contributions from the former Soviet Union and its successor states in 1991 had created financial distress for UNESCO. The director general presented a report from an independent commission appointed to evaluate UNESCO, which described the organization as having made progress in ending waste and inefficiency.

The 27th General Conference, held October 1993 in Paris, unanimously reelected Mayor to a second term, as recommended by the Executive Board. The conference also approved a $455 million biennial budget for 1994–1995, with priorities to include literacy, special educational programs for women and children, environmental and antidrug projects, and journalist training courses. Not coincidentally, much of the UNESCO emphasis reflected well-known interests of the U.S. Bill Clinton administration, which was described as adopting a more positive attitude toward the organization. Consequently, in early 1994, U.S. State Department officials said they had suggested the United States rejoin UNESCO, although not until 1997 because of budget considerations. A highlight of UNESCO activity later in the year was the readmission in December of South Africa, which had withdrawn from the organization in 1956 because of criticism of its apartheid policies. The United Kingdom rejoined on July 1, 1997.

In a secret ballot on October 20, 1999, Japan's Koichiro Matsuura defeated ten candidates for the Executive Board's endorsement to succeed Director General Mayor for a six-year term. His nomination coincided with release of an independent audit of UNESCO that uncovered mismanagement, corruption, and financial irregularities, including millions of dollars in payments to consultants and advisers who were deemed unqualified. In September 12, 2002, U.S. president George W. Bush announced to the UN General Assembly that the United States would rejoin UNESCO following an 18-year estrangement, stating, "This organization has been reformed and America will participate fully in its mission." Bush later pledged a $60 million reentry fee, returning the United States as the largest contributor to UNESCO. In October 2003 the United States was elected to serve on the 58-member Executive Board. In 2007 Montenegro joined and Singapore rejoined after walking out 22 years previously in protest of agency mismanagement. In 2011 South Sudan and Palestine joined the organization (see "Activities").

Structure. The General Conference, which usually meets every odd-dated year, has final responsibility for approving the budget, electing the director general, and deciding overall policy. Each member state has one vote; decisions are usually made by a simple majority, although some questions, such as amendments to UNESCO's constitution, require a two-thirds majority.

The Executive Board is charged with general oversight of the UNESCO program and the budget; the board examines drafts of both covering the ensuing two-year period and submits them, with its own recommendations, to the General Conference. Previously elected by, and from, General Conference participants, the members of the board under a 1991 constitutional revision are now the representatives of 58 governments selected by the conference to control board seats.

The Secretariat, which is headed by a director general selected for a six-year term by the General Conference (on recommendation of the Executive Board), is responsible for executing the program and applying the decisions of those two bodies. A distinctive feature of UNESCO's constitutional structure is the role of the national commissions. Comprising representatives of governments and nongovernmental organizations in the member states, the commissions were initially intended to act as advisory bodies for UNESCO's program. However, they have also come to serve as liaison agents between the Secretariat and the diverse educational, scientific, and cultural activities in the participant states.

Activities. UNESCO's program of activities derives from its broad mandate to "maintain, increase and diffuse knowledge," to "give fresh impulse to popular education and to the spread of knowledge," and to "collaborate in the work of advancing the mutual knowledge and understanding of peoples." Within this mandate it (1) holds international conferences, conducts expert studies, and disseminates factual information concerning education, the natural and social sciences, cultural activities, and mass communication; (2) promotes the free flow of ideas by word and image; (3) encourages the exchange of persons and of publications and other informational materials; (4) attempts to ensure conservation and protection of books, works of art, and monuments of historical and scientific significance; and (5) collaborates with member states in developing educational, scientific, and cultural programs.

To promote intellectual cooperation, UNESCO has granted financial assistance to many international nongovernmental organizations engaged in the transfer of knowledge. It has also attempted to encourage the exchange of ideas by convening major conferences on such topics as life-long education, oceanographic research, problems of youth, eradication of illiteracy, and cultural and scientific policy. To further cooperation in science and technology, UNESCO was instrumental in the establishment of the European Organization for Nuclear Research (CERN, see separate entry) in 1954, the International Brain Research Organization (IBRO) in 1960, the International Cell Research Organization in 1962, the program on Man and the Biosphere (MAB) that currently involves more than 140 countries, the International Geological Correlation Program, the International Hydrological Program (IHP), and a Coastal Regions and Small Islands (CSI) endeavor. In addition, UNESCO provides the secretariat for the Intergovernmental Oceanographic Commission (ICO).

UNESCO has paid particular attention to the human genome, establishing in 1993 a bioethics program that led to the adoption of the Universal Declaration on the Human Genome and Human Rights in 1997, which banned human reproductive cloning. (For more information, please see the 2012 *Handbook.*) UNESCO's developmental efforts also focus on modernizing educational facilities, training teachers, combating illiteracy, improving science and social science teaching, and training scientists and engineers. The International Bureau of Education (IBE) in Geneva, which dates from 1925, became part of UNESCO in 1969, while the International Institute for Educational Planning (IIEP) and the Intergovernmental Committee for Physical Education and Sport (ICPES), both located in Paris, France, were established by the organization in 1963 and 1978, respectively. Other educational units include the Caribbean Network of Educational Innovation for Development, located in Kingston, Jamaica; the European Center for Higher Education in Bucharest, Romania; the International Institute for Higher Education in Latin America and the Caribbean in Caracas, Venezuela; the Institute for Education in Hamburg, Germany; and the Institute for Information Technologies in Education in Moscow, Russia. (For more on educational initiatives, please see the 2012 *Handbook.*)

In social sciences, UNESCO focuses its attention on diverse issues such as human rights, ethics in science and technology, peace and disarmament, environment and population issues, and socioeconomic conditions. The 1978 General Conference adopted the Declaration on Race and Racial Prejudice that rejected the concept that any racial or ethnic group was inherently inferior or superior. UNESCO's *Medium-Term Report* for 2002–2007 reinforced the 2001 Universal Declaration on Cultural Diversity that tasks UNESCO with a three-part, six-year strategy to implement standards to protect cultural diversity, promote cross-cultural dialogue, and enhance links between culture and development. Since 1946, UNESCO has worked to preserve cultural heritage. Director General Matsuura decried the Taliban's willful destruction in March 2001 of the stone Buddhas of Bamiyan in Afghanistan as a "crime against culture." Additionally, UNESCO has taken steps to prevent the illicit traffic of artifacts following extensive looting in Baghdad, Iraq, after the fall of Saddam Hussein's regime in 2003 and has also worked to preserve dying languages. Similarly, UNESCO warned museums and international art dealers in August 2011 to be alert for items that might have been looted during the civil war in Libya. The February 2009 edition of UNESCO's *Atlas of the World's Languages in Danger of Disappearing* caused some comment. It listed the Manx Gaelic and Cornish languages as extinct. This brought letters of protest from schoolchildren on the Isle of Man, written in the supposedly dead language, as well as complaints from Cornish speakers. Both languages were reclassified as "critically endangered."

In communications, UNESCO has attempted to advance the free flow of information and book development, expand the use of media, assist countries in developing the media they need, and disseminate UN ideals. Since 1976 the General Information Program (PGI) has concentrated on improving the organization and dissemination of scientific and technical information. The Intergovernmental Informatics Program (IIP) has directed its attention to policy considerations and training in computer-based knowledge dissemination. Also under the communications arm of UNESCO is the ICO, which built an early-warning system for tsunamis in the Indian Ocean following the December 2004 tsunami that killed more than 200,000 people in the region.

The 33rd General Conference was held on October 17–20, 2005, in Paris. It adopted a budget of $610 million, with an additional $25 million in extra-budgetary voluntary funding. It also adopted the Convention on the Protection and Promotion of the Diversity of Cultural Expressions, the International Convention against Doping in Sport, and the Universal Declaration on Bioethics and Human Rights. The convention on cultural diversity was intended, among other things, to support national movie industries, and was opposed by the United States. The director general agreed that the organization should, for the time being, concentrate on implementing standards that had been recently promulgated, rather than on creating new ones.

With enough countries ratifying support, the Convention for the Safeguarding of the Intangible Heritage entered into force in 2006. The convention requires member nations to take steps to protect oral and cultural traditions, traditional craft-making, and performing arts and includes funding for preservation efforts and two official registry lists.

Additionally, another report entitled *Case Studies on Climate Change and World Heritage* that year found that world heritage sites, including coral reefs and archaeological sites sensitive to changes in humidity and precipitation, can be threatened by the effects of climate change.

At the 34th General Conference on October 16 to November 2, 2007, in Paris, Matsuura recommended recruiting a financial comptroller to strengthen internal agency monitoring. The conference also adopted a strategy for 2008–2013 of "attaining lifelong quality education for all"; furthering sustainable development through science and technology; and creating activities directed towards youth, least developed nations, and small island states. A 2008–2009 budget of $631 million was adopted, with educational programs receiving the largest share, followed by the natural and social science sectors, and then culture.

The conference also approved a resolution directing the director general to explore the role UNESCO could play in preserving the memory of the Holocaust and preventing all forms of its denial in reaction to Iranian president Mahmoud Ahmadinejad's calling the Holocaust "a myth" earlier in the year. In other measures in 2007, UNESCO called for Israel to end archaeological excavation work near the al-Aqsa mosque in Jerusalem out of concern Islam's third holiest site could be damaged, and listed the Galapagos Islands in the Pacific Ocean as an endangered world heritage site because of the growing pressure of tourism. It also renamed the Nazi concentration camp Auschwitz Birkenau as the German Nazi Concentration and Extermination Camp to clearly identify Germany's responsibility after a lobbying effort by Poland. UNESCO designated the Iraqi city of Samarra as an endangered world cultural treasure after insurgent attacks destroyed a number of the city's holy sites.

The state of education was summarized in a 2007 UNESCO report called *Corrupt Schools, Corrupt Universities: What Can Be Done.* The report found that illegal registration fees, academic fraud (including fake university degrees available on the Internet), embezzlement, and other corrupt practices were seriously undermining educational systems around the world.

The creation of World Heritage sites and institutions was productive in 2008, but some efforts were controversial. Cambodia attempted to register the temple of Preyah Vihear as a World Heritage site, but the temple stands on ground that is disputed between Thailand and Cambodia. The ground is recognized as Cambodian, but the only access is through Thai territory. Thailand did not object to Cambodia's action, but wanted to manage the area jointly with Cambodia. UNESCO's position was that the two countries must resolve their differences before the site could be registered. Occasional violent clashes continued at the site through 2008 and into late 2009, but both sides declared they would not allow the conflict to escalate.

Also in 2008 Egypt's culture minister, Farouk HOSNY, a potential candidate to be UNESCO's next director general, was attacked with the allegation that he had made statements against Israel. He denied the accusation and said he "dreamed" of visiting Israel after ties with the Palestinians were normalized. Also controversial was UNESCO's decision to recognize Jerusalem as "the capital of Arab culture" in 2009. The celebration was to include all Jerusalem, not just the present Arab part of the city. Eventually, Hosny was beaten out by Irina Bokova, the former external affairs minister of Bulgaria. Hosny declared that he had lost because of "Zionist pressures." Bokova was elected and sworn in at the 35th General Conference, held October 6–23, 2009, in Paris. She was the first woman and the first person from Eastern Europe to become director general. The conference adopted a budget only nominally larger than that of the previous biennium, with education as its priority, and it welcomed the Faroe Islands as a new associate member. Also at the conference, UNESCO approved Africa and gender equality as two of its main priorities for support.

In other action, UNESCO declared, in a November 2008 report, that the world was likely to miss the goal of providing elementary education for all children by 2015. In June 2009 it deleted Dresden, Germany, from the list of World Heritage Sites, to which it had been added in 2004, because of a new bridge that UNESCO deemed unsuitable. In December delegations from 50 states adopted the Belém Framework for Action, which outlined a variety of measures to promote lifelong learning among populations and to reduce illiteracy around the world by 50 percent from the levels of 2000 by 2015.

The UNESCO budget for 2010–2011 increased to $653 million, an increase of $22 million, or 3.5 percent, over the previous cycle. A January 2010 UNESCO report warned that the global economic crisis would undermine developing countries' efforts to improve education, especially in light of international aid reductions by wealthy states. UNESCO estimated that 72 million children were not in school, a number that was reduced from 105 million a decade ago. Nonetheless, UNESCO also predicted that by 2015, 56 million children would remain out of school, the majority of those female. In September UNESCO signed an agreement with the Al Jazeera satellite news network to collaborate on initiatives to promote freedom of expression and of the media in the Arab world. The effort revolved around programs to increase awareness and to undertake research on the barriers to freedom of speech. At the end of 2010, UNESCO's List of World Heritage in Danger noted that 34 recognized sites in 27 countries were threatened.

In a controversial vote in October 2011, UNESCO members admitted Palestine to full membership, on equal terms with entities that have undisputed national status. This decision occurred after the United States threatened to veto Palestine's request for full membership in the UN. The UNESCO vote was 107 in favor, 14 against, with 52 abstentions. The United States and Israel were strongly opposed, and Washington announced that it would immediately stop contributing to the agency (the United States provided about 22 percent of UNESCO's annual budget). Israel did likewise. On October 11, at the end of the UNESCO general conference, director-general Bokova announced a worldwide appeal for contributions to replace the United States' contribution. She addressed the appeal to governments, other institutions, even to individuals—anyone who cared to contribute. The loss of contributions led to a $205 million deficit by 2012 and prompted the agency to suspend some programs.

In response to the Arab Spring, UNESCO launched a range of programs. In 2011 the organization conducted a series of workshops and training sessions for journalists from the Middle East and North Africa. In addition, UNESCO and Interpol initiated a program to catalog heritage sites in Egypt and other states and assist new governments in developing adequate security procedures for sites and objects. UNESCO also conducted gender and equity training for newly elected officials.

Director-General Bokova was nominated for a second term in April 2013 by UNESCO's exceuctive board, defeating Rachad Farah (Djibouti) and Joseph Maïla (Lebanon). A June UNESCO report found that the number of children without access to primary education fell from 61 million in 2010 to 57 million in 2011. Concurrently there was a 6 percent drop in interational aid for primary education, with the United Kingdom overtaking the United States as the world's largest single donor as the latter continued to cut its foreign aid budget. In August UNESCO and the EU announced a program of expanded cooperation on education, culture, resources, freedom of expression, and water and oceans. Specific action items included efforts to safeguard unique cultural artifacts in areas of conflict and initiatives to strengthen journalism and media in developing nations.

UNITED NATIONS INDUSTRIAL DEVELOPMENT ORGANIZATION

(UNIDO)

Established: By General Assembly resolution of November 17, 1966, effective January 1, 1967. UNIDO became a UN Specialized Agency January 1, 1986, as authorized by a resolution of the Seventh Special Session of the General Assembly on September 16, 1975, based on a revised constitution adopted April 8, 1979.

Purpose: To review and promote the coordination of UN activities in the area of industrial development, with particular emphasis on industrialization in less developed countries, including both agro-based or agro-related industries and basic industries.

Headquarters: Vienna, Austria.

Principal Organs: General Conference (all members), Industrial Development Board (53 members), Program and Budget Committee (27 members), Secretariat.

Web site: www.unido.org

Director General: Li Yong (China).

Membership: (172): See Appendix C. (Canada withdrew as of December 31, 1993, the United States withdrew as of December 31, 1996, and Australia withdrew as of December 31, 1997. The United Kingdom, which in 1996 had announced its intention to withdraw, reversed its decision in 1997 and remained a member and then announced it would stop funding UNIDO in 2012 (see "Activities").

Origin and development. The creation of a comprehensive organization responsible for UN efforts in the field of industrial development was proposed to the General Assembly in 1964 by the first UN Conference on Trade and Development (UNCTAD). The General Assembly endorsed the proposal in 1965 and, through a 1966 resolution effective January 1, 1967, established UNIDO as a semi-autonomous Special Body of the General Assembly with budgetary and programmatic ties to other special bodies, such as UNCTAD and the UN Development Program (UNDP).

During its first General Conference in Vienna in 1971, UNIDO appealed for greater independence, particularly in light of the UNDP's extensive budgetary control. The plea was reiterated at the second General Conference, held in 1975 in Lima, Peru, and later that year the General Assembly, in an unprecedented move, authorized the change in status from a Special Body to a Specialized Agency, subject to the development and ratification of a UNIDO constitution. After extensive negotiations, representatives from 82 countries participating in a conference of plenipotentiaries held on March 19–April 8, 1979 in Vienna adopted such a document, and the ratification process, which was to take six years, began.

The 1980 conference proved to be highly confrontational, with the industrialized countries objecting not only to the call for the establishment of a 20-year, $300 billion global development fund, but to what they considered political provisions—including statements condemning colonialism and racism—in the New Delhi Declaration drafted by the developing countries' Group of 77. The disagreement between rich and poor continued at the 1984 conference, little being achieved apart from a renewed call for capital mobilization in support of industrial progress in the third world.

Although 120 governments ratified the UNIDO constitution by March 1985, it was not until June 21 that the minimum of 80 formal notifications of such action had been tendered, in part because of an insistence by Eastern European countries that they be guaranteed a deputy director generalship. Subsequently, a General Conference met in Vienna on August 12–17 and December 9–13 to pave the way for launching the organization as the UN's 16th Specialized Agency.

In the early 1990s observers described the organization as facing "a leadership and identity crisis," underscored by its failure to approve either of two proposed restructuring plans. Members' arrears also continued to be a major concern, with dozens of countries losing voting rights for nonpayment of dues. On March 30, 1993, a special session of the General Conference appointed Mauricio de María y Campos of Mexico as UNIDO director general, the former director general, Domingo L. Siazon Jr., having resigned to take a position in the Philippine government. The new director general called for an "urgent restructuring," with emphasis placed on helping companies in developing countries to become internationally competitive via an expanded private sector and global cooperation in the transfer of technology. Many of the recommendations were endorsed in the Yaoundé Declaration issued following the fifth General Conference, held December 6–9 in Yaoundé, Cameroon.

Despite its restructuring, UNIDO's future remained in jeopardy as a review of overlapping UN bodies proceeded. It was reported in early 1995 that a UN report had recommended the dismantling of UNIDO, a proposal endorsed by the world's leading industrialized countries during their midyear summit. Consequently, the United States announced at UNIDO's sixth General Conference in December that it would withdraw from the organization at the end of 1996. UNIDO subsequently continued to restructure its operations, cutting a number of senior managers, reducing its overall workforce by more than one-third from its 1993 total, and slashing its budget.

The 1997 General Conference endorsed the Business Plan for the Future Role and Functions of UNIDO, under which the organization's overall goals in meeting the needs of developing countries and economies in transition were defined as "the three Es": competitive economy, productive employment, and sound environment. The conference approved the nomination of a new director general, Carlos Magariños of Argentina, making him the youngest director general in UN history. Magariños was widely credited for revamping the organization's structure and was reelected to a second four-year term at the December 2001 conference.

At the 11th session of the UNIDO General Conference, held on November 28–December 2, 2005, in Vienna, Magariños was succeeded by Kandeh Yumkella of Sierra Leone. Li Yung of China was elected to succeed Yumkella on June 24, 2013, defeating five other candidates.

Structure. The General Conference, which meets every two years, establishes UNIDO policy and is responsible for final approval of its biennial budgets. The Industrial Development Board (IDB), which meets annually, exercises wide-ranging "policy review" authority, and its recommendations exert significant influence on the decisions of the conference. The Program and Budget Committee also meets annually to conduct extensive preliminary budget preparations.

The Secretariat, comprising some 700 employees, is headed by a director general appointed by the General Conference upon the recommendation of the IDB. The 1985 General Conference decided to name five deputy directors general, thus permitting greater regional/bloc representation. However, the 1993 General Conference approved a streamlined staff structure that eliminated the deputy directors general and instead named eight managing directors. In late 1997 UNIDO decided to reduce the number of divisions to three. In February 2002 the Secretariat instituted a new organizational structure with three divisions: Program Development and Technical Cooperation, Program Coordination and Field Operations, and Administration. Staff was also streamlined (143 posts abolished), and there was a significant reduction in the number of committees.

UNIDO activity in most developing countries is coordinated by a resident senior industrial development field adviser or a resident junior professional officer. In addition, expert advisers or consultantsare hired from throughout the world to work temporarily on many of the development projects administered by UNIDO. As of 2013, 50 countries had regional offices with some 2,500 contract personnel working in the field, along with the organization's 700 permanent staff.

Activities. UNIDO serves both as a technical cooperation agency and as a global forum. Its research, analysis, statistical compilation, dissemination of information, and training provide general support for industrial development throughout the world. In addition, the organization operates (usually in conjunction with other UN affiliates and national governments) hundreds of field projects per year in such areas as planning, feasibility study, research and development for specific proposals, and installation of pilot industrial plants.

UNIDO facilities include 17 Investment and Technology Promotion Offices, which encourage contacts between businessmen and governments in developing or transitional countries and industrial and financial leaders in developed countries; 10 closely associated International Technology Centers; 5 Investment Promotion Units in Africa and the Near East; 35 National Cleaner Production Centers under a program jointly organized with the UN Environment Program (UNEP); and 59 Subcontracting and Partnership Exchanges in more than 30 countries to link local manufacturers with the global market. UNIDO was also instrumental in the creation of the International Center for Genetic Engineering and Biotechnology, with bases in Trieste, Italy, and New Delhi, India; the International Center for Science and High Technology in Trieste; the Center for the Application of Solar Energy in Perth, Australia; the International Center for Small Hydro Power in Hangzhou, China; the International Center for Materials Evaluation Technology in Taejon, South Korea; and the International Center for Hydrogen Energy Technology in Istanbul, Turkey. Special UNIDO funds include the Industrial Development Fund (IDF), established in 1978 to provide financing for innovative development projects outside the criteria of existing financial services, and the Working Capital Fund, established in 1986.

In November 2001 the organization launched the Africa Investment Promotion Agency Network that focused on spurring domestic and foreign investment in 14 countries in sub-Saharan Africa. However, in July 2004 UNIDO released a report stating that the poorest African nations were "seriously off-track" for meeting the 2015 poverty reduction deadline set by the UN. Environmental sustainability has also emerged as a major theme of UNIDO's efforts. In addition to establishing the National Cleaner Production Centers Program in conjunction with the UNEP, it continues to serve as one of the UN's four implementing agencies for the Montreal Protocol on ozone-depleting chemicals and has been active in the Kyoto Protocol, which was implemented in February 2005 in an effort to combat greenhouse gases and global warming (see the discussion of both protocols in the UNEP article).

In late 1999 UNIDO held the first UNIDO Forum on Sustainable Industrial Development in Vienna, Austria, in tandem with the eighth General Conference to address the effects of economic integration in developing economies; the impact of globalization; environmental challenges to sustainable development; and the status of the recently initiated UNIDO Partnership Program, which is an effort to coordinate local and intergovernmental entities, both public and private, in assisting small- and medium-sized enterprises (SMEs).

The tenth General Conference was held in December 2003 in Vienna, where the main objective was to discuss the organization's role in fulfilling the Millennium Development Goals (MDGs) set by the UN in the environmental and developmental areas. At the 2005 11th General Conference, UNIDO adopted a strategic long-term vision statement and a medium-term program framework to cover the years 2006–2009. The 2007 General Conference took place on December 3–7 in Vienna. The Secretariat noted that member countries continued to be in arrears for payment of membership dues.

So-called south-south cooperation has become a key policy focus in recent years in an effort to promote trade and increased production capacities between advanced developing countries and poorer nations with emerging economies. To that end, UNIDO planned on opening industrial cooperation centers in China, Egypt, Brazil, and South Africa to enhance business networks. The first center opened in New Delhi, India, in February 2007, and a second in Beijing in July 2008.

In 2007 UNIDO hosted the International Conference on Biofuels in Kuala Lumpur, Malaysia, the first in a three-year series of conferences aimed at developing industrial conversion processes and uses of biofuels. UNIDO signed several agreements with India to promote SMEs in 2007 and 2008. However India was warned about its overreliance on fossil fuels and was encouraged to generate one-fifth of its electricity from renewable sources in the current UNIDO-India plan period, 2007–2012.

In April 2008 Director General Yumkella urged Africa to industrialize as a way to combat poverty and urged Nigeria to take the lead in this effort. In June UNIDO and Microsoft announced plans to set up a computer refurbishment operation in Uganda, with the twin aims of reducing pollution from discarded computers and of putting more and cheaper computers in African hands. In September UNIDO told India that it should aim to generate one fifth of the capacity expansion in its current economic plan (that covers 2007–2012) from renewable energy, thus alleviating its effect on climate change. In November UNIDO signed a Memorandum of Understanding (MOU) with China for cooperation in clean industrial development. On December 12, 2008, Samoa joined UNIDO as its 173rd member.

In January 2009 UNIDO signed an MOU for increased cooperation with the Eurasian Economic Community, an offshoot of the Commonwealth of Independent States (CIS, see separate article). In UNIDO's Industrial Development Report 2009, released February 24, 2009, it argued against using the world economic crisis as an excuse for returning to protectionism. Poor countries needed to move beyond trading raw materials and into manufacturing, it said. In June 2009 UNIDO announced the expansion of a joint program with the technology company Hewlett-Packard. This program would build additional IT training centers in Africa and the Middle East.

UNIDO's *Annual Report 2009* noted improving global trends in energy efficiency. Energy usage was 33 percent less intense in 2009 than in 1970, reflecting more energy efficient appliances, lights, and other electronic devices. In addition, UNIDO estimated that 15 percent of the economic stimulus packages adopted around the world contained "green" or eco-friendly components. In 2009 UNIDO expended $139 million on projects, a rise from the $124 million the year before. UNIDO approved 247 of 385 projects submitted that year. By the end of 2009, the organization had secured an additional $355 million for future projects.

In 2010 Japan pledged $10.6 million to support UNIDO economic development programs in Africa and Afghanistan. In addition, Italy pledged more than $3.5 million for UNIDO projects in Iraq. In February 2011 the United Kingdom announced that, as of January 1, 2013, it would no longer provide financial support to UNIDO (and would presumably leave the organization at that time). The United Kingdom had provided 9 percent of the organization's budget (€7.2 million). A UK report declared that UNIDO's mission did not sufficiently coincide with the United Kingdom's foreign aid goals.

In July and August 2011 UNIDO was embroiled in a dispute involving Nepal and China. In July Hu Yuandong, the chief UNIDO representative in China, signed an agreement with the Hong Kong–based Asia Pacific Exchange and Cooperation Foundation (APECF) to help develop a visitor center and cultural complex in Lumbini, Nepal, the birthplace of Buddha. Both the UNIDO main office and Nepal itself repudiated the arrangement, as neither had been consulted. Nepal felt the deal was a threat to its sovereignty. The deal might also have had significant geopolitical impact, as it would likely have introduced a large Chinese presence at a site close to the border between India and China. On October 27 Tuvalu became the 174th member of UNIDO.

In May 2012 UNIDO and Italy agreed to launch a program to promote sustainable development and renewable energy in developing countries. Meanwhile, Germany announced it would provide €1 million to support UNIDO efforts to bolster the pharmaceutical industry in Africa. In June UNIDO and Microsoft agreed to extend and expand a partnership program to use technology for education and employment training. The initiative would continue until 2015.

The 2013 report, the *Industrial Competitiveness of Nations: Looking Back, Looking Ahead,* utilized UNIDO's competitive industrial performace index to determine that developed nations such as the United States, Japan, and the EU states, still retained an advantage over developing states. Japan ranked first, followed by Germany and the United States. However, China made significant progress rising to 7th, the highest of any developing state, from 23rd the previous year. UNIDO's budget for 2014–2015 was $239.6 million.

WORLD BANK

Established: The World Bank Group consists of five component entities; the International Bank for Reconstruction and Development (IBRD, the oldest, established in 1945), the International Finance Corporation (IFC), the International Development Association (IDA), the Multilateral Investment Guarantee Agency (MIGA), and the International Center for Settlement of Investment Disputes (ICSID).

Purpose: To promote the international flow of capital for productive purposes, initially the rebuilding of nations devastated by World War II. The main objective of the bank at present is to offer loans at reasonable terms to member developing countries willing to engage in projects that will ultimately increase their productive capacities and reduce poverty.

Headquarters: Washington, D.C., United States.

Principal Organs: Board of Governors (all members), Executive Directors (25).

Web site: www.worldbank.org

President: Jim Yong Kim (United States).

Membership (188): See Appendix C.

Working Language: English.

Origin and development. The origins, development, and activities of the World Bank Group's three major components are discussed below.

INTERNATIONAL BANK FOR RECONSTRUCTION AND DEVELOPMENT, A MEMBER OF THE WORLD BANK GROUP

(IBRD)

Established: By Articles of Agreement signed in Bretton Woods, New Hampshire, July 22, 1944, effective December 27, 1945; began operation June 25, 1946. The IBRD became a UN Specialized Agency by agreement with the Economic and Social Council (approved by the General Assembly on November 15, 1947).

Purpose: To promote the international flow of capital for productive purposes, initially the rebuilding of nations devastated by World War II. The main objective of the bank at present is to offer loans at reasonable terms to member developing countries willing to engage in projects that will ultimately increase their productive capacities and reduce poverty.

Headquarters: Washington, D.C., United States.

Principal Organs: Board of Governors (all members), Executive Directors (25).

Web site: www.worldbank.org/ibrd

Membership (188): See Appendix C.

Working Language: English.

Origin and development. The International Bank for Reconstruction and Development was one of the two main products of the United Nations Monetary and Financial Conference held July 1–22, 1944, in Bretton Woods, New Hampshire. The bank was conceived as a center for mobilizing and allocating capital resources for the reconstruction of war-torn states and for the expansion of world production and trade; its sister institution, the International Monetary Fund (IMF), was created to maintain order in the field of currencies and exchange rates and thus to prevent a repetition of the financial chaos of the 1930s. The Articles of Agreement of the two institutions were annexed to the Final Act of the Bretton Woods Conference and went into effect December 27, 1945, following ratification by the required 28 states.

With the commencement of the U.S.-sponsored European Recovery Program in 1948, the focus of IBRD activities began to shift toward economic development. Accordingly, two affiliated institutions—the International Finance Corporation (IFC) and the International Development Association (IDA), created in 1956 and 1960, respectively (see separate entries)—were established within the IBRD's framework to undertake developmental responsibilities for which the IBRD itself was not qualified under its Articles of Agreement. In 1985 the IBRD approved a charter for another affiliate, the Multilateral Investment Guarantee Agency (MIGA), to provide borrowers with protection against noncommercial risks such as war, uncompensated expropriations, or repudiation of contracts by host governments without adequate legal redress for affected parties. The MIGA, operating as a distinct legal and financial entity, came into being on April 12, 1988, with about 54 percent of its initial $1.1 billion in authorized capital having been subscribed. As of 2013 there were 179 MIGA members.

The IBRD and IDA have long been referred to as the World Bank, or as the World Bank Group when considered in conjunction with affiliate organizations the IFC, the MIGA, and the International Center for Settlement of Investment Disputes (ICSID). The IBRD is responsible for lending to middle-income and creditworthy poor countries, while IDA extends grants and interest-free loans to the world's poorest countries. Loan statistics for both the IBRD and the IDA are given in this article.

Structure. All of the IBRD's powers are formally vested in the Board of Governors, which consists of a governor and an alternate appointed by each member state. The IBRD governors, who are usually finance ministers or equivalent national authorities, serve concurrently as governors of the IMF, as well as of the IFC, the IDA, and the MIGA, assuming that a given country's affiliations extend beyond the parent organization. The board meets each fall to review the operations of these institutions within the framework of a general examination of the world financial and economic situation. One meeting in three is held away from Washington, D.C.

Most powers of the Board of Governors are delegated to the IBRD's 25 executive directors, who meet at least once a month at the bank's headquarters and are responsible for the general conduct of its operations. Five of the directors are separately appointed by those members holding the largest number of shares of capital stock (France, Germany, Japan, the United Kingdom, and the United States). The others are individually elected for two-year terms by the remaining IBRD members, who are divided into 19 essentially geographical groupings, each of which selects one director. (Since Saudi Arabia by itself constitutes one of the geographical entities, its "election" of a director amounts, in practical terms, to an appointment. Similarly, China and the Russian Federation have single directors.) Each director is entitled to cast as a unit the votes of those members who elected him.

The bank operates on a weighted voting system that is largely based on individual country subscriptions (themselves based on IMF quotas), but with poorer states being accorded a slightly disproportionate share. As of 2013, the leading subscribers were the United States, with 16.03 percent (15.17 percent of voting power); Japan, 8.93 (8.46); China, 5.75 (5.46); Germany, 4.72 (4.49); France and the United Kingdom, 4.21 (4.01); Canada, 3.15 (3.00); India, 3.06 (2.92); Italy 2.53 (2.42); and Russia, 2.47 (2.37).

The president of the IBRD is elected to a renewable five-year term by the executive directors, serves as their chair, and is responsible for conducting the business of the bank as well as that of the IDA and the IFC. In accordance with the wishes of the U.S. government, Robert McNamara was replaced upon his retirement in June 1981 by Alden W. Clausen, a former president of the Bank of America, who restructured the bank's upper echelon to reflect his preference for collegial management and delegation of authority. On June 30, 1986, Clausen was succeeded by Barber B. Conable Jr., who had served on a number of financial committees in the course of ten consecutive terms in the U.S. House of Representatives. In May 1987 Conable announced a major reorganization within the bank to clarify and strengthen the roles of the president and senior management. Another change was the creation of country departments to oversee all aspects of individual lending projects; Conable also ordered a controversial review of all bank positions, which ultimately yielded about 350 redundancies.

Following the announcement of Conable's retirement, the executive directors in April 1991 approved the appointment of Lewis T. Preston, former chair of the board of J. P. Morgan and Morgan Guaranty Trust Company, as the next president, effective August 31. Preston's selection was seen as reflecting the insistence of the United States on additional private sector involvement by the bank and greater commercial bank influence in debt reduction negotiations. Like his predecessor, Preston instituted a number of structural changes early in his term that appeared to further concentrate power in the president's hands. Three senior vice presidents were eliminated and the remaining sixteen vice presidents were ordered to report directly to the president. Preston died on May 4, 1995, and was succeeded on June 1 by James D. Wolfensohn, a prominent New York investment banker. Administrative reforms continued under Wolfensohn, who in December 1996 appointed two new managing directors. Wolfensohn was succeeded in June 2005 by Paul Wolfowitz, previously the U.S. deputy secretary of defense. After implementing a string of controversial anticorruption measures, Wolfowitz resigned after two years in office under conflict-of-interest charges. He was replaced in July 2007 by former U.S. deputy secretary of state Robert Zoellick, then a vice chair of leading New York investment house Goldman Sachs. Zoellick was replaced by Dartmouth College president Jim Yong Kim on July 1, 2012.

Activities. The IBRD describes itself as structured like a cooperative. It is the organ of the World Bank that "works with middle-income and creditworthy poorer countries to promote sustainable, equitable and job-creating growth, reduce poverty and address issues of regional and global importance." Most funds available for lending are obtained by direct borrowing on world financial markets. Only a small percentage of the capital subscription of the member states represents paid-in capital in dollars, other currencies, or demand notes; the balance is "callable capital" that is subject to call by the bank only when needed to meet obligations incurred through borrowing or through guaranteeing loans. Most of the bank's operating funds are obtained by issuing interest-bearing bonds and notes to public and private investors.

The Articles of Agreement state that the IBRD can make loans only for productive purposes for which funds are not obtainable in the private market on reasonable terms. Loans are long-term (generally repayable over as much as 20 years, with a five-year grace period) and are available only to member states, their political subdivisions, and enterprises located in the territories of member states (in which case, the states involved must guarantee the projects).

In order to maintain the bank's financial strength and integrity as a borrower in the world capital markets, the executive directors agreed on July 2, 1982, to switch from the bank's traditional fixed-interest policy to a variable-interest policy. This action, taken in conjunction with the bank's borrowing operations in short-term capital markets, was intended to enable the bank to charge interest rates that more accurately reflect the institution's current capital costs. Under the revised system, interest rates are adjusted each January 1 and July 1 to reflect the cost of funds in a pool of bank borrowings from the preceding six-month period, plus a 0.5 percent surcharge. The bank has also initiated currency swap arrangements as an additional method of reducing its overall borrowing costs.

In the field of aid coordination, the bank has taken the lead in promoting a multilateral approach to the development problems of particular states by organizing groups of potential donors to work out long-range comprehensive plans for assistance. In addition, the bank has worked on projects with a large number of multilateral financial agencies, including the African Development Bank, the Asian Development Bank, the Inter-American Development Bank, the European Development Fund, and the Arab Fund for Economic and Social Development.

IBRD technical-assistance activities are directed toward overcoming the shortage of skills that tends to hamper economic growth in less developed states. The bank finances and organizes numerous pre-investment studies, ranging from those aimed at determining the feasibility of particular projects to sector studies directed toward formulating investment programs in such major fields as power and transport. It also sends expert missions to assist members in designing development programs and adopting policies conducive to economic growth, while the Economic Development Institute, the IBRD staff college, helps train senior officials of less developed states in development techniques.

In April 1993 it was reported that an internal review had acknowledged a "significant failure rate" within the bank's operations, with about 20 percent of the loans active in 1991 having "major problems." Although the design of some projects and the bank's follow-up procedures were criticized, the failures were primarily attributed to poor economic conditions during the 1980s in Africa, Latin America, and parts of Asia.

In July 1993 the leaders of the world's seven leading industrialized nations agreed during a summit in Tokyo to offer Moscow an aid package that included up to $1 billion in World Bank lending. Initial approvals were constrained by Moscow's difficulty in controlling government spending and inflation, coupled with economic and political turmoil within many of its newly independent neighbors. However, an improved situation led to what was expected to be at least $2 billion in additional lending.

In mid-1994 the bank embarked on another major project: the coordination of $2.4 billion in pledges from international donors for the Gaza Strip and Jericho, where the new Palestinian National Authority had recently been installed. Much of the Palestinian aid was earmarked for infrastructure development, a focus of the 1994 *World Development Report.*

For the fiscal year July 1, 1993, through June 30, 1994, bank officials said that progress had been made in monitoring loan performance and in integrating environmental concerns into IBRD activity. In addition, the bank established the three-member Independent Inspection Panel to investigate complaints about specific loans. However, the changes did not placate many of the bank's critics, environmentalists in particular continuing to assail the IBRD's "obsolete" industrial development policies. Questions also continued over the bank's role in the external debt problems facing many developing countries, highlighted by the fact that the IBRD in 1993–1994 took in $731 million more in repayments than it disbursed in new funds.

Lending approvals increased in fiscal year July 1, 1994, through June 30, 1995, totaling $16.9 billion for 134 projects. However, a decline in lending was expected under new bank president Wolfensohn, who proposed significant changes for the IBRD, including a shift away from "megaprojects" that often had proven difficult for developing countries to manage after they had been completed. In their stead, Wolfensohn said the bank should concentrate on small, environmentally sound projects that offered direct benefits to the poor. He also urged the bank to devote much more of its energy and resources to the promotion of private investment in developing countries and spearheaded the establishment of a new debt relief program, the Heavily Indebted Poor Countries (HIPC) debt-reduction initiative, for the poorest developing nations, most of which are African.

In March 1997 the Executive Board approved a Strategic Compact with the goal of increasing the World Bank's efficiency and effectiveness through "fundamental reform." Among the substantive goals of the 30-month program were the reduction of overhead and administrative costs, decentralization of the bank's operation, and the development and improvement of relationships with other organizations.

In the 1997 *World Development Report,* the IBRD asserted that "effective" governments, i.e., those that are relatively free of corruption and limited in scope, are a necessary precondition for social and economic development. Furthermore, both the IBRD and IMF began to insist on effective governance as a condition for their assistance. The bank subsequently emphasized the role of local governments in fostering development, arguing that corruption at the municipal level often undermined the best intentions of national policies. In 1998 President Wolfensohn also challenged the international financial community to develop a new long-term strategy to provide relief to the poor, and asserted, among other things, that the IMF was paying insufficient attention to the human costs of its financial stabilization activities. Debate on the subject continued into the preparation of the 2000 *World Development Report,* at which time several authors objected to the overdependence on "pro-market orthodoxy." The final report appeared to favor the "reformist" camp by calling for "empowerment" of the poor and protection of "vulnerable groups." Along those same lines, Wolfensohn subsequently called for dialogue with anti-globalization protesters who had recently conducted highly publicized demonstrations against the World Bank, IMF, and World Trade Organization (WTO). At the same time, the United States continued to press the IBRD to reduce its lending to certain middle-income countries (particularly in Latin America), which, according to the United States, needed to be weaned away from World Bank lending in favor of loans from the private sector.

In 2001–2002 the IBRD called on the wealthy nations of the world to increase their assistance to developing countries substantially, particularly in view of the global economic slowdown, which had exacerbated debt problems. The bank acknowledged that the HIPC Initiative had so far come up very short in reaching the goal of "sustainable" debt for the 34 countries considered eligible for assistance. Nevertheless, bank officials maintained their hope that more than $50 billion in debt would ultimately be canceled through the program.

IBRD lending approvals increased dramatically to $21.1 billion for 151 projects in 1997–1998 and $22.2 billion for 131 projects in 1998–1999, primarily due to the financial crises in Asia and Latin America. However, after conditions improved and the private sector resumed lending to emerging market economies, IBRD approvals declined to $10.9 billion for 97 projects in 1999–2000, $10.5 billion for 91 projects in 2000–2001, and $11.5 billion for 96 projects in 2000–2002. The reduced lending also underscored the bank's increased emphasis on "quality rather than quantity" in its lending. Special assistance was provided in 2002 for countries that had suffered particularly strong "economic shocks" in the wake of the September 11, 2001, attacks in the United States and the economic downturn that had begun even prior to those events. As of mid-2002, cumulative IBRD lending had reached over $370 billion for more than 4,600 projects.

In May 2004 the Group of Eight (G-8) pledged to continue the HPIC Debt Initiative, then scheduled to expire at the end of the year. It was estimated that some 25 countries had qualified for debt relief to date. Meanwhile, President Wolfensohn blamed the industrialized countries for the collapse of WTO negotiations in 2003, arguing that developing countries deserved a stronger voice in the global economy. Wolfensohn also said it was "unacceptable" that unprecedented military spending around the world was impeding efforts to help the poor.

In March 2005 the U.S. George W. Bush administration announced that Wolfensohn's successor would be Paul Wolfowitz, the U.S. deputy secretary of defense who had recently attracted attention as one of the main architects of the U.S.-led overthrow of the Saddam Hussein regime in Iraq. Considering the global antipathy to the war, the appointment was viewed as controversial. However, Wolfowitz pledged that he would not direct the World Bank as a vehicle for promoting U.S. policy and would maintain his predecessor's emphasis on reducing poverty.

In July 2005 the IBRD announced it would provide $500 million in loans for "priority sectors" in Iraq. It was the first bank lending to Iraq in three decades. In its *World Development Report* for 2006, issued September 2005, the bank declared that reducing inequality by liberal economic actions was the key to reducing poverty, while admitting that such inequality had risen. It suggested that the world's richest countries should abandon subsidies and encourage freer migration of skilled workers from developing countries. The report endorsed a decision by the G-8 countries at their July 2005 summit in Scotland to cancel some $55 billion in debt from the world's poorest countries.

Meanwhile, controversy surrounding Wolfowitz mounted as staff reportedly resented his heavy use of outside advisers. The anti-corruption measures he imposed in developing countries, one of his major pledges coming into office, came under increasing criticism. Also, a December 2006 report by the bank's Independent Evaluation Group (IEG) noted that many of the anti-corruption policies were failing because they lacked broad-based political consensus and were often implemented at the expense of poverty reduction and job creation goals. In March 2007 the World Bank executive board adopted a new policy that reined in the president's ability to cut funding without first consulting the board and allowed the bank to deal with independent groups in a country when it cut off loans to that country's government.

Two months later, Wolfowitz came under personal scrutiny over his role in engineering the promotion and salary raise of his companion, a female bank employee. He resigned in June 2007 amid calls for better internal controls and a more open and transparent hiring process for the bank president. Less influential member nations also renewed calls for more voting and decision-making powers. In July 2007 the bank appointed as president U.S. nominee Robert Zoellick, a former U.S. deputy secretary of state and U.S. trade representative. Zoellick announced a major policy shift in the bank's lending strategy that would boost funding for agricultural projects as a more effective means towards poverty reduction.

In advance of the World Bank and IMF annual meeting in October 2007, Zoellick called on wealthy nations to significantly increase their financial support for poor nations as part of a plan to more than double the bank's funding in grants and credits for poor countries under the IDA. He directed the IBRD and the IFC to increase contributions to the IDA as well.

In September, the bank's executive board simplified and reduced loan charges by a quarter percentage point for the 79 creditworthy countries funded by the IBRD. The change was part of an effort to increase the relevancy and attractiveness of the IBRD, which has faced competition from private sector lending sources.

As the price of food increased dramatically, causing distress in many countries of the world, the World Bank took a new interest in farming. The 2007 edition of the *World Development Report* stressed the importance of agriculture as the fastest way of improving a poor nation's economy, and the 2008 food crisis drove the point home. In April 2008 Zoellick announced, and the World Bank endorsed, a "new deal" action plan to pump more money into agricultural economies. On April 29 the UN set up an emergency task force to deal with the food situation, the members drawn from interested UN agencies and the World Bank.

The World Bank reported providing $47 billion in loans during the 2009 fiscal year, with $33 billion coming from the IBRD and $14 billion from the IDA. It provided $25 billion for 2008 (IBRD $14 billion and IDA $11 billion) and $25 billion for 2007 (IBRD $13 billion and IDA $12 billion).

During 2009 the World Bank issued various statements about the global financial crisis. On April 24 it published a report declaring that the United States and the EU were leading the world in a new round of protectionism. Also in April Zoellick warned of a "human catastrophe" unless more was done to combat the economic crisis. By September 2009 the organization warned that, while things might be going better for the world's rich, the poor were in no way recovering.

In March 2009 the World Bank launched a commission to investigate its own operations and suggest ways in which it might improve. The commission, headed by former Mexican president Ernesto Zedillo, released its report in October 2009. Among other suggestions, the Zedillo commission recommended restructuring the bank's governing bodies, strengthening management accountability, and making the selection of a president "merit-based, transparent, and open." Through 2009, the IBRD was funding 126 projects around the world.

At the IMF–World Bank spring meeting in April 2010, the capitalization of the World Bank was bolstered for the first time since 1988. The capital for the IBRD was increased to $86.2 billion as part of an agreement whereby developing states agreed to increase their capitalization in exchange for greater voting power, elevating the share of votes held by developing states from 44 percent to 47.2 percent. China was the greatest beneficiary. Its vote share would rise from 2.8 percent to 4.2 percent. In June Tuvalu became the 187th member of the IBRD. MIGA's *World Investment and Political Risk 2010* reported that foreign direct investment into developing countries would increase by 17 percent, but that political instability remained the main concern for investors and hampered an even greater inflow of funds.

Through 2011 the World Bank approved $42 billion in new loans and grants, with the IBRD accounting for $26 billion and the IDA $16 billion. Meanwhile, the administrative budget of the World Bank was $1.8 billion. In response to famine in the Horn of Africa and drought in other areas, the organization increased assistance for agriculture from $4.1 billion in 2008 to $8 billion in 2011. Along with the promulgation of a new long-term development plan for Africa, the World Bank provided a record $7 billion in loans and aid to the continent. In April 2012 South Sudan became the 188th member of the IBRD. By year's end, the IBRD had outstanding loans to 77 countries. Of the 188 members of the IBRD, 62 remained eligible to borrow from the institution, while 143 were able to borrow from either the IBRD or the IDA at the beginning of 2013.

In 2013 the IBRD had more than 100 offices worldwide and a staff of more than 9,000. In May 2013 Standard and Poor's reaffirmed the IBRD's credit rating as "AAA," although the organization's operating income decreased to $783 million in 2012, down from $1.02 billion the previous year. In addition, the IBRD had a net operating loss in 2012 of $676 million, down from a surplus of $930 million in 2011. Through June of 2013, IBRD revenues were again positive for the year, at $218 million. One result was that the board of governors approved in August, the transfer of $147 million to the general reserve.

INTERNATIONAL DEVELOPMENT ASSOCIATION, A MEMBER OF THE WORLD BANK GROUP

(IDA)

Established: By Articles of Agreement concluded in Washington, D.C., January 26, 1960, effective September 24, 1960. The IDA became a UN Specialized Agency by agreement with the Economic and Social Council (approved by the General Assembly on March 27, 1961).

Purpose: To assist in financing economic development in less developed member states by providing development credits on special terms, with particular emphasis on projects not attractive to private investors.

Headquarters: Washington, D.C., United States.

Web site: www.worldbank.org/ida

Membership (172): See Appendix C.

Working Language: English.

Origin and development. The IDA was established in response to an increasing awareness during the latter 1950s that the needs of less developed states for additional capital resources could not be fully satisfied through existing lending institutions and procedures. This was particularly true of the very poor states, which urgently needed finance on terms more concessionary than those of the International Bank for Reconstruction and Development (IBRD). Thus, in 1958 the United States proposed the creation of an institution with authority to provide credits on special terms in support of approved development projects for which normal financing was not available. Following approval by the Board of Governors of the IBRD, the IDA was established as an affiliate of that institution and was given a mandate to provide development financing, within the limits of its resources, on terms more flexible than those of conventional loans and less burdensome to the balance of payments of recipient states. Today, the IBRD and the IDA together are generally known as the World Bank.

The authorized capital of the IDA was initially fixed at $1 billion, of which the United States contributed $320 million. Members of the institution were divided by the IDA Articles of Agreement into two groups in accordance with their economic status and the nature of their contributions to the institution's resources. Part I (high-income) states pay their entire subscription in convertible currencies, all of which may be used for IDA credits; Part II (low-income) states pay only 10 percent of their subscriptions in convertible currencies and the remainder in their own currencies. Part I countries account for about 97 percent of total subscriptions and supplementary resources (special voluntary contributions and transfers from IBRD net earnings). As of 2012, leading Part I contributors were the United States, with 10.71 percent of voting power under the IDA's weighted system; Japan, 8.55 percent; United Kingdom, 5.58 percent; Germany, 5.53; France, 3.79 percent; and Canada, 2.58 percent. Leading Part II contributors are Saudi Arabia, 3.19 percent; India, 2.88 percent; and China, 2.06 percent. The weighted voting system has sometimes been criticized as unfair to smaller, poorer countries.

Structure. As an affiliate of the IBRD, the IDA has no separate institutions; its directors, officers, and staff are those of the IBRD.

Activities. The IDA is the single largest multilateral source of concessional assistance for low-income countries. Countries that had a 2012 annual per capita income of less than $1,175, had limited or no ability to borrow from the IBRD, and had good performance in implementation of IDA economic and social policies could qualify for IDA funds. IDA also provides grants to countries at risk of debt distress. To date, IDA credits and grants have totaled more than $238 billion, with the largest share, about 50 percent, directed to Africa.

Under conditions revised as part of the IDA's eighth replenishment, credits are extended for terms as long as 40 years for the least developed countries and 20 and 35 years for other countries. Credits are free of interest but there is a 0.75 percent annual service charge on disbursed credits (a 0.50 percent "commitment fee" on undisbursed credits was eliminated July 1, 1988). All credits carry a ten-year grace period, with complete repayment of principal due over the remaining 20 or 35 years of the loans.

Most IDA credits have been provided for projects to improve physical infrastructure such as road and rail systems, electrical generation and transmission facilities, irrigation and flood-control installations, educational facilities, telephone exchanges and transmission lines, and industrial plants. Loans have also been extended for rural development projects designed specifically to raise the productivity of the rural-dwelling poor. These credits often cut across sector lines.

Negotiations for the 12th replenishment, covering the period from July 1999 to June 2002, were concluded in November 1998 when, during a meeting in Copenhagen, Denmark, donor countries agreed to a $20.5 billion infusion of funds to the IDA, $11.6 billion from the donors themselves. An apparent reduction in funding from the 11th replenishment was explained by changes in exchange rates and became a 13 percent increase when the funds were measured in special drawing rights (SDRs). (For more information on previous replenishments, please see the 2013 *Handbook.*)

Borrowing countries and representatives of nongovernmental organizations were invited for the first time to participate in discussions regarding the 13th replenishment. The IDA also invited public comment on the negotiations, which culminated in a three-year (July 2002 to June 2005) replenishment of $23 billion. It was agreed that about 20 percent of overall IDA resources would henceforth be allocated in the form of grants rather than loans. (The United States had called for a 50 percent grant level on the theory that lending to date had done little to combat poverty while piling debt on developing countries.) Donors also insisted that future IDA assistance be tied to measurable progress on the part of recipient countries in areas such as education and health. Similar linkage was also endorsed to reward countries that encouraged good governance, free trade, and environmental protection.

Negotiations for the 14th replenishment (for July 2006–June 2009) concluded in April 2005 in Athens, Greece. Under this agreement, $34 billion was made available to the world's 81 poorest countries, which includes $18 billion in new contributions from 40 donor countries. At almost a 25 percent increase, it was the largest expansion of IDA resources in 20 years. Additionally, the countries facing the most difficult debt problems, mostly in sub-Saharan Africa, are receiving all of their financial support in grants. Less debt-burdened countries are receiving mostly highly concessional long-term loans, or a mixture of grants and loans. Since the replenishment the IDA has approved loans that include funding for a mining project in Mauritania, electrical power generation projects in Ghana and Benin, and for educational projects in Albania.

In 2005 the IDA revised and enhanced a system to manage the success of its projects and review progress of recipient nations. Indicators such as growth and poverty reduction, governance and investment climate, infrastructure development, and human development criteria such as health and education were considered. In the 15th replenishment, completed in December 2007, to cover years 2009–2011, the IDA was to receive more than $41 billion as part of a stepped-up effort to meet 2015 Millennium Development Goals in a program designated as IDA15 Replenishment. The vast majority of funding increases were to go to Africa and South Asia, the regions farthest away from attaining poverty reduction goals. Additionally, World Bank president Robert Zoellick offered a new proposal to raise funding for the IDA from private sector businesses and foundations and pledged to focus on agricultural initiatives as a means to battle poverty. The number of IDA programs in member countries increased from 78 in 2008 to 104 in 2009. In Africa, a joint IDA–International Finance Corporation initiative provided new funding to develop small- and medium-sized companies. The IFC provided $3 million and the IDA, $1 million, for the project.

In 2010 IDA commitments totaled $14.5 billion, with pledges of $13 billion from contributing states. India was the largest recipient of IDA aid, at $2.6 billion, followed by: Vietnam, $1.4 billion; Tanzania, $943; Ethiopia, $890 million; and Nigeria, $890 million. Through 2010, 45 countries had contributed $41.6 billion to the IDA15 Replenishment project which financed programs between 2008 and 2011. The UK was the largest donor to the effort, providing 14.1 percent of the total, followed by the United States at 12.2 percent and Japan at 10 percent. In the effort, China, Cyprus, Egypt, Estonia, Latvia, and Lithuania became donors to the IDA for the first time (China and Egypt having previously been recipient countries). In response to the January earthquake in Haiti, the IDA announced a special $30 million grant to aid in recovery. Meanwhile, the IDA agreed in June to debt relief of $4.6 billion for Liberia and in July to support debt relief of $12.3 billion for the Democratic Republic of the Congo, among other debt initiatives.

At a donor meeting in Brussels December 14–15, 2010, it was agreed to replenish the IDA with a record US $49.3 billion funding package, an 18 percent increase over the previous replenishment three years previously. The agreement was noteworthy for having strong pledges from both traditional and new donors, contributions through prepayments from countries that used to borrow interest-free loans from IDA, and contributions from World Bank and IFC net income. Observers felt that such a replenishment, at a time of considerable economic stress for donors, was a testament to IDA's track record of delivering results and value for money.

In February 2011 the IDA approved an additional $420 million for protection of basic services in Ethiopia. In July it announced over $500 million in aid to the victims of drought in the Horn of Africa. In August it announced a grant of $19 million "to strengthen the capacity of Afghanistan's Central Bank to foster a sound financial system." Through 2011 the IDA launched 230 new initiatives, worth $16.3 billion. Approximately 50 percent of the projects were in Africa. In addition, 17 percent of the funding came in the form of grants. An IDA report found that from 2000 to 2010, the organization, among other activities, recruited or trained more than 3 million teachers, provided immunization for 310 million people, and provided assistance to improve access to clean water and sanitation for 113 million people.

In the fiscal year that ended on June 31, 2013, the IDA commited $16.3 billion to 160 new projects, 15 percent of which were grants. By 2013, 82 countries, with a combined population of 2.5 billion, were eligible for funding from the IDA. Neogitations for the 17th Replenishment began in March 2013 at a conference in Paris. At the meeting, participants endorsed the priorites of climate change, gender equality, and support for fragile and conflict-affected states. The meeting also backed new guidelines for states to graduate from the IDA to the IBRD. Subsequent sessions were held in Managua, Nicaragua, in July, and Washington, D.C., in October.

INTERNATIONAL FINANCE CORPORATION

(IFC)

Established: By Articles of Agreement concluded in Washington, D.C., May 25, 1955, effective July 20, 1956. The IFC became a UN Specialized Agency by agreement with the Economic and Social Council (approved by the General Assembly on February 20, 1957).

Purpose: To further economic development by encouraging the growth of productive private enterprise in member states, particularly the less developed areas. Its investment is usually in private or partially governmental enterprises.

Headquarters: Washington, D.C., United States.

Web site: www.ifc.org

Membership (184): See Appendix C.

Working Language: English.

Origin and development. A suggestion that an international agency be formed to extend loans to private enterprises without government guarantees and to undertake equity investments in participation with other investors was made in 1951 by the U.S. International Development Advisory Board. That summer the UN Economic and

Social Council requested that the International Bank for Reconstruction and Development (IBRD) investigate the possibility of creating such an agency, and a staff report was submitted to the UN secretary general in April 1952. The General Assembly in late 1954 requested the IBRD to draw up a charter, and the following April the bank formally submitted a draft for consideration. The IFC came into being on July 20, 1956, when 31 governments representing a sufficient percentage of total capital subscriptions accepted the Articles of Agreement.

Structure. As an affiliate of the IBRD, and thus a member of the World Bank Group, the IFC shares the same institutional structure. The president of the IBRD is also president of the IFC, and those governors and executive directors of the IBRD whose states belong to the IFC hold identical positions in the latter institution. The corporation has its own operating and legal staff but draws on the bank for administrative and other services. An executive vice president directs daily operations. As is true of the IBRD and the IDA, the IFC employs a weighted voting system based on country subscriptions, but with less developed states holding a disproportionate share of voting power.

IFC investments are handled through sectors, or industry departments, that process transactions and provide regional departments with expertise. They include Agribusiness; Global Financial Markets; Global Manufacturing and Services; Health and Education; Information and Communication Technologies; Infrastructure; Oil, Gas, Mining, and Chemicals; Private Equity and Investment Funds; and Subnational Finance. The corporation divides its 3,400 employees roughly in half between field offices (some 51 percent) and agency headquarters (some 49 percent). In 2013 there were field offices in 80 countries.

Activities. The IFC concentrates its efforts in three principal areas: project finance; resource mobilization; and financial, technical, and other advisory services. It conducts its own investment program, investigates the soundness of proposed projects to furnish expert advice to potential investors, and generally seeks to promote conditions conducive to the flow of private investment into development tasks. Investments, in the form of share subscriptions and long-term loans, are made in projects of economic priority to less developed member states where sufficient private capital is not available on reasonable terms and when the projects offer acceptable prospects for adequate returns. The IFC also carries out standby and underwriting arrangements and, under a policy adopted in July 1968, may give support in the pre-investment stage of potential projects by helping to pay for feasibility studies and for coordinating industrial, technical, and financial components, including the search for business sponsors. In addition, the IFC may join other investment groups interested in backing pilot or promotional companies, which then carry out the necessary studies and negotiations needed to implement the projects. The corporation neither seeks nor accepts government guarantees in its operations.

For changes to authorized capital, and for other activities, prior to 1994, see the 2011 *Handbook*. On January 1, 1994, Jannik Landbaek of Norway, previously vice president of the Nordic Investment Bank (NIB), took over as IFC executive vice president. Peter Woicke of Germany, a former investment banker for J. P. Morgan for 29 years, succeeded him on January 1, 1999. During his five-year tenure, Woicke was credited for making the IFC "operate less like an international bureaucracy and more like a private-sector financial institution." Under a massive reorganization, Woicke shifted the IFC's resources away from large corporations in developed countries to smaller local companies that became increasingly involved in the global market. In 2004 the corporation had a record $982 million in operation profits, nearly 90 percent more than in 2003, with 80 percent of business involving small companies. Woicke also made strides in tightening corporate governance. Following his retirement in January 2005, Woicke was succeeded by Assad Jabre of Lebanon, who served as acting executive vice president until the permanent appointment of Lars H. Thunnel of Sweden, effective January 1, 2006. On August 12, 2012, Jin-Yong Cai of China, was appointed executive vice president.

The IFC has also continued to emphasize good corporate governance and greater loan transparency, due in part to the corporate scandals that erupted in the United States and elsewhere in the early 2000s. In November 2002, the IFC created three new environmental funds to encourage private sector investors to be aware of environmental and social issues in emerging markets. They include the Environmental Opportunities Facility to provide funding for innovative projects addressing local environmental concerns, the Sustainable Financial Markets Facility to address environmentally and socially responsible lending and investments, and the Corporate Citizenship Facility to work more closely with project sponsors. In November 2003, the IFC also established guidelines, known as the Equator Principles, to ensure banks invest in projects that are both environmentally and socially sound. In 2006 the IFC began programs to improve labor standards in global supply chains in partnership with the International Labour Organization. Under World Bank Group president Robert Zoellick's direction in 2007, the IFC began integrating financing with the bank's public sector arms. In late 2007, the IFC contributed $1.75 billion to the International Development Association (IDA) for private-sector development in the poorest nations; the program was slated to run through 2010.

The IFC also doubled the size of its global trade financing program to $1 billion in 2007 in order to boost trade among small- and medium-sized import and export businesses. In recent years the program has focused increasingly on investment projects in the poorest nations and post-conflict areas, such as the Democratic Republic of the Congo, Liberia, Lebanon, and Sierra Leone. In October 2007, the IFC announced the launch of the new $5 billion Global Emergency Markets Local Currency Bond Fund to help countries develop local currency bond markets to attract more private investment and allow poor nations to borrow using their own currencies. In an innovative development, in May 2008 the IFC announced a partnership with Standard Chartered Bank to issue notes backed by loans to microfinance institutions in Africa and Asia. These notes establish a new product to provide investors with access to microfinance as an asset class, and it will enable Standard Chartered to expand its lending to the microfinance sector.

The IFC reported investments of $11.4 billion for the 2008 fiscal year, with an additional $4.7 billion raised from outside sources for 372 projects in 85 countries. It also reported that it provided advisory services in 97 countries. The 2009 fiscal year saw some contraction in light of the global financial crisis. IFC financing for private sector development totaled $14.5 billion, including $4.0 billion obtained through syndications, structured finance, and crisis-related initiatives, down from the record $19 billion high of the previous year. IFC invested in 447 projects during the year, of which half were in IDA countries.

As part of its response to the economic crisis, in May 2009 IFC took an unprecedented step in launching a subsidiary to act as a fund manager for third-party capital. The new unit, called IFC Asset Management Company, LLC, initially was to manage a $3 billion IFC Recapitalization Fund, which was designed to protect emerging-markets banks from the effects of the global downturn. Now, it will also manage a new $1 billion private equity fund that will allow national pension funds, sovereign funds, and other sovereign investors from IFC's shareholder countries to support investments in IFC transactions in Africa, Latin America, and the Caribbean.

In 2010 the IFC allocated $18 billion to projects, $12.7 billion from its own accounts, the rest secured through donor states or cooperative financing arrangements. The IFC launched 528 new projects, an 18 percent increase over the previous year. By the end of the year, the IFC had ongoing projects in 58 countries and the newly formed Asset Management Company had raised $950 million. In response to the global financial crisis, the IFC committed more than $11 billion to financial stabilization and recovery projects. This included $6 billion from the IFC, $2 billion raised in additional funding from donor states, and the remainder from matching finance programs. Investments in clean energy grew substantially to account for 15 percent of the total services portfolio.

In February 2011 the IFC launched a new fund of up to €150 million to purchase carbon credits to help reduce greenhouse-gas emissions, extend carbon markets, and increase access to finance for projects that promote environmentally friendly economic growth. The IFC was to invest up to €15 million, the remainder to come from European energy companies and power utilities. On March 23 it announced that it had become the first multilateral development bank to sign the United Nations Principles for Responsible Investment, as part of its efforts to mobilize capital for investments that are environmentally and socially responsible and adhere to high standards of corporate governance.

In August 2011 the IFC announced that fiscal 2011 had been a record year for its support of trade flows in emerging markets, with more than half the total volume of $4.6 billion supporting trade in the world's poorest countries. During 2011 the IFC invested more than $1.7 billion in programs to address climate change. For instance, the IFC provided assistance for a project to build windpower farms in a remote area of the Gobi Desert. Meanwhile the IFC reported income of

$2.2 billion in 2011, up from $1.9 billion the previous year. Grants to the IFC were $600 million, an increase from $200 million in 2010.

The IFC's 2013 annual report highlighted the expansion of the organization's programs and support for developing states. The IFC provided a record $25 billion for private sector development, of which $5 billion went to sub-Saharan Africa, and $2 billion to South Asia. In addition, the IFC increased the assets of its subsidiary venture capital group, the IFC Management Company, by $5.5 billion. IFC projects in 2012–2013 provided employment for 2.7 million, along with power for 52.2 million, and water for 42 million.

WORLD HEALTH ORGANIZATION

(WHO)

Established: By constitution signed in New York, United States, July 22, 1946, effective April 7, 1948. WHO became a UN Specialized Agency by agreement with the Economic and Social Council (approved by the General Assembly on November 15, 1947, with effect from September 1, 1948).

Purpose: To aid in "the attainment by all peoples of the highest possible levels of health."

Headquarters: Geneva, Switzerland.

Principal Organs: World Health Assembly (all members), Executive Board (32 experts), Regional Committees (all regional members), Secretariat.

Web site: www.who.int/en

Director General: Margaret Chan (Hong Kong SAR).

Membership (194, plus 2 Associate Members): See Appendix C.

Official Languages: Arabic, Chinese, English, French, Russian, Spanish.

Origin and development. Attempts to institutionalize international cooperation in health matters originated as early as 1851 but reached full fruition only with establishment of WHO. The need for a single international health agency was emphasized in a special declaration of the UN Conference on International Organization held in 1945 in San Francisco, California, and the constitution of WHO was adopted at the specially convened International Health Conference held in June–July 1946 in New York. Formally established on April 8, 1948, WHO also took over the functions of the International Office of Public Health, established in 1907; those of the League of Nations Health Organization; and the health activities of the UN Relief and Rehabilitation Administration (UNRRA).

A turning point in WHO's evolution occurred in 1976. As a result of decisions reached during that year's World Health Assembly, it began to reorient its work so that by 1980 a full 60 percent of its regular budget would be allocated for technical cooperation and for the provision of services to member states. In addition, all nonessential expenditures were to be eliminated, resulting in a reduction of several hundred administrative positions. (For more information on events prior to 1980, please see the 2012 *Handbook.*)

Controversy at the 32nd World Health Assembly was generated by an abortive attempt by Arab representatives to suspend Israeli membership. The United States, objecting to politicization of the organization, warned that it would probably withdraw from WHO if the proposal were adopted. At the 33rd assembly in May 1980, Arab members succeeded in gaining approval of a resolution that declared "the establishment of Israeli settlements in the occupied Arab territories, including Palestine, a source of "serious damage" to the inhabitants' health. Moreover, the conferees condemned the "inhuman practices to which Arab prisoners and detainees are subject in Israeli prisons." A clause that would have denied Israel's membership rights was deleted from a resolution before the 35th assembly in May 1982, after the United States had again threatened withdrawal.

In 1989 a proposal to grant membership to the Palestine Liberation Organization (PLO) received strong backing from Arab states and many developing countries but was condemned by the United States, which threatened to withhold its WHO contribution. The assembly deferred the question and in 1990 postponed action "indefinitely," although it increased direct assistance to Palestinians. Currently, Palestine has observer status in the WHO. Taiwan has been denied membership eight times, most recently in 2004, because China claims sovereignty and has successfully blocked its bids.

The 1994 assembly received a director general's report outlining recent budgetary and accounting reforms, with even stricter controls subsequently being recommended by some WHO members. At the same session the assembly reinstated South Africa, under suspension since 1964, to full membership privileges.

Controversy broke out over Director General Nakajima at the 1995 assembly. WHO's external auditor told the assembly that the WHO Secretariat failed to cooperate with his inquiry into alleged fraud, waste, and financial impropriety. Consequently, the assembly rejected Nakajima's request for a 16 percent increase in the WHO regular budget, approving instead a total of $842.7 million for the 1996–1997 biennium, an increase of only 2.5 percent. At the 1998 World Health Assembly, Dr. Gro Harlem Brundtland, former prime minister of Norway, was elected director general, effective in July. In August 2002 Brundtland announced she would not run for reelection, adding that she was content with the progress WHO had made during her tenure. (Brundtland is widely credited for coining the term "sustainable development.") Lee Jong-Wook, a South Korean doctor with expertise on vaccines and diseases associated with poverty, was selected as director general in January 2003. In May 2006 Dr. Lee died suddenly, and was replaced in an acting capacity by his deputy, Dr. Anders Nordström of Sweden. In November 2006 the assembly appointed Margaret Chan as director general. Chan was the former health director of Hong Kong during the severe acute respiratory syndrome (SARS) outbreak and had worked for three years at WHO in various high level posts.

Structure. The World Health Assembly, in which all members are represented, is the principal political organ of WHO. At its annual sessions, usually held at WHO headquarters in May, the assembly approves the organization's long-range work program as well as its annual program and budget. International health conventions may be approved and recommended to governments by a two-thirds majority vote. The assembly similarly adopts technical health regulations that come into force immediately for those governments that do not specifically reject them.

The Executive Board is composed of 32 members who, although designated by governments selected by the assembly, serve in an individual expert capacity rather than as governmental representatives. Meeting at least twice a year, the board prepares the assembly agenda and oversees implementation of assembly decisions. The Secretariat is headed by a director general designated by the assembly on recommendation of the board.

WHO is the least centralized of the UN Specialized Agencies, much of its program centering on six regional organizations: Southeast Asia (headquartered in New Delhi, India); the Eastern Mediterranean (Cairo, Egypt); the Western Pacific (Manila, Philippines); the Americas (Washington, D.C.); Africa (Brazzaville, Congo); and Europe (Copenhagen, Denmark). Each of the six has a regional committee of all members in the area and an office headed by a regional director.

Activities. Generally considered one of the more successful UN agencies, WHO acts as a guiding authority on international health work, actively promotes cooperation in health matters, sets global health standards, and works toward development and transfer of health-related technology and information. Since the early 1980s WHO has accepted as a leading principle "Health for All," which in its most recent incarnation entails the equitable distribution of health resources coupled with universal access to essential health services. In addition, WHO has increasingly emphasized that the public itself needs to make wiser choices, including adherence to healthier lifestyles, to escape "the avoidable burden of disease." WHO identified ten major avoidable health risks in its October 2002 annual report that are responsible for 56 million deaths each year, including hunger, unprotected sex, high blood pressure, smoking, alcohol, contaminated water or poor sanitation, high cholesterol, nutritional deficiencies, and obesity. As part of a landmark strategy to combat obesity, the organization encouraged governments to increase taxes on foods with high sugar, salt, and saturated fat content, which prompted strong opposition from the sugar industry in 2004. However, the nonbinding strategy was ultimately adopted in May 2004 and endorses a series of policy guidelines.

The organization is perhaps best known for its highly successful immunization programs, beginning with its coordination of the worldwide smallpox vaccination campaign that by 1980 had eradicated the disease. WHO announced in January 2002 that the destruction of the remaining smallpox stocks would be postponed for up to three years to give researchers more time to develop new treatments and vaccines for the disease after terrorist attacks sparked fears that the virus could be used as a weapon. Following the September 11, 2001, terrorist attacks in the United States, U.S. president George W. Bush's administration stockpiled the vaccine. In 1974 WHO also embarked, in conjunction with the UN Children's Fund (UNICEF), on a worldwide campaign to immunize children against measles, poliomyelitis, diphtheria, pertussis (whooping cough), tetanus, and tuberculosis (TB); hepatitis B was added in 1992, as was yellow fever in relevant geographical areas. In June 2002 WHO declared Europe free of polio, marking it as the third region worldwide to be certifiably free of the disease.

Soon after taking office, Director General Brundtland set about reorganizing WHO, reducing its programs from 50 to 35 and placing them in nine clusters. Subsequent restructuring brought the number of clusters down to eight and then to six in a further realignment in October 2007 under Director General Chan.

WHO organizes its clusters into broad areas of disease management. The Health Security and Environment cluster, formerly named the Communicable Disease cluster, includes the Department of Epidemic and Pandemic Alert and Response; the Department of Protection of the Human Environment; and the Department of Food Safety, Zoonoses [diseases transmitted through contact with animals], and Food-borne Diseases. The changes reflect an expansion in the agency's scope to encompass environmental hazards and foodborne diseases as a result of implementation in 2007 of the International Health Regulations (IHR) of 2005.

The Noncommunicable Diseases and Mental Health cluster, which retained its name under the realignment, has a broad mandate that includes issues regarding aging, psychiatric and other mental disorders, substance abuse, tobacco use, violence and injury prevention, and oral health as well as such "lifestyle" diseases as diabetes, avoidable blindness, cardiovascular disease, and cancer. The 1999 World Health Assembly opened negotiations on the Framework Convention on Tobacco Control (FCTC), and tumultuous negotiations continued until May 2003 when all of the 192 member countries ultimately adopted the landmark treaty. The United States, a reluctant supporter, was the last country to sign on because of contentious language on advertising that the United States said could violate constitutional rights to free speech. The treaty regulates that health warnings must be no less than 30 percent the size of a cigarette pack, bans terms such as "light" and "low tar," encourages higher taxes on tobacco products, and condemns certain marketing methods. The treaty went into force in February 2005 and has been ratified by 146 countries. A second FCTC meeting of signatory countries in July 2007 in Bangkok, Thailand, reviewed further changes to the tobacco treaty, including the development of protocols to curb illicit trade in tobacco products and exposure to second-hand smoke.

The HIV/AIDS, TB, Malaria, and Neglected Tropical Diseases cluster includes the Department of Neglected Tropical Diseases. Longstanding WHO efforts to eradicate polio and control maladies such as "river blindness" (onchocerciasis), lymphatic filariasis, "Chagas disease" (American trypanosomiasis), guinea-worm disease (dracunculiasis), leprosy, and Buruli ulcer fall under this cluster. In October 2006 the agency announced new guidelines to tackle "neglected" tropical diseases, which would include the use of inexpensive, preventative drugs in both healthy and infected people.

Additionally, the cluster handles the Department of HIV/AIDS, a major focus of WHO attention since the 1993 World Health Assembly called for a coordinated attack against the condition. In early 1996 WHO became one of the original cosponsoring agencies of the resultant Joint UN Program on HIV/AIDS (UNAIDS), which later set a millennium development goal of reversing the spread of the disease by 2015. Since then, a number of coordinated efforts to track the spread of the disease and provide treatment to ailing populations have been formed. The "3 by 5" program launched in 2003 by UNAIDS had a target of providing 3 million people with antiretroviral treatment by the end of 2005. In July 2004 WHO officials said they would meet that target, but by 2005 it became clear that the agency would far fall short. High drug prices and delivery problems were blamed for the agency's delivery of drugs to only 1 million people.

In September 2003 WHO announced it would organize a drug- buying facility for AIDS treatments to make it easier for developing countries to access treatments. Additionally, in 2005 the Global Price Reporting Mechanism for Antiretroviral Drugs was created to screen and share drug prices with procurement agencies to allow price comparisons for optimal purchasing.

Subsequent efforts on handling HIV/AIDS have moved toward the goal of providing universal access to prevention and treatment programs. The June 2006 General Assembly set a new goal of achieving such access by 2010. However, the release later that year of the *UNAIDS/WHO 2006 AIDS Epidemic Update* suggested the task would be more difficult than anticipated, reporting a resurgence in new HIV infection rates in some countries that were previously stable or in decline. Though the largest number of infection rates continued to be in sub-Saharan Africa, the report stated that Eastern Europe and Central Asia had HIV growth rates of more than 50 percent in some areas. In 2006, 2.9 million people died of AIDS-related illnesses globally, and 4.3 million were newly infected, according to the report. Though there was "a positive trend in young people's sexual behaviors," the report noted that many HIV prevention programs were not reaching people most at risk.

However, an April 2007 progress report on universal access found some encouraging trends. Nearly one-third of those living with HIV/AIDS in low- and middle-income countries were receiving treatment. Antiretroviral drug prices in those same countries had reduced from one-third to one-half between the years 2003–2006. The signs of progress were offset by a warning that treatment needed to be greatly expanded to account for a steep increase in future need. It also outlined the emergence of an alarming growth in drug-resistant tuberculosis in settings of high HIV prevalence.

In other areas, WHO's Information, Evidence, and Research cluster focuses on epidemiology, statistics, quality assurance, access to care, cost-effectiveness, health system reform, and regulatory and legislative matters. It also publishes the *Bulletin of the World Health Organization* and the annual *World Health Report.* The cluster includes the Special Program for Research and Training in Tropical Diseases and the newly created Department on Ethics, Equity, Trade, and Human Rights. The latter handles information on bioethics and ethical aspects of health care delivery and research. Additionally, WHO publishes the *International Pharmacopoeia* and the *WHO Model List of Essential Drugs* (more than 330 in the 2007 edition), establishes drug standards, and assists in the formulation of national drug policies.

The 1998 *World Health Report* noted that there had been impressive advances in global health, with average life expectancy increasing from 48 in 1950 to 66. Despite these gains, the report also estimated that 40 percent of all deaths were premature. The 1999 *World Health Report,* acknowledging financial and other constraints in delivery of health care, recommended that priority be given to helping poorer countries combat infectious disease and malnutrition. The report also proposed that developed countries set clear health service priorities and attempt to provide universal coverage for the selected conditions. This new "universalism" has as a founding principle that "if services are to be provided for all, then not all services can be provided."

In June 2000 WHO published a report, *Overcoming Microbial Resistance,* which focused on the growing problem of multidrug-resistant tuberculosis, pneumonia, typhoid, AIDS, and sexually transmitted diseases. In October WHO joined governments, private firms, and charitable organizations in establishing a research program, budgeted at $150 million for the first five years, to develop a new drug against TB, which continues to claim some 2 million lives annually.

In May 2002 WHO announced it was taking the first steps to becoming the global watchdog over unconventional medicine, or non-Western treatments, as at least 80 percent of the world's poorest countries use them. The organization seeks to catalog all folk remedies.

WHO played a significant role during the SARS outbreak in 2003, which centered in China and caused the deaths of at least 78 people worldwide. To stem the outbreak, WHO urged airports in affected cities to screen ill passengers and connected a network of 11 laboratories in nine countries to identify the agent causing the illness and devise treatments—a rapid response strategy considered unprecedented for the organization. However, research efforts were temporarily hindered when Chinese officials repeatedly denied WHO experts access to the Guangdong Province, where the disease was believed to have originated. China eventually relented and provided data, although not full access, to WHO. By June 2003 the organization announced that the SARS outbreak was over in Vietnam and in Hong Kong.

The following month WHO approved sweeping new powers to respond to international health threats such as SARS. The resolution established round-the-clock communication between countries, allows WHO to use nonofficial sources of information such as reports from nongovernmental organizations or the news media to respond to threats, authorizes the organization to issue global alerts, and authorizes the director general to send teams to conduct on-the-spot studies to ensure countries take adequate measures to stop diseases from spreading.

In recent years WHO has been active in coordinating tsunami relief, has continued its efforts against the spread of avian influenza, and has seen the world's first global health treaty, the Framework Convention on Tobacco Control, come into force (February 2005). The organization subsequently decided to hire only nonsmokers.

In an external development that could have a significant impact on WHO's future activities, American financier Warren Buffet announced in July 2006 that he was giving $31 billion of his fortune to the Bill and Melinda Gates Foundation, a philanthropy dedicated to "bringing innovations in health and learning to the global community." Some commentators suggested that this gift would create a private health-related charity with a larger budget than WHO.

The 2007 *World Health Report* focused on public health in a time of environmental changes and diseases that spread rapidly around the world. It called for complete implementation of the IHR as well as increased global cooperation and surveillance in public health matters. In a related effort, in October 2007 WHO announced support for a campaign to register every birth in the world, pointing out the dangers to which unregistered children are subject.

The 61st World Health Assembly, held May 19–24, 2008, in Geneva, was attended by a record number of participants. It endorsed a six-year plan to deal with noncommunicable diseases, which are considered the leading threats to human health in the early twenty-first century. It also called for a draft strategy by 2010 to deal with the harmful use of alcohol and requested more information about the health aspects of migrant environments. Assembly participants asked member states to work decisively against the effects of climate change and to utilize education and legislation to eliminate female genital mutilation.

The year 2008 was notable for the increasing danger from diseases that had been thought completely or nearly extinct, coupled with a decline in childhood immunization rates in advanced countries. WHO warned about the spread of drug-resistant tuberculosis, which had grown to account for 20 percent of all cases. But it noted that a cheap, rapid test for the condition was had become available. WHO sent vaccine to Paraguay to combat a yellow fever outbreak and to the Sahel when polio emerged in the region, but it was able to declare Somalia free of tuberculosis and Zimbabwe of polio. A June 2008 report declared that there was no longer the threat of an AIDS pandemic among heterosexuals, except in Africa. In September 2008 WHO criticized China for initially not doing more to stop the sale of melamine-tainted milk products; the organization then issued guidelines to help affected countries assess and deal with the problem.

In a sign that some stability was returning to Iraq, in July 2008 the WHO office in Baghdad reopened. In October 2008 WHO scientific experts agreed to a research agenda to develop an evidence-based framework for action on human health in a time of climate change.

The 2008 *World Health Report,* published in October of that year, noted inequities in health care around the world, even between areas of the same country a few miles apart, and recommended a renewed emphasis on primary medicine. A December 2008 report pointed out that essential medicines were out many people's reach. The May 2009 World Health Assembly was dominated by concerns about the H1N1 strain of influenza, which threatened to become a pandemic. It also noted efforts to fight new strains of drug-resistant tuberculosis. On June 12, 2009, Director General Chan declared H1N1 influenza to be pandemic.

In September 2009 a WHO-sponsored study found the leading causes of death among children and young adults to be road accidents, suicide, and complications from childbirth. By October 2009, with a vaccine against H1N1 influenza becoming available, the WHO advised that in most cases people over ten years of age need only receive a single dose in order to be protected.

A cholera outbreak in Haiti following the January 2010 earthquake, and other outbreaks in Pakistan and central Africa, led the WHO global task force on cholera control to issue new guidelines for the treatment and prevention of the disease. The task force noted that there are 3–5 million cases and 100,000–200,000 deaths every year from cholera, but that 80 percent of cases can be effectively treated with oral rehydration medicines. In March WHO launched a campaign to vaccinate 85 million children against polio in central and west Africa, in a partnership with the Red Cross and Red Crescent societies. The project was funded by $30 million from Rotary International. Global efforts to vaccinate children against polio had reduced the number of cases from 350,000 in 1988 to 1,600 in 2009. Also in March a WHO report warned that drug-resistant strains of tuberculosis accounted for 3.6 percent of all cases, or 440,000 people, a new record. WHO officials announced in April that the organization's efforts to publicize the H1N1 influenza pandemic were flawed and created confusion. WHO did report that the H1N1 pandemic killed 17,770 people. In August Chan declared the pandemic to be over.

In April 2011 the WHO warned that the world was losing the battle against antibiotic-resistant infections. It reported that in the EU alone over 25,000 people die each year of infections that have become resistant to all medications. The worst of the "superbugs" originated in India or Pakistan, and the WHO warned people who were thinking of traveling to these countries for inexpensive surgery to do extreme diligence on the hospitals where they would be treated. The only long-term solution that the WHO could offer was a worldwide effort to develop more and better antibiotics, if the world was to avoid a pandemic of untreatable diseases.

The 64th World Health Assembly, held May 16–24, 2011, in Geneva, put off a decision about finally destroying all stocks of live smallpox virus. This destruction had been provisionally scheduled for 2016, but the WHO agreed to put off any discussion until 2014. The disease is believed to have been eradicated, but the United States and Russia oppose final destruction, wanting to do more research in case smallpox should reappear, perhaps as a biological weapon. Iran favored destruction. The matter has been under debate since 1986. In July the WHO called for a ban on blood tests for active tuberculosis. It stated that such tests were 50 percent unreliable, both as to false negatives and false positives, and were as much of a threat to world health as the disease itself.

The WHO staff proposed a budget of $4.8 billion for 2012–2013; however, the organization's executive board revised the budget downward to $3.95 billion in light of the global economic crisis and concurrent constraints on donor funding. Programs in Africa would receive 25.2 percent of the funding, followed by Southeast Asia at 10.9 percent and the Eastern Mediterranean at 9.1 percent. In May 2012, Chan was elected for a second term by the General Assembly.

In June 2013 the WHO published the first comprehensive, global report on gender violence. The study estimated that 35 percent of women have experienced gender violence, the majority of which was committed by intimate partners. For instance, intimate partners were responsible for 38 percent of all murders of women. In its *World Health Statistics 2013* the WHO found that significant progress had been made on child mortality, with 27 countries having achieved their Millennium Development Goals ahead of the 2015 target. One major factor was an increase in measles vaccinations, which by 2011 covered about 84 percent of all children. Between 2000 and 2011, measles deaths decreased by 71 percent.

WORLD INTELLECTUAL PROPERTY ORGANIZATION

(WIPO)

Established: By a convention signed in Stockholm, Sweden, July 14, 1967, entering into force April 26, 1970. WIPO became a UN Specialized Agency by a General Assembly resolution on December 17, 1974.

Purpose: To ensure administrative cooperation among numerous intellectual property "unions" and to promote, by means of cooperation among states and international organizations, the protection of "intellectual property," including literary, artistic, and scientific works; the contents of broadcasts, films, and photographs; and all types of inventions, industrial designs, and trademarks.

Headquarters: Geneva, Switzerland.

Principal Organs: General Assembly (172 members), Conference (all members), Coordination Committee (80 members), Program and Budget Committee (41 members), Permanent Committee on Cooperation for Development Related to Intellectual Property (all members), Standing Committee on Information Technologies (all state members plus seven nonvoting organizations), International Bureau.

Web site: www.wipo.int/portal/index.html.en

Director General: Dr. Francis Gurry (Australia).

Membership (186): See Appendix C.

Working Languages: Arabic, Chinese, English, French, Portuguese, Russian, Spanish.

Origin and development. The origins of WIPO can be traced to the establishment of the Paris Convention on the Protection of Industrial Property in 1883 and the Berne Convention for the Protection of Literary and Artistic Works in 1886. Both conventions provided for separate international bureaus, or secretariats, which were united in 1893 and functioned under various names, the last being the United International Bureau for the Protection of Intellectual Property (BIRPI). The BIRPI still has a legal existence, but for practical purposes is indistinguishable from WIPO. WIPO also assumed responsibility for administering a number of smaller unions based on other multilateral agreements and for coordinating subsequent negotiations on additional agreements. In December 1974 WIPO became the UN's 14th Specialized Agency.

In September 1977 the Coordination Committee agreed to ban South Africa from future meetings because of its apartheid policy, but a move to exclude it from the organization was narrowly defeated in 1979. South Africa's full membership privileges were restored in 1994 in concert with similar steps throughout the UN system.

Structure. The General Assembly, comprising states that are parties to the WIPO Convention and are also members of the Paris and/or Berne conventions, is the organization's highest authority. In addition, the WIPO Conference, comprising all parties to WIPO's convention, serves as a forum for discussion of all matters relating to intellectual property and has authority over WIPO's activities and budget.

The International Bureau is the WIPO secretariat, which also services the Paris Convention, the Berne Convention, and other such unions. With regard to WIPO, the International Bureau is controlled by the General Assembly and the WIPO Conference, while in regard to the unions it is governed by the separate assemblies and conferences of representatives of each. The Paris and Berne unions elect executive committees, whose joint membership constitutes the Coordination Committee of WIPO, which meets annually. The General Assembly, the WIPO Conference, and the Coordination Committee meet in September and October once every two years and in an extraordinary session in alternate years.

A September 1998 extraordinary WIPO Conference session approved formation of the Permanent Committee on Cooperation for Development Related to Intellectual Property (PCIPD), which combined the functions and programs of the Permanent Committee for Development Cooperation Related to Industrial Property (PC/IP) and the Permanent Committee for Development Cooperation Related to Copyright and Neighboring Rights (PC/CR), both of which had been established in the 1970s. The former had as its mandate aiding in the transfer of technology from highly industrialized to developing countries; the latter had been responsible for promoting and facilitating the dissemination of literary, scientific, and artistic works protected under the rights of authors and of performing artists, producers, and broadcast organizations. All WIPO states may participate in the PCIPD, which held its first session in May–June 1999, and in the Standing Committee on Information Technologies (SCIT), which was created in 1998 as successor to the Permanent Committee on Industrial Property Information (PCIPI). The SCIT, in part, serves as a forum for, and provides technical advice on, WIPO's overall information strategy. In January 2001 the SCIT established two working groups to aid its mission, one responsible for information technology and the other for standards and documentation.

The Arbitration and Mediation Center was created in 1994 to help resolve intellectual property disputes, and in 1998 the WIPO Worldwide Academy was formed, with many training courses now available through electronic media. The March 1998 assemblies of the member states of WIPO decided to form two new independent advisory boards: the Policy Advisory Commission (PAC), which identifies issues of interest to WIPO and provides policy recommendations, and the Industrial Advisory Commission, mandated to improve WIPO's relationships with its industrial and market sector constituents.

Unlike most UN agencies, which are supported by levies on members, WIPO is mostly self-financed through charges for its services. In addition to its member states, WIPO includes 68 intergovernmental organizations and 271 non-governmental organizations as accredited observers for meetings and other activities.

Activities. WIPO administers 24 international treaties dealing with the two main categories of intellectual property: copyright (involving written material, film, recording, and other works of art) and industrial property (covering inventions, patents, trademarks, and industrial designs). The most important treaty in the copyright field is the 156-member Berne Convention, most recently amended in 1979. It requires signatories to give copyright protection to works originating in other member states and establishes minimum standards for such protection.

The principal treaty affecting industrial property is the 167-member Paris Convention, under which a member state must give the same protection to nationals of other contracting states as it gives to its own. The convention contains numerous additional regulations, some of which were the subject of contentious revision conferences during the 1980s. Discord most frequently involved attempts by developing countries to shorten protection periods in order to facilitate the transfer of technology and speed up the development of product manufacturing.

In addition to its administrative function, WIPO spearheads the review and revision of treaties already under its jurisdiction, while encouraging the negotiation of new accords where needed. Among the issues under study during the past decade were piracy and counterfeiting of sound and audiovisual recordings; standards for regulating the cable television industry; expansion of copyright protection for dramatic, choreographic, and musical works; and protection in new fields such as biotechnology. WIPO has also promoted expanded activity under the Patent Cooperation Treaty (PCT), established in 1970 to help inventors and industries obtain patent protection in foreign countries by filing single international applications rather than separate applications for each country. As of October 2013, 148 countries had acceded to the treaty. Following four years of increased application levels, the PCT hit a major milestone in January 2005 when its millionth application was filed, prompting a ceremony and celebration at its Geneva headquarters. On June 1, 2000, WIPO adopted the new Patent Law Treaty (PLT) at the conclusion of a three-week diplomatic conference. The PLT simplified and harmonized patent filings by applying many PCT procedures at the national level. As of October 2013, the treaty had been signed by 59 countries. The PLT was ratified by the United States on September 18, 2013.

Faced with myriad new issues arising from the rapid growth in popular use of personal computers, CD-ROM players, advanced video machines, and other systems based on digital technology, representatives of some 160 nations met in Geneva in December 1996 to update WIPO copyright guidelines. After three weeks of often difficult negotiations, the conference adopted two new treaties designed to protect intellectual property while guaranteeing fair access to information on the part of consumers. One accord (the WIPO Copyright Treaty) provides specific new regulations regarding literary and artistic works that can be reproduced in seconds on personal computers. The second agreement (the WIPO Performances and Phonograms Treaty—WPPT) extended copyright protection to recording artists and producers, except in regard to audiovisual products, about which consensus could not be reached and further negotiations were planned. As of October 2012, 91 countries had signed the WPPT. The two treaties went into effect in 2002, despite disagreements in the United States and Europe over whether they stimulated or stifled creativity on the Internet. (For information on the Internet Corporation for Assigned Names and Numbers (ICANN) and the Uniform Domain Name Dispute Resolution Policy (UDRP), please see the 2013 *Handbook.*)

In July 2000 the SCIT passed an implementation plan for WIPOnet, which facilitates the secure online exchange of information by the global intellectual property community. Access to various WIPO programs and activities, including the recently established Intellectual Property Digital Library (IPDL) system, are incorporated into WIPOnet, which permits online filing of applications under the PTC. Establishment of WIPOnet was a key element in a nine-point "digital agenda" drawn up at the First International Conference on Electronic Commerce and Intellectual Property in September 1999.

In 2003 U.S.-led opposition scrapped a WIPO convention for talks on information sharing to promote innovation. Major U.S. lobbying interests, including Microsoft and the Business Software Alliance, reportedly prompted the United States to pull the plug on the convention despite the urging of more than 60 international academics and researchers, who called on WIPO to convene the meeting in 2004. The group contends that the United States' proliferation of patents (accounting for about one-third registered with the PCT) hinder scientific advances and innovations.

In November 2004 WIPO announced some progress during three-day negotiations on a treaty to protect broadcasters' rights for digital technologies. Negotiators failed to reach consensus over whether protection should extend to webcasts, the scope of the treaty, and whether protection rights should be 50 years or fewer. The proposed broadcast treaty, an update to the 1961 Rome Convention on the Protection of Performers, Producers of Phonograms, and Broadcasting Organizations, was the subject of a June 2006 WIPO meeting held in Barcelona, Spain. Criticized for being held on short notice with little publicity, the meeting produced no agreements on matters of copyright protection for the broadcasters of television simulcasts and material on the Internet, including podcasts. The broadcast treaty was addressed again at WIPO's September 2006 General Assembly meeting, but a lack of agreement on how to proceed continued.

The Singapore Treaty on the Law of Trademarks was adopted in March 2006 at a special diplomatic conference. The treaty, an update to the 1994 Trademark Law Treaty, widened the scope of trademark law to include nontraditional marks such as holograms; three-dimensional marks; and nonvisible marks of sound, smell, taste, and feel. The treaty also simplified and standardized administrative rules for trademark applications.

The needs of the developing world have become a growing part of WIPO. In 2004 Argentina and Brazil advocated a proposal to reform WIPO's practices to stimulate innovation in developing countries and reorient the agency towards development goals rather than protecting property rights. The proposal, cosponsored by 12 member states, called for more transparency, participation, and accountability in the organization. However, WIPO negotiations the following year on the creation of a development agenda for the agency stalled and were not resolved until late 2007 at the WIPO General Assembly meeting held in Geneva September 27–October 3. The assembly agreed on a 45-point development agenda to address the needs of the developing world in the agency's technical assistance and capacity-building programs; it also established a framework for treaty-making that takes development issues into account and created the Committee on Development and Intellectual Property to implement the agenda. A less happy development at this meeting was the attempt by the United States and some European countries to remove the director general, Kamil Idris, of Sudan. The countries that objected to Idris blocked approval of the organization's 2008–2008 budget. Idris had been accused of financial and other irregularities, and his management was said to have damaged WIPO's credibility. He eventually agreed to step down a year early, the budget was finally adopted on March 31, 2008, and on September 24, 2008, Dr. Francis Gurry of Australia was elected director general for a six-year term. On October 1, 2008, the United States ratified the Singapore Treaty.

Further meetings during 2008 refined WIPO's new development agenda. Some observers wondered whether the plan would change the organization's focus to favor the interests of small nations as much as had been anticipated. In other matters, the organization received requests from Indonesia and from the European Union to develop intellectual property (IP) standards for the protection of folklore. The issue was discussed at the 13th session of its Intergovernmental Committee on Intellectual Property and Genetic Resources, Traditional Knowledge and Folklore, held in October 2008. Gurry declared that in this, as in all WIPO efforts, he expected to see results. On December 12, 2008, WIPO announced a program of strategic change, to concentrate on nine goals relating to improving respect for IP and for WIPO. The organization committed itself to working from a balanced budget henceforward. The organization also began a comprehensive review of the international patent system.

In July 2009 WIPO announced that it would open an arbitration and mediation center in Singapore early in 2010. In October 2009 Nigeria began working with WIPO to have a similar office opened in Abuja, its capital. WIPO's income for the 2008–2009 cycle was $626.2 million, with expenditures of $600.8 million.

In its 2010 overview of activities, WIPO reported that in 2010 there were 4.2 million patents throughout the world that had not been processed. In response, a WIPO working group issued a series of recommendations to address the backlog, including the increased use of information technology and new software to streamline the process. The expanded use of electronic processing had already reduced the costs of patent filing by 21 percent globally. The United States, Germany, and Japan remained the top nations for patent filings in 2010.

In March 2011 WIPO reported that in 2010 trademark holders filed 2,696 cybersquatting cases covering 4,370 domain names with the Arbitration and Mediation Center (WIPO Center). This was a 28 percent increase over the number for 2009. In May WIPO announced a partnership with the Paris-based International Council of Museums (ICOM), to mediate disputes concerning museums and cultural heritage. The annual WIPO Assemblies, held September 26–October 5, 2011, closed with a decision to call a diplomatic conference to negotiate a treaty on the rights of artists in audiovisual performances.

In 2011 WIPO's new headquarters in Geneva was completed using green technology and building design. In 2012 WIPO reported that PCT applications increased by 5.7 percent (rising to 164,300 for the year). Once again, the United States, Japan, and Germany dominated the applications. However, China moved into fourth place with a 55.6 percent increase in its filings. Concurrently, international trademark filings also increased, rising by 12.8 percent. Germany, the United States, and France had the largest number of applications.

WIPO reported in 2012 that administrative reforms had allowed the organization to reduce its operating budget from $707.3 million to $696.2 million through reductions in travel, equipment rentals, and alterations to payments policies to outside vendors. In June 2012 the Beijing Treaty on Audiovisual Performances was adopted at the WIPO Conference on the Protection of Audiovisual Performances. The accord strengthened the rights of performers and was finalized after 12 years of talks. Through 2013 there were 55 signatories to the treaty and 30 ratifications.

UNITED NATIONS: RELATED ORGANIZATION

INTERNATIONAL ATOMIC ENERGY AGENCY

(IAEA)

Established: By statute signed in New York, United States, October 26, 1956, effective July 29, 1957. A working relationship with the United Nations was approved by the General Assembly on November 14, 1957.

Purpose: To "seek to accelerate and enlarge the contribution of atomic energy to peace, health and prosperity throughout the world" and to ensure that such assistance "is not used in such a way as to further any military purposes."

Headquarters: Vienna, Austria.

Principal Organs: General Conference (all members), Board of Governors (35 members), Secretariat.

Web site: www.iaea.org

Director General: Yukiya Amano (Japan).

Membership (159): See Appendix C.

Official Languages: Arabic, Chinese, English, French, Russian, Spanish. All are also working languages.

Origin and development. In a 1953 address before the UN General Assembly, U.S. president Dwight Eisenhower urged the establishment of an international organization devoted exclusively to the peaceful uses of atomic energy. The General Assembly endorsed the essentials of the U.S. proposal on December 4, 1954, and 70 governments signed the Statute of the IAEA on October 26, 1956. Following ratification by 26 governments, the statute entered into force July 29, 1957.

Although the statute makes no provision for expelling member states, a two-thirds majority may vote for suspension upon recommendation of the Executive Board. This procedure was followed in 1972, when the membership of the Republic of China was suspended and the People's Republic of China took its place. (International safeguards on the Republic of China's subsequent extensive atomic development have been possible only because that government still allows agency controls.)

A decision at the 26th General Conference in September 1982 to reject the Israeli delegation's credentials led to a walkout by the United States and 15 other countries. The conference charged that Israel had violated IAEA principles and undermined the agency's safeguards with its preemptive attack on Iraq's Osirak nuclear facility in June 1981. The United States, which supplies 25 percent of the agency's regular budget, announced that it would suspend its payments and contributions while reassessing its membership. Following Director General Hans Blix's certification of Israel's continued membership in March 1983, Washington paid $8.5 million in back dues and resumed full participation in the agency.

South Africa signed the Treaty on the Non-Proliferation of Nuclear Weapons (NPT) in July 1991, agreeing to open plants for IAEA inspection and forgo the development of nuclear weapons. In March 1993 South African president F. W. de Klerk acknowledged that his country had developed nuclear weapons in the late 1970s but said they had all been dismantled after his inauguration in 1989. Pretoria subsequently invited the IAEA to verify the claim, and in late 1993 the agency's inspectors concluded that South Africa was indeed the first country ever to abandon nuclear weapon capability.

Following conclusion of the 1990–1991 Persian Gulf conflict, the UN Security Council asked the IAEA to investigate Iraq's nuclear weapons capability, which led to an unprecedented determination that Baghdad had violated its safeguards agreement with the IAEA by concealing a weapons-related program. After the removal from Iraq of all declared weapons-grade nuclear materials, the IAEA, in cooperation with the UN Security Council's Special Commission (UNSCOM), attempted to maintain a monitoring and verification program that frequently put it in conflict with the Iraqi government (see "Activities" and the article on Iraq).

Structure. The General Conference is the highest policymaking body at which all members are entitled to be represented. It meets annually at the organization's headquarters, usually in the latter part of September. Conference responsibilities include final approval of the agency's budget and program, approval of the appointment of the director general, and election of 22 members of the Board of Governors. Decisions on financial questions, amendments to the statute, and suspension from membership require a two-thirds majority; other matters are decided by a simple majority.

The Board of Governors, which normally meets five times a year, is vested with general authority for carrying out the functions of the IAEA. Of its 35 members, 22 are elected by the General Conference with due regard to equitable representation by geographic areas, while 13 are designated by the outgoing Board of Governors as the leaders in nuclear technology and production of atomic source material. Decisions are usually by simple majority, although budget approval and a few other matters require a two-thirds majority.

The IAEA Secretariat is headed by a director general appointed for a four-year term by the Board of Governors with the approval of the General Conference. The director general is responsible for the appointment, organization, and functioning of the staff, under the authority and subject to the control of the board. He also prepares the initial annual budget estimates for submission by the board to the General Conference. The Secretariat includes six departments: Technical Cooperation, Nuclear Energy, Nuclear Safety and Security, Management, Nuclear Sciences and Applications, and Safeguards. The Office of External Relations and Policy Coordination and the Office of Internal Audit also report to the director general.

In 2013 the IAEA approved a budget for 2014 of €349.8 million ($472 million). The IAEA's staff consists of more than 2,300 personnel stationed in more than 100 countries.

Activities. The IAEA differs from President Eisenhower's original concept in that it has not become a major center for distributing fissionable material. Its activities in promoting the peaceful uses of atomic energy fall into four main areas: (1) nuclear research and development, (2) health and safety standards, (3) technical assistance, and (4) administration of a safeguards program to ensure that atomic materials are not diverted from peaceful to military uses.

Included in IAEA operations are the IAEA Marine Environment Laboratory in Monaco; the International Centre for Theoretical Physics in Trieste, Italy (administered jointly with the UN Educational, Scientific and Cultural Organization); the International Nuclear Information System, which provides a comprehensive bibliographic database on peaceful applications of nuclear science and technology; the IAEA/World Health Organization Network of Secondary Standard Dosimetry Laboratories; and a large multidisciplinary nuclear research laboratory in Seibersdorf, Austria. The IAEA also coordinates the work of physicists from the European Union, Japan, Russia, and the United States on a planned thermonuclear fusion reactor. (France was chosen in 2005 as the site of the new reactor, which is scheduled to begin operation in 2016.) In addition, the IAEA administers a number of multilateral conventions on nuclear matters, including civil liability for nuclear damage and the protection of nuclear material from theft, sabotage, and other hazards, such as those posed during international transport.

In the wake of the world's worst-ever nuclear accident at the Chernobyl Nuclear Power Plant in the USSR in April 1986, nuclear safety drew increased attention. Special IAEA sessions evaluated the immediate implications of the accident and laid the groundwork for full assessment of its long-term radiological consequences. A new convention establishing an early warning system for such accidents went into force in October 1986, while a convention for the provision of assistance in the case of nuclear or radiological emergency went into force in February 1987.

In addition to nuclear power plant safety, IAEA symposia have addressed such topics as the management of spent fuel and radioactive waste, a proposed global radiation monitoring system, issues specific to "aging" nuclear plants, food irradiation, and new uranium mining techniques. The IAEA has also continued its extensive involvement in research and development projects in such areas as nuclear medicine, radiation-induced plant mutation to increase crop yield and resistance to disease, and insect control through large-scale release of radioactively sterilized male insects. In 2009 the IAEA announced that its scientists were working on such a technique with mosquitoes to combat malaria.

IAEA technical assistance to developing countries involves not only offering training programs and fellowships, but also bringing together customers and suppliers of such specialized services as plant maintenance and oversight safety. In 2009 more than 4,000 experts and lecturers carried out project assignments, and nearly 2,500 individuals participated in IAEA training courses.

The IAEA is probably most closely associated with its role as administrator of the safeguards system for containing the proliferation of nuclear weapons, although critics have often argued that manpower deficiencies, a lack of reliable monitoring equipment, and political influence, particularly in imposing effective sanctions, have undermined its credibility. The Treaty on the Non-Proliferation of Nuclear Weapons (NPT), signed July 1, 1968, and effective March 5, 1970, obligates signatory states (189, the exceptions being India, Israel, and Pakistan) that possess no nuclear weapons to accept safeguards as set forth in agreements concluded with the agency. After the May 1974 surprise nuclear explosion by India, the IAEA initiated a major effort to tighten controls. Specifically, the director general called upon the governments of states possessing nuclear weapons to accept outside inspection when they conducted nuclear tests for peaceful purposes. Subsequently, the United Kingdom (1978), the United States (1980), France (1981), the Soviet Union (1985), and China (1985) concluded agreements with the IAEA regarding application of safeguards and inspection of certain civilian nuclear facilities.

The agency also provides safeguard regimes for the Treaty for the Prohibition of Nuclear Weapons in Latin America and the Caribbean (Tlatelolco Treaty), which dates from 1967; the South Pacific Nuclear-Free Zone Treaty (Rarotonga Treaty), concluded in 1985; the African Nuclear-Weapon-Free Zone Treaty (Pelindaba Treaty), concluded in 1996; and the Treaty on the Southeast Asia Nuclear Weapon-Free Zone (Treaty of Bangkok), which entered into force in 1997.

In May 1995 NPT signatories convened in New York to determine if the treaty was to be extended indefinitely or for a fixed period of time. Although the United States and other nuclear powers strongly supported the indefinite option, a number of developing countries initially announced their preference for a fixed extension in order to gain leverage on several nuclear issues. The indefinite extension was finally approved after contentious discussions.

Consequently, in June 1995 the IAEA Board of Governors adopted new guidelines to permit broader inspections with little or even no advance notice. Two years later, under U.S. pressure for even stricter controls, the Board of Governors at its May 15–16, 1997, meeting adopted a model protocol granting IAEA inspectors greater access to members' nuclear facilities and sites. As of November 2009, 136 countries had signed the resultant Protocols Additional to Safeguards Agreements.

At the 1997 IAEA General Conference, held in late September and early October, Dr. Mohamed ElBaradei's appointment as successor to Director General Blix was approved.

The May 1998 nuclear weapons tests conducted by India and Pakistan drew immediate criticism from the IAEA. Although Argentina, Brazil, and Iran were believed to have the necessary technology to make weapons, an agency spokesman stated that, like the current regime in South Africa, none had shown any inclination to do so.

The September 1998 General Conference, in addition to calling for North Korea's compliance, focused its attention on Iraq, which had suspended its cooperation the preceding August after having engaged in a series of disputes with weapons inspectors. In November it was announced that the inspectors would be withdrawn in view of pending air strikes by the United States and the United Kingdom. Although the IAEA declared late in 1998 that it had found no evidence of Iraqi nuclear weapons production, it warned that Baghdad's failure to cooperate made drawing any conclusion difficult.

The April–May 2000 Third Review Conference on the NPT confirmed the importance of IAEA safeguards as a "fundamental pillar of the non-proliferation regime." During the 44th annual IAEA General Conference on September 18–22, 2000, a number of Arab states repeated a proposal for a nuclear-weapon-free zone in the Middle East, knowing full well that Israel was not ready to accept such a proposal. Israel indicated that it was firmly committed to the concept "in the proper context and time," but an obvious concern of the Israeli government was the projection that Iran might have nuclear weapons capacity by 2005 and a missile delivery system capable of hitting Israel within a decade.

The General Conference also called on North Korea and Iraq to come into full compliance with their obligations under the NPT and, in the case of Iraq, to permit renewed inspections under Security Council resolutions. Although Iraq permitted the IAEA in January 2000 to resume inspections of its declared nuclear material stocks in Tuwaitha, in accordance with its NPT safeguards agreement, from December 1998 Baghdad had not allowed verification and monitoring inspections ordered by the Security Council.

In December 2002 IAEA director general ElBaradei accused North Korea of "nuclear brinkmanship" after Korean technicians reopened a reactor that had been shut down in 1994. Pyongyang subsequently demanded a "nonaggression" agreement from the United States and several of North Korea's neighbors in exchange for closing the reactor. In early 2003 the IAEA board condemned North Korea for expelling the IAEA's weapons inspectors and dismantling IAEA monitoring cameras. (North Korea withdrew from the NPT in April 2003.) Regarding its other major focus of attention, the IAEA in early 2003 reported that it did not believe that Iraq had resumed its nuclear weapons program, as suspected by the United States.

Pressure mounted in 2003 for the IAEA to take a greater supervisory role in the matter of Iran's alleged "non-disclosed" nuclear program. ElBaradei urged Iran to "demonstrate full transparency," and in October Iran agreed to expanded inspections, although angrily insisting that all its nuclear activities were for civilian purposes only. In November 2004 the IAEA board noted Iran had made "good progress" on the issue, although Washington continued to insist on a harder line regarding inspections.

In November 2003 the IAEA called upon the UN to develop a system of multinational control over the production of nuclear material that could be used to make weapons. ElBaradei also subsequently proposed that significant additional resources be allocated to guard uranium stockpiles. (The agency estimated that more than 40 countries had the necessary knowledge to produce nuclear weapons.)

Early in 2005 the U.S. administration signaled its opposition to a third term for ElBaradei. However, the director general otherwise received strong international support and was reelected at the September General Conference. This conference, held September 26–30 in Vienna, focused on the dangers of nuclear proliferation, essentially acknowledging that it would be impossible to prevent states from developing nuclear weapons if they really wanted to do so. Attendees noted a revived interest in nuclear power for electricity generation—a development that was not foreseen even a year or so previously—spurred by the run-up in oil prices and increased concern about global warning. In November 2005 the IAEA and ElBaradei jointly won the Nobel Peace Prize.

Since that time world attention has been focused on the nuclear ambitions of North Korea and Iran. In 2006 and 2007 the IAEA inspected nuclear sites in both countries, served as a primary source of information to international bodies on the evidence behind their nuclear ambitions, and engaged in high-level talks concerning the suspension of nuclear programs. Significant developments over that time period included North Korea's first nuclear test in October 2006, reportedly an underground nuclear explosion, and Iran's further attempts at uranium enrichment. However, UN Security Council sanctions against both countries and the high-level talks resulted in some acquiescence on the part of North Korea and Iran to IAEA inspections. In the summer of 2007, IAEA inspectors gained access to North Korea's nuclear facilities at Yongbyon for the first time since 2002 and entered a heavy water research reactor in Arak, Iran, which the agency had previously been banned from viewing. By late 2007, North Korea had reportedly shut down its nuclear reactor in exchange for shipments of heavy fuel oil and access to an overseas bank account that had been frozen. However, the situation with Iran steadily deteriorated into late 2007 with the IAEA unable to negotiate full access to information on Iran's nuclear program. The IAEA announced in May that Iran could develop a nuclear weapon in three to eight years, and by October the United States imposed the toughest sanctions against Iran in 30 years.

The IAEA's 51st General Conference on September 17–21, 2007, saw a confrontation between Arab and Western states over a resolution to create a nuclear-free zone in the Middle East, aimed at Israel. The non-binding resolution, in the past typically introduced by Arab states but later withdrawn under U.S. pressure, passed this time in a vote of 53 to 2 (the United States and Israel voting against) with 43 abstentions (many of them European states). The move was seen as a sign of growing international tension over the Middle East and an effort by Arab nations to deflect pressure from Iran by pointing the finger at Israel, which has not signed the NPT and is generally believed to have nuclear weapons.

In other measures, the IAEA launched the International Decommissioning Network (IDN), an initiative aimed at sharing information and resources for use in shutting down the more than 350 nuclear installations that are approaching the end of their operational life span.

Also in 2007, Director General ElBaradei highlighted the agency's finances as cause for concern, noting at a July Board of Governors meeting and later at the General Conference that the 2008–2009 budget of €291 million ($396 million) put the agency in a state of "financial vulnerability." He also said the IAEA lacked essential equipment to verify covert nuclear activities and would not be able to respond to another disaster on the scale of the 1986 Chernobyl accident.

In mid-2007, ElBaradei drew the ire of the United States, France, and the United Kingdom for engaging in so-called freelance diplomacy after he agreed on a "work plan" with Iran under which key questions about its nuclear program would be answered. The states' position was to demand immediate compliance from Iran on the suspension of uranium enrichment or face tougher sanctions. A November report on Iran's compliance concluded that, although Iran was not completely forthcoming about its nuclear program and continued to enrich uranium in defiance of the UN, there was no positive evidence that the country was working on a nuclear weapon. Western states' rejoinder to this was that it was cheaper to buy, rather than make, commercial-grade uranium, and the only reason for Iran to enrich its own was to build a bomb. The picture was further clouded by a U.S. intelligence estimate, released in December 2007, stating that Iran had halted its nuclear weapons program in 2003. ElBaradei said that Iran was "somewhat vindicated."

In a February 22, 2008, report to the UN Security Council, ElBaradei said that although Iran had recently been more open about its activities, it was not possible to say with complete confidence that it was not working on a bomb. The IAEA had confronted Iran with documents from the United States suggesting that it was working on matters peripheral to nuclear bomb-making (such as developing long-range missiles), but Iran dismissed these as forgeries or irrelevant. The United States and France said the report bolstered the case for further sanctions against Iran. On March 4, 2008, the Security Council approved a relatively mild new round of sanctions against Iran, the strongest that Russia and China would support. A September 15, 2008, report by the IAEA said that it had made no more progress in discovering Iran's nuclear intentions, as that country was being uncooperative.

A February 2009 IAEA report stated that Iran had built up a stockpile of fissile material. On June 17, 2009, ElBaradei said he felt that Iran was interested in having a bomb, mainly to increase its importance on the international stage. In August 2009 Iran's position appeared to soften, with IAEA inspectors given access to two nuclear facilities after several months of requests. By early September the IAEA itself seemed uncertain about Iran's intentions, but on September 25 Iran informed the IAEA that it had built a second nuclear enrichment plant, previously secret, and promised to open it to IAEA inspection. In early October 2009 Iran began a new round of negotiations and seemed more willing to cooperate. On October 21, 2009, a draft agreement was announced whereby Iran would send nuclear material abroad for enrichment. Iran seemed to react positively, but on November 2 it asked the IAEA to establish a committee to review its details. Proof of Iran's ultimate intentions remained elusive.

The IAEA also tried to determine Syria's nuclear position. In September 2007 Israel had attacked Al-Kibar, a Syrian site which it claimed was being used to develop nuclear weapons. In April 2008 the United States released material which, it claimed, showed that Syria was indeed engaging in nuclear development at the site and that it had received help from North Korea. The IAEA asked to investigate, and Syria agreed to let it inspect Al-Kibar, but no other sites. On September 22 the IAEA said it had found no radioactivity at Al-Kibar, but it was still waiting for permission to investigate other sites. Matters were delayed further by the September 25, 2008, assassination of the IAEA's chief liaison in the Syrian government. In November 2008 and again in February 2009 the IAEA announced that it had found radioactive traces at Al-Kibar. The Syrian government said the radioactive material could have come from IAEA inspectors' clothing, or from the 2007 Israeli attack—something that the IAEA said was very unlikely.

On July 18, 2008, the IAEA confirmed that North Korea had shut down its nuclear reactor at Yongbyon, along with certain other facilities, thus beginning to fulfill its part of an international agreement. But through the late summer and early fall, North Korea complained that the United States was not keeping its end of the agreement. On September 24 North Korea said it was removing the seals from the Yongbyon plant, and that the IAEA would have no further access there. In April 2009 North Korea tested a long-range missile. Following general international condemnation of this test, North Korea announced that it was withdrawing from all nuclear negotiations and ordered all IAEA personnel out of the country.

From late 2007 through most of 2008, India was trying to gain IAEA approval for a deal with the United States allowing India to receive commercial nuclear technology. India already has nuclear weapons, and has not signed the NPT. France in particular was pressing for nuclear commerce with India, while Pakistan and the Indian political left were opposed. On July 10, 2008, the Indian government gave the IAEA its detailed plans for safeguarding nuclear technology. On July 22 the Indian government survived a no-confidence vote on the issue, and on August 1 the IAEA board approved the deal.

In other matters, the IAEA had difficulty electing a successor to ElBaradei, whose term in office was to end in November 2009. A March 2009 meeting of the board failed to elect either Yukiya Amano, a Japanese diplomat generally considered favorable to U.S. positions, or Abdul Samad Minty of South Africa, an arms control specialist who was felt to be more sympathetic to the interests of poorer countries. The matter was deferred to a board meeting on July 2, 2009, where Amano was elected.

Amano immediately took a tougher stance with Iran than his predecessor had done. By the March 2010 IAEA board meeting he declared that Iran was "not cooperating" with the IAEA, and the peaceful nature of Iran's program "could not be confirmed." In May Iran accepted an arrangement, mediated by Brazil and Turkey, for sending 1,200 kg of low-enriched uranium to Russia and France, where it would be converted into medical-grade material before being returned to Iran. The agreement did not address the concerns of the United States and others that Iran might have other enriched uranium left over. In June the UN imposed a new set of sanctions on Iran.

In August Iran began loading fuel at its first nuclear power station. The plant was Russian-operated, and observers saw little "proliferation risk "from it. Questions remained about other facilities, but while the IAEA continued to deplore Iran's lack of cooperation, nothing could be proved. These concerns remained, and as of late 2011, an IAEA report noted "serious concerns" and credible information regarding activities relevant to the development of a nuclear device.

In March 2011, following a 9.0 magnitude earthquake and tsunami along the Pacific coast of Japan, the Fukushima Nuclear Power Plant suffered equipment failures and meltdowns that led to the release of radioactive materials and the evacuation of residents from the surrounding area; this was the worst nuclear disaster since Chernobyl in 1986. Amano first visited the plant March 17–19 for high level consultations, though the IAEA's response to the accidents later drew criticism from the international science community. In June 2011, the IAEA pledged broad support for plans to strengthen international peer-reviewed safety checks; as of December 2011, the Fukushima Nuclear Power Plant was declared stable.

The importance of nuclear reactor safety and security was highlighted at the 55th International Atomic Energy General Conference in Vienna September 19–23, 2011. Addressing the IAEA, U.S. Energy Secretary Steven Chu outlined U.S. President Obama's nuclear agenda: promoting the peaceful use of nuclear energy, strengthening the nuclear proliferation regime, and pursuing nuclear disarmament and enhancing nuclear security. The IAEA continues to assess the extraordinary disaster in Japan.

In 2012 the IAEA reported that 32 percent of the world's 435 nuclear power plants were more than 30 years old and that many had outlived their original design lives. Consequently, the agency underscored the need for increased maintenance and service and replacement plans. Meanwhile, tensions over Iran's nuclear program continued. An IAEA team traveled to Iran in January 2012 for what were described as "good" talks. Iran subsequently offered to restart negotiations. Amano visited Tehran in May and paved the way for a new round of discussions between Iran and the five permanent members of the Security Council, plus Germany (the so-called P5+1). Talks in May and June failed to resolve the major differences between Iran and the P5+1. In September the IAEA reported that Iran had more than doubled its uranium enrichment centrifuges, from 1,064 to 2,140 at it Fordow nuclear facility. The agency also declared that its investigation of the Iranian nuclear site had been hampered by "extensive activities," including the demolition of buildings and the removal of equipment and earth. In 2012 Dominica, Fiji, Papua New Guinea, Rwanda, Togo, and Trinidad and Tobago joined the IAEA.

In 2013 the Bahamas, Brunei, and Swaziland were approved by the General Conference for IAEA membership. In February 2013 Iran rejected a P5+1 proposal to close its Fordow nuclear plant in exchange for the easing of some economic sanctions. In July, the Board of Governors approved the creation of the Working Group on Financing the Agency's Activities and charged the group with exploring new means to ensure secure funding for the IAEA in the future. The board also approved a goal of raising €69.2 million ($90.3 million) in contributions for the technical cooperation fund. In March, Amano reported that Iran continued to fail to cooperate with efforts to investigate the country's nuclear program. The election in June of moderate cleric Hassan Rouhani as president of Iran led to speculation about a possible breakthrough in negotiations between Tehran and the P5+1 (see entry on Iran).

WORLD TRADE ORGANIZATION (WTO)

Established: By the Marrakesh Agreement signed in Marrakesh, Morocco, on April 15, 1994, effective January 1, 1995.

Purpose: To administer the agreements contained in the Final Act of the Uruguay Round of the General Agreement on Tariffs and Trade (GATT); to provide conciliation mechanisms to resolve trade conflicts between members and, if necessary, adjudicate disputes; to provide a forum for ongoing negotiations in pursuit of further lowering and/or elimination of tariffs and other trade barriers.

Headquarters: Geneva, Switzerland.

Principal Organs: Ministerial Conference (all members), General Council (all members), Trade Policy Review Body, Dispute Settlement Body, Appellate Body, Council on Trade in Goods, Council on Trade in Services, Council on the Trade-Related Aspects of Intellectual Property Rights, Secretariat.

Web site: www.wto.org

Director General: Roberto Azevêdo (Brazil).

Membership (159): Albania, Angola, Antigua and Barbuda, Argentina, Armenia, Australia, Austria, Bahrain, Bangladesh, Barbados, Belgium, Belize, Benin, Bolivia, Botswana, Brazil, Brunei, Bulgaria, Burkina Faso, Burundi, Cambodia, Cameroon, Canada, Cape Verde, Central African Republic, Chad, Chile, China, China: Hong Kong, China: Macao, Colombia, Democratic Republic of the Congo, Republic of the Congo, Costa Rica, Côte d'Ivoire, Croatia, Cuba, Cyprus, Czech Republic, Denmark, Djibouti, Dominica, Dominican Republic, Ecuador, Egypt, El Salvador, Estonia, European Communities, Fiji, Finland, France, Gabon, Gambia, Georgia, Germany, Ghana, Greece, Grenada, Guatemala, Guinea, Guinea Bissau, Guyana, Haiti, Honduras, Hungary, Iceland, India, Indonesia, Ireland, Israel, Italy, Jamaica, Japan, Jordan, Kenya, Republic of Korea, Kuwait, Kyrgyzstan, Latvia, Laos, Lesotho, Liechtenstein, Lithuania, Luxembourg, Macedonia, Madagascar, Malawi, Malaysia, Maldives, Mali, Malta, Mauritania, Mauritius, Mexico, Moldova, Mongolia, Montenegro, Morocco, Mozambique, Myanmar, Namibia, Nepal, Netherlands, New Zealand, Nicaragua, Niger, Nigeria, Norway, Oman, Pakistan, Panama, Papua New Guinea, Paraguay, Peru, Philippines, Poland, Portugal, Qatar, Russian Federation, Romania, Rwanda, St. Kitts and Nevis, St. Lucia,

St. Vincent and the Grenadines, Samoa, Saudi Arabia, Senegal, Sierra Leone, Singapore, Slovakia, Slovenia, Solomon Islands, South Africa, Spain, Sri Lanka, Suriname, Swaziland, Sweden, Switzerland, Taiwan (Separate Customs Territory of Taiwan, Penghu, Kinmen, and Matsu), Tajikistan, Tanzania, Thailand, Togo, Tonga, Trinidad and Tobago, Tunisia, Turkey, Uganda, Ukraine, United Arab Emirates, United Kingdom, United States, Uruguay, Vanuatu, Venezuela, Vietnam, Zambia, Zimbabwe.

Observer governments (25): Afghanistan, Algeria, Andorra, Azerbaijan, Bahamas, Belarus, Bhutan, Bosnia and Herzegovina, Comoro Islands, Equatorial Guinea, Ethiopia, Holy See, Iran, Iraq, Kazakhstan, Lebanon, Liberia, Libya, Sao Tomé and Principe, Serbia, Seychelles, Sudan, Syria, Uzbekistan, Yemen.

Official Languages: English, French, Spanish.

Origin and development. The World Trade Organization (WTO) was the product of a series of negotiation developing from the General Agreement on Tariffs and Trade (GATT), signed in 1947. GATT was not designed to set up a permanent international organization but merely to provide a temporary framework for tariff negotiations pending the establishment of a full-fledged International Trade Organization (ITO) under United Nations (UN) auspices. A charter establishing an ITO responsible for developing and administering a comprehensive international commercial policy was drafted at the UN Conference on Trade and Employment, which met November 1947–March 1948 in Havana, Cuba. However, the so-called Havana Charter never went into effect, principally because some opposition from the United States blocked the required treaty approval by the U.S. Senate. Failure to create an ITO left GATT as the only available instrument for seeking agreement on rules for the conduct of international trade. (Since the general agreement was not cast as a treaty, it did not require formal ratification by the United States and could be implemented solely by executive action.)

The broad objective of GATT was to contribute to general economic progress through the acceptance of agreed rights and obligations governing the conduct of trade relations. Four main principles, from which detailed rules emerged, underlay the General Agreement: (1) nondiscriminatory trade with fair import and export duties for all countries; (2) the protection of domestic industries occurring only through customs tariffs; (3) undertaking consultations to avoid damage to the trading interests of other contracting parties; and (4) the provision of a framework for negotiating the reduction of tariffs and other barriers to trade, as well as a structure for embodying the results of such negotiations in a legal instrument.

Reducing tariffs through multilateral negotiations and agreements was one of the principal techniques employed by GATT. Eight major tariff-negotiating conferences were completed under GATT auspices. Little substantive progress toward an international trade organization came from the first seven rounds of negotiation. The eighth and final round of the negotiations, convened in September 1986 and ending in December 1993 finally brought about an agreement for the establishment of the World Trade Organization (WTO).

The objectives of the final negotiations in Uruguay were by far the most ambitious ever attempted by GATT. The Uruguay Round sought extensive liberalization and proposed negotiations in important new areas such as agricultural subsidies, investment, and intellectual property rights. While progress was made in most areas by 1988, negotiations stalled because of a disagreement between the United States and the European Community (EC) over a proposal to eliminate all trade-restricting farm subsidies within ten years. GATT officials warned that extensive compromise was required by all participants if a final package was to be adopted in Brussels in December 1990, as scheduled. Despite optimism for a deal, a deadlock was declared in Brussels on December 7, and negotiations were suspended indefinitely.

Although the outcome remained in doubt until the very end, the Uruguay Round Final Act was approved by GATT's Trade Negotiations Committee on December 15, 1993, after a series of last-minute compromises, primarily between the United States and the European Union (EU), which watered down or eliminated some of the most contentious areas, such as television and film exemptions from the intellectual property agreement. The long-standing impasse on agricultural subsidies eased, however, as the EU and the United States agreed to reduce subsidies substantially over the next six years. In addition, the signatories accepted what was expected eventually to amount to tariff reductions of about 40 percent on a wide range of goods, including agricultural products. Just as significantly, by providing for creation of the WTO, the GATT members committed themselves to a much more authoritative dispute settlement procedure. (For a more detailed discussion of GATT and the eight rounds of negotiations, see *Political handbook of the World* 2012.)

On April 15, 1994, in Marrakesh, Morocco, ministers from more than 100 countries formally endorsed the Uruguay Round agreements and called for the establishment of the WTO by January 1, 1995. While ratification of the Uruguay Round agreements proceeded more slowly than anticipated, a surge late in 1994 led to the convening on December 6 in Geneva of the Implementation Conference, which authorized the official launching of the WTO on January 1, 1995. The WTO was launched with 76 members and GATT countries being eligible for automatic membership upon their acceptance of the Uruguay Round Agreement and completion of other ratification procedures. As of mid-2012, the WTO had 157 members, while working parties had been established to address WTO membership requests from 26 other countries.

To the consternation of the WTO's most ardent supporters, the first few months of the grouping's existence were marked by astruggle among members over the director general's post, GATT's Peter Sutherland having agreed to serve only temporarily once the WTO was launched. Three major candidates emerged to succeed Sutherland: Carlos Salinas de Gortari, the former president of Mexico who was strongly supported by the United States; Renato Ruggiero, an Italian diplomat favored by the EU; and South Korea's Kim Chul Su, backed by Japan and other Asian countries. No inclination toward compromise was apparent in any of the three camps until Salinas was essentially forced to withdraw in the wake of growing criticism over his government's handling of Mexico's recent currency crisis. Washington subsequently threw its support to Ruggiero, although only after an agreement had been reached that he would serve only one four-year term (to April 30, 1999) and that the next director general would be a non-European.

One of Ruggiero's first stated priorities was to promote conclusion of a WTO agreement covering financial services, which was one of the three major areas left unresolved by GATT's Uruguay Round. In July 1995 more than 30 countries signed an accord governing trade in financial services; however, the United States, the world leader in the area, refused to sign on the ground that access to foreign markets would still be too restricted. Consequently, the agreement was implemented only until November 1997, pending further efforts to achieve U.S. endorsement of a permanent pact of broader scope. A permanent pact was finally accepted by the Committee on Trade in Financial Services on December 12, 1997. Seventy members submitted new or revised plans liberalizing their financial markets, joining the 32 who already had turned in their proposals. The agreement came into effect in 1999, the United States being one of 67 countries to have signed and ratified the document.

Attention subsequently focused on activity within the initial WTO arbitration panels. In early 1996 a WTO panel (and ultimately the Appellate Body) ruled in favor of Venezuela and Brazil in their contention that U.S. environmental regulations on gasoline were being unfairly applied to their exports, while U.S. refiners had been given an extension of time to conform to the new standards. Washington announced its intention to comply with the WTO verdict in June.

Although the high rate of "out-of-court" settlements generally pleased WTO proponents, some member states argued that the trend reflected capitulation on behalf of the developing countries to the demands of industrialized nations. Their contention that the organization remained a "rich man's club" reportedly received informal attention during the first biennial meeting of the WTO's Ministerial Conference in December 1996, particularly when the developed countries rejected a proposal from Director General Ruggiero that they consider eliminating the tariffs on all imports from the 40 poorest nations in the world. The most significant practical development at the 1996 session appeared to be the approval of the U.S.-sponsored Information Technology Agreement (ITA) for the gradual elimination of tariffs on computers and other high-tech products by January 1, 2000. The agreement took effect on July 1, 1997, by which time some 40 states had signed on.

Proposed membership expansion also remained a focus of WTO attention. Of the nearly 30 accession requests under consideration in 1996, the most significant were those from Russia and China. The United States and other Western nations had announced they would support China's entry, provided Beijing reduced its tariffs and dismantled other trade barriers.

In September 1997 the Appellate Body ruled on a dispute initiated by Ecuador, Guatemala, Honduras, Mexico, and the United States against the EU's banana importation regime, which gave preferential market access to African, Caribbean, and Pacific (ACP) countries. The Appellate Body upheld the findings of a panel in agreeing that these preferences were "inconsistent with the WTO rules." The EU said it would accept the Appellate Body's verdict but expressed concern over the potential effects it could have on ACP countries. The dispute nevertheless continued into 1998, with the United States claiming late in the year that a modified regime was still inadequate and announcing it would seek WTO approval for levying sanctions on EU goods. In early 1999 both sides agreed to allow the dispute panel that had heard the original case to arbitrate the matter. In April the panel again ruled in favor of the United States.

In February 1998, an agreement opening up the telecommunications market entered into force. Also during the year, the WTO held its second Ministerial Conference in Geneva in May, at which time a number of poor countries claimed they were not benefiting from liberalized trade.

A contentious search for a successor to Director General Ruggiero dragged into 1999, and when his term expired on April 30, the office fell vacant. Principal candidates were Michael Moore, a former prime minister of New Zealand, and Supachai Panitchpakdi, a deputy prime minister of Thailand. A compromise agreement provided for Moore to serve a special three-year term (effective July 22) with Panitchpakdi to succeed Moore for a three-year term in 2002. Substantial controversy also surrounded the third meeting of the WTO's Ministerial Conference on November 30–December 3, 1999, in Seattle, Washington. Internal disputes (such as disagreements among the EU, the United States, and others over agricultural subsidies) also marred the session, which ended without a final communiqué. No agreement was reached again in 2001 in regard to a timetable and agenda for a proposed ninth round of trade negotiations.

After several years of disastrous public relations and growing concern over its future effectiveness, the WTO attempted to chart a positive course by launching the Doha Development Round at the fourth meeting of the Ministerial Conference in Doha, Qatar, in November 2001. The new trade negotiations were originally scheduled for completion by 2005, although vague language about agricultural subsidies in the Doha document concerned many analysts. Other major developments at Doha included the acceptance of China as a WTO member (effective December 11), a decision that facilitated Taiwan's admission on January 1, 2002.

In January 2002 the WTO Appellate Body endorsed a 2001 dispute tribunal's ruling that the United States was in violation of WTO agreements by providing tax breaks for U.S. companies in regard to income earned in foreign countries. The EU, which had pursued the complaint, was authorized to impose a staggering $4 billion in retaliatory tariffs, although no such action was taken while the United States and EU attempted to reach a negotiated settlement. That dispute, coupled with severe criticism from the EU, Japan, and China over Washington's decision in March to apply substantial tariffs on imported steel, contributed to a continued sense of malaise within the WTO as Director General Panitchpakdi took office in September 2002.

In March 2003 a WTO dispute panel ruled against the United States regarding its steel tariffs, and Washington lifted the tariffs in November after a WTO appeals panel upheld the original decision. The WTO also ruled against the United States in 2004 on the issues of U.S. subsidies to cotton farmers (followed by a second ruling against the United States in 2007) and the so-called Byrd Amendment that paid out anti-dumping duties collected by the United States directly to private firms. In October 2004 a WTO panel began its assessment of one of the WTO's largest and most complex cases to date—the disputes over U.S. and EU aid to their largest aircraft manufacturers (Boeing and Airbus, respectively). A dispute involving U.S. tax breaks for U.S. companies in regard to income earned abroad subsequently came to a conclusion when the U.S. Congress, after two years, finally approved legislation to comply with the WTO findings.

In January 2005 Director General Panitchpakdi announced that he did not intend to seek a second term. In May EU trade commissioner Pascal Lamy was named to the post, effective September of that year.

There were hopes that a significant agreement on the Doha Round might come at the sixth Ministerial Conference, held December 13–18, 2005, in Hong Kong, but that did not happen. Instead there was a modest agreement that the EU would end farm export subsidies by 2013 and the United States would reduce subsidies for cotton exports. It was generally recognized, however, that the conference produced only marginal benefit for poorer countries. In June 2006 Director General Lamy organized what amounted to an emergency meeting of any WTO members who cared to attend in an attempt to broker a broader resolution of the disputes over cutting tariffs and subsidies in agriculture and opening markets for industrial goods. The meeting aimed to produce template agreements known as "modalities" for this purpose. The meeting, held in Geneva beginning June 28, effectively collapsed by July 1, with no agreements reached and many delegations going home early.

A series of trade complaints was filed with the WTO in 2006 and 2007, in some cases to gain leverage in the continuing Doha talks. Canada took the lead, backed by more than a half dozen countries, in challenging the United States on farm subsidies in early 2007, saying Washington's aid to farmers exceeds WTO limits. Ongoing cases involving the EU's banana import regime and U.S. cotton subsidies were still before the WTO as contentious negotiations on a trade deal stretched through 2007 and into 2008. (Both cases were subsequently decided against the EU and the United States, respectively.)

With the faltering of talks again in the fall of 2006, observers cautioned that the WTO risked losing credibility. After months of small group consultations into the spring of 2007, four key trade powers (the United States, the EU, India, and Brazil) attempted to hammer out a deal in Potsdam, Germany, on June 19–21. The talks again collapsed with India and Brazil complaining that the United States and the EU were demanding too much access to industrial goods markets in exchange for too little cutting of tariffs and subsidies on their agricultural goods. When talks resumed among key WTO trade members in 2008, the issues were no different: agricultural subsidies in the most developed countries versus protection for industries and services in the rest. The talks collapsed in late July 2008 for much the same reasons as the previous year.

Growing frustration with China's slow progress in implementing trade accords has been reflected in a series of complaints filed with the WTO in recent years. China's fifth anniversary in the WTO in 2006 was marked by U.S. calls to open its banking and financial sectors further. Subsequently, the United States, faced with discontent over its growing trade imbalance with China, led complaints against China concerning inadequate efforts in fighting piracy and counterfeiting; restrictions on the sale of U.S. films, books, and software; and allegations that China was giving tax breaks to exporters in a wide range of industries. In July 2008 China lost its first case before the WTO, a complaint over discrimination against foreign-made auto parts.

A number of issues regarding WTO membership have occurred in recent years. Vietnam's communist-run legislature cleared up remaining hurdles, notably the removal of quotas on garment exports, and joined the WTO in November 2007. Ukraine's 14-year effort at accession continued to progress, and it became a full member at the end of 2008.

Russia, whose economy is the largest outside the WTO, worked throughout 2006 and 2007 on deals to lift remaining trade restrictions. By the end of 2007, the possibility of Russia's accession narrowed to two remaining issues with the EU, namely export duties on timber and a reform of railway fees that have favored Russian ports. Georgia declared in May of that year that it would block Russia's admission until Russia ceased supporting the breakaway Georgian provinces of Abkhazia and South Ossetia. The fighting between Russia and Georgia in August 2008 only worsened the situation.

On November 15, 2008, the Group of Twenty (G-20, see separate article) meeting in Washington, D.C., to discuss the world financial crisis committed its members not to take any actions for twelve months that might raise new trade barriers, or otherwise interfere with the WTO's work against protectionism. The G-20 also agreed to "strive to reach agreement this year on modalities that leads to a successful conclusion to the WTO's Doha Development Agenda with an ambitious and balanced outcome." On December 12, 2008, Lamy declared, after consultation with the United States, India, China, Brazil, and the EU, that there was insufficient basis to restart talks on the Doha Round. For more on activities since 2008, see "Recent Activities," below.

Structure. The WTO's supreme organ is the Ministerial Conference, in which each member state has one vote. It is mandated to meet at least every two years. Between ministerial sessions, oversight is the responsibility of the General Council, also composed of delegates from all member states. The General Council additionally acts as the Dispute Settlement Body, which establishes panels to adjudicate disputes brought before the WTO. Decisions of the panels can be appealed by either party in a dispute to the WTO Appellate Body, whose seven members are appointed by the Dispute Settlement Body. In addition, the General Council also acts as the Trade Policy Review Body, which conducts regular evaluations of the trade practices of all WTO members. Subcouncils have been established on trade in goods, trade in services, and the trade-related aspects of intellectual property rights. Permanent committees reporting directly to the General Council include Trade and Environment; Trade and Development; Regional Trade Agreements; Balance of Payments Restrictions; and Budget, Finance, and Administration. The Trade Negotiations Committee, which also reports directly to the General Council, was established in connection with the launching of the Doha Development Round of negotiations in 2001. The WTO governing bodies are assisted by the Secretariat, which is headed by a director general selected for a four-year term by consensus of the WTO members at the ministerial level.

Although its founding treaty stipulated that the WTO would be accorded privileges and immunities similar to those of the Specialized Agencies affiliated with the United Nations, the organization was not officially designated as a Specialized Agency. However, the organization cooperates extensively with a number of UN-affiliated bodies as well as other non-UN organizations. In addition, the WTO signed a cooperation agreement with the IMF in April 1997.

Recent Activities. In January 2009 the WTO issued a statement, bearing on a U.S. complaint against China's allegedly lax attitude toward pirated DVDs and other intellectual property, that was highly critical of China's position. The WTO recommended that China bring its copyright law "into conformity with its obligations." On August 12, 2009, the WTO ruled definitively in favor of the United States on the bulk of the complaint. Shortly thereafter China announced an appeal. On November 6, 2009, the WTO announced that it had received its 400th request for settlement of a dispute. On June 20, 2010, the organization handed down a decision in the Boeing-Airbus case. The decision was marginally in favor of the U.S. position. In July the EU announced an appeal. The appeal upheld the initial ruling of the panel, and in April 2012, the United States called for a DSB to be established concerning the EU's enforcement of the ruling, claiming that the EU had failed to make sufficient changes.

In 2010 Russia moved close to membership in the WTO. On June 24 U.S. president Barack Obama stated that the United States now supported Russia's accession. That Russia planned to form a customs union with Belarus and Kazakhstan (also candidates for WTO membership) had for some time been considered an obstacle. When that union came about in early June 2010, however, it seemed not to be an insuperable barrier.

U.S. protests against Chinese manipulation of the value of its currency, said by some to be undervalued by as much as 25 percent against the dollar, showed signs in 2010 of reaching the WTO. There was debate in U.S. economic and political circles as to whether a WTO challenge would be wise, and what the long-term results might be, win or lose. The U.S. trade representative said that he was investigating whether China was illegally subsidizing its clean-energy industries, and that a WTO complaint might be forthcoming. In December 2010 the WTO declared that EU punitive tariffs on Chinese metal products were inappropriate and had to be altered. Concurrently, the WTO ruled that U.S. tariffs on Chinese tires were appropriate.

In February 2011 Canada sought WTO arbitration in a dispute against the EU over its ban on Canadian seal imports. On April 14 at the Brazil, Russia, India, China, and South Africa (BRICS) summit, the group issued the Sanya Declaration, which called for Russia's admittance to the WTO. In October Vanuatu's membership bid was endorsed by the WTO. However, domestic opposition to the WTO prompted delays in the necessary membership legislation. Meanwhile, at the 2011 Ministerial Conference held on December 16 Russian membership in the WTO was finally approved, pending domestic ratification. Montenegro and Samoa were also approved as new members. Moscow subsequently called for Russian to become one of the official languages of the WTO. All three states acceded to the WTO treaty shortly after the conference. Montenegro ratified the treaty on April 29, 2012, and Samoa followed on May 10. Russian President Vladimir Putin signed the treaty ratification on July 21, 2012, ending the long process of Russian membership negotiations. Russia became the 156th member of the WTO. As of August 2012, no discussions have been initiated concerning the acceptance of Russian as an official language. Russia joined the WTO's Information Technology Agreement in September 2013.

In February 2012, the General Council met for a regular meeting, at which time they discussed, among other things, the need for progress in the Doha Round of negotiations in the upcoming year. The director general noted that the member states should not allow progress to be hindered all together, even if major progress could not be made.

After overcoming delays on the domestic front, Vanuatu announced its ratification of the WTO treaty during a General Council meeting held July 25–27. Vanuatu became the 157th member state. The most significant action to come out of the General Council meeting was a new protocol that eased the membership guidelines for the 40 poorest countries in the world. The new guidelines will allow easier accession to the WTO treaty for the Least Developed Countries by increasing flexibility on the percentage of tariff lines, easing the requirements for various sectors of industry, and creating a transition period following accession. Director General Lamy also echoed his earlier call for progress on the Doha Round of negotiations. He told the member states that, "The ball lies in your court," and cautioned against the "all or nothing" mentality of many states at the negotiating table.

In November the EU and 10 Latin American states signed an agreement ending their dispute over bananas. The agreement lowered the EU's import tariff on bananas and established annual maximum tariff rates until 2017. The banana dispute was the longest running series of disputes in GATT/WTO history, dating back to 1992.

Early 2013 saw the accession of two more states to the WTO—Laos and Tajikistan. Laos ratified the WTO treaty on January 3, having had its membership deal approved by the General Council in October 2012. Upon ratification, Laos entered the WTO as the 158th member on February 2. From a more regional approach, Laos became the last of the ASEAN member states to join the WTO's international trading framework, allowing for improved cooperation between the two organizations. The General Council approved Tajikistan's membership deal on December 10, 2012, and the Central Asian state ratified the agreement on January 31, 2013. According to protocol, they entered the WTO 30 days later on March 3.

On May 14, 2013, the General Council appointed Roberto Azevêdo of Brazil as the next Director-General of the WTO to replace Pascal Lamy, who had served as Director-General for the last eight years. Azevêdo becomes the first South American and first individual from the Western Hemisphere to serve as Director-General of GATT/WTO. Azevêdo took office effective September 1. After a meeting on the Serbian accession process in June, the committee appeared confident that Serbia could finalize its accession by the end of the year, lacking only the enactment of a few outstanding pieces of legislation and the completion of its bilateral negotiations.

The ninth ministerial conference is scheduled for December in Bali. Many representatives, including WTO Director-General Azevêdo, have expressed the opinion that the Bali meeting is pivotal for the future of the Doha Round of negotiations and the continued leadership of the WTO. Also on the agenda for the Bali meeting is final approval of WTO accession for Afghanistan and Bosnia and Herzegovina.

APPENDIXES

APPENDIX A CHRONOLOGY OF MAJOR INTERNATIONAL POLITICAL EVENTS: 1945–2013

1945, **May 8.** Proclamation of end of the war in Europe.
June 26. United Nations Charter signed in San Francisco.
August 6. United States drops atomic bomb on Hiroshima, Japan.
September 2. Surrender of Japan.

1946, **July 29–October 15.** Peace Conference meets in Paris, France.
December 30. UN Atomic Energy Commission approves U.S. proposal for world control of atomic weapons.

1947, **February 10.** Peace treaties signed with Bulgaria, Finland, Hungary, Italy, and Romania.
June 5. Marshall Plan inaugurated.
October 30. General Agreement on Tariffs and Trade (GATT) negotiated in Geneva, Switzerland.

1948, **March 17.** Brussels Treaty signed by Belgium, France, Luxembourg, Netherlands, United Kingdom.
March 20. Soviet representatives walk out of Allied Control Council for Germany.
April 16. Organization for European Economic Cooperation (OEEC) established in Paris, France.
April 30. Organization of American States (OAS) Charter signed in Bogotá, Colombia.
May 14. State of Israel proclaimed.
May 12, July 24–1949. Berlin blockade.
December 10. UN General Assembly adopts Universal Declaration of Human Rights.

1949, **January 25.** Council for Mutual Economic Assistance (CMEA) established in Moscow, USSR.
April 4. Treaty establishing North Atlantic Treaty Organization (NATO) signed in Washington.
May 4. Statute establishing Council of Europe signed in London, United Kingdom.

1950, **January 31.** U.S. president Harry S. Truman orders construction of hydrogen bomb.
June 27. United States intervenes in Korean War.

1951, **April 18.** Treaty establishing European Coal and Steel Community signed by Belgium, France, Federal Republic of Germany, Italy, Luxembourg, Netherlands.
September 1. Anzus Pact signed in San Francisco, by Australia, New Zealand, and the United States.
September 8. Peace Treaty signed by Japan and non-Communist Allied powers in San Francisco.

1952, **May 27.** European Defense Community (EDC) Charter signed by Belgium, France, Federal Republic of Germany, Italy, Luxembourg, Netherlands.
November 1. United States explodes hydrogen bomb in Eniwetok Atoll.

1953, **March 5.** Death of Joseph Stalin.
December 8. U.S. president Dwight D. Eisenhower proposes international control of atomic energy.

1954, **September 8.** Treaty establishing Southeast Asia Treaty Organization (SEATO) signed in Manila, Philippines.
October 23. Allied occupation of West Germany ends.

1955, **May 6.** Western European Union (WEU) inaugurated by admission of Italy and Federal Republic of Germany to Brussels Treaty.
May 9. Federal Republic of Germany admitted to NATO.
May 14. Warsaw Pact signed by East European communist governments.

1956, **July 26.** Egypt nationalizes Suez Canal.
October 23–November 22. Anticommunist rebellion in Hungary suppressed by Soviet troops.
October 29–November 6. Suez crisis.

1957, **March 25.** Rome Treaty establishing European Economic Community (EEC) and European Atomic Energy Community (Euratom) signed.

1960, **May 1.** U-2 incident.
May 3. European Free Trade Association (EFTA) of "Outer Seven" (Austria, Denmark, Norway, Sweden, Switzerland, Portugal, United Kingdom) established.
May 14. Beginning of Sino-Soviet dispute.
December 14. Charter of Organization for Economic Cooperation and Development (OECD) to replace OEEC signed in Paris, France.

1961, **April 17–20.** Bay of Pigs invasion of Cuba.
August 15. Start of construction of Berlin Wall between East and West Germany.
September 1–6. First conference of Nonaligned Nations in Belgrade, Yugoslavia.

1962, **October 22–28.** Cuban missile crisis.

1963, **January 29.** France vetoes British bid for admission to EEC.
May 25. Organization of African Unity (OAU) Charter adopted in Addis Ababa, Ethiopia.
August 5. Limited Nuclear Test-Ban Treaty signed in Moscow, USSR.

1964, **May 28.** Palestine Liberation Organization (PLO) established.

1965, **February 21.** Decision to merge European Economic Community (EEC), European Coal and Steel Community (ECSC), and European Atomic Energy Community (Euratom).

1966, **March 11.** France withdraws troops from NATO.

1967, **January 27.** Treaty governing exploration and use of outer space signed by the United States, USSR, and 60 other nations.
June 5. Beginning of Arab-Israeli War.
June 17. China explodes its first hydrogen bomb.

1968, **January 16.** Britain announces withdrawal of forces from Persian Gulf and Far East.
May 13. Beginning of Vietnam peace talks in Paris, France.
June 4. Nuclear Nonproliferation Treaty approved by UN General Assembly.
August 20–21. Warsaw Pact forces occupy Czechoslovakia.
August 25. France explodes its first hydrogen bomb.
September 12. Albania withdraws from Warsaw Pact.
October 5. Outbreak of civil rights violence in Londonderry, Northern Ireland.

1969, **April 28.** Charles de Gaulle resigns as French president.
July 21. United States lands first men on moon.
November 17–December 22. Initiation of Strategic Arms Limitation Talks (SALT) between the United States and USSR.

1970, **March 2.** Rhodesia issues unilateral declaration of independence from Britain.

1971, **November 12.** U.S. president Richard Nixon announces end of U.S. offensive action in Vietnam.

1972, **February 21–28.** U.S. president Richard Nixon visits China.
May 22–29. U.S. president Richard Nixon visits Soviet Union.

1973, **January 1.** Denmark, Ireland, and the United Kingdom enter European Communities.
February 12. Last U.S. ground troops leave Vietnam.
October 6–22. Fourth Arab-Israeli war.
October 17. Arab embargo launched on oil shipments to United States and other Western nations (embargo ends March 18, 1974).

1974, **January 18.** Egypt and Israel sign agreement on disengagement of forces along Suez Canal.

1975, **February 28.** First Lomé (Togo) Convention signed between EEC and developing African, Caribbean, and Pacific (ACP) states.
May 28. Treaty establishing Economic Community of West African States (ECOWAS) signed in Lagos, Nigeria.
June 5. Suez Canal reopened to international shipping.
July 30–August 1. Conference on Security and Cooperation in Europe (CSCE) concludes in Helsinki, Finland.
September 4. Agreement between Egypt and Israel provides for Israeli withdrawal in Sinai and establishment of UN buffer zone.
November 20. Death of Spain's Gen. Francisco Franco.

1976, **June 17.** Outbreak of racial violence in Soweto, South Africa.
July 3–4. Israeli raid on Entebbe Airport, Uganda.
September 9. Death of China's Mao Zedong.

1977, **June 30.** Southeast Asia Treaty Organization (SEATO) dissolved.
November 19–21. Egyptian president Anwar Sadat visits Israel.

1978, **September 9–17.** President Anwar Sadat and Prime Minister Menachem Begin meet with U.S. President Jimmy Carter at Camp David.

1979, **January 1.** People's Republic of China and United States establish diplomatic relations.
January 16. Shah of Iran goes into exile.
March 26. Egyptian-Israeli peace treaty signed in Washington.
November 4. Iranian students seize U.S. embassy in Tehran.
December 27. Soviet military forces support coup in Afghanistan.

1980, **April 18.** Zimbabwe (formerly Rhodesia) declared legally independent.
May 4. Death of Yugoslavian president Josip Broz Tito.
September 22. Iraqi invasion of Iran initiates Iran-Iraq war.
October 24. Independent trade union (Solidarity) officially registered in Poland.

1981, **January 1.** Greece enters European Communities.

January 20. Iran frees remaining U.S. hostages.
October 6. Egyptian president Anwar Sadat assassinated.
December 13. Martial law declared in Poland.
December 14. Occupied Golan Heights placed under Israeli law.

1982, **April 2–July 15.** Falkland Islands (Islas Malvinas) war between Argentina and the United Kingdom.
June 6. Israeli invasion of Lebanon.
August 21–September 1. PLO forces evacuate Beirut, Lebanon.
November 10. Soviet leader Leonid Brezhnev dies.

1983, **September 1.** USSR shoots down Korean Air Lines Boeing 747 passenger plane.
October 25. United States, in concert with six Caribbean states, invades Grenada (last troops withdrawn December 12).

1984, **October 31.** Indian prime minister Indira Gandhi assassinated.

1985, **March 11.** Mikhail S. Gorbachev named general secretary of Soviet Communist Party.
October 7. Palestinian terrorists seize Italian cruise ship Achille Lauro.
November 15. Ireland and the United Kingdom sign accord granting Irish Republic consultative role in governance of Northern Ireland.
November 19–21. U.S. president Ronald Reagan and Soviet leader Gorbachev hold summit meeting in Geneva.

1986, **January 1.** Spain and Portugal enter European Communities.
January 28. U.S. space shuttle Challenger, on 25th shuttle mission, breaks apart after lift-off.
February 7. Jean-Claude Duvalier flees from Haiti to France, ending nearly three decades of his family's rule.
February 25. General Secretary Mikhail Gorbachev calls for sweeping reforms in Soviet economic system.
February 25. Corazon Aquino inaugurated as Philippines president following disputed election February 7; after holding rival inauguration, Ferdinand Marcos flies to Hawaii.
April 15. U.S. aircraft bomb Tripoli and Benghazi in response to alleged Libyan-backed terrorist activity in Europe.
April 26. Explosion in Chernobyl, USSR, power plant results in worst nuclear accident in history.
November 25. Attorney General Edwin Meese says $10–$30 million paid by Iran for U.S. arms was diverted by Lt. Col. Oliver North to Nicaraguan insurgents.

1987, **June 11.** Margaret Thatcher becomes first prime minister in modern British history to lead her party to a third consecutive electoral victory.
August 7. Five Central American presidents sign regional peace plan proposed by Oscar Arias of Costa Rica.
September 1. Erich Honecker becomes first East German head of state to visit West Germany.
October 19. U.S. stock market crashes, with Dow Jones Industrial Average falling 508.32 points in one session; foreign markets plummet the next day.
December 8. U.S. president Ronald Reagan and Soviet general secretary Mikhail Gorbachev sign INF treaty calling for elimination of entire class of nuclear weapons.
December 9. Intifada begins among Palestinians in the Gaza Strip, spreading to the West Bank the following day.

1988, **April 14.** Afghanistan, Pakistan, Soviet Union, United States conclude agreement on Soviet withdrawal from Afghanistan (withdrawal completed February 15, 1989).
June 28. Soviet general secretary Mikhail Gorbachev proposes wide-ranging changes in Soviet political system.
August 17. Pakistan's president Zia ul-Haq dies in plane crash.
August 20. Cease-fire begins in Iran-Iraq war.
November 15. Yasir Arafat issues PLO statement declaring an independent state of Palestine.
December 22. Angola, Cuba, South Africa sign agreements providing for Cuban withdrawal from Angola and transition to independence for Namibia.

1989, **January 7.** Japanese emperor Hirohito dies.
January 19. Conference on Security and Cooperation in Europe concludes 26-month meeting in Vienna, Austria, with expansion of 1975 Helsinki Final Act to emphasize freedom of religion, information, travel, and privacy.
March 10. U.S. treasury secretary Nicholas Brady announces "Brady Plan" for commercial banks to make voluntary reductions in outstanding Third World debts and for the IMF and World Bank to provide debt-reduction assistance to debtor nations that adopt market-oriented reforms.
March 26. Soviet Union holds nationwide contested elections.
April 17. Solidarity relegalized by court action 12 days after reaching agreement with Polish government on political reforms.
May 13. Students demanding meeting with Chinese leaders begin hunger strike after occupying Beijing's Tiananmen Square.
May 15–18. Soviet leader Mikhail Gorbachev goes to China for the first Sino-Soviet summit in 20 years; antigovernment protests break out in more than 20 Chinese cities, including a demonstration by an estimated 1 million people in Tiananmen Square.
June 4. Many deaths reported as troops clear Tiananmen Square.
June 4–18. Solidarity sweeps two-stage, partially open election in Poland.
June 6. Iranian Ayatollah Khomeini dies.
November 9. East German government permits citizens to leave without special permits, thus effectively opening the country's borders, including the Berlin Wall.
December 20. U.S. forces invade Panama.
December 25. Romanian president Nicolae Ceauşescu and his wife executed.

1990, **March 11.** Lithuania becomes first Soviet republic to issue declaration of independence.
March 13. Soviet Congress of People's Deputies revokes monopoly status of Communist Party.
March 15. Soviet Congress of People's Deputies elects Mikhail Gorbachev to new office of executive president.
March 21. Namibia becomes independent.
June 7. Warsaw Pact leaders meeting in Moscow declare the West is no longer an "ideological enemy."
August 2. Iraq invades Kuwait.
August 6. UN Security Council votes to impose mandatory economic sanctions on Iraq. United States deploys troops to Gulf in defense of Saudi Arabia ("Operation Desert Shield").
September 7. Liberian president Samuel Doe killed by rebels.
October 3. East and West Germany unite as the Federal Republic of Germany.
November 19. NATO and Warsaw Pact leaders sign Conventional Forces in Europe (CFE) treaty.
November 21. CSCE summit participants sign Charter of Paris for a New Europe devoid of East-West division and committed to democracy and human rights.
November 29. UN Security Council authorizes U.S.-led forces "to use all means necessary" to secure Iraq's unconditional withdrawal from Kuwait.

1991, **January 16.** "Operation Desert Storm" air attacks initiated against Iraq.
February 27. U.S. president George H. W. Bush announces liberation of Kuwait; Iraq agrees to cease-fire.
March 26. Presidents of Argentina, Brazil, Paraguay, and Uruguay sign treaty in Asunción, Paraguay, creating Southern Cone Common Market (Mercosur).
April 11. UN Security Council officially declares end of Gulf war after receiving Iraq's acceptance of permanent cease-fire terms.
May 26. Zviad Gamsakhurdia of Georgia becomes first freely elected leader of a Soviet republic.
May 28. Ethiopian civil war ends as rebel forces occupy Addis Ababa.
June 12. Boris Yeltsin elected president of the Russian Soviet Federative Socialist Republic.
June 25. Croatia and Slovenia declare independence from Yugoslavia.
June 28. Communist Council for Mutual Economic Assistance (Comecon) agrees to disband. The Warsaw Treaty Organization (WTO) follows suit July 1.
July 17. U.S. president George H. W. Bush and Soviet president Mikhail Gorbachev reach agreement on Strategic Arms Reduction Treaty (START), signed July 31.
August 19–21. Hard-line Soviet leaders are defeated in coup attempt.
August 20. Estonia declares independence; other Soviet republics follow with similar declarations.
August 24. Mikhail Gorbachev resigns as general secretary of the Soviet Communist Party.
August 29. Supreme Soviet bans Communist Party activities.
September 7. Croatia and Slovenia formally secede from Yugoslavia; Macedonia declares independence September 8.
December 8. Leaders of Russia, Ukraine, and Belarus announce dissolution of the Soviet Union.
December 9–11. EC leaders agree on treaty for political and monetary union during meeting in Maastricht, Netherlands.
December 21. Eleven former Soviet republics launch Commonwealth of Independent States (CIS).
December 25. Mikhail Gorbachev resigns as Soviet president.

1992, **February 7.** EC's Maastricht Treaty formally signed.
March 2. Eight former Soviet republics admitted to UN.
April 27. Serbia and Montenegro proclaim new Federal Republic of Yugoslavia.
April 28. Islamic Jihad Council assumes power in Afghanistan following fall of Kabul to mujahidin rebels.
May 30. UN Security Council imposes sweeping sanctions against Serbia and Montenegro in response to aggression against Bosnia and Herzegovina.
August 1. First Lebanese parliamentary election in 20 years.

November 3. Arkansas governor Bill Clinton defeats incumbent U.S. president George H. W. Bush.
December 18. Kim Young Sam becomes first genuinely civilian president of South Korea after three decades of military leadership.

1993, **January 1.** Czech and Slovak Republics become separate states one day after the dissolution ("velvet divorce") of the 74-year-old Czech and Slovak Federative Republic.
January 1. Single European market established, paving the way for free movement of goods, services, capital, and people throughout all 12 EC countries.
January 3. U.S. and Russian presidents Bill Clinton and Boris Yeltsin sign second Strategic Arms Reduction Treaty (START II) under which the two nations will dismantle approximately two-thirds of their strategic nuclear warheads.
February 26. New York World Trade Center bombed by individuals linked to Islamic militants.
April 23–25. Eritrean people vote for independence (effective May 24) from Ethiopia, ending 30-year independence struggle.
April 27–28. China and Taiwan hold "unofficial" talks in Singapore, representing highest level of contact since Communists' 1949 seizure of the mainland.
May 23–28. Cambodia holds Constituent Assembly elections, first balloting since 1981.
July 18. Japanese Liberal Democratic Party loses its overall majority in the House of Representatives for first time since 1955 and is ousted from government by seven-party coalition on August 6.
September 13. Israeli-PLO peace accord signed in Washington.
October 3–4. Forces loyal to Russian President Boris Yeltsin battle with rebels opposed to his suspension of the parliament, ultimately ousting them from the parliament building.
October 8. UN General Assembly lifts economic sanctions against South Africa.
November 1. Maastricht Treaty on European Union formally enters into effect following the completion of the ratification process in October.
November 18. Interim constitution endorsed by South African multiparty negotiators.
December 15. Uruguay Round of the General Agreement on Tariffs and Trade (GATT) concludes.
December 15. Prime ministers of Ireland and United Kingdom sign "Downing Street Declaration," a 12-point document delineating principles for holding peace talks on Northern Ireland.

1994, **January 1.** European Economic Area (EEA), joining the EU and EFTA in a free market trading zone, comes into effect.
January 1. North American Free Trade Agreement (NAFTA), the first such agreement to link two industrialized countries (Canada and the United States) with a developing country (Mexico), becomes effective.
January 10. Announcement of Partnership for Peace (PfP), which affords military cooperation with, but not full-fledged defense guarantees by, NATO to nonmember countries.
February 28. In first offensive action by NATO, its fighters shoot down four Serbian warplanes for defying no-fly zone over Bosnia-Herzegovina.
March 27. Right-wing Freedom Alliance headed by Silvio Berlusconi wins Italian general election.
April 6. Presidents Juvénal Habyarimana of Rwanda and Cyprien Ntaryamire of Burundi die in downing of plane over Kilgali, Rwanda.
April 27. Multiracial constitution for South Africa comes into effect.
May 4. Israel and PLO sign accord in Cairo, Egypt, ending Israeli military rule in the Gaza Strip and Jericho.
May 6. Channel tunnel linking Britain and France formally opened by Queen Elizabeth II and President François Mitterrand.
May 10. Nelson Mandela sworn in as first black president of South Africa.
July 8. North Korean leader Kim Il Sung dies.
July 15. Over 500,000 Rwandan refugees arrive in Zaire, the initial wave of an exodus that would eventually involve more than 2 million people.
July 25. Israeli prime minister Yitzhak Rabin and Jordanian King Hussein sign declaration in Washington, ending 46-year state of war between their countries.
November 8. Republicans gain control of both houses of U.S. Congress for the first time in four decades.
December 11. Russian forces invade secessionist republic of Chechnya.

1995, **January 1.** Austria, Finland, and Sweden accede to EU.
January 1. World Trade Organization (WTO) inaugurated as successor to GATT.
April 19. Bombing of U.S. federal government building kills 168 in Oklahoma City.
May 7. Jacques Chirac (Gaullist) elected president of France in succession to François Mitterrand (Socialist).
September 5. France begins new series of underground nuclear tests in South Pacific, attracting worldwide protests.
September 28. Second accord in Israeli-PLO peace process signed in Washington, providing for extensive additional withdrawal of Israeli troops from West Bank and expansion of Palestinian self-rule.
November 4. Prime Minister Yitzhak Rabin of Israel assassinated by right-wing Jewish extremist in Tel Aviv.
November 21. U.S.-brokered peace agreement for Bosnia and Herzegovina initialed by contending parties in Dayton, Ohio (formally signed in Paris December 14).

1996, **January 20.** Yasir Arafat elected president of self-governing Palestinian Authority.
January 29. France announces permanent end to nuclear testing.
May 7. The first war crimes trial of the UN International Tribunal for the former Yugoslavia opens in The Hague.
May 18. Romano Prodi sworn in to head Italy's first left-dominated government, the 55th since World War II.
June 18. Conservative Benjamin Netanyahu becomes prime minister of Israel following election May 29.
June 28. Necmettin Erbakan appointed first avowedly Islamist prime minister of modern Turkey.
September 14. Post-Dayton elections in Bosnia and Herzegovina confirm entrenched ethnic loyalties.
September 24. China, France, Russia, the United Kingdom, and the United States sign Comprehensive Test Ban Treaty (CTBT) in UN headquarters, New York.
September 27. Afghanistan's Taliban militia seizes power in Kabul, immediately hanging ex-president Mohammad Najibullah.
December 10. Iraqi president Saddam Hussein reopens Iraqi oil pipelines under UN "oil-for-food" program.
December 17. Kofi Annan (Ghana) appointed (effective January 1, 1997) to succeed Boutros Boutros-Ghali (Egypt) as UN secretary general.
December 29. Guatemalan peace agreement ends 36-year-old guerrilla insurgency.

1997, **January 15.** Israeli prime minister Benjamin Netanyahu and Palestinian leader Yasir Arafat sign accord whereby Israel agrees to partial withdrawal from Hebron.
February 19. Deng Xiaoping, China's "paramount leader," dies.
April 22. Peruvian commandos raid the Japanese embassy in Lima, ending 126-day hostage crisis by Túpac Amaru Revolutionary Movement guerrillas.
May 1. Led by Tony Blair, Britain's Labour Party overwhelms the Conservative Party in legislative balloting and assumes power for first time in 18 years.
May 16–17. Mobutu Sese Seko, Zaire's leader for 32 years, flees the country and rebel leader Laurent Kabila pronounces the establishment of the Democratic Republic of the Congo.
May 25. Ahmad Tejan Kabbah, Sierra Leone's first democratically elected president, flees country following military coup.
July 1. China takes control of Hong Kong after Britain's 99-year lease expires.
July 2. The Bank of Thailand abandons fixed exchange rate after months of attacks on its currency (baht) by speculators, thus sparking East Asian financial crisis.
October 23. Former president of the Republic of the Congo Denis Sassou-Nguesso overthrows the nation's first democratically elected president, Pascal Lissouba.
December 9. North Korea, South Korea, China, and the United States open talks on creation of a permanent Korean peace treaty.

1998, **March 19.** Nationalist Hindu leader Atal Bihari Vajpayee sworn in as prime minister of India.
April 10. Northern Ireland power-sharing agreement reached.
May 6. Border dispute breaks out between Eritrea and Ethiopia.
May 11. India conducts underground nuclear tests.
May 21. President Haji Mohammad Suharto of Indonesia resigns and is succeeded by Vice President Bacharuddin Jusuf Habibie.
May 28. Pakistan conducts underground nuclear tests.
August 2. Rebellion launched in eastern Democratic Republic of the Congo against the Kabila government.
August 7. Terrorist bombs strike U.S. embassies in Nairobi, Kenya, and Dar es Salaam, Tanzania.
September 27. German chancellor Helmut Kohl defeated in reelection bid by Social Democrat Gerhard Schröder.
October 23. Wye accord signed by Israeli prime minister Benjamin Netanyahu and PLO leader Yasir Arafat.
October 31. Iraq announces end of cooperation with weapons inspectors from UNSCOM.

1999, **January 1.** Eleven of the 15 EU members launch Economic and Monetary Union (EMU), introducing euro for noncash payments on way toward replacement of national currencies by euro notes and coins in 2002.
February 27. Gen. Olusegun Obasanjo, former military ruler in 1970s, elected civilian president of Nigeria (inaugurated May 29, ending most recent period of military rule).

March 12. Czech Republic, Hungary, and Poland join NATO.
March 24. Responding to Serbian "ethnic cleansing" of Kosovo's Albanian population, NATO launches a campaign against Yugoslavia that is the biggest military operation in Europe since World War II.
June 7. Indonesia concludes first free national election in 45 years.
July 27. King Hassan II of Morocco dies.
August 30. East Timorese voters overwhelmingly vote for independence from Indonesia, leading to UN intervention following massive violence by anti-independence militias.
October 12. Gen. Pervez Musharraf declares himself chief executive of Pakistan, following military coup against elected government of Prime Minister Mohammad Nawaz Sharif.
October 14. U.S. Senate rejects Comprehensive Test Ban Treaty (CTBT) by 51–48 vote.
October 20. Abdurrahman Wahid elected president of Indonesia by People's Consultative Assembly.
December 19. Portugal returns Macao to China, ending 442 years of rule.
December 31. U.S. officially returns Panama Canal to Panama, ending 89 years of Canal Zone control.
December 31. Boris Yeltsin resigns Russian presidency and is succeeded in an acting capacity by Prime Minister Vladimir Putin.

2000, **March 18.** Chen Shui-bian elected as first non-Kuomintang president of Taiwan.
March 26. Vladimir Putin elected president of Russia.
April 6. Zimbabwe's Parliament passes controversial Land Acquisition Act, permitting uncompensated appropriation of white-owned farms and redistribution of farmland to blacks.
May 19. Armed coup launched against multiethnic government of Fiji.
May 24. Israel withdraws final troops from "security zone" in Lebanon, ending 22 years of occupation.
June 10. President Hafiz al-Assad of Syria dies.
June 13. Chairman Kim Jong Il of North Korea and President Kim Dae Jung of South Korea begin historic three-day summit in Pyongyang, North Korea.
July 2. Vicente Fox of National Action Party wins Mexican presidential election, ending 71 years of rule by Institutional Revolutionary Party.
September 28. Visit by Israeli opposition leader Ariel Sharon to Temple Mount (Haram al-Sharif) triggers new Palestinian intifada.
October 7. Vojislav Koštunica sworn in as president of Yugoslavia following capitulation of President Slobodan Milošević, who lost September 24 election.
November 17. Alberto Fujimori, having fled to Japan, resigns as president of Peru.
December 12. Eritrea and Ethiopia sign peace agreement, ending 19-month border war.
December 13. U.S. Vice President Al Gore, despite plurality of popular votes, concedes November 7 presidential election to George W. Bush, one day after Supreme Court decision effectively ended vote recounting in electorally decisive Florida.

2001, **January 7.** Nineteen years after coming to power by coup, Ghana's Jerry Rawlings hands over presidency to newly elected John Kufuor.
January 16. President Laurent Kabila of Democratic Republic of Congo assassinated.
January 20. Philippine vice president Gloria Macapagal Arroyo assumes presidency, protests having forced her predecessor, Joseph Estrada, from office.
February 6. Ariel Sharon wins special prime ministerial election in Israel, defeating Prime Minister Ehud Barak by wide margin.
April 26. Junichiro Koizumi, after unexpected victory in intraparty presidential balloting, sworn in as Japan's prime minister.
May 13. Former prime minister Silvio Berlusconi leads center-right alliance to victory in Italian general election.
June 28. Former Yugoslav president Slobodan Milošević indicted for crimes against humanity and other offenses and handed over to International Criminal Tribunal for the former Yugoslavia.
July 1. Crown Prince Dipendra of Nepal kills King Birendra and other members of royal family before committing suicide.
July 16. Russia and China conclude 20-year treaty of friendship and cooperation.
July 23. Peace agreement signed in Arusha, Tanzania, in latest effort to end eight-year civil war in Burundi.
July 23. Indonesia's People's Consultative Assembly unanimously removes President Abdurrahman Wahid from office and elects Vice President Megawati Sukarnoputri as his successor.
August 30. Bougainville secessionists sign peace agreement with Papua New Guinea government, ending 12-year conflict.
September 11. In the worst terrorist attacks in U.S. history, al-Qaida terrorists fly hijacked commercial airliners into New York's World Trade Center and the Pentagon outside Washington, D.C., causing more than 2,500 deaths.
September 23. Irish Republican Army (IRA) announces first confirmed "decommissioning" of weaponry, thereby preventing collapse of Northern Ireland power-sharing government.
October 7. U.S.-led air assault begins against al-Qaida bases and Taliban regime in Afghanistan in response to September 11 attacks.
October 29–November 10. Meeting in Marrakesh, Morocco, 164 countries negotiate final text of Kyoto Protocol to 1992 Framework Convention on Climate Change.
December 5. Hamid Karzai appointed head of interim Afghan government by factions meeting in Bonn, Germany; two days later Taliban surrenders Kandahar, its final stronghold.
December 12. China accedes to WTO.
December 20. Argentine president Fernando de la Rúa resigns in response to civil disturbances precipitated by government efforts aimed at controlling mounting financial crisis.

2002, **January 1.** The euro becomes legal tender in 12 European states.
April 4. UNITA and Angolan government sign cease-fire agreement ending civil war that dates from Angola's independence from Portugal in 1975.
April 11. International Criminal Court wins ratification by 60th UN member state, triggering its entry into force in sixty days, or July 1. United States does not ratify treaty, citing jeopardy to American citizens overseas.
April 14. Former guerilla leader José Gusmão elected first president of Timor-Leste (East Timor).
May 13. U.S. president George W. Bush and Russian president Vladimir Putin announce pact to cut nuclear arsenals by up to two-thirds over ten years.
May 20. International community recognizes Timor-Leste's independence from Indonesia.
June 13. Thirty-year-old Anti-Ballistic Missile Treaty lapses six months after President George W. Bush announced U.S. withdrawal.
June 13. Hamid Karzai elected interim president of Afghanistan.
June 16. Israel begins construction of 217-mile barrier in West Bank to thwart attacks.
July 1. International Criminal Court convenes in The Hague.
July 8. More than 30 African leaders meet in Durban to establish the African Union (AU) as the successor to the OAU.
July 30. President Paul Kagame of Rwanda and President Joseph Kabila of the Democratic Republic of the Congo sign peace agreement.
October 14. UK's secretary of state for Northern Ireland assumes powers of the suspended Northern Ireland Executive after Ulster Unionist Party withdraws its support from the Assembly.
November 21. Bulgaria, Estonia, Latvia, Lithuania, Romania, and Slovenia join NATO.
November 27. After a nearly four year hiatus, UN weapons inspectors return to Iraq to search for weapons of mass destruction.
December 4. Israeli prime minister Ariel Sharon endorses U.S. proposal for a Palestinian state in parts of the West Bank and Gaza Strip.

2003, **January 9.** North Korea withdraws from nuclear nonproliferation treaty.
January 27. Chief UN weapons inspector Hans Blix cites Iraq for noncooperation while Mohamed El-Baradei, the head of the International Atomic Energy Agency (IAEA) reports no evidence found of Iraqi nuclear weapons production.
February 4. Parliament of Federal Republic of Yugoslavia adopts new constitution renaming the country Serbia and Montenegro.
March 19. United States and allies attack Iraq.
April 9. Baghdad falls to U.S. forces.
May 22. Security Council Resolution 1483 ends economic sanctions on Iraq and recognizes United States and United Kingdom as occupying powers.
June 5. Israeli prime minister Ariel Sharon and Palestinian prime minister Mahmoud Abbas commit during summit in Aqaba, Jordan, to "roadmap" peace plan proposed by the United States.
June 6. French peacekeepers deploy in the Democratic Republic of the Congo to quell tribal warfare.
August 4. Peacekeepers from West African states arrive in Liberia to quell fighting between government and antigovernment forces.
August 7. Liberian president Charles Taylor resigns.
August 11. NATO takes command of peacekeeping operations in Afghanistan in first such mission outside Europe in alliance history.
September 14. Sweden's voters buck government to reject euro—56.1 percent to 41.8 percent—thereby retaining krona as national currency.
December 13. U.S. military captures Saddam Hussein.
December 19. Libyan leader Muammar Abu Minyar al-Qadhafi pledges to abandon pursuit of weapons of mass destruction.

2004, **January 4.** Afghan loya jirga approves constitution of Islamic Republic of Afghanistan.
February 29. Haitian president Jean Bertrand Aristide resigns and goes into exile.
March 12. South Korean National Assembly impeaches President Roh Moo Hyun for election law violations.

April 28. U.S. news program *60 Minutes II* broadcasts photos of U.S. troops abusing prisoners in Iraq's Abu Ghraib prison, publicizing an investigation under way in the military.
May 1. Ten countries—Cyprus, Czech Republic, Estonia, Hungary, Latvia, Lithuania, Malta, Poland, Slovak Republic, and Slovenia—join European Union, bringing the number of member states to 25.
May 9. Chechen president Akhmad Kadyrov assassinated in Grozny.
May 26. Conflict between Arabs and blacks continues in Darfur region of Sudan despite accord between Islamic government and Sudan People's Liberation Army.
June 28. U.S. administrator in Iraq L. Paul Bremer III transfers sovereignty to Iraqi Prime Minister Iyad Allawi.
November 3. Interim president Hamid Karzai declared official winner of Afghan presidential election.
November 11. Long-time Palestinian leader and Palestinian Authority president Yasir Arafat dies.
November 27. Ukrainian parliament nullifies results of November 21 election runoff, citing election fraud; Prime Minister Viktor Yanukovich claims a narrow 3 percent margin over challenger Viktor Yushchenko.
December 26. Yushchenko defeats Yanukovich in Ukrainian presidential runoff.
December 26. Tsunami hits Southeast Asia, killing an estimated 225,000 people and affecting a dozen states in Asia and Africa.

2005, **January 30.** Iraqis vote for representatives to national and provincial assemblies in first democratic elections since 1953.
February 1. King Gyanendra Bir Bikram Shah Dev of Nepal declares a state of emergency, dissolves coalition government, and arrests leading politicians, citing his constitutional authority and the lack of progress toward holding elections.
February 14. Former prime minister of Lebanon Rafik al-Hariri and others die in a car bomb explosion, leading to anti-Syria demonstrations and international pressure on Syria to withdraw its troops from the country.
February 16. Kyoto Protocol to UN Framework Convention on Climate Change takes effect. United States is not a party to the agreement.
March 16. Israel turns over control of Jericho to Palestinians.
April 2. Pope John Paul II dies.
April 19. Conclave of cardinals elects Cardinal Joseph Ratzinger of Germany as pope. Ratzinger takes the name Benedict XVI.
April 26. Last Syrian troops leave Lebanon, ending 29-year stay.
June 16. After a proposed European constitution is voted down in nationwide referendums in Netherlands and France, leaders of EU halt efforts to ratify.
August 1. King Fahd ibn Abd al-Aziz Al Saud of Saudi Arabia dies; Prince Abdullah assumes the throne.
August 10. Iran removes UN seals it voluntarily accepted at nuclear production sites eight months previously and begins converting raw uranium into gas for enrichment.
August 15. Indonesia and the Free Aceh Movement sign a peace accord ending 30 years of civil war.
August 15. Israel begins withdrawing more than 8,700 Jewish settlers from the Gaza Strip, enabling Palestinians to assume control of the area.
August 29. Hurricane Katrina lashes U.S. city of New Orleans, flooding the city and coastal areas, and killing over 1,500; federal emergency response is widely criticized.
September 18. Afghanistan holds its first democratic parliamentary elections in more than 25 years.
October 10. German legislative parties agree to resolve their September parliamentary election disputes by creating a Grand Coalition that includes Angela Merkel as Germany's first woman chancellor.
October 15. Iraqis endorse new constitution with 79 percent "yes" vote.
November 21. Voters defeat proposed new constitution in Kenya.
December 15. Iraq elects its first permanent parliament since the removal of President Saddam Hussein.
December 18. Bolivia holds its presidential election after the resignation of President Carlos Mesa in June; Evo Morales, the candidate of the Movement to Socialism, wins with 51.1 percent of the vote.
December 23. Lech Kaczyński sworn in as president of Poland after winning the election on the second runoff.

2006, **January 4.** Israeli leader Ariel Sharon suffers a second, catastrophic stroke and slips into a coma. Ehud Olmert named acting prime minister.
January 15. Ellen Johnson-Sirleaf sworn in as president of Liberia, thereby becoming Africa's first female president.
January 15. In a runoff election, center-left candidate Michelle Bachelet wins 53 percent of the vote to become Chile's first female president.
January 25. Hamas wins a majority in elections to the Palestinian Legislative Council, ending Fatah's dominance.
February 28. Former opposition leader Milorad Dodik confirmed as prime minister of the Serb Republic of Bosnia and Herzegovina.
April 23. Prime Minister Ferenc Gyurcsány's coalition, led by the Hungarian Socialist Party, wins runoff parliamentary elections.
April 27. Following weeks of demonstrations in Nepal in opposition to King Gyanendra's continued absolute power, consensus candidate Girija Prasad Koirala is appointed prime minister.
May 4. Ehud Olmert, leader of the recently launched Kadima party, forms a coalition government in Israel following the Knesset balloting on March 28 in which Kadima secured a plurality of seats.
May 5. The Sudanese government and the leader of Darfur's main rebel group agree to a cease-fire after three years of hostilities and the displacement of an estimated 2 million people.
May 17. Romano Prodi, leader of the new Union coalition, returns to the premiership of Italy after the Union secured a majority of the seats in the legislative poll of April 9–10.
May 20. Nurad Jawad al-Maliki forms national unity government in Iraq.
May 26. Nepal's prime minister Girija Prasad Koirala and rebel Maoist leader Prachanda sign a cease-fire code of conduct, bringing a degree of political stability to the country.
June 3. Former Yugoslav republic of Montenegro declares independence from Serbia.
June 27. Economic reformer and Communist Party chief Nguyen Minh Triet elected president of Vietnam after the country's top three leaders officially retire.
July 12. The Lebanese Shiite Muslim group Hezbollah kills three Israeli soldiers and captures two others during a raid into Israel; Israel subsequently responds with air-strike bombing of Lebanon to which Hezbollah retaliates by launching rockets and missiles into Israel.
August 3. Viktor Yanukovych of the pro-Russian Party of Regions named prime minister of Ukraine following protracted negotiations with the Orange Revolution parties.
August 14. Israel and Hezbollah declare a cease-fire.
September 19. A military coup led by Gen. Sonthi Boonyaratkalin, with the support of the royal family and numerous citizens, overthrows Prime Minister Thaksin Shinawatra of Thailand.
October 8. North Korea announces its first successful underground nuclear weapons test, prompting widespread international condemnation and UN sanctions.
October 27. After failed talks with the West, Iran restarts its nuclear program, claiming its reactors are for peaceful purposes, despite concerns expressed by the UN and Western nations.
November 21. The Nepalese government signs a Comprehensive Peace Agreement with former Maoist insurgents.
December 1. Conservative Felipe Calderón inaugurated as president of Mexico amid controversy over his victory against leftist Andrés Manuel López Obrador in balloting on July 6.
December 5. The Fijian military, led by Commander Frank Bainimarama, takes over the government of Prime Minister Laisenia Qarase in the country's fourth coup in 20 years.
December 6. Joseph Kabila sworn in as president of the Democratic Republic of the Congo, making him the nation's first elected president in 40 years.
December 14. In Bhutan, King Jigme Singye Wangchuk abdicates the throne in favor of his son, Crown Prince Jigme Khesar Namgyal Wangchuk.
December 23. Resolution 1737 is unanimously approved by the UN Security Council, imposing sanctions on Iran for failing to comply with resolution 1696, which prohibited it from enrichment activities.
December 24–28. Ethiopia formally admits to having troops engaged in battle within the borders of Somalia. Somali government forces, backed by Ethiopian troops, retake the capital, Mogadishu, from the Islamic Courts Union.
December 30. Former Iraqi president Saddam Hussein hanged, having been found guilty of crimes against humanity by an Iraqi tribunal on November 5.

2007, **January 1.** Romania and Bulgaria become members of the EU.
January 1. Ban Ki Moon, theretofore the foreign minister of South Korea, succeeds Kofi Annan as secretary general of the UN.
January 10. Sandinista leader Daniel Ortega returns to the presidency of Nicaragua.
March 4. Peace agreement signed in Côte d'Ivoire, preparing the groundwork for formation of a new national unity government.
March 17. The Palestinian Legislative Council approves a Fatah/Hamas unity government led by Ismail Haniyeh of Hamas.
April 1. Former Maoist insurgents join the cabinet in Nepal.
May 6. Conservative Nicolas Sarkozy wins the French presidential runoff election with 53.1 percent of the vote over Socialist Ségolène Royal.
May 8. Limited self-rule returns to Northern Ireland based on the St. Andrews Agreement of October 2006 and subsequent agreements between unionist and republican/nationalist parties.
May 12. Su Tseng-Chang resigns as the premier of the Republic of China (Taiwan) following a loss in a presidential primary election; President Chen Shui-bian replaces him with Chang Chun-hsiung on May 14.

June 14. Palestinian president Mahmoud Abbas dissolves the Palestinian government and installs emergency rule in the wake of Hamas's recent takeover of the Gaza Strip.
July 18. IAEA inspectors confirm the closure of all five nuclear reactors in North Korea as six-party talks resume in Beijing.
June 27. Gordon Brown succeeds Tony Blair as prime minister of the United Kingdom.
August 28. Abdullah Gul of the Justice and Development Party is elected as the first Islamist president of Turkey.
October 28. Argentine first lady Cristina Kirchner elected to succeed her husband, Nestor Kirchner, as president.
November 7. Georgian president Mikhail Saakashvili declares a state of emergency amid protests calling for his resignation.
November 29. Pervez Musharraf sworn in for another five-year term as Pakistan's president after relinquishing his military posts.
December 2. Russian president Vladimir Putin's party secures 70 percent of the vote in Russian parliamentary elections.
December 3. Kevin Rudd of the Australian Labor Party becomes prime minister, succeeding John Howard of the Liberal Party of Australia.
December 18. Yulia Tymoshenko returns as prime minister of Ukraine to head a coalition government dominated by the Orange Revolution parties, which secured a slim majority in the legislative poll of September 30 that was prompted by intense conflict between President Viktor Yushchenko and Prime Minister Viktor Yanukovych.
December 23. Thailand's People Power Party (supportive of ousted prime minister Thaksin Shinawatra) wins the Thai parliamentary elections.
December 27. Former Pakistani prime minister Benazir Bhutto assassinated at a campaign rally.
December 30. Kenya's election commission declares incumbent Mwai Kibaki the winner of the December 27 national election, sparking violent protests from opposition party supporters, who charge that the election was rigged.

2008, **January 22.** The military's Council for National Security in Thailand announces its dissolution and acceptance of the December legislative election results.
January 24. Italian prime minister Romano Prodi offers his resignation following no-confidence vote in the Senate.
January 28. Samak Sundaravej, considered a "proxy" for former prime minister Thaksin Shinawatra, elected prime minister by Thailand's House of Representatives.
February 3. Pro-Western president Boris Tadić reelected in Serbia over nationalist rival Tomislav Nikolić.
February 17. Prime Minister Hashim Thaçi declares Kosovo independent, prompting fierce criticism from Serbia and Russia but quick recognition from the United States, the United Kingdom, France, Germany, Japan, and others.
February 18. Opposition parties dominate legislative elections in Pakistan in what is generally perceived as a referendum on the rule of President Musharraf.
February 24. Raúl Castro confirmed as president of Cuba's Council of State and Council of Ministers after Fidel Castro had announced that he would not accept reelection to those posts.
February 27. Israel launches air and ground offensive in Gaza Strip.
February 28. Dimitrios Christofias, leader of the Progressive Party of the Working People, inaugurated as the first communist president of Cyprus.
March 2. Dmitri Medvedev elected president of Russia as Vladimir Putin's handpicked successor.
March 22. Ma Ying-jeou of the Nationalist Party (Kuomintang) elected president of Taiwan.
March 24. The lower house in Pakistan elects Yusuf Raza Gilani, an ally of the late Benazir Bhutto, as prime minister of Pakistan.
April 8. President Ahmadinejad of Iran announces plans for additional uranium enrichment.
April 9. New constitution, providing for a multiparty system headed by a president and a bicameral legislature, proposed by Myanmar's military junta.
April 10. Maoists secure legislative victory in Nepal.
April 13. Power-sharing cabinet announced in Kenya; Mwai Kibaki remains president and opposition leader Raila Odinga named prime minister.
April 15. The Iraqi Accord Front, a Sunni coalition, returns to the Shiite-dominated Iraqi cabinet.
April 20. Fernando Lugo is elected president of Paraguay, ending more than 60 years of rule by the Colorado Party.
April 27. Coalition government collapses in Hungary.
May 2. Election commission in Zimbabwe declares that opposition candidate Tsvangirai won only 48 percent of the vote in the March 29 balloting, thereby necessitating a runoff between him and President Mugabe, who finished second in the first round.
May 7. Brian Cowen of Fianna Fáil elected prime minister by the lower house of the legislature in Ireland, following Bertie Ahern's resignation from the post (effective May 6) amid corruption investigations.
May 8. Former president Vladimir Putin confirmed as prime minister by the Russian State Duma.
May 21. Supporters of Georgian president Mikhail Saakashvili dominate legislative balloting.
May 25. Gen. Michel Suleiman elected president of Lebanon by the National Assembly as part of the May 21 agreement designed to stem strife between Hezbollah (and other Shiite groups) and progovernment forces. Prime Minister Fouad Siniroa subsequently forms a new cabinet that includes members of Hezbollah.
May 28. Nepal's Constituent Assembly agrees to abolish the monarchy and establish a federal republic.
June 2. Bhutan's National Assembly approves draft constitution transferring power from the king to a government formed by the leading legislative party.
June 18. Israel and Hamas initiate a cease-fire.
June 26. The interim prime minister of Nepal announces his resignation as efforts to establish a transitional government falter.
June 27. Pro-European coalition government announced in Serbia.
June 27. Zimbabwean president Robert Mugabe wins highly controversial second-round presidential balloting after first-round leader Morgan Tsvangirai withdraws to protest violence against his supporters in the run-up to the election.
July 27. Ruling Cambodian People's Party wins two-thirds majority in legislative elections.
August 6. Military coup overthrows the government in Mauritania.
August 7. Georgian forces enter South Ossetia, triggering massive response by Russia in which Russian forces move deeply into Georgia proper. Russia subsequently recognizes the independence of South Ossetia and Abkhazia.
August 15. Maoist Pushpa Kamal Dahal elected prime minister of Nepal.
August 18. Pakistani president Musharraf resigns.
August 19. Zambian president Levy Mwanawasa dies.
September 1. Japanese prime minister Fukuda resigns; Taro Aso elected leader of the Liberal Democratic Party on September 22 and installed as prime minister on September 24.
September 1. Massive crowds demonstrate in Thailand against Prime Minister Samak, prompting him to impose a state of emergency.
September 5. Senate in Haiti approves government of new prime minister Michèle Pierre-Louis.
September 5–6. The Popular Movement for the Liberation of Angola dominates the first legislative balloting since 1992.
September 7. U.S. government approves takeover of two privately owned (albeit government-sponsored) mortgage companies as an unprecedented financial intervention develops, in which Congress ultimately authorizes a $700 billion bailout of banking system in the midst of a global "credit crisis" and steep declines in the stock market.
September 8. Asif Ali Zardari, the widower of Benazir Bhutto, elected president of Pakistan in a vote by the federal legislature and provincial assemblies.
September 9. Thai prime minister Samak forced to resign; succeeded on September 17 by Somchai Wongsawat, the brother-in-law of former prime minister Thaksin.
September 20. South African President Mbeki agrees to resign under pressure from the African National Congress (ANC); Kgalema Motlanthe, deputy leader of the ANC, elected as Mbeki's successor by the National Assembly on September 25.
September 28. Far-right parties gain ground in early legislative elections in Austria but ruling centrist parties form new coalition government on December 2.
September 28. New constitution (proposed by the leftist government) endorsed in national referendum in Ecuador.
September 29. Government in Iceland forced to nationalize the country's third largest bank as value of the krona plummets in midst of global financial crisis.
October 8. Malaysian prime minister Abdullah announces he will resign in March 2009 in the wake of his party's poor performance in the March 2008 legislative elections.
October 26. Tzipi Livni declares her efforts to form a new coalition government in Israel unsuccessful, setting the stage for new legislative elections in early 2009.
October 26. Fighting intensifies in eastern Democratic Republic of the Congo, ultimately displacing 250,000 people.
November 4. Barack Obama elected president of the United States, and his Democratic Party extends its legislative control.
November 7. Mass demonstrations in Georgia demand resignation of President Mikhail Saakashvili.

November 8. Opposition National Party wins legislative balloting in New Zealand; party leader John Key forms coalition government on November 17.

November 25. Referendum in Greenland approves extension of self-rule in anticipation of eventual independence.

December 2. Thailand's Constitutional Court prompts expulsion of Prime Minister Somchai via ruling that his People Power Party committed fraud in the 2007 elections; opposition leader Abhisit Vejjajiva elected prime minister by the legislature on December 15.

December 22. President Lansana Conté of Guinea dies; military leaders assume power in a bloodless coup the following day and install Capt. Moussa Dadis Camara as president of a ruling National Council for Democracy and Development.

December 28. Israel launches air strikes on Gaza following resumption of Hamas rocket attacks.

December 29. The Awami League, a former opposition party led by former prime minister Sheikh Hasina Wajed, wins an overwhelming victory in legislative elections in Bangladesh.

2009, **January 3.** Ground offensive into Gaza launched by Israel, which announces unilateral cease-fire January 17.

January 19. Left-wing opposition gains legislative victory in El Salvador.

January 26. Iceland's government collapses; minority interim government formed February 1 under Jóhanna Sigurðardóttir, the country's first female prime minister.

January 26. Violent antigovernment protests begin in Madagascar as supporters of Andry Rajoelina, the mayor of Antananarivo, demand the resignation of President Marc Ravalomanana; both sides subsequently claim to be in control of the country.

February 11. Morgan Tsvangirai sworn in as prime minister to head national unity government in Zimbabwe.

February 15. Voters in Venezuela approve constitutional revision eliminating presidential term limits.

February 20. Declining economic conditions trigger collapse of Latvian government.

March 2. President João Bernardo Vieira assassinated by "rogue" army troops in Guinea-Bissau; the army denies a coup has occurred.

March 15. Opposition leader Mauricio Funes elected president of El Salvador.

March 17. Marc Ravalomanana steps down as president of Madagascar after army supports Andry Rajoelina in power struggle.

March 27. Center-right government falls in Czech Republic after losing confidence motion over its handling of economic affairs.

March 29. Ruling pro-European coalition wins early legislative elections in Montenegro.

March 31. Likud's Benjamin Netanyahu sworn in as leader of center-right government in Israel.

April 3. Najib Razak inaugurated as prime minister of Malaysia following the resignation of Abdullah Badawi, whose government had been under year-long pressure.

April 5. Official results of legislative elections in Moldova give majority to the ruling Communist Party of Moldova, prompting massive protests, charges of fraud, and, ultimately, new elections.

April 10. Fiji's president Ratu Iloilo abrogates 1997 constitution in wake of earlier Court of Appeals ruling that called for new elections; Iloilo revokes all judicial appointments, declares himself head of state, and says elections will not be held until 2014.

April 22. African National Congress wins another solid legislative majority in South Africa; ANC leader Jacob Zuma elected president of South Africa by the legislature on May 6.

April 26. Rafael Correa reelected as president of Ecuador, and his left-wing Country Alliance secures legislative plurality.

May 3. Conservative business leader Ricardo Martinelli Berrocal elected president of Panama; his four-party coalition secures legislative majority.

May 18. Sri Lankan military announces final victory over the separatist Liberation Tigers of Tamil Eelam after 26 years of conflict.

May 23. Madhave Kumar Nepal elected prime minister of Nepal following resignation of Pushpa Kamal Dahal, who had been embroiled in a dispute with the military.

June 2. Greenland's legislative elections won by leftist, proindependence opposition.

June 7. Anti-Syrian, pro-Western alliance wins legislative majority in Lebanon.

June 8. President Omar Bongo, Gabon's president since 1967, dies of natural causes.

June 12. Incumbent Mahmoud Ahmadinejad declared winner of presidential election in Iran, prompting massive protests alleging fraud, followed by a violent government crackdown on dissidents.

June 28. President Mel Zelaya ousted in Honduras, prompting widespread international condemnation of his opponents.

July 5. Center-right opposition gains plurality in legislative balloting in Bulgaria; Boiko Borisov, theretofore mayor of Sofia, named prime minister on July 27.

July 5. Opposition Institutional Revolutionary Party and allies win majority in elections to the Mexican Chamber of Deputies.

July 10. Peruvian prime minister Yehude Simon resigns following antigovernment protests.

July 18. Mohamed Ould Abdelaziz, who led the 2008 coup in Mauritania, elected president in first-round balloting disputed as fraudulent by his opponents.

July 29. The ruling Communist Party of Moldova loses its majority in rerun of legislative elections (originally held in April); Vladimir Filat sworn in as head of a four-party, pro-EU coalition government on September 25.

August 20. Presidential elections held in Afghanistan; incumbent Hamid Karzai is later credited with a first-round victory, prompting widespread accusations of fraud.

August 30. Opposition Democratic Party of Japan wins legislative elections in Japan, ending longtime dominance of Liberal Democratic party.

September 1. Fiji suspended from the Commonwealth for government's refusal to negotiate a new election schedule with the opposition.

September 3. Ali-Ben Bongo Ondimba, son of the late president Bongo, declared winner of the August 30 presidential election in Gabon.

September 7. Premier Liu Chao-shiuan resigns as Taiwan's premier following criticism of his government's response to a recent typhoon.

September 25. Western leaders accuse Iran of operating a secret uranium enrichment facility.

October 4. Opposition Panhellenic Socialist Movement (PASOK) scores landslide victory in legislative elections in Greece; PASOK leader George Papandreou forms new government October 7.

October 20. Supporters of President Mamadou Tandja, benefiting from opposition boycott, gain all seats in early legislative balloting in Niger; Niger suspended from ECOWAS on October 21.

November 1. Abdullah Abdullah, who finished second to incumbent Hamid Karzai in the disputed presidential balloting in Afghanistan in August, withdraws from run-off; Karzai is inaugurated for another term on November 20.

November 9. Prime Minister Saad Hariri forms unity government (which includes Hezbollah) in Lebanon after months of wrangling.

November 11. Jean-Max Bellerive named prime minister of Haiti.

November 27–29. Ruling South West Africa People's Organization (SWAPO) wins landslide victory in presidential and legislative elections in Namibia.

November 29. José Mujica, a former leader of the Tupamaros guerrillas and the candidate of the ruling Progressive Encounter–Broad Front, elected president of Uruguay.

November 29. Central bank of United Arab Emirates bails out Dubai, which had earlier roiled world financial markets by asking for a moratorium on $59 billion in debt.

November 29. Iran approves construction of new uranium enrichment plants, prompting U.S. threats of additional sanctions.

November 29. Porfirio Lobo Sosa elected president of Honduras.

December 1. U.S. president Barack Obama announces that 30,000 additional troops will be sent to Afghanistan.

December 1. EU's Lisbon Treaty enters into force; Herman Van Rompuy, former prime minister of Belgium, to become the first permanent president of the European Council under the EU's revamped and expanded institutional structure.

December 3. Guinea's president Moussa Camara seriously wounded in assassination attempt by an aide.

December 6. Incumbent Traian Băsescu narrowly reelected president of Romania in disputed balloting.

December 8. Japan announces new $80 billion stimulus package.

December 7–8. Antigovernment protests continue in Iran; more than 200 people arrested.

December 18. Power-sharing plan abandoned in Madagascar.

December 29. Sudan's legislature approves law authorizing a 2011 independence referendum in southern Sudan.

2010, **January 10.** Center-left opposition candidate Ivo Josipović elected president of Croatia.

January 12. Earthquake in Haiti kills more than 200,000 people and leaves 1 million homeless.

January 17. Right-wing businessman Sebastián Piñera elected president of Chile.

February 7. Pro-Russian former prime minister Viktor Yanukovych, elected president of Ukraine.

February 7. Laura Chinchilla, the candidate of the ruling National Liberation Party, becomes the first woman to be elected president of Costa Rica.

February 13. U.S./UK/Afghan forces launch massive anti-Taliban campaign in Afghanistan's Helmand Province.

February 18. Military coup in Niger seizes power from President Mamadou Tandja.
February 23. Government collapses in Netherlands over the issue of extension of the Dutch mission in Afghanistan.
March 3. Greek prime minister George Papandreou warns of the country's potential bankruptcy and initiates severe austerity measures.
March 4. Incumbent Faure Gnassingbé reelected president of Togo.
March 7. Legislative elections in Iraq portend long negotiations on formation of a new government as Prime Minister Nuri al-Maliki's alliance vies with the alliance of former prime minister Ayad Allawi for plurality status.
March 24. United States and Russia announce agreement on a new treaty to reduce the deployment of nuclear weapons by 30 percent.
April 7. Protest demonstrations prompt President Kurmanbek Bakiyev to flee Kyrgyzstan's capital, and opposition coalition selects Roza Otunbayeva to lead provisional government. (Bakiyev officially resigns on April 15.)
April 10. Polish president Lech Kaczyński and 95 others (including many national officials) die in plane crash in Russia.
April 11–15. Umar Hassan Ahmad al-Bashir reelected president of Sudan in balloting boycotted by much of the opposition.
April 11 and 25. Right-wing opposition alliance secures overwhelming victory in legislative balloting in Hungary after the incumbent government is accused of economic incompetence.
April 12–13. Algeria, Mali, Mauritania, and Niger approve joint regional antiterrorism activity aimed primarily at al-Qaida in the Islamic Maghreb.
April 15. Legislature in Pakistan approves restoration of 1973 constitution, thereby giving back to the prime minister authority assumed by President Musharraf in 2003.
April 18. Derviş Eroğlu, considered a skeptic in regard to Cypriot reunification, elected president of the Turkish Republic of Northern Cyprus.
April 19. Djibouti's legislature approves constitutional revision permitting President Ismail Guelleh to run for a third term.
April 22. Belgium's government resigns (but remains in caretaker capacity) over issue of proposed new electoral districts.
May 5. Junta in Niger announces constitutional referendum and new elections will be held by February 2011.
May 5. Nigerian president Umaru Yar'Adua dies and is succeeded by Vice President Goodluck Jonathan.
May 6. Opposition Conservative Party wins plurality in elections to the UK House of Commons, permitting Conservative leader David Cameron to form a coalition government with the Liberal Democrats on May 11.
May 9. U.S.-mediated proximity talks begin between officials from Israel and the Palestinian Authority.
May 10. Benigno Aquino III, the son of the late former president Corazon Aquino, elected president of the Philippines.
May 23. Ruling Ethiopian People's Revolutionary Democratic Front and its allies win 534 of 547 seats in lower-house balloting in Ethiopia.
May 25. Electoral coalition led by former dictator Désiré Bouterse wins legislative plurality in Suriname, leading to Bouterse's election to the presidency by the National Assembly on July 19.
May 26. Kamla-Persad Bissessar becomes the first female prime minister of Trinidad and Tobago following the legislative victory of her opposition coalition on May 24.
May 28–29. Ruling three-party center-right government wins majority in lower-house balloting in Czech Republic, although the opposition Czech Social Democratic Party leads all parties.
May 31. Israeli naval forces intercept aid ships headed for Gaza, killing nine people and attracting widespread international criticism.
June 8. Finance Minister Naoto Kan appointed prime minister of Japan following the resignation on June 2 of Yukio Hatoyama in the face of plummeting popular approval.
June 9. Opposition People's Party for Freedom and Democracy secures one-seat plurality in lower-house balloting in Netherlands, while the anti-immigration Party for Freedom dramatically increases its representation.
June 10–14. Fighting in southern Kyrgyzstan between Kyrgyz and Uzbek ethnic groups leaves an estimated 2,000 dead and 400,000 displaced.
June 12. Center-left party of Prime Minister Robert Fico wins plurality in lower-house balloting in Slovakia, but losses by other parties in his coalition leave the government without a majority.
June 13. New Flemish Alliance, a party devoted to eventual independence for Flanders, wins pluralities in voting for both legislative houses in Belgium.
June 20. Juan Manuel Santos, the candidate of the ruling Social Party of National Unity, elected president of Colombia.
June 24. Julia Gillard named Australia's first female prime minister after successfully challenging Prime Minister Kevin Rudd for leadership of Australian Labor Party.
June 27. Voters in Kyrgyzstan approve a new constitution that establishes a parliamentary republic with limited presidential powers.
July 4. Bronisław Komorowski, the speaker of the lower house of the legislature, elected president of Poland in second-round balloting over Jarosław Kaczyński, the twin of the late president.
July 9. Iveta Radičová appointed as Slovakia's first female prime minister.
July 29. South Korean prime minister Chung Un Chan resigns in view of the poor results for his party in local elections in June.
August 27. New constitution in Kenya limits presidential authority and expands civil rights.
August 31. U.S. president Barack Obama announces the end of U.S. combat operations in Iraq, although an estimated 50,000 U.S. troops remain in Iraq in a support role.
September 12. Constitutional reforms proposed by Turkey's ruling Justice and Development Party approved in national referendum.
September 18. Legislative elections in Afghanistan marred by violence and irregularities.
September 19. Far-right anti-immigration party enters Swedish legislature for first time.
October 10. Netherlands Antilles dissolves, with Curaçao and St. Maarten becoming autonomous "countries" within the Kingdom of the Netherlands, which retains authority over defense and foreign affairs.
October 10. Party supportive of former president Bakiyev wins narrow plurality in legislative balloting in Kyrgyzstan.
October 23. David Thompson, the prime minister of Barbados, dies.
October 31. Dilma Rousseff elected Brazil's first female president.
November 2. In a major setback for the Obama administration, the Republican Party gains control of the U.S. House of Representatives.
November 7. Opposition leader Alpha Conté elected president of Guinea.
November 7. In Myanmar's first national election since 1990, junta-supportive Union Solidarity and Development Party wins an overwhelming victory at all levels. The results are widely condemned internationally.
November 13. Aung San Suu Kyi, Myanmar's most prominent antijunta leader, is released upon expiration of her most recent period of house arrest.
November 22. Ireland's prime minister Brian Cowen solicits $100 billion financial rescue package from the EU and IMF and announces he will call early elections as soon as the 2011 budget is passed.
November 28. Incumbent Laurent Gbagbo and opposition leader Alassana Ouattara both claim victory in second round of presidential balloting in Côte d'Ivoire.
November 28 and December 5. In controversial two-stage parliamentary balloting, Egypt's ruling National Democratic Party wins 420 of 508 directly elected seats.
December 13. Prime Minister Michael Somare of Papua New Guinea, facing charges involving financial irregularities, steps down, with Sam Abal, the deputy prime minister, becoming acting prime minister.
December 17. Kyrgyzstan's legislature endorses politically diverse three-party coalition government led by Prime Minister Almazbek Atambayev of the Social Democratic Party of Kyrgyzstan.
December 19. Belarusan president Alyaksandr Lukashenka wins reelection, capturing 79.6 percent of the vote, according to the official count, against nine challengers.
December 21. Prime Minister al-Maliki forms coalition government in Iraq with support of major legislative groupings.

2011, **January 1.** Estonia becomes the 17th member of the Eurozone when it officially adopts the euro as its currency.
January 9-15. Voters in South Sudan endorse independence in a referendum.
January 10. Basque separatists declare a unilateral cease-fire with Spain after 40 years of conflict.
January 12. The Lebanese government of Prime Minister Saad Hariri falls after 11 Hezbollah and allied cabinet members resign.
January 14. Tunisian president Gen. Zine El-Abidine Ben Ali flees the country amid violent protests. The fall of Ben Ali's government marks the beginning of the Arab Spring uprisings, which spread throughout the region.
January 23. Gen. François Bozizé Yangouvonda Aníbal is reelected president of the Central African Republican. In Portugal, president Cavaco Silva wins reelection.
January 26. Violent police clashes with protesters in Syria mark the beginning of the Syrian Uprising.
February 1. Marouf al-Bakhit is appointed prime minister by King Abdullah II in response to calls for political reform and in an effort to counter anti-regime protests.
February 3. After seven months of protected negotiations, Jhala Nath Khanal is elected prime minister of Nepal by the parliament.
February 4. In Myanmar, Prime minister Thein Sein is elected president by the legislature.
February 11. Egyptian president Husni Mubarak resigns after weeks of protests which kill more than 800 and injure more than 6,000. An interim government, dominated by the Supreme Council of the Armed Forces and led by Field Marshal Mohammad Hussein Tantawi is installed.

February 14. Pearl Uprising begins in Bahrain with massive protests by the majority Shiite population against the Sunni-led regime.
February 15. Anti-government protests in Libya are met with harsh military force, sparking the Libyan Revolution.
February 18. Lt. Gen. Yoweri Kaguta Museveni is reelected president of Uganda, securing more than 68 percent of the vote.
February 22. Behgjet Pacolli is elected president of Kosovo by the National Assembly in the third round of balloting. Incumbent prime minister Hashim Thaçi is reappointed.
March 5. Mustafa Abdel Jalil is appointed to head Libya's National Transitional Council, the main anti-regime umbrella organization.
March 9. Enda Kenny is elected prime minister of Ireland by the parliament, following legislative elections on February 25.
March 11. An earthquake of magnitude 9.0, and a subsequent tsunami, hit the east coast of Japan, leading to the meltdown of the Fukushima Daiichi nuclear power plant and claiming more than 18,000 lives.
March 17. UN Security Council approves a no-fly zone over Libya in an attempt to reduce civilian casualties; two days later, an international coalition begins enforcement of the no-fly zone and launched attacks on Libyan military targets. Živko Budimir is elected president of the Federation of Bosnia-Herzegovina by the House of Peoples, while Nermin Nikšić becomes prime minister.
March 18. Rosario Fernández Figueroa is appointed prime minister of Peru following the resignation of José Antonio Chang Escobedo.
March 20. In disputed run-off balloting, singer Michel Martelly is elected president of Haiti.
March 28. The constitutional court of Kosovo rules that that the election of president Pacolli on February 22 was unconstitutional. Pacolli leaves office and is replaced on an interim basis by the speaker of the parliament Jakup Krasniqi.
March 29. Syrian president Bashar al-Assad accepts the resignation of his cabinet in response to widespread protests.
April 3. Nursultan Nazarbayev is reelected president of Kazakhstan in disputed balloting that was boycotted by opposition parties. In Mali, Cissé Mariam Kaïdama Sidibé is appointed prime minister, becoming the country's first woman chief executive.
April 4. Prime minister Sir Michael Somare of Papua New Guinea is suspended from office for 14 days following his conviction on misconduct charges. After his suspension, Somare declined to return to office, citing medical reasons, and Sam Abal becomes interim prime minister.
April 11. Former Côte d'Ivoire president Laurent Gbagbo is captured by rebel forces, ending a four month civil war.
April 15. Tertius Zongo is dismissed as prime minister of Burkina Faso by president Blaise Compaoré. Luc Adolphe Tiao is appointed to replace Zongo and forms a new government on April 22.
April 16. Incumbent president Goodluck Jonathan wins presidential polling in Nigeria, but his victory is met by widespread violence in the mainly Muslim north of the country.
April 17. The National Coalition Party wins legislative elections in Finland and forms a coalition government, led by prime minister Jyrki Katainen who is sworn into office on June 22.
May 1. Osama bin Laden, founder and leader of al-Qaida, is killed by U.S. special operations forces in his compound near Islamabad, Pakistan.
May 2. Canada's Conservative Party, led by incumbent prime minister Stephen Harper, wins a majority in parliamentary balloting.
May 15. Egyptian foreign minister Nabil al-Arabi is selected as the new secretary general of the Arab League and takes office on July 1.
May 28. After being vacant through successive governments since 1998, the post of prime minister is filled in Benin with the appointment of Pascal Irénée Koupaki.
May 29. Sergey Bagapsh, the president of the breakaway Georgian republic of Abkhazia, dies in office and is succeeded on an interim basis by vice president Aleksandr Ankvab, who is elected to a full term on August 27.
June 2. In the second round of presidential balloting by the Latvian parliament, Andris Berzins defeats incumbent Valdis Zatlers.
June 5. Ollanta Humala is elected president of Peru in run-off balloting. The Social Democrat Party wins legislative elections in Portugal and party leader Pedro Passos Coelho forms a new government on June 15.
June 15. The Laotian parliament reelects Choummaly Sayasone president, and Thongsing Thammavong as prime minister.
July 9. Republic of South Sudan gains independence from Sudan and Salva Kiir is inaugurated as president of the new nation. South Sudan joins the UN five days later.
July 21. EU leaders agree to extend emergency debt repayment by Ireland, Greece and Portugal from seven to fifteen years and cut interest rates on the loans.
July 25. Troung Tan Sang is elected president of Vietnam by the national Assembly. Prime minister Nguyen Tan Dung is reappointed the following day.
July 28. Political independent Salomón Lerner Ghitis is appointed prime minister of Peru.
August 2. Peter O'Neill is elected prime minister of Papua New Guinea by the Parliament.
August 5. Yingluck Shinawatra is elected prime minister by the legislature, following elections on July 3 in which her For Thais Party secured 265 of the 500 seats in the House of Representatives.
August 7. Independent Manuel Pinto da Costa wins run-off balloting in Sao Tome and Principe's presidential election.
August 14. Jhala Nath Khanal resigns as prime minister of Nepal. He is succeeded 15 days later by Baburam Bhattarai.
August 21. Manuel Inocêncio Sousa is elected president of Cape Verde in the second round of presidential polling.
August 23. Libyan leader Muammar al-Qadhafi's government is overthrown as rebel forces take Tripoli.
August 26. Japanese prime minister Naoto Kan resigns in the wake of widespread unpopularity over his government's management of the relief efforts following the March earthquake. Yoshihiko Noda is elected to succeed him by the legislature.
September 4. After rejecting two previous nominees, the Haitian assembly approves Garry Conille as prime minister.
September 20. African Union officially recognizes the National Transitional Council as Libya's legitimate governing body. In Zambia, Michael Sata defeats incumbent president Rupiah Banda.
September 23. Palestinian president Mahmud Abbas submits a bid for full UN membership for Palestine.
October 20. Muammar al-Qadhafi is captured and killed outside Sirte, Libya, ending the Libyan Revolution.
October 23. In Bulgaria, Rosen Plevneliev is elected president in run-off balloting. Jamaican prime minister Bruce Golding resigns and Andrew Holness is named to replace him.
October 27. Michael D. Higgins is elected president of Ireland.
October 28. Omer Berizky is named prime minister of Madagascar, following the resignation of Col. Albert Camille Vital on October 17. The moderate Islamist party Ennahda wins a plurality in Tunisia's national election, claiming 90 seats in the 217-seat Constituent Assembly.
November 1. Abdurrahim el-Keib is appointed prime minister of Libya.
November 6. In run-off balloting, Otto Pérez Molina wins Guatemala's presidential election. In Nicaragua, Daniel Ortega is reelected president.
November 11. Lucas Papademos becomes prime minister of Greece following the resignation of George Papandreou.
November 12. Syria is suspended from the Arab League because of continuing government repression in that country's civil war.
November 16. Mario Monti becomes the prime minister of Italy after Silvio Berlusconi resigns.
November 24. Gambian president Yahya Jammeh is reelected with more than 71 percent of the vote. Kamal Ganzouri is appointed prime minister of Egypt.
November 25. In Morocco, the Islamist Justice and Development Party wins a plurality in legislative elections and party leader Abdelillah Benkirane is appointed prime minister four days later.
November 27. Muhammad Salim Basindwah is name prime minister of Yemen.
November 28. Joseph Kabila is reelected president of the Democratic Republic of the Congo. Prime minister Sheikh Nasser Muhammad al-Ahmad al-SABAH and his government resigns, and Sheikh Jabir Mubarak Al Hamad Al Sabah is named to lead a new government.
December 3. Donald Ramotar is inaugurated as president of Guyana.
December 4. A center-left coalition wins legislative polling in Croatia; Zoran Milanović forms a coalition government and is sworn in as prime minister on December 23. In disputed balloting in Russia, prime minister Vladimir Putin's United Russia Party wins a plurality.
December 6. Socialist Party leader Elio di Rupo is sworn in as prime minister of Belgium at the head of a coalition government after 541 days of negotiations.
December 17. North Korean leader Kim Jong-il dies of a heart attack and is succeeded by his son Kim Jong-un.
December 20. Mariano Rajoy is elected prime minister of Spain by the legislature following elections in which his People's Party won 186 of 350 seats.

2012, **January 9.** President Malam Bacai Sanhá of Guinea-Bissau dies while abroad seeking medical treatment. He is succeeded by Raimundo Pereira as interim president.
January 13. Anote Tong wins a third term as president of Kiribati.
January 22. In a national referendum, Croatia votes to join the European Union; the country is expected to accede in summer 2013.
January 23. The European Union joins the United States in imposing an oil embargo on Iran, to be phased in starting in July, in an attempt to dissuade the Iranian government from pursuing its nuclear ambitions.

January 30. A new EU fiscal pact goes into effect, with the UK and Czech Republic abstaining; the agreement calls for greater control over EU nations' budgetary practices and extended cooperation among the member states on dealing with current and future eurozone fiscal crises.

February 5. Sauli Niinistö of Finland's National Coalition Party wins the presidency in the second round of voting, marking an end of 30 years of rule by the Social Democrats.

February 12. Turkmenistan holds its fourth presidential election, returning President Gurbanguly Berdimuhamedow to office with about 97 percent of the vote. At the time of the election, Turkmenistan has only one political party, and many observers express cynicism about the outcome.

February 17. German president Christian Wulff resigns in the face of prosecution for corruption when he was prime minister of Lower Saxony.

February 18. Constitutional amendments that would have made Russian a second official language of Latvia are defeated in a national referendum.

February 19. Iran halts oil exports to France and Britain in response to the January 23 sanctions imposed by the United States and European Union.

February 27. In the face of widespread protests, Yemeni President Ali Abdullah Saleh steps down in favor of his vice president, Abd Rubbuh Mansur Al-Hadi.

March 2. Iran holds the first round of parliamentary elections (runoffs held on May 4). Amid criticisms that reformist candidates were denied registration in the election, conservative allies of Supreme Religious Leader Ayatollah Seyed Ali Khameni won the majority of seats.

March 7. The United Democratic Party (UDP) returned to power in Belize, lead by Dean Barrow. However, the UDP did lose eight seats in parliament to the opposition, the People's United Party.

March 11. In legislative elections in El Salvador, the opposition party Nationalist Republican Alliance (ARENA) narrowly defeated the Farabundo Marti National Liberaton Front (FMLN). Analysts expect that the leftist administration of President Muricio Funes will find it challenging to work with the right-wing ARENA.

March 22. Amadou Toumani Touré is removed as president of Mali in a military coup, orchestrated by a group of soldiers calling themselves the Committee for the Reestablishment of Democracy and the Restoration of the State. After several weeks in hiding, Touré announces his formal resignation and leaves for Senegal. The presidential election scheduled for April 29 is postponed.

March 26. Macky Sall defeats incumbent Senegal president Abdoulaye Wade.

March 31. Sir Anerood Jugnauth resigns as president of Mauritius. Vice President Monique Ohsah Bellepeau serves as acting president until Rajkeswur Purryag is elected as new president on July 21.

April 1. In parliamentary elections in Myanmar, the National League for Democracy wins in a landslide. In response, in July President Barack Obama will announce the lifting of sanctions as a sign for support for gradual democratic reform in that country.

April 2. Hungarian president Pál Schmitt resigns. An election is scheduled for May 2; János Áder of the Fidesz party wins with about 68 percent of the vote.

April 5. President Bingu wa Mutharika of Malawi dies of a heart attack. He is succeeded by Joyce Banda, who becomes Malawi's first female president.

April 12. In Guinea-Bissau, a military junta takes over, arresting interim president Raimundo Pereira and former prime minister Carlos Gomes Júnior; Júnior was expected to win a presidential runoff election that was to take place ten days later.

April 13. Flouting widespread international criticism, North Korea launches a long-range rocket, suspected to be part of the country's desire to become a nuclear power; the rocket fails shortly after launch, however.

April 17. After the March coup in Mali, Cheick Modibo Diarra becomes interim prime minister, and Dioncouna Traore becomes interim president.

April 26. The Special Court for Sierra Leone finds former Liberian president Charles Taylor guilty of 11 counts of crimes against humanity and aiding and abetting war crimes, including murder, rape, and torture.

May 6. Socialist François Hollande is elected President of France, defeating Nicolas Sarkozy.

May 6. Greece holds an early election for the Hellenic Parliament, in an attempt to create a coalition government to deal with the economic crisis.

May 7. Vladmir Putin is inaugurated as president of Russia amid widespread protests.

May 18. Joachim Gauck is elected president of Germany; he was the candidate of the governing coalition.

May 19. The blind Chinese dissident Chen Guangcheng arrives in the United States after escaping house arrest and seeking refuge in the U.S. embassy in Beijing.

May 20. Former military leader José Maria Vasconcelos, better known as Taur Matan Ruak ("Two Sharp Eyes"), is inaugurated president of Timor-Leste, after prevailing in the second round of voting in April.

May 20. In a close election in the Dominican Republic, Danilo Medina of the Dominication Liberation Party (PLD) is elected president, succeeding Leonel Fernàndez, also of the PLD.

May 20. In Serbia, Tomislav Nikolić emerges as the winner of the presidential election, and Nikolić's right-wing Serbian Progressive Party wins 73 seats in the National Assembly.

May 22. The military steps aside in Guinea-Bissau; a transitional council holds power until elections can take place.

May 22. NATO countries reaffirm support of Afghan government while also promising to withdraw troops by the end of 2014.

May 28. Members of the UN Security Council unanimously condemn the Syrian government's use of heavy weaponry and massive force in Houla, near Homs, which resulted in the deaths of over a hundred people, most of them women and children. Several countries—including France, the United Kingdom, Germany, Canada, and Australia—protest diplomatically by expelling senior Syrian diplomats.

June 2. Canada's newly elected Parliament convenes, led by Andrew Scheer as speaker.

June 17. The Greek election in May having not resulted in a functioning government, a second election for the Hellenic Parliament is held. The New Democracy (ND) party receives 30 percent of the vote, followed by the Syrizia Unionist Social front (27 percent), the Pan-Hellenic Socialist Movement with 12 percent, and the remaining percentages are split by four other parties. The ND invites all parties to participate in the new unity government, with noted exception of the ultra-right wing Golden Dawn party.

June 22. Syria shoots down a Turkish military plane, killing its two pilots. Syrian officials claim they thought it was an Israeli plane, but the Turkish government rejects this explanation and threatens to retaliate.

June 24. In Egypt, Mohamed Morsi of the Freedom and Justice Party is declared the winner of the presidential election.

June 30. Ólafur Ragnar Grímsson wins a record fifth term as president of Iceland.

July 1. In Mexico's general election, Enrique Peña Nieto of the Institutional Revolutionary Party (PRI) wins the presidency. Allegations of electoral misconduct result in a partial recount, but the Nieto's election is confirmed.

July 24. Ghana's president John Atta Mills dies, and he is succeeded by his vice president, John Dramani Mahama.

July 27. The 2012 Summer Olympics commence, with 204 nations participating.

July 30. The UN Security Council calls for a return to constitutional rule in Guinea-Bissau.

August 17. A new UN-Arab League envoy, seasoned Algerian diplomat Lakhdar Brahimi, is appointed to deal with the conflict in Syria succeeding Kofi Annan, who resigns due to frustration with the international community's lack of agreement on solutions to the crisis.

August 20. After 21 years in power, Ethiopian prime minister Meles Zenawi dies from an undisclosed illness. His deputy, Hailemariam Desalegn, is his designated successor.

August 21. Newly reappointed prime minister Cheick Modibo Diarra of Mali establishes a new coalition government amidst widespread rebellion and reported atrocities in the northern part of the country.

September 2. Angola's ruling party, the Popular Movement for the Liberation of Angola (MPLA), is declared the victor in Angola's third election since independence in 1979.

September 7. Canada closes its embassy in Iran and ousts Iranian diplomats from Ottawa, ending formal diplomatic relations with Iran.

September 11. The moderate Hassan Sheikh Mohamud becomes president of Somalia, defeating former president Sheikh Sharif Sheikh Ahmed in a runoff election.

September 11. In Bengahzi, Libya, a terrorist attack on the American consulate results in the deaths of four American diplomats, including Ambassador Christopher Stevens.

September 12. The German constitutional court upholds the European Stability Mechanism (ESM), clearing the way for the EU to institute the ESM's loan program to ailing eurozone economies, such as Italy and Spain.

October 25. Prime Minister of Georgia Bidzina Ivanishvili is inaugurated along with a new government.

November 6. U.S. President Barack Obama is reelected to a second term, while the Democrats expanded their majority in the Senate but the Republicans held the House.

November 13. Israel launches air strikes against a number of targets in Gaza, killing a top Hamas commander.

December 7. John Mahama of the National Democratic Congress is reelected president of Ghana.

December 11. Cheick Modibo Diarra, prime minister of Mali, and his cabinet are forced to resign in what is described as a "mini-coup."

December 16. Japan's Liberal Democratic Party, led by former prime minister Shinzo Abe, wins an overwhelming majority, returning the party to power after three years as the opposition.

December 19. Park Geun Hye of the New Frontier Party becomes the first woman to be elected president of the Republic of Korea.

December 21. A new government is formed in Romania. Incumbent prime minister Victor Ponta returns to his job with an expanded cabinet.

2013, January 11. French forces lead an international military intervention in Mali against Islamist militants.

January 12. Milos Zeman of the Party of Citizens' Rights is elected president of the Czech Republic in the country's first direct presidential elections. In the Central African Republic, Prime Minister Nicolas Tiangaye is named prime minister and appoints a new government on February 3.

January 21. Prime minister Emmanuel Nadingar of Chad resigns and is replaced by Djimrangar Dadnadiji, who names a new cabinet five days later.

January 23. In Jordan, promonarchy candidates win an absolute majority in parliamentary balloting.

January 28. Queen Beatrix of the Netherlands announces her resignation; she is succeeded by her oldest son, Willem-Alexander, on April 30.

February 2. Following Israeli legislative elections on January 22, Benjamin Netanyahu again becomes prime minister of a center-right coalition government.

February 11. Pope Benedict XVI announces he will resign, effective February 28.

February 12. North Korea conducts a nuclear weapons test, prompting international condemnation and new sanctions.

February 17. Incumbent Ecuadorean President Rafael Correa is reelected with 57.2 percent of the vote for a third term.

February 19. Following growing unrest in Tunisia, Interim Prime Minister Hamadi Jebali (*Nahda*) resigns and is replaced by Ali Laarayedh of the same party.

February 18. Jiang Yi-huah, Nationalist Party, is appointed prime minister of China, succeeding Sean Chen-Chun, Nationalist Party, who resigned on February 1.

February 24. Nicos Anastasiadis of the Democratic Rally is elected president of Cyprus in runoff balloting; he names a coalition government four days later.

February 24–25. In Italy, a center-left coalition led by Pier Luigi Bersani wins a majority in the Chamber of Deputies but fails to secure a majority in the Senate, leading to prolonged negotiations over the formation of a coalition government.

March 4. In spite of an indictment by the International Criminal Court for allegedly inciting election violence in 2007–2008, Uhuru Kenyattat (the National Alliance) is elected president of Kenya; the balloting was the first since constitutional changes eliminated the post of prime minister.

March 5. Venezuelan President Hugo Chávez dies in office and is succeeded by Vice President Nicolás Maduro on March 8.

March 13. Jorge Mario Bergoglio of Argentina is elected pope by a conclave on the fifth ballot; Bergoglio takes the papal name Frances, becoming the first Jesuit pope and the first from the Western Hemisphere.

Xi Jinping is elected president of China by the National People's Congress. Two days later, Li Keqiang is elected premier, and a new cabinet is named the following day.

March 16. After becoming the first Pakistani parliament to complete its full term, the assembly is dissolved; Prime Minister Raja Pervaiz Ashraf resigns and is replaced by Mir Hazar Khan Khoso, who leads a caretaker government.

March 20. President Zillur Rahman of Bangladesh dies and is replaced on an interim basis by the speaker of the parliament Abdul Hamid; Hamid is subsequently elected president in his own right by the parliament on April 22.

March 24. President François Bozizé of the Central African Republic is overthrown and forced to flee when rebels seize Bangui; Michel Djotodia is proclaimed president and reappoints the incumbent prime minister Nicolas Tiangaye as the head of a coalition government.

March 25. Canada announces it is withdrawing from the UN Convention to Combat Desertification. The EU and IMF announce a new economic bailout package for Cyprus.

March 31. Abdoulkader Kamil Mohamed is appointed prime minister of Djibouti following legislative balloting on February 22.

April 1. Pak Pong Ju becomes premier of North Korea.

April 2. The Arms Trade Treaty is approved by the UN General Assembly.

April 7. Democratic Party of Socialists candidate Filip Vujanovic is elected president of Montenegro with 52.2 percent of the vote.

April 10. After losing a no-confidence vote in March, Prime Minister Vlad Filat is reappointed to form a new government in Moldova; subsequently, the constitutional court rules Filat ineligible, prompting President Nicolae Timofti to name Iurie Leanca as interim prime minister on April 23.

April 18. Giorgio Napolitano becomes the first Italian president to be reelected for a second term; two days after the election, Democratic Party leader Pier Luigi Bersani resigns after failing to form a coalition government.

April 21. Horacio Cartes's election as president of Paraguay returns the Colorado Party to power after four years; the party also wins the most seats in both houses of the legislature.

April 24. In Italy, Enrico Letta of the Democratic Party is nominated by the president as prime minister; four days later, he is sworn in to lead a coalition government that included all of the major political parties.

April 25. The UN Security Council approves the creation of a peacekeeping force in Mali.

April 28. Center-right parties win legislative balloting in Iceland, and Sigmundur Davíð Gunnlaugsson becomes prime minister on May 23 of a coalition government.

April 28. Takehiko Nakao of Japan becomes president of the Asian Development Bank.

May 5. The ruling Barisan coalition wins legislative elections in Malaysia, and incumbent Najib Abdul Razak remains prime minister.

May 11. The Pakistan Muslim League-Nawaz wins a majority in parliamentary balloting; party leader Muhammad Nawaz Sharif is elected prime minister by the legislature on June 5.

May 12. In legislative polling in Bulgaria, Citizens for European Development of Bulgaria wins a plurality, and party leader Plamen Oresharski is elected prime minister of a coalition government by the parliament on May 29.

May 15. Iurie Leanca is nominated as prime minister of Moldova and formally approved by the parliament on May 30.

May 26. The Democratic Party of Equatorial Guinea wins 99 of 100 seats in the lower house of parliament and 54 of 55 elected seats in the upper chamber.

June 5. The Assembly of the Turkish Republic of Northern Cyprus (TRNC) passes a vote of no-confidence on Prime Minister İrsen Küçük, who resigns; Sibel Siber becomes the first woman prime minister of the TRNC on June 13 after she is named to lead an interim government.

June 6. Rami Hamdallah becomes prime minister of Palestine but resigns on June 20; Hamdallah remains interim prime minister until September, when he again forms a new government. U.S. security contractor Edward Snowden reveals information about the broad scope of U.S. intelligence operations and flees to Hong Kong and then Russia.

June 14. Moderate cleric Hassan Rouhani wins the Iranian presidential election.

June 17. Czech prime minister Petr Necas resigns and is succeeded by Jiri Rusnok on June 25.

June 25. The emir of Qatar, Sheikh Hamad ibn Khalifah al Thani abdicates and is succeeded by his son, Crown Prince Sheikh Tamin ibn Hamad al Thani; the new emir names Sheikh Abdullah ibn Nasser ibn Khalifah al Thani as prime minister the following day.

Nouri Abusahmain is elected president of the Libyan transitional General National Congress.

June 26. Australian Prime Minister Julia Gillard resigns after being defeated by former prime minister Kevin Rudd in a contest for leadership of the Labor Party; Rudd is sworn in as prime minister the following day.

July 1. Croatia joins the European Union.

July 2. The Egyptian military overthrows President Mohamed Morsi and suspends the constitution; Abdi Mansour, the chief of the country's constitutional court, is named interim president; on July 9, Hazem al Beblawi is named as prime minister.

July 21. King Albert II of Belgium abdicates and is succeeded by Crown Prince Philippe.

July 28. The Republic Turkish Party-United Forces wins parliamentary elections in the Turkish Republic of Northern Cyprus; Özkan Yorgancioğlu is named prime minister on September 2.

In disputed balloting in Cambodia, the ruling Cambodian People's Party wins a majority in the Assembly; Incumbent Prime Minister Hun Sen is reelected by the legislature on September 23.

July 30. Mamnoon Hussain of the Pakistan Muslim League-Nawaz is elected president of Pakistan in indirect balloting by the parliament and regional assemblies.

July 31. In disputed balloting, Robert Mugabe is reelected president of Zimbabwe; Mugabe's party, the Zimbabwe African National Union-Patriotic Front, retains its absolute majority parliament in concurrent legislative balloting.

August 7. Czech Prime Minister Jiri Rusnok loses a vote of no confidence and resigns, along with his government, on August 13.
August 11. Ibrahim Boubacar Keita wins runoff balloting in Mali's presidential election and is sworn into office on September 4.
August 21. Reports emerge that the Syrian government used chemical weapons against rebels and civilians.
September 1. Roberto Carvalho de Azevêdo of Brazil becomes director general of the World Trade Organization.
September 7. The Liberal Party wins parliamentary elections in Australia, and party leader Tony Abbott becomes prime minister.
September 9. In Norway, the Labor Party wins the most seats in parliament but fails to secure a majority; Erna Solberg of the Conservative Party forms a coalition government on October 16.
September 21. Al Shabab militants attack a shopping mall in Nairobi, Kenya, killing 62 and injuring more than 170.
September 22. German Chancellor Angela Merkel's Christian Democratic Union wins parliamentary elections but falls short of a majority, securing 311 of 631 seats. Merkel forms a coalition with the Social Democrats and is sworn in for a third term on December 17.
September 28. The UN Security Council adopts a resolution requiring Syria to destroy its chemical weapons stockpiles under the auspices of the UN. The destruction of the country's chemical weapons begins on October 6.
September 29. In Austria, the Social Democratic Party wins a plurality in legislative balloting and begins negotiations with its coalition partner, the Austrian People's party.
September 30. The ruling Cameroon People's Democratic Movement wins parliamentary balloting in Cameroon.
October 7. Mulatu Teshome is elected president of Ethiopia by a unanimous vote in the legislature.
October 9. Incumbent president of Azerbaijan Ilham Aliyev is reelected with 84.6 percent of the vote.
November 17. Former president Michelle Bachelet's center-left coalition wins legislative balloting in Chile; Bachelet wins runoff presidential balloting on December 15.
November 24. Juan Orlando Hernandez of the ruling National Party (NP) is elected president of Honduras, while the NP retains a plurality in Congress in concurrent legislative balloting.
November 17. Following the collapse of a supermarket in Riga, Lativa, which killed 54, Prime Minister Valdis Dombrovskis resigns.
December 4. Xavier Bettel of the Democratic Party is sworn in and becomes the first openly gay prime minister of Luxembourg.
December 15. The pro-presidential Rally for Mali wins a plurality of 66 of 147 seats following the second round of balloting, which along with 16 seats secured by allied parties provides Malian President Ibrahim Keïta with a parliamentary majority.
December 20. In Madagascar, Hery Rajaonarimampianina wins disputed runoff balloting in the first elections since former president Marc Ravalomanana was forced from power in 2009.
December 21. In the second round of legislative voting in Mauritania, the ruling Union for the Republic party secures an absolute majority of 75 of 146 seats.

APPENDIX B
CHRONOLOGY OF MAJOR INTERNATIONAL CONFERENCES SPONSORED BY THE UNITED NATIONS: 1946–2013

1946, June 19–July 22 (New York, New York). International Health Conference. Adopted constitution of the World Health Organization.

1947–1948, November 21–March 24 (Havana, Cuba). Conference on Trade and Employment. Drafted a charter that would have established an International Trade Organization under UN auspices but that never went into effect because of U.S. opposition.

1948, February 19–March 6 (Geneva, Switzerland). Maritime Conference. Drafted and approved a convention leading to establishment of the Inter-Governmental Maritime Consultative Organization, later the International Maritime Organization.

March 23–April 21 (Geneva, Switzerland). Conference on Freedom of Information. Adopted conventions on the gathering and international transmission of news, the institution of an international right of correction, and freedom of information.

August 23–September 19 (Geneva, Switzerland). Conference on Road and Motor Transport. Drafted and adopted the Convention on Road Traffic and a Protocol on Road Signs and Signals superseding obsolete 1926 and 1931 conventions.

1949, August 17–September 6 (Lake Success, New York). Scientific Conference on the Conservation and Utilization of Resources. Discussed the costs and benefits of practical application of technical knowledge.

1950, March 15–April 6 (Lake Success, New York). Conference on Declaration of Death of Missing Persons. Adopted a convention calling for international cooperation in alleviating the legal problems burdening individuals whose families disappeared in World War II but whose deaths could not be established with certainty.

1953, May 11–June 18 (New York, New York). Opium Conference. Adopted a protocol to control the production, trade, and use of opium.

1954, May 11–June 4 (New York, New York). Conference on Customs Formalities for the Temporary Importation of Road Motor Vehicles and for Tourism. Adopted a convention establishing custom facilities for touring and a convention establishing import regulations for road motor vehicles.

August 31–September 10 (Rome, Italy). World Population Conference. Provided a forum for an exchange of views and experiences among experts on a wide variety of questions connected with population.

September 13–23 (New York, New York). Conference of Plenipotentiaries Relating to the Status of Stateless Persons. Drafted and approved a convention putting stateless people on equal footing with nationals of a contracting state in some matters and giving them the same privileges as those generally granted to aliens in others.

1955, April 18–May 10 (Rome, Italy). International Technical Conference on the Conservation of the Living Resources of the Sea. Discussed the conservation of fish and other marine resources.

August 8–20 (Geneva, Switzerland). First International Conference on the Peaceful Uses of Atomic Energy. Surveyed all major aspects of the topic.

1958, February 24–April 27 (Geneva, Switzerland). First UN Conference on the Law of the Sea. Failed to agree on the issue of the width of the territorial sea.

September 1–12 (Geneva, Switzerland). Second International Conference on the Peaceful Uses of Atomic Energy. Addressed, among other things, the issues of nuclear power reactors, fusion power, application of radioactive isotopes, nuclear power station accidents, and risks involved with exposure to radiation in industrial settings.

1960, March 17–April 26 (Geneva, Switzerland). Second UN Conference on the Law of the Sea. Failed to adopt any substantive measures regarding the questions of the breadth of territorial seas and fishery limits.

1961, January 24–March 25 (New York, New York). Plenipotentiary Conference for the Adoption of a Single Convention on Narcotic Drugs. Adopted the convention, which replaced international control instruments with one treaty and extended the control system to the cultivation of plants that are grown for the raw materials of natural drugs.

August 21–31 (Rome, Italy). Conference on New Sources of Energy. Discussed the recent breakthrough in knowledge of geothermal energy, the need for more intensive wind surveys, and applications of solar energy.

1962, August 6–22 (Bonn, Federal Republic of Germany). Technical Conference on the International Map of the World on Millionth Scale. Reviewed and revised the International Map of the World.

1963, February 4–20 (Geneva, Switzerland). Conference on the Application of Science and Technology for the Benefit of Less Developed Areas. Discussed relevant proposals for accelerating development.

1964, March 23–June 16 (Geneva, Switzerland). UN Conference on Trade and Development (UNCTAD). Subsequently established as a Special Body of the General Assembly convening quadrennially (see under UN General Assembly: Special Bodies).

August 31–September 9 (Geneva, Switzerland). Third International Conference on the Peaceful Uses of Atomic Energy. Focused exclusively on nuclear power as a commercially competitive energy source.

1965, August 30–September 10 (Belgrade, Yugoslavia). Second World Population Conference. Gathered international experts to discuss population problems, especially as they related to development.

1967, September 4–22 (Geneva, Switzerland). Conference on the Standardization of Geographical Names. Subsequent conferences have been held every five years.

1968, March 26–May 24; reconvened **April 9–May 22, 1969** (Vienna, Austria). Conference on Law of Treaties. Adopted the Vienna Convention on the Law of Treaties.

April 22–May 13 (Tehran, Iran). International Conference on Human Rights. Adopted the Proclamation of Tehran and 29 resolutions reviewing and evaluating progress since the adoption of the Universal Declaration of Human Rights in 1948 and formulating further measures to be taken.

August 14–27 (Vienna, Austria). First Conference on the Exploration and Peaceful Uses of Outer Space. Examined the practical benefits to be derived from space research and exploration as well as how the United Nations might help make those benefits widely available and enable nonspace powers to cooperate in international space activities.

1971, January 11–February 21 (Vienna, Austria). Conference for the Adoption of a Protocol on Psychotropic Substances. Adopted the instrument after renaming it a convention.

September 6–16 (Geneva, Switzerland). Fourth International Conference on the Peaceful Uses of Atomic Energy. Discussed the ramifications of the rapid increase in nuclear power generation.

1972, June 5–16 (Stockholm, Sweden). Conference on the Human Environment. Resulted in establishment of the United Nations Environment Program (UNEP).

1973, December 3–15 (New York, New York). Third UN Conference on the Law of the Sea; reconvened for ten additional sessions, the last in three parts in **1982, March 8–April 30** and **September 22–24** (New York) and **December 6–10** (Montego Bay, Jamaica). Drafted and adopted the UN Convention on the Law of the Sea (UNCLOS).

1974, May 20–June 14 (New York, New York). Conference on Proscription (Limitation) in the International Sale of Goods. Adopted Convention on the Limitation Period in the International Sale of Goods.

August 19–30 (Bucharest, Romania). World Population Conference. Adopted, as the first international governmental meeting on population (previous World Population Conferences were for scientific discussion only), the World Population Plan of Action, including guidelines for national population policies.

November 5–16 (Rome, Italy). World Food Conference. Adopted the Universal Declaration on the Eradication of Hunger and Malnutrition and called on the General Assembly to create the World Food Council to coordinate programs to give the world (particularly less developed states) more and better food.

1975, February 4–March 14 (Vienna, Austria). Conference on the Representation of States in their Relations with International Organizations (of a Universal Character). Adopted convention of the same name.

May 5–30 (Geneva, Switzerland). Review Conference of the Parties to the Treaty on the Nonproliferation of Nuclear Weapons. Reaffirmed support for the treaty and called for more effective implementation of its provisions.

June 19–July 1, 1975 (Mexico City, Mexico). World Conference of the International Women's Year. Adopted the Declaration of Mexico on the Equality of Women and Their Contribution to Development and Peace, 1975, and the World Plan of Action for the Implementation of the Objectives of the International Women's Year.

1976, January 5–8 (Dakar, Senegal). International Conference on Namibia and Human Rights. Condemned South Africa's occupation of Namibia.

May 31–June 11 (Vancouver, British Columbia). Conference on Human Settlements. Issued recommendations for assuring the basic requirements of human habitation (shelter, clean water, sanitation, and a decent physical environment), plus the opportunity for cultural and personal growth.

June 14–17 (Geneva, Switzerland). World Employment Conference. Adopted, subject to reservations by some countries, a Declaration of Principles and a Program of Action regarding employment and related issues.

1977, January 10–February 4 (Geneva, Switzerland). Conference of Plenipotentiaries on Territorial Asylum. Failed to adopt a convention defining groups of people to be covered by a proposed convention within this category or on the allowable activities of refugees in the country of asylum.

March 14–25 (Mar del Plata, Argentina). Water Conference. Approved resolutions dealing with water use, health, and pollution control as well as training and research in water management.

April 4–May 6; reconvened **July 31–August 23, 1978** (Vienna, Austria). Conference on the Succession of States in Respect to Treaties. Adopted a convention elaborating uniform principles for such succession.

May 16–21 (Maputo, Mozambique). International Conference in Support of the Peoples of Zimbabwe and Namibia. Drafted a Declaration and Program of Action to mobilize international support for the right to self-determination by the people of the two territories.

June 20–July 1 (Geneva, Switzerland). Review Conference of the Parties to the Treaty on the Prohibition of the Emplacement of Nuclear Weapons and Other Weapons of Mass Destruction on the Seabed and the Ocean Floor and in the Subsoil Thereof. Reaffirmed interest in avoiding an arms race on the seabed and concluded that signatory states had faithfully observed the conditions of the treaty, which was concluded by a non-UN conference in 1970 and entered into force in 1972. (Similar conclusions were reached by review conferences in Geneva on **September 12–23, 1983,** and on **September 19–28, 1989.**)

August 22–26 (Lagos, Nigeria). World Conference for Action against Apartheid (cosponsored by the Organization of African Unity). Called for international support for efforts to eliminate apartheid and enable the South African people to attain their "inalienable right" to self-determination.

August 29–September 9 (Nairobi, Kenya). Conference on Desertification. Adopted a plan of action addressing desertification, improvement of land management, antidrought measures, and related science and technology.

1978, February 12–March 11; reconvened **March 19–April 8, 1979** (Vienna, Austria). Conference on the Establishment of the United Nations Industrial Development Organization (UNIDO) as a Specialized Agency. Recommended such establishment and adopted a constitution for UNIDO.

March 6–31 (Hamburg, Federal Republic of Germany). Conference on an International Convention on the Carriage of Goods by Sea. Adopted a convention designed to balance the risks of carriers and cargo owners.

August 14–25 (Geneva, Switzerland). First World Conference to Combat Racism and Racial Discrimination. Adopted a declaration and program of action recommending comprehensive and mandatory sanctions against South Africa, as well as measures to prevent multinational corporations from investing in territories "subject to racism, colonialism, and foreign domination."

August 30–September 12 (Buenos Aires, Argentina). Conference on Technical Cooperation among Developing Countries. Discussed, but did not endorse, the proposed creation of an independent, but UN-funded, body to foster technical cooperation among developing countries.

October 16–November 11; reconvened six times through 1985 (Geneva, Switzerland). Conference on an International Code of Conduct on the Transfer of Technology.

1979, July 12–20 (Rome, Italy). World Conference on Agrarian Reform and Rural Development. Adopted a declaration of principles and a program of action to abolish poverty and hunger.

August 20–31 (Vienna, Austria). Conference on Science and Technology for Development. Endorsed recommendations to promote financial and institutional arrangements for freer technology flow to developing nations.

September 10–28; reconvened **September 15–October 10, 1980** (Geneva, Switzerland). Convention on Prohibitions or Restrictions on the Use of Certain Conventional Weapons Which May Be Deemed to Be Excessively Injurious or to Have Indiscriminate Effects. Adopted a convention banning such weapons.

November 12–30; reconvened **May 24, 1980** (Geneva, Switzerland). Conference on International Multimodal Transportation. Adopted a convention on the legal obligations of multimodal transport operators.

November 19–December 8; reconvened **April 8–22, 1980** (Geneva, Switzerland). Conference on Restrictive Business Practices. Adopted the Set of Multilaterally Agreed Equitable Principles and Rules for the Control of Restrictive Business Practices.

1980, March 3–21 (Geneva, Switzerland). First Review Conference of States Parties to the Convention on the Prohibition of the Development, Production and Stockpiling of Bacteriological (Biological) and Toxin Weapons and on Their Destruction. Reaffirmed commitment to the convention (signed in 1972 and entered into force in 1975) and declared a "determination to exclude the possibility of bacteriological agents and toxins being used as weapons."

March 10–April 11 (Vienna, Austria). Conference on Contracts for International Sale of Goods. Adopted a convention to govern the sale of goods between parties in different countries, replacing the two Hague conventions of 1964.

July 14–30 (Copenhagen, Denmark). World Conference of the UN Decade for Women: Equality, Development, and Peace. Adopted a program of action for the second half of the decade.

August 11–September 7 (Geneva, Switzerland). Second Review Conference of the Parties to the Treaty on the Nonproliferation of Nuclear Weapons. Failed to agree on a final document.

1981, April 9–10 (Geneva, Switzerland). First International Conference on Assistance to African Refugees. Urged that international priority be given to the African refugee problem and received $560 million in pledges to assist the estimated 5 million people in that category.

May 20–27 (Paris, France). International Conference on Sanctions against Racist South Africa. Proposed sanctions against South Africa and discussed the situation in Namibia.

August 10–21 (Nairobi, Kenya). Conference on New and Renewable Sources of Energy. Promoted the development and utilization of nonconventional energy sources, particularly by developing countries.

September 1–14 (Paris, France). Conference on the Least Developed Countries. Adopted a substantial new program of action to assist the economies of the world's 31 poorest states.

1982, July 26–August 6 (Vienna, Austria). World Assembly on Aging. Adopted an international plan of action aimed at providing the growing number of older people with economic and social security.

August 9–21 (Vienna, Austria). Second Conference on the Exploration and Peaceful Uses of Outer Space. Recommended that the General Assembly adopt measures to accelerate the transfer of peaceful space technology, to expand access to space and its resources for developing countries, and to establish a UN information service on the world's space programs.

1983, March 1–April 8 (Vienna, Austria). Conference on the Succession of States in Respect of State Property, Archives, and Debts. Adopted a convention on the subject.

April 25–29 (Paris, France). International Conference in Support of Namibian People for Independence. Reaffirmed Namibia's right to independence.

June 27–29 (London, United Kingdom). International Conference for Sanctions against Apartheid in Sports. Reviewed progress in the campaign for a sports boycott of South Africa.

August 1–12 (Geneva, Switzerland). Second World Conference to Combat Racism and Racial Discrimination. Adopted a program of action against racism, racial discrimination, and apartheid.

August 29–September 7 (Geneva, Switzerland). International Conference on the Question of Palestine. Adopted the Geneva Declaration on Palestine and a Program of Action for the Achievement of Palestinian Rights.

1984, July 9–11 (Geneva, Switzerland). Second International Conference on Assistance to African Refugees. Declared that caring for African refugees was a global responsibility and proposed long-term solutions to the problem.

July 16–August 3 (Geneva, Switzerland); reconvened **January 28–February 15,** and **July 8–9, 1985** (Geneva), and **January 20–February 8, 1986** (New York). Conference on Conditions for the Registration of Ships. Adopted a convention designed to assure "genuine links" between ships and their flags of state.

August 6–14 (Mexico City, Mexico). International Conference on Population. Adopted Mexico City Declaration on Population and Development covering a wide range of population policy proposals, including further implementation of the 1974 World Population Plan of Action.

September 10–21 (Geneva, Switzerland). Review Conference of the Parties to the Convention on the Prohibition of Military or Any Other Hostile Use of Environmental Modification Techniques. Noted the effectiveness of the convention, which went into effect in 1978.

1985, March 11–12 (Geneva, Switzerland). International Conference on the Emergency Situation in Africa. Mobilized international aid to drought-stricken states in Africa.

May 7–9 (Arusha, Tanzania). International Conference on Women and Children Under Apartheid. Condemned South Africa for the effects of its policies on black women and children.

May 15–18 (Paris, France). Second International Conference on the Sports Boycott against South Africa. Supported the position that South Africa should not be readmitted to the Olympic games until apartheid ends.

July 15–27 (Nairobi, Kenya). World Conference to Review and Appraise the Achievement of the UN Decade for Women. Assessed steps taken over the past decade to improve the situation of women and drafted the Nairobi Forward Looking Strategies for the Achievement of Women.

August 27–September 21 (Geneva, Switzerland). Third Review Conference of the Parties to the Treaty on the Nonproliferation of Nuclear Weapons. Called for resumption of talks toward a comprehensive multilateral nuclear test ban treaty.

September 11–13 (New York, New York). Conference on the Intensification of International Action for the Independence of Namibia. Rejected U.S. policy of "constructive engagement" with South Africa and urged boycott of Namibian and South African products.

November 4–15 (Geneva, Switzerland). Conference to Review All Aspects of the Set of Multilaterally Agreed Equitable Principles and Rules for the Control of Restrictive Business Practices. Failed to agree on proposals to improve and further develop the principles.

November 13–18 (New York, New York). World Conference on the International Youth Year, 1985. Endorsed guidelines for youth and asked member states and other interested organizations to ensure that the year's activities be reinforced and maintained.

1986, February 18–March 21 (Vienna, Austria). Conference on the Law of Treaties between States and International Organizations or between International Organizations. Adopted a convention delineating the manner in which international organizations should conclude, adopt, enforce, and observe treaties.

June 16–20 (Paris, France). World Conference on Sanctions against Racist South Africa. Called for comprehensive economic sanctions against South Africa.

July 7–11 (Vienna, Austria). International Conference for the Immediate Independence of Namibia. Called for the adoption and imposition of sanctions against South Africa and the implementation of the UN plan for the independence of Namibia.

September 8–16 (Geneva, Switzerland). Second Review Conference of States Parties to the Convention on the Prohibition of the Development, Production and Stockpiling of Bacteriological (Biological) and Toxin Weapons and on Their Destruction. Adopted a final act designed to strengthen confidence in the convention, to reduce "the occurrence of ambiguities, doubts, or suspicion" involving bacteriological activities, and to enhance international cooperation in peaceful microbiology use.

1987, February 10–13 (Nairobi, Kenya). Safe Motherhood Conference (cosponsored by the World Bank, World Health Organization, and UN Fund for Population Activities).

March 23–April 10 (Geneva, Switzerland). Conference for Promotion of International Cooperation in the Peaceful Uses of Nuclear Energy. Failed to reach consensus.

June 17–26 (Vienna, Austria). International Conference on Drug Abuse and Illicit Trafficking. Adopted a declaration committing all participants to "vigorous action" to reduce drug supply and demand and approved a handbook of guidelines to assist governments and organizations in reaching a total of 35 "action targets."

August 24–September 11 (New York, New York). International Conference on the Relationship between Disarmament and Development. Recommended that a portion of resources released by disarmament be allocated to social and economic development.

1988, August 22–24 (Oslo, Norway). International Conference on the Plight of Refugees, Returnees, and Displaced Persons in Southern Africa. Adopted a plan of action to improve the economic and social conditions of the populations under consideration.

November 25–December 20 (Geneva, Switzerland). Plenipotentiary Conference to Adopt the New Convention Against Illicit Traffic in Narcotic Drugs and Psychotropic Substances. Adopted the Convention.

1989, January 7–11 (Paris, France). Conference of States Parties to the 1925 Geneva Protocol and Other Interested States on the Prohibition of Chemical Weapons. Called for early conclusion of a convention that would prohibit the development, production, stockpiling, and use of all chemical weapons and provide for the destruction of all such existing weapons.

May 29–31 (Guatemala City, Guatemala). International Conference on Central American Refugees. Adopted a three-year, $380 million program to aid an estimated two million refugees, displaced persons, and returnees in seven countries.

June 13–14 (Geneva, Switzerland). International Conference on Indochinese Refugees. Adopted a plan of action designed to promote a "lasting multilateral solution" to the problem of refugees and asylum-seekers from Laos and Vietnam.

1990, March 5–9 (Jomtien, Thailand). World Conference on Education for All: Meeting Basic Learning Needs. Adopted Declaration on Education for All.

April 9–11 (London, United Kingdom). World Ministerial Summit to Reduce the Demand for Drugs and to Combat the Cocaine Threat (organized in association with the United Kingdom). Adopted a declaration by which 124 nations pledged to give higher priority to curtailing illicit drug demand.

August 20–September 15 (Geneva, Switzerland). Fourth Review Conference of Parties to the Treaty on the Nonproliferation of Nuclear Weapons. Failed to reach agreement on a final declaration.

September 3–14 (Paris, France). Second Conference on the Least Developed Countries. Adopted a new program of action stressing bilateral assistance in the form of grants or highly concessional loans from developed nations.

September 29–30 (New York, New York). World Summit for Children. Adopted a ten-point program to promote the well-being of children through political action "at the highest level."

October 29–November 7 (Geneva, Switzerland). World Climate Conference. Urged developed nations to establish targets for the reduction in the emission of "greenhouse" gases, such as carbon dioxide, to curtail a possible warming of the global atmosphere.

November 26–December 7 (Geneva, Switzerland). Second Conference to Review All Aspects of the Set of Multilaterally Agreed Equitable Principles and Rules for the Control of Restrictive Business Practices. Urged developing countries to adopt national legislation on restrictive business practices.

1991, January 7–18 (New York, New York). Amendment Conference of the States Parties to the 1963 Treaty Banning Nuclear Weapon Tests in the Atmosphere, in Outer Space, and Under Water. Decided further work was needed before a proposed amendment could be adopted that would convert the treaty into a comprehensive test ban treaty.

September 9–17 (Geneva, Switzerland). Third Review Conference of the States Parties to the Convention on the Prohibition of the Development, Production and Stockpiling of Bacteriological (Biological) and Toxin Weapons and on Their Destruction. Called for full implementation of the convention without the placement of constraints on economic and technological development and international cooperation in peaceful biological activities.

1992, June 3–14 (Rio de Janeiro, Brazil). UN Conference on Environment and Development. Adopted Rio Declaration on Environment and Development and several other documents designed to promote global environmental cleanup and "sustainable" development.

October 15–16 (New York, New York). International Conference on Aging. Reviewed progress on the 1982 International Plan of Action on Aging.

1993, June 14–25 (Vienna, Austria). World Conference on Human Rights. Adopted nonbinding Declaration and Program of Action affirming the "universal nature" of human rights and recommending, among other things, that the General Assembly appoint a UN High Commissioner for Human Rights.

July 12–30; reconvened **March 14–31** and **August 15–26, 1994,** and **March 27–April 12** and **July 24–August 4, 1995** (New York, New York). UN Conference on Straddling Fish Stocks and Highly Migratory Fish Stocks. Adopted global treaty (opened for signature December 4, 1995) binding signatories to adopt measures to conserve and otherwise manage high-seas fisheries and to settle fishing disputes peacefully.

October 5–6 (Tokyo, Japan). International Conference on African Development (sponsored in conjunction with Japan and the U.S.-based Global Coalition of Africa). Adopted a declaration intended to "refocus" attention on African problems, such as heavy debt burden, rapid population growth, drought, hunger, and political instability.

1994, April 25–May 6 (Bridgetown, Barbados). Global Conference on the Sustainable Development of Small Island Developing States. Adopted a program of action to guide the environmental and development policies of small island states and issued the "Barbados Declaration" calling on the international community to support those states in combating rising sea levels, the loss of reefs and rain forests, shortages of fresh water, and import dependency.

May 23–27 (Yokohama, Japan). World Conference on Natural Disaster Reduction. Adopted the Yokohama Strategy for a Safer World: Guidelines for Natural Disaster Prevention, Preparedness, and Mitigation, designed to put recent technological advances at the service of disaster-prone regions of the world.

September 5–13 (Cairo, Egypt). International Conference on Population and Development. Adopted a program of action aimed at stabilizing the world's population at about 7.27 billion in 2015.

October 18 (New York, New York). International Conference on Families. Convened by the UN General Assembly to discuss activities in regard to the International Year of the Family, 1994.

November 21–23 (Naples, Italy). World Ministerial Conference on Organized Transnational Crime. Adopted the Naples Political Declaration and Global Action Plan, proposing, among other things, the establishment of an international convention on transnational crime, greater cooperation among national law enforcement agencies, and greater "transparency" of banks and other financial enterprises that can be used to "launder" money.

1995, March 6–13 (Copenhagen, Denmark). World Summit for Social Development. Adopted the Copenhagen Declaration and Program of Action recommending measures to be taken by national governments, the United Nations, and other international organizations in pursuit of "social development and social justice."

April 7–May 12 (New York, New York). Review and Extension Conference of the Parties to the Treaty on the Nonproliferation of Nuclear Weapons. Agreed to extend treaty "indefinitely" and strengthen its review process.

September 4–15 (Beijing, China). Fourth World Conference on Women. Adopted the Beijing Declaration and Platform for Action delineating nonbinding guidelines for national policies designed to enhance the status of women and to promote international cooperation in the same regard.

September 25–October 13 (Vienna, Austria); reconvened **April 22–May 3, 1996** (Geneva, Switzerland). Review Conference of States Parties to the 1980 Convention on Prohibitions or Restrictions on the Use of Certain Conventional Weapons Which May Be Deemed to Be Excessively Injurious or to Have Indiscriminate Effects. Failed to reach agreement on a proposed complete ban on land mines but adopted stricter controls on their use and export and agreed to extend the provisions of the convention to domestic conflicts; banned the use of blinding laser weapons.

1996, **June 3–14** (Istanbul, Turkey). Second UN Conference on Human Settlements. Adopted a declaration urging national governments to implement policies designed to meet their citizens' "right to adequate housing" and to establish comprehensive plans to manage urban development.

November 13–17 (Rome, Italy). World Food Summit. Adopted a declaration asserting the "fundamental right of everyone to be free from hunger" and recommending national policies that will guarantee "access to safe and nutritious food."

November 25–December 6 (Geneva, Switzerland). Fourth Review Conference of States Parties to the Convention on the Prohibition of the Development, Production and Stockpiling of Bacteriological (Biological) and Toxin Weapons and on Their Destruction. Supported continuing work by an ad hoc group designing a verification protocol for the convention.

1997, **June 23–27** (New York, New York). Second UN Conference on Environment and Development. Reviewed implementation (or lack thereof) of commitments made at the 1992 conference.

December 1–11 (Kyoto, Japan). Third Conference of the Parties to the UN Framework Convention on Climate Change. Issued Kyoto Protocol in which 38 industrialized countries agreed to cut the emission of greenhouse gases to combat global warming.

1998, **June 15–July 18** (Rome, Italy). UN Conference of Plenipotentiaries on the Establishment of an International Criminal Court. Voted to establish an International Criminal Court under UN auspices.

August 8–12 (Lisbon, Portugal). World Conference of Ministers Responsible for Youth. Adopted the Lisbon Declaration on Youth Policies and Programs, pledging to act on youth participation, development, peace, education, employment, health, and drug and substance abuse.

1999, **July 19–30** (Vienna, Austria). Third Conference on the Exploration and Peaceful Uses of Outer Space. Adopted the Vienna Declaration on Space and Human Development.

2000, **April 24–May 19** (New York, New York). Review Conference of the Treaty on the Nonproliferation of Nuclear Weapons. Concluded with a commitment by China, France, Russia, the United Kingdom, and the United States to the "total elimination" of their nuclear arsenals.

September 6–8 (New York, New York). Millennium Summit. Adopted the Millennium Declaration, which reaffirmed the role of the United Nations and its charter as "indispensable foundations of a more peaceful, prosperous, and just world."

November 13–25 (The Hague, Netherlands). World Conference on Climate Change. Failed to conclude a treaty to meet the greenhouse gas emissions requirements called for by the 1997 Kyoto Protocol.

December 12–15 (Palermo, Italy). High-Level Political Signing Conference for the UN Convention against Transnational Organized Crime. Opened for signature the first legally binding UN convention on crime.

2001, **May 14–20** (Brussels, Belgium). Third Conference on the Least Developed Countries. Adopted a plan of action for 2001–2010 that emphasized good governance, capacity-building, the role of trade in development, environmental protection, and the mobilization of financial resources.

July 9–20 (New York, New York). UN Conference on the Illicit Trade in Small Arms and Light Weapons in All Its Aspects. Adopted a program of action to prevent, combat, and eradicate illicit trade in small arms and light weapons (SALW) at national, regional, and global levels.

August 31–September 7 (Durban, South Africa). World Conference against Racism, Racial Discrimination, Xenophobia, and Related Intolerance. Adopted the Durban Declaration and Program of Action, in which states were urged to end enslavement and slavery-like practices, to promote and protect human rights, and to prosecute perpetrators of racist and other discriminatory acts against Africans, indigenous peoples, migrants, refugees, and other victims.

November 19–December 7; reconvened **November 11–22, 2002** (Geneva, Switzerland). Fifth Review Conference of States Parties to the Convention on the Prohibition of the Development, Production and Stockpiling of Bacteriological (Biological) and Toxin Weapons and on Their Destruction. Adopted a three-year work plan focusing on national measures to implement prohibitions; enhancement of international capabilities in responding to, investigating, and mitigating the effects of biological attacks and suspicious disease outbreaks; and adoption of a code of conduct for scientists.

December 11–21 (Geneva, Switzerland). Second Review Conference of the States Parties to the Convention on Prohibitions or Restrictions on the Use of Certain Conventional Weapons Which May Be Deemed to Be Excessively Injurious or to Have Indiscriminate Effects. Addressed various proposals to strengthen the convention, including extending its application to domestic as well as international conflicts and exploring how to deal with such explosive remnants of war as cluster bombs, shells, and munitions.

2002, **March 18–22** (Monterrey, Mexico). International Conference on Financing for Development. Adopted the Monterrey Consensus on promoting development through such means as increasing foreign direct investment and official development assistance, improving market access, fighting corruption, and reducing debt.

April 8–12 (Madrid, Spain). Second World Assembly on Aging. Adopted the International Plan of Action on Aging 2002, which identified three priority areas: older persons and development, the extension of health and well-being into old age, and enhancement of enabling and supportive environments for the aged.

June 10–13 (Rome, Italy). World Food Summit: Five Years Later. Reviewed the "disappointingly slow" progress since the 1996 summit and called for an international alliance against hunger.

August 26–September 4 (Johannesburg, South Africa). World Summit on Sustainable Development. Set new targets for sustainable development in a variety of areas.

2003, **August 28–29** (Almaty, Kazakhstan). International Ministerial Conference of Landlocked and Transit Developing Countries and Donor Countries and International Financial and Development Institutions on Transit Transport Cooperation. Adopted the Almaty Program of Action, addressing rail, road, and air transportation, as well as communications, pipelines, and means of facilitating international trade.

December 9–11 (Merida, Mexico). High-Level Political Conference for the Signature of the United Nations Convention Against Corruption. Ninety-four countries signed the Convention Against Corruption (previously approved by the General Assembly) requiring signatories (upon ratification) to criminalize a range of corrupt activities and to cooperate with other signatories in combating corruption.

December 10–12 (Geneva, Switzerland). World Summit on the Information Society (Phase One). Adopted the Geneva Declaration of Principles and Geneva Plan of Action in support of the creation of a "people-centered, inclusive, and development-oriented information society," with a particular emphasis on reducing the "information gap" between developed and developing countries.

2004, **February 9–20** (Kuala Lumpur, Malaysia). Conference of the Parties to the Convention on Biological Diversity. Addressed the biological diversity of mountain ecosystems, technology transfer and cooperation, and the proposed reduction of the rate of loss of biodiversity.

June 24 (New York, New York). Global Compact Leaders Summit. Participants (including more than 1,200 corporations as well as representatives from labor and civil society) recommitted themselves to the Global Compact (introduced by UN Secretary General Kofi Annan in 1999 to promote responsible "corporate citizenship") and agreed to add anticorruption efforts (particularly aimed at extortion and bribery) to the compact's guiding principles.

November 29–December 3 (Nairobi, Kenya). First Review Conference of the State Parties to the Convention on the Prohibition of the Use, Stockpiling, Production, and Transfer of Anti-personnel Mines and on their Destruction. Adopted a 70-point action plan for the coming five-year period.

2005, **January 18–22** (Kobe, Japan). World Conference on Disaster Reduction. Addressed the issues of investing in disaster preparedness and enhancing risk assessment, particularly in view of the devastating tsunami in the Indian Ocean.

April 18–25 (Bangkok, Thailand). Eleventh UN Conference on Crime Prevention and Criminal Justice. Addressed organized crime, terrorism, human trafficking, money-laundering, corruption, cyber-crime, and "restorative" justice.

May 2–27 (New York, New York). Review Conference of the Parties to the Treaty on the Nonproliferation of Nuclear Weapons. Failed to reach consensus on proposed steps for strengthening the treaty despite the recent increase in the spread of nuclear weapons.

September 14–16 (New York, New York). World Summit. Adopted a compromise declaration regarding proposed UN reform and steps to be taken in pursuit of a broad range of security and development goals.

September 21–23 (New York, New York). Conference on Facilitating the Entry into Force of the Comprehensive Nuclear Test-Ban Treaty. Reiterated that cessation of all nuclear weapon tests remains necessary in the pursuit of nuclear disarmament, despite the lack of progress toward the treaty entering into force (ratification from 11 countries still required).

November 16–18 (Tunis, Tunisia). World Summit on the Information Society (Phase Two). Monitored progress regarding the action plan approved in 2003 and endorsed the creation of an advisory body (comprised of representatives from government, business, and civil society) to review issues surrounding the Internet.

2006, **March 20–31** (Curitiba, Brazil). Conference of the Parties to the Convention on Biological Diversity. Addressed threats posed by genetically-modified trees and urged caution in applying that technology.

November 7–17 (Geneva, Switzerland). Third Review Conference of the States Parties to the Convention on Prohibitions or Restrictions on the Use of Certain Conventional Weapons Which May Be Deemed to Be Excessively Injurious or to Have Indiscriminate Effects. Welcomed the entry into force of a protocol requiring signatories to mark and clear mines and other "explosive remnants of war."

November 20–December 8 (Geneva, Switzerland). Sixth Review Conference of the States Parties to the Convention on the Prohibition of the Development, Production and Stockpiling of Bacteriological (Biological) and Toxin Weapons and on Their Destruction. Approved a general framework for future discussions and negotiations regarding the effective implementation and strengthening of the Convention.

December 10–14 (Amman, Jordan). Conference of the Parties to the United Nations Convention against Corruption, first session. Adopted a self-assessment plan (in view of criticism regarding a perceived lack of implementation of the Convention) and pledged additional aid to developing countries to combat corruption.

2007, **July 5–6** (Geneva, Switzerland). Second Global Compact Leaders Summit. Adopted a 21-point declaration designed to enhance implementation of the Global Compact regarding corporate citizenship.

October 1–3 (Davos, Switzerland). Second International Conference on Climate Change and Tourism. Agreed that the tourism industry must "respond rapidly" to climate change by curbing greenhouse gas emissions and urged tourists to assess the environmental impact of their travels.

December 3–14 (Bali, Indonesia). United Nations Climate Change Conference. Launched negotiations on a successor to the Kyoto Protocol.

2008, **January 28–February 1** (Bali, Indonesia). Conference of the Parties to the United Nations Convention against Corruption, second session. Reviewed implementation of the convention and discussed asset recovery procedures, the need for mutual legal assistance mechanisms, various ways to strengthen coordination and enhance technical assistance, and the issue of bribery as it relates to officials of public international organizations.

June 3–6 (Rome, Italy). High-Level Conference on World Food Security: the Challenges of Climate Change and Bioenergy. Called upon the international community to increase food assistance, particularly to the least developed countries and those adversely affected by escalating food prices.

November 29–December 2 (Doha, Qatar). Follow-up International Conference on Financing for Development to Review the Implementation of the Monterrey Consensus. Adopted the Doha Declaration on Financing for Development, which affirmed the Monterrey Consensus and called on the UN to examine how the ongoing world financial and economic crisis is affecting development.

2009, **April 20–24** (Geneva, Switzerland). Durban Review Conference. Evaluated progress toward goals set by the 2001 World Conference against Racism, Racial Discrimination, Xenophobia, and Related Intolerance and called for greater "political will" to combat racism. (Canada, Israel, the United States, and five other countries boycotted the conference out of concern over possible anti-Israeli and/or anti-Western "polemics," while additional countries walked out of the conference during a controversial speech by Iranian President Mahmoud Ahmadinejad.)

June 24–30 (New York, New York). Conference on the World Financial and Economic Crisis and Its Impact on Development. Called for reform of "deficiencies" in the regulation and supervision of the international financial system.

September 24–25 (New York, New York). Conference on Facilitating the Entry into Force of the Comprehensive Nuclear Test-Ban Treaty. Called upon China, Egypt, Indonesia, Iran, Israel, and the United States (who have signed but not ratified the treaty) and North Korea, India, and Pakistan (who have not signed the treaty) to complete accession to the treaty, which cannot enter into force without their ratification. (The delegation from the United States, attending such conferences for the first time in a decade, announced plans for the Obama administration to seek Senate ratification of the treaty.)

November 16–18 (Rome, Italy). World Food Summit on Food Security. Adopted declaration pledging to promote greater domestic and international funding for agriculture in an effort to combat hunger, estimated to affect 1 billion people; few leaders from the world's wealthy nations attend.

December 7–18 (Copenhagen, Denmark). Climate Change Conference (Conference of the Parties to the United Nations Framework Convention on Climate Change and the Parties to the 1997 Kyoto Protocol). Adopted the Copenhagen Document, which called for cooperation in reducing greenhouse gases and for greater assistance to developing countries to pursue clean energy but which did not include specific, legally binding targets.

2010, **May 3–28** (New York, New York). Review Conference of the Parties to the Treaty on the Non-Proliferation of Nuclear Weapons. Focused on promoting and strengthening safeguards; advancing the peaceful use of nuclear energy, safety, and security; strengthening the review process; and engaging with civil society to promote NPT norms and disarmament education.

September 20–22 (New York, New York). Summit on Millennial Development Goals. Reaffirmed the 2015 Millennial Development Goals and adopted an action plan for achieving them. Heads of state and government and representatives of the private sector, civil society, foundations, and various international organizations pledged $40 billion over five years to improving the health of women and children.

October 18–29 (Nagoya, Japan). Tenth Conference of Parties to the Convention on Biological Diversity. In support of the International Year for Biodiversity, reviewed progress toward the 2010 goals and revised the Strategic Plan. Focused in-depth attention on inland waterways, marine and coastal areas, mountains, protected areas, the sustainable use of biodiversity, and the relationship of biodiversity to climate change.

November 9–12 (Vientiane, Laos). First Meeting of Parties to the Convention on Cluster Munitions. Approved a 66-point action plan committing signatories to "implement fully all of the obligations under the convention," which had entered into force on August 1, and specified deadlines, budgets, and targets related to such matters as stockpile destruction, clearance and risk education, and transparency.

2011, **May 9–13** (Istanbul, Turkey). Fourth United Nations Conference on the Least Developed Countries. Reviewed progress on the 10-year Least Developed Countries (LDC) Plan approved at the 2001 Third UN LDC Conference in Brussels, Belgium. The 2011 conference called for the number of LDCs to be reduced from 48 to 24 by 2020.

June 20–24 (Vienna, Austria). International Atomic Energy Agency (IAEA) Ministerial Conference on Nuclear Safety. Approved a declaration on nuclear safety that incorporated lessons learned in the aftermath of the March 11, 2011, Fukushima Daiichi nuclear power plant disaster.

September 19–20 (New York). High Level Meeting on Prevention and Control of Non-Communicable Diseases. Approved declaration calling for governments to take action to reduce deaths from non-communicable diseases, including cancer, cardiovascular disease, chronic respiratory diseases, and diabetes. The declaration urged governments to reduce tobacco consumption and unhealthy dietary patterns through economic measures such as increased taxes and limitations on advertising, while encouraging healthy lifestyles.

November 28–December 9 (Durban, South Africa). Climate Change Conference (Conference of the Parties to the United Nations Framework Convention on Climate Change and the Parties to the 1997 Kyoto Protocol). Reaffirmed a commitment to establish the Green Climate Fund that would provide $100 billion annually to help lesser developed countries mitigate climate change. Attendees also agreed to finalize a new global climate change treaty by 2015, to be implemented in 2020.

2012, **January 25–29** (Davos-Klosters, Switzerland). World Economic Forum Annual Meeting. Focused on rebalancing and deleveraging the global economy. Developed a plan by which developed countries may prevent recession and emerging countries may curb inflation, avoiding future economic bubbles.

June 18 (Rio de Janeiro, Brazil). First BioTrade Congress. Focused on biodiversity and the role of the Green Economy in relation to sustainable development and poverty alleviation. Sought increased political support for sustainable development.

June 18–19 (Los Cabos, Mexico). G-20 Summit. Focused predominantly on the European financial crisis. Leaders agreed upon various plans to promote strong, sustainable, balanced growth for the faltering European economy as well as for the global economy. Also discussed food security and environmental issues pertaining to the economy.

July 22–27 (Washington, D.C.). XIX International AIDS Conference. Placed new emphasis on preventing transmission of the disease as a new strategy to complement treatment and care initiatives. Focused on the use of microbicides to kill the virus and help prevent the spread of AIDS.

November 26–December 7 (Doha, Qatar). The UN Climate Change Conference (also known as COP18) was held in Doha. After two weeks of contentious negotiation and frequent deadlock, delegates to COP18 resolved to keep the Kyoto protocols in effect until 2020, with the goal of limiting global warming to 2°C.

2013, **January 30** (Kuwait City, Kuwait). International Humanitarian Pledging Conference for Syria. Representatives from UN member states pledged $1.54 billion to bolster humanitarian relief efforts in Syria and provide support for refugees in neighboring states in response to the largest short-term emergency funding appeals ever issued by the world body. National representatives also called for the UN Security Council to play a larger role in ending the ongoing Syrian civil war.

February 20–22 (Geneva, Switzerland). Global Forum on the Effects of the Global Economic Crisis on the Civil Aviation Industry. Sponsored by the International Labor Organization (ILO), the summit called for greater cooperation between the ILO and the International Civil Aviation Organization (ICAO). The meeting also endorsed the need to develop a "sustainable civil aviation industry."

March 8–28 (New York, New York). Final UN Conference on the Arms Trade Treaty. The summit finalized the text of the UN Arms Trade Treaty, which sought to regulate the international trade in weapons and munitions. The treaty was subsequently approved by the General Assembly on April 2, on a vote of 154 in favor, 3 opposed, and 23 abstentions.

September 25 (New York, New York). Special Event Achieving the Millennium Development Goals (MDG). World leaders reaffirmed their commitment to the MDGs and called for increased development assistance to the poorest nations. In addition member states pledged to hold a high-level meeting in 2015 to finalize new goals.

November 11–22 (Warsaw, Poland). UN Climate Change Conference (also known as COP 19). The main goal of the conference was to establish specific steps to limit greenhouse emissions. However, the contentious meeting was unable to reach consensus on a formal plan; instead, attendees agreed that all states should develop national plans by 2015 to reduce greenhouse emissions, with an implementation goal of 2020.

APPENDIX C
MEMBERSHIP OF THE UNITED NATIONS AND ITS SPECIALIZED AND RELATED AGENCIES

ORGANIZATION[a]	UN	FAO	IAEA	IBRD	ICAO	IDA	IFAD	IFC	ILO	IMF	IMO	ITU	UNESCO	UNIDO	UPU	WHO	WIPO	WMO
Members[b]	193	194[c]	159[d]	188[e]	191[f]	172[g]	172[h]	184[i]	185	188[j]	170[k]	193[l]	195[m]	172	192[n]	194[o]	186[p]	191[q]
COUNTRIES																		
Afghanistan	1946	x	x	x	x	x	C	x	x	x		x	x	x	x	x	x	x
Albania	1955	x	x	x	x	x	C	x	x	x	x	x	x	x	x	x	x	x
Algeria	1962	x	x	x	x	x	B	x	x	x	x	x	x	x	x	x	x	x
Andorra	1993	x			x							x	x			x	x	
Angola	1976	x	x	x	x	x	C	x	x	x	x	x	x	x	x	x	x	x
Antigua and Barbuda	1981	x		x	x		C	x	x	x	x	x	x		x	x	x	x
Argentina	1945	x	x	x	x	x	C	x	x	x	x	x	x	x	x	x	x	x
Armenia	1992	x	x	x	x	x	C	x	x	x		x	x	x	x	x	x	x
Australia	1945	x	x	x	x	x		x	x	x	x	x	x		x	x	x	x
Austria	1955	x	x	x	x	x	A	x	x	x	x	x	x	x	x	x	x	x
Azerbaijan	1992	x	x	x	x	x	C	x	x	x	x	x	x	x	x	x	x	x
Bahamas	1973	x		x	x	x	C	x	x	x	x	x	x	x	x	x	x	x
Bahrain	1971	x	x	x	x			x	x	x	x	x	x	x	x	x	x	x
Bangladesh	1974	x	x	x	x	x	C	x	x	x	x	x	x	x	x	x	x	x
Barbados	1966	x		x	x	x	C	x	x	x	x	x	x	x	x	x	x	x
Belarus	1945	x	x	x	x			x	x	x		x	x	x	x	x	x	x
Belgium	1945	x	x	x	x	x	A	x	x	x	x	x	x	x	x	x	x	x
Belize	1981	x	x	x	x	x	C	x	x	x	x	x	x	x	x	x	x	x
Benin	1960	x	x	x	x	x	C	x	x	x	x	x	x	x	x	x	x	x
Bhutan	1971	x		x	x	x	C	x		x		x	x	x	x	x	x	x
Bolivia	1945	x	x	x	x	x	C	x	x	x	x	x	x	x	x	x	x	x
Bosnia and Herzegovina	1992	x	x	x	x	x	C	x	x	x	x	x	x	x	x	x	x	x
Botswana	1966	x	x	x	x	x	C	x	x	x		x	x	x	x	x	x	x
Brazil	1945	x	x	x	x	x	C	x	x	x	x	x	x	x	x	x	x	x
Brunei Darussalam	1984	x		x	x				x	x	x	x	x		x	x	x	x
Bulgaria	1955	x	x	x	x			x	x	x	x	x	x	x	x	x	x	x
Burkina Faso	1960	x	x	x	x	x	C	x	x	x		x	x	x	x	x	x	x
Burundi	1962	x	x	x	x	x	C	x	x	x		x	x	x	x	x	x	x
Cambodia	1955	x	x	x	x	x	C	x	x	x	x	x	x	x	x	x	x	x
Cameroon	1960	x	x	x	x	x	C	x	x	x	x	x	x	x	x	x	x	x
Canada	1945	x	x	x	x	x	A	x	x	x	x	x	x		x	x	x	x
Cape Verde	1975	x		x	x	x	C	x	x	x	x	x	x	x	x	x	x	x
Central African Republic	1960	x	x	x	x	x	C	x	x	x		x	x	x	x	x	x	x
Chad	1960	x	x	x	x	x	C	x	x	x		x	x	x	x	x	x	x
Chile	1945	x	x	x	x	x	C	x	x	x	x	x	x	x	x	x	x	x
China	1945	x	x	x	x	x	C	x	x	x	x	x	x	x	x	x	x	x
Colombia	1945	x	x	x	x	x	C	x	x	x	x	x	x	x	x	x	x	x
Comoros	1975	x		x	x	x	C	x	x	x	x	x	x	x	x	x	x	x
Democratic Republic of the Congo	1960	x	x	x	x	x	C	x	x	x	x	x	x	x	x	x	x	x
Republic of the Congo	1960	x	x	x	x	x	C	x	x	x	x	x	x	x	x	x	x	x
Costa Rica	1945	x	x	x	x	x	C	x	x	x	x	x	x	x	x	x	x	x
Côte d'Ivoire	1960	x	x	x	x	x	C	x	x	x	x	x	x	x	x	x	x	x
Croatia	1992	x	x	x	x	x	C	x	x	x	x	x	x	x	x	x	x	x
Cuba	1945	x	x		x		C		x		x	x	x	x	x	x	x	x
Cyprus	1960	x	x	x	x	x	C	x	x	x	x	x	x	x	x	x	x	x
Czech Republic[r]	1993	x	x	x	x	x		x	x	x	x	x	x	x	x	x	x	x
Denmark	1945	x	x	x	x	x	A	x	x	x	x	x	x	x	x	x	x	x
Djibouti	1977	x		x	x	x	C	x	x	x	x	x	x	x	x	x	x	x
Dominica	1978	x		x		x	C	x	x	x	x	x	x	x	x	x	x	x
Dominican Republic	1945	x	x	x	x	x	C	x	x	x	x	x	x	x	x	x	x	x
Ecuador	1945	x	x	x	x	x	C	x	x	x	x	x	x	x	x	x	x	x
Egypt	1945	x	x	x	x	x	C	x	x	x	x	x	x	x	x	x	x	x
El Salvador	1945	x	x	x	x	x	C	x	x	x	x	x	x	x	x	x	x	x
Equatorial Guinea	1968	x		x	x	x	C	x	x	x	x	x	x	x	x	x	x	
Eritrea	1993	x	x	x	x	x	C	x	x	x	x	x	x	x	x	x	x	x

ORGANIZATION[a]	UN	FAO	IAEA	IBRD	ICAO	IDA	IFAD	IFC	ILO	IMF	IMO	ITU	UNESCO	UNIDO	UPU	WHO	WIPO	WMO
Estonia	1991	x	x	x	x	x	A	x	x	x	x	x	x		x	x	x	x
Ethiopia	1945	x	x	x	x	x	C	x	x	x	x	x	x	x	x	x	x	x
Fiji	1970	x	x	x	x	x	C	x	x	x	x	x	x	x	x	x	x	x
Finland	1955	x	x	x	x	x	A	x	x	x	x	x	x	x	x	x	x	x
France	1945	x	x	x	x	x	A	x	x	x	x	x	x	x	x	x	x	x
Gabon	1960	x	x	x	x	x	B	x	x	x	x	x	x	x	x	x	x	x
Gambia	1965	x		x	x	x	C	x	x	x	x	x	x	x	x	x	x	x
Georgia	1992	x	x	x	x	x	C	x	x	x	x	x	x	x	x	x	x	x
Germany[s]	1973	x	x	x	x	x	A	x	x	x	x	x	x	x	x	x	x	x
Ghana	1957	x	x	x	x	x	C	x	x	x	x	x	x	x	x	x	x	x
Greece	1945	x	x	x	x	x	A	x	x	x	x	x	x	x	x	x	x	x
Grenada	1974	x		x	x	x	C	x	x	x	x	x	x	x	x	x	x	
Guatemala	1945	x	x	x	x	x	C	x	x	x	x	x	x	x	x	x	x	x
Guinea	1958	x		x	x	x	C	x	x	x	x	x	x	x	x	x	x	x
Guinea-Bissau	1974	x		x	x	x	C	x	x	x	x	x	x	x	x	x	x	x
Guyana	1966	x		x	x	x	C	x	x	x	x	x	x	x	x	x	x	x
Haiti	1945	x	x	x	x	x	C	x	x	x	x	x	x	x	x	x	x	x
Honduras	1945	x	x	x	x	x	C	x	x	x	x	x	x	x	x	x	x	x
Hungary	1955	x	x	x	x	x	A	x	x	x	x	x	x	x	x	x	x	x
Iceland	1946	x	x	x	x	x	A	x	x	x	x	x	x		x	x	x	x
India	1945	x	x	x	x	x	C	x	x	x	x	x	x	x	x	x	x	x
Indonesia	1950	x	x	x	x	x	B	x	x	x	x	x	x	x	x	x	x	x
Iran	1945	x	x	x	x	x	B	x	x	x	x	x	x	x	x	x	x	x
Iraq	1945	x	x	x	x	x	B	x	x	x	x	x	x	x	x	x	x	x
Ireland	1955	x	x	x	x	x	A	x	x	x	x	x	x	x	x	x	x	x
Israel	1949	x	x	x	x	x	C	x	x	x	x	x	x	x	x	x	x	x
Italy	1955	x	x	x	x	x	A	x	x	x	x	x	x	x	x	x	x	x
Jamaica	1962	x	x	x	x		C	x	x	x	x	x	x	x	x	x	x	x
Japan	1956	x	x	x	x	x	A	x	x	x	x	x	x	x	x	x	x	x
Jordan	1955	x	x	x	x	x	C	x	x	x	x	x	x	x	x	x	x	x
Kazakhstan	1992	x	x	x	x	x	C	x	x	x	x	x	x	x	x	x	x	x
Kenya	1963	x	x	x	x	x	C	x	x	x	x	x	x	x	x	x	x	x
Kiribati	1999	x		x	x	x	C	x	x	x	x	x	x		x	x	x	x
Democratic People's Republic of Korea	1991	x			x		C				x	x	x	x	x	x	x	x
Republic of Korea	1991	x	x	x	x	x	C	x	x	x	x	x	x	x	x	x	x	x
Kuwait	1963	x	x	x	x	x	B	x	x	x	x	x	x	x	x	x	x	x
Kyrgyzstan	1992	x	x	x	x	x	C	x	x	x		x	x	x	x	x	x	x
Laos	1955	x	x	x	x	x	C	x	x	x		x	x	x	x	x	x	x
Latvia	1991	x	x	x	x	x		x	x	x	x	x	x		x	x	x	x
Lebanon	1945	x	x	x	x	x	C	x	x	x	x	x	x	x	x	x	x	x
Lesotho	1966	x	x	x	x	x	C	x	x	x		x	x	x	x	x	x	x
Liberia	1945	x	x	x	x	x	C	x	x	x	x	x	x	x	x	x	x	x
Libya	1955	x	x	x	x	x	B	x	x	x	x	x	x	x	x	x	x	x
Liechtenstein	1990		x									x			x		x	
Lithuania	1991	x	x	x	x	x		x	x	x	x	x	x		x	x	x	x
Luxembourg	1945	x	x	x	x	x	A	x	x	x	x	x	x	x	x	x	x	x
Macedonia	1993	x	x	x	x	x	C	x	x	x	x	x	x	x	x	x	x	x
Madagascar	1960	x	x	x	x	x	C	x	x	x	x	x	x	x	x	x	x	x
Malawi	1964	x	x	x	x	x	C	x	x	x	x	x	x	x	x	x	x	x
Malaysia	1957	x	x	x	x	x	C	x	x	x	x	x	x	x	x	x	x	x
Maldives	1965	x		x	x	x	C	x	x	x	x	x	x	x	x	x	x	x
Mali	1960	x	x	x	x	x	C	x	x	x		x	x	x	x	x	x	x
Malta	1964	x	x	x	x		C	x	x	x	x	x	x	x	x	x	x	x
Marshall Islands	1991	x	x	x	x	x	C	x	x	x	x	x	x			x		
Mauritania	1961	x	x	x	x	x	C	x	x	x	x	x	x	x	x	x	x	x
Mauritius	1968	x	x	x	x	x	C	x	x	x	x	x	x	x	x	x	x	x
Mexico	1945	x	x	x	x	x	C	x	x	x	x	x	x	x	x	x	x	x
Federated States of Micronesia	1991	x		x	x	x		x		x		x	x			x		x
Moldova	1992	x	x	x	x	x	C	x	x	x	x	x	x	x	x	x	x	
Monaco	1993	x	x		x						x	x	x	x	x	x	x	x

ORGANIZATION[a]	UN	FAO	IAEA	IBRD	ICAO	IDA	IFAD	IFC	ILO	IMF	IMO	ITU	UNESCO	UNIDO	UPU	WHO	WIPO	WMO
Mongolia	1961	x	x	x	x	x	C	x	x	x	x	x	x	x	x	x	x	x
Montenegro[t]	2006	x	x	x	x	x		x	x	x	x	x	x	x	x	x	x	x
Morocco	1956	x	x	x	x	x	C	x	x	x	x	x	x	x	x	x	x	x
Mozambique	1975	x	x	x	x	x	C	x	x	x	x	x	x	x	x	x	x	x
Myanmar (Burma)	1948	x	x	x	x	x	C	x	x	x	x	x	x	x	x	x	x	x
Namibia	1990	x	x	x	x		C	x	x	x	x	x	x	x	x	x	x	x
Nauru	1999	x			x		C					x	x		x	x		
Nepal	1955	x	x	x	x	x	C	x	x	x	x	x	x	x	x	x	x	x
Netherlands	1945	x	x	x	x	x	A	x	x	x	x	x	x	x	x	x	x	x
New Zealand	1945	x	x	x	x	x	A	x	x	x	x	x	x	x**	x	x	x	x
Nicaragua	1945	x	x	x	x	x	C	x	x	x	x	x	x	x	x	x	x	x
Niger	1960	x	x	x	x	x	C	x	x	x		x	x	x	x	x	x	x
Nigeria	1960	x	x	x	x	x	B	x	x	x	x	x	x	x	x	x	x	x
Norway	1945	x	x	x	x	x	A	x	x	x	x	x	x	x	x	x	x	x
Oman	1971	x	x	x	x	x	C	x	x	x	x	x	x	x	x	x	x	x
Pakistan	1947	x	x	x	x	x	C	x	x	x	x	x	x	x	x	x	x	x
Palau	1994	x	x	x	x	x		x	x	x	x		x			x		
Panama	1945	x	x	x	x	x	C	x	x	x	x	x	x	x	x	x	x	x
Papua New Guinea	1975	x	x	x	x	x	C	x	x	x	x	x	x	x	x	x	x	x
Paraguay	1945	x	x	x	x	x	C	x	x	x	x	x	x	x	x	x	x	x
Peru	1945	x	x	x	x	x	C	x	x	x	x	x	x	x	x	x	x	x
Philippines	1945	x	x	x	x	x	C	x	x	x	x	x	x	x	x	x	x	x
Poland	1945	x	x	x	x	x		x	x	x	x	x	x	x	x	x	x	x
Portugal	1955	x	x	x	x	x	A	x	x	x	x	x	x	x	x	x	x	x
Qatar	1971	x	x	x	x		B	x	x	x	x	x	x	x	x	x	x	x
Romania	1955	x	x	x	x		C	x	x	x	x	x	x	x	x	x	x	x
Russia[u]	1945	x	x	x	x	x		x	x	x	x	x	x	x	x	x	x	x
Rwanda	1962	x	x	x	x	x	C	x	x	x		x	x	x	x	x	x	x
St. Kitts and Nevis	1983	x		x	x	x	C	x	x	x	x	x	x	x	x	x	x	
St. Lucia	1979	x		x	x	x	C	x	x	x	x	x	x	x	x	x	x	x
St. Vincent and the Grenadines	1980	x		x	x	x	C		x	x	x	x	x	x	x	x	x	
Samoa	1976	x		x	x	x	C	x	x	x	x	x	x	x	x	x	x	x
San Marino	1992	x		x	x				x	x	x	x	x		x	x	x	
Sao Tome and Principe	1975	x		x	x	x	C	x	x	x	x	x	x	x	x	x	x	x
Saudi Arabia	1945	x	x	x	x	x	B	x	x	x	x	x	x	x	x	x	x	x
Senegal	1960	x	x	x	x	x	C	x	x	x	x	x	x	x	x	x	x	x
Serbia[t]	1945	x	x	x	x	x		x	x	x	x	x	x	x	x	x	x	x
Seychelles	1976	x	x	x	x		C	x	x	x	x	x	x	x	x	x	x	x
Sierra Leone	1961	x	x	x	x	x	C	x	x	x	x	x	x	x	x	x	x	x
Singapore	1965		x	x	x	x		x	x	x	x	x	x		x	x	x	x
Slovakia[r]	1993	x	x	x	x	x		x	x	x	x	x	x	x	x	x	x	x
Slovenia	1992	x	x	x	x	x		x	x	x	x	x	x	x	x	x	x	x
Solomon Islands	1978	x		x	x	x	C	x	x	x	x	x	x		x	x		x
Somalia	1960	x		x	x	x	C	x	x	x	x	x	x	x	x	x	x	x
South Africa	1945	x	x	x	x	x	C	x	x	x	x	x	x	x	x	x	x	x
South Sudan	2011			x	x	x	x	x	x	x		x	x		x	x		
Spain	1955	x	x	x	x	x	A	x	x	x	x	x	x	x	x	x	x	x
Sri Lanka	1955	x	x	x	x	x	C	x	x	x	x	x	x	x	x	x	x	x
Sudan	1956	x	x	x	x	x	C	x	x	x	x	x	x	x	x	x	x	x
Suriname	1975	x		x	x		C	x	x	x	x	x	x	x	x	x	x	x
Swaziland	1968	x		x	x	x	C	x	x	x		x	x	x	x	x	x	x
Sweden	1946	x	x	x	x	x	A	x	x	x	x	x	x	x	x	x	x	x
Switzerland	2002	x	x	x	x	x	A	x	x	x	x	x	x	x	x	x	x	x
Syria	1945	x	x	x	x	x	C	x	x	x	x	x	x	x	x	x	x	x
Tajikistan	1992	x	x	x	x	x	C	x	x	x		x	x	x	x	x	x	x
Tanzania	1961	x	x	x	x	x	C	x	x	x	x	x	x	x	x	x	x	x
Thailand	1946	x	x	x	x	x	C	x	x	x	x	x	x	x	x	x	x	x
Timor-Leste (East Timor)	2002	x		x	x	x	C	x	x	x	x	x	x	x	x	x		x
Togo	1960	x	x	x	x	x	C	x	x	x	x	x	x	x	x	x	x	x
Tonga	1999	x		x	x	x	C	x		x	x	x	x	x	x	x	x	x

ORGANIZATION[a]	UN	FAO	IAEA	IBRD	ICAO	IDA	IFAD	IFC	ILO	IMF	IMO	ITU	UNESCO	UNIDO	UPU	WHO	WIPO	WMO
Trinidad and Tobago	1962	x	x	x	x	x	C	x	x	x	x	x	x	x	x	x	x	x
Tunisia	1956	x	x	x	x	x	C	x	x	x	x	x	x	x	x	x	x	x
Turkey	1945	x	x	x	x	x	C	x	x	x	x	x	x	x	x	x	x	x
Turkmenistan	1992	x		x	x			x	x	x	x	x	x	x	x	x	x	x
Tuvalu	2000	x		x		x	C		x	x	x	x	x	x	x	x		x
Uganda	1962	x	x	x	x	x	C	x	x	x	x	x	x	x	x	x	x	x
Ukraine	1945	x	x	x	x	x		x	x	x	x	x	x	x	x	x	x	x
United Arab Emirates	1971	x	x	x	x	x	B	x	x	x	x	x	x	x	x	x	x	x
United Kingdom	1945	x	x	x	x	x	A	x	x	x	x	x	x	x	x	x	x	x
United States	1945	x	x	x	x	x	A	x	x	x	x	x	x		x	x	x	x
Uruguay	1945	x	x	x	x		C	x	x	x	x	x	x	x	x	x	x	x
Uzbekistan	1992	x	x	x	x	x	C	x	x	x		x	x	x	x	x	x	x
Vanuatu	1981	x		x	x	x	C	x	x	x	x	x	x	x	x	x	x	x
Venezuela	1945	x	x	x	x		B	x	x	x	x	x	x	x	x	x	x	x
Vietnam	1977	x	x	x	x	x	C	x	x	x	x	x	x	x	x	x	x	x
Yemen[v]	1990	x	x	x	x	x	C	x	x	x	x	x	x	x	x	x	x	x
Zambia	1964	x	x	x	x	x	C	x	x	x		x	x	x	x	x	x	x
Zimbabwe	1980	x	x	x	x	x	C	x	x	x	x	x	x	x	x	x	x	x

[a] The following abbreviations are used: UN—United Nations; FAO—Food and Agriculture Organization; IAEA—International Atomic Energy Agency; IBRD—International Bank for Reconstruction and Development; ICAO—International Civil Aviation Organization; IDA—International Development Association; IFAD—International Fund for Agricultural Development; IFC—International Finance Corporation; ILO—International Labour Organisation; IMF—International Monetary Fund; IMO—International Maritime Organization; ITU—International Telecommunication Union; UNESCO—United Nations Educational, Scientific and Cultural Organization; UNIDO—United Nations Industrial Development Organization; UPU—Universal Postal Union; WHO—World Health Organization; WIPO—World Intellectual Property Organization; WMO—World Meteorological Organization. Dates are those of each member's admission to the United Nations.

[b] Totals for all columns beginning with FAO include non-UN members.

[c] The 194 members of FAO include the following not listed in the table: Cook Islands, European Union, and Niue. Faroe Islands and Tokelau are associate members.

[d] The 159 members of IAEA include the following not listed in the table: Holy See (Vatican City State). As of September 2013 Bahamas, Brunei, Cape Verde, Swaziland, Togo, San Marino, and Tonga had been approved for membership but had not yet deposited the necessary legal instruments with the IAEA.

[e] The 188 members of IBRD include the following not listed in the table: Kosovo.

[f] The 191 members of ICAO include the following not listed in the table: Cook Islands.

[g] The 172 members of IDA include the following not listed in the table: Kosovo.

[h] The 172 members of IFAD are divided into three categories: List A, primarily OECD members; List B, primarily members of the Organization of Petroleum Exporting Countries; and List C, developing states. List C is subdivided into sublist C_1, Africa; sublist C_2, Europe, Asia, and the Pacific; and sublist C_3, Latin America and the Caribbean. Members include the following not listed in the table: Cook Islands and Niue.

[i] The 184 members of IFC include the following not listed in the table: Kosovo.

[j] The 188 members of IMF include the following not listed in the table: Anguilla, Curaçao, Netherlands Antilles, Macao, Kosovo, and Sint Maarten.

[k] The 170 members of the IMO include the following not listed in the table: Cook Islands. The IMO also has three associate members: Faroe Islands, Hong Kong, and Macao.

[l] The 193 members of ITU include the following not listed in the table: Holy See (Vatican City State).

[m] The 195 members of UNESCO include the following not listed in the table: Cook Islands and Niue. UNESCO also has eight associate members: Aruba, British Virgin Islands, Cayman Islands, Curaçao, Faroe Islands, Macao, Netherlands Antilles, Sint Maarten, and Tokelau.

[n] The 192 members of UPU include the following not listed in the table: Holy See (Vatican City State), Aruba, Curaçao, and Sint Maarten, and Overseas Territories of the United Kingdom.

[o] The 194 members of WHO include the following not listed in the table: Cook Islands and Niue. WHO also has two associate members: Puerto Rico and Tokelau.

[p] The 186 members of WIPO include the following not listed in the table: Holy See (Vatican City State).

[q] The 191 members of WMO include the following (not listed in the table), which maintain their own meteorological services: British Caribbean Territories, Cook Islands, Curaçao, French Polynesia, Sint Maarten, Hong Kong, Macao, and New Caledonia.

[r] Czechoslovakia was a member from the founding of the UN in 1945 until that nation's dissolution on January 1, 1993. The Czech Republic and Slovakia were admitted separately on January 19.

[s] German Democratic Republic and Federal Republic of Germany admitted separately to the UN in 1973; merged as Federal Republic of Germany in 1990.

[t] The status of the Yugoslavian seat was in question from September 1992 until the admission of the Federal Republic of Yugoslavia in October 2000 (see article on UN: General Assembly for further information). During that period Yugoslavian participation was not permitted in some specialized and related agencies of the United Nations. Serbia and Montenegro (the successor to the Federal Republic of Yugoslavia) participated in all such UN agencies except the IFAD until it split in mid-2006. Serbia kept membership status in the UN and its specialized and related agencies; Montenegro was required to reapply for memberships.

[u] Russia assumed the seat formerly held by the Union of Soviet Socialist Republics following the USSR's dissolution on December 8, 1991.

[v] Merger of the two Yemens; the former Yemen Arab Republic joined the UN in 1947 and the former People's Democratic Republic of Yemen in 1967.

** "On 13 December 2012, the government of New Zealand deposited with the secretary general an instrument of denunciation of the above constitution. In accordance with article 6 (2) of the Constitution, the denunciation will take effect on the last day of the fiscal year following that during which such instrument was deposited, that is, on December 31, 2013."

APPENDIX D
SERIALS LIST

Africa Confidential
Africa Research Bulletin (Economic Series)
Africa Research Bulletin (Political Series)
Asian News Digest
BBC News: Country Profiles
Caribbean Insight
CARICOM Reports
Central America Report
The Christian Science Monitor
Constitutions of the Countries of the World
The Economist
The Europa World Year Book
Financial Times
Freedom House: Country Reports
Human Rights Watch: Reports
IAEA Bulletin
IMF Article IV Reports
IMF Balance of Payments Statistics
IMF Direction of Trade Statistics
IMF Government Finance Statistics
IMF International Financial Statistics
IMF Survey
IMF World Economic Outlook
Indian Ocean Newsletter
International Foundation for Electoral Systems, Election Guide
Interparliamentary Union: Women in National Parliaments
Keesing's Record of World Events
Latin America Regional Reports
Latin America Weekly Report
Le Monde (Paris)
NATO Review
The New York Times
Pacific Island Report
People in Power
Permanent Missions to the United Nations
Radio Free Europe/Radio Liberty
Reporters Without Borders Annual Report
Statistical Abstract of the United States
Transparency International: Corruption Perceptions Index
UN Chronicle
UN Handbook
UN Population and Vital Statistics Report
UN Statistical Yearbook
UNESCO Statistical Yearbook
US CIA Heads of State and Cabinet Members
US Department of State, Diplomatic List
The Washington Post
World Bank Atlas
World Bank Country Reports
World Development Report
World Trade Organization: World Trade Report

PUBLISHING HISTORY OF THE POLITICAL HANDBOOK

A Political Handbook of Europe: 1927, ed. Malcolm W. Davis. Council on Foreign Relations.

A Political Handbook of the World: 1928, ed. Malcolm W. Davis and Walter H. Mallory. Harvard University Press and Yale University Press.

Political Handbook of the World: 1929, ed. Malcolm W. Davis and Walter H. Mallory. Yale University Press.

Political Handbook of the World: 1930–1931, ed. Walter H. Mallory. Yale University Press.

Political Handbook of the World: 1932–1962, ed. Walter H. Mallory. Harper & Brothers.

Political Handbook and Atlas of the World: 1963–1967, ed. Walter H. Mallory. Harper & Row.

Political Handbook and Atlas of the World: 1968, ed. Walter H. Mallory. Simon and Schuster.

Political Handbook and Atlas of the World: 1970, ed. Richard P. Stebbins and Alba Amoia. Simon and Schuster.

The World This Year: 1971–1973 (supplements to the *Political Handbook and Atlas of the World: 1970*), ed. Richard P. Stebbins and Alba Amoia. Simon and Schuster.

Political Handbook of the World: 1975, ed. Arthur S. Banks and Robert S. Jordan. McGraw-Hill.

Political Handbook of the World: 1976–1979, ed. Arthur S. Banks. McGraw-Hill.

Political Handbook of the World: 1980–1983, ed. Arthur S. Banks and William R. Overstreet. McGraw-Hill.

Political Handbook of the World: 1984–1995, ed. Arthur S. Banks. CSA Publications.

Political Handbook of the World: 1995–1997, ed. Arthur S. Banks, Alan J. Day, and Thomas C. Muller. CSA Publications.

Political Handbook of the World: 1998–1999, ed. Arthur S. Banks and Thomas C. Muller. CSA Publications.

Political Handbook of the World: 2000–2002, ed. Arthur S. Banks, Thomas C. Muller, and William R. Overstreet. CSA Publications.

Political Handbook of the World: 2005–2006, ed. Arthur S. Banks, Thomas C. Muller, and William R. Overstreet. CQ Press.

Political Handbook of the World: 2007, ed. Arthur S. Banks, Thomas C. Muller, and William R. Overstreet. CQ Press.

Political Handbook of the World: 2008, ed. Arthur S. Banks, Thomas C. Muller, and William R. Overstreet. CQ Press.

Political Handbook of the World: 2009, ed. Arthur S. Banks, Thomas C. Muller, William R. Overstreet, and Judith F. Isacoff. CQ Press.

Political Handbook of the World: 2010, ed. Arthur S. Banks, Thomas C. Muller, William R. Overstreet, and Judith F. Isacoff. CQ Press.

Political Handbook of the World: 2011, ed. Thomas C. Muller, William R. Overstreet, Judith F. Isacoff, Tom Lansford. CQ Press.

Political Handbook of the World: 2012–2014, ed. Tom Lansford. CQ Press.

(All editions published before 2007 were annual, except for 1982–1983 and 1984–1985, which were biennial, and 2000–2002 and 2005–2006, which were triennial.)